BEST'S® PUBLICATIONS & SERVICES

RATINGS & ANALYSIS PRODUCTS

Best's Insurance Reports®
- Property/Casualty — US & Canada
- Life/Health — US & Canada
- Non-US

Best's Capital Adequacy Ratio Adjustment System — P/C, US

Best's Capital Adequacy Ratio Model — Universal

Best's Rating Reference Guide
- Property/Casualty — US
- Life/Health — US

Best's Key Rating Guide®
- Property/Casualty — US & Canada
- Life/Health — US & Canada

FINANCIAL DATA PRODUCTS

Best's Statement File
- Property/Casualty — US
- Life/Health — US

Best's State/Line (P/C Lines) — US
Best's State/Line (Life Lines) — L/H — US
Best's State/Line (A&H Lines) — L/H — US
Best's Insurance Expense Exhibit — P/C — US
Best's Schedule D — P/C & L/H — US
Best's Schedule F — P/C — US
Best's Schedule P — P/C — US
Best's Schedule S — L/H — US
Best's Credit Ratings and Data Feed

Best's Statement File
- Global
- Property/Casualty — Canada
- Life/Health — Canada
- United Kingdom
- Middle East North Africa
- Asia-Pacific
- Latin America

Best's Aggregates & Averages
- Property/Casualty — US & Canada
- Life/Health — US & Canada

ONLINE CENTERS

Best's Agent Center™
Best's Property/Casualty Center
Best's Directories of Insurance Professionals
Best's Health Center
Best's Library Center
Best's Regulatory Center

Best's Underwriting & Loss Control Center
Best's Life/Health Center
Best's Consumer Insurance Center
Best's Captive Center
Best's Title & Mortgage Guaranty Center
Best's Reinsurance Center

NEWS PRODUCTS

Best's Review®
Best's Insurance News & Analysis
Understanding the Insurance Industry

BestWire®
BestDay®
Best's Special Reports
Best's Statistical Studies

RISK ASSESSMENT PRODUCTS

Best's Underwriting Guide

Best's Loss Control Manual

DIRECTORIES

Best's Directory of Recommended Insurance Attorneys
Best's Directory of Recommended Insurance Adjusters
Best's Directory of Recommended Expert Service Providers
Best's Directory of Third Party Administrators
Best's Directory of Insurance Auditors

REGULATORY FILING SOFTWARE

BestESP® Services — US

BestESP® Services — UK

RATE FILING INFORMATION

Best's State Rate Filings® — P/C — US

SPECIAL SERVICES

Best's Custom Data Services
BestAlert® Service
Member Center

Best's Online Account
Best's Product Training Workshops

CORPORATE PROGRAMS & SERVICES

Article Reprints
BestMark Program
Best's Preferred Publisher Program
Best's Rating Referral Program

Certificate Programs
Corporate Complimentary Subscription Program

ONLINE REPORTS

AMB Credit Reports
Best's Key Rating Guide Presentation Reports
Best's Market Share Reports

Best's Executive Summary Reports
Best's Rating Reports

For a full list of products and services, call or write:
A.M. Best Company, Customer Service, Ambest Road, Oldwick, NJ 08858 USA
Phone: (908) 439-2200, ext. 5742 • Fax: (908) 439-3296
www.ambest.com/sales

TABLE OF CONTENTS

Volume I
Preface . . . . vii-x
DIRECTORY OF RECOMMENDED INSURANCE ATTORNEYS
Alphabetical Firm Index 1-73
General Defense
United States — AL-OK 75-1216

Volume II
Preface vii-x
DIRECTORY OF RECOMMENDED INSURANCE ATTORNEYS (Continued)
General Defense
United States — OR-WY 1217-1598
United States Possessions and Commonwealths 1599-1604
Canada 1605-1616
Other Countries 1617-1625
Subrogation 1627-1668
Regulatory and Compliance 1669-1674
Investigation and Adjustment 1675-1680
Digest of Insurance Laws Appreciation 1681-1686

DIRECTORY OF RECOMMENDED INSURANCE ADJUSTERS
Alphabetical Company Index 1-29
United States 31-598
State Association Rosters
California 82-83
New York 374
Pennsylvania 458
United States Possessions and Commonwealths 599-601
Canada 603-606
Other Countries 607-610

DIRECTORY OF RECOMMENDED EXPERT SERVICE PROVIDERS
Introduction/Table of Contents 1
Alphabetical Company Index 3-13
Geographical Company Index 15-25
Expert Service Providers 27-194

Get the latest listing information for all directories at:
www.ambest.com/directories

The most current information for any listee is always accessible free of charge.

The following information may be found at **www.ambest.com/directories**:
United States and Canada: Officials Having Charge of Insurance Affairs and Motor Vehicle Officials
States Requiring Adjuster License
Corporate Structures
Conference Report on Fair Insurance Claims Adjustment
National Association of Independent Insurance Adjusters Code of Ethics
NAIIA and CIAA Contact Information

TABLE OF CONTENTS

Volume I
Preface .... xiii-x

DIRECTORY OF RECOMMENDED INSURANCE ATTORNEYS
Alphabetical Firm Index 1-72
General Indexes
United States – USA-OK 75-1278

Volume II
Preface xiii
DIRECTORY OF RECOMMENDED INSURANCE ATTORNEYS (continued)
General Indexes
United States – OK-WY 1279-1596
United States – Possessions and Commonwealths 1599-1604
Canada 1605-1616
Other Countries 1619-1625
Subject Index 1627-1668
Regulations and Compliance 1669-1674
Insurance and Arbitration 1675-1678
Digest of Insurance Laws Appreciation 1681-1686

DIRECTORY OF RECOMMENDED INSURANCE ADJUSTERS
Alphabetical Company Index 1689
United States 31-57
State Association Rosters
California 58-83
New York 84
Pennsylvania 85
Possessions, Possessions and Commonwealths 100-003
Canada 604-605
Other Countries 606-610

DIRECTORY OF RECOMMENDED EXPERT SERVICE PROVIDERS
Introduction/Table of Contents
Alphabetical Company Index 3b
Geographical Company Index E-2
Expert Service Providers C-2136

For the latest listing information on all directories in
www.ambest.com/directories

The most current information for any listing is always accessible free of charge.

The following information may be found at www.ambest.com/directories:
United States and Canada Official Florida Superintendent, Insurance and Motor Vehicle Officials
State Insurance Arbitrator Rosters
Corporate Structure
Conference Report on Bad Insurance Claims Arbitration
Various Associations of Independent Insurance Adjusters Code of Ethics
VALA and CMA Code of Arbitration

A.M. BEST'S DIRECTORY OF RECOMMENDED INSURANCE ATTORNEYS AND ADJUSTERS

PREFACE
2015 EDITION

An explanation of Best's Directories of Recommended Insurance Attorneys and Adjusters system and procedures

Section	Topic	Page
I	Introduction	vii
II	Sources of Information	viii
III	Objective of Best's Recommended Listings	viii
IV	Qualifications for Attorney Listings	ix
V	Qualifications for Adjuster Listings	ix
VI	Qualifications for Expert Service Providers Listings	ix
VII	Definitions	x

SECTION I

INTRODUCTION

A.M. Best Company, Inc. (A.M. Best), is a global, full-service credit rating agency dedicated to serving the financial and health care services industries. It began assigning credit ratings in 1906, making it the first of today's credit rating agencies to use symbols to differentiate the relative creditworthiness of companies. Within the insurance sector, Best's Credit Ratings cover property casualty, life, annuity, reinsurance, captive, title and health insurance companies and health maintenance organizations (HMOs). A.M. Best provides the most comprehensive insurance ratings coverage of any credit rating agency, with reports and ratings maintained on over 11,000 insurance entities worldwide, in approximately 130 countries. A.M. Best is also a well-known and highly regarded source of information and commentary on global insurance trends and issues through a host of other products and services.

The insurance industry has possibly the greatest need of any single business for highly specialized and reliable legal services. A.M. Best Company is pleased to publish **Best's Directories of Recommended Insurance Attorneys and Adjusters** to meet the needs of this industry. This resource is an annual publication restricted to attorneys, adjusters and expert service providers. Inclusion in the publication is limited to individuals and firms recommended by representatives of insurance companies, insurance pools or self-insurers and who meet the standards of the A.M. Best Company as to reputation, character and experience.

The use of the word "recommended" in the title should not be construed to indicate that the publishers presume to pass upon the legal qualifications or the merits of attorneys, adjusters or expert service providers. Rather, it indicates that all listees are recommended by the insurance industry clients that they serve. All applications and submitted feedback are reviewed by the A.M. Best Company. Representation is open to any attorney, adjuster and/or expert service provider individual or firm who can meet these requirements; we do not permit exclusive or limited representation.

Since 1928, the A.M. Best Company has serviced the insurance industry by publishing Best's Directory of Recommended Insurance Attorneys (Volumes I and II). This publication was the result of requests made by insurance officials for information and suggestions as to a national reference source of competent insurance attorneys to handle their litigation, adjustments and investigations and other needs. The purpose of this product is to identify those firms which have demonstrated their reliability in handling insurance defense litigation, subrogation, investigation and adjustment, regulatory and compliance and other matters significant to the business of insurance.

Best's Directory of Recommended Insurance Adjusters (Volume II) has been published since 1930. The purpose of this publication is to identify those independent adjusters throughout the United States, Canada and other countries which have demonstrated their reliability in handling insurance claims. All firms must be recommended by claims representatives of insurance companies and self-insurers who are not affiliated with the proposed adjusting firm. The class of business for which the adjuster has been recommended is indicated in each listing.

We are pleased to offer in this publication Best's Directory of Recommended Expert Service Providers in Volume II. The Expert Service Providers Section was first printed in the 1972-1973 Edition of the attorney directory. Shorthand reporters comprised the only category this first year. Categories added the second year included Investigators, Consultants and Testing Laboratories. Today Best's Directory of Recommended Expert Service Providers boasts experts in over 42 categories. The purpose of this product is to identify those individuals and firms throughout the United States, Canada and other countries worldwide which have demonstrated their reliability in providing expert services to law firms, insurance companies, non-insurance companies and independent adjusters.

We feel confident that this two-volume set will be of service and value to the legal and claim representatives of the insurance industry when they need to locate and select highly qualified, competent and capable firms. By maintaining its traditionally high standards, **Best's Directories of Recommended Insurance Attorneys and Adjusters** will continue to serve as the industry's authoritative and most reputable source for providing this information. To help maintain these standards the publisher earnestly solicits your comments and suggestions.

A.M. Best Company

SECTION II
SOURCES OF INFORMATION

The primary sources of the information presented in this publication are the listees themselves as well as the insurance industry clients they represent. Listings include type of practice, firm profile, biographical information, contact information and verified client lists.

To be listed in this directory, each home office must apply for a listing and be recommended by the claims departments of insurance companies, non-insurance companies or self-insurers and their claims divisions, or trucking and transportation companies that they serve. The formal application to apply for a listing requests information about the applicant including personnel, contact data and description of practice or services. The application also requests the company name, contact person, mailing address, phone and fax numbers and e-mail addresses of individuals working for client companies and contacts that can readily provide A.M. Best Company with feedback on the services provided to them. A verification letter is then sent which asks that the company comment on the type of work, quality and volume of work that the applicant provides for them. A.M. Best Company reviews the comments and endorsements of these companies before accepting a firm into the publication. The A.M. Best Company is deeply appreciative of the cooperation of both the insurance companies and non-insurance companies that provide the necessary feedback in preparing this work. Without their assistance this work could not have been completed.

While the information received from these companies is obtained from sources believed to be reliable, its accuracy is not guaranteed. We do not monitor the claims departments of these companies and therefore cannot attest to their accuracy.

Listings in this publication are reviewed annually by each home office decision-making person or persons. The print Directory is released in late December or early January each year.

SECTION III
OBJECTIVE OF BEST'S RECOMMENDED LISTINGS

The objective of Best's Directories of Recommended Insurance Attorneys and Adjusters is not to rate any individual or firm, but to provide to the insurance industry a list of firms that have been recommended by their own clients and which are most qualified to handle their litigation, adjusting or expert service needs. Based on client endorsements, the companies presented in this publication are considered to be the best equipped to perform quality service for the companies seeking outside guidance and professional assistance.

All firms are considered for admission into the directory, regardless of firm size and geographical location. Users of this directory may choose to select a firm based on firm size, client list, type of practice the firm specializes in or location. However, all firms listed and recommended are considered to be of equal status.

SECTION IV
QUALIFICATIONS FOR LISTEES IN THE DIRECTORY OF ATTORNEYS

- The firm shall have satisfactorily served insurance companies, insurance pools, and/or self-insurers and be recommended to us by these companies

for the services performed in connection with their insurance work.
- At least one principal firm member must have a minimum experience of five (5) years in the practice of insurance law or its equivalent.
- Complete the Confidential Firm Report form for Best's Directory of Recommended Insurance Attorneys.
- Submit to the customary A.M. Best Company investigation of the candidate's reputation, character, experience, reliability, type of practice and office facility as determined by the formal application, verification responses and listing requirements forms.
- The staff must provide answering service administered by the applicant's staff during business hours. (800 numbers, answering services, call forwarding and automatic switchovers are acceptable).
- List the firm in the building directory except in the circumstance of the applicant's private residence serving as the firm's place of occupancy.
- Identify the firm on the principal door to the main office of the firm.
- The firm must sign an automatically renewable Contract for listing in Best's Directory of Recommended Insurance Attorneys.

SECTION V

QUALIFICATIONS FOR LISTEES IN THE DIRECTORY OF ADJUSTERS

- The firm shall have satisfactorily served insurance companies, insurance pools, and/or self-insurers and be recommended to us by these companies for the services performed in connection with their claims work.
- At least one principal firm member must have a minimum experience of five (5) years as a claims adjuster.
- Complete the Confidential Firm Report form for Best's Directory of Recommended Insurance Adjusters.
- Submit to the customary A.M. Best Company review of the candidate's reputation, character, experience, reliability, type of practice and office facilities as determined by the formal application, verification responses and listing requirements forms.
- The staff must provide answering service administered by the applicant's staff during business hours. (800 numbers, answering services, call forwarding and automatic switchovers are acceptable).
- List the firm in the building directory except in the circumstance of the applicant's private residence serving as the firm's place of occupancy.
- Identify the firm on the principal door to the main office of the firm.
- The firm must sign an automatically renewable Contract for listing in Best's Directory of Recommended Insurance Adjusters.

SECTION VI

QUALIFICATIONS FOR LISTEES IN THE DIRECTORY OF EXPERT SERVICE PROVIDERS

- The firm shall have satisfactorily served insurance companies, insurance pools, and/or self-insurers and law firms and be recommended to us by these companies for the services performed in connection with their expert services.
- At least one principal firm member must have a minimum experience of five (5) years in their field of expertise.
- Complete the Confidential Firm Report form for Best's Directory of Recommended Expert Service Providers.
- Submit to the customary A.M. Best Company investigation of the candidate's reputation, character, experience, reliability, type of practice and office facility as determined by the formal application, verification responses and listing requirements forms.
- The staff must provide answering service administered by the applicant's staff during business hours. (800 numbers, answering services, call forwarding and automatic switchovers are acceptable).
- List the firm in the building directory except in the circumstance of the applicant's private residence serving as the firm's place of occupancy.
- Identify the firm on the principal door to the main office of the firm.
- The firm must sign an automatically renewable Contract for listing in Best's Directory of Recommended Expert Service Providers section.

SECTION VII

DEFINITIONS

Listing Types

Main or Home Office Listing: For the purpose of this publication, a home office is the primary decision-making entity of the corporation that is listed and recommended. This entity is responsible for submitting all paperwork and reviewing all listing content on an annual basis. Any separate and unique physical location in either a corporate office structure or residence with office space is eligible for consideration as a home office listing.

Branch Office Listing: An affiliate office or location that works under the guidance and supervision of a home office is considered to be a branch office. While a firm or company can have only one home office listing, it may have multiple branch offices listings. A separate and unique physical location is required for consideration as a branch office listing.

Service Area Listing: With a Service Area Listing, a firm or company can present limited information in a city or town in which they do business. The listing refers the user back to either the home or branch office listing.

General Defense Listing for Law Firms: Listings in this section are open to firms that handle the defense of all types of liability cases including but not limited to personal injury, product liability and construction suits.

Subrogation Listings for Law Firms: These listings are available to firms that practice subrogation, which is an action instituted by the first party carrier to recover the amount paid under the policy to a third party.

Investigation and Adjustment Listing for Law Firms: These listings are open to firms that initiate and administer accident investigation, procurement of statements from principals, witnesses and policy, prescribe and direct appropriate photography, and negotiate settlements.

Regulatory and Compliance Listing for Law Firms: These listings are open to firms that administrate codes of being in accordance with established guidelines, specifications or legislation.

Organization Types

Law Firms: Firms that specialize primarily in the defense of insurance companies and non-insurance companies that have the need to outsource for litigation or legal needs.

Independent Adjusters: Adjusters that service insurance companies and non-insurance companies such as trucking, freight and transportation in their needs related to damage assessment.

Expert Service Providers: Individuals or firms that serve the insurance industry, law firms and independent adjusters by providing services such as litigation support, expert testimony, claims support or testing and analysis. There are over 42 categories represented in this section of the publication.

Legal and Claims Officials: The names and titles of the main officials in the offices of insurance companies. These Officials are only avzailable in the on-line version of the Directory.

Corporate Structures: These are listings of the combined groups of insurance companies followed by individual members of these groups. These listings are only available in the on-line version of the Directory.

BEST'S DIRECTORY OF RECOMMENDED INSURANCE ATTORNEYS

2015 Edition

Best's Attorneys Listings
are as of publication date November 3, 2014

For Current Listings and Information access www.ambest.com/directories

Published Continuously since 1928

A.M. BEST COMPANY
Oldwick, New Jersey 08858 USA • (908) 439-2200 • Fax: (908) 439-2688
www.ambest.com

BEST'S
DIRECTORY OF
RECOMMENDED
INSURANCE ATTORNEYS

2015 Edition

Best's Attorney's Listings
are as of publication date, November 3, 2014

For current Listings and Information access: www.ambest.com/directories

Published Continuously since 1928

A.M. BEST COMPANY
Oldwick, New Jersey 08858, U.S.A. (908) 439-2200 Fax: (908) 439-3698
www.ambest.com

Best's Directories of Recommended Insurance Attorneys and Adjusters
2015
Volume I - Attorneys

Alphabetical Firm Index

A

Abbey, Adams, Byelick & Mueller, L.L.P.
St. Petersburg, Florida, *General Defense* 412
Tampa, Florida, *General Defense* 418

Abowitz, Timberlake & Dahnke, P.C.
Oklahoma City, Oklahoma, *General Defense* 1193

Abrahams Kaslow & Cassman LLP
Omaha, Nebraska, *General Defense* 926

Abrams & Lafargue, L.L.C.
Shreveport, Louisiana, *General Defense* 710

Acosta
Miami, Florida, *General Defense* 379

Law Offices Benjamin Acosta, Jr.
San Juan, Puerto Rico, *General Defense* 1600

Adams & Gaffaney, LLP
Post Falls, Idaho, *General Defense* 488

Adams Hoefer Holwadel, LLC
New Orleans, Louisiana, *General Defense* 685

Adams, Stepner, Woltermann & Dusing, P.L.L.C.
Covington, Kentucky, *General Defense* 615
Florence, Kentucky, *General Defense* 617

Adams & Sullivan, P.C., L.L.O.
Papillion, Nebraska, *General Defense* 933

Adler, Cohen, Harvey, Wakeman & Guekguezian LLP
Boston, Massachusetts, *General Defense* 748

Adler Pollock & Sheehan P.C.
Boston, Massachusetts, *General Defense* 749
Providence, Rhode Island, *General Defense* 1284

Adsuar Muñiz Goyco Seda & Perez-Ochoa, P.S.C.
San Juan, Puerto Rico, *General Defense* 1600
San Juan, Puerto Rico, *Regulatory and Compliance* 1673

Aeton Law Partners LLP
Middletown, Connecticut, *General Defense* 312

Affleck Greene McMurtry LLP
Toronto, Ontario, *General Defense* 1610

Afridi & Angell
Dubai, United Arab Emirates, *General Defense* 1623

Ahlers & Cooney, P.C.
Des Moines, Iowa, *General Defense* 583

Alber Crafton, PSC
Louisville, Kentucky, *General Defense* 632
Troy, Michigan, *General Defense* 807
Westerville, Ohio, *General Defense* 1187

Frederick G. Aldrich LLC
Grand Junction, Colorado, *General Defense* 296

Alexander & Angelas, P.C.
Detroit, Michigan, *General Defense* 782

Alexander & Vann, LLP
Thomasville, Georgia, *General Defense* 464

ATTORNEYS - ALPHABETICAL FIRM INDEX

Allen, Kopet & Associates, PLLC
    Birmingham, Alabama, *General Defense* 80
    Fort Lauderdale, Florida, *General Defense* 350
    Tallahassee, Florida, *General Defense* 416
    Atlanta, Georgia, *General Defense* 435
    Chicago, Illinois, *General Defense* 499
    Indianapolis, Indiana, *General Defense* 560
    Lexington, Kentucky, *General Defense* 621
    Jackson, Mississippi, *General Defense* 842
    St. Louis, Missouri, *General Defense* 886
    Charlotte, North Carolina, *General Defense* 1119
    Raleigh, North Carolina, *General Defense* 1131
    Columbia, South Carolina, *General Defense* 1305
    Chattanooga, Tennessee, *General Defense* 1334
    Jackson, Tennessee, *General Defense* 1342
    Knoxville, Tennessee, *General Defense* 1346
    Nashville, Tennessee, *General Defense* 1357
    Bristol, Virginia, *General Defense* 1495

Allen Law Firm, P.C.
    Little Rock, Arkansas, *General Defense* 166

Alper & McCulloch
    San Francisco, California, *General Defense* 245
    San Francisco, California, *Subrogation* 1631

Al Rowaad Advocates & Legal Consultancy
    Dubai, United Arab Emirates, *General Defense* 1623

Altman, Spence, Mitchell & Brown, P.C.
    Fairfax, Virginia, *General Defense* 1498

James R. Alvillar & Associates
    Grand Junction, Colorado, *General Defense* 296

Ambrose, Wilson, Grimm & Durand, LLP
    Knoxville, Tennessee, *General Defense* 1346

A M Lawyers
    Dallas, Texas, *General Defense* 1387

Ancel, Glink, Diamond, Bush, DiCianni & Krafthefer, P.C.
    Chicago, Illinois, *General Defense* 499

Anderson Crawley & Burke, pllc
    Jackson, Mississippi, *General Defense* 843

Anderson & Gilbert, L.C.
    St. Louis, Missouri, *General Defense* 886

Anderson, Johnson, Lawrence & Butler, L.L.P.
    Fayetteville, North Carolina, *General Defense* 1123

Anderson, Julian & Hull, LLP
    Boise, Idaho, *General Defense* 476

Anderson, Murphy & Hopkins, L.L.P.
    Little Rock, Arkansas, *General Defense* 166

Anderson Reynolds & Lynch, LLP
    New Britain, Connecticut, *General Defense* 314

Anderson Reynolds & Stephens, LLC
    Charleston, South Carolina, *General Defense* 1295

Anderson, Walker & Reichert, LLP
    Macon, Georgia, *General Defense* 456

Andrews Skinner, P.S.
    Seattle, Washington, *General Defense* 1533

Anselmi & Mierzejewski, P.C.
    Bloomfield Hills, Michigan, *General Defense* 780

ATTORNEYS - ALPHABETICAL FIRM INDEX

Anstandig, McDyer & Yurcon, P.C.
    Pittsburgh, Pennsylvania, *General Defense* 1265

Appelbaum & Associates, P.C.
    Atlanta, Georgia, *General Defense* 435

Archer Norris
    Walnut Creek, California, *General Defense* 266

Armienti, DeBellis, Guglielmo & Rhoden, LLP
    New York, New York, *General Defense* 1060

Armstrong Teasdale LLP
    Jefferson City, Missouri, *General Defense* 872
    Kansas City, Missouri, *General Defense* 874
    St. Louis, Missouri, *General Defense* 887

Law Offices of Kenneth L. Aron
    Manalapan, New Jersey, *General Defense* 976

Asbury Law Firm
    Abilene, Texas, *General Defense* 1371

Ashford & Wriston
    Honolulu, Hawaii, *General Defense* 470

Law Offices of James F. Aspell, P.C.
    Hartford, Connecticut, *General Defense* 306

Aspelmeier, Fisch, Power, Engberg & Helling, P.L.C.
    Burlington, Iowa, *General Defense* 580

Atkinson & Brownell, P.A.
    Miami, Florida, *General Defense* 380

Atkinson, Haskins, Nellis, Brittingham, Gladd & Fiasco
    Tulsa, Oklahoma, *General Defense* 1204

Atkin Winner & Sherrod
    Las Vegas, Nevada, *General Defense* 937

Atlas, Hall & Rodriguez, L.L.P.
    McAllen, Texas, *General Defense* 1452

Atwill & Montgomery, Attorneys at Law, LLC
    Columbia, Missouri, *General Defense* 870

Atwood, Malone, Turner & Sabin, P.A.
    Roswell, New Mexico, *General Defense* 1016

Audilett Kastner PC
    Tucson, Arizona, *General Defense* 152

Aultman Law Firm, Ltd.
    Gulfport, Mississippi, *General Defense* 835
    Hattiesburg, Mississippi, *General Defense* 839

Austin & Sparks, P.C.
    Atlanta, Georgia, *General Defense* 436

Avery Dooley & Noone, LLP
    Boston, Massachusetts, *General Defense* 749

Axilon Law Group, PLLC
    Bozeman, Montana, *General Defense* 904

Axley Brynelson, LLP
    Madison, Wisconsin, *General Defense* 1574

B

Babcock, Scott & Babcock, PC
    Salt Lake City, Utah, *General Defense* 1474

Babin & Seeger, LLP
    Santa Rosa, California, *General Defense* 263

ATTORNEYS - ALPHABETICAL FIRM INDEX

Backus · Carranza
Las Vegas, Nevada, *General Defense* 937

Bacon, Thornton, Palmer, L.L.P.
Greenbelt, Maryland, *General Defense* 740

Bahret & Associates Co., L.P.A.
Toledo, Ohio, *General Defense* 1186

Bailey & Dixon, L.L.P.
Raleigh, North Carolina, *General Defense* 1131
Raleigh, North Carolina, *Regulatory and Compliance* 1672

Bailey, Kelleher & Johnson, P.C.
Albany, New York, *General Defense* 1022

Baird Lightner Millsap, P.C.
Springfield, Missouri, *General Defense* 883

Baker, Dublikar, Beck, Wiley & Mathews
Canton, Ohio, *General Defense* 1160

Baker, Kinsman, Hollis, Clelland & Hogue, P.C.
Chattanooga, Tennessee, *General Defense* 1335

Baker, O'Kane, Atkins & Thompson
Knoxville, Tennessee, *General Defense* 1346

Baker, Ravenel & Bender, L.L.P.
Columbia, South Carolina, *General Defense* 1305
Columbia, South Carolina, *Subrogation* 1660

Balaban, Levinson & Costigan, P.C.
Denver, Colorado, *General Defense* 277

The Bale Law Firm, PLLC
Sugar Land, Texas, *General Defense* 1465

Balestreri Potocki & Holmes
San Diego, California, *General Defense* 236
San Diego, California, *Subrogation* 1631

Ball, Ball, Matthews & Novak, P.A.
Mobile, Alabama, *General Defense* 108
Montgomery, Alabama, *General Defense* 119

Bancroft, McGavin, Horvath & Judkins, P.C.
Fairfax, Virginia, *General Defense* 1499
Fairfax, Virginia, *Subrogation* 1663

Emile Banks & Associates, LLC
Milwaukee, Wisconsin, *General Defense* 1577

Barbanel & Treuer, P.C.
Los Angeles, California, *General Defense* 197

Barker & Cook, PA
Tampa, Florida, *General Defense* 419

Barnaba & Marconi, LLP
Trenton, New Jersey, *General Defense* 999
Trenton, New Jersey, *Subrogation* 1648

Barnes, Alford, Stork & Johnson, L.L.P.
Columbia, South Carolina, *General Defense* 1306

Barnum & Clinton, PLLC
Norman, Oklahoma, *General Defense* 1192

Barnwell Whaley Patterson & Helms, L.L.C.
Charleston, South Carolina, *General Defense* 1296

Barret, Haynes, May & Carter P.S.C.
Hazard, Kentucky, *General Defense* 620

Barrett & McNagny LLP
Fort Wayne, Indiana, *General Defense* 558

ATTORNEYS - ALPHABETICAL FIRM INDEX

Barrickman, Allred & Young, LLC
    Atlanta, Georgia, *General Defense* 436

Barron & Pruitt, LLP
    Las Vegas, Nevada, *General Defense* 938
    Orem, Utah, *General Defense* 1474

Barron & Redding, P.A.
    Panama City, Florida, *General Defense* 404

Barry Law Firm, PLLC
    Philadelphia, Pennsylvania, *General Defense* 1247

Barth Sullivan Behr
    Buffalo, New York, *General Defense* 1034
    Syracuse, New York, *General Defense* 1103

Bass, Berry & Sims PLC
    Nashville, Tennessee, *General Defense* 1357

The Bassett Firm
    Dallas, Texas, *General Defense* 1388

Bassett Law Firm, LLP
    Fayetteville, Arkansas, *General Defense* 158

Bass Law
    Oklahoma City, Oklahoma, *General Defense* 1194

Batson Nolan, PLC
    Clarksville, Tennessee, *General Defense* 1337

Baty, Holm, Numrich & Otto, P.C.
    Kansas City, Missouri, *General Defense* 874

Bauman Law Firm, P.C.
    St. Louis, Missouri, *General Defense* 888

Bauman Loewe Witt & Maxwell, PLLC
    Scottsdale, Arizona, *Subrogation* 1628

Bayer & Carey, P.C.
    Denver, Colorado, *General Defense* 278

Beckham & Beckham, P.A.
    Miami, Florida, *General Defense* 380
    Miami, Florida, *Subrogation* 1633

Beckstedt & Associates
    Christiansted, St. Croix, Virgin Islands, *General Defense* 1603

Bee Ready Fishbein Hatter & Donovan, LLP
    Mineola, New York, *General Defense* 1054

Beirne, Maynard & Parsons, LLP
    New Orleans, Louisiana, *General Defense* 686
    Dallas, Texas, *General Defense* 1389
    Houston, Texas, *General Defense* 1424
    San Antonio, Texas, *General Defense* 1461

Belgrade and O'Donnell, P.C.
    Chicago, Illinois, *General Defense* 500

Belsky & Associates
    San Diego, California, *General Defense* 237

Bennett & Guthrie, P.L.L.C.
    Winston-Salem, North Carolina, *General Defense* 1143

Bennett, Lotterhos, Sulser & Wilson, P.A.
    Jackson, Mississippi, *General Defense* 843

Benoit, Alexander, Harwood & High, LLP
    Twin Falls, Idaho, *General Defense* 489

ATTORNEYS - ALPHABETICAL FIRM INDEX

Bensinger, Cotant & Menkes, P.C.
    Gaylord, Michigan, *General Defense* 792
    Marquette, Michigan, *General Defense* 800

Law Offices of Karin A. Bentz, P.C.
    Charlotte Amalie, St. Thomas, Virgin Islands, *General Defense* 1601

Berchem, Moses & Devlin, PC
    Bridgeport, Connecticut, *General Defense* 302

Berk, Merchant & Sims, PLC
    Coral Gables, Florida, *General Defense* 345

Berman Berman Berman Schneider & Lowary LLP
    Los Angeles, California, *General Defense* 197

Bernard & Merrill, PLLC
    Manchester, New Hampshire, *General Defense* 950

Berrett & Hanna, L.C.
    Phoenix, Arizona, *General Defense* 145
    Phoenix, Arizona, *Subrogation* 1628
    Salt Lake City, Utah, *General Defense* 1475
    Salt Lake City, Utah, *Subrogation* 1663

Bersenas Jacobsen Chouest Thomson Blackburn LLP
    Toronto, Ontario, *General Defense* 1610

Best & Sharp
    Tulsa, Oklahoma, *General Defense* 1205

Best, Vanderlaan & Harrington
    Chicago, Illinois, *General Defense* 500
    Joliet, Illinois, *General Defense* 536
    Naperville, Illinois, *General Defense* 541
    Rockford, Illinois, *General Defense* 544

Bienvenu, Foster, Ryan & O'Bannon, LLC
    New Orleans, Louisiana, *General Defense* 686

Biggs, Ingram & Solop, PLLC
    Jackson, Mississippi, *General Defense* 843

Billet & Associates, L.L.C.
    Philadelphia, Pennsylvania, *General Defense* 1247

Billing, Cochran, Lyles, Mauro & Ramsey, P.A.
    Fort Lauderdale, Florida, *General Defense* 350
    West Palm Beach, Florida, *General Defense* 426

Roy H. Binder & Associates, LLC
    Wayne, New Jersey, *Subrogation* 1649

Bishop | Barry | Drath
    San Francisco, California, *General Defense* 246

Bishop & Hummert
    Dallas, Texas, *General Defense* 1389

Black McLaren Jones Ryland & Griffee, PC
    Memphis, Tennessee, *General Defense* 1351

Blake, Cassels & Graydon LLP
    Toronto, Ontario, *General Defense* 1611
    Toronto, Ontario, *Regulatory and Compliance* 1673

Blake, Kirchner, Symonds, Larson, Kennedy & Smith, P.C.
    Detroit, Michigan, *General Defense* 782

Blaney McMurtry LLP
    Toronto, Ontario, *General Defense* 1611

Bledsoe, Cathcart, Diestel, Pedersen & Treppa LLP
    San Francisco, California, *General Defense* 247

Bleyer and Bleyer
    Marion, Illinois, *General Defense* 537

ATTORNEYS - ALPHABETICAL FIRM INDEX

Bliss, Wilkens & Clayton
    Anchorage, Alaska, *General Defense* 138
    Tucson, Arizona, *General Defense* 153

Bloom, Murr, Accomazzo & Siler, PC
    Denver, Colorado, *General Defense* 278

Boeggeman, George & Corde, P.C.
    Albany, New York, *General Defense* 1022
    White Plains, New York, *General Defense* 1112

Boehl Stopher & Graves, LLP
    Lexington, Kentucky, *General Defense* 621
    Louisville, Kentucky, *General Defense* 633
    Paducah, Kentucky, *General Defense* 643
    Pikeville, Kentucky, *General Defense* 645

BOEHM BROWN HARWOOD, P.A.
    Orlando, Florida, *General Defense* 394

Boggs, Avellino, Lach & Boggs, LLC
    St. Louis, Missouri, *General Defense* 888
    St. Louis, Missouri, *Subrogation* 1645

Bolen, Parker, Brenner & Lee, Ltd.
    Alexandria, Louisiana, *General Defense* 648

Thomas M. Bona, P.C.
    White Plains, New York, *General Defense* 1112

Bonezzi Switzer Polito & Hupp Co. L.P.A.
    St. Petersburg, Florida, *General Defense* 413
    Cincinnati, Ohio, *General Defense* 1161
    Cleveland, Ohio, *General Defense* 1165

Boornazian, Jensen & Garthe
    Oakland, California, *General Defense* 215

Borowsky & Borowsky, LLC
    Shrewsbury, New Jersey, *General Defense* 994

Borton Petrini, LLP
    Bakersfield, California, *General Defense* 180
    Fresno, California, *General Defense* 187
    Los Angeles, California, *General Defense* 198
    Modesto, California, *General Defense* 213
    Sacramento, California, *General Defense* 229
    San Bernardino, California, *General Defense* 235
    San Diego, California, *General Defense* 237
    San Francisco, California, *General Defense* 248
    San Jose, California, *General Defense* 256
    Seal Beach, California, *General Defense* 263

Bosch Killman VanderWal, P.C.
    Grand Rapids, Michigan, *General Defense* 792
    Grand Rapids, Michigan, *Subrogation* 1643

Boston & Hughes, P.C.
    Houston, Texas, *General Defense* 1425

Bottaro, Morefield, Kubin & Yocum, P.C.
    Leawood, Kansas, *General Defense* 598

Bouvier Partnership, LLP
    Buffalo, New York, *General Defense* 1034
    Buffalo, New York, *Subrogation* 1651

Bowen, Radabaugh & Milton, P.C.
    Troy, Michigan, *General Defense* 807

ATTORNEYS - ALPHABETICAL FIRM INDEX

Bowles Rice LLP
    Lexington, Kentucky, *General Defense* 622
    Pittsburgh, Pennsylvania, *General Defense* 1265
    Charleston, West Virginia, *General Defense* 1553
    Martinsburg, West Virginia, *General Defense* 1562
    Morgantown, West Virginia, *General Defense* 1563
    Parkersburg, West Virginia, *General Defense* 1565

Boyd & Jenerette, P.A.
    Jacksonville, Florida, *General Defense* 369

Law Offices of Kurt Boyd
    Woodland Hills, California, *General Defense* 268

Boyer, Hebert, Abels & Angelle, LLC
    Baton Rouge, Louisiana, *General Defense* 653

Boylan Associates, P.C.
    Springfield, Vermont, *General Defense* 1489

Brackett & Ellis
    Fort Worth, Texas, *General Defense* 1418

Bradham, Benson, Lindley, Blevins, Bayliss & Wyatt of Florida East Coast, P.L.L.C.
    Fort Lauderdale, Florida, *General Defense* 351

Bradley Moore Primason Cuffe & Weber, LLP
    Lynn, Massachusetts, *General Defense* 767

Bradley & Riley PC
    Cedar Rapids, Iowa, *General Defense* 581
    Cedar Rapids, Iowa, *Investigation and Adjustment* 1677

Brady Law, Chartered
    Boise, Idaho, *General Defense* 478

Braff, Harris & Sukoneck
    Livingston, New Jersey, *General Defense* 974

Brasfield, Freeman, Goldis & Cash, P.A.
    St. Petersburg, Florida, *General Defense* 414

Brault Graham, LLC
    Rockville, Maryland, *General Defense* 741

Brault Palmer Steinhilber & Robbins LLP
    Fairfax, Virginia, *General Defense* 1499

Breaud & Meyers, P.L.C.
    Lafayette, Louisiana, *General Defense* 666

Breazeale, Sachse & Wilson, L.L.P.
    Baton Rouge, Louisiana, *General Defense* 654

Brennan, Harris & Rominger LLP
    Savannah, Georgia, *General Defense* 460

Brennan, Wasden & Painter, LLC
    Savannah, Georgia, *General Defense* 461

Brenner, Evans & Millman, P.C.
    Richmond, Virginia, *General Defense* 1512
    Richmond, Virginia, *Subrogation* 1664

Brenner, Monroe, Scott & Anderson, Ltd.
    Chicago, Illinois, *General Defense* 501

Bressler, Amery & Ross, PC
    Morristown, New Jersey, *General Defense* 978

Brewer, Krause, Brooks, Chastain & Burrow, PLLC
    Nashville, Tennessee, *General Defense* 1357

Brewster, Morhous, Cameron, Caruth, Moore, Kersey & Stafford, PLLC
    Bluefield, West Virginia, *General Defense* 1552

ATTORNEYS - ALPHABETICAL FIRM INDEX

Briggs and Morgan
    Minneapolis, Minnesota, *General Defense* 818

Brinson, Askew, Berry, Seigler, Richardson & Davis, LLP
    Rome, Georgia, *General Defense* 459

Britton, Smith, Peters & Kalail Co., L.P.A.
    Cleveland, Ohio, *General Defense* 1167

Brock Person Guerra Reyna, P.C.
    San Antonio, Texas, *General Defense* 1461

The Brophy Law Firm, P.C.
    Houston, Texas, *General Defense* 1426

Brotherton Ford Berry & Weaver, PLLC
    Greensboro, North Carolina, *General Defense* 1126

Brown & Adams, LLC
    Columbus, Georgia, *General Defense* 453

Albert T. Brown, Jr.
    Cincinnati, Ohio, *General Defense* 1161

Brown & Burnes
    Toronto, Ontario, *General Defense* 1611
    Toronto, Ontario, *Subrogation* 1666

Brown & Fortunato, P.C.
    Amarillo, Texas, *General Defense* 1372

Browning, Kaleczyc, Berry & Hoven, P.C.
    Bozeman, Montana, *General Defense* 905
    Great Falls, Montana, *General Defense* 908
    Helena, Montana, *General Defense* 911
    Missoula, Montana, *General Defense* 916

Brown Jacobson P.C.
    Norwich, Connecticut, *General Defense* 321

Brown Law Firm, P.C.
    Billings, Montana, *General Defense* 900
    Missoula, Montana, *General Defense* 916

Brown Moskowitz & Kallen, P.C.
    Summit, New Jersey, *General Defense* 997

Brown & Ruprecht, PC
    Kansas City, Missouri, *General Defense* 875

Brown Sims, P.C.
    Miami, Florida, *General Defense* 381
    New Orleans, Louisiana, *General Defense* 687
    Gulfport, Mississippi, *General Defense* 835
    Houston, Texas, *General Defense* 1426

Brownson & Ballou PLLP
    Minneapolis, Minnesota, *General Defense* 819

Brunini, Grantham, Grower & Hewes, PLLC
    Jackson, Mississippi, *General Defense* 844

Bryan, Nelson, Schroeder, Castigliola & Banahan, PLLC
    Pascagoula, Mississippi, *General Defense* 857

Bryant Barnes Blair & Benoit, LLP
    Christiansted, St. Croix, Virgin Islands, *General Defense* 1603

Buchhammer & Kehl, P.C.
    Cheyenne, Wyoming, *General Defense* 1592

Buckley & Buckley, L.L.C.
    St. Louis, Missouri, *General Defense* 889

Buckman & Gray
    Tulsa, Oklahoma, *General Defense* 1206

ATTORNEYS - ALPHABETICAL FIRM INDEX

Budd Larner, P.C.
    Short Hills, New Jersey, *General Defense* 993

Budow and Noble, P.C.
    Bethesda, Maryland, *General Defense* 738

Buglione, Hutton & DeYoe, L.L.C.
    Wayne, New Jersey, *General Defense* 1002

Bullard & Associates, P.C.
    Oklahoma City, Oklahoma, *General Defense* 1194
    Oklahoma City, Oklahoma, *Subrogation* 1655

Bullivant Houser Bailey PC
    San Francisco, California, *General Defense* 248
    Portland, Oregon, *General Defense* 1223
    Seattle, Washington, *General Defense* 1534

Bunnell & Woulfe P.A.
    Fort Lauderdale, Florida, *General Defense* 352

Burchak Law Office
    Yakima, Washington, *General Defense* 1548
    Yakima, Washington, *Subrogation* 1664

Burgess Roberts LLC
    Birmingham, Alabama, *General Defense* 80

Burke, Scolamiero, Mortati & Hurd, LLP
    Albany, New York, *General Defense* 1023

Burr, Pease & Kurtz
    Anchorage, Alaska, *General Defense* 138

Burt Barr & Associates, L.L.P.
    Dallas, Texas, *General Defense* 1390

Busch and Busch, LLP
    New Brunswick, New Jersey, *General Defense* 985

Busch, Zurbuch & Thompson, PLLC
    Elkins, West Virginia, *General Defense* 1557

Bush & Ramirez, L.L.C.
    Houston, Texas, *General Defense* 1427

Bush Rudnicki Shelton PC
    Arlington, Texas, *General Defense* 1374

Bussey & Lauve, LLC
    Alexandria, Louisiana, *General Defense* 648

Butler, Snow, O'Mara, Stevens & Cannada, PLLC
    Ridgeland, Mississippi, *General Defense* 859

Butt, Thornton & Baehr, P.C.
    Albuquerque, New Mexico, *General Defense* 1006
    Albuquerque, New Mexico, *Subrogation* 1650

Buyck, Sanders & Simmons, LLC
    Charleston, South Carolina, *General Defense* 1297

Byrne & Anderson, LLP
    Boston, Massachusetts, *General Defense* 750

C

Cabaniss, Johnston, Gardner, Dumas & O'Neal, LLP
    Birmingham, Alabama, *General Defense* 81
    Mobile, Alabama, *General Defense* 109

Cain & White, LLP
    Colorado Springs, Colorado, *General Defense* 274

Caldwell & Kearns
    Harrisburg, Pennsylvania, *General Defense* 1238

ATTORNEYS - ALPHABETICAL FIRM INDEX

Callahan & Fusco, LLC
Roseland, New Jersey, *General Defense* 991
New York, New York, *General Defense* 1060

Call & Hanson, P.C.
Anchorage, Alaska, *General Defense* 139

Cameron, Hodges, Coleman, LaPointe & Wright, P.A.
Daytona Beach, Florida, *General Defense* 346
Ocala, Florida, *General Defense* 392
Orlando, Florida, *General Defense* 395

Campbell & Campbell
Chattanooga, Tennessee, *General Defense* 1336

Campbell Campbell Edwards & Conroy
Boston, Massachusetts, *General Defense* 751

Campbell & Chadwick, P.C.
Dallas, Texas, *General Defense* 1391

Campoli & Monteleone
North Adams, Massachusetts, *General Defense* 768
Pittsfield, Massachusetts, *General Defense* 768

Cantrill Skinner Lewis Casey & Sorensen, LLP
Boise, Idaho, *General Defense* 478
Boise, Idaho, *Subrogation* 1635

Canty Lutz Delaquis Grant
Saint John, New Brunswick, *General Defense* 1609

Law Offices of Douglas L. Capdeville, P.C.
Christiansted, St. Croix, Virgin Islands, *General Defense* 1604

Carey Perkins LLP
Boise, Idaho, *General Defense* 479
Boise, Idaho, *Investigation and Adjustment* 1677
Idaho Falls, Idaho, *General Defense* 485

Carney Badley Spellman, P.S.
Seattle, Washington, *General Defense* 1534

Carr Law Office, LLC
Akron, Ohio, *General Defense* 1158

Carr Maloney P.C.
Washington, District of Columbia, *General Defense* 334

Carroll McNulty & Kull LLC
Basking Ridge, New Jersey, *General Defense* 957

Carroll Warren & Parker PLLC
Jackson, Mississippi, *General Defense* 844
Jackson, Mississippi, *Subrogation* 1645
Houston, Texas, *General Defense* 1427
Houston, Texas, *Subrogation* 1662

Casarino Christman Shalk Ransom & Doss, P.A.
Wilmington, Delaware, *General Defense* 328

Cascone & Kluepfel, LLP
Garden City, New York, *General Defense* 1042

Case Linden P.C.
Kansas City, Missouri, *General Defense* 875
St. Louis, Missouri, *General Defense* 889

Case Lombardi & Pettit
Honolulu, Hawaii, *General Defense* 470
Honolulu, Hawaii, *Subrogation* 1635

Cassiday Schade LLP
Chicago, Illinois, *General Defense* 502

2015 BEST'S DIRECTORIES OF RECOMMENDED INSURANCE ATTORNEYS AND ADJUSTERS — *For Current Listings access www.ambest.com/directories* — 13

ATTORNEYS - ALPHABETICAL FIRM INDEX

Castagna Scott, LLP
Austin, Texas, *General Defense* 1374

Catalano Gallardo & Petropoulos, LLP
Jericho, New York, *General Defense* 1047

Catania, Mahon, Milligram & Rider, PLLC
Newburgh, New York, *General Defense* 1093

Cathcart & Dooley
Oklahoma City, Oklahoma, *General Defense* 1195
Oklahoma City, Oklahoma, *Subrogation* 1656

Catri, Holton, Kessler & Kessler, P.A.
Fort Lauderdale, Florida, *General Defense* 352
Fort Lauderdale, Florida, *Subrogation* 1633

Cavett & Fulton
Tucson, Arizona, *General Defense* 153

Cella - Flanagan, P.C.
New Haven, Connecticut, *General Defense* 314

Cesari, Werner & Moriarty
San Francisco, California, *General Defense* 249

Chamberlain D'Amanda
Rochester, New York, *General Defense* 1098

Chamberlain McHaney
Austin, Texas, *General Defense* 1375
Austin, Texas, *Subrogation* 1661
San Antonio, Texas, *General Defense* 1462
San Antonio, Texas, *Subrogation* 1663

Chamblee, Ryan, Kershaw & Anderson, P.C.
Dallas, Texas, *General Defense* 1391

Chance & McCann, L.L.C.
Bridgeton, New Jersey, *General Defense* 961

Cheadle Law
Nashville, Tennessee, *General Defense* 1358

Cheek Law Firm, P.L.L.C.
Oklahoma City, Oklahoma, *General Defense* 1195

Chee, Markham & Feldman
Honolulu, Hawaii, *General Defense* 471

Chelus, Herdzik, Speyer & Monte, P.C.
Buffalo, New York, *General Defense* 1035

Cherry, Seymour & Baronian, P.C.
Richmond, Virginia, *General Defense* 1512

Childs, Hester & Love, P.A.
Jacksonville, Florida, *General Defense* 370

Chisenhall, Nestrud & Julian, P.A.
Little Rock, Arkansas, *General Defense* 167

Choate, Hall & Stewart LLP
Boston, Massachusetts, *General Defense* 751

Christensen Ehret
Sacramento, California, *General Defense* 229
Torrance, California, *General Defense* 264
Chicago, Illinois, *General Defense* 505

Kevin Christensen & Associates, LLC
New Orleans, Louisiana, *General Defense* 687

ATTORNEYS - ALPHABETICAL FIRM INDEX

Cipriani & Werner, P.C.
   Wilmington, Delaware, *General Defense* 329
   Marlton, New Jersey, *General Defense* 976
   Harrisburg, Pennsylvania, *General Defense* 1239
   Philadelphia, Pennsylvania, *General Defense* 1248
   Pittsburgh, Pennsylvania, *General Defense* 1265
   Scranton, Pennsylvania, *General Defense* 1274
   Charleston, West Virginia, *General Defense* 1553
   Wheeling, West Virginia, *General Defense* 1566

Citron & Citron
   Santa Monica, California, *General Defense* 262

Civerolo, Gralow, Hill & Curtis
   Albuquerque, New Mexico, *General Defense* 1008

Clark, Butler, Walsh & Hamann
   Waterloo, Iowa, *General Defense* 590

Clark, Hunt, Ahern & Embry
   Cambridge, Massachusetts, *General Defense* 765
   Cambridge, Massachusetts, *Subrogation* 1642

Clark, Mize & Linville, Chartered
   Salina, Kansas, *General Defense* 604

Clarkson, Walsh, Terrell & Coulter, P.A.
   Greenville, South Carolina, *General Defense* 1315

Clausen Miller P.C.
   Chicago, Illinois, *General Defense* 506
   Chicago, Illinois, *Subrogation* 1635

Clawson & Staubes, LLC
   Charlotte, North Carolina, *General Defense* 1119
   Charleston, South Carolina, *General Defense* 1297
   Columbia, South Carolina, *General Defense* 1307
   Greenville, South Carolina, *General Defense* 1316

Cleary Shahi & Aicher, P.C.
   Rutland, Vermont, *General Defense* 1487

Clements & Knock, LLP
   San Diego, California, *General Defense* 238

Clifford & Brown
   Bakersfield, California, *General Defense* 181

Cline Williams
   Fort Collins, Colorado, *General Defense* 295
   Aurora, Nebraska, *General Defense* 922
   Lincoln, Nebraska, *General Defense* 923
   Omaha, Nebraska, *General Defense* 927
   Scottsbluff, Nebraska, *General Defense* 933

Clinton & Clinton
   Irvine, California, *General Defense* 189
   Long Beach, California, *General Defense* 195
   Los Angeles, California, *General Defense* 199
   Sacramento, California, *General Defense* 229
   San Diego, California, *General Defense* 238
   San Francisco, California, *General Defense* 250

Clyde & Co
   Montreal, Quebec, *General Defense* 1613
   Montreal, Quebec, *Subrogation* 1667

Cobb Martinez Woodward PLLC
   Dallas, Texas, *General Defense* 1391

Law Offices of Glenn R. Cochran
   Princeton, New Jersey, *General Defense* 990
   Princeton, New Jersey, *Subrogation* 1648

ATTORNEYS - ALPHABETICAL FIRM INDEX

J. M. Cohen, LLC
    Philadelphia, Pennsylvania, *Subrogation* 1657

Cohen & Lombardo, P.C.
    Buffalo, New York, *General Defense* 1037

Coleman Lochmiller & Bond
    Elizabethtown, Kentucky, *General Defense* 616

Coleman Talley LLP
    Valdosta, Georgia, *General Defense* 465

Cole & Moore P.S.C.
    Bowling Green, Kentucky, *General Defense* 612

Coles, Baldwin & Kaiser, LLC
    Bridgeport, Connecticut, *General Defense* 303

Law Offices of Collier-Magar, P.C.
    Indianapolis, Indiana, *General Defense* 560

Collins Collins Muir + Stewart LLP
    Pasadena, California, *General Defense* 220

Collins Einhorn Farrell PC
    Southfield, Michigan, *General Defense* 802

Collins, Fitzpatrick & Schoene, LLP
    White Plains, New York, *General Defense* 1113

Colodny Fass, P.A.
    Fort Lauderdale, Florida, *General Defense* 353
    Fort Lauderdale, Florida, *Regulatory and Compliance* 1670
    Tallahassee, Florida, *General Defense* 416
    Tallahassee, Florida, *Regulatory and Compliance* 1670

Colquhoun & Colquhoun
    Morristown, New Jersey, *General Defense* 979
    Morristown, New Jersey, *Subrogation* 1648

Ronald H. Colvin, P.A.
    Spartanburg, South Carolina, *General Defense* 1321

Congdon Flaherty O'Callaghan Reid Donlon Travis & Fishlinger
    Uniondale, New York, *General Defense* 1106
    Uniondale, New York, *Subrogation* 1654

Conklin & Conklin, LLC
    Chicago, Illinois, *General Defense* 509

Conlin, McKenney & Philbrick, P.C.
    Ann Arbor, Michigan, *General Defense* 778

Connors & Connors, PC
    Staten Island, New York, *General Defense* 1102

Connors & Corcoran PLLC
    Rochester, New York, *General Defense* 1099

Connor Weber & Oberlies
    Philadelphia, Pennsylvania, *General Defense* 1249

Conradi Anderson, PLLC
    Kalispell, Montana, *General Defense* 914

Conroy Simberg
    Fort Myers, Florida, *General Defense* 361
    Hollywood, Florida, *General Defense* 366
    Jacksonville, Florida, *General Defense* 370
    Miami, Florida, *General Defense* 381
    Naples, Florida, *General Defense* 390
    Orlando, Florida, *General Defense* 395
    Pensacola, Florida, *General Defense* 406
    Tallahassee, Florida, *General Defense* 416
    Tampa, Florida, *General Defense* 419
    West Palm Beach, Florida, *General Defense* 426

ATTORNEYS - ALPHABETICAL FIRM INDEX

Conway, Farrell, Curtin & Kelly, P.C.
New York, New York, *General Defense* 1061

Cook, Netter, Cloonan, Kurtz & Murphy, P.C.
Kingston, New York, *General Defense* 1048

CooleySublett PLC
Roanoke, Virginia, *General Defense* 1519

Cooney, Scully and Dowling
Hartford, Connecticut, *General Defense* 306

Cooney Trybus Kwavnick Peets
Fort Lauderdale, Florida, *General Defense* 354

Cooper Levenson, P.A.
Atlantic City, New Jersey, *General Defense* 956

Cooper & Scully, P.C.
San Francisco, California, *General Defense* 250
Dallas, Texas, *General Defense* 1392
Houston, Texas, *General Defense* 1427
Sherman, Texas, *General Defense* 1465

Corette Black Carlson & Mickelson
Butte, Montana, *General Defense* 906

Cornelius & Collins, LLP
Nashville, Tennessee, *General Defense* 1359

Cornell & Gollub
Boston, Massachusetts, *General Defense* 752

Coronado Katz LLC
Kansas City, Missouri, *General Defense* 876

Corrigan & Chandler LLC
Charleston, South Carolina, *General Defense* 1298

Cosio Law Group
Miami, Florida, *General Defense* 381

Cosmich Simmons & Brown, PLLC
Jackson, Mississippi, *General Defense* 845

Cottrell Solensky & Semple, P.A.
Newark, New Jersey, *General Defense* 986

Coughlin Betke LLP
Boston, Massachusetts, *General Defense* 752

Michael I. Coulson, P.A.
Jacksonville, Florida, *General Defense* 371

Countryman & McDaniel
Los Angeles, California, *General Defense* 199

Cousineau McGuire Chartered
Minneapolis, Minnesota, *General Defense* 820

Cowsert & Avery, LLP
Athens, Georgia, *General Defense* 435

Cox, Zwerner, Gambill & Sullivan, LLP
Terre Haute, Indiana, *General Defense* 576

Craig & Craig, LLC
Mattoon, Illinois, *General Defense* 538
Mount Vernon, Illinois, *General Defense* 540

Craig, Terrill, Hale & Grantham, L.L.P.
Lubbock, Texas, *General Defense* 1449

Cranfill Sumner & Hartzog LLP
Raleigh, North Carolina, *General Defense* 1133

Cray Huber Horstman Heil & VanAusdal LLC
Chicago, Illinois, *General Defense* 509

ATTORNEYS - ALPHABETICAL FIRM INDEX

Cresswell, Echeguren, Rodgers & Harvey
    Oakland, California, *General Defense* 217

Crim & Bassler L.L.P.
    Atlanta, Georgia, *General Defense* 436

Crivello Carlson, S.C.
    Milwaukee, Wisconsin, *General Defense* 1578

Cross, Gunter, Witherspoon & Galchus, P.C.
    Little Rock, Arkansas, *General Defense* 168

Crossley McIntosh Collier Hanley & Edes, PLLC
    Wilmington, North Carolina, *General Defense* 1141

Crowley Fleck PLLP
    Billings, Montana, *General Defense* 901
    Bozeman, Montana, *General Defense* 905
    Butte, Montana, *General Defense* 907
    Helena, Montana, *General Defense*. 912
    Kalispell, Montana, *General Defense* 915
    Missoula, Montana, *General Defense* 917
    Bismarck, North Dakota, *General Defense* 1146
    Williston, North Dakota, *General Defense* 1154
    Casper, Wyoming, *General Defense* 1590
    Cheyenne, Wyoming, *General Defense*. 1592
    Sheridan, Wyoming, *General Defense* 1598

Cuisinier & Farahvar, Ltd.
    Chicago, Illinois, *General Defense* 510

Cummings, King & MacDonald
    Boston, Massachusetts, *General Defense*. 753

Law Offices of Joseph F. Cunningham & Associates, PLC
    Washington, District of Columbia, *General Defense* 335
    Arlington, Virginia, *General Defense* 1494

The Law Offices of Craig P. Curcio
    Middletown, New York, *General Defense* 1053

Curley & Curley, P.C.
    Braintree, Massachusetts, *General Defense* 764

CURL & GLASSON, P.L.C.
    Tucson, Arizona, *General Defense* 153

Currie Johnson Griffin & Myers, P.A.
    Biloxi, Mississippi, *General Defense*. 830
    Jackson, Mississippi, *General Defense* 846

D

Dabney and Dabney
    Vicksburg, Mississippi, *General Defense* 865

Daily & Woods, P.L.L.C.
    Fort Smith, Arkansas, *General Defense* 161

Dalan, Katz & Siegel, P.L.
    Clearwater, Florida, *General Defense* 344

Dale and Klein, L.L.P
    McAllen, Texas, *General Defense* 1454

Daley & Heft, LLP
    San Diego, California, *General Defense* 238

Daniels Law Firm, PLLC
    Charleston, West Virginia, *General Defense* 1554

Davenport, Evans, Hurwitz & Smith, LLP
    Sioux Falls, South Dakota, *General Defense* 1329

Davenport, Files & Kelly
    Monroe, Louisiana, *General Defense*. 682

ATTORNEYS - ALPHABETICAL FIRM INDEX

Davids & Cohen, P.C.
Wellesley, Massachusetts, *General Defense* 772

Davidson, Fuller & Sloan, LLP
Atlanta, Georgia, *General Defense* 437

Davis, Clark, Butt, Carithers & Taylor, PLC
Fayetteville, Arkansas, *General Defense* 159

Law Office of Dale L. Davis
Springfield, Missouri, *General Defense* 883

Davis Hatley Haffeman & Tighe, P.C.
Great Falls, Montana, *General Defense* 909

Davison Rugeley, LLP
Wichita Falls, Texas, *General Defense* 1471

Davis, Parry & Tyler
Philadelphia, Pennsylvania, *General Defense* 1250

Davis & Young
Cleveland, Ohio, *General Defense* 1168

Deacy and Deacy, LLP
Kansas City, Missouri, *General Defense* 876

Dean, Ringers, Morgan and Lawton, P.A.
Orlando, Florida, *General Defense* 396

Deasey, Mahoney & Valentini, LTD
Haddonfield, New Jersey, *General Defense* 971
Media, Pennsylvania, *General Defense* 1246
Philadelphia, Pennsylvania, *General Defense* 1250

Declues, Burkett & Thompson, LLP
Huntington Beach, California, *General Defense* 188

Degan, Blanchard & Nash
Baton Rouge, Louisiana, *General Defense* 654
New Orleans, Louisiana, *General Defense* 687

Deisch, Marion & Klaus, P.C.
Denver, Colorado, *General Defense* 279
Denver, Colorado, *Subrogation* 1632

DeKoter, Thole & Dawson, P.L.C.
Sibley, Iowa, *General Defense* 588

Dell Graham, P.A.
Gainesville, Florida, *General Defense* 364

Del Sole & Del Sole, L.L.P.
New Haven, Connecticut, *General Defense* 315
Wallingford, Connecticut, *General Defense* 325

Demarest e Almeida Advogados
Sao Paulo, Brazil, *General Defense* 1618

Dennis, Jackson, Martin & Fontela, P.A.
Tallahassee, Florida, *General Defense* 416

Denton & Keuler, LLP
Paducah, Kentucky, *General Defense* 644

DeRouen Law Firm
New Orleans, Louisiana, *General Defense* 688

Desmarais, Ewing & Johnston, PLLC
Manchester, New Hampshire, *General Defense* 951

Deusner & Kennedy
Selmer, Tennessee, *General Defense* 1367

Devine, Millimet & Branch, P.A.
Manchester, New Hampshire, *General Defense* 952

ATTORNEYS - ALPHABETICAL FIRM INDEX

Devlin Associates, P.C.
    Philadelphia, Pennsylvania, *General Defense* 1252
    Philadelphia, Pennsylvania, *Subrogation* 1657

Dewhirst & Dolven, LLC
    Colorado Springs, Colorado, *General Defense* 275
    Denver, Colorado, *General Defense* 279
    Fort Collins, Colorado, *General Defense* 295
    Grand Junction, Colorado, *General Defense* 297
    Dallas, Texas, *General Defense* 1393
    Port Isabel, Texas, *General Defense* 1459
    Salt Lake City, Utah, *General Defense* 1475

D'Hondt de Caritat & Partners
    Brussels, Belgium, *General Defense* 1618

Dickie, McCamey & Chilcote, P.C.
    Wilmington, Delaware, *General Defense* 329
    Haddonfield, New Jersey, *General Defense* 971
    Charlotte, North Carolina, *General Defense* 1120
    Raleigh, North Carolina, *General Defense* 1133
    Cleveland, Ohio, *General Defense* 1170
    Columbus, Ohio, *General Defense* 1178
    Steubenville, Ohio, *General Defense* 1186
    Harrisburg, Pennsylvania, *General Defense* 1240
    Philadelphia, Pennsylvania, *General Defense* 1252
    Pittsburgh, Pennsylvania, *General Defense* 1266
    Lancaster, South Carolina, *General Defense* 1318
    Wheeling, West Virginia, *General Defense* 1566

Dickinson Wright PLLC
    Phoenix, Arizona, *General Defense* 146
    Ann Arbor, Michigan, *General Defense* 779
    Detroit, Michigan, *General Defense* 783
    Lansing, Michigan, *General Defense* 798
    Troy, Michigan, *General Defense* 809
    Nashville, Tennessee, *General Defense* 1360

Diepenbrock & Cotter, LLP
    Sacramento, California, *General Defense* 230

Dinsmore & Shohl LLP
    Chicago, Illinois, *General Defense* 510
    Lexington, Kentucky, *General Defense* 622
    Cincinnati, Ohio, *General Defense* 1162

Dix & Associates, P.L.L.C.
    Murfreesboro, Tennessee, *General Defense* 1356

The Dixon Law Firm
    Denver, Colorado, *General Defense* 280

Doherty & Progar LLC
    Chicago, Illinois, *General Defense* 511

Doherty, Wallace, Pillsbury & Murphy, P.C.
    Springfield, Massachusetts, *General Defense* 770

Dolden Wallace Folick LLP
    Kelowna, British Columbia, *General Defense* 1606
    Vancouver, British Columbia, *General Defense* 1606
    Toronto, Ontario, *General Defense* 1612

Donahue, Durham & Noonan, P.C.
    Guilford, Connecticut, *General Defense* 306

Donnell, Abernethy & Kieschnick, PC
    Corpus Christi, Texas, *General Defense* 1384
    Edinburg, Texas, *General Defense* 1413

ATTORNEYS - ALPHABETICAL FIRM INDEX

Donohue, Sabo, Varley & Huttner, LLP
    Albany, New York, *General Defense*..1024
    Albany, New York, *Subrogation*...1650

Dorsey & Whitney LLP
    New York, New York, *General Defense*..1061

Dover Dixon Horne PLLC
    Little Rock, Arkansas, *General Defense*..169

Doyen Sebesta Ltd., LLP
    Houston, Texas, *General Defense*..1428

Drake, Loeb, Heller, Kennedy, Gogerty, Gaba & Rodd PLLC
    New Windsor, New York, *General Defense*...1059

Drake, Narup & Mead, P.C.
    Springfield, Illinois, *General Defense*..546

Drew Eckl & Farnham, LLP
    Atlanta, Georgia, *General Defense*..437

Dubyak Connick Thompson Sammon & Bloom, LLC
    Cleveland, Ohio, *General Defense*...1170

Dudley, Topper and Feuerzeig, L.L.P.
    Charlotte Amalie, St. Thomas, Virgin Islands, *General Defense*.................1602

Dukes, Ryan, Meyer, & Freed Ltd.
    Danville, Illinois, *General Defense*...530

Dunlap & Soderland, P.S.
    Seattle, Washington, *General Defense*..1536

Dunn & Dunn P.C.
    Salt Lake City, Utah, *General Defense*..1476

Dunn, Nutter & Morgan L.L.P.
    Texarkana, Texas, *General Defense*...1467
    Texarkana, Texas, *Subrogation*..1663

Durbin, Larimore & Bialick
    Oklahoma City, Oklahoma, *General Defense*......................................1196

Robert C. Duthie, III, P.C.
    Durango, Colorado, *General Defense*..293

Dutton Brock LLP
    Toronto, Ontario, *General Defense*...1612

Dyer, Brown
    London, Ontario, *General Defense*...1610

Dynan & Associates, P.S.
    Seattle, Washington, *General Defense*..1536
    Tacoma, Washington, *General Defense*..1547

E

S. Wayne Easterling
    Hattiesburg, Mississippi, *General Defense*..839

Ebeltoft . Sickler . Lawyers PLLC
    Dickinson, North Dakota, *General Defense*..1147

Eccleston and Wolf
    Washington, District of Columbia, *General Defense*..............................335
    Baltimore, Maryland, *General Defense*..728
    Fairfax, Virginia, *General Defense*...1500

Eckenrode - Maupin
    St. Louis, Missouri, *General Defense*..890

Eckert - Kost, LLP
    Rhinelander, Wisconsin, *General Defense*..1582

ATTORNEYS - ALPHABETICAL FIRM INDEX

Edelstein Law, LLP
  Philadelphia, Pennsylvania, *General Defense* 1252

Eggleston & Briscoe, LLP
  Houston, Texas, *General Defense* 1428
  Houston, Texas, *Subrogation* 1662

Eiche & Frakes, S.C.
  Milwaukee, Wisconsin, *General Defense* 1580

Ekvall & Byrne, L.L.P.
  Dallas, Texas, *General Defense* 1394

Elam & Burke, P.A.
  Boise, Idaho, *General Defense* 480

Elardo, Bragg, Appel & Rossi, P.C.
  Phoenix, Arizona, *General Defense* 146

Ellis, Buckholts & Hicks
  Duncan, Oklahoma, *General Defense* 1191

Elverson Vasey
  Des Moines, Iowa, *General Defense* 584

Ely & Isenberg, L.L.C.
  Birmingham, Alabama, *General Defense* 82

Engles, Ketcham, Olson & Keith, P.C.
  Omaha, Nebraska, *General Defense* 927
  Omaha, Nebraska, *Subrogation* 1645

Ennis, Baynard, Morton & Medlin, P.A.
  Wilmington, North Carolina, *General Defense* 1141
  Wilmington, North Carolina, *Subrogation* 1655

Ensz & Jester, P.C.
  Kansas City, Missouri, *General Defense* 877

Epperson & Owens
  Salt Lake City, Utah, *General Defense* 1476

Ericksen Arbuthnot
  Bakersfield, California, *General Defense* 183
  Fresno, California, *General Defense* 188
  Los Angeles, California, *General Defense* 199
  Oakland, California, *General Defense* 217
  Sacramento, California, *General Defense* 231
  San Francisco, California, *General Defense* 250
  San Jose, California, *General Defense* 257
  Walnut Creek, California, *General Defense* 266

Erickson & Sederstrom, P.C.
  Omaha, Nebraska, *General Defense* 928

Erickson, Thorpe & Swainston, Ltd.
  Reno, Nevada, *General Defense* 943

Eskins, King & Marney, P.C.
  Memphis, Tennessee, *General Defense* 1351

Esty & Buckmir, LLC
  New Haven, Connecticut, *General Defense* 316

Evans & Clesi, PLC
  New Orleans, Louisiana, *General Defense* 689

Evans & Co.
  Durango, Colorado, *General Defense* 294
  New Orleans, Louisiana, *General Defense* 689
  Farmington, New Mexico, *General Defense* 1014
  Greensboro, North Carolina, *General Defense* 1126
  Houston, Texas, *General Defense* 1430
  Jackson, Wyoming, *General Defense* 1595

ATTORNEYS - ALPHABETICAL FIRM INDEX

Evans, Philp LLP
    Hamilton, Ontario, *General Defense* 1610

F

Fahl & Associates, P.C.
    Houston, Texas, *General Defense* 1430

Fain, Major & Brennan, P.C.
    Atlanta, Georgia, *General Defense* 438

Faircloth, Melton & Keiser, LLC
    Alexandria, Louisiana, *General Defense* 649
    Baton Rouge, Louisiana, *General Defense* 654

Fanning Harper Martinson Brandt & Kutchin, P.C.
    Dallas, Texas, *General Defense* 1395

Fann & Rea, P.C.
    Birmingham, Alabama, *General Defense* 82
    Birmingham, Alabama, *Investigation and Adjustment* 1676

Farmer Case & Fedor
    San Diego, California, *General Defense* 239

Farrell, White & Legg, PLLC
    Huntington, West Virginia, *General Defense* 1558

Faure Holden Attorneys at Law, P.C.
    Great Falls, Montana, *General Defense* 909

F&B Law Firm, P.C.
    Huntsville, Alabama, *General Defense* 104

Fee, Smith, Sharp & Vitullo, LLP
    Dallas, Texas, *General Defense* 1396

Feikens, Stevens, Kennedy & Galbraith, P.C.
    Detroit, Michigan, *General Defense* 783

Feirich/Mager/Green/Ryan
    Carbondale, Illinois, *General Defense* 494

Feldman Kieffer, LLP
    Buffalo, New York, *General Defense* 1038

Felt, Martin, Frazier & Weldon, P.C.
    Billings, Montana, *General Defense* 902

Fenchel, Doster & Buck, P.L.C.
    Algona, Iowa, *General Defense* 580

Fenley & Bate, L.L.P.
    Livingston, Texas, *General Defense* 1449
    Lufkin, Texas, *General Defense* 1451

Ferguson & Ferguson
    Bloomington, Indiana, *General Defense* 554

Ferguson, Schetelich & Ballew, P.A.
    Baltimore, Maryland, *General Defense* 729

Ferry, Joseph & Pearce, P.A.
    Wilmington, Delaware, *General Defense* 330

Fertig & Gramling
    Fort Lauderdale, Florida, *General Defense* 354

Fetherston, Edmonds, LLP
    Salem, Oregon, *General Defense* 1227

Fields, Howell, Athans & McLaughlin LLP
    Atlanta, Georgia, *General Defense* 439

Fillmore Riley LLP
    Winnipeg, Manitoba, *General Defense* 1607
    Winnipeg, Manitoba, *Subrogation* 1665

ATTORNEYS - ALPHABETICAL FIRM INDEX

Finan Law Offices
North Kingstown, Rhode Island, *General Defense* 1284

Fine & Hatfield
Evansville, Indiana, *General Defense* 556

Fine & Wyatt P.C.
Scranton, Pennsylvania, *General Defense* 1275

Finley, Alt, Smith, Scharnberg, Craig, Hilmes & Gaffney P.C.
Des Moines, Iowa, *General Defense* 584

Firestein & Firestein
Los Angeles, California, *Subrogation* 1630

Fischl, Culp, McMillin, Chaffin, Bahner & Long, L.L.P.
Ardmore, Oklahoma, *General Defense* 1190

Fisher Kanaris, P.C.
Chicago, Illinois, *General Defense* 511
Chicago, Illinois, *Subrogation* 1636

Fitch, Johnson, Larson & Held, P.A.
Minneapolis, Minnesota, *General Defense* 820

Fitzgerald, Schorr, Barmettler & Brennan, P.C., L.L.O.
Omaha, Nebraska, *General Defense* 929

Fitzhugh & Elliott, P.C.
Houston, Texas, *General Defense* 1431

Fitzpatrick & Hunt, Tucker, Collier, Pagano, Aubert, LLP
Los Angeles, California, *General Defense* 200
Princeton, New Jersey, *General Defense* 990
New York, New York, *General Defense* 1061

Flanagan and DiBernardo, LLP
Lancaster, Pennsylvania, *General Defense* 1245

Flanigan, Lasley & Moore, LLP
Carthage, Missouri, *General Defense* 870

Fletcher, Farley, Shipman, & Salinas, L.L.P.
Austin, Texas, *General Defense* 1376
Dallas, Texas, *General Defense* 1397

Flom Law Office, P.A.
Fargo, North Dakota, *General Defense* 1148

Flournoy & Galvagni, P.C.
Pittsfield, Massachusetts, *General Defense* 769

Floyd Pflueger & Ringer, P.S.
Seattle, Washington, *General Defense* 1536

Law Offices of Richard A. Fogel, P.C.
Islip, New York, *General Defense* 1046

Fogle Keller Purdy, PLLC
Louisville, Kentucky, *General Defense* 634
Louisville, Kentucky, *Subrogation* 1640

Forbes, Foster & Pool, LLC
Savannah, Georgia, *General Defense* 462

Ford, Parshall & Baker
Columbia, Missouri, *General Defense* 871

Forrester & Brim, LLP
Gainesville, Georgia, *General Defense* 455

Forrester & Clark
Baton Rouge, Louisiana, *General Defense* 655

ATTORNEYS - ALPHABETICAL FIRM INDEX

Forry Ullman
- Bethlehem, Pennsylvania, *General Defense* ... 1233
- King of Prussia, Pennsylvania, *General Defense* ... 1243
- Philadelphia, Pennsylvania, *General Defense* ... 1253
- Reading, Pennsylvania, *General Defense* ... 1273

Forsberg & Umlauf, P.S.
- Seattle, Washington, *General Defense* ... 1537

Foster & Company
- Fredericton, New Brunswick, *General Defense* ... 1608

Foster, Meadows & Ballard, P.C.
- Detroit, Michigan, *General Defense* ... 784
- Detroit, Michigan, *Subrogation* ... 1643

Foster Swift Collins & Smith, P.C.
- Lansing, Michigan, *General Defense* ... 798

Foulston Siefkin LLP
- Wichita, Kansas, *General Defense* ... 607

Fountain, Bruce & Mellencamp, PLLC
- The Woodlands, Texas, *General Defense* ... 1468

Fowler Bell PLLC
- Lexington, Kentucky, *General Defense* ... 622

The Fowler Law Firm, PC
- Austin, Texas, *General Defense* ... 1376

Fowler, Schimberg & Flanagan, P.C.
- Denver, Colorado, *General Defense* ... 280

Frailey, Chaffin, Cordell, Perryman, Sterkel, McCalla & Brown, L.L.P.
- Chickasha, Oklahoma, *General Defense* ... 1190
- Chickasha, Oklahoma, *Subrogation* ... 1655

Franke & Salloum, PLLC
- Gulfport, Mississippi, *General Defense* ... 835

Franke Schultz & Mullen, P.C.
- Kansas City, Missouri, *General Defense* ... 877
- Springfield, Missouri, *General Defense* ... 883

Franklin, Cooper & Marcus PLLC
- Chattanooga, Tennessee, *General Defense* ... 1336
- Chattanooga, Tennessee, *Subrogation* ... 1660

Franklin, Gordon & Hobgood
- Madisonville, Kentucky, *General Defense* ... 642

Fredrickson, Mazeika & Grant, LLP
- San Diego, California, *General Defense* ... 239

Freise and Ferguson PLLC
- Seattle, Washington, *General Defense* ... 1538

French & Casey, LLP
- New York, New York, *General Defense* ... 1062

Frenkel Lambert Weiss Weisman & Gordon, LLP
- Bay Shore, New York, *General Defense* ... 1029

Freund, Freeze & Arnold, A Legal Professional Association
- Fort Mitchell, Kentucky, *General Defense* ... 617
- Cincinnati, Ohio, *General Defense* ... 1162
- Columbus, Ohio, *General Defense* ... 1178
- Dayton, Ohio, *General Defense* ... 1181

Friedenthal, Heffernan & Klein, LLP
- Pasadena, California, *General Defense* ... 220

Friedlander Misler, PLLC
- Washington, District of Columbia, *General Defense* ... 335

ATTORNEYS - ALPHABETICAL FIRM INDEX

Friedman, Dazzio, Zulanas & Bowling, P.C.
  Birmingham, Alabama, *General Defense* 83

Frith Anderson & Peake, P.C.
  Roanoke, Virginia, *General Defense* 1519
  Roanoke, Virginia, *Subrogation* 1664
  Roanoke, Virginia, *Investigation and Adjustment* 1679

Frye Law Firm, P.A.
  Little Rock, Arkansas, *General Defense* 169

Fuerste, Carew, Juergens & Sudmeier, P.C.
  Dubuque, Iowa, *General Defense* 586

Fulcher Hagler LLP
  Augusta, Georgia, *General Defense* 449

Fuller and Vaughn
  Kingsport, Tennessee, *General Defense* 1345

Fuller & Williamson, LLP
  Sioux Falls, South Dakota, *General Defense* 1331

Furniss, Davis, Rashkind and Saunders, P.C.
  Norfolk, Virginia, *General Defense* 1506

G

Gabert, Williams, Konz & Lawrynk, LLP
  Appleton, Wisconsin, *General Defense* 1570
  Appleton, Wisconsin, *Subrogation* 1665

GableGotwals
  Oklahoma City, Oklahoma, *General Defense* 1198
  Tulsa, Oklahoma, *General Defense* 1206

Gaglione, Dolan & Kaplan
  Los Angeles, California, *General Defense* 200

Gaines Gault Hendrix P.C.
  Birmingham, Alabama, *General Defense* 84
  Huntsville, Alabama, *General Defense* 105

Galbraith, Delie & James, P.C.
  Detroit, Michigan, *General Defense* 784

Gallagher Kane Amai, Attorneys at Law
  Honolulu, Hawaii, *General Defense* 471

Gallagher Sharp
  Cleveland, Ohio, *General Defense* 1171

Gallagher, Walker, Bianco & Plastaras, LLP
  Mineola, New York, *General Defense* 1054

Gallo Vitucci Klar LLP
  Hackensack, New Jersey, *General Defense* 969
  New York, New York, *General Defense* 1062

Galloway, Johnson, Tompkins, Burr & Smith
  Mobile, Alabama, *General Defense* 109
  Pensacola, Florida, *General Defense* 406
  Tampa, Florida, *General Defense* 419
  Atlanta, Georgia, *General Defense* 440
  Lafayette, Louisiana, *General Defense* 666
  Mandeville, Louisiana, *General Defense* 674
  New Orleans, Louisiana, *General Defense* 690
  Gulfport, Mississippi, *General Defense* 836
  St. Louis, Missouri, *General Defense* 890
  Houston, Texas, *General Defense* 1431

Galloway, Wettermark, Everest & Rutens, LLP
  Mobile, Alabama, *General Defense* 109

ATTORNEYS - ALPHABETICAL FIRM INDEX

Gannam, Gnann & Steinmetz LLC
Savannah, Georgia, *General Defense* 463

Garan Lucow Miller, P.C.
Merrillville, Indiana, *General Defense* 570
Ann Arbor, Michigan, *General Defense* 779
Detroit, Michigan, *General Defense* 785
Flint, Michigan, *General Defense* 791
Grand Rapids, Michigan, *General Defense* 793
Lansing, Michigan, *General Defense* 799
Marquette, Michigan, *General Defense* 800
Port Huron, Michigan, *General Defense* 802
Traverse City, Michigan, *General Defense* 807
Troy, Michigan, *General Defense* 809

Gardner, Willis, Sweat & Handelman, LLP
Albany, Georgia, *General Defense* 434

Garlington, Lohn & Robinson, PLLP
Missoula, Montana, *General Defense* 917

Thomas D. Garlitz, PLLC
Charlotte, North Carolina, *General Defense* 1120

Garofalo, Schreiber & Storm, Chartered
Chicago, Illinois, *General Defense* 512

Garrett & Jensen
Riverside, California, *General Defense* 226

Gartner + Bloom, P.C.
New York, New York, *General Defense* 1063

Garvey, Ballou & Rogalski
Toms River, New Jersey, *General Defense* 997

Gasco Goodhue St-Germain S.E.N.C.R.L./L.L.P.
Montreal, Quebec, *General Defense* 1613

Gascoyne & Bullion, PC
Sugar Land, Texas, *General Defense* 1466

Gass Weber Mullins LLC
Milwaukee, Wisconsin, *General Defense* 1580

Gaudry, Ranson, Higgins & Gremillion, L.L.C.
Baton Rouge, Louisiana, *General Defense* 655
Gretna, Louisiana, *General Defense* 664

Gault, Nye & Quintana, L.L.P.
Brownsville, Texas, *General Defense* 1382
Corpus Christi, Texas, *General Defense* 1385
Edinburg, Texas, *General Defense* 1413

Kelly A. Genova, PC
Albuquerque, New Mexico, *General Defense* 1009

Gentry Locke Rakes & Moore, LLP
Roanoke, Virginia, *General Defense* 1520
Roanoke, Virginia, *Subrogation* 1664

Georgeson Angaran Chtd.
Reno, Nevada, *General Defense* 944

German, Gallagher & Murtagh
Philadelphia, Pennsylvania, *General Defense* 1253

Gerstenblatt Law Offices, Ltd.
Providence, Rhode Island, *General Defense* 1285

Ghantous Law Corporation
San Ramon, California, *General Defense* 260

Giarmarco, Mullins & Horton, P.C.
Detroit, Michigan, *General Defense* 785
Troy, Michigan, *General Defense* 809

ATTORNEYS - ALPHABETICAL FIRM INDEX

Gibbs Armstrong Borochoff Mullican & Hart, P.C.
Tulsa, Oklahoma, *General Defense* 1207

Gibbs Pool and Turner, P.C.
Jefferson City, Missouri, *General Defense* 872

Gieger, Laborde & Laperouse, L.L.C.
New Orleans, Louisiana, *General Defense* 690
Houston, Texas, *General Defense* 1431

Michael Gillion, P.C.
Mobile, Alabama, *General Defense* 110
Mobile, Alabama, *Subrogation* 1628

Glasgow & Veazey
Nashville, Tennessee, *General Defense* 1360

Gleason, Dunn, Walsh & O'Shea
Albany, New York, *General Defense* 1024

Glenn Robinson & Cathey PLC
Roanoke, Virginia, *General Defense* 1521

Glover, Blount & Hyatt
Augusta, Georgia, *General Defense* 451

Glowacki & Imbrigiotta, LPA
Cleveland, Ohio, *General Defense* 1173
Cleveland, Ohio, *Subrogation* 1655

Godfrey & Kahn, S.C.
Madison, Wisconsin, *General Defense* 1574

Goehring Rutter & Boehm
Pittsburgh, Pennsylvania, *General Defense* 1268

Goetz & Eckland PA
Minneapolis, Minnesota, *General Defense* 821

Goffstein, Raskas, Pomerantz, Kraus & Sherman, L.L.C.
St. Louis, Missouri, *General Defense* 890

Goicoechea, Di Grazia, Coyle & Stanton, Ltd.
Elko, Nevada, *General Defense* 936
Elko, Nevada, *Subrogation* 1646

Alan C. Gold, P.A.
Miami, Florida, *General Defense* 381

Gold, Albanese & Barletti
Boston, Massachusetts, *General Defense* 753
Morristown, New Jersey, *General Defense* 980
Red Bank, New Jersey, *General Defense* 990

Goldberg Simpson LLC
Louisville, Kentucky, *General Defense* 635

Golden and Walters, PLLC
Lexington, Kentucky, *General Defense* 623

Golding Holden & Pope, L.L.P.
Charlotte, North Carolina, *General Defense* 1120

Goldstein and Peck, P.C.
Bridgeport, Connecticut, *General Defense* 303

Gold, Weems, Bruser, Sues & Rundell
Alexandria, Louisiana, *General Defense* 649

Gonnerman Reinert, LLC
St. Louis, Missouri, *General Defense* 891

Goodell, Stratton, Edmonds & Palmer, L.L.P.
Topeka, Kansas, *General Defense* 605
Topeka, Kansas, *Subrogation* 1639

ATTORNEYS - ALPHABETICAL FIRM INDEX

Goodman, Allen & Filetti, PLLC
    Charlottesville, Virginia, *General Defense* 1495
    Norfolk, Virginia, *General Defense* 1507
    Richmond, Virginia, *General Defense* 1513

Goodman & Jacobs LLP
    New York, New York, *General Defense* 1064

Goodman McGuffey Lindsey & Johnson, LLP
    Atlanta, Georgia, *General Defense* 440

Gordon Arata McCollam Duplantis & Eagan, LLC
    New Orleans, Louisiana, *General Defense* 692

Gordon Davis Johnson & Shane, P.C.
    El Paso, Texas, *General Defense* 1414

Gordon, Muir & Foley, LLP
    Hartford, Connecticut, *General Defense* 307

Gorman & Williams
    Baltimore, Maryland, *General Defense* 729
    Baltimore, Maryland, *Subrogation* 1641

Gough, Shanahan, Johnson & Waterman, PLLP
    Helena, Montana, *General Defense* 913

Governo Law Firm LLC
    Boston, Massachusetts, *General Defense* 753
    Boston, Massachusetts, *Regulatory and Compliance* 1671

Grace, Matthews & Debro LLC
    Huntsville, Alabama, *General Defense* 105

Graham Curtin
    Morristown, New Jersey, *General Defense* 980

S. Granot & Co.
    Tel Aviv, Israel, *General Defense* 1620

Grant, Genovese & Baratta, LLP
    Irvine, California, *General Defense* 190

Gray & Associates, L.L.C.
    Birmingham, Alabama, *General Defense* 84

Green Chesnut & Hughes PLLC
    Lexington, Kentucky, *General Defense* 623

Law Offices of Kenneth N. Greenfield
    San Diego, California, *General Defense* 240

Green & Green, Lawyers
    Dayton, Ohio, *General Defense* 1182

Green, Lundgren & Ryan, P.C.
    Cherry Hill, New Jersey, *General Defense* 962

Gregory and Meyer, P.C.
    Troy, Michigan, *General Defense* 810
    Troy, Michigan, *Subrogation* 1643

Grier, Cox & Cranshaw, LLC
    Columbia, South Carolina, *General Defense* 1307

Griffith Law Firm
    Oxford, Mississippi, *General Defense* 856

The Griffith Law Group, LLP
    McAllen, Texas, *General Defense* 1454

Griffith, Strickler, Lerman, Solymos & Calkins
    York, Pennsylvania, *General Defense* 1281
    York, Pennsylvania, *Subrogation* 1660

Grimm, Vranjes & Greer LLP
    San Diego, California, *General Defense* 240

ATTORNEYS - ALPHABETICAL FIRM INDEX

Groh Eggers, LLC
Anchorage, Alaska, *General Defense* 139

Gross McGinley, LLP
Allentown, Pennsylvania, *General Defense* 1230

Gross, Minsky & Mogul, P.A.
Bangor, Maine, *General Defense* 714

Gross & Welch P.C., L.L.O.
Omaha, Nebraska, *General Defense* 929
Omaha, Nebraska, *Subrogation* 1646

Grower, Ketcham, Rutherford, Bronson, Eide & Telan, P.A.
Orlando, Florida, *General Defense* 397

Gruvman, Giordano & Glaws, LLP
New York, New York, *General Defense* 1065

Guebert Bruckner PC
Albuquerque, New Mexico, *General Defense* 1009

Guglielmo, Marks, Schutte, Terhoeve & Love, L.L.P.
Baton Rouge, Louisiana, *General Defense* 655

Gunning & LaFazia Inc.
Providence, Rhode Island, *General Defense* 1285

Gunty & McCarthy
Chicago, Illinois, *General Defense* 513
Edwardsville, Illinois, *General Defense* 531

Gust Rosenfeld P.L.C.
Phoenix, Arizona, *General Defense* 146

Gwertzman, Lefkowitz & Burman
New York, New York, *General Defense* 1065
New York, New York, *Subrogation* 1651

H

Hacker Murphy, LLP
Latham, New York, *General Defense* 1049

Hackney Grover Hoover & Bean
East Lansing, Michigan, *General Defense* 790

Hagelin Kent LLC
Buffalo, New York, *General Defense* 1038

Hager & Dowling
Santa Barbara, California, *General Defense* 261

Hailey, McNamara, Hall, Larmann & Papale, L.L.P.
Metairie, Louisiana, *General Defense* 675
Gulfport, Mississippi, *General Defense* 836

Hale Sides LLC
Birmingham, Alabama, *General Defense* 85

Hall, Estill, Hardwick, Gable, Golden & Nelson, P.C.
Tulsa, Oklahoma, *General Defense* 1207

Hallett & Perrin, PC
Dallas, Texas, *General Defense* 1398

Hall & Evans, L.L.C.
Denver, Colorado, *General Defense* 281
Billings, Montana, *General Defense* 903

Law Office of Eric J. Halverson, Jr.
Metairie, Louisiana, *General Defense* 678

Halverson & Mahlen, P.C.
Billings, Montana, *General Defense* 903

ATTORNEYS - ALPHABETICAL FIRM INDEX

Hampton & Royce, L.C.
Salina, Kansas, *General Defense* 604

Hanft Fride, P.A.
Duluth, Minnesota, *General Defense* 816

Hanna, Brophy, MacLean, McAleer & Jensen, LLP
Bakersfield, California, *General Defense* 183
Fresno, California, *General Defense* 188
Los Angeles, California, *General Defense* 201
Oakland, California, *General Defense* 218
Orange, California, *General Defense* 219
Redding, California, *General Defense* 223
Riverside, California, *General Defense* 227
Sacramento, California, *General Defense* 231
Salinas, California, *General Defense* 235
San Francisco, California, *General Defense* 251
Santa Rosa, California, *General Defense* 263
Stockton, California, *General Defense* 264

Hanna & Plaut, L.L.P.
Austin, Texas, *General Defense* 1377

Hanson Curran LLP
Providence, Rhode Island, *General Defense* 1285

Hanson Lulic & Krall, LLC
Minneapolis, Minnesota, *General Defense* 821
Minneapolis, Minnesota, *Subrogation* 1644

Hardin, Kundla, McKeon & Poletto, P.A.
Springfield, New Jersey, *General Defense* 996

Hardy Erich Brown & Wilson
Sacramento, California, *General Defense* 231

Harman, Claytor, Corrigan & Wellman, P.C.
Richmond, Virginia, *General Defense* 1514

Harris & Bunch, LLC
Marietta, Georgia, *General Defense* 458

Harris, Karstaedt, Jamison & Powers, P.C.
Denver, Colorado, *General Defense* 283

Harrison & Hull, L.L.P.
McKinney, Texas, *General Defense* 1456
McKinney, Texas, *Investigation and Adjustment* 1679

Harvey Kruse, P.C.
Flint, Michigan, *General Defense* 791
Grand Rapids, Michigan, *General Defense* 793
Troy, Michigan, *General Defense* 811
Troy, Michigan, *Subrogation* 1644

Harville Law Offices PLLC
Louisville, Kentucky, *General Defense* 636

Hassell-Legal, P.A.
Daytona Beach, Florida, *General Defense* 347
Daytona Beach, Florida, *Subrogation* 1633

Hassett & Donnelly, P.C.
Hartford, Connecticut, *General Defense* 308
Boston, Massachusetts, *General Defense* 755
Worcester, Massachusetts, *General Defense* 774

Hayes, Harkey, Smith & Cascio, L.L.P.
Monroe, Louisiana, *General Defense* 683
New Orleans, Louisiana, *General Defense* 693

Hayes and Windish, P.C.
Woodstock, Vermont, *General Defense* 1489

ATTORNEYS - ALPHABETICAL FIRM INDEX

Haynsworth Sinkler Boyd, P.A.
    Charleston, South Carolina, *General Defense*..1298

Haywood, Denny & Miller, L.L.P.
    Durham, North Carolina, *General Defense*..1122
    Durham, North Carolina, *Subrogation*...1654

Heard & Medack, P.C.
    Houston, Texas, *General Defense*..1432

Hebbler & Giordano, L.L.C.
    Metairie, Louisiana, *General Defense*...678

Heidman Law Firm, L.L.P.
    Sioux City, Iowa, *General Defense*..588
    Sioux City, Iowa, *Subrogation*...1639

Heifetz Rose, LLP
    Needham, Massachusetts, *General Defense*...767

Helmsing, Leach, Herlong, Newman & Rouse, P.C.
    Mobile, Alabama, *General Defense*...110

Henderson, Franklin, Starnes & Holt
    Fort Myers, Florida, *General Defense*...362

Henrichsen Siegel, P.L.L.C.
    Washington, District of Columbia, *General Defense*...336
    Washington, District of Columbia, *Subrogation*..1633
    Jacksonville, Florida, *General Defense*..371
    Jacksonville, Florida, *Subrogation*...1633

Hensen & Cook-Olson, LLC
    Littleton, Colorado, *General Defense*...297

Henson & Talley, L.L.P.
    Greensboro, North Carolina, *General Defense*...1127
    Greensboro, North Carolina, *Subrogation*...1654

HeplerBroom LLC
    Chicago, Illinois, *General Defense*..515
    Edwardsville, Illinois, *General Defense*...531
    Springfield, Illinois, *General Defense*..547
    St. Louis, Missouri, *General Defense*...892

Hermann Cahn & Schneider LLP
    Cleveland, Ohio, *General Defense*..1173

Heyl, Royster, Voelker & Allen
    Chicago, Illinois, *General Defense*..515
    Edwardsville, Illinois, *General Defense*...531
    Peoria, Illinois, *General Defense*..542
    Rockford, Illinois, *General Defense*..544
    Springfield, Illinois, *General Defense*..547
    Urbana, Illinois, *General Defense*..549

Hicks Law Firm, PLLC
    Hattiesburg, Mississippi, *General Defense*..840

Hicks & Llamas, P.C.
    El Paso, Texas, *General Defense*..1414

Hicks & Smith, PLLC
    Columbus, Mississippi, *General Defense*...832

Philip Hicky, II, Ltd.
    Forrest City, Arkansas, *General Defense*...161

Hightower, Stratton, Wilhelm, P.A.
    Miami, Florida, *General Defense*..381
    Orlando, Florida, *General Defense*..399
    St. Petersburg, Florida, *General Defense*..414
    West Palm Beach, Florida, *General Defense*...427

ATTORNEYS - ALPHABETICAL FIRM INDEX

Hill, Betts & Nash, LLP
    Fort Lauderdale, Florida, *General Defense* 355
    New York, New York, *General Defense* 1065

Hill & Beyer
    Lafayette, Louisiana, *General Defense* 666

Hill Fulwider, P.C.
    Indianapolis, Indiana, *General Defense* 561

Hill, Hill, Carter, Franco, Cole & Black, P.C.
    Montgomery, Alabama, *General Defense* 121

Hill, Rugh, Keller & Main
    Orlando, Florida, *General Defense* 399

Hiltgen & Brewer, P.C.
    Oklahoma City, Oklahoma, *General Defense* 1199
    Oklahoma City, Oklahoma, *Subrogation* 1656

Hinkle, Hensley, Shanor & Martin, L.L.P.
    Roswell, New Mexico, *General Defense* 1017
    Santa Fe, New Mexico, *General Defense* 1018
    Midland, Texas, *General Defense* 1457

Hoagland, Fitzgerald & Pranaitis
    Alton, Illinois, *General Defense* 492

Hodge & Hodge
    Charlotte Amalie, St. Thomas, Virgin Islands, *General Defense* 1602

Hodge & James
    Harlingen, Texas, *General Defense* 1423

Hodosh, Spinella & Angelone
    Providence, Rhode Island, *General Defense* 1286

Hoffman, Luhman & Masson, PC
    Lafayette, Indiana, *General Defense* 570
    Lafayette, Indiana, *Subrogation* 1638

Hoffman Roth & Matlin, L.L.P.
    New York, New York, *General Defense* 1066

Hohmann, Taube & Summers, L.L.P.
    Austin, Texas, *General Defense* 1377

Holcombe Bomar, P.A.
    Spartanburg, South Carolina, *General Defense* 1321

Hollins Law
    Irvine, California, *General Defense* 190

Holmes Weddle & Barcott, P.C.
    Anchorage, Alaska, *General Defense* 139

Holt Mynatt Martinez PC
    Las Cruces, New Mexico, *General Defense* 1015

Holtsford Gilliland Higgins Hitson & Howard, P.C.
    Mobile, Alabama, *General Defense* 111
    Montgomery, Alabama, *General Defense* 123

Hood Law Firm, LLC
    Charleston, South Carolina, *General Defense* 1299

Horan Lloyd, A Professional Corporation
    Monterey, California, *General Defense* 214

Horger & Connor
    Orangeburg, South Carolina, *General Defense* 1320

Hornthal, Riley, Ellis and Maland, L.L.P.
    Elizabeth City, North Carolina, *General Defense* 1122

ATTORNEYS - ALPHABETICAL FIRM INDEX

Sherry L. Horowitz, Attorney At Law
    Bala Cynwyd, Pennsylvania, *General Defense* 1232
    Bala Cynwyd, Pennsylvania, *Subrogation* 1656

Horvath & Weaver, P.C.
    Chicago, Illinois, *General Defense* 515
    Chicago, Illinois, *Subrogation* 1636
    Chicago, Illinois, *Investigation and Adjustment* 1677

Hosp, Gilbert & Bergsten
    Pasadena, California, *General Defense* 221

The House Law Firm, P.C.
    Tempe, Arizona, *General Defense* 152

House Reynolds & Faust, LLP
    Carmel, Indiana, *General Defense* 555

Howard & Howard, P.C.
    Virginia Beach, Virginia, *General Defense* 1525

Howard, Kohn, Sprague & Fitzgerald
    Hartford, Connecticut, *General Defense* 308

Howard, Tate, Sowell, Wilson Leathers & Johnson, PLLC
    Nashville, Tennessee, *General Defense* 1361

Howard & Whatley, P.C.
    Savannah, Georgia, *General Defense* 463

Howser, Newman & Besley, LLC
    Columbia, South Carolina, *General Defense* 1308

Hubbard, McIlwain & Brakefield, PC
    Tuscaloosa, Alabama, *General Defense* 131

Hudgins Law Firm, P.C.
    Alexandria, Virginia, *General Defense* 1493

Hudson, Potts & Bernstein L.L.P.
    Monroe, Louisiana, *General Defense* 684

Huelat Mack & Kreppein P.C.
    Michigan City, Indiana, *General Defense* 572

Hueston McNulty, P.C.
    Florham Park, New Jersey, *General Defense* 968
    New York, New York, *General Defense* 1067

Hughes Gorski Seedorf Odsen & Tervooren, LLC
    Anchorage, Alaska, *General Defense* 140
    Anchorage, Alaska, *Subrogation* 1628

Hughes, Socol, Piers, Resnick & Dym Ltd.
    Chicago, Illinois, *General Defense* 515

Hull Barrett, PC
    Augusta, Georgia, *General Defense* 451

Hume Smith Geddes Green & Simmons, LLP
    Indianapolis, Indiana, *General Defense* 562

Hunter, Barker & Fancher, LLP
    Corpus Christi, Texas, *General Defense* 1385

The Hunt Law Group, LLC
    Chicago, Illinois, *General Defense* 516

Hunt Suedhoff Kalamaros LLP
    Fort Wayne, Indiana, *General Defense* 559
    Indianapolis, Indiana, *General Defense* 563
    South Bend, Indiana, *General Defense* 574
    St. Joseph, Michigan, *General Defense* 806

Hurlburt, Monrose & Ernest
    Lafayette, Louisiana, *General Defense* 667

ATTORNEYS - ALPHABETICAL FIRM INDEX

The Hustead Law Firm
   Denver, Colorado, *General Defense* 284

Hyatt & Weber, P.A.
   Annapolis, Maryland, *General Defense* 726

I

Inglish & Monaco, P.C.
   Jefferson City, Missouri, *General Defense* 873

Ivone, Devine & Jensen, LLP
   Lake Success, New York, *General Defense* 1049

J

James, Carter & Coulter, PLC
   Little Rock, Arkansas, *General Defense* 169
   Little Rock, Arkansas, *Subrogation* 1629

James, Dark & Brill
   Kalamazoo, Michigan, *General Defense* 796

Jampol Zimet LLP
   Los Angeles, California, *General Defense* 201

Jardine, Baker, Hickman & Houston, PLLC
   Phoenix, Arizona, *General Defense* 147

The Javier Law Firm, LLC
   New Orleans, Louisiana, *General Defense* 693

Jeansonne & Remondet, L.L.C.
   Lafayette, Louisiana, *General Defense* 667

Jelliffe, Ferrell, Doerge & Phelps
   Harrisburg, Illinois, *General Defense* 534

Jenkins Fenstermaker, PLLC
   Huntington, West Virginia, *General Defense* 1559

Jennings Teague
   Oklahoma City, Oklahoma, *General Defense* 1199

Law Offices of Garrett L. Joest, L.L.C.
   Toms River, New Jersey, *General Defense* 997

Johns, Flaherty & Collins, S.C.
   La Crosse, Wisconsin, *General Defense* 1573

Johnson, Berg & Saxby, PLLP
   Kalispell, Montana, *General Defense* 915

Johnson & Jones, P.C.
   Tulsa, Oklahoma, *General Defense* 1208

Johnson & Legislador, PLC
   Cedar Rapids, Iowa, *General Defense* 581

Johnson & Lindberg, P.A.
   Minneapolis, Minnesota, *General Defense* 822
   Minneapolis, Minnesota, *Subrogation* 1644

Johnson Schachter & Lewis, A PLC
   Sacramento, California, *General Defense* 232

Johnson & Webbert, L.L.P.
   Augusta, Maine, *General Defense* 714

Johnson, Yacoubian & Paysse, APLC
   New Orleans, Louisiana, *General Defense* 693

Johnstone Adams, L.L.C.
   Bay Minette, Alabama, *General Defense* 79
   Birmingham, Alabama, *General Defense* 85
   Mobile, Alabama, *General Defense* 112

ATTORNEYS - ALPHABETICAL FIRM INDEX

Johnston Legal Group PC
    Oklahoma City, Oklahoma, *General Defense*........1200
    Fort Worth, Texas, *General Defense*........1420
    Houston, Texas, *General Defense*........1432
    San Antonio, Texas, *General Defense*........1463

Jones, Cork & Miller, LLP
    Macon, Georgia, *General Defense*........457

Jones Gledhill Fuhrman Gourley, P.A.
    Boise, Idaho, *General Defense*........481

Jones, Hamilton & Lay, PLC
    Dyersburg, Tennessee, *General Defense*........1339

Jones, Jackson & Moll, PLC
    Fort Smith, Arkansas, *General Defense*........162

Jones Morrison, LLP
    Stamford, Connecticut, *General Defense*........322
    New York, New York, *General Defense*........1067
    White Plains, New York, *General Defense*........1113

Jones Walker LLP
    Birmingham, Alabama, *General Defense*........86
    Mobile, Alabama, *General Defense*........113
    Baton Rouge, Louisiana, *General Defense*........656
    Lafayette, Louisiana, *General Defense*........667
    New Orleans, Louisiana, *General Defense*........694
    Jackson, Mississippi, *General Defense*........848
    Olive Branch, Mississippi, *General Defense*........856

The Law Offices of Matthew J. Jowanna, P.A.
    Tampa, Florida, *General Defense*........420

Juge, Napolitano, Guilbeau, Ruli & Frieman
    Metairie, Louisiana, *General Defense*........679

Jump & Associates, P.C.
    Chicago, Illinois, *General Defense*........517

Juneau David
    Lafayette, Louisiana, *General Defense*........668

K

Kahn, Dees, Donovan & Kahn, LLP
    Evansville, Indiana, *General Defense*........556
    Evansville, Indiana, *Subrogation*........1637

Kalbaugh, Pfund & Messersmith, P.C.
    Fairfax, Virginia, *General Defense*........1500
    Norfolk, Virginia, *General Defense*........1507
    Richmond, Virginia, *General Defense*........1515
    Roanoke, Virginia, *General Defense*........1522

Kane Russell Coleman & Logan PC
    Dallas, Texas, *General Defense*........1398
    Houston, Texas, *General Defense*........1433

Kantrow, Spaht, Weaver & Blitzer
    Baton Rouge, Louisiana, *General Defense*........656

Karel & Hicks, P.C.
    Dallas, Texas, *General Defense*........1399

Karpinski, Colaresi & Karp
    Baltimore, Maryland, *General Defense*........731

Kasdorf, Lewis & Swietlik, S.C.
    Green Bay, Wisconsin, *General Defense*........1572
    Milwaukee, Wisconsin, *General Defense*........1581

The Law Offices of Robert B. Katz & Associates
    Woodland Hills, California, *General Defense*........268

ATTORNEYS - ALPHABETICAL FIRM INDEX

Kaufman Kaufman & Miller LLP
    Encino, California, *General Defense* 186

Kaufman, Payton & Chapa
    Detroit, Michigan, *General Defense* 785
    Farmington Hills, Michigan, *General Defense* 790
    Grand Rapids, Michigan, *General Defense* 793

Kaufman, Semeraro & Leibman, LLC
    Fort Lee, New Jersey, *General Defense* 968
    Fort Lee, New Jersey, *Subrogation* 1647

Law Offices of Kay & Andersen, LLC
    Madison, Wisconsin, *General Defense* 1575

Kay Casto & Chaney PLLC
    Charleston, West Virginia, *General Defense* 1554
    Morgantown, West Virginia, *General Defense* 1564

Kazen, Meurer & Perez, L.L.P.
    Laredo, Texas, *General Defense* 1446

Keleher & McLeod, P.A.
    Albuquerque, New Mexico, *General Defense* 1009

Keller Rohrback L.L.P.
    Seattle, Washington, *General Defense* 1538

Kelly Grimes Pietrangelo & Vakil, P.C.
    Media, Pennsylvania, *General Defense* 1246

Kelly, Rode & Kelly, LLP
    Mineola, New York, *General Defense* 1055
    Riverhead, New York, *General Defense* 1097

Kelly & Smith, P.C.
    Houston, Texas, *General Defense* 1433
    Houston, Texas, *Subrogation* 1662

Kemp Smith LLP
    El Paso, Texas, *General Defense* 1415

Kennedy Lillis Schmidt & English
    New York, New York, *General Defense* 1067

Kenny, Snowden & Norine
    Redding, California, *General Defense* 223

Kent, Anderson & Bush, P.C.
    Tyler, Texas, *General Defense* 1468

Kent Law
    Las Vegas, Nevada, *General Defense* 939
    Reno, Nevada, *General Defense* 945

Kent & McBride, P.C.
    Philadelphia, Pennsylvania, *General Defense* 1254

Keogh, Cox & Wilson, Ltd.
    Baton Rouge, Louisiana, *General Defense* 657

Kerby Law Firm, L.L.C.
    Columbus, Mississippi, *General Defense* 832

Kerley, Walsh, Matera & Cinquemani, P.C.
    Seaford, New York, *General Defense* 1102

Kerrick Bachert PSC
    Bowling Green, Kentucky, *General Defense* 613
    Bowling Green, Kentucky, *Subrogation* 1640
    Elizabethtown, Kentucky, *General Defense* 617
    Elizabethtown, Kentucky, *Subrogation* 1640

Kerr, Irvine, Rhodes & Ables
    Oklahoma City, Oklahoma, *General Defense* 1200
    Oklahoma City, Oklahoma, *Regulatory and Compliance* 1672

ATTORNEYS - ALPHABETICAL FIRM INDEX

Kersten Brownlee Hendricks L.L.P.
Fort Dodge, Iowa, *General Defense* 587

Kessler & Collins, PC
Dallas, Texas, *General Defense* 1399

Kiernan, Plunkett & Redihan LLP
Providence, Rhode Island, *General Defense* 1287

Kightlinger & Gray, LLP
Evansville, Indiana, *General Defense* 557
Evansville, Indiana, *Subrogation* 1637
Indianapolis, Indiana, *General Defense* 563
Indianapolis, Indiana, *Subrogation* 1638
Merrillville, Indiana, *General Defense* 571
Merrillville, Indiana, *Subrogation* 1638
New Albany, Indiana, *General Defense* 573
New Albany, Indiana, *Subrogation* 1639
Louisville, Kentucky, *General Defense* 636
Louisville, Kentucky, *Subrogation* 1640

King, Deep & Branaman
Henderson, Kentucky, *General Defense* 620

Kinkle, Rodiger & Spriggs
Riverside, California, *General Defense* 227

Kipp & Christian, P.C.
Salt Lake City, Utah, *General Defense* 1476

Kirkpatrick & Startzel, P.S.
Spokane, Washington, *General Defense* 1546

Kirton & McConkie
Salt Lake City, Utah, *General Defense* 1477

Kitch Drutchas Wagner Valitutti & Sherbrook
Detroit, Michigan, *General Defense* 785

Klasing & Williamson, P.C.
Birmingham, Alabama, *General Defense* 86

Kluczynski, Girtz & Vogelzang
Grand Rapids, Michigan, *General Defense* 794

Knox McLaughlin Gornall & Sennett, P.C.
Erie, Pennsylvania, *General Defense* 1235

Knudsen Law Firm
Lincoln, Nebraska, *General Defense* 924

Koepke & Hiltabrand
Springfield, Illinois, *General Defense* 547

Kopon Airdo, LLC
Chicago, Illinois, *General Defense* 517

Mark T. Koss
Oklahoma City, Oklahoma, *Subrogation* 1656

Kovarik, Ellison & Mathis, P.C.
Scottsbluff, Nebraska, *General Defense* 933

Kramer & Connolly
Baltimore, Maryland, *General Defense* 731

Kramer Rayson LLP
Knoxville, Tennessee, *General Defense* 1347

Law Offices of Steven G. Kraus
Warren, New Jersey, *Subrogation* 1649

Krenek & Heinemeyer, P.C.
San Antonio, Texas, *General Defense* 1464
San Antonio, Texas, *Subrogation* 1663

ATTORNEYS - ALPHABETICAL FIRM INDEX

Krez & Flores, LLP
New York, New York, *General Defense* 1067

Kriz, Jenkins, Prewitt & Jones, P.S.C.
Lexington, Kentucky, *General Defense* 624

Kubicki Draper
Miami, Florida, *General Defense* 382

Law Offices of Charles E. Kutner, LLP
New York, New York, *General Defense* 1068

L

LaBarge, Campbell & Lyon L.L.C.
Chicago, Illinois, *General Defense* 518

Lamar, Archer & Cofrin, LLP
Atlanta, Georgia, *General Defense* 442

Lambert Coffin
Portland, Maine, *General Defense* 717
Portland, Maine, *Investigation and Adjustment* 1678

Lamp Bartram Levy Trautwein & Perry, PLLC
Huntington, West Virginia, *General Defense* 1560

Landoe, Brown, Planalp & Reida, P.C.
Bozeman, Montana, *General Defense* 905

Landrum & Shouse LLP
Lexington, Kentucky, *General Defense* 624
Louisville, Kentucky, *General Defense* 637

Law Offices of John C. Lane
Sparta, New Jersey, *General Defense* 995
New York, New York, *General Defense* 1068

Laney & Foster, P.C.
Birmingham, Alabama, *General Defense* 87

Law Offices of Paul A. Lange, LLC
Stratford, Connecticut, *General Defense* 324

Langhenry, Gillen, Lundquist & Johnson, LLC
Chicago, Illinois, *General Defense* 518
Chicago, Illinois, *Subrogation* 1636
Joliet, Illinois, *General Defense* 536
Joliet, Illinois, *Subrogation* 1636
Princeton, Illinois, *General Defense* 542
Princeton, Illinois, *Subrogation* 1636
Rockford, Illinois, *General Defense* 545
Rockford, Illinois, *Subrogation* 1637
Wheaton, Illinois, *General Defense* 550
Wheaton, Illinois, *Subrogation* 1637

Lanier Ford Shaver & Payne P.C.
Huntsville, Alabama, *General Defense* 106

LaRose & LaRose
Poughkeepsie, New York, *General Defense* 1096

Larsen Christensen & Rico, PLLC
Salt Lake City, Utah, *General Defense* 1478

Larson & Blumreich, Chartered
Topeka, Kansas, *General Defense* 606

Larzelere Picou Wells Simpson Lonero, LLC
Metairie, Louisiana, *General Defense* 680

LaSalle & Associates, P.C.
Providence, Rhode Island, *General Defense* 1287

Laser Law Firm, P.A.
Little Rock, Arkansas, *General Defense* 170

ATTORNEYS - ALPHABETICAL FIRM INDEX

Lash & Associates, P.C.
    Wellesley, Massachusetts, *General Defense* 773
    Wellesley, Massachusetts, *Subrogation* 1643

Lathrop & Rutledge, P.C.
    Cheyenne, Wyoming, *General Defense* 1593

Lavery, de Billy L.L.P.
    Montreal, Quebec, *General Defense* 1614

The Law Offices of Composto & Composto
    Brooklyn, New York, *General Defense* 1032

Law Offices of Redenbaugh, Mohr, & Redenbaugh
    Storm Lake, Iowa, *General Defense* 589

Law Offices of Robert A. Stutman, P.C.
    Anaheim, California, *Subrogation* 1629

Lawrence, Worden, Rainis & Bard, P.C.
    Melville, New York, *General Defense* 1051

Laxalt & Nomura, Ltd.
    Las Vegas, Nevada, *General Defense* 939
    Reno, Nevada, *General Defense* 945

Laxton Glass LLP
    Toronto, Ontario, *General Defense* 1612
    Toronto, Ontario, *Subrogation* 1666

Leake & Stokes
    Asheville, North Carolina, *General Defense* 1118
    Asheville, North Carolina, *Subrogation* 1654
    Marshall, North Carolina, *General Defense* 1131

Jeffrey Leavell, S.C.
    Racine, Wisconsin, *General Defense* 1582

The Ledbetter Law Firm, P.L.C.
    Cottonwood, Arizona, *General Defense* 144

Lederer Weston Craig, P.L.C.
    Cedar Rapids, Iowa, *General Defense* 581
    West Des Moines, Iowa, *General Defense* 592

The Lee Law Group, PC
    Irvine, California, *General Defense* 191

Lee Smart, P.S., Inc.
    Seattle, Washington, *General Defense* 1539

Leininger, Smith, Johnson, Baack, Placzek & Allen
    Grand Island, Nebraska, *General Defense* 922

Leiter & Belsky, P.A.
    Fort Lauderdale, Florida, *General Defense* 355

Lennon, Miller, O'Connor & Bartosiewicz, PLC
    Kalamazoo, Michigan, *General Defense* 796

Leritz Plunkert & Bruning, P.C.
    St. Louis, Missouri, *General Defense* 892

LeVangie Law Group
    Sacramento, California, *General Defense* 233

Levene Gouldin & Thompson, LLP
    Binghamton, New York, *General Defense* 1031

Levine, Orr & Geracioti, PLLC
    Nashville, Tennessee, *General Defense* 1361

Levy & Pruett
    Decatur, Georgia, *General Defense* 454

Levy Wheeler Waters
    Denver, Colorado, *General Defense* 285

ATTORNEYS - ALPHABETICAL FIRM INDEX

Lewis Baach PLLC
Washington, District of Columbia, *General Defense* 336

Lewis Hansen Law Firm
Salt Lake City, Utah, *General Defense* 1478

Lewis Roca Rothgerber LLP
Phoenix, Arizona, *General Defense* 148
Colorado Springs, Colorado, *General Defense* 276
Denver, Colorado, *General Defense* 285

Lewis, Thomason, King, Krieg & Waldrop, P.C.
Knoxville, Tennessee, *General Defense* 1349
Memphis, Tennessee, *General Defense* 1351
Nashville, Tennessee, *General Defense* 1362

Lewis Wagner, LLP
Indianapolis, Indiana, *General Defense* 564
Indianapolis, Indiana, *Subrogation* 1638

Leyden, Capotorto, Ritacco & Corrigan, P.C.
Toms River, New Jersey, *General Defense* 998
Toms River, New Jersey, *Subrogation* 1648

Lindabury, McCormick, Estabrook & Cooper, P.C.
Westfield, New Jersey, *General Defense* 1003

Lindhorst & Dreidame Co., L.P.A.
Cincinnati, Ohio, *General Defense* 1162

Lipe Lyons Murphy Nahrstadt & Pontikis Ltd.
Chicago, Illinois, *General Defense* 519

Lippman & Ouellette, L.L.C.
New Haven, Connecticut, *General Defense* 316

Lippman & Reed, PLLC
Tucson, Arizona, *Subrogation* 1629

Livingston Law Firm
Walnut Creek, California, *General Defense* 266

Lobman, Carnahan, Batt, Angelle & Nader
New Orleans, Louisiana, *General Defense* 696

Locher, Pavelka, Dostal, Braddy & Hammes, L.L.C.
Omaha, Nebraska, *General Defense* 930

Locke Lord LLP
Los Angeles, California, *General Defense* 202
San Francisco, California, *General Defense* 251
Washington, District of Columbia, *General Defense* 337
Atlanta, Georgia, *General Defense* 443
Chicago, Illinois, *General Defense* 519
New Orleans, Louisiana, *General Defense* 697
New York, New York, *General Defense* 1068
Austin, Texas, *General Defense* 1378
Dallas, Texas, *General Defense* 1400
Houston, Texas, *General Defense* 1433
London, United Kingdom, *General Defense* 1623

Logan Logan & Watson, L.C.
Prairie Village, Kansas, *General Defense* 603

London Fischer LLP
Irvine, California, *General Defense* 192
Irvine, California, *Subrogation* 1630
Irvine, California, *Investigation and Adjustment* 1676
Woodland Hills, California, *General Defense* 269
Woodland Hills, California, *Subrogation* 1632
Woodland Hills, California, *Investigation and Adjustment* 1676
New York, New York, *General Defense* 1069
New York, New York, *Subrogation* 1651
New York, New York, *Investigation and Adjustment* 1678

ATTORNEYS - ALPHABETICAL FIRM INDEX

Long Blumberg, LLP
    Walnut Creek, California, *General Defense* 267
    Las Vegas, Nevada, *General Defense* 939

Lopez Peterson, PLLC
    Laredo, Texas, *General Defense* 1447

Loughlin FitzGerald, P.C.
    Wallingford, Connecticut, *General Defense* 325

Loughran & Corbett, Attorneys, Inc.
    Watertown, Massachusetts, *General Defense* 772

Lowe Mobley Lowe & LeDuke
    Haleyville, Alabama, *General Defense* 103
    Hamilton, Alabama, *General Defense* 103

Law Offices of Robert D. Lowry
    Eugene, Oregon, *General Defense* 1221

Lowther Johnson Attorneys at Law, L.L.C.
    Springfield, Missouri, *General Defense* 883

Lubell Rosen, LLC
    Fort Lauderdale, Florida, *General Defense* 356

Lugenbuhl, Wheaton, Peck, Rankin & Hubbard
    New Orleans, Louisiana, *General Defense* 697
    New Orleans, Louisiana, *Subrogation* 1641
    Houston, Texas, *General Defense* 1434

Luks & Santaniello LLC
    Boca Raton, Florida, *General Defense* 342
    Fort Lauderdale, Florida, *General Defense* 356
    Jacksonville, Florida, *General Defense* 371
    Miami, Florida, *General Defense* 383
    Orlando, Florida, *General Defense* 400
    Tampa, Florida, *General Defense* 420

Philip M. Lustbader & David Lustbader, P.A.
    Livingston, New Jersey, *General Defense* 975
    Livingston, New Jersey, *Subrogation* 1647

Lynch, Cox, Gilman & Goodman P.S.C.
    Louisville, Kentucky, *General Defense* 638

Lyne, Woodworth & Evarts LLP
    Boston, Massachusetts, *General Defense* 755

Law Offices of Terry Lynn PLLC
    Charlottesville, Virginia, *General Defense* 1495

M

MacVean, Lewis, Sherwin & McDermott, P.C.
    Middletown, New York, *General Defense* 1053

Maddin, Hauser, Roth & Heller, P.C.
    Southfield, Michigan, *General Defense* 802

Madewell, Jared, Halfacre & Williams
    Cookeville, Tennessee, *General Defense* 1338

Maestas & Suggett, P.C.
    Albuquerque, New Mexico, *General Defense* 1010
    Albuquerque, New Mexico, *Subrogation* 1650

Magnani & Buck Ltd.
    Chicago, Illinois, *General Defense* 521

Magruder & Sumner
    Rome, Georgia, *General Defense* 460

Malapero Prisco Klauber & Licata LLP
    Paramus, New Jersey, *General Defense* 989

ATTORNEYS - ALPHABETICAL FIRM INDEX

Malapero & Prisco LLP
   New York, New York, *General Defense* 1071

Mallory & Friedman, PLLC
   Concord, New Hampshire, *General Defense* 950

Mangum, Wall, Stoops & Warden, P.L.L.C.
   Flagstaff, Arizona, *General Defense* 144
   Flagstaff, Arizona, *Subrogation* 1628

Manion Gaynor & Manning LLP
   Boston, Massachusetts, *General Defense* 756

Manning, Fulton & Skinner, P.A.
   Raleigh, North Carolina, *General Defense* 1133

Manz Swanson Hall Willson Fogarty & Gellis, P.C.
   Kansas City, Missouri, *General Defense* 878

Marcus & Myers, P.A.
   Orlando, Florida, *General Defense* 400

Marianas Legal Strategy Group, LLC
   Saipan, Mariana Islands, *General Defense* 1600

Markow Walker, P.A.
   Jackson, Mississippi, *General Defense* 849
   Ocean Springs, Mississippi, *General Defense* 855
   Oxford, Mississippi, *General Defense* 857

Marnen Mioduszewski Bordonaro Wagner & Sinnott, LLC
   Erie, Pennsylvania, *General Defense* 1236

Marra, Evenson & Bell, P.C.
   Great Falls, Montana, *General Defense* 909

Marshall, Conway & Bradley, P.C.
   Jersey City, New Jersey, *General Defense* 973
   New York, New York, *General Defense* 1072

Marshall Dennehey Warner Coleman & Goggin
   Wilmington, Delaware, *General Defense* 330
   Fort Lauderdale, Florida, *General Defense* 357
   Jacksonville, Florida, *General Defense* 371
   Orlando, Florida, *General Defense* 400
   Tampa, Florida, *General Defense* 420
   Cherry Hill, New Jersey, *General Defense* 963
   Roseland, New Jersey, *General Defense* 992
   Melville, New York, *General Defense* 1052
   New York, New York, *General Defense* 1073
   Westchester, New York, *General Defense* 1110
   Cincinnati, Ohio, *General Defense* 1163
   Cleveland, Ohio, *General Defense* 1173
   Allentown, Pennsylvania, *General Defense* 1230
   Doylestown, Pennsylvania, *General Defense* 1234
   Erie, Pennsylvania, *General Defense* 1237
   Harrisburg, Pennsylvania, *General Defense* 1240
   King of Prussia, Pennsylvania, *General Defense* 1243
   Philadelphia, Pennsylvania, *General Defense* 1255
   Pittsburgh, Pennsylvania, *General Defense* 1268
   Scranton, Pennsylvania, *General Defense* 1275

Martens & Associates, P.S.
   Seattle, Washington, *General Defense* 1541

Martin, Disiere, Jefferson & Wisdom, L.L.P.
   Austin, Texas, *General Defense* 1379
   Dallas, Texas, *General Defense* 1401
   Houston, Texas, *General Defense* 1434

Martin & Seibert, L.C.
   Martinsburg, West Virginia, *General Defense* 1562

ATTORNEYS - ALPHABETICAL FIRM INDEX

Mason Associates, P.C.
    Smithfield, Rhode Island, *General Defense* 1290

Massey, Higginbotham, Vise & Phillips, P.A.
    Jackson, Mississippi, *General Defense* 850

Mateer Goff & Honzel LLP
    Rockford, Illinois, *General Defense* 545

Matthews, Higgins, Hausfeld & Fenimore
    Mobile, Alabama, *General Defense* 114
    Panama City, Florida, *General Defense* 405
    Pensacola, Florida, *General Defense* 406
    Pensacola, Florida, *Subrogation* 1634

Matthews, Sanders & Sayes
    Little Rock, Arkansas, *General Defense* 171

Matthews, Stein, Shiels, Pearce, Knott, Eden & Davis, L.L.P.
    Dallas, Texas, *General Defense* 1402
    Dallas, Texas, *Subrogation* 1661

Matthews & Zahare, P.C.
    Anchorage, Alaska, *General Defense* 141
    Anchorage, Alaska, *Subrogation* 1628

Mattingly Law Firm
    Houston, Texas, *General Defense* 1437
    Houston, Texas, *Subrogation* 1662

Matushek, Nilles & Sinars, L.L.C.
    Chicago, Illinois, *General Defense* 521

May, Adam, Gerdes & Thompson
    Pierre, South Dakota, *General Defense* 1328

Maybank Law Firm, L.L.C.
    Charleston, South Carolina, *General Defense* 1301

Mayfield, Turner, O'Mara & Donnelly, P.C.
    Cherry Hill, New Jersey, *General Defense* 964

May & Johnson, P.C.
    Sioux Falls, South Dakota, *General Defense* 1331

Mazanec, Raskin & Ryder Co., L.P.A.
    Cleveland, Ohio, *General Defense* 1174
    Columbus, Ohio, *General Defense* 1178

Mazzara & Small, P.C.
    Bohemia, New York, *General Defense* 1031

McAloon & Friedman, P.C.
    New York, New York, *General Defense* 1074

McAnany, Van Cleave & Phillips, P.A.
    Kansas City, Kansas, *General Defense* 595

McAnany, Van Cleave & Phillips, P.C.
    Springfield, Missouri, *General Defense* 884
    St. Louis, Missouri, *General Defense* 893
    Omaha, Nebraska, *General Defense* 931
    Tulsa, Oklahoma, *General Defense* 1209

McAtee Law Office
    Tulsa, Oklahoma, *General Defense* 1209

McBrayer, McGinnis, Leslie & Kirkland, PLLC
    Washington, District of Columbia, *General Defense* 337

McBrayer, McGinnis, Leslie & Kirkland, PLLC
    Frankfort, Kentucky, *General Defense* 618
    Frankfort, Kentucky, *Regulatory and Compliance* 1671
    Frankfort, Kentucky, *Investigation and Adjustment* 1678

ATTORNEYS - ALPHABETICAL FIRM INDEX

McBrayer, McGinnis, Leslie & Kirkland, PLLC
Lexington, Kentucky, *General Defense* 625

McCabe, Collins, McGeough & Fowler, LLP
Mineola, New York, *General Defense* 1056

McCabe & Mack LLP
Poughkeepsie, New York, *General Defense* 1096
Poughkeepsie, New York, *Subrogation* 1653

McCathern
Dallas, Texas, *General Defense* 1403
Dallas, Texas, *Subrogation* 1661

McClellan, Powers, Ehmling & Rogers, P.C.
Gallatin, Tennessee, *General Defense* 1340

McCollum, Crowley, Moschet, Miller & Laak, Ltd.
Minneapolis, Minnesota, *General Defense* 822

McConnaughhay, Duffy, Coonrod, Pope & Weaver, P.A.
Fort Lauderdale, Florida, *General Defense* 358
Gainesville, Florida, *General Defense* 365
Jacksonville, Florida, *General Defense* 373
Ocala, Florida, *General Defense* 393
Panama City, Florida, *General Defense* 406
Pensacola, Florida, *General Defense* 407
Sarasota, Florida, *General Defense* 411
Tallahassee, Florida, *General Defense* 417

McConnell Fleischner Houghtaling, LLC
Denver, Colorado, *General Defense* 286

McCormick, Fitzpatrick, Kasper & Burchard, P.C.
Burlington, Vermont, *General Defense* 1484

McCormick Law Firm
Williamsport, Pennsylvania, *General Defense* 1280

McCullough, Campbell & Lane LLP
Chicago, Illinois, *General Defense* 522

McDaniel Acord, PLLC
Tulsa, Oklahoma, *General Defense* 1210

McDermott & Bonenberger, P.L.L.C.
Wheeling, West Virginia, *General Defense* 1566

McDermott & McGee
Millburn, New Jersey, *General Defense* 978

Law Offices of Bruce S. McDonald
Albuquerque, New Mexico, *General Defense* 1011

McDonald Kuhn, PLLC
Memphis, Tennessee, *General Defense* 1352
Memphis, Tennessee, *Subrogation* 1660

McDonald, Tinker, Skaer, Quinn & Herrington
Wichita, Kansas, *General Defense* 607

McDonough, O'Shaughnessy, Whaland & Meagher, PLLC
Manchester, New Hampshire, *General Defense* 952

McElroy, Deutsch, Mulvaney & Carpenter, LLP
Morristown, New Jersey, *General Defense* 982

McElroy, Hodges & Caldwell
Abingdon, Virginia, *General Defense* 1492

McGowan & Jacobs, LLC
Hamilton, Ohio, *General Defense* 1183

McGown & Markling Co., L.P.A.
Akron, Ohio, *General Defense* 1158

ATTORNEYS - ALPHABETICAL FIRM INDEX

McKay, Cauthen, Settana & Stubley, P.A.
    Columbia, South Carolina, *General Defense* 1309

McKay, de Lorimier & Acain
    Los Angeles, California, *General Defense* 202

McKellar, Tiedeken & Scoggin, LLC
    Cheyenne, Wyoming, *General Defense* 1593

McKenna & McCormick
    Providence, Rhode Island, *General Defense* 1288

McKenna Storer
    Chicago, Illinois, *General Defense* 523
    Woodstock, Illinois, *General Defense* 552

McKenry Dancigers Dawson, P.C.
    Norfolk, Virginia, *General Defense* 1508

McKercher LLP
    Regina, Saskatchewan, *General Defense* 1616
    Saskatoon, Saskatchewan, *General Defense* 1616

McKibben & Villarreal, L.L.P.
    Corpus Christi, Texas, *General Defense* 1386

McLeod, Fraser & Cone LLC
    Walterboro, South Carolina, *General Defense* 1324

McMahon Berger
    Collinsville, Illinois, *General Defense* 530
    St. Louis, Missouri, *General Defense* 893

McMahon Surovik Suttle, P.C.
    Abilene, Texas, *General Defense* 1371

McMillan LLP
    Toronto, Ontario, *Regulatory and Compliance* 1673

McMillan, McCorkle, Curry & Bennington, LLP
    Arkadelphia, Arkansas, *General Defense* 156

McNabb, Bragorgos & Burgess, PLLC
    Memphis, Tennessee, *General Defense* 1353

McNeal, Schick, Archibald & Biro Co., L.P.A.
    Cleveland, Ohio, *General Defense* 1176

McNees Wallace & Nurick LLC
    Harrisburg, Pennsylvania, *General Defense* 1241

Meier, Bonner, Muszynski, O'Dell & Harvey, P.A.
    Orlando, Florida, *General Defense* 401

Melick & Porter
    Boston, Massachusetts, *General Defense* 757

Melnick & Melnick
    Youngstown, Ohio, *General Defense* 1188

Mendes & Mount, LLP
    New York, New York, *General Defense* 1075

Methfessel & Werbel
    Edison, New Jersey, *General Defense* 966
    Edison, New Jersey, *Subrogation* 1646
    New York, New York, *General Defense* 1075
    New York, New York, *Subrogation* 1652
    Wayne, Pennsylvania, *General Defense* 1280
    Wayne, Pennsylvania, *Subrogation* 1660

Meyer Orlando LLC
    Houston, Texas, *General Defense* 1438

Meyers McConnell Reisz Siderman
    Los Angeles, California, *General Defense* 203

ATTORNEYS - ALPHABETICAL FIRM INDEX

Meyer, Unkovic & Scott, LLP
Pittsburgh, Pennsylvania, *General Defense* 1270

Charles G. Michaels
Denver, Colorado, *Subrogation* 1632

Midkiff, Muncie & Ross, P.C.
Richmond, Virginia, *General Defense* 1516

Millberg Gordon Stewart PLLC
Raleigh, North Carolina, *General Defense* 1134

Al Miller
Central City, Kentucky, *General Defense* 615

Miller Bonham, LLP
Atlanta, Georgia, *Subrogation* 1634

Miller, James, Miller & Hornsby, L.L.P.
Texarkana, Texas, *General Defense* 1467

Milligan & Coleman PLLP
Greeneville, Tennessee, *General Defense* 1341

The Milligan Law Firm, PC
Mount Pleasant, South Carolina, *General Defense* 1318

Mills & Associates
Las Vegas, Nevada, *General Defense* 939

Milton, Laurence & Dixon, L.L.P.
Worcester, Massachusetts, *General Defense* 775

Miniat & Wilson, LPC
Tucson, Arizona, *General Defense* 154
Tucson, Arizona, *Subrogation* 1629

Mintzer Sarowitz Zeris Ledva & Meyers, LLP
Wilmington, Delaware, *General Defense* 331
Miami, Florida, *General Defense* 383
Tampa, Florida, *General Defense* 421
Cherry Hill, New Jersey, *General Defense* 965
Hicksville, New York, *General Defense* 1046
New York, New York, *General Defense* 1076
Philadelphia, Pennsylvania, *General Defense* 1258
Pittsburgh, Pennsylvania, *General Defense* 1270
Wheeling, West Virginia, *General Defense* 1567

Mitchell, Brisso, Delaney & Vrieze, LLP
Eureka, California, *General Defense* 186

Mitchell & DeSimone
Boston, Massachusetts, *General Defense* 758
Boston, Massachusetts, *Subrogation* 1642
Worcester, Massachusetts, *General Defense* 775
Worcester, Massachusetts, *Subrogation* 1643

Mitchell Gallagher P.C.
Williamsport, Pennsylvania, *General Defense* 1280

Mixon & Worsham, PLC
Jonesboro, Arkansas, *General Defense* 164

Moen Sheehan Meyer, Ltd.
La Crosse, Wisconsin, *General Defense* 1573

Mollis & Mollis, Inc.
Newport Beach, California, *General Defense* 215

Molod Spitz & DeSantis, P.C.
Jersey City, New Jersey, *General Defense* 973
New York, New York, *General Defense* 1076
New York, New York, *Subrogation* 1652

ATTORNEYS - ALPHABETICAL FIRM INDEX

Momkus McCluskey, LLC
    Chicago, Illinois, *General Defense* 524
    Lisle, Illinois, *General Defense* 537

Monahan & Associates, P.C.
    Boston, Massachusetts, *General Defense* 758
    Boston, Massachusetts, *Subrogation* 1642

Monnet, Hayes, Bullis, Thompson & Edwards
    Oklahoma City, Oklahoma, *General Defense* 1201

Montgomery, Kolodny, Amatuzio & Dusbabek, L.L.P.
    Denver, Colorado, *General Defense* 287

Montgomery Little & Soran, P.C.
    Denver, Colorado, *General Defense* 288

Moore & Elia, LLP
    Boise, Idaho, *General Defense* 482

Moore, O'Connell & Refling, P.C.
    Bozeman, Montana, *General Defense* 906

Moore, Rader, Fitzpatrick and York, P.C.
    Cookeville, Tennessee, *General Defense* 1338

Moore Strickland
    Chicago, Illinois, *General Defense* 524

Morales Fierro & Reeves
    Pleasant Hill, California, *General Defense* 222
    Las Vegas, Nevada, *General Defense* 940

Morgan, Minnock, Rice & James
    Salt Lake City, Utah, *General Defense* 1478

Moriarty & Associates, P.C.
    Wakefield, Massachusetts, *General Defense* 771
    Worcester, Massachusetts, *General Defense* 776

Morin & Barkley LLP
    Charlottesville, Virginia, *General Defense* 1496

Morley Law Firm, Ltd.
    Grand Forks, North Dakota, *General Defense* 1151

Morris & Morris, P.A.
    West Palm Beach, Florida, *General Defense* 427
    West Palm Beach, Florida, *Regulatory and Compliance* 1671
    West Palm Beach, Florida, *Subrogation* 1634

Morris & Morris, P.C.
    Richmond, Virginia, *General Defense* 1517

Morrison & Morrison
    Detroit, Michigan, *General Defense* 788

Morrissey, Bove & Ebbott
    Flint, Michigan, *General Defense* 791

Morrow, Romine & Pearson, P.C.
    Montgomery, Alabama, *General Defense* 124

Morrow & White
    Costa Mesa, California, *General Defense* 184
    Walnut Creek, California, *General Defense* 267

Morrow Willnauer Klosterman Church, LLC
    Kansas City, Missouri, *General Defense* 879
    St. Louis, Missouri, *General Defense* 894
    Omaha, Nebraska, *General Defense* 931

Moseley Prichard Parrish Knight & Jones
    Jacksonville, Florida, *General Defense* 373

ATTORNEYS - ALPHABETICAL FIRM INDEX

Mouledoux, Bland, Legrand & Brackett, L.L.C.
New Orleans, Louisiana, *General Defense* 698
New Orleans, Louisiana, *Subrogation* 1641

Moulton Bellingham PC
Billings, Montana, *General Defense* 903

Mounce, Green, Myers, Safi, Paxson & Galatzan
El Paso, Texas, *General Defense* 1416

Mozley, Finlayson & Loggins LLP
Atlanta, Georgia, *General Defense* 443
Atlanta, Georgia, *Subrogation* 1634

Mulherin, Rehfeldt & Varchetto, P.C.
Wheaton, Illinois, *General Defense* 550

Mullikin, Larson & Swift LLC
Jackson, Wyoming, *General Defense* 1596

Mullins, Harris & Jessee
Norton, Virginia, *General Defense* 1510

Mulvey, Oliver, Gould & Crotta
New Haven, Connecticut, *General Defense* 317

Munro Smigliani & Jordan, LLP
San Diego, California, *General Defense* 241

Munson, Rowlett, Moore & Boone, P.A.
Little Rock, Arkansas, *General Defense* 171

Murchison & Cumming, LLP
Irvine, California, *General Defense* 194
Los Angeles, California, *General Defense* 204
San Diego, California, *General Defense* 241
San Francisco, California, *General Defense* 251
Las Vegas, Nevada, *General Defense* 940

Murphy, Campbell, Alliston & Quinn
Sacramento, California, *General Defense* 233

Murphy Collette Murphy
Moncton, New Brunswick, *General Defense* 1609
Moncton, New Brunswick, *Subrogation* 1666

Murphy & Decker, P.C.
Denver, Colorado, *General Defense* 289

Murphy, Genello & Murphy, P.C.
Scranton, Pennsylvania, *General Defense* 1276
Scranton, Pennsylvania, *Subrogation* 1659
Stroudsburg, Pennsylvania, *General Defense* 1278
Stroudsburg, Pennsylvania, *Subrogation* 1659

Murphy & Riley, P.C.
Boston, Massachusetts, *General Defense* 759

Murphy & Spagnuolo, P.C.
Lansing, Michigan, *General Defense* 799

Murray, Craven & Inman, L.L.P.
Fayetteville, North Carolina, *General Defense* 1124

Murray, Morin & Herman, P.A.
Tampa, Florida, *General Defense* 421

N

Nageley, Meredith & Miller, Inc.
Sacramento, California, *General Defense* 234

Nall & Miller, LLP
Atlanta, Georgia, *General Defense* 444

ATTORNEYS - ALPHABETICAL FIRM INDEX

Nance, McCants and Massey
    Aiken, South Carolina, *General Defense* 1294

Napier Gault Schupbach & Moore, PLC
    Louisville, Kentucky, *General Defense* 638

Napierski, VanDenburgh, Napierski, & O'Connor, LLP
    Albany, New York, *General Defense* 1025
    Albany, New York, *Subrogation* 1651

Naschitz, Brandes, Amir & Co.
    Tel Aviv, Israel, *General Defense* 1620
    Tel Aviv, Israel, *Subrogation* 1668

Nash, Spindler, Grimstad & McCracken LLP
    Manitowoc, Wisconsin, *General Defense* 1575

Nathan, Bremer, Dumm & Myers, P.C.
    Denver, Colorado, *General Defense* 289

W. Paul Needham, P.C.
    Boston, Massachusetts, *General Defense* 760

Neil, Dymott, Frank, McFall & Trexler
    San Diego, California, *General Defense* 241

Nelson Terry Morton DeWitt Paruolo & Wood
    Edmond, Oklahoma, *General Defense* 1191

Nelson Zentner Sartor and Snellings, LLC
    Monroe, Louisiana, *General Defense* 684

Law Offices of Bohdan Neswiacheny
    Fort Lauderdale, Florida, *General Defense* 358
    Orange Park, Florida, *General Defense* 393
    Sarasota, Florida, *General Defense* 411

Neville, Richards & Wuller, LLC
    Belleville, Illinois, *General Defense* 492

Newman Myers Kreines Gross Harris, P.C.
    New York, New York, *General Defense* 1077

Nicklaus & Associates, P.A.
    Miami, Florida, *General Defense* 383

Nicoletti Gonson Spinner LLP
    New York, New York, *General Defense* 1078
    Hackensack, New Jersey, *General Defense* 969

Niedner, Bodeux, Carmichael, Huff, Lenox, Pashos and Simpson, L.L.P.
    St. Charles, Missouri, *General Defense* 885

Nielsen, Haley & Abbott LLP
    Los Angeles, California, *General Defense* 205
    San Francisco, California, *General Defense* 252

Niles, Barton & Wilmer, LLP
    Baltimore, Maryland, *General Defense* 732

Nilles Law Firm
    Fargo, North Dakota, *General Defense* 1149

Norman, Wood, Kendrick & Turner
    Birmingham, Alabama, *General Defense* 88

Northcraft, Bigby & Biggs, P.C.
    Seattle, Washington, *General Defense* 1541

The Notzon Law Firm
    Laredo, Texas, *General Defense* 1448

Nowell Amoroso Klein Bierman, P.A.
    Hackensack, New Jersey, *General Defense* 970

ATTORNEYS - ALPHABETICAL FIRM INDEX

Law Offices of George W. Nowell
   San Francisco, California, *General Defense* 252
   San Francisco, California, *Subrogation* 1632

Law Offices of David C. Numrych PC
   Washington, District of Columbia, *General Defense* 337

Nuzzo & Roberts, L.L.C.
   New Haven, Connecticut, *General Defense* 317

O

O'Bannon & O'Bannon, L.L.C.
   Florence, Alabama, *General Defense* 101

Obert Law Group, P.A.
   Jackson, Mississippi, *General Defense* 850

O'Brien, Rulis and Bochicchio, LLC
   Philadelphia, Pennsylvania, *General Defense* 1259
   Pittsburgh, Pennsylvania, *General Defense* 1270

O'Bryan, Brown & Toner, PLLC
   Louisville, Kentucky, *General Defense* 638

O'Bryon & Schnabel, PLC
   New Orleans, Louisiana, *General Defense* 699

O'Connell & O'Connell, LLC
   Rockville, Maryland, *General Defense* 742

O'Connor & Campbell, P.C.
   Phoenix, Arizona, *General Defense* 148

O'Connor Kimball LLP
   Cherry Hill, New Jersey, *General Defense* 966
   Philadelphia, Pennsylvania, *General Defense* 1259

O'Connor, O'Connor, Bresee & First, P.C.
   Albany, New York, *General Defense* 1026

Offutt Nord Burchett, PLLC
   Huntington, West Virginia, *General Defense* 1560

Ogden Murphy Wallace, P.L.L.C.
   Seattle, Washington, *General Defense* 1542
   Wenatchee, Washington, *General Defense* 1548

O'Hara Halvorsen Humphries, PA
   Jacksonville, Florida, *General Defense* 374

Ohrenstein & Brown, LLP
   Garden City, New York, *General Defense* 1043
   New York, New York, *General Defense* 1079

Oland & Co.
   Kelowna, British Columbia, *General Defense* 1606
   Kelowna, British Columbia, *Subrogation* 1665

Oldenettel & McCabe
   Houston, Texas, *General Defense* 1438

Olson, Cannon, Gormley Angulo & Stoberski
   Las Vegas, Nevada, *General Defense* 940

O'Malley, Harris, Durkin & Perry, P.C.
   Scranton, Pennsylvania, *General Defense* 1277

O'Meara, Leer, Wagner & Kohl, P.A.
   Minneapolis, Minnesota, *General Defense* 823
   Minneapolis, Minnesota, *Subrogation* 1644

O'Neill & Jackson
   Fort Worth, Texas, *General Defense* 1420

ATTORNEYS - ALPHABETICAL FIRM INDEX

Oppegard & Quinton
　Moorhead, Minnesota, *General Defense* 826

Osborn, Reed & Burke, LLP
　Rochester, New York, *General Defense* 1099

Ostendorf Tate Barnett, LLP
　New Orleans, Louisiana, *General Defense* 700

Ouellette, Deganis & Gallagher, LLC
　Cheshire, Connecticut, *General Defense* 304

Overturf McGath & Hull, P.C.
　Denver, Colorado, *General Defense* 290

Owens & Millsaps, LLP
　Tuscaloosa, Alabama, *General Defense* 132

P

Page, Mannino, Peresich & McDermott, P.L.L.C.
　Biloxi, Mississippi, *General Defense* 830
　Jackson, Mississippi, *General Defense* 851
　Gulfport, Mississippi, *General Defense* 837

Pajares & Schexnaydre, L.L.C.
　Mandeville, Louisiana, *General Defense* 674

Law Office of John M. Palm, LLC
　Gibbsboro, New Jersey, *General Defense* 969

The Parker Firm, PC
　Tyler, Texas, *General Defense* 1469

Parker, Heitz & Cosgrove, PLLC
　Billings, Montana, *General Defense* 904

Parker, Lawrence, Cantrell & Smith
　Nashville, Tennessee, *General Defense* 1363

Parsons, Lee & Juliano, P.C.
　Birmingham, Alabama, *General Defense* 89

Partridge Snow & Hahn LLP
　Providence, Rhode Island, *General Defense* 1288

Paterson, MacDougall LLP
　Toronto, Ontario, *General Defense* 1612

Patterson and Sciarrino, L.L.P.
　Bayside, New York, *General Defense* 1030

Patterson Buchanan Fobes & Leitch, Inc., PS
　Seattle, Washington, *General Defense* 1542

Patterson Dilthey LLP
　Raleigh, North Carolina, *General Defense* 1135

Patterson Law Firm, L.L.P.
　Des Moines, Iowa, *General Defense* 585

Paule, Camazine & Blumenthal
　St. Louis, Missouri, *General Defense* 894

Paul Frank + Collins P.C.
　Burlington, Vermont, *General Defense* 1485

Paulsen, Malec & Malartsik, Ltd.
　Wheaton, Illinois, *General Defense* 552

Paxton & Smith, P.A.
　West Palm Beach, Florida, *General Defense* 427

Payne & Jones, Chartered
　Overland Park, Kansas, *General Defense* 600

ATTORNEYS - ALPHABETICAL FIRM INDEX

Peabody & Arnold LLP
    Boston, Massachusetts, *General Defense*..760

Peacock, Keller & Ecker, LLP
    Washington, Pennsylvania, *General Defense*...1279

Pearlman, Borska & Wax, LLP
    Los Angeles, California, *General Defense*..205

The Peisner Girsh Group LLP
    Short Hills, New Jersey, *General Defense*..994
    New York, New York, *General Defense*..1079

Pender & Coward
    Virginia Beach, Virginia, *General Defense*..1525

Perkins & Associates, L.L.C.
    Shreveport, Louisiana, *General Defense*...710

Perkins Thompson, P.A.
    Portland, Maine, *General Defense*..718

Perrier & Lacoste, LLC
    New Orleans, Louisiana, *General Defense*...700

Perrine, Redemann, Berry, Taylor & Sloan PLLC
    Tulsa, Oklahoma, *General Defense*...1210
    Tulsa, Oklahoma, *Subrogation*...1656

Perry, Atkinson, Balhoff, Mengis & Burns, L.L.C.
    Baton Rouge, Louisiana, *General Defense*..659

Pessin Katz Law, P.A.
    Baltimore, Maryland, *General Defense*...732

Peterson Farris Byrd & Parker
    Amarillo, Texas, *General Defense*...1373
    Amarillo, Texas, *Subrogation*..1661
    Lubbock, Texas, *General Defense*..1451

Peters & Wasilefski
    Harrisburg, Pennsylvania, *General Defense*...1241
    Harrisburg, Pennsylvania, *Subrogation*...1657

Petkoff and Feigelson, PLLC
    Memphis, Tennessee, *General Defense*..1354

Petruccelli, Martin & Haddow, LLP
    Portland, Maine, *General Defense*..718

Pett Furman, PL
    Boca Raton, Florida, *General Defense*...342

Phelps Dunbar LLP
    Mobile, Alabama, *General Defense*...114
    Tampa, Florida, *General Defense*...422
    Baton Rouge, Louisiana, *General Defense*..659
    New Orleans, Louisiana, *General Defense*...701
    Gulfport, Mississippi, *General Defense*..837
    Jackson, Mississippi, *General Defense*..851
    Tupelo, Mississippi, *General Defense*..863
    Raleigh, North Carolina, *General Defense*...1135
    Dallas, Texas, *General Defense*..1404
    Houston, Texas, *General Defense*...1438
    London, United Kingdom, *General Defense*...1624

Phelps, Jenkins, Gibson & Fowler, LLP
    Tuscaloosa, Alabama, *General Defense*...133

Phillips Akers Womac, P.C.
    Houston, Texas, *General Defense*...1440

Phillips & Associates
    San Luis Obispo, California, *General Defense*.......................................259

ATTORNEYS - ALPHABETICAL FIRM INDEX

Phillips Haffey PC
   Missoula, Montana, *General Defense* 918

Phillips Parker Orberson & Arnett, P.L.C.
   Louisville, Kentucky, *General Defense* 639

Pierce Herns Sloan & Wilson, LLC
   Charleston, South Carolina, *General Defense* 1301

Law Office of Donald M. Pilger
   San Diego, California, *General Defense* 243

Pillinger Miller Tarallo, LLP
   Elmsford, New York, *General Defense* 1041
   Elmsford, New York, *Subrogation* 1651
   Syracuse, New York, *General Defense* 1103
   Syracuse, New York, *Subrogation* 1653

Pino & Associates, LLP
   White Plains, New York, *General Defense* 1114
   White Plains, New York, *Subrogation* 1654

Pinto Coates Kyre & Bowers, PLLC
   Greensboro, North Carolina, *General Defense* 1127
   Greensboro, North Carolina, *Subrogation*. 1654

Plant, Christensen & Kanell, P.C.
   Salt Lake City, Utah, *General Defense* 1479

Plauché Maselli Parkerson L.L.P.
   New Orleans, Louisiana, *General Defense* 703

Plauché, Smith & Nieset, LLC
   Lake Charles, Louisiana, *General Defense* 671
   Lake Charles, Louisiana, *Subrogation* 1641

Podvey, Meanor, Catenacci, Hildner, Cocoziello & Chattman, P.C.
   Newark, New Jersey, *General Defense* 987
   Newark, New Jersey, *Subrogation* 1648

Pollack Law Firm, P.C.
   Indianapolis, Indiana, *General Defense* 566

William J. Pollinger, P.A.
   Hackensack, New Jersey, *General Defense* 971
   Hackensack, New Jersey, *Subrogation* 1647

Poole & Shaffery, LLP
   Los Angeles, California, *General Defense* 207

Porteous, Hainkel and Johnson, L.L.P.
   New Orleans, Louisiana, *General Defense* 704

Porter, Porter & Hassinger, P.C.
   Birmingham, Alabama, *General Defense* 90

Post & Post, LLC
   Berwyn, Pennsylvania, *General Defense* 1232

Powell, Birchmeier & Powell
   Tuckahoe, New Jersey, *General Defense* 1000
   Woodbury, New Jersey, *General Defense* 1004

Powers McNalis Torres Teebagy Luongo
   West Palm Beach, Florida, *General Defense*. 428

Powers, Sellers & Chapoton, L.L.P.
   Baton Rouge, Louisiana, *General Defense* 661

PPGMR Law, PLLC
   Little Rock, Arkansas, *General Defense* 173

Pratt Vreeland Kennelly Martin & White Ltd.
   Rutland, Vermont, *General Defense* 1487

ATTORNEYS - ALPHABETICAL FIRM INDEX

Preis PLC
    Lafayette, Louisiana, *General Defense* 669
    New Orleans, Louisiana, *General Defense* 705
    Houston, Texas, *General Defense* 1440

Law Offices of Michael E. Pressman
    Warren, New Jersey, *General Defense* 1002
    Brooklyn, New York, *General Defense* 1033
    Long Island City, New York, *General Defense* 1050
    New York, New York, *General Defense* 1080

Preti, Flaherty, Beliveau & Pachios, LLP
    Portland, Maine, *General Defense* 718

Pretzel & Stouffer Chartered
    Chicago, Illinois, *General Defense* 525

Clifton S. Price, II
    Birmingham, Alabama, *General Defense* 91

Prince & Keating, LLP
    Las Vegas, Nevada, *General Defense* 941

Protogyrou & Rigney, PLC
    Norfolk, Virginia, *General Defense* 1508

Provizer & Phillips, P.C.
    Bingham Farms, Michigan, *General Defense* 780

Provosty & Gankendorff, L.L.C.
    New Orleans, Louisiana, *General Defense* 705

Provosty, Sadler, deLaunay, Fiorenza & Sobel
    Alexandria, Louisiana, *General Defense* 652

Prutting & Lombardi
    Audubon, New Jersey, *General Defense* 957

Pullin, Fowler, Flanagan, Brown & Poe, PLLC
    Beckley, West Virginia, *General Defense* 1552
    Charleston, West Virginia, *General Defense* 1555
    Martinsburg, West Virginia, *General Defense* 1563
    Morgantown, West Virginia, *General Defense* 1564

Purcell & Ingrao, P.C.
    Mineola, New York, *General Defense* 1057

Purcell & Wardrope, Chartered
    Chicago, Illinois, *General Defense* 526

Pyka Lenhardt Schnaider Zell
    Santa Ana, California, *General Defense* 260

Q

The Quinn Law Firm, LLC
    Milford, Connecticut, *General Defense* 313
    Milford, Connecticut, *Subrogation* 1633

R

Daniel W. Raab, P.A.
    Miami, Florida, *General Defense* 384

Rabalais & Hebert
    Lafayette, Louisiana, *General Defense* 670
    Lafayette, Louisiana, *Subrogation* 1641

Racine Olson Nye Budge & Bailey, Chartered
    Boise, Idaho, *General Defense* 482
    Pocatello, Idaho, *General Defense* 487

Radey Law Firm
    Tallahassee, Florida, *General Defense* 417
    Tallahassee, Florida, *Regulatory and Compliance* 1670

ATTORNEYS - ALPHABETICAL FIRM INDEX

Raggio, Cappel, Chozen & Berniard
    Lake Charles, Louisiana, *General Defense* ... 672

Ragsdale Liggett PLLC
    Raleigh, North Carolina, *General Defense* ... 1136
    Raleigh, North Carolina, *Regulatory and Compliance* ... 1672

Rainey & Austin, P. C.
    Mobile, Alabama, *General Defense* ... 115

Rainey, Kizer, Reviere & Bell, P.L.C.
    Jackson, Tennessee, *General Defense* ... 1342
    Jackson, Tennessee, *General Defense* ... 1342
    Memphis, Tennessee, *General Defense* ... 1355

Rammelkamp Bradney, P.C.
    Jacksonville, Illinois, *General Defense* ... 534
    Springfield, Illinois, *General Defense* ... 548

Ramsden & Lyons, LLP
    Coeur d'Alene, Idaho, *General Defense* ... 484

Ramsey & Murray, P.C.
    Houston, Texas, *General Defense* ... 1440

Ray, McChristian & Jeans, P.C.
    Albuquerque, New Mexico, *General Defense* ... 1011
    El Paso, Texas, *General Defense* ... 1417
    Fort Worth, Texas, *General Defense* ... 1421
    San Antonio, Texas, *General Defense* ... 1464

Raymond Law Group LLC
    Glastonbury, Connecticut, *General Defense* ... 305

Reardon & Sclafani, P.C.
    Tarrytown, New York, *General Defense* ... 1105

Reed Armstrong Mudge & Morrissey P.C.
    Edwardsville, Illinois, *General Defense* ... 532

Reed McClure
    Seattle, Washington, *General Defense* ... 1543

Regan & Kiely LLP
    Boston, Massachusetts, *General Defense* ... 761

Regnier, Taylor, Curran & Eddy
    Hartford, Connecticut, *General Defense* ... 309

Reid, Burge, Prevallet & Coleman
    Blytheville, Arkansas, *General Defense* ... 157

Reminger Co., L.P.A.
    Indianapolis, Indiana, *General Defense* ... 566
    Cincinnati, Ohio, *General Defense* ... 1164
    Cleveland, Ohio, *General Defense* ... 1177
    Columbus, Ohio, *General Defense* ... 1179

Rendigs, Fry, Kiely & Dennis, L.L.P.
    Cincinnati, Ohio, *General Defense* ... 1165

Rettig Osborne Forgette, L.L.P.
    Kennewick, Washington, *General Defense* ... 1531

Rexach & Pico
    San Juan, Puerto Rico, *General Defense* ... 1601

Reynolds, DeMarco & Boland, Ltd.
    Providence, Rhode Island, *General Defense* ... 1289

Rhoads & Sinon LLP
    Harrisburg, Pennsylvania, *General Defense* ... 1242

Rhodes, Hieronymus, Jones, Tucker & Gable, PLLC
    Tulsa, Oklahoma, *General Defense* ... 1211

ATTORNEYS - ALPHABETICAL FIRM INDEX

Rice Dolan & Kershaw
    Providence, Rhode Island, *General Defense* 1289

Richards & Connor, PLLP
    Tulsa, Oklahoma, *General Defense* 1212

Richardson Plowden & Robinson, P.A.
    Myrtle Beach, South Carolina, *General Defense* 1319

Richardson, Whitman, Large & Badger
    Bangor, Maine, *General Defense* 715
    Portland, Maine, *General Defense* 719

Richardson, Wyly, Wise, Sauck & Hieb, LLP
    Aberdeen, South Dakota, *General Defense* 1328

Richards & Simpson
    Denver, Colorado, *General Defense* 291

Righi Law Group
    Phoenix, Arizona, *General Defense* 149

Riker Danzig Scherer Hyland & Perretti LLP
    Morristown, New Jersey, *General Defense* 983
    Trenton, New Jersey, *General Defense* 1000

Rimac Martin, PC
    San Francisco, California, *General Defense* 252

Ritsema & Lyon, P.C.
    Denver, Colorado, *General Defense* 291

Ritter, Robinson, McCready & James, Ltd.
    Toledo, Ohio, *General Defense* 1186

Rivkin Radler LLP
    Uniondale, New York, *General Defense* 1107

Roach, Brown, McCarthy & Gruber, P.C.
    Buffalo, New York, *General Defense* 1038

Roberts Law Firm
    Mendocino, California, *General Defense* 212

Robertson & Associates, APC
    San Diego, California, *General Defense* 243
    Seattle, Washington, *General Defense* 1544

Robinson and Havens, PSC
    Lexington, Kentucky, *General Defense* 626

Robinson, Kriger & McCallum
    Portland, Maine, *General Defense* 720

ROBINSON SHEPPARD SHAPIRO L.L.P.
    Montreal, Quebec, *General Defense* 1615

Rocap Musser LLP
    Indianapolis, Indiana, *General Defense* 566

Rocco Law Firm, P.L.L.C.
    Phoenix, Arizona, *Investigation and Adjustment* 1676

Roderick Linton Belfance, LLP
    Akron, Ohio, *General Defense* 1159

L. C. Rodrigo Abogados
    Madrid, Spain, *General Defense* 1622

Roeca Luria Hiraoka LLP
    Honolulu, Hawaii, *General Defense* 471

Law Office of David J. E. Roe
    Mount Prospect, Illinois, *General Defense* 540

Roemer Wallens Gold & Mineaux LLP
    Albany, New York, *General Defense* 1027

ATTORNEYS - ALPHABETICAL FIRM INDEX

The Law Office of Lawrence N. Rogak, LLC
    Oceanside, New York, *General Defense* 1094

Roig, Tutan, Rosenberg, Martin & Stoller, Zumpano & Bellido
    Deerfield Beach, Florida, *General Defense* 349

Roland Legal PLLC
    Lexington, Kentucky, *General Defense* 627

Ropers, Majeski, Kohn & Bentley
    Los Angeles, California, *General Defense* 207
    Redwood City, California, *General Defense* 224
    San Francisco, California, *General Defense* 253
    San Jose, California, *General Defense* 257
    Boston, Massachusetts, *General Defense* 761
    New York, New York, *General Defense* 1080

The Rosen Law Firm
    Portland, Oregon, *General Defense* 1224
    Portland, Oregon, *Subrogation* 1656

Rose Padden Petty Taylor & Lilly, L.C.
    Fairmont, West Virginia, *General Defense* 1558

Law Offices of Virgil L. Roth, PC
    Los Angeles, California, *General Defense* 208

Rubin, Rudman, Chamberlain and Marsh
    Yarmouth Port, Massachusetts, *General Defense* 776

Rucker and Rucker, P.C.
    Murfreesboro, Tennessee, *General Defense* 1356

Rushton, Stakely, Johnston & Garrett, P.A.
    Montgomery, Alabama, *General Defense* 125

Russell, English, Scoma & Beneke, P.C.
    Princeton, Illinois, *General Defense* 543

Russo & Toner, LLP
    New York, New York, *General Defense* 1081
    Trevose, Pennsylvania, *General Defense* 1278

Rutledge, Manion, Rabaut, Terry & Thomas, P.C.
    Detroit, Michigan, *General Defense* 788

Ryals, Donaldson & Agricola, P.C.
    Montgomery, Alabama, *General Defense* 127

Law Offices of Greg J. Ryan, APLC
    San Diego, California, *General Defense* 244

Ryan Ryan Deluca LLP
    Stamford, Connecticut, *General Defense* 322

Ryan Smith & Carbine, Ltd.
    Rutland, Vermont, *General Defense* 1488

Ryberg Law Firm, S.C.
    Eau Claire, Wisconsin, *General Defense* 1571

Rynearson, Suess, Schnurbusch & Champion, L.L.C.
    St. Louis, Missouri, *General Defense* 894

S

Sachs, Maitlin, Fleming & Greene
    West Orange, New Jersey, *General Defense* 1002
    West Orange, New Jersey, *Subrogation* 1649

St. Denis & Davey, P.A.
    Jacksonville, Florida, *General Defense* 375

Sandberg Phoenix & von Gontard P.C.
    St. Louis, Missouri, *General Defense* 895

ATTORNEYS - ALPHABETICAL FIRM INDEX

Sanders + Parks, P.C.
    Phoenix, Arizona, *General Defense* 150

Sanders, Bruin, Coll & Worley, P.A.
    Roswell, New Mexico, *General Defense* 1017

Sanders Warren & Russell LLP
    Overland Park, Kansas, *General Defense* 600
    Kansas City, Missouri, *General Defense* 879
    Springfield, Missouri, *General Defense* 884

Sands Anderson PC
    Richmond, Virginia, *General Defense* 1518

Saretsky Katz Dranoff & Glass, L.L.P.
    New York, New York, *General Defense* 1082

Sarrail, Castillo & Hall, LLP
    Burlingame, California, *General Defense* 183

Sasser & Inglis, P.C.
    Boise, Idaho, *General Defense* 482

Saunders & Schmieler, P.C.
    Silver Spring, Maryland, *General Defense* 744

Savage Baum & Glass
    Tulsa, Oklahoma, *General Defense* 1213

Scalley Reading Bates Hansen & Rasmussen, P.C.
    Salt Lake City, Utah, *General Defense* 1480

Schafer & Schafer
    New Orleans, Louisiana, *General Defense* 706

Schaffer, Lax, McNaughton & Chen
    Los Angeles, California, *General Defense* 208

Schechner Marcus LLP
    Springfield, New Jersey, *General Defense* 997

Schiller Osbourn Barnes & Maloney, PLLC
    Louisville, Kentucky, *General Defense* 640

Schnitter Ciccarelli Mills, PLLC
    East Amherst, New York, *General Defense* 1041

Scholz, Loos, Palmer, Siebers & Duesterhaus LLP
    Quincy, Illinois, *General Defense* 543

Schonfeld, Bertsche & Preciado, LLP
    San Diego, California, *General Defense* 244

Schuermans & Schuermans
    Antwerp, Belgium, *General Defense* 1618

Schulman, LeRoy & Bennett, P.C.
    Nashville, Tennessee, *General Defense* 1364

Schwartz, Bon, Walker & Studer, L.L.C.
    Casper, Wyoming, *General Defense* 1590

Schwartz Law Group
    Boca Raton, Florida, *General Defense* 342

Scott & Kienzle, P.A.
    Albuquerque, New Mexico, *General Defense* 1012
    Albuquerque, New Mexico, *Subrogation* 1650

Scott, Sullivan, Streetman & Fox, P.C.
    Birmingham, Alabama, *General Defense* 91

Scott, Sullivan, Streetman & Fox, P.C.
    Mobile, Alabama, *General Defense* 116

Scott, Sullivan, Streetman & Fox, P.C.
    Jackson, Mississippi, *General Defense* 852

ATTORNEYS - ALPHABETICAL FIRM INDEX

Scott Venturo LLP
    Calgary, Alberta, *General Defense* ... 1606

SCP Bouckaert Ormen Passemard Sportes "BOPS"
    Paris, France, *General Defense* ... 1619
    Paris, France, *Regulatory and Compliance* ... 1674
    Paris, France, *Subrogation* ... 1667

Scrudder, Bass, Quillian, Horlock, Taylor & Lazarus, LLP
    Atlanta, Georgia, *General Defense* ... 446

Seacrest, Karesh, Tate & Bicknese, LLP
    Atlanta, Georgia, *General Defense* ... 447

Secrest, Hill, Butler & Secrest, P.C.
    Tulsa, Oklahoma, *General Defense* ... 1213

Secrest, Wardle, Lynch, Hampton, Truex and Morley, P.C.
    Grand Rapids, Michigan, *General Defense* ... 795
    Lansing, Michigan, *General Defense* ... 799
    Troy, Michigan, *General Defense* ... 812

Seibels Law Firm, P.A.
    Charleston, South Carolina, *General Defense* ... 1302

Seidel, Baker & Tilghman, P.A.
    Salisbury, Maryland, *General Defense* ... 743

Semmes, Bowen & Semmes
    Baltimore, Maryland, *General Defense* ... 733

Serkland Law Firm
    Fargo, North Dakota, *General Defense* ... 1150

Law Offices of Gordon P. Serou, Jr., L.L.C.
    New Orleans, Louisiana, *General Defense* ... 707

SettlePou
    Dallas, Texas, *General Defense* ... 1405

Severson & Werson
    San Francisco, California, *General Defense* ... 253

Sewell, O'Brien & Neal, PLLC
    Louisville, Kentucky, *General Defense* ... 641

Shafer, Davis, O'Leary & Stoker, Inc.
    Odessa, Texas, *General Defense* ... 1457

Shafer Glazer, LLP
    New York, New York, *General Defense* ... 1084

Shaffer & Shaffer, PLLC
    Madison, West Virginia, *General Defense* ... 1562

Law Office of Patrick J. Shannon
    Pittsburgh, Pennsylvania, *General Defense* ... 1271

Shealy, Crum & Pike, P.C.
    Dothan, Alabama, *General Defense* ... 99

Sheffy, Mazzaccaro, DePaolo & Denigris, LLP
    Southington, Connecticut, *General Defense* ... 322

Shepherd, Scott, Clawater & Houston, L.L.P.
    Houston, Texas, *General Defense* ... 1441

Sheppard, Mullin, Richter & Hampton LLP
    Costa Mesa, California, *General Defense* ... 185
    Los Angeles, California, *General Defense* ... 210
    San Diego, California, *General Defense* ... 244
    San Francisco, California, *General Defense* ... 254

Shields | Mott L.L.P.
    New Orleans, Louisiana, *General Defense* ... 707

ATTORNEYS - ALPHABETICAL FIRM INDEX

Shipley Law Group
    Chicago, Illinois, *General Defense* 527

Shively & Lannin, P.C., L.L.O.
    Lincoln, Nebraska, *General Defense* 924

Shuman, McCuskey & Slicer, PLLC
    Charleston, West Virginia, *General Defense* 1556
    Morgantown, West Virginia, *General Defense* 1564

Shuttleworth Williams, PLLC
    Memphis, Tennessee, *General Defense* 1355

Shutts & Bowen LLP
    Miami, Florida, *General Defense* 384

Siciliano, Ellis, Dyer & Boccarosse PLC
    Fairfax, Virginia, *General Defense* 1501

Siegel, Moreno & Stettler, APC
    San Diego, California, *General Defense* 244

Siemion Huckabay, P.C.
    Southfield, Michigan, *General Defense* 803

Simmons Olsen Law Firm, P.C.
    Scottsbluff, Nebraska, *General Defense* 934

Simoncini & Associates
    San Jose, California, *General Defense* 258

Andrew C. Simpson, P.C.
    Christiansted, St. Croix, Virgin Islands, *General Defense* 1604

Sirote & Permutt, P.C.
    Birmingham, Alabama, *General Defense* 92
    Huntsville, Alabama, *General Defense* 107
    Mobile, Alabama, *General Defense* 117

Skaggs & Guerra
    McAllen, Texas, *General Defense* 1455

Skellenger Bender, P.S.
    Seattle, Washington, *General Defense* 1544

Skelton, Taintor & Abbott
    Auburn, Maine, *General Defense* 714
    Auburn, Maine, *Subrogation* 1641

Skiles Law Office Chartered
    Madison, Wisconsin, *General Defense* 1575

Sliwa & Lane
    Buffalo, New York, *General Defense* 1039

Sloane and Walsh
    Boston, Massachusetts, *General Defense* 762
    Boston, Massachusetts, *Subrogation* 1642

Slutsky, McMorris & Meehan, LLP
    Stamford, Connecticut, *General Defense* 324

Smiling, Wangsgard, Smiling & Burgess
    Tulsa, Oklahoma, *General Defense* 1215

Smith & Carr, P.C.
    Houston, Texas, *General Defense* 1442

Smith, Cohen & Horan, PLC
    Fort Smith, Arkansas, *General Defense* 162

Smith Duggan Buell & Rufo LLP
    Boston, Massachusetts, *General Defense* 763

Smith Fisher Maas & Howard, P.C.
    Indianapolis, Indiana, *General Defense* 567

ATTORNEYS - ALPHABETICAL FIRM INDEX

Smith Freed & Eberhard, P.C.
    Portland, Oregon, *General Defense* 1225
    Seattle, Washington, *General Defense* 1545

Smith & Glauser, P.C.
    Salt Lake City, Utah, *General Defense* 1480

Smith Law Firm
    Reno, Nevada, *Regulatory and Compliance* 1671

Smith Law Group
    Tucson, Arizona, *General Defense* 154

Smith Marshall, LLP
    Cleveland, Ohio, *General Defense* 1177

Smith Mazure Director Wilkins Young & Yagerman, P.C.
    Somerville, New Jersey, *General Defense* 994
    Somerville, New Jersey, *Subrogation* 1648
    Mineola, New York, *General Defense* 1058
    Mineola, New York, *Subrogation* 1651
    New York, New York, *General Defense* 1084
    New York, New York, *Subrogation* 1652

Smith & Pace, PC
    Birmingham, Alabama, *General Defense* 93

Smith Smith & Feeley LLP
    Irvine, California, *General Defense* 194

Smith, Sovik, Kendrick & Sugnet, P.C.
    Buffalo, New York, *General Defense* 1040
    Syracuse, New York, *General Defense* 1103
    Uniondale, New York, *General Defense* 1110

Smith & Tomkins
    Nashville, Tennessee, *General Defense* 1364

Smith, Walsh, Clarke & Gregoire, PLLP
    Great Falls, Montana, *General Defense* 910

Snellgrove, Langley, Culpepper, Williams & Mullally
    Jonesboro, Arkansas, *General Defense* 164

Sniffen & Spellman, P.A.
    Tallahassee, Florida, *General Defense* 417

Sobel Law Group LLC
    Burlington, New Jersey, *General Defense* 962
    Huntington, New York, *General Defense* 1046
    New York, New York, *General Defense* 1086

Law Offices of Douglas R. Soderland
    Seattle, Washington, *General Defense* 1545

Sodoro Daly Shomaker & Selde PC LLO
    Omaha, Nebraska, *General Defense* 931

Sonneborn Rutter & Cooney, P.A.
    West Palm Beach, Florida, *General Defense* 429

Southeast Law Group, P.A.
    Daytona Beach, Florida, *General Defense* 347
    Lake Mary, Florida, *General Defense* 378

Sowell Gray Stepp & Laffitte, L.L.C.
    Columbia, South Carolina, *General Defense* 1309

Spangler, Jennings & Dougherty, P.C.
    Indianapolis, Indiana, *General Defense* 568
    Merrillville, Indiana, *General Defense* 571
    Merrillville, Indiana, *Subrogation* 1639

Speyer & Perlberg, LLP
    Melville, New York, *General Defense* 1053

ATTORNEYS - ALPHABETICAL FIRM INDEX

Spooner & Much, P.C.
    Portland, Oregon, *General Defense* 1226
    Salem, Oregon, *General Defense* 1227

Spoon Gordon Ballew PC
    Missoula, Montana, *General Defense* 919

Spragins, Barnett and Cobb, PLC
    Jackson, Tennessee, *General Defense* 1344

Sreenan Law, P.A.
    Miami, Florida, *General Defense* 385

Stackhouse, Nexsen & Turrietta, PLLC
    Norfolk, Virginia, *General Defense* 1509

Stacy & Conder, LLP
    Dallas, Texas, *General Defense* 1406

Stafford, Stewart & Potter
    Alexandria, Louisiana, *General Defense* 652

Staines & Eppling
    Metairie, Louisiana, *General Defense* 681

Stark & Knoll Co. LPA
    Akron, Ohio, *General Defense* 1159

M. Susie Starnes & Associates
    Cleveland, Tennessee, *General Defense* 1338

Statham Allega and Jessen, LLP
    Evansville, Indiana, *General Defense* 557

Stauffer & Nathan, P.C.
    Tulsa, Oklahoma, *General Defense* 1215

Steed Dunnill Reynolds Murphy Lamberth LLP
    Rockwall, Texas, *General Defense* 1459

Stein Monast L.L.P.
    Quebec, Quebec, *General Defense* 1615

Stelzner, Winter, Warburton, Flores, Sanchez & Dawes, P.A.
    Albuquerque, New Mexico, *General Defense* 1012
    Jackson, Wyoming, *General Defense* 1596

Stephenson & Dickinson, P.C.
    Las Vegas, Nevada, *General Defense* 941

Steptoe & Johnson PLLC
    Lexington, Kentucky, *General Defense* 627
    Columbus, Ohio, *General Defense* 1180
    Canonsburg, Pennsylvania, *General Defense* 1233
    Meadville, Pennsylvania, *General Defense* 1246
    Bridgeport, West Virginia, *General Defense* 1553
    Bridgeport, West Virginia, *Investigation and Adjustment* 1679
    Charleston, West Virginia, *General Defense* 1557
    Charleston, West Virginia, *Investigation and Adjustment* 1680
    Huntington, West Virginia, *General Defense* 1561
    Martinsburg, West Virginia, *General Defense* 1563
    Morgantown, West Virginia, *General Defense* 1565
    Morgantown, West Virginia, *Investigation and Adjustment* 1680
    Wheeling, West Virginia, *General Defense* 1567

Stern & Montana, LLP
    New York, New York, *General Defense* 1086

Stiff, Keith & Garcia, LLC
    Albuquerque, New Mexico, *General Defense* 1013

Stinnett & Masters LLP
    Colorado Springs, Colorado, *General Defense* 276

Clark D. Stith
    Rock Springs, Wyoming, *General Defense* 1597

ATTORNEYS - ALPHABETICAL FIRM INDEX

Stockton, Barker & Mead, LLP
Troy, New York, *General Defense* 1105

Stoloff & Silver, L.L.P.
Monticello, New York, *General Defense* 1058

Strachan Strachan & Simon, P.C.
Salt Lake City, Utah, *General Defense* 1481

Strasburger & Price, LLP
Dallas, Texas, *General Defense* 1406

Stratton Law Firm, P.S.C.
Pikeville, Kentucky, *General Defense* 645

Strawinski & Stout, P.C.
Atlanta, Georgia, *General Defense* 447

Strong & Hanni
Salt Lake City, Utah, *General Defense* 1481

Stuart Law Firm, PLLC
Raleigh, North Carolina, *General Defense* 1137
Raleigh, North Carolina, *Regulatory and Compliance* 1672
Raleigh, North Carolina, *Subrogation* 1655

Sturgill, Turner, Barker & Moloney, PLLC
Lexington, Kentucky, *General Defense* 627

Law Offices of Robert A. Stutman, P.C.
Palm Desert, California, *Subrogation* 1630
San Diego, California, *Subrogation* 1631
San Francisco, California, *Subrogation* 1632
Cherry Hill, New Jersey, *Subrogation* 1646
New York, New York, *Subrogation* 1652
Philadelphia, Pennsylvania, *Subrogation* 1657

Suarez & Suarez
Jersey City, New Jersey, *General Defense* 973

Sucre Arias & Reyes
Panama City, Panama, Republic of, *General Defense* 1622

Sullivan and Graber
Morristown, New Jersey, *General Defense* 984
New York, New York, *General Defense* 1087

Sullivan, Forr, Stokan, Huff & Kormanski
Altoona, Pennsylvania, *General Defense* 1231

Sullivan, Ward, Asher & Patton, P.C.
Southfield, Michigan, *General Defense* 804

Sundahl, Powers, Kapp & Martin, L.L.C.
Cheyenne, Wyoming, *General Defense* 1594

Susman, Duffy & Segaloff, P.C.
New Haven, Connecticut, *General Defense* 318

Sutton | Booker P.C.
Littleton, Colorado, *General Defense* 298

Swain & Dipolito LLP
Long Beach, California, *General Defense* 196

Swanson & Warcup, Ltd.
Grand Forks, North Dakota, *General Defense* 1152
Grand Forks, North Dakota, *Subrogation* 1655

Swartz Law Offices
New York, New York, *General Defense* 1087

Sweeny, Wingate & Barrow
Columbia, South Carolina, *General Defense* 1310

ATTORNEYS - ALPHABETICAL FIRM INDEX

Sweet Pasquarelli, PC
 New Brunswick, New Jersey, *General Defense* 985
 New Brunswick, New Jersey, *Subrogation* 1648

Swetman Baxter Massenburg, LLC
 New Orleans, Louisiana, *General Defense* 707
 Hattiesburg, Mississippi, *General Defense* 840

Swisher & Cohrt, P.L.C.
 Waterloo, Iowa, *General Defense* 591
 Waterloo, Iowa, *Investigation and Adjustment* 1678

T

Tatum, Tatum & Riedel Law Firm
 Danville, Arkansas, *General Defense* 157

Taunton, Snyder & Slade, P.C.
 Houston, Texas, *General Defense* 1442
 Houston, Texas, *Subrogation* 1662
 Houston, Texas, *Investigation and Adjustment* 1679

Taylor Dunham L.L.P.
 Austin, Texas, *General Defense* 1380

Taylor, Keller & Oswald, PLLC
 Lexington, Kentucky, *General Defense* 628
 London, Kentucky, *General Defense* 630

Taylor, Pigue, Marchetti & Blair, PLLC
 Nashville, Tennessee, *General Defense* 1364
 Nashville, Tennessee, *Subrogation* 1661

Taylor Ritter, P.C.
 Birmingham, Alabama, *General Defense* 93

Taylor, Stafford, Clithero, FitzGerald & Harris, LLP
 Springfield, Missouri, *General Defense* 884

Tekell, Book, Allen & Morris, LLP
 Houston, Texas, *General Defense* 1443

Tentinger Law Firm, P.A.
 Apple Valley, Minnesota, *General Defense* 816

Terwilliger, Wakeen, Piehler & Conway, S.C.
 Wausau, Wisconsin, *General Defense* 1585

Testa Heck Scrocca & Testa, PA
 Vineland, New Jersey, *General Defense* 1001
 Vineland, New Jersey, *Subrogation* 1649

Tharpe & Howell, LLP
 Los Angeles, California, *General Defense* 210

Theriault & Joslin, P.C.
 Montpelier, Vermont, *General Defense* 1486

Thibodeau, Johnson & Feriancek, PLLP
 Duluth, Minnesota, *General Defense* 817

Thiebaud Remington Thornton Bailey LLP
 Dallas, Texas, *General Defense* 1407

Thomas, DeGrood & Witenoff, P.C.
 Southfield, Michigan, *General Defense* 806

Thomas, Mamer & Haughey, LLP
 Champaign, Illinois, *General Defense* 497

Thompson & Bowie, LLP
 Portland, Maine, *General Defense* 720

Thompson, Coe, Cousins & Irons, L.L.P.
 Dallas, Texas, *General Defense* 1407
 Dallas, Texas, *Regulatory and Compliance* 1672

ATTORNEYS - ALPHABETICAL FIRM INDEX

Thompson & Colegate LLP
Riverside, California, *General Defense* 227

Thompson Dorfman Sweatman LLP
Winnipeg, Manitoba, *General Defense* 1608

Thompson & Reilley, P.C.
Houston, Texas, *General Defense* 1445

Thomson, Rhodes & Cowie, P.C.
Pittsburgh, Pennsylvania, *General Defense* 1271

Thorndal, Armstrong, Delk, Balkenbush & Eisinger
Las Vegas, Nevada, *General Defense* 942
Reno, Nevada, *General Defense* 947

Thorner, Kennedy & Gano, P.S.
Yakima, Washington, *General Defense* 1548

Thrasher, Pelish, Franti & Heaney, Ltd.
Rice Lake, Wisconsin, *General Defense* 1583

Threlkeld & Associates
Indianapolis, Indiana, *General Defense* 568

Thuillez, Ford, Gold, Butler & Monroe, LLP
Albany, New York, *General Defense* 1027

Tiemeier & Stich, P.C.
Denver, Colorado, *General Defense* 292

Tighe & Cottrell, P.A.
Wilmington, Delaware, *General Defense* 331

Timberlake, Smith, Thomas & Moses, P.C.
Staunton, Virginia, *General Defense* 1523

Timmermier, Gross & Prentiss
Omaha, Nebraska, *General Defense* 932

Tollefson Bradley Mitchell & Melendi, LLP
Dallas, Texas, *General Defense* 1411

Tooms & Dunaway, PLLC
London, Kentucky, *General Defense* 631

Torvinen, Jones & Routh, S.C.
Superior, Wisconsin, *General Defense* 1584

Touchstone, Bernays, Johnston, Beall, Smith & Stollenwerck, L.L.P.
Dallas, Texas, *General Defense* 1411

Towle Denison Smith & Maniscalco LLP
Los Angeles, California, *General Defense* 211

Towne, Ryan & Partners, P.C.
Albany, New York, *General Defense* 1028

Traub Lieberman Straus & Shrewsberry LLP
Los Angeles, California, *General Defense* 211
St. Petersburg, Florida, *General Defense* 414
Chicago, Illinois, *General Defense* 528
Red Bank, New Jersey, *General Defense* 990
Hawthorne, New York, *General Defense* 1044
New York, New York, *General Defense* 1087
London, United Kingdom, *General Defense* 1625

Traynor Law Firm, PC
Devils Lake, North Dakota, *General Defense* 1147
Minot, North Dakota, *General Defense* 1153

Trevett, Cristo, Salzer & Andolina, P.C.
Rochester, New York, *General Defense* 1099

Trevino, Valls & Haynes, L.L.P.
Laredo, Texas, *General Defense* 1448

ATTORNEYS - ALPHABETICAL FIRM INDEX

Tropio & Morlan
    Woodland Hills, California, *General Defense* 271

Trotta, Trotta & Trotta
    New Haven, Connecticut, *General Defense* 319

The Truitt Law Firm
    Covington, Louisiana, *General Defense* 663

Tucker Holmes, P.C.
    Denver, Colorado, *General Defense* 292

Tucker Law Group
    Bangor, Maine, *General Defense* 715

Tucker, Robin & Merker, LLC
    Chicago, Illinois, *General Defense* 528

Tuesley Hall Konopa, LLP
    South Bend, Indiana, *General Defense* 575

Tupper, Grimsley & Dean, P.A.
    Beaufort, South Carolina, *General Defense* 1294

Law Offices of Kenneth W. Turner
    Sacramento, California, *Subrogation* 1630

Turner, Padget, Graham & Laney, P.A.
    Charleston, South Carolina, *General Defense* 1303
    Columbia, South Carolina, *General Defense* 1311
    Florence, South Carolina, *General Defense* 1313
    Greenville, South Carolina, *General Defense* 1316
    Myrtle Beach, South Carolina, *General Defense* 1319

Turner, Reid, Duncan, Loomer & Patton, P.C.
    Springfield, Missouri, *General Defense* 885

Tyan & Zgheib
    Beirut, Lebanon, *General Defense* 1622

The Tyra Law Firm, P.C.
    Indianapolis, Indiana, *General Defense* 568

U

Underberg & Kessler LLP
    Rochester, New York, *General Defense* 1100

Ungarino & Eckert, L.L.C.
    Metairie, Louisiana, *General Defense* 682

Upshaw, Williams, Biggers & Beckham, L.L.P.
    Greenwood, Mississippi, *General Defense* 833
    Hernando, Mississippi, *General Defense* 841
    Ridgeland, Mississippi, *General Defense* 861

Urgo & Nugent, Ltd.
    Chicago, Illinois, *General Defense* 529

V

Vandeventer Black LLP
    Norfolk, Virginia, *General Defense* 1509

Varner, Parker & Sessums, P.A.
    Vicksburg, Mississippi, *General Defense* 866

Robert T. Varney & Associates
    Bloomington, Illinois, *General Defense* 494

Vaughan & DeMuro
    Colorado Springs, Colorado, *General Defense* 276

Veon Law Firm, P.A.
    Texarkana, Arkansas, *General Defense* 177

ATTORNEYS - ALPHABETICAL FIRM INDEX

Vernis & Bowling of Atlanta, LLC
  Atlanta, Georgia, *General Defense* 448

Vernis & Bowling of Birmingham, LLC
  Birmingham, Alabama, *General Defense* 94

Vernis & Bowling of Broward, P.A.
  Fort Lauderdale, Florida, *General Defense* 359

Vernis & Bowling of Central Florida, P.A.
  Daytona Beach, Florida, *General Defense* 348

Vernis & Bowling of Charlotte, PLLC
  Charlotte, North Carolina, *General Defense* 1121

Vernis & Bowling of Miami, P.A.
  Miami, Florida, *General Defense* 386

Vernis & Bowling of North Florida, P.A.
  Jacksonville, Florida, *General Defense* 375

Vernis & Bowling of Northwest Florida, P.A.
  Pensacola, Florida, *General Defense* 407

Vernis & Bowling of Palm Beach, P.A.
  North Palm Beach, Florida, *General Defense* 392

Vernis & Bowling of Southern Alabama, LLC
  Mobile, Alabama, *General Defense* 117

Vernis & Bowling of Southern Mississippi, PLLC
  Gulfport, Mississippi, *General Defense* 838

Vernis & Bowling of Southwest Florida, P.A.
  Fort Myers, Florida, *General Defense* 363

Vernis & Bowling of the Florida Keys, P.A.
  Islamorada, Florida, *General Defense* 369
  Key West, Florida, *General Defense* 377

Vernis & Bowling of the Gulf Coast, P.A.
  Clearwater, Florida, *General Defense* 344

Vernis & Bowling of the Gulf Coast, P.A. (Tampa)
  Tampa, Florida, *General Defense* 424

Vickers, Riis, Murray and Curran, L.L.C.
  Mobile, Alabama, *General Defense* 117

Vogel Law Firm
  Bismarck, North Dakota, *General Defense* 1146
  Fargo, North Dakota, *General Defense* 1150

Vogl Meredith Burke LLP
  San Francisco, California, *General Defense* 254

Vorys, Sater, Seymour and Pease LLP
  Columbus, Ohio, *General Defense* 1180
  Columbus, Ohio, *Regulatory and Compliance* 1672

W

Waddell, Cole & Jones, PLLC
  Jonesboro, Arkansas, *General Defense* 165
  Jonesboro, Arkansas, *Investigation and Adjustment* 1676

Wade Clark Mulcahy
  New York, New York, *General Defense* 1088
  New York, New York, *Subrogation* 1653

Wade, Palmer & Shoemaker, P.A.
  Pensacola, Florida, *General Defense* 408

Wadleigh, Starr & Peters, P.L.L.C.
  Manchester, New Hampshire, *General Defense* 952

ATTORNEYS - ALPHABETICAL FIRM INDEX

Wagner, Luloff & Adams, P.L.L.C.
Yakima, Washington, *General Defense* 1549

Wagstaff & Cartmell, LLP
Kansas City, Missouri, *General Defense* 880

Wagstaff LLP
Abilene, Texas, *General Defense* 1371

Waite, McWha & Heng
North Platte, Nebraska, *General Defense* 925
North Platte, Nebraska, *Subrogation* 1645
North Platte, Nebraska, *Investigation and Adjustment* 1678

Waldeck Law Firm P.A.
Minneapolis, Minnesota, *General Defense* 825
Minneapolis, Minnesota, *Subrogation* 1644

Waldeck & Patterson, P.A.
Prairie Village, Kansas, *General Defense* 603
Kansas City, Missouri, *General Defense* 881

Waldon, Adelman, Castilla, Hiestand & Prout, LLP
Atlanta, Georgia, *General Defense* 448

Waldrep Stewart & Kendrick, LLP
Birmingham, Alabama, *General Defense* 94

Walker, Allen, Grice, Ammons & Foy, L.L.P.
Goldsboro, North Carolina, *General Defense* 1125

Walker, Brown & Brown, P.A.
Hernando, Mississippi, *General Defense* 842

Walker, Ferguson & Ferguson
Oklahoma City, Oklahoma, *General Defense* 1201

Walker & Williams, P.C.
Belleville, Illinois, *General Defense* 493

Wallace, Morris, Barwick, Landis & Stroud, P.A.
Kinston, North Carolina, *General Defense* 1130

Walsh McKean Furcolo LLP
San Diego, California, *General Defense* 245

The Waltz Law Group
New Orleans, Louisiana, *General Defense* 708

Law Offices of Ward, Anderson, Porritt & Bryant, PLC
Bloomfield Hills, Michigan, *General Defense* 781
Toledo, Ohio, *General Defense* 1187

Ward, Hocker & Thornton, PLLC
Lexington, Kentucky, *General Defense* 628

The Ward Law Firm, P.A.
Spartanburg, South Carolina, *General Defense* 1322

Waters, McCluskey & Boehle
El Segundo, California, *General Defense* 185

Watkins & McNeilly, PLLC
Nashville, Tennessee, *General Defense* 1365
Nashville, Tennessee, *Subrogation* 1661

Watson, Blanche, Wilson & Posner
Baton Rouge, Louisiana, *General Defense* 661

Watts, Donovan & Tilley, P.A.
Little Rock, Arkansas, *General Defense* 173

Weatherbee Law Office, P.A.
Bangor, Maine, *General Defense* 716

Webb, Burnett, Cornbrooks, Wilber, Vorhis, Douse & Mason, L.L.P.
Salisbury, Maryland, *General Defense* 743

ATTORNEYS - ALPHABETICAL FIRM INDEX

Webb Sanders & Williams PLLC
   Gulfport, Mississippi, *General Defense* 839
   Tupelo, Mississippi, *General Defense* 864

Webster, Henry, Lyons, Bradwell, Cohan & Black, P.C.
   Auburn, Alabama, *General Defense* 79
   Birmingham, Alabama, *General Defense* 95
   Montgomery, Alabama, *General Defense* 128

Wechsler & Cohen, LLP
   New York, New York, *General Defense* 1089

Welch & Smith, P.C.
   Oklahoma City, Oklahoma, *General Defense* 1202

Wells Marble & Hurst, PLLC
   Ridgeland, Mississippi, *General Defense* 861
   Oxford, Mississippi, *General Defense* 857

Weston - Patrick, P.A.
   Boston, Massachusetts, *General Defense* 764

West & Rose
   Kingsport, Tennessee, *General Defense* 1345

Wharton Aldhizer & Weaver PLC
   Harrisonburg, Virginia, *General Defense* 1502
   Staunton, Virginia, *General Defense* 1524

Wharton, Levin, Ehrmantraut & Klein, P.A.
   Annapolis, Maryland, *General Defense* 726

Wheatley, Segler, Osby & Miller, LLC
   Yukon, Oklahoma, *General Defense* 1216

Wheeler & Arey, P.A.
   Waterville, Maine, *General Defense* 723

Wheeler Trigg O'Donnell LLP
   Denver, Colorado, *General Defense* 292

Wheeler Upham
   Grand Rapids, Michigan, *General Defense* 795

Wheeler, Wheeler, Morgan, Faulkner & Brown
   Oklahoma City, Oklahoma, *General Defense* 1203

White Arnold & Dowd, P.C.
   Birmingham, Alabama, *General Defense* 95

White, Fleischner & Fino, LLP
   Holmdel, New Jersey, *General Defense* 972
   Holmdel, New Jersey, *Subrogation* 1647
   New York, New York, *General Defense* 1090
   New York, New York, *Subrogation* 1653

Whiteford, Taylor & Preston L.L.P.
   Washington, District of Columbia, *General Defense* 338
   Baltimore, Maryland, *General Defense* 734

White & Rhodes, P.C.
   Nashville, Tennessee, *General Defense* 1366

White-Shaver, P.C.
   Dallas, Texas, *General Defense* 1412
   Houston, Texas, *General Defense* 1445
   Tyler, Texas, *General Defense* 1469

Whiteside Law Firm
   Lubbock, Texas, *General Defense* 1451

White and Williams LLP
   Philadelphia, Pennsylvania, *General Defense* 1260

White and Wojda
   Alpena, Michigan, *General Defense* 778

ATTORNEYS - ALPHABETICAL FIRM INDEX

Wicker Smith O'Hara McCoy & Ford P.A.
   Fort Lauderdale, Florida, *General Defense* 360
   Jacksonville, Florida, *General Defense* 375
   Miami, Florida, *General Defense* 387
   Naples, Florida, *General Defense* 390
   Orlando, Florida, *General Defense* 402
   Tampa, Florida, *General Defense* 424
   West Palm Beach, Florida, *General Defense* 430

Widman, Cooney, Wilson, McGann & Fitterer, L.L.C.
   Ocean, New Jersey, *General Defense* 988

Wiederhold & Moses, P.A.
   West Palm Beach, Florida, *General Defense* 431

Wiedner & McAuliffe, Ltd.
   Chicago, Illinois, *General Defense* 529

Wilbraham, Lawler & Buba
   Wilmington, Delaware, *General Defense* 332
   Haddonfield, New Jersey, *General Defense* 972
   New York, New York, *General Defense* 1092
   Philadelphia, Pennsylvania, *General Defense* 1261
   Pittsburgh, Pennsylvania, *General Defense* 1272

Law Office of W. Mark Wilczynski, P.C.
   Charlotte Amalie, St. Thomas, Virgin Islands, *General Defense* 1602

Wild, Carey & Fife
   San Francisco, California, *General Defense* 255

Wiles Law Group, LLC
   Portland, Oregon, *General Defense* 1226

Wiley Rein LLP
   Washington, District of Columbia, *General Defense* 338

Wilkes Law Firm, P.A.
   Charleston, South Carolina, *General Defense* 1303
   Spartanburg, South Carolina, *General Defense* 1323

Wilkinson, Carmody & Gilliam
   Shreveport, Louisiana, *General Defense* 711

Willcox, Buyck & Williams, P.A.
   Florence, South Carolina, *General Defense* 1314
   Myrtle Beach, South Carolina, *General Defense* 1320

Williams & Petro Co., LLC
   Columbus, Ohio, *General Defense* 1181

Williams, Porter, Day & Neville, P.C.
   Casper, Wyoming, *General Defense* 1591

Williams, Robinson, Rigler & Buschjost, P.C.
   Rolla, Missouri, *General Defense* 882

Williams Venker & Sanders LLC
   St. Louis, Missouri, *General Defense* 896

Willman & Silvaggio, LLP
   Pittsburgh, Pennsylvania, *General Defense* 1272

Wilmer & Lee, P.A.
   Athens, Alabama, *General Defense* 78
   Huntsville, Alabama, *General Defense* 107

Wilson, Bave, Conboy, Cozza & Couzens, P.C.
   White Plains, New York, *General Defense* 1115

Wilson Smith Cochran Dickerson P.S.
   Seattle, Washington, *General Defense* 1546

Wimberly, Lawson, Steckel, Schneider & Stine, P.C.
   Atlanta, Georgia, *General Defense* 449

ATTORNEYS - ALPHABETICAL FIRM INDEX

Winder & Counsel, PC
    Salt Lake City, Utah, *General Defense* 1482

Winthrop & Weinstine, P.A.
    Minneapolis, Minnesota, *General Defense* 826
    Minneapolis, Minnesota, *Regulatory and Compliance* 1671

Withers, Gough, Pike, Pfaff & Peterson, LLC
    Wichita, Kansas, *General Defense* 608

Wolff, Helies, Spaeth & Lucas
    Manasquan, New Jersey, *General Defense* 976

Wolf, Horowitz & Etlinger, L.L.C.
    Hartford, Connecticut, *General Defense* 310

Woodley, Williams Law Firm, L.L.C.
    Lake Charles, Louisiana, *General Defense* 673

Wood, Ris & Hames, P.C.
    Denver, Colorado, *General Defense* 293

Wright & Associates, P.A.
    Portland, Maine, *General Defense* 722

Wright, Constable & Skeen, L.L.P.
    Baltimore, Maryland, *General Defense* 736

Wright & Greenhill, P.C.
    Austin, Texas, *General Defense* 1381

James B. Wright & Associates, P.C.
    Anchorage, Alaska, *General Defense* 141

Wright & Martin, L.L.P.
    Ridgeland, Mississippi, *General Defense* 862

Wright & O'Donnell, P.C.
    Iselin, New Jersey, *General Defense* 972
    Philadelphia, Pennsylvania, *General Defense* 1262

Y

Yamamura & Shimazu
    Honolulu, Hawaii, *General Defense* 472

Yaron & Associates
    Oakland, California, *General Defense* 218

Yates, McLamb & Weyher, L.L.P.
    Raleigh, North Carolina, *General Defense* 1138

York Williams, L.L.P.
    Charlotte, North Carolina, *General Defense* 1121

Yost & Baill, L.L.P.
    Minneapolis, Minnesota, *Subrogation* 1644

Yost & Tretta
    Philadelphia, Pennsylvania, *General Defense* 1262

Young & Alexander Co., L.P.A.
    Dayton, Ohio, *General Defense* 1182

Young, Bill, Roumbos & Boles, P.A.
    Miami, Florida, *General Defense* 389
    Pensacola, Florida, *General Defense* 409

Young Clement Rivers, LLP
    Charleston, South Carolina, *General Defense* 1304

Young & McNelis, LLC
    Dover, Delaware, *General Defense* 328

Young Moore and Henderson P.A.
    Raleigh, North Carolina, *General Defense* 1138

ATTORNEYS - ALPHABETICAL FIRM INDEX

Young, Thagard, Hoffman, Smith, Lawrence & Shenton, LLP
  Valdosta, Georgia, *General Defense* 466

Yules & Yules, LLC
  New Haven, Connecticut, *General Defense* 320

Z

Zalewski, Klinner & Kramer, LLP
  Wausau, Wisconsin, *General Defense* 1586

Zarwin Baum DeVito Kaplan Schaer Toddy, P.C.
  Jersey City, New Jersey, *General Defense* 973
  Marlton, New Jersey, *General Defense* 977
  Harrisburg, Pennsylvania, *General Defense* 1242
  Philadelphia, Pennsylvania, *General Defense* 1263

Zeanah, Hust, Summerford & Williamson, L.L.C.
  Tuscaloosa, Alabama, *General Defense* 134

Zeigler Cohen & Koch
  Indianapolis, Indiana, *General Defense* 569

Zender Thurston, P.S.
  Bellingham, Washington, *General Defense* 1530

Zizik, Powers, O'Connell, Spaulding & Lamontagne, P.C.
  Hyannis, Massachusetts, *General Defense* 767
  Westwood, Massachusetts, *General Defense* 773
  Providence, Rhode Island, *General Defense* 1290

Zuber & Company LLP
  Toronto, Ontario, *General Defense* 1613

Zunka, Milnor & Carter, Ltd.
  Charlottesville, Virginia, *General Defense* 1496

Best's Directories of
Recommended Insurance Attorneys and Adjusters
2015
Volume I - Attorneys
General Defense

United States
AL - OK

ALABAMA

CAPITAL: MONTGOMERY

COUNTIES AND COUNTY SEATS

County	County Seat	County	County Seat	County	County Seat
Autauga	Prattville	Dallas	Selma	Marion	Hamilton
Baldwin	Bay Minette	DeKalb	Fort Payne	Marshall	Guntersville
Barbour	Clayton	Elmore	Wetumpka	Mobile	Mobile
Bibb	Centreville	Escambia	Brewton	Monroe	Monroeville
Blount	Oneonta	Etowah	Gadsden	Montgomery	Montgomery
Bullock	Union Springs	Fayette	Fayette	Morgan	Decatur
Butler	Greenville	Franklin	Russellville	Perry	Marion
Calhoun	Anniston	Geneva	Geneva	Pickens	Carrollton
Chambers	Lafayette	Greene	Eutaw	Pike	Troy
Cherokee	Centre	Hale	Greensboro	Randolph	Wedowee
Chilton	Clanton	Henry	Abbeville	Russell	Phenix City
Choctaw	Butler	Houston	Dothan	St. Clair	Ashville
Clarke	Grove Hill	Jackson	Scottsboro	Shelby	Columbiana
Clay	Ashland	Jefferson	Birmingham	Sumter	Livingston
Cleburne	Heflin	Lamar	Vernon	Talladega	Talladega
Coffee	Elba	Lauderdale	Florence	Tallapoosa	Dadeville
Colbert	Tuscumbia	Lawrence	Moulton	Tuscaloosa	Tuscaloosa
Conecuh	Evergreen	Lee	Opelika	Walker	Jasper
Coosa	Rockford	Limestone	Athens	Washington	Chatom
Covington	Andalusia	Lowndes	Hayneville	Wilcox	Camden
Crenshaw	Luverne	Macon	Tuskegee	Winston	Double Springs
Cullman	Cullman	Madison	Huntsville		
Dale	Ozark	Marengo	Linden		

In the text that follows "†" indicates County Seats.

Our files contain additional verified data on the firms listed herein. This additional information is available on request.

A.M. BEST COMPANY

ALABAMA — ALEXANDER CITY

ALEXANDER CITY 14,875 Tallapoosa Co.

Refer To

Holtsford Gilliland Higgins Hitson & Howard, P.C.
4001 Carmichael Road, Suite 300
Montgomery, Alabama 36106
   Telephone: 334-215-8585
   Toll Free: 800-932-6964
   Fax: 334-215-7101
Mailing Address: P.O. Box 4128, Montgomery, AL 36103-4128

Insurance Defense, Automobile, Professional Liability, Product Liability, Civil Rights, Toxic Torts, General Liability, Environmental Law, Workers' Compensation, Construction Law, Coverage Issues, Governmental Entity Defense, Forestry Law

SEE COMPLETE LISTING UNDER MONTGOMERY, ALABAMA (55 MILES)

ANDALUSIA † 9,015 Covington Co.

Refer To

Rushton, Stakely, Johnston & Garrett, P.A.
184 Commerce Street
Montgomery, Alabama 36104
   Telephone: 334-206-3100
   Fax: 334-262-6277
Mailing Address: P.O. Box 270, Montgomery, AL 36101-0270

Insurance Defense, Trial and Appellate Practice, Accountants and Attorneys Liability, Administrative Law, Advertising Injury, Agent and Brokers Errors and Omissions, Appellate Practice, Arbitration, Automobile Tort, Bad Faith, Business Law, Casualty Insurance Law, Class Actions, Commercial Litigation, Complex Litigation, Construction Litigation, Contract Disputes, Copyright and Trademark Law, Coverage Analysis, Declaratory Judgments, Directors and Officers Liability, Employment Law, Environmental Law, Family Law, Fidelity and Surety, Fraud, Health Care, Health Care Professional Licensure Defense, Insurance Litigation, Labor and Employment, Law Enforcement Liability, Legal Malpractice, Medical Devices, Medical Malpractice, Pharmaceutical, Premises Liability, Primary and Excess Insurance, Product Liability, Professional Errors and Omissions, Professional Liability, Surety, Title Insurance, Uninsured and Underinsured Motorist, Workers' Compensation, Wrongful Death

SEE COMPLETE LISTING UNDER MONTGOMERY, ALABAMA (89 MILES)

ATHENS † 21,897 Limestone Co.

Wilmer & Lee, P.A.

315 West Market Street
Athens, Alabama 35611
   Telephone: 256-232-2010
   Fax: 256-230-0610
   E-Mail: wilmerlee@wilmerlee.com
   www.wilmerandlee.com

Insurance Defense, Commercial Law, Mediation, Employment Practices Liability, Workers' Compensation, Professional Liability, Errors and Omissions, Health Care, Construction Litigation, Insurance Coverage, Governmental and Civil Rights Litigation

Firm Profile: The present firm was founded in 1991 by partners from one of Huntsville's oldest law firms. In 2004 the firm merged with one of Athens, Alabama's oldest law firms, Patton, Legge & Cole. In 2007 Lawrence Weaver, a member of one of Decatur, Alabama's oldest law firms, joined the present firm and opened a Decatur, Alabama office. Since its inception, Wilmer & Lee has grown to over 28 lawyers, and has four office locations, making it one of the largest firms in North Alabama. We offer a full array of legal services from a business and insurance focus, including litigation, corporate law, labor and employment, civil rights, banking and commercial law, insurance defense, workers' compensation, real estate law, government contracting, health care law, bankruptcy, trade secrets litigation, governmental relations, utility law, and other emerging areas of the law.

We pride ourselves as being client-friendly and accountable. We believe that it is vitally important to have satisfied clients. To that end, the firm is committed to its goals of providing the highest quality legal services while controlling the costs of those services. Each of our firm's attorneys has demonstrated academic excellence and significant experience in a wide range of legal and

Wilmer & Lee, P.A., Athens, AL — (Continued)

business settings. Our firm's lawyers include: a past State Bar President, past and present Bar Examiners, past and present Bar Commissioners, former counsel to the Governor, former State Supreme Court and Federal Law Clerks, former Army Judge Advocate Attorneys, and former National Labor Relations Board counsel. Six of our attorneys have attained additional degrees, Master of Law degrees (L.L.M.s), in their areas of concentration.

The firm has attorneys that are licensed to practice law in Alabama, Tennessee, Mississippi, and several other states. Additionally, the firm has attorneys admitted to practice in front of the United States Supreme Court, the United States Court of Federal Claims, the United States Tax Court, the United States Court of Appeals for the Armed Forces, the United States Court of Appeals for the Eleventh Circuit, the United States Court of Appeals for the Fifth Circuit, and all United States District Courts in Alabama.

Insurance Clients

ACE USA
Alfa Insurance Company
American Modern Insurance Group, Inc.
Chubb Group of Insurance Companies
Coastal Insurance Exchange
Cotton States Mutual Insurance Company
CUMIS Insurance Society, Inc.
Fireman's Fund Insurance Company
General Star Management Company
Lafayette Insurance Company
Mercury Insurance Company
Nautilus Insurance Company
St. Paul Insurance Company
State Auto Insurance Company
Tower Group Companies
Travelers Insurance Companies
Western Heritage Insurance
Zurich North America
Alabama Municipal Insurance Corporation
Assurance Company of America
Auto-Owners Insurance Company
CNA Global Specialty Lines
CNA Insurance Companies
Colony Insurance Company
COUNTRY Mutual Insurance Company
Federated Mutual Insurance Company
General Casualty Company
GuideOne Insurance
The Harleysville Insurance
Liberty Mutual Insurance Company
Nationwide Insurance
OneBeacon Insurance Group
Sentry Insurance
State Farm Fire and Casualty Company
United Fire Group
Zurich American Insurance Group

Non-Insurance Clients

Alabama Gas Corporation
Alabama Power Company
Alabama Rural Water Association
Athens-Limestone Hospital
AT&T
City of Madison
Energen Corporation
Ford Motor Credit Company
Inergy Propane, LLC
Limestone County Water and Sewer Authority
Specialty Risk Services, Inc. (SRS)
Alabama Insurance Guaranty Association
Athens Industrial Development Board
City of Huntsville
Costco
E & O Professionals
Huntsville Housing Authority
Limestone County Commission
Owens Corning Corporation
Premier Insurance Adjusters, Inc.

Resident Partners

P. Michael Cole — 1953 — The University of Alabama, B.A., 1975; Cumberland School of Law of Samford University, J.D., 1978; New York University, L.L.M., 1979 — Admitted to Bar, 1978, Alabama; U.S. Court of Appeals for the District of Columbia and Eleventh Circuits — Member Limestone County Bar Association (President, 1982-1983) — Municipal Court Judge, City of Athens, 1980; Special Assistant Attorney General, 1979; Selected to Alabama Super Lawyers — E-mail: mcole@wilmerlee.com

T. Mark Maclin — 1974 — The University of North Alabama, B.S., 1997; The University of Mississippi School of Law, J.D., 2000 — Admitted to Bar, 2000, Alabama; 2001, Mississippi — E-mail: mmaclin@wilmerlee.com

(See listing under Huntsville, AL for additional information)

BAY MINETTE   ALABAMA

AUBURN   53,380 Lee Co.

Webster, Henry, Lyons, Bradwell, Cohan & Black, P.C.
822 North Dean Road, Suite 300
Auburn, Alabama 36830-9402
   Telephone: 334-264-9472
   Fax: 334-887-0983
   E-Mail: randy@websterhenry.com
   www.websterhenry.com

Insurance Defense, Automobile Liability, Construction Law, Employment Law, Premises Liability, Product Liability, Workers' Compensation

(See listing under Montgomery, AL for additional information)

The following firms also service this area.

Rushton, Stakely, Johnston & Garrett, P.A.
184 Commerce Street
Montgomery, Alabama 36104
   Telephone: 334-206-3100
   Fax: 334-262-6277

Mailing Address: P.O. Box 270, Montgomery, AL 36101-0270

Insurance Defense, Trial and Appellate Practice, Accountants and Attorneys Liability, Administrative Law, Advertising Injury, Agent and Brokers Errors and Omissions, Appellate Practice, Arbitration, Automobile Tort, Bad Faith, Business Law, Casualty Insurance Law, Class Actions, Commercial Litigation, Complex Litigation, Construction Litigation, Contract Disputes, Copyright and Trademark Law, Coverage Analysis, Declaratory Judgments, Directors and Officers Liability, Employment Law, Environmental Law, Family Law, Fidelity and Surety, Fraud, Health Care, Health Care Professional Licensure Defense, Insurance Litigation, Labor and Employment, Law Enforcement Liability, Legal Malpractice, Medical Devices, Medical Malpractice, Pharmaceutical, Premises Liability, Primary and Excess Insurance, Product Liability, Professional Errors and Omissions, Professional Liability, Surety, Title Insurance, Uninsured and Underinsured Motorist, Workers' Compensation, Wrongful Death

SEE COMPLETE LISTING UNDER MONTGOMERY, ALABAMA (59 MILES)

BAY MINETTE   † 8,044 Baldwin Co.

Johnstone Adams, L.L.C.
Dahlberg Building, 104 Hand Avenue
Bay Minette, Alabama 36507
   Telephone: 251-937-9473
   Fax: 251-937-9475
   www.JohnstoneAdams.com

(Mobile, AL Office*: One St. Louis Centre, 1 St. Louis Street, Suite 4000, 36602, P.O. Box 1988, 36633)
   (Tel: 251-432-7682)
   (Fax: 251-432-2800)
   (www.Johnstoneadams.com)
(Birmingham, AL Office*: 2020 Canyon Road, Suite 100, 35216)
   (Tel: 205-871-7733)
   (Fax: 205-871-7387)

Insurance Defense, Admiralty and Maritime Law, Automobile, Aviation, Bad Faith, Casualty, Construction Litigation, Employer Liability, ERISA, Fire, Fraud, Health, Life Insurance, Product Liability, Professional Liability, Surety, Workers' Compensation, Co-Employee

Resident Partner

Charles C. Simpson, III — 1950 — Duke University, A.B., 1972; The University of Alabama, J.D., 1979 — Order of the Coif — Admitted to Bar, 1979,

Johnstone Adams, L.L.C., Bay Minette, AL   (Continued)
Alabama — Member American and Baldwin County (President, 1988-1989) Bar Associations; Alabama State Bar; Alabama Defense Lawyers Association; Defense Research Institute

(See listing under Mobile, AL for additional information)

The following firms also service this area.

Ball, Ball, Matthews & Novak, P.A.
107 Saint Francis Street, Suite 1590
Mobile, Alabama 36602
   Telephone: 251-338-2721
   Fax: 251-338-2722

Mailing Address: P.O. Box 2648, Mobile, AL 36652

Insurance Defense, Medical Malpractice, Aviation, Bad Faith, Personal Injury, Construction Litigation, Employment Law, Product Liability, Property, Pharmaceutical, Medical Devices, Complex Litigation, Governmental Entity Defense, Workers' Compensation, Mediation, Arbitration, Trial and Appellate Practice, State and Federal Courts, Insurance Coverage Analysis, Automobile Injury, Motor Carrier Defense

SEE COMPLETE LISTING UNDER MOBILE, ALABAMA (37 MILES)

Galloway, Wettermark, Everest & Rutens, LLP
3263 Cottage Hill Road
Mobile, Alabama 36606
   Telephone: 251-476-4493
   Fax: 251-479-5566

Mailing Address: P.O. Box 16629, Mobile, AL 36616-0629

Insurance Defense, Admiralty and Maritime Law, Casualty, Fire, Life Insurance, Surety, Workers' Compensation, Governmental Liability, Product Liability, Civil Rights, Commercial Litigation, Construction Law, Professional Liability, Trial and Appellate Practice, State and Federal Courts, Title VII Defense, Medical Liability

SEE COMPLETE LISTING UNDER MOBILE, ALABAMA (29 MILES)

Michael Gillion, P.C.
74 Midtown Park West, Suite 105
Mobile, Alabama 36606
   Telephone: 251-471-9494
   Fax: 251-471-1722

Mailing Address: P.O. Box 161423, Mobile, AL 36616-2423

Insurance Defense, Automobile, Homeowners, Workers' Compensation, Subrogation, Insurance Contract and Coverage Litigation

SEE COMPLETE LISTING UNDER MOBILE, ALABAMA (29 MILES)

Holtsford Gilliland Higgins Hitson & Howard, P.C.
29000 U.S. Highway 98, Suite A-302
Daphne, Alabama 36526-7263
   Telephone: 251-447-0234
   Fax: 251-447-0212

Insurance Defense, Automobile, Professional Liability, Product Liability, Civil Rights, Toxic Torts, General Liability, Environmental Law, Workers' Compensation, Construction Law, Governmental Entity Defense

SEE COMPLETE LISTING UNDER MOBILE, ALABAMA (29 MILES)

Vernis & Bowling of Southern Alabama, LLC
61 St. Joseph Street, 11th Floor
Mobile, Alabama 36602
   Telephone: 251-432-0337
   Fax: 251-432-0244

Civil Litigation, Insurance Law, Workers' Compensation, Premises Liability, Labor and Employment, Civil Rights, Commercial Litigation, Complex Litigation, Product Liability, Directors and Officers Liability, Errors and Omissions, Construction Law, Construction Defect, Environmental Liability, Personal and Commercial Vehicle, Appellate Practice, Admiralty and Maritime Law, Real Estate, Family Law, Elder Law, Liability Defense, SIU/Fraud Litigation, Education Law (ESE/IDEA), Property and Casualty (Commercial and Personal Lines), Long-Haul Trucking Liability, Government Law, Public Law, Criminal, White Collar, Business Litigation

SEE COMPLETE LISTING UNDER MOBILE, ALABAMA (29 MILES)

ALABAMA   BIRMINGHAM

Vickers, Riis, Murray and Curran, L.L.C.
RSA Trustmark Building, 21st Floor
107 St. Francis Street
Mobile, Alabama 36602
  Telephone: 251-432-9772
  Fax: 251-432-9781
Mailing Address: P.O. Box 2568, Mobile, AL 36652-2568

Insurance Defense, Insurance Coverage, Construction Law, Admiralty and Maritime Law, Professional Liability, Environmental Law, Employment Law, Governmental Liability, Toxic Torts, Product Liability, Workers' Compensation, Business Automobile and Trucking, Education

SEE COMPLETE LISTING UNDER MOBILE, ALABAMA (29 MILES)

BIRMINGHAM   † 212,237 Jefferson Co.

Allen, Kopet & Associates, PLLC

3180 Cahaba Heights Road
Birmingham, Alabama 35243
  Telephone: 205-972-8989
  Fax: 205-972-8934

(See listing under Chattanooga, TN for additional information)

Burgess Roberts LLC

2017 Morris Avenue, Suite 100
Birmingham, Alabama 35203
  Telephone: 205-870-8611
  Fax: 205-870-8688
  E-Mail: sroberts@burgessroberts.com
  www.burgessroberts.com

Established: 2013

Architects and Engineers, Automobile, Automobile Liability, Bad Faith, Breach of Contract, Business Litigation, Casualty Defense, Casualty Insurance Law, Commercial General Liability, Commercial Litigation, Construction Litigation, Coverage Issues, Defense Litigation, Design Professionals, Dram Shop, Employer Liability, Employment Law, Engineering and Construction, Extra-Contractual Liability, Fidelity and Surety, General Liability, Insurance Coverage Litigation, Insurance Defense, Insurance Litigation, Labor and Employment, Mass Tort, Mold Litigation, Negligence, Premises Liability, Product Liability, Property and Casualty, Property Defense, Self-Insured Defense, State and Federal Courts, Transportation, Trial and Appellate Practice, Trucking Law, Trucking Litigation, Uninsured and Underinsured Motorist, Workers' Compensation, Wrongful Death, Wrongful Termination

Firm Profile: Burgess Roberts LLC is a full service insurance defense law firm handling cases in all jurisdictions throughout the state of Alabama.

Insurance Clients

ACE Agribusiness
American Mining Insurance Company
Automobile Dealers Association of Alabama Workers' Compensation Self-Insurance Fund
Catlin, Inc.
Chubb Insurance Company
The Dodson Group
Great West Casualty Company
GuideOne Insurance
The Infinity Group
Insurance Link
Integon Casualty Insurance Company
ITT Hartford
Key Risk Insurance Company
Markel Brokers and Underwriters
Allstate Insurance Company
American Specialty Insurance Company
Automotive After Market Fund
Bituminous Insurance Companies
Carolina Casualty Insurance Company
Cincinnati Insurance Company
Employers Insurance Company
GRE Insurance Group
Harleysville Mutual Insurance Company
InsureMax Insurance Company
Investors Insurance Company of America
John Deere Insurance Company
Life Insurance Company of Georgia

Burgess Roberts LLC, Birmingham, AL   **(Continued)**

Meadowbrook Insurance Group
Old Republic Life Insurance Company
Protective Insurance Company
Reliance Insurance Company
Sagamore Insurance Company
Sentry Insurance a Mutual Company
Travelers Insurance
Workmen's Auto Insurance Company
Northbrook Property and Casualty Insurance Company
Preferred Employers Insurance Company
Safeco Insurance
St. Paul Fire and Marine Insurance Company
Southern Group Indemnity, Inc.
Unity Health Services
XL Group

Insurance Guaranty Fund Clients

Alabama Insurance Guaranty Association
Arkansas Guaranty Association
Illinois Insurance Guaranty Fund

Representative Clients

AccuStaff, Inc.
Air Wisconsin Airlines Company
Alabama Retail Association
Anderson Trucking Service
Burlington Coat Factory
Dean Foods
Hatch Mott MacDonald
Labor Finders, Inc.
Lowe's Companies, Inc.
Magna International
Midwest Logistic Systems
PJ United, Inc.
Randstad Temporary Employment Services
Taft Coal
Transport South, Inc.
Trinity Industries, Inc.
Advance Auto Parts, Inc.
Alabama General Contractors
AlphaStar Insurance Services
Applebee's, Inc.
CVS Pharmacy, Inc.
Fred's, Inc.
Hilb, Rogal and Hamilton Company
LTD Financial
Michaels Stores, Inc.
Pavan, Inc.
RaceTrac Petroleum, Inc.
Russell Corporation
Square D Company
Temp Force, Inc.
TravelCenters of America, LLC
Warrior Tractor & Equipment Company

Third Party Administrators

Attenta, Inc.
Crawford & Company
Cunningham Lindsey U.S., Inc.
GAB Robins North America, Inc.
HCC Employer Services, Inc.
Insurance Servicing & Adjusting Company
Millennium Risk Managers, LLC
Sedgwick Claims Management Services, Inc.
State Claims Adjusters
Ward North America, Inc.
York Risk Services Group, Inc.
Constitution State Service Company
Custard Insurance Adjusters, Inc.
Gallagher Bassett Services, Inc.
Insurance Claims Management, Inc.
ITT Specialty Risk Services, Inc.
North American Risk Services
Southern Risk Services, Inc.
Specialty Risk Services, Inc. (SRS)
Stirling Cooke Insurance Services Inc.

Members

Tom Burgess — 1948 — The University of Alabama, B.A., 1970; Birmingham School of Law, J.D., 1980 — Admitted to Bar, 1981, Alabama; U.S. District Court, Middle, Northern and Southern Districts of Alabama; U.S. Court of Appeals for the Federal, Fifth and Eleventh Circuits; U.S. Supreme Court — Member American and Birmingham Bar Associations; Alabama State Bar — Practice Areas: Architects and Engineers; Automobile Liability; Bad Faith; Business Litigation; Casualty Insurance Law; Complex Litigation; Construction Accidents; Contract Disputes; Coverage Litigation; Design Professionals; Dram Shop; Engineering and Construction; Extra-Contractual Litigation; Insurance Coverage Litigation; Mold Litigation; Pharmacy Defense; Premises Liability; Product Liability Defense; Professional Errors and Omissions; Self-Insured Defense; Tort Litigation; Trucking Litigation; Uninsured and Underinsured Motorist; Workers' Compensation; Wrongful Death — Tel: 205-278-8617 — E-mail: tburgess@burgessroberts.com

Scott M. Roberts — 1965 — Auburn University, B.A., 1987; The University of Alabama, J.D., 1990 — Admitted to Bar, 1990, Alabama; 2003, Tennessee; 1990, U.S. District Court, Middle, Northern and Southern Districts of Alabama; 2006, U.S. Court of Appeals, Eleventh Circuit — Member Tennessee and Birmingham Bar Associations; Alabama State Bar; Alabama Defense Lawyers Association; Defense Research Institute; Atlanta Claims Association; Alabama Workers' Compensation Claims Association; Trucking Industry Defense Association — Practice Areas: Automobile Litigation; Bad Faith; Business Litigation; Casualty Insurance Law; Commercial General Liability; Commercial Transportation Litigation; Complex Litigation; Contracts; Dram Shop; Employer Liability; Employment Litigation; Fraud; Litigation Defense; Premises Liability; Premise Litigation; Product Liability; Property and Casualty; Retail and Restaurant Defense; Self-Insured Defense; Tort Claims Defense; Trial Practice; Trucking Litigation; Uninsured and Underinsured

BIRMINGHAM ALABAMA

Burgess Roberts LLC, Birmingham, AL (Continued)

Motorist; Wrongful Death; Wrongful Termination; Workers' Compensation — Tel: 205-795-3527 — E-mail: sroberts@burgessroberts.com

Associates

Ethan Dettling — 1969 — Auburn University, B.A., 1992; Seattle University School of Law, J.D., 1995 — Admitted to Bar, 1995, Alabama — Member American and Birmingham Bar Associations; Alabama State Bar — Practice Areas: Appellate Practice; Architects and Engineers; Automobile Litigation; Bad Faith; Construction Litigation; Design Professionals; Dram Shop; Employment Litigation; Engineering and Construction; General Defense Civil Litigation; Insurance Coverage Litigation; Mold Litigation; Pharmacy Defense; Premises Liability; Self-Insured Defense; Tort Litigation; Trucking Litigation; Uninsured and Underinsured Motorist; Workers' Compensation; Wrongful Death; Wrongful Termination — Tel: 205-278-8611

J. Kerry Burgess — 1972 — San Francisco Conservatory of Music, B.M., 1994; Birmingham School of Law, J.D., 2006 — Admitted to Bar, 2006, Alabama; U.S. District Court, Middle, Northern and Southern Districts of Alabama; U.S. Court of Appeals, Eleventh Circuit — Member American and Birmingham Bar Associations; Alabama State Bar — Practice Areas: Appellate Practice; Architects and Engineers; Automobile Litigation; Bad Faith; Breach of Contract; Business Litigation; Commercial Litigation; Complex Litigation; Construction Litigation; Contracts; Coverage Litigation; Design Professionals; Dram Shop Liability; Employment Litigation; Engineers; Extra-Contractual Litigation; General Civil Litigation; Homeowners; Insurance Coverage Litigation; Mold Litigation; Personal Injury Litigation; Premises Liability; Property and Casualty; Retail and Restaurant Defense; Self-Insured Defense; Tort Litigation; Trucking Litigation; Uninsured and Underinsured Motorist; Workers' Compensation; Wrongful Death — Tel: 205-278-8629

Scott Holmes — 1975 — The University of Alabama, B.S. (cum laude), 1997; Troy University, M.A. (summa cum laude), 2001; The University of Alabama, J.D. (cum laude), 2004 — Admitted to Bar, 2004, Alabama; 2005, Mississippi; 2004, U.S. District Court, Middle, Northern and Southern Districts of Alabama; 2005, U.S. Court of Appeals, Fifth Circuit — Practice Areas: Architects and Engineers; Automobile Litigation; Bad Faith; Casualty Insurance Law; Civil Trial Practice; Employment Law; General Defense Civil Litigation; Insurance Defense; Litigation Defense; Personal Injury Defense; Premises Liability; Tort Litigation; Trucking Litigation; Workers' Compensation — Tel: 205-795-3538

Amanda L. Mink — 1977 — Samford University, B.S., 2001; J.D. (Dean's List), 2008 — Admitted to Bar, 2008, Alabama; U.S. District Court, Middle, Northern and Southern Districts of Alabama — Member Alabama State Bar — Practice Areas: Appellate Practice; Automobile Liability; Employment Law; Insurance Defense; Premises Liability; Product Liability; Trucking Litigation; Workers' Compensation — Tel: 205-795-3541 — E-mail: amink@burgessroberts.com

Cabaniss, Johnston, Gardner, Dumas & O'Neal, LLP

2001 Park Place North, Suite 700
Birmingham, Alabama 35203
Telephone: 205-716-5200
Fax: 205-716-5389
E-Mail: info@cabaniss.com
www.cabaniss.com

(Mobile, AL Office*: 63 South Royal Street, Suite 700, 36602)
(Tel: 251-415-7300)
(Fax: 251-415-7350)

Established: 1887

Insurance Defense, Employment Law, Professional Liability, Personal Injury, Workers' Compensation, Environmental Law, Product Liability, Construction Law, Insurance Coverage, Complex Litigation, Admiralty and Maritime Law, Trial and Appellate Practice, State and Federal Courts

Firm Profile: Recognized as the oldest continuous law practice in Birmingham and one of the oldest continuous practices in Alabama, Cabaniss, Johnston, Gardner, Dumas & O'Neal has a distinguished history and a growing future. With offices in Birmingham and Mobile, the firm offers a state-wide civil practice in the general areas of litigation, employment, corporate, taxation and environmental law.

Cabaniss, Johnston, Gardner, Dumas & O'Neal, LLP, Birmingham, AL (Continued)

Insurance Clients

Blue Cross and Blue Shield of Alabama
Liberty Mutual Insurance
Employers Reinsurance Corporation

Members of the Firm

Lucien D. Gardner, Jr. — (1903-1988)

Forney Johnston — (1879-1965)

M. Camper O'Neal — (1907-1989)

Edward H. Cabaniss — (1857-1936)

William F. Gardner — (1934-2007)

Crawford S. McGivaren, Jr. — Vanderbilt University, A.B. (magna cum laude), 1965; Harvard University, LL.B., 1968 — Phi Beta Kappa; Omicron Delta Kappa — Admitted to Bar, 1968, Alabama

Sydney F. Frazier, Jr. — The University of Alabama, B.A., 1969; J.D., 1972 — Phi Delta Phi; Omicron Delta Kappa; Jasons — Admitted to Bar, 1972, Alabama

Benjamen T. Rowe — The University of Alabama, B.S., 1967; J.D., 1972 — Omicron Delta Kappa; Order of the Coif; Jasons — Admitted to Bar, 1972, Alabama — Resident Mobile, AL Office

Patrick H. Sims — The University of Alabama, B.A., 1971; J.D., 1974 — Omicron Delta Kappa; Order of the Coif — Admitted to Bar, 1974, Alabama — Resident Mobile, AL Office

Donald J. Stewart — The University of Alabama, B.A., 1971; J.D., 1975 — Omicron Delta Kappa; Jasons — Admitted to Bar, 1975, Alabama — Resident Mobile, AL Office

Roy J. Crawford — Troy State University, B.S. (summa cum laude), 1971; The University of Alabama, J.D., 1977; New York University, LL.M., 1980 — Omicron Delta Kappa; Order of the Coif; Jasons — Admitted to Bar, 1977, Alabama

F. Gerald Burnett — The University of Mississippi, B.B.A., 1968; J.D. (with distinction), 1972; Georgetown University Law Center, LL.M., 1977 — Omicron Delta Kappa; Phi Alpha Delta — Admitted to Bar, 1972, Mississippi; 1979, District of Columbia; Alabama

David S. Dunkle — Virginia Military Institute, B.A. (with honors), 1966; The University of North Carolina, J.D., 1969; Georgetown University Law Center, LL.M., 1970 — Admitted to Bar, 1969, North Carolina; 1980, Alabama

C. Fred Daniels — Auburn University, B.S., 1970; The University of Alabama, J.D., 1973; New York University, LL.M., 1974 — Admitted to Bar, 1973, Alabama

G. Thomas Sullivan — Emory University, B.A., 1974; Cumberland School of Law of Samford University, J.D., 1977; The University of Alabama School of Law, LL.M., 1996 — Admitted to Bar, 1977, Alabama

Carolyn L. Duncan — University of Montevallo, B.M., 1971; M.M.E., 1975; Cumberland School of Law of Samford University, J.D., 1978 — Admitted to Bar, 1978, Alabama

Leonard Wertheimer, III — University of Virginia, B.A., 1969; Emory University, J.D., 1972 — Admitted to Bar, 1972, Alabama

David L. Kane — The University of Alabama, B.S., 1970; The Wharton School of the University of Pennsylvania, M.S., 1971; Duke University, J.D. (with distinction), 1978 — Omicron Delta Kappa; Order of the Coif — Admitted to Bar, 1978, Georgia; 1982, Alabama — Resident Mobile, AL Office

R. Boyd Miller — The University of Alabama, B.A., 1974; J.D., 1979 — Omicron Delta Kappa; Order of the Coif — Admitted to Bar, 1979, Alabama — Resident Mobile, AL Office

R. Carlton Smyly — Birmingham-Southern College, B.A. (summa cum laude), 1979; University of Virginia, J.D., 1982 — Phi Beta Kappa; Omicron Delta Kappa — Admitted to Bar, 1982, Alabama

Steve A. Tucker — Samford University, B.A. (cum laude), 1974; Southern Baptist Theological Seminary, M.Div., 1979; University of Kentucky, J.D. (with distinction), 1984 — Order of the Coif — Admitted to Bar, 1984, Alabama

Sandy G. Robinson — The University of Alabama, B.S. (magna cum laude), 1981; J.D., 1984 — Order of the Coif; Phi Delta Phi — Admitted to Bar, 1984, Alabama — Resident Mobile, AL Office

Herbert H. West, Jr. — The University of Alabama, B.S. (summa cum laude), 1984; Vanderbilt University, J.D., 1987 — Beta Gamma Sigma — Admitted to Bar, 1987, Alabama

ALABAMA BIRMINGHAM

Cabaniss, Johnston, Gardner, Dumas & O'Neal, LLP, Birmingham, AL (Continued)

Melanie Merkle Atha — Birmingham-Southern College, B.A. (magna cum laude), 1986; Vanderbilt University, J.D., 1990 — Mortar Board; Phi Delta Phi — Admitted to Bar, 1990, Alabama

John M. Graham — The University of Alabama, B.S. (magna cum laude), 1989; J.D., 1992 — Phi Beta Kappa; Order of the Coif — Admitted to Bar, 1992, Alabama

Ian D. Rosenthal — University of Michigan, B.A. (with high distinction), 1992; University of Virginia School of Law, J.D., 1996 — Admitted to Bar, 1996, Alabama; 1997, Florida — Resident Mobile, AL Office

Michael E. Turner — The University of North Carolina at Chapel Hill, B.A., 1993; Wake Forest University, J.D. (cum laude), 1996 — Order of the Coif — Admitted to Bar, 1996, Alabama

Jarrod J. White — Stetson University, B.B.A. (magna cum laude), 1994; The University of Alabama, J.D. (summa cum laude), 1997 — Order of the Coif; Omicron Delta Kappa — Admitted to Bar, 1997, Alabama; 1998, Mississippi — Resident Mobile, AL Office

Diane Babb Maughan — Baylor University, B.A. (magna cum laude), 1996; The University of Alabama, J.D. (summa cum laude), 1999 — Phi Beta Kappa; Order of the Coif; Recipient, Dean M. Leigh Harrison Award; Hugo L. Black Scholar; Member, Bench and Bar — Law Clerk to the Honorable Perry O. Hooper, Sr., Chief Justice, Supreme Court of Alabama, 1999-2000 — Member, 1997-1998, and Articles Editor, 1998-1999, Alabama Law Review — Admitted to Bar, 1999, Alabama; 2001, U.S. District Court, Northern District of Alabama; U.S. Court of Appeals, Eleventh Circuit — Member American and Birmingham Bar Associations; Alabama State Bar

Amy Bell Nelson — Auburn University, B.S. (magna cum laude), 1998; Samford University, M.B.A., 2001; Cumberland School of Law of Samford University, J.D. (cum laude), 2001 — Curia Honoris; Cordell Hull Teaching Fellow — Cumberland Law Review (1999-2001) — Admitted to Bar, 2001, Alabama; U.S. District Court, Middle District of Alabama

Annette Lanning Kinderman — Amherst College, B.A., 1991; Washington and Lee University, J.D. (magna cum laude), 1996 — Law Clerk to the Honorable Sam C. Pointer, Jr., Chief Judge, Northern District of Alabama, 1996-1997 — Notes and Comments Editor, Washington and Lee University Law Review, 1995-1996 — Admitted to Bar, 1996, Alabama — Member American and Birmingham Bar Associations; Alabama State Bar

George L. Morris, IV — Millsaps College, B.S. (cum laude), 1997; Cumberland School of Law of Samford University, J.D. (magna cum laude), 2005 — Phi Kappa Phi; Curia Honoris; Cordell Hull Teaching Fellow; Presidential Scholarship (2002-2005); George M. Steward Banking Award — Admitted to Bar, 2005, Alabama; U.S. District Court, Middle, Northern and Southern Districts of Alabama — Member American and Birmingham Bar Associations; Alabama State Bar; Defense Research Institute; Alabama Defense Lawyers Association — Top Attorneys in Birmingham-Rising Star by Birmingham Magazine

Rebecca D. Parks — Loyola University, B.A. (magna cum laude), 1992; The University of Alabama, J.D. (summa cum laude), 1995 — Admitted to Bar, 1995, Illinois; 1996, Alabama — Resident Mobile, AL Office

Nancy W. Ball — Birmingham-Southern College, B.S. (cum laude), 2004; The University of Mississippi School of Law, J.D. (summa cum laude), 2007; The University of Alabama School of Law, LL.M. Taxation (magna cum laude), 2014 — Admitted to Bar, 2007, Alabama

Associates

Jason W. Bobo
Matthew M. Couch
Jade E. Sipes
Jack K. West
J. Wesley Fain
Rachel E. Kelly
Lance W. Palmer

Of Counsel

K.W. Michael Chambers — The University of Alabama, B.A., 1975; J.D., 1979 — Admitted to Bar, 1979, Alabama; 1988, District of Columbia; New York — Languages: French, Spanish — Resident Mobile, AL Office

Ely & Isenberg, L.L.C.

2100-B South Bridge Parkway, Suite 380
Birmingham, Alabama 35209
 Telephone: 205-313-1200
 Fax: 205-313-1201
 E-Mail: jisenberg@elylawllc.com
 www.elylawllc.com

Ely & Isenberg, L.L.C., Birmingham, AL (Continued)
(Auburn, AL Office: Hudson Building, Suite 223, 165 East Magnolia Street, 36830)
 (Tel: 334-821-1755)
 (Fax: 334-821-1753)

Insurance Coverage, Insurance Defense, Extra-Contractual Liability, General Liability, Property, Marine, Inland Marine, Business Interruption, Public Sector, Flood, Excess and Umbrella, Litigation, Commercial Litigation, Construction Law, State and Federal Courts, Employment/Non-Competition

Firm Profile: ELY & ISENBERG, LLC is a civil litigation law firm with offices in Birmingham and Auburn, Alabama. Our firm represents businesses and individuals throughout the state and federal courts of Alabama, with a specific focus on insurance coverage and claims litigation across multiple lines of business. Our attorneys have experience in coverage matters and litigation involving liability, property (both commercial and personal), marine, inland marine, public sector, business interruption, flood, and excess/umbrella coverage. In addition, we routinely represent insurers in bad-faith and extra-contractual cases and complex declaratory judgment actions in both state and federal courts throughout Alabama. We also pride ourselves on providing coverage opinions and advice to insurers during the claims process in order to assist in-house counsel and claims professionals in navigating coverage issues in the pre-litigation context. Finally, our attorneys have broad experience representing individuals and businesses as retained counsel by insurers when coverage is not at issue.

Insurance Clients

ACE Insurance Limited   Travelers Indemnity Company

Firm Members

Emily W. Bynum — Rhodes College, B.A., 2001; Cumberland School of Law of Samford University, J.D., 2006 — Admitted to Bar, 2006, Alabama; U.S. District Court, Middle, Northern and Southern Districts of Alabama

Brenen G. Ely — Auburn University, B.A. (magna cum laude), 1991; The University of Alabama School of Law, J.D., 1994 — Admitted to Bar, 1994, Alabama; U.S. District Court, Middle, Northern and Southern Districts of Alabama; U.S. Court of Appeals, Eleventh Circuit

Candace L. Hudson — Angelo State University, B.A. (cum laude), 1994; Cumberland School of Law of Samford University, J.D., 2000 — Admitted to Bar, 2000, Alabama; 2002, U.S. District Court, Middle, Northern and Southern Districts of Alabama; U.S. Court of Appeals, Eleventh Circuit

Joel S. Isenberg — Tulane University, B.A. (Phi Beta Kappa, cum laude), 1990; Cumberland School of Law of Samford University, J.D. (magna cum laude), 1994 — Articles Editor, Cumberland Law Review — Admitted to Bar, 1994, Alabama; 1997, District of Columbia; 2008, Georgia; Tennessee; 1994, U.S. District Court, Middle, Northern and Southern Districts of Alabama; 1997, U.S. Court of Appeals, Eleventh Circuit; 2000, U.S. Court of Appeals, Sixth Circuit

Susan Haygood McCurry — Randolph-Macon Woman's College, A.B., 1992; Cumberland School of Law of Samford University, J.D., 1996 — Admitted to Bar, 1996, Alabama; Georgia; 1998, South Carolina; 1996, U.S. District Court, Middle District of Alabama; 1999, U.S. District Court, Northern and Southern Districts of Alabama; U.S. Court of Appeals, Eleventh Circuit; 2008, U.S. District Court, Middle District of Georgia

Devona J. Segrest — University of South Alabama, B.A., 1996; Cumberland School of Law of Samford University, J.D., 1999 — Admitted to Bar, 2000, Alabama; U.S. District Court, Middle, Northern and Southern Districts of Alabama

Seth T. Hunter — The University of Mississippi, B.A., 2007; Cumberland School of Law of Samford University, J.D., 2010 — Admitted to Bar, 2010, Alabama; 2011, Tennessee; U.S. District Court, Middle, Northern and Southern Districts of Alabama

Fann & Rea, P.C.

1200 Providence Park, Suite 200
Birmingham, Alabama 35242
 Telephone: 205-991-5045
 Fax: 205-991-3866
 E-Mail: FannReaPC@FannRea.com

Established: 1995

BIRMINGHAM ALABAMA

Fann & Rea, P.C., Birmingham, AL (Continued)

Insurance Defense, Automobile, Aviation, General Liability, Professional Liability, Property and Casualty, Workers' Compensation, Employment Law

Insurance Clients

AIG Aviation, Inc.
Safety National Casualty Corporation
Union Automobile Indemnity Company
MSI Preferred Insurance Company
The St. Paul Companies
Trinity Universal Insurance Company

Non-Insurance Clients

AAA Plumbing Pottery Corporation
E-Z Serve
Fontaine Specialized, Inc.
Gold Kist, Inc.
Hilb, Rogal and Hamilton Company
Integrated Claims Strategies, Inc.
Madix, Inc.
O'Steen Adjusting Services, Inc.
Variety Wholesalers, Inc.
Weyerhaeuser Company
CT-South, Inc.
Cunningham Lindsey Claims Management, Inc.
GAB Robins North America, Inc.
Group Dekko International, Inc.
Hill Insurance Services, Inc.
Huffman Risk Management, Inc.
ITT Specialty Risk Services, Inc.
Old Republic Risk Service, Inc.
Shaw Industries, Inc.
Waffle House, Inc.

Partners

Robert P. Fann — 1953 — Florida State University, B.S., 1976; Cumberland School of Law of Samford University, J.D., 1985 — Admitted to Bar, 1985, Alabama; Georgia; 1986, Florida; District of Columbia; 1986, U.S. District Court, Middle and Northern Districts of Alabama; U.S. Court of Appeals, Eleventh Circuit; 1990, U.S. District Court, Southern District of Alabama — Member American and Birmingham Bar Associations; Alabama State Bar; State Bar of Georgia; The District of Columbia Bar; Alabama Self-Insurers Association; Georgia Self-Insurers Association; Workers' Compensation Claims Association; Alabama Claims Association; Alabama Defense Lawyers Association; Defense Research Institute — Licensed Property Casualty and Life Agent, State of Florida, 1976-1982; Multi-Line Claims Adjuster, State of Florida, 1980-1982

Patricia K. Rea — 1952 — Jacksonville State University, B.S. (with honors and distinction), 1974; Cumberland School of Law of Samford University, J.D. (summa cum laude), 1984 — Admitted to Bar, 1984, Alabama; 1985, U.S. District Court, Northern District of Alabama; 1985, U.S. Court of Appeals, Eleventh Circuit; 1990, U.S. Supreme Court; 1995, U.S. District Court, Middle District of Alabama — Member American Bar Association; Alabama State Bar; Alabama Claims Association; Alabama Self-Insurers Association; Alabama Defense Lawyers Association; Defense Research Institute; Alabama Workers' Compensation Claims Association — Multi-Line Claims Adjuster, 1975-1980; Claims Supervisor, 1980-1981

(This firm is also listed in the Investigation and Adjustment section of this directory)

Friedman, Dazzio, Zulanas & Bowling, P.C.

3800 Corporate Woods Drive
Birmingham, Alabama 35242
Telephone: 205-278-7000
Fax: 205-278-7001
Toll Free: 800-419-1808
www.friedman-lawyers.com

(Montgomery, AL Office: 401 Madison Avenue, 36104)

Established: 1998

Friedman, Dazzio, Zulanas & Bowling, P.C., Birmingham, AL (Continued)

Insurance Defense, Bad Faith, Fraud, Coverage Issues, ERISA, Workers' Compensation, Subrogation, Automobile, Product Liability, General Liability, Truck Liability, Professional Liability, Errors and Omissions, Property Damage, Bodily Injury, Litigation, Appellate Practice, State and Federal Courts, Medical Malpractice, Insurance Regulation, Construction Litigation, Employment Practices Liability, Premises Liability, Securities, Antitrust, Intellectual Property, Transportation, Commercial Transactions, Harassment and Discrimination (Title VII)

Firm Profile: FRIEDMAN, DAZZIO, ZULANAS & BOWLING, P.C. is a general civil practice firm, exclusively committed to the trial and resolution of civil litigation and commercial transactions.

Insurance Clients

Alabama Home Builders Self Insurers Fund
Amerisafe Insurance Group
Chubb Group of Insurance Companies
FCCI Insurance Group
Infinity Insurance Company
Lancer Insurance Company
Maxum Specialty Insurance Group
Nobel Insurance Company
State Auto Insurance Companies
State Volunteer Mutual Insurance Company
Zurich American Insurance Group
American Trucking and Transportation Insurance Company
COUNTRY Mutual Insurance Company
Federated Mutual Insurance Company
Liberty Mutual Group
Mountain Life Insurance Company
Physicians Mutual Insurance Company
USAA Group
Utica Mutual Insurance Company

Members of the Firm

Jeffrey E. Friedman — The University of Tennessee, B.A., 1980; Cumberland School of Law of Samford University, J.D., 1985 — Admitted to Bar, 1986, Alabama — E-mail: jfriedman@friedman-lawyers.com

P. Thomas Dazzio, Jr. — Auburn University, B.S., 1989; M.S., 1991; The University of Alabama School of Law, J.D., 1993 — Admitted to Bar, 1993, Alabama — E-mail: tdazzio@friedman-lawyers.com

Christopher J. Zulanas — University of Notre Dame, B.B.A., 1992; Cumberland School of Law of Samford University, J.D., 1995 — Admitted to Bar, 1995, Alabama — E-mail: czulanas@friedman-lawyers.com

J. Michael Bowling — The University of Alabama, B.S., 1992; The University of Alabama School of Law, J.D., 1996 — Admitted to Bar, 1996, Alabama — E-mail: mbowling@friedman-lawyers.com

Joel A. Williams — Washington and Lee University, B.A., 1975; Cumberland School of Law of Samford University, J.D., 1978 — Admitted to Bar, 1978, Alabama — E-mail: jwilliams@friedman-lawyers.com

James W. Moss — Auburn University, B.S., 1991; Cumberland School of Law of Samford University, J.D., 1998 — Admitted to Bar, 1998, Alabama — E-mail: jmoss@friedman-lawyers.com

Jess S. Boone — Vanderbilt University, B.A., 1995; The University of Alabama School of Law, J.D., 1998 — Admitted to Bar, 1998, Alabama — E-mail: jboone@friedman-lawyers.com

Michael J. Douglas — Auburn University, B.A., 1997; Cumberland School of Law of Samford University, J.D., 2001 — Admitted to Bar, 2001, Alabama — E-mail: mdouglas@friedman-lawyers.com

H. Spence Morano — The University of Alabama, B.S., 1998; Cumberland School of Law of Samford University, J.D., 2001 — Admitted to Bar, 2001, Alabama — E-mail: smorano@friedman-lawyers.com

Lee T. Patterson — Auburn University, B.A., 1999; Cumberland School of Law of Samford University, J.D., 2002 — Admitted to Bar, 2002, Alabama — E-mail: lpatterson@friedman-lawyers.com

David T. Gordon — Auburn University, B.A., 1999; Cumberland School of Law of Samford University, J.D., 2002 — Admitted to Bar, 2002, Alabama — E-mail: dgordon@friedman-lawyers.com

Associates

Gwendolyn Arendall Gordon
Matthew D. Conn
Joseph L. Kerr, Jr.
Charles A. Nelson, II

Of Counsel

Charles E. Sharp
Jamie Johnston

ALABAMA   BIRMINGHAM

Gaines Gault Hendrix P.C.

3500 Blue Lake Drive, Suite 425
Birmingham, Alabama 35243
   Telephone: 205-980-5888
   Fax: 205-402-4900
   www.ggh-law.com

(Huntsville, AL Office*: 309 Franklin Street, 35801)
   (Tel: 256-532-1957)
   (Fax: 256-532-1958)

Established: 1996

Insurance Defense, Bad Faith, Fraud, Coverage Issues, Litigation, Subrogation, Personal Injury, Workers' Compensation, Product Liability, Property, Arson, Theft, Discrimination, Medical Malpractice, Professional Malpractice, Nursing Home Liability, Education Law, Title VII

Insurance Clients

ACE USA	Auto-Owners Insurance Company
Berkley Risk Administrators Company, LLC	Broadspire Services, Inc.
Colony Management Services, Inc.	CNA Insurance Company
ESIS	Employers Reinsurance Corporation
Farmers Insurance Company	GAB Robins North America, Inc.
GMAC Insurance	Guarantee Insurance Company
GuideOne Insurance	ITT Specialty Risk Services, Inc.
MetLife Insurance Company	Nationwide Insurance
Republic Western Insurance Company	Robinson-Adams Insurance, Inc.
Sedgwick Claims Management Services, Inc.	St. Paul Fire and Marine Insurance Company
State Farm Fire and Casualty Company	Southern United Fire Insurance Company
21st Century Insurance Company	State Farm Mutual Automobile Insurance Company
Westport Insurance Company	

Non-Insurance Clients

Fred's Stores of Tennessee	Portico Magazine
Publix Super Markets, Inc.	

Partners

Ronald J. Gault — 1970 — Mississippi State University, B.A., 1992; The University of Alabama, J.D., 1997 — Admitted to Bar, 1997, Alabama; U.S. District Court, Middle and Northern Districts of Alabama; U.S. Court of Appeals, Eleventh Circuit

Ralph D. Gaines, III — 1954 — Stetson University, B.B.A., 1976; Florida State University, M.S., 1977; The University of Alabama School of Law, J.D., 1983 — Admitted to Bar, 1983, Arkansas; Alabama; U.S. District Court, Middle, Northern and Southern Districts of Alabama — Member American, Talladega County and Birmingham Bar Associations; Alabama State Bar; Alabama Defense Lawyers Association; Atlanta Claims Association

Tracy Hendrix — 1970 — The University of Alabama, B.S. (magna cum laude), 1992; J.D., 1995 — Admitted to Bar, 1995, Alabama; U.S. District Court, Middle and Northern Districts of Alabama

Julie Davis Pearce — 1972 — Lenoir-Rhyne College, B.A. (cum laude), 1994; Cumberland School of Law of Samford University, J.D. (with honors), 1997 — Admitted to Bar, 1997, Alabama; U.S. District Court, Middle and Northern Districts of Alabama; 1999, U.S. Court of Appeals, Eleventh Circuit — Member Alabama State Bar; Shelby County and Birmingham Bar Associations

Marcus "Marc" A. Jaskolka — 1974 — The University of Tennessee at Martin, B.S. (cum laude), 1997; Cumberland School of Law of Samford University, J.D., 2000 — Admitted to Bar, 2000, Alabama; U.S. District Court, Middle, Northern and Southern Districts of Alabama; U.S. Court of Appeals, Eleventh Circuit — Member Alabama State Bar; Birmingham Bar Association; Alabama Defense Lawyers Association

Associates

Travis I. Keith — 1982 — Auburn University, B.S., 2004; Cumberland School of Law of Samford University, J.D., 2008 — Admitted to Bar, 2008, Alabama; U.S. District Court, Northern District of Alabama — Member American and Birmingham Bar Associations; Alabama State Bar

Gaines Gault Hendrix P.C., Birmingham, AL (Continued)

Lee H. Stewart — 1968 — University of Kentucky, B.S., 1992; Cumberland University School of Law, J.D., 1996 — Admitted to Bar, 1996, Alabama; U.S. District Court, Northern and Southern Districts of Alabama — Member American and Birmingham Bar Associations; Alabama State Bar

Charles T. Buchanan — 1984 — Colorado State University, B.S., 2006; Cumberland University School of Law, J.D., 2012 — Admitted to Bar, 2012, Alabama

Christopher "Drew" McNutt — 1985 — The University of Alabama, B.S., 2007; Cumberland School of Law at Samford University, J.D., 2010 — Admitted to Bar, 2010, Alabama; 2011, Tennessee — Member Alabama State Bar; Birmingham Bar Association

James "Bernie" B. Brannan, III — 1985 — The University of Mississippi, B.A. (magna cum laude), 2007; The University of Alabama, J.D., 2010 — Admitted to Bar, 2010, Alabama; 2012, U.S. District Court, Northern District of Alabama — Member Alabama State Bar; Birmingham Bar Association; Litigation Counsel of America

Michael E. Eldridge — 1986 — Auburn University, B.A., 2009; Cumberland School of Law of Samford University, J.D., 2012 — Admitted to Bar, 2012, Alabama; U.S. District Court, Northern District of Alabama — Member Alabama State Bar; Birmingham Bar Association

Daniel J. Newton — 1984 — Auburn University, B.A., 2007; Washington and Lee University School of Law, J.D., 2011 — Admitted to Bar, 2011, Alabama; 2012, Georgia; U.S. District Court, Middle, Northern and Southern Districts of Alabama; U.S. District Court, Middle and Northern Districts of Georgia — Member Alabama State Bar; Birmingham Bar Association

Kristen S. Osborne — 1985 — Birmingham-Southern College, B.A. (summa cum laude), 2007; Central European University, M.A., 2008; The University of Alabama School of Law, J.D. (magna cum laude), 2012 — Admitted to Bar, 2012, Alabama; 2013, U.S. District Court, Northern District of Alabama — Member Alabama State Bar; Birmingham Bar Association (Crisis Relief Committee) — Languages: French, Hungarian

Gerri Plain — 1968 — University of South Carolina, B.A., 1991; Southern Wesleyan University, M.S., 2006; Cumberland School of Law of Samford University, J.D. (cum laude), 2012 — Admitted to Bar, 2012, Alabama; U.S. District Court, Northern District of Alabama — Member Alabama State Bar; Huntsville-Madison County Bar Association; Madison County Volunteer Lawyers Program — Certified Professional in Human Resources (PHR)

Gray & Associates, L.L.C.

3800 Colonnade Parkway, Suite 350
Birmingham, Alabama 35243
   Toll Free: 866-968-0900
   Telephone: 205-968-0900
   Fax: 205-968-6534
   Mobile: 205-601-7997
   E-Mail: wgratty@aol.com
   www.grayattorneys.com

Established: 1999

Insurance Defense, Trial Practice, Appellate Practice

Firm Profile: Gray & Associates, L.L.C. handles a wide range of complex and multi-faceted cases, appeals, negotiations and mediations that call for an expert's understanding and focus on strategy, tactics, legal precedents and technology, as well as a full understanding of the community in which clients live and work.

Insurance Clients

Alfa Financial Corporation	Alfa Life Insurance Corporation
Alfa Mutual Insurance Company	Chartis
Chubb Group of Insurance Companies	Cincinnati Insurance Company
	Cincinnati Life Insurance Company
Executive Risk Indemnity Inc.	Federal Insurance Company
General Star National Insurance Company	Hartford Insurance Company
Travelers	Liberty National Life Insurance Company

Non-Insurance Clients

Alfa Builders	Alfa Corporation
Alfa Realty Company	Bill Lunsford Construction Co., Inc.
Groome Transportation, Inc.	

Gray & Associates, L.L.C., Birmingham, AL (Continued)

National Management Resources
Turner Pine, LLC
Southern States Police Benevolent Association, Inc.

Owner

William P. Gray, Jr. — 1943 — The University of Alabama, B.S., 1965; The University of Alabama School of Law, J.D., 1968 — Kappa Sigma, Phi Alpha Delta Legal Fraternity — Admitted to Bar, 1968, Alabama; 1972, U.S. District Court, Northern District of Alabama; 1981, U.S. Court of Appeals, Eleventh Circuit; 1995, U.S. District Court, Middle District of Alabama; 1995, U.S. Supreme Court — Member Alabama State Bar; Birmingham, Tuscaloosa and Montgomery Bar Associations; Council on Litigation Management; Alabama Defense Lawyers Association — "The Ten Commandments and the Ten Amendments: A Case Study in Religious Freedom in Alabama," Alabama Law Review (Volume 49, Winter 1998, Number 2) — Reported Cases: William P. Gray, Jr. has been involved in hundreds of litigated cases, having tried around 100 jury cases to conclusion having won an overwhelming number of them. Numerous Appellate Cases, the two most recent appeals to the Alabama Sup.Ct. resulted in reversals on all counts and verdicts being rendered on behalf of our defendants saving multi-millions of dollars. — Former Chief Legal Advisor to Governor of State of Alabama (1995-1998); He was involved in the completion of the Mercedes location in the State of Alabama and was instrumental in securing and bringing the $450 million Boeing Delta IV Booster Facility to Decatur, Alabama; Best Insurance Defense Lawyers in Birmingham by Birmingham Bar Association (2014) — U.S. Air Force Captain, Staff Judge Advocate, Lockbourne AFB, Ohio — E-mail: wgratty@aol.com

Associate Counsel

Douglas N. Robertson — 1977 — Samford University, B.A. (magna cum laude), 2000; The University of Alabama School of Law, J.D. (magna cum laude), 2004 — Admitted to Bar, 2004, Alabama; U.S. District Court, Middle and Northern Districts of Alabama; Supreme Court of Alabama — Member Alabama State Bar; Birmingham Bar Association; Alabama Defense Lawyers Association — Practice Areas: Insurance Defense; Trial Practice; Employment Discrimination; Civil Litigation — E-mail: dnrobert24@gmail.com

John David Gray — 1983 — The University of Alabama, B.S., 2006; The University of Alabama School of Law, J.D., 2009 — Lamda Sigma Phi — Admitted to Bar, 2009, Alabama; U.S. District Court, Middle and Northern Districts of Alabama; Supreme Court of Alabama — Member American and Birmingham Bar Associations; Alabama State Bar; Alabama Defense Lawyers Association (Young Lawyers Division) — Languages: Spanish — Practice Areas: Civil Litigation; Insurance Defense — E-mail: jdgratty@gmail.com

Thomas A. Treadwell, Sr. — 1974 — Samford University, B.S., 1997; Cumberland School of Law at Samford University, J.D. (cum laude), 2000 — Admitted to Bar, 2000, Alabama; 2013, Kentucky; 2000, U.S. District Court, Middle District of Alabama; 2001, U.S. District Court, Northern and Southern Districts of Alabama; U.S. Court of Appeals, Eleventh Circuit — Member Kentucky, Birmingham and Montgomery County Bar Associations; Alabama State Bar; Association of Corporate Counsel; Fellow, Council on Litigation Management; Alabama Life and Disability Insurance Guaranty Association (Chairman, 2009-2013; Secretary, 2006-2009); Association of Alabama Life Insurance Companies (President, 2009-2012; Vice President, 2006-2009); American Council of Life Insurers (Litigation Committee); Alabama Legislature's Open Records Study Task Force (2006); Alabama Defense Lawyers Association — Comment, "Austin Hill Country Realty, Inc. v. Palisades Plaza, Inc.: The Commercial Landlords' Duty to Mitigate Upon Tenants' Breach, " 22 AM. J. TRIAL ADVOC. 695 (1999) — Thomas A. Treadwell, Sr. has spent the majority of his career in corporate environments, most recently as Assistant General Counsel for a large multi-line insurance company, where he managed litigation, advised management on labor and employment and employee benefits issues, served as counsel to the company's life insurance subsidiary, and maintained a general corporate practice. — Practice Areas: Civil Litigation; Insurance; Employment; Corporate Law; Contracts; Life Insurance; Property and Casualty; Regulatory and Compliance; Legislative Law — E-mail: tat@grayattorneys.com

Hale Sides LLC

600 Financial Center
505 20th Street North
Birmingham, Alabama 35203
   Telephone: 205-453-9800
   Fax: 205-453-9801
   E-Mail: rglaze@halesides.com
   http://halesides.com

(Fairhope, AL Office: 103 Kennedy Place, 308 Magnolia Avenue, 36532) (Tel: 251-517-6004)

Established: 2009

Civil Trial Practice, State and Federal Courts, Insurance Defense, Insurance Coverage Litigation, Personal Injury, Workers' Compensation, Architects and Engineers, Professional Malpractice, Municipal Liability, Product Liability, Arson, Fidelity and Surety, Corporate Law, Commercial Transactions, Banking, Employment Discrimination, Civil Rights, Construction, Lender Liability, Business Development, Constitutional Law

Firm Profile: The attorneys of Hale Sides LLC have more than 50 years combined experience successfully handling litigation and business matters with the highest standards of professionalism, precision and efficiency. We maintain a core focus on providing trusted, experienced counsel, and aggressive, ethical resolution of complex claims against businesses, employees, insureds, insurers, trust plan administrators, individuals, municipal entities and their agents.

Insurance Clients

Alabama Municipal Insurance Corporation
Chubb Group of Insurance Companies

Non-Insurance Clients

Houchens Food Group, Inc.
TMT America, Inc.
HPS North America, Inc.

Managing Partners

Thomas S. Hale — Vanderbilt University, B.A., 1979; Cumberland School of Law of Samford University, J.D., 1983 — Admitted to Bar, 1983, Tennessee; 1984, Alabama; U.S. District Court, Middle, Northern and Southern Districts of Alabama; U.S. District Court, Eastern, Middle and Western Districts of Tennessee; U.S. Court of Appeals, Fourth, Ninth and Eleventh Circuits; U.S. Supreme Court — Member American, Tennessee and Birmingham Bar Associations; Alabama State Bar; Alabama Municipal Attorneys Association; National Journal of Trial Advocacy; Alabama Defense Lawyers Association; Defense Research Institute; American Association for Justice; Alabama Trial Lawyers Association — Resident Birmingham, AL and Fairhope, AL Office

Terry A. Sides — The University of Alabama, B.S., 1982; Cumberland School of Law of Samford University, J.D., 1985 — Admitted to Bar, 1985, Alabama; 2007, Tennessee; U.S. District Court, Middle, Northern and Southern Districts of Alabama; U.S. Court of Appeals, Eleventh Circuit; U.S. Supreme Court — Member American (Former Member, Federal Courts Committee, Judicial Administration Division-Lawyers Conference), Tennessee and Birmingham Bar Associations; Alabama State Bar; Defense Research Institute (Governmental Liability Committee); Master Bencher American Inn of Court; Alabama Defense Lawyers Association

Associates

Richard D. Whitaker
Catherine "Ree" Glaze
Erin Fleming
Jesse R. Cash

Johnstone Adams, L.L.C.

2020 Canyon Road, Suite 100
Birmingham, Alabama 35216
   Telephone: 205-871-7733
   Fax: 205-871-7387
   www.JohnstoneAdams.com

ALABAMA — BIRMINGHAM

Johnstone Adams, L.L.C., Birmingham, AL (Continued)

(Mobile, AL Office*: One St. Louis Centre, 1 St. Louis Street, Suite 4000, 36602, P.O. Box 1988, 36633)
 (Tel: 251-432-7682)
 (Fax: 251-432-2800)
 (www.Johnstoneadams.com)
(Bay Minette, AL Office*: Dahlberg Building, 104 Hand Avenue, P.O. Box 729, 36507)
 (Tel: 251-937-9473)
 (Fax: 251-937-9475)

Insurance Defense, Admiralty and Maritime Law, Bad Faith, Casualty, Fire, Health, Accident, Fraud, Life Insurance, Workers' Compensation, Governmental Liability, Product Liability, Civil Rights, ERISA, Title VIII Defense

(See listing under Mobile, AL for additional information)

Jones Walker LLP

One Federal Place
1819 5th Avenue North, Suite 1100
Birmingham, Alabama 35203
 Telephone: 205-244-5200
 Fax: 205-244-5400
 E-Mail: info@joneswalker.com
 www.joneswalker.com

(New Orleans, LA Office*: 201 St. Charles Avenue, 70170-5100)
 (Tel: 504-582-8000)
 (Fax: 504-582-8583)
(Mobile, AL Office*: RSA Battle House Tower, 11 North Water Street, Suite 1200, 36602, P.O. Box 46, 36601)
 (Tel: 251-432-1414)
 (Fax: 251-433-4106)
(Baton Rouge, LA Office*: Four United Plaza, 8555 United Plaza Boulevard, 70809)
 (Tel: 225-248-2000)
 (Fax: 225-248-2010)
(Lafayette, LA Office*: 600 Jefferson Street, Suite 1600, 70501)
 (Tel: 337-593-7600)
 (Fax: 337-593-7601)
(Jackson, MS Office*: 190 East Capitol Street, Suite 800, 39201, P.O. Box 427, 39205-0427)
 (Tel: 601-949-4900)
 (Fax: 601-949-4804)
(Olive Branch, MS Office*: 6897 Crumpler Boulevard, Suite 100, 38654)
 (Tel: 662-895-2996)
 (Fax: 662-895-5480)

Accountants, Admiralty and Maritime Law, Agent/Broker Liability, Antitrust, Appellate Practice, Asbestos Litigation, Aviation, Bankruptcy, Cargo, Class Actions, Commercial Litigation, Complex Litigation, Construction Law, Contracts, Directors and Officers Liability, Disability, Employment Law, Energy, Entertainment Law, Environmental Law, ERISA, Errors and Omissions, Health Care, Insurance Coverage, Insurance Defense, Intellectual Property, International Law, Labor and Employment, Life Insurance, Medical Malpractice, Mergers and Acquisitions, Motor Carriers, Oil and Gas, Personal Injury, Product Liability, Professional Liability, Regulatory and Compliance, Toxic Torts, Workers' Compensation

Firm Profile: Since 1937, Jones Walker LLP has grown to become one of the largest law firms in the southeastern U.S. We serve local, regional, national, and international business interests in a wide range of markets and industries. Today, we have more than 375 attorneys in 19 offices.

Jones Walker is committed to providing proactive legal services to major multinational, public, and private corporations; *Fortune* 500® companies; money center banks and worldwide insurers; and family and emerging businesses located in the United States and abroad.

Jones Walker LLP, Birmingham, AL (Continued)

Firm Members

Emily Sides Bonds — Jacksonville State University, B.A. (with distinction), 1987; The University of Alabama School of Law, J.D., 1990 — Hugo Black L. Scholar; Sam H. Hammer Scholarship; Urban State Government Award — Alabama Law Review — Admitted to Bar, 1990, Alabama; 2003, Mississippi; U.S. District Court, Middle, Northern and Southern Districts of Alabama; U.S. District Court, Northern and Southern Districts of Mississippi; U.S. Court of Appeals, Fifth and Eleventh Circuits; U.S. Supreme Court — Member American Bar Association; Alabama State Bar; Alabama Defense Lawyers Association — Reported Cases: Philadelphia American Life Insurance Company v. Bender, 893 So. 2d 1104 (Ala. 2004); Densmore v. Jefferson County, 813 So. 2d 844 (Ala. 2001); Ex Parte Foster, 758 So. 2d 516 (Ala. 1999); Georgia Power Company v. Partin, 727 So. 2d 2 (Ala. 1998); Boone v. Health Strategies, Inc., 2007 WL 2332696 (M.D. Ala. August 15, 2007); English v. Capital Risk Management, 2001 WL 910412 (M.D. Ala. 2001); Maloof v. John Hancock Life Insurance Co., et al., 60 So. 3d 263 (Ala. 2010) — Alabama Super Lawyers 2012; The Best Lawyers in America® 2012 — E-mail: ebonds@joneswalker.com

Steven F. Casey — The University of Alabama, B.S., 1975; Cumberland School of Law at Samford University, J.D. (cum laude), 1979 — Editor-in-Chief, Cumberland Law Review — Admitted to Bar, 1979, Alabama; U.S. District Court, Middle, Northern and Southern Districts of Alabama; U.S. Court of Appeals, Fifth and Eleventh Circuits; U.S. Supreme Court — Member Federation of Defense and Corporate Counsel; Alabama Defense Lawyers Association; Defense Research Institute — "Generic Pharmaceutical Liability - Challenges and Changes," The International Comparative Legal Guide to: Product Liability, May, 2012 — Alabama Super Lawyers; The Best Lawyers in America — E-mail: scasey@joneswalker.com

J. David Moore — University of Virginia, B.A. (with distinction, Phi Beta Kappa), 1994; J.D., 1997 — Admitted to Bar, 1997, Alabama; 2003, Mississippi; 1997, U.S. District Court, Middle, Northern and Southern Districts of Alabama; U.S. District Court, Northern and Southern Districts of Mississippi; U.S. Court of Appeals, Fourth, Fifth and Eleventh Circuits — Member American Bar Association; The Mississippi Bar; Alabama State Bar — E-mail: dmoore@joneswalker.com

Vernon L. Wells, II — Auburn University, B.S. (summa cum laude), 1967; Harvard Law School, J.D., 1971 — Admitted to Bar, 1971, Georgia; 1973, Alabama; U.S. District Court, Middle, Northern and Southern Districts of Alabama; U.S. Court of Appeals, Eleventh Circuit — Member American Bar Association; Alabama State Bar; State Bar of Georgia; Alabama Defense Lawyers Association; Defense Research Institute — Reported Cases: Mallard v. Countrywide Home Loans, Inc., 730 So. 2d 118; Georgia Power Co. v. Partin, 727 So. 2d 2; Precise Engineering, Inc. v. LaCombe, 624 So. 2d. 1339; Spain v. Brown & Williamson Tobacco Corp., 363 F.3d 1183; Ruiz de Molina v. Merritt & Furmam Ins. Agency, Inc., 207 F.3d 1351; Gomer ex rel. Gomer v. Philip Morris, Inc., 106 F. Supp. 2d 1262 — Alabama Super Lawyers; Best Lawyers in America — Staff Judge Advocate, U.S. Air Force (1972-1975) — E-mail: vwells@joneswalker.com

(See Listing under New Orleans, LA for a List of Firm Clients and Additional Information)

Klasing & Williamson, P.C.

1601 Providence Park
Birmingham, Alabama 35242
 Telephone: 205-980-4733
 Fax: 205-980-4737
 E-Mail: danklasing@bellsouth.net

Established: 1995

Insurance Coverage, Insurance Defense, First and Third Party Defense, Arson, Fraud, Construction Law

Insurance Clients

AAA Insurance	Allstate Insurance Company
American Modern Insurance Group, Inc.	American National Property and Casualty Company
Auto-Owners Insurance Company	Donegal Insurance Group
EMC Insurance Companies	State Auto Insurance Company

BIRMINGHAM ALABAMA

Klasing & Williamson, P.C., Birmingham, AL (Continued)

Partners

Daniel R. Klasing — Auburn University, B.S., 1983; The University of Alabama School of Law, J.D., 1991 — Admitted to Bar, 1991, Alabama; U.S. District Court, Middle, Northern and Southern Districts of Alabama; U.S. Court of Appeals, Eleventh Circuit — Member The Alabama Bar; Birmingham Bar Association (Chair, Public Service Committee, 1997); Alabama Defense Lawyers Association; Defense Research Institute

Sue Elizabeth Williamson — The University of Alabama at Birmingham, B.S., 1971; Birmingham School of Law, J.D. (cum laude), 1985 — Admitted to Bar, 1985, Alabama; U.S. District Court, Middle, Northern and Southern Districts of Alabama; U.S. Court of Appeals, Eleventh Circuit — Member Birmingham Bar Association; Alabama Association of Arson Investigators (Board of Directors, 1988-present; President, 1999; Treasurer, 2000-present); Lawrence Bradley Award, 1999 & 2009; National Association of Professional Insurance Investigators (NSPII); International Association of Arson Investigators

Warren Hunter Burke, Jr. — The University of Alabama School of Law, J.D., 1991 — Admitted to Bar, 1991, Alabama

David Alexander Bright — Cumberland School of Law at Samford University, J.D., 1999 — Admitted to Bar, 1999, Alabama

Associate

Jonathan G. Wells — Cumberland School of Law at Samford University, J.D., 2007 — Admitted to Bar, 2007, Alabama

Laney & Foster, P.C.

Two Perimeter Park South, Suite 426 East
Birmingham, Alabama 35243
Telephone: 205-298-8440
Fax: 205-298-8441
www.laneyfoster.com

Established: 2000

Defense Litigation, Product Liability Defense, Professional Liability, Construction Law, Architects and Engineers, Insurance Defense, Errors and Omissions, Construction Defect, General Practice

Firm Profile: Both Mr. Laney and Mr. Foster have been in full-service professional liability practice (Mr. Laney, 38 years; Mr. Foster, 28 years) involving defense for all types of professionals. Beginning about 26 years ago, Mr. Laney began focusing on design liability and was joined by Mr. Foster in 1992. The firm has cases in State and Federal courts all over the state of Alabama and parts of Florida from Pensacola to Jacksonville. The scope of liability claims defended include bodily injury, economic loss and construction and design "defects," brought by owners, third parties, general contractors and subcontractors. They include damage claims of all types. The Florida work is heavily associated with the high-rise costal condo developments which frequently spawn lawsuits in the Gulf Coast areas of Alabama and Florida. In addition to design liability, the firm also represents accountants in the defense of accounting liability cases in Alabama and Florida.

Our lawyers perform contract reviews routinely for design professionals and advise regarding contract language and also attend contract negotiation meetings with clients. Our attorneys routinely speak to lawyers as well as architects, engineers, contractors and developers at seminars involving construction disputes and legal issues.

Corporate Clients

NHB/MasterBrand Cabinets, Inc.
Volkert & Associates, Inc.

Insurance Clients

Argo Pro
CAMICO Mutual Insurance Company
Everest National Insurance Company
Hudson Insurance Group
Navigators Insurance Company
ProSight Specialty Insurance Company
Travelers Insurance Companies
Beazley Group
CNA Insurance Company
Endurance American Specialty
The Hanover Insurance Companies
Houston Casualty Company
Liberty International Underwriters
OneBeacon Professional Insurance
QBE Insurance Corporation
RLI Insurance Company

Laney & Foster, P.C., Birmingham, AL (Continued)

Shareholders

John M. Laney, Jr. — **Founding Shareholder** — The University of Alabama, B.A., 1968; Cumberland School of Law of Samford University, J.D., 1971 — Admitted to Bar, 1972, Alabama; 1998, Florida; 1972, U.S. District Court, Middle, Northern and Southern Districts of Alabama; U.S. Court of Appeals, Fifth and Eleventh Circuits — Member American Bar Association (Forum on Construction Industry; Architect & Engineer Liability Committee; Business Litigation Committee); Birmingham Bar Association; Alabama Defense Lawyers Association; International Association of Defense Counsel; Defense Research Institute; Florida Defense Lawyers Association; Professional Liability Underwriting Society — AV Preeminent Peer Review Rated by Martindale Hubbell; Top Attorneys in Alabama by Business Alabama (2012); Super Lawyers — Practice Areas: Insurance Defense; Product Liability Defense; Professional Liability; Architects and Engineers; Errors and Omissions; Construction Law; Construction Litigation; Accountant Liability — Tel: 205-986-4408 — E-mail: jmlaney@laneyfoster.com

Roger C. Foster — **Founding Shareholder** — The University of Alabama at Birmingham, B.S., 1978; The University of Alabama School of Law, J.D., 1982 — Admitted to Bar, 1982, Alabama; U.S. District Court, Middle, Northern and Southern Districts of Alabama; U.S. Court of Appeals, Fifth and Eleventh Circuits — Member American and Birmingham Bar Associations; International Association of Defense Counsel; Alabama Defense Lawyers Association; Defense Research Institute; Professional Liability Underwriting Society — AV Preeminent Peer Review Rated by Martindale Hubbell — Practice Areas: Insurance Defense; Product Liability Defense; Professional Liability; Architects and Engineers; Errors and Omissions; Construction Law; Construction Litigation; Accountant Liability — Tel: 205-986-4405 — E-mail: rcfoster@laneyfoster.com

Forrest L. Adams, II — The University of Alabama, B.S., 1998; The University of Alabama School of Law, J.D., 2001 — Admitted to Bar, 2001, Alabama; 2003, Florida; U.S. District Court, Middle, Northern and Southern Districts of Alabama — Member American and Birmingham Bar Associations; Alabama Defense Lawyers Association; Florida Defense Lawyers Association; Professional Liability Underwriting Society — Practice Areas: Insurance Defense; Professional Liability; Architects and Engineers; Errors and Omissions; Construction Law; Construction Litigation; Product Liability; Accountant Liability — Tel: 205-986-4404 — E-mail: fladams@laneyfoster.com

Gregory S. Manning — West Georgia College, B.S., 1998; Cumberland School of Law of Samford University, J.D., 2001 — Admitted to Bar, 2001, Florida; 2002, Alabama; U.S. District Court, Northern District of Alabama — Member American and Birmingham Bar Associations; Alabama Defense Lawyers Association; Florida Defense Lawyers Association; Defense Research Institute; Professional Liability Underwriting Society — Practice Areas: Insurance Defense; Professional Liability; Architects and Engineers; Errors and Omissions; Construction Law; Premises Liability; Product Liability; Construction Litigation; Accountant Liability — Tel: 205-986-4407 — E-mail: gsmanning@laneyfoster.com

John C. DeShazo — Auburn University, B.S., 2000; The University of Alabama at Tuscaloosa, J.D., 2004 — Admitted to Bar, 2004, Alabama; 2009, Florida — Member American (Forum on Construction Industry) and Birmingham (Workers' Compensation Section) Bar Associations; Alabama Defense Lawyers Association; Florida Defense Lawyers Association; Defense Research Institute; Professional Liability Underwriting Society — Practice Areas: Insurance Defense; Professional Liability; Architects and Engineers; Errors and Omissions; Construction Law; Construction Litigation; Workers' Compensation; Accountant Liability — Tel: 205-986-4410 — E-mail: jdeshazo@laneyfoster.com

Associate

Clark E. Bowers — Samford University, B.S., 2007; The University of Alabama School of Law, J.D., 2010 — Law Clerk, Alabama Court of Criminal Appeals Judge — Admitted to Bar, 2010, Alabama; 2012, Florida — Member American and Birmingham Bar Associations — Practice Areas: Insurance Defense; Professional Liability; Architects and Engineers; Errors and Omissions; Construction Law; Product Liability; Construction Litigation; Accountant Liability

| ALABAMA | BIRMINGHAM |

Norman, Wood, Kendrick & Turner

Ridge Park Place, Suite 3000
1130 22nd Street South
Birmingham, Alabama 35205
Telephone: 205-328-6643
Fax: 205-251-5479
E-Mail: name@nwkt.com
www.nwkt.com

Insurance Defense, Trial Practice, Appellate Practice, State and Federal Courts, Property and Casualty, Product Liability, Professional Liability, Fire, Surety, Bonds, Life Insurance, Subrogation, Transportation, Insurance Coverage, Automobile, Trucking Law, Commercial Vehicle, Common Carrier, Construction Law, Health Care

Firm Profile:

About NWKT

NWKT is a boutique litigation firm specializing in high quality trial advocacy and litigation management. NWKT also has a strong creditor's rights and bankruptcy practice.

NWKT and its predecessors have represented clients in all aspects of litigation since the 1930's. NWKT handles a broad spectrum of clients and matters in areas that include appellate advocacy, bad faith litigation, business and commercial litigation, complex litigation, construction litigation, creditor's rights and bankruptcy, insurance litigation and coverage, long-term care and nursing home litigation, medical malpractice, product liability, professional liability, transportation litigation and toxic tort litigation. Today, the firm continues to build on its history of excellence, with an eye toward the future.

Trial Experience

NWKT lawyers have always been active trial lawyers. We have tried cases across Alabama in both Federal and State courts. The size of our firm dictates that all of our lawyers establish and maintain the highest skills and qualities necessary to defend the most complex cases. As technology changes, NWKT incorporates these changes into the practice of law. We have developed a state-of-the-art mock courtroom in our office to serve as training ground for our lawyers.

NWKT is committed to excellence in the courtroom. Each lawyer who practices civil defense litigation is a graduate of the International Association of Defense Counsel Trial Academy. NWKT lawyers also serve as coaches for mock trial and moot court teams at the University of Alabama School of Law and Samford University's Cumberland School of Law.

Litigation Management

NWKT lawyers are trial experts. Because of that we know the life of a file all the way through verdict and appeal, we are able to advise our clients how to most effectively manage their litigation and risk. NWKT knows how to achieve resolutions at the right time during the litigation. We pride ourselves on accurately and effectively assessing our client's exposure and providing case assessments that reflect the real world risk in the courtroom. We look at the metrics of the litigation, including time to resolution, cost budget, expected resolution value, and verdict and liability estimates to come up with a strategy that achieves the best result for our clients.

Global Reach

NKWT is a member of The Harmonie Group, an affiliation of independent law firms throughout the country. Harmonie links us to other leading law firms and provides us and our clients ready access to legal services in other jurisdictions. Our affiliation with The Harmonie Group also provides clients with 24/7 access to counsel through its Emergency Hotline—1-877-247-3659.

We are also affiliated through Harmonie with Canadian Litigation Counsel, a network of Canadian firms with similar practices.

NWKT lawyers are active in many local, national, and international organizations, including: the International Association of Defense Counsel, Federation of Defense and Corporate Counsel, American Board of Trial

Norman, Wood, Kendrick & Turner, Birmingham, AL
(Continued)

Advocates, Defense Research Institute, American Bankruptcy Institute, Alabama Defense Lawyers Association, and the Alabama State Bar.

Insurance Clients

Adesa, Inc.
Arch Insurance Company
Centennial Casualty Company
CIGNA Property and Casualty Insurance Company
The Doctors Company
Economical Insurance Group
Farm Bureau Insurance Companies
Generali - US Branch
Kingsway General Insurance Company
Lombard Insurance Company
Nationwide Indemnity Company
New Hampshire Insurance Company
Penn Millers Insurance Company
QBE Insurance Company
Tennessee Farmers Insurance Companies
Westfield Insurance Company
Amerisure Insurance Company
Auction Insurance
Chubb Executive Risk, Inc.
CNA Surety Corporation
Darwin Professional Underwriters, Inc.
Erie Insurance Company
First Professionals Insurance Company
Liberty Insurance Holdings
Lloyd's
NAMIC Insurance Company, Inc.
Nationwide Insurance
Ohio Casualty Insurance Company
OneBeacon Professional Partners, Inc.
Response Insurance Company
Truck Insurance Exchange
United Services Automobile Association (USAA)

Non-Insurance Clients

Affirmative Risk Management, Inc.
American Home Products, Inc.
Arctic Cat, Inc.
Birmingham/Jefferson County Transit Authority
Conair Corporation
Executive Risk Management Associates
Insurance Auto Auctions, Inc.
Knight Transportation Company
Lennox International, Inc.
NaphCare, Inc.
The Petroleum Group
Robinson-Adams Insurance, Inc.
Universal Adjusters, Inc.
Alabama Hospital Association Trust
Baptist Health System, Inc.
Brookwood Medical Center
Coastal Insurance Enterprises, Inc.
Employers Drug Program Management, Inc.
Frontier Trucking
J. H. Fletcher & Co.
Laidlaw International, Inc.
Mine Safety Appliances Company
Performance Food Group
Quest Diagnostics Incorporated
UAB Professional Liability Trust Fund

Partners

Robert D. Norman — (Deceased)

William C. Wood — (Retired)

Thomas A. Kendrick — 1960 — Auburn University, B.A., 1982; Cumberland School of Law of Samford University, J.D., 1985 — Admitted to Bar, 1985, Alabama; U.S. District Court, Middle, Northern and Southern Districts of Alabama; U.S. Court of Appeals, Eleventh Circuit; 1991, U.S. Supreme Court — Member American and Birmingham Bar Associations; Alabama State Bar; International Association of Defense Counsel; Defense Research Institute; Alabama Defense Lawyers Association; American Board of Trial Advocates — Practice Areas: Medical Malpractice; Nursing Home Liability; Product Liability; Hospitals; Insurance Coverage — E-mail: tkendrick@nwkt.com

Kile T. Turner — 1967 — The University of New Mexico, B.B.A., 1990; Cumberland School of Law of Samford University, J.D., 1994 — Admitted to Bar, 1994, Alabama; 1995, U.S. District Court, Middle, Northern and Southern Districts of Alabama; U.S. Court of Appeals, Eleventh Circuit — Member American and Birmingham Bar Associations; Alabama State Bar; Defense Research Institute (Chair, Young Lawyers Committee); Alabama Defense Lawyers Association; Federation of Defense and Corporate Counsel — Practice Areas: Commercial Law; Insurance Coverage; Insurance Litigation; Medical Malpractice; Nursing Home Liability; Transportation; Product Liability; Toxic Torts — E-mail: kturner@nwkt.com

Mark Peery Williams — 1958 — The University of Alabama, B.S., 1981; The University of Alabama School of Law, J.D., 1984 — Law Clerk, Chief vs. Bankruptcy, Judge, George S. Wright, 1985-1986 — University of Alabama Law Review — Admitted to Bar, 1984, Alabama; 1985, U.S. Court of Appeals, Eleventh Circuit; 1986, U.S. District Court, Middle, Northern and Southern Districts of Alabama; 2003, U.S. Supreme Court — Member American and Birmingham Bar Associations; Alabama State Bar — Certified in Creditors Rights and Business Bankruptcy, American Board of Certification — Practice Areas: Bankruptcy; Commercial Litigation; Construction Litigation; Creditor Rights — E-mail: mpwilliams@nwkt.com

Celeste P. Larson — 1972 — Auburn University, B.A., 1994; Cumberland School of Law of Samford University, J.D., 1998 — Admitted to Bar, 1999,

BIRMINGHAM   ALABAMA

Norman, Wood, Kendrick & Turner, Birmingham, AL (Continued)

Alabama; 2010, Tennessee; 1999, U.S. District Court, Middle, Northern and Southern Districts of Alabama; U.S. Court of Appeals, Eleventh Circuit — Member American and Birmingham Bar Associations; Alabama State Bar; Alabama Defense Lawyers Association; Defense Research Institute — Practice Areas: Medical Malpractice; Transportation; Insurance Litigation; Construction Litigation — E-mail: clarson@nwkt.com

Matthew W. Robinett — 1973 — Hampden-Sydney College, B.A., 1995; Cumberland School of Law of Samford University, J.D., 1998 — Admitted to Bar, 1998, Alabama; U.S. District Court, Middle, Northern and Southern Districts of Alabama; U.S. Court of Appeals, Eleventh Circuit — Member Alabama State Bar; Birmingham Bar Association; Defense Research Institute; Alabama Defense Lawyers Association — Practice Areas: Insurance Defense; Transportation; Asbestos Litigation; Mass Tort; Toxic Torts — E-mail: mrobinett@nwkt.com

James L. Pattillo — 1974 — Furman University, B.A., 1997; University of Florida, M.A.M.C. (with distinction), 1999; Cumberland School of Law of Samford University, J.D., 2002 — Admitted to Bar, 2002, Alabama; U.S. District Court, Middle, Northern and Southern Districts of Alabama — Member American and Birmingham Bar Associations; Alabama State Bar; Alabama Defense Lawyers Association; Defense Research Institute — Practice Areas: Insurance Law; Transportation; Medical Malpractice — E-mail: jpattillo@nwkt.com

Holly S. Bell — 1978 — The University of Alabama, B.S., 2000; Cumberland School of Law of Samford University, J.D., 2003 — Admitted to Bar, 2003, Alabama; U.S. District Court, Middle, Northern and Southern Districts of Alabama; U.S. Court of Appeals, Eleventh Circuit — Member American and Birmingham Bar Associations; Alabama State Bar; Alabama Defense Lawyers Association; Defense Research Institute — Practice Areas: Insurance Litigation; Medical Malpractice; Nursing Home Liability — E-mail: hbell@nwkt.com

William H. McKenzie, IV — 1980 — The University of Mississippi, B.B.A., 2002; The University of Mississippi School of Law, J.D., 2005 — Admitted to Bar, 2005, Alabama; 2006, U.S. District Court, Middle, Northern and Southern Districts of Alabama; U.S. District Court, Northern and Southern Districts of Mississippi; U.S. Court of Appeals, Fifth and Eleventh Circuits — Member American and Birmingham Bar Associations; Alabama State Bar; The Mississippi Bar; Alabama Defense Lawyers Association; Defense Research Institute — E-mail: whm@nwkt.com

W.M. Bains Fleming, III — 1980 — Washington and Lee University, B.A., 2003; Cumberland School of Law of Samford University, J.D., 2007 — President, Cumberland School of Law, Class of 2007; Order of Barristers — Admitted to Bar, 2007, Alabama; U.S. District Court, Middle, Northern and Southern Districts of Alabama; 2008, U.S. Court of Appeals, Eleventh Circuit — Member American and Birmingham Bar Associations; Alabama State Bar; Defense Research Institute; Alabama Defense Lawyers Association — Practice Areas: Toxic Torts; Mass Tort; Product Liability; Medical Malpractice; Insurance Defense — E-mail: bfleming@nwkt.com

Parsons, Lee & Juliano, P.C.

600 Vestavia Parkway, Suite 300
Birmingham, Alabama 35216
   Telephone: 205-326-6600
   Fax: 205-324-7097
   Toll Free: 866-585-1572
   E-Mail: info@pljpc.com
   www.pljpc.com

Established: 1986

Insurance Defense, Trial and Appellate Practice, State and Federal Courts, Medical Malpractice, Professional Malpractice, Automobile Liability, Truck Liability, Product Liability, Municipal Liability, Civil Rights, Premises Liability, Class Actions, Bad Faith, Fraud, Workers' Compensation, Self-Insured, Health Care Liability, Construction Litigation, Mediation, Toxic Torts, Environmental and Toxic Injury

Firm Profile: Our firm, since its inception, has maintained its specialization in civil litigation. It works with clients to provide full and complete representation in state and federal courts throughout Alabama and across the Southeast. Parsons, Lee & Juliano prides itself on providing clients with the highest caliber of representation during all stages of litigation. Its attorneys are experienced in not only "litigating" cases, but also taking cases to trial when necessary. Of course, not all cases are appropriate for trial, and Parsons, Lee & Juliano routinely employs alternative dispute resolution procedures, such as mediation and arbitration, to obtain favorable resolutions for its clients. In addition, the firm regularly handles appeals before the Alabama Supreme Court, the Alabama Court of Civil Appeals, the U.S. Courts of Appeals, and the U.S. Supreme Court.

The firm and its staff concentrate their efforts across a wide array of practice areas including appellate litigation, construction litigation, healthcare law, insurance coverage issues, insurance defense, intellectual property, medical malpractice, municipal governmental liability, premises liability, product liability, toxic torts, and workers' compensation. The firm is especially pleased with the dedicated support staff it has developed over the years. This staff enables the firm to provide clients with an exemplary level of representation while also being mindful of the expenses of present-day litigation. Parsons, Lee & Juliano also provides its attorneys and staff with stateof-the-art technology which allows it to utilize the latest and most effective techniques for presentation of materials, whether it be for trial, discovery, document management, or teaching functions. In addition, this technology allows the attorneys of Parsons, Lee & Juliano to communicate efficiently and effectively with clients.

Parsons, Lee & Juliano enjoys the highest rating afforded by the legal association's oldest and most well-known rating organization, Martindale-Hubbell.

Insurance Clients

ACE USA	Allied World Assurance Company
American Association of Orthodontists Insurance Company	American Resources Insurance Company, Inc.
Ameriprise Auto & Home Insurance	Axis Capital, Inc.
Children's of Alabama	Capson Physicians Insurance Company
Coastal Insurance Risk Retention Group Inc.	Dryvit Systems, Inc.
ESIS	EMC Insurance Companies
First Mercury Insurance Company	Fireman's Fund/Interstate Insurance Group
Fortress Insurance Company	GAB Robins, Inc.
IAT Specialty	Jackson County Healthcare Authority
Markel Southwest Underwriters, Inc.	The Medical Protective Company
Music Insurance Company	National Indemnity Company
Nationwide Insurance	Nautilus Insurance Company
OMS National Insurance Company	OneBeacon Insurance Group
Red Clay Risk Retention Group, Inc.	Rite Aid Corporation
	Scottsdale Insurance Company
Sentry Select Insurance Company	Tokio Marine Management, Inc.
Tower Group Companies	Travelers Insurance Companies
Tudor Insurance Company	Union Standard Insurance Group
United Fire & Casualty Company	Western Heritage Insurance Company
Western World Insurance Company	

Non-Insurance Clients

Baptist Health System, Inc.	Cullman Regional Medical Center
Joy Mining Machinery	Marshall Health System
Mazda Motor Corporation	STO Corp.
Wal-Mart Stores, Inc.	

Firm Members

Robert E. Parsons — 1933 — The University of Alabama, B.S., 1955; The University of Alabama School of Law, J.D., 1957 — Admitted to Bar, 1957, Alabama; U.S. District Court, Middle, Northern and Southern Districts of Alabama; U.S. Court of Appeals, Fifth and Eleventh Circuits; U.S. Supreme Court — Member American and Birmingham Bar Associations; Alabama State Bar; Defense Research Institute; Alabama Defense Lawyers Association; International Association of Defense Counsel — Lt. Col., U.S. Air Force Staff Judge Advocate [Retired] — Practice Areas: Automobile Liability; Truck Liability; Medical Malpractice Defense; Product Liability — E-mail: rparsons@pljpc.com

Jasper P. Juliano — 1952 — The University of Alabama, B.A., 1974; The University of Alabama School of Law, J.D., 1977 — Alabama Super Lawyer (2008; 2009) — Admitted to Bar, 1977, Alabama; U.S. District Court, Middle, Northern and Southern Districts of Alabama; U.S. Court of Appeals, Fifth and Eleventh Circuits; U.S. Supreme Court — Member American and

ALABAMA   BIRMINGHAM

Parsons, Lee & Juliano, P.C., Birmingham, AL
(Continued)

Birmingham Bar Associations; Alabama State Bar; Advisory Board, Continuing Legal Education for Cumberland School of Law; American Board of Trial Advocates (President, Alabama Chapter, 2005); Board Member, Southeastern Region of the American Board of Trial Advocates (SEABOTA), 2005; Alabama Defense Lawyers Association; Federation of Defense and Corporate Counsel; Defense Research Institute — Practice Areas: Health Care; Medical Malpractice Defense; Product Liability Defense; Professional Liability — E-mail: jjuliano@pljpc.com

Mark W. Lee — 1952 — The University of Alabama, B.S., 1974; Cumberland School of Law of Samford University, J.D. (cum laude), 1977 — Admitted to Bar, 1977, Alabama; U.S. District Court, Middle, Northern and Southern Districts of Alabama; U.S. Court of Appeals, Eleventh Circuit; 1982, U.S. Supreme Court — Member American and Birmingham Bar Associations; Alabama State Bar; Alabama Defense Lawyers Association; Defense Research Institute; American Board of Trial Advocates — Practice Areas: Health Care; Insurance Coverage; Medical Malpractice Defense; Product Liability Defense — E-mail: mlee@pljpc.com

Marda Walters Sydnor — 1953 — Auburn University, B.A., 1975; Cumberland School of Law of Samford University, J.D., 1980 — Admitted to Bar, 1980, Alabama; Virginia; U.S. District Court, Middle, Northern and Southern Districts of Alabama; U.S. Court of Appeals, Eleventh Circuit — Member American and Birmingham (President, 2005-2006; President-Elect, 2004-2005; Secretary/Treasurer, 2003-2004; Executive Committee, 1999-2002; Chairman, Grievance Committee, Membership Committee, Board-Legal Aid Society; Young Lawyers Section Executive Committee) Bar Associations; Alabama State Bar; Virginia State Bar; Alabama Defense Lawyers Association; Defense Research Institute; International Association of Defense Counsel; American Board of Trial Advocates — Practice Areas: Premises Liability; Product Liability — E-mail: msydnor@pljpc.com

David A. Lee — 1961 — The University of Alabama at Birmingham, B.A., 1983; Cumberland School of Law of Samford University, J.D., 1986 — Admitted to Bar, 1986, Alabama; U.S. District Court, Middle, Northern and Southern Districts of Alabama; U.S. Court of Appeals, Eleventh Circuit; U.S. Supreme Court — Member American and Birmingham Bar Associations; Alabama State Bar; Alabama Defense Lawyers Association; Alabama Trial Lawyers Association; Defense Research Institute; American Board of Trial Advocates — Practice Areas: Appellate Practice; Automobile Liability; Truck Liability; Municipal Liability; Product Liability; Toxic Torts; Environmental Litigation — E-mail: dlee@pljpc.com

Deborah Ann Wakefield — 1966 — Rhodes College, B.A., 1988; Cumberland School of Law of Samford University, J.D., 1993 — Admitted to Bar, 1993, Alabama; 1994, U.S. District Court, Middle and Northern Districts of Alabama; U.S. Court of Appeals, Eleventh Circuit — Member American and Birmingham (Young Lawyers Executive Director, 1995-1999) Bar Associations; Alabama State Bar; Alabama Defense Lawyers Association; Defense Research Institute; American Board of Trial Advocates — Practice Areas: Medical Malpractice Defense; Premises Liability — E-mail: dwakefield@pljpc.com

John M. Bergquist — 1959 — Samford University, B.S., 1981; Cumberland School of Law of Samford University, J.D., 1992 — Admitted to Bar, 1992, Alabama; U.S. District Court, Middle, Northern and Southern Districts of Alabama; U.S. Court of Appeals, Eleventh Circuit; U.S. Supreme Court — Member American and Birmingham Bar Associations; Alabama State Bar; Alabama Defense Lawyers Association; Defense Research Institute — Practice Areas: Product Liability; Construction Law; Premises Liability — E-mail: jbergquist@pljpc.com

Paul J. DeMarco — 1967 — Auburn University, B.A. (cum laude), 1990; The University of Alabama School of Law, J.D., 1993 — Admitted to Bar, 1993, Alabama; U.S. District Court, Middle, Northern and Southern Districts of Alabama; U.S. Court of Appeals, Eleventh Circuit — Member Alabama State Bar; Birmingham Bar Association; Birmingham Bar Foundation (President); Alabama Defense Lawyers Association; Defense Research Institute — Workers' Compensation Committee for Continuing Legal Education for the University of Alabama School of Law; State of Alabama House of Representatives — Practice Areas: Workers' Compensation; Premises Liability; Automobile Liability; Truck Liability — E-mail: pdemarco@pljpc.com

J. Alex Wyatt, III — 1974 — Spring Hill College, B.S., 1996; The University of Alabama School of Law, J.D., 1999 — Admitted to Bar, 1999, Alabama; 2000, U.S. District Court, Middle and Southern Districts of Alabama; U.S. Court of Appeals, Eleventh Circuit — Member American and Birmingham Bar Associations; Alabama State Bar; Alabama Defense Lawyers Association; Defense Research Institute — Practice Areas: Appellate Practice; Mediation; Medical Malpractice Defense; Product Liability Defense; Toxic Torts; Environmental Litigation — E-mail: awyatt@pljpc.com

Parsons, Lee & Juliano, P.C., Birmingham, AL
(Continued)

Paul M. Juliano — 1978 — The University of Alabama at Birmingham, B.A. (cum laude), 2000; Cumberland School of Law of Samford University, J.D., 2004 — Admitted to Bar, 2004, Alabama; U.S. District Court, Middle and Northern Districts of Alabama — Member American and Birmingham (Executive Committee, Young Lawyers Section, 2006-2007) Bar Associations; Alabama State Bar; Alabama Defense Lawyers Association; Defense Research Institute — 2014 Board Member for Legal Leaders of Greater Birmingham — Practice Areas: Medical Malpractice Defense; Premises Liability; Toxic Torts; Environmental Litigation — E-mail: pjuliano@pljpc.com

Miles E. Gresham, Jr. — 1980 — The University of Mississippi, B.A., 2003; The University of Alabama School of Law, J.D. (magna cum laude), 2006 — Admitted to Bar, 2006, Alabama; U.S. District Court, Middle, Northern and Southern Districts of Alabama — Member American and Birmingham Bar Associations; Alabama State Bar; Alabama Defense Lawyers Association; Defense Research Institute — Practice Areas: Medical Malpractice Defense; Premises Liability; Toxic Torts; Environmental Litigation — E-mail: mgresham@pljpc.com

Adrienne D. Scott — 1986 — North Carolina State University, B.A., 2008; The University of Alabama School of Law, J.D., 2011 — Admitted to Bar, 2011, Tennessee; 2012, Alabama; U.S. District Court, Northern District of Alabama — Member American, Birmingham and Magic City Bar Associations; Alabama Defense Lawyers Association — E-mail: ascott@pljpc.com

Porter, Porter & Hassinger, P.C.

215 North 21st Street, Suite 1000
Birmingham, Alabama 35203
Telephone: 205-322-1744
Fax: 205-322-1750

Established: 1931

Insurance Defense, General Liability, Product Liability, Casualty, Errors and Omissions, Workers' Compensation, Construction Law, Employment Practices Liability, Public Entities, Administrative Law

Firm Profile: The present firm was founded by Irvine C. Porter in 1931 as a full service corporate law firm. Over the years, the firm has evolved into a small but effective litigation group emphasizing prompt service and rapid deployment of necessary resources to meet immediate needs of its large client base. The lead attorneys have a great deal of experience in acting as lead trial counsel as well as local and liaison counsel in both statewide and area wide trial litigation and appellate litigation.

The firm practices extensively in the area of Products Liability, Motor Carrier, Public Entity, Employment Practices, Administrative Procedure and Workers Compensation, all on the management and defense side. James Porter is a recognized expert in the multi-disciplined area of counseling and defending public entities, officers and officials. David Hassinger is considered an expert in the area of workers compensation, and has lectured extensively on the subject. Both Mr. Porter and Mr. Hassinger have extensive experience in the defense of product liability claims involving firearms, ammunition and outdoor equipment.

Representative Insurance Clients

AIG - Chartis	Alabama Municipal Insurance
Houston Casualty Company	Corporation
Liberty Mutual Insurance Company	Millennium Risk Managers, LLC
St. Paul Travelers	

Representative Non Insurance Clients

Asplundh Tree Expert Co.	Brasfield & Gorrie, LLC
City of Alabaster	Industrial Chemicals, Inc.
Interarms-North American Group	Remington Arms Company
Smith & Wesson	Sturm, Ruger & Company, Inc.

Firm Members

Irvine C. Porter — (1910-1995)

James W. Porter, II — The University of Alabama, B.A., 1971; Cumberland School of Law of Samford University, J.D., 1974 — Phi Delta Phi — Law Clerk to Chief Judge Virgil Pittman, U.S. District Court, Southern District of Alabama, 1975-1977 — Admitted to Bar, 1974, Alabama; 1974, U.S. District Court, Middle, Northern and Southern Districts of Alabama; 1974, U.S.

BIRMINGHAM ALABAMA

Porter, Porter & Hassinger, P.C., Birmingham, AL
(Continued)

Court of Appeals, Eleventh Circuit — Member American and Birmingham Bar Associations; Alabama State Bar; Association of Transportation Practitioners; International Municipal Lawyer's Association (Local Government Fellow); Alabama Defense Lawyers Association — Practice Areas: Litigation; Administrative Law; Governmental Liability; Employment Practices Liability — E-mail: jwporterii@pphlaw.net

David S. Hassinger — The University of Alabama, B.S., 1972; Cumberland School of Law of Samford University, J.D., 1975 — Phi Delta Phi — Admitted to Bar, 1975, Alabama; 1975, U.S. District Court, Northern and Southern Districts of Alabama; 1975, U.S. Court of Appeals, Eleventh Circuit — Member American and Birmingham Bar Associations; Alabama State Bar; Alabama Defense Lawyers Association — Practice Areas: General Defense; Workers' Compensation

Associates

Karen R. Berhow — The University of Alabama, B.A. (magna cum laude), 2000; The University of Alabama School of Law, J.D. (cum laude), 2003 — Phi Beta Kappa — Admitted to Bar, 2003, Alabama; 2003, U.S. District Court, Middle and Northern Districts of Alabama — Member American and Birmingham Bar Associations; Alabama State Bar — Practice Areas: Workers' Compensation; Insurance Defense; General Liability — E-mail: kberhow@pphlaw.net

Hobart H. Arnold III — 1972 — Auburn University, B.S., 1994; The University of Alabama School of Law, J.D., 2003 — Admitted to Bar, 2003, Alabama; 2005, U.S. District Court, Northern and Southern Districts of Alabama — Member Alabama State Bar; Birmingham Bar Association — Practice Areas: Workers' Compensation; Litigation; Insurance Defense; General Liability — E-mail: barnold@pphlaw.net

Richard W. Kinney III — Kenyon College, B.A., 1999; Cumberland School of Law at Samford University, J.D., 2005; Samford University, M.S., 2005 — Admitted to Bar, 2005, Alabama; U.S. District Court, Middle, Northern and Southern Districts of Alabama; U.S. Court of Appeals, Eleventh Circuit — Practice Areas: Civil Defense; Insurance Defense; Municipal Law; Employment Law

Clifton S. Price, II
Kracke & Price
8107 Parkway Drive
Leeds, Alabama 35094
Telephone: 205-699-5000
Fax: 205-699-3333

Established: 1984

Insurance Defense, Automobile, Workers' Compensation, Personal Injury, Property Defense

Insurance Clients

Acceptance Insurance Company
Millennium Risk Managers, LLC
Safeway Insurance Company
Clarendon National Insurance Company
The St. Paul Companies

Non-Insurance Clients

Associated General Contractors
Commercial Truck Claims
Attenta, Inc.
Deep South Surplus, Inc.

Clifton S. Price, II — 1958 — Samford University, B.S., 1981; Cumberland School of Law of Samford University, J.D., 1984 — Sigma Nu Phi — Admitted to Bar, 1984, Alabama; 1985, U.S. District Court, Middle and Northern Districts of Alabama; 1985, U.S. Court of Appeals, Eleventh Circuit; 1985, U.S. Supreme Court — Member Alabama State Bar; Birmingham Bar Association (Bar Bulletin and Municipal Courts Committees); Alabama Defense Lawyers Association; Alabama Workers' Compensation Claims Association — Municipal Judge, City of Leeds

Scott, Sullivan, Streetman & Fox, P.C.
2450 Valleydale Road
Birmingham, Alabama 35244-2015
Toll Free: 800-955-8678
Telephone: 205-967-9675
Fax: 205-967-7563
www.sssandf.com

(Mobile, AL Office: 56 Saint Joseph Street, 36602)
(Tel: 251-433-1346)
(Fax: 251-433-1086)
(Ridgeland, MS Office: 725 Avignon Drive, 39157)
(Tel: 601-607-4800)
(Fax: 601-607-4801)

Established: 1982

Insurance Defense, Litigation, Product Liability, Professional Malpractice, Workers' Compensation, Medical Malpractice, Trial Practice, State and Federal Courts, Personal Injury, Automobile Liability, Toxic Torts, Premises Liability, Professional Liability, Errors and Omissions, Environmental Litigation, Bad Faith, Employment Discrimination, Hospital, Nursing Home and Health Care Facility Liability, Architects and Engineers Malpractice, Drug and Medical Devises Liability, Mental Health Litigation

Insurance Clients

ACE USA
AIG Technical Services, Inc.
American International Recovery, Inc.
Arrowpoint Capital Corporation
Broadspire Services, Inc.
California State Automobile Association
CNA
Crawford & Company
Farmland Mutual Insurance Company
First Mercury Insurance Company
GAB Robins North America, Inc.
GuideOne Insurance
Indiana Farmers Mutual Insurance Company
Lumber Insurance Companies
Markel Insurance Company
Ohio Casualty Group
Professional Underwriters Liability Insurance Company
Sedgwick Claims Management Services, Inc.
Specialty Risk Services, Inc. (SRS)
AIG Claim Services, Inc.
Alabama Insurance Guaranty Association
Amica Mutual Insurance Company
Atlanta Casualty Company
Builders Insurance Group
Cambridge Integrated Services
Carolina Casualty Insurance Company
The Doctors Company
Fireman's Fund Insurance Company
GAB Business Services, Inc.
Gallagher Bassett Services, Inc.
Hanover Insurance Company
Kemper Insurance Companies
Lexington Insurance Company
Management Services, USA
Medmarc, Inc.
Philadelphia Insurance Company
RSKCo
St. Paul Travelers
Southeastern Claims Services, Inc.
Southern Insurance Company
York Claims Service, Inc.

Non-Insurance Clients

American Medical Systems, Inc.
American Printing Company
Big Warrior Corporation
Campania Management Company, Inc.
Ellis Paving & Construction
Howmedica, Inc.
Invacare Corporation
Martin Gas Transport, Inc.
Parke-Davis
R. E. M. Directional, Inc.
Warner-Lambert Company
Wellborn Cabinet, Inc.
American Optical Corporation
AmeriSpec Inspection Service
Blue Bell Creameries, L.P.
Contemporary Panels, Inc.
C.R. Bard, Inc.
Fidelity National Information Services, Inc.
Lowe's Companies, Inc.
Milner Milling, Inc.
Pfizer, Inc.
Universal Forest Products, Inc.
Waste Management, Inc.

Firm Members

William A. Scott, Jr. — The University of Alabama, B.S., 1965; Cumberland School of Law of Samford University, J.D., 1968 — Admitted to Bar, 1968, Alabama; 1987, Tennessee; U.S. District Court, Middle, Northern and Southern Districts of Alabama; U.S. Court of Appeals, Eleventh Circuit — Member American, Tennessee, Jefferson County, Shelby County and Birmingham Bar Associations; Alabama State Bar; Alabama Defense Lawyers Association; Association of Trial Lawyers of America; Defense Research Institute;

Scott, Sullivan, Streetman & Fox, P.C., Birmingham, AL (Continued)

International Association of Defense Counsel — Martindale-Hubbell AV Preeminent — E-mail: scott@sssandf.com

Carroll H. Sullivan — 1950 — Auburn University, B.S., 1972; Cumberland School of Law of Samford University, J.D. (cum laude), 1975 — Admitted to Bar, 1975, Alabama — Member American and Mobile Bar Associations; Alabama State Bar; International Association of Defense Counsel; Alabama Defense Lawyers Association; Defense Research Institute — Resident Mobile, AL Office

James P. Streetman, III — 1953 — Auburn University, B.S., 1976; Mississippi College School of Law, J.D., 1979 — Admitted to Bar, 1979, Mississippi; 2001, Mississippi Band of Choctaw Indians Tribal Bar; 1979, U.S. Court of Appeals, Fifth Circuit; 1980, U.S. District Court, Northern and Southern Districts of Mississippi; 1989, U.S. Supreme Court — Member American and Hinds County Bar Association; The Mississippi Bar; Mississippi Claims Association; Mississippi Defense Lawyers Association; Defense Research Institute; Federation of Defense and Corporate Counsel — Resident Jackson, MS Office

Anthony N. Fox — 1958 — Maryville College, B.A., 1980; Cumberland School of Law of Samford University, J.D. (cum laude), 1983 — Admitted to Bar, 1983, Alabama; U.S. District Court, Middle, Northern and Southern Districts of Alabama; U.S. Court of Appeals, Eleventh Circuit; U.S. Supreme Court; Poarch Creek Indian Tribal Court — Member Alabama State Bar (Workers' Compensation Section); Alabama Claims Association; Alabama Defense Lawyers Association; Alabama Workers' Compensation Claims Association — E-mail: fox@sssandf.com

Joseph E. Stott — 1969 — The University of Alabama, B.A., 1992; University of Connecticut School of Law, J.D. (magna cum laude), 1995 — Phi Delta Phi — Associate Editor, Connecticut Insurance Law Journal — Admitted to Bar, 1995, Georgia; 1996, Alabama; U.S. District Court, Middle and Northern Districts of Alabama; 1998, U.S. Court of Appeals, Eleventh Circuit; 1999, U.S. District Court, Southern District of Alabama; 2000, U.S. District Court, Northern District of Georgia; 2005, U.S. District Court, Middle District of Georgia — Member American and Birmingham Bar Associations; State Bar of Georgia; Alabama State Bar; Alabama Claims Association — Practice Areas: Civil Litigation — E-mail: stott@sssandf.com

Freddie N. Harrington, Jr. — 1970 — James Madison University, B.S., 1992; Cumberland School of Law of Samford University, J.D., 1996 — Phi Delta Phi — U.S Attorney Externship; Merit Award for Legal Research and Writing; Nominated, Governing Board of Editors of the American Biographical Institute, Man of the Year — Admitted to Bar, 1996, Alabama; 1996, Alabama Court of Appeals; Supreme Court of Alabama; 1997, U.S. District Court, Northern District of Alabama; 1999, U.S. Court of Appeals, Eleventh Circuit; 2000, U.S. District Court, Southern District of Alabama; 2002, U.S. District Court, Middle District of Alabama; 2005, U.S. Supreme Court — Member American, Shelby County and Birmingham Bar Associations; Alabama State Bar; Defense Research Institute; Alabama Defense Lawyers Association — Martindale-Hubbell AV Preeminent — Practice Areas: Civil Litigation — E-mail: harrington@sssandf.com

Associates

M. Jansen Voss — 1980 — Birmingham-Southern College, B.A., 2002; The University of Alabama, M.B.A., 2006; The University of Alabama School of Law, J.D., 2006 — Admitted to Bar, 2007, Alabama; U.S. District Court, Middle, Northern and Southern Districts of Alabama; Supreme Court of Alabama — Member American, Shelby County and Birmingham (Crisis Relief Committee) Bar Associations; Alabama State Bar; The Mississippi Bar; Alabama Defense Lawyers Association; Defense Research Institute — Reported Cases: Ex parte U.S.A. Water Ski, _So. 3d_Ala. (2013); Ex parte Northwest Alabama Mental Health Center, 68 So. 3d 792 (Ala. 2011); Ex parte L D Transportation, 70 So. 3d 322 (Ala. 2011) — Practice Areas: Medical Malpractice; Insurance Agent Errors & Omissions; Employment Law; General Civil Litigation — E-mail: voss@sssandf.com

Robert M. Ronnlund — 1983 — The University of Alabama, B.A. (magna cum laude), 2005; The University of Alabama School of Law, J.D., 2008 — Phi Beta Kappa; Phi Delta Phi — Admitted to Bar, 2008, Alabama; U.S. District Court, Middle, Northern and Southern Districts of Alabama — Member American Bar Association (Litigation, Tort Trial and Insurance Sections); Alabama State Bar; Alabama Defense Lawyers Association; Defense Research Institute

Tim R. Smith — 1972 — The University of Texas at Tyler, B.S., 2008; Cumberland School of Law of Samford University, J.D. (cum laude), 2011 — Admitted to Bar, 2011, Alabama; 2012, U.S. District Court, Middle, Northern and Southern Districts of Alabama — Member American Bar Association;

Scott, Sullivan, Streetman & Fox, P.C., Birmingham, AL (Continued)

Alabama State Bar; Alabama Defense Lawyers Association — E-mail: smith@sssandf.com

Sirote & Permutt, P.C.

2311 Highland Avenue South
Birmingham, Alabama 35205
Telephone: 205-930-5100
Fax: 205-930-5101
E-Mail: bham@sirote.com
www.sirote.com

(Huntsville, AL Office*: 305 Church Street, Suite 800, 35801, P.O. Box 18248, 35804-8248)
 (Tel: 256-536-1711)
 (Fax: 256-518-3681)
 (E-Mail: huntsville@sirote.com)
(Mobile, AL Office*: One St. Louis Centre, Suite 1000, 36602-3918, P.O. Drawer 2025, 36652)
 (Tel: 251-432-1671)
 (Fax: 251-434-0196)
 (E-Mail: mobile@sirote.com)
(Pensacola, FL Office: 1115 East Gonzalez Street, 32503)
 (Tel: 850-462-1500)
 (Fax: 850-462-1599)
(Fort Lauderdale, FL Office: 200 East Broward Boulevard, Suite 900, 33301)
 (Tel: 954-828-1100)
 (Fax: 954-828-1101)

Established: 1946

Insurance Defense, Life and Health, Casualty, Product Liability, Fire, Fraud, Surety

Firm Profile: Sirote & Permutt is at the forefront of the legal profession in Alabama and Florida, serving our clients with a full range of legal services of the highest quality, prepared in a fair and timely manner. For more than half a century this diverse team of professionals has cultivated a tradition of excellence, anticipating the needs of our clients and meeting those needs in new and innovative ways. Sirote & Permutt serves our clients with 125 attorneys in Birmingham, Huntsville and Mobile, Alabama and Fort Lauderdale and Pensacola, Florida.

Insurance Clients

Alabama Insurance Guaranty Association
Allianz Global Risks U.S. Insurance Company
American Colonial Insurance Company
Certain Underwriters at Lloyd's
Chubb Group of Insurance Companies
Fireman's Fund Insurance Company
Hermitage Insurance Company
Integon Casualty Insurance Company
MIC General Insurance Corporation
Nationwide Insurance
Prudential Insurance Company of America
Titan Indemnity Company
Travelers Property Casualty Insurance Company

Alabama Municipal Insurance Corporation
Allianz Insurance Company
Allianz Underwriters Insurance Company
American United Life Insurance Company
CNA Insurance Company
Coregis Insurance Company
Great American Insurance Group
Guaranty National Insurance Company
Lincoln National Health & Casualty Insurance Company
National American Insurance Company
Penn National Insurance Company
Safeco Insurance Companies
St. Paul Fire and Marine Insurance Company
Universal Life Insurance Company
UNUM Life Insurance Company of America

Non-Insurance Clients

AIG Claim Services, Inc.
IBM, Inc.
Palomar International Corporation, L.L.C.

CRC Insurance Services, Inc.
ITT Financial Corporation
Schindler Elevator Corporation

Sirote & Permutt, P.C., Birmingham, AL (Continued)

Firm Members

Robert R. Baugh — The University of Alabama, B.S., 1979; The University of Alabama School of Law, J.D., 1982 — Admitted to Bar, 1982, Alabama; 2006, Mississippi; 2008, Georgia — Member American and Birmingham Bar Associations — Practice Areas: Bad Faith; Insurance Litigation; Civil Litigation; Labor and Employment; Product Liability — Tel: 205-930-5307 — E-mail: rbaugh@sirote.com

Christopher A. Bottcher — The University of Alabama, B.S., 1991; Cumberland School of Law of Samford University, J.D., 1996 — Admitted to Bar, 1996, Alabama — Member American and Birmingham Bar Associations — Practice Areas: Insurance Law; Civil Trial Practice; Product Liability; Commercial Litigation; Business Law — Tel: 205-930-5279 — E-mail: cbottcher@sirote.com

Kristen S. Cross — The University of Alabama, B.A., 1990; The University of Alabama School of Law, J.D., 1999 — Admitted to Bar, 1999, Alabama — Member Birmingham Bar Association — Practice Areas: Civil Trial Practice; Litigation; Insurance Defense; Class Actions; Appellate Practice — Tel: 205-930-5136 — E-mail: kcross@sirote.com

J. Mason Davis, Jr. — Talladega College, A.B., 1956; State University of New York at Buffalo Law School, J.D., 1959 — Admitted to Bar, 1959, New York; 1960, Alabama — Member National, American and Birmingham Bar Associations — Practice Areas: Litigation; Insurance Law — Tel: 205-930-5134 — E-mail: mdavis@sirote.com

Charles R. Driggars — Troy State University, B.S., 1978; The University of Alabama School of Law, J.D., 1981 — Admitted to Bar, 1981, Alabama — Member American and Birmingham Bar Associations — Practice Areas: Insurance Law; Appellate Practice; Toxic Torts; Litigation; Civil Trial Practice; Environmental Law — Tel: 205-930-5155 — E-mail: cdriggars@sirote.com

Jaime Erdberg — The University of Alabama at Birmingham, B.A., 1999; The University of Alabama School of Law, J.D., 2004 — Admitted to Bar, 2004, Alabama — Member Birmingham Bar Association — Practice Areas: Litigation — Tel: 205-930-5189 — E-mail: jerdberg@sirote.com

Gaile Pugh Gratton — Spelman College, B.A., 1980; Harvard Law School, J.D., 1983 — Admitted to Bar, 1983, Alabama — Member National, American, Birmingham and Magic City Bar Associations — Practice Areas: Litigation; Administrative Law; Civil Trial Practice; Labor and Employment — Tel: 205-930-5320 — E-mail: ggratton@sirote.com

J. Rushton McClees — The University of Alabama, B.S., 1983; The University of Alabama School of Law, J.D., 1986 — Admitted to Bar, 1986, Alabama — Member American and Birmingham Bar Associations — Practice Areas: Litigation — Tel: 205-930-5106 — E-mail: rmcclees@sirote.com

Kerry P. McInerney — Birmingham-Southern College, B.A., 1992; Wayne State University, M.A., 1994; Cumberland School of Law of Samford University, J.D., 1998 — Admitted to Bar, 1998, Alabama — Member American and Birmingham Bar Associations — Practice Areas: Civil Trial Practice; Appellate Practice — Tel: 205-930-5388 — E-mail: kmcinerney@sirote.com

George "Jack" M. Neal Jr. — The University of Alabama, B.S., 1971; Cumberland School of Law of Samford University, J.D., 1977 — Admitted to Bar, 1977, Alabama — Member Birmingham Bar Association — Practice Areas: Civil Trial Practice; Commercial Litigation; Mediation — Tel: 205-930-5252 — E-mail: jneal@sirote.com

Stephen B. Porterfield — Auburn University, B.S., 1985; Cumberland School of Law of Samford University, J.D., 1988 — Admitted to Bar, 1988, Alabama — Member American Bar Association — Practice Areas: Civil Trial Practice; Class Actions; Business Law; Commercial Law; Litigation — Tel: 205-930-5278 — E-mail: sporterfield@sirote.com

C. Lee Reeves — The University of Alabama, A.B., 1966; The University of Alabama School of Law, J.D., 1968; The George Washington University Law School, LL.M., 1969 — Admitted to Bar, 1968, Alabama — Member American and Birmingham Bar Associations — Practice Areas: Labor and Employment; Litigation; Product Liability — Tel: 205-930-5183 — E-mail: lreeves@sirote.com

Kyle T. Smith — Mississippi State University, B.A., 1992; The University of Alabama School of Law, J.D., 1995 — Admitted to Bar, 1995, Alabama — Member American and Birmingham Bar Associations — Practice Areas: Civil Trial Practice; Litigation; Labor and Employment; Workers' Compensation — Tel: 205-930-5190 — E-mail: ksmith@sirote.com

James S. Williams — Washington and Lee University, B.A., 1988; Cumberland School of Law of Samford University, J.D., 1991 — Admitted to Bar, 1991, Alabama — Member American and Birmingham Bar Associations — Practice Areas: Litigation; Insurance Defense; Personal Injury; Product Liability — Tel: 205-930-5178 — E-mail: jwilliams@sirote.com

Smith & Pace, PC

2000A SouthBridge Parkway, Suite 405
Birmingham, Alabama 35209
Telephone: 205-802-2214
Fax: 205-879-4445
E-Mail: info@smith-pace.com
www.smith-pace.com

Insurance Defense, Truck Liability, Insurance Coverage, Extra-Contractual Liability, General Liability, Professional Liability, Commercial Litigation, Construction Liability, Errors and Omissions, Excess and Umbrella, Automobile, Property Damage, Insurance Regulation, Product Liability, Marine, Workers' Compensation, Subrogation, Arbitration, Mediation, Appellate Practice, Fraud/Bad Faith, Employment Liability, Harrassment/Discrimination, Municipal

Insurance Clients

AFLAC, Inc.
First Mercury Insurance Company
Liberty Mutual
North River Insurance Company
RLI/Mt. Hawley Insurance Company
Crum & Forster/United States Fire Insurance Company
Markel Corporation
ProSight Specialty Insurance Company
Travelers

Non-Insurance Clients

FedEx Freight
Tyson Foods, Inc.

Partners

Carol Ann Smith — Birmingham-Southern College, B.A. (magna cum laude), 1971; The University of Alabama, J.D., 1975; New York University, LL.M., 1977 — Admitted to Bar, 1975, Alabama; U.S. District Court, Middle, Northern and Southern Districts of Alabama; U.S. Court of Appeals, Eleventh Circuit; U.S. Supreme Court

David R. Pace — The University of Alabama, B.A. (magna cum laude), 1984; J.D., 1987 — Admitted to Bar, 1987, Alabama; U.S. District Court, Middle, Northern and Southern Districts of Alabama; U.S. Court of Appeals, Eleventh Circuit

Associates

A. Mark Bahakel — Birmingham-Southern College, B.A., 2000; The University of Alabama, J.D., 2003 — Admitted to Bar, 2003, Alabama; U.S. District Court, Middle, Northern and Southern Districts of Alabama; U.S. Court of Appeals, Eleventh Circuit

Justin B. Lamb — Birmingham-Southern College, B.A., 2000; The University of Alabama, J.D., 2003 — Admitted to Bar, 2003, Alabama; U.S. District Court, Middle, Northern and Southern Districts of Alabama

Wilson B. Coffman, III — The University of Alabama, B.A. (cum laude), 2010; Cumberland School of Law of Samford University, J.D., 2013 — Admitted to Bar, 2013, Alabama; U.S. District Court, Middle, Northern and Southern Districts of Alabama

Christopher Doty — University of Montevallo, B.A. (magna cum laude), 2002; Cumberland School of Law of Samford University, J.D. (magna cum laude), 2014 — Admitted to Bar, 2014, Alabama; U.S. District Court, Middle, Northern and Southern Districts of Alabama

Of Counsel

Lisa B. Singer — Brown University, A.B. (with honors), 1987; University of Virginia, J.D., 1990 — Admitted to Bar, 1993, Alabama; U.S. District Court for the District of Columbia; U.S. District Court, Northern District of Alabama

Taylor Ritter, P.C.

600 Title Building, 6th Floor
300 North Richard Arrington Jr. Boulevard
Birmingham, Alabama 35203
Telephone: 205-252-3300
Fax: 205-252-3378

Taylor Ritter, P.C., Birmingham, AL (Continued)

(Orange Beach, AL Office: 26192 Canal Road, 36561-3903, P.O. Box 489, 36561)
 (Tel: 251-981-8430)
 (Fax: 251-981-8425)

Established: 1990

General Defense Civil Litigation, Automobile Accidents, Slip and Fall, Fraud, Bad Faith, Professional Liability, Construction Litigation, Product Liability, Premises Liability, Workers' Compensation, Opinions, Declaratory Judgments, Litigation Coverage Issues, Condominium Law, Defense of Insureds and Insurance Companies, General Business Litigation

Insurance Clients

Admiral Insurance Company
Millennium Risk Managers, LLC
Penn National Insurance Company
United Fire & Casualty Company
Markel Underwriting Managers, Inc.
RLI/Mt. Hawley Insurance Company

Non-Insurance Clients

Baldwin County Sewer Service
Jefferson County Truck Growers Association

Partners

Bert P. Taylor — 1949 — The University of Alabama, B.S., 1971; The University of Alabama School of Law, J.D., 1974 — Farrah Law Society — Member, Alabma Law Review — Admitted to Bar, 1974, Alabama; U.S. District Court, Northern District of Alabama; 1984, U.S. Court of Appeals, Eleventh Circuit; 1990, U.S. District Court, Middle and Southern Districts of Alabama; Alabama Court of Appeals — Member Alabama State Bar; Birmingham and Baldwin County Bar Associations; Alabama Defense Lawyers Association — Resident Orange Beach, AL Office — Tel: 251-981-8430 — Fax: 251-981-8425 — E-mail: bert@taylorritter.com

Tommy C. Ritter, Jr. — 1972 — Washington and Lee University, B.A. (magna cum laude, Phi Beta Kappa), 1994; The University of Alabama School of Law, J.D., 1997 — Admitted to Bar, 1997, Alabama; U.S. District Court, Middle, Northern and Southern Districts of Alabama; Alabama Court of Appeals — Member Alabama State Bar — E-mail: tritter@taylorritter.com

Associates

Peter A. DeSarro, III — 1954 — Jacksonville State University, B.S., 1982; Birmingham School of Law, J.D., 1988 — Admitted to Bar, 1990, Alabama; U.S. District Court, Middle and Northern Districts of Alabama; Alabama Court of Appeals — Member Alabama State Bar; Baldwin County Bar Association; Alabama Workers' Compensation Organization — Resident Orange Beach, AL Office — E-mail: pad@taylorritter.com

Natalie A. Daugherty — 1979 — The University of Alabama, B.A., 2001; The University of Alabama School of Law, J.D., 2004 — Admitted to Bar, 2004, Alabama; U.S. District Court, Middle, Northern and Southern Districts of Alabama; Alabama Court of Appeals — Member American, Baldwin County and Mobile Bar Associations; Alabama State Bar — Resident Orange Beach, AL Office — E-mail: natalie@taylorritter.com

Vernis & Bowling of Birmingham, LLC

3300 Cahaba Road, Suite 200
Birmingham, Alabama 35223
 Telephone: 205-445-1026
 Fax: 205-445-1036
 E-Mail: info@law-alabama.com
 www.law-alabama.com

Established: 1970

Vernis & Bowling of Birmingham, LLC, Birmingham, AL (Continued)

Civil Litigation, Insurance Law, Workers' Compensation, Premises Liability, Labor and Employment, Civil Rights, Commercial Litigation, Complex Litigation, Product Liability, Directors and Officers Liability, Errors and Omissions, Construction Law, Construction Defect, Environmental Liability, Personal and Commercial Vehicle, Appellate Practice, Admiralty and Maritime Law, Real Estate, Family Law, Elder Law, Liability Defense, SIU/Fraud Litigation, Education Law (ESE/IDEA), Property and Casualty (Commercial and Personal Lines), Long-Haul Trucking Liability, Government Law, Public Law, Criminal, White Collar, Business Litigation

Firm Profile: Since 1970, VERNIS & BOWLING has represented individuals, businesses, professionals, insurance carriers, self-insureds, brokers, underwriters, agents, PEOs and insured. We provide cost effective, full service, legal representation that consistently exceeds the expectations of our clients. With 115 attorneys throughout 16 offices located in Florida, Georgia, Alabama, North Carolina and Mississippi the firm is able to provide the benefits of a large organization, including a management team, consistent policies and representation to ensure personal service and local representation to our clients.

Firm Members

William F. Smith, II — 1962 — The University of Alabama, B.S. (with honors), 1984; The University of Alabama School of Law, J.D., 1987 — Sigma Gamma Epsilon — Admitted to Bar, 1987, Alabama; 1988, U.S. District Court, Northern District of Alabama; 1997, U.S. District Court, Middle District of Alabama; 1999, U.S. Court of Appeals, Eleventh Circuit; 2004, U.S. District Court, Southern District of Alabama — Member Birmingham Bar Association

John B. Welsh — Auburn University, B.A., 1999; The University of Alabama, J.D., 2002 — Academic Excellence Scholarship — Admitted to Bar, 2002, Alabama; U.S. District Court, Middle and Northern Districts of Alabama — Practice Areas: Appellate Practice; Civil Trial Practice; General Civil Litigation; Workers' Compensation

Chelsey A. Mitchell — 1985 — The University of Alabama, B.S. (summa cum laude), 2007; Cumberland School of Law at Samford University, J.D., 2010 — Admitted to Bar, 2010, Alabama; U.S. District Court, Middle, Northern and Southern Districts of Alabama — Member Alabama State Bar; Birmingham Bar Association

James A. Potts II — 1977 — Auburn University, B.S. (Dean's List), 1999; The University of Alabama School of Law, J.D., 2003 — Admitted to Bar, 2003, Alabama; 2004, U.S. District Court, Northern District of Alabama — Member Birmingham Bar Association

(See listing under Miami, FL for additional information)

Waldrep Stewart & Kendrick, LLP

2323 Second Avenue North
Birmingham, Alabama 35203
 Telephone: 205-254-3216
 Toll Free: 800-476-5128
 Fax: 205-327-8395
 E-Mail: morse@wskllc.com
 E-Mail: dolan@wskllc.com
 www.wskllc.com

Corporate Law, Labor and Employment, Environmental Law, Insurance Defense, Insurance Coverage, Automobile, Trucking Law, Natural Resources Law, Public Sector Law, Taxation, Construction Litigation

Firm Profile: Our Firm is comprised of highly qualified litigators who represent the Firm's clients in a broad range of cases including insurance coverage analysis, litigation, insurance fraud, claims for bad faith and declaratory judgments. Our lawyers have a level of skill which is reached only by their complete devotion of time and energy in such areas as representing insurance companies in builders risk insurance, professional indemnity

BIRMINGHAM   ALABAMA

Waldrep Stewart & Kendrick, LLP, Birmingham, AL
(Continued)

insurance, malpractice insurance, commercial general liability insurance, workman's compensation insurance, consequential loss insurance, personal injury, employment insurance, insurance defense, insurance coverage, and auto/trucking. Our broad-based experience allows us to address issues to the insurance industry that might arise. Our combined experience gives us the knowledge and understanding to meet the needs of our clients in the insurance industry and enables us to work closely with our clients to reach positive outcomes.

Insurance Clients

ACE USA/ESIS, Inc.
Argonaut Insurance Company
Auto-Owners Insurance Company
Church Mutual Insurance Company
Golden Bear Management Corporation
North American Risk Services
Quanta Risk Management
RiverStone Claims Management, LLC
US Administrator Claims
AON Recovery, Inc.
Attorneys Insurance Mutual of Alabama, Inc.
GAB Robins, Inc.
The Hartford
Mendota Insurance Company
North American Specialty Insurance Company
St. Paul Travelers
State Auto Insurance Companies
Zurich North America

Non-Insurance Clients

Axiometrics, Inc.
Broadspire Services, Inc.
Creative Risk Solutions, Inc.
Federal Express Corporation, Risk Management Department
R & J Trucking, Inc.
Southern Haulers, Inc.
Technical Specialties, Inc.
Broadspire, a Crawford Company
Cambridge Integrated Services
Diocese of the Southern States
First Choice Personnel, Inc.
R.E.M., Inc.
Sedgwick Claims Management Services, Inc.
Veterans Oil, Inc.

Firm Members

Michael G. Kendrick — The University of Alabama at Tuscaloosa, B.S., 1972; Cumberland School of Law of Samford University, J.D., 1977 — Delta Kappa Epsilon; Phi Delta Phi — Admitted to Bar, 1977, Alabama; U.S. District Court, Middle, Northern and Southern Districts of Alabama; U.S. Court of Appeals, Fifth and Eleventh Circuits; 1984, U.S. Supreme Court — Member American and Birmingham Bar Associations; Alabama State Bar; Alabama Municipal Attorneys Association; National Association of College and University Attorneys; International Municipal Lawyers Association — Chairman, Birmingham Racing Commission (1987-2009); Association of Racing Commissioners International (Past Chairman, Board of Directors); Homewood City Council (1980-1985); Homewood City Attorney (1985-Present); Alabama Super Lawyers (2010-Present); AV Rated by Martindale-Hubble; Selected "Top Attorney" by Peers, Birmingham Magazine (2014) — E-mail: kendrick@wskllc.com

Judith E. Dolan — Boston College, B.A. (magna cum laude), 1980; New England School of Law, J.D., 1985 — Law Review, New England School of Law — Admitted to Bar, 1985, Massachusetts; 1986, New Hampshire; 1988, Alabama; U.S. District Court, Middle, Northern and Southern Districts of Alabama; U.S. Court of Appeals, Eleventh Circuit — Member Alabama State Bar; Massachusetts, New Hampshire and Birmingham Bar Associations; Alabama Claims Association; Fellow, Litigation Counsel of America; The Women's Network; Claims and Litigation Management Alliance; Defense Research Institute; Alabama Defense Lawyers Association; Alabama Workers' Compensation Claims Association; Atlanta Claims Association — Selected "Top Attorney" by Peers, Birmingham Magazine (2012, 2014) — E-mail: dolan@wskllc.com

Wayne Morse, Jr. — Birmingham-Southern College, B.S. (Dean's Honor List), 1972; Cumberland School of Law of Samford University, J.D. (Dean's Honor List), 1976 — Phi Delta Phi; Omicron Delta Kappa — Admitted to Bar, 1976, Alabama; 2004, Tennessee; U.S. District Court, Middle, Northern and Southern Districts of Alabama; U.S. Court of Appeals, Eleventh Circuit; U.S. Supreme Court; U.S. Tax Court — Member American and Birmingham Bar Associations; Alabama State Bar; Fellow, Litigation Counsel of America; Fellow, American Bar Foundation; Inns of Court — Author: "Death Actions for Federal Rights Violations in Alabama," Vol 29, No. 1, Cumberland Law Review; "ABC's of ERISA: An Alabama Perspective," Vol. 57, No. 7, The Alabama Lawyer, November 1996; Chapter on Opening Statements "Trying Your First Case: A Practitioner's Guide," American Bar Association, August 1, 2014 — Super Lawyers; AV Rated by Martindale-Hubbell; Adjunct Professor, Birmingham School of Law; Selected "Top Attorney" by Peers, Birmingham Magazine — E-mail: morse@wskllc.com

K. Mark Parnell — Jacksonville State University, B.A., 1983; Cumberland

Waldrep Stewart & Kendrick, LLP, Birmingham, AL
(Continued)

School of Law of Samford University, J.D., 1987 — Special honors in Political Science, Jacksonville State University — Associate Editor, Cumberland Law Review — Admitted to Bar, 1987, Alabama; U.S. District Court, Middle, Northern and Southern Districts of Alabama; 1994, U.S. Supreme Court — Member American and Birmingham Bar Associations; Alabama State Bar; Alabama Association of Municipal Attorneys; American Water Works Association — 2011 President/Chairman, Alabama Leadership Council for the American Diabetes Association — E-mail: parnell@wskllc.com

Leslie M. Klasing — Birmingham-Southern College, B.S. (magna cum laude), 1989; The University of Alabama School of Law, J.D., 1992 — Admitted to Bar, 1992, Alabama; 1994, U.S. District Court, Middle, Northern and Southern Districts of Alabama; 1997, U.S. Court of Appeals, Eleventh Circuit — Member American and Birmingham Bar Associations; Alabama State Bar; Atlanta Claims Association — E-mail: klasing@wskllc.com

Webster, Henry, Lyons, Bradwell, Cohan & Black, P.C.

Two Perimeter Park South, Suite 445 East
Birmingham, Alabama 35243
Telephone: 205-380-3480
Fax: 205-380-3485
E-Mail: kim@websterhenry.com
www.websterhenry.com

Insurance Defense, Automobile Liability, Construction Law, Employment Law, Premises Liability, Product Liability, Workers' Compensation

(See listing under Montgomery, AL for additional information)

White Arnold & Dowd, P.C.

2025 Third Avenue North, Suite 500
Birmingham, Alabama 35203
Telephone: 205-323-1888
Fax: 205-323-8907
www.whitearnolddowd.com

General Civil Trial and Appellate Practice, Insurance Defense, Insurance Coverage, Extra-Contractual Liability, Personal Injury, Product Liability, Drug, Medical Devices, Environmental Law, Employment Law, Toxic Torts, State and Federal Courts

Insurance Clients

Alfa Insurance Corporation
Auto-Owners Insurance Company
GuideOne Insurance
Munich Reinsurance America, Inc.
American Alternative Insurance Corporation
Harleysville Insurance Company
OneBeacon Insurance

Non-Insurance Clients

Resolute Management, Inc. NE
VFIS Claims Management

Insurance Practice Group

Connie Ray Stockham — 1954 — The University of Alabama, B.S. (summa cum laude), 1976; The University of Alabama School of Law, J.D., 1979 — Law Clerk to Judge James Hancock, U.S. District Court, Northern District of Alabama — Admitted to Bar, 1979, Alabama; U.S. District Court, Middle, Northern and Southern Districts of Alabama; U.S. Court of Appeals, Eleventh Circuit — Member American and Birmingham Bar Associations; Alabama State Bar; Alabama Defense Lawyers Association; Defense Research Institute

Thomas E. Walker — 1955 — The University of Alabama, B.A. (summa cum laude), 1978; The University of Alabama School of Law, J.D., 1981 — Alabama Law Review — Admitted to Bar, 1981, Alabama; U.S. District Court, Middle, Northern and Southern Districts of Alabama; U.S. Court of Appeals, Eleventh Circuit — Member American and Birmingham Bar Associations; Alabama State Bar; Defense Research Institute

ALABAMA | BREWTON

White Arnold & Dowd, P.C., Birmingham, AL (Continued)

Associates

Lisha Li Graham — 1985 — Auburn University, B.S., 2006; Cumberland University School of Law, J.D., 2009 — Auburn Senior Honors Scholar; American Journal of Trial Advocacy, Herbert W. Peterson National Trial Team — Admitted to Bar, 2009, Alabama — Member American and Birmingham Bar Associations; Alabama State Bar

John K. Pocus — 1984 — The University of Alabama at Birmingham, B.A. (summa cum laude), 2006; The University of Alabama School of Law, J.D., 2012 — Admitted to Bar, 2012, Alabama — Member American and Birmingham Bar Associations; Alabama State Bar — Fulbright Teaching Fellow, Andorra, 2007

William Chambers Waller — 1987 — The University of Alabama, B.S., 2010; Cumberland University School of Law, J.D., 2013 — American Journal of Trial Advocacy, Senior Associate Editor, Herbert W. Peterson National Trial Team — Admitted to Bar, 2013, Alabama — Member American and Birmingham Bar Associations; Alabama State Bar

Of Counsel

Richard J. Stockham, III — 1954 — Vanderbilt University, B.A., 1986; Birmingham School of Law, LL.B., 1985 — Admitted to Bar, 1986, Alabama; U.S. District Court, Middle and Northern Districts of Alabama; U.S. Court of Appeals, Eleventh Circuit; 1996, U.S. Supreme Court — Member Alabama State Bar; Birmingham Bar Association

Shareholders

Stephen R. Arnold
Kitty Rogers Brown
Rebecca G. DePalma
Linda G. Flippo
Karen M. Hennecy
T. Shane Smith
J. Mark White

William M. Bowen, Jr.
U. W. Clemon
Augusta S. Dowd
Laura S. Gibson
Hope S. Marshall
Sidney C. Summey, Jr.

Associate Attorneys

C. Burton Dunn, Jr.

Hannah C. Thompson

The following firms also service this area.

Hill, Hill, Carter, Franco, Cole & Black, P.C.
425 South Perry Street
Montgomery, Alabama 36104
Telephone: 334-834-7600
Fax: 334-263-5969

Mailing Address: P.O. Box 116, Montgomery, AL 36101-0116

Appellate Practice, Aviation, Business Law, Casualty, Commercial Litigation, Discrimination, Education Law, Employment Law, Insurance Defense, Insurance Fraud, Law Enforcement Liability, Product Liability, Professional Liability, State and Federal Courts, Surety, Transportation, Trial Practice, Workers' Compensation, Insurance Coverage Opinions and Litigation

SEE COMPLETE LISTING UNDER MONTGOMERY, ALABAMA (92 MILES)

Owens & Millsaps, LLP
Attorneys at Law
2606 8th Street
Tuscaloosa, Alabama 35401
Toll Free: 866-790-2889
Telephone: 205-750-0750
Telephone: 205-759-8582
Fax: 205-750-0355

Mailing Address: P.O. Box 2487, Tuscaloosa, AL 35403-2487

Insurance Defense, Medical Malpractice, Legal Malpractice, Dental Malpractice, Coverage Issues, Comprehensive General Liability, Product Liability, Construction Law, Employment Practices Liability, Environmental Liability

SEE COMPLETE LISTING UNDER TUSCALOOSA, ALABAMA (56 MILES)

Phelps, Jenkins, Gibson & Fowler, LLP
1201 Greensboro Avenue
Tuscaloosa, Alabama 35401
Telephone: 205-345-5100
Fax: 205-758-4394, 205-391-6658

Mailing Address: P.O. Box 020848, Tuscaloosa, AL 35402-0848

Employment Litigation, General Defense, Medical Malpractice, School Law, Workers' Compensation, Personal Injury

SEE COMPLETE LISTING UNDER TUSCALOOSA, ALABAMA (56 MILES)

Rushton, Stakely, Johnston & Garrett, P.A.
184 Commerce Street
Montgomery, Alabama 36104
Telephone: 334-206-3100
Fax: 334-262-6277

Mailing Address: P.O. Box 270, Montgomery, AL 36101-0270

Insurance Defense, Trial and Appellate Practice, Accountants and Attorneys Liability, Administrative Law, Advertising Injury, Agent and Brokers Errors and Omissions, Appellate Practice, Arbitration, Automobile Tort, Bad Faith, Business Law, Casualty Insurance Law, Class Actions, Commercial Litigation, Complex Litigation, Construction Litigation, Contract Disputes, Copyright and Trademark Law, Coverage Analysis, Declaratory Judgments, Directors and Officers Liability, Employment Law, Environmental Law, Family Law, Fidelity and Surety, Fraud, Health Care, Health Care Professional Licensure Defense, Insurance Litigation, Labor and Employment, Law Enforcement Liability, Legal Malpractice, Medical Devices, Medical Malpractice, Pharmaceutical, Premises Liability, Primary and Excess Insurance, Product Liability, Professional Errors and Omissions, Professional Liability, Surety, Title Insurance, Uninsured and Underinsured Motorist, Workers' Compensation, Wrongful Death

SEE COMPLETE LISTING UNDER MONTGOMERY, ALABAMA (92 MILES)

BREWTON † 5,408 Escambia Co.

Refer To

Galloway, Wettermark, Everest & Rutens, LLP
3263 Cottage Hill Road
Mobile, Alabama 36606
Telephone: 251-476-4493
Fax: 251-479-5566

Mailing Address: P.O. Box 16629, Mobile, AL 36616-0629

Insurance Defense, Admiralty and Maritime Law, Casualty, Fire, Life Insurance, Surety, Workers' Compensation, Governmental Liability, Product Liability, Civil Rights, Commercial Litigation, Construction Law, Professional Liability, Trial and Appellate Practice, State and Federal Courts, Title VII Defense, Medical Liability

SEE COMPLETE LISTING UNDER MOBILE, ALABAMA (77 MILES)

Refer To

Michael Gillion, P.C.
74 Midtown Park West, Suite 105
Mobile, Alabama 36606
Telephone: 251-471-9494
Fax: 251-471-1722

Mailing Address: P.O. Box 161423, Mobile, AL 36616-2423

Insurance Defense, Automobile, Homeowners, Workers' Compensation, Subrogation, Insurance Contract and Coverage Litigation

SEE COMPLETE LISTING UNDER MOBILE, ALABAMA (77 MILES)

Refer To

Johnstone Adams, L.L.C.
One St. Louis Centre
1 St. Louis Street, Suite 4000
Mobile, Alabama 36602
Telephone: 251-432-7682
Fax: 251-432-2800

Mailing Address: P.O. Box 1988, Mobile, AL 36633

Insurance Defense, Admiralty and Maritime Law, Automobile, Aviation, Bad Faith, Casualty, Construction Litigation, Employer Liability, ERISA, Fire, Fraud, Health, Life Insurance, Product Liability, Professional Liability, Surety, Workers' Compensation, Co-Employee

SEE COMPLETE LISTING UNDER MOBILE, ALABAMA (77 MILES)

CENTREVILLE   ALABAMA

Refer To
Vernis & Bowling of Southern Alabama, LLC
61 St. Joseph Street, 11th Floor
Mobile, Alabama 36602
   Telephone: 251-432-0337
   Fax: 251-432-0244

Civil Litigation, Insurance Law, Workers' Compensation, Premises Liability, Labor and Employment, Civil Rights, Commercial Litigation, Complex Litigation, Product Liability, Directors and Officers Liability, Errors and Omissions, Construction Law, Construction Defect, Environmental Liability, Personal and Commercial Vehicle, Appellate Practice, Admiralty and Maritime Law, Real Estate, Family Law, Elder Law, Liability Defense, SIU/Fraud Litigation, Education Law (ESE/IDEA), Property and Casualty (Commercial and Personal Lines), Long-Haul Trucking Liability, Government Law, Public Law, Criminal, White Collar, Business Litigation

SEE COMPLETE LISTING UNDER MOBILE, ALABAMA (77 MILES)

Refer To
Vickers, Riis, Murray and Curran, L.L.C.
RSA Trustmark Building, 21st Floor
107 St. Francis Street
Mobile, Alabama 36602
   Telephone: 251-432-9772
   Fax: 251-432-9781

Mailing Address: P.O. Box 2568, Mobile, AL 36652-2568

Insurance Defense, Insurance Coverage, Construction Law, Admiralty and Maritime Law, Professional Liability, Environmental Law, Employment Law, Governmental Liability, Toxic Torts, Product Liability, Workers' Compensation, Business Automobile and Trucking, Education

SEE COMPLETE LISTING UNDER MOBILE, ALABAMA (77 MILES)

BUTLER † 1,894 Choctaw Co.

Refer To
Ball, Ball, Matthews & Novak, P.A.
445 Dexter Avenue, Suite 9045
Montgomery, Alabama 36104
   Telephone: 334-387-7680
   Fax: 334-387-3222

Mailing Address: P.O. Box 2148, Montgomery, AL 36102-2148

Insurance Defense, Medical Malpractice, Aviation, Bad Faith, Personal Injury, Construction Litigation, Employment Law, Product Liability, Property, Pharmaceutical, Medical Devices, Complex Litigation, Governmental Entity Defense, Workers' Compensation, Mediation, Arbitration, Trial and Appellate Practice, State and Federal Courts, Insurance Coverage Analysis, Automobile Injury, Motor Carrier Defense

SEE COMPLETE LISTING UNDER MONTGOMERY, ALABAMA (149 MILES)

Refer To
Phelps, Jenkins, Gibson & Fowler, LLP
1201 Greensboro Avenue
Tuscaloosa, Alabama 35401
   Telephone: 205-345-5100
   Fax: 205-758-4394, 205-391-6658

Mailing Address: P.O. Box 020848, Tuscaloosa, AL 35402-0848

Employment Litigation, General Defense, Medical Malpractice, School Law, Workers' Compensation, Personal Injury

SEE COMPLETE LISTING UNDER TUSCALOOSA, ALABAMA (103 MILES)

Refer To
Vickers, Riis, Murray and Curran, L.L.C.
RSA Trustmark Building, 21st Floor
107 St. Francis Street
Mobile, Alabama 36602
   Telephone: 251-432-9772
   Fax: 251-432-9781

Mailing Address: P.O. Box 2568, Mobile, AL 36652-2568

Insurance Defense, Insurance Coverage, Construction Law, Admiralty and Maritime Law, Professional Liability, Environmental Law, Employment Law, Governmental Liability, Toxic Torts, Product Liability, Workers' Compensation, Business Automobile and Trucking, Education

SEE COMPLETE LISTING UNDER MOBILE, ALABAMA (111 MILES)

CAMDEN † 2,020 Wilcox Co.

Refer To
Vickers, Riis, Murray and Curran, L.L.C.
RSA Trustmark Building, 21st Floor
107 St. Francis Street
Mobile, Alabama 36602
   Telephone: 251-432-9772
   Fax: 251-432-9781

Mailing Address: P.O. Box 2568, Mobile, AL 36652-2568

Insurance Defense, Insurance Coverage, Construction Law, Admiralty and Maritime Law, Professional Liability, Environmental Law, Employment Law, Governmental Liability, Toxic Torts, Product Liability, Workers' Compensation, Business Automobile and Trucking, Education

SEE COMPLETE LISTING UNDER MOBILE, ALABAMA (128 MILES)

CARROLLTON † 1,019 Pickens Co.

Refer To
Owens & Millsaps, LLP
Attorneys at Law
2606 8th Street
Tuscaloosa, Alabama 35401
   Toll Free: 866-790-2889
   Telephone: 205-750-0750
   Telephone: 205-759-8582
   Fax: 205-750-0355

Mailing Address: P.O. Box 2487, Tuscaloosa, AL 35403-2487

Insurance Defense, Medical Malpractice, Legal Malpractice, Dental Malpractice, Coverage Issues, Comprehensive General Liability, Product Liability, Construction Law, Employment Practices Liability, Environmental Liability

SEE COMPLETE LISTING UNDER TUSCALOOSA, ALABAMA (35 MILES)

Refer To
Phelps, Jenkins, Gibson & Fowler, LLP
1201 Greensboro Avenue
Tuscaloosa, Alabama 35401
   Telephone: 205-345-5100
   Fax: 205-758-4394, 205-391-6658

Mailing Address: P.O. Box 020848, Tuscaloosa, AL 35402-0848

Employment Litigation, General Defense, Medical Malpractice, School Law, Workers' Compensation, Personal Injury

SEE COMPLETE LISTING UNDER TUSCALOOSA, ALABAMA (35 MILES)

CENTREVILLE † 2,778 Bibb Co.

Refer To
Owens & Millsaps, LLP
Attorneys at Law
2606 8th Street
Tuscaloosa, Alabama 35401
   Toll Free: 866-790-2889
   Telephone: 205-750-0750
   Telephone: 205-759-8582
   Fax: 205-750-0355

Mailing Address: P.O. Box 2487, Tuscaloosa, AL 35403-2487

Insurance Defense, Medical Malpractice, Legal Malpractice, Dental Malpractice, Coverage Issues, Comprehensive General Liability, Product Liability, Construction Law, Employment Practices Liability, Environmental Liability

SEE COMPLETE LISTING UNDER TUSCALOOSA, ALABAMA (35 MILES)

Refer To
Phelps, Jenkins, Gibson & Fowler, LLP
1201 Greensboro Avenue
Tuscaloosa, Alabama 35401
   Telephone: 205-345-5100
   Fax: 205-758-4394, 205-391-6658

Mailing Address: P.O. Box 020848, Tuscaloosa, AL 35402-0848

Employment Litigation, General Defense, Medical Malpractice, School Law, Workers' Compensation, Personal Injury

SEE COMPLETE LISTING UNDER TUSCALOOSA, ALABAMA (35 MILES)

CHATOM † 1,288 Washington Co.

Refer To

Galloway, Wettermark, Everest & Rutens, LLP
3263 Cottage Hill Road
Mobile, Alabama 36606
   Telephone: 251-476-4493
   Fax: 251-479-5566

Mailing Address: P.O. Box 16629, Mobile, AL 36616-0629

Insurance Defense, Admiralty and Maritime Law, Casualty, Fire, Life Insurance, Surety, Workers' Compensation, Governmental Liability, Product Liability, Civil Rights, Commercial Litigation, Construction Law, Professional Liability, Trial and Appellate Practice, State and Federal Courts, Title VII Defense, Medical Liability

   SEE COMPLETE LISTING UNDER MOBILE, ALABAMA (62 MILES)

Refer To

Michael Gillion, P.C.
74 Midtown Park West, Suite 105
Mobile, Alabama 36606
   Telephone: 251-471-9494
   Fax: 251-471-1722

Mailing Address: P.O. Box 161423, Mobile, AL 36616-2423

Insurance Defense, Automobile, Homeowners, Workers' Compensation, Subrogation, Insurance Contract and Coverage Litigation

   SEE COMPLETE LISTING UNDER MOBILE, ALABAMA (62 MILES)

Refer To

Holtsford Gilliland Higgins Hitson & Howard, P.C.
29000 U.S. Highway 98, Suite A-302
Daphne, Alabama 36526-7263
   Telephone: 251-447-0234
   Fax: 251-447-0212

Insurance Defense, Automobile, Professional Liability, Product Liability, Civil Rights, Toxic Torts, General Liability, Environmental Law, Workers' Compensation, Construction Law, Governmental Entity Defense

   SEE COMPLETE LISTING UNDER MOBILE, ALABAMA (72 MILES)

Refer To

Johnstone Adams, L.L.C.
One St. Louis Centre
1 St. Louis Street, Suite 4000
Mobile, Alabama 36602
   Telephone: 251-432-7682
   Fax: 251-432-2800

Mailing Address: P.O. Box 1988, Mobile, AL 36633

Insurance Defense, Admiralty and Maritime Law, Automobile, Aviation, Bad Faith, Casualty, Construction Litigation, Employer Liability, ERISA, Fire, Fraud, Health, Life Insurance, Product Liability, Professional Liability, Surety, Workers' Compensation, Co-Employee

   SEE COMPLETE LISTING UNDER MOBILE, ALABAMA (62 MILES)

Refer To

Vickers, Riis, Murray and Curran, L.L.C.
RSA Trustmark Building, 21st Floor
107 St. Francis Street
Mobile, Alabama 36602
   Telephone: 251-432-9772
   Fax: 251-432-9781

Mailing Address: P.O. Box 2568, Mobile, AL 36652-2568

Insurance Defense, Insurance Coverage, Construction Law, Admiralty and Maritime Law, Professional Liability, Environmental Law, Employment Law, Governmental Liability, Toxic Torts, Product Liability, Workers' Compensation, Business Automobile and Trucking, Education

   SEE COMPLETE LISTING UNDER MOBILE, ALABAMA (62 MILES)

CLANTON † 8,619 Chilton Co.

Refer To

Holtsford Gilliland Higgins Hitson & Howard, P.C.
4001 Carmichael Road, Suite 300
Montgomery, Alabama 36106
   Telephone: 334-215-8585
   Toll Free: 800-932-6964
   Fax: 334-215-7101

Mailing Address: P.O. Box 4128, Montgomery, AL 36103-4128

Insurance Defense, Automobile, Professional Liability, Product Liability, Civil Rights, Toxic Torts, General Liability, Environmental Law, Workers' Compensation, Construction Law, Coverage Issues, Governmental Entity Defense, Forestry Law

   SEE COMPLETE LISTING UNDER MONTGOMERY, ALABAMA (40 MILES)

CLAYTON † 3,008 Barbour Co.

Refer To

Morrow, Romine & Pearson, P.C.
122 South Hull Street
Montgomery, Alabama 36104
   Telephone: 334-262-7707
   Fax: 334-262-7742

Mailing Address: P.O. Box 4804, Montgomery, AL 36103

Civil Trial Practice, Insurance Law, Medical Malpractice, Product Liability, Environmental Coverage, Personal Injury, Litigation, Mediation, Trial Practice, Appellate Practice, State and Federal Courts, Handicap and Employment Discrimination, Diving Accidents

   SEE COMPLETE LISTING UNDER MONTGOMERY, ALABAMA (80 MILES)

COLUMBIANA † 4,197 Shelby Co.

Refer To

Fann & Rea, P.C.
1200 Providence Park, Suite 200
Birmingham, Alabama 35242
   Telephone: 205-991-5045
   Fax: 205-991-3866

Insurance Defense, Automobile, Aviation, General Liability, Professional Liability, Property and Casualty, Workers' Compensation, Employment Law

   SEE COMPLETE LISTING UNDER BIRMINGHAM, ALABAMA (40 MILES)

DEMOPOLIS 7,483 Marengo Co.

Refer To

Phelps, Jenkins, Gibson & Fowler, LLP
1201 Greensboro Avenue
Tuscaloosa, Alabama 35401
   Telephone: 205-345-5100
   Fax: 205-758-4394, 205-391-6658

Mailing Address: P.O. Box 020848, Tuscaloosa, AL 35402-0848

Employment Litigation, General Defense, Medical Malpractice, School Law, Workers' Compensation, Personal Injury

   SEE COMPLETE LISTING UNDER TUSCALOOSA, ALABAMA (61 MILES)

DOTHAN — ALABAMA

Refer To
Rushton, Stakely, Johnston & Garrett, P.A.
184 Commerce Street
Montgomery, Alabama 36104
 Telephone: 334-206-3100
 Fax: 334-262-6277
Mailing Address: P.O. Box 270, Montgomery, AL 36101-0270

Insurance Defense, Trial and Appellate Practice, Accountants and Attorneys Liability, Administrative Law, Advertising Injury, Agent and Brokers Errors and Omissions, Appellate Practice, Arbitration, Automobile Tort, Bad Faith, Business Law, Casualty Insurance Law, Class Actions, Commercial Litigation, Complex Litigation, Construction Litigation, Contract Disputes, Copyright and Trademark Law, Coverage Analysis, Declaratory Judgments, Directors and Officers Liability, Employment Law, Environmental Law, Family Law, Fidelity and Surety, Fraud, Health Care, Health Care Professional Licensure Defense, Insurance Litigation, Labor and Employment, Law Enforcement Liability, Legal Malpractice, Medical Devices, Medical Malpractice, Pharmaceutical, Premises Liability, Primary and Excess Insurance, Product Liability, Professional Errors and Omissions, Professional Liability, Surety, Title Insurance, Uninsured and Underinsured Motorist, Workers' Compensation, Wrongful Death

SEE COMPLETE LISTING UNDER MONTGOMERY, ALABAMA (100 MILES)

DOTHAN † 65,496 Houston Co.

Shealy, Crum & Pike, P.C.
2346 West Main Street, Suite 1
Dothan, Alabama 36301
 Telephone: 334-677-3000
 Fax: 334-677-0030
 E-Mail: info@scplaw.us
 www.shealycrumandpike.com

(Tuscaloosa, AL Office: 701 Rice Mine Road North, 35406-2312)

Insurance Defense, Medical Malpractice Defense, Product Liability Defense, Casualty Defense, Workers' Compensation, Employment Practices, General Liability, Automobile Liability, Civil Rights Defense, Public Liability, Fire, Bad Faith, Construction Insurance Defense

Firm Profile: The law firm of Shealy, Crum and Pike, P.C., has over 70 years of experience in defending insurance claims and is proud of having held the AV® Preeminent(TM) Peer Review Rating by Martindale-Hubbell® since 2008. Our attorneys have the knowledge and expertise you need to achieve the best outcome for your situation. The firm actively tries cases throughout the State of Alabama and also has experience in Georgia and Florida

Insurance Clients
Alabama Municipal Insurance Corporation
Medical Mutual Insurance Company
Lexington Insurance Company/AIG
Millennium Risk Managers, LLC
York Claims Service, Inc.

Non-Insurance Clients
Shaw Industries Group, Inc.

Members

Steadman S. Shealy, Jr. — The University of Alabama, B.S. (cum laude), 1980; J.D., 1984 — Admitted to Bar, 1984, Alabama — Member American and Houston County Bar Associations; Alabama State Bar; Alabama Defense Lawyers Association — Toastmasters International Communication and Leadership Award, April, 1989, for Service to the Community, State and Industry; AV® Preeminent(TM) Peer Review Rating by Martindale-Hubbell® — Practice Areas: Insurance Defense; Product Liability Defense; Casualty Defense; Employment Practices; Workers' Compensation; General Liability; Automobile Liability; Civil Rights Defense; Public Liability; Fire; Bad Faith; Medical Malpractice

Richard E. Crum — Auburn University, B.A., 1991; Cumberland School of Law of Samford University, J.D., 1994 — Admitted to Bar, 1994, Alabama; 1995, Florida; 1996, Georgia — Member American and Houston County Bar Associations; Alabama State Bar; Alabama Defense Lawyers Association — AV® Preeminent(TM) Peer Review Rating by Martindale-Hubbell® —

Shealy, Crum & Pike, P.C., Dothan, AL (Continued)

 Practice Areas: Medical Malpractice Defense; Workers' Compensation; Insurance Defense; Product Liability Defense; Casualty Defense; Employment Practices; General Liability; Automobile Liability; Civil Rights Defense; Public Liability; Fire; Bad Faith

James H. Pike — Washington and Lee University, B.A. (magna cum laude), 1992; J.D. (magna cum laude), 1995 — Admitted to Bar, 1995, Alabama — Member American Bar Association; Alabama State Bar; Alabama Defense Lawyers Association; Defense Research Institute — AV® Preeminent(TM) Peer Review Rating by Martindale-Hubbell® — Practice Areas: Insurance Defense; Product Liability Defense; Casualty Defense; Employment Practices; General Liability; Automobile Liability; Civil Rights Defense; Public Liability; Fire; Bad Faith

Associates
Robin Cobb Freeman
Joey Hornsby
Kelly Harmon
Amy Mendheim Swindall

The following firms also service this area.

Ball, Ball, Matthews & Novak, P.A.
445 Dexter Avenue, Suite 9045
Montgomery, Alabama 36104
 Telephone: 334-387-7680
 Fax: 334-387-3222
Mailing Address: P.O. Box 2148, Montgomery, AL 36102-2148

Insurance Defense, Medical Malpractice, Aviation, Bad Faith, Personal Injury, Construction Litigation, Employment Law, Product Liability, Property, Pharmaceutical, Medical Devices, Complex Litigation, Governmental Entity Defense, Workers' Compensation, Mediation, Arbitration, Trial and Appellate Practice, State and Federal Courts, Insurance Coverage Analysis, Automobile Injury, Motor Carrier Defense

SEE COMPLETE LISTING UNDER MONTGOMERY, ALABAMA (104 MILES)

Hill, Hill, Carter, Franco, Cole & Black, P.C.
425 South Perry Street
Montgomery, Alabama 36104
 Telephone: 334-834-7600
 Fax: 334-263-5969
Mailing Address: P.O. Box 116, Montgomery, AL 36101-0116

Appellate Practice, Aviation, Business Law, Casualty, Commercial Litigation, Discrimination, Education Law, Employment Law, Insurance Defense, Insurance Fraud, Law Enforcement Liability, Product Liability, Professional Liability, State and Federal Courts, Surety, Transportation, Trial Practice, Workers' Compensation, Insurance Coverage Opinions and Litigation

SEE COMPLETE LISTING UNDER MONTGOMERY, ALABAMA (107 MILES)

Holtsford Gilliland Higgins Hitson & Howard, P.C.
4001 Carmichael Road, Suite 300
Montgomery, Alabama 36106
 Telephone: 334-215-8585
 Toll Free: 800-932-6964
 Fax: 334-215-7101
Mailing Address: P.O. Box 4128, Montgomery, AL 36103-4128

Insurance Defense, Automobile, Professional Liability, Product Liability, Civil Rights, Toxic Torts, General Liability, Environmental Law, Workers' Compensation, Construction Law, Coverage Issues, Governmental Entity Defense, Forestry Law

SEE COMPLETE LISTING UNDER MONTGOMERY, ALABAMA (107 MILES)

ALABAMA

Rushton, Stakely, Johnston & Garrett, P.A.
184 Commerce Street
Montgomery, Alabama 36104
 Telephone: 334-206-3100
 Fax: 334-262-6277

Mailing Address: P.O. Box 270, Montgomery, AL 36101-0270

Insurance Defense, Trial and Appellate Practice, Accountants and Attorneys Liability, Administrative Law, Advertising Injury, Agent and Brokers Errors and Omissions, Appellate Practice, Arbitration, Automobile Tort, Bad Faith, Business Law, Casualty Insurance Law, Class Actions, Commercial Litigation, Complex Litigation, Construction Litigation, Contract Disputes, Copyright and Trademark Law, Coverage Analysis, Declaratory Judgments, Directors and Officers Liability, Employment Law, Environmental Law, Family Law, Fidelity and Surety, Fraud, Health Care, Health Care Professional Licensure Defense, Insurance Litigation, Labor and Employment, Law Enforcement Liability, Legal Malpractice, Medical Devices, Medical Malpractice, Pharmaceutical, Premises Liability, Primary and Excess Insurance, Product Liability, Professional Errors and Omissions, Professional Liability, Surety, Title Insurance, Uninsured and Underinsured Motorist, Workers' Compensation, Wrongful Death

SEE COMPLETE LISTING UNDER MONTGOMERY, ALABAMA (107 MILES)

Vernis & Bowling of Southern Alabama, LLC
61 St. Joseph Street, 11th Floor
Mobile, Alabama 36602
 Telephone: 251-432-0337
 Fax: 251-432-0244

Civil Litigation, Insurance Law, Workers' Compensation, Premises Liability, Labor and Employment, Civil Rights, Commercial Litigation, Complex Litigation, Product Liability, Directors and Officers Liability, Errors and Omissions, Construction Law, Construction Defect, Environmental Liability, Personal and Commercial Vehicle, Appellate Practice, Admiralty and Maritime Law, Real Estate, Family Law, Elder Law, Liability Defense, SIU/Fraud Litigation, Education Law (ESE/IDEA), Property and Casualty (Commercial and Personal Lines), Long-Haul Trucking Liability, Government Law, Public Law, Criminal, White Collar, Business Litigation

SEE COMPLETE LISTING UNDER MOBILE, ALABAMA (205 MILES)

DOUBLE SPRINGS † 1,083 Winston Co.

Refer To
Lowe Mobley Lowe & LeDuke
1210 21st Street
Haleyville, Alabama 35565
 Telephone: 205-486-5296
 Fax: 205-486-4531

Mailing Address: P.O. Box 576, Haleyville, AL 35565

General Civil Trial and Appellate Practice, Insurance Defense, Legal Malpractice, Medical Malpractice, Product Liability, Workers' Compensation, Employment Law

SEE COMPLETE LISTING UNDER HALEYVILLE, ALABAMA (15 MILES)

ENTERPRISE † 26,562 Coffee Co.

Refer To
Morrow, Romine & Pearson, P.C.
122 South Hull Street
Montgomery, Alabama 36104
 Telephone: 334-262-7707
 Fax: 334-262-7742

Mailing Address: P.O. Box 4804, Montgomery, AL 36103

Civil Trial Practice, Insurance Law, Medical Malpractice, Product Liability, Environmental Coverage, Personal Injury, Litigation, Mediation, Trial Practice, Appellate Practice, State and Federal Courts, Handicap and Employment Discrimination, Diving Accidents

SEE COMPLETE LISTING UNDER MONTGOMERY, ALABAMA (87 MILES)

DOUBLE SPRINGS

EUFAULA 13,137 Barbour Co.

Refer To
Ball, Ball, Matthews & Novak, P.A.
445 Dexter Avenue, Suite 9045
Montgomery, Alabama 36104
 Telephone: 334-387-7680
 Fax: 334-387-3222

Mailing Address: P.O. Box 2148, Montgomery, AL 36102-2148

Insurance Defense, Medical Malpractice, Aviation, Bad Faith, Personal Injury, Construction Litigation, Employment Law, Product Liability, Property, Pharmaceutical, Medical Devices, Complex Litigation, Governmental Entity Defense, Workers' Compensation, Mediation, Arbitration, Trial and Appellate Practice, State and Federal Courts, Insurance Coverage Analysis, Automobile Injury, Motor Carrier Defense

SEE COMPLETE LISTING UNDER MONTGOMERY, ALABAMA (87 MILES)

Refer To
Holtsford Gilliland Higgins Hitson & Howard, P.C.
4001 Carmichael Road, Suite 300
Montgomery, Alabama 36106
 Telephone: 334-215-8585
 Toll Free: 800-932-6964
 Fax: 334-215-7101

Mailing Address: P.O. Box 4128, Montgomery, AL 36103-4128

Insurance Defense, Automobile, Professional Liability, Product Liability, Civil Rights, Toxic Torts, General Liability, Environmental Law, Workers' Compensation, Construction Law, Coverage Issues, Governmental Entity Defense, Forestry Law

SEE COMPLETE LISTING UNDER MONTGOMERY, ALABAMA (80 MILES)

Refer To
Morrow, Romine & Pearson, P.C.
122 South Hull Street
Montgomery, Alabama 36104
 Telephone: 334-262-7707
 Fax: 334-262-7742

Mailing Address: P.O. Box 4804, Montgomery, AL 36103

Civil Trial Practice, Insurance Law, Medical Malpractice, Product Liability, Environmental Coverage, Personal Injury, Litigation, Mediation, Trial Practice, Appellate Practice, State and Federal Courts, Handicap and Employment Discrimination, Diving Accidents

SEE COMPLETE LISTING UNDER MONTGOMERY, ALABAMA (80 MILES)

Refer To
Rushton, Stakely, Johnston & Garrett, P.A.
184 Commerce Street
Montgomery, Alabama 36104
 Telephone: 334-206-3100
 Fax: 334-262-6277

Mailing Address: P.O. Box 270, Montgomery, AL 36101-0270

Insurance Defense, Trial and Appellate Practice, Accountants and Attorneys Liability, Administrative Law, Advertising Injury, Agent and Brokers Errors and Omissions, Appellate Practice, Arbitration, Automobile Tort, Bad Faith, Business Law, Casualty Insurance Law, Class Actions, Commercial Litigation, Complex Litigation, Construction Litigation, Contract Disputes, Copyright and Trademark Law, Coverage Analysis, Declaratory Judgments, Directors and Officers Liability, Employment Law, Environmental Law, Family Law, Fidelity and Surety, Fraud, Health Care, Health Care Professional Licensure Defense, Insurance Litigation, Labor and Employment, Law Enforcement Liability, Legal Malpractice, Medical Devices, Medical Malpractice, Pharmaceutical, Premises Liability, Primary and Excess Insurance, Product Liability, Professional Errors and Omissions, Professional Liability, Surety, Title Insurance, Uninsured and Underinsured Motorist, Workers' Compensation, Wrongful Death

SEE COMPLETE LISTING UNDER MONTGOMERY, ALABAMA (80 MILES)

FLORENCE ALABAMA

EUTAW † 2,934 Greene Co.
Refer To

Owens & Millsaps, LLP
Attorneys at Law
2606 8th Street
Tuscaloosa, Alabama 35401
   Toll Free: 866-790-2889
   Telephone: 205-750-0750
   Telephone: 205-759-8582
   Fax: 205-750-0355

Mailing Address: P.O. Box 2487, Tuscaloosa, AL 35403-2487

Insurance Defense, Medical Malpractice, Legal Malpractice, Dental Malpractice, Coverage Issues, Comprehensive General Liability, Product Liability, Construction Law, Employment Practices Liability, Environmental Liability

SEE COMPLETE LISTING UNDER TUSCALOOSA, ALABAMA (35 MILES)

Refer To

Phelps, Jenkins, Gibson & Fowler, LLP
1201 Greensboro Avenue
Tuscaloosa, Alabama 35401
   Telephone: 205-345-5100
   Fax: 205-758-4394, 205-391-6658

Mailing Address: P.O. Box 020848, Tuscaloosa, AL 35402-0848

Employment Litigation, General Defense, Medical Malpractice, School Law, Workers' Compensation, Personal Injury

SEE COMPLETE LISTING UNDER TUSCALOOSA, ALABAMA (35 MILES)

EVERGREEN † 3,944 Conecuh Co.
Refer To

Ball, Ball, Matthews & Novak, P.A.
445 Dexter Avenue, Suite 9045
Montgomery, Alabama 36104
   Telephone: 334-387-7680
   Fax: 334-387-3222

Mailing Address: P.O. Box 2148, Montgomery, AL 36102-2148

Insurance Defense, Medical Malpractice, Aviation, Bad Faith, Personal Injury, Construction Litigation, Employment Law, Product Liability, Property, Pharmaceutical, Medical Devices, Complex Litigation, Governmental Entity Defense, Workers' Compensation, Mediation, Arbitration, Trial and Appellate Practice, State and Federal Courts, Insurance Coverage Analysis, Automobile Injury, Motor Carrier Defense

SEE COMPLETE LISTING UNDER MONTGOMERY, ALABAMA (84 MILES)

Refer To

Michael Gillion, P.C.
74 Midtown Park West, Suite 105
Mobile, Alabama 36606
   Telephone: 251-471-9494
   Fax: 251-471-1722

Mailing Address: P.O. Box 161423, Mobile, AL 36616-2423

Insurance Defense, Automobile, Homeowners, Workers' Compensation, Subrogation, Insurance Contract and Coverage Litigation

SEE COMPLETE LISTING UNDER MOBILE, ALABAMA (92 MILES)

Refer To

Vickers, Riis, Murray and Curran, L.L.C.
RSA Trustmark Building, 21st Floor
107 St. Francis Street
Mobile, Alabama 36602
   Telephone: 251-432-9772
   Fax: 251-432-9781

Mailing Address: P.O. Box 2568, Mobile, AL 36652-2568

Insurance Defense, Insurance Coverage, Construction Law, Admiralty and Maritime Law, Professional Liability, Environmental Law, Employment Law, Governmental Liability, Toxic Torts, Product Liability, Workers' Compensation, Business Automobile and Trucking, Education

SEE COMPLETE LISTING UNDER MOBILE, ALABAMA (92 MILES)

FAIRHOPE 15,326 Baldwin Co.
Refer To

Ball, Ball, Matthews & Novak, P.A.
107 Saint Francis Street, Suite 1590
Mobile, Alabama 36602
   Telephone: 251-338-2721
   Fax: 251-338-2722

Mailing Address: P.O. Box 2648, Mobile, AL 36652

Insurance Defense, Medical Malpractice, Aviation, Bad Faith, Personal Injury, Construction Litigation, Employment Law, Product Liability, Property, Pharmaceutical, Medical Devices, Complex Litigation, Governmental Entity Defense, Workers' Compensation, Mediation, Arbitration, Trial and Appellate Practice, State and Federal Courts, Insurance Coverage Analysis, Automobile Injury, Motor Carrier Defense

SEE COMPLETE LISTING UNDER MOBILE, ALABAMA (18 MILES)

FAYETTE † 4,619 Fayette Co.
Refer To

Owens & Millsaps, LLP
Attorneys at Law
2606 8th Street
Tuscaloosa, Alabama 35401
   Toll Free: 866-790-2889
   Telephone: 205-750-0750
   Telephone: 205-759-8582
   Fax: 205-750-0355

Mailing Address: P.O. Box 2487, Tuscaloosa, AL 35403-2487

Insurance Defense, Medical Malpractice, Legal Malpractice, Dental Malpractice, Coverage Issues, Comprehensive General Liability, Product Liability, Construction Law, Employment Practices Liability, Environmental Liability

SEE COMPLETE LISTING UNDER TUSCALOOSA, ALABAMA (41 MILES)

Refer To

Phelps, Jenkins, Gibson & Fowler, LLP
1201 Greensboro Avenue
Tuscaloosa, Alabama 35401
   Telephone: 205-345-5100
   Fax: 205-758-4394, 205-391-6658

Mailing Address: P.O. Box 020848, Tuscaloosa, AL 35402-0848

Employment Litigation, General Defense, Medical Malpractice, School Law, Workers' Compensation, Personal Injury

SEE COMPLETE LISTING UNDER TUSCALOOSA, ALABAMA (41 MILES)

FLORENCE † 39,319 Lauderdale Co.

O'Bannon & O'Bannon, L.L.C.
402 South Pine Street
Florence, Alabama 35630
   Telephone: 256-767-6731
   Fax: 256-766-5390
   E-Mail: firm@obannonlaw.com

Established: 1985

Insurance Defense, Product Liability, General Liability, Automobile Liability, Casualty, Life and Health, Medical Malpractice

Insurance Clients

Auto-Owners Insurance Company
Companion Property and Casualty Group
Jefferson-Pilot Corporation
State Auto Insurance Companies
Chrysler Insurance Company
Great River Insurance Company
IAT Specialty
Motorists Mutual Insurance Company

Partners and Senior Attorneys

A. Stewart O'Bannon, III — 1955 — The University of North Alabama, B.A., 1976; Birmingham School of Law, J.D., 1982 — Admitted to Bar, 1982, Alabama; 1982, U.S. District Court, Northern District of Alabama; 1982, U.S. Court of Appeals, Eleventh Circuit — Member American and Lauderdale

ALABAMA

O'Bannon & O'Bannon, L.L.C., Florence, AL (Continued)

County Bar Associations; Alabama State Bar; Alabama Defense Lawyers Association — E-mail: stewiii@obannonlaw.com

Firm Member

Larry M. Carr — 1981 — The University of Alabama at Birmingham, B.A., 2003; Cumberland School of Law at Samford University, J.D., 2009; University of East Anglia, LL.M., 2011 — Admitted to Bar, 2009, Alabama; 2010, Tennessee — Member American Bar Association; Alabama State Bar — E-mail: lmcarr@obannonlaw.com

The following firms also service this area.

Webb Sanders & Williams PLLC
363 North Broadway
Tupelo, Mississippi 38804
  Telephone: 662-844-2137
  Fax: 662-842-3863

Mailing Address: P.O. Box 496, Tupelo, MS 38802-0496

Insurance Defense, Insurance Coverage, Automobile, Property, Fire, Arson, Fraud, First Party Matters, Bad Faith, Special Investigations, Product Liability, Automobile Liability, Uninsured and Underinsured Motorist, Professional Malpractice, Medical Malpractice, Workers' Compensation, General Liability, Premises Liability, Defense Litigation, Corporate Law, Commercial Law, Commercial Litigation, Real Estate, Transportation, Environmental Law, Toxic Torts, Bankruptcy, Creditor Rights, Labor and Employment, ERISA, Construction Litigation, Fidelity and Surety, Insurance Fraud, General Civil Practice, Trial Practice, Appellate Practice, Employment Discrimination, Coverage Analysis, Coverage Issues

SEE COMPLETE LISTING UNDER TUPELO, MISSISSIPPI (89 MILES)

FOLEY 14,618 Baldwin Co.

Refer To

Vernis & Bowling of Southern Alabama, LLC
61 St. Joseph Street, 11th Floor
Mobile, Alabama 36602
  Telephone: 251-432-0337
  Fax: 251-432-0244

Civil Litigation, Insurance Law, Workers' Compensation, Premises Liability, Labor and Employment, Civil Rights, Commercial Litigation, Complex Litigation, Product Liability, Directors and Officers Liability, Errors and Omissions, Construction Law, Construction Defect, Environmental Liability, Personal and Commercial Vehicle, Appellate Practice, Admiralty and Maritime Law, Real Estate, Family Law, Elder Law, Liability Defense, SIU/Fraud Litigation, Education Law (ESE/IDEA), Property and Casualty (Commercial and Personal Lines), Long-Haul Trucking Liability, Government Law, Public Law, Criminal, White Collar, Business Litigation

SEE COMPLETE LISTING UNDER MOBILE, ALABAMA (35 MILES)

GREENSBORO † 2,497 Hale Co.

Refer To

Phelps, Jenkins, Gibson & Fowler, LLP
1201 Greensboro Avenue
Tuscaloosa, Alabama 35401
  Telephone: 205-345-5100
  Fax: 205-758-4394, 205-391-6658

Mailing Address: P.O. Box 020848, Tuscaloosa, AL 35402-0848

Employment Litigation, General Defense, Medical Malpractice, School Law, Workers' Compensation, Personal Injury

SEE COMPLETE LISTING UNDER TUSCALOOSA, ALABAMA (38 MILES)

FOLEY

GROVE HILL † 1,570 Clarke Co.

Refer To

Galloway, Wettermark, Everest & Rutens, LLP
3263 Cottage Hill Road
Mobile, Alabama 36606
  Telephone: 251-476-4493
  Fax: 251-479-5566

Mailing Address: P.O. Box 16629, Mobile, AL 36616-0629

Insurance Defense, Admiralty and Maritime Law, Casualty, Fire, Life Insurance, Surety, Workers' Compensation, Governmental Liability, Product Liability, Civil Rights, Commercial Litigation, Construction Law, Professional Liability, Trial and Appellate Practice, State and Federal Courts, Title VII Defense, Medical Liability

SEE COMPLETE LISTING UNDER MOBILE, ALABAMA (84 MILES)

Refer To

Michael Gillion, P.C.
74 Midtown Park West, Suite 105
Mobile, Alabama 36606
  Telephone: 251-471-9494
  Fax: 251-471-1722

Mailing Address: P.O. Box 161423, Mobile, AL 36616-2423

Insurance Defense, Automobile, Homeowners, Workers' Compensation, Subrogation, Insurance Contract and Coverage Litigation

SEE COMPLETE LISTING UNDER MOBILE, ALABAMA (84 MILES)

Refer To

Holtsford Gilliland Higgins Hitson & Howard, P.C.
29000 U.S. Highway 98, Suite A-302
Daphne, Alabama 36526-7263
  Telephone: 251-447-0234
  Fax: 251-447-0212

Insurance Defense, Automobile, Professional Liability, Product Liability, Civil Rights, Toxic Torts, General Liability, Environmental Law, Workers' Compensation, Construction Law, Governmental Entity Defense

SEE COMPLETE LISTING UNDER MOBILE, ALABAMA (92 MILES)

Refer To

Johnstone Adams, L.L.C.
One St. Louis Centre
1 St. Louis Street, Suite 4000
Mobile, Alabama 36602
  Telephone: 251-432-7682
  Fax: 251-432-2800

Mailing Address: P.O. Box 1988, Mobile, AL 36633

Insurance Defense, Admiralty and Maritime Law, Automobile, Aviation, Bad Faith, Casualty, Construction Litigation, Employer Liability, ERISA, Fire, Fraud, Health, Life Insurance, Product Liability, Professional Liability, Surety, Workers' Compensation, Co-Employee

SEE COMPLETE LISTING UNDER MOBILE, ALABAMA (84 MILES)

Refer To

Vickers, Riis, Murray and Curran, L.L.C.
RSA Trustmark Building, 21st Floor
107 St. Francis Street
Mobile, Alabama 36602
  Telephone: 251-432-9772
  Fax: 251-432-9781

Mailing Address: P.O. Box 2568, Mobile, AL 36652-2568

Insurance Defense, Insurance Coverage, Construction Law, Admiralty and Maritime Law, Professional Liability, Environmental Law, Employment Law, Governmental Liability, Toxic Torts, Product Liability, Workers' Compensation, Business Automobile and Trucking, Education

SEE COMPLETE LISTING UNDER MOBILE, ALABAMA (84 MILES)

HAYNEVILLE   ALABAMA

HALEYVILLE 4,173 Winston Co.

Lowe Mobley Lowe & LeDuke
1210 21st Street
Haleyville, Alabama 35565
   Telephone: 205-486-5296
   Fax: 205-486-4531
   E-Mail: jbl@lowemobleylowe.com
   www.lowemobleylowe.com

(Hamilton, AL Office*: 109 1st Avenue SW, P.O. Box 819, 35570)
  (Tel: 205-921-5296)
  (Fax: 205-921-9090)

Established: 1971

General Civil Trial and Appellate Practice, Insurance Defense, Legal Malpractice, Medical Malpractice, Product Liability, Workers' Compensation, Employment Law

Firm Profile: For more detailed information regarding firm profile, insurance clients and representative clients see the Firm Website.

Insurance Clients

American Bankers Insurance Company of Florida
Attorneys Insurance Mutual of the South, Inc., Risk Retention Group
Chubb Group
Continental Insurance Company
Liberty Mutual Insurance Company
Motors Insurance Corporation
Mutual Savings Fire Insurance Company
National Union Fire Insurance Company
Progressive Insurance
Sentry Claims Services
Standard Fire Insurance Company
State Farm Fire and Casualty Company
Travelers
Unisun Insurance Company
United Casualty Insurance Company of America
American Underwriters Group
Arch Insurance Group
Auto-Owners Insurance Company
Cambridge Integrated Services
CNA Insurance Company
Integon Life Insurance Corporation
Lumbermen's Underwriting Alliance
Mutual Savings Life Insurance Company
North Carolina Farm Bureau
OneBeacon Professional Insurance
St. Paul Insurance Company
Southern Guaranty Insurance Company
Time Insurance Company n.k.a. Assurant Health
Travelers Property Casualty Corporation

Non-Insurance Clients

Alabama Power Company
First National Bank
Strategic Comp
Underwriters Adjusting Company
Cavalier Homes, Inc.
NTN-Bower Corporation
Traders & Farmers Bank

Firm Members

John W Lowe — 1941 — Samford University, B.S.B.A., 1967; Cumberland School of Law of Samford University, J.D., 1969 — Admitted to Bar, 1970, Alabama — Member Alabama State Bar — Practice Areas: Corporate Law; Insurance Defense; Banking; Commercial Litigation; Medical Malpractice; Wills and Estate Litigation

Jeffery A. Mobley — 1961 — The University of Alabama, B.S., 1983; Cumberland School of Law of Samford University, J.D., 1986 — Admitted to Bar, 1986, Alabama — Member Alabama State Bar; Alabama Associations of School Boards; Alabama Defense Lawyers Association — Practice Areas: Civil Litigation; Legal Malpractice; Product Liability; Medical Malpractice; Municipal Law; School Law; Insurance Coverage; Insurance Defense; Fraud; Mediation; Arbitration; Personal Injury; Property; Corporate Litigation

Jonathan Blake Lowe — 1969 — The University of Alabama, B.S., 1991; Cumberland School of Law of Samford University, J.D., 1994 — Admitted to Bar, 1994, Alabama — Member Alabama State Bar; Alabama Defense Lawyers Association; Alabama Workers' Compensation Claims Association — Practice Areas: General Civil Litigation; Insurance Defense; Corporate Law; Employment Law; Product Liability; Workers' Compensation; Banking; Commercial Litigation; Personal Injury; Contract Litigation; General Liability; Automobile Liability; Family Law; Wills and Estate Litigation

HAMILTON † 6,885 Marion Co.

Lowe Mobley Lowe & LeDuke
109 1st Avenue SW
Hamilton, Alabama 35570
   Telephone: 205-921-5296
   Fax: 205-921-9090
   E-Mail: jbl@lowemobleylowe.com
   www.lowemobleylowe.com

(Haleyville, AL Office*: 1210 21st Street, P.O. Box 576, 35565)
  (Tel: 205-486-5296)
  (Fax: 205-486-4531)

Established: 1971

General Civil Trial and Appellate Practice, Insurance Defense, Legal Malpractice, Medical Malpractice, Product Liability, Workers' Compensation, Employment Law

Firm Member

Matthew LeDuke — 1971 — The University of Alabama, B.S., 1993; M.A., 1994; The University of Alabama School of Law, J.D., 2006 — Admitted to Bar, 2006, Alabama — Member Alabama State Bar; Alabama Defense Lawyers Association — Practice Areas: Employment Law; Insurance Defense; Workers' Compensation; Family Law; Property; General Civil Litigation

(See listing under Haleyville, AL for additional information)

The following firms also service this area.

Webb Sanders & Williams PLLC
363 North Broadway
Tupelo, Mississippi 38804
   Telephone: 662-844-2137
   Fax: 662-842-3863
Mailing Address: P.O. Box 496, Tupelo, MS 38802-0496

Insurance Defense, Insurance Coverage, Automobile, Property, Fire, Arson, Fraud, First Party Matters, Bad Faith, Special Investigations, Product Liability, Automobile Liability, Uninsured and Underinsured Motorist, Professional Malpractice, Medical Malpractice, Workers' Compensation, General Liability, Premises Liability, Defense Litigation, Corporate Law, Commercial Law, Commercial Litigation, Real Estate, Transportation, Environmental Law, Toxic Torts, Bankruptcy, Creditor Rights, Labor and Employment, ERISA, Construction Litigation, Fidelity and Surety, Insurance Fraud, General Civil Practice, Trial Practice, Appellate Practice, Employment Discrimination, Coverage Analysis, Coverage Issues

SEE COMPLETE LISTING UNDER TUPELO, MISSISSIPPI (48 MILES)

HAYNEVILLE † 932 Lowndes Co.

Refer To
Ball, Ball, Matthews & Novak, P.A.
445 Dexter Avenue, Suite 9045
Montgomery, Alabama 36104
   Telephone: 334-387-7680
   Fax: 334-387-3222
Mailing Address: P.O. Box 2148, Montgomery, AL 36102-2148

Insurance Defense, Medical Malpractice, Aviation, Bad Faith, Personal Injury, Construction Litigation, Employment Law, Product Liability, Property, Pharmaceutical, Medical Devices, Complex Litigation, Governmental Entity Defense, Workers' Compensation, Mediation, Arbitration, Trial and Appellate Practice, State and Federal Courts, Insurance Coverage Analysis, Automobile Injury, Motor Carrier Defense

SEE COMPLETE LISTING UNDER MONTGOMERY, ALABAMA (29 MILES)

ALABAMA

HUNTSVILLE

Refer To

Morrow, Romine & Pearson, P.C.
122 South Hull Street
Montgomery, Alabama 36104
  Telephone: 334-262-7707
  Fax: 334-262-7742

Mailing Address: P.O. Box 4804, Montgomery, AL 36103

Civil Trial Practice, Insurance Law, Medical Malpractice, Product Liability, Environmental Coverage, Personal Injury, Litigation, Mediation, Trial Practice, Appellate Practice, State and Federal Courts, Handicap and Employment Discrimination, Diving Accidents

SEE COMPLETE LISTING UNDER MONTGOMERY, ALABAMA (22 MILES)

Refer To

Rushton, Stakely, Johnston & Garrett, P.A.
184 Commerce Street
Montgomery, Alabama 36104
  Telephone: 334-206-3100
  Fax: 334-262-6277

Mailing Address: P.O. Box 270, Montgomery, AL 36101-0270

Insurance Defense, Trial and Appellate Practice, Accountants and Attorneys Liability, Administrative Law, Advertising Injury, Agent and Brokers Errors and Omissions, Appellate Practice, Arbitration, Automobile Tort, Bad Faith, Business Law, Casualty Insurance Law, Class Actions, Commercial Litigation, Complex Litigation, Construction Litigation, Contract Disputes, Copyright and Trademark Law, Coverage Analysis, Declaratory Judgments, Directors and Officers Liability, Employment Law, Environmental Law, Family Law, Fidelity and Surety, Fraud, Health Care, Health Care Professional Licensure Defense, Insurance Litigation, Labor and Employment, Law Enforcement Liability, Legal Malpractice, Medical Devices, Medical Malpractice, Pharmaceutical, Premises Liability, Primary and Excess Insurance, Product Liability, Professional Errors and Omissions, Professional Liability, Surety, Title Insurance, Uninsured and Underinsured Motorist, Workers' Compensation, Wrongful Death

SEE COMPLETE LISTING UNDER MONTGOMERY, ALABAMA (22 MILES)

HUNTSVILLE † 180,105 Madison Co.

F&B Law Firm, P.C.
213 Greene Street
Huntsville, Alabama 35801
  Telephone: 256-536-0095
  Fax: 256-536-4440
  www.fb-pc.com

Established: 1999

Insurance Defense, Self-Insured, Workers' Compensation, General Civil Practice, Business Law, Corporate Law, Commercial Law, Commercial Litigation, Municipal Law, Appellate Practice, Employment Law, Personal Injury, Premises Liability, Construction Litigation, Railroad Law, Police Civil Liability Defense, Municipal Litigation

Firm Profile: Originating in March of 1999 by lawyer Michael L. Fees, the firm of F&B Law Firm, P.C. (formerly known as Fees & Burgess, P.C.), is an experienced Huntsville law firm with a practice emphasis in the representation of government, business, and insurance companies in litigation and litigation avoidance and in handling its clients' sophisticated corporate needs. The firm has three driving objectives: first and foremost, to deliver excellent quality legal services for good value; second, to ensure an office atmosphere that promotes the progress and well-being of its employees; and finally, to be and remain on the cutting-edge of technology in the representation of its clients. Although there are many aspects of this law firm that set it apart from other law firms, one key feature of the firm is most prominent—its professional and capable lawyers and staff. Quality of product being critical to the firm's effort and continued success, the firm is committed to hiring only the best employees; and even for those, it encourages and promotes further education and training, all to ensure an excellent product for good value.

Insurance Clients

A.G.D. Insurance, L.L.C.
AIG Aerospace
AIG
AIG Aviation, Inc.

F&B Law Firm, P.C., Huntsville, AL (Continued)

AIG Construction Risk Management Group
Allianz Global Corporate & Specialty
Alabama Municipal Insurance Corporation
The Hanover Insurance Companies
Kansas City Life Insurance Company

Non-Insurance Clients

ADTRAN, Inc.
ALATEC, Inc.
Bowhead Holding Company
Cadence Bank, N.A.
C & C Fabrication, Inc.
Consolidated Construction Company
Daniel & Yeager, Inc.
Dynetics, Inc.
Electro-Motive Diesel, Inc.
EPE Corporation
Flint River Animal Hospital
Honor Tone Limited
IPC
Nextek, Inc.
Pearce Construction Company
Progress Rail Services Corporation
Summa Technology, Inc.
UPS
Valuetronics Holdings Limited
Westwind Technologies, Inc.
Work Force Housing, LLC
Air Essentials, Inc.
Benchmark Electronics, Inc.
Brockwell Technologies, Inc.
Caterpillar Inc.
C-MAC Microcircuits, ULC
Corradi USA, Inc.
Cove Retail, Tenancy in Common
Digium, Inc.
E. Cornell Malone Corporation
Electronic Source Company
Eye Solutions Technologies, L.L.C.
Global Recruiters of Huntsville
Intergraph Government Solutions
Martin & Cobey Construction Co., Inc.
PESA Switching Systems, Inc.
Reed Contracting Services, Inc.
Summit 7 Systems, Inc.
Valleycrest Landscape Development, Inc.
Wiregrass Construction Company, Inc.

Self-Insured Clients

City of Huntsville, Alabama

Shareholders

Michael L. Fees — 1954 — The University of Alabama in Huntsville, B.A., 1977; The University of Alabama School of Law, J.D., 1980 — Managing Editor, Alabama Law Review — Admitted to Bar, 1980, Alabama; U.S. District Court, Southern District of Alabama; 1981, U.S. Court of Appeals, Fifth and Eleventh Circuits; 1983, U.S. District Court, Northern District of Alabama; 1986, U.S. Court of Appeals, Sixth Circuit; 1987, U.S. District Court, Middle District of Alabama; 1993, U.S. Supreme Court — Member Alabama State Bar; Huntsville-Madison County Bar Association; Madison County American Inn of Court (First President; Former Member); Alabama Association of Municipal Attorneys; Alabama Self-Insurers Association — Practice Areas: Appellate Practice; Business Litigation; Class Actions; Commercial Law; Construction Law; Government Contracts; Insurance Defense; Labor and Employment; Litigation; Municipal Law — E-mail: mfees@fb-pc.com

Allen L. Anderson — 1972 — Wofford College, B.A./B.S. (cum laude), 1994; Cumberland School of Law of Samford University, J.D., 1997 — Associate Editor, Cumberland Law Review — Admitted to Bar, 1997, Alabama; U.S. District Court, Middle and Northern Districts of Alabama; 1998, U.S. District Court, Southern District of Alabama; U.S. Court of Appeals, Eleventh Circuit; 2009, U.S. Court of Federal Claims — Member Alabama State Bar; Huntsville-Madison County Bar Association; National Contract Management Association; Society for Human Resource Management; Alabama Contractors Association; Alabama Road Builders Association; Associated Builders and Contractors; Institute of Supply Management — Practice Areas: Appellate Practice; Business Litigation; Class Actions; Commercial Law; Construction Law; Government Contracts; Insurance Defense; Labor and Employment; Litigation; Municipal Law — E-mail: anderson@fb-pc.com

Jeffrey L. Roth — 1956 — University of Cincinnati, B.S., 1979; University of Dayton School of Law, J.D., 1982 — Admitted to Bar, 1982, Ohio; 1984, Alabama; 1985, U.S. District Court, Northern District of Alabama; 2009, U.S. Court of Federal Claims — Member Federal, American, Ohio State and Huntsville-Madison County Bar Associations; Alabama State Bar; Society for Human Resource Mangement; National Contract Management Association; Institute of Supply Management — Speaker: Alabama Employment Law Letter's "FMLA Master Class for Alabama Employers"; "Employment Records, Retention, Retrieval and Destruction: The Advanced Interactive Workshop for Alabama Employers" — Classes Taught: Instructor, IPC EMS Program Management Training & Certification (CEPM); Instructor, Certified Commercial Contract Manager (CCCM), NCMA — Certified Professional Contract Manager (CPCM), National Contract Management Association (NCMA); NCMA Certified Instructor/Developer — Practice Areas: Business Law; Corporate Law; Railroad Law; Labor and Employment; Technology; Government Contracts — E-mail: jroth@fb-pc.com

Stacy L. Moon — 1968 — University of Montevallo, B.A. (summa cum laude), 1990; Cumberland School of Law of Samford University, J.D. (magna cum

F&B Law Firm, P.C., Huntsville, AL (Continued)

laude), 1998 — Admitted to Bar, 1998, Alabama; U.S. District Court, Middle, Northern and Southern Districts of Alabama; U.S. Court of Appeals, Eleventh Circuit — Member Alabama State Bar; Huntsville-Madison County Bar Association; Associated Builders and Contractors; Defense Research Institute (Committees: Law Practice Management, Employment & Labor Law, Commercial Litigation, Construction Law, Lawyers Professionalism and Ethics, Trial Tactics) — Languages: Spanish — Practice Areas: Insurance Defense; Commercial Litigation; Employment Law; Premises Liability; Construction Litigation; Municipal Liability; Business Litigation; Personal Injury Defense — E-mail: smoon@fb-pc.com

Associates

Ryan G. Blount — 1980 — Tulane University, B.A. (cum laude), 2002; Tulane University Law School, J.D. (cum laude), 2005 — Admitted to Bar, 2005, Alabama; 2007, U.S. District Court, Northern District of Alabama; 2013, U.S. Court of Appeals, Eleventh Circuit — Member Alabama State Bar; Huntsville-Madison County Bar Association; National Contract Management Association — Certified Commercial Contract Manager (CCCM), NCMA — Practice Areas: Business Law; Corporate Law; Railroad Law; Labor and Employment; Technology; Government Contracts; Commercial Litigation; Municipal Liability — E-mail: rblount@fb-pc.com

Allison B. Chandler — Mississippi State University, B.A. (summa cum laude), 2007; The University of Mississippi School of Law, J.D. (magna cum laude), 2010 — Associate Editor, Mississippi Law Journal — Admitted to Bar, 2010, Alabama; 2011, U.S. District Court, Northern District of Alabama; 2012, U.S. Court of Appeals, Eleventh Circuit — Member Alabama State Bar; Huntsville-Madison County Bar Association — Practice Areas: Insurance Defense; Commercial Litigation; Employment Law; Premises Liability; Construction Litigation; Municipal Liability; Personal Injury Defense — E-mail: achandler@fb-pc.com

Gaines Gault Hendrix P.C.

309 Franklin Street
Huntsville, Alabama 35801
Telephone: 256-532-1957
Fax: 256-532-1958
www.ggh-law.com

(Birmingham, AL Office*: 3500 Blue Lake Drive, Suite 425, 35243)
 (Tel: 205-980-5888)
 (Fax: 205-402-4900)

Insurance Defense, Bad Faith, Fraud, Coverage Issues, Litigation, Subrogation, Personal Injury, Workers' Compensation, Product Liability, Property, Arson, Theft, Discrimination, Medical Malpractice, Professional Malpractice, Nursing Home Liability, Education Law, Title VII

Members

Shelley D. Lewis — 1977 — Birmingham-Southern College, B.A., 1999; Cumberland School of Law of Samford University, J.D., 2004 — Admitted to Bar, 2004, Alabama

Thomas C. Phelps III — 1980 — The University of Alabama, B.A. (cum laude), 2003; Cumberland School of Law of Samford University, J.D., 2006 — Cumberland Law Review — Admitted to Bar, 2006, Alabama; 2007, U.S. District Court, Northern District of Alabama; 2009, U.S. District Court, Southern District of Alabama

(See listing under Birmingham, AL for additional information)

Grace, Matthews & Debro LLC

108 North Jefferson Street
Huntsville, Alabama 35801
 Telephone: 256-534-0491
 Fax: 256-534-0493
 E-Mail: gem@graceattys.com
 www.GraceAttys.com

Established: 1988

Grace, Matthews & Debro LLC, Huntsville, AL (Continued)

Insurance Defense, Automobile, General Liability, Product Liability, Property and Casualty, Legal Malpractice, Municipal Liability, Construction Litigation, Trial and Appellate Practice, Coverage Analysis, Declaratory Judgments

Firm Profile: The firm has a talented, diverse team of experienced litigators. The practice focuses primarily on civil litigation from automobile accidents, construction, products liability, municipal to professional liability. The firm handles cases throughout North Alabama and in Federal Court for the Northern District. Our attorneys are experienced in and out of the courtroom, with mediation as well as arbitration.

Insurance Clients

Alabama Municipal Insurance Corporation	Alfa Mutual Insurance Company
Armed Forces Insurance	American Claims Service
Auto-Owners Insurance Company	Attorneys Insurance Mutual of Alabama, Inc.
The Cincinnati Insurance Companies	Erie Insurance Company
Global Indemnity Group	Farm Bureau Insurance Company
Indiana Farm Bureau	Hastings Mutual Insurance Company
Liberty Mutual Insurance	Pennsylvania Lumbermens Mutual Insurance Company
Shelter Insurance Companies	State Farm Fire and Casualty Company
State Auto Insurance Company	United National Insurance Company
State Farm Mutual Automobile Insurance Company	
Windsor Insurance Company	

Non-Insurance Clients

American Board of Funeral Service Education
Town of Gurley

State of Alabama Department of Human Resources

Members of the Firm

Gary K. Grace — 1949 — The University of Alabama, B.S., 1971; The University of Alabama School of Law, J.D., 1974 — Phi Delta Phi; Tau Beta Pi — Admitted to Bar, 1974, Alabama; 1975, U.S. Court of Appeals, Fifth Circuit; 2012, U.S. Court of Appeals for the Federal and Eleventh Circuits — Member American and Huntsville-Madison County Bar Associations; Alabama State Bar; Master Bencher, American Inns of Court; Counselor, Madison County Chapter, American Inns of Court; Alabama Defense Lawyers Association; Defense Research Institute — Certified Mediator, Alabama Center for Dispute Resolution

Jennifer M. Matthews — 1969 — Baylor University, B.A., 1990; Baylor Law School, J.D., 1992 — Phi Delta Phi — Admitted to Bar, 1992, Texas; 1993, Alabama; 1998, U.S. District Court, Northern District of Alabama; 2008, U.S. Supreme Court; 2012, U.S. Court of Appeals for the Federal and Eleventh Circuits — Member Alabama State Bar; State Bar of Texas; Huntsville-Madison County Bar Association; Alabama Defense Lawyers Association

John Mark Debro — 1968 — Alabama A & M University, B.A., 1991; Cumberland School of Law of Samford University, J.D., 1999 — Admitted to Bar, 1999, Alabama; U.S. District Court, Middle, Northern and Southern Districts of Alabama; U.S. Court of Appeals, Eleventh Circuit; 2002, U.S. Supreme Court — Member American and Huntsville-Madison County (Treasurer, 2007) Bar Associations; Alabama State Bar; Alabama Lawyers Association (Northern District Representative, 2006-Present); Alabama State Bar Editorial Board (Alabama Lawyer, 2007-2008); Alabama Defense Lawyers Association — U.S. Naval Reserve [1986-1999]

Associates

Bree T. Wilbourn — 1976 — The University of Alabama in Huntsville, B.A. (Dean's List), 1999; Cumberland School of Law of Samford University, J.D., 2003 — Admitted to Bar, 2003, Tennessee; 2006, Alabama; 2005, U.S. District Court, Middle District of Tennessee; 2006, U.S. District Court, Northern District of Alabama — Member American and Huntsville-Madison County Bar Associations; Alabama State Bar; Alabama Defense Lawyers Association

Kevin D. Hon — 1986 — Emory University School of Law, J.D., 2011 — Admitted to Bar, 2013, Alabama; U.S. District Court, Northern District of Alabama — Member Alabama State Bar; Huntsville-Madison County Bar Association

M. Frank Tatom II — 1958 — The University of Alabama, J.D., 1989 — Admitted to Bar, 1989, Alabama; 1990, U.S. District Court, Northern District of

ALABAMA — HUNTSVILLE

Grace, Matthews & Debro LLC, Huntsville, AL (Continued)

Alabama; U.S. Court of Appeals, Eleventh Circuit — Member Alabama State Bar; Huntsville-Madison County Bar Association

Lanier Ford Shaver & Payne P.C.

2101 West Clinton Avenue, Suite 102
Huntsville, Alabama 35805
Telephone: 256-535-1100
Fax: 256-533-9322
E-Mail: info@LanierFord.com
www.LanierFord.com

Established: 1988

Insurance Defense, Trial and Appellate Practice, State and Federal Courts, Corporate Law, Health, Insurance Law, Medical Malpractice, Labor and Employment, Product Liability, Workers' Compensation, Business Law, Commercial General Liability, Contract Disputes, Accident, Accident and Health, Alternative Dispute Resolution, Americans with Disabilities Act, Automobile, Bad Faith, Bodily Injury, Casualty Defense, Civil Rights, Commercial Vehicle, Comprehensive General Liability, Construction Accidents, Copyright and Trademark Law, Coverage Analysis, Defense Litigation, Dental Malpractice, Discrimination, Dram Shop, Employment Discrimination, Employment Law (Management Side), ERISA, Fraud, Health Care, Homeowners, Hospital Malpractice, Hospitals, Intellectual Property, Jail/Prison Defense, Law Enforcement Liability, Legal Malpractice, Medical Liability, Medical Negligence, Mergers and Acquisitions, Municipal Law, Municipal Liability, Nursing Home Liability, Personal Injury, Premises Liability, Professional Malpractice, Property Liability, Public Entities, Real Estate, School Law, Securities, Securities and Shareholders' Claims, Sexual Harassment, Slip and Fall, Technology, Truck Liability, Trucks/Heavy Equipment, Uninsured and Underinsured Motorist, Wrongful Death, Wrongful Termination, Breach of Contract, Civil Litigation, Civil Trial Practice, Commercial Law, Contracts, Eminent Domain, Employment Law, Estate Planning, General Civil Trial and Appellate Practice, Litigation, Malpractice, Mediation, Probate, Professional Liability, Professional Liability (Non-Medical) Defense, Professional Negligence, Public Liability, Public Officials Liability, Restaurant Liability, Title Insurance, Tort, Tort Liability, Tort Litigation, Trucking Law

Firm Profile: Lanier Ford Shaver & Payne P.C. was established in 1988 as a result of a merger between Ford, Caldwell, Ford & Payne and Lanier & Shaver, Huntsville's two oldest law firms. This merger gave the north Alabama area a well-rounded Huntsville-based law firm which provides client services in virtually all major areas of law through 12 practice groups including litigation, alternative dispute resolution, real estate, tax, and corporate services. The firm's clients include many local, national and international businesses, as well as a number of local governmental entities. The firm's intellectual property practice group includes attorneys registered to practice before the U.S. Patent and Trademark Office.

Insurance Clients

AIG Claim Services, Inc.
Alabama Risk Management
Catlin Underwriting Agency U.S., Inc.
CNA Insurance Companies
Crum & Forster Insurance Group
Kindred Healthcare
Liberty Mutual Insurance Company
ProAssurance Corporation
Travelers Property Casualty Corporation
Alabama Municipal Insurance Corporation
CIGNA Property and Casualty Insurance Company
Coregis Group
Government Employees Insurance Company
Mutual Assurance Company
The St. Paul Companies
Trident Insurance Services
United Services Automobile Association (USAA)

Shareholders

W. Stanley Rodgers — 1940 — The University of Alabama, B.S., 1962; The University of Alabama School of Law, LL.B., 1964 — Admitted to Bar, 1964, Alabama — Member American and Huntsville-Madison County Bar Associations; Alabama State Bar; Alabama Defense Lawyers Association; Fellow, American College of Trial Lawyers; American Board of Trial Advocates — E-mail: wsr@LanierFord.com

J.R. Brooks — 1945 — The University of Alabama, B.A., 1968; The University of Alabama School of Law, J.D., 1971 — Admitted to Bar, 1971, Alabama — Member American and Huntsville-Madison County Bar Associations; Alabama State Bar; Alabama Council of School Board Attorneys — E-mail: jrb@LanierFord.com

George W. Royer Jr. — 1947 — The University of Alabama, B.A., 1969; The University of Alabama School of Law, J.D., 1972 — Admitted to Bar, 1972, Alabama — Member American and Huntsville-Madison County Bar Associations; Alabama State Bar — E-mail: gwr@LanierFord.com

William W. Sanderson Jr. — 1954 — The University of Alabama, B.A. (cum laude), 1976; M.P.A., 1979; The University of Alabama School of Law, J.D., 1979 — Admitted to Bar, 1979, Alabama — Member American and Huntsville-Madison County Bar Associations; Alabama State Bar; Alabama Municipal Attorneys Association; Alabama Council of School Board Attorneys; Alabama Defense Lawyers Association — E-mail: wws@LanierFord.com

D. Edward Starnes, III — 1956 — The University of Alabama, B.S. (cum laude), 1979; The University of Alabama School of Law, J.D., 1982 — Admitted to Bar, 1982, Alabama — Member American Bar Association; Alabama State Bar; Alabama Defense Lawyers Association — E-mail: des@LanierFord.com

George E. Knox Jr. — 1964 — Birmingham-Southern College, B.A., 1987; Cumberland School of Law of Samford University, J.D., 1990 — Admitted to Bar, 1990, Alabama — Member American and Huntsville-Madison County Bar Associations; Alabama State Bar; American College of Trial Lawyers; American Board of Trial Advocates; Alabama Defense Lawyers Association — E-mail: gek@LanierFord.com

Daniel F. Beasley — 1959 — Abilene Christian University, B.A. (summa cum laude), 1981; University of Miami School of Law, J.D., 1984 — Admitted to Bar, 1984, Florida; 1998, Alabama; 1999, Tennessee — Member Tennessee and Huntsville-Madison County Bar Associations; Alabama State Bar; The Florida Bar; National Board of Trial Advocates; International Association of Defense Counsel; Alabama Defense Lawyers Association; Tennessee Defense Lawyers Association; Defense Research Institute — E-mail: dfb@LanierFord.com

P. Scott Arnston — 1969 — The University of Alabama, B.A. (cum laude), 1991; The University of Alabama School of Law, J.D. (magna cum laude), 1994 — Admitted to Bar, 1994, Alabama; 2009, Tennessee — Member American and Huntsville-Madison County Bar Associations; Alabama State Bar; Alabama Defense Lawyers Association — E-mail: psa@LanierFord.com

John M. Heacock, Jr.
Johnnie F. Vann
Y. Albert Moore, III
Paul A. Pate
Paul B. Seeley
J. Clark Pendergrass
Robert N. Bailey, II
Ann I. Dennen*
Corey W. Jenkins
C. Greogry Burgess
Charles A. Ray IV
John R. Wynn
Elizabeth W. Abel
Jeffrey T. Kelly
Rodney C. Lewis
Richard J. Marsden
Taylor P. Brooks
George P. Kobler*
W. Graham Burgess
David J. Canupp
Terry R. Bynum

Associates

Mr. J. Dale Gipson
Scott W. Faulkner
Laura W. Harper
Travis S. Jackson
Karen A. Lynn
Tracy A. Marion
W. Ty. Stafford*
Lauren B. Houseknecht
Mary Ellen Gill
Christopher M. Pape
Michael W. Rich
Brad A. Chynoweth

*Registered Patent Attorney

HUNTSVILLE ALABAMA

Sirote & Permutt, P.C.

305 Church Street, Suite 800
Huntsville, Alabama 35801
    Telephone: 256-536-1711
    Fax: 256-518-3681
    E-Mail: huntsville@sirote.com
    www.sirote.com

(Birmingham, AL Office*: 2311 Highland Avenue South, 35205, P.O. Box 55727, 35255)
    (Tel: 205-930-5100)
    (Fax: 205-930-5101)
    (E-Mail: bham@sirote.com)
(Mobile, AL Office*: One St. Louis Centre, Suite 1000, 36602-3918, P.O. Drawer 2025, 36652)
    (Tel: 251-432-1671)
    (Fax: 251-434-0196)
    (E-Mail: mobile@sirote.com)
(Pensacola, FL Office: 1115 East Gonzalez Street, 32503)
    (Tel: 850-462-1500)
    (Fax: 850-462-1599)
(Fort Lauderdale, FL Office: 200 East Broward Boulevard, Suite 900, 33301)
    (Tel: 954-828-1100)
    (Fax: 954-828-1101)

Established: 1946

Insurance Defense, Life and Health, Casualty, Product Liability, Fire, Fraud, Surety

Firm Profile: Sirote & Permutt is at the forefront of the legal profession in Alabama and Florida, serving our clients with a full range of legal services of the highest quality, prepared in a fair and timely manner. For more than half a century this diverse team of professionals has cultivated a tradition of excellence, anticipating the needs of our clients and meeting those needs in new and innovative ways. Sirote & Permutt serves our clients with 125 attorneys in Birmingham, Huntsville and Mobile, Alabama and Fort Lauderdale and Pensacola, Florida.

Firm Members

John P. Burbach — Auburn University, B.S., 1981; The University of Alabama School of Law, J.D., 1984 — Admitted to Bar, 1984, Alabama — Member Huntsville-Madison County Bar Association — Practice Areas: Personal Injury; Workers' Compensation; Labor and Employment; Insurance Law; Civil Trial Practice; Municipal Law — Tel: 256-518-3677 — E-mail: jburbach@sirote.com

Julian D. Butler — The University of Alabama, B.S., 1961; The University of Alabama School of Law, LL.B., 1963 — Admitted to Bar, 1963, Alabama — Member American and Huntsville Bar Associations — Practice Areas: Labor and Employment — Tel: 256-518-3675 — E-mail: jbutler@sirote.com

(See listing under Birmingham, AL for additional information)

Wilmer & Lee, P.A.

100 Washington Street, Suite 200
Huntsville, Alabama 35801
    Telephone: 256-533-0202
    Fax: 256-533-0302
    E-Mail: info@wilmerlee.com
    www.wilmerandlee.com

(Athens, AL Office*: 315 West Market Street, 35611, P.O. Box 710, 35612)
    (Tel: 256-232-2010)
    (Fax: 256-230-0610)
    (E-Mail: wilmerlee@wilmerlee.com)

Wilmer & Lee, P.A., Huntsville, AL (Continued)

Insurance Defense, Commercial Law, Mediation, Employment Practices Liability, Workers' Compensation, Professional Liability, Errors and Omissions, Health Care, Construction Litigation, Insurance Coverage, Governmental and Civil Rights Litigation

Firm Profile: The present firm was founded in 1991 by partners from one of Huntsville's oldest law firms. In 2004 the firm merged with one of Athens, Alabama's oldest law firms, Patton, Legge & Cole. In 2007 Lawrence Weaver, a member of one of Decatur, Alabama's oldest law firms, joined the present firm and opened a Decatur, Alabama office. In March, 2010, four attorneys from Spurrier, Rice & Forbes, a Huntsville, Alabama firm whose insurance defense roots go back for over fifty years, joined the firm's insurance defense practice. Since its inception, Wilmer & Lee has grown to over 31 lawyers, and has four office locations, making it one of the largest firms in North Alabama. We offer a full array of legal services from a business and insurance focus, including litigation, corporate law, labor and employment, civil rights, banking and commercial law, insurance defense, workers' compensation, real estate law, government contracting, health care law, bankruptcy, trade secrets litigation, governmental relations, utility law and other emerging areas of the law.

We pride ourselves as being client-friendly and accountable. We believe that it is vitally important to have satisfied clients. To that end, the firm is committed to its goals of providing the highest quality legal services while controlling the costs of those services. Each of our firm's attorneys has demonstrated academic excellence and significant experience in a wide range of legal and business settings. Our firm's lawyers include: a past State Bar President, past and present Bar Examiners, past and present Bar Commissioners, former counsel to the Governor, former State Supreme Court and Federal Law Clerks, former Army Judge Advocate Attorneys, and former National Labor Relations Board counsel. Six of our attorneys have attained additional degrees, Master of Law degrees (L.L.M.s), in their areas of concentration.

The firm has attorneys that are licensed to practice law in Alabama, Tennessee, Mississippi and several other states. Additionally, the firm has attorneys admitted to practice in the United States Supreme Court, the United States Court of Federal Claims, the United States Tax Court, the United States Court of Appeals for the Armed Forces, the United States Court of Appeals for the Eleventh Circuit, the United States Court of Appeals for the Fifth Circuit, the United States Court of Appeals for the Sixth Circuit, and all United States District Courts in Alabama.

Insurance Clients

ACE USA	Alabama Municipal Insurance Corporation
Alfa Insurance Company	Assurance Company of America
American Modern Insurance Group, Inc.	Auto-Owners Insurance Company
Chubb Group of Insurance Companies	CNA Global Specialty Lines
	CNA Insurance Companies
Coastal Insurance Exchange	Cotton States Mutual Insurance Company
COUNTRY Mutual Insurance Company	CUMIS Insurance Society, Inc.
Federated Mutual Insurance Company	Fireman's Fund Insurance Company
General Casualty Insurance Company	General Star Management Company
GuideOne Insurance	The Harleysville Insurance
Lafayette Insurance Company	Liberty Mutual Insurance Company
Mercury Insurance Company	Nationwide Insurance
Nautilus Insurance Company	OneBeacon Insurance Group
St. Paul Travelers Insurance Companies	Sentry Insurance
	State Auto Insurance Company
State Farm Fire and Casualty Company	Tower Group Companies
	United Fire Group
Western Heritage Insurance	Zurich American Insurance Group
Zurich North America	

Non-Insurance Clients

Alabama Gas Corporation	Alabama Insurance Guaranty Association
Alabama Power Company	
Alabama Rural Water Association	Athens Industrial Development Board
Athens-Limestone Hospital	
AT&T	City of Huntsville
City of Madison	Costco
Energen Corporation	E & O Professionals
Ford Motor Credit Company	Huntsville Housing Authority
Inergy Propane, LLC	Limestone County Commission

ALABAMA

Wilmer & Lee, P.A., Huntsville, AL (Continued)

Limestone County Water and Sewer Authority
Specialty Risk Services, Inc. (SRS)
Owens Corning Corporation
Premier Insurance Adjusters, Inc.

Partners

John A. Wilmer — 1947 — The University of Alabama, B.S., 1969; Cumberland School of Law of Samford University, J.D., 1972; New York University, LL.M., 1973 — Legal Intern, National Labor Relations Board, 1971 — Admitted to Bar, 1973, Pennsylvania; 1986, Alabama; U.S. District Court, Northern District of Alabama; U.S. Court of Appeals, Eleventh Circuit; U.S. Supreme Court — Member American (Labor and Employment Law Section), Pennsylvania and Huntsville-Madison County Bar Associations; Alabama State Bar (Executive Committee, Labor and Employment Law Section, 1990-1991) — Equal Employment Opportunity Commission, 1969-1972; Attorney, National Labor Relations Board, 1973-1974; Labor Counsel: Combustion Engineering, Inc., 1975-1975, Gulton Industries, Inc., 1975-1981; Special Assistant Attorney General, Alabama, 1987-Present — Practice Areas: Labor and Employment; Civil Rights; Employment Discrimination

Robert V. Wood, Jr. — 1957 — Vanderbilt University, B.A., 1979; The University of Alabama School of Law, J.D., 1982 — Phi Delta Phi; Associate Justice, Honor Court — Admitted to Bar, 1982, Alabama; U.S. District Court, Northern District of Alabama; U.S. Supreme Court — Member Alabama State Bar; Huntsville-Madison County Bar Association; Alabama Defense Lawyers Association; Defense Research Institute — Practice Areas: Civil Litigation; Commercial Litigation; Construction Litigation; Professional Malpractice; Professional Errors and Omissions; Insurance Defense

Benjamin R. Rice — 1947 — Samford University, A.B., 1969; Cumberland School of Law of Samford University, J.D., 1972 — Admitted to Bar, 1973, Alabama; U.S. District Court, Northern District of Alabama; U.S. Supreme Court — Member Alabama State Bar; Huntsville-Madison County Bar Associations; Defense Research Institute; Alabama Defense Lawyers Association — Practice Areas: Civil Litigation; Commercial Litigation; Construction Litigation; Insurance Defense; Mediation; Professional Errors and Omissions; Professional Malpractice

LAFAYETTE † 3,234 Chambers Co.

Refer To

Rushton, Stakely, Johnston & Garrett, P.A.
184 Commerce Street
Montgomery, Alabama 36104
Telephone: 334-206-3100
Fax: 334-262-6277

Mailing Address: P.O. Box 270, Montgomery, AL 36101-0270

Insurance Defense, Trial and Appellate Practice, Accountants and Attorneys Liability, Administrative Law, Advertising Injury, Agent and Brokers Errors and Omissions, Appellate Practice, Arbitration, Automobile Tort, Bad Faith, Business Law, Casualty Insurance Law, Class Actions, Commercial Litigation, Complex Litigation, Construction Litigation, Contract Disputes, Copyright and Trademark Law, Coverage Analysis, Declaratory Judgments, Directors and Officers Liability, Employment Law, Environmental Law, Family Law, Fidelity and Surety, Fraud, Health Care, Health Care Professional Licensure Defense, Insurance Litigation, Labor and Employment, Law Enforcement Liability, Legal Malpractice, Medical Devices, Medical Malpractice, Pharmaceutical, Premises Liability, Primary and Excess Insurance, Product Liability, Professional Errors and Omissions, Professional Liability, Surety, Title Insurance, Uninsured and Underinsured Motorist, Workers' Compensation, Wrongful Death

SEE COMPLETE LISTING UNDER MONTGOMERY, ALABAMA (90 MILES)

LINDEN † 2,123 Marengo Co.

Refer To

Owens & Millsaps, LLP
Attorneys at Law
2606 8th Street
Tuscaloosa, Alabama 35401
Toll Free: 866-790-2889
Telephone: 205-750-0750
Telephone: 205-759-8582
Fax: 205-750-0355

Mailing Address: P.O. Box 2487, Tuscaloosa, AL 35403-2487

Insurance Defense, Medical Malpractice, Legal Malpractice, Dental Malpractice, Coverage Issues, Comprehensive General Liability, Product Liability, Construction Law, Employment Practices Liability, Environmental Liability

SEE COMPLETE LISTING UNDER TUSCALOOSA, ALABAMA (70 MILES)

LAFAYETTE

Refer To

Phelps, Jenkins, Gibson & Fowler, LLP
1201 Greensboro Avenue
Tuscaloosa, Alabama 35401
Telephone: 205-345-5100
Fax: 205-758-4394, 205-391-6658

Mailing Address: P.O. Box 020848, Tuscaloosa, AL 35402-0848

Employment Litigation, General Defense, Medical Malpractice, School Law, Workers' Compensation, Personal Injury

SEE COMPLETE LISTING UNDER TUSCALOOSA, ALABAMA (70 MILES)

LIVINGSTON † 3,485 Sumter Co.

Refer To

Owens & Millsaps, LLP
Attorneys at Law
2606 8th Street
Tuscaloosa, Alabama 35401
Toll Free: 866-790-2889
Telephone: 205-750-0750
Telephone: 205-759-8582
Fax: 205-750-0355

Mailing Address: P.O. Box 2487, Tuscaloosa, AL 35403-2487

Insurance Defense, Medical Malpractice, Legal Malpractice, Dental Malpractice, Coverage Issues, Comprehensive General Liability, Product Liability, Construction Law, Employment Practices Liability, Environmental Liability

SEE COMPLETE LISTING UNDER TUSCALOOSA, ALABAMA (62 MILES)

Refer To

Phelps, Jenkins, Gibson & Fowler, LLP
1201 Greensboro Avenue
Tuscaloosa, Alabama 35401
Telephone: 205-345-5100
Fax: 205-758-4394, 205-391-6658

Mailing Address: P.O. Box 020848, Tuscaloosa, AL 35402-0848

Employment Litigation, General Defense, Medical Malpractice, School Law, Workers' Compensation, Personal Injury

SEE COMPLETE LISTING UNDER TUSCALOOSA, ALABAMA (62 MILES)

MARION † 3,686 Perry Co.

Refer To

Phelps, Jenkins, Gibson & Fowler, LLP
1201 Greensboro Avenue
Tuscaloosa, Alabama 35401
Telephone: 205-345-5100
Fax: 205-758-4394, 205-391-6658

Mailing Address: P.O. Box 020848, Tuscaloosa, AL 35402-0848

Employment Litigation, General Defense, Medical Malpractice, School Law, Workers' Compensation, Personal Injury

SEE COMPLETE LISTING UNDER TUSCALOOSA, ALABAMA (58 MILES)

MOBILE † 195,111 Mobile Co.

Ball, Ball, Matthews & Novak, P.A.
107 Saint Francis Street, Suite 1590
Mobile, Alabama 36602
Telephone: 251-338-2721
Fax: 251-338-2722

Insurance Defense, Medical Malpractice, Aviation, Bad Faith, Personal Injury, Construction Litigation, Employment Law, Product Liability, Property, Pharmaceutical, Medical Devices, Complex Litigation, Governmental Entity Defense, Workers' Compensation, Mediation, Arbitration, Trial and Appellate Practice, State and Federal Courts, Insurance Coverage Analysis, Automobile Injury, Motor Carrier Defense

Ball, Ball, Matthews & Novak, P.A., Mobile, AL
(Continued)

Firm Members

William D. Montgomery, Jr. — 1975 — University of Montevallo, B.A. (cum laude), 1998; The University of Alabama, J.D., 2001 — Admitted to Bar, 2001, Alabama; 2002, Florida; U.S. District Court, Middle and Southern Districts of Alabama — Member Mobile and Baldwin County Bar Associations; Alabama Defense Lawyers Association; Defense Research Institute — Practice Areas: Personal Injury; Construction Litigation; Workers' Compensation; Transportation; Trucking Law — E-mail: monty@ball-ball.com

Benjamin Heinz — 1976 — Duke University, B.A., 1998; The University of Alabama, J.D., 2001 — Admitted to Bar, 2001, Alabama; Mississippi; U.S. District Court, Southern District of Alabama; U.S. District Court, Northern and Southern Districts of Mississippi — Practice Areas: Appellate Practice; Business Law; Insurance Law; Construction Law; Medical Malpractice; Real Estate — E-mail: bheinz@ball-ball.com

Associate

D. Kirby Howard, Jr. — The University of Alabama, B.A., 2003; Cumberland University School of Law, J.D., 2006 — Admitted to Bar, 2006, Alabama; U.S. District Court, Middle, Northern and Southern Districts of Alabama — Member American and Mobile Bar Associations; Alabama State Bar; Alabama Defense Lawyers Association (Young Lawyers Board of Directors) — Reported Cases: Tucker v. Wal-Mart Stores, Inc., 2012 Ala. Civ. App. LEXIS 33; Sconiers v. Wal-Mart Stores, Inc., 2011 U.S. Dist. LEXIS 74034 — Practice Areas: Insurance Defense; Premises Liability; Construction Defect; Insurance Coverage; Medical Malpractice — E-mail: khoward@ball-ball.com

(See listing under Montgomery, AL for additional information)

Cabaniss, Johnston, Gardner, Dumas & O'Neal, LLP

63 South Royal Street, Suite 700
Mobile, Alabama 36602
Telephone: 251-415-7300
Fax: 251-415-7350
E-Mail: info@cabaniss.com
www.cabaniss.com

(Birmingham, AL Office*: 2001 Park Place North, Suite 700, 35203, P.O. Box 830612, 35283-0612)
(Tel: 205-716-5200)
(Fax: 205-716-5389)

Established: 1887

Insurance Defense, Employment Law, Professional Liability, Personal Injury, Workers' Compensation, Environmental Law, Product Liability, Construction Law, Insurance Coverage, Complex Litigation, Admiralty and Maritime Law, Trial and Appellate Practice, State and Federal Courts

(See listing under Birmingham, AL for additional information)

Galloway, Johnson, Tompkins, Burr & Smith

56 St. Joseph Street, Suite 502
Mobile, Alabama 36602
Telephone: 251-438-7850
Fax: 251-438-7875
E-Mail: straweek@gallowayjohnson.com
www.gallowayjohnson.com

Galloway, Johnson, Tompkins, Burr & Smith, Mobile, AL
(Continued)

(Additional Offices: New Orleans, LA*; Lafayette, LA*; Pensacola, FL*; St. Louis, MO*; Houston, TX*; Mandeville, LA*; Gulfport, MS*; Tampa, FL*; Atlanta, GA*)

Maritime, Automobile Liability, Bad Faith, Class Actions, Construction, Energy, Employment, Insurance Coverage, Insurance Defense, Product Liability, Professional Liability, Property, Transportation, General Casualty, Title Resolution, Environmental

(See listing under New Orleans, LA for additional information)

Galloway, Wettermark, Everest & Rutens, LLP

3263 Cottage Hill Road
Mobile, Alabama 36606
Telephone: 251-476-4493
Fax: 251-479-5566
E-Mail: lawyers@gallowayllp.com

Established: 1953

Insurance Defense, Admiralty and Maritime Law, Casualty, Fire, Life Insurance, Surety, Workers' Compensation, Governmental Liability, Product Liability, Civil Rights, Commercial Litigation, Construction Law, Professional Liability, Trial and Appellate Practice, State and Federal Courts, Title VII Defense, Medical Liability

Insurance Clients

ACE/USA Insurance Company
Aetna Life and Casualty Company
Alfa Mutual Insurance Company
American Hardware Mutual Insurance Company
American National Property and Casualty Company
American States Insurance Company
Canadian Universal Insurance Company
Colonial Penn Insurance Company
Dairyland Insurance Company
Employers Insurance Company of Texas Group
Florida Farm Bureau General Insurance Company
Insurance Company of North America
J. C. Penney Casualty Insurance Company
Motors Insurance Corporation
Preferred Risk Insurance Company
Reliance Insurance Company
Southeastern Fidelity Insurance Company
Aetna Insurance Company
Alabama Municipal Insurance Corporation
American Liberty Life Insurance Company
American Southern Insurance Company
Atlanta Life Insurance Company
Auto-Owners Insurance Company
Chubb Group of Insurance Companies
Connecticut General Life Insurance Company
ESIS
Federated Guaranty Life Insurance Company
General Mutual Insurance Company
International Indemnity Company
Mississippi Farm Bureau Casualty Insurance Company
Occidental Fire & Casualty Company of North Carolina
Reserve Insurance Company

Non-Insurance Clients

City of Atmore
City of Saraland
Mobile Greyhound Park
City of Mobile
Mobile County

Partners

Thomas M. Galloway, Jr. — 1948 — The University of Alabama, B.S.C.E., 1970; The University of Alabama School of Law, J.D., 1973 — Admitted to Bar, 1973, Alabama — Member American and Mobile County Bar Associations; Alabama State Bar; Alabama Defense Lawyers Association; Federation of Defense and Corporate Counsel — E-mail: tgalloway@gallowayllp.com

Lawrence M. Wettermark — 1951 — University of Notre Dame, A.B., 1973; The University of Alabama School of Law, J.D., 1976 — Admitted to Bar, 1976, Alabama — Member American and Mobile County (Executive Committee) Bar Associations; Alabama State Bar — Atmore City Attorney — E-mail: lwettermark@gallowayllp.com

ALABAMA MOBILE

Galloway, Wettermark, Everest & Rutens, LLP, Mobile, AL (Continued)

Robert M. Galloway — 1951 — The University of Alabama, B.A., 1973; The University of Alabama School of Law, J.D., 1976; New York University, LL.M., 1977 — Phi Delta Phi; Bench and Bar — Admitted to Bar, 1976, Alabama — Member American and Mobile County Bar Associations; Alabama State Bar — E-mail: bgalloway@gallowayllp.com

Mark J. Everest — 1954 — University of South Alabama, B.A., 1975; The University of Alabama School of Law, J.D., 1978 — Admitted to Bar, 1978, Alabama — Member Alabama State Bar; Mobile County Bar Association; Alabama Defense Lawyers Association; Defense Research Institute — E-mail: meverest@gallowayllp.com

Andrew J. Rutens — 1966 — Florida State University, B.A., 1988; Cumberland School of Law of Samford University, J.D., 1992 — Admitted to Bar, 1992, Alabama; 1994, Florida; 1992, U.S. District Court, Southern District of Alabama; 1995, U.S. Court of Appeals, Eleventh Circuit; 1996, U.S. Supreme Court — Member The Florida Bar; Alabama State Bar; Mobile County Bar Association; Defense Research Institute — Saraland City Attorney — E-mail: arutens@gallowayllp.com

Associates

Alicia J. Corley — 1978 — Spring Hill College, B.A., 2000; Paul M Hebert Law School at Louisiana State University, J.D./B.C.L., 2003 — Admitted to Bar, 2003, Louisiana; 2007, Alabama — Member Louisiana State and Mobile County Bar Associations; Alabama State Bar; Defense Research Institute — E-mail: acorley@gallowayllp.com

J. Willis Garrett III — 1981 — Spring Hill College, B.A., 2004; The University of Alabama School of Law, J.D., 2007 — Admitted to Bar, 2007, Alabama; U.S. District Court, Southern District of Alabama — Member Alabama State Bar; Mobile County Bar Association — E-mail: jgarrett@gallowayllp.com

Melissa P. Hunter — 1982 — Birmingham-Southern College, B.A., 2005; The University of Alabama School of Law, 2008 — Admitted to Bar, 2008, Alabama — Member Alabama State Bar; Mobile County Bar Association — E-mail: mhunter@gallowayllp.com

Michael Gillion, P.C.

74 Midtown Park West, Suite 105
Mobile, Alabama 36606
  Telephone: 251-471-9494
  Fax: 251-471-1722
  Mobile: 251-510-9494
  E-Mail: mgillion@gillionlaw.com

Established: 1999

Insurance Defense, Automobile, Homeowners, Workers' Compensation, Subrogation, Insurance Contract and Coverage Litigation

Insurance Clients

Atlanta Casualty Company
Clarendon Insurance Company
Encompass Insurance
Infinity Insurance Company
Southern United Fire Insurance Company
Auto-Owners Insurance Company
CNA Insurance Company
The Hartford
Safeway Insurance Company
Zurich North America

Non-Insurance Clients

Cunningham Lindsey U.S., Inc.
Deep South Surplus, Inc.

Michael Gillion — 1946 — The University of Alabama, B.A., 1968; J.D., 1971 — Phi Alpha Delta — Admitted to Bar, 1971, Alabama; 1978, Florida; 1988, Mississippi; 1975, U.S. Supreme Court; U.S. District Court, Middle, Northern and Southern Districts of Alabama; U.S. District Court, Northern and Southern Districts of Mississippi; U.S. Court of Appeals, Fifth and Eleventh Circuits — Member American, Baldwin County, Jackson County and Mobile Bar Associations; Alabama State Bar; The Florida Bar; The Mississippi Bar; Mississippi Defense Lawyers Association — Practice Areas: Trial Practice — E-mail: mgillion@gillionlaw.com

(This firm is also listed in the Subrogation section of this directory)

Helmsing, Leach, Herlong, Newman & Rouse, P.C.

LaClede Building, Suite 2000
150 Government Street
Mobile, Alabama 36602
  Telephone: 251-432-5521
  Fax: 251-432-0633
  www.helmsinglaw.com

Established: 1976

Alternative Dispute Resolution, Appellate Practice, Arbitration, Automobile Liability, Aviation, Bad Faith, Bankruptcy, Business and Real Estate Transactions, Business Bankruptcy, Business Formation, Business Law, Business Litigation, Business Transactions, Captive Company Matters, Casualty Defense, Church Law, Civil Trial Practice, Commercial Litigation, Complex Litigation, Construction Defect, Construction Liability, Construction Litigation, Contract Disputes, Coverage Analysis, Coverage Issues, Creditor Rights, Defense Litigation, Directors and Officers Liability, Eminent Domain, Employment Law, Estate Planning, General Civil Trial and Appellate Practice, General Liability, Hospital Malpractice, Hospitals, Insurance Coverage, Insurance Defense, Insurance Litigation, Land Use, Legal Malpractice, Litigation, Malpractice, Medical Devices, Medical Liability, Medical Malpractice, Medical Negligence, Municipal Law, Pharmaceutical, Premises Liability, Probate, Product Liability, Professional Liability, Professional Malpractice, Professional Negligence, Property, Property and Casualty, Railroad Law, Real Estate, Real Property, Religious Institutions, Transactional Law, Wills, Wrongful Death

Firm Profile: As a full service firm of medium size, we combine the characteristics of a smaller firm's vigor and personality with the quality, capability and efficiency attributed to larger groups. Since 1976, we have been advisors and counselors to businesses, professionals, families, and individuals.

Insurance Clients

American National Property and Casualty Company
GEICO
State Farm Fire and Casualty Company
United States Aviation Underwriters, Inc.
Baldwin Mutual Insurance Company, Inc.
St. Paul Travelers
State Farm Mutual Automobile Insurance Company

Non-Insurance Clients

Alabama Power Company
Black & Decker (U.S.), Inc.
Cessna Aircraft Company
Emerson Electric Company
Florida Gas Transmission Co., LLC
Huttig Building Products, Inc.
International Paper Company
Johnson & Johnson
Matrixx Initiatives, Inc.
Mobile Infirmary Medical Center
Providence Hospital
Schlumberger Technologies, Inc.
Southern Cancer Center, P.C.
Union Pacific Railroad Company
Utilities Board of the City of Foley
Ascension Health
Brunswick Corporation
City of Foley, Alabama
Evonik Industries
GlaxoSmithKline
GreatAmerica Leasing Company
Infirmary Health Systems, Inc.
International Shipholding, Inc.
Keystone RV Company
MoBay Storage Hub, LLC
Parsons & Whittemore Enterprises Corp.
The Sherwin-Williams Company
Stihl Incorporated
University of Mobile
Wal-Mart Stores, Inc.

Third Party Administrators

Advocat, Inc./Diversicare Management Services
Western Litigation, Inc.
Littleton Group
Sedgwick CMS

Shareholders

T.K. Jackson, III — **Of Counsel** — Rice University; The University of Alabama, B.S., 1966; LL.B., 1967; LL.M. Taxation, 1983 — Admitted to Bar, 1983, Alabama — Member American Bar Association (Sections: Corporate, Banking and Business Law, Real Property, Probate and Trust Law, Natural

Helmsing, Leach, Herlong, Newman & Rouse, P.C., Mobile, AL (Continued)

Resources Law, Taxation); Alabama State Bar (Sections: Real Property, Probate and Trust; Chairman, Oil, Gas and Mineral Section, 1979-1989); Mobile County Bar Association; The Maritime Law Association of the United States

John N. Leach, Jr. — Of Counsel — 1941 — Vanderbilt University, B.A. (cum laude), 1963; University of Virginia, LL.B., 1966 — Law Clerk to U.S. District Judge Virgil Pittman, Southern District of Alabama, 1966-1968 — Admitted to Bar, 1966, Alabama; U.S. District Court, Southern District of Alabama; 1968, U.S. Court of Appeals, Fifth Circuit; 1975, U.S. District Court, Northern District of Alabama; 1981, U.S. Court of Appeals, Eleventh Circuit — Member American and Mobile County Bar Associations; Alabama State Bar; Fellow, American College of Trial Lawyers; Alabama Defense Lawyers Association; Defense Research Institute — E-mail: jnl@helmsinglaw.com

Warren C. Herlong, Jr. — 1948 — The University of Alabama, B.A., 1970; University of Edinburgh (Roman Law), 1989; University of Virginia, J.D., 1974 — Admitted to Bar, 1974, Alabama; U.S. District Court, Middle, Northern and Southern Districts of Alabama; U.S. Court of Appeals, Fifth and Eleventh Circuits; U.S. Court of Federal Claims; U.S. Supreme Court — Member American (Section on Litigation), Mobile County and Baldwin County Bar Associations; Alabama State Bar; International Right-of-Way Association; Owner's Council of America; Alabama Defense Lawyers Association — E-mail: wch@helmsinglaw.com

James B. Newman — 1948 — Vanderbilt University, B.A., 1970; Cumberland University School of Law, J.D. (magna cum laude), 1976 — Law Clerk to U.S. District Judge W. Brevard Hand, 1976-1977 — Managing Editor, Cumberland Law Review, 1975-1976 — Admitted to Bar, 1976, Alabama; 1977, U.S. District Court, Middle, Northern and Southern Districts of Alabama; U.S. Court of Appeals, Fifth and Eleventh Circuits; U.S. District Court, Northern District of Florida — Member American and Mobile County Bar Associations; Alabama State Bar (President, Litigation Section, 1999); Alabama Defense Lawyers Association (Past Director); Defense Research Institute — E-mail: jbn@helmsinglaw.com

Robert H. Rouse — 1955 — Louisiana State University, B.A., 1977; The University of Alabama, J.D., 1980; New York University, LL.M., 1981 — Admitted to Bar, 1980, Alabama; 1981, U.S. District Court, Southern District of Alabama; U.S. Tax Court — Member American and Mobile County Bar Associations; Alabama State Bar — E-mail: rhr@helmsinglaw.com

Joseph P. H. Babington — 1959 — University of Notre Dame, B.A. (with highest honors), 1981; University of Virginia, J.D., 1984 — Phi Beta Kappa — Admitted to Bar, 1984, Louisiana; 1988, Alabama; 1984, U.S. District Court, Eastern District of Louisiana; 1985, U.S. Court of Appeals, Fifth Circuit; 1987, U.S. District Court, Middle and Western Districts of Louisiana; 1988, U.S. District Court, Southern District of Alabama; 1991, U.S. Court of Appeals, Eleventh Circuit; 1994, U.S. District Court, Middle and Northern Districts of Alabama; 1998, U.S. Supreme Court — Member American, Louisiana State and Mobile County Bar Associations; Alabama State Bar; Alabama Defense Lawyers Association (Board of Directors, Young Lawyers Section); Chairman, Annual Trial Academy, 1990-1995; Louisiana Association of Defense Counsel; Defense Research Institute; Trial Attorneys of America — E-mail: jpb@helmsinglaw.com

R. Alan Alexander — 1956 — University of South Alabama, B.S., 1978; Samford University, J.D., 1984 — Delta Theta Phi — Associate Editor, American Journal of Trial Advocacy — Admitted to Bar, 1984, Alabama; 1984, U.S. District Court, Middle and Southern Districts of Alabama; 1984, U.S. District Court, Northern District of Alabama; 2004, U.S. Supreme Court — Member American and Mobile (Ethics and Inter-professional Relations Committees, 1984-present) Bar Associations; Alabama State Bar (Disciplinary Rules Committee, 1997, 1984-present); Defense Research Institute (Medical Malpractice Committee, 1985-present); Alabama Defense Lawyers Association (Chairman, Personal Injury Section; President, 2006-2007, 1985-present); American Health Lawyers Association (1996-present); International Association of Defense Counsel — E-mail: raa@helmsinglaw.com

John T. Dukes — 1969 — Washington and Lee University, B.A. (cum laude), 1991; The University of Alabama, J.D. (cum laude), 1994 — Farrah Law Society — Alabama Law Review — Admitted to Bar, 1994, Alabama; U.S. District Court, Middle, Northern and Southern Districts of Alabama; U.S. Court of Appeals, Eleventh Circuit; U.S. Supreme Court — Member American and Mobile County Bar Associations; Alabama State Bar — E-mail: jtd@helmsinglaw.com

Jeffery J. Hartley — 1964 — Spring Hill College, B.S., 1987; The University of Alabama, J.D., 1990 — Admitted to Bar, 1990, Alabama; U.S. District Court, Middle, Northern and Southern Districts of Alabama; U.S. Court of Appeals, Eleventh Circuit — Member American and Mobile County Bar Associations; State Bar of Alabama; American Bankruptcy Institute; National

Helmsing, Leach, Herlong, Newman & Rouse, P.C., Mobile, AL (Continued)

Association of Chapter 13 Trustees; Federal Panel of Neutrals, Southern District of Alabama — E-mail: jjh@helmsinglaw.com

J. Casey Pipes — 1971 — Washington and Lee University, B.A., 1993; The University of Alabama, J.D. (cum laude), 1996 — Admitted to Bar, 1996, Alabama; U.S. District Court, Middle, Northern and Southern Districts of Alabama; U.S. Court of Appeals, Eleventh Circuit — Member American, Baldwin and Mobile County Bar Associations; Alabama Association of Municipal Attorneys; International Right-of-Way Association — E-mail: jcp@helmsinglaw.com

Russell C. Buffkin — 1969 — Spring Hill College, B.S., 1992; M.B.A., 1996; The University of Alabama, J.D. (cum laude), 1999 — Admitted to Bar, 1999, Alabama; U.S. District Court, Middle, Northern and Southern Districts of Alabama; 2000, U.S. Court of Appeals, Eleventh Circuit — Member American and Mobile Bar Associations; Alabama State Bar (Board of Directories, Young Lawyers Section); Alabama Defense Lawyers Association; Defense Research Institute; International Association of Defense Counsel; Trial Attorneys of America — E-mail: rcb@helmsinglaw.com

Patrick C. Finnegan — 1962 — National University of Ireland, Galway, B.S., 1983; Queens College of the City University of New York, B.S., 1990; Fordham University, J.D., 1995 — Admitted to Bar, 1995, New York; 2003, Alabama; U.S. District Court, Middle, Northern and Southern Districts of Alabama; U.S. District Court, Eastern and Southern Districts of New York; U.S. Court of Appeals, Eleventh Circuit — Member American, New York State and Mobile County Bar Associations; Alabama State Bar; Alabama Defense Lawyers Association — E-mail: pcf@helmsinglaw.com

A. Edwin Stuardi, III — 1968 — Spring Hill College, B.S., 1990; Loyola University, J.D., 1994 — Admitted to Bar, 1994, Alabama; 1997, Mississippi; U.S. District Court, Northern and Southern Districts of Mississippi; U.S. District Court, Middle, Northern and Southern Districts of Alabama; U.S. Court of Appeals, Fifth Circuit — Member Alabama State Bar; The Mississippi Bar; Mobile County Bar Association — E-mail: aes@helmsinglaw.com

Christopher T. Conte — 1977 — University of South Alabama, B.A. (with honors), 1999; Samford University, J.D. (with honors), 2003 — Admitted to Bar, 2003, Alabama; 2004, Mississippi; U.S. District Court, Middle, Northern and Southern Districts of Alabama; U.S. District Court, Northern and Southern Districts of Mississippi — Member American and Mobile Bar Associations; Alabama State Bar; The Mississippi Bar; Alabama Defense Lawyers Association — E-mail: ctc@helmsinglaw.com

Leslie G. Weeks — 1971 — The University of Alabama, B.A., 1994; J.D. (cum laude), 1999; New York University, LL.M., 2000 — Admitted to Bar, 1999, Florida; Alabama; U.S. District Court, Southern District of Alabama — Member American Bar Association; The Florida Bar; Alabama State Bar — E-mail: lgw@helmsinglaw.com

Thomas Ryan Luna — 1978 — Lambuth University, B.S., 2000; Samford University, J.D., 2002 — Admitted to Bar, 2003, Alabama; U.S. District Court, Middle, Northern and Southern Districts of Alabama — Member Alabama State Bar; Mobile Bar Association; Alabama Defense Lawyers Association; Defense Research Institute — E-mail: trl@helmsinglaw.com

Associate

Samuel C. Rosten — 1986 — Hampden-Sydney College, B.A. (summa cum laude), 2009; The University of Alabama School of Law, J.D. (cum laude), 2012 — Admitted to Bar, 2012, Alabama; 2013, U.S. District Court, Middle, Northern and Southern Districts of Alabama; U.S. Court of Federal Claims — E-mail: scr@helmsinglaw.com

Holtsford Gilliland Higgins Hitson & Howard, P.C.

29000 U.S. Highway 98, Suite A-302
Daphne, Alabama 36526-7263
 Telephone: 251-447-0234
 Fax: 251-447-0212
 E-Mail: info@hglawpc.com
 www.hglawpc.com

(Montgomery, AL Office*: 4001 Carmichael Road, Suite 300, 36106, P.O. Box 4128, 36103-4128)
 (Tel: 334-215-8585)
 (Toll Free: 800-932-6964)
 (Fax: 334-215-7101)

ALABAMA   MOBILE

Holtsford Gilliland Higgins Hitson & Howard, P.C., Mobile, AL (Continued)

Insurance Defense, Automobile, Professional Liability, Product Liability, Civil Rights, Toxic Torts, General Liability, Environmental Law, Workers' Compensation, Construction Law, Governmental Entity Defense

Firm Members & Associates

Kenneth A. Hitson, Jr. — 1964 — The University of Alabama, B.A., 1986; Cumberland School of Law of Samford University, J.D., 1989 — Phi Alpha Delta — Law Clerk to the Honorable H. Randall Thomas, Circuit Judge, Fifteenth Judicial Circuit of Alabama — Admitted to Bar, 1989, Alabama; U.S. District Court, Middle and Southern Districts of Alabama — Member Alabama State Bar; Montgomery County Bar Association; Alabama District Attorneys Association; Alabama Defense Lawyers Association; Defense Research Institute — E-mail: khitson@hglawpc.com

Steven P. Savarese, Jr. — The University of Alabama, B.S. (with special honors), 2003; The University of Alabama School of Law, J.D., 2006 — Admitted to Bar, 2006, Alabama; Florida; Mississippi; U.S. District Court, Northern and Southern Districts of Alabama; U.S. District Court, Southern District of Mississippi — Member Alabama State Bar; Mobile County (Executive Committee, Young Lawyers' Section; Bench & Bar Committee) and Baldwin County (Volunteer Lawyer Program) Bar Associations; Alabama Defense Lawyers Association — E-mail: ssavarese@hglawpc.com

(See listing under Montgomery, AL for additional information)

Johnstone Adams, L.L.C.

One St. Louis Centre
1 St. Louis Street, Suite 4000
Mobile, Alabama 36602
Telephone: 251-432-7682
Fax: 251-432-2800
www.Johnstoneadams.com

(Bay Minette, AL Office*: Dahlberg Building, 104 Hand Avenue, P.O. Box 729, 36507)
(Tel: 251-937-9473)
(Fax: 251-937-9475)
(www.JohnstoneAdams.com)
(Birmingham, AL Office*: 2020 Canyon Road, Suite 100, 35216)
(Tel: 205-871-7733)
(Fax: 205-871-7387)
(www.JohnstoneAdams.com)

Established: 1897

Insurance Defense, Admiralty and Maritime Law, Automobile, Aviation, Bad Faith, Casualty, Construction Litigation, Employer Liability, ERISA, Fire, Fraud, Health, Life Insurance, Product Liability, Professional Liability, Surety, Workers' Compensation, Co-Employee

Firm Profile: For more than a century, the firm has evolved with the changing times from generalists to lawyers with concentrated areas of practice, and it continues to represent many clients whom it has served for the majority of that period.

Insurance Clients

Alabama Insurance Guaranty Association
American Mutual Liability Insurance Company
Auto-Owners Insurance Company
Avizent
Banner Life Insurance Company
Chicago Insurance Company
Chicago Title Insurance Company
Combined Insurance Company of America
Connecticut General Life Insurance Company
Allstate Life Insurance Company
American Interstate Insurance Company
American Pioneer Life Insurance Company
AXIS Pro
Benefit Trust Life Insurance Company
Cincinnati Insurance Company
Commonwealth Life Insurance Company
EMC Insurance Company
Essex Insurance Company

Johnstone Adams, L.L.C., Mobile, AL (Continued)

Farmers Mutual Exchange
Fireman's Fund Insurance Company
General Accident Group
Globe Life and Accident Insurance Company
The Guardian Life Insurance Company of America
The Hartford Insurance Group
Imperial Casualty and Indemnity Company
John Hancock Life Insurance Company
Life Insurance Company of Virginia
Lincoln National Life Insurance Company
Metropolitan Property and Casualty Insurance Company
Minnesota Life Insurance Company
Mutual Benefit Life Insurance Company
National Standard Life Insurance Company
New England Mutual Life Insurance Company
Northeastern Fire Insurance Company of Pennsylvania
Old Republic National Title Insurance Company
Pacific Mutual Insurance Company
PACO Assurance Company, Inc.
Penn National Insurance Company
Peter J. McBreen & Associates, Inc.
Puritan Life Insurance Company
St. Paul Travelers Insurance Companies
Shipowners' Mutual Protection & Indemnity Association
Standard Steamship Owners Protection & Indemnity Association
Transamerica Group/AEGON USA, Inc.
USAA Insurance Company
U.S. Risk Insurance Group, Inc.
World Insurance Company
Zurich Insurance Company
Federal Insurance Company
First Specialty Insurance Corporation
George Washington Life Insurance Company
Gray & Company
Hanover Insurance Company
Harleysville Insurance Company
Hartford Life Insurance Company
Integon Life Insurance Corporation
J. C. Penney Life Insurance
Kemper Insurance Companies
Life Investors Insurance Company of America
Meadowbrook Insurance Group
Metropolitan Life Insurance Company
Midland National Life Insurance Company
Mississippi Valley Title Insurance Company
Mutual Savings Life Insurance Company
The Netherlands Insurance Company
New York Life Insurance Company
The Northwestern Mutual Life Insurance Company
Pacific Employers Insurance Company
Penn Mutual Life Insurance Company
Phoenix Life Insurance Company
Professional Claims Managers, Inc.
Royal Insurance Group
Security Insurance Company of Hartford
Springfield Life Insurance Company, Inc.
State Auto Insurance Companies
State Mutual Life Assurance Company
Transport Indemnity Company
Travelers Property Casualty Corporation
West of England Ship Owners Mutual Insurance Association (Luxembourg)

Non-Insurance Clients

ExxonMobil Corporation
Orion Capital Companies
Transport Agency, Inc.
John L. McWhorter & Associates, Inc.

Firm Members

Ben H. Harris, Jr. — 1937 — Davidson College, A.B., 1959; The University of Alabama, J.D., 1962 — Admitted to Bar, 1962, Alabama; U.S. Court of Appeals, Fifth and Eleventh Circuits; U.S. Supreme Court — Member American (Board of Governors, 1992-1994) and Mobile Bar Associations; Alabama State Bar (President, 1987-1988); Alabama Judicial Conference (1988-1991); Fellow, American Bar Foundation; Alabama Defense Lawyers Association; Defense Research Institute — Practice Areas: Civil Litigation; Workers' Compensation

William H. Hardie, Jr. — 1938 — Yale University, B.E., 1959; University of Virginia, LL.B., 1963 — Admitted to Bar, 1963, Virginia; 1964, New York; 1966, Alabama; U.S. Court of Appeals, Second, Fifth and Eleventh Circuits; U.S. Supreme Court — Member American, Virginia, New York State and Mobile Bar Associations; Alabama State Bar; Defense Research Institute — Practice Areas: Arbitration; Civil Litigation; Product Liability; Insurance Coverage Litigation

I. David Cherniak — 1942 — The University of North Carolina; The University of Alabama, A.B., 1963; LL.B., 1965 — Admitted to Bar, 1965, Alabama; U.S. Court of Appeals, Fifth, Seventh and Eleventh Circuits — Member American (Forum on the Construction Industry) and Mobile Bar Associations; Alabama State Bar; American Arbitration Association — Practice Areas: Construction Law; Real Estate; Bankruptcy; Civil Litigation

Wade B. Perry, Jr — 1946 — Davidson College, A.B., 1968; Vanderbilt University, J.D., 1971 — Admitted to Bar, 1971, Alabama; U.S. Court of Appeals, Fifth and Eleventh Circuits — Member American and Mobile Bar

MOBILE — ALABAMA

Johnstone Adams, L.L.C., Mobile, AL (Continued)

Associations; American Health Lawyers Association; Alabama Defense Lawyers Association; Defense Research Institute — Assistant U.S. Attorney, Middle District of Alabama (1971-1975) — Practice Areas: Health Care; Hospitals; Insurance Law; Employment Law; Civil Litigation

Alan C. Christian — 1955 — The University of Alabama, B.A., 1977; J.D., 1979 — Admitted to Bar, 1980, Alabama; U.S. Court of Appeals, Fifth and Eleventh Circuits; U.S. Claims Court; U.S. Supreme Court; U.S. Tax Court — Member American and Mobile Bar Associations; Alabama State Bar; The Maritime Law Association of the United States; Southeastern Admiralty Law Institute — Practice Areas: Civil Litigation; Environmental Law; Banking; Oil and Gas; Admiralty and Maritime Law

Celia J. Collins — 1954 — Reading University; Randolph-Macon Woman's College, B.A., 1977; Vanderbilt University, J.D., 1980 — Admitted to Bar, 1980, Alabama; U.S. Court of Appeals, Fifth and Eleventh Circuits — Member American and Mobile Bar Associations; Alabama State Bar (Vice President, Board of Bar Commissioners, 2003-2004); Alabama Defense Lawyers Association; Defense Research Institute — Practice Areas: Employment Law; Workers' Compensation; Civil Litigation

R. Gregory Watts — 1954 — University of Notre Dame, B.A., 1976; The University of Alabama, J.D., 1979; Emory University, LL.M., 1981 — Phi Beta Kappa — Admitted to Bar, 1979, Alabama; U.S. Court of Appeals, Eleventh Circuit; U.S. Tax Court — Member American and Mobile Bar Associations; Alabama State Bar — Practice Areas: Probate; Estate Planning; Corporate Law; Commercial Law

Charles C. Simpson, III — 1950 — Duke University, A.B., 1972; The University of Alabama, J.D., 1979 — Order of the Coif — Admitted to Bar, 1979, Alabama; U.S. Court of Appeals, Eleventh Circuit — Member American and Baldwin County (President, 1988-1989) Bar Associations; Alabama State Bar; Alabama Defense Lawyers Association; Defense Research Institute — Practice Areas: Business Litigation; Insurance Litigation; Arbitration; Real Estate Litigation; Business and Real Estate Transactions; Title Insurance

Tracy P. Turner — 1963 — Auburn University, B.S.B.A. (magna cum laude), 1985; The University of Alabama, J.D., 1989 — Order of the Coif — Law Clerk to U.S. District Judge W. Brevard Hand, Southern District of Alabama, 1989-1991 — Admitted to Bar, 1989, Alabama; U.S. District Court, Northern and Southern Districts of Alabama; U.S. Court of Appeals, Eleventh Circuit — Member Defense Research Institute — Practice Areas: Civil Litigation; Labor and Employment; Workers' Compensation; Insurance Defense; Municipal Law

Lawrence J. Seiter — 1964 — Louisiana State University, B.A., 1987; J.D., 1991 — Phi Kappa Phi; Order of the Coif — Admitted to Bar, 1991, Alabama; U.S. District Court, Middle, Northern and Southern Districts of Alabama; U.S. Court of Appeals, Eleventh Circuit; U.S. Supreme Court — Member American and Mobile Bar Associations; Alabama State Bar; Defense Research Institute — Practice Areas: Civil Litigation; Commercial Litigation; Construction Litigation; Insurance Law; Workers' Compensation

E. Russell March, III — 1967 — Birmingham-Southern College, B.A., 1989; Samford University, J.D., 1993 — Admitted to Bar, 1993, Alabama; U.S. District Court, Middle, Northern and Southern Districts of Alabama; U.S. Court of Appeals, Eleventh Circuit — Member American and Mobile Bar Associations; Alabama State Bar — Practice Areas: Civil Litigation; Commercial Law; Bankruptcy; Creditor Rights; Guardian and Conservatorships; Copyright and Trademark Law

Rick A. LaTrace — 1972 — Saint Louis University, B.A./B.A. (summa cum laude), 1997; Illinois Institute of Technology, Chicago-Kent College of Law, J.D. (with honors), 2002 — Phi Beta Kappa — Admitted to Bar, 2002, Alabama; 2003, Florida; 2003, Mississippi; U.S. District Court, Middle, Northern and Southern Districts of Alabama; U.S. District Court, Northern District of Florida; U.S. District Court, Northern and Southern Districts of Mississippi; U.S. Court of Appeals, Fifth and Eleventh Circuits — Member American and Mobile Bar Associations; Alabama State Bar; American Immigration Lawyers Association; Defense Research Institute — Practice Areas: Immigration Law; Commercial Litigation; Landlord and Tenant Law; Real Estate

Associates

Spencer H. Larche — 1983 — Spring Hill College, B.S. (summa cum laude), 2005; Marquette University Law School, J.D. (magna cum laude), 2008 — Admitted to Bar, 2008, Wisconsin; 2012, Alabama; U.S. District Court, Eastern District of Wisconsin; U.S. Court of Appeals, Seventh Circuit — Member American and Mobile Bar Associations; State Bar of Wisconsin; American Immigration Lawyers Association; American Health Lawyers Association — Practice Areas: Business Law; Corporate Law; Health Care; Banking; Real Estate; Business and Real Estate Transactions

Emily A. Crow — 1988 — The University of Alabama, B.A. (Phi Beta Kappa, summa cum laude), 2010; The University of Alabama School of Law, J.D.,

Johnstone Adams, L.L.C., Mobile, AL (Continued)

2013 — Admitted to Bar, 2013, Alabama — Member American Bar Association; Alabama State Bar; Alabama Defense Lawyers Association — Practice Areas: Civil Litigation

Jessica L. Welch — 1987 — Spring Hill College, B.S. (summa cum laude), 2008; The University of Alabama School of Law, J.D., 2011; Georgetown University Law Center, LL.M. Taxation, 2012 — Admitted to Bar, 2011, Alabama; U.S. District Court, Southern District of Alabama — Member American and Mobile Bar Associations; Alabama State Bar — Practice Areas: Estate and Tax Planning; Civil Litigation

Of Counsel

Charles B. Bailey, Jr. — 1929 — Sewanee, The University of the South, B.A., 1951; University of Virginia; The University of Alabama, LL.B., 1954; New York University, LL.M., 1957 — Admitted to Bar, 1954, Alabama — Member American and Mobile Bar Associations; Alabama State Bar; American College of Real Estate Lawyers — Practice Areas: Real Property; Probate; Trusts

E. Watson Smith — 1940 — Auburn University, B.S., 1962; Duke University, LL.B., 1965; New York University, LL.M., 1968 — Admitted to Bar, 1965, Alabama; U.S. Supreme Court; U.S. Tax Court; U.S. Court of Appeals, Eleventh Circuit — Member American and Mobile Bar Associations; Alabama State Bar; American Health Lawyers Association — Practice Areas: Corporate Law; Employee Benefits; ERISA; Health Care; Hospitals

Jones Walker LLP

RSA Battle House Tower
11 North Water Street, Suite 1200
Mobile, Alabama 36602
  Telephone: 251-432-1414
  Fax: 251-433-4106
  E-Mail: info@joneswalker.com
  www.joneswalker.com

(New Orleans, LA Office*: 201 St. Charles Avenue, 70170-5100)
  (Tel: 504-582-8000)
  (Fax: 504-582-8583)
(Baton Rouge, LA Office*: Four United Plaza, 8555 United Plaza Boulevard, 70809)
  (Tel: 225-248-2000)
  (Fax: 225-248-2010)
(Lafayette, LA Office*: 600 Jefferson Street, Suite 1600, 70501)
  (Tel: 337-593-7600)
  (Fax: 337-593-7601)
(Birmingham, AL Office*: One Federal Place, 1819 5th Avenue North, Suite 1100, 35203)
  (Tel: 205-244-5200)
  (Fax: 205-244-5400)
(Jackson, MS Office*: 190 East Capitol Street, Suite 800, 39201, P.O. Box 427, 39205-0427)
  (Tel: 601-949-4900)
  (Fax: 601-949-4804)
(Olive Branch, MS Office*: 6897 Crumpler Boulevard, Suite 100, 38654)
  (Tel: 662-895-2996)
  (Fax: 662-895-5480)

Accountants, Admiralty and Maritime Law, Agent/Broker Liability, Antitrust, Appellate Practice, Asbestos Litigation, Aviation, Bankruptcy, Cargo, Class Actions, Commercial Litigation, Complex Litigation, Construction Law, Contracts, Directors and Officers Liability, Disability, Employment Law, Energy, Entertainment Law, Environmental Law, ERISA, Errors and Omissions, Health Care, Insurance Coverage, Insurance Defense, Intellectual Property, International Law, Labor and Employment, Life Insurance, Medical Malpractice, Mergers and Acquisitions, Motor Carriers, Oil and Gas, Personal Injury, Product Liability, Professional Liability, Regulatory and Compliance, Toxic Torts, Workers' Compensation

Firm Profile: Since 1937, Jones Walker LLP has grown to become one of the largest law firms in the southeastern U.S. We serve local, regional, national, and international business interests in a wide range of markets and industries. Today, we have more than 375 attorneys in 19 offices.

ALABAMA — MOBILE

Jones Walker LLP, Mobile, AL (Continued)

Jones Walker is committed to providing proactive legal services to major multinational, public, and private corporations; *Fortune 500®* companies; money center banks and worldwide insurers; and family and emerging businesses located in the United States and abroad.

Firm Members

Ben H. Harris, III — The University of the South, B.A., 1986; The University of Alabama School of Law, J.D., 1989 — Order of the Coif — Admitted to Bar, 1989, Alabama; 1991, District of Columbia; 2007, Florida; Texas — Member The District of Columbia Bar; Alabama State Bar; The Florida Bar; State Bar of Texas — E-mail: bharris@joneswalker.com

James Rebarchak — Spring Hill College, B.S. (cum laude), 1977; The University of Alabama School of Law, J.D., 1982 — Admitted to Bar, 1982, Alabama; 2004, Mississippi; 1982, U.S. District Court, Middle, Northern and Southern Districts of Alabama; 2004, U.S. District Court, Northern and Southern Districts of Mississippi; U.S. Court of Appeals, Fifth and Eleventh Circuits; U.S. Supreme Court — Member American (Labor and Employment Law and Litigation Sections) and Mobile Bar Associations; Alabama State Bar; The Mississippi Bar; Alabama Defense Lawyers Association; Alabama Workers' Compensation Claims Association; Defense Research Institute; National Association of Railroad Trial Counsel — E-mail: jrebarchak@joneswalker.com

(See Listing under New Orleans, LA for a List of Firm Clients and Additional Information)

Matthews, Higgins, Hausfeld & Fenimore

910 Government Street
Mobile, Alabama 36604
 Telephone: 251-434-6711
 Fax: 850-434-2600
 www.matthewshigginslaw.com

(Pensacola, FL Office*: 114 East Gregory Street, 32502-4970, P.O. Box 13145, 32591-3145)
 (Tel: 850-434-2200)
 (Fax: 850-434-2600)
 (E-Mail: lmatthews@matthewshigginslaw.com)
(Panama City, FL Office*: 475 Harrison Avenue, Suite 200, 32401)
 (Tel: 850-769-7200)
 (Fax: 850-434-2600)

Established: 2011

Personal Injury, Wrongful Death, Defense Litigation, Insurance Coverage, Commercial Litigation, Automobile Liability, Premises Liability, Product Liability, Professional Malpractice, Subrogation, Employment Law, Bad Faith, Casualty Defense, Real Estate Litigation, Construction Litigation, Directors and Officers Liability, Insurance Defense, Mediation, Condominium Litigation

Managing Shareholder

Larry A. Matthews — 1954 — University of Florida, B.S. (with honors), 1976; Florida State University, J.D. (with honors), 1981 — Admitted to Bar, 1982, Florida; 1994, Alabama; 1982, U.S. District Court, Middle and Northern Districts of Florida; 1994, U.S. Court of Appeals, Eleventh Circuit; 1998, U.S. Supreme Court — Member The Florida Bar; Alabama State Bar; Florida Defense Lawyers Association; American Board of Trial Advocates; American Inns of Court — Florida Bar Board Certified Civil Trial Lawyer; Certified Circuit Court Mediator; Certified Public Accountant (Inactive) — E-mail: lmatthews@matthewshigginslaw.com

Shareholders

Raymond F. Higgins III — 1957 — Virginia Military Institute, B.S. (with distinction), 1979; Florida State University, J.D. (with honors), 1998 — Admitted to Bar, 1998, Florida; U.S. District Court, Northern District of Florida — Member The Florida Bar; Escambia/Santa Rosa Bar Association — E-mail: rhiggins@matthewshigginslaw.com

M. Kevin Hausfeld — 1972 — University of West Florida, B.S. (magna cum laude), 1998; University of Florida College of Law, J.D. (with honors), 2004 — Admitted to Bar, 2005, Florida; 2009, Alabama; U.S. District Court,

Matthews, Higgins, Hausfeld & Fenimore, Mobile, AL (Continued)

Northern District of Florida — Member The Florida Bar; Alabama State Bar; Florida Justice Association; Million Dollar Advocates Forum — E-mail: khausfeld@matthewshigginslaw.com

Michael Fenimore — 1978 — University of Florida, B.S. (with honors), 2001; Saint Louis University School of Law, J.D., 2005 — Admitted to Bar, 2005, Florida; 2006, Missouri; U.S. District Court, Northern District of Florida — Member Escambia-Santa Rosa County (Young Lawyers' Division) and Pensacola (Young Professionals) Bar Assocaitions — E-mail: mfenimore@matthewshigginslaw.com

Firm Member

Thomas R. Jenkins — 1949 — Eastern Illinois University, B.S. (with honors), 1975; M.B.A., 1979; Florida State University, J.D. (with high honors), 1982 — Phi Delta Phi; Order of Coif — Admitted to Bar, 1982, Florida; 1994, Alabama; 1982, U.S. District Court, Middle and Northern Districts of Florida; 1983, U.S. Court of Appeals, Eleventh Circuit — Member The Florida Bar; Alabama State Bar; Florida Defense Lawyers Association — Florida Bar Board Certified Civil Trial Lawyer; Certified Circuit Court Mediator

(See listing under Pensacola, FL for additional information)

Phelps Dunbar LLP

2 North Royal Street
Mobile, Alabama 36602
 Telephone: 251-432-4481
 Fax: 251-433-1820
 E-Mail: info@phelps.com
 www.phelpsdunbar.com

(New Orleans, LA Office*: Canal Place, 365 Canal Street, Suite 2000, 70130-6534)
 (Tel: 504-566-1311)
 (Fax: 504-568-9130)
(Baton Rouge, LA Office*: II City Plaza, 400 Convention Street, Suite 1100, 70802-5618, P.O. Box 4412, 70821-4412)
 (Tel: 225-346-0285)
 (Fax: 225-381-9197)
(Jackson, MS Office*: 4270 I-55 North, 39211-6391, P.O. Box 16114, 39236-6114)
 (Tel: 601-352-2300)
 (Fax: 601-360-9777)
(Tupelo, MS Office*: One Mississippi Plaza, 201 South Spring Street, Seventh Floor, 38804, P.O. Box 1220, 38802-1220)
 (Tel: 662-842-7907)
 (Fax: 662-842-3873)
(Gulfport, MS Office*: NorthCourt One, 2304 19th Street, Suite 300, 39501)
 (Tel: 228-679-1130)
 (Fax: 228-679-1131)
(Houston, TX Office*: One Allen Center, 500 Dallas Street, Suite 1300, 77002)
 (Tel: 713-626-1386)
 (Fax: 713-626-1388)
(Tampa, FL Office*: 100 South Ashley Drive, Suite 1900, 33602-5311)
 (Tel: 813-472-7550)
 (Fax: 813-472-7570)
(London, United Kingdom Office*: Lloyd's, Suite 725, Level 7, 1 Lime Street, EC3M 7DQ)
 (Tel: 011-44-207-929-4765)
 (Fax: 011-44-207-929-0046)
(Raleigh, NC Office*: 4140 Parklake Avenue, Suite 100, 27612-3723)
 (Tel: 919-789-5300)
 (Fax: 919-789-5301)
(Southlake, TX Office*(See Dallas listing): 115 Grand Avenue, Suite 222, 76092)
 (Tel: 817-488-3134)
 (Fax: 817-488-3214)

Insurance Law

MOBILE — ALABAMA

Phelps Dunbar LLP, Mobile, AL (Continued)

Insurance Clients

Acceptance Casualty Insurance Company
Aegis Janson Green Insurance Services Inc.
AIG
Columbus
Alabama Municipal Insurance Corporation
AmTrust Underwriters, Inc.
Arch Insurance Company (Europe) Ltd.
Aspen Insurance UK Limited
Associated Aviation Underwriters
Bankers Insurance Group
Berkley Select, LLC
Bluebonnet Life Insurance Company
Britannia Steam Ship Insurance Association Ltd.
CNA
Commercial Union Insurance Company
Companion Property and Casualty Group
ELCO Administrative Services
Endurance Services, Ltd.
Erie Insurance Company
Evanston Insurance Company
Fidelity National Financial
First Premium Insurance Group, Inc.
GE Insurance Solutions
General & Cologne Life Reinsurance of America
General Star Indemnity Company
Glencoe Group
Global Special Risks, Inc.
Great American Insurance Companies
Gulf Insurance Group
The Hartford Insurance Group
Homesite Group, Inc.
ICAT Boulder Claims
Infinity Insurance Company
Lexington Insurance Company
Liberty Mutual Group
Louisiana Farm Bureau Mutual Insurance Company
Louisiana Workers' Compensation Corporation
Markel
MetLife Auto & Home
NAS Insurance Group
Nautilus Insurance Company
Old American Insurance Company
Pharmacists Mutual Insurance Company
RenaissanceRe
Republic Western Insurance Company
St. Paul Travelers
Scottsdale Insurance Company
Sentry Insurance
Southern Farm Bureau Casualty Insurance Company
State National Insurance Company, Inc.
Terra Nova Insurance Company Limited
United States Fidelity and Guaranty Company
Victoria Insurance Group
West of England Ship Owners Mutual Insurance Association (Luxembourg)
Zurich

ACE Group of Insurance and Reinsurance Companies
Aetna Insurance Company
AFLAC - American Family Life Assurance Company of
Allstate Insurance Company
American Family Life Assurance Company of Columbus
Argonaut Insurance Company
Aspen Insurance
Aspen Re
AXIS Insurance
Beazley
Bituminous Insurance Company
Blue Cross & Blue Shield of Mississippi
Chartis Insurance
Chubb Group of Insurance Companies
Commonwealth Insurance Company
Cotton States Insurance
Criterion Claim Solutions
Employers Reinsurance Corporation
Esurance Insurance Company
Farmers Insurance Group
Fireman's Fund Insurance Company
Foremost Insurance Company
General American Life Insurance Company
General Reinsurance Corporation
General Star Management Company
Golden Rule Insurance Company
Great Southern Life Insurance Company
Hanover Insurance Group
Hermitage Insurance Company
Houston Casualty Company
Indian Harbor Insurance Company
Ironshore Insurance, Ltd.
Liberty International Underwriters
Life Insurance Company of Alabama
Louisiana Health Insurance Association
Lyndon Property Insurance Company
Munich-American Risk Partners
Nationwide Insurance
The Navigators Group, Inc.
OneBeacon Insurance Group
Prime Syndicate
QBE
Republic Insurance Company
RLI Insurance Company
Royal & SunAlliance
SCOR Global P&C
Sedgwick Claims Management Services, Inc.
SR International Business Insurance Company, Ltd.
Steamship Mutual Underwriting Association Limited
Torus
Underwriters at Lloyd's, London
Unitrin Business Insurance
Vesta Eiendom AS
Western Heritage Insurance Company
Westport Insurance Corporation
XL Insurance Group

Members of the Firm

William J. Gamble, Jr. — The University of North Carolina at Chapel Hill, B.A. (with honors), 1995; The University of Alabama School of Law, J.D., 1999 — Admitted to Bar, 1999, Alabama; 2000, Florida; 1999, U.S. District Court, Middle, Northern and Southern Districts of Alabama; 2000, U.S. District Court, Northern and Southern Districts of Florida; 2001, U.S. Court of Appeals, Eleventh Circuit — Member American, Escambia/Santa Rosa Counties and Mobile Bar Associations; Alabama State Bar; The Florida Bar; Alabama Defense Lawyers Association — Alabama State Court Mediator Roster

Allen E. Graham — The University of Alabama, B.S., 1988; Tulane University Law School, J.D., 1990; LL.M., 1991 — Admitted to Bar, 1990, Alabama; 1992, Mississippi; 1991, U.S. District Court, Southern District of Alabama; 1992, U.S. Court of Appeals, Fifth and Eleventh Circuits; 1993, U.S. District Court, Southern District of Mississippi — Member Alabama State Bar; The Mississippi Bar; Council for Litigation Management; Alabama Defense Lawyers Association; Southeastern Admiralty Law Institute; Defense Research Institute — Registered Mediator, Alabama Center for Dispute Resolution

Richard B. Johnson — Auburn University, B.A. (magna cum laude), 1999; The University of Alabama School of Law, J.D., 2002 — Admitted to Bar, 2002, Alabama; 2003, Mississippi; U.S. District Court, Southern District of Mississippi; U.S. District Court, Southern District of Alabama — Member The Mississippi Bar; Alabama State Bar; Mobile and Baldwin Bar Associations; Defense Research Institute

Joseph J. Minus, Jr. — The University of Alabama, B.S., 1981; Cumberland School of Law of Samford University, J.D., 1985 — Admitted to Bar, 1985, Alabama; U.S. District Court, Northern and Southern Districts of Alabama; 1992, U.S. Court of Appeals, Eleventh Circuit — Member Alabama State Bar; Alabama Association for Municipal Attorneys; Alabama Defense Lawyers Association; Defense Research Institute

A. Kelly Sessoms, III — The University of Georgia, B.S., 1989; The University of Mississippi School of Law, J.D., 1992 — Admitted to Bar, 1992, Mississippi; Alabama; U.S. District Court, Northern and Southern Districts of Mississippi; U.S. District Court, Middle, Northern and Southern Districts of Alabama; U.S. Court of Appeals, Fifth Circuit; 1996, U.S. Supreme Court — Member The Mississippi Bar; Alabama State Bar; Jackson County and Mobile Bar Associations; Mississippi Defense Lawyers Association; International Association of Defense Counsel

Cooper C. Thurber — The University of Mississippi, B.A., 1966; The University of Alabama School of Law, J.D., 1970 — Admitted to Bar, 1970, Alabama; Mississippi; U.S. District Court, Middle, Northern and Southern Districts of Alabama; 1972, U.S. Court of Appeals, Fifth and Eleventh Circuits; 1975, U.S. Supreme Court — Member Alabama State Bar; Mobile Bar Association; National Conference of Bar Presidents; Alabama Defense Lawyers Association; American Board of Trial Advocates; Federation of Defense and Corporate Counsel

Counsel

Ashley S. Fincher — Auburn University, B.A., 1998; Emory University School of Law, J.D., 2001 — Admitted to Bar, 2001, Alabama; U.S. District Court, Middle, Northern and Southern Districts of Alabama; U.S. Court of Appeals, Eleventh Circuit — Member Alabama State Bar

William E. Shreve, Jr. — Davidson College, A.B., 1984; The University of Alabama School of Law, J.D., 1987 — Admitted to Bar, 1987, Alabama; U.S. District Court, Middle, Northern and Southern Districts of Alabama; 1989, U.S. Court of Appeals, Fifth and Eleventh Circuits; 1994, U.S. Supreme Court — Member American and Mobile Bar Associations; Alabama State Bar; Alabama Defense Lawyers Association

(See listing under New Orleans, LA for additional information)

Rainey & Austin, P. C.

1495 University Boulevard S, Suite C
Mobile, Alabama 36609
  Telephone: 251-433-8088
  Fax: 251-433-8011
  E-Mail: bhaustin@lor-lawyers.com
  www.lorlaw.com

General Civil Practice, Product Liability, Professional Liability, Premises Liability, Workers' Compensation, Construction Litigation, Toxic Torts, Insurance Law, Employment Law, Negligence

Insurance Clients

Allstate Insurance Company
Amerisure Companies

ALABAMA — MOBILE

Rainey & Austin, P. C., Mobile, AL (Continued)

Argonaut Insurance Company
Clarendon National Insurance Company
Seaboard Underwriters, Inc.
Travelers Insurance Companies
Zurich American Insurance Group
Auto-Owners Insurance Company
Coregis Insurance Company
Preferred Risk Mutual Insurance Company
United States Fidelity and Guaranty Company

Non-Insurance Clients

Evergreen Transportation
J.B. Hunt Transport Services, Inc.
GAB Robins North America, Inc.
Landstar System, Inc.

Partners

L. Bratton Rainey, III — 1963 — Spring Hill College, B.A. (cum laude), 1984; Jones Law School, J.D. (magna cum laude), 1988 — Law Clerk to Hon. Janie Shores and Hon. Richard L. Jones, Alabama Supreme Court, 1988-1990 — Admitted to Bar, 1989, Alabama; 1990, U.S. District Court, Southern District of Alabama; U.S. Court of Appeals, Eleventh Circuit; 1995, U.S. District Court, Middle District of Alabama — Member American and Mobile Bar Associations; Alabama State Bar; Association of Trial Lawyers of America — E-mail: lbrainey@lor-lawyers.com

Brigg H. Austin — 1981 — Birmingham-Southern College, B.S., 2003; The University of Alabama School of Law, J.D., 2006 — Admitted to Bar, 2006, Alabama; U.S. District Court, Northern and Southern Districts of Alabama — Member American and Mobile Bar Associations; Alabama Defense Lawyers Association — E-mail: bhaustin@lor-lawyers.com

Associate

Joshua J. Bates — 1980 — University of South Alabama, B.S. (Dean's List), 2005; Mississippi College School of Law, J.D./M.B.A. (Trial Advocacy), 2010 — Tau Kappa Epsilon, Phi Alpha Delta — Law Clerk to Hon. Judge Sarah Stewart, 13th Judicial Circuit of Alabama; Office of the Staff Judge Advocate, Joint Force Headquarters, Jackson MS — Admitted to Bar, 2011, Alabama; 2011, Alabama Court of Appeals — Member Alabama State Bar; Mobile Bar Association — Mississippi Army National Guard, 1st Lieut. JAG Officer

Scott, Sullivan, Streetman & Fox, P.C.

Regions Bank Building, 10th Floor
56 St. Joseph Street
Mobile, Alabama 36602
 Telephone: 251-433-1346
 Fax: 251-433-1086
 Toll Free: 800-239-6733
 www.scottsullivanlaw.com

Established: 1986

Insurance Defense, Insurance Litigation, Product Liability, Medical Malpractice, Professional Malpractice, Workers' Compensation, Trial Practice, State and Federal Courts

Insurance Clients

Alabama Insurance Guaranty Association
American Southern Insurance Company
Crawford & Company
Custard Claims Management Service
Farmers Insurance Group
First Mercury Insurance Company
GAB Robins North America, Inc.
General Star National Insurance Company
Global Indemnity Group, Inc.
The Hartford Insurance Group
IAT Reinsurance Company
Lexington Insurance Company
Medmarc Mutual Insurance Company
National American Insurance Company
Republic Claims Service
RSUI Group, Inc.
Sentry Claims Services
Alterra-Markel Corp.
American International Group, Inc.
Argo Insurance Company
Cincinnati Insurance Company
Crum & Forster Insurance Group
The Doctors Company
ESIS
Fireman's Fund Insurance Company
Gay & Taylor, Inc.
Georgia Casualty & Surety Company
Hanover Insurance Company
Homesite Group, Inc.
John Deere Insurance Company
Lumber Insurance Companies
Metropolitan Property and Casualty Insurance Company
Nationwide Insurance
Philadelphia-Tokio Marine Specialty Insurance Company
Seaboard Underwriters, Inc.
Shand Morahan & Company, Inc.

Scott, Sullivan, Streetman & Fox, P.C., Mobile, AL (Continued)

Shelter Insurance Companies
Southern Risk Services, Inc.
Transport Insurance Company
United States Liability Insurance Group
Vanliner Insurance Company
Zurich American Insurance Group
Southern Heritage Insurance Company
Travelers Insurance Companies
Universal Underwriters Insurance Company
York Claims Service, Inc.

Firm Members

Carroll H. Sullivan — 1950 — Auburn University, B.S., 1972; Cumberland School of Law of Samford University, J.D. (cum laude), 1975 — Admitted to Bar, 1975, Alabama; 1982, U.S. District Court, Middle, Northern and Southern Districts of Alabama; 1982, U.S. Court of Appeals, Eleventh Circuit — Member American and Mobile Bar Associations; Alabama State Bar (Chairman, Litigation Section, 1988-1989); Alabama Defense Lawyers Association; Defense Research Institute — E-mail: csullivan@scottsullivanlaw.com

William A. Scott, Jr. — 1943 — The University of Alabama, B.S., 1965; Cumberland School of Law of Samford University, J.D., 1968 — Admitted to Bar, 1968, Alabama; 1987, Tennessee — Member American and Birmingham Bar Associations; Alabama State Bar; Alabama Defense Lawyers Association; Association of Trial Lawyers of America; Defense Research Institute; International Association of Defense Counsel — Resident Birmingham, AL Office — E-mail: wscott@sssandf.com

James P. Streetman, III — 1953 — Auburn University, B.S., 1976; Mississippi College School of Law, J.D., 1979 — Admitted to Bar, 1979, Mississippi; 2001, Mississippi Band of Choctaw Indians Tribal Bar; 1979, U.S. Court of Appeals, Fifth Circuit; 1980, U.S. District Court, Northern and Southern Districts of Mississippi; 1989, U.S. Supreme Court — Member American and Hinds County Bar Association; The Mississippi Bar; Mississippi Claims Association; Mississippi Defense Lawyers Association; Defense Research Institute; Federation of Defense and Corporate Counsel — Resident Jackson, MS Office — E-mail: JStreetman@sssf-ms.com

Anthony N. Fox — 1958 — Maryville College, B.A., 1980; Cumberland School of Law of Samford University, J.D. (cum laude), 1983 — Admitted to Bar, 1983, Alabama; U.S. District Court, Middle and Northern Districts of Alabama; U.S. Court of Appeals, Eleventh Circuit — Member Alabama State Bar (Workers' Compensation Section); Alabama Claims Association; Alabama Defense Lawyers Association; Alabama Workers' Compensation Claims Association — Resident Birmingham, AL Office — E-mail: Fox@sssandf.com

George M. Zoghby — 1966 — Spring Hill College, B.S., 1988; Cumberland School of Law of Samford University, J.D., 1992 — Admitted to Bar, 1992, Alabama; U.S. District Court, Southern District of Alabama — Member American and Mobile Bar Associations; Mobile Young Lawyers Association — E-mail: gzoghby@scottsullivanlaw.com

Christopher L. George — 1959 — Auburn University, B.S., 1981; Cumberland School of Law of Samford University, J.D. (magna cum laude), 1993 — Admitted to Bar, 1993, Alabama; 1994, Florida; 1993, U.S. District Court, Middle and Southern Districts of Alabama — Member American and Mobile Bar Associations; Alabama State Bar — E-mail: cgeorge@scottsullivanlaw.com

Carter R. Hale — 1974 — Hampden-Sydney College, B.S., 1996; Cumberland School of Law of Samford University, J.D., 1999 — Admitted to Bar, 2002, Alabama; U.S. District Court, Southern District of Alabama — Member American and Mobile Bar Associations; Alabama State Bar — E-mail: chale@scottsullivanlaw.com

Wade G. Manor — Auburn University, B.S., 1991; Mississippi College School of Law, J.D., 1995 — Admitted to Bar, 1996, Mississippi; U.S. District Court, Northern and Southern Districts of Mississippi; U.S. Court of Appeals, Fifth Circuit; Mississippi Band of Choctaw Indians Tribal Bar — Member American Bar Association; The Mississippi Bar; Defense Research Institute — E-mail: wmanor@sssf-ms.com

Joseph E. Stott — The University of Alabama at Tuscaloosa, B.A., 1992; University of Connecticut at Hartford, J.D. (magna cum laude), 1995 — Law Clerk to Hon. Judge Michael Sheldon, Superior Court, State of Connecticut — Admitted to Bar, 1995, Georgia; 1996, Alabama; U.S. District Court, Northern and Southern Districts of Georgia; U.S. District Court, Middle and Southern Districts of Alabama; U.S. District Court, Middle and Northern Districts of Georgia; Alabama Court of Appeals; Supreme Court of Alabama; Supreme Court of Georgia — Member Alabama State Bar; State Bar of Georgia — Practice Areas: Malpractice; Employment Practices; Automobile Accidents; Product Liability; General Defense Civil Litigation — E-mail: Stott@sssandf.com

Sirote & Permutt, P.C.

One St. Louis Centre, Suite 1000
Mobile, Alabama 36602-3918
 Telephone: 251-432-1671
 Fax: 251-434-0196
 E-Mail: mobile@sirote.com
 www.sirote.com

(Birmingham, AL Office*: 2311 Highland Avenue South, 35205, P.O. Box 55727, 35255)
 (Tel: 205-930-5100)
 (Fax: 205-930-5101)
 (E-Mail: bham@sirote.com)
(Huntsville, AL Office*: 305 Church Street, Suite 800, 35801, P.O. Box 18248, 35804-8248)
 (Tel: 256-536-1711)
 (Fax: 256-518-3681)
 (E-Mail: huntsville@sirote.com)
(Pensacola, FL Office: 1115 East Gonzalez Street, 32503)
 (Tel: 850-462-1500)
 (Fax: 850-462-1599)
(Fort Lauderdale, FL Office: 200 East Broward Boulevard, Suite 900, 33301)
 (Tel: 954-828-1100)
 (Fax: 954-828-1101)

Established: 1946

Insurance Defense, Life and Health, Casualty, Product Liability, Fire, Fraud, Surety

Firm Profile: Sirote & Permutt is at the forefront of the legal profession in Alabama and Florida, serving our clients with a full range of legal services of the highest quality, prepared in a fair and timely manner. For more than half a century this diverse team of professionals has cultivated a tradition of excellence, anticipating the needs of our clients and meeting those needs in new and innovative ways. Sirote & Permutt serves our clients with 125 attorneys in Birmingham, Huntsville and Mobile, Alabama and Fort Lauderdale and Pensacola, Florida.

Firm Member

T. Julian Motes — Auburn University, B.S., 1980; The University of Alabama School of Law, J.D., 1983 — Admitted to Bar, 1983, Alabama — Member Mobile Bar Association — Practice Areas: Business Law; Civil Trial Practice; Labor and Employment; Product Liability; Workers' Compensation — Tel: 251-434-0130 — E-mail: jmotes@sirote.com

Attorney

John Pierce — Birmingham-Southern College, B.S., 1988; The University of Alabama School of Law, J.D., 1991 — Admitted to Bar, 1991, Alabama — Member Mobile Bar Association — Practice Areas: Civil Trial Practice; Construction Litigation; ERISA; Labor and Employment; Product Liability Defense — Tel: 251-434-0102 — E-mail: jpierce@sirote.com

(See listing under Birmingham, AL for additional information)

Vernis & Bowling of Southern Alabama, LLC

61 St. Joseph Street, 11th Floor
Mobile, Alabama 36602
 Telephone: 251-432-0337
 Fax: 251-432-0244
 E-Mail: info@law-alabama.com
 www.law-alabama.com

(Vernis & Bowling of Palm Beach, P.A.*: 884 U.S. Highway #1, North Palm Beach, FL, 33408-5408)
 (Tel: 561-775-9822)
 (Fax: 561-775-9821)
 (E-Mail: gjvernis@florida-law.com)
 (www.national-law.com)

Vernis & Bowling of Southern Alabama, LLC, Mobile, AL
(Continued)

(Vernis & Bowling of Broward, P.A.*(See Fort Lauderdale listing): 5821 Hollywood Boulevard, First Floor, Hollywood, FL, 33021)
 (Tel: 954-927-5330)
 (Fax: 954-927-5320)
 (E-Mail: info@florida-law.com)
 (www.national-law.com)
(Vernis & Bowling of Northwest Florida, P.A.*: 315 South Palafox Street, Pensacola, FL, 32502)
 (Tel: 850-433-5461)
 (Fax: 850-432-0166)
 (E-Mail: info@florida-law.com)
 (www.national-law.com)
(Vernis & Bowling of Southern Mississippi, PLLC*: 2501 14th Street, Suite 207, Gulfport, MS, 39501)
 (Tel: 225-539-0021)
 (Fax: 228-539-0022)

Established: 1970

Civil Litigation, Insurance Law, Workers' Compensation, Premises Liability, Labor and Employment, Civil Rights, Commercial Litigation, Complex Litigation, Product Liability, Directors and Officers Liability, Errors and Omissions, Construction Law, Construction Defect, Environmental Liability, Personal and Commercial Vehicle, Appellate Practice, Admiralty and Maritime Law, Real Estate, Family Law, Elder Law, Liability Defense, SIU/Fraud Litigation, Education Law (ESE/IDEA), Property and Casualty (Commercial and Personal Lines), Long-Haul Trucking Liability, Government Law, Public Law, Criminal, White Collar, Business Litigation

Firm Profile: VERNIS & BOWLING represents individuals, businesses, insurance carriers and self-insureds. With 115 offices located in Florida, Georgia, Alabama, North Carolina & Mississippi,we provide cost effective, full service legal representation that consistently exceeds the expectations of our clients.

Resident Attorneys

James T. Patterson — Cumberland University School of Law, J.D., 2000 — Admitted to Bar, 2000, Alabama; Florida — 'AV' Rated by Martindale-Hubbell — E-mail: jpatterson@national-law.com

John "Jack" Janecky — The University of Alabama School of Law, J.D., 1975 — Admitted to Bar, 1975, Alabama; Florida — 'AV' Rated by Martindale-Hubbell — E-mail: jjanecky@national-law.com

Christopher B. Estes — Spring Hill College, B.S. (cum laude), 1995; The University of Alabama School of Law, J.D. (cum laude), 1998 — Admitted to Bar, 1998, Alabama; Mississippi — E-mail: cestes@national-law.com

Ryan T. Northrup — Cumberland University School of Law, J.D. (cum laude), 1998 — Admitted to Bar, 1998, Alabama; Florida — E-mail: rnorthrup@national-law.com

Russell D. Johnson — Mississippi College School of Law, J.D., 2010 — Admitted to Bar, 2010, Alabama — E-mail: rjohnson@national-law.com

(See listing under North Palm Beach, FL for additional information)

Vickers, Riis, Murray and Curran, L.L.C.

RSA Trustmark Building, 21st Floor
107 St. Francis Street
Mobile, Alabama 36602
 Telephone: 251-432-9772
 Fax: 251-432-9781
 www.vickersriis.com

Established: 1956

ALABAMA | MOBILE

Vickers, Riis, Murray and Curran, L.L.C., Mobile, AL
(Continued)

Insurance Defense, Insurance Coverage, Construction Law, Admiralty and Maritime Law, Professional Liability, Environmental Law, Employment Law, Governmental Liability, Toxic Torts, Product Liability, Workers' Compensation, Business Automobile and Trucking, Education

Insurance Clients

ACE Westchester Specialty Group
Alabama Municipal Insurance Corporation
The American Protection and Indemnity Club
Argo Pro
The Cincinnati Insurance Companies
Crum & Forster Insurance
Farmers Insurance Company
General Casualty Insurance Company
Harco National Insurance Company
Liberty International Underwriters
Maxum Specialty Insurance Group
National Indemnity Company
North Pointe Insurance Company
QBE Insurance Corporation
The St. Paul Companies
Trident Insurance Services
Underwriters at Lloyd's, London
Westport Insurance Company
AIG
American Mining Insurance Company
American Reliable Insurance Company
Chubb Group of Insurance Companies
CNA Insurance Company
DPIC Companies, Inc.
Fireman's Fund Insurance Company
Generali - US Branch
HDI-Gerling Marine
Lexington Insurance Company
Liberty Mutual Insurance
National Fire and Marine Insurance Company
Pan-American Life Insurance Company
Starr Indemnity & Liability Company
Utica National Insurance Company
Zurich North America

Non-Insurance Clients

Anchor Managing General Agency
Cottingham & Butler Claims Services, Inc.
Gallagher Bassett Services, Inc.
Hancock Bank
HRH Risk Services
Marine Office of America Corporation (MOAC)
McLarens Toplis North America, Inc.
Prime, Inc.
Regions Financial Corporation
Roman Catholic Archdiocese of Mobile
Spring Hill College
Syngenta Crop Protection, Inc.
BASF Corporation
Crane Co.
Foster Wheeler Corporation
Goulds Pumps
Holcim, (US) Inc.
International Paper Company
Martin Energy Services, LLC
McKinney Petroleum Equipment, Inc.
O'Charley's, Inc.
RAM Aircraft, LP
Retif Oil & Fuel, LLC
Sedgwick Claims Management Services, Inc.
Steiner Shipyard, Inc.

Firm Members

J. Manson Murray — 1930 — The University of Alabama, B.S., 1952; LL.B., 1953 — Admitted to Bar, 1953, Alabama — Member Alabama State Bar; Mobile Bar Association (President, 1975)

Edwin J. Curran, Jr. — 1932 — The University of Alabama, B.S., 1953; LL.B., 1955 — Admitted to Bar, 1955, Alabama — Member Alabama State Bar

J.W. Goodloe, Jr. — 1942 — The University of Alabama, B.S., 1964; LL.B., 1967 — Admitted to Bar, 1967, Alabama — Member Alabama State Bar; Southeastern Admiralty Law Institute; The Maritime Law Association of the United States

E.L. McCafferty, III — 1946 — The University of Alabama, B.A., 1967; J.D., 1970 — Law Clerk, Alabama Supreme Court, 1970-1971 — Admitted to Bar, 1970, Alabama — Member Alabama State Bar; Claims and Litigation Management Alliance; International Association of Defense Counsel; Trucking Industry Defense Association; Defense Research Institute; Alabama Defense Lawyers Association — Practice Areas: Insurance Defense; Litigation; Professional Liability — E-mail: elm@vickersriis.com

Z.M.P. Inge, Jr. — 1949 — University of Virginia, B.A., 1971; The University of Alabama, J.D., 1974; New York University, LL.M., 1975 — Admitted to Bar, 1974, Alabama — Member Alabama State Bar

Frank Grey Redditt, Jr. — 1950 — The University of Alabama, B.S., 1972; J.D., 1975 — Admitted to Bar, 1975, Alabama; 1992, Texas; 2013, New York — Member American and New York State Bar Associations; Alabama State Bar; State Bar of Texas; American Inns of Court; Defense Research Institute — Practice Areas: Insurance Defense; Environmental Litigation; Education Law — E-mail: greditt@vickersriis.com

Vickers, Riis, Murray and Curran, L.L.C., Mobile, AL
(Continued)

Thomas E. Sharp, III — 1951 — The University of Alabama, B.S., 1973; J.D., 1976 — Admitted to Bar, 1976, Alabama — Member Alabama State Bar; Southeastern Admiralty Law Institute; The Maritime Law Association of the United States — Practice Areas: Maritime Law — E-mail: tsharp@vickersriis.com

Ronald P. Davis — 1951 — The University of Alabama, B.A., 1973; J.D., 1976; New York University, LL.M., 1977 — Admitted to Bar, 1976, Alabama — Member Alabama State Bar

J. Marshall Gardner — 1957 — University of South Alabama, B.A. (cum laude), 1979; The University of Alabama, J.D., 1982 — Order of the Coif; Hugo L. Black Scholar — Admitted to Bar, 1982, Alabama — Member Alabama State Bar; Defense Research Institute — Practice Areas: Product Liability; Commercial Litigation; Liability Defense — E-mail: mgardner@vickersriis.com

Mark L. Redditt — 1955 — University of South Alabama, B.A., 1979; The University of Alabama, J.D., 1982 — Admitted to Bar, 1983, Alabama — Member Mobile Bar Association; Defense Research Institute; Alabama Defense Lawyers Association — Practice Areas: Governmental Entity Defense; Litigation — E-mail: mredditt@vickersriis.com

C. Richard Wilkins — 1963 — The University of Alabama, B.S., 1985; J.D., 1988 — Law Clerk to the Honorable W. B. Hand, U.S. District Court, Southern District of Alabama, 1988-1990 — Admitted to Bar, 1988, Alabama — Member Alabama State Bar; Southern Admiralty Law Institute; Defense Research Institute — Practice Areas: Insurance Coverage; Litigation — E-mail: rwilkins@vickersriis.com

Timothy Allen Clarke — 1966 — Spring Hill College, B.S., 1988; The University of Alabama, J.D., 1992; Columbia Law School, Certified Litigation Management Professional (CLMP), 2011 — Admitted to Bar, 1993, Alabama — Member Alabama State Bar; Claims and Litigation Management Alliance; Defense Research Institute; Alabama Defense Lawyers Association — Practice Areas: Toxic Torts; Insurance Defense — E-mail: tclarke@vickersriis.com

Associates

Melody M. Zeidan — 1983 — The University of Alabama, B.A., 2004; Vanderbilt University, J.D., 2007 — Admitted to Bar, 2007, Alabama — Languages: Spanish — Practice Areas: Labor and Employment; Education Law — E-mail: mzeidan@vickersriis.com

H. Finn Cox, Jr. — 1985 — Spring Hill College, B.A., 2007; Cumberland University, J.D., 2010 — Cumberland Law Review — Admitted to Bar, 2010, Alabama — Languages: Spanish — Practice Areas: Litigation — E-mail: fcox@vickersriis.com

---

The following firms also service this area.

Hill, Hill, Carter, Franco, Cole & Black, P.C.
425 South Perry Street
Montgomery, Alabama 36104
  Telephone: 334-834-7600
  Fax: 334-263-5969

Mailing Address: P.O. Box 116, Montgomery, AL 36101-0116

Appellate Practice, Aviation, Business Law, Casualty, Commercial Litigation, Discrimination, Education Law, Employment Law, Insurance Defense, Insurance Fraud, Law Enforcement Liability, Product Liability, Professional Liability, State and Federal Courts, Surety, Transportation, Trial Practice, Workers' Compensation, Insurance Coverage Opinions and Litigation

SEE COMPLETE LISTING UNDER MONTGOMERY, ALABAMA (200 MILES)

MONTGOMERY | ALABAMA

Rushton, Stakely, Johnston & Garrett, P.A.
184 Commerce Street
Montgomery, Alabama 36104
  Telephone: 334-206-3100
  Fax: 334-262-6277

Mailing Address: P.O. Box 270, Montgomery, AL 36101-0270

Insurance Defense, Trial and Appellate Practice, Accountants and Attorneys Liability, Administrative Law, Advertising Injury, Agent and Brokers Errors and Omissions, Appellate Practice, Arbitration, Automobile Tort, Bad Faith, Business Law, Casualty Insurance Law, Class Actions, Commercial Litigation, Complex Litigation, Construction Litigation, Contract Disputes, Copyright and Trademark Law, Coverage Analysis, Declaratory Judgments, Directors and Officers Liability, Employment Law, Environmental Law, Family Law, Fidelity and Surety, Fraud, Health Care, Health Care Professional Licensure Defense, Insurance Litigation, Labor and Employment, Law Enforcement Liability, Legal Malpractice, Medical Devices, Medical Malpractice, Pharmaceutical, Premises Liability, Primary and Excess Insurance, Product Liability, Professional Errors and Omissions, Professional Liability, Surety, Title Insurance, Uninsured and Underinsured Motorist, Workers' Compensation, Wrongful Death

SEE COMPLETE LISTING UNDER MONTGOMERY, ALABAMA (174 MILES)

MONROEVILLE † 6,519 Monroe Co.

Refer To
Ball, Ball, Matthews & Novak, P.A.
107 Saint Francis Street, Suite 1590
Mobile, Alabama 36602
  Telephone: 251-338-2721
  Fax: 251-338-2722

Mailing Address: P.O. Box 2648, Mobile, AL 36652

Insurance Defense, Medical Malpractice, Aviation, Bad Faith, Personal Injury, Construction Litigation, Employment Law, Product Liability, Property, Pharmaceutical, Medical Devices, Complex Litigation, Governmental Entity Defense, Workers' Compensation, Mediation, Arbitration, Trial and Appellate Practice, State and Federal Courts, Insurance Coverage Analysis, Automobile Injury, Motor Carrier Defense

SEE COMPLETE LISTING UNDER MOBILE, ALABAMA (89 MILES)

Refer To
Michael Gillion, P.C.
74 Midtown Park West, Suite 105
Mobile, Alabama 36606
  Telephone: 251-471-9494
  Fax: 251-471-1722

Mailing Address: P.O. Box 161423, Mobile, AL 36616-2423

Insurance Defense, Automobile, Homeowners, Workers' Compensation, Subrogation, Insurance Contract and Coverage Litigation

SEE COMPLETE LISTING UNDER MOBILE, ALABAMA (87 MILES)

Refer To
Johnstone Adams, L.L.C.
One St. Louis Centre
1 St. Louis Street, Suite 4000
Mobile, Alabama 36602
  Telephone: 251-432-7682
  Fax: 251-432-2800

Mailing Address: P.O. Box 1988, Mobile, AL 36633

Insurance Defense, Admiralty and Maritime Law, Automobile, Aviation, Bad Faith, Casualty, Construction Litigation, Employer Liability, ERISA, Fire, Fraud, Health, Life Insurance, Product Liability, Professional Liability, Surety, Workers' Compensation, Co-Employee

SEE COMPLETE LISTING UNDER MOBILE, ALABAMA (87 MILES)

Refer To
Vickers, Riis, Murray and Curran, L.L.C.
RSA Trustmark Building, 21st Floor
107 St. Francis Street
Mobile, Alabama 36602
  Telephone: 251-432-9772
  Fax: 251-432-9781

Mailing Address: P.O. Box 2568, Mobile, AL 36652-2568

Insurance Defense, Insurance Coverage, Construction Law, Admiralty and Maritime Law, Professional Liability, Environmental Law, Employment Law, Governmental Liability, Toxic Torts, Product Liability, Workers' Compensation, Business Automobile and Trucking, Education

SEE COMPLETE LISTING UNDER MOBILE, ALABAMA (87 MILES)

MONTGOMERY † 205,764 Montgomery Co.

Ball, Ball, Matthews & Novak, P.A.
445 Dexter Avenue, Suite 9045
Montgomery, Alabama 36104
  Telephone: 334-387-7680
  Fax: 334-387-3222
  E-Mail: firm@ball-ball.com
  www.ball-ball.com

(Mobile, AL Office*: 107 Saint Francis Street, Suite 1590, 36602, P.O. Box 2648, 36652)
  (Tel: 251-338-2721)
  (Fax: 251-338-2722)

Established: 1890

Insurance Defense, Medical Malpractice, Aviation, Bad Faith, Personal Injury, Construction Litigation, Employment Law, Product Liability, Property, Pharmaceutical, Medical Devices, Complex Litigation, Governmental Entity Defense, Workers' Compensation, Mediation, Arbitration, Trial and Appellate Practice, State and Federal Courts, Insurance Coverage Analysis, Automobile Injury, Motor Carrier Defense

Firm Profile: Ball, Ball, Matthews & Novak, P.A., and its predecessors have represented clients throughout Alabama since the 1890's and is one of the oldest law firms in the State of Alabama. The firm has represented insurance carriers almost since its inception and still handles all facets of litigation that arise from that representation. With offices in Montgomery and Mobile, the firm offers a state-wide practice with attorneys defending suits involving products liability, medical malpractice and professional liability claims, industrial accidents, construction matters, automobile and personal injury, governmental entity defense, and trucking defense. The firm also handles all types of casualty, property insurance claims, transportation liability, coverage questions, professional errors and omissions, liquor liability, bankruptcy and creditor's rights, employment matters, and workers compensation claims and litigation.

Members of the firm are also committed to the advancement of the interests of our clients beyond defending litigation assigned to us which is represented by our high level of participation in defense bar associations. Lawyers in our firm are participating members of the Federation of Defense and Corporate Counsel, American College of Trial Attorneys, Alabama Defense Lawyers Association, Defense Research Institute, Transportation Lawyers Association, Trucking Defense Association, Property Loss Research Bureau, as well as the Alabama State Bar and American Bar Association. Several of our attorneys have authored papers appearing in various defense publications and have served as speakers at continuing legal education programs.

Insurance Clients

ACE USA	Affirmative Risk Management, Inc.
AIG Aviation, Inc.	AIG Insurance Company
Alabama Workers' Compensation Self-Insurer's Guaranty Association	Alfa Mutual Insurance Company
	American Equity Insurance Company
American Southern Insurance Company	American Specialty Insurance Services, Inc.
Amerisure Insurance Company	Associated Aviation Underwriters

Ball, Ball, Matthews & Novak, P.A., Montgomery, AL (Continued)

Atlantic Mutual Companies
Baldwin Mutual Insurance Company, Inc.
Burlington Insurance Company
Chubb Group of Insurance Companies
Claims Management Services, Inc.
Continental General Insurance Company
Cotton States Mutual Insurance Company
Crawford & Company
Empire Fire and Marine Insurance Company
Employers Reinsurance Corporation
First Specialty Insurance Corporation
General Casualty Insurance Company
Government Employees Insurance Company
Gulf Insurance Company
Harbor Insurance Company
Hartford Accident and Indemnity Company
Horace Mann Insurance Company
Independent Fire Insurance Company
Medical Protective Insurance Services
Northwestern National Insurance Company
Philadelphia Insurance Company
St. Paul Fire and Marine Insurance Company
Travelers Insurance Companies
Trident Insurance Services
Union Standard Insurance Company
USAA Casualty Insurance Company
York STB, Inc.
Auto-Owners Insurance Company
Bankers Insurance Group
Berkley Specialty Underwriting Managers, LLC
CIGNA Group
CJW & Associates
Commercial Union Assurance Company plc
Coregis Insurance Company
COUNTRY Insurance & Financial Services
EMC Insurance Company
Employers Claim Management, Inc.
ESIS
Farmers Insurance Group
Foremost Insurance Company
Gallagher Bassett Services, Inc.
Georgia Casualty & Surety Company
Gray Insurance Company
Great American Insurance Company
Harco National Insurance Company
HDI-Gerling America Insurance Company
MAG Mutual Insurance Company
Meadowbrook Insurance Company
Michigan Mutual Insurance Company
Pennsylvania Lumbermens Mutual Insurance Company
Safeco Insurance
Sheffield Risk Management
Southern General Insurance Company
Union Fidelity Life Insurance Company
United States Aviation Underwriters, Inc.
XL Insurance
Zurich American Insurance Company

Non-Insurance Clients

Alabama Association of REALTORS
Asphalt Contractors, Inc.
Boulder Claims
Community Health Systems, Inc.
The Goodyear Tire & Rubber Company
Montgomery Area Mental Health Authority, Inc.
Sears, Roebuck and Co.
Store Room Fasteners, Inc.
Alabama Retail Comp
Allstate Beverage Company, LLC
Bell Helicopter Textron Inc.
BridgeWorks Commercial Management
Hyundai Motor Manufacturing Alabama, LLC
Ryder System, Inc.
SCA, Inc.
SMART Alabama, LLC

Firm Members

John R. Matthews, Jr. — (1925-2004)

Richard A. Ball, Jr. — 1938 — The University of Alabama, LL.B., 1962 — Admitted to Bar, 1962, Alabama; 1970, U.S. District Court, Middle, Northern and Southern Districts of Alabama; U.S. Court of Appeals, Fifth and Eleventh Circuits — Member Alabama State Bar; Montgomery County Bar Association; International Association of Defense Counsel; Alabama Defense Lawyers Association — Practice Areas: Civil Litigation; Corporate Law; Business Law — E-mail: rball@ball-ball.com

Tabor Robert Novak, Jr. — 1944 — Washington and Lee University, B.A., 1966; LL.B., 1969 — Admitted to Bar, 1970, Alabama — Member American and Montgomery County Bar Associations; Alabama State Bar; Alabama Defense Lawyers Association; American College of Trial Lawyers; Federation of Defense and Corporate Counsel — Assistant Attorney General, Alabama, 1970; Alabama Super Lawyers (2011, 2012) — Practice Areas: General Defense; Malpractice; Product Liability; Professional Liability; Appellate Practice; Corporate Law — E-mail: tnovak@ball-ball.com

Clyde C. Owen, Jr. — 1950 — University of Virginia, B.A., 1972; The University of Alabama, J.D., 1976 — Admitted to Bar, 1976, Alabama; U.S. District Court, Middle, Northern and Southern Districts of Alabama; U.S. Court of Appeals, Eleventh Circuit; 1990, U.S. Supreme Court — Member Alabama State Bar; Montgomery County Bar Association; Alabama Defense Lawyers

Ball, Ball, Matthews & Novak, P.A., Montgomery, AL (Continued)

Association; Defense Research Institute — Practice Areas: Insurance Litigation; Coverage Analysis; Appellate Practice; Probate; Estate Planning — E-mail: ccowen@ball-ball.com

C. Winston Sheehan, Jr. — 1947 — Sewanee, The University of the South, B.A. (cum laude), 1969; The University of Alabama, J.D., 1972 — Admitted to Bar, 1972, Alabama; U.S. District Court, Middle, Northern and Southern Districts of Alabama; U.S. Court of Appeals, Eleventh Circuit; 1974, U.S. Supreme Court — Member American and Montgomery County Bar Associations; Alabama State Bar; Alabama Defense Lawyers Association; Defense Research Institute; Trucking Industry Defense Association — Assistant Attorney General, Alabama, 1977 — Practice Areas: Civil Rights; Governmental Liability; Product Liability; Employment Law; Trucking Law; Insurance Defense — E-mail: wsheehan@ball-ball.com

William H. Brittain II — 1947 — The University of Alabama, B.A., 1970; Cumberland School of Law of Samford University, J.D. (cum laude), 1979 — Admitted to Bar, 1980, Alabama — Member Alabama State Bar; Montgomery County Bar Association; Alabama Defense Lawyers Association — Practice Areas: Product Liability; Professional Liability; Insurance Defense — E-mail: bbrittain@ball-ball.com

E. Hamilton Wilson, Jr. — 1951 — The University of Alabama, B.A., 1974; Cumberland School of Law of Samford University, J.D., 1977 — Phi Delta Phi — Admitted to Bar, 1977, Alabama; U.S. District Court, Middle, Northern and Southern Districts of Alabama; U.S. Court of Appeals, Eleventh Circuit; 1981, U.S. Supreme Court — Member Alabama State Bar; Montgomery County Bar Association (President, Young Lawyers Section and Member, Board of Directors, 1982); Defense Research Institute; Alabama Defense Lawyers Association; Federation of Defense and Corporate Counsel — Adjunct Professor in Business Law, Auburn University of Montgomery, 1980-1982; Fair Hearing Officer, State of Alabama, 1979-1983; Special Assistant Attorney General, 1980; Alabama House of Representatives Member, 1982-1983; Alabama Super Lawyers (2011, 2012) — Practice Areas: Civil Litigation; Insurance Litigation; Malpractice; Corporate Law; Professional Liability — E-mail: hwilson@ball-ball.com

Richard E. Broughton — 1951 — The University of Alabama, B.S.Ch.E., 1973; J.D., 1980 — Admitted to Bar, 1980, Alabama; U.S. District Court, Middle, Northern and Southern Districts of Alabama; U.S. Court of Appeals, Eleventh Circuit — Member American and Montgomery County Bar Associations; Alabama State Bar; Alabama Defense Lawyers Association — Practice Areas: Product Liability; Insurance Defense; Aviation; Trucking Litigation — E-mail: rbroughton@ball-ball.com

T. Cowin Knowles — 1960 — The University of Alabama, B.S., 1982; J.D., 1985 — Phi Delta Phi — Admitted to Bar, 1985, Alabama; U.S. District Court, Middle, Northern and Southern Districts of Alabama; U.S. Court of Appeals, Eleventh Circuit — Member American and Montgomery County (Board of Directors) Bar Associations; Alabama State Bar; Alabama Trucking Association; Alabama Defense Lawyers Association; Defense Research Institute; Transportation Lawyers Association — Practice Areas: Workers' Compensation; Trucking Law; Product Liability; Civil Litigation; Premises Liability — E-mail: cknowles@ball-ball.com

Gerald C. Swann, Jr. — 1960 — The University of Alabama, B.A., 1983; Cumberland School of Law of Samford University, J.D., 1986 — Admitted to Bar, 1986, Alabama; U.S. District Court, Middle, Northern and Southern Districts of Alabama; U.S. Court of Appeals, Eleventh Circuit — Member Alabama State Bar; Montgomery County Bar Association; Alabama Defense Lawyers Association (Board of Directors); Alabama Defense Lawyers (Board Member, Young Lawyers Section); Defense Research Institute — Certified Graduate Associate Alabama Homebuilder; 10 Hour OSHA Safety Certification; Associate Member, Alabama Association of General Contractors — Practice Areas: Construction Litigation; General Civil Practice; Product Liability — E-mail: gswann@ball-ball.com

Mark T. Davis — 1961 — The University of Alabama, B.A., 1983; J.D., 1986 — Admitted to Bar, 1986, Alabama — Member Alabama State Bar; Montgomery County Bar Association; Alabama Defense Lawyers Association — Practice Areas: Property; Corporate Law; Premises Liability; Construction Litigation — E-mail: mdavis@ball-ball.com

Benjamin Saxon Main — 1971 — Auburn University, B.S., 1993; The University of Alabama, J.D., 1997 — Admitted to Bar, 1997, Alabama; U.S. District Court, Middle and Northern Districts of Alabama; U.S. Court of Appeals, Eleventh Circuit — Member American and Montgomery County Bar Associations; Alabama State Bar; American, Alabama and Montgomery County Inn of Court; American Judicature Society — Alabama Super Lawyers Rising Stars (2010) — Practice Areas: Real Estate; Civil Litigation; Appellate Practice; Administrative Law — E-mail: smain@ball-ball.com

Ball, Ball, Matthews & Novak, P.A., Montgomery, AL
(Continued)

Emily C. Marks — 1973 — Spring Hill College, B.A. (magna cum laude), 1995; The University of Alabama, J.D., 1998 — John A. Campbell Moot Court Board; Bench & Bar Legal Honor Society — Senior Editor, Law & Psychology Review — Admitted to Bar, 1998, Alabama; U.S. District Court, Middle, Northern and Southern Districts of Alabama; 2002, U.S. Court of Appeals, Eleventh Circuit — Member Alabama State Bar (Volunteer Lawyers Program Chair); Montgomery County Bar Association; Hugh Maddox Inn of Court; Society of Human Resource Managers (SHRM); Alabama Defense Lawyers Association; Defense Research Institute — Languages: French — Practice Areas: Labor and Employment; Civil Rights; Appellate Practice — E-mail: emarks@ball-ball.com

W. Evans Brittain — 1974 — The University of Alabama, B.S., 1996; J.D., 2000 — Admitted to Bar, 2000, Alabama; U.S. District Court, Middle and Northern Districts of Alabama; U.S. Court of Appeals, Eleventh Circuit — Member Alabama State Bar; Montgomery County Bar Association; Alabama Defense Lawyers Association — Alabama Super Lawyers Rising Stars (2011, 2012) — Practice Areas: Insurance Defense; Insurance Law; Commercial Litigation; Employment Law — E-mail: ebrittain@ball-ball.com

William D. Montgomery, Jr. — 1975 — University of Montevallo, B.A. (cum laude), 1998; The University of Alabama, J.D., 2001 — Admitted to Bar, 2001, Alabama; 2002, Florida; U.S. District Court, Middle and Southern Districts of Alabama — Member Mobile and Baldwin County Bar Associations; Alabama Defense Lawyers Association; Defense Research Institute — Practice Areas: Personal Injury; Construction Litigation; Trucking Law; General Civil Practice — Resident Mobile, AL Office — E-mail: monty@ball-ball.com

W. Christopher Waller, Jr. — 1979 — The University of Alabama, B.S., 2001; Cumberland School of Law of Samford University, J.D., 2004 — Order of the Barristers — Admitted to Bar, 2004, Alabama; U.S. District Court, Middle and Northern Districts of Alabama — Member American (Litigation Section) and Montgomery County (Board of Directors, Young Lawyers Section) Bar Associations; Alabama State Bar (Young Lawyer Executive Committee and Treasurer); Alabama Defense Lawyers Association; Defense Research Institute — Alabama Super Lawyers Rising Stars (2010); University of Alabama Alumni Association, Montgomery County (President) — Practice Areas: Pharmaceutical; Insurance Litigation; Product Liability; Medical Malpractice; Dental Malpractice — E-mail: cwaller@ball-ball.com

Holbrook ("Brooke") E. Reid — 1981 — Birmingham-Southern College, B.A. (magna cum laude, Phi Beta Kappa), 2003; The University of Alabama, J.D., 2006 — Admitted to Bar, 2006, Alabama — Member American and Montgomery County Bar Associations; Alabama State Bar (Young Lawyer's Section) — Practice Areas: Civil Litigation; Workers' Compensation; Labor and Employment — E-mail: bemfinger@ball-ball.com

John W. Marsh — 1981 — The University of Alabama, B.A. (cum laude), 2004; J.D., 2007 — Admitted to Bar, 2007, Alabama; U.S. District Court, Middle District of Alabama — Member American and Montgomery County Bar Associations; Alabama State Bar; Alabama Defense Lawyers Association — Practice Areas: Civil Litigation; Insurance Litigation; Workers' Compensation — E-mail: jmarsh@ball-ball.com

Associates

Benjamin Heinz — 1976 — Duke University, B.A., 1998; The University of Alabama, J.D., 2001 — Admitted to Bar, 2001, Alabama; Mississippi; U.S. District Court, Southern District of Alabama; U.S. District Court, Northern and Southern Districts of Mississippi — Practice Areas: Appellate Practice; Business Law; Insurance Law; Construction Law; Medical Malpractice; Real Estate — E-mail: bheinz@ball-ball.com

D. Kirby Howard, Jr. — The University of Alabama, B.A., 2003; Cumberland University School of Law, J.D., 2006 — Admitted to Bar, 2006, Alabama; U.S. District Court, Middle, Northern and Southern Districts of Alabama — Member American and Mobile Bar Associations; Alabama State Bar; Alabama Defense Lawyers Association (Young Lawyers Board of Directors) — Reported Cases: Tucker v. Wal-Mart Stores, Inc., 2012 Ala. Civ. App. LEXIS 33; Sconiers v. Wal-Mart Stores, Inc., 2011 U.S. Dist. LEXIS 74034 — Practice Areas: Insurance Defense; Premises Liability; Construction Defect; Insurance Coverage; Medical Malpractice — E-mail: khoward@ball-ball.com

Miland F. Simpler, III — The University of Alabama, B.A. (magna cum laude), 2010; The University of Alabama School of Law, J.D., 2013 — Phi Beta Kappa Society; Omicron Delta Kappa — Admitted to Bar, 2013, Alabama; U.S. District Court, Middle, Northern and Southern Districts of Alabama — Practice Areas: Civil Defense; Insurance Litigation; Workers' Compensation — E-mail: msimpler@ball-ball.com

Ball, Ball, Matthews & Novak, P.A., Montgomery, AL
(Continued)

Of Counsel

Allison Alford Ingram — 1967 — The University of Alabama, B.S. (magna cum laude), 1989; J.D., 1992 — Pegasus Trust Scholar of the Inner Temple, London, England — Law Clerk to the Honorable W. Harold Albritton, U.S. District Court, Middle District of Alabama, 1992-1993 — Admitted to Bar, 1992, Alabama; U.S. District Court, Middle, Northern and Southern Districts of Alabama; U.S. Court of Appeals, Eleventh Circuit — Member Alabama State Bar; Montgomery County Bar Association; Alabama Defense Lawyers Association; Defense Research Institute — Practice Areas: Employment Law; Litigation; Civil Rights; Defense Litigation — E-mail: ala@ball-ball.com

Hill, Hill, Carter, Franco, Cole & Black, P.C.

425 South Perry Street
Montgomery, Alabama 36104
Telephone: 334-834-7600
Fax: 334-263-5969
E-Mail: thefirm@hillhillcarter.com
www.hillhillcarter.com

Established: 1924

Appellate Practice, Aviation, Business Law, Casualty, Commercial Litigation, Discrimination, Education Law, Employment Law, Insurance Defense, Insurance Fraud, Law Enforcement Liability, Product Liability, Professional Liability, State and Federal Courts, Surety, Transportation, Trial Practice, Workers' Compensation, Insurance Coverage Opinions and Litigation

Firm Profile: Hill, Hill, Carter, Franco, Cole & Black, P.C. was founded in 1924 by Thomas B. Hill, Jr. who was later joined by William Inge Hill, James Stovall and James J. Carter to form the firm, Hill, Hill, Stovall & Carter. The present firm evolved from growth and diversification primarily in the fields of litigation, business, taxation and estates and real estate. Various members have served as presidents of the Alabama State Bar Association, bar commissioners, and interim appellate and trial court judicial appointments. The firm is a proud member of the Claims and Litigation Management Alliance.

The firm has emphasized diversification and specialization in all fields. Its business section includes practice in federal, state and local taxation, estate planning, banking, probate, bankruptcy, employee benefits, construction, real estate and corporate work.

The litigation section practices in all fields of general litigation including insurance defense, product liability, professional liability, aviation, municipal defense, civil rights, construction, commercial, corporate litigation and employment law.

Although the size of the firm and complexity of practice have increased over the years, its objectives have remained unchanged. These objectives are predicated to legal excellence, integrity and welfare of clients.

Insurance Clients

Acceptance Insurance Company
Alabama Home Builders Self Insurers Fund
Alabama Trucking Association Workers' Compensation Fund
American General Life Insurance Company
American Public Life Insurance Company
Associated Aviation Underwriters
CIGNA Property and Casualty Insurance Company
Economy Preferred Insurance Company
George Washington Life Insurance Company
AIG Aviation, Inc.
Alabama Municipal Insurance Corporation
Alfa Insurance Group
American Fidelity Assurance Company
American Heritage Life Insurance Company
AMEX Assurance Company
Blue Cross and Blue Shield of Alabama
The Dodson Group
FCCI Insurance Group
Foremost Insurance Company
Great American Insurance Company

ALABAMA MONTGOMERY

Hill, Hill, Carter, Franco, Cole & Black, P.C., Montgomery, AL (Continued)

Hanover Insurance Company
Integon General Insurance Corporation
Midland National Life Insurance Company
Motorists Mutual Insurance Company
Mutual Savings Life Insurance Company
National Union Fire Insurance Company of Pittsburgh, PA
North American Company for Life and Health Insurance
Northland Insurance Company
Occidental Fire & Casualty Company of North Carolina
Prudential Property and Casualty Insurance Company
Regis Insurance Company
Scottsdale Insurance Company
Star Insurance Company
Transamerica Group/AEGON USA, Inc.
Imperial Casualty and Indemnity Company
Meadowbrook Insurance Group
Monumental General Casualty Company
Mutual of Omaha Insurance Company
National Casualty Company
National General Insurance Company
New England Mutual Life Insurance Company
Northbrook Property and Casualty Insurance Company
Ohio Casualty Group
The Ohio National Life Insurance Company
Reciprocal of America
Republic American Life Insurance Company
State Farm Group
Transport Insurance Company
U.S. Specialty Insurance Company

Lead Counsel for

Housing Authority of the City of Montgomery

Non-Insurance Clients

Absolute Amusement
Alabama Gas Corporation
Alabama League of Municipalities
American Gaming Systems, LLC
Big Lots Stores, Inc.
Capitol Adjustment Company, Inc.
Crawford & Company
Diamond Games
Elwood Staffing
GAB Robins North America, Inc.
General Telephone Company of the South
Greenetrack, Inc.
Innisfree Hotels
Jefferson County Racing Association
KM Administrative Services
Lion Outsourcing Management LLC
The Merchants Company
RoyOMartin Lumber Company, Inc.
Target Promotions, Inc.
Video Gaming Technologies
Alabama Association of School Boards
Ambassador Personnel
Autauga County Board of Education
Construction Materials, Inc.
Cummins Engine Company, Inc.
Elmore County Board of Education
Fountainbleau Management Services, LLC
Genpak, LLC
Globe Metallurgical, Inc.
Hartselle City Board of Education
Insurance Servicing & Adjusting Company
JLT Insurance Services Company
Lancer Claims Services, Inc.
Macon County Greyhound Park
Marinco, Inc.
Montgomery County Board of Education
St. James School
Troy City Board of Education
Winn-Dixie Stores, Inc.

Third Party Administrators

Alabama Risk Management for Schools
Business Insurance Group, LLC
Gallagher Bassett Services, Inc.
Sedgwick Group
Strategic Comp
Associated Claims Administrators, Inc.
Construction Claims Management
North American Risk Services
Sheffield Risk Management
York Risk Services Group, Inc.

Firm Members

John M. Bolton III — 1951 — University of Virginia, B.A., 1974; Cumberland School of Law of Samford University, J.D., 1977 — Admitted to Bar, 1977, Alabama — Member Montgomery County Bar Association; International Association of Gaming Attorneys; Alabama Defense Lawyers Association; Defense Research Institute — Practice Areas: Civil Litigation; Insurance Defense; Complex Commercial Litigation; Gaming Law; Amusement Law — E-mail: jbolton@hillhillcarter.com

Robert W. Bradford, Jr. — 1944 — David Lipscomb College, B.A., 1972; Vanderbilt University Law School, J.D., 1975 — Associate Editor, Vanderbilt Law Review, 1975 — Admitted to Bar, 1975, Alabama; U.S. District Court, Middle, Northern and Southern Districts of Alabama; U.S. Court of Appeals, Fifth and Eleventh Circuits; 1983, U.S. Supreme Court — Member International Association of Defense Counsel — Editorial Board, The Alabama Lawyers — Alabama Super Lawyer (2011, 2012, 2013, & 2014) — United States Navy [1966-1970] — Practice Areas: Aviation; Commercial Litigation; Product Liability; Insurance Law; Insurance Litigation — E-mail: rwbradford@hillhillcarter.com

Hill, Hill, Carter, Franco, Cole & Black, P.C., Montgomery, AL (Continued)

Elizabeth Brannen Carter — 1970 — Troy State University, B.S. (summa cum laude), 1991; Cumberland School of Law of Samford University, J.D., 1994 — Admitted to Bar, 1994, Alabama — Member Alabama State Bar; Montgomery County Bar Association; American Journal of Trial Advocacy; Defense Research Institute - The Voice of Defense Bar; Alabama Defense Lawyers Association; American Trial Lawyers Association — Practice Areas: Employment Law; Commercial Litigation; Business Litigation — E-mail: ecarter@hillhillcarter.com

Shawn Junkins Cole — 1967 — The University of Alabama, B.A., 1990; Cumberland School of Law of Samford University, J.D., 1993 — Admitted to Bar, 1993, Alabama; U.S. District Court, Middle, Northern and Southern Districts of Alabama — Member Alabama State Bar; Montgomery County Bar Association; Alabama Workers' Compensation Defense Association; Alabama Workers' Compensation Organization (AWCO); Alabama Trucking Association; Hugh Maddox Inn of Court; Alabama Defense Lawyers Association — Assistant Attorney General (1993-1995) — Practice Areas: Workers' Compensation; Insurance Defense; Insurance Litigation — E-mail: scole@hillhillcarter.com

Royal C. Dumas — 1972 — Southern Methodist University, M.M., 2002; The University of Alabama School of Law, J.D., 2007 — Admitted to Bar, 2007, Alabama; 2008, Mississippi — Member American and Montgomery County (Board of Directors) Bar Associations; Alabama State Bar (Chair, Pro Bono Task Force; Pro Bono Long Range Planning Task Force); Alabama Defense Lawyers Association; Defense Research Institute — Practice Areas: Civil Litigation; Insurance Defense; Environmental Law — E-mail: rdumas@hillhillcarter.com

David W. Henderson — 1974 — Faulkner University, B.S., 1996; Faulkner University, Thomas Goode Jones School of Law, J.D., 2002 — Admitted to Bar, 2002, Alabama — Member Alabama State Bar; Montgomery County Bar Association; Montgomery Area Chamber of Commerce; American Inns of Court (Hugh Maddox Chapter); Defense Research Institute; International Association of Defense Counsel — E-5 Sergeant, United States Marine Corps Reserve [1994-2000] — Practice Areas: Insurance Defense; Litigation; Defense Litigation; Product Liability; Workers' Compensation — E-mail: dwhenderson@hillhillcarter.com

Felicia Long — 1978 — Auburn University, B.A., 2000; Faulkner University, Thomas Goode Jones School of Law, J.D., 2003 — Admitted to Bar, 2003, Alabama; U.S. District Court, Middle and Southern Districts of Alabama; U.S. Court of Appeals, Eleventh Circuit; U.S. Supreme Court — Member Alabama State Bar; Montgomery County Bar Association (Board of Directors); American Inns of Court t(Hugh Maddox Chapter); Alabama Defense Lawyers Association — Practice Areas: Civil Litigation; Insurance Defense; Commercial Litigation; Complex Litigation; Construction Litigation — E-mail: flong@hillhillcarter.com

Randall Morgan — 1949 — Auburn University, B.A., 1971; University of Maryland School of Law, J.D., 1974 — Admitted to Bar, 1974, Alabama — Practice Areas: Litigation; Civil Rights; Municipal Law; Product Liability; Professional Liability — E-mail: rmorgan@hillhillcarter.com

James R. Seale — 1944 — Emory University; The University of Alabama, B.A., 1966; The University of Alabama School of Law, J.D., 1969 — Admitted to Bar, 1969, Alabama; 1973, Florida; 1981, U.S. Supreme Court — Member Alabama State Bar (Board of Commissioners, 1987-1992); Executive Committee, 1988-1990; Disciplinary Commission, 1990-1992; President, 1993-1994); Montgomery County Bar Association (President, 1986; Board of Directors and Secretary,1982-1985); Southern Conference of Bar Presidents (President 1993-1994); Alabama Council of School Board Attorneys (President, 1999-2000) — Captain, Judge Advocate General, United States Air Force [1969-1972]; Major, United States Air Force Reserves [1972-1982] — Practice Areas: Construction Law; Employment Law; School Law; Civil Litigation; Professional Liability; Education Law — E-mail: jrs@hillhillcarter.com

Pamela B. Slate — 1966 — Birmingham-Southern College, B.S., 1990; The University of Alabama at Birmingham, B.S., 1990; Cumberland School of Law at Samford University, J.D., 1993 — Admitted to Bar, 1993, Alabama; 1995, Mississippi — Practice Areas: Complex Litigation; Commercial Litigation; Antitrust; Mass Tort; Class Actions — E-mail: pslate@hillhillcarter.com

Charlanna W. Spencer — 1974 — Auburn University, B.A., 1996; Cumberland School of Law of Samford University, J.D., 1999 — Admitted to Bar, 1999, Alabama; U.S. District Court, Middle, Northern and Southern Districts of Alabama; U.S. Court of Appeals, Eleventh Circuit — Member Alabama State Bar; Montgomery County Bar Association; Hugh Maddox Inn of Court; Alabama Defense Lawyers Association; Defense Research Institute —

MONTGOMERY ALABAMA

Hill, Hill, Carter, Franco, Cole & Black, P.C., Montgomery, AL (Continued)

Practice Areas: Commercial Litigation; Complex Commercial Litigation; Legislative Law; Gaming Law; Amusement Law; Appellate Practice — E-mail: cspencer@hillhillcarter.com

Erika Perrone Tatum — 1971 — Florida State University, B.A., 1993; Cumberland University School of Law, J.D., 1996 — Admitted to Bar, 1996, Georgia; 1999, Alabama; U.S. District Court, Middle, Northern and Southern Districts of Alabama — Member Montgomery County Bar Association; National School Board Association Council of School Attorneys; Alabama Council of School Board Attorneys; Alabama Defense Lawyers Association — Practice Areas: Education Law; Civil Litigation — E-mail: etatum@hillhillcarter.com

Jayne Harrell Williams — 1974 — Florida A&M University, B.A., 1995; Georgetown University Law Center, J.D., 2000 — Admitted to Bar, 2001, Alabama — Member Alabama State Bar; Montgomery County Bar Association; Alabama Council for School Board Attorneys; National School Board Association Council of School Attorneys; Alabama Defense Lawyers Association — Practice Areas: Appellate Practice; School Law; Employment Discrimination — E-mail: jhwilliams@hillhillcarter.com

Associate

James E. Beck III — 1983 — Sewanee, The University of the South, B.A. (magna cum laude), 2006; The University of Alabama School of Law, J.D., 2009 — Admitted to Bar, 2009, Alabama — Member Alabama State Bar (Volunteer Lawyers Program); Montgomery County Bar Association (Pro Bono Clinic); American Inns of Court (Hugh Maddox Chapter); Alabama Defense Lawyers Association; Defense Research Institute — Practice Areas: Litigation; Insurance Litigation; Business Litigation; Commercial Litigation — E-mail: jbeck@hillhillcarter.com

Of Counsel

William I. Hill, II — 1938 — The University of Alabama, B.A., 1960; The University of Alabama School of Law, J.D., 1962 — Admitted to Bar, 1962, Alabama — Member Alabama State Bar; Montgomery County Bar Association; Defense Research Institute; International Association of Defense Counsel — Captain, Judge Advocate General Corps, U.S. Army [1962-1964] — Practice Areas: Civil Litigation; Commercial Litigation; Insurance Coverage & Defense; Insurance Litigation; Product Liability — E-mail: whill@hillhillcarter.com

T. Bowen Hill, III — 1929 — The University of Alabama School of Law, LL.B., 1953 — Award of Merit from the Alabama State Bar for Services as Member and Chairman of the State Grievance Committee — Admitted to Bar, 1953, Alabama — Member Montgomery County Bar Association (President, 1968); American College of Mortage Attorneys; Alabama State Bar Grievance Committee (Past Member & Chairman); AAA Alabama (Board of Directors) — AV Rated by Martindale-Hubbell (1974-present) — Practice Areas: Estate Planning; Probate; Real Estate — E-mail: tbhill@hillhillcarter.com

Holtsford Gilliland Higgins Hitson & Howard, P.C.

4001 Carmichael Road, Suite 300
Montgomery, Alabama 36106
Telephone: 334-215-8585
Toll Free: 800-932-6964
Fax: 334-215-7101
E-Mail: info@hglawpc.com
www.hglawpc.com

(Daphne, AL Office*(See Mobile listing): 29000 U.S. Highway 98, Suite A-302, 36526-7263)
(Tel: 251-447-0234)
(Fax: 251-447-0212)

Established: 1989

Insurance Defense, Automobile, Professional Liability, Product Liability, Civil Rights, Toxic Torts, General Liability, Environmental Law, Workers' Compensation, Construction Law, Coverage Issues, Governmental Entity Defense, Forestry Law

Holtsford Gilliland Higgins Hitson & Howard, P.C., Montgomery, AL (Continued)

Firm Profile: Our Mission is to be the preeminent law firm in our coverage territory. We plan to accomplish our mission by handling every case with a sense of urgency, in a cost effective manner and in a form that meets or exceeds all expectations.

Holtsford Gilliland's focus is resolving claims involving business, governmental and insurance related issues through litigation, negotiation, mediation and arbitration.

Insurance Clients

Alabama Municipal Insurance Corporation
American International Group, Inc.
CNA Insurance Company
Crum & Forster Insurance
Federated Mutual Insurance Company
International Indemnity Company
Lumber Mutual Insurance Company
Northbrook Property and Casualty Insurance Company
Shand Morahan & Company, Inc.
Southern Heritage Insurance Company
Tokio Marine and Fire Insurance Company, Ltd.
United States Fidelity and Guaranty Company
Westco Claims Management Services, Inc.
Alfa Insurance Corporation
All Risk Claims Service, Inc.
Auto-Owners Insurance Company
Continental National Indemnity Company
General Casualty Companies
Great American Insurance Company
Mississippi Valley Title Insurance Company
Ohio Casualty Group
Progressive Insurance Company
Skandia U.S. Insurance Company
State Farm Group
State of Alabama Employees General Liability Trust Fund
Travelers Property Casualty Corporation
Wausau General Insurance Company
Zurich American Insurance Group

Non-Insurance Clients

Coastal Chemical Corporation
Trinity Companies

Firm Members

Alex L. Holtsford, Jr. — 1959 — The University of Alabama, B.S., 1981; Cumberland School of Law of Samford University, J.D. (cum laude), 1985 — Admitted to Bar, 1985, Alabama; 1986, U.S. District Court, Middle District of Alabama; 1988, U.S. District Court, Northern District of Alabama; 1989, U.S. Court of Appeals, Eleventh Circuit — Member American and Montgomery County (Board of Directors, President) Bar Associations; Alabama State Bar; Alabama Defense Lawyers Association (Board of Directors, Past President) — Professor, Faulkner University School of Law, Appellate Advocacy and Conflicts of Law, 1986-1997 — E-mail: aholtsford@hglawpc.com

Floyd R. Gilliland, Jr. — 1939 — Arkansas Tech University, B.S., 1962; University of Arkansas, M.S., 1964; Mississippi State University, Ph.D., 1967; Faulkner University, Thomas Goode Jones School of Law, J.D., 1992 — Phi Kappa Phi; Sigma Xi; Gamma Sigma Delta — Admitted to Bar, 1993, Alabama; U.S. District Court, Middle, Northern and Southern Districts of Alabama; U.S. Court of Appeals, Eleventh Circuit — Member American and Montgomery County Bar Associations; Alabama State Bar; American Agricultural Law Association; Alabama Defense Lawyers Association — E-mail: fgilliland@hglawpc.com

Steven A. Higgins — 1967 — The University of Georgia, B.B.A., 1989; The University of Alabama School of Law, J.D., 1992 — Mu Kappa Tau; Alpha Kappa Psi — Law Clerk to Justice Hugh Maddox, Alabama Supreme Court, 1992-1993 — Admitted to Bar, 1992, Alabama; U.S. District Court, Middle, Northern and Southern Districts of Alabama; U.S. Court of Appeals, Eleventh Circuit — Member Alabama State Bar; Montgomery County Bar Association; Alabama Defense Lawyers Association — E-mail: thiggins@hglawpc.com

Kenneth A. Hitson, Jr. — 1964 — The University of Alabama, B.A., 1986; Cumberland School of Law of Samford University, J.D., 1989 — Phi Alpha Delta — Law Clerk to the Honorable H. Randall Thomas, Circuit Judge, Fifteenth Judicial Circuit of Alabama — Admitted to Bar, 1989, Alabama; U.S. District Court, Middle and Southern Districts of Alabama — Member Alabama State Bar; Montgomery County Bar Association; Alabama District Attorneys Association; Alabama Defense Lawyers Association; Defense Research Institute — E-mail: khitson@hglawpc.com

Rick A. Howard — 1967 — The University of North Alabama, B.S., 1989; Christian Brothers College, M.B.A., 1993; Cumberland School of Law of Samford University, J.D., 1997 — Admitted to Bar, 1997, Alabama; U.S. District Court, Middle District of Alabama; U.S. Court of Appeals, Eleventh

ALABAMA MONTGOMERY

Holtsford Gilliland Higgins Hitson & Howard, P.C., Montgomery, AL (Continued)

Circuit — Member Alabama State Bar; Montgomery County Bar Association; Alabama Defense Lawyers Association — E-mail: rhoward@hglawpc.com

David P. Stevens — 1970 — Washington and Lee University, B.A. (cum laude), 1992; Cumberland School of Law of Samford University, J.D., 1995 — Law Clerk to Justice Terry L. Butts, Alabama Supreme Court, 1995-1996 — Admitted to Bar, 1995, Alabama; U.S. District Court, Middle District of Alabama — Member Alabama State Bar; Montgomery County Bar Association; Alabama Defense Lawyers Association — E-mail: dstevens@hglawpc.com

Jay S. Tuley — 1973 — Auburn University, B.A., 1995; The University of Alabama School of Law, J.D. (with honors), 1998 — Phi Gamma Delta — Senior Editor, Journal of the Legal Profession, 1997-1998 — Admitted to Bar, 1998, Alabama; U.S. District Court, Middle, Northern and Southern Districts of Alabama; U.S. Court of Appeals, Eleventh Circuit — Member American and Montgomery County Bar Associations; Alabama Defense Lawyers Association — E-mail: jtuley@hglawpc.com

S. Mark Dukes — 1957 — Vanderbilt University, B.A., 1979; Georgetown University, M.A., 1988; The University of Alabama School of Law, J.D., 1995 — Admitted to Bar, 1995, Alabama; U.S. District Court, Middle and Northern Districts of Alabama; 2002, U.S. District Court, Southern District of Alabama; 2007, U.S. Court of Appeals, Eleventh Circuit — Member Alabama State Bar; Montgomery County Bar Association; Alabama Defense Lawyers Association; Defense Research Institute — U.S. Army [1979-1983]; Captain, U.S. Army Reserve, Military Intelligence [1983-1992] — E-mail: mdukes@hglawpc.com

Murry S. Whitt — 1973 — Auburn University, B.S. (magna cum laude), 1996; The University of Georgia School of Law, J.D., 1999 — Admitted to Bar, 1999, Alabama — Legal Counsel, U.S. Air Force — E-mail: mwhitt@hglawpc.com

April W. McKay — 1976 — Auburn University, B.S. (cum laude), 1998; The University of Alabama School of Law, J.D. (cum laude), 2002 — Admitted to Bar, 2002, Alabama; U.S. District Court, Middle, Northern and Southern Districts of Alabama; U.S. Court of Appeals, Eleventh Circuit — Member American Bar Association; Alabama State Bar; Defense Research Institute; Alabama Defense Lawyers Association — E-mail: amckay@hglawpc.com

Associates

Megan K. McCarthy — 1978 — Sewanee, The University of the South, B.S., 2001; University of Baltimore School of Law, J.D., 2004 — Law Clerk to the Honorable C. Clark Raley, Seventh Judicial Circuit of Maryland — Executive Editor, University of Baltimore Law Review — Admitted to Bar, 2004, Maryland; 2005, Alabama; U.S. District Court, Middle District of Alabama — E-mail: mmccarthy@hglawpc.com

Jarred E. Kaplan — 1978 — The University of Alabama, B.A., 2001; Faulkner University, Thomas Goode Jones School of Law, J.D., 2006 — Admitted to Bar, 2006, Alabama — Member American and Montgomery County Bar Associaitons; Alabama State Bar — E-mail: jkaplan@hglawpc.com

Rebecca L. Chambliss — Auburn University, B.S. (cum laude), 2005; Cumberland University School of Law, J.D., 2010 — Admitted to Bar, 2010, Alabama — Member American, Montgomery County and Birmingham Bar Associations; Alabama State Bar; Alabama Defense Lawyers Association; Defense Research Institute — E-mail: rchambliss@hglawpc.com

Alex (Trey) L. Holtsford III — The University of Alabama, B.A., 2009; The University of Alabama School of Law, J.D., 2013 — Phi Alpha Theta History Honor Society — Senior Editor, Law and Psychology Law Review — Admitted to Bar, 2013, Alabama — Member Alabama State Bar; Montgomery County Bar Association — E-mail: tholtsford@hglawpc.com

Joseph VanZandt — 1986 — Faulkner University, B.S. (summa cum laude, with honors), 2009; Faulkner University, Thomas Goode Jones School of Law, J.D., 2012 — Admitted to Bar, 2012, Alabama; U.S. District Court, Middle, Northern and Southern Districts of Alabama — Member Alabama State Bar — E-mail: jvanzandt@hglawpc.com

Of Counsel

Joana S. Ellis — 1959 — Samford University; Auburn University at Montgomery, B.S., 1979; The University of Alabama School of Law, J.D., 1983 — Admitted to Bar, 1983, Alabama — E-mail: jellis@hglawpc.com

Morrow, Romine & Pearson, P.C.
122 South Hull Street
Montgomery, Alabama 36104
   Telephone: 334-262-7707
   Fax: 334-262-7742
   E-Mail: rsmorrow@mrplaw.com

Civil Trial Practice, Insurance Law, Medical Malpractice, Product Liability, Environmental Coverage, Personal Injury, Litigation, Mediation, Trial Practice, Appellate Practice, State and Federal Courts, Handicap and Employment Discrimination, Diving Accidents

Firm Profile: The law firm of Morrow, Romine & Pearson, P.C., was founded in 1987 by Roger S. Morrow and Wesley Romine who had formerly been associates or law partners in two prior firms. They have practiced together since 1980. Joel H. Pearson became a member of the firm in 1989. Mallory M. Combest became an associate attorney with the firm in 2013. The firm's practice is directed to the representation of litigants in both state and federal courts. The firm is also engaged in appellate practice, administrative law proceedings and arbitration and mediation practice.

Insurance Clients

American Mining Insurance Company
Auto-Owners Group
Chubb Group of Insurance Companies
FARA Insurance Services
Pennsylvania Lumbermens Mutual Insurance Company
Armed Forces Insurance Exchange
Attorneys Insurance Mutual of the South, Inc.
Claim Professionals Liability Insurance Company, A RRG
Owners Insurance Company
State Auto Insurance Group

Shareholders

Roger S. Morrow — 1954 — Birmingham-Southern College, B.S., 1976; The University of Alabama, J.D., 1979 — Order of the Coif — Law Clerk to Justice T. Eric Embry, Alabama Supreme Court, 1979-1980 — Senior Editor, Journal of the Legal Profession, 1978-1979 — Admitted to Bar, 1979, Alabama; 1981, U.S. District Court, Middle, Northern and Southern Districts of Alabama; U.S. Court of Appeals, Eleventh Circuit; 1986, U.S. Supreme Court — Member Federal, American and Montgomery County Bar Associations; Alabama State Bar; Defense Research Institute; Alabama Defense Lawyers Association — Special Assistant Attorney General, Alabama, 1987-1990; Deputy Attorney General, Alabama, 1993-1995 — Certified Mediator and Arbitrator

Wesley Romine — 1950 — Auburn University, B.A., 1972; The University of Alabama, J.D., 1977 — Law Clerk to Judge Robert P. Bradley, Alabama Court of Civil Appeals, 1977-1978 — Managing Editor, Journal of the Legal Profession, 1976-1977 — Admitted to Bar, 1977, Alabama; 1978, U.S. District Court, Middle, Northern and Southern Districts of Alabama; U.S. Court of Appeals, Eleventh Circuit; 1986, U.S. Supreme Court — Member American and Montgomery County Bar Associations; Alabama State Bar; American Arbitration Association (Arbitrator); The Financial Industry Regulatory Authority (Arbitrator and Mediator) — Mediator, United States Arbitration of the South, 1988-Present; Deputy Attorney General, Alabama, 1993-1995

Joel H. Pearson — 1958 — University of South Alabama, B.S., 1981; The University of Alabama, J.D., 1984 — Omicron Delta Kappa; Phi Delta Phi — Admitted to Bar, 1985, Alabama; U.S. District Court, Middle, Northern and Southern Districts of Alabama; U.S. Court of Appeals, Eleventh Circuit; 1991, U.S. Supreme Court — Member American and Montgomery County Bar Associations; Alabama State Bar

Associate

Mallory M. Combest — The University of Alabama, B.A. (cum laude, with honors), 2007; The University of Alabama School of Law, J.D., 2010 — Admitted to Bar, 2010, Alabama; U.S. District Court, Middle, Northern and Southern Districts of Alabama; U.S. Court of Appeals, Eleventh Circuit — Member American and Montgomery County Bar Associations; Alabama State Bar; Defense Research Institute; Alabama Defense Lawyers Association

Rushton, Stakely, Johnston & Garrett, P.A.

184 Commerce Street
Montgomery, Alabama 36104
Telephone: 334-206-3100
Fax: 334-262-6277
E-Mail: lmcglaun@rushtonstakely.com
www.rushtonstakely.com

Established: 1890

Insurance Defense, Trial and Appellate Practice, Accountants and Attorneys Liability, Administrative Law, Advertising Injury, Agent and Brokers Errors and Omissions, Appellate Practice, Arbitration, Automobile Tort, Bad Faith, Business Law, Casualty Insurance Law, Class Actions, Commercial Litigation, Complex Litigation, Construction Litigation, Contract Disputes, Copyright and Trademark Law, Coverage Analysis, Declaratory Judgments, Directors and Officers Liability, Employment Law, Environmental Law, Family Law, Fidelity and Surety, Fraud, Health Care, Health Care Professional Licensure Defense, Insurance Litigation, Labor and Employment, Law Enforcement Liability, Legal Malpractice, Medical Devices, Medical Malpractice, Pharmaceutical, Premises Liability, Primary and Excess Insurance, Product Liability, Professional Errors and Omissions, Professional Liability, Surety, Title Insurance, Uninsured and Underinsured Motorist, Workers' Compensation, Wrongful Death

Firm Profile: Rushton, Stakely, Johnston & Garrett, P.A. was founded in 1890 in Montgomery, Alabama. The Firm has practiced under its present name since 1942 and is presently composed of over 30 attorneys. The Firm's litigation practice is substantially defense oriented in the areas of professional liability, antitrust, commercial business disputes, labor and employment law, media, pharmaceutical and medical device defense, products liability, insurance defense, fraud and securities cases. The Firm also has attorneys who specialize in health care matters representing hospitals, physician groups, surgical centers and other providers.

Representative Clients

Acceptance Insurance Company
Alfa Mutual Insurance Company Columbus
Allied Van Lines
American Family Life Assurance Company of New York
American Hardware Mutual Insurance Company
American Modern Home Insurance Company
American Specialty Insurance & Risk Services, Inc.
Amerisure Companies
Arthur J. Gallagher Risk Management Services, Inc.
Attorneys Insurance Mutual of the South, Inc.
Canal Insurance Company
Cincinnati Insurance Company
CNA Insurance Companies
Companion Property and Casualty Group
Continental Insurance Company
DCS North America, LLC
Employers Insurance Company of Wausau
Essex Insurance Company
Farmers Insurance Group
Federated Rural Electric Insurance Exchange
Fidelity and Deposit Company of Maryland
Fireman's Fund Insurance Company
Georgia Mutual Insurance
Glovis Alabama, LLC
The Guardian Life Insurance Company of America
Hanover Insurance Company
AFLAC - American Family Life Assurance Company of
American Family Insurance Company
American General Life Insurance Company
American International Group, Inc.
American Safety Claims Services, Inc.
American States Insurance Company
Amica Mutual Insurance Company
Aspen Specialty Insurance Company
Auto-Owners Insurance Company
Averitt Express, Inc.
Central United Life Insurance Company
Colonial Life and Accident Insurance Company
Consumers Insurance Company
CUMIS Insurance Society, Inc.
Employers Claim Management, Inc.
Employers Reinsurance Corporation
Federated Insurance Company
The Fidelity and Casualty Company of New York
Fidelity Security Life Insurance Company
Gallagher Bassett Services, Inc.
General Insurance Company of America
Great American Insurance Company
Gulf Insurance Company
INAPRO
Insurance Corporation of America
John Hancock Life Insurance Company
Lexington Insurance Company
Liberty Mutual Insurance Company
Markel Corporation
Maryland American General Insurance Company
Metropolitan Insurance Company
National Bonding and Accident Insurance Company
National Health Insurance Company
New Hampshire Insurance Company
Overnite Transportation Company
Protective Life Insurance Company
QBE North America
Safeco Insurance Company of America
The St. Paul Companies
Southeastern Fidelity Insurance Company
Southern Railway Company
State Farm Insurance Companies
TIG Specialty Insurance Company
Union Standard Insurance Company
United States Fidelity and Guaranty Company
Universal Underwriters Insurance Company
Western Casualty and Surety Company
Windsor Insurance Company
Integon General Insurance Corporation
Lawyers Title Insurance Corporation
Life Insurance Company of Georgia
Medical Assurance, Inc., A ProAssurance Company
Metropolitan Property and Casualty Insurance Company
National Fire and Marine Insurance Company
National Indemnity Company
New York Life Insurance Company
ProAssurance Group
Provident Life and Accident Insurance Company
Safeway Insurance Company of Alabama
Security Insurance Group
Southern Home Insurance Company
State Auto Insurance Companies
Superior Insurance Company
Travelers Insurance Companies
United Educators - Education's Own Insurance Company
Universal Guaranty Life Insurance Company
Vanliner Insurance Company
Wausau Insurance Companies
Western World Insurance Company

President

Thomas H. Keene — 1948 — The University of Alabama, B.S., 1970; M.B.A., 1971; J.D., 1974 — Admitted to Bar, 1974, Alabama — Member American and Montgomery County Bar Associations; Alabama State Bar; American Board of Trial Advocates (Advocate); International Academy of Trial Lawyers; Fellow, American College of Trial Lawyers; Alabama Defense Lawyers Association; Defense Research Institute — Best Lawyers in America (Listed Every Year since Inception; Named 2012 & 2013 Montgomery Personal Injury Litigation - Defendants Lawyer of the Year); Alabama Super Lawyers (Listed 2008-2014; Included in Top 50 Lawyers in Alabama); Chambers USA (Ranked Band 1 - Litigation 2012-2014) — Practice Areas: Professional Liability; Medical Malpractice; Health Care Liability; Health Care Professional Licensure Defense; Medical Devices; Commercial Litigation; Insurance Defense; Labor and Employment; Pharmaceutical — E-mail: thk@rushtonstakely.com

Partners/Shareholders

J. Theodore Jackson, Jr. — 1944 — Samford University, B.A., 1966; University of Virginia, LL.B., 1969 — 2013 Corporate INTL Magazine Legal Award in Energy Law - Lawyer of the Year in Alabama — Admitted to Bar, 1969, Alabama — Member American and Montgomery County Bar Associations; Alabama State Bar — Listed in Best Lawyers in America (2014 and Every Year Since Inception) — Practice Areas: Energy; Corporate Law; Environmental Law; Estate Planning; Mergers and Acquisitions — E-mail: jtj@rushtonstakely.com

James W. Garrett, Jr. — 1946 — The University of Alabama, B.A., 1968; J.D., 1971 — Admitted to Bar, 1971, Alabama — Member Alabama State Bar; Montgomery County Bar Association; Alabama Defense Lawyers Association; Defense Research Institute — Best Lawyers in America (2013 Montgomery Insurance Lawyer of the Year) — Practice Areas: Insurance Defense; Alternative Dispute Resolution; Mediation — E-mail: jwg@rushtonstakely.com

Jeffrey W. Blitz — 1951 — The University of Alabama, B.S., 1973; J.D., 1976 — Admitted to Bar, 1976, Alabama — Member American and Montgomery County Bar Associations; Alabama State Bar; American College of Mortgage Attorneys — Best Lawyers in America (Listed for over 12 years; Named Lawyer of the Year in Real Estate for the Montgomery Area (2010-2012); Alabama Super Lawyers (2008-2014); Listed in Birmingham Business Journal "Leading Lawyers of Alabama"; Ranked Band 1 in Real Estate by Chambers USA — Practice Areas: Real Estate; Commercial Transactions — E-mail: jwb@rushtonstakely.com

ALABAMA — MONTGOMERY

Rushton, Stakely, Johnston & Garrett, P.A., Montgomery, AL (Continued)

Dennis R. Bailey — 1953 — Auburn University, B.A., 1975; Samford University, J.D. (cum laude), 1979 — Admitted to Bar, 1979, Alabama — Member Alabama State Bar; Montgomery County Bar Association; American Board of Trial Advocates; Defense Research Institute; Alabama Defense Lawyers Association — Best Lawyers in America (Listed 2011-2014; Named Lawyer of the Year in Products Liability Litigation for the Montgomery Area 2012) — Practice Areas: Commercial Litigation; Media & Intellectual Property; Product Liability; Insurance Defense; Appellate Practice; Environmental Law; Labor and Employment — E-mail: drb@rushtonstakely.com

Ronald G. Davenport — 1947 — Huntingdon College, B.A., 1970; The University of Alabama, J.D., 1975 — Admitted to Bar, 1975, Alabama — Member Alabama State Bar; Montgomery County Bar Association; American Board of Trial Advocates; Alabama Defense Lawyers Association; Defense Research Institute — Author: "Alabama Automobile Insurance Law," Thomson-West, 1989 and 2002 — Best Lawyers in America (2005-2014); Alabama Super Lawyers (2009-2014) — Practice Areas: Insurance Defense; Insurance Coverage; Professional Liability; Commercial Litigation; Product Liability; Alternative Dispute Resolution; Mediation; Pharmaceutical — E-mail: rgd@rushtonstakely.com

Fred W. Tyson — 1956 — The University of Alabama, B.S., 1978; Samford University, J.D., 1982 — Admitted to Bar, 1982, Alabama — Member Alabama State Bar; Montgomery County Bar Association; Fellow, American College of Trial Lawyers; American Board of Trial Advocates; Alabama Defense Lawyers Association; Defense Research Institute — Best Lawyers in America (Listed 2005-2014; Named 2013 Montgomery Medical Malpractice Lawyer of the Year); Alabama Super Lawyers (2009-2014) — Practice Areas: Professional Liability; Medical Malpractice; Health Care; Health Care Professional Licensure Defense; Insurance Defense — E-mail: fwt@rushtonstakely.com

T. Kent Garrett — 1954 — Huntingdon College, B.A., 1976; The University of Alabama, J.D., 1979 — Admitted to Bar, 1980, Florida; 1981, Alabama — Member Alabama State Bar; The Florida Bar; Montgomery County Bar Association; Alabama Defense Lawyers Association; Defense Research Institute — Practice Areas: Insurance Defense; Insurance Coverage — E-mail: tkg@rushtonstakely.com

Frank J. Stakely — 1962 — The University of Alabama, B.S., 1984; J.D., 1987 — Admitted to Bar, 1987, Alabama — Member Alabama State Bar; Montgomery County Bar Association; American College of Trial Lawyers; American Board of Trial Advocates; Alabama Defense Lawyers Association; Defense Research Institute — Best Lawyers in America (Listed 2008-2014; Named 2014 Lawyer of the Year in Personal Injury Litigation - Defendants) — Practice Areas: Professional Liability; Medical Malpractice; Insurance Defense; Product Liability; Pharmaceutical — E-mail: fjs@rushtonstakely.com

William S. Haynes — 1962 — The University of Alabama, B.A., 1984; J.D., 1987 — Admitted to Bar, 1987, Alabama — Member Alabama State Bar; Montgomery County Bar Association; American Board of Trial Advocates; Alabama Defense Lawyers Association; Defense Research Institute — Best Lawyers in America (Listed over 10 Years); Alabama Super Lawyers (Listed 2008-2010; Listed in Top 25 Women Attorneys in Alabama 2010) — Practice Areas: Professional Liability; Medical Malpractice; Health Care; Health Care Professional Licensure Defense; Insurance Defense — E-mail: wsh@rushtonstakely.com

Helen Crump Wells — 1943 — The University of Alabama, B.S., 1965; Samford University, J.D. (summa cum laude), 1988 — Admitted to Bar, 1988, Alabama — Member Alabama State Bar; Montgomery County Bar Association; American College of Trust & Estate Counsel — Best Lawyers in America; Alabama Super Lawyers; Martindale-Hubbell Bar Register of Preeminent Women Lawyers (2012-2013) — Practice Areas: Estate Planning; Corporate Law; Business Formation; Mergers and Acquisitions — E-mail: hcw@rushtonstakely.com

Paul M. James, Jr. — 1964 — Washington and Lee University, B.A., 1986; Samford University, J.D., 1992 — Admitted to Bar, 1992, Alabama — Member Alabama State Bar; Montgomery County Bar Association; Alabama Defense Lawyers Association; Defense Research Institute — Best Lawyers in America (2010-2014) — Practice Areas: Insurance Defense; Insurance Coverage; Commercial Litigation; Labor and Employment — E-mail: pmj@rushtonstakely.com

Christopher S. Simmons — 1967 — The University of Alabama, B.S., 1989; J.D., 1992; New York University, LL.M., 1993 — Admitted to Bar, 1992, Alabama — Member Alabama State Bar; Montgomery County Bar Association — Best Lawyers in America (Listed over 12 Years; Named 2013 Montgomery Litigation & Controversy - Tax Lawyer of the Year) — Practice Areas: Corporate Law; Health Care; Energy; Mergers and Acquisitions; Estate Planning — E-mail: css@rushtonstakely.com

Robert C. Ward, Jr. — (1956-2014)

Daniel L. Lindsey, Jr. — 1966 — Auburn University, B.S., 1988; The University of Alabama, J.D., 1994; New York University, LL.M., 1995 — Admitted to Bar, 1994, Alabama — Member Alabama State Bar — Listed in Best Lawyers in America (2013 Montgomery Trusts & Estates Lawyer of the Year) — Practice Areas: Corporate Law; Business Formation; Mergers and Acquisitions; Estate Planning — E-mail: dll@rushtonstakely.com

Patrick M. Shegon — 1970 — Auburn University at Montgomery, B.S. (summa cum laude), 1992; The University of Alabama, J.D. (summa cum laude), 1995 — Admitted to Bar, 1995, Alabama — Member American and Montgomery County Bar Associations; Alabama State Bar; American Board of Trial Advocates; Alabama Defense Lawyers Association; Defense Research Institute — Best Lawyers in America (2009-2014); Alabama Super Lawyers Rising Stars (2010); Benchmark Litigation Future Star (2012) — Practice Areas: Professional Liability; Medical Malpractice; Health Care; Health Care Professional Licensure Defense; Insurance Defense; Product Liability — E-mail: pms@rushtonstakely.com

William I. Eskridge — 1968 — The University of Alabama, B.S., 1991; J.D., 1995 — Best Lawyers in America — Admitted to Bar, 1995, Alabama — Member Alabama State Bar; Montgomery County Bar Association — Practice Areas: Real Estate; Commercial Transactions; Environmental Law — E-mail: wie@rushtonstakely.com

L. Peyton Chapman III — 1970 — Washington and Lee University, B.A., 1992; The University of Alabama, J.D., 1996 — Admitted to Bar, 1996, Alabama — Member Alabama State Bar; Montgomery County Bar Association; International Association of Defense Counsel; Alabama Defense Lawyers Association; Defense Research Institute — Best Lawyers in America; Alabama Super Lawyers — Practice Areas: Professional Liability; Medical Malpractice; Health Care; Health Care Professional Licensure Defense; Insurance Defense; Product Liability — E-mail: lpc@rushtonstakely.com

Benjamin C. Wilson — 1970 — The University of Alabama, B.A., 1993; J.D., 1996 — Admitted to Bar, 1996, Alabama — Member Alabama State Bar; Montgomery County Bar Association; Alabama Defense Lawyers Association; Defense Research Institute — Practice Areas: Professional Liability; Medical Malpractice; Health Care; Insurance Defense; Labor and Employment; Pharmaceutical; Product Liability — E-mail: bcw@rushtonstakely.com

Alan T. Hargrove, Jr. — 1972 — Birmingham-Southern College, B.A., 1994; The University of Alabama, J.D., 1999 — Admitted to Bar, 1999, Alabama — Member Federal and Montgomery County Bar Associations; Alabama State Bar; Alabama Defense Lawyers Association; Defense Research Institute — Practice Areas: Insurance Coverage; Insurance Defense; Pharmaceutical; Commercial Litigation; Product Liability; Labor and Employment — E-mail: ath@rushtonstakely.com

R. Austin Huffaker, Jr. — 1973 — Vanderbilt University, B.E. (cum laude), 1996; The University of Alabama, J.D. (magna cum laude), 1999 — Admitted to Bar, 1999, Alabama — Member Federal (President, Montgomery Chapter) and Montgomery County Bar Associations; Alabama State Bar; Alabama Defense Lawyers Association; Defense Research Institute — Alabama Super Lawyers — Practice Areas: Commercial Litigation; Appellate Practice; Labor and Employment; Administrative Law; Insurance Defense; Product Liability; Professional Liability; Pharmaceutical — E-mail: rah2@rushtonstakely.com

Richard L. McBride, Jr. — 1970 — Princeton University, B.A., 1993; The University of Alabama, J.D., 1999; New York University, LL.M., 2000 — Admitted to Bar, 1999, Alabama — Member Alabama State Bar; Montgomery County Bar Association — Practice Areas: Government Affairs; Corporate Law; Business Formation; Estate Planning; Health Care; Mergers and Acquisitions; Energy — E-mail: rlm@rushtonstakely.com

James R. Dickens Jr. — 1978 — Auburn University, B.S., 2000; The University of Alabama, J.D. (cum laude), 2003 — Admitted to Bar, 2003, Alabama — Member Alabama State Bar; Montgomery County Bar Association — Practice Areas: Real Estate; Commercial Transactions; Environmental Law — E-mail: jrd@rushtonstakely.com

R. Mac Freeman, Jr. — 1975 — Birmingham-Southern College, B.A., 1997; Samford University, J.D., 2002 — Admitted to Bar, 2002, Alabama — Member Federal and Montgomery County Bar Associations; Alabama State Bar; Alabama Defense Lawyers Association; Defense Research Institute — Alabama Super Lawyers Rising Star 2012 — Practice Areas: Insurance Coverage; Insurance Defense; Professional Liability; Product Liability — E-mail: rmf@rushtonstakely.com

MONTGOMERY ALABAMA

Rushton, Stakely, Johnston & Garrett, P.A., Montgomery, AL (Continued)

R. Brett Garrett — 1978 — The University of Alabama, B.S., 2000; Samford University, J.D., 2004 — Admitted to Bar, 2004, Alabama — Member Federal and Montgomery County Bar Associations; Alabama State Bar; Defense Research Institute — Practice Areas: Professional Liability; Medical Malpractice; Insurance Defense; Commercial Litigation — E-mail: bg@rushtonstakely.com

T. Grant Sexton, Jr. — 1979 — The University of Alabama, B.A., 2001; Oklahoma City University, J.D., 2004 — Admitted to Bar, 2004, Oklahoma; 2006, District of Columbia; Alabama — Member Oklahoma and Montgomery County Bar Associations; Alabama State Bar; Alabama Defense Lawyers Association — Future Star (Benchmark Litigation 2009); Alabama Super Lawyers Rising Star - Personal Injury Defense (2009-2014) — Practice Areas: Professional Liability; Medical Malpractice; Commercial Litigation; Insurance Defense; Product Liability — E-mail: gsexton@rushtonstakely.com

Associates

Bethany L. Bolger — 1979 — The University of Alabama, B.A. (magna cum laude), 2000; Boston College, J.D., 2003 — Admitted to Bar, 2005, Alabama — Member Federal and Montgomery County Bar Associations; Alabama State Bar; Alabama Defense Lawyers Association; Defense Research Institute — Practice Areas: Appellate Practice; Labor and Employment; Media & Intellectual Property; Insurance Defense; Professional Liability — E-mail: bbolger@rushtonstakely.com

Stephen P. Dees — 1982 — The University of Alabama, B.A. (with honors), 2004; J.D., 2007 — Admitted to Bar, 2007, Alabama — Member Alabama State Bar; Montgomery Bar Association; Alabama Defense Lawyers Association; Defense Research Institute — Practice Areas: Professional Liability; Medical Malpractice; Insurance Coverage; Insurance Defense; Appellate Practice; Commercial Litigation — E-mail: sdees@rushtonstakely.com

J. Evans Bailey — 1982 — The University of Georgia, B.A. (cum laude), 2005; The University of Alabama, J.D., 2008 — Admitted to Bar, 2008, Alabama — Member Alabama State Bar; Montgomery County Bar Association; Alabama Defense Lawyers Association; Defense Research Institute — Practice Areas: Commercial Litigation; Insurance Defense; Labor and Employment; Product Liability; Professional Liability; Appellate Practice — E-mail: jbailey@rushtonstakely.com

J. Ladd Davis — Auburn University, B.S., 2003; Samford University, J.D., 2009 — Admitted to Bar, 2010, Alabama — Member Alabama State Bar; Montgomery County Bar Association — Practice Areas: Real Estate; Commercial Transactions; Bankruptcy; Creditor Rights — E-mail: ldavis@rushtonstakely.com

Jessica P. Trotman — The University of Alabama at Birmingham, B.A. (magna cum laude), 2004; The University of Mississippi, J.D. (cum laude), 2009 — Admitted to Bar, 2010, Alabama; U.S. District Court, Middle, Northern and Southern Districts of Alabama — Member Alabama State Bar; Montgomery County Bar Association; Alabama Defense Lawyers Association; Defense Research Institute — Practice Areas: Insurance Defense; Media & Intellectual Property; Professional Liability — E-mail: jpitts@rushtonstakely.com

Amanda Craft Hines — The University of Alabama, B.S. (cum laude), 2000; The University of Alabama School of Law, J.D., 2003 — Judicial Extern to Hon. Sharon Lovelace Blackburn — Admitted to Bar, 2003, Alabama — Member Federal, American and Montgomery County Bar Associations; Alabama State Bar; Alabama Defense Lawyers Association (Young Lawyers Board, 2012-2013) — Practice Areas: General Civil Litigation; Insurance Defense; Medical Malpractice Defense; Professional Liability; Labor and Employment; Family Law — E-mail: ach@rushtonstakely.com

Philip A. Sellers, II — The University of Georgia, B.A. (magna cum laude), 2006; Cumberland University School of Law, J.D. (cum laude), 2012 — Admitted to Bar, 2012, Alabama — Member Alabama State Bar; Montgomery County Bar Association; Alabama Volunteer Lawyers Program; Alabama Defense Lawyers Association; Defense Research Institute — Practice Areas: Insurance Defense; Health Care; Medical Malpractice Defense; Professional Liability; Labor and Employment — E-mail: pas@rushtonstakely.com

J C Love III — 1978 — Moorehouse College, B.A. (cum laude), 2002; Boston College Law School, J.D., 2005 — Admitted to Bar, 2005, Georgia; 2013, Alabama — Member Georgia State Bar; Alabama State Bar; Montgomery County Bar Association; Alabama Defense Lawyers Association; Defense Research Institute — Practice Areas: Health Care Liability; Medical Malpractice Defense; Insurance Defense — E-mail: jcl@rushtonstakely.com

Of Counsel

Richard B. Garrett — 1947 — Emory University; The University of Alabama, B.A., 1969; J.D., 1972 — Admitted to Bar, 1972, Alabama — Member Alabama State Bar; Defense Research Institute — Listed in Best Lawyers in America — Practice Areas: Insurance Defense; Professional Liability; Mediation — E-mail: rbg@rushtonstakely.com

Ryals, Donaldson & Agricola, P.C.

60 Commerce Street
Suite 1400
Montgomery, Alabama 36104
Telephone: 334-834-5290
Fax: 334-834-5297
Toll Free: 866-570-6488
E-Mail: rda@rdafirm.com
www.rdafirm.com

Established: 2008

Commercial Litigation, Insurance Defense, Product Liability, Insurance Coverage, Title Insurance, Construction Litigation, Professional Liability, Employer Liability

Firm Profile: Ryals, Donaldson & Agricola is a full service law firm which concentrates its practice in civil litigation. Solving problems for our clients through diligent, attentive, and creative strategies, both inside and outside the courtroom, allows our clients to get back to what they do best, their business.

Ninety-nine years of combined experience has taught us that this approach to the practice of law is the key to successful representation of our clients.

Insurance Clients

Alfa Mutual Insurance Company
Alterra Specialty Insurance Company
Argonaut Specialty Insurance
Baldwin & Lyons, Inc.
Encompass Insurance
Fireman's Fund Insurance Company
First Mercury Insurance Company
The Hartford Insurance Group
Markel Insurance Company
Nationwide Insurance
Sagamore Insurance Company
State Farm Insurance Company
United States Liability Insurance Company
Allstate Insurance Company
Argo Group
Argonaut Insurance Company
Assurant Insurance Group
Colony Insurance Company
Esurance
First American Title Insurance Company
The Harleysville Insurance
Investors Title Insurance Company
Max Specialty Insurance Company
Omni Insurance Company
SPARTA Insurance
Titan Auto Insurance Claims
Victoria Insurance Company
Western Heritage Insurance Company

Non-Insurance Clients

Alabama Probate Judges Association
Bentley for Governor, Inc.
Franklin Resources Group, LLC
JMR Architecture, P.C.
JP60 Mont., LLC
RealtySouth
Security Pest Control, Inc.
Assisted Living Association of Alabama
Clyde Chambliss for State Senate
Gil Manufacturing, Inc.
JP-One St. Louis, L.P.
Porters Termonox, Inc.
Risk Enterprise Management, Ltd.
TitleSouth, LLC

Firm Members

J. Lenn Ryals — 1958 — Auburn University at Montgomery, B.S., 1989; M.B.A., 1991; Faulkner University, Thomas Goode Jones School of Law, J.D., 1994 — Admitted to Bar, 1995, Alabama; U.S. District Court, Middle, Northern and Southern Districts of Alabama — Member Alabama State Bar; Montgomery County Bar Association; Alabama Defense Lawyers Association — E-mail: lryals@rdafirm.com

M. Andrew Donaldson — 1971 — Troy State University, B.S., 1994; Faulkner University, Thomas Goode Jones School of Law, J.D. (magna cum laude), 1997 — Admitted to Bar, 1998, Alabama; U.S. District Court, Middle, Northern and Southern Districts of Alabama; U.S. Bankruptcy Court, Northern District of Alabama — Member Montgomery County Bar Associations; Alabama State Bar; Alabama Defense Lawyers Association — Practice Areas:

Ryals, Donaldson & Agricola, P.C., Montgomery, AL (Continued)

Administrative Law; Business Litigation; Dram Shop; General Civil Litigation; Insurance Coverage & Defense; Insurance Defense; Pesticide Litigation — E-mail: adonaldson@rdafirm.com

Algert S. Agricola, Jr. — 1952 — Tulane University of Louisiana, B.A., 1974; The University of Alabama School of Law, J.D., 1978 — Admitted to Bar, 1978, Alabama; U.S. District Court, Middle, Northern and Southern Districts of Alabama; U.S. District Court, Western District of Tennessee; U.S. Court of Appeals, Fourth, Fifth, Sixth, Eighth and Eleventh Circuits; U.S. Supreme Court — Member Alabama State Bar; Montgomery County Bar Association; Alabama Defense Lawyers Association — E-mail: aagricola@rdafirm.com

Of Counsel

John S. Plummer — 1957 — The University of Alabama, B.S., 1982; Cumberland School of Law of Samford University, J.D., 1985 — Admitted to Bar, 1986, Florida; 2000, Alabama — Member The Florida Bar; Alabama State Bar; Montgomery County Bar Association; Alabama Defense Lawyers Association — E-mail: jplummer@rdafirm.com

Webster, Henry, Lyons, Bradwell, Cohan & Black, P.C.

105 Tallapoosa Street Suite 101
Montgomery, Alabama 36104
Telephone: 334-264-9472
Fax: 334-264-9599
E-Mail: randy@websterhenry.com
www.websterhenry.com

(Auburn, AL Office*: 822 North Dean Road, Suite 300, 36830-9402)
(Tel: 334-264-9472)
(Fax: 334-887-0983)
(Birmingham, AL Office*: Two Perimeter Park South, Suite 445 East, 35243)
(Tel: 205-380-3480)
(Fax: 205-380-3485)
(E-Mail: kim@websterhenry.com)
(Mobile, AL Office: 1252 Dauphin Street, 36604, P.O. Box 239, 36014)

Established: 2001

Insurance Defense, Automobile Liability, Construction Law, Employment Law, Premises Liability, Product Liability, Workers' Compensation

Insurance Clients

Affirmative Insurance Company
Alfa Mutual Insurance Company
American National Property and Casualty Company
EMC Insurance Company
Georgia Farm Bureau Mutual Insurance Company
Lafayette Insurance Company
Michigan Mutual Insurance Company
State Farm Mutual Automobile Insurance Company
Wausau General Insurance Company
Alabama Municipal Insurance Corporation
Athens Insurance
Auto-Owners Insurance Company
Farmers Insurance Group
GMAC Insurance Group
Integon General Insurance Corporation
St. Paul Insurance Company
State Farm Fire and Casualty Company
USAgencies Direct Insurance Company

Non-Insurance Clients

Bruno's Supermarkets, Inc.
Construction Claims Management
First South Farm Credit PCA
The Krystal Company
Southeastern Boll Weevil Eradication Foundation, Inc.
U.S. Foodservice
Wadsworth-Phillips Contractors, Inc.
City of Lanett
Engle Martin & Associates
Helena Chemical Company
Pace Runners, Inc.
Sylvest Farms, Inc.
Transportation Claims Specialist, LC

Webster, Henry, Lyons, Bradwell, Cohan & Black, P.C., Montgomery, AL (Continued)

Members

William H. Webster — 1968 — The University of Alabama, B.A. (summa cum laude), 1989; The University of Alabama School of Law, J.D., 1992 — Phi Beta Kappa; Mortar Board; Omicron Delta Kappa; Phi Kappa Phi — National Merit Scholar; Hugo Black Scholar. Recipient, Trial Advocacy Award — Law Clerk to the Honorable Eric G. Bruggink, U.S. Court of Appeals Court of Federal Claims, 1992-1993 — Editorial Board, Alabama Law Review — Admitted to Bar, 1992, Alabama; 1993, U.S. Court of Federal Claims; 1995, U.S. District Court, Middle, Northern and Southern Districts of Alabama; 1997, U.S. Court of Appeals, Eleventh Circuit; 1998, U.S. Supreme Court — Member American and Montgomery County Bar Associations; Alabama State Bar; Alabama Defense Lawyers Association — Staff Attorney to the Honorable William E. Robertson, Alabama Court of Civil Appeals, 1993-1994 — E-mail: will@websterhenry.com

D. Mitchell Henry — 1967 — Auburn University, B.A., 1988; M.A., 1990; The University of Alabama School of Law, J.D., 1993 — Bench and Bar Recipient: Trial Advocacy Award; Dean Thomas W. Christopher Award, Journal of The Legal Profession — Admitted to Bar, 1993, Alabama; U.S. District Court, Middle, Northern and Southern Districts of Alabama — Member American and Montgomery County Bar Associations; Alabama State Bar; Hugh Maddox Inns of Court; Alabama Defense Lawyers Association — E-mail: mitch@websterhenry.com

T. Randall Lyons — 1965 — Auburn University, B.A., 1987; Cumberland School of Law of Samford University, J.D., 1990 — Phi Alpha Delta — Admitted to Bar, 1990, Alabama; 1991, U.S. District Court, Middle, Northern and Southern Districts of Alabama; 1992, U.S. Court of Appeals, Eleventh Circuit — Member American and Montgomery County Bar Associations; Alabama State Bar; Alabama Defense Lawyer Association (Board of Directors); Defense Research Institute — Cumberland Trial Advocacy Board — E-mail: randy@websterhenry.com

John R. Bradwell — 1963 — Auburn University, B.A., 1985; The University of Alabama School of Law, J.D., 1988 — Admitted to Bar, 1988, Alabama — E-mail: jrbradwell@websterhenry.com

Michael J. Cohan — 1965 — The Citadel, B.S., 1986; Cumberland School of Law of Samford University, J.D., 1993 — Admitted to Bar, 1993, Alabama; Georgia — E-mail: mcohan@websterhenry.com

Robert C. Black, Jr. — 1964 — The University of the South, B.A., 1987; Cumberland School of Law of Samford University, J.D., 1991 — Admitted to Bar, 1991, Alabama — E-mail: robert@websterhenry.com

Scott M. Speagle — 1973 — Birmingham-Southern College, B.A., 1996; The University of Alabama at Birmingham, B.S., 1997; M.A., 1998; M.Ed., 2000; Cumberland School of Law of Samford University, J.D. (cum laude), 2003 — Admitted to Bar, 2003, Alabama — E-mail: scott@websterhenry.com

Kimberly S. DeShazo — 1979 — Birmingham-Southern College, B.S. (magna cum laude), 2001; The University of Alabama School of Law, J.D., 2004 — Bench and Bar Honor Society, 2003-2004; Law and Psychology Review — Admitted to Bar, 2004, Alabama; 2009, Florida; 2011, Mississippi; 2004, U.S. District Court, Middle, Northern and Southern Districts of Alabama; 2009, Florida Court of Appeals; 2011, Mississippi State Courts; Mississippi Supreme Court — Member American and Montgomery County Bar Associations; Alabama State Bar; Alabama Defense Lawyers Association — E-mail: kim@websterhenry.com

Thomas M. McCarthy — 1979 — Auburn University, B.A., 2001; University of Maryland School of Law, J.D., 2004 — Admitted to Bar, 2004, Maryland; 2005, Alabama; 2008, U.S. District Court, Middle, Northern and Southern Districts of Alabama — Member Maryland State and Montgomery County Bar Associations; Alabama Defense Lawyers Association — E-mail: tmccarthy@websterhenry.com

Frank "Chip" E. Bankston — 1966 — Auburn University, B.A., 1988; The University of Alabama School of Law, J.D., 1993 — Admitted to Bar, 1993, Alabama; U.S. District Court, Middle, Northern and Southern Districts of Alabama; U.S. Court of Appeals, Eleventh Circuit — Member Montgomery County Bar Association; Defense Research Institute; Alabama Defense Lawyers Association; Commercial Law League of America — E-mail: fbankston@websterhenry.com

Of Counsel

Keri D. Simms — 1964 — The University of Alabama, B.S. (magna cum laude), 1986; The University of Alabama School of Law, J.D., 1989 — Admitted to Bar, 1989, Alabama; 2009, Florida; 2010, Tennessee; 2012, Georgia; 1989, U.S. District Court, Middle, Northern and Southern Districts of Alabama — Member Alabama Defense Lawyers Association; Defense Research Institute — E-mail: ksimms@websterhenry.com

OZARK / ALABAMA

Webster, Henry, Lyons, Bradwell, Cohan & Black, P.C., Montgomery, AL *(Continued)*

Thomas S. Duck — 1960 — The University of Alabama at Birmingham, B.S., 1985; Cumberland School of Law of Samford University, J.D., 1988 — Admitted to Bar, 1988, Alabama; U.S. District Court, Middle, Northern and Southern Districts of Alabama; U.S. Court of Appeals, Eleventh Circuit — Member Alabama Defense Lawyers Association; Defense Research Institute — E-mail: duck@websterhenry.com

Paul V. Russell Jr — 1978 — The University of Alabama, B.A., 2000; The University of Alabama School of Law, J.D., 2003 — Admitted to Bar, 2003, Alabama; U.S. District Court, Middle District of Alabama; 2004, U.S. District Court, Northern and Southern Districts of Alabama — Member Alabama Defense Lawyers Association; Defense Research Institute — E-mail: vrussell@websterhenry.com

Associates

Stanley S. Sasser — 1984 — The University of Alabama, B.S. (cum laude), 2006; Cumberland University School of Law, J.D., 2009 — Admitted to Bar, 2009, Alabama; U.S. District Court, Middle District of Alabama — Member Alabama Defense Lawyers Association — E-mail: ssasser@websterhenry.com

Kayla W. Frisby — 1985 — Faulkner University, B.S. (summa cum laude), 2006; The University of Alabama School of Law, J.D., 2010 — Admitted to Bar, 2011, Alabama; U.S. District Court, Middle, Northern and Southern Districts of Alabama — Member Montgomery County Bar Association; Alabama Defense Lawyers Association — E-mail: kfrisby@websterhenry.com

Jeremy W. Richter — 1982 — Tennessee Temple University, B.S. (cum laude), 2004; The University of Alabama, M.A., 2007; Cumberland School of Law of Samford University, J.D., 2012 — Admitted to Bar, 2012, Alabama — E-mail: jrichter@websterhenry.com

Jason E. Lee — 1978 — Auburn University, B.Civ.Eng., 2002; Samford University School of Business, M.B.A., 2008; Cumberland University School of Law, J.D., 2014 — Admitted to Bar, 2014, Alabama — E-mail: jlee@websterhenry.com

---

The following firms also service this area.

Vernis & Bowling of Southern Alabama, LLC
61 St. Joseph Street, 11th Floor
Mobile, Alabama 36602
Telephone: 251-432-0337
Fax: 251-432-0244

Civil Litigation, Insurance Law, Workers' Compensation, Premises Liability, Labor and Employment, Civil Rights, Commercial Litigation, Complex Litigation, Product Liability, Directors and Officers Liability, Errors and Omissions, Construction Law, Construction Defect, Environmental Liability, Personal and Commercial Vehicle, Appellate Practice, Admiralty and Maritime Law, Real Estate, Family Law, Elder Law, Liability Defense, SIU/Fraud Litigation, Education Law (ESE/IDEA), Property and Casualty (Commercial and Personal Lines), Long-Haul Trucking Liability, Government Law, Public Law, Criminal, White Collar, Business Litigation

SEE COMPLETE LISTING UNDER MOBILE, ALABAMA (169 MILES)

OPELIKA † 26,477 Lee Co.

Refer To

Holtsford Gilliland Higgins Hitson & Howard, P.C.
4001 Carmichael Road, Suite 300
Montgomery, Alabama 36106
Telephone: 334-215-8585
Toll Free: 800-932-6964
Fax: 334-215-7101
Mailing Address: P.O. Box 4128, Montgomery, AL 36103-4128

Insurance Defense, Automobile, Professional Liability, Product Liability, Civil Rights, Toxic Torts, General Liability, Environmental Law, Workers' Compensation, Construction Law, Coverage Issues, Governmental Entity Defense, Forestry Law

SEE COMPLETE LISTING UNDER MONTGOMERY, ALABAMA (63 MILES)

Refer To

Rushton, Stakely, Johnston & Garrett, P.A.
184 Commerce Street
Montgomery, Alabama 36104
Telephone: 334-206-3100
Fax: 334-262-6277
Mailing Address: P.O. Box 270, Montgomery, AL 36101-0270

Insurance Defense, Trial and Appellate Practice, Accountants and Attorneys Liability, Administrative Law, Advertising Injury, Agent and Brokers Errors and Omissions, Appellate Practice, Arbitration, Automobile Tort, Bad Faith, Business Law, Casualty Insurance Law, Class Actions, Commercial Litigation, Complex Litigation, Construction Litigation, Contract Disputes, Copyright and Trademark Law, Coverage Analysis, Declaratory Judgments, Directors and Officers Liability, Employment Law, Environmental Law, Family Law, Fidelity and Surety, Fraud, Health Care, Health Care Professional Licensure Defense, Insurance Litigation, Labor and Employment, Law Enforcement Liability, Legal Malpractice, Medical Devices, Medical Malpractice, Pharmaceutical, Premises Liability, Primary and Excess Insurance, Product Liability, Professional Errors and Omissions, Professional Liability, Surety, Title Insurance, Uninsured and Underinsured Motorist, Workers' Compensation, Wrongful Death

SEE COMPLETE LISTING UNDER MONTGOMERY, ALABAMA (63 MILES)

OZARK † 14,907 Dale Co.

Refer To

Ball, Ball, Matthews & Novak, P.A.
445 Dexter Avenue, Suite 9045
Montgomery, Alabama 36104
Telephone: 334-387-7680
Fax: 334-387-3222
Mailing Address: P.O. Box 2148, Montgomery, AL 36102-2148

Insurance Defense, Medical Malpractice, Aviation, Bad Faith, Personal Injury, Construction Litigation, Employment Law, Product Liability, Property, Pharmaceutical, Medical Devices, Complex Litigation, Governmental Entity Defense, Workers' Compensation, Mediation, Arbitration, Trial and Appellate Practice, State and Federal Courts, Insurance Coverage Analysis, Automobile Injury, Motor Carrier Defense

SEE COMPLETE LISTING UNDER MONTGOMERY, ALABAMA (82 MILES)

Refer To

Rushton, Stakely, Johnston & Garrett, P.A.
184 Commerce Street
Montgomery, Alabama 36104
Telephone: 334-206-3100
Fax: 334-262-6277
Mailing Address: P.O. Box 270, Montgomery, AL 36101-0270

Insurance Defense, Trial and Appellate Practice, Accountants and Attorneys Liability, Administrative Law, Advertising Injury, Agent and Brokers Errors and Omissions, Appellate Practice, Arbitration, Automobile Tort, Bad Faith, Business Law, Casualty Insurance Law, Class Actions, Commercial Litigation, Complex Litigation, Construction Litigation, Contract Disputes, Copyright and Trademark Law, Coverage Analysis, Declaratory Judgments, Directors and Officers Liability, Employment Law, Environmental Law, Family Law, Fidelity and Surety, Fraud, Health Care, Health Care Professional Licensure Defense, Insurance Litigation, Labor and Employment, Law Enforcement Liability, Legal Malpractice, Medical Devices, Medical Malpractice, Pharmaceutical, Premises Liability, Primary and Excess Insurance, Product Liability, Professional Errors and Omissions, Professional Liability, Surety, Title Insurance, Uninsured and Underinsured Motorist, Workers' Compensation, Wrongful Death

SEE COMPLETE LISTING UNDER MONTGOMERY, ALABAMA (76 MILES)

Refer To

Vernis & Bowling of Southern Alabama, LLC
61 St. Joseph Street, 11th Floor
Mobile, Alabama 36602
Telephone: 251-432-0337
Fax: 251-432-0244

Civil Litigation, Insurance Law, Workers' Compensation, Premises Liability, Labor and Employment, Civil Rights, Commercial Litigation, Complex Litigation, Product Liability, Directors and Officers Liability, Errors and Omissions, Construction Law, Construction Defect, Environmental Liability, Personal and Commercial Vehicle, Appellate Practice, Admiralty and Maritime Law, Real Estate, Family Law, Elder Law, Liability Defense, SIU/Fraud Litigation, Education Law (ESE/IDEA), Property and Casualty (Commercial and Personal Lines), Long-Haul Trucking Liability, Government Law, Public Law, Criminal, White Collar, Business Litigation

SEE COMPLETE LISTING UNDER MOBILE, ALABAMA (227 MILES)

PHENIX CITY † 32,822 Russell Co.

Refer To
Ball, Ball, Matthews & Novak, P.A.
445 Dexter Avenue, Suite 9045
Montgomery, Alabama 36104
  Telephone: 334-387-7680
  Fax: 334-387-3222

Mailing Address: P.O. Box 2148, Montgomery, AL 36102-2148

Insurance Defense, Medical Malpractice, Aviation, Bad Faith, Personal Injury, Construction Litigation, Employment Law, Product Liability, Property, Pharmaceutical, Medical Devices, Complex Litigation, Governmental Entity Defense, Workers' Compensation, Mediation, Arbitration, Trial and Appellate Practice, State and Federal Courts, Insurance Coverage Analysis, Automobile Injury, Motor Carrier Defense

SEE COMPLETE LISTING UNDER MONTGOMERY, ALABAMA (83 MILES)

Refer To
Holtsford Gilliland Higgins Hitson & Howard, P.C.
4001 Carmichael Road, Suite 300
Montgomery, Alabama 36106
  Telephone: 334-215-8585
  Toll Free: 800-932-6964
  Fax: 334-215-7101

Mailing Address: P.O. Box 4128, Montgomery, AL 36103-4128

Insurance Defense, Automobile, Professional Liability, Product Liability, Civil Rights, Toxic Torts, General Liability, Environmental Law, Workers' Compensation, Construction Law, Coverage Issues, Governmental Entity Defense, Forestry Law

SEE COMPLETE LISTING UNDER MONTGOMERY, ALABAMA (81 MILES)

Refer To
Rushton, Stakely, Johnston & Garrett, P.A.
184 Commerce Street
Montgomery, Alabama 36104
  Telephone: 334-206-3100
  Fax: 334-262-6277

Mailing Address: P.O. Box 270, Montgomery, AL 36101-0270

Insurance Defense, Trial and Appellate Practice, Accountants and Attorneys Liability, Administrative Law, Advertising Injury, Agent and Brokers Errors and Omissions, Appellate Practice, Arbitration, Automobile Tort, Bad Faith, Business Law, Casualty Insurance Law, Class Actions, Commercial Litigation, Complex Litigation, Construction Litigation, Contract Disputes, Copyright and Trademark Law, Coverage Analysis, Declaratory Judgments, Directors and Officers Liability, Employment Law, Environmental Law, Family Law, Fidelity and Surety, Fraud, Health Care, Health Care Professional Licensure Defense, Insurance Litigation, Labor and Employment, Law Enforcement Liability, Legal Malpractice, Medical Devices, Medical Malpractice, Pharmaceutical, Premises Liability, Primary and Excess Insurance, Product Liability, Professional Errors and Omissions, Professional Liability, Surety, Title Insurance, Uninsured and Underinsured Motorist, Workers' Compensation, Wrongful Death

SEE COMPLETE LISTING UNDER MONTGOMERY, ALABAMA (81 MILES)

PRATTVILLE † 33,960 Autauga Co.

Refer To
Ball, Ball, Matthews & Novak, P.A.
445 Dexter Avenue, Suite 9045
Montgomery, Alabama 36104
  Telephone: 334-387-7680
  Fax: 334-387-3222

Mailing Address: P.O. Box 2148, Montgomery, AL 36102-2148

Insurance Defense, Medical Malpractice, Aviation, Bad Faith, Personal Injury, Construction Litigation, Employment Law, Product Liability, Property, Pharmaceutical, Medical Devices, Complex Litigation, Governmental Entity Defense, Workers' Compensation, Mediation, Arbitration, Trial and Appellate Practice, State and Federal Courts, Insurance Coverage Analysis, Automobile Injury, Motor Carrier Defense

SEE COMPLETE LISTING UNDER MONTGOMERY, ALABAMA (21 MILES)

Refer To
Morrow, Romine & Pearson, P.C.
122 South Hull Street
Montgomery, Alabama 36104
  Telephone: 334-262-7707
  Fax: 334-262-7742

Mailing Address: P.O. Box 4804, Montgomery, AL 36103

Civil Trial Practice, Insurance Law, Medical Malpractice, Product Liability, Environmental Coverage, Personal Injury, Litigation, Mediation, Trial Practice, Appellate Practice, State and Federal Courts, Handicap and Employment Discrimination, Diving Accidents

SEE COMPLETE LISTING UNDER MONTGOMERY, ALABAMA (14 MILES)

Refer To
Rushton, Stakely, Johnston & Garrett, P.A.
184 Commerce Street
Montgomery, Alabama 36104
  Telephone: 334-206-3100
  Fax: 334-262-6277

Mailing Address: P.O. Box 270, Montgomery, AL 36101-0270

Insurance Defense, Trial and Appellate Practice, Accountants and Attorneys Liability, Administrative Law, Advertising Injury, Agent and Brokers Errors and Omissions, Appellate Practice, Arbitration, Automobile Tort, Bad Faith, Business Law, Casualty Insurance Law, Class Actions, Commercial Litigation, Complex Litigation, Construction Litigation, Contract Disputes, Copyright and Trademark Law, Coverage Analysis, Declaratory Judgments, Directors and Officers Liability, Employment Law, Environmental Law, Family Law, Fidelity and Surety, Fraud, Health Care, Health Care Professional Licensure Defense, Insurance Litigation, Labor and Employment, Law Enforcement Liability, Legal Malpractice, Medical Devices, Medical Malpractice, Pharmaceutical, Premises Liability, Primary and Excess Insurance, Product Liability, Professional Errors and Omissions, Professional Liability, Surety, Title Insurance, Uninsured and Underinsured Motorist, Workers' Compensation, Wrongful Death

SEE COMPLETE LISTING UNDER MONTGOMERY, ALABAMA (14 MILES)

SELMA † 20,756 Dallas Co.

Refer To
Ball, Ball, Matthews & Novak, P.A.
445 Dexter Avenue, Suite 9045
Montgomery, Alabama 36104
  Telephone: 334-387-7680
  Fax: 334-387-3222

Mailing Address: P.O. Box 2148, Montgomery, AL 36102-2148

Insurance Defense, Medical Malpractice, Aviation, Bad Faith, Personal Injury, Construction Litigation, Employment Law, Product Liability, Property, Pharmaceutical, Medical Devices, Complex Litigation, Governmental Entity Defense, Workers' Compensation, Mediation, Arbitration, Trial and Appellate Practice, State and Federal Courts, Insurance Coverage Analysis, Automobile Injury, Motor Carrier Defense

SEE COMPLETE LISTING UNDER MONTGOMERY, ALABAMA (55 MILES)

Refer To
Holtsford Gilliland Higgins Hitson & Howard, P.C.
4001 Carmichael Road, Suite 300
Montgomery, Alabama 36106
  Telephone: 334-215-8585
  Toll Free: 800-932-6964
  Fax: 334-215-7101

Mailing Address: P.O. Box 4128, Montgomery, AL 36103-4128

Insurance Defense, Automobile, Professional Liability, Product Liability, Civil Rights, Toxic Torts, General Liability, Environmental Law, Workers' Compensation, Construction Law, Coverage Issues, Governmental Entity Defense, Forestry Law

SEE COMPLETE LISTING UNDER MONTGOMERY, ALABAMA (48 MILES)

TUSCALOOSA — ALABAMA

Refer To

Rushton, Stakely, Johnston & Garrett, P.A.
184 Commerce Street
Montgomery, Alabama 36104
Telephone: 334-206-3100
Fax: 334-262-6277

Mailing Address: P.O. Box 270, Montgomery, AL 36101-0270

Insurance Defense, Trial and Appellate Practice, Accountants and Attorneys Liability, Administrative Law, Advertising Injury, Agent and Brokers Errors and Omissions, Appellate Practice, Arbitration, Automobile Tort, Bad Faith, Business Law, Casualty Insurance Law, Class Actions, Commercial Litigation, Complex Litigation, Construction Litigation, Contract Disputes, Copyright and Trademark Law, Coverage Analysis, Declaratory Judgments, Directors and Officers Liability, Employment Law, Environmental Law, Family Law, Fidelity and Surety, Fraud, Health Care, Health Care Professional Licensure Defense, Insurance Litigation, Labor and Employment, Law Enforcement Liability, Legal Malpractice, Medical Devices, Medical Malpractice, Pharmaceutical, Premises Liability, Primary and Excess Insurance, Product Liability, Professional Errors and Omissions, Professional Liability, Surety, Title Insurance, Uninsured and Underinsured Motorist, Workers' Compensation, Wrongful Death

SEE COMPLETE LISTING UNDER MONTGOMERY, ALABAMA (48 MILES)

Refer To

Vernis & Bowling of Southern Alabama, LLC
61 St. Joseph Street, 11th Floor
Mobile, Alabama 36602
Telephone: 251-432-0337
Fax: 251-432-0244

Civil Litigation, Insurance Law, Workers' Compensation, Premises Liability, Labor and Employment, Civil Rights, Commercial Litigation, Complex Litigation, Product Liability, Directors and Officers Liability, Errors and Omissions, Construction Law, Construction Defect, Environmental Liability, Personal and Commercial Vehicle, Appellate Practice, Admiralty and Maritime Law, Real Estate, Family Law, Elder Law, Liability Defense, SIU/Fraud Litigation, Education Law (ESE/IDEA), Property and Casualty (Commercial and Personal Lines), Long-Haul Trucking Liability, Government Law, Public Law, Criminal, White Collar, Business Litigation

SEE COMPLETE LISTING UNDER MOBILE, ALABAMA (164 MILES)

TROY † 18,033 Pike Co.

Refer To

Ball, Ball, Matthews & Novak, P.A.
445 Dexter Avenue, Suite 9045
Montgomery, Alabama 36104
Telephone: 334-387-7680
Fax: 334-387-3222

Mailing Address: P.O. Box 2148, Montgomery, AL 36102-2148

Insurance Defense, Medical Malpractice, Aviation, Bad Faith, Personal Injury, Construction Litigation, Employment Law, Product Liability, Property, Pharmaceutical, Medical Devices, Complex Litigation, Governmental Entity Defense, Workers' Compensation, Mediation, Arbitration, Trial and Appellate Practice, State and Federal Courts, Insurance Coverage Analysis, Automobile Injury, Motor Carrier Defense

SEE COMPLETE LISTING UNDER MONTGOMERY, ALABAMA (50 MILES)

Refer To

Rushton, Stakely, Johnston & Garrett, P.A.
184 Commerce Street
Montgomery, Alabama 36104
Telephone: 334-206-3100
Fax: 334-262-6277

Mailing Address: P.O. Box 270, Montgomery, AL 36101-0270

Insurance Defense, Trial and Appellate Practice, Accountants and Attorneys Liability, Administrative Law, Advertising Injury, Agent and Brokers Errors and Omissions, Appellate Practice, Arbitration, Automobile Tort, Bad Faith, Business Law, Casualty Insurance Law, Class Actions, Commercial Litigation, Complex Litigation, Construction Litigation, Contract Disputes, Copyright and Trademark Law, Coverage Analysis, Declaratory Judgments, Directors and Officers Liability, Employment Law, Environmental Law, Family Law, Fidelity and Surety, Fraud, Health Care, Health Care Professional Licensure Defense, Insurance Litigation, Labor and Employment, Law Enforcement Liability, Legal Malpractice, Medical Devices, Medical Malpractice, Pharmaceutical, Premises Liability, Primary and Excess Insurance, Product Liability, Professional Errors and Omissions, Professional Liability, Surety, Title Insurance, Uninsured and Underinsured Motorist, Workers' Compensation, Wrongful Death

SEE COMPLETE LISTING UNDER MONTGOMERY, ALABAMA (49 MILES)

Refer To

Vernis & Bowling of Southern Alabama, LLC
61 St. Joseph Street, 11th Floor
Mobile, Alabama 36602
Telephone: 251-432-0337
Fax: 251-432-0244

Civil Litigation, Insurance Law, Workers' Compensation, Premises Liability, Labor and Employment, Civil Rights, Commercial Litigation, Complex Litigation, Product Liability, Directors and Officers Liability, Errors and Omissions, Construction Law, Construction Defect, Environmental Liability, Personal and Commercial Vehicle, Appellate Practice, Admiralty and Maritime Law, Real Estate, Family Law, Elder Law, Liability Defense, SIU/Fraud Litigation, Education Law (ESE/IDEA), Property and Casualty (Commercial and Personal Lines), Long-Haul Trucking Liability, Government Law, Public Law, Criminal, White Collar, Business Litigation

SEE COMPLETE LISTING UNDER MOBILE, ALABAMA (183 MILES)

TUSCALOOSA † 90,468 Tuscaloosa Co.

Hubbard, McIlwain & Brakefield, PC
808 Lurleen Wallace Boulevard North
Tuscaloosa, Alabama 35401
Telephone: 205-345-6789
Fax: 205-759-1195
E-Mail: cmcilwain@hubbardfirm.com
www.hsmbb.com

Established: 1938

Insurance Defense, Coverage Issues, Trial Practice, Automobile, Professional Malpractice, Product Liability, Fidelity, Surety, Fire, Casualty, Life Insurance, Accident, Health, Bad Faith, Workers' Compensation, Aviation, ERISA, Subrogation, Investigations, Employment Discrimination, Civil Rights, Building and Construction, Lender Liability, Defamation

Firm Profile: One of the oldest law firms in Alabama, Hubbard, McIlwain, & Brakefield, P.C., is also among the most technologically advanced and efficient. As a result, it is called on to represent clients in legal proceedings throughout the state and achieves its client's interests in a highly professional and expert manner.

Insurance Clients

American Fidelity Insurance Company	Atlantic American Corp.
The Bankers Life	Auto-Owners Insurance Company
Commercial Standard Insurance Company	Chubb Group of Insurance Companies
Farmers Insurance Group	Commercial Union-North British Group
Federated Guaranty Life Insurance Company	Fireman's Fund Insurance Company
General Guaranty Insurance Company	Georgia Casualty & Surety Company
Great West Casualty Company	Hanover Insurance Company
The Hartford Insurance Group	Home Insurance Company
Horace Mann Insurance Company	International Insurance Company
John Deere Insurance Company	John Hancock Life Insurance Company
Media/Professional Insurance	Motors Insurance Corporation
Monticello Insurance Company	National Grange Mutual Insurance Company
National Casualty Company	Northwestern Mutual Insurance Association
Nationwide Insurance	
North Carolina Farm Bureau Insurance Group	
Ohio Casualty Group	Penn National Insurance
Protective Corporation	Ranger Insurance Company
Republic National Life Insurance Company	Royal Insurance Company
Scottsdale Insurance Company	Safeco Life Insurance Company
State Automobile Mutual Insurance Company	Southern Insurance Underwriters
Transport Indemnity Company	Time Insurance Company n.k.a. Assurant Health
Universal Underwriters Insurance Company	United States Fidelity and Guaranty Company
Vanliner Insurance Company	Utica Mutual Insurance Company
West American Insurance Company	Victoria Insurance Company

ALABAMA | TUSCALOOSA

Hubbard, McIlwain & Brakefield, PC, Tuscaloosa, AL
(Continued)

Non-Insurance Clients

Alabama Life & Disability Insurance Guaranty Association
Boone Newspaper Group
Gallagher Bassett Services, Inc.
London Agency, Inc.
Ryder Truck Rental, Inc.
Southern Fire Adjusters
American Transit Corporation
Beatrice Foods
City of Tuscaloosa
GFC Construction, Inc.
Penn Threshermens
South Central Bell Telephone Company

Attorneys

Perry Hubbard — (1921-1991)

Christopher Lyle McIlwain, Sr. — 1955 — The University of Alabama, B.A., 1977; J.D., 1980 — Law and Psychology Review — Admitted to Bar, 1980, Alabama; 1980, U.S. District Court, Northern District of Alabama; 1981, U.S. Court of Appeals, Eleventh Circuit; 1984, U.S. Supreme Court — Member American and Tuscaloosa County Bar Associations; Alabama State Bar; Alabama Defense Lawyers Association; Defense Research Institute — Author: "The Comprehensive General Liability Policy in Alabama-Coverage Provisions," 48 Alabama Lawyer 326, 1987; "Building Contractor's Recovery for Incomplete Performance," 51 Alabama Lawyer 230, 1990; "Clear as Mud: An Insurer's Rights and Duties Where Coverage Under a Liability Policy is Questionable," 27 Cumberland Law Review 31, 1997; "The Qualified Immunity Defense in the Eleventh Circuit and Its Application to Excessive Force Claims," 49 Alabama Law Review 941, 1998; "Better Late Than Never: Notice Requirements in Liability Insurance Policies," 19 Alabama Defense Lawyers Association Journal 8, 2003; Minimum Standards for Adjusting Liability Insurance Claims in Alabama, 20 Alabama Defense Lawyers Association Journal 10, 2004; "The Professional Services Exclusion in Alabama: A Trap For the Unwary Insurer," 25 Alabama Defense Lawyers Association Journal 31, 2009; "Necromancing the Stone: Conjuring the Alabama Common Law Collateral Source Rule Back To Life," 27 Ala. Def. Lawyers Assoc. J. 35 2011; "A Coverage Checklist For Alabama CGL Policies" 2012 — Practice Areas: Litigation

W. Marcus Brakefield — 1957 — The University of Alabama, B.S., 1979; Tulane University, M.B.A., 1983; The University of Alabama, J.D., 1987 — Phi Delta Phi — Admitted to Bar, 1987, Alabama; 1988, U.S. District Court, Middle, Northern and Southern Districts of Alabama — Member American and Tuscaloosa County Bar Associations; Alabama State Bar (Past Chairman, Commercial Law Section) — Practice Areas: Commercial Law

Associates

Edwin L. Parker — 1961 — The University of Mississippi, B.A., 1983; J.D., 1986; Washington University, LL.M. Taxation, 1994 — Admitted to Bar, 1986, Mississippi; 1997, Alabama; 1986, U.S. District Court, Northern and Southern Districts of Mississippi; U.S. Court of Appeals, Fifth Circuit — Member American and Tuscaloosa Bar Associations; Alabama State Bar; The Mississippi Bar — Assistant Staff Judge Advocate (1986-1990) — Practice Areas: Estate Planning; Probate; Trusts; Real Estate

C. Collin Rich — 1986 — The University of Alabama, B.A. (magna cum laude), 2008; J.D., 2011 — Admitted to Bar, 2011, Alabama; U.S. District Court, Middle, Northern and Southern Districts of Alabama — Member Alabama State Bar; Tuscaloosa County Bar Association — Practice Areas: Civil Litigation; Creditor Rights; Probate; Estate Planning; Real Estate

Owens & Millsaps, LLP
Attorneys at Law

2606 8th Street
Tuscaloosa, Alabama 35401
Toll Free: 866-790-2889
Telephone: 205-750-0750
Telephone: 205-759-8582
Fax: 205-750-0355
E-Mail: jowens@theowensfirm.com
E-Mail: pat@theowensfirm.com
www.theowensfirm.com

Established: 1994

Owens & Millsaps, LLP, Attorneys at Law, Tuscaloosa, AL
(Continued)

Insurance Defense, Medical Malpractice, Legal Malpractice, Dental Malpractice, Coverage Issues, Comprehensive General Liability, Product Liability, Construction Law, Employment Practices Liability, Environmental Liability

Firm Profile: Owens & Millsaps, LLP is a successor firm to Owens & Almond, LLP. Owens & Almond, LLP was a successor firm to Owens & Carver and Owens, Carver & Almond. John Owens and Susie Carver withdrew from the firm of Phelps, Owens, Jenkins, Gibson & Fowler in 1994 and formed Owens & Carver. The Phelps, Owens firm had been established by Sam Phelps and John Owens in 1969. Over the next 25 years it grew into a firm of over 15 attorneys.

Owens & Carver became Owens, Carver & Almond in 1997 when Brad Almond was made a partner. The firm became Owens & Almond in 1998 when Susie Carver decided to leave the private practice of law to serve as Assistant Dean and Director of Law Career Services at The University of Alabama School of Law. Owens & Almond became Owens & Millsaps in 2003 when Brad Almond left the firm. The current partners of the firm are John A. Owens, Apsilah Owens Millsaps and Susie Taylor Carver. In early January 2003, Susie Carver rejoined the firm. Rebecca Young joined the firm in 2009 as an associate and Nicholas Dagostino in 2012 as an associate.

In 1998, the firm acquired the Minor-Searcy House. The house was built in 1832 by Henry Minor, who served as reporter for and as Clerk of the Alabama Supreme Court. After considerable restoration work the firm opened for business there on December 28, 1999. The Minor-Searcy House has a long and interesting history and was the subject of a feature article in "Old Tuscaloosa Magazine" in 1999. The firm looks forward to many years of practicing in and preserving this historic building.

Insurance Clients

Cincinnati Insurance Company
Royal & SunAlliance Group
MAG Mutual Insurance Company
Zurich American Insurance Company

Non-Insurance Clients

Alawest-AL, LLC
Duckworth Morris Agency, Inc.
Northern Tool & Equipment Company
Southeastern Claims Services, Inc.
Warrior Tractor & Equipment Company
DSI Transport
First National Bank of Central Alabama
Richardson Meats
Southern Risk Services, Inc.
Weyerhaeuser Company

Partners

John A. Owens — 1939 — The University of Alabama, B.S., 1961; The University of Alabama School of Law, LL.B. (with distinction), 1967 — Omicron Delta Kappa; Phi Alpha Delta; Farrah Order of Jurisprudence/Farrah Order of the Coif Alumni Association (Past President, 1994-1995); University of Alabama Distinguished Alumnus Award (2012) — Admitted to Bar, 1967, Alabama; U.S. District Court, Northern District of Alabama; 1974, U.S. District Court, Southern District of Alabama; 1978, U.S. Court of Appeals, Fifth Circuit; 1981, U.S. Court of Appeals, Eleventh Circuit; 1990, U.S. Supreme Court — Member American and Tuscaloosa County Bar Associations; Alabama State Bar (Vice President, 1991-1992; President-Elect, 1994-1995; President, 1995-1996); Board of Bar Commissioners for Tuscaloosa County in Place No. 2, 1987-1994; Tuscaloosa County Trial Lawyers Association; Master of the Bench; Tuscaloosa Chapter of American Inns of Court; Fellow, Alabama Bar Foundation (President Elect, 2003-2005; President, 2005-2007); Farrah Law Society (President, 2001-2002); International Association of Defense Counsel; Alabama Trial Lawyers Association; Alabama Defense Lawyers Association; Fellow, American Bar Foundation — E-mail: jowens@theowensfirm.com

Apsilah Owens Millsaps — 1966 — Dartmouth College, B.A., 1988; The University of Alabama School of Law, J.D., 1992 — Bench and Bar Legal Honor Society; Hugo Black Scholar — University of Alabama Law Review — Admitted to Bar, 1992, Alabama; U.S. District Court, Middle and Northern Districts of Alabama; 1993, U.S. Court of Appeals, Eleventh Circuit — Member American and Tuscaloosa County Bar Associations; Alabama State Bar (Task Force on Women in the Law, 1995-1998; Young Lawyers' Executive Committee, 1996-2002; Women's Section, Member 1999-Present, President 2007-2009); Farrah Law Society — E-mail: millsaps@theowensfirm.com

TUSCALOOSA   ALABAMA

Owens & Millsaps, LLP, Attorneys at Law, Tuscaloosa, AL (Continued)

Susie Taylor Carver — 1949 — The University of Alabama, B.A., 1971; The University of Alabama School of Law, J.D., 1986 — Admitted to Bar, 1986, Alabama; U.S. District Court, Northern District of Alabama; 1989, U.S. Court of Appeals, Fifth and Eleventh Circuits; 1990, U.S. Supreme Court; 1992, U.S. District Court, Middle District of Alabama — Member American and Tuscaloosa County Bar Associations; Alabama State Bar; American Association for Justice — E-mail: scarver@theowensfirm.com

Associates

Rebecca A. Young — 1985 — The University of Alabama, B.A. (magna cum laude), 2006; The University of Alabama School of Law, J.D., 2009 — Admitted to Bar, 2009, Alabama; U.S. District Court, Middle and Northern Districts of Alabama; 2013, U.S. Court of Appeals, Eleventh Circuit — Member Alabama State Bar; Tuscaloosa County Bar Association; Defense Research Institute — E-mail: ryoung@theowensfirm.com

Nicholas Dagostino — 1985 — Canisius College, B.A., 2007; M.S., 2009; The University of Alabama School of Law, J.D., 2012 — Alabama Law Review Best Senior Editor Award (2011-2012); Best Papers (Advanced Constitutional Law and Mediation Practice and Procedure); Eagle Scout — Admitted to Bar, 2012, Alabama; U.S. District Court, Northern District of Alabama — Member Tuscaloosa County Bar Association — E-mail: nickdagostino@theowensfirm.com

Phelps, Jenkins, Gibson & Fowler, LLP

1201 Greensboro Avenue
Tuscaloosa, Alabama 35401
  Telephone: 205-345-5100
  Fax: 205-758-4394, 205-391-6658
  E-Mail: receptionist@pjgf.com
  www.phelpsjenkins.com

Established: 1968

Employment Litigation, General Defense, Medical Malpractice, School Law, Workers' Compensation, Personal Injury

Firm Profile: Phelps, Jenkins, Gibson, & Fowler, L.L.P., one of West Alabama's largest and oldest law firms, provides a broad range of legal services to individual, corporate, and institutional clients statewide. The firm is large enough to offer diverse legal expertise yet small enough to be hands-on, with senior partners directly involved in a high percentage of cases.

The firm was organized in 1968 by the late Sam Phelps, as a successor to Mize, Spiro, and Phelps, a Tuscaloosa firm founded in the 1940s. Since its inception, the Phelps firm has evolved to include a well-balanced mix of attorneys who practice in virtually all areas of the law.

Attorneys in the firm's litigation department practice in both state and federal courts. The firm's trial practice is primarily in the state courts of Tuscaloosa, Jefferson, Bibb, Choctaw, Clarke, Fayette, Greene, Hale, Lamar, Marengo, Marion, Pickens, Sumter, and Walker counties, as well as the Northern, Middle, and Southern Districts of the federal court system in Alabama. Appellate work is handled in the Alabama Court of Civil Appeals, the Alabama Supreme Court, the Fifth and Eleventh Circuits of the United States Court of Appeals, and the United States Supreme Court.

Insurance Clients

Aetna Insurance Company
Alabama Municipal Insurance Corporation
Allstate Insurance Company
American Automobile Insurance Company
American Insurance Company
American Mutual Fire Insurance Company of Kentucky
Associated Indemnity Corporation
Carolina Casualty Insurance Company
Cincinnati Insurance Company
CNA HealthPro
Compass Insurance Company
Continental Insurance Company
Aetna Life and Casualty Company
Alabama Reassurance Company
Allied World National Assurance Company
American General Insurance Company
American International Group, Inc.
Anchor Casualty Insurance Company
Auto-Owners Insurance Company
Champion Insurance Company
Chubb Group of Insurance Companies
Coastal Insurance Company
Consolidated Mutual Insurance Company

Phelps, Jenkins, Gibson & Fowler, LLP, Tuscaloosa, AL (Continued)

Crum & Forster Insurance Group
Fireman's Fund Insurance Company
Freedom Specialty Insurance Company
Gulf Insurance Company
Hartford Financial Products
Horace Mann Educators Corporation
Hudson Specialty Insurance Company
Liberty National Life Insurance Company
North American Indemnity Company
Pennsylvania Life Insurance Company
Pilot Life Insurance Company
Safeco Insurance
Security Insurance Group
Southern Fire & Casualty Company
Travelers Bond & Financial Products
Wells Fargo Insurance Services
Westfield Companies
The Equitable Life Assurance Society of the United States
Forum Insurance Company
Great American Insurance Company
Hanover Insurance Company
Healthcare Worker's Compensation Self-Insurance Fund
Integon Life Insurance Corporation
International Service Underwriters
National Indemnity Company
The New Southland National Life Insurance Company
Northern Assurance Company of America
Pennsylvania National Mutual Casualty Insurance Company
The St. Paul Companies
Shelter Insurance Companies
Southern Pilot Insurance Company
Stonewall Insurance Company
United Services Automobile Association (USAA)
Western Casualty and Surety Company

Non-Insurance Clients

ABH Enterprises, Inc.
American International Adjustment Company
Bank of Tuscaloosa
Chilton Shelby Mental Health Center
Community Newspaper Holdings, Inc.
Fayette Medical Center
First National Bank of Central Alabama
Harrison Construction Company, Inc.
Indian Rivers Mental Health Center
Jack Marshall Foods, Inc.
Mid-States Asphalt
Northport Medical Center
PTS, Inc.
Ready Mix USA
R. L. Zeigler Packing, Inc.
S. T. Bunn Construction Company, Inc.
Tuscaloosa City Board of Education
USA Healthcare, LLC
WCFT-TV
Alabama Department of Mental Health
ARD Logistics-Alabama, LLC
Bryant Bank
City of Northport
City of Tuscaloosa
DCH Regional Medical Center
Dixie Pulp & Paper, Inc.
First Federal Bank
General Motors Acceptance Corporation
Heritage Health Care & Rehab, Inc.
Hospice of West Alabama
Innomotive Systems U.S.
Knight Sign Industries, Inc.
Norfolk Southern Corporation
Pickens County Medical Center
The Radiology Clinic
Restore Therapy, LLC
Sears, Roebuck and Co.
Stresscrete
TotalCom, Inc.
Tuscaloosa County Sales Tax Board
Walls Newspaper Consultants, Inc.
ZF Industries, Inc.

Sam M. Phelps — (1932-2011)

James J. Jenkins — 1942 — The University of Alabama, B.A., 1964; LL.B., 1967 — Admitted to Bar, 1967, Alabama; U.S. District Court, Northern District of Alabama; 2000, U.S. District Court, Southern District of Alabama — Member American and Tuscaloosa County Bar Associations; Alabama State Bar; International Association of Defense Lawyers; Defense Research Institute; Alabama Defense Lawyers Association — AV Rated by Martindale Hubbell; Selected as an Alabama Super Lawyer (since 2008); Top Attorneys in Alabama by Business Alabama (since 2011) — Alabama Registered Mediator — E-mail: jjenkins@pjgf.com

J. Russell Gibson, III — 1947 — The University of Alabama, B.A., 1971; J.D., 1973 — Admitted to Bar, 1974, Alabama; U.S. District Court, Middle, Northern and Southern Districts of Alabama; U.S. Court of Appeals, Fifth and Eleventh Circuits — Member American and Tuscaloosa County Bar Associations; Alabama State Bar; Alabama Association of School Board Attorneys; Alabama Defense Lawyers Association — AV Rated by Martindale Hubbell — E-mail: rgibson@pjgf.com

Randolph M. Fowler — 1949 — The University of Alabama, B.A., 1971; J.D., 1975 — Admitted to Bar, 1975, Alabama; U.S. District Court, Northern District of Alabama; 1988, U.S. District Court, Southern District of Alabama — Member American and Tuscaloosa County Bar Associations; Alabama State Bar — AV Rated by Martindale Hubbell — E-mail: rfowler@pjgf.com

Farley A. Poellnitz — 1957 — The University of Alabama, B.S., 1980; J.D., 1984; Boston University, LL.M., 1985 — Admitted to Bar, 1984, Alabama;

Phelps, Jenkins, Gibson & Fowler, LLP, Tuscaloosa, AL (Continued)

U.S. District Court, Northern District of Alabama; U.S. Tax Court — Member American and Tuscaloosa Bar Associations; Alabama State Bar — E-mail: fpoellnitz@pjgf.com

A. Courtney Crowder — 1958 — The University of Alabama, B.S., 1980; J.D., 1983 — Admitted to Bar, 1983, Alabama; U.S. District Court, Middle, Northern and Southern Districts of Alabama; U.S. Court of Appeals, Eleventh Circuit; U.S. Supreme Court — Member American and Tuscaloosa County Bar Associations; Alabama State Bar; Tuscaloosa County Inns of Court; Alabama Defense Lawyers Association; Defense Research Institute — AV Rated by Martindale Hubbell — E-mail: accrowder@pjgf.com

Bruce H. Henderson — Rhodes College, B.A., 1980; University of Memphis, J.D., 1982 — Admitted to Bar, 1983, Tennessee; 1997, Alabama; U.S. District Court, Middle, Northern and Southern Districts of Alabama; U.S. District Court, Middle and Western Districts of Tennessee; U.S. Court of Appeals, Eleventh Circuit; U.S. Supreme Court — Member American, Tennessee (Labor and Employment Law Sections) and Tuscaloosa County Bar Associations; Alabama State Bar (Labor and Employment Law Section); Tuscaloosa Human Resource Professionals; Alabama Defense Lawyers Association — AV Rated by Martindale Hubbell; 2013 Top Rated Lawyer in Labor & Employment by American Lawyer Media — Alabama Registered Mediator; Alabama Registered Arbitrator — E-mail: bhenderson@pjgf.com

Stephen E. Snow — 1968 — The University of Alabama, B.A., 1990; J.D. (cum laude), 1993; University of Florida, LL.M., 1994 — Admitted to Bar, 1993, Alabama — Member American and Tuscaloosa County Bar Associations; Alabama State Bar — E-mail: ssnow@pjgf.com

W. David Ryan — 1967 — The University of Alabama, B.A., 1990; J.D., 1993 — Admitted to Bar, 1993, Alabama; U.S. District Court, Northern District of Alabama; U.S. Court of Appeals, Eleventh Circuit; U.S. Supreme Court — Member American and Tuscaloosa County Bar Associations; Alabama State Bar; Alabama Council of School Board Attorneys — E-mail: dryan@pjgf.com

Terri Olive Tompkins — 1973 — The University of Alabama, B.A., 1995; J.D., 1999 — Phi Beta Kappa — Alabama Law Review — Admitted to Bar, 1999, Alabama; 2001, U.S. District Court, Middle, Northern and Southern Districts of Alabama; U.S. Court of Appeals, Eleventh Circuit — Member Tuscaloosa County Bar Association (Past President); Alabama Board of Bar Commissioners; Alabama Defense Lawyers Association — Alabama Super Lawyers - Rising Star — E-mail: ttompkins@pjgf.com

Jessica K. Boyd — The University of Alabama, B.A., 2010; The University of Alabama School of Law, J.D. (summa cum laude), 2013 — Admitted to Bar, 2013, Alabama; U.S. District Court, Northern District of Alabama — Member Tuscaloosa County Bar Association — E-mail: jboyd@pjgf.com

Zeanah, Hust, Summerford & Williamson, L.L.C.

2330 University Boulevard, 7th Floor
Tuscaloosa, Alabama 35401
Telephone: 205-349-1383
Fax: 205-391-1319
E-Mail: bhust@zeanahhust.com
www.zeanahhust.com

Established: 1959

Insurance Defense, Trial Practice, Employment Law, Workers' Compensation

Firm Profile: This firm was founded by Olin W. Zeanah in 1959. The firm practices in all central and western counties, as well as three federal districts. The firm maintains a general practice with emphasis on insurance defense, corporate, real estate, and banking litigation. The firm is active in state and local bar activities as well as the local Inn of Court. Mr. Hust is a past president of the Inn of Court, as well as past president of the Tuscaloosa County Bar Association and is a Fellow in the American College of Trial Lawyers. Mr. Summerford is a member of the Board of Directors of the Alabama Defense Lawyers Association. Ms. Williamson is the chair of the Workers Compensation section of the State Bar.

Insurance Clients

Alfa Mutual Insurance Company	Amerisure Insurance Company
Audubon Insurance Company	Bituminous Insurance Companies

Zeanah, Hust, Summerford & Williamson, L.L.C., Tuscaloosa, AL (Continued)

Chubb Group of Insurance Companies	CIGNA Property and Casualty Insurance Company
Empire Fire and Marine Insurance Company	Kodiak Insurance Company
	Liberty Mutual Insurance Company

Non-Insurance Clients

Alabama Power Company	Construction Claims Management
Drummond Company	Michelin North America, Inc.
NorthStar Emergency Medical Services, Inc.	The Westervelt Company

Partners

Olin W. Zeanah — (1922-1987)

Wilbor J. Hust, Jr. — 1946 — The University of Alabama, J.D., 1971 — University of Alabama Law Review — Admitted to Bar, 1971, Alabama; 1976, U.S. Court of Federal Claims; 1978, U.S. Supreme Court; U.S. District Court, Middle, Northern and Southern Districts of Alabama — Member American and Tuscaloosa County (Past President) Bar Associations; Alabama State Bar; Tuscaloosa Inns of Court (Past President); Fellow, American College of Trial Lawyers; Alabama Defense Lawyers Association; Defense Research Institute

E. Clark Summerford — 1950 — The University of Alabama, B.S., 1972; M.A., 1975; J.D., 1978 — Admitted to Bar, 1978, Alabama; 1986, U.S. District Court, Northern District of Alabama — Member American and Tuscaloosa County Bar Associations; Alabama State Bar; Alabama Defense Lawyers Association (Board of Directors); Defense Research Institute (Board of Directors); Association of Defense Trial Attorneys

Beverly Smith Williamson — 1965 — The University of Alabama, B.A. (cum laude), 1989; J.D., 1992 — Phi Beta Kappa — Admitted to Bar, 1992, Alabama; U.S. District Court, Northern and Southern Districts of Alabama — Member American and Tuscaloosa County Bar Associations; Alabama State Bar (Vice-Chair, Worker's Compensation Section); Alabama Defense Lawyers Association; Defense Research Institute

Associate Attorney

Joseph T. Cox III — 1986 — The University of Alabama, B.A. (magna cum laude), 2008; The University of Alabama School of Law, J.D., 2011 — Admitted to Bar, 2011, Alabama; U.S. District Court, Northern District of Alabama — Member American and Tuscaloosa County Bar Associations

---

The following firms also service this area.

Hill, Hill, Carter, Franco, Cole & Black, P.C.
425 South Perry Street
Montgomery, Alabama 36104
Telephone: 334-834-7600
Fax: 334-263-5969

Mailing Address: P.O. Box 116, Montgomery, AL 36101-0116

Appellate Practice, Aviation, Business Law, Casualty, Commercial Litigation, Discrimination, Education Law, Employment Law, Insurance Defense, Insurance Fraud, Law Enforcement Liability, Product Liability, Professional Liability, State and Federal Courts, Surety, Transportation, Trial Practice, Workers' Compensation, Insurance Coverage Opinions and Litigation

SEE COMPLETE LISTING UNDER MONTGOMERY, ALABAMA (105 MILES)

Phelps, Jenkins, Gibson & Fowler, LLP
1201 Greensboro Avenue
Tuscaloosa, Alabama 35401
Telephone: 205-345-5100
Fax: 205-758-4394, 205-391-6658

Mailing Address: P.O. Box 020848, Tuscaloosa, AL 35402-0848

Employment Litigation, General Defense, Medical Malpractice, School Law, Workers' Compensation, Personal Injury

SEE COMPLETE LISTING UNDER TUSCALOOSA, ALABAMA

TUSKEGEE † 9,865 Macon Co.

Refer To
Rushton, Stakely, Johnston & Garrett, P.A.
184 Commerce Street
Montgomery, Alabama 36104
  Telephone: 334-206-3100
  Fax: 334-262-6277

Mailing Address: P.O. Box 270, Montgomery, AL 36101-0270

Insurance Defense, Trial and Appellate Practice, Accountants and Attorneys Liability, Administrative Law, Advertising Injury, Agent and Brokers Errors and Omissions, Appellate Practice, Arbitration, Automobile Tort, Bad Faith, Business Law, Casualty Insurance Law, Class Actions, Commercial Litigation, Complex Litigation, Construction Litigation, Contract Disputes, Copyright and Trademark Law, Coverage Analysis, Declaratory Judgments, Directors and Officers Liability, Employment Law, Environmental Law, Family Law, Fidelity and Surety, Fraud, Health Care, Health Care Professional Licensure Defense, Insurance Litigation, Labor and Employment, Law Enforcement Liability, Legal Malpractice, Medical Devices, Medical Malpractice, Pharmaceutical, Premises Liability, Primary and Excess Insurance, Product Liability, Professional Errors and Omissions, Professional Liability, Surety, Title Insurance, Uninsured and Underinsured Motorist, Workers' Compensation, Wrongful Death

SEE COMPLETE LISTING UNDER MONTGOMERY, ALABAMA (42 MILES)

UNION SPRINGS † 3,980 Bullock Co.

Refer To
Ball, Ball, Matthews & Novak, P.A.
445 Dexter Avenue, Suite 9045
Montgomery, Alabama 36104
  Telephone: 334-387-7680
  Fax: 334-387-3222

Mailing Address: P.O. Box 2148, Montgomery, AL 36102-2148

Insurance Defense, Medical Malpractice, Aviation, Bad Faith, Personal Injury, Construction Litigation, Employment Law, Product Liability, Property, Pharmaceutical, Medical Devices, Complex Litigation, Governmental Entity Defense, Workers' Compensation, Mediation, Arbitration, Trial and Appellate Practice, State and Federal Courts, Insurance Coverage Analysis, Automobile Injury, Motor Carrier Defense

SEE COMPLETE LISTING UNDER MONTGOMERY, ALABAMA (40 MILES)

Refer To
Morrow, Romine & Pearson, P.C.
122 South Hull Street
Montgomery, Alabama 36104
  Telephone: 334-262-7707
  Fax: 334-262-7742

Mailing Address: P.O. Box 4804, Montgomery, AL 36103

Civil Trial Practice, Insurance Law, Medical Malpractice, Product Liability, Environmental Coverage, Personal Injury, Litigation, Mediation, Trial Practice, Appellate Practice, State and Federal Courts, Handicap and Employment Discrimination, Diving Accidents

SEE COMPLETE LISTING UNDER MONTGOMERY, ALABAMA (48 MILES)

VERNON † 2,000 Lamar Co.

Refer To
Owens & Millsaps, LLP
Attorneys at Law
2606 8th Street
Tuscaloosa, Alabama 35401
  Toll Free: 866-790-2889
  Telephone: 205-750-0750
  Telephone: 205-759-8582
  Fax: 205-750-0355

Mailing Address: P.O. Box 2487, Tuscaloosa, AL 35403-2487

Insurance Defense, Medical Malpractice, Legal Malpractice, Dental Malpractice, Coverage Issues, Comprehensive General Liability, Product Liability, Construction Law, Employment Practices Liability, Environmental Liability

SEE COMPLETE LISTING UNDER TUSCALOOSA, ALABAMA (60 MILES)

Refer To
Phelps, Jenkins, Gibson & Fowler, LLP
1201 Greensboro Avenue
Tuscaloosa, Alabama 35401
  Telephone: 205-345-5100
  Fax: 205-758-4394, 205-391-6658

Mailing Address: P.O. Box 020848, Tuscaloosa, AL 35402-0848

Employment Litigation, General Defense, Medical Malpractice, School Law, Workers' Compensation, Personal Injury

SEE COMPLETE LISTING UNDER TUSCALOOSA, ALABAMA (60 MILES)

WETUMPKA † 6,528 Elmore Co.

Refer To
Ball, Ball, Matthews & Novak, P.A.
445 Dexter Avenue, Suite 9045
Montgomery, Alabama 36104
  Telephone: 334-387-7680
  Fax: 334-387-3222

Mailing Address: P.O. Box 2148, Montgomery, AL 36102-2148

Insurance Defense, Medical Malpractice, Aviation, Bad Faith, Personal Injury, Construction Litigation, Employment Law, Product Liability, Property, Pharmaceutical, Medical Devices, Complex Litigation, Governmental Entity Defense, Workers' Compensation, Mediation, Arbitration, Trial and Appellate Practice, State and Federal Courts, Insurance Coverage Analysis, Automobile Injury, Motor Carrier Defense

SEE COMPLETE LISTING UNDER MONTGOMERY, ALABAMA (15 MILES)

Refer To
Morrow, Romine & Pearson, P.C.
122 South Hull Street
Montgomery, Alabama 36104
  Telephone: 334-262-7707
  Fax: 334-262-7742

Mailing Address: P.O. Box 4804, Montgomery, AL 36103

Civil Trial Practice, Insurance Law, Medical Malpractice, Product Liability, Environmental Coverage, Personal Injury, Litigation, Mediation, Trial Practice, Appellate Practice, State and Federal Courts, Handicap and Employment Discrimination, Diving Accidents

SEE COMPLETE LISTING UNDER MONTGOMERY, ALABAMA (19 MILES)

Refer To
Rushton, Stakely, Johnston & Garrett, P.A.
184 Commerce Street
Montgomery, Alabama 36104
  Telephone: 334-206-3100
  Fax: 334-262-6277

Mailing Address: P.O. Box 270, Montgomery, AL 36101-0270

Insurance Defense, Trial and Appellate Practice, Accountants and Attorneys Liability, Administrative Law, Advertising Injury, Agent and Brokers Errors and Omissions, Appellate Practice, Arbitration, Automobile Tort, Bad Faith, Business Law, Casualty Insurance Law, Class Actions, Commercial Litigation, Complex Litigation, Construction Litigation, Contract Disputes, Copyright and Trademark Law, Coverage Analysis, Declaratory Judgments, Directors and Officers Liability, Employment Law, Environmental Law, Family Law, Fidelity and Surety, Fraud, Health Care, Health Care Professional Licensure Defense, Insurance Litigation, Labor and Employment, Law Enforcement Liability, Legal Malpractice, Medical Devices, Medical Malpractice, Pharmaceutical, Premises Liability, Primary and Excess Insurance, Product Liability, Professional Errors and Omissions, Professional Liability, Surety, Title Insurance, Uninsured and Underinsured Motorist, Workers' Compensation, Wrongful Death

SEE COMPLETE LISTING UNDER MONTGOMERY, ALABAMA (19 MILES)

ALASKA

CAPITAL: JUNEAU

JUDICIAL DISTRICTS

First Judicial District . . . . . . Juneau and Ketchikan
Second Judicial District . . . . Nome
Third Judicial District . . . . Anchorage
Fourth Judicial District . . . . Fairbanks

Our files contain additional verified data on the firms listed herein. This additional information is available on request.

A.M. BEST COMPANY

ANCHORAGE 260,283

Bliss, Wilkens & Clayton
An Association of LLCs

500 L Street, Suite 200
Anchorage, Alaska 99501
  Telephone: 907-276-2999
  Fax: 907-276-2956
  E-Mail: atc@bwclawyers.com
  www.bwclawyers.com

(Oro Valley, AZ Office*(See Tucson listing): 1846 East Innovation Park Drive, 85755)
  (Tel: 520-318-5599)
  (Fax: 907-276-2956)

Established: 1999

Aviation, Civil Trial Practice, Appeals, Business Law, Insurance Law, Probate, Elder Law, Corporate Law, Medical Staff Review

Firm Profile: Bliss, Wilkens & Clayton is a team of seasoned advocates with a single objective: To discover and obtain the best possible outcome for each client. We draw upon decades of experience in courtrooms, boardrooms and communities across Alaska and Arizona. We seek to understand the diverse and unique objectives of every client, and are prepared to help each client realize a positive outcome best suited for their particular circumstance.

The firm is a member of the Legal Netlink Alliance, which offers clients access to a multi-state and International network of top quality law firms.

Bliss, Wilkens & Clayton enjoys a Martindale-Hubbell rating of AV.

Insurance Clients

AAA Alaska Insurance Company
Associated Aviation Underwriters
California Casualty Management Company
Great American Insurance Company
Horace Mann Insurance Company
St. Paul Fire and Marine Insurance Company
United States Aviation Underwriters, Inc.
American States Insurance Company
Chartis Aerospace
Farm Bureau Mutual Insurance Company
Home Insurance Company
Providence Washington Insurance Company
Sequoia Insurance Company
Westport Insurance Company

Non-Insurance Clients

Alaska Airlines, Inc.

Members

Ronald L. Bliss — 1949 — University of Michigan, B.S., 1970; Gonzaga University School of Law, J.D. (cum laude), 1975 — Admitted to Bar, 1975, Washington; Alaska; Arizona; U.S. District Court, District of Alaska; U.S. Court of Appeals, Ninth Circuit; U.S. Supreme Court — Member Alaska and Washington State Bar Associations (inactive); Aircraft Owners and Pilots Association; Lawyer-Pilots Bar Association

James K. Wilkens — 1954 — St. Olaf College, B.A., 1977; Drake University Law School, J.D. (with honors), 1980 — Order of the Coif; Order of the Barristers; Phi Alpha Delta — Admitted to Bar, 1980, Iowa; Alaska; Arizona; U.S. District Court, District of Alaska; U.S. District Court, District of Arizona; U.S. Court of Appeals, Ninth Circuit; U.S. Supreme Court; U.S. Tax Court — Member American, Iowa State and Alaska Bar Associations; Defense Counsel of Alaska; Aircraft Owners and Pilots Association; Defense Research Institute; Lawyer-Pilots Bar Association

Alfred Clayton, Jr. — 1962 — Linfield College, B.A. (magna cum laude), 1984; Willamette University College of Law, J.D. (summa cum laude), 1991 — Admitted to Bar, 1991, Alaska; Arizona; U.S. District Court, District of Alaska; U.S. Court of Appeals, Ninth Circuit; U.S. Supreme Court — Member Alaska Bar Association; Aircraft Owners and Pilots Association

Burr, Pease & Kurtz

810 N Street, Suite 300
Anchorage, Alaska 99501
  Telephone: 907-276-6100
  Fax: 907-258-2530
  Toll Free: 800-474-4275
  E-Mail: bpk@bpk.com
  www.bpk.com

Established: 1957

Insurance Defense, Negligence, Product Liability, Medical Malpractice, Legal Malpractice, Aviation, Admiralty and Maritime Law, Business Law, Construction Law, Employment Law, Environmental Law, Personal Injury, Oil and Gas, Professional Liability, Workers' Compensation

Firm Profile: Burr, Pease & Kurtz has represented individuals and businesses in Alaska since 1957. The firm offers expertise in a variety of legal disciplines for national, international and local clients with interests throughout the state and takes pride in its reputation for delivering the highest quality legal services.

Insurance Clients

CNA Insurance Companies
GMAC Insurance
Hartford Insurance Company
The Travelers Companies, Inc.
Darwin Professional Underwriters, Inc.
Liberty Mutual Insurance Company
Zurich American Insurance Company

Non-Insurance Clients

Alyeska Pipeline Service Company
Arctic Slope Regional Corporation
BP Amoco
Design PT
Johnson & Johnson
North Star Terminal & Stevedore Company
Olgoonik Corporation
Waters Petroleum
Anchorage Fueling and Service Company
Brews Brothers
ESI Corporation
Morgan Stanley Dean Witter
Norton Sound Economic Development Corporation
Polar Tankers, Inc.
Wirum Properties

Firm Members

Nelson G. Page — Portland State University, B.S. (cum laude), 1975; Georgetown University Law Center, J.D. (cum laude), 1978 — Admitted to Bar, 1978, Oregon; 1979, Alaska; U.S. District Court, District of Alaska; 1981, U.S. Court of Appeals, Ninth Circuit; U.S. Supreme Court — Member American, Alaska and Anchorage Bar Association; Oregon State Bar — Practice Areas: Professional Malpractice; Product Liability; Personal Injury; Environmental Law; Commercial Law; General Civil Litigation; Contract Disputes; Construction Law; Arbitration; Mediation; Contracts

David W. Pease — Yale University, B.A., 1982; Northeastern University School of Law, J.D., 1985 — Admitted to Bar, 1987, Alaska; U.S. District Court, District of Alaska — Member Alaska Bar Association — Practice Areas: Contract Disputes; Product Liability; Insurance Defense; Environmental Law; General Civil Litigation; Commercial Law; Personal Injury; Contracts

Michael W. Seville — Oregon State University, B.S. (with high honors), 1984; Arizona State University College of Law, J.D., 1988 — Admitted to Bar, 1988, Alaska; U.S. District Court, District of Alaska — Member Alaska Bar Association — Practice Areas: Insurance Defense; Contract Disputes; Personal Injury; Environmental Law; Commercial Law; Employment Litigation; General Civil Litigation; Construction Litigation; Product Liability; Oil and Gas; Contracts

Thomas P. Owens, III — Duke University, B.A., 1987; Duke Law School, J.D., 1990 — Admitted to Bar, 1990, Alaska — Member Alaska Bar Association — Practice Areas: Commercial Law; Employment Defense; Contract Disputes; General Civil Litigation

Leonard R. Anderson — Brigham Young University, B.S., 1991; Gonzaga University School of Law, J.D., 1994 — Admitted to Bar, 1994, Alaska; U.S. District Court, District of Alaska; 1996, U.S. Tax Court; 2001, U.S. Court of Appeals, Ninth Circuit — Member Alaska Bar Association; Anchorage Bar Association — Practice Areas: Contract Disputes; Employment Law; Business Law; Real Estate Transactions; Wage and Hour Law; Estate Planning; Wills; Probate; Guardian and Conservatorships

ANCHORAGE   ALASKA

Burr, Pease & Kurtz, Anchorage, AK   (Continued)

Nora G. Barlow — University of California, Berkeley, B.A., 1986; University of the Pacific, McGeorge School of Law, J.D. (Order of the Coif), 1991 — Admitted to Bar, 1993, Alaska; 1991, California — Member Alaska Bar Association; Anchorage Bar Association — Practice Areas: Workers' Compensation

Bruce E. Davison — Michigan State University, B.S. Civ. & Envir. Engr., 1974; M.S. Civil/Structural Engr., 1974; Thomas M. Cooley Law School, J.D. (cum laude), 1982 — Admitted to Bar, 1982, Alaska; 1990, Washington — Member Alaska Bar Association; Washington Bar Association; Defense Research Institute — Professional Engineer, State of Alaska — Practice Areas: Construction Law

Associate

Martha T. Tansik — American University, B.A., 2002; Seattle University School of Law, J.D., 2010 — Admitted to Bar, 2011, Alaska — Member Alaska Bar Association — Practice Areas: Workers' Compensation

Of Counsel

Constance E. Livsey — Northland College, B.S., 1980; University of Oregon School of Law, J.D., 1984 — Admitted to Bar, 1984, Alaska; 1994, U.S. Supreme Court — Member Alaska and American Bar Associations

Peter C. Ginder — Dartmouth College, A.B., 1968; University of Denver College of Law, J.D., 1974 — Admitted to Bar, 1974, Alaska — Member American, Alaska and Anchorage Bar Associations; American College of Trust and Estate Counsel — Practice Areas: Commercial Law; Probate; Estate Planning; Real Estate

Retired

John C. Siemers	Donald A. Burr
Theodore M. Pease, Jr.	Lloyd S. Kurtz
Arden E. Page	Charles P. Flynn
Ann C. Liburd	

Call & Hanson, P.C.

413 G Street
Anchorage, Alaska 99501-2126
 Telephone: 907-258-8864
 Fax: 907-258-8865
 E-Mail: mjh@chklaw.net

Established: 2004

Insurance Defense, Automobile, Homeowners, Commercial Law, Product Liability, Professional Liability, Insurance Coverage, Bad Faith, General Liability, Bodily Injury, Policy Construction and Interpretation, Governmental Liability, Regulatory and Compliance, Appellate Practice, Personal Injury

Insurance Clients

Alaska National Insurance Company	Allstate Indemnity Company
Cottingham & Butler Claims, Inc.	Cornhusker Casualty Company
Horace Mann Insurance Group	GEICO Insurance Companies
National Casualty Company	Markel American Insurance Company
Scottsdale Insurance Company	State Farm Insurance Companies
United Services Automobile Association (USAA)	

Non-Insurance Clients

Alaska Municpal League Joint Insurance Association, Inc.

Shareholders

Blake H. Call — 1962 — University of Oregon, B.S., 1984; Willamette University College of Law, J.D. (Class President), 1989 — Admitted to Bar, 1989, Alaska; U.S. District Court, District of Alaska — Member Alaska Bar Association; Defense Counsel of Alaska (Past President, 2001-2004); Defense Research Institute (State Representative) — Author: "Analyzing Medical Records," Alaska Litigation Paralegal — E-mail: bhc@chklaw.net

Michael J. Hanson — 1961 — Western Washington University, B.A., 1983; University of Puget Sound School of Law, J.D. (cum laude), 1986 — Admitted to Bar, 1986, Alaska; U.S. District Court, District of Alaska; 1987, U.S.

Call & Hanson, P.C., Anchorage, AK   (Continued)

Court of Appeals, Ninth Circuit — Member Alaska Bar Association — E-mail: mjh@chklaw.net

Of Counsel

Susan D. Mack — 1948 — University of Alaska, B.A. (cum laude), 1977; Seattle University School of Law, J.D. (cum laude), 1984 — Admitted to Bar, 1984, Alaska; 1985, U.S. District Court, District of Alaska — Member Alaska Bar Association; Defense Counsel of Alaska — E-mail: sdm@chklaw.net

Groh Eggers, LLC

2600 Cordova Street, Suite 110
Anchorage, Alaska 99503-2745
 Telephone: 907-562-6474
 Fax: 907-562-6044
 E-Mail: devined@groheggers.com
 www.groheggers.com

Personal Injury, Wrongful Death, Discrimination, Employment Law, Title Insurance, Product Liability, Construction Law, Transportation

Insurance Clients

AIG Aviation, Inc.	Fidelity Title Insurance Agency
Old Republic Title Company	

Non-Insurance Clients

Alyeska Pipeline Service Company	ARCTEC Alaska
Harris Corporation	Mat-Su Title Insurance Agency
Northrim Bank	Prudential Jack White Real Estate
Tesoro Northstore Company	

Partners

Kenneth P. Eggers — 1946 — University of California, Berkeley, B.S., 1968; University of California, Los Angeles, J.D., 1973 — Phi Beta Kappa — Order of the Coif — Admitted to Bar, 1973, Alaska; 1976, U.S. Court of Appeals, Ninth Circuit; U.S. Supreme Court — Member American Bar Association (General Practice, Labor and Employment Law, Business Law and Litigation Sections); Alaska Bar Association (Secretary, 1987-1988; Board of Governors, 1986-1989; Employment Law Section); Anchorage Bar Association (First Vice President, 1975-1976; Board of Directors, 1980-1982; 1989-1992); Alaska Bar Foundation (Trustee, 1999; President, 2000-Present)

David A. Devine — 1951 — Colorado State University, B.A., 1974; University of Denver, J.D., 1978 — Admitted to Bar, 1979, Alaska; U.S. District Court, District of Alaska; 1982, U.S. Court of Appeals, Ninth Circuit; 1986, U.S. Supreme Court; 1992, U.S. Court of Appeals, Fifth Circuit — Member Alaska and Anchorage (Torts Section; Employment Law Section; Executive Committee, 1988-1994; Fee Arbitration Committee, 1995-Present) Bar Associations; Defense Research Institute; Association of Trial Lawyers of America

Holmes Weddle & Barcott, P.C.

701 West Eighth Avenue, Suite 700
Anchorage, Alaska 99501-3408
 Telephone: 907-274-0666
 Fax: 907-277-4657
 E-Mail: rweddle@hwb-law.com
 www.hwb-law.com

(Seattle, WA Office: 999 Third Avenue, Suite 2600, 98104)
 (Tel: 206-292-8008)

Insurance Defense, Admiralty and Maritime Law, Casualty, Surety, Workers' Compensation, Medical Malpractice, Product Liability, Construction Law, Contracts, Labor Relations Law

Insurance Clients

The ACE Group	Alaska National Insurance Company
ARECA Insurance Exchange	
Canal Insurance Company	CNA Insurance Companies
Empire Fire and Marine Insurance Company	The Hartford Insurance Group
	Liberty Mutual Insurance Company

ALASKA   ANCHORAGE

Holmes Weddle & Barcott, P.C., Anchorage, AK
(Continued)

Mattei Insurance Services, Inc. Progressive Insurance Company
Umialik Insurance Company

Non-Insurance Clients

Bank of America, N.A.   Costco Wholesale Corporation
CSX Lines, Inc.   E & O Professionals
Glencoe Group Services, Inc.   Lamorte Burns & Company, Inc.
RSKCo

Resident Members

Randall J. Weddle — 1944 — Indiana University, B.S., 1966; Indiana University School of Law, J.D. (cum laude), 1971 — Order of the Coif — Admitted to Bar, 1972, Alaska; U.S. District Court, District of Alaska; U.S. Court of Appeals, Ninth Circuit — Member Alaska Bar Association; The Maritime Law Association of the United States — E-mail: rweddle@hwb-law.com

Timothy A. McKeever — 1950 — Dartmouth College, A.B. (cum laude, with high distinction in Government); The George Washington University Law School, J.D. (with honors), 1975 — Admitted to Bar, 1976, Alaska; 1980, U.S. District Court, District of Alaska; U.S. Court of Appeals, Ninth Circuit — Member American and Alaska Bar Associations — Staff Attorney and Administrative Assistant for Senator Ted Stevens, 1975-1980 — E-mail: tmckeever@hwb-law.com

Matthew D. Regan — 1963 — University of Washington, B.A., 1985; George H. Atkinson School of Management, Willamette University, M.M., 1989; Willamette University College of Law, J.D., 1989 — Admitted to Bar, 1990, Alaska; U.S. District Court, District of Alaska — Member American Bar Association (District Representative, Alaska and Hawaii Young Lawyers Division Executive Council, 1993-1994; Tort, Insurance Practice and Business Law Sections); Alaska and Anchorage (Board of Directors, Young Lawyers Section, 1990-1995; Secretary, 1992-1993; Treasurer, 1993-1994) Bar Associations; The Maritime Law Association of the United States — E-mail: mregan@hwb-law.com

David M. Freeman — 1950 — University of Washington, B.A., 1972; University of Puget Sound School of Law, J.D., 1977 — Admitted to Bar, 1978, Alaska; 1989, U.S. Court of Federal Claims; 1990, U.S. Court of Appeals, Ninth Circuit — Member American and Alaska Bar Associations — E-mail: dfreeman@hwb-law.com

Grant E. Watts — 1953 — Weber State College, B.S., 1983; University of Idaho College of Law, J.D., 1985 — Admitted to Bar, 1986, Alaska; 1987, U.S. Court of Federal Claims — Member American and Alaska Bar Associations — E-mail: gwatts@hwb-law.com

Rebecca Holdiman-Miller — 1978 — Northwest Missouri State University, B.S., 2000; The University of Iowa College of Law, J.D., 2003 — Admitted to Bar, 2006, Alaska; U.S. District Court, District of Alaska — E-mail: rholdiman@hwb-law.com

Scott M. Kendall — 1975 — Western Washington University, B.A., 2000; University of Washington School of Law, J.D., 2003 — Admitted to Bar, 2003, Alaska; U.S. District Court, District of Alaska — E-mail: smkendall@hwb-law.com

Resident Associates

Alexander K. M. Vasauskas — 1950 — University of Illinois at Chicago, B.A., 1973; Loyola University School of Law, J.D., 1980 — Admitted to Bar, 1980, Alaska; U.S. District Court, District of Alaska — E-mail: avasauskas@hwb-law.com

Adam R. Sadoski — 1983 — Pacific University, B.S. (Dean's List), 2006; Seattle University School of Law, J.D., 2010 — Beta Beta Beta National Biological Honors Society; American Bar Association National Appellate Advocacy Competition Team — Admitted to Bar, 2010, Alaska — Member American and Alaska Bar Associations — E-mail: asadoski@hwb-law.com

Jayme D. Keller — 1982 — Western Washington University, B.A., 2004; University of Miami School of Law, J.D., 2007 — Dean's Merit Scholar — Admitted to Bar, 2008, Washington; 2009, Alaska; 2011, Georgia — Member Alaska and Washington State Bar Associations; State Bar of Georgia — E-mail: jkeller@hwb-law.com

Stacey C. Stone — 1984 — Pacific Lutheran University, B.A., 2006; Gonzaga University School of Law, J.D., 2009 — Admitted to Bar, 2010, Alaska — E-mail: sstone@hwb-law.com

Resident Of Counsel

Timothy M. Stone — 1946 — University of Michigan, B.A., 1968; University of Michigan Law School, J.D., 1973 — Admitted to Bar, 1973, Alaska; U.S. District Court, District of Alaska — E-mail: tstone@hwb-law.com

Holmes Weddle & Barcott, P.C., Anchorage, AK
(Continued)

James N. Reeves — 1945 — Dartmouth College, B.A., 1967; University of Minnesota Law School, J.D., 1970 — Admitted to Bar, 1970, Minnesota; 1972, Alaska; U.S. District Court, District of Alaska; U.S. Court of Appeals for the District of Columbia and Ninth Circuits; U.S. Supreme Court — Member Alaska Bar Association — E-mail: jreeves@hwb-law.com

Hughes Gorski Seedorf Odsen & Tervooren, LLC

3900 "C" Street, Suite 1001
Anchorage, Alaska 99503
Toll Free: 800-478-7522
Telephone: 907-274-7522
Fax: 907-263-8320
E-Mail: kcolbo@hglawfirm.net
www.hglawfirm.net

Established: 1939

Insurance Defense, Insurance Coverage, Bad Faith, Product Liability, Commercial Litigation, General Defense

Insurance Clients

Aetna Life and Casualty Company   Century Surety Company
Colonial Insurance Group   CUMIS Insurance Society, Inc.
CUNA Mutual Group   ESIS
First Mercury Syndicate, Inc.   National Indemnity Company
Western World Insurance
 Company

Members

James M. Gorski — 1951 — University of Washington, B.A., 1974; Willamette University College of Law, J.D., 1977 — Admitted to Bar, 1977, Alaska; U.S. District Court, District of Alaska; 1979, U.S. Court of Appeals, Ninth Circuit; 1984, U.S. Supreme Court — Member American Bar Association (Corporation, Banking and Business Law Section; Municipal Law Section); Alaska and Anchorage Bar Associations

James M. Seedorf — 1948 — Eastern Washington State College, B.S. (magna cum laude), 1970; M.S., 1972; University of Washington School of Law, J.D., 1977 — Admitted to Bar, 1977, Alaska; 2004, Washington — Member Alaska and Washington State Bar Associations

Steven S. Tervooren — 1955 — Oregon State University, B.S. (with highest honors), 1976; University of Oregon School of Law, J.D., 1979 — Admitted to Bar, 1979, Alaska — Member Alaska Bar Association; Defense Research Institute; Association of Defense Trial Attorneys

Kimberlee A. Colbo — 1966 — University of Southern California, A.B. (cum laude), 1988; University of Washington School of Law, J.D., 1992 — Admitted to Bar, 1992, Alaska; U.S. District Court, District of Alaska — Member American (Litigation and Tort Section) and Alaska (Fee Arbitration Committee) Bar Associations; Defense Counsel of Alaska (President); Association of Defense Trial Attorneys; Defense Research Institute

Paul S. Wilcox — 1948 — University of California, Berkeley, B.A., 1970; University of California, Hastings College of the Law, J.D., 1975 — Admitted to Bar, 1975, California; 1976, Alaska; 1975, U.S. District Court, Northern District of California; 1979, U.S. Court of Appeals, Ninth Circuit — Member State Bar of California; Alaska and Anchorage Bar Association

Jimmy E. White — 1962 — University of Alaska, B.S. (cum laude), 1995; Mercer University Walter F. George School of Law, J.D. (cum laude), 1999 — Admitted to Bar, 1999, Georgia; 2005, Alaska; 1999, U.S. District Court, Northern District of Georgia; 2000, U.S. Court of Appeals, Eleventh Circuit; 2007, U.S. District Court, District of Alaska — Member Alaska Bar Association; State Bar of Georgia; Defense Research Institute; Association of Defense Trial Attorneys

(Revisors of the Alaska Insurance Law Digest for this Publication)

(This firm is also listed in the Subrogation section of this directory)

Matthews & Zahare, P.C.

911 West 8th Avenue, Suite 400
Anchorage, Alaska 99501
   Telephone: 907-276-1516
   Fax: 907-276-8955
   Toll Free: 888-796-2925
   E-Mail: mzlaw@matthewszahare.com

Established: 1994

Insurance Defense, Coverage Issues, Admiralty and Maritime Law, Automobile, Casualty, General Liability, Personal Injury, Product Liability, Property, Professional Liability, Bad Faith, Agent and Brokers Errors and Omissions, Construction Litigation, Premises Liability, Subrogation

Insurance Clients

AAA Alaska Insurance Company
Allianz of America, Inc.
CNA Insurance Company
CSAA Insurance Group
Employers Reinsurance Corporation
The Hartford Insurance Group
Nautilus Insurance Group
Providence Washington Insurance Companies
Westport Insurance Corporation
Alaska National Insurance Company
Coregis Insurance Company
Darwin National Assurance Company
GE Global Insurance Group
Nationwide Insurance Company of America
Swiss Reinsurance Company
Utica National Insurance Group

Non-Insurance Clients

Alaska USA Federal Credit Union
Northern Adjusters, Inc.
First Insurance Funding Corp.

Partners

Thomas A. Matthews — 1959 — University of California, Berkeley, B.S., 1982; Northwestern School of Law of Lewis & Clark College, J.D., 1985 — Admitted to Bar, 1985, Alaska; U.S. District Court, District of Alaska; 1986, U.S. Tax Court; 1987, U.S. Court of Appeals, Ninth Circuit; U.S. Supreme Court — Member American Bar Association (Litigation, Tort and Insurance Practice Sections); Alaska Bar Association (Ethics Committee); Defense Counsel of Alaska; Alaska Co-Chair, Claims & Litigation Management Alliance (f/k/a Council on Litigation Management); International Society of Primerus Law Firms; Defense Research Institute — Author: "Products Liability in Alaska," Alaska Law Review 1, June 1993; Contributing Faculty Member, "A Practical Guide to Federal Court Rules and Procedure in Alaska - Current Update on Federal Rules of Civil Procedure," National Business Institute, Inc.; "Bad Faith Litigation in Alaska," National Business Institute, 2005 — AV Rating

A. Michael Zahare — 1959 — Northwest Nazarene University, B.A. (summa cum laude), 1981; University of Washington, J.D., 1984 — Admitted to Bar, 1984, Alaska; U.S. District Court, District of Alaska; 1991, U.S. Court of Appeals, Ninth Circuit; 1997, U.S. Supreme Court — Member American and Alaska Bar Associations

Of Counsel

Kenneth G. Hannam — 1952 — University of Oregon, B.A., 1977; J.D., 1983 — Admitted to Bar, 1983, Alaska; U.S. District Court, District of Alaska; U.S. Court of Appeals, Ninth Circuit

(This firm is also listed in the Subrogation section of this directory)

James B. Wright & Associates, P.C.

500 "L" Street, Suite 101
Anchorage, Alaska 99501
   Telephone: 907-277-6175
   Fax: 907-277-6181
   E-Mail: jimw@wrightlaw.org
   www.wright-law.com

Established: 1999

James B. Wright & Associates, P.C., Anchorage, AK
(Continued)

Tort, Insurance Law, First and Third Party Defense, Construction Law, Product Liability, Automobile, Homeowners, Professional Negligence, Environmental Law, Bad Faith, Arbitration, Mediation, Alternative Dispute Resolution, both Defense and Coverage

Insurance Clients

Admiral Insurance Company
American States Insurance Company
Chubb Group of Insurance Companies
MetLife Auto & Home
Progressive Insurance Company
United America Indemnity Group
Windsor Insurance Company
American Modern Home Insurance Company
Atlanta Casualty Company
Great American Insurance Company
Penn-America Insurance Company
Safeco Insurance
United National Insurance Company

Senior Partner

James Bryan Wright — 1955 — University of Puget Sound, B.A. (with honors), 1978; College of William & Mary, Marshall-Wythe School of Law, J.D., 1982 — Phi Delta Phi — Admitted to Bar, 1983, Alaska; 1983, U.S. District Court, District of Alaska; 1988, U.S. Court of Appeals, Ninth Circuit; 1994, U.S. Supreme Court — Member American Bar Association (Tort and Insurance Practice Section, 1988-Present); Alaska Bar Association (Fee Arbitration Panel, 1994-Present; Mediation Panel 2001-Present); Defense Research Institute — E-mail: jimw@wrightlaw.org

Associate

David W. Murrills — 1968 — DeVry Institute of Technology, B.S., 1989; Northwestern School of Law of Lewis & Clark College, J.D. (cum laude), 1992 — Admitted to Bar, 1992, Oregon; 1993, Alaska; U.S. District Court, District of Alaska; U.S. Court of Appeals, Ninth Circuit — E-mail: d.murrills@wrightlaw.org

FAIRBANKS 31,535

Refer To

Burr, Pease & Kurtz
810 N Street, Suite 300
Anchorage, Alaska 99501
   Telephone: 907-276-6100
   Fax: 907-258-2530
   Toll Free: 800-474-4275

Insurance Defense, Negligence, Product Liability, Medical Malpractice, Legal Malpractice, Aviation, Admiralty and Maritime Law, Business Law, Construction Law, Employment Law, Environmental Law, Personal Injury, Oil and Gas, Professional Liability, Workers' Compensation

SEE COMPLETE LISTING UNDER ANCHORAGE, ALASKA (350 MILES)

HOMER 5,003

Refer To

Holmes Weddle & Barcott, P.C.
701 West Eighth Avenue, Suite 700
Anchorage, Alaska 99501-3408
   Telephone: 907-274-0666
   Fax: 907-277-4657

Insurance Defense, Admiralty and Maritime Law, Casualty, Surety, Workers' Compensation, Medical Malpractice, Product Liability, Construction Law, Contracts, Labor Relations Law

SEE COMPLETE LISTING UNDER ANCHORAGE, ALASKA (125 MILES)

ALASKA   JUNEAU

JUNEAU 30,711
Refer To
Burr, Pease & Kurtz
810 N Street, Suite 300
Anchorage, Alaska 99501
   Telephone: 907-276-6100
   Fax: 907-258-2530
   Toll Free: 800-474-4275

Insurance Defense, Negligence, Product Liability, Medical Malpractice, Legal Malpractice, Aviation, Admiralty and Maritime Law, Business Law, Construction Law, Employment Law, Environmental Law, Personal Injury, Oil and Gas, Professional Liability, Workers' Compensation

SEE COMPLETE LISTING UNDER ANCHORAGE, ALASKA (865 MILES)

KENAI 7,100
Refer To
Holmes Weddle & Barcott, P.C.
701 West Eighth Avenue, Suite 700
Anchorage, Alaska 99501-3408
   Telephone: 907-274-0666
   Fax: 907-277-4657

Insurance Defense, Admiralty and Maritime Law, Casualty, Surety, Workers' Compensation, Medical Malpractice, Product Liability, Construction Law, Contracts, Labor Relations Law

SEE COMPLETE LISTING UNDER ANCHORAGE, ALASKA (75 MILES)

PALMER 5,937
Refer To
Holmes Weddle & Barcott, P.C.
701 West Eighth Avenue, Suite 700
Anchorage, Alaska 99501-3408
   Telephone: 907-274-0666
   Fax: 907-277-4657

Insurance Defense, Admiralty and Maritime Law, Casualty, Surety, Workers' Compensation, Medical Malpractice, Product Liability, Construction Law, Contracts, Labor Relations Law

SEE COMPLETE LISTING UNDER ANCHORAGE, ALASKA (43 MILES)

ARIZONA

CAPITAL: PHOENIX

COUNTIES AND COUNTY SEATS

County	County Seat	County	County Seat	County	County Seat
Apache	St. Johns	Greenlee	Clifton	Pima	Tuscon
Cochise	Bisbee	La Paz	Parker	Pinal	Florence
Coconino	Flagstaff	Maricopa	Phoenix	Santa Cruz	Nogales
Gila	Globe	Mohave	Kingman	Yavapai	Prescott
Graham	Safford	Navajo	Holbrook	Yuma	Yuma

In the text that follows "†" indicates County Seats.

Our files contain additional verified data on the firms listed herein. This additional information is available on request.

A.M. BEST COMPANY

ARIZONA   CASA GRANDE

CASA GRANDE   48,571 Pinal Co.
Refer To
Cavett & Fulton
A Professional Corporation
6035 East Grant Road
Tucson, Arizona 85712
　　Telephone: 520-733-0100
　　Fax: 520-733-1800

Medical Malpractice, Nursing Home Liability, Professional Liability, Insurance Defense, Medical Devices, Product Liability

SEE COMPLETE LISTING UNDER TUCSON, ARIZONA (72 MILES)

COTTONWOOD   11,265 Yavapai Co.

The Ledbetter Law Firm, P.L.C.
1003 North Main Street
Cottonwood, Arizona 86326
　　Telephone: 928-649-8777
　　Fax: 928-649-8778
　　E-Mail: jledbetter@ledbetterlawaz.com
　　www.ledbetterlawaz.com

Established: 2001

Automobile, Commercial Law, General Liability, Professional Liability, Property and Casualty, Investigation and Adjustment, Indian Law, Business Formation, Employment Law, Risk Management Consulting, Medical Malpractice Defense

Firm Profile: The Ledbetter Law Firm, P.L.C. believes that the formula for success is as simple as it is demanding. Achieving success is not altered by trends or technology. Success comes from hard work, inspiration, and attention to detail. These values guide the lawyers of the Ledbetter Law Firm. Our attorneys are focused on these timeless vaulues and on the satisfaction of obtaining the best possible results for our clients.

We understand that client service and satisfaction require thorough, skilled preparation. Our goal is to maintain the high level of respect and trust our clients have in us.

Insurance Clients

Allstate Insurance Company	Arizona School Risk Retention Trust
Ohio Casualty Group	Southwest General Insurance Company
Progressive Insurance	
State Farm Fire and Casualty Company	Titan Insurance Company
Victoria Insurance Company	Zurich Insurance Company

Non-Insurance Clients

Chevron Mining, Inc.	Flagstaff Medical Center, Inc.
Kingman Hospital, Inc.	Northern Arizona Healthcare, Inc.
Sedona Medical Center	Verde Valley Medical Center, Inc.

Partner

James E. Ledbetter — Grand Canyon College, B.A. (summa cum laude), 1983; Arizona State University College of Law, J.D., 1989 — Pedrick Scholar; Dubois Scholar; Order of the Barristers; National Moot Court Team — Admitted to Bar, 1989, Arizona; U.S. District Court, District of Arizona; U.S. Court of Appeals, Ninth Circuit; U.S. Supreme Court; 1993, White Mountain Apache Tribal Court; Navajo Nation Court; 1995, Hopi Tribal Court; San Carlos Apache Tribal Court — Member Navajo Nation Bar Association; Arizona Association of Defense Counsel; Defense Research Institute

Senior Counsel

Scott J. Hergenroether — The University of Arizona, B.A. Political Science, 1984; The University of Arizona College of Law, J.D., 1987 — Admitted to Bar, 1987, Arizona; U.S. District Court, District of Arizona; U.S. Court of Appeals, Ninth Circuit — Member American Bar Association; State Bar of Arizona; Defense Research Institute

The Ledbetter Law Firm, P.L.C., Cottonwood, AZ
(Continued)

Associates

Patricia A. Prekup — Arizona State University, B.S. (cum laude), 1987; Thomas M. Cooley Law School, J.D., 1994 — Admitted to Bar, 1994, New Mexico; 1996, U.S. Court of Appeals, Ninth Circuit; 1997, U.S. Court of Appeals, Tenth Circuit

Kelley J. Ruda — Clemson University, B.S. (summa cum laude), 2004; Florida Coastal School of Law, J.D. (magna cum laude), 2007 — Admitted to Bar, 2007, Arizona; 2010, U.S. District Court, District of Arizona

Tosca G. Henry — Southern Adventist University, B.A., 1998; The University of Arizona, James E. Rogers College of Law, J.D., 2010 — Admitted to Bar, 2010, Arizona; U.S. District Court, District of Arizona; Yavapai-Apache Tribal Court — Languages: Spanish, Italian, French

Jonathan C. Linford — Brigham Young University, B.A., 2007; The University of Arizona, James E. Rogers College of Law, J.D. (Dean's List), 2011 — — Admitted to Bar, 2011, Arizona; 2012, U.S. District Court, District of Arizona; White Mountain Apache Tribal Court — Languages: French

The following firms also service this area.

Mangum, Wall, Stoops & Warden, P.L.L.C.
100 North Elden
Flagstaff, Arizona 86001
　　Telephone: 928-779-6951
　　Fax: 928-773-1312
　　Mailing Address: P.O. Box 10, Flagstaff, AZ 86002

Insurance Defense

SEE COMPLETE LISTING UNDER FLAGSTAFF, ARIZONA (71 MILES)

FLAGSTAFF   † 65,870 Coconino Co.

Mangum, Wall, Stoops & Warden, P.L.L.C.
100 North Elden
Flagstaff, Arizona 86001
　　Telephone: 928-779-6951
　　Fax: 928-773-1312
　　E-Mail: mangumwall@mwswlaw.com
　　www.flagstaffattorneys.com

Established: 1955

Insurance Defense

Insurance Clients

Aetna Life and Casualty Company	Auto-Owners Insurance Company
Bankers Life Insurance Company	Cincinnati Insurance Company
Colonial Penn Insurance Company	Commercial Union Insurance Company
Dairyland Insurance Company	
Empire Fire and Marine Insurance Company	Employers Mutual Companies
Fireman's Fund Insurance Company	Federated Insurance Company
	GEICO Direct
Great West Casualty Company	Great American Insurance Company
Guaranty National Insurance Company	Insurance Company of the West
	National Indemnity Company
National Union Fire Insurance Company	Nationwide Mutual Insurance Company
New Hampshire Insurance Company	Ohio Casualty Insurance Company
Reliance Insurance Company	Progressive Insurance Company
Sentry Insurance	St. Paul Travelers
United Services Automobile Association (USAA)	Travelers Insurance Companies
	United States Fidelity and Guaranty Company
Utah Home Fire Insurance Company	VASA North Atlantic Insurance Company
Zurich North America	

Members

Kenneth H. Brendel — 1967 — Arizona State University, B.S., 1994; University of the Pacific, McGeorge School of Law, J.D., 1998 — Admitted to Bar, 1998, Arizona; 2000, U.S. District Court, District of Arizona; 2000, Hopi Tribal Court; 2001, Navajo Nation Court; 2002, U.S. Court of Appeals, Ninth

Mangum, Wall, Stoops & Warden, P.L.L.C., Flagstaff, AZ
(Continued)

Circuit; 2004, White Mountain Apache Tribal Court; 2006, U.S. Supreme Court — Member American and Coconino County Bar Associations; State Bar of Arizona; Arizona Trial Lawyers Association; American Trial Lawyers Association; Defense Research Institute — E-mail: kbrendel@mwswlaw.com

Brandon J. Kavanagh — 1974 — Georgetown University, B.A. (cum laude), 1994; The George Washington University Law School, J.D., 1997 — Admitted to Bar, 1997, Maryland; 1999, Arizona; U.S. District Court, District of Arizona; U.S. Court of Appeals, Ninth Circuit — Member American and Maricopa County Bar Associations; State Bar of Arizona (Chair, Business Law Section, 2008-2009) — E-mail: bkavanagh@mwswlaw.com

Kellie A. Peterson — 1978 — Gonzaga University, B.B.A., 2000; The University of Montana School of Law, J.D., 2003 — Admitted to Bar, 2003, Arizona; U.S. District Court, District of Arizona; 2004, U.S. Court of Appeals, Ninth Circuit; 2005, Navajo Nation Court — Member Federal and Coconino County Bar Associations — E-mail: kpeterson@mwswlaw.com

Associates

Jeffrey D. Dollins — 1969 — University of Massachusetts, B.A., 1991; Willamette University College of Law, J.D., 1995 — Admitted to Bar, 1996, Arizona; U.S. District Court, District of Arizona — Member State Bar of Arizona; Coconino County Bar Association; Arizona Council of School Attorneys; National School Boards Association Council of School Attorneys — Assistant Attorney General, December 2005-January 2009 — E-mail: jdollins@mwswlaw.com

James D. Griffith — 1960 — Western Illinois University, B.A., 2006; Phoenix School of Law, J.D., 2009 — Admitted to Bar, 2011, Arizona; 2012, U.S. District Court, District of Arizona — E-mail: jgriffith@mwswlaw.com

Christina A. Parry — 1975 — Arizona State University, B.A. (summa cum laude, with honors), 1998; M.P.A., 2000; J.D., 2003 — Admitted to Bar, 2004, Arizona; U.S. District Court, District of Arizona — E-mail: cparry@mwswlaw.com

Thomas E. Dietrich — 1980 — The University of Arizona, B.A. (cum laude), 2003; University of California, Hastings College of the Law, J.D., 2007 — Admitted to Bar, 2007, California; 2014, Arizona; 2007, U.S. District Court, Central, Eastern, Northern and Southern Districts of California; 2013, U.S. District Court, Eastern District of Texas — Member Orange County and Coconino County Bar Associations — E-mail: tdietrich@mwswlaw.com

Of Counsel

H. K. Mangum — (1908-1993)

Robert W. Warden — (1930-2012)

Eliza Read — John Carroll University, B.A., 1990; Case Western Reserve University, J.D., 1997 — Admitted to Bar, 1997, Arizona; 2000, U.S. District Court, District of Arizona — Member State Bar of Arizona (Chair, Mental Health & Elder Law Section, 2006-2007); Coconino County Bar Association; National Academy of Elder Law Attorneys — E-mail: eread@mwswlaw.com

Daniel J. Stoops, Retired
Douglas J. Wall, Retired
Stephen K. Smith, Retired
A. Dean Pickett, Retired

(This firm is also listed in the Subrogation section of this directory)

The following firms also service this area.

The Ledbetter Law Firm, P.L.C.
1003 North Main Street
Cottonwood, Arizona 86326
   Telephone: 928-649-8777
   Fax: 928-649-8778

Automobile, Commercial Law, General Liability, Professional Liability, Property and Casualty, Investigation and Adjustment, Indian Law, Business Formation, Employment Law, Risk Management Consulting, Medical Malpractice Defense

SEE COMPLETE LISTING UNDER COTTONWOOD, ARIZONA (69 MILES)

HOLBROOK † 5,053 Navajo Co.

Refer To

The Ledbetter Law Firm, P.L.C.
1003 North Main Street
Cottonwood, Arizona 86326
   Telephone: 928-649-8777
   Fax: 928-649-8778

Automobile, Commercial Law, General Liability, Professional Liability, Property and Casualty, Investigation and Adjustment, Indian Law, Business Formation, Employment Law, Risk Management Consulting, Medical Malpractice Defense

SEE COMPLETE LISTING UNDER COTTONWOOD, ARIZONA (157 MILES)

Refer To

Mangum, Wall, Stoops & Warden, P.L.L.C.
100 North Elden
Flagstaff, Arizona 86001
   Telephone: 928-779-6951
   Fax: 928-773-1312

Mailing Address: P.O. Box 10, Flagstaff, AZ 86002

Insurance Defense

SEE COMPLETE LISTING UNDER FLAGSTAFF, ARIZONA (90 MILES)

KINGMAN † 28,068 Mohave Co.

Refer To

The Ledbetter Law Firm, P.L.C.
1003 North Main Street
Cottonwood, Arizona 86326
   Telephone: 928-649-8777
   Fax: 928-649-8778

Automobile, Commercial Law, General Liability, Professional Liability, Property and Casualty, Investigation and Adjustment, Indian Law, Business Formation, Employment Law, Risk Management Consulting, Medical Malpractice Defense

SEE COMPLETE LISTING UNDER COTTONWOOD, ARIZONA (213 MILES)

Refer To

Mangum, Wall, Stoops & Warden, P.L.L.C.
100 North Elden
Flagstaff, Arizona 86001
   Telephone: 928-779-6951
   Fax: 928-773-1312

Mailing Address: P.O. Box 10, Flagstaff, AZ 86002

Insurance Defense

SEE COMPLETE LISTING UNDER FLAGSTAFF, ARIZONA (149 MILES)

PAGE 7,247 Coconino Co.

Refer To

Mangum, Wall, Stoops & Warden, P.L.L.C.
100 North Elden
Flagstaff, Arizona 86001
   Telephone: 928-779-6951
   Fax: 928-773-1312

Mailing Address: P.O. Box 10, Flagstaff, AZ 86002

Insurance Defense

SEE COMPLETE LISTING UNDER FLAGSTAFF, ARIZONA (137 MILES)

PHOENIX † 1,445,632 Maricopa Co.

Berrett & Hanna, L.C.

2355 East Camelback Road, Suite 618
Phoenix, Arizona 85016
   Toll Free: 866-681-4878
   Telephone: 602-576-7000
   Fax: 602-516-7006
   E-Mail: info@berrettandhanna.com

ARIZONA   PHOENIX

Berrett & Hanna, L.C., Phoenix, AZ   (Continued)

(Salt Lake City, UT Office*: 405 South Main Street, Suite 1050, 84111)
  (Toll Free: 800-230-9609)
  (Tel: 801-531-7733)
  (Fax: 801-531-7711)

Insurance Defense, Coverage Issues, Employment Law, Subrogation, Personal Injury, Property Damage, Product Liability, Automobile, Bodily Injury, Asbestos Litigation

Firm Profile: The law firm of Berrett & Associates, L.C. practices law in the states of Utah and Arizona. We have comprehensive knowledge of insurance defense, transportation claims and litigation. Our firm has earned a reputation as a fair and aggressive firm with the skills and resources necessary to successfully undertake multi-million dollar cases.

(See listing under Salt Lake City, UT for additional information)

(This firm is also listed in the Subrogation section of this directory)

Dickinson Wright PLLC

1850 North Central Avenue, Suite 1400
Phoenix, Arizona 85004
  Telephone: 602-285-5000
  Fax: 602-285-5100
  E-Mail: Fortiz@dickinsonwright.com
  www.dickinson-wright.com

(Detroit, MI Office*: 500 Woodward Avenue, Suite 4000, 48226-3425)
  (Tel: 313-223-3500)
  (Fax: 313-223-3598)
  (www.dickinsonwright.com)
(Ann Arbor, MI Office*: 350 South Main Street, Suite 300, 48104)
  (Tel: 734-623-7075)
  (Fax: 734-623-1625)
(Lansing, MI Office*: 215 South Washington Square, Suite 200, 48933-1816)
  (Tel: 517-371-1730)
  (Fax: 517-487-4700)
(Nashville, TN Office*: 424 Church Street, Suite 1401, 37219)
  (Tel: 615-244-6538)
  (Fax: 615-256-8386)
(Troy, MI Office*: 2600 West Big Beaver Road, Suite 300, 48084-3312)
  (Tel: 248-433-7200)
  (Fax: 248-433-7274)

Disability, Life Insurance, Medical Malpractice, Health Care, Coverage Issues, Personal Injury, Commercial Litigation, Employment Litigation, ERISA, Accountant Malpractice, Construction Litigation, Directors and Officers Liability

Firm Profile: Dickinson Wright has long been a preferred provider of sophisticated, cost-effective legal services to insurers in the life, health, disability, property, casualty, and alternative insurance (self-insured programs, risk pools, and captives) fields. Our insurance team also represents governmental entities, captive insurers and assigned-risk pools.

Firm Members

Victoria L. Orze — Arizona State University College of Law, J.D., 1987 — Admitted to Bar, 1987, Arizona; U.S. District Court, District of Arizona; U.S. Court of Appeals, Ninth Circuit — Bankruptcy Appellate Panel for the Ninth Circuit — Practice Areas: Coverage Issues; Commercial Litigation; Employment Litigation — Tel: 602-220-4542 — E-mail: vorze@dickinsonwright.com

Frederick M. Cummings — Georgetown University Law Center, J.D., 1984 — Admitted to Bar, 1986, Arizona; U.S. District Court, District of Arizona; U.S. District Court, Eastern District of Virginia; U.S. Court of Appeals, Fourth and Ninth Circuits — Practice Areas: Medical Malpractice; Health Care; Personal Injury — Tel: 602-285-5027 — E-mail: fcummings@dickinsonwright.com

(See listing under Detroit, MI for additional information)

Elardo, Bragg, Appel & Rossi, P.C.

3001 East Camelback Road, Suite 130
Phoenix, Arizona 85016
  Telephone: 602-889-0272
  Fax: 602-294-0909
  E-Mail: jelardo@ebarlaw.com
  www.ebarlaw.com

(San Diego, CA Office: 655 West Broadway, Suite 900, 92101-8590)

Established: 2004

Alternative Dispute Resolution, Automobile Liability, Bad Faith, Extra-Contractual Liability, Business Litigation, Commercial Litigation, Construction Litigation, Insurance Coverage, Fraud, Legal Malpractice, Professional Liability, Product Liability, Trucking, Transportation, Wrongful Death, Personal Injury, General Civil Litigation

Firm Profile: Elardo, Bragg, Appel & Rossi, P.C. is a firm that provides knowledge and innovation to a wide array of clients. The firm is dedicated to defending its clients with the utmost professionalism and competence.

Insurance Clients

Acuity Insurance Company	ANPAC
Electric Insurance Company	Financial Pacific Insurance
GAINSCO Auto Insurance	Company
Permanent General Insurance	Safe Auto Insurance Company
Group	Sentry/Dairyland Insurance
State Auto Insurance Company	Company

Non-Insurance Clients

City of Phoenix   Cox Communications

Partners

John A. Elardo — Southern Methodist University, B.A., 1986; Drake University, J.D./M.B.A., 1993 — Admitted to Bar, 1993, Arizona; U.S. District Court, District of Arizona — Member Council on Litigation Management — Practice Areas: Insurance Coverage; Construction Defect; Dram Shop; Bad Faith; Premises Liability; Product Liability; Professional Negligence; Medical Malpractice; Alternative Dispute Resolution; Legal Malpractice; Trucking; Transportation — E-mail: jelardo@ebarlaw.com

Venessa J. Bragg — Arizona State University, B.A. (magna cum laude), 2003; J.D., 2007 — Admitted to Bar, 2008, Arizona; 2009, U.S. District Court, District of Arizona — Practice Areas: Insurance Defense; Construction Defect; Dram Shop; Professional Negligence; Personal Injury; Premises Liability; Trucking; Commercial Litigation — E-mail: vbragg@ebarlaw.com

Marc A. Appel — Eastern Washington University, B.A., 1982; Seattle University School of Law, J.D., 1986 — Admitted to Bar, 1986, Arizona; U.S. District Court, District of Arizona; U.S. Court of Appeals, Ninth Circuit; U.S. Supreme Court — Member State Bar of Arizona; Risk and Insurance Management Society — Practice Areas: Governmental Entity Defense; Motor Vehicle; Premises Liability; Construction Defect; Product Liability; Bad Faith; Trucking; General Liability — E-mail: marc.appel@ebarlaw.com

Michael A. Rossi — Arizona State University, B.S., 1994; Capital University Law School, J.D., 1998 — Admitted to Bar, 1998, Arizona; Supreme Court of Arizona; 2002, U.S. District Court, District of Arizona; 2004, U.S. Supreme Court — Practice Areas: Wrongful Death; Product Liability; Personal Injury; Construction Defect; Trucking Litigation; Insurance Coverage; Premises Liability; Governmental Entity Defense; Commercial Litigation — E-mail: mrossi@ebarlaw.com

Associates

Gary A. Kester	Amanda E. Nelson
Gianni Pattas	April A. Hancock
Jeffrey D. Harris	Jonathan L. Sullivan
Rochelle D. Prins	

Gust Rosenfeld P.L.C.

One East Washington Street, Suite 1600
Phoenix, Arizona 85004-2553
   Telephone: 602-257-7422
   Fax: 602-254-4878
   E-Mail: attorneys@gustlaw.com
   www.gustlaw.com

(Tucson, AZ Office: One South Church Avenue, Suite 1900, 85701-1627)
   (Tel: 520-628-7070)
   (Fax: 520-624-3849)

Established: 1921

Insurance Defense, Life Insurance, Insurance Coverage, Product Liability, Construction Liability, Automobile Liability, Title Insurance

Firm Profile: Founded in 1921, Gust Rosenfeld has more than 60 attorneys providing legal counsel to individuals, public and private corporations and units of local government. Well known for its insurance and litigation practices, the firm also maintains significant practices in the areas of real estate, environmental, public law, corporate, litigation, employment, finance, creditors' rights and franchise law.

Insurance Clients

- American Family Insurance Company
- Catholic Mutual Group
- ELCO Administrative Services
- Kemper Insurance Companies
- SECURA Insurance Companies
- ASI Underwriters
- Canal Insurance Company
- The Cincinnati Companies
- Federated Rural Electric Insurance Exchange
- Western Heritage Insurance Company

Members

Peter Collins, Jr. — 1947 — The Ohio State University Moritz College of Law, J.D., 1978 — Admitted to Bar, 1978, Ohio; 1989, Arizona — Resident Tucson, AZ Office

Craig A. McCarthy — 1963 — Willamette University College of Law, J.D., 1989 — Admitted to Bar, 1990, Arizona

Dean C. Robertson — 1955 — Seattle University School of Law, J.D., 1983 — Admitted to Bar, 1984, Washington; 1999, Arizona

Wendy N. Weigand — 1967 — Cleveland State University, Cleveland-Marshall College of Law, J.D., 1993 — Admitted to Bar, 1993, Ohio; 1994, Illinois; 1998, Arizona

Michael S. Woodlock — 1960 — University of San Diego School of Law, J.D. (cum laude), 1986 — Admitted to Bar, 1986, California; 1999, Arizona — Resident Tucson, AZ Office

(Revisors of the Arizona Insurance Law Digest for this Publication)

Jardine, Baker, Hickman & Houston, PLLC

3300 North Central Avenue, Suite 2600
Phoenix, Arizona 85012
   Telephone: 602-200-9777
   Fax: 602-200-9114
   E-Mail: bjardine@jbhhlaw.com

Established: 1998

Insurance Defense, General Liability, Personal Injury, Commercial Vehicle, Workers' Compensation, ERISA, Product Liability, Agent/Broker Liability, Accountant Malpractice, Legal Malpractice, Complex Litigation, Public Entities, Insurance Coverage, Trial and Appellate Practice, State and Federal Courts, Representation before the State Industrial Commission, Group Health and Disability, Attorney

Firm Profile: The firm of Jardine, Baker, Hickman & Houston was founded in 1998 with a commitment to excellence in the representation of parties in civil litigation. Its four founding members had many years of trial and litigation experience in a variety of practice areas including insurance coverage, bad faith and tort defense, municipal and other political subdivision liability defense, medical malpractice, professional malpractice, construction, environmental, products liability, employment and labor law, workers' compensation and intellectual property.

Insurance Clients

- AIG Claim Services, Inc.
- American Re-Insurance Company
- Arthur J. Gallagher & Company
- Auto-Owners Insurance Company
- Broadspire
- Century-National Insurance Company
- Fireman's Fund Insurance Company
- Liberty Mutual Insurance
- Markel Southwest
- Medical Protective Insurance Services
- OccuSure Workers' Compensation Specialist
- Republic Indemnity Company of America
- Royal & SunAlliance Group
- SCF Arizona
- SECURA Insurance Companies
- Southwest Risk Services, Inc.
- State Farm Insurance Company
- United Services Automobile Association (USAA)
- Vanguard Group, Inc.
- Zenith Insurance Company
- Zurich
- AIMCO Risk Management
- Arizona Municipal Risk Retention Pool
- Avizent
- Cambridge Integrated Services
- Chartis
- The Doctors Company
- Hartford Insurance Company
- Liberty Mutual
- Lumbermen's Underwriting Alliance
- Mutual Insurance Company of Arizona
- Ohio Insurance Group
- Pinnacle Risk Management Services
- Republic Insurance Company
- Safeco Select Markets
- SeaBright Insurance Company
- Sedgwick Claims Management Services, Inc.
- Travelers Insurance Companies
- UnumProvident Group
- Valley Schools Insurance Trust
- Wausau General Insurance Company

Non-Insurance Clients

- The Alliance
- City of Phoenix
- C.R. England, Inc.
- Qwest Communications
- Rural/Metro Corporation
- State of Arizona
- Tradesmen International, Inc.
- Valley Physical Medicine & Rehabilitation
- Banner Health
- City of Prescott
- Maricopa County
- Rinker Materials Corporation
- Southwest Ambulance
- Swift Transportation Company, Inc.
- Vanguard Health Services
- Walgreen Co.

Partners

Gerald T. Hickman — (1958-2008)

Bradley R. Jardine — 1952 — Brigham Young University, B.A., 1975; J. Reuben Clark Law School, Brigham Young University, J.D., 1978 — J. Reuben Clark Law Review — Admitted to Bar, 1978, Arizona; U.S. District Court, District of Arizona; 1986, U.S. Supreme Court; 1990, U.S. Court of Appeals, Ninth Circuit — Member State Bar of Arizona; Maricopa County Bar Association; Arizona Association of Defense Counsel (Board of Directors); Arizona Association of School Boards; Defense Research Institute (State Representative); International Association of Defense Counsel — Certified Specialist, Personal Injury and Wrongful Death Litigation, State Bar of Arizona — Practice Areas: Civil Litigation; Wrongful Death; Construction Law; Negligence; Product Liability — E-mail: bjardine@jbhhlaw.com

Stephen C. Baker — 1957 — Northern Arizona University, B.S. (magna cum laude), 1980; The University of Arizona, J.D. (with high distinction), 1983 — Order of the Coif — Admitted to Bar, 1983, Arizona; U.S. District Court, District of Arizona — Member State Bar of Arizona; Maricopa County Bar Association; Arizona Workers' Compensation Claims Association; Arizona Self-Insured Association; President, Arizona Association of Workers' Compensation Defense Counsel; Arizona Association of Defense Counsel — Certified Specialist, Workers' Compensation, State Bar of Arizona — Practice Areas: Workers' Compensation — E-mail: sbaker@jbhhlaw.com

Jardine, Baker, Hickman & Houston, PLLC, Phoenix, AZ (Continued)

Scott H. Houston — 1961 — University of California, Los Angeles, B.A. (with honors), 1983; Arizona State University, J.D. (with honors), 1986 — Admitted to Bar, 1986, Arizona; U.S. District Court, District of Arizona — Member State Bar of Arizona; Maricopa County Bar Association; Arizona Association of Defense Counsel — Certified Specialist, Workers' Compensation Law, State Bar of Arizona — Practice Areas: Workers' Compensation — E-mail: shouston@jbhhlaw.com

Kendall D. Steele — 1961 — Brigham Young University; University of Calgary, B.A., 1985; The University of Utah, J.D., 1988 — Admitted to Bar, 1988, Arizona; 1989, Nevada — Member State Bar of Arizona; State Bar of Nevada — Languages: Spanish — Practice Areas: Tort; Product Liability; Professional Liability; Commercial Liability; Intellectual Property — E-mail: ksteele@jbhhlaw.com

K. Casey Kurth — 1962 — Wabash College, B.A., 1984; The University of Tulsa, J.D., 1987 — American Jurisprudence Award — Admitted to Bar, 1987, Arizona; U.S. District Court, District of Arizona — Member State Bar of Arizona — Certified Specialist, Workers' Compensation Law, State Bar of Arizona — Practice Areas: Workers' Compensation — E-mail: ckurth@jbhhlaw.com

John E. Drazkowski — 1956 — The University of Arizona, B.S.Ch.E., 1979; University of Pennsylvania, Mgt., 1990; Tulane University Law School, J.D. (magna cum laude), 1997 — Order of the Coif — Admitted to Bar, 1997, Arizona; 1998, U.S. District Court, Eastern District of Texas; 1999, U.S. District Court, District of Arizona — Member State Bar of Arizona; Maricopa County Bar Association — Practice Areas: Litigation; Medical Malpractice; Environmental Law; Product Liability — E-mail: jdrazkowski@jbhhlaw.com

Michael Warzynski — 1962 — University of Wisconsin-Madison, B.A., 1985; Arizona State University, J.D., 1989 — Admitted to Bar, 1989, Arizona; 1993, U.S. District Court, District of Arizona; U.S. Court of Appeals, Ninth Circuit — Member State Bar of Arizona; Maricopa County Bar Association — Practice Areas: Litigation; Insurance Defense; Construction Defect; Product Liability; Governmental Liability — E-mail: mwarzynski@jbhhlaw.com

Neil C. Alden — 1950 — Arizona State University, B.A., 1972; J.D. (magna cum laude), 1975 — Admitted to Bar, 1975, Arizona; U.S. District Court, District of Arizona, 1988, U.S. Court of Appeals, Ninth Circuit — Member State Bar of Arizona; American Board of Trial Advocates; Arizona Association of Defense Counsel; Fellow, American College of Trial Lawyers — Practice Areas: Medical Malpractice — E-mail: nalden@jbhhlaw.com

Curtis M. Bergen — 1964 — Arizona State University, B.A., 1989; J.D. (cum laude), 1992 — Admitted to Bar, 1993, Arizona; 1995, U.S. District Court, District of Arizona — Member State Bar of Arizona; Maricopa County and Pima County Bar Associations; Arizona Association of Defense Counsel; Arizona Association of Defense Counsel — Languages: Spanish, Catalan — Practice Areas: Drug; Medical Devices; Medical Malpractice; Nursing Home Liability — E-mail: cbergen@jbhhlaw.com

Terrence Kurth — 1951 — University of Notre Dame, B.A., 1973; Arizona State University College of Law, J.D., 1980 — Admitted to Bar, 1980, Arizona; U.S. District Court, District of Arizona — Member State Bar of Arizona (Past Co-Chair, Workers' Compensation Section) — Former Administrative Law Judge, Industrial Commission of Arizona (1985-1987) — Certified Workers' Compensation Specialist by the State Bar of Arizona — Practice Areas: Workers' Compensation — E-mail: tkurth@jbhhlaw.com

Stephen M. Venezia — DePauw University, B.A., 1976; Southern Methodist University, M.B.A., 1976; American Graduate School of International Management, M.I.M., 1977; The John Marshall Law School in Chicago, J.D., 1984 — Admitted to Bar, 1984, Illinois; 1985, Arizona; 1988, U.S. District Court, District of Arizona — Member American, Illinois State and Maricopa County Bar Associations; State Bar of Arizona; Defense Research Institute; Arizona Association of Defense Counsel — Workers' Compensation Specialist by Arizona State Bar — Languages: German — Practice Areas: Workers' Compensation — E-mail: syenezia@jbhhlaw.com

Charles G. Rehling — 1951 — The University of Arizona, B.A., 1973; J.D., 1977 — Admitted to Bar, 1977, Arizona; U.S. District Court, District of Arizona; U.S. Court of Appeals, Ninth Circuit — Member State Bar of Arizona — Practice Areas: Workers' Compensation; Employment Law — E-mail: crehling@jbhhlaw.com

Lewis Roca Rothgerber LLP

201 East Washington Street, Suite 1200
Phoenix, Arizona 85004
 Telephone: 602-262-5311
 Fax: 602-262-5747
 E-Mail: info@LRRLaw.com
 www.LRRLaw.com

Insurance Law, Accident and Health, Aviation, Construction Defect, Environmental Coverage, Insurance Coverage, Insurance Defense, Life Insurance, Property and Casualty, Regulatory and Compliance

Partners

Ann-Martha Andrews — University of Maryland, College Park, B.A. (cum laude), 1986; University of Notre Dame, J.D., 1989 — Admitted to Bar, 1989, Arizona; 2001, Nevada; 1989, U.S. District Court, District of Arizona; U.S. Court of Appeals, Ninth Circuit; Supreme Court of Arizona; 2001, U.S. District Court, District of Nevada; Supreme Court of Nevada

Stephen Bressler — Duke University, B.A. (cum laude), 1980; The University of Arizona, J.D., 1983 — Admitted to Bar, 1983, Arizona — Member Federal, American (TIPS Insurance Coverage Committee; TIPS Insurance Committee, Former Chair and Life, Health and Disability Subcommittee) and Maricopa County Bar Associations; Defense Research Institute (Drug and Medical Device; Life, Health and Disability and Technology (Arizona Representative) Committees); Arizona Association of Defense Counsel (Products Liability Committee, Former Chair) — Speaker on various issues in these areas, including disability litigation and coverage for the controversial high dose chemotherapy with autologous bone marrow transplant and other insurance issues

Kristina N. Holmstrom — University of Nevada, Las Vegas, B.A., 2001; William S. Boyd School of Law, University of Nevada, Las Vegas, J.D., 2001 — Admitted to Bar, 2004, Arizona; 2006, Nevada — Member American Bar Association (Health Life & Disability Subcommittee); Litigation Section, Insurance Coverage Litigation Committee, Co-Chair); Defense Research Institute (Life Health and Disability Committee and Liaison to Alternative Dispute Resolution Committee); Arizona Association of Defense Counsel (Board of Directors); Volunteer Lawyers' Program (2004-2007)

Steven Hulsman — Malone College, B.A. (summa cum laude), 1983; The Ohio State University Moritz College of Law, J.D. (Order of the Coif), 1986 — Admitted to Bar, 1986, Arizona; 2006, Nevada — Member Maricopa County Bar Association; Arizona Trial Lawyers Association; Arizona Association of Defense Counsel — Weekend Missions to Rocky Point, Advisory Board Member; Speaker at various churches in Arizona; Mountain Park Community Church, Former Chairman of the Board; Crisis Pregnancy Centers of Greater Phoenix, Former Chairman of the Board

O'Connor & Campbell, P.C.

7955 South Priest Drive
Tempe, Arizona 85284-1050
 Telephone: 602-241-7000
 Fax: 602-241-7039
 www.occlaw.com

Established: 1999

Insurance Defense, Bad Faith, Coverage Analysis, Errors and Omissions, Discrimination, Motor Vehicle, Product Liability, Professional Liability, Property and Casualty, Fidelity and Surety, Business Law, Construction Defect, ERISA, Governmental Liability, Health Care, Homeowners, Labor and Employment, Securities, Transportation, Personal Injury, Wrongful Death, Dram Shop, Liquor Liability, Premises Liability, Professional Malpractice, Alternative Dispute Resolution, Arbitration, Mediation, Coverage Litigation, Harassment, Automobile Accidents, Elder Abuse, Short Trials

Firm Profile: After years of practicing law at large firms, Daniel J. O'Connor and Dan Campbell began practicing law together in 1999. They have over 40 years of collective experience between them, which includes hundreds of

O'Connor & Campbell, P.C., Phoenix, AZ (Continued)

trials, arbitration and mediations. The firm's practice focuses on civil trial and appellate work in all aspects of personal injury, products liability and insurance litigation, as well as commercial, real estate, construction law and defects, and labor litigation. The firm is Arizona counsel for several of our national clients and regularly appear in matters throughout the southwest region of the United States on their behalf.

Insurance Clients

ACUITY	Allied Insurance Company
Auto-Owners Insurance Company	Chubb & Son, Inc.
Colorado Casualty Insurance Company	Commonwealth Insurance Company
GAB Robins, Inc.	Liberty Mutual Insurance Company
Rainier Insurance Company	

Non-Insurance Clients

Ace Haulers, Inc.	Corporate Express Delivery Systems, Inc.
FedEx	
Kohler Company	Los Abrigados Resort & Spa
Navajo Express, Inc.	Savers, Inc.
Wyndham International	

Partners

Daniel J. O'Connor, Jr. — 1956 — Illinois Benedictine College, B.A., 1978; The John Marshall Law School, J.D., 1984 — Admitted to Bar, 1985, Arizona; 1989, U.S. District Court, District of Arizona; U.S. Court of Appeals, Ninth Circuit — Member American (Tort and Insurance Law Section) and Maricopa County Bar Associations; State Bar of Arizona; Arizona Insurance Claims Association; Arizona Association of Defense Counsel; Defense Research Institute — Instructor, Mesa Community College, 1986; Judge Pro Tem, Maricopa County Superior Court, 1996-Present — Practice Areas: Automobile Liability; Automobile Tort; Bad Faith; Carrier Defense; Casualty Defense; Casualty Insurance Law; Civil Litigation; Civil Rights; Civil Trial Practice; Commercial and Personal Lines; Commercial General Liability; Commercial Liability; Commercial Litigation; Common Carrier; Complex Litigation; Comprehensive General Liability; Construction Accidents; Construction Defect; Construction Law; Construction Liability; Construction Litigation; Contractors Liability; Declaratory Judgments; Defense Litigation; Discrimination; Dram Shop; Employer Liability; General Civil Trial and Appellate Practice; General Defense; General Liability; Governmental Liability; Homeowners; Insurance Agents; Insurance Coverage; Insurance Defense; Insurance Fraud; Insurance Litigation; Intentional Torts; Law Enforcement Liability; Litigation; Litigation and Counseling; Managed Care Liability; Mold and Mildew Claims; Motor Carriers; Motor Vehicle; Municipal Law; Municipal Liability; Negligence; Nursing Home Liability; Personal and Commercial Vehicle; Personal Injury; Personal Liability; Personal Lines; Physical Damage; Policy Construction and Interpretation; Premises Liability; Product Liability; Professional Liability; Professional Liability (Non-Medical) Defense; Professional Negligence; Property and Casualty; Property Damage; Property Defense; Property Liability; Property Loss; Protection and Indemnity; Public Entities; Public Liability; Public Officials Liability; Punitive Damages; Restaurant Liability; Risk Management; School Law; Self-Insured; Self-Insured Defense; Sexual Harassment; Slip and Fall; Sports and Entertainment Liability; State and Federal Courts; Subrogation; Surety; Surety Bonds; Tort; Tort Liability; Tort Litigation; Trial and Appellate Practice; Trial Practice; Truck Liability; Trucking Law; Trucks/Heavy Equipment; Uninsured and Underinsured Motorist; Wrongful Death; Wrongful Termination — Tel: 602-241-7002 — E-mail: daniel.oconnor@occlaw.com

John Daniel Campbell — 1953 — Arizona State University, B.S. (magna cum laude), 1975; University of Nebraska College of Law, J.D., 1978 — Admitted to Bar, 1978, Arizona; 1983, Nebraska; 1978, U.S. District Court, District of Arizona; U.S. Court of Appeals, Ninth Circuit — Member State Bar of Arizona; Nebraska State and Maricopa County (Alternative Dispute Resolution Section) Bar Associations; Arizona Insurance Claims Association; Arizona Association of Defense Counsel — Seminar Instructor, NBI, Insurance Coverage, 1998 — Certified Arbitrator, American Arbitration Association — Tel: 602-241-7025 — E-mail: dan.campbell@occlaw.com

Michael R. Altaffer — 1954 — East Texas State University, B.S., 1978; Texas Tech University School of Law, J.D., 1984 — Associate Editor, Texas Tech Law Review, 1983-1984 — Admitted to Bar, 1985, Arizona; U.S. District Court, District of Arizona — Member American and Maricopa County Bar Associations; State Bar of Arizona; Arizona Association of Defense Counsel; Defense Research Institute — "Admiralty Law," Texas Tech Law Review, 5th Circuit Symposium, 1983, Co-Author: "Criminal Law," Texas Tech Law Review, 5th Circuit Symposium, 1984 — Reported Cases: Western Agricultural Ins. Co. v. Industrial Indemnity Ins. Co., 172 Ariz. 592, 838 P.2d 1353

O'Connor & Campbell, P.C., Phoenix, AZ (Continued)

(App. 1992); Unispec Development Corp. v. Harwood K. Smith & Partners, et. al., 124 F.R.D. 211 (D. Ariz. 1988) — Tel: 602-241-7003 — E-mail: michael.altaffer@occlaw.com

Associates

Shane P. Dyet — 1974 — Utah State University, B.S., 2001; University of Denver Sturm College of Law, J.D., 2005 — Admitted to Bar, 2006, Arizona; Supreme Court of Arizona; 2007, U.S. District Court, District of Arizona; U.S. Court of Appeals, Ninth Circuit — Member Arizona State Bar — E-mail: shane.dyet@occlaw.com

Christopher S. Mihalik — 1972 — Arizona State University, B.A. (magna cum laude), 2003; Seattle University School of Law, J.D. (cum laude), 2008 — Admitted to Bar, 2009, Arizona; 2009, U.S. District Court, District of Arizona; Supreme Court of Arizona — E-mail: scott.mihalik@occlaw.com

Susanne Luse — 1968 — University of Phoenix, B.S./B.A., 1996; The University of Arizona, James E. Rogers College of Law, J.D., 2000 — Admitted to Bar, 2000, Arizona; 2001, U.S. District Court, District of Arizona — Member State Bar of Arizona; Pima County Bar Association (Board Member, Young Lawyers Division, 2001-2004); Tucson Defense Bar; Association of Defense Counsel — Practice Areas: Civil Litigation; Commercial Litigation; Construction Litigation; Insurance Fraud — E-mail: susanne.luse@occlaw.com

Mike Roberts — Arizona State University, B.S. (cum laude), 2003; Creighton University School of Law, J.D. (magna cum laude), 2009 — Admitted to Bar, 2011, Arizona

James E. Doman Jr — University of Arkansas, B.S., 2000; University of Arkansas School of Law, J.D. (cum laude), 2003 — Admitted to Bar, 2003, Arkansas

Bradley J. Biggs — 1978 — Arizona State University, B.A., 2003; Thomas Jefferson School of Law, J.D., 2007 — Admitted to Bar, 2008, Arizona

Righi Law Group

2111 East Highland Avenue, Suite B440
Phoenix, Arizona 85016
Telephone: 602-385-6776
Fax: 602-385-6777
E-Mail: beth@righilaw.com
www.righilaw.com

Premises Liability, Construction Defect, Professional Liability, Professional Malpractice, Product Liability, Municipal Liability, Governmental Liability, Insurance Defense, Bad Faith, Liquor Liability, Slip and Fall, Health Care Liability, Wrongful Death, Construction Site Accidents, Business Torts, Retail & Hospitality Liability

Insurance Clients

ACE USA	Allegiant Insurance Company
American Safety Claims Services, Inc.	Brotherhood Mutual Insurance Company
Colony Specialty	EMC Insurance Companies
Engle Martin & Associates	Lexington Insurance Company
Markel West, Inc.	Maxum Specialty Insurance Group
National Fire and Marine Insurance Company	

Founding Members

Richard L. Righi — Miami University, B.S., 1989; Capital University Law School, J.D., 1992 — Admitted to Bar, 1992, Ohio; 1993, Arizona; 2001, U.S. District Court, District of Arizona; 2001, U.S. Court of Appeals, Ninth Circuit — Member State Bar of Arizona; Maricopa County Bar Association (Construction Law Section, Former Member, Board of Directors); Arizona Association of Defense Counsel (President, 2011); Fellow, Federation of Defense and Corporate Counsel; Defense Research Institute; American Board of Trial Advocates — AV Preeminent T Rated by Martindale-Hubbell; Southwest Super Lawyer — Practice Areas: Construction Defect; Professional Liability; Casualty; Personal Injury; Insurance Litigation; Bad Faith; Commercial Litigation; Product Liability

Elizabeth S. Fitch — Arizona State University, B.S. (cum laude), 1982; Arizona State University College of Law, J.D., 1985 — Admitted to Bar, 1985, Arizona; 1985, U.S. District Court, District of Arizona; 1985, U.S. Court of

ARIZONA   PHOENIX

Righi Law Group, Phoenix, AZ (Continued)

Appeals, Ninth Circuit — Member State Bar of Arizona; Maricopa County Bar Association; Arizona Association of Defense Counsel (President, 2000) (Executive Committee, 1996-2000); Claims Litigation Management Alliance; Arizona Insurance Claims Association — Reported Cases: Monthofer Investments v. Allen, 943 P.2d 782 — AV Preeminent T Rated by Martindale-Hubbell; Southwest Super Lawyer; Top Valley Construction Lawyer, North Valley Magazine; Superb Lawyer, AVVO — Practice Areas: Casualty; Professional Liability; Construction Defect; Civil Litigation; Professional Malpractice; Insurance Defense; Bad Faith; Governmental Liability; Personal Injury

Partner

Chris H. Begeman — Dordt College, B.A., 2003; Thomas M. Cooley Law School, J.D. (magna cum laude), 2006 — Admitted to Bar, 2006, Arizona; 2010, New Mexico; 2011, U.S. District Court, District of Arizona — Member State Bar of Arizona; State Bar of New Mexico; Arizona Association of Defense Counsel — Southwest Super Lawyer Rising Star — Practice Areas: Construction Defect; Personal Injury; Complex Litigation; General Liability; Insurance Litigation; Bad Faith; Product Liability; Toxic Torts

Senior Associates

Melissa Lin — The University of Arizona, B.S. (cum laude), 2001; The University of Arizona College of Law, J.D., 2004 — Admitted to Bar, 2005, Arizona; 2011, California; 2004, U.S. Patent and Trademark Office; 2011, U.S. District Court, District of Arizona — Member State Bar of Arizona; State Bar of California; Arizona Association of Defense Counsel; Defense Research Institute — AV Preeminent Rated by Martindale-Hubbell; Southwest Super Lawyer Rising Star; Lawyers of Color Inaugural Western Region Hot List — Practice Areas: General Liability; Construction Defect; Complex Litigation; Product Liability; Personal Injury

Benjamin Hodgson — Arizona State University, B.S. (summa cum laude), 1993; University of Michigan Law School, J.D./M.B.A., 1997 — Admitted to Bar, 1997, Arizona; U.S. District Court, District of Arizona — Member State Bar of Arizona; Maricopa County Bar Association — Languages: French — Practice Areas: Insurance Defense; Personal Injury; Commercial Litigation; Construction Defect

Associate

K. Michelle Ronan — Arizona State University, B.S., 2007; The University of Arizona, J.D., 2011 — Admitted to Bar, 2011, Arizona; 2013, U.S. District Court, District of Arizona — Member American and Maricopa County Bar Associations; State Bar of Arizona; Defense Research Institute; Arizona Association of Defense Counsel — Practice Areas: Tort Litigation; Construction Defect; Personal Injury

Sanders + Parks, P.C.
Attorneys at Law

3030 North Third Street, Suite 1300
Phoenix, Arizona 85012
  Telephone: 602-532-5600
  Fax: 602-532-5700
  www.SandersParks.com

Established: 1973

Sanders + Parks, P.C., Attorneys at Law, Phoenix, AZ (Continued)

Accountants and Attorneys Liability, Administrative Law, Agent/Broker Liability, Alternative Dispute Resolution, Appellate Practice, Automobile Liability, Aviation, Bad Faith, Business Law, Casualty Defense, Civil Litigation, Civil Rights, Civil Trial Practice, Commercial General Liability, Commercial Law, Commercial Litigation, Construction Litigation, Contracts, Corporate Law, Coverage Analysis, Declaratory Judgments, Directors and Officers Liability, Dram Shop, Employment Law, Environmental Law, ERISA, Errors and Omissions, Excess and Umbrella, Health Care, Hospital Malpractice, Insurance Coverage, Insurance Coverage Litigation, Insurance Defense, Insurance Litigation, Intellectual Property, Jail/Prison Defense, Litigation, Medical Devices, Medical Malpractice, Municipal Liability, Nursing Home Liability, Patent Infringement Litigation, Personal Injury, Premises Liability, Product Liability, Professional Negligence, Property and Casualty, Public Entities, Real Estate, School Law, Subrogation, Tort Litigation, Trademark Infringement, Trade Secrets, Trial and Appellate Practice, Uninsured and Underinsured Motorist, Wrongful Death, Architects and Engineers Liability, Class Action Defense, Copyright Law and Trademark Law

Firm Profile: For over four decades, the Phoenix-based law firm of Sanders & Parks P.C. has represented individuals and businesses throughout the United States. Through the years, our lawyers have maintained our dedication to quality service and personal attention while adapting to new ideas and incorporating fresh perspectives. We work toward efficient and practical solutions with our clients, bringing the skills of a big firm with the accessibility of a small firm. We want our clients to know that we understand just how important value is.

Insurance Clients

ACE	ACE/ESIS
ACE/AGRA	Admiral Insurance Company
AIG	AIG Aerospace
Allianz Insurance Company	Allied World Assurance Company
Arch Insurance Group	Armed Forces Insurance
Burlington Insurance Company	Capson Physicians Insurance Company
Carolina Casualty Insurance Company	Catlin US
Chubb Group of Insurance Companies	Copperpoint Mutual Insurance Company
Fidelity National Insurance Company	Fireman's Fund Insurance Company
Great American Custom Insurance Services	Great American Insurance Group
The Insurance Professionals	Institute of London Underwriters
James River Insurance Company	Ironshore, Inc.
Memotec, Inc.	Medmarc Mutual Insurance Company
Munich Reinsurance America, Inc.	Mutual Insurance Company of Arizona
National Unity Insurance Company	Oregon Mutual Insurance Company
NCMIC Insurance Company	
Preferred Physicians Medical Risk Retention Group, Inc.	ProAssurance Group
Professional Risk Management	QBE North America
Safeco Insurance	Scottsdale Insurance Company
Shand Morahan & Company, Inc.	STARR Companies
State National Insurance Company, Inc.	Stonington Insurance Company
	Swiss Re
Travelers	TRISTAR Risk Management
United States Aircraft Insurance Group	USAA
XL Select Professional	XL Aviation

Non-Insurance Clients

Banner Health	Centric Elevator Corporation
City of Phoenix	Claims Management Services, Inc.
Comtech EF Data Corporation	Dignity Health
GAB Robins North America, Inc.	Gallagher Bassett Services, Inc.
Honeywell International, Inc.	Innovative Risk Management
JPMorgan Chase Bank, N.A.	Kitchell Contractors, Inc.
Lancer Claims Services, Inc.	Leo A. Daly Company
The Lincoln Electric Company	Littleton Group
Macy's	Mansfield Plumbing
Maricopa County	Maricopa County Community College District
McGough Construction	
Monitor Liability Managers, Inc.	Motorola, Inc.

PHOENIX ARIZONA

Sanders + Parks, P.C., Attorneys at Law, Phoenix, AZ (Continued)

National Bank of Arizona
Phoenix Union High School District
Schneider Electric USA
State of Arizona
Trek Bicycle Corporation
Washington Elementary School District
Overhead Door Corporation
Pinnacle Risk Management Services
Sequoia Charter Schools
Tempe Union High School District
Tyco International, Ltd.
W.M. Grace Construction, Inc.
Yarway Companies

Firm Members

Frank A. Parks — (Retired)

Robert J. Bruno — 1946 — Syracuse University, B.A., 1968; Albany Law School of Union University, J.D., 1972 — Admitted to Bar, 1973, Arizona; New York — Member State Bar of Arizona; Maricopa County Bar Association; Bar of the Supreme Court of the United States; Arizona Association of Defense Counsel; Defense Research Institute; American Board of Trial Advocates — Southwest Super Lawyer 2014 — Certified Specialist in Injury and Wrongful Death Litigation by State Bar of Arizona — Practice Areas: Insurance Law; Personal Injury; Commercial Litigation; Professional Liability; Product Liability — E-mail: Robert.Bruno@SandersParks.com

Winn L. Sammons — 1950 — Northern Arizona University, B.S., 1974; University of San Diego, J.D. (cum laude), 1978 — Admitted to Bar, 1978, Arizona; 1978, California; 1978, U.S. District Court, District of Arizona; 1990, U.S. Court of Appeals, Ninth Circuit — Member American and Maricopa County Bar Associations; State Bar of Arizona; State Bar of California; Arizona Association of Defense Counsel; Defense Research Institute — Southwest Super Lawyers 2014 — Practice Areas: Alternative Dispute Resolution — E-mail: Winn.Sammons@SandersParks.com

Garrick L. Gallagher — 1959 — University of Pennsylvania, B.A., 1981; The University of Arizona, J.D., 1984 — Admitted to Bar, 1985, Arizona; U.S. District Court, District of Arizona; U.S. Court of Appeals, Ninth Circuit; U.S. Supreme Court — Member State Bar of Arizona (Board of Governors, 1991-1992; Young Lawyers Division, Executive Council Member, 1987-1992; President, 1991-1992); Maricopa County Bar Association; Arizona Association of Defense Counsel; Defense Research Institute — Southwest Super Lawyer 2010 - 2014; Recognized by Super Lawyers as one of the Top 50 Attorneys in Arizona 2014 — Practice Areas: Complex Litigation; Civil Litigation; Insurance Law; Insurance Litigation; Insurance Coverage; Personal Injury; Bad Faith; Product Liability; Excess and Umbrella; Excess and Surplus Lines — E-mail: Garrick.Gallagher@SandersParks.com

Mark G. Worischeck — 1961 — The University of Arizona, B.S. (with distinction), 1983; Washington University in St. Louis, J.D., 1986 — Admitted to Bar, 1986, Arizona; 1986, U.S. District Court, District of Arizona; 1986, U.S. Court of Appeals for the District of Columbia and Ninth Circuits; 1996, U.S. Supreme Court — Member Federal and Maricopa County Bar Associations; State Bar of Arizona; Aviation Insurance Association; Claims and Litigation Management Alliance; Fellow, The Trial Lawyer Honorary Society; Litigation Counsel of America; Lawyer-Pilots Bar Association; Defense Research Institute; Arizona Association of Defense Counsel; American Board of Trial Advocates — Southwest Super Lawyer 2010-2014; Recognized by Super Lawyers as one of the Top 50 Attorneys in Arizona 2011-2014; Selected for Best Lawyers in America 2013-2015 — Practice Areas: Aviation; Insurance Defense; Product Liability; Bad Faith; Insurance Coverage; Professional Liability (Non-Medical) Defense — E-mail: Mark.Worischeck@SandersParks.com

Rick Neeley Bryson — 1957 — Brigham Young University, B.A., 1981; J.D. (cum laude), 1984 — Recipient, Jesse A. Udall Distinguished Service Award, J. Ruben Clark Law Society Arizona; Scribes Award, Outstanding Student Law Review Article — Judicial Clerkship to Hon. Robert H. McWilliams, U.S. Court of Appeals, Tenth Circuit — Executive Editor, BYU Law Review (1983 - 1984) — Admitted to Bar, 1986, Arizona; U.S. District Court, District of Arizona; U.S. Court of Appeals, Ninth and Tenth Circuits; U.S. Supreme Court — Member American Bar Association (Chairperson, Citizenship Education Committee, Young Lawyers Division 1990-1992 Speaker); State Bar of Arizona (CLE Seminar Forms Chairperson and Speaker); Maricopa County Bar Association (CLE Seminar Forms Chairperson and Speaker); Arizona Management Society (President, 1991-1993); Bringing Hope to Single Mom's Foundation Arizona (Co-Founder and President, 2002-2005); J. Reuben Clark Law Society (Chairperson, Litigation Section 12011-13); — Author: "Right to Sue Under Section 4 of the Clayton Act," Brigham Young University Law Review, 1982 — Adjunct Professor, Insurance Law, ASU Law School, (2006); Judge Pro Tem, Arizona Court of Appeals (1993-1995); Chairperson and Speaker, ABA, State Bar of Arizona and Maricopa County Bar, CLE Seminars on Employment Law Litigation and Appellate Litigation; Southwest Super Lawyer 2014 — Languages: Italian — Practice Areas: Commercial Litigation; Intellectual Property; Employment Law; Appellate Practice; Insurance Coverage; Bad Faith; Insurance Defense; Patent and Trademark — E-mail: Rick.Bryson@SandersParks.com

Robin E. Burgess — 1966 — Wellesley College, B.A. (cum laude), 1988; Georgetown University, J.D., 1991 — Admitted to Bar, 1991, Virginia; 1993, Arizona; 1991, U.S. Court of Appeals, Fourth Circuit; 1993, U.S. District Court, District of Arizona; U.S. Court of Appeals, Ninth Circuit — Member State Bar of Arizona — Southwest Super Lawyer 2014; Recognized by Super Lawyers as one of the Top 25 Women in 2014 — Practice Areas: Health; Medical Malpractice; Professional Liability; Product Liability; Personal Injury; Civil Litigation; Municipal Liability; Employment Law — E-mail: Robin.Burgess@SandersParks.com

J. Steven Sparks — 1967 — Northern Arizona University, B.S.B.A. (with honors), 1989; University of the Pacific, McGeorge School of Law, J.D., 1993 — Admitted to Bar, 1993, California; 1994, Arizona; 1993, U.S. District Court, Eastern District of California; 1994, U.S. District Court, District of Arizona; 2004, U.S. Court of Appeals, Ninth Circuit — Member State Bar of California; State Bar of Arizona; Arizona Association of Defense Counsel; Defense Research Institute — Practice Areas: Insurance Defense; Commercial Litigation; Insurance Coverage; Bad Faith; Public Entities; Trucking Law; Accident; Personal Injury; School Law; Product Liability; Accountants and Attorneys Liability — E-mail: Steve.Sparks@SandersParks.com

Gerald Gregory Eagleburger — 1944 — Arizona State University, B.S., 1966; The University of Texas at Austin, J.D., 1969 — Admitted to Bar, 1969, Texas; 1971, Arizona; 1975, California — E-mail: Greg.Eagleburger@SandersParks.com

James C. Goodwin — 1969 — Colorado State University, B.A., 1992; M.A., 1994; The University of Arizona, J.D., 1996 — Member, Arizona Law Review — Admitted to Bar, 1997, Arizona; 2002, U.S. District Court, District of Arizona — Member State Bar of Arizona; Maricopa County Bar Association; Arizona Association of Defense Counsel — E-mail: James.Goodwin@SandersParks.com

J. Arthur Eaves — 1973 — University of Arkansas at Little Rock, B.A., 1996; J.D., 1999 — Admitted to Bar, 1999, Arizona; 2003, U.S. District Court, District of Arizona — E-mail: Artie.Eaves@SandersParks.com

Jeffrey L. Smith — 1976 — University of Wyoming, B.A., 1998; Florida Coastal School of Law, J.D., 2003 — Admitted to Bar, 2004, Florida; 2005, Arizona; 2006, U.S. District Court, District of Arizona; 2008, U.S. Court of Appeals for the District of Columbia and Ninth Circuits — Member Claims and Litigation Management Alliance; Defense Research Institute; Arizona Association of Defense Counsel — AV Rated; Southwest Super Lawyers Rising Stars (2012-2014) — Practice Areas: Insurance Coverage; Liability Defense; Product Liability Defense; Dram Shop Liability; Marine Liability — E-mail: Jeffrey.Smith@SandersParks.com

The following firms also service this area.

Cavett & Fulton
A Professional Corporation
6035 East Grant Road
Tucson, Arizona 85712
Telephone: 520-733-0100
Fax: 520-733-1800

Medical Malpractice, Nursing Home Liability, Professional Liability, Insurance Defense, Medical Devices, Product Liability

SEE COMPLETE LISTING UNDER TUCSON, ARIZONA (119 MILES)

The House Law Firm, P.C.
4500 South Lakeshore Drive, Suite 300
Tempe, Arizona 85282
Telephone: 480-756-1500
Fax: 480-775-0418

Insurance Defense, Civil Litigation, Business Law, Personal Injury, Litigation, Automobile Negligence Defense

SEE COMPLETE LISTING UNDER TEMPE, ARIZONA (12 MILES)

ARIZONA — PRESCOTT

PRESCOTT † 39,843 Yavapai Co.

Refer To

The Ledbetter Law Firm, P.L.C.
1003 North Main Street
Cottonwood, Arizona 86326
  Telephone: 928-649-8777
  Fax: 928-649-8778

Automobile, Commercial Law, General Liability, Professional Liability, Property and Casualty, Investigation and Adjustment, Indian Law, Business Formation, Employment Law, Risk Management Consulting, Medical Malpractice Defense

SEE COMPLETE LISTING UNDER COTTONWOOD, ARIZONA (42 MILES)

Refer To

Mangum, Wall, Stoops & Warden, P.L.L.C.
100 North Elden
Flagstaff, Arizona 86001
  Telephone: 928-779-6951
  Fax: 928-773-1312
Mailing Address: P.O. Box 10, Flagstaff, AZ 86002

Insurance Defense

SEE COMPLETE LISTING UNDER FLAGSTAFF, ARIZONA (93 MILES)

SEDONA 10,031 Coconino Co.

Refer To

The Ledbetter Law Firm, P.L.C.
1003 North Main Street
Cottonwood, Arizona 86326
  Telephone: 928-649-8777
  Fax: 928-649-8778

Automobile, Commercial Law, General Liability, Professional Liability, Property and Casualty, Investigation and Adjustment, Indian Law, Business Formation, Employment Law, Risk Management Consulting, Medical Malpractice Defense

SEE COMPLETE LISTING UNDER COTTONWOOD, ARIZONA (20 MILES)

Refer To

Mangum, Wall, Stoops & Warden, P.L.L.C.
100 North Elden
Flagstaff, Arizona 86001
  Telephone: 928-779-6951
  Fax: 928-773-1312
Mailing Address: P.O. Box 10, Flagstaff, AZ 86002

Insurance Defense

SEE COMPLETE LISTING UNDER FLAGSTAFF, ARIZONA (54 MILES)

SIERRA VISTA 43,888 Cochise Co.

Refer To

Cavett & Fulton
A Professional Corporation
6035 East Grant Road
Tucson, Arizona 85712
  Telephone: 520-733-0100
  Fax: 520-733-1800

Medical Malpractice, Nursing Home Liability, Professional Liability, Insurance Defense, Medical Devices, Product Liability

SEE COMPLETE LISTING UNDER TUCSON, ARIZONA (74 MILES)

ST. JOHNS † 3,269 Apache Co.

Refer To

Mangum, Wall, Stoops & Warden, P.L.L.C.
100 North Elden
Flagstaff, Arizona 86001
  Telephone: 928-779-6951
  Fax: 928-773-1312
Mailing Address: P.O. Box 10, Flagstaff, AZ 86002

Insurance Defense

SEE COMPLETE LISTING UNDER FLAGSTAFF, ARIZONA (150 MILES)

TEMPE 161,719 Maricopa Co.

The House Law Firm, P.C.
4500 South Lakeshore Drive, Suite 300
Tempe, Arizona 85282
  Telephone: 480-756-1500
  Fax: 480-775-0418
  E-Mail: drh@houselawfirm.com
  www.houselawfirm.com

Established: 2006

Insurance Defense, Civil Litigation, Business Law, Personal Injury, Litigation, Automobile Negligence Defense

Firm Profile: The House Law Firm is dedicated to providing winning, action-driven, yet cost-effective representation to our clients. Thoughtful strategies at case inception and strong, experienced litigation and negotiation skills combine to ensure our clients of the highest quality advocacy and result.

For over fifteen years, Donald R. House has represented a multitude of individuals, corporations, partnerships, insurers and government agencies in civil litigation. With a proven trial, arbitration and mediation record, the firm is uniquely qualified to provide superior advocacy to clients.

Insurance Clients

Arizona Automobile Insurance Company
GAINSCO, Inc.
Western General Insurance Company
Coast National Insurance Company
EMC Insurance Company
Legacy Insurance Services, Inc.
Western National Mutual Group

Firm Member

Donald R. House — Arizona State University, B.S. (magna cum laude), 1992; Arizona State University College of Law, J.D., 1994 — Admitted to Bar, 1995, Arizona; 1996, New Mexico; 1995, U.S. District Court, District of Arizona; U.S. Court of Appeals, Ninth Circuit — Member State Bar of Arizona (Litigation Section); Arizona Association of Defense Counsel (Past Board Member) — Board of Directors, ARC of Tempe — U.S. Coast Guard [1984-1989] — E-mail: drh@houselawfirm.com

TUCSON † 520,116 Pima Co.

Audilett Kastner PC
335 North Wilmot Road, Suite 500
Tucson, Arizona 85711
  Telephone: 520-748-2440
  Fax: 520-748-2469
  E-Mail: john@audilettkastner.com
  www.audilettkastner.com

Established: 1996

Insurance Defense, Wrongful Death, Bodily Injury, Civil Rights, Employment Law (Management Side), Employment Discrimination, Construction Defect, Insurance Coverage, Defense of Government Entities, Constitutional Torts, General Litigation

Firm Profile: The law firm of Audilett Kastner PC offers the traditional client-service values of excellence, professionalism, thorough communication and zealous advocacy according to the highest ethical standards. For over twenty-five years our lawyers have dedicated themselves to high quality representation. Your case will be handled by one of our partners, Daryl Audilett or John Kastner, both rated AV Preeminent.

Insurance Clients

Allstate Insurance Company
Travelers Insurance
Arizona Counties Insurance Pool

TUCSON   ARIZONA

Audilett Kastner PC, Tucson, AZ   (Continued)
Shareholders

Daryl A. Audilett — 1956 — Northern Arizona University, B.S. (summa cum laude), 1979; The University of Arizona, J.D. (with distinction), 1983 — Admitted to Bar, 1983, Arizona; U.S. District Court, District of Arizona; U.S. Court of Appeals, Ninth Circuit; U.S. Supreme Court — Member Federal, American and Pima County Bar Associations; State Bar of Arizona; Tucson Defense Bar; Arizona Association of Defense Counsel (Board of Directors) — Certified Specialist in Personal Injury and Wrongful Death, State of Arizona

John J. Kastner, Jr. — 1969 — University of Wisconsin-Madison, B.A., 1991; Hamline University School of Law, J.D. (cum laude), 1996 — Articles Editor, Hamline University Law Review — Admitted to Bar, 1996, Minnesota; 2002, Arizona; U.S. District Court, District of Arizona; U.S. Court of Appeals, Ninth Circuit — Member American, Minnesota State, Pima County and Tucson Bar Associations; State Bar of Arizona; Morris K. Udall Chapter of the Inns of Court; Defense Research Institute; Arizona Association of Defense Counsel — Reported Cases: State v. Wagner, 637 N.W.2d 330 (Minn.Ct.App. 2001)

Bliss, Wilkens & Clayton
An Association of LLCs

1846 East Innovation Park Drive
Oro Valley, Arizona 85755
  Telephone: 520-318-5599
  Fax: 907-276-2956
  www.bwclawyers.com

(Anchorage, AK Office*: 500 L Street, Suite 200, 99501)
  (Tel: 907-276-2999)
  (Fax: 907-276-2956)
  (E-Mail: atc@bwclawyers.com)

Aviation, Civil Trial Practice, Appeals, Business Law, Insurance Law, Probate, Elder Law, Corporate Law, Medical Staff Review

(See listing under Anchorage, AK for additional information)

Cavett & Fulton
A Professional Corporation

6035 East Grant Road
Tucson, Arizona 85712
  Telephone: 520-733-0100
  Fax: 520-733-1800
  E-Mail: info@cavettandfulton.com
  www.cavettandfulton.com

Established: 1989

Medical Malpractice, Nursing Home Liability, Professional Liability, Insurance Defense, Medical Devices, Product Liability

Firm Profile: Cavett and Fulton, P.C., founded in 1989, is a civil litigation firm with emphasis on the defense of medical professionals, hospitals and nursing homes. The firm size has been maintained to ensure personalized representation. We are accustomed to meeting and exceeding insurance carrier guidelines.

Insurance Clients

The Doctors Company	GEICO-Government Employees Insurance Company
Medical Insurance Exchange of California	The Medical Protective Company
Medicus Insurance Company	Mutual Insurance Company of Arizona

Non-Insurance Clients

Life Care Legal and Risk Services, LLC	Tucson Medical Center
	Tucson Orthopaedic Institute, P.C.

Cavett & Fulton, A Professional Corporation, Tucson, AZ   (Continued)
Firm Members

Dan Cavett — Emory University, B.A., 1968; The University of Arizona, J.D., 1971 — Order of the Coif — Admitted to Bar, 1971, Georgia; Arizona; 1975, U.S. District Court, District of Arizona — Member State Bar of Arizona; Pima County Bar Association; American Board of Trial Advocates (President, Tucson Chapter, 1990-1991) — Captain, USAF, JAGC [1972-1975] — Practice Areas: Medical Malpractice; Professional Liability; Civil Litigation — E-mail: dan@cavettandfulton.com

Anne M. Fulton-Cavett — The University of Arizona, B.A., 1991; The Catholic University of America, Columbus School of Law, J.D., 1995 — Thurgood Marshall Inn of Court (1994-1995); Morris K. Udall Inn of Court (1998) — Admitted to Bar, 1995, Arizona; 1995, U.S. District Court, District of Arizona; 2009, U.S. Supreme Court — Member State Bar of Arizona; Pima County Bar Association; Arizona Women Lawyers Association — Languages: Spanish — Practice Areas: Medical Malpractice; Nursing Home Litigation; Professional Liability; Civil Litigation — E-mail: anne@cavettandfulton.com

CURL & GLASSON, P.L.C.

485 South Main Avenue, Building 1
Tucson, Arizona 85701
  Telephone: 520-884-7777 (Option 2)
  Fax: 520-620-0921
  E-Mail: david@curllaw.com, doug@curllaw.com, jcp@curllaw.com
  www.curllaw.com

Insurance Defense, Personal Injury, Motor Vehicle, Product Liability, Homeowners, Fire, Environmental Liability, Premises Liability, Real Estate, Civil Appeals

Firm Profile: Curl & Glasson, P.L.C., provides individual and business clients with litigation experience and expertise. The firm focuses its practice in the areas of insurance defense, civil litigation, and appeals. We know Pima County, the judges, the juries and the lawyers.

Insurance Clients

Deans & Homer	GEICO
Horace Mann Insurance Company	Lloyd's of London
SECURA Insurance Companies	State Farm Fire and Casualty Company
State Farm Mutual Automobile Insurance Company	

Non-Insurance Clients

City of Tucson

Partners

David L. Curl — 1951 — University of Illinois, A.B., 1973; Southern Illinois University School of Law, J.D., 1977 — Order of Barristers; Member, Moot Court Board, 1976-1977 — Admitted to Bar, 1977, Illinois (Inactive); 1980, Arizona; 1988, Texas (Inactive) — Member State Bar of Arizona; Tucson Defense Bar Association (Past President); Litigation Counsel of America; Arizona Finest Lawyers; Arizona Association of Defense Counsel; Defense Research Institute — Author: "What Civil Court Judges Want You to Know"; "Overcoming Complex Issues in UM/UIM Law" — Certified Specialist, Injury and Wrongful Death Litigation, Arizona Board of Legal Specialization — Practice Areas: Insurance Defense; Civil Trial Practice; Personal Injury; Construction Law — E-mail: david@curllaw.com

Douglas W. Glasson — 1955 — Illinois Wesleyan University, B.A., 1978; Southern Illinois University School of Law, J.D., 1991 — Admitted to Bar, 1991, Illinois (Inactive); 1998, Arizona — Member State Bar of Arizona; Pima County Bar Association; Tucson Defense Bar Association (Past President); Arizona Association of Defense Counsel — Chartered Property and Casualty Underwriter (CPCU), 2001; Chartered Financial Consultant (ChFC), 2003 — Practice Areas: Insurance Defense; Civil Trial Practice — E-mail: doug@curllaw.com

Associate

J.C. Patrascioiu — 1977 — The University of Arizona, B.S., 2001; The University of Arizona, James E. Rogers College of Law, J.D., 2006 — Admitted

CURL & GLASSON, P.L.C., Tucson, AZ (Continued)

to Bar, 2006, Arizona — Member State Bar of Arizona; Pima County Bar Association; Tucson Defense Bar Association (Secretary) — Practice Areas: Insurance Defense; Civil Trial Practice — E-mail: jcp@curllaw.com

Miniat & Wilson, LPC

550 West Ina Road, Suite 101
Tucson, Arizona 85704
   Telephone: 520-742-1177
   Fax: 877-399-4343
   Mobile: 520-419-8484
   E-Mail: kmin@dakotacom.net
   www.miniatwilson.com

Established: 1988

Insurance Defense, General Liability, Product Liability, Property and Casualty, Workers' Compensation, Subrogation, Business Law

Firm Profile: After practicing many years with established insurance defense firms in Arizona and California, Kevin Miniat and Jerald Wilson formed their litigation partnership to continue in the insurance defense field. The firm focuses on defense of liability claims, arising from negligence, strict liability, breach of professional duty, deprivation of civil rights, and breach of contract. Both partners invite any inquiries.

Insurance Clients

Acadia Insurance Company	Alpine Insurance Company
American Bankers Insurance Company of Florida	American Medical Security Group, Inc.
American Medical Security Insurance Company	American Reliable Insurance Company
Assurant Insurance Group	Continental Insurance Company
Coregis Indemnity Company	Great American Insurance Company
Home Insurance Company	Motorists Mutual Insurance Company
Jefferson Insurance Company	
Preferred Risk Insurance Company	
Travelers Insurance Companies	Unigard Insurance Company
United National Group	

Non-Insurance Clients

Dealer Cover, Inc.	Innovative Risk Management, Inc.
Sedgwick Group of Arizona, Inc.	Tucson Unified School District
Western Claims, Inc.	

Firm Members

Kevin E. Miniat — 1950 — The University of Arizona, B.S., 1972; J.D., 1975 — Admitted to Bar, 1975, Arizona; 1976, Illinois; 1975, U.S. District Court, District of Arizona; 1975, U.S. District Court, Northern District of Illinois — Member Illinois State and Pima County Bar Associations; State Bar of Arizona; Tucson Defense Bar Association; Defense Research Institute — Certified Personal Injury and Wrongful Death Specialist — E-mail: kmin@dakotacom.net

Jerald R. Wilson — 1963 — The University of Iowa, B.S., 1985; The University of Arizona, J.D., 1989 — Admitted to Bar, 1989, California; 1994, Arizona — Member Tucson Defense Bar Association; Defense Research Institute — E-mail: jerwil@dakotacom.net

(This firm is also listed in the Subrogation section of this directory)

Smith Law Group

Davis House
262 North Main Avenue
Tucson, Arizona 85701
   Telephone: 520-547-1600
   Fax: 520-547-1605
   www.lawyers.com/smithlawgroup

Medical Malpractice, Legal Malpractice, Professional Liability, Insurance Defense, Product Liability, Administrative Law

Smith Law Group, Tucson, AZ (Continued)

Firm Profile: Smith Law Group has extensive experience representing physicians, attorneys, and other defendants before juries as well as administrative bodies. Located in historic Davis House, Smith Law Group is a "digital" firm that uses computer technology, including scanning and presentation software, to prepare and present its cases effectively and efficiently throughout Arizona and Nevada.

Insurance Clients

Mutual Insurance Company of Arizona	OMS National Insurance Company

Non-Insurance Clients

Planned Parenthood Federation of America, Inc.	Specialty Claims, Incorporated
University Physicians Healthcare	University Medical Center

Firm Member

Christopher J. Smith — 1957 — University of Massachusetts, B.A., 1979; The University of Arizona, J.D., 1985 — Admitted to Bar, 1985, Arizona; 2005, Nevada; 1985, U.S. District Court, District of Arizona; U.S. Court of Appeals, Ninth Circuit; 2005, U.S. Supreme Court — Member American and Pima County (President, 2005-2006) Bar Associations; State Bar of Arizona; American Board of Trial Advocates (Vice President, Tucson Chapter) — E-mail: chris.smith@smithlawgroup.com

Associate

Cathleen M. Dooley — 1972 — University of Nevada, Las Vegas, B.A., 1993; M.A., 1995; The University of Arizona, Ph.D., 2001; J.D., 2003 — Admitted to Bar, 2003, Arizona — Member State Bar of Arizona; Arizona Women Lawyers Association — E-mail: cathleen.dooley@smithlawgroup.com

WILLIAMS   3,023 Coconino Co.

Refer To

Mangum, Wall, Stoops & Warden, P.L.L.C.
100 North Elden
Flagstaff, Arizona 86001
   Telephone: 928-779-6951
   Fax: 928-773-1312
Mailing Address: P.O. Box 10, Flagstaff, AZ 86002

Insurance Defense

SEE COMPLETE LISTING UNDER FLAGSTAFF, ARIZONA (33 MILES)

WINSLOW   9,655 Navajo Co.

Refer To

Mangum, Wall, Stoops & Warden, P.L.L.C.
100 North Elden
Flagstaff, Arizona 86001
   Telephone: 928-779-6951
   Fax: 928-773-1312
Mailing Address: P.O. Box 10, Flagstaff, AZ 86002

Insurance Defense

SEE COMPLETE LISTING UNDER FLAGSTAFF, ARIZONA (59 MILES)

YUMA   † 93,064 Yuma Co.

Refer To

Cavett & Fulton
A Professional Corporation
6035 East Grant Road
Tucson, Arizona 85712
   Telephone: 520-733-0100
   Fax: 520-733-1800

Medical Malpractice, Nursing Home Liability, Professional Liability, Insurance Defense, Medical Devices, Product Liability

SEE COMPLETE LISTING UNDER TUCSON, ARIZONA (244 MILES)

ARKANSAS

CAPITAL: LITTLE ROCK

COUNTIES AND COUNTY SEATS

County	County Seat
Arkansas	De Witt & Stuttgart
Ashley	Hamburg
Baxter	Mountain Home
Benton	Bentonville
Boone	Harrison
Bradley	Warren
Calhoun	Hampton
Carroll	Berryville & Eureka Springs
Chicot	Lake Village
Clark	Arkadelphia
Clay	Corning & Piggott
Cleburne	Heber Springs
Cleveland	Rison
Columbia	Magnolia
Conway	Morrilton
Craighead	Jonesboro & Lake City
Crawford	Van Buren
Crittenden	Marion
Cross	Wynne
Dallas	Fordyce
Desha	Arkansas City
Drew	Monticello
Faulkner	Conway
Franklin	Charleston & Ozark
Fulton	Salem

County	County Seat
Garland	Hot Springs
Grant	Sheridan
Greene	Paragould
Hempstead	Hope
Hot Spring	Malvern
Howard	Nashville
Independence	Batesville
Izard	Melbourne
Jackson	Newport
Jefferson	Pine Bluff
Johnson	Clarksville
Lafayette	Lewisville
Lawrence	Walnut Ridge
Lee	Marianna
Lincoln	Star City
Little River	Ashdown
Logan	Booneville & Paris
Lonoke	Lonoke
Madison	Huntsville
Marion	Yellville
Miller	Texarkana
Mississippi	Blytheville & Osceola
Monroe	Clarendon
Montgomery	Mount Ida
Nevada	Prescott

County	County Seat
Newton	Jasper
Ouachita	Camden
Perry	Perryville
Phillips	Helena
Pike	Murfreesboro
Poinsett	Harrisburg
Polk	Mena
Pope	Russellville
Prairie	Des Arc & De Valls
Pulaski	Little Rock
Randolph	Pocahontas
St. Francis	Forrest City
Saline	Benton
Scott	Waldron
Searcy	Marshall
Sebastian	Fort Smith & Greenwood
Sevier	De Queen
Sharp	Ash Flat
Stone	Mountain View
Union	El Dorado
Van Buren	Clinton
Washington	Fayetteville
White	Searcy
Woodruff	Augusta
Yell	Danville & Dardanelle

In the text that follows "†" indicates County Seats.

Our files contain additional verified data on the firms listed herein. This additional information is available on request.

A.M. BEST COMPANY

ARKADELPHIA † 10,714 Clark Co.

McMillan, McCorkle, Curry & Bennington, LLP

929 Main Street
Arkadelphia, Arkansas 71923
   Telephone: 870-246-2468
   Fax: 870-246-3851
   E-Mail: curry@mtmc-law.com
   www.mmcb-lawarkansas.com

Established: 1865

Insurance Defense, Workers' Compensation, Product Liability, Medical Malpractice, Coverage Issues

Insurance Clients

Allstate Insurance Company	CGU Group
Columbia Mutual Insurance Company	Commercial Union Assurance Company plc
EMC Insurance Companies	Fidelity and Deposit Company of Maryland
Fireman's Fund Insurance Company	Liberty Mutual Insurance Company
Lumbermens Mutual Casualty Company	OneBeacon Insurance
Provident Life and Accident Insurance Company	Preferred Risk Mutual Insurance Company
Travelers Insurance Companies	St. Paul Insurance Company
	Trinity Universal Insurance Company

Non-Insurance Clients

Silvey Companies

Partners

Otis H. Turner — (1927-2000)

Toney D. McMillan — (1942-2009)

Ed W. McCorkle — 1944 — University of Arkansas, B.A., 1966; J.D., 1969 — Admitted to Bar, 1968, Arkansas — Member American and Arkansas Bar Associations

F. Thomas Curry — 1957 — Henderson State University, B.A., 1979; University of Arkansas at Little Rock, J.D., 1982 — Admitted to Bar, 1982, Arkansas — Member American, Arkansas and Clark County Bar Associations; Arkansas Association of Defense Counsel; International Association of Defense Counsel — U.S. Army, 1982-1987; Judge Advocate General Corps, USAR, 1987-2009

Madeline L. Bennington — 1968 — The University of Mississippi, B.A., 1989; Washington University, J.D., 1994 — Admitted to Bar, 1994, Missouri; 1999, Arkansas; 1994, U.S. Court of Appeals, Eighth Circuit — Member American, Arkansas and Clark County Bar Associations; The Missouri Bar; Bar Association of Metropolitan St. Louis

Associate

Philip McCorkle — 1973 — University of Arkansas, B.S.B.A., 1996; M.B.A., 1999; J.D., 2002 — Admitted to Bar, 2002, Arkansas; U.S. District Court, Eastern and Western Districts of Arkansas — Member American and Arkansas Bar Associations

The following firms also service this area.

Dunn, Nutter & Morgan L.L.P.
3601 Richmond Road
Texarkana, Texas 75503
   Telephone: 903-793-5651
   Fax: 903-794-5651

Insurance Defense, Casualty, Fire, Workers' Compensation, Life Insurance, Accident and Health, Medical Liability, Legal Malpractice, Professional Malpractice, Employment Law, Subrogation, Commercial Litigation, Banking

SEE COMPLETE LISTING UNDER TEXARKANA, TEXAS (78 MILES)

ASHDOWN † 4,723 Little River Co.

Refer To

Dunn, Nutter & Morgan L.L.P.
3601 Richmond Road
Texarkana, Texas 75503
   Telephone: 903-793-5651
   Fax: 903-794-5651

Insurance Defense, Casualty, Fire, Workers' Compensation, Life Insurance, Accident and Health, Medical Liability, Legal Malpractice, Professional Malpractice, Employment Law, Subrogation, Commercial Litigation, Banking

SEE COMPLETE LISTING UNDER TEXARKANA, TEXAS (20 MILES)

BATESVILLE † 10,248 Independence Co.

Refer To

Snellgrove, Langley, Culpepper, Williams & Mullally
111 East Huntington, Second Floor
Jonesboro, Arkansas 72401
   Telephone: 870-932-8357
   Fax: 870-932-5488

Mailing Address: P.O. Box 1346, Jonesboro, AR 72403

Insurance Defense, Personal Injury, Commercial Law, Workers' Compensation, Product Liability, Real Estate, Corporate Law, Banking Law

SEE COMPLETE LISTING UNDER JONESBORO, ARKANSAS (74 MILES)

Refer To

Waddell, Cole & Jones, PLLC
310 East Street, Suite A
Jonesboro, Arkansas 72401
   Telephone: 870-931-1700
   Fax: 870-931-1800, 870-931-1810

Mailing Address: P.O. Box 1700, Jonesboro, AR 72403

Insurance Defense, Trial and Appellate Practice, Property and Casualty, General Liability, Toxic Torts, Errors and Omissions, Product Liability, Construction Law, Surety, Life and Health, Medical Malpractice, Arson, Fraud, Transportation, Aviation, Agriculture, Workers' Compensation, Employment Discrimination

SEE COMPLETE LISTING UNDER JONESBORO, ARKANSAS (74 MILES)

BENTONVILLE † 35,301 Benton Co.

Refer To

Davis, Clark, Butt, Carithers & Taylor, PLC
19 East Mountain Street
Fayetteville, Arkansas 72701
   Telephone: 479-521-7600
   Fax: 479-521-7661

Mailing Address: P.O. Box 1688, Fayetteville, AR 72702-1688

Insurance Defense, Automobile, General Liability, Workers' Compensation, Product Liability, Legal Malpractice, Medical Malpractice, Environmental Law, Employer Liability, Life Insurance, Surety, Construction Law, Immigration Law

SEE COMPLETE LISTING UNDER FAYETTEVILLE, ARKANSAS (30 MILES)

Refer To

Smith, Cohen & Horan, PLC
1206 Garrison Avenue
Fort Smith, Arkansas 72901
   Telephone: 479-782-1001
   Fax: 479-782-1279

Mailing Address: P.O. Box 10205, Fort Smith, AR 72917-0205

Insurance Defense, Automobile Liability, Transportation, Product Liability, Subrogation, Employment Law, Environmental Law, General and Product Liability

SEE COMPLETE LISTING UNDER FORT SMITH, ARKANSAS (82 MILES)

DANVILLE   ARKANSAS

BLYTHEVILLE † 15,620 Mississippi Co.

Reid, Burge, Prevallet & Coleman

417 North Broadway
Blytheville, Arkansas 72315
  Toll Free: 888-673-9640
  Telephone: 870-763-4586
  Fax: 870-763-4642
  E-Mail: rbpc@sbcglobal.net
  www.lawyers.com/rbpclaw

Established: 1925

Insurance Defense, Trial and Appellate Practice, Insurance Coverage, Insurance Fraud, Examinations Under Oath, General Civil Practice

Firm Profile: Formed in 1925, Reid, Burge, Prevallet & Coleman has an established civil litigation, insurance and business practice that provides quality and efficient legal services for a wide variety of clients. We represent many individuals, insurance companies, and other business concerns throughout Northeastern Arkansas. Our firm offers the experience and resources to handle a wide variety of matters, including insurance defense, workers' compensation, insurance coverage analysis, insurance fraud, examinations under oath, general civil litigation, complex litigation, and a general civil practice.

Insurance Clients

AXA Equitable Life Insurance Company
COUNTRY Mutual Insurance Company
GEICO
Great West Casualty Company
Hartford Accident and Indemnity Company
National Security Group, Inc.
State Farm Group
Transport Insurance Company
United States Fidelity and Guaranty Company
Cameron Insurance Companies
Country Companies
Fireman's Fund Insurance Company
The Glens Falls Insurance Company
ICW Group
Lafayette Insurance Company
Pacific National Insurance Company
Travelers Insurance Companies
Western Insurance Group

Non-Insurance Clients

Aviation Repair Technologies (ART)
Nucor Corporation
Royal Silvey Group
Blytheville Public Schools
Farmers Bank & Trust
Nucor-Yamato Steel Company
SISCO Self Insured Services Company

Partners

Max B. Reid — (1895-1959)

Dan M. Burge — (1927-2010)

Richard A. Reid — 1932 — University of Arkansas, B.S.B.A., 1955; J.D., 1957 — Admitted to Bar, 1957, Arkansas; U.S. District Court, Eastern District of Arkansas; U.S. Court of Military Appeals; 1965, U.S. Supreme Court — Member American and Arkansas Bar Associations; Commercial Law League of America — E-mail: rreid_rbpc@sbcglobal.net

Donald E. Prevallet — 1934 — Valparaiso University, A.B., 1956; LL.B./J.D., 1958 — Admitted to Bar, 1959, Missouri; 1963, Arkansas; 1960, U.S. District Court, Eastern District of Missouri; 1961, U.S. Court of Military Appeals; 1962, U.S. District Court, Eastern District of Arkansas; 1965, U.S. Supreme Court — Member Arkansas Bar Association; The Missouri Bar; Arkansas Association of Defense Counsel — E-mail: don.rbpc@sbcglobal.net

Robert L. Coleman — 1955 — University of Arkansas, B.A., 1977; J.D., 1980 — Phi Beta Kappa; Phi Alpha Delta; Omicron Delta Kappa; Blue Key and Lambda Chi Alpha — Admitted to Bar, 1980, Arkansas; 1980, U.S. District Court, Eastern District of Arkansas; 1988, U.S. Supreme Court — Member Arkansas and Blytheville Bar Associations; Arkansas Association of Defense Counsel (President, 2000-2001); American Board of Trial Advocates; American Association for Justice; Defense Research Institute — Listed in Mid-South Superlawyers; Named among Top 100 Trial Lawyers by National Trial Lawyers Association — E-mail: rbpc@sbcglobal.net

The following firms also service this area.

Snellgrove, Langley, Culpepper, Williams & Mullally
111 East Huntington, Second Floor
Jonesboro, Arkansas 72401
  Telephone: 870-932-8357
  Fax: 870-932-5488

Mailing Address: P.O. Box 1346, Jonesboro, AR 72403

Insurance Defense, Personal Injury, Commercial Law, Workers' Compensation, Product Liability, Real Estate, Corporate Law, Banking Law

SEE COMPLETE LISTING UNDER JONESBORO, ARKANSAS (55 MILES)

Waddell, Cole & Jones, PLLC
310 East Street, Suite A
Jonesboro, Arkansas 72401
  Telephone: 870-931-1700
  Fax: 870-931-1800, 870-931-1810

Mailing Address: P.O. Box 1700, Jonesboro, AR 72403

Insurance Defense, Trial and Appellate Practice, Property and Casualty, General Liability, Toxic Torts, Errors and Omissions, Product Liability, Construction Law, Surety, Life and Health, Medical Malpractice, Arson, Fraud, Transportation, Aviation, Agriculture, Workers' Compensation, Employment Discrimination

SEE COMPLETE LISTING UNDER JONESBORO, ARKANSAS (55 MILES)

BOONEVILLE † 3,990 Logan Co.

Refer To

Daily & Woods, P.L.L.C.
58 South Sixth
Fort Smith, Arkansas 72901
  Telephone: 479-782-0361
  Fax: 479-782-6160

Mailing Address: P.O. Box 1446, Fort Smith, AR 72902

Insurance Defense

SEE COMPLETE LISTING UNDER FORT SMITH, ARKANSAS (39 MILES)

CAMDEN † 12,183 Ouachita Co.

Refer To

McMillan, McCorkle, Curry & Bennington, LLP
929 Main Street
Arkadelphia, Arkansas 71923
  Telephone: 870-246-2468
  Fax: 870-246-3851

Mailing Address: P.O. Box 607, Arkadelphia, AR 71923

Insurance Defense, Workers' Compensation, Product Liability, Medical Malpractice, Coverage Issues

SEE COMPLETE LISTING UNDER ARKADELPHIA, ARKANSAS (58 MILES)

CHARLESTON † 2,494 Franklin Co.

Refer To

Daily & Woods, P.L.L.C.
58 South Sixth
Fort Smith, Arkansas 72901
  Telephone: 479-782-0361
  Fax: 479-782-6160

Mailing Address: P.O. Box 1446, Fort Smith, AR 72902

Insurance Defense

SEE COMPLETE LISTING UNDER FORT SMITH, ARKANSAS (24 MILES)

DANVILLE † 2,409 Yell Co.

Tatum, Tatum & Riedel Law Firm

522 Main Street
Danville, Arkansas 72833
  Telephone: 479-495-2649
  Fax: 479-495-7992

ARKANSAS

Tatum, Tatum & Riedel Law Firm, Danville, AR
(Continued)

Established: 1967

Insurance Defense, Medical Malpractice, Product Liability

Insurance Clients

Automobile Club Inter-Insurance Exchange
Ohio Insurance Group
Travelers Property Casualty Corporation
CIGNA Insurance Company
Cincinnati Insurance Company
State Auto Insurance Company

Non-Insurance Clients

Arkwest Communications
Chambers Bancshares, Inc.
Petit Jean Poultry, Inc.
The Bridgeway Hospital
First Western Bancshares, Inc.
Universal Health Services, Inc.

Firm Members

Tom Tatum, Sr. — 1941 — Arkansas Polytechnic University, B.S., 1964; University of Arkansas, J.D., 1967 — Admitted to Bar, 1967, Arkansas; 1967, U.S. District Court, Eastern and Western Districts of Arkansas; U.S. Court of Appeals, Eighth Circuit; U.S. Supreme Court — Member Arkansas Bar Association; Arkansas Trial Lawyers Association

Tom Tatum II — 1969 — Arkansas Polytechnic University, B.S., 1991; University of Arkansas, J.D., 1993 — Admitted to Bar, 1994, Arkansas; 1994, U.S. District Court, Eastern and Western Districts of Arkansas; U.S. Court of Appeals, Eighth Circuit — Member American and Arkansas Bar Associations; Arkansas Trial Lawyers Association; National District Attorneys Association — Prosecuting Attorney, 15th Judicial District, 2001-Present

John C. Riedel — 1971 — Arkansas Polytechnic University, B.S., 1993; University of Arkansas, J.D., 1997 — Admitted to Bar, 1997, Arkansas; U.S. District Court, Eastern and Western Districts of Arkansas — Member Arkansas and Yell County Bar Associations; Arkansas Trial Lawyers Association

DE QUEEN † 6,594 Sevier Co.

Refer To

Dunn, Nutter & Morgan L.L.P.
3601 Richmond Road
Texarkana, Texas 75503
Telephone: 903-793-5651
Fax: 903-794-5651

Insurance Defense, Casualty, Fire, Workers' Compensation, Life Insurance, Accident and Health, Medical Liability, Legal Malpractice, Professional Malpractice, Employment Law, Subrogation, Commercial Litigation, Banking

SEE COMPLETE LISTING UNDER TEXARKANA, TEXAS (53 MILES)

EL DORADO † 18,884 Union Co.

Refer To

Dunn, Nutter & Morgan L.L.P.
3601 Richmond Road
Texarkana, Texas 75503
Telephone: 903-793-5651
Fax: 903-794-5651

Insurance Defense, Casualty, Fire, Workers' Compensation, Life Insurance, Accident and Health, Medical Liability, Legal Malpractice, Professional Malpractice, Employment Law, Subrogation, Commercial Litigation, Banking

SEE COMPLETE LISTING UNDER TEXARKANA, TEXAS (88 MILES)

Refer To

McMillan, McCorkle, Curry & Bennington, LLP
929 Main Street
Arkadelphia, Arkansas 71923
Telephone: 870-246-2468
Fax: 870-246-3851
Mailing Address: P.O. Box 607, Arkadelphia, AR 71923

Insurance Defense, Workers' Compensation, Product Liability, Medical Malpractice, Coverage Issues

SEE COMPLETE LISTING UNDER ARKADELPHIA, ARKANSAS (83 MILES)

DE QUEEN

Refer To

Munson, Rowlett, Moore & Boone, P.A.
Regions Center
400 West Capitol, Suite 1900
Little Rock, Arkansas 72201
Telephone: 501-374-6535
Fax: 501-374-5906

Arson, Asbestos, Aviation, Bad Faith, Casualty, Catastrophic Injury, Civil Appeals, Civil Litigation, Class Actions, Commercial Litigation, Complex Litigation, Construction Litigation, Employment Law, Environmental Litigation, Fraud, Hospital Malpractice, Insurance Coverage, Insurance Defense, Mediation, Medical Devices, Medical Malpractice, Negligence, Personal Injury, Premises Liability, Product Liability, Professional Malpractice, School Law, Self-Insured Defense, Subrogation, Toxic Torts, Transportation, Trucking Litigation, Workers' Compensation, Wrongful Death

SEE COMPLETE LISTING UNDER LITTLE ROCK, ARKANSAS (116 MILES)

FAYETTEVILLE † 73,580 Washington Co.

Bassett Law Firm, LLP
221 North College Avenue
Fayetteville, Arkansas 72702
Telephone: 479-521-9996
Fax: 479-521-9600
E-Mail: blf@bassettlawfirm.com
www.bassettlawfirm.com

Established: 1981

Insurance Defense, Trial and Appellate Practice, State and Federal Courts, Casualty, Fire, Life, Workers' Compensation, Product Liability, Construction Law, Asbestos, Environmental Law, Medical Malpractice, Automobile, Commercial Law

Firm Profile: Bassett Law Firm LLP is located in Fayetteville, Arkansas. The firm's concentration is in trial insurance defense litigation. The firm performs a variety of legal services in the states of Arkansas, Oklahoma, and Missouri. The firm is preeminently rated by legal publisher Martindale-Hubble, and has been recognized by the national publication Corporate Counsel as a full service law firm. Members of the firm participate in and are lecturers at continuing legal education seminars, and are also active in professional association activities and civic affairs.

Insurance Clients

Alfa Vision Insurance Corp.
Amerisure Insurance Company
Cameron Insurance Companies
Chartis Insurance
Colony Insurance Company
General Casualty Insurance Company
James River Insurance Company
Mendota Insurance Company
National American Insurance Company
Regions Claims Management
Sagamore Insurance Company
Sedgwick Claims Management
State Auto Insurance Company
Tokio Marine and Fire Insurance Company, Ltd.
American Family Insurance Group
Arch Insurance Company c/o ESIS AGL Claims
Cincinnati Insurance Company
Gallagher Bassett Services, Inc.
Hanover Insurance Group
Hartford Insurance Company
Lexington Insurance Company/AIG
Northland Insurance Company
Ramsey Krug Farrell & Lensing
Risk Management Resources
S.B. Howard & Company, Inc.
Sentry Insurance Company
State Volunteer Mutual Insurance Company
Travelers Insurance Company

Non-Insurance Clients

Community Health Systems, Inc.
Simmons Foods, Inc.
Tyson Foods, Inc.
Monsanto Company
Sisters of Mercy Health System

Firm Members

William W. Bassett, Jr. — (1926-2006)

J. David Wall — (1967-2006)

Woodson W. Bassett III — 1951 — University of Arkansas, B.A., 1974; University of Arkansas School of Law, J.D., 1977 — Admitted to Bar, 1977, Arkansas — Member Arkansas and Washington County (President, 1987-1988) Bar Associations; American Board of Trial Advocates; American College of

FAYETTEVILLE   ARKANSAS

Bassett Law Firm, LLP, Fayetteville, AR (Continued)

Trial Lawyers; International Academy of Trial Lawyers — Practice Areas: Personal Injury; Civil Litigation; Product Liability; Criminal Law; Corporate Law; Environmental Litigation; Agriculture; Employment Discrimination; Business Litigation; Sports Law — E-mail: wbassett@bassettlawfirm.com

Tod C. Bassett — 1955 — University of Arkansas, B.A., 1977; University of Arkansas School of Law, J.D., 1980 — Admitted to Bar, 1980, Arkansas — Member Arkansas and Washington County Bar Associations; American Inns of Court; Defense Counsel of Arkansas; Defense Research Institute — Practice Areas: Personal Injury; Civil Litigation; Product Liability; Workers' Compensation; Corporate Law; Employment Law; Insurance Law — E-mail: tbassett@bassettlawfirm.com

Wm. Robert Still, Jr. — 1956 — Arkansas State University, B.A., 1978; University of Arkansas School of Law, J.D., 1983 — Phi Alpha Delta — Admitted to Bar, 1983, Arkansas; 1996, Missouri — Member American (Tort and Insurance Practice Section), Arkansas and Washington County (President, 1992) Bar Associations; Defense Counsel of Arkansas; Barrister, American Inns of Court; Arkansas Workers' Compensation Commission; Equal Employment Opportunity Commission — Practice Areas: Product Liability; Personal Injury; General Civil Litigation; Environmental Law; Disability; Aviation; Insurance Law; Business Law; Employment Discrimination; Corporate Law — E-mail: bstill@bassettlawfirm.com

Walker Dale Garrett — 1953 — Hendrix College, B.A., 1975; University of Arkansas School of Law, J.D., 1978 — Delta Theta Phi — Associate Editor, University of Arkansas Law Review (1978) — Admitted to Bar, 1978, Arkansas; 1995, Missouri — Member Arkansas and Washington County Bar Associations; The Missouri Bar; Defense Counsel of Arkansas; Arkansas Bar Foundation; Defense Research Institute; American Board of Trial Advocates; American College of Trial Lawyers — Practice Areas: Product Liability; Personal Injury; Legal Malpractice; Medical Malpractice; Insurance Law; Civil Litigation — E-mail: dgarrett@bassettlawfirm.com

Curtis L. Nebben — 1954 — University of Arkansas, B.S.B.A., 1977; University of Arkansas School of Law, J.D., 1980 — Associate Editor, University of Arkansas Law Review (1980) — Admitted to Bar, 1980, Arkansas — Member American, Arkansas and Washington County Bar Associations; Defense Counsel of Arkansas; Defense Research Institute — Practice Areas: Personal Injury; Civil Litigation; Workers' Compensation; Employment Discrimination; Business Litigation — E-mail: cnebben@bassettlawfirm.com

Earl Buddy Chadick, Jr. — 1944 — University of Arkansas, B.S.B.A., 1983; University of Arkansas School of Law, J.D., 1986 — Admitted to Bar, 1986, Arkansas — Member American, Arkansas and Washington County (President, 2003-2004) Bar Associations — Practice Areas: Asbestos Litigation; Product Liability; Personal Injury; Civil Litigation; Workers' Compensation — E-mail: bchadick@bassettlawfirm.com

Vincent O. Chadick — 1969 — Georgetown University, A.B., 1991; University of Arkansas School of Law, J.D., 1993; LL.M., 2007 — Admitted to Bar, 1994, Arkansas; Oklahoma — Member American, Arkansas, Oklahoma and Washington County Bar Associations — Practice Areas: Commercial Law; Agriculture — E-mail: vchadick@bassettlawfirm.com

James M. Graves — 1969 — University of Arkansas, B.S.B.A., 1992; University of Arkansas School of Law, J.D. (with high honors), 1995 — University of Arkansas Law Review (1994-1995) — Admitted to Bar, 1995, Arkansas; Oklahoma; 1996, Missouri — Member American, Arkansas, Oklahoma and Washington County Bar Associations; The Missouri Bar — Practice Areas: Mergers and Acquisitions; Business Litigation; Commercial Litigation; Commercial Law; Business Law; Environmental Law; Environmental Litigation; Agriculture — E-mail: jgraves@bassettlawfirm.com

Scott Edward Wray — 1969 — University of Arkansas, B.S.B.A., 1993; University of Arkansas School of Law, J.D., 1996 — Phi Delta Phi; Golden Key — Admitted to Bar, 1996, Arkansas; 1997, Oklahoma — Member Arkansas, Oklahoma and Washington County Bar Associations — Practice Areas: Commercial Litigation; Business Law; Business Litigation; Employment Discrimination; Insurance Law; Insurance Defense; Product Liability; Business Transactions — E-mail: swray@bassettlawfirm.com

Shannon L. Fant — 1971 — University of Arkansas, B.A., 1994; University of Arkansas School of Law, J.D., 1997 — Admitted to Bar, 1997, Arkansas; Oklahoma — Member Arkansas, Oklahoma and Washington County Bar Associations — Practice Areas: Insurance Law; Civil Litigation; Medical Malpractice; Product Liability — E-mail: sfant@bassettlawfirm.com

Dale W. Brown — 1978 — University of Arkansas, B.S.B.A., 2000; University of Arkansas School of Law, J.D. (cum laude), 2004 — Admitted to Bar, 2004, Arkansas — Member Arkansas Bar Association; Putnam Inn of Court — Practice Areas: Civil Litigation; Insurance Defense; Premises Liability; Workers' Compensation; Commercial Litigation — E-mail: dbrown@bassettlawfirm.com

Bassett Law Firm, LLP, Fayetteville, AR (Continued)

Joel I. Farthing — 1981 — University of Arkansas, B.S./B.A., 2004; University of Arkansas School of Law, J.D. (Dean's List), 2007 — Admitted to Bar, 2007, Arkansas — Member Arkansas Bar Association — Practice Areas: Insurance Defense; Tort; Commercial Litigation; Wrongful Death; Personal Injury; Automobile; Construction Accidents; Premises Liability; Product Liability — E-mail: jfarthing@bassettlawfirm.com

Associates

Grace K. Johnson — 1964 — Bradley University, B.S., 1986; University of Arkansas School of Law, J.D. (with high honors), 2009 — University of Arkansas Law Review — Admitted to Bar, 2009, Arkansas — Member Arkansas Bar Association; Putnam Inn of Court — Practice Areas: Business Law; Commercial Law; Business Transactions; Hospitality; Entertainment Law; Copyright and Trademark Law; Corporate Law; Civil Litigation; Employment Law; Insurance Law — E-mail: gjohnson@bassettlawfirm.com

John W. Murry — 1985 — University of Arkansas, B.A., 2008; University of Arkansas School of Law, J.D., 2011 — Admitted to Bar, 2011, Arkansas — Practice Areas: Business Litigation; Commercial Law; Corporate Law; Insurance Defense; Civil Litigation; Criminal Law — E-mail: wmurry@bassettlawfirm.com

Davis, Clark, Butt, Carithers & Taylor, PLC

19 East Mountain Street
Fayetteville, Arkansas 72701
Telephone: 479-521-7600
Fax: 479-521-7661
www.davis-firm.com

(Springdale, AR Office: 1712 West Sunset, Suite E, 72762)
(Tel: 479-717-2278)
(Fax: 479-717-2302)

Established: 1953

Insurance Defense, Automobile, General Liability, Workers' Compensation, Product Liability, Legal Malpractice, Medical Malpractice, Environmental Law, Employer Liability, Life Insurance, Surety, Construction Law, Immigration Law

Firm Profile: Since 1953 this firm has provided a broad range of quality legal services in northwest Arkansas and on a state-wide and regional basis. Two of the firm's partners are Fellows in the American College of Trial Lawyers and five partners are recognized by Best Lawyers in America and Super Lawyers as litigators. The firm's scope of practice extends from all types of personal injury and commercial trials and appeals to business, bankruptcy and tax matters, representing a broad array of clients ranging from local individuals, businesses and institutions to major insurance and Fortune 500 companies.

All members of this firm are admitted to practice before the U.S. District Court, Eastern and Western Districts of Arkansas and the U.S. Court of Appeals, Eighth Circuit and are members of the Washington County and Arkansas Bar Associations. Two lawyers are American College of Trial Lawyers and four are listed in litigation specialties in Best Lawyers of America.

Insurance Clients

AAO Services, Inc.
American Safety Claims Services, Inc.
Canal Insurance Company
Chartis
CNA Insurance Companies
Colonia Insurance Company
Consumers Insurance Company
EMC Insurance Companies
Employers Mutual Companies
Farm Bureau Mutual Insurance Company of Arkansas, Inc.
Hanover Insurance Company
The Harleysville Insurance
Lafayette Insurance Company
NCMIC Insurance Company

AIGDC - A Division of AIU Holdings, Inc.
Arkansas Mutual Insurance Company
Chubb Group of Insurance Companies
Colony Insurance Group
Deep South Surplus, Inc.
Empire Insurance Company
Essex Insurance Company
Federated Insurance Company
Glatfelter Claims Management, Inc.
K & K Insurance Group, Inc.
The Medical Protective Company
North Pointe Insurance Company

ARKANSAS — FAYETTEVILLE

Davis, Clark, Butt, Carithers & Taylor, PLC, Fayetteville, AR (Continued)

Pennsylvania Lumbermens Mutual Insurance Company
State Volunteer Mutual Insurance Company
Zurich American Insurance Company
Southern Farm Bureau Casualty Insurance Company
Travelers Insurance Companies
United Fire Group

Non-Insurance Clients

Allens, Inc.
Coldwell Banker Faucette Real Estate, Inc.
Ozark Orthopedic & Sports Medicine Clinic, Ltd.
Western Federal Credit Union
Arvest Bank Group, Inc.
J.V. Manufacturing, Inc.
Kawasaki Motors Corporation, U.S.A.
Washington Regional Medical Center

Partners

Sidney P. Davis, Jr. — 1931 — Henderson State Teachers College, B.S., 1953; University of Arkansas, J.D. (with high honors), 1960 — Admitted to Bar, 1960, Arkansas; U.S. District Court, Eastern and Western Districts of Arkansas; U.S. Court of Appeals, Eighth Circuit — Member Arkansas and Washington County Bar Associations; Arkansas Association of Defense Counsel; Fellow, American College of Trial Lawyers — Lecturer in Law (Insurance), 1961-1980 — Practice Areas: General Civil Practice; Insurance Defense; Coverage Issues; Medical Negligence — E-mail: sdavis@davis-firm.com

Constance G. Clark — 1955 — University of Arkansas, B.A. (with honors), 1976; J.D. (with honors), 1979 — Admitted to Bar, 1979, Arkansas; U.S. District Court, Eastern and Western Districts of Arkansas; U.S. Court of Appeals, Eighth Circuit; U.S. Supreme Court — Member Arkansas and Washington County Bar Associations — Practice Areas: Business Law; Commercial Law; General Civil Practice; Workers' Compensation — E-mail: cclark@davis-firm.com

William Jackson Butt, II — 1950 — University of Virginia, B.A., 1972; The George Washington University, J.D. (with honors), 1975; LL.M. Taxation, 1979 — Admitted to Bar, 1975, Virginia; 1981, Arkansas; U.S. District Court, Eastern District of Arkansas; U.S. Court of Appeals, Eighth Circuit; U.S. Supreme Court — Member Arkansas and Washington County Bar Associations — Practice Areas: Business Law; Commercial Litigation; Trust and Estate Litigation — E-mail: jbutt@davis-firm.com

Kelly P. Carithers — 1955 — University of Arkansas, B.A., 1977; J.D., 1980 — Admitted to Bar, 1980, Arkansas; U.S. District Court, Eastern and Western Districts of Arkansas; U.S. Court of Appeals, Eighth Circuit — Member Arkansas and Washington County Bar Associations; Arkansas Association of Defense Counsel — Adjunct Professor, University of Arkansas School of Law, 2006-Present — Practice Areas: Medical Negligence; Employment Law; Professional Negligence; Professional Liability — E-mail: kcarithers@davis-firm.com

Don A. Taylor — 1964 — Hendrix College, B.A., 1986; University of Arkansas at Little Rock, J.D. (with high honors), 1989 — Admitted to Bar, 1989, Arkansas; U.S. District Court, Eastern and Western Districts of Arkansas; U.S. Court of Appeals, Eighth Circuit — Member Arkansas and Washington County Bar Associations; Arkansas Association of Defense Counsel; Defense Research Institute; International Association of Defense Counsel; Fellow, American College of Trial Lawyers — Practice Areas: General Civil Practice; Insurance Defense; Insurance Coverage; Product Liability; Medical Negligence — E-mail: dtaylor@davis-firm.com

Casey Dorman Lawson — 1978 — University of Arkansas, B.S.B.A. (summa cum laude), 2000; J.D. (magna cum laude), 2003 — Admitted to Bar, 2003, Arkansas; U.S. District Court, Eastern and Western Districts of Arkansas — Member Arkansas and Washington County Bar Associations — Practice Areas: Business Law; Estate Planning; Administrative Law — E-mail: clawson@davis-firm.com

Joshua D. McFadden — 1978 — John Brown University, B.S. (magna cum laude), 2001; M.B.A., 2004; University of Arkansas, J.D. (magna cum laude), 2007 — Associate Editor, Arkansas Law Review, 2006-2007 — Admitted to Bar, 2007, Arkansas; 2013, Oklahoma; 2007, U.S. District Court, Eastern and Western Districts of Arkansas — Member Arkansas (Committees: House Advisory; Long Range Planning; Judicial and Law Reform) and Washington County Bar Associations; Delegate, Arkansas Bar Association House of Delegates; Arkansas Association of Defense Counsel — Practice Areas: General Civil Practice; Commercial Litigation; Insurance Defense; Collections; Creditor Rights; Bankruptcy; Real Estate — E-mail: jmcfadden@davis-firm.com

Colin M. Johnson — 1980 — University of Arkansas, B.S., 2002; J.D. (cum laude), 2007 — Admitted to Bar, 2007, Arkansas; U.S. District Court, Eastern and Western Districts of Arkansas; U.S. Court of Appeals, Eighth Circuit — Member Arkansas and Washington County Bar Associations; Arkansas Association of Defense Counsel; Defense Research Institute — Practice Areas: Civil Defense; Medical Negligence; Dental Malpractice; Insurance Defense; Insurance Coverage — E-mail: cjohnson@davis-firm.com

Associates

J. David Dixon — 1972 — University of Arkansas, B.S./B.A., 1994; Oklahoma State University, M.S.H.A., 1997; University of Arkansas, J.D. (cum laude), 2005 — Admitted to Bar, 2005, Arkansas; U.S. District Court, Eastern and Western Districts of Arkansas — Member Arkansas and Washington County Bar Associations; Society for Human Resource Management — Practice Areas: General Civil Practice; Employment Law; Construction Law; Insurance Defense; Workers' Compensation — E-mail: ddixon@davis-firm.com

William F. Clark — 1985 — Vanderbilt University, B.A. (cum laude), 2007; University of Arkansas, J.D. (magna cum laude), 2010 — Admitted to Bar, 2010, Arkansas; U.S. District Court, Eastern and Western Districts of Arkansas — Member Arkansas and Washington County Bar Associations; Delegate, Arkansas Bar Association House of Delegates; Arkansas Association of Defense Counsel — Practice Areas: General Civil Litigation; Insurance Defense; Creditor Rights; Bankruptcy; Commercial Litigation — E-mail: wclark@davis-firm.com

K. Drew Devenport — Rockhurst University, B.A., 2009; University of Arkansas, J.D., 2012 — Admitted to Bar, 2012, Arkansas — Member Arkansas and Washington County Bar Associations; American Immigration Lawyers Association — Executive Office for Immigration Review (EOIR), 2013 — Practice Areas: Immigration Law — Resident Springdale, AR Office — E-mail: ddevenport@davis-firm.com

Andrew D. Curtis — 1987 — Ouachita Baptist University, B.A. (summa cum laude), 2009; University of Arkansas, M.A., 2011; J.D. (cum laude), 2013 — Admitted to Bar, 2014, Arkansas; U.S. District Court, Eastern and Western Districts of Arkansas — Member Arkansas and Washington County Bar Associations — Practice Areas: General Civil Litigation; Insurance Defense; Commercial Litigation — E-mail: acurtis@davis-firm.com

---

The following firms also service this area.

Daily & Woods, P.L.L.C.
58 South Sixth
Fort Smith, Arkansas 72901
   Telephone: 479-782-0361
   Fax: 479-782-6160
Mailing Address: P.O. Box 1446, Fort Smith, AR 72902

Insurance Defense

SEE COMPLETE LISTING UNDER FORT SMITH, ARKANSAS (58 MILES)

Munson, Rowlett, Moore & Boone, P.A.
Regions Center
400 West Capitol, Suite 1900
Little Rock, Arkansas 72201
   Telephone: 501-374-6535
   Fax: 501-374-5906

Arson, Asbestos, Aviation, Bad Faith, Casualty, Catastrophic Injury, Civil Appeals, Civil Litigation, Class Actions, Commercial Litigation, Complex Litigation, Construction Litigation, Employment Law, Environmental Litigation, Fraud, Hospital Malpractice, Insurance Coverage, Insurance Defense, Mediation, Medical Devices, Medical Malpractice, Negligence, Personal Injury, Premises Liability, Product Liability, Professional Malpractice, School Law, Self-Insured Defense, Subrogation, Toxic Torts, Transportation, Trucking Litigation, Workers' Compensation, Wrongful Death

SEE COMPLETE LISTING UNDER LITTLE ROCK, ARKANSAS (203 MILES)

Smith, Cohen & Horan, PLC
1206 Garrison Avenue
Fort Smith, Arkansas 72901
   Telephone: 479-782-1001
   Fax: 479-782-1279
Mailing Address: P.O. Box 10205, Fort Smith, AR 72917-0205

Insurance Defense, Automobile Liability, Transportation, Product Liability, Subrogation, Employment Law, Environmental Law, General and Product Liability

SEE COMPLETE LISTING UNDER FORT SMITH, ARKANSAS (58 MILES)

FORT SMITH   ARKANSAS

Waddell, Cole & Jones, PLLC
310 East Street, Suite A
Jonesboro, Arkansas 72401
  Telephone: 870-931-1700
  Fax: 870-931-1800, 870-931-1810
Mailing Address: P.O. Box 1700, Jonesboro, AR 72403

Insurance Defense, Trial and Appellate Practice, Property and Casualty, General Liability, Toxic Torts, Errors and Omissions, Product Liability, Construction Law, Surety, Life and Health, Medical Malpractice, Arson, Fraud, Transportation, Aviation, Agriculture, Workers' Compensation, Employment Discrimination

SEE COMPLETE LISTING UNDER JONESBORO, ARKANSAS (289 MILES)

FORDYCE † 4,300 Dallas Co.

Refer To
McMillan, McCorkle, Curry & Bennington, LLP
929 Main Street
Arkadelphia, Arkansas 71923
  Telephone: 870-246-2468
  Fax: 870-246-3851
Mailing Address: P.O. Box 607, Arkadelphia, AR 71923

Insurance Defense, Workers' Compensation, Product Liability, Medical Malpractice, Coverage Issues

SEE COMPLETE LISTING UNDER ARKADELPHIA, ARKANSAS (51 MILES)

FORREST CITY † 15,371 St. Francis Co.

Philip Hicky, II, Ltd.
2216 North Washington Street
Forrest City, Arkansas 72335
  Telephone: 870-633-4611
  Fax: 870-633-6848

Insurance Defense, Carrier Defense, Automobile, Aviation, General Liability, Product Liability, Workers' Compensation, Surety, Life Insurance, Accident and Health, Medical Malpractice

Insurance Clients

Aetna Life and Casualty Company	American Home Assurance Company
Avemco Insurance Company	Farm Bureau Mutual Insurance Company of Arkansas, Inc.
Empire Fire and Marine Insurance Company	Federated Insurance Company
Federated Guaranty Life Insurance Company	Firemen's Insurance Company of Newark, New Jersey
Gulf Life Insurance Company	Home Insurance Company
Hartford Accident and Indemnity Company	Homestead Insurance Company
Horace Mann Insurance Group	Indiana Lumbermens Mutual Insurance Company
Integon Life Insurance Corporation	John Hancock Life Insurance Company
Interstate Insurance Group	Midwest Mutual Insurance Company
Life Insurance Company of Georgia	Omaha Property and Casualty Insurance Company
National Aviation Underwriters	Security Insurance Company of Hartford
Old Republic Life Insurance Company	Southern Farm Bureau Life Insurance Company
SECURA Insurance Companies	Transport Life Insurance Company
Southern Farm Bureau Casualty Insurance Company	United Insurance Company of America
Time Insurance Company n.k.a. Assurant Health	United States Fidelity and Guaranty Company
United Family Life Insurance Company	Western Fire Insurance Company
United States Aviation Underwriters, Inc.	Zurich American Insurance Group
United States Fire Insurance Company	

Non-Insurance Clients

American Aviation Adjusters	American Claim Service, Inc.
Aviation Adjustment Bureau	Global Aviation Insurance Services
Loss Management Services, Inc.	

Philip Hicky, II, Ltd., Forrest City, AR   (Continued)
President

Philip Hicky, II — 1942 — Sewanee, The University of the South; University of Arkansas, B.A., 1964; University of Arkansas School of Law, J.D., 1966 — Admitted to Bar, 1966, Arkansas; U.S. District Court, District of Arkansas; U.S. Court of Appeals, Eighth Circuit; U.S. Supreme Court; U.S. Claims Court — Member American, Arkansas and St. Francis County Bar Associations; Arkansas Supreme Court, Committee of Rules of Civil Procedure; Defense Research Institute; Arkansas Association of Defense Counsel — E-mail: philhicky@philiphickyltd.com

The following firms also service this area.

McNabb, Bragorgos & Burgess, PLLC
81 Monroe Avenue, Sixth Floor
Memphis, Tennessee 38103-5402
  Telephone: 901-624-0640
  Toll Free: 888-251-8000
  Fax: 901-624-0650

Insurance Defense, Trucking Litigation, Fire, Casualty, Malpractice, Fraud, Litigation, Marine, Product Liability, Workers' Compensation, Automobile, Mass Tort, Personal Injury, Commercial Law, Premises Liability, Subrogation, Construction Law, Nursing Home Defense

SEE COMPLETE LISTING UNDER MEMPHIS, TENNESSEE (46 MILES)

Snellgrove, Langley, Culpepper, Williams & Mullally
111 East Huntington, Second Floor
Jonesboro, Arkansas 72401
  Telephone: 870-932-8357
  Fax: 870-932-5488
Mailing Address: P.O. Box 1346, Jonesboro, AR 72403

Insurance Defense, Personal Injury, Commercial Law, Workers' Compensation, Product Liability, Real Estate, Corporate Law, Banking Law

SEE COMPLETE LISTING UNDER JONESBORO, ARKANSAS (63 MILES)

Waddell, Cole & Jones, PLLC
310 East Street, Suite A
Jonesboro, Arkansas 72401
  Telephone: 870-931-1700
  Fax: 870-931-1800, 870-931-1810
Mailing Address: P.O. Box 1700, Jonesboro, AR 72403

Insurance Defense, Trial and Appellate Practice, Property and Casualty, General Liability, Toxic Torts, Errors and Omissions, Product Liability, Construction Law, Surety, Life and Health, Medical Malpractice, Arson, Fraud, Transportation, Aviation, Agriculture, Workers' Compensation, Employment Discrimination

SEE COMPLETE LISTING UNDER JONESBORO, ARKANSAS (63 MILES)

FORT SMITH † 86,209 Sebastian Co.

Daily & Woods, P.L.L.C.
58 South Sixth
Fort Smith, Arkansas 72901
  Telephone: 479-782-0361
  Fax: 479-782-6160
  E-Mail: dcarson@dailywoods.com

Established: 1912

Insurance Defense

Insurance Clients

America First Insurance	American International Adjustment Company
American International Group, Inc.	Crockett Adjustment
American States Insurance Company	The Hartford Insurance Group
International Aviation Underwriters	John Hancock Property and Casualty Insurance Company

ARKANSAS

Daily & Woods, P.L.L.C., Fort Smith, AR (Continued)

Kemper Insurance Companies
Metropolitan Life Insurance Company
Mutual of Omaha Insurance Company
Ohio Casualty Insurance Company
OneBeacon Insurance
Provident Life and Accident Insurance Company
Stonewall Insurance Company
Union Standard Insurance Company
Wausau Insurance Companies
Lumbermen's Underwriting Alliance
Metropolitan Property and Casualty Insurance Company
New York Life Insurance Company
Pharmacists Mutual Insurance Company
Security Mutual Insurance Company
United Services Automobile Association (USAA)
Zurich North America

Partners

Jerry L. Canfield — 1946 — University of Arkansas, B.A., 1968; J.D. (with highest honors), 1970 — Admitted to Bar, 1970, Arkansas; U.S. District Court, Eastern and Western Districts of Arkansas — Member American, Arkansas and Sebastian County Bar Associations

Thomas A. Daily — 1946 — Sewanee, The University of the South, B.A., 1967; University of Arkansas, J.D. (with honors), 1970 — Admitted to Bar, 1970, Arkansas; U.S. District Court, Eastern and Western Districts of Arkansas — Member American, Arkansas and Sebastian County Bar Associations

Wyman R. Wade, Jr. — 1946 — Florida State University, B.A., 1969; University of Arkansas, M.A., 1975; J.D. (with honors), 1979 — Admitted to Bar, 1979, Arkansas; U.S. District Court, Eastern and Western Districts of Arkansas — Member American, Arkansas and Sebastian County (President, 1993-1994) Bar Associations

Douglas M. Carson — 1955 — University of Arkansas, B.A., 1979; J.D., 1982 — Admitted to Bar, 1983, Arkansas; U.S. District Court, Eastern and Western Districts of Arkansas — Member American Bar Association (Tort and Insurance Practice Section); Arkansas and Sebastian County Bar Associations; Defense Research Institute; Arkansas Association of Defense Counsel

Robert Briggs — 1966 — Providence College, B.A.; University of Arkansas, J.D., 2001 — Admitted to Bar, 2001, Arkansas; 2002, Oklahoma; U.S. District Court, Eastern and Western Districts of Arkansas — Member Arkansas, Oklahoma and Sebastian County Bar Associations

C. Michael Daily — 1977 — Hendrix College, B.A., 1999; University of Arkansas at Little Rock, M.B.A., 2002; University of Arkansas at Little Rock School of Law, B.A., 2005 — Admitted to Bar, 2005, Arkansas; Oklahoma; U.S. District Court, Eastern and Western Districts of Arkansas — Member American, Arkansas, and Sebastian County Bar Associations — Arkansas Certified Mediator, Civil and Probate

L. Matthew Davis — 1973 — University of Arkansas at Little Rock, B.A., 1998; Arkansas Tech University, M.A., 2002; Oklahoma City University School of Law, J.D., 2006 — Admitted to Bar, 2007, Arkansas; U.S. District Court, Eastern and Western Districts of Arkansas

Of Counsel

James E. West — 1928 — University of Arkansas, J.D., 1952 — Admitted to Bar, 1952, Arkansas — Member American, Arkansas (President, 1973-1974) and Sebastian County (President, 1961) Bar Associations

Jones, Jackson & Moll, PLC

401 North Seventh Street
Fort Smith, Arkansas 72901
 Telephone: 479-782-7203
 Fax: 479-782-9460
 E-Mail: rjackson@jjmlaw.com
 www.jjmlaw.com

Established: 1970

Insurance Defense, Trial and Appellate Practice, Casualty, Compensation, Fire, Product Liability, Construction Litigation, Professional Liability, Automobile, Commercial Litigation

Insurance Clients

American Family Insurance Company
Catlin Specialty Insurance Company
Great American Insurance Group
Automobile Club Inter-Insurance Exchange
CNA Insurance Companies
Colony Insurance Company
Nautilus Insurance Company

FORT SMITH

Jones, Jackson & Moll, PLC, Fort Smith, AR (Continued)

Shelter Insurance Companies
Utah Home Fire Insurance Company

Non-Insurance Clients

Fort Chaffee Redevelopment Authority
Sutherland Lumber Company
Ryder Truck Rental, Inc.
Sparks Health System
Wyndham Vacation Resorts, Inc.

Firm Members

Robert L. Jones, Jr. — (1922-2004)

Randolph C. Jackson — 1952 — University of Arkansas, B.A., 1974; J.D., 1977 — Admitted to Bar, 1977, Arkansas; 2005, Oklahoma — Member American (Litigation, Tort and Insurance Practice Law Sections), Arkansas and Sebastian County (President, 2001-2002) Bar Associations; International Association of Defense Counsel; Defense Research Institute; Arkansas Association of Defense Counsel; American Board of Trial Advocates — E-mail: rjackson@jjmlaw.com

Michael T. Newman — 1964 — University of Arkansas, B.A., 1987; M.A., 1990; University of Missouri, J.D., 1998 — Admitted to Bar, 1999, Missouri; 2001, Arkansas; 2003, Oklahoma — Member Arkansas (Uniform Laws Committe), Oklahoma and Sebastian County Bar Associations; The Missouri Bar; Defense Research Institute — Presentations: "Civil Procedure Update," Sebastian County and Arkansas Bar Associations 2012; "Closing Arguments/Trial Ethics," NBI 2013 — Practice Areas: Civil Litigation; Insurance Defense; Appeals — E-mail: mnewman@jjmlaw.com

Smith, Cohen & Horan, PLC

1206 Garrison Avenue
Fort Smith, Arkansas 72901
 Telephone: 479-782-1001
 Fax: 479-782-1279
 www.schfirm.com

Established: 1930

Insurance Defense, Automobile Liability, Transportation, Product Liability, Subrogation, Employment Law, Environmental Law, General and Product Liability

Insurance Clients

Berkshire Hathaway Homestate Companies
Zurich American Insurance Group
Mid-Continent Group
XL Select Professional

Firm Members

Don A. Smith — 1936 — The University of Oklahoma, B.B.A., 1958; LL.B., 1960 — Admitted to Bar, 1960, Oklahoma; 1962, Arkansas; 1960, U.S. District Court, Eastern District of Oklahoma; U.S. Supreme Court; 1962, U.S. District Court, Western District of Arkansas; U.S. Court of Appeals, Eighth, Ninth and Tenth Circuits — Member Oklahoma, Arkansas and Sebastian County Bar Associations; Transportation Lawyers Association

Robert Y. Cohen II — 1950 — Hendrix College, B.A., 1972; University of Arkansas, J.D., 1975; Southern Methodist University, LL.M., 1976 — Admitted to Bar, 1975, Arkansas; 1977, U.S. District Court, Eastern and Western Districts of Arkansas; 1980, U.S. Court of Appeals, Eighth Circuit — Member American, Arkansas and Sebastian County Bar Associations

Matthew Horan — 1950 — University of Arkansas, B.A., 1973; Harvard University, J.D., 1976 — Admitted to Bar, 1976, Arkansas; U.S. District Court, Eastern District of Oklahoma; U.S. District Court, Western District of Arkansas; U.S. Court of Appeals, Fifth, Seventh, Eighth and Tenth Circuits — Member Arkansas and Sebastian County Bar Associations — State Board of Law Examiners (1995-2001)

Stephen C. Smith — 1976 — Villanova University, B.A., 1999; Vermont Law School, J.D., 2002; M.S.E.L., 2002 — Admitted to Bar, 2003, Arkansas; U.S. District Court, Eastern and Western Districts of Arkansas — Member Arkansas (House of Delegates) and Sebastian County Bar Associations

Eric L. Pendergrass — 1981 — University of Arkansas, B.S.A., 2003; J.D., 2006; LL.M., 2007 — Admitted to Bar, 2006, Arkansas; 2007, Oklahoma; U.S. District Court, Eastern and Western Districts of Arkansas — Member Arkansas (Agricultural Law Section) and Sebastian County Bar Associations; American Agricultural Lawyers Association

HELENA
ARKANSAS

The following firms also service this area.

Davis, Clark, Butt, Carithers & Taylor, PLC
19 East Mountain Street
Fayetteville, Arkansas 72701
  Telephone: 479-521-7600
  Fax: 479-521-7661
Mailing Address: P.O. Box 1688, Fayetteville, AR 72702-1688

Insurance Defense, Automobile, General Liability, Workers' Compensation, Product Liability, Legal Malpractice, Medical Malpractice, Environmental Law, Employer Liability, Life Insurance, Surety, Construction Law, Immigration Law

SEE COMPLETE LISTING UNDER FAYETTEVILLE, ARKANSAS (58 MILES)

Munson, Rowlett, Moore & Boone, P.A.
Regions Center
400 West Capitol, Suite 1900
Little Rock, Arkansas 72201
  Telephone: 501-374-6535
  Fax: 501-374-5906

Arson, Asbestos, Aviation, Bad Faith, Casualty, Catastrophic Injury, Civil Appeals, Civil Litigation, Class Actions, Commercial Litigation, Complex Litigation, Construction Litigation, Employment Law, Environmental Litigation, Fraud, Hospital Malpractice, Insurance Coverage, Insurance Defense, Mediation, Medical Devices, Medical Malpractice, Negligence, Personal Injury, Premises Liability, Product Liability, Professional Malpractice, School Law, Self-Insured Defense, Subrogation, Toxic Torts, Transportation, Trucking Litigation, Workers' Compensation, Wrongful Death

SEE COMPLETE LISTING UNDER LITTLE ROCK, ARKANSAS (155 MILES)

Waddell, Cole & Jones, PLLC
310 East Street, Suite A
Jonesboro, Arkansas 72401
  Telephone: 870-931-1700
  Fax: 870-931-1800, 870-931-1810
Mailing Address: P.O. Box 1700, Jonesboro, AR 72403

Insurance Defense, Trial and Appellate Practice, Property and Casualty, General Liability, Toxic Torts, Errors and Omissions, Product Liability, Construction Law, Surety, Life and Health, Medical Malpractice, Arson, Fraud, Transportation, Aviation, Agriculture, Workers' Compensation, Employment Discrimination

SEE COMPLETE LISTING UNDER JONESBORO, ARKANSAS (257 MILES)

GREENWOOD † 8,952 Sebastian Co.
Refer To

Daily & Woods, P.L.L.C.
58 South Sixth
Fort Smith, Arkansas 72901
  Telephone: 479-782-0361
  Fax: 479-782-6160
Mailing Address: P.O. Box 1446, Fort Smith, AR 72902

Insurance Defense

SEE COMPLETE LISTING UNDER FORT SMITH, ARKANSAS (18 MILES)

HARRISBURG † 2,288 Poinsett Co.
Refer To

Snellgrove, Langley, Culpepper, Williams & Mullally
111 East Huntington, Second Floor
Jonesboro, Arkansas 72401
  Telephone: 870-932-8357
  Fax: 870-932-5488
Mailing Address: P.O. Box 1346, Jonesboro, AR 72403

Insurance Defense, Personal Injury, Commercial Law, Workers' Compensation, Product Liability, Real Estate, Corporate Law, Banking Law

SEE COMPLETE LISTING UNDER JONESBORO, ARKANSAS (21 MILES)

Refer To

Waddell, Cole & Jones, PLLC
310 East Street, Suite A
Jonesboro, Arkansas 72401
  Telephone: 870-931-1700
  Fax: 870-931-1800, 870-931-1810
Mailing Address: P.O. Box 1700, Jonesboro, AR 72403

Insurance Defense, Trial and Appellate Practice, Property and Casualty, General Liability, Toxic Torts, Errors and Omissions, Product Liability, Construction Law, Surety, Life and Health, Medical Malpractice, Arson, Fraud, Transportation, Aviation, Agriculture, Workers' Compensation, Employment Discrimination

SEE COMPLETE LISTING UNDER JONESBORO, ARKANSAS (21 MILES)

HARRISON † 12,943 Boone Co.
Refer To

Davis, Clark, Butt, Carithers & Taylor, PLC
19 East Mountain Street
Fayetteville, Arkansas 72701
  Telephone: 479-521-7600
  Fax: 479-521-7661
Mailing Address: P.O. Box 1688, Fayetteville, AR 72702-1688

Insurance Defense, Automobile, General Liability, Workers' Compensation, Product Liability, Legal Malpractice, Medical Malpractice, Environmental Law, Employer Liability, Life Insurance, Surety, Construction Law, Immigration Law

SEE COMPLETE LISTING UNDER FAYETTEVILLE, ARKANSAS (77 MILES)

Refer To

Munson, Rowlett, Moore & Boone, P.A.
Regions Center
400 West Capitol, Suite 1900
Little Rock, Arkansas 72201
  Telephone: 501-374-6535
  Fax: 501-374-5906

Arson, Asbestos, Aviation, Bad Faith, Casualty, Catastrophic Injury, Civil Appeals, Civil Litigation, Class Actions, Commercial Litigation, Complex Litigation, Construction Litigation, Employment Law, Environmental Litigation, Fraud, Hospital Malpractice, Insurance Coverage, Insurance Defense, Mediation, Medical Devices, Medical Malpractice, Negligence, Personal Injury, Premises Liability, Product Liability, Professional Malpractice, School Law, Self-Insured Defense, Subrogation, Toxic Torts, Transportation, Trucking Litigation, Workers' Compensation, Wrongful Death

SEE COMPLETE LISTING UNDER LITTLE ROCK, ARKANSAS (142 MILES)

HELENA † 6,323 Phillips Co.
Refer To

Snellgrove, Langley, Culpepper, Williams & Mullally
111 East Huntington, Second Floor
Jonesboro, Arkansas 72401
  Telephone: 870-932-8357
  Fax: 870-932-5488
Mailing Address: P.O. Box 1346, Jonesboro, AR 72403

Insurance Defense, Personal Injury, Commercial Law, Workers' Compensation, Product Liability, Real Estate, Corporate Law, Banking Law

SEE COMPLETE LISTING UNDER JONESBORO, ARKANSAS (104 MILES)

Refer To

Waddell, Cole & Jones, PLLC
310 East Street, Suite A
Jonesboro, Arkansas 72401
  Telephone: 870-931-1700
  Fax: 870-931-1800, 870-931-1810
Mailing Address: P.O. Box 1700, Jonesboro, AR 72403

Insurance Defense, Trial and Appellate Practice, Property and Casualty, General Liability, Toxic Torts, Errors and Omissions, Product Liability, Construction Law, Surety, Life and Health, Medical Malpractice, Arson, Fraud, Transportation, Aviation, Agriculture, Workers' Compensation, Employment Discrimination

SEE COMPLETE LISTING UNDER JONESBORO, ARKANSAS (104 MILES)

ARKANSAS — HOPE

HOPE † 10,095 Hempstead Co.

Refer To

Dunn, Nutter & Morgan L.L.P.
3601 Richmond Road
Texarkana, Texas 75503
  Telephone: 903-793-5651
  Fax: 903-794-5651

Insurance Defense, Casualty, Fire, Workers' Compensation, Life Insurance, Accident and Health, Medical Liability, Legal Malpractice, Professional Malpractice, Employment Law, Subrogation, Commercial Litigation, Banking

SEE COMPLETE LISTING UNDER TEXARKANA, TEXAS (35 MILES)

Refer To

McMillan, McCorkle, Curry & Bennington, LLP
929 Main Street
Arkadelphia, Arkansas 71923
  Telephone: 870-246-2468
  Fax: 870-246-3851

Mailing Address: P.O. Box 607, Arkadelphia, AR 71923

Insurance Defense, Workers' Compensation, Product Liability, Medical Malpractice, Coverage Issues

SEE COMPLETE LISTING UNDER ARKADELPHIA, ARKANSAS (46 MILES)

HOT SPRINGS † 35,193 Garland Co.

Refer To

Dunn, Nutter & Morgan L.L.P.
3601 Richmond Road
Texarkana, Texas 75503
  Telephone: 903-793-5651
  Fax: 903-794-5651

Insurance Defense, Casualty, Fire, Workers' Compensation, Life Insurance, Accident and Health, Medical Liability, Legal Malpractice, Professional Malpractice, Employment Law, Subrogation, Commercial Litigation, Banking

SEE COMPLETE LISTING UNDER TEXARKANA, TEXAS (112 MILES)

Refer To

Munson, Rowlett, Moore & Boone, P.A.
Regions Center
400 West Capitol, Suite 1900
Little Rock, Arkansas 72201
  Telephone: 501-374-6535
  Fax: 501-374-5906

Arson, Asbestos, Aviation, Bad Faith, Casualty, Catastrophic Injury, Civil Appeals, Civil Litigation, Class Actions, Commercial Litigation, Complex Litigation, Construction Litigation, Employment Law, Environmental Litigation, Fraud, Hospital Malpractice, Insurance Coverage, Insurance Defense, Mediation, Medical Devices, Medical Malpractice, Negligence, Personal Injury, Premises Liability, Product Liability, Professional Malpractice, School Law, Self-Insured Defense, Subrogation, Toxic Torts, Transportation, Trucking Litigation, Workers' Compensation, Wrongful Death

SEE COMPLETE LISTING UNDER LITTLE ROCK, ARKANSAS (59 MILES)

HOT SPRINGS NATIONAL PARK 35,750 Garland Co.

Refer To

McMillan, McCorkle, Curry & Bennington, LLP
929 Main Street
Arkadelphia, Arkansas 71923
  Telephone: 870-246-2468
  Fax: 870-246-3851

Mailing Address: P.O. Box 607, Arkadelphia, AR 71923

Insurance Defense, Workers' Compensation, Product Liability, Medical Malpractice, Coverage Issues

SEE COMPLETE LISTING UNDER ARKADELPHIA, ARKANSAS (45 MILES)

JONESBORO † 67,263 Craighead Co.

Mixon & Worsham, PLC

505 Union Street
Jonesboro, Arkansas 72401
  Telephone: 870-935-8600
  Fax: 870-935-8622
  E-Mail: dmixon@mixonlawfirm.com

Insurance Defense, Errors and Omissions, Automobile Liability, General Liability, Education law, Product Liability

Firm Profile: We have defended civil trials for insurance companies and represented individuals, corporations, and public entities in litigation and appellate practice for over three decades. We provide the kind of personalized attention to specific requirements that clients appreciate.

Insurance Clients

ACE Westchester Specialty Group
Hallmark Insurance Company
State Auto Insurance Company
The Cincinnati Insurance Companies

Non-Insurance Clients

Arkansas School Risk Management Association
Nestle USA, Inc.

Attorneys

Donn Mixon — 1949 — University of Arkansas, B.A., 1974; J.D., 1976 — Admitted to Bar, 1976, Arkansas; 1976, U.S. District Court, District of Arkansas; U.S. Court of Appeals, Eighth Circuit; 1983, U.S. Supreme Court — Member American, Arkansas and Craighead County Bar Associations; National Council of School Attorneys; Arkansas Association of Defense Counsel; Defense Research Institute — E-mail: dmixon@mixonlawfirm.com

Rebecca Worsham — 1983 — University of Arkansas, B.A., 2005; J.D., 2009 — Recipient: Joe C. Barrett Award (Top Grade, Commercial Transactions), 2009; Ranked in Top 11% of Law school class — Admitted to Bar, 2009, Arkansas; U.S. District Court, District of Arkansas; U.S. Court of Appeals, Eighth Circuit — Member American, Arkansas, and Craighead County Bar Associations — E-mail: rworsham@mixonlawfirm.com

Snellgrove, Langley, Culpepper, Williams & Mullally

111 East Huntington, Second Floor
Jonesboro, Arkansas 72401
  Telephone: 870-932-8357
  Fax: 870-932-5488
  www.jonesborolawfirm.com

Established: 1954

Insurance Defense, Personal Injury, Commercial Law, Workers' Compensation, Product Liability, Real Estate, Corporate Law, Banking Law

Firm Profile: The law firm of Snellgrove, Langley, Culpepper, Williams & Mullally has been providing legal services in Northeast Arkansas since 1954. The firm is committed to providing quality legal representation.

Insurance Clients

The Hartford Insurance Group
Pharmacists Mutual Companies
United Fire & Casualty Group
OrionAuto, Inc.
State Farm Insurance Companies

Non-Insurance Clients

Bank of Salem
Evolve Bank & Trust
Piggott State Bank
Centennial Bank
"K" Line America, Inc.
Regions Bank

Partners

Frank Snellgrove, Jr. — (1921-2008)

JONESBORO   ARKANSAS

Snellgrove, Langley, Culpepper, Williams & Mullally, Jonesboro, AR (Continued)

Stanley R. Langley — (1940-2011)

Malcolm Culpepper — 1954 — University of Arkansas, B.S.B.A., 1979; J.D., 1982 — Admitted to Bar, 1982, Arkansas — Member Arkansas and Craighead County Bar Associations — Practice Areas: Corporate Law; Banking; Commercial Law — E-mail: mculpepper@snellgrovefirm.com

Todd Williams — 1960 — Arkansas State University, B.S., 1982; University of Arkansas, J.D. (with honors), 1985 — Admitted to Bar, 1985, Arkansas — Member Arkansas and Craighead County Bar Associations — Practice Areas: Insurance Defense; Personal Injury; Workers' Compensation; Commercial Litigation; Mediation — E-mail: twilliams@snellgrovefirm.com

Michael E. Mullally — 1958 — University of Arkansas at Little Rock, B.A., 1982; J.D., 1985 — Admitted to Bar, 1985, Arkansas; 1986, Texas — Member American, Arkansas and Craighead County Bar Associations; State Bar of Texas; Arkansas Association of Defense Counsel; Defense Research Institute; International Association of Defense Counsel — Practice Areas: Personal Injury; Insurance Defense; Product Liability — E-mail: mmullally@snellgrovefirm.com

Matthew S. Modelevsky — 1977 — Arkansas State University, B.A., 2001; University of Arkansas, J.D. (with honors), 2004 — Recipient, Best Oralist Award, Fall Moot Court; Best Oralist Award, Benjamin J. Altheimer Moot Court — Admitted to Bar, 2004, Arkansas — Member Arkansas and Craighead County Bar Associations; Board of Advocates — Practice Areas: Personal Injury; Insurance Defense; Commercial Law — E-mail: matt@snellgrovefirm.com

Waddell, Cole & Jones, PLLC

310 East Street, Suite A
Jonesboro, Arkansas 72401
Telephone: 870-931-1700
Fax: 870-931-1800, 870-931-1810
www.wcjfirm.com

Insurance Defense, Trial and Appellate Practice, Property and Casualty, General Liability, Toxic Torts, Errors and Omissions, Product Liability, Construction Law, Surety, Life and Health, Medical Malpractice, Arson, Fraud, Transportation, Aviation, Agriculture, Workers' Compensation, Employment Discrimination

Insurance Clients

Acceptance Insurance Company
Aetna Insurance Company
Allstate Insurance Company
Cameron Insurance Companies
Century Insurance Group
CNA Insurance Company
Columbia Insurance Group
Direct Insurance Company
Equity Fire and Casualty Insurance Company
Fireman's Fund Insurance Company
Great American Insurance Company
Grinnell Mutual Group
Hartford Insurance Company
Horace Mann Insurance Group
Housing Authority Risk Retention Group, Inc.
Indiana Lumbermens Mutual Insurance Company
Liberty Mutual Insurance Company
Metropolitan Life Insurance Company
National General Insurance Company
Northland Insurance Company
Pacific Specialty Insurance Company
PMA Insurance Group
Progressive Insurance Group
Resolute Management, Inc.
Safeco Surety
ACE USA
Aetna Life and Casualty Company
American Western Home Insurance Company
Chubb Group of Insurance Companies
Continental Western Insurance Company
Essex Insurance Company
Federated Insurance Company
Founders Insurance Company
Grain Dealers Mutual Insurance Company
Great West Casualty Company
GuideOne Insurance
Heritage Mutual Insurance Company
Houston General Insurance Company
The Infinity Group
Lafayette Insurance Company
Medmarc Insurance Group
Mitsui Sumitomo Insurance Company
National Interstate Insurance Company
Occidental Fire & Casualty Company of North Carolina
Penn Millers Insurance Company
Pride National Insurance Company
Prudential Property and Casualty Insurance Company
The St. Paul Companies

Waddell, Cole & Jones, PLLC, Jonesboro, AR (Continued)

Southern Pioneer Property and Casualty Insurance Company
TransGuard Insurance Company of America, Inc.
United National Insurance Company
Utica National Insurance Group
Western World Insurance Company
State Auto Insurance Company
Statesman National Life Insurance Company
Travelers Insurance Companies
USAA Casualty Insurance Company
Wells Fargo Insurance Services
Westport Insurance Company
Zurich North America

Non-Insurance Clients

Chrysler Group LLC
Hytrol Conveyor Company, Inc.
O'Reilly Auto Parts
St. Bernards Health Care
DENSO Manufacturing
Nucor-Yamato Steel Company
Riceland Foods, Inc.

Firm Members

Ralph W. Waddell — 1960 — Arkansas State University, B.A., 1982; University of Arkansas, J.D. (with high honors), 1985 — Arkansas Law Review, 1984-1985 — Admitted to Bar, 1985, Arkansas; U.S. District Court, Eastern and Western Districts of Arkansas; U.S. Court of Appeals, Eighth Circuit — Member American, Arkansas and Craighead County Bar Associations — Mid-South Super Lawyer; Best Lawyers in America — Practice Areas: Commercial Law; Real Estate; Health Care; Business Organizations — E-mail: rwaddell@wcjfirm.com

Paul D. Waddell — 1962 — Arkansas State University, B.A., 1984; University of Arkansas, J.D. (with honors), 1987 — Research Editor, Law Review — Admitted to Bar, 1987, Arkansas; U.S. District Court, Eastern and Western Districts of Arkansas — Member American Bar Association; Arkansas Bar Association (House of Delegates, 2000-2001); Craighead County Bar Association (President, 2007-2008); Arkansas Association of Defense Counsel (President, 2007-2008); Defense Research Institute; International Association of Defense Counsel — Mid-South Super Lawyers (Employment Law and Medical Malpractice); Best Lawyers in America — Practice Areas: Medical Malpractice; Employment Law; Personal Injury; Insurance Defense; Catastrophic Injury — E-mail: pwaddell@wcjfirm.com

Kevin W. Cole — 1967 — Arkansas Tech University, B.A., 1990; University of Arkansas, J.D., 1993 — Phi Alpha Delta — Admitted to Bar, 1993, Arkansas; U.S. District Court, Eastern and Western Districts of Arkansas; U.S. Court of Appeals, Eighth Circuit — Member American, Arkansas and Craighead County Bar Associations; Arkansas Association of Defense Counsel; International Association of Defense Counsel; Defense Research Institute — Practice Areas: Insurance Defense; Insurance Coverage; Product Liability; Toxic Torts; Errors and Omissions; Transportation — E-mail: kcole@wcjfirm.com

Robert S. Jones — 1968 — Saint Louis University, B.S.B.A. (summa cum laude), 1990; Owen Graduate School of Management, M.B.A., 1994; Vanderbilt University, J.D., 1994; Georgetown University, LL.M., 1995 — Admitted to Bar, 1995, Arkansas — Member American, Arkansas, and Craighead County Bar Associations — Practice Areas: Estate Planning — E-mail: rjones@wcjfirm.com

Robert J. Gibson — 1967 — University of Arkansas, B.A., 1989; University of Arkansas at Little Rock, J.D., 1993 — Admitted to Bar, 1993, Arkansas; 1994, U.S. District Court, Eastern and Western Districts of Arkansas — Member American and Craighead County Bar Associations — Practice Areas: Commercial Law; Bankruptcy; Creditor Rights; Real Estate; Probate — E-mail: rgibson@wcjfirm.com

S. Shane Baker — 1975 — Arkansas State University, B.A., 1998; University of Arkansas, J.D., 2001 — Admitted to Bar, 2001, Arkansas; U.S. District Court, Eastern and Western Districts of Arkansas — Member American, Arkansas and Craighead County Bar Associations; Arkansas Association of Defense Counsel — Practice Areas: Litigation; Insurance Defense; Insurance Coverage; Trucking Law; Premises Liability — E-mail: sbaker@wcjfirm.com

Brandy L. Brown — 1976 — University of Arkansas, B.S.B.A., 1999; J.D. (cum laude), 2002; LL.M., 2003 — Admitted to Bar, 2002, Arkansas; 2003, U.S. District Court, Eastern and Western Districts of Arkansas — Member American, Arkansas and Craighead County Bar Associations; American Agricultural Law Association — Practice Areas: Agriculture; Commercial Law; Real Estate — E-mail: bbrown@wcjfirm.com

Associates

Pamela A. Haun — 1973 — Arkansas State University, B.S. (summa cum laude, with honors), 1996; University of Memphis, J.D. (magna cum laude), 2001 — Admitted to Bar, 2001, Arkansas; 2001, Tennessee; U.S. District

ARKANSAS

Waddell, Cole & Jones, PLLC, Jonesboro, AR
(Continued)

Court, Eastern and Western Districts of Arkansas — Member American, Arkansas, Tennessee and Craighead County Bar Associations — Certified Public Accountant, 1997 (Arkansas) — Practice Areas: Commercial Law; Estate Planning; Trusts; Wills; Probate; Family Law — E-mail: phaun@wcjfirm.com

W. Curt Hawkins — 1983 — Lyon College, B.A. (cum laude), 2006; St. Thomas University School of Law, J.D. (magna cum laude), 2009; New York University School of Law, LL.M. Taxation (magna cum laude), 2010 — Admitted to Bar, 2010, Arkansas; U.S. District Court, Eastern and Western Districts of Arkansas — Member American and Craighead County Bar Associations — Practice Areas: Wills; Trusts; Estate Planning; Commercial Transactions; Probate — E-mail: wchawkins@wcjfirm.com

Nathan A. Read — Lyon College, B.A./B.S. (magna cum laude), 2002; The George Washington University, M.A., 2004; Temple University, J.D., 2008 — Notes and Comments Editor, Temple International Comparative Law Journal — Admitted to Bar, 2008, Pennsylvania; 2008, New Jersey; 2012, Arkansas; U.S. District Court, District of New Jersey; U.S. District Court, Eastern District of Pennsylvania — Member American and Craighead County Bar Associations — Practice Areas: Litigation; Medical Malpractice; Employment Law; Insurance Defense; Antitrust

Justin E. Parkey — 1983 — Harding University, B.B.A. (summa cum laude), 2005; Pepperdine University School of Law, J.D., 2008 — Admitted to Bar, 2008, Arkansas — Member American and Craighead County Bar Associations — Practice Areas: Commercial Litigation; Employment Law; Medical Malpractice; Insurance Defense; Appeals — E-mail: jparkey@wcjfirm.com

Nathan C. Looney — University of Arkansas, B.A. (summa cum laude), 2009; University of Arkansas, Clinton School of Public Service, M.P.S., 2012; University of Arkansas at Little Rock, William H. Bowen School of Law, J.D., 2012 — Admitted to Bar, 2012, Arkansas — Practice Areas: Litigation; Medical Malpractice; Employment Law; Insurance Defense — E-mail: nlooney@wcjfirm.com

Samuel T. Waddell — 1988 — University of Arkansas, Fayetteville, B.S./B.A. (magna cum laude), 2011; University of Arkansas School of Law, J.D. (magna cum laude), 2014 — Editor-in-Chief, Arkansas Law Review, 2013-2014 — Admitted to Bar, 2014, Arkansas

(This firm is also listed in the Investigation and Adjustment section of this directory)

The following firms also service this area.

McNabb, Bragorgos & Burgess, PLLC
81 Monroe Avenue, Sixth Floor
Memphis, Tennessee 38103-5402
Telephone: 901-624-0640
Toll Free: 888-251-8000
Fax: 901-624-0650

Insurance Defense, Trucking Litigation, Fire, Casualty, Malpractice, Fraud, Litigation, Marine, Product Liability, Workers' Compensation, Automobile, Mass Tort, Personal Injury, Commercial Law, Premises Liability, Subrogation, Construction Law, Nursing Home Defense

SEE COMPLETE LISTING UNDER MEMPHIS, TENNESSEE (70 MILES)

Munson, Rowlett, Moore & Boone, P.A.
Regions Center
400 West Capitol, Suite 1900
Little Rock, Arkansas 72201
Telephone: 501-374-6535
Fax: 501-374-5906

Arson, Asbestos, Aviation, Bad Faith, Casualty, Catastrophic Injury, Civil Appeals, Civil Litigation, Class Actions, Commercial Litigation, Complex Litigation, Construction Litigation, Employment Law, Environmental Litigation, Fraud, Hospital Malpractice, Insurance Coverage, Insurance Defense, Mediation, Medical Devices, Medical Malpractice, Negligence, Personal Injury, Premises Liability, Product Liability, Professional Malpractice, School Law, Self-Insured Defense, Subrogation, Toxic Torts, Transportation, Trucking Litigation, Workers' Compensation, Wrongful Death

SEE COMPLETE LISTING UNDER LITTLE ROCK, ARKANSAS (138 MILES)

LEWISVILLE

Reid, Burge, Prevallet & Coleman
417 North Broadway
Blytheville, Arkansas 72315
Toll Free: 888-673-9640
Telephone: 870-763-4586
Fax: 870-763-4642
Mailing Address: P.O. Box 107, Blytheville, AR 72316-0107

Insurance Defense, Trial and Appellate Practice, Insurance Coverage, Insurance Fraud, Examinations Under Oath, General Civil Practice

SEE COMPLETE LISTING UNDER BLYTHEVILLE, ARKANSAS (55 MILES)

LEWISVILLE † 1,280 Lafayette Co.

Refer To

Dunn, Nutter & Morgan L.L.P.
3601 Richmond Road
Texarkana, Texas 75503
Telephone: 903-793-5651
Fax: 903-794-5651

Insurance Defense, Casualty, Fire, Workers' Compensation, Life Insurance, Accident and Health, Medical Liability, Legal Malpractice, Professional Malpractice, Employment Law, Subrogation, Commercial Litigation, Banking

SEE COMPLETE LISTING UNDER TEXARKANA, TEXAS (36 MILES)

LITTLE ROCK † 193,524 Pulaski Co.

Allen Law Firm, P.C.
212 Center Place, Ninth Floor
Little Rock, Arkansas 72201
Telephone: 501-374-7100
Fax: 501-374-1611
E-Mail: hwallen@allenlawfirmpc.com
www.lawyers.com/allenlawfirm

Business Litigation, Class Actions, Insurance Coverage, Insurance Defense, Appeals, Administrative Law

Insurance Clients

ACE American Insurance Company	Kansas City Life Insurance Company

H. William Allen — Washington University, J.D., 1969 — Admitted to Bar, 1969, Arkansas; Illinois (Inactive); Missouri (Inactive)

Associate

Willie S. Haley — University of Arkansas, J.D., 2009 — Admitted to Bar, 2009, Arkansas

Anderson, Murphy & Hopkins, L.L.P.
400 West Capitol Avenue, Suite 2400
Little Rock, Arkansas 72201-4851
Telephone: 501-372-1887
Fax: 501-372-7706
E-Mail: littleton@amhfirm.com
www.andersonmurphyhopkins.com

Established: 1980

Insurance Defense, Casualty, General Liability, Product Liability, Workers' Compensation, Fire, Surety, Medical Malpractice, Professional Malpractice, Nursing Home Liability

Firm Profile: Founded in 1980, Anderson, Murphy & Hopkins, L.L.P., specializes in defense of civil litigation. The firm operates on the premise that clients recognize and appreciate individualized and prompt service and attention. Members of the firm feel that its size, specialization, and use of state-of-the-art technology enable it to respond quickly and aggressively to the needs of its clients.

LITTLE ROCK   ARKANSAS

Anderson, Murphy & Hopkins, L.L.P., Little Rock, AR
(Continued)

Partners in the firm have been recognized annually in U.S. News Best Lawyers, Best Lawyers in America, and Mid-South Super Lawyers.

Insurance Clients

Allstate Insurance Company
Auto-Owners Insurance Company
Bituminous Insurance Companies
Colony Insurance Company
FirstComp Insurance Company
Harleysville Insurance Company
The Hartford Insurance Group
Liberty Mutual Insurance
MetLife Auto & Home
Pharmacists Mutual Insurance Company
St. Paul Fire and Marine Insurance Company
State Volunteer Mutual Insurance Company
XL Design Professional
American Physicians Insurance Company
CNA Insurance Companies
The Doctors Insurance
Hallmark Specialty Insurance Company
Liberty International Underwriters
The Medical Protective Companies
Nationwide Mutual Insurance Company
ProAssurance Company
Scottsdale Insurance
Specialty Risk Services
Union Standard Insurance Company
Zurich American Insurance Company

Non-Insurance Clients

Baptist Health System, Inc.
Rebsamen Insurance, Inc.
Perennial Business Services, LLC
Sisters of Mercy Health System

Firm Members

Randy P. Murphy — 1955 — University of Arkansas at Monticello, B.A. (with honors), 1978; University of Arkansas at Little Rock, J.D., 1988 — Admitted to Bar, 1988, Arkansas; 1988, U.S. District Court, Eastern and Western Districts of Arkansas; 1988, U.S. Court of Appeals, Eighth Circuit — Member American, Arkansas and Pulaski County Bar Associations; Arkansas Association of Defense Counsel; Defense Research Institute — Practice Areas: Insurance Defense; Product Liability; Premises Liability; Workers' Compensation; Personal Injury; Property and Casualty; Environmental Law — E-mail: murphy@amhfirm.com

Mariam T. Hopkins — 1963 — Henderson State University, B.S.E. (with honors), 1985; University of Arkansas at Little Rock, J.D. (with high honors), 1988 — University of Arkansas at Little Rock Law Journal — Admitted to Bar, 1988, Arkansas; 1988, U.S. District Court, Eastern and Western Districts of Arkansas; 1994, U.S. Court of Appeals, Eighth Circuit; 1995, U.S. Supreme Court — Member American, Arkansas and Pulaski County Bar Associations; Arkansas Association of Women Lawyers; Henry Woods Inn of Court; Association of the Bar of the United States Court of Appeals for the Eighth Circuit; Eagle International Associates; Arkansas Association of Defense Counsel; Defense Research Institute; International Association of Defense Counsel; American Board of Trial Advocates; Fellow, American College of Trial Lawyers — Author: "Criminal Procedure Survey," 10 University of Arkansas at Little Rock Law Journal 149, 1987-1988 — Practice Areas: Insurance Defense; Medical Malpractice; Nursing Home Liability; Professional Liability — E-mail: hopkins@amhfirm.com

Michael P. Vanderford — 1967 — Austin College; University of Arkansas, B.A., 1990; J.D., 1993 — Delta Theta Phi — Note and Comment Editor, University of Arkansas Law Review — Admitted to Bar, 1993, Arkansas; 1993, U.S. District Court, Eastern and Western Districts of Arkansas; 1994, U.S. Court of Appeals, Eighth Circuit — Member American, Arkansas and Pulaski County (Insurance and Litigation Sections) Bar Associations; Arkansas Association of Defense Counsel; Defense Research Institute — President, Board of Directors, Little Rock Children's Protection Center (2007-2013) — Practice Areas: Insurance Defense; Product Liability; Premises Liability; Construction Law — E-mail: vanderford@amhfirm.com

David A. Littleton — 1959 — The University of Texas at Arlington, B.B.A., 1988; University of Arkansas at Little Rock, J.D. (with high honors), 1996 — Associate Managing Editor, University of Arkansas at Little Rock Law Journal — Admitted to Bar, 1996, Arkansas; 1996, U.S. District Court, Eastern and Western Districts of Arkansas; 1996, U.S. Court of Appeals, Eighth Circuit; 2002, U.S. Supreme Court — Member American, Arkansas and Pulaski County Bar Associations; Henry Woods Inn of Court; Defense Research Institute; Arkansas Association of Defense Counsel; National Association of Railroad Trial Counsel — Practice Areas: Insurance Defense; Medical Malpractice; Legal Malpractice; Dental Malpractice; Railroad Law; Nursing Home Liability — E-mail: littleton@amhfirm.com

Scott D. Provencher — 1971 — University of Arkansas, B.A., 1993; J.D. (with high honors), 1996 — Note and Comment Editor, Arkansas Law Review — Admitted to Bar, 1996, Arkansas; 1998, U.S. District Court, Eastern and Western Districts of Arkansas; 1998, U.S. Court of Appeals, Eighth

Anderson, Murphy & Hopkins, L.L.P., Little Rock, AR
(Continued)

Circuit — Member American, Arkansas and Pulaski County Bar Associations; William R. Overton Inn of Court; Defense Research Institute; Arkansas Association of Defense Counsel — Practice Areas: Insurance Defense; Medical Malpractice; Pharmaceutical; Product Liability; Legal Malpractice; Personal Injury — E-mail: provencher@amhfirm.com

Julia M. Hancock — 1973 — Creighton University, B.S. (magna cum laude), 1995; University of Arkansas at Little Rock, J.D. (with high honors), 2000 — Associate Survey and Comments Editor, University of Arkansas at Little Rock Law Journal — Admitted to Bar, 2000, Arkansas; 2001, U.S. District Court, Eastern and Western Districts of Arkansas; 2001, U.S. Court of Appeals, Eighth Circuit; 2007, U.S. Supreme Court — Member American, Arkansas and Pulaski County Bar Associations; Arkansas Association of Women Lawyers; Defense Research Institute; Arkansas Association of Defense Counsel — Practice Areas: Insurance Defense; Nursing Home Liability; Professional Liability; Medical Malpractice — E-mail: hancock@amhfirm.com

Jason J. Campbell — 1975 — University of Arkansas, B.S.B.A., 1997; J.D., 2001 — Admitted to Bar, 2001, Arkansas; 2001, U.S. District Court, Eastern and Western Districts of Arkansas; 2001, U.S. Court of Appeals, Eighth Circuit — Member American, Arkansas and Pulaski County Bar Associations; Henry Woods Inn of Court; Eagle International Associates; National Retail and Restaurant Defense Association; Claims and Litigation Management Alliance; Arkansas Association of Defense Counsel; Defense Research Institute — Practice Areas: Insurance Defense; Architects and Engineers; Construction Law; Nursing Home Liability; Medical Malpractice; Commercial Law — E-mail: campbell@amhfirm.com

Mark Wankum — 1983 — University of Central Arkansas, B.A. (summa cum laude), 2005; University of Arkansas at Little Rock, J.D. (with high honors), 2008 — Admitted to Bar, 2008, Arkansas; U.S. District Court, Eastern and Western Districts of Arkansas; U.S. Court of Appeals, Eighth Circuit — Member American, Arkansas and Pulaski County Bar Associations — Practice Areas: Litigation; Appellate Advocacy; Medical Malpractice; Property and Casualty; Insurance Coverage — E-mail: wankum@amhfirm.com

Associate

Tony A. DiCarlo III — 1979 — Loyola University, B.Mus. (Dean's List, Academic and Dean's Scholarships), 2001; Loyola Law School, J.D./Graduate Diploma in Civil Law (Dean's List, Academic and Dean's Scholarships), 2004 — Admitted to Bar, 2005, Louisiana; 2006, Arkansas; 2007, U.S. District Court, Eastern and Western Districts of Arkansas — Member American, Louisiana State, Arkansas and Pulaski County Bar Associations; Arkansas Association of Defense Counsel — Practice Areas: Commercial Litigation; Medical Malpractice Defense; Insurance Defense

Of Counsel

Overton S. Anderson — 1943 — Southern Methodist University, B.B.A., 1965; J.D., 1968 — Admitted to Bar, 1968, Texas; 1973, Arkansas; 1973, U.S. District Court, Eastern and Western Districts of Arkansas; 1973, U.S. Court of Appeals, Eighth Circuit; 1977, U.S. Supreme Court — Member American (Litigation Section), Arkansas and Pulaski County Bar Associations; State Bar of Texas; William R. Overton Inn of Court; Arkansas Association of Defense Counsel; International Association of Defense Counsel; Defense Research Institute; Fellow, American College of Trial Lawyers — Associate Editor, Southwestern Law Journal — E-mail: anderson@amhfirm.com

(Revisors of the Arkansas Insurance Law Digest for this Publication)

Chisenhall, Nestrud & Julian, P.A.

400 West Capitol Avenue, Suite 2840
Little Rock, Arkansas 72201
  Telephone: 501-372-5800
  Fax: 501-372-4941
  E-Mail: chelmich@cnjlaw.com
  www.cnjlaw.com

Established: 1989

ARKANSAS — LITTLE ROCK

Chisenhall, Nestrud & Julian, P.A., Little Rock, AR (Continued)

Business Law, Casualty Insurance Law, Class Actions, Drug, Product Liability, Professional Errors and Omissions, Property, Toxic Torts, Hazardous Waste, Environmental Law, Corporate Law, Commercial Law, Civil Litigation, Workers' Compensation, Multi-Party Litigation, Device Litigation, Public Utility Law

Firm Profile: Chisenhall, Nestrud & Julian, P.A. is a Little Rock-based law firm. Our attorneys have diverse backgrounds, which allow us to offer services in numerous fields, including environmental law, public utility law, corporate and commercial transactions, and litigation.

Our level of service has been widely recognized through our full service representation of both nationally based and locally owned corporations. We have defended both insured and self insured claims, negotiated complex corporate and commercial transactions, and handled utility law matters. Our environmental practice has long been acknowledged as the leader in the state.

Our commitment to providing expert legal service isn't limited to the courtroom or the boardroom. Our attorneys have authored numerous books and articles, and are often called upon to give lectures and seminars. We have been recognized by our peers as the best in our fields.

Insurance Clients

Century Insurance Group
XL Insurance Company, Ltd.
Kemper Insurance Company

Non-Insurance Clients

Aeropres Corporation
Brinker International, Inc.
ECS Claims Services
Sandwell Engineering
Albemarle Corporation
Deltic Timber Corporation
LSB Industries

Partners

Lawrence E. Chisenhall, Jr. — 1948 — University of Arkansas, B.S.B.A., 1971; J.D., 1974 — Admitted to Bar, 1974, Arkansas; U.S. District Court, Eastern and Western Districts of Arkansas; U.S. Court of Appeals, Eighth Circuit — Member American and Pulaski County Bar Associations — E-mail: lchisenhall@cnjlaw.com

Charles R. Nestrud — 1951 — The University of Iowa, B.S.I.E., 1974; University of Arkansas, J.D., 1977 — Arkansas Law Review — Admitted to Bar, 1977, Arkansas; U.S. District Court, Eastern and Western Districts of Arkansas; U.S. Court of Appeals, Eighth Circuit; U.S. Supreme Court — Member American Bar Association (Natural Resources, Energy & Environmental Law Section); Arkansas Bar Association (Chairman, Environmental Section, 1998); Fellow, American College of Environmental Lawyers — Special Counsel, Arkansas Statewide Health Coordinating Council, 1983 — E-mail: cnestrud@cnjlaw.com

Jim L. Julian — 1954 — Arkansas State University, B.A., 1976; University of Arkansas, J.D., 1979 — Phi Delta Phi — Admitted to Bar, 1979, Arkansas; U.S. District Court, Eastern and Western Districts of Arkansas; U.S. Court of Appeals, Eighth Circuit — Member American Bar Association (Litigation, Natural Resources Law Sections); Arkansas Bar Association (President, 2010-2011; Board of Governors, 2002-2008); Pulaski County Bar Association; International Association of Defense Counsel; Arkansas Association of Defense Counsel; Fellow, American College of Trial Lawyers — Author: "Insurance Coverage for Environmental Cleanup Costs Under Comprehensive General Liability Policies," University of Arkansas at Little Rock Law Journal, Volume 19, Number 1, Fall 1996 — Outstanding Lawyer Citizen Award, Arkansas Bar Association, 2001 — E-mail: jjulian@cnjlaw.com

Mark W. Hodge — 1972 — Ouachita Baptist University, B.A. (cum laude), 1994; University of Arkansas at Little Rock, J.D. (with honors), 1997 — Admitted to Bar, 1997, Arkansas; U.S. District Court, Eastern and Western Districts of Arkansas; U.S. Court of Appeals, Eighth Circuit — Member American Bar Association (Business Law Section, Young Lawyers Division); Arkansas Bar Association (Young Lawyers Section, Chair, 2004-2005; Business Law Section) — Author: "Supreme Court Upholds Thirty-Day Moratorium on Targeted Direct Mail by Plaintiffs Lawyers in Florida Bar v. Went For It, Inc.," 19 University of Arkansas at Little Rock Law Journal 131 — E-mail: mhodge@cnjlaw.com

Associate

Malcolm N. Means — 1987 — Sewanee, The University of the South, B.A., History (magna cum laude), 2009; University of Arkansas School of Law,

Chisenhall, Nestrud & Julian, P.A., Little Rock, AR (Continued)

J.D. (magna cum laude), 2012 — Editorial Board, Arkansas Law Review — Admitted to Bar, 2012, Arkansas — Member American and Arkansas Bar Associations — "Private Pipeline, Public Use? Arkansas's Eminent Domain Jurisprudence," 64 Arkansas Law Review 809 — E-mail: mmeans@cnjlaw.com

Cross, Gunter, Witherspoon & Galchus, P.C.

500 President Clinton Avenue, Suite 200
Little Rock, Arkansas 72201
  Telephone: 501-371-9999
  Fax: 501-371-0035
  www.cgwg.com

(Springdale, AR Office: 6801 Isaac's Orchard Road, Suite 213, P.O. Box 9630 , 72762)
  (Tel: 479-443-6978)
  (Fax: 479-443-7697)

Established: 1997

Insurance Defense, Labor and Employment, Product Liability, Workers' Compensation, Construction Law, Transportation, Health Care, Corporate Law, Immigration, Business Law

Firm Profile: Cross, Gunter, Witherspoon & Galchus, P.C. (CGWG) is dedicated to employment defense and the representation of management. CGWG's team of attorneys are highly adept in handling a wide range of labor and employment defense matters, including discrimination litigation, labor law and employment defense litigation, development of constructive employee relations, employment-related immigration issues, Workers' Compensation, insurance defense, transportation law, health care law, collective bargaining, construction law, products liability, corporate and business law, benefits advice, employment contracts, and the development of company employment policies and procedures. The Firm regularly represents clients before the Equal Employment Opportunity Commission, National Labor Relations Board, Occupational Safety and Health Administration, Office of Federal Contract Compliance Program and the Wage and Hour Division of the U.S. Department of Labor. CGWG's preventive law strategies and exceptional educational programs help companies minimize legal exposure and navigate workplace challenges.

Insurance Clients

American Modern Insurance
  Group, Inc.
Chubb Group of Insurance
  Companies
EMC Insurance Companies
Hartford Insurance Company
Metropolitan Life Insurance
  Company
Prime Insurance Company
RSUI Group, Inc.
Travelers
Underwriters Safety and Claims
Zurich American Insurance Group
Bituminous Casualty Corporation
Cherokee Insurance Company
Cincinnati Financial Corporation
CNA Insurance Company
Great West Casualty Company
Liberty Mutual Group
Mid-Continent Group
New York Life Insurance
  Company
Sentry Insurance a Mutual
  Company
Wausau General Insurance
  Company

Directors

J. Bruce Cross — 1950 — University of Notre Dame, B.A., 1971; University of Arkansas, J.D., 1974 — Admitted to Bar, 1974, Arkansas — E-mail: bcross@cgwg.com

Carolyn B. Witherspoon — 1950 — University of Arkansas at Little Rock, B.A., 1974; J.D. (with honors), 1978 — Admitted to Bar, 1978, Arkansas — E-mail: cspoon@cgwg.com

Donna S. Galchus — 1946 — University of Missouri-Saint Louis, B.S. (cum laude), 1968; Washington University, M.A., 1971; University of Arkansas at Little Rock, J.D., 1980 — Admitted to Bar, 1980, Arkansas — E-mail: dgalchus@cgwg.com

M. Stephen Bingham — 1952 — University of Missouri-Columbia, B.A., 1974; University of Arkansas at Little Rock, J.D., 1983 — Admitted to Bar, 1983, Arkansas — E-mail: sbingham@cgwg.com

LITTLE ROCK ARKANSAS

Cross, Gunter, Witherspoon & Galchus, P.C., Little Rock, AR (Continued)

Associate

Cynthia W. Kolb — Miami University, B.A. Economics (with honors), 1994; Case Western Reserve University School of Law, J.D., 1997 — Admitted to Bar, 1997, Ohio; 2000, Arkansas; U.S. District Court, Eastern and Western Districts of Arkansas; U.S. District Court, Northern District of Ohio; U.S. Court of Appeals, Eighth Circuit — E-mail: ckolb@cgwg.com

Dover Dixon Horne PLLC

Metropolitan Bank Building
425 West Capitol, Suite 3700
Little Rock, Arkansas 72201
   Telephone: 501-375-9151
   Fax: 501-375-6484
www.doverdixonhorne.com

Administrative Law, Civil Litigation, Commercial Litigation, Construction Law, ERISA, Litigation, Insurance Law, Insurance Defense, Regulatory and Compliance, Tort Litigation, Workers' Compensation

Firm Profile: Dover Dixon Horne is dedicated to providing quality legal services in an efficient and cost effective manner. We represent many different sizes and types of businesses, including manufacturing, retail and service enterprises. Our services include advising clients on the organization of start-up businesses and advice on the type of entity most advantageous for the client, including corporations, partnerships or limited liability companies.

Insurance Clients

AFLAC, Inc.
Equity Insurance Group
Sentry Insurance a Mutual Company
Utica Mutual Insurance Company
Arkansas Blue Cross and Blue Shield, A Mutual Insurance Company
Southern Pioneer Life Insurance Company

Non-Insurance Clients

J.B. Hunt Transport Services, Inc.
USAble Life

Firm Members

Allan W. Horne — 1932 — Henderson State University; University of Arkansas, LL.B., 1960 — Admitted to Bar, 1960, Arkansas — Arkansas Insurance Commisioner, 1968-1970 — Practice Areas: Regulatory and Compliance; Administrative Law; ERISA; Insurance Defense; Civil Litigation; Health; Life Insurance — E-mail: ahorne@ddh-ar.com

Cyril Hollingsworth — 1942 — Rhodes College, B.A., 1964; University of Virginia, J.D., 1967 — Admitted to Bar, 1967, Arkansas — Member, Board of Directors, City of Little Rock, 1989-1992 — Practice Areas: Litigation; Construction Law; Insurance Defense — E-mail: chollingsworth@ddh-ar.com

Joseph H. Purvis — 1946 — Hendrix College, B.A., 1968; University of Arkansas, J.D., 1976 — Admitted to Bar, 1976, Arkansas — Practice Areas: Workers' Compensation; Insurance Litigation; Tort Litigation — E-mail: jpurvis@ddh-ar.com

Gary B. Rogers — 1956 — University of Central Arkansas, B.B.A., 1979; University of Arkansas at Little Rock, J.D., 1981 — Admitted to Bar, 1982, Arkansas — Member Trucking Industry Defense Association — Practice Areas: Commercial Litigation; Litigation; Insurance Defense — E-mail: grogers@ddh-ar.com

Mark H. Allison — 1957 — Ouachita Baptist University, B.A., 1979; Arkansas State University, M.A., 1982; University of Arkansas at Little Rock, J.D., 1985 — Admitted to Bar, 1985, Arkansas; 1985, U.S. District Court, Eastern and Western Districts of Arkansas; U.S. Court of Appeals, Eighth Circuit; 1992, U.S. Supreme Court — Member American and Arkansas Bar Associations — Practice Areas: Environmental Law; Insurance Defense — E-mail: mallison@ddh-ar.com

Michael G. Smith — 1955 — University of Maryland, College Park, B.A., 1977; University of Arkansas, J.D. (with honors), 1981 — Admitted to Bar, 1981, Arkansas; 1991, Texas; 1981, U.S. Court of Appeals, Eighth Circuit — Member Arkansas Bar Association — Practice Areas: Insurance Defense — E-mail: msmith@ddh-ar.com

Dover Dixon Horne PLLC, Little Rock, AR (Continued)

Thomas S. Stone — 1943 — University of Arkansas, B.A., 1965; J.D., 1967 — Admitted to Bar, 1967, Arkansas; 1967, U.S. District Court, Eastern and Western Districts of Arkansas; 1970, U.S. Court of Appeals, Eighth Circuit — Member American and Arkansas (Fellow) Bar Associations; Fellow, Arkansas Bar Foundation — Practice Areas: Product Liability; Health; Automobile; Professional Liability — E-mail: tstone@ddh-ar.com

Frye Law Firm, P.A.

4901 Fairway Avenue, Suite D
North Little Rock, Arkansas 72116
   Telephone: 501-753-9300
   Fax: 501-753-8212
   E-Mail: fryebill@hotmail.com

Established: 1989

Insurance Defense, Property, Casualty, Workers' Compensation, Coverage Issues, Opinions, Subrogation, Litigation, Personal Injury

Insurance Clients

Alternative Insurance Management Services, Inc.
AmTrust North America
Atlantic Risk Management, Inc.
CNA Insurance Company
Connecticut Specialty Insurance Company
EMC Insurance Companies
FirstComp Insurance Company
Integon National Insurance Company
Midwest Builders Casualty Mutual Company
Old Republic Insurance Company
Praetorian Insurance Company
Sagamore Insurance Company
Superior National Insurance Group
Zenith Insurance Company
American Family Insurance Company
Argonaut Insurance Company
Cincinnati Insurance Company
Companion Property and Casualty Group
Continental Western Group
Erie Insurance Group
The Hartford Insurance Group
LCTA Workers' Comp
Liberty Mutual Insurance Company
National American Insurance Company
PHICO Insurance Company
Protective Insurance Company
South Valley Claims, Inc.
Union Standard Insurance Company

Non-Insurance Clients

Able Erectors
Asplundh Tree Expert Company
Broadspire
Builder's Association
GAB Robins North America, Inc.
Insurisk Management Services
Lennox Industries, Inc.
Midwestern Insurance Alliance
Pilgrim's Pride Corporation
Risk Management Solutions
RSKCo
Trissel Graham & Toole, Inc.
APIC-WCT Risk Service
Berkley Risk Administrators Company, LLC
Custom Packaging Company, Inc.
Gallagher Bassett Services, Inc.
Kemper Claims
Midlands Claim Administrators, Inc.
Premier Control Services
RSI, Inc.
Sedgwick CMS
VeriClaim, Inc.

Partner

William C. Frye — 1958 — University of Arkansas, B.A. (cum laude), 1980; J.D., 1983 — Delta Theta Phi — Admitted to Bar, 1983, Arkansas; U.S. District Court, Eastern and Western Districts of Arkansas; U.S. Court of Appeals, Eighth Circuit — Member American, Arkansas (Workers' Compensation Section Chair) and Pulaski County Bar Associations; Arkansas Trial Lawyers Association; Defense Research Institute — Speaker, The Association of Trial Lawyers of America (1998); Speaker, Arkansas Worker's Compensation (2004); Speaker, National Business Institute (1996-2014) — U.S. Army Reserve, 1987-2000 — Practice Areas: Workers' Compensation; Insurance Litigation; Personal Injury; Subrogation — E-mail: fryebill@hotmail.com

James, Carter & Coulter, PLC

Arvest Bank Building, Suite 400
500 Broadway
Little Rock, Arkansas 72201
   Telephone: 501-372-1414
   Fax: 501-372-1659
   E-Mail: dcarter@jamescarterlaw.com
   www.jamescartercoulterlaw.com

ARKANSAS — LITTLE ROCK

James, Carter & Coulter, PLC, Little Rock, AR (Continued)

Insurance Defense, Professional Negligence, Accountant Malpractice, Product Liability, Insurance Coverage, Motor Vehicle, Accident, Employment Discrimination, Construction Law, Environmental Law, Title VII

Insurance Clients

Crum & Forster Insurance
Great American Insurance Companies
Hanover Insurance Company
Mutual Marine Office, Inc.
OneBeacon Insurance
TIG Insurance Company
TIG Insurance Group
United Auto Group, Inc.
United Services Automobile Association (USAA)
1st Auto & Casualty Insurance Company
Great American Insurance Company
North River Insurance Company
Royal & SunAlliance Insurance Company
Tudor Insurance Company
United Automobile Insurance Company
United States Fire Insurance Company

Non-Insurance Clients

American Management, Inc.
Cummins Engine Company, Inc.
Imerys Talc America, Inc.
Cavell USA, Inc.
Gallagher Bassett Services, Inc.
RiverStone Claims Management, LLC

Members

Paul J. James — 1957 — University of Arkansas, B.A., 1979; J.D., 1982 — Phi Alpha Delta — Admitted to Bar, 1983, Arkansas; U.S. District Court, Eastern and Western Districts of Arkansas; 1988, U.S. Court of Appeals, Eighth Circuit — Member American (Litigation Section), Arkansas and Pulaski County Bar Associations; William R. Overton Inn of Court (Secretary-Treasurer, 1993-1997; Counselor, 2000-; Master); American Board of Trial Advocates

Daniel R. Carter — 1953 — Kansas State University, B.A., 1975; M.R.C.P., 1977; University of Arkansas, J.D., 1980 — Phi Alpha Delta — Admitted to Bar, 1980, Arkansas; U.S. District Court, Eastern and Western Districts of Arkansas; 1982, U.S. Court of Appeals, Eighth Circuit; 1992, U.S. Supreme Court — Member American Bar Association (Litigation Section); Arkansas Bar Association (Secretary-Treasurer, 1996-Present; Executive Council, House of Delegates, Civil Procedure Committee); Pulaski County Bar Association (Secretary-Treasurer, 1984-1988; President, 1991-1992; Board of Directors, 1992-1993); William R. Overton Inn of Court (Master); Defense Research Institute; Arkansas Association of Defense Counsel

John D. Coulter — 1966 — Reed College, B.A., 1992; Boston College, J.D., 1998 — Admitted to Bar, 1998, Arkansas; U.S. District Court, Eastern and Western Districts of Arkansas; U.S. Court of Appeals, Eighth Circuit

Associate

Jeff Priebe — 1975 — University of Arkansas, B.S. (cum laude), 1998; J.D., 2001 — Admitted to Bar, 2001, Arkansas; 2010, Tennessee; 2011, Kentucky; Oklahoma; 2012, Illinois; 2013, Missouri; 2001, U.S. District Court, Eastern and Western Districts of Arkansas; U.S. Court of Appeals, Eighth Circuit; 2004, U.S. Supreme Court — Member Arkansas, Illinois State, Tennessee, Oklahoma and Pulaski County Bar Associations; Arkansas Trial Lawyers Association

(This firm is also listed in the Subrogation section of this directory)

Laser Law Firm, P.A.

101 South Spring Street, Suite 300
Little Rock, Arkansas 72201-2488
Telephone: 501-376-2981
Fax: 501-376-2417
E-Mail: partners@laserlaw.com
www.laserlaw.com

Established: 1952

Insurance Defense

Firm Profile: The Laser Law Firm, P.A., was founded by Sam Laser and two other original partners in 1952. For over the last 60 years, the firm has been principally engaged in a civil defense practice specializing in all areas of corporate and insurance defense litigation, serving virtually all 75 counties in the state of Arkansas. The Firm presently consists of 4 partners, 1 associate, 2 of counsel and 2 paralegals.

The firm's reported cases include *Farm Bureau Policy Holders v. Farm Bureau Mutual Insurance Company*, 335 Ark. 285, 984 S.W.2d 6 (1998); *National Security Fire & Casualty v. Barnes*, 65 Ark. App. 13, 984 S.W.2d 80 (1999); *Gourley v. Crossett School District*, 333 Ark. 178, 986 S.W.2d 56 (1998); *Scott-Huff Insurance Agency v. Sandusky*, 318 Ark. 613, 887 S.W.2d 516 (1994).

Insurance Clients

AIG - Chartis
Allstate Property & Casualty Insurance Company
Arkansas Insurance Adjusting Company
Automobile Club Inter-Insurance Exchange
Chartis/AIG Domestic Claims Inc.
Chartis - The Truck Insurance Group
Crawford & Company
Farm Bureau Mutual Insurance Company of Arkansas, Inc.
GEICO
Great American Insurance Company
Lancer Insurance Company
National Interstate Insurance Company
Penn Millers Insurance Company
Progressive Commercial Auto Group
Sentry Select Insurance Company
Southern Farm Bureau Casualty Insurance Company
State Farm Mutual Automobile Insurance Company
Western Heritage Insurance Company
Allstate Insurance Company
Ameriprise Auto & Home Insurance
Auto Club Family Insurance Company
Burlington Insurance Company
Chartis
Chartis Claims, Inc.
Church Mutual Insurance Company
CNA Insurance Companies
Encompass Insurance Company
Farmers Insurance Group
Gallagher Bassett Services, Inc.
General Star
Harco National Insurance Company
Lexington Insurance Company
Nationwide Mutual Insurance Company
Progressive Casualty Insurance Company
Scottsdale Insurance Company
Shelter Mutual Insurance Company
Specialty Risk Services, Inc. (SRS)
State Farm Insurance Company
Traders Insurance Company
United States Liability Insurance Group
York Insurance Services Group, Inc.

Non-Insurance Clients

Arkansas Department of Education
Terminix International Company, L.P.
Pilot Travel Centers, LLC

Partners

Dan F. Bufford — 1945 — Ouachita Baptist University, B.A., 1967; University of Arkansas School of Law, J.D., 1972 — Admitted to Bar, 1972, Arkansas — Member American, Arkansas and Pulaski County Bar Associations; National School Boards Association; Defense Research Institute; Arkansas Association of Defense Counsel — E-mail: dbufford@laserlaw.com

Kevin Staten — 1960 — University of Arkansas, B.A., 1982; University of Arkansas School of Law, J.D., 1985 — Admitted to Bar, 1985, Arkansas — Member Arkansas and Pulaski County Bar Associations; Arkansas Association of Defense Counsel; American Judicature Society — E-mail: kstaten@laserlaw.com

Brian A. Brown — 1962 — Rhodes College, B.A. (cum laude), 1984; University of Arkansas at Little Rock School of Law, J.D., 1988 — Admitted to Bar, 1988, Arkansas — Member American, Arkansas and Pulaski County Bar Associations — E-mail: bbrown@laserlaw.com

Keith M. McPherson — 1963 — Centenary College of Louisiana, B.A., 1986; University of Nebraska at Omaha, M.A., 1989; University of Arkansas at Little Rock School of Law, J.D., 1991 — Admitted to Bar, 1991, Arkansas; 1993, U.S. District Court, Eastern District of Arkansas — Member Arkansas Bar Association — E-mail: kmcpherson@laserlaw.com

Associate

Brent A. Correll — 1977 — University of Missouri, B.S., 1999; M.B.A., 2003; University of Missouri School of Law, J.D., 2003 — Admitted to Bar, 2003, Kansas; 2003, Missouri — Member Arkansas and Kansas Bar Associations; The Missouri Bar; American Inns of Court — E-mail: bcorrell@laserlaw.com

Of Counsel

Sam Laser — (1919-2010)

LITTLE ROCK   ARKANSAS

Laser Law Firm, P.A., Little Rock, AR   (Continued)

James M. Duckett — 1939 — University of Arkansas, B.S.Ch.E., 1963; University of Arkansas School of Law, J.D., 1973 — Admitted to Bar, 1973, Arkansas — Member Arkansas and Pulaski County Bar Associations — E-mail: jduckett@laserlaw.com

William Lavender — 1938 — University of Arkansas, B.S.E., 1962; University of Arkansas School of Law, J.D., 1971 — Admitted to Bar, 1971, Arkansas; 1987, Texas; U.S. District Court, Eastern District of Texas; U.S. District Court, Eastern and Western Districts of Arkansas; U.S. Court of Appeals, Fifth and Eighth Circuits; U.S. Supreme Court; U.S. Claims Court — Member American and Arkansas Bar Associations; State Bar of Texas

Matthews, Sanders & Sayes

825 West Third Street
Little Rock, Arkansas 72201
  Telephone: 501-378-0717
  Fax: 501-375-2924
  E-Mail: news@msslawfirm.com

Established: 1984

Motor Vehicle, Workers' Compensation, Product Liability, Civil Trial Practice, State and Federal Courts, Insurance Law, Commercial Litigation, Personal Injury

Insurance Clients

Association of Arkansas Counties	Canal Insurance Company
Columbia Insurance Group	Equity Insurance Company
Progressive Insurance	Shelter Insurance Companies
State Auto Insurance Company	State Farm Insurance Companies

Partners

Gail O. Matthews — 1937 — University of Arkansas, B.S.B.A., 1959; J.D., 1960 — Admitted to Bar, 1960, Arkansas — Member American, Arkansas and Pulaski County Bar Associations; Arkansas Trial Lawyers Association; Defense Counsel Bar of Arkansas; American Board of Trial Advocates; Defense Research Institute — Practice Areas: Workers' Compensation; Civil Trial Practice; Personal Injury; Product Liability; Insurance Law — E-mail: rsanders@msslawfirm.com

Roy Gene Sanders — 1950 — University of Arkansas, B.S.B.A., 1972; J.D., 1975 — Admitted to Bar, 1975, Arkansas — Member American and Arkansas Bar Associations; Pulaski County Criminal Defense Lawyers Association; Association of Trial Lawyers of America; American Board of Trial Advocates — Practice Areas: Civil Trial Practice; Personal Injury; Product Liability; Insurance Law — E-mail: rsanders@msslawfirm.com

James Melton Sayes — 1951 — Olivet Nazarene College, B.A., 1973; University of Arkansas, J.D., 1977 — Admitted to Bar, 1977, Arkansas — Member American, Arkansas and Pulaski County Bar Associations; Arkansas Trial Lawyers Association; Defense Counsel Bar of Arkansas; Defense Research Institute; Association of Trial Lawyers of America; American Board of Trial Advocates — Practice Areas: Civil Trial Practice; Commercial Litigation; Personal Injury; Product Liability; Insurance Law — E-mail: msayes@msslawfirm.com

Associates

Doralee Idleman Chandler — 1973 — University of Central Arkansas, B.S., 1994; University of Arkansas, J.D., 1998 — Phi Delta Phi (President, 1997-1998) — Admitted to Bar, 1998, Arkansas — Member Arkansas and Pulaski County Bar Associations — Practice Areas: Insurance Law; Civil Trial Practice; Personal Injury; Insurance Defense — E-mail: dchandler@msslawfirm.com

William R. Sanders — 1983 — University of Arkansas, Fayetteville, B.B.A. (cum laude), 2005; University of Arkansas, J.D. (cum laude), 2008 — Admitted to Bar, 2008, Arkansas — Member Arkansas and Pulaski County Bar Associations — Practice Areas: Insurance Litigation; Insurance Law; Insurance Defense; Personal Injury; Civil Trial Practice — E-mail: wsanders@msslawfirm.com

Munson, Rowlett, Moore & Boone, P.A.

Regions Center
400 West Capitol, Suite 1900
Little Rock, Arkansas 72201
  Telephone: 501-374-6535
  Fax: 501-374-5906
  E-Mail: administrator@mrmblaw.com
  www.mrmblaw.com

Established: 1984

Arson, Asbestos, Aviation, Bad Faith, Casualty, Catastrophic Injury, Civil Appeals, Civil Litigation, Class Actions, Commercial Litigation, Complex Litigation, Construction Litigation, Employment Law, Environmental Litigation, Fraud, Hospital Malpractice, Insurance Coverage, Insurance Defense, Mediation, Medical Devices, Medical Malpractice, Negligence, Personal Injury, Premises Liability, Product Liability, Professional Malpractice, School Law, Self-Insured Defense, Subrogation, Toxic Torts, Transportation, Trucking Litigation, Workers' Compensation, Wrongful Death

Firm Profile: Munson, Rowlett, Moore & Boone, P.A., was established in 1984 as a firm primarily concentrating in civil litigation. Although the firm has grown extensively, and the breadth of our practice has increased significantly, the firm's principal focus remains civil litigation. We take great pride in our record as experienced trial and appellate attorneys who strive to provide nothing but the finest in legal representation in all litigation matters. The firm has grown to become one of the largest law firms in the state of Arkansas. We provide statewide service, representing individuals and small and large businesses in a wide variety of matters.

Insurance Clients

AIG	Allstate Insurance Company
American Modern Home Insurance Company	American National Property and Casualty Company
Baldwin & Lyons, Inc.	Bituminous Insurance Companies
Farmers Insurance Group	Great West Casualty Company
Hallmark Specialty Underwriters, Inc.	Liberty Mutual Insurance Company
	Markel Insurance Company
MDOW Insurance	QBE Specialty Insurance Company
The Republic Group	St. Paul Travelers
Sedgwick Group	Shelter Insurance Companies
State Auto Insurance Company	State Farm Fire and Casualty Company
State Farm Mutual Automobile Insurance Company	Underwriters at Lloyd's, London

Non-Insurance Clients

Aurora Pump Company	Catholic Health Initiatives
Coca-Cola Enterprises Inc.	Community Health Services
DeZurik Corporation	National Park Medical Center
St. Mary's Regional Medical Center	St. Vincent Health Systems
	Scapa Waycross, Inc.
Tyson Foods, Inc.	U-Haul International, Inc.

Third Party Administrators

Affirmative Risk Management, Inc.	Cottingham & Butler Claims Services, Inc.
Jaeger + Haines	
Meadowbrook Claims Service	

Transportation Clients

Con-way Enterprise Services, Inc.	CRST International, Inc.
FedEx Freight East	Greyhound Lines, Inc.
J.B. Hunt Transport, Inc.	Old Dominion Freight Line, Inc.
Prime, Inc.	Tango Transport, LLC

Shareholders

Bruce Munson — 1948 — University of Arkansas, B.S.B.A. (with honors), 1970; J.D. (with honors), 1977 — Delta Theta Phi; Advocacy Award, International Academy of Trial Lawyers; The Best Lawyers in America, 2003-present; William R. Overton Inn of Court, Emeritus; Order of the Barristers; Mid-South Super Lawyer 2007-present; Martindale-Hubbell Peer Review Rating AV Preeminent — Arkansas Law Review, 1976-1977 — Admitted to Bar, 1978, Arkansas; U.S. District Court, Eastern and Western Districts of Arkansas; U.S. Court of Appeals, Eighth Circuit — Member Arkansas and Pulaski County Bar Associations; Fellow, Arkansas Bar Foundation; Defense Research Institute (Insurance Law and Aviation Law

Munson, Rowlett, Moore & Boone, P.A., Little Rock, AR (Continued)

Committees); American Board of Trial Advocates; Arkansas Association of Defense Counsel; International Association of Defense Counsel; Trucking Industry Defense Association — Captain/Pilot, U.S. Air Force, 1970-1975 — Practice Areas: Personal Injury; Transportation; Trucking Law; Commercial Litigation; Medical Malpractice; Product Liability; Insurance Defense; Aviation; Wrongful Death; Arson; Insurance Fraud; Mediation — E-mail: bruce.munson@mrmblaw.com

Beverly A. Rowlett — 1953 — Arkansas State University, B.A. (with high honors), 1974; University of Arkansas, J.D. (with high honors), 1977; University of Illinois, LL.M., 1980 — The Best Lawyers in America, 1999-present; Martindale-Hubbell Peer Review Rating AV Preeminent; Mid-South Super Lawyers, 2007-present including Top 50: Women Mid-South Super Lawyers, 2012, 2013 — Articles and Associate Editor, Arkansas Law Review, 1976-1977 — Admitted to Bar, 1977, Arkansas; U.S. District Court, Eastern and Western Districts of Arkansas; U.S. Court of Appeals, Eighth Circuit — Member American, Arkansas and Pulaski County Bar Associations; Fellow, Arkansas Bar Foundation; Defense Research Institute; Arkansas Association of Defense Counsel; International Association of Defense Counsel — "Survey of Tennessee Property Law," 48 Tennessee Law Review 53, 1980; "Aesthetic Regulation Under the Police Power: The New General Welfare and the Presumption of Constitutionality," 34 Vand. L. Rev. 603, 1981 — Special Associate Justice, Arkansas Supreme Court, 1995; Teaching Assistant, University of Illinois College of Law, 1977-1978; Assistant Professor of Law, University of Tennessee College of Law, 1978-1981; Board of Directors, Arkansas Law Review and Bar Association Journal, Inc., 1986-1997 — Practice Areas: Insurance Defense; Insurance Coverage; Bad Faith; Extra-Contractual Litigation; Appeals; Commercial Litigation; Complex Litigation; General Liability; Class Actions — E-mail: beverly.rowlett@mrmblaw.com

John E. Moore — 1952 — University of Central Arkansas, B.S. (with honors), 1974; University of Arkansas, J.D., 1981 — The Best Lawyers in America, 2005-present; Mid-South Super Lawyers, 2006-present including Top 50: Arkansas Super Lawyers, 2013; Martindale-Hubbell Peer Review Rating AV Preeminent — Admitted to Bar, 1982, Arkansas; U.S. District Court, Eastern and Western Districts of Arkansas; U.S. Court of Appeals, Eighth Circuit — Member Arkansas Bar Association; American College of Trial Lawyers; Defense Research Institute; Arkansas Association of Defense Counsel; International Association of Arson Investigators — Federal Bureau of Investigations (1974-1978); Lecturer, Bad Faith and other Insurance-Related Topics — Practice Areas: Insurance Defense; Bad Faith; Extra-Contractual Litigation; Arson; Insurance Fraud; Class Actions; Premises Liability; Product Liability — E-mail: john.moore@mrmblaw.com

Tim Boone — 1960 — Arkansas Tech University, B.S. (with high honors), 1982; University of Arkansas at Little Rock, William H. Bowen School of Law, J.D., 1986 — Alpha Chi; Phi Alpha Delta; The Best Lawyers in America, 2005-present; Martindale-Hubbell Peer Review Rating AV Preeminent — Admitted to Bar, 1986, Arkansas; U.S. District Court, Eastern and Western Districts of Arkansas; U.S. Court of Appeals, Eighth Circuit — Member Arkansas and Pulaski County Bar Associations; Henry Woods Inn of Court; Defense Research Institute; Arkansas Association of Defense Counsel; American Inns of Court; American Health Lawyers Association — Practice Areas: Medical Malpractice; Hospital Malpractice; Medical Devices; Product Liability; Insurance Defense — E-mail: tim.boone@mrmblaw.com

Mark S. Breeding — University of Arkansas at Little Rock, B.A., 1986; University of Arkansas at Little Rock, William H. Bowen School of Law, J.D. (with honors), 1989 — Associate Research Editor, University of Arkansas at Little Rock Law Review — Admitted to Bar, 1989, Arkansas; U.S. District Court, Eastern and Western Districts of Arkansas — Member Arkansas Bar Association; Defense Research Institute; Federation of Defense and Corporate Counsel; Arkansas Association of Defense Counsel — Deputy Prosecuting Attorney, Pulaski County, 1989-1993; The Best Lawyers in America, 2015; Martindale-Hubbell® Peer Review Rating™ AV® Preeminent — Practice Areas: Insurance Defense; Arson; Insurance Fraud; Bad Faith; Extra-Contractual Litigation; Medical Malpractice; Product Liability; Premises Liability; Personal Injury — E-mail: mark.breeding@mrmblaw.com

Richard Shane Strabala — 1974 — University of Arkansas, B.S.A., 1997; University of Arkansas at Little Rock, William H. Bowen School of Law, J.D. (with high honors), 2000 — Assistant Editor, University of Arkansas at Little Rock Law Review (1998-2000) — Admitted to Bar, 2000, Arkansas; U.S. District Court, Eastern and Western Districts of Arkansas; U.S. Court of Appeals, Eighth Circuit — Member American, Arkansas and Pulaski County Bar Associations; American Trial Lawyers Association — Martindale-Hubbell® Peer Review Rating™ AV® Preeminent — Practice Areas: Insurance Defense; Insurance Coverage; Corporate Litigation; General Defense; Product Liability; Commercial Litigation; Workers' Compensation — E-mail: shane.strabala@mrmblaw.com

Sarah E. Cullen — 1977 — Lyon College, B.A., 2000; University of Arkansas at Little Rock, William H. Bowen School of Law, J.D. (with honors), 2003 — Phi Alpha Delta; William R. Overton Inn of Court, Associate; Lyon College President's Council; Martindale-Hubbell Peer Review Rating AV Preeminent; Mid-South Super Lawyers, 2013-present; Mid-South Super Lawyers Rising Star, 2012 — University of Arkansas at Little Rock Law Review (2002-2003) — Admitted to Bar, 2003, Arkansas; U.S. District Court, Eastern and Western Districts of Arkansas; U.S. Court of Appeals, Eighth Circuit; U.S. Supreme Court — Member Arkansas and Pulaski County Bar Associations; Arkansas Association of Defense Counsel; Defense Research Institute — Mentor, University of Arkansas at Little Rock Academic Success Program; Speaker, Arkansas Association of Arson Investigators, 2007; Speaker, Lorman: Auto Insurance - UM, UIM, and Accident Litigation; Effective Depositions, 2007-2008; and Medical Records, 2010 — Practice Areas: Medical Malpractice; Arson; Insurance Fraud; Insurance Coverage; Class Actions; Medical Devices; Product Liability; Insurance Defense — E-mail: sarah.cullen@mrmblaw.com

Kara B. Mikles — 1974 — University of Arkansas at Little Rock, B.A., 2000; University of Arkansas, J.D. (with honors), 2003 — Phi Delta Phi; Board of Advocates, 2002-2003; Martindale-Hubbell Peer Review Rating BV Distinguished — Admitted to Bar, 2003, Arkansas; U.S. District Court, Eastern and Western Districts of Arkansas; U.S. Court of Appeals, Eighth Circuit — Member Arkansas and Pulaski County Bar Associations — National Moot Court Traveling Team — Practice Areas: Insurance Defense; Trucking Law; Transportation; Trucking Litigation; Construction Law; Premises Liability; Product Liability; Construction Defect — E-mail: kara.mikles@mrmblaw.com

Mary Carole Crane — Ouachita Baptist University, B.A. (with honors), 2002; The University of Mississippi School of Law, J.D. (with honors), 2005 — Mid-South Super Lawyers Rising Star (2009, 2012); Martindale-Hubbell Peer Review Rating BV Distinguished — Admitted to Bar, 2005, Arkansas; U.S. District Court, Eastern and Western Districts of Arkansas — Member American, Arkansas and Pulaski County Bar Associations; Henry Woods Inn of Court; Arkansas Association of Defense Counsel — Speaker, Arkansas School Board Association Annual CLE, 2010, 2012; Arkansas Bar Association Paralegal Committee — Practice Areas: Insurance Defense; School Law; Medical Malpractice; Civil Litigation — E-mail: mc.crane@mrmblaw.com

Senior Counsel

Elizabeth Fletcher — 1959 — University of Arkansas at Little Rock, B.A., 1986; University of Arkansas at Little Rock, William H. Bowen School of Law, J.D. (with honors), 1989 — Arkansas Bar Foundation Legal Writing Award; Phi Delta Phi (Treasurer, 1988); Martindale-Hubbell Peer Review Rating BV Distinguished — Associate Case Note Editor and Assistant Research Editor, 1988; Case Note Editor, 1989, University of Arkansas at Little Rock Law Review — Admitted to Bar, 1989, Arkansas; 1991, Texas; 2001, District of Columbia; U.S. District Court, Eastern and Western Districts of Arkansas; U.S. District Court, Eastern and Northern Districts of Texas; U.S. Court of Appeals, Fifth and Eighth Circuits — Member Arkansas Bar Association; State Bar of Texas; William R. Overton Inn of Court (Pupil, 1989-1991); Defense Research Institute — "Protecting Your Business Patrons from Criminals," Arkansas Business Law Journal, 1996; "A.R.C.P. Rule Number 11," The Arkansas Lawyer, April 1990 — Practice Areas: Complex Litigation; Professional Malpractice; Employment Law; Product Liability; Insurance Coverage; Insurance Defense; Catastrophic Injury; Premises Liability — E-mail: elizabeth.fletcher@mrmblaw.com

Jane M. Yocum — 1958 — Vanderbilt University, B.A., 1980; Louis D. Brandeis School of Law, University of Louisville, J.D., 1988 — Martindale-Hubbell Peer Review Rating BV Distinguished — Law Clerk to Hon. Chief Justice George Cracraft, Arkansas Court of Appeals, 1989-1992 — Admitted to Bar, 1989, Arkansas; U.S. District Court, Eastern and Western Districts of Arkansas; U.S. Court of Appeals, Eighth Circuit — Member Arkansas and Pulaski County Bar Associations; Defense Research Institute (Toxic Tort and Environmental Law Committees) — Member, Journal of Family Law, 1986-1987; Manuscript Editor, Journal of Family Law, 1987-1988 — Practice Areas: Asbestos Litigation; Toxic Torts; Product Liability — E-mail: jane.yocum@mrmblaw.com

Associates

Ashleigh Dale Phillips — 1982 — University of Arkansas at Little Rock, B.A. (with high honors), 2005; University of Arkansas at Little Rock, William H. Bowen School of Law, J.D. (with high honors), 2008 — Henry Woods Inn of Court, Member — Associate Research Editor and Associate Technical Notes Editor, University of Arkansas at Little Rock Law Review, 2007 — Admitted to Bar, 2008, Arkansas; U.S. District Court, Eastern and Western Districts of

LITTLE ROCK   ARKANSAS

Munson, Rowlett, Moore & Boone, P.A., Little Rock, AR
(Continued)

Arkansas; U.S. Court of Appeals, Eighth Circuit — Member American, Arkansas and Pulaski County Bar Associations; Arkansas Association of Women Lawyers; Henry Woods Inn of Court; Defense Research Institute; American Inns of Court; Arkansas Association of Defense Counsel — Practice Areas: Insurance Defense; Insurance Coverage; Civil Appeals; Commercial Litigation; Class Actions; Product Liability; Employment Law — E-mail: ashleigh.phillips@mrmblaw.com

Amy Tracy — Evangel University, B.S. (with high honors), 2007; University of Arkansas at Little Rock, William H. Bowen School of Law, J.D. (with honors), 2010 — Executive Editor, 2009-2010; Associate Research Editor, University of Arkansas at Little Rock Law Review, 2008-2009 — Admitted to Bar, 2010, Arkansas; U.S. District Court, Eastern and Western Districts of Arkansas — Member Arkansas and Pulaski County Bar Associations; Defense Research Institute; Arkansas Association of Defense Counsel — Author: "Great Google-y Moogley: The Effect and Enforcement of Click Fraud and Online Advertising," 32 UALR L. Rev. 347, 2010; "College Athletic Department and Professional League Discipline and the Legal System's Penalties and Remedies," 9 VA Sports & Entertainment L.J. 254, 2010 — Arkansas Supreme Court Certified Mediator, 2010-present — Practice Areas: Insurance Defense; Insurance Coverage; Trucking Law; Transportation; Product Liability; Premises Liability; Subrogation; Construction Law; Administrative Law; Arson; Insurance Fraud; Bad Faith; Civil Litigation — E-mail: amy.tracy@mrmblaw.com

Jacquelyn B. Harrison — University of Arkansas, B.S., 2009; University of Arkansas School of Law, J.D., 2012 — Ben J. Altheimer Moot Court Competition Chair, 2012; Board of Advocates; Davis, Clark, Butt, Carithers & Taylor, PLC, Appellate Advocacy Award, 2012; Phi Alpha Delta — Admitted to Bar, 2012, Arkansas; U.S. District Court, Eastern and Western Districts of Arkansas — Member Arkansas and Pulaski County Bar Associations; Defense Research Institute; Arkansas Association of Defense Counsel — Committee Member, Easter Seals Fashion Event — Practice Areas: Insurance Defense; Premises Liability; Personal Injury; Product Liability; Medical Malpractice — E-mail: jacquelyn.harrison@mrmblaw.com

Cody Kees — University of Arkansas, B.S. (with honors), 2009; J.D. (with honors), 2012 — Delta Theta Phi; William R. Overton Inns of Court; University of Arkansas Young Alumni Board; Board of Advocates, Client Counseling Chairperson — Admitted to Bar, 2012, Arkansas; U.S. District Court, Eastern and Western Districts of Arkansas — Member American, Arkansas and Pulaski County Bar Associations; Arkansas Trial Lawyers Association; National Counsel of School Attorneys; Defense Research Institute; Arkansas Association of Defense Counsel — Legislative Extern, Senator John Boozman, 2011; Speaker, Arkansas School Board Association: "Trademarking Your School Mascot," 2013, and "Understanding the Affordable Care Act," 2014; Arkansas Children's Hospital Committee for the Future (Executive Committee) — Practice Areas: Insurance Defense; Trucking Law; Medical Malpractice; School Law; Government Affairs; Arson; Insurance Fraud; Workers' Compensation — E-mail: cody.kees@mrmblaw.com

Emily M. Runyon — Texas Christian University, B.B.A. (with honors), 2002; University of Arkansas, J.D., 2005 — Phi Delta Phi; National Trial Competition Traveling Team; Honor Counsel — Judicial Law Clerk, Arkansas Supreme Court, 2005-2014 — Admitted to Bar, 2005, Arkansas — Member Arkansas and Pulaski Bar Associations; Arkansas Association of Women Lawyers; Arkansas Association of Defense Counsel; Defense Research Institute — Speaker, Appeals CLE (2009, 2013) — Practice Areas: Insurance Defense; Insurance Coverage; Civil Litigation; Civil Appeals — E-mail: emily.runyon@mrmblaw.com

PPGMR Law, PLLC

101 Morgan Keegan Drive, Suite A
Little Rock, Arkansas 72202
Telephone: 501-603-9000
Fax: 501-603-0556
www.ppgmrlaw.com

(El Dorado, AR Office: 100 East Church Street, 71730, P.O. Box 1718, 71731-1718)
(Tel: 870-862-5523)
(Fax: 870-862-9443)

Insurance Defense, Casualty, Fire, Life Insurance, Surety, Accident and Health

PPGMR Law, PLLC, Little Rock, AR   (Continued)
Insurance Clients

Lafayette Insurance Company
MetLife Auto & Home
Pennsylvania Lumbermens Mutual Insurance Company
Southern Farm Bureau Casualty Insurance Company
The Vision Insurance Group

Liberty Mutual Insurance Company
Nautilus Insurance Company
Sedgwick Claims Management Services, Inc.
State Auto Insurance Company
United Fire Group

Non-Insurance Clients

BHP Billiton
Goodrich Corporation
Smackover State Bank

General Motors Corporation
Medical Center of South Arkansas

Members of the Firm

Brian H. Ratcliff — 1962 — Hendrix College, B.A., 1985; University of Arkansas at Little Rock, J.D., 1988 — Admitted to Bar, 1988, Arkansas; 1988, U.S. District Court, Eastern and Western Districts of Arkansas — Member American Bar Association; Arkansas Bar Association (President-Elect, 2013-2014); Arkansas Bar Foundation (President 2008-2009); Arkansas Association of Defense Counsel (President, 2001-2002); Defense Research Institute (State Representative, 2003-2005); American Board of Trial Advocates — Resident El Dorado, AR Office — E-mail: brian@ppgmrlaw.com

Chase A. Carmichael — 1982 — Ouachita Baptist University, B.A. (cum laude, with honors), 2005; University of Arkansas, J.D., 2008 — Admitted to Bar, 2008, Arkansas — Member American and Arkansas Bar Associations — Resident El Dorado, AR Office — E-mail: chase@ppgmrlaw.com

R. Scott Morgan — 1960 — University of Arkansas, Fayetteville, B.S. Business Admin., 1982; University of Arkansas at Little Rock School of Law, J.D., 1986 — Admitted to Bar, 1986, Arkansas; U.S. District Court, Eastern and Western Districts of Arkansas; U.S. Court of Appeals, Eighth Circuit — Member American and Arkansas Bar Associations; Defense Research Institute; Arkansas Association of Defense Counsel — E-mail: scott@ppgmrlaw.com

Watts, Donovan & Tilley, P.A.

200 River Market Avenue, Suite 200
Little Rock, Arkansas 72201
Telephone: 501-372-1406
Fax: 501-372-1209
Emer/After Hrs: 501-664-4388
E-Mail: richard.watts@wdt-law.com
www.wdt-law.com

Established: 2000

Arson, Automobile, Bodily Injury, Construction Law, Disability, Insurance Defense, General Liability, Personal Liability, Property and Casualty

Firm Profile: The law firm of Watts, Donovan & Tilley is a litigation firm providing services to corporations and insurance companies in central Arkansas. The firm's tenacity in the courtroom is its defining characteristic.

We are principally a civil defense firm specializing in various areas of corporate and insurance defense litigation. Richard Watts, David Donovan and Jim Tilley have bench and jury trial experience in all types of civil defense litigation, including arson, aviation, fraud, medical malpractice, professional responsibility, civil rights, education, municipal, business and commercial torts, products liability, premises liability, chemical and occupational exposure, toxic tort, environmental litigation and general corporate litigation. The firm also provides insurance coverage analysis, declaratory judgment, and bad faith litigation services to its insurance clients.

The firm's clients include most of the major insurance companies doing business in Arkansas as well as manufacturers, health care providers, construction companies, food service corporations, governmental and educational entities, and self-insured clients. We represent property, casualty, excess and surplus lines and professional liability insurers in all aspects of insurance law, including coverage analysis, prosecution of coverage actions, defenses of bad faith litigation, monitoring underlying claims, evaluation and

ARKANSAS

Watts, Donovan & Tilley, P.A., Little Rock, AR
(Continued)

litigation of suspected fraudulent claims, and subrogation. Our expertise in defending fraud and arson litigation is well known.

Insurance Clients

Audubon Insurance Company
Crum & Forster Insurance
EMC Insurance Companies
Liberty Mutual Group
Nationwide Insurance
OMS National Insurance Company
The St. Paul Companies
State Farm Fire and Casualty Company
Sun Life Assurance Company of Canada
Unitrin, Inc.
Continental General Insurance Company
Farm Bureau Insurance Companies
MetLife Insurance Company
Northwestern Mutual Group
Progressive Insurance Companies
St. Paul Fire and Marine Insurance Company
State Farm Insurance Company
Travelers Property Casualty Corporation
UnumProvident Corporation

Non-Insurance Clients

HCC Administrators

Partners

Richard N. Watts — 1954 — University of Arkansas, B.S., 1975; J.D., 1982 — Admitted to Bar, 1982, Arkansas; 1989, Texas — Member Amercian, Arkansas and Pulaski County Bar Assocations; State Bar of Texas; American Board of Trial Advocates; American College of Trial Lawyers; Defense Research Institute — Practice Areas: Arson; Asbestos Litigation; Automobile; Aviation; Business Law; Commercial Law; Environmental Law; Insurance Defense; Personal Injury; Product Liability

David M. Donovan — 1955 — Broward Community College; University of Kentucky, B.A., 1977; University of Arkansas, J.D. (with honors), 1981 — Admitted to Bar, 1981, Arkansas; 1986, Arizona — Member American, Arkansas and Pulaski County Bar Associations; State Bar of Arizona; National Association of Dealer Counsel; Defense Research Institute; American Board of Trial Advocates; American College of Trial Lawyers — Practice Areas: Bad Faith; Business Law; Commercial Litigation; Construction Litigation; Disability; ERISA; Insurance Coverage; Insurance Defense; Medical Malpractice; Product Liability; Professional Liability; Employment Law; Trucking Law

James W. Tilley — 1955 — University of Arkansas, B.A., 1977; University of Arkansas at Little Rock School of Law, J.D., 1980 — Admitted to Bar, 1980, Arkansas — Member American, Arkansas and Pulaski County Bar Associations; American Board of Trial Advocates; Arkansas Association of Defense Counsel; Defense Research Institute — Practice Areas: Automobile; Arson; Insurance Fraud; Insurance Coverage; Premises Liability; Product Liability

Michael Harrison — University of Arkansas, B.A., 1995; University of Arkansas at Little Rock School of Law, J.D., 1998 — Admitted to Bar, 1998, Arkansas

Staci Carson — University of Arkansas at Little Rock, B.A. (summa cum laude), 1999; University of Arkansas at Little Rock School of Law, J.D. (with honors), 2003 — Admitted to Bar, 2003, Arkansas

The following firms also service this area.

McNabb, Bragorgos & Burgess, PLLC
81 Monroe Avenue, Sixth Floor
Memphis, Tennessee 38103-5402
Telephone: 901-624-0640
Toll Free: 888-251-8000
Fax: 901-624-0650

Insurance Defense, Trucking Litigation, Fire, Casualty, Malpractice, Fraud, Litigation, Marine, Product Liability, Workers' Compensation, Automobile, Mass Tort, Personal Injury, Commercial Law, Premises Liability, Subrogation, Construction Law, Nursing Home Defense

SEE COMPLETE LISTING UNDER MEMPHIS, TENNESSEE (130 MILES)

MAGNOLIA

Snellgrove, Langley, Culpepper, Williams & Mullally
111 East Huntington, Second Floor
Jonesboro, Arkansas 72401
Telephone: 870-932-8357
Fax: 870-932-5488

Mailing Address: P.O. Box 1346, Jonesboro, AR 72403

Insurance Defense, Personal Injury, Commercial Law, Workers' Compensation, Product Liability, Real Estate, Corporate Law, Banking Law

SEE COMPLETE LISTING UNDER JONESBORO, ARKANSAS (129 MILES)

Waddell, Cole & Jones, PLLC
310 East Street, Suite A
Jonesboro, Arkansas 72401
Telephone: 870-931-1700
Fax: 870-931-1800, 870-931-1810

Mailing Address: P.O. Box 1700, Jonesboro, AR 72403

Insurance Defense, Trial and Appellate Practice, Property and Casualty, General Liability, Toxic Torts, Errors and Omissions, Product Liability, Construction Law, Surety, Life and Health, Medical Malpractice, Arson, Fraud, Transportation, Aviation, Agriculture, Workers' Compensation, Employment Discrimination

SEE COMPLETE LISTING UNDER JONESBORO, ARKANSAS (129 MILES)

MAGNOLIA † 11,577 Columbia Co.

Refer To

Dunn, Nutter & Morgan L.L.P.
3601 Richmond Road
Texarkana, Texas 75503
Telephone: 903-793-5651
Fax: 903-794-5651

Insurance Defense, Casualty, Fire, Workers' Compensation, Life Insurance, Accident and Health, Medical Liability, Legal Malpractice, Professional Malpractice, Employment Law, Subrogation, Commercial Litigation, Banking

SEE COMPLETE LISTING UNDER TEXARKANA, TEXAS (52 MILES)

MALVERN † 10,318 Hot Spring Co.

Refer To

McMillan, McCorkle, Curry & Bennington, LLP
929 Main Street
Arkadelphia, Arkansas 71923
Telephone: 870-246-2468
Fax: 870-246-3851

Mailing Address: P.O. Box 607, Arkadelphia, AR 71923

Insurance Defense, Workers' Compensation, Product Liability, Medical Malpractice, Coverage Issues

SEE COMPLETE LISTING UNDER ARKADELPHIA, ARKANSAS (29 MILES)

MARIANNA † 4,115 Lee Co.

Refer To

Snellgrove, Langley, Culpepper, Williams & Mullally
111 East Huntington, Second Floor
Jonesboro, Arkansas 72401
Telephone: 870-932-8357
Fax: 870-932-5488

Mailing Address: P.O. Box 1346, Jonesboro, AR 72403

Insurance Defense, Personal Injury, Commercial Law, Workers' Compensation, Product Liability, Real Estate, Corporate Law, Banking Law

SEE COMPLETE LISTING UNDER JONESBORO, ARKANSAS (79 MILES)

MARION † 12,345 Crittenden Co.

Refer To

Snellgrove, Langley, Culpepper, Williams & Mullally
111 East Huntington, Second Floor
Jonesboro, Arkansas 72401
  Telephone: 870-932-8357
  Fax: 870-932-5488
Mailing Address: P.O. Box 1346, Jonesboro, AR 72403

Insurance Defense, Personal Injury, Commercial Law, Workers' Compensation, Product Liability, Real Estate, Corporate Law, Banking Law

SEE COMPLETE LISTING UNDER JONESBORO, ARKANSAS (57 MILES)

Refer To

Waddell, Cole & Jones, PLLC
310 East Street, Suite A
Jonesboro, Arkansas 72401
  Telephone: 870-931-1700
  Fax: 870-931-1800, 870-931-1810
Mailing Address: P.O. Box 1700, Jonesboro, AR 72403

Insurance Defense, Trial and Appellate Practice, Property and Casualty, General Liability, Toxic Torts, Errors and Omissions, Product Liability, Construction Law, Surety, Life and Health, Medical Malpractice, Arson, Fraud, Transportation, Aviation, Agriculture, Workers' Compensation, Employment Discrimination

SEE COMPLETE LISTING UNDER JONESBORO, ARKANSAS (57 MILES)

MENA † 5,737 Polk Co.

Refer To

Daily & Woods, P.L.L.C.
58 South Sixth
Fort Smith, Arkansas 72901
  Telephone: 479-782-0361
  Fax: 479-782-6160
Mailing Address: P.O. Box 1446, Fort Smith, AR 72902

Insurance Defense

SEE COMPLETE LISTING UNDER FORT SMITH, ARKANSAS (80 MILES)

MOUNTAIN HOME † 12,448 Baxter Co.

Refer To

Davis, Clark, Butt, Carithers & Taylor, PLC
19 East Mountain Street
Fayetteville, Arkansas 72701
  Telephone: 479-521-7600
  Fax: 479-521-7661
Mailing Address: P.O. Box 1688, Fayetteville, AR 72702-1688

Insurance Defense, Automobile, General Liability, Workers' Compensation, Product Liability, Legal Malpractice, Medical Malpractice, Environmental Law, Employer Liability, Life Insurance, Surety, Construction Law, Immigration Law

SEE COMPLETE LISTING UNDER FAYETTEVILLE, ARKANSAS (126 MILES)

Refer To

Snellgrove, Langley, Culpepper, Williams & Mullally
111 East Huntington, Second Floor
Jonesboro, Arkansas 72401
  Telephone: 870-932-8357
  Fax: 870-932-5488
Mailing Address: P.O. Box 1346, Jonesboro, AR 72403

Insurance Defense, Personal Injury, Commercial Law, Workers' Compensation, Product Liability, Real Estate, Corporate Law, Banking Law

SEE COMPLETE LISTING UNDER JONESBORO, ARKANSAS (121 MILES)

NASHVILLE † 4,627 Howard Co.

Refer To

Dunn, Nutter & Morgan L.L.P.
3601 Richmond Road
Texarkana, Texas 75503
  Telephone: 903-793-5651
  Fax: 903-794-5651

Insurance Defense, Casualty, Fire, Workers' Compensation, Life Insurance, Accident and Health, Medical Liability, Legal Malpractice, Professional Malpractice, Employment Law, Subrogation, Commercial Litigation, Banking

SEE COMPLETE LISTING UNDER TEXARKANA, TEXAS (50 MILES)

NEWPORT † 7,879 Jackson Co.

Refer To

Snellgrove, Langley, Culpepper, Williams & Mullally
111 East Huntington, Second Floor
Jonesboro, Arkansas 72401
  Telephone: 870-932-8357
  Fax: 870-932-5488
Mailing Address: P.O. Box 1346, Jonesboro, AR 72403

Insurance Defense, Personal Injury, Commercial Law, Workers' Compensation, Product Liability, Real Estate, Corporate Law, Banking Law

SEE COMPLETE LISTING UNDER JONESBORO, ARKANSAS (46 MILES)

Refer To

Waddell, Cole & Jones, PLLC
310 East Street, Suite A
Jonesboro, Arkansas 72401
  Telephone: 870-931-1700
  Fax: 870-931-1800, 870-931-1810
Mailing Address: P.O. Box 1700, Jonesboro, AR 72403

Insurance Defense, Trial and Appellate Practice, Property and Casualty, General Liability, Toxic Torts, Errors and Omissions, Product Liability, Construction Law, Surety, Life and Health, Medical Malpractice, Arson, Fraud, Transportation, Aviation, Agriculture, Workers' Compensation, Employment Discrimination

SEE COMPLETE LISTING UNDER JONESBORO, ARKANSAS (46 MILES)

OSCEOLA † 7,757 Mississippi Co.

Refer To

Reid, Burge, Prevallet & Coleman
417 North Broadway
Blytheville, Arkansas 72315
  Toll Free: 888-673-9640
  Telephone: 870-763-4586
  Fax: 870-763-4642
Mailing Address: P.O. Box 107, Blytheville, AR 72316-0107

Insurance Defense, Trial and Appellate Practice, Insurance Coverage, Insurance Fraud, Examinations Under Oath, General Civil Practice

SEE COMPLETE LISTING UNDER BLYTHEVILLE, ARKANSAS (18 MILES)

Refer To

Snellgrove, Langley, Culpepper, Williams & Mullally
111 East Huntington, Second Floor
Jonesboro, Arkansas 72401
  Telephone: 870-932-8357
  Fax: 870-932-5488
Mailing Address: P.O. Box 1346, Jonesboro, AR 72403

Insurance Defense, Personal Injury, Commercial Law, Workers' Compensation, Product Liability, Real Estate, Corporate Law, Banking Law

SEE COMPLETE LISTING UNDER JONESBORO, ARKANSAS (58 MILES)

ARKANSAS

OZARK † 3,684 Franklin Co.
Refer To
Daily & Woods, P.L.L.C.
58 South Sixth
Fort Smith, Arkansas 72901
  Telephone: 479-782-0361
  Fax: 479-782-6160
Mailing Address: P.O. Box 1446, Fort Smith, AR 72902

Insurance Defense

SEE COMPLETE LISTING UNDER FORT SMITH, ARKANSAS (40 MILES)

PARAGOULD † 26,113 Greene Co.
Refer To
Reid, Burge, Prevallet & Coleman
417 North Broadway
Blytheville, Arkansas 72315
  Toll Free: 888-673-9640
  Telephone: 870-763-4586
  Fax: 870-763-4642
Mailing Address: P.O. Box 107, Blytheville, AR 72316-0107

Insurance Defense, Trial and Appellate Practice, Insurance Coverage, Insurance Fraud, Examinations Under Oath, General Civil Practice

SEE COMPLETE LISTING UNDER BLYTHEVILLE, ARKANSAS (45 MILES)

Refer To
Snellgrove, Langley, Culpepper, Williams & Mullally
111 East Huntington, Second Floor
Jonesboro, Arkansas 72401
  Telephone: 870-932-8357
  Fax: 870-932-5488
Mailing Address: P.O. Box 1346, Jonesboro, AR 72403

Insurance Defense, Personal Injury, Commercial Law, Workers' Compensation, Product Liability, Real Estate, Corporate Law, Banking Law

SEE COMPLETE LISTING UNDER JONESBORO, ARKANSAS (23 MILES)

Refer To
Waddell, Cole & Jones, PLLC
310 East Street, Suite A
Jonesboro, Arkansas 72401
  Telephone: 870-931-1700
  Fax: 870-931-1800, 870-931-1810
Mailing Address: P.O. Box 1700, Jonesboro, AR 72403

Insurance Defense, Trial and Appellate Practice, Property and Casualty, General Liability, Toxic Torts, Errors and Omissions, Product Liability, Construction Law, Surety, Life and Health, Medical Malpractice, Arson, Fraud, Transportation, Aviation, Agriculture, Workers' Compensation, Employment Discrimination

SEE COMPLETE LISTING UNDER JONESBORO, ARKANSAS (23 MILES)

PARIS † 3,532 Logan Co.
Refer To
Daily & Woods, P.L.L.C.
58 South Sixth
Fort Smith, Arkansas 72901
  Telephone: 479-782-0361
  Fax: 479-782-6160
Mailing Address: P.O. Box 1446, Fort Smith, AR 72902

Insurance Defense

SEE COMPLETE LISTING UNDER FORT SMITH, ARKANSAS (42 MILES)

PIGGOTT † 3,849 Clay Co.
Refer To
Reid, Burge, Prevallet & Coleman
417 North Broadway
Blytheville, Arkansas 72315
  Toll Free: 888-673-9640
  Telephone: 870-763-4586
  Fax: 870-763-4642
Mailing Address: P.O. Box 107, Blytheville, AR 72316-0107

Insurance Defense, Trial and Appellate Practice, Insurance Coverage, Insurance Fraud, Examinations Under Oath, General Civil Practice

SEE COMPLETE LISTING UNDER BLYTHEVILLE, ARKANSAS (50 MILES)

PINE BLUFF † 49,083 Jefferson Co.
Refer To
Munson, Rowlett, Moore & Boone, P.A.
Regions Center
400 West Capitol, Suite 1900
Little Rock, Arkansas 72201
  Telephone: 501-374-6535
  Fax: 501-374-5906

Arson, Asbestos, Aviation, Bad Faith, Casualty, Catastrophic Injury, Civil Appeals, Civil Litigation, Class Actions, Commercial Litigation, Complex Litigation, Construction Litigation, Employment Law, Environmental Litigation, Fraud, Hospital Malpractice, Insurance Coverage, Insurance Defense, Mediation, Medical Devices, Medical Malpractice, Negligence, Personal Injury, Premises Liability, Product Liability, Professional Malpractice, School Law, Self-Insured Defense, Subrogation, Toxic Torts, Transportation, Trucking Litigation, Workers' Compensation, Wrongful Death

SEE COMPLETE LISTING UNDER LITTLE ROCK, ARKANSAS (43 MILES)

POCAHONTAS † 6,608 Randolph Co.
Refer To
Snellgrove, Langley, Culpepper, Williams & Mullally
111 East Huntington, Second Floor
Jonesboro, Arkansas 72401
  Telephone: 870-932-8357
  Fax: 870-932-5488
Mailing Address: P.O. Box 1346, Jonesboro, AR 72403

Insurance Defense, Personal Injury, Commercial Law, Workers' Compensation, Product Liability, Real Estate, Corporate Law, Banking Law

SEE COMPLETE LISTING UNDER JONESBORO, ARKANSAS (36 MILES)

Refer To
Waddell, Cole & Jones, PLLC
310 East Street, Suite A
Jonesboro, Arkansas 72401
  Telephone: 870-931-1700
  Fax: 870-931-1800, 870-931-1810
Mailing Address: P.O. Box 1700, Jonesboro, AR 72403

Insurance Defense, Trial and Appellate Practice, Property and Casualty, General Liability, Toxic Torts, Errors and Omissions, Product Liability, Construction Law, Surety, Life and Health, Medical Malpractice, Arson, Fraud, Transportation, Aviation, Agriculture, Workers' Compensation, Employment Discrimination

SEE COMPLETE LISTING UNDER JONESBORO, ARKANSAS (36 MILES)

PRESCOTT † 3,296 Nevada Co.
Refer To
McMillan, McCorkle, Curry & Bennington, LLP
929 Main Street
Arkadelphia, Arkansas 71923
  Telephone: 870-246-2468
  Fax: 870-246-3851
Mailing Address: P.O. Box 607, Arkadelphia, AR 71923

Insurance Defense, Workers' Compensation, Product Liability, Medical Malpractice, Coverage Issues

SEE COMPLETE LISTING UNDER ARKADELPHIA, ARKANSAS (31 MILES)

TEXARKANA / ARKANSAS

ROGERS 55,964 Benton Co.
Refer To
Davis, Clark, Butt, Carithers & Taylor, PLC
19 East Mountain Street
Fayetteville, Arkansas 72701
   Telephone: 479-521-7600
   Fax: 479-521-7661
Mailing Address: P.O. Box 1688, Fayetteville, AR 72702-1688

Insurance Defense, Automobile, General Liability, Workers' Compensation, Product Liability, Legal Malpractice, Medical Malpractice, Environmental Law, Employer Liability, Life Insurance, Surety, Construction Law, Immigration Law

SEE COMPLETE LISTING UNDER FAYETTEVILLE, ARKANSAS (15 MILES)

SPRINGDALE 69,797 Washington Co.
Refer To
Davis, Clark, Butt, Carithers & Taylor, PLC
19 East Mountain Street
Fayetteville, Arkansas 72701
   Telephone: 479-521-7600
   Fax: 479-521-7661
Mailing Address: P.O. Box 1688, Fayetteville, AR 72702-1688

Insurance Defense, Automobile, General Liability, Workers' Compensation, Product Liability, Legal Malpractice, Medical Malpractice, Environmental Law, Employer Liability, Life Insurance, Surety, Construction Law, Immigration Law

SEE COMPLETE LISTING UNDER FAYETTEVILLE, ARKANSAS (10 MILES)

TEXARKANA † 29,919 Miller Co.

Veon Law Firm, P.A.
2710 Arkansas Boulevard
Texarkana, Arkansas 71854
   Telephone: 870-774-7390
   Fax: 870-773-3690
   E-Mail: robert.veon@veonfirm.com
   www.veonfirm.com

Established: 2003

Insurance Defense, Product Liability, Premises Liability, Dram Shop, Construction Law, Automobile, Negligence, Insurance Coverage, Bad Faith, Uninsured and Underinsured Motorist, Commercial Litigation, Litigation, Automotive Products Liability, Business Litigation, Carrier Defense, Class Actions, Intellectual Property

Firm Profile: Veon Law Firm, P.A. is a law firm dedicated to the principles of integrity, leadership and results. With offices located in Texarkana, Arkansas the firm is strategically located to serve clients in all State and Federal courts throughout Texas and Arkansas. The attorneys at Veon Law Firm are committed to offering strong, effective and aggressive representation of their client's needs.

Insurance Clients

ACE USA
American Management Corporation
The Cincinnati Companies
CUNA Mutual Group
ESIS
GMAC Insurance
Greenwich Insurance Company
Harbor Specialty Insurance Company
James River Insurance Company
K & K Insurance Group, Inc.
Midlands Underwriting Managers, Inc.
National General Insurance Company
Superior Insurance Company
AIG Specialty Auto
Balboa Insurance Company
Bituminous Insurance Company
Clarendon National Insurance Company
First Mercury Insurance Company
Great American Insurance Company
Infinity/Leader Insurance Companies
Kemper Services Group
Lexington Insurance Company
Motorists Group-American Hardware Mutual
Nationwide Insurance
Royal & SunAlliance Insurance Company

Veon Law Firm, P.A., Texarkana, AR   (Continued)
TIG Specialty Insurance Company
XL Winterthur International Insurance Company

Non-Insurance Clients

Allen Engineering Company
Best Buy Company
Cantrell Machine Company
Control Concepts, Inc
Fleming Companies, Inc.
Gallagher Bassett Services, Inc.
Landstar Ranger, Inc.
Novation, LLC/VHA, Inc.
Philip Services Corporation
Rhino Linings USA, Inc.
SER of Texas, LLC
Swift Transportation Company, Inc.
Atlantic Risk Management, Inc.
Burger King Corporation
CMI Terex Corp.
DBSI Group of Companies
Frito-Lay, Inc.
Irby Construction Company
Louisiana-Pacific Corporation
Penn Warranty Corp.
Quanta Services, Inc.
Sedgwick Claims Management Services, Inc.
Sysco Corporation

Partner

Robert T. Veon — 1963 — Grove City College, B.A., 1986; University of Arkansas School of Law, J.D., 1990 — Admitted to Bar, 1990, Pennsylvania; 1991, Texas; Arkansas; 1990, U.S. District Court, Eastern District of Pennsylvania; 1991, U.S. District Court, Eastern District of Texas; U.S. District Court, Eastern and Western Districts of Arkansas; 1994, U.S. Court of Appeals, Third, Fifth and Eighth Circuits; 2002, U.S. District Court, Middle District of Pennsylvania; 2004, U.S. District Court, Northern District of Texas; 2005, U.S. District Court, Southern District of Texas — Member American and Arkansas Bar Associations; State Bar of Texas; International Association of Defense Counsel; Defense Research Institute; Arkansas Association of Defense Counsel; Texas Association of Defense Counsel

---

The following firms also service this area.

Dunn, Nutter & Morgan L.L.P.
3601 Richmond Road
Texarkana, Texas 75503
   Telephone: 903-793-5651
   Fax: 903-794-5651

Insurance Defense, Casualty, Fire, Workers' Compensation, Life Insurance, Accident and Health, Medical Liability, Legal Malpractice, Professional Malpractice, Employment Law, Subrogation, Commercial Litigation, Banking

SEE COMPLETE LISTING UNDER TEXARKANA, TEXAS

McMillan, McCorkle, Curry & Bennington, LLP
929 Main Street
Arkadelphia, Arkansas 71923
   Telephone: 870-246-2468
   Fax: 870-246-3851
Mailing Address: P.O. Box 607, Arkadelphia, AR 71923

Insurance Defense, Workers' Compensation, Product Liability, Medical Malpractice, Coverage Issues

SEE COMPLETE LISTING UNDER ARKADELPHIA, ARKANSAS (77 MILES)

Munson, Rowlett, Moore & Boone, P.A.
Regions Center
400 West Capitol, Suite 1900
Little Rock, Arkansas 72201
   Telephone: 501-374-6535
   Fax: 501-374-5906

Arson, Asbestos, Aviation, Bad Faith, Casualty, Catastrophic Injury, Civil Appeals, Civil Litigation, Class Actions, Commercial Litigation, Complex Litigation, Construction Litigation, Employment Law, Environmental Litigation, Fraud, Hospital Malpractice, Insurance Coverage, Insurance Defense, Mediation, Medical Devices, Medical Malpractice, Negligence, Personal Injury, Premises Liability, Product Liability, Professional Malpractice, School Law, Self-Insured Defense, Subrogation, Toxic Torts, Transportation, Trucking Litigation, Workers' Compensation, Wrongful Death

SEE COMPLETE LISTING UNDER LITTLE ROCK, ARKANSAS (144 MILES)

VAN BUREN † 22,791 Crawford Co.

Refer To
Daily & Woods, P.L.L.C.
58 South Sixth
Fort Smith, Arkansas 72901
   Telephone: 479-782-0361
   Fax: 479-782-6160
Mailing Address: P.O. Box 1446, Fort Smith, AR 72902

Insurance Defense

SEE COMPLETE LISTING UNDER FORT SMITH, ARKANSAS (5 MILES)

WALDRON † 3,618 Scott Co.

Refer To
Daily & Woods, P.L.L.C.
58 South Sixth
Fort Smith, Arkansas 72901
   Telephone: 479-782-0361
   Fax: 479-782-6160
Mailing Address: P.O. Box 1446, Fort Smith, AR 72902

Insurance Defense

SEE COMPLETE LISTING UNDER FORT SMITH, ARKANSAS (48 MILES)

WALNUT RIDGE † 4,890 Lawrence Co.

Refer To
Snellgrove, Langley, Culpepper, Williams & Mullally
111 East Huntington, Second Floor
Jonesboro, Arkansas 72401
   Telephone: 870-932-8357
   Fax: 870-932-5488
Mailing Address: P.O. Box 1346, Jonesboro, AR 72403

Insurance Defense, Personal Injury, Commercial Law, Workers' Compensation, Product Liability, Real Estate, Corporate Law, Banking Law

SEE COMPLETE LISTING UNDER JONESBORO, ARKANSAS (22 MILES)

Refer To
Waddell, Cole & Jones, PLLC
310 East Street, Suite A
Jonesboro, Arkansas 72401
   Telephone: 870-931-1700
   Fax: 870-931-1800, 870-931-1810
Mailing Address: P.O. Box 1700, Jonesboro, AR 72403

Insurance Defense, Trial and Appellate Practice, Property and Casualty, General Liability, Toxic Torts, Errors and Omissions, Product Liability, Construction Law, Surety, Life and Health, Medical Malpractice, Arson, Fraud, Transportation, Aviation, Agriculture, Workers' Compensation, Employment Discrimination

SEE COMPLETE LISTING UNDER JONESBORO, ARKANSAS (22 MILES)

WEST MEMPHIS 26,245 Crittenden Co.

Refer To
Munson, Rowlett, Moore & Boone, P.A.
Regions Center
400 West Capitol, Suite 1900
Little Rock, Arkansas 72201
   Telephone: 501-374-6535
   Fax: 501-374-5906

Arson, Asbestos, Aviation, Bad Faith, Casualty, Catastrophic Injury, Civil Appeals, Civil Litigation, Class Actions, Commercial Litigation, Complex Litigation, Construction Litigation, Employment Law, Environmental Litigation, Fraud, Hospital Malpractice, Insurance Coverage, Insurance Defense, Mediation, Medical Devices, Medical Malpractice, Negligence, Personal Injury, Premises Liability, Product Liability, Professional Malpractice, School Law, Self-Insured Defense, Subrogation, Toxic Torts, Transportation, Trucking Litigation, Workers' Compensation, Wrongful Death

SEE COMPLETE LISTING UNDER LITTLE ROCK, ARKANSAS (135 MILES)

Refer To
Reid, Burge, Prevallet & Coleman
417 North Broadway
Blytheville, Arkansas 72315
   Toll Free: 888-673-9640
   Telephone: 870-763-4586
   Fax: 870-763-4642
Mailing Address: P.O. Box 107, Blytheville, AR 72316-0107

Insurance Defense, Trial and Appellate Practice, Insurance Coverage, Insurance Fraud, Examinations Under Oath, General Civil Practice

SEE COMPLETE LISTING UNDER BLYTHEVILLE, ARKANSAS (60 MILES)

Refer To
Snellgrove, Langley, Culpepper, Williams & Mullally
111 East Huntington, Second Floor
Jonesboro, Arkansas 72401
   Telephone: 870-932-8357
   Fax: 870-932-5488
Mailing Address: P.O. Box 1346, Jonesboro, AR 72403

Insurance Defense, Personal Injury, Commercial Law, Workers' Compensation, Product Liability, Real Estate, Corporate Law, Banking Law

SEE COMPLETE LISTING UNDER JONESBORO, ARKANSAS (62 MILES)

WYNNE † 8,367 Cross Co.

Refer To
Snellgrove, Langley, Culpepper, Williams & Mullally
111 East Huntington, Second Floor
Jonesboro, Arkansas 72401
   Telephone: 870-932-8357
   Fax: 870-932-5488
Mailing Address: P.O. Box 1346, Jonesboro, AR 72403

Insurance Defense, Personal Injury, Commercial Law, Workers' Compensation, Product Liability, Real Estate, Corporate Law, Banking Law

SEE COMPLETE LISTING UNDER JONESBORO, ARKANSAS (47 MILES)

Refer To
Waddell, Cole & Jones, PLLC
310 East Street, Suite A
Jonesboro, Arkansas 72401
   Telephone: 870-931-1700
   Fax: 870-931-1800, 870-931-1810
Mailing Address: P.O. Box 1700, Jonesboro, AR 72403

Insurance Defense, Trial and Appellate Practice, Property and Casualty, General Liability, Toxic Torts, Errors and Omissions, Product Liability, Construction Law, Surety, Life and Health, Medical Malpractice, Arson, Fraud, Transportation, Aviation, Agriculture, Workers' Compensation, Employment Discrimination

SEE COMPLETE LISTING UNDER JONESBORO, ARKANSAS (47 MILES)

CALIFORNIA

CAPITAL: SACRAMENTO

COUNTIES AND COUNTY SEATS

County	County Seat
Alameda	Oakland
Alpine	Markleeville
Amador	Jackson
Butte	Oroville
Calaveras	San Andreas
Colusa	Colusa
Contra Costa	Martinez
Del Norte	Crescent City
El Dorado	Placerville
Fresno	Fresno
Glenn	Willows
Humboldt	Eureka
Imperial	El Centro
Inyo	Independence
Kern	Bakersfield
Kings	Hanford
Lake	Lakeport
Lassen	Susanville
Los Angeles	Los Angeles
Madera	Madera
Marin	San Rafael
Mariposa	Mariposa
Mendocino	Ukiah
Merced	Merced
Modoc	Alturas
Mono	Bridgeport
Monterey	Salinas
Napa	Napa
Nevada	Nevada City
Orange	Santa Ana
Placer	Auburn
Plumas	Quincy
Riverside	Riverside
Sacramento	Sacramento
San Benito	Hollister
San Bernardino	San Bernardino
San Diego	San Diego
San Francisco	San Francisco
San Joaquin	Stockton
San Luis Obispo	San Luis Obispo
San Mateo	Redwood City
Santa Barbara	Santa Barbara
Santa Clara	San Jose
Santa Cruz	Santa Cruz
Shasta	Redding
Sierra	Downieville
Siskiyou	Yreka
Solano	Fairfield
Sonoma	Santa Rosa
Stanislaus	Modesto
Sutter	Yuba City
Tehama	Red Bluff
Trinity	Weaverville
Tulare	Visalia
Tuolumne	Sonora
Ventura	Ventura
Yolo	Woodland
Yuba	Marysville

In the text that follows "†" indicates County Seats.

Our files contain additional verified data on the firms listed herein. This additional information is available on request.

A.M. BEST COMPANY

CALIFORNIA

ALAMEDA 73,812 Alameda Co.

Refer To

Bledsoe, Cathcart, Diestel, Pedersen & Treppa LLP
601 California Street, 16th Floor
San Francisco, California 94108
  Telephone: 415-981-5411
  Fax: 415-981-0352

Civil Trial Practice, State and Federal Courts, Product Liability, Insurance Defense, Insurance Coverage, Personal Injury, Construction Law, Employment Law, Business Law, Environmental Law, Landlord Tenant, Commercial Transportation, Copyright Litigation, Banking and Finance, Lender Liability

SEE COMPLETE LISTING UNDER SAN FRANCISCO, CALIFORNIA (8 MILES)

Refer To

Borton Petrini, LLP
660 Las Gallinas Avenue, Suite B
San Rafael, California 94903
  Telephone: 415-677-0730
  Fax: 415-677-0737

Commercial Litigation, Construction Litigation, General Civil Litigation, Intellectual Property, Professional Liability, Public Entities

SEE COMPLETE LISTING UNDER SAN FRANCISCO, CALIFORNIA (8 MILES)

ALTURAS † 2,827 Modoc Co.

Refer To

Kenny, Snowden & Norine
A Law Corporation
2701 Park Marina Drive
Redding, California 96001
  Telephone: 530-225-8990
  Fax: 530-225-8944
  Toll Free: 800-655-6677
Mailing Address: Box 994608, Redding, CA 96099-4608

Insurance Defense, Medical Malpractice, Product Liability, Defense Litigation, Civil Trial Practice, Casualty, Professional Errors and Omissions, Employment Law, Public Entities, Real Estate, Land Use, Water Law, Equine Law

SEE COMPLETE LISTING UNDER REDDING, CALIFORNIA (146 MILES)

ANAHEIM 336,265 Orange Co.

Refer To

Grant, Genovese & Baratta, LLP
2030 Main Street, Suite 1600
Irvine, California 92614-7257
  Telephone: 949-660-1600
  Fax: 949-660-6060

General Civil Litigation, Bad Faith, Insurance Coverage, Construction Defect, Directors and Officers Liability, Employment Law, Environmental Law, Intellectual Property, Homeowners' Associations, Earth Movement, Toxic Torts

SEE COMPLETE LISTING UNDER IRVINE, CALIFORNIA (13 MILES)

BAKERSFIELD † 347,483 Kern Co.

Borton Petrini, LLP
5060 California Avenue, Suite 700
Bakersfield, California 93309
  Telephone: 661-322-3051
  Fax: 661-322-4628
  E-Mail: knelson@bortonpetrini.com
  www.bortonpetrini.com

(Fresno, CA Office*: 2444 Main Street, Suite 150, 93721)
  (Tel: 559-268-0117)
  (Fax: 559-237-7995)
  (E-Mail: bpfrs@bortonpetrini.com)
(Los Angeles, CA Office*: 626 Wilshire Boulevard, Suite 975, 90017)
  (Tel: 213-624-2869)
  (Fax: 213-489-3930)
  (E-Mail: bpla@bortonpetrini.com)

Borton Petrini, LLP, Bakersfield, CA (Continued)
(Modesto, CA Office*: 201 Needham Street, 95354, P.O. Box 3384, 95353)
  (Tel: 209-576-1701)
  (Fax: 209-527-9753)
  (E-Mail: bpmod@bortonpetrini.com)
(Sacramento, California*: 3110 Gold Canal Drive, Suite A, Rancho Cordova, CA, 95670, P.O. Box 277790, 95827)
  (Tel: 916-858-1212)
  (Fax: 916-858-1252)
  (E-Mail: bpsac@bortonpetrini.com)
(San Bernardino, California*: 1461 Ford Street, Suite 201, Redlands, CA, 92373, P.O Box 11207, 92423)
  (Tel: 909-381-0527)
  (Fax: 909-381-0658)
  (E-Mail: bpsbdo@bortonpetrini.com)
(San Diego, CA Office*: 1320 Columbia Street, Suite 210, 92101)
  (Tel: 619-232-2424)
  (Fax: 619-531-0794)
  (E-Mail: bpsd@bortonpetrini.com)
(San Rafael, CA Office*(See San Francisco listing): 660 Las Gallinas Avenue, Suite B, 94903)
  (Tel: 415-677-0730)
  (Fax: 415-677-0737)
  (E-Mail: bpsf@bortonpetrini.com)
(San Jose, CA Office*: 95 South Market Street, Suite 400, 95113)
  (Tel: 408-535-0870)
  (Fax: 408-535-0878)
  (E-Mail: bpsj@bortonpetrini.com)
(Orange County*: 3020 Old Ranch Parkway, Suite 300, Seal Beach, CA, 90740)
  (Tel: 562-596-2300)
  (Fax: 562-596-2322)
  (E-Mail: bpoc@bortonpetrini.com)

Established: 1899

Administrative Law, Admiralty and Maritime Law, Agriculture, Appellate Practice, Bad Faith, Banking, Bankruptcy, Business Law, Business Litigation, Casualty Insurance Law, Church Law, Collections, Commercial Law, Contracts, Corporate Law, Coverage Issues, Creditor Rights, Eminent Domain, Employment Litigation, Environmental Law, Estate Planning, Family Law, Fire, Health Care, Insurance Coverage, Insurance Defense, Intellectual Property, Labor and Employment, Land Use, Oil and Gas, Personal Injury, Premises Liability, Probate, Product Liability, Professional Errors and Omissions, Property, Public Entities, Real Estate, Religious Institutions, Sports and Entertainment Liability, Toxic Torts, Transactional Law, Transportation, Unlawful Detainer Representing Landlords

Firm Profile: Since 1899, Borton Petrini, LLP, has offered high quality legal services in all of the practice areas described above through its California network of 10 regional offices. The mission of Borton Petrini, LLP is to treat every file as though we were representing ourselves and paying the bill for that representation.

Insurance Clients

ACE American Insurance Company	AIG Claim Services, Inc.
ALLIED Insurance	AIMS - Acclamation Insurance Management Services
American Claims Management, Inc.	American National Property and Casualty Company
American Reliable Insurance Company	American Safety Insurance Services, Inc.
Ameriprise Auto & Home Insurance	Arrowpoint Capital Corporation
Berkley Risk Administrators Company, LLC	Balboa Insurance Group
Berkshire Hathaway, Inc.	Berkshire Hathaway Homestate Companies
Chartis Marine Adjusters, Inc.	Brotherhood Mutual Insurance Company
Chubb Group of Insurance Companies	Claims Resource Management, Inc.
	Crum & Forster

Borton Petrini, LLP, Bakersfield, CA (Continued)

Essex Insurance Company
Great American Insurance Company
Kaufman, Borgeest & Ryan LLP
Lexington Insurance Company
Markel American Insurance Company
OneBeacon Insurance
QBE Agri
Royal & SunAlliance
Sedgwick Claims Management Services, Inc.
Special District Risk Management Authority
Wawanesa Mutual Insurance Company
Gallagher Bassett Insurance Company
Housing Authority Risk Retention Group, Inc.
Magna Carta Companies
Markel Shand, Inc.
Navigators Insurance Company
Professional Indemnity Agency
Risk Enterprise Management, Ltd.
St. Paul Travelers Insurance Companies
Seneca Insurance Company, Inc.
Specialty Claims Management
Travelers/Aetna Insurance
XL Insurance
Zurich American Insurance Company

Non-Insurance Clients

Albertsons, Inc.
City of Atwater
City of Livingston
City of Oakdale
City of Turlock
Dameron Hospital Association
Fiesta Mexicana Markets
Fry's Electronics
Lotus Communications
Rosedale Ranch, LLC
AT&T
City of Lathrop
City of Modesto
City of Riverbank
The Corky McMillin Companies
E.R.A. East West Realty & Investment, Inc.
Housing Authority of the County of Stanislaus

Firm Members

Fred E. Borton — (1877-1948)
James Petrini — (1897-1978)
Harry M. Conron — (1907-1971)
Kenneth D. Pinsent — (1953-1984)
Richard E. Hitchcock — (1925-2001)
John F. Petrini — (1944-2008)

Managing Partner

Diana L. Christian — 1979 — University of Oregon, B.A., 2001; Thomas Jefferson School of Law, J.D. (cum laude), 2004 — Admitted to Bar, 2005, California — Member State Bar of California; Kern County Bar Association — E-mail: dchristian@bortonpetrini.com

Partners

Calvin R. Stead — 1947 — Humboldt State University, A.B., 1970; The University of Texas, M.S., 1979; University of San Diego School of Law, J.D., 1986 — Admitted to Bar, 1987, California — Member State Bar of California; Kern County Bar Association — Editor, Construction Law Newsletter; Editor, Trucking Law Newsletter — Board of Directors and Officer, Kern Home Builders Association; Greater Bakersfield Chamber of Commerce (Chairman's Circle, Government Review Council); Bakersfield Rotary — Certified Mediator — E-mail: cstead@bortonpetrini.com

James J. Braze — 1946 — University of Southern California, B.S. Mech. Engr. (cum laude), 1968; University of Alaska, M.S., 1971; Golden Gate University School of Law, LL.M., 1997; Loyola Law School, J.D., 1977 — Tau Beta Pi; Pi Tau Sigma — Admitted to Bar, 1977, California; 1979, U.S. District Court, Eastern District of California; 1985, U.S. District Court, Central District of California; 1990, U.S. District Court, Northern District of California; 1991, U.S. District Court, Southern District of California; 1993, U.S. Court of Appeals, Ninth Circuit; 1998, U.S. Tax Court — Member American (Taxation, Business, and Energy Sections) and Kern County Bar Associations; State Bar of California; Association of Defense Counsel, Northern California — Graduate Leadership, Bakersfield Class of 2013; Greater Bakersfield Chamber of Commerce: AV Preeminent Rating, Martindale Hubbell — Registered Professional Engineer, California, 1972 — E-mail: jbraze@bortonpetrini.com

Gail S. Braze — 1945 — Fresno State University, B.A., 1978; Whittier Law School, J.D., 1989 — Admitted to Bar, 1989, California — Member State Bar of California; Kern County and Sonoma County Bar Associations; Kern County Women's Lawyers Association (Secretary & Treasurer) — Commission for the Status of Women, Sonoma County; Board of Directors of Boys & Girls, Petaluma, CA; Business Network International (Member); St. John Lutheran Church Fellowship-Petaluma, CA (Chairman) — E-mail: gbraze@bortonpetrini.com

Michael J. Stump — 1968 — University of California, Davis, B.A., 1993; University of California, Hastings College of the Law, J.D., 1997 — Admitted to Bar, 1997, California; 2012, Idaho; U.S. District Court, Eastern and Southern Districts of California; 2003, U.S. Court of Appeals, Ninth Circuit — Member American and Kern County Bar Associations; State Bar of California; Idaho State Bar — Editor, California Business Counsel Magazine; Editor, California Defense Magazine — E-mail: mstump@bortonpetrini.com

Senior Counsel

Michael D. Worthing — 1954 — California State College at Bakersfield, B.A., 1976; University of the Pacific, McGeorge School of Law, J.D., 1980 — Admitted to Bar, 1980, California; 1989, U.S. District Court, Central and Eastern Districts of California; 1990, U.S. District Court, Northern and Southern Districts of California — Member State Bar of California; Kern County Bar Association — Author: "The Peculiar Rule of Peculiar Risk: Do You Know It When You See It," California Defense Magazine (Winter, 1992); "Interpreting Indemnity Contracts," Bakersfield Business Conference Syllabus (1993); "The Ever Growing Thicket of California Civil Code Section 2782," Construction Defect Journal, January 6, 2012 — E-mail: mworthing@bortonpetrini.com

Associates

Andrew M. Morgan — 1979 — Brigham Young University, B.A., 2006; S.J. Quinney College of Law, The University of Utah, J.D., 2009 — Admitted to Bar, 2009, California — Member State Bar of California — E-mail: amorgan@bortonpetrini.com

Kyle W. Holmes — University of California at Irvine, B.A., 2009; University of the Pacific, McGeorge School of Law, J.D., 2012; Lewis & Clark Law School, LL.M., 2013 — Admitted to Bar, 2012, California — Member State Bar of California; Kern County Bar Association — E-mail: kholmes@bortonpetrini.com

Of Counsel

George F. Martin — 1944 — Sacramento State College, B.A., 1968; University of California, Davis School of Law, J.D., 1971 — Kern County Bar Association Bench & Award - Recipient (1996) — Admitted to Bar, 1972, California; U.S. District Court, Eastern District of California; U.S. Court of Appeals, Ninth Circuit; 1976, U.S. District Court, Central District of California; 1977, U.S. District Court, Southern District of California; 1996, U.S. Supreme Court — Member American and Kern County Bar Associations; State Bar of California — Editor-in-Chief: Verdict Legal Journal (1984-1988); California Defense Journal (1988-1992); California Business Counsel (1996-2000); Editor, Insurance Bar List Annual Summary of California Law (1992-2002) — Association for California Tort Reform (Board of Directors, 1983-1984); California Defense Counsel (Board of Directors, 1983-1984); Bakersfield Business Conference (Founder, Organizer, 1985-present); Bakersfield Memorial Hospital (Board of Directors, 1987-1992); Greater Bakersfield Chamber of Commerce (Board of Directors, 1988-2005; President, 1991; Chairman's Circle; Political Action Committee); Central California Heart Institute (President, 1990-1992); California State University at Bakersfield Foundation (Board of Directors, 1992-present; Chairman, 1997-1999); Witkin Legal Institute (Founding Member, Board of Directors, 1996-present; Chairman, Board of Directors, 1998-present); Kern County Economic Development Corporation (Board of Directors, 1995-2001; Chairman's Circle, 2001-present); Automobile Club of Southern California (Advisory Board, 1997-2003); California Pacific School of Law (Dean, 1992-1994; Chairman, Board of Trustees, 1994-1997); Borton Petrini LLP (Firm Managing Partner, 1977-2002); University of California at Merced Ambassadors (Board of Directors, 2002-2004); Community Foundation Serving Kern County (Board of Directors, 2002-2004) — E-mail: gmartin@bortonpetrini.com

Clifford & Brown
A Professional Corporation

1430 Truxtun Avenue, Suite 900
Bakersfield, California 93301
Telephone: 661-322-6023
Fax: 661-322-3508
E-Mail: cblaw@clifford-brownlaw.com
www.clifford-brownlaw.com

Established: 1966

CALIFORNIA — BAKERSFIELD

Clifford & Brown, A Professional Corporation, Bakersfield, CA (Continued)

General Civil Practice, State and Federal Courts, Civil Litigation, Business Law, Negligence, Product Liability, Professional Negligence, Insurance Law, Agriculture, Oil and Gas, Environmental Law, Real Estate, Creditors' Rights, Land Use, Water, Music Law, Estate Planning, Probate, Corporation

Insurance Clients

- Allstate Insurance Company
- Beta Healthcare Group
- California Fair Services Authority
- Constitution State Insurance Company
- Farmers Insurance Group
- Foremost Insurance Company
- Great West Casualty Company
- Kemper Insurance Companies
- Nationwide Insurance
- Northbrook Insurance Company
- Prudential Property and Casualty Insurance Company
- Royal & SunAlliance
- The St. Paul Companies
- Special District Risk Management Authority
- Transamerica Insurance Company
- Truck Insurance Exchange
- Viking Insurance Company
- Westport Insurance Company
- Wilshire Insurance Company
- American National Property and Casualty Company
- CIGNA Property and Casualty Insurance Company
- Coregis/Crum & Forster Managers Group
- GMAC Insurance
- Insurance Company of the West
- Lawyers Mutual Insurance Company
- Progressive Casualty Insurance Company
- Reliance Insurance Company
- Safeco Insurance
- Southern California Physicians Insurance Exchange
- State Farm Insurance Company
- Travelers Insurance Companies
- 21st Century Insurance Company
- Westchester Fire Insurance Company

Non-Insurance Clients

- Catholic Healthcare West
- The Vons Companies, Inc.

Partners

Stephen T. Clifford — 1940 — University of California, Davis, B.S., 1963; University of California, Hastings College of the Law, LL.B., 1966 — Admitted to Bar, 1966, California; U.S. District Court, Eastern District of California; U.S. Court of Appeals, Ninth Circuit — Member State Bar of California; Kern County Bar Association; American Board of Trial Advocates; Fellow, American College of Trial Lawyers; National Association of Railroad Trial Counsel; Defense Research Institute — Practice Areas: Civil Litigation — E-mail: sclifford@clifford-brownlaw.com

Robert D. Harding — 1949 — University of California, B.A., 1970; University of California, Hastings College of the Law, J.D., 1974 — Admitted to Bar, 1974, California; 1974, U.S. District Court, Eastern, Northern and Southern Districts of California — Member State Bar of California; Kern County Bar Association; American Board of Trial Advocates; Association of Defense Counsel, Northern California; Association of Southern California Defense Counsel; Defense Research Institute — Practice Areas: Civil Litigation — E-mail: rharding@clifford-brownlaw.com

Arnold J. Anchordoquy — 1948 — Saint Mary's College, B.A., 1970; University of the Pacific, McGeorge School of Law, J.D., 1973 — Admitted to Bar, 1973, California; U.S. District Court, Eastern, Northern and Southern Districts of California — Member State Bar of California; Kern County Bar Association; American Board of Trial Advocates (President, San Joaquin Chapter, 2002); Association of Defense Counsel, Northern California — Practice Areas: Civil Litigation — E-mail: aanchordoquy@clifford-brownlaw.com

Patrick J. Osborn — 1951 — University of California, Riverside, B.A., 1973; University of the Pacific, McGeorge School of Law, J.D., 1977 — Admitted to Bar, 1977, California; 1977, U.S. District Court, Eastern District of California; 1979, U.S. District Court, Central District of California — Member State Bar of California; Kern County Bar Association; American Board of Trial Advocates; Fellow, American College of Trial Lawyers; Defense Research Institute; Association of Defense Counsel; Trial Attorneys of America — Board Certified Civil Trial Advocate by the National Board of Trial Advocacy — Practice Areas: Civil Litigation — E-mail: posborn@clifford-brownlaw.com

Michael L. O'Dell — 1955 — San Diego State University, B.A., 1977; University of California, Hastings College of the Law, J.D., 1980 — Admitted to Bar, 1980, California; 1980, U.S. District Court, Central and Eastern Districts of California — Member American and Kern County Bar Associations; State Bar of California; Association of Southern California Defense Counsel (Member, 1980-present; Board of Directors, 2003-2006) — Practice Areas: Civil Litigation; Business Law — E-mail: modell@clifford-brownlaw.com

Grover H. Waldon — 1958 — California State University, Sacramento, B.S., 1980; University of the Pacific, McGeorge School of Law, J.D. (with distinction), 1983 — Admitted to Bar, 1983, California; 1983, U.S. District Court, Eastern District of California; 1984, U.S. District Court, Central District of California; U.S. Court of Appeals, Ninth Circuit — Member State Bar of California; Kern County Bar Association — Practice Areas: Business Law; Civil Litigation — E-mail: gwaldon@clifford-brownlaw.com

John R. Szewczyk — 1957 — University of California, San Diego, B.A., 1980; Loyola Law School Los Angeles, J.D. (cum laude), 1983 — Admitted to Bar, 1983, California; 1984, U.S. District Court, Eastern District of California — Member American and Kern County Bar Associations; State Bar of California (Litigation and Employment Law Sections) — Practice Areas: Civil Litigation; Employment Law; Appellate Practice — E-mail: jszewczyk@clifford-brownlaw.com

Stephen H. Boyle — 1953 — University of California, Santa Barbara, B.A., 1975; California Western School of Law, J.D. (cum laude), 1978; University of San Diego, LL.M., 1984 — Admitted to Bar, 1978, California; 1978, U.S. District Court, Southern District of California; 1986, U.S. Tax Court — Member State Bar of California; Kern County Bar Association; Christian Legal Society — Practice Areas: Business Law — E-mail: sboyle@clifford-brownlaw.com

James B. Wiens — 1949 — University of California, Berkeley, B.A., 1971; California Western School of Law, J.D., 1977 — Admitted to Bar, 1978, California; 1982, U.S. District Court, Eastern and Southern Districts of California — Member State Bar of California; Kern County Bar Association — Practice Areas: Business Law; Agriculture — E-mail: jweins@clifford-brownlaw.com

Richard G. Zimmer — 1956 — Rochester Institute of Technology, B.S. (with highest honors), 1979; California Western School of Law, J.D., 1982 — Admitted to Bar, 1982, North Carolina; 1983, California; 1982, U.S. District Court, Western District of North Carolina — Member State Bar of California; North Carolina State Bar; Kern County Bar Association; American Board of Trial Advocates — Kern County Deputy District Attorney, 1982-1987 — Practice Areas: Civil Litigation; Business Law — E-mail: rzimmer@clifford-brownlaw.com

Charles D. Melton — 1962 — University of the Pacific, B.S. (cum laude), 1984; University of California, Hastings College of the Law, J.D., 1987 — Judicial Extern for Judge William R. Channel, California Court of Appeals, First District (1986) — Admitted to Bar, 1987, California; 1987, U.S. District Court, Eastern, Northern and Southern Districts of California; U.S. Court of Appeals, Ninth Circuit — Member State Bar of California; Kern County Bar Association — Practice Areas: Commercial Law; Business Law; Mergers and Acquisitions — E-mail: cmelton@clifford-brownlaw.com

T. Mark Smith — 1966 — Claremont McKenna College, B.A. (magna cum laude), 1988; University of California, Los Angeles, J.D., 1992 — Phi Alpha Delta — Admitted to Bar, 1992, California; 1993, U.S. District Court, Central District of California; 1995, U.S. District Court, Eastern District of California — Member State Bar of California; Kern County Bar Association — Practice Areas: Business Law; Commercial Litigation — E-mail: msmith@clifford-brownlaw.com

Daniel T. Clifford — 1974 — University of Oregon, B.A., 1997; University of the Pacific, McGeorge School of Law, J.D., 2003 — Admitted to Bar, 2003, California — Member Association of Southern California Defense Counsel — Practice Areas: Business Law; Personal Injury — E-mail: dclifford@clifford-brownlaw.com

Associates

Winifred Thomson Hoss — 1951 — University of California, Berkeley; University of California, Davis, B.S. (with honors), 1976; University of California Davis School of Law, J.D., 1981 — Admitted to Bar, 1981, California; 1981, U.S. District Court, Eastern District of California — Member State Bar of California; Kern County Bar Association; Kern County Women Lawyers Association (President, 1985) — Practice Areas: Business Law; Agriculture; Oil and Gas — E-mail: whoss@clifford-brownlaw.com

Victoria M. Trichell — 1977 — Bakersfield College, A.S., 1997; University of California, San Diego, B.A. (cum laude), 1999; University of San Diego School of Law, J.D., 2002 — Admitted to Bar, 2002, Virginia; 2004, California; 2002, U.S. Court of Appeals, Fourth Circuit — Member Kern County Bar Association — E-mail: vtrichell@clifford-brownlaw.com

Nicholas J. Street — 1980 — University of California, Santa Barbara, B.S., 2002; Whittier Law School, J.D., 2006 — Clerk, United States Attorney's Office, Eastern District of California — Senior Member, Whittier Journal of Child and Family Advocacy — Admitted to Bar, 2007, California — Member

Clifford & Brown, A Professional Corporation, Bakersfield, CA (Continued)

American Bar Association; State Bar of California — E-mail: nstreet@clifford-brownlaw.com

Marc E. Denison — 1976 — Texas A&M University, B.S., 1999; University of San Francisco School of Law, J.D., 2007 — Admitted to Bar, 2007, California — Practice Areas: Business Law; Business Transactions; Estate Planning; Probate; Real Estate; Labor and Employment — E-mail: mdenison@clifford-brownlaw.com

Joseph Werner — 1985 — Chapman University, B.A., 2007; Chapman University School of Law, J.D. (magna cum laude), 2011 — Admitted to Bar, 2011, California; 2012, U.S. District Court, Eastern District of California — Member Kern County Bar Association — Practice Areas: Civil Litigation — E-mail: jwerner@clifford-brownlaw.com

Roman Macias — 1988 — University of California, Los Angeles, B.A., 2010; Chapman University School of Law, J.D., 2013 — Admitted to Bar, 2013, California — E-mail: rmarcias@clifford-brownlaw.com

Jeffrey P. Travis — 1986 — University of California, Los Angeles, B.A., 2008; University of Houston, J.D./M.B.A., 2011 — Admitted to Bar, 2013, California — E-mail: jtravis@clifford-brownlaw.com

Of Counsel

Anthony L. Leggio — 1952 — University of the Pacific, B.A. (summa cum laude), 1974; University of the Pacific, McGeorge School of Law, J.D. (with distinction), 1977 — Admitted to Bar, 1977, California — Member American and Kern County Bar Associations; State Bar of California — Practice Areas: Business Law; Litigation — E-mail: aleggio@clifford-brownlaw.com

Ericksen Arbuthnot

1830 Truxtun Avenue, Suite 200
Bakersfield, California 93301-5022
  Telephone: 661-633-5080
  Fax: 661-633-5089
  www.ericksenarbuthnot.com

(Oakland, CA Office*: 155 Grand Avenue, Suite 1050, 94612-3768)
  (Tel: 510-832-7770)
  (Fax: 510-832-0102)
(Fresno, CA Office*: 2440 West Shaw Avenue, Suite 101, 93711-3300)
  (Tel: 559-449-2600)
  (Fax: 559-449-2603)
(Los Angeles, CA Office*: 835 Wilshire Boulevard, Suite 500, 90017-2656)
  (Tel: 213-489-4411)
  (Fax: 213-489-4332)
(Sacramento, CA Office*: 100 Howe Avenue, Suite 110S, 95825-8200)
  (Tel: 916-483-5181)
  (Fax: 916-483-7558)
(San Francisco, CA Office*: 100 Bush Street, Suite 900, 94104-3950)
  (Tel: 415-362-7126)
  (Fax: 415-362-6401)
(San Jose, CA Office*: 152 North Third Street, Suite 700, 95112-5560)
  (Tel: 408-286-0880)
  (Fax: 408-286-0337)
(Walnut Creek, CA Office*: 570 Lennon Lane, 94598-2415)
  (Tel: 925-947-1702)
  (Fax: 925-947-4921)

Administrative Law, Business Law, Construction Law, Employment Law, Environmental Law, Health Care, Managed Care Liability, Insurance Coverage, Insurance Fraud, Personal Injury, Premises Liability, Product Liability, Professional Liability, Medical Malpractice, Public Entities, Appellate Law

Resident Partner

David J. Frankenberger — **Managing Partner** — University of California, Santa Barbara, B.A., 1993; California Western School of Law, J.D., 1995 — Admitted to Bar, 1996, California; 1997, U.S. District Court, Central District of California; 1998, U.S. District Court, Eastern District of California — Member American Bar Association; State Bar of California — E-mail: dfrankenberger@ericksenarbuthnot.com

(See listing under Oakland, CA for additional information)

Hanna, Brophy, MacLean, McAleer & Jensen, LLP

1800 - 30th Street, Suite 210
Bakersfield, California 93301
  Telephone: 661-397-1212
  Fax: 661-836-2327
  E-Mail: www.hannabrophy.com

Established: 1943

Insurance Defense, Workers' Compensation, Subrogation, Labor and Employment, Employment Law, Litigation

Office Managing Partner

Don L. Powelson — University of San Francisco School of Law, J.D., 1976 — Admitted to Bar, 1976, California — Member State Bar of California; California Workers' Compensation Defense Attorneys Association

(See listing under Oakland, CA for additional information)

The following firms also service this area.

Mollis & Mollis, Inc.
4621 Teller Avenue, Suite 200
Newport Beach, California 92660
  Telephone: 949-222-0735
  Fax: 949-955-0252

Insurance Defense, Civil Trial Practice, Business Law, Construction Law, Corporate Law, Appeals, Labor Law, Environmental Law, Real Estate, Estate Planning, Trusts, Probate, Trust and Estate Litigation, Taxation, Trust Settlement

SEE COMPLETE LISTING UNDER NEWPORT BEACH, CALIFORNIA (157 MILES)

BERKELEY 112,580 Alameda Co.

Refer To

Borton Petrini, LLP
660 Las Gallinas Avenue, Suite B
San Rafael, California 94903
  Telephone: 415-677-0730
  Fax: 415-677-0737

Commercial Litigation, Construction Litigation, General Civil Litigation, Intellectual Property, Professional Liability, Public Entities

SEE COMPLETE LISTING UNDER SAN FRANCISCO, CALIFORNIA (12 MILES)

BURLINGAME 28,806 San Mateo Co.

Sarrail, Castillo & Hall, LLP

700 Airport Boulevard, Suite 420
Burlingame, California 94010-1931
  Telephone: 650-685-9200
  Fax: 650-685-9206
  Mobile: 650-393-0141
  E-Mail: jsarrail@sch-lawfirm.net

Established: 1971

Insurance Defense, Civil Litigation, Appellate Practice, Insurance Litigation, Insurance Coverage, Bad Faith, Product Liability, Construction Law, Premises Liability, General Liability, Fire, Fraud, Common Carrier

Firm Profile: The firm emphasizes the aggressive defense and successful trial of cases. If a new file is not susceptible to early resolution, it is prepared for

CALIFORNIA

Sarrail, Castillo & Hall, LLP, Burlingame, CA (Continued)

successful disposition at trial. We recognize the necessity for competent preparation and the high cost of litigation: discovery tools are used to prepare for trial and not to prolong litigation. The firm also proactively assists the insurance industry in avoiding claims and exposure to bad faith by offering instructions, seminars, and publications in proper claims handling.

Insurance coverage analysis, bad faith defense and appellate work are areas of expertise offered to insurance carriers, as well. The industry has retained the firm as national/regional, state and local counsel in such matters as albuterol, fen/phen, and latex.

The firm takes pride in its superior work product, ethical responsibilities, and client input to achieve client satisfaction.

Insurance Clients

Fairmont Insurance Company
Fire Insurance Exchange
Jewelers Mutual Insurance Company
Penn-America Insurance Company
Truck Insurance Exchange
United National Insurance Company
Zurich American Insurance Group
Farmers Insurance Exchange
General Reinsurance Corporation
Medmarc Mutual Insurance Company
TIG Insurance Company
Unigard Insurance Company
Unitrin Auto & Home Insurance Company

Non-Insurance Clients

ProClaim America Incorporated
Schifrin, Gagnon & Dickey, Inc.
Risk Retention Services, Inc.

Firm Members

Stephen W. Hall — (1955-1993)

Ivanka F. Ackbari — 1947 — University of California, Berkeley, B.A., 1975; University of California, Berkeley Boalt Hall School of Law, J.D., 1978 — Law Clerk to the Honorable Judge Broussard, the Honorable Judge McKibben, and for Alameda Superior Court — Admitted to Bar, 1978, California — Member San Mateo County Bar Association

Catherine P. Johnson — 1960 — University of California, Berkeley, B.A., 1982; University of San Francisco School of Law, J.D., 2000 — Admitted to Bar, 2001, California

Firm Managing Partner

James A. Sarrail — 1943 — Northwestern University, B.A., 1965; University of San Francisco School of Law, J.D., 1968 — Admitted to Bar, 1969, California; U.S. District Court, Central, Eastern, Northern and Southern Districts of California; U.S. Court of Appeals, Ninth Circuit; U.S. Supreme Court — Member State Bar of California; Bar Association of San Francisco; San Mateo County Bar Association; Association of Defense Counsel, Northern California; Defense Research Institute

Executive Partners

Monica Castillo — 1963 — University of California, Berkeley, B.A., 1985; University of California, Hastings College of the Law, J.D., 1989 — Admitted to Bar, 1989, California — Member San Mateo County Bar Association

Jonathan S. Larsen — 1959 — Brigham Young University, B.A., 1984; University of California, Hastings College of the Law, J.D., 1987 — Admitted to Bar, 1987, California; 1988, U.S. District Court, Central District of California; 1989, U.S. District Court, Eastern, Northern and Southern Districts of California — Member Bar Association of San Francisco

CHICO   86,187 Butte Co.

Refer To

Borton Petrini, LLP
3110 Gold Canal Drive, Suite A
Rancho Cordova, California 95670
   Telephone: 916-858-1212
   Fax: 916-858-1252
Mailing Address: P.O. Box 277790, Sacramento, CA 95827

Construction Defect, Construction Law, Employment Litigation, Personal Injury, Product Liability, Professional Liability

SEE COMPLETE LISTING UNDER SACRAMENTO, CALIFORNIA (90 MILES)

Refer To

**Kenny, Snowden & Norine
A Law Corporation**
2701 Park Marina Drive
Redding, California 96001
   Telephone: 530-225-8990
   Fax: 530-225-8944
   Toll Free: 800-655-6677
Mailing Address: Box 994608, Redding, CA 96099-4608

Insurance Defense, Medical Malpractice, Product Liability, Defense Litigation, Civil Trial Practice, Casualty, Professional Errors and Omissions, Employment Law, Public Entities, Real Estate, Land Use, Water Law, Equine Law

SEE COMPLETE LISTING UNDER REDDING, CALIFORNIA (74 MILES)

COSTA MESA   109,960 Orange Co.

Morrow & White

535 Anton Boulevard, Suite 1150
Costa Mesa, California 92626
   Telephone: 714-979-7999
   Fax: 714-979-7779
   E-Mail: billmorrow@morrowandwhitelaw.com
   www.morrowandwhitelaw.com

(Northern California*: 2977 Ygnacio Valley Road, Suite 407, Walnut Creek, CA, 94598)
   (Tel: 925-691-9270)
   (Fax: 925-287-0889)
(Inland Empire: 6185 Magnolia Avenue, Suite 305, Riverside, CA, 91507)
   (Tel: 951-274-9800)
   (Fax: 951-274-9800)

Civil Litigation, Construction Accidents, Toxic Torts, Premises Liability, Construction Defect, Professional Malpractice, Wrongful Death, Product Liability, Automobile Liability, Homeowners, Business Litigation

Insurance Clients

ACE USA
The Mattei Companies
Ranger Insurance Company
Swiss Re
Balboa Insurance Company
NovaPro Risk Solutions
RiverStone Insurance

Non-Insurance Clients

ACCO Engineered Systems
Integrated Trucking & Logistics
Landmark Companies
Maxon Corporation
Allied Security Services, Inc.
Koll Construction, LP
Maxim Crane Works
Reliable Contractors, Inc.

Partners

William D. Morrow — Claremont Men's College, B.A., 1977; Oxford University, England, 1980; Pepperdine University School of Law, J.D., 1981 — Admitted to Bar, 1982, California; U.S. District Court, Central and Southern Districts of California

Christopher A. White — University of California, Berkeley, B.S. (Departmental Honors), 1987; Loyola Law School Los Angeles, J.D. (Dean's Award), 1990 — Admitted to Bar, 1991, California; U.S. District Court, Central District of California

Joanna M. Gonzalez-Konetzke — Texas A&M University, B.S., 1994; University of Colorado Law School, J.D., 2004 — Admitted to Bar, 2004, California; U.S. District Court, Central District of California

Associates

Alexander Z. Stephanik
Glenn H. Morimoto
Lily S. Yee
Samin T. Zamanian
William J. Peniston
Frederick M. Heiser
Jonathon D. Sayre
Michael E. Israel
Tara S. Hizon

EL SEGUNDO   CALIFORNIA

Sheppard, Mullin, Richter & Hampton LLP

650 Town Center Drive, Fourth Floor
Costa Mesa, California 92626
   Telephone: 714-513-5100
   www.sheppardmullin.com

Established: 1927

Antitrust, Bad Faith, Class Actions, Complex Litigation, Insurance Litigation, Trial and Appellate Practice

Firm Profile: Sheppard, Mullin, Richter & Hampton LLP represents clients in a wide variety of insurance-related litigation matters. The firm represents insurance companies, producers and third party administrators in all types of litigation, ranging from class actions and complex multi-party litigation to single insured disputes, and assists insurer clients in administrative and regulatory proceedings.

Special Counsel

Jeffrey C. Crowe — Whittier Law School, J.D. (magna cum laude), 2001 — Judicial Extern for Presiding Justice David G. Sills, Court of Appeal, Fourth Appellate District, Division Three — Admitted to Bar, California; U.S. District Court, Central, Eastern and Southern Districts of California; U.S. Court of Appeals for the Federal and Ninth Circuits — Tel: 714-424-8231 — E-mail: jcrowe@sheppardmullin.com

(See listing under Los Angeles, CA for additional information)

CRESCENT CITY † 7,643 Del Norte Co.

Refer To

**Kenny, Snowden & Norine
A Law Corporation**
2701 Park Marina Drive
Redding, California 96001
   Telephone: 530-225-8990
   Fax: 530-225-8944
   Toll Free: 800-655-6677
Mailing Address: Box 994608, Redding, CA 96099-4608

Insurance Defense, Medical Malpractice, Product Liability, Defense Litigation, Civil Trial Practice, Casualty, Professional Errors and Omissions, Employment Law, Public Entities, Real Estate, Land Use, Water Law, Equine Law
SEE COMPLETE LISTING UNDER REDDING, CALIFORNIA (230 MILES)

Refer To

**Mitchell, Brisso, Delaney & Vrieze, LLP
Attorneys at Law**
814 Seventh Street
Eureka, California 95501-1114
   Telephone: 707-443-5643
   Fax: 707-444-9586
Mailing Address: P.O. Drawer 1008, Eureka, CA 95502

Insurance Defense, Personal Injury, Product Liability, Professional Liability
SEE COMPLETE LISTING UNDER EUREKA, CALIFORNIA (82 MILES)

DELANO 53,041 Kern Co.

Refer To

Borton Petrini, LLP
5060 California Avenue, Suite 700
Bakersfield, California 93309
   Telephone: 661-322-3051
   Fax: 661-322-4628
Mailing Address: P.O. Box 2026, Bakersfield, CA 93303-2026

Administrative Law, Admiralty and Maritime Law, Agriculture, Appellate Practice, Bad Faith, Banking, Bankruptcy, Business Law, Business Litigation, Casualty Insurance Law, Church Law, Collections, Commercial Law, Contracts, Corporate Law, Coverage Issues, Creditor Rights, Eminent Domain, Employment Litigation, Environmental Law, Estate Planning, Family Law, Fire, Health Care, Insurance Coverage, Insurance Defense, Intellectual Property, Labor and Employment, Land Use, Oil and Gas, Personal Injury, Premises Liability, Probate, Product Liability, Professional Errors and Omissions, Property, Public Entities, Real Estate, Religious Institutions, Sports and Entertainment Liability, Toxic Torts, Transactional Law, Transportation, Unlawful Detainer Representing Landlords
SEE COMPLETE LISTING UNDER BAKERSFIELD, CALIFORNIA (31 MILES)

EL SEGUNDO 16,654 Los Angeles Co.

Waters, McCluskey & Boehle

200 North Sepulveda Boulevard, Suite 300
El Segundo, California 90245
   Telephone: 310-396-3411
   Fax: 310-450-0925
   E-Mail: wmb@wmboehle.com
   www.wmboehle.com

(San Jose, CA Office: 111 North Market Street, 95113)
(Tel: 408-912-2017)

Established: 1963

Civil Litigation, Bodily Injury, Complex Litigation, Coverage Issues, General Liability, Property Damage, Slip and Fall, Product Liability, Construction Defect, Environmental Law, Toxic Torts, Bad Faith, Automobile Liability, Wrongful Death, Business Law

Firm Profile: Waters, McCluskey & Boehle has provided superior legal services in civil litigation, insurance defense and appellate work for over forty years. The firm services Los Angeles, Orange, Riverside, San Bernardino, Ventura, Santa Barbara, San Luis Obispo and San Diego counties.

Insurance Clients

Chubb & Son, Inc.	Colony Specialty Insurance
First Financial Insurance Company	Company
St. Paul Travelers	Tower Group

Non-Insurance Clients

American Claim Service, Inc.   Del Taco, Inc.

Retired

Richard A. Wall

In Memoriam

Fritz B. Hax

Partners

Wayne J. Boehle — 1943 — Loyola University of Los Angeles, B.A., 1965; Southwestern University School of Law, J.D., 1970 — Admitted to Bar, 1971, California; 1971, U.S. District Court, Central District of California; 1985, U.S. Supreme Court — Member State Bar of California; Los Angeles County Bar Association; American Board of Trial Advocates; Association of Southern California Defense Counsel; Defense Research Institute — Practice Areas: Automobile; Civil Litigation; Construction Accidents; Fire; Personal Injury; Wrongful Death; Business Law — E-mail: wboehle@wmboehle.com

Gregg W. Brugger — 1958 — University of California, Los Angeles, B.A. (summa cum laude), 1979; University of California, Los Angeles School of Law, J.D., 1983 — Admitted to Bar, 1983, California; U.S. District Court,

Waters, McCluskey & Boehle, El Segundo, CA (Continued)

Central District of California — Member State Bar of California; Los Angeles County Bar Association; Association of Southern California Defense Counsel — Practice Areas: Bad Faith; Civil Litigation; Construction Defect; Insurance Coverage — E-mail: gbrugger@wmboehle.com

Kevin G. McCluskey — 1954 — University of California, Los Angeles, B.A., 1979; Southwestern University School of Law, J.D. (with honors), 1985 — Admitted to Bar, 1985, California; 1985, U.S. District Court, Southern District of California — Member State Bar of California; Los Angeles County Bar Association; Association of Southern California Defense Counsel — Practice Areas: Civil Litigation; Construction Defect; Personal Injury; Product Liability; Toxic Torts; Wrongful Death; Environmental Law — E-mail: kmccluskey@wmboehle.com

Michael T. Montgomery — 1953 — Loyola Marymount University, A.A., 1973; Ventura College of Law, J.D., 1989 — Admitted to Bar, 1989, California — Member State Bar of California; Los Angeles County Bar Association; Association of Southern California Defense Counsel — Practice Areas: Civil Litigation; Construction Defect; Product Liability — E-mail: mmontgomery@wmboehle.com

Junior Partners

Kirk M. Olson   Darin W. Flagg

Associates

Michael P. Ong

ENCINO 40,000 Los Angeles Co.

Kaufman Kaufman & Miller LLP

16633 Ventura Boulevard, Suite 500
Encino, California 91436
  Telephone: 818-788-5767
  Fax: 818-788-2992
  E-Mail: lmiller@kaufmanmiller.com
  www.kaufmanmiller.com

Established: 2004

Employment Law, Employment Litigation, Employer Liability, Employee Benefits, Employment Practices, Employment Discrimination, Trade Secrets, Sexual Harassment, Workers' Compensation, Wrongful Termination, Business and Civil Litigation

Firm Profile: Kaufman Kaufman & Miller LLP provides superior legal representation for clients located throughout the San Fernando Valley, Los Angeles and surrounding counties. Our team is composed of the best lawyers in the Southern California area with over 45 years of boardroom and courtroom experience.

Non-Insurance Clients

Able Freight Services Inc.
Battery-Biz, Inc.
Mikawaya
Phuman, Inc.
Quallion LLC
West Coast Center for Orthopedic Surgery and Sports Medicine
Amkar, Inc.
Bayless Engineering, Inc.
Ophthalmology Associates of the Valley
Simply Right
Wireless Plus, Inc.

Principals

Bruce M. Kaufman — Southwestern University School of Law, J.D., 1964 — Admitted to Bar, 1964, California; U.S. District Court, Central and Southern Districts of California — Member Los Angeles County (Past Member, Judicial Appointments and Election Committees) and San Fernando Valley (Past Trustee) Bar Associations

Jack E. Kaufman — University of Southern California, B.S., 1965; Whittier Law School, J.D., 1971 — Admitted to Bar, 1971, California; U.S. District Court, Central District of California; U.S. Supreme Court — Member Los Angeles County (Past Member, Judicial Election Committee) and San Fernando Valley (Business Law Section) Bar Associations — U.S. House of Representatives (Former Member, Business Advisory Committee); Goodwill Industries (Board of Directors)

Kaufman Kaufman & Miller LLP, Encino, CA (Continued)

Mitchell F. Kaufman — University of California, Santa Barbara, B.A., 1987; Loyola Law School Los Angeles, J.D., 1991 — Admitted to Bar, 1991, California; U.S. District Court, Central District of California — Member Los Angeles County and San Fernando Valley Bar Associations — Languages: Spanish

Lee A. Miller — University of California, Santa Barbara, B.A., 1988; Pepperdine University School of Law, J.D., 1991 — Judicial Clerk for the Honorable Pamela A. Rymer, U.S. Court of Appeals, Ninth Circuit — Lead Articles Editor, Pepperdine Law Review — Admitted to Bar, 1991, California; U.S. District Court, Central District of California — Member Los Angeles County and San Fernando Valley Bar Associations

---

ESCONDIDO 143,911 San Diego Co.

Refer To

Borton Petrini, LLP
1320 Columbia Street, Suite 210
San Diego, California 92101
  Telephone: 619-232-2424
  Fax: 619-531-0794

Admiralty and Maritime Law, Bad Faith, Casualty Insurance Law, Construction Law, Coverage Issues, Labor and Employment, Professional Liability

SEE COMPLETE LISTING UNDER SAN DIEGO, CALIFORNIA (18 MILES)

EUREKA † 27,191 Humboldt Co.

Mitchell, Brisso, Delaney & Vrieze, LLP
Attorneys at Law

814 Seventh Street
Eureka, California 95501-1114
  Telephone: 707-443-5643
  Fax: 707-444-9586
  E-Mail: general@mitchelllawfirm.com
  www.mitchelllawfirm.com

Insurance Defense, Personal Injury, Product Liability, Professional Liability

Insurance Clients

Allied Insurance Company
Associated Aviation Underwriters
The California Casualty Indemnity Exchange
CGU Group
CIGNA Property and Casualty Insurance Company
Continental National Insurance Group
Farmers Insurance Company
Golden Bear Insurance Company
Grange Insurance Association
Hartford Insurance Company
Home Insurance Company
National Union Fire Insurance Company
The St. Paul Companies
State Farm Insurance Company
Viking Insurance Company of Wisconsin
Allstate Insurance Company
Automobile Club of Southern California
California State Automobile Association
Colony Insurance Group
Continental Insurance Company
Employers Fire Insurance Company
Fireman's Fund Insurance Company
Great American Insurance Company
Lawyers Mutual Insurance Company
Penn-America Group, Inc.
Sequoia Insurance Company
Travelers Insurance Companies
Wausau Insurance Companies

Non-Insurance Clients

County of Humboldt
Redwood Empire Municipal Insurance Fund
Hospital Corporation of America
St. Joseph Health System
Trindel (Trinity County & Del Norte County)

Firm Members

Walter J. Carter — (1949-1993)

R. C. Dedekam — (Retired)

Clifford B. Mitchell — 1927 — Humboldt State University; Stanford University, A.B., 1950; Stanford Law School, J.D., 1953 — Admitted to Bar, 1953, California — Member American and Humboldt County Bar Associations; State Bar of California; Association of Defense Counsel, Northern California;

Mitchell, Brisso, Delaney & Vrieze, LLP, Attorneys at Law, Eureka, CA (Continued)

Fellow, American College of Trial Lawyers; Association of Insurance Attorneys

Nancy K. Delaney — 1950 — Humboldt State University, A.B., 1972; M.A., 1973; University of California, Hastings College of the Law, J.D., 1976 — Admitted to Bar, 1976, California — Member State Bar of California; Humboldt County Bar Association; American Board of Trial Advocates; Association of Defense Counsel, Northern California

Paul A. Brisso — 1952 — California State University, Humboldt, B.A. (magna cum laude), 1973; University of the Pacific, McGeorge School of Law, J.D. (with great distinction), 1978 — Admitted to Bar, 1978, California — Member State Bar of California; Humboldt County Bar Association; Association of Defense Counsel, Northern California; American Board of Trial Advocates; Defense Research Institute; Association of Insurance Attorneys; Fellow, American College of Trial Lawyers — Judicial Attorney to Justice George N. Zenovich, California Fifth District Court of Appeals, 1978-1979 — E-mail: pbrisso@mitchelllawfirm.com

John M. Vrieze — 1952 — University of Miami, B.S. (cum laude), 1974; Humboldt State University, M.A., 1980; University of Oregon School of Law, J.D., 1984 — Admitted to Bar, 1984, California — Member American and Humboldt County Bar Associations; State Bar of California; Association of Defense Counsel, Northern California

William F. Mitchell — 1956 — Occidental College, B.A., 1985; Santa Clara University, J.D., 1991 — Admitted to Bar, 1992, California — Member State Bar of California; Humboldt County Bar Association

Russell S. Gans — 1969 — Saint Mary's College, B.A. (cum laude), 1992; University of Oregon School of Law, J.D., 1996 — Admitted to Bar, 1996, California; U.S. District Court, Northern District of California — Member State Bar of California (Real Property Section); Humboldt County Bar Association

Nicholas R. Kloeppel — 1970 — University of California, Riverside, B.A., 1992; University of the Pacific, McGeorge School of Law, J.D., 1996 — Admitted to Bar, 1996, California — Member State Bar of California; Humboldt County Bar Association

The following firms also service this area.

Kenny, Snowden & Norine
A Law Corporation
2701 Park Marina Drive
Redding, California 96001
   Telephone: 530-225-8990
   Fax: 530-225-8944
   Toll Free: 800-655-6677
Mailing Address: Box 994608, Redding, CA 96099-4608

Insurance Defense, Medical Malpractice, Product Liability, Defense Litigation, Civil Trial Practice, Casualty, Professional Errors and Omissions, Employment Law, Public Entities, Real Estate, Land Use, Water Law, Equine Law

SEE COMPLETE LISTING UNDER REDDING, CALIFORNIA (148 MILES)

Roberts Law Firm
45011 Calpella Street
Mendocino, California 95460-2360
   Telephone: 707-937-0503
   Fax: 707-937-2916
Mailing Address: P.O. Box 2360, Mendocino, CA 95460-2360

Insurance Defense, Civil Litigation, Construction Defect, Premises Liability, Product Liability, Real Estate Errors and Omissions, Professional Negligence, Class Actions, Bad Faith, Automobile and Truck Liability, Agriculture and Wine Litigation, Class Action Defense Litigation

SEE COMPLETE LISTING UNDER MENDOCINO, CALIFORNIA (146 MILES)

FAIRFIELD † 105,321 Solano Co.

Refer To
Babin & Seeger, LLP
3550 Round Barn Boulevard, Suite 201
Santa Rosa, California 95403
   Telephone: 707-526-7370
   Fax: 707-526-0307
Mailing Address: P.O. Box 11626, Santa Rosa, CA 95406

Insurance Defense, Motor Vehicle, Commercial Law, General Liability, Product Liability, Property Damage, Construction Defect, Contracts, Environmental Law, Insurance Coverage, Workers' Compensation, Personal Injury, Professional Malpractice

SEE COMPLETE LISTING UNDER SANTA ROSA, CALIFORNIA (53 MILES)

Refer To
Boornazian, Jensen & Garthe
A Professional Corporation
555 12th Street, 18th Floor
Oakland, California 94607
   Telephone: 510-834-4350
   Fax: 510-839-1897
Mailing Address: P.O. Box 12925, Oakland, CA 94604-2925

Insurance Defense, Trial Practice, Product Liability, Legal Malpractice, Professional Malpractice, Medical Malpractice, Insurance Coverage, Construction Law

SEE COMPLETE LISTING UNDER OAKLAND, CALIFORNIA (38 MILES)

FRESNO † 494,665 Fresno Co.

Borton Petrini, LLP
2444 Main Street, Suite 150
Fresno, California 93721
   Telephone: 559-268-0117
   Fax: 559-237-7995
   E-Mail: bpfrs@bortonpetrini.com
   www.bortonpetrini.com

Established: 1899

Agriculture, Business Litigation, Casualty Insurance Law, Commercial Law, Contracts, Coverage Issues, Insurance Defense, Labor and Employment, Premises Liability, Product Liability, Professional Errors and Omissions, Public Entities, Transportation

Firm Profile: Since 1899, Borton Petrini, LLP, has offered high quality legal services in all of the practice areas described above through its California network of 10 regional offices. The mission of Borton Petrini, LLP is to treat every file as though we were representing ourselves and paying the bill for that representation.

Managing Attorney

Bryan C. Doss — 1967 — University of California, Davis, B.A., 1991; San Joaquin College of Law, J.D., 2007 — Admitted to Bar, 2009, California; U.S. District Court, Eastern District of California — Member State Bar of California; Fresno County and Kings County Bar Associations — E-mail: bdoss@bortonpetrini.com

Associates

Elizabeth E. Waldow — 1952 — George Mason University, B.S., 1975; San Joaquin College of Law, J.D. (with distinction), 2009 — Admitted to Bar, 2009, California — Member Federal, American and Fresno County Bar Associations; State Bar of California; Fresno County Women Lawyers (Board, 2012-Present); Association of Defense Counsel, Northern California — Fresno Fig Garden Rotary; San Joaquin College of Law Alumni Board Member — E-mail: ewaldow@bortonpetrini.com

Kyle R. Roberson — 1981 — California State Polytechnic University at San Luis Obispo, B.S., 2005; San Joaquin College of Law, J.D. (with distinction), 2012 — Admitted to Bar, 2012, California — Member State Bar of California; Fresno County Bar Association — Author: "One Fish, Two Fish, More Fish, No Water: Granting an Exemption Under the Endangered Species Act

CALIFORNIA — HANFORD

Borton Petrini, LLP, Fresno, CA (Continued)

due to Economic Woes in the Central Valley," San Joaquin Agricultural Law Review, Vol. 19 — E-mail: kroberson@bortonpetrini.com

Ericksen Arbuthnot

2440 West Shaw Avenue, Suite 101
Fresno, California 93711-3300
  Telephone: 559-449-2600
  Fax: 559-449-2603
  www.ericksenarbuthnot.com

(Oakland, CA Office*: 155 Grand Avenue, Suite 1050, 94612-3768)
  (Tel: 510-832-7770)
  (Fax: 510-832-0102)
(Bakersfield, CA Office*: 1830 Truxtun Avenue, Suite 200, 93301-5022)
  (Tel: 661-633-5080)
  (Fax: 661-633-5089)
(Los Angeles, CA Office*: 835 Wilshire Boulevard, Suite 500, 90017-2656)
  (Tel: 213-489-4411)
  (Fax: 213-489-4332)
(Sacramento, CA Office*: 100 Howe Avenue, Suite 110S, 95825-8200)
  (Tel: 916-483-5181)
  (Fax: 916-483-7558)
(San Francisco, CA Office*: 100 Bush Street, Suite 900, 94104-3950)
  (Tel: 415-362-7126)
  (Fax: 415-362-6401)
(San Jose, CA Office*: 152 North Third Street, Suite 700, 95112-5560)
  (Tel: 408-286-0880)
  (Fax: 408-286-0337)
(Walnut Creek, CA Office*: 570 Lennon Lane, 94598-2415)
  (Tel: 925-947-1702)
  (Fax: 925-947-4921)

Administrative Law, Business Law, Construction Law, Employment Law, Environmental Law, Health Care, Managed Care Liability, Insurance Coverage, Insurance Fraud, Personal Injury, Premises Liability, Product Liability, Professional Liability, Medical Malpractice, Public Entities, Appellate Law

Resident Partners

David J. Frankenberger — **Managing Partner** — University of California, Santa Barbara, B.A., 1993; California Western School of Law, J.D., 1995 — Admitted to Bar, 1996, California; 1997, U.S. District Court, Central District of California; 1998, U.S. District Court, Eastern District of California — Member American Bar Association; State Bar of California — E-mail: dfrankenberger@ericksenarbuthnot.com

Of Counsel

Michael D. Ott — University of California, San Diego, B.A. (with honors), 1971; University of California, Riverside, 1971-1972; The University of Iowa College of Law, J.D. (magna cum laude), 1974 — Admitted to Bar, 1975, California; 1977, Oregon (Inactive); 1982, U.S. Supreme Court — Member American, Fresno County and Madera County Bar Associations; State Bar of California; Association of Trial Lawyers of America — Judge Pro Tem, Madera County Superior Court, 1986-1988 — E-mail: mott@ericksenarbuthnot.com

Associate Attorneys

Timothy McCaughey — University of Santa Clara, J.D., 1977 — Admitted to Bar, 1978, California — E-mail: tmccaughey@ericksenarbuthnot.com
Charlotte Konczal — San Joaquin College of Law, J.D., 2000 — Admitted to Bar, 2001, California — E-mail: ckonczal@ericksenarbuthnot.com
Maribel Hernandez — San Joaquin College of Law, J.D., 2004 — Admitted to Bar, 2008, California — E-mail: mhernandez@ericksenarbuthnot.com
Chester Wells — California Polytechnic State University, B.S., 2005; San Joaquin College of Law, J.D., 2012 — Admitted to Bar, 2012, California

(See listing under Oakland, CA for additional information)

Hanna, Brophy, MacLean, McAleer & Jensen, LLP

1141 West Shaw Avenue, Suite 101
Fresno, California 93711
  Telephone: 559-435-9823
  Fax: 559-435-9098
  www.hannabrophy.com

Established: 1943

Insurance Defense, Workers' Compensation, Subrogation, Labor and Employment, Employment Law, Litigation

Office Managing Partner

Richard W. Krum — University of Santa Clara School of Law, J.D., 1980 — Admitted to Bar, 1980, California — Member Fresno County Bar Association; California Workers' Compensation Defense Attorneys Association

(See listing under Oakland, CA for additional information)

HANFORD † 53,967 Kings Co.

Refer To

Borton Petrini, LLP
2444 Main Street, Suite 150
Fresno, California 93721
  Telephone: 559-268-0117
  Fax: 559-237-7995

Agriculture, Business Litigation, Casualty Insurance Law, Commercial Law, Contracts, Coverage Issues, Insurance Defense, Labor and Employment, Premises Liability, Product Liability, Professional Errors and Omissions, Public Entities, Transportation

SEE COMPLETE LISTING UNDER FRESNO, CALIFORNIA (31 MILES)

HAYWARD 144,186 Alameda Co.

Refer To

Boornazian, Jensen & Garthe
A Professional Corporation
555 12th Street, 18th Floor
Oakland, California 94607
  Telephone: 510-834-4350
  Fax: 510-839-1897

Mailing Address: P.O. Box 12925, Oakland, CA 94604-2925

Insurance Defense, Trial Practice, Product Liability, Legal Malpractice, Professional Malpractice, Medical Malpractice, Insurance Coverage, Construction Law

SEE COMPLETE LISTING UNDER OAKLAND, CALIFORNIA (17 MILES)

Refer To

Borton Petrini, LLP
660 Las Gallinas Avenue, Suite B
San Rafael, California 94903
  Telephone: 415-677-0730
  Fax: 415-677-0737

Commercial Litigation, Construction Litigation, General Civil Litigation, Intellectual Property, Professional Liability, Public Entities

SEE COMPLETE LISTING UNDER SAN FRANCISCO, CALIFORNIA (25 MILES)

HUNTINGTON BEACH 189,992 Orange Co.

Declues, Burkett & Thompson, LLP

17011 Beach Boulevard, Suite 400
Huntington Beach, California 92647-7455
  Telephone: 714-843-9444
  Fax: 714-843-9452
  E-Mail: lgalloway@dbtlaw.com
  www.dbtlaw.com

IRVINE   CALIFORNIA

Declues, Burkett & Thompson, LLP, Huntington Beach, CA (Continued)

Established: 1996

Negligence, Intentional Torts, Construction Defect, Product Liability, Premises Liability, Sexual Harassment, Wrongful Termination, Civil Rights, Construction Accidents, Employer Liability, Employment Practices Liability, Employment Law, Motor Vehicle Negligence, Business Torts

Firm Profile: Declues, Burkett & Thompson, LLP, a firm of experienced trial lawyers, was formed in January, 1996. The principal partners, however, have practiced together for over 25 years, providing stability and a wealth of experience to the firm.

Insurance Clients

Markel Corporation
Workmen's Auto Insurance Company
Republic Western Insurance Company

Non-Insurance Clients

Alliance of Schools for Cooperative Insurance Programs
Keenan & Associates
Special District Risk Management Authority
California Joint Powers Insurance Authority
Orange County Department of Education

Members of the Firm

Michael E. Burkett — (1944-2006)

J. Michael Declues — University of Southern California, B.A., 1972; J.D., 1975 — Hale Moot Court — Admitted to Bar, 1975, California; U.S. District Court, Central District of California; U.S. Court of Appeals, Ninth Circuit — Member American and Orange County Bar Associations; State Bar of California

Jeffrey P. Thompson — Claremont McKenna College, B.A., 1983; Loyola Law School, J.D., 1988 — St. Thomas Moore Honor Society; Recipient, American Jurisprudence Award, International Law — Admitted to Bar, 1988, California; U.S. District Court, Central, Eastern, Northern and Southern Districts of California; U.S. Court of Appeals, Ninth Circuit; U.S. Supreme Court — Member State Bar of California

Glenn S. Goldby — Northern Arizona University, B.S., 1975; Southwestern University, J.D., 1978 — Phi Alpha Theta — Admitted to Bar, 1979, California; 1991, Arizona; U.S. District Court, Central, Eastern and Southern Districts of California — Member American and Orange County Bar Associations; State Bars of California and Arizona; Association of Southern California Defense Counsel; Association of Business Trial Lawyers

Jeffrey A. Smith — Emory University; The London School of Economics and Political Science, B.A., 1975; University of Florida, J.D., 1978 — Admitted to Bar, 1980, California; 1982, Florida; U.S. District Court, Central and Southern Districts of California — Member State Bar of California; The Florida Bar; American Board of Trial Advocates; Association of Southern California Defense Counsel

Associates

Gregory A. Wille
Jennifer K. Berneking
Steven J. Lowery
Cary K. Quan
Patricia A. Lynch
Fernando A. Vicente

INDIO   76,036 Riverside Co.

Refer To
Borton Petrini, LLP
1461 Ford Street, Suite 201
Redlands, California 92373
   Telephone: 909-381-0527
   Fax: 909-381-0658
Mailing Address: P.O Box 11207, San Bernardino, CA 92423

Coverage Issues, Insurance Defense, Labor and Employment, Product Liability, Professional Errors and Omissions, Public Entities

SEE COMPLETE LISTING UNDER SAN BERNARDINO, CALIFORNIA (76 MILES)

Refer To
Kinkle, Rodiger & Spriggs Professional Corporation
3333 Fourteenth Street
Riverside, California 92501-3809
   Telephone: 951-683-2410
   Toll Free: 800-235-2039
   Fax: 951-683-7759

Insurance Defense, Self-Insured, General Liability, Product Liability, Automobile, Premises Liability, Public Entities, Construction Law, Professional Liability, Coverage Issues, Bad Faith, Civil Trial Practice, Appellate Practice, Federal Courts

SEE COMPLETE LISTING UNDER RIVERSIDE, CALIFORNIA (75 MILES)

Refer To
Thompson & Colegate LLP
3610 Fourteenth Street
Riverside, California 92501
   Telephone: 951-682-5550
   Fax: 951-781-4012

Mailing Address: P.O. Box 1299, Riverside, CA 92502

Insurance Defense, Medical Malpractice, Automobile Liability, General Liability, Construction Litigation, Coverage Issues, Personal Injury, Product Liability, Premises Liability, Employment Law, Commercial Litigation, Bankruptcy, Alternative Dispute Resolution, Appellate Practice, Complex Litigation, Real Estate

SEE COMPLETE LISTING UNDER RIVERSIDE, CALIFORNIA (75 MILES)

IRVINE   212,375 Orange Co.

Clinton & Clinton
2030 Main Street, Suite 1300
Irvine, California 92614
   Telephone: 949-260-9083
   Fax: 949-260-9084
   E-Mail: dclinton@clinton-clinton.com
   www.clinton-clinton.com

(Long Beach, CA Office*: 100 Oceangate, Suite 1400, 90802)
   (Tel: 562-216-5000)
   (Fax: 562-216-5001)
(Los Angeles, CA Office*: 5757 West Century Boulevard, Suite 700, 90045)
   (Tel: 310-242-8615)
   (Fax: 310-242-8612)
(San Diego, CA Office*: 525 "B" Street, Suite 1500, 92101)
   (Tel: 619-858-4728)
   (Fax: 619-858-4729)
(San Francisco, CA Office*: 201 Spear Street, Suite 1100, 94105)
   (Tel: 415-230-5368)
   (Fax: 415-230-5369)
(Sacramento, CA Office*: 770 'L' Street, Suite 950, 95814)
   (Tel: 916-361-6060)
   (Fax: 916-361-6061)
(Calabasas, CA Office: 23480 Park Sorrento, Suite 219A, 91302)
   (Tel: 562-216-5000)
   (Fax: 562-216-5001)
(Birmingham, AL Office: 1 Chase Corporate Center, Suite 400, 35244)
   (Tel: 205-313-6329)
   (Fax: 562-216-5001)
(Cumming, GA Office: 410 Peachtree Parkway, Building 400, Suite 4245, 30041)
   (Tel: 678-341-5134)
   (Fax: 562-216-5001)
(Philadelphia, PA Office: 1315 Walnut Street, Suite 601, 19107)
   (Tel: 267-800-1897)
   (Fax: 267-800-1898)
(Nashville, TN Office: 2400 Crestmoor Road, 37215)
   (Tel: 615-386-7040)
   (Fax: 562-216-5001)
(Austin, TX Office: 12912 Hill Country Boulevard, Suite F210, 78738)
   (Tel: 512-200-7055)
   (Fax: 512-266-3655)

CALIFORNIA — IRVINE

Clinton & Clinton, Irvine, CA (Continued)

(Ft. Worth, TX Office: 109 East Third Street, Suite 350, 76102)
  (Tel: 817-900-8210)
  (Fax: 817-900-8221)
(Houston, TX Office: 480 North Sam Houston Parkway East, 77060-3528)
  (Tel: 713-659-0054)
  (Fax: 281-447-5733)

Asbestos Litigation, Automobile, Automotive Products Liability, Civil Litigation, Civil Rights, Civil Trial Practice, Commercial Litigation, Common Carrier, Complex Litigation, Construction Defect, Dental Malpractice, Employment Law, Environmental Law, Insurance Defense, Hospital Malpractice, Law Enforcement Liability, Legal Malpractice, Mass Tort, Medical Devices, Medical Malpractice, Pharmaceutical, Premises Liability, Product Liability, Retail Liability, Sexual Harassment, Slip and Fall, Special Investigative Unit Claims, Sports and Entertainment Liability, Toxic Torts, Truck Liability, Workers' Compensation

(See listing under Long Beach, CA for additional information)

Grant, Genovese & Baratta, LLP

2030 Main Street, Suite 1600
Irvine, California 92614-7257
  Telephone: 949-660-1600
  Fax: 949-660-6060
  E-Mail: jmb@ggb-law.com
  www.ggb-law.com

Established: 1999

General Civil Litigation, Bad Faith, Insurance Coverage, Construction Defect, Directors and Officers Liability, Employment Law, Environmental Law, Intellectual Property, Homeowners' Associations, Earth Movement, Toxic Torts

Firm Profile: Grant, Genovese & Baratta, LLP is one of Orange County's preeminent business, insurance and real estate litigation and transaction boutique law firms.

Insurance Clients

California Capital Insurance Company	CastlePoint National Insurance Company
Commerce West Insurance Company	The Medical Protective Company
State Farm Insurance Companies	Nationwide Insurance
Tower Group, Inc.	Sure Products Insurance Agency

Partners

James M. Baratta — University of California, Los Angeles, B.A. (cum laude, with honors), 1969; Loyola Law School Los Angeles, J.D. (cum laude) 1972 — Admitted to Bar, 1972, California; U.S. District Court, Central, Eastern, Northern and Southern Districts of California — Member State Bar of California; Orange County Bar Association (Masters Division); Defense Research Institute (Insurance Law Committee); American Board of Trial Advocates; American College of Trial Lawyers; Litigation Counsel of America; Association of Southern California Defense Counsel

Lance D. Orloff — University of California, Davis, A.B. (with honors), 1981; Loyola Law School Los Angeles, J.D., 1984 — Admitted to Bar, 1984, California — Member American and Los Angeles County Bar Associations; State Bar of California; American Board of Trial Advocates Inns of Court, Los Angeles Chapter; Association of Southern California Defense Counsel

Robin A. Webb — University of Southern California, B.A. (magna cum laude), 1989; University of Southern California School of Law, J.D., 1992 — Admitted to Bar, 1992, California — Member State Bar of California; Orange County and Los Angeles County Bar Associations; Litigation Counsel of America; Diversity Law Institute; The Trial Institute; Association of Southern California Defense Counsel

Jason S. Roberts — Indiana University-Bloomington, B.A., 1997; Loyola Law School Los Angeles, J.D., 2002 — Admitted to Bar, 2002, California —

Grant, Genovese & Baratta, LLP, Irvine, CA (Continued)

Member State Bar of California; Orange County Bar Association; Association of Southern California Defense Counsel

Hollins Law

2601 Main Street
Penthouse Suite 1300
Irvine, California 92614
  Telephone: 714-558-9119
  Fax: 714-558-9091
  Toll Free: 866-513-5033
  E-Mail: info@hollins-law.com
  www.hollins-law.com

Established: 1981

Appellate Practice, Catastrophic Injury, Construction Litigation, Employment Litigation, Insurance Litigation, Intellectual Property, Professional Liability, Business Law and Litigation, Class Action Litigation, Community Association Law, Creditor's Rights Law and Collection Litigation, Environmental Law and Litigation, Governmental/Public Entity Litigation

Firm Profile: The hallmark of Hollins Law is our trial practice. Due to our unequaled skill and experience with the trial process and dedication to our clients' needs, the talented Hollins Law attorneys are often called upon to assist or replace other attorneys for trial. Constantly praised by judges, juries, peers and even adversaries for our aggressive yet ethical presentation and attention to detail, we have earned our reputation for fearless trial advocacy.

Insurance Clients

American Safety Insurance Company	Arch Specialty Insurance Company
Fire Insurance Exchange	Farmers Insurance Exchange
Liberty Mutual Insurance	Great American Insurance Company
Mid-Century Insurance Company	Truck Insurance Exchange
21st Century Insurance Company	United States Liability Insurance Company

Non-Insurance Clients

Campagnolo North America Inc.	Fleming & Hall Administrators, Inc.
KSL II Management Operations, LLC	Henry Schein, Inc.
Shanghai Linzheng Import & Export Co., Ltd.	Stemtech International, Inc.
United Rentals, Inc.	Time Warner Cable
	Zim American Integrated Shipping Services Co., Inc.

Principals

Andrew S. Hollins — The University of Tennessee, B.S., 1973; Woodland University, Mid-Valley College of Law, J.D., 1978 — Awarded "Trial Lawyer of the Year" by the American Board of Trial Advocates - O.C. Chapter, 2005; Awarded "Super Lawyer" - 2009-2015 by Super Lawyers™; "Won the "Wiley W. Manuel Award" by the State Bar of California, 1992; Featured in The Verdict, a publication of the Southern California Defense Counsel, for successive defense verdicts in a row; Recognized by the State Board of Governors and the Orange County Bar Association for pro bono legal services. — Admitted to Bar, 1978, California; U.S. District Court, Central, Eastern, Northern and Southern Districts of California; U.S. Court of Federal Claims — Member State Bar of California; Orange County Bar Association; Association of Southern California Defense Counsel; Defense Research Institute; Association of Trial Lawyers of America; American Board of Trial Advocates — Presentations: "Masters in Trial": Defense Team Coordinator, American Board of Trial Advocates, five-time presenter; "Technology in the Courtroom", American Board of Trial Advocates; "Cumis and Its Progeny" January 2011; Super Lawyer, 2009-2014 — Practice Areas: Insurance Litigation; Catastrophic Injury; Public Entities — E-mail: ahollins@hollins-law.com

Kathleen Mary Kushi Carter — Saint Anselm College, B.A., 1988; Vermont Law School, J.D. (cum laude), 1991; Pepperdine University, M.B.A., 2007 — Admitted to Bar, 1992, California; U.S. District Court, Central, Eastern,

IRVINE   CALIFORNIA

Hollins Law, Irvine, CA   (Continued)

Northern and Southern Districts of California; U.S. Court of Federal Claims; 1999, U.S. Court of Appeals, Ninth Circuit; 2005, U.S. District Court, Southern District of Indiana — Member State Bar of California; Orange County and Los Angeles County Bar Associations; American Board of Trial Advocates — Presentations: "998 Offer Post-Verdict Valuation - How It Really Works," September, 2005, "Cumis and Its Progeny," January 2011; National Association of Professional and Executive Women; BUZZ, An Executive Women's Think Tank; National Association of Minority & Women Owned Law Firms; Women's Business Enterprise National Council — Practice Areas: Class Actions; Business Litigation; Business Law; Employment Litigation — E-mail: kcarter@hollins-law.com

Partners

Christine R. Arnold — Stanford University, B.A., 2000; California Western School of Law, J.D. (magna cum laude), 2005 — Admitted to Bar, 2005, California; 2006, U.S. District Court, Central District of California — Member American Bar Association; Orange County Bar Association — Super Lawyers Rising Stars, 2013 and 2014 — Practice Areas: Employment Litigation; Business Law; Business Litigation; Class Actions — E-mail: carnold@hollins-law.com

Tamara M. Heathcote — Ashland College, B.S., 1987; University of Southern California School of Law, J.D., 1997 — Moot Court Honors Program — Admitted to Bar, 1997, California; U.S. District Court, Central, Eastern and Northern Districts of California; U.S. Court of Appeals, Ninth Circuit — Member State Bar of California; Orange County Bar Association; Society of Toxicology — Presentations: "Solving Water Intrusion and Mold Problems," Lorman Education Services - August, 2005; "Science of Mold and Deposing the Scientific Expert," MCLE - February, 2006; "Ethics Seminar," MCLE - 1998 — Advanced Certification in Medical Technology — Practice Areas: Environmental Law; Environmental Litigation; Construction Litigation; Intellectual Property — E-mail: theathcote@hollins-law.com

Scott W. Monroe — Gettysburg College, B.A. (magna cum laude), 2003; Pepperdine University School of Law, J.D., 2007 — Dean's List; Dean's Commendation List; Classics Honors Fraternity; Trial Team, A.A.J. Trial Competition; Trial Team, San Diego Defense Lawyers Trial Competition; Moot Court; Honors Trial Advocate, Highest Distinction Award — Admitted to Bar, 2007, California; U.S. District Court, Central District of California — Member Orange County and Los Angeles Bar Associations — Practice Areas: Insurance Litigation; Catastrophic Injury; Business Law; Business Litigation — E-mail: smonroe@hollins-law.com

Associates

Braden A. Bennett — University of Southern California, B.A. (cum laude), 2004; University of San Diego School of Law, J.D., 2009 — Admitted to Bar, 2009, California; U.S. District Court, Central District of California — Member Orange County Bar Association — Practice Areas: Business Litigation; Construction Litigation; Catastrophic Injury; Business Law — E-mail: bbennett@hollins-law.com

Ronnie Chow — University of California, Irvine, B.A., 1996; University of San Diego School of Law, J.D., 1999 — Admitted to Bar, California; U.S. District Court, Central District of California — Languages: Mandarin Chinese — Practice Areas: Collections; Creditor's Rights — E-mail: rchow@hollins-law.com

Brieanna M. Dolmage — University of California, Irvine, B.S., 2003; Whittier Law School, J.D., 2007 — Admitted to Bar, 2008, California; U.S. District Court, Central District of California — Member Orange County Bar Association — Practice Areas: Insurance Litigation; Business Law; Business Litigation — E-mail: bdolmage@hollins-law.com

Jang H. Kang — University of California, Santa Barbara, B.A., 1999; William S. Boyd School of Law, University of Nevada, Las Vegas, J.D., 2009 — Admitted to Bar, 2009, Nevada; 2010, California; 2011, U.S. District Court, Central District of California — Member Orange County Bar Association — Practice Areas: Insurance Litigation; Construction Litigation; Business Law; Business Litigation — E-mail: jkang@hollins-law.com

Jonathan T. Little — Point Loma College, B.A., 2000; American University, Washington College of Law, J.D., 2005 — Admitted to Bar, 2005, California; U.S. District Court, Central, Northern and Southern Districts of California — Member State Bar of California; Orange County Bar Association — Practice Areas: Catastrophic Injury; Environmental Litigation; Employment Litigation; Employment Law — E-mail: jlittle@hollins-law.com

Andrew J. Ulwelling — University of California at Irvine, B.A., 1998; Western State University College of Law, J.D., 2010 — Admitted to Bar, 2010, California; U.S. District Court, Central District of California — Member Orange County Bar Association — Practice Areas: Insurance Litigation; Catastrophic

Hollins Law, Irvine, CA   (Continued)

Injury; Collections; Creditor's Rights — E-mail: aulwelling@hollins-law.com

Richard W. Zevnik — University of California, Los Angeles, B.A., 1976; Loyola Law School, J.D., 1985 — Admitted to Bar, 1985, California; U.S. District Court, Central, Eastern, Northern and Southern Districts of California; U.S. District Court, District of Arizona; U.S. Court of Appeals, Ninth Circuit — Member Orange County and Los Angeles County Bar Associations — Practice Areas: Business Litigation; Appellate Practice; Business Law — E-mail: rzevnik@hollins-law.com

The Lee Law Group, PC

17310 Red Hill Avenue, Suite 350
Irvine, California 92614
Telephone: 949-271-9333
Fax: 949-271-9334
E-Mail: tlee@leefirm.com
www.leefirm.com

Accident, Agent/Broker Liability, Alternative Dispute Resolution, Amusements, Architects and Engineers, Automobile, Bodily Injury, Business Law, Church Law, Construction Law, Contractors Liability, Governmental Liability, Hospitality, Mold Litigation, Municipal Liability, Personal and Commercial Vehicle, Personal Liability, Premises Liability, Product Liability, Professional Liability, Property Damage, Public Liability, Real Estate, Restaurant Liability, Retail Liability, Slip and Fall, Special Investigative Unit Claims, State and Federal Courts, Tort Litigation, Trial and Appellate Practice, Trucking, Wrongful Death, Auto Dealer Liability, Catastrophic Injuries, Golf and Bowling, Parks and Recreation, Pool Construction Liability

Insurance Clients

ALLIED Insurance	AutoOne Insurance Company
Canterbury Financial Group	Clarendon Insurance Company
Cornerstone National Insurance Company	Delos Insurance
	Discover Re
Esurance	Financial Pacific Insurance Company
Inscorp	
Monticello Insurance Company	Nations Insurance Company
Philadelphia Insurance Company	Praetorian Insurance Company
QBE	RLI Insurance Company
Scottsdale Insurance Company	Sirius Insurance Company
Suncoast Insurance	Topa Insurance Company
United Fire & Casualty Company	

Non-Insurance Clients

Brennan Electric, Inc.	California Pools & Spas
EXL Structural Enginners, Inc	PV Pools
Swan Pools of Southern California	VeriClaim, Inc.

Third Party Administrators

Adventist Risk Management, Inc.	AFA Insurance Services
American Claims Management, Inc.	BRAC
	BridgeWorks Commercial Management
Claims Control, Inc.	
Crawford & Company	Gallagher Bassett Services, Inc.
HDR Insurance Services	McLarens Young International
Multi State Claims Services	NIF Insurance Services
NovaPro Risk Solutions	Pearl Insurance
Specialty Claims Management	State Claims Administrators
Ward North America, Inc.	

Transportation Clients

SafeFleet Insurance Services

Senior Partner

Ted M. Lee — University of California, Irvine, B.A., 1987; Boston University School of Law, J.D., 1991 — Phi Alpha Delta; Phi Gamma Delta — Admitted to Bar, 1992, California; 1993, U.S. District Court, Central, Eastern, Northern and Southern Districts of California — Member American and Orange County Bar Associations; Defense Research Institute; Association of Southern California Defense Counsel; American Trial Lawyers Association; Association of Trial Lawyers of America

CALIFORNIA — IRVINE

London Fischer LLP

2505 McCabe Way, Suite 100
Irvine, California 92614
 Telephone: 949-252-0550
 Fax: 949-252-0553
 E-Mail: REndres@LondonFischer.com
 www.londonfischer.com

(New York, NY Office*: 59 Maiden Lane, 39th Floor Reception, 10038)
 (Tel: 212-972-1000)
 (Fax: 212-972-1030)
 (E-Mail: VPetrungaro@LondonFischer.com)
(Woodland Hills, CA Office*: 21550 Oxnard Street, 3rd Floor, 91367)
 (Tel: (818) 224-6068)
 (Fax: (818) 224-6061)
 (E-Mail: DLeMontree@LondonFischer.com)
 (www.LondonFischer.com)

Established: 1991

Construction Law, Professional Liability, Admiralty and Maritime Law, Civil Rights, Commercial Litigation, Directors and Officers Liability, Employment Law, Environmental Law, Fidelity and Surety, Insurance Coverage, Insurance Regulation, Marine Insurance, Mass Tort, Municipal Liability, Product Liability, Property Loss, Reinsurance, Subrogation, Toxic Torts, Transportation, Trucking Law, Employment Litigation and Counseling, Catastrophic Loss Investigations and Litigation, National Appellate Practice, National Trial Practice, Professional Contracts and Disputes

Retired

James L. Fischer — Member American Bar Association (Member, Sections on Local Government, Tort and Insurance Law and Litigation); New York State (Member, Sections on Insurance, Negligence and Compensation Law and Trial Lawyers), and Westchester County Bar Associations; Association of the Bar of the City of New York — "Minimum Contacts, Shaffer's Unified Jurisdictional Test," 12 Valp. Law Review 25

Partner

Bernard London — 1950 — New York University, B.S., 1972; The College of Insurance, St. John's University, 1973; St. John's University School of Law, J.D., 1977 — Admitted to Bar, 1978, New York; U.S. District Court, Eastern, Northern, Southern and Western Districts of New York; U.S. Court of Appeals, Second Circuit; U.S. Court of Federal Claims — Member New York State Bar Association (Committees on Professional Liability, Reinsurance and Litigation); Defense Research Institute — Author and Lecturer on Construction and Insurance Law; Author of Municipal Zoning Codes, Professional Liability Insurance and Construction Law — Trustee, Village of Lloyd Harbor, 1999; Police Commissioner, Village of Lloyd Harbor; Selected for inclusion in the New York Super Lawyers list, 2009, 2010, 2011, 2012, 2013 and 2014 — E-mail: BLondon@LondonFischer.com

Daniel Zemann, Jr. — 1953 — Fairleigh Dickinson University, B.A., 1975; South Texas College of Law, J.D., 1983 — Admitted to Bar, 1983, Texas; 1987, New York; 1983, U.S. Court of Appeals, Fifth Circuit; U.S. District Court, Eastern and Southern Districts of Texas; 1991, U.S. District Court, Eastern and Southern Districts of New York; 1997, U.S. Court of Appeals, Second Circuit — Member New York State Bar Association; State Bar of Texas — Practice Areas: Construction Litigation; Insurance Coverage; General Liability; Professional Liability; Trial and Appellate Practice; Construction Claims; Construction Defect; Product Liability Defense — E-mail: DZemann@LondonFischer.com

Richard S. Endres — 1963 — State University of New York at Albany, B.S., 1985; California Western School of Law, J.D. (magna cum laude), 1989 — Admitted to Bar, 1989, California; 1990, New York; 1989, U.S. District Court, Southern District of California; 1990, U.S. District Court, Eastern and Southern Districts of New York; 2003, U.S. District Court, Central and Northern Districts of California; U.S. Court of Appeals, Ninth Circuit — Member New York State Bar Association (Sections on Product Liability, Torts and Insurance, Construction, Trial Lawyers); State Bar of California (Sections on Product Liability, Torts and Insurance, Construction, Business Litigation); Los Angeles County and Orange County Bar Associations; Professional Liability Underwriting Society — Practice Areas: Advertising Injury; Agent/Broker Liability; Bad Faith; Bodily Injury; Carrier Defense;

London Fischer LLP, Irvine, CA (Continued)

Casualty Insurance Law; Catastrophic Injury; Commercial Insurance; Comprehensive General Liability; Construction Accidents; Coverage Analysis; Declaratory Judgments; Directors and Officers Liability; Errors and Omissions; Excess and Surplus Lines; Excess and Umbrella; Extra-Contractual Liability; Extra-Contractual Litigation; Fire Loss; Insurance Coverage Litigation; Insurance Defense; Medical Product Liability; Premises Liability; Product Liability; Professional Errors and Omissions; Property and Casualty; Property Damage; Risk Management — E-mail: REndres@LondonFischer.com

John E. Sparling — 1962 — St. Joseph's College, B.A., 1984; Hofstra University School of Law, J.D., 1987 — Hofstra Law Review, Staff Writer, 1985-1986, Assistant Editor, 1986-1987 — Admitted to Bar, 1988, New York; New York for Multiple Pro Hac Vice Admissions; 1988, U.S. District Court, Eastern, Northern, Southern and Western Districts of New York — Member American Bar Association (Committees on Litigation, Tort and Insurance Practice and Real Property, Probate and Trust Law); New York State Bar Association; Council on Litigation Management (Frequent Lecturer and Education Committee Member); New York County Lawyers Association — Reported Cases: Burack v. Tower Ins. Co. of New York, 12 A.D.3d 167, 784 N.Y.S.2d 53; Owusu v. Hearst Communications, Inc., 52 A.D.3d 285, 860 N.Y.S.2d 38; Harsch v. City of New York, 78 A.D.3d 781, 910 N.Y.S.2d 540; Mahoney v. Turner Const. Co., 61 A.D.3d 101, 872 N.Y.S.2d 433; Gropper v. St. Luke's Hospital Center, 234 A.D.2d 171, 651 N.Y.S.2d 469; Guiga v. JLS Construction Co., 255 A.D.2d 244, 685 N.Y.S.2d 1; Jani v. City of New York, 284 A.D.2d 304,725 N.Y.S.2d 388; Isola v. JWP Forest Electric Corp., 262 A.D.2d 95, 691 N.Y.S.2d 492; Ilardi v. Inte-Fac Corp., 290 A.D.2d 490, 736 N.Y.S.2d 401; Juliano v. Prudential Securities Incorporated, 287 A.D.2d 260, 731 N.Y.S.2d 142; Bachrow v. Turner Construction Company, 46 A.D.3d 388, 848 N.Y.S.2d 86; Miranda v. City of New York, 281 A.D.2d 403, 721 N.Y.S.2d 391; Yofi Book Publishing, Inc. v. Wil-Brook Realty Corp., 287 A.D.2d 712, 732 N.Y.S.2d 238; Longwood Central School District v. American Employers Insurance Company, 35 A.D.3d 550, 827 N.Y.S.2d 194; Smolik v. Turner Construction Company, 48 A.D.3d 452, 851 N.Y.S.2d 616; Gonzalez v. Turner Construction Company, 29 A.D.3d 630, 815 N.Y.S.2d 179; Schalansky v. McSpedon, 236 A.D.2d 461, 654 N.Y.S.2d 584; Wojcik v. 42nd Street Development Project, Inc., 386 F. Supp.2d 442, So. Dist. N.Y. 2005 — Appointed "Steering Committee Counsel" in the mass tort litigation entitled: In Re World Trade Center Disaster Site Litigation, with over 10,000 plaintiffs surrounding the clean-up of the 9/11 disaster in 2001; Lecturer, Council on Litigation Management in New Orleans (Topic: Litigation Management - Protecting Catastrophic Losses with Appropriate Investigation and Experts); Lecturer, Ace North America in Jersey City, NJ (Topic: Key Coverage Issues: Property); World Trade Center Clean-Up/Air Inhalation Litigation - Played critical role along with the WTC Captive and the entire WTC defense team in ultimately facilitating the execution of the global $712 million settlement agreement that included the overwhelming majority of the police officer, firefighter, sanitation and construction worker debris removal and recovery plaintiffs in the WTC Disaster Site litigation; Worked closely with Turner, lobbyists and Congress to effectuate the recent passage of the 9/11 Health and Compensation Act (the so-called Zadroga Bill) that reopens the Victim's Compensation Fund with an additional $2.3 billion in compensation for economic losses and injuries and establishes a 5 year $4.3 billion program to provide medical monitoring/screening to eligible responders and community members and also providing clients with a limitation on liability for the remaining lawsuits that did not enter into the settlement and future cases that are filed. Represents Insurance Brokers, Insurance Carriers and Insureds in complex insurance coverage and litigation matters; consultation in regulatory, insurance policy drafting and interpretation issues, insurance program recommendations and consultation; handled insurance coverage actions and policy interpretation for over twenty years. — Practice Areas: Construction Litigation; General Liability; Insurance Coverage; Insurance Defense; Product Liability; Trial and Appellate Practice; Contract Disputes; Employment Discrimination; Mass Tort; Premises Liability; Property Damage; Toxic Torts; Construction Accidents; Construction Defect; Fire and Water Subrogation — E-mail: JSparling@LondonFischer.com

James Walsh — 1967 — Fordham University, B.A. (magna cum laude), 1989; University of Pennsylvania Law School, J.D., 1992 — Admitted to Bar, 1993, New York; U.S. District Court, Eastern and Southern Districts of New York — Reported Cases: Klewinowski v. City of New York, 103 A.D.3d 547, 959 N.Y.S.2d 493 (1st Dep't 2013); In re Ancillary Receivership of Reliance Insurance Company. O'Brien & Gere Technical Services, Inc. v. New York Liquidation Bureau (Reliance Insurance Company in Liquidation) 81 A.D.3d 533, 918 N.Y.S.2d 25 (1st Dep't 2011); In the Matter of Continental Casualty Company v. Tibor Lecei, 47 A.D.3d 509, 850 N.Y.S.2d 76 (1st Dep't 2008); Romang v. Welsbach Electric Corp., 47 A.D.3d 789 (2d Dep't 2008); Travelers Indemnity Co. v. Bally Total Fitness Holding Corp., 448

IRVINE **CALIFORNIA**

London Fischer LLP, Irvine, CA (Continued)

F.Supp.2d 976 (N.D. Ill. 2006); Mickey's Rides-N-More Inc. v. Anthony Viscuso Brokerage Inc., 17 A.D.3d 308, 792 N.Y.S.2d 750 (2d Dep't 2005); Gannon v. JWP Forest Electric Corp., 275 A.D.2d 231, 712 N.Y.S.2d 494 (1st Dep't 2000) — Practice Areas: Construction Litigation; Insurance Coverage; Insurance Defense; Professional Liability; Directors and Officers Liability; Reinsurance; Errors and Omissions; Arbitration; General Liability — E-mail: JWalsh@LondonFischer.com

Anthony F. Tagliagambe — 1953 — Columbia University, B.A. (cum laude), 1975; Albany Law School of Union University, J.D., 1978 — Admitted to Bar, 1979, New York; U.S. District Court, Eastern and Southern Districts of New York — Member New York State Bar Association; Federation of Defense and Corporate Counsel (Elected Member, Chairman of the Premises and Security Liability Section) — Author: "Defendant's Strategies for Summation in a Labor Law Case," NYSBA CLE, December 2011; "Cross-Examination of the Liability Expert," NYSBA CLE Construction Site Accidents, December 2009; "Food for Thought: Defending the Food Purveyor When the Meal Turns Bad," Federation of Defense and Corporate Counsel Quarterly, Fall 2008; "An Employee By Any Other Name is Still An Employee: Determining Employment Status Under New York Law," New York State Bar Journal, February 1992 — Reported Cases: Mas v. Two Bridges, 75 N.Y.2d 680, 55 N.Y.S.2d 669, 554 N.E.2d 1257; Abbadessa v. Sprint, 291 A.D.2d 363, 736 N.Y.S.2d 881 (Mem), 2002 N.Y. Slip Op. 01067 N.Y.A.D. 2 Dept. Feb. 4, 2002; Allen v. Village of Farmingdale, 282 A.D.2d 485, 723 N.Y.S.2d 219 2001 N.Y. Slip Op. 02991, N.Y.A.D. 2 Dept. Apr. 09, 2001; Colon v. BIC USA, Inc., 199 F. Supp. 2d 53, So. Dist. N.Y. 2001; Uzdavines v. Metropolitan Baseball Club Inc., 115 Misc. 2d 343, 454 N.Y.S.2d 238, N.Y. City Civ. Ct., August 25, 1982 — Lecturer, New York State Bar Association, New York City Bar, Practicing Law Institute, Federation of Defense and Corporate Counsel (Topics: Cross Exam of Experts, Defending Product Liability Actions, Defending Construction Cases, Handling Catastrophic Injury Cases, Litigating Food Safety Cases); Selected for inclusion in the New York Super Lawyers list, 2007, 2008, 2009, 2010, 2011, 2012, 2013 and 2014 — Practice Areas: Construction Litigation; Product Liability; Negligence; Medical Malpractice; Municipal Liability — E-mail: ATagliagambe@LondonFischer.com

Clifford B. Aaron — 1958 — Franklin & Marshall College, B.A. (cum laude), 1980; Villanova University School of Law, J.D., 1983 — Admitted to Bar, 1984, New York; 2010, Tennessee; U.S. District Court, Eastern, Southern and Western Districts of New York — Member American Bar Association; New York County Lawyers Association (Treasurer, Product Liability Subcommittee of Tort Division); Defense Research Institute — Assistant District Attorney, Bronx County, New York, 1983-1988; Adjunct Professor, New York Law School, 1992-1995; Lecturer, DRI Electronic Discovery Abuse, 1999, San Francisco, CA; Lecturer, New York County Lawyers Association Continuing Legal Education (2004-Present); DRI Steering Committee on Trial Tactics; DRI Mock Trial Faculty and Participant (2014), Miami, FL; Selected for inclusion in the New York Super Lawyers list, 2009, 2010, 2011, 2012, 2013 and 2014 — Practice Areas: Product Liability; General Liability; Insurance Defense; Catastrophic Injury — E-mail: CAaron@LondonFischer.com

Virginia Goodman Futterman — 1957 — Marymount College, B.A. (magna cum laude), 1979; St. John's University School of Law, J.D., 1982 — Admitted to Bar, 1983, New York; U.S. District Court, Eastern, Northern, Southern and Western Districts of New York — Member New York State Bar Association; Defense Research Institute — Mediator, Eastern and Southern Districts of New York — Practice Areas: Defense Litigation; Product Liability; Personal Injury; Premises Liability; Construction Litigation; Asbestos Litigation; Employment Discrimination — E-mail: VFutterman@LondonFischer.com

Brian A. Kalman — 1968 — State University of New York at Binghamton, B.A. (with honors), 1990; Boston University School of Law, J.D., 1993 — Admitted to Bar, 1993, New Jersey; 1994, New York; 1995, U.S. District Court, Eastern and Southern Districts of New York; 1999, U.S. District Court, Northern District of New York; 2006, U.S. District Court, Western District of New York — Reported Cases: UTC Fire & Security Americas Corp. v. NCS Power, Inc. 844 F.Supp. 2d 366 (S.D.N.Y. 2012), Auriemma v. Biltmore Theatre 82 A.D. 3d 1, 917 N.Y.S.2d 130 (1st Dept. 2011), Gayle v. National Railroad Passenger Corp. 701 F.Supp. 2d 556 (S.D.N.Y. 2010), Astudillo v. City of New York, 71 A.D. 3d 709, 895 N.Y.S.2d 731 (2d Dep't 2010), Mann v. Dambrosio, 58 A.D.3d 701, 873 N.Y.S.2d 317 (2d Dep't 2009); Heimbuch v. Grumman Corp. 51 A.D.3d 865, 858 N.Y.S.2d 378 (2d Dep't 2008); Meza v. Consolidated Edison Co. of New York, 50 A.D.3d 452, 854 N.Y.S.2d 646 (1st Dep't 2008); Seabury v. County of Dutchess, 38 A.D.3d 752, 832 N.Y.S.2d 269 (2d Dep't 2007); Singh v. Kolcas, 283 A.D.2d 350, 725 N.Y.S.2d 37 (1st Dep't 2001) — Selected for inclusion in the New York Super Lawyers list, 2009, 2010, 2011, 2012, 2013 and 2014; Lecturer,

London Fischer LLP, Irvine, CA (Continued)

New York County Lawyers Association Continuing Education, 2012-Present — Practice Areas: Product Liability; Construction Law; General Liability — E-mail: BKalman@LondonFischer.com

Spiro K. Bantis — 1960 — New York University, B.A., 1982; Temple University Beasley School of Law, J.D., 1985 — Admitted to Bar, 1986, New York; U.S. District Court, Eastern and Southern Districts of New York — Member Bar Association of the City of New York — General Counsel, Gulf Insurance Company (Retired); Board Member, Insurance Federation of New York; Board Member, Atrium Insurance Corporation — Certified Arbitrator - ARIAS-US — Practice Areas: Insurance Corporate Practice; Insurance Coverage; Insurance Law; Insurance Regulation — E-mail: SBantis@LondonFischer.com

Perry I. Kreidman — Colgate University, B.S. (cum laude), 1973; New York University School of Law, J.D., 1976 — Admitted to Bar, 1977, New York — Member American Bar Association — Lectured and written on insurance and reinsurance coverage and claims in the U.S., Bermuda, and England — Practice Areas: Insurance Coverage; Reinsurance; Litigation; Arbitration; Professional Liability; Architects and Engineers; Directors and Officers Liability — E-mail: PKreidman@LondonFischer.com

Michael J. Carro — 1960 — Queens College, B.A., 1983; Pace University School of Law, J.D., 1987 — Phi Alpha Delta — Admitted to Bar, 1988, New York; 1989, U.S. District Court, Eastern and Southern Districts of New York — Member New York State Bar Association — Practice Areas: Personal Injury; Labor and Employment; Medical Malpractice; Premises Liability; Product Liability; Toxic Torts — E-mail: MCarro@LondonFischer.com

Matthew K. Finkelstein — 1970 — Franklin & Marshall College, B.A., 1991; St. Johns University School of Law, J.D. (cum laude), 1996 — Admitted to Bar, 1998, New York; 2000, U.S. District Court, Eastern and Southern Districts of New York; 2009, U.S. Court of Appeals, Second Circuit — Member New York State Bar Association — Practice Areas: Construction Accidents; Construction Defect; General Liability; Motor Vehicle; Premises Liability; Product Liability; Professional Liability — E-mail: MFinkelstein@LondonFischer.com

Christopher Ruggiero — 1979 — Manhattanville College, B.A. (summa cum laude), 2001; Brooklyn Law School, J.D. (Dean's List), 2004 — Brooklyn Journal of International Law, Staff Writer 2002-2003, Notes and Comments Editor, 2003-2004 — Admitted to Bar, 2005, New York; District of Columbia; U.S. District Court, Eastern and Southern Districts of New York — Member New York State Bar Association; Claims and Litigation Management Alliance; New York County Lawyers Association — Reported Cases: In Re World Trade Center Disaster Site Litigation; Baumann v. Metropolitan Life Ins. Co., 17 A.D.3d 260, 793 N.Y.S.2d 410 (1st Dep't 2005); Mayo v. Metropolitan Opera Ass'n, Inc., 108 A.D.422 (1st Dep't 2013) — Practice Areas: Automobile; Construction Litigation; Insurance Coverage; Mass Tort; Premises Liability; Property Damage — Tel: CRuggiero@LondonFischer.com

Daniel W. London — 1979 — University of Pennsylvania, B.A., 2001; Brooklyn Law School, J.D., 2005 — Admitted to Bar, 2005, New Jersey; 2006, New York; 2005, U.S. District Court, District of New Jersey; U.S. District Court, Eastern and Southern Districts of New York — Practice Areas: Commercial Litigation; Insurance Coverage; Insurance Law; Insurance Regulation — E-mail: DLondon@LondonFischer.com

James T. H. Deaver — 1961 — The Wharton School of the University of Pennsylvania, B.S., 1985; Temple University School of Law, J.D. (cum laude), 1991; New York University School of Law, LL.M., 1992 — Admitted to Bar, 1993, New York; U.S. District Court, Eastern and Southern Districts of New York — Reported Cases: Representative Cases: Appalachian Ins. Co. v. General Electric Co., 796 N.Y.S.2d 609 (N.Y. App. Div. 1st Dep't, 2005); Bridgestone/Firestone North American Tire, LLC v. Sompo Japan Ins. Co. of America, Civ. Ac. No. 3-02-1117 (M.D.Tenn)(case filed 2002) — Practice Areas: Insurance Coverage Litigation — E-mail: JDeaver@LondonFischer.com

Darren Le Montree — 1972 — University of California, Los Angeles, B.A. Political Science, 1994; Southwestern University School of Law, J.D. (cum laude), 1998 — Admitted to Bar, 1998, California; U.S. District Court, Central, Eastern, Northern and Southern Districts of California — Member Los Angeles County Bar Assocation — Reported Cases: Feldman v. Illinois Union Ins. Co., 198 Cal.App. 4th 1495 (2011) — Practice Areas: Commercial Litigation; Employment Litigation; Insurance Coverage; Professional Liability — E-mail: DLemontree@LondonFischer.com

(Associates not listed)

(See listing under New York, NY for additional information)

(This firm is also listed in the Subrogation, Investigation and Adjustment section of this directory)

CALIFORNIA   LAKEPORT

Murchison & Cumming, LLP
18201 Von Karman Avenue, Suite 1100
Irvine, California 92612
   Telephone: 714-972-9977
   Fax: 714-972-1404

Civil Litigation, Business Transactions

(See listing under Los Angeles, CA for additional information)

Smith Smith & Feeley LLP
16330 Bake Parkway
Irvine, California 92618
   Telephone: 949-263-5920
   Fax: 949-263-5925
   www.insurlaw.com

Insurance Coverage, Insurance Litigation, Bad Faith, Property, General Liability, Commercial and Personal Lines, Primary and Excess Insurance, Examinations Under Oath, Trial Practice, Arbitration, Appellate Practice

Firm Profile: Smith Smith & Feeley LLP is a law firm devoted to insurance coverage analysis and litigation. The firm's mission is to provide all clients with prompt, innovative and cost-effective solutions to insurance claims and litigation, while adhering to the highest professional standards.

Insurance Clients

Allstate Insurance Company	Capital Insurance Group
Contractors Insurance Company of North America Inc. (RRG)	Fireman's Fund Insurance Company
First American Property Casualty Insurance Company / First American Specialty Insurance Company	Great American Insurance Company
	Hanover Insurance Group
	The Hartford
Interinsurance Exchange of the Automobile Club	Liberty Mutual Insurance Company
	Markel International Insurance Company, Ltd.
Mercury Insurance Group	
Oregon Mutual Insurance Company	State Farm General Insurance Company
Stillwater Insurance Group, Inc.	Underwriters at Lloyd's, London

John E. Feeley — Fairfield University, B.S., 1981; Southwestern University School of Law, J.D., 1984 — Admitted to Bar, 1984, California; U.S. District Court, Central and Southern Districts of California; U.S. Court of Appeals, Ninth Circuit — Member American Bar Association (Trial, Tort and Insurance Practice Section); Orange County Bar Association (Insurance Law Section); Defense Research Institute — Practice Areas: Insurance Coverage; Bad Faith — E-mail: jfeeley@insurlaw.com

Stephen E. Smith — California Lutheran College, B.A. (summa cum laude), 1982; University of Southern California School of Law, J.D., 1985 — Admitted to Bar, 1985, California; U.S. District Court, Central and Southern Districts of California; U.S. Court of Appeals, Ninth Circuit — Member American Bar Association (Trial, Tort and Insurance Practice Section); Orange County Bar Association (Insurance Law Section); California Conference of Arson Investigators; Association of Southern California Defense Counsel — Practice Areas: Insurance Coverage; Bad Faith — E-mail: ssmith@insurlaw.com

Phillip E. Smith — California Lutheran College, B.A. (summa cum laude), 1982; Loyola Law School, J.D., 1985 — Admitted to Bar, 1985, California; U.S. District Court, Central and Southern Districts of California; U.S. Court of Appeals, Ninth Circuit — Member American Bar Association (Trial, Tort and Insurance Practice Section); Orange County Bar Association (Insurance Law Section); Association of Southern California Defense Counsel — Practice Areas: Insurance Coverage; Bad Faith — E-mail: psmith@insurlaw.com

Smith Smith & Feeley LLP, Irvine, CA   *(Continued)*

Amy C. Baghramian — Duke University, B.A. (cum laude), 1997; University of California, Davis School of Law, J.D. (Order of the Coif), 2002 — Admitted to Bar, 2002, California — E-mail: abaghramian@insurlaw.com

Michael L. Bean — University of California, Santa Barbara, B.A. (cum laude), 2006; Pepperdine University School of Law, J.D., 2009 — Admitted to Bar, 2009, California; U.S. District Court, Central, Eastern and Northern Districts of California — Member Orange County Bar Association (Insurance Law Section) — E-mail: mbean@insurlaw.com

Edwin B. Brown — Brigham Young University, B.A., 1976; Loyola Law School Los Angeles, J.D., 1979 — Admitted to Bar, 1979, California; U.S. District Court, Central, Eastern and Southern Districts of California; U.S. Court of Appeals, Ninth Circuit — Member Orange County Bar Association (Insurance Law Section) — E-mail: ebrown@insurlaw.com

Lois S. Kim — University of California, Los Angeles, B.A., 2005; University of San Diego School of Law, J.D., 2009 — Admitted to Bar, 2009, California; U.S. District Court, Central and Southern Districts of California — Member Orange County Bar Association (Insurance Law Section) — E-mail: lkim@insurlaw.com

Scott P. Ward — University of Washington, B.A. (Phi Beta Kappa, cum laude), 1991; University of California, Los Angeles School of Law, J.D., 1995 — Phi Beta Kappa — Admitted to Bar, 1995, California; U.S. District Court, Central District of California; U.S. Court of Appeals, Ninth Circuit — Member American and Orange County (Insurance Law Section) Bar Associations; Association of Southern California Defense Counsel — E-mail: sward@insurlaw.com

(Revisors of the California Insurance Law Digest for this Publication)

LAKEPORT † 4,753 Lake Co.

Refer To
Babin & Seeger, LLP
3550 Round Barn Boulevard, Suite 201
Santa Rosa, California 95403
   Telephone: 707-526-7370
   Fax: 707-526-0307

Mailing Address: P.O. Box 11626, Santa Rosa, CA 95406

Insurance Defense, Motor Vehicle, Commercial Law, General Liability, Product Liability, Property Damage, Construction Defect, Contracts, Environmental Law, Insurance Coverage, Workers' Compensation, Personal Injury, Professional Malpractice

SEE COMPLETE LISTING UNDER SANTA ROSA, CALIFORNIA (68 MILES)

Refer To
Roberts Law Firm
45011 Calpella Street
Mendocino, California 95460-2360
   Telephone: 707-937-0503
   Fax: 707-937-2916

Mailing Address: P.O. Box 2360, Mendocino, CA 95460-2360

Insurance Defense, Civil Litigation, Construction Defect, Premises Liability, Product Liability, Real Estate Errors and Omissions, Professional Negligence, Class Actions, Bad Faith, Automobile and Truck Liability, Agriculture and Wine Litigation, Class Action Defense Litigation

SEE COMPLETE LISTING UNDER MENDOCINO, CALIFORNIA (85 MILES)

LANCASTER 156,633 Los Angeles Co.

Refer To
Borton Petrini, LLP
626 Wilshire Boulevard, Suite 975
Los Angeles, California 90017
   Telephone: 213-624-2869
   Fax: 213-489-3930

Business Litigation, Civil Litigation, Construction Law, Employment Law, Employment Litigation, Trust and Estate Litigation

SEE COMPLETE LISTING UNDER LOS ANGELES, CALIFORNIA (72 MILES)

LONG BEACH — CALIFORNIA

LONG BEACH 462,257 Los Angeles Co.

Clinton & Clinton

100 Oceangate, Suite 1400
Long Beach, California 90802
 Telephone: 562-216-5000
 Fax: 562-216-5001
 E-Mail: dclinton@clinton-clinton.com
 www.clinton-clinton.com

(Los Angeles, CA Office*: 5757 West Century Boulevard, Suite 700, 90045)
 (Tel: 310-242-8615)
 (Fax: 310-242-8612)
(San Diego, CA Office*: 525 "B" Street, Suite 1500, 92101)
 (Tel: 619-858-4728)
 (Fax: 619-858-4729)
(San Francisco, CA Office*: 201 Spear Street, Suite 1100, 94105)
 (Tel: 415-230-5368)
 (Fax: 415-230-5369)
(Sacramento, CA Office*: 770 'L' Street, Suite 950, 95814)
 (Tel: 916-361-6060)
 (Fax: 916-361-6061)
(Irvine, CA Office*: 2030 Main Street, Suite 1300, 92614)
 (Tel: 949-260-9083)
 (Fax: 949-260-9084)
(Calabasas, CA Office: 23480 Park Sorrento, Suite 219A, 91302)
 (Tel: 562-216-5000)
 (Fax: 562-216-5001)
(Birmingham, AL Office: 1 Chase Corporate Center, Suite 400, 35244)
 (Tel: 205-313-6329)
 (Fax: 562-216-5001)
(Cumming, GA Office: 410 Peachtree Parkway, Building 400, Suite 4245, 30041)
 (Tel: 678-341-5134)
 (Fax: 562-216-5001)
(Philadelphia, PA Office: 1315 Walnut Street, Suite 601, 19107)
 (Tel: 267-800-1897)
 (Fax: 267-800-1898)
(Nashville, TN Office: 2400 Crestmoor Road, 37215)
 (Tel: 615-386-7040)
 (Fax: 562-216-5001)
(Austin, TX Office: 12912 Hill Country Boulevard, Suite F210, 78738)
 (Tel: 512-200-7055)
 (Fax: 512-266-3655)
(Ft. Worth, TX Office: 109 East Third Street, Suite 350, 76102)
 (Tel: 817-900-8210)
 (Fax: 817-900-8221)
(Houston, TX Office: 480 North Sam Houston Parkway East, 77060-3528)
 (Tel: 713-659-0054)
 (Fax: 281-447-5733)

Established: 1994

Insurance Defense, Asbestos Litigation, Automobile, Automotive Products Liability, Civil Litigation, Civil Rights, Civil Trial Practice, Commercial Litigation, Common Carrier, Complex Litigation, Construction Defect, Dental Malpractice, Employment Law, Environmental Law, Hospital Malpractice, Law Enforcement Liability, Legal Malpractice, Mass Tort, Medical Devices, Medical Malpractice, Pharmaceutical, Premises Liability, Product Liability, Retail Liability, Sexual Harassment, Slip and Fall, Special Investigative Unit Claims, Sports and Entertainment Liability, Toxic Torts, Truck Liability, Workers' Compensation

Firm Profile: Clinton & Clinton's capabilities are illustrated through their outstanding trial and settlement record. Clinton & Clinton utilize an aggressive and comprehensive approach in the litigation of its cases to achieve its client's goals. Specifically, we are committed to achieving results through the use of a detailed and innovative evaluation of each individual case and a practical assessment of how to most beneficially resolve each matter. Our attorneys possess the requisite experience, common sense and personal initiative to

Clinton & Clinton, Long Beach, CA (Continued)

effectively manage all cases through settlement, trial and appeal and have the ability to adopt to evolving client expectations as litigation progresses.

Throughout the litigation of each case, Clinton & Clinton emphasizes the importance of consistent contact with our clients to allow them to be informed regarding the litigation process and to allow them to be flexible in their case resolution goals. We recognize that litigation costs are an important factor in the successful resolution of cases and Clinton & Clinton was founded with the goal of providing the highest quality legal representation in a cost-efficient and service-oriented manner to insurance companies and self-insured corporations throughout the country.

We are experienced civil litigators skilled in advocacy and dedicated to providing our clients with the highest quality legal representation. Our formula of common sense litigation combined with a zeal to win creates results.

Insurance Clients

ACE USA	Ameriprise Auto & Home Insurance
Charter Insurance Group	Cunningham Lindsey Claims Management, Inc.
Chartis Insurance	
ESIS	
Financial Indemnity Company	Gallagher Bassett Services, Inc.
Kemper Insurance Companies	Liberty Mutual Insurance Company
Sedgwick CMS	Sentry Insurance
Travelers Property Casualty Corporation	Zurich North America

Non-Insurance Clients

Ace Hardware Corporation	Applebee's, Inc.
Ball-Foster Glass Container Company	Berwind Corporation Company
	CertainTeed Corporation
City of Los Angeles Police Department	Clausing Industries
	Colonial Abrasives, Inc.
Constitution State Service Company	Ecology Auto Parts, Inc.
	FedEx Corporation
Felsted	Furon Company
H.J. Heinz Company	International Church of the Foursquare Gospel
Interstate Hotels and Resorts	
Live Nation, Inc.	Nestle USA, Inc.
The Norton Company	Orscheln
Pentair, Inc.	Pilgrim's Pride Corporation
Praxair, Inc.	Ralphs Grocery Company
Saint-Gobain Corporation	Seacliff Seafood, Inc.
Sierra Leasing Company	True Value Company
Wisdom Industries	

Founder

David A. Clinton — 1964 — University of California, Los Angeles, B.A., 1987; Loyola Marymount University, Loyola Law School, J.D., 1990 — Admitted to Bar, 1990, California; 1991, U.S. District Court, Central District of California — Member State Bar of California; Los Angeles County and Orange County Bar Associations; Association of Southern California Defense Counsel; American Board of Trial Advocates; Defense Research Institute; Federation of Defense and Corporate Counsel — Practice Areas: Environmental Litigation; Employment Law; Product Liability; Premises Liability; General Civil Litigation — E-mail: dclinton@clinton-clinton.com

Firm Members

Holly Gagas — California State University, Northridge, B.A., 1990; Whittier Law School, J.D., 1995 — Admitted to Bar, 1996, California; 2003, U.S. District Court, Southern District of California — Practice Areas: Toxic Torts; Employment Law; General Civil Litigation — E-mail: hgagas@clinton-clinton.com

Marlon D'Oyen — 1974 — University of California, San Diego, B.A., 1996; Whittier Law School, J.D., 2001 — Admitted to Bar, 2002, California — Practice Areas: Product Liability; Automobile Liability; Toxic Torts; Insurance Defense; Premises Liability — E-mail: mdoyen@clinton-clinton.com

Todd M. Austin — California State University, Fullerton, B.A., 1999; Whittier Law School, J.D., 2004 — Admitted to Bar, 2004, California; U.S. District Court, Central District of California — Member Los Angeles County and Orange County Bar Associations — Practice Areas: Product Liability; Premises Liability — E-mail: taustin@clinton-clinton.com

Dana Ulise — University of California, Santa Barbara, B.A., 2000; Loyola Law School, J.D., 2003 — Admitted to Bar, 2003, California; U.S. District Court, Central District of California — Practice Areas: Professional Liability; Product Liability; Insurance Defense; Premises Liability — E-mail: dulise@clinton-clinton.com

Clinton & Clinton, Long Beach, CA (Continued)

Adrienne Marie Stover — 1971 — California State University, Fullerton, B.A., 1995; Southwestern University School of Law, J.D., 2002 — Admitted to Bar, 2002, California; U.S. District Court, Central District of California — Member Los Angeles County Bar Association — Languages: Spanish — Practice Areas: Toxic Torts; Employment Law; Insurance Corporate Practice; Product Liability; General Civil Litigation; Premises Liability — E-mail: astover@clinton-clinton.com

Jaison T. Benjamin — Hunter College, B.A., 2000; Southwestern University School of Law, J.D., 2004 — Admitted to Bar, 2005, California; U.S. District Court, Central District of California — Member Beverly Hills Bar Association — Practice Areas: Product Liability; Insurance Defense; Automobile Liability; General Civil Practice; Premises Liability — E-mail: jbenjamin@clinton-clinton.com

Bruce Markarian — Oxnard College, A.A., 1994; California State College at Northridge, B.A., 1996; Ventura College of Law; Santa Barbara College of Law, J.D., 1999 — Admitted to Bar, 2000, California — Practice Areas: Workers' Compensation — E-mail: bmarkarian@clinton-clinton.com

Matthew Warren — University of Southern California, B.S., 1999; Whittier Law School, J.D., 2005 — Admitted to Bar, 2009, California — Practice Areas: Contracts; Business Law; Premises Liability; Product Liability; Toxic Torts — E-mail: mwarren@clinton-clinton.com

Kristine M. Best — The University of Alabama at Birmingham, B.S., 1995; Birmingham School of Law, J.D., 1998 — Admitted to Bar, 1998, Alabama — Practice Areas: Asbestos Litigation; Automobile Liability; Bad Faith; Casualty Defense; Commercial General Liability; Construction Defect; General Civil Practice; Insurance Coverage Litigation; Premises Liability; Product Liability; Toxic Torts

Laurie C. Book — University of California, San Diego, B.A. (cum laude), 2008; University of California at Los Angeles School of the Law, J.D., 2011 — Admitted to Bar, 2011, California — Practice Areas: Asbestos Litigation; Automobile Tort; Employment Law; General Civil Litigation; Premises Liability; Product Liability; Toxic Torts

Mark B. Brueggemann — The University of Iowa, B.S. Mech. Engr., 1992; Whittier Law School, J.D., 1995 — Admitted to Bar, 1996, California; U.S. District Court, Central District of California — Practice Areas: Commercial Law; Construction Defect; General Civil Litigation; Premises Liability; Product Liability; Real Estate Litigation

Scott B. Cloud — Pepperdine University, B.A., 1985; Pepperdine University School of Law (Dean's Scholar), 1989 — Admitted to Bar, 1989, California; U.S. District Court, Central District of California — Member Association of Southern California Defense Counsel; Defense Research Institute — Practice Areas: Commercial Law; Construction Defect; Fraud; General Liability; Premises Liability; Product Liability

Mark J. Downton — Xavier University, B.A., 1996; The University of Tennessee College of Law, J.D. (Order of the Coif), 1999 — Admitted to Bar, 1999, Tennessee; U.S. Court of Appeals, Sixth Circuit; U.S. Supreme Court — Practice Areas: Automobile Liability; Business Litigation; Employment Law; General Civil Litigation; Insurance Defense; Premises Liability; Product Liability

Charles Karlin — Pomona College, B.A., 1986; Southwestern University School of Law, J.D., 1990 — Admitted to Bar, 1990, California; U.S. District Court, Central District of California — Practice Areas: Premises Liability; Product Liability; Real Estate Litigation

Patrick McIntyre — Vassar College, B.A., 2007; Loyola Law School Los Angeles, J.D., 2010 — Admitted to Bar, 2010, California — Practice Areas: Automobile Liability; Construction Defect; General Civil Litigation; Insurance Defense; Premises Liability; Product Liability

Christopher T. Olsen — Elon College, B.A., 1986; Pepperdine University School of Law, J.D., 1989 — Admitted to Bar, 1989, California — Member Association of Southern California Defense Counsel; Defense Research Institute — Practice Areas: Civil Defense; Commercial Litigation; Construction Defect; Environmental Law; Premises Liability

Jessica A. Putonti — University of Connecticut, B.S., 1997; University of Connecticut School of Law, J.D., 2003 — Admitted to Bar, 2003, Texas — Member Defense Research Institute; Texas Association of Defense Counsel — Practice Areas: Admiralty and Maritime Law; Cargo; Civil Litigation; Contract Disputes; Insurance Defense; Premises Liability

Christopher Willis — Harding University, B.B.A., 1990; St. Mary's University School of Law, J.D. (Dean's List), 1994 — Admitted to Bar, 1995, Georgia; U.S. District Court, Northern District of Georgia; U.S. Court of Appeals, Eleventh Circuit — Practice Areas: Criminal Law; General Civil Litigation; Insurance Defense; Mediation

John F. McDevitt — Saint Joseph's University, B.S., 1970; New England School of Law, J.D., 1973 — Admitted to Bar, 1974, Pennsylvania

Clinton & Clinton, Long Beach, CA (Continued)

Lori L. Vieira — California State University, Chico, B.A., 1997; Loyola Law School Los Angeles, J.D., 2000 — Admitted to Bar, 2000, California; U.S. District Court, Central District of California — Practice Areas: Automobile; Bodily Injury; Casualty Defense; Commercial General Liability; Complex Tort Litigation; Construction Defect; Insurance Defense; Premises Liability; Product Liability; Wrongful Death — E-mail: lvieira@clinton-clinton.com

Of Counsel

DeWitt W. Clinton — 1936 — Loyola Marymount University, B.A., 1958; Loyola Marymount University, Loyola Law School, J.D., 1961 — Admitted to Bar, 1962, California; 1961, U.S. Court of Military Appeals; 1963, U.S. District Court, Central District of California; U.S. Court of Federal Claims; U.S. Supreme Court — Member State Bar of California

James R. Tedford, II — 1968 — University of California, Irvine, B.A., 1991; Whittier Law School, J.D., 1994 — Admitted to Bar, 1994, California; U.S. District Court, Central District of California — Member Pasadena and Los Angeles Bar Associations; Los Angeles County Criminal Defense Attorneys; Association of Southern California Defense Counsel; Defense Research Institute

C. Robert Dorsett, Jr. — Southwest Texas State University, B.A., 1990; Texas Wesleyan University School of Law, J.D., 2000 — Admitted to Bar, 2001, Texas — Practice Areas: Automobile Liability; Environmental Law; General Civil Litigation; Hospitality; Premises Liability; Product Liability; Real Estate

Brian T. Swift — Seton Hall University, B.S., 1985; Widener University, M.B.A., 1992; Widener University School of Law, J.D., 1991 — Admitted to Bar, 1998, Texas; New Jersey; Pennsylvania

Darla Cunningham — Kent State University, B.A. (magna cum laude), 1976; Southern Methodist University Law School, 1980 — Admitted to Bar, 1981, California — Practice Areas: Employment Discrimination; Employment Law; Sexual Harassment

Doug Dubois — Baylor University, B.A./B.B.A., 1989; University of Houston Law Center, J.D., 2003 — Admitted to Bar, 2003, Texas — Practice Areas: Business Litigation; Commercial Litigation; Insurance Defense; Premises Liability; Product Liability; Trucking Liability

J.C. Johnson — Tarleton State University, B.S., 1991; Texas A&M International University, M.B.A., 1994; Texas Wesleyan University School of Law, J.D., 2011 — Admitted to Bar, 2011, Texas — Practice Areas: Commercial Litigation; General Civil Litigation; Liability Defense; Real Estate Litigation

Swain & Dipolito LLP

555 East Ocean Boulevard, Suite 600
Long Beach, California 90802
Telephone: 562-983-7833
Fax: 562-983-7835
E-Mail: admin@swaindipolito.com
www.swaindipolito.com

Established: 1993

General Liability, Insurance Defense, Transportation, Admiralty and Maritime Law, Business Law, Marine, Motor Vehicle, Trucks/Heavy Equipment, Cargo, Warehouse

Firm Profile: Swain & Dipolito LLP focuses on admiralty law, maritime law, transportation law, and insurance law. Since 1993, the firm has provided efficient and effective legal representation for its clients in state and federal courts throughout the State of California.

Insurance Clients

Canal Insurance Company Chartis Insurance
Chubb & Son, Inc. Markel Corporation
Navigators Insurance Company Northland Insurance Company
Thomas Miller Insurance Services

Firm Members

Michael L. Swain — Franklin & Marshall College, B.A., 1980; Tulane University Law School, J.D. (cum laude), 1983 — Law Clerk to Chief Judge Nauman S. Scott, U.S. District Court, Western District of Louisiana — Admitted to Bar, 1983, Louisiana; 1987, California — Member State Bar of California; Louisiana State Bar Association; The Maritime Law Association of the United States

LOS ANGELES   CALIFORNIA

Swain & Dipolito LLP, Long Beach, CA   (Continued)

Frank X. Dipolito — State University of New York Maritime College, B.S., 1972; Loyola Law School, J.D., 1988 — St. Thomas More Honor Society — Admitted to Bar, 1988, California — Member State Bar of California; The Maritime Law Association of the United States — U.S. Coast Guard Master's License; American Master Mariners

Associates

John G. Nursall — University of Southern California, B.A., 1975; M.A., 1978; Ph.D., 1987; Pepperdine University School of Law, J.D., 1987 — Admitted to Bar, 1988, California — Member State Bar of California

Ross Landau — Dartmouth College, A.B., 2003; Tulane University Law School, J.D. (cum laude), 2008 — Admitted to Bar, 2008, California — Member American Bar Association

Of Counsel

Cheryl F. Gertler — University of California, Los Angeles, B.A., 1979; University of California, Davis School of Law, J.D., 1982 — Admitted to Bar, 1982, California; 1987, Illinois — Member State Bar of California; American Immigration Lawyers Association — Languages: Japanese

The following firms also service this area.

Pyka Lenhardt Schnaider Zell
837 North Ross Street
Santa Ana, California 92701
   Telephone: 714-835-9011
   Fax: 714-667-7806
Mailing Address: P.O. Box 1558, Santa Ana, CA 92702-1558

Automobile, Business Litigation, Catastrophic Injury, Civil Litigation, Civil Rights, Construction Accidents, Construction Defect, Labor and Employment, Municipal Liability, Personal Injury, Police Liability Defense, Premises Liability, Product Liability, Professional Liability, Public Entities, School Law, Trucking, Uninsured and Underinsured Motorist, Wrongful Death, Wrongful Termination, Homeowners Association Litigation, Utility Defense

SEE COMPLETE LISTING UNDER SANTA ANA, CALIFORNIA (22 MILES)

LOS ANGELES † 3,792,621 Los Angeles Co.

Barbanel & Treuer, P.C.

1925 Century Park East, Suite 350
Los Angeles, California 90067-2731
   Telephone: 310-282-8088
   Fax: 310-282-8779
   E-Mail: abarbanel@btlawla.com
   www.btlawla.com

Insurance Coverage, Professional Liability, Employers' Liability, Bad Faith Liability, Cyber/Information Technology Liability

Firm Profile: BT attorneys have a high level of expertise in insurance law. BT represents clients in all regions of the country and abroad. BT renders advice and is trial counsel on wide variety of first party and third party coverage issues, bad faith liability, claims handling practices, insurance fraud, rescission, agent/broker issues, and regulatory matters.

Insurance Clients

ACE, Lloyd's London
General Star Management Company

Beazley Group, Lloyd's London
Markel Service, Incorporated

Partners

Alan H. Barbanel — Northeastern University, B.S. (magna cum laude), 1978; University of San Diego, J.D., 1982 — Phi Alpha Delta, Member, 1980-1982 — San Diego Law Review, Lead Articles Editor, 1981-1982 — Admitted to Bar, 1983, California; 1983, U.S. District Court, Central, Eastern, Northern and Southern Districts of California; U.S. Court of Appeals, Ninth Circuit — Member American (Member, Torts and Insurance Practice Section), Los Angeles County and San Diego County Bar Associations; State Bar of California (Vice Chair, Insurance Law Committee, 2014-2015); Defense Research Institute; Professional Liability Underwriting Society

Barbanel & Treuer, P.C., Los Angeles, CA   (Continued)

Stephen D. Treuer — Hampshire College, B.A., 1976; University of California, Berkeley, M.A., 1980; University of California, Berkeley Boalt Hall School of Law, J.D., 1984 — Admitted to Bar, 1984, Arizona; 1988, California; U.S. District Court, Central, Northern and Southern Districts of California; U.S. Court of Appeals, Ninth Circuit — Member State Bar of Arizona; State Bar of California

Berman Berman Berman Schneider & Lowary LLP

11900 West Olympic Boulevard, Suite 600
Los Angeles, California 90064-1151
   Telephone: 310-447-9000
   Fax: 310-447-9011
   E-Mail: rsberman@b3law.com
   www.b3law.com

(Riverside, CA Office: 3890 Tenth Street, Second Floor, 92501)
   (Tel: 951-682-8300)
   (Fax: 951-682-8331)

Established: 1994

Insurance Defense, Insurance Coverage, Construction Defect, Product Liability, Employment Law, Professional Liability, Legal, Insurance Agents, Agent/Broker Liability, Medical Malpractice Defense, Design Professionals, Accountants, Trucking Law, Transportation, Real Estate Agents, Brokers and Appraisers, Elder Care, Monitoring Counsel, Litigation Management, California Insurance Regulations and Consulting to Insurance Industry

Firm Profile: The firm brings together an experienced, seasoned staff. The firm strives to maintain a high caliber of client service, emphasizing a strong sensitivity to containing litigation costs while providing high quality legal service.

Insurance Clients

Burlington Insurance Company
The Colony Group
General Agents Insurance Company of America, Inc.
Markel Insurance Company
Mid-Continent Group
Resurgens Specialty Underwriting, Inc.
Savers Property and Casualty Insurance Company
United National Group
Williamsburg National Insurance Company

Church Insurance Company
First Financial Insurance Company
Gulf Insurance Group
Lexington Insurance Company
Media/Professional Insurance
Philadelphia Insurance Company
St. Paul Fire and Marine Insurance Company
Star Insurance Company
Travelers Property Casualty Insurance Company

Non-Insurance Clients

Associated Claims Enterprises, Inc.
Crest Financial Corporation

Blair & Company Claims Adjusters
RSA Surplus Lines Insurance Services, Inc.

Partners

Ronald S. Berman — 1938 — University of California, Los Angeles, B.S., 1960; M.B.A., 1964; Loyola Law School, J.D., 1970 — St. Thomas Moore Honor Society — Admitted to Bar, 1972, California; U.S. District Court, Central, Eastern and Northern Districts of California — Member American (Torts and Insurance Section and Standing Committee on Lawyers' Professional Liability, Law Practice Management and Litigation Sections) and Los Angeles County Bar Associations; General Counsel, Professional Liability Underwriting Society, 1987-1996; JD/MBA Association of Los Angeles; General Counsel, California Association of Independent Insurance Adjusters, 1993, 1995; City of Hope National Insurance Industry Council (Practice Management & Technology Section) — Author: "Defending Another Attorney," Case & Comment, March/April 1988; "Mistakes That Don't Have to Happen," Insurance Advocate, April 9, 1988; Co-Author: "The Non-Client Plaintiff," The Malpractice Prevention Reporter; Co-Author: "Insurance Producer Liability in Plain Language"; Co-Author: "Real Estate Agent & Appraiser Liability in Plain Language" — Captain, U.S. Army Reserve, 1968 — E-mail: rsberman@b3law.com

Berman Berman Berman Schneider & Lowary LLP, Los Angeles, CA (Continued)

Evan A. Berman — 1964 — University of Washington, B.A., 1987; Pepperdine University School of Law, J.D., 1990 — Admitted to Bar, 1990, California; 1991, U.S. District Court, Central District of California — Member American Bar Association — E-mail: eaberman@b3law.com

Stephanie Berman Schneider — 1968 — University of California, Los Angeles, B.A. (magna cum laude), 1990; Loyola Law School Los Angeles, J.D., 1993 — Phi Beta Kappa — Chief Articles Editor, Loyola Law School Los Angeles Entertainment Law Journal — Admitted to Bar, 1993, California; U.S. District Court, Central District of California — Member American and Los Angeles County Bar Associations; Professional Liability Underwriting Society (Southern California Steering Committee Chairperson, 1997-1999; Education Committee); National Association of Insurance Women (President, South Bay Chapter, 2000-2001); City of Hope National Insurance Industry Council — Author: "View At Your Own Risk: Gang Movies and Spectator Violence," 12 Loyola Law School Los Angeles Entertainment Law Journal, 477 — E-mail: sjschneider@b3law.com

Spencer A. Schneider — 1969 — University of California, Los Angeles, B.A. (with high honors), 1991; University of California Davis School of Law, J.D., 1994 — American Jurisprudence Award — Admitted to Bar, 1994, California; U.S. District Court, Central, Eastern, Northern and Southern Districts of California — Member American Bar Association (Tort and Insurance Practice Section); State Bar of California; Association of Southern California Defense Counsel — E-mail: saschneider@b3law.com

Mark Lowary — 1966 — California State University, Fullerton, B.A., 1989; Southwestern University School of Law, J.D., 1993 — Admitted to Bar, 1993, California — E-mail: mclowary@b3law.com

Senior Litigation Counsel

James W. McCord — 1941 — The Ohio State University, B.S., 1963; The Ohio State University Moritz College of Law, J.D., 1966 — Admitted to Bar, 1966, Ohio; 1970, California; 1966, U.S. District Court, Central District of Ohio; 1970, U.S. District Court, Central District of California; 1972, U.S. District Court, Eastern District of California — Member Los Angeles County Bar Association — E-mail: jwmccord@b3law.com

Associates

Karen E. Adelman — 1974 — University of California, Berkeley, B.A., 1996; University of California, Hastings College of the Law, J.D., 1999 — American Jurisprudence Awards — Member and Contributor, Hastings International and Comparative Law Review — Admitted to Bar, 2001, California; 2001, U.S. District Court, Central District of California; 2003, U.S. District Court, Northern and Southern Districts of California — Member American, Los Angeles County and Beverly Hills Bar Associations — E-mail: keadelman@b3law.com

Patricia L. Blanton — 1958 — Roanoke College, B.A. (cum laude), 1980; Pepperdine University School of Law, J.D., 1983 — Admitted to Bar, 1984, California; 1990, Virginia; 1988, U.S. District Court, Central District of California — E-mail: plbanton@b3law.com

David R. Casady — University of California, Riverside, B.A., 1998; University of La Verne College of Law, J.D. (cum laude), 2010 — CALI Award Recipient; Dean's List — Admitted to Bar, 2010, California — Member State Bar of California — Three year Scholar, University of La Verne Academic Tutoring Program — Practice Areas: General Liability; Civil Litigation — Resident Riverside, CA Office — Tel: 951-682-8300 — Fax: 951-682-8331

Michael D. Didszun — 1967 — California State University, Northridge, B.A., 1996; Southwestern School of Law, J.D., 1999 — Admitted to Bar, 1999, California; 2004, U.S. District Court, Eastern, Northern and Southern Districts of California — E-mail: mddidszun@b3law.com

Joyce Helock Furzer — 1955 — University of California, Los Angeles, B.A. (cum laude), 1979; Loyola Law School, J.D. — Admitted to Bar, 1983, California; 1985, U.S. District Court, Central District of California; U.S. Court of Appeals, Ninth Circuit; 1992, U.S. District Court, Southern District of California — E-mail: jhfurzer@b3law.com

Brian T. Gravdal — University of Northern Iowa, B.A. (Dean's List), 1993-1997; Southwestern University School of Law, J.D., 2001-2005 — Admitted to Bar, 2005, California; 2006, Illinois; U.S. District Court, Eastern District of California; U.S. Court of Appeals, Ninth Circuit — Member American, Los Angeles County and Riverside County Bar Associations; Illinois Association of Defense Trial Counsel; Defense Research Institute — Author: "Illinois Appellate Court Strikes Down Legislation Revising Gross Weight Limits for Commercial Vehicles, but Decision Temporarily Stayed," SmithAmundsen Transportation Alert, February 2011; "FMCSA Prohibits Texting by Commercial Motor Vehicle Drivers," SmithAmundsen

Berman Berman Berman Schneider & Lowary LLP, Los Angeles, CA (Continued)

Transportation Alert, September 27, 2010; Co-Author: "Federal and State Trends Toward Prohibition of Texting While Driving," SmithAmundsen Transportation Alert, January 4, 2011; Contributor, USLAW Network Compendium of Law, 2009; "The Illinois Supreme Court Introduces New Element of Compensable Damages: Shortened Life Expectancy," IDC QUARTERLY, Vol. 18, No. 4, 52 (4th Qtr. 2008); "The Inter-American Commission on Human Rights' Quixotic and Unjustified Expansion of its Authority and the American Declaration of the Rights and Duties of Man: The Case of Michael Domingues," 11 SW. J. OF L. & TRADE AM. 257 (2005) — Reported Cases: Summary Judgments: 2006, Wrongful Death; 2012, Traumatic Brain Injury (TBI) — Second Chair 13 day jury trial, TBI/Cook Co, IL, 2011 — Resident Riverside, CA Office — Tel: 951-682-8300 — Fax: 951-682-8331

Kelly M. Henry — California State College at San Bernardino, B.A., 1996; Western State University College of Law, J.D., 2001 — Admitted to Bar, 2001, California — Resident Riverside, CA Office — Tel: 951-682-8300 — Fax: 951-682-8331

Howard J. Smith — 1968 — State University of New York, B.A., 1990; Whittier Law School, J.D., 1993 — Admitted to Bar, 1993, California; U.S. District Court, Central and Eastern Districts of California — E-mail: hjsmith@b3law.com

Vanessa H. Ticas — University of California, Riverside, B.A. Political Science (cum laude), 2003; University of La Verne College of Law, J.D., 2010 — Admitted to Bar, 2010, California — Languages: Spanish — E-mail: vhticas@b3law.com

Kevin E. Magennis — San Diego State University, B.A. Economics, 2007; California Western School of Law, J.D., 2012 — Admitted to Bar, 2012, California — Member American, Orange County, San Diego and Los Angeles Bar Associations; California Western Student Bar Association (President, 2011-2012) — E-mail: kemagennis@b3law.com

Angela Young Park — Georgetown University, B.A., 2008; University of Maryland Francis King Carey School of Law, J.D., 2012 — Admitted to Bar, 2012, California; U.S. District Court, Central District of California — Member American and National Asian Pacific American Bar Associations; Asian Pacific American Lawyers of the Inland Empire — Languages: Korean — E-mail: aypark@b3law.com

Jessica Elihu — University of California, Los Angeles, B.A., History (magna cum laude), 2010; Southwestern Law School, J.D., 2012 — Admitted to Bar, 2012, California; U.S. District Court, Central District of California — Member State Bar of California (Business Law Section) — Languages: Farsi — E-mail: jelihu@b3law.com

Borton Petrini, LLP

626 Wilshire Boulevard, Suite 975
Los Angeles, California 90017
Telephone: 213-624-2869
Fax: 213-489-3930
E-Mail: bpla@bortonpetrini.com
www.bortonpetrini.com

Established: 1899

Business Litigation, Civil Litigation, Construction Law, Employment Law, Employment Litigation, Trust and Estate Litigation

Firm Profile: Since 1899, Borton Petrini, LLP, has offered high quality legal services in all of the practice areas described above through its California network of 10 regional offices. The mission of Borton Petrini, LLP is to treat every file as though we were representing ourselves and paying the bill for that representation.

Managing Partner

Rosemarie Suazo Lewis — 1962 — University of Southern California, B.A., 1983; Western State University College of Law, J.D., 1991 — Admitted to Bar, 1992, California; U.S. District Court, Central, Eastern, Northern and Southern Districts of California — Member National Hispanic, Mexican-American and Los Angeles County Bar Associations; State Bar of California; Women Lawyers Association of Los Angeles; University of Southern California Commerce Associates; Association of Southern California Defense Counsel — Languages: Spanish — E-mail: rlewis@bortonpetrini.com

LOS ANGELES CALIFORNIA

Borton Petrini, LLP, Los Angeles, CA (Continued)
Partners

Matthew J. Trostler — 1966 — University of Southern California, B.A., 1988; California Western School of Law, J.D., 1991 — Phi Delta Phi — Admitted to Bar, 1991, California; 1991, U.S. District Court, Central District of California — Member State Bar of California; American Board of Trial Advocates — E-mail: mtrostler@bortonpetrini.com

Edward J. Morales — 1961 — University of California, Los Angeles, B.A., 1986; Loyola Law School, J.D., 1992 — Admitted to Bar, 1995, California — Member State Bar of California; Los Angeles County Bar Association — E-mail: emorales@bortonpetrini.com

Attorneys

Randy A. Lopez — 1982 — University of California, Irvine, B.A., 2004; The University of Arizona, James E. Rogers College of Law, J.D., 2007 — Admitted to Bar, 2007, California; 2007, U.S. District Court, Central District of California — Member Student Bar Association (Vice President 2005-2006; President, 2006-2007); Young Professionals of Pasadena — City of Los Angeles, The University of Arizona & James E. Rogers College of Law (Law Ambassador) — Languages: Spanish — E-mail: rlopez@bortonpetrini.com

Samire K. Elhouty — 1984 — University of California, Los Angeles, B.A., 2008; Cornell University Law School, J.D., 2011 — Admitted to Bar, 2012, California — Member State Bar of California — Editorial Board, California Bar's Business Law News; Lifetime Member, UCLA Alumni Association — E-mail: selhouty@bortonpetrini.com

Clinton & Clinton

5757 West Century Boulevard, Suite 700
Los Angeles, California 90045
Telephone: 310-242-8615
Fax: 310-242-8612
E-Mail: dclinton@clinton-clinton.com
www.clinton-clinton.com

(Long Beach, CA Office*: 100 Oceangate, Suite 1400, 90802)
 (Tel: 562-216-5000)
 (Fax: 562-216-5001)
(San Diego, CA Office*: 525 "B" Street, Suite 1500, 92101)
 (Tel: 619-858-4728)
 (Fax: 619-858-4729)
(San Francisco, CA Office*: 201 Spear Street, Suite 1100, 94105)
 (Tel: 415-230-5368)
 (Fax: 415-230-5369)
(Sacramento, CA Office*: 770 'L' Street, Suite 950, 95814)
 (Tel: 916-361-6060)
 (Fax: 916-361-6061)
(Irvine, CA Office*: 2030 Main Street, Suite 1300, 92614)
 (Tel: 949-260-9083)
 (Fax: 949-260-9084)
(Calabasas, CA Office: 23480 Park Sorrento, Suite 219A, 91302)
 (Tel: 562-216-5000)
 (Fax: 562-216-5001)
(Birmingham, AL Office: 1 Chase Corporate Center, Suite 400, 35244)
 (Tel: 205-313-6329)
 (Fax: 562-216-5001)
(Cumming, GA Office: 410 Peachtree Parkway, Building 400, Suite 4245, 30041)
 (Tel: 678-341-5134)
 (Fax: 562-216-5001)
(Philadelphia, PA Office: 1315 Walnut Street, Suite 601, 19107)
 (Tel: 267-800-1897)
 (Fax: 267-800-1898)
(Nashville, TN Office: 2400 Crestmoor Road, 37215)
 (Tel: 615-386-7040)
 (Fax: 562-216-5001)
(Austin, TX Office: 12912 Hill Country Boulevard, Suite F210, 78738)
 (Tel: 512-200-7055)
 (Fax: 512-266-3655)
(Ft. Worth, TX Office: 109 East Third Street, Suite 350, 76102)
 (Tel: 817-900-8210)
 (Fax: 817-900-8221)

Clinton & Clinton, Los Angeles, CA (Continued)
(Houston, TX Office: 480 North Sam Houston Parkway East, 77060-3528)
 (Tel: 713-659-0054)
 (Fax: 281-447-5733)

Asbestos Litigation, Automobile, Automotive Products Liability, Civil Litigation, Civil Rights, Civil Trial Practice, Commercial Litigation, Common Carrier, Complex Litigation, Construction Defect, Dental Malpractice, Employment Law, Environmental Law, Insurance Defense, Hospital Malpractice, Law Enforcement Liability, Legal Malpractice, Mass Tort, Medical Devices, Medical Malpractice, Pharmaceutical, Premises Liability, Product Liability, Retail Liability, Sexual Harassment, Slip and Fall, Special Investigative Unit Claims, Sports and Entertainment Liability, Toxic Torts, Truck Liability, Workers' Compensation

(See listing under Long Beach, CA for additional information)

Countryman & McDaniel

LAX Airport Center
5959 West Century Boulevard, 9th Floor
Los Angeles, California 90045
Telephone: 310-342-6500
Fax: 310-342-6505
E-Mail: info@cargolaw.com
www.CargoLaw.com

Admiralty and Maritime Law, Aviation, Equipment Charter, Coverage Disputes, Business Formation, Regulatory Support, Cargo, Commercial Litigation, Arbitration

Firm Profile: The Law Office of Countryman & McDaniel is a maritime, aviation, trade and transportation practice serving the logistics industry since 1978.

Representative Insurance Clients

Avalon Risk Management	Integro Insurance Brokers
Munich Re Underwriting Limited, Watkins Syndicate	Navigators Management Company
ProSight Specialty Insurance Company	Pac Global Insurance Brokerage, Inc.
UPINSCO, Inc.	Roanoke Trade Services, Inc.

Representative Non Insurance Clients

United Parcel Service Co, UPS Airlines	UPS Supply Chain Solutions

Partners

Michael S. McDaniel — Loyola University School of Law, J.D., 1975 — Admitted to Bar, 1975, California

Byron E. Countryman — Southwestern University School of Law, J.D., 1974 — Admitted to Bar, 1975, California

Associates

Christoph M. Wahner Bruce A. Lindsay

Ericksen Arbuthnot

835 Wilshire Boulevard, Suite 500
Los Angeles, California 90017-2656
Telephone: 213-489-4411
Fax: 213-489-4332
www.ericksenarbuthnot.com

(Oakland, CA Office*: 155 Grand Avenue, Suite 1050, 94612-3768)
 (Tel: 510-832-7770)
 (Fax: 510-832-0102)
(Bakersfield, CA Office*: 1830 Truxtun Avenue, Suite 200, 93301-5022)
 (Tel: 661-633-5080)
 (Fax: 661-633-5089)

CALIFORNIA

LOS ANGELES

Ericksen Arbuthnot, Los Angeles, CA (Continued)

(Fresno, CA Office*: 2440 West Shaw Avenue, Suite 101, 93711-3300)
  (Tel: 559-449-2600)
  (Fax: 559-449-2603)
(Sacramento, CA Office*: 100 Howe Avenue, Suite 110S, 95825-8200)
  (Tel: 916-483-5181)
  (Fax: 916-483-7558)
(San Francisco, CA Office*: 100 Bush Street, Suite 900, 94104-3950)
  (Tel: 415-362-7126)
  (Fax: 415-362-6401)
(San Jose, CA Office*: 152 North Third Street, Suite 700, 95112-5560)
  (Tel: 408-286-0880)
  (Fax: 408-286-0337)
(Walnut Creek, CA Office*: 570 Lennon Lane, 94598-2415)
  (Tel: 925-947-1702)
  (Fax: 925-947-4921)

Administrative Law, Business Law, Construction Law, Employment Law, Environmental Law, Health Care, Managed Care Liability, Insurance Coverage, Insurance Fraud, Personal Injury, Premises Liability, Product Liability, Professional Liability, Medical Malpractice, Public Entities, Appellate Law

Resident Partners

Mark L. Kiefer — **Managing Partner** — University of California, Los Angeles, B.A. (magna cum laude), 1981; University of Santa Clara School of Law, J.D., 1984 — Admitted to Bar, 1984, California; U.S. District Court, Northern District of California; 1987, U.S. District Court, Central District of California — Member American Bar Association; State Bar of California; Association of Southern California Defense Counsel — E-mail: mkiefer@ericksenarbuthnot.com

George J. Hernandez, Jr. — **Assistant Managing Partner** — California State University, Northridge, B.A., 1997; Northwestern School of Law of Lewis & Clark College, J.D., 1980 — Admitted to Bar, 1983, California; 1984, U.S. District Court, Central, Eastern, Northern and Southern Districts of California — Member American, Los Angeles County, Hispanic National and Mexican American Bar Associations; State Bar of California; Southern California Defense Counsel — Languages: American Sign Language, French, Italian, Spanish — E-mail: ghernandez@ericksenarbuthnot.com

Lisa P. Gruen — **Partner** — University of Michigan, B.A. (with honors), 1980; Wayne State University Law School, J.D., 1984 — Admitted to Bar, 1984, California; U.S. District Court, Southern District of California; 1986, U.S. District Court, Central District of California — Member State Bar of California; Los Angeles County Bar Association; Defense Research Institute (Product Liability Committee) — E-mail: lgruen@ericksenarbuthnot.com

Angela G. Kim — **Partner** — University of California, Los Angeles, B.A., 1991; California Western School of Law, J.D., 1994 — Admitted to Bar, 1995, California; U.S. District Court, Central District of California — Member State Bar of California — E-mail: akim@ericksenarbuthnot.com

Norma Pedroza Chavez — **Partner** — Wellesley College, B.A., 1989; Boston University Law School, J.D., 1992 — Admitted to Bar, 1995, California — Member State Bar of California — E-mail: nchavez@ericksenarbuthnot.com

Resident Associates

Dale Arakawa — Southwestern University School of Law, J.D., 2006 — Admitted to Bar, 2007, California — E-mail: darakawa@ericksenarbuthnot.com

Paul Green — University of Southern California School of Law, LL.M., 2006 — Admitted to Bar, 2005, California — E-mail: pgreen@ericksenarbuthnot.com

Mark Licker — University of Southern California, J.D., 1979 — Admitted to Bar, 1979, California — E-mail: mlicker@ericksenarbuthnot.com

Abby Moscatel — Southwestern School of Law, J.D., 2010 — Admitted to Bar, 2011, California — E-mail: amoscatel@ericksenarbuthnot.com

(See listing under Oakland, CA for additional information)

Fitzpatrick & Hunt, Tucker, Collier, Pagano, Aubert, LLP

US Bank Tower
633 West Fifth Street, 60th Floor
Los Angeles, California 90071
  Telephone: 213-873-2100
  Fax: 213-873-2125
  www.fitzhunt.com

Alternative Dispute Resolution, Appellate Practice, Arbitration, Aviation, Class Actions, First and Third Party Defense, Insurance Litigation, International Law, Mediation, Product Liability, Reinsurance, Toxic Torts, Mass Disasters

Firm Profile: Fitzpatrick & Hunt specializes in products liability defense and claims prevention. Among the experienced product and services defense lawyers in our Firm are those with degrees and backgrounds in engineering and other technical fields. We provide advisory consultation to worldwide insurance markets and product manufacturers.

Equity Partners

James W. Hunt — Siena College, B.S., 1966; Seton Hall University School of Law, J.D., 1976 — Admitted to Bar, 1976, New Jersey; 1977, New York; 1986, California — Tel: 213-873-2150 — E-mail: james.hunt@fitzhunt.com

Alan H. Collier — Abilene Christian University, B.A. (summa cum laude), 1987; Pepperdine University School of Law, J.D. (cum laude), 1990 — Admitted to Bar, 1990, California — Tel: 213-873-2121 — E-mail: alan.collier@fitzhunt.com

Garth W. Aubert — University of Southern California, B.A., 1989; University of the Pacific, McGeorge School of Law, J.D., 1992 — Admitted to Bar, 1992, California — Tel: 213-873-2111 — E-mail: garth.aubert@fitzhunt.com

Partners

Christopher S. Hickey — University of California, Los Angeles, B.A., 1990; University of San Diego School of Law, J.D., 1998 — Admitted to Bar, 1998, California — Tel: 213-873-2147 — E-mail: christopher.hickey@fitzhunt.com

Mark Irvine — University of California, Los Angeles, B.A., 1985; University of the Pacific, McGeorge School of Law, J.D., 1988 — Admitted to Bar, 1988, California — Tel: 213-873-2131 — E-mail: mark.irvine@fitzhunt.com

Suzanne N. McNulty — University of Massachusetts, B.A., 1982; University of San Diego School of Law, J.D., 1988 — Admitted to Bar, 1989, California — Tel: 213-873-2120 — E-mail: suzanne.mcnulty@fitzhunt.com

Darrell M. Padgette — Northern Arizona University, B.S., 1995; University of Dayton School of Law, J.D., 1998 — Admitted to Bar, 1998, California — Tel: 213-873-2172 — E-mail: darrell.padgette@fitzhunt.com

Associates

Stephanie N. Gonzalez
Courtney P. McIntire
Brian J. Headman
Jennifer M. Vagle

(See listing under New York, NY for additional information)

Gaglione, Dolan & Kaplan
A Professional Corporation

Trident Center
11377 West Olympic Boulevard
Los Angeles, California 90064-1625
  Telephone: 310-231-1600
  Fax: 310-231-1610
  www.gaglionedolan.com

(Woodland Hills, CA Office: 20750 Ventura Boulevard, Suite 238, 91364)
  (Tel: 818-704-1464)
  (Fax: 818-704-1564)

Established: 1994

LOS ANGELES   CALIFORNIA

Gaglione, Dolan & Kaplan, A Professional Corporation, Los Angeles, CA (Continued)

Insurance Defense, Professional Liability (Non-Medical) Defense, Property and Casualty, Construction Defect, Coverage Issues, Employment Practices Liability, Agent and Brokers Errors and Omissions, Legal Malpractice, Architects and Engineers, Community Association Law

Insurance Clients

ACE USA	Allied World Assurance Company
American International Group, Inc.	AXIS Pro
Bankers Insurance Company	First Community Insurance Company
Great American Insurance Company	Hartford Insurance Company
Lawyers Mutual Insurance Company	Lexington Insurance Company
	Liberty International Underwriters
Markel Insurance Company	ProSight Specialty Insurance Company
Savers Property and Casualty Insurance Company	Star Insurance Company
Tudor Insurance Company	United States Liability Insurance Group

Non-Insurance Clients

Associated Claims Enterprises, Inc.	Insurance Management Solutions Group
Lancer Claims Services, Inc.	Specialty Claims Management, LLC
Lawyer's Protector Plan	
Superior Claim Services	
TRISTAR Risk Management	

Partners

Claudia L. Gaglione — 1958 — St. John's University, B.S. (summa cum laude), 1979; University of Southern California School of Law, J.D., 1982 — Phi Alpha Delta — Admitted to Bar, 1982, California; U.S. District Court, Central District of California; U.S. Court of Appeals, Ninth Circuit — Member Professional Liability Underwriting Society — E-mail: cgaglione@gaglionedolan.com

Robert T. Dolan — 1957 — Boston College, B.A., 1979; Pepperdine University School of Law, J.D., 1983 — Admitted to Bar, 1983, California; U.S. District Court, Central District of California; 1984, U.S. Court of Appeals, Ninth Circuit — Member Association of Southern California Defense Counsel; Defense Research Institute — E-mail: rdolan@gaglionedolan.com

Jeffrey S. Kaplan — 1967 — University of California, Berkeley, B.A., 1989; Loyola Law School Los Angeles, J.D., 1993 — Admitted to Bar, 1993, California; U.S. District Court, Central and Eastern Districts of California — Member Los Angeles County Bar Association; Professional Liability Underwriting Society; Defense Research Institute — E-mail: jkaplan@gaglionedolan.com

Associates

Lindsay McMenamin — 1949 — University of Illinois, B.S., 1972; Southwestern University School of Law, J.D., 2000 — Admitted to Bar, 2000, California; U.S. District Court, Central District of California — Member Los Angeles County Bar Association — E-mail: lmcmenamin@gaglionedolan.com

Jack M. LaPedis — 1967 — University of California, Irvine, B.A., 1991; Pepperdine University School of Law, J.D., 1995 — Admitted to Bar, 1995, California; U.S. District Court, Central District of California; U.S. Court of Appeals, Ninth Circuit — Member Los Angeles County Bar Association; Association of Southern California Defense Counsel — E-mail: jlapedis@gaglionedolan.com

June Poyourow — 1957 — State University of New York at Buffalo, B.A., 1979; Southwestern University School of Law, J.D., 1984 — Admitted to Bar, 1985, California; U.S. District Court, Central District of California — Member Beverly Hills and Los Angeles County Bar Associations — E-mail: jpoyourow@gaglionedolan.com

Kaiulani S. Lie — 1974 — Illinois State University, B.S., 1995; Tulane University Law School, J.D. (Environmental Law), 1999 — Admitted to Bar, 2000, California; U.S. District Court, Central District of California — Member Association of Southern California Defense Counsel — E-mail: klie@gaglionedolan.com

Steven F. Bauer — 1956 — University of Southern California, B.S., 1978; University of California, Hastings College of the Law, J.D., 1981 — Admitted to Bar, 1981, California — Member Los Angeles County Bar Association (Real Property Section; Title Insurance Subsection); California Land Title Association (Litigation Committee) — E-mail: sbauer@gaglionedolan.com

Gaglione, Dolan & Kaplan, A Professional Corporation, Los Angeles, CA (Continued)

Of Counsel

Martina A. Silas — University of Tampa, B.S., 1978; Whittier Law School, J.D. (Valedictorian), 1985 — American Jurisprudence Awards for Outstanding Achievement in: Contracts, Legal Writing, Business Torts, Uniform Commercial Code, Copyright Law, Criminal Law, Criminal Procedure, Family Law, Real Property & Wills & Trusts; Nominated: National Trial Lawyer of the Year, Trial Lawyers for Public Justice, 2000 — Admitted to Bar, 1985, California; 1986, U.S. District Court, Central District of California; U.S. District Court, Southern District of California; U.S. District Court, Eastern District of California; U.S. Court of Appeals, Ninth Circuit — Reported Cases: Published opinions as lead appellate or amicus curiae counsel: State Farm Fire & Casualty Co. v. Superior Court (Aegea), 215 Cal. App. 3d 1435 (1989); Torres v. Parkhouse Tire Service, Inc., 26 Cal. 4th 995 (2001); Cavalier v. Random House, Inc., 297 F.3d 815 (9th Cir. 2002); Nemarnik v. Los Angeles Kings Hockey Club, L.P., 103 Cal. App. 4th 631 (2002) — Guest Instructor on Insurance Bad Faith, State Farm Fire & Casualty Company and Farmers Insurance Group, 1986-1996; Instructor on Bad Faith and Punitive Damages, American Conference Institute — E-mail: msilas1@aol.com

Hanna, Brophy, MacLean, McAleer & Jensen, LLP

606 South Olive Street, Suite 1020
Los Angeles, California 90014
Telephone: 213-943-4800
Fax: 213-943-4081
www.hannabrophy.com

Established: 1943

Insurance Defense, Workers' Compensation, Subrogation, Labor and Employment, Employment Law, Litigation

Office Managing Partner

Philip E. Dunn — San Fernando College of Law, J.D., 1976 — Admitted to Bar, 1977, California — Member American and Los Angeles County Bar Associations; State Bar of California; California Trial Lawyers Association; Association of Trial Lawyers of America

(See listing under Oakland, CA for additional information)

Jampol Zimet LLP

800 Wilshire Boulevard, Suite 1400
Los Angeles, California 90017-2623
Telephone: 213-689-8500
Fax: 213-689-8501
E-Mail: mzimet@jzlaw.com
www.jzlaw.com

Agent/Broker Liability, Arbitration, Construction Defect, Insurance Coverage, Legal Malpractice, Employment Practices, Nursing Home Liability, Legal Liability

Firm Profile: Insurers entrust Jampol Zimet LLP to defend their insureds because we provide exceptional and consistent results inexpensively. We are comprised of a small group of skilled attorneys who appreciate that their job is to resolve claims reasonably and quickly.

Insurance Clients

Allied World Assurance Company	AmTrust North America
Arch Insurance Group	Atrium Underwriting PLC
Darwin Professional Underwriters, Inc.	Gallagher Bassett Services, Inc.
	Monitor Liability Managers, Inc.
U.S. Liability Insurance Company	

Non-Insurance Clients

Lancer Claims Services, Inc.	Midlands Claim Administrators, Inc.
NAS Insurance Services, Inc.	

Jampol Zimet LLP, Los Angeles, CA (Continued)

Partners

Alan R. Jampol — University of California, B.A., 1969; University of California, Los Angeles School of Law, J.D., 1972 — Admitted to Bar, 1972, California; 1972, U.S. District Court, Northern and Southern Districts of California — Member American and Los Angeles County Bar Associations; Professional Liability Underwriting Society; Association of Southern California Defense Counsel — AV Rated, Martindale-Hubbell

Marc J. Zimet — Texas State University, B.B.A., 1987; University of La Verne College of Law, J.D., 1995 — Admitted to Bar, 1996, California; 2008, Massachusetts; 1996, U.S. District Court, Southern District of California; 1997, U.S. District Court, Northern District of California; 2001, U.S. Supreme Court — Member American and Los Angeles County Bar Associations; Defense Research Institute; Association of Southern California Defense Counsel; Professional Liability Underwriting Society — AV Rated, Martindale-Hubbell

Locke Lord LLP

300 South Grand Avenue, Suite 2600
Los Angeles, California 90071-3119
   Telephone: 213-485-1500
   Fax: 213-485-1200
   www.lockelord.com

(Chicago, IL Office*: 111 South Wacker Drive, 60606-4410)
   (Tel: 312-443-0700)
   (Fax: 312-443-0336)
(Atlanta, GA Office*: Terminus 200, Suite 1200, 3333 Piedmont Road NE, 30305)
   (Tel: 404-870-4600)
   (Fax: 404-872-5547)
(Austin, TX Office*: 600 Congress Avenue, Suite 2200, 78701-2748)
   (Tel: 512-305-4700)
   (Fax: 512-305-4800)
(Dallas, TX Office*: 2200 Ross Avenue, Suite 2200, 75201)
   (Tel: 214-740-8000)
   (Fax: 214-740-8800)
(Houston, TX Office*: 2800 JPMorgan Chase Tower, 600 Travis, 77002-3095)
   (Tel: 713-226-1200)
   (Fax: 713-223-3717)
(London, United Kingdom Office*: 201 Bishopsgate, DX 567 London/City, EC2M 3AB)
   (Tel: +44 (0) 20 7861 9000 (Int'l))
   (Tel: 011 44 207861 9000 (US))
   (Fax: +44 (0) 20 7785 6869 201 (Bishopsgate))
(New Orleans, LA Office*: 601 Poydras, Suite 2660, 70130)
   (Tel: 504-558-5100)
   (Fax: 504-558-5200)
(New York, NY Office*: Three World Financial Center, Floor 20, 10281)
   (Tel: 212-415-8600)
   (Fax: 212-303-2754)
(Sacramento, CA Office: 500 Capitol Mall, Suite 1800, 95814)
   (Tel: 916-554-0240)
   (Fax: 916-554-5440)
(San Francisco, CA Office*: 44 Montgomery Street, Suite 2400, 94104)
   (Tel: 415-318-8810)
   (Fax: 415-676-5816)
(Washington, DC Office*: 701 8th Street, N.W., Suite 700, 20001)
   (Tel: 202-521-4100)
   (Fax: 202-521-4200)
(Hong Kong, China-PRC Office: 21/F Bank of China Tower, 1 Garden Road, Central)
   (Tel: +852 3465 0600)
   (Fax: +852 3014 0991)

Locke Lord LLP, Los Angeles, CA (Continued)

Antitrust, Arbitration, Aviation, Business Law, Class Actions, Construction Law, Corporate Law, Directors and Officers Liability, Employee Benefits, Environmental Law, Health Care, Insurance Law, Intellectual Property, Labor and Employment, Land Use, Admiralty and Maritime Law, Mergers and Acquisitions, Product Liability, Railroad Law, Regulatory and Compliance, Reinsurance, Securities, Technology, Transportation, Appellate, Long Term Care

Partners

Carey S. Barney — 1955 — Brigham Young University, B.S. (summa cum laude), 1979; The University of Chicago, J.D., 1982 — Admitted to Bar, 1982, Illinois; 2000, California — Member American, Illinois State and Chicago Bar Associations; State Bar of California — Languages: Finnish — Practice Areas: Insurance Law; Corporate Law; Regulatory and Compliance

C. Guerry Collins — 1944 — Yale University, B.A., 1966; University of Southern California School of Law, J.D., 1984 — Admitted to Bar, 1984, California; 1984, U.S. District Court, Central and Northern Districts of California; 1985, U.S. District Court, Southern District of California; 1988, U.S. District Court, Eastern District of California; 1988, U.S. Court of Appeals, Ninth Circuit — Member State Bar of California; Los Angeles County Bar Association — Practice Areas: Commercial Litigation; Excess and Reinsurance; Insurance Law

Mitchell J. Popham — 1958 — La Pierce College; University of California, Los Angeles, B.A. (magna cum laude), 1981; Loyola Law School, J.D. (cum laude), 1986 — Admitted to Bar, 1986, California; 1986, U.S. District Court, Central District of California; 1986, U.S. Court of Appeals, Ninth Circuit — Member American and Los Angeles County Bar Associations; State Bar of California — Practice Areas: Environmental Law; Insurance Law; Product Liability

Michael F. Perlis — Georgetown University, B.S.F.S. (magna cum laude), 1968; Georgetown University Law Center, J.D., 1971 — Admitted to Bar, 1971, District of Columbia; 1980, California; 1994, New York — Southern California Super Lawyer, Southern California Super Lawyers Magazine (2005-2012) — Practice Areas: Business Litigation; Dispute Resolution; Insurance; Securities

Karen R. Palmersheim — University of California, Berkeley, B.A., 1988; Southwestern University School of Law, J.D. (magna cum laude, Dean's List), 1994 — Articles Editor, Law Review Executive Board, American Jurisprudence Awards, Constitutional Law and Legal Ethics, Southwestern University Law Review — Admitted to Bar, 1994, California; U.S. District Court, Central, Northern and Southern Districts of California; U.S. Court of Appeals, Ninth Circuit; Supreme Court of California — Member Los Angeles County (Health Law) Bar Association; Women in Health Administration of Southern California; American Health Lawyers Association — Pasadena Magazine, Top Attorney (2010, 2011, 2012); Super Lawyers, Rising Star (2006); Who's Who in America (2006) — Practice Areas: Administrative Law; Business Litigation; Dispute Resolution; Class Actions; Health Care; Insurance; Labor and Employment

Senior Counsel

Patricia Arias Musitano   Susan J. Welde
Cary Economou   Richard Johnson

Of Counsel

Jonathan F. Bank

Associates

Kelly Biggins   Michelle Ferrara
Phillip Hosp   Silvia Huang
Lilian Khanjiah

(See listing under Chicago, IL for additional information)

McKay, de Lorimier & Acain

3250 Wilshire Boulevard, Suite 603
Los Angeles, California 90010
   Telephone: 213-386-6900
   Fax: 213-381-1762
   E-Mail: pdelorimier@mdalaw.net
   www.mdalaw.net

McKay, de Lorimier & Acain, Los Angeles, CA
(Continued)

Insurance Law, Personal Injury, Premises Liability, Product Liability, Civil Litigation, Construction Defect, International Law, Tort, Legal Malpractice, Professional Liability

Insurance Clients

AXA Corporate Solutions
Church Mutual Insurance Company
Grange Insurance Group
Progressive Insurance Companies
Safeco Insurance Companies
AXA Group
General Casualty Company
Harleysville Insurance Company
QBE Regional Insurance
Swiss Reinsurance America Corporation

Non-Insurance Clients

Club Med Sales, Inc.

Partners

John P. McKay — California State University, Fullerton, B.A., 1963; Pepperdine University School of Law, J.D., 1968 — Admitted to Bar, 1969, California; 1969, U.S. District Court, Central and Northern Districts of California; 1977, U.S. Court of Appeals, Ninth Circuit; 1977, U.S. Supreme Court; 1985, U.S. District Court, Eastern District of California; 2003, U.S. District Court, Southern District of California — Member American (Torts and Insurance Practice Section), Los Angeles County and Orange County Bar Associations; State Bar of California; Robert A. Banyad Inn of Court; Panel of Arbitrators, American Arbitration Association; Founding Fellow of Litigation Counsel of America; Association of Southern California Defense Counsel; American Board of Trial Advocates; Defense Research Institute — Reported Cases: Doe v. California Lutheran High School Association (2009) 170 Cal.App.4th 828; Wiener v. Southcoast Childcare Centers, Inc. (2004) 32 Cal.4th 1138; Federal Deposit Insurance Corporation v. British-American Insurance Company, LTD (1987) 828 F.2d 1439; Cynthia Baldwin v. Harold Johnson, et al. (1979) 123 Cal.App.3rd 275; Nadine Peterson v. Superior Court of Riverside (1995) 10 Cal.4th 1183 — Los Angeles Superior Court (Panel of Arbitrators); Orange County Superior Court, Judge Pro Tem (1985-Present); Southern California Super Lawyers (2006-2013) — Certified Specialist in Trial Advocacy, The National Board of Trial Advocacy (2000-2010) — Practice Areas: Church Law; Insurance Coverage Litigation; Insurance Defense; Tort Claims Defense; Product Liability Defense — E-mail: jmckay@mdalaw.net

Paul A. de Lorimier — California State University, Los Angeles, B.A., 1978; Southwestern University School of Law, J.D., 1982 — Admitted to Bar, 1983, California; 1984, U.S. District Court, Central District of California; 1984, U.S. Court of Appeals, Ninth Circuit; 1986, U.S. District Court, Eastern District of California; 2000, U.S. District Court, Northern District of California; 2003, U.S. District Court, Southern District of California — Member American Bar Association; State Bar of California; Association of Southern California Defense Counsel — Reported Cases: Northland Insurance Company v. Briones (2000) 81 Cal.App.4th 796; Guardian Angel Polish National Catholic Church v. Grotnik (2004) 118 Cal.App.4th 919 — Litigation Counsel of America, Associate Fellow — Practice Areas: Church Law; Product Liability Defense; Insurance Coverage Litigation; Insurance Defense; Tort Claims Defense — E-mail: pdelorimier@mdalaw.net

Michael P. Acain — Loyola Marymount University, B.A. (cum laude), 1996; Loyola Law School, J.D., 1999 — Admitted to Bar, 1999, California; 2000, U.S. District Court, Central District of California; 2003, U.S. District Court, Northern and Southern Districts of California — Member American and Los Angeles Bar Assocations; Philippine American Bar Association of Los Angeles; State Bar of California — Reported Cases: Doe v. California Lutheran High School Association (2009) 170 Cal.App.4th 828; Wiener v. Southcoast Childcare Centers, Inc. (2004) 32 Cal.4th 1138 — Practice Areas: Church Law; Product Liability Defense; Insurance Defense; Tort Claims Defense; Insurance Coverage Litigation — E-mail: macain@mdalaw.net

Associates

Janet S. Yoon — University of California, Los Angeles, B.A. (with honors), 2006; Loyola Law School Los Angeles, J.D., 2009 — Admitted to Bar, 2009, California; 2010, U.S. District Court, Central District of California; 2013, U.S. District Court, Southern District of California — Member State Bar of California — Practice Areas: Church Law; Insurance Defense — E-mail: jyoon@mdalaw.net

James Wright — California State University, Fullerton, B.A., History (Dean's List), 2006; Western State University College of Law, J.D., 2012 — Admitted to Bar, 2014, California; 2014, U.S. District Court, Central and Southern Districts of California — Member American, Los Angeles County and Orange County Bar Associations; State Bar of California; American Bar Foundation — Practice Areas: Civil Litigation; Personal Injury; Premises Liability; Product Liability; Church Law; Property Damage; Insurance Law; Intentional Torts; Employment Discrimination; Wrongful Termination — E-mail: jwright@mdalaw.net

Of Counsel

Michael A. Byrne — University of Wisconsin, B.A., 1964; Loyola University Chicago School of Law, J.D., 1967 — Admitted to Bar, 1969, California; 1972, U.S. District Court, Central District of California; 1976, U.S. District Court, Northern District of California; 1977, U.S. Court of Appeals, Ninth Circuit; 1977, U.S. Supreme Court; 1983, U.S. Court of Appeals, Fifth Circuit; 1985, U.S. District Court, Eastern District of California; 1987, U.S. District Court, Southern District of California — Member State Bar of California; Los Angeles Superior Court, Panel of Arbitrators — Reported Cases: Jacqueline R. v. Household of Faith Family Church (2002) 97 Cal.App.4th 198 — Lecturer, Southern California Defense Counsel; Los Angeles Superior Court Crash Program, Settlement Officer — Practice Areas: Church Law; Product Liability; Insurance Coverage Litigation; Insurance Defense; Tort Claims Defense — E-mail: mbyrne@mdalaw.net

Meyers McConnell Reisz Siderman

11620 Wilshire Boulevard, Suite 800
Los Angeles, California 90025
  Telephone: 310-312-0772
  Fax: 310-312-0656
  E-Mail: mm@meyersmcconnell.com
  www.meyersmcconnell.com

(New York, NY Office: 750 3rd Avenue, 9th Floor, 10017)
  (Tel: 212-572-8384)
  (Fax: 212-572-8304)
(Las Vegas, NV Office: 1745 Village Center Circle, 89134)
  (Tel: 702-253-1377)
  (Fax: 702-248-6192)

Established: 1980

Product Liability, Architects and Engineers, Attorneys, Agents and Brokers Errors and Omissions, Construction Defect, Employment Practices, General Liability, Commercial Litigation, Mediation, Risk Management, Loss Prevention Consultation

Firm Profile: In over thirty years of practice, MMRS has developed a broad range of Attorney/Design Professional, E&O, PL, EPL, Construction and CGL clients across the USA, Japan and Canada. Offices in LA, LV and NY emphasize diversity, efficiency and a commitment to experienced lawyers affording personal and timely service and communication.

Insurance Clients

Aioi Nissay Dowa Insurance Co., Ltd.
Aviva Insurance Company of Canada
Berkley Specialty Underwriting Managers, LLC
Lexington Insurance Company
Navigators Management Company
OneBeacon Insurance
Sompo Japan Nipponkoa Insurance Inc.
Arch Insurance Company
Aspen Specialty Insurance Solutions, LLC
AXIS Professional Insurance
Dongbu Insurance
Hiscox USA
Mitsui Sumitomo Insurance Group
Navigators Pro
Samsung Fire & Marine Insurance Company, Ltd.
Zurich American Insurance Group

Non-Insurance Clients

Converse Professional Group
Panasonic Corporation of North America
Toshiba Corporation
IPD Global Inc.
Sega Entertainment U.S.A., Inc.
Sengoku L.A., Ltd.
The Viking Corporation

Principals

John W. McConnell III — 1949 — University of Southern California, B.A. (cum laude), 1971; California Western School of Law, J.D., 1974 — California Western Law Review — Admitted to Bar, 1974, California; U.S. District

CALIFORNIA — LOS ANGELES

Meyers McConnell Reisz Siderman, Los Angeles, CA (Continued)

Court, Central, Eastern and Southern Districts of California — Member American Bar Association; State Bar of California; Product Liability Advisory Council; Association of Southern California Defense Counsel; Defense Research Institute — Practice Areas: Product Liability; Construction Defect; Professional Liability; General Liability; Mediation — E-mail: mcconnell@meyersmcconnell.com

Frederick S. Reisz — 1964 — Franklin & Marshall College, B.A., 1986; Pepperdine University School of Law, J.D., 1989 — Admitted to Bar, 1989, California; U.S. District Court, Central District of California; U.S. Court of Appeals, Ninth Circuit — Member State Bar of California; Defense Research Institute — Practice Areas: Professional Liability; Construction Defect; Product Liability; General Liability — E-mail: reisz@meyersmcconnell.com

Lori E. Siderman — 1969 — University of California, Santa Barbara, B.A. (with honors), 1991; University of the Pacific, McGeorge School of Law, J.D., 1994 — Admitted to Bar, 1994, California; 2000, Nevada; U.S. District Court, Central District of California; U.S. Court of Appeals, Ninth Circuit — Member American Bar Association; State Bar of California; State Bar of Nevada; Defense Research Institute — California Real Estate Broker — Practice Areas: Professional Liability; Construction Defect; Product Liability; General Liability; Real Estate — E-mail: siderman@meyersmcconnell.com

Associates

Daniel A. Eisenberg
Jieun Choi
Kenton L. Robinson
Scott G. Greene
Joseph K. Bakshandeh
Russell B. Brown
S. Seth Kershaw

Of Counsel

Jeffrey G. Meyers
Robert P. Dickerson
Andrew Feldman

Murchison & Cumming, LLP

801 South Grand Avenue, 9th Floor
Los Angeles, California 90017
Telephone: 213-623-7400
Fax: 213-623-6336
E-Mail: marketing@murchisonlaw.com
www.murchisonlaw.com

(Additional Offices: San Diego, CA*; Irvine, CA*; Las Vegas, NV*; San Francisco, CA*)

Established: 1930

Appellate Practice, Arbitration, Business Litigation, Business and Real Estate Transactions, Casualty, Class Actions, Construction Law, Directors and Officers Liability, Employment Law, Environmental Law, General Liability, Health, Hospitality, Insurance Law, International Law, Mediation, Product Liability, Professional Liability, Toxic Torts, Transportation, Emerging Risks & Specialty Tort Litigation, Long Term Care Facilities for the Elderly, Law & Motion, Management Protection, Training/Education and Other Client Services, Utilities, Vertical Transportation, White Collar Crime, Wildland Fire Litigation

Firm Profile: Murchison & Cumming, LLP is a premier civil litigation firm specializing in the defense of domestic and international companies and individuals doing business in California and Nevada, as well as the representation of clients in business transactions and litigation throughout the U.S.

Corporate Clients

American Power Conversion
Daimler Trucks North America, LLC
Fujifilm USA
Great Dane Trailers
Cessna Aircraft Company
Del Taco Risk Management
Denny's, Inc.
Global Aerospace, Inc.
Haupt Pharma AG

Murchison & Cumming, LLP, Los Angeles, CA (Continued)

Hertz Claim Management
Jarden Corporation
Mitsubishi Electric & Electronics USA, Inc.
Res-Care, Inc.
Southern California Edison Company
Universal Health Services, Inc.
Hyatt Corporation
Jons Marketplace
Nissan Motor Corporation
PACCAR, Inc.
Schneider Electric
Strategic Hotels & Resorts, Inc.
Tenet Healthcare Corporation
The Vons Companies, Inc.

Insurance Clients

Allianz Global Corporate & Specialty
American Claims Service, Inc.
Argo Pro US
AXA Insurance Company
AXIS U.S. Insurance
Catlin Specialty Insurance Company
Chubb Services Corporation
Clarendon National Insurance Company
Crum & Forster
Electric Insurance Company
Endurance U.S. Insurance Operations
Fireman's Fund Insurance Companies
Great American Insurance Companies
Interested Underwriters at Lloyds of London
Lawyer's Protector Plan
Life Care Legal and Risk Services, LLC
Midland Claims Administrators, Inc.
OneBeacon Insurance
QBE North America
Royal & SunAlliance
Specialty Risk Services
TM Claims Service, Inc.
Tokio Marine & Nichido Fire Insurance Co., Ltd
Zurich North America
Allianz Versicherungs - AG
Alterra Specialty
Arch Insurance Group
Avizent Risk Management Solutions
Burlington Insurance Company
Century Surety Company
Chubb Group of Insurance Companies
Colony Insurance Company
Contractors Bonding and Insurance Company (CBIC), an RLI Company
Farmers Insurance Group
Federated Insurance Company
First Mercury Insurance Company
Gothaer Versicherungsbank VVaG
The Hartford
HDI-Gerling America Insurance Company
James River Insurance Company
Lexington Insurance Company
Markel Insurance Companies
Meadowbrook Insurance Group
NBIS Claims and Risk Management, Inc.
PMA Insurance Group
RiverStone Claims Management, LLC
Strickland Insurance Group
Tokio Marine Management, Inc.
United States Liability Insurance Group

Senior Partners

Friedrich W. Seitz — Co-Chair, International Law, Business Litigation and Product Liability/Utilities; Chair, Wildland Fire Litigation — 1941 — University of Southern California, B.A., 1965; Southwestern University School of Law, J.D., 1971 — Admitted to Bar, 1972, California — Practice Areas: Product Liability; Aviation; Business Law; Business Litigation; International Law; Transportation

Michael B. Lawler — Co-Chair, Employment Law — 1942 — Loyola University, B.B.A., 1964; Southwestern University School of Law, J.D., 1971 — Admitted to Bar, 1972, California; 2000, Colorado; 2001, District of Columbia — Practice Areas: Complex Litigation; General Liability; Employment Law; Construction Law; Nursing Home Liability; Health

Kenneth H. Moreno — Partner-in-Charge, San Diego Office; Co-Chair, Employment Law Group, Management Protection — 1956 — University of California, Los Angeles, B.A., 1979; University of Southern California School of Law, J.D., 1982 — Admitted to Bar, 1983, California — Practice Areas: Directors and Officers Liability; Labor and Employment; Nursing Home Liability; Medical Malpractice; General Liability; Professional Liability; Environmental Law; Business Litigation; Business Transactions; Health

Dan L. Longo — Managing Partner, Orange County Office; Co-Chair, Professional Liability, Health Law — 1956 — University of Southern California, B.A., 1978; Loyola Law School Los Angeles, J.D., 1982 — Admitted to Bar, 1982, California — Practice Areas: General Liability; Medical Malpractice; Legal Malpractice; Nursing Home Liability; Medical Liability; Employment Law; Sexual Harassment; Discrimination; Professional Liability; Health

Jean M. Lawler — Co-Chair, International Law — 1954 — Loyola Marymount University, B.B.A., 1976; Loyola Law School Los Angeles, J.D., 1979 — Admitted to Bar, 1979, California; 1981, Oregon — Practice Areas: Insurance Coverage; Civil Litigation; Contracts; Regulatory and Compliance; Bad Faith; Insurance Litigation; Arbitration; Mediation

Edmund G. Farrell, III — Partner-in-Charge, Los Angeles Office; Chair, Appellate Law; Co-Chair, Professional Liability — 1955 — University of California, San Diego, B.S., 1978; Santa Clara University School of Law,

LOS ANGELES | CALIFORNIA

Murchison & Cumming, LLP, Los Angeles, CA
(Continued)

J.D., 1982 — Admitted to Bar, 1983, California — Practice Areas: Appellate Practice; Professional Liability

Guy R. Gruppie — Co-Chair, Emerging Risks & Specialty Tort Litigation; Senior Member, Product Liability and General Liability Practice Groups — 1962 — University of Southern California, B.A., 1988; Loyola Law School Los Angeles, J.D., 1991 — Admitted to Bar, 1991, California — Practice Areas: General Liability; Casualty; Product Liability; Risk Management; Tort Litigation

Richard C. Moreno — Chair, Transportation Law; Co-Chair, Product Liability/Utilities — 1970 — University of Southern California, B.A., 1994; Whittier Law School, J.D., 1997 — Admitted to Bar, 1997, California — Practice Areas: Transportation; Product Liability

William D. Naeve — Co-Chair, Management Protection, Directors & Officers, Hospitality, Employment Law and Class Action & Consumer Litigation Practice Groups — 1953 — University of California, Los Angeles, B.A., 1976; Western State University College of Law, J.D., 1979 — Admitted to Bar, 1980, California; 2001, Nevada — Practice Areas: Management Protection; Directors and Officers Liability; Employment Law; Class Actions; Consumer Litigation

Partners

Gina Bazaz
Jean A. Dalmore
Melissa W. Eisenberg
Scott J. Loeding
Heather L. Mills
Michael J. Nunez
Robert H. Panman
Matthew H. Printz
Jefferson S. Smith
Ellen M. Tipping
Bryan M. Weiss
Bradley T. Wibicki
David A. Winkle
Russell S. Wollman
Cooper W. Collins
Malena Dobal
Scott L. Hengesbach
Michael D. McEvoy
Mhare O. Mouradian
Gina E. Och
John H. Podesta
Heidi C. Quan
William J. Snyder
Kasey C. Townsend
Eric P. Weiss
James S. Williams
Matthew K. Wisinski
Corine Zygelman

Associate Partners

Todd A. Chamberlain
Paul R. Flaherty
Terry L. Kesinger
Carolyn A. Matthews
Nancy N. Potter
Robert M. Scherk
J. Lynn Feldner
Joseph Kang
Pamela J. Marantz
Daniel G. Pezold
Gregory A. Sargenti

Associates

Lisa D. Angelo
Abraham Berger
Sarai L. Brown
Dawn L. Davis
Mark M. Gnesin
Scott R. Jackman
Joon Y. Kim
Chantel E. Lafrades
German A. Marcucci
Nichole Murray
Matthew D. Pearson
Anita Sreerama
Mary C. Trinh
Carolynn K. Beck
Rachel K. Brilliant
Joyce E. Clifford
Mary Jane Dellafiora
Dustun H. Holmes
James N. Kahn
Katelyn M. Knight
Jennifer K. Letulle
Steven J. McEvoy
Georgiana A. Nikias
Nanette G. Reed
Dana L. Tom
Bryan J. Ure

Of Counsel

William T. Delhagen
David M. Hall
Steven C. Spronz
Joseph Fox
Benjamin H. Seal, II
B. Casey Yim

Senior Counsel

James P. Collins
Michael D. McEvoy

Nielsen, Haley & Abbott LLP

606 South Olive Street, Suite 1800
Los Angeles, California 90014
Telephone: 213-239-9009
Fax: 213-239-9007

(San Rafael, CA Office*(See San Francisco listing): 100 Smith Ranch Road, Suite 350, 94903-5595)
(Tel: 415-693-0900)
(Fax: 415-693-9674)
(E-Mail: jnielsen@nielsenhaley.com)
(www.nielsenhaley.com)

Insurance Coverage, Fidelity, Surety, Tort Litigation, Business Law, Appellate Practice, Employment Law, Bad Faith, Product Liability, Professional Liability

Mary N. Abbott — University of California, Davis, B.A., 1973; University of the Pacific, McGeorge School of Law, J.D., 1976 — Admitted to Bar, 1977, California

August L. Lohuaru — University of California, Los Angeles, B.A., 1995; University of San Francisco, J.D., 2002 — Admitted to Bar, 2002, California

James C. Nielsen — University of California, Davis, B.A., 1980; University of Virginia, J.D., 1983 — Admitted to Bar, 1983, California; 2000, Nevada — Certified Specialist, Appellate Law, State Bar of California Board of Legal Specialization, 1996

(See listing under San Francisco, CA for additional information)

Pearlman, Borska & Wax, LLP

15910 Ventura Boulevard, 18th Floor
Encino, California 91436
Telephone: 818-501-4343
Fax: 818-386-5700
E-Mail: bsp@4pbw.com
www.pbw-law.com

(Oxnard, CA Office: 500 East Esplanade Drive, Suite 510, 93036)
(Tel: 805-604-1134)
(Fax: 805-604-1194)
(Glendale, CA Office: 330 North Brand Boulevard, Suite 250, 91203)
(Tel: 818-245-4285)
(Fax: 818-245-4291)
(Gardena, CA Office: 1411 West 190th Street, Suite 225, 90248)
(Tel: 310-856-4729)
(Fax: 310-436-0525)
(San Diego, CA Office: 5935 Cornerstone Court West, Suite #250, 92121)
(Tel: 858-875-5500)
(Fax: 858-875-5540)

Established: 1984

Workers' Compensation, Employment Law, Insurance Defense, Subrogation

Insurance Clients

Berkley Specialty Underwriting Managers, LLC
Employers Direct Insurance Company
GMIS/Springfield Insurance Company
Electric Insurance Company
Employers Compensation Insurance Company
ESIS/ACE USA Group
OneBeacon Insurance
Republic Indemnity Company of America

Non-Insurance Clients

Able Building Maintenance Company
K.V. Mart Company
SelectRemedy Staffing
University of Southern California
American Airlines, Inc.
Bank of America, N.A.
RJN Investigations, Inc.
Tampa Bay Buccaneers

Pearlman, Borska & Wax, LLP, Los Angeles, CA
(Continued)

Partners

Barry S. Pearlman — 1956 — University of California, Los Angeles, B.S., 1978; Southwestern University School of Law, J.D., 1980 — Admitted to Bar, 1981, California; 1982, U.S. District Court, Central District of California — Member State Bar of California; Los Angeles County Bar Association; California Workers' Compensation Defense Attorneys' Association (President, 2000-2005); Southern California Workers' Compensation Defense Attorneys Association (President, 1999-2003, 2004-2005) — E-mail: bsp@4pbw.com

Elliot F. Borska — 1954 — American University, B.A., 1975; California State University, Long Beach, M.S., 1979; Southwestern University School of Law, J.D., 1982 — Admitted to Bar, 1983, California; U.S. District Court, Central District of California — Member California Workers' Compensation Defense Attorneys' Association — E-mail: efb@4pbw.com

Steven H. Wax — 1950 — California State University, Northridge, B.A.; Southwestern University School of Law, J.D., 1976 — Admitted to Bar, 1976, California — Member California Workers' Compensation Defense Attorneys' Association — Certified Workers' Compensation Specialist — E-mail: shw@4pbw.com

Dean S. Brown — 1963 — University of California, Santa Barbara, B.A., 1985; Whittier Law School, J.D., 1989 — Admitted to Bar, 1990, California — Member California Workers' Compensation Defense Attorneys' Association — E-mail: dsb@4pbw.com

Neil D. Schwartz — 1949 — The University of Arizona, B.A., 1972; University of West Los Angeles School of Law, J.D., 1976 — Associate Editor, West Los Angeles Law Review — Admitted to Bar, 1977, California; U.S. District Court, Central District of California — Member State Bar of California; California Workers' Compensation Defense Attorneys' Association — Arbitrator, Los Angeles County Superior Court, State of California Workers' Compensation Appeals Board — E-mail: nds@4pbw.com

Yvonne E. Lang — 1969 — University of California, Irvine, B.A., 1991; University of La Verne College of Law, J.D., 1996 — Admitted to Bar, 1997, California; U.S. Court of Appeals, Ninth Circuit — Member California Workers' Compensation Defense Attorneys' Association — E-mail: yel@4pbw.com

Jeffrey S. Stern — 1954 — California State University, Northridge, B.A. (with honors), 1976; Loyola Law School, J.D., 1981 — Admitted to Bar, 1981, California; 1982, U.S. District Court, Central District of California — Member San Fernando Valley Bar Association (Executive Committee, Workers' Compensation); California Workers' Compensation Defense Attorneys' Association — E-mail: jss@4pbw.com

Rudy R. Grob — 1962 — University of Virginia, 1983-1985; University of California, Los Angeles, B.A., 1987; Southwestern University School of Law, J.D., 1990 — Admitted to Bar, 1990, California; U.S. District Court, Central, Eastern, Northern and Southern Districts of California — Member State Bar of California; California Workers' Compensation Defense Attorneys' Association — E-mail: rrg@4pbw.com

Noel A. Olins — 1972 — California State University, Northridge, B.A., 1998; Chapman University School of Law, J.D., 2002 — Admitted to Bar, 2002, California — Member Los Angeles County and San Fernando Valley Bar Associations; California Workers' Compensation Defense Attorney's Association — E-mail: nao@4pbw.com

Associates

Bonnie V. Stern — 1971 — University of California, Santa Barbara, B.A., 1993; University of San Diego School of Law, J.D., 1997 — Admitted to Bar, 1997, California — Member San Fernando Valley Bar Association (Workers' Compensation Section); California Workers' Compensation Defense Attorneys' Association — E-mail: bvs@4pbw.com

Brian Dreyfus — 1971 — Loyola Marymount University, B.A., 1992; Whittier Law School, J.D., 1995 — Admitted to Bar, 1995, California; U.S. District Court, Central District of California — Member American Bar Association; State Bar of California; California Workers' Compensation Defense Attorneys' Association — E-mail: bd@4pbw.com

Meline H. Sirounian — 1971 — The Pennsylvania State University, B.A. (with honors), 1994; Loyola Law School, J.D., 1998 — Phi Alpha Delta — Admitted to Bar, 2001, California — Member California Workers' Compensation Defense Attorneys' Association — E-mail: mhs@4pbw.com

Mark E. Joseph — 1947 — Queens College, B.A., 1968; New York Law School, J.D., 1972 — Admitted to Bar, 1973, New York; 1974, California; 1980, U.S. District Court, Central District of California — Member California Workers' Compensation Defense Attorneys' Association — E-mail: mej@4pbw.com

Pearlman, Borska & Wax, LLP, Los Angeles, CA
(Continued)

Robert B. Heller — 1950 — University of California, Santa Barbara, B.A., 1976; California Polytechnic State University, B.S., 1980; Loyola Law School, J.D., 1984 — Admitted to Bar, 1985, California — Member State Bar of California; California Workers' Compensation Defense Attorneys Association — E-mail: rbh@4pbw.com

Charles B. Ressler — 1950 — California State University, Northridge, B.S., 1973; Whittier Law School, J.D., 1979 — Admitted to Bar, 1979, California; 1983, U.S. District Court, Central District of California — Member California Workers' Compensation Defense Attorney's Association — E-mail: cbr@4pbw.com

Karinneh Aslanian — 1973 — University of California, Los Angeles, B.A., 1995; University of La Verne College of Law, J.D., 2000 — Admitted to Bar, 2000, California — Member California Workers' Compensation Attorney's Association — E-mail: ka@4pbw.com

Jack M. Cohen — 1950 — University of California, Riverside, B.A., 1973; San Fernando College of Law, J.D., 1976 — Admitted to Bar, 1976, California — Member California Workers' Compensation Defense Attorney's Association — Certified Workers' Compensation Specialist — E-mail: jmc@4pbw.com

Howard R. Daniels-Stock — 1954 — Adelphi University, B.A., 1976; Gonzaga University School of Law, J.D., 1979 — Admitted to Bar, 1980, California — Member California Workers' Compensation Defense Attorney's Association — E-mail: hrds@4pbw.com

Raymond F. Correio — 1946 — Chapman College, B.A. (Departmental Honors), 1971; University of the Pacific, McGeorge School of Law, J.D., 1978 — Moot Court Honors Board; Moot Court Honors, Top Oral Argument and Brief — Admitted to Bar, 1985, California — Member California Workers' Compensation Defense Attorney's Association — E-mail: rfc@4pbw.com

Brian A. Penney — 1971 — California State University, San Bernardino, B.S., 1993; University of Houston Law Center, J.D., 1999 — Admitted to Bar, 2000, California; U.S. District Court, Central District of California — Member California Workers' Compensation Defense Attorneys' Association — E-mail: bap@4pbw.com

Christine L. Renten — 1972 — University of Southern California, B.A./B.A., 1994; Southwestern University School of Law, J.D., 1999 — Admitted to Bar, 2000, California; U.S. District Court, Central District of California — Member American and Los Angeles County Bar Associations; California Workers' Compensation Defense Attorneys' Association — E-mail: clr@4pbw.com

M. Christina Ramirez — 1949 — California State University, Long Beach, B.A., 1972; University of Southern California School of Education, M.S.Ed., 1974; University of California at Los Angeles School of the Law, J.D., 1983 — Admitted to Bar, 1985, California; 1986, U.S. District Court, Central, Eastern, Northern and Southern Districts of California; 2011, U.S. Supreme Court — Member Hispanic National Bar Association; California Workers' Compensation Defense Attorneys' Association — E-mail: mcr@4pbw.com

Anahid N. Silah — 1969 — University of California, Los Angeles, B.A. (cum laude), 1993; Loyola Law School Los Angeles, J.D., 1996 — Admitted to Bar, 1996, California — Member California Workers' Compensation Defense Attorneys' Association — E-mail: ans@4pbw.com

Gary P. Andre — 1950 — Michigan State University, B.S., 1972; University of San Fernando Valley, J.D., 1980 — Admitted to Bar, 1983, California — Member Los Angeles County Bar Association; California Workers' Compensation Defense Attorneys' Association — E-mail: gpa@4pbw.com

Nicole G. Minkow — 1972 — University of California, Riverside, B.A., 1994; Loyola Law School, J.D., 1997 — Admitted to Bar, 1997, California; U.S. District Court, Central and Southern Districts of California — E-mail: ngm@4pbw.com

Olivia M. Gordon — 1975 — University of Southern California, B.A., 1998; Southwestern University School of Law, J.D., 2001 — Admitted to Bar, 2003, California — Member California Workers' Compensation Defense Attorneys' Association — E-mail: omg@4pbw.com

Sarah J. Jaffe — 1977 — Baylor University, B.B.A., 2000; Thomas Jefferson School of Law, J.D., 2006 — Admitted to Bar, 2007, California — E-mail: sjj@4pbw.com

H. David Hwang — 1969 — University of Pennsylvania, B.A., 1991; University of California, Hastings College of the Law, J.D., 2001 — Admitted to Bar, 2002, California — Member California Workers' Compensation Defense Attorneys' Association — E-mail: hdh@4pbw.com

Michelle Sauntry — 1955 — University of California, Santa Barbara, B.A., 1987; Loyola Law School, J.D. — Admitted to Bar, 2002, California; U.S. District Court, Central District of California — Member California Workers' Compensation Defense Attorneys' Association — E-mail: ms@4pbw.com

Pearlman, Borska & Wax, LLP, Los Angeles, CA (Continued)

Ani Baghdassarian — 1982 — University of California, Santa Barbara; Ventura College of Law, J.D. — Admitted to Bar, 2012, California — Member California Workers' Compensation Defense Attorneys' Association — E-mail: AB@4pbw.com

Shepard Jacobson — 1966 — Cornell University, B.A.; Loyola Law School, J.D. — Admitted to Bar, 1993, California — Member California Workers' Compensation Defense Attorneys' Association — E-mail: SAJ@4pbw.com

Corinne Spencer — University of California, San Diego, B.A., 2009; University of San Francisco School of Law, J.D., 2012 — Admitted to Bar, 2012, California; U.S. District Court, Central District of California — E-mail: cds@4pbw.com

Justin Borska — University of California, Santa Barbara, B.A., 2008; University of West Los Angeles School of Law, J.D., 2011 — Admitted to Bar, 2012, California; U.S. District Court, Central District of California — E-mail: jib@4pbw.com

Gelareh Fassazadeh — University of California, Los Angeles, B.A. Economics, 2005; University of La Verne College of Law, J.D., 2010 — Admitted to Bar, 2011, California — E-mail: gf@4pbw.com

Ada Rodriguez — University of California, Santa Barbara, B.A., 1995; American College of Law, J.D., 2001 — Admitted to Bar, 2003, California — Tel: amr@4pbw.com

David Alpern — The Evergreen State College, B.A., 1994; University of California, Hastings College of the Law, J.D., 2001 — Admitted to Bar, 2001, California; 2002, U.S. District Court, Central District of California; U.S. Court of Appeals for the Federal and Ninth Circuits — E-mail: dba@4pbw.com

Julie Feng — 1977 — University of California, Santa Barbara, B.A. (Phi Beta Kappa, cum laude), 1999; Loyola Law School, J.D., 2002 — Admitted to Bar, 2003, California — E-mail: jf@4pbw.com

Maureen Blair — California State University, Northridge, B.A., 2000; Southwestern Law School, J.D., 2004 — Admitted to Bar, 2005, California — E-mail: mtb@4pbw.com

Richard Park — 1973 — University of California, Berkeley, B.A., 1997; Southwestern Law School, J.D., 2008 — Admitted to Bar, 2009, California; U.S. District Court, Central District of California — E-mail: rjp@4pbw.com

Roshanack Yaghobi — 1980 — University of California, Irvine, B.A., 2002; Chapman University School of Law, J.D., 2005 — Admitted to Bar, 2008, California — E-mail: ry@4pbw.com

Poole & Shaffery, LLP

400 South Hope Street
Suite 1100
Los Angeles, California 90071
Telephone: 213-439-5390
Fax: 213-439-0183
E-Mail: info@pooleshaffery.com
www.pooleshaffery.com

(Santa Clarita, CA Office: 25350 Magic Mountain Parkway, Second Floor, 91355)
 (Tel: 661-290-2991)
 (Fax: 661-290-3338)
(Villa Park, CA Office: 1421 North Wanda Road, Suite 180, 92867)
 (Tel: 714-974-8941)
 (Fax: 714-974-8972)
(San Francisco, CA Office: 1 Sansome Street, Suite 3500, 94104)
 (Tel: 415-852-5440)
 (Toll Free: 888-595-5963)
(Walnut Creek, CA Office: 500 Ygnacio Valley Road, Suite 325, 94596)
 (Tel: 925-627-3200)
 (Toll Free: 888-595-5963)

Tort Litigation, Employment Litigation, Business Litigation, Toxic Torts, Construction Defect, Product Liability, Environmental Law, Commercial General Liability

Firm Profile: Comprised of 20 attorneys with extensive trial experience, Poole & Shaffery, LLP specializes in effective and efficient litigation case management including, where appropriate, steering cases to early resolution in order to eliminate potential risk and to minimize attorneys' fees. In addition to its successful early settlement of cases when warranted, the firm is proud of its jury trial victories in federal and California state courts. The firm has also obtained significant victories through complex law and motion practice, which includes obtaining hundreds of dismissals of the firm's clients in exchange for a waiver of costs. The firm's established reputation for trial success has led numerous clients to retain the firm to try cases on short notice, or to settle cases with difficult or complex liability issues.

Insurance Clients

AIG	The Hartford
Liberty Mutual Group	Travelers

Firm Members

David S. Poole — 1955 — University of California, Los Angeles, A.B. (cum laude), 1977; University of Southern California School of Law, J.D., 1980 — Phi Eta Sigma; Pi Gamma Mu — Admitted to Bar, 1980, California; 1985, U.S. Court of Federal Claims; 1988, U.S. Court of Appeals, Ninth Circuit; U.S. Supreme Court — Member State Bar of California — Deputy Attorney General, State of California Department of Justice, 1980-1984; Judge Pro Tem, Los Angeles Superior Court

John H. Shaffery — 1959 — Florida Institute of Technology, School of Aeronautics, B.S., 1982; Southwestern University School of Law, J.D., 1991 — Admitted to Bar, 1992, California; U.S. District Court, Central, Eastern, Northern and Southern Districts of California; U.S. Supreme Court — Member State Bar of California

J. Kevin Moore — 1961 — University of Virginia, B.A., 1983; Wake Forest University School of Law, J.D., 1986 — Admitted to Bar, 1991, California; 1996, Virginia (Inactive); U.S. District Court, Eastern District of Virginia; U.S. District Court, Eastern and Northern Districts of California; U.S. Court of Appeal for the Federal Circuit; U.S. Court of Appeals, Fourth and Ninth Circuits; U.S. Claims Court — Member Association of Defense Counsel of Northern California and Nevada

Ropers, Majeski, Kohn & Bentley
A Professional Corporation

515 South Flower Street, Suite 1100
Los Angeles, California 90071
 Telephone: 213-312-2000
 Fax: 213-312-2001
 www.rmkb.com

(Redwood City, CA Office*: 1001 Marshall Street, Suite 500, 94063)
 (Tel: 650-364-8200)
 (Fax: 650-780-1701)
(San Francisco, CA Office*: 150 Spear Street, Suite 850, 94105)
 (Tel: 415-543-4800)
 (Fax: 415-972-6301)
(San Jose, CA Office*: 50 West San Fernando Street, Suite 1400, 95113)
 (Tel: 408-287-6262)
 (Fax: 408-918-4501)
(New York, NY Office*: 750 Third Avenue, 25th Floor, 10017)
 (Tel: 212-668-5927)
 (Fax: 212-668-5929)
(Boston, MA Office*: Ten Post Office Square, 8th Floor South, 02109)
 (Tel: 617-850-9087)
 (Fax: 617-850-9088)

Established: 1950

Antitrust, Appellate Practice, Business Litigation, Commercial Litigation, Civil Rights, Class Actions, Complex Litigation, Construction Law, Corporate Law, Elder Abuse, Employment Law, Entertainment Law, Environmental Law, ERISA, Estate Planning, Governmental Entity Defense, Health Care, Intellectual Property, International Law, Mergers and Acquisitions, Personal Injury, Premises Liability, Product Liability, Professional Liability, Real Estate, Toxic Torts, Asset Protection, Banking/Consumer Credit, Catastrophic Injury, Cost Control, Elder Rights, Fee Disputes, Insurance Services, IT and Business Process Outsourcing, Litigation Management, Non-Profit, Proposition 65, Special Education Law, Taxation, Wealth Management

CALIFORNIA   LOS ANGELES

Ropers, Majeski, Kohn & Bentley, A Professional Corporation, Los Angeles, CA (Continued)

Partners

Stephen J. Erigero — 1959 — Loyola Marymount University, B.A., 1982; University of California, Hastings College of the Law, J.D. (summa cum laude), 1985 — Phi Delta Phi — Admitted to Bar, 1985, California; 2010, Nevada; 1985, U.S. District Court, Central, Eastern, Northern and Southern Districts of California — Member State Bar of California; Risk Insurance Management Society; Defense Research Institute; Association of Southern California Defense Counsel — Practice Areas: Business Litigation; Commercial Litigation; Construction Litigation; Class Actions; Environmental Litigation; Insurance Litigation

Gerald G. Knapton — 1940 — Brown University; University of California, Berkeley, A.B. (with highest honors), 1973; University of California, Los Angeles School of Law, J.D., 1976 — Phi Beta Kappa — Admitted to Bar, 1977, California; 1978, U.S. District Court, Central, Eastern, Northern and Southern Districts of California; 1979, U.S. Court of Appeals, Ninth Circuit; 1998, U.S. Court of Appeals, Third Circuit — Member State Bar of California — Practice Areas: Litigation

Kim Karelis — 1953 — Winona State University, B.S., 1976; Southwestern University School of Law, J.D. (cum laude), 1993 — American Jurisprudence Award — Southwestern University Law Review — Admitted to Bar, 1994, California; 1995, U.S. District Court, Central and Northern Districts of California; U.S. Court of Appeals, Ninth Circuit — Member State Bar of California — Practice Areas: Litigation; Insurance Litigation

Arnold E. Sklar — 1946 — University of California, Los Angeles, B.A., 1968; University of Southern California School of Law, J.D., 1971 — Admitted to Bar, 1972, California — Member State Bar of California — Practice Areas: Business Litigation; Commercial Litigation; Corporate Law; Intellectual Property

Michael T. Ohira — 1957 — California State University, Long Beach, B.S., 1981; Loyola Law School, J.D., 1986 — Admitted to Bar, 1986, California; U.S. District Court, Central, Northern and Southern Districts of California — Member State Bar of California; Japanese American Bar Association — Practice Areas: Insurance Law; Coverage Issues; Bad Faith; Product Liability

Lawrence Borys — 1950 — University of California, Los Angeles, B.A., 1971; University of California, Los Angeles School of Law, J.D., 1974 — Admitted to Bar, 1974, California; U.S. District Court, Central and Southern Districts of California; U.S. Court of Appeals, Ninth Circuit — Member Association of Southern California Defense Counsel; Defense Research Institute; Federation of Defense and Corporate Counsel — Practice Areas: Construction Litigation; Premises Liability; Product Liability; Insurance Law; Bad Faith

Ivan L. Tjoe — 1974 — University of California, Berkeley, B.A. (with honors), 1996; University of California, Hastings College of the Law, J.D., 1999 — Admitted to Bar, 1999, California; U.S. District Court, Central, Eastern, Northern and Southern Districts of California; U.S. Court of Appeals for the Federal and Ninth Circuits — Practice Areas: Business Litigation; Commercial Litigation; Entertainment Law; International Law; Intellectual Property; Corporate Governance; Product Liability

Tim M. Agajanian — 1961 — University of Southern California, B.S., 1983; Southwestern Law School, J.D., 1986 — Admitted to Bar, 1987, California — Member Association of Defense Trial Attorneys — Practice Areas: Business Litigation; Commercial Litigation; Intellectual Property; Toxic Torts; Environmental Litigation; Insurance Litigation; Corporate Law

Associates

Pascale Gagnon
Alan J. Hart
Gary S. Spitzer
Stephen M. Shaner
E. Lacey Rice
Jamie M. Kurtz
Jeff W. Poole

Of Counsel

Tahereh S. Mahmoudian — 1958 — University of California, Irvine, B.S., 1985; University of California, Davis, M.B.A., 2001; University of California, Davis School of Law, J.D., 2001 — Admitted to Bar, 2001, California; U.S. District Court, Central District of California — Languages: Farsi, Turkish — Practice Areas: Business Litigation; Commercial Litigation; Environmental Litigation; Insurance Litigation; Appellate Practice

Kathleen Duggan — 1951 — California State University, San Jose, B.S., 1973; P.H.N., 1973; Golden Gate University School of Law, J.D., 1982 — Admitted to Bar, 1982, California; U.S. District Court, Northern District of California — Member State Bar of California; San Mateo County Bar Association; Bar Association of San Francisco — Practice Areas: Dental Malpractice; Medical Malpractice; Health Care; Product Liability

(See listing under Redwood City, CA for additional information)

Law Offices of Virgil L. Roth, PC

625 Fair Oaks Avenue, Suite 255
South Pasadena, California 91030
Telephone: 626-441-1165
Fax: 626-441-1166
Add'l Phone: 626-441-1178
E-Mail: vroth@vlrlaw.com
www.vlrlaw.com

Established: 1996

Personal Injury, Property Damage, Class Actions, Intellectual Property, Professional Liability, Construction Defect, Insurance Defense, Premises Liability, Mass Tort, Complex Litigation, Mediation, Toxic Torts, Product Liability, Commercial Litigation

Firm Profile: The Law Offices of Virgil L. Roth is a full-service civil litigation and business transaction law firm based in Los Angeles, California and operating statewide. Specializing in insurance defense, the firm also represents clients in a wide variety of complex litigation and class action matters.

Insurance Clients

Essex Insurance Company
Golden Bear Insurance Company
Markel Insurance Company
State Farm General Insurance Company
Global Aerospace, Inc.
Hudson Insurance Group
Nationwide Mutual Insurance Company
Wausau Insurance Companies

Third Party Administrators

Engle Martin Claims Administrative Services (EMCAS, Inc.)

Principal

Virgil L. Roth — 1945 — Goshen College, B.A., 1967; University of Notre Dame Law School, J.D. (cum laude), 1976 — Admitted to Bar, 1976, California — Member American Bar Association; Defense Research Institute; Association of Southern California Defense Counsel

Attorneys

Anthony DiMonte — 1971 — University of Illinois, B.A., 1993; Chicago-Kent College of Law, J.D., 1996 — Admitted to Bar, 1996, Illinois; 1998, California

Charles D. Ferrari — 1958 — California State University, Northridge, B.A., 1983; University of California Davis School of Law, J.D., 1987 — Admitted to Bar, 1987, California; 1992, Oregon

Gregory Kim — 1970 — University of California, Los Angeles, B.A., 1992; Loyola University Law School, J.D., 1996 — Admitted to Bar, 1996, California

Vanessa C. Deniston — 1985 — University of Massachusetts Amherst, B.A., 2007; Suffolk University Law School, J.D., 2010 — Admitted to Bar, 2012, California

Schaffer, Lax, McNaughton & Chen
A Professional Corporation

515 South Figueroa Street, Suite 1400
Los Angeles, California 90071
Telephone: 213-337-1000
Fax: 213-337-1010
www.slmclaw.com

(Newport Beach, CA Office: 4590 MacArthur Boulevard, Suite 290, 92660)
(Tel: 949-724-0300)
(Fax: 949-724-8504)

LOS ANGELES / CALIFORNIA

Schaffer, Lax, McNaughton & Chen, A Professional Corporation, Los Angeles, CA (Continued)

Established: 1987

Litigation, Appellate Practice, State and Federal Courts, Administrative Law, Regulatory and Compliance, Insurance Coverage, Product Liability, Bad Faith, Business Law, Construction Law, Toxic Torts, Environmental Law, Professional Liability, Transportation, Medical Liability, Employment Law, Governmental Compliance, Medical Products, Appearances before Administrative and Regulatory Agencies

Insurance Clients

American Home Assurance Company
Anchor Claims Services, Inc.
Crawford & Company
Fireman's Fund Insurance Company
General Star Management Company
Lexington Insurance Company
National Union Fire Insurance Company
New Hampshire Insurance Company
St. Paul Fire and Marine Insurance Company
Transamerica Insurance Company
Zurich American Insurance Group
American International Group, Inc.
American International Underwriters
Employers Insurance Company of Wausau
GAB Robins North America, Inc.
Granite State Insurance Company
Lancer Insurance Company
Liberty Mutual Fire Insurance Company
Nationwide Indemnity Company
Nobel Insurance Company
OneBeacon Insurance
Sedgwick Claims Management Services, Inc.
VeriClaim, Inc.

Non-Insurance Clients

American Medical Systems, Inc.
Mohawk Industries, Inc.
Professional Service Industries, Inc.
Hyatt Corporation
NAS Group
Sullivan and Curtis

Managing Partner

Clifford L. Schaffer — University of Southern California, B.S.M.E., 1962; University of California, Berkeley Boalt Hall School of Law, LL.B., 1966 — Admitted to Bar, 1967, California; 1967, U.S. District Court, Central District of California; U.S. Court of Appeals, Ninth Circuit — Member State Bar of California; Los Angeles County Bar Association; Director, Association of Southern California Defense Counsel, 1992-1993; Defense Research Institute — California Deputy Attorney General, 1967-1969 — E-mail: cliff@slmclaw.com

Partners/Shareholders

Stephen A. Lax — State University of New York at Stony Brook, B.A., 1972; M.S.W., 1976; Loyola Law School Los Angeles, J.D. (cum laude), 1979 — Loyola Law Review, 1977-1978 — Admitted to Bar, 1979, California; 1980, U.S. District Court, Central District of California; 1982, U.S. Court of Appeals, Ninth Circuit — Member State Bar of California; Los Angeles County Bar Association; Association of Southern California Defense Counsel; Defense Research Institute — E-mail: laxs@slmclaw.com

Kevin J. McNaughton — Baruch College, City University of New York, B.A., 1975; Brooklyn Law School, J.D., 1978 — Admitted to Bar, 1979, New York; 1980, California; 1980, U.S. Court of Appeals, Second Circuit; U.S. District Court, Eastern and Southern Districts of New York; 1983, U.S. Court of Appeals, Ninth Circuit; U.S. District Court, Central and Northern Districts of California; 1985, U.S. District Court, Southern District of California; 1986, U.S. District Court, Eastern District of California — Member Federal, American, New York State and Los Angeles County Bar Associations; State Bar of California; Association of Southern California Defense Counsel — E-mail: kevin@slmclaw.com

Alexander J. Chen — University of California, San Diego, B.A. (cum laude), 1978; University of California, Hastings College of the Law, J.D., 1981 — Admitted to Bar, 1982, California; 1982, U.S. District Court, Central District of California; U.S. Court of Appeals, Ninth Circuit — Member American and Los Angeles County Bar Associations; State Bar of California; Association of Southern California Defense Counsel — E-mail: chena@slmclaw.com

Jill A. Franklin — Occidental College, B.A., 1980; Loyola Law School Los Angeles, J.D., 1986 — Admitted to Bar, 1987, California; 1987, U.S. District Court, Central District of California; 1995, U.S. District Court, District of Arizona — Member State Bar of California; Los Angeles County Bar Association; Association of Southern California Defense Counsel — E-mail: franklinj@slmclaw.com

John H. Horwitz — University of California, Irvine, B.A., 1972; University of California, Los Angeles, M.A., 1978; Loyola Law School Los Angeles, J.D., 1988 — Admitted to Bar, 1988, California; 1990, U.S. District Court, Central District of California; 1993, U.S. District Court, Southern District of California; 1994, U.S. Court of Appeals, Ninth Circuit — Member American, Los Angeles County and Wilshire (Board Member) Bar Associations; State Bar of California; Los Angeles Trial Lawyers Association; Association of Southern California Defense Counsel — E-mail: horwitzj@slmclaw.com

Kara A. Pape — Loyola Marymount University, B.A., 1984; Loyola Law School, J.D., 1987 — Admitted to Bar, 1987, California — Member State Bar of California; Los Angeles County Bar Association; Association of Southern California Defense Counsel — E-mail: papek@slmclaw.com

David M. Frishman — Illinois State University, B.S., 1984; Southwestern University School of Law, J.D., 1987 — Admitted to Bar, 1987, California; 1987, U.S. District Court, Central District of California; U.S. Court of Appeals, Ninth Circuit — Member American and Los Angeles County Bar Associations; State Bar of California; Association of Southern California Defense Counsel — E-mail: frishmand@slmclaw.com

Russell A. Franklin — Occidental College, B.S., 1975; Loyola Law School Los Angeles, J.D., 1996 — Admitted to Bar, 1997, California; 1997, U.S. District Court, Central District of California — Member State Bar of California; Los Angeles County Bar Association; Association of Southern California Defense Counsel — E-mail: franklinr@slmclaw.com

David R. Highman — California State University, Fullerton, B.A., 1970; Southwestern University School of Law, J.D., 1977 — Admitted to Bar, 1978, California; U.S. Court of Appeals, Ninth Circuit; U.S. Supreme Court — Member State Bar of California; Los Angeles and Orange County Bar Associations; Association of Southern California Defense Counsel; Defense Research Institute — E-mail: highmand@slmclaw.com

Jane E. Carey — University of California, Santa Barbara, B.S., 1982; Santa Clara University School of Law, J.D., 1988 — Admitted to Bar, 1988, California; U.S. District Court, Eastern, Northern and Southern Districts of California; U.S. Court of Appeals, Ninth Circuit — Member State Bar of California; Orange County and Los Angeles County Bar Associations; Association of Southern California Defense Counsel — E-mail: careyj@slmclaw.com

Associates

Brian Buron — University of Washington, B.S.B.A., 1994; Seattle University School of Law, J.D., 1997 — Admitted to Bar, 1997, Washington; 2001, California; 2003, U.S. District Court, Western District of Washington — Member Washington State and Los Angeles County Bar Associations; State Bar of California; Association of Southern California Defense Counsel — Practice Areas: Insurance Defense — E-mail: buronb@slmclaw.com

Yaron Dunkel — University of California, Los Angeles, B.A., 1997; Loyola Law School, J.D. (with highest honors), 2001 — Golden Key — Admitted to Bar, 2001, California; U.S. District Court, Central District of California — Member State Bar of California; Los Angeles County Bar Association; Association of Southern California Defense Counsel — Author: "Medical Privacy Rights in Anonymous Data," 23 Loy. LA Intl. & Corp. L. Rev. 41 — E-mail: dunkely@slmclaw.com

Katrina J. Valencia — Villa Julie College, B.A., 1998; Whittier Law School, J.D., 2002 — Admitted to Bar, 2004, California — Member State Bar of California; Los Angeles County Bar Association; Association of Southern California Defense Counsel — E-mail: valenciak@slmclaw.com

Cynthia A. Kitchen — University of California, Los Angeles, B.A., 1996; Pepperdine University School of Law, J.D., 1999 — Admitted to Bar, 1999, California — Member State Bar of California; Los Angeles County Bar Association; Association of Southern California Defense Counsel — E-mail: kitchenc@slmclaw.com

Ankita A. Patel — University of California, Berkeley, B.A./B.S., 2004; Santa Clara University School of Law, J.D., 2007 — Admitted to Bar, 2007, California — Member American, Los Angeles County and Orange County Bar Associations; South Asian Bar Association; Association of Southern California Defense Counsel — Languages: Gujarati, Hindi — E-mail: patela@slmclaw.com

Farrell C. Covell — University of California, Berkeley, B.A., 1998; Loyola Law School, J.D., 2003 — Admitted to Bar, 2003, California; 2009, Washington; 2003, U.S. District Court, Central District of California — Member

CALIFORNIA — LOS ANGELES

Schaffer, Lax, McNaughton & Chen, A Professional Corporation, Los Angeles, CA (Continued)

State Bar of California; Washington State, Los Angeles County and Beverly Hills Bar Associations — E-mail: covellc@slmclaw.com

Of Counsel

Richard P. Dieffenbach — Albright College, B.A.E. (cum laude), 1978; Washington University School of Law, J.D. (cum laude), 1981 — Admitted to Bar, 1982, California — Member State Bar of California; Los Angeles County Bar Association; Association of Southern California Defense Counsel — E-mail: richardd@slmclaw.com

Sheppard, Mullin, Richter & Hampton LLP

333 South Hope Street, Forty-Third Floor
Los Angeles, California 90071
Telephone: 213-620-1780
Fax: 213-620-1398
www.sheppardmullin.com

(Century City, CA Office: 1901 Avenue of the Stars, Suite 1600, 90067)
(Tel: 310-228-3700)
(San Francisco, CA Office*: Four Embarcadero Center, 17th Floor, 94111)
(Tel: 415-434-9100)
(Palo Alto, CA Office: 390 Lytton Avenue, 94301)
(Tel: 650-815-2600)
(Costa Mesa, CA Office*: 650 Town Center Drive, Fourth Floor, 92626)
(Tel: 714-513-5100)
(San Diego, CA Office: 12275 El Camino Real, Suite 200, 92130)
(Tel: 858-720-8900)
(San Diego, CA Office*: 501 West Broadway, 19th Floor, 92101)
(Tel: 619-338-6500)
(Chicago, IL Office: Three First National Plaza, 70 West Madison Street, 48th Floor, 60602)
(Tel: 312-499-6300)
(New York, NY Office: 30 Rockefeller Plaza, 10112)
(Tel: 212-653-8700)
(Washington, DC Office: 2099 Pennsylvania Avenue, N.W., Suite 100, 20006)
(Tel: 202-747-1900)
(London, Sheppard Mullin (UK) LLP: One London Wall, London, United Kingdom, EC2Y 5EB)
(Tel: 44.20.7199.5996)
(Brussels, Belgium Office: Place du Champ de Mars 2, Marsveldplein, 1050)
(Tel: 32.2.289.29.89)
(Beijing, China-PRC Office: 15F, China World Office 1, No. 1 Jian Guo Man Wai Avenue, Chaoyang District, 100004)
(Tel: 86.10.5706.7500)
(Shanghai, China-PRC: 26th Floor, Wheelock Square, 1717 Nanjing Road West, Jing An District, Shanghai, China-PRC, 200040)
(Tel: (86 21) 2321 6000)
(Seoul, Korea-South Office: West Tower, 23rd Floor, Mirae Asset Center 1 Building, 26 Euljiro 5-gil, Jung-ug, 100-210)
(Tel: 02-6030-3000)

Established: 1927

Antitrust, Bad Faith, Class Actions, Complex Litigation, Insurance Litigation, Trial and Appellate Practice

Firm Profile: Sheppard, Mullin, Richter & Hampton LLP represents clients in a wide variety of insurance-related litigation matters. The firm represents insurance companies, producers and third party administrators in all types of litigation, ranging from class actions and complex multi-party litigation to single insured disputes, and assists insurer clients in administrative and regulatory proceedings.

Insurance Clients

Certain Underwriters at Lloyd's, London
CNA Insurance Companies
Fidelity National Title Group

Sheppard, Mullin, Richter & Hampton LLP, Los Angeles, CA (Continued)

Golden Eagle Insurance Corporation
Safeco Insurance
State Compensation Insurance Fund of California
HealthMarkets, Inc.
Liberty Mutual Insurance Company
Sierra Health Services, Inc.
State Farm Insurance Companies
Zurich American Insurance Company

Partners

Andre J. Cronthall — University of Southern California, B.S., 1981; University of Southern California School of Law, J.D., 1984 — Director, Hale Moot Court Honor's Program; Co-Founder and Co-Chairman, Federalist Society — Admitted to Bar, 1984, California; U.S. District Court, Central, Eastern, Northern and Southern Districts of California; U.S. Court of Appeals, Ninth Circuit — Member Association of Business Trial Lawyers (Board of Governors); American Board of Trial Advocates — Tel: 213-617-5474 — E-mail: acronthall@sheppardmullin.com

Frank Falzetta — Dartmouth College, B.A., 1983; University of Michigan Law School, J.D., 1986 — Admitted to Bar, 1986, California; U.S. District Court, Central and Eastern Districts of California; U.S. District Court, District of Arizona; U.S. Court of Appeals, Ninth Circuit — Tel: 213-617-4194 — E-mail: ffalzetta@sheppardmullin.com

Fred R. Puglisi — University of Minnesota Duluth, B.S. (cum laude), 1982; University of Minnesota, J.D. (Order of the Coif), 1985 — Admitted to Bar, 1985, California; U.S. District Court, Central and Northern Districts of California; U.S. Court of Appeals, Ninth Circuit — Member American (Litigation Section) and Los Angeles County Bar Associations; State Bar of California (Litigation Section); Constitutional Rights Foundation (Board Member); Association of Business Trial Lawyers (Former Board Member) — Tel: 310-228-3733 — E-mail: fpuglisi@sheppardmullin.com

Tharpe & Howell, LLP

15250 Ventura Boulevard, Ninth Floor
Sherman Oaks, California 91403
Telephone: 818-205-9955
Fax: 818-205-9944
E-Mail: dmurray@tharpe-howell.com
www.tharpe-howell.com

Established: 1977

Bad Faith, Insurance Defense, Employment Law, Transportation, Environmental, Hospitality Law

Firm Profile: For more than 34 years, hospitality groups, small businesses, major corporations, individuals and insurance companies have depended on Tharpe & Howell to deliver pragmatic, innovative, cost-effective civil litigation and transactional solutions. Offices in four western states.

Insurance Clients

Farmers Insurance Exchange
Travelers Insurance Group

Partners

Todd R. Howell — University of California, Santa Barbara, B.A., 1970; California Western School of Law, J.D., 1973 — Admitted to Bar, 1973, California

Stephanie Forman — University of Southern California, B.S., 1994; University of Southern California School of Law, J.D., 1997 — Admitted to Bar, 1998, California

Robert M. Freedman — Golden West University, B.S., 1978; Golden West University School of Law, J.D., 1980 — Admitted to Bar, 1989, California

Timothy D. Lake — University of Southern California, B.A., 1971; Southwestern University School of Law, J.D., 1974 — Admitted to Bar, 1974, California

Christopher S. Maile — University of California, Los Angeles, B.A., 1980; Loyola Marymount University, Loyola Law School, J.D., 1984 — Admitted to Bar, 1985, California

Charles D. May — Loyola Marymount University, B.A., 1977; Southwestern University School of Law, J.D., 1984 — Admitted to Bar, 1985, Idaho; 1987, California

Robert B. Salley — University of California, Santa Barbara, B.A., 1982; Whittier Law School, J.D., 1987 — Admitted to Bar, 1987, California

LOS ANGELES   CALIFORNIA

Tharpe & Howell, LLP, Los Angeles, CA   (Continued)

Paul V. Wayne — University of California, San Diego, B.A., 1977; University of San Diego School of Law, J.D., 1981 — Admitted to Bar, 1981, California

Towle Denison Smith & Maniscalco LLP

10866 Wilshire Boulevard, Suite 600
Los Angeles, California 90024
   Telephone: 310-446-5445
   Fax: 310-446-5447
   E-Mail: mdenison@tdsmlaw.com
   www.tdsmlaw.com

Civil Litigation, Commercial Litigation, Employment Law, Insurance Litigation, Professional Liability, Securities

Firm Profile: Towle Denison Smith & Maniscalco LLP currently has six lawyers. The firm's primary objective is to maintain the highest standards of professionalism while providing clients with the personal attention that often is not possible with large firms.

Insurance Clients

AXIS Insurance Company
NCMIC Group - Professional Solutions Insurance Company

Clyde & Co US LLP

Non-Insurance Clients

Adventist Health System/West
HUB International Limited

Brown & Brown, Inc.
MeadWestvaco Corporation

Firm Members

Edmund J. Towle, III — 1948 — Georgetown University, A.B., 1970; Columbia University of Law, J.D., 1973 — Admitted to Bar, 1974, California; New York; U.S. District Court, Central District of California; 1980, U.S. Court of Appeals, Ninth Circuit; 1990, U.S. District Court, District of Arizona — Member State Bar of California; Los Angeles County Bar Association; American Arbitration Association (Panel of Arbitrators) — E-mail: etowle@tdsmlaw.com

Michael C. Denison — 1947 — University of California, Los Angeles, A.B., 1969; Loyola Law School, J.D., 1974 — Admitted to Bar, 1974, California; U.S. District Court, Central and Eastern Districts of California; 1976, U.S. Court of Appeals, Ninth Circuit; 2008, U.S. Supreme Court — Member State Bar of California; Los Angeles County Bar Association — E-mail: mdenison@tdsmlaw.com

Charles G. Smith — 1960 — Stanford University, A.B., 1981; Loyola Law School, J.D., 1984 — Admitted to Bar, 1984, California; 1985, U.S. District Court, Central, Eastern, Northern and Southern Districts of California; U.S. Court of Appeals, Ninth Circuit; 1989, U.S. Supreme Court; 1997, U.S. Court of Appeals for the Federal Circuit — Member State Bar of California; Los Angeles County Bar Association — E-mail: csmith@tdsmlaw.com

James P. Maniscalco — 1969 — University of California, Berkeley, B.A., 1991; University of Southern California School of Law, J.D., 1995 — Admitted to Bar, 1995, California; 2009, Nevada; 1995, U.S. District Court, Central District of California; 1998, U.S. District Court, Northern District of California; 2003, U.S. District Court, Southern District of California — Member State Bar of California; State Bar of Nevada; Los Angeles County Bar Association — E-mail: jmaniscalco@tdsmlaw.com

Traub Lieberman Straus & Shrewsberry LLP

626 Wilshire Boulevard, Suite 800
Los Angeles, California 90017
   Telephone: 213-624-4500

(Hawthorne, NY Office*: Mid-Westchester Executive Park, Seven Skyline Drive, 10532)
   (Tel: 914-347-2600)
   (Fax: 914-347-8898)
   (www.traublieberman.com)
   (E-Mail: swolfe@traublieberman.com)

Traub Lieberman Straus & Shrewsberry LLP, Los Angeles, CA   (Continued)

(Red Bank, NJ Office*: 322 Highway 35, 07701)
   (Tel: 732-985-1000)
   (Fax: 732-985-2000)
   (www.traublieberman.com)
(St. Petersburg, FL Office*: 360 Central Avenue, 33701)
   (Tel: 727-898-8100)
   (Fax: 727-895-4838)
   (www.traublieberman.com)
(Chicago, IL Office*: 303 West Madison, Suite 1200, 60606)
   (Tel: 312-332-3900)
   (Fax: 312-332-3908)
   (www.traublieberman.com)
(London, United Kingdom Office*: Gallery 4, 12 Leadenhall Street, EC3V1LP)
   (Tel: +44 (0) 020 7816 5856)
(New York, NY Office*: 100 Park Avenue, 16th Floor, 10017)
   (Tel: 646-227-1700)
   (www.traublieberman.com)

Established: 2012

Appellate Practice, Bad Faith, Civil Rights, Complex Litigation, Construction Law, Coverage Issues, Environmental Law, Extra-Contractual Litigation, General Liability, Insurance Coverage, Labor and Employment, Medical Malpractice, Premises Liability, Product Liability, Professional Liability, Technology, Toxic Torts, Transportation, Trucking Law

Partners

Robert D. Dennison — University of California, B.A., 1979; University of West Los Angeles School of Law, J.D., 1986 — Admitted to Bar, 1979, California; U.S. District Court, Central, Eastern, Northern and Southern Districts of California — E-mail: rdennison@traublieberman.com

Kevin P. McNamara — University of California, Berkeley, B.A., 1992; Pepperdine University School of Law, J.D. (cum laude), 1995 — Admitted to Bar, 1995, California; U.S. District Court, Central, Eastern, Northern and Southern Districts of California; U.S. District Court, Northern District of New York; U.S. Court of Appeals, Ninth Circuit — E-mail: kmcnamara@traublieberman.com

Mario Mennano — California State University, Northridge, B.A., 1996; The University of Oklahoma College of Law, J.D. (cum laude), 1999 — Admitted to Bar, 1999, California; U.S. District Court, Central District of California — E-mail: mmennano@traublieberman.com

Associates

Justin A. Bubion
Natalie Hernandez

Giuseppe Castaldi
Neal K. Kojima

(See listing under Hawthorne, NY for additional information)

The following firms also service this area.

Borton Petrini, LLP
3020 Old Ranch Parkway, Suite 300
Seal Beach, California 90740
   Telephone: 562-596-2300
   Fax: 562-596-2322

Business Litigation, Civil Litigation, Construction Law, Employment Law, Employment Litigation, Trust and Estate Litigation

SEE COMPLETE LISTING UNDER SEAL BEACH, CALIFORNIA (27 MILES)

CALIFORNIA

Kinkle, Rodiger & Spriggs
Professional Corporation
3333 Fourteenth Street
Riverside, California 92501-3809
  Telephone: 951-683-2410
  Toll Free: 800-235-2039
  Fax: 951-683-7759

Insurance Defense, Self-Insured, General Liability, Product Liability, Automobile, Premises Liability, Public Entities, Construction Law, Professional Liability, Coverage Issues, Bad Faith, Civil Trial Practice, Appellate Practice, Federal Courts

SEE COMPLETE LISTING UNDER RIVERSIDE, CALIFORNIA (56 MILES)

Mollis & Mollis, Inc.
4621 Teller Avenue, Suite 200
Newport Beach, California 92660
  Telephone: 949-222-0735
  Fax: 949-955-0252

Insurance Defense, Civil Trial Practice, Business Law, Construction Law, Corporate Law, Appeals, Labor Law, Environmental Law, Real Estate, Estate Planning, Trusts, Probate, Trust and Estate Litigation, Taxation, Trust Settlement

SEE COMPLETE LISTING UNDER NEWPORT BEACH, CALIFORNIA (43 MILES)

Pyka Lenhardt Schnaider Zell
837 North Ross Street
Santa Ana, California 92701
  Telephone: 714-835-9011
  Fax: 714-667-7806
Mailing Address: P.O. Box 1558, Santa Ana, CA 92702-1558

Automobile, Business Litigation, Catastrophic Injury, Civil Litigation, Civil Rights, Construction Accidents, Construction Defect, Labor and Employment, Municipal Liability, Personal Injury, Police Liability Defense, Premises Liability, Product Liability, Professional Liability, Public Entities, School Law, Trucking, Uninsured and Underinsured Motorist, Wrongful Death, Wrongful Termination, Homeowners Association Litigation, Utility Defense

SEE COMPLETE LISTING UNDER SANTA ANA, CALIFORNIA (33 MILES)

Tropio & Morlan
A Law Corporation
21700 Oxnard Street, Suite 1700
Woodland Hills, California 91367
  Telephone: 818-883-4000
  Fax: 818-883-4242

Insurance Defense, Premises Liability, Product Liability, Automobile, Fraud, Asbestos Litigation, Toxic Substances, Mass Tort, Complex Litigation, Commercial Litigation, Employment Litigation, Environmental Litigation, Environmental Liability, Environmental and Toxic Injury, Environmental Law, Toxic Tort, Environmental Regulatory Compliance, Underground Storage Tank Litigation

SEE COMPLETE LISTING UNDER WOODLAND HILLS, CALIFORNIA (25 MILES)

MADERA † 61,416 Madera Co.
Refer To
Borton Petrini, LLP
2444 Main Street, Suite 150
Fresno, California 93721
  Telephone: 559-268-0117
  Fax: 559-237-7995

Agriculture, Business Litigation, Casualty Insurance Law, Commercial Law, Contracts, Coverage Issues, Insurance Defense, Labor and Employment, Premises Liability, Product Liability, Professional Errors and Omissions, Public Entities, Transportation

SEE COMPLETE LISTING UNDER FRESNO, CALIFORNIA (23 MILES)

MADERA

MARTINEZ † 35,824 Contra Costa Co.
Refer To
Bledsoe, Cathcart, Diestel, Pedersen & Treppa LLP
601 California Street, 16th Floor
San Francisco, California 94108
  Telephone: 415-981-5411
  Fax: 415-981-0352

Civil Trial Practice, State and Federal Courts, Product Liability, Insurance Defense, Insurance Coverage, Personal Injury, Construction Law, Employment Law, Business Law, Environmental Law, Landlord Tenant, Commercial Transportation, Copyright Litigation, Banking and Finance, Lender Liability

SEE COMPLETE LISTING UNDER SAN FRANCISCO, CALIFORNIA (32 MILES)

Refer To
Boornazian, Jensen & Garthe
A Professional Corporation
555 12th Street, 18th Floor
Oakland, California 94607
  Telephone: 510-834-4350
  Fax: 510-839-1897
Mailing Address: P.O. Box 12925, Oakland, CA 94604-2925

Insurance Defense, Trial Practice, Product Liability, Legal Malpractice, Professional Malpractice, Medical Malpractice, Insurance Coverage, Construction Law

SEE COMPLETE LISTING UNDER OAKLAND, CALIFORNIA (24 MILES)

MARYSVILLE † 12,072 Yuba Co.
Refer To
Borton Petrini, LLP
3110 Gold Canal Drive, Suite A
Rancho Cordova, California 95670
  Telephone: 916-858-1212
  Fax: 916-858-1252
Mailing Address: P.O. Box 277790, Sacramento, CA 95827

Construction Defect, Construction Law, Employment Litigation, Personal Injury, Product Liability, Professional Liability

SEE COMPLETE LISTING UNDER SACRAMENTO, CALIFORNIA (54 MILES)

MENDOCINO 894 Mendocino Co.

Roberts Law Firm

45011 Calpella Street
Mendocino, California 95460-2360
  Telephone: 707-937-0503
  Fax: 707-937-2916
  E-Mail: robertslaw@mcn.org
  www.roberts-law-firm.com

Insurance Defense, Civil Litigation, Construction Defect, Premises Liability, Product Liability, Real Estate Errors and Omissions, Professional Negligence, Class Actions, Bad Faith, Automobile and Truck Liability, Agriculture and Wine Litigation, Class Action Defense Litigation

Firm Profile: The Roberts Law Firm was established in 2002 in place of the law firm of Graham & Roberts which existed for 12 years. The Roberts Law Firm offers high quality, experienced and cost effective litigation and trial services in the Redwood Empire counties of Mendocino, Humboldt, Lake and Sonoma.

Insurance Clients

AIG	Allied Insurance Company
California Insurance Group	Coast National Insurance Company
Farmers Insurance Exchange	Grange Insurance Company
Hudson Insurance Company	Mercury Insurance Group
Nationwide Group	Nonprofits' Insurance Alliance of California
Royal & SunAlliance	
Travelers Insurance	Truck Insurance Exchange
21st Century Insurance Group	Unigard Insurance Company

MODESTO • CALIFORNIA

Roberts Law Firm, Mendocino, CA (Continued)

Non-Insurance Clients

Crawford Technical Services
York Claims Service, Inc.
State of California Department of General Services

Managing Attorney

Harvey L. Roberts, Jr. — 1954 — Chaminade University of Honolulu, B.A. (magna cum laude), 1980; University of the Pacific, McGeorge School of Law, J.D., 1984 — Admitted to Bar, 1984, California; 1984, U.S. District Court, Eastern and Northern Districts of California — Member American Board of Trial Advocates

---

The following firms also service this area.

**Kenny, Snowden & Norine
A Law Corporation**
2701 Park Marina Drive
Redding, California 96001
   Telephone: 530-225-8990
   Fax: 530-225-8944
   Toll Free: 800-655-6677

Mailing Address: Box 994608, Redding, CA 96099-4608

Insurance Defense, Medical Malpractice, Product Liability, Defense Litigation, Civil Trial Practice, Casualty, Professional Errors and Omissions, Employment Law, Public Entities, Real Estate, Land Use, Water Law, Equine Law

SEE COMPLETE LISTING UNDER REDDING, CALIFORNIA (236 MILES)

MERCED † 78,958 Merced Co.

Refer To

Borton Petrini, LLP
2444 Main Street, Suite 150
Fresno, California 93721
   Telephone: 559-268-0117
   Fax: 559-237-7995

Agriculture, Business Litigation, Casualty Insurance Law, Commercial Law, Contracts, Coverage Issues, Insurance Defense, Labor and Employment, Premises Liability, Product Liability, Professional Errors and Omissions, Public Entities, Transportation

SEE COMPLETE LISTING UNDER FRESNO, CALIFORNIA (55 MILES)

Refer To

Borton Petrini, LLP
201 Needham Street
Modesto, California 95354
   Telephone: 209-576-1701
   Fax: 209-527-9753

Mailing Address: P.O. Box 3384, Modesto, CA 95353

Agriculture, Appellate Practice, Bankruptcy, Business Law, Business Litigation, Casualty Insurance Law, Contracts, Corporate Law, Eminent Domain, Estate Planning, Family Law, Insurance Defense, Labor and Employment, Premises Liability, Probate, Product Liability, Professional Errors and Omissions, Public Entities, Real Estate, Transportation, Unlawful Detainer Representing Landlords

SEE COMPLETE LISTING UNDER MODESTO, CALIFORNIA (40 MILES)

MODESTO † 201,165 Stanislaus Co.

Borton Petrini, LLP
201 Needham Street
Modesto, California 95354
   Telephone: 209-576-1701
   Fax: 209-527-9753
   E-Mail: bpmod@bortonpetrini.com
   www.bortonpetrini.com

Established: 1899

Borton Petrini, LLP, Modesto, CA (Continued)

Agriculture, Appellate Practice, Bankruptcy, Business Law, Business Litigation, Casualty Insurance Law, Contracts, Corporate Law, Eminent Domain, Estate Planning, Family Law, Insurance Defense, Labor and Employment, Premises Liability, Probate, Product Liability, Professional Errors and Omissions, Public Entities, Real Estate, Transportation, Unlawful Detainer Representing Landlords

Firm Profile: Since 1899, Borton Petrini, LLP, has offered high quality legal services in all of the practice areas described above through its California network of 10 regional offices. The mission of Borton Petrini, LLP is to treat every file as though we were representing ourselves and paying the bill for that representation.

Managing Partner

Bradley A. Post — 1959 — University of the Pacific, B.A., 1981; University of the Pacific, McGeorge School of Law, J.D., 1986 — Admitted to Bar, 1986, California; 1986, U.S. District Court, Central, Eastern, Northern and Southern Districts of California; 1986, U.S. Court of Appeals, Ninth Circuit — Member State Bar of California; Stanislaus County Bar Association (Board of Directors, Past President 1978-2006); Mid-Valley Claims Association; Modesto Claims Association; Association of Defense Counsel, Northern California — Co-Author: "Corporate Successor Liability - When Does the Burden Outweigh the Benefit," California Defense Magazine (Winter 2004) — Stanislaus County Society for Handicapped Children and Adults (Past President and Board Member); Borton Petrini LLP, Firm Managing Partner (2006-Present); Sportsmen of Stanislaus (President and Past Board Member) — E-mail: bpost@bortonpetrini.com

Partners

Cornelius J. Callahan — 1967 — The George Washington University, B.A., 1989; Pace University School of Law, J.D. (cum laude), 1995 — Editor, Pace International Law Review (1994-1995) — Admitted to Bar, 1995, New Jersey; 1996, New York; 1997, Connecticut; 1999, California; 1996, U.S. District Court, Eastern and Southern Districts of New York; 1997, U.S. District Court, District of Connecticut; 1997, U.S. District Court, District of New Jersey; 2008, U.S. District Court, Eastern and Northern Districts of California; 2013, U.S. Court of Appeals, Ninth Circuit — Member State Bar of California; Connecticut, New York State, New Jersey State and Stanislaus County Bar Associations; Wray Ladine American Inn of Court; Modesto Claims Association — Author: "Liability for Delivering Your Goods by Truck," California Defense Magazine (Fall 1999); "The Admissibility of Expert Scientific Evidence," California Defense Magazine (Summer 2004); "Slipping through the Cracks (or tripping over the crack): Liability for Uneven & Broken Sidewalks in Front of Your Property," California Defense Magazine (Summer 2004) — E-mail: ccallahan@bortonpetrini.com

John J. Hollenback, Jr. — 1950 — California State University, Sacramento, B.A., 1971; M.A., 1972; The University of Texas, J.D. (with honors), 1975 — American Jurisprudence Award in Civil Procedure - Recipient — Admitted to Bar, 1975, California — Member State Bar of California, Family Law Section; Stanislaus County Bar Association; Modesto Claims Association — Editor, Digest of California Labor Law, California Chamber of Commerce, Sacramento (1973, 1974 and 1975 Editions) — Stanislaus County Superior Court (Judge Pro Tem, 1994-2005) — Certified Specialist, Family Law, State Bar of California Board of Legal Specialization — E-mail: jhollenback@bortonpetrini.com

Jeff L. Bean — 1959 — Brigham Young University, B.S., 1985; Golden Gate University, M.B.A., 1987; Humphreys College School of Law, J.D., 1995 — Admitted to Bar, 1998, California; 2008, U.S. District Court, Eastern District of California — Member State Bar of California; Stanislaus County Bar Association (President); Modesto Claims Association — San Joaquin County Financial Elder Abuse Team (Former Member) — Languages: Spanish — E-mail: jbean@bortonpetrini.com

Tamie L. Cummins — 1962 — University of the Pacific, B.A., 2001; Humphreys College Laurence Drivon School of Law, J.D., 2007 — Admitted to Bar, 2007, California; 2008, U.S. Federal Court — Member State Bar of California; Stanislaus County Bar Association (Family Law Section); National Association of Consumer Bankruptcy Attorneys — Women's Haven Board (Past Director and Bench Bar Liason, Family Law Sections); Modesto Jr. Chamber (President, 1994-1995); City of Modesto (Past Administrative Hearing Officer) — E-mail: tcummins@bortonpetrini.com

Philip B. Avila — 1953 — California State University, Fresno, B.A., 1976; California State University, Stanislaus, M.P.A. (with distinction), 1978; University of the Pacific, McGeorge School of Law, J.D., 1982 — Admitted to Bar, 1983, California; 1983, U.S. District Court, Eastern and Northern Districts of

CALIFORNIA

Borton Petrini, LLP, Modesto, CA (Continued)

California — Member State Bar of California; Stanislaus County Bar Association; California Trial Lawyers Association; California Society of Health Care Attorneys; Stanislaus County Employer's Advisory Council; American Collectors Association; Association of Defense Counsel, Northern California — Moot Court Honors Board (Member) — E-mail: pavila@bortonpetrini.com

Associate

Stephanie Y. Wu — 1984 — California Polytechnic State University, B.A., 2006; Santa Clara University School of Law, J.D., 2009 — Comments Editor, Santa Clara High Technology Law Journal (2005-2006) — Admitted to Bar, 2010, California; 2014, Illinois; 2009, U.S. District Court, Eastern District of California; 2010, U.S. Court of Appeals, Ninth Circuit — Member American (Young Lawyers Division), Illinois State and Stanislaus County Bar Associations; State Bar of California; Wray Ladine American Inn of Court — Reported Cases: C.B. v. Sonora, 730 F.3d 816 (9th Cir. 2013); Fantozzi Bros. v. San Joaquin Tomato Growers, Inc. (2011) 201 Cal.App.4th 330 — E-mail: swu@bortonpetrini.com

Of Counsel

James J. Kroll, Jr. — 1943 — San Francisco State University, B.A., 1967; M.A., 1970; University of San Francisco School of Law, J.D., 1976 — Recipient, American Jurisprudence Award in Property, McAuliffe Honors Society — Admitted to Bar, 1976, California; 1976, U.S. District Court, Northern District of California; 1978, U.S. District Court, Eastern District of California — Member State Bar of California; Stanislaus County Bar Association — E-mail: jkroll@bortonpetrini.com

MOJAVE 4,238 Kern Co.

Refer To

Borton Petrini, LLP
5060 California Avenue, Suite 700
Bakersfield, California 93309
   Telephone: 661-322-3051
   Fax: 661-322-4628

Mailing Address: P.O. Box 2026, Bakersfield, CA 93303-2026

Administrative Law, Admiralty and Maritime Law, Agriculture, Appellate Practice, Bad Faith, Banking, Bankruptcy, Business Law, Business Litigation, Casualty Insurance Law, Church Law, Collections, Commercial Law, Contracts, Corporate Law, Coverage Issues, Creditor Rights, Eminent Domain, Employment Litigation, Environmental Law, Estate Planning, Family Law, Fire, Health Care, Insurance Coverage, Insurance Defense, Intellectual Property, Labor and Employment, Land Use, Oil and Gas, Personal Injury, Premises Liability, Probate, Product Liability, Professional Errors and Omissions, Property, Public Entities, Real Estate, Religious Institutions, Sports and Entertainment Liability, Toxic Torts, Transactional Law, Transportation, Unlawful Detainer Representing Landlords

SEE COMPLETE LISTING UNDER BAKERSFIELD, CALIFORNIA (64 MILES)

MONTEREY 27,810 Monterey Co.

Horan Lloyd, A Professional Corporation

26385 Carmel Rancho Boulevard
Carmel, California 93923
   Telephone: 831-373-4131
   Fax: 831-373-8302
   E-Mail: jpierce@horanlegal.com
   www.horanlegal.com

Property, Casualty Insurance Law, Property Damage, Product Liability, Bad Faith, Employment Law, Personal Injury, Slip and Fall, Wrongful Death, Automobile, Premises Liability, Habitability

Insurance Clients

California Capital Insurance Company
Citation Insurance Company
Mid-State Mutual Insurance Company

Non-Insurance Clients

Pacific Gas & Electric Company
SureProducts Insurance Agency
Precision Risk Management, Inc.
Tanimura & Antle

MOJAVE

Horan Lloyd, A Professional Corporation, Monterey, CA (Continued)

Jacqueline M. Pierce — 1957 — Smith College, B.A., 1979; The University of North Dakota, J.D., 1983 — Admitted to Bar, 1983, North Dakota; 1987, California — Member American and Monterey County Bar Associations; State Bar of California; Northern California Association of Defense Cousel — Languages: French

The following firms also service this area.

Borton Petrini, LLP
95 South Market Street, Suite 400
San Jose, California 95113
   Telephone: 408-535-0870
   Fax: 408-535-0878

Agriculture, Americans with Disabilities Act, Construction Defect, Employment Law, Insurance Litigation, Product Liability, Professional Liability, Toxic Torts

SEE COMPLETE LISTING UNDER SAN JOSE, CALIFORNIA (60 MILES)

NAPA † 76,915 Napa Co.

Refer To

Babin & Seeger, LLP
3550 Round Barn Boulevard, Suite 201
Santa Rosa, California 95403
   Telephone: 707-526-7370
   Fax: 707-526-0307

Mailing Address: P.O. Box 11626, Santa Rosa, CA 95406

Insurance Defense, Motor Vehicle, Commercial Law, General Liability, Product Liability, Property Damage, Construction Defect, Contracts, Environmental Law, Insurance Coverage, Workers' Compensation, Personal Injury, Professional Malpractice

SEE COMPLETE LISTING UNDER SANTA ROSA, CALIFORNIA (39 MILES)

Refer To

Bledsoe, Cathcart, Diestel, Pedersen & Treppa LLP
601 California Street, 16th Floor
San Francisco, California 94108
   Telephone: 415-981-5411
   Fax: 415-981-0352

Civil Trial Practice, State and Federal Courts, Product Liability, Insurance Defense, Insurance Coverage, Personal Injury, Construction Law, Employment Law, Business Law, Environmental Law, Landlord Tenant, Commercial Transportation, Copyright Litigation, Banking and Finance, Lender Liability

SEE COMPLETE LISTING UNDER SAN FRANCISCO, CALIFORNIA (47 MILES)

Refer To

Boornazian, Jensen & Garthe
A Professional Corporation
555 12th Street, 18th Floor
Oakland, California 94607
   Telephone: 510-834-4350
   Fax: 510-839-1897

Mailing Address: P.O. Box 12925, Oakland, CA 94604-2925

Insurance Defense, Trial Practice, Product Liability, Legal Malpractice, Professional Malpractice, Medical Malpractice, Insurance Coverage, Construction Law

SEE COMPLETE LISTING UNDER OAKLAND, CALIFORNIA (39 MILES)

Refer To

Borton Petrini, LLP
95 South Market Street, Suite 400
San Jose, California 95113
   Telephone: 408-535-0870
   Fax: 408-535-0878

Agriculture, Americans with Disabilities Act, Construction Defect, Employment Law, Insurance Litigation, Product Liability, Professional Liability, Toxic Torts

SEE COMPLETE LISTING UNDER SAN JOSE, CALIFORNIA (82 MILES)

OAKLAND CALIFORNIA

NEWPORT BEACH   85,186 Orange Co.

Mollis & Mollis, Inc.
4621 Teller Avenue, Suite 200
Newport Beach, California 92660
   Telephone: 949-222-0735
   Fax: 949-955-0252
   E-Mail: ronald@mollislaw.com
   www.mollislaw.com

Established: 2001

Insurance Defense, Civil Trial Practice, Business Law, Construction Law, Corporate Law, Appeals, Labor Law, Environmental Law, Real Estate, Estate Planning, Trusts, Probate, Trust and Estate Litigation, Taxation, Trust Settlement

Firm Profile: Mollis & Mollis, Inc. (AV rated 30 years) is made up of a group of dedicated attorneys, paralegals and legal assistants that provide excellent service to their clients.

Non-Insurance Clients

General Underground Fire   NOVA Steel, Inc.
   Protection, Inc.

Partners

Charles A. Mollis — 1959 — California State University, Long Beach, B.A. (with honors), 1980; Western State University College of Law, J.D., 1985 — American Jurisprudence Award-Corporations — Admitted to Bar, 1985, California; 1986, U.S. District Court, Central, Eastern, Northern and Southern Districts of California; U.S. Court of Appeals, Ninth Circuit; 1987, U.S. Claims Court; U.S. Tax Court; 1989, U.S. Supreme Court — Member State Bar of California

Ronald A. Mollis — 1955 — California State University, Long Beach, B.S., 1977; Western State University College of Law, J.D., 1980 — Admitted to Bar, 1981, California; 1982, U.S. District Court, Central, Eastern, Northern and Southern Districts of California; U.S. Court of Appeals, Ninth Circuit; U.S. Claims Court; U.S. Tax Court; 1985, U.S. Supreme Court — Member State Bar of California (Board of Legal Specialization Taxation Law Advisory Committee, 1989-1994, 2009-Present, Chairman, 2013-2014; Business Law Section Committee, 1995-Present); Orange County and Los Angeles County Bar Associations; American Society of International Law; Golden West College Foundation (2005-2007) — AV Rated 30 Consecutive Years — Certified Specialist, Taxation Law (30 years) by The State Bar of California Board of Legal Specialization; California Notary Public, 1979 to present; California Real Estate Broker, 1981 to present

The following firms also service this area.

Berman Berman Berman Schneider & Lowary LLP
11900 West Olympic Boulevard, Suite 600
Los Angeles, California 90064-1151
   Telephone: 310-447-9000
   Fax: 310-447-9011

Insurance Defense, Insurance Coverage, Construction Defect, Product Liability, Employment Law, Professional Liability, Legal, Insurance Agents, Agent/Broker Liability, Medical Malpractice Defense, Design Professionals, Accountants, Trucking Law, Transportation, Real Estate Agents, Brokers and Appraisers, Elder Care, Monitoring Counsel, Litigation Management, California Insurance Regulations and Consulting to Insurance Industry

   SEE COMPLETE LISTING UNDER LOS ANGELES, CALIFORNIA (39 MILES)

Grant, Genovese & Baratta, LLP
2030 Main Street, Suite 1600
Irvine, California 92614-7257
   Telephone: 949-660-1600
   Fax: 949-660-6060

General Civil Litigation, Bad Faith, Insurance Coverage, Construction Defect, Directors and Officers Liability, Employment Law, Environmental Law, Intellectual Property, Homeowners' Associations, Earth Movement, Toxic Torts

   SEE COMPLETE LISTING UNDER IRVINE, CALIFORNIA (9 MILES)

OAKLAND   † 390,724 Alameda Co.

Boornazian, Jensen & Garthe
A Professional Corporation
555 12th Street, 18th Floor
Oakland, California 94607
   Telephone: 510-834-4350
   Fax: 510-839-1897
   www.bjg.com

Established: 1974

Insurance Defense, Trial Practice, Product Liability, Legal Malpractice, Professional Malpractice, Medical Malpractice, Insurance Coverage, Construction Law

Insurance Clients

Admiral Insurance Company	Affiliated FM Insurance Company
AIMS - Acclamation Insurance Management Services	American Claims Service
	Anchor Claims Services, Inc.
Arch Insurance Group	AXA Re Property & Casualty
Broadspire	Carl Warren & Company
Clarendon America Insurance Company	Clarendon National Insurance Company
Crawford & Company	Crawford Technical Services
First Specialty Insurance Corporation	Gallagher Bassett Services, Inc.
	Hudson Insurance Company
Lloyd's Underwriters	Mattei Insurance Services, Inc.
Network Adjusters, Inc.	North American Risk Services
North American Specialty Insurance Company	QBE The Americas
	Quanta Specialty Lines Insurance Company
Risk Management Services, Inc.	
Royal & SunAlliance	Sedgwick CMS
Sirius International Insurance Corporation	Swiss Re America Group
	TRISTAR Risk Management
USF Insurance Company	Virginia Surety Company, Inc.
Western Heritage Insurance Company	Westport Insurance Corporation

Non-Insurance Clients

Administrative Office of the Courts	Amvac Chemical Corporation
County of Alameda	County of Santa Barbara
East Bay Municipal Utility District	Harley-Davidson Motor Company Group, Inc.
Target Corporation	

Shareholders

Gregory J. Rockwell — 1951 — University of San Francisco, B.A., 1973; University of San Francisco School of Law, J.D., 1975 — Admitted to Bar, 1975, California — Member State Bar of California; Alameda County Bar Association; Association of Defense Counsel, Northern California; American Board of Trial Advocates — E-mail: grockwell@bjg.com

Robert B. Lueck — 1953 — University of Southern California, A.B., 1975; University of the Pacific, McGeorge School of Law, J.D., 1978 — Admitted to Bar, 1978, California — Member State Bar of California; Alameda County and Contra Costa County Bar Associations; Association of Defense Counsel, Northern California — E-mail: rlueck@bjg.com

Alan E. Swerdlow — 1961 — University of California, Berkeley, A.B., 1984; University of the Pacific, McGeorge School of Law, J.D., 1987 — Admitted to Bar, 1987, California — Member American and Alameda County Bar Associations; State Bar of California; Association of Defense Counsel, Northern California — E-mail: aswerdlow@bjg.com

Thomas E. Mulvihill — 1958 — University of California, Berkeley, B.A., 1981; University of San Francisco School of Law, J.D., 1987 — Admitted to Bar, 1987, California — Member State Bar of California; Alameda County Bar Association; National Association of Securities Dealers (Board of Arbitrators); Association of Defense Counsel, Northern California — E-mail: tmulvihill@bjg.com

Dennis P. Fitzsimons — 1952 — University of Connecticut, B.A., 1974; Golden Gate University School of Law, J.D., 1989 — Admitted to Bar, 1989, California — Member State Bar of California; Alameda County Bar Association; Northern California Fraud Investigators Association; Association of Defense Counsel, Northern California; Defense Research Institute — E-mail: dfitzsimons@bjg.com

Boornazian, Jensen & Garthe, A Professional Corporation, Oakland, CA (Continued)

Christopher E. Brumfiel — 1972 — University of California, Davis, B.A., 1994; University of California, Hastings College of the Law, J.D., 2001 — Admitted to Bar, 2001, California — Member State Bar of California; Alameda County Bar Association — E-mail: cbrumfiel@bjg.com

Jeffrey A. Chadic — 1963 — Allan Hancock College, A.A./A.S., 1987; San Francisco State University, B.A., 1990; University of San Francisco School of Law, J.D., 1997 — Admitted to Bar, 1998, California — Member State Bar of California; Alameda County Bar Association — E-mail: jchadic@bjg.com

Principals

Alexander Rolph Moore — 1964 — University of California, Berkeley, B.A. (Dean's List), 1986; Golden Gate University School of Law, J.D., 1993 — Admitted to Bar, 1998, California — Member State Bar of California; Alameda County Bar Association — E-mail: amoore@bjg.com

Jonathan W. Heck — 1973 — University of California, Davis, B.A., 1996; Santa Clara University School of Law, J.D., 2001 — Admitted to Bar, 2001, California — Member State Bar of California; Alameda County Bar Association — E-mail: jheck@bjg.com

Emmett E. Seltzer — 1973 — Vanguard University of Southern California, B.A. (summa cum laude), 1995; University of California, Hastings College of the Law, J.D., 2003 — Admitted to Bar, 2003, California — Member State Bar of California; Alameda County Bar Association — E-mail: eseltzer@bjg.com

Tamiko A. Dunham — 1978 — University of California, Berkeley, B.A. (with high honors), 2000; University of California, Hastings College of the Law, J.D., 2004 — Admitted to Bar, 2004, California — Member State Bar of California; Alameda County Bar Association — E-mail: tdunham@bjg.com

Gregory B. Thomas — 1975 — University of Pennsylvania, B.A. (cum laude), 1997; University of San Diego School of Law, J.D., 2005 — Admitted to Bar, 2005, California — Member State Bar of California; Alameda County Bar Association — E-mail: gthomas@bjg.com

Thomas E. Borbely — 1976 — Diablo Valley College, A.A., 2001; John F. Kennedy University School of Law, J.D., 2005 — Admitted to Bar, 2005, California — Member State Bar of California; Alameda County Bar Association — E-mail: tborbely@bjg.com

Associates

Jeffrey A. Loew — 1980 — University of California, Los Angeles, B.A., 2002; Boston University School of Law, J.D., 2005 — Admitted to Bar, 2006, New York; 2010, California — Member State Bar of California; Alameda County Bar Association — E-mail: jloew@bjg.com

Roseanne C. Lazzarotto — 1980 — University of California, Berkeley, B.A., 2003; University of California, Hastings College of the Law, J.D., 2007 — Admitted to Bar, 2007, California — Member State Bar of California; Alameda County Bar Association — E-mail: rlazzarotto@bjg.com

Donnelly A. Gillen — 1983 — University of Maryland, College Park, B.A., 2005; University of California, Hastings College of the Law, J.D., 2008 — Admitted to Bar, 2008, California — Member State Bar of California; Alameda County Bar Association — E-mail: dgillen@bjg.com

Nina K. Dindral — 1983 — University of California, Berkeley, B.A., 2005; Chapman University School of Law, J.D., 2008 — Admitted to Bar, 2008, California — Member State Bar of California; Alameda County Bar Association — E-mail: ndindral@bjg.com

Anthony F. Manzo — 1975 — University of California, San Diego, B.A., 1999; University of San Francisco School of Law, J.D., 2008 — Admitted to Bar, 2008, California — Member State Bar of California; Alameda County Bar Association — E-mail: amanzo@bjg.com

Brentley P. Yim — 1983 — University of California, Riverside, B.A., 2006; University of California Davis School of Law, J.D., 2009 — Admitted to Bar, 2009, California — Member State Bar of California; Alameda County Bar Association — E-mail: byim@bjg.com

John A. Castro — 1983 — University of California, Santa Cruz, B.A. (magna cum laude), 2005; University of California, Hastings College of the Law, J.D. (cum laude), 2010 — Admitted to Bar, 2010, California — Member State Bar of California; Alameda County Bar Association — E-mail: jcastro@bjg.com

Allison L. Shrallow — 1984 — The University of Arizona, B.A., 2007; University of California, Hastings College of the Law, J.D. (magna cum laude), 2010 — Admitted to Bar, 2010, California — Member State Bar of California; Alameda County Bar Association — E-mail: ashrallow@bjg.com

Frank J. Lee — University of Illinois-Urbana-Champaign, B.A., 2006; University of California Davis School of Law, J.D., 2011 — Admitted to Bar, 2011, California — Member State Bar of California; Alameda County Bar Association — E-mail: flee@bjg.com

Patrick J. Larsen — 1984 — University of Miami, B.S., 2006; University of San Francisco School of Law, J.D., 2011 — Admitted to Bar, 2011, California — Member State Bar of California; Alameda County Bar Association — E-mail: plarsen@bjg.com

Lauren O. Miller — California Polytechnic State University, B.A. (magna cum laude), 2008; University of California, Hastings College of the Law, J.D. (magna cum laude), 2011 — Admitted to Bar, 2011, California — Member State Bar of California; Alameda County Bar Association — E-mail: lmiller@bjg.com

Paul H. Kim — 1979 — California Polytechnic State University, B.A. (cum laude), 2006; University of California, Hastings College of the Law, J.D., 2010 — Admitted to Bar, 2011, California — Member State Bar of California; Alameda County Bar Association — E-mail: pkim@bjg.com

Travis A. Brooks — Colorado College, B.A., 2006; University of the Pacific, McGeorge School of Law, J.D. (Order of the Coif), 2011 — Admitted to Bar, 2012, California — Member Alameda County Bar Association — E-mail: tbrooks@bjg.com

Jeffrey M. Mahnken — 1978 — The University of Arizona, B.A. (magna cum laude), 2001; University of the Pacific, McGeorge School of Law, J.D., 2011 — Admitted to Bar, 2012, California — Member State Bar of California; Alameda County Bar Association — E-mail: jmahnken@bjg.com

Justin A. Mallory — 1986 — University of California, Davis, B.S., 2009; University of the Pacific, McGeorge School of Law, J.D. (with distinction), 2012 — Admitted to Bar, 2012, California — Member State Bar of California; Alameda County Bar Association — E-mail: jmallory@bjg.com

Steven M. Wheat — 1984 — The University of Mississippi, B.A. (Phi Beta Kappa, magna cum laude), 2007; University of California, Hastings College of the Law, J.D. (cum laude), 2012 — Admitted to Bar, 2012, California — Member State Bar of California; Alameda County Bar Association — E-mail: swheat@bjg.com

Kevin M. Pease — University of California, Irvine, B.A., 2009; University of California Davis School of Law, J.D., 2013 — Admitted to Bar, 2013, California — Member State Bar of California; Alameda County Bar Association — E-mail: kpease@bjg.com

Zachary W. Lloyd — University of California, Los Angeles, B.A., 2008; University of California, Hastings College of the Law, J.D., 2013 — Admitted to Bar, 2013, California — Member State Bar of California; Alameda County Bar Association — E-mail: zlloyd@bjg.com

Daniel S. Maroon — University of California, Davis, B.A., 2010; University of California, Hastings College of the Law, J.D., 2013 — Admitted to Bar, 2014, California — Member State Bar of California; Alameda County Bar Association — E-mail: dmaroon@bjg.com

Of Counsel

David J. Garthe — 1946 — University of California, Davis, A.B., 1968; University of California Davis School of Law, J.D., 1971 — Admitted to Bar, 1972, California — Member American and Alameda County Bar Associations; State Bar of California; Association of Defense Counsel, Northern California; American Board of Trial Advocates — E-mail: dgarthe@bjg.com

William T. Mulvihill — 1950 — University of San Francisco, B.A., 1972; Golden Gate University School of Law, J.D., 1977 — Admitted to Bar, 1977, California; U.S. District Court, Northern District of California; 2003, U.S. District Court, Eastern District of California — Member State Bar California; Bar Association of San Francisco; Alameda County Bar Association; Association of Defense Counsel, Northern California; Defense Research Institute — ADR Panel Member: San Francisco Superior Court (1988-Present); Contra Costa Superior Court (1989-Present); Alameda Superior Court (1996-Present); Faculty Member, Personal Injury Litigation, Hastings College of Advocacy, Hastings Center for Trial & Appellate Advocacy (1988-1989) — E-mail: wmulvihill@bjg.com

Gail C. Trabish — 1955 — Georgetown University, B.S.B.A., 1976; The Catholic University of America, Columbus School of Law, J.D., 1980 — Admitted to Bar, 1982, California — Member State Bar of California; Virginia State Bar; The District of Columbia Bar; Alameda County Bar Association — E-mail: gtrabish@bjg.com

OAKLAND CALIFORNIA

Cresswell, Echeguren, Rodgers & Harvey
A Professional Corporation

180 Grand Avenue, Suite 440
Oakland, California 94612
   Telephone: 510-444-1735
   Fax: 510-444-6923
   E-Mail: office@cresswell-law.com
   www.cresswell-law.com

Established: 1949

Professional Liability, Insurance Coverage, Litigation

Insurance Clients

AXIS Pro
First Specialty Insurance Corporation
Swiss Reinsurance Company
Capitol Indemnity Corporation
Liberty Mutual Insurance
Rockhill Insurance Company
Westport Insurance Corporation

Non-Insurance Clients

Arkansas Best Corporation
Custard Insurance Adjusters, Inc.
Mattei Insurance Services, Inc.
Carl Warren & Company
Gallagher Bassett Services, Inc.
VeriClaim, Inc.

Firm Members

Robert Cresswell — (1917-1995)
Ronald D. Echeguren — University of California, Berkeley, A.B., 1973; University of California, Hastings College of the Law, J.D., 1977 — Phi Alpha Delta — Admitted to Bar, 1977, California — E-mail: recheguren@cresswell-law.com
G. Dennis Rodgers — University of California, Santa Barbara, B.A., 1980; University of California, Hastings College of the Law, J.D., 1983 — Phi Beta Kappa — Admitted to Bar, 1983, California — E-mail: drodgers@cresswell-law.com
Matthew Harvey — Santa Clara University, B.S., 2001; The University of North Carolina School of Law, J.D., 2004 — Admitted to Bar, 2004, California — E-mail: mharvey@cresswell-law.com

Associates

Lori S. Mandell
Julie A. Lemmer

Of Counsel

Elsa S. Baldwin
David R. McDonald
Julie S. James

Ericksen Arbuthnot

155 Grand Avenue, Suite 1050
Oakland, California 94612-3768
   Telephone: 510-832-7770
   Fax: 510-832-0102
   www.ericksenarbuthnot.com

(Bakersfield, CA Office*: 1830 Truxtun Avenue, Suite 200, 93301-5022)
   (Tel: 661-633-5080)
   (Fax: 661-633-5089)
(Fresno, CA Office*: 2440 West Shaw Avenue, Suite 101, 93711-3300)
   (Tel: 559-449-2600)
   (Fax: 559-449-2603)
(Los Angeles, CA Office*: 835 Wilshire Boulevard, Suite 500, 90017-2656)
   (Tel: 213-489-4411)
   (Fax: 213-489-4332)
(Sacramento, CA Office*: 100 Howe Avenue, Suite 110S, 95825-8200)
   (Tel: 916-483-5181)
   (Fax: 916-483-7558)
(San Francisco, CA Office*: 100 Bush Street, Suite 900, 94104-3950)
   (Tel: 415-362-7126)
   (Fax: 415-362-6401)
(San Jose, CA Office*: 152 North Third Street, Suite 700, 95112-5560)
   (Tel: 408-286-0880)
   (Fax: 408-286-0337)

Ericksen Arbuthnot, Oakland, CA (Continued)

(Walnut Creek, CA Office*: 570 Lennon Lane, 94598-2415)
   (Tel: 925-947-1702)
   (Fax: 925-947-4921)

Established: 1950

Administrative Law, Business Law, Construction Law, Employment Law, Environmental Law, Health Care, Managed Care Liability, Insurance Coverage, Insurance Fraud, Personal Injury, Premises Liability, Product Liability, Professional Liability, Medical Malpractice, Public Entities, Appellate Law

Firm Profile: Ericksen Arbuthnot, founded in 1950, includes a network of offices throughout California. Our lawyers handle a wide range of legal services for insurance companies and self-insured entities. This multiple office approach allows for statewide, cost-effective, uniform procedures for clients.

Insurance Clients

American International Group, Inc. (AIG)
California Insurance Guarantee Association
RLI Corp.
RSUI Group, Inc.
York Risk Services Group, Inc.
Arch Insurance Company
Broadspire Services, Inc.
James River Insurance Company
Philadelphia Insurance Companies
Rockhill Insurance Company
Sompo Japan Insurance Company of America

Non-Insurance Clients

American Professional Agency
Fortune Brands Home & Security, Inc.
Clopay, Inc.
Sears Holdings Corporation

In Memoriam

A. D. Ericksen — (1883-1969)
Preston N. Ericksen — (1921-1997)

Resident Partners

Lois A. Lindstrom — *Managing Partner* — University of Wisconsin-Madison, B.A., 1970; Golden Gate University School of Law, J.D., 1983 — Admitted to Bar, 1983, California — Member American and Contra Costa County Bar Associations; State Bar of California; Bar Association of San Francisco — E-mail: llindstrom@ericksenarbuthnot.com
Joseph J. Minioza — *Assistant Managing Partner* — University of California, Davis, B.A. (magna cum laude), 1993; University of California, Boalt Hall School of Law; University of California, Los Angeles School of Law, J.D., 1997 — Admitted to Bar, 1998, California — Member State Bar of California — E-mail: jminioza@ericksenarbuthnot.com
Brian M. Sanders — *Partner* — California State University, Fullerton, B.A. (cum laude), 1996; Loyola Marymount University, Loyola Law School, J.D., 1999 — Admitted to Bar, 2002, California — Member American Bar Association; State Bar of California — E-mail: bsanders@ericksenarbuthnot.com
Andrew Kozlow — *Partner* — University of California, Davis, B.A., 2004; Gonzaga University School of Law, J.D., 2007 — Admitted to Bar, 2007, California — E-mail: akozlow@ericksenarbuthnot.com

Of Counsel

Roger F. Allen — San Jose State University, B.A. (with distinction), 1968; M.A., 1971; Golden Gate University School of Law, J.D., 1977 — Admitted to Bar, 1977, California; U.S. District Court, Northern District of California — Member American, Alameda County and Contra Costa Bar Associations; State Bar of California — E-mail: rallen@ericksenarbuthnot.com

Resident Associates

G. Geoffrey Wood — University of Santa Clara, J.D., 1983 — Admitted to Bar, 1983, California — Member State Bar of California; Alameda County and Eastern Alameda County Bar Associations; Association of Defense Counsel of Northern California and Nevada — Practice Areas: Construction Defect; Construction Law; Litigation; Insurance Defense; Product Liability; Casualty Defense; Insurance Coverage; Real Estate; Wrongful Death; Personal Injury — E-mail: gwood@ericksenarbuthnot.com
Joseph Kim — University of San Francisco School of Law, J.D., 2007 — Admitted to Bar, 2008, California — E-mail: jkim@ericksenarbuthnot.com
Jason Mauck — University of California, Santa Barbara, B.A., 2002; California Western School of Law, J.D., 2007 — Admitted to Bar, 2008, California

Ericksen Arbuthnot, Oakland, CA (Continued)

Ross Dwyer — Santa Clara University, B.A., 2003; Santa Clara University School of Law, J.D., 2011 — Admitted to Bar, 2011, California — Languages: Spanish

(For biographical data on other personnel, see Additional Office Information)

Hanna, Brophy, MacLean, McAleer & Jensen, LLP

555 12th Street, Suite 1450
Oakland, California 94607
Telephone: 510-839-1180
Fax: 510-839-4804
www.hannabrophy.com

(Additional Offices: Bakersfield, CA*; Fresno, CA*; Los Angeles, CA*; Orange, CA*; Redding, CA*; Riverside, CA*; Rancho Cordova, CA*(See Sacramento listing); Salinas, CA*; San Francisco, CA*; Santa Rosa, CA*; Stockton, CA*)

Established: 1943

Insurance Defense, Workers' Compensation, Subrogation, Labor and Employment, Employment Law, Litigation

Firm Profile: Hanna, Brophy, MacLean, McAleer & Jensen, a limited liability partnership, specializes in workers' compensation defense and employment-related litigation. Since 1943, employers throughout California have looked to Hanna & Brophy for excellence in legal representation.

From twelve offices located throughout California, seasoned partners and experienced associates blend their expertise in the representation of our clients. Each office enjoys a regional reputation among judges and opposing counsel as a solid, aggressive legal representative of employers and insurance carriers.

From our firm's earliest days, Warren Hanna and Don Brophy established high standards. The same standards of expertise, professionalism and personal service have guided us ever since. That's why you can count on Hanna & Brophy, case after case.

Insurance Clients

California Insurance Guarantee Association
Liberty Mutual Insurance Company

Firm Managing Partner

Leslie Tuxhorn — Western State University at Fullerton, J.D. (with honors), 1990 — Admitted to Bar, 1991, California — Member State Bar of California; Shasta County Bar Association; California Workers' Compensation Defense Attorneys Association

Office Managing Partner

Michael L. Giachino — University of California, Berkeley, B.A., 1975; San Francisco Law School, J.D., 1979 — Admitted to Bar, 1980, California — Member State Bar of California

Yaron & Associates

1300 Clay Street, Suite 800
Oakland, California 94612
Telephone: 415-658-2929
Fax: 415-658-2930
E-Mail: gyaron@yaronlaw.com
www.yaronlaw.com

Established: 1999

Insurance Defense, Litigation, Insurance Coverage, Product Liability, Transportation, Construction Defect, Environmental Law, Toxic Torts, Asbestos Litigation

Yaron & Associates, Oakland, CA (Continued)

Insurance Clients

American Alternative Insurance Corporation
Chubb Group of Insurance Companies
Clarendon National Insurance Company
George Hills Company/Claremont
Munich RE America
RiverStone Claims Management, LLC
Assicurazioni Generali S.p.A.
AXA Insurance Company
Clarendon America Insurance Company
Crum & Forster Insurance
First Mercury Insurance Company
Lincoln General Insurance Company
United States Fire Insurance Company

Non-Insurance Clients

Beutler Corporation
Hathaway Dinwiddie
Todd Pacific Shipyards Corporation
Enstar (US) Inc.
Shimmick Construction
West Bay Builders, Inc.
Woodruff-Sawyer

Partners

George D. Yaron — 1954 — San Francisco State University, B.A., 1977; Golden Gate University School of Law, J.D., 1980 — Admitted to Bar, 1980, California; 1983, Oregon; 2001, Nevada; 1980, U.S. District Court, Northern District of California; 1984, U.S. District Court, Eastern District of California; 1995, U.S. District Court, Central and Southern Districts of California; 2001, U.S. District Court, District of Nevada — Member American Bar Association; Oregon State Bar; State Bars of California and Nevada; Bar Association of San Francisco; Defense Research Institute — Captain, U.S. Marine Corps, 1980-1984 — E-mail: gyaron@yaronlaw.com

James I. Silverstein — 1963 — University of California, Berkeley, B.S., 1985; Loyola Law School Los Angeles, J.D., 1989 — Admitted to Bar, 1989, California; U.S. District Court, Central, Eastern, Northern and Southern Districts of California — E-mail: jsilverstein@yaronlaw.com

David Gray Douglas — 1967 — Carleton College, B.A., 1989; Tulane University Law School, J.D. (cum laude), 1993 — Admitted to Bar, 1993, California; U.S. District Court, Northern District of California; U.S. Court of Appeals, Ninth Circuit; 1994, U.S. District Court, Central District of California; 1997, U.S. District Court, Eastern District of California; 1998, U.S. District Court, Southern District of California — Member American and Marin County Bar Associations; State Bar of California; California Young Lawyers Association (Director 1996-1999; Treasurer, 1997-1999); Defense Research Institute — Governing Board, CEB, 1997-1999; Delegate, Conference of Delegates, State Bar of California, 1999 — E-mail: ddouglas@yaronlaw.com

Keith E. Patterson — 1974 — University of Southern California, B.A. (magna cum laude), 1998; University of California, Hastings College of the Law, J.D., 2001 — Admitted to Bar, 2003, California — Member American Bar Association; Bar Association of San Francisco — E-mail: kpatterson@yaronlaw.com

Henry M. Su — 1969 — University of California, Davis, B.A., 1992; Southwestern University School of Law, J.D., 1994 — Admitted to Bar, 1994, California — E-mail: hsu@yaronlaw.com

D. David Steele — 1967 — University of California, Los Angeles, B.A., 1989; Golden Gate University School of Law, J.D., 1993 — Merit Tuition Scholar — Admitted to Bar, 1994, California; U.S. District Court, Central, Eastern, Northern and Southern Districts of California — Member The Federalist Society; Association of Defense Counsel — U.S. Navel Reserves, Honorable Discharge [1985-1993] — Languages: French — E-mail: dsteele@yaronlaw.com

Associates

Brentley P. Yim — 1983 — University of California, Riverside, B.A. (cum laude), 2006; University of California Davis School of Law, J.D., 2009 — Admitted to Bar, 2009, California; 2010, U.S. District Court, Northern District of California — E-mail: byim@yaronlaw.com

Jenna E. Settino — 1975 — University of New Hampshire, B.S., 1998; Vermont Law School, J.D., 2002 — Admitted to Bar, 2002, Massachusetts; 2005, California — E-mail: jsettino@yaronlaw.com

Craig Brinckerhoff — 1982 — University of California, Berkeley, B.A., 2005; Pepperdine University School of Law, J.D. (cum laude), 2011 — Admitted to Bar, 2011, California; 2013, U.S. District Court, Central and Northern Districts of California — Member Bar Association of San Francisco — E-mail: cbrinckerhoff@yaronlaw.com

PALM SPRINGS   CALIFORNIA

The following firms also service this area.

Borton Petrini, LLP
660 Las Gallinas Avenue, Suite B
San Rafael, California 94903
   Telephone: 415-677-0730
   Fax: 415-677-0737

Commercial Litigation, Construction Litigation, General Civil Litigation, Intellectual Property, Professional Liability, Public Entities

SEE COMPLETE LISTING UNDER SAN FRANCISCO, CALIFORNIA (8 MILES)

OCEANSIDE   167,086 San Diego Co.
Refer To

Borton Petrini, LLP
1320 Columbia Street, Suite 210
San Diego, California 92101
   Telephone: 619-232-2424
   Fax: 619-531-0794

Admiralty and Maritime Law, Bad Faith, Casualty Insurance Law, Construction Law, Coverage Issues, Labor and Employment, Professional Liability

SEE COMPLETE LISTING UNDER SAN DIEGO, CALIFORNIA (21 MILES)

ONTARIO   163,924 San Bernardino Co.
Refer To

Borton Petrini, LLP
1461 Ford Street, Suite 201
Redlands, California 92373
   Telephone: 909-381-0527
   Fax: 909-381-0658

Mailing Address: P.O Box 11207, San Bernardino, CA 92423

Coverage Issues, Insurance Defense, Labor and Employment, Product Liability, Professional Errors and Omissions, Public Entities

SEE COMPLETE LISTING UNDER SAN BERNARDINO, CALIFORNIA (24 MILES)

Refer To

Thompson & Colegate LLP
3610 Fourteenth Street
Riverside, California 92501
   Telephone: 951-682-5550
   Fax: 951-781-4012

Mailing Address: P.O. Box 1299, Riverside, CA 92502

Insurance Defense, Medical Malpractice, Automobile Liability, General Liability, Construction Litigation, Coverage Issues, Personal Injury, Product Liability, Premises Liability, Employment Law, Commercial Litigation, Bankruptcy, Alternative Dispute Resolution, Appellate Practice, Complex Litigation, Real Estate

SEE COMPLETE LISTING UNDER RIVERSIDE, CALIFORNIA (23 MILES)

ORANGE   136,416 Orange Co.

Hanna, Brophy, MacLean, McAleer & Jensen, LLP
701 South Parker Street, Suite 7400
Orange, California 92868
   Telephone: 714-598-4050
   Fax: 714-542-9697
   www.hannabrophy.com

Established: 2008

Insurance Defense, Workers' Compensation, Subrogation, Labor and Employment, Employment Law, Litigation

Office Managing Partner

Mark Lee — University of San Diego, J.D., 2001 — Admitted to Bar, 2001, California

(See listing under Oakland, CA for additional information)

The following firms also service this area.

Borton Petrini, LLP
626 Wilshire Boulevard, Suite 975
Los Angeles, California 90017
   Telephone: 213-624-2869
   Fax: 213-489-3930

Business Litigation, Civil Litigation, Construction Law, Employment Law, Employment Litigation, Trust and Estate Litigation

SEE COMPLETE LISTING UNDER LOS ANGELES, CALIFORNIA (34 MILES)

**Kinkle, Rodiger & Spriggs
Professional Corporation**
3333 Fourteenth Street
Riverside, California 92501-3809
   Telephone: 951-683-2410
   Toll Free: 800-235-2039
   Fax: 951-683-7759

Insurance Defense, Self-Insured, General Liability, Product Liability, Automobile, Premises Liability, Public Entities, Construction Law, Professional Liability, Coverage Issues, Bad Faith, Civil Trial Practice, Appellate Practice, Federal Courts

SEE COMPLETE LISTING UNDER RIVERSIDE, CALIFORNIA (35 MILES)

OXNARD   197,899 Ventura Co.
Refer To

Berman Berman Berman Schneider & Lowary LLP
11900 West Olympic Boulevard, Suite 600
Los Angeles, California 90064-1151
   Telephone: 310-447-9000
   Fax: 310-447-9011

Insurance Defense, Insurance Coverage, Construction Defect, Product Liability, Employment Law, Professional Liability, Legal, Insurance Agents, Agent/Broker Liability, Medical Malpractice Defense, Design Professionals, Accountants, Trucking Law, Transportation, Real Estate Agents, Brokers and Appraisers, Elder Care, Monitoring Counsel, Litigation Management, California Insurance Regulations and Consulting to Insurance Industry

SEE COMPLETE LISTING UNDER LOS ANGELES, CALIFORNIA (59 MILES)

PALM DESERT   48,445 Riverside Co.
Refer To

Thompson & Colegate LLP
3610 Fourteenth Street
Riverside, California 92501
   Telephone: 951-682-5550
   Fax: 951-781-4012

Mailing Address: P.O. Box 1299, Riverside, CA 92502

Insurance Defense, Medical Malpractice, Automobile Liability, General Liability, Construction Litigation, Coverage Issues, Personal Injury, Product Liability, Premises Liability, Employment Law, Commercial Litigation, Bankruptcy, Alternative Dispute Resolution, Appellate Practice, Complex Litigation, Real Estate

SEE COMPLETE LISTING UNDER RIVERSIDE, CALIFORNIA (70 MILES)

PALM SPRINGS   44,552 Riverside Co.
Refer To

Borton Petrini, LLP
1461 Ford Street, Suite 201
Redlands, California 92373
   Telephone: 909-381-0527
   Fax: 909-381-0658

Mailing Address: P.O Box 11207, San Bernardino, CA 92423

Coverage Issues, Insurance Defense, Labor and Employment, Product Liability, Professional Errors and Omissions, Public Entities

SEE COMPLETE LISTING UNDER SAN BERNARDINO, CALIFORNIA (57 MILES)

CALIFORNIA

Refer To

Kinkle, Rodiger & Spriggs Professional Corporation
3333 Fourteenth Street
Riverside, California 92501-3809
Telephone: 951-683-2410
Toll Free: 800-235-2039
Fax: 951-683-7759

Insurance Defense, Self-Insured, General Liability, Product Liability, Automobile, Premises Liability, Public Entities, Construction Law, Professional Liability, Coverage Issues, Bad Faith, Civil Trial Practice, Appellate Practice, Federal Courts

SEE COMPLETE LISTING UNDER RIVERSIDE, CALIFORNIA (56 MILES)

Refer To

Thompson & Colegate LLP
3610 Fourteenth Street
Riverside, California 92501
Telephone: 951-682-5550
Fax: 951-781-4012
Mailing Address: P.O. Box 1299, Riverside, CA 92502

Insurance Defense, Medical Malpractice, Automobile Liability, General Liability, Construction Litigation, Coverage Issues, Personal Injury, Product Liability, Premises Liability, Employment Law, Commercial Litigation, Bankruptcy, Alternative Dispute Resolution, Appellate Practice, Complex Litigation, Real Estate

SEE COMPLETE LISTING UNDER RIVERSIDE, CALIFORNIA (56 MILES)

PALO ALTO   64,403 Santa Clara Co.

Refer To

Borton Petrini, LLP
95 South Market Street, Suite 400
San Jose, California 95113
Telephone: 408-535-0870
Fax: 408-535-0878

Agriculture, Americans with Disabilities Act, Construction Defect, Employment Law, Insurance Litigation, Product Liability, Professional Liability, Toxic Torts

SEE COMPLETE LISTING UNDER SAN JOSE, CALIFORNIA (6 MILES)

PASADENA   137,122 Los Angeles Co.

Collins Collins Muir + Stewart LLP

1100 El Centro Street
South Pasadena, California 91030
Telephone: 626-243-1100
Fax: 626-243-1111
E-Mail: jkelly@ccmslaw.com
www.ccmslaw.com

(Orange, CA Office: 750 The City Drive, Suite 400, 92867)
   (Tel: 714-823-4100)
   (Fax: 714-823-4101)
(Carlsbad, CA Office: 6104 Innovation Way, 92009)
   (Tel: 760-274-2110)
   (Fax: 760-274-2111)

Insurance Defense, Litigation, Construction Law, Professional Malpractice, Public Entities, Product Liability, Premises Liability, Employment Law, Arbitration, Mediation, Complex Litigation

Insurance Clients

American States Insurance Company
Civil Service Employees Insurance Company
Hawkeye-Security Insurance Company
National Automobile and Casualty Insurance Company
Automobile Club of Southern California
CNA Insurance Company
DPIC Companies, Inc.
Lexington Insurance Company
Motors Insurance Corporation
Shand Morahan & Company, Inc.
Zurich American Insurance Company

PALO ALTO

Collins Collins Muir + Stewart LLP, Pasadena, CA
(Continued)

Non-Insurance Clients

Carl Warren & Company
GAB Robins North America, Inc.
RA&MCO Insurance Services
TCO Insurance Services
First Security Services Corporation
HCM Claim Management Corporation

Firm Members

Samuel J. Muir — Azusa Pacific University, B.A., 1976; Loyola Law School Los Angeles, J.D., 1979 — Admitted to Bar, 1979, California

Brian K. Stewart — Western Illinois University, B.A., 1983; The John Marshall Law School, J.D., 1986 — Admitted to Bar, 1986, California; 1987, Illinois

Robert H. Stellwagen, Jr. — University of California, San Diego, B.A., 1986; University of California, Hastings College of the Law, J.D., 1990 — Admitted to Bar, 1990, California

Michele L. Gamble — Santa Clara University, B.A., 1994; University of San Diego School of Law, J.D., 1996 — Admitted to Bar, 1997, California

Tomas A. Guterres — Boston University, B.A., 1987; Loyola Law School, J.D., 1990 — Admitted to Bar, 1991, California

Howard Franco, Jr. — University of Dayton, B.A. (cum laude), 1981; Pepperdine University School of Law, J.D., 1984 — Admitted to Bar, 1984, California

David E. Barker — California Lutheran University, B.A., 1994; Pepperdine University School of Law, J.D., 1997 — Admitted to Bar, 1997, California

Nicole A. Davis-Tinkham — University of California, Irvine, B.S., 2000; Southwestern University School of Law, J.D., 2003 — Admitted to Bar, 2003, California

Associates

Melinda W. Ebelhar
Eric C. Brown
James C. Jardin
Dustin D. Sichon
Catherine C. Mathers
Ryan J. Kohler
John D. Perkins
Christie Bodnar Swiss
Robert R. Walker
Erin R. Dunkerly
Kevin J. Engelien
Ryan E. Palumbo
Alexandra N. Krasovec
Desiri L. Schultze
David C. Moore
Joshua A. Cohen
Edward J. Riffle
Michael L. Wroniak
Christian E. Foy Nagy
Christian Bredeson
Ryan P. Harley
Ryan M. Deam
Niall Fordyce
Clay R. Wilkinson
Michael B. McDonald
Justin J. Morgan
Denisse O. Gastelum

Friedenthal, Heffernan & Klein, LLP

155 North Lake Avenue, Suite 430
Pasadena, California 91101-1848
Telephone: 626-628-2800
Fax: 626-628-2828
www.fhklegal.com

(San Mateo, CA Office: 1900 South Norfolk Street, Suite 350, 94403)

Defense Litigation, Automobile Accidents, Environmental Litigation, Product Liability, Premises Liability, Appellate Practice, Toxic Torts, Class Actions, Construction Defect, Complex Litigation, General Negligence, Trucking Accidents, Catastrophic Loss

Firm Profile: Friedenthal, Heffernan & Klein, LLP is a civil litigation firm composed of experienced trial lawyers with backgrounds in a wide range of practice areas. The partners founded the firm on the principle that, throughout the life of a case, they will provide their clients with superior representation that is both aggressive and cost-effective.

The firm offers corporate and individual clients the best legal resources available. Lawsuits often become more complex and expensive than necessary. Friedenthal, Heffernan & Klein prides itself on offering the kind of accurate assessment and skillful navigation that avoids unnecessary litigation, while simultaneously positioning matters for success at trial. The firm operates on a

Friedenthal, Heffernan & Klein, LLP, Pasadena, CA (Continued)

foundation of zeal for client service and a depth and breadth of experience that allows for dependably high quality representation.

Insurance Clients

The Hartford
Sedgwick CMS

Partners

Daniel R. Friedenthal — University of California, Los Angeles, B.A., 1983; Rutgers University School of Law, J.D., 1986 — Admitted to Bar, 1987, Colorado; 1988, California; 1987, U.S. District Court, District of Colorado; 1990, U.S. District Court, Central District of California; U.S. Court of Appeals, Ninth Circuit — Member American Board of Trial Advocates

Kevin N. Heffernan — University of California, San Diego, Earl Warren College, B.A., 1984; Villanova University School of Law, J.D., 1988 — Admitted to Bar, 1988, California; 1990, U.S. District Court, Central District of California — Member American Board of Trial Advocates; Defense Research Institute

Carl C. Klein, II — University of California, Los Angeles, B.A., 1984; University of San Francisco School of Law, J.D., 1991 — Admitted to Bar, 1991, California; U.S. District Court, Central, Northern and Southern Districts of California — Member Alameda, Los Angeles County and San Diego County Bar Associations

Associates

Jay D. Brown — McGill University, B.A., 1983; University of California, Los Angeles School of Law, J.D., 1989 — Admitted to Bar, 1989, California; U.S. District Court, Central and Southern Districts of California; U.S. Court of Appeals, Ninth Circuit

Benjamin M. Bartlett — University of California, San Diego, B.A. Political Science (cum laude), 2006; University of California, Davis School of Law, J.D. (Order of the Coif), 2009 — Admitted to Bar, 2009, California

Hosp, Gilbert & Bergsten

301 North Lake Avenue, Suite 410
Pasadena, California 91101
    Telephone: 626-792-2400
    Fax: 626-356-9656
    www.hosp-gilbert.com

Established: 1993

Insurance Defense, Trial and Appellate Practice, State and Federal Courts, Automobile, Common Carrier, Commercial Law, Construction Law, Coverage Issues, Employment Law, Legal Malpractice, Municipal Liability, Premises Liability, Subrogation, Toxic Torts, Earth Movement

Firm Profile: Hosp, Gilbert & Bergsten specializes in insurance defense and risk management for insurance companies, self-insureds and self-administered insurance purchasing groups. In addition to an extensive defense practice in general property and liability as well as individual tort and professional liability areas, the firm also designs client development and insurance programs for a wide range of clients.

Insurance Clients

Admiral Insurance Company
American Reliable Insurance Company
Arch Insurance Group
Avizent
Balboa Insurance Group
Century Insurance Group
CIBA Insurance Services
CMI Nixon and Company
Employers Mutual Companies
Great West Casualty Company
Mercury Insurance Group
Nationwide Agribusiness Insurance Company
RLI Transportation
Topa Insurance Company
American Claims Management, Inc.
Ameriprise Auto & Home Insurance
AXIS Insurance
Catlin Specialty Insurance Company
Claims Adjusting Group
Crum & Forster
General Star Management Company
Montpelier US Insurance Company
Nationwide Indemnity Company
Network Adjusters, Inc.
Scottsdale Insurance Company
21st Century Insurance Company

Hosp, Gilbert & Bergsten, Pasadena, CA (Continued)

Western Heritage Insurance Company
Zurich London, Ltd.

Non-Insurance Clients

Aegean Restaurant Group
Gordon Trucking, Inc.
Phoenix American Companies
T Mcgee Electric, Inc.
Z-Best Concrete
Forward Air, Inc.
International Church of the Foursquare Gospel
Westfield Companies

Firm Members

Warren L. Gilbert — 1951 — University of California, Los Angeles, A.B., 1973; Southwestern University School of Law, J.D., 1979 — Admitted to Bar, 1980, California — Member American, Los Angeles County and Pasadena Bar Associations; State Bar of California; Association of Southern California Defense Counsel; American Board of Trial Advocates — Arbitrator, Settlement Officer, Judge Pro Tem, Los Angeles County Superior Court — E-mail: wlgilbert@hosplaw.com

Robert T. Bergsten — 1968 — Boston University, B.S., 1990; Pepperdine University School of Law, J.D., 1993 — Admitted to Bar, 1993, California — Member American and Los Angeles County Bar Associations; State Bar of California; Association of Southern California Defense Counsel; Defense Research Institute — Languages: Spanish — E-mail: rbergsten@hosplaw.com

Associates

Leslie Ann Keidel — 1953 — San Diego State University, B.S., 1975; Southwestern University School of Law, J.D., 1984 — Admitted to Bar, 1984, California; 1985, U.S. District Court, Central District of California; U.S. Court of Appeals, Ninth Circuit — Member State Bar of California — E-mail: lkeidel@hosplaw.com

Bryan L. King — 1982 — University of California, Los Angeles, B.A., 2005; Pepperdine University School of Law, J.D., 2011 — Admitted to Bar, 2011, California; U.S. District Court, Central District of California — Member State Bar of California; Los Angeles Bar Association; UCLA Alumni Association — E-mail: bking@hosplaw.com

Scott Zonder — 1956 — San Francisco State University, B.A. (cum laude), 1978; Santa Clara University, J.D. (magna cum laude), 1987 — Admitted to Bar, 1987, California; U.S. District Court, Northern District of California — E-mail: szonder@hosplaw.com

Devon T. Pollard — 1982 — University of Southern California, B.A., 2004; Chapman University School of Law, J.D., 2011 — Admitted to Bar, 2011, California; U.S. District Court, Central District of California — Member American, Los Angeles County and Pasadena Bar Associations — E-mail: dpollard@hosplaw.com

Brianne R. Gardner — University of Redlands, B.A., 2002; Whittier Law School, J.D. (magna cum laude), 2010 — Admitted to Bar, 2010, California; 2011, U.S. District Court, Central District of California — E-mail: bgardner@hosplaw.com

John P. Young — 1960 — University of Missouri-Columbia, B.A., 1982; Pepperdine University School of Law, J.D. (cum laude), 1991 — Admitted to Bar, 1991, California; U.S. District Court, Central District of California; 2005, U.S. District Court, Southern District of California — Member Los Angeles County Bar Association; Association of Southern California Defense Counsel — E-mail: jyoung@hosplaw.com

Caitlin R. Johnson — 1983 — Pepperdine University - Seaver College, B.A., 2005; Pepperdine University School of Law, J.D., 2010 — Admitted to Bar, 2010, California; U.S. District Court, Central District of California — Member State Bar of California; Los Angeles County and Pasadena Bar Associations — E-mail: cjohnson@hosplaw.com

Of Counsel

F. Phillip Hosp — 1944 — University of Southern California, B.A. (with honors), 1966; Loyola Law School Los Angeles, J.D., 1969 — Phi Delta Phi — Admitted to Bar, 1970, California — Member American, Los Angeles County and Pasadena Bar Associations; State Bar of California; Insurance Brokers and Agents of the West; Association of Southern California Defense Counsel; Defense Research Institute — Mediator, Settlement Officer, Arbitrator, Judge Pro Tem, Los Angeles County Superior Court — E-mail: phosp@hosplaw.com

CALIFORNIA

The following firms also service this area.

Law Offices of Virgil L. Roth, PC
625 Fair Oaks Avenue, Suite 255
South Pasadena, California 91030
  Telephone: 626-441-1165
  Fax: 626-441-1166

Personal Injury, Property Damage, Class Actions, Intellectual Property, Professional Liability, Construction Defect, Insurance Defense, Premises Liability, Mass Tort, Complex Litigation, Mediation, Toxic Torts, Product Liability, Commercial Litigation

SEE COMPLETE LISTING UNDER LOS ANGELES, CALIFORNIA (11 MILES)

PASO ROBLES   29,793 San Luis Obispo Co.

Refer To

Borton Petrini, LLP
5060 California Avenue, Suite 700
Bakersfield, California 93309
  Telephone: 661-322-3051
  Fax: 661-322-4628

Mailing Address: P.O. Box 2026, Bakersfield, CA 93303-2026

Administrative Law, Admiralty and Maritime Law, Agriculture, Appellate Practice, Bad Faith, Banking, Bankruptcy, Business Law, Business Litigation, Casualty Insurance Law, Church Law, Collections, Commercial Law, Contracts, Corporate Law, Coverage Issues, Creditor Rights, Eminent Domain, Employment Litigation, Environmental Law, Estate Planning, Family Law, Fire, Health Care, Insurance Coverage, Insurance Defense, Intellectual Property, Labor and Employment, Land Use, Oil and Gas, Personal Injury, Premises Liability, Probate, Product Liability, Professional Errors and Omissions, Property, Public Entities, Real Estate, Religious Institutions, Sports and Entertainment Liability, Toxic Torts, Transactional Law, Transportation, Unlawful Detainer Representing Landlords

SEE COMPLETE LISTING UNDER BAKERSFIELD, CALIFORNIA (112 MILES)

PLEASANT HILL   33,152 Contra Costa Co.

Morales Fierro & Reeves

2300 Contra Costa Boulevard, Suite 310
Pleasant Hill, California 94523
  Telephone: 925-288-1776
  Fax: 925-288-1856
  E-Mail: LawOffice@mfrlegal.com
  www.mfrlegal.com

(Las Vegas, NV Office*: 600 South Tonopah Drive, Suite 300, 89106)
  (Tel: 702-699-7822)
  (Fax: 702-699-9455)
(Phoenix, AZ Office: 3420 East Shea Boulevard, Suite 200, 85028)
  (Tel: 602-258-0755)
  (Fax: 602-258-0755)

Insurance Litigation, Coverage Analysis, Insurance Coverage, Bad Faith, Subrogation, Construction Defect, Workers' Compensation, Probate, Civil Trial Practice

Firm Profile: Morales Fierro & Reeves specializes in insurance coverage advice and litigation. The firm has handled an extensive variety of coverage issues and has provided services, both in and out of litigation, involving the most complex issues arising in the field of commercial insurance.

Insurance Clients

ACE USA
HDI-Gerling America Insurance Company
Zurich North America
America First/One Beacon Insurance Company
Travelers Insurance Group

Partners

Ramiro Morales — California State University, B.S., 1988; University of San Francisco School of Law, J.D., 1993 — National Business Honor Society — Admitted to Bar, 1993, California; 1999, Nevada; 1994, Supreme Court of California; 2000, Supreme Court of Nevada; 2007, U.S. Court of Appeals,

Morales Fierro & Reeves, Pleasant Hill, CA   (Continued)

Ninth Circuit — Member Federation of Defense and Corporate Counsel — Faculty Speaker, State Bar of Nevada; Speaker, Insurance Law; Speaker, CDCMA Nevada Strategies Conference; MC2 Annual Conference; Western States Coverage — Languages: Spanish — E-mail: rmorales@mfrlegal.com

Christine M. Fierro — Santa Clara University, B.S. (magna cum laude), 1988; University of California, Berkeley, M.A., 1997; University of California, Berkeley Boalt Hall School of Law, J.D., 1997 — Admitted to Bar, 1997, California — E-mail: cfierro@mfrlegal.com

William C. Reeves — University of California, San Diego, B.A., 1993; University of California Davis School of Law, King Hall, J.D., 1996 — University of California at Davis Law Review — Admitted to Bar, 1996, California; 2002, Nevada; 2006, Arizona — E-mail: wreeves@mfrlegal.com

Marilyn A. Rogers — University of California, Berkeley, B.A., 1983; University of California, Hastings College of the Law, J.D., 1988 — Admitted to Bar, 1988, California — E-mail: mrogers@mfrlegal.com

Patrick M. Quigley — Loyola Marymount University, B.A., 1986; Pepperdine University School of Law, J.D., 1990 — Admitted to Bar, 1990, California — E-mail: pquigley@mfrlegal.com

Special Counsel

Eric D. Esser
Stacey Rocheleau

Associates

Elizabeth B. Celniker
Debra B. Branse
Aaron M. Davis
David A. Astengo
Laura Jane Coles
W. Brian Jones

PLEASANTON   70,285 Alameda Co.

Refer To

**Boornazian, Jensen & Garthe
A Professional Corporation**
555 12th Street, 18th Floor
Oakland, California 94607
  Telephone: 510-834-4350
  Fax: 510-839-1897

Mailing Address: P.O. Box 12925, Oakland, CA 94604-2925

Insurance Defense, Trial Practice, Product Liability, Legal Malpractice, Professional Malpractice, Medical Malpractice, Insurance Coverage, Construction Law

SEE COMPLETE LISTING UNDER OAKLAND, CALIFORNIA (30 MILES)

POMONA   149,058 Los Angeles Co.

Refer To

Borton Petrini, LLP
1461 Ford Street, Suite 201
Redlands, California 92373
  Telephone: 909-381-0527
  Fax: 909-381-0658

Mailing Address: P.O Box 11207, San Bernardino, CA 92423

Coverage Issues, Insurance Defense, Labor and Employment, Product Liability, Professional Errors and Omissions, Public Entities

SEE COMPLETE LISTING UNDER SAN BERNARDINO, CALIFORNIA (33 MILES)

PORTERVILLE 54,165 Tulare Co.

Refer To

Borton Petrini, LLP
5060 California Avenue, Suite 700
Bakersfield, California 93309
   Telephone: 661-322-3051
   Fax: 661-322-4628

Mailing Address: P.O. Box 2026, Bakersfield, CA 93303-2026

Administrative Law, Admiralty and Maritime Law, Agriculture, Appellate Practice, Bad Faith, Banking, Bankruptcy, Business Law, Business Litigation, Casualty Insurance Law, Church Law, Collections, Commercial Law, Contracts, Corporate Law, Coverage Issues, Creditor Rights, Eminent Domain, Employment Litigation, Environmental Law, Estate Planning, Family Law, Fire, Health Care, Insurance Coverage, Insurance Defense, Intellectual Property, Labor and Employment, Land Use, Oil and Gas, Personal Injury, Premises Liability, Probate, Product Liability, Professional Errors and Omissions, Property, Public Entities, Real Estate, Religious Institutions, Sports and Entertainment Liability, Toxic Torts, Transactional Law, Transportation, Unlawful Detainer Representing Landlords

SEE COMPLETE LISTING UNDER BAKERSFIELD, CALIFORNIA (51 MILES)

RANCHO CORDOVA 64,776 Sacramento Co.

Refer To

Borton Petrini, LLP
3110 Gold Canal Drive, Suite A
Rancho Cordova, California 95670
   Telephone: 916-858-1212
   Fax: 916-858-1252

Mailing Address: P.O. Box 277790, Sacramento, CA 95827

Construction Defect, Construction Law, Employment Litigation, Personal Injury, Product Liability, Professional Liability

SEE COMPLETE LISTING UNDER SACRAMENTO, CALIFORNIA (13 MILES)

RANCHO CUCAMONGA 165,269 San Bernardino Co.

Refer To

Borton Petrini, LLP
1461 Ford Street, Suite 201
Redlands, California 92373
   Telephone: 909-381-0527
   Fax: 909-381-0658

Mailing Address: P.O Box 11207, San Bernardino, CA 92423

Coverage Issues, Insurance Defense, Labor and Employment, Product Liability, Professional Errors and Omissions, Public Entities

SEE COMPLETE LISTING UNDER SAN BERNARDINO, CALIFORNIA (17 MILES)

RED BLUFF † 14,076 Tehama Co.

Refer To

Kenny, Snowden & Norine
A Law Corporation
2701 Park Marina Drive
Redding, California 96001
   Telephone: 530-225-8990
   Fax: 530-225-8944
   Toll Free: 800-655-6677

Mailing Address: Box 994608, Redding, CA 96099-4608

Insurance Defense, Medical Malpractice, Product Liability, Defense Litigation, Civil Trial Practice, Casualty, Professional Errors and Omissions, Employment Law, Public Entities, Real Estate, Land Use, Water Law, Equine Law

SEE COMPLETE LISTING UNDER REDDING, CALIFORNIA (30 MILES)

REDDING † 89,861 Shasta Co.

Hanna, Brophy, MacLean, McAleer & Jensen, LLP

2701 Park Marina Drive, First Floor
Redding, California 96001
   Telephone: 530-223-6010
   Fax: 530-223-0813
   www.hannabrophy.com

Established: 1943

Insurance Defense, Workers' Compensation, Subrogation, Labor and Employment, Employment Law, Litigation

Office Managing Partner

Kevin M. Roberts — California Northern School of Law, J.D., 1997 — Admitted to Bar, 1997, California — Member State Bar of California; Shasta County Bar Association — Certified Specialist, Workers' Compensation Law, State Bar of California Board of Legal Specialization

(See listing under Oakland, CA for additional information)

Kenny, Snowden & Norine
A Law Corporation

2701 Park Marina Drive
Redding, California 96001
   Telephone: 530-225-8990
   Fax: 530-225-8944
   Toll Free: 800-655-6677
   E-Mail: jnorine@lawksn.com
   www.lawksn.com

Established: 1980

Insurance Defense, Medical Malpractice, Product Liability, Defense Litigation, Civil Trial Practice, Casualty, Professional Errors and Omissions, Employment Law, Public Entities, Real Estate, Land Use, Water Law, Equine Law

Firm Profile: Kenny, Snowden & Norine serves all of Northern California, including the fourteen counties of: Shasta, Trinity, Humboldt, Lassen, Tehama, Del Norte, Siskiyou, Modoc, Mendocino, Glenn, Butte, Plumas, Sierra and Lake.

Insurance Clients

Admiral Insurance Company
ALLIED Insurance
American Bankers Insurance Company of Florida
American Motorists Insurance Company
American Safety Insurance Claims
Benchmark Insurance Company
California Casualty Management Company
Century Insurance Group
COUNTRY Financial
Crum & Forster Insurance
Cunningham Lindsey Claims Management, Inc.
Empire Insurance Group
E & O Professionals
Fireman's Fund Insurance Company
Harco National Insurance Company
Horace Mann Insurance Group
K & K Insurance Group, Inc.
AIG Claim Services, Inc.
America First/One Beacon Insurance Company
American Modern Home Insurance Company
American Reliable Insurance Company
Berkley Risk Administrators Company, LLC
Catholic Healthcare West
Chartis
Crawford & Company
Crusader Insurance Company
Dignity Health
The Doctors Company
Employers Reinsurance Corporation
Freese & Gianelli Claim Services
Gallagher Basset Services, Inc./Costco
The Hartford
Kemper Insurance Companies
Lexington Insurance Company

CALIFORNIA — REDLANDS

Kenny, Snowden & Norine, A Law Corporation, Redding, CA (Continued)

Liberty Insurance Services, Inc.
Meadowbrook Insurance Group
Mercury Casualty Company
Mutual of Omaha Group
Nautilus Insurance Company
Nonprofits' Insurance Alliance of California
Progressive Casualty Insurance Company
St. Paul Fire and Marine Insurance Company
Sequoia Insurance Company
TIG Insurance Company
Universal Underwriters Insurance Company
VELA Insurance
Wilshire Insurance Company
York Claims Service, Inc.
Lumbermens Mutual Casualty Company
Midwest Insurance Company
National Chiropractic Mutual Insurance Company
Professional Liability Insurance Company
QBE Agri
Safeco Insurance
Sentry Insurance a Mutual Company
State Farm Insurance Companies
United States Liability Insurance
USAA Casualty Insurance Company
Viking Insurance Company of Wisconsin
Zurich U.S.

Non-Insurance Clients

Save Mart Supermarkets

Firm Members

John S. Kenny — 1941 — University of San Francisco, B.A., 1963; University of California, Hastings College of the Law, J.D., 1966 — Admitted to Bar, 1966, California — Member State Bar of California; Shasta-Trinity County Bar Association; American Arbitration Association — U.S. Army [1967-1969] — Practice Areas: Environmental Litigation; Governmental Entity Defense; Municipal Law; Land Use — E-mail: jskenny@lawksn.com

Kelly J. Snowden — 1966 — San Diego State University, B.A., 1990; University of San Francisco School of Law, J.D., 1993 — Admitted to Bar, 1993, California; U.S. District Court, Northern District of California — Member State Bar of California; Shasta-Trinity County Bar Association; American Board of Trial Advocates — Practice Areas: Civil Litigation; Medical Malpractice — E-mail: ksnowden@lawksn.com

Jonz Norine — 1969 — Philipps-Universität, B.A.; California Lutheran University, B.A. (Dean's List), 1992; Hamline University School of Law, J.D. (Dean's List), 1995 — Admitted to Bar, 1996, California; U.S. District Court, Eastern and Northern Districts of California — Member State Bar of California; Shasta-Trinity County Bar Association; Association of Defense Counsel Trial Attorneys; Association of Defense Counsel — Languages: German — Practice Areas: Real Estate; Business Litigation; Employment Law; Personal Injury; Environmental Litigation; Product Liability; Premises Liability; Insurance Defense — E-mail: jnorine@lawksn.com

Associate

Linda R. Schaap — 1953 — Napa College School of Nursing, R.N., 1976; Empire College School of Law, J.D., 1994 — Top Student Award; Lifetime Academy of Science Award; West's Law High Honors Award — Admitted to Bar, 1994, California; 1995, U.S. District Court, Eastern and Northern Districts of California; 1999, U.S. Court of Appeals for the Federal and Ninth Circuits — Member State Bar of California; Shasta-Trinity County Bar Association — California Board of Registered Nursing; Missouri Board of Registered Nursing; Washington Board of Registered Nursing — Practice Areas: Civil Litigation; Medical Malpractice — E-mail: lschaap@lawksn.com

REDLANDS 68,747 San Bernardino Co.

Refer To

Thompson & Colegate LLP
3610 Fourteenth Street
Riverside, California 92501
Telephone: 951-682-5550
Fax: 951-781-4012

Mailing Address: P.O. Box 1299, Riverside, CA 92502

Insurance Defense, Medical Malpractice, Automobile Liability, General Liability, Construction Litigation, Coverage Issues, Personal Injury, Product Liability, Premises Liability, Employment Law, Commercial Litigation, Bankruptcy, Alternative Dispute Resolution, Appellate Practice, Complex Litigation, Real Estate

SEE COMPLETE LISTING UNDER RIVERSIDE, CALIFORNIA (14 MILES)

REDWOOD CITY † 76,815 San Mateo Co.

Ropers, Majeski, Kohn & Bentley
A Professional Corporation

1001 Marshall Street, Suite 500
Redwood City, California 94063
Telephone: 650-364-8200
Fax: 650-780-1701
www.rmkb.com

(Los Angeles, CA Office*: 515 South Flower Street, Suite 1100, 90071)
 (Tel: 213-312-2000)
 (Fax: 213-312-2001)
(San Francisco, CA Office*: 150 Spear Street, Suite 850, 94105)
 (Tel: 415-543-4800)
 (Fax: 415-972-6301)
(San Jose, CA Office*: 50 West San Fernando Street, Suite 1400, 95113)
 (Tel: 408-287-6262)
 (Fax: 408-918-4501)
(New York, NY Office*: 750 Third Avenue, 25th Floor, 10017)
 (Tel: 212-668-5927)
 (Fax: 212-668-5929)
(Boston, MA Office*: Ten Post Office Square, 8th Floor South, 02109)
 (Tel: 617-850-9087)
 (Fax: 617-850-9088)

Established: 1950

Antitrust, Appellate Practice, Business Litigation, Commercial Litigation, Civil Rights, Class Actions, Complex Litigation, Construction Law, Corporate Law, Elder Abuse, Employment Law, Entertainment Law, Environmental Law, ERISA, Estate Planning, Governmental Entity Defense, Health Care, Intellectual Property, International Law, Mergers and Acquisitions, Personal Injury, Premises Liability, Product Liability, Professional Liability, Real Estate, Toxic Torts, Asset Protection, Banking/Consumer Credit, Catastrophic Injury, Cost Control, Elder Rights, Fee Disputes, Insurance Services, IT and Business Process Outsourcing, Litigation Management, Non-Profit, Proposition 65, Special Education Law, Taxation, Wealth Management

Firm Profile: We pride ourselves on client relationships, pragmatic results and exceptional value. Offering premier litigation skills and a complete spectrum of business-oriented services, we solve problems, structure deals, and deliver results with complete client focus.

Insurance Clients

AIG Insurance Company
Chubb Group of Insurance Companies
Fireman's Fund Insurance Company
State Farm Insurance Companies
United Services Automobile Association (USAA)
California Casualty & Fire Insurance Company
Farmers Insurance Group
The Hartford Insurance Group
Markel Corporation
The Travelers Companies, Inc.

Partners

Frank J. Pagliaro, Jr. — 1940 — University of Vermont, B.A., 1963; Hague Academy of International Law, The Hague, Netherlands, 1965; University of Virginia School of Law, J.D., 1967 — Admitted to Bar, 1967, New York; 1970, California; 1967, U.S. District Court, Central, Eastern, Northern and Southern Districts of California; U.S. Court of Appeals, Ninth Circuit; U.S. Court of Federal Claims; U.S. Court of the Armed Forces — Member Inter-American, American, New York State and San Mateo County Bar Associations; State Bar of California; International Association of Defense Counsel; Defense Research Institute — Languages: French — Practice Areas: Construction Defect; Product Liability

Richard K. Wilson — 1949 — University of California, Berkeley, B.S., 1972; University of California, Hastings College of the Law, J.D., 1976 — Admitted to Bar, 1976, California; U.S. District Court, Central and Northern Districts of California; U.S. Court of Appeals, Ninth Circuit — Member State

Ropers, Majeski, Kohn & Bentley, A Professional Corporation, Redwood City, CA (Continued)

Bar of California; San Mateo County Bar Association; Association of Defense Counsel of Northern California and Nevada

Pamela E. Cogan — 1956 — University of Massachusetts Amherst, B.A. (cum laude), 1977; University of the Pacific, McGeorge School of Law, J.D. (cum laude), 1982 — Order of the Coif — Pacific Law Journal — Admitted to Bar, 1982, California; U.S. District Court, Eastern, Northern and Southern Districts of California; U.S. Court of Appeals, Ninth Circuit — Member American Bar Association; State Bar of California; International Association of Defense Counsel; Association of Defense Counsel of Northern California and Nevada — Practice Areas: Appellate Practice; Class Actions; Complex Litigation; ERISA; Insurance Defense; Bad Faith

Robert P. Andris, II — 1962 — San Jose State University, B.A., 1984; Santa Clara University School of Law, J.D., 1987 — Editor, Santa Clara Computer and High Technology Law Journal, Vol. 3, 1986 — Admitted to Bar, 1987, California; U.S. District Court, Central, Eastern, Northern and Southern Districts of California; U.S. Court of Appeals, Ninth Circuit; U.S. Court of Appeals for the Federal Circuit; U.S. Patent and Trademark Office — Member American Bar Association — Practice Areas: Intellectual Property; Patents; Product Liability

Todd A. Roberts — 1961 — University of Oregon, B.S., 1983; University of California, Davis School of Law, J.D., 1987 — Admitted to Bar, 1987, California; U.S. District Court, Central, Eastern, Northern and Southern Districts of California; U.S. District Court, District of Arizona; U.S. Court of Appeals, Ninth Circuit — Member Defense Research Institute; Federation of Defense and Corporate Counsel; Association of Defense Counsel of Northern California and Nevada — Practice Areas: Employment Litigation; Business Litigation; Commercial Litigation; Insurance Defense; Dispute Resolution

Susan H. Handelman — 1946 — Washington State University, B.A. (cum laude), 1985; Golden Gate University School of Law, J.D. (with honors), 1989 — Admitted to Bar, 1989, California; U.S. Court of Appeals, Ninth Circuit; U.S. Supreme Court — Member State Bar of California — Author: "When Will the Artful Pleading Doctrine Support Removal of a State Claim to Federal Court?," 18 Golden Gate Law Review 177 — Practice Areas: Appellate Practice; Insurance Defense

Chi-Hung A. Chan — 1947 — St. John's University, B.A., 1971; University of Pittsburgh, M.B.A., 1972; DePaul University; University of Santa Clara School of Law, J.D., 1981 — Admitted to Bar, 1982, California — Member American Bar Association; State Bar of California; American Immigration Lawyer Association; Hong Kong Mediation Association; Hong Kong Law Society; American Arbitration Association — Overseas Representative, Shanghai Foreign Service Company, 1995 — Languages: Mandarin Chinese, Cantonese, Taiwanese, Japanese — Practice Areas: Corporate Law; International Law; Mergers and Acquisitions

Francois G. Laugier — 1963 — Université de Montpellier, France, Master of Private Law, 1984; University of San Diego School of Law, LL.M., 1988 — Admitted to Bar, 1985, France; 1989, California — Member French-American Chamber of Commerce (Past President); French Ministry of Economy and Finance — Languages: French — Practice Areas: Corporate Law; International Law; Mergers and Acquisitions

Enrique Marinez — 1965 — Occidental College, A.B., 1987; Whittier Law School, J.D., 1992 — Admitted to Bar, 1992, California; U.S. District Court, Central District of California; 1998, U.S. District Court, Eastern, Northern and Southern Districts of California — Member Hispanic National Bar Association — Languages: Spanish — Practice Areas: Business Litigation; Commercial Litigation; Insurance Defense; Professional Liability

John M. Bentley — 1929 — University of San Francisco, B.A., 1952; University of San Francisco School of Law, LL.B., 1955 — Admitted to Bar, 1955, California; U.S. Court of Appeals, Ninth Circuit; U.S. Supreme Court — Member American and San Mateo County Bar Associations; State Bar of California; Association of Defense Counsel, Northern California; American Board of Trial Advocates; International Association of Defense Counsel; Federation of Insurance Counsel; American Board of Professional Liability Attorneys; Fellow, International Academy of Trial Lawyers; American College of Trial Lawyers

David M. McLaughlin — 1961 — University of California, Los Angeles, B.A., 1983; Santa Clara University School of Law, J.D., 1987 — Admitted to Bar, 1987, California; U.S. District Court, Central, Northern and Southern Districts of California; 1988, U.S. District Court, Eastern District of California — Member State Bar of California; San Mateo and Santa Clara County Bar Associations; Association of Defense Counsel of Northern California and Nevada — Practice Areas: Employment Litigation; Business Litigation; Commercial Litigation; Product Liability; Catastrophic Injury; Personal Injury

Ropers, Majeski, Kohn & Bentley, A Professional Corporation, Redwood City, CA (Continued)

Dean A. Pappas — 1954 — California State University, Chico, B.A., 1975; University of San Francisco School of Law, J.D., 1984 — Admitted to Bar, 1984, California; U.S. District Court, Central, Eastern, Northern and Southern Districts of California — Member State Bar of California; Santa Clara County Bar Association; Association of Defense Counsel of Northern California and Nevada — Practice Areas: Insurance Litigation; Insurance Coverage

Jennifer E. Acheson — 1955 — The University of Kansas, B.A., 1980; University of San Francisco School of Law, J.D., 1985 — Admitted to Bar, 1985, California — Member State Bar of California; San Mateo County Bar Association — Practice Areas: Appellate Practice; Insurance Litigation

Jesshill E. Love, III — Chief Operating Officer — 1970 — Connecticut College, B.A., 1993; Golden Gate University, M.B.A., 2000; Golden Gate University School of Law, J.D., 1999 — Admitted to Bar, 2000, California — Member American and Sam Mateo Bar Associations; State Bar of California — Languages: Spanish — Practice Areas: Real Estate; Intellectual Property; Estate Planning

Kristina H. Chung — 1964 — University of Michigan - Ann Arbor, B.A., 1986; Indiana University School of Law-Bloomington, J.D., 1991 — Admitted to Bar, 1993, California; Illinois — Member State Bar of California; Illinois State Bar Association — Practice Areas: Employment Litigation; Dispute Resolution

Lael D. Andara — 1972 — University of California, Santa Cruz, B.A., 1998; University of the Pacific, McGeorge School of Law, J.D., 2001 — Admitted to Bar, 2001, California; New York; District of Columbia; U.S. District Court, Northern District of California; U.S. Court of Appeals, Ninth Circuit; 2004, U.S. Court of Appeal for the Federal Circuit; 2004, U.S. District Court, Central District of California; U.S. District Court for the District of Columbia; U.S. District Court, Eastern and Southern Districts of California; U.S. District Court, District of Colorado; U.S. District Court, Eastern District of Michigan; U.S. Patent and Trademark Office — Member San Mateo County and Santa Clara County Bar Associations; American Intellectual Property Law Association — Practice Areas: Intellectual Property; Patents; Corporate Law

Robert M. Forni, Jr. — 1969 — University of Pennsylvania, B.A. (cum laude), 1992; Santa Clara University School of Law, J.D., 1995 — Admitted to Bar, 1995, California; U.S. District Court, Northern District of California; 1996, U.S. District Court, Southern District of California; 2001, U.S. District Court, Central and Eastern Districts of California; U.S. Court of Appeals, Ninth Circuit — Member State Bar of California; Bar Association of San Francisco; Golden Gate Business Association (Board of Directors); San Francisco Small Business Network (SBN) — Practice Areas: Appellate Practice; ERISA; Insurance Litigation; Bad Faith

Elise R. Vasquez — 1964 — University of California, Berkeley, A.B. (summa cum laude), 1992; Golden Gate University School of Law, J.D., 1998 — Admitted to Bar, 1999, California; U.S. District Court, Central, Eastern, Northern and Southern Districts of California — Member State Bar of California — Practice Areas: Employment Litigation; Dispute Resolution; Business Litigation; Commercial Litigation; Intellectual Property

Nicole S. Healy — University of California, Davis, B.A./B.S., 1985; University of California at Los Angeles School of the Law, J.D., 1991 — Admitted to Bar, 1992, California; U.S. District Court, Northern District of California; U.S. Court of Appeals, Fourth, Ninth, Tenth and Eleventh Circuits — Member State Bar of California — Practice Areas: Business Litigation; Commercial Litigation; Directors and Officers Liability

Brock R. Lyle — 1978 — Brigham Young University, B.A., 2002; Washington University in St. Louis School of Law, J.D., 2005 — Admitted to Bar, 2006, California; U.S. District Court, Central, Eastern, Northern and Southern Districts of California; U.S. Court of Appeals, Ninth Circuit; Supreme Court of the United States — Member San Mateo County Bar Association (Board of Directors); Barristers Club of San Mateo; J. Reuben Clark Society; BYU Manangement Society, Silicon Valley Chapter — Languages: French — Practice Areas: Business Litigation; Commercial Litigation; Corporate Law; Employment Litigation; Dispute Resolution; Insurance Litigation; Intellectual Property; International Law

Matthew D. Zumstein — 1970 — University of California, Los Angeles, B.A., 1993; University of the Pacific, McGeorge School of Law, J.D., 1998 — Admitted to Bar, 1999, California; U.S. District Court, Central, Eastern, Northern and Southern Districts of California — Member San Mateo County Bar Association; National Association of the Remodeling Industry; Defense Research Institute — United Way; San Mateo County Association of Realtors — Practice Areas: Business Litigation; Commercial Litigation; Catastrophic Injury; Personal Injury; Construction Litigation; Product Liability; Premises Liability; Toxic Torts

CALIFORNIA

Ropers, Majeski, Kohn & Bentley, A Professional Corporation, Redwood City, CA (Continued)

John G. Dooling — 1962 — University of San Francisco, B.S., 1984; San Francisco Law School, J.D., 1991 — Admitted to Bar, 1991, California; U.S. District Court, Northern District of California — Member State Bar of California; St. Thomas More Society of San Francisco; The Olympic Club of San Francisco — Licensed California Real Estate Broker; Sovereign Military Order of Malta — Practice Areas: Real Estate; Business Litigation; Commercial Litigation; Product Liability; Corporate Law; Professional Liability

Michon M. Spinelli — 1976 — Santa Clara University School of Law, J.D. (magna cum laude), 2000 — Admitted to Bar, 2002, California; Nevada — Member Bar Association of San Francisco; The McFetridge Inn of Court; Northern Nevada Women Lawyers Association; Association of Defense Counsel of Northern California and Nevada — Practice Areas: Catastrophic Injury; Product Liability; Premises Liability; Real Estate; Construction Litigation; Governmental Entity Defense

Stacy M. Tucker — 1973 — University of Illinois at Chicago, B.A. (cum laude), 1994; University of Illinois College of Law, J.D., 2001 — Admitted to Bar, 2002, California; 2011, Washington; U.S. District Court, Central, Eastern, Northern and Southern Districts of California; U.S. District Court, Eastern and Western Districts of Washington; U.S. Court of Appeals for the District of Columbia and Ninth Circuits — Member State Bar of California; Washington State Bar Association; Bar Associations of the District of Columbia and San Francisco; American Intellectual Property Law Association; American Health Lawyers Association — Practice Areas: Appellate; Bad Faith; ERISA; Intellectual Property; Business Litigation; Commercial Litigation; Insurance Litigation; Health Care

Associates

Michael D. Kanach	Blake J. Russum
Ramon A. Miyar	Jordan R. Beckerman
Norman Lau	Christopher R. Mezzetti
Colette R. Thomason	Laura L. Reidenbach

Of Counsel

Michael J. Brady — 1941 — Stanford University, A.B., 1964; Harvard Law School, LL.B., 1967 — Admitted to Bar, 1967, California — Member State Bar of California; San Mateo County Bar Association; Bar Association of San Francisco; California Academy of Appellate Lawyers; International Association of Insurance Counsel (President, 1992); Association of Defense Counsel, Northern California; Defense Research Institute; Federation of Defense and Corporate Counsel — Author: "Stop Blaming Everyone Else," (Silicon Valley biz ink, April 11, 2003); "The Arbitration That Cannot be Stopped," (Metropolitan Corporate Counsel Journal; Vol. 11, No. 6, June 2003); "A New Predictability in Punitive Damages?," (For the Defense, Vol. 45, No. 6, June 2003); "The Amazing New World of Punitive Damages," (Federation Flyer, November 2003); "Do State OSHA Regulations Apply to Homeowners?," (Federation of Insurance & Corporate Counsel, Quarterly, Vol. 54, No. 2, Winter, 2004); "State of the Law After Campbell v. State Farm: How Goes It In California and the Nation Concerning Punitive Damages?," (ADC Defense Comment, Vol. 20., No. 1, Spring 2005) — Practice Areas: Appellate Practice; Insurance Defense; Bad Faith

Steven G. Wood — 1952 — University of California, Los Angeles, B.A. (summa cum laude), 1984; University of California at Los Angeles School of the Law, J.D., 1987 — Admitted to Bar, 1987, California; U.S. District Court, Central, Eastern, Northern and Southern Districts of California; U.S. Court of Appeals, Ninth Circuit — Practice Areas: Real Estate; Corporate Law; Real Estate Agents & Brokers Liability; Directors and Officers Liability; Intellectual Property; Business Litigation; Commercial Litigation

The following firms also service this area.

Bledsoe, Cathcart, Diestel, Pedersen & Treppa LLP
601 California Street, 16th Floor
San Francisco, California 94108
  Telephone: 415-981-5411
  Fax: 415-981-0352

Civil Trial Practice, State and Federal Courts, Product Liability, Insurance Defense, Insurance Coverage, Personal Injury, Construction Law, Employment Law, Business Law, Environmental Law, Landlord Tenant, Commercial Transportation, Copyright Litigation, Banking and Finance, Lender Liability

SEE COMPLETE LISTING UNDER SAN FRANCISCO, CALIFORNIA (25 MILES)

Boornazian, Jensen & Garthe A Professional Corporation
555 12th Street, 18th Floor
Oakland, California 94607
  Telephone: 510-834-4350
  Fax: 510-839-1897
Mailing Address: P.O. Box 12925, Oakland, CA 94604-2925

Insurance Defense, Trial Practice, Product Liability, Legal Malpractice, Professional Malpractice, Medical Malpractice, Insurance Coverage, Construction Law

SEE COMPLETE LISTING UNDER OAKLAND, CALIFORNIA (35 MILES)

RIDGECREST 27,616 Kern Co.

Refer To

Borton Petrini, LLP
5060 California Avenue, Suite 700
Bakersfield, California 93309
  Telephone: 661-322-3051
  Fax: 661-322-4628
Mailing Address: P.O. Box 2026, Bakersfield, CA 93303-2026

Administrative Law, Admiralty and Maritime Law, Agriculture, Appellate Practice, Bad Faith, Banking, Bankruptcy, Business Law, Business Litigation, Casualty Insurance Law, Church Law, Collections, Commercial Law, Contracts, Corporate Law, Coverage Issues, Creditor Rights, Eminent Domain, Employment Litigation, Environmental Law, Estate Planning, Family Law, Fire, Health Care, Insurance Coverage, Insurance Defense, Intellectual Property, Labor and Employment, Land Use, Oil and Gas, Personal Injury, Premises Liability, Probate, Product Liability, Professional Errors and Omissions, Property, Public Entities, Real Estate, Religious Institutions, Sports and Entertainment Liability, Toxic Torts, Transactional Law, Transportation, Unlawful Detainer Representing Landlords

SEE COMPLETE LISTING UNDER BAKERSFIELD, CALIFORNIA (122 MILES)

RIVERSIDE † 303,871 Riverside Co.

Garrett & Jensen

3390 Orange Street
Riverside, California 92501
  Telephone: 951-781-0222
  Fax: 951-781-0221
  E-Mail: boyd@boydjensen.com
  www.boydjensen.com

Established: 1965

Personal Injury, Premises Liability, Construction Defect, Business Litigation, Amusement Industry Litigation

Non-Insurance Clients

Bosco Legal Services, Inc.	CalPRO, LLC
Ray Cammack Shows, Inc.	Choice Transportation, LP
FiberCo Inc.	International Association of
Knott's Berry Farm	Amusement Parks and
Attractions	
Lagoon Corporation	National R.V.
Six Flags Theme Parks, Inc.	Trademark Plastics, Inc.

Firm Members

Boyd F. Jensen II — The University of Utah, B.A.; Pepperdine University, J.D., 1979 — Admitted to Bar, 1979, California; 1980, Utah — Member American, Orange County and Riverside County Bar Associations; State Bar of California; Wyoming State Bar; International Association of Amusement Parks and Attractions (Safety Committee); International Amusements and Leisure Defense Association (Past President); Amusement Industry Manufacturers and Suppliers; Association of Southern California Defense Counsel; American Board of Trial Advocates — E-mail: boyd@boydjensen.com

Betty L. Fracisco — University of San Francisco, B.A. (cum laude), 1968; E.D. (cum laude), 1969; Western State University, J.D. (with honors), 1990 — Admitted to Bar, 1990, California; U.S. District Court, Central and Eastern Districts of California — Member American and Orange County Bar Associations; California Women Lawyers (Board of Governors); Orange

RIVERSIDE   CALIFORNIA

Garrett & Jensen, Riverside, CA (Continued)

County Women Lawyers Association (Past President); Association of Southern California Defense Counsel — E-mail: betty@boydjensen.com

Hanna, Brophy, MacLean, McAleer & Jensen, LLP

1500 Iowa Avenue, Suite 220
Riverside, California 92507
   Telephone: 951-779-9415
   Fax: 951-779-9494
   www.hannabrophy.com

Established: 1943

Insurance Defense, Workers' Compensation, Subrogation, Labor and Employment, Employment Law, Litigation

Office Managing Partner

Todd E. Ewing — University of San Diego School of Law, J.D., 1992 — Admitted to Bar, 1992, California — Certified Specialist, Workers' Compensation Law, State Bar of California Board of Legal Specialization

(See listing under Oakland, CA for additional information)

Kinkle, Rodiger & Spriggs
Professional Corporation

3333 Fourteenth Street
Riverside, California 92501-3809
   Telephone: 951-683-2410
   Toll Free: 800-235-2039
   Fax: 951-683-7759
   E-Mail: krsinfo@krs-law.com
   www.krs-law.com

Established: 1960

Insurance Defense, Self-Insured, General Liability, Product Liability, Automobile, Premises Liability, Public Entities, Construction Law, Professional Liability, Coverage Issues, Bad Faith, Civil Trial Practice, Appellate Practice, Federal Courts

Firm Profile: The law firm of Kinkle, Rodiger and Spriggs was organized in Los Angeles, California, in 1960 as a civil litigation defense firm handling such matters as products liability, medical and professional malpractice, automobile accidents, slip and fall cases, false arrest, construction defect and inspection cases, aviation law, flood control, government entities, law enforcement related incidents, and environmental pollution claims.

The firm is headquartered in Riverside and services all Federal, Superior and Municipal courts and Courts of Appeal in Southern California, as well as the United States Supreme Court.

Insurance Clients

Mercury Insurance Company   Progressive Casualty Insurance Company

Director

Scott B. Spriggs — 1960 — University of Southern California, B.S., 1981; Southwestern University School of Law, J.D., 1984 — Admitted to Bar, 1985, California; U.S. District Court, Central District of California — Member State Bar of California; Riverside County Bar Association; USC Alumni Association; American Board of Trial Advocates; Association of Southern California Defense Counsel — E-mail: sspriggs@krs-law.com

Associates

Michael F. Moon — 1959 — National University, B.A. (magna cum laude), 1997; Thomas Jefferson School of Law, J.D., 2000 — Admitted to Bar, 2001, California; U.S. District Court, Central and Northern Districts of California;

Kinkle, Rodiger & Spriggs, Professional Corporation, Riverside, CA (Continued)

U.S. Court of Appeals, Ninth Circuit — Member State Bar of California; Riverside County Bar Association — E-mail: mmoon@krs-law.com

David A. Poull — 1987 — University of California, Riverside, B.A. (magna cum laude), 2009; Loyola Law School, J.D., 2012 — Admitted to Bar, 2013, California — Member State Bar of California; Orange County Bar Association

Matthew C. Anderson — 1967 — Southeastern Louisiana University, B.A., 1989; Western State University College of Law, J.D., 1995 — Admitted to Bar, 1995, California; 1996, U.S. District Court, Central District of California; 1999, U.S. District Court, Southern District of California — Member American Bar Association; Association of Trial Lawyers of America — E-mail: manderson@krs-law.com

(See listing under Los Angeles, CA for additional information)

Thompson & Colegate LLP

3610 Fourteenth Street
Riverside, California 92501
   Telephone: 951-682-5550
   Fax: 951-781-4012
   E-Mail: info@tclaw.net
   www.tclaw.net

Established: 1915

Insurance Defense, Medical Malpractice, Automobile Liability, General Liability, Construction Litigation, Coverage Issues, Personal Injury, Product Liability, Premises Liability, Employment Law, Commercial Litigation, Bankruptcy, Alternative Dispute Resolution, Appellate Practice, Complex Litigation, Real Estate

Firm Profile: In 2015 Thompson & Colegate LLP celebrates its 100th anniversary as a full service law firm handling litigation and transactional matters for its clients. The firm provides a broad range of legal services to insurance carriers, educational institutions, school districts, healthcare providers, governmental entities, businesses and individuals throughout California. The firm's practice was built on a tradition of excellence and integrity in providing legal services. The firm's commitment and approach is to understand client objectives and identify the most practical ways to accomplish them. Members of the firm are regularly involved in and serve on boards for community activities and organizations.

Insurance Clients

Carl Warren & Company	CorVel Corporation
Dignity Health	Gallagher Bassett Services, Inc.
Glatfelter Claims Management, Inc.	Keenan & Associates
	Motorists Insurance Group
Norcal Mutual Insurance Company	Philadelphia Insurance Companies
Travelers Insurance Companies	Zurich Insurance Company

Non-Insurance Clients

Altura Credit Union	Alvord Unified School District
Chino Valley Unified School District	Jurupa Unified School District
	Phillips & Jordan Inc.
Provident Savings Bank	Riverside Unified School District
Security Paving Company, Inc.	Skanska USA Civil West
Visterra Credit Union	California District, Inc.

Self-Insured Clients

County of Riverside   County of San Bernardino

Partners

H. L. Thompson — (1885-1962)
Roy W. Colegate — (1906-1960)
John W. Marshall — 1946 — St. Francis College, New York, B.A., 1967; Fordham University, M.A., 1968; Pepperdine University, J.D., 1978 — Law Review — Admitted to Bar, 1978, California; U.S. District Court, Central District of California; U.S. Court of Appeals, Ninth Circuit; U.S. Supreme Court — Member State Bar of California; Riverside County Bar Association; Association of Southern California Defense Counsel (Board of Directors, 1986-1998; President, 1996); American Board of Trial Advocates (President,

CALIFORNIA — RIVERSIDE

Thompson & Colegate LLP, Riverside, CA (Continued)

Riverside/San Bernardino Chapter, 1999; California Board of Directors, 1998-2000; National Board of Directors, 1999-2000); Riverside County Barristers (President, 1981-1982); Civil and Small Claims Advisory Committee, Judicial Council of California, 2000-2003; California Defense Counsel (President, 2002; Board of Directors, 1997-2003); Federation of Defense and Corporate Counsel; American College of Trial Lawyers — E-mail: jmarshall@tclaw.net

John A. Boyd — 1954 — San Diego State University, B.S., 1976; Pepperdine University, J.D. (cum laude), 1979 — Admitted to Bar, 1979, California; 1979, U.S. Supreme Court; 1982, U.S. District Court, Central and Southern Districts of California; U.S. Bankruptcy Court, Central and Southern Districts of California; 2011, U.S. Bankruptcy Court, Eastern and Northern Districts of California — Member State Bar of California; Riverside County Bar Association — E-mail: jboyd@tclaw.net

Michael J. Marlatt — 1957 — University of Southern California; California Polytechnic State University, B.A., 1981; Pepperdine University, J.D., 1984 — Phi Alpha Delta — NASA Achievement Award Recipient; Research Associate, University of Southern California School of Medicine — Admitted to Bar, 1984, California; 1984, U.S. District Court, Central District of California; 1984, U.S. Court of Appeals, Ninth Circuit — Member State Bar of California; Riverside County Bar Association; Association of Southern California Defense Counsel (Board of Directors); California Association of Healthcare Managers (Past Bylaws Committee); American Board of Trial Advocates (Past President, San Bernardino/Riverside Chapter; Masters in Trial); Southern California Association of Healthcare Risk Managers; California Association of School Business Officials — Lecturer: University of Amsterdam Law School, Princeton University and Loma Linda University School of Medicine; Chairman, Civil Law Program, University of California at Riverside; Civil Bench and Bar Committee of the Superior Court (Attorney Member); Arbitrator, Mediator and Judge Pro Tem, Riverside Superior Court; AV-Rated, Martindale Hubbell; Listed in Super Lawyers and Best Lawyers; American Medical Association; California State Association of Counties Excess Insurance Carrier Progam — E-mail: mmarlatt@tclaw.net

Diane Mar Wiesmann — 1961 — The University of Arizona, B.A., 1983; J.D., 1986 — Admitted to Bar, 1986, California; 1998, U.S. District Court, Central District of California — Member State Bar of California; Riverside County Bar Association; Bench-Bar Coalition; Association of Southern California Defense Counsel (President 2012); Southern California Association of Healthcare Risk Management; Defense Research Institute — American Red Cross, Riverside Chapter (Board of Directors); National Charity League, Riverside Chapter — E-mail: dwiesmann@tclaw.net

Gary T. Montgomery — 1967 — Princeton University, A.B., 1989; Pepperdine University, J.D., 1993 — Admitted to Bar, 1993, California; 1993, U.S. District Court, Central District of California — Member State Bar of California; Riverside County Bar Association; Riverside County Barristers; Board of Directors, University of California at Riverside Athletic Association (2001-2007); Association of Southern California Defense Counsel (Board of Directors) — Riverside Chamber of Commerce, Downtown Division (Board of Directors) — E-mail: gmontgomery@tclaw.net

Craig M. Marshall — 1971 — University of California, Riverside, B.A. (magna cum laude, Phi Beta Kappa), 1995; Pepperdine University, M.B.A., 1998; Pepperdine University School of Law, J.D. (cum laude), 1999 — Academic All-American; Straus Institute Certificate of Dispute Resolution; Political Science Dept.-Graduating Senior Award — Admitted to Bar, 1999, California; Supreme Court of California — Member American and Riverside Bar Associations; State Bar of California — E-mail: cmarshall@tclaw.net

Associates

Lisa V. Todd — 1962 — Schiller International University, Heidelberg, Germany (Dean's List), 1982; Loyola Marymount University, B.A., 1984; University of Santa Clara, J.D., 1987 — Admitted to Bar, 1987, California; 1993, Colorado; 1989, U.S. District Court, Central District of California — Member State Bar of California; Riverside County Bar Association; Leo A. Deegan Inn of Court (1994-1996, 1997-1998); Association of Southern California Defense Counsel — E-mail: ltodd@tclaw.net

William A. Pennell — 1969 — California State Polytechnic University, B.S. Mech. Engr., 1995; Western State University, J.D., 1999 — Admitted to Bar, 2001, California; 2013, Colorado; U.S. District Court, Central District of California; 2003, U.S. Patent and Trademark Office — Member State Bar of California; Riverside County Bar Association; Association of Southern California Defense Counsel — E-mail: wpennell@tclaw.net

Susan Knock Brennecke — 1954 — Riverside City College, A.A. (with honors), 1984; University of La Verne, J.D., 2003 — Supervising Staff Editor/Senior Staff Writer, University of La Verne Journal of Juvenile Law — Admitted to Bar, 2004, California; 2004, U.S. District Court, Central District

Thompson & Colegate LLP, Riverside, CA (Continued)

of California; 2006, U.S. Court of Appeals, Ninth Circuit; 2010, U.S. Supreme Court — Member State Bar of California; Riverside County Bar Association (Past Chair, Appellate Section); Leo A. Deegan Inn of Court (2006-2009); Association of Southern California Defense Counsel (Amicus Committee) — E-mail: sbrennecke@tclaw.net

Kelly Moran — 1984 — University of California, Riverside, B.A. (cum laude), 2006; B.A.P.S. (cum laude), 2006; Pepperdine University School of Law, J.D., 2009 — Admitted to Bar, 2009, California; U.S. District Court, Central District of California — Certificate in Dispute Resolution - Pepperdine University School of Law — Languages: Spanish — E-mail: kmoran@tclaw.net

Maxine M. Morisaki — 1951 — California State University, Los Angeles, B.A., 1972; M.A., 1983; Loyola Law School, J.D., 1986 — Admitted to Bar, 1988, California; U.S. District Court, Central District of California; U.S. Court of Appeals, Ninth Circuit — Member Riverside County Bar Association — E-mail: mmorisaki@tclaw.net

Mark W. Regus — University of California, Santa Barbara, B.A. (with honors), 2008; University of California, Hastings College of the Law, J.D. (cum laude), 2011 — Witkin Award for Excellence in Civil Procedure II, Personal Injury Law and Trial Advocacy — Admitted to Bar, 2011, California; U.S. District Court, Central and Northern Districts of California — Member Riverside County and Los Angeles County Bar Associations — E-mail: mregus@tclaw.net

Binu V. Cloud — 1983 — University of California, Irvine, B.A. (cum laude), 2004; Pepperdine University School of Law, J.D., 2007 — Admitted to Bar, 2008, California; U.S. District Court, Central District of California; 2014, U.S. District Court, Eastern, Northern and Southern Districts of California — E-mail: bcloud@tclaw.net

Charmaine E. Grant — 1974 — University of California, Riverside, B.A., 1996; California Western School of Law, J.D., 2000 — Admitted to Bar, 2002, California — Member Riverside County and Western San Bernardino Bar Associations — Languages: Tagalog — E-mail: cgrant@tclaw.net

---

The following firms also service this area.

Berman Berman Berman Schneider & Lowary LLP
11900 West Olympic Boulevard, Suite 600
Los Angeles, California 90064-1151
Telephone: 310-447-9000
Fax: 310-447-9011

Insurance Defense, Insurance Coverage, Construction Defect, Product Liability, Employment Law, Professional Liability, Legal, Insurance Agents, Agent/Broker Liability, Medical Malpractice Defense, Design Professionals, Accountants, Trucking Law, Transportation, Real Estate Agents, Brokers and Appraisers, Elder Care, Monitoring Counsel, Litigation Management, California Insurance Regulations and Consulting to Insurance Industry

SEE COMPLETE LISTING UNDER LOS ANGELES, CALIFORNIA (56 MILES)

Borton Petrini, LLP
1461 Ford Street, Suite 201
Redlands, California 92373
Telephone: 909-381-0527
Fax: 909-381-0658

Mailing Address: P.O Box 11207, San Bernardino, CA 92423

Coverage Issues, Insurance Defense, Labor and Employment, Product Liability, Professional Errors and Omissions, Public Entities

SEE COMPLETE LISTING UNDER SAN BERNARDINO, CALIFORNIA (10 MILES)

Mollis & Mollis, Inc.
4621 Teller Avenue, Suite 200
Newport Beach, California 92660
Telephone: 949-222-0735
Fax: 949-955-0252

Insurance Defense, Civil Trial Practice, Business Law, Construction Law, Corporate Law, Appeals, Labor Law, Environmental Law, Real Estate, Estate Planning, Trusts, Probate, Trust and Estate Litigation, Taxation, Trust Settlement

SEE COMPLETE LISTING UNDER NEWPORT BEACH, CALIFORNIA (42 MILES)

SACRAMENTO | CALIFORNIA

Pyka Lenhardt Schnaider Zell
837 North Ross Street
Santa Ana, California 92701
   Telephone: 714-835-9011
   Fax: 714-667-7806
Mailing Address: P.O. Box 1558, Santa Ana, CA 92702-1558

Automobile, Business Litigation, Catastrophic Injury, Civil Litigation, Civil Rights, Construction Accidents, Construction Defect, Labor and Employment, Municipal Liability, Personal Injury, Police Liability Defense, Premises Liability, Product Liability, Professional Liability, Public Entities, School Law, Trucking, Uninsured and Underinsured Motorist, Wrongful Death, Wrongful Termination, Homeowners Association Litigation, Utility Defense

SEE COMPLETE LISTING UNDER SANTA ANA, CALIFORNIA (39 MILES)

SACRAMENTO † 466,488 Sacramento Co.

Borton Petrini, LLP

3110 Gold Canal Drive, Suite A
Rancho Cordova, California 95670
   Telephone: 916-858-1212
   Fax: 916-858-1252
   E-Mail: bpsac@bortonpetrini.com
   www.bortonpetrini.com

Established: 1899

Construction Defect, Construction Law, Employment Litigation, Personal Injury, Product Liability, Professional Liability

Firm Profile: Since 1899, Borton Petrini, LLP, has offered high quality legal services in all of the practice areas described above through its California network of 10 regional offices. The mission of Borton Petrini, LLP is to treat every file as though we were representing ourselves and paying the bill for that representation.

Managing Partner

Mark S. Newman — 1955 — University of California, Davis, B.A., 1977; University of the Pacific, McGeorge School of Law, J.D., 1982 — Admitted to Bar, 1982, California; 1982, U.S. District Court, Northern District of California; 1984, U.S. District Court, Eastern District of California; 2006, U.S. Court of Appeals, Ninth Circuit — Member State Bar of California; Sacramento County Bar Association; Association of Defense Counsel, Northern California — Editor, "Amicus Curious," California Defense Magazine — Unfair Claims Settlement Practices Regulations, Elder Law (Lecturer) — E-mail: mnewman@bortonpetrini.com

Partners

Elizabeth W. Lawley — 1973 — Seattle University, B.A., 1995; California Northern School of Law, J.D., 1999 — Admitted to Bar, 2000, California — Member State Bar of California; Sacramento County Bar Association — E-mail: elawley@bortonpetrini.com

Manish Parikh — 1974 — University of Delhi, B.A. (with honors), 1995; LL.B., 1999; Golden Gate University School of Law, LL.M., 2002 — Admitted to Bar, 2006, California — Member State Bar of California; Bar Council of India — International Students Association, Golden Gate University (Treasurer, 2002) — Languages: Hindi — E-mail: mparikh@bortonpetrini.com

Associates

Gino Cano — San Jose State University, B.A., 1995; University of Santa Clara School of Law, J.D., 1998 — Admitted to Bar, 1999, California — Member State Bar of California — E-mail: gcano@bortonpetrini.com

Alma Torlak — 1980 — University of Louisville, B.A., 2003; M.A., 2007; Louis D. Brandeis School of Law, University of Louisville, J.D., 2012 — Admitted to Bar, 2013, California — Member State Bar of California — E-mail: atorlak@bortonpetrini.com

Tahmina Yassine — 1986 — University of California, San Diego, B.A., 2008; University of the Pacific, McGeorge School of Law, J.D., 2012 — Admitted to Bar, 2012, California — Member State Bar of California — E-mail: tyassine@bortonpetrini.com

Borton Petrini, LLP, Sacramento, CA (Continued)

Sara A. Anderson — 1985 — University of California, Santa Cruz, B.A., 2007; Lincoln Law School of Sacramento, J.D., 2013 — Admitted to Bar, 2013, California — Member Sacramento Bar Association — E-mail: sanderson@bortonpetrini.com

Senior Counsel

Jason R. Sherlock — California State University, Sacramento, B.A., 2005; Thomas Jefferson School of Law, J.D., 2007 — Admitted to Bar, 2008, California; 2010, U.S. District Court, Eastern District of California — Member American, Sacramento County (Family Law Division) and Placer County Bar Associations; State Bar of California — E-mail: jsherlock@bortonpetrini.com

Christensen Ehret

2485 Natomas Park Drive, Suite 315
Sacramento, California 95814
   Telephone: 916-443-6909
   Fax: 916-313-0645
   www.christensenlaw.com

(Chicago, IL Office*: 135 South LaSalle Street, Suite 4200, 60603)
   (Tel: 312-634-1014)
   (Fax: 312-634-1018)
   (E-Mail: mchristensen@christensenlaw.com)
   (E-Mail: law@christensenlaw.com)
(Torrance, CA Office*: 1629 Cravens Avenue, 90501)
   (Tel: 310-222-8680)
   (Fax: 310-222-5752)

Construction Law, Employment Law, Energy, Insurance Law, Product Liability, Reinsurance, Subrogation, Maritime Law, Banking, Financial and Professional Liability

(See listing under Chicago, IL for additional information)

Clinton & Clinton

770 'L' Street, Suite 950
Sacramento, California 95814
   Telephone: 916-361-6060
   Fax: 916-361-6061
   E-Mail: dclinton@clinton-clinton.com
   www.clinton-clinton.com

(Long Beach, CA Office*: 100 Oceangate, Suite 1400, 90802)
   (Tel: 562-216-5000)
   (Fax: 562-216-5001)
(Los Angeles, CA Office*: 5757 West Century Boulevard, Suite 700, 90045)
   (Tel: 310-242-8615)
   (Fax: 310-242-8612)
(San Diego, CA Office*: 525 "B" Street, Suite 1500, 92101)
   (Tel: 619-858-4728)
   (Fax: 619-858-4729)
(San Francisco, CA Office*: 201 Spear Street, Suite 1100, 94105)
   (Tel: 415-230-5368)
   (Fax: 415-230-5369)
(Irvine, CA Office*: 2030 Main Street, Suite 1300, 92614)
   (Tel: 949-260-9083)
   (Fax: 949-260-9084)
(Calabasas, CA Office: 23480 Park Sorrento, Suite 219A, 91302)
   (Tel: 562-216-5000)
   (Fax: 562-216-5001)
(Birmingham, AL Office: 1 Chase Corporate Center, Suite 400, 35244)
   (Tel: 205-313-6329)
   (Fax: 562-216-5001)
(Cumming, GA Office: 410 Peachtree Parkway, Building 400, Suite 4245, 30041)
   (Tel: 678-341-5134)
   (Fax: 562-216-5001)

CALIFORNIA

Clinton & Clinton, Sacramento, CA (Continued)

(Philadelphia, PA Office: 1315 Walnut Street, Suite 601, 19107)
  (Tel: 267-800-1897)
  (Fax: 267-800-1898)
(Nashville, TN Office: 2400 Crestmoor Road, 37215)
  (Tel: 615-386-7040)
  (Fax: 562-216-5001)
(Austin, TX Office: 12912 Hill Country Boulevard, Suite F210, 78738)
  (Tel: 512-200-7055)
  (Fax: 512-266-3655)
(Ft. Worth, TX Office: 109 East Third Street, Suite 350, 76102)
  (Tel: 817-900-8210)
  (Fax: 817-900-8221)
(Houston, TX Office: 480 North Sam Houston Parkway East, 77060-3528)
  (Tel: 713-659-0054)
  (Fax: 281-447-5733)

Asbestos Litigation, Automobile, Automotive Products Liability, Civil Litigation, Civil Rights, Civil Trial Practice, Commercial Litigation, Common Carrier, Complex Litigation, Construction Defect, Dental Malpractice, Employment Law, Environmental Law, Insurance Defense, Hospital Malpractice, Law Enforcement Liability, Legal Malpractice, Mass Tort, Medical Devices, Medical Malpractice, Pharmaceutical, Premises Liability, Product Liability, Retail Liability, Sexual Harassment, Slip and Fall, Special Investigative Unit Claims, Sports and Entertainment Liability, Toxic Torts, Truck Liability, Workers' Compensation

(See listing under Long Beach, CA for additional information)

Diepenbrock & Cotter, LLP

1545 River Park Drive, Suite 201
Sacramento, California 95815
  Telephone: 916-565-6222
  Fax: 916-565-6220
  E-Mail: jpc@diepenbrockcotter.com
  www.diepenbrockcotter.com

(Los Angeles, CA Office: 1701 James M. Wood Boulevard, 90015)
  (Tel: 213-785-2667)
  (Fax: 213-984-4305)

Established: 1993

Transportation, Construction Defect, Public Entities, General Liability, Truck Liability, Trucks/Heavy Equipment, Insurance Defense, Insurance Coverage, Bad Faith, Admiralty and Maritime Law

Firm Profile: Diepenbrock & Cotter, LLP is a law firm specializing in civil litigation. Prior to starting Diepenbrock & Cotter, LLP, Anthony Diepenbrock was a partner in the Sacramento law firm of Greve, Clifford, Diepenbrock & Paras. In 1993 he left that law firm to form a law firm limiting its practice to civil litigation. John Cotter joined the firm in 1994. It is their belief that a smaller law firm is more attentive, efficient, and cost-conscious in handling litigation.

Centrally located in Sacramento, California, Diepenbrock & Cotter, LLP is able to service clients throughout Central and Northern California. It handles matters in all Federal, State and Appellate courts in Central and Northern California, and appears before various administrative and regulatory agencies.

The lawyers of Diepenbrock & Cotter, LLP represent clients in cases involving construction site accidents, trucking/vehicular accidents, employment litigation, professional malpractice, construction defect litigation, wrongful termination, toxic tort exposure, products liability, insurance bad faith, railroad accidents and premises liability litigation.

Diepenbrock & Cotter, LLP's goal is to provide the highest quality legal service efficiently and economically without compromising the integrity of its clients' position. The firm is dedicated to this goal and has been a pioneer in

SACRAMENTO

Diepenbrock & Cotter, LLP, Sacramento, CA (Continued)

developing non-traditional fee arrangements in order to provide cost-effective representation.

Insurance Clients

Arch Insurance Company
Converium/ZC Insurance
Hudson Insurance Company
Lancer Claims Services, Inc.
Magna Carta Companies
Praetorian Insurance Company
Public Agency Risk Sharing
  Authority of CA (PARSAC)
Clarendon National Insurance
  Company
Ironshore Specialty Insurance
  Company
Meadowbrook Insurance Group
Progressive Insurance Company
Williamsburg National Insurance
  Company

Non-Insurance Clients

Burger King Corporation
Cambridge Integrated Services
Coca-Cola Bottling Company
Enterprise Rent-A-Car Company
May Trucking Company
United Parcel Service, Inc.
Burlington Northern Santa Fe
  Railway
Dollar Rent A Car Systems, Inc.
Gordon Trucking Company, Inc.
Union Pacific Railroad Company

Partners

John P. Cotter — 1963 — University of California, Los Angeles; Pepperdine University, B.S., 1986; University of the Pacific, McGeorge School of Law, J.D., 1991 — Admitted to Bar, 1992, California; U.S. District Court, Central, Eastern and Northern Districts of California — Member State Bar of California; Association of Defense Counsel, Northern California; National Association of Railroad Trial Counsel; Trucking Industry Defense Association — E-mail: jpc@diepenbrockcotter.com

Paul R. Cotter — 1967 — University of California, Irvine, B.A., 1991; University of the Pacific, McGeorge School of Law, J.D., 1995 — Admitted to Bar, 1995, California; U.S. District Court, Central, Eastern, Northern and Southern Districts of California — E-mail: prc@diepenbrockcotter.com

Associates

Anthony R. Rossmiller — 1975 — University of Notre Dame, B.A. (cum laude), 1998; Santa Clara University School of Law, J.D., 2001 — Admitted to Bar, 2001, California; U.S. District Court, Northern District of California; U.S. Court of Appeals, Ninth Circuit — Member State Bar of California — Languages: French — E-mail: arr@diepenbrockcotter.com

Vera Cha Lu — 1975 — University of California, Los Angeles, B.S., 1997; University of California Davis School of Law, King Hall, J.D., 2001 — Admitted to Bar, 2007, California; U.S. District Court, Eastern District of California — E-mail: vyc@diepenbrockcotter.com

Brian J. O'Connor — 1962 — Santa Clara University; University of the Pacific, McGeorge School of Law, J.D., 1991 — Admitted to Bar, 1991, California — Member State Bar of California — E-mail: bjo@diepenbrockcotter.com

Joshua W. Rose — 1969 — The University of Arizona, B.A., 1993; Golden Gate University School of Law, J.D., 1996 — Admitted to Bar, 1997, California — E-mail: jrose@diepenbrockcotter.com

Glen Williams — Santa Clara University, B.S., 2004; University of the Pacific, McGeorge School of Law, J.D., 2007 — Admitted to Bar, 2008, California; U.S. District Court, Eastern District of California; 2009, U.S. District Court, Northern District of California — Member State Bar of California; Sacramento County Bar Association; Sacramento County Barristers Club; Sacramento Regional Builders Exchange — Santa Clara University (Sacramento Chapter) and McGeorge School of Law Alumni Associations

Darren S. Nakashima — University of California, Los Angeles, B.A., 2002; University of the Pacific, McGeorge School of Law, J.D., 2007 — Admitted to Bar, 2007, California; 2008, U.S. District Court, Eastern District of California; 2011, U.S. District Court, Northern District of California

Of Counsel

Anthony C. Diepenbrock — 1940 — University of Santa Clara, B.A., 1961; University of California, Hastings College of the Law, J.D., 1965 — Admitted to Bar, 1965, California; U.S. District Court, Eastern District of California — Member Association of Defense Counsel, Northern California (Board Director, 1984-1988); National Association of Railroad Trial Counsel; American Board of Trial Advocates; International Association of Defense Counsel — E-mail: td@diepenbrockcotter.com

Mary L. Diepenbrock — 1962 — Loyola Marymount University, B.A., 1984; University of the Pacific, McGeorge School of Law, J.D., 1991 — Order of the Coif — Admitted to Bar, 1991, California — E-mail: mld@diepenbrockcotter.com

SACRAMENTO   CALIFORNIA

Ericksen Arbuthnot

100 Howe Avenue, Suite 110S
Sacramento, California 95825-8200
   Telephone: 916-483-5181
   Fax: 916-483-7558
   www.ericksenarbuthnot.com

(Oakland, CA Office*: 155 Grand Avenue, Suite 1050, 94612-3768)
   (Tel: 510-832-7770)
   (Fax: 510-832-0102)
(Bakersfield, CA Office*: 1830 Truxtun Avenue, Suite 200, 93301-5022)
   (Tel: 661-633-5080)
   (Fax: 661-633-5089)
(Fresno, CA Office*: 2440 West Shaw Avenue, Suite 101, 93711-3300)
   (Tel: 559-449-2600)
   (Fax: 559-449-2603)
(Los Angeles, CA Office*: 835 Wilshire Boulevard, Suite 500, 90017-2656)
   (Tel: 213-489-4411)
   (Fax: 213-489-4332)
(San Francisco, CA Office*: 100 Bush Street, Suite 900, 94104-3950)
   (Tel: 415-362-7126)
   (Fax: 415-362-6401)
(San Jose, CA Office*: 152 North Third Street, Suite 700, 95112-5560)
   (Tel: 408-286-0880)
   (Fax: 408-286-0337)
(Walnut Creek, CA Office*: 570 Lennon Lane, 94598-2415)
   (Tel: 925-947-1702)
   (Fax: 925-947-4921)

Administrative Law, Business Law, Construction Law, Employment Law, Environmental Law, Health Care, Managed Care Liability, Insurance Coverage, Insurance Fraud, Personal Injury, Premises Liability, Product Liability, Professional Liability, Medical Malpractice, Public Entities, Appellate Law

Resident Partners

Douglas M. Kilduff — **Managing Partner, President** — University of the Pacific, B.A., 1974; University of San Francisco School of Law, J.D., 1977 — Admitted to Bar, 1977, California — Member State Bar of California — E-mail: dkilduff@ericksenarbuthnot.com

Charles S. Painter — **Assistant Managing Partner** — University of California, Davis, B.A., 1975; California Western School of Law, J.D., 1978 — Admitted to Bar, 1979, California; 1983, Oregon — Member State Bar of California; Oregon State Bar; Sacramento County Bar Association; Association of Defense Counsel, Northern California — E-mail: cpainter@ericksenarbuthnot.com

William A. Jenkins — **Partner** — California State University, Sacramento, B.A., 1979; Lincoln Law School of Sacramento, J.D., 1987 — Admitted to Bar, 1988, California; U.S. District Court, Eastern District of California — Member American and Sacramento County Bar Associations; State Bar of California — E-mail: wjenkins@ericksenarbuthnot.com

Mark S. Tratten — **Partner** — Bennington College, B.A., 1979; University of the Pacific, McGeorge School of Law, J.D., 1984 — Admitted to Bar, 1985, California — Member American Bar Association; State Bar of California — E-mail: mtratten@ericksenarbuthnot.com

Timothy P. Dailey — **Partner** — University of California, Davis, B.A., 1985; University of the Pacific, McGeorge School of Law, J.D. (with distinction), 1991 — Admitted to Bar, 1991, California; U.S. District Court, Central, Eastern and Northern Districts of California; 1992, U.S. Court of Appeals, Ninth Circuit — Member State Bar of California; Sacramento County Bar Association — E-mail: tdailey@ericksenarbuthnot.com

Resident Associates

David Leas — University of the Pacific, McGeorge School of Law, J.D., 2005 — Admitted to Bar, 2005, California — Practice Areas: Commercial Law; Legal Malpractice; Personal Injury; Consumer Law; Premises Liability — E-mail: dleas@ericsenarbuthnot.com

Gabriel Ullrich — University of California, Hastings College of the Law, J.D., 2009 — Admitted to Bar, 2009, California — E-mail: gullrich@ericksenarbuthnot.com

Graham Cridland — Truman State University, B.S., 2000; Georgetown University Law Center, J.D., 2003 — Admitted to Bar, 2006, California

(See listing under Oakland, CA for additional information)

Hanna, Brophy, MacLean, McAleer & Jensen, LLP

3100 Zinfandel Drive, Suite 400
Rancho Cordova, California 95670
   Telephone: 916-929-9411
   Fax: 916-929-0549
   www.hannabrophy.com

Insurance Defense, Workers' Compensation, Subrogation, Labor and Employment, Employment Law, Litigation

Office Managing Partner

Jeff V. Lusich — University of the Pacific, McGeorge School of Law, J.D., 1986 — Admitted to Bar, 1987, California — Member Stockton Workers' Compensation Appeals Board Bench and Bar Committee — Certified Specialist, Workers' Compensation Law, State Bar of California Board of Legal Specialization

(See listing under Oakland, CA for additional information)

Hardy Erich Brown & Wilson
A Professional Law Corporation

1000 G Street, Suite 200
Sacramento, California 95814-0894
   Telephone: 916-449-3800
   Fax: 916-449-3888
   Toll Free: 800-470-8622
   E-Mail: hebw@hebw.com
   www.hebw.com

Established: 1967

Civil Litigation, Trial and Appellate Practice, Personal Injury, Insurance Defense, Tort Litigation, Construction Law, Labor and Employment, Civil Rights, Professional Errors and Omissions, Medical Malpractice, Legal Malpractice, Product Liability, Business Law, Insurance Coverage, Business Litigation

Firm Profile: Hardy Erich Brown & Wilson, established in 1967 as Hardy Erich & Brown, has a longstanding reputation for providing quality, timely and cost effective legal services. Founded as a litigation defense firm, Hardy Erich Brown & Wilson has built upon that foundation by developing practice expertise in business litigation and counseling, real estate transactions, bankruptcy, employment law and defense of professional errors and omissions, intellectual property, products liability and personal injury claims.

Hardy Erich Brown & Wilson is organized by practice areas, providing a group-oriented approach to each case. By working in groups, the firm provides clients with the skills and experience necessary for the efficient handling of each matter.

The firm handles cases throughout California in state and federal courts, at both the trial and appellate levels. They carefully consider alternatives to litigation, including creative settlement techniques, arbitration and mediation.

Insurance Clients

AIG Aviation, Inc.	The Doctors Company
Empire Fire and Marine Insurance Company	Great West Casualty Company
	Health Care Indemnity, Inc.
Norcal Mutual Insurance Company	Old Republic Insurance Company
Sentry Insurance a Mutual Company	Travelers Insurance
	Zurich American Insurance Company

CALIFORNIA   SACRAMENTO

Hardy Erich Brown & Wilson, A Professional Law Corporation, Sacramento, CA (Continued)

Non-Insurance Clients

Catholic Healthcare West
Orber & Associates
Tahoe City Public Utility District
Crestwood Behavioral Health, Inc.
Pride Industries, Inc.

Shareholders

Richard L. Alley — 1948 — Southwest Texas State University, B.S. (with honors), 1974; Arizona State University, M.S. (with honors), 1979; Creighton University School of Law, J.D. (cum laude), 1984 — Admitted to Bar, 1984, Nebraska; 1989, California; U.S. District Court, Eastern District of California; U.S. Court of the Armed Forces — E-mail: ralley@hebw.com

John Quincy Brown, III — 1950 — University of Oregon, B.S., 1971; University of the Pacific, McGeorge School of Law, J.D., 1974 — Admitted to Bar, 1974, California — Member American Bar Association; Association of Defense Counsel, Northern California (Board of Directors, 1994-1997); California Society for Healthcare Attorneys; Diplomate, American Board of Professional Liability Attorneys; American Board of Trial Advocates (President, Sacramento Valley Chapter, 2005); Defense Research Institute; American Society of Law and Medicine — E-mail: jbrown@hebw.com

John P. Rhode — 1959 — University of Minnesota, B.A., 1981; University of Minnesota Law School, J.D., 1984 — Admitted to Bar, 1984, Minnesota; 1987, California; 1997, U.S. District Court, Eastern District of California — Member Association of Defense Counsel, Northern California — E-mail: jrhode@hebw.com

Anders R. Morrison — 1969 — Santa Rosa Junior College, A.A. (with honors), 1992; University of Colorado, B.A. (with honors), 1998; Washington University School of Law, J.D., 2001 — Admitted to Bar, 2001, Missouri; 2002, Illinois; 2002, California; 2001, U.S. District Court, Eastern and Western Districts of Missouri — Member American Bar Association — E-mail: amorrison@hebw.com

Stephen L. Ramazzini — 1963 — Stanford University, B.A., 1985; University of the Pacific, McGeorge School of Law, J.D., 1993 — Admitted to Bar, 1994, California — Member State Bar of California; Sacramento County and Los Angeles County Bar Associations; Stanford Alumni Association — E-mail: sramazzini@hebw.com

Cameron L. Cobden — 1974 — Carleton College, B.A. (with honors), 1996; College of William & Mary, Marshall-Wythe School of Law, J.D., 2000 — Admitted to Bar, 2001, California — Member American Bar Association; Association of Defense Counsel — E-mail: ccobden@hebw.com

Associates

David L. Perrault — 1944 — California State University, Sacramento, B.A., 1966; California State University, Northridge, M.A., 1969; University of the Pacific, McGeorge School of Law, J.D., 1975 — Admitted to Bar, 1975, California — Member American Bar Association (Labor and Employment Section); Association of Defense Counsel, Northern California; American Board of Trial Advocates — E-mail: dperrault@hebw.com

Danielle M. Guard — 1966 — The University of Utah, B.A., 1990; University of the Pacific, McGeorge School of Law, J.D., 1994 — Admitted to Bar, 1994, California; U.S. District Court, Eastern District of California — Member Sacramento County Bar Association (Health Care Division) — E-mail: dguard@hebw.com

Kelly F. Watson — 1964 — University of California, Los Angeles, B.S. (cum laude), 1986; University of California, Hastings College of the Law, J.D., 1990 — Admitted to Bar, 1990, California; U.S. District Court, Central, Eastern and Northern Districts of California; U.S. Court of Appeals, Ninth Circuit — Member Sacramento County Bar Association — E-mail: kwatson@hebw.com

Stephen W. Robertson — 1978 — Knox College, B.S., 2000; Valparaiso University School of Law, J.D., 2003 — Admitted to Bar, 2003, California — Member Association of Defense Counsel of Northern California and Nevada — E-mail: srobertson@hebw.com

Joseph A. Androvich — 1981 — University of California, Berkeley, B.S., 2004; University of San Francisco School of Law, J.D., 2008 — Admitted to Bar, 2008, California — Member Association of Defense Counsel of Northern California and Nevada — E-mail: jandrovich@hebw.com

Jeffrey V. Lovell — 1982 — University of San Diego, B.A. (magna cum laude), 2005; Baylor University, J.D. (cum laude), 2008 — Admitted to Bar, 2008, California — Member State Bar of California; Sacramento County Bar Association — E-mail: jlovell@hebw.com

Hardy Erich Brown & Wilson, A Professional Law Corporation, Sacramento, CA (Continued)

Of Counsel

L. Thomas Wagner — 1942 — California State University, Sacramento, B.A., 1964; University of California, Berkeley Boalt Hall School of Law, J.D., 1967 — Admitted to Bar, 1968, California — Member Association of Defense Counsel, Northern California; American Board of Trial Advocates; American Board of Professional Liability Attorneys — E-mail: twagner@hebw.com

Anthony D. Osmundson — 1943 — University of California, Los Angeles, A.B., 1964; University of California, Hastings College of the Law, J.D., 1967 — Admitted to Bar, 1968, California — Member Association of Defense Counsel, Northern California; American Board of Trial Advocates — E-mail: aosmundson@hebw.com

John Quincy Brown, Jr. — 1927 — Stanford University, A.B., 1948; University of the Pacific, McGeorge School of Law, LL.B., 1958 — Admitted to Bar, 1959, California — Member American Bar Association; American Judicature Society; Association of Defense Counsel, Northern California; American Board of Trial Advocates; Fellow, American College of Trial Lawyers; American Board of Professional Liability Attorneys — E-mail: jqbrown@hebw.com

William A. Wilson — 1935 — University of California, Berkeley, B.S., 1957; University of California, Berkeley Boalt Hall School of Law, LL.B., 1960 — Admitted to Bar, 1961, California — Member American Bar Association; Association of Defense Counsel, Northern California; Defense Research Institute; American Board of Trial Advocates; International Association of Defense Counsel — E-mail: wwilson@hebw.com

(All Attorneys are Members of the State Bar of California and Sacramento County Bar Association)

Johnson Schachter & Lewis, A PLC

2180 Harvard Street, Suite 560
Sacramento, California 95815
Telephone: 916-921-5800
Fax: 916-921-0247
E-Mail: info@jsl-law.com
www.jsl-law.com

Civil Defense, Self-Insured Defense, Public Entities, Construction Litigation, Employment Litigation, Premises Liability, Product Liability, Professional Malpractice

Firm Profile: Johnson Schachter & Lewis is an AV-rated law firm providing a broad range of legal services to national, regional and local clients throughout Northern California.

Insurance Clients

Ameriprise Insurance Company
CAMICO Mutual Insurance Company
Chubb Insurance Company
Constitution State Service Company
Electric Insurance Company
Financial Pacific Insurance Company
Jackson National Life Insurance Company
Pinnacle Risk Management Services
Wright Risk Management
Aspen Insurance
Catlin Insurance Company, Inc.
Century Insurance Company, Ltd.
CNA
CPA Mutual Insurance Company of America, A RRG
Evanston Insurance Company
Fireman's Fund Insurance Companies
Markel Insurance Company
North American Risk Services
United States Liability Insurance Group

Non-Insurance Clients

Carl Karcher Enterprises, Inc.
Thrifty Payless, Inc.

Shareholders

Robert H. Johnson — University of Redlands, B.A. (with distinction), 1964; New York University, J.D., 1967 — Admitted to Bar, 1971, California

Alesa Schachter — University of California, Los Angeles, B.A. (cum laude), 1978; University of California, Davis, J.D., 1981 — Admitted to Bar, 1981, California

SACRAMENTO   **CALIFORNIA**

Johnson Schachter & Lewis, A PLC, Sacramento, CA (Continued)

Luther R. Lewis — University of California, Davis, B.S. (with high honors), 1972; M.A.T., 1977; University of California, Berkeley, J.D., 1983 — Admitted to Bar, 1983, California

Kellie M. Murphy — University of Dayton, B.A., 1994; University of Houston, J.D. (cum laude), 1996 — Admitted to Bar, 1997, California

Jason M. Sherman — San Diego State University, B.S. (Phi Beta Kappa), 1997; Loyola Law School, J.D. (cum laude), 2006 — Admitted to Bar, 2006, California

Associates

Sander van der Heide
Craig A. Tomlins
Danielle R. Teeters

LeVangie Law Group

2021 N Street
Sacramento, California 95811-4222
  Telephone: 916-443-4849
  Fax: 916-443-4855
  E-Mail: michael.levangie@llg-law.com
  www.llg-law.com

(Carson City, NV Office: 808 West Nye Lane, Suite 204, 89703)
  (Tel: 775-297-4321)
  (Fax: 772-297-4258)

Alternative Dispute Resolution, Appellate Practice, Business Law, Construction Litigation, Employment Law, Environmental Law, Personal Injury, Product Liability, Professional Malpractice, Sports Claims Defense

Firm Profile: Our mission at LeVangie Law Group is to provide clients state-of-the-art legal advice, deliver services efficiently and cost effectively, act as a seamless extension of our clients' interests, and advocate those interests tenaciously and zealously.

Insurance Clients

Anchor General Insurance Group
Clarendon Insurance Company
Columbia Casualty Company
General Star Management Company
Hanover Insurance Group
Magnolia LTC Management Service, Inc.
St. Paul Travelers
Western General Insurance Company
AXIS U.S. Insurance
CNA HealthPro
Doctors' Company Insurance Group
GuideOne America Insurance Company
OneBeacon Professional Insurance
Philadelphia Insurance Company
United States Liability Insurance Group
Worldwide Insurance Company

Non-Insurance Clients

AAO Services, Inc.
Gallagher Bassett Services, Inc.
Hamlin & Burton Liability Management, Inc.
Riverside Health Care
Clear Channel Communications, Inc.
JTS Communities, Inc.
North American Risk Services

Partners

Michael J. Levangie — The University of Tulsa; San Francisco State University, B.A., 1988; Golden Gate University School of Law, J.D., 1992; LL.M. (with honors), 1995 — Admitted to Bar, 1992, California; U.S. District Court, Eastern and Northern Districts of California; 1997, U.S. Court of Appeals, Ninth Circuit; U.S. Supreme Court — E-mail: michael.levangie@llg-law.com

Jeffery C. Long — Arizona State University, B.A., 1997; St. John's University School of Law, J.D., 2003 — Admitted to Bar, 2003, California; 2005, Nevada; U.S. District Court, Eastern District of California — E-mail: jeffery.long@llg-law.com

Associates

Eric S. Emanuels — University of California, Los Angeles, B.A. (magna cum laude, Phi Beta Kappa), 1985; Loyola Law School, J.D., 1988 — Admitted to Bar, 1989, California; U.S. District Court, Central and Eastern Districts of

LeVangie Law Group, Sacramento, CA (Continued)

California; U.S. Court of Appeals, Ninth Circuit — E-mail: eric.emanuels@llg-law.com

Sharon B. Futerman — Boston University, B.A. (with honors), 1981; Washington University School of Law, J.D., 1984 — Admitted to Bar, 1984, Missouri; 1986, California; U.S. District Court, Eastern and Northern Districts of California; U.S. Court of Appeals, Ninth Circuit — E-mail: sharon.futerman@llg-law.com

Shawn C. Loorz — University of California, Davis, B.A., 2003; University of the Pacific, McGeorge School of Law, J.D., 2007 — Admitted to Bar, 2007, California; U.S. District Court, Eastern District of California — E-mail: shawn.loorz@llg-law.com

Bryan L. Malone — University of Nevada, Reno, B.S., 1986; Pepperdine University School of Law, J.D. (cum laude), 1989 — Admitted to Bar, 1989, California; U.S. District Court, Central, Eastern and Northern Districts of California; U.S. Court of Appeals, Ninth Circuit — E-mail: bryan.malone@llg-law.com

Laurie L. Marquis — Sonoma State University, B.A., 1988; Empire College School of Law, J.D., 1998 — Admitted to Bar, 1998, California; U.S. District Court, Eastern District of California — E-mail: laurie.marquis@llg-law.com

Anna J. Niemann — University of California, San Diego, B.A., 1973; Lincoln Law School of Sacramento, J.D., 1992 — Admitted to Bar, 1993, California; 1994, U.S. District Court, Eastern District of California — E-mail: anna.niemann@llg-law.com

Jason A. Rose — Dominican University of California, B.A. (with business department honors), 2002; University of the Pacific, McGeorge School of Law, J.D. (with great distinction), 2005 — Admitted to Bar, 2005, Nevada; 2006, Texas; 2010, California; U.S. District Court, Central and Eastern Districts of California; U.S. District Court, Eastern, Northern, Southern and Western Districts of Texas; U.S. District Court, District of Colorado; U.S. District Court, District of Nevada; U.S. Tax Court — E-mail: jason.rose@llg-law.com

Murphy, Campbell, Alliston & Quinn

8801 Folsom Boulevard, Suite 230
Sacramento, California 95826
  Telephone: 916-400-2300
  Fax: 916-400-2311
  E-Mail: gmurphy@murphycampbell.com
  www.MurphyCampbell.com

Civil Litigation, Appellate Practice, Insurance Coverage, Construction Law, Personal Injury, Business Law, Real Estate, Professional Liability

Firm Profile: Based in the California state capital, our statewide practice focuses on insurance coverage and litigation; general civil appeals; real estate, business, railroad, and professional liability litigation; estate planning; and representation of public entities including joint powers insurance authorities.

General Counsel For

Bickmore Risk Services

Insurance Clients

Beta Healthcare Group
Financial Pacific Insurance Company
Credit Union Self-Insured Group of California
Optima Healthcare Insurance Services

Non-Insurance Clients

State of California

Shareholders

George E. Murphy — 1950 — University of California, Santa Barbara, B.A., 1975; Golden Gate University School of Law, J.D., 1979 — Admitted to Bar, 1980, California; 2006, Texas; 1980, U.S. Court of Appeals, Ninth Circuit; 1983, U.S. Supreme Court — Member Sacramento County Bar Association; American Council of Appellate Lawyers — Practice Areas: Appellate Practice; Insurance Coverage; Bad Faith; Civil Litigation; Mediation — E-mail: GMurphy@MurphyCampbell.com

Mark A. Campbell — 1955 — University of California, Santa Barbara, B.A., 1977; University of the Pacific, McGeorge School of Law, J.D., 1980 — Admitted to Bar, 1980, California; U.S. District Court, Central and Northern Districts of California — Member Placer County Bar Association — Practice

Murphy, Campbell, Alliston & Quinn, Sacramento, CA (Continued)

Areas: Civil Litigation; Real Estate; Professional Liability; Intellectual Property; Business Law; Personal Injury — E-mail: MCampbell@MurphyCampbell.com

Douglas R. Alliston — 1961 — Oklahoma Christian College, B.A., 1984; University of the Pacific, McGeorge School of Law, J.D., 1988 — Admitted to Bar, 1988, California; 2006, Texas; 1989, U.S. Court of Appeals, Ninth Circuit — Member Sacramento County Bar Association; The Federalist Society — Practice Areas: Insurance Coverage; Self-Insured — E-mail: DAlliston@MurphyCampbell.com

Stephanie L. Quinn — California State University, Sacramento, B.A., 1998; University of the Pacific, McGeorge School of Law, J.D., 2001 — Admitted to Bar, 2001, California; 2012, Nevada — Member Sacramento County Bar Association — Practice Areas: Federal Employer Liability Claims (FELA); General Liability; Railroad Law; Public Entities; Labor and Employment; Litigation Defense — E-mail: SQuinn@MurphyCampbell.com

Senior Attorneys

J. Douglas Durham — 1951 — North Central College, B.A., 1974; The John Marshall Law School, J.D., 1982 — Admitted to Bar, 1982, Illinois; 1991, California; U.S. District Court, Northern District of Illinois; U.S. District Court, Eastern, Northern and Southern Districts of California; U.S. Court of Appeals, Ninth Circuit — Member Aviation Insurance Association — Practice Areas: Insurance Coverage; Litigation — E-mail: DDurham@MurphyCampbell.com

Nageley, Meredith & Miller, Inc.

8801 Folsom Boulevard, Suite 172
Sacramento, California 95826
Telephone: 916-386-8282
Fax: 916-386-8952
www.nmlawfirm.com

Established: 1972

Insurance Defense, Product Liability, Professional Negligence, Negligence, Construction Litigation, Business Law, Employment Law, State and Federal Courts

Firm Profile: The firm primarily engages in trial practice in all California state and federal courts, with an emphasis in the areas of insurance defense, products liability, and medical device defense, employment torts, business, construction, and real property litigation. In addition to litigation, the firm engages in general business practice, concentrating in the fields of construction and real estate.

Insurance Clients

American Claims Service	American Reliable Insurance Company
Automobile Club of Southern California	Berkley Risk Services, LLC
California State Automobile Association	Capital Insurance Group
CNA Insurance Company	Century-National Insurance Company
Crawford & Company	Cunningham Lindsey Claims Management, Inc.
Custard Insurance Adjusters, Inc.	Great American Insurance Companies
ESIS	
Gulf Insurance Group	Medmarc Insurance Group
Hartford Specialty Risk Services, Inc.	MetLife Insurance Company
Midland Insurance Company	Millers American Group
Murdock Claim Management Company	Nautilus Insurance Company
Peter Corrick & Associates	NovaPro Risk Solutions
RSKCo	Robert Moreno Insurance Services
Saskatchewan Government Insurance	The St. Paul Companies
Specialty Risk Services, Inc. (SRS)	Sequoia Insurance Company
Sterling Insurance Company	Sompo Japan Insurance Company of America
Travelers Indemnity Company	Superior Insurance Company
Virginia Farm Bureau Insurance Services	VELA Insurance Services (A Berkley Company)
Zurich Insurance Group	Ward North America, Inc.

Non-Insurance Clients

Bickmore & Associates, Inc.	Budget Rent-A-Car Corporation

Nageley, Meredith & Miller, Inc., Sacramento, CA (Continued)

Consolidated Stores	Foster Farms
Penske Truck Leasing	Sacramento Area Flood Control

Founding Partner

Sam Roth Nageley — (1937-2003)

Managing Partner

Gregory A. Meredith — California State University, Sacramento, B.S., 1982; University of the Pacific, McGeorge School of Law, J.D., 1985 — Admitted to Bar, 1985, California; 1985, U.S. District Court, Eastern District of California; 1987, U.S. District Court, Southern District of California — Member State Bar of California; Sacramento County Bar Association; Defense Research Institute — Associated General Contractors of California, Legal Advisory Committee; Judge Pro Tem, Sacramento Superior Court; Sacramento County Civil Service Commissioner, 2006-2011 — Practice Areas: Construction Litigation; Insurance Defense; Product Liability; Business Formation; Business and Real Estate Transactions; Business Litigation — E-mail: gmeredith@nmlawfirm.com

Firm Members

Andrea M. Miller — California State University, Long Beach, B.A., 1963; University of the Pacific, McGeorge School of Law, J.D. (with great distinction), 1979 — Clerk for Chief Judge Philip C. Wilkins, U.S. District Court, Eastern District of California — Admitted to Bar, 1979, California; 1979, U.S. District Court, Central, Eastern and Northern Districts of California; U.S. Court of Appeals for the District of Columbia and Ninth Circuits; 1983, U.S. District Court, District of Nevada; 1984, U.S. Court of Federal Claims; 1997, U.S. Supreme Court — Member Federal Bar Association; State Bar of California; Milton L. Schwartz/David L. Levi Inn of Court — President, Eastern District of California, Historical Society — Practice Areas: Medical Devices; Product Liability; Alternative Dispute Resolution — E-mail: amiller@nmlawfirm.com

Craig S. MacGlashan — Occidental College, B.A., 1973; University of Santa Clara School of Law, J.D., 1976 — Admitted to Bar, 1976, California; 1983, U.S. District Court, Eastern District of California; 1983, U.S. Supreme Court — Member State Bar of California — Practice Areas: Business Litigation; Insurance Defense; Product Liability — E-mail: cmacglashan@nmlawfirm.com

James R. Kirby II — The University of North Carolina at Chapel Hill, B.A., 1972; University of the Pacific, McGeorge School of Law, J.D. (with honors), 1979 — Clerk for Judge Thomas J. McBride and Writ Clerk, U.S. District Court, Eastern District — Admitted to Bar, 1979, California; U.S. District Court, Eastern and Northern Districts of California; U.S. Court of Appeals, Fifth and Ninth Circuits; Supreme Court of the United States — Member Federal and Sacramento County Bar Associations; Anthony M. Kennedy Inn of Court — Eastern District of California Early Neutral Evaluation Program — Practice Areas: Legal Malpractice; Insurance Defense — E-mail: jkirby@nmlawfirm.com

Janet M. Meredith — California State University, Sacramento, B.S.N., 1984; University of the Pacific, McGeorge School of Law, J.D. (with distinction), 1991 — Admitted to Bar, 1991, California; 1991, U.S. District Court, Eastern District of California; 2001, U.S. Court of Appeals, Ninth Circuit — Member Federal Bar Association; State Bar of California — Practice Areas: Medical Devices; Insurance Defense — E-mail: jmeredith@nmlawfirm.com

James C. Keowen — Santa Clara University, B.S., 1987; University of the Pacific, McGeorge School of Law, J.D., 1994 — Admitted to Bar, 1994, California; 1994, U.S. District Court, Eastern and Northern Districts of California; 2013, U.S. Court of Appeals, Ninth Circuit; 2013, U.S. Supreme Court — Member State Bar of California; Milton L. Schwartz/David L. Levi Inn of Court; Association of Defense Counsel — Practice Areas: Construction Defect; Insurance Defense — E-mail: jimkeowen@nmlawfirm.com

Andrew A. Weil — The University of Arizona, B.A. Economics (cum laude), 2009; Pennsylvania State University-Dickinson School of Law, J.D., 2012; Georgetown University Law Center, LL.M. Taxation, 2013 — Admitted to Bar, 2012, California — E-mail: aweil@nmlawfirm.com

SAN BERNARDINO   CALIFORNIA

The following firms also service this area.

Babin & Seeger, LLP
3550 Round Barn Boulevard, Suite 201
Santa Rosa, California 95403
   Telephone: 707-526-7370
   Fax: 707-526-0307

Mailing Address: P.O. Box 11626, Santa Rosa, CA 95406

Insurance Defense, Motor Vehicle, Commercial Law, General Liability, Product Liability, Property Damage, Construction Defect, Contracts, Environmental Law, Insurance Coverage, Workers' Compensation, Personal Injury, Professional Malpractice

SEE COMPLETE LISTING UNDER SANTA ROSA, CALIFORNIA (81 MILES)

Boornazian, Jensen & Garthe
A Professional Corporation
555 12th Street, 18th Floor
Oakland, California 94607
   Telephone: 510-834-4350
   Fax: 510-839-1897

Mailing Address: P.O. Box 12925, Oakland, CA 94604-2925

Insurance Defense, Trial Practice, Product Liability, Legal Malpractice, Professional Malpractice, Medical Malpractice, Insurance Coverage, Construction Law

SEE COMPLETE LISTING UNDER OAKLAND, CALIFORNIA (90 MILES)

Mollis & Mollis, Inc.
4621 Teller Avenue, Suite 200
Newport Beach, California 92660
   Telephone: 949-222-0735
   Fax: 949-955-0252

Insurance Defense, Civil Trial Practice, Business Law, Construction Law, Corporate Law, Appeals, Labor Law, Environmental Law, Real Estate, Estate Planning, Trusts, Probate, Trust and Estate Litigation, Taxation, Trust Settlement

SEE COMPLETE LISTING UNDER NEWPORT BEACH, CALIFORNIA (429 MILES)

SALINAS † 150,441 Monterey Co.

Hanna, Brophy, MacLean, McAleer & Jensen, LLP

Six Quail Run Circle, Suite 202
Salinas, California 93907
   Telephone: 831-443-6300
   Fax: 831-443-8224
   www.hannabrophy.com

Insurance Defense, Workers' Compensation, Subrogation, Labor and Employment, Employment Law, Litigation

Office Managing Partner

Bruce L. Bevacqua — The John Marshall Law School in Chicago, J.D., 1980 — Admitted to Bar, 1980, California — Member Monterey County and El Dorado County Bar Associations; California Workers' Compensation Defense Attorneys Association

(See listing under Oakland, CA for additional information)

SAN BERNARDINO † 209,924 San Bernardino Co.

Borton Petrini, LLP

1461 Ford Street, Suite 201
Redlands, California 92373
   Telephone: 909-381-0527
   Fax: 909-381-0658
   E-Mail: bpsbdo@bortonpetrini.com
   www.bortonpetrini.com

Established: 1899

Coverage Issues, Insurance Defense, Labor and Employment, Product Liability, Professional Errors and Omissions, Public Entities

Firm Profile: Since 1899, Borton Petrini, LLP, has offered high quality legal services in all of the practice areas described above through its California network of 10 regional offices. The mission of Borton Petrini, LLP is to treat every file as though we were representing ourselves and paying the bill for that representation.

Managing Partner

Daniel L. Ferguson — 1956 — California State College at Northridge, B.A., 1977; University of California, Hastings College of the Law, J.D., 1980 — Admitted to Bar, 1981, California — Member State Bar of California; San Bernardino County Bar Association; Association of Southern California Defense Counsel — E-mail: dferguson@bortonpetrini.com

Partner

Jeffrey A. Dains — 1957 — Western State University, B.S., 1985; Western State University College of Law, J.D., 1987 — Admitted to Bar, 1989, California; 1991, U.S. District Court, Southern District of California; 1991, U.S. Federal Court — Member State Bar of California — Superior Court of Riverside (Judge Pro Tem, 2006-2007); California State University at San Bernardino, Business Law (Professor, 1995-2007); California State University at Riverside (Professor, 2005-2008) — E-mail: jdains@bortonpetrini.com

Senior Counsel

Daniel L. Morgan — 1952 — California State University, Long Beach, B.A., 1976; University of Arkansas School of Law, J.D., 1992 — Phi Kappa Phi; John T. Amendt Award, California State University, Long Beach — Admitted to Bar, 1994, California; 1998, U.S. District Court, Central District of California — Member State Bar of California; San Bernardino County Bar Association — Languages: Spanish — E-mail: dmorgan@bortonpetrini.com

Of Counsel

Christopher L. Cockrell, Sr. — 1955 — University of California, Los Angeles, B.A., 1977; Southwestern University School of Law, J.D., 1980 — Phi Alpha Delta — Admitted to Bar, 1980, California; 1981, U.S. District Court, Southern District of California — Member State Bar of California — E-mail: ccockrell@bortonpetrini.com

Associate

Joseph Richardson — 1972 — University of Redlands, B.A., 1993; Northwestern University School of Law, J.D., 1996 — Admitted to Bar, 2001, California; 2001, U.S. District Court, Central District of California — Member State Bar of California; San Bernardino Bar Association; Consumer Attorneys of California; American Association for Justice — YMCA Board - Redlands (2005-2009); Redlands Community Hospital Foundation Board (Member, 2008-present); University of Redlands Alumni for Greeks (Member) — E-mail: jrichardson@bortonpetrini.com

CALIFORNIA

The following firms also service this area.

Berman Berman Berman Schneider & Lowary LLP
11900 West Olympic Boulevard, Suite 600
Los Angeles, California 90064-1151
   Telephone: 310-447-9000
   Fax: 310-447-9011

Insurance Defense, Insurance Coverage, Construction Defect, Product Liability, Employment Law, Professional Liability, Legal, Insurance Agents, Agent/Broker Liability, Medical Malpractice Defense, Design Professionals, Accountants, Trucking Law, Transportation, Real Estate Agents, Brokers and Appraisers, Elder Care, Monitoring Counsel, Litigation Management, California Insurance Regulations and Consulting to Insurance Industry

SEE COMPLETE LISTING UNDER LOS ANGELES, CALIFORNIA (59 MILES)

Kinkle, Rodiger & Spriggs Professional Corporation
3333 Fourteenth Street
Riverside, California 92501-3809
   Telephone: 951-683-2410
   Toll Free: 800-235-2039
   Fax: 951-683-7759

Insurance Defense, Self-Insured, General Liability, Product Liability, Automobile, Premises Liability, Public Entities, Construction Law, Professional Liability, Coverage Issues, Bad Faith, Civil Trial Practice, Appellate Practice, Federal Courts

SEE COMPLETE LISTING UNDER RIVERSIDE, CALIFORNIA (10 MILES)

Pyka Lenhardt Schnaider Zell
837 North Ross Street
Santa Ana, California 92701
   Telephone: 714-835-9011
   Fax: 714-667-7806

Mailing Address: P.O. Box 1558, Santa Ana, CA 92702-1558

Automobile, Business Litigation, Catastrophic Injury, Civil Litigation, Civil Rights, Construction Accidents, Construction Defect, Labor and Employment, Municipal Liability, Personal Injury, Police Liability Defense, Premises Liability, Product Liability, Professional Liability, Public Entities, School Law, Trucking, Uninsured and Underinsured Motorist, Wrongful Death, Wrongful Termination, Homeowners Association Litigation, Utility Defense

SEE COMPLETE LISTING UNDER SANTA ANA, CALIFORNIA (49 MILES)

Thompson & Colegate LLP
3610 Fourteenth Street
Riverside, California 92501
   Telephone: 951-682-5550
   Fax: 951-781-4012

Mailing Address: P.O. Box 1299, Riverside, CA 92502

Insurance Defense, Medical Malpractice, Automobile Liability, General Liability, Construction Litigation, Coverage Issues, Personal Injury, Product Liability, Premises Liability, Employment Law, Commercial Litigation, Bankruptcy, Alternative Dispute Resolution, Appellate Practice, Complex Litigation, Real Estate

SEE COMPLETE LISTING UNDER RIVERSIDE, CALIFORNIA (10 MILES)

SAN DIEGO † 1,307,402 San Diego Co.

Balestreri Potocki & Holmes

401 B Street, Suite 1470
San Diego, California 92101-4223
   Telephone: 619-686-1930
   Fax: 619-497-1052
   E-Mail: info@bph-law.com
   www.bph-law.com

Established: 1991

Construction Law, Professional Liability, Product Liability, Subrogation, Recoveries, Premises Liability, Insurance Defense, Governmental Liability, Personal Injury, Toxic Mold Litigation

SAN DIEGO

Balestreri Potocki & Holmes, San Diego, CA (Continued)

Firm Profile: Balestreri Potocki & Holmes' (BPH) model of representation focuses on determining and understanding the complexity of our client's business, interests and goals. The lawyers of BPH are dedicated to achieving a complete understanding of complex contracting, engineering, environmental and hazardous risk issues. This knowledge, combined with in-the-trenches experience, enables BPH to evaluate and formulate sound legal strategies and plans for businesses, whether encountering opportunities, managing risk, or requiring the highest quality of legal advocacy.

The firm regularly handles cases throughout California. Representative cases include: high-rise commercial and residential construction litigation; construction site injury matters on behalf of owners, builders and trades; premises liability claims for restaurants and hotels; residential construction defect litigation including SB 800 claims; public works matters of all types; contract drafting and review for affordable housing contractor; elevator and escalator claims; self-storage facility claims; products claims for manufacturer of waste water treatment plant equipment, and personal injury claims for commercial trucking entities as well as employers in on-the-job employee-related motor vehicle accidents.

BPH is qualified counsel on a wide variety of matters including construction law and related intellectual property matters, design professional liability consulting and litigation, ultra-hazardous risk management and litigation, common carrier litigation, transportation claims, premises liability, restaurant and hotel security claims, product liability, real estate law and general civil matters.

Insurance Clients

Clarendon Insurance Company
Evanston Insurance Company
Navigators Insurance Company
Tudor Insurance Company
United National Insurance Company
XL Insurance

EMC Insurance Companies
Nationwide Indemnity Company
The St. Paul/Travelers Companies, Inc.
Wausau General Insurance Company

Shareholders

Thomas A. Balestreri, Jr. — 1954 — California State University, Sacramento, B.A., 1977; University of San Diego School of Law, J.D., 1980 — Admitted to Bar, 1980, California; U.S. District Court, Southern District of California; 1982, U.S. Court of Appeals, Ninth Circuit — Member American and San Diego County Bar Associations; State Bar of California; Association of Southern California Defense Counsel; Defense Research Institute — Top San Diego Lawyers, Construction, San Diego Super Lawyers 2010-2014; Top Lawyers, Construction Law, San Diego Magazine, March 2013 — E-mail: tbalestreri@bph-law.com

Joseph P. Potocki — University of California, Irvine, B.A., 1983; California Western School of Law, J.D., 1987 — Admitted to Bar, 1988, California; U.S. District Court, Southern District of California — Member American and San Diego County Bar Associations; State Bar of California; Building Industry Association; San Diego Defense Lawyers; Association of General Contractors, San Diego Chapter; Association of Southern California Defense Counsel; Defense Research Institute — Top 25 attorneys in Construction & Real Estate Law (SDDT) 2005; Top San Diego Lawyers in Construction - Super Lawyers 2013-2014 — E-mail: jpotocki@bph-law.com

Karen A. Holmes — 1957 — San Diego State University, B.S., 1979; California Western School of Law, J.D., 1983 — Admitted to Bar, 1983, California — Member American and San Diego County Bar Associations; State Bar of California; San Diego Defense Lawyers Association; Defense Research Institute; Federation of Defense and Corporate Counsel; Association of Southern California Defense Counsel — Top 10 Attorneys, Construction & Real Estate Law, San Diego Daily Transcript 2006; Top San Diego Lawyers, Construction, San Diego Super Lawyers 2007, 2009-2012 and 2014; Top 25 Women Lawyers, San Diego Super Lawyers 2008; 2013 Top Lawyers, Professional Liability, San Diego Magazine March 2013 — E-mail: kholmes@bph-law.com

Associates

Eric J. Miersma
Matthew Stohl
Jackson Isaacs
Zachariah Rowland
Clayton T. Graham

Renee M. Botham
Danielle Ward
Anthony S. Chalifoux
Quelie M. Saechao
Peter B. Nichols

Of Counsel

Susan Sparks

(This firm is also listed in the Subrogation section of this directory)

SAN DIEGO   CALIFORNIA

Belsky & Associates

591 Camino De La Reina, Suite 640
San Diego, California 92108
　Telephone: 619-497-2900
　Fax: 619-497-2901
　Toll Free: 866-738-0279
　E-Mail: dbelsky@belskylaw.com
　www.belskylaw.com

Established: 1992

Medical Malpractice, Insurance Defense, General Civil Trial and Appellate Practice, State and Federal Courts, Negligence, Insurance Law, Legal Malpractice, Professional Malpractice, Product Liability, Tort Litigation

Insurance Clients

The Doctors Company
Medical Insurance Exchange of California
Novus/HSPRRG
MedAmerica Mutual Risk Retention Group, Inc.
Norcal Mutual Insurance Company
Professional Underwriters Liability Insurance Company

Non-Insurance Clients

Children's Specialists of San Diego
Kaiser Foundation Health Plan, Inc.
Scripps Coastal Medical Center
UniFirst Corporation
Gateway Risk Services, Inc.
The Regents of the University of California
Sharp Rees-Stealy Medical Group

Partners

Daniel S. Belsky — 1952 — University of Sheffield; Hobart College, B.A. (cum laude), 1974; University of Miami School of Law, J.D., 1977 — Law Clerk, Honorable Lewis B. Whitworth, Eleventh Judicial Circuit of Florida, 1976-1977 — Admitted to Bar, 1977, California; 1979, U.S. District Court, Southern District of California; 1995, U.S. District Court, Northern District of California — Member American (Tort and Insurance Practice Section) and San Diego County (Medical/Legal Committee) Bar Associations; State Bar of California; American Society of Healthcare Risk Management; Southern California Association for Healthcare Risk Management; San Diego Association of Healthcare Risk Management; American Board of Trial Advocates; Association of Southern California Defense Counsel; San Diego Defense Lawyers Association; Defense Research Institute — San Diego Super Lawyers; AV Rated by Martindale-Hubbell; Bar Register of Preeminent Lawyers — Practice Areas: Medical Malpractice; Tort Litigation; Personal Injury; Wrongful Death; Professional Errors and Omissions; Appellate Practice

Gabriel M. Benrubi — 1957 — San Diego State University, B.A., 1979; California Western School of Law, J.D. (cum laude), 1983 — Admitted to Bar, 1983, California; 1983, U.S. District Court, Southern District of California; 1987, U.S. District Court, Central District of California; 1995, U.S. District Court, Northern District of California — Member American and San Diego County Bar Associations; State Bar of California; San Diego Defense Lawyers Association (Board of Directors); Association of Southern California Defense Counsel — Certified to practice before General Courts Martial, U.S. Armed Forces, 1984 — LCDR, U.S. Naval Reserve, Judge Advocate General Corps.

Vincent J. Iuliano — 1963 — Suffolk University; Fairfield University, B.A., 1985; The Ohio State University Moritz College of Law, J.D., 1988 — Delta Theta Phi; Pi Sigma Alpha, Fairfield University — The Ohio State University College of Law, Law Journal — Admitted to Bar, 1988, Illinois; 1991, California; 1989, U.S. District Court, Northern District of Illinois; 1995, U.S. District Court, Southern District of California — Member American, Illinois State, San Diego County and Chicago Bar Associations; State Bar of California; Illinois Trial Lawyers Association; Association of Southern California Defense Counsel

Associates

Bruce William Boetter — 1957 — University of Illinois, B.S., 1979; San Diego State University, M.B.A., 1985; University of San Diego School of Law, J.D. (cum laude), 1997 — Admitted to Bar, 1997, California; U.S. District Court,

Belsky & Associates, San Diego, CA　　　　　**(Continued)**

Southern District of California — Member State Bar of California; San Diego County Bar Association; San Diego Defense Lawyers Association

Carolyn Balfour McCormick — 1976 — Yale University, B.A., 1998; University of San Diego School of Law, J.D., 2003 — Admitted to Bar, 2003, California; U.S. District Court, Southern District of California — Member State Bar of California; San Diego County Bar Association; San Diego Defense Lawyers Association — Practice Areas: Medical Malpractice; Wrongful Death; Civil Litigation

Nicholas R. Schechter — 1984 — University of California, Berkeley, B.A. (with honors), 2006; California Western School of Law, J.D., 2011 — Admitted to Bar, 2011, California — Member State Bar of California; San Diego County Bar Association — Practice Areas: Medical Malpractice; Personal Injury; Civil Litigation

Borton Petrini, LLP

1320 Columbia Street, Suite 210
San Diego, California 92101
　Telephone: 619-232-2424
　Fax: 619-531-0794
　E-Mail: bpsd@bortonpetrini.com
　www.bortonpetrini.com

Established: 1899

Admiralty and Maritime Law, Bad Faith, Casualty Insurance Law, Construction Law, Coverage Issues, Labor and Employment, Professional Liability

Firm Profile: Since 1899, Borton Petrini, LLP, has offered high quality legal services in all of the practice areas described above through its California network of 10 regional offices. The mission of Borton Petrini, LLP is to treat every file as though we were representing ourselves and paying the bill for that representation.

Managing Partner

Paul Kissel — 1951 — University of Miami, B.E., 1973; Florida State University, M.S.L.S., 1974; University of the Pacific, McGeorge School of Law, J.D., 1984 — Phi Delta Phi — Admitted to Bar, 1984, California; 1985, Florida; U.S. District Court, Eastern and Southern Districts of California — Member State Bar of California; The Florida Bar; San Diego County Bar Association — Author: "Peculiar Risk," California Defense Magazine (Summer 1991); "Reducing a Loss of Consortium Claim," California Defense Magazine (Spring 1993); "Mold - Hazard or Hype," California Defense Magazine (Summer 2003); "Minors' Compromises," California Defense Magazine (Winter 2004) — E-mail: pkissel@bortonpetrini.com

Partners

Jonathan P. Geen — 1960 — Columbia College, Columbia University, B.A., 1982; Northwestern School of Law, J.D., 1985 — John J. Coss Memorial Award for Scholastic Attainment, Aesthetic Appreciation and Sense of Public Responsibility - Recipient — Admitted to Bar, 1985, Illinois; 1997, California; 1988, U.S. District Court, Northern District of Illinois; 1997, U.S. Court of Appeals, Seventh Circuit; 2001, U.S. District Court, Southern District of California; 2001, U.S. Court of Appeals, Ninth Circuit — Member State Bar of California; San Diego County Bar Association — Senior Honor Society of Sachems (Member) — Languages: French — E-mail: jgeen@bortonpetrini.com

Jason A. Cohen — 1967 — George Mason University, B.A., 1991; University of San Diego School of Law, J.D., 2001 — Admitted to Bar, 2001, California; 2001, U.S. District Court, Southern District of California — Member State Bar of California; San Diego County Bar Association — Co-Author: Various Employment and Personal Injury Articles — E-mail: jcohen@bortonpetrini.com

Associate

Georgia L. Williams — 1959 — California Lutheran University, B.A., 1981; California Western School of Law, J.D., 1987 — Admitted to Bar, 1988, Pennsylvania; 1992, California; 2001, U.S. District Court, Central, Northern and Southern Districts of California — Member State Bar of California; San Diego County Bar Association; Lawyers' Club — U.S. Navy Reserve, LCDR (1984-1988) — E-mail: gwilliams@bortonpetrini.com

CALIFORNIA   SAN DIEGO

Borton Petrini, LLP, San Diego, CA   (Continued)

Senior Counsel

Robert S. Rucci — 1957 — University of California, Irvine, B.A., 1979; California Western School of Law, J.D., 1984 — Admitted to Bar, 1986, California; U.S. District Court, Central, Eastern and Southern Districts of California; Supreme Court of California — Member State Bar of California — E-mail: rrucci@bortonpetrini.com

Clements & Knock, LLP

7825 Fay Avenue, Suite 200
La Jolla, California 92037
　Telephone: 619-686-6900
　Fax: 866-433-2690
　E-Mail: rknock@cklawpro.com
　http://cklawpro.com

Established: 2000

General Civil Practice, State and Federal Courts, Trial and Appellate Practice, General Liability, Automobile, Construction Defect, Premises Liability, Business Law, Insurance Law

Firm Profile: A full service law firm serving California and providing counsel to and representation of insurers, their insureds and self-insured entities in a broad variety of civil litigation matters.

Insurance Clients

Business Alliance Insurance Company
State National Insurance Company, Inc.
Kemper Specialty
Liberty Mutual Insurance Company

Partners

Thomas V. Clements — University of California, Santa Cruz, B.A., 1980; Southwestern University School of Law, J.D. (SCALE Graduate), 1983 — Admitted to Bar, 1983, California; U.S. District Court, Central, Eastern, Northern and Southern Districts of California; Supreme Court of California — Member State Bar of California; San Diego Defense Lawyers Association — E-mail: tclements@cklawpro.com

Rick H. Knock — Albion College, B.A., 1972; Naval Postgraduate School, M.S.M.E., 1982; Thomas Jefferson School of Law, J.D., 1993 — Admitted to Bar, 1994, California; U.S. District Court, Southern District of California; U.S. Court of Appeals for the Federal and Ninth Circuits; Supreme Court of California; U.S. Patent and Trademark Office — Registered Patent Attorney, U.S. Patent and Trademark Office — Lt. Commander, U.S. Navy (retired) — E-mail: rknock@cklawpro.com

Clinton & Clinton

525 "B" Street, Suite 1500
San Diego, California 92101
　Telephone: 619-858-4728
　Fax: 619-858-4729
　E-Mail: dclinton@clinton-clinton.com
　www.clinton-clinton.com

(Long Beach, CA Office*: 100 Oceangate, Suite 1400, 90802)
　(Tel: 562-216-5000)
　(Fax: 562-216-5001)
(Los Angeles, CA Office*: 5757 West Century Boulevard, Suite 700, 90045)
　(Tel: 310-242-8615)
　(Fax: 310-242-8612)
(San Francisco, CA Office*: 201 Spear Street, Suite 1100, 94105)
　(Tel: 415-230-5368)
　(Fax: 415-230-5369)
(Sacramento, CA Office*: 770 'L' Street, Suite 500, 95814)
　(Tel: 916-361-6060)
　(Fax: 916-361-6061)
(Irvine, CA Office*: 2030 Main Street, Suite 1300, 92614)
　(Tel: 949-260-9083)
　(Fax: 949-260-9084)

Clinton & Clinton, San Diego, CA   (Continued)

(Calabasas, CA Office: 23480 Park Sorrento, Suite 219A, 91302)
　(Tel: 562-216-5000)
　(Fax: 562-216-5001)
(Birmingham, AL Office: 1 Chase Corporate Center, Suite 400, 35244)
　(Tel: 205-313-6329)
　(Fax: 562-216-5001)
(Cumming, GA Office: 410 Peachtree Parkway, Building 400, Suite 4245, 30041)
　(Tel: 678-341-5134)
　(Fax: 562-216-5001)
(Philadelphia, PA Office: 1315 Walnut Street, Suite 601, 19107)
　(Tel: 267-800-1897)
　(Fax: 267-800-1898)
(Nashville, TN Office: 2400 Crestmoor Road, 37215)
　(Tel: 615-386-7040)
　(Fax: 562-216-5001)
(Austin, TX Office: 12912 Hill Country Boulevard, Suite F210, 78738)
　(Tel: 512-200-7055)
　(Fax: 512-266-3655)
(Ft. Worth, TX Office: 109 East Third Street, Suite 350, 76102)
　(Tel: 817-900-8210)
　(Fax: 817-900-8221)
(Houston, TX Office: 480 North Sam Houston Parkway East, 77060-3528)
　(Tel: 713-659-0054)
　(Fax: 281-447-5733)

Asbestos Litigation, Automobile, Automotive Products Liability, Civil Litigation, Civil Rights, Civil Trial Practice, Commercial Litigation, Common Carrier, Complex Litigation, Construction Defect, Dental Malpractice, Employment Law, Environmental Law, Insurance Defense, Hospital Malpractice, Law Enforcement Liability, Legal Malpractice, Mass Tort, Medical Devices, Medical Malpractice, Pharmaceutical, Premises Liability, Product Liability, Retail Liability, Sexual Harassment, Slip and Fall, Special Investigative Unit Claims, Sports and Entertainment Liability, Toxic Torts, Truck Liability, Workers' Compensation

(See listing under Long Beach, CA for additional information)

Daley & Heft, LLP

462 Stevens Avenue, Suite 201
Solana Beach, California 92075
　Telephone: 858-755-5666
　Fax: 858-755-7870
　E-Mail: cshoate@daleyheft.com
　www.daleyheft.com

Established: 1980

Insurance Defense, Product Liability, Construction Defect, Employment Law, Coverage Issues

Insurance Clients

Allied, A Division of Nationwide
Philadelphia Insurance Company

Non-Insurance Clients

City of San Diego

Partners

Dennis W. Daley — 1948 — University of Washington, B.A., 1970; University of San Diego, J.D., 1976 — Admitted to Bar, 1976, California — Member American, Washington State, San Diego County and North San Diego County Bar Associations; State Bar of California

Robert R. Heft — 1950 — San Diego State University, B.A., 1973; University of San Diego, J.D., 1977 — Admitted to Bar, 1977, California — Member American, San Diego County and North San Diego County Bar Associations; State Bar of California

Daley & Heft, LLP, San Diego, CA (Continued)

Richard J. Schneider — 1959 — University of Minnesota, B.A., 1982; University of San Diego, J.D., 1985 — Admitted to Bar, 1985, California — Member State Bar of California; San Diego County Bar Association

Robert W. Brockman, Jr. — 1958 — John Carroll University, B.S., 1979; Xavier University, M.B.A., 1981; California Western University, J.D., 1985 — Admitted to Bar, 1986, California — Member State Bar of California; San Diego County and North San Diego County Bar Associations

Mitchell D. Dean — 1960 — University of California, San Diego, B.A., 1982; University of San Diego, J.D., 1986 — Admitted to Bar, 1987, California — Member American, San Diego County and North San Diego County Bar Associations; State Bar of California

David P. Berman — 1954 — University of California, San Diego, B.A., 1978; Southwestern University, J.D., 1985 — Admitted to Bar, 1986, California — Member State Bar of California; San Diego County and North San Diego County Bar Associations

Scott A. Noya — 1960 — Loyola University New Orleans, B.A., 1984; University of San Diego, J.D. (cum laude), 1988 — Admitted to Bar, 1988, California; 1991, Hawaii — Member State Bar of California; San Diego County and North San Diego County Bar Associations; International Right of Way Association

Robert H. Quayle, IV — 1966 — University of the Pacific, B.A., 1988; California Western University, J.D. (cum laude), 1991 — Admitted to Bar, 1991, California — Member State Bar of California; San Diego County and North San Diego County Bar Associations

Lee H. Roistacher — 1969 — University of Maryland, B.A., 1991; California Western University, J.D., 1995 — Admitted to Bar, 1995, California — Member State Bar of California; San Diego County Bar Association

Matthew E. Bennett — 1973 — University of California, Santa Barbara, B.A., 1995; University of San Diego, J.D., 1999 — Admitted to Bar, 1999, California — Member State Bar of California; San Diego County and North San Diego County Bar Associations

Farmer Case & Fedor

402 West Broadway
Suite 1100
San Diego, California 92101
   Telephone: 619-338-0300
   Fax: 619-338-0180
   E-Mail: cdoria@farmercase.com
   www.farmercase.com

(San Francisco, CA Office: 101 Montgomery Street, Suite 450, 94104)
   (Tel: 415-677-9816)
   (Fax: 415-677-9539)
   (E-Mail: jfarmer@farmercase.com)
(Orange County, CA Office: 20 Corporate Park, Suite 350, Irvine, 92606)
   (Tel: 714-662-5832)
   (Fax: 714-662-5927)
   (E-Mail: jfarmer@farmercase.com)
(Las Vegas, NV Office: 1100 East Bridger, Third Floor, 89125-2070)
   (Tel: 702-579-3900)
   (Fax: 702-739-3001)
   (E-Mail: tcase@farmercase.com)

Established: 1997

Construction Defect, Premises Liability, Insurance Coverage, Product Liability, Environmental Law, Business Law, Directors and Officers Liability, Professional Liability, Medical Liability, Design Professionals, Subrogation, Personal & Commercial Automobile Liability, Trucking Liability

Firm Profile: Farmer Case & Fedor brings its emphasis on value to all of the litigation and transactional legal matters we handle throughout the states of California and Nevada. To us, "value" connotes that blend of cost effectiveness and outcome that results in a sense of satisfaction with the work performed. The firm and its individual members are deeply committed to delivering value in the services they render for all of their clients.

Insurance Clients

Clarendon Insurance Company
G6 Hospitality LLC
Deep South Insurance Services
Horace Mann Insurance Company

Farmer Case & Fedor, San Diego, CA (Continued)

Infinity Insurance Company
Preferred Employers Insurance Company
Topa Insurance Company
VGM Insurance Company
Praetorian Financial Group
QBE the Americas
State Farm Mutual Automobile Insurance Company
Virginia Surety Company, Inc.

Non-Insurance Clients

Berkley Risk Services, LLC
Motel 6 Operating LP
7-Eleven, Inc.
Starr Adjustment Services, Inc.
York Pro, Inc.
California Insurance Guarantee Association
Specialty Claims Management
Tidewater Pacific Adjusters, Inc.

Partners

John T. Farmer — The University of Montana School of Law, J.D., 1977 — Admitted to Bar, 1977, Montana; 1979, California — E-mail: jfarmer@farmercase.com

Anthony T. Case — University of San Diego School of Law, J.D., 1990 — Admitted to Bar, 1990, California; 1998, Nevada — E-mail: tcase@farmercase.com

John M. Fedor — University of San Diego School of Law, J.D., 1990 — Admitted to Bar, 1990, California — E-mail: jfedor@farmercase.com

Senior Associate

Jason M. Murphy — University of San Diego School of Law, J.D., 2001 — Admitted to Bar, 2001, California

Associates

Daniel P. Fallon — University of San Diego School of Law, J.D., 2006 — Admitted to Bar, 2006, California — E-mail: dfallon@farmercase.com

Michele M. Angeles — Thomas Jefferson School of Law, J.D. (cum laude), 2003 — Admitted to Bar, 2003, California — E-mail: mangeles@farmercase.com

Alexander T. Bauer — California Western School of Law, J.D., 2009 — Admitted to Bar, 2010, California — E-mail: abauer@farmercase.com

Stacy M. Dooley — California Western University, J.D. (Dean's Honor List), 2012 — Admitted to Bar, 2013, California — E-mail: sdooley@farmercase.com

Kathryn C. Lee — California Western School of Law, J.D. (cum laude), 2009 — Admitted to Bar, 2009, California — E-mail: klee@farmercase.com

Tiffany L. Steward — Thomas Jefferson School of Law, J.D. (summa cum laude), 2011 — Admitted to Bar, 2011, California; 2012, Nevada — E-mail: tsteward@farmercase.com

Fredrickson, Mazeika & Grant, LLP

5720 Oberlin Drive
San Diego, California 92121
   Telephone: 800-231-8440
   Fax: 858-642-2001
   E-Mail: tgrant@fmglegal.com
   www.fmglegal.com

(Las Vegas, NV Office: 333 South 6th Street, Suite 230, 89101)
   (Tel: 702-384-4048)
   (Fax: 702-384-4484)
(San Francisco, CA Office: 300 Montgomery Street, Suite 410, 94104)
   (Tel: 415-957-1900)
   (Fax: 415-634-2646)
(Los Angeles, CA Office: 11755 Wilshire Boulevard, Suite 2400, 90025)
   (Tel: 818-246-2318)
   (Fax: 866-413-6263)
(Fresno, CA Office: 516 West Shaw Avenue, Suite 200, 93704)
   (Tel: 559-225-6600)
   (Fax: 559-981-1208)
(Phoenix, AZ Office: 40 North Central Avenue, Suite 1400, 85004)
   (Tel: 602-253-6323)
   (Fax: 602-391-3242)

Established: 1991

CALIFORNIA   SAN DIEGO

Fredrickson, Mazeika & Grant, LLP, San Diego, CA
(Continued)

Business Law, Construction Law, Product Liability, Personal Injury, Trucking Litigation, Professional Liability, Insurance, Pharmaceutical, Real Estate, Automobile, Environmental Law

Firm Profile: The firm's 21 attorneys provide services throughout California, Nevada and Arizona in a broad range of civil litigation matters.

Insurance Clients

ACE USA	American Claims Services, Inc.
Amlin, PLC	AmTrust North America
Arch Specialty Insurance Company	Atlas Insurance Company
Carl Warren & Company	Century Surety/Meadowbrook Insurance Group
Financial Pacific Insurance Company	Fireman's Fund Insurance Company
Liberty Mutual Group	
Lloyd's	Midlands Claim Administrators, Inc.
NAS/NAC	
NovaPro Risk Solutions	Sedgwick CMS
Specialty Claims Services, Inc.	Tower Group, Inc.
Travelers/Connecticut Specialties	York Claims Service, Inc.

Non-Insurance Clients

California Pharmacists Association	Frozen Food Express Industries, Inc.
Gale Industries	
Mansfield Plumbing Products	Masco Corporation
Milgard Manufacturing, Inc.	Western Pottery, L.L.C.

Partners

Tomas V. Mazeika — California State University, Los Angeles, B.A., 1972; Loyola Marymount University, J.D., 1975 — Admitted to Bar, 1975, California; 1997, Nevada — Resident Las Vegas, NV Office — Tel: 702-384-4048 — E-mail: tmazeika@fmglegal.com

Timothy J. Grant — San Jose State University, B.A., 1983; Magdalen College, Oxford University; University of Santa Clara, J.D., 1986 — Admitted to Bar, 1986, California — Tel: 858-642-2002 — E-mail: tgrant@fmglegal.com

Non-Equity Partners

Jacqueline F. Stein — State University of New York at Albany, B.A., 1979; Georgia State University, J.D., 1982 — Admitted to Bar, 1985, California — Tel: 858-842-2002

Peter S. Gregorovic — John Jay College of Criminal Justice of the City University of New York, B.A., 1985; California Western University, J.D., 1988 — Admitted to Bar, 1988, California — Resident Los Angeles, CA Office — Tel: 818-246-2318

John A. Cronin — University of California, Pharm.D., 1976; University of San Diego School of Law, J.D., 1987 — Admitted to Bar, 1987, California — Tel: 858-642-2002

Elliot H. Heller — University of California, Santa Barbara, B.A., 1991; Thomas Jefferson School of Law, J.D., 1993 — Admitted to Bar, 1994, California — Tel: 858-642-2002

Stephen B. Heath — Oklahoma University, B.A., 2002; Wesleyan University, J.D., 2005 — Admitted to Bar, 2005, California — Resident San Francisco, CA Office — Tel: 415-957-1900

Ronald J. Lauter — Indiana University, B.S. (magna cum laude), 1983; Indiana University School of Law-Bloomington, J.D. (cum laude), 1986 — Admitted to Bar, 1986, Arizona; 1991, California — Resident Phoenix, AZ Office — Tel: 602-253-6323

Law Offices of Kenneth N. Greenfield

16516 Bernardo Center Drive, Suite 210
San Diego, California 92128
Telephone: 858-675-0301
Fax: 858-675-0319
E-Mail: info@thegreenfieldlawfirm.com
www.thegreenfieldlawfirm.com

Established: 1988

Insurance Defense, Insurance Bad Faith, Appellate Practice, Subrogation, State and Federal Courts, Insurance Coverage Litigation and Opinions

Law Offices of Kenneth N. Greenfield, San Diego, CA
(Continued)

Firm Profile: The firm has extensive experience in both first and third party insurance matters, including insurance defense, insurance "bad faith," subrogation, and insurance appraisals.

Insurance Clients

Allstate Insurance Company	California Earthquake Authority
Farmers Home Mutual Insurance Company	Fireman's Fund Insurance Companies
General Star Management Company	North Carolina Farm Bureau Insurance Group
State Farm Insurance Company	Wawanesa General Insurance Company
Wawanesa Mutual Insurance Company	Western Home Insurance Company

Owner

Kenneth N. Greenfield — 1951 — The University of Arizona, B.A., 1978; California Western School of Law, J.D. (cum laude), 1982 — Managing Editor, Law Review — Admitted to Bar, 1982, California; 1994, U.S. District Court, Central and Southern Districts of California; 1995, U.S. Court of Appeals, Ninth Circuit — Member State Bar of California; San Diego County Bar Association; The Louis M. Welsh American Inn of Court; San Diego Defense Lawyers Association (Past President); American Board of Trial Advocates (Board of Directors, Treasurer); Association of Southern California Defense Counsel — Arbitrator, Superior and Municipal Courts, 1988-present; Judge Pro Tem, San Diego Municipal Court, 1990 — Practice Areas: Insurance Bad Faith; Civil Litigation — E-mail: kgreenfield@thegreenfieldlawfirm.com

Associates

Alexandra N. Selfridge — 1980 — University of California, San Diego, B.A., 2002; University of San Diego School of Law, J.D., 2006 — Admitted to Bar, 2006, California; 2006, U.S. District Court, Southern District of California — Member State Bar of California; San Diego Defense Lawyers Association (Vice President/President Elect) — Practice Areas: Insurance Bad Faith; Civil Litigation — E-mail: selfridge@thegreenfieldlawfirm.com

Anastasia F. Osbrink — 1983 — San Diego State University, B.A., 2008; University of California, Los Angeles School of Law, J.D., 2013 — Admitted to Bar, 2013, California; 2014, U.S. District Court, Central District of California — Member State Bar of California; San Diego Defense Lawyers Association — Practice Areas: Insurance Bad Faith; Civil Litigation — E-mail: aosbrink@thegreenfieldlawfirm.com

Grimm, Vranjes & Greer LLP

550 West C Street, Suite 1100
San Diego, California 92101-3532
Telephone: 619-231-8802
Fax: 619-233-6039
www.gvgllp.com

Established: 1976

Insurance Defense, Personal Injury, Wrongful Death, Product Liability, Bad Faith, Construction Defect, Professional Errors and Omissions, Directors and Officers Liability, Environmental Law, Toxic Torts, Premises Liability, Americans with Disabilities Act, Legal Malpractice, Employment Litigation, Insurance Coverage Litigation, Trademark and Copyright Litigation, Elder Abuse, Design Professionals Liability, Real Estate Agent and Broker Errors and Omissions, Pharmacy Errors and Omissions, Insurance Agent and Broker Errors and Omissions

Insurance Clients

AIG	Gallagher Bassett Services, Inc.
IAT Group	Lexington Insurance Company
North American Specialty Insurance Company	Occidental Fire & Casualty Company of North Carolina
Tower Group	Travelers Insurance
Wilshire Insurance Company	

Non-Insurance Clients

BASF Corporation	The Corky McMillin Companies
DPR Construction, Inc.	Rite Aid Corporation
Truly Nolen of America, Inc	

SAN DIEGO   CALIFORNIA

Grimm, Vranjes & Greer LLP, San Diego, CA (Continued)

Partners

W. Patrick Grimm — 1949 — Loyola Marymount University, B.B.A., 1972; University of San Diego, J.D., 1979 — Admitted to Bar, 1979, California; U.S. District Court, Central, Eastern, Northern and Southern Districts of California — Member State Bar of California; San Diego County Bar Association; San Diego Defense Lawyers Association

Mark Vranjes — 1956 — University of California, San Diego, B.S., 1979; University of San Diego, J.D., 1982 — Admitted to Bar, 1982, California; U.S. District Court, Central, Eastern, Northern and Southern Districts of California — Member State Bar of California; San Diego County Bar Association; San Diego Defense Lawyers Association; Defense Research Institute

Jeffrey Y. Greer — 1955 — Oregon State University; San Diego State University, B.A., 1981; Western State University, J.D., 1983 — Admitted to Bar, 1983, California; 2003, U.S. District Court, Central, Eastern, Northern and Southern Districts of California — Member State Bar of California; San Diego County Bar Association; San Diego Defense Lawyers Association

Michael B. Martin — 1961 — University of Nevada, Las Vegas, B.A., 1984; California Western University, J.D., 1987 — Admitted to Bar, 1987, Nevada; 1990, California; U.S. District Court, Central, Eastern, Northern and Southern Districts of California — Member State Bar of California; State Bar of Nevada; San Diego County and Clark County Bar Associations; San Diego Defense Lawyers Association

Eugene P. Kenny — 1953 — State University of New York at Stony Brook, B.A., 1979; University of San Diego, J.D., 1982 — Admitted to Bar, 1982, California; U.S. District Court, Central, Eastern, Northern and Southern Districts of California — Member State Bar of California; San Diego County Bar Association; San Diego Defense Lawyers Association

Gregory D. Stephan — 1959 — Franklin & Marshall College, B.A., 1981; California Western University, J.D., 1987 — Admitted to Bar, 1988, California; U.S. District Court, Central, Eastern, Northern and Southern Districts of California — Member State Bar of California; San Diego County Bar Association; San Diego Defense Lawyers Association

Lisa S. Bridgman — 1975 — University of San Diego School of Law, J.D. (magna cum laude), 2001 — Admitted to Bar, 2001, California; U.S. District Court, Central, Eastern, Northern and Southern Districts of California — Member State Bar of California; San Diego County Bar Association; San Diego Defense Lawyers Association

Munro Smigliani & Jordan, LLP

2251 San Diego Avenue, Suite B-257
San Diego, California 92110
   Telephone: 619-295-2955
   Fax: 619-295-2959
   E-Mail: info@msjlaw.com
   www.msjlaw.com

(Los Angeles, CA Office: 355 South Grand Avenue, Suite 2450, 90071)
   (Tel: 213-943-1364)
(San Francisco, CA Office: 101 California Street, Suite 2450, 94111)
   (Tel: 415-946-8859)
(Phoenix, AZ Office: 2942 North 24th Street, Suite 114-528, 85016)
   (Tel: 602-424-7457)

Professional Malpractice, Professional Negligence, Property Defense, Public Entities, Public Liability, Reinsurance, Risk Management, Self-Insured, Self-Insured Defense, Sexual Harassment, Slip and Fall, State and Federal Courts, Subrogation, Toxic Torts, Trial and Appellate Practice, Trial Practice, Truck Liability, Uninsured and Underinsured Motorist, Wrongful Death, Wrongful Termination, Real Estate, Errors and Omissions, Business Litigation, Sports and Recreation

Firm Profile: Munro Smigliani & Jordan, LLP and its predecessor firms have been involved in insurance defense and commercial litigation in Southern California since 1978. The attorneys of Munro Smigliani & Jordan, LLP are experienced trial counsel in the areas of insurance bad faith, automobile, commercial litigation, construction defect, products liability, professional liability, business litigation, real estate litigation, sports and recreation, trucking and transportation, and employment discrimination-wrongful termination.

Munro Smigliani & Jordan, LLP, San Diego, CA (Continued)

Insurance Clients

Aegis Security Insurance Company
Allstate Risk Management
Clarendon America Insurance Company
Distinguished Programs Group, LLC
Glencoe Group Services, Inc.
Ironshore Specialty Insurance Company
Lloyd's Underwriters
Preferred Contractors Insurance Company
TRISTAR Risk Management
Twenty Mile Insurance Services
West Coast Casualty Service

Aggressive Insurance
Armour Risk Management
Clarendon National Insurance Company
First Mercury Insurance Company
GAINSCO, Inc.
Harbor Specialty Insurance Company
James River Insurance Company
Network Adjusters, Inc.
RenaissanceRe
Sedgwick Claims Management Services, Inc.
Unitrin Insurance Company

Non-Insurance Clients

American Claims Management, Inc.
North American Risk Services
Precision Risk Management, Inc.
Tidewater Pacific Adjusters, Inc.

Blackhawk Claims Service, Inc.
Midlands Claim Administrators, Inc.
San Diego State University
Tuesday Morning, Inc.

Partners

Douglas J. Munro — 1960 — University of California, Santa Barbara, B.A., 1982; University of San Diego School of Law, J.D., 1989 — Admitted to Bar, 1989, California; U.S. District Court, Central, Northern and Southern Districts of California — Member San Diego County and Orange County Bar Associations — E-mail: dmunro@msjlaw.com

Paul W. Smigliani — 1965 — Lafayette College, B.A., 1987; University of San Diego, M.B.A., 1989; University of San Diego School of Law, J.D., 1994 — Admitted to Bar, 1994, California; 2012, Arizona; U.S. District Court, Central, Eastern, Northern and Southern Districts of California; U.S. Bankruptcy Court, Central and Southern Districts of California — Member State Bar of California (Board of Governors, 1999-2000); San Diego County Bar Association; San Diego Defense Lawyers Association — E-mail: psmigliani@msjlaw.com

Of Counsel

R. Michael Jordan — 1950 — California Western University; United States International University, B.A., 1971; University of Santa Clara School of Law, J.D. (magna cum laude), 1982 — Admitted to Bar, 1983, California; 1989, U.S. District Court, Central and Southern Districts of California — Member San Diego County Bar Association — E-mail: rjordan@msjlaw.com

Murchison & Cumming, LLP

Symphony Towers
750 B Street, Suite 2550
San Diego, California 92101
   Telephone: 619-544-6838
   Fax: 619-544-1568

Civil Litigation, Business Transactions

(See listing under Los Angeles, CA for additional information)

Neil, Dymott, Frank, McFall & Trexler
A Professional Law Corporation

1010 Second Avenue, Suite 2500
San Diego, California 92101-4959
   Telephone: 619-238-1712
   Fax: 619-238-1562
   E-Mail: jmcfall@neildymott.com
   www.neildymott.com

(Palm Desert, CA Office: 41-990-F Cook Street, Suite 2004, 92211)
   (Tel: 760-568-9959)
   (Fax: 760-340-0011)
   (E-Mail: strexler@neildymott.com)

CALIFORNIA   SAN DIEGO

Neil, Dymott, Frank, McFall & Trexler, A Professional Law Corporation, San Diego, CA (Continued)

(Temecula, CA Office: 43920 Margarita Road, Suite B, 92592)
(Tel: 951-303-3930)
(Fax: 951-303-3940)
(E-Mail: strexler@neildymott.com)

Established: 1964

Administrative Law, Appellate Practice, Bad Faith, Business Law, Civil Litigation, Construction Defect, Employment Law, Environmental Law, Estate Planning, Governmental Liability, Insurance Coverage, Medical Malpractice, Premises Liability, Probate, Product Liability, Trucking Litigation, Healthcare Fraud and Abuse, Professional Liability including Medical, Dental and Legal Malpractice, Trucking and Transportation

Firm Profile: Established in 1964, Neil, Dymott, Frank, McFall & Trexler APLC, has gained national recognition as one of the premier law firms in San Diego and throughout Southern California, and we have earned the highest rating for professional excellence, skill and integrity. Five of the firm's partners are members of the prestigious American Board of Trial Advocates (ABOTA) which limits eligibility to lawyers with extensive jury trial experience who are of high personal character and reputation. Lawyers of the firm have distinguished themselves as leaders of the civil bar on local, state and national levels and many serve as arbitrators, mediators and judges' pro tem. Over the years, the firm has been honored to have several lawyers appointed to both federal and state judgeships.

Insurance Clients

CNP Insurance Company
Doctors' Company Insurance Group
Hartford Accident and Indemnity Company
NCMIC Insurance Company
Occidental Fire & Casualty Company of North Carolina
RLI Insurance Company
Royal & SunAlliance USA
Safeco Insurance Companies
SCPIE Companies
United Community Insurance Company
The Dentists Insurance Company - TDIC
Fireman's Fund Insurance Company
The Medical Protective Company
North American Specialty Insurance Company
Oregon Mutual Insurance Company
Royal Surplus Lines Insurance Company
21st Century Insurance Company
Western World Insurance Company

Shareholders

Thomas M. Dymott — (1945-2002)

Michael I. Neil — 1940 — San Diego State University, B.A., 1962; University of California, Berkeley Boalt Hall School of Law, LL.B., 1966 — Admitted to Bar, 1967, California; 1970, U.S. District Court, Southern District of California; 1996, U.S. District Court, Northern District of California — Member American and San Diego County Bar Associations; American College of Trial Lawyers; American Board of Trial Advocates, Diplomat; Federation of Defense and Corporate Counsel (Vice President, 2002-2003); Association of Southern California Defense Counsel (President, 1988-1989); Defense Research Institute; California Medical-Legal Committee; Southern California Association of Healthcare Risk Management; San Diego Defense Lawyers Association — Brigadier General, U.S. Marine Corp Reserve [Retired] — Practice Areas: Professional Liability; Product Liability; Business Law; General Liability; Civil Litigation; Personal Injury — E-mail: mneil@neildymott.com

Robert W. Frank — 1955 — San Diego State University, A.B., 1977; University of California, Hastings College of the Law, J.D., 1980 — Phi Beta Kappa — Admitted to Bar, 1980, California — Member American Board of Trial Advocates; American, San Diego County and Desert Bar Associations; Association of Southern California Defense Counsel; California Medical-Legal Committee; Defense Research Institute; Professional Liability Underwriting Society; San Diego Defense Lawyers Association; Health Care Compliance Association; San Diego Association for Healthcare Risk Management; Southern California Association of Healthcare Risk Management — Practice Areas: Professional Liability; General Liability; Civil Litigation; Dental Malpractice; Medical Malpractice — E-mail: rfrank@neildymott.com

James A. McFall — 1958 — University of California, San Diego, B.A., 1981; University of California, Hastings College of the Law, J.D., 1985 — Admitted to Bar, 1985, California; 1985, U.S. District Court, Central, Eastern, Northern and Southern Districts of California; U.S. Court of Appeals, Ninth

Neil, Dymott, Frank, McFall & Trexler, A Professional Law Corporation, San Diego, CA (Continued)

Circuit — Member San Diego County Bar Association; Association of Southern California Defense Counsel; Defense Research Institute; San Diego Defense Lawyers Association; Association of Business Trial Lawyers; Professional Liability Underwriting Society — Practice Areas: Insurance Coverage; Bad Faith; Civil Litigation; Complex Litigation; Commercial Litigation — E-mail: jmcfall@neildymott.com

Sheila S. Trexler — 1950 — College of the Desert, A.D.N., 1973; University of Nevada, B.S.N., 1982; California Western School of Law, J.D., 1985 — Admitted to Bar, 1986, California; 1986, U.S. District Court, Southern District of California; 1994, U.S. Court of Appeals, Ninth Circuit — Member San Diego County and Desert Bar Associations; American Board of Trial Advocates; Association of Southern California Defense Counsel; Southern California Association of Healthcare Risk Management; American Society of Healthcare Risk Management; San Diego Organization of Healthcare Leaders; The American Association of Nurse Attorneys; Defense Research Institute; San Diego Defense Lawyers Association; Lawyers Club of San Diego; San Diego Association for Healthcare Risk Management; San Diego County Medical Society and Bar — Practice Areas: Medical Liability; Civil Litigation; Health Care; Medical Malpractice; Medical Negligence — E-mail: strexler@neildymott.com

Hugh A. McCabe — 1961 — Humboldt State University, B.A., 1984; University of the Pacific, McGeorge School of Law, J.D., 1987 — Phi Alpha Delta — Admitted to Bar, 1987, California; 1987, U.S. District Court, Central, Northern and Southern Districts of California; U.S. Court of Appeals, Ninth Circuit; 1996, U.S. Supreme Court — Member San Diego County Bar Association; Society for Human Resource Management (San Diego Chapter); Southern California Association of Health Risk Management; American Inns of Court; San Diego Defense Lawyers Association; American Board of Trial Advocates; Association of Business Trial Lawyers; Association of Southern California Defense Counsel; Defense Research Institute; Association of Defense Trial Attorneys — Practice Areas: Professional Liability; General Liability; Employment Law; Trucking Law; Transportation; Civil Litigation; Business Law — E-mail: hmccabe@neildymott.com

Clark R. Hudson — 1961 — The University of Arizona, B.A., 1983; Washburn University School of Law, J.D., 1990 — Phi Alpha Delta — Admitted to Bar, 1990, California; 1994, Arizona; 1990, U.S. District Court, Southern District of California; 1992, U.S. District Court, Central District of California — Member San Diego County Bar Association; Litigation Counsel of America; San Diego Association for Healthcare Risk Management; Southern California Association for Health Risk Management; American Board of Trial Advocates; American Inns of Court; Association of Southern California Defense Counsel; Defense Research Institute; Federation of Defense and Corporate Counsel; San Diego Defense Lawyers Association — Captain, U.S. Marine Corps, 1983-1986, 1991 — Practice Areas: Professional Liability; General Liability; Civil Litigation; Medical Malpractice — E-mail: chudson@neildymott.com

Stephen T. Sigler — 1970 — The University of Kansas, B.A., 1992; The University of Kansas School of Law, J.D., 1996 — Admitted to Bar, 1996, California; 1996, U.S. District Court, Southern District of California — Member Federal and San Diego County Bar Associations; Southern California Association for Health Risk Management; San Diego Association for Healthcare Risk Management; Association of Southern California Defense Counsel; Defense Research Institute; San Diego Defense Lawyers Association — Practice Areas: Professional Liability; General Liability; Premises Liability; Product Liability; Civil Litigation — E-mail: ssigler@neildymott.com

David P. Burke — 1971 — Saint Mary's College of California, B.A. (cum laude), 1994; Notre Dame Law School, National Institute for Trial Advocacy, J.D., 1998 — Admitted to Bar, 1999, California; U.S. District Court, Northern and Southern Districts of California; U.S. Court of Appeals, Ninth Circuit; Supreme Court of California — Member San Diego County Bar Association; San Diego Association for Healthcare Risk Management; San Diego Defense Lawyers Association; Defense Research Institute; Association of Southern California Defense Counsel — Practice Areas: Appellate Practice; Health Care; Professional Liability; Premises Liability; Product Liability — E-mail: dburke@neildymott.com

Tamara L. Glaser — 1967 — Case Western Reserve University, B.A. (cum laude), 1989; University of Pittsburgh School of Law, J.D. (cum laude), 1993 — Admitted to Bar, 1993, Pennsylvania; 1994, Florida; 1999, California; U.S. District Court, Central and Southern Districts of California — Member San Diego County Bar Association; Association of Southern California Defense Counsel; Defense Research Institute; San Diego Defense Lawyers Association — Practice Areas: Civil Litigation; Elder Abuse; Health Care; Medical Malpractice; Premises Liability; Product Liability — E-mail: tglaser@neildymott.com

SAN DIEGO   **CALIFORNIA**

Neil, Dymott, Frank, McFall & Trexler, A Professional Law Corporation, San Diego, CA   (Continued)

Jason E. Gallegos — 1972 — University of California, San Diego, B.A., 1993; University of California, Los Angeles School of Law, J.D., 1996 — Admitted to Bar, 1996, California; U.S. District Court, Central and Southern Districts of California; U.S. Supreme Court; Supreme Court of California — Member Desert Bar Association; Association of Southern California Defense Counsel; American Inns of Court — Practice Areas: Appellate; Estate Planning; General Liability; Health Care; Professional Liability; Medical Malpractice Defense — E-mail: jegallegos@neildymott.com

Matthew R. Souther — 1974 — University of Nevada, B.A., 1999; California Western School of Law, J.D., 2003 — Admitted to Bar, 2003, California; U.S. District Court, Southern District of California — Practice Areas: Medical Malpractice Defense; Health Care Liability; Administrative Law; General Defense Civil Litigation; Elder Abuse; Personal Injury; Professional Liability — E-mail: msouther@neildymott.com

Benjamin J. Howard — 1974 — U.S. Military Academy, B.S., 1996; The University of Oklahoma, M.A., 2001; The University of Iowa College of Law, J.D., 2005 — Admitted to Bar, 2005, California; U.S. District Court, Southern District of California — Practice Areas: General Civil Litigation; Medical Malpractice Defense; Personal Injury Litigation — E-mail: bhoward@neildymott.com

Law Office of Donald M. Pilger

225 Broadway, Suite 2100
San Diego, California 92101
   Telephone: 619-233-8700
   Fax: 619-233-5730
   E-Mail: dpilger@juno.com

Established: 1996

Workers' Compensation, Coverage Issues, Civil Litigation, Subrogation, Appellate Practice, Insurance Law, Employer Representation

Firm Profile: Since 1996, the Law Office of Donald M. Pilger has provided high-quality legal services, with primary focus in the field of workers' compensation defense. The firm principally represents employers and insurance carriers in defending workers' compensation claims. The firm also maintains a general civil litigation practice, including subrogation and employer representation, along with coverage issues and appellate work. The firm philosophy is to provide detailed, high-caliber legal services, from case inception through final disposition, while maintaining cost-effectiveness for the client. High value is placed on responsiveness to the client's inquiries and needs in all areas of litigation handling, with simultaneous cost control for the benefit of each client. The firm has represented the interests of such high-profile clientele as Zenith Insurance Company and Berkshire Hathaway, while also representing smaller entities and more regional insurance carriers. The firm provides services in numerous venues throughout southern California, from San Diego to Santa Barbara, and east to El Centro and San Bernardino.

Representative Clients

Golden Eagle Insurance Corporation	Highlands Insurance Group
Tristar Claims Management	Liberty Mutual Insurance Company
	Zenith Insurance Company

Donald M. Pilger — 1965 — University of Notre Dame, B.B.A., 1987; University of San Diego, J.D., 1990 — Admitted to Bar, 1991, California; 1992, Florida; 1991, U.S. District Court, Southern District of California; 1991, U.S. Court of Appeals, Ninth Circuit — Member State Bar of California; The Florida Bar (Out-of-State Practitioners' Division); San Diego County Bar Association (Workers' Compensation and General Civil Litigation Sections) — Certified AMA Impairment Rater, American Board of Independent Medical Examiners, 2007-present; Instructor, Insurance Educational Association, 1994-present; Faculty Member, National Business Institute, 1998-present; Faculty Member, Sterling Educational Service, 2003-present; Faculty Member, Lorman Educational Services, 2004-present; Recognized Lecturer on Issues of Workers' Compensation Law; Board of Directors, Harmonium, Inc. (Chairman of the Board, 2002-present)

Robertson & Associates, APC

655 West Broadway, Suite 1410
San Diego, California 92101
   Telephone: 619-531-7000
   Fax: 619-531-7007
   E-Mail: lworden@robertsonclark.com
   www.robertsonapc.com

(Seattle, WA Office*: 701 Fifth Avenue, Suite 4200, 98104)
   (Tel: 206-262-8144)
   (Fax: 206-262-8001)
   (E-Mail: info@robertsonapc.com)

Established: 2001

Insurance Coverage, Insurance Defense, Construction Defect, Professional Liability, Subrogation, Recoveries

Firm Profile: The goal at Robertson & Associates, APC is to build strong client relationships by providing exceptional legal services in an expeditious and cost-effective manner. The firm's attorneys have high academic credentials, valuable experience and a strong belief in Robertson & Associates, APC philosophy.

Insurance Clients

American Safety Claims Services, Inc.	Auto-Owners Insurance Company
Maxum Indemnity Company	AXIS Insurance
Reliant Structural Warranty Insurance Company, Inc.	OneBeacon Insurance

Non-Insurance Clients

Apex Pacific, Inc.	Blue Horizon Homes
California Sheet Metal Works, Inc.	Claims Resource Management, Inc.
C.W. Construction	Discount Glass & Mirror, Inc.
George Hills Company, Inc.	M & F Fishing
Pacific Century Homes	Saddleback Waterproofing
Sundt Construction	William Kelley & Sons California, Inc.

Principal and Shareholder

Les W. Robertson — Massachusetts College of Liberal Arts, B.A., 1981; Chicago-Kent College of Law, J.D., 1988 — Admitted to Bar, 1988, Illinois; 1989, California; 2004, Washington; 2009, Oregon; 1988, U.S. District Court, Northern District of Illinois; 1989, U.S. District Court, Central District of California; 1990, U.S. District Court, Southern District of California; 2005, U.S. District Court, Western District of Washington; 2009, U.S. District Court, Eastern District of California; 2011, U.S. Court of Appeals, Ninth Circuit; 2012, U.S. District Court, Eastern District of Washington — Member American Bar Associaion; San Diego County Bar Association (Insurance Law Section); AAA Southern California Panel of Neutrals (Construction, Commercial); Founding Panel Member of AAA Nationwide Complex Coverage Neutral Evaluation (CCNE) Panel — E-mail: lrobertson@robertsonapc.com

Associate Attorneys

Kathleen A. Harrison — Boston University, B.A., 1993; University of the Pacific, McGeorge School of Law, J.D. (with distinction), 1997 — Admitted to Bar, 1997, California; 2005, Washington; 1997, U.S. District Court, Southern District of California; 2006, U.S. District Court, Western District of Washington — Member San Diego County Bar Association — E-mail: kharrison@robertsonapc.com

Jack S. Fischer — University of Maryland, College Park, B.A. Political Science, 1988; California Western School of Law, J.D., 1993 — Admitted to Bar, 1994, California; U.S. District Court, Central, Eastern, Northern and Southern Districts of California — Member San Diego County Bar Association — E-mail: jfischer@robertsonapc.com

CALIFORNIA — SAN DIEGO

Law Offices of Greg J. Ryan, APLC

1010 Second Avenue, Suite 2500
San Diego, California 92101
   Telephone: 619-239-4848
   Fax: 619-239-8858
   E-Mail: greg@gjryan.com
   www.gjryan.com

Established: 1927

Insurance Defense, Coverage Issues, Litigation, Bad Faith, Civil Litigation, Appellate Practice

Non-Insurance Clients

American Names Association
McMillin Construction Company
Aspen Insurance Brokers
Pardee Homes

Greg J. Ryan — California Western School of Law, J.D. (cum laude), 1980 — Admitted to Bar, 1980, California; 1980, U.S. District Court, Southern District of California; 1995, U.S. Court of Appeals, Ninth Circuit; 1997, U.S. Supreme Court — Member American Bar Association; State Bar of California; U.S. Supreme Court Bar Association; Association of Southern California Defense Counsel; San Diego Defense Lawyers Association; Defense Research Institute

Schonfeld, Bertsche & Preciado, LLP

402 West Broadway, Suite 1890
San Diego, California 92101-8577
   Telephone: 619-544-8300
   Fax: 619-338-0017
   E-Mail: mmcnalley@schonfeldlaw.com
   www.schonfeldlaw.com

Appellate Practice, Commercial Litigation, Insurance Defense, Legal Malpractice, Professional Malpractice, Trial Practice

Firm Profile: Schonfeld, Bertsche & Preciado, LLP is a top rated litigation and appellate law firm with a long standing and well earned reputation for excellence and integrity. The firm handles a broad spectrum of cases throughout California, with a strong emphasis on professional liability defense.

Insurance Clients

Argo Pro
Lawyers Mutual Insurance Company

Partners

Alan H. Schonfeld — California Western School of Law, J.D., 1985 — Admitted to Bar, 1985, California

Corinne Coleman Bertsche

Cecilia Preciado

Sheppard, Mullin, Richter & Hampton LLP

501 West Broadway, 19th Floor
San Diego, California 92101
   Telephone: 619-338-6500
   www.sheppardmullin.com

Established: 1927

Antitrust, Bad Faith, Class Actions, Complex Litigation, Insurance Litigation, Trial and Appellate Practice

Firm Profile: Sheppard, Mullin, Richter & Hampton LLP represents clients in a wide variety of insurance-related litigation matters. The firm represents insurance companies, producers and third party administrators in all types of litigation, ranging from class actions and complex multi-party litigation to

Sheppard, Mullin, Richter & Hampton LLP, San Diego, CA (Continued)

single insured disputes, and assists insurer clients in administrative and regulatory proceedings.

Partners

John T. Brooks — Stanford University, B.A. (Phi Beta Kappa), 1988; Stanford Law School, J.D., 1993 — California Academy of Appellate Lawyers; Chambers USA Ranking - 2014: Band 4, 2013: Band 4, 2012: Band 4, 2011: Band 4, 2010: Band 3, 2009: Band 4 - Insurance, Insurer Firms, California — Admitted to Bar, 1993, California — Tel: 619-338-6537 — E-mail: jbrooks@sheppardmullin.com

R. Randal Crispen — University of California, Santa Barbara, B.A. (with highest honors), 1981; University of California, Berkeley Boalt Hall School of Law, J.D., 1985 — Admitted to Bar, 1985, California — Member American and San Diego County (Advisory Board, Insurance/Bad Faith Section) Bar Associations; American Inns of Court, Louis Welsh Chapter (Master); Association of Business Trial Lawyers — San Diego County Superior Court (Judge Pro Tem) — Tel: 619-338-6627 — E-mail: rcrispen@sheppardmullin.com

Charles A. Danaher — Rutgers College, B.A. (summa cum laude), 1986; Harvard University, J.D. (cum laude), 1989 — Admitted to Bar, 1989, California; 2008, Maryland — Tel: 619-338-6548 — E-mail: cdanaher@sheppardmullin.com

Marc J. Feldman — Princeton University, A.B. (cum laude, Phi Beta Kappa), 1985; Harvard University, J.D. (magna cum laude), 1989 — Admitted to Bar, 1989, California; 2009, Maryland — Member San Diego County Bar Association (Insurance Bad Faith Section, Past President); Association of Business Trial Lawyers — Tel: 619-338-6526 — E-mail: mfeldman@sheppardmullin.com

Peter H. Klee — University of California, Berkeley, A.B. (Phi Beta Kappa), 1979; University of California, Berkeley Boalt Hall School of Law, J.D., 1983 — Admitted to Bar, 1983, California — Member American Board of Trial Advocates (Associate); American College of Trial Lawyers — Tel: 619-338-6624 — E-mail: pklee@sheppardmullin.com

(See listing under Los Angeles, CA for additional information)

Siegel, Moreno & Stettler, APC

1011 Camino del Rio South, Suite 600
San Diego, California 92108
   Telephone: 619-525-7626
   Fax: 619-525-7685
   E-Mail: biwinter@siegelmoreno.com
   www.siegelmoreno.com

Litigation, Subrogation, Workers' Compensation, Fraud, Employment Law, Insurance Defense Workers' Compensation

Firm Profile: Siegel, Moreno & Stettler, APC provides personal service and attention afforded a smaller firm coupled with the capabilities and expertise of a large firm. Our firm has managed cases throughout California and has been able to meet clients' specialized defense needs on a cost effective basis.

Insurance Clients

Berkshire Hathaway Homestate Companies
Chartis/AIG Domestic Claims Inc.
Liberty Mutual Insurance Company
United America Insurance Group
California Joint Powers Insurance Authority
Everest National Insurance Company
Zenith Insurance Company

Non-Insurance Clients

Capistrano Unified School District
Kaiser Permanente
Solar Turbines, Inc.
Starwood Hotels & Resorts Worldwide, Inc.
CorVel Corporation
Sedgwick Claims Management Services, Inc.
Tristar Claims Management
York Insurance Services Group, Inc.

Partner

Steven M. Siegel — 1950 — United States International University, B.A., 1974;

SAN FRANCISCO   CALIFORNIA

Siegel, Moreno & Stettler, APC, San Diego, CA (Continued)

California Western School of Law, J.D., 1976 — Admitted to Bar, 1976, California — Member State Bar of California; San Diego County Bar Association; California Workers' Compensation Defense Attorney Association; San Diego Insurance Adjusters Association; RIMS; San Diego Defense Lawyers Association

Walsh McKean Furcolo LLP

550 West C Street, Suite 950
San Diego, California 92101
 Telephone: 619-232-8486
Fax: 619-232-2691
E-Mail: jwalsh@wmfllp.com
www.wmfllp.com

Established: 1996

Construction Defect, Insurance Coverage, Bad Faith, Toxic Torts, Product Liability, Professional Liability, Medical Malpractice, Personal Injury, General Liability, Premises Liability, Employer Liability

Firm Profile: Walsh McKean Furcolo LLP is a mid-size Martindale-Hubbell AV-rated and A.M. Best's recommended defense firm located in San Diego, California. The firm places an emphasis on the defense and trial of construction defect, professional liability, commercial and general liability, employment liability, insurance coverage, bad faith and product liability litigation.

Insurance Clients

Admiral Insurance Company
American Reliable Insurance Company
Canal Insurance Company
Interstate Insurance Group
Nationwide Indemnity Company
Riverport Insurance Company
American Bankers Insurance Company of Florida
Berkley Specialty Underwriting Managers, LLC
National Casualty Company
Nautilus Insurance Group
Scottsdale Insurance Company

Non-Insurance Clients

Advanced Geosolutions, Inc.
Dermacare
Hon Development Company
Ken Grody Ford
The Real Estate Group
Sunzone Real Estate Group, Inc.
Trusonic, Inc.
City of Long Beach
Good & Roberts, Inc.
Hughes Property Management
Nordstrom, Inc.
Secret Charm LLP
Tone Framing

Partners

John H. Walsh — California State University, Northridge, B.A. (cum laude), 1980; Loyola Law School, J.D., 1983 — Admitted to Bar, 1983, California; U.S. District Court, Central, Eastern, Northern and Southern Districts of California; U.S. District Court, Eastern District of Michigan; U.S. Court of Appeals, Ninth Circuit — Member State Bar of California; San Diego County Bar Association; Defense Research Institute; San Diego Defense Lawyers Association; Association of Southern California Defense Counsel — E-mail: jwalsh@wmfllp.com

Regan Furcolo — University of California, Irvine, B.A., 1989; Suffolk University Law School, J.D., 1992 — Admitted to Bar, 1992, California; U.S. District Court, Central, Eastern, Northern and Southern Districts of California; U.S. Court of Appeals, Ninth Circuit — Member State Bar of California; San Diego County Bar Association; San Diego Defense Lawyers Association; Association of Southern California Defense Counsel; Defense Research Institute — E-mail: rfurcolo@wmfllp.com

Thomas R. Kelleher — San Jose State University, B.A., 1987; California Western School of Law, J.D., 1995 — Admitted to Bar, 1995, California; U.S. District Court, Central and Southern Districts of California; U.S. Court of Appeals, Ninth Circuit — Member State Bar of California; San Diego County Bar Association; San Diego Defense Lawyers Association — E-mail: tkelleher@wmfllp.com

James T. Derfler — The Pennsylvania State University, B.S., 1976; The George Washington University, M.S., 1984; Thomas Jefferson School of Law, J.D., 1994 — Admitted to Bar, 1995, California; U.S. District Court, Central, Northern and Southern Districts of California — Member State Bar

Walsh McKean Furcolo LLP, San Diego, CA (Continued)

of California; San Diego County Bar Association — E-mail: jderfler@wmfllp.com

Of Counsel

Foster Furcolo Jr.   Dinah McKean

Associates

Ashley W. Christensen   Stephen M. Kerins
Christopher M. Lea   Laura E. Stewart
Lynn Trang

The following firms also service this area.

Berman Berman Berman Schneider & Lowary LLP
11900 West Olympic Boulevard, Suite 600
Los Angeles, California 90064-1151
 Telephone: 310-447-9000
 Fax: 310-447-9011

Insurance Defense, Insurance Coverage, Construction Defect, Product Liability, Employment Law, Professional Liability, Legal, Insurance Agents, Agent/Broker Liability, Medical Malpractice Defense, Design Professionals, Accountants, Trucking Law, Transportation, Real Estate Agents, Brokers and Appraisers, Elder Care, Monitoring Counsel, Litigation Management, California Insurance Regulations and Consulting to Insurance Industry

SEE COMPLETE LISTING UNDER LOS ANGELES, CALIFORNIA (124 MILES)

Pyka Lenhardt Schnaider Zell
837 North Ross Street
Santa Ana, California 92701
 Telephone: 714-835-9011
 Fax: 714-667-7806
Mailing Address: P.O. Box 1558, Santa Ana, CA 92702-1558

Automobile, Business Litigation, Catastrophic Injury, Civil Litigation, Civil Rights, Construction Accidents, Construction Defect, Labor and Employment, Municipal Liability, Personal Injury, Police Liability Defense, Premises Liability, Product Liability, Professional Liability, Public Entities, School Law, Trucking, Uninsured and Underinsured Motorist, Wrongful Death, Wrongful Termination, Homeowners Association Litigation, Utility Defense

SEE COMPLETE LISTING UNDER SANTA ANA, CALIFORNIA (89 MILES)

SAN FRANCISCO   † 805,235 San Francisco Co.

Alper & McCulloch

100 Drakes Landing Road, Suite 160
Greenbrae, California 94904-3120
 Telephone: 415-785-8814
Fax: 415-785-8831
E-Mail: daa@alpermcculloch.com
www.alpermcculloch.com

Established: 1991

Subrogation, Recoveries, Property Loss, Insurance Defense

Firm Profile: Alper & McCulloch has specialized in subrogation and defense litigation for nearly 25 years. We represent insurers, third party administrators, and self-insureds. We are dedicated to providing quality, cost effective legal services. We handle cases throughout California and beyond from our offices in the San Francisco Bay Area.

Insurance Clients

Allianz Insurance Group
Arch Insurance Company
Chubb Group of Insurance Companies
Fireman's Fund Insurance Company
Kaiser Permanente Insurance Company
Mid-Century Insurance Company
Northern Insurance Company of New York
American Re
Chubb Group
Chubb Insurance Company
Farmers Insurance Company
Foremost Insurance Company
Grange Mutual Casualty Company
Legion Indemnity Company
Markel Insurance Company
Munich Reinsurance America, Inc.
SeaBright Insurance Company
State Auto Insurance Companies

CALIFORNIA — SAN FRANCISCO

Alper & McCulloch, San Francisco, CA (Continued)

Truck Insurance Exchange
Voyager Indemnity Insurance Company
Underwriters at Lloyd's, London
Zurich North America

Non-Insurance Clients

McLarens Young International
Risk Enterprise Management, Ltd.
Quanta Risk Management
VeriClaim, Inc.

Partners

Dean A. Alper — 1955 — University of California, Santa Cruz, B.A., 1977; University of California, Hastings College of the Law, J.D., 1984 — Admitted to Bar, 1984, California; 1985, U.S. District Court, Central, Eastern, Northern and Southern Districts of California; 1985, U.S. Court of Appeals, Ninth Circuit; 1994, U.S. Court of Appeals for the District of Columbia Circuit; 1994, U.S. Supreme Court — Member State Bar of California; Bar Association of San Francisco; National Association of Subrogation Professionals — Substantive Editor: Constitutional Law Quarterly — Northern California Super Lawyer (2005, 2006, 2008, 2009, 2010, 2011, 2012, 2013, 2014); Settlement Panelist, San Francisco and Marin County Superior Courts; Arbitrator, San Francisco Superior Court; Mediator and Early Neutral Evaluator, U.S. District Court, Northern District of California; Delegate, California State Bar Convention (1993-1996) — Practice Areas: Subrogation; Insurance Defense; Business Law — E-mail: daa@alpermcculloch.com

Tracy B. McCulloch — 1959 — Pomona College, B.A., 1981; Loyola Marymount University, Loyola Law School, J.D., 1984 — Loyola Law Review — Admitted to Bar, 1984, California; 1985, U.S. District Court, Central, Northern and Southern Districts of California; 1985, U.S. Court of Appeals, Ninth Circuit — Member State Bar of California — Author: "Labor Law in the Ninth Circuit, Recent Developments," Volume 17 Loyola Law Review 496 (1984) — Licensed Real Estate Broker, California — Practice Areas: Subrogation; Insurance Defense; Business Law

Of Counsel

Philip A. Fant — 1952 — Tulane University, B.A., 1974; Tulane University Law School, J.D., 1977 — Admitted to Bar, 1977, Louisiana; 1991, California; 1977, U.S. District Court, Eastern District of Louisiana; U.S. Court of Appeals, Fifth Circuit; 1991, U.S. District Court, Central, Eastern, Northern and Southern Districts of California; U.S. Court of Appeals, Ninth Circuit — Member The Maritime Law Association of the United States — Practice Areas: Insurance Law; Admiralty and Maritime Law — E-mail: pfant@alpermcculloch.com

(This firm is also listed in the Subrogation section of this directory)

Bishop | Barry | Drath
A Professional Corporation

Watergate Tower III
2000 Powell Street, Suite 1425
Emeryville, California 94608
    Telephone: 510-596-0888
    Fax: 510-596-0899
    www.Bishop-Barry.com

Established: 1918

Insurance Defense, Construction Law, Professional Liability, Product Liability, Insurance Coverage, Bad Faith, Environmental Law, Litigation, Mediation, Alternative Dispute Resolution, Civil Litigation, Trial and Appellate Practice

Insurance Clients

AmTrust North America
Berkley Risk Services, LLC
Colony Insurance Company
General Reinsurance Corporation
Great American Insurance Company
Travelers Insurance Companies
Zurich American Insurance Company
Argo Pro
Chartis Insurance
Farmers Insurance Group
GMAC Insurance
Riverport Insurance Company
Royal & SunAlliance Group
Truck Insurance Exchange

Non-Insurance Clients

Maxson Young Associates Inc.
United States Steel Corporation

Bishop | Barry | Drath, A Professional Corporation, San Francisco, CA (Continued)

Shareholder

Nelson C. Barry — 1924 — University of California, A.B., 1949; University of California, Hastings College of the Law, J.D., 1952 — Phi Delta Phi — Admitted to Bar, 1952, California — Member American Bar Association; State Bar of California; International Association of Defense Counsel; American Board of Trial Advocates; Association of Defense Counsel, Northern California; Fellow, American College of Trial Lawyers; Fellow, International Academy of Trial Lawyers

John M. Drath — 1944 — University of Washington, B.A., 1965; University of San Francisco School of Law, J.D., 1969 — Admitted to Bar, 1971, California; 1993, Colorado; U.S. Supreme Court — Member Association of Defense Counsel, Northern California; Defense Research Institute; American Board of Trial Advocates; Federation of Defense and Corporate Counsel; American Trial Lawyers Association — Mediation Panel: Alameda, Contra Costa, Santa Clara and Marin County Superior Courts and First District Court of Appeals; The Mediation Society of San Francisco

Andrew A. Goode — 1961 — Tufts University, B.S. (cum laude), 1983; Golden Gate University School of Law, J.D., 1986 — Admitted to Bar, 1988, California; 1992, U.S. District Court, Northern District of California; 2002, U.S. District Court, Eastern District of California; U.S. District Court, Southern District of California; U.S. Court of Appeals for the Federal and Ninth Circuits — Member State Bar of California; Defense Research Institute

Jonathan R. Gross — 1958 — University of California, Santa Cruz, B.A. (with honors), 1982; University of California, Hastings College of the Law, J.D., 1985 — Admitted to Bar, 1986, California; U.S. Court of Appeals, Ninth Circuit — Member State Bar of California (Past Chair, Alternative Dispute Resolution Commitee); Defense Research Institute

Jeffrey N. Haney — 1943 — California State University, San Jose, B.A., 1965; University of Santa Clara School of Law, J.D., 1968 — Admitted to Bar, 1969, California — Member American Bar Association; State Bar of California; Association of Defense Counsel, Northern California; Defense Research Institute; American Arbitration Association — Captain, United States Air Force, Judge Advocate General Corp. [1969-1972]

Carol L. Healey — 1945 — Ohio University, A.B. (cum laude), 1967; University of California, Hastings College of the Law, J.D., 1974 — Admitted to Bar, 1974, California; 1992, U.S. District Court, Northern District of California; 2002, U.S. District Court, Eastern District of California; U.S. Court of Appeals for the District of Columbia and Ninth Circuits — Member State Bar of California, (Committee on Rules and Procedures of Court, 1982-1985; Judicial Council Advisory Committee on Rules of Court, 1985-1988); Alameda County Bar Association; Bar Association of San Francisco; Lawyer-Pilots Bar Association — Judge Pro Tem, San Francisco Municipal Court — Languages: Spanish

Peter J. Linn — University of California, Los Angeles, B.A., 1986; University of San Francisco School of Law, J.D., 1995 — Admitted to Bar, 1995, California; 1998, U.S. Court of Appeals, Ninth Circuit; 1999, U.S. District Court, Central, Eastern, Northern and Southern Districts of California; U.S. Court of Appeals, First Circuit — Member State Bar of California (Member, Employment Section); Association of Defense Trial Counsel; Defense Research Institute; Association of Defense Counsel, Northern California

Mark C. Raskoff — 1950 — Northwestern University, B.A., 1972; University of the Pacific, McGeorge School of Law, J.D., 1976 — Law Clerk to the Honorable Hugh A. Evans, U.S. Court of Appeals, Third District — Admitted to Bar, 1976, California; U.S. District Court, Eastern District of California; 1982, U.S. District Court, Central District of California; 2001, U.S. Court of Appeals, Ninth Circuit

Mary Margaret Ryan — 1949 — University of San Francisco, B.A., 1971; Golden Gate University School of Law, J.D., 1986 — Admitted to Bar, 1987, California — Member American Bar Association; State Bar of California; Association of Defense Counsel, Northern California; Defense Research Institute

Of Counsel

Sheila T. Addiego — 1967 — University of California, Berkeley, B.A., 1989; University of San Francisco School of Law, J.D., 1993 — Admitted to Bar, 1993, California

Rebecca B. Aherne — 1954 — University of California, Berkeley, B.A., 1976; San Francisco Law School, J.D., 1983 — Admitted to Bar, 1983, California; 1984, U.S. District Court, Northern District of California — Member National Association of Insurance Women

Ramon Z. Bacerdo — 1959 — University of California, Los Angeles, B.A., 1984; Hastings College, J.D., 1988 — Admitted to Bar, 1989, California —

SAN FRANCISCO | CALIFORNIA

Bishop | Barry | Drath, A Professional Corporation, San Francisco, CA (Continued)

Member American Bar Association; State Bar of California; Barrister's Association; Association of Defense Counsel, Northern California

David F. Beach — 1955 — University of California, Berkeley, B.S., 1977; University of San Diego School of Law, J.D. (magna cum laude), 1980 — Admitted to Bar, 1980, California — Member State Bar of California; Association of Defense Counsel, Northern California; Defense Research Institute

John A. Burke — 1956 — San Francisco State University, B.S. (with honors), 1982; University of San Francisco School of Law, J.D. (cum laude), 1990 — Admitted to Bar, 1990, California; 1991, U.S. District Court, Eastern and Northern Districts of California — Member State Bar of California

Aaron Hancock — 1967 — University of California, Berkeley, B.A./B.A. (magna cum laude), 1989; University of California, Davis, J.D., 1992 — Admitted to Bar, 1992, California; 1994, U.S. District Court, Central District of California; 1999, U.S. District Court, Southern District of California; 2000, U.S. District Court, Northern District of California; 2005, U.S. District Court, Eastern District of California

Victor Jacobellis — 1974 — University of Wisconsin-Madison, B.S., 1996; Loyola University Chicago, J.D., 1999; Vermont Law School, M.S.E.L. (cum laude), 2000 — Admitted to Bar, 1999, Illinois; 2011, California; 2006, U.S. District Court, Northern District of Illinois; 2012, U.S. District Court, Eastern District of California

Edward M. Lai — 1958 — University of Maryland, College Park, B.S./B.A., 1980; Golden Gate University School of Law, J.D., 1984 — Admitted to Bar, 1991, California

Vivian L. Lerche — 1959 — University of California, Berkeley, B.A., 1982; University of San Francisco School of Law, J.D., 1990 — Admitted to Bar, 1990, California — Member Asian American Bar Association of the Greater Bay Area; American Mensa; University of California, Alumni Association; University of San Francisco Alumni Association

Elaine I. Videa — 1971 — University of California, Berkeley, B.A., 1993; Golden Gate University School of Law, J.D., 2001 — Admitted to Bar, 2001, California — Member State Bar of California

Bledsoe, Cathcart, Diestel, Pedersen & Treppa LLP

601 California Street, 16th Floor
San Francisco, California 94108
Telephone: 415-981-5411
Fax: 415-981-0352
E-Mail: info@bledsoelaw.com
www.bledsoelaw.com

Established: 1947

Civil Trial Practice, State and Federal Courts, Product Liability, Insurance Defense, Insurance Coverage, Personal Injury, Construction Law, Employment Law, Business Law, Environmental Law, Landlord Tenant, Commercial Transportation, Copyright Litigation, Banking and Finance, Lender Liability

Firm Profile: Bledsoe, Cathcart, Diestel, Pedersen & Treppa LLP provide its clients with high quality legal representation throughout California. With a proven record of success in all venues, our attorneys have extensive experience in the litigation process and are highly regarded throughout the legal community.

Insurance Clients

Farmers Insurance Group	Safeco Insurance
St. Paul Travelers Property Casualty Group	State Farm Fire and Casualty Company
Topa Insurance Company	

Partners

Richard S. Diestel — 1951 — University of California, Berkeley, A.B., 1975; University of California, Hastings College of the Law, J.D., 1979 — Admitted to Bar, 1980, California; U.S. District Court, Northern and Southern Districts of California; U.S. Court of Appeals, Ninth Circuit — Member American Bar Association; State Bar of California; Bar Association of San Francisco; American Inns of Court Foundation; Association of Defense Counsel, Northern California; Defense Research Institute — Practice Areas:

Bledsoe, Cathcart, Diestel, Pedersen & Treppa LLP, San Francisco, CA (Continued)

Civil Litigation; Product Liability; Catastrophic Injury; Wrongful Death; Insurance Defense; Construction Defect; Fire Loss; Landlord and Tenant Law — E-mail: rdiestel@bledsoelaw.com

James M. Treppa — 1967 — University of California, Santa Barbara, B.A., 1989; Golden Gate University School of Law, J.D. (with highest honors), 1992 — Admitted to Bar, 1992, California; U.S. District Court, Northern District of California — Member American Bar Association; Bar Association of San Francisco; Association of Defense Counsel, Northern California; Trucking Industry Defense Association — E-mail: jtreppa@bledsoelaw.com

Alison M. Crane — 1973 — Villanova University, B.A. (cum laude), 1995; Boston University School of Law, J.D. (cum laude), 1998 — Admitted to Bar, 1998, California; U.S. District Court, Northern District of California; U.S. Court of Appeals, Ninth Circuit — Member American Bar Association; State Bar of California; Bar Association of San Francisco; Lawyer's Club of San Francisco; American Inns of Court Foundation; Queen's Bench; Association of Defense Counsel — Practice Areas: Civil Litigation; Catastrophic Injury; Wrongful Death; Product Liability; Trial Practice; Intentional Torts; Employment Law; Class Actions; Appeals; Religious Institutions — E-mail: acrane@bledsoelaw.com

Steven E. McDonald — 1959 — University of California, Berkeley, 1981; University of the Pacific, McGeorge School of Law, J.D., 1985 — Admitted to Bar, 1985, California — Member State Bar of California; Association of Defense Counsel, Northern California — E-mail: smcdonald@bledsoelaw.com

Jeffrey V. Ta — 1976 — University of California, Davis, B.A., 1999; University of San Diego School of Law, J.D., 2002 — Admitted to Bar, 2003, California — Member Asian American Bar Association; Association of Defense Counsel — Languages: Vietnamese — Practice Areas: Bodily Injury; Breach of Contract; Business Litigation; Civil Defense; Civil Litigation; Commercial General Liability; Commercial Litigation; Entertainment Law; Environmental and Toxic Injury; First and Third Party Defense; Garage Liability; General Civil Litigation; General Defense; General Liability; Homeowners; Insurance Defense; Insurance Litigation; Landlord and Tenant Law; Lender Liability Defense; Litigation; Litigation Defense; Mold and Mildew Claims; Mold Litigation; Motor Carriers; Motor Vehicle; Negligence; Personal Injury; Pollution; Product Liability; Property Damage; Property Liability; Real Estate Litigation; Real Property; Restaurant Liability; Tort Liability; Tort Litigation; Truck Liability; Trucking Litigation — E-mail: jta@bledsoelaw.com

In Memoriam

L. Jay Pedersen — (1950-2012)
Leighton M. Bledsoe — (1903-1993)
Robert S. Cathcart — (1909-2007)

Associates

James L. Shea — California State University, Sacramento, B.A., 1999; University of San Francisco School of Law, J.D., 2005 — Admitted to Bar, 2005, California — Member State Bar of California — Practice Areas: Construction Defect — E-mail: jshea@bledsoelaw.com

Davin R. Bacho — 1985 — California State University, Chico, B.S., 2007; Golden Gate University School of Law, J.D., 2011 — Admitted to Bar, 2012, California — Member State Bar of California — Practice Areas: Insurance Defense; Bodily Injury; Breach of Contract; Civil Defense; Civil Law; Civil Litigation; Civil Trial Practice; Comprehensive General Liability; Complex Commercial Litigation; Contract Disputes; Contracts; Eminent Domain; First and Third Party Defense; General Civil Litigation; General Defense; Garage Liability; Homeowners; Insurance Litigation; Intentional Torts; Landlord and Tenant Law; Litigation and Counseling; Mediation; Negligence; Personal Injury; Personal Liability; Premises Liability; Product Liability; Property Liability; Punitive Damages; Subrogation — E-mail: dbacho@bledsoelaw.com

Davis J. Reilly — 1985 — California State Polytechnic University at San Luis Obispo, B.S., 2007; Santa Clara University School of Law, J.D., 2010 — Admitted to Bar, 2010, California; 2011, Nevada — Member American Bar Association; State Bars of California and Nevada — Practice Areas: Civil Defense; Civil Litigation; Insurance Defense; Insurance; Litigation; Medical Malpractice Defense; Defense Litigation; Negligence; Personal Injury Litigation; Personal Injury; Premises Liability; Product Liability; Religious Institutions; Tort; Toxic Torts — E-mail: dreilly@bledsoelaw.com

Errol C. Dauis — 1984 — California State University, Long Beach, B.A. (cum laude), 2007; University of California Davis School of Law, King Hall, J.D., 2011 — Clerk, for the Legal Aid Foundation of Los Angeles, the Asian Law Caucus and the California Law Revision Commission; Judicial Extern, the Honorable John A. Mendez, U.S. District Court, Eastern District of

Bledsoe, Cathcart, Diestel, Pedersen & Treppa LLP, San Francisco, CA (Continued)

California — Editor in Chief, UC Davis Law Review — Admitted to Bar, 2011, California — Member State Bar of California — Practice Areas: Civil Defense; Civil Litigation; Insurance Defense; Alternative Dispute Resolution; Negligence; Personal Injury; Personal Injury Litigation; Premises Liability; Product Liability; Toxic Torts; Tort; Business Law — E-mail: edauis@bledsoelaw.com

Caitlin M. Emmett — 1987 — The University of Arizona, B.A. (summa cum laude, with honors), 2009; Golden Gate University School of Law, J.D. (cum laude, with highest honors), 2012 — Clerk, Office of General Counsel for the California State Bar — Board Member, Golden Gate University Law Review as the Ninth Circuit Survey Articles Editor — Admitted to Bar, 2012, California — Member State Bar of California — Practice Areas: Insurance Defense; Product Liability; Civil Trial Practice; Contracts; General Practice; Tort; Negligence; Litigation; Personal Injury; Premises Liability; Property — E-mail: cemmett@bledsoelaw.com

Colin W. Larson — 1984 — University of California, Santa Barbara, B.A., 2007; Golden Gate University School of Law, J.D., 2012 — Judicial Extern, Honorable Chief U.S. District Judge James Ware and Honorable Magistrate Judge James Larson — Associate Editor and Staff Writer, Golden Gate University Law Review — Admitted to Bar, 2012, California — Practice Areas: Civil Trial Practice; Construction Law; Construction Defect; Construction Litigation; Insurance Defense; Litigation; Real Estate; Negligence; General Practice; Personal Injury; Premises Liability — E-mail: clarson@bledsoelaw.com

Nicholas J. Bernate — 1986 — University of California, Santa Cruz, B.A., 2008; Santa Clara University School of Law, J.D. (Order of the Coif), 2012 — Clerk, Sonoma County Public Defender's Office and Clerked at the San Francisco City Attorney's Office — Admitted to Bar, 2012, California — Practice Areas: Consumer Law; Fraud; Insurance; Insurance Defense; Civil Trial Practice; Negligence; Personal Injury; Premises Liability; Product Liability; Tort; Toxic Torts; Premise Litigation — E-mail: nbernate@bledsoelaw.com

Tessa K. Weeks — 1984 — Washington University in St. Louis, B.A. Economics, 2006; Seton Hall University School of Law, J.D., 2009 — Judicial Law Clerk for The Honorable Fred H. Kumpf, J.S.C — Admitted to Bar, 2010, New Jersey; 2010, New York; 2014, California — Practice Areas: Alternative Dispute Resolution; Appellate Practice; Civil Trial Practice; Contracts; General Practice; Insurance; Insurance Defense; Labor and Employment; Legal Malpractice; Litigation; Negligence; Personal Injury; Personal Liability; Product Liability; Professional Liability; Property; Tort; Toxic Torts — E-mail: tweeks@bledsoelaw.com

Jacy C. Dardine — 1982 — University of California, Davis, B.A. Political Science, 2008; University of Oregon School of Law, J.D., 2013 — 2013-2014 Lane County Circuit Court - Honorable Clara L. Rigmaiden — Admitted to Bar, 2013, California — Member American and Sonoma County Bar Associations; State Bar of California — Oregon Review of International Law - Executive Editor Technology and Entrepreneurship Program - Fellow Legal Research and Writing Program - Tutor Lane County District Attorney's Office - Certified Law Student — Practice Areas: Civil Litigation — E-mail: jdardine@bledsoelaw.com

Stevie B. Newton — 1987 — University of California, Santa Barbara, B.A. (with high honors), 2009; Pepperdine University School of Law, J.D. (Dean's List), 2012 — Dean's List; Distinguished Graduate in French Major; Pi Delta Phi French Honor Society; Dean's Merit Scholarhip in Law School — Pepperdine Law Review — Admitted to Bar, 2012, California — Global Justice Practicum; Refugee Assistance in Burma nd Thailand (March 2011); International Human Rights law Program in San Jose, Costa Rica — E-mail: snewton@bledsoelaw.com

Borton Petrini, LLP

660 Las Gallinas Avenue, Suite B
San Rafael, California 94903
  Telephone: 415-677-0730
  Fax: 415-677-0737
  E-Mail: bpsf@bortonpetrini.com
  www.bortonpetrini.com

Established: 1899

Borton Petrini, LLP, San Francisco, CA (Continued)

Commercial Litigation, Construction Litigation, General Civil Litigation, Intellectual Property, Professional Liability, Public Entities

Firm Profile: Since 1899, Borton Petrini, LLP, has offered high quality legal services in all of the practice areas described above through its California network of 10 regional offices. The mission of Borton Petrini, LLP is to treat every file as though we were representing ourselves and paying the bill for that representation.

Managing Partner

Samuel L. Phillips — 1960 — University of San Francisco, B.A., 1982; J.D., 1985 — Alpha Sigma Nu; Jesuit Honor Society — Admitted to Bar, 1987, California; 1989, U.S. District Court, Eastern and Northern Districts of California; 1989, U.S. Court of Appeals, Ninth Circuit — Member State Bar of California; Santa Clara County Bar Association (Former Member; Judical Committee); William Ingram Inns of Court; Ralph M. Brown Inns of the Court (Past Founding Member); Defense Research Institute (Professionalism & Ethics Committee); Cerebal Palsy Association (Past Special Advisor); St. Thomas More Society — Author: "The Empty Chair Defense," California Defense Magazine (Fall 1995); "Should Parents be Liable for Intentional Acts of Their Children?" California Defense Magazine (Summer 1999) — Languages: Spanish — E-mail: sphillips@bortonpetrini.com

Partner

G. Kelley Reid, Jr. — 1941 — The University of Iowa; Florida State University, B.A., 1964; University of Florida College of Law, J.D., 1968 — Admitted to Bar, 1968, Florida; 1973, California; 1973, U.S. District Court, Eastern and Northern Districts of California; 1973, U.S. Court of Appeals, Ninth Circuit — Member State Bar of California; The Florida Bar; Marin County Bar Association; Marines' Memorial Association; Marin Builders Association; Federation of Defense and Corporate Counsel; Association of Defense Counsel of Northern California and Nevada; Defense Research Institute — National Football League Players Association (Arbitrator, Mediator, Contract Advisor); Marin County Superior Court (Mediator); San Francisco Superior Court (Arbitrator, Mediator, Judge Pro Tem, 1990-1996); Southern Marin Pop Warner Football (Assistant Athletic Director, 1990-1993); Ross, California (Mayor, 1992-1993 & 1996-1997, Town Councilman, 1990-1998, Treasurer, 1998 - present); Marin County Council of Mayors and Councilmembers (President, Contract Advisor, 1994-1995); Marin County Cable Rate Regulation Joint Powers Authority (Chairman, 1995-1998); Marin Conservation Corp. (Board of Directors, 1995-1998); The Frank Lloyd Wright Civic Center Conservancy Fund (Member, Board of Directors, 1998-2000); Kentfield Rehabilitation Hospital (Governing Board, 2001 - present); Barbershop Harmony Society - Marin Chapter (Member, 2008 - present); Barbershop Chorus and Quartet Group (Member, 2008-Present); Redwood High School Hall of Fame Selection Committee (2008) — U.S. Air Force, Judge Advocate General (Captain, 1969-1972) — E-mail: kreid@bortonpetrini.com

Bullivant Houser Bailey PC

601 California Street, Suite 1800
San Francisco, California 94108-2823
  Telephone: 415-352-2700
  Fax: 415-352-2701
  E-Mail: clientservices@bullivant.com
  www.bullivant.com

Established: 1998

Insurance Coverage, Complex Litigation, Trial Practice, Insurance Coverage Litigation, Insurance Litigation, Insurance, Insurance Claim Analysis and Evaluation, Insurance Defense, Insurance Law, Insurance Regulation, Marine Insurance, Marine Liability, Maritime Law, Arbitration, Mediation, Commercial Litigation, Product Liability, Directors and Officers Liability, Professional Liability, Appellate, Insurance Company Regulation and Rate Filings

SAN FRANCISCO / CALIFORNIA

Bullivant Houser Bailey PC, San Francisco, CA
(Continued)

Shareholders

Andrew B. Downs — University of California, Los Angeles School of Law, J.D., 1983 — Admitted to Bar, 1983, California; 2002, Nevada; 1985, U.S. Court of Appeals, Ninth Circuit; 1991, U.S. Supreme Court; U.S. District Court, Central, Eastern, Northern and Southern Districts of California; U.S. District Court, District of Nevada — Practice Areas: Insurance Law; Admiralty and Maritime Law; Commercial Litigation; Fidelity and Surety — Tel: 415-352-2716 — E-mail: andy.downs@bullivant.com

Jess B. Millikan — University of California, Berkeley Boalt Hall School of Law, J.D., 1980 — Admitted to Bar, 1980, California; U.S. District Court, Central, Eastern, Northern and Southern Districts of California; U.S. District Court, Eastern District of Wisconsin; U.S. Court of Appeals, Ninth and Tenth Circuits; U.S. Supreme Court — Practice Areas: Insurance Law; Admiralty and Maritime Law; Alternative Dispute Resolution — Tel: 415-352-2718 — E-mail: jess.millikan@bullivant.com

James P. Moher — University of California, Hastings College of the Law, J.D., 1982 — Admitted to Bar, 1982, California; U.S. District Court, Eastern, Northern and Southern Districts of California — Practice Areas: Commercial Litigation; Transportation — Tel: 415-352-2719 — E-mail: jim.moher@bullivant.com

Paul D. Nelson — University of Oregon School of Law, J.D., 1974 — Admitted to Bar, 1974, California; 1975, Oregon; U.S. District Court, Central, Eastern, Northern and Southern Districts of California; U.S. District Court, District of Colorado; U.S. District Court, District of Idaho; U.S. District Court, District of Oregon — Practice Areas: Appellate Practice; Business Litigation; Insurance Litigation; Insurance Coverage — Tel: 415-352-2766 — E-mail: paul.nelson@bullivant.com

Samuel H. Ruby — University of California, Berkeley Boalt Hall School of Law, J.D., 1997 — Admitted to Bar, 1997, California; U.S. Court of Appeals, Ninth Circuit — Practice Areas: Insurance Law; Admiralty and Maritime Law; Appellate Practice; Commercial Litigation — Tel: 415-352-2723 — E-mail: samuel.ruby@bullivant.com

Of Counsel

Norman J. Ronneberg Jr. — University of California, Berkeley Boalt Hall School of Law, J.D., 1975 — Admitted to Bar, 1975, California; U.S. District Court, Central, Eastern, Northern and Southern Districts of California; U.S. District Court, Eastern District of Pennsylvania; U.S. District Court, District of Arizona; U.S. Court of Appeals, Ninth Circuit; U.S. Supreme Court — Practice Areas: Admiralty and Maritime Law; Bad Faith; Coverage Issues; Jones Act; Pollution; Protection and Indemnity — Tel: 415-352-2728 — E-mail: norman.ronneberg@bullivant.com

(See listing under Portland, OR for additional information)

Cesari, Werner & Moriarty

P.O. Box 27307
San Francisco, California 94127-0307
   Telephone: 650-991-5126
   Fax: 650-991-5134
   E-Mail: dmoriarty@cwmlaw.com
   www.cwmlaw.com

Established: 1965

Insurance Defense, Casualty, Accident, Bad Faith, Construction Law, Public Entities, Product Liability, Professional Malpractice, Premises Liability, Trucking Law

Firm Profile: Cesari, Werner & Moriarty was founded in 1965 by D. Ralph Cesari and James B. Werner. Since its inception, the firm has specialized in the defense of Civil Litigation throughout California.

The firm is comprised of skilled and experienced trial attorneys who are effective courtroom advocates with an impressive jury trial track record. Our attorneys are also seasoned practitioners in cost effective advocacy, the art of arbitration, settlement and mediation.

Cesari, Werner & Moriarty, San Francisco, CA
(Continued)

The firm's expertise encompasses product liability, professional malpractice, personal injury, construction defect, premises liability, employment defense, disability law, bad faith, trucking, landlord-tenant and insurance coverage.

Insurance Clients

Allianz Insurance Company
Argo Insurance-U.S. Grocery and Retail Specialty
Kemper Insurance Company
Mercury Casualty Company
National Farmers Union Mutual Insurance Society
Navigators Management Company
Prudential Insurance Company of America
St. Paul Travelers Insurance Company
Vanliner Insurance Company
Allied Insurance Company
California Insurance Group
Grocers Insurance Company
Lancer Insurance Company
Metropolitan Life Insurance Company
Nationwide Insurance
Pacific National Insurance Company
Scottsdale Insurance Company
Transportation Insurance Company
United Services Automobile Association (USAA)

Non-Insurance Clients

Budget Rent-A-Car Corporation
Move-Pak Insurance Brokers
Covenant Transport, Inc.
Schneider National Carriers, Inc.

Firm Members

James B. Werner — (1929-1988)

D. Ralph Cesari — (1926-2009)

Dennis F. Moriarty — 1937 — St. Patrick's College, A.B., 1958; University of San Francisco, J.D., 1965 — Admitted to Bar, 1966, California — Member State Bar of California; Bar Association of San Francisco; Association of Defense Counsel, Northern California (President, 1997); Lawyers Club of San Francisco; Fellow, American College of Trial Lawyers; American Board of Trial Advocates — Tel: 650-991-5126, Ext. 17 — E-mail: dmoriarty@cwmlaw.com

Ian A. Fraser-Thomson — 1951 — University of Oregon, B.A. (magna cum laude), 1973; University of San Francisco, J.D., 1976 — Phi Beta Kappa — Admitted to Bar, 1976, California — Member American Bar Association; State Bar of California; Bar Association of San Francisco; Lawyers Club of San Francisco; Association of Defense Counsel, Northern California — Tel: 650-991-5126, Ext. 14 — E-mail: ift@cwmlaw.com

Andrew S. Werner — 1959 — Northwestern University, B.A., 1981; University of San Francisco, J.D., 1986 — Admitted to Bar, 1988, California — Member State Bar of California; Association of Defense Counsel, Northern California — Tel: 650-991-5126, Ext. 13 — E-mail: awerner@cwmlaw.com

Associates

Stephen L. Dahm — 1949 — Fairleigh Dickinson University, B.A., 1971; Golden Gate University, J.D., 1984 — Admitted to Bar, 1984, California; 1986, New Jersey; 1984, U.S. District Court, Northern District of California — Member American Bar Association (Tort, Insurance Practice and Litigation Sections, 1984-Present); New Jersey State Bar Association; State Bar of California; Lawyers Club of San Francisco; Association of Defense Counsel, Northern California — Tel: 650-991-5126, Ext. 12 — E-mail: sdahm@cwmlaw.com

Kristina L. Velarde — 1972 — Loyola Marymount University, B.A., 1994; University of San Diego, J.D., 1998 — Admitted to Bar, 1998, California — Member State Bar of California; Bar Association of San Francisco — Tel: 650-991-5126, Ext. 26 — E-mail: kvelarde@cwmlaw.com

Sean Moriarty — 1972 — University of California, Los Angeles, B.A., 1994; University of San Francisco, J.D., 1997 — Admitted to Bar, 1998, California — Member State Bar of California; Association of Defense Counsel, Northern California — Tel: 650-991-5126, Ext. 15 — E-mail: smoriarty@cwmlaw.com

Margaret M. Lesniak — 1970 — New York University, B.A., 1993; Seton Hall University, J.D., 1997 — Admitted to Bar, 2002, California — Member San Mateo County Bar Association — Tel: 650-991-5126, Ext. 29 — E-mail: mlesniak@cwmlaw.com

Hugh A. Donohoe — 1950 — St. Patrick's College, B.A., 1972; University of San Francisco, J.D., 1976 — Admitted to Bar, 1976, California; U.S. District Court, Central, Eastern and Northern Districts of California — Member Bar Association of San Francisco; Northern California Defense Counsel — St. Thomas More Award, 2010 — Tel: 650-991-5126, Ext. 11 — E-mail: hdonohoe@cwmlaw.com

Clinton & Clinton

201 Spear Street, Suite 1100
San Francisco, California 94105
Telephone: 415-230-5368
Fax: 415-230-5369
E-Mail: dclinton@clinton-clinton.com
www.clinton-clinton.com

(Long Beach, CA Office*: 100 Oceangate, Suite 1400, 90802)
(Tel: 562-216-5000)
(Fax: 562-216-5001)
(Los Angeles, CA Office*: 5757 West Century Boulevard, Suite 700, 90045)
(Tel: 310-242-8615)
(Fax: 310-242-8612)
(San Diego, CA Office*: 525 "B" Street, Suite 1500, 92101)
(Tel: 619-858-4728)
(Fax: 619-858-4729)
(Sacramento, CA Office*: 770 'L' Street, Suite 950, 95814)
(Tel: 916-361-6060)
(Fax: 916-361-6061)
(Irvine, CA Office*: 2030 Main Street, Suite 1300, 92614)
(Tel: 949-260-9083)
(Fax: 949-260-9084)
(Calabasas, CA Office: 23480 Park Sorrento, Suite 219A, 91302)
(Tel: 562-216-5000)
(Fax: 562-216-5001)
(Birmingham, AL Office: 1 Chase Corporate Center, Suite 400, 35244)
(Tel: 205-313-6329)
(Fax: 562-216-5001)
(Cumming, GA Office: 410 Peachtree Parkway, Building 400, Suite 4245, 30041)
(Tel: 678-341-5134)
(Fax: 562-216-5001)
(Philadelphia, PA Office: 1315 Walnut Street, Suite 601, 19107)
(Tel: 267-800-1897)
(Fax: 267-800-1898)
(Nashville, TN Office: 2400 Crestmoor Road, 37215)
(Tel: 615-386-7040)
(Fax: 562-216-5001)
(Austin, TX Office: 12912 Hill Country Boulevard, Suite F210, 78738)
(Tel: 512-200-7055)
(Fax: 512-266-3655)
(Ft. Worth, TX Office: 109 East Third Street, Suite 350, 76102)
(Tel: 817-900-8210)
(Fax: 817-900-8221)
(Houston, TX Office: 480 North Sam Houston Parkway East, 77060-3528)
(Tel: 713-659-0054)
(Fax: 281-447-5733)

Asbestos Litigation, Automobile, Automotive Products Liability, Civil Litigation, Civil Rights, Civil Trial Practice, Commercial Litigation, Common Carrier, Complex Litigation, Construction Defect, Dental Malpractice, Employment Law, Environmental Law, Insurance Defense, Hospital Malpractice, Law Enforcement Liability, Legal Malpractice, Mass Tort, Medical Devices, Medical Malpractice, Pharmaceutical, Premises Liability, Product Liability, Retail Liability, Sexual Harassment, Slip and Fall, Special Investigative Unit Claims, Sports and Entertainment Liability, Toxic Torts, Truck Liability, Workers' Compensation

(See listing under Long Beach, CA for additional information)

Cooper & Scully, P.C.

100 California Street, Suite 850
San Francisco, California 94111
Telephone: 415-956-9700
Fax: 415-391-0274
www.cooperscully.com

Cooper & Scully, P.C., San Francisco, CA   (Continued)

(Dallas, TX Office*: Founders Square, 900 Jackson Street, Suite 100, 75202-4426)
(Tel: 214-712-9500)
(Fax: 214-712-9540)
(Houston, TX Office*: 700 Louisiana Street, Suite 3850, 77002)
(Tel: 713-236-6800)
(Fax: 713-236-6880)
(Sherman, TX Office*: 250 East Evergreen, 75090)
(Tel: 903-813-3900)
(Fax: 903-868-1919)

Appellate Practice, Bad Faith, Class Actions, Commercial Litigation, Complex Litigation, Construction Law, Copyright and Trademark Law, Coverage Issues, Employment Law, Extra-Contractual Litigation, First and Third Party Defense, General Liability, Health, Insurance Coverage, Insurance Defense, Legal Malpractice, Malpractice, Managed Care Liability, Medical Devices, Medical Malpractice, Product Liability, Property and Casualty, Pharmaceutical, Professional Liability, Transportation, Trial and Appellate Practice

Shareholders

Derek S. Davis — 1968 — The University of Texas at Austin, B.S., 1992; Texas Tech University, J.D., 1995 — Admitted to Bar, 1995, Texas; 2006, California; U.S. District Court, Eastern, Northern, Southern and Western Districts of Texas; U.S. District Court, Eastern and Northern Districts of California — Member State Bars of Texas and California; Texas Pharmacy Association — E-mail: derek.davis@cooperscully.com

Gordon K. Wright — 1958 — Brigham Young University, B.S. (summa cum laude), 1982; Stanford Law School, J.D., 1985 — Admitted to Bar, 1985, Texas; 1991, Utah; 2006, California; 2010, Oregon; U.S. District Court, Eastern, Northern and Southern Districts of Texas; U.S. District Court, District of Utah; U.S. Court of Appeals, Fifth Circuit; U.S. Supreme Court — E-mail: gordon.wright@cooperscully.com

Associates

Komal C. Chokshi   Carol A. Treasure

(See listing under Dallas, TX for additional information)

Ericksen Arbuthnot

100 Bush Street, Suite 900
San Francisco, California 94104-3950
Telephone: 415-362-7126
Fax: 415-362-6401
www.ericksenarbuthnot.com

(Oakland, CA Office*: 155 Grand Avenue, Suite 1050, 94612-3768)
(Tel: 510-832-7770)
(Fax: 510-832-0102)
(Bakersfield, CA Office*: 1830 Truxtun Avenue, Suite 200, 93301-5022)
(Tel: 661-633-5080)
(Fax: 661-633-5089)
(Fresno, CA Office*: 2440 West Shaw Avenue, Suite 101, 93711-3300)
(Tel: 559-449-2600)
(Fax: 559-449-2603)
(Los Angeles, CA Office*: 835 Wilshire Boulevard, Suite 500, 90017-2656)
(Tel: 213-489-4411)
(Fax: 213-489-4332)
(Sacramento, CA Office*: 100 Howe Avenue, Suite 110S, 95825-8200)
(Tel: 916-483-5181)
(Fax: 916-483-7558)
(San Jose, CA Office*: 152 North Third Street, Suite 700, 95112-5560)
(Tel: 408-286-0880)
(Fax: 408-286-0337)
(Walnut Creek, CA Office*: 570 Lennon Lane, 94598-2415)
(Tel: 925-947-1702)
(Fax: 925-947-4921)

SAN FRANCISCO   CALIFORNIA

Ericksen Arbuthnot, San Francisco, CA   (Continued)

Administrative Law, Business Law, Construction Law, Employment Law, Environmental Law, Health Care, Managed Care Liability, Insurance Coverage, Insurance Fraud, Personal Injury, Premises Liability, Product Liability, Professional Liability, Medical Malpractice, Public Entities, Appellate Law

In Memoriam

Robert M. Arbuthnot — (1936-2014)

Resident Partners

Andrew P. Sclar — Managing Partner — University of California, Santa Barbara, B.A. (with honors), 1980; University of California, Hastings College of the Law, J.D., 1983 — Admitted to Bar, 1983, California — Member American Bar Association; State Bar of California; Bar Association of San Francisco — E-mail: asclar@ericksenarbuthnot.com

Albert M. T. Finch, III — Partner — Cornell University, B.A., 1989; The John Marshall Law School, J.D., 1993 — Staff Editor, The John Marshall Law Review — Admitted to Bar, 1993, Illinois; 1998, California; 1993, U.S. District Court, Northern District of Illinois; 1995, U.S. Court of Appeals, Seventh Circuit — Member State Bar of California — E-mail: tfinch@ericksenarbuthnot.com

Resident Associates

Jennifer A. Riso — The University of Tulsa College of Law, J.D., 1999 — Admitted to Bar, 1999, California — E-mail: jriso@ericksenarbuthnot.com

Jason R. Honey — University of Washington School of Law, J.D., 2010 — Admitted to Bar, 2011, California — E-mail: jhoney@ericksenarbuthnot.com

(See listing under Oakland, CA for additional information)

Hanna, Brophy, MacLean, McAleer & Jensen, LLP

251 Rhode Island Street, Suite 201
San Francisco, California 94103
   Telephone: 415-543-9110
   Fax: 415-896-0901
   www.hannabrophy.com

Established: 1943

Insurance Defense, Workers' Compensation, Subrogation, Labor and Employment, Employment Law, Litigation

Office Managing Partner

John Armanino — University of San Francisco, J.D., 1979 — Admitted to Bar, 1979, California — Member State Bar of California

(See listing under Oakland, CA for additional information)

Locke Lord LLP

44 Montgomery Street, Suite 2400
San Francisco, California 94104
   Telephone: 415-318-8810
   Fax: 415-676-5816
   www.lockelord.com

(Chicago, IL Office*: 111 South Wacker Drive, 60606-4410)
   (Tel: 312-443-0700)
   (Fax: 312-443-0336)
(Atlanta, GA Office*: Terminus 200, Suite 1200, 3333 Piedmont Road NE, 30305)
   (Tel: 404-870-4600)
   (Fax: 404-872-5547)

Locke Lord LLP, San Francisco, CA   (Continued)

(Austin, TX Office*: 600 Congress Avenue, Suite 2200, 78701-2748)
   (Tel: 512-305-4700)
   (Fax: 512-305-4800)
(Dallas, TX Office*: 2200 Ross Avenue, Suite 2200, 75201)
   (Tel: 214-740-8000)
   (Fax: 214-740-8800)
(Houston, TX Office*: 2800 JPMorgan Chase Tower, 600 Travis, 77002-3095)
   (Tel: 713-226-1200)
   (Fax: 713-223-3717)
(London, United Kingdom Office*: 201 Bishopsgate, DX 567 London/City, EC2M 3AB)
   (Tel: +44 (0) 20 7861 9000 (Int'l))
   (Tel: 011 44 207861 9000 (US))
   (Fax: +44 (0) 20 7785 6869 201 (Bishopsgate))
(Los Angeles, CA Office*: 300 South Grand Avenue, Suite 2600, 90071-3119)
   (Tel: 213-485-1500)
   (Fax: 213-485-1200)
(New Orleans, LA Office*: 601 Poydras, Suite 2660, 70130)
   (Tel: 504-558-5100)
   (Fax: 504-558-5200)
(New York, NY Office*: Three World Financial Center, Floor 20, 10281)
   (Tel: 212-415-8600)
   (Fax: 212-303-2754)
(Sacramento, CA Office: 500 Capitol Mall, Suite 1800, 95814)
   (Tel: 916-554-0240)
   (Fax: 916-554-5440)
(Washington, DC Office*: 701 8th Street, N.W., Suite 700, 20001)
   (Tel: 202-521-4100)
   (Fax: 202-521-4200)
(Hong Kong, China-PRC Office: 21/F Bank of China Tower, 1 Garden Road, Central)
   (Tel: +852 3465 0600)
   (Fax: +852 3014 0991)

Antitrust, Arbitration, Aviation, Business Law, Class Actions, Construction Law, Corporate Law, Directors and Officers Liability, Employee Benefits, Environmental Law, Health Care, Insurance Law, Intellectual Property, Labor and Employment, Land Use, Admiralty and Maritime Law, Mergers and Acquisitions, Product Liability, Railroad Law, Regulatory and Compliance, Reinsurance, Securities, Technology, Transportation, General Liability, Appellate, Long Term Care

Partner

Elizabeth A. Tosaris — Williams College, B.A. (cum laude), 1987; University of California, Hastings College of the Law, J.D., 1991 — Admitted to Bar, 1991, California; U.S. District Court, Central, Eastern and Northern Districts of California; U.S. Court of Appeals, Ninth Circuit — Practice Areas: Health Care; Insurance; Reinsurance

(See listing under Chicago, IL for additional information)

Murchison & Cumming, LLP

Embarcadero Center West
275 Battery Street, Suite 550
San Francisco, California 94111
   Telephone: 415-524-4300
   Fax: 415-391-2058

Civil Litigation, Business Transactions

(See listing under Los Angeles, CA for additional information)

Nielsen, Haley & Abbott LLP

100 Smith Ranch Road, Suite 350
San Rafael, California 94903-5595
   Telephone: 415-693-0900
   Fax: 415-693-9674
   E-Mail: jnielsen@nielsenhaley.com
   www.nielsenhaley.com

(Los Angeles, CA Office*: 606 South Olive Street, Suite 1800, 90014)
   (Tel: 213-239-9009)
   (Fax: 213-239-9007)

Established: 2001

Insurance Coverage, Fidelity, Surety, Tort Litigation, Business Law, Appellate Practice, Employment Law, Bad Faith, Product Liability, Professional Liability

Insurance Clients

CUNA Mutual Group
The Hartford
United National Group
Federated Insurance Company
TIG Insurance Company

Non-Insurance Clients

First State Management Group, Inc.
The Regents of the University of California

Jennifer S. Cohn — University of California, Los Angeles, B.A., 1989; University of California, Hastings College of the Law, J.D., 1993 — Admitted to Bar, 1994, California

Stephen W. Cusick — Hamilton College, A.B., 1975; University of California, Berkeley Boalt Hall School of Law, J.D., 1983 — Admitted to Bar, 1983, California

Peter C. Haley — University of California, Berkeley, A.B., 1964; University of California, Berkeley Boalt Hall School of Law, J.D., 1967 — Admitted to Bar, 1968, California

Tung Khuu — University of California, Berkeley, B.A., 1999; Cornell University Law School, J.D., 2002 — Admitted to Bar, 2002, California

James C. Nielsen — University of California, Davis, B.A., 1980; University of Virginia, J.D., 1983 — Admitted to Bar, 1983, California; 2000, Nevada — Certified Specialist, Appellate Law, State Bar of California Board of Legal Specialization, 1996

Thomas H. Nienow — University of California, Los Angeles, B.A., 1980; University of California, Hastings College of the Law, J.D., 1988 — Admitted to Bar, 1988, California

Law Offices of George W. Nowell

100 Montgomery Street, Suite 1990
San Francisco, California 94104-4322
   Telephone: 415-362-1333
   Fax: 415-362-1344
   Emer/After Hrs: 415-362-1333
   Mobile: 415-362-1333
   E-Mail: admin@nowelllaw.com
   www.nowelllaw.com

Established: 1985

Insurance Defense, Insurance Coverage, Subrogation, Admiralty and Maritime Law, Transportation, Aviation

Firm Profile: Founded in 1985, the firm practices in the areas of Insurance Coverage, Insurance Defense, Insurance Subrogation, Personal Injury and Jones Act Defense, Mariner License Defense, Government Torts, Transportation, Aviation, Maritime and Admiralty Law.

Insurance Clients

Chartis Marine Adjusters, Inc.
CNA Risk Management

Law Offices of George W. Nowell, San Francisco, CA
(Continued)

Great American Insurance Company
Zurich Insurance Company
Navigators Insurance Company
St. Paul Fire and Marine Insurance Company

Partner

George W. Nowell — 1949 — Stanford University, B.A. (Phi Beta Kappa), 1969; University of Pennsylvania, M.A., 1971; Stanford Law School, J.D., 1978 — Admitted to Bar, 1978, California; U.S. District Court, Central, Eastern, Northern and Southern Districts of California; U.S. Court of Appeals, Ninth Circuit; U.S. Court of Federal Claims; U.S. Court of Appeals for Veterans Claims — Member American Bar Association; State Bar of California; Bar Association of San Francisco; San Francisco Marine Claims Association; San Francisco Marine Underwriters Association (1981-Present); The Maritime Law Association of the United States — Northern California Super Lawyer (2005-2013); Pacific Admiralty Seminar (Chairman 1992; Steering Committee Member 1981-Present); Maritime Law Association of the United States (Director, 2010-2013; Proctor in Admiralty); Associate Editor, American Maritime Cases (2006-Present) — Lt., U.S. Navy [1971-1975] — E-mail: george.nowell@nowelllaw.com

Associate

John H. Cigavic, III — 1976 — James Madison University, B.A., 1998; St. John's University School of Law, J.D. (cum laude), 2003 — Admitted to Bar, 2004, New York; California; U.S. District Court, Central, Eastern, Northern and Southern Districts of California; U.S. Court of Appeals, Ninth Circuit — Member Bar Association of San Francisco; San Francisco Marine Underwriters Association; San Francisco Marine Claims Assocition; Property Claims Association of the Pacific; National Association of Insurance Women; The Maritime Law Association of the United States — Pacific Admiralty Seminar Planning Committee — E-mail: john.cigavic@nowelllaw.com

(This firm is also listed in the Subrogation section of this directory)

Rimac Martin, PC

1051 Divisadero Street
San Francisco, California 94115
   Telephone: 415-561-8440
   Fax: 415-561-8430
   www.rimacmartin.com

(Incline Village, NV Office: 803 Snead Court, P.O. Box 7028, 89450)
   (Tel: 775-833-2269)
   (Fax: 775-833-2279)

Established: 1998

Civil Trial Practice, State and Federal Courts, Insurance Law, Product Liability, Commercial Litigation, Intellectual Property, Reinsurance, Employment Law, Transportation, ERISA, Personal Injury, Securities, Transactions, International Commercial Law, Pest Control, Corporate Litigation

Insurance Clients

American Fidelity Assurance Company
Gerber Life Insurance Company
Houston Casualty Company
Mutual of Omaha Insurance Company
Sagicor at Lloyd's
Travelers Insurance Companies
UNUM Life Insurance Company of America
Aon Group Limited
CIGNA Group
HCC Specialty Underwriters, Inc.
International Risk Management Group
National Union Fire Insurance Company of Pittsburgh, PA
Unum Group

Non-Insurance Clients

A. C. Newman & Company
Coca-Cola Enterprises Inc.
Midlands Claim Administrators, Inc.
American Airlines, Inc.
Los Angeles Police Protective League
Rollins, Inc.

SAN FRANCISCO   CALIFORNIA

Rimac Martin, PC, San Francisco, CA   (Continued)

Firm Members

Joseph M. Rimac, Jr. — 1951 — Stanford University, B.A., 1973; University of Michigan Law School, J.D., 1976 — Phi Delta Phi — Admitted to Bar, 1976, California; U.S. District Court, Central, Eastern, Northern and Southern Districts of California; U.S. Court of Appeals, Fourth, Fifth, Sixth, Ninth and Eleventh Circuits; U.S. Supreme Court — Member American Bar Association; State Bar of California; Bar Association of San Francisco; Defense Research Institute

Anna Maria Martin — 1964 — California State Polytechnic University, B.S., 1987; University of the Pacific, McGeorge School of Law, J.D. (with distinction), 1991 — Admitted to Bar, 1991, California; 2000, Nevada; U.S. District Court, Central, Eastern, Northern and Southern Districts of California; U.S. Court of Appeals, Ninth Circuit; U.S. Supreme Court — Member American and Incline Village Bar Associations; State Bar of California; State Bar of Nevada; Bar Association of San Francisco; California Women Lawyers Association; Defense Research Institute — Super Lawyers for 2011-2014

Associates

William B. Reilly   Grant E. Ingram

Ropers, Majeski, Kohn & Bentley
A Professional Corporation

150 Spear Street, Suite 850
San Francisco, California 94105
   Telephone: 415-543-4800
   Fax: 415-972-6301
   www.rmkb.com

(Redwood City, CA Office*: 1001 Marshall Street, Suite 500, 94063)
   (Tel: 650-364-8200)
   (Fax: 650-780-1701)
(Los Angeles, CA Office*: 515 South Flower Street, Suite 1100, 90071)
   (Tel: 213-312-2000)
   (Fax: 213-312-2001)
(San Jose, CA Office*: 50 West San Fernando Street, Suite 1400, 95113)
   (Tel: 408-287-6262)
   (Fax: 408-918-4501)
(New York, NY Office*: 750 Third Avenue, 25th Floor, 10017)
   (Tel: 212-668-5927)
   (Fax: 212-668-5929)
(Boston, MA Office*: Ten Post Office Square, 8th Floor South, 02109)
   (Tel: 617-850-9087)
   (Fax: 617-850-9088)

Established: 1950

Antitrust, Appellate Practice, Business Litigation, Commercial Litigation, Civil Rights, Class Actions, Complex Litigation, Construction Law, Corporate Law, Elder Abuse, Employment Law, Entertainment Law, Environmental Law, ERISA, Estate Planning, Governmental Entity Defense, Health Care, Intellectual Property, International Law, Mergers and Acquisitions, Personal Injury, Premises Liability, Product Liability, Professional Liability, Real Estate, Toxic Torts, Asset Protection, Banking/Consumer Credit, Catastrophic Injury, Cost Control, Elder Rights, Fee Disputes, Insurance Services, IT and Business Process Outsourcing, Litigation Management, Non-Profit, Proposition 65, Special Education Law, Taxation, Wealth Management

Partners

George G. Weickhardt — 1944 — Harvard University, B.A. (summa cum laude), 1966; Harvard Law School, J.D. (magna cum laude), 1973 — Admitted to Bar, 1973, California; U.S. District Court, Northern District of California; U.S. Court of Appeals, Ninth Circuit; 1982, U.S. Supreme Court; 1985, U.S. District Court, Central District of California; 1987, U.S. District Court, Eastern and Southern Districts of California — Member American Bar Association — Languages: Russian — Practice Areas: Banking; Business Litigation; Commercial Litigation; Appellate Practice; Class Actions; Antitrust

Thomas H. Clarke, Jr. — 1945 — University of California, Berkeley, A.B.,

Ropers, Majeski, Kohn & Bentley, A Professional Corporation, San Francisco, CA   (Continued)

1967; The George Washington University, M.S., 1980; University of California, Berkeley Boalt Hall School of Law, J.D., 1970 — Admitted to Bar, 1971, California; District of Columbia; U.S. District Court, Central and Northern Districts of California; U.S. Court of Appeals, Ninth Circuit; U.S. Supreme Court — Member State Bar of California; The District of Columbia Bar — Practice Areas: Environmental Litigation; Business Litigation; Commercial Litigation; Class Actions; Tort Litigation; Product Liability

Terry Anastassiou — 1956 — Michigan Technological University; The George Washington University, B.A., 1983; Syracuse University; Santa Clara University School of Law, J.D., 1991 — Admitted to Bar, 1992, California; 1996, U.S. District Court, Central, Eastern, Northern and Southern Districts of California; U.S. Court of Appeals, Ninth Circuit; U.S. Court of Appeals for the Federal Circuit; U.S. Supreme Court — Member State Bar of California (Board of Legal Specialization); Bar Association of San Francisco; Hellenic Law Society — Practice Areas: Appellate Practice

Kathleen N. Strickland — Institute of European Studies; Spring Hill College, B.S. (magna cum laude); University of San Diego School of Law, J.D. — Admitted to Bar, 1975, California; 1994, Texas; 1996, Colorado; 2008, District of Columbia; 2009, New York; 1975, U.S. District Court, Central, Eastern, Northern and Southern Districts of California; U.S. Court of Appeals, Ninth Circuit — Member American and Los Angeles County (Litigation Section) Bar Associations; Bar Association of San Francisco; Product Liability Advisory Council; American Board of Trial Advocates — National Charity League — Practice Areas: Product Liability; Environmental Litigation; Class Actions; Complex Litigation; Business Litigation; Commercial Litigation

Associates

Spencer C. Martinez   Devin C. Courteau
Justin A. Zucker

Of Counsel

Todd J. Wenzel — 1966 — University of California, Los Angeles, B.A., 1988; Southwestern University School of Law, J.D., 1991 — Admitted to Bar, 1992, California; U.S. District Court, Central, Eastern, Northern and Southern Districts of California; U.S. Court of Appeals, Ninth Circuit — Member American and Napa County Bar Associations; State Bar of California; Bar Association of San Francisco; Association of Defense Counsel of Northern California and Nevada — U.S. Green Building Council, Northern California Chapter — Practice Areas: Real Estate; Business Litigation; Commercial Litigation; Product Liability

John A. Koeppel — 1947 — University of Notre Dame, B.A. (cum laude), 1969; Tufts University, M.A., 1970; University of California, Hastings College of the Law, J.D., 1976 — Admitted to Bar, 1976, California; U.S. District Court, Central, Eastern and Northern Districts of California; U.S. Supreme Court — Member State Bar of California; Bar Association of San Francisco; National Board of Trial Advocacy — Practice Areas: Business Litigation; Commercial Litigation; Catastrophic Injury; Construction Litigation; Health Care; Product Liability; Professional Liability

(See listing under Redwood City, CA for additional information)

Severson & Werson

One Embarcadero Center, Suite 2600
San Francisco, California 94111
   Telephone: 415-398-3344
   Fax: 415-956-0439
   E-Mail: rem@severson.com
   www.severson.com

(Irvine, CA Office: 19100 Von Karman, Suite 700, 92612)
   (Tel: 949-442-7110)
   (Fax: 949-442-7118)

Established: 1945

Severson & Werson, San Francisco, CA (Continued)

Appellate Practice, Antitrust, Bankruptcy, Class Actions, Commercial Law, Construction Law, Contracts, Environmental Law, Errors and Omissions, Insurance Coverage, Insurance Defense, Labor and Employment, Litigation, Product Liability, Professional Liability, Admiralty and Maritime Law, Energy, Sports Law

Firm Profile: With over 120 attorneys in two California offices, the 69 year old Firm of Severson & Werson listens closely, considers fully, and provides honest, straightforward advice and advocacy to their clients.

When Severson & Werson's clients are embroiled in litigation, their aim is not to needlessly litigate but to resolve the matter to the swiftest, surest and most successful result possible. When litigation is necessary to commence or defend, Severson & Werson strives to provide efficient results with a proven track record of trial success. Severson also recognizes that litigation is only one component of legal support necessary to serve its' clients. Severson takes great pride in its collective ability to listen to clients and provide the strategic and responsive advice which can often avoid litigation.

As a result, Severson has become a trusted advisor and counselor to many of its clients as they chart their respective business plans. For example, insurance companies, law firms, construction professionals, financial services firms, real estate companies, and many others have all come to count on Severson for practical and straightforward advice serving the immediate and long term interests of the client. In many areas such as insurance defense, insurance coverage, construction, employment practices, and professional liability, this strategic advice takes its final form in the drafting and negotiation of corporate documents and agreements integral to the success of Severson & Werson's clients.

Insurance Clients

K & K Insurance Group, Inc.
XL Design Professional
Underwriters at Lloyd's, London

Non-Insurance Clients

Police & Firemen's Insurance Association

Principals and Shareholders

Michael B. Murphy — University of Santa Clara, B.A., 1980; University of Santa Clara School of Law, J.D., 1983 — Admitted to Bar, 1983, California; Indiana; 1984, U.S. District Court, Central, Eastern, Northern and Southern Districts of California; U.S. Court of Appeals, Ninth Circuit; 1986, U.S. Court of Appeals, Seventh Circuit; 2003, U.S. District Court, District of Colorado — Member American and Indiana State Bar Associations; State Bar of California; Association of Fraternal Benefit Counsel; Association of Defense Counsel, Northern California; Professional Liability Underwriting Society; Federation of Defense and Corporate Counsel; Defense Research Institute — E-mail: mbm@severson.com

David A. Ericksen — Pacific Lutheran University, B.A. (summa cum laude), 1986; University of California, Berkeley Boalt Hall School of Law, J.D., 1990 — Admitted to Bar, 1990, Washington; 1991, California; U.S. District Court, Eastern and Northern Districts of California; U.S. Court of Appeals, Ninth Circuit — Member American and Washington State Bar Associations; State Bar of California — E-mail: dae@severson.com

Forrest Booth — Amherst College, B.A. (cum laude), 1968; Harvard Law School, J.D., 1975 — Admitted to Bar, 1976, District of Columbia; 1977, California; 1979, U.S. Supreme Court — Member State Bar of California; Bar Association of the District of Columbia; Bar Association of San Francisco; ASIA-Pacific Lawyers Association; International Bar Association; Maritime Law Association of the United States (Board of Directors) — E-mail: fb@severson.com

Joel L. Halverson — Pomona College, B.A. (cum laude), 1990; University of California, Hastings College of the Law, J.D., 1994 — Admitted to Bar, 1994, California; 2000, U.S. District Court, Central, Eastern and Northern Districts of California; 2004, U.S. Court of Appeals, Ninth Circuit — Member State Bar of California; Association of Defense Counsel of Northern California and Nevada — E-mail: jlh@severson.com

Mark D. Lonergan — Managing Partner — University of Virginia, B.A., 1984; University of Virginia School of Law, J.D., 1989 — Admitted to Bar, 1989, California — E-mail: mdl@severson.com

Jeane Struck — University of California, Santa Cruz, B.A., 1977; Santa Clara University, J.D., 1983 — Admitted to Bar, 1983, California — E-mail: js@severson.com

Severson & Werson, San Francisco, CA (Continued)

Adam H. Hutchinson — University of California, Irvine, B.A. (cum laude), 1993; Loyola Law School, J.D., 1997 — Admitted to Bar, 1997, California; 2001, U.S. District Court, Central, Eastern and Northern Districts of California; 2004, U.S. Court of Appeals, Ninth Circuit — Member American and Orange County Bar Associations; State Bar of California — E-mail: ahh@severson.com

Scott J. Hyman — Penn State University, B.A., 1987; University of the Pacific, J.D., 1990 — Admitted to Bar, 1990, California; 2013, Texas — E-mail: sjh@severson.com

Kristin L. Walker-Probst — Pepperdine University, B.A., 1995; Loyola Law School, J.D., 1999 — Admitted to Bar, 1999, California — E-mail: klw@severson.com

Of Counsel

Eric M. Crowe
Elizabeth L. Dolter
Susan Carbone Keeney
Peter C. Lyon
Cynthia L. Mitchell
Ann L. Strayer
Katherine A. Wadley

Nannette DeLara
Harry A. Hagan
Erik M. Kowalewsky
John R. Meehan
Peter B. Molgaard
Gale A. Townsley
Pamela L. Schultz

Associates

Yevgenia Wiener
Adam M. Polakoff
J. Andrew Lawson

Sheppard, Mullin, Richter & Hampton LLP

Four Embarcadero Center, 17th Floor
San Francisco, California 94111
  Telephone: 415-434-9100
  www.sheppardmullin.com

Established: 1927

Antitrust, Bad Faith, Class Actions, Complex Litigation, Insurance Litigation, Trial and Appellate Practice

Firm Profile: Sheppard, Mullin, Richter & Hampton LLP represents clients in a wide variety of insurance-related litigation matters. The firm represents insurance companies, producers and third party administrators in all types of litigation, ranging from class actions and complex multi-party litigation to single insured disputes, and assists insurer clients in administrative and regulatory proceedings.

Partner

Todd L. Padnos — Emory University, B.A., 1989; Loyola University Chicago School of Law, J.D., 1992 — Admitted to Bar, 1992, Illinois; 2000, California; U.S. District Court, Northern District of Illinois; U.S. District Court, Central, Eastern, Northern and Southern Districts of California; U.S. Court of Appeals, Second, Seventh and Ninth Circuits — Tel: 415-774-2938 — E-mail: tpadnos@sheppardmullin.com

(See listing under Los Angeles, CA for additional information)

Vogl Meredith Burke LLP

456 Montgomery Street, 20th Floor
San Francisco, California 94104-1233
  Telephone: 415-398-0200
  Fax: 415-398-2820
  E-Mail: mburke@vmbllp.com
  www.vmbllp.com

Established: 1991

SAN FRANCISCO CALIFORNIA

Vogl Meredith Burke LLP, San Francisco, CA
(Continued)

Commercial Liability, Insurance Defense, Commercial Law, Toxic Torts, Personal Lines, Employment Law, Discrimination, Professional Liability, Negligence, Insurance Coverage, Insurance Litigation, Construction Defect, Product Liability, Premises Liability, Energy, Antitrust, Appellate Advocacy, Construction Injury

Firm Profile: Established in 1992, Vogl Meredith Burke LLP is a firm comprised of trial attorneys who specialize in the defense and prosecution of complex litigated matters. The firm holds the highest "AV" rating from Martindale-Hubbel Bar Register of Preeminent Lawyers. The firm regularly handles civil litigation for individuals, businesses, and public entities throughout the State of California. Vogl Meredith Burke LLP is committed to cost-effective, yet high quality representation of clients, with an eye towards building long-term trusted relationships.

The lawyers of Vogl Meredith Burke LLP focus their practice on the defense of General Liability and Personal Injury matters, including: Motor Vehicle Accident, Construction Injury, and Products Liability cases; Employment Litigation, including Wrongful Termination, Wage and Hour, and responding to administrative claims; Insurance Coverage and Bad Faith litigation; Construction Defect; Environmental and Toxic Torts; Professional Liability; and General Business and Complex Litigation matters.

Vogl Meredith Burke LLP has been recognized as one of California's Top Ranked Law Firms® by LexisNexis® Martindale-Hubbell®. Only 222 law firms in the state have achieved this ranking.

Insurance Clients

Acuity Insurance Company	Admiral Insurance Company
AIU Insurance Company	Amica Mutual Insurance Company
Arch Insurance Company	Golden Eagle Insurance Corporation
Hanover Insurance Group	
Liberty Mutual Insurance Company	Nonprofits' Insurance Alliance of California
OneBeacon Insurance Group	
Philadelphia Indemnity Insurance Company	QBE Insurance Company
	Reliance Insurance Company
Resolute Management, Inc.	RLI/Mt. Hawley Insurance Company
Sequoia Insurance Company	
Travelers Insurance Companies	Unigard Insurance Group
United States Liability Insurance	Utica National Insurance Group
Zurich North America	

Non-Insurance Clients

California Insurance Guarantee Association	Carl Warren & Company
	Gallagher Bassett Services, Inc.
The Herrick Corporation	Maxson Young Associates Inc.
MCM Construction, Inc.	MDU Resource Group
Pacific Coast Building Products	Rudolph and Sletten, Inc.
Shimmick Construction	

Attorneys

David R. Vogl — University of San Francisco, A.B., 1965; University of California, Hastings College of the Law, J.D., 1968 — Admitted to Bar, 1968, California; 1968, U.S. Court of Appeals, Ninth Circuit — Member American Bar Association; State Bar of California; Bar Association of San Francisco; Association of Attorneys-Mediators; American Board of Trial Advocates; Association of Defense Counsel, Northern California — E-mail: dvogl@vmbllp.com

Samuel E. Meredith — Dickinson College, A.B., 1960; Golden Gate University School of Law, J.D., 1967 — Admitted to Bar, 1968, California; 1968, U.S. District Court, Eastern and Northern Districts of California; 1968, U.S. Court of Appeals, Ninth Circuit — Member State Bar of California; Bar Association of San Francisco; California Compensation Defense Attorneys Association; Association of Defense Counsel, Northern California; American Board of Trial Advocates — E-mail: smeredith@vmbllp.com

Michael S. Burke — University of California, San Diego, B.A., 1987; University of San Diego School of Law, J.D., 1990 — Admitted to Bar, 1990, California; 1990, U.S. District Court, Central and Southern Districts of California — Member Bar Association of San Francisco — E-mail: mburke@vmbllp.com

David A. Firestone — University of Nevada, B.A., 1968; University of San Francisco School of Law, J.D., 1974 — Admitted to Bar, 1974, California; U.S. District Court, Central, Eastern, Northern and Southern Districts of California; U.S. Court of Appeals, Ninth Circuit — Member State Bar of California; Bar Association of San Francisco; Association of Defense Counsel, Northern California — E-mail: dfirestone@vmbllp.com

Diane E. Pritchard — Northeastern University, B.A. (summa cum laude), 1975; Columbia University, M.A., 1976; New York University School of Law, J.D. (cum laude), 1980 — Admitted to Bar, 1981, California; U.S. District Court, Central, Eastern, Northern and Southern Districts of California; U.S. Court of Appeals, Ninth Circuit; U.S. Supreme Court — Member American Bar Association (Litigation and Antitrust Sections); Bar Association of San Francisco (Litigation and Antitrust Sections); Association of Business Trial Lawyers — E-mail: dpritchard@vmbllp.com

David J. Streza — California State University, Pomona, B.A., 1997; University of San Francisco School of Law, J.D., 2000 — Admitted to Bar, 2000, California; U.S. District Court, Eastern and Northern Districts of California; U.S. Court of Appeals, Ninth Circuit — Member American Bar Association; State Bar of California; Association of Defense Counsel, Northern California — E-mail: dstreza@vmbllp.com

E. Forrest Shyrock, Jr. — University of California, Riverside, B.A. (with honors), 1982; University of California, Hastings College of the Law, J.D., 1985 — Admitted to Bar, 1985, California; U.S. District Court, Central, Eastern and Northern Districts of California; U.S. Court of Appeals, Ninth Circuit — Member State Bar of California; Bar Association of San Francisco — E-mail: fshyrock@vmbllp.com

Nicole Lee Meredith — University of California, Irvine, B.A., 1989; Pepperdine University School of Law, J.D., 1992 — Admitted to Bar, 1992, California; 1992, U.S. District Court, Central District of California — Member American Bar Association — E-mail: nmeredith@vmbllp.com

G. Randy Kasten — Reed College, B.A., 1978; Golden Gate University School of Law, J.D., 1982 — Admitted to Bar, 1984, California; U.S. District Court, Central, Eastern, Northern and Southern Districts of California; U.S. Tax Court — Member State Bar of California; Alameda County Bar Association — Court Appointed Arbitrator; Fee Dispute Arbitrator — E-mail: rkasten@vmbllp.com

Liza C. Milanes — University of California, Los Angeles, B.A./B.S., 2000; University of California, Hastings College of the Law, J.D., 2004 — Admitted to Bar, 2005, Hawaii; 2006, California — Member American, Hawaii State, Alameda County (Member, Barristers Executive Committee, 2010-2011) and Queen's Bench Bar Associations; State Bar of California; Bar Association of San Francisco — E-mail: lmilanes@vmbllp.com

Jean N. Yeh — University of San Francisco, B.S., 1982; University of California, Berkeley; University of California, Hastings College of the Law, J.D., 1985 — Hastings Law Journal — Admitted to Bar, 1986, California; 1986, U.S. District Court, Northern District of California; 1986, U.S. Court of Appeals, Ninth Circuit — Member American Bar Association; State Bar of California; Bar Association of San Francisco; Association of Defense Counsel, Northern California — E-mail: jyeh@vmbllp.com

Corie A. Edwards — University of California, Riverside, B.A., 1993; University of California, Hastings College of the Law, J.D., 1996 — Admitted to Bar, 1996, California — Member State Bar of California; Urban Land Institute; Environmental Law Institute — Approved Discovery Facilitator, Contra Costa County Superior Court

Wild, Carey & Fife

100 Montgomery Street, Suite 1410
San Francisco, California 94104-4317
Telephone: 415-837-3101
Fax: 415-837-3111
E-Mail: nancyholliday@wcandf.com
www.wcandf.com

Established: 1980

Insurance Defense, Automobile, General Liability, Professional Liability, Property and Casualty, Product Liability, Coverage Issues, Construction Defect, Employment Law, Business Law, Insurance Bad Faith

Firm Profile: Wild Carey & Fife is a San Francisco civil litigation firm. The firm was founded in 1980 by Don Wild and has 3 partners and 3 associates. The firm's principal areas of practice include (1) non-medical professional liability; (2) major personal injury, premises liability, product liability and

CALIFORNIA SAN JOSE

Wild, Carey & Fife, San Francisco, CA (Continued)

wrongful death actions; (3) transportation litigation; (4) insurance coverage and bad faith; (5) construction defect litigation and (6) employment law.

Insurance Clients

Argo Pro	Auto-Owners Insurance Company
Berkley Risk Administrators Company, LLC	CAMICO Mutual Insurance Company
Employers Insurance Company of Wausau	Everest National Insurance Company
Golden Eagle Insurance Corporation	Hanover Insurance Group
Liberty Mutual Insurance/Specialty Liability Claims	Indemnity Insurance Corporation of DC
	National Indemnity Company

Non-Insurance Clients

K & K Insurance Group, Inc.	MRR3, Inc.
NTA, Inc.	Vela Insurance Services, LLC
Werner Enterprises, Inc.	

Partners

Donald R. Wild — 1938 — The University of Arizona, B.S. (cum laude), 1962; Loyola Law School Los Angeles, J.D., 1969 — Admitted to Bar, 1970, California; 1977, U.S. District Court, Central, Eastern and Northern Districts of California; U.S. Court of Appeals, Ninth Circuit — Member American Bar Association; National Board of Trial Advocacy; American Board of Trial Advocates; Defense Research Institute; Trucking Industry Defense Association — Practice Areas: Professional Liability; Product Liability; Personal Injury; Business Law; Employment Law; Insurance Coverage; Construction Defect; Transportation — E-mail: donaldwild@wcandf.com

John E. Carey — 1945 — Georgetown University, B.A., 1968; University of California, Hastings College of the Law, J.D., 1975 — Admitted to Bar, 1975, California — Practice Areas: Personal Injury; Business Law; Labor and Employment; Civil Rights — E-mail: johncarey@wcandf.com

Paul D. Fife — 1957 — University of California, Davis, B.A. (cum laude), 1980; University of California, Hastings College of the Law, J.D., 1984 — Admitted to Bar, 1984, California; U.S. District Court, Central, Eastern and Northern Districts of California; U.S. Court of Appeals, Ninth Circuit — Member American Bar Association (Professional Liability Litigation and Construction Litigation Committees); Bar Association of San Francisco; Professional Liability Underwriting Society; Defense Research Institute; Association of Defense Counsel, Northern California — Practice Areas: Professional Liability; Insurance Coverage; Personal Injury; Transportation; Business Law; Construction Litigation — E-mail: paulfife@wcandf.com

Associates

Terence H. Kenney — 1956 — University of California, Santa Cruz, B.A., 1978; University of North Carolina at Chapel Hill School of Law, J.D., 1982 — Admitted to Bar, 1983, North Carolina; 1984, California; U.S. District Court, Northern District of California — Practice Areas: Professional Liability; Insurance Coverage; General Civil Practice; Construction Defect; Transportation — E-mail: terencekenney@wcandf.com

William M. Henley — 1954 — University of Missouri-Columbia, B.A., 1976; University of California, Berkeley Boalt Hall School of Law, J.D., 1980 — Admitted to Bar, 1989, California; 1991, U.S. District Court, Eastern District of California; 1992, U.S. District Court, Northern District of California; U.S. Court of Appeals, Ninth Circuit — Practice Areas: Insurance Defense; Commercial Litigation; Construction Defect; Personal Injury — E-mail: williamhenley@wcandf.com

Enoch Wang — 1970 — Yale University, B.A., 1992; University of California, Hastings College of the Law, J.D., 1999 — Admitted to Bar, 2002, California; Texas; Pennsylvania; New Jersey; U.S. District Court, Northern District of California; U.S. District Court, Southern District of Texas; U.S. Court of Appeals, Ninth Circuit — Practice Areas: Professional Liability; Commercial Litigation; Construction Litigation; Insurance Coverage — E-mail: enochwang@wcandf.com

---

The following firms also service this area.

Babin & Seeger, LLP
3550 Round Barn Boulevard, Suite 201
Santa Rosa, California 95403
   Telephone: 707-526-7370
   Fax: 707-526-0307
Mailing Address: P.O. Box 11626, Santa Rosa, CA 95406

Insurance Defense, Motor Vehicle, Commercial Law, General Liability, Product Liability, Property Damage, Construction Defect, Contracts, Environmental Law, Insurance Coverage, Workers' Compensation, Personal Injury, Professional Malpractice

SEE COMPLETE LISTING UNDER SANTA ROSA, CALIFORNIA (51 MILES)

Boornazian, Jensen & Garthe
A Professional Corporation
555 12th Street, 18th Floor
Oakland, California 94607
   Telephone: 510-834-4350
   Fax: 510-839-1897
Mailing Address: P.O. Box 12925, Oakland, CA 94604-2925

Insurance Defense, Trial Practice, Product Liability, Legal Malpractice, Professional Malpractice, Medical Malpractice, Insurance Coverage, Construction Law

SEE COMPLETE LISTING UNDER OAKLAND, CALIFORNIA (13 MILES)

Mollis & Mollis, Inc.
4621 Teller Avenue, Suite 200
Newport Beach, California 92660
   Telephone: 949-222-0735
   Fax: 949-955-0252

Insurance Defense, Civil Trial Practice, Business Law, Construction Law, Corporate Law, Appeals, Labor Law, Environmental Law, Real Estate, Estate Planning, Trusts, Probate, Trust and Estate Litigation, Taxation, Trust Settlement

SEE COMPLETE LISTING UNDER NEWPORT BEACH, CALIFORNIA (426 MILES)

SAN JOSE † 945,942 Santa Clara Co.

Borton Petrini, LLP

95 South Market Street, Suite 400
San Jose, California 95113
   Telephone: 408-535-0870
   Fax: 408-535-0878
   E-Mail: bpsj@bortonpetrini.com
   www.bortonpetrini.com

Established: 1899

Agriculture, Americans with Disabilities Act, Construction Defect, Employment Law, Insurance Litigation, Product Liability, Professional Liability, Toxic Torts

Firm Profile: Since 1899, Borton Petrini, LLP, has offered high quality legal services in all of the practice areas described above through its California network of 10 regional offices. The mission of Borton Petrini, LLP is to treat every file as though we were representing ourselves and paying the bill for that representation.

Managing Partner

Samuel L. Phillips — 1960 — University of San Francisco, B.A., 1982; J.D., 1985 — Alpha Sigma Nu; Jesuit Honor Society — Admitted to Bar, 1987, California; 1989, U.S. District Court, Eastern and Northern Districts of California; 1989, U.S. Court of Appeals, Ninth Circuit — Member State Bar of California; Santa Clara County Bar Association (Former Member; Judical Committee); William Ingram Inns of Court; Ralph M. Brown Inns of the Court (Past Founding Member); Defense Research Institute (Professionalism & Ethics Committee); Cerebal Palsy Association (Past Special Advisor); St. Thomas More Society — Author: "The Empty Chair Defense," California Defense Magazine (Fall 1995); "Should Parents be Liable for Intentional Acts

SAN JOSE
CALIFORNIA

Borton Petrini, LLP, San Jose, CA (Continued)

of Their Children?" California Defense Magazine (Summer 1999) — Languages: Spanish — E-mail: sphillips@bortonpetrini.com

Partners

Lynne L. Bentley — 1962 — Santa Clara University, B.S., 1984; Santa Clara University School of Law, J.D., 1988 — Admitted to Bar, 1988, California; 1988, U.S. District Court, Northern District of California; 2014, U.S. District Court, Eastern District of California — Member State Bar of California; Santa Clara County Bar Association — Author: "Goodbye and Good Riddance," California Defense Magazine (Fall 1993) — Santa Clara University School of Law (Alumni Board Member, 1989-1998, Board of Directors, 1996-1997); Campfire Boys & Girls (Board Member, 1989-1995) — E-mail: lbentley@bortonpetrini.com

Mark W. Shem — 1965 — University of California, Davis, B.A., 1987; Temple University, J.D., 1990 — Admitted to Bar, 1991, California; 1991, U.S. District Court, Northern District of California; 1991, U.S. Court of Appeals, Ninth Circuit; 2002, U.S. District Court, Eastern District of California — Member State Bar of California (Board of Trustees, 2011-2014); Santa Clara County Bar Association (President, 2010); Defense Research Institute — International & Comparative Law Journal (Business Editor); Santa Clara County Superior Court (Judical Arbitrator, 1997-2002) — E-mail: mshem@bortonpetrini.com

Associate

Molly A. Sundstrom — 1987 — University of California, Davis, B.A., 2005; Santa Clara University, J.D., 2012 — Admitted to Bar, 2013, California; 2014, U.S. District Court, Central and Northern Districts of California — Member American Bar Association; State Bar of California; Central Coast Claims Association — E-mail: msundstrom@bortonpetrini.com

Ericksen Arbuthnot

152 North Third Street, Suite 700
San Jose, California 95112-5560
 Telephone: 408-286-0880
 Fax: 408-286-0337
 www.ericksenarbuthnot.com

(Oakland, CA Office*: 155 Grand Avenue, Suite 1050, 94612-3768)
 (Tel: 510-832-7770)
 (Fax: 510-832-0102)
(Bakersfield, CA Office*: 1830 Truxtun Avenue, Suite 200, 93301-5022)
 (Tel: 661-633-5080)
 (Fax: 661-633-5089)
(Fresno, CA Office*: 2440 West Shaw Avenue, Suite 101, 93711-3300)
 (Tel: 559-449-2600)
 (Fax: 559-449-2603)
(Los Angeles, CA Office*: 835 Wilshire Boulevard, Suite 500, 90017-2656)
 (Tel: 213-489-4411)
 (Fax: 213-489-4332)
(Sacramento, CA Office*: 100 Howe Avenue, Suite 110S, 95825-8200)
 (Tel: 916-483-5181)
 (Fax: 916-483-7558)
(San Francisco, CA Office*: 100 Bush Street, Suite 900, 94104-3950)
 (Tel: 415-362-7126)
 (Fax: 415-362-6401)
(Walnut Creek, CA Office*: 570 Lennon Lane, 94598-2415)
 (Tel: 925-947-1702)
 (Fax: 925-947-4921)

Administrative Law, Business Law, Construction Law, Employment Law, Environmental Law, Health Care, Managed Care Liability, Insurance Coverage, Insurance Fraud, Personal Injury, Premises Liability, Product Liability, Professional Liability, Medical Malpractice, Public Entities, Appellate Law

Resident Partners

Von Ryan Reyes — Managing Partner — Santa Clara University, B.A., 1996; Santa Clara University School of Law, J.D., 1999 — Admitted to Bar, 1999, California; U.S. District Court, Northern District of California — Member State Bar of California; Santa Clara County Bar Association; Association of

Ericksen Arbuthnot, San Jose, CA (Continued)

Defense Counsel, Northern California — E-mail: vreyes@ericksenarbuthnot.com

Sharon L. Hightower — Assistant Managing Partner — University of Hawaii; Saint Mary's College, B.A., 1983; Lincoln Law School, J.D., 1987 — Admitted to Bar, 1987, California; U.S. Court of Appeals, Ninth Circuit — Member American and Santa Clara County Bar Associations; State Bar of California; California Trial Lawyers Association; American Dental Hygienist Association; California Dental Hygienist Association — E-mail: shightower@ericksenarbuthnot.com

Of Counsel

Steven W. Dollar — California State University, San Jose, B.S. (magna cum laude), 1978; University of California, Hastings College of the Law, J.D., 1982 — Phi Kappa Phi — Admitted to Bar, 1982, California — Member American and Santa Clara County Bar Associations; State Bar of California — E-mail: sdollar@ericksenarbuthnot.com

Resident Associates

Felicia P. Jafferies — University of California at Irvine, B.A., 1999; University of the Pacific, McGeorge School of Law, J.D., 2006 — Admitted to Bar, 2007, California — Member State Bar of California — E-mail: fjafferies@ericksenarbuthnot.com

Nathaniel R. Lucey — College of William & Mary, B.A., 2002; Santa Clara University School of Law, J.D., 2008 — Admitted to Bar, 2008, California — Member State Bar of California (Litigation Section) — Practice Areas: Civil Litigation — E-mail: nlucey@ericksenarbuthnot.com

(See listing under Oakland, CA for additional information)

Ropers, Majeski, Kohn & Bentley
A Professional Corporation

50 West San Fernando Street, Suite 1400
San Jose, California 95113
 Telephone: 408-287-6262
 Fax: 408-918-4501
 www.rmkb.com

(Redwood City, CA Office*: 1001 Marshall Street, Suite 500, 94063)
 (Tel: 650-364-8200)
 (Fax: 650-780-1701)
(Los Angeles, CA Office*: 515 South Flower Street, Suite 1100, 90071)
 (Tel: 213-312-2000)
 (Fax: 213-312-2001)
(San Francisco, CA Office*: 150 Spear Street, Suite 850, 94105)
 (Tel: 415-543-4800)
 (Fax: 415-972-6301)
(New York, NY Office*: 750 Third Avenue, 25th Floor, 10017)
 (Tel: 212-668-5927)
 (Fax: 212-668-5929)
(Boston, MA Office*: Ten Post Office Square, 8th Floor South, 02109)
 (Tel: 617-850-9087)
 (Fax: 617-850-9088)

Established: 1950

Antitrust, Appellate Practice, Business Litigation, Commercial Litigation, Civil Rights, Class Actions, Complex Litigation, Construction Law, Corporate Law, Elder Abuse, Employment Law, Entertainment Law, Environmental Law, ERISA, Estate Planning, Governmental Entity Defense, Health Care, Intellectual Property, International Law, Mergers and Acquisitions, Personal Injury, Premises Liability, Product Liability, Professional Liability, Real Estate, Toxic Torts, Asset Protection, Banking/Consumer Credit, Catastrophic Injury, Cost Control, Elder Rights, Fee Disputes, Insurance Services, IT and Business Process Outsourcing, Litigation Management, Non-Profit, Proposition 65, Special Education Law, Taxation, Wealth Management

Ropers, Majeski, Kohn & Bentley, A Professional Corporation, San Jose, CA (Continued)

Partners

Dennis J. Ward — 1949 — University of California, Santa Barbara, B.A., 1971; Golden Gate University School of Law, J.D. (cum laude), 1977 — Admitted to Bar, 1977, California — Member State Bar of California; Santa Clara County Bar Association; American Board of Trial Advocates — Practice Areas: Catastrophic Injury; Personal Injury; Civil Rights; Elder Abuse; Employment Litigation; Dispute Resolution; Insurance Litigation; Product Liability

Michael J. Ioannou — Chairman — 1955 — University of Santa Clara, B.C.S., 1977; University of Santa Clara School of Law, J.D., 1980 — Admitted to Bar, 1980, California; U.S. District Court, Central, Eastern and Northern Districts of California — Member State Bar of California; Santa Clara County Bar Association — Practice Areas: Corporate Law; Mergers and Acquisitions; Business Litigation; Commercial Litigation; Intellectual Property; International Law; Antitrust

Stephan A. Barber — 1950 — University of California, Santa Barbara, B.A., 1972; University of the Pacific, McGeorge School of Law, J.D., 1976 — Admitted to Bar, 1976, California; U.S. District Court, Central, Eastern and Northern Districts of California; U.S. Court of Appeals, Ninth Circuit — Member State Bar of California; Santa Clara County Bar Association — National Register's Who's Who — Practice Areas: Business Litigation; Commercial Litigation; Catastrophic Injury; Personal Injury; Construction Litigation; Insurance Litigation; Professional Liability

Kevin P. Cody — 1953 — University of Santa Clara, B.S., 1975; University of Santa Clara School of Law, J.D., 1980 — Admitted to Bar, 1980, California — Member State Bar of California; Santa Clara County Bar Association; Association of Defense Counsel, Northern California — Practice Areas: Business Litigation; Commercial Litigation; Class Actions; Construction Litigation; Product Liability; Catastrophic Injury; Personal Injury

James C. Hyde — 1953 — San Jose State University, B.S., 1976; Santa Clara University School of Law, J.D., 1979 — Admitted to Bar, 1979, California; U.S. District Court, Central, Eastern and Northern Districts of California; U.S. Court of Appeals, Ninth Circuit — Member Santa Clara County Bar Association; Association of Ski Defense Attorneys; American Board of Trial Advocates — Practice Areas: Catastrophic Injury; Personal Injury; Elder Abuse; Employment Litigation; Dispute Resolution; Product Liability; Professional Liability

J. Mark Thacker — 1953 — University of Southwestern Louisiana, B.A., 1976; Santa Clara University School of Law, J.D. (magna cum laude), 1991 — Admitted to Bar, 1991, California; U.S. District Court, Eastern and Northern Districts of California; U.S. Court of Appeals, Ninth Circuit; U.S. District Court, Central District of California — Member State Bar of California; Santa Clara County Bar Association — Practice Areas: Business Litigation; Commercial Litigation; Health Care; Product Liability; Intellectual Property

Gregory M. Gentile — 1952 — Rhode Island College, B.A. (magna cum laude), 1979; Golden Gate University School of Law, J.D., 1989 — Admitted to Bar, 1990, California; U.S. District Court, Northern District of California; 2002, U.S. District Court, Eastern District of California — Member Santa Clara County Bar Association — Practice Areas: Business Litigation; Commercial Litigation; Corporate Law; ERISA; Intellectual Property; Product Liability; Professional Liability; Real Estate

Sonia M. Agee — 1969 — Boston University, B.A., 1989; Temple University School of Law, J.D., 1992; Golden Gate University School of Law, LL.M., 1995 — Admitted to Bar, 1993, California; 1994, New York; Massachusetts; 1996, District of Columbia; Washington; 1993, U.S. District Court, Northern District of California; U.S. Court of Appeals, Ninth Circuit; 2000, U.S. Tax Court — Member Santa Clara County Bar Association; Santa Clara County Estate Planning Council — Languages: Spanish, French — Practice Areas: Estate Planning; Business Litigation; Commercial Litigation; Corporate Law; Mergers and Acquisitions

Associates

Daniel P. McKinnon
Julian Pardo de Zela
Rachael E. Binder
Kimberly F. Whitfield
Enedina Cardenas
Wendy C. Krog

Ropers, Majeski, Kohn & Bentley, A Professional Corporation, San Jose, CA (Continued)

Of Counsel

Lisa E. Aguiar — 1963 — Santa Clara University, B.A./B.S., 1985; University of the Pacific, McGeorge School of Law, J.D., 1989 — Admitted to Bar, 1989, California; 2008, U.S. District Court, Central and Northern Districts of California — Member Santa Clara County Bar Association; Northern California Human Resources Association — Practice Areas: Employment Litigation; Dispute Resolution

(See listing under Redwood City, CA for additional information)

Simoncini & Associates

1694 The Alameda
San Jose, California 95126-2219
Telephone: 408-280-7711
Fax: 408-280-1330
E-Mail: kds@simoncini-law.com

Established: 1994

Insurance Defense, Construction Defect, Personal Injury, Automobile, General Liability, Public Entities, Tort Litigation

Insurance Clients

Atlantic Mutual Insurance Company
Evanston Insurance Company
Fireman's Fund Insurance Company
OneBeacon Insurance
Travelers Casualty and Surety Company
Burlington Insurance Company
CNA Insurance Company
Everest National Insurance Company
Liberty Mutual Insurance Company
TIG Insurance Company
United National Group
Zurich Insurance Company

Non-Insurance Clients

Association of Bay Area Governments
Network Adjusters, Inc.
Santa Clara Valley Transportation District
John Glenn Adjusters and Administrators, Inc.
Peninsula Corridor Joint Power Board

Kenneth D. Simoncini — 1956 — University of San Francisco, B.S., 1985; California Western School of Law, J.D., 1988 — Phi Alpha Delta — Order of Barristers — Admitted to Bar, 1989, California; 1990, District of Columbia; Minnesota; 1989, U.S. District Court, Central, Eastern, Northern and Southern Districts of California; 1990, U.S. Court of Appeals, Ninth Circuit; U.S. Supreme Court — Member State Bar of California; The District of Columbia Bar; Minnesota State, Santa Clara County and San Mateo County Bar Associations; Bar Association of San Francisco; Association of Defense Counsel, Northern California; Central Coast Claims Association, Casualty Claim; Public Agency Risk Management Association

Associates

Marilynn J. Winters — 1942 — California State University, San Francisco, B.S. (cum laude), 1971; University of California at San Francisco, M.S., 1972; University of San Diego, J.D. (cum laude), 1986 — Admitted to Bar, 1987, California; 1987, U.S. District Court, Southern District of California; 1993, U.S. District Court, Central District of California; 1994, U.S. District Court, Northern District of California; U.S. Court of Appeals, Ninth Circuit — Member State Bar of California

Kerri A. Johnson — 1963 — University of California, Santa Barbara, B.S., 1985; Santa Clara University, J.D., 1988 — Admitted to Bar, 1988, California; 1988, U.S. District Court, Northern District of California; U.S. Court of Appeals, Ninth Circuit — Member State Bar of California; Bar Association of San Francisco; Association of Defense Counsel, Northern California

SAN RAFAEL CALIFORNIA

The following firms also service this area.

Boornazian, Jensen & Garthe
A Professional Corporation
555 12th Street, 18th Floor
Oakland, California 94607
  Telephone: 510-834-4350
  Fax: 510-839-1897

Mailing Address: P.O. Box 12925, Oakland, CA 94604-2925

Insurance Defense, Trial Practice, Product Liability, Legal Malpractice, Professional Malpractice, Medical Malpractice, Insurance Coverage, Construction Law

SEE COMPLETE LISTING UNDER OAKLAND, CALIFORNIA (47 MILES)

SAN LUIS OBISPO † 45,119 San Luis Obispo Co.

Phillips & Associates

7350 Morro Road
Atascadero, California 93422
  Telephone: 805-466-6600
  Fax: 805-466-6608
  E-Mail: phillipslaw@thegrid.net
  www.rphillipslaw.com

Established: 1993

Insurance Defense, Personal and Commercial Vehicle, Premises Liability, Construction Defect, Professional Negligence, Civil Litigation

Firm Profile: The firm of Phillips & Associates was established in 1993 by Richard I. Phillips. Currently, the firm consists of Mr. Phillips, an associate attorney, paralegals and other support personnel. We are committed to providing the highest quality legal services in the most efficient and cost-saving manner possible.

Insurance Clients

Alliance United Insurance Company	Allied Group Insurance
Ameriprise Auto & Home Insurance	American National Property and Casualty Company
California Capital Insurance Company	Anchor General Insurance Company
Financial Pacific Insurance Company	Colony Insurance Company
National American Insurance Company of California	Glatfelter Insurance Group
Stillwater Insurance Group, Inc.	Legacy Pacific Insurance Services, Inc.
	Progressive Insurance Company
	Western General Insurance Company

Non-Insurance Clients

Carl Warren & Company	City of Pismo Beach
City of San Luis Obispo	Longs Drug Stores, Inc.
Ralphs Grocery Company	

Richard I. Phillips — San Francisco State University, B.A., 1965; University of California, Los Angeles, M.S.W., 1970; University of West Los Angeles, J.D., 1978 — Moot Court — Admitted to Bar, 1978, California; 1979, U.S. District Court, Central District of California — Member State Bar of California; San Luis Obispo County Bar Association; Association of Southern California Defense Counsel; Association of Defense Counsel, Northern California — Practice Areas: Insurance Defense; Professional Negligence; Civil Trial Practice

---

The following firms also service this area.

Borton Petrini, LLP
5060 California Avenue, Suite 700
Bakersfield, California 93309
  Telephone: 661-322-3051
  Fax: 661-322-4628

Mailing Address: P.O. Box 2026, Bakersfield, CA 93303-2026

Administrative Law, Admiralty and Maritime Law, Agriculture, Appellate Practice, Bad Faith, Banking, Bankruptcy, Business Law, Business Litigation, Casualty Insurance Law, Church Law, Collections, Commercial Law, Contracts, Corporate Law, Coverage Issues, Creditor Rights, Eminent Domain, Employment Litigation, Environmental Law, Estate Planning, Family Law, Fire, Health Care, Insurance Coverage, Insurance Defense, Intellectual Property, Labor and Employment, Land Use, Oil and Gas, Personal Injury, Premises Liability, Probate, Product Liability, Professional Errors and Omissions, Property, Public Entities, Real Estate, Religious Institutions, Sports and Entertainment Liability, Toxic Torts, Transactional Law, Transportation, Unlawful Detainer Representing Landlords

SEE COMPLETE LISTING UNDER BAKERSFIELD, CALIFORNIA (139 MILES)

SAN MATEO 97,207 San Mateo Co.

Refer To

Borton Petrini, LLP
660 Las Gallinas Avenue, Suite B
San Rafael, California 94903
  Telephone: 415-677-0730
  Fax: 415-677-0737

Commercial Litigation, Construction Litigation, General Civil Litigation, Intellectual Property, Professional Liability, Public Entities

SEE COMPLETE LISTING UNDER SAN FRANCISCO, CALIFORNIA (18 MILES)

Refer To

Sarrail, Castillo & Hall, LLP
700 Airport Boulevard, Suite 420
Burlingame, California 94010-1931
  Telephone: 650-685-9200
  Fax: 650-685-9206

Insurance Defense, Civil Litigation, Appellate Practice, Insurance Litigation, Insurance Coverage, Bad Faith, Product Liability, Construction Law, Premises Liability, General Liability, Fire, Fraud, Common Carrier

SEE COMPLETE LISTING UNDER BURLINGAME, CALIFORNIA (10 MILES)

SAN RAFAEL † 57,713 Marin Co.

Refer To

Babin & Seeger, LLP
3550 Round Barn Boulevard, Suite 201
Santa Rosa, California 95403
  Telephone: 707-526-7370
  Fax: 707-526-0307

Mailing Address: P.O. Box 11626, Santa Rosa, CA 95406

Insurance Defense, Motor Vehicle, Commercial Law, General Liability, Product Liability, Property Damage, Construction Defect, Contracts, Environmental Law, Insurance Coverage, Workers' Compensation, Personal Injury, Professional Malpractice

SEE COMPLETE LISTING UNDER SANTA ROSA, CALIFORNIA (38 MILES)

Refer To

Bledsoe, Cathcart, Diestel, Pedersen & Treppa LLP
601 California Street, 16th Floor
San Francisco, California 94108
  Telephone: 415-981-5411
  Fax: 415-981-0352

Civil Trial Practice, State and Federal Courts, Product Liability, Insurance Defense, Insurance Coverage, Personal Injury, Construction Law, Employment Law, Business Law, Environmental Law, Landlord Tenant, Commercial Transportation, Copyright Litigation, Banking and Finance, Lender Liability

SEE COMPLETE LISTING UNDER SAN FRANCISCO, CALIFORNIA (20 MILES)

CALIFORNIA   SAN RAMON

Refer To
Boornazian, Jensen & Garthe
A Professional Corporation
555 12th Street, 18th Floor
Oakland, California 94607
 Telephone: 510-834-4350
 Fax: 510-839-1897
Mailing Address: P.O. Box 12925, Oakland, CA 94604-2925

Insurance Defense, Trial Practice, Product Liability, Legal Malpractice, Professional Malpractice, Medical Malpractice, Insurance Coverage, Construction Law

SEE COMPLETE LISTING UNDER OAKLAND, CALIFORNIA (30 MILES)

Refer To
Borton Petrini, LLP
660 Las Gallinas Avenue, Suite B
San Rafael, California 94903
 Telephone: 415-677-0730
 Fax: 415-677-0737

Commercial Litigation, Construction Litigation, General Civil Litigation, Intellectual Property, Professional Liability, Public Entities

SEE COMPLETE LISTING UNDER SAN FRANCISCO, CALIFORNIA (20 MILES)

SAN RAMON   72,148 Contra Costa Co.

Ghantous Law Corporation

2603 Camino Ramon, Suite 200
San Ramon, California 94583
 Telephone: 925-242-2431
 Fax: 800-485-8201
 E-Mail: kghantous@glawcorp.com
 www.glawcorp.com

Established: 2009

Commercial General Liability, Personal Injury, Toxic Torts, Construction Defect, Premises Liability, Landlord-Tenant Liability, Military Housing

Firm Profile: The firm serves as California defense counsel for business and property owners, property managers, contractors, and public entities involved in general liability, contract, indemnity, construction accident/defect, bodily injury, disability access, toxic tort, insurance coverage, and landlord-tenant disputes.

Insurance Clients

AIG	Lincoln General Insurance Company

Non-Insurance Clients

Clark Pinnacle LLC	Clear Channel Communications, Inc.
Monterey Bay Military Housing, Clark Pinnacle	Pinnacle, an American Management Services Company

Karyne T. Ghantous — Owner — 1972 — University of California, Los Angeles, B.A., 1994; University of California, Hastings College of the Law, J.D., 1997 — Admitted to Bar, 1997, California; U.S. District Court, Northern District of California — Member Contra Costa County Bar Association (Board Member Women's Section, Litigation Section); California Women Lawyers Association; Defense Research Institute — San Ramon Chamber of Commerce

SANTA ANA   † 324,528 Orange Co.

Pyka Lenhardt Schnaider Zell

837 North Ross Street
Santa Ana, California 92701
 Telephone: 714-835-9011
 Fax: 714-667-7806
 E-Mail: contact@plszlaw.com
 www.plszlaw.com

Automobile, Business Litigation, Catastrophic Injury, Civil Litigation, Civil Rights, Construction Accidents, Construction Defect, Labor and Employment, Municipal Liability, Personal Injury, Police Liability Defense, Premises Liability, Product Liability, Professional Liability, Public Entities, School Law, Trucking, Uninsured and Underinsured Motorist, Wrongful Death, Wrongful Termination, Homeowners Association Litigation, Utility Defense

Firm Profile: Specializing in civil litigation, the Law Office of Pyka Lenhardt Schnaider Zell quickly and efficiently handles its clients' legal concerns by providing exceptional results for a reasonable cost. Collectively, our partners have tried over 300 cases and are proud of their successful track record.

Insurance Clients

Adventist Risk Management, Inc.	American Family Insurance
American Safety Claims Services, Inc.	CCMSI
	Corporate Claims Service, Inc.
Crum & Forster Insurance Group	Lexington Insurance Company
Liberty International Underwriters	Liberty Mutual Insurance Company
Mercury Insurance Group	Midland Claims Administrators, Inc.
Network Adjusters, Inc.	
Philadelphia Insurance Company	Precision Risk Management, Inc.
ProSight Specialty Insurance Company	Public Agency Risk Sharing Authority of CA (PARSAC)
York Risk Services Group, Inc.	

Non-Insurance Clients

City of Huntington Beach	City of Santa Ana
Los Angeles Community College District	Philip Services Corporation
	Professional Community Management, Inc., Golden Rain Foundation
San Diego Unified Port Authority	
Southern California Edison Company	Staff Pro

Managing Partner

A. J. Pyka — University of Denver, B.S., 1967; University of California, Los Angeles School of Law, J.D., 1972 — Admitted to Bar, 1972, California; 1973, U.S. District Court, Central District of California; 1987, U.S. Supreme Court — Member Orange County Bar Association; American Board of Trial Advocates — U.S. Army — Practice Areas: Civil Litigation; Insurance Defense; General Liability; Premises Liability; Automobile; Product Liability; Construction Defect; Environmental Law — E-mail: apyka@plszlaw.com

Senior Partners

David P. Lenhardt — University of California, Santa Barbara, B.A. (with honors), 1970; University of Southern California School of Law, J.D., 1973 — Admitted to Bar, 1974, California; U.S. District Court, Central District of California; 1981, U.S. Court of Appeals, Ninth Circuit; 1995, U.S. Supreme Court — Member American Board of Trial Advocates — Practice Areas: General Liability; Product Liability; Construction Defect; Professional Liability; Civil Rights; Premises Liability; Trucking — E-mail: dlenhardt@plszlaw.com

Guillermo W. Schnaider — Loyola University of Los Angeles, B.A., 1966; Loyola Law School, J.D., 1969 — Executive Editor, Loyola Law Review — Admitted to Bar, 1970, California; U.S. District Court, Central District of California; 1995, U.S. District Court, Southern District of California; 2003, U.S. Court of Appeals, Ninth Circuit — Member American Board of Trial Advocates — Languages: Spanish — Practice Areas: Civil Litigation; Insurance Defense; Uninsured and Underinsured Motorist; Premises Liability — E-mail: gschnaider@plszlaw.com

Don H. Zell — University of Redlands, B.A., 1966; Pepperdine University School of Law, J.D. (cum laude), 1971 — Admitted to Bar, 1972, California;

Pyka Lenhardt Schnaider Zell, Santa Ana, CA (Continued)

1985, U.S. District Court, Northern District of California — Member American Board of Trial Advocates — Practice Areas: Civil Trial Practice; Product Liability; General Defense — E-mail: dzell@plszlaw.com

Partners

Evelyn Levine Solis — University of Southern California, B.A., 1996; Loyola Marymount University, Loyola Law School, J.D., 2000 — Admitted to Bar, 2001, California; U.S. District Court, Central District of California; 2003, U.S. District Court, Southern District of California; U.S. Court of Appeals, Ninth Circuit; 2006, U.S. District Court, Eastern and Northern Districts of California — Practice Areas: Civil Litigation; Personal Injury; Municipal Law; Insurance Defense; Automobile Accidents; Trucking; Uninsured and Underinsured Motorist; Premises Liability — E-mail: esolis@plszlaw.com

Krista Dawkins — University of California, Los Angeles, B.A., 2002; Whittier Law School, J.D., 2005 — Admitted to Bar, 2006, California; 2007, U.S. District Court, Central, Eastern and Southern Districts of California — Practice Areas: Insurance Defense; Estate Planning; Estate Litigation — E-mail: kdawkins@plszlaw.com

Daniel J. Kolcz — Arizona State University, B.A., 2000; Pepperdine University School of Law, J.D. (cum laude), 2003 — Admitted to Bar, 2004, California; U.S. District Court, Central and Southern Districts of California — Practice Areas: Civil Litigation; Insurance Defense; General Liability; Premises Liability; Automobile; Product Liability; Construction Defect; Environmental Law; Employment Law; Business Litigation — E-mail: dkolcz@plszlaw.com

Associates

Francois Auroux
Carissa Ann Casolari
Drew D. Helms

The following firms also service this area.

Grant, Genovese & Baratta, LLP
2030 Main Street, Suite 1600
Irvine, California 92614-7257
Telephone: 949-660-1600
Fax: 949-660-6060

General Civil Litigation, Bad Faith, Insurance Coverage, Construction Defect, Directors and Officers Liability, Employment Law, Environmental Law, Intellectual Property, Homeowners' Associations, Earth Movement, Toxic Torts

SEE COMPLETE LISTING UNDER IRVINE, CALIFORNIA (6 MILES)

Mollis & Mollis, Inc.
4621 Teller Avenue, Suite 200
Newport Beach, California 92660
Telephone: 949-222-0735
Fax: 949-955-0252

Insurance Defense, Civil Trial Practice, Business Law, Construction Law, Corporate Law, Appeals, Labor Law, Environmental Law, Real Estate, Estate Planning, Trusts, Probate, Trust and Estate Litigation, Taxation, Trust Settlement

SEE COMPLETE LISTING UNDER NEWPORT BEACH, CALIFORNIA (12 MILES)

SANTA BARBARA † 88,410 Santa Barbara Co.

Hager & Dowling

319 East Carrillo Street, 2nd Floor
Santa Barbara, California 93101
Telephone: 805-966-4700
Fax: 805-966-4120
E-Mail: mail@hdlaw.com
www.hdlaw.com

(Las Vegas, NV Office: 4045 Spencer Street, Suite 408, 89119)
(Tel: 702-586-4800)
(Fax: 702-586-0831)
(E-Mail: bcarman@hdlaw.com)

Established: 1997

Hager & Dowling, Santa Barbara, CA (Continued)

Insurance Defense, Bad Faith, Insurance Coverage, Product Liability, Professional Liability, Major Litigation

Firm Profile: Here at Hager & Dowling, we offer skilled defense of tort and insurance litigation. We are above all top trial attorneys with unmatched experience and results. Our cases include bad faith, coverage, product and professional liability, automobile and general liability suits, as well as contract and construction defect cases. Our 12 attorneys and our loyal support staff provide clients high quality, cost-effective representation throughout Central and Southern California. Our lawyers have spent 50,000 hours on bad faith issues in the last five years alone. More details are available on our website, www.hdlaw.com, or by calling us.

Insurance Clients

Alliance United Insurance Company
Ameriprise Insurance Company
Chartis Claims, Inc.
Chubb Group of Insurance Companies
Frankenmuth Insurance Company
General Casualty Company
Mercury Insurance Company
The Travelers Companies, Inc.
American Family Insurance Company
California Automobile Insurance Company
Financial Indemnity Company
Fireman's Fund Insurance Company
Mercury Casualty Company
State National Insurance Company, Inc.

Firm Members

John V. Hager — 1949 — University of Southern California, B.A. (magna cum laude), 1971; J.D., 1974 — Phi Beta Kappa; Phi Kappa Phi — Admitted to Bar, 1974, California; U.S. District Court, Central District of California; 1987, U.S. Court of Appeals, Ninth Circuit — Member State Bar of California; Santa Barbara County, San Luis Obispo County and Ventura County Bar Associations; American Board of Trial Advocates; Defense Research Institute — Practice Areas: Trial Practice; Negligence; Insurance Law; Malpractice; Product Liability; Construction Law

Thomas J. Dowling — 1940 — Loyola University of Los Angeles, B.A., 1969; University of Southern California, J.D., 1972 — Phi Alpha Delta — Admitted to Bar, 1972, California — Member Federal, Los Angeles County and Ventura County Bar Associations; American Board of Trial Advocates; Association of Southern California Defense Counsel — Practice Areas: Trial Practice; Negligence; Insurance Law; Malpractice; Product Liability; Construction Law

Benjamin J. Carman — 1979 — University of Nevada, Reno, B.S. (summa cum laude), 2001; M.B.A., 2002; Santa Clara University, J.D., 2007 — Admitted to Bar, 2007, California; 2012, Nevada; 2007, California Courts of Appeal; 2010, U.S. District Court, Central District of California; 2013, U.S. District Court, District of Nevada — Member Clark County Bar Association — Practice Areas: Appellate; Bad Faith; Breach of Contract; Civil Tort; Civil Trial Practice; Commercial and Personal Lines; Commercial Litigation; Coverage Analysis; Coverage Litigation; General Civil Litigation; Homeowners; Insurance; Insurance Fraud; Insurance Litigation; Insurance Sales Practice Litigation; Patent Trademark Infringement Litigation; Property and Casualty; Tort; Trial Practice; Uninsured and Underinsured Motorist — Resident Las Vegas, NV Office — Tel: 702-586-4800

Christian B. Blasbichler — 1969 — The University of Texas at Austin, B.B.A., 1994; Seattle University, M.B.A., 2002; Willamette University, J.D., 2005 — Admitted to Bar, 2006, California — Member State Bar of California — Practice Areas: Civil Litigation; Civil Trial Practice; Insurance Coverage; Insurance Litigation

Sean D. Cooney — 1978 — Whitman College, B.A., 2001; Santa Clara University, J.D., 2007 — Admitted to Bar, 2007, California — Member State Bar of California — Languages: German — Practice Areas: Civil Litigation; Bad Faith; Insurance Litigation

Lora D. Hemphill — 1971 — University of California, Santa Barbara, B.A., 1993; Santa Barbara College of Law, J.D., 2001 — Admitted to Bar, 2001, California — Member State Bar of California — Practice Areas: Casualty Defense; Civil Litigation; Employment Law; Environmental Law; Insurance Litigation

Associates

Christine W. Chambers — 1985 — Case Western Reserve University, B.A. (maxima cum laude), 2007; Case Western Reserve University School of Law, J.D. (Dean's List), 2010 — Admitted to Bar, 2010, California — Practice Areas: Insurance Litigation; Bad Faith; Casualty

L. Renee Green — University of Florida, B.S. Business Admin. (cum laude), 2006; William S. Boyd School of Law, University of Nevada, Las Vegas,

CALIFORNIA

Hager & Dowling, Santa Barbara, CA (Continued)

J.D., 2012 — Admitted to Bar, 2012, Nevada; 2013, U.S. District Court, District of Nevada — Practice Areas: Bad Faith; Civil Trial Practice; Commercial and Personal Lines; Commercial Litigation; Consumer Law; Insurance Coverage Litigation; Insurance Defense; Insurance Law; Personal Injury Litigation; Uninsured and Underinsured Motorist — Resident Las Vegas, NV Office — Tel: 702-586-4800

Brian S. Dewey — 1974 — Ventura College, A.S., 2000; Santa Barbara College of Law, J.D. (Dean's List), 2007 — Admitted to Bar, 2007, California — Practice Areas: Civil Litigation; Civil Trial Practice; Insurance Coverage; Insurance Litigation

Amber N. Hurley — 1987 — University of Redlands, B.A. (cum laude), 2009; Chapman University School of Law, J.D., 2012 — Admitted to Bar, 2013, California — Member Santa Barbara County Bar Association — Practice Areas: Insurance Litigation; Bad Faith; Casualty Defense

Caitlin R. Maurer — University of California, Davis, B.A., 2007; Golden Gate University School of Law, J.D., 2011 — Admitted to Bar, 2011, California — Practice Areas: Civil Litigation; Insurance Coverage & Defense

Brett B. McMurdo — University of California, Davis, B.A. Political Science, 2009; University of California, Berkeley, J.D., 2013 — Admitted to Bar, 2013, California — Practice Areas: Civil Litigation; Insurance Coverage & Defense; Bad Faith

The following firms also service this area.

Borton Petrini, LLP
5060 California Avenue, Suite 700
Bakersfield, California 93309
Telephone: 661-322-3051
Fax: 661-322-4628

Mailing Address: P.O. Box 2026, Bakersfield, CA 93303-2026

Administrative Law, Admiralty and Maritime Law, Agriculture, Appellate Practice, Bad Faith, Banking, Bankruptcy, Business Law, Business Litigation, Casualty Insurance Law, Church Law, Collections, Commercial Law, Contracts, Corporate Law, Coverage Issues, Creditor Rights, Eminent Domain, Employment Litigation, Environmental Law, Estate Planning, Family Law, Fire, Health Care, Insurance Coverage, Insurance Defense, Intellectual Property, Labor and Employment, Land Use, Oil and Gas, Personal Injury, Premises Liability, Probate, Product Liability, Professional Errors and Omissions, Property, Public Entities, Real Estate, Religious Institutions, Sports and Entertainment Liability, Toxic Torts, Transactional Law, Transportation, Unlawful Detainer Representing Landlords

SEE COMPLETE LISTING UNDER BAKERSFIELD, CALIFORNIA (147 MILES)

SANTA CLARA   116,468 Santa Clara Co.

Refer To

Bledsoe, Cathcart, Diestel, Pedersen & Treppa LLP
601 California Street, 16th Floor
San Francisco, California 94108
Telephone: 415-981-5411
Fax: 415-981-0352

Civil Trial Practice, State and Federal Courts, Product Liability, Insurance Defense, Insurance Coverage, Personal Injury, Construction Law, Employment Law, Business Law, Environmental Law, Landlord Tenant, Commercial Transportation, Copyright Litigation, Banking and Finance, Lender Liability

SEE COMPLETE LISTING UNDER SAN FRANCISCO, CALIFORNIA (42 MILES)

Refer To

Borton Petrini, LLP
95 South Market Street, Suite 400
San Jose, California 95113
Telephone: 408-535-0870
Fax: 408-535-0878

Agriculture, Americans with Disabilities Act, Construction Defect, Employment Law, Insurance Litigation, Product Liability, Professional Liability, Toxic Torts

SEE COMPLETE LISTING UNDER SAN JOSE, CALIFORNIA (10 MILES)

SANTA CLARA

SANTA CRUZ   † 59,946 Santa Cruz Co.

Refer To

Borton Petrini, LLP
95 South Market Street, Suite 400
San Jose, California 95113
Telephone: 408-535-0870
Fax: 408-535-0878

Agriculture, Americans with Disabilities Act, Construction Defect, Employment Law, Insurance Litigation, Product Liability, Professional Liability, Toxic Torts

SEE COMPLETE LISTING UNDER SAN JOSE, CALIFORNIA (30 MILES)

SANTA MONICA   89,736 Los Angeles Co.

Citron & Citron
Attorneys-at-Law
3420 Ocean Park Boulevard, Suite 3030
Santa Monica, California 90405
Telephone: 310-450-6695
Fax: 310-450-3851
E-Mail: Joel.Citron@Citronlaw.com
www.Citronlaw.com

Established: 1981

Insurance Defense, Casualty, Trial Practice, Product Liability, Medical Malpractice, Professional Errors and Omissions, Personal Injury, Physical Damage, Construction Defect, Environmental Coverage, Bad Faith, Excess Liability Coverage Issues, Elder Care

Insurance Clients

California Capital Insurance Company
Country-Wide Insurance Company
Lexington Insurance Company

Non-Insurance Clients

Gallagher Bassett Services, Inc.
Hertz Claim Management
Network Adjusters, Inc.
Gregory B. Bragg & Associates, Inc.

Firm Members

Joel F. Citron — 1939 — Pomona College, B.A., 1961; University of California, Los Angeles, LL.B., 1964 — Admitted to Bar, 1964, California; 1964, U.S. District Court, Central District of California; U.S. Court of Appeals, Ninth Circuit; U.S. Supreme Court — Member State Bar of California; Los Angeles County Bar Association; Attorney Advisor, American Arbitration Association; Panel of Arbitrators, Los Angeles Superior Court Panel of Arbitrators; Association of Southern California Defense Counsel; American Arbitration Association; American Board of Trial Advocates; American Judicature Society — Practice Areas: Civil Litigation

Thomas H. Citron — 1969 — Pomona College, B.A., 1991; Western State University College of Law, J.D., 1996 — Admitted to Bar, 1996, California; U.S. District Court, Central District of California — Member American and Los Angeles County Bar Associations; State Bar of California

Associates

Katherine Auchincloss Tatikian — 1949 — Scripps College, B.A., 1970; Claremont University, M.A. (with high honors), 1975; Southwestern University School of Law, J.D., 1989 — Pi Lambda Theta; Dean's Scholar; American Jurisprudence Awards, Contracts II; Corporations Seminar; Exceptional Achievement Awards, Legal Communications Skills I and II — Admitted to Bar, 1989, California; U.S. District Court, Central, Eastern, Northern and Southern Districts of California; U.S. Court of Appeals, Ninth Circuit — Member State Bar of California

Jacqueline L. Shulman — 1954 — University of California, Santa Cruz, B.A., 1976; University of San Diego School of Law, J.D., 1983 — Admitted to Bar, 1983, California; U.S. District Court, Central District of California

Allan Enriquez — 1984 — University of Michigan, B.A., 2007; University of California, Los Angeles, J.D., 2011 — Admitted to Bar, 2011, California — Member American and Mexican American Bar Associations

Citron & Citron, Attorneys-at-Law, Santa Monica, CA (Continued)

James C. Lumsden — 1984 — Queen's University, B.S., 2007; Western State University College of Law, J.D. (magna cum laude), 2012 — Admitted to Bar, 2012, California

Paloma Carrero — 1988 — Loyola Marymount University, B.A., 2010; Loyola Law School, J.D., 2013 — Admitted to Bar, 2013, California — Languages: Spanish

SANTA ROSA † 167,815 Sonoma Co.

Babin & Seeger, LLP

3550 Round Barn Boulevard, Suite 201
Santa Rosa, California 95403
  Telephone: 707-526-7370
  Fax: 707-526-0307

Established: 1982

Insurance Defense, Motor Vehicle, Commercial Law, General Liability, Product Liability, Property Damage, Construction Defect, Contracts, Environmental Law, Insurance Coverage, Workers' Compensation, Personal Injury, Professional Malpractice

Insurance Clients

Acceptance Insurance Companies
Allied Insurance Company
American Star Insurance Company
COUNTRY Mutual Insurance Company
Financial Pacific Insurance Company
General Casualty Companies
Hanover Insurance Company
Kemper Insurance Companies
Mercury Casualty Company
MSI Preferred Insurance Company
Northland Insurance Company
St. Paul Fire and Marine Insurance Company
Travelers Group
Valley Insurance Company
Westfield Insurance Company
Zurich American Insurance Group
AIM Insurance Company
Allstate Insurance Company
Commerce West Insurance Company
Erie Insurance Group
Fireman's Fund Insurance Company
Grange Insurance Association
Houston General Insurance Company
Metropolitan Property and Casualty Insurance Company
Royal Specialty Underwriting, Inc.
Shelter Insurance Companies
Sutter Insurance Company
Unigard Insurance Group
Viking Insurance Company of Wisconsin

Non-Insurance Clients

American Insurance Adjustment Agency
Calpine Corporation
Gallagher Bassett Services, Inc.
Union Oil Company of California
Berkley Risk & Insurance Services
California Insurance Guarantee Association
National Claims Management
Western Geothermal Company

Partners

Norbert C. Babin — 1935 — University of California, Berkeley, B.A., 1957; Golden Gate University School of Law, LL.B., 1965 — Admitted to Bar, 1966, California; 1966, U.S. District Court, Northern District of California; U.S. Court of Appeals, Ninth Circuit — Member American (Tort and Insurance Practice Section) and Sonoma County Bar Associations; State Bar of California; Association of Defense Counsel, Northern California (Board of Directors, 1986-1987); Defense Research Institute; International Association of Defense Counsel — E-mail: ncb@babinseeger.com

Martin L. Seeger IV — 1948 — University of the Pacific, B.A., 1970; University of the Pacific, McGeorge School of Law, J.D., 1973 — Admitted to Bar, 1973, California; 1973, U.S. District Court, Northern District of California; U.S. Court of Appeals, Ninth Circuit — Member American and Sonoma County Bar Associations; State Bar of California; Redwood Empire Trial Lawyers Association; Association of Defense Counsel, Northern California; Defense Research Institute — Professor of Law, Empire College School of Law — E-mail: mseeger@babinseeger.com

Associate

Thomas S. Seeger — 1965 — Central Connecticut State University, B.S., 1988; Empire College School of Law, J.D., 1997 — Admitted to Bar, 2005, California — Sgt., U.S. Army, 1998-2002 — E-mail: tseeger@babinseeger.com

Hanna, Brophy, MacLean, McAleer & Jensen, LLP

101 D Street
Santa Rosa, California 95404
  Telephone: 707-576-0331
  Fax: 707-528-1834
  www.hannabrophy.com

Insurance Defense, Workers' Compensation, Subrogation, Labor and Employment, Employment Law, Litigation

(See listing under Oakland, CA for additional information)

The following firms also service this area.

Boornazian, Jensen & Garthe
A Professional Corporation
555 12th Street, 18th Floor
Oakland, California 94607
  Telephone: 510-834-4350
  Fax: 510-839-1897
Mailing Address: P.O. Box 12925, Oakland, CA 94604-2925

Insurance Defense, Trial Practice, Product Liability, Legal Malpractice, Professional Malpractice, Medical Malpractice, Insurance Coverage, Construction Law

SEE COMPLETE LISTING UNDER OAKLAND, CALIFORNIA (55 MILES)

Roberts Law Firm
45011 Calpella Street
Mendocino, California 95460-2360
  Telephone: 707-937-0503
  Fax: 707-937-2916
Mailing Address: P.O. Box 2360, Mendocino, CA 95460-2360

Insurance Defense, Civil Litigation, Construction Defect, Premises Liability, Product Liability, Real Estate Errors and Omissions, Professional Negligence, Class Actions, Bad Faith, Automobile and Truck Liability, Agriculture and Wine Litigation, Class Action Defense Litigation

SEE COMPLETE LISTING UNDER MENDOCINO, CALIFORNIA (102 MILES)

SEAL BEACH 24,168 Orange Co.

Borton Petrini, LLP

3020 Old Ranch Parkway, Suite 300
Seal Beach, California 90740
  Telephone: 562-596-2300
  Fax: 562-596-2322
  E-Mail: bpoc@bortonpetrini.com
  www.bortonpetrini.com

Established: 1899

Business Litigation, Civil Litigation, Construction Law, Employment Law, Employment Litigation, Trust and Estate Litigation

Firm Profile: Since 1899, Borton Petrini, LLP, has offered high quality legal services in all of the practice areas described above through its California network of 10 regional offices. The mission of Borton Petrini, LLP is to treat every file as though we were representing ourselves and paying the bill for that representation.

Managing Partner

Rosemarie Suazo Lewis — 1962 — University of Southern California, B.A., 1983; Western State University College of Law, J.D., 1991 — Admitted to Bar, 1992, California; U.S. District Court, Central, Eastern, Northern and Southern Districts of California — Member National Hispanic, Mexican-American and Los Angeles County Bar Associations; State Bar of California; Women Lawyers Association of Los Angeles; University of Southern

CALIFORNIA

Borton Petrini, LLP, Seal Beach, CA (Continued)

California Commerce Associates; Association of Southern California Defense Counsel — Languages: Spanish — E-mail: rlewis@bortonpetrini.com

SONOMA 10,648 Sonoma Co.

Refer To

Bledsoe, Cathcart, Diestel, Pedersen & Treppa LLP
601 California Street, 16th Floor
San Francisco, California 94108
   Telephone: 415-981-5411
   Fax: 415-981-0352

Civil Trial Practice, State and Federal Courts, Product Liability, Insurance Defense, Insurance Coverage, Personal Injury, Construction Law, Employment Law, Business Law, Environmental Law, Landlord Tenant, Commercial Transportation, Copyright Litigation, Banking and Finance, Lender Liability

SEE COMPLETE LISTING UNDER SAN FRANCISCO, CALIFORNIA (48 MILES)

SONORA † 4,903 Tuolumne Co.

Refer To

Borton Petrini, LLP
201 Needham Street
Modesto, California 95354
   Telephone: 209-576-1701
   Fax: 209-527-9753

Mailing Address: P.O. Box 3384, Modesto, CA 95353

Agriculture, Appellate Practice, Bankruptcy, Business Law, Business Litigation, Casualty Insurance Law, Contracts, Corporate Law, Eminent Domain, Estate Planning, Family Law, Insurance Defense, Labor and Employment, Premises Liability, Probate, Product Liability, Professional Errors and Omissions, Public Entities, Real Estate, Transportation, Unlawful Detainer Representing Landlords

SEE COMPLETE LISTING UNDER MODESTO, CALIFORNIA (50 MILES)

STOCKTON † 291,707 San Joaquin Co.

Hanna, Brophy, MacLean, McAleer & Jensen, LLP

306 East Main Street, Suite 307A
Stockton, California 95202
   Telephone: 209-478-6616
   Fax: 209-951-9814
www.hannabrophy.com

Established: 1943

Insurance Defense, Workers' Compensation, Subrogation, Labor and Employment, Employment Law, Litigation

Office Managing Partner

Jeff V. Lusich — University of the Pacific, McGeorge School of Law, J.D., 1986 — Admitted to Bar, 1987, California — Member Stockton Workers' Compensation Appeals Board Bench and Bar Committee — Certified Specialist, Workers' Compensation Law, State Bar of California Board of Legal Specialization

(See listing under Oakland, CA for additional information)

SONOMA

The following firms also service this area.

Borton Petrini, LLP
201 Needham Street
Modesto, California 95354
   Telephone: 209-576-1701
   Fax: 209-527-9753

Mailing Address: P.O. Box 3384, Modesto, CA 95353

Agriculture, Appellate Practice, Bankruptcy, Business Law, Business Litigation, Casualty Insurance Law, Contracts, Corporate Law, Eminent Domain, Estate Planning, Family Law, Insurance Defense, Labor and Employment, Premises Liability, Probate, Product Liability, Professional Errors and Omissions, Public Entities, Real Estate, Transportation, Unlawful Detainer Representing Landlords

SEE COMPLETE LISTING UNDER MODESTO, CALIFORNIA (30 MILES)

SUSANVILLE † 17,947 Lassen Co.

Refer To

**Kenny, Snowden & Norine
A Law Corporation**
2701 Park Marina Drive
Redding, California 96001
   Telephone: 530-225-8990
   Fax: 530-225-8944
   Toll Free: 800-655-6677

Mailing Address: Box 994608, Redding, CA 96099-4608

Insurance Defense, Medical Malpractice, Product Liability, Defense Litigation, Civil Trial Practice, Casualty, Professional Errors and Omissions, Employment Law, Public Entities, Real Estate, Land Use, Water Law, Equine Law

SEE COMPLETE LISTING UNDER REDDING, CALIFORNIA (114 MILES)

TEMECULA 100,097 Riverside Co.

Refer To

Borton Petrini, LLP
1320 Columbia Street, Suite 210
San Diego, California 92101
   Telephone: 619-232-2424
   Fax: 619-531-0794

Admiralty and Maritime Law, Bad Faith, Casualty Insurance Law, Construction Law, Coverage Issues, Labor and Employment, Professional Liability

SEE COMPLETE LISTING UNDER SAN DIEGO, CALIFORNIA (58 MILES)

TORRANCE 145,438 Los Angeles Co.

Christensen Ehret

1629 Cravens Avenue
Torrance, California 90501
   Telephone: 310-222-8680
   Fax: 310-222-5752
www.christensenlaw.com

(Chicago, IL Office*: 135 South LaSalle Street, Suite 4200, 60603)
   (Tel: 312-634-1014)
   (Fax: 312-634-1018)
   (E-Mail: mchristensen@christensenlaw.com)
   (E-Mail: law@christensenlaw.com)
(Sacramento, CA Office*: 2485 Natomas Park Drive, Suite 315, 95814)
   (Tel: 916-443-6909)
   (Fax: 916-313-0645)

Construction Law, Employment Law, Energy, Insurance Law, Product Liability, Reinsurance, Subrogation, Maritime Law, Banking, Financial and Professional Liability

(See listing under Chicago, IL for additional information)

VISTA CALIFORNIA

TULARE 59,278 Tulare Co.

Refer To

Borton Petrini, LLP
2444 Main Street, Suite 150
Fresno, California 93721
  Telephone: 559-268-0117
  Fax: 559-237-7995

Agriculture, Business Litigation, Casualty Insurance Law, Commercial Law, Contracts, Coverage Issues, Insurance Defense, Labor and Employment, Premises Liability, Product Liability, Professional Errors and Omissions, Public Entities, Transportation

SEE COMPLETE LISTING UNDER FRESNO, CALIFORNIA (46 MILES)

UKIAH † 16,075 Mendocino Co.

Refer To

Babin & Seeger, LLP
3550 Round Barn Boulevard, Suite 201
Santa Rosa, California 95403
  Telephone: 707-526-7370
  Fax: 707-526-0307

Mailing Address: P.O. Box 11626, Santa Rosa, CA 95406

Insurance Defense, Motor Vehicle, Commercial Law, General Liability, Product Liability, Property Damage, Construction Defect, Contracts, Environmental Law, Insurance Coverage, Workers' Compensation, Personal Injury, Professional Malpractice

SEE COMPLETE LISTING UNDER SANTA ROSA, CALIFORNIA (61 MILES)

Refer To

Kenny, Snowden & Norine
A Law Corporation
2701 Park Marina Drive
Redding, California 96001
  Telephone: 530-225-8990
  Fax: 530-225-8944
  Toll Free: 800-655-6677

Mailing Address: Box 994608, Redding, CA 96099-4608

Insurance Defense, Medical Malpractice, Product Liability, Defense Litigation, Civil Trial Practice, Casualty, Professional Errors and Omissions, Employment Law, Public Entities, Real Estate, Land Use, Water Law, Equine Law

SEE COMPLETE LISTING UNDER REDDING, CALIFORNIA (191 MILES)

Refer To

Roberts Law Firm
45011 Calpella Street
Mendocino, California 95460-2360
  Telephone: 707-937-0503
  Fax: 707-937-2916

Mailing Address: P.O. Box 2360, Mendocino, CA 95460-2360

Insurance Defense, Civil Litigation, Construction Defect, Premises Liability, Product Liability, Real Estate Errors and Omissions, Professional Negligence, Class Actions, Bad Faith, Automobile and Truck Liability, Agriculture and Wine Litigation, Class Action Defense Litigation

SEE COMPLETE LISTING UNDER MENDOCINO, CALIFORNIA (65 MILES)

VENTURA † 106,433 Ventura Co.

Refer To

Berman Berman Berman Schneider & Lowary LLP
11900 West Olympic Boulevard, Suite 600
Los Angeles, California 90064-1151
  Telephone: 310-447-9000
  Fax: 310-447-9011

Insurance Defense, Insurance Coverage, Construction Defect, Product Liability, Employment Law, Professional Liability, Legal, Insurance Agents, Agent/Broker Liability, Medical Malpractice Defense, Design Professionals, Accountants, Trucking Law, Transportation, Real Estate Agents, Brokers and Appraisers, Elder Care, Monitoring Counsel, Litigation Management, California Insurance Regulations and Consulting to Insurance Industry

SEE COMPLETE LISTING UNDER LOS ANGELES, CALIFORNIA (64 MILES)

Refer To

Borton Petrini, LLP
626 Wilshire Boulevard, Suite 975
Los Angeles, California 90017
  Telephone: 213-624-2869
  Fax: 213-489-3930

Business Litigation, Civil Litigation, Construction Law, Employment Law, Employment Litigation, Trust and Estate Litigation

SEE COMPLETE LISTING UNDER LOS ANGELES, CALIFORNIA (68 MILES)

Refer To

Tropio & Morlan
A Law Corporation
21700 Oxnard Street, Suite 1700
Woodland Hills, California 91367
  Telephone: 818-883-4000
  Fax: 818-883-4242

Insurance Defense, Premises Liability, Product Liability, Automobile, Fraud, Asbestos Litigation, Toxic Substances, Mass Tort, Complex Litigation, Commercial Litigation, Employment Litigation, Environmental Litigation, Environmental Liability, Environmental and Toxic Injury, Environmental Law, Toxic Tort, Environmental Regulatory Compliance, Underground Storage Tank Litigation

SEE COMPLETE LISTING UNDER WOODLAND HILLS, CALIFORNIA (40 MILES)

VICTORVILLE 115,903 San Bernardino Co.

Refer To

Borton Petrini, LLP
1461 Ford Street, Suite 201
Redlands, California 92373
  Telephone: 909-381-0527
  Fax: 909-381-0658

Mailing Address: P.O Box 11207, San Bernardino, CA 92423

Coverage Issues, Insurance Defense, Labor and Employment, Product Liability, Professional Errors and Omissions, Public Entities

SEE COMPLETE LISTING UNDER SAN BERNARDINO, CALIFORNIA (41 MILES)

VISALIA † 124,442 Tulare Co.

Refer To

Borton Petrini, LLP
2444 Main Street, Suite 150
Fresno, California 93721
  Telephone: 559-268-0117
  Fax: 559-237-7995

Agriculture, Business Litigation, Casualty Insurance Law, Commercial Law, Contracts, Coverage Issues, Insurance Defense, Labor and Employment, Premises Liability, Product Liability, Professional Errors and Omissions, Public Entities, Transportation

SEE COMPLETE LISTING UNDER FRESNO, CALIFORNIA (42 MILES)

VISTA 93,834 San Diego Co.

Refer To

Borton Petrini, LLP
1320 Columbia Street, Suite 210
San Diego, California 92101
  Telephone: 619-232-2424
  Fax: 619-531-0794

Admiralty and Maritime Law, Bad Faith, Casualty Insurance Law, Construction Law, Coverage Issues, Labor and Employment, Professional Liability

SEE COMPLETE LISTING UNDER SAN DIEGO, CALIFORNIA (45 MILES)

WALNUT CREEK 64,173 Contra Costa Co.

Archer Norris
A Professional Law Corporation
2033 North Main Street
Suite 800
Walnut Creek, California 94596
  Telephone: 925-930-6600
  Fax: 925-930-6620
  E-Mail: info@archernorris.com
  www.archernorris.com

(Los Angeles, CA Office: 777 South Figueroa Street, Suite 4250, 90017)
  (Tel: 213-437-4000)
  (Fax: 213-437-4011)
(Sacramento, CA Office: 301 University Avenue, Suite 110, 95825)
  (Tel: 916-646-2480)
  (Fax: 916-646-5696)
(Newport Beach, CA Office: 4695 MacArthur Court, Suite 350, 92660)
  (Tel: 949-975-8200)
  (Fax: 949-975-8210)
(San Francisco, CA Office: One Embarcadero Center, Suite 360, 94111)
  (Tel: 415-653-1480)
  (Fax: 415-653-1481)

Established: 1980

Appellate Practice, Asbestos Litigation, Business Law, Commercial Litigation, Construction Litigation, Design Professionals, Employment Law, Environmental Law, Errors and Omissions, First and Third Party Defense, Hazardous Waste, Health, Insurance Coverage, Insurance Defense, Intellectual Property, Land Use, Litigation, Litigation and Counseling, Marine Insurance, Medical Malpractice, Municipal Law, Product Liability, Professional Liability, Real Estate, Risk Management, Toxic Torts, Trial Practice, Admiralty and Maritime Law

Firm Profile: Archer Norris knows California and delivers solid, affordable legal counsel that is direct and on point. We resolve commercial disputes, steer groundbreaking deals, reduce risks and maximize opportunities wherever our clients need us.

A leading California law firm with more than 110 attorneys admitted to practice in 18 states, we laser-focus on your business from five strategically-located California offices. Archer Norris counsels clients in complex litigation, insurance coverage, bad faith litigation, business, health care, public entity, environmental, and real estate transactions. We think you will like the competitive edge you gain by partnering with Archer Norris.

Representative Insurance Clients

Allianz Global Corporate & Specialty
Chubb Services Corporation
Fireman's Fund Insurance Company
Liberty International Underwriters
Navigators Insurance Company
Sequoia Insurance
Zurich North America
Atain Insurance Companies
Chartis Insurance
Financial Pacific Insurance Company
Hanover Insurance Company
Nationwide Agribusiness Insurance Company
Travelers Special Liability Group

Managing Partner

Eugene C. Blackard, Jr. — 1959 — Sacramento State College, B.A., 1982; University of the Pacific, McGeorge School of Law, J.D., 1989 — Admitted to Bar, 1989, California — Member State Bar of California; Contra Costa County Bar Association — Practice Areas: Toxic Torts; Asbestos Litigation; Insurance Defense; Trial Practice

Ericksen Arbuthnot
570 Lennon Lane
Walnut Creek, California 94598-2415
  Telephone: 925-947-1702
  Fax: 925-947-4921
  www.ericksenarbuthnot.com

(Oakland, CA Office*: 155 Grand Avenue, Suite 1050, 94612-3768)
  (Tel: 510-832-7770)
  (Fax: 510-832-0102)
(Bakersfield, CA Office*: 1830 Truxtun Avenue, Suite 200, 93301-5022)
  (Tel: 661-633-5080)
  (Fax: 661-633-5089)
(Fresno, CA Office*: 2440 West Shaw Avenue, Suite 101, 93711-3300)
  (Tel: 559-449-2600)
  (Fax: 559-449-2603)
(Los Angeles, CA Office*: 835 Wilshire Boulevard, Suite 500, 90017-2656)
  (Tel: 213-489-4411)
  (Fax: 213-489-4332)
(Sacramento, CA Office*: 100 Howe Avenue, Suite 110S, 95825-8200)
  (Tel: 916-483-5181)
  (Fax: 916-483-7558)
(San Francisco, CA Office*: 100 Bush Street, Suite 900, 94104-3950)
  (Tel: 415-362-7126)
  (Fax: 415-362-6401)
(San Jose, CA Office*: 152 North Third Street, Suite 700, 95112-5560)
  (Tel: 408-286-0880)
  (Fax: 408-286-0337)

Administrative Law, Business Law, Construction Law, Employment Law, Environmental Law, Health Care, Managed Care Liability, Insurance Coverage, Insurance Fraud, Personal Injury, Premises Liability, Product Liability, Professional Liability, Medical Malpractice, Public Entities, Appellate Law

(See listing under Oakland, CA for additional information)

Livingston Law Firm
A Professional Corporation
1600 South Main Street, Suite 280
Walnut Creek, California 94596
  Telephone: 925-952-9880
  Fax: 925-952-9881
  E-Mail: info@livingstonlawyers.com,
  sangelos@livingstonlawyers.com
  www.livingstonlawyers.com

Established: 2000

General Liability, Product Liability, Professional Negligence, Trucking Law, Transportation, Premises Liability, Construction Law, Fire Loss, Property and Casualty, Appellate Practice, Insurance Coverage, Wrongful Death, Sexual Harassment, Intentional Torts

Firm Profile: At Livingston Law Firm, we bring quality, dedication and candor to every engagement, regardless of its size or complexity. From our most senior trial attorneys to our support staff, we provide our clients with the highest quality legal services in the most cost-effective manner possible.

Insurance Clients

Chubb Services Corporation
Federal Deposit Insurance Corporation
Nationwide Insurance
State Farm General Insurance Company
The Cincinnati Companies
Lancer Insurance Company
Liberty Mutual Insurance Company
PMA Insurance Group
Zurich Insurance plc

Non-Insurance Clients

Beretta U.S.A. Corp.
Broadspire, a Crawford Company

Livingston Law Firm, A Professional Corporation, Walnut Creek, CA (Continued)

Dr Pepper Snapple Group
Glimcher Realty Trust
Honda North America, Inc.
MEC Aerial Work Platforms
TASER International, Inc.
UpRight International Manufacturing Ltd.
Fabbrica D'Armi Pietro Beretta SpA
Jetro Cash & Carry
Pacific Gas & Electric Company
UniGroup, Inc.

Shareholders

Renée Welze Livingston — 1959 — University of California, Santa Barbara, B.A. (with high honors), 1982; University of San Francisco, J.D. (with honors), 1986 — Admitted to Bar, 1986, California — Member American and Contra Costa County Bar Associations; State Bar of California; Bar Association of San Francisco; Queen's Bench; National Association of Women Lawyers; National Association of Minority and Women Owned Law Firms; Claims and Litigation Management Alliance; Association of Defense Counsel; Defense Research Institute — Reported Cases: Becker v. State Farm Fire & Cas., 664 F. Supp. 460 (N.D. Cal. 1987); Bakanauskas v. Urdan, 206 Cal. App. 3d 621 (1988); Calvillo-Silva v. Home Grocery, 19 Cal. 4th 714 (1998); Jankey v. Lee (2012) 55 Cal.4th 1038, cert. denied (U.S. April 15, 2013) — Practice Areas: Wrongful Death; Product Liability; Motor Carriers; Insurance Litigation; Premises Liability; Professional Liability; Insurance Coverage; Discrimination; Fire Loss; Sexual Harassment — E-mail: rlivingston@livingstonlawyers.com

Craig A. Livingston — 1960 — University of California, Santa Barbara, B.A., 1982; University of San Francisco, J.D., 1990 — Admitted to Bar, 1990, California — Member State Bar of California; Contra Costa County Bar Association; Product Liability Advisory Council (Sustaining Member); Defense Research Institute; International Association of Defense Counsel — Reported Cases: Adames v. Sheahan, et al., 233 Ill. 2nd 276, 909 N.E. 2d 742, 2009 III. Lexis 310 (2009), cert. denied, 130 S. Ct. 1014, 2009 U.S. LEXIS 9085 (Dec. 14, 2009) — Practice Areas: Wrongful Death; Catastrophic Injury; Product Liability; General Civil Litigation; Mass Tort; Commercial Litigation — E-mail: clivingston@livingstonlawyers.com

Crystal L. Van Der Putten — 1976 — Pepperdine University, B.A. (cum laude), 1997; University of San Francisco, J.D. (magna cum laude), 2003 — Admitted to Bar, 2003, California — Member State Bar of California; Contra Costa County Bar Association; National Association of Minority and Women Owned Law Firms — Reported Cases: Jankey v. Lee (2012) 55 Cal.4th 1038, cert. denied (U.S. April 15, 2013) — Practice Areas: Civil Litigation; General Liability; Premises Liability; Commercial Litigation; Product Liability — E-mail: cvanderputten@livingstonlawyers.com

Senior Counsel

John C. Hentschel — 1964 — Fairfield University, B.A., 1986; University of San Francisco, J.D., 1990 — Admitted to Bar, 1990, California — Member State Bar of California; Contra Costa County Bar Association; Defense Research Institute — Practice Areas: General Civil Litigation; Product Liability; Premises Liability; Environmental and Toxic Injury; Personal Injury Litigation; Commercial Litigation; Fire Loss; Homeowners — E-mail: jhentschel@livingstonlawyers.com

Associates

Janell M. Alberto — 1980 — Saint Mary's College of California, B.A., 2002; Willamette University College of Law, J.D., 2005 — Admitted to Bar, 2005, California; 2006, Oregon — Member American and Contra Costa County Bar Associations; State Bar of California; Oregon State Bar; National Association of Minority and Women Owned Law Firms — Practice Areas: General Civil Litigation; Product Liability; General Liability; Commercial Litigation — E-mail: jalberto@livingstonlawyers.com

Avery K. Gordon — 1985 — Michigan State University, B.A. Political Science, 2007; Golden Gate University School of Law, J.D. (Dean's List), 2012 — Admitted to Bar, 2013, California — Member American and Contra Costa County Bar Associations; Bar Association of San Francisco; National Association of Minority and Women Owned Law Firms — Practice Areas: General Civil Litigation; Product Liability; General Liability; Commercial Liability — E-mail: agordon@livingstonlawyers.com

Long Blumberg, LLP

2950 Buskirk Avenue, Suite 315
Walnut Creek, California 94597
Telephone: 925-941-0090
Fax: 925-941-0085
E-Mail: jlong@longblumberg.com
www.longblumberg.com

(Las Vegas, NV Office*: 7674 W. Lake Mead Boulevard, Suite 245, 89128)
(Tel: 877-941-0090)
(Fax: 877-941-0085)

Established: 2002

Personal Injury, Construction Defect, Product Liability, Insurance Litigation, Asbestos, Subrogation, General Civil Litigation

Firm Profile: Over the past 25 years, Long Blumberg, LLP's experience and knowledge has given us the unique ability to skillfully handle a full range of extraordinary legal issues. We have dedicated ourselves to the highest level of legal representation and have consistently maintained a successful record.

Insurance Clients

ACE North American Claims
Contractors Bonding and Insurance Company (CBIC), an RLI Company
AXIS Insurance Company
National Claims Services, Inc.
RLI Insurance Company
US Administrator Claims

Non-Insurance Clients

Applied Industrial Technologies

Managing Partner

Joseph A. Long — University of California, Los Angeles, B.A., 1979; Golden Gate University, J.D., 1982 — Admitted to Bar, 1982, California; 1996, Nevada; 1983, U.S. District Court, Northern District of California; 1996, U.S. District Court, District of Nevada; 2003, U.S. District Court, Central and Eastern Districts of California — Member State Bars of California and Nevada; Contra Costa County Bar Association; Association of Defense Counsel of Northern California and Nevada; Defense Research Institute

Member

Jane S. Blumberg — San Francisco State University, B.A. (cum laude), 1977; M.A., 1979; Golden Gate University, J.D., 1982 — Admitted to Bar, 1985, California; U.S. District Court, Northern District of California — Member State Bar of California

Morrow & White

2977 Ygnacio Valley Road, Suite 407
Walnut Creek, California 94598
Telephone: 925-691-9270
Fax: 925-287-0889

Civil Litigation, Construction Accidents, Toxic Torts, Premises Liability, Construction Defect, Professional Malpractice, Wrongful Death, Product Liability, Automobile Liability, Homeowners, Business Litigation

(See listing under Costa Mesa, CA for additional information)

CALIFORNIA   WEAVERVILLE

The following firms also service this area.

Borton Petrini, LLP
660 Las Gallinas Avenue, Suite B
San Rafael, California 94903
   Telephone: 415-677-0730
   Fax: 415-677-0737

Commercial Litigation, Construction Litigation, General Civil Litigation, Intellectual Property, Professional Liability, Public Entities

SEE COMPLETE LISTING UNDER SAN FRANCISCO, CALIFORNIA (22 MILES)

WEAVERVILLE † 3,600 Trinity Co.

Refer To

**Kenny, Snowden & Norine
A Law Corporation**
2701 Park Marina Drive
Redding, California 96001
   Telephone: 530-225-8990
   Fax: 530-225-8944
   Toll Free: 800-655-6677

Mailing Address: Box 994608, Redding, CA 96099-4608

Insurance Defense, Medical Malpractice, Product Liability, Defense Litigation, Civil Trial Practice, Casualty, Professional Errors and Omissions, Employment Law, Public Entities, Real Estate, Land Use, Water Law, Equine Law

SEE COMPLETE LISTING UNDER REDDING, CALIFORNIA (47 MILES)

Refer To

**Mitchell, Brisso, Delaney & Vrieze, LLP
Attorneys at Law**
814 Seventh Street
Eureka, California 95501-1114
   Telephone: 707-443-5643
   Fax: 707-444-9586

Mailing Address: P.O. Drawer 1008, Eureka, CA 95502

Insurance Defense, Personal Injury, Product Liability, Professional Liability

SEE COMPLETE LISTING UNDER EUREKA, CALIFORNIA (107 MILES)

WOODLAND HILLS 59,891 Los Angeles Co.

Law Offices of Kurt Boyd

5850 Canoga Avenue, Suite 400
Woodland Hills, California 91367
   Telephone: 818-710-7122
   Fax: 818-710-7124
   E-Mail: kurtb@boydlawyer.com

Established: 1995

General Civil Litigation, Insurance Law, Personal Injury, Product Liability, Tort Law

Firm Profile: Since 1995, the Law Offices of Kurt Boyd has represented individuals, corporations, insurance carriers, self insured entities and public entities in the defense of tort based personal injury claims, including those based on product liability, premises liability, insurance coverage, employment, motor vehicle and related aspects of civil litigation.

The firm philosophy has been, and still is to provide quality legal representation at reasonable cost; keeping in mind the nature of our profession and the obligations that profession requires.

The firm actively pursues subrogation on behalf of insurance carriers, self insured entities and public entities for both property based and motor vehicle accident based losses.

The firm specializes in the investigation of suspicious or fraudulent first or third party claims, and in the conduct of Examinations Under Oath.

**Law Offices of Kurt Boyd, Woodland Hills, CA
(Continued)**

Geographically, the firm represents clients in all State and Federal Courts in the southern half of California, with the capacity to appear in State and Federal Courts throughout the State.

The firm's Woodland Hills office is particularly well located to service Santa Barbara, San Luis Obispo, Ventura, Kern, Los Angeles, San Bernardino, Riverside, Orange and San Diego Counties. We routinely appear in Fresno and Tulare Counties and throughout the California central valley.

Insurance Clients

AIG-Global Recovery Services
Rental Insurance Services

Broadspire, a Crawford Company
Workmen's Auto Insurance Company

Non-Insurance Clients

Carlson Restaurants
ELCO Administrative Services
Keenan & Associates

Cinemark USA, Inc.
Enterprise Rent-a-Car Company of Los Angeles

Kurt Boyd — University of California, Los Angeles, B.A./B.A., 1974; Southwestern University School of Law, J.D., 1978 — Admitted to Bar, 1979, California; U.S. District Court, Central District of California; U.S. Supreme Court — Member American (Tort Trial & Insurance Practice Section), Los Angeles County and San Fernando Valley Bar Associations; Defense Research Institute; Association of Southern California Defense Counsel

The Law Offices of Robert B. Katz & Associates

21800 Oxnard Street, Suite 450
Woodland Hills, California 91367
   Telephone: 818-716-6110
   Fax: 818-716-6166
   E-Mail: rob@robkatzlaw.com
   www.robkatzlaw.com

(Las Vegas, NV Office: 2300 West Sahara Avenue, Suite 800, 89102)
   (Tel: 702-435-5916)
   (Fax: 702-435-7456)

Established: 2005

General Liability, Construction Defect, Product Liability, Toxic Torts, Complex Claims

Firm Profile: Civil litigation and trial law firm specializing in construction defect, general liability, premises liability, environmental, toxic tort and business.

Corporate Clients

Associated Cement Contractors, Inc.

Hammerhead International

Insurance Clients

CNA
OneBeacon Insurance

The Hartford

Founder

Robert B. Katz — 1969 — California State University, Northridge, B.S., 1992; Golden Gate University School of Law, J.D., 1998 — Admitted to Bar, 1999, California; 2001, Nevada; 2002, Arizona; 1999, U.S. District Court, Central District of California; 2001, U.S. District Court, District of Nevada — Practice Areas: Civil Litigation; Construction Defect; Toxic Torts — E-mail: rob@robkatzlaw.com

London Fischer LLP

21550 Oxnard Street, 3rd Floor
Woodland Hills, California 91367
 Telephone: (818) 224-6068
 Fax: (818) 224-6061
 E-Mail: DLeMontree@LondonFischer.com
 www.LondonFischer.com

(New York, NY Office*: 59 Maiden Lane, 39th Floor Reception, 10038)
 (Tel: 212-972-1000)
 (Fax: 212-972-1030)
 (E-Mail: VPetrungaro@LondonFischer.com)
 (www.londonfischer.com)
(Irvine, CA Office*: 2505 McCabe Way, Suite 100, 92614)
 (Tel: 949-252-0550)
 (Fax: 949-252-0553)
 (E-Mail: REndres@LondonFischer.com)
 (www.londonfischer.com)

Construction Law, Professional Liability, Admiralty and Maritime Law, Civil Rights, Commercial Litigation, Directors and Officers Liability, Employment Law, Environmental Law, Fidelity and Surety, Insurance Coverage, Insurance Regulation, Marine Insurance, Mass Tort, Municipal Liability, Product Liability, Property Loss, Reinsurance, Subrogation, Toxic Torts, Transportation, Trucking Law, Employment Litigation and Counseling, Catastrophic Loss Investigations and Litigation, National Appellate Practice, National Trial Practice, Professional Contracts and Disputes

Retired

James L. Fischer — Member American Bar Association (Member, Sections on Local Government, Tort and Insurance Law and Litigation); New York State (Member, Sections on Insurance, Negligence and Compensation Law and Trial Lawyers), and Westchester County Bar Associations; Association of the Bar of the City of New York — "Minimum Contacts, Shaffer's Unified Jurisdictional Test," 12 Valp. Law Review 25

Partner

Bernard London — 1950 — New York University, B.S., 1972; The College of Insurance, St. John's University, 1973; St. John's University School of Law, J.D., 1977 — Admitted to Bar, 1978, New York; U.S. District Court, Eastern, Northern, Southern and Western Districts of New York; U.S. Court of Appeals, Second Circuit; U.S. Court of Federal Claims — Member New York State Bar Association (Committees on Professional Liability, Reinsurance and Litigation); Defense Research Institute — Author and Lecturer on Construction and Insurance Law; Author of Municipal Zoning Codes, Professional Liability Insurance and Construction Law — Trustee, Village of Lloyd Harbor, 1999; Police Commissioner, Village of Lloyd Harbor; Selected for inclusion in the New York Super Lawyers list, 2009, 2010, 2011, 2012, 2013 and 2014 — E-mail: BLondon@LondonFischer.com

Daniel Zemann, Jr. — 1953 — Fairleigh Dickinson University, B.A., 1975; South Texas College of Law, J.D., 1983 — Admitted to Bar, 1983, Texas; 1987, New York; 1983, U.S. Court of Appeals, Fifth Circuit; U.S. District Court, Eastern and Southern Districts of Texas; 1991, U.S. District Court, Eastern and Southern Districts of New York; 1997, U.S. Court of Appeals, Second Circuit — Member New York State Bar Association; State Bar of Texas — Practice Areas: Construction Litigation; Insurance Coverage; General Liability; Professional Liability; Trial and Appellate Practice; Construction Claims; Construction Defect; Product Liability Defense — E-mail: DZemann@LondonFischer.com

Richard S. Endres — 1963 — State University of New York at Albany, B.S., 1985; California Western School of Law, J.D. (magna cum laude), 1989 — Admitted to Bar, 1989, California; 1990, New York; 1989, U.S. District Court, Southern District of California; 1990, U.S. District Court, Eastern and Southern Districts of New York; 2003, U.S. District Court, Central and Northern Districts of California; U.S. Court of Appeals, Ninth Circuit — Member New York State Bar Association (Sections on Product Liability, Torts and Insurance, Construction, Trial Lawyers); State Bar of California (Sections on Product Liability, Torts and Insurance, Construction, Business Litigation); Los Angeles County and Orange County Bar Associations; Professional Liability Underwriting Society — Practice Areas: Advertising Injury; Agent/Broker Liability; Bad Faith; Bodily Injury; Carrier Defense; Casualty Insurance Law; Catastrophic Injury; Commercial Insurance; Comprehensive General Liability; Construction Accidents; Coverage Analysis; Declaratory Judgments; Directors and Officers Liability; Errors and Omissions; Excess and Surplus Lines; Excess and Umbrella; Extra-Contractual Liability; Extra-Contractual Litigation; Fire Loss; Insurance Coverage Litigation; Insurance Defense; Medical Product Liability; Premises Liability; Product Liability; Professional Errors and Omissions; Property and Casualty; Property Damage; Risk Management — E-mail: REndres@LondonFischer.com

John E. Sparling — 1962 — St. Joseph's College, B.A., 1984; Hofstra University School of Law, J.D., 1987 — Hofstra Law Review, Staff Writer, 1985-1986, Assistant Editor, 1986-1987 — Admitted to Bar, 1988, New York; New York for Multiple Pro Hac Vice Admissions; 1988, U.S. District Court, Eastern, Northern, Southern and Western Districts of New York — Member American Bar Association (Committees on Litigation, Tort and Insurance Practice and Real Property, Probate and Trust Law); New York State Bar Association; Council on Litigation Management (Frequent Lecturer and Education Committee Member); New York County Lawyers Association — Reported Cases: Burack v. Tower Ins. Co. of New York, 12 A.D.3d 167, 784 N.Y.S.2d 53; Owusu v. Hearst Communications, Inc., 52 A.D.3d 285, 860 N.Y.S.2d 38; Harsch v. City of New York, 78 A.D.3d 781, 910 N.Y.S.2d 540; Mahoney v. Turner Const. Co., 61 A.D.3d 101, 872 N.Y.S.2d 433; Gropper v. St. Luke's Hospital Center, 234 A.D.2d 171, 651 N.Y.S.2d 469; Guiga v. JLS Construction Co., 255 A.D.2d 244, 685 N.Y.S.2d 1; Jani v. City of New York, 284 A.D.2d 304,725 N.Y.S.2d 388; Isola v. JWP Forest Electric Corp., 262 A.D.2d 95, 691 N.Y.S.2d 492; Ilardi v. Inte-Fac Corp., 290 A.D.2d 490, 736 N.Y.S.2d 401; Juliano v. Prudential Securities Incorporated, 287 A.D.2d 260, 731 N.Y.S.2d 142; Bachrow v. Turner Construction Company, 46 A.D.3d 388, 848 N.Y.S.2d 86; Miranda v. City of New York, 281 A.D.2d 403, 721 N.Y.S.2d 391; Yofi Book Publishing, Inc. v. Wil-Brook Realty Corp., 287 A.D.2d 712, 732 N.Y.S.2d 238; Longwood Central School District v. American Employers Insurance Company, 35 A.D.3d 550, 827 N.Y.S.2d 194; Smolik v. Turner Construction Company, 48 A.D.3d 452, 851 N.Y.S.2d 616; Gonzalez v. Turner Construction Company, 29 A.D.3d 630, 815 N.Y.S.2d 179; Schalansky v. McSpedon, 236 A.D.2d 461, 654 N.Y.S.2d 584; Wojcik v. 42nd Street Development Project, Inc., 386 F. Supp.2d 442, So. Dist. N.Y. 2005 — Appointed "Steering Committee Counsel" in the mass tort litigation entitled: In Re World Trade Center Disaster Site Litigation, with over 10,000 plaintiffs surrounding the clean-up of the 9/11 disaster in 2001; Lecturer, Council on Litigation Management in New Orleans (Topic: Litigation Management - Protecting Catastrophic Losses with Appropriate Investigation and Experts); Lecturer, Ace North America in Jersey City, NJ (Topic: Key Coverage Issues: Property); World Trade Center Clean-Up/Air Inhalation Litigation - Played critical role along with the WTC Captive and the entire WTC defense team in ultimately facilitating the execution of the global $712 million settlement agreement that included the overwhelming majority of the police officer, firefighter, sanitation and construction worker debris removal and recovery plaintiffs in the WTC Disaster Site litigation; Worked closely with Turner, lobbyists and Congress to effectuate the recent passage of the 9/11 Health and Compensation Act (the so-called Zadroga Bill) that reopens the Victim's Compensation Fund with an additional $2.3 billion in compensation for economic losses and injuries and establishes a 5 year $4.3 billion program to provide medical monitoring/screening to eligible responders and community members and also providing clients with a limitation on liability for the remaining lawsuits that did not enter into the settlement and future cases that are filed. Represents Insurance Brokers, Insurance Carriers and Insureds in complex insurance coverage and litigation matters; consultation in regulatory, insurance policy drafting and interpretation issues, insurance program recommendations and consultation; handled insurance coverage actions and policy interpretation for over twenty years. — Practice Areas: Construction Litigation; General Liability; Insurance Coverage; Insurance Defense; Product Liability; Trial and Appellate Practice; Contract Disputes; Employment Discrimination; Mass Tort; Premises Liability; Property Damage; Toxic Torts; Construction Accidents; Construction Defect; Fire and Water Subrogation — E-mail: JSparling@LondonFischer.com

James Walsh — 1967 — Fordham University, B.A. (magna cum laude), 1989; University of Pennsylvania Law School, J.D., 1992 — Admitted to Bar, 1993, New York; U.S. District Court, Eastern and Southern Districts of New York — Reported Cases: Klewinowski v. City of New York, 103 A.D.3d 547, 959 N.Y.S.2d 493 (1st Dep't 2013); In re Ancillary Receivership of Reliance Insurance Company. O'Brien & Gere Technical Services, Inc. v. New York Liquidation Bureau (Reliance Insurance Company in Liquidation) 81 A.D.3d 533, 918 N.Y.S.2d 25 (1st Dep't 2011); In the Matter of Continental Casualty Company v. Tibor Lecei, 47 A.D.3d 509, 850 N.Y.S.2d 76 (1st Dep't 2008); Romang v. Welsbach Electric Corp., 47 A.D.3d 789 (2d Dep't 2008); Travelers Indemnity Co. v. Bally Total Fitness Holding Corp., 448

CALIFORNIA

WOODLAND HILLS

London Fischer LLP, Woodland Hills, CA (Continued)

F.Supp.2d 976 (N.D. Ill. 2006); Mickey's Rides-N-More Inc. v. Anthony Viscuso Brokerage Inc., 17 A.D.3d 308, 792 N.Y.S.2d 750 (2d Dep't 2005); Gannon v. JWP Forest Electric Corp., 275 A.D.2d 231, 712 N.Y.S.2d 494 (1st Dep't 2000) — Practice Areas: Construction Litigation; Insurance Coverage; Insurance Defense; Professional Liability; Directors and Officers Liability; Reinsurance; Errors and Omissions; Arbitration; General Liability — E-mail: JWalsh@LondonFischer.com

Anthony F. Tagliagambe — 1953 — Columbia University, B.A. (cum laude), 1975; Albany Law School of Union University, J.D., 1978 — Admitted to Bar, 1979, New York; U.S. District Court, Eastern and Southern Districts of New York — Member New York State Bar Association; Federation of Defense and Corporate Counsel (Elected Member, Chairman of the Premises and Security Liability Section) — Author: "Defendant's Strategies for Summation in a Labor Law Case," NYSBA CLE, December 2011; "Cross-Examination of the Liability Expert," NYSBA CLE Construction Site Accidents, December 2009; "Food for Thought: Defending the Food Purveyor When the Meal Turns Bad," Federation of Defense and Corporate Counsel Quarterly, Fall 2008; "An Employee By Any Other Name is Still An Employee: Determining Employment Status Under New York Law," New York State Bar Journal, February 1992 — Reported Cases: Mas v. Two Bridges, 75 N.Y.2d 680, 55 N.Y.S.2d 669, 554 N.E.2d 1257; Abbadessa v. Sprint, 291 A.D.2d 363, 736 N.Y.S.2d 881 (Mem), 2002 N.Y. Slip Op. 01067 N.Y.A.D. 2 Dept. Feb. 4, 2002; Allen v. Village of Farmingdale, 282 A.D.2d 485, 723 N.Y.S.2d 219 2001 N.Y. Slip Op. 02991, N.Y.A.D. 2 Dept. Apr. 09, 2001; Colon v. BIC USA, Inc., 199 F. Supp. 2d 53, So. Dist. N.Y. 2001; Uzdavines v. Metropolitan Baseball Club Inc., 115 Misc. 2d 343, 454 N.Y.S.2d 238, N.Y. City Civ. Ct., August 25, 1982 — Lecturer, New York State Bar Association, New York City Bar, Practicing Law Institute, Federation of Defense and Corporate Counsel (Topics: Cross Exam of Experts, Defending Product Liability Actions, Defending Construction Cases, Handling Catastrophic Injury Cases, Litigating Food Safety Cases); Selected for inclusion in the New York Super Lawyers list, 2007, 2008, 2009, 2010, 2011, 2012, 2013 and 2014 — Practice Areas: Construction Litigation; Product Liability; Negligence; Medical Malpractice; Municipal Liability — E-mail: ATagliagambe@LondonFischer.com

Clifford B. Aaron — 1958 — Franklin & Marshall College, B.A. (cum laude), 1980; Villanova University School of Law, J.D., 1983 — Admitted to Bar, 1984, New York; 2010, Tennessee; U.S. District Court, Eastern, Southern and Western Districts of New York — Member American Bar Association; New York County Lawyers Association (Treasurer, Product Liability Subcommittee of Tort Division); Defense Research Institute — Assistant District Attorney, Bronx County, New York, 1983-1988; Adjunct Professor, New York Law School, 1992-1995; Lecturer, DRI Electronic Discovery Abuse, 1999, San Francisco, CA; Lecturer, New York County Lawyers Association Continuing Legal Education (2004-Present); DRI Steering Committee on Trial Tactics; DRI Mock Trial Faculty and Participant (2014), Miami, FL; Selected for inclusion in the New York Super Lawyers list, 2009, 2010, 2011, 2012, 2013 and 2014 — Practice Areas: Product Liability; General Liability; Insurance Defense; Catastrophic Injury — E-mail: CAaron@LondonFischer.com

Virginia Goodman Futterman — 1957 — Marymount College, B.A. (magna cum laude), 1979; St. John's University School of Law, J.D., 1982 — Admitted to Bar, 1983, New York; U.S. District Court, Eastern, Northern, Southern and Western Districts of New York — Member New York State Bar Association; Defense Research Institute — Mediator, Eastern and Southern Districts of New York — Practice Areas: Defense Litigation; Product Liability; Personal Injury; Premises Liability; Construction Litigation; Asbestos Litigation; Employment Discrimination — E-mail: VFutterman@LondonFischer.com

Brian A. Kalman — 1968 — State University of New York at Binghamton, B.A. (with honors), 1990; Boston University School of Law, J.D., 1993 — Admitted to Bar, 1993, New Jersey; 1994, New York; 1995, U.S. District Court, Eastern and Southern Districts of New York; 1999, U.S. District Court, Northern District of New York; 2006, U.S. District Court, Western District of New York — Reported Cases: UTC Fire & Security Americas Corp. v. NCS Power, Inc. 844 F.Supp. 2d 366 (S.D.N.Y. 2012), Auriemma v. Biltmore Theatre 82 A.D. 3d 1, 917 N.Y.S.2d 130 (1st Dept. 2011), Gayle v. National Railroad Passenger Corp. 701 F.Supp. 2d 556 (S.D.N.Y. 2010), Astudillo v. City of New York, 71 A.D. 3d 709, 895 N.Y.S.2d 731 (2d Dep't 2010), Mann v. Dambrosio, 58 A.D.3d 701, 873 N.Y.S.2d 317 (2d Dep't 2009); Heimbuch v. Grumman Corp. 51 A.D.3d 865, 858 N.Y.S.2d 378 (2d Dep't 2008); Meza v. Consolidated Edison Co. of New York, 50 A.D.3d 452, 854 N.Y.S.2d 646 (1st Dep't 2008); Seabury v. County of Dutchess, 38 A.D.3d 752, 832 N.Y.S.2d 269 (2d Dep't 2007); Singh v. Kolcas, 283 A.D.2d 350, 725 N.Y.S.2d 37 (1st Dep't 2001) — Selected for inclusion in the New York Super Lawyers list, 2009, 2010, 2011, 2012, 2013 and 2014; Lecturer,

London Fischer LLP, Woodland Hills, CA (Continued)

New York County Lawyers Association Continuing Education, 2012-Present — Practice Areas: Product Liability; Construction Law; General Liability — E-mail: BKalman@LondonFischer.com

Spiro K. Bantis — 1960 — New York University, B.A., 1982; Temple University Beasley School of Law, J.D., 1985 — Admitted to Bar, 1986, New York; U.S. District Court, Eastern and Southern Districts of New York — Member Bar Association of the City of New York — General Counsel, Gulf Insurance Company (Retired); Board Member, Insurance Federation of New York; Board Member, Atrium Insurance Corporation — Certified Arbitrator - ARIAS-US — Practice Areas: Insurance Corporate Practice; Insurance Coverage; Insurance Law; Insurance Regulation — E-mail: SBantis@LondonFischer.com

Perry I. Kreidman — Colgate University, B.S. (cum laude), 1973; New York University School of Law, J.D., 1976 — Admitted to Bar, 1977, New York — Member American Bar Association — Lectured and written on insurance and reinsurance coverage and claims in the U.S., Bermuda, and England — Practice Areas: Insurance Coverage; Reinsurance; Litigation; Arbitration; Professional Liability; Architects and Engineers; Directors and Officers Liability — E-mail: PKreidman@LondonFischer.com

Michael J. Carro — 1960 — Queens College, B.A., 1983; Pace University School of Law, J.D., 1987 — Phi Alpha Delta — Admitted to Bar, 1988, New York; 1989, U.S. District Court, Eastern and Southern Districts of New York — Member New York State Bar Association — Practice Areas: Personal Injury; Labor and Employment; Medical Malpractice; Premises Liability; Product Liability; Toxic Torts — E-mail: MCarro@LondonFischer.com

Matthew K. Finkelstein — 1970 — Franklin & Marshall College, B.A., 1991; St. Johns University School of Law, J.D. (cum laude), 1996 — Admitted to Bar, 1998, New York; 2000, U.S. District Court, Eastern and Southern Districts of New York; 2009, U.S. Court of Appeals, Second Circuit — Member New York State Bar Association — Practice Areas: Construction Accidents; Construction Defect; General Liability; Motor Vehicle; Premises Liability; Product Liability; Professional Liability — E-mail: MFinkelstein@LondonFischer.com

Christopher Ruggiero — 1979 — Manhattanville College, B.A. (summa cum laude), 2001; Brooklyn Law School, J.D. (Dean's List), 2004 — Brooklyn Journal of International Law, Staff Writer 2002-2003, Notes and Comments Editor, 2003-2004 — Admitted to Bar, 2005, New York; District of Columbia; U.S. District Court, Eastern and Southern Districts of New York — Member New York State Bar Association; Claims and Litigation Management Alliance; New York County Lawyers Association — Reported Cases: In Re World Trade Center Disaster Site Litigation; Baumann v. Metropolitan Life Ins. Co., 17 A.D.3d 260, 793 N.Y.S.2d 410 (1st Dep't 2005); Mayo v. Metropolitan Opera Ass'n, Inc., 108 A.D.422 (1st Dep't 2013) — Practice Areas: Automobile; Construction Litigation; Insurance Coverage; Mass Tort; Premises Liability; Property Damage — Tel: CRuggiero@LondonFischer.com

Daniel W. London — 1979 — University of Pennsylvania, B.A., 2001; Brooklyn Law School, J.D., 2005 — Admitted to Bar, 2005, New Jersey; 2006, New York; 2005, U.S. District Court, District of New Jersey; U.S. District Court, Eastern and Southern Districts of New York — Practice Areas: Commercial Litigation; Insurance Coverage; Insurance Law; Insurance Regulation — E-mail: DLondon@LondonFischer.com

James T. H. Deaver — 1961 — The Wharton School of the University of Pennsylvania, B.S., 1985; Temple University School of Law, J.D. (cum laude), 1991; New York University School of Law, LL.M., 1992 — Admitted to Bar, 1993, New York; U.S. District Court, Eastern and Southern Districts of New York — Reported Cases: Representative Cases: Appalachian Ins. Co. v. General Electric Co., 796 N.Y.S.2d 609 (N.Y. App. Div. 1st Dep't, 2005); Bridgestone/Firestone North American Tire, LLC v. Sompo Japan Ins. Co. of America, Civ. Ac. No. 3-02-1117 (M.D.Tenn)(case filed 2002) — Practice Areas: Insurance Coverage Litigation — E-mail: JDeaver@LondonFischer.com

Darren Le Montree — 1972 — University of California, Los Angeles, B.A. Political Science, 1994; Southwestern University School of Law, J.D. (cum laude), 1998 — Admitted to Bar, 1998, California; U.S. District Court, Central, Eastern and Southern Districts of California — Member Los Angeles County Bar Assocation — Reported Cases: Feldman v. Illinois Union Ins. Co., 198 Cal.App. 4th 1495 (2011) — Practice Areas: Commercial Litigation; Employment Litigation; Insurance Coverage; Professional Liability — E-mail: DLemontree@LondonFischer.com

(See listing under New York, NY for additional information)

(This firm is also listed in the Subrogation, Investigation and Adjustment section of this directory)

Tropio & Morlan
A Law Corporation

21700 Oxnard Street, Suite 1700
Woodland Hills, California 91367
   Telephone: 818-883-4000
   Fax: 818-883-4242
   E-Mail: mail@tropiolaw.com
   www.tropiolaw.com

Established: 1995

Insurance Defense, Premises Liability, Product Liability, Automobile, Fraud, Asbestos Litigation, Toxic Substances, Mass Tort, Complex Litigation, Commercial Litigation, Employment Litigation, Environmental Litigation, Environmental Liability, Environmental and Toxic Injury, Environmental Law, Toxic Tort, Environmental Regulatory Compliance, Underground Storage Tank Litigation

Firm Profile: We are WMBE Certified and the Western States Regional Counsel for BP Toxic Tort and Personal Injury.

Insurance Clients

Motorists Group-American Hardware Mutual	OneBeacon Insurance

Non-Insurance Clients

Atlantic Richfield Company	BP America, Inc.
BP West Coast Products LLC	Castrol North America
Foseco, Inc.	Hub Construction Specialties, Inc.
Industrial Holdings Corporation	Intimate Brands Company
Keeler/Dorr-Oliver	Limited Brands, Inc.
Mitsubishi Caterpillar Forklift America Inc.	Pangborn Corporation
Tecumseh	Sedgwick Claims Management Services, Inc.
Toys "R" Us, Inc.	Trizec Realty, Inc.

Partners

Scott T. Tropio — 1957 — Arizona State University, B.A., 1979; Pepperdine University School of Law, J.D., 1983 — Admitted to Bar, 1983, California; U.S. Court of Appeals, Ninth Circuit; 1984, U.S. District Court, Central District of California; 1996, U.S. District Court, Southern District of California — Member American and Los Angeles County Bar Associations; State Bar of California; Association of Southern California Defense Counsel; Defense Research Institute

Ingrid K. Calle — 1961 — University of Southern California, B.S., 1983; University of California, Hastings College of the Law, J.D., 1986 — Admitted to Bar, 1987, California; U.S. District Court, Central District of California — Member Los Angeles County Bar Association — Managing Attorney, Legal Department, Atlantic Richfield Company, 1991-2000

Christopher J. Hammond — 1964 — California State University, Northridge, B.A., 1987; Southwestern University School of Law, J.D., 1990 — Admitted to Bar, 1990, California; 1995, U.S. District Court, Central District of California; 2007, U.S. District Court, Southern District of California — Member Los Angeles County Bar Association

Associates

Santosh Narayan — 1979 — University of California, San Diego, B.A., 2001; Vanderbilt University Law School, J.D., 2004 — Admitted to Bar, 2006, California; U.S. District Court, Central and Southern Districts of California; U.S. Court of Appeals, Ninth Circuit — Member Los Angeles Bar Association; South Asian Bar Association of Los Angeles

Angela V. Sayre — 1982 — University of California, Los Angeles, B.A., 2004; Southwestern University School of Law, J.D., 2007 — Admitted to Bar, 2007, California; U.S. District Court, Central District of California — Member Los Angeles County Bar Association

---

The following firms also service this area.

Berman Berman Berman Schneider & Lowary LLP
11900 West Olympic Boulevard, Suite 600
Los Angeles, California 90064-1151
   Telephone: 310-447-9000
   Fax: 310-447-9011

Insurance Defense, Insurance Coverage, Construction Defect, Product Liability, Employment Law, Professional Liability, Legal, Insurance Agents, Agent/Broker Liability, Medical Malpractice Defense, Design Professionals, Accountants, Trucking Law, Transportation, Real Estate Agents, Brokers and Appraisers, Elder Care, Monitoring Counsel, Litigation Management, California Insurance Regulations and Consulting to Insurance Industry

SEE COMPLETE LISTING UNDER LOS ANGELES, CALIFORNIA (23 MILES)

YREKA † 7,765 Siskiyou Co.
Refer To

Kenny, Snowden & Norine
A Law Corporation
2701 Park Marina Drive
Redding, California 96001
   Telephone: 530-225-8990
   Fax: 530-225-8944
   Toll Free: 800-655-6677

Mailing Address: Box 994608, Redding, CA 96099-4608

Insurance Defense, Medical Malpractice, Product Liability, Defense Litigation, Civil Trial Practice, Casualty, Professional Errors and Omissions, Employment Law, Public Entities, Real Estate, Land Use, Water Law, Equine Law

SEE COMPLETE LISTING UNDER REDDING, CALIFORNIA (97 MILES)

YUBA CITY † 64,925 Sutter Co.
Refer To

Kenny, Snowden & Norine
A Law Corporation
2701 Park Marina Drive
Redding, California 96001
   Telephone: 530-225-8990
   Fax: 530-225-8944
   Toll Free: 800-655-6677

Mailing Address: Box 994608, Redding, CA 96099-4608

Insurance Defense, Medical Malpractice, Product Liability, Defense Litigation, Civil Trial Practice, Casualty, Professional Errors and Omissions, Employment Law, Public Entities, Real Estate, Land Use, Water Law, Equine Law

SEE COMPLETE LISTING UNDER REDDING, CALIFORNIA (117 MILES)

COLORADO

CAPITAL: DENVER

COUNTIES AND COUNTY SEATS

County	County Seat
Adams	Brighton
Alamosa	Alamosa
Arapahoe	Littleton
Archuleta	Pagosa Springs
Baca	Springfield
Bent	Las Animas
Boulder	Boulder
Broomfield	Broomfield
Chaffee	Salida
Cheyenne	Cheyenne Wells
Clear Creek	Georgetown
Conejos	Conejos
Costilla	San Luis
Crowley	Ordway
Custer	Westcliffe
Delta	Delta
Denver	Denver
Dolores	Dove Creek
Douglas	Castle Rock
Eagle	Eagle
Elbert	Kiowa
El Paso	Colorado Springs
Fremont	Canon City
Garfield	Glenwood Springs
Gilpin	Central City
Grand	Hot Sulphur Springs
Gunnison	Gunnison
Hinsdale	Lake City
Huerfano	Walsenburg
Jackson	Walden
Jefferson	Golden
Kiowa	Eads
Kit Carson	Burlington
Lake	Leadville
La Plata	Durango
Larimer	Fort Collins
Las Animas	Trinidad
Lincoln	Hugo
Logan	Sterling
Mesa	Grand Junction
Mineral	Creede
Moffat	Craig
Montezuma	Cortez
Montrose	Montrose
Morgan	Fort Morgan
Otero	La Junta
Ouray	Ouray
Park	Fairplay
Phillips	Holyoke
Pitkin	Aspen
Prowers	Lamar
Pueblo	Pueblo
Rio Blanco	Meeker
Rio Grande	Del Norte
Routt	Steamboat Springs
Saguache	Saguache
San Juan	Silverton
San Miguel	Telluride
Sedgwick	Julesburg
Summit	Breckenridge
Teller	Cripple Creek
Washington	Akron
Weld	Greeley
Yuma	Wray

In the text that follows "†" indicates County Seats.

Our files contain additional verified data on the firms listed herein. This additional information is available on request.

A.M. BEST COMPANY

COLORADO

ALAMOSA † 8,780 Alamosa Co.
Refer To

Cain & White, LLP
1555 Quail Lake Loop, Suite 100
Colorado Springs, Colorado 80906
  Telephone: 719-575-0010
  Fax: 719-575-0020
  Toll Free: 877-282-5300

Civil Litigation, Commercial and Business Litigation, Insurance Defense Litigation, Construction Defect Defense Litigation, Bad Faith Insurance Defense Litigation, Municipal & Governmental Liability Defense, Premises Liability Defense, Trucking/Transportation Defense, EUO's/Coverage Opinions, Medical Malpractice Defense, Health Care Entity Defense, Governmental Entity Defense, Products Liability Defense, Commercial/Business Defense

SEE COMPLETE LISTING UNDER COLORADO SPRINGS, COLORADO (163 MILES)

ASPEN † 6,658 Pitkin Co.
Refer To

Deisch, Marion & Klaus, P.C.
851 Clarkson Street
Denver, Colorado 80218-3205
  Telephone: 303-837-1122
  Fax: 303-832-6750

Insurance Defense, Casualty, Errors and Omissions, Professional Liability, Municipal Liability, Product Liability, Subrogation

SEE COMPLETE LISTING UNDER DENVER, COLORADO (161 MILES)

BOULDER † 97,385 Boulder Co.
Refer To

Cain & White, LLP
1555 Quail Lake Loop, Suite 100
Colorado Springs, Colorado 80906
  Telephone: 719-575-0010
  Fax: 719-575-0020
  Toll Free: 877-282-5300

Civil Litigation, Commercial and Business Litigation, Insurance Defense Litigation, Construction Defect Defense Litigation, Bad Faith Insurance Defense Litigation, Municipal & Governmental Liability Defense, Premises Liability Defense, Trucking/Transportation Defense, EUO's/Coverage Opinions, Medical Malpractice Defense, Health Care Entity Defense, Governmental Entity Defense, Products Liability Defense, Commercial/Business Defense

SEE COMPLETE LISTING UNDER COLORADO SPRINGS, COLORADO (101 MILES)

BRECKENRIDGE † 4,540 Summit Co.
Refer To

Bayer & Carey, P.C.
1660 Downing Street
Denver, Colorado 80218
  Telephone: 303-830-8911
  Fax: 303-830-8917

Insurance Defense, Automobile Liability, Premises Liability, Construction Liability, Toxic Torts, Wrongful Death, Coverage Issues, Product Liability, Trial Practice, Appellate Practice

SEE COMPLETE LISTING UNDER DENVER, COLORADO (80 MILES)

Refer To

Deisch, Marion & Klaus, P.C.
851 Clarkson Street
Denver, Colorado 80218-3205
  Telephone: 303-837-1122
  Fax: 303-832-6750

Insurance Defense, Casualty, Errors and Omissions, Professional Liability, Municipal Liability, Product Liability, Subrogation

SEE COMPLETE LISTING UNDER DENVER, COLORADO (80 MILES)

CASTLE ROCK † 48,231 Douglas Co.
Refer To

Cain & White, LLP
1555 Quail Lake Loop, Suite 100
Colorado Springs, Colorado 80906
  Telephone: 719-575-0010
  Fax: 719-575-0020
  Toll Free: 877-282-5300

Civil Litigation, Commercial and Business Litigation, Insurance Defense Litigation, Construction Defect Defense Litigation, Bad Faith Insurance Defense Litigation, Municipal & Governmental Liability Defense, Premises Liability Defense, Trucking/Transportation Defense, EUO's/Coverage Opinions, Medical Malpractice Defense, Health Care Entity Defense, Governmental Entity Defense, Products Liability Defense, Commercial/Business Defense

SEE COMPLETE LISTING UNDER COLORADO SPRINGS, COLORADO (47 MILES)

COLORADO SPRINGS † 416,427 El Paso Co.

Cain & White, LLP
1555 Quail Lake Loop, Suite 100
Colorado Springs, Colorado 80906
  Telephone: 719-575-0010
  Fax: 719-575-0020
  Toll Free: 877-282-5300
  E-Mail: ccain@cainwhitelaw.com
  E-Mail: jwhite@cainwhitelaw.com
  www.cainwhitelaw.com

(Denver Area: The Point at Inverness, 8310 South Valley Highway, Suite 300, Englewood, CO, 80112)
(Tel: 720-279-2578)
(Fax: 720-279-2501)
(Toll Free: 877-282-5300)
(E-Mail: ccain@cainwhitelaw.com, jwhite@cainwhitelaw.com)

Established: 2002

Civil Litigation, Commercial and Business Litigation, Insurance Defense Litigation, Construction Defect Defense Litigation, Bad Faith Insurance Defense Litigation, Municipal & Governmental Liability Defense, Premises Liability Defense, Trucking/Transportation Defense, EUO's/Coverage Opinions, Medical Malpractice Defense, Health Care Entity Defense, Governmental Entity Defense, Products Liability Defense, Commercial/Business Defense

Firm Profile: The law firm of Cain & White, LLP has its primary office in Colorado Springs, Colorado, with a second office in the Denver metro area. For detailed profiles of the firm's attorneys, please go to: www.cainwhitelaw.com. We provide a broad range of legal services for insurers and business clients throughout Colorado. Cain & White's focus has always been on insurance defense; we do not do "plaintiff's work." We are your "Colorado Defense Counsel."

Our firm represents and advises clients out to, and all points within, the four corners of the State of Colorado in all areas of insurance defense litigation, including personal injury defense, construction defect defense, premises liability defense, "bad faith" claim defense, coverage issues and "EUO's", and medical malpractice defense. We also defend clients in commercial and business litigation, and products liability defense, as well as practicing in the areas of municipal and government liability defense. Our attorneys represent clients at every level of Colorado state and federal courts. Applying our wealth of successful trial and litigation experience, we can provide effective and efficient legal services anywhere in the State of Colorado.

High Profile Cases: *General Security Indemnity Company of Arizona v. Mountain States Mutual Casualty Company*, 205 P.3d 529 (Colo. App., 2009); *Sperry v. Field*, 205 P.3d 365 (Colo. 2009); *Salazar v. State Farm Mutual Automobile Insurance Co.*, 148 P.3d 278 (Colo. App., 2006); *Trigg v. State Farm Mutual Automobile Insurance Co.*, 129 P.3d 1099 (Colo. App., 2005); *Kastner v. State Farm Mutual Automobile Insurance Co.*, 56 P.3d 1144 (Colo. App., 2002).

COLORADO SPRINGS / COLORADO

Cain & White, LLP, Colorado Springs, CO (Continued)

Insurance Clients

ACE Risk Management
American National Property and Casualty Company
Ameriprise Auto & Home Insurance
Badger Mutual Insurance Company
Central Mutual Insurance Company
Cherokee Insurance Company
Encompass Insurance
Great American Insurance Company
Kemper Auto and Home
Mountain States Insurance Group
National American Insurance Company
Sentry Insurance
State Farm Life Insurance Company
TransGuard Insurance Company of America, Inc.
West Bend Mutual Insurance Company
American Claims Service
American Safety Indemnity Company
Aspen Specialty Insurance Company
Buckeye State Mutual Insurance Company
Chubb Group of Insurance Companies
GuideOne Insurance
Harco National Insurance Company
National Adjustment Bureau
Safeco Insurance
SECURA Insurance Companies
State Farm Fire and Casualty Company
State Farm Mutual Automobile Insurance Company
United Fire & Casualty Company

Non-Insurance Clients

Gallagher Bassett Services, Inc.
Ryder Logistics & Transportation
State of Colorado
Rio Claims Service, Inc.
Specialty Risk Services, Inc. (SRS)

Partners

Craig W. Cain — 1961 — Southern Illinois University Edwardsville, B.A. (with high honors), 1983; University of Illinois College of Law, J.D., 1986 — University of Illinois Moot Court Team — University of Illinois Law Review — Admitted to Bar, 1986, Colorado; U.S. District Court, District of Colorado — Member The Colorado and El Paso County Bar Associations; Colorado Defense Lawyers Association (Co-Chair, Southern Chapter, 1993-1995, 2003-2005); Defense Research Institute — Practice Areas: Insurance Defense; Bad Faith; Automobile Tort; Construction Litigation; Insurance Coverage Determination; Trucks/Heavy Equipment; Catastrophic Injury; Defense Litigation; Medical Malpractice Defense — E-mail: ccain@cainwhitelaw.com

Jennifer L. White — 1963 — Texas A&M University, B.B.A. Accounting, 1987; University of Houston Law Center, J.D., 2003 — Houston Journal of International Law — Admitted to Bar, 2003, Texas; 2006, Colorado; U.S. District Court, District of Colorado — Member American, The Colorado and El Paso County Bar Associations; State Bar of Texas; Colorado Defense Lawyers Association (Board of Directors; Chair, Southern Chapter, 2011-2013) — Practice Areas: Insurance Defense; Construction Defect; Bad Faith; Appellate Practice; Automobile Accidents; Business Law; Trucking Law; Medical Malpractice Defense; Fraud; Commercial Litigation — E-mail: jwhite@cainwhitelaw.com

Associate

Oliver A. Robinson — 1978 — University of Colorado at Colorado Springs, B.A., 2004; Washburn University School of Law, J.D. (Dean's Honors), 2010 — Admitted to Bar, 2010, Colorado; U.S. District Court, District of Colorado — Member The Colorado and El Paso County Bar Associations; Colorado Defense Lawyers Association — Practice Areas: Health Care; Personal Injury Defense; Product Liability; Medical Malpractice Defense; Civil Litigation; Trucking Law; Examinations Under Oath; Opinions; Insurance Defense Litigation; UM/IUM Bad Faith Defense; Construction Defect Litigation; Premises Liability Defense; Business and Commercial Litigation — E-mail: orobinson@cainwhitelaw.com

Dewhirst & Dolven, LLC

102 South Tejon Street, Suite 500
Colorado Springs, Colorado 80903-2236
Telephone: 719-520-1421
Fax: 719-633-3387
E-Mail: jzapf@dewhirstdolven.com
www.dewhirstdolven.com

(Denver, CO Office*: 650 South Cherry Street, Suite 600, 80246)
 (Tel: 303-757-0003)
 (Fax: 303-757-0004)

Dewhirst & Dolven, LLC, Colorado Springs, CO (Continued)

(Fort Collins, CO Office*: 1631 Greenstone Trail, 80525)
 (Tel: 970-214-9698)
 (Fax: 303-757-0003)
(Grand Junction, CO Office*: 2695 Patterson Road, Suite 2, #288, 81506)
 (Tel: 970-241-1855)
 (Fax: 970-241-1854)
(Dallas, TX Office*: III Lincoln Centre, 5430 LBJ Freeway, Suite 1200, 75240)
 (Tel: 972-789-9344)
 (Fax: 972-789-9335)
 (Mobile: 970-214-9698)
(Port Isabel, TX Office*: 400 North Yturria Street, 78578)
 (Tel: 956-433-7166)
(Salt Lake City, UT Office*: Suite 103, 2225 East Murray-Holladay Road, 84117)
 (Tel: 801-274-2717)
 (Fax: 801-274-0170)

Established: 1999

Insurance Defense, Trial and Appellate Practice, State and Federal Courts, General Liability, Automobile Liability, Construction Defect, Premises Liability, Product Liability, Professional Liability, Medical Malpractice, Dental Malpractice, Employment Law, Directors and Officers Liability, Coverage Issues, Mental Health

Firm Profile: Our attorneys have combined experience of over 250 years. The two partners, Miles Dewhirst and Thomas R. Dolven, practiced with large firms before establishing Dewhirst & Dolven, LLC.

Dewhirst & Dolven, LLC is committed to providing clients with superior legal representation while remaining sensitive to the economic interests of each case. We strive to understand our clients' business interests to assist them in obtaining business solutions through the legal process. Our priority is to establish a reputation in the legal and business community of not only being very competent attorneys but maintaining a high level of ethics and integrity. We are committed to building professional relationships with open communication, which creates an environment of team work directed at achieving successful results for our clients.

Insurance Clients

AIG
Argo Select
California Casualty Insurance Company
ESIS
Hanover Insurance Company
The Hartford
National Fire and Marine Insurance Company
OHIC Insurance Company
Santa Fe Auto Insurance Company
Wilshire Insurance Company
American Family Insurance Company
Columbia Insurance Company
Creative Risk Solutions, Inc.
Great American Insurance Company
Markel Service, Incorporated
National Indemnity Company
Nationwide Mutual Insurance Company
Scottsdale Insurance Company
Zurich North America

Non-Insurance Clients

Acme Truck Line, Inc.
Brownyard Claims Management, Inc.
Gallagher Bassett Services, Inc.
M.D.C. Holdings, Inc./Richmond American Homes
Berkley Risk Services, LLC
The Dentists Professional Liability Trust
Interstate Hotels and Resorts
Schlumberger Technologies, Inc.

Members

Thomas R. Dolven — (Deceased)

Miles M. Dewhirst — University of Nebraska, B.S., 1982; J.D., 1987 — Admitted to Bar, 1987, Colorado; 2008, Utah; 2013, Texas; 1987, U.S. District Court, District of Colorado; 2000, U.S. Court of Appeals, Tenth Circuit — Member The Colorado, El Paso County and Denver Bar Associations; Fellow, Colorado Bar Foundation; Professional Liability Defense Federation; Claims and Litigation Management Alliance; Utah Claims Adjusters Association; Utah Defense Lawyers Association; Council for National Policy; Colorado Defense Lawyers Association; Defense Research Institute; Association of Defense Trial Attorneys — Author: "Colorado Court Uninsured and Underinsured Motorist Decisions," Colorado Claims Association Newsletter, 1994; "Clergy Liability for Sexual Misconduct, Chapter 6 of Clergy Sexual

COLORADO | COLORADO SPRINGS

Dewhirst & Dolven, LLC, Colorado Springs, CO
(Continued)

Misconduct: A Systems Approach to Prevention, Intervention and Oversight," Gentle Path Press, 2011 — Intern, The White House, Washington, D.C., 1981; Staff Assistant, U.S. Department of the Interior, Office of the Solicitor, Washington, D.C., 1982-1983; Staff Assistant, U.S. Department of Justice, Land and Natural Resources Division, Environmental Enforcement Section, Washington, D.C., 1983-1984; Speaker: National Federation of Independent Business, Colorado Small Business Conference, 2002; "Informed Consent," Dentists' Professional Liability Trust Board of Directors Meeting, 2001; "Court Rulings Affecting Colorado's No-Fault Act," Colorado Claims Association Spring Meeting, 1998: Board of Directors Chair, Big Brothers Big Sisters, Pikes Peak Region; Foundation Board Member, Goodwill Industries of Colorado Springs; Leadership Program of the Rockies (LPR) — E-mail: mdewhirst@dewhirstdolven.com

Bradley W. Maudlin — 1959 — Washburn University, B.A., 1986; J.D. (with honors), 1990 — Order of Barristers — Member Washburn Law Journal — Admitted to Bar, 1990, Kansas; 2002, Colorado; 1990, U.S. District Court, District of Kansas; 1999, U.S. Court of Appeals, Tenth Circuit; 2001, U.S. District Court, District of Colorado — Member The Colorado, Kansas and El Paso County Bar Associations; Claims and Litigation Management Alliance — E-mail: bmaudlin@dewhirstdolven.com

Patrick J. Maggio — 1947 — The University of Iowa, B.A., 1969; Drake University, J.D., 1972 — Admitted to Bar, 1972, Iowa; Colorado; U.S. District Court, District of Colorado — Member The Colorado and El Paso County Bar Associations; America Arbitration Association; Professional Liability Defense Federation; Claims and Litigation Management Alliance; Association of Defense Trial Attorneys — E-mail: pjm@dewhirstdolven.com

Marilyn B. Doig — 1950 — Bradley University, B.S., 1971; Northern Illinois University, M.S.Ed., 1977; DePaul University, J.D. (with honors), 1985 — Admitted to Bar, 1985, Illinois; 1997, Colorado — Member The Colorado and El Paso County Bar Associations; Professional Liability Defense Federation; Claims and Litigation Management Alliance; Colorado Defense Lawyers Association; Defense Research Institute — E-mail: mdoig@dewhirstdolven.com

Special Counsel

Steven Jon Paul — 1958 — Creighton University, B.A., 1981; J.D., 1985 — Creighton Law Review — Admitted to Bar, 1987, Colorado; 1990, Nebraska; 1988, U.S. District Court, District of Colorado; 1992, U.S. District Court, District of Nebraska — Member The Colorado and El Paso Bar Associations; Claims and Litigation Management Alliance; Colorado Defense Lawyers Association; Defense Research Institute — E-mail: spaul@dewhirstdolven.com

Lewis Roca Rothgerber LLP
90 South Cascade Avenue, Suite 1100
Colorado Springs, Colorado 80903
Telephone: 719-386-3000
Fax: 719-386-3070
E-Mail: info@LRRLaw.com
www.LRRLaw.com

Established: 1995

Insurance Defense, Insurance Law, Regulatory and Compliance, Insurance Coverage, Property and Casualty, Life Insurance, Accident and Health, Environmental Coverage, Construction Defect, Aviation, Transactional and Litigation

Resident Partner

Troy R. Olsen — 1963 — Brigham Young University, B.S. (cum laude), 1987; University of Idaho College of Law, J.D. (cum laude), 1992 — Admitted to Bar, 1992, Colorado; 1995, U.S. District Court, District of Colorado — Member The Colorado and El Paso County Bar Associations; Colorado Defense Lawyers Association — Tel: 719-386-3000 — E-mail: tolsen@LRRLaw.com

(See listing under Denver, CO for additional information)

Stinnett & Masters LLP
2 North Cascade Avenue, Suite 500
Colorado Springs, Colorado 80903
Telephone: 719-999-5121
Fax: 719-999-5121
E-Mail: stml@stmasterslaw.com
www.stmasterslaw.com

Established: 2013

Civil Trial Practice, Medical Malpractice, Professional Liability, Product Liability, Commercial Litigation

Firm Profile: Offering national-level experience and veteran trial insight, Stinnett & Masters LLP provides defense representation in civil litigation matters throughout the states of Colorado and Texas. With a combined win rate as lead counsel in trials to verdict of better than 97%, our attorneys offer clients a proven record of courtroom success and the thorough preparation needed to achieve it. Our principal areas of defense practice include medical malpractice, professional liability, product liability and business tort claims. The firm has offices in Colorado Springs and Dallas.

Insurance Clients

ACE USA
Catholic Health Initiatives
Zurich American Insurance Company

Attorney Protective
The Medical Protective Company

Partners

Mark A. Stinnett — Texas Tech University, B.A. (with honors), 1977; The University of Texas, J.D. (with honors), 1980 — Admitted to Bar, 1980, Texas; 2008, Colorado; U.S. District Court, Eastern, Northern and Southern Districts of Texas; U.S. District Court, District of Colorado; U.S. Court of Appeals, Fifth and Tenth Circuits; Supreme Court of the United States — Member American, Colorado, El Paso County and Dallas Bar Associations; State Bar of Texas; Professional Liability Defense Federation; Life Fellow, Texas Bar Foundation; American College of Legal Medicine; American Board of Trial Advocates; American Health Lawyers Association; Colorado Defense Lawyers Association; Defense Research Institute; Texas Association of Defense Counsel — Listed in Best Lawyers in America, Medical Malpractice Law-Defense (2014-2015); Texas SuperLawyers (2003-2014) — Practice Areas: Civil Trial Practice; Medical Malpractice; Legal Malpractice; Professional Malpractice; Product Liability — E-mail: mstinnett@stmasterslaw.com

Margaret N. Masters — Stephen F. Austin State University, B.S., 1986; South Texas College of Law, J.D., 1989 — Admitted to Bar, 1989, Texas; 1998, Colorado; U.S. District Court, Northern District of Texas; U.S. District Court, District of Colorado — Member Colorado and El Paso County Bar Associations; State Bar of Texas; Professional Liability Defense Federation; Colorado Defense Lawyers Association — Practice Areas: Civil Trial Practice; Medical Malpractice; Professional Liability; Product Liability; Premises Liability — E-mail: mmasters@stmasterslaw.com

Vaughan & DeMuro
111 South Tejon Street, Suite 545
Colorado Springs, Colorado 80903
Telephone: 719-578-5500
Fax: 719-578-5504
E-Mail: info@vaughandemuro.com
www.vaughandemuro.com

(Denver, CO Office: 3900 East Mexico Avenue, Suite 620, 80210)
(Tel: 303-837-9200)
(Fax: 303-837-9400)

Established: 1992

Insurance Defense, Employment Law, Americans with Disabilities Act, General Liability, Product Liability, Automobile Liability, Governmental Liability, Construction Liability, Commercial Litigation

DENVER   COLORADO

Vaughan & DeMuro, Colorado Springs, CO   (Continued)

Insurance Clients

American Family Insurance
Colorado Counties Casualty & Property Pool
Colorado Special Districts Property and Liability Pool
First American Title Insurance Company
Travelers
American National Property and Casualty Company
Colorado Intergovernmental Risk Sharing Agency
EMC Insurance Company
OneBeacon Government Risks
State Farm Insurance Companies
Trident Insurance Services

Non-Insurance Clients

City of Colorado Springs
Crawford & Company
El Paso County
Network Adjusters, Inc.
State of Colorado
Colorado Compensation Insurance Authority/Pinnacol Assurance Company
Professional Claims Managers, Inc.

Partners

Gordon L. Vaughan — 1952 — Metropolitan State College of Denver, B.A. (magna cum laude), 1977; South Texas College of Law, J.D., 1980 — Admitted to Bar, 1980, Colorado; U.S. District Court, District of Colorado; U.S. Court of Appeals, Tenth Circuit; 1986, U.S. Supreme Court — Member American, The Colorado and El Paso County Bar Associations; Colorado Defense Lawyers Association; Defense Research Institute — E-mail: gvaughan@vaughandemuro.com

David R. DeMuro — 1948 — University of Michigan, B.A., 1970; University of Denver College of Law, J.D., 1976 — Admitted to Bar, 1976, Colorado; U.S. District Court, District of Colorado; U.S. Court of Appeals, Tenth Circuit — Member American, The Colorado and Denver Bar Associations; Colorado Defense Lawyers Association; Defense Research Institute — Resident Denver Office — E-mail: ddemuro@vaughandemuro.com

Sara Ludke Cook — 1974 — Creighton University, B.S.B.A., 1996; Creighton University School of Law, J.D., 1998 — Admitted to Bar, 1998, Colorado; U.S. District Court, District of Colorado; U.S. Court of Appeals, Tenth Circuit — Member American, The Colorado and El Paso County Bar Associations; Colorado Defense Lawyers Association; Defense Research Institute — E-mail: scook@vaughandemuro.com

Jessica Kyle Muzzio — 1970 — Seton Hall University, B.A. (summa cum laude), 1992; Rutgers University School of Law, J.D., 1995 — Admitted to Bar, 1995, New Jersey; New York; 1998, Colorado; 2004, U.S. District Court, District of Colorado; U.S. Court of Appeals, Tenth Circuit — Member American, The Colorado and El Paso County Bar Associations; Colorado Defense Lawyers Association; Defense Research Institute — E-mail: jmuzzio@vaughandemuro.com

Shelby A. Felton — 1970 — University of Nebraska-Lincoln, B.S. (cum laude), 1992; University of Nebraska College of Law, J.D., 1995 — Admitted to Bar, 1995, Wyoming; 1995, Colorado; 1996, U.S. District Court, District of Colorado; U.S. Court of Appeals, Tenth Circuit — Member American, The Colorado, and Douglas County Bar Associations; Wyoming State Bar; Defense Research Institute; Colorado Defense Lawyers Association — Resident Denver Office — E-mail: sfelton@vaughandemuro.com

Ann B. Smith — 1978 — The University of Kansas, B.A., 2000; Southern Methodist University, Dedman School of Law, J.D., 2005 — Admitted to Bar, 2005, Colorado; U.S. District Court, District of Colorado; U.S. Court of Appeals, Tenth Circuit — Member American, The Colorado and El Paso County Bar Associations; Colorado Defense Lawyers Association; Defense Research Institute — E-mail: asmith@vaughandemuro.com

Jennifer C. Madsen — 1973 — Washington University in St. Louis, B.S.B.A., 1995; University of Colorado, J.D., 2000 — Admitted to Bar, 2000, Colorado; 2002, U.S. District Court, District of Colorado; 2003, U.S. Court of Appeals, Tenth Circuit — Member American, The Colorado and Denver Bar Associations; Colorado Defense Lawyers Association; Defense Research Institute — Resident Denver Office — E-mail: jmadsen@vaughandemuro.com

Of Counsel

Steven P. Bailey — 1952 — University of Denver, B.A., 1974; Washington and Lee University School of Law, J.D. (cum laude), 1977 — Admitted to Bar, 1981, Colorado; U.S. District Court, District of Colorado; U.S. Court of Appeals, Tenth Circuit — Member American, The Colorado and El Paso County Bar Associations; Colorado Defense Lawyers Association; Defense Research Institute — E-mail: sbailey@vaughandemuro.com

---

The following firms also service this area.

Bayer & Carey, P.C.
1660 Downing Street
Denver, Colorado 80218
  Telephone: 303-830-8911
  Fax: 303-830-8917

Insurance Defense, Automobile Liability, Premises Liability, Construction Liability, Toxic Torts, Wrongful Death, Coverage Issues, Product Liability, Trial Practice, Appellate Practice

SEE COMPLETE LISTING UNDER DENVER, COLORADO (72 MILES)

Montgomery Little & Soran, P.C.
The Quadrant
5445 DTC Parkway, Suite 800
Greenwood Village, Colorado 80111
  Telephone: 303-773-8100
  Fax: 303-220-0412

Trial Practice, Appellate Practice, Insurance Defense, Accountants and Attorneys Liability, Architects and Engineers, Design Professionals, Construction Litigation, Legal Malpractice, Environmental Law, Product Liability

SEE COMPLETE LISTING UNDER DENVER, COLORADO (72 MILES)

CORTEZ † 8,482 Montezuma Co.

Refer To

Evans & Co.
823 East 4th Avenue
Durango, Colorado 81301
  Telephone: 970-375-9300
  Fax: 877-585-1401
  Toll Free: 800-EVANSCO

Aviation, Comprehensive General Liability, Construction Law, Directors and Officers Liability, Employment Practices Liability, Energy, Environmental Law, Excess and Umbrella, Insurance Coverage, Insurance Defense, Motor Carriers, Oil and Gas, Product Liability, Professional Liability, Property and Casualty, Railroad Law, Toxic Torts

SEE COMPLETE LISTING UNDER DURANGO, COLORADO (46 MILES)

DENVER † 600,158 Denver Co.

Balaban, Levinson & Costigan, P.C.
1745 Lafayette Street
Denver, Colorado 80218
  Telephone: 303-571-1234
  Fax: 303-825-7520
  E-Mail: info@ballev.com
  www.ballev.com

Established: 1979

Insurance Defense, Agent and Brokers Errors and Omissions, Bad Faith, Premises Liability, Coverage Matters

Firm Profile: We are a general practice firm, with emphasis on litigation, including commercial, insurance and real estate matters. We have a long history of representing real estate and insurance brokers, as well as other professionals in the defense of malpractice claims; construction defect claims; premises liability and bodily injury claims.

Insurance Clients

CNA Insurance Companies
Westport Insurance Corporation
Travelers Insurance Companies
Zurich American Insurance Company

Partner

Kenneth L. Levinson — 1953 — University of Colorado, B.A. (with distinction), 1974; University of Denver, J.D., 1978 — Admitted to Bar, 1978, Colorado; U.S. District Court, District of Colorado — Member The Colorado and Denver Bar Associations — Legal Authorship: Errors and Omissions Seminar, online presentation for Colorado Association of Realtors, (October 3,

COLORADO

Balaban, Levinson & Costigan, P.C., Denver, CO
(Continued)

2012); "Seven Sure-fire Ways to Get Yourself Sued, A Presentation to the Brokers of Re/Max International, Inc.," (August 19, 2005); Real Estate Broker Liability in Colorado (Lorman), April 26, 2002; Risk Management Workshop (American Home Shield, June 24, 1997); Risk Management Workshop (American Home Shield, October, 1996) [This workshop was videotaped for broadcast on the Re/Max Satellite Network]; Real Estate Law Newsletter, "E & O Insurance: Mandatory for Colorado Real Estate Professionals," 27 The Colorado Lawyer 99 (September 1998); "Legal Foundations of Errors and Omissions Claims," Seminar Materials (Lorman, January 29, 1997); Levinson, Kenneth L., "A Copyright Primer," ProSound Music Magazine, Vol. 10, No. 10 at p. 8 (Spring, 1987); Burton & Levinson, "Plaintiff's Use of Juries in Patent and Trademark Litigation," 1978 Intellectual Property Review 435 (Clark Boardman, 1978); Dorr & Levinson, "The New Copyright Act: What It Means To General Practitioners," 7 The Colorado Lawyer 1 (Jan., 1978); Contributing Author; Burton, "Jury Instructions In Intellectual Property Cases" (Bigfoot Press, 1980); Coe & Levinson, "In Defense Of Young Lawyers," Clinical Legal Education Perspective, Vol. 1, No. 2 at p. 1 (1977); Fiction: A Knight at the Opera (Uncial Press,www.uncialpress.com, 2013); The Bootleggers (Uncial Press, October 2012); A Man of His Word (Uncial Press, (2010); An Unconventional Murder (Uncial Press 2009); Final Argument, eBook, (Uncial Press, January, 2007); A Shadow In The Night (Uncial Press, June, 2007); Bootleggers, also appeared in a condensed version in Disturbing the Peace: Writings by Colorado Attorneys (Colorado and Denver Bar Associations, 2001) — Reported Cases: Gibbons v. Ludlow, 304 P.3d 249 (2013), 2013 CO 49, 2013 WL 3322676 (Colo.), rehearing denied (2013), reversing, Ludlow v. Gibbons, 2011 WL 5436481, (Colo. App., Div. 3, 2011); Adams v. Land Services, Inc., 194 P.3d 429 (Colo.App.Div. 5, 2008); Stearns v. McGuire, 354 F.Supp.2d 1188 (D.Colo. 2004), affirmed, 154 Fed. Appx. 70, 2005 U.S. App. LEXIS 24577 (10th Cir. 2005); Axtell v. Park School District R-3, 962 P.2d 319 (Colo.App.), cert. denied (1998); Golden Rule Insurance Corp. v. Greenfield, 786 F.Supp. 914 (D.Colo. 1992); Golden Rule Insurance Co. v. Lease, 755 F.Supp. 948 (D.Colo. 1991); In re Marriage of O'Brien, 759 P.2d 826 (Colo.App. 1988); Brewster v. Nandrea, 705 P.2d 1 (Colo. 1985); Bennett Waites Corp. v. Piedmont Aviation, Inc., 563 F.Supp. 810 (D.Colo. 1983); In re Marriage of Debreceni, 663 P.2d 1062 (Colo.App. 1983) — Member, Colorado Real Estate Commission Forms Committee (2006-present) — E-mail: kll@ballev.com

Associates

Cherami Ball Costigan — 1975 — Metropolitan State College of Denver, B.S., 1998; Thomas M. Cooley Law School, J.D., 2003 — Admitted to Bar, 2003, Colorado; 2005, U.S. District Court, District of Colorado — Member The Colorado and Denver Bar Associations — E-mail: cbc@ballev.com

Bernadette J. Wasilik — 1977 — University of Colorado, B.A. (summa cum laude), 2000; University of Denver, J.D., 2004 — Admitted to Bar, 2004, Colorado — Member The Colorado and Denver Bar Associations — E-mail: bjw@ballev.com

Of Counsel

Harlan G. Balaban — (1924-2013)

Bayer & Carey, P.C.

1660 Downing Street
Denver, Colorado 80218
Telephone: 303-830-8911
Fax: 303-830-8917
E-Mail: pbollard@bayerlaw.com
www.bayerlaw.com

Established: 1932

Insurance Defense, Automobile Liability, Premises Liability, Construction Liability, Toxic Torts, Wrongful Death, Coverage Issues, Product Liability, Trial Practice, Appellate Practice

Firm Profile: Bayer & Carey, PC is a full service insurance defense firm providing exceptional legal services throughout Colorado. The firm specializes in building a strong tripartite relationship among the claim representative from the insurance carrier, the client/insured, and our attorney. We provide direct communication between the attorney and the insured client, and between the attorney and the claim representative for the insurance carrier.

DENVER

Bayer & Carey, P.C., Denver, CO (Continued)

Insurance Clients

Access Insurance Company
Allmerica Financial Group/Hanover Insurance Company
Hortica, The Florists' Mutual Insurance Company
Interinsurance Exchange of the Automobile Club of Southern California
North American Risk Services
Progressive Insurance Companies
State Farm Fire and Casualty Company

ALLIED Insurance/Nationwide Insurance Company
Auto-Owners Insurance Company
COUNTRY Insurance & Financial Services
IAT Specialty
Meridian Mutual Insurance Company
Millers First Insurance Companies
OneBeacon Insurance Group
State Auto Insurance Companies
State Farm Mutual Automobile Insurance Company

Non-Insurance Clients

Beecher Carlson

Contract Freighters, Inc.

Partners

James T. Bayer — (1925-2012)

Raymond G. Carey, Jr. — (1944-1992)

Gary L. Palumbo — 1950 — University of Notre Dame, B.A. (magna cum laude), 1972; University of Colorado Law School, J.D., 1975 — Admitted to Bar, 1975, Colorado; U.S. District Court, District of Colorado; U.S. Court of Appeals, Tenth Circuit — Member The Colorado and Boulder Bar Associations; Colorado Defense Lawyers Association; Defense Research Institute; American Board of Trial Advocates — E-mail: garyp@bayerlaw.com

Laura A. Tighe — 1962 — University of Notre Dame, B.A., 1984; Creighton University School of Law, J.D., 1987 — Admitted to Bar, 1987, Colorado; U.S. District Court, District of Colorado; 1988, U.S. Court of Appeals, Tenth Circuit — Member The Colorado and Denver Bar Associations; Colorado Defense Lawyers Association; American Board of Trial Advocates

Associates

Peter M. Spiessbach — 1958 — University of Colorado, B.S., 1981; Suffolk University Law School, J.D., 1992 — Admitted to Bar, 1992, Colorado — Member The Colorado and Denver Bar Associations; Colorado Defense Lawyers Association

Teri L. Vasquez — 1967 — University of California, Los Angeles, B.A., 1989; University of California, Los Angeles School of Law, J.D., 1994 — Admitted to Bar, 1994, California; 1998, Colorado; 1994, U.S. District Court, Central District of California; U.S. Court of Appeals, Ninth Circuit; 2003, U.S. District Court, District of Colorado — Member The Colorado, Colorado Hispanic and Adams/Broomfield Bar Associations; Colorado Defense Lawyers Association

Matthew J. Weeber — 1983 — University of Colorado at Boulder, B.A., 2005; University of Colorado Law School, J.D., 2009 — Admitted to Bar, 2009, Colorado; 2010, U.S. District Court, District of Colorado — Member The Colorado Bar Association; Colorado Defense Lawyers Association

Mark W. Gerganoff — 1958 — Michigan State University, B.A., 1980; Michigan State University College of Law, J.D., 1983; University of Denver College of Law, LL.M. Taxation, 1986 — Admitted to Bar, 1983, Colorado; 1992, Wyoming; 1983, U.S. District Court, District of Colorado; 1986, U.S. Tax Court; 1994, U.S. Supreme Court — Member The Colorado Bar Association

Andrew C. Nickel — 1982 — Colorado State University, B.A., 2005; University of Colorado Law School, J.D., 2012 — Admitted to Bar, 2012, Colorado — Member The Colorado and Denver Bar Associations; Catholic Lawyers Guild

Bloom, Murr, Accomazzo & Siler, PC

410 Seventeenth Street, Suite 2400
Denver, Colorado 80202
Telephone: 303-534-2277
Fax: 303-534-1313
E-Mail: jgigax@bmas.com
www.bmas.com

Established: 1992

Life and Health, Disability, ERISA, First Party Litigation, Coverage, Substantial Subrogation Litigation, Defense and Opinions

Bloom, Murr, Accomazzo & Siler, PC, Denver, CO (Continued)

Firm Profile: Bloom Murr Accomazzo & Siler, P.C. is a Denver, Colorado law firm established in 1992 with practice in the following areas: Insurance, Tort and Commercial Litigation as well as trials and litigation in Colorado and Wyoming. Jim Gigax is the Reviewer of Colorado insurance law for Best's.

Insurance Clients

AEGON USA, LLC
Centennial Life Insurance Company
Globe Life and Accident Insurance Company
The MEGA Life and Health Insurance Company
Monarch Life Insurance Company
Mutual Life Insurance Company of New York
Trustmark Insurance Company
Union Bankers Insurance Company
Union Fidelity Life Insurance Company
Bankers United Life Assurance Company
Destiny Health Insurance Company
Kansas City Life Insurance Company
Mid America Mutual Life Insurance Company
MONY Life Insurance Company
PFL Life Insurance Company
Stonebridge Life Insurance Company
The Union Central Life Insurance Company
United Insurance Companies, Inc.

Lead Insurance Attorney

James E. Gigax — 1954 — Indiana University, A.B., 1977; Indiana University School of Law-Bloomington; University of Denver College of Law, J.D., 1980 — Denver Law Review, 1978-80 — Admitted to Bar, 1980, Colorado; Wyoming; 1981, U.S. District Court, District of Colorado; 2002, U.S. Supreme Court — Member American Bar Association (Vice-Chair, Tort and Insurance Practice Section, Health and Disability Insurance Law Committee, 1999-2006); Life Member, Million Dollar Advocates Forum — Reported Cases: Golden Rule Insurance v. Lease, 755 F. Supp. 948 (D. Colo. 1991); Myers v. Alliance For Affordable Services et al., 318 F. Supp. 2d 1055 (D.Colo. 2004); Medina v. Conseco Annuity Assurance Co., 121 P.2d 345 (Colo. App. 2005); Fabjancic v. Union Central Life Insurance Co., 2006 WL 2406268 (D.Colo.); Sierra v. Stonebridge Life Ins. Co., 2013 WL 5323083 (D. Colo. 2013); Romero v. Reiman Corp., 2012 WL 9385475, (D.Wyo. 2012) — Languages: Spanish — Practice Areas: Accident and Health; Life and Health; Trial Practice — E-mail: jgigax@bmas.com

(Revisors of the Colorado Insurance Law Digest for this Publication)

Deisch, Marion & Klaus, P.C.

851 Clarkson Street
Denver, Colorado 80218-3205
Telephone: 303-837-1122
Fax: 303-832-6750

Established: 1919

Insurance Defense, Casualty, Errors and Omissions, Professional Liability, Municipal Liability, Product Liability, Subrogation

Firm Profile: Deisch, Marion & Klaus, P.C., continues a tradition of providing exceptional legal services since its inception in 1919. The Firm's members are experienced trial lawyers who aggressively represent their clients throughout all stages of negotiation, trial, arbitration or appeal. The Firm's lawyers also represent clients in a wide variety of commercial and real estate transactions.

Clients of the Firm include insurance companies providing all lines of coverage, product manufacturers and distributors, banks, mortgage lenders, individuals with routine legal matters, and small businesses faced with a wide range of contractual and commercial issues. The Firm's depth of experience and flexibility allows it to focus on the unique circumstances facing each client.

Insurance Clients

California Indemnity Insurance Company
Colorado Casualty Insurance Company
Government Employees Insurance Company
Clarendon America Insurance Company
Deep South - Texas Farmers Insurance Group - Professional Liability
Horace Mann Insurance Group
Montgomery OneBeacon Insurance Company
Underwriters at Lloyd's, London
Sumitomo Marine and Fire Insurance Company, Ltd.
United Services Automobile Association (USAA)

Non-Insurance Clients

Safeway, Inc.

Stockholders

John M. Deisch — (1930-1998)

Michael B. Marion — (1932-2010)

Gregory K. Falls — 1959 — Colorado State University, B.S., 1981; University of Denver, J.D., 1987 — Admitted to Bar, 1988, Colorado; 1988, U.S. District Court, District of Colorado; 2006, U.S. Court of Appeals, Tenth Circuit — Member The Colorado and Denver Bar Associations; Colorado Defense Lawyers Association; Defense Research Institute — E-mail: greg_falls@deisch-marion.com

Timothy F. Marion — 1964 — University of Northern Colorado, B.S., 1987; University of Wyoming, J.D., 1991 — Admitted to Bar, 1991, Colorado; Wyoming; 1991, U.S. District Court, District of Colorado — Member The Colorado Bar Association; Wyoming State Bar; National Association of Subrogation Professionals; Defense Research Institute; Colorado Defense Lawyers Association — E-mail: tim_marion@deisch-marion.com

Donald G. Moore — 1964 — University of Colorado, B.S., 1986; University of Wyoming, J.D., 1991 — Admitted to Bar, 1991, Colorado; Wyoming; 1991, U.S. District Court, District of Colorado; 1991, U.S. District Court, District of Wyoming — Member The Colorado (Workers' Compensation Section) and Denver Bar Associations; State Bar of Wyoming; National Association of Subrogation Professionals; Colorado Defense Lawyers Association — E-mail: don_moore@deisch-marion.com

Jeffrey B. Klaus — 1957 — University of Colorado, B.A., 1980; Drake University, J.D. (with honors), 1985 — Admitted to Bar, 1985, Colorado; 1985, U.S. District Court, District of Colorado; U.S. Court of Appeals, Tenth Circuit — Member American, The Colorado and Denver Bar Associations — E-mail: jeff_klaus@deisch-marion.com

(This firm is also listed in the Subrogation section of this directory)

Dewhirst & Dolven, LLC

650 South Cherry Street, Suite 600
Denver, Colorado 80246
Telephone: 303-757-0003
Fax: 303-757-0004
www.dewhirstdolven.com

(Colorado Springs, CO Office*: 102 South Tejon Street, Suite 500, 80903-2236)
(Tel: 719-520-1421)
(Fax: 719-633-3387)
(E-Mail: jzapf@dewhirstdolven.com)
(Fort Collins, CO Office*: 1631 Greenstone Trail, 80525)
(Tel: 970-214-9698)
(Fax: 303-757-0003)
(Grand Junction, CO Office*: 2695 Patterson Road, Suite 2, #288, 81506)
(Tel: 970-241-1855)
(Fax: 970-241-1854)
(Dallas, TX Office*: III Lincoln Centre, 5430 LBJ Freeway, Suite 1200, 75240)
(Tel: 972-789-9344)
(Fax: 972-789-9335)
(Mobile: 970-214-9698)
(Port Isabel, TX Office*: 400 North Yturria Street, 78578)
(Tel: 956-433-7166)
(Salt Lake City, UT Office*: Suite 103, 2225 East Murray-Holladay Road, 84117)
(Tel: 801-274-2717)
(Fax: 801-274-0170)

Established: 2000

COLORADO DENVER

Dewhirst & Dolven, LLC, Denver, CO (Continued)

Insurance Defense, Trial and Appellate Practice, State and Federal Courts, General Liability, Automobile Liability, Construction Defect, Premises Liability, Product Liability, Professional Liability, Medical Malpractice, Dental Malpractice, Employment Law, Coverage Issues

Members

Thomas R. Dolven — (Deceased)

Miles M. Dewhirst — University of Nebraska, B.S., 1982; J.D., 1987 — Admitted to Bar, 1987, Colorado; 2008, Utah; 2013, Texas; 1987, U.S. District Court, District of Colorado; 2000, U.S. Court of Appeals, Tenth Circuit — Member The Colorado, El Paso County and Denver Bar Associations; Fellow, Colorado Bar Foundation; Professional Liability Defense Federation; Claims and Litigation Management Alliance; Utah Claims Adjusters Association; Utah Defense Lawyers Association; Council for National Policy; Colorado Defense Lawyers Association; Defense Research Institute; Association of Defense Trial Attorneys — Author: "Colorado Court Uninsured and Underinsured Motorist Decisions," Colorado Claims Association Newsletter, 1994; "Clergy Liability for Sexual Misconduct, Chapter 6 of Clergy Sexual Misconduct: A Systems Approach to Prevention, Intervention and Oversight," Gentle Path Press, 2011 — Intern, The White House, Washington, D.C., 1981; Staff Assistant, U.S. Department of the Interior, Office of the Solicitor, Washington, D.C., 1982-1983; Staff Assistant, U.S. Department of Justice, Land and Natural Resources Division, Environmental Enforcement Section, Washington, D.C., 1983-1984; Speaker: National Federation of Independent Business, Colorado Small Business Conference, 2002; "Informed Consent," Dentists' Professional Liability Trust Board of Directors Meeting, 2001; "Court Rulings Affecting Colorado's No-Fault Act," Colorado Claims Association Spring Meeting, 1998: Board of Directors Chair, Big Brothers Big Sisters, Pikes Peak Region; Foundation Board Member, Goodwill Industries of Colorado Springs; Leadership Program of the Rockies (LPR) — E-mail: mdewhirst@dewhirstdolven.com

Special Counsel

Lars F. Bergstrom — 1972 — Georgetown University, B.S., 1994; Tulane University, J.D. (cum laude), 1998 — Admitted to Bar, 1998, Colorado; 2004, Nebraska; 2002, U.S. District Court, District of Colorado; U.S. Court of Appeals, Tenth Circuit; 2004, U.S. District Court, District of Nebraska; U.S. Court of Appeals, Eighth Circuit — Member The Colorado and Denver Bar Associations; Nebraska State Bar Association; Claims and Litigation Management Alliance; Colorado Defense Lawyers Association — Major, US Army JAG CORPS [1999-2007]; Meritorious Service Medal; Army Commendation Medal; Army Achievement Medal — Languages: Swedish, German — E-mail: larsbergstrom@dewhirstdolven.com

Aldo DelPiccolo — 1958 — University of California, Los Angeles, B.A., 1981; University of Denver, J.D., 1985 — Admitted to Bar, 1985, Colorado; U.S. Court of Appeals, Tenth Circuit; 1987, U.S. District Court, District of Colorado — Member The Colorado and Denver Bar Associations; Claims and Litigation Management Alliance; Colorado Defense Lawyers Association — Languages: Italian — E-mail: adelpiccolo@dewhirstdolven.com

Sue Pray — Gonzaga University, B.S., 1979; Harvard Law School, J.D. (cum laude), 1982 — Admitted to Bar, 1982, Colorado; U.S. District Court, District of Colorado; U.S. Court of Appeals, Tenth Circuit — Member American, The Colorado, Arapahoe County (Director and Co-chair, Communications Committee) and Denver Bar Associations; Fellow, Colorado Bar Foundation; Fellow, Arapahoe County Bar Foundation; Claims and Litigation Management Alliance — E-mail: spray@dewhirstdolven.com

Jeffrey D. Bursell — 1966 — The University of Utah, B.A. (with honors), 1992; Widener University, J.D. (with honors), 1996 — Admitted to Bar, 1996, Utah; 2006, Colorado; 1996, U.S. District Court, District of Utah; 2006, U.S. District Court, District of Colorado — Member Arapahoe County and Denver Bar Associations; Colorado Claims Association; Claims and Litigation Management Alliance; Colorado Defense Lawyers Association — E-mail: jbursell@dewhirstdolven.com

George H. Parker — 1956 — Texas A&M University, B.A., 1986; University of Houston Law Center, J.D., 1988 — Admitted to Bar, 1989, Texas; 1992, Colorado; 1992, U.S. District Court, District of Colorado; 2004, U.S. Supreme Court — Member The Colorado Bar Association; Claims and Litigation Management Alliance; Colorado Defense Lawyers Association — Texas Peace Officer — Advanced Mediator — E-mail: gparker@dewhirstdolven.com

Kathleen M. Kulasza — 1954 — Georgetown University, A.B. (summa cum laude), 1976; University of Virginia, J.D., 1979 — Admitted to Bar, 1979, Colorado — Member The Colorado Bar Association; First Judicial District

Dewhirst & Dolven, LLC, Denver, CO (Continued)

Bar Association; Claims and Litigation Management Alliance — E-mail: kmkulasza@comcast.net

Associates

Robin R. Lambourn — Trinity University, B.S. (cum laude), 2003; Tulane University, J.D. (cum laude), 2006 — Recipient: CALI Awards in Law and Economics and Marine Pollution — Judicial Extern for the Honorable Sarah S. Vance, U.S. District Court, Eastern District of Louisiana; Legal Intern with the Securities and Exchange Commission — Notes and Comments Editor, Tulane Law Review — Admitted to Bar, 2006, Texas (Inactive); 2008, Colorado; 2006, U.S. District Court, Southern District of Texas — Member The Colorado and Denver Bar Associations; Claims and Litigation Management Alliance — E-mail: rlambourn@dewhirstdolven.com

Maggie Stewart — 1982 — The University of Texas, B.A., 2004; University of Denver, J.D., 2007 — Admitted to Bar, 2007, Colorado; 2010, U.S. District Court, District of Colorado — Member The Colorado and Denver Bar Associations; Claims and Litigation Management Alliance; Colorado Defense Lawyers Association — E-mail: mstewart@dewhirstdolven.com

Jason M. Cook — 1983 — Iowa State University, B.S. (with distinction), 2005; Hamline University School of Law, J.D. (cum laude), 2008 — Admitted to Bar, 2008, Colorado; 2009, U.S. Court of Appeals, Tenth Circuit; 2011, U.S. District Court, District of Colorado — Member The Colorado and Denver Bar Associations; Faculty of Federal Advocates, Young Lawyers Division — E-mail: jcook@dewhirstdolven.com

(See listing under Colorado Springs, CO for additional information)

The Dixon Law Firm

1741 High Street
Denver, Colorado 80218-1320
Telephone: 303-999-0118
Fax: 303-900-1486
E-Mail: info@strategicdefenselaw.com
www.strategicdefenselaw.com

Established: 2011

Personal Injury, Insurance Coverage Litigation, Employment Defense, Catastrophic Loss Defense

Insurance Clients

Allstate Insurance Company
National Adjustment Bureau

Helmsman Management Services, Inc.

Non-Insurance Clients

North American Van Lines

Managing Attorney

Christina L. Dixon — University of Denver, B.A., 1992; J.D., 1996 — Admitted to Bar, 1996, Colorado; U.S. District Court, District of Colorado; U.S. Court of Appeals, Tenth Circuit

Fowler, Schimberg & Flanagan, P.C.

1640 Grant Street, Suite 150
Denver, Colorado 80203
Telephone: 303-298-8603
Fax: 303-298-8748
E-Mail: lawfirm@fsf-law.com
www.fsf-law.com

Established: 1987

DENVER COLORADO

Fowler, Schimberg & Flanagan, P.C., Denver, CO
(Continued)

Insurance Law, Bad Faith, Construction Law, Coverage Analysis, Litigation, General Liability, Agent and Brokers Errors and Omissions, Legal Malpractice, Environmental Law, Employment Law, Civil Rights, Governmental Liability, Confidential Relations, Education and Governmental Entities

Insurance Clients

Berkley Regional Specialty Insurance Company
Crum & Forster Insurance
The Hartford
Mercury Insurance Company
Utica Mutual Insurance Company
Colony Specialty Insurance Company
Founders Insurance Company
Maxum Specialty Insurance Group
National Indemnity Group
Westfield Insurance Company

Partners

Daniel M. Fowler — 1950 — Monmouth College, B.A. (magna cum laude), 1972; University of Denver, J.D. (with honors), 1974 — Order of St. Ives — Associate Editor, Denver Law Journal — Admitted to Bar, 1975, Colorado; 1994, Wyoming; 1975, U.S. District Court, District of Colorado; 1994, U.S. District Court, District of Wyoming; 1997, U.S. Court of Appeals, Tenth Circuit — Member American, The Colorado and Denver Bar Associations; Federation of Defense and Corporate Counsel; Colorado Defense Lawyers Association; Defense Research Institute — E-mail: d_fowler@fsf-law.com

Timothy P. Schimberg — 1949 — University of Notre Dame, B.A. (Dean's List), 1971; Drake University, J.D. (with honors), 1980 — Admitted to Bar, 1980, Colorado; U.S. District Court, District of Colorado; U.S. Court of Appeals, Tenth Circuit — Member American Bar Association (Tort and Insurance Practice and Litigations Sections); The Colorado, Jefferson County and Denver (Board of Governors) Bar Associations; Council of School Attorneys; Colorado Association of School Boards (CASB); National School Boards Association (NSBA); Colorado Defense Lawyers Association (President, 1988; Board Member, 1985-Present; Timothy P. Schimberg Diversity Scholarship); Defense Research Institute (Colorado State Representative, 1988-1997; Director, 1998-2002) — Author: "Colorado Premises Liability Act," Colorado Claims Association Quarterly, 1995; "Overview of the ADA," Colorado Claims Association Quarterly, 1996; "School Law," National Business Institute, 1997-2000 — Super Lawyer Designation, 2009, 2010 — E-mail: t_schimberg@fsf-law.com

Timothy J. Flanagan — 1950 — University of Denver, B.A. (cum laude), 1972; J.D., 1974 — Phi Beta Kappa — Admitted to Bar, 1975, Colorado; 1995, Wyoming; 1996, Montana; 1975, U.S. District Court, District of Colorado; 1976, U.S. Court of Appeals, Tenth Circuit; 1990, U.S. Supreme Court; 1995, U.S. District Court, District of Wyoming; 1996, U.S. District Court, District of Montana — Member American, The Colorado and Denver Bar Associations — Author: "Privilege for Environmental Audits," Washington Legal Foundation, Volume 6, Number 6, February, 1991; "Insurance Coverage for Environmental Claims," 25 Colorado Law 87, February 1996; Editor: "Colorado Water Law Benchbook," CLE Colorado Inc., 2006 — Certified Civil Trial Advocate by National Board of Trial Advocacy, 1982 — E-mail: t_flanagan@fsf-law.com

Adam B. Linton — 1970 — The University of New Mexico, B.A., 1994; The University of Tulsa, J.D., 1998 — Admitted to Bar, 1999, Colorado; 2000, U.S. District Court, District of Colorado — Member American, The Colorado and Denver Bar Associations; Colorado Defense Lawyers Association; Defense Research Institute — Practice Areas: Construction Law — E-mail: a_linton@fsf-law.com

Andrew R. McLetchie — 1976 — Colby College, B.A. (Dean's List), 1999; Hofstra University, J.D. (with distinction), 2002 — Law Clerk to the Honorable Jack W. Berryhill, Jefferson County District Court, 2002-2003 — Associate Editor, Hofstra Law Review, 2001-2002. — Admitted to Bar, 2002, Colorado; 2003, U.S. District Court, District of Colorado; U.S. Court of Appeals, Tenth Circuit; Supreme Court of Colorado — Member American, The Colorado (Professional Liability Committee) and Denver Bar Associations; Faculty of Federal Advocates; Colorado Defense Lawyers Association; Defense Research Institute — Author Note: "The Case for Bright-Line Rules in Fourth Amendment Jurisprudence," 30 Hofstra Law Review 225, Winter 2002; Editor: "Whoops!" Column, The Colorado Lawyer, 2005-Present; "Colorado's New Rule on Mandatory Professional Liability Insurance Disclosure," 38 Colorado Lawyer 69, February 2009 — E-mail: a_mcletchie@fsf-law.com

Fowler, Schimberg & Flanagan, P.C., Denver, CO
(Continued)

Special Counsel

Jeffery B. Stalder — 1949 — Stanford University, B.A., 1971; University of Colorado, J.D., 1974 — Admitted to Bar, 1974, Colorado; U.S. District Court, District of Colorado — Member American Bar Association (Forum on Construction Industry, Dispute Resolution Section; Professionals for Colorado Contractors Council; Associated General Contractors of Colorado); The Colorado and Denver Bar Associations; Colorado Defense Lawyers Association — E-mail: j_stalder@fsf-law.com

Associate

Brian E. Widman — 1965 — Middlebury College (with honors), 1988; University of Denver, J.D. (cum laude), 1995 — Admitted to Bar, 1995, Colorado; U.S. District Court, District of Colorado — Member The Colorado and Denver Bar Associations; Colorado Defense Lawyers Association — E-mail: b_widmann@fsf-law.com

Hall & Evans, L.L.C.

1001 Seventeenth Street, Suite 300
Denver, Colorado 80202
Telephone: 303-628-3300
Fax: 303-628-3368
E-Mail: vargam@hallevans.com
www.hallevans.com

(Billings, MT Office*: 401 North 31st Street, Suite 1650, 59101)
(Tel: 406-969-5227)
(Fax: 406-969-5233)
(Cheyenne, WY Office: 2015 Central Avenue, Capital West Bank, 82001)
(Tel: 307-514-2567)

Established: 1932

Administrative Law, Appellate Practice, Commercial Litigation, Complex Litigation, Construction Law, Coverage Issues, Employee Benefits, Employment Law, Environmental Law, ERISA, General Liability, Health Care, Insurance Law, Insurance Litigation, Intellectual Property, Legislative Law, Life Insurance, Accident and Health, Product Liability, Professional Liability, Public Entities, Regulatory and Compliance, Reinsurance, Transportation, Workers' Compensation, Coverage Law and Litigation

Firm Profile: Established in 1932, Hall & Evans, LLC is a regional law firm which focuses on complex tort and commercial litigation as more fully described in our list of practice areas on our website. Historically, our attorneys have tried more cases to verdict than any other law firm in Colorado. There are over 1,000 published decisions in the 10th Circuit, Colorado Court of Appeals, and Colorado Supreme Court where our attorneys have appeared.

Our attorneys litigate in Colorado and are routinely involved in cases in other Rocky Mountain States, including Idaho, Montana, Nebraska, Utah, and Wyoming. Several of our attorneys serve as coordinating counsel for companies facing nationwide litigation. The firm is involved in regulatory and government affairs, public policy work on behalf of the insurance industry and enjoys positive relations with significant public entities and the state judiciary.

Our firm attorneys are active in organizations including ALFA International, DRI, FDCC, IADC NAPSLO, PLAC, PLUS, and "The Select List." We utilize our membership within these organizations to extend our resources on behalf of our clients.

Insurance Clients

ACE INA Group
AIG
American Insurance Association (AIA)
Assurant Specialty Property
AXIS U.S. Insurance
Beazley
Catlin Specialty Insurance Company
CIGNA Insurance Company
Aetna, Inc.
Allied World Assurance Company
Arch Specialty Insurance Company
Assurant Health
AXIS
Banner Life Insurance Company
Builders Insurance Group
Chubb Group of Insurance Companies
CNA Insurance Companies

COLORADO — DENVER

Hall & Evans, L.L.C., Denver, CO (Continued)

Copic Insurance Company
Farmers New World Life Insurance Company
Fireman's Fund Insurance Company
Gallagher Bassett Services, Inc.
General Star Management Company
Hanover Professionals
Hiscox USA
Ironshore, Inc.
Liberty Mutual
Markel
National Council on Compensation Insurance, Inc. (NCCI)
OneBeacon Insurance
Preferred Physicians Medical Risk Retention Group, Inc.
York Risk Services Group, Inc.
The Dentists Professional Liability Trust
Federated Rural Electric Insurance Exchange
Fort Dearborn Life Insurance Company
Guarantee Trust Life Insurance Company
The Hartford Insurance Company
Humana Inc.
Lexington Insurance Company
Lincoln Financial Group
MetLife
Navigators Pro
Northland Insurance Company
Philadelphia Insurance Companies
RLI Corp.
XL Environmental, Inc.
Zurich

Non-Insurance Clients

American Enterprise Group
BNSF Railway Company
Chrysler Group LLC
Corrections Corporation of America
Jacobs Engineering Group, Inc.
MBK Senior Living
State of Colorado
Arch Coal, Inc.
Bridgestone Americas Holding, Inc.
Costco Wholesale Corporation
Denver Health and Hospital Authority
McLane Company, Inc.
Walgreen Co.

Firm Members

Benton J. Barton — 1967 — Austin College, B.A., 1989; The University of Texas School of Law, J.D., 1992 — Admitted to Bar, 1992, Texas; 1999, Colorado; 1993, U.S. District Court, Northern District of Texas; 1995, U.S. District Court, Eastern District of Texas; 1999, U.S. District Court, District of Colorado; U.S. Court of Appeals, Fifth and Tenth Circuits; U.S. Supreme Court — Member American (Forum on the Construction Industry), Colorado and Denver Bar Associations; ALFA International, Construction Law Practice Group; Litigation Counsel of America, Trial Lawyer Honorary Society; Professional Liability Defense Federation; American Arbitration Association; Colorado Defense Lawyers Association; Defense Research Institute — Practice Areas: Alternative Dispute Resolution; Civil Litigation; Construction Litigation; Product Liability; Professional Liability — E-mail: bartonb@hallevans.com

Thomas L. Beam — 1956 — University of Nebraska, B.A. (Order of the Coif), 1978; University of Nebraska College of Law, J.D., 1987 — Admitted to Bar, 1987, Nebraska; 1988, Colorado; U.S. District Court, District of Colorado; U.S. District Court, District of Nebraska; U.S. Court of Appeals, Eighth and Tenth Circuits — Member Nebraska State, Colorado and Denver Bar Associations; National Association of Railroad Trial Counsel — Practice Areas: Transportation; Railroad Law; Trucking; Insurance Litigation — E-mail: beamt@hallevans.com

John E. Bolmer, II — 1958 — Claremont McKenna College, B.A. (cum laude), 1980; University of California, Hastings College of the Law, J.D., 1983 — Admitted to Bar, 1983, Colorado; 1984, California (Inactive); 1983, U.S. District Court, District of Colorado; U.S. Court of Appeals, Tenth Circuit — Member American (Forum on Franchising), Colorado (Business Law Section; Securities Law and Corporate Counsel Subsections) and Denver Bar Associations; American Association of Franchisees and Dealers (LegaLine Steering Committee); Professional Liability Underwriting Society — Practice Areas: Professional Liability; Business Law; Civil Litigation; Commercial Litigation; Employment Law — E-mail: bolmerj@hallevans.com

Walter J. Downing — Principia College, B.A., 1977; University of Colorado Law School, J.D., 1981 — Admitted to Bar, 1981, Colorado; 2001, Nebraska; 1981, U.S. District Court, District of Colorado; 2001, U.S. District Court, District of Nebraska; U.S. Court of Appeals, Tenth Circuit; U.S. Court of Federal Claims; U.S. Court of Veterans Appeals — Member American, Colorado (Construction and Litigation Sections) and Denver Bar Associations; Defense Research Institute; Colorado Defense Lawyers Association; National Association of Railroad Trial Counsel — Practice Areas: Administrative Law; Real Estate Litigation; Commercial Litigation; Construction Litigation; Railroad Law — E-mail: downingw@hallevans.com

Lance G. Eberhart — 1971 — The University of Iowa, B.A., 1994; Washington University School of Law, J.D., 1997 — Admitted to Bar, 1997, Missouri; 1998, Colorado; 2004, Nebraska; 1998, U.S. District Court, District of Colorado — Member Colorado and Denver Bar Associations; ALFA International; Colorado Defense Lawyers Association; Denver Metro Chamber of Commerce, Transportation Committee; North American Transportation Management Institute; Transportation Lawyers Association; Trucking Industry Defense Association — Practice Areas: Civil Litigation; Commercial Litigation; Transportation; Premises Liability; Tort Litigation — E-mail: eberhartl@hallevans.com

Alan Epstein — 1954 — University of Colorado, B.A. (Phi Beta Kappa), 1976; University of Denver College of Law, J.D., 1980 — Admitted to Bar, 1980, Colorado; U.S. District Court, District of Colorado; U.S. Court of Appeals, Tenth Circuit; U.S. Supreme Court — Member Colorado (Co-Founder and Chair, 1992-1994, Appellate Practice Subcommittee) and Denver Bar Associations; Colorado Defense Lawyers Association (Chair, Appellate Subcommittee, 1997-present); Defense Research Institute — Contributing Author: "Colorado Appellate Handbook," Third Edition, 2005 — Practice Areas: Appellate Practice — E-mail: epsteina@hallevans.com

Steven M. Hamilton — 1971 — Montana State University, B.S., 1994; The University of Montana School of Law, J.D., 1997 — Admitted to Bar, 1997, Montana; 2003, Colorado; 1997, U.S. District Court, District of Montana; 2003, U.S. District Court, District of Colorado; U.S. Court of Appeals, Ninth and Tenth Circuits — Member State Bar of Montana; ALFA International (Product Liability Steering Committee, 2008-present); Colorado Defense Lawyers Association — Practice Areas: Automotive Products Liability; Defense Litigation; Insurance Litigation; Premises Liability; Product Liability Defense — E-mail: hamiltons@hallevans.com

Michael W. Jones — 1950 — Duke University, B.A. (cum laude), 1972; University of Denver College of Law, J.D., 1974 — Admitted to Bar, 1975, Colorado; U.S. District Court, District of Colorado; U.S. Court of Appeals, Tenth Circuit — Member American, Colorado and Denver Bar Associations; American Board of Trial Advocates (Advocate; Colorado Chapter President, 2002); Colorado Defense Lawyers Association (President, 1991-1992); Federation of Insurance and Corporate Counsel (Chair, Trial Tactics Section, 1990-1993); American College of Trial Lawyers; Defense Research Institute — Practice Areas: First and Third Party Defense; Medical Malpractice Defense; Nursing Home Litigation; Product Liability Defense; Professional Malpractice — E-mail: jonesm@hallevans.com

Douglas J. Kotarek — 1961 — Brigham Young University, B.A., 1985; J. Reuben Clark Law School, Brigham Young University, J.D., 1988 — Admitted to Bar, 1988, New Mexico (Inactive); 1992, Colorado; U.S. District Court, District of Colorado; U.S. Court of Appeals, Tenth Circuit — Member Colorado (Workers' Compensation Section) and Denver Bar Associations; ALFA International (Steering Committee, Workers' Compensation Practice Group); Colorado Self-Insurers' Association (Professional Member, Executive Committee); Professionals in Workers' Compensation; Defense Research Institute; Colorado Defense Lawyers Association — Languages: Spanish — Practice Areas: Administrative Law; Insurance Law; Legislative Law; Workers' Compensation — E-mail: kotarekd@hallevans.com

Darin J. Lang — 1970 — Wichita State University, B.A. (cum laude), 1993; University of Nebraska College of Law, J.D. (cum laude), 1996 — Order of the Coif — Admitted to Bar, 1996, Nebraska; 2000, Colorado; 1996, U.S. District Court, District of Nebraska; 2000, U.S. District Court, District of Colorado; U.S. Court of Appeals, Eighth and Tenth Circuits — Member Nebraska State, Colorado and Denver Bar Associations; Colorado Self Insurers Association; Product Liability Advisory Council, Sustaining Member; Sporting Goods Manufacturers' Association, Panel Counsel; Defense Research Institute — Practice Areas: Civil Litigation; Commercial Litigation; Design Professionals; Product Liability; Transportation — E-mail: langd@hallevans.com

Kenneth H. Lyman — 1952 — University of Colorado, B.A., 1975; M.B.A., 1982; University of Colorado Law School, J.D., 1982 — Admitted to Bar, 1982, Colorado; U.S. District Court, District of Colorado; U.S. Court of Appeals, Tenth Circuit — Member American, Colorado and Denver Bar Associations; Products Liability Advisory Council, Inc; Faculty of Federal Advocates; Defense Research Institute; Colorado Defense Lawyers Association — Practice Areas: Casualty Defense; Catastrophic Injury; Civil Litigation; Commercial Litigation; Insurance Law; Product Liability — E-mail: lymank@hallevans.com

Thomas J. Lyons — 1952 — Claremont McKenna College, B.A. (cum laude), 1974; University of Colorado Law School, J.D., 1977 — Admitted to Bar, 1977, Colorado; U.S. District Court, District of Colorado; U.S. Court of Appeals, Tenth Circuit — Member American, Colorado and Denver Bar Associations; Faculty of Federal Advocates; Colorado Defense Lawyers Association — Practice Areas: Administrative Law; Alternative Dispute Resolution; Civil Litigation; Employment Law; Product Liability; Professional Liability; Public Entities — E-mail: lyonst@hallevans.com

Cristin J. Mack — Webster University, B.A. (with honors), 1997; Saint Louis University School of Law, J.D. (cum laude), 2001 — Admitted to Bar, 2001,

DENVER   COLORADO

Hall & Evans, L.L.C., Denver, CO   (Continued)

Colorado; U.S. District Court, District of Colorado; U.S. Court of Appeals, Tenth Circuit — Member American, Colorado (Litigation Section) and Denver Bar Associations; American Health Lawyers Association; Colorado Defense Lawyers Association; Defense Research Institute — Practice Areas: Accident and Health; Civil Tort; Disability; Health Care; Insurance Litigation; Life and Health; Medical Malpractice; Professional Liability — E-mail: mackc@hallevans.com

Deanne McClung — University of South Florida, B.A., 1993; University of Denver Sturm College of Law, J.D., 1996 — Admitted to Bar, 1996, Colorado; U.S. District Court, District of Colorado; U.S. Court of Appeals, Tenth Circuit; U.S. Supreme Court — Member Colorado and Denver Bar Associations; 1st Judicial District; Colorado Defense Lawyers Association; Defense Research Institute — Practice Areas: Civil Tort; Health Care; Medical Malpractice; Professional Liability

Lisa F. Mickley — The University of Texas at Dallas, B.S., 1989; The University of Utah, S.J. Quinney College of Law, J.D., 1992 — Admitted to Bar, 1992, Texas; 1994, Colorado; U.S. District Court, District of Colorado; U.S. District Court, Districts of Texas — Member American, Colorado and Douglas-Elbert County Bar Associations; State Bar of Texas; Colorado Pledge to Diversity Legal Group; Colorado Campaign for Inclusive Excellence; ALFA International — Practice Areas: Civil Litigation; Commercial Litigation; Environmental Law; Insurance Coverage Determination; Insurance Coverage Litigation; Real Estate — E-mail: mickleyl@hallevans.com

Peter C. Middleton — 1972 — University of Illinois, B.A., 1994; DePaul University College of Law, J.D., 1997 — Admitted to Bar, 1997, Illinois; 1998, Indiana; 2000, Colorado; 1997, U.S. District Court, Northern District of Illinois; 1998, U.S. District Court, Northern and Southern Districts of Indiana; 2000, U.S. District Court, District of Colorado; U.S. Court of Appeals, Tenth Circuit — Member American (Tort Trial and Insurance Practice Section), Colorado, Denver, Illinois State and Indiana State Bar Associations; American Health Lawyers Association; Colorado Defense Lawyers Association — Practice Areas: Catastrophic Injury; Health Care Liability; Primary and Excess Insurance; Premises Liability; Product Liability; Professional Liability — E-mail: middletonp@hallevans.com

S. Jane Mitchell — University of South Florida, B.A., 1983; University of Florida College of Law, J.D. (Order of the Coif), 1986 — Admitted to Bar, 1987, Florida; 1994, Colorado; U.S. District Court, District of Colorado; U.S. District Court, District of Florida; U.S. Court of Appeals, Tenth and Eleventh Circuits — Member Colorado (Intellectual Property Section) and Denver Bar Associations; Colorado Defense Lawyers Association; Professional Liability Underwriting Society — Practice Areas: Accident and Health; Disability; Health Care; Life; Medical Malpractice; Product Liability

Brian P. Molzahn — 1968 — Wheaton College, B.A., 1990; DePaul University College of Law, J.D., 1994 — Admitted to Bar, 1994, Illinois (Inactive); 2002, Colorado; 2001, U.S. District Court, Northern District of Illinois; U.S. District Court, District of Colorado; U.S. Court of Appeals, Tenth Circuit — Member American, Colorado and Denver Bar Associations; Professional Liability Defense Federation; Colorado Defense Lawyers Association — Practice Areas: Alternative Dispute Resolution; Appellate Practice; Civil Litigation; Commercial Litigation; Construction Litigation; Professional Liability — E-mail: molzahnb@hallevans.com

Richard L. Murray Jr. — Bucknell University, B.A. (cum laude), 1974; Wake Forest University School of Law, J.D., 1978 — Admitted to Bar, 1978, Colorado; U.S. District Court, District of Colorado; U.S. Court of Appeals, Tenth Circuit — Member Colorado and Denver Bar Associations — Practice Areas: Civil Litigation; Commercial Litigation; Health Care; Insurance Law; Medical Malpractice; Professional Liability — E-mail: murrayr@hallevans.com

Joyce H. Nakamura — 1957 — University of Hawaii, B.A., 1978; University of California, Hastings College of the Law, J.D., 1982; University of Denver, Master of Law (Taxation), 1983 — Admitted to Bar, 1982, Hawaii (Inactive); 1984, Colorado — Member American (Real Property, Probate and Trusts Section), Colorado (Trust, Estate and Elder Law Sections) and Denver Bar Associations; Rocky Mountain Estate Planning Council — Practice Areas: Trusts; Estate Planning; Wills and Estate Litigation; ERISA; Employee Benefits — E-mail: nakamuraj@hallevans.com

Kevin E. O'Brien — 1952 — University of Notre Dame, B.A., 1975; University of Denver College of Law, J.D., 1977 — Admitted to Bar, 1980, Colorado; U.S. District Court, District of Colorado; U.S. District Court, District of Arizona; U.S. Court of Appeals, Third and Tenth Circuits — Member American, Colorado and Denver Bar Associations; ALFA International (Corporate Secretary, Board Member, Chair Emeritus Insurance Practice Group); Colorado Defense Lawyers Association; Defense Research Institute; Federation of Defense and Corporate Counsel — Practice Areas: Civil Litigation; ERISA; Health Care; Insurance Law; Life; Accident; Health; Product Liability — E-mail: obrienk@hallevans.com

Hall & Evans, L.L.C., Denver, CO   (Continued)

Andrew D. Ringel — 1969 — Claremont McKenna College, B.A. (magna cum laude), 1991; Georgetown University Law Center, J.D. (cum laude), 1994 — Admitted to Bar, 1994, Colorado; U.S. District Court, District of Colorado; U.S. Court of Appeals, Ninth and Tenth Circuits; U.S. Supreme Court — Member American, Colorado and Denver Bar Associations; Faculty of Federal Advocates; Defense Research Institute; Colorado Defense Lawyers Association — Practice Areas: Appellate Practice; Employment Law; ERISA; Professional Errors and Omissions; Public Entities; Directors and Officers Liability; Civil Rights — E-mail: ringela@hallevans.com

Lance E. Shurteff — University of Wyoming, B.A., 1999; University of Wyoming College of Law, J.D., 2002 — Admitted to Bar, 2002, Colorado; 2004, Wyoming; U.S. District Court, District of Colorado; U.S. District Court, District of Wyoming; U.S. Court of Appeals, Tenth Circuit — Member American, Colorado and Denver Bar Associations; Wyoming State Bar; Defense Research Institute; Colorado Defense Lawyers Association — Practice Areas: Civil Litigation; Professional Liability; Casualty; Errors and Omissions; Oil and Gas; General Civil Litigation; Bodily Injury — E-mail: shurteffl@hallevans.com

Ryan L. Winter — 1973 — Kansas State University, B.A. (Phi Beta Kappa), 1996; University of Colorado Law School, J.D., 2000 — Admitted to Bar, 2000, Colorado; U.S. District Court, District of Colorado — Member Colorado and Denver Bar Associations; ALFA International (Retail Practice Group Steering Committee); Colorado Defense Lawyers Association; Defense Research Institute — Practice Areas: Alternative Dispute Resolution; Commercial Litigation; Construction Litigation; Health Care; Insurance Law; Product Liability; Professional Liability — E-mail: winterr@hallevans.com

Of Counsel

Peter F. Jones, General Counsel   Vincent A. Zarlengo

Special Counsel

Jeanne C. Baak	Christopher D. Bryan
Megan E. Coulter	Gillian Dale
Robert M. Ferm	Todd H. Fleckenstein
Daniel Furman	Keith M. Goman
J. Ryan Johnson	David M. Jones
Deborah M. Kellam	Edmund M. Kennedy
Chad M. Knight	Gary L. Kuhn
David E. Leavenworth	Robert J. McCormick
Malcolm S. Mead	Bruce A. Menk
Timothy M. Murphy	Anthony M. Nicastro
Michael A. Paul	Mark S. Ratner
Brian L. Taylor	Paige K. Treptow
Adam B. Wiens	

Associates

Nicole M. Black	Conor P. Boyle
Clinton L. Coberly	Susan F. Fisher
Bryan Gogarty	Bree A. Gorinsky
Natalie A. Gray	Christina S. Gunn
Matthew J. Hegarty	Craig H. Hensel
Jaclyn S. Laferriere	Mary K. Lanning
Alyssa L. Levy	Ian K. London
Stephaine A. Montague	Cash K. Parker
Andrew Reitman	Gina M. Rossi
Rachel E. Yeates	Erin K. Young

(Revisors of the Colorado Insurance Law Digest for this Publication)

Harris, Karstaedt, Jamison & Powers, P.C.

10333 East Dry Creek Road, Suite 300
Englewood, Colorado 80112
  Telephone: 720-875-9140
  Fax: 720-875-9141
  E-Mail: hkjp@hkjp.com
  www.hkjp.com

Established: 1994

COLORADO   DENVER

Harris, Karstaedt, Jamison & Powers, P.C., Denver, CO
(Continued)

Insurance Defense, Bad Faith, Commercial and Personal Lines, Automobile Liability, Construction Defect, Insurance Coverage, Self-Insured, Product Liability, Professional Malpractice, Trial and Appellate Practice, State and Federal Courts, Heavy Equipment, Commercial Motor Carrier, Catastrophic Injury

Firm Profile: Harris, Karstaedt, Jamison & Powers, P.C., is a team of attorneys whose combined knowledge and experience can achieve the best possible outcomes. Our firm is dedicated to working hard to represent each client in a competent and professional manner to achieve optimum results.

Our firm has built a reputation as effective civil trial attorneys with a successful history in insurance defense practice and countless other civil matters. We are familiar with all aspects of civil litigation. Whether in discovery, deposition or trial we aggressively protect our clients' interests by putting in the necessary preparation, asking hard questions and revealing the weaknesses in our opponents' positions.

Insurance Clients

ACUITY
American Family Insurance Group
Canal Insurance Company
Encompass Insurance Company
Grange Insurance Company
Horace Mann Insurance Company
Lancer Insurance Company
Maxum Insurance Company
Nationwide Group
Permanent General Assurance Corporation
Western Heritage Insurance
Allstate Insurance Company
ASI Underwriters
EMC Insurance Companies
Esurance Insurance Company
Hanover Insurance Group
Housing Authority Insurance Group
Motorists Group-American Hardware Mutual
Scottsdale Insurance Company
Sedgwick Claims Management
Western World Insurance Group

Non-Insurance Clients

Comcast Corporation
Federal Express
Valero Energy Corporation
Crawford & Company
Metro Taxi

Shareholders

Jamey W. Jamison — 1955 — University of Denver, B.A., 1977; J.D., 1980 — Admitted to Bar, 1981, Colorado — Member Denver and First Judicial District Bar Associations; Trial Attorneys of America; Defense Research Institute — Visiting Professor, Trial Tactics and Evidence, University of Denver — E-mail: jjamison@hkjp.com

James B. Powers — 1956 — University of Colorado, B.A., 1978; Drake University, J.D., 1981 — Admitted to Bar, 1981, Colorado — Member Denver Bar Association — Instructor, Bad Faith Defense, Construction Litigation Defense, CLE of Colorado — E-mail: jpowers@hkjp.com

A. Peter Gregory — 1954 — Colgate University, B.A., 1976; Washington and Lee University, J.D., 1979 — Admitted to Bar, 1981, Colorado — Member American and Denver Bar Associations; Defense Research Institute — E-mail: pgregory@hkjp.com

Heather A. Salg — 1972 — Fort Lewis College, B.A. (cum laude), 1993; University of Denver, J.D./M.B.A., 1998 — Admitted to Bar, 1998, Colorado — Member Denver Bar Association — E-mail: hsalg@hkjp.com

Anthony R. Clapp — 1965 — Colorado State University, B.A., 1990; Hamline University, J.D., 1994 — Admitted to Bar, 1996, Colorado — Member Arapahoe County Bar Association; Defense Research Institute — E-mail: tclapp@hkjp.com

Thomas H. Falivene — 1954 — University of Delaware, B.S., 1976; University of Arkansas, M.S., 1979; J.D., 1984 — Admitted to Bar, 1984, Missouri; 1990, Colorado — Member Arapahoe County Bar Association; South Metro Denver Chamber of Commerce — E-mail: tfalivene@hkjp.com

Jane Bendle Lucero — 1972 — University of Richmond, B.A., 1994; University of Denver College of Law, J.D., 1999 — Admitted to Bar, 1999, Colorado — Member Denver Bar Association — E-mail: jlucero@hkjp.com

Mark A. Neider — 1965 — University of Colorado at Boulder, B.A., 1987; University of Denver, J.D., 1996 — Admitted to Bar, 1996, Colorado — Member Denver Bar Association; Defense Research Institute — E-mail: mneider@hkjp.com

Steven J. Paul — 1958 — Creighton University, B.A., 1981; Creighton University School of Law, J.D., 1985 — Admitted to Bar, 1987, Colorado; 1990, Nebraska — Member Colorado Defense Lawyers Association — E-mail: spaul@hkjp.com

Harris, Karstaedt, Jamison & Powers, P.C., Denver, CO
(Continued)

Susan M. Stamm — 1964 — University of Colorado at Boulder, B.S., 1988; University of Denver, J.D., 1995 — Admitted to Bar, 1995, Colorado — Member Denver Bar Association; American Health Lawyers Association; Honorable Order of the Blue Goose International, Colorado Pond — E-mail: sstamm@hkjp.com

Of Counsel

Robert W. Harris — 1948 — The University of Kansas, B.A., 1970; University of Denver, J.D., 1973 — Admitted to Bar, 1973, Colorado — Member Denver Bar Association; Defense Research Institute — E-mail: bharris@hkjp.com

Arthur R. Karstaedt III — 1951 — University of Wisconsin, B.A., 1972; University of Denver, J.D., 1975 — Admitted to Bar, 1976, Colorado — Member Denver Bar Association; Defense Research Institute — E-mail: akarstaedt@hkjp.com

Associates

Emily L. P. Aguero
Patrick J. Hickey
Mark A. Sares
Cesilie J. Garles
Aaron J. Pratt

(All attorneys are members of The Colorado State Bar and the Colorado Defense Lawyers Association)

The Hustead Law Firm
A Professional Corporation

Regency Plaza One
4643 South Ulster Street, Suite 1250
Denver, Colorado 80237
   Telephone: 303-721-5000
   Telephone: 877-256-7871
   Fax: 303-721-5001
   www.thlf.com

Insurance Defense, Professional Liability, Property and Casualty, Fidelity and Surety, Errors and Omissions, Directors and Officers Liability

Firm Profile: The Hustead Law Firm was formed in 1996 by Patrick Q. Hustead, a former partner at one of Denver's largest regional law firms, Rothgerber, Appel, Powers & Johnson, LLP. The Firm represents fidelity and surety bonding companies and insurers throughout the Rocky Mountain region, and has members admitted in Montana, Wyoming, Colorado, New Mexico and South Dakota.

Insurance Clients

ACE USA
American Safety Casualty Insurance Company
Auto-Owners Insurance Company
Continental Western Group
EMC Insurance Companies
Great American Insurance Companies
Liberty Mutual Surety
National American Insurance Company
RSUI Group, Inc.
State Farm Insurance
Underwriters at Lloyd's, London
VELA Insurance Services (A Berkley Company)
American Modern Insurance Group, Inc.
Arch Insurance Company
Berkley Risk Administrators Company, LLC
Granite Re, Inc.
Hanover Insurance Company
Insurance Company of the West
Merchants Bonding Company
Navigators Pro
RLI Insurance Company
The St. Paul/Travelers Companies, Inc.
United Fire & Casualty Company
Western Surety Company
Zurich North America

Founder & President

Patrick Q. Hustead — University of Colorado, B.S., 1981; University of Paris - Sorbonne, C.P., 1984; Boston College Law School, J.D. (cum laude), 1987 — Admitted to Bar, 1987, Colorado; 1996, South Dakota; Montana; 1997, Wyoming; 1987, U.S. District Court, District of Colorado; 1988, U.S. Court of Appeals, Tenth Circuit; 1993, U.S. Supreme Court; 1996, U.S. District Court, District of Montana; U.S. District Court, District of South Dakota; 1997, U.S. District Court, District of Wyoming — Please Visit Our Website for a More Detailed Biographical Profile at www.thlf.com — E-mail: pqh@thlf.com

DENVER   **COLORADO**

The Hustead Law Firm, A Professional Corporation, Denver, CO   (Continued)

Shareholders

Christopher D. Yvars — Boston College, B.A., 1993; Syracuse University College of Law, J.D. (cum laude), 1998 — Admitted to Bar, 1998, Colorado; U.S. District Court, District of Colorado; U.S. Court of Appeals for the District of Columbia and Tenth Circuits — E-mail: cdy@thlf.com

Ryan A. Williams — Point Loma College, B.A., 1996; Chapman University School of Law, J.D., 2002 — Admitted to Bar, 2003, California; Colorado; U.S. District Court, District of Colorado — E-mail: raw@thlf.com

Associate

Christopher J. Shannon — University of Dayton, B.A., 2004; DePaul University College of Law, J.D., 2007 — Admitted to Bar, 2007, Colorado — E-mail: csh@thlf.com

Levy Wheeler Waters
Professional Corporation

Plaza Tower One
6400 South Fiddlers Green Circle, Suite 900
Greenwood Village, Colorado 80111
  Telephone: 303-796-2900
  Fax: 303-796-2081
  E-Mail: gilda@lwwlaw.com
  www.lwwlaw.com

Bad Faith, Commercial Litigation, Construction Law, Copyright and Trademark Law, Employment Law, Environmental Law, Insurance Coverage, Malpractice, Personal Injury, Professional Negligence, Civil Rights Violation

Insurance Clients

Auto-Owners Insurance Company	Bituminous Casualty Corporation
Farmers Insurance Exchange	Fire Insurance Exchange
St. Paul Travelers	Scottsdale Insurance Company
State Farm Mutual Automobile Insurance Company	

Partners

Marc R. Levy — The University of Oklahoma, B.A., 1978; J.D., 1980 — Admitted to Bar, 1981, Colorado; U.S. District Court, District of Colorado; U.S. Court of Appeals, Tenth Circuit; U.S. Supreme Court

Karen H. Wheeler — Colorado State University, B.A., 1984; University of Nebraska, J.D., 1987 — Admitted to Bar, 1987, Colorado; U.S. District Court, District of Colorado; U.S. Court of Appeals, Tenth Circuit

Brian J. Waters — California State University, Fullerton, B.A., 1990; Wake Forest University School of Law, J.D., 1994 — Admitted to Bar, 1994, Colorado; U.S. District Court, District of Colorado; U.S. Court of Appeals, Tenth Circuit

Jesse O. Brant — The University of Iowa, B.A., 1997; Creighton University School of Law, J.D., 2001 — Admitted to Bar, 2001, Colorado

Joshua R. Proctor — Colorado State University, B.A., 1998; University of San Diego School of Law, J.D., 2001 — Admitted to Bar, 2001, California (Inactive); 2002, Colorado

Associates

Kathryn E. Cobb	Heather E. Judd
Matthew W. Hall	Andrew L. Shively
Jami A. Maul	Charles C. Hall
Jeffrey H. Boxer	

Of Counsel

Kim D. Poletto — Colorado State University, B.A., 1978; Loyola Marymount University, Loyola Law School, J.D., 1983 — Admitted to Bar, 1983, California; 1984, Colorado; U.S. District Court, District of Colorado; U.S. Court of Appeals, Tenth Circuit

Lewis Roca Rothgerber LLP

One Tabor Center, Suite 3000
1200 Seventeenth Street
Denver, Colorado 80202-5855
  Telephone: 303-623-9000
  Fax: 303-623-9222
  E-Mail: info@LRRLaw.com
  www.LRRLaw.com

(Colorado Springs, CO Office*: 90 South Cascade Avenue, Suite 1100, 80903)
  (Tel: 719-386-3000)
  (Fax: 719-386-3070)
(Casper, WY Office: 123 West First Street, Suite 200, 82601-2480)
  (Tel: 307-232-0222)
  (Fax: 307-232-0077)
(Phoenix, AZ (Headquarters)*: 201 East Washington Street, Suite 1200, Phoenix, AZ, 85004)
  (Tel: 602-262-5311)
  (Fax: 602-262-5747)
(Tucson, AZ Office: One S. Church Avenue, Suite 700, 85701)
  (Tel: 520-622-2090)
  (Fax: 520-622-3088)
(Albuquerque, NM Office: 201 Third Street NW, Suite 1950, 87102)
  (Tel: 505-764-5400)
  (Fax: 505-764-5480)
(Las Vegas, NV Office: 3993 Howard Hughes Parkway, Suite 600, 89169)
  (Tel: 702-949-8200)
  (Fax: 702-949-8398)
(Reno, NV Office: 50 West Liberty Street, Suite 410, 89501)
  (Tel: 775-823-2900)
  (Fax: 775-823-2929)
(Menlo Park, CA Office: 4300 Bohannon Drive, Suite 230, 94025)
  (Tel: 650-391-1380)
  (Fax: 650-391-1395)

Established: 1903

Insurance Law, Regulatory and Compliance, Insurance Coverage, Property and Casualty, Life Insurance, Accident and Health, Environmental Coverage, Insurance Defense, Construction Defect, Aviation

Firm Profile: Lewis Roca Rothgerber is one of the largest law firms in the Western U.S. with 250 attorneys serving clients across nine offices including Denver, Colorado Springs, Phoenix, Tucson, Las Vegas, Reno, Albuquerque, Silicon Valley and Casper. The firm maintains thriving practices in litigation, real estate, business transactions, intellectual property, gaming, banking, bankruptcy, and energy/natural resources. For additional information, please visit LRRLaw.com.

We now have one of the strongest, litigation practices in the Rocky Mountain and Southwestern regions. Our firm's insurance litigation practice has demonstrated great success representing insurers in, among other things, class actions, high-stakes business litigation and bad faith cases, agent and employee terminations, reinsurance disputes, matters addressing the practices of insurers, life and health insurance, title insurance and matters related to surety and bonding. We also have a premier appellate practice that regularly handles appeals for insurers and their policyholders in cases in which we did not handle the matter in the trial court. Under certain circumstances, our firm represents insureds as part of an insurance defense practice.

In addition to our litigation experience, our regulatory practice is well-connected and we assist many insurance companies nationally with their regulatory and legislative issues and priorities. Our attorneys and lobbyists are adept at handling matters such as responding to investigations, assisting with market conduct examinations and designing, negotiating and securing regulatory approval for assumption reinsurance transactions or other material transactions. Lewis Roca Rothgerber also has extensive experience in all aspects of insurer insolvencies, including representation of state life and health guaranty associations and receivers.

COLORADO — DENVER

Lewis Roca Rothgerber LLP, Denver, CO (Continued)

Insurance Clients

AEGON USA, LLC
Aetna, Inc.
Allstate Insurance Company
American Family Mutual Insurance Company
American Heritage Life Insurance Company
Ameritas Life Insurance Company
Anthem Blue Cross and Blue Shield
Assurity Life Insurance Company
Catholic Insurance Company
CIGNA Group
Colorado Casualty Insurance Company
Colorado Choice Health
Continental Western Insurance Company
Disability Management Services, Inc.
Employers Insurance Company of Wausau
Farm Bureau Insurance Company
Fidelity and Guaranty Life Insurance Company
First American Title Insurance Company
Frankenmuth Mutual Insurance Company
Genworth Life Insurance Company
Guarantee Life Insurance Company
Guardian Trust Life Insurance Company
Hartford Life and Accident Insurance Company
Hawaii Division of Insurance
HealthMarkets, Inc.
Independent Order of Foresters
Jefferson Pilot Financial Insurance Company
Knights of Columbus
Liberty Mutual Insurance Company
Life Insurance Company of North America
Lincoln National Life Insurance Company
Massachusetts Mutual Life Insurance Company
Metropolitan Life Insurance Company
Minnesota Life Insurance Company/Securian
Modern Woodmen of America
Monumental Life Insurance Company
Mutual of Omaha Insurance Company/United of Omaha Insurance Company
National Life of Vermont
The Northwestern Mutual Life Insurance Company
Ohio State Life Insurance Company
The Prudential Insurance Company of America
Reliance Standard Life Insurance Company
Rocky Mountain Health Management Company
Security Life of Denver Insurance Company
Standard Insurance Company
Stonebridge Life Insurance Company
Symetra Assigned Benefits Service Company
Transamerica Life Insurance Company
Trustmark Insurance Company
Unum Group
Wausau Business Insurance Company
Western Reserve Life Assurance Company of Ohio
Zurich North America

Protection & Indemnity Associations

American Safety Indemnity Company
California Life & Health Insurance Guarantee Association
Hawaii Life and Disability Insurance Guaranty Association
Idaho Life and Health Insurance Guaranty Association
Illinois Health Maintenance Organization Guaranty Association
Illinois Life and Health Insurance Guaranty Association
Life & Health Insurance Protection Association - Colorado
Montana Life & Health Insurance Guaranty Association
National Organization of Life and Health Insurance Guaranty Associations
Oregon Life & Health Insurance Guaranty Association
Wyoming Life & Health Insurance Guaranty Association
Woodmen of the World Assured Life Association

Partners

Franklin D. O'Loughlin — 1951 — University of Northern Colorado, B.S., 1973; The University of Montana School of Law, J.D., 1979 — Admitted to Bar, 1979, Montana; 1981, Colorado; 1994, Wyoming; 2010, Illinois; 1979, U.S. District Court, District of Montana; 1981, U.S. District Court, District of Colorado; 1994, U.S. District Court, District of Wyoming; U.S. Court of Appeals, First, Third, Ninth and Tenth Circuits; U.S. Supreme Court — Member American Bar Association (Torts and Insurance Practice Section), The Colorado (Litigation Section), Illinois State and Denver Bar Associations; State Bar of Montana; Wyoming State Bar; International Association of Insurance Receivers; Lawyer-Pilots Bar Association; Colorado Defense Lawyers Association; Federation of Regulatory Counsel — E-mail: foloughlin@LRRLaw.com

Charles Goldberg — 1939 — University of Colorado, B.A., 1961; University of Denver College of Law, J.D., 1964 — Admitted to Bar, 1964, Colorado; U.S. District Court, District of Colorado; U.S. Court of Appeals, Tenth Circuit; U.S. Supreme Court — Member Colorado Trial Lawyers Association; Judge William E. Doyle Inn of Court; American College of Trial Lawyers — District Judge, Denver District Court, 1974-1978; Benemerenti ("To a Well Deserving Person") Medal, granted by Pope Benedict XVI, 2010; Civis Princeps (First Citizen) Award by Regis University, 2010; Colorado Attorneys' Fund for Client Protection, Chairman, Board of Trustees — E-mail: cgoldberg@LRRLaw.com

Gregory B. Kanan — 1949 — University of Colorado, B.A., 1972; University of Colorado Law School, J.D., 1975 — Order of the Coif — Admitted to Bar, 1975, Colorado; U.S. District Court, District of Colorado; U.S. Court of Appeals, Tenth Circuit; U.S. Supreme Court — Member American, The Colorado and Denver Bar Associations; American Board of Trial Advocates; National Health Lawyers Association — E-mail: gkanan@LRRLaw.com

Kris J. Kostolansky — 1954 — University of Michigan, A.B. (with high distinction), 1977; Boston University Law School, J.D. (cum laude), 1980 — Admitted to Bar, 1980, Ohio; 1984, Colorado; 1992, Wyoming; 1992, U.S. District Court, Northern District of Ohio; U.S. District Court, District of Colorado; U.S. Court of Appeals, Sixth and Tenth Circuits; U.S. Supreme Court — Member The Colorado and Denver Bar Associations; Denver Americans with Disability Act Roundtable (Founding Member) — E-mail: kkosto@LRRLaw.com

Brian J. Spano — 1962 — University of Michigan, A.B. (with distinction), 1984; University of Illinois College of Law, J.D., 1987 — Admitted to Bar, 1987, Colorado; U.S. District Court, District of Colorado; U.S. Court of Appeals, Tenth Circuit; U.S. Supreme Court — Member The Colorado and Denver Bar Associations; International Association of Insurance Receivers; Colorado Defense Lawyers Association — E-mail: bspano@LRRLaw.com

Joel A. Glover — 1966 — University of South Dakota, B.A. (cum laude), 1988; University of Minnesota Law School, J.D. (magna cum laude), 1991 — Phi Beta Kappa; Order of the Coif — Admitted to Bar, 1991, Colorado; 1993, Wyoming; 1991, U.S. District Court, District of Colorado; U.S. Court of Appeals, Tenth Circuit; 1995, U.S. District Court, District of Wyoming; 2001, U.S. Court of Appeals, Third Circuit; 2002, U.S. Court of Appeals, First Circuit; 2003, U.S. Supreme Court — Member American (Torts and Insurance Practice Section) and The Colorado Bar Associations; Wyoming State Bar; International Association of Insurance Receivers; Colorado Defense Lawyers Association; Federation of Regulatory Counsel — E-mail: jglover@LRRLaw.com

Cindy C. Oliver — 1967 — University of Colorado, B.A. (cum laude), 1989; University of Colorado Law School, J.D., 1992 — Order of the Coif — Admitted to Bar, 1992, Colorado; 2010, Illinois; 1992, U.S. District Court, District of Colorado; U.S. Court of Appeals, Tenth Circuit — Member American, The Colorado, Illinois State and Denver Bar Associations; Colorado Women's Bar Association; Colorado Defense Lawyers Association — E-mail: coliver@LRRLaw.com

Hilary D. Wells — 1974 — Colorado State University, B.A., 1994; Arizona State University College of Law, J.D., 2002 — Admitted to Bar, 2002, Colorado — Member American and The Colorado Bar Associations; Colorado Women's Bar Association — E-mail: hwells@LRRLaw.com

Tamara F. Goodlette — 1970 — Colorado College, B.A., 1992; University of Denver Sturm College of Law, J.D., 2004 — Admitted to Bar, 2004, Colorado; U.S. District Court, District of Colorado; U.S. Court of Appeals, Tenth Circuit — Member American Bar Association (Sections on: Torts and Insurance Practice; Environment, Energy, and Resources); The Colorado and Denver Bar Associations; Colorado Women's Bar Association; Faculty of Federal Advocates — E-mail: tgoodlette@LRRLaw.com

Associate

Lyndsay K. Arundel — 1983 — Georgetown University, B.A. (magna cum laude), 2005; University of Denver Sturm College of Law, J.D., 2008 — Admitted to Bar, 2008, Colorado; 2009, U.S. District Court, District of Colorado; 2010, U.S. Court of Appeals, Tenth Circuit — Member The Colorado and Denver Bar Associations; Alliance of Professional Women; Colorado Defense Lawyers Association — E-mail: laurndel@LRRLaw.com

McConnell Fleischner Houghtaling, LLC

4700 South Syracuse Street, Suite 200
Denver, Colorado 80237
Telephone: 303-480-0400
Fax: 303-458-9520
E-Mail: information@mfhlegal.com
www.mfhlegal.com

Established: 2001

DENVER COLORADO

McConnell Fleischner Houghtaling, LLC, Denver, CO
(Continued)

Insurance Litigation, Professional Liability, Medical Liability, Regulatory and Compliance, Employment Law, Complex Litigation, Commercial Litigation, Bad Faith, Construction Litigation, Directors and Officers Liability, Errors and Omissions, Insurance Defense, Health Care, Insurance Coverage

Firm Profile: Our attorneys are experienced in a wide range of legal matters. A significant percentage of our practice is in the defense of professionals and professional organizations in malpractice matters, providing legal services to health care institutions and medical practice groups and in advising and defending insurers. MFH attorneys can also assist with professional licensing and discipline matters, the defense of employment related actions and matters involving state and federal regulatory practice. We are experienced in mediation and arbitration and we have substantial trial experience in all of these areas.

Insurance Clients

ALAS
CNA
Employers Reinsurance Corporation
General Star Management Company
Lloyd's
OneBeacon Insurance Group
Safeco Insurance Companies
Safeco Select Markets
TIG Insurance Company
Westport Insurance Company
Chubb Specialty Insurance
Coregis Insurance Company
Farmers Insurance Group - Healthcare Professional Liability
Great-West Life and Annuity Insurance Company
NCMIC Insurance Company
Professionals Direct Insurance Company
Swiss Re Life & Health America, Inc.

Non-Insurance Clients

Banner Health
Centura Health
Cheyenne Regional Medical Center
One Health Plan of Colorado, Inc.
Cambridge Professional Liability Services
Exempla Saint Joseph Hospital

Firm Managing Partner

Michael T. McConnell — 1954 — University of Oregon, B.S., 1977; University of Denver Sturm College of Law, J.D., 1980 — Admitted to Bar, 1980, Colorado; 1992, Wyoming; 1980, U.S. District Court, District of Colorado; U.S. Court of Appeals, Tenth Circuit; 1998, U.S. Supreme Court — Member American, The Colorado and Denver Bar Associations; Fellow, American College of Trial Lawyers; Defense Research Institute; Colorado Defense Lawyers Association — Practice Areas: Legal Malpractice; Medical Malpractice; Appellate Practice; Civil Litigation; Insurance Law — E-mail: mmcconnell@mfhlegal.com

Firm Members

Cecelia A. Fleischner — 1959 — Lafayette College, B.A., 1980; University of Denver Sturm College of Law, J.D., 1984 — Member, The Denver Journal of International Law and Policy, 1983-1984 — Admitted to Bar, 1984, Colorado; U.S. District Court, District of Colorado; U.S. Court of Appeals, Tenth Circuit — Member American (Tort and Insurance Section), The Colorado (Litigation Section; Ethics Committee) and Denver Bar Associations; Colorado Women's Bar Association; Colorado Defense Lawyers Association; Defense Research Institute — Practice Areas: Professional Liability; Insurance Litigation; Insurance Defense; Legal Malpractice — E-mail: cfleischner@mfhlegal.com

Walter N. Houghtaling — 1955 — Norwich University, B.S., 1977; University of Denver Sturm College of Law, J.D., 1988 — Admitted to Bar, 1989, Colorado; U.S. District Court, District of Colorado; U.S. Court of Appeals, Tenth Circuit; U.S. Supreme Court — Member American, The Colorado and Denver Bar Associations; National Legal Malpractice Data Center; Professional Liability Underwriting Society — Author: Civil Procedure Section, Annual Survey of Colorado Law, 2003 — Practice Areas: Legal Malpractice; Professional Liability; Employment Law; Commercial Litigation; General Liability — E-mail: whoughtaling@mfhlegal.com

James M. Miletich — 1964 — The University of Iowa, B.A., 1986; St. Mary's University School of Law, J.D., 1994 — Admitted to Bar, 1994, Colorado; 1995, U.S. District Court, District of Colorado; U.S. Court of Appeals, Tenth Circuit — Member American, The Colorado, Arapahoe County and Denver Bar Associations; Colorado Defense Lawyers Association; Defense Research Institute — Practice Areas: Insurance Defense; Litigation; Professional Liability; Casualty — E-mail: jmiletich@mfhlegal.com

McConnell Fleischner Houghtaling, LLC, Denver, CO
(Continued)

Traci L. Van Pelt — 1965 — University of California, Davis, B.A., 1987; University of California, Hastings College of the Law, J.D., 1994 — Admitted to Bar, 1994, California; 1995, Colorado; 1994, U.S. District Court, Northern District of California; U.S. Court of Appeals, Ninth Circuit; 1995, U.S. District Court, District of Colorado; U.S. Court of Appeals, Tenth Circuit; U.S. Supreme Court — Member American, The Colorado (Ethics Committee) and Denver Bar Associations; Colorado Women's Bar Association; Colorado Defense Lawyers Association — Practice Areas: Complex Litigation; Commercial Litigation; Professional Liability; Legal Malpractice; Civil Litigation — E-mail: tvanpelt@mfhlegal.com

Robert W. Steinmetz — Boston College, B.S., 1996; University of Wisconsin Law School, J.D. (cum laude), 2002 — Admitted to Bar, 2002, Wisconsin; 2003, Colorado; 2005, U.S. District Court, District of Colorado; U.S. Court of Appeals, Tenth Circuit — Member American, The Colorado and Denver Bar Associations — Practice Areas: Professional Liability — E-mail: RSteinmetz@MFHLegal.com

Associate Attorneys

Matthew C. Miller — University of California, San Diego, B.S., 1997; University of San Francisco School of Law, J.D. (cum laude), 2007 — Admitted to Bar, 2007, California; 2009, Colorado — Practice Areas: Professional Liability — E-mail: MMiller@MFHLegal.com

Ryann B. Fogel — University of Colorado at Boulder, B.S. Business Admin., 2005; University of Denver Sturm College of Law, J.D., 2009 — Admitted to Bar, 2009, Colorado — E-mail: rfogel@mfhlegal.com

Jonthan J. Corrigan — 1984 — Gonzaga University, B.A. (magna cum laude), 2007; University of Colorado Law School, J.D., 2011 — Admitted to Bar, 2011, Colorado — E-mail: jcorrigan@mfhlegal.com

Eric D. Hevenor — 1971 — Metropolitan State College of Denver, B.S., 2003; Lewis & Clark Law School, J.D., 2007 — Admitted to Bar, 2007, Oregon; 2008, Wyoming; 2011, Colorado; U.S. District Court, District of Colorado — Practice Areas: Civil Litigation; Professional Liability (Non-Medical) Defense; Professional Licensure; Professional Malpractice; Professional Negligence; Professional Responsibility; Regulatory and Compliance — E-mail: ehevenor@mfhlegal.com

Montgomery, Kolodny, Amatuzio & Dusbabek, L.L.P.

1775 Sherman Street, Suite 2100
Denver, Colorado 80203
   Telephone: 303-592-6600
   Fax: 303-592-6666
   E-Mail: mrichey@mkadlaw.com
   www.mkadlaw.com

(Fort Collins, CO Office: 3534 John F. Kennedy Parkway, Suite B, 80525)
   (Tel: 970-221-2800)
   (Fax: 970-221-0271)
   (Toll Free: 866-803-5130)
(Cheyenne, WY Office: 109 East 17th Street, Suite 23, 82001)
   (Tel: 307-432-4028)

Insurance Law, Personal Injury, Wrongful Death, Product Liability, Construction Law, Commercial Law, Professional Malpractice, Toxic Torts, Environmental Law

Insurance Clients

Berkley Regional Specialty Insurance Company
RLI Insurance Company
Continental Western Group
Mendota Insurance Company
United Fire Group

Partners

Kevin F. Amatuzio — 1957 — University of Denver, B.A., 1980; University of Denver College of Law, J.D., 1983 — Admitted to Bar, 1983, Colorado; U.S. District Court, District of Colorado; 1989, U.S. Court of Appeals, Tenth Circuit; 2004, U.S. Supreme Court — Member American, The Colorado, Denver and Arapahoe County Bar Associations; Colorado Defense Lawyers Association (President 2002-2003, Officer 2000-2004); Association of Defense Trial Attorneys (State Chair 2000-Present); Defense Research Institute; Federation of Defense and Corporate Counsel — E-mail: kamatuzio@mkadlaw.com

Lori K. Bell   John R. Chase

COLORADO — DENVER

Montgomery, Kolodny, Amatuzio & Dusbabek, L.L.P., Denver, CO (Continued)

Peter S. Dusbabek
Max K. Jones
David C. Fawley
Thomas H. Blomstrom

Associates

Jennifer K. Morris
Claire E. Munger
Sara K. Stieben
Aaron L. Hayden
Marianne LaBorde

Of Counsel

Joel A. Kolodny, Retired
Michael C. Montgomery

Montgomery Little & Soran, P.C.

The Quadrant
5445 DTC Parkway, Suite 800
Greenwood Village, Colorado 80111
  Telephone: 303-773-8100
  Fax: 303-220-0412
  E-Mail: info@montgomerylittle.com
  www.montgomerylittle.com

Established: 1965

Trial Practice, Appellate Practice, Insurance Defense, Accountants and Attorneys Liability, Architects and Engineers, Design Professionals, Construction Litigation, Legal Malpractice, Environmental Law, Product Liability

Firm Profile: Since its founding in 1965, Montgomery Little & Soran, P.C. has provided comprehensive services in civil litigation, commercial law, real estate, and family law matters. Over the years the firm has grown both in size and in fields of practice to accommodate the diverse and changing needs of its clients. The attorneys practicing with Montgomery Little & Soran today offer a full range of services to a broad spectrum of clients ranging from major corporations and insurance companies to small businesses and private individuals.

Montgomery Little & Soran delivers fast, efficient, first-rate legal services at extremely competitive rates. The firm is dedicated to the proposition that the most effective and cost efficient legal services are provided by attorneys who maintain a high level of integrity and who communicate honestly and frankly with clients.

Insurance Clients

Attorneys Liability Protection Society
CNA Global Specialty Lines
HCC Specialty, InsPro Corporation
Lexington Insurance Company
Rice Insurance Services Company, LLC
Travelers Indemnity Company
XL Specialty Insurance Company
Beazley Insurance Company, Inc.
Chubb Specialty Insurance
Hanover Professionals
James River Insurance Company
Monitor Liability Managers, Inc.
Travelers - Architects and Engineers
XL Design Professional
Zurich American Insurance Company

Non-Insurance Clients

Brakes Plus
CorePointe Group LLC
Dillon Companies, Inc.
Gallegos Corp.
Gold Crown Management Company
Comerica Bank
CTL/Thompson, Inc.
First American Title Insurance Company
The Kroger Co.
Monaghan Farms, Inc.

Founding Members

Roy E. Montgomery — (1907-1986)

Robert R. Montgomery — 1934 — Dartmouth College, A.B., 1956; University of Denver College of Law, LL.B., 1958 — Admitted to Bar, 1959, Colorado — Member The Colorado (Litigation Council, 1994-1997) and Denver Bar Associations; Defense Lawyers Association of Colorado (President 1972-1973); American Board of Trial Advocates (Past President, Colorado); Fellow, American College of Trial Lawyers (State Chair, 1996, 1998) — Practice Areas: Commercial Litigation; Environmental Liability; Medical Malpractice; Product Liability; Professional Liability

Montgomery Little & Soran, P.C., Denver, CO (Continued)

Directors/Shareholders

David C. Little — 1934 — Santa Clara University, B.S., 1956; University of Denver College of Law, LL.B., 1958 — Admitted to Bar, 1959, Colorado — Member American, The Colorado (Ethics and Lawyer Professional Liability Committees), Arapahoe County and Denver Bar Associations; Defense Lawyers Association of Colorado; American Board of Trial Advocates (Past President, Colorado); Supreme Court Civil Rules Committee; Diplomat, National Board of Trial Advocacy; Diplomat, American Board of Professional Liability Attorneys; Supreme Court Board of Continuing Legal and Judicial Education; Supreme Court Standing Committee on Rules of Professional Conduct; International Association of Defense Counsel — Colorado SuperLawyer, 2007-2013 — Practice Areas: Commercial Litigation; Construction Litigation; Insurance Litigation; Professional Liability — E-mail: dlittle@montgomerylittle.com

James J. Soran, III — 1951 — Colorado College, B.A., 1974; University of Denver College of Law, J.D., 1977 — Admitted to Bar, 1978, Colorado — Member American, The Colorado and Denver Bar Associations; International Council of Shopping Centers — Colorado SuperLawyer, 2007-2013 — Practice Areas: Real Estate; Commercial Law — E-mail: jsoran@montgomerylittle.com

Robert J. Beattie — 1957 — State University of New York College at Cortland, B.S., 1980; University of Wyoming, M.S., 1982; University of Denver College of Law, J.D., 1985 — Admitted to Bar, 1985, Colorado; 1985, U.S. District Court, District of Colorado — Member American, The Colorado and Denver Bar Associations — Colorado SuperLawyer (2010-2011) — Practice Areas: Family Law — E-mail: rbeattie@montgomerylittle.com

Debra Piazza — 1952 — Metropolitan State College of Denver, B.S. (with honors), 1979; University of Denver College of Law, J.D., 1985 — Admitted to Bar, 1985, Colorado; 1996, U.S. District Court, District of Colorado; 1996, U.S. Court of Appeals, Tenth Circuit — Member American, The Colorado and Denver Bar Associations — Practice Areas: Commercial Law — E-mail: dpiazza@montgomerylittle.com

John Riley — 1962 — Drake University, B.A., 1984; The University of Iowa College of Law, J.D., 1989 — Admitted to Bar, 1989, Iowa; Colorado; 1989, U.S. District Court, District of Colorado; U.S. Court of Appeals, Tenth Circuit — Member American, The Colorado, Arapahoe County and Denver Bar Associations; Colorado Defense Lawyers Association; Defense Research Institute — Practice Areas: Construction Law; Personal Injury; Litigation; Insurance Defense — E-mail: jriley@montgomerylittle.com

Christopher B. Little — 1963 — University of Colorado, B.A., 1985; University of Denver College of Law, J.D., 1987 — Admitted to Bar, 1989, Colorado; District of Columbia; 1989, U.S. District Court, Northern District of California; 1989, U.S. Court of Appeals for the District of Columbia, Fifth, Tenth, Sixth, Eighth and Ninth Circuits; U.S. District Court, District of Colorado; U.S. Supreme Court — Member American, The Colorado, Arapahoe County and Denver (President, 2005-2006) Bar Associations; Colorado Defense Lawyers Association (President, 2005-2006); Defense Research Institute — Colorado SuperLawyer, 2007-2013 — Practice Areas: Complex Litigation; Employment Law; Professional Liability — E-mail: clittle@montgomerylittle.com

Frederick B. Skillern — 1951 — Dartmouth College, A.B. (cum laude), 1973; University of Colorado Law School, J.D., 1976 — Admitted to Bar, 1977, Colorado; 1977, U.S. District Court, District of Colorado; 1983, U.S. Court of Appeals, Tenth Circuit — Member American and The Colorado Bar Associations — District Judge, Eighteenth Judicial District of Colorado, 2000-2002; Colorado SuperLawyer, 2007-2013 — Practice Areas: Appellate Practice; Insurance Law; Mediation; Arbitration; Real Estate; Commercial Litigation — E-mail: fskillern@montgomerylittle.com

William J. Searfoorce, Jr. — 1966 — Temple University, B.A., 1989; Seattle University School of Law, J.D. (cum laude), 1993 — Admitted to Bar, 1994, Pennsylvania; 2000, Colorado; 1994, U.S. District Court, Eastern District of Pennsylvania; U.S. District Court, District of New Jersey; 2000, U.S. District Court, District of Colorado; U.S. Court of Appeals, Tenth Circuit — Member American, The Colorado and Denver Bar Associations; Colorado Defense Lawyers Association — Practice Areas: Civil Litigation; Construction Law; Contracts; Design Professionals — E-mail: wsearfoorce@montgomerylittle.com

Courtney J. Cline — 1978 — The University of Georgia, B.A. (magna cum laude), 2001; University of Colorado Law School, J.D., 2004 — Admitted to Bar, 2004, Colorado — Member The Colorado and Arapahoe County Bar Associations; Metropolitan Denver Interdisciplinary Committee — Super Lawyer Rising Star, 2012-2013 — E-mail: ccline@montgomerylittle.com

Montgomery Little & Soran, P.C., Denver, CO (Continued)

Shareholders

Christopher A. Taravella — 1951 — United States Air Force Academy, B.S., 1973; University of Colorado Law School, J.D., 1976; Harvard Business School, A.M., 1996 — Admitted to Bar, 1976, Colorado; 1985, Michigan; 2008, Wyoming; U.S. Patent; 1976, U.S. District Court, District of Colorado; 1976, U.S. Court of Military Appeals — Member American and The Colorado Bar Associations — Practice Areas: Commercial Law; Employment Law; Civil Litigation; Intellectual Property — E-mail: ctaravella@montgomerylittle.com

Michael R. McCormick — 1972 — University of Colorado, B.A., 1994; University of Denver College of Law, J.D., 2001 — Order of St. Ives — Admitted to Bar, 2002, Colorado; 2003, U.S. District Court, District of Colorado — Practice Areas: Eminent Domain; Real Estate; Litigation — E-mail: mmccormick@montgomerylittle.com

Nathan G. Osborn — 1981 — Texas Christian University, B.A. (Dean's List), 2003; University of Nebraska College of Law, J.D. (with distinction), 2007 — Admitted to Bar, 2007, Colorado — Member The Colorado and Douglas County Bar Associations — Practice Areas: Real Estate; Commercial Litigation; Professional Liability (Non-Medical) Defense; Personal Injury — E-mail: nosborn@montgomerylittle.com

Echo D. Ryan — 1979 — University of Northern Colorado, B.A., 2001; University of Denver College of Law, J.D., 2006 — Admitted to Bar, 2006, Colorado — Member The Colorado and Arapahoe County Bar Associations — Practice Areas: Litigation; Business Transactions — E-mail: eryan@montgomerylittle.com

Associates

Rachel L. Kranz — 1986 — University of Florida, B.A. (cum laude), 2008; University of Denver, J.D., 2011 — Admitted to Bar, 2011, Colorado; 2012, U.S. District Court, District of Colorado — Member The Colorado, Arapahoe County (Family Law Section) and Denver Bar Associations — E-mail: rkranz@montgomerylittle.com

Adrienne L. Toon — 1984 — Ohio University, B.A. (Dean's List), 2007; Case Western Reserve University School of Law, J.D., 2010 — Delores K. Hanna Women in Law Scholarship — Admitted to Bar, 2010, Colorado — Member Colorado Defense Lawyers Association — Board Member, Case Western Reserve University Colorado Alumni Chapter — Practice Areas: Civil Litigation; Business Law — E-mail: atoon@montgomerylittle.com

Shawn A. Eady — 1978 — Colorado State University, B.A., 2001; University of Denver Sturm College of Law, J.D., 2006 — Admitted to Bar, 2007, Colorado — Practice Areas: Construction Defect; Professional Liability; Insurance Coverage; Real Estate — E-mail: seady@montgomerylittle.com

Aaron Prom — 1984 — University of Florida, B.A. (Phi Beta Kappa), 2006; University of Florida, Levin College of Law, J.D. (cum laude), 2009 — Admitted to Bar, 2009, Florida; 2012, Colorado; 2013, U.S. District Court, District of Colorado — Practice Areas: Business Law; Real Estate — E-mail: aprom@montgomerylittle.com

William B. Ross — 1986 — The University of North Carolina at Chapel Hill, B.A., 2008; University of Denver Sturm College of Law, J.D., 2013 — Admitted to Bar, 2013, Colorado — E-mail: wross@montgomerylittle.com

Murphy & Decker, P.C.

4725 S. Monaco Street, Suite 110
Denver, Colorado 80237
Telephone: 303-468-5980
Fax: 303-468-5981
E-Mail: mdecker@murphydecker.com
www.murphydecker.com

Defense Litigation, Construction Defect, Personal Injury Defense

Firm Profile: At Murphy & Decker, P.C. we provide the top-quality legal representation and personal attention that our clients deserve. Our experienced lawyers provide you with the time, compassion, and determination you need to successfully handle your case.

Insurance Clients

ACE Group
The Hartford
Travelers Insurance Company
Zurich Insurance Company
CNA
SECURA Insurance, A Mutual Company

Murphy & Decker, P.C., Denver, CO (Continued)

Partners

Daniel P. Murphy — Regis College, B.S. (cum laude), 1982; University of Wyoming College of Law, J.D., 1986 — Admitted to Bar, 1986, Colorado; U.S. District Court, District of Colorado — Member The Colorado and Denver Bar Associations — E-mail: dmurphy@murphydecker.com

Michael J. Decker — Valparaiso University, B.A., 1995; Chicago-Kent College of Law, J.D. (with honors), 1998 — Admitted to Bar, 1998, Colorado; 1999, U.S. District Court, District of Colorado; U.S. Court of Appeals, Tenth Circuit — Member The Colorado and Denver Bar Associations; Colorado Defense Lawyers Association — E-mail: mdecker@murphydecker.com

Greg R. Lindsay — Brigham Young University, B.A., 1999; University of Pittsburgh School of Law, J.D., 2002 — Admitted to Bar, 2002, Colorado; 2003, U.S. District Court, District of Colorado — Member The Colorado, Arapahoe County and Denver Bar Associations; Colorado Defense Lawyers Association — Languages: Portuguese — E-mail: glindsay@murphydecker.com

Of Counsel

Eric M. Kirby — Southern Utah University, B.A., 2003; University of Denver, J.D., 2007 — Admitted to Bar, 2008, Colorado; Utah; 2009, Wyoming; U.S. District Court, District of Colorado; U.S. District Court, District of Utah; U.S. District Court, District of Wyoming — Member The Colorado, Central Utah, Arapahoe County, Denver County and Salt Lake County Bar Associations; Utah and Wyoming State Bars; Colorado Defense Lawyers Association — E-mail: ekirby@murphydecker.com

Associates

Danielle R. Bergman — The University of Virginia's College at Wise, B.A., 2006; Appalachian School of Law, J.D., 2009 — Admitted to Bar, 2009, Colorado; 2010, U.S. District Court, District of Colorado — Member The Colorado and Denver Bar Associations — E-mail: dbergman@murphydecker.com

C. Stephen Herlihy — St. Lawrence University, B.A., 2001; University of Wyoming, J.D., 2009 — Admitted to Bar, 2009, Colorado; Wyoming — E-mail: sherlihy@murphydecker.com

Sean P. Hughey — University of Washington, B.A., 2006; University of Denver Sturm College of Law, J.D., 2009 — Admitted to Bar, 2010, Colorado; 2013, U.S. District Court, District of Colorado — Member The Colorado and Denver Bar Associations — E-mail: shughey@murphydecker.com

Elizabeth A. Gillespie — Saint Mary's College, B.S. (magna cum laude), 2008; University of Missouri-Kansas City School of Law, J.D., 2011 — Admitted to Bar, 2011, Missouri; 2012, Kansas; 2013, Colorado — Member The Colorado and Kansas Bar Associations; The Missouri Bar; Missouri Organization of Defense Lawyers — E-mail: egillespie@murphydecker.com

Nathan, Bremer, Dumm & Myers, P.C.

Denver Corporate Center III, Suite 600
7900 East Union Avenue
Denver, Colorado 80237-2776
Telephone: 303-691-3737
Fax: 303-757-5106
www.nbdmlaw.com

Established: 1973

Insurance Defense, Casualty, Surety, Workers' Compensation, Insurance Law, Automobile, Product Liability, Professional Malpractice, Employment Law, Construction Defect, Governmental Defense

Insurance Clients

American Alternative Insurance Corporation
Burlington Insurance Company
American Family Insurance Company
Chubb & Son, Inc.

COLORADO

Nathan, Bremer, Dumm & Myers, P.C., Denver, CO (Continued)

CIGNA Property and Casualty Insurance Company
Colony Insurance Group
Colorado Farm Bureau Mutual Insurance Company
Colorado Special Districts Property and Liability Pool
Continental Divide Insurance Company
ESIS/ACE USA Group
Insurance Company of the West
Kemper Insurance Companies
Munich Reinsurance America, Inc.
National Fire and Marine Insurance Company
Police Officers Research Association of California
SECURA Insurance Companies
United Fire Group
York Risk Services Group, Inc.
Citation Insurance Company
Clarendon National Insurance Company/North American Risk Services
Colorado Intergovernmental Risk Sharing Agency
Companion Specialty Insurance Company
CUNA Mutual Group
Federated Mutual Insurance Company
Mountain West Farm Bureau Mutual Insurance Company
Nationwide Insurance
Orion Insurance Company
Safeco Insurance
Scottsdale Insurance Company
Sentry Insurance
Viking Insurance Company

Non-Insurance Clients

Adams County
Albertson's LLC
Asphalt Specialties Company, Inc.
AutoZone, Inc.
Berkley Risk Administrators Company, LLC
Cherry Creek School District
City of Aurora
City of Lakewood
Continental Materials Corp.
Denver Public Schools
Douglas County, CO
Hospital Shared Services
The Kroger Co.
Lockheed Martin Corporation
National Claim Services, Inc.
Qwest Communications
Rocla Concrete Tie, Inc.
Sedgwick CMS
Specialty Risk Services, Inc. (SRS)
Tradesmen International, Inc.
University of Colorado
ADP TotalSource/Specialty Risk Services
Aurora Public Schools
Avis Rent-A-Car System, LLC
Budget Rent-A-Car System, Inc.
CenturyLink, Inc.
Church of Jesus Christ of Latter Day Saints
ConAgra Beef Company
Crawford & Company
Dillon Companies, Inc.
Gallagher Bassett Services, Inc.
Isle of Capri Black Hawk, LLC
Larimer County
Mini Mart, Inc.
Penske Truck Leasing
Risk Enterprise Management, Ltd.
Sedgwick Claims Management Services, Inc.
Speedy Heavy Hauling Inc.
Transit Mix Concrete Co.
Wells Fargo

Shareholders

Peter Watson — (1923-2004)

Andrew J. Fisher — (1965-2009)

Howard W. Bremer — (Retired)

J. Andrew Nathan — 1947 — University of Colorado; University of Missouri, B.A., 1969; University of Colorado, J.D., 1972 — Admitted to Bar, 1972, Colorado — Member The Colorado and Denver Bar Associations; American Board of Trial Advocates (President, Colorado Chapter, 1990; National Board of Directors, 1990-1996); Colorado Defense Lawyers Association — Practice Areas: Civil Litigation; Employment Law; Civil Rights; Land Use; Personal Injury; Insurance Law; Professional Liability — E-mail: anathan@nbdmlaw.com

Mark H. Dumm — 1951 — University of Colorado, B.A., 1973; University of San Diego, J.D., 1978 — Admitted to Bar, 1978, Colorado; U.S. District Court, District of Colorado; U.S. Court of Appeals, Tenth Circuit — Member The Colorado and Elbert County Bar Associations; Colorado Defense Lawyers Association; Defense Research Institute — Practice Areas: Insurance Law; Product Liability; Professional Liability; Workers' Compensation; Personal Injury; Automobile Accidents; Construction Defect; Livestock Liability — E-mail: mdumm@nbdmlaw.com

Anne Smith Myers — 1954 — University of Wyoming, B.A. (with honors), 1975; University of Denver, J.D., 1978 — Phi Beta Kappa — Admitted to Bar, 1979, Colorado — Member The Colorado and Denver Bar Associations; Colorado Defense Lawyers Association — Practice Areas: Workers' Compensation — E-mail: amyers@nbdmlaw.com

Mark E. Macy — 1953 — Michigan State University, B.A., 1976; University of Detroit, J.D., 1980 — Admitted to Bar, 1981, Colorado; U.S. District Court, District of Colorado; U.S. Court of Appeals, Tenth Circuit — Member The Colorado and Jefferson County Bar Associations; Colorado Defense Lawyers Association — Practice Areas: Insurance Defense; Personal Injury; Construction Defect; Bad Faith; Employment Law; Mediation — E-mail: mmacy@nbdmlaw.com

DENVER

Nathan, Bremer, Dumm & Myers, P.C., Denver, CO (Continued)

Ellis J. Mayer — 1955 — University of Colorado, B.A., 1977; University of Denver, J.D., 1981 — Admitted to Bar, 1982, Colorado; U.S. District Court, District of Colorado; U.S. Court of Appeals, Tenth Circuit; U.S. Court of Appeals for the Federal Circuit — Member The Colorado, Douglas and Arapahoe Bar Associations; Colorado Defense Lawyers Association; American Board of Trial Advocates — Practice Areas: Automobile; Personal Injury; Premises Liability; Insurance Defense; Legal Malpractice; Construction Defect — E-mail: emayer@nbdmlaw.com

Heidi J. Hugdahl — 1963 — Colorado State University, B.A. (with distinction and honors), 1986; American University, J.D., 1990 — Phi Beta Kappa — Admitted to Bar, 1990, Colorado; U.S. District Court, District of Colorado; U.S. Court of Appeals, Tenth Circuit; U.S. Supreme Court — Member The Colorado, Denver and Women's Bar Associations; Colorado Defense Lawyers Association; Defense Research Institute — Practice Areas: Civil Litigation; Employment Law; Civil Rights; Land Use — E-mail: hhugdahl@nbdmlaw.com

Michael Robert Lancto — 1964 — Colorado State University, B.A., 1986; University of Denver, J.D., 1990 — Law Clerk to District Court Judge Michael J. Watanabe, 1990-1992 — Admitted to Bar, 1990, Colorado; 1993, U.S. District Court, District of Colorado; 1995, U.S. Court of Appeals, Tenth Circuit — Member The Colorado, Arapahoe County and Jefferson County Bar Associations; Colorado Defense Lawyers Association; Defense Research Institute — Practice Areas: Civil Litigation; Premises Liability; Construction Litigation; Liquor Liability; Insurance Law; Automobile Liability; Professional Liability — E-mail: mlancto@nbdmlaw.com

Bernard R. Woessner — 1967 — Rutgers University, B.A., 1989; University of Denver, J.D., 1994 — Admitted to Bar, 1994, Colorado; U.S. District Court, District of Colorado; U.S. Court of Appeals, Tenth Circuit; U.S. Supreme Court — Member The Colorado and Denver Bar Associations; Colorado Defense Lawyers Association; Defense Research Institute — Practice Areas: Civil Litigation; Workers' Compensation; Insurance Law; Civil Rights; Municipal Liability; Employment Law; Personal Injury — E-mail: bwoessner@nbdmlaw.com

Benjamin E. Tracy — 1970 — The University of New Mexico, B.A., 1992; University of Colorado, J.D., 1998 — Admitted to Bar, 1998, Colorado; U.S. District Court, District of Colorado; U.S. Court of Appeals, Tenth Circuit — Member The Colorado and Denver Bar Associations; Colorado Defense Lawyers Association — Practice Areas: Civil Litigation; Workers' Compensation; Construction Defect; Personal Injury — E-mail: btracy@nbdmlaw.com

Marni Nathan Kloster — 1978 — Emory University, B.B.A. (with distinction), 2000; University of Denver, J.D., 2003 — Order of St. Ives — Admitted to Bar, 2003, Colorado; U.S. District Court, District of Colorado; U.S. Court of Appeals, Tenth Circuit; U.S. Supreme Court — Member The Colorado Bar Association; Colorado Defense Lawyers Association — Practice Areas: Civil Litigation; Employment Law; Land Use; Civil Rights — E-mail: mnathan@nbdmlaw.com

Overturf McGath & Hull, P.C.

625 East 16th Avenue
Denver, Colorado 80203
Telephone: 303-860-2848
Fax: 303-860-2869
E-Mail: OMH-Office@omhlaw.com
www.omhlaw.com

Established: 1995

Professional Liability, Construction Litigation, Commercial Litigation, Environmental Litigation, Employment Litigation, Governmental Entity Defense, Personal Injury, Product Liability, Premises Liability, Intellectual Property, Insurance Bad Faith Litigation, Trucking/Transportation Litigation

Firm Profile: OMH has a proven track record of delivering timely, appropriate resolution of litigated cases. We operate on the principle that excellent results are achieved through prompt and thoughtful case analysis and identification of key fact, legal, and damages issues. Our litigation strategy for each case is uniquely tailored to target the earliest potential resolution of the case. We invite you to review our website and to contact us to discuss how our firm can serve your organization's needs.

DENVER COLORADO

Overturf McGath & Hull, P.C., Denver, CO (Continued)

Insurance Clients

Continental Western Insurance Group
Glatfelter Insurance Group
Liberty Mutual Insurance

Partners

Mark C. Overturf — University of Colorado, B.A., 1979; University of Denver College of Law, J.D., 1985 — Admitted to Bar, 1985, Colorado; 1996, Wyoming

Scott A. McGath — University of Illinois, B.S., 1981; University of Colorado Law School, J.D., 1985 — Admitted to Bar, 1985, Colorado; 1999, Wyoming

Brandon P. Hull — University of Nebraska, B.A., 1985; University of Nebraska College of Law, J.D., 1988 — Admitted to Bar, 1988, California; 1994, Colorado; 2002, Nebraska; 2009, Wyoming

Robert I. Lapidow — The University of Iowa, B.A., 1996; Hofstra University School of Law, J.D., 1999 — Admitted to Bar, 2000, New York; 2005, Colorado; 2006, Wyoming; 2007, Nebraska

Meredith L. McDonald — Emory University, B.A., 1993; Daniels College of Business, University of Denver, M.I.M., 1999; University of Denver College of Law, J.D., 1999 — Admitted to Bar, 1999, Colorado

Richard K. Rediger — University of California, Los Angeles, B.A. (cum laude), 1975; Loyola University School of Law, J.D., 1978 — Admitted to Bar, 1979, Colorado

Jason P. Rietz — Hamline University, B.A. (magna cum laude), 1993; University of Minnesota Law School, J.D. (cum laude), 1996 — Admitted to Bar, 1996, Minnesota; 2001, Colorado

M. Kate Strauss — The Pennsylvania State University, B.A./B.A. (with honors and high distinction), 2001; University of Pittsburgh School of Law, J.D. (cum laude), 2006 — Admitted to Bar, 2007, Colorado

Associates

January D. Allen — College of Charleston, B.S. (cum laude), 2000; William S. Richardson School of Law, University of Hawaii, J.D., 2005 — Admitted to Bar, 2005, Colorado

Steven W. Boatright — Rhodes College, B.A. (cum laude), 2001; University of Denver Sturm College of Law, J.D., 2009 — Admitted to Bar, 2009, Colorado

Ike M. Eckert — University of Nebraska-Lincoln, B.S. (with high distinction), 2002; William Mitchell College of Law, J.D., 2007 — Admitted to Bar, 2007, Colorado; 2012, Nebraska

Lindsey W. Jay — The University of North Carolina at Chapel Hill, B.A., 1999; University of Denver College of Law, J.D., 2002 — Admitted to Bar, 2002, Colorado

Susanne E. Rhodes — University of Notre Dame, B.A., 2000; University of Denver Sturm College of Law, J.D., 2007 — Admitted to Bar, 2007, Colorado

Of Counsel

David M. Bost — Colorado College, B.A., 1984; University of Denver College of Law, J.D., 1989 — Admitted to Bar, 1990, Colorado

Richards & Simpson

600 Grant Street, Suite 620
Denver, Colorado 80203-3527
  Telephone: 303-832-5588
  Fax: 303-832-9265
  E-Mail: msimpson@ahrs-law.com

Established: 1969

Insurance Defense, Casualty, Workers' Compensation, Professional Liability, Product Liability, Employment Law

Insurance Clients

Allstate Insurance Company
Fidelity National Insurance Company
Omaha Property and Casualty Insurance Company
Farmers Alliance Mutual Insurance Company
GEICO-Government Employees Insurance Company
Specialty Risk Services, Inc. (SRS)

Richards & Simpson, Denver, CO (Continued)

Non-Insurance Clients

Circle K Corporation
GAB Robins North America, Inc.
The Hertz Corporation
Thrifty Rent-A-Car Systems, Inc.
Dollar Rent A Car Systems, Inc.
Hertz Claim Management
Safeway, Inc.

Of Counsel

Ronald C. Hill — 1937 — University of Denver, B.A., 1959; J.D., 1962 — Admitted to Bar, 1962, Colorado — Member American, The Colorado and Denver Bar Associations; Defense Lawyers Association of Colorado; National Panel of Arbitrators; American Arbitration Association (1968-present); Defense Research Institute — E-mail: rhill@ahrs-law.com

Partners

Jeffrey J. Richards — 1955 — University of Colorado, B.A. (cum laude), 1980; The Ohio State University, J.D., 1986 — Admitted to Bar, 1986, Colorado — Member American, The Colorado and Denver Bar Associations; Colorado Defense Lawyers Association — E-mail: jrichards@ahrs-law.com

Michael S. Simpson — 1964 — Kansas State University, B.A., 1987; The University of Kansas, J.D., 1990 — Admitted to Bar, 1990, Colorado; 1990, U.S. District Court, District of Colorado — Member American, The Colorado and Denver Bar Associations; Colorado Defense Lawyers Association — E-mail: msimpson@ahrs-law.com

Ritsema & Lyon, P.C.

999 18th Street, Suite 3100
Denver, Colorado 80202
  Telephone: 303-293-3100
  Fax: 303-297-2337
  E-Mail: info@ritsema-lyon.com
  www.ritsema-lyon.com

Established: 1993

Workers' Compensation, Insurance Defense, Medicare Set Aside Trusts

Firm Profile: The attorneys of Ritsema & Lyon actively represent Colorado, Arizona, Nebraska, Utah and Wyoming employers and insurance carriers in workers' compensation and insurance defense matters. We have additional offices in: Colorado Springs, Fort Collins, Grand Junction, CO and Omaha, NE.

Insurance Clients

Gallagher Bassett Services, Inc.
Pinnacol Assurance Company

Managing Partners

Lynn P. Lyon — 1956 — University of Colorado, J.D., 1982 — Admitted to Bar, 1982, Colorado

Susan K. Reeves — 1956 — Case Western Reserve University, J.D., 1986 — Admitted to Bar, 1986, Colorado — Resident Colorado Springs, CO Office

Kim D. Starr — Nebraska Managing Partner — 1957 — South Texas College of Law, J.D., 1987 — Admitted to Bar, 1996, Nebraska; 1988, Colorado — Resident Fort Collins, CO Office

Carol A. Finley — 1961 — University of South Dakota, J.D., 1986 — Admitted to Bar, 1986, South Dakota; 1988, Colorado — Resident Grand Junction, CO Office

Nancy C. Hummel — Utah Managing Partner — 1965 — Saint Louis University School of Law, J.D., 1993 — Admitted to Bar, 2000, Colorado; 2009, Utah

Kelly F. Kruegel — Arizona Managing Partner — 1979 — Washington University in St. Louis School of Law, J.D., 2005 — Admitted to Bar, 2005, Colorado; 2011, Arizona

Tiemeier & Stich, P.C.

1000 East 16th Avenue
Denver, Colorado 80218
   Telephone: 303-531-0022
   Fax: 303-531-0021
   E-Mail: hroell@tslawpc.com
   www.tslawpc.com

Medical Malpractice Defense, Real Estate, Mechanics Liens, Appeals, Construction Law and Litigation, Landlord/Tenant Disputes

Firm Profile: When you're defending a lawsuit or contemplating one, you want lawyers who are not afraid of the courtroom. Mr. Tiemeier and Mr. Stich started their firm in 2010 because of their shared interest in taking cases to trial (if that is what is best for their client), as opposed to posturing, beating their chests, then settling at the last minute. They will give you an early assessment of your legal problem, and then work with you on how best to achieve your goals in prosecuting or defending the lawsuit. Tiemeier and Stich are trial lawyers, not just litigators. There is a difference.

Insurance Clients

Copic Insurance Company
Ophthalmic Mutual Insurance Company
Correctional Healthcare Companies, Inc.
Rice Insurance Services Company, LLC

Partners

C. Gregory Tiemeier — University of Missouri-Columbia, B.A., 1980; University of Denver College of Law, J.D., 1986 — Admitted to Bar, 1986, Colorado — Member The Colorado Bar Association

Max S. Stich — University of California, Santa Barbara, B.A., 2001; University of Denver College of Law, J.D., 2005 — Admitted to Bar, 2005, Colorado — Member The Colorado Bar Association

Associate

Daniel L. Mauk

Tucker Holmes, P.C.

7400 East Caley Avenue, Suite 300
Centennial, Colorado 80111-6714
   Telephone: 303-694-9300
   Fax: 303-694-9370
   E-Mail: board@tucker-holmes.com
   www.tucker-holmes.com

Established: 1983

Insurance Defense, Automobile, Product Liability, General Liability, Property, Coverage Issues, Opinions, Employment Law, Appellate Practice, Bad Faith, Construction Defect, Special Investigative Unit Claims

Insurance Clients

Allstate Insurance Company
California Casualty Insurance Company
CNA Insurance Companies
COUNTRY Insurance & Financial Services
Esurance Insurance Company
GuideOne Insurance
Kemper Services
MetLife Auto & Home Group
Amica Mutual Insurance Company
Chartis Insurance
Chartis International
Colorado Casualty Insurance Company
Encompass Insurance
Gallagher Bassett Services, Inc.
International Marine Underwriters
Liberty Mutual Insurance
Sedgwick Claims Management Services, Inc.

Non-Insurance Clients

Kohl's Department Stores, Inc.
Wagner Equipment Company
United Parcel Service, Inc.

Shareholders

Bradley D. Tucker — The University of Tulsa, B.S., 1987; J.D., 1990 — Phi Alpha Delta — Admitted to Bar, 1990, Oklahoma; 1993, Colorado; 1990,

Tucker Holmes, P.C., Denver, CO   (Continued)

U.S. District Court, Eastern and Northern Districts of Oklahoma; 1991, U.S. Court of Appeals, Tenth Circuit; 1996, U.S. District Court, District of Colorado — Member The Colorado, Oklahoma and Denver Bar Associations; American Board of Trial Advocates — E-mail: bdt@tucker-holmes.com

Matthew A. Holmes — Columbia University, 1984-1985; Colorado College, B.A., 1988; University of Denver, J.D., 1991 — Admitted to Bar, 1991, Colorado; 1997, New Mexico; 2006, Wyoming; 1992, U.S. District Court, District of Colorado; 1997, U.S. District Court, District of New Mexico; 2006, U.S. District Court, District of Wyoming; 2006, U.S. Court of Appeals, Tenth Circuit — Member Federal, American, The Colorado and Denver Bar Associations; State Bar of New Mexico; Wyoming State Bar; Defense Research Institute; Colorado Defense Lawyers Association; American Board of Trial Advocates; New Mexico Defense Lawyers Association — E-mail: mah@tucker-holmes.com

Associates

Kurt Henkel — Westminster College, B.A., 1989; University of Denver, J.D., 1992 — Admitted to Bar, 1992, Colorado; 1997, U.S. District Court, District of Colorado — Member The Colorado Bar Association; Colorado Defense Lawyers Association — E-mail: khh@tucker-holmes.com

Leigh C. Anderson — University of Wisconsin, B.S. (magna cum laude), 2002; The University of Tennessee College of Law, J.D., 2005 — Admitted to Bar, 2005, Tennessee; 2006, Colorado; 2006, U.S. District Court, District of Colorado — Member The Colorado and Denver Bar Associations; Colorado Defense Lawyers Association — E-mail: lca@tucker-holmes.com

Nicole L. King — Michigan State University, B.A., 2005; Vanderbilt University Law School, J.D., 2008 — Admitted to Bar, 2009, Colorado; 2009, U.S. District Court, District of Colorado; 2009, U.S. Court of Appeals, Tenth Circuit — Member The Colorado and Denver Bar Associations — E-mail: nlk@tucker-holmes.com

Michael T. Sullivan — The University of Tulsa, B.A., 2009; The University of Tulsa College of Law, J.D. (with highest honors), 2011 — Admitted to Bar, 2012, Colorado; 2014, Wyoming; 2013, U.S. District Court, District of Colorado — Member The Colorado Bar and Arapahoe Bar Associations — E-mail: mts@tucker-holmes.com

Retired

Frederick W. Long

Wheeler Trigg O'Donnell LLP

370 17th Street, Suite 4500
Denver, Colorado 80202-5647
   Telephone: 303-244-1800
   Fax: 303-244-1879
   E-Mail: info@wtotrial.com
   www.wtotrial.com

Established: 1998

Bad Faith, Breach of Contract, Personal Injury Defense, Insurance Defense, Product Liability, Professional Liability

Firm Profile: The insurance lawyers at Denver-based Wheeler Trigg O'Donnell have extensive experience representing many of the nation's largest commercial insurers, several as national or regional counsel, and their insureds at trial and on appeal. We focus our insurance practice on high-exposure litigation, including class actions, mass torts, wrongful death and serious injury cases.

Insurance Clients

Allstate Insurance
USAA

Partners

John M. Vaught — Stephen F. Austin State University, B.S., 1969; St. Mary's University School of Law, J.D. (summa cum laude), 1978 — Admitted to Bar, 1979, Colorado; U.S. District Court, District of Colorado; U.S. Court of Appeals, Tenth Circuit; U.S. Supreme Court — Practice Areas: Complex Insurance Defense; Class Actions; Securities Fraud Class Actions; Corporate Governance Issues; Liability and Director and Officer Insurance Disputes; Trade Secrets; Intellectual Property; Commercial; Antitrust Matters

Terence M. Ridley — University of Pennsylvania, B.A. Political Science (magna cum laude), 1981; University of Denver Sturm College of Law, J.D.,

Wheeler Trigg O'Donnell LLP, Denver, CO (Continued)

1985 — Admitted to Bar, 1985, Colorado; U.S. District Court, District of Colorado; U.S. Court of Appeals, Tenth Circuit; U.S. Supreme Court

Michael D. Alper — University of California, Berkeley, A.B. (with high honors), 1995; Stanford Law School, J.D., 1998 — Admitted to Bar, 1998, California; 2002, Colorado; U.S. District Court, Central and Northern Districts of California; U.S. District Court, District of Colorado; U.S. Court of Appeals, Ninth and Tenth Circuits

Associate

Evan Stephenson

Wood, Ris & Hames, P.C.

1775 Sherman Street, Suite 1600
Denver, Colorado 80203-4313
   Telephone: 303-863-7700
   Fax: 303-830-8772
   www.wrhlaw.com

Established: 1948

Insurance Defense, Civil Litigation, Trial Practice, State and Federal Courts, Corporate Law, Product Liability, Professional Malpractice, Property and Casualty, Construction Law, Workers' Compensation, Environmental Law, Toxic Substances, Coverage Issues, Subrogation

Firm Profile: Founded in 1948, Wood, Ris & Hames, P.C. developed its trademark strength in every area of civil litigation and appellate practice. The firm has grown to provide litigation expertise to both plaintiffs and defendants and also provides a full range of corporate and commercial services encompassing real estate, business, estate planning and insurance matters. The firm continues to evolve in order to better serve its clients.

Insurance Clients

Alliance Insurance Companies
Allied World Assurance Company
Bituminous Insurance Company
Carolina Casualty Insurance Company
Crum & Forster Insurance Group
Equitable General Insurance Company
Farmers Alliance Mutual Insurance Company
Fireman's Fund Insurance Company
Great American Insurance Company
Metropolitan Life Insurance Company
Prudential Insurance Company of America
Security Insurance Group
Southwestern Insurance Group
Transamerica Insurance Company
Union Standard Insurance Company
United States Liability Insurance Group
Allianz Global Corporate & Specialty
Canal Insurance Company
Chartis Insurance
Continental Western Insurance Company
The Equitable Life Assurance Society of the United States
Federated Insurance Company
Federated Mutual Insurance Company
Grange Insurance Association
Jefferson Insurance Group
Liberty Mutual Insurance Company
Mutual Marine Insurance Company
National Indemnity Company
Public Service Mutual Insurance Company
Shand Morahan & Company, Inc.
Stonington Insurance Company
Travelers Insurance Companies
United States Fire Insurance Company
U.S. Insurance Group

Non-Insurance Clients

Ace Pipe Cleaning, Inc./Carylon Corporation
FirstGroup America
Invacare Corporation
ValleyCrest Landscape Companies
The Cheesecake Factory
E & O Professionals
Gallagher Bassett Services, Inc.
OfficeMax Incorporated

Firm Members

Edward L. Wood — (1899-1974)

William K. Ris — (1915-2003)

Eugene S. Hames — (1920-2006)

Charles E. Weaver — 1944 — Washington State University, B.A., 1966; University of Colorado, J.D., 1969 — Admitted to Bar, 1969, Colorado; U.S. Court of Appeals, Tenth Circuit; 1973, U.S. Supreme Court — Member Federal, The Colorado and Denver Bar Associations; International Association of Defense Counsel — E-mail: cweaver@wrhlaw.com

Wood, Ris & Hames, P.C., Denver, CO (Continued)

Mark R. Davis — 1952 — University of Colorado, B.S.B.A., 1975; University of Denver, J.D., 1978 — Admitted to Bar, 1978, Colorado — Member The Colorado and Denver Bar Associations — E-mail: mdavis@wrhlaw.com

William A. Rogers, III — 1962 — Colby College, B.A., 1984; University of Colorado, J.D., 1990 — Admitted to Bar, 1991, Maine; 1992, Colorado — Member The Colorado, Boulder and Denver Bar Associations — E-mail: wrogers@wrhlaw.com

Andrew D. Peterson — 1975 — Iowa State University, B.A., 1998; The University of Iowa, J.D., 2001 — Phi Beta Kappa — Admitted to Bar, 2001, Colorado — Member The Colorado and Denver Bar Associations — E-mail: apeterson@wrhlaw.com

Mark J. Jachimiak — 1972 — Colorado School of Mines, B.S., 1995; University of Colorado, J.D., 1998 — Admitted to Bar, 1998, Colorado; 2000, Wyoming — Member The Colorado and Denver Bar Associations; Wyoming State Bar — E-mail: mjachimiak@wrhlaw.com

Associates

Rachel A. Morris — 1979 — Abilene Christian University, B.S., 2000; University of Nebraska, J.D., 2004 — Admitted to Bar, 2005, Colorado — Member The Colorado and Denver Bar Associations — E-mail: rmorris@wrhlaw.com

Joseph R. Kummer — 1981 — Truman State University, B.S., 2003; Marquette University, J.D., 2006 — Admitted to Bar, 2006, Wisconsin; Colorado — Member The Colorado and Denver Bar Associations — E-mail: jkummer@wrhlaw.com

Brenden L. Loy — 1981 — University of Southern California, B.A., 2003; University of Notre Dame, J.D., 2007 — Admitted to Bar, 2008, Colorado; Tennessee — Member The Colorado and Denver Bar Associations — E-mail: bloy@wrhlaw.com

Andrew K. Lavin — 1981 — Brown University, B.A., 2003; The Ohio State University, J.D., 2009 — Admitted to Bar, 2009, Colorado; U.S. District Court, District of Colorado — Member The Colorado and Denver Bar Associations — E-mail: alavin@wrhlaw.com

Carin J. Ramirez — 1976 — Michigan Technological University, B.S. (summa cum laude), 1998; Michigan State University, B.M., 2004; University of Colorado, J.D., 2010 — Admitted to Bar, 2010, Colorado; 2011, U.S. District Court, District of Colorado — Member The Colorado and Denver Bar Associations — E-mail: cramirez@wrhlaw.com

Mimi M. Tatum — 1983 — The University of Tennessee, B.A. (summa cum laude), 2004; College of William & Mary, M.A. (summa cum laude), 2007; University of Colorado, J.D., 2010 — Admitted to Bar, 2010, Colorado; Wyoming; 2011, U.S. District Court, District of Colorado — Member The Colorado and Denver Bar Associations; Colorado Defense Lawyers Association — E-mail: mtatum@wrhlaw.com

Senior Counsel

Todd E. Mackintosh — 1959 — University of Colorado, B.A., 1983; University of Denver, J.D., 1989 — Admitted to Bar, 1989, Colorado — Member The Colorado and Denver Bar Associations — E-mail: tmackintosh@wrhlaw.com

Of Counsel

F. Michael Ludwig — 1939 — Georgetown University, B.A., 1961; University of Denver, J.D., 1964 — Admitted to Bar, 1964, Colorado — Member The Colorado and Denver Bar Associations; Federation of Insurance Counsel — E-mail: Fmludwig@wrhlaw.com

Donald L. Cook — 1940 — Wittenberg University, B.A., 1962; University of Denver, J.D., 1971; LL.M., 1978 — Admitted to Bar, 1972, Colorado — Member The Colorado and Denver Bar Associations — E-mail: dcook@wrhlaw.com

DURANGO † 16,887 La Plata Co.

Robert C. Duthie, III, P.C.

1010 Main Avenue
Durango, Colorado 81301
   Telephone: 970-247-4545
   Fax: 970-247-4546
   E-Mail: bduthie@trialdurango.com

COLORADO | DURANGO

Robert C. Duthie, III, P.C., Durango, CO (Continued)

Insurance Defense, Automobile, Fire, Construction Law, Accident, First Party Matters, Bad Faith, Casualty, Civil Litigation, Commercial Litigation

Insurance Clients

Capitol Indemnity Corporation
General Accident Insurance Company
Mountain States Insurance Company
Prudential Property and Casualty Insurance Company
State Farm Mutual Automobile Insurance Company
Western Insurance Company
Commercial Union Insurance Company
Great West Casualty Company
National Fire and Marine Insurance Company
State Farm Fire and Casualty Company
United Fire & Casualty Company
United Services Automobile Association (USAA)

Principal

Robert C. Duthie, III — 1952 — University of Colorado, B.A., 1976; M.B.A., 1978; The University of Tulsa, J.D., 1981 — Admitted to Bar, 1982, Colorado; U.S. District Court, District of Colorado — Member The Colorado Bar Association; Colorado Criminal Defense Association

Associate Attorneys

Anthony C. Savastano
Ryan E. Brungard

Paralegal

Kathleen Costello

Evans & Co.

823 East 4th Avenue
Durango, Colorado 81301
Telephone: 970-375-9300
Fax: 877-585-1401
Toll Free: 800-EVANSCO
E-Mail: revans@evanslawfirm.com
www.evanslawfirm.com

(Additional Offices: New Orleans, LA*; Greensboro, NC*; Katy, TX*(See Houston listing); Farmington, NM*; Jackson, WY*)

Established: 1999

Aviation, Comprehensive General Liability, Construction Law, Directors and Officers Liability, Employment Practices Liability, Energy, Environmental Law, Excess and Umbrella, Insurance Coverage, Insurance Defense, Motor Carriers, Oil and Gas, Product Liability, Professional Liability, Property and Casualty, Railroad Law, Toxic Torts

Insurance Clients

Accident Insurance Company
AequiCap Claims Services
All Risk Claims Service, Inc.
American Family Insurance Company
American Hallmark Insurance Services, Inc.
American National Property and Casualty Company
Assicurazioni Generali S.p.A.
Atlantic Casualty Insurance Company
Bituminous Casualty Corporation
Canal Indemnity Company
Claims Management Corporation
CNA Insurance Companies
Colony Insurance Group
Continental Western Group
Deep South Surplus, Inc.
Employers Mutual Casualty Company
Essex Insurance Company
First Financial Insurance Company
Greenwich Insurance Company
ACE Westchester Specialty Group
Allianz Insurance Company
American Ambassador Casualty Company
American Fidelity Insurance Company
American Interstate Insurance Company
Anchor General Insurance Company
Atlantic Mutual Companies
Atlas Insurance Company
Boat/U.S. Marine Insurance
The Cincinnati Insurance Companies
CNA Insurance Company
Construction Insurance Company
COUNTRY Financial
Employers Insurance Company of Wausau
Erie Insurance Group
Farm Family Insurance Companies
General Security Insurance Company

Evans & Co., Durango, CO (Continued)

GuideOne Insurance
Kiln Group
Markel Insurance Company
Mountain States Insurance Group
National Grange Mutual Insurance Company
Ocean Marine Indemnity Insurance Company
Phoenix Aviation Managers, Inc.
Preferred Contractors Insurance Company
St. Paul Fire and Marine Insurance Company
Southern Insurance Company
Texas All Risk General Agency, Inc.
T.H.E. Insurance Company
Transportation Claims, Inc.
Underwriters at Lloyd's, London
Underwriters Service Company, Inc.
United National Insurance Company
United States Liability Insurance Company
Universal Underwriters Insurance Company
Wilshire Insurance Company
Zurich North America
H & W Insurance Services, Inc.
Liberty Insurance Services, Inc.
Meadowbrook Insurance Group
National Farmers Union Property & Casualty Company
Occidental Fire & Casualty Company of North Carolina
Penn National Insurance
Phoenix Indemnity Insurance Company
Professional Insurance Underwriters, Inc.
Shelter Insurance Companies
State National Companies, Inc.
Texas Select Lloyds Insurance Company
Transportation Casualty Insurance Company
Underwriters Indemnity Company
United Educators Insurance
United Fire & Casualty Company
United Specialty Insurance Company
Unitrin Property and Casualty Insurance Group
Virginia Mutual Insurance Company
XL Insurance

Non-Insurance Clients

High Country Transportation, Inc.
SAIA Motor Freight Line, Inc.
Jones Motor Group
United States Postal Service

Attorneys

Robert C. Evans — 1954 — Columbia University, B.A., 1975; University of Maryland, J.D. (with honors), 1980 — Admitted to Bar, 1980, Louisiana; Maryland; 1999, Colorado; 1980, U.S. District Court, Eastern, Middle and Western Districts of Louisiana; U.S. District Court, District of Maryland; U.S. Court of Appeals, Fifth Circuit; 1991, U.S. Court of Appeals, Eleventh Circuit — Member Louisiana State, Maryland State and New Orleans Bar Associations; The Colorado Bar Association; New Orleans Association of Defense Counsel; Louisiana Association of Defense Counsel; Lawyer-Pilots Bar Association; The Maritime Law Association of the United States; Defense Research Institute

Karen M. Worthington — 1959 — Louisiana State University, B.A. (cum laude), 1981; J.D. (with honors), 1984 — Admitted to Bar, 1984, Louisiana; 1984, U.S. District Court, Eastern, Middle and Western Districts of Louisiana; 1984, U.S. Court of Appeals, Fifth Circuit — Member Louisiana State Bar Association

Tonya Johnson Wales — 1967 — The University of Texas, B.B.A., 1990; Southern Methodist University, J.D., 1993 — Admitted to Bar, 1993, Texas; 2000, Colorado

Christopher Graham — The University of Arizona, B.A. Political Science, 1994; Arizona State University College of Law, J.D., 1998 — Admitted to Bar, 1998, Arizona; U.S. District Court, District of Arizona

Of Counsel

James Whitley — 1949 — University of Colorado, B.A., 1971; The University of New Mexico, J.D., 1978 — Admitted to Bar, 1978, New Mexico; 1998, Colorado; 1978, U.S. District Court, District of New Mexico; 1979, U.S. District Court, District of Colorado; U.S. Court of Appeals, Tenth Circuit — Member The Colorado, Southwest Colorado and San Juan County Bar Associations; State Bar of New Mexico

---

The following firms also service this area.

James R. Alvillar & Associates
101 South Third Street, Suite 100
Grand Junction, Colorado 81501
Telephone: 970-241-2500
Fax: 970-245-2312

Automobile, Casualty

SEE COMPLETE LISTING UNDER GRAND JUNCTION, COLORADO (169 MILES)

FORT COLLINS COLORADO

Cain & White, LLP
1555 Quail Lake Loop, Suite 100
Colorado Springs, Colorado 80906
   Telephone: 719-575-0010
   Fax: 719-575-0020
   Toll Free: 877-282-5300

Civil Litigation, Commercial and Business Litigation, Insurance Defense Litigation, Construction Defect Defense Litigation, Bad Faith Insurance Defense Litigation, Municipal & Governmental Liability Defense, Premises Liability Defense, Trucking/Transportation Defense, EUO's/Coverage Opinions, Medical Malpractice Defense, Health Care Entity Defense, Governmental Entity Defense, Products Liability Defense, Commercial/Business Defense

SEE COMPLETE LISTING UNDER COLORADO SPRINGS, COLORADO (313 MILES)

EAGLE † 6,508 Eagle Co.

Refer To
Bayer & Carey, P.C.
1660 Downing Street
Denver, Colorado 80218
   Telephone: 303-830-8911
   Fax: 303-830-8917

Insurance Defense, Automobile Liability, Premises Liability, Construction Liability, Toxic Torts, Wrongful Death, Coverage Issues, Product Liability, Trial Practice, Appellate Practice

SEE COMPLETE LISTING UNDER DENVER, COLORADO (130 MILES)

ENGLEWOOD 30,255 Arapahoe Co.

Refer To
Montgomery Little & Soran, P.C.
The Quadrant
5445 DTC Parkway, Suite 800
Greenwood Village, Colorado 80111
   Telephone: 303-773-8100
   Fax: 303-220-0412

Trial Practice, Appellate Practice, Insurance Defense, Accountants and Attorneys Liability, Architects and Engineers, Design Professionals, Construction Litigation, Legal Malpractice, Environmental Law, Product Liability

SEE COMPLETE LISTING UNDER DENVER, COLORADO (9 MILES)

FORT COLLINS † 143,986 Larimer Co.

Cline Williams
Wright Johnson & Oldfather, L.L.P.

330 South College Avenue
Suite 300
Fort Collins, Colorado 80524
   Telephone: 970-221-2637
   Fax: 970-221-2638

(Lincoln, NE Office*: 233 South 13th Street, 1900 US Bank Building, 68508)
   (Tel: 402-474-6900)
   (Fax: 402-474-5393)
   (www.clinewilliams.com)
(Omaha, NE Office*: One Pacific Place, Suite 600, 1125 South 103rd Street, 68124)
   (Tel: 402-397-1700)
   (Fax: 402-397-1806)
(Aurora, NE Office*: 1207 M Street, 68818, P.O. Box 510, 68818-0510)
   (Tel: 402-694-6314)
   (Fax: 402-694-6315)
(Scottsbluff, NE Office*: 416 Valley View Drive, Suite 304, 69361)
   (Tel: 308-635-1020)
   (Fax: 308-635-7010)

Casualty, Surety, Life Insurance, General Liability, Professional Liability, Property and Casualty, Medical Malpractice, Dental Malpractice

Cline Williams, Wright Johnson & Oldfather, L.L.P., Fort Collins, CO *(Continued)*

Insurance Practice Partners

Tracy A. Oldemeyer — 1971 — Creighton University, B.S.B.A. (magna cum laude), 1993; J.D./M.B.A. (cum laude), 1995 — Admitted to Bar, 1995, Nebraska; 1997, Colorado; 2004, Wyoming — E-mail: toldemeyer@clinewilliams.com

Insurance Practice Associate

Cristin M. Berkhausen — 1981 — Creighton University, B.A. (cum laude), 2003; J.D. (magna cum laude), 2007 — Admitted to Bar, 2007, Nebraska; 2012, Colorado — E-mail: cberkhausen@clinewilliams.com

(See listing under Lincoln, NE for additional information)

Dewhirst & Dolven, LLC

1631 Greenstone Trail
Fort Collins, Colorado 80525
   Telephone: 970-214-9698
   Fax: 303-757-0003
   www.dewhirstdolven.com

(Colorado Springs, CO Office*: 102 South Tejon Street, Suite 500, 80903-2236)
   (Tel: 719-520-1421)
   (Fax: 719-633-3387)
   (E-Mail: jzapf@dewhirstdolven.com)
(Denver, CO Office*: 650 South Cherry Street, Suite 600, 80246)
   (Tel: 303-757-0003)
   (Fax: 303-757-0004)
(Grand Junction, CO Office*: 2695 Patterson Road, Suite 2, #288, 81506)
   (Tel: 970-241-1855)
   (Fax: 970-241-1854)
(Dallas, TX Office*: III Lincoln Centre, 5430 LBJ Freeway, Suite 1200, 75240)
   (Tel: 972-789-9344)
   (Fax: 972-789-9335)
   (Mobile: 970-214-9698)
(Port Isabel, TX Office*: 400 North Yturria Street, 78578)
   (Tel: 956-433-7166)
(Salt Lake City, UT Office*: Suite 103, 2225 East Murray-Holladay Road, 84117)
   (Tel: 801-274-2717)
   (Fax: 801-274-0170)

Insurance Defense, Trial and Appellate Practice, State and Federal Courts, General Liability, Automobile Liability, Construction Defect, Premises Liability, Product Liability, Professional Liability, Medical Malpractice, Dental Malpractice, Employment Law, Directors and Officers Liability, Coverage Issues, Mental Health

Member

Miles M. Dewhirst — University of Nebraska, B.S., 1982; J.D., 1987 — Admitted to Bar, 1987, Colorado; 2008, Utah; 2013, Texas; 1987, U.S. District Court, District of Colorado; 2000, U.S. Court of Appeals, Tenth Circuit — Member The Colorado, El Paso County and Denver Bar Associations; Fellow, Colorado Bar Foundation; Professional Liability Defense Federation; Claims and Litigation Management Alliance; Utah Claims Adjusters Association; Utah Defense Lawyers Association; Council for National Policy; Colorado Defense Lawyers Association; Defense Research Institute; Association of Defense Trial Attorneys — Author: "Colorado Court Uninsured and Underinsured Motorist Decisions," Colorado Claims Association Newsletter, 1994; "Clergy Liability for Sexual Misconduct, Chapter 6 of Clergy Sexual Misconduct: A Systems Approach to Prevention, Intervention and Oversight," Gentle Path Press, 2011 — Intern, The White House, Washington, D.C., 1981; Staff Assistant, U.S. Department of the Interior, Office of the Solicitor, Washington, D.C., 1982-1983; Staff Assistant, U.S. Department of Justice, Land and Natural Resources Division, Environmental Enforcement Section, Washington, D.C., 1983-1984; Speaker: National Federation of Independent Business, Colorado Small Business Conference, 2002; "Informed Consent," Dentists' Professional Liability Trust Board of Directors Meeting, 2001; "Court Rulings Affecting Colorado's No-Fault Act," Colorado Claims

COLORADO

Dewhirst & Dolven, LLC, Fort Collins, CO   (Continued)

Association Spring Meeting, 1998: Board of Directors Chair, Big Brothers Big Sisters, Pikes Peak Region; Foundation Board Member, Goodwill Industries of Colorado Springs; Leadership Program of the Rockies (LPR) — E-mail: mdewhirst@dewhirstdolven.com

Special Counsel

George H. Parker — 1956 — Texas A&M University, B.A., 1986; University of Houston Law Center, J.D., 1988 — Admitted to Bar, 1989, Texas; 1992, Colorado; 1992, U.S. District Court, District of Colorado; 2004, U.S. Supreme Court — Member The Colorado Bar Association; Claims and Litigation Management Alliance; Colorado Defense Lawyers Association — Texas Peace Officer — Advanced Mediator — E-mail: gparker@dewhirstdolven.com

(See listing under Colorado Springs, CO for additional information)

The following firms also service this area.

Bayer & Carey, P.C.
1660 Downing Street
Denver, Colorado 80218
 Telephone: 303-830-8911
 Fax: 303-830-8917

Insurance Defense, Automobile Liability, Premises Liability, Construction Liability, Toxic Torts, Wrongful Death, Coverage Issues, Product Liability, Trial Practice, Appellate Practice

SEE COMPLETE LISTING UNDER DENVER, COLORADO (63 MILES)

Cain & White, LLP
1555 Quail Lake Loop, Suite 100
Colorado Springs, Colorado 80906
 Telephone: 719-575-0010
 Fax: 719-575-0020
 Toll Free: 877-282-5300

Civil Litigation, Commercial and Business Litigation, Insurance Defense Litigation, Construction Defect Defense Litigation, Bad Faith Insurance Defense Litigation, Municipal & Governmental Liability Defense, Premises Liability Defense, Trucking/Transportation Defense, EUO's/Coverage Opinions, Medical Malpractice Defense, Health Care Entity Defense, Governmental Entity Defense, Products Liability Defense, Commercial/Business Defense

SEE COMPLETE LISTING UNDER COLORADO SPRINGS, COLORADO (137 MILES)

Montgomery Little & Soran, P.C.
The Quadrant
5445 DTC Parkway, Suite 800
Greenwood Village, Colorado 80111
 Telephone: 303-773-8100
 Fax: 303-220-0412

Trial Practice, Appellate Practice, Insurance Defense, Accountants and Attorneys Liability, Architects and Engineers, Design Professionals, Construction Litigation, Legal Malpractice, Environmental Law, Product Liability

SEE COMPLETE LISTING UNDER DENVER, COLORADO (63 MILES)

FORT MORGAN   † 11,315 Morgan Co.

Refer To

Montgomery Little & Soran, P.C.
The Quadrant
5445 DTC Parkway, Suite 800
Greenwood Village, Colorado 80111
 Telephone: 303-773-8100
 Fax: 303-220-0412

Trial Practice, Appellate Practice, Insurance Defense, Accountants and Attorneys Liability, Architects and Engineers, Design Professionals, Construction Litigation, Legal Malpractice, Environmental Law, Product Liability

SEE COMPLETE LISTING UNDER DENVER, COLORADO (80 MILES)

FORT MORGAN

GLENWOOD SPRINGS   † 9,614 Garfield Co.

Refer To

Bayer & Carey, P.C.
1660 Downing Street
Denver, Colorado 80218
 Telephone: 303-830-8911
 Fax: 303-830-8917

Insurance Defense, Automobile Liability, Premises Liability, Construction Liability, Toxic Torts, Wrongful Death, Coverage Issues, Product Liability, Trial Practice, Appellate Practice

SEE COMPLETE LISTING UNDER DENVER, COLORADO (150 MILES)

GRAND JUNCTION   † 58,566 Mesa Co.

Frederick G. Aldrich LLC

601A 28-1/4 Road
Grand Junction, Colorado 81506
 Telephone: 970-245-7950
 Fax: 970-245-0664

Insurance Defense, Self-Insured Defense, Commercial Law, Premises Liability, Automobile, Employment Law, Workers' Compensation, Commercial General Liability, Construction Law, Land Development, Water Rigths

Insurance Clients

Liberty Mutual Insurance

Non-Insurance Clients

Central Distributing Company	City Market, Inc.
EnCana Oil & Gas (USA) Inc.	Grand Valley Irrigation Company
The Kroger Co.	Monument Homes Development
Sedgwick CMS	Company, LLC

Frederick G. Aldrich — 1946 — University of Washington, B.A., 1970; University of Colorado, J.D., 1973 — Admitted to Bar, 1973, Colorado; 1988, Washington; 1973, U.S. District Court, District of Colorado; 1976, U.S. Court of Appeals, Tenth Circuit; 2001, U.S. District Court, Central District of Illinois — Member American, Washington State, The Colorado (Board of Governors, 1991-1993) and Mesa County (President, 1990-1991) Bar Associations

James R. Alvillar & Associates

101 South Third Street, Suite 100
Grand Junction, Colorado 81501
 Telephone: 970-241-2500
 Fax: 970-245-2312
 E-Mail: ajr21@qwestoffice.net

Automobile, Casualty

Firm Profile: James R. Alvillar & Associates has represented insurers and their insureds throughout western Colorado for over 30 years. Counsel and staff have extensive experience in all aspects of litigation, including jury trials, arbitration and mediation.

Insurance Clients

Allstate Insurance Company	Mountain States Mutual Casualty
National Interstate Insurance	Company
Company	State Farm Fire and Casualty
State Farm Life Insurance	Company
Company	State Farm Mutual Automobile
United Fire & Casualty Company	Insurance Company
Westport Insurance Company	

Non-Insurance Clients

Greyhound Lines, Inc.

LITTLETON   COLORADO

James R. Alvillar & Associates, Grand Junction, CO
(Continued)

Firm Member

James R. Alvillar, Esq. — 1943 — University of California, Berkeley, A.B., 1970; University of California, Boalt Hall School of Law, J.D., 1973 — Admitted to Bar, 1973, Colorado; Illinois and Kansas Bar pro hac vice; 1974, U.S. District Court, District of Colorado — Deputy District Attorney Mesa County, 1974-1982

Dewhirst & Dolven, LLC

2695 Patterson Road, Suite 2, #288
Grand Junction, Colorado 81506
    Telephone: 970-241-1855
    Fax: 970-241-1854
    www.dewhirstdolven.com

(Colorado Springs, CO Office*: 102 South Tejon Street, Suite 500, 80903-2236)
    (Tel: 719-520-1421)
    (Fax: 719-633-3387)
    (E-Mail: jzapf@dewhirstdolven.com)
(Denver, CO Office*: 650 South Cherry Street, Suite 600, 80246)
    (Tel: 303-757-0003)
    (Fax: 303-757-0004)
(Fort Collins, CO Office*: 1631 Greenstone Trail, 80525)
    (Tel: 970-214-9698)
    (Fax: 303-757-0003)
(Dallas, TX Office*: III Lincoln Centre, 5430 LBJ Freeway, Suite 1200, 75240)
    (Tel: 972-789-9344)
    (Fax: 972-789-9335)
    (Mobile: 970-214-9698)
(Port Isabel, TX Office*: 400 North Yturria Street, 78578)
    (Tel: 956-433-7166)
(Salt Lake City, UT Office*: Suite 103, 2225 East Murray-Holladay Road, 84117)
    (Tel: 801-274-2717)
    (Fax: 801-274-0170)

Insurance Defense, Trial and Appellate Practice, State and Federal Courts, General Liability, Automobile Liability, Construction Defect, Premises Liability, Product Liability, Professional Liability, Medical Malpractice, Dental Malpractice, Employment Law, Directors and Officers Liability, Coverage Issues, Mental Health

Members

Miles M. Dewhirst — University of Nebraska, B.S., 1982; J.D., 1987 — Admitted to Bar, 1987, Colorado; 2008, Utah; 2013, Texas; 1987, U.S. District Court, District of Colorado; 2000, U.S. Court of Appeals, Tenth Circuit — Member The Colorado, El Paso County and Denver Bar Associations; Fellow, Colorado Bar Foundation; Professional Liability Defense Federation; Claims and Litigation Management Alliance; Utah Claims Adjusters Association; Utah Defense Lawyers Association; Council for National Policy; Colorado Defense Lawyers Association; Defense Research Institute; Association of Defense Trial Attorneys — Author: "Colorado Court Uninsured and Underinsured Motorist Decisions," Colorado Claims Association Newsletter, 1994; "Clergy Liability for Sexual Misconduct, Chapter 6 of Clergy Sexual Misconduct: A Systems Approach to Prevention, Intervention and Oversight," Gentle Path Press, 2011 — Intern, The White House, Washington, D.C., 1981; Staff Assistant, U.S. Department of the Interior, Office of the Solicitor, Washington, D.C., 1982-1983; Staff Assistant, U.S. Department of Justice, Land and Natural Resources Division, Environmental Enforcement Section, Washington, D.C., 1983-1984; Speaker: National Federation of Independent Business, Colorado Small Business Conference, 2002; "Informed Consent," Dentists' Professional Liability Trust Board of Directors Meeting, 2001; "Court Rulings Affecting Colorado's No-Fault Act," Colorado Claims Association Spring Meeting, 1998: Board of Directors Chair, Big Brothers Big Sisters, Pikes Peak Region; Foundation Board Member, Goodwill Industries of Colorado Springs; Leadership Program of the Rockies (LPR) — E-mail: mdewhirst@dewhirstdolven.com

Rick N. Haderlie — 1968 — Westminster College, B.A., 1996; The University of Montana, J.D., 2000 — Admitted to Bar, 2001, Nevada; 2002, Utah; 2003, Arizona; 2004, Colorado; 2006, Wyoming; New Mexico; 2001, U.S. District

Dewhirst & Dolven, LLC, Grand Junction, CO
(Continued)

Court, District of Nevada — Member The Colorado and El Paso County Bar Associations; State Bar of Arizona; State Bar of Nevada; Wyoming State Bar; State Bar of New Mexico; Utah Claims Adjusters Association; Utah Defense Lawyers Association; Claims and Litigation Management Alliance; Wyoming Claims Association — Certified, Trial Advocacy Skills, 2004; Insurance Agent and Broker — E-mail: rhaderlie@dewhirstdolven.com

(See listing under Colorado Springs, CO for additional information)

The following firms also service this area.

Cain & White, LLP
1555 Quail Lake Loop, Suite 100
Colorado Springs, Colorado 80906
    Telephone: 719-575-0010
    Fax: 719-575-0020
    Toll Free: 877-282-5300

Civil Litigation, Commercial and Business Litigation, Insurance Defense Litigation, Construction Defect Defense Litigation, Bad Faith Insurance Defense Litigation, Municipal & Governmental Liability Defense, Premises Liability Defense, Trucking/Transportation Defense, EUO's/Coverage Opinions, Medical Malpractice Defense, Health Care Entity Defense, Governmental Entity Defense, Products Liability Defense, Commercial/Business Defense

SEE COMPLETE LISTING UNDER COLORADO SPRINGS, COLORADO (315 MILES)

Evans & Co.
823 East 4th Avenue
Durango, Colorado 81301
    Telephone: 970-375-9300
    Fax: 877-585-1401
    Toll Free: 800-EVANSCO

Aviation, Comprehensive General Liability, Construction Law, Directors and Officers Liability, Employment Practices Liability, Energy, Environmental Law, Excess and Umbrella, Insurance Coverage, Insurance Defense, Motor Carriers, Oil and Gas, Product Liability, Professional Liability, Property and Casualty, Railroad Law, Toxic Torts

SEE COMPLETE LISTING UNDER DURANGO, COLORADO (168 MILES)

GREELEY † 92,889 Weld Co.

Refer To
Cain & White, LLP
1555 Quail Lake Loop, Suite 100
Colorado Springs, Colorado 80906
    Telephone: 719-575-0010
    Fax: 719-575-0020
    Toll Free: 877-282-5300

Civil Litigation, Commercial and Business Litigation, Insurance Defense Litigation, Construction Defect Defense Litigation, Bad Faith Insurance Defense Litigation, Municipal & Governmental Liability Defense, Premises Liability Defense, Trucking/Transportation Defense, EUO's/Coverage Opinions, Medical Malpractice Defense, Health Care Entity Defense, Governmental Entity Defense, Products Liability Defense, Commercial/Business Defense

SEE COMPLETE LISTING UNDER COLORADO SPRINGS, COLORADO (137 MILES)

LITTLETON † 41,737 Arapahoe Co.

Hensen & Cook-Olson, LLC

1510 West Canal Covit, Suite 1500
Littleton, Colorado 80120
    Telephone: 720-316-7156
    Telephone: 720-664-5464
    Fax: 720-664-6465
    E-Mail: shensen@hco-law.com

Defense Litigation, Medical Malpractice

Firm Profile: At Hensen & Cook-Olson, LLC, our goal is to provide the top-quality legal representation and personal attention that our clients deserve.

COLORADO MONTROSE

Hensen & Cook-Olson, LLC, Littleton, CO (Continued)

Our experienced lawyers provide you with the time, compassion, and determination you need to successfully handle your case.

Insurance Clients

Copic Insurance Company
Kaiser Foundation Health Plan, Inc.

Firm Members

Stephen J. Hensen — Colorado State University, B.S., 1984; Gonzaga University School of Law, J.D. (magna cum laude), 1987 — Admitted to Bar, 1987, Colorado; U.S. District Court, District of Colorado; 1989, U.S. Court of Appeals, Tenth Circuit; 1994, U.S. Supreme Court — Member Denver Bar Association (Ethics Committee); Colorado Supreme Court Bar Committee — E-mail: shensen@hco-law.com

Amy E. Cook-Olson — Millikin University, B.A., 1992; University of Denver, J.D., 1996 — Admitted to Bar, 1996, Colorado; 1997, Illinois; U.S. District Court, District of Colorado; U.S. Court of Appeals, Tenth Circuit — Member The Colorado Bar Association; Colorado Defense Lawyers Association

Special Counsel

C. Todd Drake — University of Illinois, B.A., 1990; University of Colorado at Boulder, J.D., 1996 — Admitted to Bar, 1996, Colorado; 1997, U.S. District Court, District of Colorado; U.S. Court of Appeals, Tenth Circuit — Member The Colorado (Interprofessional Committee) and Denver Bar Associations

Associate

Jessie M. Fischer — University of Colorado, B.A. (with honors and distinction), 2004; University of Denver, J.D., 2007 — Admitted to Bar, 2007, Colorado; U.S. District Court, District of Colorado; U.S. Court of Appeals, Tenth Circuit — Member The Colorado Bar Association; Colorado Defense Lawyers Association

Sutton | Booker P.C.

26 West Dry Creek Circle, Suite 375
Littleton, Colorado 80120
Telephone: 303-730-6204
Fax: 303-730-6208
E-Mail: dsutton@suttonbooker.com
www.suttonbooker.com

Personal Injury, Insurance Coverage, Bad Faith, Premises Liability, Construction, Products

Firm Profile: The lawyers of Sutton|Booker have extensive trial experience representing individuals, businesses and insurance companies. The firm has special expertise in personal injury, products liability, insurance coverage, bad faith, construction litigation and premises liability.

Insurance Clients

American Family Mutual Insurance Company
CNA
State Farm Mutual Automobile Insurance Company
American Standard Insurance Company
The Navigators Group, Inc.

Managing Attorney

Debra K. Sutton — Arkansas State University, B.S., 1976; University of Arkansas School of Law, J.D., 1983 — Admitted to Bar, 1984, Colorado — Member American, Colorado and Arapahoe County Bar Associations; Colorado Defense Lawyers Association, Former Board Member; Defense Research Institute; American Board of Trial Advocates

Partner

Jacquelyn S. Booker — Louisiana State University, B.A., 1997; University of Denver College of Law, J.D., 2000 — Admitted to Bar, 2000, Colorado — Member American, Colorado and Arapahoe County Bar Associations; Colorado Defense Lawyers Association

Associates

Scott C. James — The University of Iowa, B.B.A., 2007; University of Denver Sturm College of Law, J.D., 2010 — Admitted to Bar, 2010, Colorado —

Sutton | Booker P.C., Littleton, CO (Continued)

Member American, Colorado, Iowa State and Arapahoe County Bar Associations; Colorado Defense Lawyers Association

Katie B. Johnson — Pepperdine University, B.A. (magna cum laude), 2006; DePaul University College of Law, J.D. (summa cum laude), 2010 — Admitted to Bar, 2010, Colorado — Member American, Colorado, Colorado Women's and Denver County Bar Associations; Faculty of Federal Advocates

Ashley Larson — The University of Texas at Austin, B.S., 2006; University of Denver Sturm College of Law, J.D., 2011 — Admitted to Bar, 2011, Colorado

Of Counsel

Bruce B. McLarty — Western State College of Colorado, B.A. (summa cum laude), 1980; M.A., 1983; University of Denver College of Law, J.D., 1986 — Admitted to Bar, 1986, Colorado — Member Colorado and Denver Bar Associations; Colorado Defense Lawyers Association; Defense Research Institute

MONTROSE † 19,132 Montrose Co.

Refer To

Evans & Co.
823 East 4th Avenue
Durango, Colorado 81301
Telephone: 970-375-9300
Fax: 877-585-1401
Toll Free: 800-EVANSCO

Aviation, Comprehensive General Liability, Construction Law, Directors and Officers Liability, Employment Practices Liability, Energy, Environmental Law, Excess and Umbrella, Insurance Coverage, Insurance Defense, Motor Carriers, Oil and Gas, Product Liability, Professional Liability, Property and Casualty, Railroad Law, Toxic Torts

SEE COMPLETE LISTING UNDER DURANGO, COLORADO (107 MILES)

PAGOSA SPRINGS † 1,727 Archuleta Co.

Refer To

Evans & Co.
823 East 4th Avenue
Durango, Colorado 81301
Telephone: 970-375-9300
Fax: 877-585-1401
Toll Free: 800-EVANSCO

Aviation, Comprehensive General Liability, Construction Law, Directors and Officers Liability, Employment Practices Liability, Energy, Environmental Law, Excess and Umbrella, Insurance Coverage, Insurance Defense, Motor Carriers, Oil and Gas, Product Liability, Professional Liability, Property and Casualty, Railroad Law, Toxic Torts

SEE COMPLETE LISTING UNDER DURANGO, COLORADO (61 MILES)

PUEBLO † 106,595 Pueblo Co.

Refer To

Cain & White, LLP
1555 Quail Lake Loop, Suite 100
Colorado Springs, Colorado 80906
Telephone: 719-575-0010
Fax: 719-575-0020
Toll Free: 877-282-5300

Civil Litigation, Commercial and Business Litigation, Insurance Defense Litigation, Construction Defect Defense Litigation, Bad Faith Insurance Defense Litigation, Municipal & Governmental Liability Defense, Premises Liability Defense, Trucking/Transportation Defense, EUO's/Coverage Opinions, Medical Malpractice Defense, Health Care Entity Defense, Governmental Entity Defense, Products Liability Defense, Commercial/Business Defense

SEE COMPLETE LISTING UNDER COLORADO SPRINGS, COLORADO (42 MILES)

VAIL　　　　　　　　　　　　　　　　　　　　　　　　　　　　　　COLORADO

STEAMBOAT SPRINGS † 12,088 Routt Co.
Refer To

Cain & White, LLP
1555 Quail Lake Loop, Suite 100
Colorado Springs, Colorado 80906
　Telephone: 719-575-0010
　Fax: 719-575-0020
　Toll Free: 877-282-5300

Civil Litigation, Commercial and Business Litigation, Insurance Defense Litigation, Construction Defect Defense Litigation, Bad Faith Insurance Defense Litigation, Municipal & Governmental Liability Defense, Premises Liability Defense, Trucking/Transportation Defense, EUO's/Coverage Opinions, Medical Malpractice Defense, Health Care Entity Defense, Governmental Entity Defense, Products Liability Defense, Commercial/Business Defense

SEE COMPLETE LISTING UNDER COLORADO SPRINGS, COLORADO (227 MILES)

TELLURIDE † 2,325 San Miguel Co.
Refer To

Evans & Co.
823 East 4th Avenue
Durango, Colorado 81301
　Telephone: 970-375-9300
　Fax: 877-585-1401
　Toll Free: 800-EVANSCO

Aviation, Comprehensive General Liability, Construction Law, Directors and Officers Liability, Employment Practices Liability, Energy, Environmental Law, Excess and Umbrella, Insurance Coverage, Insurance Defense, Motor Carriers, Oil and Gas, Product Liability, Professional Liability, Property and Casualty, Railroad Law, Toxic Torts

SEE COMPLETE LISTING UNDER DURANGO, COLORADO (121 MILES)

VAIL 5,305 Eagle Co.
Refer To

Deisch, Marion & Klaus, P.C.
851 Clarkson Street
Denver, Colorado 80218-3205
　Telephone: 303-837-1122
　Fax: 303-832-6750

Insurance Defense, Casualty, Errors and Omissions, Professional Liability, Municipal Liability, Product Liability, Subrogation

SEE COMPLETE LISTING UNDER DENVER, COLORADO (97 MILES)

CONNECTICUT

CAPITAL: HARTFORD

COUNTIES

Fairfield
Hartford
Litchfield

Middlesex
New Haven
New London

Tolland
Windham

Our files contain additional verified data on the firms listed herein. This additional information is available on request.

A.M. BEST COMPANY

CONNECTICUT — BRIDGEPORT

BRIDGEPORT 144,229 Fairfield Co.

Berchem, Moses & Devlin, PC

75 Broad Street
Milford, Connecticut 06460
Telephone: 203-783-1200
Fax: 203-878-4912
Mobile: 203-530-8724
E-Mail: rbuturla@bmdlaw.com
www.bmdlaw.com

(Westport, CT Office: 27 Imperial Avenue, 06880)

Established: 1933

Insurance Defense, Automobile, Bad Faith, Common Carrier, Construction Liability, Environmental Liability, Governmental Liability, Hospitals, Legal Malpractice, Municipal Liability, Medical Malpractice, Professional Malpractice, Trial Practice, Workers' Compensation, Premises Liability, Liquor Liability, Civil Rights, Employment Practices Liability, Police Liability Defense

Firm Profile: The Litigation Department is chaired by Richard J. Buturla with seven other attorneys who litigate in all State and Federal Courts in Connecticut as well as Workers' Compensation Commission. The firm also practices in the areas of Land Use, Environmental, Real Estate, Commercial and Corporate Law, the Commission of Human Rights and Opportunity, and the Equal Employment Opportunity Commission.

Insurance Clients

Acceptance Insurance Company
AIG Insurance Company
Alterra Specialty Insurance Company
Amerisure Insurance Company
Argonaut Insurance Company
Berkshire Mutual Insurance Company
CIGNA Property and Casualty Insurance Company
Crum & Forster Insurance
The Dodson Group
Employers Insurance Company of Wausau
Farmers Insurance Company
Gulf Insurance Group
Holyoke Mutual Insurance Company in Salem
John Hancock Property and Casualty Insurance Company
Metropolitan Insurance Company
National Casualty Company
Norfolk and Dedham Mutual Fire Insurance Company
Penn-America Group, Inc.
Pennsylvania Lumbermens Mutual Insurance Company
Preferred Mutual Insurance Company
Prudential Property and Casualty Insurance Company
Safeco Insurance Companies
Security Insurance Group
Transamerica Group/AEGON USA, Inc.
Tri-State Consumer Insurance Company
Utica Mutual Insurance Company
Vermont Mutual Insurance Company
Affiliated FM Insurance Company
Allstate Insurance Company
American Family Mutual Insurance Company
Andover Group
Bankers and Shippers Insurance Company
Chrysler Insurance Company
Colonial Penn Insurance Company
Connecticut Interlocal Risk Management Agency (CIRMA)
Empire Fire and Marine Insurance Company
Erie Insurance Company
Fitchburg Mutual Insurance Company
Interstate Insurance Group
Jefferson Insurance Company
Lexington Insurance Company
Liberty International Underwriters
Michigan Mutual Insurance Company
Pawtucket Insurance Company
Peerless Insurance Company
Penn Millers Insurance Company
Pioneer Insurance Company
PMA Companies, Inc.
Providence Washington Insurance Companies
Puritan Insurance Company
Quincy Mutual Fire Insurance Company
Sentry Insurance a Mutual Company
Transport Insurance Company
United Capitol Insurance Company
United States Aviation Underwriters, Inc.
Zurich North America

Non-Insurance Clients

A.I. Transport
American International Adjustment Company
Caronia Corporation
Certified Claims Corporation
Allied Van Lines
Aviation Adjustment Bureau
Carolina Freight Carriers Corporation
Charlotte Adjusting, Inc.

Berchem, Moses & Devlin, PC, Bridgeport, CT
(Continued)

Claims Management, Inc.
Corporate Claims Management, Inc.
Crawford & Company
GAB Robins North America, Inc.
Gallagher Bassett Services, Inc.
Kellogg Company
The MacDonald Companies, Inc.
Marine Office of America Corporation (MOAC)
Network Adjusters, Inc.
Pathmark Stores, Inc.
Professional Claims Managers, Inc.
Ryder Transportation, Inc.
Scott Wetzel Services, Inc.
Specialty Risk Services, Inc. (SRS)
United States Airlines, Inc.
Constitution State Service Company
CorVel Corporation
Cunningham Lindsey Claims Management, Inc.
GatesMcDonald
Kemper Environmental Ltd.
Mahle Trumbull Plant
Marriott International, Inc.
National Car Rental
Nygren & Nygren, Inc.
Peter Pan Bus Lines
RSKCo
Safety Marking Inc.
Sedgwick Group
Underwriters Adjusting Company
Warnaco Group

Firm Members

Richard J. Buturla — 1957 — Southern Connecticut State College, B.S. (magna cum laude), 1979; Villanova University, J.D., 1982 — Associate Editor, Villanova Law Review, 1981-1982 — Admitted to Bar, 1982, Connecticut; 1982, U.S. District Court, District of Connecticut; 1982, U.S. Court of Appeals, Second Circuit — Member American and Connecticut Bar Associations; Connecticut Trial Lawyers Association; Association of Trial Lawyers of America — Town Council Chairman, Stratford, Connecticut, 1987-1989; Corporate Counsel, Derby, Connecticut, 1997-2005; Town Attorney, Cheshire, Connecticut, 2002-2003; Assistant Town Attorney, Stratford, Connecticut, 2000-2004; Town Attorney, Stratford, Connecticut, 2005-2009; Town Counsel, Seymour, Connecticut, 2011-present — Practice Areas: Trial Practice; Municipal Law; Insurance Defense — E-mail: rbuturla@bmdlaw.com

Jonathan D. Berchem — 1969 — Fairfield University, B.A., 1992; Syracuse University, J.D., 1995 — Admitted to Bar, 1995, Connecticut; 1995, Pennsylvania; 1999, U.S. Supreme Court — Member American, Connecticut and Milford Bar Associations — Town Attorney, Milford, Connecticut (2013-Present) — E-mail: jberchem@bmdlaw.com

Warren L. Holcomb — 1950 — Butler University; University of Connecticut at Storrs, B.A., 1972; Southwestern University School of Law, J.D., 1977 — Admitted to Bar, 1977, California; 1993, Connecticut; 1994, U.S. District Court, District of Connecticut — Member American and Connecticut Bar Associations; State Bar of California — E-mail: wholcomb@bmdlaw.com

Bryan L. LeClerc — 1962 — Fairfield University, B.A., 1984; University of Connecticut School of Law, J.D. (with honors), 1987 — Admitted to Bar, 1987, Connecticut; 1988, New York; 1987, U.S. District Court, District of Connecticut; 1993, U.S. District Court, Southern District of New York; 1996, U.S. Supreme Court; 2014, U.S. District Court, Eastern District of New York — Member American, Connecticut, Bridgeport and Milford Bar Associations; Connecticut Trial Lawyers Association — Fairfield Town Plan & Zoning Commission, 2007-2013, Chairman; Member, Town of Fairfield Representative Town Meeting, 1989-2007; Connecticut Yankee Council BSA, Vice President- Legal and General Counsel- 2013-Present — E-mail: bleclerc@bmdlaw.com

Brian W. Smith — 1957 — University at Buffalo, B.A. (magna cum laude), 1978; Duke University, J.D., 1981 — Phi Alpha Delta — Admitted to Bar, 1981, Connecticut; 1982, U.S. District Court, District of Connecticut — Member American, Connecticut, Milford and Bridgeport Bar Associations; American Trial Lawyers Association; Connecticut Defense Lawyers Association — Seminar Faculty: Trial Practice Seminar, Connecticut Trial Lawyers Association, 1996-Present — E-mail: bsmith@bmdlaw.com

Richard C. Buturla — 1985 — Quinnipiac University, B.A. (magna cum laude), 2007; Western New England College School of Law, J.D., 2010 — Admitted to Bar, 2010, Connecticut — E-mail: rcbuturla@bmdlaw.com

Ryan P. Driscoll — 1978 — University of Connecticut at Storrs, B.A., 2000; Seton Hall University School of Law, J.D., 2003 — Admitted to Bar, 2003, New Jersey; 2004, Connecticut; 2006, New York — Member Connecticut Bar Association — E-mail: rdriscoll@bmdlaw.com

Coles, Baldwin & Kaiser, LLC

1261 Post Road, First Floor
Fairfield, Connecticut 06824
   Telephone: 203-319-0800
   Fax: 203-319-1210
   E-Mail: kcoles@cbklaw.net
   www.cbklaw.net

Established: 1996

Insurance Defense, Casualty, First Party Matters, Professional Malpractice, Workers' Compensation, Coverage Issues, Employment Law, Discrimination, Sexual Harassment, Municipal Liability, Governmental Liability, Life and Health, Americans with Disabilities Act, Advertising Injury, Agent and Brokers Errors and Omissions, Arson, Asbestos Litigation, Automobile Liability, Bad Faith, Bodily Injury, Business Law, Carrier Defense, Casualty Insurance Law, Commercial General Liability, Construction Accidents, Construction Litigation, Declaratory Judgments, Directors and Officers Liability, ERISA, Employment Discrimination, Equal Employment Opportunity Commission, Examinations Under Oath, Fire and Allied Lines, Inland Marine, Insurance Coverage, Law Enforcement Liability, Legal Malpractice, Municipal Law, Personal Lines, Premises Liability, Professional Liability, Property and Casualty, Self-Insured Defense, Special Investigative Unit Claims, Uninsured and Underinsured Motorist, Fair Housing Act

Insurance Clients

Admiral Insurance Company	AIG Insurance Company
Allstate Insurance Company	CIT Healthcare, LLC
CNA Insurance Company	Connecticut Interlocal Risk
Continental Insurance Company	Management Agency (CIRMA)
Essex Insurance Company	Housing Authority Risk Retention
Investors Insurance Company of	Group, Inc.
America	Liberty Mutual Fire Insurance
Nautilus Insurance Company	Company
Seneca Insurance Company, Inc.	

Non-Insurance Clients

Aon Risk Services, Inc.	City of Bristol
City of Middletown	City of Milford
City of Shelton	Claims Management, Inc.
Crawford & Company	GAB Robins North America, Inc.
GatesMcDonald	The MacDonald Companies, Inc.
Marriott Claims Service	Marriott International, Inc.
Norwalk Housing Authority	RSKCo
Sedgwick Group of Connecticut,	Torrington Housing Authority
Inc.	Town of Fairfield
Wal-Mart Stores, Inc.	

Members

Kevin A. Coles — 1947 — Georgetown University, B.S.B.A., 1970; University of Houston, J.D., 1974 — American Jurisprudence Award (Tort); Order of the Barons — Admitted to Bar, 1974, Connecticut; 1974, U.S. District Court, District of Connecticut; 1977, U.S. Supreme Court; 1979, U.S. Court of Appeals, Second Circuit; 2009, U.S. Bankruptcy Court — Member Connecticut and Bridgeport (Former Chairman, Civil Litigation Committee) Bar Associations; Connecticut Trial Lawyers Association

James T. Baldwin — 1962 — The George Washington University, B.S., 1987; University of Bridgeport, J.D., 1990 — Admitted to Bar, 1990, Connecticut; 1990, U.S. District Court, District of Connecticut — Member Connecticut and Bridgeport Bar Associations (Litigation and Workers' Compensation Sections) — Executive Board Member, Quinnipiac University School of Law

John B. Kaiser — 1964 — New York University, B.A., 1987; American University, J.D., 1991 — Admitted to Bar, 1991, Connecticut; 2003, Massachusetts; 2002, U.S. District Court, District of Connecticut; 2004, U.S. District Court, District of Massachusetts — Languages: French

Associate

Catherine L. Creager — 1961 — Western Kentucky University, B.A. (magna cum laude), 1983; Carnegie Mellon University, M.A.M., 1989; Quinnipiac College, J.D., 2000 — Admitted to Bar, 2000, Connecticut; 2002, U.S. District Court, District of Connecticut

Coles, Baldwin & Kaiser, LLC, Bridgeport, CT
(Continued)
Of Counsel

David M. McHugh — 1939 — Fairfield University, B.S.S., 1962; University of Connecticut, J.D., 1965 — Admitted to Bar, 1966, Connecticut; 1985, Massachusetts; 1969, U.S. District Court, District of Connecticut; U.S. Court of Appeals, Second Circuit; U.S. Supreme Court — Author: "A Practical Guide To Estate Planning," 2000-2001

Candace Fay — 1979 — University of Connecticut, B.A., 2001; University of Connecticut School of Law, J.D., 2007 — Admitted to Bar, 2007, Connecticut; New York; U.S. District Court, District of Connecticut; U.S. District Court, Eastern and Southern Districts of New York; U.S. Court of Appeals, Second Circuit; U.S. Supreme Court — Member American, Connecticut, Fairfield County and Danbury Bar Associations; Connecticut Inns of Court

Martin McCann — 1958 — Fairfield University, B.S., 1980; Quinnipiac University School of Law, J.D., 1991 — Admitted to Bar, 1992, Connecticut; 1993, New York; U.S. District Court, District of Connecticut; U.S. Tax Court — Member American and Connecticut Bar Associations; The American Institute of Attorney-Certified Public Accountants; James Cooper Fellow, Connecticut Bar Foundation — AV-Rated, Martindale-Hubbell — Certified Public Accountant, State of Connecticut (1986)

Lynne G. Rozen — University of Pennsylvania, B.A., 1970; Quinnipiac University School of Law, J.D., 1987 — Admitted to Bar, 1987, Connecticut; 1991, U.S. District Court, District of Connecticut

Goldstein and Peck, P.C.

1087 Broad Street
Bridgeport, Connecticut 06604
   Telephone: 203-334-9421
   Fax: 203-334-6949
   E-Mail: info@goldsteinandpeck.com
   www.goldsteinandpeck.com

Established: 1975

Insurance Defense, Insurance Coverage, Property and Casualty, Automobile Liability, Premises Liability, Fire, Fraud, Investigations, Uninsured and Underinsured Motorist, Arbitration, Medical Malpractice, Legal Malpractice, Product Liability, Municipal Liability, Trial Practice, Appellate Practice

Firm Profile: Goldstein and Peck, P.C. continues a tradition of excellence in the practice of law started by David Goldstein (1898-1992) as a sole practitioner over eighty years ago. The firm itself has been in continuous existence for over fifty years. While the firm generally serves the needs of clients in Connecticut, and particularly southwestern Connecticut, including Fairfield County, the firm regularly represents clients in all areas of the state and has represented the interests of clients throughout the United States.

The firm is listed in the Martindale-Hubbell Bar Directory of Preeminent Attorneys under the category of Insurance Defense. Litigation of casualty and insurance coverage cases forms a large part of the firm's practice. With the exception of patent law and securities law (in which the firm participates only from a litigation standpoint), there are probably few areas in which the firm has not had significant involvement. While the firm has been recognized for its litigation capabilities, it does maintain a significant practice in non-litigation matters. The firm's clients range from individuals to "Fortune 500" companies.

Insurance Clients

American Modern Insurance	Colony Insurance Group
Group, Inc.	Community Association
IFA insurance Company	Underwriters of America, Inc.
Infinity Insurance Company	New Jersey Manufacturers
Strickland Insurance Group	Insurance Company

Non-Insurance Clients

Pacesetter Adjustment Company

Partners

Dennis M. Laccavole — 1953 — Fairfield University, B.S., 1975; St. John's University School of Law, J.D., 1978 — Admitted to Bar, 1978, Connecticut; 1979, New York; 1979, U.S. District Court, District of Connecticut; 1980,

Goldstein and Peck, P.C., Bridgeport, CT (Continued)

U.S. Court of Appeals, Second Circuit; 1982, U.S. Supreme Court — Member American, Connecticut and Greater Bridgeport Bar Associations; Connecticut Defense Lawyers Association (Board of Directors, 1997-2000); American Trial Lawyers Associations (Associate Membership); Connecticut Trial Lawyers Association; Defense Research Institute — Practice Areas: Insurance Defense; Property and Casualty; Uninsured Motorist Defense; Professional Liability; Municipal Liability; Insurance Coverage Litigation; Bad Faith; Extra-Contractual Liability — Tel: 203-384-5883 — E-mail: laccavoled@goldsteinandpeck.com

Associates

Keith P. Sturges — 1975 — University of Massachusetts Amherst, B.A., 1997; University of Richmond School of Law, J.D., 2000 — Admitted to Bar, 2000, Connecticut; 2005, U.S. District Court, District of Connecticut — Member Connecticut Bar Association — Practice Areas: Insurance Defense

Andrew M. McPherson — 1976 — Temple University, B.A., 2002; Rutgers University School of Law, J.D. (Dean's List), 2006 — Admitted to Bar, 2007, Connecticut — Member American and Connecticut Bar Associations; Associate Member, American Association for Justice — Practice Areas: Insurance Defense

William J. Kupinse, Jr.   Walter A. Flynn

The following firms also service this area.

Berchem, Moses & Devlin, PC
75 Broad Street
Milford, Connecticut 06460
  Telephone: 203-783-1200
  Fax: 203-878-4912

Insurance Defense, Automobile, Bad Faith, Common Carrier, Construction Liability, Environmental Liability, Governmental Liability, Hospitals, Legal Malpractice, Municipal Liability, Medical Malpractice, Professional Malpractice, Trial Practice, Workers' Compensation, Premises Liability, Liquor Liability, Civil Rights, Employment Practices Liability, Police Liability Defense

SEE COMPLETE LISTING UNDER BRIDGEPORT, CONNECTICUT (10 MILES)

Del Sole & Del Sole, L.L.P.
27 Elm Street
New Haven, Connecticut 06510
  Telephone: 203-785-8500
  Fax: 203-777-4485
Mailing Address: 46 South Whittlesey Avenue, Wallingford, CT 06492

Insurance Defense, Negligence, Product Liability, Medical Liability, Legal Malpractice, Accountant Malpractice, Dental Malpractice, Corporate Law, Subrogation, Trial Practice, State and Federal Courts, Workers' Compensation, Real Estate, Probate

SEE COMPLETE LISTING UNDER NEW HAVEN, CONNECTICUT (18 MILES)

Del Sole & Del Sole, L.L.P.
46 South Whittlesey Avenue
Wallingford, Connecticut 06492
  Telephone: 203-284-8000
  Fax: 203-284-9800

Accountant Malpractice, Corporate Law, Insurance Defense, Legal Malpractice, Medical Liability, Dental Malpractice, Negligence, Product Liability, State and Federal Courts, Subrogation, Trial Practice, Workers' Compensation, Insurance Coverage, Probate

SEE COMPLETE LISTING UNDER WALLINGFORD, CONNECTICUT (24 MILES)

Lippman & Ouellette, L.L.C.
142 Temple Street
New Haven, Connecticut 06510
  Telephone: 203-776-4546
  Fax: 203-776-4435

Insurance Defense, Automobile Liability, Personal Injury, Property Damage, Casualty, Fire, General Liability, Premises Liability, Homeowners, Commercial Liability, Trucking Liability, Dram Shop, Municipal Liability, Uninsured and Underinsured Motorist, Bad Faith, CUTPA/CUIPA, Legal Defense/Coverage Opinions, Declaratory Judgments, Subrogation, Appeals, Arbitration, Mediation and Administrative Hearings

SEE COMPLETE LISTING UNDER NEW HAVEN, CONNECTICUT (20 MILES)

Nuzzo & Roberts, L.L.C.
One Town Center
Cheshire, Connecticut 06410
  Telephone: 203-250-2000
  Fax: 203-250-3131
  Toll Free: 888-866-8297
Mailing Address: P.O. Box 747, Cheshire, CT 06410

Insurance Defense, Professional Liability, Legal Malpractice, Directors and Officers Liability, Workers' Compensation, Construction Litigation, Premises Liability, Product Liability, Toxic Torts, Trucking, Transportation, Appellate Practice, Coverage/Bad Faith Issues, Motor Vehicle Tort

SEE COMPLETE LISTING UNDER NEW HAVEN, CONNECTICUT (18 MILES)

Ryan Ryan Deluca LLP
707 Summer Street
Stamford, Connecticut 06901-1026
  Telephone: 203-357-9200
  Fax: 203-357-7915

Insurance Defense, Appellate Practice, Asbestos Litigation, Automobile Liability, Construction Law, Coverage Issues, Directors and Officers Liability, Environmental Law, Fire, Law Enforcement Liability, Legal Malpractice, Liquor Liability, Medical Malpractice, Municipal Liability, Premises Liability, Professional Liability, Railroad Law, School Law, Subrogation, Transportation, Trucking Law

SEE COMPLETE LISTING UNDER STAMFORD, CONNECTICUT (22 MILES)

Slutsky, McMorris & Meehan, LLP
396 Danbury Road, 2nd Floor
Wilton, Connecticut 06897
  Telephone: 203-762-9815
  Fax: 203-762-9864

Insurance Defense, Property, Casualty, Professional Liability, Construction Defect, Product Liability

SEE COMPLETE LISTING UNDER STAMFORD, CONNECTICUT (20 MILES)

Susman, Duffy & Segaloff, P.C.
59 Elm Street
New Haven, Connecticut 06510
  Telephone: 203-624-9830
  Fax: 203-562-8430
Mailing Address: P.O. Box 1684, New Haven, CT 06507

Insurance Defense, General Liability, Product Liability, Professional Liability, Construction Law, Fidelity and Surety

SEE COMPLETE LISTING UNDER NEW HAVEN, CONNECTICUT (18 MILES)

CHESHIRE 25,684 New Haven Co.

Ouellette, Deganis & Gallagher, LLC

143 Main Street
Cheshire, Connecticut 06410
  Telephone: 203-272-1157
  Fax: 203-250-1835
  E-Mail: info@odglaw.com
  www.odglaw.com

Established: 1996

Insurance Defense, Motor Vehicle, Premises Liability, Product Liability, Medical Malpractice, Personal Injury

Firm Profile: Ouellette, Deganis & Gallagher, LLC, represents people and businesses involved in litigation throughout Connecticut, New York and Massachusetts. We work to achieve prompt and successful results for our clients.

Insurance Clients

Arbella Insurance Group   Liberty Mutual Insurance Company

Partners

Sergio C. Deganis — Suffolk University Law School, J.D. (cum laude), 1981 — Admitted to Bar, 1981, Massachusetts; 1989, Connecticut

GLASTONBURY　　　　　　　　　　　　　　　　　　　　　　　　CONNECTICUT

Ouellette, Deganis & Gallagher, LLC, Cheshire, CT
(Continued)

Karen J. S. Gallagher — University of Connecticut School of Law, J.D., 1988 — Admitted to Bar, 1988, Connecticut

Joseph R. Grippe — Quinnipiac University School of Law, J.D. (cum laude), 2006 — Admitted to Bar, 2006, Connecticut; 2007, New York

Of Counsel

Steven A. Ouellette

DANBURY   80,893 Fairfield Co.

Refer To

Berchem, Moses & Devlin, PC
75 Broad Street
Milford, Connecticut 06460
　Telephone: 203-783-1200
　Fax: 203-878-4912

Insurance Defense, Automobile, Bad Faith, Common Carrier, Construction Liability, Environmental Liability, Governmental Liability, Hospitals, Legal Malpractice, Municipal Liability, Medical Malpractice, Professional Malpractice, Trial Practice, Workers' Compensation, Premises Liability, Liquor Liability, Civil Rights, Employment Practices Liability, Police Liability Defense

SEE COMPLETE LISTING UNDER BRIDGEPORT, CONNECTICUT (28 MILES)

Refer To

Coles, Baldwin & Kaiser, LLC
1261 Post Road, First Floor
Fairfield, Connecticut 06824
　Telephone: 203-319-0800
　Fax: 203-319-1210

Insurance Defense, Casualty, First Party Matters, Professional Malpractice, Workers' Compensation, Coverage Issues, Employment Law, Discrimination, Sexual Harassment, Municipal Liability, Governmental Liability, Life and Health, Americans with Disabilities Act, Advertising Injury, Agent and Brokers Errors and Omissions, Arson, Asbestos Litigation, Automobile Liability, Bad Faith, Bodily Injury, Business Law, Carrier Defense, Casualty Insurance Law, Commercial General Liability, Construction Accidents, Construction Litigation, Declaratory Judgments, Directors and Officers Liability, ERISA, Employment Discrimination, Equal Employment Opportunity Commission, Examinations Under Oath, Fire and Allied Lines, Inland Marine, Insurance Coverage, Law Enforcement Liability, Legal Malpractice, Municipal Law, Personal Lines, Premises Liability, Professional Liability, Property and Casualty, Self-Insured Defense, Special Investigative Unit Claims, Uninsured and Underinsured Motorist, Fair Housing Act

SEE COMPLETE LISTING UNDER BRIDGEPORT, CONNECTICUT (28 MILES)

Refer To

Lippman & Ouellette, L.L.C.
142 Temple Street
New Haven, Connecticut 06510
　Telephone: 203-776-4546
　Fax: 203-776-4435

Insurance Defense, Automobile Liability, Personal Injury, Property Damage, Casualty, Fire, General Liability, Premises Liability, Homeowners, Commercial Liability, Trucking Liability, Dram Shop, Municipal Liability, Uninsured and Underinsured Motorist, Bad Faith, CUTPA/CUIPA, Legal Defense/Coverage Opinions, Declaratory Judgments, Subrogation, Appeals, Arbitration, Mediation and Administrative Hearings

SEE COMPLETE LISTING UNDER NEW HAVEN, CONNECTICUT (35 MILES)

Refer To

Nuzzo & Roberts, L.L.C.
One Town Center
Cheshire, Connecticut 06410
　Telephone: 203-250-2000
　Fax: 203-250-3131
　Toll Free: 888-866-8297

Mailing Address: P.O. Box 747, Cheshire, CT 06410

Insurance Defense, Professional Liability, Legal Malpractice, Directors and Officers Liability, Workers' Compensation, Construction Litigation, Premises Liability, Product Liability, Toxic Torts, Trucking, Transportation, Appellate Practice, Coverage/Bad Faith Issues, Motor Vehicle Tort

SEE COMPLETE LISTING UNDER NEW HAVEN, CONNECTICUT (35 MILES)

Refer To

Ryan Ryan Deluca LLP
707 Summer Street
Stamford, Connecticut 06901-1026
　Telephone: 203-357-9200
　Fax: 203-357-7915

Insurance Defense, Appellate Practice, Asbestos Litigation, Automobile Liability, Construction Law, Coverage Issues, Directors and Officers Liability, Environmental Law, Fire, Law Enforcement Liability, Legal Malpractice, Liquor Liability, Medical Malpractice, Municipal Liability, Premises Liability, Professional Liability, Railroad Law, School Law, Subrogation, Transportation, Trucking Law

SEE COMPLETE LISTING UNDER STAMFORD, CONNECTICUT (25 MILES)

Refer To

Slutsky, McMorris & Meehan, LLP
396 Danbury Road, 2nd Floor
Wilton, Connecticut 06897
　Telephone: 203-762-9815
　Fax: 203-762-9864

Insurance Defense, Property, Casualty, Professional Liability, Construction Defect, Product Liability

SEE COMPLETE LISTING UNDER STAMFORD, CONNECTICUT (16 MILES)

GLASTONBURY   7,157 Hartford Co.

Raymond Law Group LLC
90 National Drive, Suite 3
Glastonbury, Connecticut 06033
　Telephone: 860-633-0580
　Toll Free: 866-781-3106
　Fax: 860-633-0438
　E-Mail: Info@RaymondLawGroup.com
　www.RaymondLawGroup.com

(Boston, MA Office: Park Plaza Executive Center, 20 Park Plaza, 4th Floor, 02116)
　(Tel: 617-314-6462)
　(Toll Free: 866-781-3106)
　(Fax: 617-848-2253)

Established: 2007

Property and Casualty, Commercial Law, Business Law, Employment Law, Technology, Personal Injury, Wrongful Death, Professional Negligence, Malpractice, Product Liability, Asbestos Litigation, Toxic Torts, Environmental Liability, Construction Defect, Insurance Fraud, Specialty Lines, Cyber Liability, Technology Errors & Omissions, Privacy and Data Loss, Liquor Liability

Firm Profile: Raymond Law Group LLC in Glastonbury, Connecticut, provides aggressive and professional representation in cases involving insurance, business, technology, personal injury and employment. Bruce Raymond founded the firm in 2007 after a successful career at one of the region's largest litigation and trial firms. Raymond Law Group LLC was founded on the core principles of excellent client service, lean business practices, alternative fee programs, and effective use of technology in firm management and litigation. Bruce started the firm because he believed the traditional law firm model was failing to deliver value to clients in a rapidly changing business environment. Clients ranging from individuals, corporations and insurance companies were looking for an alternative to the traditional law firm model. Raymond Law Group LLC is the alternative.

Insurance Clients

The Hartford	Hortica Insurance & Employee Benefits
OneBeacon Insurance	Propel Insurance
Plymouth Rock Assurance Corporation	Selective Insurance Company of America
State Auto Insurance Company	XL Insurance
Western World Insurance Company	

CONNECTICUT

Raymond Law Group LLC, Glastonbury, CT (Continued)

Founder & Senior Managing Partner

Bruce H. Raymond — University of Connecticut, B.A., 1986; New England School of Law, J.D. (cum laude), 1989 — Phi Alpha Delta; American Jurisprudence Award — Admitted to Bar, 1989, Connecticut; Massachusetts; U.S. District Court, District of Massachusetts; U.S. District Court, District of Connecticut — Member American Bar Association (Sections on: Intellectual Property, Tort and Insurance Practice, Litigation, and Law Office Management); Connecticut and Massachusetts Bar Associations; Connecticut Defense Lawyers Association (President; Chairman, Board of Directors); Defense Research Institute (Regional Representative, Board of Directors); Connecticut Defense Lawyers Association (President; Chairman, Board of Directors); CLM Regional Chair; Connecticut State Chair; International Association of Defense Counsel — E-mail: Raymond@RaymondLawGroup.com

Associates

Lanell Hession Allen
Sharon Sloan Kozial
Stephen Troiano
Jay M. Wolman

GUILFORD 2,603 New Haven Co.

Donahue, Durham & Noonan, P.C.

Concept Park
741 Boston Post Road, Suite 306
Guilford, Connecticut 06437
Telephone: 203-458-9168
Fax: 203-458-4424
E-Mail: tdonahue@ddnctlaw.com
www.ddnctlaw.com

Automobile, Aviation, Employment Law, Insurance Litigation, Medical Malpractice, Premises Liability, Product Liability, Trucking Law

Firm Profile: Donahue, Durham & Noonan, P.C. is a civil litigation firm with a statewide trial practice in both the Federal and State Courts. Our attorneys handle every matter with legal sophistication and thoroughness.

Insurance Clients

Allstate Insurance Company
Electric Insurance Company
FolksAmerica Reinsurance Company
National Casualty Company
Scottsdale Insurance Company
Anthem Blue Cross and Blue Shield
Hartford Life and Annuity Insurance Company
RLI Insurance Company

Principal Contact

Timothy W. Donahue — 1952 — Boston College Law School, J.D., 1978 — Admitted to Bar, 1978, Connecticut — Best Lawyers New York Area; Best Lawyers of New England; Connecticut SuperLawyer; Best Lawyers in America

HARTFORD 124,775 Hartford Co.

Law Offices of James F. Aspell, P.C.

61 South Main Street, Suite 310
Hartford, Connecticut 06107-2403
Telephone: 860-523-8783
Fax: 860-232-5525
Toll Free: 866-620-4878
Emer/After Hrs: 860-236-3655
E-Mail: jfaspell@Aspelllaw.com
www.AspellLaw.com

Established: 2004

Workers' Compensation, Subrogation, Insurance Defense

GUILFORD

Law Offices of James F. Aspell, P.C., Hartford, CT (Continued)

Firm Profile: Board Certified Worker's Compensation Specialist; Statewide Defense and Subrogation Practice

Insurance Clients

Marsh & McLennan Companies
St. Paul Fire and Marine Insurance Company

Non-Insurance Clients

City of Meriden
Golden Rule Realty, Inc.
Urban Developers
Crawford & Company
Silver Mill Tours

James F. Aspell — 1961 — Ohio Wesleyan University, B.A., 1983; Western New England College School of Law, J.D., 1986 — Admitted to Bar, 1986, Connecticut; 1986, U.S. District Court, District of Connecticut; 1992, U.S. Supreme Court — Member Connecticut (Worker's Compensation Section) and Hartford County (Medical-Legal Committee) Bar Associations; Defense Research Institute; Connecticut Defense Lawyers Association — Board Certified Workers' Compensation Specialist

Cooney, Scully and Dowling

Hartford Square North
10 Columbus Boulevard
Hartford, Connecticut 06106
Telephone: 860-527-1141
Fax: 860-247-5215
www.csd-law.com

Established: 1929

Insurance Defense, Tort Litigation, Casualty, Product Liability, Construction Law, Contracts, Bonds, Employment Law, Civil Rights, Compensation, Fire, Surety, Life Insurance, Subrogation, Railroad Law, Appellate Practice, Malpractice (Medical, Legal, Accountants, Architects, Engineers, Cosmetic, and Environmental), Corporate (Non Profit and For Profit), Utilities

Insurance Clients

The ACE Group
AIG Technical Services, Inc.
Catholic Mutual Group
Chubb Group of Insurance Companies
Darwin Professional Underwriters, Inc.
The Hartford Insurance Group
Liberty Mutual Insurance
Met-Pro Corporation
Philadelphia Insurance Company
Prime Insurance Company
Quincy Mutual Fire Insurance Company
Xchanging
Aegis Security Insurance Company
Arch Insurance Company
Chartis International
CNA Insurance Companies
Connecticut Medical Insurance Company (CMIC)
Fireman's Fund Insurance Company
Medmarc Insurance Group
OneBeacon Insurance
Phoenix Insurance Company
ProMutual Group
RLI Insurance Company
Travelers Casualty and Surety Company

Non-Insurance Clients

AT&T
Connecticut Children's Medical Center
Eastern Connecticut Health Network
GAB Robins Risk Management Services, Inc.
Genesis HealthCare
The Hartford Roman Catholic Diocesan Corporation
Natchaug Hospital
Railway Claim Services, Inc.
St. Francis Home for Children, Inc.
Saint Mary Home
St. Raphael Healthcare System
Sisters of Notre Dame de Namur
The Sisters of St. Joseph Corporation
University of Hartford
Caronia Corporation
Connecticut Psychological Association, Inc.
Engle Martin Claims Administrative Services (EMCAS, Inc.)
Gallagher Bassett Services, Inc.
Hartford Hospital
Manchester Memorial Hospital
MidState Medical Center
New Britain General Hospital
Rockville General Hospital
St. Francis Hospital & Medical Center
Sisters of Mercy of Americas Northeast Community, Inc.
Specialty Risk Services, Inc. (SRS)
State of Connecticut

HARTFORD   **CONNECTICUT**

Cooney, Scully and Dowling, Hartford, CT (Continued)

Firm Members

Louis B. Blumenfeld — University of Vermont, B.A., 1967; Boston College, J.D., 1970 — Admitted to Bar, 1970, Connecticut; 1971, U.S. District Court, District of Connecticut; 1974, U.S. Court of Appeals, Second Circuit; 1977, U.S. Supreme Court — Member Federal Circuit Bar Association; Connecticut Defense Lawyers Association

John W. Sitarz — Wesleyan University, B.A., 1969; The University of Maine, J.D., 1972 — Admitted to Bar, 1972, Connecticut; 1973, U.S. District Court, District of Connecticut; 1978, U.S. Court of Appeals, Second Circuit — Member National Diocesan Attorneys Association; American Board of Trial Advocates; Connecticut Defense Lawyers Association

Eugene A. Cooney — Saint Michael's College, B.A., 1972; University of Connecticut, J.D. (with honors), 1977 — Admitted to Bar, 1977, Connecticut; 1978, U.S. District Court, District of Connecticut; 1985, U.S. Court of Appeals, Second Circuit — Member Connecticut Defense Lawyers Association (President, 1996-1997); Connecticut Medical Defense Lawyers Association; American Health Lawyers Association; American Board of Trial Advocates

Karen Jansen Casey — University of Vermont, B.A. (with honors), 1977; University of Connecticut, J.D., 1981 — Admitted to Bar, 1981, Connecticut; 1981, U.S. District Court, District of Connecticut — Member National Diocesan Attorneys Association

Jeffrey C. Pingpank — Johns Hopkins University, B.A., 1972; University of Connecticut, J.D., 1975 — Admitted to Bar, 1975, Connecticut; 1975, U.S. District Court, District of Connecticut; 1981, U.S. Court of Appeals, Second Circuit — Member Connecticut Defense Lawyers Association

Paul T. Nowosadko — Dartmouth College, B.A., 1979; University of Connecticut, J.D. (with honors), 1983 — Admitted to Bar, 1983, Connecticut; 1984, U.S. District Court, District of Connecticut — Member Connecticut Defense Lawyers Association, Director; Connecticut Society for Health Risk Management

Herbert J. Shepardson — University of Massachusetts, B.A., 1978; Western New England College, J.D. (cum laude), 1981 — Admitted to Bar, 1981, Connecticut; 1981, U.S. District Court, District of Connecticut — Member Connecticut Defense Lawyers Association — Of Counsel, Governor M. Jodi Rell

David A. Haught — Amherst College, B.A., 1982; Suffolk University, J.D. (with honors), 1986 — Admitted to Bar, 1986, Connecticut; 1987, U.S. District Court, District of Connecticut

James T. Scully — Salve Regina University, B.A. (cum laude), 1983; Western New England College, J.D., 1987 — Admitted to Bar, 1988, Connecticut; 1988, U.S. District Court, District of Connecticut

William J. Scully — Connecticut College, B.A., 1984; Western New England College, J.D., 1987 — Admitted to Bar, 1987, Connecticut; 1988, U.S. District Court, District of Connecticut

Robert G. Clemente — Boston College, B.A. (cum laude), 1985; University of Connecticut, J.D. (with honors), 1988 — Admitted to Bar, 1988, Connecticut; 1989, U.S. District Court, District of Connecticut

Paul A. Croce, II — Hartwick College, B.A. (with honors), 1993; University of Connecticut, J.D., 1999 — Admitted to Bar, 1999, Connecticut; 2001, U.S. District Court, District of Connecticut

Jessica D. Meerbergen — Bates College, B.S., 1996; University of Connecticut, J.D. (with honors), 1999 — Admitted to Bar, 1999, Connecticut; 2000, U.S. District Court, District of Connecticut

Lorinda S. Coon — Binghamton University, B.S. (with honors), 1979; Albany Law School of Union University, J.D. (cum laude), 1984 — Admitted to Bar, 1984, Connecticut; 1985, New York; U.S. District Court, District of Connecticut; 2008, U.S. Court of Appeals, Second Circuit

David A. Post — University of Connecticut, B.A., 1999; Western New England College, J.D., 2003 — Admitted to Bar, 2003, Connecticut; 2004, U.S. District Court, District of Connecticut

Of Counsel

Patrick J. Flaherty — College of the Holy Cross, A.B., 1955; Yale University, LL.B., 1958 — Admitted to Bar, 1958, Connecticut; 1961, U.S. District Court, District of Connecticut — Member National Association of Railroad Trial Counsel (National Executive Committee, 1991-2001; Vice President, 1995)

Cooney, Scully and Dowling, Hartford, CT (Continued)

Associates

John M. O'Donnell — College of Holy Cross, B.A., 2004; University of Connecticut, J.D., 2007 — Admitted to Bar, 2007, Connecticut; 2008, Massachusetts; 2013, U.S. District Court, District of Connecticut

Kay A. Williams — University of Notre Dame, B.B.A. (magna cum laude), 2000; University of Connecticut, J.D., 2006 — Admitted to Bar, 2006, Connecticut; 2007, New York; 2008, U.S. District Court, District of Connecticut

Leah M. Nollenberger — Southern Connecticut State University, B.A., 2004; Roger Williams University School of Law, J.D. (with honors), 2010; University of Connecticut, LL.M., 2011 — Admitted to Bar, 2010, Connecticut; 2011, U.S. District Court, District of Connecticut — Member American and Connecticut Bar Associations

Jacob P. Riley — University of Connecticut at Storrs, B.A. Political Science, 2007; Western New England College School of Law, J.D., 2010 — Admitted to Bar, 2010, Connecticut

Gordon, Muir & Foley, LLP

Hartford Square North
Ten Columbus Boulevard
Hartford, Connecticut 06106-1976
   Telephone: 860-525-5361
   Fax: 860-525-4849
   www.gmflaw.com

Established: 1947

Insurance Defense, Product Liability, Professional Malpractice, Casualty, Fire, Fidelity and Surety, Construction Law, Workers' Compensation, Life Insurance, Subrogation, Insurance Law

Insurance Clients

Aetna Casualty and Surety Company
Argonaut Insurance Company
Chubb Group of Insurance Companies
ELCO Administrative Services
Employers Mutual Casualty Company
General Casualty Insurance Company
HelpPoint Claim Services by Farmers Insurance
Kemper Insurance Companies
Liberty Mutual Insurance Company
Markel Corporation
MiddleOak
Nationwide Mutual Insurance Company
Quincy Mutual Fire Insurance Company
Sedgwick CMS
Travelers Insurance Companies
United National Insurance Company

American Safety Insurance Company
Carl Warren & Company
CNA Insurance Companies
Connecticut Interlocal Risk Management Agency (CIRMA)
Fireman's Fund Insurance Companies
Greater New York Mutual Insurance Company
Integrity Administrators
James River Insurance Company
Legal Management Services
MAPFRE U.S.A. Corp.
MetLife Auto & Home
Motorists Mutual Insurance Company
Pinnacle Risk Management Services
Safeco Insurance Companies
Specialty Risk Services
Trident Insurance Services
Utica Mutual Insurance Company
Zurich American Insurance Company

Non-Insurance Clients

Crawford & Company
Gallagher Bassett Services, Inc.
The Hertz Corporation
The May Department Stores Company
Rite Aid Corporation
RSKCo
Securitas Security Services USA, Inc.
Tutor Time Child Care/Learning Center

Dick's Sporting Goods, Inc.
Gilbane Building Company
The Home Depot
Penske Truck Leasing
PepsiCo & New Bern Transportation Company
Rushford Center, Inc.
Taco Bell-Yum!
Target Corporation

Partners

Jon S. Berk — 1950 — Wesleyan University, B.A., 1972; Boston University School of Law, J.D., 1975 — Admitted to Bar, 1975, Connecticut — Member Connecticut Defense Lawyers Association; Defense Research Institute —

Gordon, Muir & Foley, LLP, Hartford, CT (Continued)

Co-Author: "Connecticut Law of Uninsured and Underinsured Motorist Coverage," a treatise widely cited by the Connecticut Courts — Connecticut Defense Lawyers Association Award of Excellence, 2010 — Practice Areas: Premise Litigation; Automobile Litigation; Professional Liability; Municipal Liability; Discrimination

William J. Gallitto — 1950 — Wesleyan University, B.A., 1972; Boston College Law School, J.D., 1976 — Admitted to Bar, 1976, Connecticut; 1979, U.S. District Court, District of Connecticut — Member Connecticut and Hartford County Bar Associations; Association of Trial Lawyers of America; Connecticut Trial Lawyers Association — Practice Areas: Employment Law; Medical Malpractice; Product Liability; Toxic Torts

Kenneth G. Williams — 1956 — University of Connecticut, B.A. (magna cum laude), 1978; J.D. (with honors), 1982 — Admitted to Bar, 1982, Connecticut — Member Connecticut Bar Association; Fellow, Connecticut Bar Foundation; Connecticut Defense Lawyers Association; Defense Research Institute — Author/Lecturer: "Lead Paint Litigation" — Practice Areas: Negligence; Personal Injury; Product Liability; Medical Malpractice; Toxic Substances; Environmental Litigation; Construction Accidents; Employment Litigation

Renee Wocl Dwyer — 1966 — Providence College, B.S. (cum laude), 1988; The Catholic University of America, Columbus School of Law, J.D., 1991 — Admitted to Bar, 1991, Connecticut; 1991, U.S. District Court, District of Connecticut — Member Connecticut Commission on Human Rights and Opportunities; Connecticut Defense Lawyers Association; Defense Research Institute — Co-Author: "Modern Premises Liability Challanges to Retail Operations," For the Defense, February, 2012 — Practice Areas: Trial Practice; Insurance Defense; Retail Liability; Employment Practices Liability; Motor Vehicle; Premises Liability; Daycare Liability

Russell N. Jarem — 1982 — Providence College, B.S. (magna cum laude), 2004; University of Connecticut School of Law, J.D., 2007 — Admitted to Bar, 2007, Connecticut; 2008, Massachusetts; 2008, U.S. District Court, District of Connecticut; 2009, U.S. Court of Appeals, Second Circuit — Member Connecticut Bar Association; Defense Research Institute — Author: "Slip & Fall in Aisle Four: Modern Premises Liability Challenges to Retail Liability" — Practice Areas: Employment Law; Municipal Liability; Retail Liability; Errors and Omissions; Insurance Defense

Of Counsel

R. Bradley Wolfe — 1948 — Haverford College, B.A., 1970; University of Connecticut, M.B.A., 2005; University of Connecticut School of Law, J.D., 1973 — Admitted to Bar, 1974, Connecticut — Member American (Tort and Insurance Practice Section, Fidelity and Surety Law Committee) and Connecticut (Construction Law Section) Bar Associations; International Association of Defense Counsel (Professional Liability and Fidelity and Surety Committees) — Practice Areas: Professional Liability; Fidelity and Surety; Construction Law

Philip J. O'Connor — 1949 — Johns Hopkins University, B.A., 1971; University of Connecticut School of Law, J.D., 1976 — Admitted to Bar, 1976, Connecticut — Member Connecticut Defense Lawyers Association (Former President, Chairman and Chairman of the Board) — Connecticut Author: "Tort Law Desk Reference," Aspen Pubulishers — Former Staff Member, Connecticut General Assembly's Judiciary Committee — Practice Areas: Product Liability; Premises Liability; Municipal Litigation; Professional Liability; Negligence; Insurance Coverage; Mold Litigation; Toxic Torts

Hassett & Donnelly, P.C.
100 Pearl Street
11th Floor
Hartford, Connecticut 06103
Telephone: 860-247-0644
Fax: 860-247-0653
www.hassettanddonnelly.com

Hassett & Donnelly, P.C., Hartford, CT (Continued)

(Additional Offices: Worcester, MA*; Boston, MA*)

Insurance Defense, Defense Litigation, Construction Litigation, Coverage Analysis, Declaratory Judgments, Bad Faith, Professional Liability, Product Liability, Premises Liability, Municipal Liability, Workers' Compensation, Civil Litigation, Commercial General Liability, Employment Law, Motor Vehicle, Negligence, Toxic Torts, Wrongful Death, Breach of Contract, Property Defense, Environmental Litigation, Business Litigation, Fire, Homeowners, First and Third Party Defense, Property and Casualty, Self-Insured Defense, Uninsured and Underinsured Motorist, Employment Law (Management Side), Trial and Appellate Practice

Partners

Sarah B. Christie — 1969 — University of Massachusetts, B.B.A. (cum laude), 1991; Georgetown University, J.D., 1994 — Admitted to Bar, 1994, Massachusetts; 1998, Connecticut; 1996, U.S. District Court, District of Massachusetts — E-mail: schristie@hassettanddonnelly.com

Scott T. Ober — 1969 — Villanova University, B.S., 1991; Vermont Law School, J.D. (cum laude), 1994 — Admitted to Bar, 1994, Massachusetts; 1995, New Hampshire; 1998, Connecticut; 2014, Vermont; 1995, U.S. District Court, District of Massachusetts; 2001, U.S. District Court, District of New Hampshire; 2007, U.S. District Court, District of Connecticut; U.S. Court of Appeals, First Circuit — E-mail: sober@hassettanddonnelly.com

Paul S. Rainville — 1965 — Providence College, B.A. (cum laude), 1988; New England School of Law, J.D., 1992 — Admitted to Bar, 1992, Massachusetts; 1993, Connecticut; 1993, U.S. District Court, District of Massachusetts — E-mail: prainville@hassettanddonnelly.com

Associates

Peter G. Barrett — 1965 — University of Hartford, B.S.B.A., 1988; Texas Southern University, J.D., 1993 — Admitted to Bar, 1994, Massachusetts; 1995, Connecticut; 1995, U.S. District Court, District of Connecticut; 1996, U.S. Bankruptcy Court — E-mail: pbarrett@hassettanddonnelly.com

Kelly A. O'Brien — 1984 — University of New Haven, B.A. (magna cum laude), 2007; Quinnipiac College School of Law, J.D. (cum laude), 2010 — Admitted to Bar, 2011, Connecticut; New York — E-mail: kobrien@hassettanddonnelly.com

Timothy A. Smith — 1982 — University of Connecticut, B.A. Political Science (magna cum laude), 2004; Quinnipiac College School of Law, J.D. (magna cum laude), 2009 — Admitted to Bar, 2009, Connecticut; 2010, New York — E-mail: tsmith@hassettanddonnelly.com

(See listing under Worcester, MA for additional information)

Howard, Kohn, Sprague & Fitzgerald
237 Buckingham Street
Hartford, Connecticut 06106
Telephone: 860-525-3101
Fax: 860-247-4201
E-Mail: hksf@HKSFlaw.com
www.hksflaw.com

(Manchester, CT Office: 99 East Center Street, 06040)
(Tel: 860-646-8075)

Established: 1786

Insurance Defense, Coverage Issues, Bad Faith, Automobile Liability, Product Liability, Homeowners, Casualty, Environmental Law, Medical Malpractice, Workers' Compensation, Admiralty and Maritime Law, Appellate Practice, Alternative Dispute Resolution, Uninsured and Underinsured Motorist, Trucking Law, Errors and Omissions, First Party Matters, Employment Practices Liability

HARTFORD

CONNECTICUT

Howard, Kohn, Sprague & Fitzgerald, Hartford, CT
(Continued)

Insurance Clients

Amica Mutual Insurance Company
Patrons Mutual Insurance Company of Connecticut
Union Mutual of Vermont Companies
Farm Family Casualty Insurance Company
Peerless Insurance Company

Partners

John Stephen Papa — 1942 — Fordham University, A.B., 1964; University of Hartford, M.S., 1976; Fordham University, J.D., 1967 — Admitted to Bar, 1967, Connecticut; District of Columbia; 1974, U.S. District Court, District of Connecticut; 1982, U.S. District Court, Southern District of New York — Member American, Connecticut, Hartford County and Manchester Bar Associations — Special Master, Superior Court, Hartford County and U.S. District Court, District of Connecticut — Judge Advocate and Military Judge, U.S. Marine Corps [1967-1970] — E-mail: jsp@hksflaw.com

James M. Moher — 1947 — Providence College, B.A. (magna cum laude), 1969; University of Connecticut, J.D., 1972 — Admitted to Bar, 1972, Connecticut; 1972, U.S. District Court, District of Connecticut — Member Connecticut and Hartford County Bar Associations; Connecticut Defense Lawyers Association — E-mail: jmm@hksflaw.com

Thomas P. Cella — 1957 — University of Connecticut, B.A., 1979; Western New England College, J.D., 1983 — Law Clerk, Superior Court, State of Connecticut (1983-1984) — Admitted to Bar, 1983, Connecticut; 1984, U.S. District Court, District of Connecticut; 2003, U.S. Court of Appeals, Second Circuit — Member American, Connecticut, Hartford County and Manchester Bar Associations; Connecticut Defense Lawyers Association; Connecticut Trial Lawyers Association; Defense Research Institute; American Trial Lawyers Association — Special Master, U.S. District Court, District of Connecticut (1988 to present); Assistant Town Attorney of Manchester, Connecticut (1986-1989, 1991 to present); Fact Finder and Attorney Trial Referee, Connecticut Superior Court — Board Certified Civil Trial Lawyer, National Board of Trial Advocacy — Practice Areas: Trial Practice; Personal Injury; Medical Malpractice; Product Liability — E-mail: tpc@hksflaw.com

Jack G. Steigelfest — 1960 — Lehigh University, B.S., 1981; University of Connecticut, J.D. (with high honors), 1984 — American Jurisprudence Awards; ASCAP Award — Judicial Law Clerk for Justice Shea, Connecticut Supreme Court (1984-1985) — Executive Editor, Connecticut Law Review (1983-1984) — Admitted to Bar, 1984, Connecticut; 1985, U.S. District Court, District of Connecticut; 1987, U.S. Court of Appeals, Second Circuit — Member American and Connecticut Bar Associations; Connecticut Defense Lawyers Association (President, Board Member, Chair of Amicus Brief Committee); Defense Research Institute (Insurance Committee); Member, Judicial Branch Task Force on Civil Jury Instructions; Member, Code of Evidence Oversight Committee — Senior Co-Editor for Civil Litigation, Connecticut Bar Journal; Author: "Withdrawal and Reinstatement of State Court Actions," 71 Conn. B.J. 389, 1997; "The Unity of Interest Rule and Peremptory Challenge in Connecticut," 69 Conn. B.J. 353, 1995; "Multiple Claims, Meager Coverage," 10 The Defense 1, 1994 — Lecturer: "Auto Insurance Law and Accident Litigation in Connecticut," Lorman 2002, 2003; "Connecticut Personal Injury Practice for Paralegals," Halfmoon 2000; "Adjusting the Automobile Injury Case in Connecticut," NBI 2000; "Developments in Tort Law," Annual Survey of Connecticut Law, The University of Connecticut Law School Alumni Association, 1999, 2000; "Bad Faith Litigation In Connecticut," NBI 1999; "Insurance Coverage Law in Connecticut," NBI 1998 — E-mail: jgs@hksflaw.com

James F. Sullivan — 1963 — Boston College, A.B. (summa cum laude), 1986; University of Connecticut, M.A. (with high honors), 1989; University of Connecticut School of Law, J.D. (with honors), 1992 — American Jurisprudence Awards — Judicial Law Clerk for Justice Callahan, Connecticut Supreme Court — Editor in Chief, Connecticut Law Review — Admitted to Bar, 1992, Connecticut; 1993, U.S. District Court, District of Connecticut — Member Federal, American and Connecticut Bar Associations; Connecticut Defense Lawyers Association — Author: "Successor Corporate Liability in Product Liability Actions," 73 Conn. B.J. 297, 1999; "The New Amendments to Fed. R. Civ. P.26," Connecticut Lawyer, 1994; "The Scope of Procedural Rule-Making," 65 Conn. B.J. 411, 1991 — Speaker Seminars: Automobile College of Law, Topic, "Examining Bio Mechanical Experts," CTLA 2001; Motion Practice, Topic, "Trial Motions," NBI, 2000, 2001 — E-mail: jfs@hksflaw.com

Todd W. Whitford — 1970 — Albright College, B.A., 1992; University of Connecticut, J.D., 1995 — Connecticut Moot Court Board (1992-1995) — Editor, Insurance Law Journal — Admitted to Bar, 1995, Connecticut; 1996, Massachusetts; 1996, U.S. District Court, District of Connecticut; 1996, U.S. District Court, District of Massachusetts; 1998, U.S. Court of Appeals, Second Circuit — Member Connecticut and Tolland County Bar Associations; Connecticut Defense Lawyers Association — Practice Areas: Civil Litigation; Insurance Law; Land Use; Personal Injury — E-mail: tww@hksflaw.com

Steven J. Barber — 1972 — Stonehill College, B.A., 1994; Western New England College School of Law, J.D., 1997 — Admitted to Bar, 1997, Connecticut; 1998, Massachusetts; 1998, U.S. District Court, District of Connecticut; 1998, U.S. District Court, District of Massachusetts — Member American, Massachusetts and Connecticut Bar Associations; Connecticut Defense Lawyers Association — Associate Editor, The Defense; Author: "Apportionment of Liability and the Non-Delegable Duty to Maintain: Can a Snow Removal Contractor Be Cited for Apportionment?," The Defense, Volume 16, No. 1, Spring 2000; "Public Sidewalk Injuries - Appellate Court Holds That Abutting Landowner Is Not Responsible for Injury to Third Person Caused by Defective Sidewalk," The Defense, Volume 16, No. 3, Winter, 2000; "Snow Remover Liability: Did the Supreme Court Resolve All the Issues in Deciding, Gazo v. City of Stamford?," The Defense, Volume 16, No. 3, Spring, 2001 — Practice Areas: Civil Litigation; Insurance Law; Personal Injury — E-mail: sjb@hksflaw.com

Associate

Greg S. Krieger — 1975 — University of Connecticut, B.A., 1997; University of Connecticut School of Law, J.D., 2001 — Admitted to Bar, 2001, Connecticut; 2005, New York; 2003, U.S. District Court, District of Connecticut — Member Connecticut Bar Association; Connecticut Defense Lawyers Association — Practice Areas: Litigation — E-mail: gsk@hksflaw.com

Of Counsel

John R. Fitzgerald — 1927 — University of Connecticut, B.A., 1951; University of Connecticut School of Law, J.D. (with high honors), 1953 — Admitted to Bar, 1953, Connecticut; 1954, U.S. District Court, District of Connecticut; 1959, U.S. Supreme Court; 1960, U.S. Court of Appeals, Second Circuit — Member American, Connecticut, Hartford County (President, 1979-1980) and Manchester (President, 1972-1973) Bar Associations; Association of Trial Lawyers of America; American Judicature Society; Defense Research Institute — Co-Author: "Connecticut Law of Torts," 3rd Edition, 1991; "Connecticut Trial Practice," 1987 — Adjunct Professor of Law, Connecticut University Law School (1953-1991) — E-mail: jrf@hksflaw.com

Robert P. Volpe — 1934 — Harvard University, B.A. (cum laude), 1956; University of Michigan, J.D., 1959 — Board of Editors, University of Michigan Law Review (1958) — Admitted to Bar, 1959, Connecticut — Member Connecticut and Hartford County Bar Associations; Connecticut Defense Lawyers Association — E-mail: rpv@hksflaw.com

Regnier, Taylor, Curran & Eddy

100 Pearl Street, Floor 10
Hartford, Connecticut 06103
Telephone: 860-249-9121
Fax: 860-527-4343
www.rtcelawhartford.com

Established: 1936

Trial Practice, Insurance Defense, Insurance Coverage, Product Liability, Medical Malpractice, Legal Malpractice, Professional Malpractice, Personal Injury, Employment Law, Municipal Liability, Toxic Torts, Premises Liability/Inadequate Security

Firm Profile: Regnier, Taylor, Curran & Eddy is a trial firm keyed to defense and insurance issues. We are not only proud of our effectiveness in the courtroom and at the negotiating table, we are equally proud of our ability to minimize the legal costs of our clients through greater efficiency and technology, and to provide our clients with more responsive and dedicated service.

Insurance Clients

Auto-Owners Insurance Company
Connecticut Interlocal Risk Management Agency (CIRMA)
ESIS
The Concord Group Insurance Companies
Discover Re
Federated Insurance

CONNECTICUT HARTFORD

Regnier, Taylor, Curran & Eddy, Hartford, CT
(Continued)

Lawyer's Protector Plan
Magna Carta Companies
The Main Street America Group
National Indemnity Company
Penn Millers Insurance Company
Trident Insurance Services of New England, Inc.
Utica First Insurance Company
Vermont Mutual Insurance Company
Lumber Mutual Insurance Company
Mutual Benefit Group
Omni Insurance Company
Pennsylvania Lumbermens Mutual Insurance Company
United Services Automobile Association (USAA)
Zurich North America

Non-Insurance Clients

Big Y Foods, Inc.
Holiday Retirement
Jo-Ann Stores, Inc.
Sedgwick Claims Management Services, Inc.
Town of West Hartford, Connecticut
Frito-Lay, Inc.
Intercontinental Hotels
Ryder Transportation, Inc.
Specialized Education Services, Inc.
Walgreen Co.

Partners

J. Ronald Regnier — (1906-1987)

Robert F. Taylor — (1930-1994)

Edmund T. Curran — (Retired)

Ralph G. Eddy — 1947 — Bowdoin College, A.B., 1969; University of Connecticut School of Law, J.D., 1972 — Phi Beta Kappa; James Bowdoin Scholar — Admitted to Bar, 1972, Connecticut; 1974, U.S. District Court, District of Connecticut; 1979, U.S. Court of Appeals, Second Circuit — Member Connecticut Bar Association — E-mail: reddy@rtcelaw.com

Lawrence L. Connelli — 1958 — University of Connecticut, B.A. (magna cum laude), 1980; University of Connecticut School of Law, J.D., 1983 — Admitted to Bar, 1983, Connecticut; 1984, U.S. District Court, District of Connecticut — Member Connecticut Bar Association — E-mail: lconnelli@rtcelaw.com

Jay F. Huntington — 1955 — Northeastern University, B.S. (cum laude), 1978; University of Santa Clara School of Law, J.D., 1981 — Admitted to Bar, 1981, California; 1987, Connecticut; 1984, U.S. District Court, Central District of California; 1988, U.S. District Court, District of Connecticut — Member Connecticut and Middlesex County Bar Associations — E-mail: jhuntington@rtcelaw.com

Sandra R. Stanfield — 1969 — Wesleyan University, B.A., 1991; University of Connecticut School of Law, J.D. (with honors), 1994 — Admitted to Bar, 1994, Connecticut; 2001, Massachusetts; 1995, U.S. District Court, District of Connecticut — Member Connecticut Bar Association; Connecticut Trial Lawyers Association — E-mail: sstanfield@rtcelaw.com

Associates

Stacey Francoline — 1973 — University of Connecticut, B.A., 1995; Hamline University School of Law, J.D., 2001 — Admitted to Bar, 2002, New York; Connecticut; U.S. District Court, District of Connecticut — Member Connecticut and New York State Bar Associations — E-mail: sfrancoline@rtcelaw.com

David A. Estabrook — 1957 — Southern New Hampshire University, B.S., 1981; Franklin Pierce Law Center, J.D., 2005 — Admitted to Bar, 2005, Connecticut; 2007, Massachusetts; U.S. District Court, District of Connecticut — Member Connecticut Bar Association — E-mail: destabrook@rtcelaw.com

Rebecca A. Hartley — 1980 — University of Connecticut, B.A. (cum laude), 2002; Suffolk University Law School, J.D. (Dean's List), 2005 — Admitted to Bar, 2005, Massachusetts; 2006, Connecticut; 2008, U.S. District Court, District of Connecticut — Member Connecticut Bar Association; Connecticut Trial Lawyers Association — Languages: Spanish — E-mail: rhartley@rtcelaw.com

Keith S. McCabe — 1966 — Trinity College, B.A., 1988; Quinnipiac College, J.D., 1991 — Admitted to Bar, 1991, Connecticut; U.S. District Court, District of Connecticut — Member Connecticut Bar Association — E-mail: kmccabe@rtcelaw.com

Wolf, Horowitz & Etlinger, L.L.C.
99 Pratt Street, Fourth Floor
Hartford, Connecticut 06103
Telephone: 860-724-6667
Fax: 860-293-1979
E-Mail: info@wolfhorowitz.com
www.wolfhorowitz.com

Insurance Defense, Litigation, Toxic Torts, Product Liability, Insurance Coverage, Malpractice, Surety, Fidelity, Construction Law, Subrogation

Firm Profile: Wolf Horowitz is a boutique litigation law firm located in downtown Hartford, Connecticut. Our primary practice areas are complex insurance defense cases, insurance coverage cases and surety and fidelity matters. Our insurance cases focus largely on bad faith claims, toxic tort defense, employment defense and construction defect cases. Our surety cases largely address construction disputes, subdivision bond claims and alleged breaches of fiduciary duty arising out of probate estates. Our fidelity cases arise out of Commercial Crime Policies and Financial Institution Bonds. We provide representation to insurance carriers, sureties and fidelity carriers in Connecticut and Massachusetts.

Insurance Clients

Acadia Insurance Company
Allied Insurance Company
Amerisure Mutual Insurance Company
Berkley Surety Group
California Casualty Management Company
Chubb & Son, Inc.
CNA Surety Corporation
Connecticut General Life Insurance Company
General Star Management Company
The Hanover Insurance Companies
HCC Surety Group
Liberty Bond Services
Liberty Mutual Insurance Company
Ohio Casualty Insurance Company
OneBeacon Insurance Group
Philadelphia Insurance Companies
State Auto Insurance Companies
State Farm Fire and Casualty Company
Travelers Property Casualty Group
ACSTAR Insurance Company
American Modern Home Insurance Company
AXIS Professional Lines
Burlington Insurance Group
Capitol Indemnity Corporation
Chartis Insurance
CIGNA Insurance Company
Colony Insurance Company
Fairmont Specialty Insurance Company
Great American Insurance Company
The Hartford
International Fidelity Insurance Company
National Union Fire Insurance Company of Pittsburgh, PA
Peerless Insurance Company
Selective Insurance Company of South Carolina
Travelers Casualty and Surety Company

Partners

Matthew Horowitz — 1952 — Tufts University, B.A. (summa cum laude), 1973; New York University School of Law, J.D., 1976 — Order of the Coif — Admitted to Bar, 1977, District of Columbia; 1978, Texas; 1984, Massachusetts; 1988, Connecticut; 1977, U.S. Court of Appeals, Fifth Circuit; 1978, U.S. District Court, Southern District of Texas; 1985, U.S. District Court, District of Massachusetts; 1988, U.S. District Court, District of Connecticut; 1990, U.S. Court of Appeals, Second Circuit — Member American Bar Association (Tort and Insurance Practice Section; Vice Chair, Fidelity and Surety Law Committee, 1997-present); Connecticut Bar Association (Construction Law Section); The District of Columbia Bar; State Bar of Texas — Author: "Forged Endorsement Claims Against Depository Banks: Defenses Available to the Insured and Coverage Implications under the Financial Institution Bond," Northeast Surety and Fidelity Claims Conference, 1997; "Ethical Consideration re: Interviewing Third Parties in the Course of a Surety Investigation," Surety Claims Institute, 1997; "Relationships and Duties Among Primary and Excess Carriers, XIV," Fidelity Journal, 2011; Editor: "The Law of Performance Bonds," American Bar Association, 2009; Co-Editor: "CGL/Builder's Risk Monograph," American Bar Association, 2004; Contributing Author: "Law of Payment Bonds," American Bar Association, 2011 — Reported Cases: Amwest Surety Insurance Co. v. United States, 870 F. Supp. 432 (D. Conn. 1994); Goldberg v. Hartford Fire Insurance Co., 269 (Conn. 550 2004); Doe v. Marshall, 459 F. Supp. 1190 (S.D. Tex. 1978) — E-mail: mhorowitz@wolfhorowitz.com

Deborah Etlinger — 1957 — University of Massachusetts, B.A., 1979; Western New England College School of Law, J.D. (cum laude), 1987 — American Jurisprudence Award — Admitted to Bar, 1987, Pennsylvania; 1988, Connecticut; 1993, Massachusetts; 1987, U.S. District Court, Eastern District

MERIDEN / CONNECTICUT

Wolf, Horowitz & Etlinger, L.L.C., Hartford, CT
(Continued)

of Pennsylvania; 1988, U.S. District Court, District of Connecticut — Member American Bar Association (Tort and Insurance Practice, Environmental Law Sections); Connecticut Bar Association (Litigation, Executive Committee, Environmental Law and Gender Equity Committees) — Contributing Author: "Law and Practice of Insurance Coverage Litigation," West Group & American Bar Association Tort and Insurance Practice Section, 2000 — Reported Cases: Published Decisions: Burlington Insurance Co. v. DeVesta, 511 F. Supp. 2d 231 (D. Conn. 2007); Acstar Insurance Co. v. Clean Harbors, Inc. F. Supp. 2d (D. Conn. 2011); Citizens Communications Co. v. Trustmark Insurance, 303 F. Supp. 2d 197 (D. Conn. 2004); Viola v. O'Dell, 108 Conn. App. 760 (2008) — E-mail: detlinger@wolfhorowitz.com

Associates

Adam J. LaFleche — 1977 — University of Massachusetts Amherst, B.A., 1999; University of Connecticut School of Law, J.D., 2002 — Admitted to Bar, 2002, Connecticut; U.S. District Court, District of Connecticut — Member American Bar Association; Connecticut Bar Association; Connecticut Defense Lawyers Association; Defense Research Institute — E-mail: ajl@wolfhorowitz

Eric D. Eddy — 1975 — Brown University, B.A. (magna cum laude), 1997; University of Connecticut School of Law, J.D. (with honors), 2000 — Admitted to Bar, 2001, Connecticut; 2003, U.S. District Court, District of Connecticut — Member American Bar Association; Connecticut Bar Association — E-mail: eeddy@wolfhorowitz.com

Miruna C. Popescu Voiculescu — 1985 — University of Connecticut, B.S., 2008; Western New England College School of Law, J.D., 2012 — Admitted to Bar, 2012, Connecticut; Massachusetts — Member American Bar Association; Connecticut Bar Association — Languages: Romanian — E-mail: mpopescu@wolfhorowitz.com

Of Counsel

Penrose Wolf — 1925 — The Pennsylvania State University, B.S., 1948; University of Connecticut School of Law, J.D., 1967 — Admitted to Bar, 1967, Connecticut; 1988, U.S. District Court, District of Connecticut — Member American Bar Association (Tort and Insurance Practice Section; Fidelity and Surety Law Committee; Forum on the Construction Industry); Connecticut Bar Association (Economics of Tort and Insurance Practice Committee); Arbitrator, National Panel of Arbitrators; American Arbitration Association — Author: "Deviations in Relet Contract," The Forum, Volume X, 1974; "New Limitations and Penalties on Surety," The Forum, Volume XVII, 1981

The following firms also service this area.

Berchem, Moses & Devlin, PC
75 Broad Street
Milford, Connecticut 06460
 Telephone: 203-783-1200
 Fax: 203-878-4912

Insurance Defense, Automobile, Bad Faith, Common Carrier, Construction Liability, Environmental Liability, Governmental Liability, Hospitals, Legal Malpractice, Municipal Liability, Medical Malpractice, Professional Malpractice, Trial Practice, Workers' Compensation, Premises Liability, Liquor Liability, Civil Rights, Employment Practices Liability, Police Liability Defense

SEE COMPLETE LISTING UNDER BRIDGEPORT, CONNECTICUT (51 MILES)

Lippman & Ouellette, L.L.C.
142 Temple Street
New Haven, Connecticut 06510
 Telephone: 203-776-4546
 Fax: 203-776-4435

Insurance Defense, Automobile Liability, Personal Injury, Property Damage, Casualty, Fire, General Liability, Premises Liability, Homeowners, Commercial Liability, Trucking Liability, Dram Shop, Municipal Liability, Uninsured and Underinsured Motorist, Bad Faith, CUTPA/CUIPA, Legal Defense/Coverage Opinions, Declaratory Judgments, Subrogation, Appeals, Arbitration, Mediation and Administrative Hearings

SEE COMPLETE LISTING UNDER NEW HAVEN, CONNECTICUT (39 MILES)

Nuzzo & Roberts, L.L.C.
One Town Center
Cheshire, Connecticut 06410
 Telephone: 203-250-2000
 Fax: 203-250-3131
 Toll Free: 888-866-8297
Mailing Address: P.O. Box 747, Cheshire, CT 06410

Insurance Defense, Professional Liability, Legal Malpractice, Directors and Officers Liability, Workers' Compensation, Construction Litigation, Premises Liability, Product Liability, Toxic Torts, Trucking, Transportation, Appellate Practice, Coverage/Bad Faith Issues, Motor Vehicle Tort

SEE COMPLETE LISTING UNDER NEW HAVEN, CONNECTICUT (40 MILES)

Susman, Duffy & Segaloff, P.C.
59 Elm Street
New Haven, Connecticut 06510
 Telephone: 203-624-9830
 Fax: 203-562-8430
Mailing Address: P.O. Box 1684, New Haven, CT 06507

Insurance Defense, General Liability, Product Liability, Professional Liability, Construction Law, Fidelity and Surety

SEE COMPLETE LISTING UNDER NEW HAVEN, CONNECTICUT (40 MILES)

LITCHFIELD 1,258 Litchfield Co.

Refer To

Berchem, Moses & Devlin, PC
75 Broad Street
Milford, Connecticut 06460
 Telephone: 203-783-1200
 Fax: 203-878-4912

Insurance Defense, Automobile, Bad Faith, Common Carrier, Construction Liability, Environmental Liability, Governmental Liability, Hospitals, Legal Malpractice, Municipal Liability, Medical Malpractice, Professional Malpractice, Trial Practice, Workers' Compensation, Premises Liability, Liquor Liability, Civil Rights, Employment Practices Liability, Police Liability Defense

SEE COMPLETE LISTING UNDER BRIDGEPORT, CONNECTICUT (46 MILES)

Refer To

Lippman & Ouellette, L.L.C.
142 Temple Street
New Haven, Connecticut 06510
 Telephone: 203-776-4546
 Fax: 203-776-4435

Insurance Defense, Automobile Liability, Personal Injury, Property Damage, Casualty, Fire, General Liability, Premises Liability, Homeowners, Commercial Liability, Trucking Liability, Dram Shop, Municipal Liability, Uninsured and Underinsured Motorist, Bad Faith, CUTPA/CUIPA, Legal Defense/Coverage Opinions, Declaratory Judgments, Subrogation, Appeals, Arbitration, Mediation and Administrative Hearings

SEE COMPLETE LISTING UNDER NEW HAVEN, CONNECTICUT (44 MILES)

MERIDEN 60,868 New Haven Co.

Refer To

Berchem, Moses & Devlin, PC
75 Broad Street
Milford, Connecticut 06460
 Telephone: 203-783-1200
 Fax: 203-878-4912

Insurance Defense, Automobile, Bad Faith, Common Carrier, Construction Liability, Environmental Liability, Governmental Liability, Hospitals, Legal Malpractice, Municipal Liability, Medical Malpractice, Professional Malpractice, Trial Practice, Workers' Compensation, Premises Liability, Liquor Liability, Civil Rights, Employment Practices Liability, Police Liability Defense

SEE COMPLETE LISTING UNDER BRIDGEPORT, CONNECTICUT (32 MILES)

CONNECTICUT

MIDDLETOWN

Refer To
Cella - Flanagan, P.C.
Attorneys and Counselors at Law
21 Washington Avenue, Suite A
North Haven, Connecticut 06473
    Telephone: 203-239-5851
    Fax: 203-234-2974

Insurance Defense, Bodily Injury, Casualty, Automobile, Malpractice, Product Liability

SEE COMPLETE LISTING UNDER NEW HAVEN, CONNECTICUT (21 MILES)

Refer To
Del Sole & Del Sole, L.L.P.
27 Elm Street
New Haven, Connecticut 06510
    Telephone: 203-785-8500
    Fax: 203-777-4485

Mailing Address: 46 South Whittlesey Avenue, Wallingford, CT 06492

Insurance Defense, Negligence, Product Liability, Medical Liability, Legal Malpractice, Accountant Malpractice, Dental Malpractice, Corporate Law, Subrogation, Trial Practice, State and Federal Courts, Workers' Compensation, Real Estate, Probate

SEE COMPLETE LISTING UNDER NEW HAVEN, CONNECTICUT (21 MILES)

Refer To
Del Sole & Del Sole, L.L.P.
46 South Whittlesey Avenue
Wallingford, Connecticut 06492
    Telephone: 203-284-8000
    Fax: 203-284-9800

Accountant Malpractice, Corporate Law, Insurance Defense, Legal Malpractice, Medical Liability, Dental Malpractice, Negligence, Product Liability, State and Federal Courts, Subrogation, Trial Practice, Workers' Compensation, Insurance Coverage, Probate

SEE COMPLETE LISTING UNDER WALLINGFORD, CONNECTICUT (5 MILES)

Refer To
Lippman & Ouellette, L.L.C.
142 Temple Street
New Haven, Connecticut 06510
    Telephone: 203-776-4546
    Fax: 203-776-4435

Insurance Defense, Automobile Liability, Personal Injury, Property Damage, Casualty, Fire, General Liability, Premises Liability, Homeowners, Commercial Liability, Trucking Liability, Dram Shop, Municipal Liability, Uninsured and Underinsured Motorist, Bad Faith, CUTPA/CUIPA, Legal Defense/Coverage Opinions, Declaratory Judgments, Subrogation, Appeals, Arbitration, Mediation and Administrative Hearings

SEE COMPLETE LISTING UNDER NEW HAVEN, CONNECTICUT (23 MILES)

Refer To
Nuzzo & Roberts, L.L.C.
One Town Center
Cheshire, Connecticut 06410
    Telephone: 203-250-2000
    Fax: 203-250-3131
    Toll Free: 888-866-8297

Mailing Address: P.O. Box 747, Cheshire, CT 06410

Insurance Defense, Professional Liability, Legal Malpractice, Directors and Officers Liability, Workers' Compensation, Construction Litigation, Premises Liability, Product Liability, Toxic Torts, Trucking, Transportation, Appellate Practice, Coverage/Bad Faith Issues, Motor Vehicle Tort

SEE COMPLETE LISTING UNDER NEW HAVEN, CONNECTICUT (21 MILES)

Refer To
Susman, Duffy & Segaloff, P.C.
59 Elm Street
New Haven, Connecticut 06510
    Telephone: 203-624-9830
    Fax: 203-562-8430

Mailing Address: P.O. Box 1684, New Haven, CT 06507

Insurance Defense, General Liability, Product Liability, Professional Liability, Construction Law, Fidelity and Surety

SEE COMPLETE LISTING UNDER NEW HAVEN, CONNECTICUT (21 MILES)

MIDDLETOWN 47,648 Middlesex Co.

Aeton Law Partners LLP
101 Centerpoint Drive
Middletown, Connecticut 06457
    Telephone: 860-724-2160
    E-Mail: info@aetonlaw.com
    www.aetonlaw.com

Established: 2012

Insurance, Business Law, Technology, Employment Law, Intellectual Property

Firm Profile: Aeton Law handles litigation and transactions throughout Connecticut involving a variety of insurance matters including general defense, subrogation, errors and omissions, cyber liability, products liability, environmental, employment and commercial. We also regularly handle matters in Massachusetts, New York and throughout the country on a select basis.

Insurance Clients

The Hartford   National Interstate Insurance Company

Partners

David Benoit — University of Connecticut, B.A., 1995; University of Connecticut School of Law, J.D., 2000 — Admitted to Bar, 2000, Connecticut; 2001, New York; U.S. District Court, District of Connecticut; U.S. District Court, Southern District of New York — Member American and Connecticut Bar Associations (Intellectual Property Section); International Association of Outsourcing Professionals; Professional Risk Managers International Association; International Trademark Associatioon; Intellectual Property Owners Association — American Mensa-Connecticut/Western Massachusetts Chapter; AV-Rated, Martindale-Hubbell, 2011-2013 — E-mail: dbb@aetonlaw.com

N. Kane Bennett — University of Connecticut, B.A., 1994; Suffolk University Law School, J.D. (cum laude), 1997 — Admitted to Bar, 1997, Massachusetts; 1999, Connecticut; U.S. District Court, District of Connecticut; 2000, U.S. District Court, District of Massachusetts; U.S. Court of Appeals, Second Circuit — Member Connecticut (Technology Committee) Bar Association; Council on Litigation Management — AV-Rated, Martindale-Hubbell, 2010-2013 — E-mail: nkb@aetonlaw.com

The following firms also service this area.

Berchem, Moses & Devlin, PC
75 Broad Street
Milford, Connecticut 06460
    Telephone: 203-783-1200
    Fax: 203-878-4912

Insurance Defense, Automobile, Bad Faith, Common Carrier, Construction Liability, Environmental Liability, Governmental Liability, Hospitals, Legal Malpractice, Municipal Liability, Medical Malpractice, Professional Malpractice, Trial Practice, Workers' Compensation, Premises Liability, Liquor Liability, Civil Rights, Employment Practices Liability, Police Liability Defense

SEE COMPLETE LISTING UNDER BRIDGEPORT, CONNECTICUT (38 MILES)

Cella - Flanagan, P.C.
Attorneys and Counselors at Law
21 Washington Avenue, Suite A
North Haven, Connecticut 06473
    Telephone: 203-239-5851
    Fax: 203-234-2974

Insurance Defense, Bodily Injury, Casualty, Automobile, Malpractice, Product Liability

SEE COMPLETE LISTING UNDER NEW HAVEN, CONNECTICUT (26 MILES)

MILFORD   CONNECTICUT

Del Sole & Del Sole, L.L.P.
27 Elm Street
New Haven, Connecticut 06510
  Telephone: 203-785-8500
  Fax: 203-777-4485
Mailing Address: 46 South Whittlesey Avenue, Wallingford, CT 06492

Insurance Defense, Negligence, Product Liability, Medical Liability, Legal Malpractice, Accountant Malpractice, Dental Malpractice, Corporate Law, Subrogation, Trial Practice, State and Federal Courts, Workers' Compensation, Real Estate, Probate

SEE COMPLETE LISTING UNDER NEW HAVEN, CONNECTICUT (26 MILES)

Del Sole & Del Sole, L.L.P.
46 South Whittlesey Avenue
Wallingford, Connecticut 06492
  Telephone: 203-284-8000
  Fax: 203-284-9800

Accountant Malpractice, Corporate Law, Insurance Defense, Legal Malpractice, Medical Liability, Dental Malpractice, Negligence, Product Liability, State and Federal Courts, Subrogation, Trial Practice, Workers' Compensation, Insurance Coverage, Probate

SEE COMPLETE LISTING UNDER WALLINGFORD, CONNECTICUT (10 MILES)

Lippman & Ouellette, L.L.C.
142 Temple Street
New Haven, Connecticut 06510
  Telephone: 203-776-4546
  Fax: 203-776-4435

Insurance Defense, Automobile Liability, Personal Injury, Property Damage, Casualty, Fire, General Liability, Premises Liability, Homeowners, Commercial Liability, Trucking Liability, Dram Shop, Municipal Liability, Uninsured and Underinsured Motorist, Bad Faith, CUTPA/CUIPA, Legal Defense/Coverage Opinions, Declaratory Judgments, Subrogation, Appeals, Arbitration, Mediation and Administrative Hearings

SEE COMPLETE LISTING UNDER NEW HAVEN, CONNECTICUT (33 MILES)

Nuzzo & Roberts, L.L.C.
One Town Center
Cheshire, Connecticut 06410
  Telephone: 203-250-2000
  Fax: 203-250-3131
  Toll Free: 888-866-8297
Mailing Address: P.O. Box 747, Cheshire, CT 06410

Insurance Defense, Professional Liability, Legal Malpractice, Directors and Officers Liability, Workers' Compensation, Construction Litigation, Premises Liability, Product Liability, Toxic Torts, Trucking, Transportation, Appellate Practice, Coverage/Bad Faith Issues, Motor Vehicle Tort

SEE COMPLETE LISTING UNDER NEW HAVEN, CONNECTICUT (26 MILES)

Susman, Duffy & Segaloff, P.C.
59 Elm Street
New Haven, Connecticut 06510
  Telephone: 203-624-9830
  Fax: 203-562-8430
Mailing Address: P.O. Box 1684, New Haven, CT 06507

Insurance Defense, General Liability, Product Liability, Professional Liability, Construction Law, Fidelity and Surety

SEE COMPLETE LISTING UNDER NEW HAVEN, CONNECTICUT (26 MILES)

MILFORD 51,271 New Haven Co.

The Quinn Law Firm, LLC
204 South Broad Street
Milford, Connecticut 06460
  Telephone: 203-877-5400
  Fax: 203-877-5416
  www.quinn-lawfirm.com

(Southbury, CT Office: 204 Playhouse Corner, 06488)
  (Tel: 203-405-3300)
  (Fax: 203-405-3301)

The Quinn Law Firm, LLC, Milford, CT (Continued)

Insurance Defense, Workers' Compensation, Personal Injury, Professional Liability, Commercial General Liability, Subrogation, Criminal Defense, Wills, Trusts, Estate Planning, Employment Litigation, Real Estate Closings, Foreclosure

Insurance Clients

Lumber Insurance Companies   Providence Washington Insurance Company

Non-Insurance Clients

Petro, Inc.

Members

Clayton J. Quinn — 1971 — The University of Arizona, B.S.B.A., 1993; Quinnipiac University, J.D., 1996 — Admitted to Bar, 1997, Connecticut; 2000, New York; 1997, U.S. District Court, District of Connecticut — Member Connecticut, New York State and Greater Bridgeport Bar Associations — Practice Areas: Workers' Compensation; Personal Injury; Insurance Defense

James T. Smith — 1970 — University of Connecticut, B.A. (cum laude), 1993; Quinnipiac University School of Law, J.D. (cum laude), 1996 — Admitted to Bar, 1996, Connecticut — Member Connecticut, Danbury and Waterbury Bar Associations — Practice Areas: Real Estate Transactions; Wills; Trusts; Estate Planning — Resident Milford/Southbury, CT Office

Of Counsel

William L. Cotter — 1957 — Georgetown University, B.S.B.A., 1980; University of Bridgeport, J.D., 1983 — Admitted to Bar, 1985, Connecticut; 1985, U.S. District Court, District of Connecticut — Member Connecticut and Bridgeport Bar Associations; Connecticut Trial Lawyers Association — Practice Areas: Insurance Defense; Personal Injury; Subrogation

Anthony J. Pantuso, III — 1963 — Rhodes College, B.S. (cum laude), 1986; University of Connecticut School of Law, J.D. (cum laude), 1992 — Admitted to Bar, 1992, Connecticut; 1993, U.S. District Court, District of Connecticut; 1996, U.S. Court of Appeals, Second Circuit; 2011, U.S. District Court, Southern District of New York — Member American, Connecticut and Milford Bar Associations; National Employment Lawyers Association; Connecticut Employment Lawyers Association — Practice Areas: Employment Litigation; Discrimination

(This firm is also listed in the Subrogation section of this directory)

The following firms also service this area.

Cella - Flanagan, P.C.
Attorneys and Counselors at Law
21 Washington Avenue, Suite A
North Haven, Connecticut 06473
  Telephone: 203-239-5851
  Fax: 203-234-2974

Insurance Defense, Bodily Injury, Casualty, Automobile, Malpractice, Product Liability

SEE COMPLETE LISTING UNDER NEW HAVEN, CONNECTICUT (11 MILES)

Del Sole & Del Sole, L.L.P.
27 Elm Street
New Haven, Connecticut 06510
  Telephone: 203-785-8500
  Fax: 203-777-4485
Mailing Address: 46 South Whittlesey Avenue, Wallingford, CT 06492

Insurance Defense, Negligence, Product Liability, Medical Liability, Legal Malpractice, Accountant Malpractice, Dental Malpractice, Corporate Law, Subrogation, Trial Practice, State and Federal Courts, Workers' Compensation, Real Estate, Probate

SEE COMPLETE LISTING UNDER NEW HAVEN, CONNECTICUT (11 MILES)

CONNECTICUT

Del Sole & Del Sole, L.L.P.
46 South Whittlesey Avenue
Wallingford, Connecticut 06492
  Telephone: 203-284-8000
  Fax: 203-284-9800

Accountant Malpractice, Corporate Law, Insurance Defense, Legal Malpractice, Medical Liability, Dental Malpractice, Negligence, Product Liability, State and Federal Courts, Subrogation, Trial Practice, Workers' Compensation, Insurance Coverage, Probate

SEE COMPLETE LISTING UNDER WALLINGFORD, CONNECTICUT (18 MILES)

Lippman & Ouellette, L.L.C.
142 Temple Street
New Haven, Connecticut 06510
  Telephone: 203-776-4546
  Fax: 203-776-4435

Insurance Defense, Automobile Liability, Personal Injury, Property Damage, Casualty, Fire, General Liability, Premises Liability, Homeowners, Commercial Liability, Trucking Liability, Dram Shop, Municipal Liability, Uninsured and Underinsured Motorist, Bad Faith, CUTPA/CUIPA, Legal Defense/Coverage Opinions, Declaratory Judgments, Subrogation, Appeals, Arbitration, Mediation and Administrative Hearings

SEE COMPLETE LISTING UNDER NEW HAVEN, CONNECTICUT (11 MILES)

Nuzzo & Roberts, L.L.C.
One Town Center
Cheshire, Connecticut 06410
  Telephone: 203-250-2000
  Fax: 203-250-3131
  Toll Free: 888-866-8297
Mailing Address: P.O. Box 747, Cheshire, CT 06410

Insurance Defense, Professional Liability, Legal Malpractice, Directors and Officers Liability, Workers' Compensation, Construction Litigation, Premises Liability, Product Liability, Toxic Torts, Trucking, Transportation, Appellate Practice, Coverage/Bad Faith Issues, Motor Vehicle Tort

SEE COMPLETE LISTING UNDER NEW HAVEN, CONNECTICUT (11 MILES)

Susman, Duffy & Segaloff, P.C.
59 Elm Street
New Haven, Connecticut 06510
  Telephone: 203-624-9830
  Fax: 203-562-8430
Mailing Address: P.O. Box 1684, New Haven, CT 06507

Insurance Defense, General Liability, Product Liability, Professional Liability, Construction Law, Fidelity and Surety

SEE COMPLETE LISTING UNDER NEW HAVEN, CONNECTICUT (11 MILES)

NEW BRITAIN 73,206 Hartford Co.

Anderson Reynolds & Lynch, LLP
1 Liberty Square, Suite 208
New Britain, Connecticut 06051
  Telephone: 860-893-0500
  Telephone: 860-767-0882 (Essex Office)
  Fax: 860-893-0550
  E-Mail: edlynch@arllawyers.com
  www.arllawyers.com

Established: 2004

Corporate Litigation, Construction Litigation, Business Litigation, Arbitration, Insurance Defense, Labor and Employment Litigation

Firm Profile: At Anderson, Reynolds, & Lynch, LLP, we dedicate ourselves to helping our clients obtain positive results in a timely and professional manner.

We have an additional office located at 11 N. Main Street, Essex, CT 06051.

Non-Insurance Clients

Barretta Construction	CWPM, LLC
Ferguson Electric	Manafort Brothers Inc.
The Mattabassett District	Tilcon, Inc.

NEW BRITAIN

Anderson Reynolds & Lynch, LLP, New Britain, CT
(Continued)

Edward T. Lynch, Jr. — Partner — Georgetown University, A.B., 1967; University of Connecticut, M.B.A., 1976; J.D., 1970 — Admitted to Bar, 1970, Connecticut; 1972, District of Columbia; 1970, U.S. District Court, District of Connecticut; 1971, U.S. Court of Appeals, Second Circuit; 1972, U.S. Supreme Court — Member American and Connecticut Bar Associations; Defense Research Institute — AV Rated Martindale Hubbell; 2013 SuperLawyer

The following firms also service this area.

Berchem, Moses & Devlin, PC
75 Broad Street
Milford, Connecticut 06460
  Telephone: 203-783-1200
  Fax: 203-878-4912

Insurance Defense, Automobile, Bad Faith, Common Carrier, Construction Liability, Environmental Liability, Governmental Liability, Hospitals, Legal Malpractice, Municipal Liability, Medical Malpractice, Professional Malpractice, Trial Practice, Workers' Compensation, Premises Liability, Liquor Liability, Civil Rights, Employment Practices Liability, Police Liability Defense

SEE COMPLETE LISTING UNDER BRIDGEPORT, CONNECTICUT (43 MILES)

Lippman & Ouellette, L.L.C.
142 Temple Street
New Haven, Connecticut 06510
  Telephone: 203-776-4546
  Fax: 203-776-4435

Insurance Defense, Automobile Liability, Personal Injury, Property Damage, Casualty, Fire, General Liability, Premises Liability, Homeowners, Commercial Liability, Trucking Liability, Dram Shop, Municipal Liability, Uninsured and Underinsured Motorist, Bad Faith, CUTPA/CUIPA, Legal Defense/Coverage Opinions, Declaratory Judgments, Subrogation, Appeals, Arbitration, Mediation and Administrative Hearings

SEE COMPLETE LISTING UNDER NEW HAVEN, CONNECTICUT (34 MILES)

Nuzzo & Roberts, L.L.C.
One Town Center
Cheshire, Connecticut 06410
  Telephone: 203-250-2000
  Fax: 203-250-3131
  Toll Free: 888-866-8297
Mailing Address: P.O. Box 747, Cheshire, CT 06410

Insurance Defense, Professional Liability, Legal Malpractice, Directors and Officers Liability, Workers' Compensation, Construction Litigation, Premises Liability, Product Liability, Toxic Torts, Trucking, Transportation, Appellate Practice, Coverage/Bad Faith Issues, Motor Vehicle Tort

SEE COMPLETE LISTING UNDER NEW HAVEN, CONNECTICUT (31 MILES)

NEW HAVEN 129,779 New Haven Co.

Cella - Flanagan, P.C.
Attorneys and Counselors at Law
21 Washington Avenue, Suite A
North Haven, Connecticut 06473
  Telephone: 203-239-5851
  Fax: 203-234-2974
  E-Mail: carlc@cfwlawyers.com
  www.cfwlawfirm.com

Established: 1976

Insurance Defense, Bodily Injury, Casualty, Automobile, Malpractice, Product Liability

Firm Profile: The firm was established in North Haven, Connecticut in 1976 and has continuously engaged in a statewide practice litigating in all state and federal courts. Each lawyer in the firm has a wide range of experience in the

NEW HAVEN / CONNECTICUT

Cella - Flanagan, P.C., Attorneys and Counselors at Law, New Haven, CT (Continued)

law and at the same time has developed particular expertise in specific areas of practice. As a result we can offer our clients specific expertise within the framework of a full service law firm.

Insurance Clients

AAA Insurance	AIG Specialty Auto
Ameriprise Auto & Home Insurance	Commerce Insurance Company
	International Surplus Lines Insurance Company
Jefferson Insurance Company	Liberty Mutual Group
Jefferson/Interstate Insurance Group	National Grange Mutual Insurance Company
Nationwide Insurance	
New Jersey Manufacturers Insurance Company	Norfolk and Dedham Mutual Fire Insurance Company
Peerless Insurance Company	Safeco/American States Insurance Company
St. Paul Fire and Marine Insurance Company	Tokio Marine Management, Inc.
United National Insurance Company	Zurich Insurance Company

Firm Members

Carl E. Cella — 1941 — Choate School, 1959; Georgetown University, A.B., 1963; University of Connecticut School of Law, J.D., 1966 — Former Law Clerk for Justice Elmer Ryan, Connecticut Supreme Court — Admitted to Bar, 1966, Connecticut; 1967, U.S. District Court, District of Connecticut; 1976, U.S. Supreme Court; 1976, U.S. Court of Appeals, Second Circuit — Member American, Connecticut and New Haven County Bar Associations; Connecticut Trial Lawyers Association — Practice Areas: Personal Injury; Product Liability; Malpractice; Premises Liability; Construction Litigation — E-mail: carlc@cfwlawyers.com

Robert Flanagan — 1969 — University of Notre Dame, B.A. (magna cum laude), 1991; University of Notre Dame Law School, J.D. (cum laude), 1994 — Admitted to Bar, 1994, Connecticut; 1998, U.S. District Court, District of Connecticut — Member American, Connecticut and New Haven County Bar Associations — Middlebury Board of Tax Review — Practice Areas: Workers' Compensation; Personal Injury; Premises Liability; Construction Litigation; Subrogation — E-mail: robertf@cfwlawyers.com

Lynn J. Cella-Coyne — 1974 — Wheaton College, B.A., 1997; Quinnipiac University School of Law, J.D., 2000 — Admitted to Bar, 2001, Connecticut — Member Connecticut and New Haven County Bar Associations — Board of Directors, Wallingford Y.M.C.A. — Practice Areas: Personal Injury — E-mail: lynnc@cfwlawyers.com

Michael Vitali — 1985 — Quinnipiac University, B.A., 2007; Quinnipiac University School of Law, J.D., 2011 — Admitted to Bar, 2011, Connecticut; 2012, U.S. District Court, District of Connecticut — E-mail: michaelv@cfwlawyers.com

Del Sole & Del Sole, L.L.P.

27 Elm Street
New Haven, Connecticut 06510
 Telephone: 203-785-8500
 Fax: 203-777-4485
 E-Mail: ddk@delsoledelsole.com
 www.delsoledelsole.com

(Wallingford, CT Office*: 46 South Whittlesey Avenue, 06492)
 (Tel: 203-284-8000)
 (Fax: 203-284-9800)

Established: 1982

Insurance Defense, Negligence, Product Liability, Medical Liability, Legal Malpractice, Accountant Malpractice, Dental Malpractice, Corporate Law, Subrogation, Trial Practice, State and Federal Courts, Workers' Compensation, Real Estate, Probate

Firm Profile: Del Sole & Del Sole is a mid-sized firm concentrating in civil litigation of all types, with an emphasis in the defense of personal injury claims. The firm provides representation to insurers, manufacturers, health care and other municipalities, professionals, national trucking companies and other corporations in diverse areas including products liability, medical and other professional negligence liability issues. The firm also practices in the

Del Sole & Del Sole, L.L.P., New Haven, CT (Continued)

areas of commercial and residential real estate, corporate law, worker's compensation and probate. It handles matters before all state and federal tribunals within the state of Connecticut, at both the trial and appellate levels, and has substantial experience in mediation and arbitration.

Insurance Clients

Acadia Insurance Company	Aetna Casualty and Surety Company
Affinity Insurance Group, Inc.	
Allstate Insurance Company	American Healthcare Indemnity Company
Chicago Insurance Company	
Chubb Group of Insurance Companies	CIGNA Property and Casualty Insurance Company
CNA Commercial Insurance Company	CNA HealthPro
	CNA Insurance Company
CNA PRO	Colonial Penn Insurance Company
Connecticut Medical Insurance Company (CMIC)	Connecticut Specialty Insurance Company
Country-Wide Insurance Company	Crown Life Insurance Company
Danbury Insurance Company	Encompass Insurance
Fidelity and Deposit Company of Maryland	Gallagher Bassett Insurance Company
Gerling-Konzern AG	Global Indemnity Group, Inc.
Greater New York Mutual Insurance Company	Hanover Insurance Company
	Harleysville Mutual Insurance Company
Hingham Group	
Home Mutual Insurance Company	Houston General Insurance Company
Integon General Insurance Corporation	
	Kemper Insurance Companies
Kendall Insurance, Inc.	Kentucky Farm Bureau Mutual Insurance Company
Lincoln Insurance Group	
Maryland Casualty Company	Merchants and Business Men's Mutual Insurance Company
Mitsui Sumitomo Insurance Group	
Motorists Mutual Insurance Company	National Continental Insurance Company
National General Insurance Company	National Interstate Insurance Company
Naughton Insurance, Inc.	Occidental Fire & Casualty Company of North Carolina
Podiatry Insurance Company of America (PICA)	Preferred Risk Financial, Inc.
The Proformance Insurance Company	Puritan Insurance Company
	Rockford Mutual Insurance Company
Safeco Insurance	
St. Paul Fire and Marine Insurance Company	SEACO Insurance Company
	Security Insurance Company of Hartford
State Auto Insurance Company	
Travelers Insurance Companies	Unisun Insurance Company
United America Indemnity Group	United Automobile Insurance Company
Utah Home Fire Insurance Company	Windsor Group
Yasuda Fire & Marine Insurance Company of America	Zurich American Insurance Company

Non-Insurance Clients

Alexsis, Inc.	All American Administrators, Inc.
ARAMARK Corporation	Associated Financial Services, Inc.
Blackard & Murphy	Boise Cascade, L.L.C.
Brown & Brown, Inc.	Cambridge Claims Service
CHC Physicians	Chesterfield Services, Inc.
City of New Haven	The Coca-Cola Company
Colony Management Services, Inc.	Connecticut Limousine Service
Constitution State Service Company	Crawford & Company
	Cunningham Lindsey U.S., Inc.
Dattco, Inc.	Edwards Super Food Stores
Executive Auto Group	First National Supermarkets, Inc.
Frozen Food Express Industries, Inc.	GAB Robins North America, Inc.
	Gulf Risk Services, Inc.
Helmsman Management Services, Inc.	Hubbell Incorporated
	J.B. Hunt Transport Services, Inc.
Liberty Insurance Services, Inc.	MAC Risk Management, Inc.
May Transit, Inc.	MiniCo, Inc.
National Alliance Brokerage Services, Inc.	Network Adjusters, Inc.
	Nissan Motor Acceptance Corporation
Office of Assistant Attorney General	
	Orion Capital Companies
Preferred Dealer Protection	Proline Carriers, Inc.
Recovery Services International, Inc.	RSKCo
	Sedgwick Claims Management Services, Inc.
Smeal Manufacturing Company	
State of Connecticut Department of Transportation	Stop & Shop, Inc.
	Temtex Industries, Inc.
Textron, Inc.	Tran-Star, Inc.
TRISTAR Risk Management	United Rentals, Inc.
Wells Fargo Insurance Services	York Claims Service, Inc.

Del Sole & Del Sole, L.L.P., New Haven, CT   (Continued)

Firm Members

Stephen P. Del Sole — 1952 — Boston College, B.A., 1974; Brooklyn Law School, J.D., 1977 — Admitted to Bar, 1977, Connecticut; 1979, U.S. District Court, District of Connecticut — Member Connecticut and New Haven County Bar Associations; Connecticut Defense Lawyers Association

Michael P. Del Sole — 1953 — Boston College, B.A. (summa cum laude), 1975; University of Connecticut, J.D. (with honors), 1979 — Recipient, American Jurisprudence Award in Civil Procedure — Law Clerk to the Judges of the Appellate Session of the Connecticut Superior Court, 1979-1980 — Admitted to Bar, 1979, Connecticut; 1980, U.S. District Court, District of Connecticut; 1993, U.S. Court of Appeals, Second Circuit — Member Connecticut and New Haven County Bar Associations; Connecticut Defense Lawyers Association; Defense Research Institute

Denise D. Kennedy — 1957 — Quinnipiac College, A.S., 1977; B.A., 1981; Quinnipiac University School of Law, J.D., 1988 — Admitted to Bar, 1990, Connecticut; 1990, U.S. District Court, District of Connecticut — Member Connecticut and New Haven County Bar Associations; Connecticut Defense Lawyers Association

Ellen M. Costello — 1947 — St. Joseph's College, B.S., 1984; Suffolk University, J.D., 1988 — Admitted to Bar, 1988, Connecticut; 1988, U.S. District Court, District of Connecticut — Member American and Connecticut Bar Associations; American Association of Nurse Attorneys; Connecticut Defense Lawyers Association

Rene Gerard Martineau — 1961 — University of Lowell, B.S. (cum laude), 1984; Western New England College, J.D. (cum laude), 1987 — Admitted to Bar, 1987, Connecticut; 1988, Massachusetts; 1988, U.S. District Court, District of Connecticut; 1992, U.S. Supreme Court; 2003, U.S. Court of Appeals, Second Circuit — Member Connecticut, Massachusetts and New Haven County Bar Associations; Connecticut Defense Lawyers Association

Of Counsel

Dominic P. Del Sole — 1926 — University of Notre Dame, B.S., 1948; University of Connecticut, LL.B., 1962 — Admitted to Bar, 1962, Connecticut; 1962, U.S. District Court, District of Connecticut — Member American, Connecticut and New Haven County Bar Associations

Edward F. Piazza — 1941 — Fordham University, B.S., 1963; Boston College, J.D., 1966 — Admitted to Bar, 1966, Connecticut — Member Connecticut and New Haven County Bar Associations

Esty & Buckmir, LLC

2340 Whitney Avenue
Hamden, Connecticut 06518
  Telephone: 203-248-5678
  Fax: 203-288-9974
  E-Mail: ebuckmir@estyandbuckmir.com
  E-Mail: mesty@estyandbuckmir.com

Established: 1998

Insurance Defense, Motor Vehicle, Uninsured and Underinsured Motorist, Premises Liability, Product Liability, Professional Liability, Medical Malpractice, Legal Malpractice, Construction Litigation, Workers' Compensation, Personal Injury

Insurance Clients

Arbella Insurance Group
Colony Insurance Company
Kemper Insurance Companies
National Indemnity Company
Providence Washington Insurance Company
Selective Insurance Company of America
Carl Warren & Company
Housing Authority Insurance, Inc.
Lumber Insurance Companies
Nationwide Insurance
The Reciprocal Group
Sagamore Insurance Company
Vermont Mutual Insurance Company

Non-Insurance Clients

Costco Companies, Inc.
Limited Brands, Inc.
Risk Services, Inc.
Sikorsky Aircraft Corporation
Yale-New Haven Hospital
Domino's Pizza, Inc.
Miller Brewing Company
ShopRite
Wakefern Food Corporation
Yale University

Esty & Buckmir, LLC, New Haven, CT   (Continued)

Partners

Miles N. Esty — 1962 — Trinity College, B.A., 1985; New York Law School, J.D., 1989 — Admitted to Bar, 1989, Connecticut; New York; 1990, U.S. District Court, Eastern and Southern Districts of New York; 1991, U.S. District Court, District of Connecticut; 1992, U.S. Court of Appeals, Second Circuit — Member Connecticut Bar Association; Connecticut Defense Lawyers Association — E-mail: mesty@estyandbuckmir.com

Elizabeth M. Buckmir — 1963 — University of Connecticut, B.A., 1985; University of Connecticut School of Law, J.D., 1988 — Admitted to Bar, 1988, Connecticut; 1989, U.S. District Court, District of Connecticut — Member Connecticut Bar Association; Connecticut Defense Lawyers Association — E-mail: ebuckmir@estyandbuckmir.com

Marla L. Seligson — 1972 — Southern Connecticut State University, B.S. (cum laude), 1994; Syracuse University College of Law, J.D. (cum laude), 1998 — Admitted to Bar, 1998, Connecticut — Member Connecticut Bar Association; Defense Lawyers Association — E-mail: mseligson@estyandbuckmir.com

Jonathan A. Beatty — 1972 — Boston College, B.A., 1996; University of Connecticut School of Law, J.D., 1999 — Admitted to Bar, 1999, Connecticut; 2000, U.S. District Court, District of Connecticut — Member Connecticut Bar Association — E-mail: jbeatty@estyandbuckmir.com

Associates

Michael D. Schweitzer — 1980 — Northeastern University, B.S.B.A. (cum laude), 2004; Quinnipiac University School of Law, J.D., 2007 — Admitted to Bar, 2007, Connecticut — Member Connecticut, Hartford and New Haven Bar Associations — E-mail: mschweitzer@estyandbuckmir.com

Saul A. Cardenas — 1981 — Florida International University, B.A., 2007; University of Miami School of Law, J.D., 2012 — Admitted to Bar, 2012, Florida; Massachusetts; 2013, Connecticut — Languages: Spanish, German — E-mail: scardenas@estyandbuckmir.com

Shane M. Mathieu — 1988 — Quinnipiac University, B.A. Physiology (cum laude), 2010; Quinnipiac University School of Law, J.D. (magna cum laude), 2013 — Admitted to Bar, 2013, Connecticut — E-mail: smathieu@estyandbuckmir.com

Thomas R. Hollowell — 1988 — University of Rhode Island, B.A. Political Science (Pi Sigma Alpha), 2009; Quinnipiac University School of Law, J.D. (cum laude), 2013 — Admitted to Bar, 2013, Massachusetts; Rhode Island; 2014, Connecticut — E-mail: thollowell@estyandbuckmir.com

Lippman & Ouellette, L.L.C.

142 Temple Street
New Haven, Connecticut 06510
  Telephone: 203-776-4546
  Fax: 203-776-4435
  E-Mail: louellette@lipplette.com
  www.lipplette.com

Established: 1995

Insurance Defense, Automobile Liability, Personal Injury, Property Damage, Casualty, Fire, General Liability, Premises Liability, Homeowners, Commercial Liability, Trucking Liability, Dram Shop, Municipal Liability, Uninsured and Underinsured Motorist, Bad Faith, CUTPA/CUIPA, Legal Defense/Coverage Opinions, Declaratory Judgments, Subrogation, Appeals, Arbitration, Mediation and Administrative Hearings

Firm Profile: Founded in 1995, and composed of experienced trial counsel in the field of insurance defense, the firm's litigation practice encompasses the handling of all types of personal injury/property damage cases involving premises liability, automobile negligence and first and third party insurance coverage cases related to: casualty, fire, general liability, premises liability, homeowners, umbrella, commercial, contract, automobile/bus/trucking accidents, dram shop, municipal liability, dog bite, trespass, assault, slander, libel, UM/UIM, bad faith, CUTPA/CUIPA, coverage opinions, declaratory judgments, subrogation and appeals. The Firm's practice also encompasses arbitrations, mediations and administrative hearings before Insurance Commissioner.

Lippman & Ouellette, L.L.C., New Haven, CT (Continued)

Insurance Clients

American Independent Insurance Company
Erie Insurance Company
GMAC Insurance Group
Lincoln Insurance Company
Lipca, Inc.
Motorists Insurance Company
National General Insurance Company
Auto Club Group
Donegal Insurance Group
Fiduciary Insurance Company
Indiana Farmers Mutual Insurance Company
Montpelier US Insurance Company
National Continental Insurance Company
United States Liability Insurance Company

Non-Insurance Clients

Town of Clinton
Town of East Haven

Partner

Lawrence A. Ouellette, Jr. — 1955 — University of Connecticut, B.A. (cum laude), 1977; Vermont Law School, J.D., 1980 — Phi Alpha Delta — Admitted to Bar, 1981, Connecticut; 1981, U.S. District Court, District of Connecticut; 1986, U.S. Court of Appeals, Second Circuit; 1987, U.S. Supreme Court — Member American (Tort and Insurance Practice Section), Connecticut and New Haven County (Committee on Civil Trials and Procedure) Bar Associations; Connecticut Defense Lawyers Association

Of Counsel

Ira H. Lippman — 1945 — University of Connecticut, B.S., 1967; Suffolk University Law School, J.D., 1970 — Admitted to Bar, 1970, Connecticut; 1986, U.S. District Court, District of Connecticut — Member American (Litigation and Law Practice Management Sections), Connecticut, New Haven County and Bridgeport Bar Associations; Connecticut Trial Lawyers Association; Connecticut Defense Lawyers Association

Mulvey, Oliver, Gould & Crotta

83 Trumbull Street
New Haven, Connecticut 06511
Telephone: 203-624-5111
Fax: 203-789-8371
E-Mail: mog@moglaw.com

Insurance Defense, Litigation, Negligence, Probate, Product Liability, Trial and Appellate Practice, Workers' Compensation

Insurance Clients

AAA Mid-Atlantic Insurance Group
Central Mutual Insurance Company
Horace Mann Insurance Company
IAT Specialty
Vermont Mutual Insurance Group
Allstate Insurance Company
Bunker Hill Insurance Company
Fireman's Fund Insurance Company
Penn Millers Insurance Company
Western World Insurance Group

Non-Insurance Clients

Avizent
Fitzpatrick & Hunt, Tucker, Collier, Pagano, Aubert, LLP
CJW & Associates
Paul C. Higgins, Inc.
Lowe's Companies, Inc.

Partners

Robert G. Oliver — 1940 — Yale University, B.A. (magna cum laude), 1962; Yale Law School, LL.B., 1965 — Admitted to Bar, 1965, Connecticut; 1971, U.S. District Court, District of Connecticut; 1974, U.S. Court of Appeals, Second Circuit; U.S. Supreme Court; U.S. Court of Military Appeals — Member Connecticut (House of Delegates, 1975-1978; Federal Practice Committee, Federal Judicial Committee, 1993-1995) and New Haven (President, 1979-1990) Bar Associations; Retired Navy and Marine Corps Judge Advocates Association; Naval Reserve Association; Military Officers Association; Connecticut Defense Lawyers Association — Federal Grievance Committee for the District of Connecticut (Member, 1997-2003; Chair, 2000-2003) — U.S. Naval Institute, Captain, Judge Advocate General's Corps, U.S. Naval Reserves [Retired] — Practice Areas: Trial Practice; State and Federal Courts; Civil Litigation; Appeals — E-mail: oliver@moglaw.com

David J. Crotta — 1960 — Fairfield University, A.B. (cum laude), 1982; University of Connecticut School of Law, J.D., 1988 — Phi Alpha Theta; Milton Horwitz Memorial Award in Torts; American Jurisprudence Award in

Mulvey, Oliver, Gould & Crotta, New Haven, CT (Continued)

Torts — Admitted to Bar, 1988, Connecticut; 1989, U.S. District Court, District of Connecticut; 1992, U.S. Court of Appeals, Second Circuit; 1998, U.S. Supreme Court — Member Connecticut (Professional Ethics Committee, 1973-Present) and New Haven County Bar Associations; Connecticut Defense Lawyers Association — Arbitrator, Connecticut Superior Court (2002-Present); Member, Grievance Panel, Ansonia-Milford Judicial District (2004-2010); Dominican Foundation (Founding Member; Board of Directors, 2004-Present; Vice President, 2009-Present); Community Soup Kitchen (Board of Directors, 2008; Vice President 2009-Present) — Practice Areas: Trial Practice; Negligence; Commercial Litigation; Civil Litigation; Appeals; Probate — E-mail: crotta@moglaw.com

James M. Hyland — 1962 — Boston College, A.B., 1984; Brooklyn Law School, J.D., 1990 — American Jurisprudence Award (Estate Administration) — Admitted to Bar, 1990, Connecticut; 1991, New York; 1992, U.S. District Court, Eastern and Southern Districts of New York; 1993, U.S. District Court, District of Connecticut — Member Connecticut, New Haven County and Bridgeport Bar Associations; Defense Research Institute; Connecticut Defense Lawyers Association — Practice Areas: Insurance Defense; Trial Practice; Workers' Compensation; Product Liability Defense; Lead Paint; Civil Litigation — E-mail: hyland@moglaw.com

Francis J. Drumm, III — 1970 — University of Connecticut, B.A., 1992; Western New England College School of Law, J.D., 2000 — Admitted to Bar, 2000, Connecticut; 2003, U.S. District Court, District of Connecticut — Member Connecticut and New Haven County Bar Associations; Connecticut Defense Lawyers Association — Practice Areas: Trial Practice; Negligence; Civil Litigation — E-mail: drumm@moglaw.com

Associates

James D. Hine, II — 1975 — University of Connecticut, B.A., 1998; The Pennsylvania State University Dickinson School of Law, J.D., 2001 — Admitted to Bar, 2002, Connecticut; 2004, U.S. District Court, District of Connecticut — Member Connecticut and New Haven Bar Associations — Practice Areas: Insurance Defense; Civil Litigation; Commercial Litigation; Negligence; Trial Practice — E-mail: hine@moglaw.com

Andrew G. Buchetto — 1985 — University of Massachusetts Amherst, B.A. (cum laude), 2007; Roger Williams University School of Law, J.D., 2010 — Admitted to Bar, 2010, Connecticut — Member Connecticut and New Haven Bar Associations — Practice Areas: Insurance Defense; Trial Practice; Workers' Compensation — E-mail: buchetto@moglaw.com

Nuzzo & Roberts, L.L.C.

One Town Center
Cheshire, Connecticut 06410
Telephone: 203-250-2000
Fax: 203-250-3131
Toll Free: 888-866-8297
E-Mail: help@nuzzo-roberts.com
www.nuzzo-roberts.com

Insurance Defense, Professional Liability, Legal Malpractice, Directors and Officers Liability, Workers' Compensation, Construction Litigation, Premises Liability, Product Liability, Toxic Torts, Trucking, Transportation, Appellate Practice, Coverage/Bad Faith Issues, Motor Vehicle Tort

Firm Profile: NUZZO & ROBERTS, L.L.C. is a full service insurance defense firm located in central Connecticut. With 23 lawyers and 35 support staff, the firm represents insurers and their insured in every court in Connecticut. In addition to representing clients for general insurance matters, the firm handles cases involving professional liability, coverage, bad faith, workers' compensation, employment, uninsured motorist and construction claims.

Insurance Clients

ACE USA/ESIS, Inc.
American International Group, Inc.
Casco Indemnity Company
CNA Insurance Company
EMC Insurance Companies
Esurance
Great American Insurance Company
Allstate Insurance Company
Assurant Specialty Property
Chubb Group of Insurance Companies
ESIS
General Casualty Company
Hanover Insurance Group
The Hartford

Nuzzo & Roberts, L.L.C., New Haven, CT (Continued)

MAC Risk Management, Inc.
Merchants Insurance Group
Monitor Liability Managers, Inc.
Nautilus Insurance Company
OneBeacon Insurance
Pharmacists Mutual Insurance Company
Swiss Reinsurance Company
Ullico Casualty Company
Xchanging
Zurich Insurance
Magna Carta Companies
Metropolitan Property and Casualty Insurance Company
Ohio Casualty Group
Patriot Risk Services, Inc.
Progressive Insurance Company
Sedgwick CMS
Tower Group Companies
Utica National Insurance Group
York Risk Services Group, Inc.

Non-Insurance Clients

Broadspire
Gallagher Bassett Services, Inc.
Whole Foods Market, Inc.
Compass Group USA, Inc.
Risk Enterprise Management, Ltd.

Managing Partners

Anthony Nuzzo, Jr. — 1944 — University of Connecticut, B.A., 1965; University of Connecticut School of Law, J.D., 1968 — Admitted to Bar, 1968, Connecticut; District of Columbia; 1969, U.S. District Court for the District of Columbia; U.S. Court of Appeals for the District of Columbia Circuit; 1971, U.S. District Court, District of Connecticut — Member American (Member, Litigation Section), Connecticut and New Haven County Bar Associations (President, 1998-1999); Connecticut Defense Lawyers Association (Past President); Defense Research and Trial Lawyers Association; Connecticut Trial Lawyers Association — Co-Author: "Uninsured/Underinsured Motorists Law in Connecticut," Volume II, Connecticut Law Tribune, Numbers 12 and 13, 1985 — Appointed Public Defender for District of Columbia, 1968-1970 — E-mail: anuzzo@nuzzo-roberts.com

Richard A. Roberts — 1959 — State University of New York at Binghamton, B.A., 1979; State University of New York at Buffalo Law School, J.D., 1983 — Moot Court Board — Admitted to Bar, 1984, New York; Connecticut; 1985, U.S. District Court, District of Connecticut; 2006, U.S. Court of Appeals, Second Circuit; 2008, U.S. Supreme Court — Member American (District Representative; Professionals, Officers and Directors Liability Committee, Tort and Insurance Practice Section) and Connecticut (Executive Committee, Young Lawyers Section) Bar Associations; New Haven Young Lawyers (President, 1989-1990); Connecticut Defense Lawyers Association; Connecticut Trial Lawyers Association; Defense Research Institute — Co-Author: "A Defense Perspective of Tort Reform," Connecticut Law Tribune, June 1995; Presenter: "Preparing and Trying the Accident Case," PESI, 1995; "Advanced Personal Injury," NBI, 2000 — Factfinder and Arbitrator, Superior Courts; Lecturer, Legal Studies, Quinnipiac College — E-mail: rroberts@nuzzo-roberts.com

Partners

David J. Weil — 1960 — Franklin & Marshall College, B.A., 1982; The George Washington University Law School, J.D., 1988 — Admitted to Bar, 1988, Connecticut; 1989, U.S. District Court, District of Connecticut — Member Connecticut Bar Association (Workers' Compensation Section, Chair) — E-mail: dweil@nuzzo-roberts.com

Jane Stoddard-Bietz — 1969 — Bowdoin College, B.A., 1991; University of Connecticut School of Law, J.D. (with honors), 1994 — Notes and Comments Editor, Connecticut Law Review — Admitted to Bar, 1994, Connecticut; 1995, U.S. District Court, District of Connecticut — E-mail: jbietz@nuzzo-roberts.com

Robert J. Chomiak, Jr. — 1971 — Boston University, B.A. (cum laude), 1993; New England School of Law, J.D., 1996 — Admitted to Bar, 1996, Connecticut; 2000, U.S. District Court, District of Connecticut — E-mail: rchomiak@nuzzo-roberts.com

Nicole C. Chomiak — 1972 — Providence College, B.S., 1994; Quinnipiac College School of Law, J.D. (cum laude), 1997 — Admitted to Bar, 1997, Connecticut; 1998, Massachusetts; U.S. District Court, District of Connecticut; 2008, U.S. Court of Appeals, Second Circuit — E-mail: nchomiak@nuzzo-roberts.com

Jane M. Carlozzi — 1956 — Wesleyan University, B.A., 1978; University of Hartford, M.B.A., 1987; University of Connecticut School of Law, J.D. (with high honors), 1998 — Admitted to Bar, 1998, Connecticut; U.S. District Court, District of Connecticut — E-mail: jcarlozzi@nuzzo-roberts.com

Michele C. Camerota — 1969 — Central Connecticut State University, B.A., 1993; University of Connecticut School of Law, J.D., 1998 — Admitted to Bar, 1998, Connecticut; 1999, U.S. District Court, District of Connecticut — E-mail: mcamerota@nuzzo-roberts.com

Jennifer J. Cavalier-Mozzer — 1972 — Bryant College, B.S., 1994; Quinnipiac College School of Law, J.D., 1999 — Admitted to Bar, 1999,

Nuzzo & Roberts, L.L.C., New Haven, CT (Continued)

Connecticut; 2003, U.S. District Court, District of Connecticut — E-mail: jcavaliermozzer@nuzzo-roberts.com

Amber J. Hines — 1973 — College of New Rochelle, B.A. (summa cum laude), 1994; Quinnipiac University School of Law, J.D. (cum laude), 1999 — Admitted to Bar, 1999, Connecticut; 2004, U.S. District Court, District of Connecticut; 2012, U.S. Court of Appeals, Second Circuit — E-mail: ahines@nuzzo-roberts.com

Nadine M. Pare — 1974 — University of Connecticut, B.A. (cum laude), 1996; Quinnipiac College School of Law, J.D., 2000 — Admitted to Bar, 2000, Connecticut; 2006, U.S. District Court, District of Connecticut — E-mail: npare@nuzzo-roberts.com

Kevin C. Hines — 1974 — University of New Haven, B.S. (summa cum laude), 1997; Western New England College School of Law, J.D. (cum laude), 2001 — Admitted to Bar, 2002, Massachusetts; Connecticut; 2003, U.S. District Court, District of Connecticut; 2010, U.S. Court of Appeals, Second Circuit — E-mail: khines@nuzzo-roberts.com

Jason K. Matthews — 1977 — Tufts University, B.A., 1999; University of Connecticut School of Law, J.D., 2002 — Admitted to Bar, 2002, Connecticut; 2006, U.S. District Court, District of Connecticut — E-mail: jmatthews@nuzzo-roberts.com

James R. Fiore — 1977 — Stonehill College, B.A., 1999; Syracuse University College of Law, J.D. (cum laude), 2002 — Admitted to Bar, 2002, Connecticut; 2006, U.S. District Court, District of Connecticut; 2012, U.S. Court of Appeals, Second Circuit — E-mail: jfiore@nuzzo-roberts.com

Senior Associate

Stacey L. Pitcher — 1979 — Fairfield University, B.A. (cum laude), 2001; University of Connecticut School of Law, J.D., 2004 — Admitted to Bar, 2004, Connecticut; 2006, U.S. District Court, District of Connecticut; 2010, U.S. Court of Appeals, Second Circuit

Associates

Kristin K. Mullins — 1972 — State University of New York at Geneseo, B.A. Political Science, 1994; State University of New York at Buffalo Law School, J.D., 1999 — Admitted to Bar, 2000, Connecticut

Kelly B. Gaertner — 1978 — Rutgers University, B.A., 2000; Seton Hall University School of Law, J.D. (cum laude), 2006 — Admitted to Bar, 2006, Connecticut; 2007, New York; U.S. District Court, District of Connecticut

James P. Henke — 1980 — State University of New York at Geneseo, B.A., 2003; University of Connecticut School of Law, J.D., 2007 — Admitted to Bar, 2007, Connecticut; 2008, New York; 2013, U.S. District Court, District of Connecticut

Sean E. Boyd — 1985 — Marshall University, B.A. (summa cum laude), 2007; Quinnipiac University School of Law, J.D. (summa cum laude), 2010 — Admitted to Bar, 2010, Connecticut; 2012, U.S. District Court, District of Connecticut

Daniel R. Labrecque — 1984 — University of Connecticut, B.A. (summa cum laude), 2007; Western New England College School of Law, J.D. (cum laude), 2010 — Admitted to Bar, 2010, Connecticut; 2012, U.S. District Court, District of Connecticut

Regina P. Armon — 1986 — Boston University, B.A. Political Science (magna cum laude), 2008; University of Connecticut School of Law, J.D. (with honors), 2011; Boston University, M.A. (magna cum laude), 2012 — Admitted to Bar, 2011, Connecticut; 2012, U.S. District Court, District of Connecticut

Laura M. Kritzman — 1982 — Central Connecticut State University, B.A., 2006; Western New England College School of Law, J.D., 2009 — Admitted to Bar, 2009, Connecticut

Natalie E. Wayne — 1985 — The University of Chicago, B.A. (with honors), 2008; University of Connecticut School of Law, J.D., 2013 — Admitted to Bar, 2013, Connecticut; Massachusetts — Member Connecticut Bar Association

Susman, Duffy & Segaloff, P.C.

59 Elm Street
New Haven, Connecticut 06510
  Telephone: 203-624-9830
  Fax: 203-562-8430
  www.susmanduffy.com

Established: 1977

NEW HAVEN
CONNECTICUT

Susman, Duffy & Segaloff, P.C., New Haven, CT
(Continued)

Insurance Defense, General Liability, Product Liability, Professional Liability, Construction Law, Fidelity and Surety

Firm Profile: Susman, Duffy & Segaloff, P.C. provides services to insurance carriers and self-insureds throughout Connecticut. In addition to general liability, the firm represents clients in the areas of product liability, toxic tort, legal and medical malpractice, design professional errors and omissions, health insurance benefit disputes, and construction law. It also advises and represents carriers on coverage issues.

Insurance Clients

Architects and Engineers Insurance Company, Inc., A RRG
Connecticut Interlocal Risk Management Agency (CIRMA)
Genesis Underwriting Management Company
Liberty Mutual Group
OneBeacon Professional Insurance
Specialty Risk Services, Inc. (SRS)
Utica National Insurance Group
CNA Insurance Company
Commercial Underwriters Insurance Company
First State Management Group, Inc.
Hartford Financial Products
North Pointe Insurance Company
Pacific Insurance Company
TIG Insurance Company

Non-Insurance Clients

Carolina Precision Plastics LLC
Illinois Tool Works, Inc.

Partners

Allen H. Duffy — (1931-1986)

Michael Susman — 1931 — University of Connecticut, B.A., 1952; University of Connecticut School of Law, LL.B., 1955 — Member, Board of Editors, University of Connecticut Law Review, 1954-1955 — Admitted to Bar, 1955, Connecticut — Member American, Connecticut and New Haven County Bar Associations — E-mail: msusman@susmanduffy.com

James H. Segaloff — 1943 — Syracuse University, A.B., 1965; University of Connecticut School of Law, LL.B., 1968 — Admitted to Bar, 1969, Connecticut — Member Connecticut and New Haven County Bar Associations — Member and Chairman, New Haven Civil Service Commission — E-mail: jsegaloff@susmanduffy.com

Joseph E. Faughnan — 1950 — Fordham University, B.A., 1972; University of Connecticut School of Law, J.D. (with honors), 1976 — Admitted to Bar, 1976, Connecticut; 1980, U.S. District Court, District of Connecticut — Member Connecticut (Academy of Continuing Professional Development, 1984-1985) and New Haven County Bar Associations; Connecticut Trial Lawyers Association — E-mail: jfaughnan@susmanduffy.com

Laura M. Sklaver — 1950 — Wellesley College, B.A., 1972; Case Western Reserve University, M.S.L.S., 1975; University of Connecticut School of Law, J.D. (with honors), 1981 — Admitted to Bar, 1981, Connecticut — Member American Bar Association; Connecticut Bar Association (Executive Committee, Business Law Section, 1994-Present; Secretary, 1996-1997; Treasurer, 1997-1998; Elder Law; Estates and Tax Sections); New Haven County Bar Association — E-mail: lsklaver@susmanduffy.com

Thomas E. Katon — 1959 — University of Pennsylvania, B.A., 1981; University of Bridgeport School of Law, J.D., 1986 — Associate Editor, University of Bridgeport Law Review — Admitted to Bar, 1986, Connecticut; 1987, U.S. District Court, District of Connecticut; 1997, U.S. Court of Appeals, Second Circuit — Member American, Connecticut, and New Haven County Bar Associations; Defense Research Institute (Professional Liability, State Liaison Business Litigation Committee); Connecticut Association of Defense Lawyers; Professional Liability Underwriting Society — Insurance Coverage Law and Bad Faith Litigation Lecturer, National Business Institute — E-mail: tkaton@susmanduffy.com

Karen Baldwin Kravetz — 1972 — Cornell University, B.S., 1994; Hofstra University School of Law, J.D., 1997 — Managing Articles Editor, Hofstra Law Review — Admitted to Bar, 1998, Connecticut; New York; U.S. District Court, District of Connecticut — Member American, Connecticut (Litigation Section) and New Haven County Bar Associations — Practice Areas: Legal Malpractice; Municipal Law; Commercial Litigation; Employment Law — E-mail: kkravetz@susmanduffy.com

Associates

Meghan K. Gallagher — 1978 — College of the Holy Cross, B.A., 2000; Quinnipiac University School of Law, J.D., 2004 — Admitted to Bar, 2004, Connecticut — Member Connecticut and New Haven County Bar Associations — E-mail: mgallagher@susmanduffy.com

Susman, Duffy & Segaloff, P.C., New Haven, CT
(Continued)

Philip G. Kent — 1971 — Boston University, B.A. (cum laude), 1993; B.S., 1993; Mercy College; Quinnipiac University School of Law, J.D. (magna cum laude), 2001 — Phi Delta Phi; Recipient, Distinguished Academic Achievement Awards: Contracts Law, 1999; Jurisprudence, 2001; Sports and Entertainment Law, 2001; Award for Excellence in Clinical Work, Advanced Tax Clinic, 2001; Dean's Scholar, 1998-2001 — Judicial Law Clerk to the Honorable Judge Socrates H. Mihalakos, Connecticut Appellate Court, 2001-2002 — Admitted to Bar, 2001, Connecticut; 2003, New York — Member American, Connecticut and New Haven County Bar Associations — Emergency Certified Teacher's License, New York, 1996-1997, 1997-1998 — E-mail: pkent@susmanduffy.com

Michael J. Pinto — 1970 — New York University, B.A., History, 1993; Quinnipiac University School of Law, J.D., 2007 — Admitted to Bar, 2007, Connecticut; 2010, New York; 2011, U.S. District Court, District of Connecticut — E-mail: mpinto@susmanduffy.com

Matthew A. Ciarleglio — 1987 — University of Connecticut, B.A. Political Science (Dean's List), 2008; Quinnipiac University School of Law, J.D. (cum laude), 2012 — Admitted to Bar, 2012, Connecticut; 2013, New York — E-mail: mciarleglio@susmanduffy.com

Jason L. Stevenson — 1984 — Boston College Carrol School of Management, B.S., 2007; University of Connecticut School of Law, J.D., 2010 — Admitted to Bar, 2011, Connecticut; 2012, New York — E-mail: jstevenson@susmanduffy.com

Trotta, Trotta & Trotta

900 Chapel Street, 12th Floor
New Haven, Connecticut 06510-2802
Telephone: 203-787-6756
Fax: 203-776-4538
E-Mail: etodd@trottalaw.com
www.trottalaw.com

Established: 1927

Insurance Defense, Subrogation, Product Liability, Litigation, Premises Liability, Workers' Compensation, Personal Injury Defense

Firm Profile: For over 87 years, our firm has tried cases for individuals, corporations, insurance companies and self-insureds. Members of our firm have been nationally recognized by the National Law Reporter, American Board of Trial Advocates and accredited by the National Board of Trial Advocates.

Insurance Clients

American Family Insurance Company
Farmers Insurance Company
Foremost Insurance Company
H & W Risk Management, Inc.
Atain Insurance Companies
Chubb Group of Insurance Companies
Gallagher Bassett Services, Inc.
Sedgwick CMS

Non-Insurance Clients

Kmart Corporation
Sears, Roebuck and Co.

Firm Members

Joseph F. Trotta — University of Connecticut School of Law, J.D., 1957 — Admitted to Bar, 1957, Connecticut; 1958, U.S. District Court, District of Connecticut; 1962, U.S. Court of Appeals, Second Circuit; 1965, U.S. Supreme Court — Member American Board of Trial Advocates

Erica W. Todd-Trotta — 1967 — University of Bridgeport School of Law, J.D., 1992 — Admitted to Bar, 1992, Connecticut; 1994, U.S. District Court, District of Connecticut; 1998, U.S. Supreme Court — Member Counsel of Litigation Management — Super Lawyer, New England/Connecticut area since 2010 — Board Ceritified, Civil Trial and Civil Pretrial Advocacy, National Board of Trial Advocates

CONNECTICUT   NEW LONDON

Yules & Yules, LLC
195 Church Street, 17th Floor
New Haven, Connecticut 06510
  Telephone: 203-789-1000
  Fax: 203-789-6320
  E-Mail: yuleslaw@yuleslaw.com
  www.Yuleslaw.com

Medical Devices, Insurance Law, Product Liability, Professional Malpractice, Workers' Compensation, Medical Malpractice

Firm Profile: Since 1938, Yules & Yules has represented insurers and self-insureds in cases involving products liability, professional malpractice, insurance, business torts, wrongful death, workers' compensation and motor carrier, rail and transportation law.

Insurance Clients

Allstate Insurance Company   Chubb Group

Firm Members

Herman Yules — (1910-1999)

Robert B. Yules — The University of Toledo College of Law, J.D., 1977 — Admitted to Bar, 1978, Connecticut; 1992, New York — Member American, Connecticut and New York State Bar Associations

Associate

Matthew S. Cahill

The following firms also service this area.

Berchem, Moses & Devlin, PC
75 Broad Street
Milford, Connecticut 06460
  Telephone: 203-783-1200
  Fax: 203-878-4912

Insurance Defense, Automobile, Bad Faith, Common Carrier, Construction Liability, Environmental Liability, Governmental Liability, Hospitals, Legal Malpractice, Municipal Liability, Medical Malpractice, Professional Malpractice, Trial Practice, Workers' Compensation, Premises Liability, Liquor Liability, Civil Rights, Employment Practices Liability, Police Liability Defense

SEE COMPLETE LISTING UNDER BRIDGEPORT, CONNECTICUT (12 MILES)

Coles, Baldwin & Kaiser, LLC
1261 Post Road, First Floor
Fairfield, Connecticut 06824
  Telephone: 203-319-0800
  Fax: 203-319-1210

Insurance Defense, Casualty, First Party Matters, Professional Malpractice, Workers' Compensation, Coverage Issues, Employment Law, Discrimination, Sexual Harassment, Municipal Liability, Governmental Liability, Life and Health, Americans with Disabilities Act, Advertising Injury, Agent and Brokers Errors and Omissions, Arson, Asbestos Litigation, Automobile Liability, Bad Faith, Bodily Injury, Business Law, Carrier Defense, Casualty Insurance Law, Commercial General Liability, Construction Accidents, Construction Litigation, Declaratory Judgments, Directors and Officers Liability, ERISA, Employment Discrimination, Equal Employment Opportunity Commission, Examinations Under Oath, Fire and Allied Lines, Inland Marine, Insurance Coverage, Law Enforcement Liability, Legal Malpractice, Municipal Law, Personal Lines, Premises Liability, Professional Liability, Property and Casualty, Self-Insured Defense, Special Investigative Unit Claims, Uninsured and Underinsured Motorist, Fair Housing Act

SEE COMPLETE LISTING UNDER BRIDGEPORT, CONNECTICUT (18 MILES)

Ryan Ryan Deluca LLP
707 Summer Street
Stamford, Connecticut 06901-1026
  Telephone: 203-357-9200
  Fax: 203-357-7915

Insurance Defense, Appellate Practice, Asbestos Litigation, Automobile Liability, Construction Law, Coverage Issues, Directors and Officers Liability, Environmental Law, Fire, Law Enforcement Liability, Legal Malpractice, Liquor Liability, Medical Malpractice, Municipal Liability, Premises Liability, Professional Liability, Railroad Law, School Law, Subrogation, Transportation, Trucking Law

SEE COMPLETE LISTING UNDER STAMFORD, CONNECTICUT (40 MILES)

NEW LONDON   27,620 New London Co.

Refer To

Berchem, Moses & Devlin, PC
75 Broad Street
Milford, Connecticut 06460
  Telephone: 203-783-1200
  Fax: 203-878-4912

Insurance Defense, Automobile, Bad Faith, Common Carrier, Construction Liability, Environmental, Governmental Liability, Hospitals, Legal Malpractice, Municipal Liability, Medical Malpractice, Professional Malpractice, Trial Practice, Workers' Compensation, Premises Liability, Liquor Liability, Civil Rights, Employment Practices Liability, Police Liability Defense

SEE COMPLETE LISTING UNDER BRIDGEPORT, CONNECTICUT (57 MILES)

Refer To

Brown Jacobson P.C.
Twenty-Two Courthouse Square
Norwich, Connecticut 06360
  Telephone: 860-889-3321
  Fax: 860-886-0673

Mailing Address: P.O. Box 391, Norwich, CT 06360-0391

Insurance Defense

SEE COMPLETE LISTING UNDER NORWICH, CONNECTICUT (14 MILES)

Refer To

Lippman & Ouellette, L.L.C.
142 Temple Street
New Haven, Connecticut 06510
  Telephone: 203-776-4546
  Fax: 203-776-4435

Insurance Defense, Automobile Liability, Personal Injury, Property Damage, Casualty, Fire, General Liability, Premises Liability, Homeowners, Commercial Liability, Trucking Liability, Dram Shop, Municipal Liability, Uninsured and Underinsured Motorist, Bad Faith, CUTPA/CUIPA, Legal Defense/Coverage Opinions, Declaratory Judgments, Subrogation, Appeals, Arbitration, Mediation and Administrative Hearings

SEE COMPLETE LISTING UNDER NEW HAVEN, CONNECTICUT (48 MILES)

Refer To

Nuzzo & Roberts, L.L.C.
One Town Center
Cheshire, Connecticut 06410
  Telephone: 203-250-2000
  Fax: 203-250-3131
  Toll Free: 888-866-8297

Mailing Address: P.O. Box 747, Cheshire, CT 06410

Insurance Defense, Professional Liability, Legal Malpractice, Directors and Officers Liability, Workers' Compensation, Construction Litigation, Premises Liability, Product Liability, Toxic Torts, Trucking, Transportation, Appellate Practice, Coverage/Bad Faith Issues, Motor Vehicle Tort

SEE COMPLETE LISTING UNDER NEW HAVEN, CONNECTICUT (49 MILES)

Refer To

Susman, Duffy & Segaloff, P.C.
59 Elm Street
New Haven, Connecticut 06510
 Telephone: 203-624-9830
 Fax: 203-562-8430
Mailing Address: P.O. Box 1684, New Haven, CT 06507

Insurance Defense, General Liability, Product Liability, Professional Liability, Construction Law, Fidelity and Surety

SEE COMPLETE LISTING UNDER NEW HAVEN, CONNECTICUT (49 MILES)

NORWALK 85,603 Fairfield Co.

Refer To

Berchem, Moses & Devlin, PC
75 Broad Street
Milford, Connecticut 06460
 Telephone: 203-783-1200
 Fax: 203-878-4912

Insurance Defense, Automobile, Bad Faith, Common Carrier, Construction Liability, Environmental Liability, Governmental Liability, Hospitals, Legal Malpractice, Municipal Liability, Medical Malpractice, Professional Malpractice, Trial Practice, Workers' Compensation, Premises Liability, Liquor Liability, Civil Rights, Employment Practices Liability, Police Liability Defense

SEE COMPLETE LISTING UNDER BRIDGEPORT, CONNECTICUT (23 MILES)

NORWICH 40,493 New London Co.

Brown Jacobson P.C.
Twenty-Two Courthouse Square
Norwich, Connecticut 06360
 Telephone: 860-889-3321
 Fax: 860-886-0673
 www.brownjacobson.com

Established: 1966

Insurance Defense

Insurance Clients

Allied World Assurance Company	Catholic Mutual Group
CCMSI	Commerce Insurance Company
ESIS	Liberty Mutual Insurance Company
Nationwide Mutual Insurance Company	New London County Mutual Insurance Company
Pennsylvania Lumbermens Mutual Insurance Company	Quincy Mutual Fire Insurance Company
Safeco Insurance	Vermont Mutual Insurance Company

Non-Insurance Clients

Lawrence + Memorial Hospital
The William W. Backus Hospital
Mashantucket Pequot Tribal Nation

Partners

Wayne G. Tillinghast — 1935 — University of Connecticut, B.S., 1957; LL.B. (with honors), 1960 — Admitted to Bar, 1960, Connecticut; 1961, U.S. District Court, District of Connecticut; 1967, U.S. Supreme Court — Member Connecticut Defense Lawyers Association (President, 1982-1983); Advocate, American Board of Trial Advocates; Fellow, American College of Trial Lawyers — Adjunct Professor of Law, Trial Practice, University of Connecticut Law School, 1979-1999 — Practice Areas: Medical Malpractice Defense — E-mail: wtillinghast@brownjacobson.com

Michael E. Driscoll — 1948 — Georgetown University, B.S., 1970; J.D., 1973 — Admitted to Bar, 1973, Connecticut; 1975, U.S. District Court, District of Connecticut; 1992, Mashantucket Pequot Tribal Court; 1997, Mohegan Gaming Disputes Court — Member Connecticut and New London County Bar Associations; Connecticut Defense Lawyers Association (President, 1992-1993); National Defense Lawyers Association; Associate, American Board of Trial Advocates; Connecticut Association of Municipal Attorneys; International Association of Defense Counsel — Practice Areas: General Civil Litigation; Insurance Defense; Municipal Law — E-mail: mdriscoll@brownjacobson.com

Brown Jacobson P.C., Norwich, CT (Continued)

David S. Williams — 1951 — University of California, Santa Barbara, B.A., 1973; University of the Pacific, McGeorge School of Law, J.D., 1978 — Admitted to Bar, 1978, California; 1979, Connecticut; 1979, U.S. District Court, District of Connecticut; 1992, Mashantucket Pequot Tribal Court; 1996, U.S. Court of Appeals, Second Circuit; 1997, Mohegan Sun Gaming Disputes Court — Member American, Connecticut and New London County Bar Associations; Connecticut Defense Lawyers Association — Practice Areas: Insurance Defense; General Civil Litigation — E-mail: dwilliams@brownjacobson.com

Jeffrey F. Buebendorf — 1961 — Hamilton College, B.A., 1983; University of Connecticut School of Law, J.D. (cum laude), 1994 — Phi Delta Phi (Past President), Trustee — Admitted to Bar, 1994, Connecticut; 1994, U.S. District Court, District of Connecticut; 1995, Mashantucket Pequot Tribal Court; 1997, Mohegan Gaming Disputes Court; 2006, U.S. Court of Appeals, Second Circuit; 2007, U.S. Supreme Court — Member American, Connecticut (Treasurer) and New London County Bar Associations; Fellow, American Bar Foundation — Practice Areas: Employment Law; General Civil Litigation — E-mail: jbuebendorf@brownjacobson.com

PUTNAM 7,214 Windham Co.

Refer To

Brown Jacobson P.C.
Twenty-Two Courthouse Square
Norwich, Connecticut 06360
 Telephone: 860-889-3321
 Fax: 860-886-0673
Mailing Address: P.O. Box 391, Norwich, CT 06360-0391

Insurance Defense

SEE COMPLETE LISTING UNDER NORWICH, CONNECTICUT (30 MILES)

Refer To

Lippman & Ouellette, L.L.C.
142 Temple Street
New Haven, Connecticut 06510
 Telephone: 203-776-4546
 Fax: 203-776-4435

Insurance Defense, Automobile Liability, Personal Injury, Property Damage, Casualty, Fire, General Liability, Premises Liability, Homeowners, Commercial Liability, Trucking Liability, Dram Shop, Municipal Liability, Uninsured and Underinsured Motorist, Bad Faith, CUTPA/CUIPA, Legal Defense/Coverage Opinions, Declaratory Judgments, Subrogation, Appeals, Arbitration, Mediation and Administrative Hearings

SEE COMPLETE LISTING UNDER NEW HAVEN, CONNECTICUT (89 MILES)

ROCKVILLE 7,474 Tolland Co.

Refer To

Berchem, Moses & Devlin, PC
75 Broad Street
Milford, Connecticut 06460
 Telephone: 203-783-1200
 Fax: 203-878-4912

Insurance Defense, Automobile, Bad Faith, Common Carrier, Construction Liability, Environmental Liability, Governmental Liability, Hospitals, Legal Malpractice, Municipal Liability, Medical Malpractice, Professional Malpractice, Trial Practice, Workers' Compensation, Premises Liability, Liquor Liability, Civil Rights, Employment Practices Liability, Police Liability Defense

SEE COMPLETE LISTING UNDER BRIDGEPORT, CONNECTICUT (63 MILES)

CONNECTICUT — SOUTHINGTON

SOUTHINGTON 28,567 Hartford Co.

Sheffy, Mazzaccaro, DePaolo & Denigris, LLP

166 North Main Street
Southington, Connecticut 06489
　Telephone: 860-620-9460
　Fax: 860-620-9348
　E-Mail: tsheffy@smddlaw.com
　www.smddlaw.com

Established: 1996

Insurance Defense, Insurance Coverage, Personal Injury, Municipal Liability, Premises Liability, Subrogation

Firm Profile: Our firm is known for the accessibility of the lawyers and our aggressive representation of our clients. We offer Flat Fee Arrangements.

Representative Insurance Clients

AutoOne Insurance Company	Infinity Insurance Company
Lloyd's	MetLife Auto & Home
Omni Insurance Company	

Founding Partner

Anthony Alan Sheffy — 1963 — Lebanon Valley College, B.S., 1985; Western New England College School of Law, J.D. (magna cum laude), 1988 — Western New England Law Review (1986-1987) — Admitted to Bar, 1988, Connecticut; 1989, U.S. District Court, District of Connecticut — Member American and Connecticut Bar Associations; Litigation Counsel of America; Connecticut Defense Lawyers Association — Founder and Editor of Recovery Magazine; Monthly Legal Column in the Southington Observer — NBI Guest Seminar Lectures: Uninsured Motorist Coverage and Depositions of Expert Witnesses; Super Lawyers' Million Dollar Advocates Forum; AV Rated, Martindale Hubbell; Connecticut Super Lawyers — Certified National Institute of Trial Advocacy — Practice Areas: Coverage Opinions; Declaratory Judgments; Personal and Commercial Lines Insurance Defense

STAMFORD 122,643 Fairfield Co.

Jones Morrison, LLP

60 Long Ridge Road, Suite 202
Stamford, Connecticut 06902
　Telephone: 203-965-7700
　www.jonesmorrisonlaw.com
　E-Mail: info@jonesmorrisonlaw.com

(Scarsdale, NY Office*(See White Plains listing): 670 White Plains Road, Penthouse, 10583)
　(Tel: 914-472-2300)
　(Fax: 914-472-2312)
(New York, NY Office*: 60 East 42nd Street, 40th Floor, 10165)
　(Tel: 212-759-2500)

Alternative Dispute Resolution, Architects and Engineers, Asbestos, Bad Faith, Bankruptcy, Business Law, Commercial Litigation, Construction Law, Creditor's Rights, Coverage Analysis, Directors and Officers Liability, Environmental Law, Errors and Omissions, Labor and Employment, Medical Malpractice, Motor Vehicle, Municipal Liability, Premises Liability, Product Liability, Professional Liability, Property Damage

---

Jones Morrison, LLP, Stamford, CT　　(Continued)

Insurance Clients

Everest National Insurance Company	GEICO
Markel Insurance Company	The Hartford
Sompo Japan Insurance Company of America	Selective Insurance Company of America
	Travelers Indemnity Company

Managing Partner

Stephen J. Jones — Williams College, B.A., 1987; Fordham University School of Law, J.D., 1993 — Admitted to Bar, 1994, New York; U.S. District Court, Eastern and Southern Districts of New York; U.S. Supreme Court — Member The Business Council of Westchester (Chairman of the Board; Executive Committee Member); United Way of Westchester and Putnam (Director); Westchester-Putnam Council of the Boys Scouts of America (Director, Executive Committee Member); Westchester County Industrial Development Agency (Board Member); Legal Services of the Hudson Valley (Past Director); Justice Court for the Village of Tarrytown, New York State Unified Court System (Past Justice); Westchester-Putnam Fordham Law Alumni (Past President); The Williams Club of New York (Past Board of Governors) — Eagle Scout — Practice Areas: Corporate Law; Commercial Transactions; Litigation; Real Estate

Partners

Daniel W. Morrison — Haverford College, B.A., 1980; Fordham University School of Law, J.D., 1984 — Admitted to Bar, 1985, New York; Connecticut; U.S. District Court, Eastern, Northern, Southern and Western Districts of New York; U.S. Supreme Court — Member American and New York State (Co-Chair, Environmental Insurance Committee) Bar Associations; Claims & Litigation Management Alliance; American Corporate Counsel Association; Westchest-Putman Fordham Law Alumni Association (Past President) — Practice Areas: Insurance Law; Product Liability; Professional Liability; Environmental Law; Construction Law; Commercial Litigation; Corporate Litigation; Real Estate; Bad Faith

Terence J. Gallagher — The Wharton School of the University of Pennsylvania, B.S., 1988; University of Pennsylvania, B.A., 1989; Pace University, M.S., 1990; University of Southern California School of Law, J.D., 1993 — Admitted to Bar, 1994, Connecticut; New York; U.S. District Court, District of Connecticut; U.S. District Court, Eastern and Southern Districts of New York; U.S. Court of Appeals, Second Circuit; U.S. Supreme Court — Member Connecticut Bar Association; Federal Bar Council — Practice Areas: Class Actions; Complex Litigation; Directors and Officers Liability; Securities; Breach of Contract

(See listing under White Plains, NY for additional information)

Ryan Ryan Deluca LLP

707 Summer Street
Stamford, Connecticut 06901-1026
　Telephone: 203-357-9200
　Fax: 203-357-7915
　E-Mail: info@ryandelucalaw.com
　www.ryandelucalaw.com

Established: 1954

Insurance Defense, Appellate Practice, Asbestos Litigation, Automobile Liability, Construction Law, Coverage Issues, Directors and Officers Liability, Environmental Law, Fire, Law Enforcement Liability, Legal Malpractice, Liquor Liability, Medical Malpractice, Municipal Liability, Premises Liability, Professional Liability, Railroad Law, School Law, Subrogation, Transportation, Trucking Law

Insurance Clients

ACE Private Risk Services	Adventist Risk Management, Inc.
AIG Technical Services, Inc.	AIX Group
Alliance of Nonprofits for Insurance	Allied World Assurance Company
Aon Risk Services, Inc.	American Contractors Insurance Group

STAMFORD   **CONNECTICUT**

Ryan Ryan Deluca LLP, Stamford, CT   (Continued)

Arch Insurance Group
Argo Insurance - U.S. Grocery & Retail
Aviva Insurance Company of Canada
Balboa Insurance Company
Central Mutual Insurance Company
Chubb Group of Insurance Companies
Church Mutual Insurance Company
Claims Services Bureau of NY
CNA Insurance Companies
Colony Specialty
Connecticut Interlocal Risk Management Agency (CIRMA)
Connecticut Medical Insurance Company (CMIC)
Coverys
Crawford & Company
Crum & Forster Insurance
Cunningham Lindsey U.S., Inc.
Endurance Services, Ltd.
ESIS
ESIS ProClaim
Esurance Insurance Company
Farmers Insurance Group
Federated Mutual Insurance Company
Fireman's Fund Insurance Company
GCAN Insurance Company
GEICO
General Star Indemnity Company
Global Indemnity Group
GuideOne
Intercare Insurance Services, Inc.
Ironshore Insurance, Ltd.
Lawyer's Protector Plan
Lexington Insurance Company
Magna Carta Companies
Markel
MetLife Auto & Home
Minnesota Lawyers Mutual Insurance Company
Mitsui Sumitomo Insurance Group
Nautilus Insurance Company
Navigators Insurance Company
Old Republic Construction Program Group
Ophthalmic Mutual Insurance Company
Philadelphia Insurance Companies
Privilege Underwriters Reciprocal Exchange (PURE)
PRMS, Inc. - Professional Risk Management Services, Inc.
Progressive Casualty Insurance Company
The Redwoods Group
RLI Transportation
Rockville Risk Management Associates
Seneca Insurance Company, Inc.
Swiss Reinsurance Company
Tower Group Companies
Travelers Insurance Companies
USAA Casualty Insurance Company
Utica Mutual Insurance Company
Westfield Insurance
Zurich American Insurance Group

Non-Insurance Clients

Ascension Health
CareOne
Davita, Inc.
Dyson-Kissner-Moran Corporation
GAMBRO Healthcare, Inc.
Genesee & Wyoming Inc.
Griffin Hospital
Hall-Brooke Hospital
Home Depot USA, Inc.
Hospital of St. Raphael
LaFarge North America, Inc.
Metro-North Railroad
Milford Hospital
Quest Diagnostics
RailAmerica, Inc.
St. Mary's Hospital
St. Vincent's Medical Center
Skanska USA Building, Inc.
Stamford Health Systems
Stamford Hospital
Toys "R" Us, Inc.
Yale-New Haven Hospital

Firm Members

Charles A. Deluca — 1950 — University of Connecticut, B.A., 1973; Brooklyn Law School, J.D. (cum laude), 1977 — Admitted to Bar, 1977, Connecticut; 1978, U.S. District Court, District of Connecticut; 1980, U.S. District Court, Eastern and Southern Districts of New York; 1985, U.S. Court of Appeals, Second Circuit — Member Fellow, American College of Trial Lawyers; Federation of Defense and Corporate Counsel; International Association of Defense Counsel — E-mail: cdeluca@ryandelucalaw.com

Daniel E. Ryan, III — 1955 — Boston College, A.B., 1977; Fordham University School of Law, J.D., 1980 — Admitted to Bar, 1981, Connecticut; 1992, New York; 1983, U.S. District Court, District of Connecticut; 1984, U.S. District Court, Eastern and Southern Districts of New York — E-mail: deryan@ryandelucalaw.com

Michael T. Ryan — 1957 — Boston College, A.B. (magna cum laude), 1979; Boston College Law School, J.D., 1982 — Admitted to Bar, 1982, Connecticut; 1983, U.S. District Court, District of Connecticut; 1984, U.S. District Court, Eastern and Southern Districts of New York; 1987, U.S. Court of Appeals, Second Circuit; 2000, U.S. Court of Appeals, First Circuit — E-mail: mtryan@ryandelucalaw.com

Kevin M. Tepas — 1947 — Holy Cross College, B.S., 1969; University of Connecticut School of Law, J.D., 1972 — Admitted to Bar, 1972, Connecticut; 1977, U.S. District Court, District of Connecticut — E-mail: kmtepas@ryandelucalaw.com

Robert C. E. Laney — 1962 — College of William & Mary, B.A., 1985; College of William & Mary, Marshall-Wythe School of Law, J.D., 1988 — Admitted to Bar, 1988, Virginia; 1990, North Carolina; 1992, Connecticut; 1988, U.S. District Court, Eastern District of Virginia; U.S. Court of Appeals, Fourth Circuit; 1991, U.S. District Court, Eastern District of North Carolina; 1992, U.S. District Court, District of Connecticut — E-mail: roblaney@ryandelucalaw.com

Ryan Ryan Deluca LLP, Stamford, CT   (Continued)

Catherine S. Nietzel — 1964 — Georgetown University, B.S.F.S., 1986; Fordham University School of Law, J.D., 1992 — Admitted to Bar, 1996, Connecticut; 1997, U.S. District Court, District of Connecticut; U.S. Court of Appeals, Second Circuit — E-mail: cnietzel@ryandelucalaw.com

Robert O. Hickey — 1964 — University of Connecticut, B.A., 1986; Quinnipiac College School of Law, J.D. (cum laude), 1997 — Admitted to Bar, 1997, Connecticut — E-mail: rohickey@ryandelucalaw.com

James J. Noonan — 1972 — Stonehill College, B.A., 1994; Quinnipiac College School of Law, J.D., 1997 — Admitted to Bar, 1997, Connecticut; 1998, New York; U.S. District Court, District of Connecticut; 1999, U.S. District Court, Southern District of New York; 2002, U.S. Supreme Court — E-mail: jjnoonan@ryandelucalaw.com

John F. Costa — 1960 — College of the Holy Cross, B.A., 1982; Brooklyn Law School, J.D., 1985 — Admitted to Bar, 1985, Connecticut; 1986, New York; U.S. District Court, District of Connecticut; U.S. District Court, Eastern and Southern Districts of New York — E-mail: jfcosta@ryandelucalaw.com

James A. Mahar — 1966 — The Pennsylvania State University, B.S., 1989; Pace University School of Law, J.D., 1995 — Admitted to Bar, 1995, Connecticut; 1996, New York — E-mail: jamahar@ryandelucalaw.com

Sally O. Hagerty — 1960 — The Ohio State University, B.S.N., 1984; The Ohio State University Moritz College of Law, 1987 — Admitted to Bar, 1987, Illinois; 1996, Connecticut — E-mail: sohagerty@ryandelucalaw.com

Beck S. Fineman — 1979 — Smith College, B.A., 2001; University of Maryland School of Law, J.D., 2006 — Admitted to Bar, 2007, Connecticut — E-mail: bsfineman@ryandelucalaw.com

Counsel

Joanne P. Sheehan — 1957 — Pace University, B.S.N. (cum laude), 1982; Pace University School of Law, J.D., 1987 — Admitted to Bar, 1987, Connecticut; 1988, New York; U.S. District Court, District of Connecticut; 1998, U.S. Supreme Court — E-mail: jpsheehan@ryandelucalaw.com

Associates

Maciej A. Piatkowski — 1971 — Georgetown University, B.A., 1993; University of Connecticut School of Law, J.D., 1997 — Admitted to Bar, 1997, Connecticut — E-mail: mapiatkowski@ryandelucalaw.com

Brian M. Candela — 1979 — Fordham University, B.A. (magna cum laude), 2001; Fordham Law School, J.D., 2004 — Admitted to Bar, 2004, Connecticut; 2005, New York — E-mail: bmcandela@ryandelucalaw.com

Michael R. Young — 1976 — State University of New York at Plattsburgh, B.A., 1998; Quinnipiac University School of Law, J.D., 2002 — Admitted to Bar, 2003, Connecticut — E-mail: mryoung@ryandelucalaw.com

John W. Cannavino Jr. — 1980 — Case Western Reserve University, B.A., 2004; University of San Francisco School of Law, J.D., 2007 — Admitted to Bar, 2007, Connecticut — E-mail: jwcannavino@ryandelucalaw.com

Liam M. West — 1978 — Hamilton College, B.A., 2000; Western New England College School of Law, J.D., 2006 — Admitted to Bar, 2007, Connecticut — E-mail: lmwest@ryandelucalaw.com

Claire E. Ryan — 1970 — Kenyon College, B.A. (cum laude), 1992; American University, Washington College of Law, J.D. (cum laude), 1999 — Admitted to Bar, 1999, Connecticut; 2000, New York; 2001, District of Columbia — E-mail: ceryan@ryandelucalaw.com

Peter E. DeMartini — 1981 — Boston College, B.A. (cum laude), 2004; Syracuse University College of Law (summa cum laude), 2008 — Admitted to Bar, 2009, New York; Massachusetts; 2010, Connecticut — E-mail: pedemartini@ryandelucalaw.com

Gina M. Von Oehsen — 1969 — Boston College, B.A., 1991; Fordham University School of Law, J.D., 1994 — Admitted to Bar, 1994, Connecticut; 1995, New York — E-mail: gmvonoehsen@ryandelucalaw.com

Nicole D. Wright — 1985 — Providence College, B.A. Political Science (magna cum laude), 2007; Hofstra University, J.D. (cum laude), 2010 — Admitted to Bar, 2011, Connecticut; New York — E-mail: ndwright@ryandelucalaw.com

Jonathan C. Zellner — 1985 — Hamilton College, B.A. (cum laude, with high distinction in Government), 2008; University of Connecticut School of Law, J.D., 2011 — Admitted to Bar, 2011, Connecticut — E-mail: jczellner@ryandelucalaw.com

Thomas J. Plumridge — 1986 — Tufts University, B.A. (magna cum laude), 2008; Quinnipiac University School of Law, J.D. (magna cum laude), 2011 — Admitted to Bar, 2011, Connecticut — E-mail: tjplumridge@ryandelucalaw.com

CONNECTICUT

Ryan Ryan Deluca LLP, Stamford, CT (Continued)

Michael C. Barbarula — 1987 — University of Connecticut at Storrs, B.A. Political Science, 2009; Penn State University, J.D., 2012 — Admitted to Bar, 2012, Connecticut — E-mail: mcbarbarula@ryandelucalaw.com

John Kanca — 1983 — Boston College, B.A. Political Science, 2006; University of Connecticut School of Law, J.D., 2009 — Admitted to Bar, 2009, Connecticut — E-mail: jkanca@ryandelucalaw.com

Shivani J. Desai — 1985 — The Cooper Union, B.E.M.E. (Dean's List), 2007; Quinnipiac College School of Law, J.D. (magna cum laude), 2011 — Admitted to Bar, 2011, Connecticut — E-mail: sjdesai@ryandelucalaw.com

Thomas S. Lambert — 1987 — Pepperdine University, B.A. Political Science (maxima cum laude), 2010; Wake Forest University School of Law, J.D., 2013 — Admitted to Bar, 2013, Connecticut — E-mail: tslambert@ryandelucalaw.com

Amanda L. Carlson — 1986 — Boston University, B.S., 2008; Quinnipiac University School of Law, J.D. (cum laude), 2011 — Admitted to Bar, 2011, Connecticut — E-mail: alcarlson@ryandelucalaw.com

Of Counsel

Charles M. McCaghey — 1940 — Manhattan College, B.A., 1962; Cornell University Law School, LL.B., 1965 — Admitted to Bar, 1965, New York; 1991, Connecticut; 1968, U.S. District Court, Southern District of New York; 1972, U.S. Court of Appeals, Second Circuit; 1978, U.S. District Court, Eastern District of New York; 1988, U.S. District Court, Western District of New York; 1992, U.S. District Court, District of Connecticut — E-mail: cmccaghey@ryandelucalaw.com

Elizabeth Ryan Lane — 1958 — Boston College, B.A. (magna cum laude), 1980; Fordham University School of Law, J.D., 1983 — Admitted to Bar, 1983, Connecticut; 1984, New York — E-mail: erlane@ryandelucalaw.com

Kieran M. Ryan — 1968 — Marquette University, B.A., 1990; Franklin Pierce Law Center, J.D., 1995 — Admitted to Bar, 1995, Connecticut; New York — E-mail: kmryan@ryandelucalaw.com

(Revisors of the Connecticut Insurance Law Digest for this Publication)

Slutsky, McMorris & Meehan, LLP

396 Danbury Road, 2nd Floor
Wilton, Connecticut 06897
Telephone: 203-762-9815
Fax: 203-762-9864
E-Mail: williammeehan@snet.net

Insurance Defense, Property, Casualty, Professional Liability, Construction Defect, Product Liability

Insurance Clients

St. Paul Reinsurance Company Limited   Underwriters at Lloyd's, London

Partner

William A. Meehan — 1955 — Stony Brook University, B.A., 1977; Fordham Law School, J.D., 1980 — Admitted to Bar, 1981, New York; 1997, Connecticut; 1983, U.S. District Court, Eastern and Southern Districts of New York; 1992, U.S. Court of Appeals, Second Circuit; 1993, U.S. Supreme Court; 1998, U.S. District Court, District of Connecticut — Member American, Connecticut and New York State Bar Associations; Professional Liability Underwriting Society

The following firms also service this area.

Berchem, Moses & Devlin, PC

75 Broad Street
Milford, Connecticut 06460
Telephone: 203-783-1200
Fax: 203-878-4912

Insurance Defense, Automobile, Bad Faith, Common Carrier, Construction Liability, Environmental Liability, Governmental Liability, Hospitals, Legal Malpractice, Municipal Liability, Medical Malpractice, Professional Malpractice, Trial Practice, Workers' Compensation, Premises Liability, Liquor Liability, Civil Rights, Employment Practices Liability, Police Liability Defense

SEE COMPLETE LISTING UNDER BRIDGEPORT, CONNECTICUT (21 MILES)

STRATFORD

Coles, Baldwin & Kaiser, LLC

1261 Post Road, First Floor
Fairfield, Connecticut 06824
Telephone: 203-319-0800
Fax: 203-319-1210

Insurance Defense, Casualty, First Party Matters, Professional Malpractice, Workers' Compensation, Coverage Issues, Employment Law, Discrimination, Sexual Harassment, Municipal Liability, Governmental Liability, Life and Health, Americans with Disabilities Act, Advertising Injury, Agent and Brokers Errors and Omissions, Arson, Asbestos Litigation, Automobile Liability, Bad Faith, Bodily Injury, Business Law, Carrier Defense, Casualty Insurance Law, Commercial General Liability, Construction Accidents, Construction Litigation, Declaratory Judgments, Directors and Officers Liability, ERISA, Employment Discrimination, Equal Employment Opportunity Commission, Examinations Under Oath, Fire and Allied Lines, Inland Marine, Insurance Coverage, Law Enforcement Liability, Legal Malpractice, Municipal Law, Personal Lines, Premises Liability, Professional Liability, Property and Casualty, Self-Insured Defense, Special Investigative Unit Claims, Uninsured and Underinsured Motorist, Fair Housing Act

SEE COMPLETE LISTING UNDER BRIDGEPORT, CONNECTICUT (21 MILES)

Lippman & Ouellette, L.L.C.

142 Temple Street
New Haven, Connecticut 06510
Telephone: 203-776-4546
Fax: 203-776-4435

Insurance Defense, Automobile Liability, Personal Injury, Property Damage, Casualty, Fire, General Liability, Premises Liability, Homeowners, Commercial Liability, Trucking Liability, Dram Shop, Municipal Liability, Uninsured and Underinsured Motorist, Bad Faith, CUTPA/CUIPA, Legal Defense/Coverage Opinions, Declaratory Judgments, Subrogation, Appeals, Arbitration, Mediation and Administrative Hearings

SEE COMPLETE LISTING UNDER NEW HAVEN, CONNECTICUT (41 MILES)

Susman, Duffy & Segaloff, P.C.

59 Elm Street
New Haven, Connecticut 06510
Telephone: 203-624-9830
Fax: 203-562-8430
Mailing Address: P.O. Box 1684, New Haven, CT 06507

Insurance Defense, General Liability, Product Liability, Professional Liability, Construction Law, Fidelity and Surety

SEE COMPLETE LISTING UNDER NEW HAVEN, CONNECTICUT (39 MILES)

Wolf, Horowitz & Etlinger, L.L.C.

99 Pratt Street, Fourth Floor
Hartford, Connecticut 06103
Telephone: 860-724-6667
Fax: 860-293-1979

Insurance Defense, Litigation, Toxic Torts, Product Liability, Insurance Coverage, Malpractice, Surety, Fidelity, Construction Law, Subrogation

SEE COMPLETE LISTING UNDER HARTFORD, CONNECTICUT (77 MILES)

STRATFORD 51,384 Fairfield Co.

Law Offices of Paul A. Lange, LLC

80 Ferry Boulevard
Stratford, Connecticut 06615
Telephone: 203-375-7724
Fax: 203-375-9397
E-Mail: pal@lopal.com
www.lopal.com

(New York, NY Office: 445 Park Avenue, 9th Floor, 10022-8632)
(Tel: 212-385-1215)
(Fax: 212-608-1215)

Established: 1992

Aviation, Insurance Defense, Coverage Issues, Employment Law

Firm Profile: The Law Offices of Paul A. Lange, LLC focuses its practice on high stakes litigation and select significant transactions typically involving

Law Offices of Paul A. Lange, LLC, Stratford, CT
(Continued)

aviation, employment, and insurance matters. Our firm is headquartered in Stratford, CT with a satellite office in Manhattan.

Underlying our success in an outstanding work product combined with the personal attention and economies of scale available only in a small, specialty firm. We pride ourselves on high quality, pragmatic, result-oriented legal representation. Our goal is to continually and creatively seek out ways to resolve matters as expeditiously as possible and provide our clients with peace of mind. Our clients require lawyers who can successfully help them meet their goals, whether those goals require careful, delicate and sensitive negotiation, aggressive high stakes litigation, or a combination of both.

Insurance Clients

Aviation Light Services Corporation
Chartis Insurance
CTC Services Aviation (LAD, Inc.)
Houston Casualty Company
Motor Transport Underwriters, Inc.
United States Aviation Underwriters, Inc.
AXA Insurance Company
Chartis Aerospace Adjustment Services, Inc.
Great West Casualty Company
Lloyd's
Phoenix Aviation Managers, Inc.

Non-Insurance Clients

American Airlines, Inc.
Atlas Air Worldwide Holdings, Inc.
Atlantic Aviation, Inc.
Southwest Airlines Company

Paul A. Lange, Esq. — 1961 — C.W. Post College, B.A., 1982; M.B.A., 1988; University of Bridgeport School of Law, J.D., 1986 — Admitted to Bar, 1986, Connecticut; 1987, New York; 1999, Massachusetts; 1988, U.S. District Court, Eastern and Southern Districts of New York; 1992, U.S. District Court, District of Connecticut; 1995, U.S. District Court, Northern and Western Districts of New York; U.S. Court of Appeals for the Federal, District of Columbia, First, Second and Third Circuits; U.S. Court of Appeals for the Armed Forces; 1996, U.S. Supreme Court; 2000, U.S. District Court, District of Massachusetts — Member American Bar Association (Tort and Insurance Practice Section; Forum Committee on Air and Space Law; Administrative Law and Regulatory Practice Section and Litigation Section; FAA Subcommittee and Chair, 1992-1997); National Transportation Safety Board Bar Association; Defense Research Institute (Co-Chair, Legislation and Case Law Panel); Aviation Insurance Association; Lawyer-Pilots Bar Association

WALLINGFORD 40,838 New Haven Co.

Del Sole & Del Sole, L.L.P.
46 South Whittlesey Avenue
Wallingford, Connecticut 06492
 Telephone: 203-284-8000
 Fax: 203-284-9800
 www.delsoledelsole.com

(New Haven, CT Office*: 27 Elm Street, 06510, 46 South Whittlesey Avenue, 06492)
 (Tel: 203-785-8500)
 (Fax: 203-777-4485)
 (E-Mail: ddk@delsoledelsole.com)

Established: 1982

Accountant Malpractice, Corporate Law, Insurance Defense, Legal Malpractice, Medical Liability, Dental Malpractice, Negligence, Product Liability, State and Federal Courts, Subrogation, Trial Practice, Workers' Compensation, Insurance Coverage, Probate

(See listing under New Haven, CT for additional information)

Loughlin FitzGerald, P.C.
150 South Main Street
Wallingford, Connecticut 06492
 Telephone: 203-265-2035
 Fax: 203-269-3487
 E-Mail: creed@lflaw.com
 www.lflaw.com

Insurance Defense, Personal Injury, Insurance Coverage, Medical Malpractice, Product Liability, Appeals

Firm Profile: Our firm serves as defense counsel statewide for several insurance companies and represents numerous self-insured corporations and entities in a wide variety of matters. The firm's expertise extends from personal and commercial lines defense and insurance coverage, to complex commercial disputes, medical malpractice, product liability, sports and leisure, as well as employment and municipal litigation.

Insurance Clients

Acadia Insurance Company
Electric Insurance Company
Empire Fire and Marine Insurance Company
MiddleOak
Preferred Mutual Insurance Company
The Travelers Companies, Inc.
United Educators Insurance
Utica First Insurance Company
American Specialty Insurance Company
Gemini Insurance Company
Hanover Insurance Company
New London County Mutual Insurance Company
Specialty Risk Services
Union Mutual Fire Insurance Company
Zurich Insurance Company

Non-Insurance Clients

AT&T Services, Inc.
The United Illuminating Company

Attorneys

John F. Conway — 1963 — Lehigh University, B.S. (cum laude), 1985; Fordham University School of Law, J.D., 1988 — Law Clerk to the Honorable J. Daniel Mahoney, U.S. Court of Appeals, Second Circuit (1988-1989) — Admitted to Bar, 1989, Connecticut; U.S. District Court, District of Connecticut — E-mail: jconway@lflaw.com

Charles P. Reed — 1964 — Northwestern University, B.A. (cum laude), 1986; University of Notre Dame Law School, J.D., 1990 — Admitted to Bar, 1990, Connecticut; U.S. District Court, District of Connecticut; 1994, U.S. Tax Court; 2002, U.S. Court of Appeals, Second Circuit — E-mail: creed@lflaw.com

W. Glen Pierson — 1969 — Princeton University, A.B. (cum laude), 1990; Georgetown University Law Center, J.D., 1995 — Admitted to Bar, 1996, New York; Connecticut; U.S. District Court, District of Connecticut — E-mail: gpierson@lflaw.com

Eileen R. Becker — 1967 — Syracuse University, A.B., 1989; Rutgers University School of Law-Camden, J.D. (magna cum laude), 1992 — Admitted to Bar, 1992, Pennsylvania; 1994, Connecticut; U.S. District Court, District of Connecticut; 2007, U.S. Court of Appeals, Second Circuit — E-mail: ebecker@lflaw.com

---

The following firms also service this area.

Del Sole & Del Sole, L.L.P.
27 Elm Street
New Haven, Connecticut 06510
 Telephone: 203-785-8500
 Fax: 203-777-4485
Mailing Address: 46 South Whittlesey Avenue, Wallingford, CT 06492

Insurance Defense, Negligence, Product Liability, Medical Liability, Legal Malpractice, Accountant Malpractice, Dental Malpractice, Corporate Law, Subrogation, Trial Practice, State and Federal Courts, Workers' Compensation, Real Estate, Probate

SEE COMPLETE LISTING UNDER NEW HAVEN, CONNECTICUT (14 MILES)

CONNECTICUT — WATERBURY

WATERBURY 110,366 New Haven Co.

Refer To

Berchem, Moses & Devlin, PC
75 Broad Street
Milford, Connecticut 06460
Telephone: 203-783-1200
Fax: 203-878-4912

Insurance Defense, Automobile, Bad Faith, Common Carrier, Construction Liability, Environmental Liability, Governmental Liability, Hospitals, Legal Malpractice, Municipal Liability, Medical Malpractice, Professional Malpractice, Trial Practice, Workers' Compensation, Premises Liability, Liquor Liability, Civil Rights, Employment Practices Liability, Police Liability Defense

SEE COMPLETE LISTING UNDER BRIDGEPORT, CONNECTICUT (29 MILES)

Refer To

Cella - Flanagan, P.C.
Attorneys and Counselors at Law
21 Washington Avenue, Suite A
North Haven, Connecticut 06473
Telephone: 203-239-5851
Fax: 203-234-2974

Insurance Defense, Bodily Injury, Casualty, Automobile, Malpractice, Product Liability

SEE COMPLETE LISTING UNDER NEW HAVEN, CONNECTICUT (21 MILES)

Refer To

Del Sole & Del Sole, L.L.P.
27 Elm Street
New Haven, Connecticut 06510
Telephone: 203-785-8500
Fax: 203-777-4485

Mailing Address: 46 South Whittlesey Avenue, Wallingford, CT 06492

Insurance Defense, Negligence, Product Liability, Medical Liability, Legal Malpractice, Accountant Malpractice, Dental Malpractice, Corporate Law, Subrogation, Trial Practice, State and Federal Courts, Workers' Compensation, Real Estate, Probate

SEE COMPLETE LISTING UNDER NEW HAVEN, CONNECTICUT (21 MILES)

Refer To

Del Sole & Del Sole, L.L.P.
46 South Whittlesey Avenue
Wallingford, Connecticut 06492
Telephone: 203-284-8000
Fax: 203-284-9800

Accountant Malpractice, Corporate Law, Insurance Defense, Legal Malpractice, Medical Liability, Dental Malpractice, Negligence, Product Liability, State and Federal Courts, Subrogation, Trial Practice, Workers' Compensation, Insurance Coverage, Probate

SEE COMPLETE LISTING UNDER WALLINGFORD, CONNECTICUT (13 MILES)

Refer To

Lippman & Ouellette, L.L.C.
142 Temple Street
New Haven, Connecticut 06510
Telephone: 203-776-4546
Fax: 203-776-4435

Insurance Defense, Automobile Liability, Personal Injury, Property Damage, Casualty, Fire, General Liability, Premises Liability, Homeowners, Commercial Liability, Trucking Liability, Dram Shop, Municipal Liability, Uninsured and Underinsured Motorist, Bad Faith, CUTPA/CUIPA, Legal Defense/Coverage Opinions, Declaratory Judgments, Subrogation, Appeals, Arbitration, Mediation and Administrative Hearings

SEE COMPLETE LISTING UNDER NEW HAVEN, CONNECTICUT (27 MILES)

Refer To

Melick & Porter
1 Liberty Square
Boston, Massachusetts 02109
Telephone: 617-523-6200
Fax: 617-523-8130

Accountants, Administrative Law, Advertising Injury, Agent/Broker Liability, Appellate Practice, Architects and Engineers, Asbestos, Automobile, Bad Faith, Commercial Litigation, Complex Litigation, Construction Litigation, Dental Malpractice, Directors and Officers Liability, Employment Practices, Environmental Law, Fire, General Liability, Health Care, Hospitality, Insurance Coverage, Insurance Defense, Lead Paint, Legal Malpractice, Life Insurance, Liquor Liability, Medical Devices, Pharmaceutical, Pollution, Premises Liability, Product Liability, Professional Liability, Property and Casualty, Public Entities, Real Estate Agents & Brokers Liability, Restaurant Liability, State and Federal Courts, Toxic Torts, Transportation, Trucking, Workers' Compensation

SEE COMPLETE LISTING UNDER BOSTON, MASSACHUSETTS (133 MILES)

Refer To

Nuzzo & Roberts, L.L.C.
One Town Center
Cheshire, Connecticut 06410
Telephone: 203-250-2000
Fax: 203-250-3131
Toll Free: 888-866-8297

Mailing Address: P.O. Box 747, Cheshire, CT 06410

Insurance Defense, Professional Liability, Legal Malpractice, Directors and Officers Liability, Workers' Compensation, Construction Litigation, Premises Liability, Product Liability, Toxic Torts, Trucking, Transportation, Appellate Practice, Coverage/Bad Faith Issues, Motor Vehicle Tort

SEE COMPLETE LISTING UNDER NEW HAVEN, CONNECTICUT (21 MILES)

Refer To

Susman, Duffy & Segaloff, P.C.
59 Elm Street
New Haven, Connecticut 06510
Telephone: 203-624-9830
Fax: 203-562-8430

Mailing Address: P.O. Box 1684, New Haven, CT 06507

Insurance Defense, General Liability, Product Liability, Professional Liability, Construction Law, Fidelity and Surety

SEE COMPLETE LISTING UNDER NEW HAVEN, CONNECTICUT (21 MILES)

DELAWARE

CAPITAL: DOVER

COUNTIES AND COUNTY SEATS

County	County Seat
Kent	Dover
New Castle	Wilmington
Sussex	Georgetown

In the text that follows "†" indicates County Seats.

Our files contain additional verified data on the firms listed herein. This additional information is available on request.

A.M. BEST COMPANY

DELAWARE

DOVER † 36,047 Kent Co.

Young & McNelis, LLC
300 South State Street
Dover, Delaware 19901
Telephone: 302-674-8822
Fax: 302-674-8251
E-Mail: jyoung@youngandmcnelis.com

Established: 1975, 2005

Insurance Defense, Automobile, Product Liability, Professional Malpractice, Fire, Casualty

Firm Profile: This firm was established in 2005 following the appointment of the previous senior partner to the Delaware Superior Court Bench, and consists of the two named partners and one associate, as well as experienced paralegal and support personnel. With few exceptions, our practice is the representation of defendants in trial and appellate civil litigation, including tort and coverage defense. We also have extensive experience in alternative dispute resolution, both as representatives of parties and as arbitrators and mediators. We have a long and well documented history of cost-effective, successful legal service to our clients. Additionally, we are engaged in both Bar Association and outside community activities extensively.

Insurance Clients

Aegis Security Insurance Company
CIGNA Property and Casualty Insurance Company
Erie Insurance Group
Farm Family Mutual Insurance Company
Harford Mutual Insurance Company
K & K Insurance Group, Inc.
Lititz Mutual Insurance Company
Millers Mutual Insurance Company
PMA Insurance Group
Scottsdale Insurance Company
T.H.E. Insurance Company
All Risk Insurance Company
Cincinnati Insurance Company
Colonial Insurance Company of California
Goodville Mutual Casualty Company
International Underwriters Insurance Company
League General Insurance Company
Penn Mutual Insurance Company
Ranger Insurance Company
State Farm Insurance Company
United Services Automobile Association (USAA)

Non-Insurance Clients

CNC Insurance Associates, Inc.
MacDonald Company, Inc.

Partners

Jeffrey A. Young — 1968 — Swarthmore College, B.A., 1991; Villanova University School of Law, J.D., 1995 — Delaware Superior Court Clerk, 1995-1996 — Editorial Board, Delaware Law Review — Admitted to Bar, 1995, Delaware; 2004, U.S. Court of Appeals, Third Circuit; 2011, Supreme Court of the United States — Member American, Delaware State (Nominating Committee; Fee Dispute Committee) and Kent County (past-President) Bar Associations; Terry-Carey American Inn of Court (past-President); Executive Board Community Legal Aid Society (past); Supreme Court Rules Committee; Permanent Advisory Committee (Delaware Lawyers' Rules of Professional Conduct; Delaware Uniform Rules of Evidence); Superior Court Civil Advisory Committee; Preliminary Review Committee (Board of Professional Responsibility); Defense Research Institute — Bayhealth Board of Directors and Planning Committee; Delaware Stadium Corporation Board Member — Certified Mediator — Practice Areas: Insurance Defense

Brian Thomas McNelis — 1965 — University of Virginia, B.A., 1987; Widener University School of Law, J.D. (cum laude), 1990 — Ruby R. Vale Clerkship, Hon. Judge Justice Henry R. Horsey, Delaware Supreme Court, 1989 — Admitted to Bar, 1990, Delaware; U.S. District Court, District of Delaware — Member Delaware State and Kent County Bar Associations; American Board of Trial Advocates — Practice Areas: Insurance Defense

Associate

Reneta L. Green-Streett — 1981 — College of William & Mary, B.A. (magna cum laude), 2003; The College of William and Mary, Marshall-Wythe School of Law, J.D., 2009 — Delaware Superior Court Law Clerk, 2009-2010 — Admitted to Bar, 2009, Delaware — Member Delaware State and Kent County Bar Associations — Practice Areas: Insurance Defense

GEORGETOWN † 6,422 Sussex Co.

Refer To
Young & McNelis, LLC
300 South State Street
Dover, Delaware 19901
Telephone: 302-674-8822
Fax: 302-674-8251

Insurance Defense, Automobile, Product Liability, Professional Malpractice, Fire, Casualty

SEE COMPLETE LISTING UNDER DOVER, DELAWARE (35 MILES)

WILMINGTON † 70,851 New Castle Co.

Casarino Christman Shalk Ransom & Doss, P.A.
405 North King Street, Suite 300
Wilmington, Delaware 19801
Telephone: 302-594-4500
Fax: 302-594-4509
E-Mail: mashlock@casarino.com
www.casarino.com

Established: 1989

Insurance Defense, General Liability, Negligence, Litigation, Workers' Compensation, Product Liability, Automobile Liability, Commercial Liability, Asbestos Litigation, Fire, Property Damage, Bankruptcy

Counsel For

RSKCo

Insurance Clients

Acadia Insurance Company
Allianz Insurance Company
American Equity Insurance Company
Ameriprise Auto & Home Insurance
Brethren Mutual Insurance Company
Chester County Mutual Insurance Company
Crawford & Company
Cumberland Insurance Group
Employers Reinsurance Corporation
GAB Robins North America, Inc.
Great American Insurance Company
Horace Mann Insurance Company
Lititz Mutual Insurance Company
National Interstate Insurance Company
Palisades Insurance Company
Progressive Insurance Companies
St. Paul Fire and Marine Insurance Company
Sentry Insurance a Mutual Company
Swiss Reinsurance America Corporation
United Services Automobile Association (USAA)
Westfield Insurance Company
Alliance of Nonprofits for Insurance
American Family Insurance Company
Auto-Owners Insurance Company
Berkley Mid-Atlantic Group
Broadspire, a Crawford Company
California Casualty Management Company
Continental Insurance Company
Crum & Forster Insurance
Donegal Mutual Insurance Company
Essex Insurance Company
Gallagher Bassett Services, Inc.
Harleysville Mutual Insurance Company
Johns Eastern Company, Inc.
Metropolitan Insurance Company
Nautilus Insurance Group
Northland Insurance Company
The Peninsula Insurance Company
Safeco Insurance Companies
Selective Insurance Company of America
State Farm Insurance Companies
Sterling National Insurance Agency
T.H.E. Insurance Company
Travelers Insurance Companies
USAA Casualty Insurance Company
Zurich North America

Non-Insurance Clients

American Express Companies
Greyhound Lines, Inc.
Ryder Truck Rental, Inc.
Cowan Systems, LLC
Pepco Holdings, Inc.
Wilmington Trust Company

Partners

Stephen P. Casarino — 1941 — University of Delaware, B.A., 1963; The

Casarino Christman Shalk Ransom & Doss, P.A., Wilmington, DE (Continued)

Catholic University of America, Columbus School of Law, LL.B., 1966 — Admitted to Bar, 1966, Delaware; 1969, U.S. District Court, District of Delaware; 1982, U.S. Court of Appeals, Third Circuit; 1991, U.S. Supreme Court — Member American and Delaware State Bar Associations; Defense Counsel of Delaware (President, 2001); Diplomate, American Board of Trial Advocates (President, Delaware Chapter, 1997); Fellow, International Society of Barristers; Defense Research Institute; Fellow, American College of Trial Lawyers; American Association for Justice — Assistant City Solicitor, Wilimington, Delaware, 1968-1969 — Captain, U.S. Army [1966-1968] — E-mail: scasarino@casarino.com

Beth H. Christman — 1955 — Central College, B.A., 1977; The George Washington University Law School, J.D., 1980 — Admitted to Bar, 1981, District of Columbia (Inactive); 1982, Delaware; 1984, Pennsylvania; 1982, U.S. District Court, District of Delaware — Member Delaware State and Pennsylvania Bar Associations; Defense Counsel of Delaware; The Delaware Association of Trial Lawyers of America; Associate, American Board of Trial Advocates (President, Delaware Chapter, 2007); Fellow, American College of Trial Lawyers — E-mail: bchristman@casarino.com

Colin M. Shalk — 1947 — University of Delaware, B.A. (with high honors), 1974; Dickinson School of Law, J.D., 1977 — Law Clerk, Superior Court of the State of Delaware, 1977-1978 — Admitted to Bar, 1978, Delaware; U.S. District Court, District of Delaware; 1979, U.S. Court of Appeals, Third Circuit; U.S. Supreme Court — Member Delaware State Bar Association (Insurance, Fee Dispute Conciliation and Mediation Committees); Defense Counsel of Delaware; Associate, American Board of Trial Advocates, Board of Professional Responsibility; Defense Research Institute — E-mail: cshalk@casarino.com

Donald M. Ransom — 1961 — University of Delaware, B.A., 1984; Villanova University School of Law, J.D., 1987 — Admitted to Bar, 1987, Delaware; 1988, Pennsylvania; U.S. District Court, District of Delaware; 1989, U.S. Court of Appeals, Third Circuit; 1992, U.S. District Court, Eastern District of Pennsylvania — Member American and Delaware State Bar Associations — E-mail: dransom@casarino.com

Kenneth M. Doss — 1965 — University of Virginia, B.A., 1987; University of Richmond, T.C. Williams School of Law, J.D., 1990 — Admitted to Bar, 1990, Delaware; 1991, Pennsylvania (Inactive); U.S. District Court, District of Delaware — Member Delaware State Bar Association (Litigation and Products Liability Sections); Pennsylvania Bar Association (Litigation Section); Defense Counsel of Delaware; Delaware Volunteer Legal Services; Defense Research Institute — E-mail: kdoss@casarino.com

Thomas P. Leff — 1950 — Case Western Reserve University, B.A. (cum laude), 1972; M.F.A., 1975; University of Maryland School of Law, J.D., 1995 — Law Clerk, Superior Court of Delaware, 1996-1998 — Admitted to Bar, 1995, Maryland; 1997, Delaware; 1996, U.S. District Court, District of Maryland; 1998, U.S. District Court, District of Delaware; 2002, U.S. Court of Appeals, Third Circuit — Member Delaware State and Maryland State Bar Associations; Defense Counsel of Delaware — E-mail: tleff@casarino.com

Associates

Matthew E. O'Byrne — 1977 — University of Delaware, B.A., 2000; Rutgers University School of Law, J.D., 2003 — Admitted to Bar, 2003, Delaware; 2004, U.S. District Court, District of Delaware — Member Delaware State Bar Association (Bankruptcy Litigation Committee) — E-mail: mobyrne@casarino.com

Sarah Brannan Cole — 1979 — Bryn Mawr College, B.A., 2001; University of Maryland School of Law, J.D., 2005 — Admitted to Bar, 2005, Delaware; 2006, U.S. District Court, District of Delaware — Member Delaware State Bar Association — E-mail: scole@casarino.com

Joel H. Fredricks — 1984 — University of Delaware, B.S., 2006; Widener University School of Law, J.D. (cum laude), 2009 — Admitted to Bar, 2009, Delaware; 2010, New Jersey; Pennsylvania; U.S. District Court, District of Delaware — E-mail: jfredricks@casarino.com

Brian T. N. Jordan — 1980 — University of Delaware, B.A., 2003; Villanova University School of Law, J.D., 2010 — Admitted to Bar, 2010, Delaware — E-mail: bjordan@casarino.com

Rachel D. Allen — 1985 — Iowa State University, B.A. (with honors), 2003; Pennsylvania State University-Dickinson School of Law, J.D., 2010 — Admitted to Bar, 2011, Delaware — E-mail: rallen@casarino.com

Cipriani & Werner, P.C.

1000 N. West Street, Suite 1200
Wilmington, Delaware 19801
Telephone: 302-401-1600

(Pittsburgh, PA Office*: 650 Washington Road, Suite 700, 15228)
(Tel: 412-563-2500)
(Fax: 412-563-2080)
(www.c-wlaw.com)
(Blue Bell, PA Office*(See Philadelphia listing): 450 Sentry Parkway, Suite 200, 19422)
(Tel: 610-567-0700)
(Fax: 610-567-0712)
(Lemoyne, PA Office*(See Harrisburg listing): 1011 Mumma Road, Suite 201, 17043)
(Tel: 717-975-9600)
(Fax: 717-975-3846)
(Scranton, PA Office*: 409 Lackawanna Avenue, Suite 402, 18503)
(Tel: 570-347-0600)
(Fax: 570-347-4018)
(Mt. Laurel, NJ Office*(See Marlton listing): 155 Gaither Drive, Suite B, 08054)
(Tel: 856-761-3800)
(Fax: 856-761-0726)
(Wheeling, WV Office*: 1144 Market Street, Suite 300, 26003)
(Tel: 304-232-3600)
(Fax: 304-232-3601)
(Charleston, WV Office*: United Center, 400 Tracy Way, 25311)
(Tel: 304-341-0500)
(Fax: 304-341-0507)

Insurance Defense, General Liability, Product Liability, Professional Liability, Workers' Compensation, Transportation, First Party Matters, Coverage Analysis, Liquor Liability, Recreation Liability, Employers' Rights

Firm Profile: Cipriani & Werner, PC is a mid-Atlantic litigation law firm that is well established in the defense of businesses and insurers.

Firm Member

Morgan A. Sack — Syracuse University, B.S., 2004; Widener University, J.D., 2007 — Admitted to Bar, 2007, Pennsylvania; New Jersey; Delaware

(See listing under Pittsburgh, PA for additional information)

Dickie, McCamey & Chilcote, P.C.

PNC Bank Center
222 Delaware Avenue, Suite 1040
Wilmington, Delaware 19801-1621
Telephone: 302-428-6133
Fax: 888-811-7144
Toll Free: 866-775-3714
E-Mail: info@dmclaw.com
www.dmclaw.com

(Additional Offices: Pittsburgh, PA*; Charlotte, NC*; Cleveland, OH*; Columbus, OH*; Haddonfield, NJ*; Camp Hill, PA*(See Harrisburg listing); Lancaster, SC*; Philadelphia, PA*; Cary, NC*(See Raleigh listing); Steubenville, OH*; Wheeling, WV*)

Established: 2007

DELAWARE   WILMINGTON

Dickie, McCamey & Chilcote, P.C., Wilmington, DE
(Continued)

Asbestos Litigation, Bad Faith, Captive Company Matters, Casualty, Commercial Litigation, Energy, Labor and Employment, Excess and Reinsurance, Extra-Contractual Litigation, Insurance Agents, Insurance Coverage, Insurance Coverage Litigation, Legal Malpractice, Medical Malpractice, Medicare Set-Aside Practice, Municipal Liability, Nursing Home Liability, Product Liability, Professional Liability, Property and Casualty, Surety, Transportation, Trucking, Uninsured and Underinsured Motorist, Workers' Compensation

Shareholder

William R. Adams — Branch Office Shareholder-in-Charge — The Pennsylvania State University, B.A., 1991; Temple University, J.D., 1994 — Admitted to Bar, 1994, Pennsylvania; 1994, New Jersey; 2007, Delaware — E-mail: wadams@dmclaw.com

(See listing under Pittsburgh, PA for additional information)

Ferry, Joseph & Pearce, P.A.

824 North Market Street, Suite 1000
Wilmington, Delaware 19801
Telephone: 302-575-1555
Fax: 302-575-1714
E-Mail: info@ferryjoseph.com
www.ferryjoseph.com

(Georgetown, DE Office: 4 West Market Street, 19947)
 (Tel: 302-856-3706)
 (Fax: 302-856-3709)
(Newark, DE Office: 111 Barksdale Professional Center, 19711)
 (Tel: 302-286-6336)
 (Fax: 302-266-9940)

Established: 1990

Insurance Defense, Workers' Compensation, Automobile, Subrogation, Litigation, Probate, Elder Law, Personal Injury, Negligence, Business Law, Damage Claims, Coverage Opinions/Litigation, Bad Faith Claims, Trust and Guardianship Litigation, Commercial and Collection Law, Bankruptcy and Reorganization, Premises Liability - Commercial, Residential, School, Municipal and Construction

Firm Profile: Founded in 1990, Ferry, Joseph & Pearce, P.A. is a Delaware law firm with a varied practice. Our goal is to provide skillful, efficient and cost effective services to our clients. To better achieve that goal, we utilize the resources and state of the art technology of a large firm while maintaining the personal service and value of a small firm.

Insurance Clients

PMA Insurance Group
State Farm Fire and Casualty Company
Selective Insurance Company of America
Zurich American Insurance Company

Partners

Robert K. Pearce — 1949 — University of Delaware, B.S., 1971; Villanova University School of Law, J.D., 1974 — Admitted to Bar, 1974, Delaware; 1977, U.S. District Court, District of Delaware; 1988, U.S. Court of Appeals, Third Circuit; 1997, U.S. Supreme Court — Member Delaware Bar Association; Delaware Trial Lawyers Association — Reported Cases: *Schadt v. Latchford*, 843 A.2d 689 (Del. 2004); *Lemos v. Willis*, 858 A.2d 955 (Del. 2004); *Fritz v. Yeager*, 790 A.2d 460 (Del. 2002) — Practice Areas: Premises Liability; Automobile; Coverage Issues; Bad Faith; Subrogation; Wills and Estate Litigation — E-mail: rpearce@ferryjoseph.com

Edward F. Kafader — 1949 — University of Delaware, B.S., 1971; Villanova University School of Law, J.D., 1976 — Admitted to Bar, 1976, Delaware; 1977, U.S. District Court, District of Delaware; 1979, U.S. Court of Appeals,

Ferry, Joseph & Pearce, P.A., Wilmington, DE
(Continued)

Third Circuit; 1980, U.S. Supreme Court; 1981, U.S. District Court, District of Maryland — Member Delaware Bar Association — Reported Cases: *Pagano v. Hadley, et al.*, 535 F. Supp. 92 (D. Del. 1982); *Oakes v. Megaw*, 565 A.2d 914 (Del. 1989); *Wilhelm v. Ryan*, 903 A. 2d. 745 (Del. 2005) — Practice Areas: Civil Litigation; Insurance Defense; Wills and Estate Litigation — E-mail: ekafader@ferryjoseph.com

David J. Ferry, Jr.
Theodore J. Tacconelli
Jason C. Powell
Michael B. Joseph
Rick S. Miller

Of Counsel

Thomas Herlihy, III
Larry D. Sullivan

Associates

Kristopher T. Starr, RN, MSN, JD
Regina M. Matozzo
Brian J. Ferry
Lisa L. Coggins
Thomas R. Riggs
Timothy S. Ferry
James Gaspero Jr.

Marshall Dennehey Warner Coleman & Goggin

Nemours Building
1007 North Orange Street, Suite 600
Wilmington, Delaware 19801
Telephone: 302-552-4300
Fax: 302-552-4340
www.marshalldennehey.com

(Philadelphia, PA Office*: 2000 Market Street, Suite 2300, 19103)
 (Tel: 215-575-2600)
 (Fax: 215-575-0856)
 (Toll Free: 800-220-3308)
 (E-Mail: marshalldennehey@mdwcg.com)
(Fort Lauderdale, FL Office*: 100 Northeast 3rd Avenue, Suite 1100, 33301)
 (Tel: 954-847-4920)
 (Fax: 954-627-6640)
(Jacksonville, FL Office*: 200 West Forsyth Street, Suite 1400, 32202)
 (Tel: 904-358-4200)
 (Fax: 904-355-0019)
(Orlando, FL Office*: Landmark Center One, 315 East Robinson Street, Suite 550, 32801-1948)
 (Tel: 407-420-4380)
 (Fax: 407-839-3008)
(Tampa, FL Office*: 201 East Kennedy Boulevard, Suite 1100, 33602)
 (Tel: 813-898-1800)
 (Fax: 813-221-5026)
(Cherry Hill, NJ Office*: Woodland Falls Corporate Park, 200 Lake Drive East, Suite 300, 08002)
 (Tel: 856-414-6000)
 (Fax: 856-414-6077)
(Roseland, NJ Office*: 425 Eagle Rock Avenue, Suite 302, 07068)
 (Tel: 973-618-4100)
 (Fax: 973-618-0685)
(New York, NY Office*: Wall Street Plaza, 88 Pine Street, 21st Floor, 10005-1801)
 (Tel: 212-376-6400)
 (Fax: 212-376-6490)
(Melville, NY Office*: 105 Maxess Road, Suite 303, 11747)
 (Tel: 631-232-6130)
 (Fax: 631-232-6184)
(Cincinnati, OH Office*: 312 Elm Street, Suite 1850, 45202)
 (Tel: 513-375-6800)
 (Fax: 513-372-6801)
(Cleveland, OH Office*: 127 Public Square, Suite 3510, 44114-1291)
 (Tel: 216-912-3800)
 (Fax: 216-344-9006)

WILMINGTON   DELAWARE

Marshall Dennehey Warner Coleman & Goggin, Wilmington, DE (Continued)

(Allentown, PA Office*: 4905 West Tilghman Street, Suite 300, 18104)
  (Tel: 484-895-2300)
  (Fax: 484-895-2303)
(Doylestown, PA Office*: 10 North Main Street, 2nd Floor, 18901-4318)
  (Tel: 267-880-2020)
  (Fax: 215-348-5439)
(Erie, PA Office*: 717 State Street, Suite 701, 16501)
  (Tel: 814-480-7800)
  (Fax: 814-455-3603)
(Camp Hill, PA Office*(See Harrisburg listing): 100 Coporate Center Drive, Suite 201, 17011)
  (Tel: 717-651-3500)
  (Fax: 717-651-9630)
(King of Prussia, PA Office*: 620 Freedom Business Center, Suite 300, 19406)
  (Tel: 610-354-8250)
  (Fax: 610-354-8299)
(Pittsburgh, PA Office*: U.S. Steel Tower, Suite 2900, 600 Grant Street, 15219)
  (Tel: 412-803-1140)
  (Fax: 412-803-1188)
(Moosic, PA Office*(See Scranton listing): 50 Glenmaura National Boulevard, 18507)
  (Tel: 570-496-4600)
  (Fax: 570-496-0567)
(Rye Brook, NY Office*(See Westchester listing): 800 Westchester Avenue, Suite C-700, 10573)
  (Tel: 914-977-7300)
  (Fax: 914-977-7301)

Established: 1995

Amusements, Sports and Recreation Liability, Asbestos and Mass Tort Litigation, Automobile Liability, Aviation and Complex Litigation, Construction Injury Litigation, Fraud/Special Investigation, General Liability, Hospitality and Liquor Liability, Maritime Litigation, Product Liability, Property Litigation, Retail Liability, Trucking & Transportation Liability, Appellate Advocacy and Post-Trial Practice, Architectural, Engineering and Construction Defect Litigation, Class Action Litigation, Commercial Litigation, Consumer and Credit Law, Employment Law, Environmental & Toxic Tort Litigation, Insurance Coverage/Bad Faith Litigation, Life, Health and Disability Litigation, Privacy and Data Security, Professional Liability, Public Entity and Civil Rights Litigation, Real Estate E&O Liability, School Leaders' Liability, Securities and Investment Professional Liability, Technology, Media and Intellectual Property Litigation, White Collar Crime, Birth Injury Litigation, Health Care Governmental Compliance, Health Care Liability, Health Law, Long-Term Care Liability, Medical Device and Pharmaceutical Liability, Medicare Set-Aside, Workers' Compensation

Firm Profile: Marshall Dennehey Warner Coleman & Goggin opened its Wilmington, Delaware office in July 1995. From this office, situated in downtown Wilmington, the firm is able to serve clients in Delaware's three counties - New Castle, Kent and Sussex. This office is situated just minutes away from Delaware's federal and state courthouses and workers' compensation offices.

Inquiries about the Wilmington office may be directed to Kevin J. Connors, Esquire, the managing attorney, at (302) 552-4302 or kjconnors@mdwcg.com.

Managing Shareholder

Kevin J. Connors — Chair, Casualty Practice Group — 1955 — University of Virginia, B.A. (with high distinction), 1977; University of Vienna, 1977-1978; Villanova University School of Law, J.D., 1981 — Rotary International Graduate Fellow — Law Clerk, Supreme Court of Delaware, Hon. John J. McNeilly, Associate Justice (1981 - 1982) — Articles Editor, Villanova Law Review (1980-1981) — Admitted to Bar, 1982, Pennsylvania; Delaware; U.S. District Court, District of Delaware; U.S. District Court, Eastern District of Pennsylvania; 1983, U.S. Court of Appeals, Third Circuit — Member Delaware State Bar Association; Defense Counsel of Delaware; Delaware Claims Association; Trial Attorneys of America; Defense

Marshall Dennehey Warner Coleman & Goggin, Wilmington, DE (Continued)

Research Institute — Author: "The Admissibility of Vehicle Photographs and the Correlation of Minimal Damages with Minimal Injuries," Defense Digest, Vol. 9, No. 4, December, 2003; "Note, Commonwealth v. Bussey," 26 Villanova Law Review 205, 1981; Seminars/Classes Taught: Strict Liability, Motor Vehicle, and Pennsylvania and Delaware Insurance law (1990-2007) — Languages: German — Practice Areas: Insurance Law; Appeals; Product Liability; Employment Law; Civil Rights; Professional Malpractice; Toxic Torts — E-mail: kjconnors@mdwcg.com

Special Counsel

Kimberly A. Harrison

Senior Counsel

Richard R. Wier, Jr.

Resident Shareholders

Tracy A. Burleigh   Armand J. Della Porta, Jr.
Thomas J. Gerard   Bradley J. Goewert
Jessica L. Julian   Gary H. Kaplan
Thomas J. Marcoz, Jr.   Elizabeth A. Saurman
Joseph Scott Shannon   Paul V. Tatlow
Douglas T. Walsh   Linda L. Wilson
Lorenza A. Wolhar

Resident Associates

Art C. Aranilla   Shannon L. Brainard
Sarah B. Cole   Joshua J. Inkell
Ana M. McCann   Kimberly A. Meany
Keri Lynn Morris-Johnston Elderidge A. Nichols, Jr.
Sarah A. Roberts   Jessica L. Tyler
Nicole T. Whetham Warner Lee Ann Wurst

(See listing under Philadelphia, PA for additional information)

Mintzer Sarowitz Zeris Ledva & Meyers, LLP

919 North Market Street, Suite 200
Wilmington, Delaware 19801
  Telephone: 302-655-2181
  Fax: 302-655-2182
  www.Defensecounsel.com

(Additional Offices: Philadelphia, PA*; Miami, FL*; Cherry Hill, NJ*; Hicksville, NY*; New York, NY*; Pittsburgh, PA*; Tampa, FL*; Wheeling, WV*)

Insurance Defense, Premises Liability, Product Liability, Environmental Law, Workers' Compensation, Coverage Issues, Asbestos Litigation, Medical Malpractice, Nursing Home Liability, Professional Liability, Trucking Law

Managing Partner

Richard D. Abrams

(See listing under Philadelphia, PA for additional information)

Tighe & Cottrell, P.A.

One Customs House
704 King Street, Suite 500
Wilmington, Delaware 19801
  Telephone: 302-658-6400
  Fax: 302-658-9836
  E-Mail: p.cottrell@tighecottrell.com
  www.tighecottrell.com

DELAWARE / WILMINGTON

Tighe & Cottrell, P.A., Wilmington, DE (Continued)

(Towson, MD Office: 1220-C East Joppa Road, Suite 505, 21286)
 (Tel: 410-321-1616)
(Woodstown, NJ Office: 13 West Avenue, P.O. Box 303, 08098)
 (Tel: 856-769-2206)
(Philadelphia, PA Office: 30 South 15th Street, 19102-4826)
 (Tel: 215-564-0101)

Established: 1993

General Liability, Professional Liability, Construction Law, Coverage Issues, Litigation, Surety Bonds, Subrogation, Malpractice

Firm Profile: Tighe & Cottrell, P.A. is a law firm specializing in litigation, insurance defense, and business practices. Our offices are located in Wilmington, DE; Philadelphia, PA; Baltimore, MD and Woodstown, NJ. Other practice areas include construction, employment and transportation law, professional and general liability, corporate transactions, commerical and residential real estate transactions, debt collection, and estate planning, asset protection and trusts.

Insurance Clients

Beazley Insurance Company, Inc.
General Star Management Company
Lexington Insurance Company
Minnesota Lawyers Mutual Insurance Company
St. Paul Travelers
State Farm Insurance Company
Zurich American Insurance Group
CNA Insurance Company
The Hartford
Leader Insurance Company
Liberty Mutual Insurance Company
OneBeacon Insurance
RLI Insurance Company
Sentry Insurance
XL Insurance

Non-Insurance Clients

The Berkely Group
RA&MCO Insurance Services
ECS Claims Administrators, Inc.
Tetra Technologies, Inc.

Partners

Michael K. Tighe — 1947 — Member American and Delaware Bar Associations; Delaware Trial Lawyers Association — (Retired)
Paul Cottrell — 1951 — University of Delaware, B.A. (magna cum laude), 1975; The University of Chicago Law School, J.D., 1978 — Admitted to Bar, 1978, Illinois; 1985, Pennsylvania; Delaware; 1987, Maryland — Tel: 302-658-6400 ext. 12 — E-mail: p.cottrell@tighecottrell.com

Directors

Melissa Arnold Rhoads — 1980 — Wheeling Jesuit University, B.A., 2002; Syracuse University College of Law, J.D., 2006 — Admitted to Bar, 2006, Delaware; 2013, Maryland — Tel: 302-658-6400 ext. 22 — E-mail: m.rhoads@tighecottrell.com
Patrick M. McGrory — 1979 — University of Delaware, B.A., 2001; The Catholic University of America, Columbus School of Law, J.D., 2005 — Admitted to Bar, 2006, New Jersey; Pennsylvania; Delaware — Tel: 302-658-6400 ext. 13 — E-mail: p.mcgrory@tighecottrell.com
Jason J. Cummings — The Richard Stockton College of New Jersey, B.A. (Dean's List), 2005; Widener University School of Law, J.D. (Dean's List), 2011 — Admitted to Bar, 2012, Pennsylvania; New Jersey; Delaware; U.S. District Court, District of New Jersey; 2013, U.S. District Court, District of Delaware — Tel: 302-658-6400 ext. 15 — E-mail: j.cummings@tighecottrell.com

(Revisors of the Delaware Insurance Law Digest for this Publication)

Wilbraham, Lawler & Buba

901 North Market Street, Suite 810
Wilmington, Delaware 19801-3090
 Telephone: 302-421-9935
 Fax: 302-421-9955
 E-Mail: bbuba@wlbdeflaw.com
 www.wlbdeflaw.com

(Philadelphia, PA Office*: 1818 Market Street, Suite 3100, 19103-3631)
 (Tel: 215-564-4141)
 (Fax: 215-564-4385)

Wilbraham, Lawler & Buba, Wilmington, DE (Continued)

(Haddonfield, NJ Office*: 24 Kings Highway West, 08033-2122)
 (Tel: 856-795-4422)
 (Fax: 856-795-4699)
(Pittsburgh, PA Office*: 603 Stanwix Street, Two Gateway Center - 17 North, 15222)
 (Tel: 412-255-0500)
 (Fax: 412-255-0505)
(New York, NY Office*: 140 Broadway, 46th Floor, 10005-1101)
 (Tel: 212-858-7575)
 (Fax: 212-943-9246)

Appellate Practice, Asbestos Litigation, Civil Trial Practice, Commercial Litigation, Insurance Defense, Toxic Torts, Workers' Compensation, Product Liability Law

Associates

Timothy A. Sullivan, III — 1978 — University of Notre Dame, B.A., 2000; Temple University School of Law, J.D., 2004 — Admitted to Bar, 2004, Pennsylvania; 2005, New Jersey; 2006, Delaware; 2005, U.S. District Court, District of New Jersey — Tel: 215-972-2836
Antranig N. Garibian — 1979 — Princeton University, B.A., 2001; Temple University School of Law, J.D., 2004 — Admitted to Bar, 2004, Pennsylvania; 2005, New Jersey; 2007, Delaware; 2005, U.S. District Court, District of New Jersey — Languages: Armenian, Russian, French — Tel: 215-972-2859

(See listing under Philadelphia, PA for additional information)

The following firms also service this area.

Young & McNelis, LLC
300 South State Street
Dover, Delaware 19901
 Telephone: 302-674-8822
 Fax: 302-674-8251

Insurance Defense, Automobile, Product Liability, Professional Malpractice, Fire, Casualty

SEE COMPLETE LISTING UNDER DOVER, DELAWARE (47 MILES)

DISTRICT OF COLUMBIA

Our files contain additional verified data on the firms listed herein. This additional information is available on request.

A.M. BEST COMPANY

DISTRICT OF COLUMBIA   *WASHINGTON*

WASHINGTON   601,723 District of Columbia

Carr Maloney P.C.

2000 L Street, NW, Suite 450
Washington, District of Columbia 20036
    Telephone: 202-310-5500
    Fax: 202-310-5555
    www.carrmaloney.com

(Baltimore, MD Office: Inner Harbor Center, 400 East Pratt Street, Suite 800, 21202)
    (Tel: 410-752-1570)
(Bethesda, MD Office: 6120 Woodmont Avenue, Suite 650, 20814)
    (Tel: 301-424-7024)
(Vienna, VA Office: Tycon Towers, 8000 Towers Crescent Drive, Suite 1350, 22182)
    (Tel: 703-691-8818)

Established: 1984

Appellate Practice, Civil Rights, Commercial Litigation, Complex Litigation, Construction Law, Directors and Officers Liability, General Liability, Government Investigations and Enforcement, Health Care, Immigration Law, Insurance Coverage, Labor and Employment, Product Liability, Professional Liability, Religious Institutions, Retailers and Chain Restaurant Litigation, Risk Management, Toxic Torts, Mass Tort, Trust and Estate Litigation

Firm Profile: Carr Maloney is a litigation firm providing comprehensive legal services throughout the mid-Atlantic region. Established in Washington, D.C. in 1984, the firm applies its extensive regional experience and highly individualized approach to the diverse needs of each client.

Insurance Clients

ACE USA
Allied World Assurance Company
Aspen Specialty Insurance Company
CAMICO Insurance Services
CNA Insurance Companies
Endurance Services, Ltd.
Farmers Insurance
Fireman's Fund Insurance Company
Hanover Insurance Company
Hartford Products
Liberty International Underwriters
Minnesota Lawyers Mutual Insurance Company
OneBeacon Insurance Group
Resolute Management, Inc.
Selective Insurance Company of America
Utica National Insurance Company
Zurich North America
ALAS
Arch Insurance Group
AXIS Insurance
Berkley Insurance Company
Catholic Mutual Group
Crum & Forster
Everest National Insurance Company
Gallagher Bassett Services, Inc.
General Star Management Company
Hudson Insurance Company
Medmarc Insurance Group
Monitor Liability Managers, LLC
Navigators
Philadelphia Insurance Company
The RiverStone Group
Swiss Re
Travelers
Vela Insurance Services, LLC

Non-Insurance Clients

A.M.E. Zion Church
Association of Financial Planners
Certified Financial Planner Board of Standards, Inc.
Marriott International, Inc.
Archdiocese of Washington
BMW of North America, Inc.
Invacare Corporation
Macy's
Overhead Door Corporation

Firm Members

William J. Carter — Virginia Polytechnic Institute and State University, B.S. (with honors), 1971; College of William & Mary, Marshall-Wythe School of Law, J.D., 1974 — Admitted to Bar, 1974, Virginia; Pennsylvania; 1980, Maryland; District of Columbia; 2004, Colorado; 1975, U.S. Court of Military Appeals; 1977, U.S. Court of Federal Claims; U.S. Supreme Court; U.S. Court of Appeals for the Federal, District of Columbia, Third, Fourth, Fifth, Sixth and Eleventh Circuits; U.S. District Court for the District of Columbia and District of Maryland — Practice Areas: Appellate Practice; Insurance Coverage; Contract Disputes

Paul J. Maloney — Washington and Lee University, 1976; The Catholic University of America, Columbus School of Law, J.D., 1981 — Admitted to Bar,

Carr Maloney P.C., Washington, DC   **(Continued)**

1982, District of Columbia; 1983, Maryland; U.S. District Court for the District of Columbia and District of Maryland — Practice Areas: Professional Malpractice; Complex Litigation; Commercial Litigation; Product Liability

Thomas L. McCally — University of Delaware, B.A., 1981; Emory University School of Law, J.D., 1984 — Admitted to Bar, 1984, Georgia; 1985, Maryland; District of Columbia; 1989, U.S. District Court, District of Maryland; U.S. Court of Appeals for the Federal, District of Columbia and Fourth Circuits — Practice Areas: Labor and Employment; Discrimination; Wrongful Termination; Religious Institutions; Civil Rights; Commercial Litigation

Kevin M. Murphy — University of Notre Dame, B.B.A., 1981; The Catholic University of America, Columbus School of Law, J.D., 1984 — Admitted to Bar, 1985, Maryland; District of Columbia — Practice Areas: Professional Malpractice; Trust and Estate Litigation; Commercial Litigation; Directors and Officers Liability

Jan E. Simonsen — Northeastern University, B.S., 1984; Vermont Law School, J.D., 1988 — Admitted to Bar, 1988, Virginia; 1989, District of Columbia; U.S. District Court for the District of Columbia; U.S. District Court, District of Maryland; U.S. District Court, Eastern District of Virginia; U.S. Court of Appeals for the District of Columbia Circuit — Practice Areas: Professional Malpractice; Toxic Torts; Mass Tort; Retailers and Chain Restaurant Litigation; Risk Management; Complex Litigation

James P. Steele — University of Delaware, B.A., 1987; The Catholic University of America, Columbus School of Law, J.D., 1992 — Admitted to Bar, 1992, Maryland; 1995, District of Columbia; U.S. District Court for the District of Columbia and District of Maryland — Practice Areas: General Liability; Professional Liability; Insurance Coverage

Dennis J. Quinn — Montclair State University, B.A. (cum laude), 1985; The George Washington University Law School, J.D., 1988 — Admitted to Bar, 1988, Pennsylvania; 1997, Virginia; District of Columbia; 1998, U.S. Court of Appeals for the District of Columbia and Fourth Circuits; U.S. District Court for the District of Columbia and Eastern District of Virginia — Practice Areas: Commercial Litigation; Product Liability; Professional Liability

Tina M. Maiolo — College of William & Mary, B.A. (cum laude), 1993; College of William & Mary, Marshall-Wythe School of Law, J.D., 1996 — Admitted to Bar, 1996, Virginia; 1997, District of Columbia; 2007, Maryland; 2000, U.S. Court of Appeals, Fourth Circuit; 2003, U.S. Supreme Court; U.S. District Court for the District of Columbia and Eastern District of Virginia — Practice Areas: Labor and Employment; Commercial Litigation; Civil Rights; Immigration Law; Discrimination

Mariana D. Bravo — Marymount University, B.S., 1990; University of Baltimore School of Law, J.D., 2000 — Admitted to Bar, 2001, Virginia; District of Columbia; U.S. District Court for the District of Columbia and Eastern and Western Districts of Virginia — Practice Areas: General Liability; Professional Malpractice; Construction Law

Kelly M. Lippincott — Drew University, B.A., 1999; American University, Washington College of Law, J.D., 2002 — Admitted to Bar, 2002, Maryland; 2004, Virginia; District of Columbia; 2003, U.S. District Court, District of Maryland; 2004, U.S. Court of Appeals, Fourth Circuit — Practice Areas: Commercial Litigation; Professional Malpractice; Product Liability; Insurance Coverage

Nat P. Calamis — Boston College, B.A., 2001; The Catholic University of America, Columbus School of Law, J.D., 2005 — Admitted to Bar, 2005, Maryland; 2007, District of Columbia — Member Maryland State Bar Association; Bar Association of the District of Columbia — Practice Areas: Litigation; Labor and Employment; Directors and Officers Liability; Professional Liability; Business Law; Commercial Litigation

Associates

Sarah R. Bagley
Sarah W. Conkright
Kristine M. Ellison
Alexander M. Gormley
Nicholas G. Hallenbeck
Katherine C. Ondeck
Andrew M. Williamson
Matthew D. Berkowitz
Suzanne E. Derr
John P. Glaws IV
Joseph E. Hainline
Erin D. Hendrixson
Tracy D. Scott
Jason C. Zappasodi

Of Counsel

Lawrence E. Carr, Jr.
Janette M. Blee
Edward J. Krill
Richard L. Schwartz

Law Offices of Joseph F. Cunningham & Associates, PLC

5039 Connecticut Avenue, Unit 3
Washington, District of Columbia 20008

Insurance Defense, Professional Liability, Workers' Compensation, Alternative Dispute Resolution, Coverage Issues, Litigation

(See listing under Arlington, VA for additional information)

Eccleston and Wolf
Professional Corporation

1629 K Street, NW
Suite 260
Washington, District of Columbia 20006
Telephone: 202-857-1696
Fax: 202-857-0762

(Additional Offices: Hanover, MD*(See Baltimore listing); Fairfax, VA*)

Insurance Defense, Premises Liability, Product Liability, Professional Malpractice, Accountants, Title Insurance, Architects and Engineers, Engineers, Agent/Broker Liability, Medical Liability, Automobile, Casualty, Aviation, Construction, Coverage, Attorneys, Employment, Physicians, Nurses, Investment Advisors

Firm Members

Aaron L. Handleman — 1946 — Marietta College, B.A. (cum laude), 1968; The George Washington University, J.D. (with honors), 1971 — Phi Beta Kappa; Omicrop Delta Kappa — Admitted to Bar, 1971, District of Columbia; 1972, Maryland; 1972, U.S. District Court for the District of Columbia; 1978, U.S. Supreme Court; 1984, U.S. Court of Appeals for the Federal Circuit; 1984, U.S. Court of Appeals, Fourth Circuit; 1988, U.S. District Court, District of Maryland — Author-Co-Contributor: American Insurance Attorneys, "Insurance & Tort Desk Reference, D.C. Section," 1990 — E-mail: handleman@ewdc.com

Justin M. Flint — The Catholic University of America, B.A. (magna cum laude), 1999; University of Baltimore School of Law, J.D. (cum laude), 2003 — Admitted to Bar, 2003, Maryland; 2005, District of Columbia; U.S. District Court for the District of Columbia and District of Maryland; U.S. Court of Appeals for the Federal and District of Columbia Circuits

Associates

Laura M.K. Hassler
B. Steven Kushnir
Diana Hamar
Channing Shor

(See listing under Baltimore, MD for additional information)

Friedlander Misler, PLLC

5335 Wisconsin Avenue, NW
Suite 600
Washington, District of Columbia 20015
Telephone: 202-872-0800
Fax: 202-857-8343
E-Mail: dvhill@dclawfirm.com
www.dclawfirm.com

Established: 1964

Insurance Defense, Workers' Compensation, Public Liability, Casualty, General Liability, Employment Law, Insurance Coverage

Friedlander Misler, PLLC, Washington, DC   (Continued)

Insurance Clients

A.C.E. Insurance Company, Ltd.
Crum & Forster Insurance Group
ESIS
Great West Casualty Company
Hanover Insurance Company
Liberty Mutual Insurance
Nationwide Insurance
Wells Fargo Insurance Services
York Claims Service, Inc.
Argonaut Insurance Company
Erie Insurance Company
First Mercury Insurance Company
GUARD Insurance Group
Hartford Specialty Risk Services, Inc.
Property & Casualty Insurance Guaranty Corporation
Zurich North America

Non-Insurance Clients

DTG, Inc.
Jamaica Central Labour Organisation
Murray Lawrence & Partners Limited (Lloyd's Underwriters)
Guardian Fire Protection Services
Metropolitan Washington Airports Authority
Vector Security
Washington Metropolitan Area Transit Authority

Partners

Jack L. Friedlander — (1914-1999)

Albert D. Misler — (1909-2000)

Jeffrey W. Ochsman — (1952-2013)

Morris Kletzkin — 1946 — University of Hartford, B.A., 1968; American University, Washington College of Law, J.D., 1971 — Admitted to Bar, 1971, District of Columbia; 1977, Maryland; 1971, U.S. District Court for the District of Columbia; 1976, U.S. Supreme Court; 1977, U.S. District Court, District of Maryland; 1980, U.S. Court of Appeals, Fourth Circuit — Member Montgomery County Bar Association — E-mail: mkletzkin@dclawfirm.com

Alan D. Sundburg — 1961 — Hamilton College, A.B., 1983; The College of William and Mary, Marshall-Wythe School of Law, J.D., 1986 — Admitted to Bar, 1987, Pennsylvania (Inactive); 1989, District of Columbia; 1991, Virginia; U.S. Court of Appeals, Fourth Circuit — E-mail: asundburg@dclawfirm.com

Todd S. Sapiro — 1967 — University of Michigan, B.A., 1989; American University, Washington College of Law, J.D., 1992 — Admitted to Bar, 1992, Maryland; 1993, District of Columbia; U.S. District Court, District of Maryland; 1997, U.S. District Court for the District of Columbia — E-mail: tsapiro@dclawfirm.com

Thomas F. Murphy — 1971 — James Madison University, B.S. (cum laude), 1993; The University of Georgia School of Law, J.D., 1996 — Admitted to Bar, 1996, Georgia; 1997, Maryland; 1999, District of Columbia; Virginia; U.S. District Court, Eastern District of Virginia; U.S. Claims Court — E-mail: tmurphy@dclawfirm.com

Robert N. Driscoll — 1968 — Georgetown University, B.S./B.A., 1990; Georgetown University Law Center, J.D., 1993 — Admitted to Bar, 1994, Massachusetts; 2004, District of Columbia; U.S. Court of Appeals for the District of Columbia Circuit; District of Columbia Court of Appeals — E-mail: rdriscoll@dclawfirm.com

Joseph W. Santini — 1976 — University of Pittsburgh, B.A., 1998; University of Richmond School of Law, J.D., 2001; Georgetown University Law Center, LL.M., 2002 — Admitted to Bar, 2001, Virginia; 2007, District of Columbia; 2002, U.S. District Court, Eastern District of Virginia; 2003, U.S. District Court, Western District of Virginia; 2005, U.S. Court of Appeals, Fourth Circuit — Member Virginia Association of Defense Attorneys — E-mail: jsantini@dclawfirm.com

Associates

Sarah M. Burton — 1980 — University of South Carolina, B.A., 2004; University of Baltimore School of Law, J.D., 2007 — Phi Alpha Delta — Admitted to Bar, 2007, Maryland; 2008, U.S. District Court, District of Maryland — Member American and Baltimore County Bar Associations; Maryland Bar Association, Inc. — E-mail: sburton@dclawfirm.com

Lindsay A. Thompson — 1978 — Virginia Polytechnic Institute and State University, B.A., 2000; The John Marshall Law School, J.D., 2007 — Admitted to Bar, 2007, Illinois; 2010, District of Columbia; 2012, Virginia; 2007, U.S. District Court, Northern District of Illinois; 2010, U.S. Court of Appeals for the Federal and Seventh Circuits — E-mail: lathompson@dclawfirm.com

Zachary Shapiro — 1983 — University of Michigan - Ann Arbor, B.A. Political Science, 2006; University of Maryland School of Law, J.D., 2010 — Admitted to Bar, 2010, Maryland; 2014, District of Columbia — E-mail: zshapiro@dclawfirm.com

DISTRICT OF COLUMBIA   **WASHINGTON**

Friedlander Misler, PLLC, Washington, DC (Continued)

Of Counsel

Robert E. Greenberg — 1949 — Herbert H. Lehman College of the City University of New York, A.B., 1970; University of Florida, Levin College of Law, J.D., 1972; Georgetown University, LL.M., 1975 — Admitted to Bar, 1972, Florida; 1973, District of Columbia; U.S. District Court for the District of Columbia; U.S. Court of Appeals for the District of Columbia Circuit; 1978, U.S. District Court, District of Maryland — Member American and Maryland State Bar Association; The District of Columbia Bar; The Florida Bar — E-mail: rgreenberg@dclawfirm.com

Henrichsen Siegel, P.L.L.C.

1150 Connecticut Avenue, N.W., Suite 900
Washington, District of Columbia 20036
Telephone: 202-293-7766
Fax: 202-379-9792
E-Mail: NHenrichsen@hslawyers.com
www.hslawyers.com

(Jacksonville, FL Office*: 1648 Osceola Street, 32204)
(Tel: 904-381-8183)
(Fax: 904-381-8191)

Established: 2000

Fidelity and Surety, Errors and Omissions, Subrogation, Construction Law, Commercial Torts

Firm Profile: Henrichsen Siegel, PLLC is a specialized litigation/trial law firm that provides quality legal services nationwide in a cost effective manner. With an emphasis on the use of technology in our practice and alternatives to hourly fee arrangements, our attorneys in offices in Washington, DC and Florida provide personalized and dedicated attention to all cases.

Insurance Clients

International Fidelity Insurance Company
XL Insurance

Travelers Casualty and Surety Company

Firm Members

Neil L. Henrichsen — 1963 — Hunter College, B.A. (cum laude), 1984; American University, M.A., 1988; American University, Washington College of Law, J.D., 1988 — Recipient, New York State Assembly Legislative Fellowship, 1984 — Admitted to Bar, 1989, New Jersey; District of Columbia; 1991, Virginia; 1997, Florida; 1990, U.S. District Court, District of Maryland; U.S. Court of Federal Claims; 1997, U.S. Supreme Court — Member American Bar Association (Member: Forum on the Construction Industry, 1991; Fidelity and Surety Law Committee, Torts and Insurance Practice Section; Litigation Section); The District of Columbia Bar; Virginia State Bar; The Florida Bar; Association of Trial Lawyers of America — Contributor: The Most Important Questions a Surety Can Ask About Performance Bonds, ABA, TIPS Section, 1997 — Practice Areas: Construction Law; Surety; Product Liability — E-mail: NHenrichsen@hslawyers.com

(This firm is also listed in the Subrogation section of this directory)

Lewis Baach PLLC

1899 Pennsylvania Avenue, NW, Suite 600
Washington, District of Columbia 20006
Telephone: 202-833-8900
Fax: 202-466-5738
E-Mail: martin.baach@lewisbaach.com
www.lewisbaach.com

(London, United Kingdom Office: One Lime Street, Room 735, EC3M 7DQ)
(Tel: +44(0)20 7327-4433)
(Fax: +44(0)20 7327-4024)
(New York, NY Office: The Chrysler Building, 405 Lexington Avenue, 32nd Floor, 10174)
(Tel: 212-826-7001)

Lewis Baach PLLC, Washington, DC (Continued)

(Buenos Aires, Argentina Office: Edificio Bouchard Plaza, Bouchard 599 Piso 20, C1106ABG)
(Tel: +54(11) 4850-1220)
(Fax: +54(11) 4850-1201)

Established: 1996

Litigation, Reinsurance, Casualty Insurance Law, Comprehensive General Liability, Contracts, Coverage Issues, Insurance Law, Directors and Officers Liability, Workers' Compensation, Professional Liability, Product Liability, Alternative Dispute Resolution, Appellate Practice, Government Relations, Business Ethics, Political Risk, Latin America, Complex Financial Disputes, International Disputes, International Insolvency and Asset Tracing

Firm Profile: LB meets its clients' dispute resolution needs-locally, nationally and globally. The focus of our practice is the resolution of disputes through negotiation, mediation, arbitration, and litigation. LB has assembled a team of accomplished lawyers. They include seasoned trial attorneys, experts in resolving complex insurance disputes, sophisticated international commercial litigators, and counsel to the largest international bank insolvency.

LB's clients include multinational, national and local companies, the London insurance market, domestic and international banks and financial services companies, and legal and accounting firms as well as individuals. Clients select LB because it has the experience, skill and depth to handle the largest and most complex matters, yet it retains the flexibility to efficiently handle matters smaller in scale.

Representative Insurance Clients

ACE Global Markets Limited (UK)
Aspen Insurance Limited
Catalina London Ltd.
Certain Underwriters at Lloyd's, London
Markel International, Ltd.

Amlin Group
Canopius Syndicate Management
Catlin Group Limited
Great American Insurance Company
Resolute Management Services, Ltd. - UK

Partners

Martin R. Baach — 1948 — Washington University, A.B., 1969; Indiana University, M.A., 1971; University of Cincinnati, J.D., 1974 — Admitted to Bar, 1974, Ohio (Inactive); 1975, District of Columbia; 2002, West Virginia; U.S. Court of Appeals, Third, Fourth, Fifth, Ninth and Eleventh Circuits; U.S. Supreme Court — Member District of Columbia Court of Appeals Board on Professional Responsibility (Member, 2002-2007; Chair, 2004-2007); U.S. District Court for the District of Columbia, Committee on Grievances (Member, 2008-Present; Vice-chair, 2012; Chair, 2013) — E-mail: martin.baach@lewisbaach.com

Eric L. Lewis — 1957 — Princeton University, A.B., 1979; Cambridge University, M.Phil. (Fulbright Scholar), 1980; Yale University, J.D., 1983 — Admitted to Bar, 1985, New York; District of Columbia — Member International Bar Association; Fellow, Congress of International Legal Studies; Elected Member, Council on Foreign Relations — E-mail: eric.lewis@lewisbaach.com

Mark J. Leimkuhler — 1960 — University of Virginia, B.A., 1982; University of Pennsylvania, J.D. (cum laude), 1986 — Admitted to Bar, 1986, Pennsylvania (Inactive); 1988, District of Columbia; 1989, U.S. District Court for the District of Columbia — E-mail: mark.leimkuhler@lewisbaach.com

Joseph L. Ruby — 1955 — Reed College, B.A., 1978; University of Rochester, M.A., 1979; Yale University, J.D., 1984 — Admitted to Bar, 1985, New York; 1988, District of Columbia; 1989, U.S. District Court for the District of Columbia; U.S. Court of Appeals for the District of Columbia Circuit — Member American Bar Association — E-mail: joseph.ruby@lewisbaach.com

Bruce R. Grace — 1957 — The University of Chicago, B.A., 1979; Columbia University, J.D., 1987 — Kent Scholar, Columbia University — Admitted to Bar, 1989, New York; 1990, District of Columbia; 1989, U.S. Court of Appeals for the District of Columbia Circuit; 1996, U.S. Court of Appeals, Third Circuit — Member American Bar Association; AIDA Reinsurance and Insurance Arbitration Society — E-mail: bruce.grace@lewisbaach.com

Manuel S. Varela — 1972 — Harvard College, A.B. (cum laude), 1994; Georgetown University, J.D., 1997 — Admitted to Bar, 1997, Maryland; 1998, District of Columbia; U.S. District Court, District of Maryland; 2001, U.S. District Court for the District of Columbia — Member International and

WASHINGTON

DISTRICT OF COLUMBIA

Lewis Baach PLLC, Washington, DC (Continued)

American Bar Associations; Spain, U.S. Chamber of Commerce — Languages: Portuguese, Spanish — E-mail: manuel.varela@lewisbaach.com

Jack B. Gordon — 1955 — State University of New York at Albany, B.A. (magna cum laude), 1976; The George Washington University, J.D. (magna cum laude), 1979 — Admitted to Bar, 1980, District of Columbia; New York; U.S. Supreme Court; U.S. Court of Appeals, Second, Fourth, Fifth, Ninth and Eleventh Circuits — Member American Bar Association; AIDA Reinsurance and Insurance Arbitration Society — E-mail: jack.gordon@lewisbaach.com

Brett A. Walter — 1972 — University of Wyoming, B.S. (Phi Beta Kappa), 1995; University of Nebraska, M.A., 1997; Duke Law School, J.D., 2000 — Admitted to Bar, 2000, Virginia; 2001, District of Columbia; U.S. District Court, Eastern District of Virginia; 2002, U.S. District Court for the District of Columbia; 2004, U.S. Court of Appeals, Fourth Circuit — Member American Bar Association — E-mail: brett.walter@lewisbaach.com

Aisha E.R. Henry — 1978 — University of Maryland, B.S., 2000; The Pennsylvania State University Dickinson School of Law, J.D., 2003 — Admitted to Bar, 2003, Maryland; 2003, District of Columbia; 2011, U.S. District Court for the District of Columbia — E-mail: aisha.henry@lewisbaach.com

Associates

Chiara Spector-Naranjo
Jessica Buckwalter
Tara Plochocki
Elizabeth Sheldon
Elizabeth Marvin

Locke Lord LLP

701 8th Street, N.W., Suite 700
Washington, District of Columbia 20001
   Telephone: 202-521-4100
   Fax: 202-521-4200
   www.lockelord.com

(Chicago, IL Office*: 111 South Wacker Drive, 60606-4410)
   (Tel: 312-443-0700)
   (Fax: 312-443-0336)
(Atlanta, GA Office*: Terminus 200, Suite 1200, 3333 Piedmont Road NE, 30305)
   (Tel: 404-870-4600)
   (Fax: 404-872-5547)
(Austin, TX Office*: 600 Congress Avenue, Suite 2200, 78701-2748)
   (Tel: 512-305-4700)
   (Fax: 512-305-4800)
(Dallas, TX Office*: 2200 Ross Avenue, Suite 2200, 75201)
   (Tel: 214-740-8000)
   (Fax: 214-740-8800)
(Houston, TX Office*: 2800 JPMorgan Chase Tower, 600 Travis, 77002-3095)
   (Tel: 713-226-1200)
   (Fax: 713-223-3717)
(London, United Kingdom Office*: 201 Bishopsgate, DX 567 London/City, EC2M 3AB)
   (Tel: +44 (0) 20 7861 9000 (Int'l))
   (Tel: 011 44 207861 9000 (US))
   (Fax: +44 (0) 20 7785 6869 201 (Bishopsgate))
(Los Angeles, CA Office*: 300 South Grand Avenue, Suite 2600, 90071-3119)
   (Tel: 213-485-1500)
   (Fax: 213-485-1200)
(New Orleans, LA Office*: 601 Poydras, Suite 2660, 70130)
   (Tel: 504-558-5100)
   (Fax: 504-558-5200)
(New York, NY Office*: Three World Financial Center, Floor 20, 10281)
   (Tel: 212-415-8600)
   (Fax: 212-303-2754)
(Sacramento, CA Office: 500 Capitol Mall, Suite 1800, 95814)
   (Tel: 916-554-0240)
   (Fax: 916-554-5440)
(San Francisco, CA Office*: 44 Montgomery Street, Suite 2400, 94104)
   (Tel: 415-318-8810)
   (Fax: 415-676-5816)

Locke Lord LLP, Washington, DC (Continued)

(Hong Kong, China-PRC Office: 21/F Bank of China Tower, 1 Garden Road, Central)
   (Tel: +852 3465 0600)
   (Fax: +852 3014 0991)

Antitrust, Arbitration, Aviation, Business Law, Class Actions, Construction Law, Corporate Law, Directors and Officers Liability, Employee Benefits, Environmental Law, Health Care, Insurance Law, Intellectual Property, Labor and Employment, Land Use, Admiralty and Maritime Law, Mergers and Acquisitions, Product Liability, Railroad Law, Regulatory and Compliance, Reinsurance, Securities, Technology, Transportation, Appellate, Long Term Care

Partners

Douglas P. Faucette — 1946 — University of Massachusetts, B.A., 1968; Suffolk University, J.D., 1971 — Admitted to Bar, 1972, District of Columbia; 1974, New York; 1996, U.S. Supreme Court — Member International, Federal and American Bar Associations — Practice Areas: Arbitration; Business Law

William J. Kelty, III — 1946 — Boston College, B.A., 1968; The University of Chicago, J.D., 1975 — Admitted to Bar, 1975, Illinois; 1975, U.S. District Court, Northern District of Illinois — Member American and Illinois State Bar Associations — Practice Areas: Insurance Law; Mergers and Acquisitions

Kirk Van Brunt — Northwest Nazarene University, B.A., 1980; Harvard Law School, J.D., 1985 — Admitted to Bar, 1985, Massachusetts; 1986, District of Columbia

Seth M. Warner — Tufts University, B.A., 1990; American University, Washington College of Law, J.D., 1994 — Admitted to Bar, 1994, District of Columbia — Languages: Spanish

Harriet Miers — Southern Methodist University, B.S., 1967; Southern Methodist University, Dedman School of Law, J.D., 1970 — Barristers; Moot Court Board — Comments Editor, Southwestern Law Journal — Admitted to Bar, 1970, Texas; District of Columbia — Practice Areas: Appellate Practice; Class Actions; Insurance Law; Government Affairs; Securities

(See listing under Chicago, IL for additional information)

McBrayer, McGinnis, Leslie & Kirkland, PLLC

1341 G Street, N.W., Suite 700
Washington, District of Columbia 20005-3131
   Telephone: 202-730-9531

Casualty Defense, Insurance Law, Insurance Defense, Personal Injury, Coverage Analysis, Civil Rights

(See listing under Lexington, KY for additional information)

Law Offices of David C. Numrych PC

4th Floor - East Wing
2200 Pennsylvania Avenue, NW
Washington, District of Columbia 20037-1701
   Telephone: 202-351-6171
   Fax: 202-280-1398
   E-Mail: david@numrychlaw.com
   www.numrychlaw.com

(Falls Church, VA Office: 3374 Lakeside View Drive, 22041-2204)

Established: 2012

DISTRICT OF COLUMBIA   **WASHINGTON**

Law Offices of David C. Numrych PC, Washington, DC
(Continued)

Aviation, Commercial Litigation, Insurance Defense, Automobile Accidents, Product Liability, Personal Injury, Professional Negligence, Medical Malpractice, Architects and Engineers, Workers' Compensation, Wrongful Death

Firm Profile: David Numrych has practiced law for more than twenty (20) years. He is licensed in the District of Columbia, Maryland, and Virginia. Through his practice, he is able to provide guidance on handling claims and civil suits that overlap these multiple jurisdictions.

Insurance Clients

AIG Insurance Company	ESIS/ACE USA Group
Sedgwick CMS	Travelers Insurance

Non-Insurance Clients

AMN Healthcare	Otis Elevator Company
United Technologies Corporation	

David C. Numrych — University of Illinois at Urbana-Champaign, B.S. (Dean's List), 1986; IIT, Chicago-Kent College of Law, J.D. (Dean's List), 1990 — Admitted to Bar, 1986, District of Columbia; 1990, Illinois; 1997, Maryland; 1998, Virginia; U.S. District Court for the District of Columbia; U.S. District Court, District of Maryland; U.S. District Court, Eastern District of Virginia — Member The District of Columbia Bar; Maryland State and Virginia State Bar Associations; Maryland Defense Counsel Organization; District of Columbia Defense Lawyers Association; Virginia Association of Defense Attorneys; Defense Research Institute — Reported Cases: James Slater v. Gloria Biehl, 793 A.2d 1268 (DC 2002); State Farm v. Enterprise, WDCLR Vol 127, No. 78, p.721 (DC 1999); National Coach Works v. Detroit Diesel, 128 F.Supp. 2nd 821 (D. Ct. MD 2001) — Recipient, Defense Research Institute DC State Leadership Award, 2009; Former Special Assistant United States Attorney — Master Advocate, Faculty Member, National Institute Trial Advocacy (NITA) — United States Air Force Judge Advocate General Corps (1991-1997); Two Commendation Medals and Meritorious Service Medal — E-mail: david@numrychlaw.com

Whiteford, Taylor & Preston L.L.P.

1025 Connecticut Avenue, N.W.
Washington, District of Columbia 20036-5405
  Telephone: 202-659-6800
  Fax: 202-331-0573

(Baltimore, MD Office*: Seven Saint Paul Street, 21202-1636)
  (Tel: 410-347-8700)
  (Toll Free: 800-987-8705)
  (Fax: 410-752-7092)
  (E-Mail: info@wtplaw.com)
  (www.wtplaw.com)
(Towson, MD Office: 1 West Pennsylvania Avenue, Suite 300, 21204-5025)
  (Tel: 410-832-2000)
  (Fax: 410-832-2015)
(Columbia, MD Office: 10500 Little Patuxent Parkway, Suite 750, 21044-3585)
  (Tel: 410-884-0700)
  (Fax: 410-884-0719)
(Falls Church, VA Office: 3190 Fairview Park Drive, Suite 300, 22042-4510)
  (Tel: 703-836-5742)
  (Fax: 703-573-1287)
(Wilmington, DE Office: The Renaissance Centre, Suite 500, 405 North King Street, 19801-3700)
  (Tel: 302-353-4144)
  (Fax: 302-661-7950)
(Bethesda, MD Office: 7501 Wisconsin Avenue, Suite 700W, 20814)
  (Tel: 301-804-3610)
  (Fax: 301-215-6359)

Whiteford, Taylor & Preston L.L.P., Washington, DC
(Continued)

(Dearborn, MI Office: Fairlane Plaza North, 290 Town Center Drive, Suite 324, 48126)
  (Tel: 313-406-5759)
  (Fax: 313-406-5840)
(Roanoke, VA Office: 114 Market Street, Suite 210, 24011)
  (Tel: 540-759-3560)
  (Fax: 540-759-3569)
(Lexington, KY Office: 120 Prosperous Place, Suite 100, 40509)
  (Tel: 859-687-6700)
  (Fax: 859-263-3239)
(Betheny Beach, DE Office: 209 Fifth Street, Suite 200, 19930)
  (Tel: 302-829-3040)
  (Fax: 302-829-3041)

General Liability, Casualty, Fire, Surety, Malpractice, Product Liability, Insurance Coverage, Environmental Law, Toxic Torts, Wrongful Termination, Intellectual Property, Professional Liability

(See listing under Baltimore, MD for additional information)

Wiley Rein LLP

1776 K Street, NW
Washington, District of Columbia 20006
  Telephone: 202-719-7000
  Fax: 202-719-7049
  E-Mail: dstandish@wileyrein.com
  www.wileyrein.com

(McLean, VA Office: 7925 Jones Branch Drive, Suite 6200, 22102)
  (Tel: 703-905-2800)
  (Fax: 703-905-2820)

Established: 1983

Accountants, Alternative Dispute Resolution, Arbitration, Architects and Engineers, Bad Faith, Casualty Insurance Law, Commercial General Liability, Complex Litigation, Coverage Issues, Directors and Officers Liability, Employment Law, Employment Practices Liability, Environmental Coverage, Excess and Surplus Lines, Insurance Agents, Insurance Law, Insurance Regulation, Product Liability, Professional Errors and Omissions, Professional Liability, Real Estate, Reinsurance, Health Insurance, Crime Insurance/Fidelity, Lawyers Professional Liability, Property Insurance, Renewable Energy Risks, Asbestos Coverage, Expert Witness/Consultation

Insurance Clients

AEGIS Insurance Services, Inc.	AIG/American International Group
Allied World Assurance Company	American Insurance Association (AIA)
Arch Insurance Group	
Aspen Specialty Insurance Company	AXA Liabilities Managers Switzerland
AXA Liabilities Managers UK	AXIS Financial Insurance Solutions
BCS Insurance Company	
Beazley Group	Berkley Professional Liability
Blue Cross & Blue Shield Association	Blue Cross and Blue Shield of Louisiana
Blue Cross Blue Shield of Nebraska	Blue Cross & Blue Shield of North Carolina
Blue Cross & Blue Shield of Rhode Island	BlueCross BlueShield of Tennessee, Inc.
Blue Shield of California Group	Capital BlueCross
CareFirst BlueCross BlueShield	Central Benefits Mutual Insurance Company
Chubb Group	
CNA Insurance Companies	Coalition against Insurance Fraud
Complex Insurance Claims Litigation Association	Evanston Insurance Company
	Farmers Insurance Company
General Star Indemnity Company	Genesis Insurance Company
Hannover Re	Hanover Insurance Company
The Hartford Insurance Group	Hawaii Medical Service Association
HCC Global Financial Products	

WASHINGTON — DISTRICT OF COLUMBIA

Wiley Rein LLP, Washington, DC (Continued)

Health Care Service Corporation
ICI Mutual Insurance Group
Liberty Mutual Insurance Company
National Insurance Crime Bureau
The Navigators Group, Inc.
Premera Blue Cross
Reliance Insurance Company
Starr Indemnity & Liability Company
Travelers Insurance Companies
Wellmark Blue Cross and Blue Sheild
Highmark Inc.
Lexington Insurance Company
Mountain State Blue Cross Blue Shield
OneBeacon Insurance
QBE the Americas Group
Resolute Management - New England
State Farm Insurance Companies
ULLICO Group
XL Professional
Zurich American Insurance Group

Partners

Rachel A. Alexander — 1971 — Rutgers College, B.A., 1993; The George Washington University, J.D. (magna cum laude), 2005 — Admitted to Bar, 2005, Maryland; 2007, District of Columbia — Practice Areas: Insurance Law; Health Care; Government Contracts — E-mail: ralexander@wileyrein.com

Kimberly A. Ashmore — 1975 — The Pennsylvania State University, B.A., 1995; University of Central Florida, M.S., 1999; The George Washington University, J.D. (with highest honors), 2005 — Admitted to Bar, 2005, Maryland; 2007, District of Columbia; U.S. District Court for the District of Columbia; U.S. District Court, District of Maryland; U.S. District Court, Northern District of Florida; U.S. Court of Appeals, Fourth and Eleventh Circuits — Practice Areas: Insurance Law — E-mail: kashmore@wileyrein.com

Mary E. Borja — 1969 — Johns Hopkins University, B.A., 1990; University of Miami, J.D. (magna cum laude), 1993 — Order of the Coif — Admitted to Bar, 1994, District of Columbia; U.S. District Court for the District of Columbia; U.S. Court of Appeals for the District of Columbia, Third, Fourth, Sixth, Tenth and Eleventh Circuits — Practice Areas: Insurance Law; Litigation — Tel: 202-719-4252 — E-mail: mborja@wileyrein.com

Thomas W. Brunner — 1945 — Columbia University, A.B. (cum laude), 1966; Yale University, J.D., 1970 — Admitted to Bar, 1973, District of Columbia; U.S. Supreme Court; U.S. Court of Appeals for the District of Columbia, First, Second, Third, Fourth, Fifth, Sixth, Seventh, Eighth, Ninth, Tenth and Eleventh Circuits — Practice Areas: Insurance Law; Litigation; Health Care — Tel: 202-719-7225 — E-mail: tbrunner@wileyrein.com

Kathryn Bucher — 1958 — University of Vermont, B.A. (cum laude), 1980; Cornell University, J.D., 1983 — Admitted to Bar, 1983, District of Columbia; 1984, U.S. District Court for the District of Columbia; 1989, U.S. Supreme Court; 1992, U.S. Court of Federal Claims — Member American Health Lawyers Association — Practice Areas: Insurance Law; Health Care — Tel: 202-719-7530 — E-mail: kbucher@wileyrein.com

John D. Cole — 1949 — Rutgers University, B.A., 1971; University of Baltimore, J.D., 1979 — Admitted to Bar, 1979, Maryland; 2003, District of Columbia; U.S. District Court, District of Maryland — ARIAS - U.S. Certified Insurance/Reinsurance Arbitrator — Practice Areas: Insurance Law; Litigation — Tel: 202-719-7333 — E-mail: jcole@wileyrein.com

Jason P. Cronic — 1968 — Tulane University, B.A. (cum laude), 1990; The University of Chicago, J.D., 1993 — Admitted to Bar, 1994, District of Columbia — Practice Areas: Insurance Law; Litigation — Tel: 202-719-7175 — E-mail: jcronic@wileyrein.com

Cara Tseng Duffield — 1974 — Harvard-Radcliffe College, A.B. (magna cum laude), 1996; The University of Chicago, J.D. (cum laude), 2000 — Recipient, Hinton Moot Court Cup — Admitted to Bar, 2002, District of Columbia; U.S. Court of Appeals, Second, Fourth, Sixth, Ninth and Eleventh Circuits — Practice Areas: Insurance Law; Litigation — Tel: 202-719-7407 — E-mail: cduffield@wileyrein.com

Benjamin C. Eggert — 1974 — University of Virginia, B.A. (with distinction), 1996; J.D., 2000 — Admitted to Bar, 2000, Virginia; 2001, District of Columbia; U.S. District Court for the District of Columbia; U.S. District Court, Eastern and Western Districts of Virginia; U.S. Court of Appeals, Fourth Circuit; U.S. Bankruptcy Court, Eastern District of Virginia — Practice Areas: Insurance Law; Litigation; Appellate Practice — Tel: 202-719-7336 — E-mail: beggert@wileyrein.com

Laura A. Foggan — 1958 — University of Pennsylvania, B.A. (magna cum laude), 1980; M.S.Ed., 1980; The George Washington University, J.D. (with high honors), 1983 — Order of the Coif — Admitted to Bar, 1983, District of Columbia; U.S. District Court for the District of Columbia; U.S. Court of Appeals for the District of Columbia, First, Second, Third, Fourth, Fifth, Sixth, Seventh, Eighth, Ninth and Tenth Circuits; U.S. Supreme Court — Member American Bar Association (Past Chair, Litigation Section, Insurance Coverage Litigation Committee); The District of Columbia Bar (Courts, Lawyers and the Administration of Justice Section); Defense Research Institute (Appellate Advocacy and Insurance Coverage Committees); Federation of Defense and Corporate Counsel — Practice Areas: Appellate Practice; Insurance Law — Tel: 202-719-3382 — E-mail: lfoggan@wileyrein.com

Dale E. Hausman — 1961 — Cornell University, B.A., 1983; Georgetown University, J.D. (magna cum laude), 1989 — Order of the Coif — Admitted to Bar, 1989, District of Columbia; U.S. District Court for the District of Columbia; U.S. District Court, Eastern District of Michigan; U.S. Court of Appeals for the District of Columbia and Fourth Circuits; District of Columbia Court of Appeals — Practice Areas: Insurance Law; Litigation — Tel: 202-719-7005 — E-mail: dhausman@wileyrein.com

Theodore A. Howard — 1956 — University of Notre Dame, B.A., 1978; Harvard University, J.D., 1981 — Admitted to Bar, 1982, District of Columbia; U.S. Supreme Court; U.S. Court of Federal Claims; U.S. District Court for the District of Columbia; U.S. Court of Appeals for the District of Columbia, Fourth, Fifth, Eighth, Ninth and Eleventh Circuits — Practice Areas: Insurance Law; Litigation — Tel: 202-719-7120 — E-mail: thoward@wileyrein.com

Richard A. Ifft — 1959 — College of William & Mary, B.A. (with high honors), 1981; Georgetown University, J.D. (magna cum laude), 1984 — Admitted to Bar, 1985, District of Columbia; 1985, Maryland; U.S. District Court for the District of Columbia; U.S. District Court, District of Maryland; U.S. Court of Appeals for the District of Columbia, Second, Fourth, Fifth, Sixth, Seventh, Eighth, Tenth and Eleventh Circuits — Practice Areas: Insurance Law; Litigation — Tel: 202-719-7170 — E-mail: rifft@wileyrein.com

Charles C. Lemley — 1960 — University of North Florida, B.A. (summa cum laude), 1989; Georgetown University, J.D. (magna cum laude), 1994 — Order of the Coif — Admitted to Bar, 1994, Florida; 1996, District of Columbia; U.S. District Court for the District of Columbia and District of Maryland; U.S. District Court, Middle, Northern and Southern Districts of Florida; U.S. District Court, Eastern District of Michigan; U.S. Court of Appeals for the District of Columbia, Third, Fourth and Eighth Circuits; U.S. Supreme Court — Practice Areas: Insurance Law; Litigation — Tel: 202-719-7354 — E-mail: clemley@wileyrein.com

Richard L. McConnell — 1952 — The University of Tennessee, B.A. (with highest honors), 1974; University of Virginia, J.D., 1977 — Order of the Coif — Law Clerk to Judge Bailey Brown, U.S. District Court, Western District of Tennessee, 1977-1978 — Admitted to Bar, 1978, District of Columbia; U.S. District Court for the District of Columbia; U.S. Court of Appeals for the District of Columbia, Second, Sixth and Eighth Circuits; District of Columbia Court of Appeals; U.S. Supreme Court — Member AIDA Reinsurance and Insurance Arbitration Society — Practice Areas: Insurance Law; Litigation; Reinsurance — Tel: 202-719-7265 — E-mail: rmcconnell@wileyrein.com

Kimberly M. Melvin — 1975 — Mary Washington College, B.A. (magna cum laude), 1997; George Mason University, J.D. (magna cum laude), 2000 — Admitted to Bar, 2000, Virginia; 2001, District of Columbia; U.S. District Court for the District of Columbia; U.S. District Court, Eastern District of Virginia; U.S. District Court, Southern District of Indiana — Practice Areas: Insurance Law; Litigation — Tel: 202-719-7403 — E-mail: kmelvin@wileyrein.com

Kirk J. Nahra — 1962 — Georgetown University, B.A. (magna cum laude), 1984; Harvard University, J.D. (cum laude), 1987 — Admitted to Bar, 1988, District of Columbia — Member American Health Lawyers Association — Practice Areas: Insurance Law; Litigation; Health Care — Tel: 202-719-7335 — E-mail: knahra@wileyrein.com

Leslie A. Platt — 1967 — Albion College, B.A. (cum laude), 1989; College of William & Mary, J.D., 1994 — Admitted to Bar, 1995, District of Columbia; New York — Practice Areas: Insurance Law; Litigation — Tel: 202-719-3174 — E-mail: lplatt@wileyrein.com

Dorthula H. Powell-Woodson — 1956 — Virginia Union University, B.A. (magna cum laude), 1978; University of Richmond, J.D., 1981 — Admitted to Bar, 1982, Virginia; 1998, District of Columbia; U.S. District Court, Eastern District of Virginia — Member American Health Lawyers Association — Practice Areas: Health Care; Insurance Law — Tel: 202-719-7150 — E-mail: dpowell-woodson@wileyrein.com

Marc E. Rindner — 1973 — University of Delaware, B.A. (cum laude), 1994; American University, Washington College of Law, J.D. (magna cum laude), 1997 — Admitted to Bar, 1997, Maryland; 1998, District of Columbia; U.S. Court of Appeals for the District of Columbia, First, Second, Fourth, Fifth and Ninth Circuits; U.S. District Court for the District of Columbia; U.S. District Court, District of Maryland; U.S. District Court, Middle District of Pennsylvania — Practice Areas: Insurance Law; Litigation — Tel: 202-719-7486 — E-mail: mrindner@wileyrein.com

Kenneth E. Ryan — 1963 — Boston College, B.A. (magna cum laude), 1985; The George Washington University, J.D., 1988 — Admitted to Bar, 1988,

DISTRICT OF COLUMBIA / WASHINGTON

Wiley Rein LLP, Washington, DC (Continued)

Massachusetts; 1989, District of Columbia; U.S. District Court for the District of Columbia; U.S. Court of Appeals for the District of Columbia and Fourth Circuits — Practice Areas: Insurance Law — Tel: 202-719-7028 — E-mail: kryan@wileyrein.com

Gary P. Seligman — 1972 — Harvard University, A.B. (magna cum laude), 1996; Washington and Lee University School of Law, J.D. (magna cum laude), 1999 — Admitted to Bar, 1999, Virginia; 2000, District of Columbia; U.S. Court of Appeals, Fourth Circuit — Practice Areas: Insurance Law; Litigation; Appellate Practice — Tel: 202-719-3587 — E-mail: gseligman@wileyrein.com

Richard A. Simpson — 1952 — Wesleyan University, B.A. (magna cum laude), 1974; The University of North Carolina, J.D. (with high honors), 1977 — Order of the Coif — Admitted to Bar, 1978, Illinois; 1987, District of Columbia; 1991, Virginia; 2000, Maryland; U.S. District Court for the District of Columbia and District of Maryland; U.S. District Court, Western District of Michigan; U.S. District Court, Eastern and Western Districts of Virginia; U.S. District Court, Northern District of Illinois; U.S. District Court, Northern District of Texas; U.S. District Court, Northern District of Florida; U.S. District Court, District of Colorado; U.S. Court of Appeals for the District of Columbia, First, Second, Third, Fourth, Fifth, Sixth, Seventh, Ninth, Tenth and Eleventh Circuits; U.S. Supreme Court — Practice Areas: Insurance Law; Litigation; Appellate Practice — Tel: 202-719-7314 — E-mail: rsimpson@wileyrein.com

William E. Smith — 1966 — Michigan State University, B.A. (with high honors), 1989; University of Michigan, J.D. (magna cum laude), 1992 — Order of the Coif — Admitted to Bar, 1992, Maryland; 1994, District of Columbia; U.S. District Court for the District of Columbia; U.S. District Court, District of Maryland; U.S. Court of Appeals, Ninth Circuit; U.S. Court of Federal Claims — Practice Areas: Insurance Law; Litigation — Tel: 202-719-7350 — E-mail: wsmith@wileyrein.com

Daniel J. Standish — 1960 — Bowdoin College, A.B. (magna cum laude), 1983; The University of Chicago, J.D., 1986 — Admitted to Bar, 1988, District of Columbia; U.S. District Court for the District of Columbia and District of Maryland; U.S. District Court, Eastern District of Wisconsin; U.S. District Court, Northern District of Illinois; U.S. District Court, Southern District of Indiana; U.S. District Court, District of Colorado; U.S. Court of Appeals for the District of Columbia, First, Second, Third, Fourth, Sixth, Seventh, Eighth, Ninth and Eleventh Circuits — Member Professional Liability Underwriting Society (Past President and Trustee); PLUS Foundation (Current Director) — Assistant U.S. Attorney for the District of Columbia, 1989-1993 — Practice Areas: Insurance Law; Litigation — Tel: 202-719-7130 — E-mail: dstandish@wileyrein.com

Sandra Tvarian Stevens — 1973 — American University, B.A. (cum laude), 1994; American University, Washington College of Law, J.D. (summa cum laude), 1997 — American Jurisprudence Award, Constitutional Process — Admitted to Bar, 1997, Illinois; 1998, District of Columbia; U.S. District Court for the District of Columbia — Practice Areas: Litigation; Insurance Law — Tel: 202-719-3229 — E-mail: sstevens@wileyrein.com

David H. Topol — 1966 — Cornell University, B.A., 1988; Yale Law School, J.D., 1992 — Admitted to Bar, 1992, Maryland; 1993, District of Columbia — Practice Areas: Insurance Law; Litigation; Appellate Practice — Tel: 202-719-7214 — E-mail: dtopol@wileyrein.com

Of Counsel

Keith S. Watson

Associates

Matthew W. Beato	Edward R. Brown
Ashley E. Eiler	Muhammad Elsayed
Milad Emam	Michael J. Gridley
John Howell	Leland H. Jones, IV
Parker J. Lavin	Mary Catherine Martin
Jason O'Brien	Pamela Okafor
Frederick H. Schutt	Karen Toto
Jennifer A. Williams	

The following firms also service this area.

Bacon, Thornton, Palmer, L.L.P.
6411 Ivy Lane
Suite 500
Greenbelt, Maryland 20770-1411
Telephone: 301-345-7001
Fax: 301-345-7075

Insurance Defense, General Liability, Casualty, Construction Defect, Product Liability, Employment Law, Retail Liability, Premises Liability, Environmental Law, Asbestos Litigation, Lead Paint, Mold and Mildew Claims

SEE COMPLETE LISTING UNDER GREENBELT, MARYLAND (12 MILES)

Gorman & Williams
36 South Charles Street, Suite 900
Baltimore, Maryland 21201-3754
Telephone: 410-528-0600
Fax: 410-528-0602

Insurance Defense, Comprehensive General Liability, Commercial Liability, Business Litigation, Business Law, Mergers and Acquisitions, Negligence, Product Liability, Insurance Coverage, Corporate Law, Antitrust, Arbitration, Mediation, Construction Law, Employment Law, Admiralty and Maritime Law, Estate Planning, Commercial Law, Patents, Tradmarks, Copyrights and Technology Licensing and Infringement, Real Property Law, Consumer Protection Law, International Trade, Estate Administration, Executive Liability, Maryland Insurance Administration Regulatory Representation, Securities Litigation

SEE COMPLETE LISTING UNDER BALTIMORE, MARYLAND (39 MILES)

Hudgins Law Firm, P.C.
515 King Street, Suite 400
Alexandria, Virginia 22314
Telephone: 703-739-3300
Fax: 703-739-3700

Accident, Accountant Malpractice, Accountants and Attorneys Liability, Agent and Brokers Errors and Omissions, Agent/Broker Liability, Appellate Practice, Automobile Liability, Automotive Products Liability, Bad Faith, Business Law, Carrier Defense, Casualty Defense, Civil Trial Practice, Commercial Litigation, Construction Litigation, Declaratory Judgments, Defense Litigation, Directors and Officers Liability, Employer Liability, Errors and Omissions, General Civil Trial and Appellate Practice, General Defense, Insurance Coverage, Insurance Defense, Insurance Law, Insurance Litigation, Intentional Torts, Law Enforcement Liability, Legal Malpractice, Medical Malpractice, Motor Vehicle, Municipal Liability, Negligence, Nursing Home Liability, Personal Injury, Premises Liability, Product Liability, Professional Errors and Omissions, Professional Liability, Property and Casualty, Securities and Investments, Self-Insured Defense, Slip and Fall, State and Federal Courts, Tort Litigation, Trial and Appellate Practice, Workers' Compensation, Wrongful Death

SEE COMPLETE LISTING UNDER ALEXANDRIA, VIRGINIA (7 MILES)

Saunders & Schmieler, P.C.
The Montgomery Center, Suite 1202
8630 Fenton Street
Silver Spring, Maryland 20910-3808
Telephone: 301-588-7717
Fax: 301-588-5073

Advertising Injury, Animal Law, Appellate Practice, Civil Rights, Class Actions, Contracts, Construction Liability, Corporate Law, Directors and Officers Liability, Environmental Law, Errors and Omissions, Insurance Coverage, Risk Management, Intellectual Property, Labor and Employment, Mass Tort, Medical Malpractice, Personal Injury, Premises Liability, Product Liability, Professional Malpractice, Sports Law, Real Estate, Self-Insured Defense, Toxic Torts, Workers' Compensation, Wrongful Death

SEE COMPLETE LISTING UNDER SILVER SPRING, MARYLAND (8 MILES)

Wright, Constable & Skeen, L.L.P.
100 North Charles Street
16th Floor
Baltimore, Maryland 21201
Telephone: 410-659-1300
Fax: 410-659-1350
Toll Free: 888-894-7602

Insurance Defense, Automobile, General Liability, Marine, Bodily Injury, Fire, Professional Malpractice, Alternative Dispute Resolution, Commercial Litigation, Construction Liability, Employment Practices Liability, Railroad Law, Fidelity and Surety, Coverage

SEE COMPLETE LISTING UNDER BALTIMORE, MARYLAND (41 MILES)

FLORIDA

CAPITAL: TALLAHASSEE

COUNTIES AND COUNTY SEATS

County	County Seat	County	County Seat	County	County Seat
Alachua	Gainesville	Hardee	Wauchula	Okeechobee	Okeechobee
Baker	Macclenny	Hendry	La Belle	Orange	Orlando
Bay	Panama City	Hernando	Brooksville	Osceola	Kissimmee
Bradford	Starke	Highlands	Sebring	Palm Beach	West Palm Beach
Brevard	Titusville	Hillsborough	Tampa	Pasco	Dade City
Broward	Fort Lauderdale	Holmes	Bonifay	Pinellas	Clearwater
Calhoun	Blountstown	Indian River	Vero Beach	Polk	Bartow
Charlotte	Punta Gorda	Jackson	Marianna	Putnam	Palatka
Citrus	Inverness	Jefferson	Monticello	St. Johns	St. Augustine
Clay	Green Cove Springs	Lafayette	Mayo	St. Lucie	Fort Pierce
Collier	Naples	Lake	Tavares	Santa Rosa	Milton
Columbia	Lake City	Lee	Fort Myers	Sarasota	Sarasota
De Soto	Arcadia	Leon	Tallahassee	Seminole	Sanford
Dixie	Cross City	Levy	Bronson	Sumter	Bushnell
Duval	Jacksonville	Liberty	Bristol	Suwannee	Live Oak
Escambia	Pensacola	Madison	Madison	Taylor	Perry
Flagler	Bunnell	Manatee	Bradenton	Union	Lake Butler
Franklin	Apalachicola	Marion	Ocala	Volusia	De Land
Gadsden	Quincy	Martin	Stuart	Wakulla	Crawfordville
Gilchrist	Trenton	Miami-Dade	Miami	Walton	De Funiak Springs
Glades	Moor Haven	Monroe	Key West	Washington	Chipley
Gulf	Port St. Joe	Nassau	Fernandina Beach		
Hamilton	Jasper	Okaloosa	Crestview		

In the text that follows "†" indicates County Seats.

Our files contain additional verified data on the firms listed herein. This additional information is available on request.

A.M. BEST COMPANY

FLORIDA

ALTAMONTE SPRINGS   41,496 Seminole Co.

Refer To

Vernis & Bowling of Central Florida, P.A.
1450 South Woodland Boulevard, Fourth Floor
DeLand, Florida 32720
   Telephone: 386-734-2505
   Fax: 386-734-3441

Civil Litigation, Insurance Law, Workers' Compensation, Premises Liability, Labor and Employment, Civil Rights, Commercial Litigation, Complex Litigation, Product Liability, Directors and Officers Liability, Errors and Omissions, Construction Law, Construction Defect, Environmental Liability, Personal and Commercial Vehicle, Appellate Practice, Admiralty and Maritime Law, Real Estate, Family Law, Elder Law, Liability Defense, SIU/Fraud Litigation, Education Law (ESE/IDEA), Property and Casualty (Commercial and Personal Lines), Long-Haul Trucking Liability, Government Law, Public Law, Criminal, White Collar, Business Litigation

SEE COMPLETE LISTING UNDER DAYTONA BEACH, FLORIDA (33 MILES)

BARTOW   † 17,298 Polk Co.

Refer To

Abbey, Adams, Byelick & Mueller, L.L.P.
360 Central Avenue, 11th Floor
St. Petersburg, Florida 33701
   Telephone: 727-821-2080
   Fax: 727-822-3970

Mailing Address: P.O. Box 1511, St. Petersburg, FL 33731

Administrative Law, Americans with Disabilities Act, Appellate Practice, Complex Litigation, General Defense, Employment Law, Bad Faith, Insurance Coverage, Insurance Fraud, Uninsured and Underinsured Motorist, Professional Malpractice, Mediation, Negligence, Personal Injury, Premises Liability, Product Liability, Subrogation, Toxic Torts, Workers' Compensation, Motor Vehicle Liability, Defense of Insureds, Sovereign Immunity and Governmental Defense

SEE COMPLETE LISTING UNDER ST. PETERSBURG, FLORIDA (62 MILES)

BOCA RATON   84,392 Palm Beach Co.

Luks & Santaniello LLC
301 Yamato Road, Suite 1234
Boca Raton, Florida 33431
   Telephone: 561-893-9088
   Fax: 561-893-9048
   www.LS-LAW.com

(Additional Offices: Fort Lauderdale, FL*; Tampa, FL*; Orlando, FL*; Jacksonville, FL*; Miami, FL*; Tallahassee, FL)

Insurance Defense, General Liability, Workers' Compensation

(See listing under Fort Lauderdale, FL for additional information)

Pett Furman, PL
2101 N.W. Corporate Boulevard, Suite 316
Boca Raton, Florida 33431
   Telephone: 561-994-4311
   Fax: 561-982-8985
   E-Mail: info@pettfurman.com
   www.pettfurman.com

Established: 2002

ERISA, Life and Health, Disability, Employment Discrimination, Commercial Litigation, Trial and Appellate Practice

Firm Profile: Based in South Florida, we handle litigation throughout the entire state and also handle select out-of-state matters. In addition, we provide counseling to our clients in an effort to avoid potential disputes before they arise. We give in-house presentations regarding "hot topics", in addition to serving as speakers at the American Bar Association, Defense Research

ALTAMONTE SPRINGS

Pett Furman, PL, Boca Raton, FL   (Continued)

Institute, International Claims Association, Eastern Claims Conference and American Conference Institute.

Insurance Clients

AEGON Insurance Group	Aetna, Inc.
Assurant Employee Benefits	Disability Reinsurance
The Guardian Life Insurance	Management Services, Inc.
Company of America	Lincoln National Life Insurance
Minnesota Life Insurance	Company
Company	Mutual of Omaha Insurance
Penn Mutual Insurance Company	Company
Phoenix Life Insurance Company	Prudential Insurance Company of
RBC Life Insurance Company	America
Trustmark Insurance Company	The Union Central Life Insurance
Unum Group	Company

Firm Members

Kristina B. Pett — The George Washington University, B.A., 1985; Temple University School of Law, J.D. (cum laude), 1989 — Admitted to Bar, 1989, Pennsylvania; 1993, Florida; 1989, U.S. District Court, Western District of Pennsylvania; 1990, U.S. Court of Appeals, Fourth Circuit; 1993, U.S. District Court, Middle and Southern Districts of Florida; 1995, U.S. Court of Appeals, Eleventh Circuit; 1999, U.S. Supreme Court; 2004, U.S. District Court, Northern District of Florida — Member American Bar Association; International Claims Association; Defense Research Institute

Wendy L. Furman — Franklin & Marshall College, B.A. (magna cum laude), 1991; University of Pittsburgh School of Law, J.D. (magna cum laude), 1994 — Order of the Coif; Phi Beta Kappa — Executive Editor, University of Pittsburgh Law Review (1993-1994) — Admitted to Bar, 1994, Pennsylvania; 1996, Florida; 1994, U.S. District Court, Western District of Pennsylvania; 1997, U.S. District Court, Middle, Northern and Southern Districts of Florida; 1998, U.S. Court of Appeals, Eleventh Circuit — Member American Bar Association; Defense Research Institute

Schwartz Law Group
6751 North Federal Highway, Suite 400
Boca Raton, Florida 33487
   Telephone: 561-395-4747
   Fax: 561-367-1550
   E-Mail: els@theschwartzlawgroup.com
   www.theschwartzlawgroup.com

Established: 2001

Appellate Practice, Bad Faith, Civil Litigation, Construction Defect, Examinations Under Oath, Maritime Law, Premise Litigation, Product Liability, Professional Liability, Subrogation, Arbitration, Appraisal, and Mediation, Business Law, Corporate Counseling, Commercial Auto Liability, Employment Law, Restrictive Non-Compete Covenants, Homeowners Claims, Insurance Coverage Disputes, Personal & Commercial, Intellectual Property, Trade Secrets, Mass Tort, Multi-District Litigation, Third Party Liability Defense, Underwriting/Claims Risk Management

Firm Profile: Steve Schwartz and the Schwartz Law Group team of professionals are dedicated to providing cost-effective, results-oriented legal services. Our attorneys have handled over 100 jury trials involving homeowners' claims, construction defects, commercial disputes, insurance first and third party coverage, bad faith litigation, and personal injury/wrongful death cases in Florida state and federal courts as well as other jurisdictions around the country. In addition to handling proceedings at the trial level, we regularly appear in state and federal appellate courts, mediations and arbitrations.

Insurance Clients

Elements Property Insurance	MSA, Old Dominion Insurance
Company	Company
St. Johns Insurance Company, Inc.	

Third Party Administrators

NCA Group, Inc.	Seibels Insurance Technology & Services

BROOKSVILLE　　　　　　　　　　　　　　　　　　　　　　　　　　　　　　　　　　　　FLORIDA

Schwartz Law Group, Boca Raton, FL (Continued)

Partner

Steven G. Schwartz — Washington and Lee University School of Law, J.D., 1978 — Admitted to Bar, 1978, Virginia; 1986, Maryland; 1991, Florida; U.S. District Court, Middle, Northern and Southern Districts of Florida; U.S. District Court, Southern District of Florida including Trial Bar; U.S. District Court, District of Maryland; U.S. District Court, Eastern and Western Districts of Virginia; U.S. Court of Appeals, Second, Fourth, Fifth and Eleventh Circuits; U.S. Claims Court; Supreme Court of the United States — Member American, Maryland and Palm Beach County Bar Associations; The Florida Bar; Virginia State Bar; American Association for Justice; Southeastern Admirality Law Institute; Supreme Court Historical Society; Council on Litigation Management

Associates

Noah S. Bender　　　　　　　　　　Andrew P. Ketterer
David J. Pascuzzi　　　　　　　　　Robert B. Gertzman

The following firms also service this area.

Conroy Simberg
3440 Hollywood Boulevard, Second Floor
Hollywood, Florida 33021
　Telephone: 954-961-1400
　Fax: 954-967-8577

Insurance Defense, Appellate Practice, Insurance Coverage, Environmental Law, Governmental Liability, Civil Rights, Wrongful Termination, Americans with Disabilities Act, Sexual Harassment, Land Use, Commercial Law, Fire, Arson, Fraud, Fidelity and Surety, Automobile Liability, Admiralty and Maritime Law, Bad Faith, Employment Law, Self-Insured, Public Entities, Product Liability, Casualty, Excess and Reinsurance, Accident and Health, Workers' Compensation, Medical Malpractice, Class Actions, Construction Defect, Construction Litigation, First Party Matters, Premises Liability, Professional Liability, Intellectual Property

SEE COMPLETE LISTING UNDER HOLLYWOOD, FLORIDA (26 MILES)

BONIFAY † 2,793 Holmes Co.

Refer To
Barron & Redding, P.A.
220 McKenzie Avenue
Panama City, Florida 32401-3129
　Telephone: 850-785-7454
　Fax: 850-785-2999
Mailing Address: P.O. Box 2467, Panama City, FL 32402-2467

Casualty, Surety, Fire, Life Insurance, Professional Liability, Product Liability, Medical Malpractice, Environmental Law, Automobile Liability, Premises Liability, Business Torts, Construction Law

SEE COMPLETE LISTING UNDER PANAMA CITY, FLORIDA (48 MILES)

BRADENTON † 49,546 Manatee Co.

Refer To
Abbey, Adams, Byelick & Mueller, L.L.P.
360 Central Avenue, 11th Floor
St. Petersburg, Florida 33701
　Telephone: 727-821-2080
　Fax: 727-822-3970
Mailing Address: P.O. Box 1511, St. Petersburg, FL 33731

Administrative Law, Americans with Disabilities Act, Appellate Practice, Complex Litigation, General Defense, Employment Law, Bad Faith, Insurance Coverage, Insurance Fraud, Uninsured and Underinsured Motorist, Professional Malpractice, Mediation, Negligence, Personal Injury, Premises Liability, Product Liability, Subrogation, Toxic Torts, Workers' Compensation, Motor Vehicle Liability, Defense of Insureds, Sovereign Immunity and Governmental Defense

SEE COMPLETE LISTING UNDER ST. PETERSBURG, FLORIDA (26 MILES)

Refer To
Barker & Cook, PA
501 East Kennedy Boulevard, Suite 790
Tampa, Florida 33602
　Telephone: 813-489-1001
　Fax: 813-489-1008
　Toll Free: 888-892-8722

Insurance Defense, Self-Insured, Trial and Appellate Practice, State and Federal Courts, First and Third Party Defense, Automobile, Casualty, Construction Law, Engineers, Malpractice, Environmental Law, General Liability, Life and Health, Medical Malpractice, Product Liability, Property, Reinsurance, Workers' Compensation, Civil Litigation, Commercial Litigation, Personal Injury, Premises Liability, Contract Disputes, Labor and Employment, Construction Disputes, Insurance Coverage Disputes

SEE COMPLETE LISTING UNDER TAMPA, FLORIDA (45 MILES)

Refer To
Brasfield, Freeman, Goldis & Cash, P.A.
2553 First Avenue North
St. Petersburg, Florida 33713
　Telephone: 727-327-2258
　Fax: 727-328-1340
Mailing Address: P.O. Box 12349, St. Petersburg, FL 33733-2349

Insurance Defense, Trial Practice, Product Liability, Professional Liability, Premises Liability, Automobile Liability, Personal Injury, Wrongful Death, Construction Defect, Insurance Coverage

SEE COMPLETE LISTING UNDER ST. PETERSBURG, FLORIDA (26 MILES)

Refer To
Vernis & Bowling of the Gulf Coast, P.A.
696 1st Avenue, 1st Floor
St. Petersburg, Florida 33701
　Telephone: 727-443-3377
　Fax: 727-443-6828

Civil Litigation, Insurance Law, Workers' Compensation, Premises Liability, Labor and Employment, Civil Rights, Commercial Litigation, Complex Litigation, Product Liability, Directors and Officers Liability, Errors and Omissions, Construction Law, Construction Defect, Environmental Liability, Personal and Commercial Vehicle, Appellate Practice, Admiralty and Maritime Law, Real Estate, Family Law, Elder Law, Liability Defense, SIU/Fraud Litigation, Education Law (ESE/IDEA), Property and Casualty (Commercial and Personal Lines), Long-Haul Trucking Liability, Government Law, Public Law, Criminal, White Collar, Business Litigation

SEE COMPLETE LISTING UNDER CLEARWATER, FLORIDA (44 MILES)

BROOKSVILLE † 7,719 Hernando Co.

Refer To
Abbey, Adams, Byelick & Mueller, L.L.P.
360 Central Avenue, 11th Floor
St. Petersburg, Florida 33701
　Telephone: 727-821-2080
　Fax: 727-822-3970
Mailing Address: P.O. Box 1511, St. Petersburg, FL 33731

Administrative Law, Americans with Disabilities Act, Appellate Practice, Complex Litigation, General Defense, Employment Law, Bad Faith, Insurance Coverage, Insurance Fraud, Uninsured and Underinsured Motorist, Professional Malpractice, Mediation, Negligence, Personal Injury, Premises Liability, Product Liability, Subrogation, Toxic Torts, Workers' Compensation, Motor Vehicle Liability, Defense of Insureds, Sovereign Immunity and Governmental Defense

SEE COMPLETE LISTING UNDER ST. PETERSBURG, FLORIDA (70 MILES)

Refer To
Cameron, Hodges, Coleman, LaPointe & Wright, P.A.
111 North Magnolia Avenue, Suite 1350
Orlando, Florida 32801-2378
　Telephone: 407-841-5030
　Fax: 407-841-1727

Insurance Law

SEE COMPLETE LISTING UNDER ORLANDO, FLORIDA (68 MILES)

BUNNELL † 2,676 Flagler Co.
Refer To

Cameron, Hodges, Coleman, LaPointe & Wright, P.A.
150 South Palmetto Avenue, # 101
Daytona Beach, Florida 32114
  Telephone: 386-257-1755
  Fax: 386-252-5601

Insurance Law

SEE COMPLETE LISTING UNDER DAYTONA BEACH, FLORIDA (23 MILES)

BUSHNELL † 2,418 Sumter Co.
Refer To

Cameron, Hodges, Coleman, LaPointe & Wright, P.A.
111 North Magnolia Avenue, Suite 1350
Orlando, Florida 32801-2378
  Telephone: 407-841-5030
  Fax: 407-841-1727

Insurance Law

SEE COMPLETE LISTING UNDER ORLANDO, FLORIDA (64 MILES)

CAPE CORAL 154,305 Lee Co.
Refer To

Vernis & Bowling of Southwest Florida, P.A.
2369 West 1st Street
Fort Myers, Florida 33901-3309
  Telephone: 239-334-3035
  Fax: 239-334-7702

Civil Litigation, Insurance Law, Workers' Compensation, Premises Liability, Labor and Employment, Civil Rights, Commercial Litigation, Complex Litigation, Product Liability, Directors and Officers Liability, Errors and Omissions, Construction Law, Construction Defect, Environmental Liability, Personal and Commercial Vehicle, Appellate Practice, Admiralty and Maritime Law, Real Estate, Family Law, Elder Law, Liability Defense, SIU/Fraud Litigation, Education Law (ESE/IDEA), Property and Casualty (Commercial and Personal Lines), Long-Haul Trucking Liability, Government Law, Public Law, Criminal, White Collar, Business Litigation

SEE COMPLETE LISTING UNDER FORT MYERS, FLORIDA (221 MILES)

CHIPLEY † 3,605 Washington Co.
Refer To

Barron & Redding, P.A.
220 McKenzie Avenue
Panama City, Florida 32401-3129
  Telephone: 850-785-7454
  Fax: 850-785-2999

Mailing Address: P.O. Box 2467, Panama City, FL 32402-2467

Casualty, Surety, Fire, Life Insurance, Professional Liability, Product Liability, Medical Malpractice, Environmental Law, Automobile Liability, Premises Liability, Business Torts, Construction Law

SEE COMPLETE LISTING UNDER PANAMA CITY, FLORIDA (52 MILES)

CLEARWATER † 107,685 Pinellas Co.

Dalan, Katz & Siegel, P.L.
2633 McCormick Drive, Suite 101
Clearwater, Florida 33759-1041
  Telephone: 727-796-1000
  Fax: 727-797-2200
  E-Mail: JK@Dalan-Katz.com
  www.Dalan-Katz.com

Insurance Defense, Fire, Casualty, Automobile, Personal Injury, Subrogation, Environmental Law, Premises Liability, Product Liability, Medical Malpractice, Employment Discrimination, Construction Defect, Insurance Coverage, Extra-Contractual Litigation, Chemical and Asbestos Exposure

Dalan, Katz & Siegel, P.L., Clearwater, FL (Continued)

Insurance Clients

AIG Life Insurance Company	Allstate Insurance Company
American Strategic Insurance Company	Amerisure Insurance Company
	Builders Insurance Group
Farmers Insurance Company	FCCI Insurance Group
Mercury Insurance Group	MetLife Auto & Home
Mid-Continent Group	Royal Insurance Company
State Farm Fire and Casualty Company	State Farm Mutual Automobile Insurance Company
US Administrator Claims	Zurich U.S.

Partners

Jeffrey M. Katz — 1966 — University of Florida, B.S.B.A., 1988; Stetson University College of Law, J.D., 1991; Emory University School of Law, LL.M., 1992 — Admitted to Bar, 1991, Florida; 1991, U.S. District Court, Middle District of Florida; 1991, U.S. Court of Appeals, Eleventh Circuit — Member American, Hillsborough County and Clearwater Bar Associations; The Florida Bar; West Coast Claims Association; Florida Defense Lawyers Association

Michael D. Siegel — 1959 — University of South Florida, B.A., 1981; Stetson University College of Law, J.D., 1984 — Admitted to Bar, 1984, Florida; 1985, U.S. District Court, Middle District of Florida; 1987, U.S. Court of Appeals, Eleventh Circuit — Member American, St. Petersburg and Clearwater Bar Associations; The Florida Bar; Pinellas County Trial Lawyers Association

Of Counsel

Rick Dalan

Vernis & Bowling of the Gulf Coast, P.A.
696 1st Avenue, 1st Floor
St. Petersburg, Florida 33701
  Telephone: 727-443-3377
  Fax: 727-443-6828
  E-Mail: info@florida-law.com
  www.florida-law.com

Established: 1970

Civil Litigation, Insurance Law, Workers' Compensation, Premises Liability, Labor and Employment, Civil Rights, Commercial Litigation, Complex Litigation, Product Liability, Directors and Officers Liability, Errors and Omissions, Construction Law, Construction Defect, Environmental Liability, Personal and Commercial Vehicle, Appellate Practice, Admiralty and Maritime Law, Real Estate, Family Law, Elder Law, Liability Defense, SIU/Fraud Litigation, Education Law (ESE/IDEA), Property and Casualty (Commercial and Personal Lines), Long-Haul Trucking Liability, Government Law, Public Law, Criminal, White Collar, Business Litigation

Firm Profile: Since 1970, VERNIS & BOWLING has represented individuals, businesses, professionals, insurance carriers, self-insureds, brokers, underwriters, agents, PEOs and insured. We provide cost effective, full service, legal representation that consistently exceeds the expectations of our clients. With 115 attorneys throughout 16 offices located in Florida, Georgia, Alabama, North Carolina and Mississippi the firm is able to provide the benefits of a large organization, including a management team, consistent policies and representation to ensure personal service and local representation to our clients.

Firm Members

Kenneth E. Amos, Jr. — 1970 — Hillsborough Community College, A.A. (with honors), 1998; University of Central Florida, B.A. (cum laude), 2000; Stetson University College of Law, J.D., 2003 — Admitted to Bar, 2004, Florida; 2009, U.S. District Court, Middle District of Florida

William C. Gula — 1981 — Florida Atlantic University, B.A. (Dean's List), 2003; Florida International University College of Law, J.D. (Dean's List), 2006 — Admitted to Bar, 2006, Florida

Matthew S. Garnett — 1978 — University of Rochester, B.A. (Dean's List), 2000; Vanderbilt University Law School, J.D., 2006 — Admitted to Bar,

CORAL GABLES   FLORIDA

Vernis & Bowling of the Gulf Coast, P.A., Clearwater, FL
(Continued)

2006, Florida; 2007, U.S. District Court, Middle and Southern Districts of Florida — Member St. Petersburg Bar Association

Kory Watson — 1986 — University of Illinois-Urbana-Champaign, B.S. (with honors), 2008; Southern Illinois University School of Law, J.D. (cum laude), 2011 — Admitted to Bar, 2012, Florida

Donald Calhall — University of Florida, B.S., 2005; M.A., 2006; Stetson University College of Law, J.D., 2013 — Admitted to Bar, 2014, Florida

Lauren Pcholinski

(See listing under Miami, FL for additional information)

The following firms also service this area.

Abbey, Adams, Byelick & Mueller, L.L.P.
360 Central Avenue, 11th Floor
St. Petersburg, Florida 33701
  Telephone: 727-821-2080
  Fax: 727-822-3970

Mailing Address: P.O. Box 1511, St. Petersburg, FL 33731

Administrative Law, Americans with Disabilities Act, Appellate Practice, Complex Litigation, General Defense, Employment Law, Bad Faith, Insurance Coverage, Insurance Fraud, Uninsured and Underinsured Motorist, Professional Malpractice, Mediation, Negligence, Personal Injury, Premises Liability, Product Liability, Subrogation, Toxic Torts, Workers' Compensation, Motor Vehicle Liability, Defense of Insureds, Sovereign Immunity and Governmental Defense

SEE COMPLETE LISTING UNDER ST. PETERSBURG, FLORIDA (20 MILES)

Barker & Cook, PA
501 East Kennedy Boulevard, Suite 790
Tampa, Florida 33602
  Telephone: 813-489-1001
  Fax: 813-489-1008
  Toll Free: 888-892-8722

Insurance Defense, Self-Insured, Trial and Appellate Practice, State and Federal Courts, First and Third Party Defense, Automobile, Casualty, Construction Law, Engineers, Malpractice, Environmental Law, General Liability, Life and Health, Medical Malpractice, Product Liability, Property, Reinsurance, Workers' Compensation, Civil Litigation, Commercial Litigation, Personal Injury, Premises Liability, Contract Disputes, Labor and Employment, Construction Disputes, Insurance Coverage Disputes

SEE COMPLETE LISTING UNDER TAMPA, FLORIDA (23 MILES)

Brasfield, Freeman, Goldis & Cash, P.A.
2553 First Avenue North
St. Petersburg, Florida 33713
  Telephone: 727-327-2258
  Fax: 727-328-1340

Mailing Address: P.O. Box 12349, St. Petersburg, FL 33733-2349

Insurance Defense, Trial Practice, Product Liability, Professional Liability, Premises Liability, Automobile Liability, Personal Injury, Wrongful Death, Construction Defect, Insurance Coverage

SEE COMPLETE LISTING UNDER ST. PETERSBURG, FLORIDA (20 MILES)

COCOA 17,140 Brevard Co.

Refer To

Cameron, Hodges, Coleman, LaPointe & Wright, P.A.
111 North Magnolia Avenue, Suite 1350
Orlando, Florida 32801-2378
  Telephone: 407-841-5030
  Fax: 407-841-1727

Insurance Law

SEE COMPLETE LISTING UNDER ORLANDO, FLORIDA (47 MILES)

CORAL GABLES 46,780 Miami-Dade Co.

Berk, Merchant & Sims, PLC
2 Alhambra Plaza, Suite 700
Coral Gables, Florida 33134
  Telephone: 786-338-2900
  Fax: 786-338-2888
  E-Mail: wberk@berklawfirm.com
  www.berklawfirm.com

Established: 2005

Bad Faith, First Party Matters, Third Party, Insurance Coverage, Insurance Defense, Property

Firm Profile: Berk, Merchant & Sims, PLC is a full service insurance firm providing assistance in coverage, liability and bad faith disputes. For additional information please visit our web site www.berklawfirm.com, or contact us at wberk@berklawfirm.com

Insurance Clients

ACE Global Markets, Ltd.	A. F. Beazley & Ors
American Integrity Insurance Company	American Strategic Insurance Company
Amlin Group	Argus Fire & Casualty Insurance Company
ARI Insurance Group	Capacity Insurance Company
Brit Insurance Limited	Chaucer Syndicates at Lloyd's, London
Catlin Group Limited	
Citizens Property Insurance Corp.	Kiln Syndicate, Lloyd's
Florida Intracoastal Underwriters, Ltd.	Lexington Insurance Company
Liberty Syndicate Management Limited	Markel International, Ltd.
	MetLife Insurance Company
Nationwide Insurance	Novae Syndicates Limited
Pure Insurance	QBE Insurance Corporation
Southern Fidelity Insurance Company	State Farm Insurance Company
	Swiss Re America Group
Tower Hill Insurance Company	Travelers of Florida
Travelers Property Casualty Company of America	Wellington Underwriting plc

Members of the Firm

William S. Berk — 1957 — Bowdoin College, A.B. (cum laude), 1979; University of Miami School of Law, J.D., 1982 — Admitted to Bar, 1982, Florida; U.S. District Court, Middle, Northern and Southern Districts of Florida; U.S. Court of Appeals, Eleventh Circuit — Member American (Torts and Insurance Practice Section) and Dade County Bar Associations; The Florida Bar; Dade County Defense Bar Association; Florida Defense Lawyers Association; Defense Research Institute; Federation of Defense and Corporate Counsel

Evelyn M. Merchant — 1949 — Florida International University, B.S., 1978; Nova Southeastern University, Shepard Broad Law Center, J.D., 1985 — Admitted to Bar, 1985, Florida; U.S. District Court, Middle and Southern Districts of Florida; U.S. Court of Appeals, Eleventh Circuit — Member American Bar Association; The Florida Bar; Ft. Lauderdale Claims Association; Florida Advisory Committee on Arson Defense; Florida Defense Lawyers Association

Melissa M. Sims — 1963 — Louisiana State University, B.A., 1986; St. Thomas University School of Law, J.D. (with honors), 1992 — Admitted to Bar, 1992, Louisiana; 1996, Florida; U.S. District Court, Eastern District of Louisiana; U.S. District Court, Middle, Northern and Southern Districts of Florida — Member Federal, American (Torts and Insurance Practice Section) and Dade County Bar Associations

Partners

Gilberto J. Barreto — 1974 — Valencia Community College, A.A., 1995; St. Thomas University, B.A., 1997; University of Florida College of Law, J.D., 2002 — Admitted to Bar, 2002, Florida; 2003, U.S. District Court, Middle and Southern Districts of Florida — Member The Florida Bar — Languages: Spanish

Patrick E. Betar — 1979 — Rhodes College, B.A./B.A., 2001; Syracuse University College of Law, M.A., 2004 — Admitted to Bar, 2005, Florida; U.S. District Court, Northern and Southern Districts of Florida — Member American and Dade County Bar Associations; The Florida Bar

Berk, Merchant & Sims, PLC, Coral Gables, FL
(Continued)

Maria Fuxa — 1962 — University of Miami School of Nursing, B.S.N., 1984; St. Thomas University School of Law, J.D., 1992 — Admitted to Bar, 1995, Florida; 2001, U.S. District Court, Southern District of Florida; U.S. Supreme Court — Member The Florida Bar; Cuban American and Dade County Bar Associations — Registered Nurse, 1985; Licensed Health Care Risk Manager — Languages: Spanish

Senior Attorney

William Xanttopoulos — 1953 — University of the Pacific, B.A., 1976; The University of Texas School of Law, J.D., 1980 — Admitted to Bar, 1981, New York; 1994, Florida; U.S. District Court, Southern District of Florida; U.S. District Court, Eastern and Southern Districts of New York; U.S. Court of Appeals, Second and Ninth Circuits — Member American Bar Association

Associates

Scott Janowitz — 1978 — University of Miami School of Law, J.D., 2005 — Admitted to Bar, 2006, Florida; 2009, U.S. District Court, Middle, Northern and Southern Districts of Florida

Jocelyn Mroz — 1984 — Valparaiso University School of Law, J.D., 2009 — Admitted to Bar, 2009, Florida — Member The Florida Bar

Raluca S. Neagu — 1975 — Johnson & Wales University, A.S. (summa cum laude), 2001; Florida International University, B.A. (magna cum laude), 2003; University of Detroit Mercy School of Law, LL.B./J.D., 2008 — Windsor Law Review of Legal and Social Issues — Admitted to Bar, 2010, Florida — Member Canadian Lawyers Association for International Human Rights; NAFSA: Association for International Educators — International Research Certification (2007) — Languages: Romanian, French, Spanish

Jonathan Tobin — 1982 — Northeastern University School of Law, J.D., 2009 — Admitted to Bar, 2009, Florida

Illon Kantro — 1981 — University of Miami, J.D., 2006 — Admitted to Bar, 2006, Florida

Alan Palma — 1978 — American University, B.A. (cum laude), 2001; University of Miami School of Law, J.D. (cum laude), 2008 — Admitted to Bar, 2009, Florida; U.S. District Court, Southern District of Florida; U.S. Court of Appeals, Eleventh Circuit

Evan Brooks — 1982 — University of Miami School of Law, J.D., 2009 — Admitted to Bar, 2009, Florida

Andrew J. Chan — 1981 — University of California, Berkeley, B.A., 2003; University of Miami School of Law, J.D., 2007 — Admitted to Bar, 2009, Florida; U.S. District Court, Southern District of Florida — Member The Florida Bar; Dade County Bar Association

Ross C. Johns — 1988 — Florida State University (Dean's List), 2010; University of Miami School of Law (cum laude), 2013 — Admitted to Bar, 2010, Florida

CRESTVIEW † 20,978 Okaloosa Co.

Refer To

Barron & Redding, P.A.
220 McKenzie Avenue
Panama City, Florida 32401-3129
   Telephone: 850-785-7454
   Fax: 850-785-2999

Mailing Address: P.O. Box 2467, Panama City, FL 32402-2467

Casualty, Surety, Fire, Life Insurance, Professional Liability, Product Liability, Medical Malpractice, Environmental Law, Automobile Liability, Premises Liability, Business Torts, Construction Law

SEE COMPLETE LISTING UNDER PANAMA CITY, FLORIDA (89 MILES)

Refer To

Vernis & Bowling of Northwest Florida, P.A.
315 South Palafox Street
Pensacola, Florida 32502
   Telephone: 850-433-5461
   Fax: 850-432-0166

Civil Litigation, Insurance Law, Workers' Compensation, Premises Liability, Labor and Employment, Civil Rights, Commercial Litigation, Complex Litigation, Product Liability, Directors and Officers Liability, Errors and Omissions, Construction Law, Construction Defect, Environmental Liability, Personal and Commercial Vehicle, Appellate Practice, Admiralty and Maritime Law, Real Estate, Family Law, Elder Law, Liability Defense, SIU/Fraud Litigation, Education Law (ESE/IDEA), Property and Casualty (Commercial and Personal Lines), Long-Haul Trucking Liability, Government Law, Public Law, Criminal, White Collar, Business Litigation

SEE COMPLETE LISTING UNDER PENSACOLA, FLORIDA (51 MILES)

DADE CITY † 6,437 Pasco Co.

Refer To

Abbey, Adams, Byelick & Mueller, L.L.P.
360 Central Avenue, 11th Floor
St. Petersburg, Florida 33701
   Telephone: 727-821-2080
   Fax: 727-822-3970

Mailing Address: P.O. Box 1511, St. Petersburg, FL 33731

Administrative Law, Americans with Disabilities Act, Appellate Practice, Complex Litigation, General Defense, Employment Law, Bad Faith, Insurance Coverage, Insurance Fraud, Uninsured and Underinsured Motorist, Professional Malpractice, Mediation, Negligence, Personal Injury, Premises Liability, Product Liability, Subrogation, Toxic Torts, Workers' Compensation, Motor Vehicle Liability, Defense of Insureds, Sovereign Immunity and Governmental Defense

SEE COMPLETE LISTING UNDER ST. PETERSBURG, FLORIDA (58 MILES)

DAYTONA BEACH 61,005 Volusia Co.

Cameron, Hodges, Coleman, LaPointe & Wright, P.A.
150 South Palmetto Avenue, # 101
Daytona Beach, Florida 32114
   Telephone: 386-257-1755
   Fax: 386-252-5601
   www.cameronhodges.com

(Orlando, FL Office*: 111 North Magnolia Avenue, Suite 1350, 32801-2378)
   (Tel: 407-841-5030)
   (Fax: 407-841-1727)
   (E-Mail: ccameron@cameronhodges.com)
(Ocala, FL Office*: 1820 Southeast 18th Avenue, #1-2, 34478)
   (Tel: 352-351-1119)
   (Fax: 352-351-0151)

Established: 1980

Insurance Law

Firm Profile: Our history of client satisfaction is a result of responsiveness to client expectations, and open communication regarding file handling and fees.

Insurance Clients

Adventist Risk Management, Inc.	AIX Group
Allstate Insurance Company	American Family Insurance Group
American Inter-Fidelity Exchange	Athens Insurance
Auto-Owners Insurance Company	Carolina Casualty Insurance Company
Chubb Group of Insurance Companies	The Concord Group Insurance Companies
Co-operative Insurance Companies	EGI Auto
Crawford & Company	Erie Insurance Group
Engle Martin & Associates	Gallagher Bassett Services, Inc.
Federated Insurance Company	The Hartford
GEICO	Lancer Insurance Company
Hertz Claim Management	Nationwide Insurance
Mid-Continent Casualty Company	

DAYTONA BEACH   *FLORIDA*

Cameron, Hodges, Coleman, LaPointe & Wright, P.A., Daytona Beach, FL (Continued)

North Carolina Farm Bureau Mutual Insurance Company
Penn Tank Lines
Sedgwick CMS
Sentry Transportation Insurance Company
United Services Automobile Association (USAA)
York Claims Service, Inc.
Pennsylvania Lumbermens Mutual Insurance Company
St. Johns Insurance Company, Inc.
The Seibels Bruce Group, Inc.
SPARTA Insurance
TRISTAR Risk Management
Wilshire Insurance Company [IAT-Group]

Non-Insurance Clients

Albertsons, Inc.
Davis Transfer Company
Enterprise Rent-A-Car Company
SuperShuttle
Central Refrigerated Services Inc.
Dollar Rent A Car Systems, Inc.
J.B. Hunt Transport Services, Inc.

Firm Member

A. Craig Cameron — 1947 — University of Pennsylvania, B.A., 1970; Stetson University, J.D., 1973 — Phi Alpha Delta — Stetson Law Review — Admitted to Bar, 1973, Florida; 1973, U.S. District Court, Middle District of Florida; 1973, U.S. Court of Appeals, Fifth Circuit; 1973, U.S. Supreme Court — Member American Bar Association; The Florida Bar; Diplomate, National Board of Trial Advocacy; Defense Research Institute; Florida Defense Lawyers Association; International Association of Defense Counsel — Florida Bar Board Certified Civil Trial Lawyer (1983-Present); Certified Civil Trial Lawyer, National Board of Trial Advocacy (1980-Present) — Practice Areas: Automobile; Premises Liability; Truck Liability; Product Liability — E-mail: ccameron@cameronhodges.com

(See Ocala and Orlando, FL listings for additional information)

Hassell-Legal, P.A.

1616 Concierge Boulevard, Suite 100
Daytona Beach, Florida 32117
   Telephone: 386-238-1357
   Fax: 386-258-7406
   E-Mail: Office@Hassell-Legal.com

Established: 1996

Insurance Defense, Automobile, Professional Liability, Product Liability, Medical Malpractice, Subrogation, Aviation, General Practice

Firm Profile: For almost thirty years, the attorneys of the firm have provided efficient and thorough legal representation to businesses, individuals and insurers. We have been involved in complex litigation and trials in both state and federal courts. We are dedicated to achieving a fair and just result for our clients, without unnecessary expenditure of time and costs.

From our many years of experience working with bodily injury claims, we are equipped to thoroughly analyze the medical aspects of those claims. We are also experienced in the assessment of technical issues arising from automobile, trucking and aviation accidents and from product liability and construction claims. The firm has ready access to nationally known expert consultants to assist with technical issues, and to present testimony on those issues at trial.

Our main office is centrally located in Daytona Beach, and from there we can quickly respond to the needs of clients throughout Florida. The firm was an early adopter of advanced technology to allow current and timely electronic communication and case updates to its clients, and the electronic presentation of documents and exhibits at trial.

Martindale-Hubbell has rated us as "AV" (the highest rating achievable).

Insurance Clients

Aetna Casualty and Surety Company
CIGNA Group
Colonial Insurance Company of California
Horace Mann Insurance Company
K & K Insurance Group, Inc.
Nationwide Group
Allstate Insurance Company
Auto-Owners Insurance Company
CNA Insurance Companies
Federated Insurance Company
Florida Farm Bureau General Insurance Company
Maryland Casualty Company
Oak Casualty Insurance Company

Hassell-Legal, P.A., Daytona Beach, FL (Continued)

Prudential Insurance Company of America
United Services Automobile Association (USAA)
Westfield Companies
State Farm Insurance Companies
TIG Insurance Company
United States Aviation Underwriters, Inc.

Non-Insurance Clients

Crawford & Company
Delta Air Lines, Inc.
Monnex Insurance Management, Inc.
Scotty's, Inc.
Daytona International Speedway
Florida Insurance Guaranty Association
Preferred Dealer Protection
Winn-Dixie Stores, Inc.

Partner

F. Bradley Hassell — 1955 — Florida Technological University, B.S.B.A., 1975; University of Florida, J.D., 1978 — Judicial Research Assistant for Judge Spencer C. Cross, Fifth District Court of Appeals, State of Florida, 1979-1980; Sr. Law Clerk to Judge Joe A. Cowart, Fifth District Court of Appeals, State of Florida, 1980-1982 — Admitted to Bar, 1978, Florida; 2013, Georgia; U.S. District Court, Middle District of Florida; U.S. Court of Appeals, Eleventh Circuit; 1998, U.S. District Court, Southern District of Florida; U.S. Supreme Court; Supreme Court of Georgia — Member The Florida Bar; Volusia County Bar Association; Florida Defense Lawyers Association; Defense Research Institute — Board Certified Civil Trial Law; Board Certified Aviation Law — E-mail: FBH@Hassell-Legal.com

Associates

Cynthia B. Beissel — 1970 — Nova Southeastern University, J.D., 2002 — Admitted to Bar, 2002, Florida; U.S. District Court, District of Florida; Florida Court of Appeals — Member The Florida Bar; Volusia County Bar Association — E-mail: CBB@Hassell-Legal.com

W. Ashby Underhill — Northwestern State University, B.S./B.A., 2006; Florida Coastal School of Law, J.D., 2010 — Admitted to Bar, 2010, Florida; 2014, U.S. District Court, Middle District of Florida — Member Volusia County and St. Johns County Bar Associations; International Air and Transportation Safety Bar Association; Lawyer-Pilots Bar Association — E-mail: WAU@Hassell-Legal.com

R. Jeremy Hill — 1975 — Stetson University, B.A., 1997; M.Ed., 1999; Ed.S., 2002; Duke Law School, M.S.L., 2004; Florida A&M University College of Law, J.D., 2008 — Admitted to Bar, 2009, Florida — E-mail: RJH@Hassell-Legal.com

(This firm is also listed in the Subrogation section of this directory)

Southeast Law Group, P.A.

104 La Costa Lane, Suite 140
Daytona Beach, Florida 32114
   Telephone: 386-274-1700
   Fax: 386-274-0220
   E-Mail: mscheihing@southeastlaw.com
   www.southeastlaw.com

(Lake Mary, FL Office*: 725 Primera Boulevard, Suite 130, 32746)
   (Tel: 386-274-1700)
   (Fax: 386-274-0220)
   (E-Mail: jkelly@southeastlaw.com)

Established: 2013

Insurance Coverage, Bad Faith, Arson, Fraud, Mediation, Sinkhole/Earth Movement, Windstorm/Hurricane/Tornado/Hail

Firm Profile: Southeast Law Group, P.A. was formed with the primary goal of exceeding client expectations in a targeted range of insurance matters and is rated AV preeminent by Martindale Hubbell. The practice combines experience with professionalism and progressive litigation management to serve its clients' interests. Southeast Law Group, P.A. is dedicated to delivering only the very best while developing relationships.

Insurance Clients

American Coastal Insurance Company
Aspen Specialty Insurance Company

FLORIDA

Southeast Law Group, P.A., Daytona Beach, FL
(Continued)

Auto Club Insurance Company of Florida
Federated National Insurance Company
GeoVera Specialty Insurance Company
State Farm Insurance
Tower Hill Insurance Group
Boulder Claims
Citizens Property Insurance Corp.
Florida Insurance Guaranty Association
The Hartford Insurance Company
Homeowners Choice Property & Casualty Insurance Company, Inc.

Partner

Michaela D. Scheihing — 1960 — Indian River Community College, A.S. (Dean's List), 1985; Barry University, B.P.S., 1988; Mercer University Walter F. George School of Law, J.D., 1991 — Admitted to Bar, 1992, Florida; U.S. District Court, Middle, Northern and Southern Districts of Florida; U.S. Court of Appeals, Eleventh Circuit — Member American and Volusia County Bar Associations; The Florida Bar; Fire Investigators of Florida, Inc., a Chapter of the IAAI (Legal Advisor); International Association of Arson Investigators; Florida Advisory Committee on Arson Prevention (Past President; Board of Directors); Windstorm Insurance Network, Inc. (Past President; Board of Directors; Wind Fellow); Property Loss Research Bureau (PLRB) — Rated AV preeminent by Martindale Hubbell — Practice Areas: First Party Defense; Arson; Fire Loss; Fraud; Bad Faith; Sinkhole/Earth Movement; Coverage Opinions

Vernis & Bowling of Central Florida, P.A.

1450 South Woodland Boulevard, Fourth Floor
DeLand, Florida 32720
Telephone: 386-734-2505
Fax: 386-734-3441
E-Mail: info@florida-law.com
www.florida-law.com

Established: 1970

Civil Litigation, Insurance Law, Workers' Compensation, Premises Liability, Labor and Employment, Civil Rights, Commercial Litigation, Complex Litigation, Product Liability, Directors and Officers Liability, Errors and Omissions, Construction Law, Construction Defect, Environmental Liability, Personal and Commercial Vehicle, Appellate Practice, Admiralty and Maritime Law, Real Estate, Family Law, Elder Law, Liability Defense, SIU/Fraud Litigation, Education Law (ESE/IDEA), Property and Casualty (Commercial and Personal Lines), Long-Haul Trucking Liability, Government Law, Public Law, Criminal, White Collar, Business Litigation

Firm Profile: Since 1970, VERNIS & BOWLING has represented individuals, businesses, professionals, insurance carriers, self-insureds, brokers, underwriters, agents, PEOs and insured. We provide cost effective, full service, legal representation that consistently exceeds the expectations of our clients. With 115 attorneys throughout 16 offices located in Florida, Georgia, Alabama, North Carolina and Mississippi the firm is able to provide the benefits of a large organization, including a management team, consistent policies and representation to ensure personal service and local representation to our clients.

Firm Members

Terry D. Dixon — 1960 — University of Florida, B.A., 1983; Mercer University, J.D., 1987 — Admitted to Bar, 1987, Florida; Georgia — Member American and Orange County Bar Associations — Resident Orlando, FL Office

Larry J. Feinstein — 1957 — University of Florida, B.S., 1979; South Texas College of Law, J.D., 1983 — Admitted to Bar, 1986, Florida — Member The Florida Bar (Workers' Compensation Section)

Timothy Kazee — The University of Toledo, B.A. (cum laude), 1999; The University of Toledo College of Law, J.D., 2002 — Admitted to Bar, 2002, Ohio; 2003, Florida

Juliet Fleming Stage — Southern Illinois University, B.S./B.A., 1985; Cumberland School of Law of Samford University, J.D., 1993 — Admitted to Bar, 1993, Florida; 1994, Alabama; U.S. District Court, Middle District of Florida; U.S. District Court, Middle District of Alabama

DE FUNIAK SPRINGS

Vernis & Bowling of Central Florida, P.A., Daytona Beach, FL
(Continued)

Elizabeth M. White — 1984 — Harvard University, B.A., 2006; University of Florida, Levin College of Law, J.D., 2012 — Admitted to Bar, 2012, Florida

Benjamin Loving

(See listing under Miami, FL for additional information)

The following firms also service this area.

Dean, Ringers, Morgan and Lawton, P.A.
201 East Pine Street, Suite 1200
Orlando, Florida 32801
Telephone: 407-422-4310
Fax: 407-648-0233

Mailing Address: P.O. Box 2928, Orlando, FL 32802

Casualty, ERISA, Health, Life Insurance, Surety, Workers' Compensation, Civil Rights, Personal Injury, Product Liability, Wrongful Death, Medical Malpractice, Employment Practices Liability, Trucking Law, Police Misconduct, Business Law, Amusement and Recreation Law

SEE COMPLETE LISTING UNDER ORLANDO, FLORIDA (55 MILES)

DE FUNIAK SPRINGS † 5,177 Walton Co.

Refer To

Barron & Redding, P.A.
220 McKenzie Avenue
Panama City, Florida 32401-3129
Telephone: 850-785-7454
Fax: 850-785-2999

Mailing Address: P.O. Box 2467, Panama City, FL 32402-2467

Casualty, Surety, Fire, Life Insurance, Professional Liability, Product Liability, Medical Malpractice, Environmental Law, Automobile Liability, Premises Liability, Business Torts, Construction Law

SEE COMPLETE LISTING UNDER PANAMA CITY, FLORIDA (62 MILES)

Refer To

Vernis & Bowling of Northwest Florida, P.A.
315 South Palafox Street
Pensacola, Florida 32502
Telephone: 850-433-5461
Fax: 850-432-0166

Civil Litigation, Insurance Law, Workers' Compensation, Premises Liability, Labor and Employment, Civil Rights, Commercial Litigation, Complex Litigation, Product Liability, Directors and Officers Liability, Errors and Omissions, Construction Law, Construction Defect, Environmental Liability, Personal and Commercial Vehicle, Appellate Practice, Admiralty and Maritime Law, Real Estate, Family Law, Elder Law, Liability Defense, SIU/Fraud Litigation, Education Law (ESE/IDEA), Property and Casualty (Commercial and Personal Lines), Long-Haul Trucking Liability, Government Law, Public Law, Criminal, White Collar, Business Litigation

SEE COMPLETE LISTING UNDER PENSACOLA, FLORIDA (76 MILES)

Refer To

Wade, Palmer & Shoemaker, P.A.
14 North Palafox Street
Pensacola, Florida 32502
Telephone: 850-429-0755
Fax: 850-429-0871
Toll Free: 888-980-0755

Mailing Address: P.O. Box 13510, Pensacola, FL 32591-3510

Insurance Defense, Automobile Liability, Product Liability, Bodily Injury, Coverage Issues, Subrogation, Property and Casualty, Construction Law, General Liability, Litigation, Employment Law, Employment Discrimination

SEE COMPLETE LISTING UNDER PENSACOLA, FLORIDA (81 MILES)

DEERFIELD BEACH   *FLORIDA*

DE LAND † 20,904 Volusia Co.

Refer To

Cameron, Hodges, Coleman, LaPointe & Wright, P.A.
150 South Palmetto Avenue, # 101
Daytona Beach, Florida 32114
   Telephone: 386-257-1755
   Fax: 386-252-5601

Insurance Law

SEE COMPLETE LISTING UNDER DAYTONA BEACH, FLORIDA (19 MILES)

Refer To

Vernis & Bowling of Central Florida, P.A.
1450 South Woodland Boulevard, Fourth Floor
DeLand, Florida 32720
   Telephone: 386-734-2505
   Fax: 386-734-3441

Civil Litigation, Insurance Law, Workers' Compensation, Premises Liability, Labor and Employment, Civil Rights, Commercial Litigation, Complex Litigation, Product Liability, Directors and Officers Liability, Errors and Omissions, Construction Law, Construction Defect, Environmental Liability, Personal and Commercial Vehicle, Appellate Practice, Admiralty and Maritime Law, Real Estate, Family Law, Elder Law, Liability Defense, SIU/Fraud Litigation, Education Law (ESE/IDEA), Property and Casualty (Commercial and Personal Lines), Long-Haul Trucking Liability, Government Law, Public Law, Criminal, White Collar, Business Litigation

SEE COMPLETE LISTING UNDER DAYTONA BEACH, FLORIDA (19 MILES)

DEERFIELD BEACH   75,018 Broward Co.

Roig, Tutan, Rosenberg, Martin & Stoller, Zumpano & Bellido

1255 South Military Trail, Suite 100
Deerfield Beach, Florida 33442
   Telephone: 954-462-0330
   Fax: 954-462-7798
   E-Mail: mmenoud@roiglawyers.com
   www.roiglawyers.com

(Miami Office: 44 W. Flagler Street, Suite 2100, Miami, FL, 33130)
   (Tel: 305-405-0997)
   (Fax: 305-405-1022)
(Orlando Office: 7380 Sand Lake Road, Suite 130, Orlando, FL, 32819)
   (Tel: 407-349-6100)
   (Fax: 407-349-6007)
(Roig, Tutan, Rosenberg, Martin, Stoller, Zumpano & Bellido: 100 S. Ashley Drive, Suite 1350, Tampa, FL, 33602)
   (Tel: 813-514-1865)
   (Fax: 813-514-1876)
(Roig, Tutan, Rosenberg, Martin, Stoller, Zumpano & Bellido: 1400 Centrepark Drive, Suite 605, West Palm Beach, FL, 33401)
   (Tel: 561-613-0394)
   (Fax: 561-613-0466)
(Roig, Tutan, Rosenberg, Martin, Stoller, Zumpano & Bellido: 113 S. Monroe Street, First Floor, Tallahassee, FL, 32301)
   (Tel: 850-391-9294)
   (Fax: 850-270-9815)
(Coral Gables Office: 500 South Dixie Highway, Suite 302, Coral Gables, FL, 33146)
   (Tel: 305-503-2990)
   (Fax: 305-774-5908)

Established: 2000

Insurance Defense, Bodily Injury, Uninsured and Underinsured Motorist, Personal Injury Protection (PIP), Premises Liability, Wrongful Death, Commercial Litigation, Appeals, Examinations Under Oath, Construction Litigation, Corporate Law, Homeowners, Property Defense, Labor and Employment, Litigation, Medical Malpractice, Real Estate, Banking, Special Investigative Unit Claims, Workers' Compensation, Coverage Disputes, Healthcare Fraud, Finance

Roig, Tutan, Rosenberg, Martin & Stoller, Zumpano & Bellido, Deerfield Beach, FL   (Continued)

Firm Profile: Roig Lawyers is an AV® Preeminent™ Peer Review Rated, minority-owned litigation law firm that is proud to be listed in the A.M. Best Directory of Recommended Insurance Attorneys. We are an aggressive, professional firm dedicated to using our combined experience and expertise to explore novel issues of the law and ongoing legal trends.

Our highly skilled and knowledgeable attorneys strive to obtain favorable results. They are supported by a carefully trained team of litigation professionals who utilize advanced technology that helps us to process case files quickly and cost-effectively.

We provide services throughout Florida from our Deerfield Beach headquarters, with additional offices in Coral Gables, Miami, Orlando, West Palm Beach, Tampa, and Tallahassee. Our areas of coverage include all Florida counties. Since our founding in 2000, we have grown to more than 100 attorneys and 200 support staff.

Insurance Clients

Florida Peninsula Insurance Company   GEICO

Founding Partner

Fernando L. Roig — University of Miami, B.A., 1985; Nova Southeastern University, Shepard Broad Law Center, J.D., 1988 — AV Peer Review Rated by Martindale-Hubbell; Governor Appointment, Fourth District Court of Appeals Judicial Nominating Committee (Two Terms, 2001); Governor Appointment, Governor's Commission for the Everglades (Two Year Term, 2000) — Admitted to Bar, 1989, Florida — Member The Florida Bar — Languages: Spanish — Practice Areas: Insurance Defense; Personal Injury Protection (PIP); Litigation; Commercial Litigation; General Liability — E-mail: froig@roiglawyers.com

Firm Managing Partner

Michael A. Rosenberg — Concordia University, B.A., 2001; St. Thomas University School of Law, J.D., 2004 — International Moot Court Competition — Articles Editor, St. Thomas Law Review — Admitted to Bar, 2004, Florida; 2006, U.S. District Court, Southern District of Florida — Member The Florida Bar; International Association of Special Investigative Units (IASIU); Claims & Litigation Management Alliance (CLM) — Languages: French, Creole — Practice Areas: Insurance Defense; Personal Injury Protection (PIP); Special Investigative Unit Claims; Fraud; Examinations Under Oath — E-mail: mrosenberg@roiglawyers.com

Partners

Jeffrey B. Tutan — Florida Southern College, B.A., 1982; Cumberland School of Law at Samford University, J.D., 1985 — Admitted to Bar, 1985, Florida — Member The Florida Bar — Head of the firm's trial division — Board Certified, Civil Trial by The Florida Bar — Practice Areas: Personal Injury Protection (PIP); Fraud; Bodily Injury; Uninsured and Underinsured Motorist; Homeowners; Litigation — E-mail: jtutan@roiglawyers.com

Jessica Z. Martin — University of Florida, B.S. (with highest honors), 2002; University of Florida, Levin College of Law, J.D. (cum laude), 2005 — Admitted to Bar, 2006, Florida — Member Federal Bar Association; The Florida Bar — Practice Areas: Insurance Defense; Personal Injury Protection (PIP) — E-mail: jmartin@roiglawyers.com

Drew A. Stoller — University of South Florida, B.A., 1994; Nova Southeastern University, Shepard Broad Law Center, J.D., 1998 — Admitted to Bar, 1998, Florida — Member The Florida Bar — Practice Areas: Insurance Defense; Personal Injury Protection (PIP) — E-mail: dstoller@roiglawyers.com

Nelson C. Bellido — Duke University, B.A., 1989; University of Florida College of Law, J.D., 1992 — Admitted to Bar, 1993, Florida; U.S. District Court, Middle and Southern Districts of Florida; U.S. Court of Appeals, Eleventh Circuit; U.S. Supreme Court — Member The Florida Bar — Appointed Chairman of the Miami-Dade Commission on Ethics & Public Trust in a unanimous vote (Present); Former Commissioner (2011-present); Florida Super Lawyers, recognized as a leader in the business litigation practice (2010-present), and one of the Top 100 Lawyers in Florida (2013); South Florida Legal Guide, Top Lawyer (2012-present); Florida Trend Magazine's Legal Elite in Complex Commercial Litigation (2006-2014); Wall Street Journal Top Attorneys in Florida (June 2011); South Florida Business Journal (2006), Best of the Bar in Complex Business Litigation (2005); Put Something Back 2004 Pro Bono Service Award, recognized for his community service; Dade County Bar Association Outstanding Service Award (2003-2004); Legal Services of Greater Miami Volunteer Service Award (2006); Business

FLORIDA

Roig, Tutan, Rosenberg, Martin & Stoller, Zumpano & Bellido, Deerfield Beach, FL (Continued)

Networking International Most Valuable Member 2007 & Outstanding Service Award 2008; American Bar Association Committee on Corporate Counsel's The In-House Counsel's Essential Toolkit (2007) — Languages: Spanish — Practice Areas: Commercial Litigation; Insurance; Product Liability — E-mail: nbellido@roiglawyers.com

Carlos A. Zumpano — Harvard University, A.B. (cum laude), 1996; University of Miami School of Law, J.D., 1999 — Admitted to Bar, 1999, Florida; U.S. District Court, Middle, Northern and Southern Districts of Florida — Member American Bar Association; The Florida Bar; Cuban-American Bar Association — AV® Preeminent™ Rated by Martindale-Hubbell, Florida Super Lawyers® (2013, 2014); Florida Rising Star for Super Lawyers® (2011, 2012) — Practice Areas: Corporate Law; Litigation; Labor and Employment — E-mail: czumpano@roiglawyers.com

DELTONA 85,182 Volusia Co.

Refer To

Vernis & Bowling of Central Florida, P.A.

1450 South Woodland Boulevard, Fourth Floor
DeLand, Florida 32720
Telephone: 386-734-2505
Fax: 386-734-3441

Civil Litigation, Insurance Law, Workers' Compensation, Premises Liability, Labor and Employment, Civil Rights, Commercial Litigation, Complex Litigation, Product Liability, Directors and Officers Liability, Errors and Omissions, Construction Law, Construction Defect, Environmental Liability, Personal and Commercial Vehicle, Appellate Practice, Admiralty and Maritime Law, Real Estate, Family Law, Elder Law, Liability Defense, SIU/Fraud Litigation, Education Law (ESE/IDEA), Property and Casualty (Commercial and Personal Lines), Long-Haul Trucking Liability, Government Law, Public Law, Criminal, White Collar, Business Litigation

SEE COMPLETE LISTING UNDER DAYTONA BEACH, FLORIDA (14 MILES)

DESTIN 12,305 Okaloosa Co.

Refer To

Wade, Palmer & Shoemaker, P.A.

14 North Palafox Street
Pensacola, Florida 32502
Telephone: 850-429-0755
Fax: 850-429-0871
Toll Free: 888-980-0755

Mailing Address: P.O. Box 13510, Pensacola, FL 32591-3510

Insurance Defense, Automobile Liability, Product Liability, Bodily Injury, Coverage Issues, Subrogation, Property and Casualty, Construction Law, General Liability, Litigation, Employment Law, Employment Discrimination

SEE COMPLETE LISTING UNDER PENSACOLA, FLORIDA (47 MILES)

FORT LAUDERDALE † 165,521 Broward Co.

Allen, Kopet & Associates, PLLC

3333 West Commercial Boulevard, Suite 210
Fort Lauderdale, Florida 33309
Telephone: 954-561-7887
Fax: 954-561-9411

(See listing under Chattanooga, TN for additional information)

Billing, Cochran, Lyles, Mauro & Ramsey, P.A.

515 East Las Olas Boulevard, Suite 600
Fort Lauderdale, Florida 33301
Telephone: 954-764-7150
Fax: 954-764-7279
Toll Free: 888-764-7150
www.billingcochran.com

DELTONA

Billing, Cochran, Lyles, Mauro & Ramsey, P.A., Fort Lauderdale, FL (Continued)

(West Palm Beach, FL Office*: 1601 Forum Place, Suite 400, 33401)
(Tel: 561-659-5930)
(Fax: 561-659-6173)

Established: 1977

General Civil Trial and Appellate Practice, State and Federal Courts, Personal Injury, Product Liability, Medical Liability, Dental Malpractice, Nursing Home Liability, Hospitals, Health Care, Workers' Compensation, Insurance Coverage, Litigation, Governmental Litigation, Funeral Service Liability Law

Insurance Clients

A.C.E. Insurance Company, Ltd.
The Doctors Company
First Professionals Insurance Company
Health Care Indemnity, Inc.
State Farm Fire and Casualty Company
Zurich North America

AIG
The Equitable Life Assurance Society of the United States
Gulf Atlantic Insurance Company
Prudential Property and Casualty Insurance Company
Travelers Insurance Companies

Non-Insurance Clients

Armor Correctional Health Services, Inc.
City of Fort Lauderdale
Florida Medical Center

Broward County Sheriff's Office
Catholic Health East
CSX Corporation
Tenet Healthcare Corporation

Partners

Steven F. Billing — (1947-1998)

Hayward D. Gay — (1943-2007)

Clark J. Cochran, Jr. — 1949 — Vanderbilt University, B.A., 1971; Florida State University, J.D. (with honors), 1974 — Recipient, American Jurisprudence Award — Admitted to Bar, 1974, Florida; 1976, U.S. District Court, Southern District of Florida; 1984, U.S. Court of Appeals, Eleventh Circuit — Member The Florida Bar (Trial Lawyers Section); Broward County Bar Association (Trial Lawyers Section); Florida Defense Lawyers Association; American Board of Trial Advocates; Trial Attorneys of America; Defense Research Institute; American Trial Lawyers Association — Assistant State Attorney, Seventeenth Judicial Circuit, 1974-1976; Assistant General Counsel, Broward County, 1977 — Practice Areas: Insurance Law; General Liability; Appellate Practice; Governmental Defense

Dennis E. Lyles — 1947 — Florida State University, B.A., 1971; J.D., 1974 — Admitted to Bar, 1974, Florida; 1976, U.S. District Court, Southern District of Florida — Member American (Tort and Insurance Practice Section; Urban, State and Local Government Section) and Broward County Bar Associations; The Florida Bar (Local Government Law and Trial Lawyers Sections); Florida Defense Lawyers Association; Defense Research Institute — Assistant State Attorney, Seventeenth Judicial Circuit, 1974-1976; Assistant General Counsel, 1977-1978, Broward County; Deputy City Attorney, City of Fort Lauderdale, 1978-1984; Appointed City Attorney, City of Fort Lauderdale, November, 1987 — Practice Areas: Governmental Defense; Real Estate; Land Use

John W. Mauro — 1953 — Boston College, B.A. (magna cum laude), 1975; University of Miami, J.D., 1978 — Admitted to Bar, 1978, Florida — Member American and Broward County Bar Associations; The Florida Bar; American Academy of Hospital Attorneys; Southeastern Defense Lawyers Association; Florida Hospital Association; Florida Defense Lawyers Association; Defense Research Institute; Association of Trial Lawyers of America; Florida Medical Malpractice Claims Council; American Board of Trial Advocates; American Trial Lawyers Association — Associate Editor, Lawyer of the Americas, Journal of International Law, 1977-1978 — Practice Areas: Medical Malpractice; Insurance Law; General Liability

William T. Craig — 1956 — University of Florida, B.S., 1978; Nova University, J.D., 1982 — Admitted to Bar, 1983, Florida; U.S. District Court, Middle and Southern Districts of Florida — Member American and Broward County Bar Associations; The Florida Bar; Defense Research Institute; Florida Defense Lawyers Association; Florida Medical Malpractice Claims Council; Trial Attorneys of America — Assistant State Attorney, Seventeenth Judicial Circuit, Florida, 1983-1987 — Practice Areas: Medical Malpractice; Insurance Law; General Liability; Product Liability; Governmental Defense

Kenneth W. Morgan, Jr. — 1959 — University of Florida, B.A., 1982; Nova University, J.D., 1986 — Admitted to Bar, 1986, Florida; 1987, U.S. District

Billing, Cochran, Lyles, Mauro & Ramsey, P.A., Fort Lauderdale, FL (Continued)

Court, Southern District of Florida — Member American and Broward County Bar Associations; The Florida Bar; Defense Research Institute; Florida Defense Lawyers Association; Florida Medical Malpractice Claims Council; Association of Trial Lawyers of America — Practice Areas: Medical Malpractice; Insurance Law; General Liability

Bruce M. Ramsey — Florida State University, B.S., 1978; University of Florida, J.D. (with honors), 1981 — Admitted to Bar, 1981, Florida — Member The Florida Bar (Chairperson, Grievance Committee; Substantive Law Committee for Patient Care/Risk Management); Palm Beach County Bar Association (Medical, Legal, Dental Liaison Committee); Palm Beach County Trial Lawyers Association; Florida Medical Malpractice Claims Council (President; Board of Governors); American Trial Lawyers Association; American Society of Law and Medicine; Academy of Florida Trial Lawyers — American College of Barristers — Practice Areas: Health; Medical Malpractice; Product Liability; Personal Injury; Nursing Home Liability; General Liability; Insurance Law — Resident West Palm Beach, FL Office

Susan F. Delegal — 1950 — University of Florida, B.A. (with honors), 1971; J.D., 1973 — Admitted to Bar, 1974, Florida; 1979, U.S. District Court, Southern District of Florida — Member American and Broward County Bar Associations; The Florida Bar (Past Chair, City, County and Local Government Law, 1999-2000); Florida Association of County Attorneys (Past President) — Board Certified, City, County and Local Government Lawyer, Florida Bar Board of Legal Specialization and Education — Practice Areas: Land Use; Governmental Defense

Gerald L. Knight — 1947 — University of Florida, B.A. (with honors), 1969; J.D. (with honors), 1973; University of Miami, LL.M., 1982 — Admitted to Bar, 1974, Florida; 1990, Colorado — Member American and Broward County Bar Associations; The Florida Bar — U.S. Army, 1969-1971 — Practice Areas: Land Use; Administrative Law; Governmental Defense

Carol J. Healy Glasgow — 1965 — Baystate Medical Center School of Nursing, R.N., 1987; Barry University, B.S.N. (magna cum laude), 1991; Nova Southeastern University, J.D., 1994 — Admitted to Bar, 1994, Florida; 1995, U.S. District Court, Southern District of Florida — Member American and Broward County Bar Associations; Defense Research Institute; Florida Defense Lawyers Association — Practice Areas: Medical Malpractice; General Liability; Nursing Home Liability

Michael V. Baxter — 1970 — Florida State University, B.S., 1992; Nova Southeastern University, J.D., 1996 — Admitted to Bar, 1996, Florida — Member Miami-Dade County and Broward County Bar Associations; Defense Research Institute; Florida Defense Lawyers Association — Assistant State Attorney, Eleventh Judicial Circuit, Miami-Dade County, 1996-1999 — Practice Areas: Personal Injury; Medical Malpractice; Insurance Defense; Product Liability; Nursing Home Liability — Resident West Palm Beach, FL Office

Michael J. Pawelczyk — 1969 — University of Illinois, B.A., 1991; Louisiana State University, J.D., 1994 — Admitted to Bar, 1994, Florida; 1995, U.S. District Court, Southern District of Florida; 2001, U.S. Court of Appeals, Eleventh Circuit — Member The Florida Bar — Practice Areas: Land Use; Governmental Defense

Andrew A. Rief — University of South Florida, B.S., 1996; University of Miami, J.D., 2000 — Admitted to Bar, 2000, Florida — Member Palm Beach County Bar Association; Defense Research Institute; Florida Defense Lawyers Association — Registered Nurse — Practice Areas: Medical Malpractice; Nursing Home Liability; Personal Injury; Product Liability; General Liability — Resident West Palm Beach, FL Office

Manuel R. Comras — 1972 — Brandeis University, B.A. (cum laude), 1995; Stetson University, J.D. (cum laude), 1997 — Admitted to Bar, 1998, Florida; 2002, U.S. District Court, Northern and Southern Districts of Florida; 2003, U.S. District Court, Middle District of Florida; 2005, U.S. Court of Appeals, Eleventh Circuit — Resident West Palm Beach, FL Office

Shirley Ann DeLune — 1956 — Indiana University, A.A., 1979; Florida Atlantic University, B.S., 1989; Nova Southeastern University, J.D., 1992 — Admitted to Bar, 1992, Florida — Member Palm Beach County Bar Association; Florida Association for Women Lawyers — Practice Areas: Civil Law; Medical Malpractice; General Liability; Professional Malpractice; Criminal Law; Personal Injury — Resident West Palm Beach, FL Office

Associates

Christine A. Brown — 1948 — Barry University, B.A., 1989; New York Law School, J.D., 1997 — Admitted to Bar, 1998, New York; 2000, Florida — Member Broward County Bar Association — Practice Areas: Insurance Defense; Medical Malpractice

Howard L. Citron — 1973 — Nova Southeastern University, B.A., 1997; J.D. (summa cum laude), 2000 — Admitted to Bar, 2000, Florida; 2006, Texas —

Billing, Cochran, Lyles, Mauro & Ramsey, P.A., Fort Lauderdale, FL (Continued)

Member American and Broward County Bar Associations — Practice Areas: Trial Practice; Medical Malpractice Defense; Premises Liability; Product Liability; Nursing Home Liability; Commercial Litigation — Resident West Palm Beach, FL Office

Scott C. Cochran — 1980 — Florida State University, B.A., 2002; J.D., 2005 — Admitted to Bar, 2005, Florida; 2006, U.S. District Court, Middle and Southern Districts of Florida; 2007, U.S. Court of Appeals, Eleventh Circuit — Member The Florida Bar; Broward County Bar Association — Practice Areas: Trial and Appellate Practice; Insurance Defense

Rachel Davant — 1975 — University of Rhode Island, B.A., 1998; Nova Southeastern University, J.D. (cum laude), 2002 — Admitted to Bar, 2002, Florida; U.S. District Court, Northern and Southern Districts of Florida — Practice Areas: Medical Malpractice; General Liability; Premises Liability; Appellate Practice

Donna M. Krusbe — 1964 — Auburn University, B.A., 1986; University of Miami, J.D., 1992 — Admitted to Bar, 1993, Florida; 1994, Illinois — Member Illinois State and Palm Beach County Bar Associations; The Florida Bar; Florida Legal Services (Board of Directors, President); Florida Defense Lawyers Association — Practice Areas: Appellate Practice; Insurance Defense; Medical Malpractice — Resident West Palm Beach, FL Office

Jeffrey R. Lawley — 1975 — Miami University, B.A., 1997; St. Thomas University, J.D., 2002 — Admitted to Bar, 2002, Florida; Tennessee; U.S. District Court, Middle and Southern Districts of Florida — Practice Areas: Trial Practice; Personal Injury; Wrongful Death; Premises Liability; Governmental Liability; Police Liability Defense; Commercial Litigation; Landlord and Tenant Law; Toxic Torts

Shawn B. McKamey — 1965 — University of Florida, B.A., 1987; Nova University, J.D., 1993 — Admitted to Bar, 1993, Florida; 1994, U.S. District Court, Southern District of Florida — Member American and Broward County Bar Associations; The Florida Bar; Defense Research Institute; Florida Defense Lawyers Association — Languages: Spanish — Practice Areas: Insurance Law; General Liability; Workers' Compensation; Admiralty and Maritime Law

Michael Lawrence Schwebel, Jr. — 1983 — University of Florida, B.A., 2004; J.D., 2007 — Admitted to Bar, 2008, Florida; U.S. District Court, Southern District of Florida; 2011, U.S. District Court, Middle and Northern Districts of Florida; U.S. Court of Appeals, Eleventh Circuit — Member American and Palm Beach County Bar Associations; Craig Barnard American Inn of Court — Practice Areas: Medical Malpractice; Premises Liability — Resident West Palm Beach, FL Office

Ginger E. Wald — 1966 — University of South Florida, B.S., 1987; University of Florida, J.D., 1990 — Admitted to Bar, 1990, Florida; 1991, Louisiana (Inactive); 2006, U.S. District Court, Southern District of Florida; 2010, U.S. Supreme Court; 2012, U.S. Court of Appeals, Eleventh Circuit — Member The Florida Bar; Broward County Bar Association; International Municipal Lawyer's Association (Code Enforcement Section, Vice Chair) — Practice Areas: Civil Litigation; Labor Law; Land Use; Zoning; Insurance Defense

Bradham, Benson, Lindley, Blevins, Bayliss & Wyatt of Florida East Coast, P.L.L.C.

1301 South Andrews Avenue, Suite 302
Fort Lauderdale, Florida 33316-1823
  Telephone: 954-462-4304
  Fax: 954-462-4554
  E-Mail: vladd@fla-esq.com
  www.fla-esq.com

(St. Petersburg, FL Office: 4141 Central Avenue, 33713)
  (Tel: 727-322-1739)
  (Fax: 727-322-1239)

Established: 2002

Insurance Defense, Trial Practice, Casualty, Automobile, General Liability, Compensation, Workers' Compensation, Governmental Liability

Insurance Clients

Kemper Insurance Companies	Merchants Bonding Company
Patriot National Insurance Group	St. Paul Travelers

FLORIDA — FORT LAUDERDALE

Bradham, Benson, Lindley, Blevins, Bayliss & Wyatt of Florida East Coast, P.L.L.C., Fort Lauderdale, FL (Continued)

Non-Insurance Clients

Claims Center
State of Florida
Gallagher Bassett & Co.
Tire Kingdom

Managing Partner

Donald H. Benson — 1944 — University of Florida, B.A., 1970; The University of Mississippi School of Law, J.D., 1974 — Admitted to Bar, 1974, Mississippi; 1975, Florida; 1975, U.S. District Court, Southern District of Florida — Member The Mississippi Bar; The Florida Bar

Founding Partner

Joseph W. Bradham, Jr.

Senior Partners

David M. Lindley
Joseph A. Bayliss, Sr.
Jerome B. Blevins
Walter C. Wyatt

Partner

Robert M. Potter, III

Associate

Jill E. Jacobs

Bunnell & Woulfe P.A.

One Financial Plaza, Suite 1000
100 Southeast Third Avenue
Fort Lauderdale, Florida 33394
   Telephone: 954-761-8600
   Fax: 954-463-6643
   E-Mail: asd@bunnellwoulfe.com
   www.bunnellwoulfe.com

Established: 1972

Medical Malpractice, Legal Malpractice, Accountant Malpractice, Product Liability, Contractors Liability, Automobile Liability, Premises Liability, Bad Faith, Appellate Practice, All Fields of Civil Trial Litigation, Health Care Litigation, Architects and Engineers Liability, Property Insurance, Arson and Fraud, Coverage Disputes, Health, Life & Disability Insurance

Firm Profile: Bunnell & Woulfe P.A. engages in all fields of civil litigation including medical, legal and accounting malpractice defense, product liability, contractors liability, automobile liability, premises, architects and engineers liability, property insurance, arson and fraud, coverage issues, insurance bad faith and appellate practice. The firm practices in all federal and state courts at all trial and appellate levels.

Insurance Clients

American Vehicle Insurance Company
Aviva Canada, Inc.
Church Mutual Insurance Company
Colony Insurance Company
Farmers Insurance Group
Florida Doctors Insurance Company
Intact Insurance Company
Premier Claims Management, LLC
Pure Insurance
TeamHealth
AMS Risk Retention
Assurant Group
Care Professional Liability Association, LLC
The Doctors Company
First Professionals Insurance Company
Gulf Atlantic Insurance Company
Missisquoi Insurance Company
Progressive Insurance Company
QBE European Operations
Zurich American Insurance Group

Non-Insurance Clients

Broward County Sheriff's Office
Howard Needles Tammen & Bergendoff
Neighborhood Health
Sheridan Healthcorp, Inc.
CNA Accountants Professional Liability
Lee County Sheriff's Office
Prison Health Services, Inc.
Western Litigation Specialists, Inc.

Bunnell & Woulfe P.A., Fort Lauderdale, FL (Continued)

Partners

Robert J. Berman — Brooklyn College, The City University of New York, B.A. (cum laude), 1972; Hofstra University School of Law, J.D., 1974 — Admitted to Bar, 1975, New York; 1992, Florida; U.S. District Court, Eastern and Southern Districts of New York

Richard T. Woulfe — Michigan State University, B.A., 1972; Washington and Lee University, J.D., 1976 — Admitted to Bar, 1976, Florida; 1986, District of Columbia; U.S. District Court, Southern District of Florida including Trial Bar; U.S. Court of Appeals, Fifth and Eleventh Circuits; U.S. Supreme Court — Florida Bar Board Certified Civil Trial Lawyer

Of Counsel

George E. Bunnell — The University of North Carolina, B.A., 1960; University of Florida College of Law, LL.B., 1962 — Admitted to Bar, 1963, Florida; U.S. District Court, Southern District of Florida including Trial Bar; U.S. Court of Appeals, Fifth and Eleventh Circuits; U.S. Supreme Court

Catri, Holton, Kessler & Kessler, P.A.

The Litigation Building, Third Floor
633 South Andrews Avenue
Fort Lauderdale, Florida 33301
   Telephone: 954-463-8593
   Fax: 954-462-1303
   E-Mail: kryan@chkklaw.com
   www.chkklaw.com

Insurance Defense, Trial and Appellate Practice, Insurance Coverage, Self-Insured, General Liability, Product Liability, Automobile Liability, Premises Liability, Construction Liability, Guardian and Conservatorships, Probate, Business Litigation, Commercial Litigation, Arbitration, Mediation

Firm Profile: Catri, Holton, Kessler & Kessler, P.A. is a firm of civil trial and appellate lawyers providing full litigation and insurance related services for all of South Florida.

The Firm's members are well known for their extensive experience in all areas of civil litigation, representing corporations, insurance companies, municipalities, governmental entities and individuals in tort, products liability, premises liability, construction liability, and commercial litigation. The five partners alone have more than 100 years of combined experience as insurance defense litigators. In recent years, the five member litigation practice has been expanded to include a broad range of litigation matters.

Catri, Holton, Kessler & Kessler's tradition of excellence includes a commitment to service the client's needs by obtaining optimum results as swiftly and economically as possible. The firm remains moderate in size to provide the personal service and economics of scale available only from a medium-sized firm.

Insurance Clients

American Trucking and Transportation Insurance Company
Chartis Insurance
Claims Services, Inc.
Deep South of Arkansas
ESIS
Grange Mutual Casualty Company
Great West Casualty Company
The Hartford Insurance Group
INS Insurance, Inc.
Lincoln General Insurance Company
Medmarc Mutual Insurance Company
Old Republic Insurance Company
Sedgwick Claims Management Services, Inc.
Specialty Claims Management, LLC
Supervalu Risk Management
Topa Insurance Company
Andover Companies
AXA Insurance Company
Broadspire
Cherokee Insurance Company
Crawford & Company
Effective Claims Management, Inc.
Gallagher Bassett Insurance Company
Harco National Insurance Company
Integrity Mutual Insurance Company
Meadowbrook Claims Service
North American Specialty Insurance Company
Pacific Specialty Insurance Company
Sentry Insurance
Specialty Risk Services, Inc. (SRS)
State Auto Insurance Companies
T.H.E. Insurance Company
Travelers Insurance

FORT LAUDERDALE, FLORIDA

Catri, Holton, Kessler & Kessler, P.A., Fort Lauderdale, FL (Continued)

Non-Insurance Clients

Albertsons, Inc.
ALDI
AV Logistics
Broward County School Board
CGI
Comcar Industries, Inc.
Delaware North Companies, Inc.
Heartland Express, Inc.
Johns Eastern Company, Inc.
Liberty Bell Agency, Inc.
Office Depot, Inc.
Payless ShoeSource
The Sports Authority
Trans West Logisitics
Tuesday Morning, Inc.
Albertson's LLC
Atlas Van Lines, Inc.
Beall's, Inc.
Cardinal Logistics Management
Claim Service & Administration
C.R. England, Inc.
Gallagher Bassett Services, Inc.
J.B. Hunt Transport, Inc.
Kohl's Department Stores, Inc.
New England Teamsters & Trucking Industry Pension Fund
Publix Super Markets, Inc.
TMC Transportation
Truck Claims, Inc.
Winn-Dixie Stores, Inc.

Members of the Firm

Charles T. Kessler — (1930-1997)

Wesley L. Catri — 1948 — John Carroll University, A.B., 1970; Cleveland-Marshall College of Law, J.D., 1973 — Admitted to Bar, 1973, Florida — Member American and Broward County Bar Associations; The Florida Bar; St. Thomas More Society; American Arbitration Association; Defense Research Institute; Florida Defense Lawyers Association; American Board of Trial Advocates — Qualified Florida Arbitrator; Certified County and Circuit Court Florida Mediator — Captain, U.S. Army Reserve, Transportation Corps — E-mail: wcatri@chkklaw.com

Raymond O. Holton — 1943 — University of Miami, B.B.A. (magna cum laude), 1971; J.D., 1973 — Selected as one of the top lawyers in South Florida by The South Florida LegalGuide — Admitted to Bar, 1974, Florida — Member The Florida Bar; Broward County Bar Associations; St. Thomas More Society; Defense Research Institute; Florida Defense Lawyers Association; American Trial Lawyers Association; American Board of Trial Advocates — Florida Supreme Court Certified Civil Mediator; Qualified Florida Arbitrator — E-mail: roholton@chkklaw.com

Paula C. Kessler — 1957 — University of Florida, B.S., 1979; Nova Southeastern University, J.D., 1983 — Admitted to Bar, 1983, Florida; 1984, U.S. District Court, Southern District of Florida — Member Federal, American and Broward County Bar Associations; The Florida Bar; Trucking Industry Defense Group; St. Thomas More Society; Stephen R. Booher American Inn of Court; Florida Defense Lawyers Association; Defense Research Institute; American Board of Trial Advocates — Certified County and Circuit Court Mediator — E-mail: paulak@chkklaw.com

Andrea L. Kessler — 1958 — University of Florida, B.A., 1981; Nova Southeastern University, J.D., 1984 — Delta Theta Phi — Admitted to Bar, 1985, Florida; 1985, U.S. District Court, Southern District of Florida — Member Federal, American and Broward County Bar Associations; The Florida Bar (Trial Lawyers Section; Real Property Probate and Trust Law Section); St. Thomas More Society; Estate Planning Counsel of Broward County (Treasurer 2008 - 2009; Secretary 2007 - 2008; Vice President, 2009-2010); Probate Rules and Procedures (Committee Member); Probate Trust and Litigation (Committee Member); Broward County Probate Committee (Co-Chair 2013-2014); Defense Research Institute; Florida Defense Lawyers Association — Florida Supreme Court Qualified Civil Arbitrator; Florida Supreme Court Certified Mediator Circuit and County — Practice Areas: Americans with Disabilities Act; Construction Litigation; General Liability; Product Liability; Probate; Guardian and Conservatorships; Arbitration; Mediation; Premises Liability; Trucking Liability; Tort Litigation — E-mail: andreak@chkklaw.com

Edwina V. Kessler — 1965 — University of Florida, B.A., 1989; Nova Southeastern University, J.D., 1994 — Admitted to Bar, 1994, Florida; 1995, U.S. District Court, Southern District of Florida; 2008, U.S. District Court, Middle District of Florida — Member Federal, American and Broward County (Board of Director, 2003-2007, 2008-2010; Young Lawyers Section) Bar Associations; The Florida Bar; Stephen Booher Inns of Court; St. Thomas More Society; Trucking Industry Defense Association; Defense Research Institute; Florida Defense Lawyers Association; Transportation Lawyers Association — Certified County and Circuit Court Florida Mediator — E-mail: edwinak@chkklaw.com

Wesley E. Catri — 1980 — John Carroll University, B.A., 2002; Nova Southeastern University, J.D., 2005 — Admitted to Bar, 2005, Florida — E-mail: wecatri@chkklaw.com

(This firm is also listed in the Subrogation section of this directory)

Colodny Fass, P.A.

One Financial Plaza, 23rd Floor
100 Southeast Third Avenue
Fort Lauderdale, Florida 33394
Telephone: 954-492-4010
Fax: 954-492-1144
E-Mail: mcolodny@colodnyfass.com
www.colodnyfass.com

(Additional Offices: Tallahassee, FL*)

Established: 1974

Insurance Litigation, Insurance Defense, Insurance Law, Bad Faith, Appellate Practice, Class Actions, Insurance Regulation, Regulatory and Compliance, Government Affairs, Reinsurance, Administrative Law, Formation and Financing, Mergers and Acquisitions, Market Conduct, Financial Examinations and Financial Issues, Surplus Lines, Rate, Form and Rule Filings, Portfolio Transfers, Assumptions, Agent and Agency Matters, Market Expansion and Withdrawal, Self-Insurance

Firm Profile: Founded in 1974, Colodny Fass' comprehensive insurance regulatory, litigation and governmental practice includes the representation of insurance companies, reinsurers, self-insurers, risk retention groups, captives, surplus lines insurers, managing general agencies, agents, reinsurance intermediaries and premium finance companies. With experience involving a wide range of licensing and compliance issues, the Firm handles formation and financing; mergers and acquisitions; adding lines of business; market expansion; market conduct and financial examinations; financial issues; statutory accounting procedures; portfolio transfers; risk-based capital levels; capital infusion issues; rate, form and rule filings; reduced collateral obligations; and agent and agency matters. It also handles the defense of major institutional class actions raising complex constitutional and federal issues. Its litigation practice group handles commercial, civil rights and employment matters at both the trial and appellate levels.

Representative Insurance Clients

Assurant Solutions
Endurance Specialty Insurance Ltd.
Guy Carpenter & Co., Inc.
Marsh & McLennan Companies
United Automobile Insurance Group
Capacity Insurance Company
ETI Financial Corporation
MacNeill Group, Inc.
Southern Oak Management, LLC

Shareholders

Mike Colodny — University of Florida, J.D., 1966 — Admitted to Bar, 1967, Florida — Member The Florida Bar; Florida Association of Professional Lobbyists — Practice Areas: Insurance Regulation; Government Affairs; Real Estate; Commercial Law — E-mail: mcolodny@colodnyfass.com

Joel S. Fass — State University of New York at Buffalo Law School, J.D. (cum laude), 1973 — Admitted to Bar, 1974, New York; 1976, Florida — Member The Florida Bar; American Trial Lawyers Association; Florida Justice Association — Practice Areas: Insurance Defense; Litigation — E-mail: jfass@colodnyfass.com

Maria Elena Abate — University of Miami, J.D. (cum laude), 1988 — Admitted to Bar, 1988, Florida — Member The Florida Bar; Claims and Litigation Management Alliance - Certified Litigation Management Professional; American Trial Lawyers Association; American Association for Justice — Languages: Spanish — Practice Areas: Insurance Law; Litigation; Appellate Practice; Civil Rights; Employment Law — E-mail: mabate@colodnyfass.com

Katherine S. Webb — Florida State University, J.D., 2003 — Admitted to Bar, 2003, Florida — Member The Florida Bar; Florida Association of Professional Lobbyists — Adjunct Professor of Insurance Law, Florida State University College of Law — Practice Areas: Government Affairs; Insurance Regulation — E-mail: kwebb@colodnyfass.com

Amy L. Koltnow — Stetson University College of Law, J.D., 1991 — Admitted to Bar, 1991, Florida — Member The Florida Bar; Claims and Litigation Management Alliance — Languages: Spanish — E-mail: akoltnow@colodnyfass.com

Colodny Fass, P.A., Fort Lauderdale, FL (Continued)

Nate Wesley Strickland — Florida State University College of Law, J.D., 1998 — Admitted to Bar, 1999, Florida — Member The Florida Bar — E-mail: wstrickland@colodnyfass.com

Partners

Sandy P. Fay — Nova Southeastern University, Shepard Broad Law Center, J.D., 1998 — Admitted to Bar, 1998, Florida — E-mail: sfay@colodnyfass.com

Megan M. Grant — University of Idaho, J.D., 1995; Tulane University, LL.M., 1998 — Admitted to Bar, 1995, Idaho; 1996, Colorado; 1999, District of Columbia; 2007, Florida — E-mail: mgrant@colodnyfass.com

Trevor B. Mask — Florida Coastal School of Law, J.D., 2002 — Admitted to Bar, 2003, Florida — E-mail: tmask@colodnyfass.com

Associates

Frank A. Alerte — New York University School of Law, J.D., 1987 — Admitted to Bar, 1988, New York; 2014, Florida — E-mail: falerte@colodnyfass.com

Sharlee Hobbs Edwards — Florida State University College of Law, J.D., 2006 — Admitted to Bar, 2006, Florida — E-mail: sedwards@colodnyfass.com

Nicole H. Fried — University of Florida College of Law, J.D., 2003 — Admitted to Bar, 2003, Florida — E-mail: nfried@colodnyfass.com

Silvia M. Gonzalez — Stetson University College of Law, J.D., 1995 — Admitted to Bar, 1995, Florida — Languages: Spanish — E-mail: sgonzalez@colodnyfass.com

Jamie B. Horne — Florida State University College of Law, J.D., 2010 — Admitted to Bar, 2011, Florida — E-mail: jhorne@colodnyfass.com

O. Karina Iñigo — St. Thomas University School of Law, J.D. (cum laude), 2007 — Admitted to Bar, 2007, Florida — E-mail: kinigo@colodnyfass.com

Adrian S. Middleton — Florida State University College of Law, 2012 — Admitted to Bar, 2013, Florida — E-mail: amiddleton@colodnyfass.com

A. Abidemi Oladipo — Florida State University College of Law, J.D., 2007 — Admitted to Bar, 2007, Florida — E-mail: aoladipo@colodnyfass.com

Charlyne M. Patterson — Florida State University College of Law, J.D., 2005 — Admitted to Bar, 2006, Florida — E-mail: cpatterson@colodnyfass.com

Matthew C. Scarfone — Michigan State University College of Law, J.D., 2010 — Admitted to Bar, 2010, Michigan; 2011, Florida — E-mail: mscarfone@colodnyfass.com

Timothy Fordham Stanfield — Florida Coastal School of Law, J.D., 2006 — Admitted to Bar, 2006, Florida — E-mail: tstanfield@colodnyfass.com

Jeffrey M. Wank — Nova Southeastern University, Shepard Broad Law Center, J.D., 2009 — Admitted to Bar, 2009, Florida — E-mail: jwank@colodnyfass.com

Devon A. Woolard — University of Florida, Levin College of Law, J.D., 2014 — Admitted to Bar, 2014, Florida — E-mail: dwoolard@colodnyfass.com

Benjamin J. Zellner — New York Law School, J.D., 2013 — Admitted to Bar, 2014, Florida — E-mail: bzellner@colodnyfass.com

Scott R. Zucker — Nova Southeastern University, Shepard Broad Law Center, J.D., 2009 — Admitted to Bar, 2009, Florida — E-mail: szucker@colodnyfass.com

Of Counsel

Jennifer C. Erdelyi — Nova Southeastern University, Shepard Broad Law Center, J.D., 2006 — Admitted to Bar, 2006, Florida — E-mail: jerdelyi@colodnyfass.com

(Revisors of Florida Insurance Law Digest for this Publication)

(This firm is also listed in the Regulatory and Compliance section of this directory)

Cooney Trybus Kwavnick Peets

1600 West Commercial Boulevard
Suite 200
Fort Lauderdale, Florida 33309
Telephone: 954-568-6669
Fax: 954-568-0085
E-Mail: jclifford@ctkplaw.com
www.ctkplaw.com

Cooney Trybus Kwavnick Peets, Fort Lauderdale, FL (Continued)

Established: 2009

Trucking Law, Product Liability, Premises Liability, Professional Liability, Medical Malpractice, Legal Malpractice, Class Actions, Mass Tort, Commercial Litigation, Appellate Practice, Insurance Coverage, Bad Faith, Automobile Negligence, Drug & Medical Device Defects, Pharmaceutical Negligence

Insurance Clients

CNA	Federated National Adjusting, Inc.
Fidelity General Insurance Company	IAT Specialty
	National Indemnity Company
Nautilus Insurance Group	State Farm Group
Wilshire Insurance Company	Zurich North America

Non-Insurance Clients

Costco Companies, Inc.	The Hertz Corporation
Ryder Truck Rental, Inc.	Target Corporation

Partners

David F. Cooney — University of Notre Dame, B.B.A. (magna cum laude), 1975; University of Notre Dame Law School, J.D., 1978 — Admitted to Bar, 1978, Florida; U.S. District Court, Middle and Southern Districts of Florida; U.S. Court of Appeals, Fifth, Eighth and Eleventh Circuits — Member Diplomate, American Board of Trial Advocates; Diplomate, Litigation Counsel of America — E-mail: dcooney@ctkplaw.com

Bruce M. Trybus — University of the Witwatersrand, Johannesburg, B.A., 1983; LL.B., 1985; Nova Southeastern University, Shepard Broad Law Center, J.D. (cum laude), 1992 — Admitted to Bar, 1993, Florida; U.S. District Court, Middle and Southern Districts of Florida — Member American and Broward County Bar Associations; Associate, American Board of Trial Advocates; Florida Defense Lawyers Association; Defense Research Institute — E-mail: btrybus@ctkplaw.com

Warren B. Kwavnick — McGill University, B.C.A. (with great distinction), 1993; Nova Southeastern University, Shepard Broad Law Center, J.D. (magna cum laude), 1996 — Admitted to Bar, 1996, Florida; U.S. District Court, Middle and Southern Districts of Florida; U.S. Court of Appeals, Eleventh Circuit — Member Broward County Bar Association; Florida Defense Lawyers Association — E-mail: wkwavnick@ctkplaw.com

Alphonso O. Peets — University of Central Florida, B.A., 1992; Nova Southeastern University, Shepard Broad Law Center, J.D., 1995 — Admitted to Bar, 1996, Florida; U.S. District Court, Middle and Southern Districts of Florida — Member Broward County and Palm Beach County Bar Associations; Florida Medical Malpractice Claims Council; Florida Defense Lawyers Association; Defense Research Institute — E-mail: apeets@ctkplaw.com

Grisell Turnau — Florida International University, B.S., 1992; Nova Southeastern University, Shepard Broad Law Center, J.D., 1998 — Phi Delta Phi — Admitted to Bar, 1998, Florida — Member Broward County Bar Association — E-mail: gturnau@ctkplaw.com

Benjamin Kashi — University of Florida, B.S. (with honors), 2001; University of Florida College of Law, J.D. (cum laude), 2004 — Admitted to Bar, 2004, Florida; U.S. District Court, Southern District of Florida — Member American Bar Association; The Florida Bar — E-mail: bkashi@ctkplaw.com

Associates

Meredith Chaiken-Weiss	Rachel Gray-Cerni
Paul Shafranski	Sterling A. McMahan

Fertig & Gramling

200 Southeast 13th Street
Fort Lauderdale, Florida 33316
Telephone: 954-763-5020, 305-945-6250 (Miami)
Fax: 954-763-5412
www.fertig.com

Coverage Issues, Admiralty and Maritime Law, Casualty, Fraud, Property, Reinsurance, Errors and Omissions, Directors and Officers Liability

FORT LAUDERDALE — FLORIDA

Fertig & Gramling, Fort Lauderdale, FL (Continued)

Insurance Clients

Acadia Insurance Company
Canopius Managing Agents Limited
Foremost Insurance Company
International Surplus Lines Insurance Company
Markel International Insurance Company, Ltd.
Norwegian Hull Club
Progressive Insurance
Royal & Sun Alliance Insurance
Underwriters at Lloyd's, London
United States Liability Insurance Company
AXIS Reinsurance Company
Chubb/Pacific Indemnity Company
Federal Insurance Company
Great Lakes Reinsurance (U.K.) PLC
Marine Insurance Company
Northern Insurance Company of New York
Private Client Group of AIU Holdings, Inc.
St. Paul Reinsurance Company Limited
Willis North America, Inc.

Non-Insurance Clients

AGF&J Claims Service, LLC
Farmer's & Zurich Marine Claims
Lazzara Yachts
Atlass Insurance Group
Hilb, Rogal and Hobbs Company

Partners

Frank R. Gramling — (Retired)

Christopher R. Fertig — Georgetown University School of Foreign Service, B.S.F.S., 1973; University of Miami School of Law, J.D., 1976 — Admitted to Bar, 1976, Florida; 1976, U.S. District Court, Middle and Southern Districts of Florida; 1976, U.S. Court of Appeals, Fifth and Eleventh Circuits; 1976, U.S. Supreme Court; 2006, U.S. District Court, Northern District of Florida — Member The Florida Bar; The Maritime Law Association of the United States — E-mail: chris.fertig@fertig.com

Darlene M. Lidondici — 1957 — John Jay College of Criminal Justice of the City University of New York, B.S., 1979; Fordham University, J.D., 1982 — Admitted to Bar, 1983, New York; 1985, Florida; 1983, U.S. District Court, Eastern and Southern Districts of New York; 1988, U.S. District Court, Southern District of Florida; U.S. District Court, Middle and Northern Districts of Florida; U.S. Court of Appeals, Eleventh Circuit — Member American Bar Association; The Florida Bar — E-mail: darlene.lidondici@fertig.com

Andrew Mescolotto — 1979 — The George Washington University, B.A., 2001; Nova Southeastern University, J.D., 2006 — Admitted to Bar, 2006, Florida — E-mail: andrew.mescolotto@fertig.com

Associates

Alexander P. Koffler — Nova Southeastern University, Shepard Broad Law Center, J.D., 2007 — Admitted to Bar, 2007, Florida — E-mail: apk@fertig.com

Seth E. Harris — University of Miami School of Law, J.D., 2009 — Admitted to Bar, 2009, Florida

Judith A. Bradshaw — 1980 — St. Thomas University School of Law, J.D., 2014 — Admitted to Bar, 2014, Florida

Hill, Betts & Nash, LLP

1515 SE 17th Street, Suite A115
Fort Lauderdale, Florida 33316
Telephone: 954-522-2271
Fax: 954-522-2355
www.hillbetts.com

(New York, NY Office*: 1 World Financial Center, 200 Liberty Street, 26th Floor, 10281)
 (Tel: 212-839-7000)
 (Fax: 212-466-0514)
 (Mobile: 917-864-9673)

Established: 2009

Insurance Defense, Personal Injury, Premises Liability, Jones Act, Longshore and Harbor Workers' Compensation, Workers' Compensation, Construction Law, Product Liability, Property Damage, Environmental Law, Inland and Ocean Marine, Coverage Issues, Reinsurance, Subrogation, Fidelity and Surety, General Passenger Claim Defense, Cruise Passenger

(See listing under New York, NY for additional information)

Leiter & Belsky, P.A.

707 Southeast Third Avenue, Third Floor
Fort Lauderdale, Florida 33316
Telephone: 954-462-3116
Fax: 954-761-8990
E-Mail: ebelsky@jlblaw.com
www.jlblaw.com

Established: 2000

Insurance Defense, Insurance Coverage, Appellate Practice, General Liability, Bad Faith, Automobile Liability, Product Liability, Construction Claims, Construction Defect, Construction Litigation, Insurance Claim Analysis and Evaluation, Insurance Coverage Determination, Insurance Coverage Litigation, Insurance Law, Insurance Litigation, Litigation, No-Fault, Personal Injury Protection (PIP), Premises Liability, Primary and Excess Insurance, Professional Liability, Self-Insured, Self-Insured Defense, Trial and Appellate Practice

Firm Profile: Leiter & Belsky, P.A. is a full service, defense oriented law firm which provides legal counsel to the insurance industry and their insureds, together with individuals and self-insured companies. In addition to litigating and evaluating personal injury, wrongful death, professional liability and products liability actions, the firm has substantial experience with first-party insurance coverage disputes and bad faith litigation. Our appellate attorneys have handled cases in every state and federal jurisdiction in Florida, as well as the United States Supreme Court. Our attorneys and staff consider communication and personal service to our clients to be of the utmost importance.

Insurance Clients

Balboa Insurance Company
GMAC Insurance
Great American Insurance Company
QBE FIRST Insurance Agency, Inc.
Zurich Insurance Company
Empire Fire and Marine Insurance Company
Infinity Insurance Group
Kemper Insurance Companies
T.H.E. Insurance Company
United Automobile Insurance Company

Non-Insurance Clients

Compass Group USA, Inc.
CorVel Corporation

Partners

Eric G. Belsky — 1962 — Nova University, B.S. (with distinction), 1990; University of Miami, J.D. (cum laude), 1993 — Phi Theta Kappa; Alpha Chi; Phi Alpha Delta — Admitted to Bar, 1993, Florida; U.S. District Court, Southern District of Florida; 1994, U.S. District Court, Middle District of Florida; 1995, U.S. District Court, Northern District of Florida; U.S. Court of Appeals, Eleventh Circuit; 1997, U.S. Supreme Court — Member The Florida Bar; Broward County Bar Association — Practice Areas: Appellate Practice; Bad Faith; Class Actions; Construction Defect; Construction Litigation; Coverage Analysis; Coverage Issues; Extra-Contractual Litigation; General Civil Trial and Appellate Practice; General Liability; Insurance Coverage — E-mail: ebelsky@jlblaw.com

Steven J. Leiter — 1967 — The University of Georgia, B.A., 1989; University of Miami, J.D. (cum laude), 1992 — Phi Delta Phi — Staff Member, 1990-1991 and Articles and Comments Editor, 1991-1992, Inter-American Law Review — Admitted to Bar, 1992, Florida; 1995, Georgia; 1992, U.S. District Court, Southern District of Florida; 2001, U.S. District Court, Middle District of Florida — Member The Florida Bar; State Bar of Georgia and Broward County Bar Association — "Abrogation of Joint and Several Liability for Non-Economic Damages," For The Defense, December 1993 — E-mail: sleiter@jlblaw.com

Charles Andrew Tharp — 1961 — Occidental College, A.B., 1983; University of Miami School of Law, J.D., 1987 — Admitted to Bar, 1988, Florida; U.S. District Court, Middle, Northern and Southern Districts of Florida — Member Broward County Bar Association; Claims and Litigation Management Alliance; Florida Defense Lawyers Association — Practice Areas: First and

FLORIDA   **FORT LAUDERDALE**

Leiter & Belsky, P.A., Fort Lauderdale, FL   (Continued)

Third Party Matters; General Liability; Professional Liability; Product Liability; Civil Trial Practice; Insurance Coverage; Coverage Analysis; Coverage Issues; Construction Defect; Construction Litigation; Bad Faith; Extra-Contractual Litigation — Tel: 954-462-3116 — E-mail: atharp@jlblaw.com

Belayne D. Guerrero

Associate

Shelby L. Cohen

Lubell Rosen, LLC

200 South Andrews Avenue, Suite 900
Fort Lauderdale, Florida 33301
Telephone: 954-880-9500
Fax: 954-755-2993
E-Mail: info@lubellrosen.com
www.lubellrosen.com

(Coral Gables, FL Office: 1 Alhambra Plaza, Suite 1410, 33134)
  (Tel: 305-655-3425)
(Upper Saddle River, NJ Office: 345 Route 17 S, 07458)
  (Tel: 866-655-3425)
(Syossett, NY: 485 Underhill Boulevard, Suite 300, Syossett, NY, 11791)
  (Tel: 516-364-3564)
(Atlanta, GA Office: The High House, 309 Sycamore Street , 30030)
  (Tel: 404-885-1220)

Established: 1999

Asset Protection, Business and Real Estate Transactional, Commercial and Construction Litigation, Employment Law, Estate Planning and Probate, Going Bare, Health Law, HIPAA Compliance, Insurance Defense, Managed Care, Medical Malpractice Defense, White Collar Criminal Defense

Firm Profile: The legal team at Lubell Rosen handles large health care-based clientele, from individual representation to large corporations. Firm Partner Steven Lubell is considered an expert in Civil Trial Law through Board Certification by The Florida Bar; firm Partner Mark Rosen is considered an expert in Health Law through Board Certification by The Florida Bar. As a medical malpractice defense firm, Lubell Rosen enforces the principals and values of providing affordable, quality legal solutions to the health care industry.

Insurance Clients

Doctors & Surgeons National RRG, Inc.
Lancet Indemnity Risk Retention Group

Partners

Steven L. Lubell — University of Michigan, B.A., 1990; University of Florida College of Law, J.D. (with honors), 1993 — Admitted to Bar, 1994, Florida; District of Columbia; New York; New Jersey; Texas; Michigan; U.S. District Court, Southern District of Florida — Member American (Health Law Section), New York State, New Jersey State, Broward County and Dade County Bar Associations; The District of Columbia and The Florida (Health Law Section; Trial Law Section) Bars; State Bars of Texas and Michigan; Florida Academy of Healthcare Attorneys; Florida Trial Lawyers Association; American Health Lawyers Association — Board Certified, Civil Trial Law; "AV" Rated by Lexis-Nexis Martindale-Hubbell — Practice Areas: Medical Malpractice Defense; Health; Administrative Law; Complex Litigation; Appellate Practice — E-mail: slubell@lubellrosen.com

Mark L. Rosen — Emory University, B.B.A., 1991; University of Florida College of Law, J.D. (with honors), 1994 — Admitted to Bar, 1994, Georgia; Florida; New York — Member American Bar Association (Health Law Section); The Florida Bar; Florida Academy of Healthcare Attorneys; Florida Hospital Association; American Health Lawyers Association — Certified Public Accountant, Florida 1993; Board Certified Health Law Lawyer, Florida Bar of Legal Specialization and Education; "AV" Rated by Lexis-Nexis Martindale-Hubbell — Practice Areas: Medical Malpractice Defense; Health; Complex Litigation — E-mail: mlr@lubellrosen.com

Firm Members

Marshall A. Adams   Bernard M. Cassidy

Lubell Rosen, LLC, Fort Lauderdale, FL   (Continued)

Sandra Greenblatt   Julia M. Ingle
Aldo Leiva   Liz Messianu
Michael O'Connor   William C. Phillippi
Kathryn Shanley   Matthew Staab
Anette Yelin

Associates

Adi Amit   Josh M. Bloom
Christiane Flewelling   Vanessa Duffey
Anthony Spano   Deborah M. Silverman
Megan C. Sincore   Ariel D. Sofro

Of Counsel

Cynthia Hibnick   Cort Neimark

Luks & Santaniello LLC

110 SE 6th Street, 20th Floor
Fort Lauderdale, Florida 33301
  Telephone: 954-761-9900
Fax: 954-761-9940
E-Mail: LS@LS-LAW.com
http://www.LS-LAW.com

(Additional Offices: Tampa, FL*; Orlando, FL*; Jacksonville, FL*; Boca Raton, FL*; Miami, FL*; Tallahassee, FL)

Established: 1995

General Liability, Wrongful Death, Automobile Liability, Premises Liability, Retail and Restaurant Defense, Negligent Security, Product Liability, Trucking Litigation, Personal Injury, Construction Liability, Employment Practices Liability, Labor and Employment, Professional Liability, Errors and Omissions, First and Third Party Defense, Insurance Law, Insurance Coverage, Bad Faith, Commercial Litigation, Creditor's Rights, ERISA, Securities and Shareholders' Claims, Admiralty and Maritime Law, Self-Insured Defense, Appellate Practice, Workers' Compensation, Medicare Set-Aside Practice

Firm Profile: Luks, Santaniello, Petrillo & Jones is a Florida Corporate & Insurance Defense Litigation firm. We defend businesses and insurers from both Liability (A/GL, A&E, BAP, CGL, D&O, E&O, E&S, P&C, PL, PLL, JUA, XS and EC) and Workers' Compensation claims. The firm has a full service Appellate team in South, Central and Northern Florida to assist with summary judgments, motions in limine, discovery objectives, trial strategy and post trial motions. We also offer Medicare reporting, MSA and Lien Resolution services. Our team of over 50 litigators reside in seven offices: Miami, Ft. Lauderdale, Boca Raton, Orlando, Tampa, Jacksonville and Tallahassee. We are members of the Claims and Litigation Management Alliance (CLM).

Insurance Clients

Northland Insurance   Tower Hill Insurance Group
United States Liability Insurance Group   XL Insurance/XL Environmental Inc.

Non-Insurance Clients

Alamo Rent-A-Car, LLC   EMCOR Group
The Home Depot   Laboratory Corporation of America
National Car Rental   Simon Property Group, Inc.

Members

Jack D. Luks — 1961 — Michigan State University, B.A., 1983; University of Miami, J.D., 1986 — Admitted to Bar, 1987, Florida; New Jersey; U.S. District Court, Middle, Northern and Southern Districts of Florida including Trial Bar

Daniel J. Santaniello — 1964 — Northeastern University, B.S., 1987; Nova Southeastern University, J.D. (summa cum laude), 1990 — Recipient of FDLA's 2010 President's Award — Admitted to Bar, 1990, Florida; Massachusetts; U.S. District Court, Middle, Northern and Southern Districts of Florida including Trial Bar; U.S. District Court, District of Massachusetts — Member Florida Defense Lawyers Association (President Elect, 2012-2013) — Co-Author: with Alvarez, Rey, "Medicare White Paper," Florida Defense

FORT LAUDERDALE   **FLORIDA**

Luks & Santaniello LLC, Fort Lauderdale, FL (Continued)

Lawyers Association, 2 June, 2011 — Florida Bar Board Certified in Civil Trial

Anthony J. Petrillo — 1965 — University of Florida, B.S., 1987; Nova Southeastern University, J.D., 1990 — Admitted to Bar, 1991, Florida; U.S. District Court, Southern District of Florida; 1996, U.S. Court of Appeals, Eleventh Circuit; 1999, U.S. District Court, Middle District of Florida — Florida Bar Board Certified in Civil Trial

Paul S. Jones — 1967 — University of Central Florida, B.A., 1993; Nova Southeastern University, J.D. (cum laude), 1998 — Admitted to Bar, 1998, Florida; 1999, U.S. District Court, Southern District of Florida; 2001, U.S. Court of Appeals, Eleventh Circuit; 2002, U.S. District Court, Middle and Northern Districts of Florida — Florida Bar Board Certified in Civil Trial

Managing Attorney

Rey Alvarez

Junior Partners

Lynn F. Gambino
Carl W. Christy
Marcella L. Garcia
Marc M. Greenberg
Michael H. Kestenbaum
David A. Lipkin
Anthony Merendino
Todd T. Springer
Andrew L. Chiera
Steven G. Hemmert
Dorsey C. Miller, III

Heather M. Calhoon
Thomas W. Farrell
Zeb I. Goldstein
Howard W. Holden
Doreen E. Lasch
Samuel A. Maroon
Joseph F. Scarpa, Jr.
James P. Waczewski
Daniel L. Fox
Matthew G. Krause

Administration

Sherri L. Bauer   Maria C. Donnelly

Associates

Marlo A. Bodach
Michael A. Graham
Katherine N. Kmiec
Derek H. Lloyd
Seth Masson
Jennifer J. Seitz
Joshua C. Vincent
Marci L. Matonis
Lisa Clary
Daniel J. Feight
Alec Masson
John F. Meade

Christopher H. Burrows
Kelly M. Klein
Joseph A. Kopacz
Allison B. Wasserman
Shana Pollack Nogues
Evgenia M. Waczewski
Paul R. Shalhoub
Luis Menendez-Aponte
Melissa A. Bensel
Patrick T. Graves
Jorge Padilla

Marshall Dennehey Warner Coleman & Goggin

100 Northeast 3rd Avenue, Suite 1100
Fort Lauderdale, Florida 33301
   Telephone: 954-847-4920
   Fax: 954-627-6640
   www.marshalldennehey.com

(Philadelphia, PA Office*: 2000 Market Street, Suite 2300, 19103)
   (Tel: 215-575-2600)
   (Fax: 215-575-0856)
   (Toll Free: 800-220-3308)
   (E-Mail: marshalldennehey@mdwcg.com)
(Wilmington, DE Office*: Nemours Building, 1007 North Orange Street, Suite 600, 19801)
   (Tel: 302-552-4300)
   (Fax: 302-552-4340)
(Jacksonville, FL Office*: 200 West Forsyth Street, Suite 1400, 32202)
   (Tel: 904-358-4200)
   (Fax: 904-355-0019)
(Orlando, FL Office*: Landmark Center One, 315 East Robinson Street, Suite 550, 32801-1948)
   (Tel: 407-420-4380)
   (Fax: 407-839-3008)

Marshall Dennehey Warner Coleman & Goggin, Fort Lauderdale, FL (Continued)

(Tampa, FL Office*: 201 East Kennedy Boulevard, Suite 1100, 33602)
   (Tel: 813-898-1800)
   (Fax: 813-221-5026)
(Cherry Hill, NJ Office*: Woodland Falls Corporate Park, 200 Lake Drive East, Suite 300, 08002)
   (Tel: 856-414-6000)
   (Fax: 856-414-6077)
(Roseland, NJ Office*: 425 Eagle Rock Avenue, Suite 302, 07068)
   (Tel: 973-618-4100)
   (Fax: 973-618-0685)
(New York, NY Office*: Wall Street Plaza, 88 Pine Street, 21st Floor, 10005-1801)
   (Tel: 212-376-6400)
   (Fax: 212-376-6490)
(Melville, NY Office*: 105 Maxess Road, Suite 303, 11747)
   (Tel: 631-232-6130)
   (Fax: 631-232-6184)
(Cincinnati, OH Office*: 312 Elm Street, Suite 1850, 45202)
   (Tel: 513-375-6800)
   (Fax: 513-372-6801)
(Cleveland, OH Office*: 127 Public Square, Suite 3510, 44114-1291)
   (Tel: 216-912-3800)
   (Fax: 216-344-9006)
(Allentown, PA Office*: 4905 West Tilghman Street, Suite 300, 18104)
   (Tel: 484-895-2300)
   (Fax: 484-895-2303)
(Doylestown, PA Office*: 10 North Main Street, 2nd Floor, 18901-4318)
   (Tel: 267-880-2020)
   (Fax: 215-348-5439)
(Erie, PA Office*: 717 State Street, Suite 701, 16501)
   (Tel: 814-480-7800)
   (Fax: 814-455-3603)
(Camp Hill, PA Office*(See Harrisburg listing): 100 Coporate Center Drive, Suite 201, 17011)
   (Tel: 717-651-3500)
   (Fax: 717-651-9630)
(King of Prussia, PA Office*: 620 Freedom Business Center, Suite 300, 19406)
   (Tel: 610-354-8250)
   (Fax: 610-354-8299)
(Pittsburgh, PA Office*: U.S. Steel Tower, Suite 2900, 600 Grant Street, 15219)
   (Tel: 412-803-1140)
   (Fax: 412-803-1188)
(Moosic, PA Office*(See Scranton listing): 50 Glenmaura National Boulevard, 18507)
   (Tel: 570-496-4600)
   (Fax: 570-496-0567)
(Rye Brook, NY Office*(See Westchester listing): 800 Westchester Avenue, Suite C-700, 10573)
   (Tel: 914-977-7300)
   (Fax: 914-977-7301)

Established: 2002

FLORIDA — FORT LAUDERDALE

Marshall Dennehey Warner Coleman & Goggin, Fort Lauderdale, FL (Continued)

Amusements, Sports and Recreation Liability, Asbestos and Mass Tort Litigation, Automobile Liability, Aviation and Complex Litigation, Construction Injury Litigation, Fraud/Special Investigation, General Liability, Hospitality and Liquor Liability, Maritime Litigation, Product Liability, Property Litigation, Retail Liability, Trucking & Transportation Liability, Appellate Advocacy and Post-Trial Practice, Architectural, Engineering and Construction Defect Litigation, Class Action Litigation, Commercial Litigation, Consumer and Credit Law, Employment Law, Environmental & Toxic Tort Litigation, Insurance Coverage/Bad Faith Litigation, Life, Health and Disability Litigation, Privacy and Data Security, Professional Liability, Public Entity and Civil Rights Litigation, Real Estate E&O Liability, School Leaders' Liability, Securities and Investment Professional Liability, Technology, Media and Intellectual Property Litigation, White Collar Crime, Birth Injury Litigation, Health Care Governmental Compliance, Health Care Liability, Health Law, Long-Term Care Liability, Medical Device and Pharmaceutical Liability, Medicare Set-Aside, Workers' Compensation

Firm Profile: The Fort Lauderdale office of Marshall Dennehey Warner Coleman & Goggin is a short distance from state and federal courthouses and ideally positioned to service clients throughout southeastern Florida. As a regional office of Marshall Dennehey, the Fort Lauderdale office is backed by the resources of a firm with more than 490 lawyers. It stands ready to assist every client-be they individuals, small businesses, large corporations or insurance carriers-by providing high-quality, result-oriented legal representation that is both innovative and cost-effective.

For additional information concerning the Fort Lauderdale office, please contact Craig S. Hudson, Esquire, its managing attorney, at (954) 847-4955 or cshudson@mdwcg.com

Managing Shareholder

Craig S. Hudson — **Supervisor, Professional Liability Practice Group, FL** — 1960 — Villanova University, B.A., 1982; Rutgers University School of Law-Camden, J.D., 1985 — Moot Court Board — Admitted to Bar, 1985, Pennsylvania; 1986, New Jersey; 2006, Florida; 1986, U.S. District Court, Eastern, Middle and Western Districts of Pennsylvania; U.S. District Court, District of New Jersey; U.S. Court of Appeals, Third Circuit; 2006, U.S. District Court, Middle and Southern Districts of Florida — Member Pennsylvania, Broward County and Palm Beach County Bar Associations; The Florida Bar; Defense Research Institute — Arthor: "Did the Florida Supreme Court Greatly Expand Tort Law At a Cost to Florida's contract Law?" Defense Digest, Vol. 19, No. 3, September 2013; "Fear The Next Hurricane More Than Florida Supreme Court's Ruling on Tiara," Claims Journal, June 2013; "Third Circuit Confirms That All Claims Concerning Medical Devices, Other Than Breach of Express Warranty Claims, Are Barred," Defense Digest, January, 1996 — Seminars/Classes Taught: Understanding the Sub-Prime Credit and Housing Crises, AIG (2008); Sub-Prime Market Collapse and Its Impact on Claims against Professionals involved in Real Estate Transactions, Gen Star (2008); Defending Construction Defect Litigation Claims in Florida, Liberty International (2007); Claims Against the Board of Directors of Condominium and Homeowner Associations, USLI (2006) — Practice Areas: Professional Liability; Architects and Engineers; Construction Defect; Employment Law; Commercial Litigation; Premises Liability — E-mail: cshudson@mdwcg.com

Special Counsel

Patrick M. DeLong

Resident Shareholders

Jonathan E. Kanov
Michael A. Packer
R. David Ravine
Andrew J. Marchese
Stephen J. Poljak

Resident Associates

Ryan D. Burns
Alan C. Nash
Chad J. Robinson
Jason L. Scarberry
Jeannie Anne Liebegott
Kerri Haley O'Brien
Danielle N. Robinson
Nneka B. Uzodinma

(See listing under Philadelphia, PA for additional information)

McConnaughhay, Duffy, Coonrod, Pope & Weaver, P.A.

500 West Cypress Creek Road, Suite 300
Fort Lauderdale, Florida 33309
 Telephone: 954-332-0050
 Fax: 954-332-0052
 www.mcconnaughhay.com

(Additional Offices: Tallahassee, FL*; Gainesville, FL*; Jacksonville, FL*; Ocala, FL*; Panama City, FL*; Pensacola, FL*; Sarasota, FL*)

Insurance Defense, Workers' Compensation, Product Liability, Labor and Employment, Civil Litigation, Trial Practice, Appellate Practice

Firm Member

Taysha L. Carmody — Villanova University, B.A., 2000; Florida State University, J.D., 2004 — Admitted to Bar, 2004, Florida — Practice Areas: Workers' Compensation

Associates

Suzanne Y. Gutierrez
Charlotte Zubizaretta

Law Offices of Bohdan Neswiacheny

2929 E Commercial Boulevard, Suite 300
Fort Lauderdale, Florida 33308
 Telephone: 954-522-5400
 Fax: 954-765-1274
 E-Mail: bnlaw@bnlaw.com
 www.bnlaw.com

(Sarasota, FL Office*: 1800 Second Street, Suite 760, 34236)
 (Tel: 941-957-3400)
 (Fax: 941-952-9103)
(Orange Park, FL Office*: 151 College Drive, Suite 1, 32065)
 (Tel: 904-276-6171)
 (Fax: 904-276-1751)

Established: 1981

Insurance Defense, Insurance Coverage, Employment Discrimination, Automotive Products Liability, Product Liability, Construction Defect, Premises Liability, Self-Insured Defense, Trial and Appellate Practice

Insurance Clients

Auto-Owners Insurance Company
Conifer Insurance Company
Harco National Insurance Company
Security First Insurance Company
Zurich North America
CNA HealthPro
Cypress Property & Casualty Insurance Company
Mid-Continent Group
United Property and Casualty Insurance Company

Non-Insurance Clients

Asbury Automotive Group
State of Florida, Division of Risk Management

Managing Member

Bohdan Neswiacheny — United States Military Academy at West Point, B.S., 1968; University of Miami, J.D., 1980 — Admitted to Bar, 1980, Florida; U.S. District Court, Middle, Northern and Southern Districts of Florida — U.S. Army, Lieutenant Colonel (Retired) — Languages: Ukrainian — Practice Areas: Insurance Defense; Insurance Coverage; Construction Defect — E-mail: bneswiacheny@bnlaw.com

FORT LAUDERDALE

Law Offices of Bohdan Neswiacheny, Fort Lauderdale, FL (Continued)

Associate

Barbra A. Stern — University of Florida, B.S., 1996; Nova Southeastern University, Shepard Broad Law Center, J.D. (cum laude), 2001 — Admitted to Bar, 2001, Florida; 2004, U.S. District Court, Middle and Southern Districts of Florida — Practice Areas: Insurance Defense; Employment Practices Liability — E-mail: bstern@bnlaw.com

Vernis & Bowling of Broward, P.A.

5821 Hollywood Boulevard, First Floor
Hollywood, Florida 33021
   Telephone: 954-927-5330
   Fax: 954-927-5320
   E-Mail: info@florida-law.com
   www.national-law.com

(Vernis & Bowling of Palm Beach, P.A.*: 884 U.S. Highway #1, North Palm Beach, FL, 33408-5408)
   (Tel: 561-775-9822)
   (Fax: 561-775-9821)
   (E-Mail: gjvernis@florida-law.com)

(Vernis & Bowling of Southern Alabama, LLC*: 61 St. Joseph Street, 11th Floor, Mobile, AL, 36602)
   (Tel: 251-432-0337)
   (Fax: 251-432-0244)
   (E-Mail: info@law-alabama.com)
   (www.law-alabama.com)

(Vernis & Bowling of Northwest Florida, P.A.*: 315 South Palafox Street, Pensacola, FL, 32502)
   (Tel: 850-433-5461)
   (Fax: 850-432-0166)

(Vernis & Bowling of Southern Mississippi, PLLC*: 2501 14th Street, Suite 207, Gulfport, MS, 39501)
   (Tel: 225-539-0021)
   (Fax: 228-539-0022)

Established: 1970

Civil Litigation, Insurance Law, Workers' Compensation, Premises Liability, Labor and Employment, Civil Rights, Commercial Litigation, Complex Litigation, Product Liability, Directors and Officers Liability, Errors and Omissions, Construction Law, Construction Defect, Environmental Liability, Personal and Commercial Vehicle, Appellate Practice, Admiralty and Maritime Law, Real Estate, Family Law, Elder Law, Liability Defense, SIU/Fraud Litigation, Education Law (ESE/IDEA), Property and Casualty (Commercial and Personal Lines), Long-Haul Trucking Liability, Government Law, Public Law, Criminal, White Collar, Business Litigation

Firm Profile: VERNIS & BOWLING represents individuals, businesses, insurance carriers and self-insureds. With 115 offices located in Florida, Georgia, Alabama, North Carolina & Mississippi, we provide cost effective, full service legal representation that consistently exceeds the expectations of our clients.

Resident Attorneys

Henry J. Roman — Florida International University, B.A., 1993; Quinnipiac College School of Law, J.D., 1996 — Admitted to Bar, 1996, Florida — Member Dade County Bar Association; The Florida Bar; Ft. Lauderdale Claims Association; South Florida Claims Association

Carlton A. Bober — Emory University, B.A. (with honors), 1986; The George Washington University Law School, J.D., 1989 — Admitted to Bar, 1989, Florida; 1992, District of Columbia; 1995, U.S. District Court, Middle and Southern Districts of Florida

Thomas W. Paradise — Tulane University, B.A., 1988; Stetson University College of Law, J.D., 1991 — Admitted to Bar, 1991, Florida; 1991, U.S. District Court, Southern District of Florida; 1991, U.S. Court of Appeals, Eleventh Circuit

FLORIDA

Vernis & Bowling of Broward, P.A., Fort Lauderdale, FL (Continued)

Nicolette N. John — University of Miami, B.S., 1997; M.S., 2002; Howard University School of Law, J.D. (cum laude), 2000 — Admitted to Bar, 2003, Florida

Jose Pete Font — Florida International University, B.S. (magna cum laude), 2001; St. Thomas University School of Law, J.D., 2003 — Admitted to Bar, 2004, Florida

Evan Zuckerman — University of Florida, B.A. (magna cum laude), 2004; University of Florida, Levin College of Law, J.D. (Dean's List), 2007 — Admitted to Bar, 2007, Florida

Joshua Bruce — University of Florida, B.S.B.A., 2005; Stetson University College of Law, J.D., 2008 — Admitted to Bar, 2008, Florida

Steven J. Getman — Florida State University, B.S., 2004; St. Thomas University School of Law, J.D., 2008 — Admitted to Bar, 2009, Florida

Frantz C. Nelson — 1979 — The University of the West Indies, B.A., 2003; Nova Southeastern University, Shepard Broad Law Center, J.D., 2006 — Admitted to Bar, 2006, Florida

Michael Odrobina — University of Miami School of Law, J.D., 2007 — Admitted to Bar, 2007, Florida

Lauren Stone — University of Central Florida, B.A., 2006; Nova Southeastern University, Shepard Broad Law Center, J.D., 2010 — Admitted to Bar, 2010, Florida

Mikiel A. Singh — University of Florida, B.A. (summa cum laude), 2007; Florida State University College of Law, J.D., 2011 — Admitted to Bar, 2011, Florida

Belinda Scott — Ithaca College, B.A. (Dean's Scholar), 2004; University of Miami School of Law, J.D. (Dean's Scholar), 2010 — Admitted to Bar, 2011, Florida — E-mail: bscott@florida-law.com

Jennifer Valentin Lopez — Boston University, B.A. (cum laude), 2004; The Catholic University of America, Columbus School of Law, J.D., 2007 — Admitted to Bar, 2007, Florida — Languages: Spanish — E-mail: jlopez@hhdefense.com

Jessica Aberman — Richard Ivey School of Business, H.B.A. (summa cum laude), 2003; University of Miami School of Law, J.D., 2007; University of Miami, School of Business, M.B.A. (summa cum laude), 2008 — Admitted to Bar, 2010, Florida; 2012, U.S. District Court, Southern District of Florida

Tierney Conklin — University of North Carolina Wilmington, B.S., 2005; Nova Southeastern University, Shepard Broad Law Center, J.D., 2011 — Pro Bono Honors Award — Admitted to Bar, 2011, Florida — E-mail: tconklin@florida-law.com

Adam Friedman — Florida State University, B.S. (cum laude), 2008; M.S., 2009; St. Thomas University School of Law, J.D. (magna cum laude), 2012 — Admitted to Bar, 2012, Florida — E-mail: afriedman@florida-law.com

Robert B. Gertzman — Florida State University, B.S. (Dean's List), 2002; University of Baltimore, M.A. (Dean's List), 2004; Nova Southeastern University, Shepard Broad Law Center, J.D. (Dean's List), 2012 — Pro Bono Honors — Admitted to Bar, 2012, Florida — E-mail: rgertzman@vernis-bowling.com

Jaimee Goode — University of Central Florida, B.A. (with honors), 2007; Florida State University College of Law, J.D., 2010 — Admitted to Bar, 2011, Florida — E-mail: jgoode@florida-law.com

Isabel Carolina Dao — University of Florida, B.A. (cum laude), 2005; New York Law School, J.D., 2009 — Admitted to Bar, 2009, Florida — E-mail: idao@florida-law.com

Ava Mahmoudi — University of Florida, B.S., 2008; Nova Southeastern University, Shepard Broad Law Center, J.D., 2011 — Pro Bono Honors Award — Admitted to Bar, 2011, Florida — E-mail: amahmoudi@florida-law.com

Katie Shenko — Florida Atlantic University, B.A., 2008; Nova Southeastern University, Shepard Broad Law Center, J.D. (Dean's List), 2012 — Moot Court — Law Review, Nova Southeastern University — Admitted to Bar, 2013, Florida — Languages: Russian — E-mail: kshenko@florida-law.com

Erin D. Sparks — The University of Alabama, B.S., 2008; The University of Alabama School of Law, J.D., 2012 — Admitted to Bar, 2013, Florida — E-mail: esparks@florida-law.com

Robert M. Pickett — Nova Southeastern University, Shepard Broad Law Center, J.D., 2011 — Admitted to Bar, 2011, Florida

Jacqueline Zewski — Nova Southeastern University, Shepard Broad Law Center, J.D., 2012 — Admitted to Bar, 2012, Florida

Deniz S. Cankaya — University of Florida, B.A. Political Science, 2007; Florida State University College of Law, J.D., 2011 — Admitted to Bar, 2012, Florida

FLORIDA / FORT LAUDERDALE

Vernis & Bowling of Broward, P.A., Fort Lauderdale, FL (Continued)

Karin N. Mathiesen — Wellesley College, B.A., 2006; Nova Southeastern University, Shepard Broad Law Center, J.D., 2012 — Admitted to Bar, 2013, Florida

Anne Solenne-Rolland — The University of Texas at Austin, B.A., 2008; University of Miami School of Law, J.D., 2012 — Admitted to Bar, 2012, Florida; 2014, U.S. District Court, Southern District of Florida — Languages: French

Aron Rudman — Florida State University, B.A. (cum laude), 2010; Nova Southeastern University, Shepard Broad Law Center, J.D., 2013 — Admitted to Bar, 2013, Florida; 2014, U.S. District Court, Southern District of Florida — Languages: Spanish, Hebrew

Max Andres Lopez — Florida International University, B.B.A., 2008; St. Thomas University School of Law, J.D., 2012 — Admitted to Bar, 2012, Florida — Languages: Spanish

Latoya Harridon-Lodge — Stephen F. Austin State University, B.A. (magna cum laude), 2009; Nova Southeastern University, Shepard Broad Law Center, J.D., 2012 — Admitted to Bar, 2013, Florida

Jaime Martin — 1990 — Arizona State University, B.A. Political Science, 2011; University of Miami School of Law, J.D., 2013 — Admitted to Bar, 2014, Florida

Alisha N. Wilson — Texas Woman's University, B.B.A., 2002; Oklahoma City University School of Law, J.D., 2010 — Admitted to Bar, 2011, Oklahoma; 2013, Florida — E-mail: awilson@national-law.com

Alan Blose   Donna Romero
Kristin Yoder

(See listing under North Palm Beach, FL for additional information)

(Distance to Listing City Fort Lauderdale, FL: 12 Miles)

Wicker Smith O'Hara McCoy & Ford P.A.

Sun Trust Center
515 East Las Olas Boulevard, Suite 1400
Fort Lauderdale, Florida 33301
   Telephone: 954-847-4800
   Fax: 954-760-9353
   www.wickersmith.com

(Coral Gables, FL Office*(See Miami listing): 2800 Ponce de Leon Boulevard, Suite 800, 33134)
   (Tel: 305-448-3939)
   (Fax: 305-441-1745)
(Jacksonville, FL Office*: Bank of America, Suite 2700, 50 North Laura Street, 32202)
   (Tel: 904-355-0225)
   (Fax: 904-355-0226)
(Naples, FL Office*: Mercato, 9128 Strada Place, Suite 10200, 34108)
   (Tel: 239-552-5300)
   (Fax: 239-552-5399)
(Orlando, FL Office*: Bank of America Center, 390 North Orange Avenue, Suite 1000, 32801)
   (Tel: 407-843-3939)
   (Fax: 407-649-8118)
(Tampa, FL Office*: 100 North Tampa Street, Suite 1800, 33602)
   (Tel: 813-222-3939)
   (Fax: 813-222-3938)
(West Palm Beach, FL Office*: Northbridge Centre, 515 North Flagler Drive, Suite 1600, 33401)
   (Tel: 561-689-3800)
   (Fax: 561-689-9206)

Established: 1952

Wicker Smith O'Hara McCoy & Ford P.A., Fort Lauderdale, FL (Continued)

General Civil Litigation, General Civil Practice, State and Federal Courts, Accountant Malpractice, Accountants and Attorneys Liability, Administrative Law, Admiralty and Maritime Law, Agent and Brokers Errors and Omissions, Appellate Practice, Automobile, Aviation, Bad Faith, Class Actions, Commercial Litigation, Complex Litigation, Construction Litigation, Environmental Law, Estate Planning, Fraud, Hospital Malpractice, Insurance Coverage, Labor and Employment, Legal Malpractice, Medical Devices, Medical Malpractice, Nursing Home Liability, Pharmaceutical, Premises Liability, Probate, Product Liability, Professional Liability, Professional Malpractice, Special Investigative Unit Claims, Real Estate, Retail Liability, Toxic Torts, Transportation, Trucking Litigation, Trusts, Workers' Compensation, Multi-District Litigation, Sexual Abuse

Firm Profile: In 1952, Idus Q. Wicker and James A. Smith formed a partnership with the goal of providing legal services of exceptional quality to their clients. They remained partners until their retirement and life-long friends. The firm they founded has expanded to seven offices located throughout Florida in Miami, Fort Lauderdale, West Palm Beach, Orlando, Tampa, Naples and Jacksonville. Although the firm has changed in size and scope, the goal of providing exceptional legal representation has remained the same.

Clients turn to Wicker Smith when they have critical and complex litigation matters because of the firm's vast experience in complex litigation filed in State and Federal Courts. Numerous major corporations have selected Wicker Smith as national and regional counsel. Supporting the litigation team is a preeminent Appellate Department, which has appeared as appellate counsel in more than 1,200 reported decisions, including several landmark opinions issued by the Supreme Court of Florida.

Wicker Smith has recognized leaders in the defense of a wide range of litigation practice areas, including products liability, medical malpractice, pharmaceutical and medical devices, catastrophic aviation accidents, legal malpractice, accounting malpractice, nursing home claims, construction litigation, as well as a variety of general negligence matters. In all such matters, communication and attention to the client's specific needs are our highest priority. The backbone of our relationship with clients is built upon integrity and stability. We strive to establish long-term relationships with our clients, built upon a partnership of communication and trust. We achieve this objective by listening to our clients, understanding their businesses and developing legal solutions to best meet their individual needs.

Firm Members

Dennis M. O'Hara — 1943 — Muhlenberg College, B.A., 1965; Villanova University, J.D., 1968 — Admitted to Bar, 1968, Pennsylvania; 1972, Florida; 1992, Colorado; 1974, U.S. District Court, Southern District of Florida including Trial Bar — Member American, Colorado, Pennsylvania, Broward County, Dade County and Lehigh County Bar Associations; The Florida Bar; International Academy of Trial Lawyers (Board of Directors 2006-2009); Special Magistrate Village of Key Biscayne; Florida Medical Malpractice Claims Council; International Association of Defense Counsel; American Society of Law and Medicine; Florida Defense Lawyers Association; Defense Research Institute — Top Defense Lawyer in Florida by Florida Trend Magazine 2004; Florida Trend Magazine's "Florida Legal Elite" 2005 & 2006; Florida Super Lawyers 2006-2012; South Florida Legal Guide "Top Lawyers" 2005-2012; Daily Business Review's Most Effective Lawyer 2007 Finalist; Best Lawyers in America 2007-2012; Benchmark Litigation's "Litigation Stars" 2010-2011 (commercial litigation & products liability) — Practice Areas: Accountant Malpractice; Aviation; Civil Litigation; Class Actions; Commercial Litigation; Medical Devices; Medical Malpractice; Pharmaceutical; Premises Liability; Product Liability — Resident Fort Lauderdale and Miami Office

Steven Y. Leinicke — 1949 — DePauw University, B.A., 1971; University of Miami, J.D., 1973 — Admitted to Bar, 1974, Florida; 1975, U.S. District Court, Southern District of Florida including Trial Bar; 1996, U.S. District Court, Middle District of Florida; 2009, U.S. District Court, Northern District of Florida — Member American and Broward County Bar Associations; The Florida Bar; Rotary International; International Association of Defense Counsel; Defense Research Institute; Federation of Defense and Corporate Counsel; American Trial Lawyers Association; Florida Medical Malpractice Claims Council — Practice Areas: Agent and Brokers Errors and Omissions;

FORT MYERS   FLORIDA

Wicker Smith O'Hara McCoy & Ford P.A., Fort Lauderdale, FL (Continued)

Automobile Liability; Civil Litigation; Construction Litigation; Medical Devices; Medical Malpractice; Pharmaceutical; Premises Liability; Product Liability

Robert C. Bauroth — 1951 — Duke University, B.A., 1973; University of Miami, J.D., 1979 — South Florida Legal Guide's Top Lawyers in Florida for Aviation & Professional Liability, 2005-2012 — Admitted to Bar, 1979, Florida; 2002, Colorado; 1979, U.S. District Court, Southern District of Florida; 2000, U.S. District Court, Middle District of Florida including Trial Bar — Member The Florida Bar; The Colorado Bar; Broward County Bar Association; Defense Research Institute — Practice Areas: Automobile Liability; Aviation; Bad Faith; Civil Litigation; Construction Law; Insurance Coverage; Premises Liability; Product Liability; Professional Liability

Robert E. Paradela — 1964 — Florida State University, B.S., 1985; J.D./M.B.A., 1989 — Admitted to Bar, 1990, Florida; U.S. District Court, Southern District of Florida; 1992, U.S. District Court, Middle District of Florida — Member American and Broward County Bar Associations; The Florida Bar; South Florida Medical Claims Council; Defense Research Institute — Languages: Spanish — Practice Areas: Automobile Liability; Civil Litigation; Medical Malpractice; Premises Liability

Jordan Cohen — 1976 — Tulane University, B.A. (cum laude), 1997; Duke University, J.D. (cum laude), 2001 — Phi Beta Kappa — Admitted to Bar, 2002, Florida; 2003, U.S. District Court, Middle, Northern and Southern Districts of Florida — Member Broward County Bar Association; The Florida Bar; Defense Research Institute — Florida Super Lawyers "Rising Star" 2009; International "Who's Who" of Product Liability Defense Lawyers, 2012 — Practice Areas: Accountant Malpractice; Aviation; Civil Litigation; Class Actions; Commercial Litigation; Medical Devices; Pharmaceutical; Product Liability; Real Estate Litigation

Shelley H. Leinicke — 1949 — DePauw University, B.A., 1971; University of Miami, J.D., 1977 — Admitted to Bar, 1977, Florida; U.S. District Court, Southern District of Florida including Trial Bar; 1981, U.S. Court of Appeals, Fifth and Eleventh Circuits; 1990, U.S. Supreme Court; 1996, U.S. District Court, Middle District of Florida; 1999, U.S. Court of Appeals for the Federal Circuit; 2002, U.S. Court of Appeals, Third Circuit — Best Lawyers in America, 2011-2012 — Practice Areas: Accountant Malpractice; Appellate Practice; Aviation; Bad Faith; Civil Litigation; Insurance Coverage; Legal Malpractice; Medical Malpractice

C. Martin Harvey — 1949 — Presbyterian College, B.A., 1970; Wake Forest University, J.D., 1973 — Admitted to Bar, 1985, Florida; 1994, U.S. District Court, Middle District of Florida — Practice Areas: Civil Litigation; Premises Liability; Workers' Compensation

Jason A. Glusman — 1975 — University of Florida, B.A., 1997; The John Marshall Law School, J.D., 2000 — Admitted to Bar, 2000, Florida; 2006, U.S. District Court, Southern District of Florida; 2007, U.S. District Court, Northern District of Florida; 2010, U.S. District Court, Middle District of Florida — Member The Florida Bar; Broward County and Palm Beach County Bar Associations; Defense Research Institute (Retail & Hospitality Substantive Law Committee — Florida Super Lawyers "Rising Star" 2009, 2011 — Practice Areas: Aviation; Civil Litigation; Commercial Litigation; Labor and Employment; Medical Devices; Pharmaceutical; Premises Liability; Professional Liability

Kathleen O. King — 1970 — University of Virginia, B.A., 1992; St. Thomas University, J.D., 1995 — Admitted to Bar, 1996, Florida; 2009, U.S. Supreme Court — Practice Areas: Automobile Liability; Civil Litigation; Medical Malpractice; Premises Liability

H. Wayne Clark, Jr. — 1974 — The University of North Carolina, B.A., 2000; Nova Southeastern University, J.D., 2004 — Admitted to Bar, 2004, Florida; 2008, U.S. District Court, Southern District of Florida

Associates

Rafferty E. Kellogg — Cornell University, B.S., 2001; University at Buffalo, J.D., 2005 — Admitted to Bar, 2005, Florida

Jonathon S. Miller — University of California, Los Angeles, B.A., 2000; Florida State University, J.D. (cum laude), 2003 — Admitted to Bar, 2003, Florida; 2004, New Jersey

James D. Murdock, II — University of Virginia, B.A., 2002; Rutgers University School of Law, J.D., 2005 — Admitted to Bar, 2005, Florida

Robert C. Streit — University of Florida, B.A., 2001; Seton Hall University School of Law, J.D., 2004 — Admitted to Bar, 2005, New Jersey; 2008, New York; 2009, Florida

Michelle H. Zeiger — Emory University, B.B.A., 2000; University of Miami, J.D., 2003 — Admitted to Bar, 2003, Florida — Languages: Spanish

Wicker Smith O'Hara McCoy & Ford P.A., Fort Lauderdale, FL (Continued)

Christopher J. Jahr — Tulane University, B.S. (magna cum laude), 2004; University of Florida College of Law, J.D. (cum laude), 2009 — Admitted to Bar, 2009, Florida

Adam G. Wasch — University of Florida, B.S.B.A. (cum laude), 2003; Florida International University College of Law, J.D., 2009 — Admitted to Bar, 2009, Florida

Patrick K. Dahl — University of Notre Dame, B.A. (cum laude), 1999; University of Notre Dame Law School, J.D. (cum laude), 2002 — Admitted to Bar, 2002, Illinois; 2010, Florida

Erik J. Gruber — Florida State University, B.S., 2008; University of Florida College of Law, J.D., 2011 — Admitted to Bar, 2011, Florida

Joseph Apatov — The Pennsylvania State University, B.A. (with honors), 2007; Duke Law School, J.D., 2011 — Admitted to Bar, 2011, Florida

(See listing under Miami, FL for additional information)

The following firms also service this area.

Beckham & Beckham, P.A.
1550 NE Miami Gardens Drive, Suite 504
Miami, Florida 33179
Telephone: 305-957-3900
Fax: 305-940-8706

Insurance Defense, Property Damage, Transportation, Product Liability, Premises Liability, Motor Carriers, Subrogation

SEE COMPLETE LISTING UNDER MIAMI, FLORIDA (25 MILES)

Shutts & Bowen LLP
201 South Biscayne Boulevard
Suite 1500
Miami, Florida 33131
Telephone: 305-358-6300
Fax: 305-381-9982
Toll Free: 800-325-2892

Insurance Defense, Life and Health, General Liability, Fraud, Reinsurance, Disability

SEE COMPLETE LISTING UNDER MIAMI, FLORIDA (27 MILES)

Wiederhold & Moses, P.A.
560 Village Boulevard, Suite 240
West Palm Beach, Florida 33409-1963
Telephone: 561-615-6775, 954-763-5630
Fax: 561-615-7225
Mailing Address: P.O. Box 3918, West Palm Beach, FL 33402

Insurance Defense, Trial Practice

SEE COMPLETE LISTING UNDER WEST PALM BEACH, FLORIDA (40 MILES)

Young, Bill, Roumbos & Boles, P.A.
One Biscayne Tower, Suite 3195
2 South Biscayne Boulevard
Miami, Florida 33131
Telephone: 305-222-7720
Fax: 305-492-7729

Insurance Defense, Coverage Issues, Complex Litigation, Bad Faith, Product Liability, Medical Malpractice, Nursing Home Liability, Construction Defect, Premises Liability, General Liability, Automobile Liability

SEE COMPLETE LISTING UNDER MIAMI, FLORIDA (28 MILES)

FORT MYERS   † 62,298 Lee Co.

Conroy Simberg
4315 Metro Parkway, Suite 250
Fort Myers, Florida 33916-7950
Telephone: 239-337-1101
Fax: 239-334-3383
E-Mail: csg@conroysimberg.com
www.conroysimberg.com

FLORIDA — FORT MYERS

Conroy Simberg, Fort Myers, FL (Continued)

Insurance Defense, Appellate Practice, Insurance Coverage, Environmental Law, Governmental Liability, Civil Rights, Wrongful Termination, Americans with Disabilities Act, Sexual Harassment, Land Use, Commercial Law, Fire, Arson, Fraud, Fidelity and Surety, Automobile Liability, Admiralty and Maritime Law, Bad Faith, Employment Law, Self-Insured, Public Entities, Product Liability, Casualty, Excess and Reinsurance, Accident and Health, Workers' Compensation, Medical Malpractice, Class Actions, Construction Defect, Construction Litigation, First Party Matters, Premises Liability, Professional Liability, Intellectual Property

(See listing under Hollywood, FL for additional information)

Henderson, Franklin, Starnes & Holt
Professional Association

1715 Monroe Street
Fort Myers, Florida 33901
Telephone: 239-344-1100
Fax: 239-344-1200
E-Mail: info@henlaw.com
www.henlaw.com

(Sanibel, FL Office: 1648 Periwinkle Way, Suite B, 33957)
  (Tel: 239-472-6700)
  (Fax: 239-472-5129)
(Bonita Springs, FL Office: 3451 Bonita Bay Boulevard, Suite 206, 34134)
  (Tel: 239-498-6222)
  (Fax: 239-498-6225)
(Naples, FL Office: 999 Vanderbilt Beach Road, Suite 200, Fifth Third Bank Building, 34108)
  (Tel: 239-325-5010)

Established: 1924

Construction Litigation, Employment Law, Municipal Law, Professional Malpractice, Tort Litigation, Workers' Compensation

Firm Profile: Henderson, Franklin, Starnes & Holt, P.A. is located in the Southwest Florida communities of Fort Myers, Bonita Springs, Sanibel and Naples*. Founded in 1924, Henderson Franklin is one of the oldest and largest law firms between Tampa and Miami.

We continue to nurture and foster the sentiments of our founders in providing dedicated and quality service to the firm's clients and to support and participate in civic and charitable organizations and community activities. These commitments have provided Henderson Franklin with a reputation of ethical conduct and professionalism.

We anticipate the future needs of our clients by planning for substantial growth in all areas of practice. The firm continues to keep pace with technological advances, affording our clients legal counsel, quickly and efficiently. Henderson Franklin is committed to the growth of the area and is ideally suited to meet the challenges of the future.

Corporate Clients

Better Roads, Inc.
Goodwill Industries of Southwest Florida
Merck & Company, Inc.
Pella Corporation
Publix Super Markets, Inc.
RWA Consulting Inc.
TRC Worldwide Engineering, Inc.
Wal-Mart Stores, Inc.
Deloitte, LLP
Hess Corporation
Johnson Engineering, Inc.
Michelin North America, Inc.
Philip Morris USA, Inc.
Radiation Therapy Services, Inc.
Stantec, Inc. (f/k/a WilsonMiller, Inc.)

Insurance Clients

ACE/ACE Westchester
Allied World Assurance Company
AIG
Amerisure Companies

Henderson, Franklin, Starnes & Holt, Professional Association, Fort Myers, FL (Continued)

Amica Mutual Insurance Company
Berkley Risk Administrators Company, LLC
Cincinnati Financial Corporation
Crawford & Company
FCCI Insurance Company
Florida Doctors Insurance Company
Gallagher Bassett Services, Inc.
Houston Casualty Company
ITT Specialty Risk Services, Inc.
Liberty Mutual Insurance
Medmarc Insurance Group
OneBeacon Insurance
PMA Insurance Group
Public Risk Management of Florida
Summit Claims Management
United States Liability Insurance Company
Beazley Group
Brown & Brown/Lawyer's Protector Plan
CNA Insurance Companies
Farmer's Insurance/21st Century Insurance Group
Florida Lawyers Mutual Insurance Company
GEICO
Hunt Insurance Group
Johns Eastern Company, Inc.
Markel Corporation
Nautilus Insurance Company
Philadelphia Insurance Company
ProAssurance Group
Rental Insurance Services
Travelers
XL Capital Group
York Claims Service, Inc.

Department Chairs

Michael J. Corso — Tort & Insurance Litigation Department Chair — 1949 — Purdue University, B.S.A.E., 1971; Villanova University, J.D., 1974 — Admitted to Bar, 1974, Pennsylvania; 1977, Florida; 1975, U.S. Court of Military Appeals; 1978, U.S. Supreme Court; U.S. District Court, Middle, Northern and Southern Districts of Florida — Member Federal, American, Collier and Lee County (President, 1984-1985) Bar Associations; The Florida Bar; Florida Defense Lawyers Association (Past President); Defense Research Institute; Federation of Defense and Corporate Counsel — National Board of Trial Advocacy Certified Civil Trial Advocate; Board Certified Civil Trial and Business Litigation Lawyer, The Florida Bar — Captain, JAG, U.S. Air Force, active duty, 1974-1978 — Practice Areas: Professional Liability (Non-Medical) Defense; Product Liability — E-mail: michael.corso@henlaw.com

David H. Roos — Workers' Compensation Department Chair — 1968 — University of South Florida, B.A., 1991; Nova Southeastern University, J.D. (cum laude), 1999 — Admitted to Bar, 1999, Florida — Member The Florida Bar; Defense Research Institute; Florida Defense Lawyers Association — Practice Areas: Workers' Compensation — E-mail: david.roos@henlaw.com

Insurance Litigation Partners

J. Matthew Belcastro — 1972 — Haverford College, B.A., 1994; University of Florida, J.D. (with honors), 1997 — Admitted to Bar, 1998, Florida; U.S. District Court, Middle District of Florida; U.S. Court of Appeals for the Federal and Eleventh Circuits; U.S. Supreme Court — Member The Florida Bar; Florida Defense Lawyers Association; Defense Research Institute — Practice Areas: Construction Litigation; Construction Defect; Contracts; Appellate Practice — E-mail: matthew.belcastro@henlaw.com

Kelly Spillman Jablonski — 1967 — Stetson University, B.A., 1988; J.D., 1991 — Admitted to Bar, 1992, Pennsylvania; 2004, Florida — Member The Florida Bar — Practice Areas: Personal Injury Litigation; Tort Claims Defense — E-mail: kelly.jablonski@henlaw.com

William O. Kratochvil — 1971 — University of Florida, B.A. (with honors), 1977; University of Florida, Levin College of Law, J.D. (with honors), 2000 — Admitted to Bar, 2000, Florida — Member The Florida Bar — United States Marine Corps — Practice Areas: Civil Rights; Construction Litigation; Insurance Litigation; Personal Injury; Tort Litigation; Wrongful Death — Tel: william.kratochvil@henlaw.com

Traci T. McKee — 1978 — University of North Florida, B.B.A. (summa cum laude), 2000; Stetson University College of Law, J.D. (summa cum laude), 2007 — Admitted to Bar, 2008, Florida; U.S. District Court, Middle District of Florida — Member The Florida Bar; Florida Defense Lawyers Association (Co-Chair, Young Lawyer's Committee); Defense Research Institute — Practice Areas: Professional Liability (Non-Medical) Defense; Tort Claims Defense — E-mail: traci.mckee@henlaw.com

Mark Schultz — 1966 — James Madison University, B.A. (summa cum laude), 1989; University of Florida, J.D., 2002 — Admitted to Bar, 2002, Florida; U.S. District Court, Middle District of Florida — Member The Florida Bar — Practice Areas: Design Professionals; Construction Litigation; Tort Claims Defense — E-mail: mark.schultz@henlaw.com

Robert C. Shearman — 1961 — Emory University, B.A., 1983; Florida State University, J.D. (cum laude), 1986 — Admitted to Bar, 1986, Florida; 1987, U.S. Court of Appeals, Eleventh Circuit; U.S. District Court, Middle and Southern Districts of Florida — Member Federal, American and Lee County Bar Associations; The Florida Bar; Florida Defense Lawyers Association; Association of Defense Trial Attorneys — Florida Bar Board Certified Civil

Henderson, Franklin, Starnes & Holt, Professional Association, Fort Myers, FL (Continued)

Trial Lawyer; Florida Supreme Court Certified Civil Mediator — Practice Areas: Employment Law; Civil Rights; Municipal Litigation; Real Estate Errors and Omissions — E-mail: robert.shearman@henlaw.com

Bruce M. Stanley, Sr. — 1948 — College of William & Mary, A.B. (with high honors), 1970; University of Virginia, J.D., 1974 — Admitted to Bar, 1974, Florida; 1975, U.S. Court of Appeals, Fifth Circuit; 1978, U.S. Supreme Court; 1981, U.S. Court of Appeals, Eleventh Circuit; U.S. District Court, Middle and Southern Districts of Florida including Trial Bar — Member The Florida Bar; Defense Research Institute; Florida Defense Lawyers Association; International Association of Defense Counsel; Lawyer-Pilots Bar Association — Florida Bar Board Certified Civil Trial Lawyer — Practice Areas: Medical Malpractice; Aviation; Administrative Law; Tort Claims Defense; Product Liability — E-mail: bruce.stanley@henlaw.com

Insurance Litigation Associates

Richard B. Akin — 1985 — Florida State University, B.S., 2006; Florida State University College of Law, J.D. (with high honors), 2009 — Admitted to Bar, 2009, Florida — Member The Florida Bar — Practice Areas: Tort Claims Defense — E-mail: richard.akin@henlaw.com

Robert Anderson — 1981 — The University of Georgia, B.A., 2006; University of Florida, Levin College of Law, J.D. (cum laude), 2009 — Admitted to Bar, 2009, Florida — Member The Florida Bar; Florida Defense Lawyers Association; Defense Research Institute — Non-Commissioned Officer, United States Marine Corps Reserve — Practice Areas: Tort Claims Defense — E-mail: robert.anderson@henlaw.com

William Boltrek III — 1975 — University at Buffalo, B.A., 1977; Quinnipiac University, J.D., 2000 — Admitted to Bar, 2012, Florida; 2000, New York — Member The Florida Bar; Defense Research Institute; Florida Defense Lawyers Association — Practice Areas: Tort Claims Defense — E-mail: william.boltrek@henlaw.com

John M. Miller — 1980 — University of Florida, B.A., 2004; Stetson University College of Law, J.D. (cum laude), 2008 — Admitted to Bar, 2008, Florida; U.S. District Court, Middle, Northern and Southern Districts of Florida — Member The Florida Bar; Florida Defense Lawyers Association; Defense Research Institute — Practice Areas: Tort Litigation; Municipal Litigation — E-mail: john.miller@henlaw.com

Stefani C. Norrbin — 1987 — Florida State University, B.A. (summa cum laude), 2008; Florida State College of Law, J.D. (magna cum laude), 2011 — Admitted to Bar, 2011, Florida — Member Florida Defense Lawyers Association; Defense Research Institute — Practice Areas: Tort Claims Defense — E-mail: stefani.norrbin@henlaw.com

Workers' Compensation

Michael E. McCabe — 1970 — Florida Gulf Coast University, B.A. (summa cum laude), 2000; University of Florida, Levin College of Law, J.D. (cum laude), 2004 — Admitted to Bar, 2004, Florida; U.S. Court of Appeals for the Federal and First Circuits — Member The Florida Bar (Workers' Compensation Section) — Former Russian Linguist — United States Navy — Practice Areas: Workers' Compensation; Appellate Practice — E-mail: michael.mccabe@henlaw.com

Mark Trank — 1956 — Yale University, B.A., 1979; University of Virginia School of Law, J.D., 1990 — Admitted to Bar, 1990, Pennsylvania (Inactive); 1991, Virginia (Inactive); 2008, Florida; U.S. District Court, Middle District of Florida; U.S. Court of Appeals, Third and Fourth Circuits — Member American Bar Association (Litigation and Labor & Employment Law Sections); The Florida Bar (Labor & Employment Section) — Practice Areas: Workers' Compensation; Education Law; Governmental Liability — E-mail: mark.trank@henlaw.com

Vernis & Bowling of Southwest Florida, P.A.

2369 West 1st Street
Fort Myers, Florida 33901-3309
   Telephone: 239-334-3035
   Fax: 239-334-7702
   E-Mail: info@florida-law.com
   www.florida-law.com

Established: 1970

Vernis & Bowling of Southwest Florida, P.A., Fort Myers, FL (Continued)

Civil Litigation, Insurance Law, Workers' Compensation, Premises Liability, Labor and Employment, Civil Rights, Commercial Litigation, Complex Litigation, Product Liability, Directors and Officers Liability, Errors and Omissions, Construction Law, Construction Defect, Environmental Liability, Personal and Commercial Vehicle, Appellate Practice, Admiralty and Maritime Law, Real Estate, Family Law, Elder Law, Liability Defense, SIU/Fraud Litigation, Education Law (ESE/IDEA), Property and Casualty (Commercial and Personal Lines), Long-Haul Trucking Liability, Government Law, Public Law, Criminal, White Collar, Business Litigation

Firm Profile: Since 1970, VERNIS & BOWLING has represented individuals, businesses, professionals, insurance carriers, self-insureds, brokers, underwriters, agents, PEOs and insured. We provide cost effective, full service, legal representation that consistently exceeds the expectations of our clients. With 115 attorneys throughout 16 offices located in Florida, Georgia, Alabama, North Carolina and Mississippi the firm is able to provide the benefits of a large organization, including a management team, consistent policies and representation to ensure personal service and local representation to our clients.

Firm Members

Steve B. Sundook — 1956 — University of Massachusetts, B.S., 1978; University of Miami, J.D., 1982 — Admitted to Bar, 1982, Florida — Member American, Dade County and Lee County Bar Associations; The Florida Bar

Terrence L. Lavy — 1967 — State University of New York, B.S. (Dean's List), 1989; Rutgers University, J.D., 1993 — Admitted to Bar, 1993, Pennsylvania; New Jersey; 2005, Florida

Cassius R. Borel — 1976 — The University of Alabama, B.A. Political Science, 1999; Nova Southeastern University, Shepard Broad Law Center, J.D., 2003 — Admitted to Bar, 2004, Florida; 2005, Alabama — Practice Areas: Automobile Liability; Workers' Compensation; Product Liability; Construction Litigation; Employment Law

Kristin L. Stocks — 1981 — The University of North Carolina, B.A. Political Science, 2003; Florida Coastal School of Law, J.D., 2007 — Admitted to Bar, 2007, Florida

Alexis Barkis

(See listing under Miami, FL for additional information)

The following firms also service this area.

Abbey, Adams, Byelick & Mueller, L.L.P.
360 Central Avenue, 11th Floor
St. Petersburg, Florida 33701
   Telephone: 727-821-2080
   Fax: 727-822-3970
Mailing Address: P.O. Box 1511, St. Petersburg, FL 33731

Administrative Law, Americans with Disabilities Act, Appellate Practice, Complex Litigation, General Defense, Employment Law, Bad Faith, Insurance Coverage, Insurance Fraud, Uninsured and Underinsured Motorist, Professional Malpractice, Mediation, Negligence, Personal Injury, Premises Liability, Product Liability, Subrogation, Toxic Torts, Workers' Compensation, Motor Vehicle Liability, Defense of Insureds, Sovereign Immunity and Governmental Defense

SEE COMPLETE LISTING UNDER ST. PETERSBURG, FLORIDA (106 MILES)

FLORIDA

Barker & Cook, PA
501 East Kennedy Boulevard, Suite 790
Tampa, Florida 33602
   Telephone: 813-489-1001
   Fax: 813-489-1008
   Toll Free: 888-892-8722

Insurance Defense, Self-Insured, Trial and Appellate Practice, State and Federal Courts, First and Third Party Defense, Automobile, Casualty, Construction Law, Engineers, Malpractice, Environmental Law, General Liability, Life and Health, Medical Malpractice, Product Liability, Property, Reinsurance, Workers' Compensation, Civil Litigation, Commercial Litigation, Personal Injury, Premises Liability, Contract Disputes, Labor and Employment, Construction Disputes, Insurance Coverage Disputes

SEE COMPLETE LISTING UNDER TAMPA, FLORIDA (120 MILES)

Young, Bill, Roumbos & Boles, P.A.
One Biscayne Tower, Suite 3195
2 South Biscayne Boulevard
Miami, Florida 33131
   Telephone: 305-222-7720
   Fax: 305-492-7729

Insurance Defense, Coverage Issues, Complex Litigation, Bad Faith, Product Liability, Medical Malpractice, Nursing Home Liability, Construction Defect, Premises Liability, General Liability, Automobile Liability

SEE COMPLETE LISTING UNDER MIAMI, FLORIDA (153 MILES)

FORT PIERCE † 41,590 St. Lucie Co.

Refer To

Conroy Simberg
3440 Hollywood Boulevard, Second Floor
Hollywood, Florida 33021
   Telephone: 954-961-1400
   Fax: 954-967-8577

Insurance Defense, Appellate Practice, Insurance Coverage, Environmental Law, Governmental Liability, Civil Rights, Wrongful Termination, Americans with Disabilities Act, Sexual Harassment, Land Use, Commercial Law, Fire, Arson, Fraud, Fidelity and Surety, Automobile Liability, Admiralty and Maritime Law, Bad Faith, Employment Law, Self-Insured, Public Entities, Product Liability, Casualty, Excess and Reinsurance, Accident and Health, Workers' Compensation, Medical Malpractice, Class Actions, Construction Defect, Construction Litigation, First Party Matters, Premises Liability, Professional Liability, Intellectual Property

SEE COMPLETE LISTING UNDER HOLLYWOOD, FLORIDA (105 MILES)

Refer To

Wiederhold & Moses, P.A.
560 Village Boulevard, Suite 240
West Palm Beach, Florida 33409-1963
   Telephone: 561-615-6775, 954-763-5630
   Fax: 561-615-7225

Mailing Address: P.O. Box 3918, West Palm Beach, FL 33402

Insurance Defense, Trial Practice

SEE COMPLETE LISTING UNDER WEST PALM BEACH, FLORIDA (56 MILES)

FORT WALTON BEACH 19,507 Okaloosa Co.

Refer To

Barron & Redding, P.A.
220 McKenzie Avenue
Panama City, Florida 32401-3129
   Telephone: 850-785-7454
   Fax: 850-785-2999

Mailing Address: P.O. Box 2467, Panama City, FL 32402-2467

Casualty, Surety, Fire, Life Insurance, Professional Liability, Product Liability, Medical Malpractice, Environmental Law, Automobile Liability, Premises Liability, Business Torts, Construction Law

SEE COMPLETE LISTING UNDER PANAMA CITY, FLORIDA (63 MILES)

FORT PIERCE

Refer To

Matthews, Higgins, Hausfeld & Fenimore
114 East Gregory Street
Pensacola, Florida 32502-4970
   Telephone: 850-434-2200
   Fax: 850-434-2600

Mailing Address: P.O. Box 13145, Pensacola, FL 32591-3145

Personal Injury, Wrongful Death, Defense Litigation, Insurance Coverage, Commercial Litigation, Automobile Liability, Premises Liability, Product Liability, Professional Malpractice, Subrogation, Employment Law, Bad Faith, Casualty Defense, Real Estate Litigation, Construction Litigation, Directors and Officers Liability, Insurance Defense, Mediation, Condominium Litigation

SEE COMPLETE LISTING UNDER PENSACOLA, FLORIDA (40 MILES)

Refer To

Vernis & Bowling of Northwest Florida, P.A.
315 South Palafox Street
Pensacola, Florida 32502
   Telephone: 850-433-5461
   Fax: 850-432-0166

Civil Litigation, Insurance Law, Workers' Compensation, Premises Liability, Labor and Employment, Civil Rights, Commercial Litigation, Complex Litigation, Product Liability, Directors and Officers Liability, Errors and Omissions, Construction Law, Construction Defect, Environmental Liability, Personal and Commercial Vehicle, Appellate Practice, Admiralty and Maritime Law, Real Estate, Family Law, Elder Law, Liability Defense, SIU/Fraud Litigation, Education Law (ESE/IDEA), Property and Casualty (Commercial and Personal Lines), Long-Haul Trucking Liability, Government Law, Public Law, Criminal, White Collar, Business Litigation

SEE COMPLETE LISTING UNDER PENSACOLA, FLORIDA (40 MILES)

Refer To

Wade, Palmer & Shoemaker, P.A.
14 North Palafox Street
Pensacola, Florida 32502
   Telephone: 850-429-0755
   Fax: 850-429-0871
   Toll Free: 888-980-0755

Mailing Address: P.O. Box 13510, Pensacola, FL 32591-3510

Insurance Defense, Automobile Liability, Product Liability, Bodily Injury, Coverage Issues, Subrogation, Property and Casualty, Construction Law, General Liability, Litigation, Employment Law, Employment Discrimination

SEE COMPLETE LISTING UNDER PENSACOLA, FLORIDA (40 MILES)

Refer To

Young, Bill, Roumbos & Boles, P.A.
Seville Tower, 7th Floor
226 South Palafox Place
Pensacola, Florida 32502
   Telephone: 850-432-2222
   Fax: 850-432-1444

Mailing Address: P.O. Drawer 1070, Pensacola, FL 32591-1070

Insurance Defense, Coverage Issues, Complex Litigation, Bad Faith, Product Liability, Medical Malpractice, Nursing Home Liability, Construction Defect, Premises Liability, General Liability, Automobile Liability

SEE COMPLETE LISTING UNDER PENSACOLA, FLORIDA (40 MILES)

GAINESVILLE † 124,354 Alachua Co.

Dell Graham, P.A.
203 Northeast First Street
Gainesville, Florida 32601
   Telephone: 352-372-4381
   Fax: 352-376-7415
   E-Mail: firm@dellgraham.com
   www.dellgraham.com

Insurance Defense, Civil Trial Practice, State and Federal Courts, Automobile, Medical Malpractice, Product Liability, Governmental Liability, Property and Casualty

GAINESVILLE   FLORIDA

Dell Graham, P.A., Gainesville, FL   (Continued)

Firm Profile: We, the lawyers and staff at the law firm of Dell Graham, are committed to providing our clients top quality legal representation in the most cost-effective manner possible. It has been that way for over 100 Years.

We concentrate our practice defending clients in civil litigation matters in North Central Florida. We represent individuals and small businesses, as well as some of America's largest health care providers and insurance companies.

At Dell Graham, our goal is to achieve the best result possible for you, our valued client. And, we pledge to do so in a highly professional and cost-effective manner.

Dell Graham. Committed to integrity, results and value.

Insurance Clients

American Modern Insurance Group, Inc.
The Equitable Life Assurance Society of the United States
Florida Police Chief's Self-Insurance Fund
General Accident Insurance Company
The Harleysville Insurance
Metropolitan Life Insurance Company
Northwestern National Insurance Company
The St. Paul Companies
Sentry Insurance a Mutual Company
State Auto Insurance Company
TIG Insurance Company
Cotton States Mutual Insurance Company
Florida Farm Bureau General Insurance Company
Florida Select Insurance Company
Gallagher Bassett Services, Inc.
Government Employees Insurance Company
Health Care Indemnity, Inc.
National Casualty Company
Nationwide Insurance
Risk Enterprise Management, Ltd.
Safeco Insurance Companies
Scottsdale Insurance Company
Southern Guaranty Insurance Company
State Farm Insurance Company
Westfield Insurance Company

Non-Insurance Clients

Alachua County School Board
Florida Community College
National Car Rental
University of Florida
City of Gainesville
MMI Companies Group
North East Florida Educational Consortium

Members of the Firm

Sam T. Dell — (1921-1992)

L. William Graham — (Retired)

Joe C. Willcox — (Retired)

W. Henry Barber, Jr. — (Retired)

John D. Jopling — 1957 — University of Florida, J.D. (with honors), 1982 — Admitted to Bar, 1982, Florida; 1984, U.S. District Court, Northern District of Florida; 1985, U.S. District Court, Middle District of Florida; 1994, U.S. Court of Appeals, Eleventh Circuit; 2003, U.S. Supreme Court — Member Federal and American Bar Associations; Fellow, American College of Trial Lawyers; Florida Defense Lawyers Association; International Association of Defense Counsel; American Board of Trial Advocates; Association of Defense Trial Attorneys — Florida Bar Board Certified Civil Trial Lawyer — E-mail: jjopling@dellgraham.com

Carl B. Schwait — 1950 — University of Rochester, B.A., 1972; University of Miami, J.D., 1976 — Inn of Court — Admitted to Bar, 1976, Florida; 1977, U.S. District Court, Southern District of Florida; 1977, U.S. Court of Appeals, Fifth and Eleventh Circuits — Member The Florida Bar (Board of Governors); Eighth Judicial Circuit Bar Association (President 2003-2004); American College of Barristers; Florida Defense Lawyers Association; National Institute of Trial Advocacy; American Board of Trial Advocates; Defense Research Institute — Florida Bar Board Certified Civil Trial Lawyer; National Board Certified Trial Advocate — Practice Areas: Civil Litigation — E-mail: cschwait@dellgraham.com

Ellen R. Gershow — 1951 — University of Wisconsin, B.A., 1973; University of Miami, J.D. (magna cum laude), 1976; University of Florida, LL.M., 1983 — Admitted to Bar, 1976, Ohio; 1977, Florida — Member The Florida Bar; Eighth Judicial Circuit Bar Association — Practice Areas: Business Law; Corporate Law — E-mail: egershow@dellgraham.com

Jennifer Cates Lester — 1967 — University of Florida, B.A., 1989; J.D. (with honors), 1992 — Admitted to Bar, 1992, Florida; 1994, U.S. District Court, Middle and Northern Districts of Florida; 1995, U.S. Court of Appeals, Eleventh Circuit — Member The Florida Bar (Health Law and Litigation Sections); Eighth Judicial Circuit Bar Association (President, Young Lawyers Division, 1996-1997; Board of Directors, 1997-2002; President, 2000-2001);

Dell Graham, P.A., Gainesville, FL   (Continued)

Florida Defense Lawyers Association; Bench/Bar Committee (2000-Present); Defense Research Institute — Practice Areas: Appellate Practice; Insurance Defense; Personal Injury; Wrongful Death — E-mail: jlester@dellgraham.com

David M. Delaney — 1971 — Baylor University, B.A., 1994; University of Florida, J.D. (with honors), 1997 — Admitted to Bar, 1997, Florida; 1999, U.S. District Court, Middle and Northern Districts of Florida — Member Federal Bar Association; The Florida Bar; Eighth Judicial Circuit Bar Association — Reported Cases: Winslow v. School Board of Alachua County, No. SC10-2459, Oral Argument Supreme Court of Florida 2012 — AV Preeminent Rating Martindale Hubbell; Florida SuperLawyers Rising Star, 2011 — Board Certified, Florida Bar Board of Legal Specialization and Education — Practice Areas: Governmental Liability; Medical Malpractice; Personal Injury — E-mail: ddelaney@dellgraham.com

Susan M. Seigle — Michigan State University, B.A. (cum laude), 1969; University of South Florida, M.Ed. (cum laude, with highest honors), 1979; University of Florida, J.D. (cum laude), 1986 — Admitted to Bar, 1986, Florida; U.S. District Court, Middle and Northern Districts of Florida; U.S. Court of Appeals, Fourth and Eleventh Circuits — Member American Bar Association; The Florida Bar; Eighth Judicial Circuit Bar Association — Certified Circuit Civil Mediator, Florida Supreme Court — Practice Areas: Commercial Litigation; Education Law; Insurance Defense; Insurance Litigation; Appeals; Business Litigation; Civil Litigation; Construction Defect — E-mail: sseigle@dellgraham.com

Associates

Kevin A. McNeill — **Senior Associate** — 1970 — University of Florida, B.A., 1997; Nova Southeastern University, J.D., 2001 — Admitted to Bar, 2002, Florida; 2004, U.S. District Court, Northern District of Florida; 2010, U.S. District Court, Middle District of Florida including Trial Bar — Practice Areas: Property Damage; Premises Liability; Insurance Defense — E-mail: kmcneill@dellgraham.com

Andrew A. Morey
Charles B. Koval
Elizabeth A. McFarland
Michael D. Pierce

McConnaughhay, Duffy, Coonrod, Pope & Weaver, P.A.

2790 NW 43rd Street, Suite 300
Gainesville, Florida 32606
Telephone: 352-378-4422
Fax: 352-378-7826
www.mcconnaughhay.com

(Additional Offices: Tallahassee, FL*; Fort Lauderdale, FL*; Jacksonville, FL*; Ocala, FL*; Panama City, FL*; Pensacola, FL*; Sarasota, FL*)

Insurance Defense, Workers' Compensation, Product Liability, Labor and Employment, Civil Litigation, Trial Practice, Appellate Practice

Firm Member

Sean S. O'Connor — University of Florida, J.D., 1990 — Admitted to Bar, 1992, Florida — Practice Areas: Workers' Compensation

Associate

Laura A. Buck

FLORIDA

HOLLYWOOD

The following firms also service this area.

Barker & Cook, PA
501 East Kennedy Boulevard, Suite 790
Tampa, Florida 33602
  Telephone: 813-489-1001
  Fax: 813-489-1008
  Toll Free: 888-892-8722

Insurance Defense, Self-Insured, Trial and Appellate Practice, State and Federal Courts, First and Third Party Defense, Automobile, Casualty, Construction Law, Engineers, Malpractice, Environmental Law, General Liability, Life and Health, Medical Malpractice, Product Liability, Property, Reinsurance, Workers' Compensation, Civil Litigation, Commercial Litigation, Personal Injury, Premises Liability, Contract Disputes, Labor and Employment, Construction Disputes, Insurance Coverage Disputes

SEE COMPLETE LISTING UNDER TAMPA, FLORIDA (128 MILES)

Vernis & Bowling of Central Florida, P.A.
1450 South Woodland Boulevard, Fourth Floor
DeLand, Florida 32720
  Telephone: 386-734-2505
  Fax: 386-734-3441

Civil Litigation, Insurance Law, Workers' Compensation, Premises Liability, Labor and Employment, Civil Rights, Commercial Litigation, Complex Litigation, Product Liability, Directors and Officers Liability, Errors and Omissions, Construction Law, Construction Defect, Environmental Liability, Personal and Commercial Vehicle, Appellate Practice, Admiralty and Maritime Law, Real Estate, Family Law, Elder Law, Liability Defense, SIU/Fraud Litigation, Education Law (ESE/IDEA), Property and Casualty (Commercial and Personal Lines), Long-Haul Trucking Liability, Government Law, Public Law, Criminal, White Collar, Business Litigation

SEE COMPLETE LISTING UNDER DAYTONA BEACH, FLORIDA (101 MILES)

HOLLYWOOD 140,768 Broward Co.

Conroy Simberg

3440 Hollywood Boulevard, Second Floor
Hollywood, Florida 33021
  Telephone: 954-961-1400
  Fax: 954-967-8577
  E-Mail: csg@conroysimberg.com
  www.conroysimberg.com

(Fort Myers, FL Office*: 4315 Metro Parkway, Suite 250, 33916-7950)
  (Tel: 239-337-1101)
  (Fax: 239-334-3383)
(Jacksonville, FL Office*: 4887 Belfort Road, Suite 103, 32256)
  (Tel: 904-296-6004)
  (Fax: 904-296-6008)
(Miami, FL Office*: 9155 South Dadeland Boulevard, Suite 1000, 33156)
  (Tel: 305-373-2888)
  (Fax: 305-373-2889)
(Naples, FL Office*: 5100 North Tamiami Trail, Suite 125, 34103)
  (Tel: 239-263-0663)
  (Fax: 239-263-0960)
(Orlando, FL Office*: 2 South Orange Avenue, Suite 300, 32801)
  (Tel: 407-649-9797)
  (Fax: 407-649-1968)
(Pensacola, FL Office*: 125 West Romana Street, Suite 320, 32502)
  (Tel: 850-436-6605)
  (Fax: 850-436-2102)
(West Palm Beach, FL Office*: 1801 Centrepark Drive East, Suite 200, 33401)
  (Tel: 561-697-8088)
  (Fax: 561-697-8664)
(Tallahassee, FL Office*: 325 John Knox Road, Atrium Building, Suite 105, 32303)
  (Tel: 850-383-9103)
  (Fax: 850-383-9109)
(Tampa, FL Office*: 201 East Kennedy Boulevard, Suite 900, 33602)
  (Tel: 813-273-6464)
  (Fax: 813-273-6465)

Conroy Simberg, Hollywood, FL (Continued)

Established: 1979

Insurance Defense, Appellate Practice, Insurance Coverage, Environmental Law, Governmental Liability, Civil Rights, Wrongful Termination, Americans with Disabilities Act, Sexual Harassment, Land Use, Commercial Law, Fire, Arson, Fraud, Fidelity and Surety, Automobile Liability, Admiralty and Maritime Law, Bad Faith, Employment Law, Self-Insured, Public Entities, Product Liability, Casualty, Excess and Reinsurance, Accident and Health, Workers' Compensation, Medical Malpractice, Class Actions, Construction Defect, Construction Litigation, First Party Matters, Premises Liability, Professional Liability, Intellectual Property

Insurance Clients

Accredited Surety & Casualty Company, Inc. Columbus
Agricultural Excess and Surplus Insurance Company
All Risk Claims Service, Inc.
American Interstate Insurance Company
American Southern Insurance Company
ARI Mutual Insurance Company
Associated Risk Services Corporation
Berkley Risk Administrators Company, LLC
Burlington Insurance Company
Capacity Insurance Company
Carl Warren & Company
CGU Insurance Company
Church Mutual Insurance Company
Claims Associates, Inc.
CNA Claim Plus
CNA Insurance Company
Colorado Casualty Insurance Company
Constitution State Service Company
Cornerstone National Insurance Company
Crum & Forster Insurance Group
Cunningham Lindsey U.S., Inc.
Electric Insurance Company
Employers Mutual Insurance Company
ESIS
Everest National Insurance Company
Executive Risk Management Associates
Farmers Insurance Group
Federated National Insurance Company
Fidelity National Title Insurance Company
First Floridian Auto and Home Insurance Company
GAB Robins North America, Inc.
Gallagher Bassett Services, Inc.
Georgia Casualty & Surety Company
Guarantee Insurance Company
Harbin Adjustment Company
HDI-Gerling America Insurance Company
Insurance Corporation of New York
Jefferson Insurance Group
Kemper Insurance Companies
Liberty Mutual Group
Lopez Claim Management
Markel Shand, Inc.
Marriott Claims Service
Mercury Insurance Company
Michigan Millers Mutual Insurance Company
Montgomery Insurance Companies

AFLAC - American Family Life Assurance Company of
AIG
Allied Adjusters, Inc.
American Claim Service, Inc.
American National Insurance Company
American States Insurance Company
Associated Claims Enterprises, Inc.
Atlantic Mutual Companies
Bankers Insurance Company
Brandan Insurance
Brownyard Claims Management, Inc.
Capitol Indemnity Corporation
Casualty Underwriters, Inc.
Chubb Group of Insurance Companies
Claims Service Bureau of New York
CNL/Insurance America, Inc.
Commerce Protective Insurance Company
Continental Loss Adjusting Services
Country-Wide Insurance Company
Crawford & Company
CSC Claims Company
Custard Insurance Adjusters, Inc.
Empire All City Insurance Company
Employers Reinsurance Corporation
Excess Insurance Company Limited
FACCA Self-Insurers Fund
F.A. Richard & Associates, Inc.
FAWA Self Insurers
Fidelity and Deposit Company of Maryland
Fireman's Fund Insurance Companies
First Southeast Risk Management
Florida Hospitality Mutual Insurance Company
General Insurance Company
Great American Insurance Company
Gulf Insurance Company
The Hartford Insurance Group
The Horace Mann Companies
ING Canada
Insurance Servicing & Adjusting Company
Johns Eastern Company, Inc.
Lexington Insurance Company
Lloyd's
Lyndon Property Insurance Company
Meadowbrook/Star Insurance
MetLife Auto & Home
Mid-Continent Group
Midwestern Insurance Company
National Casualty Company

HOLLYWOOD / FLORIDA

Conroy Simberg, Hollywood, FL (Continued)

National Chiropractic Mutual Insurance Company
National Union Fire Insurance Company of Pittsburgh, PA
New England Reinsurance Corporation
Northbrook Property and Casualty Insurance Company
Occidental Insurance Company
Old Republic Security Assurance Company
Palm Beach County Risk Management
Penn Treaty Network America Insurance Company
Pioneer State Mutual Insurance Company
Property Casualty Insurers Association of America
The Protective National Insurance Company of Omaha
QBE Reinsurance Corporation
Regal Claims Services
RSKCo Claims Services, Inc.
St. Paul Fire and Marine Insurance Company
Scott Wetzel Services, Inc.
Sedgwick CMS
Sentry Claims Services
Society National Insurance Company
Star Casualty Insurance Company, Inc.
Superior Insurance Company
Ulico Standard of America Casualty Company
United Fire Group
United States Liability Insurance Group
Universal Underwriters Group
USA Insurance Company
Ward North America, Inc.
Western Indemnity Insurance Company
X-Press Claims Service
Zenith Insurance Company
National Grange Mutual Insurance Company
Nationwide Insurance
Nautilus Insurance Company
New Hampshire Insurance Company
NOVA Casualty Company
NovaPro Risk Solutions
Ohio Casualty Insurance Company
OneBeacon Insurance
Pafco General Insurance Company
Peerless Insurance Company
Pennsylvania Lumbermens Mutual Insurance Company
Pilot Insurance Company
PMA Insurance Group
Progressive Insurance Company
Protective Adjustment Company
Protective Insurance Company
Provident General Insurance Company
R.A.C. Insurance Partners, L.L.C.
Risk Enterprise Management, Ltd.
Safeco Insurance
Savage Claims Service
Scottsdale Insurance Company
SeaBright Insurance Company
Selective Insurance Company of America
Southern Group Indemnity, Inc.
Southern Life and Health Insurance Company
State Farm Insurance Companies
Travelers Insurance Companies
United Automobile Insurance Company
United Self Insured Services
Unitrin Direct Auto Insurance
Universal Property & Casualty Insurance Company
Victoria Fire & Casualty Company
Wausau Insurance Companies
Workmen's Auto Insurance Company
York Claims Service, Inc.
Zurich North America

Non-Insurance Clients

Advanced Elevator Services, Inc.
AmCOMP/Pinnacle Benefits, Inc.
Antonucci & Associates
Atrium Companies, Inc.
Broward County Board of Commissioners
City of West Palm Beach
C.R. Vince & Associates
Devcon International Corporation
Edward D. Stone & Associates, Inc.
Florida League of Cities
Georgia-Pacific LLC
Hanson Industries
Hewitt, Coleman & Associates, Inc.
Loggins & Bennett Transport, Inc.
McAloon & Friedman, P.C.
Mendes & Mount, LLP
Motorola, Inc.
Palm Springs General Hospital
Pharmastat, LLC
Pinnacle Interiors
Professional Administrators, Inc.
Reimbursement Consultants, Inc.
Robert Plan of New York Corporation
SAIA Motor Freight Line, Inc.
Sewell, Todd & Broxton, Inc.
Siegal, Battanini & Associates
South Florida Water Management District
Tarragon Realty Investors, Inc.
Universal Health Services, Inc.
Allied Bolt, Inc.
Antares Real Estate Services
Arthur Yanoff & Company
AutoNation Incorporated
Century Development Company
City of Port St. Lucie
Continental Airlines, Inc.
De Lage Landen Financial Services
Dickerson Florida, Inc.
First State Management Group, Inc.
Florida Preferred Administrators
Hallmark Management, LLC
Hardyston Management Company
Hospital Risk Management
Ideal Homes, Inc.
Masco Corporation
McCreary Corporation
Millennium General Contractors, Inc.
Parkway Regional Medical Center
Piedmont American
PLCM Group, Inc.
Protegrity Services, Inc.
R.K. Associates
Ross Stores, Inc.
Ryder System, Inc.
School District of Palm Beach County
Siris, Ltd
Summit Claims
Symons International Group, Inc.
Tenet Healthcare Corporation
Weingarten Realty Investors

Conroy Simberg, Hollywood, FL (Continued)

Retired

Thomas W. Conroy — 1949 — University of Miami, B.B.A., 1971; Florida State University, J.D., 1974 — Admitted to Bar, 1974, Florida — Member American and Dade County Bar Associations; Southern Florida Claims Association; Defense Research Institute; Florida Defense Lawyers Association

Partners

Jonathan C. Abel — 1958 — University of Florida, B.A., 1980; J.D., 1983 — Admitted to Bar, 1983, Florida — Member The Florida Bar; Dade County Bar Association; South Florida Claims Association; Florida Defense Lawyers Association; Defense Research Institute

Jeffrey A. Blaker — 1959 — University of Miami, B.S., 1981; University of Miami School of Law, J.D., 1984 — Admitted to Bar, 1984, Florida — Member The Florida Bar

Joshua C. Canton — University of Central Florida, B.A., 1998; University of Miami School of Law, J.D., 2001 — Admitted to Bar, 2002, Florida; Georgia; District of Columbia; U.S. District Court, Middle, Northern and Southern Districts of Florida; U.S. District Court, Middle and Northern Districts of Georgia; U.S. Court of Appeals, Eleventh Circuit; Georgia Court of Appeals

Kristian S. Coad — The University of Utah, B.A., 1994; St. Thomas University School of Law, J.D., 1998 — Admitted to Bar, 1998, Florida

Stuart F. Cohen — 1968 — University of Florida, B.B.A., 1990; J.D., 1993 — Admitted to Bar, 1993, Florida; 1994, U.S. District Court, Southern District of Florida — Member Dade County Bar Association; Florida Trial Lawyers Association; American Trial Lawyers Association

Matthew J. Corker — St. John's University, B.S., 2000; Hofstra University School of Law, J.D., 2003 — Admitted to Bar, 2004, New York; 2006, Florida; 2007, U.S. District Court, Middle District of Florida

Christopher T. Corkran — The Ohio State University, B.A., 1995; St. Thomas University, J.D., 1999 — Executive Editor, Opinio Juris; Articles Editor, St. Thomas Law Review — Admitted to Bar, 1999, Florida — Member American Bar Association

Thomas R. Criss — 1955 — Florida State University, B.S., 1976; J.D., 1981 — Admitted to Bar, 1982, Florida — Member American and Broward County Bar Associations; The Florida Bar; American Trial Lawyers Association

Millard L. Fretland — 1959 — Florida State University, B.S. (magna cum laude), 1980; Washington and Lee University, J.D. (cum laude), 1983 — Admitted to Bar, 1983, Florida; 1983, U.S. District Court, Northern District of Florida — Member American Board of Trial Advocates; Defense Research Institute

Dale L. Friedman — 1947 — University of Miami, B.A., 1969; J.D. (cum laude), 1990 — Admitted to Bar, 1990, Florida; 1990, U.S. District Court, Middle and Southern Districts of Florida — Member The Florida Bar

Neal L. Ganon — 1958 — Duke University, B.A., 1980; Indiana University, J.D., 1983 — Admitted to Bar, 1983, Florida — Member The Florida Bar

Seth R. Goldberg — 1967 — Arizona State University, B.S., 1990; Nova Southeastern University, J.D., 1994 — Admitted to Bar, 1994, Florida; New York; 1995, New Jersey — Member The Florida Bar

Lawrence S. Gordon — Emory University; University of Miami, B.A. (summa cum laude), 1978; University of Miami School of Law, J.D. (magna cum laude), 1983 — Admitted to Bar, 1983, Florida; U.S. District Court, Southern District of Florida; U.S. Court of Appeals, Eleventh Circuit — Member American and Miami-Dade County Bar Associations

Jacqueline M. Gregory — Simmons College, B.A., 1980; University of Miami, M.A., 1984; J.D., 1989 — Admitted to Bar, 1989, Florida — Member The Florida Bar

Marc J. Gutterman — 1972 — Florida State University, B.A., 1994; Syracuse University, J.D., 1997 — Admitted to Bar, 1997, Florida; 1997, U.S. District Court, Middle, Northern and Southern Districts of Florida; 1998, U.S. Court of Appeals, Eleventh Circuit — Member American Bar Association (Sections: Tort and Insurance Litigation)

John E. Herndon, Jr. — 1948 — Florida State University, B.S. (cum laude), 1970; University of Miami, J.D. (cum laude), 1975 — Admitted to Bar, 1975, Florida; 1976, U.S. District Court, Middle District of Florida; 1976, U.S. Court of Appeals, Eleventh Circuit; 1989, U.S. Supreme Court — Member The Florida Bar; Defense Research Institute; Florida Defense Lawyers Association

Philip T. Hoffman, Jr. — 1960 — Florida State University, B.S. (cum laude), 1983; University of Florida, J.D., 1987 — Admitted to Bar, 1987, Florida — Member American, Broward County and Dade County Bar Associations; The Florida Bar

Conroy Simberg, Hollywood, FL (Continued)

Robert S. Horwitz — 1971 — Boston University, B.S., 1993; Nova Southeastern University, Shepard Broad Law Center, J.D. (cum laude), 1998 — Admitted to Bar, 1998, Florida; 1999, Maryland; U.S. District Court, Middle, Northern and Southern Districts of Florida; U.S. Court of Appeals, Eleventh Circuit

John A. Howard — 1959 — Bridgewater State College, B.A., 1981; University of Massachusetts Amherst, M.S., 1985; St. John's University School of Law, J.D. (magna cum laude), 1994 — St. John's University Law Review — Admitted to Bar, 1994, Connecticut; 1995, New York; 1996, Florida

Michael S. Kast — 1959 — Emory University, B.A., 1981; Emory University School of Law, J.D., 1984 — Moot Court Society, Emory University School of Law — Admitted to Bar, 1984, Florida

Hinda Klein — 1961 — University of Florida, B.S., 1982; Syracuse University, J.D., 1985 — Admitted to Bar, 1985, Florida — Member Broward County Bar Association; The Florida Bar; Booher Inns of Court

Michael Kraft — 1971 — The George Washington University, B.B.A., 1993; University of Miami School of Law, J.D., 1996 — Admitted to Bar, 1996, Florida

Scott D. Krevans — 1961 — University of Maryland, B.A., 1982; Nova University Law School, J.D., 1986 — Admitted to Bar, 1986, Florida — Member The Florida Bar (Trial Lawyers Division)

Katherine G. Letzter — 1967 — State University of New York at Stony Brook, B.S.N., 1989; Touro College, J.D., 1994 — Admitted to Bar, 1995, Florida; 1996, New Jersey; New York — Member American Bar Association; The Florida Bar

Rodney C. Lundy — 1962 — Washington and Lee University, B.S., 1985; Nova Southeastern University, J.D., 1988; College of William & Mary, LL.M., 1989 — Admitted to Bar, 1989, Florida; 1994, U.S. District Court, Middle District of Florida — Member The Florida Bar; Florida Academy of Trial Lawyers

John A. Lurvey — 1958 — University of Florida, B.A., 1980; J.D., 1984 — Admitted to Bar, 1986, Florida; 1986, U.S. District Court, Southern District of Florida — Member American and Palm Beach County Bar Associations; The Florida Bar

Thomas J. McCausland — 1955 — University of Maryland, B.A., 1978; University of Baltimore School of Law, J.D., 1981 — Admitted to Bar, 1982, Maryland; 1985, Florida; 1996, U.S. District Court, Southern District of Florida

Rachel H. Minetree — Emory & Henry College, B.A., 1998; University of Dayton School of Law, J.D., 2001 — Admitted to Bar, 2001, Florida; U.S. District Court, Middle, Northern and Southern Districts of Florida — Member American and Dade County Bar Associations

John L. Morrow — 1959 — University of Miami, B.B.A., 1981; M.B.A., 1983; Nova Southeastern University, J.D., 1987 — Admitted to Bar, 1987, Florida — Member Orange County Bar Association

Michael J. Paris — 1949 — University of Miami, B.B.A., 1971; Nova University, J.D., 1977 — Admitted to Bar, 1977, Florida; 1977, U.S. District Court, Southern District of Florida; 1977, U.S. Court of Appeals, Eleventh Circuit; 1997, U.S. District Court, Middle District of Florida

Christian Petric — 1972 — University of South Florida, B.A., 1994; University of Miami School of Law, J.D., 1999 — Admitted to Bar, 1999, Florida — Member The Florida Bar — Languages: Croatian

Jayne A. Pittman — 1972 — University of Scranton, B.A./M.A., 1994; University of Miami, J.D., 1997 — Admitted to Bar, 1997, Florida — Member American Bar Association; The Florida Bar

Steven P. Pyle — 1958 — Florida State University, B.S., 1980; Mercer University Walter F. George School of Law, J.D., 1987 — Admitted to Bar, 1987, Florida; U.S. District Court, Middle District of Florida; 1990, U.S. District Court, Northern District of Florida

Esther Zapata Ruderman — 1963 — University of Florida, B.A., 1985; J.D., 1988 — Admitted to Bar, 1989, Florida; 1990, U.S. District Court, Southern District of Florida; 1991, U.S. District Court, Middle District of Florida — Member Palm Beach County and Palm Beach County Hispanic (Past President) Bar Associations; University of Florida, Spanish American Law School Association — Languages: Spanish

Alison J. Schefer — Stetson University, B.A., 1984; University of Florida College of Law, J.D., 1986 — Admitted to Bar, 1987, New Jersey; 1990, Florida — Member American, New Jersey State and Palm Beach County Bar Associations; The Florida Bar

Joseph M. Sette — 1965 — University of California, Davis, B.A., 1987; University of the Pacific, McGeorge School of Law, J.D., 1990 — Admitted to Bar, 1990, California; 2005, Florida; 1990, U.S. District Court, Eastern District of California — Member State Bar of California

Conroy Simberg, Hollywood, FL (Continued)

Bruce F. Simberg — 1948 — Emory University, B.B.A., 1970; University of Miami, J.D., 1975 — Admitted to Bar, 1975, Florida; 1990, U.S. Supreme Court — Member American, Broward County and Dade County Bar Associations; Southern Florida Claims Association; Defense Research Institute; Florida Defense Lawyers Association; American Board of Trial Advocates; International Association of Defense Counsel

Daniel J. Simpson — 1974 — Georgia Southern University, B.A., 1996; Stetson University, J.D., 1999 — Admitted to Bar, 2000, Florida — Member The Florida Bar

Eric M. Thorn — 1973 — Stetson University College of Law, J.D., 2000 — Admitted to Bar, 2001, Florida; U.S. District Court, Middle, Northern and Southern Districts of Florida; U.S. Court of Appeals, Eleventh Circuit; U.S. Supreme Court — Member American and Hillsborough County Bar Associations; Tampa Bay Inns of Court; American Inns of Court

Christopher A. Tice — University of Florida, B.S., 1993; University of Miami, J.D., 1997 — Admitted to Bar, 1997, Florida; 2005, Georgia

Jonathan E. Walker — 1966 — University of West Florida, B.A., 1988; Cumberland School of Law of Samford University, J.D., 1997 — Admitted to Bar, 1997, Florida — Member Escambia/Santa Rosa and Okaloosa-Walton Bar Associations — Languages: Spanish

Jack A. Weiss — University of Florida, B.A., 1987; University of Florida College of Law, J.D., 1990; LL.M., 1992 — Admitted to Bar, 1991, Florida; 1993, U.S. Court of Appeals, Eleventh Circuit; 1994, U.S. District Court, Southern District of Florida; 2007, U.S. District Court, Middle District of Florida — Board Certified in Workers' Compensation

Michael K. Wilensky — 1955 — Florida State University, B.S. (cum laude), 1977; J.D., 1980 — Admitted to Bar, 1980, Florida — Member American, Dade County and Broward County Bar Associations; The Florida Bar; Florida Defense Lawyers Association; Defense Research and Trial Lawyers Association

Edward N. Winitz — 1947 — Temple University, B.B.A., 1969; The University of Toledo, J.D., 1972; Case Western Reserve Law-Medicine Center, LL.M., 1976 — Admitted to Bar, 1972, Pennsylvania; 1973, Florida; 1975, District of Columbia; 1975, U.S. Supreme Court; 1978, U.S. District Court, Southern District of Florida; 1978, U.S. Court of Appeals, Fifth Circuit — Member American, Pennsylvania, Dade County and Philadelphia Bar Associations; The Florida and District of Columbia Bars; American College of Legal Medicine; American Academy of Forensic Sciences; Pittsburgh Institute of Legal Medicine; Dade County Trial Lawyers Association; Medical Claims Defense Network; American Trial Lawyers Association; Academy of Florida Trial Lawyers; American Society of Law and Medicine

Associates

David M. Abosch	Michael A. Adams
Manuel F. Alvarez	Debrah L. Antell
Pablo M. Arrue	Xaverie L. Baxley-Hull
Neal H. Beylus	Kristian A. Bie
Chandler Black	Albert E. Blair
Jonathon C. A. Blevins	Lee C. Boeppler
Chandler E. Bonanno	Robert A. Bouvatte, Jr.
Andrew S. Bruce	James J. Cannon
Jeffrey A. Carter	Stephanie N. Carver
Cristobal A. Casal	Maria S. Chapman
Gerard J. Chiesa	R. Scott Clayton
Rina K. Clemens	Brett T. Conger
Meghan M. Cox	Elizabeth H. Crispin
Marc Crumpton, Jr.	Shannon Darsch
Christopher J. DeLorenzo	Frantz Destin, Jr.
Demetrea Dobson	Jason J. Durham
Jennifer M. Eberly	James M. Eckhart
Todd M. Feldman	Gianina Ferrando
Lorty G. Fevry	Rosalba J. Figueroa
Jennifer M. Forte	Holly Galinskie
Guillermo A. Gascue	Ashley A. Graham
Stephan M. Greco	Ari B. Gutman
Sandra Guzman	Jamie N. Haas
Michael J. Hale	Paul L. Hammond
Brian Haskell	Sharon W. Hendon
Stephanie S. Hoffman	Alex S. Hoy
Katie Marie Husta	Kacie K. Hutchinson
Matthew W. Innes	Elizabeth A. Izquierdo
Gregory Jackson	Christopher R. Jaramillo
Kyle Johnson	Jacqueline Katz
Yasmine Kirollos	Wendy Ellen Knecht
Riley M. Landy	Robert A. Lowry

JACKSONVILLE FLORIDA

Conroy Simberg, Hollywood, FL (Continued)

Dean R. Mallett
Melissa G. McDavitt
Starlene D. McGory
Timothy O. McMahon
Pamela Moody
Joshua E. Nathanson
Alina O'Connor
Dina O. Piedra
Thomas Regnier
Evan Roberts
Nicole E. Roero
David S. Rothenberg
Kelly B. Schaet
Mitchell Silver
Sarah (May) Smith
John Stroble Stevens
Michelle Karinne Suarez
Diane H. Tutt
Christopher E. Varner
Brittany L. Orlando Weisberg
Rebecca J. Williams
Brian Wisniewski
Kristen H. Matthis
Tracy L. McDuffie Jr.
Shannon P. McKenna
Daniel Mojena
Kimberly C. Mosley
Manuel Negron
Maria D. Ortiz
Amy D. Prevatt
Ryan J. Rhyce
Stephanie A. Robinson
Adam C. Rosen
Jeffrey K. Rubin
Elinis M. Sequeira
R. Lauren Smith
Richard N. Staten
Darlene Stosik
Ryan K. Todd
Jody A. Tuttle
Scott A. Wachholder
Lauren M. White
Ashley O. Wilson
Donna Zmijewski

INVERNESS † 7,210 Citrus Co.

Refer To

Abbey, Adams, Byelick & Mueller, L.L.P.
360 Central Avenue, 11th Floor
St. Petersburg, Florida 33701
  Telephone: 727-821-2080
  Fax: 727-822-3970

Mailing Address: P.O. Box 1511, St. Petersburg, FL 33731

Administrative Law, Americans with Disabilities Act, Appellate Practice, Complex Litigation, General Defense, Employment Law, Bad Faith, Insurance Coverage, Insurance Fraud, Uninsured and Underinsured Motorist, Professional Malpractice, Mediation, Negligence, Personal Injury, Premises Liability, Product Liability, Subrogation, Toxic Torts, Workers' Compensation, Motor Vehicle Liability, Defense of Insureds, Sovereign Immunity and Governmental Defense

SEE COMPLETE LISTING UNDER ST. PETERSBURG, FLORIDA (99 MILES)

Refer To

Cameron, Hodges, Coleman, LaPointe & Wright, P.A.
111 North Magnolia Avenue, Suite 1350
Orlando, Florida 32801-2378
  Telephone: 407-841-5030
  Fax: 407-841-1727

Insurance Law

SEE COMPLETE LISTING UNDER ORLANDO, FLORIDA (70 MILES)

ISLAMORADA 1,220 Monroe Co.

Vernis & Bowling of the Florida Keys, P.A.
Islamorada Professional Center
81990 Overseas Highway, Third Floor
Islamorada, Florida 33036
  Telephone: 305-664-4675
  Fax: 305-664-5414
  E-Mail: info@florida-law.com
  www.florida-law.com

Established: 1970

Vernis & Bowling of the Florida Keys, P.A., Islamorada, FL (Continued)

Civil Litigation, Insurance Law, Workers' Compensation, Premises Liability, Labor and Employment, Civil Rights, Commercial Litigation, Complex Litigation, Product Liability, Directors and Officers Liability, Errors and Omissions, Construction Law, Construction Defect, Environmental Liability, Personal and Commercial Vehicle, Appellate Practice, Admiralty and Maritime Law, Real Estate, Family Law, Elder Law, Liability Defense, SIU/Fraud Litigation, Education Law (ESE/IDEA), Property and Casualty (Commercial and Personal Lines), Long-Haul Trucking Liability, Government Law, Public Law, Criminal, White Collar, Business Litigation

Firm Profile: Since 1970, VERNIS & BOWLING has represented individuals, businesses, professionals, insurance carriers, self-insured, brokers, underwriters, agents, PEO's and insured. We provide cost effective, full service, legal representation that consistently exceeds the expectations of our clients. With 90 attorneys throughout 14 offices located in Florida, Georgia and Alabama the firm is able to provide the benefits of a large organization, including a management team, consistent policies and representation to ensure personal service and local representation to our clients.

Firm Members

Dirk M. Smits — 1966 — Tulane University, B.S.M., 1988; University of Miami School of Law, J.D., 1991 — Admitted to Bar, 1991, Florida

Scott C. Black — 1973 — Florida State University, B.S., 1995; Stetson University College of Law, J.D., 1998 — Admitted to Bar, 1998, Florida — Member American Bar Association; The Florida Bar

James W. Bowling — University of Kentucky, B.S., 1960; University of Miami School of Law, J.D., 1970 — Admitted to Bar, 1970, Florida; U.S. District Court, Southern District of Florida — Member American, Dade County and Florida Keys Bar Associations; The Florida Bar; South Florida Claims Association; Atlanta Claims Association; Defense Research Institute

Theron Simmons — 1970 — Middle Tennessee State University, B.S., 1997; St. Thomas University School of Law, J.D. (cum laude, Dean's List), 2002; Georgetown University Law Center, LL.M., 2003 — Admitted to Bar, 2003, Florida — Languages: French

Matthew Francis — 1985 — University of Florida, B.S./B.A., 2008; University of Florida College of Law, J.D., 2011 — Admitted to Bar, 2011, Florida

Mark Hruska — 1950 — University of Pittsburgh, B.A. (summa cum laude), 1972; University of Pittsburgh School of Law, J.D., 1975 — Admitted to Bar, 1975, Pennsylvania; 1986, Florida; U.S. District Court, Middle, Northern and Southern Districts of Florida

(See listing under Miami, FL for additional information)

JACKSONVILLE † 821,784 Duval Co.

Boyd & Jenerette, P.A.
The Levy Building
201 North Hogan Street, Suite 400
Jacksonville, Florida 32202-3372
  Telephone: 904-353-6241
  Fax: 904-493-3738
  E-Mail: firm@Boyd-Jenerette.com
  www.boyd-jenerette.com

(Coconut Creek, FL Office: 4443 Lyons Road Suite D-209, 33073)
  (Tel: 954-670-2198)
  (Fax: 954-467-7692)
(Savannah, GA Office: 7505 Waters Avenue, Suite D-3, 31406)
  (Tel: 912-921-8820)
  (Fax: 912-352-9042)

Established: 1952

FLORIDA — JACKSONVILLE

Boyd & Jenerette, P.A., Jacksonville, FL (Continued)

Admiralty and Maritime Law, Alternative Dispute Resolution, Appellate Practice, Automobile Liability, Bad Faith, Civil Litigation, Commercial Litigation, Construction Law, Coverage Issues, Employment Law, First Party Defense, Longshore and Harbor Workers' Compensation, Mass Tort, Personal Injury Protection (PIP), Premises Liability, Professional Liability, Transportation, Trucking Litigation, Uninsured Motorist Defense, Workers' Compensation, Asbestos, Global Settlements

Insurance Clients

Allstate Insurance Group
Amerisure Insurance Company
The Hartford Insurance Company
United Services Automobile Association (USAA)
American Indemnity Group
Auto-Owners Insurance Company
Travelers Insurance Group
Zurich Insurance

Shareholders

Glen A. McClary — University of North Florida, B.A., 1988; Florida State University, J.D. (with honors), 1992 — Admitted to Bar, 1993, Florida; U.S. District Court, Middle District of Florida

Benford L. Samuels, Jr.
Mark K. Eckels
Jane Anderson
Kristen M. Van der Linde
Robert E. Schrader, III

Partners

Peter P. Sledzik
Mary Nelson Morgan
Christopher D. Ritchie
Heather B. Carbone
Thomas A. Berger
Kristie R. Schrader
Linda Wagner Farrell
Blake J. Hood
Kenneth C. Steel III
Elizabeth B. Howard
Paul M. Woodson
Andrew Abramovich

Of Counsel

Catherine M. Bowman
Amanda J. Love

Senior Associates

Kansas R. Gooden
Michael J. Childers
Billie Jo Taylor

Associates

Jonathan M. Sang
Ariane J. Assadoghli
Kellie M. Hill
Kelly L. Downer
Pamela J. Nelson
Eric J. Netcher
Nicolle Piquet
Kathryn M. Oughton
Kelly Brannon
Nicole C. Liu
Patrick D. Hinchey
Kathleen H. Henry

Childs, Hester & Love, P.A.

1551 Atlantic Boulevard, 2nd Floor
Jacksonville, Florida 32207
Toll Free: 800-940-5299
Telephone: 904-396-3007
Fax: 904-396-3047
E-Mail: triallawyers@childslegalgroup.com
www.childslegalgroup.com

Established: 1973

Complex Litigation, Toxic Torts, Construction Litigation, Product Liability, Property and Casualty, Medical Malpractice, Professional Malpractice, Automobile, Banking Liability, Coverage and Coverage Litigation

Insurance Clients

Allied World National Assurance Company
K & K Insurance Group, Inc.
MedMal Direct Insurance Company
Argo Group US
Deep South Surplus, Inc.
MAG Mutual Insurance Company
Sedgwick Claims Management Services, Inc.

Childs, Hester & Love, P.A., Jacksonville, FL (Continued)

TransGuard Insurance Company of America, Inc.
United Fire Group
Western Litigation Specialists, Inc.

Non-Insurance Clients

Genesis Rehabilitation Hospital, Inc.
Markel Shand, Inc.

Attorneys

W. Douglas Childs — 1949 — The University of North Carolina at Chapel Hill, B.A., 1970; University of Pittsburgh, J.D., 1973 — Admitted to Bar, 1973, Florida; 1981, Georgia; 1974, U.S. District Court, Middle District of Florida; 1974, U.S. Court of Appeals, Eleventh Circuit; 1977, U.S. Supreme Court; 1981, U.S. District Court, Southern District of Georgia — Member The Florida Bar; State Bar of Georgia; Jacksonville Bar Association; American Board of Trial Advocates (Past Chapter President); Rotary International; Jacksonville Association of Defense Counsel; Defense Research Institute; Florida Defense Lawyers Association — Florida Bar Board Certified Civil Trial Lawyer — Practice Areas: Complex Litigation; Professional Liability; Product Liability; Insurance Coverage Determination; Insurance Coverage Litigation — Tel: 904-396-3007 — Fax: 904-396-3047 — E-mail: dchilds@childslegalgroup.com

Linda M. Hester — 1970 — University of Florida, B.A., 1992; J.D., 1995 — Admitted to Bar, 1995, Florida; 1998, U.S. District Court, Middle District of Florida; 1999, U.S. District Court, Northern and Southern Districts of Florida — Member The Florida Bar; Jacksonville Bar Association; Jacksonville Association of Defense Counsel — Practice Areas: Insurance Defense; Personal Injury; Civil Litigation — Tel: 904-396-3007 — Fax: 904-396-3047 — E-mail: lhester@childslegalgroup.com

Davis C. Love — 1976 — University of Florida, B.S. (with honors), 1998; J.D., 2001 — Admitted to Bar, 2001, Florida — Member The Florida Bar; Jacksonville Bar Association; Florida Association of Criminal Defense Lawyers; Defense Research Institute; Jacksonville Association of Defense Counsel; Professional Liability Defense Federation — Practice Areas: Medical Malpractice; Civil Litigation; Insurance Defense; Personal Injury; Criminal Defense — Tel: 904-396-3007 — Fax: 904-396-3047 — E-mail: dlove@childslegalgroup.com

Associate

Brian M. Pederson — University of Wisconsin, B.A., 2002; University of Florida, Levin College of Law, J.D., 2011 — Admitted to Bar, 2011, Florida — Member The Florida Bar Young Lawyers Division; The American Bar Association — Former Plaintiff's attorney — Practice Areas: Civil Litigation; Automobile Liability; Insurance Defense; Medical Malpractice Defense; Premises Liability; Product Liability — Tel: 904-396-3007 — Fax: 904-396-3047 — E-mail: bpederson@childslegalgroup.com

Conroy Simberg

4887 Belfort Road, Suite 103
Jacksonville, Florida 32256
Telephone: 904-296-6004
Fax: 904-296-6008
E-Mail: csg@conroysimberg.com
www.conroysimberg.com

Insurance Defense, Appellate Practice, Insurance Coverage, Environmental Law, Governmental Liability, Civil Rights, Wrongful Termination, Americans with Disabilities Act, Sexual Harassment, Land Use, Commercial Law, Fire, Arson, Fraud, Fidelity and Surety, Automobile Liability, Admiralty and Maritime Law, Bad Faith, Employment Law, Self-Insured, Public Entities, Product Liability, Casualty, Excess and Reinsurance, Accident and Health, Workers' Compensation, Medical Malpractice, Class Actions, Construction Defect, Construction Litigation, First Party Matters, Premises Liability, Professional Liability, Intellectual Property

(See listing under Hollywood, FL for additional information)

JACKSONVILLE   FLORIDA

Michael I. Coulson, P.A.

320 North First Street, Suite 708
Jacksonville Beach, Florida 32250
    Telephone: 904-296-9919
    Fax: 904-296-8323
    E-Mail: mcoulson@smithcoulson.com

Insurance Defense, Personal Injury, Mediation, Product Liability, Trucking Law, Premises Liability

Firm Profile: Our firm handles legal matters in the following practice areas: Civil Litigation, Insurance Defense, General Insurance Matters, Mediation, Automobile Accidents, Trucking Accidents, Catastrophic Accidents and Injuries, Head and Spinal Cord Injuries, Trucking and Transportation, Wrongful Death, Products Liability.

Insurance Clients

Auto-Owners Insurance Company
Fidelity National Property and
    Casualty Insurance Group
Security First Insurance Company
United Automobile Insurance
    Services
ESIS AGL Claims
Liberty International Underwriters
Medmarc Insurance Company
Tennessee Farm Bureau Insurance
    Company
U.S. Auto Insurance Company

Non-Insurance Clients

Air Liquide America, L.P.
Unarco Industries, Inc.
The Braun Corporation

Firm Members

Michael I. Coulson — 1949 — Washburn University, B.A., 1971; J.D., 1974 — Phi Alpha Delta — Admitted to Bar, 1975, Kansas; 1978, Florida; 1976, U.S. Court of Military Appeals; 1978, U.S. District Court, Middle and Northern Districts of Florida; U.S. Court of Appeals, Fifth and Eleventh Circuits — Member Kansas and Jacksonville Bar Associations, The Florida Bar; Jacksonville Defense Lawyers Association; Chester Bedell American Inns of Court, INN XIV; American Board of Trial Advocates — Board Certified Civil Trial Lawyer, Florida Bar Board of Legal Specialization and Education; Florida Supreme Court Certified Civil Court Mediator; U.S. District Court Certified Mediator for the Middle District of Florida — Lt. U.S. Navy JAG Corps, 1975-1978 — Practice Areas: Insurance Defense; Personal Injury; Mediation; Product Liability; Trucking Law; Premises Liability

Henrichsen Siegel, P.L.L.C.

1648 Osceola Street
Jacksonville, Florida 32204
    Telephone: 904-381-8183
    Fax: 904-381-8191
    E-Mail: NHenrichsen@hslawyers.com
    www.hslawyers.com

Established: 2000

Fidelity and Surety, Construction Law, Errors and Omissions, Subrogation, Commerical Torts, Uniform CommercialCode, Bank Negligence, Professional Malpractice

Firm Profile: Henrichsen Siegel, PLLC is a specialized litigation/trial law firm that provides quality legal services nationwide in a cost effective manner. With an emphasis on the use of technology in our practice and alternatives to hourly fee arrangements, our attorneys in offices in Washington, DC, Florida and Tennessee provide personalized and dedicated attention to all cases.

Firm Members

Neil L. Henrichsen — 1963 — Hunter College, B.A. (cum laude), 1984; American University, M.A., 1988; American University, Washington College of Law, J.D., 1988 — Recipient, New York State Assembly Legislative Fellowship, 1984 — Admitted to Bar, 1989, New Jersey; District of Columbia; 1991, Virginia; 1997, Florida; 1990, U.S. District Court, District of Maryland; U.S. Court of Federal Claims; 1997, U.S. Supreme Court — Member American Bar Association (Member; Forum on the Construction Industry, 1991; Fidelity and Surety Law Committee; Torts and Insurance Practice Section; Litigation Section); The District of Columbia Bar; Virginia State Bar;

Henrichsen Siegel, P.L.L.C., Jacksonville, FL (Continued)
The Florida Bar; Association of Trial Lawyers of America — Contributor: The Most Important Questions a Surety Can Ask About Performance Bonds, ABA, TIPS Section, 1997 — Practice Areas: Construction Law; Surety; Product Liability — E-mail: NHenrichsen@hslawyers.com

Helen H. Albee — 1967 — University of Florida, B.S.B.A. (with honors), 1989; University of Florida College of Law, J.D. (with honors), 1993 — Admitted to Bar, 1993, Florida; 2003, Georgia; 1994, U.S. District Court, Middle District of Florida; 2000, U.S. District Court, Northern and Southern Districts of Florida; 2003, U.S. Court of Federal Claims; U.S. Court of Appeals, Eleventh Circuit — Member American Bar Association (Member, Torts and Insurance Sections); The Florida Bar (Member, Real Property, Probate and Trust Law Sections; Construction Law Committee) — Practice Areas: Surety; Construction Law; Fidelity; Subrogation — E-mail: HAlbee@hslawyers.com

(See listing under Washington, DC for additional information)

(This firm is also listed in the Subrogation section of this directory)

Luks & Santaniello LLC

301 West Bay Street, Suite 1050
Jacksonville, Florida 32202
    Telephone: 904-791-9191
    Fax: 904-791-9196
    www.LS-LAW.com

(Additional Offices: Fort Lauderdale, FL*; Tampa, FL*; Orlando, FL*; Boca Raton, FL*; Miami, FL*; Tallahassee, FL)

Insurance Defense, General Liability, Workers' Compensation

(See listing under Fort Lauderdale, FL for additional information)

Marshall Dennehey Warner Coleman & Goggin

200 West Forsyth Street, Suite 1400
Jacksonville, Florida 32202
    Telephone: 904-358-4200
    Fax: 904-355-0019
    www.marshalldennehey.com

(Philadelphia, PA Office*: 2000 Market Street, Suite 2300, 19103)
    (Tel: 215-575-2600)
    (Fax: 215-575-0856)
    (Toll Free: 800-220-3308)
    (E-Mail: marshalldennehey@mdwcg.com)
(Wilmington, DE Office*: Nemours Building, 1007 North Orange Street, Suite 600, 19801)
    (Tel: 302-552-4300)
    (Fax: 302-552-4340)
(Fort Lauderdale, FL Office*: 100 Northeast 3rd Avenue, Suite 1100, 33301)
    (Tel: 954-847-4920)
    (Fax: 954-627-6640)
(Orlando, FL Office*: Landmark Center One, 315 East Robinson Street, Suite 550, 32801-1948)
    (Tel: 407-420-4380)
    (Fax: 407-839-3008)
(Tampa, FL Office*: 201 East Kennedy Boulevard, Suite 1100, 33602)
    (Tel: 813-898-1800)
    (Fax: 813-221-5026)
(Cherry Hill, NJ Office*: Woodland Falls Corporate Park, 200 Lake Drive East, Suite 300, 08002)
    (Tel: 856-414-6000)
    (Fax: 856-414-6077)
(Roseland, NJ Office*: 425 Eagle Rock Avenue, Suite 302, 07068)
    (Tel: 973-618-4100)
    (Fax: 973-618-0685)

FLORIDA — JACKSONVILLE

Marshall Dennehey Warner Coleman & Goggin, Jacksonville, FL (Continued)

(New York, NY Office*: Wall Street Plaza, 88 Pine Street, 21st Floor, 10005-1801)
 (Tel: 212-376-6400)
 (Fax: 212-376-6490)
(Melville, NY Office*: 105 Maxess Road, Suite 303, 11747)
 (Tel: 631-232-6130)
 (Fax: 631-232-6184)
(Cincinnati, OH Office*: 312 Elm Street, Suite 1850, 45202)
 (Tel: 513-375-6800)
 (Fax: 513-372-6801)
(Cleveland, OH Office*: 127 Public Square, Suite 3510, 44114-1291)
 (Tel: 216-912-3800)
 (Fax: 216-344-9006)
(Allentown, PA Office*: 4905 West Tilghman Street, Suite 300, 18104)
 (Tel: 484-895-2300)
 (Fax: 484-895-2303)
(Doylestown, PA Office*: 10 North Main Street, 2nd Floor, 18901-4318)
 (Tel: 267-880-2020)
 (Fax: 215-348-5439)
(Erie, PA Office*: 717 State Street, Suite 701, 16501)
 (Tel: 814-480-7800)
 (Fax: 814-455-3603)
(Camp Hill, PA Office*(See Harrisburg listing): 100 Coporate Center Drive, Suite 201, 17011)
 (Tel: 717-651-3500)
 (Fax: 717-651-9630)
(King of Prussia, PA Office*: 620 Freedom Business Center, Suite 300, 19406)
 (Tel: 610-354-8250)
 (Fax: 610-354-8299)
(Pittsburgh, PA Office*: U.S. Steel Tower, Suite 2900, 600 Grant Street, 15219)
 (Tel: 412-803-1140)
 (Fax: 412-803-1188)
(Moosic, PA Office*(See Scranton listing): 50 Glenmaura National Boulevard, 18507)
 (Tel: 570-496-4600)
 (Fax: 570-496-0567)
(Rye Brook, NY Office*(See Westchester listing): 800 Westchester Avenue, Suite C-700, 10573)
 (Tel: 914-977-7300)
 (Fax: 914-977-7301)

Established: 2004

Amusements, Sports and Recreation Liability, Asbestos and Mass Tort Litigation, Automobile Liability, Aviation and Complex Litigation, Construction Injury Litigation, Fraud/Special Investigation, General Liability, Hospitality and Liquor Liability, Maritime Litigation, Product Liability, Property Litigation, Retail Liability, Trucking & Transportation Liability, Appellate Advocacy and Post-Trial Practice, Architectural, Engineering and Construction Defect Litigation, Class Action Litigation, Commercial Litigation, Consumer and Credit Law, Employment Law, Environmental & Toxic Tort Litigation, Insurance Coverage/Bad Faith Litigation, Life, Health and Disability Litigation, Privacy and Data Security, Professional Liability, Public Entity and Civil Rights Litigation, Real Estate E&O Liability, School Leaders' Liability, Securities and Investment Professional Liability, Technology, Media and Intellectual Property Litigation, White Collar Crime, Birth Injury Litigation, Health Care Governmental Compliance, Health Care Liability, Health Law, Long-Term Care Liability, Medical Device and Pharmaceutical Liability, Medicare Set-Aside, Workers' Compensation

Firm Profile: As part of its continuing strategic expansion into Florida, Marshall Dennehey Warner Coleman & Goggin's latest regional Florida office was opened in Jacksonville in 2004.

The Jacksonville office practices aggressive, well-prepared defense litigation by lawyers who are accessible, practical and highly experienced. The attorneys in the Jacksonville office have a corporate, commercial and civil litigation practice. The litigation practice focuses on civil trials, administrative, appellate, commercial and constitutional law. The trial practice includes personal injury litigation, medical and other professional malpractice, construction litigation, products liability, coverage and bad faith litigation.

For additional information concerning the Jacksonville office, please contact Martin Sitler, Esquire, its managing attorney, at (904) 358-4234 or mhsitler@mdwcg.com

Managing Shareholders

Michael J. Obringer — Managing Attorney — 1949 — University of Notre Dame, B.B.A., 1971; University of Florida College of Law, J.D., 1973 — Best Lawyers in America (2008-Present) — Admitted to Bar, 1974, Florida; 1975, U.S. District Court, Middle District of Florida; 1979, U.S. Supreme Court; 1984, U.S. District Court, Northern District of Florida — Member The Florida Bar, Jacksonville Bar Association; Jacksonville Defense Lawyers Association; American Board of Trial Advocates; Florida Defense Lawyers Association; Defense Research Institute — Seminars/Classes Taught: Trial Testimony, Drug Enforcement Administration, 1976; Current Trends In Evidence, Jacksonville Sheriff's Office, 1980; Cross-Examination, Florida Defense Lawyers, 1985; Joint and Several Liability, Jacksonville Defense Lawyers, 1990; Search and Seizure Law, University of North Florida, 1998; Ethics Seminar for newly-admitted members of Florida Bar, 2008 — American Board of Trial Advocacy, Certification, 2000 — U.S. Army Reserves, Capt., 1973-1974 — Practice Areas: Professional Liability; Product Liability; Trucking Litigation; Transportation; Commercial Litigation — E-mail: mjobringer@mdwcg.com

Martin Sitler — Managing Attorney — 1961 — The Ohio State University, B.S., 1983; University of South Dakota School of Law, J.D., 1992; Judge Advocate General's School Army (TJAGSA), LL.M., 1997 — Sterling Honor Graduate (Top 5%), Univeristy of South Dakota School of Law; Deputy Circuit Military Judge, Piedmont Judicial Circuit, Navy-Marine Corps Trial Judiciary (2000-2004); Navy-Marine Corps Achievement Medals (1987, 1989, 1995); Meritorious Service Medals (1996, 2004); Legion of Merit (2004) — Admitted to Bar, 1992, South Dakota; 2004, Ohio; Pennsylvania; 2010, Florida; 1996, U.S. Court of Appeals for the Armed Forces; 2004, U.S. District Court, Western District of Pennsylvania; 2005, U.S. District Court, Northern and Southern Districts of Ohio — Member Ohio State and Akron Bar Associations; Scanlon Inn of Court; American Health Lawyers Association — Author:"The "Citadel of Privity" - A Fortress in Ohio for a Claim of Breach of Implied Warranty Under the Magnuson-Moss Warranty Act," Defense Digest, Vol. 13, No. 4, December, 2007; "A Hole in the Make-Whole Doctrine: The Ohio Supreme Court Approves an Insurance Contract that Avoids the Make-Whole Doctrine," Defense Digest, Vol. 11, No. 1, March, 2005; "Annual Review Of Developments In Instructions—2001," The Army Lawyer, August, 2002; Co-Author "The Advocacy Trainer; A Manual For Supervisors," Criminal Law Department The Judge Advocate General's School, U.S. Army, 1997-2000; Author: "The Armor: Recent Developments In Self-Incrimination Law," The Army Lawyer, May, 2000; "The Cornerstone: Recent Developments In Jurisdiction," The Army Lawyer, April, 2000; "The Art Of Trial Advocacy Note, The Art Of Storytelling," The Army Lawyer, October, 1999; "Silence Is Golden: Recent Developments In Self-Incrimination Law," The Army Lawyer, May, 1999; "The Top Ten Jurisdiction Hits Of The 1998 Term: New Developments In Jurisdiction," The Army Lawyer, April, 1999; "The Art Of Trial Advocacy Note, An Approach To Cross Examination," The Army Lawyer, July, 1998; "Widening The Door: Recent Developments In Self-Incrimination Law," The Army Lawyer, April, 1998; "The Power To Prosecute: New Developments In Courts-Martial Jurisdiction," The Army Lawyer, April, 1998; Seminars/Classes Taught: Associate Professor, Criminal Law Department, The Judge Advocate General's School, U.S. Army, Charlottesville, VA, 1997-2000 — Reported Cases: Caldwell v. Petersburg Stone Co., (Mahoning App. No. 05MA12 Dec 16, 2005) *2005 Ohio App. LEXIS 6119; Church v. Fleishour Homes, Inc., (2007), 172 Ohio App. 3d 205 — U.S. Marine Corps, Retired Lieutenant Colonel, 1984-2004 — Practice Areas: General Liability; Asbestos Litigation; Toxic Torts; Medical Malpractice; Nursing Home Liability; Insurance Coverage — E-mail: mhsitler@mdwcg.com

Senior Counsel

Pamela L. St. John Lynde

Resident Shareholders

Michael J. DeCandio
R. Thomas Roberts
James P. Hanratty
John Viggiani

JACKSONVILLE   FLORIDA

Marshall Dennehey Warner Coleman & Goggin, Jacksonville, FL (Continued)

Resident Associates

Rocco J. Carbone, III James Gonzalez
Tashia M. Small

(See listing under Philadelphia, PA for additional information)

McConnaughhay, Duffy, Coonrod, Pope & Weaver, P.A.

6816 South Point Parkway, No. 500
Jacksonville, Florida 32216
  Telephone: 904-363-1950
  Fax: 904-363-1510
  www.mcconnaughhay.com

(Additional Offices: Tallahassee, FL*; Fort Lauderdale, FL*; Gainesville, FL*; Ocala, FL*; Panama City, FL*; Pensacola, FL*; Sarasota, FL*)

Insurance Defense, Workers' Compensation, Product Liability, Labor and Employment, Civil Litigation, Trial Practice, Appellate Practice

Firm Member

Robert D. Pope — Mercer University Walter F. George School of Law, J.D., 1987 — Admitted to Bar, 1987, Florida; Georgia — Practice Areas: Workers' Compensation; Civil Litigation

Associates

Sean A. Doothard Caitlin W. Beyl

Moseley Prichard Parrish Knight & Jones

501 West Bay Street
Jacksonville, Florida 32202
  Telephone: 904-356-1306
  Fax: 904-354-0194
  E-Mail: firm@mppkj.com
  www.mppkj.com

Established: 1906

Admiralty and Maritime Law, Transportation, Labor and Employment, Insurance Law, Civil Litigation, Class Actions, Environmental Law, Personal Injury, Product Liability, Wrongful Death

Firm Profile: Headquartered in the historic port of Jacksonville, Florida, Moseley, Prichard, Parrish, Knight & Jones represents clients in marine, transportation, commercial and insurance matters, both domestic and international. Founded in 1906 as the W.E. Kay Law Firm, Moseley, Prichard, Parrish, Knight & Jones is one of Jacksonville's oldest law firms in continuous service. Legal services are provided by a professional staff of lawyers, paralegals, law clerks and legal secretaries prepared to handle the most complex legal cases.

Insurance Clients

Assuranceforeningen Gard
Britannia Steam Ship Insurance Association Ltd.
North of England Protecting and Indemnity Association, Ltd.
Through Transport Mutual Insurance Association
Western World Insurance Company
Zurich American Insurance Company

Assuranceforeningen Skuld
Chubb & Son, Inc.
London Steamship Owners Mutual Insurance Association Ltd.
The Swedish Club (SAAF)
United Kingdom Mutual Steam Ship Assurance Association Ltd.
West of England Ship Owners Protection and Indemnity Association

Non-Insurance Clients

Amtrak Atlantic Marine Florida, LLC

Moseley Prichard Parrish Knight & Jones, Jacksonville, FL (Continued)

Crowley Liner Services, Inc.
Emerson Electric Company
Norfolk Southern Corporation

CSX Transportation Inc.
Hanjin Shipping Company, Ltd.
R.J. Reynolds Tobacco Company

Firm Members

James F. Moseley — 1936 — The Citadel, A.B. (with honors), 1958; University of Florida, LL.B., 1961; J.D., 1967 — Admitted to Bar, 1961, Florida — Member American Bar Association (House of Delegates, 2002-2008); The Florida Bar (Chairman, Admiralty Law Committee, 1973-1975); Jacksonville Bar Association (President 1975-1976); Florida Council of Bar Presidents (Chairman, 1978); Federal Rules Advisory Committee (Middle District, Florida); Maritime Law Association of the United States, (President, 1996-1998; Vice President, 1992-1996; Chairman of Committee on Navigation and Coast Guard Matters, 1982-1988; Executive Committee, 1978-1981); Titulary Member Comite Maritime International; Federation of Insurance and Corporate Counsel (Chairman, Maritime Law Section, 1986-1988); International Association of Defense Counsel (Chairman, Maritime Law Committee, 1989-1991); Southeastern Admiralty Law Institute (Chairman, 1980); Fellow, American Bar Foundation; National Association of Railroad Trial Counsel; Fellow, American College of Trial Lawyers — Advisory Board, Admiralty Law Institute, Tulane University; Editor, American Maritime Cases — Practice Areas: Admiralty and Maritime Law; Insurance Defense; Litigation; Transportation — E-mail: jfmoseley@mppkj.com

Joseph W. Prichard, Jr. — 1946 — University of Florida, B.A., 1968; J.D., 1973 — Admitted to Bar, 1974, Florida — Member Jacksonville Bar Association (President, Young Lawyers Section, 1982-1983; President, 1988-1989); National Association of Railroad Trial Counsel (Executive Committee, 1987-1993); Florida Defense Lawyers Association; Defense Research Institute; American Board of Trial Advocates — Practice Areas: Personal Injury; Product Liability; Transportation — E-mail: jwprichard@mppkj.com

Robert B. Parrish — 1951 — Duke University, A.B., 1973; J.D., 1978 — Law Clerk, Hon. Gerald B. Tjoflat United States Fifth Court of Appeals (1978-1979) — Duke Law Journal (Staff 1977; Editorial Board, 1978) — Admitted to Bar, 1979, Florida — Member Federal (President, Jacksonville Chapter, 1984-1985), American and Jacksonville Bar Associations; The Florida Bar; Maritime Law Association of the United States (President, May 2012-2014); Federation of Defense and Corporate Counsel; Jacksonville Federal Bar (Jacksonville Chapter, President 1984-1985); Southeastern Admiralty Law Institute; Defense Research Institute; Fellow, American College of Trial Lawyers; International Society of Barristers — Author: Note, "Circumventing Title III: The Use of Pen Register Surveillance in Law Enforcement," Duke Law Journal , 751, 1977 — Practice Areas: Admiralty and Maritime Law; Appellate Practice; Environmental Law; Labor and Employment; Product Liability; Complex Litigation; Class Actions — E-mail: bparrish@mppkj.com

Andrew J. Knight II — 1958 — The University of Mississippi, B.B.A., 1980; University of Florida, J.D. (with honors), 1982 — Admitted to Bar, 1983, Florida; 1989, Georgia — Member Federal Bar Association (Jacksonville Chapter; President, 1997-1998); Master of the Bench Chester Bedell Inns of Court; Southeastern Admiralty Law Institute (Port Director, 1988-1989 and 2002-2003); Propeller Club of the United States (National President, 1999-2001); Maritime Law Association of the United States; Defense Research Institute; National Association of Railroad Trial Counsel — Practice Areas: Railroad Law; Admiralty and Maritime Law; Insurance Law; Litigation; Personal Injury; Product Liability — E-mail: ajknight@mppkj.com

Richard K. Jones — 1955 — Florida State University, B.S. (cum laude), 1976; J.D. (with honors), 1982 — Admitted to Bar, 1982, Florida; 1983, U.S. Tax Court — Member Federal Bar Association (President, Jacksonville Chapter, 1991-1992); International Foundation of Employee Benefit Plans; Southeastern Admiralty Law Institute (Port Director, 1990-91); Maritime Law Association of the United States — Practice Areas: Commercial Law; Contracts; Corporate Law; Estate Planning; Probate; Admiralty and Maritime Law — E-mail: rkjones@mppkj.com

James F. Moseley Jr — 1962 — Hampden-Sydney College, B.A., 1984; Cumberland School of Law of Samford University, J.D., 1987 — Order of the Barristers; Chief Justice, Moot Court Board, 1986-1987 — Admitted to Bar, 1987, Georgia; Florida — Member Jacksonville Bar Association (President, 2003-2004); Southeastern Admiralty Law Institute (Port Director, 1992-1994); Maritime Law Association of the United States (Board of Directors, 2000-Present; Chairman, Marine Ecology Committee); Master, Chester Bedell Inns of Court — Florida Bar Board Certified Admiralty and Maritime Lawyer — Practice Areas: Admiralty and Maritime Law; Insurance Law; Litigation — E-mail: jmoseleyjr@mppkj.com

Moseley Prichard Parrish Knight & Jones, Jacksonville, FL (Continued)

Phillip A. Buhler — 1962 — College of William & Mary, B.A., 1984; University of Miami, J.D., 1987; Tulane University, LL.M., 1988 — Admitted to Bar, 1988, Louisiana; 1989, Florida; District of Columbia; 1992, U.S. Court of Federal Claims; U.S. Court of International Trade; U.S. District Court, Northern and Southern Districts of Florida; U.S. District Court, Eastern and Middle Districts of Louisiana; U.S. District Court for the District of Columbia; U.S. Court of Appeals for the Federal, Fifth and Eleventh Circuits; U.S. Court of Appeals for the District of Columbia Circuit; U.S. Supreme Court — Member Federal Bar Association (President, Jacksonville Chapter, 2003-2004); Inter-American Bar Association (Council Member; Treasurer and Executive Committee Member 2008-2009; President, International Law Committee 2006-09); Maritime Law Association of the United States (Chairman, International Organizations, Conventions and Standards Committee); Southeastern Admiralty Law Institute; Propeller Club of Jacksonville (President, 2002-2003); Associated Industries of Florida (Chairman, Maritime Council); Florida Bar International Law Section (Executive Council) — Florida Bar Board Certified in International Law and Admiralty and Maritime Law; Civil Law Notary — Practice Areas: Commercial Law; Transportation; International Law; Admiralty and Maritime Law; Litigation; Environmental Law — E-mail: pabuhler@mppkj.com

Stanley M. Weston — 1960 — Florida State University, B.S. (cum laude), 1982; University of Virginia, J.D., 1985 — Admitted to Bar, 1986, Florida — Member D.W. Perkins Bar Association — Practice Areas: Insurance Law; Litigation; Personal Injury; Admiralty and Maritime Law — E-mail: smweston@mppkj.com

Tracy Alan Chesser — 1968 — The University of Georgia, B.B.A. (cum laude), 1989; University of Florida, J.D., 1993 — Admitted to Bar, 1993, Georgia; 1995, Florida — Practice Areas: Insurance Law; Personal Injury; Product Liability — E-mail: tachesser@mppkj.com

Charles M. Trippe Jr. — 1953 — Columbia University, A.B. (cum laude), 1979; J.D., 1979 — Admitted to Bar, 1980, Massachusetts; New York; 1995, Florida; 1980, U.S. District Court, Eastern and Southern Districts of New York; 1981, U.S. District Court, District of Massachusetts; U.S. Court of Appeals, First Circuit; 1986, U.S. District Court, Northern District of Ohio; U.S. Court of Appeals, Third Circuit; 1990, U.S. Court of Appeals, Second Circuit; 1996, U.S. District Court, Middle District of Florida; 2002, U.S. District Court, Northern and Southern Districts of Florida; 2004, U.S. Court of Appeals, Eleventh Circuit; U.S. Court of Appeal for the Federal Circuit; 2012, U.S. District Court for the District of Columbia — Certified Civil Mediator (2005); Certified District Court Mediator (2006) — Practice Areas: Civil Litigation — E-mail: cmtrippe@mppkj.com

Eric L. Hearn — 1970 — Florida State University, B.S. (magna cum laude), 1992; University of Miami, J.D. (magna cum laude), 1996 — 1996 - Order of the Coif — Admitted to Bar, 1996, Florida — Member Propeller Club of Jacksonville (President, 2008-2009) — Practice Areas: Business Law; Real Estate Transactions; Estate Planning; Probate; Franchise Law; Commercial Litigation — E-mail: elhearn@mppkj.com

David C. Reeves — 1967 — Wake Forest University, B.A. (cum laude), 1989; The Catholic University of America, J.D. (cum laude), 1995 — Admitted to Bar, 1995, Florida — Practice Areas: Commercial Litigation; Personal Injury; Defense Litigation; Class Actions — E-mail: dcreeves@mppkj.com

P. Michael Leahy — 1966 — United States Merchant Marine Academy, B.S., 1988; The University of Akron, J.D., 1997 — Admitted to Bar, 2001, Florida — Member Southeastern Admiralty Law Institute; The Maritime Law Association of the United States; International Association of Defense Counsel — Practice Areas: Admiralty and Maritime Law; Insurance Law; Civil Litigation; Product Liability Defense — E-mail: pmleahy@mppkj.com

Thomas C. Sullivan — 1955 — United States Naval Academy, B.S., 1977; University of Florida, J.D., 1985 — Admitted to Bar, 1985, Florida — Member The Maritime Law Association of the United States — Practice Areas: Civil Litigation — E-mail: tsullivan@mppkj.com

Associates

Shea Michael Moser — 1978 — University of Florida, B.S.B.A. (cum laude), 2002; Samford University, M.B.A., 2006; Cumberland School of Law of Samford University, J.D., 2006 — Admitted to Bar, 2006, Florida; 2008, Georgia — E-mail: smoser@mppkj.com

J. Matt Rabil — 1979 — The University of North Carolina at Chapel Hill, B.S., 2002; University of Miami, J.D., 2007 — Law Clerk for Judge Leslie B. Rothenberg, Florida 3rd District Court of Appeals (2005) — Admitted to Bar, 2007, Florida — E-mail: mrabil@mppkj.com

John W. Wallace — 1981 — Auburn University, B.A.P.S. (Pi Sigma Alpha), 2004; The University of Georgia, J.D., 2008 — Admitted to Bar, 2008, Florida; 2009, Alabama — Member Jacksonville Bar Asssociation — E-mail: jwwallace@mppkj.com

Jeffrey A. Yarbrough — 1974 — University of North Florida, B.A., 2001; University of Florida, J.D. (cum laude), 2005 — Admitted to Bar, 2005, Florida — Member Jacksonville Bar Association; Jacksonville Federal Bar Association; Chester Bedell American Inn of Court (Associate Member, 2013) — Practice Areas: Civil Litigation; Product Liability Defense — E-mail: jyarbrough@mppkj.com

Joni A. Poitier — 1980 — Vanderbilt University Law School, J.D., 2005 — Admitted to Bar, 2005, Georgia; 2006, Florida — Member Jacksonville Bar Association; Jacksonville Women Lawyers Association; Daniel Webster Perkins Bar Association; Chester Bedell American Inn of Court Associate Member (2009)

Lisa Oswell — Boston College, P.S., 1986; Suffolk University, J.D., 1989 — Admitted to Bar, 1989, Connecticut; Florida — Member The Florida Bar; Connecticut Bar Association — Practice Areas: Civil Litigation; Product Liability Defense — E-mail: loswell@mppkj.com

O'Hara Halvorsen Humphries, PA

4811 Beach Boulevard, Suite 303
Jacksonville, Florida 32207
Telephone: 904-346-3166
Fax: 904-346-5445
E-Mail: inquires@ohhlaw.com
www.ohhlaw.com

Established: 1995

Coverage Issues, Appellate Practice, Automobile Liability, Bad Faith, Construction Liability, Examinations Under Oath, Extra-Contractual Liability, Negligence, Premises Liability

Firm Profile: O'Hara Halvorsen Humphries, PA, has specialized in insurance defense litigation for more than nineteen years. Based out of Jacksonville, Florida, our firm handles all kinds of insurance defense and liability cases throughout Florida and Georgia in county, state and federal court. In addition to defending against lawsuits, we have experience prosecuting lawsuits for declaratory judgment on coverage, providing a variety of pre-suit services, and handling appeals of orders and judgments.

We draw upon years and years of experience to provide our clients with effective and cost-efficient representation. Our attorneys are highly experienced in handling various defense claims from origination through settlement negotiations, litigation, trial and appeal. Our firm goes to trial, and we have the knowledge, tools, and experience to do it well.

Included among our team are AV-rated attorneys, a Board Certified Trial Attorney, an attorney licensed to practice in both Florida and Georgia, and attorneys well-versed in appellate work. Our firm was recently invited to join the prestigious Claims and Litigation Management Alliance (CLM), and three of our attorneys were named among Jacksonville's best in 2012.

Our firm's depth of experience handling insurance defense matters combined with its state-of-the-art technology, give us the ability to help our insurance clients meet the demands of handling a high volume of claims in the most efficient and cost-effective manner possible. In addition, our medium size allows us to provide a higher level of personal service and attention, and enables us to adapt more quickly to client needs and litigation changes. We can also accommodate alternate billing options such as flat rate or flexible fee arrangements.

Insurance Clients

Amica Mutual Insurance Company
Farm Bureau Insurance Company
GEICO General Insurance Company

Auto-Owners Insurance Company
First Acceptance Services, Inc.
Infinity Insurance Company
State Farm Mutual Automobile Insurance Company

Shareholders

Deborah A. Halvorsen — University of Florida College of Law, J.D., 1992 — Admitted to Bar, 1993, Florida

JACKSONVILLE   FLORIDA

O'Hara Halvorsen Humphries, PA, Jacksonville, FL (Continued)

Jeffrey J. Humphries — Florida Coastal School of Law, J.D., 2003 — Admitted to Bar, 2004, Florida; 2009, Georgia

J. Stephen O'Hara, Jr. — Florida State University College of Law, J.D., 1977 — Admitted to Bar, 1977, Florida

Jerilynn M. O'Hara — University of Florida College of Law, J.D., 1985 — Admitted to Bar, 1986, Florida

Associates

Tiffany M. Jones
Michael P. Regan, Jr.
Kathryn N. Slade

James D. Morgan
Abby R. Dyal

St. Denis & Davey, P.A.

1300 Riverplace Boulevard, Suite 401
Jacksonville, Florida 32207
  Toll Free: 866-542-1996
  Telephone: 904-396-1996
  Fax: 904-396-1991
  E-Mail: don@sdtriallaw.com
  www.stdenisdavey.com

(Jacksonville, FL Office: 1300 Riverplace Boulevard, Suite 401, 32207)
  (Tel: 904-396-1996)
  (Fax: 904-396-1991)

Admiralty and Maritime Law, Insurance Defense, Legal Malpractice, Premises Liability, Product Liability, Professional Liability, Sports and Entertainment Liability, Automobile, Truck Liability, Manufacturer Defense, Swimming Pool Defense, Warranty Defense, Car, Boat and Motorcycle Dealer Defense

Insurance Clients

American Management Corporation
BrightClaim, Inc.
K & K Insurance Group, Inc.
Old Dominion Insurance Company
Travelers of Florida

Amica Mutual Insurance Company
AmTrust North America
CNA Insurance Company
Liberty Mutual Insurance Company
Sentry Insurance
Universal Underwriters Group

Non-Insurance Clients

Asbury Automotive
Brickell Motors
Central Florida Chrysler Jeep Dodge
Hanmar Motor Corporation
J. C. Penney Company, Inc.

Automotive Management Services, Inc.
Clay County, Florida
Grady White Boats
Home & Park Motor Homes
Keystone RV Company

Members

Donald W. St. Denis — 1962 — University of Arkansas, B.S.B.A. (with honors), 1984; University of Florida, J.D., 1988 — Admitted to Bar, 1989, Florida; 1993, U.S. District Court, Middle, Northern and Southern Districts of Florida; 1993, U.S. Court of Appeals, Eleventh Circuit; U.S. Supreme Court — Member The Florida Bar; Jacksonville Bar Association; Trial Lawyers Association; Association of Trial Lawyers of America — Board Certified Civil Trial Practice Lawyer, Florida Bar Board of Legal Specialization

Brian W. Davey — 1973 — Florida State University, B.S. (cum laude), 1995; Stetson University, J.D./M.B.A. (with honors), 1998 — Phi Alpha Delta — Admitted to Bar, 1998, Florida; 1999, U.S. District Court, Middle District of Florida; 2002, U.S. District Court, Northern and Southern Districts of Florida — Member The Florida Bar; Jacksonville Bar Association

Eric M. Bradstreet — 1978 — Jacksonville University, B.S., 2000; Florida State University College of Law, J.D. (cum laude), 2006 — Admitted to Bar, 2006, Florida; 2007, U.S. District Court, Middle and Northern Districts of Florida — Member The Florida Bar

Blaire C. Hammock — 1985 — Samford University, B.A. (summa cum laude), 2007; Cumberland School of Law of Samford University, J.D. (cum laude), 2010 — Admitted to Bar, 2010, Florida; 2013, Alabama — Member The Florida Bar; Jacksonville Bar Association

Geoffrey R. Lutz — 1979 — Yale University, B.A., 2002; University of Florida, Levin College of Law, J.D. (cum laude), 2005 — Admitted to Bar,

St. Denis & Davey, P.A., Jacksonville, FL (Continued)

2006, Florida; U.S. District Court, Middle and Northern Districts of Florida — Member The Florida Bar

Vernis & Bowling of North Florida, P.A.

4309 Salisbury Road
Jacksonville, Florida 32216
  Telephone: 904-296-6751
  Fax: 904-296-2712
  E-Mail: info@florida-law.com
  www.florida-law.com

Established: 1970

Civil Litigation, Insurance Law, Workers' Compensation, Premises Liability, Labor and Employment, Civil Rights, Commercial Litigation, Complex Litigation, Product Liability, Directors and Officers Liability, Errors and Omissions, Construction Law, Construction Defect, Environmental Liability, Personal and Commercial Vehicle, Appellate Practice, Admiralty and Maritime Law, Real Estate, Family Law, Elder Law, Liability Defense, SIU/Fraud Litigation, Education Law (ESE/IDEA), Property and Casualty (Commercial and Personal Lines), Long-Haul Trucking Liability, Government Law, Public Law, Criminal, White Collar, Business Litigation

Firm Profile: Since 1970, VERNIS & BOWLING has represented individuals, businesses, professionals, insurance carriers, self-insureds, brokers, underwriters, agents, PEOs and insured. We provide cost effective, full service, legal representation that consistently exceeds the expectations of our clients. With 115 attorneys throughout 16 offices located in Florida, Georgia, Alabama, North Carolina and Mississippi the firm is able to provide the benefits of a large organization, including a management team, consistent policies and representation to ensure personal service and local representation to our clients.

Firm Members

Leonard T. Hackett — 1964 — Stonehill College, B.A., 1986; Cleveland-Marshall College of Law, J.D. (with honors), 1996 — Admitted to Bar, 1996, Maryland; 2000, Florida — Member The Florida Bar — Lieutenant, U.S. Army (1988-1992) — Resident Florida Keys, FL Office

Lori Anne Scott — 1975 — University of South Florida, B.A., 1999; Florida Coastal School of Law, J.D. (Dean's List), 2001 — Admitted to Bar, 2002, Florida; 2004, Georgia; U.S. District Court, Middle District of Florida

Michelle L. Glass — 1972 — Columbia College, B.S., 1994; St. Thomas University School of Law, J.D., 2003 — Admitted to Bar, 2003, Florida

T. Daniel Webb — 1973 — University of Florida, B.A., 1996; Florida Coastal School of Law, J.D., 2001 — Admitted to Bar, 2001, Florida; U.S. District Court, Middle District of Florida

Matthew T. Collett — 1984 — Valparaiso University, B.A., 2006; Florida Coastal School of Law, J.D., 2009 — Admitted to Bar, 2011, Florida; U.S. District Court, Middle District of Florida — Member Jacksonville Bar Association; Florida Defense Lawyers Association; Jacksonville Association of Defense Counsel

Candace Weeks Padgett — University of North Florida, B.A., 2007; Florida Coastal School of Law, J.D., 2010 — Admitted to Bar, 2011, Florida; U.S. District Court, Middle District of Florida — Member The Florida Bar; Jacksonville Bar Association; Jacksonville Area Defense Counsel

Sean A. Douthard

(See listing under Miami, FL for additional information)

Wicker Smith O'Hara McCoy & Ford P.A.

Bank of America, Suite 2700
50 North Laura Street
Jacksonville, Florida 32202
  Telephone: 904-355-0225
  Fax: 904-355-0226
  www.wickersmith.com

Wicker Smith O'Hara McCoy & Ford P.A., Jacksonville, FL (Continued)

(Coral Gables, FL Office*(See Miami listing): 2800 Ponce de Leon Boulevard, Suite 800, 33134)
(Tel: 305-448-3939)
(Fax: 305-441-1745)
(Fort Lauderdale, FL Office*: Sun Trust Center, 515 East Las Olas Boulevard, Suite 1400, 33301)
(Tel: 954-847-4800)
(Fax: 954-760-9353)
(Naples, FL Office*: Mercato, 9128 Strada Place, Suite 10200, 34108)
(Tel: 239-552-5300)
(Fax: 239-552-5399)
(Orlando, FL Office*: Bank of America Center, 390 North Orange Avenue, Suite 1000, 32801)
(Tel: 407-843-3939)
(Fax: 407-649-8118)
(Tampa, FL Office*: 100 North Tampa Street, Suite 1800, 33602)
(Tel: 813-222-3939)
(Fax: 813-222-3938)
(West Palm Beach, FL Office*: Northbridge Centre, 515 North Flagler Drive, Suite 1600, 33401)
(Tel: 561-689-3800)
(Fax: 561-689-9206)

General Civil Litigation, General Civil Practice, State and Federal Courts, Accountant Malpractice, Accountants and Attorneys Liability, Administrative Law, Admiralty and Maritime Law, Agent and Brokers Errors and Omissions, Appellate Practice, Automobile, Aviation, Bad Faith, Class Actions, Commercial Litigation, Complex Litigation, Construction Litigation, Environmental Law, Estate Planning, Fraud, Hospital Malpractice, Insurance Coverage, Labor and Employment, Legal Malpractice, Medical Devices, Medical Malpractice, Nursing Home Liability, Pharmaceutical, Premises Liability, Probate, Product Liability, Professional Liability, Professional Malpractice, Special Investigative Unit Claims, Real Estate, Retail Liability, Toxic Torts, Transportation, Trucking Litigation, Trusts, Workers' Compensation, Multi-District Litigation, Sexual Abuse

Firm Profile: In 1952, Idus Q. Wicker and James A. Smith formed a partnership with the goal of providing legal services of exceptional quality to their clients. They remained partners until their retirement and life-long friends. The firm they founded has expanded to seven offices located throughout Florida in Miami, Fort Lauderdale, West Palm Beach, Orlando, Tampa, Naples and Jacksonville. Although the firm has changed in size and scope, the goal of providing exceptional legal representation has remained the same.

Clients turn to Wicker Smith when they have critical and complex litigation matters because of the firm's vast experience in complex litigation filed in State and Federal Courts. Numerous major corporations have selected Wicker Smith as national and regional counsel. Supporting the litigation team is a preeminent Appellate Department, which has appeared as appellate counsel in more than 1,200 reported decisions, including several landmark opinions issued by the Supreme Court of Florida.

Wicker Smith has recognized leaders in the defense of a wide range of litigation practice areas, including products liability, medical malpractice, pharmaceutical and medical devices, catastrophic aviation accidents, legal malpractice, accounting malpractice, nursing home claims, construction litigation, as well as a variety of general negligence matters. In all such matters, communication and attention to the client's specific needs are our highest priority. The backbone of our relationship with clients is built upon integrity and stability. We strive to establish long-term relationships with our clients, built upon a partnership of communication and trust. We achieve this objective by listening to our clients, understanding their businesses and developing legal solutions to best meet their individual needs.

Firm Members

Richard E. Ramsey — 1962 — New York University, B.A. (cum laude), 1984; The Catholic University of America, J.D., 1987 — Admitted to Bar, 1987, Florida; U.S. District Court, Middle District of Florida; 1988, U.S. Court of Appeals, Eleventh Circuit; 2001, U.S. Supreme Court; 2006, U.S. District Court, Northern District of Florida — Member American and Jacksonville Bar Associations; The Florida Bar (Former Member, Fourth Judicial Circuit Bar Grievance Committee); Florida Medical Malpractice Claims Council; The Big Fun Box (Board of Directors); Defense Research Institute; Florida Defense Lawyers Association — Florida Super Lawyers 2009-2012; Litigation Counsel of America, Fellow, 2010; National Board of Trial Advocacy, 2010; Jacksonville Magazine's 904 Edition, "Top Lawyers" Medical Malpractice, 2010; Jacksonville Magazine's "Order in the Court Top Law Professional" Civil Litigation, 2009 — Certified Federal Court Arbitrator; Board Certified Civil Trial Law Lawyer, Florida Bar Board of Legal Specialization and Education — Practice Areas: Agent and Brokers Errors and Omissions; Bad Faith; Civil Litigation; Construction Litigation; Insurance Coverage; Legal Malpractice; Medical Malpractice; Nursing Home Liability; Product Liability; Professional Liability

Kevin G. Mercer — 1969 — University of Florida, B.S., 1991; J.D. (with honors), 1994 — Admitted to Bar, 1994, Florida; 1994, U.S. District Court, Middle District of Florida; 1995, U.S. District Court, Northern and Southern Districts of Florida; 1995, U.S. Court of Appeals, Eleventh Circuit — Member The Florida Bar; Hillsborough County Bar Association — Florida Super Lawyers "Rising Star" 2009 — Practice Areas: Civil Litigation; Medical Malpractice; Premises Liability; Product Liability

E. Holland "Holly" Howanitz — 1979 — Oglethorpe University, B.A., 2002; Florida Coastal School of Law, J.D. (cum laude), 2004 — Admitted to Bar, 2005, Florida; Georgia; Tennessee; 2006, U.S. District Court, Middle District of Georgia; U.S. District Court, Middle District of Florida — Practice Areas: Accountant Malpractice; Agent and Brokers Errors and Omissions; Civil Litigation; Construction Litigation; Legal Malpractice; Medical Malpractice; Nursing Home Liability

Associates

S. Scott Ross — University of Louisville, B.A., 1990; St. Thomas University, J.D., 1999 — Admitted to Bar, 2000, Florida

Alexis C. Brown-Gelb — University of Miami, B.A. (magna cum laude), 2000; Nova Southeastern University, J.D. (cum laude), 2005 — Admitted to Bar, 2005, Florida

Richard L. Lasseter — Valdosta State University, B.A., 2005; Florida Coastal School of Law, J.D., 2008 — Admitted to Bar, 2008, Florida

Charlene C. Poblete — University of Florida, B.A. (magna cum laude), 2004; Florida State University, J.D., 2007 — Admitted to Bar, 2007, Florida

Shylie A. Armon — Tulane University, B.A. (magna cum laude), 2006; University of Florida College of Law, J.D. (cum laude), 2009 — Admitted to Bar, 2009, Florida — Languages: Hebrew

Jessica Prince — University of Colorado, B.A. (magna cum laude), 2006; Florida State University College of Law, J.D., 2011 — Admitted to Bar, 2011, Florida

(See listing under Miami, FL for additional information)

The following firms also service this area.

Young, Bill, Roumbos & Boles, P.A.
Seville Tower, 7th Floor
226 South Palafox Place
Pensacola, Florida 32502
Telephone: 850-432-2222
Fax: 850-432-1444
Mailing Address: P.O. Drawer 1070, Pensacola, FL 32591-1070

Insurance Defense, Coverage Issues, Complex Litigation, Bad Faith, Product Liability, Medical Malpractice, Nursing Home Liability, Construction Defect, Premises Liability, General Liability, Automobile Liability

SEE COMPLETE LISTING UNDER PENSACOLA, FLORIDA (359 MILES)

KISSIMMEE   FLORIDA

KEY LARGO   10,433 Monroe Co.

Refer To

Vernis & Bowling of the Florida Keys, P.A.
Islamorada Professional Center
81990 Overseas Highway, Third Floor
Islamorada, Florida 33036
    Telephone: 305-664-4675
    Fax: 305-664-5414

Civil Litigation, Insurance Law, Workers' Compensation, Premises Liability, Labor and Employment, Civil Rights, Commercial Litigation, Complex Litigation, Product Liability, Directors and Officers Liability, Errors and Omissions, Construction Law, Construction Defect, Environmental Liability, Personal and Commercial Vehicle, Appellate Practice, Admiralty and Maritime Law, Real Estate, Family Law, Elder Law, Liability Defense, SIU/Fraud Litigation, Education Law (ESE/IDEA), Property and Casualty (Commercial and Personal Lines), Long-Haul Trucking Liability, Government Law, Public Law, Criminal, White Collar, Business Litigation

SEE COMPLETE LISTING UNDER ISLAMORADA, FLORIDA (17 MILES)

KEY WEST   † 24,649 Monroe Co.

Vernis & Bowling of the Florida Keys, P.A.
1009 Simonton Street, Suite 3
Key West, Florida 33040
    Telephone: 305-294-7050
    Fax: 305-294-7016
    E-Mail: info@florida-law.com
    www.florida-law.com

Established: 1970

Civil Litigation, Insurance Law, Workers' Compensation, Premises Liability, Labor and Employment, Civil Rights, Commercial Litigation, Complex Litigation, Product Liability, Directors and Officers Liability, Errors and Omissions, Construction Law, Construction Defect, Environmental Liability, Personal and Commercial Vehicle, Appellate Practice, Admiralty and Maritime Law, Real Estate, Family Law, Elder Law, Liability Defense, SIU/Fraud Litigation, Education Law (ESE/IDEA), Property and Casualty (Commercial and Personal Lines), Long-Haul Trucking Liability, Government Law, Public Law, Criminal, White Collar, Business Litigation

Firm Profile: Since 1970, VERNIS & BOWLING has represented individuals, businesses, professionals, insurance carriers, self-insureds, brokers, underwriters, agents, PEOs and insured. We provide cost effective, full service, legal representation that consistently exceeds the expectations of our clients. With 115 attorneys throughout 16 offices located in Florida, Georgia, Alabama, North Carolina and Mississippi the firm is able to provide the benefits of a large organization, including a management team, consistent policies and representation to ensure personal service and local representation to our clients.

Firm Member

Dirk M. Smits

(See listing under Miami, FL for additional information)

The following firms also service this area.

Conroy Simberg
3440 Hollywood Boulevard, Second Floor
Hollywood, Florida 33021
    Telephone: 954-961-1400
    Fax: 954-967-8577

Insurance Defense, Appellate Practice, Insurance Coverage, Environmental Law, Governmental Liability, Civil Rights, Wrongful Termination, Americans with Disabilities Act, Sexual Harassment, Land Use, Commercial Law, Fire, Arson, Fraud, Fidelity and Surety, Automobile Liability, Admiralty and Maritime Law, Bad Faith, Employment Law, Self-Insured, Public Entities, Product Liability, Casualty, Excess and Reinsurance, Accident and Health, Workers' Compensation, Medical Malpractice, Class Actions, Construction Defect, Construction Litigation, First Party Matters, Premises Liability, Professional Liability, Intellectual Property

SEE COMPLETE LISTING UNDER HOLLYWOOD, FLORIDA (178 MILES)

Fertig & Gramling
200 Southeast 13th Street
Fort Lauderdale, Florida 33316
    Telephone: 954-763-5020, 305-945-6250 (Miami)
    Fax: 954-763-5412

Coverage Issues, Admiralty and Maritime Law, Casualty, Fraud, Property, Reinsurance, Errors and Omissions, Directors and Officers Liability

SEE COMPLETE LISTING UNDER FORT LAUDERDALE, FLORIDA (189 MILES)

Vernis & Bowling of the Florida Keys, P.A.
Islamorada Professional Center
81990 Overseas Highway, Third Floor
Islamorada, Florida 33036
    Telephone: 305-664-4675
    Fax: 305-664-5414

Civil Litigation, Insurance Law, Workers' Compensation, Premises Liability, Labor and Employment, Civil Rights, Commercial Litigation, Complex Litigation, Product Liability, Directors and Officers Liability, Errors and Omissions, Construction Law, Construction Defect, Environmental Liability, Personal and Commercial Vehicle, Appellate Practice, Admiralty and Maritime Law, Real Estate, Family Law, Elder Law, Liability Defense, SIU/Fraud Litigation, Education Law (ESE/IDEA), Property and Casualty (Commercial and Personal Lines), Long-Haul Trucking Liability, Government Law, Public Law, Criminal, White Collar, Business Litigation

SEE COMPLETE LISTING UNDER ISLAMORADA, FLORIDA (85 MILES)

Young, Bill, Roumbos & Boles, P.A.
One Biscayne Tower, Suite 3195
2 South Biscayne Boulevard
Miami, Florida 33131
    Telephone: 305-222-7720
    Fax: 305-492-7729

Insurance Defense, Coverage Issues, Complex Litigation, Bad Faith, Product Liability, Medical Malpractice, Nursing Home Liability, Construction Defect, Premises Liability, General Liability, Automobile Liability

SEE COMPLETE LISTING UNDER MIAMI, FLORIDA (160 MILES)

KISSIMMEE   † 59,682 Osceola Co.

Refer To

Cameron, Hodges, Coleman, LaPointe & Wright, P.A.
111 North Magnolia Avenue, Suite 1350
Orlando, Florida 32801-2378
    Telephone: 407-841-5030
    Fax: 407-841-1727

Insurance Law

SEE COMPLETE LISTING UNDER ORLANDO, FLORIDA (16 MILES)

FLORIDA

LA BELLE † 2,703 Hendry Co.

Refer To

Vernis & Bowling of Southwest Florida, P.A.
2369 West 1st Street
Fort Myers, Florida 33901-3309
 Telephone: 239-334-3035
 Fax: 239-334-7702

Civil Litigation, Insurance Law, Workers' Compensation, Premises Liability, Labor and Employment, Civil Rights, Commercial Litigation, Complex Litigation, Product Liability, Directors and Officers Liability, Errors and Omissions, Construction Law, Construction Defect, Environmental Liability, Personal and Commercial Vehicle, Appellate Practice, Admiralty and Maritime Law, Real Estate, Family Law, Elder Law, Liability Defense, SIU/Fraud Litigation, Education Law (ESE/IDEA), Property and Casualty (Commercial and Personal Lines), Long-Haul Trucking Liability, Government Law, Public Law, Criminal, White Collar, Business Litigation

SEE COMPLETE LISTING UNDER FORT MYERS, FLORIDA (31 MILES)

LAKE CITY † 12,046 Columbia Co.

Refer To

Dell Graham, P.A.
203 Northeast First Street
Gainesville, Florida 32601
 Telephone: 352-372-4381
 Fax: 352-376-7415

Insurance Defense, Civil Trial Practice, State and Federal Courts, Automobile, Medical Malpractice, Product Liability, Governmental Liability, Property and Casualty

SEE COMPLETE LISTING UNDER GAINESVILLE, FLORIDA (44 MILES)

Refer To

Vernis & Bowling of North Florida, P.A.
4309 Salisbury Road
Jacksonville, Florida 32216
 Telephone: 904-296-6751
 Fax: 904-296-2712

Civil Litigation, Insurance Law, Workers' Compensation, Premises Liability, Labor and Employment, Civil Rights, Commercial Litigation, Complex Litigation, Product Liability, Directors and Officers Liability, Errors and Omissions, Construction Law, Construction Defect, Environmental Liability, Personal and Commercial Vehicle, Appellate Practice, Admiralty and Maritime Law, Real Estate, Family Law, Elder Law, Liability Defense, SIU/Fraud Litigation, Education Law (ESE/IDEA), Property and Casualty (Commercial and Personal Lines), Long-Haul Trucking Liability, Government Law, Public Law, Criminal, White Collar, Business Litigation

SEE COMPLETE LISTING UNDER JACKSONVILLE, FLORIDA (65 MILES)

LAKE MARY 13,822 Seminole Co.

Southeast Law Group, P.A.
725 Primera Boulevard, Suite 130
Lake Mary, Florida 32746
 Telephone: 386-274-1700
 Fax: 386-274-0220
 E-Mail: jkelly@southeastlaw.com
 www.southeastlaw.com

(Daytona Beach, FL Office*: 104 La Costa Lane, Suite 140, 32114)
 (Tel: 386-274-1700)
 (Fax: 386-274-0220)
 (E-Mail: mscheihing@southeastlaw.com)

Established: 2013

Insurance Coverage, Bad Faith, Arson, Fraud, Mediation, Sinkhole/Earth Movement, Windstorm/Hurricane/Tornado/Hail

Firm Profile: Southeast Law Group, P.A. was formed with the primary goal of exceeding client expectations in a targeted range of insurance matters and is rated AV preeminent by Martindale Hubbell. The practice combines experience with professionalism and progressive litigation management to

Southeast Law Group, P.A., Lake Mary, FL   (Continued)

serve its clients' interests. Southeast Law Group, P.A. is dedicated to delivering only the very best while developing relationships.

Partners

Janice A. Kelly — 1950 — Florida State University, B.S. (Dean's List), 1972; Stetson University College of Law, J.D. (Dean's List), 1983 — Admitted to Bar, 1983, Florida; U.S. District Court, Middle, Northern and Southern Districts of Florida; U.S. Court of Appeals, Eleventh Circuit — Member Federal Bar Association; American Bar Association (TIPS; Advisory Panel); The Florida Bar; Florida Advisory Committee on Arson Prevention; Windstorm Insurance Network, Inc. (Past President; Board of Directors; Wind Fellow); Property Loss Research Bureau (PLRB); Defense Research Institute (DRI) — Rated AV preeminent by Martindale Hubbell — Practice Areas: First Party Defense; Arson; Fire Loss; Fraud; Construction Defect; Bad Faith; Sinkhole/Earth Movement; Coverage Opinions

Soobadra Gauthier — 1961 — The University of the West Indies, LL.B. (Bachelor of Laws, with honors), 1983; University of Central Florida, B.A. (magna cum laude), 1986; Stetson University College of Law, J.D. (cum laude), 1991 — Admitted to Bar, 1992, Florida; U.S. District Court, Middle and Southern Districts of Florida; U.S. Court of Appeals, Eleventh Circuit — Member American Bar Association (Advisory Panel); The Florida Bar; Florida Advisory Committee on Arson Prevention; Windstorm Insurance Network, Inc. (Conference Chair, 2016); Property Loss Research Bureau (PLRB) — Practice Areas: First Party Defense; Arson; Fire Loss; Fraud; Sinkhole/Earth Movement; Water Losses; Coverage Opinions

(See listing under Daytona Beach, FL for additional information)

The following firms also service this area.

Vernis & Bowling of Central Florida, P.A.
1450 South Woodland Boulevard, Fourth Floor
DeLand, Florida 32720
 Telephone: 386-734-2505
 Fax: 386-734-3441

Civil Litigation, Insurance Law, Workers' Compensation, Premises Liability, Labor and Employment, Civil Rights, Commercial Litigation, Complex Litigation, Product Liability, Directors and Officers Liability, Errors and Omissions, Construction Law, Construction Defect, Environmental Liability, Personal and Commercial Vehicle, Appellate Practice, Admiralty and Maritime Law, Real Estate, Family Law, Elder Law, Liability Defense, SIU/Fraud Litigation, Education Law (ESE/IDEA), Property and Casualty (Commercial and Personal Lines), Long-Haul Trucking Liability, Government Law, Public Law, Criminal, White Collar, Business Litigation

SEE COMPLETE LISTING UNDER DAYTONA BEACH, FLORIDA (27 MILES)

LAKELAND 97,422 Polk Co.

Refer To

Abbey, Adams, Byelick & Mueller, L.L.P.
360 Central Avenue, 11th Floor
St. Petersburg, Florida 33701
 Telephone: 727-821-2080
 Fax: 727-822-3970

Mailing Address: P.O. Box 1511, St. Petersburg, FL 33731

Administrative Law, Americans with Disabilities Act, Appellate Practice, Complex Litigation, General Defense, Employment Law, Bad Faith, Insurance Coverage, Insurance Fraud, Uninsured and Underinsured Motorist, Professional Malpractice, Mediation, Negligence, Personal Injury, Premises Liability, Product Liability, Subrogation, Toxic Torts, Workers' Compensation, Motor Vehicle Liability, Defense of Insureds, Sovereign Immunity and Governmental Defense

SEE COMPLETE LISTING UNDER ST. PETERSBURG, FLORIDA (58 MILES)

MIAMI   FLORIDA

Refer To
Barker & Cook, PA
501 East Kennedy Boulevard, Suite 790
Tampa, Florida 33602
   Telephone: 813-489-1001
   Fax: 813-489-1008
   Toll Free: 888-892-8722

Insurance Defense, Self-Insured, Trial and Appellate Practice, State and Federal Courts, First and Third Party Defense, Automobile, Casualty, Construction Law, Engineers, Malpractice, Environmental Law, General Liability, Life and Health, Medical Malpractice, Product Liability, Property, Reinsurance, Workers' Compensation, Civil Litigation, Commercial Litigation, Personal Injury, Premises Liability, Contract Disputes, Labor and Employment, Construction Disputes, Insurance Coverage Disputes

SEE COMPLETE LISTING UNDER TAMPA, FLORIDA (35 MILES)

Refer To
Cameron, Hodges, Coleman, LaPointe & Wright, P.A.
111 North Magnolia Avenue, Suite 1350
Orlando, Florida 32801-2378
   Telephone: 407-841-5030
   Fax: 407-841-1727

Insurance Law

SEE COMPLETE LISTING UNDER ORLANDO, FLORIDA (54 MILES)

Refer To
Vernis & Bowling of the Gulf Coast, P.A. (Tampa)
3031 North Rocky Point Drive West, Suite 185
Tampa, Florida 33607
   Telephone: 813-712-1700
   Fax: 813-712-1701

Civil Litigation, Insurance Law, Workers' Compensation, Premises Liability, Labor and Employment, Civil Rights, Commercial Litigation, Complex Litigation, Product Liability, Directors and Officers Liability, Errors and Omissions, Construction Law, Construction Defect, Environmental Liability, Personal and Commercial Vehicle, Appellate Practice, Admiralty and Maritime Law, Real Estate, Family Law, Elder Law

SEE COMPLETE LISTING UNDER TAMPA, FLORIDA (38 MILES)

LARGO 77,648 Pinellas Co.

Refer To
Vernis & Bowling of the Gulf Coast, P.A.
696 1st Avenue, 1st Floor
St. Petersburg, Florida 33701
   Telephone: 727-443-3377
   Fax: 727-443-6828

Civil Litigation, Insurance Law, Workers' Compensation, Premises Liability, Labor and Employment, Civil Rights, Commercial Litigation, Complex Litigation, Product Liability, Directors and Officers Liability, Errors and Omissions, Construction Law, Construction Defect, Environmental Liability, Personal and Commercial Vehicle, Appellate Practice, Admiralty and Maritime Law, Real Estate, Family Law, Elder Law, Liability Defense, SIU/Fraud Litigation, Education Law (ESE/IDEA), Property and Casualty (Commercial and Personal Lines), Long-Haul Trucking Liability, Government Law, Public Law, Criminal, White Collar, Business Litigation

SEE COMPLETE LISTING UNDER CLEARWATER, FLORIDA (5 MILES)

MAITLAND 15,751 Orange Co.

Refer To
Vernis & Bowling of Central Florida, P.A.
1450 South Woodland Boulevard, Fourth Floor
DeLand, Florida 32720
   Telephone: 386-734-2505
   Fax: 386-734-3441

Civil Litigation, Insurance Law, Workers' Compensation, Premises Liability, Labor and Employment, Civil Rights, Commercial Litigation, Complex Litigation, Product Liability, Directors and Officers Liability, Errors and Omissions, Construction Law, Construction Defect, Environmental Liability, Personal and Commercial Vehicle, Appellate Practice, Admiralty and Maritime Law, Real Estate, Family Law, Elder Law, Liability Defense, SIU/Fraud Litigation, Education Law (ESE/IDEA), Property and Casualty (Commercial and Personal Lines), Long-Haul Trucking Liability, Government Law, Public Law, Criminal, White Collar, Business Litigation

SEE COMPLETE LISTING UNDER DAYTONA BEACH, FLORIDA (35 MILES)

MARATHON 8,297 Monroe Co.

Refer To
Vernis & Bowling of the Florida Keys, P.A.
Islamorada Professional Center
81990 Overseas Highway, Third Floor
Islamorada, Florida 33036
   Telephone: 305-664-4675
   Fax: 305-664-5414

Civil Litigation, Insurance Law, Workers' Compensation, Premises Liability, Labor and Employment, Civil Rights, Commercial Litigation, Complex Litigation, Product Liability, Directors and Officers Liability, Errors and Omissions, Construction Law, Construction Defect, Environmental Liability, Personal and Commercial Vehicle, Appellate Practice, Admiralty and Maritime Law, Real Estate, Family Law, Elder Law, Liability Defense, SIU/Fraud Litigation, Education Law (ESE/IDEA), Property and Casualty (Commercial and Personal Lines), Long-Haul Trucking Liability, Government Law, Public Law, Criminal, White Collar, Business Litigation

SEE COMPLETE LISTING UNDER ISLAMORADA, FLORIDA (36 MILES)

MARIANNA † 6,102 Jackson Co.

Refer To
Barron & Redding, P.A.
220 McKenzie Avenue
Panama City, Florida 32401-3129
   Telephone: 850-785-7454
   Fax: 850-785-2999
Mailing Address: P.O. Box 2467, Panama City, FL 32402-2467

Casualty, Surety, Fire, Life Insurance, Professional Liability, Product Liability, Medical Malpractice, Environmental Law, Automobile Liability, Premises Liability, Business Torts, Construction Law

SEE COMPLETE LISTING UNDER PANAMA CITY, FLORIDA (52 MILES)

MELBOURNE 76,068 Brevard Co.

Refer To
Cameron, Hodges, Coleman, LaPointe & Wright, P.A.
111 North Magnolia Avenue, Suite 1350
Orlando, Florida 32801-2378
   Telephone: 407-841-5030
   Fax: 407-841-1727

Insurance Law

SEE COMPLETE LISTING UNDER ORLANDO, FLORIDA (68 MILES)

Refer To
Conroy Simberg
3440 Hollywood Boulevard, Second Floor
Hollywood, Florida 33021
   Telephone: 954-961-1400
   Fax: 954-967-8577

Insurance Defense, Appellate Practice, Insurance Coverage, Environmental Law, Governmental Liability, Civil Rights, Wrongful Termination, Americans with Disabilities Act, Sexual Harassment, Land Use, Commercial Law, Fire, Arson, Fraud, Fidelity and Surety, Automobile Liability, Admiralty and Maritime Law, Bad Faith, Employment Law, Self-Insured, Public Entities, Product Liability, Casualty, Excess and Reinsurance, Accident and Health, Workers' Compensation, Medical Malpractice, Class Actions, Construction Defect, Construction Litigation, First Party Matters, Premises Liability, Professional Liability, Intellectual Property

SEE COMPLETE LISTING UNDER HOLLYWOOD, FLORIDA (153 MILES)

MIAMI † 399,457 Miami-Dade Co.

Acosta
301 Almeria Avenue, Suite 100
Miami, Florida 33134
   Telephone: 305-858-8880
   Fax: 305-858-8084
   E-Mail: info@acostalaw.org
   www.acostalaw.org

Established: 2001

Acosta, Miami, FL (Continued)

General Liability, Premises Liability, Workers' Compensation, Personal Injury Protection (PIP), Automobile Liability, Bad Faith, Construction Accidents, Insurance Law, Insurance Coverage, Insurance Defense, Product Liability, Restaurant Liability, Self-Insured Defense, Toxic Torts, Automobile Fraud, Trucking and Rental Vehicle Litigation, Flood Insurance Defense, Fire Insurance Defense, Hotel Liability

Firm Profile: Comprised of trial attorneys dedicated to providing the insurance and self-insured industry with the highest level of service and results, the firm is large enough to handle complex multi-district litigation throughout the entire state, and small enough to provide clients with the individual service and attention their specialized area may require.

Insurance Clients

AAA Auto Club South Insurance Company
Brinker International/Liberty Mutual Group
Homeowners Choice, Inc.
QBE Insurance/Florida Intracoastal Underwriters, Ltd.
AIG International Insurance Group
American Southern Home Insurance Company
Citizens Property Insurance Corp.
Liberty Mutual Insurance Company
State Farm Insurance Company

Non-Insurance Clients

BJ's Wholesale Club, Inc.
Dollar Rent A Car Systems, Inc.
The Gap, Inc.
Cunningham Lindsey Claims Management, Inc.
MasTec, Inc.

Partners

Julio C. Acosta — 1967 — Florida International University, B.B.A., 1993; Nova Southeastern University, J.D., 1996 — Admitted to Bar, 1996, Florida; 1998, U.S. District Court, Southern District of Florida; 1999, U.S. District Court, Middle District of Florida; U.S. Court of Appeals, Eleventh Circuit — Member American, Cuban-American and Dade County (Civil Litigation Committee) Bar Associations; The Florida Bar; South Florida Claims Association; Florida Defense Lawyers Association — Languages: Spanish — E-mail: jacosta@acostalaw.org

Atkinson & Brownell, P.A.

One Biscayne Tower
2 South Biscayne Boulevard, Suite 3750
Miami, Florida 33131
  Telephone: 305-376-8840
  Fax: 305-376-8841
  E-Mail: jatkinson@atkinsonbrownell.com
  www.atkinsonbrownell.com

Insurance Defense, Insurance Coverage, Bad Faith, Construction Defect, Product Liability, Premises Liability

Insurance Clients

American Southern Insurance Company
Armed Forces Insurance
AssuranceAmerica Insurance Company
Casco Indemnity Company
General Reinsurance Corporation
Great American Insurance Companies
MAPFRE Insurance
North Pointe Insurance Company
St. Johns Insurance Company, Inc.
Star Casualty Insurance Company, Inc.
Amerisure Insurance Company
Arbella Mutual Insurance Company
Auto Club South Insurance Company
Colony Insurance Company
Granada Insurance Company
Hiscox Insurance Company
Liberty Mutual Insurance Company
National Insurance Company
Professional Claims Managers, Inc.
Southern General Insurance Company
U.S. Liability Insurance Company

Partners

John B. Atkinson — 1950 — University of Pennsylvania, B.A., 1972; University of Miami, J.D., 1975 — Admitted to Bar, 1975, Pennsylvania; 1979, Florida; 1975, U.S. District Court, Eastern District of Pennsylvania; 1976, U.S. Court of Military Appeals; 1981, U.S. District Court, Middle, Northern and Southern Districts of Florida; U.S. Court of Appeals, Fourth, Fifth and Sixth Circuits — Member American Bar Association (Tort and Insurance

Atkinson & Brownell, P.A., Miami, FL (Continued)

Practice Law Section); The Florida Bar; Pennsylvania, Dade County and Broward County Bar Associations; Defense Research Institute; Florida Defense Lawyers Association — U.S. Marine Corps Reserve (Retired, Judge Advocate, 1976-2006)

Rebecca A. Brownell — 1961 — University of South Florida, B.A., 1982; Nova Southeastern University, M.S., 1988; Nova Southeastern University, Shepard Broad Law Center, J.D., 2001 — Team Editor and Member, Nova Southeastern Moot Court Society; Executive Editor, Nova Southeastern Law Review — Admitted to Bar, 2001, Florida; U.S. District Court, Middle, Northern and Southern Districts of Florida; U.S. Court of Appeals, Eleventh Circuit — Member American (Tort and Insurance Practice Practice) and Dade County Bar Associations; The Florida Bar; Florida Defense Research Institute — Vocational Evaluation; Certified Rehabilitation Consultant

Associates

Krystina Jiron — 1978 — Loyola University New Orleans, B.A. (cum laude), 2001; Villanova University School of Law, J.D., 2005 — Admitted to Bar, 2005, Florida; U.S. District Court, Middle and Southern Districts of Florida — Languages: Spanish

Joseph V. Manzo — University of Florida, B.S., 2004; J.D., 2007 — Admitted to Bar, 2008, Florida

Viviana Arango — 1985 — Florida International University, B.A. (magna cum laude), 2007; St. Thomas School of Law, J.D. (cum laude), 2010 — Admitted to Bar, 2010, Florida

Beckham & Beckham, P.A.

1550 NE Miami Gardens Drive, Suite 504
Miami, Florida 33179
  Telephone: 305-957-3900
  Fax: 305-940-8706
  Mobile: 305-790-6587
  E-Mail: egb@beckhamlaw.com
  www.beckhamlaw.com

Established: 1990

Insurance Defense, Property Damage, Transportation, Product Liability, Premises Liability, Motor Carriers, Subrogation

Insurance Clients

Gallagher Bassett Services, Inc.
The St. Paul/Travelers Companies, Inc.
Motor Transport Underwriters, Inc.
Vanliner Insurance Company

Non-Insurance Clients

FedEx Freight East

Partners

Eugene G. Beckham — 1957 — Emory University, B.A., 1979; University of Miami School of Law, J.D., 1982 — Admitted to Bar, 1983, Florida; 1984, U.S. District Court, Southern District of Florida; 1996, U.S. District Court, Middle District of Florida — Member American Bar Association; Florida Defense Lawyers Association; Transportation Lawyers Association; Trucking Industry Defense Association; Defense Research Institute; Federation of Defense and Corporate Counsel — Languages: French

Pamela Beckham — 1958 — Barry University, B.A. (cum laude), 1978; University of Miami School of Law, J.D., 1982 — Admitted to Bar, 1982, Florida; 1984, U.S. District Court, Southern District of Florida; 1985, U.S. Court of Appeals, Eleventh Circuit; 2000, U.S. District Court, Middle District of Florida — Member American Bar Association

Robert J. Beckham, Jr. — 1956 — Emory University, B.A., 1978; Mercer University, J.D., 1982 — Admitted to Bar, 1988, Georgia; 1994, Florida; 1994, U.S. District Court, Southern District of Florida; 1996, U.S. District Court, Middle District of Florida; 1999, U.S. District Court, Northern District of Florida

"Investigation: Tractor-Trailer Accidents," For The Defense, Vol. 43, No. 3, Page 29 (2001); "Truck Drivers Failure To Cooperate After a Claim is Made: Effects of the MCS-90 Endorsement," The Brief, Vol. 28, No. 2, Page 51 (Winter, 1999)

(This firm is also listed in the Subrogation section of this directory)

MIAMI	FLORIDA

Brown Sims, P.C.

9130 South Dadeland Boulevard, Suite 1600
Miami, Florida 33156-7851
   Telephone: 305-274-5507
   Fax: 305-274-5517

Insurance Defense, Trial and Appellate Practice, Admiralty and Maritime Law, Insurance Coverage, Construction Litigation, Product Liability, Premises Liability, Negligence, Employment Law, Casualty Defense, Professional Liability, Toxic Torts, Environmental Law, Workers' Compensation, Longshore and Harbor Workers' Compensation

Conroy Simberg

9155 South Dadeland Boulevard, Suite 1000
Miami, Florida 33156
   Telephone: 305-373-2888
   Fax: 305-373-2889
   E-Mail: csg@conroysimberg.com
   www.conroysimberg.com

Insurance Defense, Appellate Practice, Insurance Coverage, Environmental Law, Governmental Liability, Civil Rights, Wrongful Termination, Americans with Disabilities Act, Sexual Harassment, Land Use, Commercial Law, Fire, Arson, Fraud, Fidelity and Surety, Automobile Liability, Admiralty and Maritime Law, Bad Faith, Employment Law, Self-Insured, Public Entities, Product Liability, Casualty, Excess and Reinsurance, Accident and Health, Workers' Compensation, Medical Malpractice, Class Actions, Construction Defect, Construction Litigation, First Party Matters, Premises Liability, Professional Liability, Intellectual Property

(See listing under Hollywood, FL for additional information)

Cosio Law Group

1430 South Dixie Highway, Suite 202
Miami, Florida 33146
   Telephone: 305-567-0503
   Fax: 305-567-9875
   E-Mail: ecosio@cosiolaw.com
   www.cosiolaw.com

Insurance Defense, Wrongful Death, Commercial Vehicle, General Liability, Professional Malpractice, Premises Liability, Product Liability, Automobile Negligence

Insurance Clients

Infinity/Leader Insurance Companies
Old Dominion Insurance Company
QBE the Americas
Markel Corporation
North Pointe Insurance Company
ProPoint Claim Services, LLC

Non-Insurance Clients

AutoZone, Inc.
Kiewit Southern
Dave & Buster's, Inc.

Firm Member

Eduardo Cosio — 1962 — University of Miami, B.B.A. (cum laude), 1984; Boston College, J.D., 1987 — Admitted to Bar, 1987, Florida — Member Cuban-American (Board of Directors, 1993-1998, President, 1997) and Dade

Cosio Law Group, Miami, FL (Continued)

County (Board of Directors, 1993-1997) Bar Associations — Languages: Spanish

Associate Litigators

Julie B. Glassman — 1969 — University of Florida, B.A., 1991; University of Miami, J.D., 1994 — Phi Beta Kappa; Moot Court Board — Member, Inter-American Law Review — Admitted to Bar, 1994, Florida

Jose Valdes — 1962 — University of Miami, B.A. (cum laude), 1985; J.D. (cum laude), 1988 — Admitted to Bar, 1988, Florida — Languages: Spanish

Alan C. Gold, P.A.

1501 Sunset Drive, 2nd Floor
Miami, Florida 33143
   Telephone: 305-667-0475
   Fax: 305-663-0799
   E-Mail: agold@acgoldlaw.com

Established: 1994

Insurance Defense, Reinsurance, Personal Injury, Regulatory and Compliance, Commercial Litigation, Fraud, Complex Litigation, Civil Litigation, General Liability, Insurance Coverage, Probate, Estate Planning

Insurance Clients

American Financial Security Life Insurance Company
Atlantic General Insurance Company
International Insurance Company
Nanseekay Life Insurance Company
American Trend Life Insurance Company
Bel-Aire Insurance Company
Century Surety Company
Marigot Insurance Company

Non-Insurance Clients

AIG Claim Services, Inc.
Claims Management, Inc.
Flips #9, Inc.
Riveria Insurance Group, Ltd.
American Way Service Corporation
Interstate Cleaning Corporation

Shareholder

Alan C. Gold — 1953 — The George Washington University, B.A., 1975; University of Miami, J.D., 1980 — Admitted to Bar, 1980, Florida; 1980, U.S. District Court, Middle, Northern and Southern Districts of Florida; 1980, U.S. Court of Appeals, Sixth, Eighth and Eleventh Circuits; 1980, U.S. Supreme Court — Member The Florida Bar

Associate

James L. Parado — 1975 — University of Florida, B.S.B.A. (cum laude), 1997; J.D., 2002; University of Miami, LL.M., 2005 — Admitted to Bar, 2002, Florida; 2003, U.S. District Court, Middle, Northern and Southern Districts of Florida — Member The Florida Bar — Practice Areas: Commercial Litigation; General Practice — E-mail: jparado@acgoldlaw.com

Hightower, Stratton, Wilhelm, P.A.

4770 Biscayne Boulevard, Suite 1200
Miami, Florida 33137
   Telephone: 305-539-0909
   Fax: 305-530-0661
   Emer/After Hrs: 305-799-3054
   E-Mail: dale@hightowerlaw.net
   www.hightowerlaw.net

(Orlando, FL Office*: 151 Southhall Lane, Suite 140, 32751)
   (Tel: 407-352-4240)
   (Fax: 407-352-4201)
(St. Petersburg, FL Office*: 200 Central Avenue, Suite 450, 33701)
   (Tel: 727-209-1373)
   (Fax: 727-209-1383)

FLORIDA   MIAMI

Hightower, Stratton, Wilhelm, P.A., Miami, FL
(Continued)

(West Palm Beach, FL Office*: 330 Clematis Street, Suite 201, 33401)
   (Tel: 561-833-2022)
   (Fax: 561-833-2140)

Established: 1992

Assault & Battery Defense, Auto and Trucking Negligence, Commercial Litigation, Construction Claims, Environmental Law, Fraud/SIU (Special Investigative Unit), General Litigation, Homeowner's Insurance, Insurance Coverage and Bad Faith, Personal Injury and Wrongful Death, Premises Liability, Product Liability, Resorts & Leisure Liability, Retail Liability

Firm Profile: Hightower, Stratton, Wilhelm is known throughout the state of Florida for its aggressive defense of America's most well known companies. The boutique defense firm was founded in 1992 by Dale R. Hightower, one of the state's most experienced and successful litigators. The firm offers personalized, immediate service to its business partners and has become known as the "go to" law firm for companies frustrated by conventional approaches. Corporate decision makers with vision and foresight have turned to Hightower, Stratton, Wilhelm for their use of cutting edge techniques that produce great results. The firm's litigation strategies are cost effective, efficient, and result in early resolutions.

Insurance Clients

ACE USA
American Southern Insurance Company
Broadspire
Cambridge Integrated Services
ESIS
Florida Insurance Guaranty Association
GAB Robins, Inc.
G4S Wackenhut
Kemper Insurance Companies
Loomis Armored U.S., Inc.
MetLife Auto & Home
Safe Auto Insurance Company
Tower Group, Inc.
United Fire Group
Xchanging
Zurich Insurance Company
American Empire Insurance Company
Ascendant Commercial Insurance, Inc.
Chartis
Explorer Insurance Company
Frontier Insurance (In Rehabilitation)
Gallagher Bassett Services, Inc.
Great American Insurance Group
Liberty Mutual Group
Markel West, Inc.
RSUI Group, Inc.
Specialty Risk Services, Inc. (SRS)
Travelers Insurance Company
U.S. Specialty Insurance Company
York STB, Inc.

Non-Insurance Clients

American Automobile Association
Ampco System Parking
BJ's Wholesale Club, Inc.
The Cheesecake Factory
C. H. Robinson Worldwide, Inc.
Denny's, Inc.
Dollar Tree Stores, Inc.
Florida Department of Transportation
Hillstone Restaurant Group, Inc.
Home Depot USA, Inc.
Hylant Group
Kohl's Department Stores, Inc.
Marriott International, Inc.
Michaels Stores, Inc.
Moen, Inc.
Penske Truck Leasing Company
Publix Super Markets, Inc.
Ratner Companies
Sodexho, Inc.
Sysco Corporation
U.S. Security Associates, Inc.
American Management Services, Inc.
Boston Market Corporation
Chipotle Mexican Grill, Inc.
Daily Express, Inc.
Dollar General Corporation
Dunbar Armored, Inc.
GE Money
Helmsman Management Services, Inc.
Horizon Freight System, Inc.
Jo-Ann Stores, Inc.
Landry's Restaurants, Inc.
Maxim Crane Works
Miller's Ale House
National Supermarkets Association
Perkins Restaurant & Bakery
Quanta Services, Inc.
Royal Caribbean Cruises, Ltd.
SUPERVALU, Inc.
Universal Forest Products, Inc.
Waste Management, Inc.

Managing Partner

Dale R. Hightower — 1958 — Florida Southern College, B.S., 1980; Cumberland School of Law of Samford University, J.D., 1983 — Admitted to Bar, 1983, Florida; 1984, U.S. District Court, Middle and Southern Districts of Florida; 1989, U.S. Supreme Court — Member The Florida Bar; Dade County Bar Association (Board of Directors, 1985-1988); South Florida Claim Association; New York Claim Association; American Trucking Association; Defense Research Institute (Trucking Law Committee); Florida Trucking Association; Council on Litigation Management; Florida

Hightower, Stratton, Wilhelm, P.A., Miami, FL
(Continued)

Restaurant and Lodging Association; Florida Defense Lawyers Association; Transportation Lawyers Association — Resident Miami, Orlando, West Palm Beach and St. Petersburg Office

Partners

Terra D. Wilhelm
Daniel M. Novigrod
Valerie P. Prochazka, Division Leader
Christopher S. Stratton
Lee A. Kantor
Nicholas D. Mermiges, Division Leader

Associate

Scott W. Plankey

Kubicki Draper

25 West Flagler Street, Penthouse
Miami, Florida 33130-1712
   Telephone: 305-374-1212
   Fax: 305-374-7846
   E-Mail: bmc@kubickidraper.com
   www.kubickidraper.com

(Fort Lauderdale, Florida)
   (Tel: 954-768-0011)
(Fort Myers/Naples, Florida)
   (Tel: 239-334-8403)
(Jacksonville, Florida)
   (Tel: 904-396-0062)
(Ocala, Florida)
   (Tel: 352-622-4222)
(Orlando, Florida)
   (Tel: 407-245-3630)
(Pensacola, Florida)
   (Tel: 850-434-0003)
(Tallahassee, Florida)
   (Tel: 850-222-5188)
(Tampa, Florida)
   (Tel: 813-204-9776)
(West Palm Beach, Florida)
   (Tel: 561-640-0303)
(Key West, Florida)
   (Tel: 305-509-7300)

Admiralty and Maritime Law, Alternative Dispute Resolution, Arbitration, Americans with Disabilities Act, Appellate Practice, Automobile, Aviation, Bad Faith, Banking, Bankruptcy, Class Actions, Construction Accidents, Construction Defect, Construction Litigation, Corporate Law, Excess, Insurance Fraud, Intellectual Property, Labor and Employment, Personal Injury Protection (PIP), Premises Liability, Probate, Product Liability, Professional Liability, Property, Real Estate, Transportation, Trucking, Special Investigations, Workers' Compensation

Firm Profile: Kubicki Draper, established in 1963, represents corporations and insurance companies throughout Florida. With over 90 attorneys and offices in Miami, Key West, Ft. Lauderdale, West Palm Beach, Ft. Myers/Naples, Orlando, Ocala, Jacksonville, Tallahassee and Pensacola, the firm covers the entire state.

Representative Clients

Allstate Insurance Company
CNA Insurance Companies
Liberty Mutual Insurance Company
Chartis Insurance/21st Century
The Hartford Insurance Group
Zurich North America

Partners

Laurie J. Adams — University of Miami, J.D. (cum laude), 1994 — Admitted to Bar, 1994, Florida

Michael J. Carney — University of Miami, J.D., 1994 — Admitted to Bar, 1994, Florida

Earleen H. Cote — Nova University, J.D., 1981 — Admitted to Bar, 1981, Florida

MIAMI   FLORIDA

Kubicki Draper, Miami, FL   (Continued)

Brad J. McCormick — St. Thomas University, J.D., 1993 — Admitted to Bar, 1993, Florida

Peter H. Murphy — University of Miami, J.D., 1975 — Admitted to Bar, 1975, Florida

Kenneth M. Oliver — Nova University, J.D., 1984 — Admitted to Bar, 1984, Florida

Gregory J. Prusak — St. Thomas University, J.D., 1987 — Admitted to Bar, 1988, Florida

Jane C. Rankin — Widener University, J.D., 1980 — Admitted to Bar, 1982, Florida

Harold A. Saul — Florida State University, J.D., 1988 — Admitted to Bar, 1988, Florida

Charles H. Watkins — University of Miami, J.D., 1992 — Admitted to Bar, 1993, Florida

Michael Balducci
Caryn L. Bellus
G. William Bissett
Joseph W. Carey
Steve W. Cornman
Sharon C. Degnan
Jarred S. Dichek
Daniel Draper, Jr.
Betsy E. Gallagher
Steven Katz
Gene Kubicki
J. Scott McMahon
Stuart C. Poage
Ed Schuster
Kendra B. Therrell
Chelsea R. Winicki

Peter S. Baumberger
Deborah J. Bergin
Carey N. Bos
Michael C. Clarke
Stephen M. Cozart
Frank Delia
Valerie A. Dondero
Angela C. Flowers
Francesca A. Ippolito-Craven
Michelle M. Krone
Betty D. Marion
Yvette M. Pace
Jorge Santeiro
Jeremy E. Slusher
Michael S. Walsh
Sean-Kelly Xenakis

Associates

Jill Aberbach
Anthony Atala
Maegan Bridwell
Stefanie D. Capps
Richard L. Cartlidge
Karly R. Christine
Patricia Concepcion
David M. Drahos
Joseph W. Etter, IV
Michael Fogarty
Ariella J. Gutman
Kenneth Jayme Idle
Rebecca C. Kay
Bryan M. Krasinski
Heather M. Lang
Jennifer Levy
Ava G. Mahmoudi
Katherine McGovern
Grayson Miller
Ralph Mora
Brian D. Orsborn
Karina I. Perez
Jennifer Remy-Estorino
Scott M. Rosso
Christopher J. Saba
LeVale W. Simpson
Michael F. Suarez
Radia Turay
Michael A. Valverde
Nicole L. Wulwick

Bretton C. Albrecht
Lucretia A.P. Barrett
Melonie Bueno
Kara M. Carper
Brian E. Chojnowski
Terron L. Clark
Jeffrey R. DeFelice
Nicole M. Ellis
Jennifer LeVine Feld
Adam Friedman
Amanda Hutchison
Sam H. Itayim
Charles Kondla
Karl W. Labertew
Stephanie Levitt
Robyn Lustgarten
Fotini Z. Manolakos
David J. Miller
Jonathan Mills
Sia Y. Nejad
Jerrod M. Paul
Joshua Polsky
Justin P. Roberts
Christin M. Russell
William A. Sabinson
Jason S. Stewart
Eric Tourian
Christopher M. Utrera
Kristin F. Wood
Alicia Zweig

Luks & Santaniello LLC
150 West Flagler Street, Suite 2750
Miami, Florida 33130
   Telephone: 305-377-8900
   Fax: 305-377-8901
   www.LS-Law.com

Luks & Santaniello LLC, Miami, FL   (Continued)

(Additional Offices: Fort Lauderdale, FL*; Tampa, FL*; Orlando, FL*; Jacksonville, FL*; Boca Raton, FL*; Tallahassee, FL)

Insurance Defense, General Liability, Workers' Compensation

(See listing under Fort Lauderdale, FL for additional information)

Mintzer Sarowitz Zeris Ledva & Meyers, LLP
The Waterford at Blue Lagoon
1000 N.W. 57th Court, Suite 300
Miami, Florida 33126
   Telephone: 305-774-9966
   Fax: 305-774-7743
   www.Defensecounsel.com

(Additional Offices: Philadelphia, PA*; Cherry Hill, NJ*; Hicksville, NY*; New York, NY*; Pittsburgh, PA*; Wilmington, DE*; Tampa, FL*; Wheeling, WV*)

Insurance Defense, Premises Liability, Product Liability, Environmental Law, Coverage Issues, Asbestos Litigation, Medical Malpractice, Nursing Home Liability, Professional Liability, Trucking Law

Managing Partner

Addison J. Meyers

(See listing under Philadelphia, PA for additional information)

Nicklaus & Associates, P.A.
4651 Ponce de Leon Boulevard, Suite 200
Miami (Coral Gables), Florida 33146
   Telephone: 305-460-9888
   Fax: 305-460-9889
   Toll Free: 888-460-9888
   Emer/After Hrs: 305-986-4879 (Mobile)
   E-Mail: edwardn@nicklauslaw.com
   www.nicklauslaw.com

(Lakeland, FL Office: 206 Easton Drive, 33803)

Established: 1995

Insurance Law, Product Liability, Admiralty and Maritime Law, Personal Injury, Professional Liability, Trucking Law, Automobile, Transportation, Contracts, Corporate Law, Arbitration, Mediation, Civil Trial Practice, State and Federal Courts, International

Firm Profile: Nicklaus & Associates, P.A., is a nationally recognized law firm in Miami, FL with clients located across the nation. The firm primarily serves institutional and corporate clients, as well as individuals in the defense of civil cases, insurance defense, coverage matters and jury and non-jury trials.

Insurance Clients

Allianz Underwriters Insurance Company
Canal Insurance Company
Cherokee Insurance Company
Cincinnati Insurance Company
First State Insurance Company
Harco National Insurance Company
Lexington Insurance Company

California Union Insurance Company
Carolina Casualty Insurance Company
Deep South Insurance Services
Forum Insurance Company
Home Insurance Company
Jackson National Life Insurance Company

FLORIDA

Nicklaus & Associates, P.A., Miami, FL (Continued)

Liberty Mutual Insurance Company
Metropolitan Property and Casualty Insurance Company
National Benefit Life Insurance Company
Pacific Insurance Company
Prudential Insurance Company of America
XL Insurance America, Inc.
Lincoln General Insurance Company
Mutual Benefit Life Insurance Company
Ohio Casualty Insurance Company
Phoenix Insurance Company
Republic National Life Insurance Company

Non-Insurance Clients

Aero Technologies
American International Adjustment Company
Commercial Carrier Corporation
C.R. England, Inc.
The Hertz Corporation
P.A.M. Transportation Services, Inc.
Sears, Roebuck and Co.
USA Truck, Inc.
Werner Enterprises, Inc.
Alexsis, Inc.
Arkansas Best Corporation
Bulk Express Transport, Inc.
Crawford & Company
Gallagher Bassett Services, Inc.
Husqvarna Outdoor Products, Inc.
Penske Truck Leasing
Ryobi Motor Products Corporation
Swift Transportation Company, Inc.
White Consolidated Industries, Inc.

Shareholder

Edward R. Nicklaus — 1945 — DePauw University, B.A., 1967; University of Louisville, J.D., 1971 — Admitted to Bar, 1971, Kentucky; Florida; 1971, U.S. District Court, Middle and Southern Districts of Florida; 1992, U.S. District Court, Northern District of Florida; U.S. Court of Appeals, Eleventh Circuit — Member Federal, American, Kentucky and Dade County Bar Associations; The Florida Bar; National Private Truck Council; National Tank Truck Carriers; American Trucking Association; Florida Trucking Association; Southeastern Admiralty Law Institute; The Maritime Law Association of the United States; International Association of Defense Counsel; Defense Research Institute; Transportation Lawyers Association; Trucking Industry Defense Association — E-mail: edwardn@nicklauslaw.com

Associates

Gustavo A. Martinez — 1965 — University of Puerto Rico, B.S., 1988; Pontifical Catholic University of Puerto Rico School of Law, J.D. (Dean's List), 1991; Tulane University Law School, LL.M., 1993 — Admitted to Bar, 1988, Puerto Rico; 2003, Florida — Officer, U.S. Army, 1987-1998

Joshua A. Golembe — 1979 — University of Wisconsin-Madison, B.A., 2002; Nova Southeastern University, J.D., 2006 — Admitted to Bar, 2007, Florida; 2010, District of Columbia; U.S. District Court, Southern District of Florida; U.S. Court of Appeals, Eleventh Circuit — Member The Florida and District of Columbia Bars — Practice Areas: Insurance Defense — E-mail: joshuag@nicklauslaw.com

Henry P. Romeu — 1986 — University of Florida, B.A. Economics, 2008; Stetson University College of Law, J.D., 2011 — Admitted to Bar, 2011, Florida; U.S. District Court, Southern District of Florida — Member The Florida Bar — Practice Areas: Insurance Defense — E-mail: henryr@nicklauslaw.com

Danielle Venezia — 1984 — Florida State University, B.S., 2006; Nova Southeastern University, J.D., 2010 — Admitted to Bar, 2012, Florida; U.S. District Court, Southern District of Florida — Member The Florida Bar — Practice Areas: Insurance Defense — E-mail: daniellev@nicklauslaw.com

Of Counsel

Timothy J. Kovac — 1972 — University of Colorado, B.A. (cum laude), 1995; Emory University School of Law, J.D., 1998 — Admitted to Bar, 1998, Florida — Member The Florida Bar

Daniel W. Raab, P.A.

Kendall Executive Center
9555 North Kendall Drive, Suite 210
Miami, Florida 33176-1978
 Telephone: 305-598-5517
Fax: 305-598-5593
 E-Mail: raabd@bellsouth.net
 www.danielraab.com

Insurance Defense, Admiralty and Maritime Law, Personal Injury, Property Damage, Insurance Coverage, Transportation, General Liability, Cargo

Daniel W. Raab, P.A., Miami, FL (Continued)

Firm Profile: Daniel W. Raab, P.A. has been serving South Florida for over 20 years. The firm has provided a wide range of legal services for commercial enterprises including but not limited to steamship companies, insurance companies, logistic companies, freight forwarders, truckers, exporters, and retailers.

Insurance Clients

Progressive Insurance
Travelers Insurance Companies
Zurich U.S.
S.E.C.U.R.E. Underwriters Risk Retention Group

Non-Insurance Clients

Crowley Liner Services, Inc.
National Loss Management

Daniel W. Raab — Johns Hopkins University, B.A. (magna cum laude), 1975; University of Miami School of Law, J.D., 1978 — Florida Legal Elite Lawyer — Admitted to Bar, 1978, Florida; U.S. District Court, Middle and Southern Districts of Florida; U.S. Court of Appeals, Fifth and Eleventh Circuits; U.S. Supreme Court — Member The Maritime Law Association of the United States (Proctor); Southeastern Admiralty Law Institute — Author: "Transportation Terms and Conditions," Claitor's Publishing Division; Contributing Author: "Goods in Transit," LexisNexis Matthew Bender — Adjunct Professor, Florida Coastal School of Law

Shutts & Bowen LLP

201 South Biscayne Boulevard
Suite 1500
Miami, Florida 33131
 Telephone: 305-358-6300
 Fax: 305-381-9982
 Toll Free: 800-325-2892
 E-Mail: info@shutts.com
 www.shutts.com

(Fort Lauderdale, FL Office: 200 East Broward Boulevard, Suite 2100, 33301)
 (Tel: 954-524-5505)
 (Fax: 954-524-5506)
(West Palm Beach, FL Office: 525 Okeechobee Boulevard, Suite 1100, 33401)
 (Tel: 561-835-8500)
 (Fax: 561-650-8530)
(Tampa, FL Office: 4301 West Boy Scout Boulevard, Suite 300, 33607)
 (Tel: 813-229-8900)
 (Fax: 813-229-8901)
(Orlando, FL Office: 300 South Orange Avenue, Suite 1000, 32801)
 (Tel: 407-423-3200)
 (Fax: 407-425-8316)
(Sarasota, FL Office: 46 North Washington Boulevard, Suite 1, 34236)
 (Tel: 941-552-3500)

Established: 1910

Insurance Defense, Life and Health, General Liability, Fraud, Reinsurance, Disability

Firm Profile: Since its establishment in 1910, Shutts & Bowen has taken great pride in its representation of the insurance industry. Currently, more than a dozen trial and appellate lawyers are members of Shutts & Bowen's Insurance Practice Group ("IPG"). Particular areas of experience include litigation relating to individual life, health and disability insurance policies, as well as issues arising under ERISA-controlled group policies. Shutts & Bowen's IPG also extensively litigates (and provides analysis and consultation on) all aspects of automobile, homeowners, and other property and casualty policies, including tort defense, coverage, bad faith, and claims handling issues. We are also frequently consulted on issues relating to directors and officers liability policies, and we regularly litigate coverage and tort issues arising under commercial general liability policies. The firm's insurance practice also includes class action defense. IPG lawyers represent insurers in state and federal trial and appellate courts throughout the state of Florida. The IPG conducts in-house training/educational seminars for its insurer clients on subjects important to the industry, including deposition and trial preparation

MIAMI   FLORIDA

Shutts & Bowen LLP, Miami, FL   (Continued)

for employees, detection and prevention of fraudulent insurance claims, the prevention of bad faith scenarios and recent developments and trends in Florida insurance law.

Insurance Clients

Aetna Life Insurance Company	Colonial Life and Accident Insurance Company
Federated National Insurance Company	First Acceptance Insurance Company, Inc.
Florida Combined Life Insurance Company	GEICO Direct
The Guardian Life Insurance Company of America	Hartford Life Insurance Company
	Massachusetts Mutual Life Insurance Company
Mercury Insurance Group	MetLife Auto & Home
Meritplan Insurance Company - Bank of America	MetLife Insurance Company
Metropolitan Life Insurance Company	Monarch Life Insurance Company
	The Northwestern Mutual Life Insurance Company
Standard Insurance Company	Swiss Re Group
Sun Life Assurance Company of Canada	Travelers Insurance Company
Trustmark Insurance Company	United Services Automobile Association (USAA)
Unum Group	
USAA Life Insurance Company	

Non-Insurance Clients

Disability Management Services, Inc.   Lincoln Financial Group

Partners

Arnold L. Berman — 1950 — Brown University, B.A., 1972; New York University, M.B.A. (with distinction), 1976; University of Miami, J.D. (cum laude), 1977 — Admitted to Bar, 1977, Florida; New Jersey; U.S. District Court, Southern District of Florida including Trial Bar; U.S. District Court, District of New Jersey — Member American, New Jersey State, Dade County and Palm Beach County Bar Associations; The Florida Bar; Defense Research and Trial Lawyers Association — E-mail: aberman@shutts.com

Jerel C. Dawson — 1969 — University of Florida, B.A., 1990; The University of Alabama, M.A., 1993; Florida State University, J.D. (magna cum laude), 1998 — Florida State University Law Review, 1996-1998 — Admitted to Bar, 1998, Florida; 1999, U.S. District Court, Southern District of Florida; 2000, U.S. District Court, Middle District of Florida; 2004, U.S. Court of Appeals, Eleventh Circuit — Member The Florida Bar

Steven M. Ebner — 1971 — State University of New York at Binghamton, B.A., 1994; Brooklyn Law School, J.D., 1997 — Admitted to Bar, 1998, New York; 1999, New Jersey; 2003, Florida; U.S. District Court, Middle, Northern and Southern Districts of Florida; U.S. District Court, Eastern and Southern Districts of New York; U.S. District Court, District of New Jersey; U.S. Supreme Court — E-mail: sebner@shutts.com

Jonathan M. Fordin — Cornell University, B.A., 1980; University of Florida, J.D., 1983 — Admitted to Bar, 1983, Florida; 1990, District of Columbia; 1991, New York; U.S. District Court, Middle, Northern and Southern Districts of Florida; U.S. Court of Appeals, Eleventh Circuit — Member American (Trial Section) and Dade County Bar Associations; Defense Research Institute — Practice Areas: Disability; ERISA; First Party Matters; Insurance Coverage Litigation; Life and Health — E-mail: jfordin@shutts.com

William J. Gallwey, III — 1947 — Louisiana State University, B.S., 1968; Duke University, J.D., 1972 — Admitted to Bar, 1972, Ohio; 1975, Florida; U.S. District Court, Middle, Northern and Southern Districts of Florida; U.S. Court of Appeals, Fifth and Eleventh Circuits — Practice Areas: ERISA; Life and Health; Disability — E-mail: wgallwey@shutts.com

Joseph M. Goldstein — 1964 — Cornell University, B.S., 1986; Nova University, J.D. (cum laude), 1989; Georgetown University, LL.M. (with distinction), 1994 — Law Clerk to Judge Patricia Fawsett, U.S. District Court, Middle District of Florida — Admitted to Bar, 1989, Florida; U.S. Court of Appeals for the Federal Circuit; U.S. District Court, Middle and Southern Districts of Florida; U.S. Court of Appeals, Eleventh Circuit — Member American, Dade County and Broward County Bar Associations; The Florida Bar — Captain, U.S. Air Force, 1990-1994 — E-mail: jgoldstein@shutts.com

Edmund T. Henry, III — 1950 — Sewanee, The University of the South, B.A., 1972; University of Florida, J.D. (with honors), 1975 — Admitted to Bar, 1975, Florida; District of Columbia; U.S. District Court, Middle and Southern Districts of Florida; U.S. Court of Appeals, Fifth and Eleventh Circuits — Member American and Dade County Bar Associations — E-mail: ehenry@shutts.com

Shutts & Bowen LLP, Miami, FL   (Continued)

Jeffrey M. Landau — City College of the City University of New York, B.S., 1968; Columbia University, M.A., 1971; Fordham University, Ph.D., 1977; University of Miami, J.D. (with honors), 1990 — Admitted to Bar, 1990, Florida; U.S. District Court, Middle, Northern and Southern Districts of Florida; U.S. Court of Appeals, Eleventh Circuit; U.S. Supreme Court — Member American and Dade County Bar Associations; Defense Research Institute (Life, Health & Disability Committee) — Practice Areas: Insurance Coverage Litigation; Life and Health; Long-Term Care; Disability; Insurance Defense — E-mail: jlandau@shutts.com

Maxine M. Long — 1943 — Bryn Mawr College, A.B. (cum laude), 1965; Georgetown University, M.S., 1971; University of Miami, J.D. (cum laude), 1979 — Admitted to Bar, 1979, Florida; U.S. District Court, Middle, Northern and Southern Districts of Florida; U.S. Court of Appeals, Eleventh Circuit — Member American and Dade County Bar Associations; The Florida Bar (Business Law Section Executive Council, Business Litigation Committee and Pro Bono Committee); Florida Bar Business Litigation Certification Committee (Chair); Florida Supreme Court Business and Contract Jury Instruction Drafting Committee — Practice Areas: Appellate; Banking; Creditor's Rights; Litigation — E-mail: mlong@shutts.com

John E. Meagher — 1960 — University of South Florida, B.A. (cum laude), 1982; Georgetown University Law Center, J.D. (cum laude), 1985 — Admitted to Bar, 1985, Florida; U.S. District Court, Middle, Northern and Southern Districts of Florida; U.S. Court of Appeals, Eleventh Circuit; U.S. Supreme Court — Member Federal District Trial and Dade County Bar Associations; The Florida Bar; Defense Research Institute (Life, Health and Disability Section; Member, Law Committee); Association of Defense Trial Attorneys — Practice Areas: Bad Faith; Disability; Insurance Coverage Litigation; Insurance Defense; Life and Health — E-mail: jmeagher@shutts.com

Ellen Novoseletsky — The George Washington University, B.A. (summa cum laude), 1995; University of Miami, J.D. (magna cum laude), 1998 — Admitted to Bar, 1998, Florida; U.S. District Court, Middle, Northern and Southern Districts of Florida — Practice Areas: Bad Faith; Insurance Coverage Litigation; Insurance Defense; Product Liability; Commercial Litigation — E-mail: enovoseletsky@shutts.com

Harold E. Patricoff, Jr. — 1959 — Stetson University, B.A. (cum laude), 1982; J.D. (cum laude), 1985 — Admitted to Bar, 1985, Florida — Member American and Dade County Bar Associations — Practice Areas: Agent/Broker Liability; Coverage Issues; Directors and Officers Liability; Disability; ERISA; General Liability; Life and Health — E-mail: hpatricoff@shutts.com

Vanessa S. Septien — University of Miami, B.A., 1994; University of Miami School of Law, J.D., 1997 — Admitted to Bar, 1997, Florida; U.S. District Court, Middle and Southern Districts of Florida — Practice Areas: Bad Faith; Employment Law; First and Third Party Matters; Insurance Coverage Litigation; Insurance Defense; Litigation; Tort Litigation — E-mail: vseptien@shutts.com

Frank A. Zacherl — 1964 — University of Notre Dame, B.A., 1987; The George Washington University, J.D., 1990 — Admitted to Bar, 1990, Florida; U.S. District Court, Middle, Northern and Southern Districts of Florida; U.S. Court of Appeals, Eleventh Circuit — Member American Bar Association; The Florida Bar (Trial Lawyers Section); Defense Research Institute — Practice Areas: Automobile; Bad Faith; Commercial General Liability; Directors and Officers Liability; First and Third Party Matters; Homeowners; Litigation; Tort Litigation — E-mail: fzacherl@shutts.com

Sreenan Law, P.A.
44 West Flagler Street
Suite 1720
Miami, Florida 33130-1808
  Telephone: 786-369-5529
  E-Mail: sreenang@bellsouth.net

Established: 1998

Civil Litigation, Product Liability, Insurance Defense, Commercial Litigation, Aviation

Insurance Clients

AIG Aviation, Inc.	Amlin Aviation
AON Corporation	Catlin, Inc.
Chartis Insurance	Global Aerospace, Inc.

Non-Insurance Clients

South African Airways	U.S. Airways, Inc.

Sreenan Law, P.A., Miami, FL (Continued)

Gregory P. Sreenan — Florida State University College of Law, J.D., 1984 — Admitted to Bar, 1985, Florida; 1990, U.S. Supreme Court — Member American Bar Association (Sections: Air and Space Law; Litigation; Products; General Liability; Consumer Law); The Florida Bar (Aviation Law Committee, 1986-; Chairman, 1991-1992, 2002-2003; Trial Lawyers Section) — Speaker and Co-Author: "Problems and Pitfalls in Litigation Involving a Foreign Party," 1991 ABA Annual Convention, Vol 25, No. 1 The Brief 59 (1995); "The 1995 SMU Air Law Symposium," Apportionment of Damages: Evolution of a Fault-Based System of Liability for Negligence, 61 J. Air L. & Comm. 365 (1996); Co-Author: "Recent Developments in Products, General Liability and Consumer Law," Torts and Insurance Law Journal, Vol. 34 #2, Cite as 34 Tort & Ins. L.J., 1999, p. 573 — Moot Court Team (President, 1983-1984 and Competition Chairperson, 1983)

Vernis & Bowling of Miami, P.A.

1680 N.E. 135th Street
Miami, Florida 33181
Telephone: 305-895-3035
Fax: 305-892-1260
E-Mail: mgandarilla@national-law.com
www.National-Law.com

(Vernis & Bowling of the Florida Keys, P.A.*: Islamorada Professional Center, 81990 Overseas Highway, Third Floor, Islamorada, FL, 33036)
(Tel: 305-664-4675)
(Fax: 305-664-5414)
(E-Mail: info@florida-law.com)
(www.florida-law.com)
(Vernis & Bowling of the Florida Keys, P.A.*: 1009 Simonton Street, Suite 3, Key West, FL, 33040)
(Tel: 305-294-7050)
(Fax: 305-294-7016)
(E-Mail: info@florida-law.com)
(www.florida-law.com)
(Vernis & Bowling of Southwest Florida, P.A.*: 2369 West 1st Street, Fort Myers, FL, 33901-3309)
(Tel: 239-334-3035)
(Fax: 239-334-7702)
(E-Mail: info@florida-law.com)
(www.florida-law.com)
(Vernis & Bowling of the Gulf Coast, P.A. (Tampa)*: 3031 North Rocky Point Drive West, Suite 185, Tampa, FL, 33607)
(Tel: 813-712-1700)
(Fax: 813-712-1701)
(E-Mail: info@florida-law.com)
(www.florida-law.com)
(Vernis & Bowling of the Gulf Coast, P.A.*(See Clearwater listing): 696 1st Avenue, 1st Floor, St. Petersburg, FL, 33701)
(Tel: 727-443-3377)
(Fax: 727-443-6828)
(E-Mail: info@florida-law.com)
(www.florida-law.com)
(Vernis & Bowling of Central Florida, P.A.*(See Daytona Beach listing): 1450 South Woodland Boulevard, Fourth Floor, DeLand, FL, 32720)
(Tel: 386-734-2505)
(Fax: 386-734-3441)
(E-Mail: info@florida-law.com)
(www.florida-law.com)
(Vernis & Bowling of North Florida, P.A.*: 4309 Salisbury Road, Jacksonville, FL, 32216)
(Tel: 904-296-6751)
(Fax: 904-296-2712)
(E-Mail: info@florida-law.com)
(www.florida-law.com)
(Vernis & Bowling of Palm Beach, P.A.: 884 U.S. Highway One, North Palm Beach, FL, 33408)
(Tel: 561-775-9822)
(Fax: 561-775-9821)
(E-Mail: info@florida-law.com)
(www.florida-law.com)

Vernis & Bowling of Miami, P.A., Miami, FL (Continued)

(Vernis & Bowling of Broward, P.A.: 5821 Hollywood Boulevard, First Floor, Hollywood, FL, 33021)
(Tel: 954-927-5330)
(Fax: 954-927-5320)
(E-Mail: info@florida-law.com)
(www.florida-law.com)
(Vernis & Bowling of Northwest Florida, P.A.: 315 South Palafox Street, Pensacola, FL, 32502)
(Tel: 850-433-5461)
(Fax: 850-432-0166)
(E-Mail: info@florida-law.com)
(www.florida-law.com)
(Vernis & Bowling of Atlanta, LLC*: 7100 Peachtree Dunwoody Road, Suite 300, Atlanta, GA, 30328)
(Tel: 404-846-2001)
(Fax: 404-846-2002)
(E-Mail: info@georgia-law.com)
(www.georgia-law.com)
(Vernis & Bowling of Birmingham, LLC*: 3300 Cahaba Road, Suite 200, Birmingham, AL, 35223)
(Tel: 205-445-1026)
(Fax: 205-445-1036)
(E-Mail: info@law-alabama.com)
(www.law-alabama.com)
(Vernis & Bowling of Southern Alabama, LLC: 61 St. Joseph Street, Eleventh Floor, Mobile, AL, 36602)
(Tel: 251-432-0337)
(Fax: 251-432-0244)
(E-Mail: info@law-alabama.com)
(www.law-alabama.com)
(Vernis & Bowling of Charlotte, PLLC*: 4701 Hedgemore Drive, Suite 812, Charlotte, NC, 28209)
(Tel: 704-910-8162)
(Fax: 704-910-8163)
(www.national-law.com)
(Vernis & Bowling of Mississippi, PLLC: 2501 14th Street, Suite 207, Gulfport, MS, 39501)
(Tel: 228-539-0021)
(Fax: 228-539-0022)

Established: 1970

Civil Litigation, Insurance Law, Workers' Compensation, Premises Liability, Labor and Employment, Civil Rights, Commercial Litigation, Automobile Liability, Complex Litigation, Product Liability, Directors and Officers Liability, Errors and Omissions, Construction Law, Construction Defect, Environmental Liability, Personal and Commercial Vehicle, Appellate Practice, Admiralty and Maritime Law, Real Estate, Family Law, Elder Law, Personal Injury Protection (PIP), Liability Defense, SIU/Fraud Litigation, Education Law (ESE/IDEA), Property and Casualty (Commercial and Personal Lines), Long-Haul Trucking Liability, Government Law, Public Law, Criminal Law, White Collar, Business Litigation

Firm Profile: Since 1970, VERNIS & BOWLING has represented individuals, businesses, professionals, insurance carriers, self-insureds, brokers, underwriters, agents, PEOs and insured. We provide cost effective, full service, legal representation that consistently exceeds the expectations of our clients. With 115 attorneys throughout 16 offices located in Florida, Georgia, Alabama, North Carolina and Mississippi the firm is able to provide the benefits of a large organization, including a management team, consistent policies and representation to ensure personal service and local representation to our clients.

Insurance Clients

AAA Chicago Motor Club Insurance Company	AAA Michigan
Admiral Insurance Company	ACE USA
Allstate Insurance Company	AIG
American Specialty Insurance Company	American Southern Insurance Company
Armed Forces Insurance Exchange	Amica Mutual Insurance Company
Atlanta Casualty Company	AssuranceAmerica Insurance Company
Auto-Owners Insurance Company	Berkley Risk Administrators Company, LLC
Broadspire	

MIAMI   FLORIDA

Vernis & Bowling of Miami, P.A., Miami, FL   (Continued)

Burlington Insurance Company
Cincinnati Insurance Company
Citizens Property Insurance Corp.
Crawford & Company
ESIS
Farmers Insurance Group
Federated Insurance Company
First Southern Insurance Company
Florida Insurance Guaranty Association
General Reinsurance Corporation
Horace Mann Insurance Company
Johns Eastern Company, Inc.
Key Risk Insurance Company
The Main Street America Group
Mendota Insurance Company
National Marine Underwriters, Inc.
Navigators Insurance Company
Northland Insurance Company
Pennsylvania Lumbermens Mutual Insurance Company
Sedgwick Group
Self-Insurers
Travelers
Universal Insurance Company
USAA
York Risk Services Group, Inc.
Capitol Preferred Insurance Company, Inc.
CNA
EMC Insurance Company
Everest Security Insurance Company
Fireman's Fund Insurance Company
GAINSCO, Inc.
Gallagher Bassett & Co.
Great American Insurance Group
Infinity Insurance Company
Kemper Insurance Company
Liberty International Underwriters
Markel Insurance Company
Mt. Hawley Insurance Company
Nationwide Insurance
New Jersey Manufacturers Insurance Company
Prepared Insurance Company
QBE the Americas
The Seibels Bruce Group, Inc.
Stillwater Insurance Group, Inc.
United States Liability Insurance Group
US Administrator Claims

Non-Insurance Clients

ABM Industries, Inc.
Arby's
Bealls Department Stores
Bekins Van Lines
Broward County School Board
CEC Entertainment, Inc.
Chick-Fil-A, Inc.
Collier County School Board
DaVita Dialysis
FedEx
Haverty's Furniture
Lee County Board of Education
Lowe's Companies, Inc.
Nassau County School Board
Panda Restaurant Group
Rent-A-Center, Inc.
State of Florida, Division of Risk Management
US Foods
AEG Live
Barnes & Noble, Inc.
Bed Bath & Beyond, Inc.
Blockbuster Entertainment Group
Burger King Corporation
The Cheesecake Factory
CKE/Hardee's
Costco Companies, Inc.
Einstein Noah Restaurant Group
The Gap, Inc.
JPMorgan Chase & Co.
Live Nation, Inc.
Monroe County School Board
Office Depot, Inc.
Red Robin
Saks Fifth Avenue
Target Stores
Trader Joe's

Firm Members

James W. Bowling — 1935 — University of Kentucky, B.S., 1960; University of Miami School of Law, J.D., 1970 — Admitted to Bar, 1970, Florida; 1970, U.S. District Court, Southern District of Florida — Member American, Dade County and Florida Keys Bar Associations; The Florida Bar; South Florida Claims Association; Atlanta Claims Association; Defense Research Institute

Robert C. Bowling — 1964 — Stetson University, B.B.A., 1987; University of Miami, J.D. (cum laude), 1990 — Phi Delta Phi — Admitted to Bar, 1990, Georgia; 1991, Florida — Member American and Dade County Bar Associations

Jerry M. Hayden — 1962 — The University of Tennessee, B.A. (cum laude), 1984; University of Miami School of Law, J.D., 1990 — Admitted to Bar, 1990, Florida — Member Workers' Compensation and Employment Law Sections of the Florida Bar Association

Mario E. Lopez — 1970 — Florida International University, B.A., 1992; Nova Southeastern University, J.D., 1995 — Admitted to Bar, 1996, Florida — Member Dade County Bar Association — Languages: Spanish

Andrew W. Bray — 1959 — University of Connecticut, B.A. (magna cum laude), 1988; University of Connecticut School of Law, J.D., 1991 — Admitted to Bar, 2004, Florida; 1991, Connecticut; 1992, U.S. District Court, District of Connecticut; 2004, U.S. District Court, Southern District of Florida — Member American and Broward County Bar Associations; Florida Defense Lawyers Association — U.S. Army

Eric J. Knuth — 1964 — Northern Michigan University, B.S., 1987; Thomas M. Cooley Law School, J.D. (cum laude, with honors), 1990 — Admitted to Bar, 1991, Michigan; 2010, Florida; 1991, U.S. District Court, Eastern and Western Districts of Michigan; 1994, U.S. District Court, Eastern District of Wisconsin — Member Lapeer County Bar Association; State Bar of Michigan; Lapeer County Optimist Club; Sons of the American Legion-Post 16 Lapeer

Vernis & Bowling of Miami, P.A., Miami, FL   (Continued)

K. Scott Dwyer — 1953 — State University of New York at Buffalo, B.A. (cum laude), 1975; The University of North Carolina at Chapel Hill, J.D., 1979 — Phi Eta Sigma — Admitted to Bar, 1980, Florida

Ramy P. Elmasri — 1979 — Texas Tech University, B.A., 2001; Texas A&M University School of Law, J.D. (Dean's List), 2005 — Admitted to Bar, 2005, Texas; 2010, Florida; 2012, U.S. District Court, Southern District of Florida — Member American and Dade County (Young Lawyers Section) Bar Associations — Languages: Spanish

Emily Smith — 1985 — Roosevelt University, B.A. (with highest honors), 2007; University of Miami School of Law, J.D. (cum laude), 2012 — Admitted to Bar, 2012, Florida

Sarah Rickey — University of South Florida, B.A., 2008; Nova Southeastern University, Shepard Broad Law Center, J.D., 2012 — Admitted to Bar, 2013, Florida

Tim West — 1985 — Texas Tech University, B.A., 2008; California State University, Long Beach, M.A., Communications, 2010; St. Thomas University School of Law, J.D., 2013 — Admitted to Bar, 2013, Florida

Jennifer E. Pelaez — 1984 — Florida International University, B.A., 2006; Florida International University College of Law, J.D., 2009 — Admitted to Bar, 2010, Florida; 2011, U.S. District Court, Southern District of Florida — Languages: Spanish

Raul Flores
Willie B. Ramhofer
Faustino Estoy
Justin D. Siegwald

Wicker Smith O'Hara McCoy & Ford P.A.

2800 Ponce de Leon Boulevard, Suite 800
Coral Gables, Florida 33134
 Telephone: 305-448-3939
 Fax: 305-441-1745
 www.wickersmith.com

(Fort Lauderdale, FL Office*: Sun Trust Center, 515 East Las Olas Boulevard, Suite 1400, 33301)
 (Tel: 954-847-4800)
 (Fax: 954-760-9353)
(Jacksonville, FL Office*: Bank of America, Suite 2700, 50 North Laura Street, 32202)
 (Tel: 904-355-0225)
 (Fax: 904-355-0226)
(Naples, FL Office*: Mercato, 9128 Strada Place, Suite 10200, 34108)
 (Tel: 239-552-5300)
 (Fax: 239-552-5399)
(Orlando, FL Office*: Bank of America Center, 390 North Orange Avenue, Suite 1000, 32801)
 (Tel: 407-843-3939)
 (Fax: 407-649-8118)
(Tampa, FL Office*: 100 North Tampa Street, Suite 1800, 33602)
 (Tel: 813-222-3939)
 (Fax: 813-222-3938)
(West Palm Beach, FL Office*: Northbridge Centre, 515 North Flagler Drive, Suite 1600, 33401)
 (Tel: 561-689-3800)
 (Fax: 561-689-9206)

Established: 1952

General Civil Litigation, General Civil Practice, State and Federal Courts, Accountant Malpractice, Accountants and Attorneys Liability, Administrative Law, Admiralty and Maritime Law, Agent and Brokers Errors and Omissions, Appellate Practice, Automobile, Aviation, Bad Faith, Class Actions, Commercial Litigation, Complex Litigation, Construction Litigation, Environmental Law, Estate Planning, Fraud, Hospital Malpractice, Insurance Coverage, Labor and Employment, Legal Malpractice, Medical Devices, Medical Malpractice, Nursing Home Liability, Pharmaceutical, Premises Liability, Probate, Product Liability, Professional Liability, Professional Malpractice, Special Investigative Unit Claims, Real Estate, Retail Liability, Toxic Torts, Transportation, Trucking Litigation, Trusts, Workers' Compensation, Multi-District Litigation, Sexual Abuse

Wicker Smith O'Hara McCoy & Ford P.A., Miami, FL
(Continued)

Firm Profile: In 1952, Idus Q. Wicker and James A. Smith formed a partnership with the goal of providing legal services of exceptional quality to their clients. They remained partners until their retirement and life-long friends. The firm they founded has expanded to seven offices located throughout Florida in Coral Gables, Fort Lauderdale, West Palm Beach, Orlando, Tampa, Naples and Jacksonville. Although the firm has changed in size and scope, the goal of providing exceptional legal representation has remained the same.

Clients turn to Wicker Smith when they have critical and complex litigation matters because of the firm's vast experience in complex litigation filed in State and Federal Courts. Numerous major corporations have selected Wicker Smith as national and regional counsel. Supporting the litigation team is a preeminent Appellate Department, which has appeared as appellate counsel in more than 1,200 reported decisions, including several landmark opinions issued by the Supreme Court of Florida.

Wicker Smith attorneys are recognized as leaders in the defense of a wide range of litigation practice areas, including products liability, medical malpractice, catastrophic aviation accidents, legal malpractice, accounting malpractice, nursing home claims, construction litigation, and commercial litigation, as well as a variety of general negligence matters. In all such matters, communication and attention to the client's specific needs are our highest priority.

The backbone of our relationship with clients is built upon integrity and stability. We strive to establish long-term relationships with our clients built upon a partnership of communication and trust. We achieve this objective by listening to our clients, understanding their businesses and developing legal solutions to best meet their individual needs. With seven offices, over 140 attorneys, and an experienced support staff of legal assistants, paralegals, investigators, nurses, and a physician, Wicker Smith can provide legal services for its clients throughout the entire State of Florida and beyond.

Insurance Clients

American Healthcare Indemnity Company
Chubb Group of Insurance Companies
Florida Intracoastal Underwriters, Ltd.
National Indemnity Company
Philadelphia Insurance Companies
ProAssurance Group
Scottsdale Insurance Company
State Farm Insurance Companies
Travelers Insurance Company
Zurich North America
Chartis
Chartis Aerospace
The Doctors Company
First Professionals Insurance Company
The Medical Protective Company
Ohio Casualty Insurance Company
Physicians Insurance Company
Safeco Insurance Company of America
Swiss Re
XL Aerospace

Non-Insurance Clients

Bob's Barricades, Inc.
Columbia Hospital
Continental Commercial Products, Inc.
Interstate Hotels Corporation
Landstar System, Inc.
Lawnwood Regional Medical Center
NCH Healthcare Systems, Inc.
Office Depot, Inc.
PRMS, Inc. - Professional Risk Management Services, Inc.
Stanley Black & Decker, Inc.
University of Miami
Wet 'n Wild
Circle K Stores, Inc., a division of Tosco Corp.
Delta Air Lines, Inc.
Health Management Associates, Inc.
La Quinta Inns, Inc.
McDonald's Corporation
Mt. Sinai Medical Center
North American Risk Services
Orlando Health
Publix Super Markets, Inc.
7-Eleven, Inc.
Tenet Healthcare Corporation
Walgreen Co.

Firm Members

Idus Q. Wicker — (1918-1986)

James A. Smith — (Retired)

Jackson F. McCoy — 1948 — University of Miami, B.B.A., 1970; J.D., 1973 — Admitted to Bar, 1973, Florida; 1975, U.S. District Court, Southern District of Florida including Trial Bar — Member American and Dade County Bar Associations; The Florida Bar; The Federal Bar; Dade County Defense Bar Association (Director,1980-1984); American Society for Healthcare Risk Management; Florida Society for Healthcare Risk Management; International Academy of Trial Lawyers (2005-present); International Association of Defense Counsel; American Society of Law and Medicine; Defense Research Institute; Florida Medical Malpractice Claims Council; American Board of Trial Advocates — Best Lawyers in America 2003-2012; Florida Super Lawyers "Top 100" Lawyers for Personal Injury Defense: Medical Malpractice, 2008-2011; Florida Super Lawyers Personal Injury Defense: Medical Malpractice, 2006-2012; Florida Monthly Top Lawyers in Florida for Personal Injury Litigation, 2003-2005; South Florida Legal Guide's Top Lawyers in Florida for Professional Liability & Medical Malpractice, 2005-2011; Florida Trend Magazine's Florida Legal Elite for Civil Trial, 2005, 2006, 2008 & 2009 — Practice Areas: Civil Litigation; Medical Malpractice

Frederick E. Hasty, III — 1950 — University of Florida, B.A., 1973; Mercer University, J.D., 1976 — Admitted to Bar, 1976, Georgia; 1978, Florida; 1976, U.S. District Court, Middle District of Georgia; 1977, U.S. Court of Appeals, Fifth Circuit; 1979, U.S. District Court, Southern District of Florida including Trial Bar; 1981, U.S. Court of Appeals, Eleventh Circuit — Member American and Dade County Bar Associations; State Bar of Georgia; The Florida Bar (Committee on Health Law, 1983-Present); Florida Hospital Association; Dade County Defense Bar Association; International Association of Defense Counsel; Florida Medical Malpractice Claims Council (General Counsel, 1985-1992); Defense Research Institute — Assistant State Attorney, Eleventh Judicial Circuit, 1979; Legal Advisor, City of Macon, Georgia, 1976-1978 — Practice Areas: Accountant Malpractice; Agent and Brokers Errors and Omissions; Bad Faith; Civil Litigation; Commercial Litigation; Construction Law; Insurance Coverage; Legal Malpractice; Medical Malpractice

Nicholas E. Christin — 1948 — University of Miami, B.B.A., 1970; M.S., 1971; J.D., 1974; LL.M., 1978 — Admitted to Bar, 1974, Florida; U.S. District Court, Southern District of Florida — Member American (Fiduciary Income Tax Committee) and Dade County Bar Associations; The Florida Bar; Florida and American Institute of Certified Public Accountants — Certified Public Accountant — Practice Areas: Accountant Malpractice; Civil Litigation; Commercial Litigation; Estate Planning; Real Estate Litigation; Wills and Estate Litigation

Leslie A. McCormick — 1962 — Clemson University, B.A., 1984; University of Miami, J.D., 1987 — Admitted to Bar, 1987, Florida; U.S. District Court, Southern District of Florida — Member American and Dade County (AD HOC Trial Practices and Procedures Committee of Dade County, 1994-2004) Bar Associations; The Florida Bar; The Federal Bar, Southern District of Florida Trial Bar; American Society for Healthcare Risk Management; Dade County Defense Bar Association (Officer, 1995-1997); Florida Hospital Association; Riviera Country Club, Coral Gables, FL (Board of Governors 2006-2010; Executive Committee 2007-2008); University of Miami School of Law Alumni Association (Presidential Appointee 2000-2001); Council on Litigation Management; Defense Research Institute — Best Lawyers in America 2010-2012; Florida Super Lawyers 2008-2012; Florida Trend's Florida Legal Elite 2008 — Practice Areas: Civil Litigation; Class Actions; Medical Devices; Medical Malpractice; Pharmaceutical

Oscar J. Cabanas — 1958 — Northwestern University, B.A., 1981; University of Miami, J.D., 1984 — Admitted to Bar, 1984, Illinois; 1985, Florida; 1984, U.S. District Court, Northern District of Illinois; U.S. Court of Appeals, Fifth Circuit; 1985, U.S. District Court, Southern District of Florida; 2004, U.S. District Court, Middle District of Florida — Member American Bar Association; The Florida Bar; American Hospital Association; Florida Hospital Association; Litigation Counsel of America; Cuban American Bar Association; American Society for Healthcare Risk Management; Florida Defense Lawyers Association; Defense Research Institute; American Board of Trial Advocates; Federation of Defense and Corporate Counsel; Transportation Lawyers Association — Florida Super Lawyers 2007-2012; Florida Trend's Florida Legal Elite, Civil Trial 2010-2011 — Languages: Spanish — Practice Areas: Civil Litigation; Medical Malpractice; Professional Malpractice; Transportation

Constantine G. Nickas — 1965 — University of Miami, B.B.A. (cum laude), 1987; J.D. (cum laude), 1990 — Admitted to Bar, 1990, Florida; 1991, U.S. District Court, Southern District of Florida including Trial Bar — Member Dade County Bar Association; The Florida Bar; Dade County Defense Bar Association; Florida Medical Malpractice Claims Institute; Defense Research Institute (Committees: Lawyers' Professionalism and Ethics, Food Liability); USLAW Network, Inc (Chair, Retail Practice Group Program) — Florida Super Lawyers 2009-2012 — Languages: Spanish, Greek — Practice Areas: Automobile Liability; Bad Faith; Civil Litigation; Insurance Coverage; Labor and Employment; Legal Malpractice; Medical Malpractice; Nursing Home Liability; Premises Liability; Product Liability; Professional Liability; Retail Liability

MIAMI   FLORIDA

Wicker Smith O'Hara McCoy & Ford P.A., Miami, FL (Continued)

William F. Fink — 1961 — University of Florida, B.S.B.A., 1984; Stetson University, J.D., 1988 — Admitted to Bar, 1988, Florida; U.S. District Court, Southern District of Florida — Member The Florida Bar; Dade County Bar Association; Dade County Defense Bar Association; Defense Research Institute (Construction Committee, Medical Malpractice Committee and Product Liability Committee); South Florida Chapter, Associated General Contractors of America; American Board of Trial Advocates — Practice Areas: Accountant Malpractice; Agent and Brokers Errors and Omissions; Automobile Liability; Bad Faith; Civil Litigation; Construction Law; Insurance Coverage; Legal Malpractice; Medical Malpractice; Premises Liability; Product Liability; Professional Liability

Michael A. Holtmann — 1962 — The University of Iowa, B.A., 1984; Creighton University, J.D., 1993 — Admitted to Bar, 1993, Florida; 1994, U.S. District Court, Southern District of Florida; 2006, U.S. District Court, Northern District of Florida — Practice Areas: Agent and Brokers Errors and Omissions; Bad Faith; Civil Litigation; Construction Law; Insurance Coverage; Medical Malpractice; Premises Liability; Professional Liability

Cary W. Capper — 1959 — Florida State University, B.S., 1982; St. Thomas University, J.D., 1991 — Admitted to Bar, 1992, Florida; 1998, U.S. District Court, Southern District of Florida — Practice Areas: Bad Faith; Civil Litigation; Insurance Coverage; Medical Malpractice; Premises Liability

Bryan B. Walton — 1972 — Washington and Lee University, B.A., 1995; The University of Alabama, J.D., 1998 — Admitted to Bar, 1998, Florida; 2000, U.S. District Court, Southern District of Florida — Practice Areas: Civil Litigation; Medical Malpractice; Nursing Home Liability; Premises Liability; Professional Liability; Retail Liability

Eric D. Diamond — 1977 — University of Miami, B.A., 1999; J.D., 2002 — Admitted to Bar, 2002, Florida; 2006, U.S. District Court, Southern District of Florida — Practice Areas: Civil Litigation; Medical Malpractice

Erik P. Crep — 1976 — Columbia University, B.A., 1999; University of Miami, J.D. (cum laude), 2004 — Admitted to Bar, 2004, Florida; 2012, U.S. District Court, Southern District of Florida — Practice Areas: Civil Litigation; Commercial Litigation; Medical Malpractice; Premises Liability; Professional Liability

Ana M. Alexander — 1964 — Florida International University, B.A., 1987; University of Miami, J.D., 1990 — Admitted to Bar, 1990, Florida; 1997, Massachusetts; 1992, U.S. District Court, Southern District of Florida; 2001, U.S. Court of Appeals, First Circuit — Languages: Spanish — Practice Areas: Automobile Liability; Civil Litigation; Construction Law; Legal Malpractice; Medical Malpractice; Nursing Home Liability; Premises Liability; Product Liability; Retail Liability

Vivianne A. Wicker — 1957 — Samford University, B.S., 1978; J.D., 1981 — Admitted to Bar, 1982, Florida; 1988, U.S. District Court, Southern District of Florida — Practice Areas: Automobile Liability; Bad Faith; Civil Litigation; Construction Law; Insurance Coverage; Premises Liability; Product Liability; Retail Liability

A. Scott Lundeen — 1954 — Vanderbilt University, B.A., 1976; University of Miami School of Law, J.D., 1985 — Admitted to Bar, 1985, Florida; 1985, U.S. District Court, Northern District of Florida — Practice Areas: Administrative Law; Automobile Liability; Civil Litigation; Construction Law; Medical Malpractice; Premises Liability; Product Liability

Damian D. Daley — University of Florida, B.A. (with honors), 2002; J.D., 2006 — Admitted to Bar, 2006, Florida; 2008, U.S. District Court, Southern District of Florida; 2009, U.S. Court of Appeals, Eleventh Circuit

Jacob J. Liro — Boston College, B.A., 2003; University of Miami, J.D., 2006 — Admitted to Bar, 2006, Florida; 2011, U.S. District Court, Southern District of Florida

Associates

Johnny D. White — Florida State University, B.S., 1998; St. Thomas University, J.D., 2003 — Admitted to Bar, 2004, Florida

Katie S. Fleischman — Tulane University, B.A. (cum laude), 1980; Nova Southeastern University, J.D. (magna cum laude), 2005 — Admitted to Bar, 2005, Florida

Heidi Nam — Northwestern University, B.S., 1999; University of Miami, J.D., 2004 — Admitted to Bar, 2004, Florida — Languages: French, Korean, Spanish

Shannon L. McCoy — Florida State University, B.S. (with honors), 2002; University of Miami, J.D., 2005 — Admitted to Bar, 2005, Florida

David R. Cook — The University of North Carolina, B.A., 2003; University of Miami, J.D., 2007 — Admitted to Bar, 2007, Florida — Languages: Spanish

Wicker Smith O'Hara McCoy & Ford P.A., Miami, FL (Continued)

Manuel A. Dieguez — University of Florida, B.A., 2004; The George Washington University, J.D., 2007 — Admitted to Bar, 2007, Florida — Languages: Spanish

Teresita M. Sierra — Florida International University, B.A., 2003; St. Thomas University, J.D., 2008 — Admitted to Bar, 2008, Florida — Languages: Spanish

John S. Leinicke — Boston University, B.A., 2004; University of Miami, J.D., 2008 — Admitted to Bar, 2009, Florida

Lynn L. Audie — Georgia State University, B.S., 1985; University of Miami School of Law, 1990 — Admitted to Bar, 1990, Florida

Drew M. Levin — University of Michigan, B.A., 2004; University of Miami School of Law, J.D., 2007 — Admitted to Bar, 2008, Florida

Anthony C. Hevia — Rollins College, B.A. (cum laude), 2003; Florida International University College of Law, J.D., 2007 — Admitted to Bar, 2007, Florida; 2009, District of Columbia — Languages: Spanish

Laura E. Shearon — Tulane University, B.A., 2002; Tulsa University School of Law, J.D., 2007 — Admitted to Bar, 2007, Florida

Brandon J. Hechtman — University of Miami, B.S.C. (magna cum laude), 2006; Florida International University College of Law, J.D., 2010 — Admitted to Bar, 2011, Florida

John C. Lukacs, Jr. — University of Florida, B.S., 2007; St. Thomas University School of Law, J.D. (cum laude), 2011 — Admitted to Bar, 2011, Florida

Jaime A. Alvarez, Jr. — Florida International University, B.A. (magna cum laude), 2006; Florida State University College of Law, J.D. (cum laude), 2009 — Admitted to Bar, 2009, Florida

Todd M. Norbraten — University of Florida, B.S.B.A., 2005; St. Thomas University School of Law, J.D., 2008 — Admitted to Bar, 2008, Florida

Nicole R. Somoano — Universidad del Sagrado Corazón, Santurce, Puerto Rico, B.A. (summa cum laude), 2000; Florida International University College of Law, J.D. (cum laude), 2005 — Admitted to Bar, 2005, Florida

Kirsten O. Erdmann — Florida State University, B.S., 1997; Florida International University College of Law, J.D., 2006 — Admitted to Bar, 2006, Florida

Young, Bill, Roumbos & Boles, P.A.

One Biscayne Tower, Suite 3195
2 South Biscayne Boulevard
Miami, Florida 33131
    Telephone: 305-222-7720
    Fax: 305-492-7729
    E-Mail: ryoung@flalawyer.net
    www.flalawyer.net

(Pensacola, FL Office*: Seville Tower, 7th Floor, 226 South Palafox Place, 32502, P.O. Drawer 1070, 32591-1070)
(Tel: 850-432-2222)
(Fax: 850-432-1444)

Insurance Defense, Coverage Issues, Complex Litigation, Bad Faith, Product Liability, Medical Malpractice, Nursing Home Liability, Construction Defect, Premises Liability, General Liability, Automobile Liability

(See listing under Pensacola, FL for additional information)

The following firms also service this area.

Catri, Holton, Kessler & Kessler, P.A.
The Litigation Building, Third Floor
633 South Andrews Avenue
Fort Lauderdale, Florida 33301
    Telephone: 954-463-8593
    Fax: 954-462-1303

Insurance Defense, Trial and Appellate Practice, Insurance Coverage, Self-Insured, General Liability, Product Liability, Automobile Liability, Premises Liability, Construction Liability, Guardian and Conservatorships, Probate, Business Litigation, Commercial Litigation, Arbitration, Mediation

SEE COMPLETE LISTING UNDER FORT LAUDERDALE, FLORIDA (25 MILES)

FLORIDA

Fertig & Gramling
200 Southeast 13th Street
Fort Lauderdale, Florida 33316
  Telephone: 954-763-5020, 305-945-6250 (Miami)
  Fax: 954-763-5412

Coverage Issues, Admiralty and Maritime Law, Casualty, Fraud, Property, Reinsurance, Errors and Omissions, Directors and Officers Liability

SEE COMPLETE LISTING UNDER FORT LAUDERDALE, FLORIDA (25 MILES)

Leiter & Belsky, P.A.
707 Southeast Third Avenue, Third Floor
Fort Lauderdale, Florida 33316
  Telephone: 954-462-3116
  Fax: 954-761-8990

Insurance Defense, Insurance Coverage, Appellate Practice, General Liability, Bad Faith, Automobile Liability, Product Liability, Construction Claims, Construction Defect, Construction Litigation, Insurance Claim Analysis and Evaluation, Insurance Coverage Determination, Insurance Coverage Litigation, Insurance Law, Insurance Litigation, Litigation, No-Fault, Personal Injury Protection (PIP), Premises Liability, Primary and Excess Insurance, Professional Liability, Self-Insured, Self-Insured Defense, Trial and Appellate Practice

SEE COMPLETE LISTING UNDER FORT LAUDERDALE, FLORIDA (25 MILES)

MILTON † 8,826 Santa Rosa Co.

Refer To

Vernis & Bowling of Northwest Florida, P.A.
315 South Palafox Street
Pensacola, Florida 32502
  Telephone: 850-433-5461
  Fax: 850-432-0166

Civil Litigation, Insurance Law, Workers' Compensation, Premises Liability, Labor and Employment, Civil Rights, Commercial Litigation, Complex Litigation, Product Liability, Directors and Officers Liability, Errors and Omissions, Construction Law, Construction Defect, Environmental Liability, Personal and Commercial Vehicle, Appellate Practice, Admiralty and Maritime Law, Real Estate, Family Law, Elder Law, Liability Defense, SIU/Fraud Litigation, Education Law (ESE/IDEA), Property and Casualty (Commercial and Personal Lines), Long-Haul Trucking Liability, Government Law, Public Law, Criminal, White Collar, Business Litigation

SEE COMPLETE LISTING UNDER PENSACOLA, FLORIDA (21 MILES)

NAPLES † 19,537 Collier Co.

Conroy Simberg

5100 North Tamiami Trail, Suite 125
Naples, Florida 34103
  Telephone: 239-263-0663
  Fax: 239-263-0960
  E-Mail: csg@conroysimberg.com
  www.conroysimberg.com

Insurance Defense, Appellate Practice, Insurance Coverage, Environmental Law, Governmental Liability, Civil Rights, Wrongful Termination, Americans with Disabilities Act, Sexual Harassment, Land Use, Commercial Law, Fire, Arson, Fraud, Fidelity and Surety, Automobile Liability, Admiralty and Maritime Law, Bad Faith, Employment Law, Self-Insured, Public Entities, Product Liability, Casualty, Excess and Reinsurance, Accident and Health, Workers' Compensation, Medical Malpractice, Class Actions, Construction Defect, Construction Litigation, First Party Matters, Premises Liability, Professional Liability, Intellectual Property

(See listing under Hollywood, FL for additional information)

Wicker Smith O'Hara McCoy & Ford P.A.

Mercato
9128 Strada Place, Suite 10200
Naples, Florida 34108
  Telephone: 239-552-5300
  Fax: 239-552-5399
  www.wickersmith.com

(Coral Gables, FL Office*(See Miami listing): 2800 Ponce de Leon Boulevard, Suite 800, 33134)
  (Tel: 305-448-3939)
  (Fax: 305-441-1745)
(Fort Lauderdale, FL Office*: Sun Trust Center, 515 East Las Olas Boulevard, Suite 1400, 33301)
  (Tel: 954-847-4800)
  (Fax: 954-760-9353)
(Jacksonville, FL Office*: Bank of America, Suite 2700, 50 North Laura Street, 32202)
  (Tel: 904-355-0225)
  (Fax: 904-355-0226)
(Orlando, FL Office*: Bank of America Center, 390 North Orange Avenue, Suite 1000, 32801)
  (Tel: 407-843-3939)
  (Fax: 407-649-8118)
(Tampa, FL Office*: 100 North Tampa Street, Suite 1800, 33602)
  (Tel: 813-222-3939)
  (Fax: 813-222-3938)
(West Palm Beach, FL Office*: Northbridge Centre, 515 North Flagler Drive, Suite 1600, 33401)
  (Tel: 561-689-3800)
  (Fax: 561-689-9206)

General Civil Litigation, General Civil Practice, State and Federal Courts, Accountant Malpractice, Accountants and Attorneys Liability, Administrative Law, Admiralty and Maritime Law, Agent and Brokers Errors and Omissions, Appellate Practice, Automobile, Aviation, Bad Faith, Class Actions, Commercial Litigation, Complex Litigation, Construction Litigation, Environmental Law, Estate Planning, Fraud, Hospital Malpractice, Insurance Coverage, Labor and Employment, Legal Malpractice, Medical Devices, Medical Malpractice, Nursing Home Liability, Pharmaceutical, Premises Liability, Probate, Product Liability, Professional Liability, Professional Malpractice, Special Investigative Unit Claims, Real Estate, Retail Liability, Toxic Torts, Transportation, Trucking Litigation, Trusts, Workers' Compensation, Multi-District Litigation, Sexual Abuse

Firm Profile: In 1952, Idus Q. Wicker and James A. Smith formed a partnership with the goal of providing legal services of exceptional quality to their clients. They remained partners until their retirement and life-long friends. The firm they founded has expanded to seven offices located throughout Florida in Miami, Fort Lauderdale, West Palm Beach, Orlando, Tampa, Naples and Jacksonville. Although the firm has changed in size and scope, the goal of providing exceptional legal representation has remained the same.

Clients turn to Wicker Smith when they have critical and complex litigation matters because of the firm's vast experience in complex litigation filed in State and Federal Courts. Numerous major corporations have selected Wicker Smith as national and regional counsel. Supporting the litigation team is a preeminent Appellate Department, which has appeared as appellate counsel in more than 1,200 reported decisions, including several landmark opinions issued by the Supreme Court of Florida.

Wicker Smith has recognized leaders in the defense of a wide range of litigation practice areas, including products liability, medical malpractice, pharmaceutical and medical devices, catastrophic aviation accidents, legal malpractice, accounting malpractice, nursing home claims, construction litigation, as well as a variety of general negligence matters. In all such matters, communication and attention to the client's specific needs are our highest priority. The backbone of our relationship with clients is built upon integrity and stability. We strive to establish long-term relationships with our clients, built upon a partnership of communication and trust. We achieve this objective by listening to our clients, understanding their businesses and developing legal solutions to best meet their individual needs.

NEW SMYRNA BEACH FLORIDA

Wicker Smith O'Hara McCoy & Ford P.A., Naples, FL (Continued)

Firm Members

Kevin W. Crews — 1968 — Florida State University, B.S., 1990; St. Thomas University, J.D., 1994 — Admitted to Bar, 1994, Florida; 1997, U.S. District Court, Northern and Southern Districts of Florida; 2000, U.S. District Court, Middle District of Florida — Member American, Dade County, Collier County and Lee County Bar Associations; The Florida Bar; American Inns of Court; Florida Medical Malpractice Claims Council; Florida Defense Lawyers Association; Defense Research Institute — Florida Trend's Legal Elite, 2011 — Practice Areas: Administrative Law; Automobile Liability; Civil Litigation; Commercial Litigation; Construction Law; Labor and Employment; Medical Malpractice; Premises Liability

Anthony J. McNicholas, III — 1945 — University of Miami, B.A., 1970; Florida State University, J.D. (with high honors), 1974 — Admitted to Bar, 1974, Florida; 1977, U.S. District Court, Northern District of Florida; 1988, U.S. District Court, Southern District of Florida; 1993, U.S. District Court, Middle District of Florida — Member American, Collier County and Palm Beach County Bar Associations; The Florida Bar; Florida Defense Lawyers Association; Defense Research Institute

Ashley P. Withers — 1974 — University of Illinois at Urbana-Champaign, B.S., 1996; DePaul University, J.D., 2001 — Admitted to Bar, 2001, Illinois; 2005, Florida — Languages: Spanish — Practice Areas: Civil Litigation; Construction Law; Medical Malpractice; Premises Liability

R. Baron Ringhofer — 1978 — The University of Arizona, B.A., 1999; Loyola University Chicago, J.D., 2002 — Admitted to Bar, 2002, Illinois; 2007, Florida; 2002, U.S. District Court, Northern District of Illinois; U.S. Court of Appeals, Seventh Circuit; 2008, U.S. District Court, Middle District of Florida

Julie A. Campbell — 1963 — The Ohio State University, B.A., 1995; Georgetown University, J.D., 1998 — Admitted to Bar, 1998, Virginia; 2001, District of Columbia; 2008, Florida; 2001, U.S. District Court for the District of Columbia; 2003, U.S. District Court, Eastern District of Virginia; 2008, U.S. District Court, Middle District of Florida

Craig Ferrante — 1956 — University of Florida, B.S.B.A. (with honors), 1977; University of Florida College of Law, J.D., 1980 — Admitted to Bar, 1981, Florida; 1987, U.S. District Court, Middle District of Florida

Associates

A. Kevin Houston — Florida State University, B.S., 1997; J.D. (cum laude), 2002 — Admitted to Bar, 2002, Florida

Tiffany N. Hampton — University of Miami, B.A., 2005; Stetson University, J.D. (cum laude), 2008 — Admitted to Bar, 2008, Florida

Brandon M. Nichols — University of Florida, B.A., 2003; Nova Southeastern University, J.D., 2007 — Admitted to Bar, 2008, Florida — Languages: Spanish

Lauren R. McBride — University of Florida, B.A. (summa cum laude), 2000; University of Florida, Levin College of Law, J.D. (cum laude), 2004 — Admitted to Bar, 2004, Florida

Odelsa "Ody" Flores-Dickman — Florida International University, B.A., 1996; Nova Southeastern University, Shepard Broad Law Center, J.D., 1999 — Admitted to Bar, 2000, Florida

David P. Fraser — Siena Heights University, B.A., 2008; Florida State University College of Law, J.D., 2011 — Admitted to Bar, 2011, Florida

(See listing under Miami, FL for additional information)

The following firms also service this area.

Abbey, Adams, Byelick & Mueller, L.L.P.
360 Central Avenue, 11th Floor
St. Petersburg, Florida 33701
Telephone: 727-821-2080
Fax: 727-822-3970

Mailing Address: P.O. Box 1511, St. Petersburg, FL 33731

Administrative Law, Americans with Disabilities Act, Appellate Practice, Complex Litigation, General Defense, Employment Law, Bad Faith, Insurance Coverage, Insurance Fraud, Uninsured and Underinsured Motorist, Professional Malpractice, Mediation, Negligence, Personal Injury, Premises Liability, Product Liability, Subrogation, Toxic Torts, Workers' Compensation, Motor Vehicle Liability, Defense of Insureds, Sovereign Immunity and Governmental Defense

SEE COMPLETE LISTING UNDER ST. PETERSBURG, FLORIDA (153 MILES)

Henderson, Franklin, Starnes & Holt Professional Association
1715 Monroe Street
Fort Myers, Florida 33901
Telephone: 239-344-1100
Fax: 239-344-1200

Mailing Address: P.O. Box 280, Fort Myers, FL 33902-0280

Construction Litigation, Employment Law, Municipal Law, Professional Malpractice, Tort Litigation, Workers' Compensation

SEE COMPLETE LISTING UNDER FORT MYERS, FLORIDA (37 MILES)

Vernis & Bowling of Southwest Florida, P.A.
2369 West 1st Street
Fort Myers, Florida 33901-3309
Telephone: 239-334-3035
Fax: 239-334-7702

Civil Litigation, Insurance Law, Workers' Compensation, Premises Liability, Labor and Employment, Civil Rights, Commercial Litigation, Complex Litigation, Product Liability, Directors and Officers Liability, Errors and Omissions, Construction Law, Construction Defect, Environmental Liability, Personal and Commercial Vehicle, Appellate Practice, Admiralty and Maritime Law, Real Estate, Family Law, Elder Law, Liability Defense, SIU/Fraud Litigation, Education Law (ESE/IDEA), Property and Casualty (Commercial and Personal Lines), Long-Haul Trucking Liability, Government Law, Public Law, Criminal, White Collar, Business Litigation

SEE COMPLETE LISTING UNDER FORT MYERS, FLORIDA (37 MILES)

Young, Bill, Roumbos & Boles, P.A.
One Biscayne Tower, Suite 3195
2 South Biscayne Boulevard
Miami, Florida 33131
Telephone: 305-222-7720
Fax: 305-492-7729

Insurance Defense, Coverage Issues, Complex Litigation, Bad Faith, Product Liability, Medical Malpractice, Nursing Home Liability, Construction Defect, Premises Liability, General Liability, Automobile Liability

SEE COMPLETE LISTING UNDER MIAMI, FLORIDA (111 MILES)

NEW PORT RICHEY 14,911 Pasco Co.

Refer To

Abbey, Adams, Byelick & Mueller, L.L.P.
360 Central Avenue, 11th Floor
St. Petersburg, Florida 33701
Telephone: 727-821-2080
Fax: 727-822-3970

Mailing Address: P.O. Box 1511, St. Petersburg, FL 33731

Administrative Law, Americans with Disabilities Act, Appellate Practice, Complex Litigation, General Defense, Employment Law, Bad Faith, Insurance Coverage, Insurance Fraud, Uninsured and Underinsured Motorist, Professional Malpractice, Mediation, Negligence, Personal Injury, Premises Liability, Product Liability, Subrogation, Toxic Torts, Workers' Compensation, Motor Vehicle Liability, Defense of Insureds, Sovereign Immunity and Governmental Defense

SEE COMPLETE LISTING UNDER ST. PETERSBURG, FLORIDA (41 MILES)

NEW SMYRNA BEACH 22,464 Volusia Co.

Refer To

Vernis & Bowling of Central Florida, P.A.
1450 South Woodland Boulevard, Fourth Floor
DeLand, Florida 32720
Telephone: 386-734-2505
Fax: 386-734-3441

Civil Litigation, Insurance Law, Workers' Compensation, Premises Liability, Labor and Employment, Civil Rights, Commercial Litigation, Complex Litigation, Product Liability, Directors and Officers Liability, Errors and Omissions, Construction Law, Construction Defect, Environmental Liability, Personal and Commercial Vehicle, Appellate Practice, Admiralty and Maritime Law, Real Estate, Family Law, Elder Law, Liability Defense, SIU/Fraud Litigation, Education Law (ESE/IDEA), Property and Casualty (Commercial and Personal Lines), Long-Haul Trucking Liability, Government Law, Public Law, Criminal, White Collar, Business Litigation

SEE COMPLETE LISTING UNDER DAYTONA BEACH, FLORIDA (25 MILES)

NORTH PALM BEACH 12,015 Palm Beach Co.

Vernis & Bowling of Palm Beach, P.A.
884 U.S. Highway #1
North Palm Beach, Florida 33408-5408
  Telephone: 561-775-9822
  Fax: 561-775-9821
  E-Mail: gjvernis@florida-law.com
  www.national-law.com

(Vernis & Bowling of Southern Alabama, LLC*: 61 St. Joseph Street, 11th Floor, Mobile, AL, 36602)
  (Tel: 251-432-0337)
  (Fax: 251-432-0244)
  (E-Mail: info@law-alabama.com)
  (www.law-alabama.com)
(Vernis & Bowling of Broward, P.A.*(See Fort Lauderdale listing): 5821 Hollywood Boulevard, First Floor, Hollywood, FL, 33021)
  (Tel: 954-927-5330)
  (Fax: 954-927-5320)
  (E-Mail: info@florida-law.com)
(Vernis & Bowling of Northwest Florida, P.A.*: 315 South Palafox Street, Pensacola, FL, 32502)
  (Tel: 850-433-5461)
  (Fax: 850-432-0166)
  (E-Mail: info@florida-law.com)
(Vernis & Bowling of Southern Mississippi, PLLC*: 2501 14th Street, Suite 207, Gulfport, MS, 39501)
  (Tel: 225-539-0021)
  (Fax: 228-539-0022)

Established: 1970

Civil Litigation, Insurance Law, Workers' Compensation, Premises Liability, Labor and Employment, Civil Rights, Commercial Litigation, Complex Litigation, Product Liability, Directors and Officers Liability, Errors and Omissions, Construction Law, Construction Defect, Environmental Liability, Personal and Commercial Vehicle, Appellate Practice, Admiralty and Maritime Law, Real Estate, Family Law, Elder Law, Liability Defense, SIU/Fraud Litigation, Education Law (ESE/IDEA), Property and Casualty (Commercial and Personal Lines), Long-Haul Trucking Liability, Government Law, Public Law, Criminal, White Collar, Business Litigation

Firm Profile: VERNIS & BOWLING represents individuals, businesses, insurance carriers and self-insureds. With 115 offices located in Florida, Georgia, Alabama, North Carolina & Mississippi, we provide cost effective, full service legal representation that consistently exceeds the expectations of our clients.

Insurance Clients

Auto-Owners Insurance Company	Burlington Insurance Company
Chrysler Insurance Company	Chubb Group of Insurance Companies
CNA Insurance Companies	Florida Insurance Guaranty Association
Crum & Forster Insurance Group	
Lexington Insurance Company	National Service Industries, Inc.
National General Insurance Company	United Automobile Insurance Group

Non-Insurance Clients

AAA Michigan	AutoNation Incorporated
Lowe's Home Centers, Inc.	State of Florida

Managing Partner

G. Jeffrey Vernis — University of South Florida, B.A., 1984; St. Thomas University School of Law, J.D., 1987 — Admitted to Bar, 1988, Florida; 1988, U.S. District Court, Southern District of Florida — Member American and Palm Beach County Bar Associations; The Florida Bar

---

Vernis & Bowling of Palm Beach, P.A., North Palm Beach, FL *(Continued)*

Firm Members

Karen Nissen — 1956 — Rollins College/University of Georgia, M.Ed., 1981; University of Florida, J.D., 1990 — Admitted to Bar, 1991, Florida — Member Federal, American and Palm Beach County Bar Associations; The Florida Bar

Ralph Mabie, Jr. — 1960 — University of Florida, B.A., 1982; J.D., 1985 — Admitted to Bar, 1985, Florida

Joseph G. Murasko — 1962 — University of Central Florida, B.S., 1984; University of San Diego, J.D., 1988 — Admitted to Bar, 1989, California; 1991, Florida; U.S. District Court, Central and Southern Districts of California; U.S. District Court, Middle and Southern Districts of Florida; U.S. Court of Appeals, Ninth Circuit

Elizabeth Cantu — Palm Beach Atlantic University, B.S., 2002; Nova Southeastern University, Shepard Broad Law Center, J.D., 2010 — Admitted to Bar, 2010, Florida — Languages: Spanish

Stephanie Showe — Florida Coastal School of Law, J.D., 2010 — Admitted to Bar, 2010, Florida

Jeffrey Alexander — University of Colorado at Boulder, B.A., 1988; Gonzaga University School of Law, J.D., 1992 — Admitted to Bar, 1992, Florida

Chioma R. Deere — Wells College, B.A. (Dean's List), 2000; Pace University School of Law, J.D. (Dean's List), 2006 — Wells College, Presidential Leadership Award — Admitted to Bar, 2008, Florida

Gina Leiser — Montclair State University, B.A., 2003; University of Miami School of Law, J.D. (cum laude), 2008 — Admitted to Bar, 2008, Florida

Lauren Walsh — University of Miami, B.A., 2005; Stetson University College of Law, J.D., 2009 — Admitted to Bar, 2009, Florida; U.S. District Court, Southern District of Florida

Miriama Roc — Bridgewater State College, B.S., 2000; New England School of Law, J.D., 2006 — Admitted to Bar, 2007, Florida; U.S. District Court, Middle, Northern and Southern Districts of Florida; U.S. Bankruptcy Court, Middle, Northern and Southern Districts of Florida — Member Broward County Bar Association; Haitian Lawyers Association — Languages: Haitian Creole

Robin M. Rumpf — 1975 — Michigan State University, B.A., 2001; New York Law School, J.D. (cum laude), 2004 — New York Law School Law Review — Admitted to Bar, 2005, Florida

Ashley Landrum — Florida State University, B.A., 2011; Michigan State University College of Law, J.D., 2014 — Admitted to Bar, 2014, Florida

OCALA † 56,315 Marion Co.

Cameron, Hodges, Coleman, LaPointe & Wright, P.A.
1820 Southeast 18th Avenue, #1-2
Ocala, Florida 34478
  Telephone: 352-351-1119
  Fax: 352-351-0151
  www.cameronhodges.com

(Orlando, FL Office*: 111 North Magnolia Avenue, Suite 1350, 32801-2378)
  (Tel: 407-841-5030)
  (Fax: 407-841-1727)
  (E-Mail: ccameron@cameronhodges.com)
(Daytona Beach, FL Office*: 150 South Palmetto Avenue, # 101, 32114)
  (Tel: 386-257-1755)
  (Fax: 386-252-5601)

Insurance Law

Firm Profile: Our history of client satisfaction is a result of responsiveness to client expectations, and open communication regarding file handling and fees.

Insurance Clients

Adventist Risk Management, Inc.	AIX Group
Allstate Insurance Company	American Family Insurance Group
American Inter-Fidelity Exchange	Athens Insurance

Cameron, Hodges, Coleman, LaPointe & Wright, P.A., Ocala, FL (Continued)

Auto-Owners Insurance Company
Chubb Group of Insurance Companies
Co-operative Insurance Companies
Crawford & Company
Engle Martin & Associates
Federated Insurance Company
GEICO
Hertz Claim Management
Nationwide Insurance
Pennsylvania Lumbermens Mutual Insurance Company
St. Johns Insurance Company, Inc.
The Seibels Bruce Group, Inc.
SPARTA Insurance
TRISTAR Risk Management
Wilshire Insurance Company [IAT-Group]
Carolina Casualty Insurance Company
The Concord Group Insurance Companies
EGI Auto
Erie Insurance Group
Gallagher Bassett Services, Inc.
The Hartford
Mid-Continent Casualty Company
North Carolina Farm Bureau Mutual Insurance Company
Penn Tank Lines
Sedgwick CMS
Sentry Transportation Insurance Company
United Services Automobile Association (USAA)
York Claims Service, Inc.

Non-Insurance Clients

Albertsons, Inc.
Davis Transfer Company
Enterprise Rent-A-Car Company
SuperShuttle
Central Refrigerated Services Inc.
Dollar Rent A Car Systems, Inc.
J.B. Hunt Transport Services, Inc.

Partners

Christopher C. Coleman — 1951 — Mercer University, B.S., 1973; Southern School of Pharmacy, B.S., 1976; Mercer University Walter F. George School of Law, J.D., 1987 — Admitted to Bar, 1987, Florida; 1987, U.S. District Court, Middle District of Florida — Member American and Marion County Bar Associations — E-mail: ccoleman@cameronhodges3.com

Virgil W. Wright, III — 1963 — Pensacola Junior College, A.A., 1988; University of West Florida, B.A., 1990; Cumberland School of Law of Samford University, J.D., 1993 — Admitted to Bar, 1993, Florida; 1996, U.S. District Court, Middle District of Florida — Member Marion County and Duval County Bar Associations — E-mail: bwright@cameronhodges3.com

Junior Partner

Bradley R. Killinger — 1977 — University of Florida, B.S.B.A., 1998; J.D., 2001 — Admitted to Bar, 2002, Florida — E-mail: bkillinger@cameronhodges3.com

(See Daytona Beach and Orlando, FL listings for additional information)

McConnaughhay, Duffy, Coonrod, Pope & Weaver, P.A.

2403 SE 17th Street, Suite 201
Ocala, Florida 34471
Telephone: 352-840-0330
Fax: 352-401-9518
www.mcconnaughhay.com

(Additional Offices: Tallahassee, FL*; Fort Lauderdale, FL*; Gainesville, FL*; Jacksonville, FL*; Panama City, FL*; Pensacola, FL*; Sarasota, FL*)

Insurance Defense, Workers' Compensation, Product Liability, Labor and Employment, Civil Litigation, Trial Practice, Appellate Practice

Associates

Jennifer T. Reimsnyder
Kristianna K. Lindgren

The following firms also service this area.

Abbey, Adams, Byelick & Mueller, L.L.P.
360 Central Avenue, 11th Floor
St. Petersburg, Florida 33701
Telephone: 727-821-2080
Fax: 727-822-3970

Mailing Address: P.O. Box 1511, St. Petersburg, FL 33731

Administrative Law, Americans with Disabilities Act, Appellate Practice, Complex Litigation, General Defense, Employment Law, Bad Faith, Insurance Coverage, Insurance Fraud, Uninsured and Underinsured Motorist, Professional Malpractice, Mediation, Negligence, Personal Injury, Premises Liability, Product Liability, Subrogation, Toxic Torts, Workers' Compensation, Motor Vehicle Liability, Defense of Insureds, Sovereign Immunity and Governmental Defense

SEE COMPLETE LISTING UNDER ST. PETERSBURG, FLORIDA (121 MILES)

Dell Graham, P.A.
203 Northeast First Street
Gainesville, Florida 32601
Telephone: 352-372-4381
Fax: 352-376-7415

Insurance Defense, Civil Trial Practice, State and Federal Courts, Automobile, Medical Malpractice, Product Liability, Governmental Liability, Property and Casualty

SEE COMPLETE LISTING UNDER GAINESVILLE, FLORIDA (37 MILES)

Vernis & Bowling of Central Florida, P.A.
1450 South Woodland Boulevard, Fourth Floor
DeLand, Florida 32720
Telephone: 386-734-2505
Fax: 386-734-3441

Civil Litigation, Insurance Law, Workers' Compensation, Premises Liability, Labor and Employment, Civil Rights, Commercial Litigation, Complex Litigation, Product Liability, Directors and Officers Liability, Errors and Omissions, Construction Law, Construction Defect, Environmental Liability, Personal and Commercial Vehicle, Appellate Practice, Admiralty and Maritime Law, Real Estate, Family Law, Elder Law, Liability Defense, SIU/Fraud Litigation, Education Law (ESE/IDEA), Property and Casualty (Commercial and Personal Lines), Long-Haul Trucking Liability, Government Law, Public Law, Criminal, White Collar, Business Litigation

SEE COMPLETE LISTING UNDER DAYTONA BEACH, FLORIDA (77 MILES)

OKEECHOBEE † 5,621 Okeechobee Co.

Refer To

Wiederhold & Moses, P.A.
560 Village Boulevard, Suite 240
West Palm Beach, Florida 33409-1963
Telephone: 561-615-6775, 954-763-5630
Fax: 561-615-7225

Mailing Address: P.O. Box 3918, West Palm Beach, FL 33402

Insurance Defense, Trial Practice

SEE COMPLETE LISTING UNDER WEST PALM BEACH, FLORIDA (62 MILES)

ORANGE PARK 8,412 Clay Co.

Law Offices of Bohdan Neswiacheny

151 College Drive, Suite 1
Orange Park, Florida 32065
Telephone: 904-276-6171
Fax: 904-276-1751
E-Mail: bnlaw@bnlaw.com
www.bnlaw.com

(Fort Lauderdale, FL Office*: 2929 E Commercial Boulevard, Suite 300, 33308)
(Tel: 954-522-5400)
(Fax: 954-765-1274)
(Sarasota, FL Office*: 1800 Second Street, Suite 760, 34236)
(Tel: 941-957-3400)
(Fax: 941-952-9103)

FLORIDA

Law Offices of Bohdan Neswiacheny, Orange Park, FL
(Continued)

Insurance Defense, Insurance Coverage, Automotive Products Liability, Construction Defect, Employment Discrimination, Premises Liability, Product Liability, Trial and Appellate Practice

Managing Member

Bohdan Neswiacheny — United States Military Academy at West Point, B.S., 1968; University of Miami, J.D., 1980 — Admitted to Bar, 1980, Florida; U.S. District Court, Middle, Northern and Southern Districts of Florida — U.S. Army, Lieutenant Colonel (Retired) — Languages: Ukrainian — Practice Areas: Insurance Defense; Insurance Coverage; Construction Defect — E-mail: bneswiacheny@bnlaw.com

Associates

James E. Kallaher — University of Missouri, B.A., 1988; Florida Coastal School of Law, J.D., 2000 — Admitted to Bar, 2001, Florida; U.S. District Court, Middle District of Florida — U.S. Naval Reserve, Commander — Practice Areas: Insurance Defense; Construction Defect — E-mail: jkallaher@bnlaw.com

Sean C. Barber — C. Newport College, College of William and Mary, B.A., 1998; Florida Coastal School of Law, J.D., 2003 — Admitted to Bar, 2003, Florida; U.S. District Court, Middle District of Florida — Practice Areas: Insurance Defense — E-mail: sbarber@bnlaw.com

(See listing under Fort Lauderdale, FL for additional information)

ORLANDO † 238,300 Orange Co.

BOEHM BROWN HARWOOD, P.A.

Suite 365
1060 Maitland Center Commons Boulevard
Maitland, Florida 32751
Telephone: 407-660-0990
Fax: 407-660-5052
www.boehmbrown.com

Established: 1976

Trial and Appellate Practice, State and Federal Courts, General Liability, Product Liability, Construction Litigation, Property Damage, Arson, Fraud, Insurance Coverage, First Party Matters, Excess and Reinsurance, Bad Faith, Windstorm, Collapse

Firm Profile: Since its founding in 1976, BOEHM BROWN HARWOOD, P.A. has represented a wide range of institutional and corporate clients in the highly specialized field of insurance coverage issues. Our firm also continues to represent commercial and individual insureds in the defense of lawsuits brought against them. Our commitment to service and excellence is reflected by the professionalism of the partners, our record of success in the insurance and defense arenas and recognition by peers through invitations to speak and publish at a variety of insurance industry conferences.

For many years, BOEHM BROWN HARWOOD, P.A. has enjoyed the reputation of being a leader in the field of first party insurance coverage issues. Our firm's attorneys actively participate in numerous national and local organizations devoted to both property insurance and other first party coverage disputes. Serving as officers, faculty and authors for publications by entities such as the Windstorm Insurance Network, Inc., the Property Insurance Law Committee of the Tort Trial and Insurance Practice Section of the American Bar Association, the Florida Advisory Committee on Arson Prevention, the Loss Executives Association, the Federation of Defense and Corporate Counsel, The American College of Coverage and Extracontractual Counsel and the Defense Research Institute, BOEHM BROWN HARWOOD, P.A. remains on the cutting edge of insurance coverage issues.

As the 21st century progresses, our firm has chosen to strongly emphasize our experience with first and third party insurance coverage issues. By concentrating our efforts in these areas, the firm's knowledge of coverage issues helps us to serve our clients in a cost-effective manner by reducing the duplication of research, as well as repetitive investigations and consultations.

ORLANDO

BOEHM BROWN HARWOOD, P.A., Orlando, FL
(Continued)

This knowledge also allows our firm to concentrate on solutions with intensity and utilize each attorney's strong work ethic and knowledge in his or her chosen areas of practice.

BOEHM BROWN HARWOOD, P.A. recognizes that the highest quality, most cost-effective legal representation is achieved through the preparation of accurate and reliable strategic plans and litigation budgets. While our firm is vigorous in the defense of lawsuits, we recognize that early resolution of claims can be beneficial to our clients. We therefore strive to use our extensive resources to avoid (or bring an efficient conclusion to) costly litigation through mediation and other alternative dispute resolution methods.

Insurance Clients

ACE Westchester Specialty Group	America First/One Beacon Insurance Company
American Coastal Insurance Company/AmRisk	American Integrity Insurance Company
American National Property and Casualty Company	Arch Insurance Group
Aspen Specialty Insurance Company	Axis Surplus Insurance Company
Chartis/Lexington Insurance Company	Boulder Claims
Essex/Markel International Insurance Company	Crum & Forster
Foremost Insurance Company	Endurance U.S. Insurance Operations
General Reinsurance Corporation	Farmers/Foremost Insurance Company
GeoVera Specialty Insurance Company	General Star Indemnity Company
Privilege Underwriters Reciprocal Exchange (PURE)	Pacific/Beazley/First State
The Travelers Companies, Inc.	Philadelphia Insurance Companies
XL Insurance	RSUI Group, Inc.
	State Auto Insurance Company
	U.S. Adjustment Corporation
	Zurich North America

Firm Members

J. Richard Boehm — Retired (2013) — 1947 — Florida State University, B.A., 1969; J.D., 1975 — Phi Delta Phi — Admitted to Bar, 1976, Florida — Member American Bar Association (Trial Tort and Insurance Practice Section); The Florida Bar (Workers' Compensation and Trial Lawyer's Section); Volusia County Bar Association (Workers' Compensation Committee); Florida Defense Lawyers Association; Defense Research Institute — State of Florida Attorney General's Office, Civil Litigation Division — Florida Bar Board Certified Civil Trial (1990-1995) and Workers' Compensation Lawyer (1988-2008); Certified Circuit Mediator

Janet L. Brown — 1951 — Cottey College, A.A., 1971; Marietta College, B.A., 1973; College of William & Mary, Marshall-Wythe School of Law, J.D., 1976 — Admitted to Bar, 1977, Florida; 1977, U.S. District Court, Middle District of Florida; 1977, U.S. Court of Appeals, Fifth Circuit; 1977, U.S. District Court, Northern District of Florida; 1980, U.S. Supreme Court; 1981, U.S. Court of Appeals, Eleventh Circuit; 1986, U.S. District Court, Southern District of Florida — Member American Bar Association (Trial Tort and Insurance Practice Section); The Florida Bar (Trial Lawyers Section); Loss Executives Association; Windstorm Insurance Network, Inc. (President, 2003); Florida Advisory Committee on Arson Prevention (President, 1982); Federation of Defense and Corporate Counsel (Regional Vice-President, 2000-2003; Director, 2003-2007); American College of Coverage and Extracontractual Counsel; Defense Research Institute — Trustee, Cottey College (2008-Present) — Florida Bar Board Certified Civil Trial Lawyer (1990-Present); Certified Circuit Mediator (1986-Present); CPCU (1987-Present) — Practice Areas: First Party Matters; Arson; Fraud; Construction Law; Extra-Contractual Litigation — E-mail: jbrown@boehmbrown.com

Susan B. Harwood — 1957 — Wake Forest University, B.A. (Phi Beta Kappa, magna cum laude), 1979; Wake Forest University School of Law, J.D., 1983 — Admitted to Bar, 1983, Florida; U.S. Court of Appeals, Eleventh Circuit; U.S. District Court, Middle and Southern Districts of Florida — Member The Florida Bar (Trial Lawyers Section); Federation of Defense and Corporate Counsel (Board of Directors, 2011-2013; Litigation Management College (Dean of Graduate Program 2011-2013; Associate Dean of Graduate Program, 2009-2011); Membership Committee, 2011-2013; Visibility Project, 2011-2013; Chair, Property Insurance Section, 2007-2009; Admissions Committee, 2006-2014; Amicus Committee, 2011-2013; Diversity Initiative Committee, 2008-2012; Chair, Exhibitors Committee, 2005-2007); Loss Executive Association; Windstorm Insurance Network, Inc. (Board of Directors, 2008-2013; Secretary, 2014); American College of Coverage and

ORLANDO — FLORIDA

BOEHM BROWN HARWOOD, P.A., Orlando, FL
(Continued)

Extracontractual Counsel — Certified Circuit Mediator — Practice Areas: Insurance Coverage; General Liability; Construction Defect; Bad Faith; Extra-Contractual Litigation — E-mail: sbharwood@boehmbrown.com

Cameron, Hodges, Coleman, LaPointe & Wright, P.A.

111 North Magnolia Avenue, Suite 1350
Orlando, Florida 32801-2378
 Telephone: 407-841-5030
 Fax: 407-841-1727
 E-Mail: ccameron@cameronhodges.com
 www.cameronhodges.com

(Daytona Beach, FL Office*: 150 South Palmetto Avenue, # 101, 32114)
 (Tel: 386-257-1755)
 (Fax: 386-252-5601)
(Ocala, FL Office*: 1820 Southeast 18th Avenue, #1-2, 34478)
 (Tel: 352-351-1119)
 (Fax: 352-351-0151)

Established: 1980

Insurance Law

Firm Profile: Our history of client satisfaction is a result of responsiveness to client expectations, and open communication regarding file handling and fees.

Insurance Clients

Adventist Risk Management, Inc.
Allstate Insurance Company
American Inter-Fidelity Exchange
Auto-Owners Insurance Company
Chubb Group of Insurance Companies
Co-operative Insurance Companies
Crawford & Company
Engle Martin & Associates
Federated Insurance Company
GEICO
Hertz Claim Management
Mid-Continent Casualty Company
North Carolina Farm Bureau Mutual Insurance Company
Penn Tank Lines
Sedgwick CMS
Sentry Transportation Insurance Company
United Services Automobile Association (USAA)
York Claims Service, Inc.
AIX Group
American Family Insurance Group
Athens Insurance
Carolina Casualty Insurance Company
The Concord Group Insurance Companies
EGI Auto
Erie Insurance Group
Gallagher Bassett Services, Inc.
The Hartford
Lancer Insurance Company
Nationwide Insurance
Pennsylvania Lumbermens Mutual Insurance Company
St. Johns Insurance Company, Inc.
The Seibels Bruce Group, Inc.
SPARTA Insurance
TRISTAR Risk Management
Wilshire Insurance Company [IAT-Group]

Non-Insurance Clients

Albertsons, Inc.
Davis Transfer Company
Enterprise Rent-A-Car Company
SuperShuttle
Central Refrigerated Services Inc.
Dollar Rent A Car Systems, Inc.
J.B. Hunt Transport Services, Inc.

Partners

A. Craig Cameron — 1947 — University of Pennsylvania, B.A., 1970; Stetson University, J.D., 1973 — Phi Alpha Delta — Stetson Law Review — Admitted to Bar, 1973, Florida; U.S. District Court, Middle District of Florida; U.S. Court of Appeals, Fifth Circuit; U.S. Supreme Court — Member American Bar Association; The Florida Bar; Diplomate, National Board of Trial Advocacy; Defense Research Institute; Florida Defense Lawyers Association; International Association of Defense Counsel — Florida Claims Manual — Florida Bar Board Certified Civil Trial Lawyer — Practice Areas: Automobile; Premises Liability; Truck Liability; Product Liability — E-mail: ccameron@cameronhodges.com

E. Peyton Hodges — 1953 — The University of Georgia, A.B., 1975; Mercer University, J.D., 1975 — Phi Delta Phi — Admitted to Bar, 1978, Florida; Georgia — Member American and Orange County Bar Associations; The Florida Bar; State Bar of Georgia; Florida Defense Lawyers Association; Defense Research Institute; International Association of Defense Counsel —

Cameron, Hodges, Coleman, LaPointe & Wright, P.A., Orlando, FL
(Continued)

Practice Areas: Automobile; Premises Liability; Product Liability — E-mail: eph@cameronhodges.com

Douglas J. LaPointe — 1968 — Florida State University, B.S. (with honors), 1990; Cumberland School of Law of Samford University, J.D., 1993 — Psi Chi National Honor Society — Admitted to Bar, 1993, Florida; 1994, U.S. District Court, Middle and Southern Districts of Florida; 1996, U.S. Court of Appeals, Eleventh Circuit — Member The Florida Bar; Association of Trial Lawyers of America; Defense Research Institute — Practice Areas: Employment Discrimination; Sexual Harassment — E-mail: dlapointe@cameronhodges.com

Junior Partners

Robert W. Mixson — 1953 — University of Florida, B.S., 1975; J.D., 1978 — Admitted to Bar, 1979, Florida; U.S. District Court, Middle District of Florida; 1982, U.S. Court of Appeals, Eleventh Circuit — Member American and Orange County Bar Associations; The Florida Bar — E-mail: rmixson@cameronhodges.com

Julia M. Pinnell — 1955 — University of Central Florida, B.A., 1988; Stetson University, J.D., 1991 — Admitted to Bar, 1991, Florida; U.S. District Court, Middle District of Florida — E-mail: jpinnell@cameronhodges.com

Associates

Tiffany M. Chill — 1973 — University of Central Florida, B.S., 1995; Stetson University, J.D./M.B.A., 1999 — Moot Court Board (1998-1999) — Admitted to Bar, 2000, Florida; U.S. District Court, Middle District of Florida — Member American Bar Association; The Florida Bar — Practice Areas: Civil Litigation; Employment Law; Employment Litigation

David A. Fifner — 1959 — Cleveland State University, Cleveland-Marshall College of Law, J.D., 1985 — Admitted to Bar, 1985, Ohio; 1987, Florida; 2001, U.S. Court of Appeals for the Federal and Eleventh Circuits; 2002, U.S. District Court, Northern District of Ohio; 2003, U.S. District Court, Middle District of Florida including Trial Bar — Member The Florida Bar — Practice Areas: Automobile; Insurance Defense; Coverage Opinions; Trucking

Gregg W. Hooth — 1968 — Thomas M. Cooley Law School, J.D., 1995 — Admitted to Bar, 1995, Florida; 1996, U.S. Court of Appeals for the Federal and Eleventh Circuits; 2006, U.S. District Court, Middle and Southern Districts of Florida — Member The Florida Bar (Labor and Employment Section) — Practice Areas: Commercial Litigation; Insurance Defense; Labor and Employment

Jonathan Thomson — University of Miami, B.B.A., 2005; Brooklyn Law School, J.D., 2009 — Admitted to Bar, 2010, Florida

Daniel R. Blundy — 1983 — University of Florida, B.S. (magna cum laude), 2005; B.A. Physiology (cum laude), 2005; Florida State University College of Law, J.D., 2008 — Admitted to Bar, 2009, Florida; 2012, U.S. District Court, Middle District of Florida — Member The Florida Bar (Young Lawyer's Division) — Practice Areas: Civil Litigation; Insurance Defense

(See Daytona Beach and Ocala, FL listings for additional information)

Conroy Simberg

2 South Orange Avenue, Suite 300
Orlando, Florida 32801
 Telephone: 407-649-9797
 Fax: 407-649-1968
 E-Mail: csg@conroysimberg.com
 www.conroysimberg.com

Insurance Defense, Appellate Practice, Insurance Coverage, Environmental Law, Governmental Liability, Civil Rights, Wrongful Termination, Americans with Disabilities Act, Sexual Harassment, Land Use, Commercial Law, Fire, Arson, Fraud, Fidelity and Surety, Automobile Liability, Admiralty and Maritime Law, Bad Faith, Employment Law, Self-Insured, Public Entities, Product Liability, Casualty, Excess and Reinsurance, Accident and Health, Workers' Compensation, Medical Malpractice, Class Actions, Construction Defect, Construction Litigation, First Party Matters, Premises Liability, Professional Liability, Intellectual Property

(See listing under Hollywood, FL for additional information)

FLORIDA   ORLANDO

Dean, Ringers, Morgan and Lawton, P.A.

201 East Pine Street, Suite 1200
Orlando, Florida 32801
    Telephone: 407-422-4310
    Fax: 407-648-0233
    www.DRML-law.com

(Tampa, FL Office: Corporate Center One at International Plaza, 2202 North West Shore Boulevard, Suite 200, 33607)
    (Tel: 813-288-4686)
    (Fax: 813-902-6575)

Established: 1978

Casualty, ERISA, Health, Life Insurance, Surety, Workers' Compensation, Civil Rights, Personal Injury, Product Liability, Wrongful Death, Medical Malpractice, Employment Practices Liability, Trucking Law, Police Misconduct, Business Law, Amusement and Recreation Law

Insurance Clients

AIG	American Empire Surplus Lines Insurance Company
American Specialty Insurance Company	Argonaut Insurance Company
Broadspire	Cambridge Integrated Services
Celtic Insurance Company	Central Mutual Insurance Company
Claims Management Services, Inc.	CNA Claim Plus
Crawford & Company	FCCI Insurance Group
FFVA Mutual Insurance Company	Florida Farm Bureau General Insurance Company
Florida Municipal Insurance Trust	
Florida Municipal Liability Self Insurers Program	GAB Robins North America, Inc.
	GatesMcDonald
Grange Insurance Association	Guarantee Insurance Company
Hanover Insurance Company	Houston General Insurance Company
Independent Order of Foresters	
Indiana Insurance Company	Jefferson-Pilot Corporation
Johns Eastern Company, Inc.	Medmarc Insurance Group
Mutual of Omaha Insurance Company	North American Risk Services
	Ohio Casualty Group
Progressive Insurance Company	Risk Enterprise Management, Ltd.
St. Paul Property & Liability Insurance	Sedgwick James
	Specialty Risk Services, Inc. (SRS)
Unisource Insurance Company	United Self Insured Services
York Claims Service, Inc.	Zurich Insurance Group

Non-Insurance Clients

Abbott Laboratories	Adventist Health Systems
Amateur Athletic Union of the United States, Inc.	Avis Budget Car Rental, LLC
	BP Company
Central Florida YMCA	City of Altamonte Springs
City of Sanford	Coca-Cola Bottling Company
Collis Roofing, Inc.	Covenant Administrators, Inc.
Dollar General Corporation	Dollar-Thrifty Automotive Group, Inc.
Estes Express Lines	
Florida League of Cities	Florida Roofers Association, Inc.
Florida Workers' Compensation Fund	Hernando County Government
	Hubbard Construction
Hughes Supply, Inc.	Hyatt Corporation
Interstate Hotels and Resorts	Morgan Tire Company
MV Transportation, Inc.	Oakley Transport
Oasis Outsourcing	Orange County Government
Orange County Sheriff	Pacific Cycle, Inc.
Pinnacle Benefits, Inc.	Protegrity Services, Inc.
Regis Corporation	Rollins College
7-Eleven, Inc.	Starwood Hotels & Resorts Worldwide, Inc.
Universal Orlando, Florida	
UPS Freight	Water Mania
Wyeth	

Founding Partner

Dale O. Morgan — 1943 — University of South Florida, B.A. (with honors), 1968; Stetson University, J.D., 1971 — Admitted to Bar, 1971, Florida; 1971, U.S. District Court, Middle District of Florida; 1979, U.S. Supreme Court; 1986, U.S. Court of Appeals for the Federal and Eleventh Circuits — Member American and Orange County Bar Associations; The Florida Bar — Florida Bar Board Certified Civil Trial Lawyer — Practice Areas: Insurance Defense — E-mail: dmorgan@drml-law.com

Dean, Ringers, Morgan and Lawton, P.A., Orlando, FL
(Continued)
Founder & Senior Managing Partner

William E. Lawton — 1949 — University of Florida, B.A. (magna cum laude), 1971; J.D. (cum laude), 1973 — Phi Beta Kappa, Phi Kappa Phi — Admitted to Bar, 1973, Florida; 1993, District of Columbia; 1973, U.S. District Court, Middle District of Florida; 1979, U.S. Supreme Court; 1985, U.S. Court of Appeals for the Federal and Eleventh Circuits; 2004, U.S. District Court, Northern District of Florida; 2004, U.S. District Court, Eastern and Middle Districts of Pennsylvania; 2005, U.S. District Court, Eastern and Northern Districts of Arkansas; 2005, U.S. District Court, Eastern and Western Districts of Washington — Member American and Orange County Bar Associations; The Florida Bar; Association of Trial Lawyers of America; Defense Research and Trial Lawyers Association; Florida Defense Lawyers Association; International Association of Defense Counsel — Florida Bar Board Certified Civil Trial Lawyer, National Board of Trial Advocacy — Practice Areas: Insurance Defense; Product Liability; Malpractice; Insurance Coverage; Business Law; Corporate Law; Construction Law; Life and Health; Disability; Professional Liability — E-mail: wlawton@drml-law.com

Partners/Shareholders

Lamar D. Oxford — 1949 — Princeton University, A.B. (cum laude), 1971; University of Florida, J.D. (cum laude), 1976 — Admitted to Bar, 1977, Florida; 1977, U.S. District Court, Middle District of Florida; 1981, U.S. District Court, Northern District of Florida; 1981, U.S. Court of Appeals, Eleventh Circuit; 1981, U.S. Supreme Court — Member The Florida Bar; Orange County Bar Association; Florida Defense Lawyers Association; Defense Research Institute — Languages: Latin — Practice Areas: Insurance Defense; Workers' Compensation; Appellate Practice; Employment Law; Personal Injury; Property Defense; Product Liability — E-mail: loxford@drml-law.com

F. Scott Pendley — 1956 — University of Florida, B.A., 1978; Mercer University, J.D., 1981 — Admitted to Bar, 1981, Georgia; 1982, Florida; 1982, U.S. District Court, Middle District of Florida; 1984, U.S. Court of Appeals, Eleventh Circuit; 1987, U.S. Supreme Court — Member The Florida Bar; State Bar of Georgia; Orange County Bar Association; Defense Research Institute; Florida Defense Lawyers Association — Florida Bar Board Certified Civil Trial Lawyer — Practice Areas: Civil Rights; Negligence; Wrongful Death; Trucking Law; Product Liability; Personal Injury; Property Damage; Law Enforcement Liability — E-mail: spendley@drml-law.com

John D. Robinson — 1957 — University of Central Florida, B.A. (cum laude), 1978; Mercer University, J.D., 1982 — American Jurisprudence Award, Administrative Law, 1982 — Admitted to Bar, 1984, Florida; 1984, U.S. District Court, Middle District of Florida; 1987, U.S. Court of Appeals, Eleventh Circuit — Member American and Orange County Bar Associations; The Florida Bar; Florida Defense Lawyers Association; Defense Research Institute — Practice Areas: Life and Health; Disability; Insurance Law; Insurance Litigation; Personal Injury; Property Damage; Product Liability; Business Law; Corporate Law; Commercial Litigation; Employment Law; Construction Law; Real Estate — E-mail: jrobinson@drml-law.com

Frank C. Wesighan — 1958 — Florida State University, B.A., 1980; University of Florida, J.D., 1982 — Award of Excellance, Orange County Legal Aid/Guardian Ad Litem Program — Admitted to Bar, 1983, Florida — Member The Florida Bar; Orange County Bar Association — Florida Bar Board Certified Workers' Compensation Lawyer — Practice Areas: Workers' Compensation — E-mail: fwesighan@drml-law.com

Jeffry J. Branham — 1957 — Florida State University, B.S., 1978; J.D. (with honors), 1982 — Admitted to Bar, 1982, Florida; 1982, U.S. Supreme Court; 1986, U.S. District Court, Middle District of Florida — Member The Florida Bar; Orange County Bar Association — Florida Bar Board Certified Workers' Compensation Lawyer — Practice Areas: Workers' Compensation — E-mail: jbranham@drml-law.com

Joseph R. Flood, Jr. — 1957 — Florida State University, B.S. (cum laude), 1979; J.D., 1982 — Admitted to Bar, 1983, Florida; 1988, U.S. District Court, Middle District of Florida; 1993, U.S. Court of Appeals, Eleventh Circuit; 1981, U.S. Claims Court — Member American, Brevard County and Orange County Bar Associations; The Florida Bar; Academy of Florida Trial Lawyers; Florida Defense Lawyers Association — Practice Areas: Civil Rights; Insurance Law; Law Enforcement Liability; Bad Faith; Personal Injury; Property Damage; Product Liability; Liquor Liability; Dram Shop — E-mail: jflood@drml-law.com

S. Renee Stephens Lundy — 1962 — University of Florida, B.A., 1982; J.D., 1985 — Admitted to Bar, 1985, Florida; 1986, U.S. District Court, Middle and Northern Districts of Florida; 1986, U.S. Court of Appeals, Eleventh Circuit; 2004, U.S. District Court, Northern and Southern Districts of Florida — Member The Florida Bar; Orange County Bar Association; Defense Research Institute; Florida Defense Lawyers Association — Practice Areas: Medical

ORLANDO FLORIDA

Dean, Ringers, Morgan and Lawton, P.A., Orlando, FL (Continued)

Malpractice; Civil Rights; Negligence; Wrongful Death; Insurance Law; Law Enforcement Liability; Bad Faith; Personal Injury; Property Damage; Premises Liability; Product Liability — E-mail: rlundy@drml-law.com

Douglas T. Noah — 1962 — Florida Southern College, B.S., 1984; Stetson University College of Law, J.D., 1990 — Admitted to Bar, 1990, Florida; 1990, U.S. District Court, Middle District of Florida; 2005, U.S. District Court, Northern and Southern Districts of Florida; U.S. Court of Appeals, Eleventh Circuit — Member The Florida Bar; Orange County Bar Association — Practice Areas: Public Entities; Employment Law; Civil Rights — E-mail: dnoah@drml-law.com

Alan D. Kalinoski — 1960 — Western Illinois University, B.A., 1982; The John Marshall Law School, J.D., 1992 — Admitted to Bar, 1992, Illinois; 1994, Florida; 1995, District of Columbia; 1992, U.S. District Court, Northern District of Illinois; 1994, U.S. District Court, Middle District of Florida; 1996, U.S. Supreme Court — Member Illinois State Bar Association; The Florida Bar; The District of Columbia Bar; Defense Research Institute; Florida Defense Lawyers Association — Practice Areas: Commercial Litigation; Corporate Law; Construction Law; Fraud; Workers' Compensation — E-mail: akalinoski@drml-law.com

G. Clay Morris — 1959 — Florida State University, B.S., 1982; Memphis State University, J.D., 1987 — Phi Delta Phi — Admitted to Bar, 1988, Florida; 1993, U.S. District Court, Middle District of Florida; 2001, U.S. Supreme Court — Member The Florida Bar; Orange County and Seminole County Bar Associations; Volie A. Williams Inns of Court; Academy of Florida Trial Lawyers; Association of Trial Lawyers of America — Practice Areas: Insurance Defense; Personal Injury; Product Liability; Civil Litigation; Insurance Law; Property; Dram Shop — E-mail: cmorris@drml-law.com

Ronald P. Greninger — 1970 — University of Florida, B.A. (with honors), 1991; Rollins College, M.B.A. (with honors), 2000; University of Florida, J.D., 1994 — Admitted to Bar, 1995, Florida; 1995, U.S. District Court, Middle District of Florida — Member The Florida Bar; Orange County Bar Association — Practice Areas: Insurance Defense; Employment Law; Workers' Compensation; Dram Shop; Commercial Litigation — E-mail: rgreninger@drml-law.com

James A. Wilkinson — 1962 — The University of Iowa, B.S., 1985; Hamline University, J.D., 1989 — Admitted to Bar, 1990, Florida; 1991, U.S. District Court, Middle District of Florida; 1992, U.S. Court of Appeals, Eleventh Circuit; 2002, U.S. Supreme Court — Member American and Orange County Bar Associations; The District of Columbia Bar; American Society for Testing and Materials; International Amusement and Leisure Defense Association; International Association of Amusement Parks and Attractions; Florida Defense Lawyers Association; Defense Research Institute — Certified Mediator, Florida — Practice Areas: Amusements; Personal Injury; Wrongful Death; Corporate Law; Property Damage; Commercial Litigation; Premises Liability; Product Liability — E-mail: jwilkinson@drml-law.com

John M. Joyce — 1960 — University of Notre Dame, B.A., 1982; Florida State University, J.D. (with high honors), 1991 — Admitted to Bar, 1992, Florida; 1994, U.S. District Court, Middle District of Florida — Member The Florida Bar; Orange County Bar Association; Defense Research Institute; Florida Defense Lawyers Association — Board Certified Workers' Compensation — Practice Areas: Workers' Compensation; Business Law; Commercial Litigation; Construction Litigation; Employment Law; Fraud; General Defense; Corporate Law; Real Estate — E-mail: jjoyce@drml-law.com

Associates

A. Lynne Ringers — 1969 — Florida State University, B.A./B.A., 1992; Mercer University, J.D., 1995 — Phi Delta Phi — Admitted to Bar, 1995, Georgia; Florida; 2006, U.S. District Court, Middle District of Florida; U.S. Supreme Court — Member State Bar of Georgia; The Florida Bar; Orange County Bar Association; Defense Research Institute; Florida Defense Lawyers Association — Practice Areas: Workers' Compensation; Personal Injury; Property Damage; Product Liability; Longshore and Harbor Workers' Compensation — E-mail: lringers@drml-law.com

Michael A. Lowe — 1971 — Brigham Young University, B.A., 1996; Mercer University, J.D., 1999 — Admitted to Bar, 1999, Florida; 1999, U.S. District Court, Middle District of Florida — Member Orange County Bar Association — Languages: Spanish — Practice Areas: Workers' Compensation; General Liability — E-mail: mlowe@drml-law.com

John T. Conner — 1972 — University of Florida, B.A., 1995; University of Central Florida, M.S., 2000; University of Florida, J.D. (with honors), 2003 — Senior Editor, Florida Law Review — Admitted to Bar, 2004, Florida; 2004, U.S. District Court, Middle and Northern Districts of Florida; U.S. Court of Appeals, Eleventh Circuit — Member The Florida Bar; Orange County Bar Association; Defense Research Institute; Florida Defense Lawyers Association — Practice Areas: Municipal Law; Amusements; Corporate Law; Civil Rights; Insurance Law; Malpractice; Property Damage; Personal Injury; Commercial Litigation; Dram Shop — E-mail: jconner@drml-law.com

Donna N. Maloney Hansen — 1979 — Brigham Young University, B.S., 2000; University of Florida, J.D., 2004 — Admitted to Bar, 2004, Florida; 2005, U.S. District Court, Middle and Northern Districts of Florida; 2005, U.S. Court of Appeals, Eleventh Circuit — Member American and Orange County Bar Associations; The Florida Bar; Defense Research Institute — Practice Areas: Civil Litigation; Construction Law; Employment Law; Life and Health; Disability; Product Liability; Professional Liability; Personal Injury; Property Damage; Automobile; Intentional Torts — E-mail: dhansen@drml-law.com

Bryan A. Lowe — 1977 — Brigham Young University, B.S., 2000; University of Florida, J.D., 2003 — Admitted to Bar, 2003, Florida; 2007, U.S. District Court, Middle District of Florida — Member The Florida Bar; Orange County Bar Associaton — Languages: Spanish — Practice Areas: Workers' Compensation; Commercial Litigation; Employment Law — E-mail: blowe@drml-law.com

Gloria A. Carr — 1962 — University of South Florida, M.A.P.A., 1993; Stetson University College of Law, J.D., 2001 — Admitted to Bar, 2002, Florida; 2007, U.S. District Court, Middle District of Florida — Member The Florida Bar; Orange County Bar Association — Practice Areas: Employment Law; Insurance Coverage; Personal Injury; Property Damage; Civil Rights; Premises Liability; Product Liability; Administrative Law — E-mail: gcarr@drml-law.com

Joshua B. Walker — 1979 — University of Central Florida, B.S. (cum laude), 2003; University of Florida, Levin College of Law, J.D. (cum laude), 2007 — Admitted to Bar, 2007, Florida; 2009, U.S. District Court, Middle, Northern and Southern Districts of Florida — Member The Florida Bar; Orange County Bar Association — Captain, Florida Army National Guard (1997-Present) — Practice Areas: Insurance Defense; Commercial Litigation; Governmental Entity Defense — E-mail: jwalker@drml-law.com

Of Counsel

Andrew L. Ringers — 1937 — Florida State University, B.S., 1959; Stetson University, J.D., 1969 — Admitted to Bar, 1969, Florida; U.S. Supreme Court

(All Attorneys are Members of Florida Defense Lawyers Association)

Grower, Ketcham, Rutherford, Bronson, Eide & Telan, P.A.

901 North Lake Destiny Road, Suite 450
Maitland, Florida 32751
Telephone: 407-423-9545
Fax: 407-425-7104
E-Mail: gk@growerketcham.com
www.growerketcham.com

Established: 1986

Civil Trial Practice, Appellate Practice, State and Federal Courts, Automobile, Corporate Law, Employment Law, Environmental Law, Insurance Litigation, Medical Malpractice, Product Liability, Workers' Compensation, Health Care Liability, Health Care Professional Licensure Defense, Long-Term Care, General Liability, Professional Liability, Governmental Entity Defense, Insurance Defense, Accountant Malpractice, Accountants and Attorneys Liability, Hospitality, Administrative Law, Trucking Litigation, Police Liability Defense, Premises Liability, Family Law, Legal Malpractice, Professional Malpractice, Civil Rights Defense

Firm Profile: Since 1986, our firm has provided leadership and guidance in civil and commercial litigation cases. As a tight-knit, client focused firm, our mission has remained unchanged to vigorously protect our clients through experienced, ethical counsel maximizing all available resources and talent to that end. Our firm is well versed in complex legal matters with attorneys who form close relationships with our clients.

Grower, Ketcham, Rutherford, Bronson, Eide & Telan, P.A., Orlando, FL (Continued)

Insurance Clients

American Safety Insurance Company
Carolina Casualty Insurance Company
Essex Insurance Company
Farmers Insurance Group
Frontier Insurance Company
Gallagher Bassett Services, Inc.
Hunt Insurance Group
Lancer Insurance Company
National Chiropractic Mutual Insurance Company
Security First Insurance Company
Sedgwick Group of Florida, Inc.
Specialty Claims, Incorporated
Travelers Insurance Companies
Western Litigation Specialists, Inc.
Avizent/Frank Gates Service Company
CNA Insurance Company
Cooperativa deSeguros Multiples de Puerto Rico
Florida Farm Bureau Insurance Companies
Horace Mann Insurance Group
Johns Eastern Company, Inc.
Markel Insurance Company
Navigators Insurance Company
Ocean Harbor Casualty Insurance Company
Service Insurance Company
T.H.E. Insurance Company
Wells Fargo Insurance Services
Zurich American Insurance Group

Non-Insurance Clients

Adventist Health Systems
Belz Enterprises
Desoto Memorial Hospital
Emergency Medical Services Association
Florida School Boards Insurance Trust
Lakeside Behavioral Healthcare
Orange County
Orange County Sheriff
The Peabody Orlando
The Schumacher Group
State of Florida, Division of Risk Management
Varsity Contractors, Inc.
AlliedBarton Security Services
City of Orlando, Florida
The Duvall Home
Florida Emergency Physicians
Florida Hospital
Gencor Industries
Ke'aki Technologies, LLC
Mears Transportation
Orange County School Board
OSI Restaurant Partners, LLC
Quality Circle for Healthcare, Inc
Seminole County School Board
Sysco Corporation
Team Health

Partners

Mason H. Grower, III — 1949 — University of Florida, B.S.B.A., 1971; University of Florida College of Law, J.D., 1975 — Admitted to Bar, 1975, Florida; 1980, U.S. District Court, Middle District of Florida; 1987, U.S. Court of Appeals, Eleventh Circuit; 1994, U.S. Supreme Court; U.S. Tax Court; U.S. Court of Military Appeals — Member American and Orange County Bar Associations; The Florida Bar; American Society for Healthcare Risk Management; Florida Hospital Association; Central Florida American Board of Trial Advocates; Florida Defense Lawyers Association; International Association of Defense Counsel; American Board of Trial Advocates; Academy of Florida Trial Lawyers; Defense Research Institute; Florida Medical Malpractice Claims Council — Florida SuperLawyers (2006-2013); Legal Aid Award of Excellence — Capt., JAGC, U.S. Air Force, 1976-1980 — Practice Areas: Medical Malpractice; General Liability; Environmental Law; Administrative Law; Hospital Malpractice; Product Liability; Toxic Torts; Wrongful Death; Health

Walter A. Ketcham, Jr. — 1948 — Stetson University, B.B.A., 1970; Stetson University College of Law, J.D., 1973 — Delta Sigma Phi; Phi Delta Phi — Admitted to Bar, 1973, Florida; U.S. District Court, Middle District of Florida; 1981, U.S. Court of Appeals, Eleventh Circuit — Member American and Orange County Bar Associations; The Florida Bar; American Academy of Trial Lawyers; American Board of Trial Advocates (Past President; Charter Member); Fellow Litigation Counsel of America; Transportation Lawyers Association; American Association for Justice — Florida SuperLawyers; Former Member of National Mock Trial Team, Dental Malpractice, American Association of Oral and Maxillofacial Surgery — Certified Civil Circuit and County Mediation — Capt., USA AG, 1973 — Practice Areas: General Liability; Insurance Defense; Insurance Coverage; Property Defense; Personal Injury; Municipal Law; Subrogation; Legal Malpractice; Premises Liability; Product Liability; Trucking Litigation

Launa K. Rutherford — 1949 — University of Central Florida, B.A. (magna cum laude), 1979; Florida State University, J.D., 1981 — Admitted to Bar, 1983, Florida; 1985, U.S. District Court, Middle District of Florida; U.S. Court of Appeals, Eleventh Circuit — Member Orange County Bar Association; Florida Guardians Association — Certified Civil Circuit and County Mediator — Practice Areas: Medical Malpractice; General Liability; Health Care; Administrative Law; Civil Rights; Antitrust; Hospitals; Nursing Home Liability

Jeanelle G. Bronson — 1951 — Rollins College, B.A., 1973; University of Florida College of Law, J.D. (with high honors), 1978 — Phi Kappa Phi — Admitted to Bar, 1978, Florida; U.S. District Court, Middle and Northern Districts of Florida; U.S. Court of Appeals, Eleventh Circuit; U.S. Supreme Court — Member National, American and Orange County Bar Associations; The Florida Bar; Paul C. Perkins Bar Association; Central Florida Association of Women Lawyers; Florida Association of Police Attorneys; Leadership Florida — Practice Areas: Civil Rights; Insurance Defense; Municipal Law; Governmental Liability; Employment Law; Administrative Law; Premises Liability; Appellate Practice

Eric R. Eide — 1963 — Valencia Community College, A.A. (with high honors), 1983; University of Florida, B.S. (with honors), 1985; J.D., 1988 — Phi Theta Kappa; Phi Kappa Phi — Admitted to Bar, 1989, Florida; U.S. District Court, Middle District of Florida — Member American and Orange County Bar Associations; The Florida Bar; Florida Defense Lawyers Association; Defense Research Institute; Transportation Lawyers Association — Practice Areas: Insurance Defense; Premises Liability; Health Care; Workers' Compensation; General Liability; Medical Malpractice; Appellate Practice; Employment Law

Patrick H. Telan — 1967 — University of Florida, B.A. (with honors), 1989; Stetson University College of Law, J.D., 1992 — Admitted to Bar, 1993, Florida; U.S. District Court, Middle and Southern Districts of Florida; 2008, U.S. Court of Appeals, Eleventh Circuit — Member American and Orange County Bar Associations; The Florida Bar; American Society of Pharmacy Law; Florida Hospital Association; Fellow, Litigation Counsel of America; Defense Research Institute; Florida Defense Lawyers Association — Practice Areas: Medical Malpractice; Health Care; Civil Litigation; Environmental Litigation; Toxic Torts

Jack E. Holt, III — 1964 — Harvard University, B.A., 1986; University of Florida, J.D. (with honors), 1991 — Admitted to Bar, 1991, Florida; 1992, U.S. District Court, Middle District of Florida; U.S. Court of Appeals, Eleventh Circuit — Member American (Tort Trial and Insurance Practice Section) and Orange County Bar Associations; The Florida Bar; Florida Hospital Association; American Health Lawyers Association — Practice Areas: Health Care; Health Care Professional Licensure Defense; Employment Law; Contracts; Americans with Disabilities Act; Appellate Practice

Charles J. Meltz — 1968 — University of Florida, B.S.B.A., 1990; J.D., 1993 — Admitted to Bar, 1993, Florida; U.S. District Court, Middle, Northern and Southern Districts of Florida; U.S. Court of Appeals, Eleventh Circuit — Practice Areas: Legal Malpractice; Accountant Malpractice; Medical Malpractice; Professional Liability; Complex Litigation; Civil Litigation; Hospitals

Philip J. Wallace — 1971 — Florida State University, B.A. (with honors), 1992; Tulane University Law School, J.D. (cum laude), 1997 — Admitted to Bar, 1997, Florida; 1999, Louisiana (Inactive); U.S. District Court, Middle District of Florida — Member Orange County Bar Association; The Florida Bar; Florida Hospital Association; Defense Research Institute — Practice Areas: Medical Malpractice; General Liability; Health Care; Civil Rights; Hospitals; Antitrust; Health; Nursing Home Liability; Health Care Professional Licensure Defense

Ramón Vázquez — 1964 — University of Puerto Rico, B.A. (magna cum laude), 1989; J.D. (cum laude), 1994 — Admitted to Bar, 1995, Puerto Rico; 2000, Florida; 2000, U.S. Court of Appeals, Eleventh Circuit; 2001, U.S. District Court, Middle, Northern and Southern Districts of Florida — Member American and Orange County Bar Associations; The Florida Bar; Florida Association of Police Attorneys — Languages: Spanish — Practice Areas: Civil Litigation; Insurance Defense; Civil Rights; Appellate Practice; Administrative Law; Governmental Liability; Commercial Litigation; Construction Law; Personal Injury; Tort

John J. Tress III — 1974 — The George Washington University, B.A. (magna cum laude), 1996; The Ohio State University Moritz College of Law, J.D., 1999 — Admitted to Bar, 1999, Florida; 2003, U.S. District Court, Middle District of Florida — Member Orange County Bar Association; The Florida Bar; American Society for Healthcare Risk Management; Defense Research Institute; Florida Defense Lawyers Association; Florida Medical Malpractice Claims Council — Practice Areas: Medical Malpractice; Health Care; General Liability; Environmental Law; Civil Litigation

T'anjuiming A. Marx — 1976 — Florida International University, B.A., 2001; University of Florida, Levin College of Law, J.D., 2005 — Phi Delta Phi — Admitted to Bar, 2006, Florida; District of Columbia; U.S. District Court, Middle District of Florida; U.S. Court of Appeals, Eleventh Circuit; 2010, U.S. Supreme Court; 2013, U.S. District Court, Southern District of Florida — Member ; American and Orange County Bar Associations; The Florida Bar; The District of Columbia Bar; Florida Defense Lawyers Association — Practice Areas: Medical Malpractice; Legal Malpractice; Premises Liability; Health Care; Hospitals; Accountant Malpractice; General Liability

ORLANDO   FLORIDA

Grower, Ketcham, Rutherford, Bronson, Eide & Telan, P.A., Orlando, FL (Continued)

Associates

Jennifer L. Phillips — 1971 — Florida State University, B.A. (cum laude), 1993; Florida State University College of Law, J.D. (with honors), 1999 — Executive Editor (1998-1999), Notes and Comments Editor (1997-1998), Florida State University Law Review — Admitted to Bar, 1999, Florida; 1999, U.S. District Court, Middle District of Florida; 2009, U.S. District Court, Southern District of Florida — Member Orange County Bar Association; The Florida Bar — Practice Areas: Medical Malpractice; Health Care; Hospitals; Wrongful Death; Personal Injury; Civil Rights Defense

Blaine A. Bizik — 1974 — Virginia Wesleyan College, B.A., 1997; University of Miami School of Law, J.D., 2000 — Admitted to Bar, 2001, Florida; 2005, U.S. District Court, Middle District of Florida; 2010, U.S. Supreme Court — Member Orange County Bar Association; The Florida Bar — Practice Areas: Insurance Defense; Workers' Compensation; Civil Trial Practice; Health Care

Emily R. Katz — 1981 — Florida State University, B.A. (with honors), 2003; University of Florida, J.D., 2008 — Dean's List; Phi Eta Sigma National Honor's Fraternity; Golden Key Honor Society. National Society of Collegiate Scholars — Admitted to Bar, 2008, Florida; U.S. District Court, Middle and Southern Districts of Florida — Member The Florida Bar; Orange County Bar Association — Recipient: Appellate Advocacy, Award of Distinction; Legal Research and Writing, Award of Distinction. Certificate in Family Law, University of Florida, 2008. — Practice Areas: Health Care; Hospitals; Medical Malpractice Defense; Premises Liability; Family Law; Civil Defense; Personal Injury Litigation

Stacey J. Waldorf — 1985 — University of Florida, B.A. (cum laude), 2007; University of Florida, Levin College of Law, J.D. (cum laude), 2010 — Admitted to Bar, 2010, Florida; U.S. District Court, Middle and Southern Districts of Florida; U.S. Court of Appeals, Eleventh Circuit — Member The Florida Bar; Orange County Bar Association — Practice Areas: Insurance Defense; Medical Malpractice; Professional Malpractice

Samantha L. Aylward — 1989 — University of Florida, B.A. (cum laude), 2010; University of Florida, Levin College of Law, J.D. (cum laude, Dean's List), 2013 — Dean's List — Executive Articles Editor, University of Florida Journal of Law and Public Policy — Admitted to Bar, 2013, Florida — Member The Florida Bar; Orange County Bar Association — Criminal Procedure Adversary Systems Book Award; Environmental Moot Court; Student Recruitment Team; Pro Bono Certificate; Community Service Certificate — Practice Areas: Workers' Compensation; Governmental Liability; Premises Liability

Laura M. Kelly — 1988 — University of Florida, B.S. (summa cum laude), 2010; University of Florida, Levin College of Law, J.D., 2013 — Dean's List; National Society of Collegiate Scholars; Omicron Delta Kappa Honor Society — Admitted to Bar, 2013, Florida; U.S. District Court, Middle District of Florida — Member The Florida Bar — Recipient: Interviewing, Counseling, and Negotiation Award of Distinction — Practice Areas: Accountant Malpractice; Legal Malpractice; Medical Malpractice Defense

Hightower, Stratton, Wilhelm, P.A.

151 Southhall Lane, Suite 140
Orlando, Florida 32751
Telephone: 407-352-4240
Fax: 407-352-4201
www.hightowerlaw.net

(Miami, FL Office*: 4770 Biscayne Boulevard, Suite 1200, 33137)
 (Tel: 305-539-0909)
 (Fax: 305-530-0661)
 (Emer/After Hrs: 305-799-3054)
 (E-Mail: dale@hightowerlaw.net)
(St. Petersburg, FL Office*: 200 Central Avenue, Suite 450, 33701)
 (Tel: 727-209-1373)
 (Fax: 727-209-1383)
(West Palm Beach, FL Office*: 330 Clematis Street, Suite 201, 33401)
 (Tel: 561-833-2022)
 (Fax: 561-833-2140)

Hightower, Stratton, Wilhelm, P.A., Orlando, FL (Continued)

Assault & Battery Defense, Auto and Trucking Negligence, Commercial Litigation, Construction Claims, Contracts, Employment Law, Environmental Law, Fraud/SIU (Special Investigative Unit), General Litigation, Homeowner's Insurance, Insurance Coverage and Bad Faith, Maritime Law, Personal Injury and Wrongful Death, Premises Liability, Product Liability, Resorts & Leisure Liability, Retail Liability

Partners

Dale R. Hightower   Michelle R. Reeves, Division Leader

Associate

H. Davis Lewis, Jr.

(See listings under Miami and West Palm Beach, FL for additional information)

Hill, Rugh, Keller & Main

390 North Orange Avenue, Suite 1610
Orlando, Florida 32802
 Telephone: 407-926-7460
 Fax: 407-926-7461
 E-Mail: jean@hrkmlaw.com
 www.hrkmlaw.com

Insurance Defense, Commercial Litigation, Premises Liability, Product Liability, Dram Shop, Liquor Liability, Insurance Coverage, Bad Faith, Intellectual Property, Construction Litigation, Auto & Commercial Auto Liability, Amusement Park Litigation

Firm Profile: Hill, Rugh, Keller & Main is a civil practice law firm comprised solely of experienced trial attorneys. The firm has an "AV" rating by the Martindale-Hubbell peer review rating system, which signifies the highest level of professional excellence a firm can achieve. Our size allows us to give each client and case the personal attention required. We work closely with our clients and are committed to providing an early evaluation of each claim and specific recommendations on the optimal and most cost-effective plan to achieve a successful result.

Insurance Clients

Tower Hill Insurance Company   Westfield Group
Workmen's Auto Insurance
 Company

Partners

Christopher T. Hill — 1964 — University of Florida, B.S.I.E. (cum laude), 1987; University of Florida College of Law, J.D., 1990 — Admitted to Bar, 1990, Florida; U.S. District Court, Middle, Northern and Southern Districts of Florida; U.S. Court of Appeals for the Federal, Ninth and Eleventh Circuits — Member American and Orange County Bar Associations; The Florida Bar; Defense Research Institute; Florida Defense Lawyers Association — Practice Areas: Insurance Defense; Commercial Litigation; Premises Liability — E-mail: chill@hrkmlaw.com

Kenneth B. Rugh — 1968 — University of Florida, B.S., 1991; Stetson University College of Law, J.D. (cum laude), 1995 — Admitted to Bar, 1995, Florida; U.S. District Court, Middle, Northern and Southern Districts of Florida — Member The Florida Bar; Orange County Bar Association; Florida Defense Lawyers Association — Practice Areas: Automobile Liability; Premises Liability; Dram Shop Liability; Liquor Liability; Product Liability; Insurance Coverage; Bad Faith — E-mail: krugh@hrkmlaw.com

Congressman Ric A. Keller — 1964 — East Tennessee State University, B.S. (summa cum laude), 1986; Vanderbilt University Law School, J.D., 1992 — Admitted to Bar, 1992, Florida; U.S. District Court, Middle District of Florida — Member The Florida Bar; Orange County Bar Association — U.S. House of Representatives, 2001-2009 — Practice Areas: Intellectual Property; Commercial Litigation; Product Liability — E-mail: rkeller@hrkmlaw.com

FLORIDA   ORLANDO

Hill, Rugh, Keller & Main, Orlando, FL   (Continued)

Steven R. Main — 1972 — Laurentian University, B.Com. (with honors), 1995; Wake Forest University School of Law, J.D., 1998 — Admitted to Bar, 1998, Florida; U.S. District Court, Middle, Northern and Southern Districts of Florida; U.S. Court of Appeals for the Federal, Second, Fourth, Fifth and Eleventh Circuits — Member The Florida Bar (Young Lawyers Division); Orange County Bar Association; Florida Defense Lawyers Association; Defense Research Institute — Practice Areas: Commercial Litigation; Construction Defect; Product Liability; Insurance Coverage; Insurance Defense; Civil Tort — E-mail: smain@hrkmlaw.com

Associates

Scott L. Reed   John D. Martin
Nick S. Patrick

Luks & Santaniello LLC

255 South Orange Avenue, Suite 750
Orlando, Florida 32801
　Telephone: 407-540-9170
　Fax: 407-540-9171
　www.LS-LAW.com

(Additional Offices: Fort Lauderdale, FL*; Tampa, FL*; Jacksonville, FL*; Boca Raton, FL*; Miami, FL*; Tallahassee, FL)

Insurance Defense, General Liability, Workers' Compensation

(See listing under Fort Lauderdale, FL for additional information)

Marcus & Myers, P.A.

1515 Park Center Drive
Suite 2G
Orlando, Florida 32835
　Telephone: 407-447-2550
　Fax: 407-447-2551
　www.marcusmyerslaw.com

Insurance Coverage, Property and Casualty, Bad Faith, Extra-Contractual Litigation, Disability, ERISA, Breach of Contract, Coverage Issues, Declaratory Judgments, Professional Liability, Life Insurance, General Liability, Special Investigative Unit Claims, Insurance Fraud, Fire Loss, Business and Real Estate Transactions, Appellate Practice

Insurance Clients

American Integrity Insurance Company
Merastar Insurance Company
Travelers Insurance Company
Unitrin Direct Auto Insurance
Great West Casualty Company
HM Life Insurance Company
Nationwide Mutual Insurance Company

Firm Members

Lee W. Marcus — 1967 — State University of New York at Albany, B.S. (cum laude), 1989; University of Florida College of Law, J.D., 1992 — Admitted to Bar, 1992, Florida; 1993, U.S. District Court, Middle District of Florida; 1995, U.S. District Court, Southern District of Florida; 1996, U.S. District Court, Northern District of Florida; U.S. Court of Appeals, Eleventh Circuit; 2004, U.S. Supreme Court — Member The Florida Bar; Orange County Bar Association; Florida Defense Lawyers Association; Defense Research Institute; Florida Advisory Committee on Arson Prevention — Circuit Civil Mediator (2008) — E-mail: lmarcus@marcusmyerslaw.com

Ernest J. Myers — 1967 — Temple University, B.B.A. (magna cum laude), 1989; University of Florida College of Law, J.D., 1992 — Admitted to Bar, 1992, Florida; 1993, U.S. District Court, Middle District of Florida; 1993, U.S. Court of Appeals, Eleventh Circuit; 2000, U.S. District Court, Northern and Southern Districts of Florida; 2001, U.S. Supreme Court — Member The Florida Bar (Charter Member of the Appellate Practice and Advocacy Section); Orange County Bar Association; Florida Defense Lawyers Association; Defense Research Institute — E-mail: emyers@marcusmyerslaw.com

Marshall Dennehey Warner Coleman & Goggin

Landmark Center One
315 East Robinson Street, Suite 550
Orlando, Florida 32801-1948
　Telephone: 407-420-4380
　Fax: 407-839-3008
　www.marshalldennehey.com

(Philadelphia, PA Office*: 2000 Market Street, Suite 2300, 19103)
　(Tel: 215-575-2600)
　(Fax: 215-575-0856)
　(Toll Free: 800-220-3308)
　(E-Mail: marshalldennehey@mdwcg.com)
(Wilmington, DE Office*: Nemours Building, 1007 North Orange Street, Suite 600, 19801)
　(Tel: 302-552-4300)
　(Fax: 302-552-4340)
(Fort Lauderdale, FL Office*: 100 Northeast 3rd Avenue, Suite 1100, 33301)
　(Tel: 954-847-4920)
　(Fax: 954-627-6640)
(Jacksonville, FL Office*: 200 West Forsyth Street, Suite 1400, 32202)
　(Tel: 904-358-4200)
　(Fax: 904-355-0019)
(Tampa, FL Office*: 201 East Kennedy Boulevard, Suite 1100, 33602)
　(Tel: 813-898-1800)
　(Fax: 813-221-5026)
(Cherry Hill, NJ Office*: Woodland Falls Corporate Park, 200 Lake Drive East, Suite 300, 08002)
　(Tel: 856-414-6000)
　(Fax: 856-414-6077)
(Roseland, NJ Office*: 425 Eagle Rock Avenue, Suite 302, 07068)
　(Tel: 973-618-4100)
　(Fax: 973-618-0685)
(New York, NY Office*: Wall Street Plaza, 88 Pine Street, 21st Floor, 10005-1801)
　(Tel: 212-376-6400)
　(Fax: 212-376-6490)
(Melville, NY Office*: 105 Maxess Road, Suite 303, 11747)
　(Tel: 631-232-6130)
　(Fax: 631-232-6184)
(Cincinnati, OH Office*: 312 Elm Street, Suite 1850, 45202)
　(Tel: 513-375-6800)
　(Fax: 513-372-6801)
(Cleveland, OH Office*: 127 Public Square, Suite 3510, 44114-1291)
　(Tel: 216-912-3800)
　(Fax: 216-344-9006)
(Allentown, PA Office*: 4905 West Tilghman Street, Suite 300, 18104)
　(Tel: 484-895-2300)
　(Fax: 484-895-2303)
(Doylestown, PA Office*: 10 North Main Street, 2nd Floor, 18901-4318)
　(Tel: 267-880-2020)
　(Fax: 215-348-5439)
(Erie, PA Office*: 717 State Street, Suite 701, 16501)
　(Tel: 814-480-7800)
　(Fax: 814-455-3603)
(Camp Hill, PA Office*(See Harrisburg listing): 100 Coporate Center Drive, Suite 201, 17011)
　(Tel: 717-651-3500)
　(Fax: 717-651-9630)
(King of Prussia, PA Office*: 620 Freedom Business Center, Suite 300, 19406)
　(Tel: 610-354-8250)
　(Fax: 610-354-8299)
(Pittsburgh, PA Office*: U.S. Steel Tower, Suite 2900, 600 Grant Street, 15219)
　(Tel: 412-803-1140)
　(Fax: 412-803-1188)

ORLANDO   FLORIDA

Marshall Dennehey Warner Coleman & Goggin, Orlando, FL (Continued)

(Moosic, PA Office*(See Scranton listing): 50 Glenmaura National Boulevard, 18507)
 (Tel: 570-496-4600)
 (Fax: 570-496-0567)
(Rye Brook, NY Office*(See Westchester listing): 800 Westchester Avenue, Suite C-700, 10573)
 (Tel: 914-977-7300)
 (Fax: 914-977-7301)

Established: 2001

Amusements, Sports and Recreation Liability, Asbestos and Mass Tort Litigation, Automobile Liability, Aviation and Complex Litigation, Construction Injury Litigation, Fraud/Special Investigation, General Liability, Hospitality and Liquor Liability, Maritime Litigation, Product Liability, Property Litigation, Retail Liability, Trucking & Transportation Liability, Appellate Advocacy and Post-Trial Practice, Architectural, Engineering and Construction Defect Litigation, Class Action Litigation, Commercial Litigation, Consumer and Credit Law, Employment Law, Environmental & Toxic Tort Litigation, Insurance Coverage/Bad Faith Litigation, Life, Health and Disability Litigation, Privacy and Data Security, Professional Liability, Public Entity and Civil Rights Litigation, Real Estate E&O Liability, School Leaders' Liability, Securities and Investment Professional Liability, Technology, Media and Intellectual Property Litigation, White Collar Crime, Birth Injury Litigation, Health Care Governmental Compliance, Health Care Liability, Health Law, Long-Term Care Liability, Medical Device and Pharmaceutical Liability, Medicare Set-Aside, Workers' Compensation

Firm Profile: The Marshall Dennehey Warner Coleman & Goggin Orlando office is situated in the heart of downtown, overlooking Lake Eola. The Orlando office is mere blocks from state and federal courthouses and ideally positioned to service clients throughout central and northeast Florida. Its reach includes Jacksonville, Ocala, Gainesville, Daytona, the Space Coast, I-4 corridor and all points between. This office provides experienced legal representation in venues including the United States District Court for the Middle District of Florida and the state Circuit Courts of Orange, Seminole, Osceola, Brevard, Volusia, Flagler, St. Johns, Duval, Nassau, Clay, Putnam, Marion, Alachua, Lake, Polk, Indian River, St. Lucie, Martin, Palm Beach and Okeechobee Counties.

For additional information concerning the Orlando office, please contact Cynthia Kohn, Esquire, its managing attorney, at (407) 420-4388 or cjkohn@mdwcg.com

Managing Shareholders

Cynthia Kohn — Managing Attorney — 1962 — Duquesne University, B.A./M.A., 1984; Temple University School of Law, J.D., 1988 — Admitted to Bar, 1988, Pennsylvania, 2004, Florida; U.S. District Court, Eastern and Middle Districts of Pennsylvania; U.S. District Court, Middle, Northern and Southern Districts of Florida — Member American, Pennsylvania (Former Member, Zone 2 Representative, Young Lawyers Division), Orange County, Lehigh County (Former Member and Board of Directors; Former Co-Chair, Young Lawyers Division; Former Co-Chair, Medical Society Liaison) and Northampton County (Former Member) Bar Associations, The Florida Bar; Women Lawyers of Lehigh County (Former Member and Program Director) — Practice Areas: Professional Liability; Retail Liability; Liquor Liability; Dram Shop — E-mail: cjkohn@mdwcg.com

Resident Shareholders

Bradley P. Blystone   Thomas F. Brown
Adam C. Herman   Janice L. Merrill

Resident Associates

April C. Collins   Andrea L. Diederich
Robert Garcia   Chanel A. Mosley
Amanda J. Podlucky   Jodi M. Ruberg

(See listing under Philadelphia, PA for additional information)

Meier, Bonner, Muszynski, O'Dell & Harvey, P.A.

260 Wekiva Springs Road, Suite 2000
Longwood, Florida 32779
 Telephone: 407-872-7774
 Fax: 407-872-7997
 E-Mail: info@fltrialteam.com
 www.fltrialteam.com

Established: 1997

Insurance Defense, Construction Defect, Automobile Liability, Premises Liability, Governmental Liability, Product Liability, Aviation, Property and Casualty, Personal Injury, General Liability, Employment Litigation, Professional Malpractice, Errors and Omissions, Mediation, Arbitration, Aircraft Hull Subrogation, Federal Civil Rights, State Tort Actions, Insurance Disputes

Firm Profile: The firm has dedicated its practice entirely to aggressive trial and appellate advocacy in State and Federal courts within Florida, as well as the 11th Circuit Court of Appeals. The firm provides legal services both before and after initiation of suit to insurance companies, corporations, individuals, TPA's, and governmental entities throughout the entire Central Florida area. Experienced legal assistants and paralegals are on staff to assist in the investigation and preparation of cases.

Insurance Clients

Aerospace Claims Management Group
Chubb Group of Insurance Companies
Fireman's Fund Insurance Company
Mid-Continent Casualty Company
Western World Insurance Company

Auto-Owners Insurance Company
Chartis Aerospace
Coregis Insurance Company
Crum & Forster Insurance
James River Insurance Company
Markel Insurance Company
Swiss Re
Zurich American Insurance Company

Non-Insurance Clients

Florida League of Cities   Phoenix Aviation Managers, Inc.
Starr Aviation Agency, Inc.

Partners

George A. Meier III — 1947 — Colgate University, B.A., 1969; The Ohio State University Moritz College of Law, J.D. (cum laude), 1972 — Admitted to Bar, 1972, Ohio; 1977, Florida; U.S. District Court, Middle District of Florida; 1989, U.S. Court of Appeals, Eleventh Circuit; U.S. Supreme Court — Member American and Orange County Bar Associations; The Florida Bar; Florida Association of Police Attorneys; Florida Defense Lawyers Association; Defense Research Institute — U.S. Air Force JAG, 1973-1977 — Practice Areas: Premises Liability; Product Liability; Motor Vehicle; General Liability — E-mail: gam@fltrialteam.com

Robert E. Bonner — 1954 — The Ohio State University, B.A., 1976; University of Florida, J.D. (with honors), 1981 — Phi Delta Phi — Admitted to Bar, 1981, Florida; 1982, U.S. District Court, Middle District of Florida; U.S. Court of Appeals, Eleventh Circuit; 1989, U.S. Supreme Court; U.S. District Court, Southern District of Florida — Member The Florida Bar; Seminole County Bar Association; Florida Association of Policy Attorneys; Florida Defense Lawyers Association — Board Certified Civil Trial Lawyer — Practice Areas: Governmental Liability; Law Enforcement Liability; Employment Litigation — E-mail: reb@fltrialteam.com

Alexander Muszynski, III — 1958 — Valencia Community College, A.A., 1978; University of Central Florida, B.A., 1980; Florida State University, J.D., 1983 — Admitted to Bar, 1984, Florida; U.S. District Court, Middle District of Florida; 1985, U.S. Court of Appeals, Eleventh Circuit; 2007, U.S. District Court, Northern and Southern Districts of Florida — Member Orange County and Lawyer-Pilots Bar Associations; Aviation Insurance Association; Aircraft Owners and Pilots Association; Helicopter Association International Legal Referral Counsel; Defense Research Institute; Florida Defense Lawyers Association — Practice Areas: Aviation; Premises Liability; Motor Vehicle; General Liability — E-mail: am3@fltrialteam.com

Donald L. O'Dell — 1944 — University of Missouri-Kansas City, B.A., 1972; J.D., 1976 — Admitted to Bar, 1978, Florida; U.S. District Court, Middle District of Florida; 1981, U.S. Court of Appeals, Eleventh Circuit — Member The Florida Bar — Certified Circuit Court Mediator, Florida Supreme

FLORIDA

Meier, Bonner, Muszynski, O'Dell & Harvey, P.A., Orlando, FL (Continued)

Court — Practice Areas: Errors and Omissions; Professional Malpractice; Municipal Liability; Law Enforcement Liability; Premises Liability; State and Federal Courts; Coverage Analysis — E-mail: dlo@fltrialteam.com

Veronica L. Harvey — 1950 — Indiana University, B.G.S. (cum laude), 1989; North Carolina Central University School of Law, J.D., 1996 — Phi Delta Phi — Admitted to Bar, 1996, North Carolina; 1998, Florida; U.S. District Court, Middle District of Florida — Member American, North Carolina, Durham County and Seminole County Bar Associations; The Florida Bar; Fourteenth Judicial District and Family Law Associations; Florida Association of Police Attorneys; Florida Defense Lawyers Association — Certified Circuit Court Mediator and Arbitrator, State of Florida; Certified Dispute Resolution Board — Practice Areas: Construction Defect; General Liability; Automobile Liability; Mediation; Arbitration — E-mail: vlh@fltrialteam.com

John Bengier — 1950 — West Virginia University, B.S. (magna cum laude), 1972; J.D., 1975 — Admitted to Bar, 1975, West Virginia; 1995, Georgia; 1996, North Carolina; 1998, Florida; U.S. District Court, Middle District of Florida — Member The Florida Bar; Orange County Bar Association — U.S. Marine Corps, Colonel (Retired) — Practice Areas: Automobile; Insurance Defense; Nursing Home Liability; Premises Liability; Product Liability — E-mail: jeb@fltrialteam.com

Atheseus R. Lockhart — 1970 — Columbia College, B.S.B.A., 2000; Florida State University College of Law, J.D., 2003 — Admitted to Bar, 2003, Florida — Member National Bar and Orange County Bar Associations; The Florida Bar — Practice Areas: Personal Injury; General Civil Practice; Construction Litigation — E-mail: arl@fltrialteam.com

Associates

Cameron E. Shackelford — 1955 — Rollins College, B.A., 1977; Roy E. Crummer Graduate School of Business, M.B.A. (with honors), 2002; Rutgers University School of Law, J.D., 1998 — Beta Gamma Sigma — Admitted to Bar, 2003, Florida; 2004, U.S. District Court, Middle District of Florida — Member Seminole County Bar Association; The Florida Bar; Lawyer-Pilots Bar Association — Lt. Col. (Retired) U.S. Air Force 1979-1999 — Practice Areas: Aviation; Civil Trial Practice; Insurance Defense — E-mail: ces@fltrialteam.com

David R. Lane — 1970 — University of Florida, B.A., 1994; Tulane University Law School, J.D. (Admiralty), 2001 — Admitted to Bar, 2002, Florida; 2003, Texas; 2004, Louisiana; 2003, U.S. District Court, Middle, Northern and Southern Districts of Florida; U.S. Court of Appeals, Eleventh Circuit — E-mail: drl@fltrialteam.com

Wicker Smith O'Hara McCoy & Ford P.A.

Bank of America Center
390 North Orange Avenue, Suite 1000
Orlando, Florida 32801
   Telephone: 407-843-3939
   Fax: 407-649-8118
   www.wickersmith.com

(Coral Gables, FL Office*(See Miami listing): 2800 Ponce de Leon Boulevard, Suite 800, 33134)
   (Tel: 305-448-3939)
   (Fax: 305-441-1745)
(Fort Lauderdale, FL Office*: Sun Trust Center, 515 East Las Olas Boulevard, Suite 1400, 33301)
   (Tel: 954-847-4800)
   (Fax: 954-760-9353)
(Jacksonville, FL Office*: Bank of America, Suite 2700, 50 North Laura Street, 32202)
   (Tel: 904-355-0225)
   (Fax: 904-355-0226)
(Naples, FL Office*: Mercato, 9128 Strada Place, Suite 10200, 34108)
   (Tel: 239-552-5300)
   (Fax: 239-552-5399)
(Tampa, FL Office*: 100 North Tampa Street, Suite 1800, 33602)
   (Tel: 813-222-3939)
   (Fax: 813-222-3938)
(West Palm Beach, FL Office*: Northbridge Centre, 515 North Flagler Drive, Suite 1600, 33401)
   (Tel: 561-689-3800)
   (Fax: 561-689-9206)

ORLANDO

Wicker Smith O'Hara McCoy & Ford P.A., Orlando, FL (Continued)

General Civil Litigation, General Civil Practice, State and Federal Courts, Accountant Malpractice, Accountants and Attorneys Liability, Administrative Law, Admiralty and Maritime Law, Agent and Brokers Errors and Omissions, Appellate Practice, Automobile, Aviation, Bad Faith, Class Actions, Commercial Litigation, Complex Litigation, Construction Litigation, Environmental Law, Estate Planning, Fraud, Hospital Malpractice, Insurance Coverage, Labor and Employment, Legal Malpractice, Medical Devices, Medical Malpractice, Nursing Home Liability, Pharmaceutical, Premises Liability, Probate, Product Liability, Professional Liability, Professional Malpractice, Special Investigative Unit Claims, Real Estate, Retail Liability, Toxic Torts, Transportation, Trucking Litigation, Trusts, Workers' Compensation, Multi-District Litigation, Sexual Abuse

Firm Profile: In 1952, Idus Q. Wicker and James A. Smith formed a partnership with the goal of providing legal services of exceptional quality to their clients. They remained partners until their retirement and life-long friends. The firm they founded has expanded to seven offices located throughout Florida in Miami, Fort Lauderdale, West Palm Beach, Orlando, Tampa, Naples and Jacksonville. Although the firm has changed in size and scope, the goal of providing exceptional legal representation has remained the same.

Clients turn to Wicker Smith when they have critical and complex litigation matters because of the firm's vast experience in complex litigation filed in State and Federal Courts. Numerous major corporations have selected Wicker Smith as national and regional counsel. Supporting the litigation team is a preeminent Appellate Department, which has appeared as appellate counsel in more than 1,200 reported decisions, including several landmark opinions issued by the Supreme Court of Florida.

Wicker Smith has recognized leaders in the defense of a wide range of litigation practice areas, including products liability, medical malpractice, pharmaceutical and medical devices, catastrophic aviation accidents, legal malpractice, accounting malpractice, nursing home claims, construction litigation, as well as a variety of general negligence matters. In all such matters, communication and attention to the client's specific needs are our highest priority. The backbone of our relationship with clients is built upon integrity and stability. We strive to establish long-term relationships with our clients, built upon a partnership of communication and trust. We achieve this objective by listening to our clients, understanding their businesses and developing legal solutions to best meet their individual needs.

Firm Members

Richards H. Ford — 1954 — University of Florida, B.A. (with honors), 1976; Boston University, J.D., 1979 — Admitted to Bar, 1979, Florida; 1981, U.S. District Court, Southern District of Florida including Trial Bar; 1989, U.S. District Court, Middle and Northern Districts of Florida; 1996, U.S. Court of Appeals, Eleventh Circuit — Member American and Orange County Bar Associations; The Florida Bar (Health Law Section); Florida Defense Lawyers Association (Board of Directors, 2004-2006); Florida Hospital Association; Central Florida Medical Malpractice Claims Council (President, 1998); Florida Health Care Association; USLAW Network (Board of Directors); International Association of Defense Counsel; American Board of Trial Advocates; Defense Research Institute; Fellow, American Bar Foundation; Transportation Lawyers Association; Federation of Defense and Corporate Counsel — Assistant State Attorney, 1980-1983; Florida Trend's Florida Legal Elite for 2004-2007 & 2009; Florida Super Lawyers 2006-2012; Best Lawyers in America, 2012 — Board Certified Civil Trial Attorney, Florida Bar Board of Legal Specialization and Education; Board Certified as a Civil Trial Advocate by the National Board of Trial Advocacy; Board Certified as a Civil Pretrial Practice Advocate by The National Board of Civil Pretrial Practice Advocacy — Practice Areas: Accountant Malpractice; Automobile Liability; Civil Litigation; Class Actions; Construction Law; Legal Malpractice; Medical Malpractice; Nursing Home Liability; Premises Liability; Product Liability; Real Estate Litigation; Transportation

Kurt M. Spengler — 1962 — University of Florida, B.S., 1984; J.D., 1987 — Admitted to Bar, 1987, Florida; 1988, U.S. District Court, Middle and Southern Districts of Florida — Member The Florida Bar; Orange County Bar Association; Transportation Law Association; Defense Research Institute; American Board of Trial Advocates — Florida Super Lawyers 2008-2012; Florida Trend's Florida Legal Elite, Transporation 2009-2011 and Civil Trial

Wicker Smith O'Hara McCoy & Ford P.A., Orlando, FL (Continued)

2007 & 2008; Best of the Bar 2006-Orlando Business Journal — Board Certified Civil Trial Law Lawyer, Florida Bar Board of Legal Specialization and Education — Practice Areas: Automobile Liability; Civil Litigation; Medical Malpractice; Premises Liability; Transportation

Barbara A. Flanagan — 1960 — Wake Forest University, B.A. (magna cum laude), 1982; Tulane University, J.D., 1985 — Admitted to Bar, 1985, Florida; 1988, U.S. District Court, Middle District of Florida — Member The Florida Bar; Orange County Bar Association — Practice Areas: Civil Litigation; Nursing Home Liability; Premises Liability; Professional Liability; Retail Liability

Clay H. Coward — 1957 — University of Colorado at Boulder, B.S. (with honors), 1979; University of Florida, J.D. (with honors), 1983 — Admitted to Bar, 1983, Florida; 1984, U.S. District Court, Middle District of Florida; 1985, U.S. Court of Appeals, Eleventh Circuit — Practice Areas: Accountant Malpractice; Automobile Liability; Civil Litigation; Legal Malpractice; Medical Malpractice

Raymond E. Watts, Jr. — 1964 — University of Florida, B.A., 1986; Mercer University, J.D., 1989 — Admitted to Bar, 1989, Florida; 2007, Arizona; 1989, U.S. District Court, Middle District of Florida; 1989, U.S. Court of Appeals, Eleventh Circuit — Member Orange County Bar Association; The Florida Bar; State Bar of Arizona; Florida Defense Lawyers Association; Defense Research Institute — U.S. Army Reserves, JAG Corps. 1986-1992 — Practice Areas: Civil Litigation; Construction Law; Medical Malpractice; Nursing Home Liability; Premises Liability

Joseph P. Menello — 1973 — Florida State University, B.A. (cum laude), 1994; J.D. (cum laude), 1998 — Admitted to Bar, 1998, Florida; 1998, U.S. District Court, Middle District of Florida — Member The Florida Bar; Orange County Bar Association; Florida Healthcare Association; Central Florida Medical Malpractice Claims Council, Inc. — Florida Super Lawyers "Rising Star" 2009-2012 — Practice Areas: Automobile Liability; Civil Litigation; Medical Malpractice; Premises Liability; Professional Liability; Retail Liability; Transportation

Michael R. D'Lugo — 1967 — Columbia University, B.A., 1989; Boston University, J.D., 1994 — Admitted to Bar, 1994, Florida; 1995, U.S. District Court, Middle District of Florida; 1996, U.S. Court of Appeals, Eleventh Circuit; 2001, U.S. Supreme Court

Kevin K. Chase — 1967 — Mississippi State University, B.A., 1990; The University of Mississippi, J.D., 1994 — Admitted to Bar, 1994, Florida; U.S. District Court, Middle District of Florida; U.S. Court of Appeals, Eleventh Circuit — Practice Areas: Automobile Liability; Civil Litigation; Medical Malpractice

Patrick M. DeLong — 1968 — University of Notre Dame, B.A. (cum laude), 1990; J.D., 1993 — Admitted to Bar, 1993, Florida; 1994, U.S. District Court, Middle District of Florida; 2000, U.S. District Court, Northern and Southern Districts of Florida; 2010, U.S. Court of Appeals, Eleventh Circuit — Languages: Spanish — Practice Areas: Civil Litigation; Class Actions; Commercial Litigation; Medical Malpractice; Premises Liability; Real Estate Litigation

Michael C. Tyson — 1963 — Rollins College, B.A., 1985; Florida State University, J.D., 1990 — Admitted to Bar, 1990, Florida; U.S. District Court, Middle District of Florida — Certified Civil Mediator — Practice Areas: Appellate Practice; Bad Faith; Civil Litigation; Insurance Coverage; Medical Malpractice; Premises Liability; Retail Liability

Chad E. Leeper — 1981 — University of Florida, B.A. (with high honors), 2004; Mercer University, J.D., 2007 — Admitted to Bar, 2007, Florida; 2011, Georgia; 2008, U.S. District Court, Middle District of Florida

Associates

Steven L. Meints — University of Nebraska-Lincoln, B.A., 1993; J.D., 1997 — Admitted to Bar, 1998, Kansas; 1999, Nebraska; 2002, Florida; 2009, North Carolina; 2012, District of Columbia

Stephen D. Houser — Purdue University, B.S. (with honors), 1974; University of Florida, J.D., 1984 — Admitted to Bar, 1985, Florida

Logan J. Young — University of Central Florida, B.A., 2000; Florida Coastal School of Law, J.D., 2004 — Admitted to Bar, 2005, Florida

Lindsey E. Freeman — University of Florida, B.A. (cum laude), 2004; St. Thomas University, J.D., 2007 — Admitted to Bar, 2007, Florida

Robert R. Saunders — Rollins College, B.A., 1986; Hofstra University School of Law, J.D., 1991 — Admitted to Bar, 1991, Florida

Randall M. Bolinger — Shippensburg University, B.A. (summa cum laude), 1979; William & Mary School of Law, J.D., 1984 — Admitted to Bar, 1984, Florida; 1994, Pennsylvania (Inactive); 2006, Virginia (Inactive)

Wicker Smith O'Hara McCoy & Ford P.A., Orlando, FL (Continued)

R. Gavin Mackinnon — The George Washington University, B.S., 1992; Chicago-Kent College of Law, J.C.L., 1998 — Admitted to Bar, 2000, Florida; 1998, Illinois

Patrick L. Mixson — University of Florida, B.A., 2007; University of Florida, Levin College of Law, J.D. (with honors), 2010 — Admitted to Bar, 2010, Florida

Deborah E. Frimmel — Villanova University, B.S. (cum laude), 1990; Nova Southeastern University, Shepard Broad Law Center, J.D. (with honors), 1996 — Admitted to Bar, 1996, Florida; 2003, U.S. Virgin Islands

Spensyr A. Mayfield — Rollins College, B.A. (cum laude), 2004; Brooklyn Law School, J.D., 2008 — Admitted to Bar, 2010, Florida; 2009, New York

Scharome R. Deaton — University of North Florida, B.S., 2000; West Virginia University College of Law, J.D., 2003 — Admitted to Bar, 2000, Florida; 2003, Florida

Michael J. Quinn — University of Florida, B.A., 2006; Florida State University College of Law, J.D., 2010 — Admitted to Bar, 2010, Florida

Spencer M. Diamond — The University of Georgia, B.B.A. (magna cum laude), 2008; University of Florida College of Law, J.D. (cum laude), 2011 — Admitted to Bar, 2011, Florida

Varun Ramnarine — University of Florida, B.S.B.A., 2008; University of Florida College of Law, J.D., 2011 — Admitted to Bar, 2011, Florida

Brian W. Rush — University of Florida, B.A. (cum laude), 2008; University of Florida College of Law, J.D., 2011 — Admitted to Bar, 2011, Florida

Jennifer Nicole Yencarelli — University of Florida, B.S. (summa cum laude), 2005; Florida Coastal School of Law, J.D. (magna cum laude), 2008 — Admitted to Bar, 2008, Florida

Melissa T. Woodward — New York University, B.A., 1993; New York Law School, J.D., 2000 — Admitted to Bar, 2001, New York; 2006, Florida

Margalie F. Reyes — Florida International University, B.A. (cum laude), 2007; Barry University School of Law, J.D., 2011 — Admitted to Bar, 2011, Florida

(See listing under Miami, FL for additional information)

The following firms also service this area.

Shutts & Bowen LLP
201 South Biscayne Boulevard
Suite 1500
Miami, Florida 33131
   Telephone: 305-358-6300
   Fax: 305-381-9982
   Toll Free: 800-325-2892

Insurance Defense, Life and Health, General Liability, Fraud, Reinsurance, Disability

SEE COMPLETE LISTING UNDER MIAMI, FLORIDA (232 MILES)

Vernis & Bowling of Central Florida, P.A.
1450 South Woodland Boulevard, Fourth Floor
DeLand, Florida 32720
   Telephone: 386-734-2505
   Fax: 386-734-3441

Civil Litigation, Insurance Law, Workers' Compensation, Premises Liability, Labor and Employment, Civil Rights, Commercial Litigation, Complex Litigation, Product Liability, Directors and Officers Liability, Errors and Omissions, Construction Law, Construction Defect, Environmental Liability, Personal and Commercial Vehicle, Appellate Practice, Admiralty and Maritime Law, Real Estate, Family Law, Elder Law, Liability Defense, SIU/Fraud Litigation, Education Law (ESE/IDEA), Property and Casualty (Commercial and Personal Lines), Long-Haul Trucking Liability, Government Law, Public Law, Criminal, White Collar, Business Litigation

SEE COMPLETE LISTING UNDER DAYTONA BEACH, FLORIDA (55 MILES)

FLORIDA

Young, Bill, Roumbos & Boles, P.A.
Seville Tower, 7th Floor
226 South Palafox Place
Pensacola, Florida 32502
   Telephone: 850-432-2222
   Fax: 850-432-1444
   Mailing Address: P.O. Drawer 1070, Pensacola, FL 32591-1070

Insurance Defense, Coverage Issues, Complex Litigation, Bad Faith, Product Liability, Medical Malpractice, Nursing Home Liability, Construction Defect, Premises Liability, General Liability, Automobile Liability

SEE COMPLETE LISTING UNDER PENSACOLA, FLORIDA (451 MILES)

ORMOND BEACH   38,137 Volusia Co.
Refer To
Vernis & Bowling of Central Florida, P.A.
1450 South Woodland Boulevard, Fourth Floor
DeLand, Florida 32720
   Telephone: 386-734-2505
   Fax: 386-734-3441

Civil Litigation, Insurance Law, Workers' Compensation, Premises Liability, Labor and Employment, Civil Rights, Commercial Litigation, Complex Litigation, Product Liability, Directors and Officers Liability, Errors and Omissions, Construction Law, Construction Defect, Environmental Liability, Personal and Commercial Vehicle, Appellate Practice, Admiralty and Maritime Law, Real Estate, Family Law, Elder Law, Liability Defense, SIU/Fraud Litigation, Education Law (ESE/IDEA), Property and Casualty (Commercial and Personal Lines), Long-Haul Trucking Liability, Government Law, Public Law, Criminal, White Collar, Business Litigation

SEE COMPLETE LISTING UNDER DAYTONA BEACH, FLORIDA (6 MILES)

PALATKA   † 10,558 Putnam Co.
Refer To
Cameron, Hodges, Coleman, LaPointe & Wright, P.A.
150 South Palmetto Avenue, # 101
Daytona Beach, Florida 32114
   Telephone: 386-257-1755
   Fax: 386-252-5601

Insurance Law

SEE COMPLETE LISTING UNDER DAYTONA BEACH, FLORIDA (54 MILES)

Refer To
Dell Graham, P.A.
203 Northeast First Street
Gainesville, Florida 32601
   Telephone: 352-372-4381
   Fax: 352-376-7415

Insurance Defense, Civil Trial Practice, State and Federal Courts, Automobile, Medical Malpractice, Product Liability, Governmental Liability, Property and Casualty

SEE COMPLETE LISTING UNDER GAINESVILLE, FLORIDA (46 MILES)

PALM HARBOR   57,439 Pinellas Co.
Refer To
Vernis & Bowling of the Gulf Coast, P.A.
696 1st Avenue, 1st Floor
St. Petersburg, Florida 33701
   Telephone: 727-443-3377
   Fax: 727-443-6828

Civil Litigation, Insurance Law, Workers' Compensation, Premises Liability, Labor and Employment, Civil Rights, Commercial Litigation, Complex Litigation, Product Liability, Directors and Officers Liability, Errors and Omissions, Construction Law, Construction Defect, Environmental Liability, Personal and Commercial Vehicle, Appellate Practice, Admiralty and Maritime Law, Real Estate, Family Law, Elder Law, Liability Defense, SIU/Fraud Litigation, Education Law (ESE/IDEA), Property and Casualty (Commercial and Personal Lines), Long-Haul Trucking Liability, Government Law, Public Law, Criminal, White Collar, Business Litigation

SEE COMPLETE LISTING UNDER CLEARWATER, FLORIDA (9 MILES)

ORMOND BEACH

PANAMA CITY   † 36,484 Bay Co.

Barron & Redding, P.A.
220 McKenzie Avenue
Panama City, Florida 32401-3129
   Telephone: 850-785-7454
   Fax: 850-785-2999
   E-Mail: barronredding@barronredding.com
   www.barronredding.com

Established: 1969

Casualty, Surety, Fire, Life Insurance, Professional Liability, Product Liability, Medical Malpractice, Environmental Law, Automobile Liability, Premises Liability, Business Torts, Construction Law

Insurance Clients

Acceptance Insurance Companies	ACE USA
AIG Insurance Company	Alfa Insurance Corporation
Auto-Owners Insurance Company	Chicago Insurance Company
Crum & Forster Insurance	Farmers Insurance Group
First American Title Insurance Company	The Hartford Insurance Group
MAG Mutual Insurance Company	Liberty Bankers Life Insurance Company
Mid-Continent Group	State Farm Insurance Companies
T.H.E. Insurance Company	Tower Hill Insurance Group
Ullico Casualty Company	Wells Fargo Insurance Services
Westcor Land Title Insurance Company	

Of Counsel

Benjamin W. Redding — 1933 — University of Florida, B.S.F., 1955; J.D. (with honors), 1966 — Phi Delta Phi — Admitted to Bar, 1967, Florida; U.S. District Court, Northern District of Florida; U.S. Court of Appeals, Eleventh Circuit; U.S. Supreme Court — Member American and Bay County Bar Associations; The Florida Bar; Florida Bar Board of Governors, 1976-1980 — Lieutenant, JG USNR, 1956-1959 — Practice Areas: Real Estate; Trusts; Wills; Probate — E-mail: bredding@barronredding.com

John M. Fite — 1946 — Florida Presbyterian College, B.A. (with high honors), 1968; Vanderbilt University, J.D., 1974 — Order of the Coif — Associate Editor & Editorial Board, Vanderbilt Law Review, 1973-1974 — Admitted to Bar, 1975, Florida — Member Bay County Bar Association; The Florida Bar; American Inns of Court — Patrick Wilson Fellow — Certified Circuit Court Mediator — U.S. Army, 1968-1972 — Practice Areas: Personal Injury; Product Liability; Medical Malpractice; Civil Litigation; Mediation — E-mail: jfite@barronredding.com

Partners

J. Robert Hughes — 1943 — Virginia Military Institute, B.A., 1965; University of Florida, J.D., 1968 — Phi Delta Phi — Admitted to Bar, 1968, Florida — Member The Florida Bar; Bay County Bar Association; St. Andrews Bay American Inn of Court — Captain, U.S. Military Intelligence, U.S. Army, 1968-1970 — Practice Areas: Real Estate; Commercial Law; Land Use; Corporate Law — E-mail: jhughes@barronredding.com

Clifford W. Sanborn — 1958 — Florida State University, B.S., 1980; J.D. (with high honors), 1984 — Order of the Coif — Admitted to Bar, 1984, Florida — Member American and Bay County Bar Associations; The Florida Bar (Young Lawyers' Division, Board of Governors 1990-1995; Executive Committee; Chair, Florida Bar Journal Committee; Chair, Long Range Planning Committee; Trial Lawyers Section, Executive Council, 2002-present; Board of Governors, 2004-2010); Fourteenth Judicial Circuit Grievance Committee, 1998-2001; Florida Defense Lawyers Association; American Inns of Court — Practice Areas: Litigation; Commercial Law; Construction Litigation; Product Liability; Business Litigation — E-mail: csanborn@barronredding.com

Roland W. Kiehn — 1963 — University of Miami, B.A., 1987; Florida State University, J.D. (with honors), 1990 — Admitted to Bar, 1990, Florida — Member The Florida Bar; American and Bay County (Vice President, 1993-1994) Bar Associations; Northern District of Florida Bankruptcy Bar Association (Board Member 1993-1997; President 1995-1996, 2006-2007; Secretary/Treasurer 2005-2006); St. Andrews Bay American Inn of Court (Secretary/Treasurer 1997-2007; President 2007-present); Fourteenth Judicial Circuit Grievance Committee (January 2001-2004); Fourteenth Judicial

Barron & Redding, P.A., Panama City, FL   (Continued)

Circuit Nominating Commission (2003-present); American Bankruptcy Institute — Practice Areas: Real Estate; Bankruptcy; Creditor Rights; Contracts; Business Law; Corporate Law; Litigation; Construction Law; Health Care — E-mail: rkiehn@barronredding.com

Brian D. Leebrick — 1974 — University of Florida, B.A. (with honors), 1996; J.D. (with high honors), 1999 — Phi Betta Kappa — Order of the Coif — Admitted to Bar, 1999, Florida — Member American and Bay County Bar Associations; The Florida Bar (Member, Executive Council, Real Property, Probate & Trust Law Section); St. Andrews Bay American Inn of Court — Co-author, "Transferable Development Rights and Alternatives After Suitum," 30 Urb. Law. 441, 1998 — Practice Areas: Real Estate; Commercial Law; Contracts; Corporate Law; Construction Law; Health Care — E-mail: bleebrick@barronredding.com

Michael P. Dickey — 1964 — University of Southern California, A.B., 1986; Troy State University, M.S., 1993; The University of Georgia School of Law, J.D. (magna cum laude), 1997 — Admitted to Bar, 1997, Florida — Member American (Litigation and Dispute Resolution Sections) and Bay County Bar Associations; The Florida Bar (Former chair, Code and Rules of Evidence Committee; Civil Procedure Rules Committee); Florida Board of Bar Examiners (Grader, Member 2006-08); St. Andrews Bay American Inn of Court (Barrister, Group Leader) — Author, "ADR Gone Wild: Is It Time for a Federal Mediation Exclusionary Rule," 25 Ohio State Journal on Dispute Resolution, 2010; "The Florida Evidence Code and the Separation of Powers Doctrine: How to Distinguish Substance and Procedure Now That It Matters," 34 Stetson Law Review 109, Fall 2004; "Conflict of Laws and the Dangerous Instrumentality Doctrine in Florida," Trial Advocate Quarterly, Fall 1999; "Crawford v Washington: Testimonial Hearsay meets the Confrontation Clause," Bulletin of the ABA Committee on Trial Evidence, Fall 2004; "Demand Letters and Diversity Jurisdiction," Bulletin of the ABA Committee on Trial Evidence, Spring 2006; Editor, "Receiverships in Florida, Florida Civil Practice Before Trial," 6th ed.; "Evidence in Florida," 2007 ed. — Certified Circuit Court Mediator — Practice Areas: Commercial Litigation; Construction Law; Tort Litigation; Alternative Dispute Resolution; Mediation; Entertainment Law — E-mail: mdickey@barronredding.com

Theodore "Ted" R. Howell — 1980 — University of Florida, B.S. (cum laude), 2002; J.D. (magna cum laude), 2005 — Phi Delta Phi — Order of the Coif — Admitted to Bar, 2005, Florida; 2006, Alabama — Member American Bar Association; The Florida Bar; Alabama State Bar; Defense Research Institute — Journal of Law and Public Policy — Practice Areas: Personal Injury; Commercial Litigation; Construction Litigation; Product Liability — E-mail: thowell@barronredding.com

Holly K. Melzer — 1981 — University of Florida, B.S. (cum laude), 2003; J.D. (cum laude), 2006 — Admitted to Bar, 2006, Florida — Member American and Bay County Bar Associations; American Bankruptcy Institute; Northern District of Florida Bankruptcy Bar Association; American Inns of Court — Practice Areas: Commercial Litigation; Creditor Rights; Business Transactions; Commercial Transactions; Real Estate; Bankruptcy — E-mail: hmelzer@barronredding.com

Associates

Jeffrey S. Carter — 1975 — Middle Tennessee State University, B.S. (summa cum laude), 2007; The University of Tennessee College of Law, J.D. (cum laude), 2010 — Admitted to Bar, 2011, Florida; 2011, Tennessee; U.S. District Court, Northern District of Florida — Member The Florida Bar (Entertainment, Arts, and Sports Law Section); Tennessee Bar Association (Entertainment, Arts, and Sports Law Section); American Society of Composers, Authors and Publications; St. Andrews American Inn of Court; Florida Bar Unlicensed Practice of Law Committee, Fourteenth Judicial Circuit — "Strictly Business: A Historical Narrative and Commentary on Rock and Roll Business Practices" 78 Tenn.L.Rev 213, 2010; Acknowledged contributor, "George Kuney & Brian Krumm, The Entrepreneurial Law Clinic Handbook," West's American Casebook Series, 2013 — Leadership Bay Class of 2013 — Practice Areas: Commercial Litigation; Business Transactions; Bankruptcy; Personal Injury; Probate; Entertainment Law; Intellectual Property; Insurance Defense; Construction Litigation; Banking; Creditor's Rights — E-mail: jcarter@barronredding.com

Justin N. Rost — 1978 — University of Michigan - Ann Arbor, B.A., 2000; University of Miami School of Law, J.D. (Dean's Scholar), 2003 — Admitted to Bar, 2003, Florida; 2009, Kentucky — Member Kentucky, Bay County and Louisville Bar Associations; The Florida Bar; St. Andrews Bay American Inn of Court — Practice Areas: Commercial Litigation; Tort Litigation; Appellate Practice; Insurance Coverage; Bad Faith; Health Care; Criminal Defense — E-mail: jrost@barronredding.com

Paul A. Blay — 1984 — University of California, Davis, B.A. Economics (with honors), 2008; University of Florida, Levin College of Law, J.D. (cum laude, Dean's List), 2014 — Admitted to Bar, 2014, Florida — Member American

Barron & Redding, P.A., Panama City, FL   (Continued)

and Bay County Bar Associations; The Florida Bar; American Inns of Court, St. Andrews Bay Chapter; Northern District of Florida Bankruptcy Bar Association — Practice Areas: Bankruptcy; Business Transactions; Commercial Transactions; Commercial Litigation — E-mail: pblay@barronredding.com

Matthews, Higgins, Hausfeld & Fenimore

475 Harrison Avenue, Suite 200
Panama City, Florida 32401
  Telephone: 850-769-7200
  Fax: 850-434-2600
  www.matthewshigginslaw.com

(Pensacola, FL Office*: 114 East Gregory Street, 32502-4970, P.O. Box 13145, 32591-3145)
  (Tel: 850-434-2200)
  (Fax: 850-434-2600)
  (E-Mail: lmatthews@matthewshigginslaw.com)
(Mobile, AL Office*: 910 Government Street, 36604)
  (Tel: 251-434-6711)
  (Fax: 850-434-2600)

Established: 1997

Personal Injury, Wrongful Death, Defense Litigation, Insurance Coverage, Commercial Litigation, Automobile Liability, Premises Liability, Product Liability, Professional Malpractice, Subrogation, Employment Law, Bad Faith, Casualty Defense, Real Estate Litigation, Construction Litigation, Directors and Officers Liability, Insurance Defense, Mediation, Condominium Litigation

Managing Shareholder

Larry A. Matthews — 1954 — University of Florida, B.S. (with honors), 1976; Florida State University, J.D. (with honors), 1981 — Admitted to Bar, 1982, Florida; 1994, Alabama; 1982, U.S. District Court, Middle and Northern Districts of Florida; 1994, U.S. Court of Appeals, Eleventh Circuit; 1998, U.S. Supreme Court — Member The Florida Bar; Alabama State Bar; Florida Defense Lawyers Association; American Board of Trial Advocates; American Inns of Court — Florida Bar Board Certified Civil Trial Lawyer; Certified Circuit Court Mediator; Certified Public Accountant (Inactive) — E-mail: lmatthews@matthewshigginslaw.com

Shareholders

Raymond F. Higgins III — 1957 — Virginia Military Institute, B.S. (with distinction), 1979; Florida State University, J.D. (with honors), 1998 — Admitted to Bar, 1998, Florida; U.S. District Court, Northern District of Florida — Member The Florida Bar; Escambia/Santa Rosa Bar Association — E-mail: rhiggins@matthewshigginslaw.com

M. Kevin Hausfeld — 1972 — University of West Florida, B.S. (magna cum laude), 1998; University of Florida College of Law, J.D. (with honors), 2004 — Admitted to Bar, 2005, Florida; 2009, Alabama; U.S. District Court, Northern District of Florida — Member The Florida Bar; Alabama State Bar; Florida Justice Association; Million Dollar Advocates Forum — E-mail: khausfeld@matthewshigginslaw.com

Michael Fenimore — 1978 — University of Florida, B.S. (with honors), 2001; Saint Louis University School of Law, J.D., 2005 — Admitted to Bar, 2005, Florida; 2006, Missouri; U.S. District Court, Northern District of Florida — Member Escambia-Santa Rosa County (Young Lawyers' Division) and Pensacola (Young Professionals) Bar Assocaitions — E-mail: mfenimore@matthewshigginslaw.com

Firm Member

Thomas R. Jenkins — 1949 — Eastern Illinois University, B.S. (with honors), 1975; M.B.A., 1979; Florida State University, J.D. (with high honors), 1982 — Phi Delta Phi; Order of Coif — Admitted to Bar, 1982, Florida; 1994, Alabama; 1982, U.S. District Court, Middle and Northern Districts of Florida; 1983, U.S. Court of Appeals, Eleventh Circuit — Member The Florida Bar; Alabama State Bar; Florida Defense Lawyers Association — Florida Bar Board Certified Civil Trial Lawyer; Certified Circuit Court Mediator

(See listing under Pensacola, FL for additional information)

McConnaughhay, Duffy, Coonrod, Pope & Weaver, P.A.

306 East Nineteenth Street
Panama City, Florida 32401
  Telephone: 850-784-2599
  Fax: 850-769-5461
  www.mcconnaughhay.com

(Additional Offices: Tallahassee, FL*; Fort Lauderdale, FL*; Gainesville, FL*; Jacksonville, FL*; Ocala, FL*; Pensacola, FL*; Sarasota, FL*)

Insurance Defense, Workers' Compensation, Product Liability, Labor and Employment, Civil Litigation, Trial Practice, Appellate Practice

Firm Members

Patrick E. Weaver — South Texas College of Law, J.D., 1987 — Admitted to Bar, 1989, Florida — Practice Areas: Workers' Compensation

Tracey J. Hyde — Florida State University College of Law, J.D. (with honors), 1994 — Admitted to Bar, 1994, Florida; 1995, Maryland — Practice Areas: Workers' Compensation; Longshore and Harbor Workers' Compensation

Associates

Teresa F. Cummings   Jennifer L. Gutai

The following firms also service this area.

Vernis & Bowling of Northwest Florida, P.A.
315 South Palafox Street
Pensacola, Florida 32502
  Telephone: 850-433-5461
  Fax: 850-432-0166

Civil Litigation, Insurance Law, Workers' Compensation, Premises Liability, Labor and Employment, Civil Rights, Commercial Litigation, Complex Litigation, Product Liability, Directors and Officers Liability, Errors and Omissions, Construction Law, Construction Defect, Environmental Liability, Personal and Commercial Vehicle, Appellate Practice, Admiralty and Maritime Law, Real Estate, Family Law, Elder Law, Liability Defense, SIU/Fraud Litigation, Education Law (ESE/IDEA), Property and Casualty (Commercial and Personal Lines), Long-Haul Trucking Liability, Government Law, Public Law, Criminal, White Collar, Business Litigation

SEE COMPLETE LISTING UNDER PENSACOLA, FLORIDA (103 MILES)

Wade, Palmer & Shoemaker, P.A.
14 North Palafox Street
Pensacola, Florida 32502
  Telephone: 850-429-0755
  Fax: 850-429-0871
  Toll Free: 888-980-0755

Mailing Address: P.O. Box 13510, Pensacola, FL 32591-3510

Insurance Defense, Automobile Liability, Product Liability, Bodily Injury, Coverage Issues, Subrogation, Property and Casualty, Construction Law, General Liability, Litigation, Employment Law, Employment Discrimination

SEE COMPLETE LISTING UNDER PENSACOLA, FLORIDA (103 MILES)

Young, Bill, Roumbos & Boles, P.A.
Seville Tower, 7th Floor
226 South Palafox Place
Pensacola, Florida 32502
  Telephone: 850-432-2222
  Fax: 850-432-1444

Mailing Address: P.O. Drawer 1070, Pensacola, FL 32591-1070

Insurance Defense, Coverage Issues, Complex Litigation, Bad Faith, Product Liability, Medical Malpractice, Nursing Home Liability, Construction Defect, Premises Liability, General Liability, Automobile Liability

SEE COMPLETE LISTING UNDER PENSACOLA, FLORIDA (103 MILES)

PENSACOLA † 51,923 Escambia Co.

Conroy Simberg
125 West Romana Street, Suite 320
Pensacola, Florida 32502
  Telephone: 850-436-6605
  Fax: 850-436-2102
  E-Mail: csg@conroysimberg.com
  www.conroysimberg.com

Insurance Defense, Appellate Practice, Insurance Coverage, Environmental Law, Governmental Liability, Civil Rights, Wrongful Termination, Americans with Disabilities Act, Sexual Harassment, Land Use, Commercial Law, Fire, Arson, Fraud, Fidelity and Surety, Automobile Liability, Admiralty and Maritime Law, Bad Faith, Employment Law, Self-Insured, Public Entities, Product Liability, Casualty, Excess and Reinsurance, Accident and Health, Workers' Compensation, Medical Malpractice, Class Actions, Construction Defect, Construction Litigation, First Party Matters, Premises Liability, Professional Liability, Intellectual Property

(See listing under Hollywood, FL for additional information)

Galloway, Johnson, Tompkins, Burr & Smith
118 East Garden Street
Pensacola, Florida 32502
  Telephone: 850-436-7000
  Fax: 850-436-7099
  E-Mail: tburr@gallowayjohnson.com
  www.gallowayjohnson.com

(Additional Offices: New Orleans, LA*; Lafayette, LA*; St. Louis, MO*; Houston, TX*; Mandeville, LA*; Gulfport, MS*; Tampa, FL*; Mobile, AL*; Atlanta, GA*)

Maritime, Automobile Liability, Bad Faith, Class Actions, Construction, Energy, Employment, Insurance Coverage, Insurance Defense, Product Liability, Professional Liability, Property, Transportation, General Casualty, Title Resolution, Environmental

(See listing under New Orleans, LA for additional information)

Matthews, Higgins, Hausfeld & Fenimore
114 East Gregory Street
Pensacola, Florida 32502-4970
  Telephone: 850-434-2200
  Fax: 850-434-2600
  E-Mail: lmatthews@matthewshigginslaw.com
  www.matthewshigginslaw.com

(Panama City, FL Office*: 475 Harrison Avenue, Suite 200, 32401)
  (Tel: 850-769-7200)
  (Fax: 850-434-2600)
(Mobile, AL Office*: 910 Government Street, 36604)
  (Tel: 251-434-6711)
  (Fax: 850-434-2600)

Established: 1992

Matthews, Higgins, Hausfeld & Fenimore, Pensacola, FL (Continued)

Personal Injury, Wrongful Death, Defense Litigation, Insurance Coverage, Commercial Litigation, Automobile Liability, Premises Liability, Product Liability, Professional Malpractice, Subrogation, Employment Law, Bad Faith, Casualty Defense, Real Estate Litigation, Construction Litigation, Directors and Officers Liability, Insurance Defense, Mediation, Condominium Litigation

Firm Profile: Matthews, Higgins, Hausfeld & Fenimore, is a team of attorneys, support staff, specialists, subject-matter experts, and technical consultants specializing in insurance defense and related matters. We handle litigation involving almost every type of civil matter, including general liability matters for insurance companies, businesses, and governmental entities. We represent clients in cases throughout the Florida Panhandle and Southern Alabama. We provide a practical, aggressive approach to litigation, while mindful of the need to manage fees and costs.

Insurance Clients

Allstate Floridian Indemnity Company
American Specialty Insurance & Risk Services, Inc.
Chubb Group of Insurance Companies
CNA Insurance Companies
Founders Insurance Company
Global Indemnity Group, Inc.
Interstate Insurance Group
Markel American Insurance Company
RSKCo
TIG Insurance Company
United States Liability Insurance Company
American Modern Insurance Group, Inc.
Central Mutual Insurance Company
Chartis Insurance
Clarendon National Insurance Company
FCCI Insurance Company
Frankenmuth Mutual Insurance Company
Liberty Mutual Insurance Company
Naughton Insurance, Inc.
Nautilus Insurance Company
St. Paul Insurance Company
Union Standard Insurance Group

Non-Insurance Clients

Florida Department of Financial Services
Smurfit-Stone Container Corporation
Okaloosa County
Santa Rosa County
WTI Transport, Inc.

Managing Shareholder

Larry A. Matthews — 1954 — University of Florida, B.S. (with honors), 1976; Florida State University, J.D. (with honors), 1981 — Admitted to Bar, 1982, Florida; 1994, Alabama; 1982, U.S. District Court, Middle and Northern Districts of Florida; 1994, U.S. Court of Appeals, Eleventh Circuit; 1998, U.S. Supreme Court — Member The Florida Bar; Alabama State Bar; Florida Defense Lawyers Association; American Board of Trial Advocates; American Inns of Court — Florida Bar Board Certified Civil Trial Lawyer; Certified Circuit Court Mediator; Certified Public Accountant (Inactive) — E-mail: lmatthews@matthewshigginslaw.com

Shareholders

Raymond F. Higgins III — 1957 — Virginia Military Institute, B.S. (with distinction), 1979; Florida State University, J.D. (with honors), 1998 — Admitted to Bar, 1998, Florida; U.S. District Court, Northern District of Florida — Member The Florida Bar; Escambia/Santa Rosa Bar Association — E-mail: rhiggins@matthewshigginslaw.com

M. Kevin Hausfeld — 1972 — University of West Florida, B.S. (magna cum laude), 1998; University of Florida College of Law, J.D. (with honors), 2004 — Admitted to Bar, 2005, Florida; 2009, Alabama; U.S. District Court, Northern District of Florida — Member The Florida Bar; Alabama State Bar; Florida Justice Association; Million Dollar Advocates Forum — E-mail: khausfeld@matthewshigginslaw.com

Michael Fenimore — 1978 — University of Florida, B.S. (with honors), 2001; Saint Louis University School of Law, J.D., 2005 — Admitted to Bar, 2005, Florida; 2006, Missouri; U.S. District Court, Northern District of Florida — Member Escambia-Santa Rosa County (Young Lawyers' Division) and Pensacola (Young Professionals) Bar Assocaitions — E-mail: mfenimore@matthewshigginslaw.com

Firm Member

Thomas R. Jenkins — 1949 — Eastern Illinois University, B.S. (with honors), 1975; M.B.A., 1979; Florida State University, J.D. (with high honors),

1982 — Phi Delta Phi; Order of Coif — Admitted to Bar, 1982, Florida; 1994, Alabama; 1982, U.S. District Court, Middle and Northern Districts of Florida; 1983, U.S. Court of Appeals, Eleventh Circuit — Member The Florida Bar; Alabama State Bar; Florida Defense Lawyers Association — Florida Bar Board Certified Civil Trial Lawyer; Certified Circuit Court Mediator

(This firm is also listed in the Subrogation section of this directory)

McConnaughhay, Duffy, Coonrod, Pope & Weaver, P.A.

316 South Baylen Street, Suite 500
Pensacola, Florida 32502
 Telephone: 850-434-7122
 Fax: 850-435-0924
 www.mcconnaughhay.com

(Additional Offices: Tallahassee, FL*; Fort Lauderdale, FL*; Gainesville, FL*; Jacksonville, FL*; Ocala, FL*; Panama City, FL*; Sarasota, FL*)

Insurance Defense, Workers' Compensation, Product Liability, Labor and Employment, Civil Litigation, Trial Practice, Appellate Practice

Firm Members

Susan N. Marks — Florida State University, J.D. (cum laude), 1996 — Admitted to Bar, 1996, Florida — Practice Areas: Workers' Compensation

Timothy R. Whitney — Florida State University, J.D. (with honors), 1997 — Admitted to Bar, 1997, California; 1998, Florida — Practice Areas: Workers' Compensation; Civil Litigation

Associates

Wheeler H. Bryant   Patrick W. Luna

Vernis & Bowling of Northwest Florida, P.A.

315 South Palafox Street
Pensacola, Florida 32502
 Telephone: 850-433-5461
 Fax: 850-432-0166
 E-Mail: info@florida-law.com
 www.national-law.com

(Vernis & Bowling of Palm Beach, P.A.*: 884 U.S. Highway #1, North Palm Beach, FL, 33408-5408)
 (Tel: 561-775-9822)
 (Fax: 561-775-9821)
 (E-Mail: gjvernis@florida-law.com)
(Vernis & Bowling of Southern Alabama, LLC*: 61 St. Joseph Street, 11th Floor, Mobile, AL, 36602)
 (Tel: 251-432-0337)
 (Fax: 251-432-0244)
 (E-Mail: info@law-alabama.com)
 (www.law-alabama.com)
(Vernis & Bowling of Broward, P.A.*(See Fort Lauderdale listing): 5821 Hollywood Boulevard, First Floor, Hollywood, FL, 33021)
 (Tel: 954-927-5330)
 (Fax: 954-927-5320)
(Vernis & Bowling of Southern Mississippi, PLLC*: 2501 14th Street, Suite 207, Gulfport, MS, 39501)
 (Tel: 225-539-0021)
 (Fax: 228-539-0022)

Established: 1970

FLORIDA   PENSACOLA

Vernis & Bowling of Northwest Florida, P.A., Pensacola, FL (Continued)

Civil Litigation, Insurance Law, Workers' Compensation, Premises Liability, Labor and Employment, Civil Rights, Commercial Litigation, Complex Litigation, Product Liability, Directors and Officers Liability, Errors and Omissions, Construction Law, Construction Defect, Environmental Liability, Personal and Commercial Vehicle, Appellate Practice, Admiralty and Maritime Law, Real Estate, Family Law, Elder Law, Liability Defense, SIU/Fraud Litigation, Education Law (ESE/IDEA), Property and Casualty (Commercial and Personal Lines), Long-Haul Trucking Liability, Government Law, Public Law, Criminal, White Collar, Business Litigation

Firm Profile: VERNIS & BOWLING represents individuals, businesses, insurance carriers and self-insureds. With 115 offices located in Florida, Georgia, Alabama, North Carolina & Mississippi, we provide cost effective, full service legal representation that consistently exceeds the expectations of our clients.

Resident Attorneys

John A. Unzicker — 1947 — California State University, B.S.M.E., 1970; University of Miami School of Law, J.D. (cum laude), 1981 — Phi Kappa Phi — Admitted to Bar, 1981, Florida; 1989, Alabama

Stephanie D. Alexander — 1949 — California State University, Fullerton, B.A., 1974; Florida State University, J.D. (cum laude), 1998 — Admitted to Bar, 1998, Florida — Resident Pensacola Office

Michelle Hendrix — University of Southern Mississippi, B.A., 1996; Tulane University Law School, J.D., 1999 — Admitted to Bar, 1999, Florida; 1999, U.S. District Court, Middle and Northern Districts of Florida; 1999, Supreme Court of Florida; 1999, Supreme Court of Alabama

Lawrence J. Obin, II — 1974 — MacMurray College, B.S., 1996; Thomas M. Cooley Law School, J.D., 2001 — Admitted to Bar, 2002, Florida; 2005, U.S. District Court, Northern District of Florida

Charles M. Hughes — 1929 — Louisiana State University, B.S., 1951; Louisiana State University Law Center, J.D., 1957 — Admitted to Bar, 1957, Louisiana — Member American, Louisiana State and Washington Parish Bar Associations; International Association of Defense Counsel; Federation of Insurance Counsel; Louisiana Association of Defense Counsel; Defense Research Institute

William J. Thames — Florida State University, B.S., 1987; University of Florida College of Law, J.D., 1990 — Admitted to Bar, 1990, Florida

Wade, Palmer & Shoemaker, P.A.

14 North Palafox Street
Pensacola, Florida 32502
    Telephone: 850-429-0755
    Fax: 850-429-0871
    Toll Free: 888-980-0755
    E-Mail: wps@wpslawyers.com
    www.wpslawyers.com

Established: 1997

Insurance Defense, Automobile Liability, Product Liability, Bodily Injury, Coverage Issues, Subrogation, Property and Casualty, Construction Law, General Liability, Litigation, Employment Law, Employment Discrimination

Insurance Clients

Admiral Insurance Company
Broadspire, a Crawford Company
Cincinnati Insurance Company
Claims Management Services, Inc.
CRES Insurance Services, LLC
CUMIS Insurance Society, Inc.
Fireman's Fund Insurance Company
Auto-Owners Insurance Company
Burlington Insurance Group
Citizens Property Insurance Corp.
Companion Property and Casualty Group
Encompass Insurance Company
First Acceptance Services, Inc.
Gallagher Bassett Services, Inc.

Wade, Palmer & Shoemaker, P.A., Pensacola, FL (Continued)

General Star Management Company
Harco National Insurance Company
The Infinity Group
Medmarc, Inc.
Network Adjusters, Inc.
Occidental Fire & Casualty Company
The Seibels Bruce Group, Inc.
Tower Hill Insurance Group
United States Liability Insurance Group
Western World/Tudor Insurance Company
GMAC Insurance
Great American Insurance Company
The Horace Mann Companies
Markel Insurance Company
Nationwide Insurance
NOVA Casualty Company
RSKCo
Scottsdale Insurance Company
T.H.E. Insurance Company
Tudor Insurance Company
Unitrin Direct Insurance Company
U.S. Auto Insurance Services
Zurich North America

Non-Insurance Clients

CGI
FedEx
Select Medical Corporation
Winn-Dixie Stores, Inc.
EFCO Corporation
ResortQuest International, Inc
State of Florida, Division of Risk Management

Senior Partners

Linda H. Wade — 1961 — University of Florida, B.S., 1982; Cumberland School of Law of Samford University, J.D., 1986 — Admitted to Bar, Florida; Kentucky; U.S. District Court, Middle and Northern Districts of Florida; U.S. Court of Appeals, Eleventh Circuit; U.S. Supreme Court — Member The Florida Bar; The Florida Bar, Civil Trial Certification Committee, (2004 - 2007), Assistant Chair (2007); Commonwealth of Kentucky; American and Escambia/Santa Rosa Bar Associations; American Board of Trial Advocates, Vice President, Northwest Florida Chapter (2007), President, Northwest Florida Chapter (2010); American Inns of Court, Pensacola, FL (1991-1993,1997-1999); Judicial Nomination Committee, First Circuit (2001-2002, 2002-2006, Co-Chairman, 2004); Member, Claims & Litigation Management Alliance (CLM); Fellow, Litigation Counsel of America; Florida Defense Lawyers Association; Defense Research Institute — Co-Author: "A Man in a Wheelchair and His Lawyers Go Into A Bar: Serial ADA Litigation is No Joke", Florida Defense Lawyers Association, Trial Advocate Quarterly - Fall 2006 — Board Certified Civil Trial Lawyer — Practice Areas: Employment Law; Civil Trial Practice; Bad Faith; Wrongful Death; Professional Liability; Personal Injury — E-mail: lwade@wpslawyers.com

Robert C. Palmer III — 1955 — Davidson College, B.A., 1977; Florida State University, J.D., 1980 — Phi Delta Phi — Admitted to Bar, 1981, Florida; U.S. District Court, Middle and Northern Districts of Florida; U.S. Court of Appeals, Eleventh Circuit; U.S. Supreme Court — Member American Bar Association; Escambia-Santa Rosa Bar Association; The Florida Bar, Trial Lawyers Section, Executive Counsel (1998-2006), Chair (2007-2008), Civil Procedure Rules Committee (1995-2002), Civil Trial Certification Committee (2004-2010), Chair (2007-2008), Young Lawyers Division of the Florida Bar, Board of Governors, (1985-1992), President (1991-1992); The Florida Bar Foundation, Director (1992-1997); Florida Defense Lawyers Association, Secretary (2002-2003), Board of Directors, (1996-2002); Florida Chapter of American Board of Trial Advocates, President - Elect (2013-2014); Florida Chapter of American Board of Trial Advocates, President - Elect (2013-2014); Member, Claims & Litigation Management Alliance (CLM); Defense Research Institute; International Association of Defense Counsel — Board Certified Civil Trial Lawyer, , Florida Bar Board of Legal Specialization and Education — Practice Areas: Construction Litigation; Product Liability Defense; Professional Liability; Personal Injury; Civil Trial Practice — E-mail: bpalmer@wpslawyers.com

Gregory M. Shoemaker — 1960 — University of Nebraska-Lincoln, B.A., 1983; J.D., 1986 — Admitted to Bar, 1986, Nebraska; 1991, Florida; 1986, U.S. District Court, District of Nebraska; 1991, U.S. District Court, Northern District of Florida — Member The Florida Bar; Escambia/Santa Rosa Bar Association — Practice Areas: Insurance Coverage & Defense; Construction Litigation; Civil Litigation — E-mail: gshoemaker@wpslawyers.com

Partner

Elizabeth Nicole Palmer — 1975 — University of Virginia, B.A., 1997; East Tennessee State University, M.B.A., 2000; Mercer University, J.D. (cum laude), 2003 — Admitted to Bar, 2003, Georgia; 2005, Florida; 2005, Virginia; U.S. District Court, Northern District of Florida — Member The Florida Bar; Virginia State Bar; State Bar of Georgia; Escambia/Santa Rosa Bar Association — Author: "Update on Recent Trends in Medical Malpractice and How Impacted By Senate Bill 3: Georgia Tort Reform," G.D.L.A. Law Journal, 2005 — Practice Areas: Insurance Defense; Construction Litigation; General Liability — E-mail: npalmer@wpslawyers.com

PENSACOLA   FLORIDA

Wade, Palmer & Shoemaker, P.A., Pensacola, FL
(Continued)

Associate

J. Matthew Shook — Mississippi State University, B.A., 2001; Florida State University, J.D., 2011 — Admitted to Bar, 2011, Florida; U.S. District Court, Middle, Northern and Southern Districts of Florida — Member The Florida Bar — E-mail: mshook@wpslawyers.com

Young, Bill, Roumbos & Boles, P.A.

Seville Tower, 7th Floor
226 South Palafox Place
Pensacola, Florida 32502
 Telephone: 850-432-2222
 Fax: 850-432-1444
 E-Mail: ryoung@flalawyer.net
 www.flalawyer.net

(Miami, FL Office*: One Biscayne Tower, Suite 3195, 2 South Biscayne Boulevard, 33131)
 (Tel: 305-222-7720)
 (Fax: 305-492-7729)

Established: 1994

Insurance Defense, Coverage Issues, Complex Litigation, Bad Faith, Product Liability, Medical Malpractice, Nursing Home Liability, Construction Defect, Premises Liability, General Liability, Automobile Liability

Firm Profile: Young, Bill, Roumbos & Boles, P.A. is a 20 attorney law firm founded in 1994. The firm maintains a full support staff including legal assistants and paralegals.

Young, Bill, Roumbos & Boles, P.A. is a trial firm. All lawyers in the firm are actively engaged in trial practice. In the representation and defense of its clients, it is Young, Bill, Roumbos & Boles, P.A.'s belief that proper trial preparation and a reputation in the community for being willing to go forward to trial on appropriate cases is essential to obtaining good results. Although not all cases are appropriate for trial and not all cases should be tried, it is an abiding belief of the firm that consistently good results cannot be achieved for a client unless the firm has established a reputation in the community as a group of aggressive trial lawyers with above average abilities.

The attorneys at Young, Bill, Roumbos & Boles, P.A. specialize in all aspects of Insurance defense practice, including bad faith litigation, coverage litigation, products liability, construction defect, automobile negligence, premises liability, nursing home malpractice and medical malpractice. The firm has lawyers admitted to practice in all state courts of Florida, Georgia, Texas and Alabama, all federal courts of Florida, including trial bars, the United States Fifth Circuit Court of Appeals and the United States Eleventh Circuit Court of Appeals, and the United States Supreme Court.

Insurance Clients

The ACE Group
AIG Insurance Company
Bankers Insurance Company
California Casualty Group
CNA Insurance Companies
Crawford & Company
FAWA Self Insurers
GAB Business Services, Inc.
GAINSCO, Inc.
General Accident Insurance Company
Investors Underwriting Managers, Inc.
Northern Life Insurance Company
North Pointe Insurance Company
Paradigm Insurance Company
Ron Coleman & Associates, Ltd.
RSKCo
Southeastern Security Insurance Company
Travelers Group
United Underwriting

A.C.E. Insurance Company, Ltd.
Atlantic Mutual Insurance Company
Chubb Group of Insurance Companies
The Doctors Company
First Floridian Auto and Home Insurance Company
GEICO Direct
Gulf Insurance Company
The Hartford
Mid-Continent Group
Midland Risk Insurance Company
Northland Insurance Company
Omni Insurance Company
Reliant American Insurance Company
Sentry Claims Services
Southern Heritage Insurance Company
United Equitable Insurance Company

Young, Bill, Roumbos & Boles, P.A., Pensacola, FL
(Continued)

Uni-Ter Underwriting Management Corporation

York Claims Service, Inc.
Zurich U.S.

Non-Insurance Clients

Chase Manhattan Bank
Enterprise Leasing Company / ELCO
Healthprime, Inc.
The Pensacola News Journal

Coca-Cola Enterprises Inc.
Frito-Lay, Inc.
Gannett Corporation
Ogden Services Corporation
Protegrity Services, Inc.

Partners

B. Richard Young — 1959 — Florida State University, B.A. (magna cum laude), 1981; Florida State University College of Law, J.D. (cum laude), 1984 — Admitted to Bar, 1984, Florida; 1985, U.S. District Court, Middle and Southern Districts of Florida; 1986, U.S. Court of Appeals, Fifth Circuit; 1990, U.S. Court of Appeals, Eleventh Circuit; 1994, U.S. District Court, Northern District of Florida; 2000, U.S. Supreme Court — Member The Florida Bar; Escambia/Santa Rosa Bar Associations — National Board of Trial Advocacy — Board Certified Civil Trial Lawyer, Florida Bar Board of Legal Specialization; Board Certified Civil Trial Advocate, National Board of Trial Advocacy; Board Certified Civil Pretrial Practice Advocate, National Board of Trial Advocacy — Practice Areas: Bad Faith; Insurance Defense; Product Liability; Medical Malpractice; Construction Litigation; Nursing Home Liability — E-mail: ryoung@flalawyer.net

Michael T. Bill — 1968 — Auburn University, B.S., 1990; University of Florida College of Law, J.D. (with honors), 1993 — Admitted to Bar, 1994, Florida; U.S. District Court, Middle and Northern Districts of Florida; 1997, U.S. District Court, Southern District of Florida; U.S. Court of Appeals, Eleventh Circuit — Member The Florida Bar — Practice Areas: Construction Litigation; Insurance Coverage; Bad Faith; Insurance Defense; Product Liability; Insurance Litigation — E-mail: mbill@flalawyer.net

Peter S. Roumbos — 1958 — University of Notre Dame, B.A., 1980; University of Florida, B.A., 1981; University of Florida College of Law, J.D., 1985 — Admitted to Bar, 1986, Florida; U.S. District Court, Southern District of Florida; U.S. Court of Appeals, Fifth Circuit; 1994, U.S. District Court, Middle District of Florida; 1997, U.S. District Court, Northern District of Florida; 2009, U.S. Court of Appeals, Eleventh Circuit — Member The Florida Bar — Practice Areas: Automobile Liability; Civil Trial Practice; Insurance Defense; Product Liability; Bad Faith — E-mail: proumbos@flalawyer.net

B.B. Boles III — 1958 — Pensacola Junior College, A.A., 1978; University of West Florida, B.A. (cum laude), 1980; Florida State University College of Law, J.D., 1982 — Admitted to Bar, 1983, Florida; 2005, U.S. District Court, Northern District of Florida — Member The Florida Bar; Escambia/Santa Rosa Bar Association — Practice Areas: Construction Litigation; Insurance Defense; Automobile Liability — E-mail: bboles@flalawyer.net

Brentt E. Palmer — 1976 — Spring Hill College, B.S., 2000; Mercer University Walter F. George School of Law, J.D., 2003; DePaul University College of Law, LL.M., 2004 — Phi Delta Phi — Admitted to Bar, 2003, Florida; 2006, Georgia; 2007, Alabama; 2006, U.S. District Court, Middle and Northern Districts of Florida; 2009, U.S. Court of Appeals, Eleventh Circuit — Member Escambia/Santa Rose Bar Association — Practice Areas: Bad Faith; Insurance Defense; Liability Defense; Automobile Liability — E-mail: bpalmer@flalawyer.net

Associates

Megan M. Hall — 1981 — Grand Valley State University; Palm Beach Atlantic University, B.A. (Dean's List), 2003; Florida State University College of Law, J.D. (Dean's List), 2007 — Admitted to Bar, 2007, Florida; U.S. District Court, Middle District of Florida; 2008, U.S. District Court, Northern and Southern Districts of Florida; U.S. Court of Appeals, Eleventh Circuit — Practice Areas: Bad Faith; Insurance Coverage — E-mail: mhall@flalawyer.net

Adam A. Duke — 1984 — Florida State University, B.S., 2005; Florida State University College of Law, J.D., 2008 — Admitted to Bar, 2008, Florida; U.S. District Court, Middle, Northern and Southern Districts of Florida; 2010, U.S. Court of Appeals, Eleventh Circuit — Practice Areas: Bad Faith; Insurance Coverage — E-mail: aduke@flalawyer.net

Jordan M. Thompson — 1982 — Earlham College, B.A., 2006; Florida State University College of Law, J.D., 2010 — Admitted to Bar, 2011, Florida; 2012, U.S. District Court, Middle, Northern and Southern Districts of Florida — Practice Areas: Bad Faith; Insurance Coverage — E-mail: jthompson@flalawyer.net

M. Justin Lusko — 1981 — University of Florida, B.S./B.A., 2004; Florida Coastal School of Law, J.D., 2007 — Admitted to Bar, 2008, Florida; 2012,

FLORIDA

Young, Bill, Roumbos & Boles, P.A., Pensacola, FL (Continued)

U.S. District Court, Middle, Northern and Southern Districts of Florida — Member American and Escambia Santa Rosa Bar Associations; American Inns of Court — Practice Areas: Bad Faith; Insurance Coverage; Insurance Defense

Katina M. Hardee — 1973 — University of West Florida, B.A., 2002; Mississippi College of Law, J.D. (cum laude), 2005 — Admitted to Bar, 2005, Florida; 2012, U.S. District Court, Middle, Northern and Southern Districts of Florida — Practice Areas: Bad Faith; Insurance Defense; Insurance Coverage

Megan E. Alexander — 1983 — University of Florida, B.A., 2005; New England School of Law, J.D., 2008 — Admitted to Bar, 2008, Florida; 2009, U.S. District Court, Southern District of Florida; 2010, U.S. Court of Appeals, Eleventh Circuit; 2013, U.S. District Court, Middle and Northern Districts of Florida — Practice Areas: Bad Faith; Insurance Defense; Insurance Coverage

Amanda L. Kidd — 1986 — Western Kentucky University, B.A. (summa cum laude), 2008; Florida Coastal School of Law, J.D., 2011 — Admitted to Bar, 2011, Florida; 2013, U.S. District Court, Middle, Northern and Southern Districts of Florida — Member Escambia, Santa Rosa County Bar Association; American Inns of Court — Practice Areas: Bad Faith; Insurance Coverage

Lauren A. Harris — 1986 — University of North Texas, B.A.A.S., 2006; Texas Wesleyan University School of Law, J.D., 2011 — Admitted to Bar, 2012, Texas — Practice Areas: Bad Faith; Insurance Coverage

Cody S. Pflueger — 1982 — Shippensburg University, B.S., 2005; Pennsylvania State University-Dickinson School of Law, J.D., 2009 — Admitted to Bar, 2009, Pennsylvania; 2010, New Jersey; 2011, Florida; 2013, U.S. District Court, Southern District of Florida — Practice Areas: Bad Faith; Insurance Coverage

Michel A. Morgan — 1982 — Florida Atlantic University, B.A., 2004; University of Maryland, B.S., 2007; Nova Southeastern University, Shepard Broad Law Center, J.D., 2012 — Admitted to Bar, 2012, Florida; U.S. District Court, Southern District of Florida — Practice Areas: Bad Faith; Insurance Coverage

Carlos E. Nunez — 1989 — Florida International University, B.A. Economics (cum laude), 2009; University of Miami School of Law, J.D. (cum laude), 2013 — Admitted to Bar, 2014, Florida — Languages: Spanish — Practice Areas: Bad Faith; Insurance Coverage

Stephanie A. McQueen — 1986 — Florida Gulf Coast University, B.S., 2008; Stetson University College of Law, J.D., 2012 — Admitted to Bar, 2013, Florida — Practice Areas: Bad Faith; Insurance Coverage

Lisa S. Kass — 1988 — University of Florida, B.S. (cum laude), 2011; Nova Southeastern University, J.D. (cum laude), 2014 — Admitted to Bar, 2014, Florida — Practice Areas: Bad Faith; Insurance Coverage

Courtney Smith — 1981 — University of West Florida, B.A. (cum laude), 2005; Cumberland University School of Law, J.D., 2008 — Admitted to Bar, 2009, Florida; 2010, U.S. District Court, Northern District of Florida — Practice Areas: Bad Faith; Insurance Defense; Appellate; Litigation

The following firms also service this area.

Barron & Redding, P.A.
220 McKenzie Avenue
Panama City, Florida 32401-3129
Telephone: 850-785-7454
Fax: 850-785-2999

Mailing Address: P.O. Box 2467, Panama City, FL 32402-2467

Casualty, Surety, Fire, Life Insurance, Professional Liability, Product Liability, Medical Malpractice, Environmental Law, Automobile Liability, Premises Liability, Business Torts, Construction Law

SEE COMPLETE LISTING UNDER PANAMA CITY, FLORIDA (103 MILES)

PLANTATION

Helmsing, Leach, Herlong, Newman & Rouse, P.C.
LaClede Building, Suite 2000
150 Government Street
Mobile, Alabama 36602
Telephone: 251-432-5521
Fax: 251-432-0633

Mailing Address: P.O. Box 2767, Mobile, AL 36652

Alternative Dispute Resolution, Appellate Practice, Arbitration, Automobile Liability, Aviation, Bad Faith, Bankruptcy, Business and Real Estate Transactions, Business Bankruptcy, Business Formation, Business Law, Business Litigation, Business Transactions, Captive Company Matters, Casualty Defense, Church Law, Civil Trial Practice, Commercial Litigation, Complex Litigation, Construction Defect, Construction Liability, Construction Litigation, Contract Disputes, Coverage Analysis, Coverage Issues, Creditor Rights, Defense Litigation, Directors and Officers Liability, Eminent Domain, Employment Law, Estate Planning, General Civil Trial and Appellate Practice, General Liability, Hospital Malpractice, Hospitals, Insurance Coverage, Insurance Defense, Insurance Litigation, Land Use, Legal Malpractice, Litigation, Malpractice, Medical Devices, Medical Liability, Medical Malpractice, Medical Negligence, Municipal Law, Pharmaceutical, Premises Liability, Probate, Product Liability, Professional Liability, Professional Malpractice, Professional Negligence, Property, Property and Casualty, Railroad Law, Real Estate, Real Property, Religious Institutions, Transactional Law, Wills, Wrongful Death

SEE COMPLETE LISTING UNDER MOBILE, ALABAMA (55 MILES)

PLANTATION 82,934 Broward Co.

Refer To

Vernis & Bowling of the Florida Keys, P.A.
Islamorada Professional Center
81990 Overseas Highway, Third Floor
Islamorada, Florida 33036
Telephone: 305-664-4675
Fax: 305-664-5414

Civil Litigation, Insurance Law, Workers' Compensation, Premises Liability, Labor and Employment, Civil Rights, Commercial Litigation, Complex Litigation, Product Liability, Directors and Officers Liability, Errors and Omissions, Construction Law, Construction Defect, Environmental Liability, Personal and Commercial Vehicle, Appellate Practice, Admiralty and Maritime Law, Real Estate, Family Law, Elder Law, Liability Defense, SIU/Fraud Litigation, Education Law (ESE/IDEA), Property and Casualty (Commercial and Personal Lines), Long-Haul Trucking Liability, Government Law, Public Law, Criminal, White Collar, Business Litigation

SEE COMPLETE LISTING UNDER ISLAMORADA, FLORIDA (107 MILES)

PORT CHARLOTTE 54,392 Charlotte Co.

Refer To

Vernis & Bowling of Southwest Florida, P.A.
2369 West 1st Street
Fort Myers, Florida 33901-3309
Telephone: 239-334-3035
Fax: 239-334-7702

Civil Litigation, Insurance Law, Workers' Compensation, Premises Liability, Labor and Employment, Civil Rights, Commercial Litigation, Complex Litigation, Product Liability, Directors and Officers Liability, Errors and Omissions, Construction Law, Construction Defect, Environmental Liability, Personal and Commercial Vehicle, Appellate Practice, Admiralty and Maritime Law, Real Estate, Family Law, Elder Law, Liability Defense, SIU/Fraud Litigation, Education Law (ESE/IDEA), Property and Casualty (Commercial and Personal Lines), Long-Haul Trucking Liability, Government Law, Public Law, Criminal, White Collar, Business Litigation

SEE COMPLETE LISTING UNDER FORT MYERS, FLORIDA (249 MILES)

PORT ST. JOE † 3,445 Gulf Co.

Refer To

Barron & Redding, P.A.
220 McKenzie Avenue
Panama City, Florida 32401-3129
Telephone: 850-785-7454
Fax: 850-785-2999

Mailing Address: P.O. Box 2467, Panama City, FL 32402-2467

Casualty, Surety, Fire, Life Insurance, Professional Liability, Product Liability, Medical Malpractice, Environmental Law, Automobile Liability, Premises Liability, Business Torts, Construction Law

SEE COMPLETE LISTING UNDER PANAMA CITY, FLORIDA (37 MILES)

SARASOTA FLORIDA

PUNTA GORDA † 16,641 Charlotte Co.
Refer To
Abbey, Adams, Byelick & Mueller, L.L.P.
360 Central Avenue, 11th Floor
St. Petersburg, Florida 33701
  Telephone: 727-821-2080
  Fax: 727-822-3970

Mailing Address: P.O. Box 1511, St. Petersburg, FL 33731

Administrative Law, Americans with Disabilities Act, Appellate Practice, Complex Litigation, General Defense, Employment Law, Bad Faith, Insurance Coverage, Insurance Fraud, Uninsured and Underinsured Motorist, Professional Malpractice, Mediation, Negligence, Personal Injury, Premises Liability, Product Liability, Subrogation, Toxic Torts, Workers' Compensation, Motor Vehicle Liability, Defense of Insureds, Sovereign Immunity and Governmental Defense

SEE COMPLETE LISTING UNDER ST. PETERSBURG, FLORIDA (90 MILES)

Refer To
Vernis & Bowling of Southwest Florida, P.A.
2369 West 1st Street
Fort Myers, Florida 33901-3309
  Telephone: 239-334-3035
  Fax: 239-334-7702

Civil Litigation, Insurance Law, Workers' Compensation, Premises Liability, Labor and Employment, Civil Rights, Commercial Litigation, Complex Litigation, Product Liability, Directors and Officers Liability, Errors and Omissions, Construction Law, Construction Defect, Environmental Liability, Personal and Commercial Vehicle, Appellate Practice, Admiralty and Maritime Law, Real Estate, Family Law, Elder Law, Liability Defense, SIU/Fraud Litigation, Education Law (ESE/IDEA), Property and Casualty (Commercial and Personal Lines), Long-Haul Trucking Liability, Government Law, Public Law, Criminal, White Collar, Business Litigation

SEE COMPLETE LISTING UNDER FORT MYERS, FLORIDA (23 MILES)

QUINCY † 7,972 Gadsden Co.
Refer To
Barron & Redding, P.A.
220 McKenzie Avenue
Panama City, Florida 32401-3129
  Telephone: 850-785-7454
  Fax: 850-785-2999

Mailing Address: P.O. Box 2467, Panama City, FL 32402-2467

Casualty, Surety, Fire, Life Insurance, Professional Liability, Product Liability, Medical Malpractice, Environmental Law, Automobile Liability, Premises Liability, Business Torts, Construction Law

SEE COMPLETE LISTING UNDER PANAMA CITY, FLORIDA (81 MILES)

ROCKLEDGE 24,926 Brevard Co.
Refer To
Cameron, Hodges, Coleman, LaPointe & Wright, P.A.
111 North Magnolia Avenue, Suite 1350
Orlando, Florida 32801-2378
  Telephone: 407-841-5030
  Fax: 407-841-1727

Insurance Law

SEE COMPLETE LISTING UNDER ORLANDO, FLORIDA (48 MILES)

SANFORD † 53,570 Seminole Co.
Refer To
Cameron, Hodges, Coleman, LaPointe & Wright, P.A.
111 North Magnolia Avenue, Suite 1350
Orlando, Florida 32801-2378
  Telephone: 407-841-5030
  Fax: 407-841-1727

Insurance Law

SEE COMPLETE LISTING UNDER ORLANDO, FLORIDA (20 MILES)

Refer To
Vernis & Bowling of Central Florida, P.A.
1450 South Woodland Boulevard, Fourth Floor
DeLand, Florida 32720
  Telephone: 386-734-2505
  Fax: 386-734-3441

Civil Litigation, Insurance Law, Workers' Compensation, Premises Liability, Labor and Employment, Civil Rights, Commercial Litigation, Complex Litigation, Product Liability, Directors and Officers Liability, Errors and Omissions, Construction Law, Construction Defect, Environmental Liability, Personal and Commercial Vehicle, Appellate Practice, Admiralty and Maritime Law, Real Estate, Family Law, Elder Law, Liability Defense, SIU/Fraud Litigation, Education Law (ESE/IDEA), Property and Casualty (Commercial and Personal Lines), Long-Haul Trucking Liability, Government Law, Public Law, Criminal, White Collar, Business Litigation

SEE COMPLETE LISTING UNDER DAYTONA BEACH, FLORIDA (23 MILES)

SARASOTA † 51,917 Sarasota Co.

McConnaughhay, Duffy, Coonrod, Pope & Weaver, P.A.
2601 Cattlemen Road, Suite 402
Sarasota, Florida 34232
  Telephone: 941-955-6141
  Fax: 941-955-6244
  www.mcconnaughhay.com

(Additional Offices: Tallahassee, FL*; Fort Lauderdale, FL*; Gainesville, FL*; Jacksonville, FL*; Ocala, FL*; Panama City, FL*; Pensacola, FL*)

Insurance Defense, Workers' Compensation, Product Liability, Labor and Employment, Civil Litigation, Trial Practice, Appellate Practice

Firm Members

E. Louis Stern — Florida State University, J.D., 1987 — Admitted to Bar, 1987, Florida — Practice Areas: Workers' Compensation

Jacqueline B. Steele — Florida State University College of Law, J.D. (with honors), 1994 — Admitted to Bar, 1995, Florida — Practice Areas: Workers' Compensation

Associates

Melissa A. Volk   Katherine A. Moum
Mia H. Hong

Law Offices of Bohdan Neswiacheny
1800 Second Street, Suite 760
Sarasota, Florida 34236
  Telephone: 941-957-3400
  Fax: 941-952-9103
  E-Mail: bnlaw@bnlaw.com
  www.bnlaw.com

(Fort Lauderdale, FL Office*: 2929 E Commercial Boulevard, Suite 300, 33308)
  (Tel: 954-522-5400)
  (Fax: 954-765-1274)
(Orange Park, FL Office*: 151 College Drive, Suite 1, 32065)
  (Tel: 904-276-6171)
  (Fax: 904-276-1751)

Insurance Defense, Employment Discrimination, Automotive Products Liability, Product Liability, Trial and Appellate Practice

Managing Attorney

Mark R. Kapusta — Stetson University, B.A., 1986; Stetson University College of Law, J.D., 1989 — Admitted to Bar, 1989, Florida; 1989, U.S. District Court, Middle District of Florida — Practice Areas: Insurance Defense; Construction Defect; Employment Discrimination; Premises Liability — E-mail: mkapusta@bnlaw.com

FLORIDA

Law Offices of Bohdan Neswiacheny, Sarasota, FL
(Continued)

Associate

Sean P. O'Sullivan — Florida State University, B.S. (Dean's List), 2008; University of Miami School of Law, J.D., 2012 — Admitted to Bar, 2012, Florida — Practice Areas: Insurance Defense

(See listing under Fort Lauderdale, FL for additional information)

The following firms also service this area.

Abbey, Adams, Byelick & Mueller, L.L.P.
360 Central Avenue, 11th Floor
St. Petersburg, Florida 33701
Telephone: 727-821-2080
Fax: 727-822-3970

Mailing Address: P.O. Box 1511, St. Petersburg, FL 33731

Administrative Law, Americans with Disabilities Act, Appellate Practice, Complex Litigation, General Defense, Employment Law, Bad Faith, Insurance Coverage, Insurance Fraud, Uninsured and Underinsured Motorist, Professional Malpractice, Mediation, Negligence, Personal Injury, Premises Liability, Product Liability, Subrogation, Toxic Torts, Workers' Compensation, Motor Vehicle Liability, Defense of Insureds, Sovereign Immunity and Governmental Defense

SEE COMPLETE LISTING UNDER ST. PETERSBURG, FLORIDA (37 MILES)

Barker & Cook, PA
501 East Kennedy Boulevard, Suite 790
Tampa, Florida 33602
Telephone: 813-489-1001
Fax: 813-489-1008
Toll Free: 888-892-8722

Insurance Defense, Self-Insured, Trial and Appellate Practice, State and Federal Courts, First and Third Party Defense, Automobile, Casualty, Construction Law, Engineers, Malpractice, Environmental Law, General Liability, Life and Health, Medical Malpractice, Product Liability, Property, Reinsurance, Workers' Compensation, Civil Litigation, Commercial Litigation, Personal Injury, Premises Liability, Contract Disputes, Labor and Employment, Construction Disputes, Insurance Coverage Disputes

SEE COMPLETE LISTING UNDER TAMPA, FLORIDA (52 MILES)

Brasfield, Freeman, Goldis & Cash, P.A.
2553 First Avenue North
St. Petersburg, Florida 33713
Telephone: 727-327-2258
Fax: 727-328-1340

Mailing Address: P.O. Box 12349, St. Petersburg, FL 33733-2349

Insurance Defense, Trial Practice, Product Liability, Professional Liability, Premises Liability, Automobile Liability, Personal Injury, Wrongful Death, Construction Defect, Insurance Coverage

SEE COMPLETE LISTING UNDER ST. PETERSBURG, FLORIDA (37 MILES)

Vernis & Bowling of the Gulf Coast, P.A.
696 1st Avenue, 1st Floor
St. Petersburg, Florida 33701
Telephone: 727-443-3377
Fax: 727-443-6828

Civil Litigation, Insurance Law, Workers' Compensation, Premises Liability, Labor and Employment, Civil Rights, Commercial Litigation, Complex Litigation, Product Liability, Directors and Officers Liability, Errors and Omissions, Construction Law, Construction Defect, Environmental Liability, Personal and Commercial Vehicle, Appellate Practice, Admiralty and Maritime Law, Real Estate, Family Law, Elder Law, Liability Defense, SIU/Fraud Litigation, Education Law (ESE/IDEA), Property and Casualty (Commercial and Personal Lines), Long-Haul Trucking Liability, Government Law, Public Law, Criminal, White Collar, Business Litigation

SEE COMPLETE LISTING UNDER CLEARWATER, FLORIDA (63 MILES)

SEBRING

SEBRING † 10,491 Highlands Co.

Refer To

Cameron, Hodges, Coleman, LaPointe & Wright, P.A.
111 North Magnolia Avenue, Suite 1350
Orlando, Florida 32801-2378
Telephone: 407-841-5030
Fax: 407-841-1727

Insurance Law

SEE COMPLETE LISTING UNDER ORLANDO, FLORIDA (80 MILES)

Refer To

Vernis & Bowling of Southwest Florida, P.A.
2369 West 1st Street
Fort Myers, Florida 33901-3309
Telephone: 239-334-3035
Fax: 239-334-7702

Civil Litigation, Insurance Law, Workers' Compensation, Premises Liability, Labor and Employment, Civil Rights, Commercial Litigation, Complex Litigation, Product Liability, Directors and Officers Liability, Errors and Omissions, Construction Law, Construction Defect, Environmental Liability, Personal and Commercial Vehicle, Appellate Practice, Admiralty and Maritime Law, Real Estate, Family Law, Elder Law, Liability Defense, SIU/Fraud Litigation, Education Law (ESE/IDEA), Property and Casualty (Commercial and Personal Lines), Long-Haul Trucking Liability, Government Law, Public Law, Criminal, White Collar, Business Litigation

SEE COMPLETE LISTING UNDER FORT MYERS, FLORIDA (84 MILES)

ST. AUGUSTINE † 12,975 St. Johns Co.

Refer To

Vernis & Bowling of North Florida, P.A.
4309 Salisbury Road
Jacksonville, Florida 32216
Telephone: 904-296-6751
Fax: 904-296-2712

Civil Litigation, Insurance Law, Workers' Compensation, Premises Liability, Labor and Employment, Civil Rights, Commercial Litigation, Complex Litigation, Product Liability, Directors and Officers Liability, Errors and Omissions, Construction Law, Construction Defect, Environmental Liability, Personal and Commercial Vehicle, Appellate Practice, Admiralty and Maritime Law, Real Estate, Family Law, Elder Law, Liability Defense, SIU/Fraud Litigation, Education Law (ESE/IDEA), Property and Casualty (Commercial and Personal Lines), Long-Haul Trucking Liability, Government Law, Public Law, Criminal, White Collar, Business Litigation

SEE COMPLETE LISTING UNDER JACKSONVILLE, FLORIDA (41 MILES)

ST. PETERSBURG 244,769 Pinellas Co.

Abbey, Adams, Byelick & Mueller, L.L.P.
360 Central Avenue, 11th Floor
St. Petersburg, Florida 33701
Telephone: 727-821-2080
Fax: 727-822-3970
E-Mail: attorneys@abbeyadams.com
www.abbeyadams.com

(Tampa, FL Office*: 5001 West Cypress Street, 33607)
(Tel: 813-223-7800)

Established: 1982

Administrative Law, Americans with Disabilities Act, Appellate Practice, Complex Litigation, General Defense, Employment Law, Bad Faith, Insurance Coverage, Insurance Fraud, Uninsured and Underinsured Motorist, Professional Malpractice, Mediation, Negligence, Personal Injury, Premises Liability, Product Liability, Subrogation, Toxic Torts, Workers' Compensation, Motor Vehicle Liability, Defense of Insureds, Sovereign Immunity and Governmental Defense

Firm Profile: The Firm was established in St. Petersburg, Florida in 1982 for the defense of Liability, Malpractice, Workers' Compensation, Employment

ST. PETERSBURG — FLORIDA

Abbey, Adams, Byelick & Mueller, L.L.P., St. Petersburg, FL (Continued)

Claims and Appeals. The lawyers with Abbey, Adams, Byelick & Mueller, L.L.P., from their main office in St. Petersburg and a satellite office in Tampa, represent organizations, employers, governments, individuals, insurance companies and their insureds in a broad spectrum of litigation. The Firm maintains the highest rating of "AV" with the Martindale-Hubbell Law Directory. Also, many of the lawyers are Certified Specialist by the Florida Bar in Civil Trial Practice and Workers' Compensation Law.

Insurance Clients

- ACE USA
- Alfa Mutual Insurance Company
- American Insurance Company
- American Premier Insurance Company
- Ameriprise Auto & Home Insurance
- Atlantic Mutual Insurance Company
- Brotherhood Mutual Insurance Company
- Claims Control Corporation
- EMC Insurance Companies
- ESIS
- Farmers Commercial Insurance
- FFVA Mutual Insurance Company
- First Colony Life Insurance Company
- Florida Family Insurance Company
- Florida Insurance Guaranty Association
- Florists' Insurance Company
- Gallagher Bassett Services, Inc.
- GMAC Insurance
- The Hartford
- Interstate Insurance Company
- Johns Eastern Company, Inc.
- The Main Street America Group
- Meadowbrook Insurance Group
- Metropolitan Insurance Company
- MMG Insurance Company
- Motorists Mutual Insurance Company
- Old Dominion Insurance Company
- Pekin Insurance Company
- Providence Property and Casualty Insurance Company
- Scottsdale Insurance Company
- Security First Managers, LLC
- Southern Oak Management, LLC
- State Auto Insurance Companies
- Technology Insurance Company, Inc.
- Transportation Casualty Insurance Company
- United Automobile Insurance Company
- United Self Insured Services
- Universal Property & Casualty Insurance Company
- West Bend Mutual Insurance Company
- Zenith Insurance Company
- Zurich American Insurance Company
- Agway Insurance Company
- ALLIED Mutual Insurance Company
- American United Life Insurance Company
- AmerUs Life Insurance Company
- Amstar Insurance Company
- Bankers Insurance Company
- Broadspire
- Cannon Cochran Management Services, Inc.
- Crawford & Company
- Erie Insurance Company
- Everest National Insurance Company
- Fireman's Fund Insurance Company
- First Insurance Network, Inc.
- Florida Farm Bureau
- Florida Workers' Compensation Insurance Guaranty Association
- GAB Robins, Inc.
- Genesis Indemnity Insurance Company
- Holyoke Mutual Insurance Company in Salem
- Kentucky Farm Bureau Insurance Companies
- Mercury Casualty Company
- Michigan Commercial Insurance Mutual
- Nationwide Insurance
- New England Life Insurance Company
- PMA Insurance Group
- Risk Management Services, Inc.
- Rockford Mutual Insurance Company
- Sedgwick Claims Management Services, Inc.
- Stonewall Insurance Company
- Tennessee Farmers Mutual Insurance Company
- Travelers
- Unisun Insurance Company
- United Insurance Company of America
- United States Liability Insurance Group
- VGM Insurance Company
- Western National Insurance Group
- Western-Southern Life Assurance Company

Non-Insurance Clients

- Abbott Laboratories
- Allied Automotive Group
- A-1 Contract Staffing, Inc.
- City of Dunedin, Florida
- Climate Design
- Cox Target Media
- Diocese of St. Petersburg
- Eaton Corporation
- Intrepid Powerboats, Inc.
- Lakeland Tigers Food Service
- Nestle USA, Inc.
- Pinellas County Schools
- Professional Business Owners Association
- School Board of Manatee County
- Scott Wetzel Services, Inc.
- Able Staffing & Leasing
- Angels Baseball L.P.
- Chevron U.S.A., Inc.
- City of Sarasota
- Cottingham and Butler, Inc.
- Crown Chicago Industries (CCI)
- Eaton Aerospace
- Film Technologies International
- Johnson Brothers Corporation
- Motor Transport Underwriters, Inc.
- Philadelphia Phillies
- Pinnacle Benefits, Inc.
- Progress Energy
- Protegrity Services, Inc.
- School District of Hillsborough County

Abbey, Adams, Byelick & Mueller, L.L.P., St. Petersburg, FL (Continued)

- SISCO
- Southern Fire Adjusters
- State of Florida, Division of State Fire Marshall
- Tampa Bay Rays
- USA Benefits Group
- Washington Nationals Major League Baseball
- SouthEast Personnel Leasing, Inc.
- State of Florida, Division of Risk Management
- Statewide Adjusters, Inc.
- Toronto Blue Jays
- Val-Pak

Partners

Jeffrey M. Adams — 1958 — Oral Roberts University, B.A. (cum laude), 1981; Stetson University College of Law, J.D., 1984 — Admitted to Bar, 1985, Florida; Illinois — Member The Florida Bar (Trial Lawyers Section); Illinois State Bar Association (Tort Law and Insurance Law Sections); Hillsborough County and St. Petersburg Bar Associations; Florida Defense Lawyers Association (Board of Directors) — E-mail: jadams@abbeyadams.com

David J. Abbey
V. Joseph Mueller
Deborah L. Eldridge
Robert P. Byelick
John D. Kiernan

Associates

Allison G. Mawhinney
Martin G. Deptula
Samantha A. Satish
Michael C. Auchampau
Michael P. Falkowski
Blair H. Clarke

Bonezzi Switzer Polito & Hupp Co. L.P.A.

City Center
100 2nd Avenue South, Suite 502-S
St. Petersburg, Florida 33701-4313
Telephone: 727-826-0909
Fax: 727-826-0914
E-Mail: wbonezzi@bsphlaw.com
www.bsphlaw.com

(Cleveland, OH Office*: 1300 East 9th Street, Suite 1950, 44114-1501)
- (Tel: 216-875-2767)
- (Fax: 216-875-1570)
- (Toll Free: 800-875-2767)
- (E-Mail: jvanwagner@bsphlaw.com)

(Cincinnati, OH Office*: 201 East Fifth Street, Suite 1900, 45202)
- (Tel: 513-766-9444)
- (Fax: 513-766-9301)
- (E-Mail: pmccartney@bsphlaw.com)

Established: 1998

Environmental Law, Long-Term Care, Premises Liability, Medical Malpractice, Nursing Home Liability, Product Liability, Civil Litigation, Commercial Litigation, Professional Negligence, Assisted Living, General Insurance Defense

Firm Profile: Our Florida trial practice is managed by William D. Bonezzi, a lawyer who has devoted his career to trial work since 1973. Mr. Bonezzi has tried in excess of 200 cases defending physicians and other medical providers across the United States. Mr. Bonezzi's experience and diligence in the courtroom has been recognized by colleagues, medical providers and insurance carriers throughout the country.

Our Florida attorneys have developed a litigation practice focused on representing the interests of doctors, surgeons and other medical providers throughout Florida. Our Florida attorneys specialize in challenges faced by uninsured physicians in medical malpractice litigation and have been successful in obtaining positive results due to hard work and case preparation.

Shareholder

William D. Bonezzi

(See listing under Cleveland, OH for additional information)

FLORIDA — ST. PETERSBURG

Brasfield, Freeman, Goldis & Cash, P.A.

2553 First Avenue North
St. Petersburg, Florida 33713
  Telephone: 727-327-2258
  Tampa Direct Line: 813-224-0430
  Fax: 727-328-1340
  E-Mail: ccranston@brasfieldlaw.net
  www.brasfieldlaw.com

Established: 1975

Insurance Defense, Trial Practice, Product Liability, Professional Liability, Premises Liability, Automobile Liability, Personal Injury, Wrongful Death, Construction Defect, Insurance Coverage

Firm Profile: Full-service litigation defense law firm focusing on insurance defense representation with 40 years of experience. We have the skills and agility to provide each client with aggressive representation. An AV® Preeminent TM Rated litigation firm.

Insurance Clients

Amerisure Companies
Direct General Insurance Company
Esurance
First Mercury Insurance Company
GuideOne Insurance
Mercury General Group
Nationwide Insurance
Progressive American Insurance Company
RLI Insurance Company
Tennessee Farmers Insurance Companies
Wells Fargo Insurance Services
Xchanging
Auto-Owners Insurance Company
ESIS
First Acceptance Insurance Company, Inc.
HealthSmart
National Loss Management
Pennsylvania Lumbermens Mutual Insurance Company
RiverStone Claims Management, LLC
United Fire & Casualty Company
Universal Underwriters Insurance Company

Non-Insurance Clients

Albertsons, Inc.
Cornerstone Bank
Gibson & Associates
Safeguard Properties
Yellow Corporation
Cintas Corporation
Genuine Parts Company
HeartCare
Synovus Bank

Firm Members

J. Scott Brasfield — 1946 — The University of Mississippi, J.D., 1970 — Admitted to Bar, 1970, Mississippi; 1974, Florida — Member American and Pinellas County Bar Associations; The Florida Bar; Mississippi State Bar — E-mail: jsbrasfield@brasfieldlaw.net

Stuart J. Freeman — 1952 — Penn State University, B.A., 1974; Stetson University, J.D., 1977 — Admitted to Bar, 1977, Florida; 1978, Pennsylvania; 1977, U.S. District Court, Middle District of Florida; 1977, U.S. Court of Appeals, Eleventh Circuit; 1990, U.S. Court of Federal Claims — Member American (Tort and Insurance Section) and Pennsylvania Bar Associations; The Florida Bar (Trial Lawyers Section); St. Petersburg Bar Association; Florida Defense Lawyers Association; Defense Research Institute; American Board of Trial Advocates — Member, Adjunct Faculty, Stetson University College of Law — Florida Bar Board Certified Civil Trial Lawyer; Board Certified Civil Trial Advocate by National Board of Trial Advocacy — Practice Areas: General Defense; Insurance Defense; Casualty Defense; Property and Casualty; Civil Litigation; Insurance Coverage; Construction Defect — E-mail: sjfreeman@brasfieldlaw.net

Joshua D. Goldis — 1972 — University of Florida, B.A., 1994; Valparaiso University, J.D., 1998 — Admitted to Bar, 1999, Florida — E-mail: jdgoldis@brasfieldlaw.net

Cary A. Cash — University of South Alabama, B.S., 1998; Stetson University College of Law, J.D. (cum laude), 2005 — Recipient, Judge Alexander Paskay Bankruptcy Award; Recipient, William F. Blews Award, pro bono service; Recipient, Raphael Steinhardt Award; Recipient, American Cancer Society's Most Inspirational Cancer Survivor Award (1999) — Law Clerk, Hon. Paul M. Glenn, Chief Judge U.S. Bankruptcy Court Middle District of Florida — Admitted to Bar, 2005, Florida; U.S. District Court, Middle District of Florida — Member The Florida Bar (Mobile Home and RV Committee; Real Property Probate and Trust Law Sections); Pinellas County Trial Lawyers Association (President); Barney Masterson's Inn of Court (Executive Officer); Masonic Lodge, Mastor Mason; Historic Kenwood Neighborhood Association — Certified Mediator, Florida County Court — Practice

Brasfield, Freeman, Goldis & Cash, P.A., St. Petersburg, FL (Continued)

Areas: Personal Injury; Real Estate; Bankruptcy; Construction Law; Contracts; Construction Litigation; Environmental Litigation; Civil Litigation — E-mail: cary.cash@brasfieldlaw.net

Hightower, Stratton, Wilhelm, P.A.

200 Central Avenue, Suite 450
St. Petersburg, Florida 33701
  Telephone: 727-209-1373
  Fax: 727-209-1383
  www.hightowerlaw.net

(Miami, FL Office*: 4770 Biscayne Boulevard, Suite 1200, 33137)
  (Tel: 305-539-0909)
  (Fax: 305-530-0661)
  (Emer/After Hrs: 305-799-3054)
  (E-Mail: dale@hightowerlaw.net)
(Orlando, FL Office*: 151 Southhall Lane, Suite 140, 32751)
  (Tel: 407-352-4240)
  (Fax: 407-352-4201)
(West Palm Beach, FL Office*: 330 Clematis Street, Suite 201, 33401)
  (Tel: 561-833-2022)
  (Fax: 561-833-2140)

Assault & Battery Defense, Auto and Trucking Negligence, Commercial Litigation, Construction Claims, Employment Law, Environmental Law, Fraud/SIU (Special Investigative Unit), General Litigation, Homeowner's Insurance, Insurance Coverage and Bad Faith, Personal Injury and Wrongful Death, Premises Liability, Product Liability, Resorts & Leisure Liability, Retail Liability

Partners

Dale R. Hightower
Kyle Y. Murphy, Division Leader
Terra D. Wilhelm

(See listing under Miami, FL for additional information)

Traub Lieberman Straus & Shrewsberry LLP

360 Central Avenue
St. Petersburg, Florida 33701
  Telephone: 727-898-8100
  Fax: 727-895-4838
  www.traublieberman.com

(Hawthorne, NY Office*: Mid-Westchester Executive Park, Seven Skyline Drive, 10532)
  (Tel: 914-347-2600)
  (Fax: 914-347-8898)
  (E-Mail: swolfe@traublieberman.com)
(Red Bank, NJ Office*: 322 Highway 35, 07701)
  (Tel: 732-985-1000)
  (Fax: 732-985-2000)
(Chicago, IL Office*: 303 West Madison, Suite 1200, 60606)
  (Tel: 312-332-3900)
  (Fax: 312-332-3908)
(Los Angeles, CA Office*: 626 Wilshire Boulevard, Suite 800, 90017)
  (Tel: 213-624-4500)
(London, United Kingdom Office*: Gallery 4, 12 Leadenhall Street, EC3V1LP)
  (Tel: +44 (0) 020 7816 5856)
(New York, NY Office*: 100 Park Avenue, 16th Floor, 10017)
  (Tel: 646-227-1700)

Established: 2007

STUART

Traub Lieberman Straus & Shrewsberry LLP, St. Petersburg, FL (Continued)

Appellate Practice, Bad Faith, Extra-Contractual Litigation, Civil Rights, Complex Litigation, Construction Law, Environmental Law, General Liability, Insurance Coverage, Labor and Employment, Premises Liability, Product Liability, Professional Liability, Technology, Toxic Torts, Trucking Law, Transportation, Medical Malpractice

Partners

Lauren S. Curtis — Duke University, B.A., 1995; Florida State University College of Law, J.D., 1998 — Admitted to Bar, 1998, Florida; U.S. District Court, Middle, Northern and Southern Districts of Florida; U.S. Court of Appeals for the District of Columbia and Eleventh Circuits — E-mail: lcurtis@traublieberman.com

Frank E. Dylong — Williams College, B.A., 1986; University of Miami School of Law, J.D., 1992 — Admitted to Bar, 1982, Florida; U.S. District Court, Middle District of Florida — Member St. Petersburg Bar Association — E-mail: fdylong@traublieberman.com

C. Ryan Jones — The University of Georgia, B.B.A. Accounting, 2001; Stetson University College of Law, J.D. (cum laude), 2006 — Admitted to Bar, 2006, Florida — Member American and Hillsborough County Bar Associations; The Florida Bar — E-mail: crjones@traublieberman.com

Michael K. Kiernan — St. Leo College, B.A., 1980; Drake University Law School, J.D., 1983 — Admitted to Bar, 1983, Florida; Iowa; U.S. District Court, Southern District of Iowa; U.S. District Court, Middle District of Florida; U.S. Supreme Court — Member The Florida Bar (Trial Lawyers Section; Civil Procedure Rules Committee, 2003, 2009); Iowa State and St. Petersburg Bar Associations; Federation of Defense and Corporate Counsel; Defense Research Institute; Florida Defense Lawyers Association — E-mail: mkiernan@traublieberman.com

Scot E. Samis — Hamilton College, A.B. (cum laude), 1981; Stetson University College of Law, J.D. (cum laude), 2004 — Admitted to Bar, 2004, Florida — Member The Florida Bar (Appellate Practice Section); St. Petersburg Bar Association — Adjunct Professor of Law, Stetson University, 1994-2004; Trustee and Vice President, Community Law Program; Pro Bono legal clinic through the Community Law Program; Volunteer, Society of St. Vincent de Paul — E-mail: ssamis@traublieberman.com

Burks A. Smith III — Stetson University, B.B.A., 2002; Stetson University College of Law, J.D. (cum laude), 2005 — Admitted to Bar, 2005, Florida; U.S. District Court, Middle District of Florida — Member St. Petersburg Bar Association; The Order of Barristers — E-mail: bsmith@traublieberman.com

Senior Counsel

Rebecca Levy-Sachs — Rutgers University, Livingston College, B.A., 1973; Rutgers University School of Law, J.D., 1978 — Admitted to Bar, 1978, Florida; New Jersey — Member American and New Jersey State Bar Associations; The Florida Bar; Defense Research Institute; Federation of Defense and Corporate Counsel; Florida Defense Lawyers Association; Florida Advisory Committee on Arson Prevention; American Bar Foundation — E-mail: rlevysachs@traublieberman.com

Associates

Ryan S. Burke
W. Daniel Finlayson
John Henley
Michael F. Lenhardt
Samuel Cooley
Bradley T. Guldalian
Katherine L. Koener
Christina M. Mallatt

(See listing under Hawthorne, NY for additional information)

The following firms also service this area.

Barker & Cook, PA
501 East Kennedy Boulevard, Suite 790
Tampa, Florida 33602
Telephone: 813-489-1001
Fax: 813-489-1008
Toll Free: 888-892-8722

Insurance Defense, Self-Insured, Trial and Appellate Practice, State and Federal Courts, First and Third Party Defense, Automobile, Casualty, Construction Law, Engineers, Malpractice, Environmental Law, General Liability, Life and Health, Medical Malpractice, Product Liability, Property, Reinsurance, Workers' Compensation, Civil Litigation, Commercial Litigation, Personal Injury, Premises Liability, Contract Disputes, Labor and Employment, Construction Disputes, Insurance Coverage Disputes

SEE COMPLETE LISTING UNDER TAMPA, FLORIDA (24 MILES)

Vernis & Bowling of the Gulf Coast, P.A.
696 1st Avenue, 1st Floor
St. Petersburg, Florida 33701
Telephone: 727-443-3377
Fax: 727-443-6828

Civil Litigation, Insurance Law, Workers' Compensation, Premises Liability, Labor and Employment, Civil Rights, Commercial Litigation, Complex Litigation, Product Liability, Directors and Officers Liability, Errors and Omissions, Construction Law, Construction Defect, Environmental Liability, Personal and Commercial Vehicle, Appellate Practice, Admiralty and Maritime Law, Real Estate, Family Law, Elder Law, Liability Defense, SIU/Fraud Litigation, Education Law (ESE/IDEA), Property and Casualty (Commercial and Personal Lines), Long-Haul Trucking Liability, Government Law, Public Law, Criminal, White Collar, Business Litigation

SEE COMPLETE LISTING UNDER CLEARWATER, FLORIDA (20 MILES)

STUART † 15,593 Martin Co.

Refer To

Paxton & Smith, P.A.
1615 Forum Place, Suite 500
West Palm Beach, Florida 33401
Telephone: 561-684-2121
Fax: 561-684-6855

Accountants and Attorneys Liability, Antitrust, Appellate Practice, Arbitration, Architects and Engineers, Automobile, Bad Faith, Bodily Injury, Business Law, Business Litigation, Church Law, Civil Litigation, Commercial General Liability, Commercial Litigation, Construction Accidents, Construction Defect, Construction Litigation, Contracts, Coverage Analysis, Coverage Issues, Defense Litigation, Design Professionals, Directors and Officers Liability, Discrimination, Employment Litigation, Engineering and Construction, Environmental Coverage, Environmental Law, Errors and Omissions, Examinations Under Oath, Excess and Surplus Lines, Extra-Contractual Litigation, Governmental Liability, Insurance Coverage, Insurance Defense, School Law, Negligent Security, Personal Injury, Premises Liability, Product Liability, Real Estate, Sexual Harassment, Subrogation, Surety, Toxic Torts, Wrongful Death, Child Abuse, Libel & Slander

SEE COMPLETE LISTING UNDER WEST PALM BEACH, FLORIDA (37 MILES)

Refer To

Vernis & Bowling of Palm Beach, P.A.
884 U.S. Highway #1
North Palm Beach, Florida 33408-5408
Telephone: 561-775-9822
Fax: 561-775-9821

Civil Litigation, Insurance Law, Workers' Compensation, Premises Liability, Labor and Employment, Civil Rights, Commercial Litigation, Complex Litigation, Product Liability, Directors and Officers Liability, Errors and Omissions, Construction Law, Construction Defect, Environmental Liability, Personal and Commercial Vehicle, Appellate Practice, Admiralty and Maritime Law, Real Estate, Family Law, Elder Law, Liability Defense, SIU/Fraud Litigation, Education Law (ESE/IDEA), Property and Casualty (Commercial and Personal Lines), Long-Haul Trucking Liability, Government Law, Public Law, Criminal, White Collar, Business Litigation

SEE COMPLETE LISTING UNDER NORTH PALM BEACH, FLORIDA (31 MILES)

FLORIDA   TALLAHASSEE

Refer To
Wiederhold & Moses, P.A.
560 Village Boulevard, Suite 240
West Palm Beach, Florida 33409-1963
   Telephone: 561-615-6775, 954-763-5630
   Fax: 561-615-7225
Mailing Address: P.O. Box 3918, West Palm Beach, FL 33402

Insurance Defense, Trial Practice

SEE COMPLETE LISTING UNDER WEST PALM BEACH, FLORIDA (37 MILES)

TALLAHASSEE † 181,376 Leon Co.

Allen, Kopet & Associates, PLLC
2868 Remington Green Circle, Suite B
Tallahassee, Florida 32308
   Telephone: 850-385-5612
   Fax: 850-385-2679

(See listing under Chattanooga, TN for additional information)

Colodny Fass, P.A.
215 S. Monroe Street, Ste. 701
Tallahassee, Florida 32301
   Telephone: 850-577-0398
   Fax: 850-577-0385
   www.colodnyfass.com

(Additional Offices: Fort Lauderdale, FL*)

Insurance Litigation, Insurance Defense, Commercial Litigation, Government Affairs, Insurance Regulation, Appellate Practice

(See listing under Fort Lauderdale, FL for additional information)

(Revisors of Florida Insurance Law Digest for this Publication)

(This firm is also listed in the Regulatory and Compliance section of this directory)

Conroy Simberg
325 John Knox Road
Atrium Building, Suite 105
Tallahassee, Florida 32303
   Telephone: 850-383-9103
   Fax: 850-383-9109
   E-Mail: csg@conroysimberg.com
   www.conroysimberg.com

Insurance Defense, Appellate Practice, Insurance Coverage, Environmental Law, Governmental Liability, Civil Rights, Wrongful Termination, Americans with Disabilities Act, Sexual Harassment, Land Use, Commercial Law, Fire, Arson, Fraud, Fidelity and Surety, Automobile Liability, Admiralty and Maritime Law, Bad Faith, Employment Law, Self-Insured, Public Entities, Product Liability, Casualty, Excess and Reinsurance, Accident and Health, Workers' Compensation, Medical Malpractice, Class Actions, Construction Defect, Construction Litigation, First Party Matters, Premises Liability, Professional Liability, Intellectual Property

(See listing under Hollywood, FL for additional information)

Dennis, Jackson, Martin & Fontela, P.A.
1591 Summit Lake Drive, Suite 200
Tallahassee, Florida 32317
   Telephone: 850-422-3345
   Fax: 850-422-1325
   www.djmf-law.com

Established: 1992

Insurance Defense, Bodily Injury, Civil Rights, Commercial Vehicle, General Liability, Governmental Liability, Legal Malpractice, Medical Malpractice, Professional Liability, Wrongful Termination

Firm Profile: Dennis, Jackson, Martin & Fontela, P.A. was organized in 1992 for the purpose of providing effective and efficient legal representation to its clients. The firm handles litigation matters with an emphasis on professional and governmental liability. It currently consists of six partners, three associates and eight litigation support personnel.

Insurance Clients

Anesthesiologists' Professional Assurance Company
COUNTRY Financial
The Doctors Company
Florida Lawyers Indemnity Group, Inc.
National American Insurance Company
Sedgwick Group
Travelers
Auto-Owners Insurance Company
Chubb Group of Insurance Companies
Farmers Group, Inc.
Gulf Atlantic Insurance Company
MAG Mutual Insurance Company
ProAssurance Casualty Company
Scottsdale Insurance Company
Sheridan Healthcorp, Inc.
U.S. Liability Insurance Company

Non-Insurance Clients

Florida Association of Counties Trust
Florida Electric Cooperatives Association, Inc.
Professional Risk Management Services, Inc.
Florida Department of Insurance/Division of Risk Management
Florida Municipal Liability Self Insurers Program
Western Litigation Specialists, Inc.

Partners/Shareholders

Craig A. Dennis — 1954 — University of Florida, B.S. (with honors), 1976; M.A., 1977; Florida State University, J.D. (with honors), 1982 — Admitted to Bar, 1983, Florida; 1987, U.S. District Court, Northern District of Florida; 1988, U.S. District Court, Middle District of Florida; U.S. Court of Appeals, Eleventh Circuit — Member American and Tallahassee Bar Associations; The Florida Bar; Defense Research Institute; Florida Defense Lawyers Association — Certified Circuit Civil Mediator — Practice Areas: Professional Liability; Construction Law; Automobile Liability; Health Care — E-mail: craig@djmf-law.com

William T. Jackson — 1963 — Clarkson University, B.S. (with distinction), 1985; Florida State University, J.D. (with honors), 1991 — Judicial Law Clerk, The Honorable Anne C. Booth, State of Florida, First District Court of Appeals — Admitted to Bar, 1992, Florida; 1997, U.S. District Court, Northern District of Florida — Member Tallahassee Bar Association — Practice Areas: Medical Malpractice; Premises Liability; Employment Law; Appellate — E-mail: bill@djmf-law.com

William Peter Martin — 1950 — Oglethorpe University, B.A., 1974; University of Connecticut School of Law, J.D., 1989 — Admitted to Bar, 1990, Florida; 1991, U.S. District Court, Middle and Northern Districts of Florida; 1991, U.S. Court of Appeals, Eleventh Circuit — Member American Bar Association; The Florida Bar — Board Certified in Civil Trial Law — Practice Areas: Professional Liability; Employment Law — E-mail: peter@djmf-law.com

Rogelio J. Fontela — 1964 — Loyola University New Orleans, B.B.A. (summa cum laude), 1986; Florida State University, J.D. (with high honors), 1992 — Admitted to Bar, 1994, Florida; 1994, U.S. District Court, Middle and Northern Districts of Florida — Member American and Tallahassee Bar Associations; The Florida Bar; Defense Research Institute; Florida Defense Lawyers Association — Languages: Spanish — Practice Areas: Professional Liability — E-mail: roger@djmf-law.com

Partners

Tiffany Rohan-Williams — 1965 — University of Florida, B.S., 1988; St. Thomas University School of Law, J.D. (with honors), 1996 — Admitted to Bar, 1997, Florida — Member Tallahassee Women Lawyers Association —

Dennis, Jackson, Martin & Fontela, P.A., Tallahassee, FL (Continued)

Practice Areas: Contracts; Medical Malpractice; Nursing Home Liability — E-mail: tiffany@djmf-law.com

Maria A. Santoro — 1960 — Florida State University, B.S., 1982; Thomas M. Cooley Law School, J.D., 1986 — Admitted to Bar, 1987, Florida; 1988, U.S. District Court, Southern District of Florida; 1996, U.S. District Court, Northern District of Florida; 2007, U.S. District Court, Middle District of Florida — Member American Bar Association; The Florida Bar; American Inns of Court; Florida Bar Committee on Professionalism; American Trial Lawyers Association; Florida Supreme Court Task Force on Management of Litigation involving Complex Cases — "AV" Rating, Martindale-Hubbell; "AV" Preeminent Women Lawyers, Martindale-Hubbell; Adjunct Professor, Florida State University, College of Law, Tallahassee — Certified Court Mediatior, Supreme Court of Florida — Languages: Spanish — Practice Areas: Medical Malpractice; Employment; Personal Injury; Premises Liability — E-mail: maria@djmf-law.com

Associates

William B. Carter Jr. Michael R. Fidrych

Of Counsel

Lawrence Hardy

McConnaughhay, Duffy, Coonrod, Pope & Weaver, P.A.

1709 Hermitage Boulevard, Suite 200
Tallahassee, Florida 32308
Telephone: 850-222-8121
Fax: 850-222-4359
www.mcconnaughhay.com

(Additional Offices: Fort Lauderdale, FL*; Gainesville, FL*; Jacksonville, FL*; Ocala, FL*; Panama City, FL*; Pensacola, FL*; Sarasota, FL*)

Established: 1976

Insurance Defense, Workers' Compensation, Product Liability, Labor and Employment, Civil Litigation, Trial Practice, Appellate Practice

Insurance Clients

Bituminous Insurance Company	CNA Insurance Company
Florida Municipal Insurance Trust	Liberty Mutual Insurance Company
Travelers	

Non-Insurance Clients

ADP TotalSource	Costco Companies, Inc.
Florida League of Cities	McKenzie Tank Lines, Inc.
North American Risk Services	PBOA, Inc.

Firm Members

James N. McConnaughhay — Florida State University, J.D., 1969 — Admitted to Bar, 1969, Florida — Board Certified Workers' Compensation — Practice Areas: Workers' Compensation; Civil Litigation; Administrative Law

Brian S. Duffy — Florida State University, J.D. (with honors), 1974 — Admitted to Bar, 1974, Florida — Member Board Certified Civil Trial — Practice Areas: Civil Litigation; Employment Litigation; Product Liability

R. Stephen Coonrod — Florida State University, J.D., 1988 — Admitted to Bar, 1988, Florida — Board Certified Workers' Compensation Lawyer — Practice Areas: Workers' Compensation; Civil Litigation; Litigation

M. Kemmerly Thomas — The University of Mississippi, J.D., 1991 — Admitted to Bar, 1991, Florida; 2009, Georgia — Board Certified in Workers' Compensation — Practice Areas: Workers' Compensation

Christopher G. McCue — Stetson University College of Law, J.D., 1999 — Admitted to Bar, 1999, Florida — Practice Areas: Workers' Compensation; Civil Litigation

Jeff F. Dodson — The University of Mississippi School of Law, J.D., 1982 — Admitted to Bar, 1983, Florida; Mississippi — Practice Areas: Civil Litigation; Product Liability

Charles J. Schreiber, Jr. — University of Florida College of Law, J.D., 1988 — Admitted to Bar, 1990, Florida — Practice Areas: Civil Litigation; Commercial Litigation

McConnaughhay, Duffy, Coonrod, Pope & Weaver, P.A., Tallahassee, FL (Continued)

Associates

Matthew G. Hawk	Jason C. Taylor
Marianna R. Sarkisyan	Joe G. Durrett
Marissa S. Pyle	

Radey Law Firm

301 South Bronough Street, Suite 200
Tallahassee, Florida 32301
Telephone: 850-425-6654
Fax: 850-425-6694
E-Mail: info@radeylaw.com
www.radeylaw.com

Established: 2003

Regulatory and Compliance, Corporate Law, Insurance Litigation, Company Licensing, Market Conduct and Financial Examinations, Rate and Form Filings

Firm Profile: Based in Tallahassee, Florida, the Radey Law Firm is an AV-rated firm consisting of lawyers who practice regularly before a variety of state agencies and in all state and federal courts. Our professionals provide advice and counsel in connection with the formation, licensure, and acquisition or merger of regulated companies. We have also worked closely with companies seeking to expand or contract their business operations. We have assisted with hundreds of rate and form filings, all areas of statutory compliance, and our litigation team handles administrative, civil, and appellate litigation. Operating in Florida requires an understanding of residual markets, unfair trade practice laws, and reinsurance facilities such as the Florida Hurricane Catastrophe Fund. Our insurance team has the experience necessary to assist the insurance industry with the full range of issues arising in the Florida market.

Insurance Clients

AXIS Insurance	Chubb Group of Insurance Companies

Shareholders

Karen Asher-Cohen	Bert L. Combs
Travis L. Miller	David A. Yon
Thomas A. Crabb	

(This firm is also listed in the Regulatory and Compliance section of this directory)

Sniffen & Spellman, P.A.

123 North Monroe Street
Tallahassee, Florida 32301
Telephone: 850-205-1996
Fax: 850-205-3004
E-Mail: rsniffen@sniffenlaw.com
www.sniffenlaw.com

Labor and Employment, Civil Rights, Professional Liability, Premises Liability, Insurance Defense, Commercial Litigation, Education Law, Local Government, Special Education Litigation, Law Enforcement Liability

Insurance Clients

ACE Westchester Specialty Group	Allied World National Assurance Company
Avemco Insurance Company, Rockwood Programs	Beazley Group, Lloyd's London
Chartis	CUNA Mutual Group
Farmers Insurance Group	Freedom Specialty Insurance Company
Lexington Insurance Company	
LVL Claims Services, LLC	Philadelphia Insurance Companies
Thomas T. North, Inc	

FLORIDA

Sniffen & Spellman, P.A., Tallahassee, FL (Continued)

Principal

Robert J. Sniffen — University of Florida, B.A., 1990; Stetson University College of Law, J.D., 1993 — Admitted to Bar, 1994, Florida — Board Certified Labor and Employment Law Lawyer, Florida Bar Board of Legal Specialization and Education — E-mail: rsniffen@sniffenlaw.com

Shareholder

Michael P. Spellman — University of Florida, B.A., 1987; Florida State University College of Law, J.D. (with honors), 1991 — Admitted to Bar, 1992, Florida — E-mail: mspellman@sniffenlaw.com

Associates

Lisa A. Barclay
Jeffrey D. Slanker
Hetal H. Desai
Todd C. Hunter
Terry J. Harmon
Maureen McCarthy Daughton
Kenyetta M. Mullins

Of Counsel

Mark Knowles Logan
John R. Eubanks, Jr.

The following firms also service this area.

Barron & Redding, P.A.
220 McKenzie Avenue
Panama City, Florida 32401-3129
Telephone: 850-785-7454
Fax: 850-785-2999

Mailing Address: P.O. Box 2467, Panama City, FL 32402-2467

Casualty, Surety, Fire, Life Insurance, Professional Liability, Product Liability, Medical Malpractice, Environmental Law, Automobile Liability, Premises Liability, Business Torts, Construction Law

SEE COMPLETE LISTING UNDER PANAMA CITY, FLORIDA (98 MILES)

Young, Bill, Roumbos & Boles, P.A.
Seville Tower, 7th Floor
226 South Palafox Place
Pensacola, Florida 32502
Telephone: 850-432-2222
Fax: 850-432-1444

Mailing Address: P.O. Drawer 1070, Pensacola, FL 32591-1070

Insurance Defense, Coverage Issues, Complex Litigation, Bad Faith, Product Liability, Medical Malpractice, Nursing Home Liability, Construction Defect, Premises Liability, General Liability, Automobile Liability

SEE COMPLETE LISTING UNDER PENSACOLA, FLORIDA (189 MILES)

TAMPA † 335,709 Hillsborough Co.

Abbey, Adams, Byelick & Mueller, L.L.P.

5001 West Cypress Street
Tampa, Florida 33607
 Telephone: 813-223-7800
 E-Mail: attorneys@abbeyadams.com
 www.abbeyadams.com

(St. Petersburg, FL Office*: 360 Central Avenue, 11th Floor, 33701, P.O. Box 1511, 33731)
 (Tel: 727-821-2080)
 (Fax: 727-822-3970)

Established: 1982

Administrative Law, Americans with Disabilities Act, Appellate Practice, Complex Litigation, General Defense, Employment Law, Bad Faith, Insurance Coverage, Insurance Fraud, Uninsured and Underinsured Motorist, Professional Malpractice, Mediation, Negligence, Personal Injury, Premises Liability, Product Liability, Subrogation, Toxic Torts, Workers' Compensation, Motor Vehicle Liability, Defense of Insureds, Sovereign Immunity and Governmental Defense

---

TAMPA

Abbey, Adams, Byelick & Mueller, L.L.P., Tampa, FL (Continued)

Insurance Clients

ACE USA
Alfa Mutual Insurance Company
Allstate Insurance Company
American Insurance Company
American Premier Insurance Company
Ameriprise Auto & Home Insurance
Atlanta Casualty Company
Bankers Insurance Company
Broadspire
Cambridge Integrated Services
Cannon Cochran Management Services, Inc.
Claims Control Corporation
Colorado Western Insurance Company
Crawford & Company
EMC Insurance Companies
Erie Insurance Company
ESIS
Farmers Commercial Insurance
FFVA Mutual Insurance Company
First Colony Life Insurance Company
Florida Family Insurance Company
Florida Insurance Guaranty Association
Florida Preferred Administrators
Florida Workers' Compensation Insurance Guaranty Association
GAB Robins, Inc.
GatesMcDonald
GMAC Insurance
Gulf Insurance Company
HDI-Gerling America Insurance Company
Interstate Insurance Company
Johns Eastern Company, Inc.
Liberty Mutual Group
The Main Street America Group
Meadowbrook Insurance Group
Metropolitan Insurance Company
MMG Insurance Company
Motorists Mutual Insurance Company
Nationwide Insurance
Old Dominion Insurance Company
Packard Claims Administration
PHICO Insurance Company
Progressive Insurance Company
Prudential Property and Casualty Insurance Company
Risk Management Services, Inc.
Rockford Mutual Insurance Company
Safety National Casualty Corporation
Security First Managers, LLC
Southern Fire Adjusters
Southern Oak Management, LLC
State Auto Insurance Companies
Stonewall Insurance Company
Tennessee Farmers Mutual Insurance Company
Transportation Casualty Insurance Company
United Automobile Insurance Company
United Self Insured Services
United States Liability Insurance Group
West Bend Mutual Insurance Company
Willis Administrative Services Corporation
Zurich American Insurance Company
Agway Insurance Company
ALLIED Mutual Insurance Company
American International Group, Inc.
American United Life Insurance Company
AmerUs Life Insurance Company
Amstar Insurance Company
Atlantic Mutual Insurance Company
Brotherhood Mutual Insurance Company
Cincinnati Insurance Company
Citizens Property Insurance Corp.
CNA Insurance Companies
Commercial Risk Management, Inc.
Delta Casualty Company
Employers Reinsurance Corporation
Everest National Insurance Company
Fireman's Fund Insurance Company
First Insurance Network, Inc.
Florida Farm Bureau
Florida Life and Health Insurance Guaranty Association
Florida Restaurant Insurance Service Company
Florists' Insurance Company
Gallagher Bassett Services, Inc.
Genesis Indemnity Insurance Company
The Hartford
Holyoke Mutual Insurance Company in Salem
John Deere Insurance Company
Kentucky Farm Bureau Insurance Companies
Maryland Automobile Insurance Fund
Michigan Commercial Insurance Mutual
Motor Transport Underwriters, Inc.
National Service Industries, Inc.
New England Life Insurance Company
Pekin Insurance Company
PMA Insurance Group
Providence Property and Casualty Insurance Company
Republic Western Insurance Company
Royal Palm Insurance Company
Safeco Insurance
Scottsdale Insurance Company
Scott Wetzel Services, Inc.
Sedgwick Claims Management Services, Inc.
Specialty Risk Services, Inc. (SRS)
Statewide Adjusters, Inc.
Technology Insurance Company, Inc.
TransGuard Insurance Company of America, Inc.
Unisun Insurance Company
United Insurance Company of America
United Services Automobile Association (USAA)
VGM Insurance Company
Western National Insurance Group
Western-Southern Life Assurance Company
Zenith Insurance Company

Non-Insurance Clients

Abbott Laboratories
Allied Automotive Group
Able Staffing & Leasing
Angels Baseball L.P.

Abbey, Adams, Byelick & Mueller, L.L.P., Tampa, FL (Continued)

A-1 Contract Staffing, Inc.
CatManDo, Inc.
City of Dunedin, Florida
Climate Design
Cox Target Media
Delta Air Lines, Inc.
Diocese of St. Petersburg
Eaton Corporation
Film Technologies International
Greater Tampa Bay Auto Auction
Intrepid Powerboats, Inc.
Johnson Brothers Corporation
Lakeland Tigers Food Service
New York Yankees
Pinellas County Schools
Polk County Board of County Commissioners
Progress Energy
School Board of Manatee County
SouthEast Personnel Leasing, Inc.
State of Florida, Division of Risk Management
Tampa Bay Rays
Unisource Administrators, Inc.
Val-Pak
WCASC
Wendy's International, Inc.
Burger King Corporation
Chevron U.S.A., Inc.
City of Sarasota
Cottingham and Butler, Inc.
Crown Chicago Industries (CCI)
Dillard's, Inc.
Eaton Aerospace
EOS Comp, L.L.C.
Florida Progress
Intergovernment Risk Management Department for the City of Ocala/Marion County
Nestle USA, Inc.
Philadelphia Phillies
Pinnacle Benefits, Inc.
Professional Business Owners Association
Protegrity Services, Inc.
School District of Hillsborough County
State of Florida, Division of State Fire Marshall
Toronto Blue Jays
USA Benefits Group
Washington Nationals Major League Baseball

Partners

David J. Abbey
Robert P. Byelick
V. Joseph Mueller
Deborah L. Eldridge
Jeffrey M. Adams, Managing Partner
John D. Kiernan

Associates

Allison G. Mawhinney
Martin G. Deptula
Blair H. Clarke
Michael C. Auchampau
Michael P. Falkowski
Samantha A. Satish

Barker & Cook, PA

501 East Kennedy Boulevard, Suite 790
Tampa, Florida 33602
  Telephone: 813-489-1001
  Fax: 813-489-1008
  Toll Free: 888-892-8722
  E-Mail: chris@barkercook.com
  www.barkercook.com

Established: 2000

Insurance Defense, Self-Insured, Trial and Appellate Practice, State and Federal Courts, First and Third Party Defense, Automobile, Casualty, Construction Law, Engineers, Malpractice, Environmental Law, General Liability, Life and Health, Medical Malpractice, Product Liability, Property, Reinsurance, Workers' Compensation, Civil Litigation, Commercial Litigation, Personal Injury, Premises Liability, Contract Disputes, Labor and Employment, Construction Disputes, Insurance Coverage Disputes

Insurance Clients

American International Group, Inc.
CNA Insurance Company
Guarantee Trust Life Insurance Company
Investors Insurance Company of America
Mutual Benefit Group
Travelers Insurance Companies
American International Group-Claims Services, Inc.
Gulf Insurance Group-Atlanta
Gulf Insurance Group-Texas
Lexington Insurance Company
Markel Insurance Company
National Insurance Company

Non-Insurance Clients

Crawford & Company
GatesMcDonald
Deep South Surplus, Inc.
RSKCo

Barker & Cook, PA, Tampa, FL (Continued)

Partners

Chris A. Barker — 1965 — Birmingham-Southern College, B.A. (magna cum laude), 1987; The University of Alabama, J.D., 1990 — Phi Alpha Delta — Admitted to Bar, 1990, Alabama; 1991, Florida; 1991, U.S. District Court, Southern District of Alabama; 1991, U.S. District Court, Northern District of Florida; 1992, U.S. District Court, Middle District of Alabama; 1993, U.S. District Court, Middle District of Florida; 1993, U.S. Court of Appeals, Eleventh Circuit; 1998, U.S. District Court, Southern District of Florida; 2003, U.S. District Court, Northern District of Alabama; 2004, U.S. Supreme Court — Member American and Hillsborough County Bar Associations; The Florida Bar; Alabama State Bar — Editor-in-Chief, The Column - Legal Newspaper, 1989-1990; Associate Editor, The Law and Psychology Review, 1988-1990 — E-mail: chris@barkercook.com

William J. Cook — 1968 — Virginia Tech, B.A., 1990; Stetson University College of Law, J.D. (cum laude), 1993 — Finalist in 1992-1993 Scribes Note and Comment Competition — Member, Notes Editor, Stetson Law Review, 1992-1993 — Admitted to Bar, 1993, Florida; 1993, U.S. District Court, Middle District of Florida; 2001, U.S. District Court, Southern District of Florida — Member American and Hillsborough County Bar Associations; The Florida Bar — Author: "From Insider Trading to Unfair Trading: Chestman II and Rule 14e-3," 22 Stetson Law Review 171, 1992 — E-mail: wcook@barkercook.com

Conroy Simberg

201 East Kennedy Boulevard, Suite 900
Tampa, Florida 33602
  Telephone: 813-273-6464
  Fax: 813-273-6465
  E-Mail: csg@conroysimberg.com
  www.conroysimberg.com

Insurance Defense, Appellate Practice, Insurance Coverage, Environmental Law, Governmental Liability, Civil Rights, Wrongful Termination, Americans with Disabilities Act, Sexual Harassment, Land Use, Commercial Law, Fire, Arson, Fraud, Fidelity and Surety, Automobile Liability, Admiralty and Maritime Law, Bad Faith, Employment Law, Self-Insured, Public Entities, Product Liability, Casualty, Excess and Reinsurance, Accident and Health, Workers' Compensation, Medical Malpractice, Class Actions, Construction Defect, Construction Litigation, First Party Matters, Premises Liability, Professional Liability, Intellectual Property

(See listing under Hollywood, FL for additional information)

Galloway, Johnson, Tompkins, Burr & Smith

620 Twiggs Street, Suite 303
Tampa, Florida 33602
  Telephone: 813-977-1200
  Fax: 813-977-1288
  E-Mail: phowell@gallowayjohnson.com
  www.gallowayjohnson.com

(Additional Offices: New Orleans, LA*; Lafayette, LA*; Pensacola, FL*; St. Louis, MO*; Houston, TX*; Mandeville, LA*; Gulfport, MS*; Mobile, AL*; Atlanta, GA*)

Maritime, Automobile Liability, Bad Faith, Class Actions, Construction, Energy, Employment, Insurance Coverage, Insurance Defense, Product Liability, Professional Liability, Property, Transportation, General Casualty, Title Resolution, Environmental

(See listing under New Orleans, LA for additional information)

The Law Offices of Matthew J. Jowanna, P.A.

2521 Windguard Circle
Wesley Chapel, Florida 33544-7346
   Telephone: 813-929-7300
   Fax: 813-929-7325
   E-Mail: Info@Jowanna.com
   www.FloridaInsuranceDefense.com

Firm Profile: The Law Offices of Matthew J. Jowanna, P.A. is a civil litigation and trial law firm. The Firm has received Martindale-Hubbell's highest rating, ("AV"). The Firm is also listed in the Bar Register of Preeminent Lawyers.

Insurance Clients

American Southwest Insurance Managers, Inc.
Seneca Insurance Company, Inc.
State of Florida, Division of Risk Management
Armed Forces Insurance
Chubb Group of Insurance Companies

Founding Partner & Managing Shareholder

Matthew J. Jowanna — University of South Florida, B.A., 1989; Nova Southeastern University, Shepard Broad Law Center, J.D. (summa cum laude), 1994; University of Notre Dame, LL.M. (magna cum laude), 2010 — Senior Staff Member, Nova Law Review — Admitted to Bar, Florida; U.S. District Court, Middle District of Florida; U.S. Court of Appeals, Eleventh Circuit; U.S. Supreme Court — Member The Florida Bar; Hillsborough County Bar Association — "AV" Rated by Martindale-Hubbell — E-mail: MJJ@Jowanna.com

Luks & Santaniello LLC

100 North Tampa Street, Suite 2120
Tampa, Florida 33602
   Telephone: 813-226-0081
   Fax: 813-226-0082
   www.LS-LAW.com

(Additional Offices: Fort Lauderdale, FL*; Orlando, FL*; Jacksonville, FL*; Boca Raton, FL*; Miami, FL*; Tallahassee, FL)

Insurance Defense, General Liability, Workers' Compensation

(See listing under Fort Lauderdale, FL for additional information)

Marshall Dennehey Warner Coleman & Goggin

201 East Kennedy Boulevard, Suite 1100
Tampa, Florida 33602
   Telephone: 813-898-1800
   Fax: 813-221-5026
   www.marshalldennehey.com

(Philadelphia, PA Office*: 2000 Market Street, Suite 2300, 19103)
   (Tel: 215-575-2600)
   (Fax: 215-575-0856)
   (Toll Free: 800-220-3308)
   (E-Mail: marshalldennehey@mdwcg.com)
(Wilmington, DE Office*: Nemours Building, 1007 North Orange Street, Suite 600, 19801)
   (Tel: 302-552-4300)
   (Fax: 302-552-4340)

Marshall Dennehey Warner Coleman & Goggin, Tampa, FL (Continued)

(Fort Lauderdale, FL Office*: 100 Northeast 3rd Avenue, Suite 1100, 33301)
   (Tel: 954-847-4920)
   (Fax: 954-627-6640)
(Jacksonville, FL Office*: 200 West Forsyth Street, Suite 1400, 32202)
   (Tel: 904-358-4200)
   (Fax: 904-355-0019)
(Orlando, FL Office*: Landmark Center One, 315 East Robinson Street, Suite 550, 32801-1948)
   (Tel: 407-420-4380)
   (Fax: 407-839-3008)
(Cherry Hill, NJ Office*: Woodland Falls Corporate Park, 200 Lake Drive East, Suite 300, 08002)
   (Tel: 856-414-6000)
   (Fax: 856-414-6077)
(Roseland, NJ Office*: 425 Eagle Rock Avenue, Suite 302, 07068)
   (Tel: 973-618-4100)
   (Fax: 973-618-0685)
(New York, NY Office*: Wall Street Plaza, 88 Pine Street, 21st Floor, 10005-1801)
   (Tel: 212-376-6400)
   (Fax: 212-376-6490)
(Melville, NY Office*: 105 Maxess Road, Suite 303, 11747)
   (Tel: 631-232-6130)
   (Fax: 631-232-6184)
(Cincinnati, OH Office*: 312 Elm Street, Suite 1850, 45202)
   (Tel: 513-375-6800)
   (Fax: 513-372-6801)
(Cleveland, OH Office*: 127 Public Square, Suite 3510, 44114-1291)
   (Tel: 216-912-3800)
   (Fax: 216-344-9006)
(Allentown, PA Office*: 4905 West Tilghman Street, Suite 300, 18104)
   (Tel: 484-895-2300)
   (Fax: 484-895-2303)
(Doylestown, PA Office*: 10 North Main Street, 2nd Floor, 18901-4318)
   (Tel: 267-880-2020)
   (Fax: 215-348-5439)
(Erie, PA Office*: 717 State Street, Suite 701, 16501)
   (Tel: 814-480-7800)
   (Fax: 814-455-3603)
(Camp Hill, PA Office*(See Harrisburg listing): 100 Coporate Center Drive, Suite 201, 17011)
   (Tel: 717-651-3500)
   (Fax: 717-651-9630)
(King of Prussia, PA Office*: 620 Freedom Business Center, Suite 300, 19406)
   (Tel: 610-354-8250)
   (Fax: 610-354-8299)
(Pittsburgh, PA Office*: U.S. Steel Tower, Suite 2900, 600 Grant Street, 15219)
   (Tel: 412-803-1140)
   (Fax: 412-803-1188)
(Moosic, PA Office*(See Scranton listing): 50 Glenmaura National Boulevard, 18507)
   (Tel: 570-496-4600)
   (Fax: 570-496-0567)
(Rye Brook, NY Office*(See Westchester listing): 800 Westchester Avenue, Suite C-700, 10573)
   (Tel: 914-977-7300)
   (Fax: 914-977-7301)

Established: 2000

TAMPA   FLORIDA

Marshall Dennehey Warner Coleman & Goggin, Tampa, FL (Continued)

Amusements, Sports and Recreation Liability, Asbestos and Mass Tort Litigation, Automobile Liability, Aviation and Complex Litigation, Construction Injury Litigation, Fraud/Special Investigation, General Liability, Hospitality and Liquor Liability, Maritime Litigation, Product Liability, Property Litigation, Retail Liability, Trucking & Transportation Liability, Appellate Advocacy and Post-Trial Practice, Architectural, Engineering and Construction Defect Litigation, Class Action Litigation, Commercial Litigation, Consumer and Credit Law, Employment Law, Environmental & Toxic Tort Litigation, Insurance Coverage/Bad Faith Litigation, Life, Health and Disability Litigation, Privacy and Data Security, Professional Liability, Public Entity and Civil Rights Litigation, Real Estate E&O Liability, School Leaders' Liability, Securities and Investment Professional Liability, Technology, Media and Intellectual Property Litigation, White Collar Crime, Birth Injury Litigation, Health Care Governmental Compliance, Health Care Liability, Health Law, Long-Term Care Liability, Medical Device and Pharmaceutical Liability, Medicare Set-Aside, Workers' Compensation

Firm Profile: Our firm established its first office in Florida in Tampa in April 2000. Since that time, the office has experienced consistent growth. Currently, the attorneys in our Tampa office handle professional liability, product liability, and property and casualty claims.

This office is located in the heart of downtown Tampa, within walking distance of the Hillsborough County and federal courthouses. From this location, we are able to provide legal services to our clients in the Northern, Middle, and Southern Federal District Courts, as well as the counties of Citrus, Sumter, Hernando, Pasco, Pinellas, Hillsborough, Manatee, Hardee, Sarasota, DeSoto, Highlands, Glades, Charlotte and Lee.

For additional information regarding the Tampa, Florida office, please feel free to contact Russell S. Buhite, Esquire, the managing attorney of this office at (813) 898-1827 or rsbuhite@mdwcg.com

Managing Shareholder

Russell S. Buhite — Rice University, B.A. (cum laude), 1984; Washington University in St. Louis School of Law, J.D., 1987 — Phi Delta Phi — Florida Super Lawyers, 2006-2007; Best Lawyers in America (2011-Present); Florida Trend's Legal Elite (2011) — Law Clerk, U.S. Magistrate Judge Elizabeth Jenkins, Middle District of Florida, Tampa Division, 1989-1991 — Associate Editor, Journal of Urban and Contemporary Law — Admitted to Bar, 1988, Missouri; 1989, Florida; U.S. District Court, Middle, Northern and Southern Districts of Florida — Member American and Hillsborough County Bar Associations; Defense Research Institute (Life, Health and Disability Insurance Committee); Florida Defense Lawyers Association — Author: "ERISA Survey of Federal Circuits," ABA, Tort Trial and Insurance Practice Section, Health and Disability Insurance Law Committee, 2005, 2007, 2010 Ed.; "Watts v. Bell South Telecommunications, the 11th Circuit Breaks From the Pack on Exhaustion of Administrative Remedies," Spring, 2003, ABA TIPS Newsletter; "The Facts of the Matter - Standard of Review of ERISA Plan Administrator's Factual Determinations," Life and Health News, Defense Research Institute, Summer, 1996; "Insurance Policy Application Misrepresentation and their Consequences Under Florida Law," 15 Trial Advocate Quarterly, No. 2, April, 1996; "Appraising the Appraisal Process," 14 Trial Advocate Quarterly, No. 2, April 1995; "Recent Development, Random Urinalysis and the Fourth Amendment, Can They Co-exist?" 33 J.Urb. & Comtemp. L. 801, 1988; "Private Healthcare Exchanges Grow in Populatiry While Affordable Care Act Struggles," ABA TIPS Section's Tortsource Maganzine, Vol. 16, No. 2, Winter 2014; "Righting the Ship in the Nick of Time? Congress Reauthorizes NFIP," WestLaw Journal, Volume 22, Issue 52, October 2012; Co-Author: "11th Circuit Chapter of ERISA Survey of Federal Circuits," ABAPublishing, 2012 Edition; "11th Circuit Chapter of the 5th Edition of The ERISA Survey of Federal Circuits," published by the ABA TIPS Section, 2014 — Seminars/Classes Taught: "Supplementation of the Administrative Record with Additional Evidence in ERISA Litigation," American Bar Association's 40th Annual TIPS Mid-Winter Symposium on Insurance and Employee Benefits, January 16-18, 2014; "What Insurance Lawyers Need To Know About New Long Term Insurance Products," ExecSense Webinar, May 2011; "What Insurance Lawyers Need To Know About The Impact of State of Florida v. U.S. Department of Health & Human Services (N.D. FL. Jan. 31, 2011) On The Survival of The Patient Protection and Affordable Care Act,: ExecSense Webinar, March 2011; "Directors and Officers Liability Insurance," Fowler White Boggs Banker Business Department Seminar; "Insurance Coverage Law in Florida," National Business Institute, 1994-1997 — Languages: French — Practice Areas: Professional Liability; Insurance Coverage; Life and Health; Disability; ERISA; Health Care Liability; Agent and Brokers Errors and Omissions — E-mail: rsbuhite@mdwcg.com

Senior Counsel

Terrance A. Bostic

Resident Shareholders

Michael G. ArchibaldJanice L. Merrill

Resident Associates

John W. HeilmanSamuel C. Higginbottom
Haley R. MapleLindsay McCormick

(See listing under Philadelphia, PA for additional information)

Mintzer Sarowitz Zeris Ledva & Meyers, LLP

8166 Woodland Center Boulevard
Tampa, Florida 33614-2418
 Telephone: 813-449-4400
 Fax: 813-449-4401
 www.Defensecounsel.com

(Additional Offices: Philadelphia, PA*; Miami, FL*; Cherry Hill, NJ*; Hicksville, NY*; New York, NY*; Pittsburgh, PA*; Wilmington, DE*; Wheeling, WV*)

Insurance Defense, Premises Liability, Product Liability, Environmental Law, Workers' Compensation, Coverage Issues, Asbestos Litigation, Medical Malpractice, Nursing Home Liability, Professional Liability, Trucking Law

Managing Partner

David R. Bolen

(See listing under Philadelphia, PA for additional information)

Murray, Morin & Herman, P.A.

Bank of America Plaza, Suite 1810
101 East Kennedy Boulevard
Tampa, Florida 33602-5148
 Telephone: 813-222-1800
 Fax: 813-222-1801
 E-Mail: jmurray@mmhlaw.com
 www.mmhlaw.com

(Miami, FL Office: 255 Alhambra Circle, Suite 750, 33134)
 (Tel: 305-441-1180)
 (Fax: 305-441-1801)
(Harrison, NY Office: 500 Mamaroneck Avenue, Suite 320, 10528)
 (Tel: 914-705-4568)
 (Fax: 914-705-4578)

Established: 2000

Appellate, Automobile Liability, Automobile, Trucking, Aviation, Commercial Litigation, Construction Law, General Defense, Insurance Coverage, Insurance Litigation, Mediation, Personal Injury, Product Liability, Professional Liability, Subrogation

Murray, Morin & Herman, P.A., Tampa, FL (Continued)

Firm Profile: Murray, Morin & Herman, P.A. is an AV® rated, full service civil litigation firm representing clients throughout the state of Florida, New York, the Southeastern United States, and Central and South America. We handle civil, trial and appellate matters in all Florida, New York, Alabama, Mississippi and Georgia state courts, as well as federal courts with an emphasis on aviation, transportation, general insurance defense litigation, product liability, insurance coverage, personal injury and wrongful death, professional negligence, construction litigation, and commercial litigation.

Insurance Clients

ACE Group
Allianz
Arch Insurance Group
Century Insurance Group
Chartis Insurance
CJW & Associates
Gallagher Bassett Services, Inc.
Global Aerospace Underwriting Managers, Ltd.
Houston Casualty Company
Phoenix Aviation Managers, Inc.
Professional Claims Managers, Inc.
QBE European Operations
Starr Adjustment Services, Inc.
Travelers Syndicate Management, Ltd.
Aerospace Claims Management Group
Burns & Wilcox Ltd.
Certain Underwriters at Lloyd's, London
GAB Robins/Aviation LS
Gibson & Associates
Hamlin & Burton Liability Management
National Interstate Insurance Company
Providence Washington Insurance Company
T.H.E. Insurance Company
XL Specialty Insurance Company

Non-Insurance Clients

American Airlines, Inc.
Cannon Cochran Management Services, Inc.
Hillsborough County Aviation Authority
Virgin Atlantic Airways, Ltd.
BBA Aviation PLC
City of Lake Wales
Federal Express
Kelowna Flightcraft Group of Companies

Members

John M. Murray — 1946 — Auburn University, B.S., 1968; Memphis State University, J.D., 1972 — Admitted to Bar, 1973, Florida; 1999, Alabama; 1976, U.S. District Court, Middle, Northern and Southern Districts of Florida; 1976, U.S. Supreme Court; 1999, U.S. District Court, Middle District of Alabama; 2002, U.S. District Court, Southern District of Alabama — Member American Board of Trial Advocates; Aviation Insurance Association; Counsel on Aviation Accreditation; Defense Research Institute; Federation of Defense and Corporate Counsel (FDCC); Florida Aviation Trades Association; Fellow, International Academy of Trial Lawyers; Florida Bar Aviation Law Committee — Certified Flight Instructor; Pilot; Martindale-Hubbell® AV Rated — Board Certified Civil Trial Law; Board Certified Aviation Law — Languages: Spanish — Practice Areas: Aviation; Insurance Law; Product Liability — E-mail: jmurray@mmhlaw.com

David P. Herman — 1961 — The University of Arizona, B.S., 1986; University of Miami, J.D., 1989 — Admitted to Bar, 1990, Florida; 1990, U.S. District Court, Middle and Southern Districts of Florida; 1990, Federal Trial Bar — Member Aviation Insurance Association; Defense Research Institute — Martindale-Hubbell® AV Rated — Practice Areas: Aviation; Insurance Law; Product Liability — Resident Miami, FL Office — E-mail: dherman@mmhlaw.com

Christopher S. Morin — 1969 — University of South Florida, B.A. (magna cum laude), 1994; M.A. (summa cum laude), 1995; Stetson University College of Law, J.D. (magna cum laude), 1999 — Admitted to Bar, 1999, Florida; 1999, U.S. District Court, Middle, Northern and Southern Districts of Florida — Member Aviation Insurance Association (Director, Attorneys Division); Defense Research Institute; Florida Aviation Law Committee — Aircraft Owners Pilots Association Panel Attorney; Pilot — U.S. Navy, 1987-1990 — Practice Areas: Aviation; Insurance Defense; Product Liability — E-mail: cmorin@mmhlaw.com

Christopher E. Doran — 1969 — University of South Florida, B.A., 1991; Stetson University College of Law, J.D., 1997 — Admitted to Bar, 1997, Florida; 2001, U.S. District Court, Middle District of Florida; 2003, U.S. District Court, Northern and Southern Districts of Florida — Member The Florida Bar — Practice Areas: Automobile; Trucking; Construction Law; Insurance Defense; Product Liability — E-mail: cdoran@mmhlaw.com

Of Counsel

Raymond L. Mariani — 1961 — Boston University, B.S., 1984; Georgetown University Law Center, J.D., 1987 — Admitted to Bar, 1988, New York; 1989, District of Columbia; 2013, Texas; U.S. District Court, Eastern, Northern, Southern and Western Districts of New York; U.S. District Court, Northern District of Illinois; U.S. Court of Appeals, Second and Third Circuits — Certified Mediator — Practice Areas: Contracts; Product Liability; Insurance Coverage; Alternative Dispute Resolution — Resident Harrison, NY Office — E-mail: rmariani@mmhlaw.com

Associates

Rollin M. Smith — 1970 — University of Florida, B.S.B.A., 1994; J.D., 1998 — Admitted to Bar, 1999, Florida; 2001, U.S. District Court, Southern District of Florida — Member Caribbean Bar Association — Languages: French — Resident Miami, FL Office — E-mail: rsmith@mmhlaw.com

Michael G. Shannon — 1956 — University of Miami, B.A. (cum laude), 1981; J.D. (cum laude), 1987 — Admitted to Bar, 1988, Florida; U.S. District Court, Middle, Northern and Southern Districts of Florida; 1989, U.S. Court of Appeals, Eleventh Circuit; 1997, U.S. Court of Appeal for the Federal Circuit — Resident Miami, FL Office — E-mail: mshannon@mmhlaw.com

Jennifer M. Clark — 1980 — University of Florida, B.A. (with honors), 2002; J.D., 2005 — Admitted to Bar, 2005, Florida; 2006, U.S. District Court, Middle District of Florida; 2007, U.S. District Court, Northern and Southern Districts of Florida — Member Defense Research Institute; International Aviation Women's Association; Tampa Bay Inn of Court — E-mail: jclark@mmhlaw.com

George H. Featherstone — 1976 — University of Florida, B.A., 1999; Tulane University Law School, J.D., 2002 — Admitted to Bar, 2002, Florida; 2004, U.S. District Court, Middle District of Florida — Member Defense Research Institute — E-mail: gfeatherstone@mmhlaw.com

Christopher D. Cloud — 1980 — Florida State University, B.S.P.S., 2002; Mississippi College of Law, J.D., 2005 — Admitted to Bar, 2005, Mississippi; 2006, Florida; U.S. District Court, Northern and Southern Districts of Mississippi; U.S. District Court, Southern District of Florida; U.S. Court of Appeals, Fifth Circuit — E-mail: ccloud@mmhlaw.com

Nathan M. Wheat — 1975 — Syracuse University, B.A. (magna cum laude), 1996; Vanderbilt University Law School, J.D., 1999 — Admitted to Bar, 1999, Georgia; 2010, Florida; U.S. District Court, Middle and Northern Districts of Georgia; U.S. District Court, Southern District of Florida; U.S. Court of Appeals, Eleventh Circuit — Member State Bar of Georgia (Aviation Law Section); Aircraft Owners and Pilots Association — Pilot — E-mail: nwheat@mmhlaw.com

Laurence M. Krutchik — 1982 — Northeastern University, B.SC.J., 2004; Nova Southeastern University, Shepard Broad Law Center, J.D., 2009 — Admitted to Bar, 2009, Florida; U.S. District Court, Middle and Southern Districts of Florida — Member Defense Research Institute (Assistant Newsletter Editor, Aerospace Law Committee) — Resident Miami, FL Office — E-mail: lkrutchik@mmhlaw.com

Richard D. Giglio — 1972 — College of William & Mary, B.A., 1994; Villanova University School of Law, J.D., 1997 — Admitted to Bar, 1997, Florida; U.S. District Court, Middle and Southern Districts of Florida — Martindale-Hubbell® AV Rating — E-mail: rgiglio@mmhlaw.com

Phelps Dunbar LLP

100 South Ashley Drive, Suite 1900
Tampa, Florida 33602-5311
Telephone: 813-472-7550
Fax: 813-472-7570
E-Mail: info@phelps.com
www.phelpsdunbar.com

(New Orleans, LA Office*: Canal Place, 365 Canal Street, Suite 2000, 70130-6534)
  (Tel: 504-566-1311)
  (Fax: 504-568-9130)
(Baton Rouge, LA Office*: II City Plaza, 400 Convention Street, Suite 1100, 70802-5618, P.O. Box 4412, 70821-4412)
  (Tel: 225-346-0285)
  (Fax: 225-381-9197)
(Jackson, MS Office*: 4270 I-55 North, 39211-6391, P.O. Box 16114, 39236-6114)
  (Tel: 601-352-2300)
  (Fax: 601-360-9777)
(Tupelo, MS Office*: One Mississippi Plaza, 201 South Spring Street, Seventh Floor, 38804, P.O. Box 1220, 38802-1220)
  (Tel: 662-842-7907)
  (Fax: 662-842-3873)

TAMPA — FLORIDA

Phelps Dunbar LLP, Tampa, FL (Continued)

(Gulfport, MS Office*: NorthCourt One, 2304 19th Street, Suite 300, 39501)
  (Tel: 228-679-1130)
  (Fax: 228-679-1131)
(Houston, TX Office*: One Allen Center, 500 Dallas Street, Suite 1300, 77002)
  (Tel: 713-626-1386)
  (Fax: 713-626-1388)
(Mobile, AL Office*: 2 North Royal Street, 36602, P.O. Box 2727, 36652-2727)
  (Tel: 251-432-4481)
  (Fax: 251-433-1820)
(London, United Kingdom Office*: Lloyd's, Suite 725, Level 7, 1 Lime Street, EC3M 7DQ)
  (Tel: 011-44-207-929-4765)
  (Fax: 011-44-207-929-0046)
(Raleigh, NC Office*: 4140 Parklake Avenue, Suite 100, 27612-3723)
  (Tel: 919-789-5300)
  (Fax: 919-789-5301)
(Southlake, TX Office*(See Dallas listing): 115 Grand Avenue, Suite 222, 76092)
  (Tel: 817-488-3134)
  (Fax: 817-488-3214)

Insurance Law

Insurance Clients

- Acceptance Casualty Insurance Company
- Aegis Janson Green Insurance Services Inc.
- AIG
- Columbus
- Alabama Municipal Insurance Corporation
- AmTrust Underwriters, Inc.
- Arch Insurance Company (Europe) Ltd.
- Aspen Insurance UK Limited
- Associated Aviation Underwriters
- Bankers Insurance Group
- Berkley Select, LLC
- Bluebonnet Life Insurance Company
- Britannia Steam Ship Insurance Association Ltd.
- CNA
- Commercial Union Insurance Company
- Companion Property and Casualty Group
- ELCO Administrative Services
- Endurance Services, Ltd.
- Erie Insurance Company
- Evanston Insurance Company
- Fidelity National Financial
- First Premium Insurance Group, Inc.
- GE Insurance Solutions
- General & Cologne Life Reinsurance of America
- General Star Indemnity Company
- Glencoe Group
- Global Special Risks, Inc.
- Great American Insurance Companies
- Gulf Insurance Group
- The Hartford Insurance Group
- Homesite Group, Inc.
- ICAT Boulder Claims
- Infinity Insurance Company
- Lexington Insurance Company
- Liberty Mutual Group
- Louisiana Farm Bureau Mutual Insurance Company
- Louisiana Workers' Compensation Corporation
- Markel
- MetLife Auto & Home
- NAS Insurance Group
- Nautilus Insurance Company
- ACE Group of Insurance and Reinsurance Companies
- Aetna Insurance Company
- AFLAC - American Family Life Assurance Company of
- Allstate Insurance Company
- American Family Life Assurance Company of Columbus
- Argonaut Insurance Company
- Aspen Insurance
- Aspen Re
- AXIS Insurance
- Beazley
- Bituminous Insurance Company
- Blue Cross & Blue Shield of Mississippi
- Chartis Insurance
- Chubb Group of Insurance Companies
- Commonwealth Insurance Company
- Cotton States Insurance
- Criterion Claim Solutions
- Employers Reinsurance Corporation
- Esurance Insurance Company
- Farmers Insurance Group
- Fireman's Fund Insurance Company
- Foremost Insurance Company
- General American Life Insurance Company
- General Reinsurance Corporation
- General Star Management Company
- Golden Rule Insurance Company
- Great Southern Life Insurance Company
- Hanover Insurance Group
- Hermitage Insurance Company
- Houston Casualty Company
- Indian Harbor Insurance Company
- Ironshore Insurance, Ltd.
- Liberty International Underwriters
- Life Insurance Company of Alabama
- Louisiana Health Insurance Association
- Lyndon Property Insurance Company
- Munich-American Risk Partners
- Nationwide Insurance
- The Navigators Group, Inc.
- Old American Insurance Company
- Pharmacists Mutual Insurance Company
- RenaissanceRe
- RLI Insurance Company
- Royal & SunAlliance
- St. Paul Travelers
- SCOR Global P&C
- Sedgwick Claims Management Services, Inc.
- SR International Business Insurance Company, Ltd.
- Steamship Mutual Underwriting Association Limited
- Torus
- Underwriters at Lloyd's, London
- Unitrin Business Insurance
- Vesta Eiendom AS
- Western Heritage Insurance Company
- Westport Insurance Corporation
- XL Insurance Group
- OneBeacon Insurance Group
- Prime Syndicate
- QBE
- Republic Western Insurance Company
- St. Paul Reinsurance Company Limited
- Scottsdale Insurance Company
- Sentry Insurance
- Southern Farm Bureau Casualty Insurance Company
- State National Insurance Company, Inc.
- Terra Nova Insurance Company Limited
- United States Fidelity and Guaranty Company
- Victoria Insurance Group
- West of England Ship Owners Mutual Insurance Association (Luxembourg)
- Zurich

Members of the Firm

A. Brian Albritton — New College of the University of South Florida, B.A., 1979; Harvard Divinity School, M.T.S., 1982; Boston College Law School, J.D. (with honors), 1988 — Law Clerk to Hon. U.S. District Judge William Terrell Hodges, M.D. Florida (1988-1990) — Admitted to Bar, 1988, Florida; U.S. District Court, Middle and Southern Districts of Florida; U.S. Court of Appeals, Eleventh Circuit; U.S. Supreme Court — Member Federal, American, and Hillsborough County Bar Associations; Hillsborough County Association of Criminal Defense Lawyers; Florida Association of Criminal Defense Lawyers

Jessica Kirkwood Alley — Stetson University, B.A., 1995; Florida State University, J.D. (with honors), 1999 — Admitted to Bar, 1999, Florida; U.S. District Court, Middle and Southern Districts of Florida — Member The Florida Bar; Hillsborough County Bar Association (Young Lawyers Division); Hillsborough Association for Women Lawyers

Michael H. Ashy — Florida State University, B.S., 1990; University of San Diego School of Law, M.I.B., 1995; J.D., 1995 — Admitted to Bar, 1996, Florida; U.S. District Court, Middle, Northern and Southern Districts of Florida

Karl J. Brandes — University of California, Berkeley, A.B., 1977; Golden Gate University School of Law, J.D., 1981 — Admitted to Bar, 1981, Florida; U.S. District Court, Middle and Southern Districts of Florida; U.S. Court of Appeals, Eleventh Circuit; U.S. Supreme Court — Member Federal, American and Hillsborough County Bar Associations; The Florida Bar — Arbitrator, U.S. District Court, Middle District of Florida — State and Federal Court Mediator

Michael P. Brundage — Florida State University, B.S. (with honors), 1981; Stetson University College of Law, J.D. (cum laude), 1986 — Admitted to Bar, 1986, Florida; U.S. District Court, Middle, Northern and Southern Districts of Florida; U.S. Court of Appeals, Eleventh Circuit; U.S. Tax Court — Member Federal and Hillsborough Colunty Bar Association; The Florida Bar; Tampa Bay Bankruptcy Bar Association; American Bankruptcy Institute — Board Certified in Business Bankruptcy Law by the American Board of Certification

Bret M. Feldman — University of Florida, B.A. (with honors), 1996; M.A./J.D. (with honors), 2000 — Admitted to Bar, 2000, Florida; U.S. District Court, Middle District of Florida — Member American and Hillsborough County Bar Associations; The Florida Bar — Board Certified in Construction Law by The Florida Bar Board of Legal Specialization

Robert R. Hearn — Vanderbilt University, B.A., 1990; Tulane University Law School, J.D. (cum laude), 1995 — Law Clerk to Hon. U.S. Magistrate Judge Mark A. Pizzo, U.S. District Court, Middle District of Florida — Admitted to Bar, 1995, Florida; U.S. District Court, Middle and Southern Districts of Florida; U.S. Court of Appeals, Eleventh Circuit — Member The Florida Bar; Hillsborough County Bar Association

Michael S. Hooker — University of Virginia, B.A. (with high distinction), 1976; Indiana University, M.A. (with high distinction), 1979; University of Virginia, J.D., 1981 — Admitted to Bar, 1981, Florida; U.S. District Court, Middle and Southern Districts of Florida; U.S. Court of Appeals for the Federal and Eleventh Circuits; U.S. Supreme Court — Member Federal and Hillsborough County Bar Associations; The Florida Bar

Lawrence P. Ingram — University of South Florida, B.A. (cum laude), 1987; Stetson University, J.D. (cum laude), 1990 — Admitted to Bar, 1990, Florida; U.S. District Court, Northern and Southern Districts of Florida; U.S. Supreme

Phelps Dunbar LLP, Tampa, FL (Continued)

Court — Member Federal, American and Hillsborough County Bar Associations; The Florida Bar; Academy of Florida Trial Lawyers

Matthew L. Litsky — Columbia University, B.A., 1987; New York Law School, J.D., 1991 — Admitted to Bar, 1992, New York; 1993, Florida; 2004, Texas; U.S. District Court, Middle, Northern and Southern Districts of Florida; U.S. District Court, District of the Virgin Islands; U.S. Court of Appeals, Fourth and Eleventh Circuits — Member New York State and Virgin Islands Bar Associations; The Florida Bar; State Bar of Texas — Resident Tampa, FL and London, United Kingdom Office

Dennis M. McClelland — Florida State University, B.S. (summa cum laude), 1993; University of Florida, J.D. (Order of the Coif), 1996 — Admitted to Bar, 1996, Florida; U.S. District Court, Middle, Northern and Southern Districts of Florida; U.S. Court of Appeals, Fifth and Eleventh Circuits; U.S. Supreme Court — Member American and Hillsborough County Bar Associations; The Florida Bar; Wage and Hour Defense Institute — Board Certified Specialist, Labor and Employment Law by The Florida Bar

Patricia A. McLean — Vanderbilt University, B.A., 1990; Loyola University New Orleans College of Law, J.D. (magna cum laude), 1997 — Admitted to Bar, 1997, Florida; 1998, U.S. District Court, Middle, Northern and Southern Districts of Florida; 2001, U.S. Court of Appeals, Eleventh Circuit — Member American and Hillsborough County Bar Associations; The Florida Bar — Resident Tampa, FL and London, United Kingdom Office

John D. Mullen — New College of the University of South Florida, B.A., 1989; New York University School of Law, J.D., 1994 — Admitted to Bar, 1994, Florida; U.S. District Court, Middle, Northern and Southern Districts of Florida; U.S. Court of Appeals, Eleventh Circuit; U.S. Supreme Court — Member The Florida Bar; Hillsborough County Bar Association

John E. Phillips — University of South Florida, B.A. (summa cum laude), 1986; Boston University School of Law, J.D. (cum laude), 1989 — Admitted to Bar, 1989, Florida; U.S. District Court, Middle, Northern and Southern Districts of Florida; U.S. Court of Appeals, Ninth and Eleventh Circuits — Member American and Hillsborough County Bar Associations; The Florida Bar

Reed L. Russell — Wake Forest University, B.S., 1991; The Catholic University of America, J.D. (Valedictorian), 1999 — Admitted to Bar, 1999, Florida; District of Columbia; U.S. District Court, Middle, Northern and Southern Districts of Florida; U.S. Court of Appeals, Fourth and Eleventh Circuits — Member American and Hillsborough County Bar Associations; The Florida Bar; Wage and Hour Defense Institute; Litigation Counsel of America — Former Major, U.S. Army National Guard; Veteran of Operation Iraqi Freedom

Seth M. Schimmel — Tufts University, B.A. (magna cum laude), 1990; Vanderbilt University Law School, J.D. (Order of the Coif), 1993 — Admitted to Bar, 1993, Florida; U.S. District Court, Middle and Southern Districts of Florida; U.S. Court of Appeals, Eleventh Circuit — Member American and Hillsborough County Bar Associations; The Florida Bar

Counsel

Sharon C. Britton — American University, B.A. (magna cum laude), 1989; Georgetown University Law Center, J.D. (cum laude), 1992 — Admitted to Bar, 1992, Florida; New York; U.S. District Court, Eastern and Southern Districts of New York; U.S. District Court, Middle District of Florida — Member The Florida Bar

Guy P. McConnell — University of Cincinnati, B.B.A. (summa cum laude), 1980; University of Michigan Law School, J.D., 1983 — Admitted to Bar, 1985, Florida; U.S. District Court, Middle District of Florida; U.S. District Court, Eastern District of Michigan — Member The Florida Bar; Hillsborough County Bar Association

Timothy P. Shusta — The University of Maine, B.A., 1974; Stetson University College of Law, J.D., 1984 — Admitted to Bar, 1984, Florida; U.S. District Court, Middle, Northern and Southern Districts of Florida; U.S. Court of Appeals, Eleventh Circuit; U.S. Supreme Court — Member American and Hillsborough County Bar Associations; The Florida Bar; Southeastern Admiralty Law Institute; The Maritime Law Association of the United States

(See listing under New Orleans, LA for additional information)

Vernis & Bowling of the Gulf Coast, P.A. (Tampa)

3031 North Rocky Point Drive West, Suite 185
Tampa, Florida 33607
   Telephone: 813-712-1700
   Fax: 813-712-1701
   E-Mail: info@florida-law.com
   www.florida-law.com

Civil Litigation, Insurance Law, Workers' Compensation, Premises Liability, Labor and Employment, Civil Rights, Commercial Litigation, Complex Litigation, Product Liability, Directors and Officers Liability, Errors and Omissions, Construction Law, Construction Defect, Environmental Liability, Personal and Commercial Vehicle, Appellate Practice, Admiralty and Maritime Law, Real Estate, Family Law, Elder Law

Firm Profile: Since 1970, VERNIS & BOWLING has represented individuals, businesses, professionals, insurance carriers, self-insureds, brokers, underwriters, agents, PEOs and insured. We provide cost effective, full service, legal representation that consistently exceeds the expectations of our clients. With 115 attorneys throughout 16 offices located in Florida, Georgia, Alabama, North Carolina and Mississippi the firm is able to provide the benefits of a large organization, including a management team, consistent policies and representation to ensure personal service and local representation to our clients.

Firm Members

Christopher Blain — 1974 — Lake Forest College, B.A., 1996; Barry University School of Law, J.D., 2002 — Admitted to Bar, 2003, Florida

Birdy V. Vanasupa — School of the Art Institute of Chicago, B.F.A., 1995; Thomas M. Cooley Law School, J.D., 2007 — Admitted to Bar, 2009, Florida; U.S. District Court, Middle District of Florida

Donna L. Kerfoot — 1948 — The University of Iowa, B.A. (with distinction), 1970; M.S.W., 1972; Stetson University College of Law, J.D. (cum laude), 1985 — Admitted to Bar, 1985, Florida; U.S. District Court, Middle District of Florida — Member Sarasota County Bar Association; The Florida Bar; Sarasota Bradenton Claims Association; Florida Defense Lawyers Association — Practice Areas: Workers' Compensation

R. Ryan Sainz — 1985 — University of South Florida, B.A., 2009; Barry University School of Law, J.D., 2013 — Barry University Book Award (Highest Honors): Trial Advocacy, Motions & Depositions — Admitted to Bar, 2013, Florida; U.S. District Court, Middle District of Florida — 2012 ABA Chicago Mock Trial National Champion

Bradley Mitseff   Courtney Newton

(See listing under Miami, FL for additional information)

Wicker Smith O'Hara McCoy & Ford P.A.

100 North Tampa Street, Suite 1800
Tampa, Florida 33602
   Telephone: 813-222-3939
   Fax: 813-222-3938
   www.wickersmith.com

(Coral Gables, FL Office*(See Miami listing): 2800 Ponce de Leon
   Boulevard, Suite 800, 33134)
   (Tel: 305-448-3939)
   (Fax: 305-441-1745)
(Fort Lauderdale, FL Office*: Sun Trust Center, 515 East Las Olas
   Boulevard, Suite 1400, 33301)
   (Tel: 954-847-4800)
   (Fax: 954-760-9353)
(Jacksonville, FL Office*: Bank of America, Suite 2700, 50 North Laura
   Street, 32202)
   (Tel: 904-355-0225)
   (Fax: 904-355-0226)
(Naples, FL Office*: Mercato, 9128 Strada Place, Suite 10200, 34108)
   (Tel: 239-552-5300)
   (Fax: 239-552-5399)

TAMPA FLORIDA

Wicker Smith O'Hara McCoy & Ford P.A., Tampa, FL
(Continued)

(Orlando, FL Office*: Bank of America Center, 390 North Orange Avenue, Suite 1000, 32801)
 (Tel: 407-843-3939)
 (Fax: 407-649-8118)
(West Palm Beach, FL Office*: Northbridge Centre, 515 North Flagler Drive, Suite 1600, 33401)
 (Tel: 561-689-3800)
 (Fax: 561-689-9206)

General Civil Litigation, General Civil Practice, State and Federal Courts, Accountant Malpractice, Accountants and Attorneys Liability, Administrative Law, Admiralty and Maritime Law, Agent and Brokers Errors and Omissions, Appellate Practice, Automobile, Aviation, Bad Faith, Class Actions, Commercial Litigation, Complex Litigation, Construction Litigation, Environmental Law, Estate Planning, Fraud, Hospital Malpractice, Insurance Coverage, Labor and Employment, Legal Malpractice, Medical Devices, Medical Malpractice, Nursing Home Liability, Pharmaceutical, Premises Liability, Probate, Product Liability, Professional Liability, Professional Malpractice, Special Investigative Unit Claims, Real Estate, Retail Liability, Toxic Torts, Transportation, Trucking Litigation, Trusts, Workers' Compensation, Multi-District Litigation, Sexual Abuse

Firm Profile: In 1952, Idus Q. Wicker and James A. Smith formed a partnership with the goal of providing legal services of exceptional quality to their clients. They remained partners until their retirement and life-long friends. The firm they founded has expanded to seven offices located throughout Florida in Miami, Fort Lauderdale, West Palm Beach, Orlando, Tampa, Naples and Jacksonville. Although the firm has changed in size and scope, the goal of providing exceptional legal representation has remained the same.

Clients turn to Wicker Smith when they have critical and complex litigation matters because of the firm's vast experience in complex litigation filed in State and Federal Courts. Numerous major corporations have selected Wicker Smith as national and regional counsel. Supporting the litigation team is a preeminent Appellate Department, which has appeared as appellate counsel in more than 1,200 reported decisions, including several landmark opinions issued by the Supreme Court of Florida.

Wicker Smith has recognized leaders in the defense of a wide range of litigation practice areas, including products liability, medical malpractice, pharmaceutical and medical devices, catastrophic aviation accidents, legal malpractice, accounting malpractice, nursing home claims, construction litigation, as well as a variety of general negligence matters. In all such matters, communication and attention to the client's specific needs are our highest priority. The backbone of our relationship with clients is built upon integrity and stability. We strive to establish long-term relationships with our clients, built upon a partnership of communication and trust. We achieve this objective by listening to our clients, understanding their businesses and developing legal solutions to best meet their individual needs.

Firm Members

James R. Brown — 1950 — The University of North Carolina, B.A., 1973; Cumberland School of Law of Samford University, J.D., 1976 — Admitted to Bar, 1976, Florida; 1977, U.S. District Court, Southern District of Florida including Trial Bar; 2003, U.S. District Court, Middle District of Florida — Member Hillsborough County Bar Association; The Florida Bar; Defense Research Institute; American Board of Trial Advocates; Florida Defense Lawyers Association — Practice Areas: Automobile Liability; Civil Litigation; Construction Law; Legal Malpractice; Premises Liability; Product Liability; Retail Liability; Transportation

Michael E. Reed — 1956 — Central State University, B.S., 1979; Amber University, M.B.A., 1985; Oklahoma City University, J.D., 1992 — Admitted to Bar, 1992, Florida; U.S. District Court, Middle District of Florida; 2003, U.S. District Court, Southern District of Florida; 2007, U.S. District Court, Northern District of Florida — Member The Florida Bar; Hillsborough County Bar Association; Defense Research Institute; Florida Defense Lawyers Association — Practice Areas: Agent and Brokers Errors and Omissions; Bad Faith; Civil Litigation; Commercial Litigation; Insurance Coverage; Medical Malpractice; Premises Liability; Product Liability; Retail Liability; Transportation

Wicker Smith O'Hara McCoy & Ford P.A., Tampa, FL
(Continued)

Erin M. Diaz — 1972 — West Virginia University, B.S. (summa cum laude), 1994; The University of North Dakota, J.D. (with honors), 2001 — Admitted to Bar, 2001, North Dakota; 2002, Minnesota; 2003, Florida; 2001, U.S. District Court, District of North Dakota; 2005, U.S. District Court, Middle District of Florida; 2007, U.S. District Court, Northern District of Florida — Florida Super Lawyers "Rising Star", 2009 — Captain, U.S. Air Force (inactive reserves) — Practice Areas: Civil Litigation; Medical Malpractice; Nursing Home Liability; Premises Liability; Product Liability; Transportation

Lindsay T. Brigman — 1978 — Auburn University, B.A. (summa cum laude), 2000; University of Florida, J.D., 2003 — Admitted to Bar, 2003, Florida; 2004, U.S. District Court, Southern District of Florida

Associates

Wendy B. Accardi — University of South Florida, B.A., 1995; Oklahoma City University School of Law, J.D. (cum laude), 2002 — Admitted to Bar, 2002, Florida

Meghan L. Dewitt — University of Florida, B.A. (cum laude), 2005; Stetson University College of Law, J.D. (magna cum laude), 2007 — Admitted to Bar, 2008, Florida

Jennifer D. Burby — University of Florida, B.A. (with honors), 2004; University of Florida, Levin College of Law, J.D., 2007 — Admitted to Bar, 2008, Florida

Christopher A. Cazin — University of Florida, B.A., 2002; Stetson University College of Law, J.D., 2007 — Admitted to Bar, 2007, Florida

Susanne M. Suiter — Metropolitan State College of Denver, B.S., 2002; Oklahoma City University School of Law, J.D. (magna cum laude), 2009 — Admitted to Bar, 2009, Florida

Brian P. Haskell — University of South Florida, B.A. (magna cum laude), 1999; Stetson University College of Law, J.D./M.B.A. (cum laude), 2002 — Admitted to Bar, 2002, Florida

Susan M. Wilson — Hillsborough Community College, A.S.N., 1977; University of Tampa, B.S.N., 1987; Notre Dame Law School, National Institute for Trial Advocacy, J.D., 1998 — Admitted to Bar, 1998, Indiana; 2002, Florida

Lisset G. Hanewicz — Florida International University, B.A., 1999; M.B.A., 2001; University of Florida College of Law, J.D. (cum laude), 2004 — Admitted to Bar, 2005, Florida

Sara J. Carter — Florida State University, B.S., 2000; Florida Coastal School of Law, J.D., 2005 — Admitted to Bar, 2005, Florida

William G. Hyland, Jr. — The University of Alabama, B.A., 1980; Cumberland School of Law of Samford University, J.D., 1983 — Admitted to Bar, 1984, Florida; Alabama; District of Columbia; 1993, Colorado

(See listing under Miami, FL for additional information)

The following firms also service this area.

Brasfield, Freeman, Goldis & Cash, P.A.
2553 First Avenue North
St. Petersburg, Florida 33713
 Telephone: 727-327-2258
 Fax: 727-328-1340
Mailing Address: P.O. Box 12349, St. Petersburg, FL 33733-2349

Insurance Defense, Trial Practice, Product Liability, Professional Liability, Premises Liability, Automobile Liability, Personal Injury, Wrongful Death, Construction Defect, Insurance Coverage

SEE COMPLETE LISTING UNDER ST. PETERSBURG, FLORIDA (21 MILES)

Dean, Ringers, Morgan and Lawton, P.A.
201 East Pine Street, Suite 1200
Orlando, Florida 32801
 Telephone: 407-422-4310
 Fax: 407-648-0233
Mailing Address: P.O. Box 2928, Orlando, FL 32802

Casualty, ERISA, Health, Life Insurance, Surety, Workers' Compensation, Civil Rights, Personal Injury, Product Liability, Wrongful Death, Medical Malpractice, Employment Practices Liability, Trucking Law, Police Misconduct, Business Law, Amusement and Recreation Law

SEE COMPLETE LISTING UNDER ORLANDO, FLORIDA (85 MILES)

FLORIDA

Shutts & Bowen LLP
201 South Biscayne Boulevard
Suite 1500
Miami, Florida 33131
  Telephone: 305-358-6300
  Fax: 305-381-9982
  Toll Free: 800-325-2892

Insurance Defense, Life and Health, General Liability, Fraud, Reinsurance, Disability

SEE COMPLETE LISTING UNDER MIAMI, FLORIDA (249 MILES)

Vernis & Bowling of the Gulf Coast, P.A.
696 1st Avenue, 1st Floor
St. Petersburg, Florida 33701
  Telephone: 727-443-3377
  Fax: 727-443-6828

Civil Litigation, Insurance Law, Workers' Compensation, Premises Liability, Labor and Employment, Civil Rights, Commercial Litigation, Complex Litigation, Product Liability, Directors and Officers Liability, Errors and Omissions, Construction Law, Construction Defect, Environmental Liability, Personal and Commercial Vehicle, Appellate Practice, Admiralty and Maritime Law, Real Estate, Family Law, Elder Law, Liability Defense, SIU/Fraud Litigation, Education Law (ESE/IDEA), Property and Casualty (Commercial and Personal Lines), Long-Haul Trucking Liability, Government Law, Public Law, Criminal, White Collar, Business Litigation

SEE COMPLETE LISTING UNDER CLEARWATER, FLORIDA (23 MILES)

Young, Bill, Roumbos & Boles, P.A.
Seville Tower, 7th Floor
226 South Palafox Place
Pensacola, Florida 32502
  Telephone: 850-432-2222
  Fax: 850-432-1444

Mailing Address: P.O. Drawer 1070, Pensacola, FL 32591-1070

Insurance Defense, Coverage Issues, Complex Litigation, Bad Faith, Product Liability, Medical Malpractice, Nursing Home Liability, Construction Defect, Premises Liability, General Liability, Automobile Liability

SEE COMPLETE LISTING UNDER PENSACOLA, FLORIDA (441 MILES)

TAVERNIER 2,136 Monroe Co.

Refer To

Vernis & Bowling of the Florida Keys, P.A.
Islamorada Professional Center
81990 Overseas Highway, Third Floor
Islamorada, Florida 33036
  Telephone: 305-664-4675
  Fax: 305-664-5414

Civil Litigation, Insurance Law, Workers' Compensation, Premises Liability, Labor and Employment, Civil Rights, Commercial Litigation, Complex Litigation, Product Liability, Directors and Officers Liability, Errors and Omissions, Construction Law, Construction Defect, Environmental Liability, Personal and Commercial Vehicle, Appellate Practice, Admiralty and Maritime Law, Real Estate, Family Law, Elder Law, Liability Defense, SIU/Fraud Litigation, Education Law (ESE/IDEA), Property and Casualty (Commercial and Personal Lines), Long-Haul Trucking Liability, Government Law, Public Law, Criminal, White Collar, Business Litigation

SEE COMPLETE LISTING UNDER ISLAMORADA, FLORIDA (10 MILES)

TITUSVILLE † 43,761 Brevard Co.

Refer To

Cameron, Hodges, Coleman, LaPointe & Wright, P.A.
111 North Magnolia Avenue, Suite 1350
Orlando, Florida 32801-2378
  Telephone: 407-841-5030
  Fax: 407-841-1727

Insurance Law

SEE COMPLETE LISTING UNDER ORLANDO, FLORIDA (40 MILES)

Refer To

Cameron, Hodges, Coleman, LaPointe & Wright, P.A.
150 South Palmetto Avenue, # 101
Daytona Beach, Florida 32114
  Telephone: 386-257-1755
  Fax: 386-252-5601

Insurance Law

SEE COMPLETE LISTING UNDER DAYTONA BEACH, FLORIDA (45 MILES)

VERO BEACH † 15,220 Indian River Co.

Refer To

Wiederhold & Moses, P.A.
560 Village Boulevard, Suite 240
West Palm Beach, Florida 33409-1963
  Telephone: 561-615-6775, 954-763-5630
  Fax: 561-615-7225

Mailing Address: P.O. Box 3918, West Palm Beach, FL 33402

Insurance Defense, Trial Practice

SEE COMPLETE LISTING UNDER WEST PALM BEACH, FLORIDA (70 MILES)

WEST PALM BEACH † 99,919 Palm Beach Co.

Billing, Cochran, Lyles, Mauro & Ramsey, P.A.

1601 Forum Place, Suite 400
West Palm Beach, Florida 33401
  Telephone: 561-659-5930
  Fax: 561-659-6173
  www.billingcochran.com

(Fort Lauderdale, FL Office*: 515 East Las Olas Boulevard, Suite 600, 33301)
  (Tel: 954-764-7150)
  (Fax: 954-764-7279)
  (Toll Free: 888-764-7150)

Established: 1977

General Civil Trial and Appellate Practice, State and Federal Courts, Personal Injury, Product Liability, Medical Liability, Dental Malpractice, Nursing Home Liability, Hospitals, Health Care, Workers' Compensation, Insurance Coverage, Litigation, Governmental Litigation, Funeral Service Liability Law

(See listing under Fort Lauderdale, FL for additional information)

Conroy Simberg

1801 Centrepark Drive East, Suite 200
West Palm Beach, Florida 33401
  Telephone: 561-697-8088
  Fax: 561-697-8664
  E-Mail: csg@conroysimberg.com
  www.conroysimberg.com

Insurance Defense, Appellate Practice, Insurance Coverage, Environmental Law, Governmental Liability, Civil Rights, Wrongful Termination, Americans with Disabilities Act, Sexual Harassment, Land Use, Commercial Law, Fire, Arson, Fraud, Fidelity and Surety, Automobile Liability, Admiralty and Maritime Law, Bad Faith, Employment Law, Self-Insured, Public Entities, Product Liability, Casualty, Excess and Reinsurance, Accident and Health, Workers' Compensation, Medical Malpractice, Class Actions, Construction Defect, Construction Litigation, First Party Matters, Premises Liability, Professional Liability, Intellectual Property

(See listing under Hollywood, FL for additional information)

WEST PALM BEACH   FLORIDA

Hightower, Stratton, Wilhelm, P.A.

330 Clematis Street, Suite 201
West Palm Beach, Florida 33401
　Telephone: 561-833-2022
　Fax: 561-833-2140
　www.hightowerlaw.net

(Miami, FL Office*: 4770 Biscayne Boulevard, Suite 1200, 33137)
　(Tel: 305-539-0909)
　(Fax: 305-530-0661)
　(Emer/After Hrs: 305-799-3054)
　(E-Mail: dale@hightowerlaw.net)
(Orlando, FL Office*: 151 Southhall Lane, Suite 140, 32751)
　(Tel: 407-352-4240)
　(Fax: 407-352-4201)
(St. Petersburg, FL Office*: 200 Central Avenue, Suite 450, 33701)
　(Tel: 727-209-1373)
　(Fax: 727-209-1383)

Assault & Battery Defense, Auto and Trucking Negligence, Commercial Litigation, Construction Claims, Environmental Law, Fraud/SIU (Special Investigative Unit), General Litigation, Homeowner's Insurance, Insurance Coverage and Bad Faith, Personal Injury and Wrongful Death, Premises Liability, Product Liability, Resorts & Leisure Liability, Retail Liability

Partners

Dale R. Hightower	Christopher S. Stratton
Lee A. Kantor	Scott A. Kantor

(See listings under Miami and Orlando, FL for additional information)

Morris & Morris, P.A.

777 South Flagler Drive, Suite 800-West Tower
West Palm Beach, Florida 33401
　Telephone: 561-838-9811
　Fax: 561-828-9351
　E-Mail: momorris@morris-morris.com
　www.morris-morris.com

Established: 2004

Insurance Law, Insurance Fraud, Subrogation, Appellate Practice, Special Investigation Unit Claims, Insurance Regulatory and Administrative Law, Insurance Mediation

Firm Profile: Morris & Morris, P.A. represents carriers in multi-state federal and state litigation involving loss-sensitive coverage issues and collections and defense, as well as administrative and regulatory matters. Appellate representation in the Firm's areas of concentration is also available.

Insurance Clients

Ascendant Commercial Insurance, Inc.	FCCI Insurance Company
Liberty Mutual Insurance Company	Guarantee Insurance Company
Ullico Casualty Company	Munich Re Group
	Wausau Underwriters Insurance Company

Mary Morris — University of Maryland, B.A., 1981; Golden Gate University, J.D., 1990 — Admitted to Bar, 1990, California; 1991, District of Columbia; 1993, Maryland; 1994, North Carolina; 1995, Florida; 1990, U.S. District Court, Northern District of California; 1990, U.S. Court of Appeals, Ninth Circuit; 1991, U.S. District Court, Eastern District of California; 1997, U.S. District Court, Southern District of Florida; 1998, U.S. District Court, Northern District of Florida; 2001, U.S. District Court, District of Maryland; 2012, U.S. District Court, Central District of California — Member Association of Certified Fraud Examiners — Practice Areas: Insurance Regulation; Administrative Law; Appeals

Michael R. Morris — University of Miami, B.S. (with honors), 1992; Ball State University, M.A., 2001; University of Miami, J.D., 1995; University of Edinburgh, LL.M. (with high distinction), 2008 — Admitted to Bar, 1995, Florida; 1997, U.S. District Court, Middle District of Florida; 2009, U.S. District Court, Southern District of Florida; 2011, U.S. Court of Appeals, Eleventh Circuit — Member Palm Beach County and Palm Beach Bar Associations; The Florida Bar — Author: "Bitzer's Model of the Rhetorical Situation as Examined Through Restoration Rhetoric of the Posse Comitatus and the Republic of Texas," 2001 — Practice Areas: Insurance Law; Appeals

Mitchel J. Krouse — City University of New York, B.S., 1980; New York Law School, J.D., 1983; University of Miami School of Law, LL.M., 1984 — Admitted to Bar, 1984, New York; 1989, Florida; 1985, U.S. District Court, Eastern and Southern Districts of New York; 1994, U.S. District Court, Southern District of Florida; 1997, U.S. District Court, Middle District of Florida; 1998, U.S. District Court, Northern District of Florida — Practice Areas: Insurance Law; Regulatory and Compliance; Administrative Law

(This firm is also listed in the Subrogation, Regulatory and Compliance section of this directory)

Paxton & Smith, P.A.

1615 Forum Place, Suite 500
West Palm Beach, Florida 33401
　Telephone: 561-684-2121
　Fax: 561-684-6855
　E-Mail: mail@paxsmith.com
　www.paxsmith.com

Established: 1977

Accountants and Attorneys Liability, Antitrust, Appellate Practice, Arbitration, Architects and Engineers, Automobile, Bad Faith, Bodily Injury, Business Law, Business Litigation, Church Law, Civil Litigation, Commercial General Liability, Commercial Litigation, Construction Accidents, Construction Defect, Construction Litigation, Contracts, Coverage Analysis, Coverage Issues, Defense Litigation, Design Professionals, Directors and Officers Liability, Discrimination, Employment Litigation, Engineering and Construction, Environmental Coverage, Environmental Law, Errors and Omissions, Examinations Under Oath, Excess and Surplus Lines, Extra-Contractual Litigation, Governmental Liability, Insurance Coverage, Insurance Defense, School Law, Negligent Security, Personal Injury, Premises Liability, Product Liability, Real Estate, Sexual Harassment, Subrogation, Surety, Toxic Torts, Wrongful Death, Child Abuse, Libel & Slander

Insurance Clients

Amerisure Insurance Company	First Mercury Insurance Company
Great American Custom Insurance Services	Horace Mann Insurance Group
Mid-Continent Group	Liberty Mutual Group
Teachers Insurance Company	The St. Paul Companies
Zurich U.S. Maryland Casualty	Travelers Insurance Companies

Non-Insurance Clients

Florida Power & Light Company	G.L. Homes
Ranger Construction Industries, Inc.	State of Florida, Division of Risk Management
Thomasville\Furniture Brands	

In Memoriam

Ralph B. Paxton — (1923-2009)

Retired

Morgan S. Bragg

FLORIDA WEST PALM BEACH

Paxton & Smith, P.A., West Palm Beach, FL (Continued)

Firm Members

Clark W. Smith — 1952 — University of Florida, B.A., 1974; J.D., 1977 — Admitted to Bar, 1977, Florida; 1977, U.S. District Court, Southern District of Florida — Member The Florida Bar; Palm Beach County Bar Association — Practice Areas: Construction Law; Commercial Litigation; Bodily Injury; Wrongful Death; Insurance Defense; Insurance Coverage; Bad Faith — E-mail: cws@paxsmith.com

Thomas B. Miller — 1959 — Auburn University, B.A., 1984; Cumberland School of Law of Samford University, J.D. (magna cum laude), 1988 — Admitted to Bar, 1988, Alabama; 1992, Florida; 1989, U.S. District Court, Middle, Northern and Southern Districts of Alabama; 1989, U.S. Court of Appeals, Eleventh Circuit; 1993, U.S. District Court, Southern District of Florida; 1997, U.S. District Court, Middle District of Florida — Member Alabama State Bar; The Florida Bar; Palm Beach County Bar Association — Practice Areas: Construction Litigation; Personal Injury; Insurance Law; Commercial Litigation — E-mail: tbm@paxsmith.com

Mark C. Charter — 1956 — Western Michigan University, B.S., 1979; Thomas M. Cooley Law School, J.D. (cum laude), 1982 — Admitted to Bar, 1982, Michigan; 1983, Florida; 1983, U.S. District Court, Western District of Michigan — Member American Bar Association; The Florida Bar; State Bar of Michigan — Practice Areas: Construction Litigation; Personal Injury; Automobile — E-mail: mcc@paxsmith.com

Of Counsel

Michele I. Nelson — 1952 — Miami Christian College, B.S., 1975; University of Miami School of Law, J.D. (with honors), 1984 — Admitted to Bar, 1984, Florida — Member The Florida Bar; Palm Beach County Bar Association; Florida Association for Women Laywers — Practice Areas: Construction Law; Appeals; Insurance Coverage — E-mail: min@paxsmith.com

Michael B. Davis — 1944 — Loyola University New Orleans, B.A., 1966; Northwestern University, J.D. (cum laude), 1969 — Admitted to Bar, 1969, Florida; 1970, U.S. District Court, Southern District of Florida; 1970, U.S. Court of Appeals, Fifth Circuit; 1975, U.S. Supreme Court; 1981, U.S. District Court, Middle and Northern Districts of Florida; 1981, U.S. Court of Appeals, Eleventh Circuit; 1983, U.S. Court of Appeals for the District of Columbia Circuit — Member The Florida Bar; Palm Beach County Bar Association — Practice Areas: Appeals; Civil Rights; Land Use; Antitrust; Commercial Law — E-mail: mbd@paxsmith.com

Powers McNalis Torres Teebagy Luongo

1601 Belvedere Road, Suite 500 South
West Palm Beach, Florida 33406
Telephone: 561-588-3000
Fax: 561-588-3705
www.powersmcnalis.com

(Miami Lakes, FL Office: The Promenade, 15100 NW 67th Avenue, Suite 410, 33014)
(Tel: 786-257-2830)

(Tampa, FL Office: One Urban Centre at Westshore, 4830 West Kennedy Boulevard., Suite 600, 33609)
(Tel: 813-769-3700)

Established: 1983

Arbitration, Arson, Bad Faith, Builders Risk, Examinations Under Oath, General Liability, Inland Marine, Subrogation, Appellate, Construction Litigation, Professional Liability, Fraud, Product Liability, Premises Liability, Negligent Security, Catastrophe Claims, Tort Defense, Auto and Transportation, Personal Injury/Wrongful Death, Coverage Analysis and Investigations

Firm Profile: For over 30 years Powers McNalis Torres Teebagy Luongo has been a leading South Florida law firm handling all aspects of Insurance Law, Civil Litigation, and Business Law. We provide a full range of legal services throughout the State of Florida to our domestic and international clients. Our mission is to render professional service of uncompromising quality to every client. The client's needs in each matter guide the actions we take on the client's behalf. The client's complete satisfaction is our goal.

Powers McNalis Torres Teebagy Luongo provides full representation to our clients. We represent our clients before federal, state and local courts, both at

Powers McNalis Torres Teebagy Luongo, West Palm Beach, FL (Continued)

the trial and appellate levels. We also represent clients before administrative agencies and in alternative dispute resolution. Our firm understands the challenges clients confront when legal issues arise, and we are aware of the need to maintain close, regular contact.

Our clientele encompasses insurance carriers, brokers, underwriters, agents and other businesses. Although a major part of our practice involves the insurance industry, we serve numerous and varied clients in a wide variety of legal matters. Our clients include established companies or organizations, as well as emerging and start-up companies engaged in traditional and progressive ventures.

Our areas of practice for both personal and commercial lines include fraud investigation and defense, arson investigation and defense, examinations under oath, general property coverage and defense, catastrophe/large loss claims, appraisals and arbitration, liability coverage and defense, insurance bad faith, construction litigation, environmental litigation, appeals, recovery/subrogation, inland marine, cargo and transportation coverage and litigation, commercial litigation, and business counseling.

Insurance Clients

Allstate Insurance Company
Arch Specialty Insurance Company
Capacity Insurance Company
Chubb Group of Insurance Companies
FCCI Insurance Group
Florida Family Insurance Company
Hermitage Insurance Company
Homeowners Choice, Inc.
Lloyd's and London Market Underwriters
St. Johns Insurance Company, Inc.
State Farm Insurance Company
Utica National Insurance Group
American Mercury Insurance Company
Chartis Insurance Private Client Group
Elements Property Insurance Company
Florida Farm Bureau Casualty Insurance Company
Ironshore Insurance, Ltd.
Mercury Insurance Group
Nationwide Insurance Companies
Seneca Insurance Company
Tower Group
Zurich American Insurance Company

Retired

Brian C. Powers — 1953 — University of Miami, B.B.A., 1974; J.D., 1977 — Admitted to Bar, 1977, Florida; 1977, U.S. District Court, Southern District of Florida including Trial Bar; 2001, U.S. District Court, Middle District of Florida — Member Federal, American (Torts and Insurance Practice Section; Property Insurance Sub-committee) and Illinois State Bar Associations; The Florida Bar; Palm Beach County Claims Associaiton; International Association of Arson Investigators; Florida Defense Lawyers Association; Defense Research Institute

Partners

Daniel M. McNalis — 1952 — University of Illinois, B.S. (cum laude), 1974; The John Marshall Law School, J.D., 1979 — Admitted to Bar, 1979, Illinois; 1986, Florida; 1979, U.S. District Court, Northern District of Illinois; 1986, U.S. District Court, Southern District of Florida; 2001, U.S. District Court, Middle District of Florida — Member Federal, American (Torts and Insurance Practice Section), Illinois State, Palm Beach County and Chicago Bar Associations; The Florida Bar (Advisory Committee on Arson Prevention); International Association of Arson Investigators

Anna D. Torres — 1964 — San Diego State University, B.A., 1985; Stanford Law School, J.D., 1988 — Admitted to Bar, 1988, California; 1996, Florida; 1989, U.S. District Court, Southern District of California; 1994, U.S. Court of Appeals, Ninth Circuit; 1996, U.S. District Court, Southern District of Florida; 1999, U.S. District Court, Middle and Northern Districts of Florida; 2003, U.S. Court of Appeals for the Federal and Eleventh Circuits — Member American Bar Association; Claims and Litigation Management Alliance; Loss Executives Association; National Association of Surplus Lines Offices; Property and Liability Resource Bureau — Languages: Spanish

Steven C. Teebagy — 1966 — The University of Texas, B.B.A., 1991; California Western School of Law, J.D. (cum laude), 1995 — Admitted to Bar, 1995, Florida; 2001, U.S. District Court, Middle District of Florida — Member The Florida Bar; Palm Beach County Bar Association — U.S. Marine Corp Reserve, 1985-1991

Stephanie H. Luongo — 1960 — Fashion Institute of Technology, State University of New York, A.A.S., 1980; Emerson College, B.S. (cum laude), 1982; Simmons College, M.S., 1985; New England School of Law, J.D. (with honors), 1992 — Admitted to Bar, 1992, Massachusetts; 2002, Florida; 1995, U.S. District Court, District of Massachusetts; 1995, U.S. Court of Appeals, First Circuit; 2004, U.S. District Court, Southern District of Florida; 2004,

WEST PALM BEACH   FLORIDA

Powers McNalis Torres Teebagy Luongo, West Palm Beach, FL (Continued)

U.S. Court of Appeals, Eleventh Circuit; 2004, U.S. Supreme Court; 2005, U.S. District Court, Middle District of Florida; 2006, U.S. District Court, Northern District of Florida — Member Federal, American and Palm Beach County Bar Associations; The Florida Bar; Claims and Litigation Management Alliance; South Florida Claims Association; Florida Association of Women Lawyers

Deidrie A. Buchanan — 1981 — Boston University, B.A. (cum laude), 2003; Boston University School of Law, J.D., 2006 — Admitted to Bar, 2006, Florida; 2008, U.S. District Court, Middle and Southern Districts of Florida

Junior Partners

Courtney A. Siders — 1977 — The University of Iowa, B.B.A. (with honors), 2000; DePaul University College of Law, J.D. (with honors), 2003 — Admitted to Bar, 2003, Illinois; 2010, Florida; 2011, U.S. District Court, Middle, Northern and Southern Districts of Florida; U.S. Court of Appeals, Eleventh Circuit — Member The Florida Bar; Palm Beach County Bar Association (Young Lawyers Division); National Association of Subrogation Professionals

Inlv Gabay — 1980 — York University, B.A. (with honors), 2003; Thomas M. Cooley Law School, J.D. (cum laude), 2006 — Admitted to Bar, 2007, Florida; 2011, District of Columbia; 2012, New York; 2008, U.S. District Court, Southern District of Florida; 2009, U.S. District Court, Middle District of Florida — Languages: Hebrew

Crystalin C. Medeiros — 1980 — Northeastern University, B.A. (Dean's List), 2003; St. Thomas University School of Law, J.D. (magna cum laude, Dean's List), 2008 — Political Science Honor Society; Phi Delta Phi — Admitted to Bar, 2008, Florida; 2014, U.S. District Court, Southern District of Florida

Sonneborn Rutter & Cooney, P.A.

1400 Centrepark Boulevard, Suite 400
West Palm Beach, Florida 33401-7403
Telephone: 561-684-2000
Fax: 561-684-2312
E-Mail: bws@srcke.com

Established: 1983

Civil Trial Practice, Civil Litigation, State and Federal Courts, Insurance Defense, Health Care, Health Care Professional Licensure Defense, Medical Malpractice Defense, Medical Liability, Liability Defense, Product Liability, Dental Malpractice, Hospital Malpractice, Toxic Substances, Mass Tort, Casualty, Appellate Practice, Family Law, Mediation

Firm Profile: Sonneborn Rutter & Cooney,PA is located in West Palm Beach serving clients throughout Florida. Legal counsel is offered in all areas of litigation, with special emphasis on medical, legal, professional malpractice, nursing home, ACLF liability, medical staff disputes, employment issues, administrative law and professional licensing proceedings. Members of the firm also practice in areas of HIPPA Compliance and Hospital transactional law. The firm provides transactional representation to hospitals and physicians regarding third party contracting and functions as general counsel to a number of hospitals and corporations.

The firm's attorneys offer years of experience with extensive trial practice. This quality is supported by a staff which includes nurses, Certified Paralegals and experienced legal assistants.

Insurance Clients

Chubb Group	The Doctors Company
Farmers Insurance Group	First Professionals Insurance Company
Florida Doctors Insurance Company	Hanover Insurance Company
Medical Assurance Company, Inc.	Scottsdale Insurance Company
Western Indemnity Insurance Company	Zurich American Specialties

Non-Insurance Clients

Bethesda Hospital	Boca Raton Regional Hospital
Coastal Group	Hendry Regional Corporation Health
TeamHealth	

Sonneborn Rutter & Cooney, P.A., West Palm Beach, FL (Continued)

Partners/Shareholders

Barbara W. Sonneborn — 1946 — Washington University, B.A., 1968; M.A., 1969; University of Miami, J.D., 1976 — Kappa Delta Pi; Mortar Board — Admitted to Bar, 1976, Florida; 1977, U.S. District Court, Southern District of Florida; U.S. Court of Appeals, Fifth Circuit — Member American and Palm Beach County Bar Associations; The Florida Bar (Executive Council, Trial Lawyers Section); Florida Association of Hospital Attorneys; International Academy of Trial Lawyers; American Board of Trial Advocates; Florida Defense Lawyers Association — Co-Author: "The Hospital's Risk from Innkeeper to Insurer," Florida Bar Journal, Volume 60, No. 7, Pages 35-37 July-August, 1986 — Board Certified Civil Trial Lawyer by The Florida Bar; Board Certified in Civil Trial Advocacy by National Board of Trial Advocacy, Florida Bar Board of Legal Specialization and Education — Practice Areas: Civil Litigation; Medical Malpractice Defense; Hospital Law; Health Care; Health Care Professional Licensure Defense; Insurance Defense; Employment Law; Product Liability Defense — E-mail: bws@srcke.com

R. William Rutter, Jr. — 1942 — University of Florida, B.S., 1964; M.A., 1965; National Judicial College, University of Nevada, Reno, Graduate, 1979; University of Florida, J.D., 1967 — Phi Alpha Delta — Admitted to Bar, 1968, Florida; 1969, U.S. District Court, Southern District of Florida; 1969, U.S. Court of Appeals, Fifth Circuit — Member American and Palm Beach County Bar Associations; The Florida Bar (Judicial Administration Rules Committee, 1986-1987) — County Attorney, Palm Beach County, 1972-1978; Circuit Court Judge, 1978-1988; Administrative Judge, Civil Division, 1985-1987 and Chief Judge, 1987-1988, Circuit Court, Palm Beach County — Practice Areas: Civil Litigation; Probate; Family Law; Mediation; Alternative Dispute Resolution; Contracts — E-mail: rwr@srcke.com

Rosemary Cooney — 1954 — University of Virginia, B.A. (with distinction), 1976; Stetson University, J.D. (cum laude), 1978 — Sigma Nu Phi — Admitted to Bar, 1979, Florida; 1979, U.S. District Court, Southern District of Florida — Member American and Palm Beach County Bar Associations; The Florida Bar; Association of Trial Lawyers of America; Florida Defense Lawyers Association; Florida Medical Malpractice Claims Council — Certified Circuit Mediator by the Florida Supreme Court — Practice Areas: Civil Litigation; Medical Malpractice Defense; Family Law; Insurance Defense; Product Liability Defense — E-mail: rc@srcke.com

Partners

Michael D. Burt — 1960 — The Ohio State University, B.A. (Phi Delta Kappa), 1982; Case Western Reserve University, J.D., 1985 — Admitted to Bar, 1985, Ohio (Inactive); 1987, Florida; 1986, U.S. Air Force Court of Appeals; U.S. Air Force Court of Military Review; 1990, U.S. Supreme Court; 1996, U.S. District Court, Middle District of Florida; 2005, U.S. District Court, Southern District of Florida — Member American and Palm Beach County Bar Associations — Air Force Commendation Medals (2); National Defense Service Medal (Operation Desert Shield/Desert Storm); Meritorious Service Medal (MSM) — Florida Board Certified Civil Trial Law — Commissioned Officer, U.S. Air Force (1985-1994) — Practice Areas: Civil Litigation; Medical Malpractice Defense; Hospital Law; Product Liability Defense; Health Care Professional Licensure Defense; Employment Law — E-mail: mburt@srcke.com

William T. Viergever — University of Central Florida, B.S., 1993; University of Miami, J.D. (cum laude), 1996 — Admitted to Bar, 1996, Florida; 1998, California; U.S. District Court, Middle and Southern Districts of Florida; U.S. Court of Appeals, Eleventh Circuit; U.S. Supreme Court — Member The Florida Bar; State Bar of California — Practice Areas: Appellate Practice; Civil Litigation; Contracts; Product Liability — E-mail: wtv@srcke.com

Senior Attorneys

Sharon (Minnie) L. Urbanek — 1950 — West Liberty State College, B.S. Business Admin., 1998; West Virginia University, J.D., 2002 — Admitted to Bar, 2002, West Virginia (Inactive); 2004, Florida; 2005, U.S. District Court, Southern District of Florida — Member The Florida Bar; Palm Beach County Bar Association — Practice Areas: Civil Litigation; Medical Malpractice; Health Care; Insurance Defense; Liability Defense; Hospital Law — E-mail: minnieu@srcke.com

Steven M. Lury — 1958 — University of Rhode Island, B.A., 1980; George Mason University, J.D., 1987 — Admitted to Bar, 1987, Florida; U.S. District Court, District of Florida; U.S. Court of Appeals, Eleventh Circuit — Member American and Palm Beach County Bar Associations; The Florida Bar; American Society of Law and Medicine; Defense Research Institute — Practice Areas: Civil Litigation; Medical Malpractice; Health Care; Nursing

Sonneborn Rutter & Cooney, P.A., West Palm Beach, FL (Continued)

Home Litigation; Insurance Defense; Liability Defense — E-mail: slury@srcke.com

John D. Heffling — 1960 — University of Florida, B.A., 1981; Rollins College, M.S., 1982; University of Florida, J.D., 1985 — Admitted to Bar, 1985, Florida; 1995, U.S. District Court, Middle and Southern Districts of Florida — Member The Florida Bar; Palm Beach County Bar Association — Practice Areas: Civil Trial Practice; Business Litigation — E-mail: jheffling@srcke.com

Associates

Lisa M. Munoz — 1979 — Florida State University, B.A., 2000; St. Thomas School of Law, J.D., 2003 — Admitted to Bar, 2003, Florida; 2005, U.S. District Court, Southern District of Florida — Member The Florida Bar; Palm Beach County Bar Association; Hispanic Bar Association — Languages: Spanish, Portuguese — Practice Areas: Medical Malpractice; Wrongful Death; Automobile Liability; Civil Litigation — E-mail: lmunoz@srcke.com

Timothy D. Kenison — 1976 — University of Florida, B.A., 1997; Temple University, J.D., 2003 — Admitted to Bar, 2003, Pennsylvania; 2004, Florida; U.S. District Court, Southern District of Florida — Member The Florida Bar; Palm Beach County Bar Association — Practice Areas: Civil Litigation; Insurance Defense; Medical Malpractice Defense; Premises Liability — E-mail: tkenison@srcke.com

Wicker Smith O'Hara McCoy & Ford P.A.

Northbridge Centre
515 North Flagler Drive, Suite 1600
West Palm Beach, Florida 33401
Telephone: 561-689-3800
Fax: 561-689-9206
www.wickersmith.com

(Coral Gables, FL Office*(See Miami listing): 2800 Ponce de Leon Boulevard, Suite 800, 33134)
(Tel: 305-448-3939)
(Fax: 305-441-1745)

(Fort Lauderdale, FL Office*: Sun Trust Center, 515 East Las Olas Boulevard, Suite 1400, 33301)
(Tel: 954-847-4800)
(Fax: 954-760-9353)

(Jacksonville, FL Office*: Bank of America, Suite 2700, 50 North Laura Street, 32202)
(Tel: 904-355-0225)
(Fax: 904-355-0226)

(Naples, FL Office*: Mercato, 9128 Strada Place, Suite 10200, 34108)
(Tel: 239-552-5300)
(Fax: 239-552-5399)

(Orlando, FL Office*: Bank of America Center, 390 North Orange Avenue, Suite 1000, 32801)
(Tel: 407-843-3939)
(Fax: 407-649-8118)

(Tampa, FL Office*: 100 North Tampa Street, Suite 1800, 33602)
(Tel: 813-222-3939)
(Fax: 813-222-3938)

General Civil Practice, State and Federal Courts, Appellate Practice, Medical Malpractice, Hospital Malpractice, Nursing Home Liability, Aviation, Professional Liability, Accountants and Attorneys Liability, Product Liability, Pharmaceutical, Medical Devices, Premises Liability, Special Investigative Unit Claims, Fraud, Toxic Torts, Environmental Law, Labor and Employment, Construction Litigation, Workers' Compensation, Commercial Litigation, Admiralty and Maritime Law, Automobile, Bad Faith, Complex Litigation, Insurance Coverage, Real Estate, Multi-District Litigation, Sexual Abuse, Trusts, Estate Planning

Firm Profile: In 1952, Idus Q. Wicker and James A. Smith formed a partnership with the goal of providing legal services of exceptional quality to their clients. They remained partners until their retirement and life-long friends. The firm they founded has expanded to seven offices located throughout Florida in Miami, Fort Lauderdale, West Palm Beach, Orlando, Tampa, Naples and Jacksonville. Although the firm has changed in size and scope, the goal of providing exceptional legal representation has remained the same.

Clients turn to Wicker Smith when they have critical and complex litigation matters because of the firm's vast experience in complex litigation filed in State and Federal Courts. Numerous major corporations have selected Wicker Smith as national and regional counsel. Supporting the litigation team is a preeminent Appellate Department, which has appeared as appellate counsel in more than 1,200 reported decisions, including several landmark opinions issued by the Supreme Court of Florida.

Wicker Smith has recognized leaders in the defense of a wide range of litigation practice areas, including products liability, medical malpractice, pharmaceutical and medical devices, catastrophic aviation accidents, legal malpractice, accounting malpractice, nursing home claims, construction litigation, as well as a variety of general negligence matters. In all such matters, communication and attention to the client's specific needs are our highest priority. The backbone of our relationship with clients is built upon integrity and stability. We strive to establish long-term relationships with our clients, built upon a partnership of communication and trust. We achieve this objective by listening to our clients, understanding their businesses and developing legal solutions to best meet their individual needs.

Firm Members

J.J. Wicker, II — 1950 — University of Florida, B.S., 1972; Samford University, M.B.A., 1975; Cumberland School of Law of Samford University, J.D., 1975 — Admitted to Bar, 1976, Florida; 1983, U.S. District Court, Southern District of Florida including Trial Bar; 1982, U.S. Court of Appeals, Eleventh Circuit; 2008, U.S. District Court, Middle District of Florida — Member American and Palm Beach County Bar Associations; The Florida Bar; USLAW Network: Transportation Rapid Response; Florida Defense Lawyers Association; Defense Research Institute; American Board of Trial Advocates; Transportation Lawyers Association — Florida Trend Legal Elite 2005 — Practice Areas: Automobile Liability; Bad Faith; Civil Litigation; Construction Law; Insurance Coverage; Medical Malpractice; Premises Liability; Product Liability; Professional Liability; Retail Liability; Transportation

Adam W. Rhys — 1962 — Trinity College, B.A., 1984; Brooklyn Law School, J.D., 1992 — Admitted to Bar, 1993, New York; New Jersey; 1997, Florida; 1993, U.S. District Court, Eastern District of New York; 2006, U.S. District Court, Southern District of Florida — Member The Florida Bar; New York State and Palm Beach County Bar Associations; Florida Defense Lawyers Association; Defense Research Institute — Practice Areas: Civil Litigation; Medical Malpractice; Premises Liability

Mark H. Ruff, Jr — 1977 — Flagler College, B.A. (cum laude), 1999; University of Florida, J.D., 2002 — Admitted to Bar, 2002, Florida; 2003, U.S. District Court, Southern District of Florida; 2006, U.S. District Court, Northern District of Florida — Practice Areas: Automobile Liability; Civil Litigation; Construction Law; Premises Liability; Product Liability; Retail Liability; Transportation

Antonia M. Smillova — 1965 — University of Sofia, M.Ed. (with high honors), 1991; University of Florida, M.S.N. (with high honors), 1998; J.D. (with high honors), 2003 — Admitted to Bar, 2003, Florida — Florida Super Lawyers "Rising Stars", 2010-2011 — Languages: Bulgarian, Russian — Practice Areas: Accountant Malpractice; Civil Litigation; Legal Malpractice; Medical Malpractice; Premises Liability

Amy M. DeMartino — 1976 — Florida Atlantic University, B.A. (cum laude), 1997; University of Florida, J.D. (with honors), 2001 — Admitted to Bar, 2002, Florida; 2003, U.S. District Court, Southern District of Florida; 2009, U.S. District Court, Middle District of Florida — Practice Areas: Civil Litigation; Construction Law; Premises Liability

Rachel Studley — 1969 — Florida International University, B.A. (cum laude), 1999; University of Florida, J.D., 2002 — Admitted to Bar, 2002, Florida; 2006, U.S. District Court, Southern District of Florida; 2008, U.S. District Court, Middle District of Florida — Practice Areas: Automobile Liability; Civil Litigation; Premises Liability; Professional Liability; Retail Liability; Transportation

Traci L. Glickman — Pace University, B.S. (summa cum laude), 1994; J.D., 1998 — Admitted to Bar, 1998, Connecticut; 1999, New York; 2002, Florida; 2004, U.S. District Court, Southern District of Florida

Associates

Concetta G. Camacho — University of Florida, B.A. (cum laude), 2004; J.D. (cum laude), 2007 — Admitted to Bar, 2007, Florida — Languages: Italian

WEST PALM BEACH   FLORIDA

Wicker Smith O'Hara McCoy & Ford P.A., West Palm Beach, FL (Continued)

Nicholas S. Seamster — Florida State University, B.S., 2003; St. Thomas University, J.D. (cum laude), 2008 — Admitted to Bar, 2008, Florida

Michael J. Stewart — University of Central Florida, B.S.B.A. (summa cum laude), 2007; University of Florida, Levin College of Law, J.D. (cum laude), 2010 — Admitted to Bar, 2010, Florida

Heather L. Stover — University of Florida, B.A., 2007; The George Washington University Law School, J.D., 2010 — Admitted to Bar, 2011, Florida

Tara L. Stephens — University of Kentucky, B.A. (magna cum laude), 2008; University of Florida College of Law, J.D., 2011 — Admitted to Bar, 2011, Florida; 2012, Kentucky

Amanda Ritucci — University of Florida, B.A. (summa cum laude), 2008; College of William & Mary, Marshall-Wythe School of Law, J.D., 2011 — Admitted to Bar, 2011, Florida

(See listing under Miami, FL for additional information)

Wiederhold & Moses, P.A.

560 Village Boulevard, Suite 240
West Palm Beach, Florida 33409-1963
   Telephone: 561-615-6775, 954-763-5630
   Fax: 561-615-7225

Established: 1982

Insurance Defense, Trial Practice

Insurance Clients

Agricultural Excess and Surplus Insurance Company
American Security Insurance Company
Berkley Risk Administrators Company, LLC
Carolina Casualty Insurance Company
Florida Farm Bureau General Insurance Company
GuideOne Insurance
Midlands Claim Administrators, Inc.
Ohio Casualty Group
Reliant American General Agency
Scottsdale Insurance Company
Sedgwick Claims Management Services, Inc.
Specialty Claims Services, Inc.
U.S. Security Insurance Company, Inc.
American Claims Services, Inc.
American International Group, Inc.
American Southern Insurance Company
Berkley Risk Services, LLC
Canal Insurance Company
Claims Management Services, Inc.
Commercial Underwriters Insurance Company
Great American Insurance Company
Nationwide Insurance
Naughton Insurance, Inc.
Professional Claims Managers, Inc.
St. Paul Fire and Marine Insurance Company
Southern Farm Bureau Casualty Group
Specialty Risk Services
Western and Southern Life Insurance Company

Local Counsel For

R.J. Reynolds Tobacco Company

Non-Insurance Clients

Brink's, Inc.
Fiberglass Water Flumes
Palm Beach Newspapers
Catalfumo Construction & Development, Inc.
Pat Salmon & Sons

Firm Members

John P. Wiederhold — 1945 — University of Florida, B.A./B.S., 1967; J.D., 1969 — Admitted to Bar, 1970, Florida; 1972, U.S. District Court, Southern District of Florida; 1973, U.S. Court of Appeals, Fifth Circuit; 1981, U.S. Court of Appeals, Eleventh Circuit — Member Federal, American and Palm Beach County Bar Associations; The Florida Bar — Florida Bar Board Certified Civil Trial Lawyer, 1986 — Captain, U.S. Army, 1970-1972

Robert D. Moses — 1949 — University of South Florida, B.A., 1971; University of Florida, J.D., 1974 — Admitted to Bar, 1974, Florida; 1975, U.S. District Court, Northern District of Florida; 1978, U.S. District Court, Southern District of Florida — Member American and Palm Beach County Bar Associations; The Florida Bar — Florida Bar Board Certified Civil Trial Lawyer

Wiederhold & Moses, P.A., West Palm Beach, FL (Continued)

Associates

Gregory A. Kummerlen — 1977 — University of Central Florida, B.A., 1999; University of Florida, J.D., 2002 — Admitted to Bar, 2002, Florida; 2004, U.S. District Court, Southern District of Florida — Member The Florida Bar; Palm Beach County Bar Association

Brett M. Waronicki

The following firms also service this area.

Catri, Holton, Kessler & Kessler, P.A.
The Litigation Building, Third Floor
633 South Andrews Avenue
Fort Lauderdale, Florida 33301
   Telephone: 954-463-8593
   Fax: 954-462-1303

Insurance Defense, Trial and Appellate Practice, Insurance Coverage, Self-Insured, General Liability, Product Liability, Automobile Liability, Premises Liability, Construction Liability, Guardian and Conservatorships, Probate, Business Litigation, Commercial Litigation, Arbitration, Mediation

SEE COMPLETE LISTING UNDER FORT LAUDERDALE, FLORIDA (40 MILES)

Fertig & Gramling
200 Southeast 13th Street
Fort Lauderdale, Florida 33316
   Telephone: 954-763-5020, 305-945-6250 (Miami)
   Fax: 954-763-5412

Coverage Issues, Admiralty and Maritime Law, Casualty, Fraud, Property, Reinsurance, Errors and Omissions, Directors and Officers Liability

SEE COMPLETE LISTING UNDER FORT LAUDERDALE, FLORIDA (40 MILES)

Leiter & Belsky, P.A.
707 Southeast Third Avenue, Third Floor
Fort Lauderdale, Florida 33316
   Telephone: 954-462-3116
   Fax: 954-761-8990

Insurance Defense, Insurance Coverage, Appellate Practice, General Liability, Bad Faith, Automobile Liability, Product Liability, Construction Claims, Construction Defect, Construction Litigation, Insurance Claim Analysis and Evaluation, Insurance Coverage Determination, Insurance Coverage Litigation, Insurance Law, Insurance Litigation, Litigation, No-Fault, Personal Injury Protection (PIP), Premises Liability, Primary and Excess Insurance, Professional Liability, Self-Insured, Self-Insured Defense, Trial and Appellate Practice

SEE COMPLETE LISTING UNDER FORT LAUDERDALE, FLORIDA (40 MILES)

Shutts & Bowen LLP
201 South Biscayne Boulevard
Suite 1500
Miami, Florida 33131
   Telephone: 305-358-6300
   Fax: 305-381-9982
   Toll Free: 800-325-2892

Insurance Defense, Life and Health, General Liability, Fraud, Reinsurance, Disability

SEE COMPLETE LISTING UNDER MIAMI, FLORIDA (66 MILES)

Vernis & Bowling of Palm Beach, P.A.
884 U.S. Highway #1
North Palm Beach, Florida 33408-5408
   Telephone: 561-775-9822
   Fax: 561-775-9821

Civil Litigation, Insurance Law, Workers' Compensation, Premises Liability, Labor and Employment, Civil Rights, Commercial Litigation, Complex Litigation, Product Liability, Directors and Officers Liability, Errors and Omissions, Construction Law, Construction Defect, Environmental Liability, Personal and Commercial Vehicle, Appellate Practice, Admiralty and Maritime Law, Real Estate, Family Law, Elder Law, Liability Defense, SIU/Fraud Litigation, Education Law (ESE/IDEA), Property and Casualty (Commercial and Personal Lines), Long-Haul Trucking Liability, Government Law, Public Law, Criminal, White Collar, Business Litigation

SEE COMPLETE LISTING UNDER NORTH PALM BEACH, FLORIDA (9 MILES)

FLORIDA

Young, Bill, Roumbos & Boles, P.A.
One Biscayne Tower, Suite 3195
2 South Biscayne Boulevard
Miami, Florida 33131
  Telephone: 305-222-7720
  Fax: 305-492-7729

Insurance Defense, Coverage Issues, Complex Litigation, Bad Faith, Product Liability, Medical Malpractice, Nursing Home Liability, Construction Defect, Premises Liability, General Liability, Automobile Liability

SEE COMPLETE LISTING UNDER MIAMI, FLORIDA (71 MILES)

WINTER PARK   27,852 Orange Co.

Refer To
Cameron, Hodges, Coleman, LaPointe & Wright, P.A.
111 North Magnolia Avenue, Suite 1350
Orlando, Florida 32801-2378
  Telephone: 407-841-5030
  Fax: 407-841-1727

Insurance Law

SEE COMPLETE LISTING UNDER ORLANDO, FLORIDA (3 MILES)

Refer To
Vernis & Bowling of Central Florida, P.A.
1450 South Woodland Boulevard, Fourth Floor
DeLand, Florida 32720
  Telephone: 386-734-2505
  Fax: 386-734-3441

Civil Litigation, Insurance Law, Workers' Compensation, Premises Liability, Labor and Employment, Civil Rights, Commercial Litigation, Complex Litigation, Product Liability, Directors and Officers Liability, Errors and Omissions, Construction Law, Construction Defect, Environmental Liability, Personal and Commercial Vehicle, Appellate Practice, Admiralty and Maritime Law, Real Estate, Family Law, Elder Law, Liability Defense, SIU/Fraud Litigation, Education Law (ESE/IDEA), Property and Casualty (Commercial and Personal Lines), Long-Haul Trucking Liability, Government Law, Public Law, Criminal, White Collar, Business Litigation

SEE COMPLETE LISTING UNDER DAYTONA BEACH, FLORIDA (38 MILES)

GEORGIA

CAPITAL: ATLANTA

COUNTIES AND COUNTY SEATS

County	County Seat	County	County Seat	County	County Seat
Appling	Baxley	Evans	Claxton	Newton	Covington
Atkinson	Pearson	Fannin	Blue Ridge	Oconee	Watkinsville
Bacon	Alma	Fayette	Fayetteville	Oglethorpe	Lexington
Baker	Newton	Floyd	Rome	Paulding	Dallas
Baldwin	Milledgeville	Forsyth	Cumming	Peach	Fort Valley
Banks	Homer	Franklin	Carnesville	Pickens	Jasper
Barrow	Winder	Fulton	Atlanta	Pierce	Blackshear
Bartow	Cartersville	Gilmer	Ellijay	Pike	Zebulon
Ben Hill	Fitzgerald	Glascock	Gibson	Polk	Cedartown
Berrien	Nashville	Glynn	Brunswick	Pulaski	Hawkinsville
Bibb	Macon	Gordon	Calhoun	Putnam	Eatonton
Bleckly	Cochran	Grady	Cairo	Quitman	Georgetown
Brantley	Nahunta	Greene	Greensboro	Rabun	Clayton
Brooks	Quitman	Gwinnett	Lawrenceville	Randolph	Cuthbert
Bryan	Pembroke	Habersham	Clarkesville	Richmond	Augusta
Bulloch	Statesboro	Hall	Gainesville	Rockdale	Conyers
Burke	Waynesboro	Hancock	Sparta	Schley	Ellaville
Butts	Jackson	Haralson	Buchanan	Screven	Sylvania
Calhoun	Morgan	Harris	Hamilton	Seminole	Donalsonville
Camden	Woodbine	Hart	Hartwell	Spalding	Griffin
Candler	Metter	Heard	Franklin	Stephens	Toccoa
Carroll	Carrollton	Henry	McDonough	Stewart	Lumpkin
Catoosa	Ringgold	Houston	Perry	Sumter	Americus
Charlton	Folkston	Irwin	Ocilla	Talbot	Talbotton
Chatham	Savannah	Jackson	Jefferson	Taliaferro	Crawfordville
Chattahoochee	Cusseta	Jasper	Monticello	Tatnall	Reidsville
Chattooga	Summerville	Jeff Davis	Hazlehurst	Taylor	Butler
Cherokee	Canton	Jefferson	Louisville	Telfair	McRea
Clarke	Athens	Jenkins	Millen	Terrell	Dawson
Clay	Fort Gaines	Johnson	Wrightsville	Thomas	Thomasville
Clayton	Jonesboro	Jones	Gray	Tift	Tifton
Clinch	Homerville	Lamar	Barnesville	Toombs	Lyons
Cobb	Marietta	Lanier	Lakeland	Towns	Haiwasee
Coffee	Douglas	Laurens	Dublin	Truetlen	Soperton
Colquitt	Moultrie	Lee	Leesburg	Troup	LaGrange
Columbia	Appling	Liberty	Hinesville	Turner	Ashburn
Cook	Adel	Lincoln	Lincolnton	Twiggs	Jeffersonville
Coweta	Newnan	Long	Ludowici	Union	Blairsville
Crawford	Knoxville	Lowndes	Valdosta	Upson	Thomaston
Crisp	Cordele	Lumpkin	Dahlonega	Walker	La Fayette
Dade	Trenton	Macon	Oglethorpe	Walton	Monroe
Dawson	Dawsonville	Madison	Danielsville	Ware	Waycross
Decatur	Bainbridge	Marion	Buena Vista	Warren	Warrenton
De Kalb	Decatur	McDuffie	Thomson	Washington	Sandersville
Dodge	Eastman	McIntosh	Darien	Wayne	Jesup
Dooly	Vienna	Meriwether	Greenville	Webster	Preston
Dougherty	Albany	Miller	Colquitt	Wheeler	Alamo
Douglas	Douglasville	Mitchell	Camilla	White	Cleveland
Early	Blakely	Monroe	Forsyth	Whitfield	Dalton
Echols	Statenville	Montgomery	Mount Vernon	Wilcox	Abbeville
Effingham	Springfield	Morgan	Madison	Wilkes	Washington
Elbert	Elberton	Murray	Chatsworth	Wilkinson	Irwinton
Emanuel	Swainsboro	Muscogee	Columbus	Worth	Sylvester

In the text that follows "†" indicates County Seats.

Our files contain additional verified data on the firms listed herein. This additional information is available on request.

A.M. BEST COMPANY

ALBANY † 77,434 Dougherty Co.

Gardner, Willis, Sweat & Handelman, LLP

2408 Westgate Drive
Albany, Georgia 31707
 Telephone: 229-883-2441
 Fax: 229-888-8148
 E-Mail: gwsh@gwsh-law.com
 gwsh-law.com

(Atlanta, GA Office: 400 Colony Square, Suite 200, 1201 Peachtree Street N.E., 30361)
 (Tel: 404-874-9588)
 (Fax: 229-888-8148)

Established: 1976

Insurance Defense, Workers' Compensation, Trucking Law, General Liability, Employment Litigation, Business Litigation

Insurance Clients

State Farm Insurance Company

Non-Insurance Clients

City of Albany
Miller Brewing Company
Coats & Clark, Inc.
State of Georgia

Partners

Sherman Willis — Georgia State University, B.B.A., 1971; Emory University, J.D., 1973 — Phi Delta Phi — Admitted to Bar, 1974, Georgia — Member Dougherty Circuit Bar Association; State Bar of Georgia — E-mail: Sherman.Willis@gwsh-law.com

Donald A. Sweat — Georgia Institute of Technology, B.S. (summa cum laude), 1974; The University of Georgia, J.D. (cum laude), 1976 — Phi Eta Sigma; Pi Mu Epsilon; Phi Kappa Phi — Admitted to Bar, 1976, Georgia; 1976, U.S. District Court, Middle and Northern Districts of Georgia; 1976, U.S. Court of Appeals, Eleventh Circuit; 1976, Georgia Court of Appeals; 1976, Supreme Court of Georgia — Member State Bar of Georgia; Dougherty Circuit Bar Association — E-mail: Donald.Sweat@gwsh-law.com

Todd S. Handelman — University of Illinois, B.A. (magna cum laude), 1986; The University of Georgia, J.D., 1989 — Phi Beta Kappa — Admitted to Bar, 1989, Georgia; 1989, U.S. District Court, Middle District of Georgia — Member State Bar of Georgia; Dougherty Circuit Bar Association; Georgia Self-Insureds Association — E-mail: Todd.Handelman@gwsh-law.com

Gail S. Pursel — The University of Georgia, B.A. (magna cum laude), 1983; J.D., 1986 — Phi Beta Kappa — Admitted to Bar, 1986, Georgia; 1986, U.S. District Court, Middle District of Georgia — Member American and Dougherty Circuit Bar Associations; State Bar of Georgia; Atlanta Claims Association — E-mail: Gail.Pursel@gwsh-law.com

Deena Plaire-Haas — Mercer University, B.B.A. (summa cum laude), 1990; J.D., 1993 — Admitted to Bar, 1993, Georgia; 1994, U.S. District Court, Middle District of Georgia; 1993, Georgia Court of Appeals; 1993, Supreme Court of Georgia — Member State Bar of Georgia; Dougherty Circuit Bar Association — E-mail: Deena.Plaire-Haas@gwsh-law.com

Glenn M. Booker — Southeastern Louisiana University, B.A., 1979; M.B.A., 1982; Mercer University, J.D., 1991; University of Florida, LL.M., 1992 — Admitted to Bar, 1992, Georgia; 1993, U.S. Supreme Court; 1994, U.S. District Court, Middle District of Georgia; 1999, Georgia Court of Appeals — Member State Bar of Georgia; Dougherty Circuit Bar Association; Georgia Society of Certified Public Accountants; Institute of Business Appraisers — Certified Public Accountant; Certified Business Appraiser — E-mail: Glenn.Booker@gwsh-law.com

Mark L. Pickett — Vanderbilt University, B.S., 1986; Vanderbilt University Law School, J.D., 1990 — Law Clerk to Hon. Jean Hoefer Toal, Associate Justice, South Carolina Supreme Court, 1991 — Admitted to Bar, 1991, South Carolina; 1995, Georgia; U.S. District Court, Middle District of Georgia; U.S. District Court, District of South Carolina; South Carolina Court of Appeals; Georgia Superior and State Courts; Supreme Court of South Carolina — Member American and Dougherty Circuit Bar Associations; State Bar of Georgia; South Carolina Bar — E-mail: Mark.Pickett@gwsh-law.com

Gardner, Willis, Sweat & Handelman, LLP, Albany, GA (Continued)

Associates

Amanda K. Goff — Georgia Southern University, B.A., 2001; Florida Coastal School of Law, J.D., 2005 — Phi Alpha Delta Legal Fraternity — Admitted to Bar, 2006, Florida; 2009, Georgia; U.S. District Court, Middle District of Georgia; Georgia Court of Appeals — Member State Bar of Georgia; The Florida Bar; Dougherty Circuit Bar Association — E-mail: Amanda.Goff@gwsh-law.com

Kimberly L. Guthrie — The University of Alabama, B.S. (magna cum laude), 2001; The University of Mississippi School of Law, J.D., 2005 — Admitted to Bar, 2005, Mississippi; 2006, Alabama; 2012, Georgia — Member State Bar of Georgia; Alabama State Bar; The Mississippi Bar; Dougherty Circuit Bar Association — E-mail: Kimberly.Guthrie@gwsh-law.com

Cara Fiore — The University of Georgia, B.S. (magna cum laude), 2008; J.D. (cum laude), 2012 — Admitted to Bar, 2012, Georgia — Member State Bar of Georgia; Dougherty Circuit Bar Association — E-mail: Cara.Fiore@gwsh-law.com

Smith N. Wilson — The University of Mississippi, B.A., 2006; University of Memphis, J.D., 2010 — Admitted to Bar, 2010, Georgia — Member Dougherty Circuit Bar Association — E-mail: Smith.Wilson@gwsh-law.com

The following firms also service this area.

Gannam, Gnann & Steinmetz LLC
Christian J. Steinmetz III
425 East President Street, Suite A
Savannah, Georgia 31401
 Telephone: 912-232-1192
 Fax: 912-238-9917

Civil Litigation, General Liability, Professional Liability, Property Damage, Coverage Issues, Insurance Defense

SEE COMPLETE LISTING UNDER SAVANNAH, GEORGIA (215 MILES)

Jones, Cork & Miller, LLP
SunTrust Bank Building, Suite 500
435 Second Street, 5th Floor
Macon, Georgia 31201-2724
 Telephone: 478-745-2821
 Fax: 478-743-9609

Mailing Address: P.O. Box 6437, Macon, GA 31208-6437

Insurance Defense, Automobile, Fire, Casualty, Surety, Life Insurance, Workers' Compensation, Medical Malpractice, Product Liability, Civil Rights, Governmental Liability, Business Law, Class Actions, Complex Litigation, Construction Law, Employment Law, Engineers, Environmental Law, Hospitals, Railroad Law, Self-Insured

SEE COMPLETE LISTING UNDER MACON, GEORGIA (103 MILES)

AMERICUS † 17,041 Sumter Co.

Refer To
Jones, Cork & Miller, LLP
SunTrust Bank Building, Suite 500
435 Second Street, 5th Floor
Macon, Georgia 31201-2724
 Telephone: 478-745-2821
 Fax: 478-743-9609

Mailing Address: P.O. Box 6437, Macon, GA 31208-6437

Insurance Defense, Automobile, Fire, Casualty, Surety, Life Insurance, Workers' Compensation, Medical Malpractice, Product Liability, Civil Rights, Governmental Liability, Business Law, Class Actions, Complex Litigation, Construction Law, Employment Law, Engineers, Environmental Law, Hospitals, Railroad Law, Self-Insured

SEE COMPLETE LISTING UNDER MACON, GEORGIA (68 MILES)

ATLANTA   GEORGIA

ATHENS † 85,855 Clarke Co.

Cowsert & Avery, LLP
2405 West Broad Street, Suite 250
Athens, Georgia 30606
　Telephone: 706-543-7700
　Fax: 706-543-7731
　E-Mail: craig.avery@cowsertavery.com
　cowsertavery.com

Insurance Defense, Workers' Compensation, Business Litigation, Personal Injury, Probate, Wills and Estate Litigation, Criminal Defense

Firm Profile: Finding the right lawyer is not always easy. Dealing with legal matters can be intimidating, and you need an attorney you can trust to protect you and your interests. That is what you get at the Athens/Metro Atlanta, Georgia law firm of Cowsert & Avery, LLP. Our experienced litigators have been successfully representing clients throughout Northeast Georgia since 1983-together, we have more than 125 years of combined experience.

At Cowsert & Avery, LLP, our skilled trial lawyers prepare every case for the courtroom. When it is possible to settle a case without going to trial we do so, however, we do not take chances with your future. We approach each case with integrity and we are not afraid to provide candid advice-even if it is not what you want to hear.

Insurance Clients

Auto-Owners Insurance Company
GEICO
Pharmacists Mutual Insurance Company
Cincinnati Insurance Company
Georgia Farm Bureau Mutual Insurance Company
Progressive Insurance Company

Non-Insurance Clients

Georgia Power Company
St. Mary's Health Care System

Firm Members

Bill Cowsert — Presbyterian College, B.S. (cum laude), 1980; The University of Georgia School of Law, J.D., 1983 — Admitted to Bar, 1983, Georgia — Member American Bar Association; State Bar of Georgia; Western Circuit Bar Association; Defense Research Institute; Georgia Defense Lawyers Association — AV Rated, Martindale-Hubbell; Georgia Super Lawyer, Atlanta Magazine, 2008; State Senator, Georgia District 46 — Practice Areas: Civil Litigation; Insurance Defense; Product Liability; Wrongful Death; Medical Malpractice; Commercial Litigation

Craig C. Avery — University of Kentucky, B.A., 1978; The John Marshall Law School, J.D. (cum laude), 1983 — Admitted to Bar, 1983, Georgia; U.S. District Court, Middle and Northern Districts of Georgia — Member State Bar of Georgia; American and Gwinnett County Bar Associations; Western Circuit Bar Association (Past President); Georgia Legal Services Program (Volunteer); Georgia Defense Lawyers Association (Vice President); Defense Research Institute — AV Rated, Martindale-Hubbell; Georgia Super Lawyer (2011, 2012, 2013) — Practice Areas: Civil Litigation; Insurance Law

M. Steven Heath — The University of Georgia, B.B.A. (magna cum laude), 1974; The University of Georgia School of Law, J.D. (cum laude), 1977 — Editorial Staff, Georgia Law Review — Admitted to Bar, 1977, Georgia; U.S. District Court, Middle and Northern Districts of Georgia; U.S. Court of Appeals, Eleventh Circuit — Member American Bar Association; State Bar of Georgia; Western Circuit Bar Association; Georgia Defense Lawyers Association — A.V. Peer Review Rated, Martindale Hubbell; Best Lawyers in America — Practice Areas: Insurance Defense; Workers' Compensation; General Civil Litigation; Commercial Litigation; Business Litigation; Medical Malpractice

Susan S. Elder — Florida State University, B.A., 1992; University of South Carolina, M.H.R., 1996; University of South Carolina School of Law, J.D., 1996 — Admitted to Bar, 1996, Georgia — Member State Bar of Georgia; Western Circuit Bar Association; Georgia Defense Lawyers Association — Practice Areas: Insurance Defense; Business Law; Probate; Estate Planning

Matthew A. Moseley — The University of Georgia, B.A., 1993; Cumberland University School of Law, J.D., 1997 — Admitted to Bar, 1997, Georgia; 1999, U.S. District Court, Middle District of Georgia; 2008, U.S. District

Cowsert & Avery, LLP, Athens, GA   (Continued)
Court, Northern District of Georgia — Member Western Circuit Bar Association (President 2010-2011); Georgia Defense Lawyers Association — Practice Areas: Civil Litigation; Commercial Litigation; Insurance Defense

Pamela H. Dillard — Valdosta State University, B.A., 1985; The University of Georgia School of Law, J.D., 1988 — Admitted to Bar, 1988, Georgia — Member State Bar of Georgia; Western Judicial Circuit Bar Association — Practice Areas: Insurance Defense; Real Estate

Michael Broun — The University of Georgia, B.A., 2003; The University of Mississippi School of Law, J.D. (magna cum laude), 2006 — Phi Delta Phi Legal Fraternity — Associate Articles Editor, Mississippi Law Journal — Admitted to Bar, 2006, Georgia — Ole Miss Moot Court Board; Federalist Society — Practice Areas: Civil Trial Practice; Insurance Law; Premises Liability; Commercial Litigation; Appellate Practice; Criminal Law

Colin Moriarty — College of William & Mary, B.A., 1995; Southwestern University School of Law, J.D., 2005 — Admitted to Bar, 2005, California; 2006, Georgia — Practice Areas: Civil Litigation; Criminal Defense

Ben Avery — The John Marshall Law School, J.D., 2012 — Admitted to Bar, 2013, Georgia — Member State Bar of Georgia; Western Judicial Circuit Bar Association

ATLANTA † 420,003 Fulton Co.

Allen, Kopet & Associates, PLLC
900 Circle 75 Parkway SE, Suite 1695
Atlanta, Georgia 30339
　Telephone: 770-435-7260
　Fax: 770-432-3512

(See listing under Chattanooga, TN for additional information)

Appelbaum & Associates, P.C.
9 Lenox Pointe NE, Suite B
Atlanta, Georgia 30324
　Telephone: 404-841-1275
　Fax: 404-841-0248
　E-Mail: eaa@aps-law.com

Established: 1991

Insurance Defense, Motor Vehicle, Civil Rights, Employment Law, Premises Liability, Professional Negligence, Workers' Compensation, Civil Litigation, General Liability, Product Liability

Insurance Clients

American Family Insurance Company
American Mercury Insurance Company
Southern United Fire Insurance Company
American Interstate Insurance Company
American Southern Insurance Company
Underwriters at Lloyd's, London

Non-Insurance Clients

Metropolitan Atlanta Rapid Transit Authority (MARTA)
RSKCo
Midway Insurance Management International
State of Georgia

Eve A. Appelbaum — 1954 — The George Washington University, B.A. (summa cum laude), 1976; The University of Texas at Austin, J.D. (with honors), 1982 — Phi Beta Kappa — Admitted to Bar, 1982, Georgia; U.S. District Court, Middle and Northern Districts of Georgia; U.S. Court of Appeals, Eleventh Circuit

Associates

Paul A. Henefeld — 1975 — The University of Georgia, B.A. (cum laude), 1998; Emory University, J.D., 2001 — Admitted to Bar, 2001, Georgia

Brian T. Mohs — 1980 — Georgia Institute of Technology, B.S. (with highest honors), 2002; Georgia State University College of Law, J.D., 2008 — Admitted to Bar, 2008, Georgia

GEORGIA ATLANTA

Austin & Sparks, P.C.
2974 Lookout Place, Suite 200
Atlanta, Georgia 30305-3272
  Telephone: 404-869-0100
  Fax: 404-869-0200
  E-Mail: jaustin@austinsparks.com

Established: 1996

Insurance Defense, Automobile, Motor Carriers, Product Liability, Premises Liability, Coverage Issues

Insurance Clients

American Southern Insurance Company	Canal Insurance Company
Motorists Mutual Insurance Company	Hallmark Insurance Company
	Star Casualty Insurance Company, Inc.

Founding Partners

John B. Austin — 1957 — Georgia Southern College, B.S., 1978; Georgia State University, J.D., 1985 — Phi Delta Phi — Editor, Georgia State University Law Review — Admitted to Bar, 1985, Georgia; U.S. District Court, Middle and Northern Districts of Georgia; U.S. Court of Appeals, Eleventh Circuit; 2012, U.S. District Court, Southern District of Georgia — Member State Bar of Georgia; Atlanta Bar Association; Georgia Defense Lawyers Association — Certified, Georgia Office of Dispute Resolution — E-mail: jaustin@austinsparks.com

John T. Sparks — 1958 — The University of Mississippi, B.A., 1980; M.A., 1984; J.D. (cum laude), 1987 — Admitted to Bar, 1987, Georgia; 1987, U.S. District Court, Middle, Northern and Southern Districts of Georgia; 1987, U.S. Court of Appeals, Eleventh Circuit — Member State Bar of Georgia; Atlanta Bar Association; Lawyers Club of Atlanta — E-mail: jsparks@austinsparks.com

Barrickman, Allred & Young, LLC
5775 Glenridge Drive NE, Suite E100
Atlanta, Georgia 30328-5386
  Telephone: 404-252-2230
  Fax: 404-252-3376
  E-Mail: wbb@bayatl.com
  www.bayatl.com

Insurance Defense, Product Liability, Insurance Coverage, Premises Liability, Construction Law, Employment Law, Workers' Compensation, Arbitration, Mediation

Firm Profile: The law firm of Barrickman, Allred & Young, LLC, was formed in 1999 in Atlanta, Georgia and the three partners have over 85 years of combined experience in the area of civil litigation. The partners are committed to providing quality legal services at a reasonable cost.

Insurance Clients

American Resources Insurance Company, Inc.	Auto Club South Insurance Company
Bituminous Insurance Companies	Equity Insurance Company
Federated Insurance Company	Florists' Mutual Insurance Company
Great American Insurance Group	Liberty Mutual Group
Kemper Services Group	Liberty Mutual Insurance Group
Liberty Mutual Insurance	Peerless Insurance Company
Ohio Casualty Company	Safeco/Liberty Mutual Insurance Companies
Penn National Insurance Company	
Tower Group, Inc.	United States Liability Insurance Group
United Fire & Casualty Group	
Unitrin, Inc.	
Wausau/Liberty Mutual Insurance Company	

Partners

W. Bruce Barrickman — University of Kentucky, B.A., 1975; J.D., 1978 — Admitted to Bar, 1979, Kentucky; 1987, Georgia — Practice Areas: Insurance Defense; Construction Litigation; Commercial General Liability; Product Liability; Premises Liability; Employment Law; Professional Liability; Truck Liability; Arbitration; Mediation

Barrickman, Allred & Young, LLC, Atlanta, GA
(Continued)

William Allred — The University of Georgia, B.A., 1982; College of William & Mary, M.A., 1989; Western New England College School of Law, J.D., 1986 — Admitted to Bar, 1986, Massachusetts; 1988, Georgia — Practice Areas: Civil Litigation; Insurance Defense; Commercial Litigation; Product Liability; Arbitration; Mediation

F. Scott Young — The University of Georgia, B.A., 1985; M.A., 1987; Georgia State University College of Law, J.D., 1991 — Admitted to Bar, 1991, Georgia — Practice Areas: Insurance Defense; Workers' Compensation; Construction Law; Arbitration; Mediation; Business Law

Crim & Bassler L.L.P.
100 Galleria Parkway, Suite 1510
Atlanta, Georgia 30339
  Telephone: 770-956-1813
  Fax: 770-955-5976
  www.crimbassler.com

Insurance Defense, General Liability, Personal Injury, Construction Defect

Insurance Clients

ACCC Insurance Company	American Claims Services, Inc.
American Service Insurance Company	Atlantic Casualty Insurance Company
Burlington Insurance Company	Canal Indemnity Company
Canal Insurance Company	Federated Rural Electric Insurance Exchange
First Financial Insurance Company	
Founders Insurance Company	Fulcrum Insurance Company
Golden Isles Insurance Company	InsureMax Insurance Group
Markel American Insurance Company	Omni Insurance Company
	Progressive Insurance Company
Safe Auto Insurance Company	Safeway Insurance Company
Selective Insurance Company of America	Southern Casualty Insurance Company
Southern General Insurance Company	Southern Insurance Underwriters
	Strickland Insurance Group
Tower Risk Management	Underwriters at Lloyd's, London
Unique Insurance Company	Universal Insurance Company
Western Heritage Insurance Company	

Firm Members

Candler Crim, Jr. — 1931 — The University of Alabama, J.D., 1956 — Admitted to Bar, 1956, Alabama; 1962, Georgia — Member American and Atlanta Bar Associations; Alabama State Bar; State Bar of Georgia; Advocates Club; Lawyers Club of Atlanta

Harry W. Bassler — 1948 — Emory University, B.A., 1970; J.D., 1973 — Admitted to Bar, 1974, Georgia — Member State Bar of Georgia; Atlanta Bar Association; Lawyers Club of Atlanta; Georgia Defense Lawyers Association

Thomas S. Bechtel — 1962 — The University of Georgia, A.B., 1985; Mercer University, J.D., 1988 — Admitted to Bar, 1988, Georgia — Member State Bar of Georgia; Cobb County Bar Association; Georgia Defense Lawyers Association

Associates

Janet C. Allen — 1959 — Stetson University, B.A., 1981; Georgia State University, J.D., 1996 — Phi Delta Phi — Admitted to Bar, 1996, Georgia — Member American and Atlanta Bar Associations; State Bar of Georgia; Georgia Defense Lawyers Association

Anne D. Gower — 1976 — The University of Georgia, B.S. (cum laude), 1998; Whittier Law School, J.D. (magna cum laude), 2002 — Admitted to Bar, 2002, Georgia — Member State Bar of Georgia

Jason D. Darneille — 1977 — Vanderbilt University, B.A., 1999; The University of Alabama School of Law, J.D., 2002 — Admitted to Bar, 2002, Alabama; 2008, Georgia — Member State Bar of Georgia; Alabama State Bar

Alexandra M. Svoboda — 1977 — The University of Georgia, B.A., 2000; Mercer University, J.D. (cum laude), 2007 — Admitted to Bar, 2007, Georgia — Member Atlanta Bar Association; Georgia Defense Lawyers Association

Caroline C. Owings — 1981 — Southern Methodist University, B.A., 2003; Cumberland School of Law of Samford University, J.D., 2009 — Admitted to Bar, 2009, Georgia — Member State Bar of Georgia

Davidson, Fuller & Sloan, LLP

10475 Medlock Bridge Road, Suite 820
Johns Creek, Georgia 30097
 Telephone: 770-622-4700
 Fax: 770-622-4705
 E-Mail: info@dfslaw.com
 www.dfslaw.com

Established: 1983

Business Litigation, Business Transactions, Real Estate Litigation, Commercial Real Estate Law, Eminent Domain, Estate Planning, Trademark, Commercial Leases, Labor and Employment, Catastrophic Injury and Death

Firm Profile: When addressing legal issues, an ideal resolution must come from comprehensive knowledge, tested experience and total understanding of all issues involved in a case. We have decades of experience including 20 plus years representing the founder of the largest casual full service restaurant chains in the nation.

Non-Insurance Clients

Apple Creek Management Company, Inc dba Applebee's
Hallmark Developers, Inc.
Neighborhood Restaurant Partners, LLC dba Applebee's
BF Saul Company
Bullock Communities
Indel, Inc.
Provident Group
Vanatage Products Corporation

Partners

William M. Davidson — Georgia State University, B.B.A. (with honors), 1973; Atlanta Law School, J.D., 1979 — Admitted to Bar, 1979, Georgia

Stephen P. Fuller — Atlanta Law School, J.D. (magna cum laude), 1983 — Admitted to Bar, 1983, Georgia

Donnie R. Sloan, Jr. — Georgia Institute of Technology, B.S., 1968; The University of Georgia School of Law, J.D. (cum laude), 1971; Harvard Law School, LL.M., 1975 — Admitted to Bar, 1971, Georgia

Drew Eckl & Farnham, LLP

880 West Peachtree Street
Atlanta, Georgia 30309
 Telephone: 404-885-1400
 Fax: 404-876-0992
 www.deflaw.com

(Brunswick, GA Office: 777 Gloucester Street, Suite 303, 31520)
 (Tel: 912-280-9662)
 (Fax: 912-267-0654)

Established: 1983

Appellate Practice, Casualty Insurance Law, Collections, Commercial Law, Commercial Vehicle, Construction Litigation, Employment Law, First Party Matters, Health Care Liability, Insurance Coverage, Property Defense, Professional Malpractice, Reinsurance, Sports and Entertainment Liability, Subrogation, Workers' Compensation

Firm Profile: For over 25 years, Drew Eckl & Farnham has developed a reputation for providing uncompromising service to local, regional and national clients. As experts in risk management litigation, our professionals are renowned for their abilities in and out of the courtroom. There is no civil, corporate or individual matter, large or small, that our diverse personnel cannot handle.

Insurance Clients

Auto-Owners Insurance Company
Church Mutual Insurance Company

Drew Eckl & Farnham, LLP, Atlanta, GA   (Continued)

CNA Insurance Companies
GEICO General Insurance Company
Hanover Insurance Company
Liberty Mutual Insurance Company
Nautilus Insurance Company
Sedgwick Group of Georgia, Inc.
Commerce Mutual Insurance Company, Inc.
Georgia Administrative Services, Inc.
Maryland Casualty Company
Safeco Insurance Companies
Zurich American Insurance Group

Non-Insurance Clients

Ford Motor Company
Georgia-Pacific LLC
General Motors Corporation

Partners

John A. Ferguson, Jr. — University of Virginia, B.A. (with distinction), 1973; The University of Georgia, J.D., 1976 — Admitted to Bar, 1976, Georgia — Practice Areas: Workers' Compensation — E-mail: jferguson@deflaw.com

John P. Reale — Trinity College, B.A., 1971; Vanderbilt University, J.D., 1976 — Admitted to Bar, 1976, Georgia — Practice Areas: Casualty Insurance Law; Insurance Coverage; Reinsurance; Sports and Entertainment Liability; Workers' Compensation — E-mail: jreale@deflaw.com

Stevan A. Miller — University of Virginia, B.A. (with high distinction), 1974; J.D., 1977 — Admitted to Bar, 1977, Georgia — Practice Areas: Casualty Insurance Law; Construction Litigation; Health Care Liability; Insurance Coverage; Personal and Commercial Vehicle; Professional Malpractice; Reinsurance — E-mail: smiller@deflaw.com

H. Michael Bagley — Emory University, B.A., 1977; The University of Georgia, J.D., 1980 — Admitted to Bar, 1980, Georgia — Practice Areas: First Party Defense; Workers' Compensation — E-mail: mbagley@deflaw.com

Hall F. McKinley, III — Princeton University, B.A., 1978; The University of Georgia, J.D., 1981 — Admitted to Bar, 1981, Georgia — Practice Areas: Casualty Insurance Law; Commercial Vehicle; Construction Litigation; Health Care Liability; Professional Malpractice — E-mail: hmckinley@deflaw.com

G. Randall Moody — Georgia State University, B.S., 1978; Mercer University Walter F. George School of Law, J.D. (cum laude), 1982 — Admitted to Bar, 1982, Georgia — Practice Areas: Casualty Insurance Law; Commercial Liability; Commercial Vehicle; Health Care Liability; Insurance Coverage; Professional Malpractice; Reinsurance — E-mail: rmoody@deflaw.com

Paul W. Burke — Sewanee, The University of the South, B.A., 1980; Stetson University, J.D. (cum laude), 1983 — Admitted to Bar, 1983, Florida; 1984, Georgia; 2001, Alabama — Practice Areas: Collections; Commercial Law; Commercial Vehicle; Construction Litigation; First Party Matters; Health Care Liability; Insurance Coverage; Professional Malpractice; Reinsurance; Subrogation — E-mail: pburke@deflaw.com

Daniel C. Kniffen — Mercer University, B.A. (magna cum laude), 1981; Mercer University Walter F. George School of Law, J.D. (cum laude), 1984 — Admitted to Bar, 1984, Georgia — Practice Areas: Employment Law; Workers' Compensation — E-mail: dkniffen@deflaw.com

John C. Bruffey, Jr. — The University of North Carolina at Chapel Hill, B.A., 1979; University of Cambridge, England; Campbell University School of Law, J.D., 1984 — Admitted to Bar, 1984, Georgia — Practice Areas: Workers' Compensation — E-mail: jbruffey@deflaw.com

John G. Blackmon, Jr. — The Citadel, B.S., 1976; Mercer University, J.D. (cum laude), 1986 — Admitted to Bar, 1986, Georgia — Practice Areas: Workers' Compensation — E-mail: jblackmon@deflaw.com

Gary R. Hurst — College of the Holy Cross, B.A., 1975; The University of Georgia, M.P.A., 1985; Rutgers University School of Law-Camden, J.D., 1978 — Admitted to Bar, 1978, Georgia — Practice Areas: Workers' Compensation — E-mail: ghurst@deflaw.com

Katherine D. Dixon — Emory University, B.A., 1983; The University of Georgia, J.D. (cum laude), 1990 — Admitted to Bar, 1990, Georgia — Practice Areas: Workers' Compensation — E-mail: kdixon@deflaw.com

Bruce A. Taylor, Jr. — St. Andrews Presbyterian College, B.A., 1974; Emory University School of Law, J.D., 1978 — Admitted to Bar, 1978, Georgia — Practice Areas: Casualty Insurance Law; Commercial Law; Commercial Vehicle; Construction Law — E-mail: btaylor@deflaw.com

Joseph C. Chancey — Mercer University, B.A. (cum laude), 1982; Florida State University, J.D. (with highest honors), 1985 — Order of the Coif - admitted to Bar, 1985, Georgia — Practice Areas: Appellate; Commercial Law; Employment Law; Property Defense; Real Estate Agents & Brokers Liability — E-mail: jchancey@deflaw.com

David A. Smith — The University of Georgia, B.B.A. (with honors), 1980; J.D., 1983 — Admitted to Bar, 1983, Georgia — Practice Areas: Workers' Compensation — E-mail: dsmith@deflaw.com

GEORGIA — ATLANTA

Drew Eckl & Farnham, LLP, Atlanta, GA (Continued)

James P. Anderson — Georgia Institute of Technology, B.I.E., 1987; Georgia State University, J.D., 1991 — Admitted to Bar, 1991, Georgia — Captain, Judge Advocate, U.S. Marine Corps, 1988-1995 — Languages: French — Practice Areas: Workers' Compensation — E-mail: janderson@deflaw.com

Julie Y. John — The University of Tennessee, B.S. (with high honors), 1984; Cumberland School of Law of Samford University, J.D. (cum laude), 1987 — Admitted to Bar, 1987, Georgia — Practice Areas: Workers' Compensation — E-mail: jjohn@deflaw.com

Sandra S. Cho — Emory University, B.A., 1990; American University, Washington College of Law, J.D., 1994 — Admitted to Bar, 1995, Georgia — Languages: French — Practice Areas: Workers' Compensation — E-mail: scho@deflaw.com

Barbara A. Marschalk — University of South Carolina, B.A. (cum laude), 1995; Georgia State University College of Law, J.D., 1998 — Admitted to Bar, 1998, Georgia — Practice Areas: Casualty Insurance Law; Health Care Liability; Professional Malpractice — E-mail: bmarschalk@deflaw.com

Brian T. Moore — University of Michigan; University of Copenhagen; DePauw University, B.A., 1997; The University of Tennessee College of Law, J.D., 2000 — Admitted to Bar, 2000, Tennessee; 2001, Georgia — Practice Areas: Appellate; Casualty Insurance Law; Collections; Commercial Law; Construction Litigation; Insurance Coverage; Reinsurance; Subrogation — E-mail: bmoore@deflaw.com

Robert L. Welch — State University of West Georgia, A.B. (cum laude), 1985; The University of Georgia School of Law, J.D. (cum laude), 1989; Georgia State University, M.S., 1998 — Admitted to Bar, 1989, Georgia — Practice Areas: Casualty Insurance Law; Commercial Law; Reinsurance; Workers' Compensation — E-mail: rwelch@deflaw.com

Michael L. Miller — The University of Alabama, B.S. (with honors), 1990; The University of Georgia School of Law, J.D., 1994 — Admitted to Bar, 1994, Georgia — Practice Areas: Casualty Insurance Law; Commercial Vehicle; Construction Litigation; Insurance Coverage; Reinsurance — E-mail: mmiller@deflaw.com

Andrew D. Horowitz — Johns Hopkins University, B.A., 1989; Emory University, J.D., 1994 — Admitted to Bar, 1994, Georgia; New Jersey; New York — Practice Areas: Casualty Insurance Law; Commercial Vehicle; Construction Litigation; Insurance Coverage; Reinsurance — E-mail: ahorowitz@deflaw.com

J.C. Roper, Jr. — Samford University, B.S., 1992; Cumberland School of Law of Samford University, J.D., 1995 — Admitted to Bar, 2000, Georgia — Practice Areas: Workers' Compensation — E-mail: jroper@deflaw.com

Burke A. Noble — University of Maryland, B.A., 1993; Mercer Law School, J.D., 1998 — Admitted to Bar, 1998, Georgia — Practice Areas: Construction Litigation; Commercial Vehicle; Casualty Insurance Law — E-mail: bnoble@deflaw.com

Brian W. Johnson — Samford University, B.A., 1997; Cumberland School of Law of Samford University, J.D., 2000 — Admitted to Bar, 2000, Georgia — Practice Areas: Casualty Insurance Law; Commercial Law — E-mail: bjohnson@deflaw.com

Douglas K. Burrell — The University of Iowa, B.A., 1986; M.B.A., 1994; The University of Iowa College of Law, J.D., 1994 — Admitted to Bar, 1995, Iowa; 2001, Georgia — Practice Areas: Casualty Insurance Law; Commercial Law; Commercial Vehicle; Construction Litigation — E-mail: dburrell@deflaw.com

Karen K. Karabinos — Mercer University Walter F. George School of Law, J.D. (cum laude), 1986 — Admitted to Bar, 1986, Georgia; 1991, Texas — Practice Areas: Casualty Insurance Law; First Party Matters — E-mail: kkarabinos@deflaw.com

Gary D. Beelen — College of William & Mary, B.A., 1984; The University of Akron School of Law, J.D., 1998 — Admitted to Bar, 1998, Ohio; 1999, Georgia — Practice Areas: Construction Litigation; Commercial Law; Property Defense; Real Estate Agents & Brokers Liability — E-mail: gbeelen@deflaw.com

Jeffrey S. Ward — Minnesota State University, Mankato, B.A. (cum laude), 1992; Arizona State University, M.S., 1995; The University of Georgia School of Law, J.D. (cum laude), 2002 — Admitted to Bar, 2002, Georgia — Practice Areas: Casualty Insurance Law; Health Care Liability; Professional Malpractice; Workers' Compensation — E-mail: jward@deflaw.com

Of Counsel

Charles L. Drew — Retired — The University of Georgia, LL.B., 1954 — Admitted to Bar, 1954, Georgia

W. Wray Eckl — University of Vienna; University of Notre Dame, B.A. (cum laude), 1959; University of Virginia, LL.B., 1962 — Admitted to Bar, 1962, Virginia; Alabama; 1964, Georgia — Practice Areas: Casualty Insurance Law; Professional Malpractice; Health Care Liability — E-mail: weckl@deflaw.com

Clayton H. Farnham — The University of Georgia School of Law, LL.B., 1967 — Admitted to Bar, 1968, Georgia — Practice Areas: First Party Matters; Subrogation

Melanie C. Eyre — Michigan State University, B.A. (with high honors), 1977; The George Washington University Law School, J.D. (with honors), 1987 — Admitted to Bar, 1995, Georgia — Practice Areas: Casualty Insurance Law; Health Care Liability; Professional Malpractice — E-mail: meyre@deflaw.com

Jeffrey A. Burmeister — University of Michigan, B.A., 1988; Marquette University Law School, J.D., 1992 — Admitted to Bar, 1988, Wisconsin; 1992, Georgia — Practice Areas: Casualty Insurance Law; Construction Litigation; Insurance Coverage; Reinsurance — E-mail: jburmeister@deflaw.com

Leslie P. Becknell — Georgia State University College of Law, J.D., 1989 — Admitted to Bar, 1989, Georgia — Practice Areas: Casualty Insurance Law; Commercial Vehicle; Construction Litigation; Insurance Coverage; Reinsurance — E-mail: lbecknell@deflaw.com

Senior Associates

Douglas G. Smith Jr. — The University of Georgia School of Law, J.D., 1991 — Admitted to Bar, 1991, Georgia — Practice Areas: Casualty Insurance Law; Commercial Vehicle; Insurance Coverage; Reinsurance — E-mail: dgsmith@deflaw.com

Robert D. Goldsmith — The University of Georgia School of Law, J.D., 1980 — Admitted to Bar, 1980, Georgia — Practice Areas: Casualty Insurance Law; Employment Law; Workers' Compensation — E-mail: rgoldsmith@deflaw.com

(Revisors of the Georgia Insurance Law Digest for this Publication)

Fain, Major & Brennan, P.C.

100 Glenridge Point Parkway, Suite 500
Atlanta, Georgia 30342-1440
Telephone: 404-688-6633
Fax: 404-420-1544
E-Mail: sbanks@fainmajor.com
www.fainmajor.com

Established: 1977

Insurance Law, Automobile, Motor Carriers, Premises Liability, Product Liability, Litigation, Personal Injury, Wrongful Death, Construction Litigation, Food Services

Firm Profile: Fain, Major & Brennan, P.C. is one of Georgia's premier litigation defense firms, specializing in civil litigation practice, including motor vehicle and trucking litigation, insurance coverage disputes, wrongful death, premises and professional liability defense. We represent many insurance companies and businesses throughout the state.

Insurance Clients

AAA Automobile Club
Acuity Insurance
American Family Insurance Group
BITCO Insurance Companies
Crawford & Company
Donegal Insurance Group
The Hartford
Indiana Lumbermens Mutual Insurance Company
North Carolina Farm Bureau Mutual Insurance Company
Sedgwick CMS
Sentry Claims Services
Westfield Companies

ACCC Insurance Company
Allstate Insurance Company
Baldwin & Lyons Group
Century Surety/Meadowbrook Insurance Group
Hanover Insurance Group
Housing Authority Insurance Group
National Farmers Union Casualty Group
Pennsylvania Lumbermens Mutual Insurance Company
USAA
Zurn Industries, Inc.

Non-Insurance Clients

Avis Budget Group, Inc.
Hardee's Food Systems, Inc.
LandAir Transport, Inc.

Budget Rent-A-Car Corporation
The Hertz Corporation
Publix Super Markets, Inc.

Fain, Major & Brennan, P.C., Atlanta, GA (Continued)

In Memoriam
Donald M. Fain — (1931-1999)

Partners

Gene A. Major — 1954 — Michigan State University, B.A. (with high honors), 1975; The University of Georgia, J.D., 1979 — Admitted to Bar, 1979, Georgia; U.S. District Court, Middle, Northern and Southern Districts of Georgia; U.S. Court of Appeals, Fifth and Eleventh Circuits — Member American and Atlanta Bar Associations; State Bar of Georgia; Association of Transportation Practitioners; Atlanta Claims Association; Georgia Defense Lawyers Association; Defense Research Institute — Georgia Super Lawyer; AV Rated by Martindale Hubbell

Thomas E. Brennan — 1961 — Marquette University, B.S., 1983; Wake Forest University, J.D., 1986 — Order of the Barristers; National Moot Court — Admitted to Bar, 1986, Georgia; U.S. District Court, Middle, Northern and Southern Districts of Georgia; U.S. Court of Appeals for the Federal and Eleventh Circuits — Member American and Atlanta Bar Associations; State Bar of Georgia; Georgia Defense Lawyers Association; Defense Research Institute; Transportation Lawyers Association — AV Rated by Martindale Hubbell

James W. Hardee — 1965 — Auburn University, B.S., 1987; Cumberland School of Law of Samford University, J.D., 1990 — Admitted to Bar, 1990, Florida; 2000, Georgia — Member Atlanta and Jacksonville Bar Associations; The Florida Bar; State Bar of Georgia; Atlanta Claims Association; American Association for Justice — Past GDLA Education Coordinator; AV Rated by Martindale Hubbell; Distinguished Community Service Award; Top Lawyers in Georgia by Atlanta Magazine

Associates

James F. Taylor III — 1967 — The University of Georgia, A.B. (cum laude), 1988; Georgia State University, J.D., 1993 — Admitted to Bar, 1993, Georgia; U.S. District Court, Northern District of Georgia; 1994, U.S. District Court, Middle District of Georgia; U.S. Court of Appeals for the Federal and Eleventh Circuits — Member American and Atlanta (Tort Insurace Practice Section, Chairman 2004-2005) Bar Associations; State Bar of Georgia; Southern Loss Association; Atlanta Claims Association; Defense Research Institute; Georgia Defense Lawyers Association

Jennifer L. Nichols — Vanderbilt University, B.A., 2001; University of Miami School of Law, J.D., 2004 — Admitted to Bar, 2004, Georgia; U.S. District Court, Middle District of Georgia; U.S. Court of Appeals for the Federal and Eleventh Circuits; Supreme Court of Georgia; Georgia Court of Appeals — Member American and Atlanta Bar Associations; State Bar of Georgia (Co-Chair, Women in the Profession Committee, Young Lawyers Division, 2012-2014) — Reported Cases: Mucyo v. Publix Super Markets, Inc., 301 Ga. App. 599, 688 S.E. 2d 372 (2009) — Achievement Award for Outstanding Service to the Profession, Young Lawyers Division, State Bar of Georgia (2012-2013); Executive Committee of The Red Shoe Society of Atlanta (Ronald McDonald House Charities) — Practice Areas: Insurance Defense; Premise Litigation; Construction Litigation

Richard W. Brown — 1958 — Boston College, B.A. (summa cum laude), 1984; Duke University, J.D. (with honors), 1987 — Phi Beta Kappa — Duke University Law Review — Admitted to Bar, 1987, Ohio (Inactive); 1989, Georgia; U.S. District Court, Northern District of Georgia; 1994, U.S. District Court, Middle District of Georgia; U.S. Court of Appeals, Eleventh Circuit — Member State Bar of Georgia — BV Rated by Martindale Hubbell — United States Air Force, 1976-1980

Elliot D. Tiller — The University of Georgia, B.S. (summa cum laude), 1995; The University of Georgia School of Law, J.D. (cum laude), 1998 — Admitted to Bar, 1998, Georgia; 1999, U.S. District Court, Middle, Northern and Southern Districts of Georgia — Member Atlanta Bar Association; Defense Research Institute — Reported Cases: Arnold v. Neal, 320 Ga. App. 289, 738 S.E.2d 707 (2013); Perkins v. Kranz, 316 Ga. App.171, 728 S.E.2d 804 (2012); Behforouz v. Vakil, 281 GA APP 603, 636 S.E.2d 674 (2006) — BV Rated by Martindale Hubbell — Practice Areas: Insurance Defense; Tort

Jason Pettus — Middle Tennessee State University, B.A., 2001; Cumberland School of Law at Samford University, J.D. (Dean's Award), 2004 — Admitted to Bar, 2004, Georgia; 2005, U.S. District Court, Middle and Northern Districts of Georgia — Member Georgia Defense Lawyers Association — Reported Cases: Dominic v. Eurocar Classics, 2011 WL 2697056, July 13, 2011 — 2010-2011 Chairperson for the GDLA Contruction Subcommittee — Practice Areas: Construction Liability; Premises Liability; General Liability; Insurance Coverage

Sean L. Gill — The University of Alabama at Birmingham, B.S. (cum laude, with honors), 2002; Case Western Reserve University School of Law, J.D.,

Fain, Major & Brennan, P.C., Atlanta, GA (Continued)

2005 — Georgia Super Lawyers Rising Stars 2011 and 2012 — Admitted to Bar, 2005, Georgia; U.S. District Court, Middle and Northern Districts of Georgia; Georgia Court of Appeals; U.S. Court of Appeals, Eleventh Circuit; Supreme Court of Georgia

Mitchel S. Evans — Georgia Institute of Technology, B.S.Mech.Engr., 1986; Georgia State University, J.D., 1991 — Admitted to Bar, 1991, Georgia; 1993, U.S. District Court, Middle and Southern Districts of Georgia; Georgia Court of Appeals; Supreme Court of Georgia — Reported Cases: Canada v. Shropshire, 232 Ga. App. 341; Hitchcock v. McPhail, 221 Ga. App. 299

Dale C. Ray Jr — Georgia State University, B.S. (magna cum laude), 1979; The University of Georgia School of Law, J.D. (cum laude), 1982 — Admitted to Bar, 1982, Georgia; U.S. District Court, Northern District of Georgia; 2000, U.S. Court of Appeals for the Federal and Eleventh Circuits; 1996, U.S. District Court, Middle District of Georgia

Of Counsel

Jessica E. Sanford — 1975 — New York University, B.A., 1997; University of Miami School of Law, J.D., 2000 — Admitted to Bar, 2000, Florida; 2002, District of Columbia; 2004, Georgia; 2005, U.S. District Court, Northern and Southern Districts of Georgia

Fields, Howell, Athans & McLaughlin LLP

191 Peachtree Street NE, Suite 4600
Atlanta, Georgia 30303-1740
Telephone: 404-214-1250
Fax: 404-214-1251
E-Mail: info@fieldshowell.com
www.fieldshowell.com

(Tennessee Office: Republic Centre, Suite 600, 633 Chestnut Street, Chattanooga, TN, 37450)
(Tel: 423-424-5263)

Established: 2004

Insurance Coverage, Tort Litigation, Property, Casualty, Professional Liability, Motor Carriers, Commercial General Liability, Construction Defect, Environmental Liability, Aviation, Reinsurance, Commercial Litigation

Firm Profile: Fields Howell focuses on complex insurance matters and commercial litigation. Fields Howell attorneys have successfully handled numerous suits and arbitrations involving insurance coverage disputes under third-party, first-party, professional liability, errors and omissions, and construction defect policies. Clients also retain the firm's attorneys regularly to handle reinsurance disputes, arbitrations, and program audits. Insurers frequently retain Fields Howell to defend cases involving class actions, professional liability, toxic torts, aviation, personal injury, and wrongful death. Additionally, Fields Howell attorneys frequently handle complex commercial litigation involving class actions, toxic torts, injunctive relief, and contract disputes. Fields Howell attorneys provide quality work at more modest rates and with better service. Fields Howell clients know they are a priority and that their individual needs and concerns will be addressed.

Insurance Clients

ACE USA	American Western Home Insurance Company
Aspen Specialty Insurance Company	AXIS Specialty Insurance Company
Berkley Select, LLC	Fireman's Fund Insurance Company
CNA	Hanover Insurance Group
Great American Insurance Company	ProSight Specialty Insurance Company
Markel Corporation	XL America Group
RSUI Group, Inc.	
Underwriters at Lloyd's, London	

Non-Insurance Clients

Burns & Wilcox Ltd.

Fields, Howell, Athans & McLaughlin LLP, Atlanta, GA
(Continued)
Partners

Michael J. Athans — State University of New York at Buffalo, B.A. (cum laude), 1979; University at Buffalo Law School, J.D., 1982 — Admitted to Bar, 1982, Georgia

Paul L. Fields, Jr. — Wake Forest University, B.A., 1985; The University of Georgia, J.D. (cum laude), 1988 — Moot Court Board — Law Review (1986-1987); Vice Chairman — Admitted to Bar, 1988, Georgia

Joseph C. Gebara — University of Southern California, B.S., 1986; J. Reuben Clark Law School, Brigham Young University, J.D. (cum laude), 1990 — Admitted to Bar, 1990, Arizona; 1991, California; 2013, Georgia

Ann T. Kirk — Emory University, B.A., 2000; Northwestern University School of Law, J.D., 2003 — Admitted to Bar, 2003, Illinois; 2006, Georgia

Jonathan D. Kramer — Bucknell University, B.A., 1997; Indiana University School of Law, J.D., 2000 — Admitted to Bar, 2000, Georgia

Gregory L. Mast — Tennessee Office Representative — The George Washington University, B.A., 1999; Emory University, J.D. (with honors), 2003 — Admitted to Bar, 2003, Georgia; 2012, Tennessee — Resident Atlanta, GA & Chattanooga, TN Office

Robert E. McLaughlin — The University of Georgia, B.A. (cum laude), 1986; Boston College Law School, J.D., 1989 — Admitted to Bar, 1989, Georgia

Jennifer W. Wolak — State University of New York at Buffalo, B.A. (cum laude), 1997; Syracuse University College of Law, J.D., 2000 — Admitted to Bar, 2001, New York; Georgia

Richard E. Zelonka, Jr. — University of Florida, B.A., 1997; M.E.S.S., 1999; The University of Mississippi, J.D. (cum laude), 2003 — Admitted to Bar, 2003, Florida; 2005, Georgia

Associates

D. Austin Bersinger — University of South Carolina Honors College, B.A. (cum laude), 2007; The University of Georgia School of Law, J.D. (cum laude), 2011 — Admitted to Bar, 2011, Georgia

Caitlin M. Crist — Georgia Institute of Technology, B.S., 2007; The University of Georgia School of Law, J.D., 2010 — Admitted to Bar, 2010, Georgia; 2011, Alabama

Jocelyn C. DeMars — University of Notre Dame, B.A., 2005; The University of Toledo College of Law, J.D. (cum laude), 2010 — Admitted to Bar, 2010, Ohio

E. Helen Eisenstein — The University of Georgia, B.B.A. (summa cum laude), 2003; The University of Georgia School of Law, J.D. (cum laude), 2006 — Admitted to Bar, 2006, Georgia

Brandon R. Gossett — The University of Georgia, B.A. (cum laude, with honors), 2010; The University of Georgia School of Law, J.D. (cum laude), 2013 — Admitted to Bar, 2013, Georgia

Samantha T. Lemery — University of Wisconsin, B.S., 2004; Emory University School of Law, J.D., 2008 — Admitted to Bar, 2008, Georgia

Colleen V. McCaffrey — Vanderbilt University, B.A. (cum laude), 2010; The University of Georgia School of Law, J.D. (magna cum laude, Order of the Coif), 2013 — Admitted to Bar, 2013, Georgia

Keshia L. Williams — Duke University, B.A., 2008; The University of Tennessee College of Law, J.D. (magna cum laude), 2012 — Admitted to Bar, 2012, Georgia; 2013, Tennessee

Galloway, Johnson, Tompkins, Burr & Smith

990 Hammond Drive, Suite 770
Atlanta, Georgia 30328
  Telephone: 678-951-1500
  E-Mail: tladouceur@gallowayjohnson.com
  www.gallowayjohnson.com

(Additional Offices: New Orleans, LA*; Lafayette, LA*; Pensacola, FL*; St. Louis, MO*; Houston, TX*; Mandeville, LA*; Gulfport, MS*; Tampa, FL*; Mobile, AL*)

Maritime, Automobile Liability, Bad Faith, Class Actions, Construction, Energy, Employment, Insurance Coverage, Insurance Defense, Product Liability, Professional Liability, Property, Transportation, General Casualty, Title Resolution, Environmental

(See listing under New Orleans, LA for additional information)

Goodman McGuffey Lindsey & Johnson, LLP

3340 Peachtree Road NE
Suite 2100
Atlanta, Georgia 30326-1084
  Telephone: 404-264-1500
  Fax: 404-264-1737
  E-Mail: gmlj@gmlj.com
  www.gmlj.com

(Orlando, FL Office: 201 South Orange Avenue, Suite 1010, 32801-3477)
  (Tel: 407-478-1247)
  (Fax: 407-478-1527)
(Savannah, GA Office: 532 Stephenson Avenue, Suite 200, 31405)
  (Tel: 912-355-6433)
  (Fax: 912-355-6434)
(Charlotte, NC Office: 11006 Rushmore Drive, Suite 270, 28277-3606)
  (Tel: 704-887-4985)
  (Fax: 704-887-4983)
(Sarasota, FL Office: 6751 Professional Parkway West, Suite 103, 34240)
  (Tel: (941) 953-4411)
  (Fax: (941) 953-4410)
(Raleigh, NC Office: 4208 Six Forks Road, Suite 1000, 10th Floor, 27609-5738)
  (Tel: 912-210-5402)
  (Fax: 404-264-1737)
(Charleston, SC Office: 4000 S. Faber Place Drive, Suite 300, 29405-1084)
  (Tel: 843-849-6440)
  (Fax: 843-849-6433)

Established: 1990

Alternative Dispute Resolution, Automobile Litigation, Bodily Injury, Construction Defect, Construction Litigation, Employer Liability, Employment Law, Environmental Litigation, Governmental Liability, Municipal Liability, Insurance Coverage & Defense, Insurance Coverage, Bad Faith, Medical Malpractice, Premises Liability, Product Liability, Professional Liability, Property Liability, Sexual Harassment, Subrogation, Uninsured and Underinsured Motorist, Workers' Compensation

Firm Profile: Goodman McGuffey Lindsey & Johnson LLP, founded in 1990, is a mid-sized civil and commercial litigation firm with offices in Atlanta and Savannah, Georgia; Orlando and Sarasota, Florida; Charlotte and Raleigh, North Carolina and Charleston, South Carolina. With substantial experience in a wide array of corporate and business litigation, our expertise includes commercial matters, products and tort liability, construction, insurance, class action and employment disputes. We are currently active in several states throughout the Southeast.

Insurance Clients

ACE/ESIS
Brotherhood Mutual Insurance Company
Cincinnati Insurance Company
GAB Robins North America, Inc.
Safeco Insurance
The Travelers Companies
Zurich American Insurance Company

Berkshire Hathaway Homestate Companies
Capitol Indemnity Corporation
Crawford & Company
GuideOne Insurance
Sedgwick Claims Management Services, Inc.

Non-Insurance Clients

Best Buy Company
CareSouth Home Health Services, Inc.
The Pepsi Bottling Group, Inc.
Skansa Construction Company
United Parcel Service, Inc.

Blue Bird Corporation
Frito-Lay, Inc.
Holder Construction Company
Rome Tool & Die Company
Super Transport, Inc.

Goodman McGuffey Lindsey & Johnson, LLP, Atlanta, GA (Continued)

Equity Partners

C. Wade McGuffey, Jr. — The University of Georgia, B.B.A., 1973; J.D. (cum laude), 1976 — Admitted to Bar, 1976, Georgia; 1977, Florida; 1976, U.S. District Court, Middle District of Georgia; 1977, U.S. Court of Appeals, Fifth Circuit; 1979, U.S. Supreme Court; 1981, U.S. District Court, Northern District of Georgia — Member American Bar Association; The Florida Bar; State Bar of Georgia (Workers' Compensation Section); Atlanta Bar Association (Workers' Compensation Section, Board of Directors, 1994-1996; Secretary/Treasurer, 1997; Chair-Elect, 1998; Chairman, 1999); Georgia Self-Insurers Association; Independent Insurance Agents of Georgia (YAC Honorary Life Member); Georgia Defense Lawyers Association; Defense Research Institute; Atlanta Claims Association; Lawyers Club of Atlanta — Editor, "An Employer's Guide to the Georgia Workers' Compensation Law," 2nd edition, 1993; Contributor, Employer Liability, Georgia Workers' Compensation: A Reference Manual for Group Self-Insurance Funds, 1995 — Faculty, Trial Academy, Georgia Defense Lawyers Association, 1987 — Certified Mediator; Certified Workers' Compensation Professional — Practice Areas: Employer Liability; Workers' Compensation; Employment Law — E-mail: wmcguffey@gmlj.com

Edward H. Lindsey, Jr. — Davidson College, B.A., 1981; The University of Georgia, J.D., 1984 — Admitted to Bar, 1984, Georgia; U.S. District Court, Middle and Northern Districts of Georgia; 1985, U.S. Court of Appeals, Eleventh Circuit — Member American and Atlanta Bar Associations; State Bar of Georgia (Litigation and Insurance Sections); Lawyer's Club of Atlanta; Atlanta Volunteer Lawyers Foundation (Board of Directors, 1996-Present); Atlanta Claims Association; Georgia Defense Lawyers Association — Certified Mediator — Practice Areas: Environmental Law; Insurance Defense; Insurance Fraud; Personal Injury; Property — E-mail: elindsey@gmlj.com

James F. Cook, Jr. — Georgia Institute of Technology, B.S., 1975; The University of Georgia, J.D. (cum laude), 1984 — Admitted to Bar, 1984, Georgia — Member State Bar of Georgia; Atlanta Bar Association; Defense Lawyers Association of Georgia; Lawyers Club of Atlanta; Defense Research Institute — Practice Areas: Insurance Defense — E-mail: jcook@gmlj.com

Teri Alpert Zarrillo — Emory University, B.A., 1990; J.D., 1993 — Admitted to Bar, 1993, Georgia; Florida — Member The Florida Bar; State Bar of Georgia; Atlanta Trial Lawyers Association; Association of Trial Lawyers of America; Lawyers Club of Atlanta; Atlanta Claims Association — Practice Areas: Subrogation; Workers' Compensation — E-mail: tzarrillo@gmlj.com

Robert M. Darroch — Barry College, B.A. (summa cum laude), 1977; Emory University, J.D., 1980 — Admitted to Bar, 1980, Georgia; Florida — Member State Bar of Georgia; The Florida Bar — Practice Areas: Construction Litigation; Premises Liability; Product Liability; Construction Defect; Insurance Coverage; Bad Faith; Uninsured Motorist Defense — Resident Sarasota, FL Office — E-mail: rdarroch@gmlj.com

Robert A. Luskin — Centre College of Kentucky, B.A., 1998; Mercer University, J.D., 2001 — Admitted to Bar, 2001, Georgia; 2009, Tennessee — Member Atlanta Bar Association; State Bar of Georgia — Practice Areas: Construction Litigation; Employer Liability; Governmental Liability; Municipal Liability; Premises Liability; Product Liability; Subrogation; Construction Defect; Employment Law; Insurance Coverage; Bad Faith; Professional Liability; Uninsured Motorist Defense — E-mail: rluskin@gmlj.com

Partners

Judy Farrington Aust — Samford University, B.M.E., 1978; The University of Georgia School of Law, J.D., 1985 — Barrister, Joseph Henry Lumpkin Inn of Court — Admitted to Bar, 1985, Georgia — Member State Bar of Georgia; DeKalb County, Decatur and Atlanta (Task Force Juris; Chair, Board of Directors, Litigation Section) Bar Associations; Lawyers Club of Atlanta; Georgia Defense Lawyers Association — Speaker: "Trial and Discovery Procedure," "Employment Law," and "Professionalism"; Faculty, Atlanta College of Trial Advocacy — Practice Areas: Construction Litigation; Employer Liability; Governmental Liability; Municipal Liability; Medical Malpractice; Premises Liability; Employment Law; Insurance Coverage; Bad Faith; Professional Liability — E-mail: jaust@gmlj.com

Frederick R. Green — University of Michigan, A.B., 1990; University of Detroit Mercy School of Law, J.D., 1994 — Admitted to Bar, 1994, Michigan; 1995, Georgia; 2008, North Carolina; 1994, U.S. District Court, Eastern District of Michigan; 1995, U.S. District Court, Northern District of Georgia; U.S. Court of Appeals, Eleventh Circuit; 1996, U.S. Court of Appeals, Sixth Circuit — Member Atlanta Bar Association; State Bar of Michigan; State Bar of Georgia — Languages: German — Practice Areas: Premises Liability; Product Liability; Workers' Compensation; Professional Liability — E-mail: fgreen@gmlj.com

Goodman McGuffey Lindsey & Johnson, LLP, Atlanta, GA (Continued)

Peter D. Muller — The University of Georgia, A.B.J., 1984; J.D., 1987 — Admitted to Bar, 1987, Georgia; U.S. District Court, Middle and Southern Districts of Georgia; U.S. Court of Appeals, Eleventh Circuit; Supreme Court of the United States; Supreme Court of Georgia — Member Savannah Bar Association; Georgia Defense Lawyers Association — Practice Areas: Construction Litigation; Employer Liability; Governmental Liability; Municipal Liability; Medical Liability; Premises Liability; Construction Defect; Employment Law; Property Damage; Professional Liability; Uninsured Motorist Defense — Resident Savannah, GA Office — E-mail: pmuller@gmlj.com

Edwin L. Hamilton — Charleston Southern University, B.S., 1982; Mercer University Walter F. George School of Law, J.D. (with honors), 1988 — Admitted to Bar, 1988, Georgia — Member State Bar of Georgia; Association of Corporate Counsel; Georgia Defense Lawyers Association; Defense Research Institute — Practice Areas: Construction Litigation; Premises Liability; Product Liability; Construction Defect; Property Damage — Resident Savannah, GA Office — E-mail: ehamilton@gmlj.com

Adam E. Whitten — Brigham Young University, B.S., 1999; The University of North Carolina at Chapel Hill, J.D., 2003 — Admitted to Bar, 2003, North Carolina — Member North Carolina and Mecklenburg County Bar Associations — Practice Areas: Employer Liability; Premises Liability; Product Liability; Subrogation; Workers' Compensation; Elder Law; Construction Defect; Employment Law; Insurance Coverage; Bad Faith; Property Damage; Uninsured Motorist Defense — Resident Charlotte, NC Office — E-mail: awhitten@gmlj.com

Adam C. Joffe — The University of Georgia, B.B.A., 2000; Georgia State University College of Law, J.D., 2003 — Admitted to Bar, 2003, Georgia — Member State Bar of Georgia — Practice Areas: Construction Litigation; Premises Liability; Construction Defect; Insurance Coverage; Bad Faith; Property Damage; Uninsured Motorist Defense — E-mail: ajoffe@gmlj.com

Charles W. Barrow — The University of Georgia, B.A.; Mercer University Walter F. George School of Law, J.D., 1976 — Admitted to Bar, 1976, Georgia — Member Georgia State Bar; Savannah Bar Association — Practice Areas: Governmental Liability; Municipal Liability; Workers' Compensation — Resident Savannah, GA Office — E-mail: cbarrow@gmlj.com

Joshua S. Stein — The University of Georgia, B.A. (cum laude), 2001; The University of Georgia School of Law, J.D., 2004 — Admitted to Bar, 2005, Georgia — Member American Bar Association; State Bar of Georgia — Practice Areas: Construction Litigation; Premises Liability; Product Liability; Uninsured Motorist Defense — E-mail: jstein@gmlj.com

Stephanie F. Glickauf — Georgetown University, B.A., 1996; The University of Georgia School of Law, J.D., 1999 — Admitted to Bar, 1999, Georgia; U.S. District Court, Northern District of Georgia; Georgia Court of Appeals; U.S. Court of Appeals, Eleventh Circuit; Georgia Superior and State Courts; U.S. Supreme Court of Georgia — Member Atlanta Bar Association; Atlanta Claims Association — Practice Areas: Construction Defect; Insurance Coverage; Bad Faith — E-mail: sglickauf@gmlj.com

David M. Havlicek — University of Central Florida, B.A., 1993; Nova Southeastern University, Shepard Broad Law Center, J.D., 2000 — Admitted to Bar, 2000, Florida — Member The Florida Bar (Workers' Compensation Section) — Practice Areas: Governmental Liability; Municipal Liability; Workers' Compensation — Resident Orlando, FL Office — E-mail: dhavlicek@gmlj.com

Jennifer Jerzak Blackman — University of Virginia, B.A.; Wake Forest University, J.D., 1997 — Admitted to Bar, 1997, North Carolina — Member North Carolina State Bar; North Carolina and Wake County Bar Associations; North Carolina Association of Defense Attorneys — Practice Areas: Premises Liability; Workers' Compensation — Resident Raleigh, NC Office — E-mail: jblackman@gmlj.com

Jeff K. Stinson — The University of Georgia, A.B.J., 2000; Georgia State University College of Law, J.D., 2003 — Admitted to Bar, 2003, Georgia — Member Atlanta Bar Association — Practice Areas: Subrogation; Workers' Compensation; Employment Law — E-mail: jstinson@gmlj.com

Andrew N. Bernardini — State University of New York at Plattsburgh, B.A., 1996; Albany Law School of Union University, J.D., 2000 — Admitted to Bar, 2000, North Carolina — Member North Carolina and Mecklenburg County Bar Associations — Practice Areas: Workers' Compensation — Resident Charlotte, NC Office — E-mail: abernardini@gmlj.com

D. Scott Porch, IV — The University of Tennessee, B.S., 1994; University of Memphis, J.D., 1999 — Admitted to Bar, 1999, Tennessee; 2006, Georgia — Member American and Savannah Bar Associations; Georgia Defense Lawyers Association; Defense Research Institute — Practice Areas: Workers' Compensation — Resident Savannah, GA Office — E-mail: sporch@gmlj.com

GEORGIA — ATLANTA

Goodman McGuffey Lindsey & Johnson, LLP, Atlanta, GA (Continued)

Of Counsel

William S. Goodman — (Retired)

Kraig N. Johnson — (Retired)

W. Davis Hewitt — Vanderbilt University, B.A., 1972; The University of Georgia, J.D., 1975 — Admitted to Bar, 1975, Georgia; U.S. District Court, Middle, Northern and Southern Districts of Georgia; U.S. Court of Appeals, Eleventh Circuit; U.S. Supreme Court — Member American Bar Association; State Bar of Georgia — Former Attorney General, State of Georgia — Practice Areas: Construction Litigation; Employer Liability; Governmental Liability; Municipal Liability; Medical Malpractice; Premises Liability; Product Liability; Subrogation; Construction Defect; Elder Law; Employment Law; Professional Liability; Uninsured Motorist Defense — E-mail: whewitt@gmlj.com

Associates

David M. Abercrombie — 1970 — Georgia State University, B.S.B.A. (summa cum laude), 1999; Emory University School of Law, J.D., 2003 — Admitted to Bar, 2003, Georgia — Member American and Atlanta Bar Associations; State Bar of Georgia — Practice Areas: Construction Litigation; Medical Malpractice; Premises Liability; Product Liability; Subrogation; Construction Defect; Insurance Coverage; Bad Faith; Professional Liability; Uninsured Motorist Defense — E-mail: dabercrombie@gmlj.com

Chad W. Bickerton — New College of Florida, B.A., 2009; University of Florida College of Law, J.D. (with honors), 2012 — Admitted to Bar, 2011, Florida; Alabama — Practice Areas: Automobile Liability; Construction Defect; Construction Litigation; Insurance Coverage & Defense; Subrogation — Resident Sarasota, FL Office — E-mail: cbickerton@gmlj.com

R. Tyler Bryant — The University of Georgia, B.A. (summa cum laude), 2005; The University of Georgia School of Law, J.D. (cum laude), 2008 — Admitted to Bar, 2008, Georgia — Member State Bar of Georgia — Practice Areas: Construction Litigation; Construction Defect; Insurance Coverage; Bad Faith; Uninsured Motorist Defense — E-mail: tbryant@gmlj.com

Michael A. Cannon — The University of North Carolina at Charlotte, B.A., 2003; Roger Williams University School of Law, J.D., 2007 — Admitted to Bar, 2007, North Carolina; U.S. District Court, Eastern and Western Districts of North Carolina — Member North Carolina and Mecklenburg County Bar Associations; North Carolina Association of Defense Attorneys — Practice Areas: Construction Litigation; Employer Liability; Premises Liability; Product Liability; Subrogation; Workers' Compensation; Employment Law; Insurance Coverage; Bad Faith; Uninsured Motorist Defense — Resident Charlotte, NC Office — E-mail: mcannon@gmlj.com

Kristen S. Cawley — The University of Georgia, B.B.A. (magna cum laude, with high honors), 2004; Georgia State University College of Law, J.D., 2007 — Admitted to Bar, 2007, Georgia — Member State Bar of Georgia — Practice Areas: Construction Litigation; Premises Liability; Product Liability; Construction Defect; Insurance Coverage; Bad Faith; Uninsured Motorist Defense — E-mail: kcawley@gmlj.com

Neal B. Childers — Mars Hill College, B.A., 1981; Mercer University, J.D. (cum laude), 1988 — Admitted to Bar, 1984, Georgia; U.S. District Court, Middle, Northern and Southern Districts of Georgia; Georgia Court of Appeals; U.S. Court of Appeals, Eleventh Circuit; Georgia Superior and State Courts; Supreme Court of Georgia; U.S. Supreme Court — Member Atlanta Bar Association — Practice Areas: Governmental Liability; Municipal Liability; Subrogation; Workers' Compensation; Professional Liability — E-mail: nchilders@gmlj.com

Sean B. Cox — The University of Georgia, B.S., 2004; Georgia State University College of Law, J.D. (with honors), 2008 — Admitted to Bar, 2008, Georgia; 2012, South Carolina — Member Atlanta Bar Association — Practice Areas: Construction Litigation; Employer Liability; Premises Liability; Product Liability; Construction Defect; Elder Law; Employment Law; Insurance Coverage; Bad Faith; Uninsured Motorist Defense — E-mail: scox@gmlj.com

Rosetta Davidson — North Carolina Agricultural and Technical State University, B.A., 2004; Thomas M. Cooley Law School, J.D., 2008 — Admitted to Bar, 2008, North Carolina — Member North Carolina State Bar — Practice Areas: Workers' Compensation — Resident Charlotte, NC Office — E-mail: rdavidson@gmlj.com

Phillip B. Hairston — Georgia Institute of Technology, B.S., 2009; Washington University School of Law, J.D., 2013 — Admitted to Bar, 2013, Georgia — Member Atlanta Bar Association — Practice Areas: Workers' Compensation — E-mail: phairston@gmlj.com

James T. Hankins, III — The University of Georgia, B.A. (with honors), 2003; The University of Georgia School of Law, J.D. (with honors), 2008 — Admitted to Bar, 2008, Georgia — Member State Bar of Georgia — Practice Areas: Premises Liability; Subrogation; Construction Defect; Insurance Coverage; Bad Faith; Professional Liability — E-mail: jhankins@gmlj.com

Rachel E. Hudgins — Emory University, B.A., 2008; The University of Georgia School of Law, J.D. (cum laude), 2012 — Admitted to Bar, 2013, Georgia — Member Atlanta Bar Association — Practice Areas: Construction Defect; Construction Litigation; Employment Law; Premises Liability; Product Liability; Professional Liability; Uninsured and Underinsured Motorist — E-mail: rhudgins@gmlj.com

Nathan J. Kaplan — Vanderbilt University, B.A., 2004; Florida State College of Law, J.D., 2013 — Admitted to Bar, 2013, Florida — Practice Areas: Workers' Compensation — E-mail: nkaplan@gmlj.com

Zachary J. Nelson — The University of Georgia, B.A., 2007; University of Florida College of Law, J.D. (cum laude), 2011 — Admitted to Bar, 2011, Georgia — Practice Areas: Construction Litigation; Employer Liability; Premises Liability; Product Liability; Employment Law; Insurance Coverage; Bad Faith; Professional Liability — E-mail: znelson@gmlj.com

Kevin C. Patrick — The University of Georgia, B.A. (magna cum laude, with high honors); Mercer University Walter F. George School of Law, J.D., 2008 — Admitted to Bar, 2008, Georgia; District of Columbia — Member State Bar of Georgia (Young Lawyers Division); Atlanta Bar Association — Practice Areas: Premises Liability; Product Liability; Insurance Coverage; Bad Faith — E-mail: kpatrick@gmlj.com

Brett A. Smith — Indiana University, B.A., 2006; Barry University School of Law, J.D., 2010 — Admitted to Bar, 2011, Florida — Member The Florida Bar — Practice Areas: Construction Litigation; Employer Liability; Governmental Liability; Municipal Liability; Premises Liability; Construction Defect; Insurance Coverage; Bad Faith; Uninsured Motorist Defense — Resident Sarasota, FL Office — E-mail: bsmith@gmlj.com

Lamar, Archer & Cofrin, LLP

The Hurt Building, Suite 900
50 Hurt Plaza
Atlanta, Georgia 30303
Telephone: 404-577-1777
Fax: 404-577-9490
laclaw.net

Established: 1981

Premises Liability, Self-Insured Defense, Directors and Officers Liability, Trucking Litigation, Legal Malpractice, Accountant Malpractice, Equine Law, Architects and Engineers, Accountants and Attorneys Liability, Bad Faith, Business Litigation, Coverage Analysis, Coverage Issues, Real Estate Agents & Brokers Liability, Real Estate Litigation, Truck Liability

Firm Profile: Celebrating its 33rd year, Lamar, Archer & Cofrin continues to provide its insurance and self insured clients with proven expertise and results in trucking liability, professional malpractice, directors and officers liability, premises and product liability defense, equine law and insurance coverage analysis and litigation.

Insurance Clients

Berkley Underwriting Partners, LLC	Chartis Insurance
Empire Fire and Marine Insurance Company	CNA Insurance Companies
Hanover Insurance Company	First State Management Group, Inc.
Lexington Insurance Company	Interstate Insurance Group
Zurich North America	StarNet Insurance Company

Non-Insurance Clients

Belk, Inc.	Buffets, Inc.
Charles Machine Works	Diversified Trucking Corporation
Lend Lease Trucks, Inc.	Parking Company of America, Inc.
Premier Trailer Leasing	Sentinel Real Estate Corporation
Wills Trucking, Inc.	

Partners

Robert C. Lamar — 1950 — Emory University, 1969; University of Kentucky,

Lamar, Archer & Cofrin, LLP, Atlanta, GA (Continued)

B.A., 1972; Emory University, J.D., 1976 — Legislative Fellow, U.S. Senator Sam Nunn, 1974-1975 — Admitted to Bar, 1976, Georgia; 1976, U.S. District Court, Northern District of Georgia; 1977, U.S. Court of Appeals, Fifth Circuit; 1981, U.S. Court of Appeals, Eleventh Circuit; 1983, U.S. Court of Appeals, Sixth Circuit — Member American and Atlanta Bar Associations; State Bar of Georgia; Atlanta Claims Association; Lawyers Club of Atlanta

Burke O. Archer — 1948 — The University of North Carolina, B.S., 1970; Rutgers University, J.D. (with honors), 1975 — Admitted to Bar, 1975, Georgia; 1977, U.S. District Court, Northern District of Georgia; 1977, U.S. Court of Appeals, Fifth Circuit; 1981, U.S. Court of Appeals, Eleventh Circuit — Member Federal, American and Atlanta Bar Associations; State Bar of Georgia

David H. Cofrin — 1948 — Cornell University, 1967; Jacksonville University, B.A., 1970; University of Notre Dame, J.D., 1978 — Admitted to Bar, 1978, Georgia; 1982, U.S. District Court, Northern District of Georgia; 1982, U.S. Court of Appeals, Eleventh Circuit — Member American and Atlanta Bar Associations; State Bar of Georgia — Lieutenant, U.S. Navy, 1970-1973, Lieutenant J. G., USNR

David W. Davenport — 1952 — The University of Oklahoma, B.A., 1974; Emory University, J.D., 1979 — Delta Theta Phi — Admitted to Bar, 1979, Georgia; 1979, U.S. District Court, Northern District of Georgia; 1980, U.S. Court of Appeals, Ninth Circuit; 1981, U.S. Court of Appeals, Fifth and Eleventh Circuits — Member State Bar of Georgia; Atlanta Lawyers Club (Secretary, 1995-1995; Executive Committee, 1996-1998; Second Vice President, 1998-1999; Vice President/President Elect, 1999-2000; President, 2000-2001; Chairman, 2001-2002); Atlanta Claims Association

Associates

Katherine E. Decker — 1971 — University of Notre Dame, B.A. (cum laude), 1994; Georgia State University, J.D. (cum laude), 1999 — Admitted to Bar, 1999, Georgia; 1999, U.S. District Court, Northern District of Georgia; 1999, U.S. Court of Appeals, Eleventh Circuit — Member State Bar of Georgia

Keith A. Pittman — 1956 — Emory University, B.A. (cum laude), 1979; The University of Georgia School of Law, J.D., 1993 — Order of the Coif — Admitted to Bar, 1993, Georgia; U.S. Court of Appeals, Eleventh Circuit; U.S. District Court, Middle and Northern Districts of Georgia

Counsel

Brian J. O'Shea — 1953 — The University of Georgia, B.B.A. (magna cum laude), 1975; University of Notre Dame, J.D., 1978 — Admitted to Bar, 1978, Georgia; 1978, U.S. District Court, Northern District of Georgia; 1995, U.S. Court of Appeals, Eleventh Circuit — Member State Bar of Georgia — Assistant Attorney General, State of Georgia, 1979-1981

Locke Lord LLP

Terminus 200, Suite 1200
3333 Piedmont Road NE
Atlanta, Georgia 30305
 Telephone: 404-870-4600
 Fax: 404-872-5547
 www.lockelord.com

(Chicago, IL Office*: 111 South Wacker Drive, 60606-4410)
 (Tel: 312-443-0700)
 (Fax: 312-443-0336)
(Austin, TX Office*: 600 Congress Avenue, Suite 2200, 78701-2748)
 (Tel: 512-305-4700)
 (Fax: 512-305-4800)
(Dallas, TX Office*: 2200 Ross Avenue, Suite 2200, 75201)
 (Tel: 214-740-8000)
 (Fax: 214-740-8800)
(Houston, TX Office*: 2800 JPMorgan Chase Tower, 600 Travis, 77002-3095)
 (Tel: 713-226-1200)
 (Fax: 713-223-3717)
(London, United Kingdom Office*: 201 Bishopsgate, DX 567 London/City, EC2M 3AB)
 (Tel: +44 (0) 20 7861 9000 (Int'l))
 (Tel: 011 44 207861 9000 (US))
 (Fax: +44 (0) 20 7785 6869 201 (Bishopsgate))

Locke Lord LLP, Atlanta, GA (Continued)

(Los Angeles, CA Office*: 300 South Grand Avenue, Suite 2600, 90071-3119)
 (Tel: 213-485-1500)
 (Fax: 213-485-1200)
(New Orleans, LA Office*: 601 Poydras, Suite 2660, 70130)
 (Tel: 504-558-5100)
 (Fax: 504-558-5200)
(New York, NY Office*: Three World Financial Center, Floor 20, 10281)
 (Tel: 212-415-8600)
 (Fax: 212-303-2754)
(Sacramento, CA Office: 500 Capitol Mall, Suite 1800, 95814)
 (Tel: 916-554-0240)
 (Fax: 916-554-5440)
(San Francisco, CA Office*: 44 Montgomery Street, Suite 2400, 94104)
 (Tel: 415-318-8810)
 (Fax: 415-676-5816)
(Washington, DC Office*: 701 8th Street, N.W., Suite 700, 20001)
 (Tel: 202-521-4100)
 (Fax: 202-521-4200)
(Hong Kong, China-PRC Office: 21/F Bank of China Tower, 1 Garden Road, Central)
 (Tel: +852 3465 0600)
 (Fax: +852 3014 0991)

Antitrust, Arbitration, Aviation, Business Law, Class Actions, Construction Law, Corporate Law, Directors and Officers Liability, Employee Benefits, Environmental Law, Health Care, Insurance Law, Intellectual Property, Labor and Employment, Land Use, Admiralty and Maritime Law, Mergers and Acquisitions, Product Liability, Railroad Law, Regulatory and Compliance, Reinsurance, Securities, Technology, Transportation, Litigation, Appellate, Long Term Care

Partners

Brian T. Casey — 1962 — Auburn University, B.S.B.A. (summa cum laude), 1984; Emory University, M.L., 1992; The Ohio State University, J.D., 1987 — Admitted to Bar, 1988, Georgia — Member Association of Life Insurance Council; Atlanta Association for Corporate Growth; Georgia Electronic Commerce Association — Practice Areas: Corporate Law; Mergers and Acquisitions

Neil H. Dickson — 1959 — University of Michigan, B.S., 1981; State University of New York at Buffalo, J.D., 1984 — Admitted to Bar, 1984, Georgia — Practice Areas: Corporate Law

Elizabeth J. Campbell — Furman University, B.A. (cum laude), 1999; The University of Texas School of Law, J.D. (with distinction), 2003 — Admitted to Bar, 2003, Georgia; Florida

Senior Counsel

Larry Davie   Lori Bibb

Of Counsel

Thomas D. Sherman   Randall Johnson

Associate

Alexandra Dishun

(See listing under Chicago, IL for additional information)

Mozley, Finlayson & Loggins LLP

One Premier Plaza, Suite 900
5605 Glenridge Drive
Atlanta, Georgia 30342
 Telephone: 404-256-0700
 Fax: 404-250-9355
 www.mfllaw.com

Established: 1977

Mozley, Finlayson & Loggins LLP, Atlanta, GA
(Continued)

Insurance Defense, Aviation, Construction Law, Employment Law, Environmental Law, Fidelity and Surety, General Liability, Property Liability, Fire and Allied Lines, Product Liability, Property Damage, Toxic Torts, Subrogation, Workers' Compensation, Coverage Issues, Bankruptcy, Corporate Law, Commercial Litigation, Real Estate, Restrictive Covenants

Firm Profile: Mozley, Finlayson & Loggins LLP is a mid-sized law firm founded in 1977. The majority of the partners at the firm have practiced law from 20 to 40 years, with the result being that each matter is normally handled by lawyers with more experience than their opponents in litigation. The firm blends this depth of experience with the ability to keep fees in a reasonable and attractive range. Innovative and alternative fee arrangements are encouraged, with the goal always being thorough and competent legal work at a fair and competitive rate.

Insurance Clients

ACE USA
American Benefit Plan Administrators
Argo Group US
Chartis Aerospace
Chubb Group of Insurance Companies
Companion Commercial Insurance c/o National Claim Services
ESIS Casualty Claims
Federal Insurance Company
Fireman's Fund Insurance Company
Grange Mutual Casualty Company
Horace Mann Insurance Company
Liberty Mutual Insurance Company
Lincoln General Insurance Company
National Claims Services, Inc.
National Union Fire Insurance Company
OneBeacon Insurance Group, Ltd.
RSUI Group, Inc.
Sedgwick Claims Management Services, Inc.
Starr Adjustment Services, Inc.
Underwriters at Lloyd's, London
Victoria Fire & Casualty Company
Virginia Surety Company, Inc.
Westpoint Insurance Group
Zurich American Insurance Group
Allianz Global Corporate & Specialty
Amerisure Companies
Berkley Risk Administrators Company, LLC
Cincinnati Insurance Company
CNA Reinsurance Company Limited
Donegal Insurance Group
FCCI Insurance Group
FFVA Mutual Insurance Company
GAB Robins North America, Inc.
Global Aerospace, Inc.
The Hartford Insurance Group
Jewelers Mutual Insurance Company
MetLife Auto & Home
Metropolitan Property and Casualty Insurance Company
Nationwide Insurance Company of North Carolina
Occidental Fire & Casualty Company of North Carolina
Safeco Insurance Companies
Southern Insurance Company of Virginia
Travelers Insurance Company
United States Liability Insurance Company
Wausau General Insurance Company

Non-Insurance Clients

Air Cargo Express, Inc.
Atlanta Airlines Terminal Corporation
Atlantic Companies
BAH Express, Inc.
BankSouth
BellSouth Telecommunications, Inc. d/b/a/ AT&T Georgia
The Brickman Group, Ltd.
CarMax
Deere & Company
Epps Air Service, Inc.
Grady Health System
HealthPlan Services, Inc.
J.D. Byrider Systems, Inc.
Level 3 Communications, Inc.
McNeilus Truck and Manufacturing, Inc.
Nix-Fowler Constructors, Inc.
The Parkes Companies
Sterling Healthcare
United Parcel Service, Inc.
Willett Honda
Altus Healthcare & Hospice, Inc.
Atlanta Air Salvage, Inc.
Atlanta Regional Commission
Avita Community Partners
Bank of North Georgia
The Beasley Group
Billy Howell Ford Lincoln-Mercury
B & W Cartage
Crown Diamond
Discrete Wireless, Inc.
Fuzebox, LLC
Growers Marketing Service, Inc.
The Hyman Companies, Inc.
Komatsu America Corp.
McGriff Transportation, Inc.
Metropolitan Atlanta Rapid Transit Authority (MARTA)
Osborn Transportation, Inc.
Peach State Trucking, LLC
Uniglobe Courier Services, Inc
Weingarten Realty Investors
YRC Worldwide, Inc.

Firm Members

J. Arthur Mozley — Emory University, LL.B., 1965 — Admitted to Bar, 1965, Georgia — E-mail: amozley@mfllaw.com

Mozley, Finlayson & Loggins LLP, Atlanta, GA
(Continued)

Robert M. Finlayson, II
William D. Harrison
Wayne D. Taylor
Edward C. Bresee, Jr.
Anne M. Landrum
Deborah S. Cameron
Brian J. Duva
Joseph J. Burton, Jr.
John R. Lowery
Sewell K. Loggins
C. David Hailey
Lawrence B. Domenico
William J. Rawls, II
Jennifer T. McLean
John L. McKinley, Jr.
James G. Coyle
Rosemary S. Armstrong
Allison E. Maloney

Associates

Aaron A. Miller
Michelle A. Sherman
Bridgette E. Eckerson
Janine D. Willis
Andrew Capobianco
Arthur J. Park
Richard S. Bruno
Sharon P. Horne

Of Counsel

Joe Hardy

(This firm is also listed in the Subrogation section of this directory)

Nall & Miller, LLP
235 Peachtree Street, NE
Suite 1500, North Tower
Atlanta, Georgia 30303
Telephone: 404-522-2200
Fax: 404-522-2208
www.nallmiller.com

Established: 1952

Insurance Defense, Medical Malpractice, Motor Carriers, Premises Liability, Product Liability, Professional Liability

Firm Profile: Nall & Miller, LLP is one of Atlanta's oldest and most respected law firms, representing global corporations, medical professionals and individuals, alike. For over sixty years, we have delivered exceptional client service by applying creative and cost-efficient legal strategies to both resolve and try cases. We are recognized for our experienced trial lawyers who litigate routine to highly complex cases. Nall & Miller maintains a strong regional practice in Georgia and the Southeast, as well as representing clients throughout the United States, Canada, and the U.S. Virgin Islands. Several of our attorneys are recognized as Super Lawyers and are Martindale Hubbell AV Rated.

Insurance Clients

ACE Westchester Specialty Group
Berkshire Hathaway Homestate Companies
Burlington Insurance Company
Cypress Insurance Company
Harbor Pacific Insurance Company
Jewelers Mutual Insurance Company
National American Insurance Company of California
PACO Assurance Company, Inc.
Ranger Insurance Company
RenaissanceRe Holdings, Ltd.
Seneca Insurance Company, Inc.
Stonington Insurance Company
Western Litigation, Inc.
Aviva Life Insurance Company
Blue Cross and Blue Shield of Georgia, Inc.
Celina Mutual Insurance Company
First Financial Insurance Company
James River Insurance Company
Lincoln General Insurance Company
North American Specialty Insurance Company
Preferred Risk Mutual Insurance Company
Security Mutual Casualty Company
Shelter Insurance Companies
West Bend Mutual Insurance Company

National Counsel

CHG Healthcare Services, Inc.
Podiatry Insurance Company of America (PICA)
Corizon Health, Inc.
SpecialtyCare, Inc.

National Product Counsel

Whirlpool Corporation

Nall & Miller, LLP, Atlanta, GA (Continued)

Non-Insurance Clients

Airgas, Inc.
Anchor Hospital
Black & Decker Corporation
Cardinal Logistics Management
Claims Management Services, Inc.
Criterion Claim Solutions
Damon Corporation
Dutchmen Manufacturing, Inc.
Forward Air, Inc.
Gulf Claims Service
Lancer Claims Services, Inc.
Landair Transportation Inc.
Landstar Ranger, Inc.
Monaco Coach Corporation
Osborn Transportation, Inc.
Penske Truck Leasing Company
The Podiatry Institute, Inc.
Staples, Inc.
State Bar of Georgia
Switzerland Claims Management, Inc.
Universal Health Services of Delaware, Inc. - Central Region
Winnebago Industries, Inc.
Alliance Shippers, Inc.
Benson Media, Inc.
Broan-NuTone LLC
CBT Truck Brokerage, Inc.
Coachmen Recreational Vehicle Company, LLC
Discount Tire Company, Inc.
EmCare
Georgia Osteopathic Hospital, Inc.
Hamlin & Burton Liability Management
Landstar Inway, Inc.
Laurel Heights Hospital
Morbark, Inc.
Peachford Behavioral Health Systems of Atlanta
Risk Management Claim Services, Inc.
Subaru of America, Inc.
Talbott Recovery Campus
Tempco Electric Heater Corporation
US Xpress, Inc.

Partners

George R. Neuhauser — The University of Georgia, J.D., 1978 — Admitted to Bar, 1978, Georgia; U.S. District Court, Northern District of Georgia; U.S. Court of Appeals, Eleventh Circuit — Member American and Atlanta Bar Associations; State Bar of Georgia; Product Liability Advisory Council; Defense Research Institute; Trial Attorneys of America; Georgia Defense Lawyers Association — Practice Areas: Alternative Dispute Resolution; Catastrophic Injury; Pharmaceutical; Product Liability; Toxic Torts; Trial Practice — E-mail: gneuhauser@nallmiller.com

Robert L. Goldstucker — The University of Georgia, J.D., 1977 — Admitted to Bar, 1977, Georgia; 2002, Nevada; 2007, Iowa; 2008, Washington; U.S. District Court, Middle, Northern and Southern Districts of Georgia; U.S. District Court, District of Massachusetts; U.S. District Court, District of South Carolina; U.S. District Court, District of New Mexico; U.S. District Court, Northern District of Oklahoma; U.S. District Court, Northern District of Mississippi; U.S. District Court, District of Colorado; U.S. District Court, Western District of Michigan; 1977, Georgia Court of Appeals; 1977, U.S. Court of Appeals, Fourth, Fifth, Tenth and Eleventh Circuits — Member American and Atlanta Bar Associations; State Bar of Georgia (Chairperson, Product Liability Section, 1991-1995); Defense Research Institute — Practice Areas: Alternative Dispute Resolution; Catastrophic Injury; Governmental Liability; Trial Practice — E-mail: bgoldstucker@nallmiller.com

Kenneth P. McDuffie — Mercer University, J.D., 1976 — Admitted to Bar, 1976, Georgia; U.S. District Court, Middle and Northern Districts of Georgia; U.S. Court of Appeals, Eleventh Circuit; Georgia Court of Appeals; Supreme Court of the United States; Supreme Court of Georgia — Member State Bar of Georgia — Practice Areas: Business Law; Catastrophic Injury; Construction Litigation; E-Discovery; Governmental Liability; Health Care; Insurance; Premises Liability; Product Liability; Professional Liability; Trial Practice — E-mail: kmcduffie@nallmiller.com

Michael D. Hostetter — Emory University, J.D., 1987 — Admitted to Bar, 1987, Georgia; 2008, Tennessee; U.S. District Court, Middle, Northern and Southern Districts of Georgia; U.S. Court of Appeals, Eleventh Circuit; Georgia Court of Appeals; U.S. Supreme Court; Supreme Court of Georgia; Tennessee Supreme Court — Member American and Atlanta Bar Associations; State Bar of Georgia; Georgia Academy of Hospital Attorneys; Georgia Society for Healthcare Risk Management; Professional Liability Defense Federation; Defense Research Institute; Federation of Defense and Corporate Counsel; Georgia Defense Lawyers Association; International Association of Arson Investigators; Transportation Lawyers Association; Trucking Industry Defense Association — Practice Areas: Catastrophic Injury; Health Care; Motor Carriers; Premises Liability; Product Liability; Professional Liability — E-mail: mhostetter@nallmiller.com

Mary A. Palma — Emory University School of Law, J.D., 1994 — Admitted to Bar, 1994, Georgia; U.S. District Court, Middle and Northern Districts of Georgia; U.S. Court of Appeals, Eleventh Circuit; Georgia Court of Appeals — Member American and Atlanta Bar Associations; State Bar of Georgia; Defense Research Institute — Practice Areas: Appellate Practice; Business Law; E-Discovery; Health Care; Insurance; Product Liability; Toxic Torts; Trial Practice — E-mail: mpalma@nallmiller.com

Nall & Miller, LLP, Atlanta, GA (Continued)

Mark D. Lefkow — Emory University, J.D., 2000 — Admitted to Bar, 2000, Georgia; U.S. District Court, Northern District of Georgia; U.S. District Court, Western District of Michigan; U.S. Court of Appeals, Eleventh Circuit; Georgia Court of Appeals — Member American and Atlanta Bar Associations; State Bar of Georgia — Practice Areas: Appellate Practice; Business Law; Catastrophic Injury; Construction Litigation; Governmental Liability; Health Care; Insurance; Motor Carriers; Professional Liability; Trial Practice — E-mail: mlefkow@nallmiller.com

Adriane Y. Sammons — The University of Georgia, J.D., 1999 — Admitted to Bar, 2000, Georgia; U.S. District Court, Middle and Northern Districts of Georgia; U.S. Court of Appeals, Eleventh Circuit; Georgia Court of Appeals — Member American and Atlanta Bar Associations; State Bar of Georgia; National Association of Fire Investigators; Defense Research Institute; Georgia Defense Lawyers Association — Practice Areas: Appellate Practice; Catastrophic Injury; Health Care; Insurance; Nursing Home Litigation; Pharmaceutical; Premises Liability; Product Liability; Professional Liability; Toxic Torts; Trial Practice — E-mail: asammons@nallmiller.com

Laura D. Eschleman — The University of Georgia, J.D. (cum laude), 2005 — Admitted to Bar, 2005, Georgia; 2009, Alabama; 2011, Missouri; U.S. District Court, Northern District of Georgia; U.S. Court of Appeals, Eleventh Circuit; Supreme Court of Georgia — Member American and Atlanta Bar Associations; State Bar of Georgia; Alabama State Bar; The Missouri Bar; Defense Research Institute; Professional Liability Underwriting Society; Alabama Defense Lawyers Association; Georgia Defense Lawyers Association — Practice Areas: Business Law; Catastrophic Injury; Construction Litigation; Insurance; Motor Carriers; Premises Liability; Product Liability; Professional Liability; Trial Practice — E-mail: leschleman@nallmiller.com

Amanda L. Matthews — Georgia State University, J.D., 2006 — Admitted to Bar, 2006, Georgia; U.S. District Court, Middle and Northern Districts of Georgia; U.S. Court of Appeals, Eleventh Circuit; Georgia Court of Appeals; Supreme Court of Georgia — Member American and Atlanta Bar Associations; State Bar of Georgia; Georgia Society for Healthcare Risk Management; Professional Liability Defense Federation; Defense Research Institute; American Health Lawyers Association; Trucking Industry Defense Association; Transportation Lawyers Association — Practice Areas: Catastrophic Injury; Construction Litigation; Health Care; Insurance; Motor Carriers; Nursing Home Litigation; Premises Liability; Product Liability; Professional Liability; Toxic Torts; Trial Practice; Wills and Estate Litigation — E-mail: amatthews@nallmiller.com

Clinton F. Fletcher — Emory University School of Law, J.D., 2001 — Admitted to Bar, 2001, Georgia; U.S. District Court, Northern and Southern Districts of Georgia; U.S. Court of Appeals, Eleventh Circuit; Supreme Court of Georgia — Member American and Atlanta Bar Associations; State Bar of Georgia; Defense Research Institute — Practice Areas: Business Law; Motor Carriers; Premises Liability; Product Liability — E-mail: cfletcher@nallmiller.com

Meghan R. Davidson — Georgia State University, J.D., 2006 — Admitted to Bar, 2006, Georgia; U.S. District Court, Middle and Northern and Southern Districts of Georgia; U.S. Court of Appeals, Eleventh Circuit; Georgia Court of Appeals; Supreme Court of Georgia — Member State Bar of Georgia; Atlanta Bar Association; Georgia Defense Lawyers Association; Defense Research Institute — Practice Areas: Governmental Liability; Health Care; Insurance; Premises Liability; Product Liability; Toxic Torts; Trial Practice — E-mail: mdavidson@nallmiller.com

Associates

Patrick N. Arndt — The University of Georgia School of Law, J.D., 2008 — Admitted to Bar, 2008, Georgia; U.S. District Court, Middle District of Georgia; Georgia Court of Appeals; Supreme Court of Georgia — Practice Areas: Construction Litigation; Governmental Liability; Health Care; Motor Carriers; Product Liability; Professional Liability; Trial Practice — E-mail: parndt@nallmiller.com

Matthew F. Boyer — Tulane University Law School, J.D., 2004 — Admitted to Bar, 2004, Georgia; U.S. District Court, Middle, Northern and Southern Districts of Georgia; U.S. Court of Appeals, Eleventh Circuit; Georgia Court of Appeals; Supreme Court of Georgia — Practice Areas: Construction Litigation; Governmental Liability; Insurance; Motor Carriers

Benjamin H. Pierman — The University of Mississippi School of Law, J.D., 2005 — Admitted to Bar, 2006, Georgia; U.S. District Court, Middle, Northern and Southern Districts of Georgia; Supreme Court of Georgia — Member State Bar of Georgia — Practice Areas: Business Law; Governmental Liability; Motor Carriers; Premises Liability; Product Liability — E-mail: bpierman@nallmiller.com

GEORGIA — ATLANTA

Nall & Miller, LLP, Atlanta, GA (Continued)

Rachael K. Goldstucker — New York University School of Law, J.D., 2011 — Admitted to Bar, 2012, New York — Member American Bar Association — Practice Areas: Insurance — E-mail: rachaelgoldstucker@nallmiller.com

Michael T. Davis — The University of Georgia School of Law, J.D., 2012 — Admitted to Bar, 2012, Georgia — Member State Bar of Georgia — Practice Areas: Governmental Liability — E-mail: mdavis@nallmiller.com

Of Counsel

Teresa W. Pendergrast — The University of Georgia School of Law, J.D., 1984 — Admitted to Bar, 1984, Georgia; U.S. District Court, Northern District of Georgia; Georgia Court of Appeals; Supreme Court of Georgia — Member State Bar of Georgia — Practice Areas: Business Law; Governmental Liability; Insurance; Professional Liability — E-mail: tpendergrast@nallmiller.com

Scrudder, Bass, Quillian, Horlock, Taylor & Lazarus, LLP

900 Circle 75 Parkway, Suite 850
Atlanta, Georgia 30339
Telephone: 770-612-9200
Fax: 770-612-9201
E-Mail: kshelton@scrudderbass.com
www.scrudderbass.com

Established: 1981

Product Liability, Construction Law, Construction Litigation, Premises Liability, Subrogation, Toxic Torts, Professional Errors and Omissions, Life and Health, Disability, ERISA, Workers' Compensation, Commercial Litigation, Business Litigation, Civil Rights, Employment Discrimination, Equal Employment Opportunity Commission, Commercial Property Loss Litigation, Health Care and Medical Malpractice Defense, Automobile Products Litigation, Automobile Dealership Defense, Insurance Coverage and Contract Litigation, Corporate Transactions, Corporate Contract Litigation, Automobile and Trucking Liability Litigation

Firm Profile: Scrudder, Bass, Quillian, Horlock, Taylor & Lazarus LLP, located in metropolitan Atlanta, has a statewide practice that concentrates on civil litigation, dispute resolution, and administrative claims inclusive of products liability, medical malpractice, professional malpractice, toxic torts, construction, workers' compensation, contract and insurance disputes and other civil and commercial matters for over 30 years. While specializing in civil litigation, the firm routinely counsels clients on a wide range of matters outside the context of litigation. As a natural result of the firm's extensive litigation practice, its attorneys are highly experienced in all forms of alternative dispute resolution, including arbitration, mediation, and administrative practice. The firm's attorneys are all licensed to practice in all state and federal trial and appellate courts in the State of Georgia. Individual members of the firm are also licensed in New York, South Carolina, and Florida.

Various members are listed in the Bar Register of Preeminent Lawyers in the areas of commercial law, insurance defense law, civil trial practice, and personal injury law. Individual members are actively involved with both the Defense Research Institute and the Georgia Defense Lawyers Association.

Insurance Clients

American Home Assurance Company
Chartis Insurance Group
Commerce and Industry Insurance Company
Crawford & Company
Gallagher Bassett Services, Inc.
GUARD Insurance Group
Hanover Insurance Company
Broadspire
Burlington Insurance Company
CNA Insurance Company
Constitution State Insurance Company
ESIS
Georgia Casualty & Surety Company
The Hartford Insurance Group
Lexington Insurance Company
National American Insurance Company
New Hampshire Insurance Company
Verizon Wireless
Massachusetts Indemnity and Life Insurance Company
National Union Fire Insurance Company
Sedgwick Claims Management Services, Inc.

Non-Insurance Clients

Black Clawson Company
Brentwood Services, Inc.
Continental General Tire Company
Frozen Food Express Industries, Inc.
HFIC Management Company, Inc.
John Wieland Homes, Inc.
Live Nation, Inc.
McMaster-Carr Supply Company
Northside Hospital
ServiceMaster Company
Southern Mills, Inc.
Terminix International Company, L.P.
Bowman Transportation, Inc.
Chestatee Regional Hospital
Federated Department Stores, Inc.
General Fibers & Fabrics, Inc.
Grady Health System
House of Blues Legal Department
Kellogg's
Lowe's Companies, Inc.
NALCO Company
St. Joseph's Hospital of Atlanta, Inc.
SunLink Health Systems, Inc.
UtiliQuest/STS
Waffle House, Inc.

Partners

Henry E. Scrudder, Jr. — **Managing Partner** — The University of Tennessee, B.A., 1976; Duke University, J.D., 1979 — Phi Beta Kappa; Moot Court Board — Admitted to Bar, 1979, Georgia — Member State Bar of Georgia; Atlanta Bar Association; Georgia Defense Lawyers Association (Board of Directors, 1994-); Defense Research Institute

Glenn S. Bass — Clark University, B.A., 1979; Emory University, J.D., 1982 — Admitted to Bar, 1982, Georgia — Member State Bar of Georgia; Atlanta Bar Association; Georgia Defense Lawyers Association; Defense Research Institute

Alfred A. Quillian, Jr. — Georgia Southern College, B.B.A. (cum laude), 1980; The University of Georgia, J.D., 1983 — Admitted to Bar, 1983, Georgia — Member State Bar of Georgia; Atlanta Bar Association

William W. Horlock, Jr. — The University of Georgia, B.B.A., 1985; Emory University, J.D., 1989 — Admitted to Bar, 1989, Georgia; 1990, South Carolina — Member State Bar of Georgia; South Carolina Bar; Atlanta Bar Association; Georgia Defense Lawyers Association; Defense Research Institute

Jane C. Taylor — Auburn University, B.S., 1984; Cumberland School of Law of Samford University, J.D., 1988 — Associate Editor, American Journal of Trial Advocacy, 1987-1988 — Admitted to Bar, 1988, Georgia — Member State Bar of Georgia; Atlanta Bar Association; Georgia Defense Lawyers Association; Defense Research Institute

Matthew P. Lazarus — Duke University, B.A., 1993; Emory University, J.D., 1996 — Law Clerk for the Superior Court Judges of the Cherokee Judicial Circuit (1996-1998) — Admitted to Bar, 1996, Georgia — Member State Bar of Georgia; Atlanta Bar Association

Chiaka U. Adele — University of Nigeria, LL.B. (with honors), 1992; University of London, England, LL.M. (with honors), 1994; Nigerian Law School, B.L. (with honors), 1993; Emory University, J.D. (with high honors), 2001 — Admitted to Bar, 1996, New York; 2001, Georgia — Member State Bar of Georgia; Atlanta Bar Association

Keith Whitesides — The University of Alabama, B.S. (summa cum laude), 1989; Emory University, J.D. (with distinction), 1993 — Admitted to Bar, 1993, Georgia

Teddy Sutherland — The University of Georgia, B.A., 1999; J.D., 2002 — Admitted to Bar, 2002, Georgia — Member State Bar of Georgia; Atlanta Bar Association; Georgia Defense Lawyers Association

Associates

Rodney W. Hood — College of Charleston, B.A. (summa cum laude), 2000; The University of Chicago, J.D., 2004 — Admitted to Bar, 2004, Georgia — Member State Bar of Georgia; Atlanta Bar Association

Trisha Godsey — The Pennsylvania State University, B.A., 1998; Emory University, J.D., 2001 — Admitted to Bar, 2001, Georgia — Member State Bar of Georgia; Atlanta Bar Association

David C. Rhodes — Emory University, B.A., 2006; New York Law School, J.D., 2009 — Admitted to Bar, 2009, California; 2010, Georgia

C. Ryan Cooper — Valdosta State University, B.A. (summa cum laude), 2006; Florida State University, J.D., 2010 — Admitted to Bar, 2010, Florida; 2011, Georgia — Member Atlanta Bar Association

Scrudder, Bass, Quillian, Horlock, Taylor & Lazarus, LLP, Atlanta, GA (Continued)

Jeffrey Putnam — The University of Georgia, 2008; Cumberland School of Law at Samford University, 2013 — Admitted to Bar, 2013, Georgia

Of Counsel

Colleen P. O'Neill — Agnes Scott College, B.A. (with honors), 1984; Emory University, J.D., 1989 — Admitted to Bar, 1989, Georgia — Member State Bar of Georgia; Atlanta Bar Association

Seacrest, Karesh, Tate & Bicknese, LLP

56 Perimeter Center, East, Suite 450
Atlanta, Georgia 30346
   Telephone: 770-804-1800
   Fax: 770-804-1400
   E-Mail: INFO@sktblaw.com
   www.sktblaw.com

Established: 1977

Insurance Defense, Automobile, General Liability, Product Liability, Property and Casualty, Fidelity and Surety, Professional Liability, Medical Malpractice, Public Entities

Insurance Clients

Accredited Surety & Casualty Company, Inc.	AIG Personal Lines Claims
American States Insurance Company	American Southern Insurance Company
Atlanta Casualty Company	AssuranceAmerica Insurance Company
Broadspire, a Crawford Company	Columbia Insurance Group
Everest Security Insurance Company	Farmers Insurance
Independent Fire Insurance Company	Great American Insurance Company
Maxum Indemnity Company	Infinity Insurance Company
Permanent General Insurance Group	OneBeacon Insurance
21st Century Insurance Company	Sedgwick Claims Management Services, Inc.
	York Claims Service, Inc.

Non-Insurance Clients

Atlantic Companies   London Agency, Inc.

Firm Members

Edwin A. Tate, II — 1955 — State University of New York at Binghamton, B.A. (with honors), 1977; Emory University, J.D., 1980 — Phi Beta Kappa; Pi Sigma Alpha; Phi Delta Phi — Moot Court Board — Admitted to Bar, 1980, Georgia — Member State Bar of Georgia; Atlanta Bar Association; Georgia Defense Lawyers Association

Karsten Bicknese — 1958 — Ludwig-Maximillians University, 1979; Duke University, A.B. (magna cum laude), 1980; The University of Georgia, J.D., 1983 — Admitted to Bar, 1983, Georgia — Member American (Litigation Section) and Atlanta Bar Associations; State Bar of Georgia; Georgia Defense Lawyers Association — Languages: German

Of Counsel

Gary L. Seacrest — 1946 — The Pennsylvania State University, B.S., 1968; Emory University, J.D. (with distinction), 1975 — Admitted to Bar, 1975, Georgia — Member State Bar of Georgia; Atlanta Bar Association; Georgia Defense Lawyers Association; Defense Research Institute

Retired

Sanford R. Karesh

Strawinski & Stout, P.C.

Tower Place 100
3340 Peachtree Road Northeast, Suite 1445
Atlanta, Georgia 30326
   Toll Free: 877-540-1995
   Telephone: 404-264-9955
   Fax: 404-264-1450
   E-Mail: jss@strawlaw.com
   www.strawlaw.com

Aviation, Insurance Coverage, Insurance Defense, Motor Carriers, Pharmaceutical, Premises Liability, Professional Liability (Non-Medical) Defense, Product Liability, Transportation, Trucking Law

Firm Profile: Focused on liability defense litigation, the firm of Strawinski & Stout, P.C. was founded on the principle of providing clients with the industry-specific experience, superb advocacy, and the dedication to success that sets this firm apart.

Whether defending individuals, major retailers, local and national corporations, or insurance companies, the lawyers and staff at Strawinski & Stout bring the same attention to detail and unflagging commitment to excellence in pursuit of an efficient and cost-effective resolution to each case.

From offices in the Buckhead area of Atlanta, Georgia the attorneys of Strawinski & Stout are committed to working closely with clients throughout the U.S., developing individual litigation plans designed specifically for the client's needs, and keeping clients up to date during each stage of the process.

Insurance Clients

ACE USA	AIG Aerospace Insurance Services, Inc.
Allianz Aviation Managers, LLC	Avemco Insurance Company
The AOPA Legal Services Plan	Catlin, Inc.
Baldwin & Lyons, Inc.	Discover Re
Daily Underwriters of America	Fireman's Fund Insurance Company
Esurance Insurance Company	
Global Aerospace, Inc.	National American Insurance Company
Hallmark Insurance Company Effective Claims Management, Inc.	NCMIC Insurance Company
Occidental Fire & Casualty Company of North Carolina	Pharmacists Mutual Insurance Company
Phoenix Aviation Managers, Inc.	Royal & SunAlliance USA
State Farm Fire and Casualty Company	United States Aviation Underwriters, Inc.
U.S. Specialty Insurance Company	XL Aerospace

Non-Insurance Clients

Airtex Products, LP/United Components, Inc.	Delta Air Lines, Inc.
Kmart Corporation	Forward Air, Inc.
Sears Holdings Corporation	Roadsprint, Inc.

Partners

James S. Strawinski — 1949 — Duke University, A.B., 1971; Southern Illinois University Edwardsville, M.B.A., 1975; Emory University School of Law, J.D., 1979 — Phi Alpha Delta — Admitted to Bar, 1979, Georgia; Georgia Court of Appeals; 1980, Supreme Court of Georgia; U.S. District Court, Middle and Northern Districts of Georgia; U.S. Court of Appeals, Eleventh Circuit; U.S. Supreme Court — Member State Bar of Georgia (Chairman, Aviation Section, 1987, 1994); Atlanta Bar Association; National Transportation Safety Board Bar Association; Aviation Insurance Association; Georgia Defense Lawyers Association; Lawyer-Pilots Bar Association; Lawyers Club of Atlanta; Atlanta Claims Association; Trucking Industry Defense Association; Defense Research Institute — Georgia Jurisprudence, Personal Injury and Torts; Author: "Aviation Accidents", Vol. 14, Ch.29; "Where is the ACAA Today? Tracing the law developing from the Air Carrier Access Act of 1986," Southern Methodist University School of Law, Journal of Air Law and Commerce, Vol. 68, No. 2, Spring 2003; "Pre-Impact Pain and Suffering," Georgia State Bar Journal, Vol. 26, No.2, November 1989 — Judge, 2009 William W. Daniel National Invitational Mock Trial Competition — USAF, Active Duty, 1971-1976; Major, USAFR 1977-1985 — Practice Areas: Aviation; Insurance Law; Motor Carriers; Pharmaceutical; Premises Liability; Professional Liability (Non-Medical) Defense; Truck Liability — E-mail: JSS@strawlaw.com

GEORGIA ATLANTA

Strawinski & Stout, P.C., Atlanta, GA (Continued)

Nicole Wolfe Stout — 1972 — The University of Tennessee, B.A., 1995; Emory University School of Law, J.D., 1998 — Admitted to Bar, 1998, Georgia; U.S. District Court, Northern District of Georgia; U.S. District Court, Middle District of Georgia; U.S. Court of Appeals, Eleventh Circuit; Supreme Court of Georgia — Member State Bar of Georgia; Atlanta Bar Association; International Aviation Women's Association (IAWA); Atlanta Claims Association; Georgia Defense Lawyers Association; Lawyers Club of Atlanta; Defense Research Institute — Author: "Privileges and Immunities Available for Self-Critical Analysis and Reporting: Legal, Practical and Ethical Considerations," Journal of Air Law & Commerce, Vol. 69, No.3, Summer 2004; "Parameters of the Passenger-Carrier Relationship in Commercial Travel," Pre-Flight, State Bar of Georgia Aviation Law Section, Summer 2005; "The Tripartite Relationship," Pre-Flight, State Bar of Georgia Aviation Law Section, Winter 2006 — Practice Areas: Aviation; Truck Liability; Defense Litigation; Insurance Coverage; Legal Malpractice; Professional Liability; Premises Liability; Insurance Defense — E-mail: NWS@strawlaw.com

Associates

Jay M. O'Brien — 1979 — Hobart College, B.A., 2002; Nova University Law School, J.D. (magna cum laude), 2005 — Admitted to Bar, 2005, Florida; 2006, Georgia; U.S. District Court, Middle, Northern and Southern Districts of Georgia; U.S. Bankruptcy Court, Northern District of Georgia; Georgia Court of Appeals; U.S. Court of Appeals, Eleventh Circuit; Supreme Court of Georgia — Member State Bar of Georgia; The Florida Bar; Atlanta Claims Association; Georgia Defense Lawyers Association — Practice Areas: Aviation; Motor Carriers; Premises Liability; Professional Liability (Non-Medical) Defense; Truck Liability; Product Liability — E-mail: JMO@strawlaw.com

Daniel G. Cheek — 1980 — Furman University, B.S., 2003; Georgia State University College of Law, J.D. (magna cum laude), 2007 — Admitted to Bar, 2007, Georgia — Practice Areas: Aviation; Insurance Defense; Trucking; Premises Liability — E-mail: DGC@strawlaw.com

Vernis & Bowling of Atlanta, LLC

7100 Peachtree Dunwoody Road, Suite 300
Atlanta, Georgia 30328
  Telephone: 404-846-2001
  Fax: 404-846-2002
  E-Mail: info@georgia-law.com
  www.georgia-law.com

Established: 1970

Civil Litigation, Insurance Law, Workers' Compensation, Premises Liability, Labor and Employment, Civil Rights, Commercial Litigation, Complex Litigation, Product Liability, Directors and Officers Liability, Errors and Omissions, Construction Law, Construction Defect, Environmental Liability, Personal and Commercial Vehicle, Appellate Practice, Admiralty and Maritime Law, Real Estate, Family Law, Elder Law, Liability Defense, SIU/Fraud Litigation, Education Law (ESE/IDEA), Property and Casualty (Commercial and Personal Lines), Long-Haul Trucking Liability, Government Law, Public Law, Criminal, White Collar, Business Litigation

Firm Profile: Since 1970, VERNIS & BOWLING has represented individuals, businesses, professionals, insurance carriers, self-insureds, brokers, underwriters, agents, PEOs and insured. We provide cost effective, full service, legal representation that consistently exceeds the expectations of our clients. With 115 attorneys throughout 16 offices located in Florida, Georgia, Alabama, North Carolina and Mississippi the firm is able to provide the benefits of a large organization, including a management team, consistent policies and representation to ensure personal service and local representation to our clients.

Firm Members

Ian N. Matthes — Georgia State University, B.A., 1994; The University of Georgia School of Law, J.D., 1997 — Admitted to Bar, 1997, Georgia; U.S. District Court, Middle, Northern and Southern Districts of Georgia

Jeffrey P. Raasch — 1957 — University of Virginia, B.A., 1979; Cumberland School of Law of Samford University, J.D., 1983 — Admitted to Bar, 1983,

Vernis & Bowling of Atlanta, LLC, Atlanta, GA (Continued)

Virginia; 1985, Georgia; 2004, Tennessee; 1983, U.S. District Court, Eastern and Western Districts of Virginia; 1995, U.S. District Court, Middle, Northern and Southern Districts of Georgia — U.S.A.F. Captain, Judge Advocate General Corps 1983-1988

David W. Willis — Workers' Compensation — 1974 — Wake Forest University, B.A., 1996; Mercer Law School, J.D., 1999 — Admitted to Bar, 1999, Georgia; 2003, Florida; 1999, U.S. District Court, Northern District of Georgia; 2010, U.S. Court of Appeals, Eleventh Circuit

Joel R. Cope — 1968 — Vanderbilt University, B.A., 1991; Mercer University Walter F. George School of Law, J.D., 1996 — Admitted to Bar, 1996, Georgia; U.S. District Court, Northern District of Georgia

Alisa W. Ellenburg — 1963 — The University of Georgia, B.A., 1981; Vanderbilt University Law School, J.D., 1997 — Admitted to Bar, 1997, Tennessee; 1998, Georgia; 1997, U.S. District Court, Middle District of Tennessee; 1998, U.S. District Court, Middle, Northern and Southern Districts of Georgia

J. Scott Bell — Liability Department Head — 1964 — The University of Texas, B.A., 1988; American University, Washington College of Law, J.D., 1993 — Admitted to Bar, 2004, Georgia; Tennessee; U.S. District Court, Northern District of Georgia; 2006, U.S. District Court, Middle District of Georgia

Andrew Nelson — 1961 — University of South Carolina, B.A. Political Science, 1983; University of South Carolina School of Law, J.D., 1989 — Admitted to Bar, 1989, Georgia — Member State Bar of Georgia; Atlanta Bar Association

William P. Lee — 1982 — Georgia State University, B.A., 2005; Georgia State University College of Law, J.D., 2011 — Admitted to Bar, 2011, Georgia

(See listing under Miami, FL for additional information)

Waldon, Adelman, Castilla, Hiestand & Prout, LLP

900 Circle 75 Parkway, Suite 1040
Atlanta, Georgia 30339
  Telephone: 770-953-1710
  Fax: 770-933-9162
  E-Mail: jadelman@wachp.com
  www.wachp.com

Insurance Defense, Insurance Coverage, Bad Faith, Motor Vehicle, Truck Liability, General Liability

Insurance Clients

AssuranceAmerica Insurance Company	Canal Insurance Company
Farmers Insurance Group	Direct General Insurance Company
GAINSCO Auto Insurance	First Acceptance Insurance Company, Inc.
Grange Insurance Company	Grocers Insurance Company
Infinity Property & Casualty Group	Omni Insurance Company
Sedgwick CMS	Southern General Insurance Company
State Farm Insurance Companies	

Non-Insurance Clients

DHL Express (USA), Inc.

Partners

Jonathan M. Adelman — 1969 — The University of Georgia, B.B.A., 1992; Georgia State University, J.D., 1995 — Admitted to Bar, 1995, Georgia; 1995, U.S. District Court, Northern District of Georgia — Member State Bar of Georgia; Atlanta Bar Association; Defense Research Institute; Atlanta Claims Association — Practice Areas: Insurance Defense; Insurance Coverage; Bad Faith; Motor Vehicle; Trucking Law — E-mail: jadelman@hwc-law.com

Hilliard V. Castilla — 1962 — Jackson State University, B.S. (cum laude), 1982; University of Virginia, J.D., 1985 — Admitted to Bar, 1986, Mississippi; 1987, Georgia; 1988, U.S. Court of Appeals, Fourth Circuit; 1994, U.S. Court of Appeals, Eleventh Circuit — Member Atlanta and Gate City Bar Associations — Practice Areas: Insurance Defense; Sports and Entertainment Liability

AUGUSTA   GEORGIA

Waldon, Adelman, Castilla, Hiestand & Prout, LLP, Atlanta, GA (Continued)

Trevor G. Hiestand — 1970 — University of Wisconsin-Madison, B.A. (with distinction), 1993; Emory University, J.D., 1996 — Admitted to Bar, 1996, Georgia; U.S. District Court, Northern District of Georgia — Practice Areas: Insurance Defense — E-mail: thiestand@hwc-law.com

Kimberly A. McNamara — 1975 — Auburn University, B.A./B.A. (magna cum laude), 1998; M.A., 1999; Washington State University, J.D., 2002 — Admitted to Bar, 2002, Georgia; 2002, U.S. District Court, Northern District of Georgia; 2006, U.S. District Court, Middle District of Georgia — Languages: French — Practice Areas: Insurance Defense — E-mail: kmcnamara@hwc-law.com

Daniel C. Prout, Jr. — 1966 — Wake Forest University, B.A. (cum laude), 1988; The University of Alabama, J.D., 1991 — Admitted to Bar, 1991, Georgia; 1991, U.S. District Court, Northern District of Georgia — Member State Bar of Georgia — Practice Areas: Insurance Defense — E-mail: dcprout@hwc-law.com

Russell D. Waldon — 1957 — Georgia State University, B.A. (with honors), 1978; Emory University School of Law, J.D. (with distinction), 1982 — Order of the Coif, Order of Barristers — Admitted to Bar, 1982, Georgia; U.S. District Court, Northern District of Georgia; 2001, U.S. Supreme Court — Practice Areas: Insurance Defense — E-mail: rwaldon@hwc-law.com

All of the lawyers are admitted to the Georgia Court of Appeals and the Georgia Supreme Court

Wimberly, Lawson, Steckel, Schneider & Stine, P.C.

Lenox Towers, Suite 400
3400 Peachtree Road, NE
Atlanta, Georgia 30326
   Telephone: 404-365-0900
   Fax: 404-261-3707
   www.wimlaw.com

Labor and Employment, Administrative Law, Alternative Dispute Resolution, ERISA, Arbitration, Mediation, Litigation Defense Management (All Forums), OFCCP

Firm Profile: Wimberly, Lawson, Steckel & Stine, P.C. is an Atlanta based litigation firm with affiliate offices in Athens and Savannah, Georgia, Nashville, Cookeville, Knoxville, and Morristown, Tennessee and Greenville, South Carolina. Our practice is primarily defense of labor and employment litigation, including extensive work in NLRB, EEOC, OSHA, FLSA, OFCCP, and employment contract issues. In addition, we deal with construction related matters from both a contractor's and owner's perspective.

Representative Insurance Clients

Atlanta General Insurance/Markel Corporation

Representative Non Insurance Clients

American Cancer Society, Inc.   AmeriFleet Transportation, Inc.
Carey Executive Limousine   Claxton Poultry Company
Johnson & Johnson   Pilgrim's Pride Corporation
Sysco Corporation   Tip Top Poultry, Inc.
United Bank

Firm Members

Paul Oliver — Yale University, B.A., 1971; Harvard Law School, J.D., 1974 — Admitted to Bar, 1974, Georgia — Member American, National and Gate City Bar Associations; State Bar of Georgia — Adjunct Professor of Litigation, Georgia State University (1988-1999); Master of the Bench, Bleckley American Inn of Court — Practice Areas: Business Litigation; Contract Disputes; Deceptive Trade Practices; Dispute Resolution; Employment Litigation; Employment Practices Liability; Trial and Appellate Practice — E-mail: po@wimlaw.com

Rhonda L. Klein — Michigan State University, B.A. (cum laude), 1979; The George Washington University, J.D. (with honors), 1982 — Admitted to Bar, 1982, Michigan; 1983, Illinois; 1986, Georgia — Member American (Labor and Employment Section) and Atlanta Bar Associations; State Bar of Georgia (Labor and Employment Section); Lawyers Club of Atlanta — Practice

Wimberly, Lawson, Steckel, Schneider & Stine, P.C., Atlanta, GA (Continued)

Areas: Employment Law; Employment Discrimination; Americans with Disabilities Act; Sexual Harassment; Employment Litigation; Employment Practices Liability; Trade Secrets; Dispute Resolution; Trial and Appellate Practice — E-mail: rlk@wimlaw.com

Jonathan Gaul — University of Virginia, B.A., 1991; Emory University, J.D. (with honors), 1995 — Admitted to Bar, 1995, Georgia — Practice Areas: Alternative Dispute Resolution; Arbitration; Breach of Contract; Builders Risk; Commercial General Liability; Construction Accidents; Construction Claims; Construction Defect; Construction Law; Construction Liability; Construction Litigation; Contract Disputes; Contractors Liability; Contracts; Design Professionals; Dispute Resolution; Engineering and Construction; Engineers; Errors and Omissions; General Liability; Government Affairs; Governmental Liability; Mechanics Liens; Mold and Mildew Claims; Mold Litigation; Professional Errors and Omissions; Professional Liability (Non-Medical) Defense; Professional Negligence; Professional Malpractice; Property; Property Damage; Surety; Surety Bonds; Trade Secrets; Trial and Appellate Practice — E-mail: jdg@wimlaw.com

Kathleen Jennings — Cornell University College of Arts and Sciences, B.A. (with distinction), 1984; New York University School of Law, J.D., 1987 — Admitted to Bar, 1987, New York; 1988, Georgia — Member New York State Bar Association; State Bar of Georgia (Labor and Employment Section) — Practice Areas: Litigation; Labor and Employment; Employment Discrimination; Sexual Harassment — E-mail: kjj@wimlaw.com

Elizabeth Dorminey — The University of Georgia, B.A. (magna cum laude), 1976; J.D., 1981; Columbia University, LL.M., 1984 — Admitted to Bar, 1981, Georgia; 1984, Connecticut; 1985, New York — Practice Areas: Labor and Employment — E-mail: ekd@wimlaw.com

James L. Hughes — Lambuth College, B.B.A. (magna cum laude), 1979; Vanderbilt University, J.D., 1982 — Admitted to Bar, 1982, Texas; 1987, Georgia — Practice Areas: ERISA; Immigration Law; Labor and Employment — E-mail: jlh@wimlaw.com

Raymond Perez, II — Loyola University, B.A. (magna cum laude), 2002; Emory University School of Law, J.D., 2005 — Admitted to Bar, 2005, Georgia — Practice Areas: Immigration Law; Labor and Employment — E-mail: rp@wimlaw.com

Les A. Schneider — Lehigh University, B.A., 1972; Emory University, J.D., 1975 — Admitted to Bar, 1976, Georgia — Practice Areas: Labor and Employment — E-mail: las@wimlaw.com

Martin A. Steckel — The University of Georgia, A.B., 1968; J.D., 1972 — Admitted to Bar, 1972, Georgia — Practice Areas: Labor and Employment — E-mail: mhs@wimlaw.com

J. Larry Stine — The University of Georgia, B.S. (cum laude), 1972; J.D. (cum laude), 1975 — Admitted to Bar, 1975, Georgia — Practice Areas: Labor and Employment — E-mail: jls@wimlaw.com

Mark A. Waschak — Georgia Institute of Technology, B.S., 1986; M.S., 1990; Georgia State University, J.D., 1992 — Admitted to Bar, 1992, Georgia — E-mail: maw@wimlaw.com

James W. Wimberly — The University of Georgia, B.B.A. (cum laude), 1965; J.D., 1968; Harvard University, LL.M., 1969 — Admitted to Bar, 1967, Georgia — Practice Areas: Labor and Employment — E-mail: jww@wimlaw.com

Peter H. Steckel — Georgia State University, B.A., History, 2000; The John Marshall Law School, J.D., 2013 — Admitted to Bar, 2013, Georgia — E-mail: phs@wimlaw.com

AUGUSTA † 44,639 Richmond Co.

Fulcher Hagler LLP

One 10th Street, Suite 700
Augusta, Georgia 30901
   Telephone: 706-724-0171
   E-Mail: scook@fulcherlaw.com
   www.fulcherlaw.com

Established: 1946

General Civil Practice, Insurance Law, Trial Practice, Appellate Practice

GEORGIA / AUGUSTA

Fulcher Hagler LLP, Augusta, GA (Continued)

Insurance Clients

Alternative Service Concepts, LLC
Broadspire
Chartis Insurance
Crawford & Company
The Doctors Company
Georgia Interlocal Risk Management Agency (GIRMA)
Grange Mutual Casualty Company
MAG Mutual Insurance Company
Safeco Insurance
South Carolina Farm Bureau Mutual Insurance Company
Trident Insurance Company
American National Property and Casualty Company
The Cincinnati Insurance Companies
Gallagher Bassett Services, Inc.
Government Employees Insurance Company
GuideOne Insurance
The Medical Protective Company
Sedgwick Claims Management Services, Inc.
T.H.E. Insurance Company
Underwriters Safety and Claims

Partners

William M. Fulcher — (1902-1993)

Ronald C. Griffeth — (1935-1998)

William C. Reed — (1929-2007)

Michael B. Hagler — (1955-2014)

Gould B. Hagler — (Retired)

David H. Hanks — (Retired)

Robert C. Hagler — 1953 — Furman University, B.A., 1975; Cumberland University School of Law, J.D. (cum laude), 1979 — Admitted to Bar, 1979, Georgia — Member American and Augusta Bar Associations; State Bar of Georgia; Review Panel for Ethics Violations, 1990-1993; — Appointed Attorney, Development Authority of Richmond County — Practice Areas: Business Law; Commercial Litigation; Probate Litigation; Bond Law; Securities Fraud — Fax: 706-396-3607 — E-mail: rhagler@fulcherlaw.com

James William Purcell — 1951 — The University of Georgia, B.A. (cum laude), 1973; J.D., 1975 — Admitted to Bar, 1975, Georgia; U.S. District Court, Middle, Northern and Southern Districts of Georgia; U.S. Court of Appeals, Eleventh Circuit; U.S. Supreme Court — Member State Bar of Georgia; Augusta Bar Association (President, 2000); Judicial Nominating Commission (For the State of Georgia, 2003-2010); National Association of Railroad Trial Counsel; Georgia Defense Lawyers Association — Practice Areas: Litigation; Medical Malpractice — Fax: 706-396-3613 — E-mail: jpurcell@fulcherlaw.com

J. Arthur Davison — 1956 — The University of Georgia, B.B.A. (cum laude), 1978; J.D., 1981 — Admitted to Bar, 1981, Georgia; 1982, South Carolina; 1981, U.S. District Court, Southern District of Georgia; U.S. Court of Appeals, Eleventh Circuit; 1982, U.S. District Court, District of South Carolina; 1998, U.S. Court of Appeals, Fourth Circuit — Member State Bar of Georgia; South Carolina Bar; Augusta Bar Association (President, 2008); Fellow, Lawyers Foundation of Georgia; Defense Research Institute; Georgia Defense Lawyers Association — Practice Areas: Litigation — Fax: 706-396-3619 — E-mail: adavison@fulcherlaw.com

Mark C. Wilby — 1956 — Augusta College, B.A. (cum laude), 1979; The University of Georgia, J.D., 1986 — Admitted to Bar, 1986, Georgia; South Carolina; U.S. District Court, Southern District of Georgia; U.S. District Court, District of South Carolina; 1995, U.S. District Court, Northern District of Georgia — Member State Bar of Georgia; South Carolina Bar; Augusta Bar Association; Georgia Defense Lawyers Association; National Association of Railroad Trial Counsel — Practice Areas: Litigation; Railroad Law; Family Law — Fax: 706-396-3621 — E-mail: mwilby@fulcherlaw.com

N. Staten Bitting, Jr. — 1953 — Furman University, B.A., 1975; Stetson University, J.D. (cum laude), 1978 — Admitted to Bar, 1978, Florida; 1989, Georgia; U.S. District Court, Southern District of Georgia; U.S. Supreme Court — Member State Bar of Georgia; The Florida Bar; Augusta Bar Association; Georgia Defense Lawyers Association (President, 2009 - 2010); Defense Research Institute — Special Assistant Attorney General, State of Georgia (1996-present) — Practice Areas: Civil Trial Practice; Workers' Compensation; Appellate Practice; Mediation — Fax: 706-396-3627 — E-mail: sbitting@fulcherlaw.com

Scott W. Kelly — 1967 — The University of Georgia, B.B.A. (cum laude), 1990; J.D., 1993 — Admitted to Bar, 1993, Georgia; U.S. District Court, Southern District of Georgia; 1996, U.S. District Court, Northern District of Georgia; 1997, U.S. Court of Appeals, Eleventh Circuit; 2001, U.S. District Court, Middle District of Georgia — Member State Bar of Georgia; Augusta Bar Association; Georgia Defense Lawyers Association; Defense Research Institute; National Association of Railroad Trial Counsel — Practice Areas: Litigation; Civil Rights; Personal Injury; Commercial Litigation; Premises Liability — Fax: 706-396-3623 — E-mail: skelly@fulcherlaw.com

Elizabeth Ann McLeod — 1969 — Mercer University, B.A. (summa cum laude), 1991; Mercer Law School, J.D. (cum laude), 1994 — Admitted to Bar, 1994, Georgia; 2004, South Carolina; 1994, U.S. District Court, Southern District of Georgia; 1996, U.S. District Court, Northern District of Georgia; U.S. Court of Appeals, Eleventh Circuit — Member State Bar of Georgia; South Carolina Bar; Augusta Bar Association; National Association of Railroad Trial Counsel; Georgia Defense Lawyers Association — Practice Areas: Litigation; Railroad Law; Employment Law; Insurance Defense — Fax: 706-396-3631 — E-mail: emcleod@fulcherlaw.com

Russell V. Mobley — 1963 — Augusta College, B.B.A., 1986; Georgia State University, J.D., 1991; University of Florida, LL.M., 1992 — Admitted to Bar, 1991, Georgia — Member State Bar of Georgia; Augusta Bar Association; Georgia Society of Certified Public Accountants; University Health Care Foundation; Augusta Estate Planning Council (President) — Certified Public Accountant — Practice Areas: Corporate Law; Estate Planning; Elder Law; Tax Controversy; Business Succession — Fax: 706-396-3636 — E-mail: rmobley@fulcherlaw.com

Susan Carter Mulherin — Auburn University, B.A., 1977; University of South Carolina Aiken, A.S.N.-R.N., 1985; University of Richmond, J.D. (cum laude), 1998 — Admitted to Bar, 1998, Georgia; U.S. District Court, Northern and Southern Districts of Georgia — Member State Bar of Georgia; Augusta Bar Association; Augusta Family Law Bar Association; Georgia Defense Lawyers Association; Defense Research Institute — Registered Nurse — Practice Areas: Medical Malpractice; Family Law; Litigation — Fax: 706-396-3604 — E-mail: smulherin@fulcherlaw.com

Mary Bryan Robbins — 1955 — Augusta College, B.A., 1978; Case Western Reserve University School of Law, J.D., 1998 — Admitted to Bar, 1998, Georgia — Member State Bar of Georgia (Fiduciary, Business and Real Property Sections); Augusta Bar Association; American Health Lawyers Association — Practice Areas: Health; Corporate Law; Business Law; Employment Law; Estate Planning; Trust Administration — Fax: 706-396-3605 — E-mail: mrobbins@fulcherlaw.com

Sonja R. Tate — 1971 — The University of Georgia, A.B., 1993; J.D., 1996 — Admitted to Bar, 1996, Georgia; 1999, South Carolina; U.S. District Court, District of South Carolina; 2000, U.S. District Court, Southern District of Georgia; 2001, U.S. Court of Appeals, Fourth Circuit; 2002, U.S. District Court, Northern District of Georgia; U.S. Court of Appeals, Eleventh Circuit; 2010, U.S. Supreme Court — Member Augusta and Aiken Bar Associations; Georgia Association Women Lawyers; Defense Research Institute; Georgia Defense Lawyers Association — Practice Areas: Insurance Defense; Litigation; Insurance Law; Railroad Law — Fax: 706-396-3625 — E-mail: state@fulcherlaw.com

Michael N. Loebl — 1973 — The University of Georgia, B.A. (summa cum laude), 1997; The University of Georgia School of Law, J.D. (magna cum laude), 2000 — Phi Beta Kappa, Order of the Coif — Admitted to Bar, 2001, Georgia; 2005, South Carolina; U.S. District Court, District of South Carolina; U.S. District Court, Middle, Northern and Southern Districts of Georgia; U.S. Court of Appeals, Third, Fourth, Ninth and Eleventh Circuits; South Carolina Court of Appeals; Georgia Court of Appeals; U.S. Supreme Court; Supreme Court of Georgia; Supreme Court of South Carolina — Practice Areas: Litigation — Fax: 706-396-3630 — E-mail: mloebl@fulcherlaw.com

John E. Price — 1979 — The University of North Carolina, B.A. (with distinction), 2001; College of William & Mary, Marshall-Wythe School of Law, J.D., 2004 — Admitted to Bar, 2005, Georgia; U.S. District Court, Middle, Northern and Southern Districts of Georgia; U.S. Court of Appeals, Eleventh Circuit; Supreme Court of Georgia — Member Augusta Bar Association; Defense Research Institute; National Association of Railroad Trial Counsel; Georgia Defense Lawyers Association — Practice Areas: Litigation; Railroad Law; Insurance Defense; Governmental Liability; Employment Discrimination; Civil Rights — Fax: 706-393-3645 — E-mail: jprice@fulcherlaw.com

Scott D. Lewis — 1969 — University of South Carolina, B.S., 1991; Emory University, M.B.A., 1998; University of South Carolina, MSACCY, Taxation, 2004; University of South Carolina School of Law, J.D., 2008 — Admitted to Bar, 2008, Georgia; 2010, South Carolina — Member Augusta Bar Association; Augusta Estate Planning Council; Georgia Society of CPA's — Board Member, Georgia-Carolina Counsel of the Boy Scouts of America — Practice Areas: Estate Planning; Probate; Guardian and Conservatorships; Elder Law; Trusts; Corporate Business Law; Tax Law; Personal Asset Protection; Business & Real Estate Transactions — Fax: 706-396-3624 — E-mail: slewis@fulcherlaw.com

Associates

Dorothy H. Hogg
Steven L. Sanders
Kyle B. Waddell
Andrew A. Murdison
P. Kyle Perry

AUGUSTA, GEORGIA

Glover, Blount & Hyatt

429 Walker Street
Augusta, Georgia 30901
Telephone: 706-722-3786
Fax: 706-722-7145
E-Mail: gbpc@comcast.net

Established: 1982

Insurance Law, Defense Litigation

Insurance Clients

Grange Mutual Insurance Company
The Infinity Group
Liberty Mutual Insurance Company
Progressive Insurance Group
South Carolina Farm Bureau Mutual Insurance Company
Southern Trust Insurance Company
State Auto Insurance Company
State Farm Insurance Company
USAA Casualty Insurance Company
Hartford Insurance Company
Kemper Specialty
National General Insurance Company
Southern General Insurance Company
Southern United Fire Insurance Company
United Insurance Company of America

Non-Insurance Clients

Gallagher Bassett Services, Inc.
Universal Security Insurance Company
Georgia Insurers Insolvency Pool

Firm Members

Gary A. Glover — 1941 — The University of Georgia, B.A., 1964; Mercer Law School, J.D., 1972 — Admitted to Bar, 1972, Georgia — Member Georgia Defense Lawyers Association

Percy J. Blount — 1940 — Southwestern at Memphis; The University of Georgia, A.B., 1963; Memphis State University, J.D., 1966 — Admitted to Bar, 1967, Georgia

Jennie M. Hyatt — Stephen F. Austin State University, B.A.A.S. (magna cum laude), 1998; South Texas College of Law, J.D., 2004 — Admitted to Bar, 2004, Georgia; 2005, U.S. District Court, Southern District of Georgia

Hull Barrett, PC

801 Broad Street, Seventh Floor
Augusta, Georgia 30901
Telephone: 706-722-4481
Fax: 706-722-9779
E-Mail: ClientRelations@HullBarrett.com
www.HullBarrett.com

(Aiken, SC Office: 111 Park Avenue, S.W., 29801, P.O. Box 517, 29802-0517)
(Tel: 803-648-4213)
(Fax: 803-648-2601)
(Evans, GA Office: 7004 Evans Town Center Boulevard, Suite 300, 30809)
(Tel: 706-722-4481)
(Fax: 706-650-0925)

Established: 1916

General Civil Practice, Trial and Appellate Practice, Corporate Law, Securities, Insurance Law, Construction Law, Employment Law, Health Care, Environmental Law, Technology, Medical Malpractice, Product Liability, Class Actions, Media, Communications and First Amendment, Local Government

Firm Profile: As a firm and as individuals, we believe we can better represent our clients by working collaboratively. At Hull Barrett we strive for excellence, which is why you will find a team of experienced, knowledgeable and competent staff. Our past and current members have served on the federal and state trial courts, as state legislators and city council members, as members of the state bar governing bodies, as presidents of state and local bar organizations, as members of the Georgia Board of Bar Examiners, and on numerous bar committees and court advisory committees. We are experienced to serve as mediators or arbitrators in alternative dispute resolution proceedings and have a long history of public service to the states of Georgia and South Carolina and their organized bars.

Hull Barrett is engaged in a general civil practice providing a broad range of legal services with an emphasis on general litigation, trials & appeals; securities & corporate law; mergers, acquisitions & public offerings; local government law & eminent domain actions; health care; computer & technology law; internet ventures; trademark & copyright law; taxation; public finance; commercial real estate; construction law & disputes; employment law; banking law; medical malpractice defense; insurance law; trusts, estate planning & probate; First Amendment & media law and environmental matters. We represent a broad client base of major corporations, small businesses, professional entities, financial & lending institutions, local governments, public authorities, public utilities, railroad companies, insurance companies, health care institutions & individuals.

Insurance Clients

Allied Insurance Company
American Specialty Insurance Services, Inc.
Empire Fire and Marine Insurance Company
Federated Mutual Insurance Company
Hudson Healthcare
John Hancock Life Insurance Company
MAG Mutual Insurance Company
Massachusetts Mutual Life Insurance Company
Nationwide Group
Pennsylvania Lumbermens Mutual Insurance Company
York Insurance Company
American Indemnity Company
AmTrust North America
The Doctors Company
Employers Reinsurance Corporation
First Professionals Insurance Company
Interstate Life & Accident Company
Life Insurance Company of Georgia
Monumental Life Insurance Company
Penn Millers Insurance Company
United Life Insurance Company
Vermont Life Insurance Company

Non-Insurance Clients

Atlanta Gas Light Company
The BOC Group
Community Newspapers
Georgia Power Company
Housing Authority of the City of Augusta
Merry Land Properties, Inc.
Morris Communications Corporation
Procter & Gamble Company
Southern Bell Telephone & Telegraph Company
BellSouth Telecommunications, Inc.
CVS Pharmacy, Inc.
Georgia Press Association
MCG Health, Inc.
The Medical College Of Georgia Physicians Practice Group Foundation
Norfolk Southern Corporation
Regions Bank
SunTrust Banks, Inc.
Trinity Hospital of Augusta

Partners

Patrick J. Rice — Spring Hill College, B.S., 1963; The University of Georgia, LL.B., 1966 — Georgia Super Lawyers; Top 100 Georgia Super Lawyers; State Bar of Georgia's Chief Justice Thomas O. Marshall Professionalism Award; Paul C. Harris Fellow of Rotary International — Admitted to Bar, 1966, Georgia — Member Augusta Bar Association; State Bar of Georgia; Georgia Defense Lawyers Association; Augusta Area Trial Lawyers Association; Federation of Insurance Counsel; American College of Trial Lawyers; Defense Research Institute; Fellow, American Bar Foundation — Practice Areas: Class Actions; Medical Malpractice; Product Liability; Commercial Litigation; Trial Practice; Health; Professional Liability; Eminent Domain; Insurance Coverage; Land Use; Business Formation; Intellectual Property — E-mail: PRice@HullBarrett.com

Douglas D. Batchelor, Jr. — University of Virginia, A.B., 1966; University of Florida, J.D., 1968 — Georgia Super Lawyers; Georgia Trend's Legal Elite — Admitted to Bar, 1969, Georgia; Florida; 1988, South Carolina — Member American and Augusta Bar Associations; State Bar of Georgia; The Florida Bar; South Carolina Bar — Practice Areas: Corporate Law; Hospitals; Bonds; Governmental Liability; Eminent Domain; Health Care; Land Use; Business Formation; Insurance Coverage — E-mail: DBatchelor@HullBarrett.com

David E. Hudson — Mercer University, A.B. (summa cum laude), 1968; Harvard Law School, J.D. (cum laude), 1971 — Chief Justice's Commission on Professionalism Benham Award; Georgia's Super Lawyers; Top 100 Georgia Super Lawyers — Law Clerk to Honorable Griffin B. Bell, Fifth Circuit Court

GEORGIA / AUGUSTA

Hull Barrett, PC, Augusta, GA (Continued)

of Appeals, 1971-1972 — Admitted to Bar, 1972, Georgia — Member Augusta Bar Association; State Bar of Georgia; Fellow, American College of Trial Lawyers — Civil Justice Reform Committee, Southern District of Georgia, Chair, 1991-1994; Georgia Board of Bar Examiners. — Captain, United States Army (1972-1974) — Practice Areas: Trial Practice; Construction Law; Commercial Litigation; Trial and Appellate Practice; Alternative Dispute Resolution; Mediation; Arbitration; Class Actions; Health Care; Insurance Coverage; Probate; Product Liability; Employment Law; Intellectual Property — E-mail: DHudson@HullBarrett.com

Neal W. Dickert — Wofford College, B.A., 1968; University of South Carolina, M.B.A., 1969; J.D., 1974 — Paul C. Harris Fellow of Rotary International — Admitted to Bar, 1974, South Carolina; 1975, Georgia; U.S. District Court, Middle and Southern Districts of Georgia; U.S. District Court, District of South Carolina; U.S. Court of Appeals, Eleventh Circuit — Member American and Augusta Bar Associations; State Bar of Georgia; South Carolina Bar — Author: "Georgia Handbook on Foundations and Objections," Thomson-West, 2003 — U.S. Army - Bronze Star — Practice Areas: Mediation; Arbitration; Alternative Dispute Resolution; Probate; Product Liability; Class Actions; Insurance Coverage; Construction Litigation; Trial and Appellate Practice; Environmental Litigation — E-mail: NDickert@HullBarrett.com

William H. Tucker — DePauw University, B.A., 1974; University of South Carolina, J.D., 1978 — Phi Delta Phi — Admitted to Bar, 1978, South Carolina — Member American and Aiken County (Secretary, 1981) Bar Associations; South Carolina Bar — Gold Key; Assistant Solicitor, Second Judicial Circuit of South Carolina, 1978-1980 — Practice Areas: Corporate Law; Real Estate; Estate Planning; Probate; Business Formation; Wills; Trusts; Land Use — Resident Aiken, SC Office — Tel: 803-648-4213 — E-mail: WTucker@HullBarrett.com

Mark S. Burgreen — Erskine College, A.B. (summa cum laude), 1982; University of South Carolina, J.D., 1985; New York University, LL.M., 1986 — Admitted to Bar, 1985, South Carolina; 1986, Georgia — Member American and Augusta Bar Associations; State Bar of Georgia; South Carolina Bar — Practice Areas: Corporate Law; Probate; Securities; Wills; Trusts; Mergers and Acquisitions; Bonds — E-mail: MBurgreen@HullBarrett.com

George R. Hall — Presbyterian College, B.A. (summa cum laude), 1983; University of South Carolina, J.D., 1986 — Order of the Coif; Order of the Wig and Robe; Blue Key; Georgia Super Lawyers — Admitted to Bar, 1986, South Carolina; 1987, Georgia — Member American and Augusta (President, 2007) Bar Associations; State Bar of Georgia; South Carolina Bar; Georgia Defense Lawyers Association; National Association of Railroad Trial Counsel; Defense Research Institute; American Board of Trial Advocates; Atlanta Claims Association — Practice Areas: Commercial Litigation; Tort; Trial Practice; Product Liability; Professional Liability; Alternative Dispute Resolution; Arbitration; Mediation; Civil Rights; Land Use — E-mail: GHall@HullBarrett.com

James B. Ellington — The University of Georgia, A.B. (summa cum laude), 1984; The University of Georgia School of Law, J.D. (magna cum laude), 1987 — Order of the Coif; Litigation Counsel of America, Fellow; University of Georgia Blue Key Young Alumnus Award; Georgia Super Lawyers — Law Clerk to the Honorable Dudley H. Bowen Jr., U.S. District Judge, 1987-1988 — Georgia Law Review, Executive Research Editor — Admitted to Bar, 1987, Georgia — Member American and Augusta Bar Associations; State Bar of Georgia — Practice Areas: Employment Litigation; Appellate Practice; Civil Rights; Employment Law; Trial Practice; Intellectual Property; Professional Liability; Governmental Liability — E-mail: JEllington@HullBarrett.com

William J. Keogh, III — Duke University, B.A., 1988; Emory University, J.D., 1991 — Recent Publication Editor, Emory International Law Review — Admitted to Bar, 1991, Georgia; 1991, U.S. District Court, Northern and Southern Districts of Georgia — Member American and Augusta Bar Associations; State Bar of Georgia — Practice Areas: Construction Law; Commercial Litigation; Eminent Domain; Land Use — E-mail: WKeogh@HullBarrett.com

Ralph E. Hanna, III — West Virginia University, B.S.E.E., 1988; University of South Carolina, J.D. (cum laude), 1993 — Admitted to Bar, 1993, South Carolina; Georgia; 1994, U.S. District Court, Northern and Southern Districts of Georgia; U.S. Court of Appeals, Fourth and Eleventh Circuits; U.S. Supreme Court — Member American and Augusta Bar Associations; State Bar of Georgia; South Carolina Bar — Practice Areas: Commercial Law; Corporate Law — Resident Aiken, SC Office — Tel: 803-648-4213 — E-mail: RHanna@HullBarrett.com

Darren G. Meadows — The University of Georgia, B.B.A., 1990; Georgia State University, J.D., 1994 — Admitted to Bar, 1994, Georgia — Member American, Atlanta and Augusta Bar Associations; State Bar of Georgia —

Hull Barrett, PC, Augusta, GA (Continued)

Practice Areas: Environmental Law; Corporate Law — E-mail: DMeadows@HullBarrett.com

Thomas L. Cathey — Duke University, B.A. (cum laude), 1997; The University of North Carolina, J.D., 2000 — Admitted to Bar, 2000, North Carolina; 2001, Georgia; 2010, South Carolina — Practice Areas: Commercial Litigation; Employment Law — E-mail: TCathey@HullBarrett.com

Davis A. Dunaway — The University of Georgia, B.B.A., 2000; J.D. (cum laude), 2003 — Georgia Super Lawyers Rising Star — Admitted to Bar, 2003, Georgia; U.S. District Court, Middle and Southern Districts of Georgia; U.S. Court of Appeals, Eleventh Circuit — Member Augusta Bar Association; Young Lawyers of Augusta (President); Georgia Defense Lawyers Association; Defense Research Institute — Practice Areas: Trial Practice; Tort; Commercial Litigation; Construction Law — E-mail: DDunaway@HullBarrett.com

J. Christopher Driver — Medical College of Georgia, B.S. (summa cum laude), 1997; The University of Georgia, J.D. (cum laude), 2002 — Admitted to Bar, 2002, Georgia; 2010, South Carolina — Practice Areas: Labor and Employment — E-mail: CDriver@HullBarrett.com

Christopher A. Cosper — The University of Georgia, B.S. (summa cum laude), 2001; The University of Georgia School of Law, J.D. (summa cum laude), 2004 — Georgia Super Lawyers Rising Star — Law Clerk, Hon. B. Avant Edenfield, United States District Court, Southern District of Georgia. — Admitted to Bar, 2005, Georgia; 2006, South Carolina — Practice Areas: Class Actions; Construction Litigation; Medical Malpractice; Commercial Litigation — E-mail: CCosper@HullBarrett.com

Michael E. Fowler, Jr. — The University of Georgia, B.A., 1995; Cumberland School of Law of Samford University, J.D., 2000 — Admitted to Bar, 2000, Alabama; Georgia; South Carolina — Practice Areas: Real Estate Transactions; Business Formation; Business Transactions; Business and Real Estate Transactions; Commercial Real Estate Law — E-mail: MFowler@HullBarrett.com

Associates

Paul K. Simons Jr. — E-mail: PSimons@HullBarrett.com
Brian S. Coursey — E-mail: BCoursey@HullBarrett.com
Brooks K. Hudson — E-mail: BHudson@HullBarrett.com
Mary Runkle Smith — E-mail: mrunkle.smith@hullbarrett.com

Of Counsel

J. Milton Martin Jr. — E-mail: MMartin@HullBarrett.com
N. Shannon Gentry Lanier — E-mail: SLanier@HullBarrett.com

The following firms also service this area.

Allen, Kopet & Associates, PLLC
900 Circle 75 Parkway SE, Suite 1695
Atlanta, Georgia 30339
  Telephone: 770-435-7260
  Fax: 770-432-3512
Mailing Address: P.O. Box 724077, Atlanta, GA 31139

SEE COMPLETE LISTING UNDER ATLANTA, GEORGIA (146 MILES)

Gannam, Gnann & Steinmetz LLC
Christian J. Steinmetz III
425 East President Street, Suite A
Savannah, Georgia 31401
  Telephone: 912-232-1192
  Fax: 912-238-9917

Civil Litigation, General Liability, Professional Liability, Property Damage, Coverage Issues, Insurance Defense

SEE COMPLETE LISTING UNDER SAVANNAH, GEORGIA (127 MILES)

COLUMBUS   GEORGIA

BAINBRIDGE † 12,697 Decatur Co.

Refer To

Alexander & Vann, LLP
411 Gordon Avenue
Thomasville, Georgia 31792
   Telephone: 229-226-2565
   Fax: 229-228-0444

Governmental Liability, Insurance Defense, Automobile, Product Liability, Medical Malpractice, Legal Malpractice, Architects and Engineers, Workers' Compensation, Surety, Life Insurance, Accident, Property Damage, Litigation

SEE COMPLETE LISTING UNDER THOMASVILLE, GEORGIA (41 MILES)

Refer To

Gardner, Willis, Sweat & Handelman, LLP
2408 Westgate Drive
Albany, Georgia 31707
   Telephone: 229-883-2441
   Fax: 229-888-8148

Mailing Address: P.O. Drawer 71788, Albany, GA 31708-1788

Insurance Defense, Workers' Compensation, Trucking Law, General Liability, Employment Litigation, Business Litigation

SEE COMPLETE LISTING UNDER ALBANY, GEORGIA (58 MILES)

BAXLEY † 4,400 Appling Co.

Refer To

Brennan, Harris & Rominger LLP
2 East Bryan Street, Suite 1300
Savannah, Georgia 31401
   Telephone: 912-233-3399
   Fax: 912-236-4558

Mailing Address: P.O. Box 2784, Savannah, GA 31402

Insurance Law, Admiralty and Maritime Law, Casualty, Surety, Life Insurance, Workers' Compensation

SEE COMPLETE LISTING UNDER SAVANNAH, GEORGIA (97 MILES)

BRUNSWICK † 15,383 Glynn Co.

Refer To

Brennan, Harris & Rominger LLP
2 East Bryan Street, Suite 1300
Savannah, Georgia 31401
   Telephone: 912-233-3399
   Fax: 912-236-4558

Mailing Address: P.O. Box 2784, Savannah, GA 31402

Insurance Law, Admiralty and Maritime Law, Casualty, Surety, Life Insurance, Workers' Compensation

SEE COMPLETE LISTING UNDER SAVANNAH, GEORGIA (75 MILES)

Refer To

Forbes, Foster & Pool, LLC
7505 Waters Avenue, Suite D-14
Savannah, Georgia 31406
   Telephone: 912-352-1190
   Fax: 912-352-1471

Mailing Address: P.O. Box 13929, Savannah, GA 31416-0929

Insurance Defense, Appellate Practice, Automobile, General Liability, Product Liability, Property and Casualty, Toxic Torts, Life Insurance, Professional Malpractice, Medical Malpractice, Errors and Omissions, Employment Discrimination

SEE COMPLETE LISTING UNDER SAVANNAH, GEORGIA (75 MILES)

Refer To

Gannam, Gnann & Steinmetz LLC
Christian J. Steinmetz III
425 East President Street, Suite A
Savannah, Georgia 31401
   Telephone: 912-232-1192
   Fax: 912-238-9917

Civil Litigation, General Liability, Professional Liability, Property Damage, Coverage Issues, Insurance Defense

SEE COMPLETE LISTING UNDER SAVANNAH, GEORGIA (78 MILES)

CAIRO † 9,607 Grady Co.

Refer To

Alexander & Vann, LLP
411 Gordon Avenue
Thomasville, Georgia 31792
   Telephone: 229-226-2565
   Fax: 229-228-0444

Governmental Liability, Insurance Defense, Automobile, Product Liability, Medical Malpractice, Legal Malpractice, Architects and Engineers, Workers' Compensation, Surety, Life Insurance, Accident, Property Damage, Litigation

SEE COMPLETE LISTING UNDER THOMASVILLE, GEORGIA (17 MILES)

CAMILLA † 5,360 Mitchell Co.

Refer To

Alexander & Vann, LLP
411 Gordon Avenue
Thomasville, Georgia 31792
   Telephone: 229-226-2565
   Fax: 229-228-0444

Governmental Liability, Insurance Defense, Automobile, Product Liability, Medical Malpractice, Legal Malpractice, Architects and Engineers, Workers' Compensation, Surety, Life Insurance, Accident, Property Damage, Litigation

SEE COMPLETE LISTING UNDER THOMASVILLE, GEORGIA (35 MILES)

CLAXTON † 2,746 Evans Co.

Refer To

Brennan, Harris & Rominger LLP
2 East Bryan Street, Suite 1300
Savannah, Georgia 31401
   Telephone: 912-233-3399
   Fax: 912-236-4558

Mailing Address: P.O. Box 2784, Savannah, GA 31402

Insurance Law, Admiralty and Maritime Law, Casualty, Surety, Life Insurance, Workers' Compensation

SEE COMPLETE LISTING UNDER SAVANNAH, GEORGIA (60 MILES)

COLUMBUS † 189,885 Muscogee Co.

Brown & Adams, LLC

The Rothschild Building
1214 1st Avenue, Suite 400
Columbus, Georgia 31901
   Telephone: 706-653-6109
Fax: 706-653-9472
E-Mail: jbrown@brownadamsllc.com
www.brownadamsllc.com

Automobile Liability, Insurance Coverage, Medical Malpractice, Construction Law, Personal Injury, Premises Liability, Product Liability, Property, Transportation

Firm Profile: Brown & Adams, LLC focuses on civil defense litigation and dispute resolution. Our attorneys' experience, training and diverse backgrounds have made us one of the leading trial firms in Southwest Georgia and Southeast Alabama. Our core areas of practice are: Construction Litigation, General Liability Litigation, Health Care Litigation, Automobile Liability, and Trucking and Transportation Litigation. As our Firm grows, we stress the importance of our founding principles: zealous and cost effective legal representation and a committment to maintaining the highest level of professionalism.

Insurance Clients

Alfa Mutual Insurance Company	Anchor Managing General Agency
Auto-Owners Insurance Company	Canal Insurance Company
Cincinnati Insurance Company	Cotton States Insurance Companies
FCCI Insurance Group	Liberty Mutual Group
Progressive Insurance Company	USAA

GEORGIA

Brown & Adams, LLC, Columbus, GA (Continued)

Partners

Jeffrey A. Brown — North Georgia College, B.S., 1989; Cumberland School of Law of Samford University, J.D., 1993 — Admitted to Bar, 1993, Alabama; 1993, Georgia — Member Alabama State Bar; State Bar of Georgia; Alabama Claims Association; Alabama Defense Lawyers Association; Defense Research Institute; Georgia Defense Lawyers Association — Captain, Georgia Army National Guard, JAGC (1985-2005) — Practice Areas: General Liability; Insurance Coverage; Premises Liability; Construction Litigation; Medical Malpractice; Automobile Liability

Clayton M. Adams — Vanderbilt University, B.A., 1998; The University of Alabama School of Law, J.D., 2001 — Admitted to Bar, 2001, Alabama; 2002, Georgia — Member Alabama State Bar; State Bar of Georgia; Alabama Defense Lawyers Association; Georgia Defense Lawyers Association; Defense Research Institute — Practice Areas: General Liability; Health Care; Medical Malpractice; Insurance Coverage; Premises Liability; Trucking; Transportation; Automobile Liability

Richard A. Marchetti — University of Notre Dame, A.B., 1964; Emory University School of Law, J.D., 1966 — Admitted to Bar, 1966, Georgia — Member American and Columbus Bar Associations; State Bar of Georgia; Georgia Defense Lawyers Association (President, 1988-1989) — Practice Areas: Litigation; Insurance Defense; Workers' Compensation; Product Liability; Professional Liability; Automobile Liability; Trucking; Transportation; Insurance Coverage; Premises Liability

Associates

Martin H. Drake
Bryan G. Forsyth
Benjamin W. Wallace
Anderson D. Robinson

CORDELE † 11,147 Crisp Co.

Refer To

Gardner, Willis, Sweat & Handelman, LLP
2408 Westgate Drive
Albany, Georgia 31707
   Telephone: 229-883-2441
   Fax: 229-888-8148

Mailing Address: P.O. Drawer 71788, Albany, GA 31708-1788

Insurance Defense, Workers' Compensation, Trucking Law, General Liability, Employment Litigation, Business Litigation

SEE COMPLETE LISTING UNDER ALBANY, GEORGIA (39 MILES)

Refer To

Jones, Cork & Miller, LLP
SunTrust Bank Building, Suite 500
435 Second Street, 5th Floor
Macon, Georgia 31201-2724
   Telephone: 478-745-2821
   Fax: 478-743-9609

Mailing Address: P.O. Box 6437, Macon, GA 31208-6437

Insurance Defense, Automobile, Fire, Casualty, Surety, Life Insurance, Workers' Compensation, Medical Malpractice, Product Liability, Civil Rights, Governmental Liability, Business Law, Class Actions, Complex Litigation, Construction Law, Employment Law, Engineers, Environmental Law, Hospitals, Railroad Law, Self-Insured

SEE COMPLETE LISTING UNDER MACON, GEORGIA (65 MILES)

DARIEN † 1,975 McIntosh Co.

Refer To

Brennan, Harris & Rominger LLP
2 East Bryan Street, Suite 1300
Savannah, Georgia 31401
   Telephone: 912-233-3399
   Fax: 912-236-4558

Mailing Address: P.O. Box 2784, Savannah, GA 31402

Insurance Law, Admiralty and Maritime Law, Casualty, Surety, Life Insurance, Workers' Compensation

SEE COMPLETE LISTING UNDER SAVANNAH, GEORGIA (63 MILES)

CORDELE

DECATUR † 19,335 DeKalb Co.

Levy & Pruett
Two Decatur TownCenter
125 Clairemont Avenue, Suite 550
Decatur, Georgia 30030
   Telephone: 404-371-8857
   Fax: 404-371-8882
   E-Mail: info@levypruett.com
   www.levypruett.com

Insurance Defense, Insurance Coverage, Governmental Liability, Premises Liability, Product Liability, Business Litigation, Construction Litigation, Medical Malpractice Defense

Firm Profile: The skilled professionals at Levy & Pruett collectively represent four decades of legal expertise. With passion and purpose, we prepare the most effective, compelling cases possible for our clients. We offer a broad spectrum of legal services and have a dynamic team of seasoned trial lawyers who use state-of-the-art courtroom technology. From the initial consultation to the final outcome, every client gets our very best.

Corporate Clients

Jowers and Company, Inc
Tidwell Construction Company

Insurance Clients

American Southern Insurance Company
Georgia Farm Bureau Mutual Insurance Company
USAA Investment Management Company
COUNTRY Mutual Insurance Company
IAT Specialty
Midwest Claims Service

Non-Insurance Clients

CJW & Associates
The Hillshire Brands Company
Continental Tire North America, Inc.

Third Party Administrators

Carl Warren & Company
Gallagher Bassett Services, Inc.
Crawford & Company

Transportation Clients

ELCO Administrative Services
Georgia Department of Transportation

Firm Members

Susan J. Levy — Cornell University, B.A., 1985; Emory University School of Law, J.D. (Dean's List), 1988 — Law Clerk for Hon. Jack T. Camp, U.S. District Court — Admitted to Bar, 1988, Georgia — Member State Bar of Georgia; DeKalb County Bar Association; Council on Litigation Management; Defense Research Institute; Georgia Defense Lawyers Association — Author: "A Practitioner's View of the Georgia Tort Claims Act," Volume 30, Number 1, Georgia State Bar Journal 24 (1993) — Emory Law Trial Techniques (Instructor); Special Assistant Attorney General, State of Georgia; Georgia Super Lawyers, 2010-2011

H. Lee Pruett — Mercer University, B.A., 1978; Georgia State University College of Law, J.D., 1990 — Admitted to Bar, 1990, Georgia — Member DeKalb County and Atlanta Bar Associations; State Bar of Georgia; Atlanta Claims Association; Council on Litigation Management — Author: "Defending the Server of Alcohol in Bar Fight Cases," Georgia Defense Lawyers Association Law Journal, 2001

DONALSONVILLE † 2,650 Seminole Co.
Refer To
Alexander & Vann, LLP
411 Gordon Avenue
Thomasville, Georgia 31792
 Telephone: 229-226-2565
 Fax: 229-228-0444

Governmental Liability, Insurance Defense, Automobile, Product Liability, Medical Malpractice, Legal Malpractice, Architects and Engineers, Workers' Compensation, Surety, Life Insurance, Accident, Property Damage, Litigation

SEE COMPLETE LISTING UNDER THOMASVILLE, GEORGIA (63 MILES)

DOUGLAS † 11,589 Coffee Co.
Refer To
Brennan, Harris & Rominger LLP
2 East Bryan Street, Suite 1300
Savannah, Georgia 31401
 Telephone: 912-233-3399
 Fax: 912-236-4558

Mailing Address: P.O. Box 2784, Savannah, GA 31402

Insurance Law, Admiralty and Maritime Law, Casualty, Surety, Life Insurance, Workers' Compensation

SEE COMPLETE LISTING UNDER SAVANNAH, GEORGIA (126 MILES)

DUBLIN † 16,201 Laurens Co.
Refer To
Brennan, Harris & Rominger LLP
2 East Bryan Street, Suite 1300
Savannah, Georgia 31401
 Telephone: 912-233-3399
 Fax: 912-236-4558

Mailing Address: P.O. Box 2784, Savannah, GA 31402

Insurance Law, Admiralty and Maritime Law, Casualty, Surety, Life Insurance, Workers' Compensation

SEE COMPLETE LISTING UNDER SAVANNAH, GEORGIA (118 MILES)

Refer To
Jones, Cork & Miller, LLP
SunTrust Bank Building, Suite 500
435 Second Street, 5th Floor
Macon, Georgia 31201-2724
 Telephone: 478-745-2821
 Fax: 478-743-9609

Mailing Address: P.O. Box 6437, Macon, GA 31208-6437

Insurance Defense, Automobile, Fire, Casualty, Surety, Life Insurance, Workers' Compensation, Medical Malpractice, Product Liability, Civil Rights, Governmental Liability, Business Law, Class Actions, Complex Litigation, Construction Law, Employment Law, Engineers, Environmental Law, Hospitals, Railroad Law, Self-Insured

SEE COMPLETE LISTING UNDER MACON, GEORGIA (50 MILES)

EVANS 29,011 Columbia Co.
Refer To
Hull Barrett, PC
801 Broad Street, Seventh Floor
Augusta, Georgia 30901
 Telephone: 706-722-4481
 Fax: 706-722-9779

Mailing Address: P.O. Box 1564, Augusta, GA 30903-1564

General Civil Practice, Trial and Appellate Practice, Corporate Law, Securities, Insurance Law, Construction Law, Employment Law, Health Care, Environmental Law, Technology, Medical Malpractice, Product Liability, Class Actions, Media, Communications and First Amendment, Local Government

SEE COMPLETE LISTING UNDER AUGUSTA, GEORGIA (13 MILES)

FITZGERALD † 9,053 Ben Hill Co.
Refer To
Brennan, Harris & Rominger LLP
2 East Bryan Street, Suite 1300
Savannah, Georgia 31401
 Telephone: 912-233-3399
 Fax: 912-236-4558

Mailing Address: P.O. Box 2784, Savannah, GA 31402

Insurance Law, Admiralty and Maritime Law, Casualty, Surety, Life Insurance, Workers' Compensation

SEE COMPLETE LISTING UNDER SAVANNAH, GEORGIA (149 MILES)

FORSYTH † 3,788 Monroe Co.
Refer To
Jones, Cork & Miller, LLP
SunTrust Bank Building, Suite 500
435 Second Street, 5th Floor
Macon, Georgia 31201-2724
 Telephone: 478-745-2821
 Fax: 478-743-9609

Mailing Address: P.O. Box 6437, Macon, GA 31208-6437

Insurance Defense, Automobile, Fire, Casualty, Surety, Life Insurance, Workers' Compensation, Medical Malpractice, Product Liability, Civil Rights, Governmental Liability, Business Law, Class Actions, Complex Litigation, Construction Law, Employment Law, Engineers, Environmental Law, Hospitals, Railroad Law, Self-Insured

SEE COMPLETE LISTING UNDER MACON, GEORGIA (24 MILES)

GAINESVILLE † 33,804 Hall Co.

Forrester & Brim, LLP
459 E. E. Butler Parkway, S.E.
Gainesville, Georgia 30501
 Telephone: 770-531-0800
 Fax: 770-536-7789

Established: 1988

Insurance Defense, Medical Malpractice, Professional Liability, Product Liability, General Civil Litigation, Commercial Law, Motor Vehicle Liability, General Liability

Insurance Clients

Berkley Mid-Atlantic Group
Cotton States Mutual Insurance Company
Hanover Insurance Company
Integon General Insurance Corporation
MAG Mutual Insurance Company
Norcal Mutual Insurance Company
Penn-America Insurance Company
Preferred Physicians Medical Risk Retention Group, Inc.
Progressive Insurance Company
Southern Trust Insurance Company
State Farm Fire and Casualty Company
Unisun Insurance Company

Berkley Southeast Insurance Group
The Doctors Company
Government Employees Insurance Company
Jefferson-Pilot Life Insurance Company
Medical Mutual Insurance Company
Pennsylvania Lumbermens Mutual Insurance Company
ProAssurance Company
Southern General Insurance Company
State Farm Mutual Automobile Insurance Company
United Services Automobile Association (USAA)

Non-Insurance Clients

COUNTRY Financial
Rabun Gap-Nacoochee School

Emory Healthcare
Riverside Military Academy

Firm Members

Weymon H. Forrester — 1942 — Emory University, A.B., 1964; Emory University School of Law, LL.B., 1966 — Admitted to Bar, 1966, Georgia; 1966, U.S. District Court, Middle and Northern Districts of Georgia; 1966, U.S. Court of Appeals, Eleventh Circuit; 1969, U.S. Supreme Court — Member

Forrester & Brim, LLP, Gainesville, GA (Continued)

State Bar of Georgia; Gainesville-Northeastern Bar Association; Georgia Defense Lawyers Association; Fellow, American College of Trial Lawyers — E-mail: wforrester@forbrim.com

James E. Brim, III — 1952 — Emory University, B.A. (with high honors), 1975; The University of Georgia School of Law, J.D. (cum laude), 1979 — Admitted to Bar, 1979, Georgia; 1979, U.S. District Court, Middle, Northern and Southern Districts of Georgia; 1979, U.S. Court of Appeals, Eleventh Circuit — Member State Bar of Georgia; Gainesville-Northeastern Bar Association; Georgia Defense Lawyers Association; Fellow, American College of Trial Lawyers — E-mail: jbrim@forbrim.com

Associates

Elizabeth Farrar Latta — 1982 — The University of Georgia, B.A. (magna cum laude), 2005; Mercer University Walter F. George School of Law, J.D., 2008 — Admitted to Bar, 2008, Georgia; 2009, U.S. District Court, Northern District of Georgia — Member State Bar of Georgia; Gainesville-Northeastern Bar Association — E-mail: elatta@forbrim.com

Jason F. Carter — 1982 — The University of Georgia, B.A., Business Administration (magna cum laude), 2004; The University of Georgia School of Law, J.D., 2010 — Admitted to Bar, 2011, Georgia — Member State Bar of Georgia; Gainesville-Northeastern Bar Association — E-mail: jcarter@forbrim.com

Quinn Curtis Bennett — 1986 — Valdosta State University, B.A. Political Science (summa cum laude), 2009; The University of Georgia School of Law, J.D., 2012 — Admitted to Bar, 2012, Georgia — Member Sate Bar of Georgia; Gainesville-Northeastern Bar Association — E-mail: qbennett@forbrim.com

GRIFFIN † 23,643 Spalding Co.

Refer To

Jones, Cork & Miller, LLP
SunTrust Bank Building, Suite 500
435 Second Street, 5th Floor
Macon, Georgia 31201-2724
Telephone: 478-745-2821
Fax: 478-743-9609

Mailing Address: P.O. Box 6437, Macon, GA 31208-6437

Insurance Defense, Automobile, Fire, Casualty, Surety, Life Insurance, Workers' Compensation, Medical Malpractice, Product Liability, Civil Rights, Governmental Liability, Business Law, Class Actions, Complex Litigation, Construction Law, Employment Law, Engineers, Environmental Law, Hospitals, Railroad Law, Self-Insured

SEE COMPLETE LISTING UNDER MACON, GEORGIA (52 MILES)

HINESVILLE † 33,437 Liberty Co.

Refer To

Brennan, Harris & Rominger LLP
2 East Bryan Street, Suite 1300
Savannah, Georgia 31401
Telephone: 912-233-3399
Fax: 912-236-4558

Mailing Address: P.O. Box 2784, Savannah, GA 31402

Insurance Law, Admiralty and Maritime Law, Casualty, Surety, Life Insurance, Workers' Compensation

SEE COMPLETE LISTING UNDER SAVANNAH, GEORGIA (41 MILES)

Refer To

Forbes, Foster & Pool, LLC
7505 Waters Avenue, Suite D-14
Savannah, Georgia 31406
Telephone: 912-352-1190
Fax: 912-352-1471

Mailing Address: P.O. Box 13929, Savannah, GA 31416-0929

Insurance Defense, Appellate Practice, Automobile, General Liability, Product Liability, Property and Casualty, Toxic Torts, Life Insurance, Professional Malpractice, Medical Malpractice, Errors and Omissions, Employment Discrimination

SEE COMPLETE LISTING UNDER SAVANNAH, GEORGIA (41 MILES)

JESUP † 10,214 Wayne Co.

Refer To

Brennan, Harris & Rominger LLP
2 East Bryan Street, Suite 1300
Savannah, Georgia 31401
Telephone: 912-233-3399
Fax: 912-236-4558

Mailing Address: P.O. Box 2784, Savannah, GA 31402

Insurance Law, Admiralty and Maritime Law, Casualty, Surety, Life Insurance, Workers' Compensation

SEE COMPLETE LISTING UNDER SAVANNAH, GEORGIA (60 MILES)

LOUISVILLE † 2,493 Jefferson Co.

Refer To

Glover, Blount & Hyatt
429 Walker Street
Augusta, Georgia 30901
Telephone: 706-722-3786
Fax: 706-722-7145

Insurance Law, Defense Litigation

SEE COMPLETE LISTING UNDER AUGUSTA, GEORGIA (46 MILES)

LUDOWICI † 1,703 Long Co.

Refer To

Brennan, Harris & Rominger LLP
2 East Bryan Street, Suite 1300
Savannah, Georgia 31401
Telephone: 912-233-3399
Fax: 912-236-4558

Mailing Address: P.O. Box 2784, Savannah, GA 31402

Insurance Law, Admiralty and Maritime Law, Casualty, Surety, Life Insurance, Workers' Compensation

SEE COMPLETE LISTING UNDER SAVANNAH, GEORGIA (56 MILES)

LYONS † 4,367 Toombs Co.

Refer To

Brennan, Harris & Rominger LLP
2 East Bryan Street, Suite 1300
Savannah, Georgia 31401
Telephone: 912-233-3399
Fax: 912-236-4558

Mailing Address: P.O. Box 2784, Savannah, GA 31402

Insurance Law, Admiralty and Maritime Law, Casualty, Surety, Life Insurance, Workers' Compensation

SEE COMPLETE LISTING UNDER SAVANNAH, GEORGIA (83 MILES)

MACON † 91,351 Bibb Co.

Anderson, Walker & Reichert, LLP

577 Mulberry Street, Suite 500
Macon, Georgia 31201
Telephone: 478-743-8651
Fax: 478-743-9636
E-Mail: bjh@awrlaw.com
www.awrlaw.com

Established: 1849

Fire, Casualty, Surety, Life Insurance, Disability, Medical Malpractice, Workers' Compensation, General Liability, Defense Litigation, Business Law

Insurance Clients

Allstate Insurance Company	Atlantic Casualty Insurance Company
CNA Insurance Company	

Anderson, Walker & Reichert, LLP, Macon, GA
(Continued)

Esurance
Horace Mann Insurance Company
Liberty Life Insurance Company
Maquire Insurance Group
Penn Millers Insurance Company
Safeco Insurance Companies
Florists' Mutual Insurance Company
Liberty Mutual Insurance Company
Nationwide Insurance
Philadelphia Insurance Companies

Of Counsel

Thomas L. Bass — 1938 — Duke University, B.A., 1960; LL.B., 1963 — Admitted to Bar, 1963, Georgia

William J. Self — 1949 — The University of Georgia, B.B.A. Accounting, 1971; The University of Georgia School of Law, J.D., 1974 — Admitted to Bar, 1974, Georgia

S. Phillip Brown — 1941 — Mercer University Walter F. George School of Law, LL.B., 1967 — Admitted to Bar, 1967, Georgia — Retired, Superior Court Judge

Partners

Albert P. Reichert, Jr. — 1939 — Emory University, A.B. (with honors), 1961; Harvard University, LL.B., 1964 — Admitted to Bar, 1963, Georgia

Eugene S. Hatcher — 1944 — Georgia Institute of Technology, B.S.I.M., 1968; Mercer University, J.D., 1981 — Admitted to Bar, 1981, Georgia

Robert A. B. Reichert — **Temporary Leave of Absence/Currently Mayor, Macon-Bibb County** — 1948 — The University of Georgia, B.S.A., 1978; Mercer University, J.D., 1981 — Admitted to Bar, 1981, Georgia

Jonathan A. Alderman — 1961 — The University of Georgia, B.A. (summa cum laude), 1983; J.D. (cum laude), 1986 — Admitted to Bar, 1986, Georgia

Associate

Allen E. Orr — 1988 — The University of Georgia, A.B.J. (with high honors), 2006; Wake Forest University School of Law, J.D., 2013 — Admitted to Bar, 2013, Georgia

Jones, Cork & Miller, LLP

SunTrust Bank Building, Suite 500
435 Second Street, 5th Floor
Macon, Georgia 31201-2724
   Telephone: 478-745-2821
   Fax: 478-743-9609
   E-Mail: contact@jonescork.com
   www.jonescork.com

Established: 1872

Insurance Defense, Automobile, Fire, Casualty, Surety, Life Insurance, Workers' Compensation, Medical Malpractice, Product Liability, Civil Rights, Governmental Liability, Business Law, Class Actions, Complex Litigation, Construction Law, Employment Law, Engineers, Environmental Law, Hospitals, Railroad Law, Self-Insured

Firm Profile: Jones, Cork & Miller, LLP is one of the largest law firms in Georgia outside of Atlanta and legal representation reaches throughout the State. Our goal in each legal engagement is to achieve a successful result for our client while maintaining the highest standards of excellence and ethics.

District Counsel For

CSX Transportation Inc.

General Counsel For

Baldwin County School District
L. E. Schwartz & Son, Inc.
Pulaski County School District
SunTrust Bank, Middle Georgia
Wesleyan College
Cherokee Brick & Tile Company
Nu-Way Weiners, Inc.
South Georgia Annual Conference of the United Methodist Church

Insurance Clients

Acceptance Insurance Company of Georgia
AssuranceAmerica Insurance Company
Alfa Vision Insurance Corp.
American Southern Insurance Company
Bituminous Casualty Corporation

Jones, Cork & Miller, LLP, Macon, GA   (Continued)

Cincinnati Insurance Company
Direct Adjusting Company, Inc.
Foremost Insurance Company
James River Insurance Company
Mercury Insurance Group
Occidental Fire & Casualty Company of North Carolina
Progressive Insurance Group
Southern General Insurance Company
Southern Trust Insurance Company
Stratford Insurance Company
Tudor Insurance Company
Western World Insurance Company
Deep South Insurance Services
Farmers Insurance Exchange
GE Life and Annuity Assurance Company
Middle Georgia Mutual Insurance Company
Omni Insurance Company
QBE the Americas Group
Southern Mutual Insurance Company
State Farm Fire and Casualty Company
21st Century Insurance Company

Local Counsel For

AT&T Southeast
BB&T
CIT Group/Business Credit, Inc.
Genworth Financial, Inc.
Georgia Transmission Corporation
Green Group Holdings, LLC
Oconee Regional Medical Center
Rheem Manufacturing Company
YKK (U.S.A.), Inc.
BASF Corporation
Bibb County School District
Educational Credit Management Corporation
Goody Products, Inc.
KaMin LLC
Republic Services, Inc.
Taylor Memorial Hospital

Regional Counsel For

Georgia Power Company
Howard Sheppard, Inc.

Partners

Timothy K. Adams — 1938 — Emory University, A.B., 1960; University of Virginia, LL.B., 1963 — Phi Alpha Delta; Omicron Delta Kappa — Order of the Coif — Admitted to Bar, 1962, Georgia — Member Macon Bar Association (President, 1972) — E-mail: tim.adams@jonescork.com

H. Jerome Strickland — 1940 — Auburn University; Mercer University, LL.B., 1964 — Tau Kappa Alpha; Phi Alpha Delta — Admitted to Bar, 1963, Georgia — Member Macon Bar Association; Georgia Bar Foundation; American Judicature Society; Fellow, American College of Trial Lawyers — Assistant Solicitor General, Macon Judicial Circuit of Georgia, 1966-1968 — E-mail: jerome.strickland@jonescork.com

W. Warren Plowden, Jr. — 1944 — Davidson College, A.B., 1965; Mercer University, LL.B. (magna cum laude), 1968 — Delta Theta Phi — Law Clerk to Honorable Griffin B. Bell, U.S. Circuit Judge, Fifth Circuit, 1970-1971 — Admitted to Bar, 1968, Georgia; 1971, U.S. Court of Appeals, Eleventh Circuit; 1978, U.S. District Court, Middle District of Georgia; 1978, U.S. Supreme Court — Member Macon Bar Association — E-mail: warren.plowden@jonescork.com

Rufus D. Sams, III — 1947 — Rensselaer Polytechnic Institute; Mercer University, J.D. (cum laude), 1971 — Phi Delta Phi — Board of Editors, Mercer Law Review, 1970-1971 — Admitted to Bar, 1971, Georgia — Member Macon Bar Association; State Bar of Georgia; Georgia Defense Lawyers Association — E-mail: dee.sams@jonescork.com

Steve L. Wilson — 1947 — Emory University, A.B., 1969; The University of Georgia, J.D., 1972 — Phi Delta Phi — Articles Editor, Georgia Law Review, 1971-1972 — Admitted to Bar, 1972, Georgia — Member Macon Bar Association — E-mail: steve.wilson@jonescork.com

Thomas C. Alexander — 1950 — The University of Georgia, B.B.A. (cum laude), 1973; Mercer University Walter F. George School of Law, J.D. (cum laude), 1976 — Phi Delta Phi — Editorial Board, Mercer Law Review, Fifth Circuit Survey Editor, 1975-1976 — Admitted to Bar, 1976, Georgia — Member Macon Bar Association (President, 1986-1987); Fellow, Georgia Bar Foundation; Georgia Defense Lawyers Association; Association of Defense Trial Attorneys — Co-Author: Handbook on Georgia Medical Malpractice Law, The Harrison Company, 1991 — E-mail: tom.alexander@jonescork.com

Robert C. Norman, Jr. — 1955 — Furman University, A.B. (magna cum laude), 1977; The University of Georgia, J.D. (cum laude), 1980 — Phi Beta Kappa; Phi Kappa Phi; Phi Delta Phi — Admitted to Bar, 1980, Georgia — Member Macon Bar Association (President, 2000); Georgia Defense Lawyers Association; Georgia Defense Lawyers Association — E-mail: bob.norman@jonescork.com

Howard J. Strickland, Jr. — 1963 — The Citadel, B.A., 1985; The University of Georgia, J.D., 1988 — Admitted to Bar, 1988, Georgia — Member Macon Bar Association — E-mail: jay.strickland@jonescork.com

Cater C. Thompson — 1959 — Mercer University, B.A. (summa cum laude), 1980; J.D. (cum laude), 1983 — Alpha Lambda Delta; Phi Kappa Phi; Phi

GEORGIA

Jones, Cork & Miller, LLP, Macon, GA (Continued)

Delta Phi — Mercer Law Review, 1981-1983 — Admitted to Bar, 1983, Georgia — Member Macon Bar Association — E-mail: cater.thompson@jonescork.com

Thomas W. Joyce — 1958 — Wofford College, A.B., 1980; Mercer University, J.D. (cum laude), 1989 — Phi Kappa Phi — Mercer University Law Review, 1988-1989 — Admitted to Bar, 1989, Georgia — Member Macon Bar Association — E-mail: tom.joyce@jonescork.com

Brandon A. Oren — 1964 — Bob Jones University, B.A., 1986; The University of Georgia, J.D., 1989 — Order of the Barristers — Admitted to Bar, 1989, Georgia — Member Macon Bar Association; American Inn of Court, 1988-1989 — E-mail: brandon.oren@jonescork.com

Jeffery O. Monroe — 1973 — The University of Georgia, B.A. (cum laude), 1996; J.D., 2000 — Admitted to Bar, 2001, Georgia; 2001, U.S. District Court, Middle and Northern Districts of Georgia — Member Macon Bar Association; University of Georgia Young Law Alumni Committee — E-mail: jeffery.monroe@jonescork.com

Sharon Hurt Reeves — 1970 — The University of Georgia, A.B.J. (cum laude), 1991; J.D., 1995 — Mock Trial Board, Chair, 1994-1995; Order of the Barristers — Admitted to Bar, 1995, Georgia; 1995, U.S. District Court, Middle District of Georgia — Member Macon Bar Association — Joseph Lumpkin Inn of Court — E-mail: sharon.reeves@jonescork.com

Callie Dickson Bryan — 1977 — The University of Georgia, B.A. (cum laude), 1999; Georgia State University College of Law, J.D., 2002 — Admitted to Bar, 2002, Georgia; 2002, U.S. District Court, Middle District of Georgia; 2003, U.S. District Court, Northern District of Georgia — Member Macon Bar Association — E-mail: callie.bryan@jonescork.com

Eugene S. Hatcher, Jr. — 1971 — The University of Alabama, B.A., 1994; Mercer University, J.D., 1997 — Admitted to Bar, 1997, Georgia — Member Macon Bar Association — E-mail: gene.hatcher@jonescork.com

J. Patrick Goff — 1979 — Mercer University, B.B.A. (cum laude), 2001; Mercer University Walter F. George School of Law, J.D., 2004 — Admitted to Bar, 2005, Georgia; 2005, U.S. District Court, Middle and Northern Districts of Georgia — Member Macon (Young Lawyers Division) Bar Association — E-mail: patrick.goff@jonescork.com

Of Counsel

Carr G. Dodson — 1937 — The University of Georgia, B.A., 1959; LL.B., 1961 — Admitted to Bar, 1961, Georgia — Member Macon Bar Association (President, 1976); Fellow, American College of Trial Lawyers — Representative, General Assembly of Georgia, 1967-1971; Minority Leader, 1970-1971 — E-mail: carr.dodson@jonescork.com

Emeritus

Hubert C. Lovein, Jr. — 1946 — Emory University, A.B. (magna cum laude), 1968; The University of Georgia, J.D. (magna cum laude), 1971 — Phi Beta Kappa; Omicron Delta Kappa; Phi Delta Phi — Admitted to Bar, 1971, Georgia; 1971, U.S. District Court, Middle, Northern and Southern Districts of Georgia; 1971, U.S. Court of Appeals, Fifth and Eleventh Circuits; 1971, U.S. Supreme Court — Member Federal and Macon (President, 1982) Bar Associations; State Bar of Georgia (Board of Governors, 1996); Fellow, American College of Trial Lawyers — E-mail: hu.lovein@jonescork.com

Associates

Canon B. Hill — 1979 — The University of Georgia, A.B.J. (cum laude), 2002; Mercer University Walter F. George School of Law, J.D., 2005 — Admitted to Bar, 2006, Georgia — Member Macon Bar Association; Twaliga Bus Association — Practice Areas: School Law; Employment Law — E-mail: canon.hill@jonescork.com

Christopher J. Arnold — 1982 — The University of Georgia, B.B.A. (cum laude), 2005; Mercer University Walter F. George School of Law, J.D., 2008 — Admitted to Bar, 2008, Georgia — E-mail: chris.arnold@jonescork.com

Hays B. McQueen — 1984 — The University of Georgia, B.A.P.S., 2006; Mercer University Walter F. George School of Law, J.D. (cum laude), 2010 — Admitted to Bar, 2010, Georgia; Georgia Superior Court — Member American and Macon Bar Associations — Practice Areas: Business Litigation; Insurance Defense; Litigation; Self-Insured Defense; Trial and Appellate Practice — E-mail: hays.mcqueen@jonescork.com

Reneé S. Rainey — 1985 — Presbyterian College, B.S. (maxima cum laude), 2007; Mercer University Walter F. George School of Law, J.D., 2010 — Admitted to Bar, 2010, Georgia; Georgia Superior Court — Member State Bar of Georgia; Macon Bar Association — Practice Areas: General Practice; Appellate Practice — E-mail: renee.sherrin@jonescork.com

Collier W. McKenzie — 1985 — The University of Georgia, B.A., 2007; Mercer University Walter F. George School of Law, J.D., 2011 — Admitted to

Jones, Cork & Miller, LLP, Macon, GA (Continued)

Bar, 2011, Georgia — Practice Areas: Business Law; Commercial Litigation; Litigation; Personal Injury

---

The following firms also service this area.

Gannam, Gnann & Steinmetz LLC
Christian J. Steinmetz III
425 East President Street, Suite A
Savannah, Georgia 31401
Telephone: 912-232-1192
Fax: 912-238-9917

Civil Litigation, General Liability, Professional Liability, Property Damage, Coverage Issues, Insurance Defense

SEE COMPLETE LISTING UNDER SAVANNAH, GEORGIA (166 MILES)

MARIETTA † 56,579 Cobb Co.

Harris & Bunch, LLC
142 South Park Square
Marietta, Georgia 30060
Telephone: 678-483-8657
Fax: 770-499-1365
E-Mail: fharris@harrisandbunch.com
www.harrisandbunch.com

Established: 1995

Insurance Defense, Professional Malpractice, Product Liability, Business Law, Corporate Law, Insurance Litigation, Contract Litigation, Civil Rights Defense

Insurance Clients

Apollo Casualty Company
GAB Robins North America, Inc.
Gulf Insurance Company
Peerless Insurance Company
United Financial Casualty Company

Chrysler Insurance Company
Greenwich Insurance Company
Hanover Insurance Company
Tennessee Farmers Mutual Insurance Company

Self-Insured Clients

Budget Group, Inc.
Dollar Rent A Car Systems, Inc.
Snappy Car Rental
Thrifty Rent-A-Car Systems, Inc.
Toyota Rent-A-Car

Cobb County Police Department
Enterprise Rent-A-Car Company
State of Georgia Department of Administrative Services

Third Party Administrators

Cambridge Integrated Services
Cunningham Lindsey Claims Management, Inc.

Crawford & Company
York STB, Inc.

Partners

Frank P. Harris — 1956 — The University of Tennessee, B.A. (summa cum laude), 1977; J.D., 1981 — Phi Delta Phi; Phi Beta Kappa — Admitted to Bar, 1981, Tennessee; 1982, Georgia; 1982, U.S. District Court, Middle, Northern and Southern Districts of Georgia; 1982, U.S. Court of Appeals, Eleventh Circuit; 2008, U.S. Supreme Court — Member American, Tennessee and Cobb County Bar Associations; State Bar of Georgia; Georgia Defense Lawyers Association; Atlanta Claims Association — E-mail: fharris@harrisandbunch.com

Jeffrey D. Bunch — 1960 — Mercer University at Macon, B.B.A., 1982; M.B.A., 1985; Mercer University, J.D., 1985 — Admitted to Bar, 1985, Georgia; 1985, U.S. District Court, Northern District of Georgia — Member State Bar of Georgia; Cobb County Bar Association; Georgia Defense Lawyers Association — E-mail: jbunch@harrisandbunch.com

METTER † 4,130 Candler Co.
Refer To

Brennan, Harris & Rominger LLP
2 East Bryan Street, Suite 1300
Savannah, Georgia 31401
   Telephone: 912-233-3399
   Fax: 912-236-4558

Mailing Address: P.O. Box 2784, Savannah, GA 31402

Insurance Law, Admiralty and Maritime Law, Casualty, Surety, Life Insurance, Workers' Compensation

SEE COMPLETE LISTING UNDER SAVANNAH, GEORGIA (64 MILES)

MILLEDGEVILLE † 17,715 Baldwin Co.
Refer To

Jones, Cork & Miller, LLP
SunTrust Bank Building, Suite 500
435 Second Street, 5th Floor
Macon, Georgia 31201-2724
   Telephone: 478-745-2821
   Fax: 478-743-9609

Mailing Address: P.O. Box 6437, Macon, GA 31208-6437

Insurance Defense, Automobile, Fire, Casualty, Surety, Life Insurance, Workers' Compensation, Medical Malpractice, Product Liability, Civil Rights, Governmental Liability, Business Law, Class Actions, Complex Litigation, Construction Law, Employment Law, Engineers, Environmental Law, Hospitals, Railroad Law, Self-Insured

SEE COMPLETE LISTING UNDER MACON, GEORGIA (30 MILES)

MILLEN † 3,120 Jenkins Co.
Refer To

Glover, Blount & Hyatt
429 Walker Street
Augusta, Georgia 30901
   Telephone: 706-722-3786
   Fax: 706-722-7145

Insurance Law, Defense Litigation

SEE COMPLETE LISTING UNDER AUGUSTA, GEORGIA (50 MILES)

PEMBROKE † 2,196 Bryan Co.
Refer To

Brennan, Harris & Rominger LLP
2 East Bryan Street, Suite 1300
Savannah, Georgia 31401
   Telephone: 912-233-3399
   Fax: 912-236-4558

Mailing Address: P.O. Box 2784, Savannah, GA 31402

Insurance Law, Admiralty and Maritime Law, Casualty, Surety, Life Insurance, Workers' Compensation

SEE COMPLETE LISTING UNDER SAVANNAH, GEORGIA (35 MILES)

PERRY † 13,839 Houston Co.
Refer To

Jones, Cork & Miller, LLP
SunTrust Bank Building, Suite 500
435 Second Street, 5th Floor
Macon, Georgia 31201-2724
   Telephone: 478-745-2821
   Fax: 478-743-9609

Mailing Address: P.O. Box 6437, Macon, GA 31208-6437

Insurance Defense, Automobile, Fire, Casualty, Surety, Life Insurance, Workers' Compensation, Medical Malpractice, Product Liability, Civil Rights, Governmental Liability, Business Law, Class Actions, Complex Litigation, Construction Law, Employment Law, Engineers, Environmental Law, Hospitals, Railroad Law, Self-Insured

SEE COMPLETE LISTING UNDER MACON, GEORGIA (28 MILES)

QUITMAN † 3,850 Brooks Co.
Refer To

Alexander & Vann, LLP
411 Gordon Avenue
Thomasville, Georgia 31792
   Telephone: 229-226-2565
   Fax: 229-228-0444

Governmental Liability, Insurance Defense, Automobile, Product Liability, Medical Malpractice, Legal Malpractice, Architects and Engineers, Workers' Compensation, Surety, Life Insurance, Accident, Property Damage, Litigation

SEE COMPLETE LISTING UNDER THOMASVILLE, GEORGIA (27 MILES)

REIDSVILLE † 4,944 Tattnall Co.
Refer To

Brennan, Harris & Rominger LLP
2 East Bryan Street, Suite 1300
Savannah, Georgia 31401
   Telephone: 912-233-3399
   Fax: 912-236-4558

Mailing Address: P.O. Box 2784, Savannah, GA 31402

Insurance Law, Admiralty and Maritime Law, Casualty, Surety, Life Insurance, Workers' Compensation

SEE COMPLETE LISTING UNDER SAVANNAH, GEORGIA (75 MILES)

RICHMOND HILL 9,281 Bryan Co.
Refer To

Brennan, Harris & Rominger LLP
2 East Bryan Street, Suite 1300
Savannah, Georgia 31401
   Telephone: 912-233-3399
   Fax: 912-236-4558

Mailing Address: P.O. Box 2784, Savannah, GA 31402

Insurance Law, Admiralty and Maritime Law, Casualty, Surety, Life Insurance, Workers' Compensation

SEE COMPLETE LISTING UNDER SAVANNAH, GEORGIA (17 MILES)

ROME † 36,303 Floyd Co.

Brinson, Askew, Berry, Seigler, Richardson & Davis, LLP

615 West First Street
Rome, Georgia 30161
   Telephone: 706-291-8853, 800-201-7166
   Fax: 706-234-3574
   E-Mail: law@brinson-askew.com
   www.brinson-askew.com

Established: 1975

Casualty, Commercial Law, Complex Litigation, Class Actions, Errors and Omissions, Carrier Defense, Automobile, General Liability, Product Liability, Litigation, Professional Malpractice, Civil Rights, Trial Practice, Appellate Practice, State and Federal Courts

Firm Profile: The firm was founded in 1975. With 19 lawyers, it continues to grow and expand its wide range of services. The firm's forte is litigation, trials and appeals. With over 330 years of combined trial and appellate experience in federal and state courts over the State, the firm's lawyers handle a variety of cases, including complex business and class actions, products liability, personal injury, professional liability, employment and governmental actions. The former Chief Justice of the Supreme Court of Georgia has now become of Counsel to the Firm.

Insurance Clients

Alfa Insurance Corporation
AmTrust Group

American Independent Insurance Company

GEORGIA

Brinson, Askew, Berry, Seigler, Richardson & Davis, LLP, Rome, GA (Continued)

Canal Insurance Company
CIGNA Property and Casualty Insurance Company
Commercial Union Assurance Company plc
Frankenmuth Insurance Company
Georgia Farm Bureau Mutual Insurance Company
Hanover Insurance Group
MAG Mutual Insurance Company
Montgomery Insurance Companies
Pennsylvania Lumbermens Mutual Insurance Company
Southern Farm Bureau Life Insurance Company
Travelers Property Casualty Corporation
Unitrin, Inc.
Wausau Underwriters Insurance Company
Carolina Casualty Insurance Company
The Cincinnati Insurance Companies
Electric Mutual Liability Insurance Company
Georgia Interlocal Risk Management Agency (GIRMA)
Health Care Indemnity, Inc.
Medical Assurance Company, Inc.
National Union Fire Insurance Company
Safeco Insurance Company of America
Southern Mutual Insurance Company
United States Fidelity and Guaranty Company

Firm Members

Robert L. Berry — 1946 — Emory University, A.B., 1968; The University of Georgia, J.D., 1973 — Admitted to Bar, 1973, Georgia; U.S. District Court, Middle and Northern Districts of Georgia — Member American and Rome Bar Associations; State Bar of Georgia; American Academy of Health Care Attorneys; Georgia Academy of Healthcare Attorneys; Georgia Defense Lawyers Association; Defense Research Institute; Fellow, American College of Trial Lawyers — Practice Areas: Insurance Defense; Medical Malpractice — E-mail: bberry@brinson-askew.com

J. Anderson Davis — 1957 — The University of Georgia, A.B., 1979; J.D., 1984 — Admitted to Bar, 1984, Georgia; U.S. District Court, Middle and Northern Districts of Georgia; 1992, U.S. Supreme Court — Member American and Rome Bar Associations; State Bar of Georgia; Leadership Georgia; Georgia Defense Lawyers Association; Defense Research Institute; Atlanta Claims Association; Lawyers Club of Atlanta; American Board of Trial Advocates — City Attorney for Rome, Georgia — Practice Areas: Complex Litigation; Trial Practice; Class Actions; Product Liability; Municipal Law; Personal Injury — E-mail: adavis@brinson-askew.com

C. King Askew
Joseph M. Seigler, Jr.
Wright W. Smith
I. Stewart Duggan
Kristy L. Treadaway
Samuel L. Lucas
Robert M. Brinson
Thomas D. Richardson
Mark M. J. Webb
Stephen B. Moseley
A. Franklin Beacham, III

Associates

Alison S. Warren
Lee B. Carter
David M. Brearley

Of Counsel

Norman S. Fletcher
Kimberly M. Moseley
Frank H. Jones

Magruder & Sumner

701 Broad Street, Suite 300
Rome, Georgia 30161
  Telephone: 706-291-7050
  Fax: 706-291-9881
  E-Mail: law@magrudersumner.com
  www.magrudersumner.com

Established: 1994

Insurance Law

Insurance Clients

American General Life and Accident Insurance Company
Argonaut Great Central Insurance Company
Anthem Life Insurance Company of Florida
Cotton States Mutual Insurance Company

SAVANNAH

Magruder & Sumner, Rome, GA (Continued)

General Casualty Insurance Company
Liberty Mutual Insurance Company
Liberty National Life Insurance Company
Motorists Mutual Insurance Company
Northwestern National Insurance Company
State Auto Insurance Company
Universal Underwriters Insurance Company
Infinity Property & Casualty Group
John Hancock Life Insurance Company
Metropolitan Life Insurance Company
North Carolina Farm Bureau Mutual Insurance Company
Ohio Casualty Group
Ohio Mutual Insurance Company
State Farm Insurance Companies

Non-Insurance Clients

AAA Michigan
Georgia Insurers Insolvency Pool
AT&T, Inc.
Ryder Truck Rental, Inc.

Partners

Karl M. Kothe — (1937-2002)

Dudley B. Magruder, Jr. — (1914-1995)

J. Clinton Sumner, Jr. — 1939 — Tulane University, B.A., 1961; University of Virginia, LL.B., 1964 — Admitted to Bar, 1964, Georgia; 1965, U.S. District Court, Northern District of Georgia — Member American and Rome Bar Associations; State Bar of Georgia; Federation of Defense and Corporate Counsel; Georgia Defense Lawyers Association; Association of Defense Trial Attorneys — Practice Areas: Litigation

Associates

J. Andrew Owens — 1963 — The University of Georgia, A.B.J., 1985; Berry College, M.B.A., 1990; University of Memphis, J.D., 1994 — Admitted to Bar, 1994, Georgia; Tennessee; 1995, U.S. District Court, Northern District of Georgia — Member American and Rome Bar Associations; State Bar of Georgia; Georgia Defense Lawyers Association — Practice Areas: Insurance Defense

Susan D. Taylor — 1970 — University of South Alabama, B.A. (magna cum laude), 1995; The University of Georgia, J.D., 1999 — Admitted to Bar, 1999, Georgia; 2000, U.S. District Court, Northern District of Georgia — Member State Bar of Georgia; Rome Bar Association; Georgia Defense Lawyers Association — Practice Areas: Insurance Defense

Stephen Paul Woodard — 1969 — Covenant College, B.S., 1996; Mercer University, J.D., 2001 — Admitted to Bar, 2001, Georgia; 2002, U.S. District Court, Northern District of Georgia — Member State Bar of Georgia; Rome Bar Association — Practice Areas: Insurance Defense

SAVANNAH † 136,286 Chatham Co.

Brennan, Harris & Rominger LLP

2 East Bryan Street, Suite 1300
Savannah, Georgia 31401
  Telephone: 912-233-3399
  Fax: 912-236-4558
  E-Mail: attys@bhrlegal.com

Insurance Law, Admiralty and Maritime Law, Casualty, Surety, Life Insurance, Workers' Compensation

Insurance Clients

Carolina Casualty Insurance Company
Employers Reinsurance Corporation
GEICO Insurance Companies
Grange Mutual Casualty Company
GUARD Insurance Group
Liberty Mutual Insurance Company
Progressive Insurance
Signal Mutual Indemnity Association
State Farm Insurance Companies
Underwriters at Lloyd's, London
U.S. Auto Insurance Company
Companion Property and Casualty Insurance Company
Everest Security Insurance Company
Georgia Farm Bureau Mutual Insurance Company
Hartford Accident and Indemnity Company
Selective Insurance Company of America
Southern Mutual Insurance Company
United Services Automobile Association (USAA)

Non-Insurance Clients

Ceres Marine Terminals, Inc.
Signal Administration, Inc.
Sears, Roebuck and Co.

Brennan, Harris & Rominger LLP, Savannah, GA
(Continued)

Partners

G. Mason White — 1960 — The University of Georgia, B.S. (with honors), 1982; J.D., 1985 — Admitted to Bar, 1985, Georgia — Member American and Savannah Bar Associations; State Bar of Georgia; Georgia Defense Lawyers Association; The Maritime Law Association of the United States; Defense Research Institute; Association of Defense Trial Attorneys

T. Langston Bass, Jr. — 1966 — Duke University, B.A., 1989; Mercer University Walter F. George School of Law, J.D., 1993 — Admitted to Bar, 1993, Georgia — Member American and Savannah Bar Associations; State Bar of Georgia; The Maritime Law Association of the United States; Southeastern Admiralty Law Institute

Edward R. Stabell, III — 1964 — The University of Georgia, B.A., 1988; Valdosta State College, M.A., 1989; Mercer University Walter F. George School of Law, J.D., 1992 — Admitted to Bar, 1992, Georgia — Member American and Savannah Bar Associations; Georgia Defense Lawyers Association

James D. Kreyenbuhl — 1972 — The University of Georgia, A.B. (magna cum laude), 1994; Georgia State University College of Law, J.D. (cum laude), 1997 — Admitted to Bar, 1997, Georgia; 1997, U.S. District Court, Southern District of Georgia — Member American and Savannah (Young Lawyers Section) Bar Associations; State Bar of Georgia

Associates

Katherine Stein — 1980 — The University of Georgia, B.A. (summa cum laude), 2003; J.D., 2006 — Admitted to Bar, 2006, Georgia — Member State Bar of Georgia; Savannah Bar Association

Britton G. White — 1981 — Emmanuel College, B.S. (magna cum laude), 2002; The University of Georgia School of Law, J.D., 2006 — Admitted to Bar, 2006, Georgia

Leslie J. Thompson — 1973 — Auburn University, B.A. (magna cum laude), 1995; The University of Alabama School of Law, J.D., 1999 — University of Alabama Law Review — Admitted to Bar, 1999, Georgia — Member State Bar of Georgia; Glynn County and Chatham County Bar Associations

Matthew J. Jones — 1986 — The University of Georgia, B.A., History (cum laude), 2010; Mercer University Walter F. George School of Law, J.D., 2013 — Admitted to Bar, 2013, Georgia; U.S. District Court, Southern District of Georgia — Member State Bar of Georgia; Savannah Bar Association

Of Counsel

Edward T. Brennan — 1927 — Georgetown University, A.B., 1950; University of Virginia, LL.B., 1953 — Admitted to Bar, 1953, Georgia — Member State Bar of Georgia; Savannah Bar Association; The Maritime Law Association of the United States; Southeastern Admiralty Law Institute; Association of Defense Trial Attorneys; Defense Research Institute

Richard J. Harris — 1938 — Emory University, B.A., 1960; University of Virginia, LL.B., 1962 — Admitted to Bar, 1961, Georgia — Member American and Savannah Bar Associations; State Bar of Georgia; Southeastern Admiralty Law Institute; Association of Defense Trial Attorneys; Defense Research Institute

In Memoriam

Richard A. Rominger — (1946-2013)

Brennan, Wasden & Painter, LLC

411 East Liberty Street
Savannah, Georgia 31401
 Telephone: 912-232-6700
 Fax: 912-232-0799
 E-Mail: attorneys@brennanwasden.com
 www.brennanwasden.com

(Augusta, GA Office: 801 Broad Street, Suite 501, 30901)
 (Tel: 706-250-7373)
 (Fax: 706-550-0614)

Established: 1989

Brennan, Wasden & Painter, LLC, Savannah, GA
(Continued)

Insurance Defense, Automobile, Casualty, Professional Liability, Product Liability, Medical Malpractice, Workers' Compensation, Employment Discrimination

Insurance Clients

American Equity Insurance Company
American Horizon Insurance Company
American Southern Insurance Company
Atlantic Mutual Insurance Company
Caronia Corporation
Chubb Group of Insurance Companies
Empire Indemnity Insurance Company
FPIC Insurance Group
Georgia Insurers Insolvency Pool
MAG Mutual Insurance Company
The Medical Protective Company
Metropolitan Insurance Company
NCMIC Insurance Company
ProMutual Group
Royal Insurance Company
Safeco Life Insurance Company
Sentry Insurance a Mutual Company
Travelers Insurance Companies
Underwriters Service Company, Inc.
VASA North Atlantic Insurance Company
Zurich Direct Underwriters

American Family Home Insurance Company
American National Lawyers Insurance Reciprocal
Anesthesiologists' Professional Assurance Company
Brotherhood Mutual Insurance Company
Catholic Mutual Group
Doctors Insurance Reciprocal Risk Retention Group
E & O Professionals
Erie Insurance Group
Gallagher Bassett Services, Inc.
Grocers Insurance Company
Medical Claims Management Group
National Interstate Insurance Company
Reliance National Insurance Company
St. Paul Fire and Marine Insurance Company
State Volunteer Mutual Insurance Company
United States Fidelity and Guaranty Company
Western Heritage Insurance Company
Zurich Insurance Company

Non-Insurance Clients

Catholic Diocese of Savannah
Chatham Area Transit Authority
Comcar Industries, Inc.
Georgia Ear Institute
Memorial Health University Medical Center, Inc.
The Price Communications Group
St. Joseph's/Candler Health System
US Antenna
Yamaha Motor Corporation, U.S.A.

Champion International Corporation
Embarq Corp.
Islands Moving & Rentals
New South Federal Savings Bank
Pep Boys, Inc.
Re-Bars, Inc.
Seacrest Partners
Vanguard Group, Inc.

Firm Members

Wiley A. Wasden III — 1959 — Sewanee, The University of the South, B.A., 1981; The University of Georgia, J.D., 1984 — Phi Delta Phi — Admitted to Bar, 1984, Georgia; U.S. District Court, Northern and Southern Districts of Georgia; 1991, U.S. Claims Court; 1992, U.S. Court of Appeals, Eleventh Circuit — Member State Bar of Georgia (Executive Council, Young Lawyers Section, 1987-1989); Savannah Bar Association; Georgia Insurance Defense Lawyers Association (Board, 1991-present); American Academy of Hospital Attorneys; Georgia Society of Hospital Attorneys; Defense Research Institute — Editor, Georgia Defense Lawyer Journal, 1997; Co-Author: "Recent Developments in Georgia Premises Liablity Law: Criminal Activity Cases," Georgia Defense Lawyers Association Journal, 1996

Joseph P. Brennan — 1946 — Spring Hill College, B.S., 1968; The University of Georgia, J.D., 1977 — Admitted to Bar, 1977, Georgia; 1978, U.S. District Court, Southern District of Georgia — Member State Bar of Georgia; Savannah Bar Association; Georgia Insurance Defense Lawyers Association; Savannah Claims Association; Atlanta Claims Association; American Board of Trial Advocates — Lieutenant Colonel, Georgia Air National Guard

Marvin W. McGahee — 1957 — Georgia State University, B.S. (magna cum laude), 1978; The University of Georgia, J.D., 1981 — Admitted to Bar, 1981, Georgia; 1994, South Carolina; 1985, U.S. District Court, Southern District of Georgia; 1989, U.S. Court of Appeals, Eleventh Circuit — Member South Carolina Bar; State Bar of Georgia (Insurance Defense Section, Workers' Compensation Section); Savannah Bar Association

W. Richard Dekle — 1968 — Mercer University, B.A., 1990; Mercer University Walter F. George School of Law, J.D., 1993 — Admitted to Bar, 1993, Georgia — Member State Bar of Georgia; Savannah Bar Association; Georgia Defense Lawyers Association; Defense Research Institute

GEORGIA   SAVANNAH

Brennan, Wasden & Painter, LLC, Savannah, GA
(Continued)

Tracie Macke — 1963 — Emory & Henry College, B.A. (cum laude), 1985; Washington and Lee University School of Law, J.D., 1988 — Admitted to Bar, 1988, Tennessee; 1989, Georgia; 1993, Texas — Member State Bar of Georgia; Savannah Bar Association

J. Curt Thomas — 1976 — Georgia State University, B.S., 2001; Mercer University Walter F. George School of Law, J.D., 2005 — Admitted to Bar, 2005, Georgia; 2008, South Carolina — Member Savannah Bar Association

James V. Painter — 1968 — State University of New York at Buffalo, B.S., 1991; The University of Georgia School of Law, J.D., 1994 — Admitted to Bar, 1994, Georgia; 1997, South Carolina; New York; U.S. District Court, Southern District of Georgia; U.S. District Court, District of South Carolina — Member American, New York State and Augusta Bar Associations; State Bar of Georgia; South Carolina Bar; Georgia Defense Lawyers Association; Defense Research Institute — Resident Augusta, GA Office

F. Michael Taylor — 1955 — The University of Georgia, B.A., 1981; Mercer University Walter F. George School of Law, J.D. (cum laude), 1988 — Managing Editor, Mercer Law Review — Admitted to Bar, 1988, Georgia; South Carolina; U.S. District Court, Northern and Southern Districts of Georgia; U.S. Court of Appeals, Fourth and Eleventh Circuits; Georgia Court of Appeals; Supreme Court of Georgia — Member American and Augusta Bar Associations; State Bar of Georgia; South Carolina Bar; Atlanta Claims Association; Defense Research Institute; Georgia Defense Lawyers Association — Resident Augusta, GA Office

Junior Partners

B. Nicole Smith — 1974 — The University of Georgia, A.B.J. (with high honors), 1996; J.D., 2000 — Admitted to Bar, 2000, Georgia; U.S. District Court, Middle, Northern and Southern Districts of Georgia — Member Atlanta and Savannah Bar Associations; Young Lawyers Association

Sally Haskell Perkins — 1979 — The University of North Carolina at Chapel Hill, A.B., 2001; The University of Georgia, J.D., 2004 — Admitted to Bar, 2005, Georgia — Member Georgia State Bar; Atlanta and Savannah Bar Associations

Sandra Vinueza Foster — 1973 — Armstrong Atlantic State University, B.A., 1994; Mercer University Walter F. George School of Law, J.D., 1997 — Admitted to Bar, 1998, Georgia; Georgia Court of Appeals; Supreme Court of Georgia — Member State Bar of Georgia; Savannah Bar Association; Georgia Defense Lawyers Association; Georgia Association for Women Lawyers

Robert S. D. Pace — 1976 — Oglethorpe University, B.S., 1999; Mercer University Walter F. George School of Law, J.D. (Dean's List), 2003 — Moot Court Board; Ryals Scholar — Admitted to Bar, 2003, Georgia; 2006, U.S. District Court, Middle and Southern Districts of Georgia; 2009, Georgia Court of Appeals; Supreme Court of Georgia — Member Savannah Bar Association — Hugh Lawson Oral Advocacy Competition Finalist

William E. Dillard III — 1955 — The University of Georgia, B.B.A., 1982; The University of Georgia School of Law, J.D., 1987 — Admitted to Bar, 1987, Georgia — Member American and Savannah Bar Associations — Chartered Property & Casualty Underwriter (1987)

T. Daniel Tucker — 1977 — Clayton College & State University, B.A., 2001; Mercer University, J.D., 2004 — Admitted to Bar, 2004, Georgia; 2005, U.S. District Court, Middle and Southern Districts of Georgia — Member State Bar of Georgia; Savannah Bar Association; Georgia Defense Lawyers Association

Travis D. Windsor — 1974 — The University of Georgia, B.A., 1997; Mercer University, J.D., 2002 — Mercer University Law Review — Admitted to Bar, 2002, Georgia; 2006, U.S. District Court, Southern District of Georgia; 2011, U.S. District Court, Northern District of Georgia

Associate

Amanda DiOrio Lynde — 1982 — University of Notre Dame, B.A., 2004; University of Dayton School of Law, J.D., 2008 — Admitted to Bar, 2008, Illinois; 2012, Georgia; 2010, U.S. District Court, Northern District of Illinois; 2012, U.S. District Court, Northern District of Georgia — Member Augusta Bar Association; Georgia Defense Lawyers Association — Resident Augusta, GA Office

Forbes, Foster & Pool, LLC
7505 Waters Avenue, Suite D-14
Savannah, Georgia 31406
  Telephone: 912-352-1190
  Fax: 912-352-1471
  Emer/After Hrs: 912-695-1011
  E-Mail: salty@ffp-law.com

Established: 1991

Insurance Defense, Appellate Practice, Automobile, General Liability, Product Liability, Property and Casualty, Toxic Torts, Life Insurance, Professional Malpractice, Medical Malpractice, Errors and Omissions, Employment Discrimination

Insurance Clients

AIG
Audubon Insurance Company
CNA Risk Management
COUNTRY Mutual Insurance Company
First Mercury Insurance Company
Fortis Insurance Company
Gallagher Bassett Services, Inc.
K & K Insurance Group, Inc.
Life Investors Insurance Company of America
Minnesota Life Insurance Company
National Lloyds Insurance Company
Philadelphia Insurance Company
Sedgwick Claims Management Services, Inc.
Tennessee Farmers Mutual Insurance Company
Veterans Life Insurance Company
Western Heritage Insurance Company
Arch Insurance Group
Clarendon National Insurance Company
Crawford & Company
Fireman's Fund Insurance Company
GAB Robins North America, Inc.
Kemper Insurance Companies
Lexington Insurance Company
Lincoln National Life Insurance Company
Mutual Service Insurance Companies
Onyx Insurance Group
PFL Life Insurance Company
Providian Life and Health Insurance Company
Southern Farm Bureau Life Insurance Company
United States Liability Insurance Company
York Claims Service, Inc.

Non-Insurance Clients

Allstate Settlement Corporation
American National Red Cross
Dean Foods
Frito-Lay, Inc.
Lowe's Companies, Inc.
McKenzie Tank Lines, Inc.
OUM & Associates
PepsiCo, Inc.
Rite Aid Corporation
Wal-Mart Stores, Inc.
Allwaste, Inc.
Arizona Chemical
Dentist's Advantage
GAF Materials Corporation
Lowe's Home Centers, Inc.
North American Risk Services
The Pepsi Bottling Group, Inc.
Quaker Oats Company
Safety-Kleen Systems, Inc.
Wells Fargo Bank, N.A. formerly Wachovia Bank, N.A.

Partners

Morton G. Forbes — 1938 — Wofford College, A.B., 1962; The University of Georgia, LL.B., 1965 — Pi Kappa Phi; Phi Alpha Delta — Admitted to Bar, 1965, Georgia; 1965, U.S. District Court, Middle, Northern and Southern Districts of Georgia; 1965, U.S. Court of Appeals, Fourth and Eleventh Circuits — Member American and Savannah (President, 1992-1993) Bar Associations; State Bar of Georgia; Georgia Defense Lawyers Association (President, 1991-1992); Defense Research Institute (Board of Directors, 1999-2002, State Representative, 1992-1999); Savannah Claims Association; Fellow, Federation of Defense and Corporate Counsel; Alabama Defense Lawyers Association (Honorary); Fellow, Lawyer Foundation of Georgia; Council on Litigation Management; International Association of Defense Counsel; Atlanta Claims Association; American Judicature Society — Practice Areas: Product Liability; Toxic Torts — E-mail: salty@ffp-law.com

John A. Foster — 1961 — Newberry College, B.A., 1984; Campbell University, J.D., 1988 — Omicron Delta Kappa — Admitted to Bar, 1988, Georgia; 1989, U.S. District Court, Southern District of Georgia; 1991, U.S. Court of Appeals, Eleventh Circuit — Member State Bar of Georgia; Savannah Bar Association; American Judicature Society; Federation of Defense and Corporate Counsel; Georgia Defense Lawyers Association (President, 2005-2006); Council on Litigation Management; Defense Research Institute — Practice Areas: Insurance Law; Transportation — E-mail: jfoster@ffp-law.com

Forbes, Foster & Pool, LLC, Savannah, GA (Continued)

Scot V. Pool — 1971 — Emory University, B.A. (cum laude), 1993; The University of Georgia, J.D., 1996 — Phi Beta Kappa; Pi Sigma Alpha — Georgia Journal of International and Comparative Law, Editorial Board, 1994-1995; Articles Editor, 1995-1996 — Admitted to Bar, 1996, Georgia; 1996, U.S. District Court, Southern District of Georgia; 1996, U.S. Court of Appeals, Eleventh Circuit — Member State Bar of Georgia; Savannah Bar Association; Council on Litigation Management; Georgia Defense Lawyers Association; Defense Research Institute — Adjunct Professor, College of Business Administration, Georgia Southern University, Legal Environment of Business, Building Construction Law (2003-Present) — Practice Areas: Insurance Law; Employment Law — E-mail: svpool@ffp-law.com

Gannam, Gnann & Steinmetz LLC
Christian J. Steinmetz III

425 East President Street, Suite A
Savannah, Georgia 31401
Telephone: 912-232-1192
Fax: 912-238-9917
E-Mail: cjs@ggsattorneys.com
www.ggsattorneys.com

Civil Litigation, General Liability, Professional Liability, Property Damage, Coverage Issues, Insurance Defense

Firm Profile: Insurance defense representation at an affordable value with personal service and immediate access. My clients get what they pay for, my legal advice and work. I provide insurers with value without compromising performance.

Insurance Clients

Northland Insurance Company
United States Liability Insurance Company
Sedgwick Claims Management Services, Inc.
Utica National Insurance Company

Non-Insurance Clients

Bonitz of Georgia, Inc
Goodwill of the Coastal Empire, Inc.
Wilmington Plantation Owners Association, Inc.
Chatham County, Georgia
Memorial Day School Inc.
Starwood Hotels & Resorts Worldwide, Inc.

Christian J. Steinmetz III — 1966 — University of Virginia, B.A., 1988; Mercer Law School, J.D., 1993 — Admitted to Bar, 1993, Georgia; 1994, U.S. District Court, Middle and Southern Districts of Georgia — Member Savannah Bar Association; Georgia Defense Lawyers Association; Federation of Defense and Corporate Counsel

Howard & Whatley, P.C.

325 Tattnall Street
Savannah, Georgia 31401
Telephone: 912-234-1000
Fax: 912-236-5700
E-Mail: tom.whatley@howardandwhatley.com

Established: 1991

Insurance Defense, Automobile, General Liability, Workers' Compensation, Premises Liability, Commercial Vehicle Liability

Firm Profile: Howard & Whatley, P.C. is a civil litigation firm handling matters throughout Middle and Southern Georgia. The firm's practice focuses principally on the representation of businesses and insurers, liability defense, insurance coverage and business tort cases.

Insurance Clients

Bituminous Insurance Companies
Hortica
Kemper Insurance Companies
Underwriters Safety and Claims
CCMSI - Cannon Claims Management Services, Inc.
Penn Millers Insurance Company

Howard & Whatley, P.C., Savannah, GA (Continued)

Non-Insurance Clients

Briggs & Stratton Corporation
DOAS Risk Management
Great Dane Trailers, Inc.
Sedgwick Claims Management Services, Inc.
Coca Cola Bottling Company United, Inc.
St. Joseph's/Candler Health System
Southeastern Claims Services, Inc.
The Waggoners

Partners

Thomas G. Whatley, Jr. — The University of Georgia, B.B.A., 1983; Emory University School of Law, J.D., 1986 — Admitted to Bar, 1986, Georgia; 1986, U.S. District Court, Middle, Northern and Southern Districts of Georgia; U.S. Court of Appeals, Eleventh Circuit — Member State Bar of Georgia; Savannah and Atlanta Bar Associations; Georgia Defense Lawyers Association; Georgia Self-Insurers Association; Lawyers Foundation of Georgia; Defense Research Institute; Atlanta Claims Association — Practice Areas: Insurance Defense; Automobile Liability; Commercial Vehicle; Premises Liability; Workers' Compensation — E-mail: tom.whatley@howardandwhatley.com

Molly M. Howard — The University of Georgia, A.B. (magna cum laude), 1976; J.D., 1979 — Admitted to Bar, 1979, Georgia; 1979, U.S. District Court, Middle, Northern and Southern Districts of Georgia — Member State Bar of Georgia; Savannah Bar Association; Georgia Self-Insurers Association; Georgia Defense Lawyers Association — E-mail: molly.howard@howardandwhatley.com

SOPERTON † 3,115 Treutlen Co.

Refer To

Brennan, Harris & Rominger LLP
2 East Bryan Street, Suite 1300
Savannah, Georgia 31401
Telephone: 912-233-3399
Fax: 912-236-4558

Mailing Address: P.O. Box 2784, Savannah, GA 31402

Insurance Law, Admiralty and Maritime Law, Casualty, Surety, Life Insurance, Workers' Compensation

SEE COMPLETE LISTING UNDER SAVANNAH, GEORGIA (97 MILES)

SPRINGFIELD † 2,852 Effingham Co.

Refer To

Brennan, Harris & Rominger LLP
2 East Bryan Street, Suite 1300
Savannah, Georgia 31401
Telephone: 912-233-3399
Fax: 912-236-4558

Mailing Address: P.O. Box 2784, Savannah, GA 31402

Insurance Law, Admiralty and Maritime Law, Casualty, Surety, Life Insurance, Workers' Compensation

SEE COMPLETE LISTING UNDER SAVANNAH, GEORGIA (35 MILES)

Refer To

Forbes, Foster & Pool, LLC
7505 Waters Avenue, Suite D-14
Savannah, Georgia 31406
Telephone: 912-352-1190
Fax: 912-352-1471

Mailing Address: P.O. Box 13929, Savannah, GA 31416-0929

Insurance Defense, Appellate Practice, Automobile, General Liability, Product Liability, Property and Casualty, Toxic Torts, Life Insurance, Professional Malpractice, Medical Malpractice, Errors and Omissions, Employment Discrimination

SEE COMPLETE LISTING UNDER SAVANNAH, GEORGIA (35 MILES)

GEORGIA — ST. MARYS

ST. MARYS 17,121 Camden Co.

Refer To

Brennan, Harris & Rominger LLP
2 East Bryan Street, Suite 1300
Savannah, Georgia 31401
   Telephone: 912-233-3399
   Fax: 912-236-4558

Mailing Address: P.O. Box 2784, Savannah, GA 31402

Insurance Law, Admiralty and Maritime Law, Casualty, Surety, Life Insurance, Workers' Compensation

SEE COMPLETE LISTING UNDER SAVANNAH, GEORGIA (112 MILES)

ST. SIMONS ISLAND 12,026 Glynn Co.

Refer To

Brennan, Harris & Rominger LLP
2 East Bryan Street, Suite 1300
Savannah, Georgia 31401
   Telephone: 912-233-3399
   Fax: 912-236-4558

Mailing Address: P.O. Box 2784, Savannah, GA 31402

Insurance Law, Admiralty and Maritime Law, Casualty, Surety, Life Insurance, Workers' Compensation

SEE COMPLETE LISTING UNDER SAVANNAH, GEORGIA (81 MILES)

STATESBORO † 28,422 Bulloch Co.

Refer To

Brennan, Harris & Rominger LLP
2 East Bryan Street, Suite 1300
Savannah, Georgia 31401
   Telephone: 912-233-3399
   Fax: 912-236-4558

Mailing Address: P.O. Box 2784, Savannah, GA 31402

Insurance Law, Admiralty and Maritime Law, Casualty, Surety, Life Insurance, Workers' Compensation

SEE COMPLETE LISTING UNDER SAVANNAH, GEORGIA (53 MILES)

Refer To

Forbes, Foster & Pool, LLC
7505 Waters Avenue, Suite D-14
Savannah, Georgia 31406
   Telephone: 912-352-1190
   Fax: 912-352-1471

Mailing Address: P.O. Box 13929, Savannah, GA 31416-0929

Insurance Defense, Appellate Practice, Automobile, General Liability, Product Liability, Property and Casualty, Toxic Torts, Life Insurance, Professional Malpractice, Medical Malpractice, Errors and Omissions, Employment Discrimination

SEE COMPLETE LISTING UNDER SAVANNAH, GEORGIA (53 MILES)

Refer To

Gannam, Gnann & Steinmetz LLC
Christian J. Steinmetz III
425 East President Street, Suite A
Savannah, Georgia 31401
   Telephone: 912-232-1192
   Fax: 912-238-9917

Civil Litigation, General Liability, Professional Liability, Property Damage, Coverage Issues, Insurance Defense

SEE COMPLETE LISTING UNDER SAVANNAH, GEORGIA (54 MILES)

SWAINSBORO † 7,277 Emanuel Co.

Refer To

Brennan, Harris & Rominger LLP
2 East Bryan Street, Suite 1300
Savannah, Georgia 31401
   Telephone: 912-233-3399
   Fax: 912-236-4558

Mailing Address: P.O. Box 2784, Savannah, GA 31402

Insurance Law, Admiralty and Maritime Law, Casualty, Surety, Life Insurance, Workers' Compensation

SEE COMPLETE LISTING UNDER SAVANNAH, GEORGIA (90 MILES)

SYLVANIA † 2,956 Screven Co.

Refer To

Brennan, Harris & Rominger LLP
2 East Bryan Street, Suite 1300
Savannah, Georgia 31401
   Telephone: 912-233-3399
   Fax: 912-236-4558

Mailing Address: P.O. Box 2784, Savannah, GA 31402

Insurance Law, Admiralty and Maritime Law, Casualty, Surety, Life Insurance, Workers' Compensation

SEE COMPLETE LISTING UNDER SAVANNAH, GEORGIA (63 MILES)

Refer To

Glover, Blount & Hyatt
429 Walker Street
Augusta, Georgia 30901
   Telephone: 706-722-3786
   Fax: 706-722-7145

Insurance Law, Defense Litigation

SEE COMPLETE LISTING UNDER AUGUSTA, GEORGIA (63 MILES)

THOMASVILLE † 18,413 Thomas Co.

Alexander & Vann, LLP

411 Gordon Avenue
Thomasville, Georgia 31792
   Telephone: 229-226-2565
   Fax: 229-228-0444

Established: 1941

Governmental Liability, Insurance Defense, Automobile, Product Liability, Medical Malpractice, Legal Malpractice, Architects and Engineers, Workers' Compensation, Surety, Life Insurance, Accident, Property Damage, Litigation

Firm Profile: Alexander & Vann, LLP is a firm of eleven attorneys representing a number of insurers, including The Travelers Insurance Companies, the CNA Companies, Georgia Farm Bureau Mutual Insurance Company and The State Farm Insurance Companies. The firm is engaged in an area defense practice which covers southwest Georgia, and the firm handles not only traditional motor vehicle liability cases, but also the defense of local governments, medical malpractice and hospital liability work, and products liability cases. The firm represents the City of Thomasville, Georgia, and the Thomas County School System. Partners in the firm are members of Defense Research Institute, the International Association of Defense Counsel, the Georgia Defense Lawyers Association and similar organizations.

Insurance Clients

Argonaut Insurance Company
Atlanta Casualty Company
Auto-Owners Insurance Company
Canal Insurance Company
Chubb Group of Insurance
   Companies
Cotton States Mutual Insurance
   Company

Association County
   Commissioners of Georgia
   (ACCG-IRMA)
Carolina Casualty Insurance
   Company
CNA Insurance Companies
Employers Insurance Company of
   Wausau

VALDOSTA | GEORGIA

Alexander & Vann, LLP, Thomasville, GA (Continued)

Georgia Farm Bureau Mutual Insurance Company
Georgia Mutual Insurance
Hartford Accident and Indemnity Company
Nationwide Insurance
New York Life Insurance Company
Southern Insurance Underwriters
State Farm Insurance Companies
Zurich Insurance Company
Georgia Interlocal Risk Management Agency (GIRMA)
Guaranty National Insurance Company
Interstate Life & Accident Company
Ohio Casualty Group
Southern Guaranty Insurance Company
Travelers Insurance Company

Partners

W. W. Alexander — (Deceased)

Heyward Vann — (Deceased)

William C. Sanders — 1945 — Mercer University, A.B., 1967; J.D. (cum laude), 1975 — Admitted to Bar, 1975, Georgia; U.S. District Court, Middle District of Georgia — Member State Bar of Georgia; Georgia Defense Lawyers Association; Defense Research Institute

George R. Lilly, II — 1958 — The University of Georgia, B.A., 1980; Mercer University, J.D., 1983 — Admitted to Bar, 1983, Georgia; U.S. District Court, Middle District of Georgia

Thomas H. Vann, Jr. — 1944 — The University of Georgia, B.A., 1966; Mercer University, J.D., 1969; New York University, LL.M. (Taxation), 1973 — Admitted to Bar, 1970, Georgia

John Turner Holt — 1949 — The University of Georgia, B.A., 1971; J.D., 1974 — Admitted to Bar, 1974, Georgia; U.S. District Court, Middle District of Georgia

James Hillman Smith — 1959 — The University of Georgia, B.A., 1981; J.D., 1983 — Admitted to Bar, 1984, Georgia; Florida — Practice Areas: Real Estate; Commercial Leases

Raleigh W. Rollins — 1968 — The University of Georgia, B.A., 1991; The University of Georgia School of Law, J.D., 1995 — Admitted to Bar, 1994, Georgia; U.S. District Court, Middle District of Georgia

J. Renee Hall Oliveto — 1976 — Valdosta State University, B.A. (with honors), 1997; The University of Georgia, J.D., 2002 — Admitted to Bar, 2003, Georgia

Timothy C. Sanders — 1975 — Mercer University, A.B., 1997; J.D., 2003 — Admitted to Bar, 2003, Georgia

James A. Garland — 1976 — The University of Georgia, B.A., 1999; Mercer University, J.D., 2002 — Admitted to Bar, 2002, Georgia; U.S. District Court, Middle District of Georgia

Associate

Rachel Cook Beverly — 1971 — Washington and Lee University, B.A., 1994; Florida State University, J.D. (with honors), 2000 — Admitted to Bar, 2001, Georgia

THOMSON † 6,778 McDuffie Co.

Refer To

Glover, Blount & Hyatt
429 Walker Street
Augusta, Georgia 30901
Telephone: 706-722-3786
Fax: 706-722-7145

Insurance Law, Defense Litigation

SEE COMPLETE LISTING UNDER AUGUSTA, GEORGIA (30 MILES)

TIFTON † 16,350 Tift Co.

Refer To

Gardner, Willis, Sweat & Handelman, LLP
2408 Westgate Drive
Albany, Georgia 31707
Telephone: 229-883-2441
Fax: 229-888-8148
Mailing Address: P.O. Drawer 71788, Albany, GA 31708-1788

Insurance Defense, Workers' Compensation, Trucking Law, General Liability, Employment Litigation, Business Litigation

SEE COMPLETE LISTING UNDER ALBANY, GEORGIA (43 MILES)

VALDOSTA † 54,518 Lowndes Co.

Coleman Talley LLP
910 North Patterson Street
Valdosta, Georgia 31601
Telephone: 229-242-7562
Fax: 229-333-0885
www.colemantalley.com

(Atlanta, GA Office: 3475 Lenox Road, Suite 400, 30326)
(Tel: 770-698-9556)
(Fax: 770-698-9729)

Established: 1937

Insurance Law, Insurance Coverage & Defense, Medical Malpractice Defense

Firm Profile: With a legal practice historically concentrated in civil trial defense and corporate law, the firm of Coleman Talley LLP currently serves clients within a wide array of legal practice areas, including experience in the following: general civil practice, insurance defense, workers' compensation, medical and professional malpractice defense, municipal law, construction law, commercial transactions, corporate and business law and litigation.

Founded in 1937 on traditional principles of integrity and trustworthiness, supported through the years by generational expertise in civil litigation defense and business law, we have grown in recent years to 32 lawyers practicing in Atlanta and Valdosta, Georgia.

Insurance Clients

American Family Home Insurance Company
American Mutual Fire Insurance Company of Kentucky
Georgia Casualty & Surety Company
Kemper Insurance Companies
MAG Mutual Insurance Company
Metropolitan Property and Casualty Insurance Company
Reserve Life Insurance Company
St. Paul Insurance Company
Senior Life Insurance Company
TeamHealth
Tift Area Captive Insurance Company
American Motorists Insurance Company
Bituminous Insurance Companies
GAB Robins North America, Inc.
Grange Mutual Insurance Company
Hanover Insurance Company
Liberty Mutual Insurance Company
Medicus Insurance Company
Nautilus Insurance Company
Powell Insurance Group, LLLP
Safeco Insurance
Sedgwick Group of Georgia, Inc.
Southern General Insurance Company
TPA Captive Insurance Company

Non-Insurance Clients

Atlanta Gas Light Company
Stowe Associates
City of Valdosta

Partners

Wade H. Coleman — 1940 — Vanderbilt University, B.A., 1962; The University of Georgia, J.D., 1965 — Admitted to Bar, 1964, Georgia; 1964, U.S. District Court, Middle District of Georgia; 1965, U.S. Court of Appeals, Eleventh Circuit — Member American and Valdosta Bar Associations; State Bar of Georgia; International Association of Defense Counsel; Georgia Defense Lawyers Association; American College of Trial Lawyers — Practice Areas: Professional Malpractice; Insurance Defense; Medical Malpractice Defense — E-mail: wade.coleman@colemantalley.com

George T. Talley — 1944 — University of South Carolina, B.S., 1965; J.D., 1968 — Admitted to Bar, 1968, Georgia; South Carolina; U.S. District Court, Middle and Northern Districts of Georgia; U.S. Court of Appeals, Eleventh Circuit — Member American and Valdosta Bar Associations; State Bar of Georgia; South Carolina Bar; Georgia Defense Lawyers Association — City Attorney, Valdosta, 1976-present — Practice Areas: Insurance Defense; Workers' Compensation — E-mail: george.talley@colementalley.com

Edward F. Preston — 1954 — Michigan State University, B.S., 1975; University of Michigan Law School, J.D., 1977 — Admitted to Bar, 1978, Michigan; 1987, Georgia — Member State Bar of Georgia; Valdosta Bar Association — Practice Areas: Insurance Defense — E-mail: ed.preston@colemantalley.com

William E. Holland — 1962 — The University of Georgia, 1985; Mercer University, J.D., 1988 — Admitted to Bar, 1988, Georgia; 1988, U.S. District

GEORGIA — VALDOSTA

Coleman Talley LLP, Valdosta, GA (Continued)

Court, Middle District of Georgia; 1991, U.S. District Court, Southern District of Georgia — Member State Bar of Georgia; Valdosta Bar Association — Practice Areas: Insurance Defense — E-mail: bill.holland@colemantalley.com

Gregory T. Talley — 1968 — The University of Georgia, B.A., 1991; Mercer University, J.D. (cum laude), 1995 — Admitted to Bar, 1995, Georgia; 1995, U.S. District Court, Middle District of Georgia — Member State Bar of Georgia; Valdosta Bar Association — Practice Areas: Insurance Defense; Medical Malpractice — E-mail: greg.talley@colemantalley.com

Timothy M. Tanner — 1974 — The University of Georgia, B.B.A., 1997; Mercer University Walter F. George School of Law, J.D., 2001 — Admitted to Bar, 2001, Georgia; 2002, Alabama; 2002, U.S. District Court, Middle and Northern Districts of Georgia; U.S. District Court, Middle and Northern Districts of Alabama — Member State Bar of Georgia; Alabama Trial Lawyers Association; Georgia Defense Lawyers Association — Practice Areas: Insurance Defense; Municipal Law — E-mail: tim.tanner@colemantalley.com

C. Hansell Watt, IV — Rhodes College, B.A., 2000; Mercer University, J.D. (cum laude), 2004 — Admitted to Bar, 2004, Georgia; U.S. District Court, Middle and Northern Districts of Georgia; U.S. Court of Appeals, Eleventh Circuit; Georgia Superior and State Courts; Supreme Court of Georgia — Member State Bar of Georgia — Practice Areas: Insurance Defense; Medical Malpractice Defense — E-mail: hansell.watt@colemantalley.com

Eric A. Collins — Concord College, B.S. (cum laude), 1986; West Virginia University College of Law, J.D., 1989 — Admitted to Bar, 1989, West Virginia (Inactive); 2008, Georgia — Member State Bar of Georgia; West Virginia State Bar — Practice Areas: Insurance Defense; Workers' Compensation — E-mail: eric.collins@colemantalley.com

Associate

Beau Howell — Auburn University, B.A. (summa cum laude), 2005; The University of Georgia School of Law, J.D. (cum laude), 2008 — Admitted to Bar, 2008, Georgia — Practice Areas: Insurance Defense; Medical Malpractice Defense — E-mail: beau.howell@colemantalley.com

Of Counsel

Annette K. McBrayer — North Carolina State University, B.A. (Accounting), 1978; Emory University, J.D./M.B.A., 1983 — Admitted to Bar, 1983, Georgia — Member State Bar of Georgia; Atlanta Bar Association — Elected, Board of Directors Georgia Association of Fraud Prevention and Awareness Coalition (June 2011) — Practice Areas: Insurance Coverage & Defense — E-mail: annette.mcbrayer@colemantalley.com

Young, Thagard, Hoffman, Smith, Lawrence & Shenton, LLP

801 Northwood Park Drive
Valdosta, Georgia 31602
 Telephone: 229-242-2520
 Fax: 229-242-5040
 E-Mail: ythsl@youngthagard.com
 www.youngthagard.com

Established: 1960

Insurance Defense, Medical Malpractice, Product Liability, Personal Injury, Property Damage, Civil Rights, Employment Law, Workers' Compensation

Insurance Clients

Allstate Insurance Company	Auto-Owners Insurance Company
Cincinnati Insurance Company	CNA Insurance Company
Colquitt EMC	Cotton States Mutual Insurance Company
Empire Fire and Marine Insurance Company	Encompass Insurance
Frankenmuth Mutual Insurance Company	Georgia Farm Bureau Mutual Insurance Company
Georgia Interlocal Risk Management Agency (GIRMA)	Government Employees Insurance Company
Great Central Insurance Company	Lloyd's
MAG Mutual Insurance Company	Nationwide Group
Scottsdale Insurance Company	Sentry Insurance
Southern General Insurance Company	South Georgia Medical Center
	State Auto Insurance Company
State Farm Insurance Companies	State of Georgia Department of Administrative Services
USAA	

Young, Thagard, Hoffman, Smith, Lawrence & Shenton, LLP, Valdosta, GA (Continued)

Firm Members

F. Thomas Young — (1935-2008)

Cam U. Young — (1913-1998)

James B. Thagard — 1954 — Valdosta State College, B.A., 1977; Cumberland School of Law of Samford University, J.D., 1980 — Admitted to Bar, 1980, Georgia; 1986, U.S. District Court, Middle District of Georgia; 1986, U.S. Court of Appeals, Eleventh Circuit — Member American and Valdosta (President, 1995) Bar Associations; Association of Defense Trial Attorneys; Defense Research Institute; Georgia Defense Lawyers Association — Assistant District Attorney, Southern Judicial Circuit, 1980-1985 — Practice Areas: Litigation — E-mail: jamesthagard@youngthagard.com

Daniel C. Hoffman — 1960 — University of Wisconsin, B.B.A. (magna cum laude), 1981; University of Notre Dame, J.D. (cum laude), 1984 — Admitted to Bar, 1984, Wisconsin; 1986, Georgia; 1986, U.S. District Court, Middle District of Georgia; 1990, U.S. Court of Appeals, Eleventh Circuit; 1999, U.S. Supreme Court — Member American Bar Association; Association of Defense Trial Attorneys — Practice Areas: Litigation; Workers' Compensation — E-mail: danhoffman@youngthagard.com

J. Holder Smith, Jr. — 1968 — Emory University, B.A. (with distinction), 1990; The University of Georgia, J.D. (cum laude), 1993 — Admitted to Bar, 1993, Georgia; 1993, U.S. District Court, Middle District of Georgia — E-mail: jaysmith@youngthagard.com

Matthew Russell Lawrence — 1971 — The University of Georgia, B.A., 1993; Georgia State University, J.D., 1996 — Admitted to Bar, 1996, Georgia; 1996, U.S. District Court, Middle District of Georgia; 2002, U.S. Court of Appeals, Eleventh Circuit — Practice Areas: Litigation — E-mail: mattlawrence@youngthagard.com

Charles A. Shenton, IV — 1978 — Valdosta State University, B.A., 2000; Mississippi College School of Law, J.D., 2003 — Admitted to Bar, 2003, Georgia; 2005, U.S. District Court, Middle District of Georgia — Member Valdosta Bar Association — Practice Areas: Litigation — E-mail: chadshenton@youngthagard.com

Brian J. Miller — 1982 — The University of Georgia, B.B.A. (cum laude), 2004; The University of Alabama School of Law, J.D., 2008 — Admitted to Bar, 2008, Georgia — Practice Areas: Litigation; Workers' Compensation — E-mail: brianmiller@youngthagard.com

Leslie Kennerly — 1980 — Vanderbilt University, B.A., 2002; University of South Carolina, J.D., 2005 — Admitted to Bar, 2005, Georgia; 2006, U.S. District Court, Middle District of Georgia — Member State Bar of Georgia — Practice Areas: Litigation — E-mail: lesliekennerly@youngthagard.com

William J. Purvis — 1987 — The University of Georgia, B.A. Political Science, 2009; Mercer University Walter F. George School of Law, J.D. (cum laude), 2012 — Admitted to Bar, 2012, Georgia — Member Valdosta Bar Association; Georgia Defense Lawyers Association — Practice Areas: Litigation — E-mail: justinpurvis@youngthagard.com

Crystal S. Lang — 1986 — Armstrong Atlantic State University, B.A. Arts and Culture, 2007; Mercer University Walter F. George School of Law, J.D., 2011 — Admitted to Bar, 2011, Georgia; 2011, Georgia Superior and State Courts; 2012, Georgia Court of Appeals; 2012, Supreme Court of Georgia — Member State Bar of Georgia — Practice Areas: Litigation

---

The following firms also service this area.

Gannam, Gnann & Steinmetz LLC
Christian J. Steinmetz III
425 East President Street, Suite A
Savannah, Georgia 31401
 Telephone: 912-232-1192
 Fax: 912-238-9917

Civil Litigation, General Liability, Professional Liability, Property Damage, Coverage Issues, Insurance Defense

SEE COMPLETE LISTING UNDER SAVANNAH, GEORGIA (168 MILES)

VIDALIA   10,473 Toombs Co.
Refer To

Brennan, Harris & Rominger LLP
2 East Bryan Street, Suite 1300
Savannah, Georgia 31401
   Telephone: 912-233-3399
   Fax: 912-236-4558

Mailing Address: P.O. Box 2784, Savannah, GA 31402

Insurance Law, Admiralty and Maritime Law, Casualty, Surety, Life Insurance, Workers' Compensation

SEE COMPLETE LISTING UNDER SAVANNAH, GEORGIA (98 MILES)

WARNER ROBINS   66,588 Houston Co.
Refer To

Jones, Cork & Miller, LLP
SunTrust Bank Building, Suite 500
435 Second Street, 5th Floor
Macon, Georgia 31201-2724
   Telephone: 478-745-2821
   Fax: 478-743-9609

Mailing Address: P.O. Box 6437, Macon, GA 31208-6437

Insurance Defense, Automobile, Fire, Casualty, Surety, Life Insurance, Workers' Compensation, Medical Malpractice, Product Liability, Civil Rights, Governmental Liability, Business Law, Class Actions, Complex Litigation, Construction Law, Employment Law, Engineers, Environmental Law, Hospitals, Railroad Law, Self-Insured

SEE COMPLETE LISTING UNDER MACON, GEORGIA (18 MILES)

WASHINGTON   † 4,134 Wilkes Co.
Refer To

Glover, Blount & Hyatt
429 Walker Street
Augusta, Georgia 30901
   Telephone: 706-722-3786
   Fax: 706-722-7145

Insurance Law, Defense Litigation

SEE COMPLETE LISTING UNDER AUGUSTA, GEORGIA (56 MILES)

WAYCROSS   † 14,649 Ware Co.
Refer To

Brennan, Harris & Rominger LLP
2 East Bryan Street, Suite 1300
Savannah, Georgia 31401
   Telephone: 912-233-3399
   Fax: 912-236-4558

Mailing Address: P.O. Box 2784, Savannah, GA 31402

Insurance Law, Admiralty and Maritime Law, Casualty, Surety, Life Insurance, Workers' Compensation

SEE COMPLETE LISTING UNDER SAVANNAH, GEORGIA (109 MILES)

WAYNESBORO   † 5,766 Burke Co.
Refer To

Brennan, Harris & Rominger LLP
2 East Bryan Street, Suite 1300
Savannah, Georgia 31401
   Telephone: 912-233-3399
   Fax: 912-236-4558

Mailing Address: P.O. Box 2784, Savannah, GA 31402

Insurance Law, Admiralty and Maritime Law, Casualty, Surety, Life Insurance, Workers' Compensation

SEE COMPLETE LISTING UNDER SAVANNAH, GEORGIA (97 MILES)

Refer To

Glover, Blount & Hyatt
429 Walker Street
Augusta, Georgia 30901
   Telephone: 706-722-3786
   Fax: 706-722-7145

Insurance Law, Defense Litigation

SEE COMPLETE LISTING UNDER AUGUSTA, GEORGIA (25 MILES)

WOODBINE   † 1,412 Camden Co.
Refer To

Brennan, Harris & Rominger LLP
2 East Bryan Street, Suite 1300
Savannah, Georgia 31401
   Telephone: 912-233-3399
   Fax: 912-236-4558

Mailing Address: P.O. Box 2784, Savannah, GA 31402

Insurance Law, Admiralty and Maritime Law, Casualty, Surety, Life Insurance, Workers' Compensation

SEE COMPLETE LISTING UNDER SAVANNAH, GEORGIA (95 MILES)

HAWAII

CAPITAL: HONOLULU

COUNTIES AND COUNTY SEATS

County	County Seat
Hawaii	Hilo
Honolulu	Honolulu
Kalawao	
Kauai	Lihue
Maui	Wailuku

In the text that follows "†" indicates County Seats.

Our files contain additional verified data on the firms listed herein. This additional information is available on request.

A.M. BEST COMPANY

HONOLULU † 371,657 Honolulu Co.

Ashford & Wriston

Alii Place, 14th Floor
1099 Alakea Street
Honolulu, Hawaii 96813
Telephone: 808-539-0400
Fax: 808-533-4945
Toll Free: 800-458-6806
E-Mail: kherring@awlaw.com
www.ashfordwriston.com

Established: 1955

Title Insurance, Insurance Coverage, Subrogation, Commercial General Liability, Insurance Defense, Personal Injury Defense

Insurance Clients

Fidelity National Title Insurance Company
Ticor Title Insurance Company
Old Republic Title Insurance Group
Title Guaranty of Hawaii, Inc.

Non-Insurance Clients

The Wackenhut Corporation

Partners

Paul S. Aoki — University of Hawaii, B.A., 1969; The George Washington University, J.D., 1973 — Admitted to Bar, 1973, Hawaii

Rosemary T. Fazio — Fordham University, B.A. (magna cum laude), 1971; University of Toronto, M.A., 1974; University of Hawaii, M.S.W., 1975; J.D., 1978 — Admitted to Bar, 1978, Hawaii; 1983, U.S. Supreme Court

Michael W. Gibson — University of Wisconsin, B.B.A., 1970; University of California, Hastings College of the Law, J.D., 1973 — Admitted to Bar, 1974, Hawaii; California

Kevin W. Herring — University of Hawaii, B.B.A. (with distinction), 1993; Case Western Reserve University, J.D. (cum laude), 1996 — Admitted to Bar, 1996, Hawaii; U.S. District Court, District of Hawaii

Francis P. Hogan — United States Military Academy at West Point, B.S., 1972; Stanford University, J.D., 1980 — Admitted to Bar, 1980, Hawaii

Wayne P. Nasser — University of Santa Clara, B.B.A. (cum laude), 1968; University of California, J.D., 1971 — Admitted to Bar, 1971, Hawaii; 1975, U.S. Supreme Court; 1978, U.S. Court of Federal Claims

Case Lombardi & Pettit
A Law Corporation

Mauka Tower, Suite 2600
737 Bishop Street
Honolulu, Hawaii 96813
Telephone: 808-547-5400
Fax: 808-523-1888
E-Mail: info@caselombardi.com
www.caselombardi.com

Established: 1888

Insurance Defense, Directors and Officers Liability, Professional Liability, Professional Errors and Omissions, Employment Practices Liability, Title Insurance, Casualty, Coverage Issues, Bad Faith, Securities, Commercial Law, Construction Litigation, Product Liability, Subrogation, Investigation and Adjustment, Automobile, Civil Litigation, Bankruptcy, Collections, Business Law, Health Care, ERISA, Real Estate, Land Use, Administrative Law

Firm Profile: Tracing its roots back to 1888, Case Lombardi & Pettit is committed to providing outstanding and cost effective client and legal services throughout Hawaii. The firm is located in Honolulu on the island of Oahu.

Case Lombardi & Pettit, A Law Corporation, Honolulu, HI (Continued)

Case Lombardi & Pettit is a full service law firm offering litigation and dispute resolution, bankruptcy, real estate, business, employee benefits, health care, tax, estate planning, and probate services.

The Litigation and Dispute Resolution Practice Group is comprised of a team of skillful, experienced, successful, and zealous litigators and trial lawyers. Attorneys from the firm who practice litigation and dispute resolution are creative and conscientious in their representation of clients involved in commercial and civil disputes, insurance defense, complex litigation, financial, business, real estate, and construction matters, and employment and civil rights cases. The attorneys regularly appear in all federal and state courts in Hawaii, both at the trial and appellate levels, before administrative and regulatory agencies, and in mediation and arbitration proceedings. Lawyers in this Group are committed to achievement by mediation or negotiated settlement, arbitration award, and if necessary, verdict at trial.

Insurance Clients

Allied World Assurance Company
CNA Insurance Company
First American Title Insurance Company
Infinity Insurance Company
Travelers Construction
United National Insurance Company
Chubb Specialty Insurance
Commonwealth Land Title Insurance Company
Great American Insurance Company
Underwriters at Lloyd's, London

Directors

Lissa H. Andrews — University of Hawaii at Manoa, B.S.W., 1980; University of Hawaii at Manoa, William S. Richardson School of Law, J.D., 1983 — Admitted to Bar, 1983, Hawaii; U.S. District Court, District of Hawaii; 1986, U.S. Court of Appeals, Ninth Circuit; 1997, U.S. Supreme Court — Member Hawaii State Bar Association — Practice Areas: Directors and Officers Liability; Professional Liability; Commercial Litigation — E-mail: landrews@caselombardi.com

Michael L. Lam — Creighton University, B.A., 1981; University of Santa Clara, J.D., 1986 — Admitted to Bar, 1986, Hawaii; 1986, U.S. District Court, District of Hawaii — Member American and Hawaii State Bar Associations — Practice Areas: Construction Law; Construction Litigation; Commercial Litigation; Business Litigation; Premises Liability; Product Liability; Real Estate; Insurance; Personal Injury Litigation; Real Estate Transactions; Commercial Leases; Employment Law — E-mail: mlam@caselombardi.com

Michael R. Marsh — Blackburn University, B.A., 1969; The George Washington University, J.D., 1973 — Admitted to Bar, 1973, Hawaii; 1973, U.S. District Court, District of Hawaii; 1980, U.S. Court of Appeals, Ninth Circuit — Member Hawaii State Bar Association — Practice Areas: Construction Claims; Surety; Commercial Litigation; Subrogation; Intellectual Property; Employment Practices Liability — E-mail: mmarsh@caselombardi.com

Mark G. Valencia — University of Hawaii West Oahu, B.A., 1993; Southern Methodist University, J.D., 1996 — Admitted to Bar, 1996, Hawaii; U.S. District Court, District of Hawaii — Member American and Hawaii State Bar Associations — U.S. Army, Sergeant (1989-1993); U.S. Army, Reserve Captain (2010-Present) — Practice Areas: Civil Litigation; Employment Law; Errors and Omissions; Civil Rights; Discrimination — E-mail: mvalencia@caselombardi.com

John D. Zalewski — University of Minnesota, B.S., 1980; University of Wisconsin-Madison, J.D., 1986 — Admitted to Bar, 1986, Wisconsin; 1988, Hawaii; 1988, U.S. District Court, District of Hawaii; 2003, U.S. Court of Appeals, Ninth Circuit — Member Federal, American and Hawaii State Bar Associations; Defense Research Institute — Certified Public Accountant — Practice Areas: Insurance Defense; Directors and Officers Liability; Professional Liability; Employment Practices Liability; Title Insurance; Casualty; Subrogation — E-mail: jzalewski@caselombardi.com

Of Counsel

Frederick W. Rohlfing III — Dartmouth College, B.A. (magna cum laude), 1978; The University of Chicago, J.D., 1983 — Admitted to Bar, 1983, Hawaii; 1983, U.S. District Court, District of Hawaii; 1983, U.S. Court of Appeals, Ninth Circuit — Member Hawaii State Bar Association — Practice Areas: Business Litigation; Insurance Coverage — E-mail: frohlfing@caselombardi.com

(This firm is also listed in the Subrogation section of this directory)

HONOLULU — HAWAII

Chee, Markham & Feldman
Suite 2700 American Savings Bank Tower
1001 Bishop Street
Honolulu, Hawaii 96813
   Telephone: 808-523-0111
   Fax: 808-523-0115
   E-Mail: kchee@cheemarkham.com

Established: 1985

Insurance Defense, Premises Liability, Malpractice, Product Liability, Coverage Analysis, Subrogation, Real Estate, Business Litigation, Construction Defect, Contracts

Insurance Clients

American Hallmark Insurance Company of Texas
Burlington Insurance Company
Carl Warren & Company
Dongbu Insurance
Endurance U.S. Insurance Operations
Fireman's Fund Insurance Company
Hawaii Employers' Mutual Insurance Company
Northland Insurance Company
Quanta Services, Inc.
Sagicor Claims Management, Inc.
Travelers Casualty and Surety Company
York Risk Services Group, Inc.
Amica Mutual Insurance Company
AmTrust North America
Capitol Indemnity Corporation
Chicago Insurance Company
DTRIC Insurance Company Limited
Essex Insurance Company
Global Aerospace, Inc.
The Hawaiian Insurance & Guaranty Company, Limited
Mitsui Sumitomo Insurance Group
QBE North America
Riverport Insurance Company
Sompo Japan Insurance Company of America
United Educators Insurance

Non-Insurance Clients

Costco Wholesale Corporation
Safeway, Inc.

Partners

Kevin S. W. Chee — 1952 — Dartmouth College, B.A. (magna cum laude), 1974; University of California, Berkeley Boalt Hall School of Law, J.D., 1977 — Phi Beta Kappa — Admitted to Bar, 1977, California; 1978, Hawaii; 1978, U.S. District Court, Northern District of California; 1978, U.S. District Court, District of Hawaii; 1978, U.S. Court of Appeals, Ninth Circuit — Member Hawaii State Bar Association; The State Bar of California; Hawaii Defense Lawyers Association — E-mail: kchee@cheemarkham.com

Gregory K. Markham — 1957 — University of Colorado, B.A. (cum laude), 1979; University of Colorado Law School, J.D., 1983 — Admitted to Bar, 1983, Hawaii; U.S. District Court, District of Hawaii; U.S. Court of Appeals, Ninth Circuit; U.S. Supreme Court — Member American and Hawaii State (President-Elect) Bar Associations — Best Lawyers in America; Hawaii Super Lawyer; Honolulu Rotary Club; Martindale-Hubbell®, AV Rated; Former President, Hawaii Justice Foundation — E-mail: gmarkham@cheemarkham.com

Keith K. Kato — 1965 — Washington University, B.A., 1987; J.D., 1990 — Admitted to Bar, 1990, Hawaii; 1990, U.S. District Court, District of Hawaii — Member American and Hawaii State Bar Associations — E-mail: kkato@cheemarkham.com

Kale Feldman — 1958 — University of Hawaii, B.A., 1981; University of California, Hastings College of the Law, J.D., 1984 — Admitted to Bar, 1984, Hawaii; U.S. Court of Appeals, Ninth Circuit — Member American Bar Association (Forum on Construction Industry; Panel of Arbitrators and Mediators; Panel of Distinguished Neutrals for Dispute Prevention & Resolution, Inc.) — E-mail: kfeldman@cheemarkham.com

Daniel T. Kim — 1962 — Washington University, A.B. (Dean's List), 1984; William S. Richardson School of Law, J.D., 1987 — Moot Court Board — Articles Editor, University of Hawaii Law Review — Admitted to Bar, 1987, Hawaii; 1989, District of Columbia; 1988, U.S. Court of Appeals, Ninth Circuit; 1996, U.S. Supreme Court — E-mail: dkim@cheemarkham.com

Associates

Devon I. Peterson — 1975 — University of Hawaii at Manoa, B.S./B.A. (Phi Beta Kappa), 1997; William S. Richardson School of Law, J.D., 2002 — Admitted to Bar, 2002, Hawaii — E-mail: dpeterson@cheemarkham.com

Mari L. Tsukayama — William S. Richardson School of Law, University of Hawaii, J.D., 2012 — Admitted to Bar, 2013, Hawaii

Gallagher Kane Amai, Attorneys at Law
A Law Corporation
745 Fort Street, Suite 1550
Honolulu, Hawaii 96813-3817
   Telephone: 808-531-2023
   Fax: 808-531-2408
   E-Mail: gka@insurlawhawaii.com
   www.insurlawhawaii.com

Established: 1996

Insurance Defense, Bodily Injury, General Liability, Insurance Coverage, Workers' Compensation, Products Defense

Firm Profile: GALLAGHER KANE AMAI is a civil litigation firm with emphasis on insurance defense and the defense of self-insured individuals and corporations. The firm is most active in the areas of general liability, product liability, construction defects, workers' compensation, insurance coverage, bad faith litigation, trust and estate litigation, commercial litigation, toxic torts, automobile and personal lines litigation, and other areas of civil litigation. GKA's philosophy emphasizes quality of performance and speed of response. The firm's blend of experience assures that civil litigation of all magnitudes can be handled effectively and efficiently. At the same time, the firm's size assures clients that they will receive personal and individual attention on each case from GKA's trusted partners and attorneys.

Insurance Clients

Allstate Insurance Company
DTRIC Insurance Company Limited
Global Indemnity (formerly United American Insurance Group and Penn-America Insurance Company)
Liberty Mutual Group
W.R. Berkley Corporation
Chartis Claims, Inc.
Fairmont Specialty Group
Farmers Insurance Group
Government Employees Insurance Company
Hartford Insurance Company
Island Insurance Company, Ltd.
Nautilus Insurance Group
Zurich North America

Principals

J. Patrick Gallagher — 1955 — Cornell College, B.A. (cum laude), 1977; University of Notre Dame, J.D., 1980 — Admitted to Bar, 1983, Hawaii; 1980, U.S. District Court, Northern District of Illinois; 1980, U.S. Court of Appeals, Ninth Circuit; 1983, U.S. District Court, District of Hawaii — Member Hawaii State Bar Association; Hawaii Defense Lawyers Association; Defense Research Institute — Practice Areas: General Liability; Trial Practice; Insurance Coverage — E-mail: pgallagher@insurlawhawaii.com

Joelle Segawa Kane — 1969 — University of Washington, B.A. (with honors), 1991; William S. Richardson School of Law, J.D., 1995 — Phi Alpha Delta — Admitted to Bar, 1995, Hawaii; 1995, U.S. District Court, District of Hawaii — Member American and Hawaii State Bar Associations; Native Hawaiian Bar Association (Legislative and Lobbying Committee); Hawaii Womens Lawyers — Practice Areas: Estate Litigation; Insurance Defense — E-mail: jkane@insurlawhawaii.com

Jacqueline W.S. Amai — 1966 — University of Hawaii, B.A., 1988; William S. Richardson School of Law, J.D., 1992 — Admitted to Bar, 1992, Hawaii; 1992, U.S. District Court, District of Hawaii — Member Hawaii State Bar Association — Practice Areas: Workers' Compensation — E-mail: jamai@insurlawhawaii.com

Leah M. Reyes — 1973 — University of Hawaii, B.A., 1995; Seattle University School of Law, J.D., 2000 — Admitted to Bar, 2000, Hawaii — Member Federal Bar Association; Hawaii State Bar Association — Practice Areas: Construction Defect; Toxic Torts; Product Liability; Insurance Coverage — E-mail: lreyes@insurlawhawaii.com

Roeca Luria Hiraoka LLP
A Limited Liability Law Partnership
900 Davies Pacific Center
841 Bishop Street
Honolulu, Hawaii 96813
   Telephone: 808-538-7500
   Fax: 808-521-9648
   E-Mail: rlh@rlhlaw.com
   www.rlhlaw.com

Roeca Luria Hiraoka LLP, A Limited Liability Law Partnership, Honolulu, HI (Continued)

Established: 1988

Insurance Defense, Automobile, Product Liability, Professional Liability, Medical Malpractice, Aviation, Bad Faith, Coverage Issues, Construction Litigation, Civil Litigation, Commercial Litigation, Extra-Contractual Litigation, Insurance Coverage, Insurance Litigation, Medical Liability, General Civil Litigation

Insurance Clients

- Attorneys Liability Protection Society (ALPS)
- Chartis Aerospace
- The Doctors Company
- Fairmont Specialty Group
- Farmers Insurance Company
- Founders Insurance Company
- Gallagher Bassett Services, Inc.
- Global Aerospace, Inc.
- Great American Custom Insurance Services
- HAPI's Physicians' Indemnity Plan
- Island Insurance Company, Ltd.
- James River Insurance Company
- Nautilus Insurance Group
- OMS National Insurance Company
- Philadelphia Insurance Company
- Prime Insurance Syndicate, Inc.
- Progressive Casualty Insurance Company
- RSUI Group, Inc.
- Sedgwick Claims Management Services, Inc.
- Sun Life Assurance Company of Canada
- Western World Insurance Company
- AXIS Insurance
- Century Insurance Group
- CNA Insurance Companies
- DTRIC Insurance Company Limited
- Fireman's Fund Insurance Company
- General Star Management Company
- Great American Insurance Company
- HDI-Gerling America Insurance Company
- Medical Insurance Exchange of California
- Ophthalmic Mutual Insurance Company
- Professional Underwriters Liability Insurance Company
- RiverStone Claims Management, LLC
- Shand Morahan & Company, Inc.
- Sumitomo Marine and Fire Insurance Company, Ltd.
- The Travelers Companies, Inc.
- Zurich American Insurance Group

Non-Insurance Clients

- Baxter Healthcare Corporation
- Corrections Corporation of America
- The Gentry Companies
- Hard Rock Cafe International
- Hawaiian Electric Company, Inc.
- Honolulu Board of Water Supply
- Kmart Corporation
- State of Hawaii
- United States Olympic Committee
- Constructors Hawaii Inc.
- County of Maui
- D.R. Horton, Inc.
- Goodfellow Brothers, Inc.
- Hawaiian Dredging Construction Co., Inc.
- Kaanapali Land, LLC
- Sears Holdings Management Corporation
- Walgreen Co.

Partners

Arthur F. Roeca — 1948 — University of California, Los Angeles, B.A., 1970; Southwestern University, J.D. (cum laude), 1975 — Admitted to Bar, 1975, California; 1976, Hawaii; 1976, U.S. District Court, District of Hawaii; U.S. Court of Appeals, Ninth Circuit — Member American (Tort and Insurance Practice and Litigation Sections) and Hawaii State Bar Associations; State Bar of California; Hawaii Defense Lawyers Association; Defense Research Institute — US Army, 1970-1972

Keith K. Hiraoka — 1958 — University of Hawaii, B.A. (with distinction), 1980; University of California, Berkeley Boalt Hall School of Law, J.D., 1983 — Phi Beta Kappa; Phi Kappa Phi — Admitted to Bar, 1983, Hawaii; 1983, U.S. District Court, District of Hawaii; 1988, U.S. Court of Appeals, Ninth Circuit — Member American (Tort and Insurance Practice and Litigation Sections) and Hawaii State Bar Associations; Hawaii Defense Lawyers Association; Defense Research Institute — Guest Lecturer, Civil Procedure, Evidence, University of Hawaii William S. Richardson School of Law

April Luria — 1955 — Purdue University, B.S., 1977; Indiana University School of Law, J.D., 1984 — Admitted to Bar, 1984, Indiana; 1988, Hawaii; 1984, U.S. District Court, Northern and Southern Districts of Indiana; 1988, U.S. District Court, District of Hawaii; U.S. Court of Appeals, Ninth Circuit — Member American, Indiana State and Hawaii State Bar Association — Deputy Prosecuting Attorney, City and County of Honolulu; 1991-1994

James Shin — 1968 — The University of Iowa, B.A., 1991; The University of Iowa College of Law, J.D., 1994 — Admitted to Bar, 1994, Hawaii; U.S. District Court, District of Hawaii; 1996, U.S. Court of Appeals, Ninth Circuit — Member Hawaii State Bar Association

Roeca Luria Hiraoka LLP, A Limited Liability Law Partnership, Honolulu, HI (Continued)

Shannon Wack — 1956 — University of Hawaii, B.B.A., 1987; University of Hawaii at Manoa, William S. Richardson School of Law, J.D., 1990 — American Jurisprudence Award Advanced Legal Writing, 1989 — Admitted to Bar, 1990, Hawaii; U.S. District Court, District of Hawaii; 1994, U.S. Court of Appeals, Ninth Circuit — Member Hawaii State Bar Association (Chair, Delivery of Legal Services to the Public Committee; Access to Justice Commissioner); Hawaii Womens Lawyers — Practice Areas: Commercial Law; Construction Litigation; Insurance Defense

Associates

Norman K. Odani — 1976 — University of California, Riverside, B.A., 1998; University of the Pacific, McGeorge School of Law, J.D., 2001 — Admitted to Bar, 2002, California; 2007, Hawaii — Member State Bar of California; Hawaii State Bar Association

Mark J. Kaetsu — 1984 — University of Hawaii, B.A., 2007; University of Hawaii at Manoa, J.D., 2010 — Admitted to Bar, 2010, Hawaii; U.S. District Court, District of Hawaii — Member Hawaii State Bar Association

Of Counsel

Lois H. Yamaguchi — 1957 — University of Washington, B.A./B.S., 1980; University of Hawaii at Manoa, Graduate Certificate, Public Administration, 1986; University of California, Hastings College of the Law, J.D., 1990 — Law Clerk, Hon. Robert G. Klein, First Circuit Court, State of Hawaii (1990-1991) — Admitted to Bar, 1990, Hawaii — Member Hawaii State Bar Association; Defense Research Institute (Hawaii State Representative, 2009-present)

Jodie D. Roeca — 1956 — University of California, Santa Barbara, B.A., 1977; William S. Richardson School of Law, University of Hawaii, J.D., 1985 — Law Clerk to the Honorable Edward H. Nakamura, Hawaii Supreme Court, 1984 — Comments Editor, Hawaii Law Review, 1984-1985 — Admitted to Bar, 1985, Hawaii; 1996, U.S. Court of Appeals, Ninth Circuit — Member Hawaii State and Native Hawaiian Bar Associations; Hawaii Women Lawyers Association — Deputy Prosecuting Attorney, City and County of Honolulu, 1985-1987

William J. Nagle III — College of the Holy Cross, B.A., 1969; Pepperdine University School of Law, J.D., 1977 — Admitted to Bar, 1977, California; 1978, Hawaii; U.S. District Court, District of Hawaii; 1986, U.S. Court of Appeals, Ninth Circuit — Perdiem Judge, Hawaii Family Court (1999-Present) — U.S. Navy (1969-1972); U.S. Coast Guard (1977-1981)

Yamamura & Shimazu
Attorneys at Law, A Law Corporation

Central Pacific Plaza
220 South King Street, Suite 1770
Honolulu, Hawaii 96813
  Telephone: 808-523-6969
  Fax: 808-599-5580
  E-Mail: pyamamur@hawaiiantel.net

Established: 2002

Insurance Defense, Automobile, General Liability, Product Liability, Casualty, Coverage Issues, Professional Liability, Construction Litigation

Firm Profile: Yamamura & Shimazu is a trial and dispute resolution law firm composed of attorneys with substantial experience in the trial of jury cases. Our concentration is trial and appellate advocacy in State and Federal Courts, arbitration and other alternative dispute resolution forums. Our attorneys are actively involved in the preparation and trial of civil cases of all kinds including personal injury, commercial, property damage, coverage disputes and other areas including first and third party disputes. The firm's practice covers the entire State of Hawaii.

The firm handles self-insured risks. It also deals with third-party administrators. As such, the philosophy of the firm has always been to handle litigation in a cost effective and expeditious manner to the satisfaction of both insured and insurers.

HONOLULU

HAWAII

Yamamura & Shimazu, Attorneys at Law, A Law Corporation, Honolulu, HI (Continued)

Insurance Clients

Argonaut Great Central Insurance Company
Church Insurance Company
Church Mutual Insurance Company
Global Indemnity Group, Inc.
Grinnell Mutual Reinsurance Company
Nationwide Insurance
Navigators Insurance Company
Royal Specialty Underwriting, Inc.
Scottsdale Insurance Company
Verus Underwriting Managers, LLC
CGU Insurance Company
Chubb Group of Insurance Companies
Colony Specialty Insurance Company
National Casualty Company
National Farmers Union Standard Insurance Company
Northland Insurance Company
Royal SunAlliance Surplus Lines Insurance Services

Non-Insurance Clients

Cambridge Integrated Services
Diamond Parking Services, LLC
Exel Transportation Services, Inc.
FedEx Corporation
PBR Hawaii
Sedgwick Claims Management Services, Inc.
Carl Warren & Company
Executive Risk Management Associates
Gallagher Bassett Services, Inc.
Petco Animal Supplies, Inc.
Specialty Risk Services, Inc. (SRS)
Target Corporation

Partners

Paul T. Yamamura — 1952 — University of Hawaii, B.A., 1974; M.A., 1977; J.D., 1981 — Admitted to Bar, 1981, Hawaii; 1981, U.S. Court of Appeals, Ninth Circuit; 1981, U.S. Supreme Court — Member American and Hawaii State Bar Associations; Hawaii Defense Lawyers Association; Defense Research Institute; International Association of Defense Counsel

Wesley D. Shimazu — 1964 — University of Hawaii, B.B.A., 1987; University of California, Hastings College of the Law, J.D., 1992 — Admitted to Bar, 1992, California; 1993, Hawaii; 1992, U.S. District Court, Northern District of California; 1992, U.S. Court of Appeals, Ninth Circuit; 1994, U.S. District Court, District of Hawaii — Member Hawaii State Bar Association

IDAHO

CAPITAL: BOISE

COUNTIES AND COUNTY SEATS

County	County Seat
Ada	Boise
Adams	Council
Bannock	Pocatello
Bear Lake	Paris
Benewah	St. Maries
Bingham	Blackfoot
Blaine	Hailey
Boise	Idaho City
Bonner	Sandpoint
Bonneville	Idaho Falls
Boundary	Bonners Ferry
Butte	Arco
Camas	Fairfield
Canyon	Caldwell
Caribou	Soda Springs
Cassia	Burley
Clark	Dubois
Clearwater	Orofino
Custer	Challis
Elmore	Mountain Home
Franklin	Preston
Fremont	St. Anthony
Gem	Emmett
Gooding	Gooding
Idaho	Grangeville
Jefferson	Rigby
Jerome	Jerome
Kootenai	Coeur d' Alene
Latah	Moscow
Lemhi	Salmon
Lewis	Nezperce
Lincoln	Shoshone
Madison	Rexburg
Minidoka	Rupert
Nez Perce	Lewiston
Oneida	Malad City
Owyhee	Murphy
Payette	Payette
Power	American Falls
Shoshone	Wallace
Teton	Driggs
Twin Falls	Twin Falls
Valley	Cascade
Washington	Weiser

In the text that follows "†" indicates County Seats.

Our files contain additional verified data on the firms listed herein. This additional information is available on request.

A.M. BEST COMPANY

AMERICAN FALLS † 4,457 Power Co.

Refer To
Racine Olson Nye Budge & Bailey, Chartered
201 East Center
Pocatello, Idaho 83201
  Telephone: 208-232-6101
  Toll Free: 877-232-6101
  Fax: 208-232-6109

Mailing Address: P.O. Box 1391, Pocatello, ID 83204-1391

Insurance Defense, Coverage Issues, Product Liability, Bad Faith, Automobile, Trial Practice, Appellate Practice

SEE COMPLETE LISTING UNDER POCATELLO, IDAHO (24 MILES)

BLACKFOOT † 11,899 Bingham Co.

Refer To
Carey Perkins LLP
980 Pierview Drive, Suite B
Idaho Falls, Idaho 83405
  Telephone: 208-529-0000
  Fax: 208-529-0005

Mailing Address: P.O. Box 51388, Idaho Falls, ID 83405

Civil Trial Practice, Insurance Defense, Product Liability

SEE COMPLETE LISTING UNDER IDAHO FALLS, IDAHO (27 MILES)

Refer To
Racine Olson Nye Budge & Bailey, Chartered
201 East Center
Pocatello, Idaho 83201
  Telephone: 208-232-6101
  Toll Free: 877-232-6101
  Fax: 208-232-6109

Mailing Address: P.O. Box 1391, Pocatello, ID 83204-1391

Insurance Defense, Coverage Issues, Product Liability, Bad Faith, Automobile, Trial Practice, Appellate Practice

SEE COMPLETE LISTING UNDER POCATELLO, IDAHO (24 MILES)

BOISE † 125,738 Ada Co.

Anderson, Julian & Hull, LLP

C.W. Moore Plaza
250 South 5th Street, Suite 700
Boise, Idaho 83702
  Telephone: 208-344-5800
  Fax: 208-344-5510
  E-Mail: ajh@ajhlaw.com
  www.ajhlaw.com

Established: 1998

Insurance Defense, Trial Practice, Aviation, Personal Injury, Professional Malpractice, Health Care, Workers' Compensation, Commercial Litigation, Business Law, Construction Law, Product Liability, Employment Law, Environmental Law, Hazardous Waste, Appellate Practice, Pollution, Contracts, Insurance Coverage, Surety, Civil Rights, Transportation, Automobile, Fire, Tort Litigation, Casualty, Inland Marine, Property, Subrogation, Investigation and Adjustment, Alternative Dispute Resolution, Natural Resources, Governmental Entitites

Firm Profile: Anderson, Julian & Hull, LLP offers a general litigation and commercial practice with an emphasis in insurance defense, education law, worker's compensation, commercial disputes, real estate, construction, professional liability, employment, personal injury, governmental liability, ERISA, civil rights, environmental, products liability, immigration and naturalization matters. We focus our practice on all aspects of insurance defense litigation, including general liability and worker's compensation disputes. Our attorneys possess extensive trial experience in a wide variety of

Anderson, Julian & Hull, LLP, Boise, ID (Continued)

cases ranging from personal injury and property damage matters, to the most complex civil-rights or commercial disputes.

Insurance Clients

American Home Assurance Company
American Specialty Insurance Company
Associated Loggers Exchange
Attorneys Liability Protection Society (ALPS)
Cambridge Integrated Services
Catholic Mutual Relief Society of America
Cincinnati Insurance Company
CNA HealthPro
Continental Western Group
Country-Wide Insurance Company
Design Professionals Insurance Company
ERC Group
ESIS
Farm Bureau Mutual Insurance Company
Fireman's Fund Insurance Companies
Fremont Indemnity Company
GAB Robins North America, Inc.
General Casualty Companies
George Hills Company, Inc.
Great Southwest Fire Insurance Company
Hanover Insurance Company
Hartford Life and Accident Insurance Company
The Horace Mann Companies
Idaho Counties Risk Management Program
Insurance Company of North America
Insurance Services Network
John Deere Insurance Company
Kempes Insurance
Liberty Mutual Insurance
Lloyd's
Lumber Insurance Companies
Maxson Young Associates Inc.
Millers Insurance Group
Mutual of Omaha Group
National American Insurance Company of California
National Interstate Insurance Company
Nationwide Group
Nautilus Insurance Company
New Hampshire Insurance Company
Ohio Casualty Group
Omaha Property and Casualty Insurance Company
Philadelphia Indemnity Insurance Company
Preferred Risk Mutual Insurance Company
Providence Washington Insurance Companies
Republic Western Insurance Company
Risk Co.
Risk Management Services, Inc.
The St. Paul Companies
Scottsdale Insurance Company
Sentry Claims Services
Sentry Select Insurance Company
TIG Insurance Company
Trident Insurance Services
Unigard Insurance Group
Universal Underwriters Group
USLIFE Credit Life Insurance Company
Viking Insurance Company of Wisconsin
Washington Casualty Company
Westport Insurance Corporation

American International Group, Inc.
American National Property and Casualty Company
Amica Mutual Insurance Company
Atlantic Mutual Companies
Birmingham Fire Insurance Company of Pennsylvania
CAMICO Mutual Insurance Company
Chubb Group of Insurance Companies
CNA Insurance Companies
Coregis Insurance Company
Crawford & Company
EMC Insurance Companies
Employee Benefits Insurance Company
Everest National Insurance Company
Federated Insurance Company
Fleming & Hall Administrators, Inc.
Frontier Insurance Company
Gallagher Bassett Services, Inc.
General Fire and Casualty Company
Gryphon Insurance Group
Guaranty National Insurance Company
Hartford Life Insurance Company
Home Insurance Company
HSBC Gibbs North America, Ltd.
Idaho State Insurance Fund
Industrial Indemnity Company
Insurance Company of the State of Pennsylvania
Interstate Insurance Group
Kemper Insurance Company
K & K Insurance Group, Inc.
Liberty Northwest Insurance Corporation
Markel Insurance Company
Millers American Group
Mutual of Enumclaw Insurance Company
National Casualty Company
National Farmers Union Property & Casualty Company
National Union Fire Insurance Company of Pittsburgh, PA
Network Adjusters, Inc.
North American Risk Services
NOVA Casualty Company
Old Republic Insurance Company
OneBeacon Insurance
Oregon Mutual Insurance Company
Pinnacle Risk Management Services
Progressive Insurance Group
Rain and Hail Insurance Service, Inc.
Rice Insurance Services Company, LLC
Risk Enterprise Management, Ltd.
Safeco Insurance
St. Paul Fire and Marine Group
Sedgwick Claims Management Services, Inc.
State Farm Insurance Companies
Travelers Insurance Companies
21st Century Insurance Company
Unitrin Property and Casualty Insurance Group
Valley Insurance Company
VeriClaim, Inc.
Virginia Surety Company, Inc.
Ward North America, Inc.
Wausau Underwriters Insurance Company

Anderson, Julian & Hull, LLP, Boise, ID (Continued)

Willis Group
Zurich American Insurance Company
XL Insurance

Non-Insurance Clients

AMEC, Inc.
AmeriTel Inns, Inc.
Associated Construction Concepts, Inc.
Cambridge HealthCare Delivery Services
Century 21 Chisholm Realty
Clima-Tech
CSHQA Architects / Engineers / Planners
Fred A. Moreton & Company
Hayes Lemmerz International, Inc.
Idaho Intermountain Claims
IHDS Corporation
Integrated Healthcare Delivery Services, Inc.
J.R. Simplot Company
KM Administrative Services
M. A. Mortenson Company
The Mattei Companies
Medical Center Physicians, P.A.
National Registered Agent Service, Inc.
North American Construction, Inc.
OMI/CH2M Hill
Petro Corporation
Rock Shox, Inc.
St. Luke's Regional Medical Center
Skinner Earl & Associates, Inc.
Spears Manufacturing Company
Sunshine Mining Company
Swift Transportation Company, Inc.
Transportation Claims, Inc.
TruGreen-Chemlawn
W & H Pacific
American General Finance
Applied Risk Services
Briggs Engineering
Bureau of Risk Management, State of Idaho
Capital Motors, Inc.
Chevron Energy Solutions
Corporate Visions, Inc.
Davis Medical
Fidelity Investments Institutional Operations Company
Home Depot USA, Inc.
Idaho Waste Systems, Inc.
IMO, Inc.
Intermountain Lumber, Inc.
Intermountain Water, Inc.
J-U-B Engineers, Inc.
Lombard-Conrad Architects, P.A.
Materials Testing and Inspection
Medeva Pharmaceuticals
Mercy Medical Center
NCI Building Systems, Inc.
Nonpariel Corporation
Northwest Trading, Inc.
Orion Capital Companies
Ringle Components, Inc.
Rockwell Architecture Planning
Saltzer Medical Group
Singer Asset Finance Company
Snide & Associates
State of Idaho
Swift, Currie, McGhee & Hiers, LLP
T & J Properties LLC
Trout Architects
U-Haul International, Inc.

Partners

Robert A. Anderson — 1951 — The University of Utah, B.S. (magna cum laude), 1973; University of Colorado, J.D., 1977 — Admitted to Bar, 1977, Idaho; 1977, U.S. District Court, District of Idaho; 1977, U.S. Court of Appeals, Ninth Circuit — Member American Bar Association (Tort and Insurance Sections); State Bar of Idaho, Fourth District Bar (President, 1990-1991); Idaho Association of Defense Counsel; Defense Research Institute — Regional Editor: DRI Publication "For the Defense;" DRI Publication "Covered Events;" "DRI Construction Law Committee Newsletter" — Lecturer: American Society of Professional Engineers; American Institute of Architects; Associated General Contractors; Consulting Engineers of Idaho; National Business Institute Seminar, and Idaho Law Foundation. Moderator: Seminar on Insurance Fraud in Idaho. Chairman, Interest on Lawyers' Trust Accounts Committee, 1993-2000; Super Lawyers, Mountain States Super Lawyers (Construction Litigation, Insurance Coverage) 2009, 2010, 2011, 2012; Super Lawyers, Corporate Counsel Edition (Insurance Coverage) 2010; Best Lawyers (Construction Law, Personal Injury Litigation, Commercial Litigation, Insurance Law, Litigation-Construction) 2008-2013 — Practice Areas: Insurance Defense; Construction Litigation; Trial Practice; Professional Malpractice; Commercial Litigation; Insurance Coverage; Appellate Practice — E-mail: raanderson@ajhlaw.com

Brian K. Julian — 1954 — Utah State University, B.S. (cum laude), 1976; University of Idaho College of Law, J.D. (cum laude), 1978 — Phi Alpha Delta — Managing Editor, University of Idaho Law Review — Admitted to Bar, 1979, Idaho; 1979, U.S. District Court, District of Idaho; 1982, U.S. Court of Appeals, Ninth Circuit; 1984, U.S. Supreme Court — Member American and Boise Bar Associations; Idaho State Bar; Boise Adjuster Association; NSBA Council of School Attorneys; Advocate Member, American Board of Trial Advocates; Defense Research Institute — Author and Speaker: various continuing legal education seminars and employee training sessions concerning employment discrimination, civil rights, damages, punitive damages, sexual harassment, Americans With Disabilities Act, and governmental tort liability — Super Lawyers, Mountain States Super Lawyers (Employment & Labor) 2009, 2010, 2011, 2012; Super Lawyers, Corporate Counsel Edition (Employment & Labor) 2009, 2010; Best Lawyers (Insurance Law, Personal Injury, Litigation, Labor and Employment Law, Commercial Litigation)

Anderson, Julian & Hull, LLP, Boise, ID (Continued)

2008-2013 — Practice Areas: Trial Practice; Insurance Defense; Employment Law; Civil Rights; Product Liability; Professional Malpractice; Premises Liability; Appellate Practice — E-mail: bjulian@ajhlaw.com

Alan K. Hull — 1947 — University of Idaho, B.S., 1969; University of Idaho College of Law, J.D. (with high honors), 1973 — Editor-in-Chief, University of Idaho Law Review — Admitted to Bar, 1973, Idaho; 1973, U.S. District Court, District of Idaho — Practice Areas: Workers' Compensation — E-mail: akhull@ajhlaw.com

Chris H. Hansen — 1957 — Boise State University, B.B.A., 1979; University of Idaho College of Law, J.D., 1983 — Admitted to Bar, 1983, Idaho; 1983, U.S. District Court, District of Idaho; Washington State Court — Member Idaho State Bar (Litigation Section); Washington State Bar Association; Boise Adjuster Association; Trucking Industry Defense Association — Best Lawyers (Personal Injury Litigation) 2008-2013 — Practice Areas: Insurance Defense; Trial Practice; Professional Malpractice; Accountant Malpractice; Legal Malpractice; Real Estate; Product Liability; Personal Injury; Employment Law — E-mail: chhansen@ajhlaw.com

Phillip J. Collaer — 1956 — University of Idaho, B.S., 1979; Gonzaga University, J.D., 1985 — Phi Alpha Delta — Admitted to Bar, 1985, Idaho; 1988, U.S. District Court, District of Idaho; 1994, U.S. Court of Appeals, Ninth Circuit; 1994, U.S. Supreme Court — Member Idaho State Bar; Boise Bar Association; Boise Adjusters Association; American Inns of Court, Inn No. 130 — Super Lawyers, Mountain States Super Lawyers (Professional Liability-Defense) 2012; Best Lawyers (Personal Injury Litigation-Defendants) 2013; Prosecuting Attorney, Ada County, 1985-1989 — Practice Areas: Insurance Defense; Real Estate; Appellate Practice; Employment Law; Agriculture — E-mail: pcollaer@ajhlaw.com

Michael P. Stefanic II — 1963 — Colorado College, B.A., 1985; University of Idaho College of Law, J.D., 1989 — National Moot Court Team, 1988-1989 — Admitted to Bar, 1989, Idaho; 1992, Colorado; 1989, U.S. District Court, District of Idaho — Member Idaho State Bar (Board Member, Professional Conduct); The Colorado Bar Association; Idaho Motor Transportation Association; Boise Adjusters Association (President, 2001); Conference of Freight Counsel; American Inns of Court, Inn No. 130; Idaho Association of Defense Counsel; Defense Research Institute — Best Lawyers (Product Liability Litigation and Personal Injury Litigation-Defendants) 2011-2013 — Practice Areas: Insurance Defense; Trucking Law; Construction Litigation; Commercial Law — E-mail: mstefanic@ajhlaw.com

Amy G. White — 1967 — The Pennsylvania State University, B.S., 1989; University of the Pacific, McGeorge School of Law, J.D., 1992 — Phi Delta Phi — Law Clerk, Honorable Gerald F. Schroeder and the Honorable Thomas F. Neville, District Court, Fourth Judicial District, County of Ada — Admitted to Bar, 1992, Pennsylvania; 1994, Idaho; 1993, U.S. District Court, Western District of Pennsylvania; 1994, U.S. District Court, District of Idaho; 1995, U.S. Court of Appeals, Ninth Circuit — Member Federal (Idaho Chapter) and Pennsylvania Bar Associations; Idaho State Bar; American Inns of Court, Inn Number 130; Boise Adjusters' Association; Defense Research Institute — Best Lawyers (Education Law) 2009-2013 — Practice Areas: Insurance Defense; Employment Law; Premises Liability — E-mail: agwhite@ajhlaw.com

Mark D. Sebastian — 1968 — Boise State University, B.A., 1996; University of Idaho College of Law, J.D., 1999 — Phi Delta Phi — Board of Student Advocates — Admitted to Bar, 1999, Idaho; 1999, U.S. District Court, District of Idaho; 2006, U.S. Court of Appeals, Ninth Circuit — Member Idaho State Bar — Practice Areas: Commercial Litigation; Construction Law; Employment Law; Insurance Defense; Personal Injury — E-mail: msebastian@ajhlaw.com

Matthew O. Pappas — 1975 — University of Idaho, B.S., 1997; University of Idaho College of Law, J.D., 2000 — Admitted to Bar, 2000, Idaho; 2000, U.S. District Court, District of Idaho — Member Idaho State Bar; American Inns of Court — E-mail: mpappas@ajhlaw.com

Associates

Rachael M. O'Bar — 1967 — University of West Florida, B.A., 1994; Cumberland School of Law of Samford University, J.D., 1998 — Phi Kappa Phi Historian — Recipient, Presidential Scholar; Scholar of Merit; — Admitted to Bar, 1998, Idaho; U.S. District Court, District of Idaho — Member Idaho State Bar — Practice Areas: Workers' Compensation; Insurance Defense — E-mail: robar@ajhlaw.com

Robert A. Mills — 1971 — Brigham Young University, B.S., 2000; Thomas M. Cooley Law School, J.D. (cum laude), 2003 — Admitted to Bar, 2003, Maryland; 2005, Idaho; U.S. District Court, District of Idaho; U.S. District Court, District of Maryland — Practice Areas: Insurance Defense; Commercial Transactions; Personal Injury; Construction Law — E-mail: rmills@ajhlaw.com

Anderson, Julian & Hull, LLP, Boise, ID (Continued)

Bret A. Walther — 1960 — Cleveland State University, B.S., 1985; Boston University School of Law, J.D., 1992 — Editor-In-Chief, Boston University Public Interest Law Journal (1992) — Admitted to Bar, Idaho; U.S. District Court, District of Idaho — Trustee, Boise City Zoo (Current) — Captain, U.S. Marine Corps (1985-1989) — Practice Areas: Insurance Defense; Personal Injury; Education Law — E-mail: bwalther@ajhlaw.com

Yvonne A. Dunbar — 1980 — University of Florida, B.A. (with honors), 2002; University of California, Berkeley Boalt Hall School of Law, J.D., 2005 — Law Clerk, Hon. Justice Jim Jones, Idaho Supreme Court — Admitted to Bar, 2005, Idaho; U.S. District Court, District of Idaho — Member Federal Bar Association; State Bar of Idaho; Idaho Women's Lawyers; Lawyers Assistance Program (Professionalism & Ethics Section; Young Lawyers Section) — Practice Areas: Insurance Defense; Commercial Litigation; Construction Litigation — E-mail: ydunbar@ajhlaw.com

Andrew S. Jorgensen — 1979 — Idaho State University, B.A. (with high honors), 2003; Brigham Young University, M.A. (with honors), 2005; University of Idaho College of Law, J.D. (summa cum laude), 2011 — Law Clerk, Honorable Darla Williamson and Honorable Lynn Norton, Idaho Fourth Judicial District — Admitted to Bar, 2011, Idaho — Practice Areas: Education Law; Insurance Defense; Commercial Transactions; Personal Injury; Construction Law — E-mail: ajorgensen@ajhlaw.com

Tracy J. Crane — 1974 — Idaho State University, B.S., 1996; M.S., 2000; University of Idaho College of Law, J.D. (summa cum laude), 2003 — Managing Editor and Outstanding Member, Idaho Law Review — Admitted to Bar, 2003, Idaho; U.S. District Court, District of Idaho; Idaho Court of Appeals; Idaho Supreme Court — "Mountain States Rising Star", Super Lawyers (2008, 2009, 2011 and 2012); Special Recognition for Pro Bono Service, *The Advocate*, February 2007 — Practice Areas: Commercial Litigation; Business Litigation; Tort; Insurance Litigation; Employment Litigation; Complex Litigation; Construction Litigation — E-mail: tcrane@ajhlaw.com

Andrea J. Fontaine — 1980 — University of Idaho, B.S. (cum laude), 2002; University of Idaho College of Law, J.D. (cum laude), 2005 — Admitted to Bar, 2005, Idaho; 2006, U.S. District Court, District of Idaho; 2007, U.S. Court of Appeals, Ninth Circuit — Member Idaho State Bar — Languages: French — Practice Areas: Employment Law; Education Law; Civil Rights — E-mail: ajfontaine@ajhlaw.com

Scott W. Marotz — Counsel — 1955 — Boise State University, B.A.A., 1978; University of Idaho College of Law, J.D., 1981 — Admitted to Bar, 1981, Idaho — Practice Areas: Civil Litigation; Education Law; Employment; Business Law; Agriculture; Commercial Litigation; Civil Rights — E-mail: smarotz@ajhlaw.com

Brady Law, Chartered

St. Mary's Crossing
2537 West State Street, Suite 200
Boise, Idaho 83702
Telephone: 208-345-8400
Fax: 208-322-4486
E-Mail: bradylaw@bradylawoffice.com
www.bradylawoffice.com

Defense Litigation, Alternative Dispute Resolution, Mediation, Arbitration, Workers' Compensation, Subrogation

Firm Profile: The primary emphasis of the firm is to represent and serve insurance and self-insured companies. Quality representation of our clients is the firm's uncompromised principle. When a case is referred to this firm for defense, it is our belief that the best defense of a case is a cooperative effort between the insured, the company and the defense attorney.

Insurance Clients

Allied/Nationwide Insurance Company
American Family Mutual Insurance Company
Balboa Insurance Group
California Casualty Auto and Home Insurance
COUNTRY Insurance & Financial Services
Federated Insurance Company
GuideOne Insurance
American Empire Surplus Lines Insurance Company
American Hardware Mutual Insurance Company
Burlington Insurance Group
Chartis Aerospace
Colony Insurance Company
Employers Insurance Company
Farmland Mutual Insurance Company
Nautilus Insurance Group

Brady Law, Chartered, Boise, ID (Continued)

Ohio Casualty Insurance Company
Oregon Mutual Insurance Company
Western Heritage Insurance Company
Oregon Insurance Guaranty Association
Scottsdale Insurance Company

Non-Insurance Clients

Sinclair Oil Corporation
Sun Valley Company

Members

Andrew E. Schepp — (1971-2011)

Michael G. Brady — 1946 — University of Idaho, B.A., 1968; University of Idaho College of Law, J.D., 1970 — Phi Alpha Delta — Admitted to Bar, 1970, Idaho; 1999, Utah; 2002, Washington; 2004, Oregon; U.S. District Court, District of Idaho; U.S. District Court, District of Utah; U.S. District Court, Eastern and Western Districts of Washington; U.S. District Court, District of Oregon; U.S. Court of Appeals, Ninth Circuit — Member Washington State and Boise Bar Associations; Idaho, Utah and Oregon State Bars; Idaho Lawyers Association; Risk and Insurance Management Society, Inc.; Idaho Mediation Association; Boise Adjusters Association; Idaho Tort Reform Coalition Committee; Idaho Association of Defense Counsel; Defense Research Institute; American Trial Lawyers Association; American Arbitration Association — Visiting Professor, Insurance Law, University of Idaho Law School (1994); State of Idaho Assistant Attorney General, 1970-1971 — Practice Areas: Insurance Defense; Insurance Coverage; Extra-Contractual Litigation; Bad Faith; Aviation; Complex Litigation; Commercial Litigation; Arbitration; Mediation

Kyle D. Duren — 1970 — University of Idaho, B.S., 1992; University of Idaho College of Law, J.D., 1996 — Law Clerk, Hon. William Hart, U.S. District Court, District of Idaho (1996-1998) — Admitted to Bar, 1998, Idaho; U.S. District Court, District of Idaho — Member American and Boise Bar Associations; Idaho State Bar; Idaho Association of Defense Counsel — Practice Areas: Insurance Defense; Agriculture; Commercial Litigation

Glenda M. Talbutt — 1963 — University of South Carolina, B.S., 1984; University of Oregon School of Law, J.D., 1997 — Law Clerk, Hon. Byron Johnson, Idaho Supreme Court, 1997-1999 — Admitted to Bar, 1997, Idaho; 2007, Oregon; 1997, U.S. District Court, District of Idaho — Member Boise Bar Association; Idaho and Oregon State Bars; Idaho Women Lawyers Association — Practice Areas: Insurance Defense; Civil Litigation; Family Law

Eric D. Fredericksen — 1976 — University of Idaho College of Law, J.D., 2000 — Admitted to Bar, 2002, Idaho; U.S. District Court, District of Idaho — Member Idaho State Bar; Idaho Association of Criminal Defense Lawyers — State of Idaho Appellate Public Defender 2003 - 2012 — Practice Areas: Appellate Practice; Criminal Defense

Jason S. Thompson — University of Idaho, B.S., 2008; University of Idaho College of Law, J.D., 2012 — Admitted to Bar, 2012, Idaho; U.S. District Court, District of Idaho — Member Idaho State Bar — Practice Areas: Insurance Defense; Workers' Compensation; Creditor's Rights; Bankruptcy

Daniel R. Page — University of Idaho, B.S., 2009; William & Mary School of Law, J.D., 2012 — Admitted to Bar, 2012, Idaho; 2013, U.S. District Court, District of Idaho

Cantrill Skinner Lewis Casey & Sorensen, LLP

1423 Tyrell Lane
Boise, Idaho 83706
Telephone: 208-344-8035
Fax: 208-345-7212
E-Mail: cssklaw@cssklaw.com
www.cssklaw.com

Established: 1980

Insurance Defense, Casualty, General Liability, Product Liability, Property Damage, Bodily Injury, Workers' Compensation, General Civil Trial and Appellate Practice, Subrogation, Employer Liability, Medical Malpractice, Insurance Coverage, Automobile Insurance, Commercial Insurance, Fire Insurance

Firm Profile: Since 1980, insurance defense litigation, both trial and appellate practice, insurance coverage analysis, and litigation have been the principal strength of the firm. Regardless whether the matter is large or small, or

Cantrill Skinner Lewis Casey & Sorensen, LLP, Boise, ID (Continued)

whether it involves negotiations or trial, members of the firm approach every aspect of a case with a high regard for personal service to the client.

Insurance Clients

American States Insurance Company
Empire Fire and Marine Insurance Company
Hartford Casualty Insurance Company
Idaho State Insurance Fund
Mutual of Enumclaw Insurance Company
United Fire & Casualty Company
The Cincinnati Insurance Companies
Farmers Insurance Group
Hartford Accident and Indemnity Company
Hartford Fire Insurance Company
Liberty Mutual Insurance Company
Safeco Insurance
Twin City Fire Insurance Company

Firm Members

Willis E. Sullivan, III — (1941-2001)

John L. King — (1942-2008)

David W. Cantrill — 1942 — Idaho State University, B.A., 1966; University of Idaho College of Law, J.D., 1970 — Admitted to Bar, 1970, Idaho; 1970, U.S. District Court, District of Idaho; 1970, U.S. Court of Appeals, Ninth Circuit; 1977, U.S. Supreme Court — Member Idaho State Bar; American College of Trial Lawyers; Defense Research Institute

Gardner W. Skinner, Jr. — 1944 — University of Santa Clara, B.A., 1966; University of Idaho, J.D., 1970 — Admitted to Bar, 1970, Idaho; 1970, U.S. District Court, District of Idaho; 1975, U.S. Court of Appeals, Ninth Circuit — Member Idaho State Bar

Robert D. Lewis — 1953 — University of Colorado at Boulder, B.A. (magna cum laude), 1977; University of Idaho, J.D., 1980 — Admitted to Bar, 1981, Idaho; 1981, U.S. District Court, District of Idaho; 1986, U.S. Court of Appeals, Ninth Circuit; 1994, U.S. Court of Appeals, Tenth Circuit — Member Idaho State Bar; Defense Research Institute

Clinton O. Casey — 1963 — University of Idaho, B.S., 1986; University of San Francisco, J.D., 1990 — Admitted to Bar, 1990, California; 1991, Idaho; 1991, U.S. District Court, District of Idaho; 1995, U.S. Court of Appeals, Ninth Circuit — Member Idaho State Bar; American Inns of Court; Defense Research Institute; Idaho Association of Defense Counsel

Dean C. Sorensen — 1972 — The University of Utah, B.S., 1994; University of Idaho College of Law, J.D. (cum laude), 1998 — Admitted to Bar, 1999, Idaho; 1999, U.S. District Court, District of Idaho — Member American Bar Association; Idaho State Bar

Daniel J. Skinner — 1970 — University of Oregon, B.A., 1993; Boise State University, M.A., 1998; University of Idaho, J.D., 2005 — Admitted to Bar, 2005, Idaho; 2007, U.S. District Court, District of Idaho — Member Idaho State Bar; Defense Research Institute — Member Idaho Association of Criminal Defense Lawyers

(This firm is also listed in the Subrogation section of this directory)

Carey Perkins LLP

300 North 6th Street, Suite 200
Boise, Idaho 83702
   Telephone: 208-345-8600
   Fax: 208-345-8660
   E-Mail: info@careyperkins.com
   www.careyperkins.com

(Idaho Falls, ID Office*: 980 Pierview Drive, Suite B, P.O. Box 51388, 83405)
   (Tel: 208-529-0000)
   (Fax: 208-529-0005)

Carey Perkins LLP, Boise, ID (Continued)

Insurance Defense, Accountants and Attorneys Liability, Agent and Brokers Errors and Omissions, Agriculture, Alternative Dispute Resolution, Appellate Practice, Architects and Engineers, Arson, Asbestos Litigation, Automobile Liability, Aviation, Bad Faith, Business Law, Civil Litigation, Civil Rights, Commercial Litigation, Complex Litigation, Comprehensive General Liability, Construction Litigation, Dental Malpractice, Design Professionals, Directors and Officers Liability, ERISA, Employer Liability, Employment Practices Liability, Environmental Law, General Civil Trial and Appellate Practice, Governmental Liability, Health Care, Insurance Law, Insurance Coverage, Insurance Fraud, Insurance Litigation, Legal Malpractice, Litigation and Counseling, Medical Malpractice, Municipal Liability, Nursing Home Liability, Pharmaceutical, Product Liability, Professional Malpractice, Public Entities, Public Liability, School Law, Self-Insured Defense, Sexual Harassment, Subrogation, Toxic Torts, Truck Liability, Trucks/Heavy Equipment, Uninsured and Underinsured Motorist, Workers' Compensation, Wrongful Death, Wrongful Termination

Firm Profile: A regional law firm established and headquartered in Boise, Idaho with offices located to service several western states. The Boise office manages large litigation actions and coverage analyses throughout the intermountain west region, and represents clients throughout Idaho, and eastern Oregon. The Idaho Falls office represents clients throughout Idaho and western Wyoming. The firm has attorneys licensed in Idaho, Oregon, Utah Washington and Wyoming.

Insurance Clients

ACE USA
Allianz Insurance Company
American Bankers Insurance Company of Florida
American International Group, Inc.
Amica Mutual Insurance Company
Appalachian Insurance Company
Atlanta International Insurance Company
Automobile Club Insurance Company
Bankers Life and Casualty Company
California Casualty Insurance Company
Capitol Indemnity Corporation
Centennial Insurance Company
CIGNA Group
The Cincinnati Insurance Companies
CNA Insurance Companies
Colonial Penn Insurance Company
Colorado Casualty Insurance Company
COUNTRY Casualty Insurance Company
CUMIS Insurance Society, Inc.
Eagle Star Insurance Company, Ltd.
Employers Mutual Casualty Company
Farm Bureau Mutual Insurance Company
Farmers Home Mutual Insurance Company
Federated Mutual Insurance Company
Fireman's Fund Insurance Companies
Fortis, Inc.
Gallagher Bassett Services, Inc.
General Star Management Company
Grange Insurance Association
Great West Casualty Company
Guarantee Insurance Company
Hallmark Insurance Company
The Hartford Insurance Group
Homestead Insurance Company
Affiliated FM Insurance Company
Allstate Insurance Company
American Home Assurance Company
American States Insurance Company
Armco Insurance Group
Atlantic Mutual Companies
Attorneys Liability Protection Society
Auto-Owners Insurance Company
Bituminous Insurance Companies
British Aviation Insurance Company Ltd.
California State Automobile Association
Chubb Group of Insurance Companies
Civil Service Employees Insurance Company
Colonial Life and Accident Insurance Company
Compass Insurance Company
Consumers Insurance Company
Country-Wide Insurance Company
Crum & Forster Insurance Group
Dairyland Insurance Company
Employers Insurance Company of Wausau
Equity Insurance Group
Essex Insurance Company
Farmers Alliance Mutual Insurance Company
Farmers Insurance Group
Farmland Mutual Insurance Company
Financial Indemnity Company
First State Insurance Company
Foremost Insurance Company
GAINSCO, Inc.
GEICO
Gibraltar National Insurance Company
Great American Insurance Company
Guarantee Trust Life Insurance Company
Hawkeye-Security Insurance Company

Carey Perkins LLP, Boise, ID (Continued)

Horace Mann Insurance Company
Houston General Insurance Company
Indiana Insurance Company
Insurance Company of the West
Insurance Corporation of British Columbia
Jefferson Insurance Company
Kemper Insurance Companies
Lawyers Mutual Insurance Company
Liberty Northwest Insurance Corporation
Lumbermen's Underwriting Alliance
Markel Insurance Company
Maryland Casualty Company
MetLife Auto & Home Group
Mid-Century Insurance Company
Middlesex Mutual Assurance Company
Mt. Hawley Insurance Company
National American Insurance Company
National Casualty Company
National Chiropractic Mutual Insurance Company
National Farmers Union Property & Casualty Company
National Merit Insurance Company
National Union Fire Insurance Company
Nationwide Insurance Company
New Hampshire Insurance Company
NOVA Casualty Company
Ohio Casualty Group
Occidental Fire & Casualty Company of North Carolina
Old Reliable Casualty Company
Oregon Mutual Insurance Company
Old Republic Insurance Company
Pacific Employers Insurance Company
Parthenon Insurance Company
PRMS, Inc. - Professional Risk Management Services, Inc.
Progressive Insurance Group
Protective Life Insurance Company
Prudential Insurance Company of America
Rockwood Casualty Insurance Company
Safeco Insurance
Sentry Insurance Group
Sequoia Insurance Company
State Farm Insurance Companies
Stonewall Insurance Company
Sublimity Insurance Company
Tokio Marine Management, Inc.
Transamerica Group/AEGON USA, Inc.
Travelers Insurance Companies
Twin City Fire Insurance Company
Underwriters at Lloyd's, London
Unigard Insurance Group
United States Fidelity and Guaranty Company
United States Fire Insurance Company
Unitrin Insurance Company
USAA Casualty Insurance Company
Utica Mutual Insurance Company
Valley Insurance Company
Vanliner Insurance Company
Viking Insurance Company of Wisconsin
Western Heritage Insurance Company
Zurich American Insurance Company

Non-Insurance Clients

E.R. Squibb & Sons, Inc.
Greyhound Lines, Inc.
North American Van Lines
State of Idaho

Managing Partner

Hans A. Mitchell — University of Oregon, B.A., 1991; Willamette University College of Law, J.D., 1996 — Admitted to Bar, 1996, Oregon; 1997, Idaho — Languages: Spanish — Tel: 208-345-8600 — Fax: 208-345-8660 — E-mail: hamitchell@careyperkins.com

Firm Members

E. B. Smith — (1896-1975)

Leslie S. Brown — University of Puget Sound, B.A., 1991; University of the Pacific, McGeorge School of Law, J.D. (with honors), 1997 — Admitted to Bar, 1997, Idaho — Tel: 208-345-8600 — Fax: 208-345-8660 — E-mail: lsbrown@careyperkins.com

Donald F. Carey — Mesa State College, B.A., 1984; University of Wyoming, J.D., 1991 — Admitted to Bar, 1991, Idaho; 1992, Wyoming — Resident Idaho Falls, ID Office — Tel: 208-529-0000 — Fax: 208-529-0005 — E-mail: dfcarey@careyperkins.com

Marisa S. Crecelius — University of Idaho, B.A., 2002; University of Idaho College of Law, 2008 — Admitted to Bar, 2008, Idaho — Tel: 208-345-8600 — Fax: 208-345-8660 — E-mail: mscrecelius@careyperkins.com

David W. Knotts — Indiana University, B.A. (with honors and highest distinction), 1977; The University of North Carolina, M.A., 1982; University of Oregon, J.D., 1985 — Order of the Coif — Admitted to Bar, 1986, Idaho — Tel: 208-345-8600 — Fax: 208-345-8660 — E-mail: dwknotts@careyperkins.com

Aubrey D. Lyon — Lewis & Clark College, B.A., 2001; Lewis & Clark Law School, J.D., 2009 — Admitted to Bar, 2009, Oregon; 2010, Idaho — Tel: 208-345-8600 — Fax: 208-345-8660 — E-mail: adlyon@careyperkins.com

Bruce R. McAllister — University of Minnesota, B.A., 1976; J.D., 1980 — Admitted to Bar, 1980, Idaho — Tel: 208-345-8600 — Fax: 208-345-8660 — E-mail: brmcallister@careyperkins.com

David S. Perkins — The University of Utah, B.S., 1988; University of Idaho,

Carey Perkins LLP, Boise, ID (Continued)

J.D., 1991 — Admitted to Bar, 1991, Idaho — Member Transportation Lawyers Association — Tel: 208-345-8600 — Fax: 208-345-8660 — E-mail: dsperkins@careyperkins.com

Carsten A. Peterson — Utah State University, B.S., 1998; University of Idaho, J.D., 2001 — Admitted to Bar, 2001, Idaho — Tel: 208-345-8600 — Fax: 208-345-8660 — E-mail: capeterson@careyperkins.com

Jessica E. Pollack — University of Idaho, B.A., 2007; University of Idaho College of Law, J.D., 2011 — Admitted to Bar, 2011, Idaho — Tel: 208-345-8600 — Fax: 208-345-8660 — E-mail: jepollack@careyperkins.com

William G. Pope — Brigham Young University, B.A., 1994; J.D., 1997 — Admitted to Bar, 1997, Washington; 2001, Idaho — Tel: 208-345-8600 — Fax: 208-345-8660 — E-mail: wgpope@careyperkins.com

Dina L. Sallak — Wellesley College, B.A., 1989; University of Idaho College of Law, J.D., 2008 — Admitted to Bar, 2008, Idaho — Resident Idaho Falls, ID Office — Tel: 208-529-0000 — Fax: 208-529-0005 — E-mail: dlsallak@careyperkins.com

Richard L. Stubbs — Carleton College, B.A., 1979; Northwestern School of Law of Lewis & Clark College, J.D., 1984 — Admitted to Bar, 1984, Idaho — Member International Association of Defense Counsel — Tel: 208-345-8600 — Fax: 208-345-8660 — E-mail: rlstubbs@careyperkins.com

Erica J. White — Boise State University, B.A., 2000; University of Idaho, J.D., 2006 — Admitted to Bar, 2006, Idaho — Tel: 208-345-8600 — Fax: 208-345-8660 — E-mail: ejwhite@careyperkins.com

Tracy L. Wright — Auburn University, B.A., 1993; University of Idaho College of Law, J.D., 2008 — Admitted to Bar, 2008, Idaho — Fax: 208-345-8660 — E-mail: tlwright@careyperkins.com

William K. Fletcher — Northern Arizona University, B.S. (cum laude), 2004; University of Idaho College of Law, J.D., 2008 — Admitted to Bar, 2008, Idaho — Tel: 208-345-8600 — Fax: 208-345-8660 — E-mail: wkfletcher@careyperkins.com

(This firm is also listed in the Investigation and Adjustment section of this directory)

Elam & Burke, P.A.

251 East Front Street, Suite 300
Boise, Idaho 83702
Telephone: 208-343-5454
Fax: 208-384-5844
Toll Free: 866-343-5681
E-Mail: eblaw@elamburke.com
www.elamburke.com

Established: 1928

Agent and Brokers Errors and Omissions, Appellate Practice, Arbitration, Automobile Liability, Aviation, Bad Faith, Business Law, Carrier Defense, Civil Litigation, Class Actions, Construction Litigation, Coverage Issues, Defense Litigation, Environmental Law, Extra-Contractual Litigation, Fire Loss, First and Third Party Defense, Insurance Defense, Health, Insurance Coverage, Insurance Litigation, Life Insurance, Mediation, Medical Malpractice, Municipal Law, Product Liability, Professional Liability, Punitive Damages, Self-Insured Defense, Trial and Appellate Practice, Workers' Compensation

Firm Profile: Elam & Burke has been a leader in the Idaho legal community since its founding in 1928. We offer a full array of legal services on a regional basis. We are located in Idaho's state capital, in close proximity to both federal and state courts and numerous administrative agencies. Over time, we have developed a wide range of specialized capabilities to meet our client's needs, although our cornerstone remains our litigation, commercial, and business practice. The firm's clients include those in the corporate, business, banking, governmental, and insurance fields.

Insurance Clients

ACE American Insurance Company
Atlantic Mutual Insurance Company

BOISE   IDAHO

Elam & Burke, P.A., Boise, ID   (Continued)

Attorneys Liability Protection Society
CAMICO Mutual Insurance Company
Certain Underwriters at Lloyd's, London
Global Aerospace, Inc.
Idaho State Insurance Fund
Northwest Physicians Insurance Company
Philadelphia Insurance Companies
Sublimity Insurance Company
Banner Life Insurance Company
Berkshire Hathaway Homestate Companies
Capitol Indemnity Corporation
CNA Insurance Companies
Farmers Insurance Group
The Hartford
Indemnity Insurance Company of North America
Old Republic Insurance Company
Regence BlueShield of Idaho
United Heritage Life Insurance Company

Shareholders and Associates

Laurel E. Elam — (1888-1974)

Carl A. Burke — (1898-1961)

Ryan P. Armbruster — 1951 — Bradley University, B.A., 1973; University of Denver, J.D., 1975 — Admitted to Bar, 1976, Idaho; 1976, U.S. District Court, District of Idaho; 1979, U.S. Court of Appeals, Ninth Circuit — Member American Bar Association; Idaho State Bar; Idaho Municipal Attorneys (Associate Member); Defense Research Institute

William G. Dryden — 1953 — Brown University; Stanford University, B.A. (with distinction), 1975; Willamette University, J.D., 1978 — Admitted to Bar, 1978, Idaho; 1978, U.S. District Court, District of Idaho; 1987, U.S. Court of Appeals, Ninth Circuit — Member Idaho State Bar; Defense Research Institute; Idaho Association of Defense Counsel; Federation of Defense and Corporate Counsel; American Inns of Court — Languages: Spanish

James A. Ford — 1960 — The University of Montana, B.S., 1982; University of Idaho, J.D., 1985 — Admitted to Bar, 1985, Idaho; 1985, U.S. District Court, District of Idaho — Member American Bar Association; Idaho State Bar; Defense Research Institute; Idaho Association of Defense Counsel; American Inns of Court; International Association of Defense Counsel

Jeffrey A. Thomson — 1959 — University of Idaho, B.S., 1981; J.D., 1985 — Admitted to Bar, 1985, Idaho; 1985, U.S. District Court, District of Idaho; 1987, U.S. Court of Appeals, Ninth Circuit — Member Idaho State Bar; Idaho Association of Defense Counsel

Loren C. Ipsen — 1950 — Harvard University, B.A. (magna cum laude), 1972; University of California, Hastings College of the Law, J.D., 1975 — Admitted to Bar, 1975, Idaho; 1975, U.S. District Court, District of Idaho; 1975, U.S. Court of Appeals, Ninth Circuit; 1975, U.S. Tax Court — Member Idaho State Bar; American College of Trust and Estate Counsel

Joshua S. Evett — 1965 — Macalester College, B.A. (cum laude), 1987; University of California, Hastings College of the Law, J.D., 1994 — Admitted to Bar, 1996, California; 1997, Idaho; 1997, U.S. District Court, District of Idaho — Member American Bar Association; Idaho State Bar; State Bar of California; Idaho Trial Lawyers Association; Idaho Association of Defense Counsel — Languages: German

Jon M. Bauman — 1953 — The University of Utah, B.A. (magna cum laude), 1976; M.A., 1980; University of Idaho, J.D., 1982 — Phi Beta Kappa — Admitted to Bar, 1982, Idaho; 1985, Utah; 1982, U.S. District Court, District of Idaho; 1985, U.S. District Court, District of Utah; 2003, U.S. Court of Appeals, Ninth Circuit — Member Idaho State Bar (Workers' Compensation Section); Utah State Bar; Idaho Association of Defense Counsel

Matthew L. Walters — 1975 — The University of Montana, B.A. (cum laude), 1997; University of Idaho, J.D., 2002 — Admitted to Bar, 2002, Idaho; 2002, U.S. District Court, District of Idaho — Member Idaho State Bar (Employment and Labor Law Section); Association of Ski Defense Attorneys; Idaho Association of General Contractors

Joseph N. Pirtle — 1978 — University of Idaho, B.S., 2001; J.D., 2004 — Admitted to Bar, 2004, Idaho; 2010, Oregon; 2004, U.S. District Court, District of Idaho; 2006, U.S. Court of Appeals, Ninth Circuit — Member Idaho State Bar; Idaho Association of Defense Counsel; Oregon Association of Defense Counsel — Serving the following cities in eastern Oregon: Ontario, Vale, Baker City, La Grande, Pendleton, Canyon City, Enterprise and Burns.

John J. Burke — 1955 — Weber State University, A.S., 1981; B.S. (magna cum laude), 1989; The University of Utah, J.D., 1992 — Admitted to Bar, 1992, Idaho; U.S. District Court, District of Idaho; 1995, U.S. Court of Appeals, Ninth Circuit — Member Idaho State Bar; American Bar Association; International Association of Defense Counsel; Defense Research Institute; Idaho Association of Defense Counsel; American Health Lawyers Association — A.M. Best Law Digest Revisor

Meghan S. Conrad — 1977 — Colgate University, B.A., 1999; University of Idaho, J.D., 2004 — Admitted to Bar, 2004, Idaho; 2004, U.S. District Court,

Elam & Burke, P.A., Boise, ID   (Continued)

District of Idaho — Member Idaho State Bar; Idaho Association of Defense Counsel

Matthew C. Parks — 1973 — Providence College, B.A., 1994; The University of Mississippi, J.D., 2006 — Admitted to Bar, 2006, Idaho; U.S. District Court, District of Idaho — Member American Bar Association; Idaho State Bar

Craig R. Yabui — 1974 — The University of Montana, B.A., 1999; University of Idaho, J.D., 2007 — Admitted to Bar, 2007, Idaho — Member Idaho State Bar; Idaho Association of Defense Counsel

Jade C. Stacey — 1977 — Boise State University, B.A., 2004; University of Idaho, J.D., 2008 — Admitted to Bar, 2009, Idaho; U.S. District Court, District of Idaho — Member Idaho State Bar

Robert A. Berry — 1987 — University of Idaho, J.D., 2007 — Admitted to Bar, 2007, Idaho; U.S. District Court, District of Idaho; U.S. Court of Appeals, Ninth Circuit — Member American and Idaho State Bar Associations

Jaclyn T. Hovda — 1988 — California State University, Fullerton, B.A. (magna cum laude), 2010; University of Idaho College of Law, J.D., 2013 — Admitted to Bar, 2013, Idaho — Member Idaho Association of Defense Counsel; Defense Research Institute

Of Counsel

James D. LaRue — 1946 — University of Idaho, B.A., 1968; J.D., 1975 — Order of Barristers — Idaho Law Review, 1974-1975 — Admitted to Bar, 1975, Idaho; 1975, U.S. District Court, District of Idaho — Member Idaho State Bar (Litigation Section); Idaho Association of Defense Counsel (Past President); Fellow, American College of Trial Lawyers; Defense Research Institute; Federation of Defense and Corporate Counsel

(Revisors of the Idaho Insurance Law Digest for this Publication)

Jones Gledhill Fuhrman Gourley, P.A.

225 North 9th Street, Suite 820
Boise, Idaho 83702
 Telephone: 208-331-1170
 Fax: 208-331-1529
 E-Mail: info@idalaw.com
 www.idalaw.com

Established: 1996

Insurance Defense, Coverage Issues, Bad Faith, Automobile, Construction Law, General Liability, Environmental Law, Product Liability, Subrogation, Real Estate, Estate Planning, Employment Law, Bankruptcy, Civil Litigation, Business Law, Corporate Law, Domestic Relations

Insurance Clients

American Family Mutual Insurance Company
Fidelity National Title Group
Fireman's Fund Insurance Company
MetLife Insurance Company
Old Republic Insurance Company
Travelers Insurance Company
United National Insurance Company
Austin Mutual Insurance Company
Colorado Casualty Insurance Company
Liberty Mutual Insurance Company
Liberty Northwest Group
North Pacific Insurance Company
QBE the Americas
United America Indemnity Group

Non-Insurance Clients

CNH America LLC
The Hershey Company
Illinois Tool Works, Inc.
May Trucking Company
Sanofi-aventis LLC
United Parcel Service, Inc.
Walgreen Co.
Freightliner, LLC
Hubbell Incorporated
Macy's
Phoenix Aviation Managers, Inc.
Sedgwick CMS
Varsity Contractors, Inc.

Shareholders

William A. Fuhrman — 1954 — Boise State University, B.A. (magna cum laude), 1978; University of Idaho, J.D. (summa cum laude), 1982 — Admitted to Bar, 1982, Idaho; 1982, U.S. District Court, District of Idaho; 1982, U.S. Court of Appeals, Ninth Circuit — Member American Bar Association;

Jones Gledhill Fuhrman Gourley, P.A., Boise, ID
(Continued)

Idaho State Bar (Litigation Section); Defense Research Institute; Idaho Association of Defense Counsel — Author: "Insurance Law in Idaho," Business Institute, 1994; "Uninsured and Underinsured Motorist Insurance in Idaho," Idaho Law Foundation, 1996 — E-mail: bfuhrman@idalaw.com

Christopher P. Graham — 1972 — Boise State University, B.A., 1995; University of Idaho College of Law, J.D. (cum laude), 2000 — Admitted to Bar, 2000, Idaho; U.S. District Court, District of Idaho; 2009, U.S. Court of Appeals, Tenth Circuit; 2012, U.S. Court of Appeals, Ninth Circuit — Member American Bar Association; Idaho State Bar; Idaho Association of Defense Counsel; Defense Research Institute — Co-Author with Douglas R. Nash, "The Importance of Being Honest-Exploring the Need for Tribal Court Approval for Search Warrants Executed in Indian Country after State v. Matthews", 38 Idaho L. Rev. 581 (2002); Co-Author with Douglas R. Nash, "Cobell v. Norton-Indian Trust Fund Management Takes Center Stage", The Advocate (March 2003) — E-mail: cgraham@idalaw.com

Moore & Elia, LLP

Key Financial Center
702 West Idaho Street, Suite 800
Boise, Idaho 83702
 Telephone: 208-336-6900
 Fax: 208-336-7031
 Toll Free: 1-800-346-4896
 E-Mail: mike@melawfirm.net
 melawfirm.net

Automobile, Product Liability, Civil Rights, Aviation, Commercial Law, General Liability, Insurance Coverage, Litigation, Coverage Analysis, Premises Liability, Governmental Entity Defense, Nursing Home Defense

Insurance Clients

American Family Insurance
Federated Insurance Company
Idaho Counties Risk Management Program
Sedgwick Claims Management Services, Inc.
Trident Insurance Company
Unigard Insurance Group
United States Aviation Underwriters, Inc.
Chartis Aerospace
Global Aerospace, Inc.
Northland Insurance Company
ProAssurance Company
State Farm Insurance Company
Travelers Property Casualty Insurance Company
United Services Automobile Association (USAA)
XL Insurance

Self-Insured Clients

Kindred Healthcare
State of Idaho

Partners

Michael W. Moore — 1951 — University of Idaho, B.A./B.S., 1973; J.D., 1976 — Phi Beta Kappa, Pi Gamma Mu, Phi Kappa Phi — Idaho Law Review — Admitted to Bar, 1976, Idaho; 1976, U.S. Court of Appeals, Ninth Circuit; 1982, U.S. Court of Federal Claims; U.S. District Court, District of Idaho — Member Federal and Fourth District Bar Associations; Idaho State Bar; Idaho Association of Defense Counsel; Defense Research Institute

Michael J. Elia — 1962 — Gonzaga University, B.A. (magna cum laude), 1984; University of Washington, J.D., 1987 — Admitted to Bar, 1987, California; 1992, Washington; 1994, Idaho; 1987, U.S. District Court, Southern District of California; 1994, U.S. District Court, District of Idaho; 1997, U.S. Court of Appeals, Ninth Circuit — Member Federal Bar Association; State Bar of California; Washington State Bar Association; Idaho State Bar (Litigation Section); Defense Research Institute; Idaho Association of Defense Counsel

Non-Equity Partners

Steven R. Kraft — 1965 — Boise State University, B.S., 1990; University of Puget Sound, J.D. (cum laude), 1993 — Admitted to Bar, 1993, Idaho; 2000, U.S. District Court, District of Idaho; 2001, U.S. Court of Appeals, Ninth Circuit — Member Federal Bar Association; Idaho State Bar; Defense Research Institute; Idaho Association of Defense Counsel

Brady J. Hall — 1978 — University of Idaho, B.A., 2000; J.D., 2004 — University of Idaho Law Review — Admitted to Bar, 2007, Colorado; 2008, Idaho; U.S. District Court, District of Idaho; U.S. Court of Appeals, Ninth

Moore & Elia, LLP, Boise, ID (Continued)

Circuit — Member Federal Bar Association; Idaho State Bar; Idaho Association of Defense Counsel; Defense Research Institute

Associates

Craig Stacey — 1972 — Boise State University, B.A., 2004; University of Idaho, J.D., 2008 — Admitted to Bar, 2009, Idaho; 2010, U.S. District Court, District of Idaho — Member American Bar Association; Idaho State Bar; Boise Adjusters Association; Idaho Association of Defense Counsel; Defense Research Institute

Chris F. Brown — 1984 — Wesleyan University, B.A., 2007; University of Idaho, J.D., 2013 — Admitted to Bar, 2013, Idaho; U.S. District Court, District of Idaho — Member Federal Bar Association; Idaho State Bar; Idaho Association of Defense Counsel; Defense Research Institute

Racine Olson Nye Budge & Bailey, Chartered

101 South Capitol, Suite 300
Boise, Idaho 83702
 Telephone: 208-395-0011
 Fax: 208-433-0167
 www.racinelaw.net

(Pocatello, ID Office*: 201 East Center, 83201, P.O. Box 1391, 83204-1391)
 (Tel: 208-232-6101)
 (Toll Free: 877-232-6101)
 (Fax: 208-232-6109)
 (E-Mail: racine@racinelaw.net)
(Idaho Falls, ID Office: 477 Shoup Avenue, 83402)
 (Tel: 208-528-6101)
 (Fax: 208-528-6109)

Insurance Defense, Coverage Issues, Product Liability, Bad Faith, Automobile, Trial Practice, Appellate Practice

(See listing under Pocatello, ID for additional information)

Sasser & Inglis, P.C.

1902 West Judith Lane, Suite 100
Boise, Idaho 83705
 Telephone: 208-344-8474
 Fax: 208-344-8479
 E-Mail: si@sasseringlis.com
 www.sasseringlis.com

Established: 1982

Insurance Law, Insurance Defense, Appellate Practice, Automobile, Aviation, Bad Faith, Casualty, Construction Law, Coverage Issues, Entertainment Law, Intellectual Property, Municipal Law, Product Liability, Professional Malpractice, Transportation, Trucking Law, Trial Practice

Insurance Clients

Allstate Insurance Company
American Hardware Mutual Insurance Company
Badger Mutual Insurance Company
Berkley North Pacific Group, LLC
Canal Insurance Company
Chartis Insurance
CNA Insurance Companies
Continental Insurance Companies
Continental Western Group
Dairyland Insurance Company
Gateway Insurance Company
Great Northwest Insurance Company
Gulf Insurance Group
American Family Insurance Group
AMEX Life Assurance Company
Attorneys Liability Protection Society
CAMICO Mutual Insurance Company
CIGNA Group
Commercial Union Insurance Company
CUMIS Insurance Society, Inc.
Esurance
Grange Mutual Insurance Company
Guaranty National Insurance Company
The Hartford

Sasser & Inglis, P.C., Boise, ID (Continued)

Horace Mann Insurance Company
INAPRO
Lancer Insurance Company
National Casualty Company
National Union Fire Insurance Company
Ohio Casualty Insurance Company
OUM Group
The Principal Financial Group
Royal & SunAlliance USA
Sentry Insurance
Underwriters at Lloyd's, London
Universal Underwriters Group
Wilshire Insurance Company [IAT-Group]
Idaho Counties Risk Management Program
Mammoet Canada Western Ltd.
National Interstate Insurance Company
Nobel Insurance Company
Orion Auto Group
Pioneer Title Insurance Company
Reliance Insurance Company
Safeco Insurance
State Farm Insurance Companies
Unigard Insurance Company
Viking Insurance Company of Wisconsin

Non-Insurance Clients

Albertsons, Inc.
Crawford & Company
Intermountain Claims, Inc.
Pacific Intermountain Express Company
Ruan Transportation Corporation
SUPERVALU, Inc.
Baxter International, Inc.
FedEx Freight, Inc.
Lithia Motors, Inc.
PIE Nationwide, Inc.
Rio Tinto
Ryder System, Inc.

Partners

M. Michael Sasser — 1948 — University of Idaho, J.D., 1974 — Admitted to Bar, 1974, Idaho — Member American Bar Association; Idaho State Bar; Idaho Association of Defense Counsel; Defense Research Institute

Associates

Clay M. Shockley
Matthew R. Harrison
Angela C. Sasser

BURLEY † 10,345 Casia Co.

Refer To

Carey Perkins LLP
980 Pierview Drive, Suite B
Idaho Falls, Idaho 83405
   Telephone: 208-529-0000
   Fax: 208-529-0005

Mailing Address: P.O. Box 51388, Idaho Falls, ID 83405

Civil Trial Practice, Insurance Defense, Product Liability

SEE COMPLETE LISTING UNDER IDAHO FALLS, IDAHO (124 MILES)

Refer To

Racine Olson Nye Budge & Bailey, Chartered
201 East Center
Pocatello, Idaho 83201
   Telephone: 208-232-6101
   Toll Free: 877-232-6101
   Fax: 208-232-6109

Mailing Address: P.O. Box 1391, Pocatello, ID 83204-1391

Insurance Defense, Coverage Issues, Product Liability, Bad Faith, Automobile, Trial Practice, Appellate Practice

SEE COMPLETE LISTING UNDER POCATELLO, IDAHO (79 MILES)

CALDWELL † 46,237 Canyon Co.

Refer To

Carey Perkins LLP
300 North 6th Street, Suite 200
Boise, Idaho 83702
   Telephone: 208-345-8600
   Fax: 208-345-8660

Mailing Address: P.O. Box 519, Boise, ID 83701-0519

Insurance Defense, Accountants and Attorneys Liability, Agent and Brokers Errors and Omissions, Agriculture, Alternative Dispute Resolution, Appellate Practice, Architects and Engineers, Arson, Asbestos Litigation, Automobile Liability, Aviation, Bad Faith, Business Law, Civil Litigation, Civil Rights, Commercial Litigation, Complex Litigation, Comprehensive General Liability, Construction Litigation, Dental Malpractice, Design Professionals, Directors and Officers Liability, ERISA, Employer Liability, Employment Practices Liability, Environmental Law, General Civil Trial and Appellate Practice, Governmental Liability, Health Care, Insurance Law, Insurance Coverage, Insurance Fraud, Insurance Litigation, Legal Malpractice, Litigation and Counseling, Medical Malpractice, Municipal Liability, Nursing Home Liability, Pharmaceutical, Product Liability, Professional Malpractice, Public Entities, Public Liability, School Law, Self-Insured Defense, Sexual Harassment, Subrogation, Toxic Torts, Truck Liability, Trucks/Heavy Equipment, Uninsured and Underinsured Motorist, Workers' Compensation, Wrongful Death, Wrongful Termination

SEE COMPLETE LISTING UNDER BOISE, IDAHO (26 MILES)

CASCADE † 939 Valley Co.

Refer To

Anderson, Julian & Hull, LLP
C.W. Moore Plaza
250 South 5th Street, Suite 700
Boise, Idaho 83702
   Telephone: 208-344-5800
   Fax: 208-344-5510

Mailing Address: P.O. Box 7426, Boise, ID 83707-7426

Insurance Defense, Trial Practice, Aviation, Personal Injury, Professional Malpractice, Health Care, Workers' Compensation, Commercial Litigation, Business Law, Construction Law, Product Liability, Employment Law, Environmental Law, Hazardous Waste, Appellate Practice, Pollution, Contracts, Insurance Coverage, Surety, Civil Rights, Transportation, Automobile, Fire, Tort Litigation, Casualty, Inland Marine, Property, Subrogation, Investigation and Adjustment, Alternative Dispute Resolution, Natural Resources, Governmental Entitites

SEE COMPLETE LISTING UNDER BOISE, IDAHO (80 MILES)

Refer To

Carey Perkins LLP
300 North 6th Street, Suite 200
Boise, Idaho 83702
   Telephone: 208-345-8600
   Fax: 208-345-8660

Mailing Address: P.O. Box 519, Boise, ID 83701-0519

Insurance Defense, Accountants and Attorneys Liability, Agent and Brokers Errors and Omissions, Agriculture, Alternative Dispute Resolution, Appellate Practice, Architects and Engineers, Arson, Asbestos Litigation, Automobile Liability, Aviation, Bad Faith, Business Law, Civil Litigation, Civil Rights, Commercial Litigation, Complex Litigation, Comprehensive General Liability, Construction Litigation, Dental Malpractice, Design Professionals, Directors and Officers Liability, ERISA, Employer Liability, Employment Practices Liability, Environmental Law, General Civil Trial and Appellate Practice, Governmental Liability, Health Care, Insurance Law, Insurance Coverage, Insurance Fraud, Insurance Litigation, Legal Malpractice, Litigation and Counseling, Medical Malpractice, Municipal Liability, Nursing Home Liability, Pharmaceutical, Product Liability, Professional Malpractice, Public Entities, Public Liability, School Law, Self-Insured Defense, Sexual Harassment, Subrogation, Toxic Torts, Truck Liability, Trucks/Heavy Equipment, Uninsured and Underinsured Motorist, Workers' Compensation, Wrongful Death, Wrongful Termination

SEE COMPLETE LISTING UNDER BOISE, IDAHO (80 MILES)

IDAHO — COEUR D'ALENE

COEUR D'ALENE † 44,137 Kootenai Co.

Ramsden & Lyons, LLP

700 Northwest Boulevard
Coeur d'Alene, Idaho 83814
Toll Free: 800-352-0813
Telephone: 208-664-5818
Fax: 208-664-5884
E-Mail: firm@ramsdenlyons.com
www.ramsdenlyons.com

Established: 1994

Insurance Defense, Coverage Analysis, Medical Malpractice Defense, Personal Injury Litigation, Professional Liability, Fire Loss, Product Liability, Civil Litigation, Commercial Litigation, Construction Law, Education Law, Employment Law, Real Estate Litigation, Water Law, Environmental & Natural Resources Law, Business Law & Formation, Creditor Representation, Eminent Domain & Condemnation, Mining Law, Public Agency & Municipal Law, Real Estate Development, Wills, Trusts, & Estates, Defense of Housing & Access Discrimination Claims

Firm Profile: Serving both Idaho and Washington, the attorneys at Ramsden & Lyons, LLP provide comprehensive and effective legal representation to individuals and businesses in a wide range of practice areas.

Insurance Clients

ACE Westchester Specialty Group
Admiral Insurance Company
ALLIED Mutual Insurance Company
Associated Claims Enterprises, Inc.
AXIS Insurance
Capitol Indemnity Corporation
CNA Insurance Companies
Coregis Insurance Company
The Doctors Company
Effective Claims Management, Inc.
EMC Insurance Company
Fidelity National Insurance Company
Gem State Insurance Company
Guaranty National Insurance Company
Hartford Financial Products
Hudson Insurance Company
Liberty Northwest Insurance Corporation
National Fire and Marine Insurance Company
Northwest Physicians Insurance Company
Progressive Insurance Company
Rice Insurance Services Company, LLC
State Farm Insurance Company
State Farm Mutual Automobile Insurance Company
Tribal First
USAA Insurance Company
Viking Insurance Company of Wisconsin
ACUITY
Allied Group Insurance
American Financial Group
Amica Mutual Insurance Company
Attorneys Liability Protection Society
CIGNA Insurance Company
Contractors Bonding and Insurance Company (CBIC), an RLI Company
Electric Insurance Company
Federated Insurance Company
Financial Indemnity Company
Frontier Insurance Company
Grange Insurance Group
GuideOne Mutual Insurance Company
Horace Mann Insurance Company
Liberty Mutual Insurance Company
Meadowbrook Insurance Group
Motorists Insurance Company
National Indemnity Company
Northland Insurance Company
Professional Underwriters Agency, Inc.
Regence BlueShield
Safeco Insurance
Specialty Claims Management, LLC
Sublimity Insurance Company
Travelers Insurance Companies
Unitrin Insurance Company
Utah Medical Insurance Association
Zurich American Insurance Company

Non-Insurance Clients

Beckett & Lee, LLP
Coastal Community Bank
Coeur d'Alene School District No. 271
Essential Metals Corporation
GMAC Real Estate Northwest
Hecla Mining Company
Kiemle & Hagood Company
Knight Transportation, Inc.
Century 21 - Beutler & Associates
Coeur d'Alene Mines Corporation
Coldwell Banker Schneidmiller Realty
Forest Capital Partners
Gordon Trucking Inc.
Keller Williams Realty Coeur d'Alene
Lakeshore Realty

Ramsden & Lyons, LLP, Coeur d'Alene, ID (Continued)

Moscow Realty
Panhandle Health District
Shelter Associates, Inc.
Silver Royal Apex, Inc.
Spokane Adjuster's Association
Tomlinson Sotheby's North Idaho
United Mine Services, Inc.
Westslope Properties
North Idaho College
RE/MAX By the Lake
Shoshone Silver Mining Company
Southwood Pharmaceuticals, Inc.
Swift Transportation Company, Inc.
WaterStone Bank
Windermere Real Estate

Managing Partner

Marc A. Lyons — University of Idaho, B.S. (cum laude), 1977; J.D., 1983 — Admitted to Bar, 1983, Idaho; 1991, Washington; 1983, U.S. District Court, District of Idaho; 1985, U.S. Court of Appeals, Ninth Circuit; 1992, U.S. District Court, Eastern District of Washington; 1998, U.S. Supreme Court — Member Idaho State Bar; Washington State Bar Association; Kootenai County Bar Association; Idaho Society of Certified Public Accountants; Defense Research Institute

Partners

Michael E. Ramsden — University of Washington, B.A., 1976; University of Idaho, J.D., 1978 — Admitted to Bar, 1979, Idaho; 1986, Washington; 1979, U.S. District Court, District of Idaho; 1987, U.S. District Court, Eastern District of Washington; 1998, U.S. Court of Appeals, Ninth Circuit — Member Idaho State Bar; Washington State Bar Association; Kootenai County Bar Association; Spokane Adjusters Association; Litigation Counsel of America; Defense Research Institute; International Association of Defense Counsel; American College of Trial Lawyers

Douglas S. Marfice — University of Nebraska, B.A., 1986; J.D., 1989 — Admitted to Bar, 1989, Idaho; 1996, Washington; 1989, U.S. District Court, District of Idaho; 1996, U.S. District Court, Eastern District of Washington — Member Idaho State Bar; Washington State Bar Association; Kootenai County Bar Association

Michael A. Ealy — University of Idaho, B.S., 1989; J.D., 1997 — Admitted to Bar, 1997, Idaho; 1999, Washington; 1997, U.S. District Court, District of Idaho; 2001, U.S. District Court, Eastern District of Washington — Member Idaho State Bar; Washington State Bar Association; Kootenai County Bar Association

Terrance R. Harris — Eastern Washington University, B.A., 1987; Gonzaga University, J.D. (summa cum laude), 1991 — Admitted to Bar, 1996, Idaho; 2009, Washington; 1996, U.S. District Court, District of Idaho — Member Idaho State Bar; Washington State Bar Association; Kootenai County Bar Association; First Judicial District Bar Association

Associates

Christopher D. Gabbert — University of Idaho, B.A., 1999; Washington State University, M.B.A., 2003; University of Idaho College of Law, J.D., 2003 — Admitted to Bar, 2003, Idaho; 2003, U.S. District Court, District of Idaho — Member Idaho State Bar; Kootenai County Bar Association

Theron J. De Smet — University of Idaho, B.S., 2005; University of Idaho College of Law, J.D., 2009 — Admitted to Bar, 2009, Idaho; U.S. District Court, District of Idaho — Member Idaho State Bar; Kootenai County Bar Association; First District Bar Association

Megan S. O'Dowd — Boise State University, B.A. (cum laude), 2005; University of Idaho College of Law, J.D. (summa cum laude), 2010 — Admitted to Bar, 2010, Idaho; 2010, U.S. District Court, District of Idaho — Member Idaho State Bar; Kootenai County Bar Association

Lukas D. O'Dowd — Boise State University, B.S., 2004; University of Idaho College of Law, J.D., 2010 — Admitted to Bar, 2010, Idaho; U.S. District Court, District of Idaho — Member Idaho State Bar; Kootenai County Bar Association

Of Counsel

William F. Boyd — Oregon State University, B.S., 1962; University of Idaho College of Law, L.L.L./L.L.B., 1965 — Admitted to Bar, 1965, Idaho; U.S. District Court, District of Idaho; 1975, U.S. Court of Appeals, Ninth Circuit; 1976, U.S. Court of Appeals, Tenth Circuit; 1977, U.S. Supreme Court; 1981, U.S. Court of Appeals for the District of Columbia Circuit — Member Idaho State Bar; Kootenai County Bar Association; First Judicial District Bar Association

KETCHUM   IDAHO

HAILEY † 7,960 Blaine Co.

Refer To

Anderson, Julian & Hull, LLP
C.W. Moore Plaza
250 South 5th Street, Suite 700
Boise, Idaho 83702
 Telephone: 208-344-5800
 Fax: 208-344-5510

Mailing Address: P.O. Box 7426, Boise, ID 83707-7426

Insurance Defense, Trial Practice, Aviation, Personal Injury, Professional Malpractice, Health Care, Workers' Compensation, Commercial Litigation, Business Law, Construction Law, Product Liability, Employment Law, Environmental Law, Hazardous Waste, Appellate Practice, Pollution, Contracts, Insurance Coverage, Surety, Civil Rights, Transportation, Automobile, Fire, Tort Litigation, Casualty, Inland Marine, Property, Subrogation, Investigation and Adjustment, Alternative Dispute Resolution, Natural Resources, Governmental Entitites

SEE COMPLETE LISTING UNDER BOISE, IDAHO (143 MILES)

Refer To

Carey Perkins LLP
300 North 6th Street, Suite 200
Boise, Idaho 83702
 Telephone: 208-345-8600
 Fax: 208-345-8660

Mailing Address: P.O. Box 519, Boise, ID 83701-0519

Insurance Defense, Accountants and Attorneys Liability, Agent and Brokers Errors and Omissions, Agriculture, Alternative Dispute Resolution, Appellate Practice, Architects and Engineers, Arson, Asbestos Litigation, Automobile Liability, Aviation, Bad Faith, Business Law, Civil Litigation, Civil Rights, Commercial Litigation, Complex Litigation, Comprehensive General Liability, Construction Litigation, Dental Malpractice, Design Professionals, Directors and Officers Liability, ERISA, Employer Liability, Employment Practices Liability, Environmental Law, General Civil Trial and Appellate Practice, Governmental Liability, Health Care, Insurance Law, Insurance Coverage, Insurance Fraud, Insurance Litigation, Legal Malpractice, Litigation and Counseling, Medical Malpractice, Municipal Liability, Nursing Home Liability, Pharmaceutical, Product Liability, Professional Malpractice, Public Entities, Public Liability, School Law, Self-Insured Defense, Sexual Harassment, Subrogation, Toxic Torts, Truck Liability, Trucks/Heavy Equipment, Uninsured and Underinsured Motorist, Workers' Compensation, Wrongful Death, Wrongful Termination

SEE COMPLETE LISTING UNDER BOISE, IDAHO (143 MILES)

Refer To

Racine Olson Nye Budge & Bailey, Chartered
201 East Center
Pocatello, Idaho 83201
 Telephone: 208-232-6101
 Toll Free: 877-232-6101
 Fax: 208-232-6109

Mailing Address: P.O. Box 1391, Pocatello, ID 83204-1391

Insurance Defense, Coverage Issues, Product Liability, Bad Faith, Automobile, Trial Practice, Appellate Practice

SEE COMPLETE LISTING UNDER POCATELLO, IDAHO (158 MILES)

IDAHO FALLS † 56,813 Bonneville Co.

Carey Perkins LLP
980 Pierview Drive, Suite B
Idaho Falls, Idaho 83405
 Telephone: 208-529-0000
 Fax: 208-529-0005
 E-Mail: info@careyperkins.com
 www.careyperkins.com

(Boise, ID Office*: 300 North 6th Street, Suite 200, 83702, P.O. Box 519, 83701-0519)
 (Tel: 208-345-8600)
 (Fax: 208-345-8660)

Civil Trial Practice, Insurance Defense, Product Liability

Carey Perkins LLP, Idaho Falls, ID   (Continued)
Managing Partner

Donald F. Carey — Mesa State College, B.A., 1984; University of Wyoming, J.D., 1991 — Admitted to Bar, 1991, Idaho; 1992, Wyoming — Resident Idaho Falls, ID Office — Tel: 208-529-0000 — Fax: 208-529-0005 — E-mail: dfcarey@careyperkins.com

(See Boise, ID listing for Personnel and Client information)

The following firms also service this area.

Anderson, Julian & Hull, LLP
C.W. Moore Plaza
250 South 5th Street, Suite 700
Boise, Idaho 83702
 Telephone: 208-344-5800
 Fax: 208-344-5510

Mailing Address: P.O. Box 7426, Boise, ID 83707-7426

Insurance Defense, Trial Practice, Aviation, Personal Injury, Professional Malpractice, Health Care, Workers' Compensation, Commercial Litigation, Business Law, Construction Law, Product Liability, Employment Law, Environmental Law, Hazardous Waste, Appellate Practice, Pollution, Contracts, Insurance Coverage, Surety, Civil Rights, Transportation, Automobile, Fire, Tort Litigation, Casualty, Inland Marine, Property, Subrogation, Investigation and Adjustment, Alternative Dispute Resolution, Natural Resources, Governmental Entitites

SEE COMPLETE LISTING UNDER BOISE, IDAHO (280 MILES)

Racine Olson Nye Budge & Bailey, Chartered
201 East Center
Pocatello, Idaho 83201
 Telephone: 208-232-6101
 Toll Free: 877-232-6101
 Fax: 208-232-6109

Mailing Address: P.O. Box 1391, Pocatello, ID 83204-1391

Insurance Defense, Coverage Issues, Product Liability, Bad Faith, Automobile, Trial Practice, Appellate Practice

SEE COMPLETE LISTING UNDER POCATELLO, IDAHO (50 MILES)

KETCHUM 2,689 Blaine Co.

Refer To

Carey Perkins LLP
300 North 6th Street, Suite 200
Boise, Idaho 83702
 Telephone: 208-345-8600
 Fax: 208-345-8660

Mailing Address: P.O. Box 519, Boise, ID 83701-0519

Insurance Defense, Accountants and Attorneys Liability, Agent and Brokers Errors and Omissions, Agriculture, Alternative Dispute Resolution, Appellate Practice, Architects and Engineers, Arson, Asbestos Litigation, Automobile Liability, Aviation, Bad Faith, Business Law, Civil Litigation, Civil Rights, Commercial Litigation, Complex Litigation, Comprehensive General Liability, Construction Litigation, Dental Malpractice, Design Professionals, Directors and Officers Liability, ERISA, Employer Liability, Employment Practices Liability, Environmental Law, General Civil Trial and Appellate Practice, Governmental Liability, Health Care, Insurance Law, Insurance Coverage, Insurance Fraud, Insurance Litigation, Legal Malpractice, Litigation and Counseling, Medical Malpractice, Municipal Liability, Nursing Home Liability, Pharmaceutical, Product Liability, Professional Malpractice, Public Entities, Public Liability, School Law, Self-Insured Defense, Sexual Harassment, Subrogation, Toxic Torts, Truck Liability, Trucks/Heavy Equipment, Uninsured and Underinsured Motorist, Workers' Compensation, Wrongful Death, Wrongful Termination

SEE COMPLETE LISTING UNDER BOISE, IDAHO (132 MILES)

IDAHO

Refer To

Racine Olson Nye Budge & Bailey, Chartered
201 East Center
Pocatello, Idaho 83201
 Telephone: 208-232-6101
 Toll Free: 877-232-6101
 Fax: 208-232-6109

Mailing Address: P.O. Box 1391, Pocatello, ID 83204-1391

Insurance Defense, Coverage Issues, Product Liability, Bad Faith, Automobile, Trial Practice, Appellate Practice

SEE COMPLETE LISTING UNDER POCATELLO, IDAHO (170 MILES)

LEWISTON † 31,894 Nez Perce Co.

Refer To

Ramsden & Lyons, LLP
700 Northwest Boulevard
Coeur d'Alene, Idaho 83814
 Toll Free: 800-352-0813
 Telephone: 208-664-5818
 Fax: 208-664-5884

Mailing Address: P.O. Box 1336, Coeur d'Alene, ID 83816-1336

Insurance Defense, Coverage Analysis, Medical Malpractice Defense, Personal Injury Litigation, Professional Liability, Fire Loss, Product Liability, Civil Litigation, Commercial Litigation, Construction Law, Education Law, Employment Law, Real Estate Litigation, Water Law, Environmental & Natural Resources Law, Business Law & Formation, Creditor Representation, Eminent Domain & Condemnation, Mining Law, Public Agency & Municipal Law, Real Estate Development, Wills, Trusts, & Estates, Defense of Housing & Access Discrimination Claims

SEE COMPLETE LISTING UNDER COEUR D'ALENE, IDAHO (116 MILES)

MALAD CITY † 2,095 Oneida Co.

Refer To

Racine Olson Nye Budge & Bailey, Chartered
201 East Center
Pocatello, Idaho 83201
 Telephone: 208-232-6101
 Toll Free: 877-232-6101
 Fax: 208-232-6109

Mailing Address: P.O. Box 1391, Pocatello, ID 83204-1391

Insurance Defense, Coverage Issues, Product Liability, Bad Faith, Automobile, Trial Practice, Appellate Practice

SEE COMPLETE LISTING UNDER POCATELLO, IDAHO (57 MILES)

MONTPELIER 2,597 Bear Lake Co.

Refer To

Racine Olson Nye Budge & Bailey, Chartered
201 East Center
Pocatello, Idaho 83201
 Telephone: 208-232-6101
 Toll Free: 877-232-6101
 Fax: 208-232-6109

Mailing Address: P.O. Box 1391, Pocatello, ID 83204-1391

Insurance Defense, Coverage Issues, Product Liability, Bad Faith, Automobile, Trial Practice, Appellate Practice

SEE COMPLETE LISTING UNDER POCATELLO, IDAHO (87 MILES)

MOSCOW † 23,800 Latah Co.

Refer To

Ramsden & Lyons, LLP
700 Northwest Boulevard
Coeur d'Alene, Idaho 83814
 Toll Free: 800-352-0813
 Telephone: 208-664-5818
 Fax: 208-664-5884

Mailing Address: P.O. Box 1336, Coeur d'Alene, ID 83816-1336

Insurance Defense, Coverage Analysis, Medical Malpractice Defense, Personal Injury Litigation, Professional Liability, Fire Loss, Product Liability, Civil Litigation, Commercial Litigation, Construction Law, Education Law, Employment Law, Real Estate Litigation, Water Law, Environmental & Natural Resources Law, Business Law & Formation, Creditor Representation, Eminent Domain & Condemnation, Mining Law, Public Agency & Municipal Law, Real Estate Development, Wills, Trusts, & Estates, Defense of Housing & Access Discrimination Claims

SEE COMPLETE LISTING UNDER COEUR D'ALENE, IDAHO (84 MILES)

MOUNTAIN HOME † 14,206 Elmore Co.

Refer To

Carey Perkins LLP
300 North 6th Street, Suite 200
Boise, Idaho 83702
 Telephone: 208-345-8600
 Fax: 208-345-8660

Mailing Address: P.O. Box 519, Boise, ID 83701-0519

Insurance Defense, Accountants and Attorneys Liability, Agent and Brokers Errors and Omissions, Agriculture, Alternative Dispute Resolution, Appellate Practice, Architects and Engineers, Arson, Asbestos Litigation, Automobile Liability, Aviation, Bad Faith, Business Law, Civil Litigation, Civil Rights, Commercial Litigation, Complex Litigation, Comprehensive General Liability, Construction Litigation, Dental Malpractice, Design Professionals, Directors and Officers Liability, ERISA, Employer Liability, Employment Practices Liability, Environmental Law, General Civil Trial and Appellate Practice, Governmental Liability, Health Care, Insurance Law, Insurance Coverage, Insurance Fraud, Insurance Litigation, Legal Malpractice, Litigation and Counseling, Medical Malpractice, Municipal Liability, Nursing Home Liability, Pharmaceutical, Product Liability, Professional Malpractice, Public Entities, Public Liability, School Law, Self-Insured Defense, Sexual Harassment, Subrogation, Toxic Torts, Truck Liability, Trucks/Heavy Equipment, Uninsured and Underinsured Motorist, Workers' Compensation, Wrongful Death, Wrongful Termination

SEE COMPLETE LISTING UNDER BOISE, IDAHO (45 MILES)

NAMPA 81,557 Canyon Co.

Refer To

Carey Perkins LLP
300 North 6th Street, Suite 200
Boise, Idaho 83702
 Telephone: 208-345-8600
 Fax: 208-345-8660

Mailing Address: P.O. Box 519, Boise, ID 83701-0519

Insurance Defense, Accountants and Attorneys Liability, Agent and Brokers Errors and Omissions, Agriculture, Alternative Dispute Resolution, Appellate Practice, Architects and Engineers, Arson, Asbestos Litigation, Automobile Liability, Aviation, Bad Faith, Business Law, Civil Litigation, Civil Rights, Commercial Litigation, Complex Litigation, Comprehensive General Liability, Construction Litigation, Dental Malpractice, Design Professionals, Directors and Officers Liability, ERISA, Employer Liability, Employment Practices Liability, Environmental Law, General Civil Trial and Appellate Practice, Governmental Liability, Health Care, Insurance Law, Insurance Coverage, Insurance Fraud, Insurance Litigation, Legal Malpractice, Litigation and Counseling, Medical Malpractice, Municipal Liability, Nursing Home Liability, Pharmaceutical, Product Liability, Professional Malpractice, Public Entities, Public Liability, School Law, Self-Insured Defense, Sexual Harassment, Subrogation, Toxic Torts, Truck Liability, Trucks/Heavy Equipment, Uninsured and Underinsured Motorist, Workers' Compensation, Wrongful Death, Wrongful Termination

SEE COMPLETE LISTING UNDER BOISE, IDAHO (22 MILES)

POCATELLO   IDAHO

POCATELLO † 54,255 Bannock Co.

Racine Olson Nye Budge & Bailey, Chartered

201 East Center
Pocatello, Idaho 83201
    Telephone: 208-232-6101
    Toll Free: 877-232-6101
    Fax: 208-232-6109
    E-Mail: racine@racinelaw.net
    www.racinelaw.net

(Boise, ID Office*: 101 South Capitol, Suite 300, 83702)
    (Tel: 208-395-0011)
    (Fax: 208-433-0167)
(Idaho Falls, ID Office: 477 Shoup Avenue, 83402)
    (Tel: 208-528-6101)
    (Fax: 208-528-6109)

Established: 1940

Insurance Defense, Coverage Issues, Product Liability, Bad Faith, Automobile, Trial Practice, Appellate Practice

Firm Profile: Founded in 1940, Racine, Olson, Nye, Budge and Bailey, Chartered, is one of the Idaho's larger firms and understands that the needs of each client are unique. With offices in Pocatello, Boise and Idaho Falls, this firm tailors services to meet the needs of our clients. We also assist clients in Wyoming. We strive to continue to provide excellence in service at a reasonable cost.

Insurance Clients

American Mutual Insurance Company
Colonial Penn Insurance Company
Continental Western Insurance Company
Farm Bureau Mutual Insurance Company
Farmers Home Group
Farmers Insurance Group
Great American Insurance Company
The Hartford Insurance Group
Jefferson Insurance Group
MetLife Insurance Company
National Chiropractic Mutual Insurance Company
Old Reliable Casualty Company
Prudential of America Group
Reliance Insurance Company
Specialty Risk Services, Inc. (SRS)
Transamerica Insurance Company
Transit Casualty Company
Underwriters Adjusting Company
United Pacific Insurance Company
Chubb/Pacific Indemnity Company
Cincinnati Insurance Company
Commercial Union Insurance Companies
CUMIS Insurance Society, Inc.
Farmers Alliance Mutual Insurance Company
Farmers Insurance Company of Idaho
Guaranty National Insurance Company
Iowa Mutual Insurance Company
Kemper Insurance Companies
Milbank Insurance Company
North American Risk Services
North Pacific Insurance Company
Preferred Risk Mutual Insurance Company
Sentry Insurance Group
State of Idaho, Bureau of Risk Management
Transport Indemnity Company
Unigard Insurance Company
USAA Casualty Insurance Company

Non-Insurance Clients

FMC Corporation
Monsanto Company
Idaho State University

Firm Members

W. Marcus W. Nye — 1945 — Harvard University, A.B., 1967; University of Idaho, J.D. — Admitted to Bar, 1974, Idaho — Member American Bar Association (House of Delegates, 1988-2000; Board of Governors, 1997-2000); Idaho State Bar (President, 1987-1988); Idaho Association of Insurance Defense Counsel (Past President); American College of Trial Lawyers

Randall C. Budge — 1951 — University of Idaho, J.D., 1976 — Admitted to Bar, 1976, Idaho — Member American and Sixth Judicial District Bar Associations; Idaho State Bar

John A. Bailey, Jr. — 1954 — University of Idaho, J.D., 1980 — Admitted to Bar, 1980, Idaho — Member American and Sixth Judicial District Bar Associations; Idaho State Bar (Board of Commissioners, 1997-2000, President, 1999-2000); Defense Research Institute

Racine Olson Nye Budge & Bailey, Chartered, Pocatello, ID (Continued)

John R. Goodell — 1956 — Georgetown University, A.B., 1977; Southern Illinois University School of Law, J.D., 1981 — Admitted to Bar, 1981, Illinois; 1982, Idaho; 1991, Wyoming — Member American and Illinois State Bar Associations; Idaho State Bar; Wyoming State Bar; Sixth Judicial District Bar Association

John B. Ingelstrom — 1953 — Idaho State University, B.S., 1977; University of Idaho, J.D., 1980 — Admitted to Bar, 1980, Idaho — Member American and Sixth Judicial District Bar Associations; Idaho State Bar

Daniel C. Green — Weber State College, A.B.; Brigham Young University, J.D., 1984 — Admitted to Bar, 1984, Idaho; 2004, Utah — Member American and Sixth Judicial Bar Associations; Idaho State Bar

Brent O. Roche — 1955 — Idaho State University, B.A., 1977; University of Washington, J.D., 1980 — Admitted to Bar, 1980, Idaho — Member American and Sixth Judical District Bar Associations; Idaho State Bar; Idaho Trial Lawyers Association

Kirk B. Hadley — 1960 — University of Idaho, B.S., 1982; J.D., 1985 — Admitted to Bar, 1988, Idaho — Member Idaho State Bar; Sixth Judicial District Bar Association

Fred J. Lewis — 1959 — The University of Utah, B.A., 1959; University of Idaho, J.D., 1988 — Admitted to Bar, 1988, Idaho — Member Idaho State Bar; Sixth Judicial District Bar Association

Eric L. Olsen — 1965 — Brigham Young University, B.S., 1990; University of Idaho, J.D., 1993; University of Florida, LL.M., 1997 — Admitted to Bar, 1993, Idaho — Member Idaho State Bar

Conrad J. Aiken — 1944 — Wittenberg University, A.B., 1973; Duke University, J.D., 1977 — Admitted to Bar, 1969, Ohio; 1971, Kentucky; 1975, Colorado; 1977, Idaho — Member Idaho State Bar; Kentucky State Bar Association

Richard A. Hearn — 1948 — The University of Alabama, Ph.D., 1974; M.D., 1976; Georgetown University Law Center, J.D. (magna cum laude), 1991 — Admitted to Bar, 1994, District of Columbia; 1997, Idaho; 1994, U.S. District Court for the District of Columbia; 1997, U.S. District Court, District of Idaho — Member The District of Columbia Bar; Idaho State Bar

Lane V. Erickson — 1970 — Idaho State University, B.A., 1996; University of Idaho, J.D., 1999 — Admitted to Bar, 1999, Idaho — Member Idaho State Bar; Utah State Bar

Frederick J. Hahn III — 1963 — University of Idaho, B.A., 1986; University of Idaho College of Law, J.D., 1990 — Admitted to Bar, 1990, Idaho; 2007, Wyoming; 1990, U.S. District Court, District of Idaho; 1992, U.S. Court of Appeals, Ninth Circuit; 1999, U.S. Supreme Court; 2003, U.S. Court of Federal Claims; 2008, U.S. District Court, District of Wyoming — Member American Bar Association; Idaho State Bar — Languages: German — Practice Areas: Commercial Litigation; Contracts; Construction Litigation

Patrick N. George — 1977 — Brigham Young University, B.S., 1996; University of Idaho, J.D., 1999 — Admitted to Bar, 1999, Idaho

Scott J. Smith — 1976 — Brigham Young University, B.S., 1995; University of Idaho College of Law, J.D. (magna cum laude), 1999 — Admitted to Bar, 1999, Idaho; 1999, U.S. District Court, District of Idaho

Joshua D. Johnson — 1971 — Southern Oregon University, B.A., 1993; The John Marshall Law School, J.D., 1997 — Admitted to Bar, 1997, Illinois; 2004, Idaho; 1997, U.S. District Court, Northern District of Illinois; 2004, U.S. District Court, District of Idaho

Stephen J. Muhonen — 1971 — Idaho State University, A.A., 1992; B.A., 1999; University of Idaho, J.D., 2002 — Admitted to Bar, 2003, Idaho; U.S. District Court, District of Idaho

David E. Alexander — 1961 — Trinity University, B.S., 1983; Washington University, J.D., 1990 — Admitted to Bar, 1992, Idaho — Member Idaho State Bar; The Missouri Bar

Carol T. Volyn — 1975 — Montana State University, B.A., 1997; University of Idaho College of Law, J.D., 2001 — Admitted to Bar, 2001, Idaho; 2005, Washington — Member Washington State and Sixth Judicial District Bar Associations; Idaho State Bar

Nolan E. Wittrock — 1987 — Boise State University, B.A. Political Science (with honors), 2009; University of Idaho College of Law, J.D., 2012 — Admitted to Bar, 2012, Idaho

Rachel A. Miller — 1983 — Brigham Young University, Idaho, B.S. (cum laude), 2008; J. Reuben Clark Law School, Brigham Young University, J.D. (cum laude), 2011 — Admitted to Bar, 2011, Idaho

Associates

Jonathan M. Volyn — 1976 — Walla Walla College, B.A. (cum laude), 1998; University of Idaho College of Law, J.D., 2001 — Admitted to Bar, 2001,

Racine Olson Nye Budge & Bailey, Chartered, Pocatello, ID (Continued)

Idaho; 2005, Washington; U.S. District Court, District of Idaho; U.S. District Court, Eastern District of Washington

Thomas J. Budge — 1977 — Idaho State University, B.B.A., 2003; University of Idaho, J.D., 2006 — Admitted to Bar, 2006, Idaho

Brent L. Whiting — 1971 — Ricks College, A.A.S., 1994; Idaho State University, B.A. (magna cum laude), 1997; The University of Montana, J.D. (cum laude), 2002 — Admitted to Bar, 2002, Idaho; U.S. District Court, District of Idaho — Member American Bar Association; Idaho State Bar

Dave Bagley — 1973 — Brigham Young University, B.A., 1999; University of Idaho, J.D., 2005; University of Florida, LL.M., 2006 — Admitted to Bar, 2006, Idaho; U.S. District Court, District of Idaho — Member American Bar Association; Idaho State Bar

Jason E. Flaig — 1978 — Brigham Young University, B.S., 2003; University of Idaho College of Law, J.D., 2008 — Admitted to Bar, 2009, Idaho; U.S. District Court, District of Idaho

Aaron A. Crary — Western Washington University, B.S., 2003; University of Idaho, J.D., 2008 — Admitted to Bar, 2010, Idaho

John J. Bulger — 1960 — The University of Montana, B.A., 1984; J.D., 1988 — Law Clerk, Montana Supreme Court (1989-1990) — Admitted to Bar, 2010, Idaho

Brett R. Cahoon — 1982 — The University of Utah, B.A., 2006; Washington State University, M.B.A., 2010; University of Idaho, J.D., 2010 — Admitted to Bar, 2011, Idaho — Member Idaho State Bar

Of Counsel

William D. Olson — 1933 — Washington University, J.D., 1959 — Admitted to Bar, 1959, Idaho — Member American and Sixth Judicial District Bar Associations; Idaho State Bar (Character and Fitness Committee); Idaho Insurance Defense Counsel Association

Founder

Louis F. Racine, Jr. — (1917-2005)

The following firms also service this area.

Anderson, Julian & Hull, LLP
C.W. Moore Plaza
250 South 5th Street, Suite 700
Boise, Idaho 83702
   Telephone: 208-344-5800
   Fax: 208-344-5510

Mailing Address: P.O. Box 7426, Boise, ID 83707-7426

Insurance Defense, Trial Practice, Aviation, Personal Injury, Professional Malpractice, Health Care, Workers' Compensation, Commercial Litigation, Business Law, Construction Law, Product Liability, Employment Law, Environmental Law, Hazardous Waste, Appellate Practice, Pollution, Contracts, Insurance Coverage, Surety, Civil Rights, Transportation, Automobile, Fire, Tort Litigation, Casualty, Inland Marine, Property, Subrogation, Investigation and Adjustment, Alternative Dispute Resolution, Natural Resources, Governmental Entitites

SEE COMPLETE LISTING UNDER BOISE, IDAHO (233 MILES)

POST FALLS   27,574 Kootenai Co.

Adams & Gaffaney, LLP

1810 East Schneidmiller Avenue, Suite 301
Post Falls, Idaho 83854
   Telephone: 208-457-9281
   Fax: 208-457-8390
   E-Mail: rradams@adamsgaffaney.com
   www.adamsgaffaney.com

Insurance Defense, Insurance Coverage Disputes, Guardian ad Litem, Government Law, Mediation, Appellate Practice, Professional Malpractice

Firm Profile: With more than 40 years of collective experience, the partners at Adams & Gaffaney, LLP possess the skills and expertise to handle even the most complex civil litigation and appellate matters. On behalf of insurance companies and their insureds alike, we provide thorough, cost-effective representation, personally handling every aspect of our clients' cases from start to finish.

Insurance Clients

Allstate Insurance Company
GEICO
Nationwide Insurance
Western Heritage Insurance Company
EMC Insurance Companies
James River Insurance Company
Scottsdale Insurance Company

Non-Insurance Clients

City of Coeur d'Alene
On Site For Seniors
Worley Fire District
Northern Lakes Fire District
State of Idaho, Bureau of Risk Management

Firm Members

Randall R. Adams — University of Southern California, B.A., 1979; University of Idaho College of Law, J.D., 1983 — Law Clerk, Hon. Roger Swanstrom, Idaho Court of Appeals — Admitted to Bar, 1983, Idaho; 1995, Washington — Member Idaho State Bar; Washington State Bar Association

Jennifer D. Gaffaney — Gonzaga University, B.A., 1998; Gonzaga University School of Law, J.D., 2002 — Law Clerk, Hon. Neal Q. Rielly, Spokane Superior Court — Admitted to Bar, 2002, Washington; 2003, Idaho — Member Idaho State Bar; Washington State Bar Association

---

PRESTON   † 5,204 Franklin Co.

Refer To

Racine Olson Nye Budge & Bailey, Chartered
201 East Center
Pocatello, Idaho 83201
   Telephone: 208-232-6101
   Toll Free: 877-232-6101
   Fax: 208-232-6109

Mailing Address: P.O. Box 1391, Pocatello, ID 83204-1391

Insurance Defense, Coverage Issues, Product Liability, Bad Faith, Automobile, Trial Practice, Appellate Practice

SEE COMPLETE LISTING UNDER POCATELLO, IDAHO (69 MILES)

REXBURG   † 25,484 Madison Co.

Refer To

Carey Perkins LLP
980 Pierview Drive, Suite B
Idaho Falls, Idaho 83405
   Telephone: 208-529-0000
   Fax: 208-529-0005

Mailing Address: P.O. Box 51388, Idaho Falls, ID 83405

Civil Trial Practice, Insurance Defense, Product Liability

SEE COMPLETE LISTING UNDER IDAHO FALLS, IDAHO (27 MILES)

RUPERT   † 5,554 Minidoka Co.

Refer To

Racine Olson Nye Budge & Bailey, Chartered
201 East Center
Pocatello, Idaho 83201
   Telephone: 208-232-6101
   Toll Free: 877-232-6101
   Fax: 208-232-6109

Mailing Address: P.O. Box 1391, Pocatello, ID 83204-1391

Insurance Defense, Coverage Issues, Product Liability, Bad Faith, Automobile, Trial Practice, Appellate Practice

SEE COMPLETE LISTING UNDER POCATELLO, IDAHO (73 MILES)

SALMON † 3,112 Lemhi Co.
Refer To

Carey Perkins LLP
980 Pierview Drive, Suite B
Idaho Falls, Idaho 83405
   Telephone: 208-529-0000
   Fax: 208-529-0005

Mailing Address: P.O. Box 51388, Idaho Falls, ID 83405

Civil Trial Practice, Insurance Defense, Product Liability

SEE COMPLETE LISTING UNDER IDAHO FALLS, IDAHO (207 MILES)

SODA SPRINGS † 3,058 Caribou Co.
Refer To

Racine Olson Nye Budge & Bailey, Chartered
201 East Center
Pocatello, Idaho 83201
   Telephone: 208-232-6101
   Toll Free: 877-232-6101
   Fax: 208-232-6109

Mailing Address: P.O. Box 1391, Pocatello, ID 83204-1391

Insurance Defense, Coverage Issues, Product Liability, Bad Faith, Automobile, Trial Practice, Appellate Practice

SEE COMPLETE LISTING UNDER POCATELLO, IDAHO (60 MILES)

SUN VALLEY 1,406 Blaine Co.
Refer To

Racine Olson Nye Budge & Bailey, Chartered
201 East Center
Pocatello, Idaho 83201
   Telephone: 208-232-6101
   Toll Free: 877-232-6101
   Fax: 208-232-6109

Mailing Address: P.O. Box 1391, Pocatello, ID 83204-1391

Insurance Defense, Coverage Issues, Product Liability, Bad Faith, Automobile, Trial Practice, Appellate Practice

SEE COMPLETE LISTING UNDER POCATELLO, IDAHO (165 MILES)

TWIN FALLS † 44,125 Twin Falls Co.

Benoit, Alexander, Harwood & High, LLP

126 Second Avenue North
Twin Falls, Idaho 83303
   Telephone: 208-733-5463
   Fax: 208-734-1438
   E-Mail: mollerup@benoitlaw.com
   www.benoitlaw.com

Established: 1919

Insurance Defense, Bad Faith, Employment Litigation, Mediation, Product Liability, Malpractice

Firm Profile: Founded in 1919 by Harry Benoit, the law firm known as Benoit, Alexander, Harwood & High L.L.P. has enjoyed a long and distinguished history, and has retained a commitment to high quality and exemplary service throughout. Since its founding, the philosophy of providing fair, efficient legal services at a reasonable price has guided the firm.

Insurance Clients

Arch Insurance Company
Farm Bureau Insurance Company
Farmers Alliance Mutual Insurance Company
Bureau of Risk Management, State of Idaho

Partners

Robert M. Harwood — University of Idaho College of Law, J.D., 1971 — Admitted to Bar, 1971, Idaho

Benoit, Alexander, Harwood & High, LLP, Twin Falls, ID (Continued)

Thomas B. High — The University of Utah, B.S. (with honors), 1973; University of Idaho College of Law, J.D., 1979 — Admitted to Bar, 1979, Idaho

Bren E. Mollerup — The University of Utah, B.S. (with honors), 2004; Drake University Law School, J.D. (with honors), 2008 — Admitted to Bar, 2008, Idaho

Of Counsel

J. Robert Alexander

The following firms also service this area.

Anderson, Julian & Hull, LLP
C.W. Moore Plaza
250 South 5th Street, Suite 700
Boise, Idaho 83702
   Telephone: 208-344-5800
   Fax: 208-344-5510

Mailing Address: P.O. Box 7426, Boise, ID 83707-7426

Insurance Defense, Trial Practice, Aviation, Personal Injury, Professional Malpractice, Health Care, Workers' Compensation, Commercial Litigation, Business Law, Construction Law, Product Liability, Employment Law, Environmental Law, Hazardous Waste, Appellate Practice, Pollution, Contracts, Insurance Coverage, Surety, Civil Rights, Transportation, Automobile, Fire, Tort Litigation, Casualty, Inland Marine, Property, Subrogation, Investigation and Adjustment, Alternative Dispute Resolution, Natural Resources, Governmental Entitites

SEE COMPLETE LISTING UNDER BOISE, IDAHO (130 MILES)

Carey Perkins LLP
300 North 6th Street, Suite 200
Boise, Idaho 83702
   Telephone: 208-345-8600
   Fax: 208-345-8660

Mailing Address: P.O. Box 519, Boise, ID 83701-0519

Insurance Defense, Accountants and Attorneys Liability, Agent and Brokers Errors and Omissions, Agriculture, Alternative Dispute Resolution, Appellate Practice, Architects and Engineers, Arson, Asbestos Litigation, Automobile Liability, Aviation, Bad Faith, Business Law, Civil Litigation, Civil Rights, Commercial Litigation, Complex Litigation, Comprehensive General Liability, Construction Litigation, Dental Malpractice, Design Professionals, Directors and Officers Liability, ERISA, Employer Liability, Employment Practices Liability, Environmental Law, General Civil Trial and Appellate Practice, Governmental Liability, Health Care, Insurance Law, Insurance Coverage, Insurance Fraud, Insurance Litigation, Legal Malpractice, Litigation and Counseling, Medical Malpractice, Municipal Liability, Nursing Home Liability, Pharmaceutical, Product Liability, Professional Malpractice, Public Entities, Public Liability, School Law, Self-Insured Defense, Sexual Harassment, Subrogation, Toxic Torts, Truck Liability, Trucks/Heavy Equipment, Uninsured and Underinsured Motorist, Workers' Compensation, Wrongful Death, Wrongful Termination

SEE COMPLETE LISTING UNDER BOISE, IDAHO (130 MILES)

Racine Olson Nye Budge & Bailey, Chartered
201 East Center
Pocatello, Idaho 83201
   Telephone: 208-232-6101
   Toll Free: 877-232-6101
   Fax: 208-232-6109

Mailing Address: P.O. Box 1391, Pocatello, ID 83204-1391

Insurance Defense, Coverage Issues, Product Liability, Bad Faith, Automobile, Trial Practice, Appellate Practice

SEE COMPLETE LISTING UNDER POCATELLO, IDAHO (116 MILES)

ILLINOIS

CAPITAL: SPRINGFIELD

COUNTIES AND COUNTY SEATS

County	County Seat
Adams	Quincy
Alexander	Cairo
Bond	Greenville
Boone	Belvidere
Brown	Mount Sterling
Bureau	Princeton
Calhoun	Hardin
Carroll	Mount Carroll
Cass	Virginia
Champaign	Urbana
Christian	Taylorville
Clark	Marshall
Clay	Louisville
Clinton	Carlyle
Coles	Charleston
Cook	Chicago
Crawford	Robinson
Cumberland	Toledo
De Kalb	Sycamore
De Witt	Clinton
Douglas	Tuscola
Du Page	Wheaton
Edgar	Paris
Edwards	Albion
Effingham	Effingham
Fayette	Vandalia
Ford	Paxton
Franklin	Benton
Fulton	Lewistown
Gallatin	Shawneetown
Greene	Carrolton
Grundy	Morris
Hamilton	McLeansboro
Hancock	Carthage
Hardin	Elizabethtown
Henderson	Oquawka
Henry	Cambridge
Iroquois	Watseka
Jackson	Murphysboro
Jasper	Newton
Jefferson	Mount Vernon
Jersey	Jerseyville
Jo Daviess	Galena
Johnson	Vienna
Kane	Geneva
Kankakee	Kankakee
Kendall	Yorkville
Knox	Galesburg
Lake	Waukegan
La Salle	Ottawa
Lawrence	Lawrenceville
Lee	Dixon
Livingston	Pontiac
Logan	Lincoln
Macon	Decatur
Macoupin	Carlinville
Madison	Edwardsville
Marion	Salem
Marshall	Lacon
Mason	Havana
Massac	Metropolis
McDonough	Macomb
McHenry	Woodstock
McLean	Bloomington
Menard	Petersburg
Mercer	Aledo
Monroe	Waterloo
Montgomery	Hillsboro
Morgan	Jacksonville
Moultrie	Sullivan
Ogle	Oregon
Peoria	Peoria
Perry	Pinckneyville
Piatt	Monticello
Pike	Pittsfield
Pope	Golconda
Pulaski	Mound City
Putnam	Hennepin
Randolph	Chester
Richland	Olney
Rock Island	Rock Island
St. Clair	Belleville
Saline	Harrisburg
Sangamon	Springfield
Schuyler	Rushville
Scott	Winchester
Shelby	Shelbyville
Stark	Toulon
Stephenson	Freeport
Tazewell	Pekin
Union	Jonesboro
Vermilion	Danville
Wabash	Mount Carmel
Warren	Monmouth
Washington	Nashville
Wayne	Fairfield
White	Carmi
Whiteside	Morrison
Will	Joliet
Williamson	Marion
Winnebago	Rockford
Woodford	Eureka

In the text that follows "†" indicates County Seats.

Our files contain additional verified data on the firms listed herein. This additional information is available on request.

A.M. BEST COMPANY

ALTON 27,865 Madison Co.

Hoagland, Fitzgerald & Pranaitis

401 Market Street
Alton, Illinois 62002
   Telephone: 618-465-7745
   Fax: 618-465-3744
   Toll Free: 866-830-1066
   E-Mail: hfp@il-mo-lawfirm.com
   www.hoaglandlawfirm.com

Insurance Defense

Insurance Clients

American Family Insurance Group
Chartis Inc.
Gallagher Bassett Services, Inc.
St. Paul Travelers
Badger Mutual Insurance Company
Cincinnati Insurance Company
OneBeacon Insurance
Zurich American Insurance Company

Non-Insurance Clients

Crown Cork and Seal Company, Inc.
Simon Property Group, Inc.
SSM Health Care
Madison County, Illinois-Self-Insured
Specialty Tires of America, Inc.

Partners

William H. Hoagland — 1940 — University of Michigan, A.B., 1962; University of Illinois, LL.B., 1965 — Admitted to Bar, 1965, Illinois; 1965, U.S. District Court, Southern District of Illinois — Member Illinois State, Madison County and Alton-Wood River (President, 1985) Bar Associations; Illinois Association of Defense Trial Counsel — Practice Areas: Insurance Law; Personal Injury — E-mail: billhoag@il-mo-lawfirm.com

R. Emmett Fitzgerald — 1926 — University of Notre Dame, B.A. (cum laude), 1950; LL.B. (cum laude), 1952 — Admitted to Bar, 1952, Illinois; 1952, U.S. District Court, Southern District of Illinois; 1952, U.S. Supreme Court — Member Illinois State and Alton-Wood River Bar Associations; National Lawyers Association — Practice Areas: Corporate Law; Banking; Commercial Law; Probate; Real Estate — E-mail: refitz@il-mo-lawfirm.com

Alphonse J. Pranaitis — 1948 — University of Illinois, B.S. (with honors), 1970; Saint Louis University, J.D., 1975 — Admitted to Bar, 1975, Illinois; 2004, Missouri; 1977, U.S. District Court, Central and Southern Districts of Illinois; 1979, U.S. Court of Appeals, Seventh Circuit; 1987, U.S. Supreme Court; 2005, U.S. District Court, Eastern District of Missouri; 2005, U.S. Court of Appeals, Eighth Circuit — Member American, Illinois State, Madison County and Alton-Wood River Bar Associations; Bar Association of Central and Southern Districts of Illinois; Fellow, American College of Trial Lawyers; Illinois Association of Defense Trial Counsel; Defense Research Institute — Practice Areas: Construction Accidents; Medical Malpractice; Motor Vehicle; Product Liability; Legal Malpractice — E-mail: alpran@il-mo-lawfirm.com

Stephen J. Maassen — 1951 — Central College, B.A., 1973; Valparaiso University, J.D., 1977 — Admitted to Bar, 1977, Indiana; 1978, Illinois; 1999, Missouri; 1977, U.S. District Court, Northern and Southern Districts of Indiana; 1978, U.S. District Court, Southern District of Illinois; 1981, U.S. Court of Appeals, Seventh Circuit; 2006, U.S. District Court, Eastern District of Missouri — Member Illinois State, Indiana State, Madison County, Alton-Wood River and Metropolitan St. Louis Bar Associations; The Missouri Bar; Illinois Association of Defense Trial Counsel; Defense Research Institute; Fellow, American Bar Foundation; International Association of Defense Counsel — Practice Areas: Class Actions; Construction Accidents; Insurance Coverage; Product Liability; Toxic Torts — E-mail: maassen@il-mo-lawfirm.com

Scott D. Bjorseth — 1964 — University of Missouri, B.J., 1987; Southern Illinois University, J.D. (cum laude), 1990 — Admitted to Bar, 1990, Illinois; 1991, Missouri; 1991, U.S. District Court, Central and Southern Districts of Illinois; 1991, U.S. District Court, Western District of Missouri; 1995, U.S. District Court, Northern District of Illinois; 2002, U.S. District Court, Eastern District of Missouri; 2003, U.S. Court of Appeals, Eighth Circuit — Member Illinois State, Madison County and Alton-Wood River Bar Associations; The Missouri Bar; Illinois Association of Defense Trial Counsel; Defense Research Institute — Practice Areas: Motor Vehicle; Construction Accidents;

Hoagland, Fitzgerald & Pranaitis, Alton, IL (Continued)

Toxic Torts; Personal Injury; General Defense; Civil Litigation; Insurance Law — E-mail: scottb@il-mo-lawfirm.com

Associate

David A. Schott — 1981 — Butler University, B.A. (with honors), 2003; Southern Illinois University, J.D. (cum laude), 2005 — Admitted to Bar, 2006, Illinois; 2006, Missouri; 2006, U.S. District Court, Southern District of Illinois; 2007, U.S. District Court, Eastern and Western Districts of Missouri; 2010, U.S. District Court, Central District of Illinois; 2013, U.S. Court of Appeals, Seventh Circuit — Member American, Illinois State, Madison County, Alton-Wood River and Metropolitan St. Louis Bar Associations; Illinois Association of Defense Trial Counsel; Defense Research Institute — Practice Areas: Insurance Litigation; Commercial Litigation; Family Law; Personal Injury; Bankruptcy; Medical Malpractice Defense — E-mail: dschott@il-mo-lawfirm.com

Of Counsel

Karl K. Hoagland, Jr. — *Retired* — 1933 — University of Pennsylvania, B.S., 1955; University of Illinois, LL.B., 1958 — Admitted to Bar, 1958, Illinois; 1958, U.S. District Court, Southern District of Illinois — Member Illinois State, Madison County and Alton-Wood River Bar Associations

BELLEVILLE † 44,478 St. Clair Co.

Neville, Richards & Wuller, LLC

5 Park Place Professional Centre
Illinois Street and Fullerton Road
Belleville, Illinois 62226
   Telephone: 618-277-0900
   Fax: 618-277-0970
   E-Mail: cbray@nrw-law.com
   www.nrw-law.com

(Springfield, IL Office: 415 South Seventh Street, 62701)
   (Tel: 217-788-0900)
   (Fax: 217-788-0901)

Established: 1994

Insurance Defense, Professional Negligence, Product Liability, Premises Liability, Automobile, Bodily Injury, Fraud, Arson, Coverage Issues, Medical Malpractice, General Liability

Insurance Clients

American Physicians Capital, Inc.
The Doctors Company
GE Insurance Solutions
Hudson Insurance Group
The St. Paul Companies
CNA Insurance Companies
Economy Fire & Casualty Company
Rockford Mutual Insurance Company

Non-Insurance Clients

Illinois State Medical Society
St. Louis University Hospital System

Partners

James E. Neville — 1955 — Saint Louis University, B.S., 1977; J.D., 1980 — Admitted to Bar, 1980, Illinois; 1982, Missouri — E-mail: jneville@nrw-law.com

Timothy S. Richards — 1956 — Augustana College, A.B., 1978; Southern Illinois University, J.D. (cum laude), 1981 — Admitted to Bar, 1982, Illinois; 1983, Missouri — E-mail: trichards@nrw-law.com

Robert G. Wuller, Jr. — 1947 — University of Notre Dame, A.B., 1969; Saint Louis University, J.D., 1972 — Admitted to Bar, 1972, Illinois; 1983, Missouri — E-mail: bwuller@nrw-law.com

Matthew C. Zittel — 1971 — McKendree College, B.B.A. (cum laude), 1994; Southern Illinois University School of Law, J.D., 1997 — Admitted to Bar, 1997, Illinois; 1998, Missouri — E-mail: mzittel@nrw-law.com

Christopher B. Bortz — 1974 — Purdue University, B.A., 1996; Saint Louis University School of Law, J.D., 1999 — Admitted to Bar, 2000, Illinois; Missouri — E-mail: cbortz@nrw-law.com

BELLEVILLE   ILLINOIS

Neville, Richards & Wuller, LLC, Belleville, IL (Continued)

Associate

Lucas J. Dalton — 1980 — Southeast Missouri State University, B.S., 2002; Saint Louis University, J.D., 2005 — Admitted to Bar, 2005, Illinois; 2006, Missouri — Member St. Clair County Bar Association — E-mail: ldalton@nrw-law.com

Walker & Williams, P.C.

4343 West Main Street
Belleville, Illinois 62226
   Telephone: 618-277-1000, 618-274-1000
   Fax: 618-233-1637
   Emer/After Hrs: 618-398-6854
   E-Mail: lab@wawpc.net

Trial and Appellate Practice, State and Federal Courts, Insurance Defense, Class Actions, Insurance Coverage, Casualty Defense, Fire, Bodily Injury, Wrongful Death, Personal Lines, Governmental Liability, Civil Rights, Product Liability, Professional Liability, Automobile, Examinations Under Oath, Toxic Torts, Environmental Law

Firm Profile: Walker and Williams, P.C., was established in the 1930's in East St. Louis before moving to Belleville in 1969. Its insurance defense practice includes personal injury, property damage, first and third-party cases, class actions, coverage issues, automobile, premises and products liability, insurance fraud, toxic torts, environmental law and federal and state civil rights law and governmental liability. The firm maintains its primary office at Belleville. The firm provides insurance defense throughout Southern Illinois south of Springfield, and in the St. Louis, Missouri region.

Insurance Clients

Amerisure Insurance Company
Farmers Insurance Group
Governmental Interinsurance Exchange
National Fire and Casualty Company
OneBeacon Insurance Group
Travelers Indemnity Company
Travelers, Special Liability Group
Constitutional Casualty Company
Fireman's Fund Insurance Companies
Madison Mutual Insurance Company
Nautilus Insurance Company
Standard Mutual Insurance Company
United States Liability Insurance Group

Non-Insurance Clients

Alton & Southern Railway Company
Harley-Davidson Motor Company, Inc.
Chicago Pneumatic Tool Company, Inc.
Northrop Grumman Corporation

Firm Members

Ralph D. Walker — (1906-1988)

Wayne P. Williams — (1904-1990)

John B. Gunn — (1933-2001)

David B. Stutsman — **Retired** — 1929 — The University of Oklahoma; Washington University; University of Illinois, B.S., 1951; LL.B., 1953 — Phi Alpha Delta — Admitted to Bar, 1953, Illinois; 1966, U.S. Court of Appeals, Seventh Circuit; 1966, U.S. District Court, Southern District of Illinois — Member St. Clair County (President, 1971-1972) and East St. Louis Bar Associations; Fellow, American College of Trial Lawyers; American Board of Trial Advocates

Donald J. Dahlmann — 1948 — Southern Illinois University, B.A., 1970; Saint Louis University, J.D., 1973 — Admitted to Bar, 1973, Illinois; 1977, U.S. District Court, Southern District of Illinois; 1977, U.S. Supreme Court — Member Illinois State and St. Clair County (President, 1997-1998) Bar Associations; Illinois Association of Defense Trial Counsel; American Board of Trial Advocates; Defense Research Institute — Assistant St. Clair County State's Attorney, 1973-1975 — E-mail: djd@wawpc.net

Dale L. Bode — 1945 — Southern Illinois University; University of Missouri, J.D., 1976 — Admitted to Bar, 1976, Illinois; 1985, Missouri; 1978, U.S. District Court, Southern District of Illinois — Member Illinois State and Madison County Bar Associations; Illinois Association of Defense Trial Counsel; American Board of Trial Advocates; Defense Research Institute — E-mail: dlb@wawpc.net

Walker & Williams, P.C., Belleville, IL (Continued)

James C. Cook — 1951 — University of Illinois, B.A., 1973; Loyola University Chicago, J.D., 1976 — Law Clerk to Justice John T. Reardon, Illinois Appelate Court, Fourth District, 1976-1978 — Admitted to Bar, 1976, Illinois; 1984, Missouri; 1978, U.S. District Court, Central District of Illinois; 1979, U.S. District Court, Southern District of Illinois; 1979, U.S. Court of Appeals, Seventh Circuit; 1979, U.S. Supreme Court; 2002, U.S. Court of Appeals, Eighth Circuit — Member Illinois State and Peoria Bar Associations; Bar Association of the Central and Southern Federal Districts of Illinois (Director and Secretary 2001-2005; President 2005-Present); The Bar Association of Metropolitan St. Louis; Illinois Association of Defense Trial Counsel; Defense Research Institute — E-mail: jcc@wawpc.net

Paul P. Waller III — 1955 — University of Notre Dame, B.A., 1977; Saint Louis University, J.D., 1980 — Law Clerk to William Beatty, U.S. District Judge, Southern District of Illinois, 1980-1981 — Admitted to Bar, 1980, Illinois; 1987, Missouri; 1981, U.S. District Court, Southern District of Illinois; 1987, U.S. Court of Appeals, Seventh Circuit — Member American, Illinois State and St. Clair County Bar Associations — E-mail: ppw@wawpc.net

Leslie G. Offergeld — 1962 — University of Illinois, B.A., 1984; Southern Illinois University School of Law, J.D., 1987 — Admitted to Bar, 1987, Illinois; 1988, Missouri; 1987, U.S. District Court, Southern District of Illinois; 1988, U.S. Court of Appeals, Seventh Circuit; 1991, U.S. Supreme Court — Member American, Illinois State and St. Clair County Bar Associations; The Missouri Bar; Bar Association of the Central and Southern Federal Districts of Illinois; The Bar Association of Metropolitan St. Louis — E-mail: lgo@wawpc.net

Christian Cagas — 1968 — University of Illinois, B.S., 1990; Saint Louis University, J.D., 1999 — Admitted to Bar, 2002, Illinois; 2004, Missouri; 2003, U.S. District Court, Southern District of Illinois; 2004, U.S. District Court, Eastern District of Missouri — Member American, Illinois State and St. Clair County Bar Associations; The Missouri Bar; The Bar Association of Metropolitan St. Louis; Illinois Association of Defense Trial Counsel; Defense Research Institute — E-mail: ccc@wawpc.net

Elizabeth A. Dahlmann — 1983 — Purdue University, B.A., 2006; Southern Illinois University Carbondale, J.D., 2010 — Admitted to Bar, 2010, Illinois; 2011, Missouri — Member American, Illinois State and St. Clair County Bar Associations; Defense Research Institute — E-mail: ead@wawpc.net

---

The following firms also service this area.

Anderson & Gilbert, L.C.
515 Olive Street, Suite 704
St. Louis, Missouri 63101-1800
   Telephone: 314-721-2777
   Fax: 314-721-3515
   Toll Free: 800-721-2858

Insurance Defense, Trial and Appellate Practice, Medical Malpractice, Product Liability, Asbestos Litigation, Coverage Issues, State and Federal Courts, Toxic Torts, Truck Liability, Latex and Drug Product Liability

SEE COMPLETE LISTING UNDER ST. LOUIS, MISSOURI (16 MILES)

HeplerBroom LLC
130 North Main Street
Edwardsville, Illinois 62025
   Telephone: 618-656-0184
   Fax: 618-656-1364

Mailing Address: P.O. Box 510, Edwardsville, IL 62025-0510

Antitrust, Insurance Defense, Product Liability, Toxic Torts, Property and Casualty, Class Actions, Legal Malpractice, Commercial Litigation, Pharmaceutical, General Liability, Asbestos Litigation, Medical Malpractice, Workers' Compensation, Employment Litigation, Insurance Coverage, Transportation, Automobile, Trucking Law, Agent and Brokers Errors and Omissions, Personal Injury, Skilled Nursing Facilities, Construction Liability, White Collar Criminal Defense, Qui Tam/False Claims Act Litigation

SEE COMPLETE LISTING UNDER EDWARDSVILLE, ILLINOIS (36 MILES)

ILLINOIS

Hoagland, Fitzgerald & Pranaitis
401 Market Street
Alton, Illinois 62002
  Telephone: 618-465-7745
  Fax: 618-465-3744
  Toll Free: 866-830-1066
Mailing Address: P.O. Box 130, Alton, IL 62002

Insurance Defense

SEE COMPLETE LISTING UNDER ALTON, ILLINOIS (38 MILES)

Williams Venker & Sanders LLC
Bank of America Tower
100 North Broadway, 21st Floor
St. Louis, Missouri 63102
  Telephone: 314-345-5000
  Fax: 314-345-5055

Premises Liability, Product Liability, Professional Liability, Property and Casualty

SEE COMPLETE LISTING UNDER ST. LOUIS, MISSOURI (15 MILES)

BELVIDERE † 25,585 Boone Co.

Refer To

Mateer Goff & Honzel LLP
401 West State Street, Suite 400
Rockford, Illinois 61101
  Telephone: 815-965-7745
  Fax: 815-965-7749

Insurance Law, Fire, Casualty Insurance Law, Defense Litigation, Trial and Appellate Practice

SEE COMPLETE LISTING UNDER ROCKFORD, ILLINOIS (15 MILES)

BENTON † 7,087 Franklin Co.

Refer To

Craig & Craig, LLC
P.O. Box 1545
Mount Vernon, Illinois 62864
  Telephone: 618-244-7511
  Fax: 618-244-7628

Professional Liability, Workers' Compensation, Product Liability, Civil Rights, Dram Shop, Premises Liability, Automobile Liability, Fire, Casualty, Surety, Life Insurance, Uninsured and Underinsured Motorist, Employment Law, Intellectual Property, Family Law, Criminal Defense, Mediation

SEE COMPLETE LISTING UNDER MOUNT VERNON, ILLINOIS (22 MILES)

Refer To

Feirich/Mager/Green/Ryan
2001 West Main Street
Carbondale, Illinois 62901
  Telephone: 618-529-3000
  Fax: 618-529-3008
Mailing Address: P.O. Box 1570, Carbondale, IL 62903-1570

Insurance Defense, Medical Negligence, Casualty, Construction Litigation, Product Liability, Workers' Compensation, Civil Rights, Trial Practice, Appellate Practice, Professional Liability, Subrogation, Coverage Issues

SEE COMPLETE LISTING UNDER CARBONDALE, ILLINOIS (32 MILES)

Refer To

Jelliffe, Ferrell, Doerge & Phelps
108 East Walnut Street
Harrisburg, Illinois 62946
  Telephone: 618-253-7153, 618-253-7647
  Fax: 618-252-1843
Mailing Address: P.O. Box 406, Harrisburg, IL 62946

Insurance Law, Negligence, Personal Injury, Workers' Compensation, Product Liability, General Civil Practice, State and Federal Courts, Trial Practice, Appellate Practice, All Tort Litigation

SEE COMPLETE LISTING UNDER HARRISBURG, ILLINOIS (30 MILES)

BLOOMINGTON † 76,610 McLean Co.

Robert T. Varney & Associates

121 North Main Street, 4th Floor
Bloomington, Illinois 61701
  Telephone: 309-827-4444
  Fax: 309-828-3536
  E-Mail: rvarney@varneylaw.com
  www.varneylaw.com

Established: 2001

Insurance Law, Personal Lines, General Liability, Asbestos Litigation, Environmental Law, Trucking Law

Firm Profile: Robert T. Varney & Associates is a law firm dedicated to providing cost-effective legal representation to corporations, businesses and the risk industry. We are a civil trial firm with experience focused on commercial litigation, employment, transportation, environmental law, and insurance defense.

Insurance Clients

COUNTRY Mutual Insurance
  Company

Non-Insurance Clients

Amtrak   Chevron U.S.A., Inc.
Target Corporation

Firm Managing Partner

Robert Varney — 1961 — University of Illinois, B.S., 1983; University of Illinois College of Law, J.D., 1986 — Admitted to Bar, 1987, Illinois; 1994, Massachusetts; 2008, Missouri — E-mail: rvarney@varneylaw.com

Associate Attorneys

John O'Brien   Michael Butts

The following firms also service this area.

Drake, Narup & Mead, P.C.
107 East Allen Street, Suite 100
Springfield, Illinois 62704
  Telephone: 217-528-9776
  Fax: 217-528-9401

Insurance Defense, Malpractice, Casualty, Automobile, Fire Loss, Coverage Issues, Professional Liability, Construction Law, Truck Liability, Product Liability, Subrogation, Mediation

SEE COMPLETE LISTING UNDER SPRINGFIELD, ILLINOIS (60 MILES)

Langhenry, Gillen, Lundquist & Johnson, LLC
33 North Dearborn, Suite 1600
Chicago, Illinois 60602
  Telephone: 312-704-6700
  Fax: 312-704-6777

Medical Malpractice, General Liability, Subrogation, Coverage Issues, Opinions, Declaratory Judgments, Automobile, Property Damage, Personal Injury, Premises Liability, Product Liability, Defense Litigation, Employment Discrimination, Class Actions, Construction Litigation

SEE COMPLETE LISTING UNDER CHICAGO, ILLINOIS (46 MILES)

CARBONDALE 25,902 Jackson Co.

Feirich/Mager/Green/Ryan

2001 West Main Street
Carbondale, Illinois 62901
  Telephone: 618-529-3000
  Fax: 618-529-3008
  E-Mail: managingpartner@fmgr.com
  www.fmgr.com

CARBONDALE ILLINOIS

Feirich/Mager/Green/Ryan, Carbondale, IL (Continued)

Established: 1909

Insurance Defense, Medical Negligence, Casualty, Construction Litigation, Product Liability, Workers' Compensation, Civil Rights, Trial Practice, Appellate Practice, Professional Liability, Subrogation, Coverage Issues

Firm Profile: Feirich/Mager/Greer/Ryan is the foremost insurance defense firm in the tri-state region of Southern Illinois, Southeast Missouri, and Western Kentucky. It owes its success to the long-standing relationships the firm establishes with its clients. Every attorney in the firm is geared to serving the client's interest with all of the professionalism and responsiveness that a modern and diverse law firm can provide. The foundation of Feirich/Mager/Green/Ryan is the partnership established by Charles E. Feirich and Jack W.W. Barr in 1909 and which served as district council to the Illinois Central Railroad Company. The firm continues to grow in members and clientele, and today serves the legal needs of business, industry, and banking and insurance throughout Southern Illinois, Southeast Missouri, and Western Kentucky.

Insurance Clients

Allied Insurance Company
ASU Risk Management Services, Ltd.
Bituminous Insurance Company
Cannon Cochran Management Services, Inc.
Chrysler Life Insurance Company of Arizona
CNA
COUNTRY Mutual Insurance Company
Employers Reinsurance Corporation
Farmers Insurance Group
Florists' Insurance Company
General Accident Insurance Company
Hanover Insurance Company
Illinois Fair Plan Association
Indiana Insurance Company
Jackson National Life Insurance Company
Kentucky Associated General Contractors Self-Insurers Fund
Metropolitan Property and Casualty Insurance Company
Nationwide Agribusiness Insurance Company
Northland Insurance Company
Providian Direct Insurance Property & Casualty Group
Randolph Mutual Insurance Company
Safeco Insurance Companies
Scottsdale Insurance Company
Sentry Insurance a Mutual Company
Transport Life Insurance Company
Travelers Indemnity Company
Viking Insurance Company of Wisconsin
Western Indemnity Insurance Company
Zurich American Insurance Company
American States Insurance Company
Bishop Township Mutual Insurance Company
Capitol Indemnity Corporation
Central States Health & Life Company of Omaha
Chubb Insurance Company
Continental Insurance Company
Diamond Insurance Company
Employers Mutual Companies
The Equitable Life Assurance Society of the United States
Federated Insurance Company
GAB Robins North America, Inc.
General Casualty Companies
Great Central Insurance Company
Illinois Casualty Company
Illinois Insurance Guaranty Fund
Iuka Mutual Insurance Company
Jefferson County Mutual Insurance Company
The Merchants Property Insurance Company of Indiana
National General Insurance Company
North Central Life Insurance Company
OHIC Insurance Company
Prudential Insurance Company of America
Rockford Mutual Insurance Company
St. Paul Insurance Company
Sentry Insurance
State Auto Insurance Company
Tokio Marine and Fire Insurance Company, Ltd.
Travelers Insurance Companies
West Bend Mutual Insurance Company
Westfield Companies
Willis Group

Non-Insurance Clients

Aid Association for Lutherans
Illinois Compensation Trust
Illinois Municipal League Risk Management Association
Management Services, Inc.
Southern Illinois Counties Insurance Trust
Associated Physicians Management Company, Inc.
Illinois Parks Association Risk Services
Rogers Adjustment Services
Southern Illinois Regional Social Services, Inc.

Partners

John K. Feirich — (1909-1998)
T. Richard Mager — (1934-2002)

Feirich/Mager/Green/Ryan, Carbondale, IL (Continued)

Richard A. Green — 1946 — University of Illinois, J.D., 1972 — Admitted to Bar, 1972, Illinois; 1972, U.S. District Court, Southern District of Illinois — Member American, Illinois State and Jackson County Bar Associations — Adjunct Professor, Southern Illinois University School of Law (1981-1996) — Practice Areas: Arbitration; Mediation — E-mail: rgreen@fmgr.com

John C. Ryan — 1951 — Southern Illinois University, J.D., 1976 — Admitted to Bar, 1976, Illinois; 1994, Kentucky; 1998, Missouri; U.S. District Court, Southern District of Illinois — Member American, Illinois State and Jackson County Bar Associations — Practice Areas: Insurance Defense; Medical Malpractice; Municipal Liability — E-mail: jryan@fmgr.com

Michael F. Dahlen — 1949 — DePaul University, J.D., 1974 — Admitted to Bar, 1974, Illinois; 1994, Kentucky; 1989, Supreme Court of Illinois; U.S. District Court, Northern and Southern Districts of Illinois; U.S. Court of Appeals, Seventh and Eighth Circuits; 2011, Missouri State Court — Member American, Illinois State and Jackson County Bar Associations; Kentucky Bar Association; Defense Research Institute; Illinois Association of Defense Trial Counsel — Practice Areas: Appellate Practice; Medical Malpractice; Insurance Defense; Civil Litigation — E-mail: mdahlen@fmgr.com

Kevin L. Mechler — 1957 — Southern Illinois University, B.S., 1979; J.D., 1982 — Admitted to Bar, 1982, Illinois; 1994, Kentucky; 1982, U.S. District Court, Central District of Illinois — Member American Bar Association (Tort and Insurance Section); Illinois State Bar Association (Insurance and Workers' Compensation Sections); Kentucky Bar Association; Jackson County Bar Association — Practice Areas: Workers' Compensation — E-mail: kmechler@fmgr.com

John S. Rendleman, III — 1958 — Southern Illinois University Edwardsville, B.A., 1984; Southern Illinois University Carbondale, J.D., 1987 — Admitted to Bar, 1987, Illinois; 1987, U.S. District Court, Southern District of Illinois — Member American, Illinois State and Jackson County Bar Associations — Practice Areas: Commercial Litigation; Corporate Law; Real Estate — E-mail: jrendleman@fmgr.com

Pieter N. Schmidt — 1956 — Southern Illinois University, B.A., 1981; J.D., 1988 — Admitted to Bar, 1988, Illinois; 1988, U.S. District Court, Southern District of Illinois — Member American, Illinois State and Jackson County Bar Associations — Practice Areas: Workers' Compensation; Insurance Defense — E-mail: pschmidt@fmgr.com

R. James Giacone — 1973 — Southeast Missouri State University, B.S.B.A., 1995; University of Missouri, J.D., 1998 — Admitted to Bar, 1998, Illinois; 2002, U.S. District Court, Southern District of Illinois — Member American and Illinois State Bar Associations — Practice Areas: Insurance Defense; Workers' Compensation — E-mail: rgiacone@fmgr.com

Cheryl L. Intravaia — 1968 — University of Illinois, B.A., 1990; Southern Illinois University, J.D., 2001 — Admitted to Bar, 2002, Illinois; 2002, U.S. District Court, Southern District of Illinois — Member American and Illinois State Bar Associations — Practice Areas: Corporate Law; Workers' Compensation — E-mail: cintravaia@fmgr.com

Kara L. Jones — 1969 — Saint Louis University, B.S.B.A. (magna cum laude), 1991; Southern Illinois University, J.D., 1994 — Admitted to Bar, 1994, Illinois; 1995, U.S. District Court, Southern District of Illinois — Member American, Illinois State and Jackson County Bar Associations — Practice Areas: Appellate Practice; Insurance Defense; Medical Malpractice — E-mail: kjones@fmgr.com

Thomas R. Frenkel — 1953 — National Registry of Emergency Medical Technicians, 1973; Southern Illinois University, B.A. Physiology, 1975; J.D., 2000 — Admitted to Bar, 2000, Illinois; 2002, Minnesota; District of Columbia; 2007, Missouri; 2000, U.S. District Court, Southern District of Illinois; 2001, U.S. Court of Appeals, Seventh Circuit; 2002, U.S. Court of Appeals for the District of Columbia Circuit — Member American, Illinois State and Jackson County Bar Associations; Defense Research Institute; Illinois Association of Defense Trial Counsel; Transportation Lawyers Association — Practice Areas: Insurance Defense; Medical Malpractice; Insurance Coverage — E-mail: tfrenkel@fmgr.com

Associates

Angela M. Povolish — 1977 — Elmira College, B.A. (summa cum laude), 1998; Southern Illinois University, M.A., 2001; Washington University School of Law, J.D., 2005; Southern Illinois University, Ph.D., 2008 — Admitted to Bar, 2005, Illinois — Practice Areas: Real Estate — E-mail: apovolish@fmgr.com

Jonathan A. Mitchell — 1973 — Baylor University, B.B.A., 1996; The University of Oklahoma, J.D. (with honors), 2001 — Order of the Coif; Order of the Barristers — Admitted to Bar, 2001, Oklahoma; 2004, Illinois; 2006, U.S. District Court, Southern District of Illinois; 2010, U.S. Court of Appeals,

ILLINOIS

Feirich/Mager/Green/Ryan, Carbondale, IL (Continued)

Seventh Circuit — Lieutenant Commander, U.S. Navy Reserve, Judge Advocate General's Corp (2000-present) — Practice Areas: Insurance Defense; Workers' Compensation; Family Law — E-mail: jmitchell@fmgr.com

Brandy L. Johnson — 1976 — Southern Illinois University School of Law, J.D. (magna cum laude, with honors), 2003 — Admitted to Bar, 2003, Illinois; 2004, Missouri; U.S. District Court, Eastern District of Missouri; U.S. Court of Appeals, Eighth Circuit; 2005, U.S. District Court, Southern District of Illinois — Member Illinois State Bar Association (Standing Committee for Disability Law); The Missouri Bar; Missouri Organization of Defense Lawyers — Practice Areas: Workers' Compensation; Employment Law; Appellate — E-mail: bjohnson@fmgr.com

D Brian Smith — 1980 — Southern Illinois University School of Law, J.D., 2005 — Admitted to Bar, 2005, Illinois — Member Illinois State Bar Association — National School Board Association Council of School Attorneys; Illinois State Board of Education Council of School Attorneys — Practice Areas: Workers' Compensation; Civil Litigation; School Law — E-mail: bsmith@fmgr.com

Bentley J. Bender — 1979 — Washington University in St. Louis School of Law, J.D. (Dean's List), 2004; M.L.T., 2007 — Admitted to Bar, 2004, Illinois; 2005, Louisiana; 2007, Missouri; 2009, U.S. District Court, Central and Southern Districts of Illinois; U.S. District Court, Eastern District of Missouri; 2011, U.S. District Court, Northern District of Illinois — Member American, Illinois State and Jefferson County Bar Associations; The Missouri Bar; Bankruptcy Association of Southern Illinois — Practice Areas: Estate Planning; Tax Litigation; Business Law; Business Formation — E-mail: bbender@fmgr.com

CARLINVILLE † 5,917 Macoupin Co.

Refer To

Neville, Richards & Wuller, LLC
5 Park Place Professional Centre
Illinois Street and Fullerton Road
Belleville, Illinois 62226
Telephone: 618-277-0900
Fax: 618-277-0970
Mailing Address: P.O. Box 23977, Belleville, IL 62226-0070

Insurance Defense, Professional Negligence, Product Liability, Premises Liability, Automobile, Bodily Injury, Fraud, Arson, Coverage Issues, Medical Malpractice, General Liability

SEE COMPLETE LISTING UNDER BELLEVILLE, ILLINOIS (55 MILES)

Refer To

Rammelkamp Bradney, P.C.
232 West State
Jacksonville, Illinois 62650
Telephone: 217-245-6177
Fax: 217-243-7322
Mailing Address: P.O. Box 550, Jacksonville, IL 62651-0550

Insurance Law, Fire Loss, Arson, First Party Matters, Litigation, Declaratory Judgments, Workers' Compensation, Americans with Disabilities Act, Civil Rights, Construction Litigation, Employment Practices Liability, Trial and Appellate Practice

SEE COMPLETE LISTING UNDER JACKSONVILLE, ILLINOIS (45 MILES)

CARLYLE † 3,281 Clinton Co.

Refer To

Craig & Craig, LLC
P.O. Box 1545
Mount Vernon, Illinois 62864
Telephone: 618-244-7511
Fax: 618-244-7628

Professional Liability, Workers' Compensation, Product Liability, Civil Rights, Dram Shop, Premises Liability, Automobile Liability, Fire, Casualty, Surety, Life Insurance, Uninsured and Underinsured Motorist, Employment Law, Intellectual Property, Family Law, Criminal Defense, Mediation

SEE COMPLETE LISTING UNDER MOUNT VERNON, ILLINOIS (38 MILES)

CARLINVILLE

Refer To

Neville, Richards & Wuller, LLC
5 Park Place Professional Centre
Illinois Street and Fullerton Road
Belleville, Illinois 62226
Telephone: 618-277-0900
Fax: 618-277-0970
Mailing Address: P.O. Box 23977, Belleville, IL 62226-0070

Insurance Defense, Professional Negligence, Product Liability, Premises Liability, Automobile, Bodily Injury, Fraud, Arson, Coverage Issues, Medical Malpractice, General Liability

SEE COMPLETE LISTING UNDER BELLEVILLE, ILLINOIS (30 MILES)

CARMI † 5,240 White Co.

Refer To

Craig & Craig, LLC
P.O. Box 1545
Mount Vernon, Illinois 62864
Telephone: 618-244-7511
Fax: 618-244-7628

Professional Liability, Workers' Compensation, Product Liability, Civil Rights, Dram Shop, Premises Liability, Automobile Liability, Fire, Casualty, Surety, Life Insurance, Uninsured and Underinsured Motorist, Employment Law, Intellectual Property, Family Law, Criminal Defense, Mediation

SEE COMPLETE LISTING UNDER MOUNT VERNON, ILLINOIS (47 MILES)

Refer To

Jelliffe, Ferrell, Doerge & Phelps
108 East Walnut Street
Harrisburg, Illinois 62946
Telephone: 618-253-7153, 618-253-7647
Fax: 618-252-1843
Mailing Address: P.O. Box 406, Harrisburg, IL 62946

Insurance Law, Negligence, Personal Injury, Workers' Compensation, Product Liability, General Civil Practice, State and Federal Courts, Trial Practice, Appellate Practice, All Tort Litigation

SEE COMPLETE LISTING UNDER HARRISBURG, ILLINOIS (35 MILES)

Refer To

Kahn, Dees, Donovan & Kahn, LLP
501 Main Street, Suite 305
Evansville, Indiana 47708
Telephone: 812-423-3183
Fax: 812-423-3841
Mailing Address: P.O. Box 3646, Evansville, IN 47735-3646

Asbestos Litigation, Automobile, Construction Law, Coverage Issues, Environmental Law, Insurance Defense, General Liability, Labor and Employment, Mass Tort, Medical Malpractice, Personal Injury, Premises Liability, Product Liability, Property, Public Entities, Self-Insured, Subrogation, Workers' Compensation

SEE COMPLETE LISTING UNDER EVANSVILLE, INDIANA (46 MILES)

CARROLLTON † 2,484 Greene Co.

Refer To

Hoagland, Fitzgerald & Pranaitis
401 Market Street
Alton, Illinois 62002
Telephone: 618-465-7745
Fax: 618-465-3744
Toll Free: 866-830-1066
Mailing Address: P.O. Box 130, Alton, IL 62002

Insurance Defense

SEE COMPLETE LISTING UNDER ALTON, ILLINOIS (35 MILES)

CHAMPAIGN — ILLINOIS

Refer To
Rammelkamp Bradney, P.C.
232 West State
Jacksonville, Illinois 62650
Telephone: 217-245-6177
Fax: 217-243-7322

Mailing Address: P.O. Box 550, Jacksonville, IL 62651-0550

Insurance Law, Fire Loss, Arson, First Party Matters, Litigation, Declaratory Judgments, Workers' Compensation, Americans with Disabilities Act, Civil Rights, Construction Litigation, Employment Practices Liability, Trial and Appellate Practice

SEE COMPLETE LISTING UNDER JACKSONVILLE, ILLINOIS (30 MILES)

CARTHAGE † 2,605 Hancock Co.

Refer To
Rammelkamp Bradney, P.C.
232 West State
Jacksonville, Illinois 62650
Telephone: 217-245-6177
Fax: 217-243-7322

Mailing Address: P.O. Box 550, Jacksonville, IL 62651-0550

Insurance Law, Fire Loss, Arson, First Party Matters, Litigation, Declaratory Judgments, Workers' Compensation, Americans with Disabilities Act, Civil Rights, Construction Litigation, Employment Practices Liability, Trial and Appellate Practice

SEE COMPLETE LISTING UNDER JACKSONVILLE, ILLINOIS (70 MILES)

CHAMPAIGN   81,055 Champaign Co.

Thomas, Mamer & Haughey, LLP

30 E. Main Street, Suite 500
Champaign, Illinois 61820-3629
Telephone: 217-351-1500
Fax: 217-351-2017, 217-351-2169, 217-355-0087
E-Mail: tmh@tmh-law.com
www.tmh-law.com

Established: 1946

Insurance Defense, Trial and Appellate Practice, Product Liability, Directors and Officers Liability, Legal Malpractice, Medical Malpractice, Workers' Compensation, Commercial Litigation, Civil Rights, Defense Litigation, Construction Law, Municipal Law, Employment Litigation, Real Estate, General Practice, State and Federal Courts, Probate, Trusts, Business Law, Commercial Law, Employment Discrimination, Employment Law, Elder Law, Professional Malpractice, Health Care, Governmental Defense, Patents, Copyright and Trademark Law, Personal Injury, Litigation, Criminal Defense, Guardian and Conservatorships

Firm Profile: Founded in 1946 by attorneys James G. Thomas and Wallace Mulliken, the law firm of Thomas, Mamer & Haughey, LLP today ranks as one of the top firms in Central Illinois.

The key elements of this success are people- among the best in their respective fields- carefully and specifically chosen for the expertise they bring to the firm's practice and clients. These individuals share the firm's long-standing commitment to provide a complete range of services in a timely manner at a fair price.

Because each attorney in the firm concentrates in three to four specific areas of law, Thomas, Mamer & Haughey, LLP can accommodate most legal service requests.

Although this specific concentration is vital to a superior understanding of each legal situation, the attorneys and staff of Thomas, Mamer & Haughey, LLP also work together in teams to achieve the best possible results for their clients. The innate value in this continual sharing of ideas, opinions and counsel has always been recognized.

Thomas, Mamer & Haughey, LLP, Champaign, IL (Continued)

It is a trait that has made Thomas, Mamer & Haughey, LLP the respected law firm it is today and an attribute that is assuring its place for tomorrow.

Insurance Clients

AHRMA - Assisted Housing Risk Management Association
Broadspire
Cambridge Integrated Services
Cannon Cochran Management Services, Inc.
Chubb Group of Insurance Companies
Claims One
Claims Resource Management, Inc.
Country Companies
Crimco (Carle Risk Management Company)
Employers Mutual Casualty Company
Farmers Insurance Company
Fremont Compensation Insurance Company
GMAC Insurance
Harco National Insurance Company
Health Alliance Plan
HIH America Compensation and Liability Insurance Company
ISBA Mutual Insurance Company
Lumbermen's Underwriting Alliance
MIC General Insurance Corporation
Mutual Insurance Company, Inc.
NHRMA Mutual Insurance Company
PersonalCare HMO
Progressive Insurance Company
Safeco/American States Insurance Company
State Auto Insurance Companies
Transportation Claims, Inc.
United Heartland Life Insurance Company
West Bend Mutual Insurance Company
Western Reserve Group
Westfield Companies
Auto-Owners Group
Bituminous Insurance Companies
Brotherhood Mutual Insurance Company
Capitol Indemnity Corporation
Chicago Motor Club Insurance Company
The Cincinnati Insurance Companies
CNA
Crawford & Company
The Doctors Company
EBI Companies
Employers Security Insurance Company
Federated Insurance Company
Frontier Insurance Company
Gallagher Bassett Services, Inc.
Grocers Insurance Company
The Hartford Insurance Group
Hastings Mutual Insurance Company
Illinois State Medical Insurance Services, Inc.
Jefferson Insurance Group
Medicus Insurance Company
Medmarc Insurance Group
Minnesota Fire and Casualty Company
Mutual Service Insurance Companies
Ohio Mutual Insurance Group
ProAssurance Group
ProNational Insurance Company
Sedgwick Claims Management Services, Inc.
Superior Insurance Group
Travelers Insurance Companies
Unitrin, Inc.
Wausau General Insurance Company
Western Litigation Specialists, Inc.
Western States Insurance Company
Zurich Insurance Company

Non-Insurance Clients

The Carle Foundation Hospital
City of Champaign
Illinois Provider Trust
Martin Boyer Company
State Universities Retirement System
Citizens Management, Inc.
City of Decatur
Kraft Foods, Inc.
Quaker Oats Company
University of Illinois

Of Counsel

Roger E. Haughey — 1928 — University of Illinois, J.D., 1951 — Admitted to Bar, 1952, Illinois — Member American, Illinois State and Champaign County Bar Associations — Practice Areas: Real Estate; Estate Planning — E-mail: haughey@tmh-law.com

George S. Miller — 1928 — Northwestern University, B.S., 1950; Harvard Law School, LL.B., 1955; J.D., 1969 — Admitted to Bar, 1956, Illinois — Member Illinois State and Champaign County Bar Associations — Retired Circuit Judge, 6th Judicial Circuit, State of Illinois

Partners

Lott H. Thomas — 1934 — DePauw University, B.A., 1956; University of Illinois, J.D., 1962 — Admitted to Bar, 1962, Illinois — Member American, Illinois State and Champaign County Bar Associations — Practice Areas: Probate; Trusts; Real Estate — E-mail: lthomas@tmh-law.com

William J. Brinkmann — 1948 — University of Illinois, B.S., 1970; J.D., 1974 — Admitted to Bar, 1974, Illinois; 1987, U.S. District Court, Central District of Illinois; U.S. Court of Appeals, Seventh Circuit; 1988, U.S. Supreme Court — Member American Bar Association (Insurance, Negligence and Compensation Law Sections); Illinois State and Champaign County Bar Associations; International Association of Defense Counsel; Defense Research Institute; Illinois Association of Defense Trial Counsel; Fellow, American College of

ILLINOIS

Thomas, Mamer & Haughey, LLP, Champaign, IL (Continued)

Trial Lawyers — Practice Areas: Employment Law; Professional Liability — E-mail: wjbrinkm@tmh-law.com

David A. Bailie — 1948 — Westminster College, B.A. (cum laude), 1970; University of Illinois, J.D., 1975 — Admitted to Bar, 1975, Illinois; 1979, U.S. District Court, Central and Southern Districts of Illinois; U.S. Court of Appeals, Seventh Circuit; 1982, U.S. Supreme Court — Member American, Illinois State and Champaign County Bar Associations; Federation of Defense and Corporate Counsel; Defense Research Institute; Illinois Association of Defense Trial Counsel — Practice Areas: Professional Liability — E-mail: bailie@tmh-law.com

Richard R. Harden — 1958 — Knox College, B.A. (cum laude), 1980; University of Illinois, J.D. (cum laude), 1983 — Admitted to Bar, 1983, Illinois — Member Illinois State and Champaign County Bar Associations; Defense Research Institute (Member, Council on Litigation Management); Illinois Association of Defense Trial Counsel — Illinois Leading Lawyers, 2005-2013; Illinois Super Lawyers, 2006 — Practice Areas: Medical Malpractice; Tort; Insurance Defense — E-mail: riharden@tmh-law.com

David E. Krchak — 1950 — University of Illinois, B.A. (with high honors), 1973; Northwestern University, 1974; University of Illinois, J.D., 1980 — Admitted to Bar, 1980, Illinois; 1982, U.S. District Court, Central, Northern and Southern Districts of Illinois; 1983, U.S. Court of Appeals, Seventh Circuit — Member American Bar Association; Illinois State Bar Association (Chair, Employment Law Section, 1998-1999); Champaign County Bar Association (Board of Governors, 1986-1987; Board of Directors, Chamber of Commerce) — Practice Areas: Employment Law; Labor and Employment; Civil Rights — E-mail: krchak@tmh-law.com

Bruce E. Warren — 1954 — University of Illinois, B.A., 1977; Southern Illinois University, M.A., 1983; J.D., 1986 — Admitted to Bar, 1986, Illinois; 1987, U.S. District Court, Southern District of Illinois; U.S. Court of Appeals, Seventh Circuit; 1991, U.S. District Court, Central District of Illinois — Member Illinois State and Champaign County Bar Associations; Illinois Association of Defense Trial Counsel — E-mail: nottd@tmh-law.com

John M. Sturmanis — 1967 — Southern Illinois University, B.A., 1989; J.D., 1992 — Phi Delta Phi — Admitted to Bar, 1992, Illinois; 1995, U.S. District Court, Central District of Illinois; U.S. Court of Appeals, Seventh Circuit — Member Illinois State and Champaign County Bar Associations — Practice Areas: Civil Litigation; Defense Litigation; Workers' Compensation — E-mail: jms@tmh-law.com

Kenneth D. Reifsteck — 1965 — Parkland College, A.A.S., 1986; Illinois State University, B.S., 1988; Southern Illinois University School of Law, J.D., 1991 — Phi Delta Phi — Admitted to Bar, 1991, Illinois; 1992, U.S. District Court, Central and Southern Districts of Illinois; U.S. Court of Appeals, Seventh Circuit; 1999, U.S. Supreme Court — Member Illinois State and Champaign County Bar Associations; Illinois Association of Defense Trial Counsel — Practice Areas: Insurance Defense; Workers' Compensation — E-mail: kdr@tmh-law.com

Melissa A. Thomas — 1969 — University of Illinois, B.S., 1991; University of Illinois College of Law, J.D., 1994 — Admitted to Bar, 1994, Illinois; 2002, U.S. District Court, Central District of Illinois — Member American, Illinois State and Champaign County Bar Associations — Practice Areas: Estate Planning; Elder Law — E-mail: mat@tmh-law.com

James D. Green — 1961 — Illinois Wesleyan University, B.S., 1983; Saint Louis University School of Law, J.D., 1989 — Admitted to Bar, 1989, Missouri; 1990, Illinois; 1993, U.S. District Court, Central District of Illinois; 1994, U.S. Court of Appeals, Seventh Circuit — Member Illinois State and Champaign County Bar Associations; The Missouri Bar; Illinois Supreme Court Rules Committee (2012-present); Champaign City Council (1999-2005); Champaign Plan Commission (1997-1999); Clark-Lindsey Village (Board of Directors, 2012-present); Robeson Meadows Homeowner's Association (President, 2010-2012); Illinois Association of Defense Trial Counsel — Practice Areas: Litigation; Insurance Defense; Real Estate — E-mail: jim@tmh-law.com

Denise Knipp Bates — 1978 — University of Illinois at Urbana-Champaign, B.A., 2000; Loyola University Chicago School of Law, J.D., 2003 — Admitted to Bar, 2003, Illinois; U.S. District Court, Central District of Illinois — Member Illinois State and Champaign County Bar Associations; East Central Illinois Women Attorney Association; Champaign County Association of Realtors — Languages: Spanish — Practice Areas: Real Estate; Estate Planning; Probate; Civil Litigation; Corporate Law; Guardian and Conservatorships — E-mail: dkb@tmh-law.com

Associates

Eric S. Chovanec — 1983 — University of Illinois, B.S., 2006; DePaul University College of Law, J.D., 2009 — Admitted to Bar, 2009, Illinois — Member

CHAMPAIGN

Thomas, Mamer & Haughey, LLP, Champaign, IL (Continued)

American, Illinois State and Champaign County Bar Associations — Practice Areas: Workers' Compensation; Civil Litigation — E-mail: Eric@tmh-law.com

Seth D. Baker — 1985 — St. John Fisher College, B.A., 2007; University of Illinois at Urbana-Champaign, J.D., 2012 — Admitted to Bar, 2012, Illinois; 2013, U.S. District Court, Central District of Illinois; U.S. Bankruptcy Court, Central, Northern and Southern Districts of Illinois — Member American, Illinois State and Champaign County Bar Associations; Illinois Association of Defense Trial Counsel — Practice Areas: Civil Litigation; Premises Liability; General Liability; Professional Liability; Bankruptcy; Trademark — E-mail: Seth@tmh-law.com

Austin J. Hill — 1986 — University of Illinois at Urbana-Champaign, B.A., 2008; The John Marshall Law School, J.D., 2013 — Admitted to Bar, 2013, Illinois — Member American, Illinois State and Champaign County Bar Associations — Practice Areas: Estate Planning; Probate; Real Estate; Business Law — E-mail: ajhill@law-tmh.com

The following firms also service this area.

Craig & Craig, LLC
1807 Broadway Avenue
P.O. Box 689
Mattoon, Illinois 61938
Telephone: 217-234-6481
Fax: 217-234-6486
Fax: 217-258-8292

Automobile Liability, Casualty, Civil Rights, Dram Shop, Employment Practices Liability, Family Law, Fire, Insurance Coverage, Intellectual Property, Mediation, Product Liability, Premises Liability, Professional Liability, Surety, Uninsured and Underinsured Motorist, Workers' Compensation

SEE COMPLETE LISTING UNDER MATTOON, ILLINOIS (45 MILES)

Dukes, Ryan, Meyer, & Freed Ltd.
146 North Vermilion Street
Danville, Illinois 61832
Telephone: 217-442-0384
Fax: 217-442-0009

Insurance Defense, Personal Injury, Property Damage, Automobile, Homeowners, General Practice, Criminal Law

SEE COMPLETE LISTING UNDER DANVILLE, ILLINOIS (35 MILES)

Langhenry, Gillen, Lundquist & Johnson, LLC
33 North Dearborn, Suite 1600
Chicago, Illinois 60602
Telephone: 312-704-6700
Fax: 312-704-6777

Medical Malpractice, General Liability, Subrogation, Coverage Issues, Opinions, Declaratory Judgments, Automobile, Property Damage, Personal Injury, Premises Liability, Product Liability, Defense Litigation, Employment Discrimination, Class Actions, Construction Litigation

SEE COMPLETE LISTING UNDER CHICAGO, ILLINOIS (50 MILES)

Rammelkamp Bradney, P.C.
232 West State
Jacksonville, Illinois 62650
Telephone: 217-245-6177
Fax: 217-243-7322

Mailing Address: P.O. Box 550, Jacksonville, IL 62651-0550

Insurance Law, Fire Loss, Arson, First Party Matters, Litigation, Declaratory Judgments, Workers' Compensation, Americans with Disabilities Act, Civil Rights, Construction Litigation, Employment Practices Liability, Trial and Appellate Practice

SEE COMPLETE LISTING UNDER JACKSONVILLE, ILLINOIS (119 MILES)

CHICAGO   ILLINOIS

CHARLESTON † 21,838 Coles Co.
Refer To
Craig & Craig, LLC
1807 Broadway Avenue
P.O. Box 689
Mattoon, Illinois 61938
   Telephone: 217-234-6481
   Fax: 217-234-6486
   Fax: 217-258-8292

Automobile Liability, Casualty, Civil Rights, Dram Shop, Employment Practices Liability, Family Law, Fire, Insurance Coverage, Intellectual Property, Mediation, Product Liability, Premises Liability, Professional Liability, Surety, Uninsured and Underinsured Motorist, Workers' Compensation

SEE COMPLETE LISTING UNDER MATTOON, ILLINOIS (10 MILES)

CHESTER † 8,586 Randolph Co.
Refer To
Neville, Richards & Wuller, LLC
5 Park Place Professional Centre
Illinois Street and Fullerton Road
Belleville, Illinois 62226
   Telephone: 618-277-0900
   Fax: 618-277-0970
Mailing Address: P.O. Box 23977, Belleville, IL 62226-0070

Insurance Defense, Professional Negligence, Product Liability, Premises Liability, Automobile, Bodily Injury, Fraud, Arson, Coverage Issues, Medical Malpractice, General Liability

SEE COMPLETE LISTING UNDER BELLEVILLE, ILLINOIS (40 MILES)

CHICAGO † 2,695,598 Cook Co.

Allen, Kopet & Associates, PLLC
33 North La Salle Street, Suite 2110
Chicago, Illinois 60602
   Telephone: 312-229-1327
   Fax: 312-229-1328

(See listing under Chattanooga, TN for additional information)

Ancel, Glink, Diamond, Bush, DiCianni & Krafthefer, P.C.
140 South Dearborn Street, Suite 600
Chicago, Illinois 60603
   Telephone: 312-782-7606
   Fax: 312-782-0943
   E-Mail: sdiamond@ancelglink.com
   www.ancelglink.com

(Vernon Hills, IL Office: 175 East Hawthorn Parkway, Suite 145, 60061)
   (Tel: 847-247-7400)
(Bloomington, IL Office: 207 West Jefferson Street, Suite 402, 61701)
   (Tel: 309-828-1990)
(West Suburban Office: 1979 Mill Street, Suite 207, Naperville, IL, 60563)
   (Tel: 630-596-4610)
(Crystal Lake, IL Office: 4 East Terra Cotta Avenue, 60014)
   (Tel: 815-477-8980)

Established: 1931

Insurance Defense, Automobile, General Liability, Professional Liability, Product Liability, Directors and Officers Liability, Land Use, Employment Law, Public Officials Liability, Civil Rights, Property Damage, Workers' Compensation, Construction Law

Insurance Clients

Apex Insurance Company
Brit Insurance Services USA, Inc.

Ancel, Glink, Diamond, Bush, DiCianni & Krafthefer, P.C., Chicago, IL   (Continued)

Cannon Cochran Management Services, Inc.
HCC Public Risk Claim Service, Inc.
Municipal Insurance Cooperative Agency
Selective Insurance Group, Inc.
Summit Risk Services, Inc.
Utica National Insurance Group
Gallagher Bassett Services, Inc.
General Star Indemnity Company
High-Level Excess Liability Pool
McHenry County Municipal Risk Management Agency
Nugent Risk Management Service
Suburban Schools Cooperative Insurance Pool

Non-Insurance Clients

Chicago Park District
Illinois Municipal League
Rexam PLC
City of Waukegan
NuCare Services Corp.

Partners

Stewart H. Diamond — 1941 — The University of Chicago, A.B., 1961; Oxford University, England, Post-Graduate Research, 1965; The University of Chicago, J.D., 1963 — Admitted to Bar, 1963, Illinois; 1963, U.S. District Court, Northern District of Illinois; 1972, U.S. Supreme Court; 1974, U.S. Court of Appeals, Seventh Circuit — Member Illinois State and Chicago Bar Associations — Editor, IICLE, Illinois Municipal Law and Practice, 2008; Illinois School Law, 2005 — E-mail: sdiamond@ancelglink.com

Robert K. Bush — 1952 — College of William & Mary, B.A., 1974; Wesleyan University; Boston University, J.D., 1977 — Admitted to Bar, 1977, Illinois; 1978, Indiana; 1977, U.S. District Court, Northern District of Illinois — Member American (Litigation Section), Illinois State and Chicago Bar Associations; Illinois Worker's Compensation Lawyers Association — E-mail: rbush@ancelglink.com

Thomas G. DiCianni — University of Illinois, B.A., 1976; DePaul University, J.D., 1980 — Admitted to Bar, 1980, Illinois; 1988, Arizona; 1980, U.S. District Court, Central, Northern and Southern Districts of Illinois; 1987, U.S. Court of Appeals, Seventh Circuit — Member Illinois State, DuPage County and Chicago Bar Associations; American Board of Trial Advocates — E-mail: tdicianni@ancelglink.com

Keri-Lyn J. Krafthefer — University of Illinois at Urbana-Champaign, B.S., 1985; The John Marshall Law School, J.D., 1988 — Admitted to Bar, 1988, Illinois; 1988, U.S. District Court, Northern District of Illinois; 1988, U.S. Court of Appeals, Seventh Circuit; 1988, U.S. Supreme Court — E-mail: kkrafthefer@ancelglink.com

Derke J. Price — 1963 — Wheaton College, B.A., 1985; Harvard Law School, J.D., 1988 — Admitted to Bar, 1988, Illinois — Member American and Chicago Bar Associations — E-mail: dprice@ancelglink.com

Darcy L. Proctor — 1963 — Loyola University Chicago, B.A., 1985; Loyola University Chicago School of Law, J.D., 1988 — Admitted to Bar, 1988, Illinois; 1988, U.S. District Court, Northern District of Illinois; 1990, U.S. Court of Appeals, Seventh Circuit — Member American, Illinois State and Chicago Bar Associations — E-mail: dproctor@ancelglink.com

Ellen K. Emery — Northern Illinois University, B.S., 1978; The John Marshall Law School, J.D., 1982 — Admitted to Bar, 1982, Illinois; 1982, U.S. District Court, Central and Northern Districts of Illinois including Trial Bar; 1982, U.S. Court of Appeals, Seventh Circuit — Member Illinois State Bar Association; The Florida Bar

Lucy B. Bednarek — 1974 — Loyola University Chicago, B.S. (magna cum laude, with honors), 1996; Indiana University School of Law, J.D., 1999 — Admitted to Bar, 1999, Illinois; 1999, U.S. District Court, Northern District of Illinois — Member Illinois State and Chicago Bar Associations; Women's Bar Association of Illinois — E-mail: lbednarek@ancelglink.com

W. Britton Isaly — University of Michigan, B.A., 1992; Chicago-Kent College of Law, J.D., 1995 — Admitted to Bar, 1995, Illinois; 1995, U.S. District Court, Northern District of Illinois — Member Illinois State and Chicago Bar Associations — E-mail: wisaly@ancelglink.com

Associates

Pedro Fregoso, Jr. — 1977 — University of Illinois at Chicago, B.A., 2001; DePaul University College of Law, J.D., 2004 — Moot Court, 2003 Best Oralist — Admitted to Bar, 2005, Illinois; 2009, U.S. District Court, Eastern and Northern Districts of Illinois — Member Illinois State and Chicago Bar Associations; Hispanic Lawyers Association of Illinois — Languages: Spanish — E-mail: pfregoso@ancelglink.com

Brent O. Denzin — University of Michigan, B.A./B.S., 2001; University of Wisconsin Law School, J.D. (cum laude, with honors), 2005 — Admitted to Bar, 2005, Illinois; U.S. District Court, Northern District of Illinois; U.S. Court of Appeals, Seventh Circuit — Member American and Illinois State

Ancel, Glink, Diamond, Bush, DiCianni & Krafthefer, P.C., Chicago, IL (Continued)

Bar Associations; American Planning Association — E-mail: bdenzin@ancelglink.com

Erin M. Baker — 1986 — DePaul University, B.A. (cum laude), 2008; DePaul University College of Law, J.D., 2011 — Admitted to Bar, 2011, Illinois; 2012, Missouri — E-mail: ebaker@ancelglink.com

Of Counsel

David L. Ader — 1943 — University of Illinois, A.B., 1964; Northwestern University, J.D., 1967 — Admitted to Bar, 1967, Illinois; 1968, U.S. District Court, Northern District of Illinois; 1970, U.S. Court of Appeals, Seventh Circuit; 1972, U.S. Supreme Court; 1981, U.S. District Court, Central District of Illinois — Member Federal, American, Illinois State and Chicago Bar Associations; Arbitrator, American Arbitration Association — E-mail: dader@ancelglink.com

Gregory S. Mathews — 1955 — Yale University, B.A., 1977; Indiana University, J.D., 1980 — Admitted to Bar, 1980, Illinois; 1980, U.S. District Court, Northern District of Illinois — Member Illinois State and Chicago Bar Associations — E-mail: gmathews@ancelglink.com

Belgrade and O'Donnell, P.C.

20 North Wacker Drive, Suite 1900
Chicago, Illinois 60606
    Telephone: 312-422-1700
    312-623-4550
    Fax: 312-422-1717
    Toll Free: 800-360-9559
    Emer/After Hrs: 312-422-1700
    Mobile: 312-613-1455
    E-Mail: sbelgrade@bodpc.com
    www.belgradeodonnelllaw.com

Established: 1983

Admiralty and Maritime Law, Construction Accidents, Construction Litigation, Premises Liability, Insurance Coverage, Bodily Injury, Product Liability, Property Loss, Automobile, Truck Liability, Transportation

Firm Profile: Founded as a litigation firm, Belgrade and O'Donnell is recognized for its trial ability. The firm has substantial knowledge and expertise in a wide range of insurance defense matters, including injury and death claims involving construction and other employment-related accidents, products liability, premises liability, admiralty and maritime and other general negligence claims. The firm has also litigated a variety of complex property loss claims, transportation claims, and disputes regarding insurance policy coverage and interpretation. The firm's experience includes litigation and appeals in both the state and federal courts of Illinois and throughout the Midwest.

Each attorney's experience and dedication to the practice of law is representative of the firm's philosophy to provide tenacious, yet efficient and affordable legal representation of the highest quality.

Insurance Clients

ACE USA	AIG - Chartis
Arch Insurance Group	CNA Insurance Company
Indiana Insurance Company	Liberty Mutual Insurance Company
OneBeacon Insurance	Osprey Underwriting Agency Ltd.
St. Paul Fire and Marine Insurance Company	Steamship Mutual Management Services Ltd.
Wausau Business Insurance Company	Zurich North America

Firm Members

Steven B. Belgrade — 1950 — Loyola University Chicago, B.A., 1972; Loyola University Chicago School of Law, J.D., 1975 — Admitted to Bar, 1975, Illinois; 1999, Indiana; 1975, U.S. District Court, Northern District of Illinois including Trial Bar; 1979, U.S. Supreme Court; 1989, U.S. District Court, Central District of Illinois; 1994, U.S. District Court, Western District of Michigan; 1996, U.S. Court of Appeals, Sixth and Seventh Circuits; U.S. Court of Appeals for the District of Columbia Circuit; 1999, U.S. District Court, Northern and Southern Districts of Indiana; U.S. District Court, Eastern District of Wisconsin; 2001, U.S. Court of Appeals, Eighth Circuit; 2004, U.S. District Court, Eastern District of Missouri — Member Federal, American, Indiana State, Illinois State and Chicago Bar Associations; American Institute of Marine Underwriters; Chicago Ocean Marine Association; The Maritime Law Association of the United States; American Board of Trial Advocates; Transportation Lawyers Association; Defense Research Institute — Practice Areas: Insurance Defense; Insurance Coverage; Admiralty and Maritime Law; Construction Accidents; Transportation; Appellate Practice — E-mail: sbelgrade@bodpc.com

John A. O'Donnell — 1956 — St. John's University, B.A., 1978; Loyola University, J.D., 1981 — Admitted to Bar, 1981, Illinois; 1999, Indiana; 1981, U.S. District Court, Northern District of Illinois including Trial Bar; 1989, U.S. District Court, Central District of Illinois; 1993, U.S. Court of Appeals, Seventh Circuit; 1994, U.S. District Court, Western District of Michigan; 1996, U.S. Court of Appeals, Sixth Circuit; 1999, U.S. District Court, Northern and Southern Districts of Indiana; 2002, U.S. Court of Appeals, Eighth Circuit; 2004, U.S. District Court, Eastern District of Missouri — Member Illinois State, Indiana State and Chicago Bar Associations; American Institute of Marine Underwriters; The Maritime Law Association of the United States — Practice Areas: Insurance Defense; Construction Accidents; Admiralty and Maritime Law; Premises Liability; Trucking Law — E-mail: jodonnell@bodpc.com

George M. Velcich — 1955 — University of Notre Dame, B.A., 1977; Loyola University Chicago, J.D., 1980 — Admitted to Bar, 1980, Illinois; 1980, U.S. District Court, Northern District of Illinois including Trial Bar; 1992, U.S. District Court, Central District of Illinois; 1993, U.S. Court of Appeals, Seventh Circuit; 1996, U.S. District Court, Western District of Michigan; 2001, U.S. District Court, Eastern District of Michigan; 2002, U.S. District Court, Northern District of Indiana — Member Chicago Bar Association — Practice Areas: Negligence; Insurance Coverage; Construction Accidents; Admiralty and Maritime Law — E-mail: gvelcich@bodpc.com

Patrick J. Cullinan — 1959 — Loyola University Chicago, B.A., 1981; The John Marshall Law School, J.D., 1986 — Admitted to Bar, 1986, Illinois; 2001, Indiana; 1987, U.S. District Court, Northern District of Illinois including Trial Bar; 1993, U.S. Court of Appeals, Seventh Circuit; 1998, U.S. District Court, Southern District of Illinois; 2001, U.S. District Court, Northern and Southern Districts of Indiana — Member Chicago Bar Association — Practice Areas: Negligence; Construction Liability; Admiralty and Maritime Law — E-mail: pcullinan@bodpc.com

Associates

Ross M. Kucera — 1967 — Michigan State University, B.A., 1992; DePaul University College of Law, J.D., 2002 — Admitted to Bar, 2002, Illinois — Practice Areas: Insurance Defense; Premises Liability — E-mail: rkucera@bodpc.om

Richard P. Girzadas — 1965 — The George Washington University, B.A., 1987; The John Marshall Law School, J.D., 1997; Tulane University Law School, LL.M., 1998 — Admitted to Bar, 1997, Illinois; 2001, Indiana; 1999, U.S. District Court, Northern District of Illinois; 2001, U.S. District Court, Northern and Southern Districts of Indiana; U.S. Court of Appeals, Seventh Circuit — U.S. Army Reserve — Practice Areas: Insurance Defense; Insurance Coverage; Professional Malpractice; Admiralty and Maritime Law — E-mail: rgirzadas@bodpc.com

Stephanie T. Potter — 1978 — University of Illinois at Urbana-Champaign, B.A. (Bronze Tablet), 1999; The John Marshall Law School in Chicago, J.D. (Valedictorian, summa cum laude), 2011 — Admitted to Bar, 2011, Illinois; 2012, U.S. District Court, Northern District of Illinois

Best, Vanderlaan & Harrington

25 East Washington Street, Suite 800
Chicago, Illinois 60602
    Telephone: 312-819-1100
    Fax: 312-819-8062
    E-Mail: BVH@Bestfirm.com
    www.bestfirm.com

(Naperville, IL Office*: 400 East Diehl Road, Suite 280, 60563)
    (Tel: 630-752-8000)
    (Fax: 630-752-8763)
(Joliet, IL Office*: 1000 Essington Road, 60435)
    (Tel: 815-740-1500)
    (Fax: 815-740-6304)

CHICAGO   ILLINOIS

Best, Vanderlaan & Harrington, Chicago, IL (Continued)

(Rockford, IL Office*: 129 South Phelps Avenue, Suite 800, 61108)
(Tel: 815-964-9500)
(Fax: 815-964-8778)

Established: 1999

Medical Malpractice, General Liability, Coverage Issues, Opinions, Declaratory Judgments, Automobile, Property Damage, Personal Injury, Premises Liability, Product Liability, Defense Litigation, Employment Discrimination, Class Actions, Construction Litigation, Professional Malpractice, Commercial Litigation, Construction Defect, Construction Liability, Dram Shop, Labor and Employment, Insurance Coverage, Professional Liability, Toxic Torts, Trucking, Consumer Fraud Litigation, Governmental Law, Housing Authorities-Compliance and Litigation

Firm Profile: We are an AV rated firm with several attorneys being members of the Leading Lawyers Network. Our clients, many of whom have worked with us over many years, benefit from our vast experience & dedication to achieving results at reasonable rates. Our priorities are efficient case management & effective communication. We are accessible to you when you need us.

Insurance Clients

AAA Chicago Motor Club Insurance Company
IAT Reinsurance Company
Liberty Mutual Insurance
Park District Risk Management Agency
Safeco Insurance
Tower Group Companies
Unitrin Insurance Company
Zurich Direct Underwriters
Zurich North America

EMC Insurance Companies
Erie Insurance Company
Illinois Casualty Company
Lloyd's of London
RIMCO - Risk & Insurance Management Company
Society Insurance
Travelers
Western National Mutual Insurance Company

Non-Insurance Clients

Illinois Insurance Guaranty Fund   Northwest Community Hospital

Self-Insured Clients

AHRMA - Assisted Housing Risk Management Association
Intergovernmental Risk Management Agency

Illinois Municipal League Risk Management Association
Management Services, Inc.
Township Officials of Illinois Risk Management Association

Partners

James F. Best — 1949 — Drake University, B.S., 1971; J.D., 1974 — Admitted to Bar, 1974, Illinois; U.S. District Court, Central, Northern and Southern Districts of Illinois — Member Illinois State, DuPage County (Chairman, Civil Law and Practice Committee, 1985-1987, 1991) and Chicago Bar Associations; Defense Research Institute; Illinois Defense Counsel — Super Lawyer; Illinois Leading Lawyer — Practice Areas: Civil Litigation; Coverage Issues; Opinions; Declaratory Judgments; Insurance Defense; Medical Malpractice — E-mail: jbest@bestfirm.com

Lori A. Vanderlaan — **Managing Partner** — 1968 — University of Illinois, B.A. (with honors), 1989; The John Marshall Law School, J.D. (magna cum laude), 1995 — Admitted to Bar, 1995, Illinois; 2012, California; U.S. District Court, Central and Northern Districts of Illinois; U.S. Court of Appeals, Seventh Circuit; U.S. Supreme Court — Member Illinois State and DuPage County Bar Associations; Defense Research Institute — Illinois Leading Lawyers — Practice Areas: Civil Litigation; Insurance Defense; Opinions; Coverage Analysis; Employment Discrimination — E-mail: lvanderlaan@bestfirm.com

Alison Harrington — 1971 — The University of Iowa, B.S., 1994; Marquette University, J.D., 1997 — Admitted to Bar, 1997, Illinois; Wisconsin; U.S. District Court, Central and Northern Districts of Illinois — Member Illinois State Bar Association; Defense Research Institute — Illinois Leading Lawyer — Practice Areas: Civil Litigation; Insurance Defense; Medical Malpractice; Employment Discrimination — E-mail: aharrington@bestfirm.com

John C. Kreamer — 1973 — Coe College, B.A. (cum laude), 1996; DePaul University, J.D. (with honors), 1999 — Admitted to Bar, 1999, Illinois; U.S. District Court, Central and Northern Districts of Illinois — Member American, Illinois State and DuPage County Bar Associations; Defense Research

Best, Vanderlaan & Harrington, Chicago, IL (Continued)

Institute — Practice Areas: Civil Litigation; Personal Injury; Real Estate; Estate Planning; Employment Discrimination — E-mail: jckreamer@bestfirm.com

Scott McKenna — 1970 — Loyola University Chicago, B.A., 1993; Illinois Institute of Technology, Chicago-Kent College of Law, J.D., 1996 — Admitted to Bar, 1996, Illinois — Member Illinois State and Chicago Bar Associations; Illinois Trial Lawyers Association — Practice Areas: Civil Litigation; Employment Discrimination; Insurance Defense — E-mail: smckenna@bestfirm.com

Adam F. Haussermann — 1972 — Wake Forest University, B.A., 1994; DePaul University College of Law, J.D., 2001 — Admitted to Bar, 2002, Illinois — Member Illinois State and Chicago Bar Associations — Practice Areas: General Liability; Insurance Coverage; Medical Malpractice; Employment Discrimination — E-mail: ahaussermann@bestfirm.com

Adam M. Stefancic — 1974 — University of Illinois at Urbana-Champaign, B.S., 1996; The John Marshall Law School, J.D., 2000 — Admitted to Bar, 2000, Illinois; U.S. District Court, Central and Northern Districts of Illinois — Member Illinois State and Chicago Bar Associations — Practice Areas: Asbestos Litigation; Toxic Torts; Civil Litigation; Insurance Defense — E-mail: astefancic@bestfirm.com

Thomas J. Costello, III — 1979 — University of Illinois at Urbana-Champaign, B.S., 2001; J.D. (cum laude), 2004 — Admitted to Bar, 2004, Illinois — Member American and Illinois State Bar Associations — Practice Areas: Civil Litigation; Insurance Coverage; General Liability — E-mail: tcostello@bestfirm.com

Kimberlee Massin — 1968 — Illinois State University, B.S., 1990; Southwestern University School of Law, J.D. (SCALE Graduate), 1993 — Admitted to Bar, 1993, Illinois — Member Illinois State and Will County Bar Associations — Practice Areas: Dram Shop; Insurance Defense — E-mail: kmassin@bestfirm.com

Fritz V. Wilson — 1977 — Northwestern University, B.S. (with honors), 2000; George Mason University School of Law, J.D., 2004 — Admitted to Bar, 2004, Illinois; U.S. District Court, Northern District of Illinois — Member American (Litigation Section), Illinois State, DuPage County and Chicago Bar Associations — Practice Areas: Civil Litigation; Estate Planning; Real Estate; Insurance Defense — E-mail: fwilson@bestfirm.com

Allie M. Burnet — 1976 — Boston University, B.S., 1998; DePaul University College of Law, J.D. (cum laude), 2002 — Admitted to Bar, 2002, Illinois; U.S. District Court, Central, Northern and Southern Districts of Illinois; U.S. District Court, Northern District of Indiana; U.S. Court of Appeals, Eighth Circuit — Member American and Chicago Bar Associations — E-mail: aburnet@bestfirm.com

(See Joliet, Rockford and Naperville, IL Listings for additional information)

Brenner, Monroe, Scott & Anderson, Ltd.

33 North Dearborn Street, Suite 300
Chicago, Illinois 60602
  Telephone: 312-781-1970
  Fax: 312-781-9202
  www.brennerlawfirm.com

Insurance Defense, Trial Practice, Casualty, Professional Malpractice, Automobile, Product Liability, Insurance Coverage, Appellate Practice

Firm Profile: Brenner, Monroe, Scott & Anderson, Ltd. has offices in the Chicago loop. The firm concentrates its practice in litigation and trial work. The firm has represented clients throughout Illinois and Northern Indiana. The firm takes pride in its record of success, and the personalized service that we provide for our clients. Clients of Brenner, Monroe, Scott & Anderson, Ltd. are primarily insurers and managers of self-insured ventures with high standards and expectation of efficient, high-quality legal work. We strive to provide early and accurate evaluations of our cases to our clients, to thoroughly and vigorously prepare them for trial, to keep the client informed of the status of their case, and to use our experience and hard work to obtain a favorable result on behalf of the client.

Insurance Clients

AAO Services, Inc.
Continental Western Group

Allied Professionals Insurance Company

Brenner, Monroe, Scott & Anderson, Ltd., Chicago, IL (Continued)

The Dentists Insurance Company - TDIC
Medicus Insurance Company
NCMIC Group
ISBA Mutual Insurance Company
ISMIE Mutual Insurance Company
Nationwide Insurance
Scottsdale Insurance Company

Non-Insurance Clients

Bass Pro Shops, Inc./Tracker Marine Group
Western Litigation, Inc.
ELCO Administrative Services
NuCare Services Corp.

Third Party Administrators

Experix

Partners

Sheldon A. Brenner — President — 1944 — DePaul University, J.D., 1969 — Admitted to Bar, 1969, Illinois — Member Illinois State Bar Association; Illinois Association of Defense Trial Counsel — E-mail: sbrenner@brennerlawfirm.com

Randall C. Monroe — Secretary — 1959 — Valparaiso University, B.A. (with distinction), 1981; University of Illinois at Urbana-Champaign, J.D., 1984 — Admitted to Bar, 1984, Illinois — Member American, Illinois State and Chicago Bar Associations — Practice Areas: Litigation; Trial Practice — E-mail: rmonroe@brennerlawfirm.com

Mary Kay Scott — Vice President — 1959 — University of Illinois at Urbana-Champaign, B.A., 1981; J.D., 1984 — Admitted to Bar, 1984, Illinois — Member The Society of Trial Lawyers; American and Illinois State Bar Associations; The Society of Trial Lawyers; Defense Research Institute — Martindale-Hubbell AV Rated — E-mail: mscott@brennerlawfirm.com

Amy L. Anderson — Treasurer — 1965 — University of Illinois at Urbana-Champaign, B.A., 1987; J.D., 1990 — Admitted to Bar, 1990, Illinois — Member Illinois State Bar Association; The Society of Trial Lawyers; Defense Research Institute — E-mail: aanderson@brennerlawfirm.com

Teresa R. Maher, D.D.S. — 1955 — Illinois Institute of Technology, Chicago-Kent College of Law, J.D., 1990 — Admitted to Bar, 1990, Illinois — E-mail: tmaher@brennerlawfirm.com

Joshua C. Bell — 1974 — Illinois State University, B.S., 1996; The John Marshall Law School, J.D., 1999 — Admitted to Bar, 1999, Illinois — E-mail: jbell@brennerlawfirm.com

Associate

Austin C. Monroe — 1987 — Lindenwood University, B.A., 2009; Pennsylvania State University-Dickinson School of Law, J.D., 2012 — Admitted to Bar, 2012, Illinois — Member Illinois State and Chicago Bar Associations — E-mail: amonroe@brennerlawfirm.com

Cassiday Schade LLP

20 North Wacker Drive, Suite 1000
Chicago, Illinois 60606-2903
Telephone: 312-641-3100
Fax: 312-444-1669
E-Mail: info@cassiday.com
www.cassiday.com

(Naperville, IL Office: 2056 Westings Avenue, Suite 250, 60563)
(Tel: 630-328-2970)
(Fax: 630-328-2979)
(Libertyville, IL Office: 1870 Winchester Road, Suite 148, 60048)
(Tel: 847-932-6922)
(Fax: 847-932-6947)
(Rockford, IL Office: 120 West State Street, Suite 401, 61101)
(Tel: 815-962-8301)
(Fax: 815-962-8401)
(Crown Point, IN Office: 2100 North Main Street, Suite 300, 46307)
(Tel: 219-663-5575)
(Fax: 219-663-5382)
(Milwaukee, WI Office: 111 East Wisconsin Avenue, Suite 2100, 53202)
(Tel: 414-224-1086)
(Fax: 414-290-6781)

Cassiday Schade LLP, Chicago, IL (Continued)

Established: 1979

Accountant Liability, Appellate, Arbitration, Architects and Engineers, Commercial Law, Construction Law, Employment Law, Environmental and Toxic Injury, Family Law, Health Care, Insurance Law, Legal Liability, Long-Term Care, Mediation, Medical Liability, Medicare Set-Aside Practice, Nursing Home Liability, Product Liability, Professional Liability, Transportation, Workers' Compensation

Firm Profile: Cassiday Schade LLP is a law firm with experience in virtually all areas of civil litigation, representing a diverse client base in a variety of industries including insurance, health and long-term care, manufacturing, construction, professional services and transportation. In addition to trial and appellate work our attorneys are retained in cases involving alternative dispute resolution. We handle cases throughout Illinois, Indiana and Wisconsin as well as mass litigation in multiple states as national or regional counsel for clients facing nationwide exposures.

Representative Clients

Illinois State Medical Insurance Services, Inc.
Skyjack, Inc.
Pepper Construction Company
PIC Wisconsin
University of Chicago Hospitals

Managing Partners

Joseph A. Giannelli — The John Marshall Law School, J.D., 1982 — Admitted to Bar, 1982, Illinois; U.S. District Court, Northern District of Illinois including Trial Bar; U.S. District Court, Central District of Illinois; U.S. District Court, Northern District of Indiana — Member Illinois State Bar Association; Illinois Association of Defense Trial Counsel; Defense Research Institute — Practice Areas: Medical Liability; Professional Liability; Nursing Home Liability; Long-Term Care; Construction Law; Commercial Law; Product Liability — Tel: 312-444-2487 — E-mail: jgiannelli@cassiday.com

Bradford D. Roth — Illinois Institute of Technology, Chicago-Kent College of Law, J.D. (with high honors), 1979 — Admitted to Bar, 1979, Illinois; Wisconsin; U.S. District Court, Central and Northern Districts of Illinois including Trial Bar; U.S. District Court, Eastern and Western Districts of Wisconsin; U.S. District Court, Northern District of Indiana; U.S. Court of Appeals, Seventh Circuit — Member Illinois State and Chicago Bar Associations; Illinois Association and Health Systems Association; Illinois Association of Defense Trial Counsel; Defense Research Institute — Practice Areas: Professional Liability; Product Liability; Commercial Litigation; Environmental and Toxic Injury; Medical Liability; Construction Law; Legal Liability — Tel: 312-444-2480 — E-mail: broth@cassiday.com

Partners

James D. Ahern — The John Marshall Law School, J.D., 1989 — Admitted to Bar, 1989, Illinois; U.S. District Court, Northern District of Illinois; U.S. Court of Appeals, Seventh Circuit; Supreme Court of Illinois — Practice Areas: Construction Law; Professional Liability; Insurance Law; Product Liability; Environmental and Toxic Injury; Medicare Set-Aside Practice; Workers' Compensation; Accountant Liability; Architects and Engineers; Legal Liability; Medical Liability — Tel: 312-444-1666 — E-mail: jahern@cassiday.com

Erik L. Andersen — IIT, Chicago-Kent College of Law, J.D. (with honors), 1998 — Admitted to Bar, 1998, Illinois; U.S. District Court, Northern District of Illinois — Practice Areas: Professional Liability; Product Liability; Commercial Law; Construction Law; Employment Law; Environmental and Toxic Injury — Tel: 312-444-1611 — E-mail: eandersen@cassiday.com

Melissa A. Anderson — IIT, Chicago-Kent College of Law, J.D. (with honors), 2002 — Admitted to Bar, 2002, Illinois; U.S. District Court, Northern District of Illinois; Supreme Court of Illinois — Practice Areas: Appellate; Commercial Law; Insurance Law — Tel: 312-444-2494 — E-mail: manderson@cassiday.com

Ryan T. Armour — Northern Illinois University College of Law, J.D. (cum laude), 2005 — Admitted to Bar, 2005, Illinois; U.S. District Court, Northern District of Illinois; Supreme Court of Illinois — Practice Areas: Construction Law; Insurance Law; Medical Liability; Product Liability — Tel: 815-962-8382 — E-mail: rarmour@cassiday.com

Richard A. Barrett, Jr. — Georgetown University, J.D., 1976 — Admitted to Bar, 1976, Illinois; 1981, U.S. District Court, Northern District of Illinois including Trial Bar — Certified Arbitrator, DuPage County — Practice Areas:

CHICAGO ILLINOIS

Cassiday Schade LLP, Chicago, IL (Continued)

Medical Liability; Professional Liability; Commercial Law; Mediation; Arbitration; Construction Law; Product Liability; Transportation — Tel: 312-444-2461 — E-mail: rbarrett@cassiday.com

Marc Benjoya — IIT, Chicago-Kent College of Law, J.D., 1983 — Admitted to Bar, 1983, Illinois; 1998, Wisconsin; U.S. District Court, Central and Northern Districts of Illinois including Trial Bar; U.S. Court of Appeals, Seventh Circuit; U.S. District Court, Southern District of Indiana; U.S. District Court, Eastern District of Wisconsin; Supreme Court of Illinois; Supreme Court of Wisconsin — Practice Areas: Medical Liability; Nursing Home Liability; Long-Term Care; Commercial Law; Construction Law; Employment Law; Professional Liability; Legal Liability; Product Liability — Resident Libertyville, IL and Milwaukee, WI Office — Tel: 847-932-6930 — E-mail: mbenjoya@cassiday.com

Ehren V. Bilshausen — The John Marshall Law School, J.D., 2002 — Admitted to Bar, 2002, Illinois; U.S. District Court, Northern District of Illinois; Supreme Court of Illinois — Practice Areas: Construction Law; Transportation — Tel: 312-739-3283 — E-mail: ebilshausen@cassiday.com

Jennifer A. Bollow — Loyola University Chicago School of Law, J.D. (cum laude), 1998 — Admitted to Bar, 1998, Illinois; U.S. District Court, Northern District of Illinois; Supreme Court of Illinois — Arbitrator, Circuit Court of DuPage County — Practice Areas: Medical Liability; Nursing Home Liability; Long-Term Care; Professional Liability — Resident Naperville Office — Tel: 630-328-2983 — E-mail: jbollow@cassiday.com

Thomas P. Boylan — Loyola University Chicago School of Law, J.D., 1986 — Admitted to Bar, 1986, Illinois; U.S. District Court, Northern District of Illinois; Supreme Court of Illinois — Practice Areas: Construction Law; Product Liability; Commercial Law — Tel: 312-444-2463 — E-mail: tboylan@cassiday.com

Mark M. Brennan — Loyola University Chicago School of Law, J.D., 1993 — Admitted to Bar, 1993, Illinois; U.S. District Court, Northern District of Illinois; Supreme Court of Illinois — Practice Areas: Commercial Law; Medical Liability; Product Liability; Professional Liability — Tel: 312-444-2485 — E-mail: mbrennan@cassiday.com

Scott J. Brown — Boston University School of Law, J.D., 1991 — Admitted to Bar, 1991, Illinois; U.S. District Court, Northern District of Illinois including Trial Bar; U.S. District Court, Southern District of Indiana; Supreme Court of Illinois — Practice Areas: Commercial Law; Employment Law; Environmental and Toxic Injury; Medical Liability; Product Liability; Professional Liability; Accountant Liability; Architects and Engineers; Legal Liability — Tel: 312-444-1613 — E-mail: sbrown@cassiday.com

Kyle R. Burkhardt — The John Marshall Law School, J.D., 1997 — Admitted to Bar, 1997, Illinois; U.S. District Court, Northern District of Illinois; Supreme Court of Illinois — Practice Areas: Commercial Law; Medical Liability; Product Liability; Transportation — Tel: 312-444-1685 — E-mail: kburkhardt@cassiday.com

Robert S. Burtker — IIT, Chicago-Kent College of Law, J.D., 1981 — Admitted to Bar, 1981, Illinois; U.S. District Court, Northern District of Illinois; Supreme Court of Illinois — Practice Areas: Medical Liability — Tel: 312-444-2465 — E-mail: rburtker@cassiday.com

Bradford A. Burton — The John Marshall Law School, J.D. (Dean's List), 1983 — Admitted to Bar, 1983, Illinois; U.S. District Court, Northern District of Illinois — Practice Areas: Construction Law; Environmental and Toxic Injury; Product Liability — Tel: 312-444-1673 — E-mail: bburton@cassiday.com

Brook M. Carey — Loyola University Chicago School of Law, J.D. (cum laude), 2003 — Admitted to Bar, 2003, Illinois; U.S. District Court, Northern District of Illinois; U.S. District Court, Central District of Illinois — Practice Areas: Commercial Law; Construction Law; Medical Liability — Resident Naperville, IL Office — Tel: 630-328-2988 — E-mail: bcarey@cassiday.com

Stacey A. Cischke — Loyola University Chicago School of Law, J.D., 2000 — Admitted to Bar, 2000, Illinois; U.S. District Court, Northern District of Illinois; Supreme Court of Illinois — Practice Areas: Medical Liability — Tel: 312-444-1815 — E-mail: scischke@cassiday.com

Susan E. Conner — Loyola University Chicago School of Law, J.D., 1984 — Admitted to Bar, 1984, Illinois; U.S. District Court, Northern District of Illinois — Practice Areas: Medical Liability — Tel: 312-444-2458 — E-mail: sconner@cassiday.com

Michael J. Cucco — Loyola University Chicago School of Law, J.D., 1986 — Admitted to Bar, 1986, Illinois; U.S. District Court, Northern District of Illinois including Trial Bar; Supreme Court of Illinois — Practice Areas: Medical Liability; Environmental and Toxic Injury; Professional Liability; Legal Liability; Product Liability — Tel: 312-444-1661 — E-mail: mcucco@cassiday.com

Cassiday Schade LLP, Chicago, IL (Continued)

Christopher M. Daddino — Loyola University Chicago School of Law, J.D., 1991 — Admitted to Bar, 1991, Illinois; U.S. District Court, Northern District of Illinois; Supreme Court of Illinois — Practice Areas: Professional Liability; Legal Liability; Medical Liability; Nursing Home Liability; Transportation — Tel: 312-444-2499 — E-mail: cdaddino@cassiday.com

J. Randall Davis — The John Marshall Law School, J.D., 1983 — Admitted to Bar, 1983, Illinois; 1999, Wisconsin; U.S. District Court, Northern District of Illinois; U.S. Court of Appeals, Seventh Circuit; U.S. District Court, Eastern District of Wisconsin; U.S. Court of Appeals, Eighth Circuit; Supreme Court of Illinois — Co-Author: "Sexual Harassment and Age Discrimination," Risk Management Magazine (Feb. 2002); Co-Author: "Liability Issues in Wake of ENRON," Risk Management Magazine (Feb. 2003) — Practice Areas: Construction Law; Commercial Law; Insurance Law; Medical Liability; Nursing Home Liability; Product Liability; Professional Liability; Accountant Liability; Architects and Engineers — Resident Libertyville, IL Office — Tel: 847-932-6931 — E-mail: jdavis@cassiday.com

Andrew T. Fleishman — IIT, Chicago-Kent College of Law, J.D., 1995 — Admitted to Bar, 1995, Illinois; U.S. District Court, Northern District of Illinois; Supreme Court of Illinois — Practice Areas: Construction Law; Medical Liability; Nursing Home Liability; Long-Term Care; Product Liability; Professional Liability; Transportation — Resident Libertyville, IL Office — Tel: 847-932-6924 — E-mail: afleishman@cassiday.com

James A. Foster — University of Illinois College of Law, J.D., 1983 — Admitted to Bar, 1983, Illinois; Supreme Court of Illinois; U.S. District Court, Northern District of Illinois including Trial Bar — Practice Areas: Product Liability; Transportation — Tel: 312-444-2479 — E-mail: jfoster@cassiday.com

Catherine L. Garvey — DePaul University College of Law, J.D., 1990 — Certificate in Health and Hospital Law — Admitted to Bar, 1990, Illinois; U.S. District Court, Northern District of Illinois; Supreme Court of Illinois — Registered Nurse in Illinois — Practice Areas: Medical Liability; Nursing Home Liability; Product Liability; Professional Liability; Legal Liability — Tel: 312-444-1618 — E-mail: cgarvey@cassiday.com

Jean M. Golden — Loyola University Chicago School of Law, J.D., 1977 — Admitted to Bar, 1977, Illinois; U.S. District Court, Northern District of Illinois; Supreme Court of Illinois; Supreme Court of the United States — Practice Areas: Commercial Law; Construction Law; Insurance Law — Tel: 312-444-2489 — E-mail: jgolden@cassiday.com

John D. Hackett — DePaul University College of Law, J.D., 1987 — Admitted to Bar, 1987, Illinois; U.S. District Court, Northern District of Illinois; Supreme Court of Illinois — Chartered Property and Underwriters Society, Chicago Chapter — Chartered Property and Casualty Underwriters (CPU) Designation, 1999; Associate in Risk Management Designation, 2000 — Practice Areas: Commercial Law; Construction Law; Employment Law; Insurance Law; Professional Liability — Tel: 312-444-1615 — E-mail: jhackett@cassiday.com

Michael J. Hennig — The John Marshall Law School, J.D. (with high distinction), 1981 — Admitted to Bar, 1981, Illinois; U.S. District Court, Northern District of Illinois; U.S. Court of Appeals, Seventh Circuit; U.S. District Court, Eastern District of Wisconsin; Supreme Court of Illinois — Practice Areas: Construction Law; Environmental and Toxic Injury; Medical Liability; Nursing Home Liability; Product Liability; Professional Liability — Tel: 312-444-2490 — E-mail: mhennig@cassiday.com

Jeffrey A. Hesser — DePaul University College of Law, J.D., 1998 — Admitted to Bar, 1998, Illinois; U.S. District Court, Northern District of Illinois; U.S. Supreme Court; Supreme Court of Illinois — Practice Areas: Commercial Litigation; Medical Liability; Professional Liability — Tel: 312-444-2473 — E-mail: jhesser@cassiday.com

Brian J. Hickey — DePaul University College of Law, J.D., 1988 — Admitted to Bar, 1988, Illinois; U.S. District Court, Northern District of Illinois including Trial Bar; U.S. District Court, Northern District of Indiana; Supreme Court of Illinois — Languages: Spanish — Practice Areas: Construction Law; Medical Liability; Nursing Home Liability; Long-Term Care; Product Liability; Professional Liability — Resident Naperville, IL Office — Tel: 630-328-2980 — E-mail: bhickey@cassiday.com

Patricia J. Hogan — University of Illinois College of Law, J.D. (cum laude), 1990 — Admitted to Bar, 1990, Illinois; U.S. District Court, Northern District of Illinois; Supreme Court of Illinois — Practice Areas: Construction Law — Tel: 312-444-1665 — E-mail: phogan@cassiday.com

Richard C. Huettel — DePaul University College of Law, J.D., 1985 — Admitted to Bar, 1985, Illinois; U.S. District Court, Northern District of Illinois; Supreme Court of Illinois — Practice Areas: Professional Liability; Product Liability; Medical Liability; Nursing Home Liability; Long-Term Care — Tel: 312-444-2467 — E-mail: rhuettel@cassiday.com

ILLINOIS / CHICAGO

Cassiday Schade LLP, Chicago, IL (Continued)

Jamie L. Hull — The John Marshall Law School, J.D., 2000 — Admitted to Bar, 2001, Illinois; U.S. District Court, Northern District of Illinois; U.S. Court of Appeals, Seventh Circuit; Supreme Court of Illinois — Practice Areas: Appellate; Commercial Law; Insurance Law — Tel: 312-444-1891 — E-mail: jhull@cassiday.com

Sandra G. Iorio-Power — Marquette University Law School, J.D. (cum laude, Dean's List), 1994 — Admitted to Bar, 1994, Illinois; Wisconsin; U.S. District Court, Northern District of Illinois; U.S. District Court, Eastern District of Wisconsin; Supreme Court of Illinois; Supreme Court of Wisconsin — Practice Areas: Commercial Law; Medical Liability — Tel: 312-444-1662 — E-mail: siorio-power@cassiday.com

Paul T. Kleppetsch — The John Marshall Law School, J.D. (cum laude), 2003 — Admitted to Bar, 2003, Illinois; U.S. District Court, Northern District of Illinois; U.S. District Court; Supreme Court of Illinois — Practice Areas: Construction Law; Product Liability; Transportation — Tel: 312-739-3286 — E-mail: pkleppetsch@cassiday.com

James W. Kopriva — Lewis University College of Law, J.D., 1979 — Admitted to Bar, 1979, Illinois; U.S. District Court, Northern District of Illinois including Trial Bar; Supreme Court of Illinois — Practice Areas: Medical Liability; Environmental and Toxic Injury — Tel: 312-444-2495 — E-mail: jkopriva@cassiday.com

Brandon J. Kroft — DePaul University College of Law, J.D., 1999 — Admitted to Bar, 1999, Illinois; 2002, Indiana; U.S. District Court, Central and Northern Districts of Illinois; U.S. District Court, Northern District of Indiana; Supreme Court of Illinois; Supreme Court of Indiana — Army Reserve and National Guard — Practice Areas: Construction Law; Insurance Law; Product Liability; Transportation — Resident Chesterton, IN and Chicago, IL Office — Tel: 219-663-5575 — E-mail: bkroft@cassiday.com

Robin B. Levin — The John Marshall Law School in Chicago, J.D., 1999 — Admitted to Bar, 1999, Illinois; U.S. District Court, Northern District of Illinois; U.S. Court of Appeals, Seventh Circuit; Supreme Court of Illinois — Practice Areas: Medical Liability; Product Liability; Professional Liability; Legal Liability; Transportation — Resident Libertyville, IL Office — Tel: 847-932-6926 — E-mail: rlevin@cassiday.com

Anthony J. Longo — The John Marshall Law School, J.D. (Dean's Scholar), 2004 — Admitted to Bar, 2004, Illinois; U.S. District Court, Northern District of Illinois; Supreme Court of Illinois — Practice Areas: Appellate; Construction Law; Medical Liability — Tel: 312-444-1898 — E-mail: alongo@cassiday.com

Yaro M. Melnyk — IIT, Chicago-Kent College of Law, J.D. (with honors), 1999 — Admitted to Bar, 2000, Illinois; U.S. District Court, Northern District of Illinois; Supreme Court of Illinois — Practice Areas: Construction Law; Product Liability; Transportation; Professional Liability; Accountant Liability — Tel: 312-444-1687 — E-mail: ymelnyk@cassiday.com

Jonathan P. Mincieli — St. John's University School of Law, J.D. (cum laude), 1996 — Admitted to Bar, 1997, New York; 2000, New Jersey; 2001, Illinois; U.S. District Court, Eastern, Southern and Western Districts of New York; U.S. District Court, Northern District of Indiana; U.S. District Court, Central and Northern Districts of Illinois; Supreme Court of Illinois; Supreme Court of New Jersey; Supreme Court of the State of New York — Practice Areas: Construction Law; Medical Liability — Resident Naperville, IL Office — Tel: 630-328-2984 — E-mail: jmincieli@cassiday.com

Tanya B. Park — Valparaiso University School of Law, J.D., 1998 — Admitted to Bar, 1998, Illinois; U.S. District Court, Central and Northern Districts of Illinois; Supreme Court of Illinois — Languages: Spanish, German — Practice Areas: Medical Liability; Product Liability; Professional Liability; Legal Liability — Tel: 312-444-1816 — E-mail: tpark@cassiday.com

Heather F. Pfeffer — DePaul University College of Law, J.D., 2005 — Admitted to Bar, 2005, Illinois; Supreme Court of Illinois; U.S. District Court, Northern District of Illinois — Practice Areas: Medical Liability; Product Liability — Tel: 312-444-1879 — E-mail: hpfeffer@cassiday.com

William W. Ranard — University of Missouri-Columbia School of Law, J.D., 1992 — Admitted to Bar, 1992, Illinois; 1993, Missouri; 1999, Wisconsin; U.S. District Court, Northern District of Illinois; U.S. District Court, Northern District of Indiana; Supreme Court of Illinois; Supreme Court of Wisconsin — Practice Areas: Medical Liability; Nursing Home Liability; Long-Term Care; Construction Law; Insurance Law; Product Liability; Professional Liability; Transportation — Resident Rockford, IL Office — Tel: 815-962-8357 — E-mail: wranard@cassiday.com

Tami J. Reding-Brubaker — IIT, Chicago-Kent College of Law, J.D. (cum laude), 1983 — Admitted to Bar, 1983, Illinois; U.S. District Court, Northern District of Illinois including Trial Bar; Supreme Court of Illinois — Practice Areas: Construction Law; Employment Law; Medical Liability; Product Liability — Resident Libertyville, IL Office — Tel: 847-932-6927 — E-mail: treding@cassiday.com

Cassiday Schade LLP, Chicago, IL (Continued)

John J. Reid — IIT, Chicago-Kent College of Law, J.D., 1996 — Admitted to Bar, 1996, Illinois; 2005, Wisconsin; U.S. District Court, Northern District of Illinois including Trial Bar; U.S. District Court, Eastern District of Wisconsin; U.S. Bankruptcy Court, Eastern District of Wisconsin; U.S. Bankruptcy Court, Western District of Wisconsin; Supreme Court of Illinois; Supreme Court of Wisconsin — Practice Areas: Commercial Law; Medical Liability; Nursing Home Liability; Long-Term Care; Professional Liability; Transportation — Resident Libertyville, IL and Milwaukee, WI Office — Tel: 847-932-6928 — E-mail: jreid@cassiday.com

Kimberly L. Robinson — Northern Illinois University College of Law, J.D., 1989 — Admitted to Bar, 1989, Illinois; U.S. District Court, Northern District of Illinois; Supreme Court of Illinois — United Way, Diversity Alliance — Practice Areas: Medical Liability — Tel: 312-444-2472 — E-mail: krobinson@cassiday.com

Mark A. Sansone — Valparaiso University School of Law, J.D., 2000 — Admitted to Bar, 2000, Illinois; U.S. District Court, Northern District of Illinois; Supreme Court of Illinois — Practice Areas: Construction Law; Medical Liability — Resident Naperville, IL Office — Tel: 630-328-2985 — E-mail: msansone@cassiday.com

Jennifer Burke Santoro — Indiana University School of Law, J.D., 1997 — Admitted to Bar, 1997, Illinois; U.S. District Court, Northern District of Illinois; Supreme Court of Illinois — Medicare Set-Aside Certified Consultant; National Alliance of Medicare Set-Aside Professionals (NAMSAP) — Practice Areas: Workers' Compensation; Commercial Law; Construction Law; Medicare Set-Aside Practice; Medical Liability; Environmental and Toxic Injury — Tel: 312-444-1872 — E-mail: jburke@cassiday.com

Rudolf G. Schade, Jr. — The John Marshall Law School, J.D. (with honors), 1968 — Admitted to Bar, 1968, Illinois; U.S. District Court, Northern District of Illinois including Trial Bar; Supreme Court of Illinois — Languages: German — Practice Areas: Commercial Law; Construction Law; Professional Liability; Accountant Liability; Architects and Engineers; Legal Liability; Product Liability; Mediation; Arbitration; Medical Liability; Nursing Home Liability; Long-Term Care — Tel: 312-444-2456 — E-mail: rschade@cassiday.com

Therese S. Seeley — DePaul University College of Law, J.D., 1982 — Admitted to Bar, 1982, Illinois; U.S. District Court, Northern District of Illinois including Trial Bar; Supreme Court of Illinois — Practice Areas: Construction Law; Medical Liability; Product Liability; Transportation — Resident Naperville, IL Office — Tel: 630-328-2981 — E-mail: tseeley@cassiday.com

John N. Seibel — University of Detroit Mercy School of Law, J.D. (magna cum laude), 1978 — Admitted to Bar, 1981, Illinois; U.S. District Court, Northern District of Illinois including Trial Bar; Supreme Court of Illinois — Practice Areas: Medical Liability; Professional Liability; Nursing Home Litigation; Long-Term Care — Tel: 312-444-2482 — E-mail: jseibel@cassiday.com

Stephanie Rachford Stomberg — Loyola University Chicago School of Law, J.D., 1997 — Admitted to Bar, 1997, Illinois; U.S. District Court, Northern District of Illinois; Supreme Court of Illinois — Practice Areas: Commercial Law; Environmental and Toxic Injury; Medical Liability; Product Liability; Professional Liability; Legal Liability — Tel: 312-444-1660 — E-mail: sstomberg@cassiday.com

Douglas Strohm — The University of Iowa College of Law, J.D., 1990 — Admitted to Bar, 1990, Illinois; U.S. District Court, Northern District of Illinois; Supreme Court of Illinois — Practice Areas: Construction Law; Environmental and Toxic Injury; Product Liability; Professional Liability; Transportation — Resident Naperville, IL Office — Tel: 630-328-2982 — E-mail: dstrohm@cassiday.com

Robert H. Summers, Jr. — The John Marshall Law School, J.D., 1991 — Admitted to Bar, 1991, Illinois; U.S. District Court, Northern District of Illinois; U.S. District Court, Eastern and Western Districts of Arkansas; Supreme Court of Illinois — Practice Areas: Construction Law; Employment Law; Medical Liability; Product Liability; Professional Liability; Legal Liability; Transportation — Tel: 312-444-1892 — E-mail: rsummers@cassiday.com

Trisha K. Tesmer — DePaul University College of Law, J.D., 2001 — Admitted to Bar, 2001, Illinois; Supreme Court of Illinois; U.S. District Court, Northern District of Illinois including Trial Bar; U.S. Supreme Court; U.S. Court of Appeals, Seventh Circuit — Practice Areas: Appellate; Commercial Law; Employment Law; Environmental and Toxic Injury; Medical Liability — Tel: 312-444-1870

Christine L. Trimarco — The John Marshall Law School in Chicago, J.D., 1997 — Admitted to Bar, 1998, Illinois; U.S. District Court, Northern District of Illinois; Supreme Court of Illinois — Practice Areas: Construction Law; Product Liability; Professional Liability — Tel: 312-444-1614 — E-mail: ctrimarco@cassiday.com

CHICAGO ILLINOIS

Cassiday Schade LLP, Chicago, IL (Continued)

Luisa F. Trujillo — Washington University School of Law, J.D., 1993; DePaul University College of Law, LL.M., 1999 — Admitted to Bar, 1993, Illinois; U.S. District Court, Northern District of Illinois; Supreme Court of Illinois — Languages: Spanish — Practice Areas: Medical Liability; Nursing Home Liability; Long-Term Care; Professional Liability — Tel: 312-444-1663 — E-mail: ltrujillo@cassiday.com

Lisa Velez — University of California at Los Angeles School of the Law, J.D., 1997 — Admitted to Bar, 1998, Illinois; Supreme Court of Illinois; U.S. District Court, Northern District of Illinois — Practice Areas: Medical Liability; Nursing Home Liability; Long-Term Care; Product Liability — Tel: 312-444-2475 — E-mail: lvelez@cassiday.com

Bruce M. Wall — IIT, Chicago-Kent College of Law, J.D., 1976 — Admitted to Bar, 1976, Illinois; U.S. District Court, Northern District of Illinois; U.S. Court of Appeals, Seventh Circuit; U.S. District Court, Southern District of Illinois; Supreme Court of Illinois; U.S. District Court, Northern District of Indiana — Practice Areas: Product Liability; Medical Liability; Construction Law; Mediation; Arbitration — Tel: 312-444-2483 — E-mail: bwall@cassiday.com

Matthew H. Weller — IIT, Chicago-Kent College of Law, J.D., 2002 — Admitted to Bar, 2002, Illinois; U.S. District Court, Northern District of Illinois; Supreme Court of Illinois — Practice Areas: Construction Law; Medical Liability; Nursing Home Litigation; Long-Term Care; Product Liability; Professional Liability; Transportation; Workers' Compensation — Tel: 312-739-3289 — E-mail: mweller@cassiday.com

Sally J. Zimmerman — Northern Illinois University College of Law, J.D., 1991 — Admitted to Bar, 1991, Illinois; 2013, Wisconsin; U.S. District Court, Northern District of Illinois; Supreme Court of Illinois; Supreme Court of Wisconsin — Registered Nurse, (Illinois) — Practice Areas: Medical Malpractice; Professional Liability; Nursing Home Litigation — Resident Libertyville, IL Office — Tel: 847-932-6925 — E-mail: szimmerman@cassiday.com

Of Counsel

Lisa L. Curshellas
Don Pesce
Maria L. Vertuno
Constance R. O'Neill
Julie A. Teuscher

Associates

Jessica D. Allan
Lindsay R. Boyd
Daniel J. Broderick, Jr.
Alex E. Campos
Myriah F. Conaughty
Cliff Demosthene
Matthew A. Eliaser
Lea Ann C. Fracasso
Stephen J. Gorski
Jacquelyn M. Hill
Anne M. Junia
Blair Kipnis
Jillian A. Mikrut
James F. Maruna
Henry Ortiz
Michael D. Pisano
Daniel J. Pylman
Margaret A. Shipitalo
Whitney K. Siehl
Rachel S. Stern
Carrie Lynn P. Vine
Daniel Basler
Matthew H. Brandabur
Todd R. Burgett
Jonathan E. Cavins
Brian C. Cuttone
Lindsay Drecoll Brown
Thomas A. Fitzgerald
Heather T. Gilbert
Patrick E. Halliday
Kimberly M. Hume
Jamie R. Kauther
Joseph J. Lombardo
Michael P. Moothart
Ronald Neroda
Joseph A. Panatera
Laura S. Platt
William H. Schramm
Victoria S. Shoemaker
Matthew S. Sims
Lynsey A. Stewart
John J. Vitanovec

Christensen Ehret

135 South LaSalle Street, Suite 4200
Chicago, Illinois 60603
Telephone: 312-634-1014
Fax: 312-634-1018
E-Mail: mchristensen@christenlaw.com
E-Mail: law@christenlaw.com
www.christensenlaw.com

(Torrance, CA Office*: 1629 Cravens Avenue, 90501)
 (Tel: 310-222-8680)
 (Fax: 310-222-5752)

Christensen Ehret, Chicago, IL (Continued)

(Sacramento, CA Office*: 2485 Natomas Park Drive, Suite 315, 95814)
 (Tel: 916-443-6909)
 (Fax: 916-313-0645)

Established: 1994

Construction Law, Employment Law, Energy, Insurance Law, Product Liability, Reinsurance, Subrogation, Maritime Law, Banking, Financial and Professional Liability

Insurance Clients

QBE Underwriting Agency, Ltd.   Zurich Specialties London Limited

Non-Insurance Clients

Walsh Group

Partners

Mark E. Christensen — Wheaton College, B.A. (with high honors), 1977; Northwestern University, J.D. (cum laude), 1982 — Admitted to Bar, 1982, Illinois; 2003, California; 2009, New York; 2010, Texas; 1982, U.S. District Court, Northern District of Illinois including Trial Bar; 1988, U.S. Court of Appeals, Sixth and Seventh Circuits; 1989, U.S. Supreme Court; 1992, U.S. District Court, District of North Dakota; 1993, U.S. District Court, Eastern and Western Districts of Michigan; 1993, U.S. District Court, Western District of Wisconsin; 1994, U.S. District Court, Southern District of Illinois; 2007, U.S. Court of Appeals, Third Circuit; 2008, U.S. Court of Federal Claims — Member American and Illinois State Bar Associations; State Bar of California; National Association of Railroad Trial Counsel (Treasurer, Secretary and President, Illinois Division, 1992-1994) — E-mail: mchristensen@christensenlaw.com

John B. Ehret — Cornell University, B.M.E., 1952; Northwestern University, J.D., 1958 — Admitted to Bar, 1958, Illinois; U.S. District Court, Northern District of Illinois; U.S. Court of Federal Claims — Member American, Illinois State and Chicago Bar Associations — E-mail: jehret@christensenlaw.com

Nathan A. Hall — Hillsdale College, B.A., 2000; University of Notre Dame Law School, J.D., 2003 — Admitted to Bar, 2003, Ohio; 2004, Michigan; 2012, Illinois; U.S. District Court, Northern and Southern Districts of Ohio; U.S. District Court, Eastern and Western Districts of Michigan; U.S. District Court, Northern District of Illinois — E-mail: nhall@christensenlaw.com

Michael D. Hirsch — University of California, Davis, B.A., 1991; Whittier Law School, J.D., 1996 — Admitted to Bar, 1996, California; U.S. District Court, Central District of California; 2000, U.S. District Court, Southern District of California — Member State Bar of California — Resident Torrance, CA Office — E-mail: mhirsch@christensenlaw.com

Jack C. Hsu — The University of Chicago, A.B., 1990; Indiana University, J.D., 1993 — Admitted to Bar, 1993, Illinois; 2003, California; 2009, New York; 2009, Wisconsin; 1993, U.S. District Court, Northern District of Illinois; 2002, U.S. Court of Appeals, Sixth Circuit; 2003, U.S. District Court, Central, Northern and Southern Districts of California; U.S. Court of Appeals, Seventh Circuit; 2007, U.S. Court of Appeals, Third Circuit; 2008, U.S. Court of Federal Claims; 2009, U.S. Court of Appeals, Ninth Circuit — Member American Bar Association (Vice Chair, Economics of Tort and Insurance Law Practice Section, 1998-2001); Illinois State Bar Association; State Bar of California; Defense Research Institute — E-mail: jhsu@christensenlaw.com

Katherine Amelotte Jones — Lawrence University, B.A. (cum laude), 1994; Washington and Lee University, J.D., 1998 — Admitted to Bar, 1998, West Virginia; 2002, Illinois; 2006, New York; 2009, Wisconsin; 1998, U.S. District Court, Southern District of West Virginia; 1999, U.S. Court of Appeals, Fourth Circuit; 2002, U.S. Court of Appeals, Third Circuit; 2003, U.S. District Court, Northern District of Illinois — Member American and Illinois State Bar Associations — E-mail: kjones@christensenlaw.com

Jeffrey D. Naffziger — The University of Iowa, B.A., 1996; Loyola University Chicago School of Law, J.D., 2001 — Admitted to Bar, 2001, Illinois; 2011, Indiana; 2002, U.S. District Court, Northern District of Illinois; 2003, U.S. District Court, Central District of Illinois — Member Chicago Council of Lawyers — E-mail: jnaffziger@christensenlaw.com

Edward E. Sipes — Arizona State University, B.S., 1991; University of La Verne, J.D., 1994 — Admitted to Bar, 1994, California; 1994, U.S. District Court, Central, Northern and Southern Districts of California; U.S. Court of Appeals, Ninth Circuit — Member State Bar of California — Resident Torrance, California Office — E-mail: esipes@christensenlaw.com

ILLINOIS   **CHICAGO**

Christensen Ehret, Chicago, IL   (Continued)

Associates

Paal Bakstad — University of California, Santa Barbara, B.S., 1991; Pepperdine University School of Law, J.D., 1996 — Admitted to Bar, 1996, California — Resident Torrance, CA Office — E-mail: pbakstad@christensenlaw.com

Christopher C. Cassidy — Harvard University, B.A., 1991; Vermont Law School, J.D., 1994 — Admitted to Bar, 1994, Vermont; 2004, Illinois; U.S. District Court, Northern District of Illinois — E-mail: ccassidy@christensenlaw.com

Paul S. Cooley — Loyola Marymount University, B.A., 1987; Loyola Law School, J.D., 1990 — Admitted to Bar, 1990, California; U.S. District Court, Central District of California — Resident Torrance, CA Office — E-mail: pcooley@christensenlaw.com

Bradley V. DeBlanc — University of California, Davis, B.A., 1994; Southwestern University School of Law, J.D., 1997 — Admitted to Bar, 1997, California; U.S. District Court, Central District of California — Resident Torrance, CA Office — E-mail: bdeblanc@christensenlaw.com

Rachel M. Garcia — Indiana University, B.A., 2003; DePaul University College of Law, J.D., 2006 — Admitted to Bar, 2006, Illinois; U.S. District Court, Northern District of Illinois — E-mail: rgarcia@christensenlaw.com

Kathleen M. Gilbert — Northwestern University School of Law, J.D., 2002 — Admitted to Bar, 2002, California; 2003, Illinois; U.S. District Court, Eastern District of California — Resident Sacramento, CA Office — E-mail: kgilbert@christensenlaw.com

Marcella S. Novellano — Miami University, B.A., 2001; Boston University School of Law, J.D., 2004 — Admitted to Bar, 2004, Ohio (Inactive); 2006, Illinois; U.S. District Court, Northern District of Illinois; 2009, U.S. District Court, Eastern District of Michigan — E-mail: mnovellano@christensenlaw.com

Stephanie J. Rocco — Merrimack College, B.S., 2003; Quinnipiac College, J.D., 2007 — Admitted to Bar, 2007, Connecticut; 2008, New York; 2013, Illinois; U.S. District Court, District of Connecticut; U.S. District Court, Northern District of Illinois — E-mail: srocco@christensenlaw.com

Kevin J. Rodriguez — University of California, Los Angeles, B.A., 1999; University of San Diego School of Law, J.D., 2002 — Admitted to Bar, 2003, California; 2007, U.S. District Court, Central District of California — Member State Bar of California — Resident Torrance, CA Office — E-mail: krodriguez@christensenlaw.com

Kelly A. Seelig — University of California, San Diego, B.A., 1999; Loyola Law School, J.D., 2003 — Admitted to Bar, 2003, California; U.S. District Court, District of Connecticut; U.S. District Court, Northern District of Illinois — E-mail: ksellig@christensenlaw.com

Scott J. Sterling — University of California, Davis, B.A., 1998; Loyola Law School, J.D., 2002 — Admitted to Bar, 2002, California; U.S. District Court, Central District of California — Member State Bar of California — Resident Torrance, CA Office — E-mail: ssterling@christensenlaw.com

Jennifer K. Stinnett — University of North Texas, B.B.A., 1993; Southwestern University School of Law, J.D., 2003 — Admitted to Bar, 2003, California; U.S. District Court, Central and Eastern Districts of California — Member American and Los Angeles Bar Associations — Resident Sacramento, CA Office — E-mail: jstinnett@christensenlaw.com

Matthew E. Szwajkowski — Northwestern University, B.S., 2000; Cornell University Law School, J.D., 2004 — Admitted to Bar, 2005, New York; 2007, Illinois; U.S. District Court, Eastern and Southern Districts of New York; U.S. District Court, Northern District of Illinois — E-mail: mszwajkowski@christensenlaw.com

Steven Tsuyuki — San Jose University, B.A., 1991; University of the Pacific, McGeorge School of Law, J.D., 2004 — Admitted to Bar, 2008, California — Resident Sacramento, CA Office — E-mail: stsuyuki@christensenlaw.com

Kirsten Radler Waack — Duquesne University, B.A. (cum laude), 1991; Wake Forest University, J.D., 1994 — Phi Alpha Delta — Law Clerk to Judge John W. Reece, Ohio Ninth District Court of Appeals (1995-1997); Justice Deborah L. Cook, Ohio Supreme Court (1998-1999) — Admitted to Bar, 1994, Ohio; 1999, Illinois; U.S. District Court, Northern District of Illinois; U.S. District Court, Northern District of Ohio; 2002, U.S. Court of Appeals, Sixth Circuit; 2007, U.S. Court of Appeals, Third Circuit — Member Illinois State, Ohio State and Chicago Bar Associations — Co-Editor In Chief, The Jurist — E-mail: kwaack@christensenlaw.com

Michael S. Weisenbach — Eastern Michigan University, B.S., 2006; The Ohio State University Moritz College of Law, J.D., 2009 — Admitted to Bar, 2009, Michigan; 2014, Illinois — E-mail: mweisenbach@christensenlaw.com

James W. Whitemyer — University of California, Santa Barbara, B.A., 1991; Pepperdine University School of Law, J.D., 1996 — Admitted to Bar, 1996,

Christensen Ehret, Chicago, IL   (Continued)

California; U.S. District Court, Central, Northern and Southern Districts of California; U.S. Court of Appeals, Ninth Circuit — Resident Torrance, CA Office — E-mail: jwhitemyer@christensenlaw.com

Joshua H. Willert — University of California, Davis, B.A., 1998; University of the Pacific, McGeorge School of Law, J.D. (with distinction), 2004 — Admitted to Bar, 2004, California; U.S. District Court, Eastern District of California; 2005, U.S. District Court, Northern District of California; 2009, U.S. Court of Appeals, Ninth Circuit — Member State Bar of California — Resident Sacramento, CA Office — E-mail: jwillert@christensenlaw.com

Counsel

James A. Knox — Southern Methodist University, B.A., 1980; The University of Texas School of Law, J.D., 1984 — Admitted to Bar, 1984, Texas; 1985, Oklahoma; 1987, Illinois; U.S. District Court, Central, Northern and Southern Districts of Illinois; U.S. District Court, Western District of Michigan; U.S. District Court, Eastern District of Wisconsin; U.S. District Court, Western District of Oklahoma; U.S. Court of Appeals, Seventh, Tenth and Eleventh Circuits — E-mail: jknox@christensenlaw.com

Clausen Miller P.C.

10 South LaSalle Street
Chicago, Illinois 60603-1098
  Telephone: 312-855-1010
  Fax: 312-606-7777
  Toll Free: 800-826-3505
  E-Mail: info@clausen.com
  www.clausen.com

(Additional Offices: Irvine, CA; Florham Park, NJ; New York, NY; London, United Kingdom; Rome, Italy; Brussels, Belgium; Shanghai, China-PRC; Düsseldorf, Germany; Paris, France)

Established: 1936

Fidelity and Surety, Medical Malpractice, Professional Liability, Subrogation, Admiralty and Maritime Law, Employment Law, Intellectual Property, Premises Liability, Product Liability, Transportation, Appellate Practice, Banking, Bankruptcy, Business Litigation, Commercial Litigation, Construction Litigation, Corporate Law, Directors and Officers Liability, Environmental Coverage, Estate Planning, Toxic Torts, Securities, Reinsurance, Real Estate, Municipal Law, Municipal Liability, Mass Tort, Insurance Coverage, International Law, Health Care Liability, Insurance Law, Insurance Litigation, Insurance Policy Enforcement, Insurance Regulation, Insurance Claim Analysis and Evaluation, Insurance Corporate Practice, Insurance Defense, First Party Matters, Mold Litigation, Appellate, Intellectual Property, Healthcare Fraud

Firm Profile: Founded over 75 years ago, Clausen Miller represents businesses, insurers, and professionals through strategic, cost-effective litigation and counseling across the nation and around the globe. With over 130 attorneys practicing in four U.S. offices, Shanghai, China and London, England, Clausen Miller serves as international, national, regional and local counsel to numerous insurance companies, corporations and financial clients. In addition, the Firm partners with Clausen Miller Europe, a multi-national partnership with English, French, Italian, Belgian, German and American affiliates.

While maintaining the firm's core practice of serving and representing the insurance industry, particularly with regard to analyzing coverage under policies, defending insurers when sued and prosecuting subrogation actions for or on behalf of insurers, the firm counsels clients on a broad range of commercial litigation, insurance and liability issues.

Insurance Clients

Fireman's Fund Insurance Company
The Hartford Insurance Group
Industrial Risk Insurers
Lloyd's

Great American Insurance Companies
Illinois State Medical Insurance Services, Inc.
Ohio Casualty Group

CHICAGO ILLINOIS

Clausen Miller P.C., Chicago, IL (Continued)

Old Republic Insurance Company
St. Paul Fire and Marine Insurance Company
Royal Specialty Underwriting, Inc.
Zurich American Insurance Company

Partners

W. Gregory Aimonette — DePauw University, B.A., 1994; Northern Illinois University College of Law, J.D., 1997 — Admitted to Bar, 1998, Illinois — E-mail: waimonette@clausen.com

Ivar R. Azeris — University of Illinois, B.A., 1970; Boston College, J.D., 1973 — Admitted to Bar, 1974, Illinois — E-mail: iazeris@clausen.com

Alec M. Barinholtz*** — Northern Illinois University, B.S., 1979; Southwestern University School of Law, J.D. (magna cum laude), 1988 — Admitted to Bar, 1988, California — Resident Irvine, CA Office — Tel: 949-260-3100 — E-mail: abarinholtz@clausen.com

Diane M. Baron — Northwestern University, B.S. (with high honors), 1981; Northwestern University School of Law, J.D., 1984 — Admitted to Bar, 1984, Illinois; 1997, New York — E-mail: dbaron@clausen.com

Michael W. Basil — University of Michigan, B.A., 1990; Loyola University, M.B.A., 2001; Saint Louis University School of Law, J.D. (with honors), 1995 — Admitted to Bar, 1995, Missouri; 1996, Illinois — E-mail: mbasil@clausen.com

Colleen A. Beverly — University of Illinois, B.S., 1996; DePaul University College of Law, J.D. (Dean's List), 1999 — Admitted to Bar, 1999, Illinois — E-mail: cbeverly@clausen.com

James J. Bigoness — St. Joseph's College, B.S., 1976; DePaul University, J.D., 1982 — Admitted to Bar, 1982, Illinois — E-mail: jbigoness@clausen.com

Paul Bozych — University of Illinois, B.A., 1985; DePaul University College of Law, J.D. (with honors), 1988 — Admitted to Bar, 1988, Illinois — E-mail: pbozych@clausen.com

Paul W. Daugherity — Iowa State University, B.S., 1997; State University of New York at Albany, M.A., 2000; DePaul University College of Law, J.D., 2005 — Admitted to Bar, 2005, Illinois — E-mail: pdaugherity@clausen.com

Michael L. Duffy — Miami University, B.A. (magna cum laude, Phi Beta Kappa), 1997; The Ohio State University Moritz College of Law, J.D., 2000 — Admitted to Bar, 2000, Illinois — E-mail: mduffy@clausen.com

Rodd E. Elges — Illinois State University, B.S., 1988; Northern Illinois University, M.A., 1991; The John Marshall Law School, J.D., 1998 — Admitted to Bar, 1998, Illinois — E-mail: relges@clausen.com

Margaret Hupp Fahey — University of Missouri-Columbia, B.J. (with high honors), 1983; University of Illinois, J.D., 1986 — Admitted to Bar, 1986, Illinois — E-mail: mfahey@clausen.com

Ian R. Feldman*** — State University of New York at Binghamton, B.A. (cum laude), 1993; Hofstra University School of Law, J.D., 1996 — Admitted to Bar, 1997, New York; New Jersey; 1999, California — Resident Irvine, CA Office — Tel: 949-260-3100 — E-mail: ifeldman@clausen.com

Joseph J. Ferrini — Loyola University Chicago, B.A., 1999; Loyola University Chicago School of Law, J.D. (magna cum laude), 2007 — Admitted to Bar, 2007, Illinois — E-mail: jferrini@clausen.com

Dennis D. Fitzpatrick — Marquette University, B.A., 1986; DePaul University, J.D., 1989 — Admitted to Bar, 1989, Illinois; 1991, District of Columbia; 1992, Minnesota; Wisconsin — E-mail: dfitzpatrick@clausen.com

George K. Flynn — Illinois State University, B.S., 1993; Thomas M. Cooley Law School, J.D., 1997 — Admitted to Bar, 1997, Illinois — E-mail: gflynn@clausen.com

Steven J. Fried** — Yeshiva University, B.A., 1987; New York University, J.D., 1990 — Admitted to Bar, 1991, New York — Resident New York, NY Office — Tel: 212-805-3900 — E-mail: sfried@clausen.com

Brian Gitnik** — State University of New York, B.S., 1997; St. John's University School of Law, J.D., 2000 — Admitted to Bar, 2000, New York; 2003, Connecticut — Resident New York, NY Office — Tel: 212-805-3900 — E-mail: bgitnik@clausen.com

Michael W. Goodin*** — University of California, B.S., 1976; University of the Pacific, McGeorge School of Law, J.D., 1989 — Admitted to Bar, 1989, California — Resident Irvine, CA Office — Tel: 949-260-3100 — E-mail: mgoodin@clausen.com

Thomas S. Gozdziak — Bradley University, B.S., 1990; The John Marshall Law School, J.D., 1995 — Admitted to Bar, 1995, Illinois — E-mail: tgozdziak@clausen.com

Michael R. Grimm, Sr. — University of Illinois, B.A. (with honors), 1973; The John Marshall Law School, J.D. (with distinction), 1978 — Admitted to Bar, 1978, Illinois — E-mail: mgrimm@clausen.com

Clausen Miller P.C., Chicago, IL (Continued)

John T. Groark — Loyola University, B.S., 1976; The John Marshall Law School, J.D., 1979; DePaul University, LL.M., 1984 — Admitted to Bar, 1979, Illinois — E-mail: jgroark@clausen.com

Betsy Grover — University of Wisconsin, B.A., 1998; Washington University, J.D., 2001 — Admitted to Bar, 2001, Illinois — E-mail: bgrover@clausen.com

William J. Hacker — DePaul University, B.S., 1973; The John Marshall Law School, J.D., 1976 — Admitted to Bar, 1976, Illinois — E-mail: whacker@clausen.com

Jay D. Harker*** — Brigham Young University, B.S. (magna cum laude), 1990; University of California, Berkeley Boalt Hall School of Law, J.D., 1993 — Admitted to Bar, 1993, California — Resident Irvine, CA Office — Tel: 949-260-3100 — E-mail: jharker@clausen.com

Kimberly A. Hartman — Clemson University, B.A. (cum laude), 1999; University of Maryland School of Law, J.D., 2002 — Admitted to Bar, 2002, Illinois; Maryland — E-mail: khartman@clausen.com

David M. Heilmann — University of Illinois, B.S., 1984; DePaul University College of Law, J.D., 1987 — Admitted to Bar, 1987, Illinois — E-mail: dheilmann@clausen.com

J. Ryan Hemingway — University of California, Los Angeles, B.A. (magna cum laude), 1996; Southwestern University School of Law, J.D., 1999 — Admitted to Bar, 1999, California — Languages: Mandarin Chinese — Resident Shanghai, China Office — Tel: 862151175428 — E-mail: rhemingway@clausen.com

Christopher Henson — Millsaps College, B.A., 1991; Southern Illinois University Law School, J.D., 1995 — Admitted to Bar, 1996, Illinois — E-mail: chenson@clausen.com

Harvey R. Herman — University of Michigan, B.A., 1977; University of Michigan Law School, J.D., 1982 — Admitted to Bar, 1982, Illinois — E-mail: hherman@clausen.com

Celeste A. Hill — University of Illinois, B.A. (Phi Beta Kappa), 1982; Northwestern University School of Law, J.D., 1986 — Admitted to Bar, 1986, Illinois — E-mail: chill@clausen.com

James M. Hoey — Purdue University, B.S.M.E., 1974; Loyola University Chicago School of Law, J.D., 1977 — Admitted to Bar, 1977, Illinois — E-mail: jhoey@clausen.com

Richard G. Howser — University of Illinois, B.A., 1973; Loyola University Chicago, J.D., 1977 — Admitted to Bar, 1977, Illinois — E-mail: rhowser@clausen.com

John M. Hynes — Northwestern University, B.A., 1976; Loyola University, J.D., 1979 — Admitted to Bar, 1979, Illinois — E-mail: jhynes@clausen.com

Andrew C. Jacobson****** — University of Rochester, B.A., 1973; New England School of Law, J.D., 1976 — Admitted to Bar, 1977, Massachusetts; New York; 1988, New Jersey — Resident New York, NY and Florham Park, NJ Office — Tel: 212-805-3900 — E-mail: ajacobson@clausen.com

Richard M. Kaplan — Johns Hopkins University, B.A., 1972; Northwestern University School of Law, J.D., 1975 — Admitted to Bar, 1975, Illinois — E-mail: rkaplan@clausen.com

Edward M. Kay — Loyola University, B.A., 1974; Northern Illinois University College of Law, J.D., 1979 — Admitted to Bar, 1979, Illinois — E-mail: ekay@clausen.com

Kimbley A. Kearney — Saint Mary's College, B.A., 1980; Tulane University of Louisiana, M.B.A., 1984; J.D. (cum laude), 1984 — Admitted to Bar, 1984, Louisiana; 1991, Illinois; New York — E-mail: kkearney@clausen.com

Melinda S. Kollross — DePaul University, B.A. (with highest honors), 1989; Illinois Institute of Technology, Chicago-Kent College of Law, J.D. (with high honors), 1992 — Admitted to Bar, 1992, Illinois; 1999, New York — E-mail: mkollross@clausen.com

Ilene M. Korey — University of Colorado at Boulder, B.A., 1979; DePaul University College of Law, J.D., 1983 — Admitted to Bar, 1983, Illinois — E-mail: ikorey@clausen.com

Bradford S. Krause — University of Illinois at Urbana-Champaign, B.A., 1994; DePaul University College of Law, J.D., 1997 — Admitted to Bar, 1997, Illinois — E-mail: bkrause@clausen.com

Eric T. Krejci** — Binghamton University, B.A. (cum laude), 1996; Brooklyn Law School, J.D., 1999 — Admitted to Bar, 1999, New York — Resident New York, NY Office — Tel: 212-805-3900 — E-mail: ekrejci@clausen.com

Tyler Jay Lory** — University of Rochester, B.A., 1978; Boston College Law School, J.D., 1981 — Admitted to Bar, 1981, Illinois; 1989, New York —

Clausen Miller P.C., Chicago, IL (Continued)

Resident New York, NY Office — Tel: 212-805-3900 — E-mail: tlory@clausen.com

Mindy M. Medley — Washington University in St. Louis, B.A., 1998; Washington University in St. Louis School of Law, J.D., 2001 — Admitted to Bar, 2001, Illinois — E-mail: mmedley@clausen.com

Courtney E. Murphy** — Fordham University, B.A., 1990; New York Law School, J.D., 1994 — Admitted to Bar, 1994, New Jersey; 1995, New York — Resident New York, NY Office — Tel: 212-805-3900 — E-mail: cmurphy@clausen.com

Jack J. Murphy — University of Notre Dame, B.A. (with honors), 2003; Loyola University Chicago School of Law, J.D., 2006 — Admitted to Bar, 2006, Illinois — E-mail: jmurphy@clausen.com

Richard L. Murphy — University of Notre Dame, B.A., 1973; Boston College Law School, J.D., 1976 — Admitted to Bar, 1976, Illinois — E-mail: rmurphy@clausen.com

Todd M. Murphy — University of Notre Dame, B.A., 1996; The John Marshall Law School, J.D. (cum laude), 2003 — Admitted to Bar, 2003, Illinois — E-mail: tmurphy@clausen.com

Paige M. Neel — Indiana University-Bloomington, B.A., 1998; Indiana University School of Law-Bloomington, J.D., 2001 — Admitted to Bar, 2001, Illinois; Indiana — Tel: pneel@clausen.com

Steven N. Novosad — Southern Illinois University, B.S., 1977; The John Marshall Law School, J.D., 1984 — Admitted to Bar, 1984, Illinois — E-mail: snovosad@clausen.com

Margaret J. Orbon — Saint Mary's College, B.A., 1973; Loyola University Chicago School of Law, J.D., 1976 — Admitted to Bar, 1976, Illinois — E-mail: morbon@clausen.com

Monica C. Palermo — University of Michigan - Ann Arbor, B.A., 1999; Loyola University Chicago School of Law, J.D. (Dean's List), 2002 — Admitted to Bar, 2003, Illinois — E-mail: mpalermo@clausen.com

Mark D. Paulson — Southern Illinois University, B.A., 1987; The John Marshall Law School, J.D. (cum laude), 1992 — Admitted to Bar, 1992, Illinois — E-mail: mpaulson@clausen.com

Amy Rich Paulus — Northwestern University, B.A., 1985; Northern Illinois University College of Law, J.D. (magna cum laude), 1989 — Admitted to Bar, 1989, Illinois — E-mail: apaulus@clausen.com

Erin E. Pellegrino — Illinois Benedictine College, B.A. (magna cum laude), 1994; The John Marshall Law School, J.D. (cum laude), 1998 — Admitted to Bar, 1998, Illinois — E-mail: epellegrino@clausen.com

Carl M. Perri****** — St. Bonaventure University, B.A., 1994; New York Law School, J.D., 1999 — Admitted to Bar, 1999, New York; New Jersey — Resident New York, NY and Florham Park, NJ Office — Tel: 212-805-3900 — E-mail: cperri@clausen.com

William P. Pistorius — University of Illinois, B.A., 1984; DePaul University College of Law, J.D., 1987 — Admitted to Bar, 1987, Illinois — E-mail: wpistorius@clausen.com

Dean S. Rauchwerger — Washington University in St. Louis, B.A., 1981; Washington University in St. Louis School of Law, J.D., 1984 — Admitted to Bar, 1984, Connecticut; 1985, New York; Illinois — E-mail: drauchwerger@clausen.com

Robert L. Reifenberg — Saint Mary's College, B.A. (cum laude), 1978; Northern Illinois University College of Law, J.D., 1981 — Admitted to Bar, 1981, Illinois — E-mail: rreifenberg@clausen.com

Brian J. Riordan — Eastern Illinois University, B.A., 1993; Loyola University Chicago School of Law, J.D., 1996 — Admitted to Bar, 1996, Illinois — E-mail: briordan@clausen.com

P. Scott Ritchie — Purdue University, B.S., 1983; DePaul University College of Law, J.D., 1989 — Admitted to Bar, 1989, Illinois — E-mail: pritchie@clausen.com

Thomas H. Ryerson — Northwestern University, B.A., 1973; Loyola University Chicago School of Law, J.D., 1976 — Admitted to Bar, 1976, Illinois — E-mail: tryerson@clausen.com

Don R. Sampen — Northwestern University, B.A., 1972; Northwestern University School of Law, J.D. (magna cum laude), 1975 — Admitted to Bar, 1975, Illinois — E-mail: dsampen@clausen.com

Dominick W. Savaiano — University of Illinois, B.A., 1978; Loyola University Chicago School of Law, J.D., 1981 — Admitted to Bar, 1981, Illinois — E-mail: dsavaiano@clausen.com

Christopher T. Scanlon** — Fordham University, B.A., 1988; St. John's University School of Law, J.D. (cum laude), 1996 — Admitted to Bar, 1997, New Jersey; New York — Resident New York, NY Office — Tel: 212-805-3900 — E-mail: cscanlon@clausen.com

Clausen Miller P.C., Chicago, IL (Continued)

Martin C. Sener — Northwestern University, B.S.E., 1981; The John Marshall Law School, J.D., 1984 — Admitted to Bar, 1984, Illinois — E-mail: msener@clausen.com

Ruth V. Simon****** — Queens College, B.A., 1971; Temple University Beasley School of Law, J.D., 1974 — Admitted to Bar, 1983, New York; 1985, New Jersey; District of Columbia — Resident Florham Park, NJ and New York, NY Office — Tel: 973-410-4130 — E-mail: rsimon@clausen.com

Mary F. Stafford — University of Illinois, B.A., 1973; The John Marshall Law School, J.D. (with highest honors), 1976 — Admitted to Bar, 1976, Illinois — E-mail: mstafford@clausen.com

Robert A. Stern****** — Union College, B.A., 1987; Boston University Law School, J.D., 1990 — Admitted to Bar, 1991, New York; 1998, Massachusetts; 2003, New Jersey — Resident New York, NY and Florham Park, NJ Office — E-mail: rstern@clausen.com

James R. Swinehart — University of Notre Dame, B.A. (cum laude), 1979; The University of Toledo College of Law, J.D., 1982 — Admitted to Bar, 1982, Illinois — E-mail: jswinehart@clausen.com

Joseph W. Szalyga** — Binghamton University, B.A., 2000; Brooklyn Law School, J.D., 2003 — Admitted to Bar, 2003, New York — Resident New York, NY Office — Tel: 212-805-3900 — E-mail: jszalyga@clausen.com

Andrew S. Turkish****** — Bowdoin College, B.A. (cum laude), 1986; Boston University School of Law, J.D., 1989 — Admitted to Bar, 1989, New Jersey; New York — Resident Florham Park, NJ & New York, NY Office — Tel: 973-410-4130 — E-mail: aturkish@clausen.com

Anthony P. Ulm — University of Illinois at Urbana-Champaign, B.A., 1994; Southern Illinois University School of Law, J.D., 1997 — Admitted to Bar, 1997, Illinois — E-mail: aulm@clausen.com

Michelle R. Valencic — Ohio University, B.A. (summa cum laude), 1992; Case Western Reserve University, M.S.S.A. (cum laude), 1996; Case Western Reserve University School of Law, J.D. (cum laude), 1996 — Admitted to Bar, 1996, Ohio; 1997, Illinois — E-mail: mvalencic@clausen.com

Matthew J. Van Dusen** — University of Central Florida, B.S., 1999; Quinnipiac University School of Law, J.D. (cum laude), 2003 — Admitted to Bar, 2003, Connecticut; New Jersey; New York — Resident New York, NY Office — Tel: 212-805-3900 — E-mail: mvandusen@clausen.com

Sava Alexander Vojcanin — DePauw University, B.A., 1985; Washington University School of Law, J.D., 1988 — Admitted to Bar, 1988, Illinois — E-mail: svojcanin@clausen.com

Robert E. Wilens — University of Michigan - Ann Arbor, B.G.S., 1987; Washington University School of Law, J.D., 1990 — Admitted to Bar, 1990, Illinois; 1997, Missouri — E-mail: rwilens@clausen.com

Mark W. Zimmerman — Southern Illinois University, B.S., 1983; DePaul University, J.D. (with honors), 1993 — Admitted to Bar, 1993, Illinois — E-mail: mzimmerman@clausen.com

Jacob R. Zissu** — United States Naval Academy, B.S., 1996; The Catholic University of America, Columbus School of Law, J.D., 2004 — Admitted to Bar, 2004, New York — Resident New York, NY Office — Tel: 212-805-3900 — E-mail: jzissu@clausen.com

Jane Beacham*****   Douglas A. Greer
Jonathan C. Hall*****   John P. Startin*****

Senior Counsel

Paul V. Esposito — St. Norbert College, B.A., 1972; Loyola University Chicago School of Law, J.D. (magna cum laude), 1975 — Admitted to Bar, 1975, Illinois — E-mail: pesposito@clausen.com

Of Counsel

Norman Chimenti — Yale University, B.A. (Dean's List), 1962; Yale Law School, LL.B., 1967 — Admitted to Bar, 1967, Illinois — Member Illinois State, DuPage County and Chicago Bar Associations — U.S. Marine Corps (1963-1968); American Spirit Honor Medal — Tel: 312-855-1010 — E-mail: nchimenti@clausen.com

Gilbert J. Schroeder — DePaul University, B.A., 1967; DePaul University College of Law, J.D., 1970 — Admitted to Bar, 1970, Illinois — E-mail: gschroeder@clausen.com

Associates

Ms. Rebecca Ahdoot**   Elise Allen
Lyndsey C. Bechtel**   Dawn Brehony**
Daniel R. Bryer   Thomas J. Byrne*****
Serena Cesani**   Nicholas A. Corsano**
John De Filippis**   William Dickinson

CHICAGO   ILLINOIS

Clausen Miller P.C., Chicago, IL   (Continued)

Allison K. Ferrini
Lynn M. Geerdes
Nathalie C. Hackett******
Timothy F. Jacobs
Thomas D. Jacobson**
Kelly A. Jorgensen
John D. Kendzior
Kathleen M. Klein
Matthew Leis**
Aruna Limoli*****
Nicholas J. Marino
Maura Lutz Morgan
Mark J. Perry**
R. Mick Rubio***
Erin K. Schreiber
Scott R. Shinkan
Mark Sobczak
Sheila M. Totorp***
Kenneth R. Wysocki
Michael V. Furlong
Mara Goltsman**
Emily N. Holmes
Michael W. Jacobson
Kathleen A. Johnson
Elizabeth T. Jozefowicz
Alexander Kharash**
Katharina Kraatz-Dunkel*****
Christopher J. Liegel
Marc P. Madonia**
Tatiana Markovitch*****
Theodore Mottola**
Adam J. Petit**
Louise Ryder*****
Matthew E. Schweiger
G. Brent Sims***
Mark Soloman**
Joshua A. Wolkomir

**Resident New York City, NY Office
***Resident Irvine, CA Office
****Resident Florham Park, NJ Office
*****Resident London, England Office
******Resident New York, NY and Florham Park, NJ Offices

(This firm is also listed in the Subrogation section of this directory)

Conklin & Conklin, LLC

53 West Jackson Boulevard, Suite 1150
Chicago, Illinois 60604
  Telephone: 312-341-9500
  Fax: 312-341-9151

(Bangor, MI Office: P.O. Box 189, 49013)

General Civil Trial and Appellate Practice, General Liability, Personal Injury, Product Liability, Construction Law, Commercial Litigation, Insurance Coverage, Eminent Domain, Inland Marine, Property and Casualty, Dram Shop, Business and Real Estate Transactions, Liquor and Operational Licensing

Firm Profile: Since 1928, when the late Clarence R. Conklin was admitted to practice law in Illinois, a tradition of father to son to grandson has kept the Conklin name in the forefront of the legal community servicing the legal needs of the business and insurance community of Chicago. Combining youthful vigor and mature wisdom Conklin & Conklin, LLC moves forward in this century with same dedication, determination and creative thinking that has characterized its prior firms for more then 70 years. From its principal attorneys to its many experienced associate attorneys, the firm is a unified team. Frequently asked to take on difficult, complex or high risk cases, the firm focuses its varied talents and experiences to do whatever is required for its clients.

The partners and associate attorneys of Conklin & Conklin, LLC have a breadth of experience in all aspects of insurance law. The firm handles both first and third party claims, coverage interpretation, and subrogation. The Firm has handeld cases in all courts of Illinois and Michigan, both at the trial and appeals. Founded in 1969, the firm has grown and developed along with the rapidly changing laws applicable to insurance. In addition to its insurance work, the firm has a general litigation, corporate, real estate, administrative law, eminent domain and commercial licensing practice.

Insurance Clients

Markel Insurance Company
North American Capacity
  Insurance Company
NAS Insurance Group

Non-Insurance Clients

The Blackstone Group
Illinois Department of
  Transportation
The Walt Disney Company
Hilton Hotels Corporation
Illinois State Toll Highway
  Authority

Conklin & Conklin, LLC, Chicago, IL   (Continued)
Partners

Thomas W. Conklin, Sr. — 1938 — Yale University, B.A., 1960; The University of Chicago, J.D., 1963 — Admitted to Bar, 1996, Michigan; 1964, U.S. District Court, Central, Northern and Southern Districts of Illinois; U.S. Court of Appeals, Seventh Circuit; 1996, U.S. District Court, Eastern and Western Districts of Michigan — Practice Areas: Insurance Defense; Complex Litigation; Insurance Coverage

Thomas W. Conklin — 1964 — University of Illinois at Chicago, B.A., 1987; Loyola University Chicago, J.D. (magna cum laude), 1996 — Admitted to Bar, 1996, Illinois; U.S. District Court, Northern District of Illinois; Illinois State Court; 2007, U.S. Court of Appeals for the District of Columbia and Seventh Circuits — Practice Areas: Complex Litigation; Corporate Law; Litigation; Insurance Coverage; Eminent Domain; Construction Litigation; Personal Injury; Real Estate — E-mail: twconklin@aol.com

Cray Huber Horstman Heil & VanAusdal LLC

303 West Madison, Suite 2200
Chicago, Illinois 60606
  Telephone: 312-332-8450
  Fax: 312-332-8451
  E-Mail: attorneys@crayhuber.com
  www.crayhuber.com

Established: 1999

Commercial Litigation, Insurance Defense, Coverage Issues, General Liability, Subrogation, Breach of Contract, Malpractice, Construction Liability, Medical Malpractice, Personal Injury, Personal Liability, Product Liability

Firm Profile: Cray Huber Horstman Heil & VanAusdal LLC was formed in 1999 for the purpose of improving the quality and efficiency of defense litigation services through the use of emerging technology and more experienced lawyers. The founding partners of the firm have more than 100 years of experience in defending lawsuits in state and federal courts across the country. Cray Huber focuses its counseling and litigation practice in commercial disputes, product liability, professional liability, insurance coverage, construction liability, medical liability, transportation, premises liability and civil appeals.

Insurance Clients

Lancer Insurance Company
ProAssurance Group

Firm Members

Daniel K. Cray — 1956 — Illinois State University, B.S. (with high honors), 1978; University of Illinois, J.D., 1981 — Admitted to Bar, 1981, Illinois — Member American, Illinois State and DuPage County Bar Associations; Defense Research Institute; Illinois Association of Defense Trial Counsel; International Association of Defense Counsel

Michael D. Huber — 1960 — Wabash College, A.B. (cum laude), 1982; Indiana University, J.D. (cum laude), 1985 — Delta Theta Pi — Admitted to Bar, 1985, Illinois; 1996, Indiana; 1985, U.S. District Court, Northern and Southern Districts of Illinois; 1996, U.S. District Court, Northern and Southern Districts of Indiana — Member Illinois State, Indiana State and Chicago Bar Associations; Defense Research Institute; International Association of Defense Counsel; Trucking Industry Defense Association

James K. Horstman — 1953 — DePauw University, B.A., 1975; Yale University, M.A.R., 1977; Washington University, J.D., 1980 — Admitted to Bar, 1980, Illinois — Member American and Illinois State Bar Associations; Appellate Lawyers Association; Defense Research Institute; Federation of Defense and Corporate Counsel; Illinois Association of Defense Trial Counsel

Rodney E. VanAusdal — 1958 — Indiana University, B.S., 1980; J.D., 1982 — Beta Gamma Sigma — Admitted to Bar, 1983, Illinois — Member American and Illinois State Bar Associations; American Society for Healthcare Risk Management; Illinois Association of Healthcare Attorneys

Stephen W. Heil — 1965 — Lewis University, B.A. (with honors), 1987; University of Illinois, J.D. (cum laude), 1990 — Admitted to Bar, 1990, Illinois; 1990, U.S. District Court, Northern District of Illinois; 1995, U.S. District Court, Central District of Illinois — Member Illinois State Bar Association; Defense Research Institute

ILLINOIS CHICAGO

Cray Huber Horstman Heil & VanAusdal LLC, Chicago, IL (Continued)

David E. Kravitz — 1968 — University of Wisconsin, B.A., 1990; Chicago-Kent College of Law, J.D., 1994 — Admitted to Bar, 1994, Illinois; U.S. District Court, Northern District of Illinois

David J. Farina — 1968 — State University of New York at Plattsburgh, B.S. (summa cum laude), 1990; The John Marshall Law School, J.D., 1994 — Admitted to Bar, 1995, Illinois; 1997, U.S. District Court, Northern District of Illinois — Member Illinois State and Chicago Bar Associations; Defense Research Institute

Summer E. Heil — 1969 — Indiana University, B.A., 1991; DePaul University College of Law, J.D., 1994 — Admitted to Bar, 1994, Illinois; U.S. District Court, Northern District of Illinois; 1994, 15th and 17th Judicial Circuit Courts of Florida

Associates

Adam C. Carter — 1976 — Augustana College, B.A., 1998; University of Illinois, J.D., 2001 — Admitted to Bar, 2001, Illinois; 2001, U.S. District Court, Northern District of Illinois

Scott D. Pfeiffer — 1973 — Southern Illinois University, B.A., 1997; The John Marshall Law School, J.D., 2000 — Admitted to Bar, 2000, Illinois; U.S. District Court, Northern District of Illinois; Supreme Court of Illinois; 2002, U.S. District Court, Northern District of Illinois including Trial Bar; 2003, U.S. District Court, Northern District of Indiana; 2004, U.S. District Court, Southern District of Illinois — Member Chicago Bar Association; National Association of Railroad Trial Counsel

Aimee K. Lipkis — 1984 — Indiana University, B.A., 2006; Michigan State University College of Law, J.D., 2009 — Admitted to Bar, 2009, Illinois — Member Chicago Bar Association

Jennifer M. Hart — The University of Mississippi, B.S., 1994; The John Marshall Law School, J.D., 1998 — Admitted to Bar, 1998, Illinois; 2009, California — Member Illinois State and Chicago Bar Associations; State Bar of California (Litigation Section)

Melissa H. Dakich — DePauw University, B.A., 1985; The John Marshall Law School, J.D., 1998 — Admitted to Bar, 1998, Illinois; 2000, U.S. District Court, Northern District of Illinois

Jennifer N. Ross — 1975 — Truman State University, B.A., 1997; Indiana University School of Law, J.D., 2000 — Admitted to Bar, 2000, Illinois; 2001, Indiana; 2000, U.S. District Court, Central and Northern Districts of Illinois — Member Illinois State and Chicago Bar Associations; American Health Lawyers Association — Certified Professional Health Care Risk Manager; Barton Certificate in Health Care Risk Management

Zachary G. Shook — 1983 — James Madison College at Michigan State University, B.A., 2006; The John Marshall Law School, J.D., 2011 — Admitted to Bar, 2011, Illinois — Member American, Illinois State and Chicago Bar Associations

Kelly V. Milam — 1982 — Michigan State University, B.A., 2005; Thomas M. Cooley Law School, J.D., 2008 — Admitted to Bar, 2008, Illinois; 2010, Indiana — Member Illinois State, Indiana State and Chicago Bar Associations

Jeanne M. Zeiger — 1952 — The University of Iowa, B.S., 1975; Washington University School of Law, J.D., 1979 — Admitted to Bar, 1979, Illinois; 1982, U.S. District Court, Northern District of Illinois; 2001, U.S. District Court, Central District of Illinois — Member Illinois State and Chicago Bar Associations

Anthony M. Sam — 1985 — Lewis University, B.S., 2007; The John Marshall Law School, J.D., 2011 — Admitted to Bar, 2011, Illinois; U.S. District Court, Northern District of Illinois — Member American, Illinois State, Cook County and Chicago Bar Associations

Chase M. Gruszka — 1987 — Loras College, B.A., 2009; The John Marshall Law School, J.D., 2013 — Admitted to Bar, 2013, Illinois — Member American, Illinois State and Chicago Bar Associations

Cuisinier & Farahvar, Ltd.

200 West Adams Street
Suite 430
Chicago, Illinois 60606
  Telephone: 312-634-0412
  Fax: 312-846-6140
  E-Mail: pcuisinier@candflaw.net
  www.cfblaw.net

Cuisinier & Farahvar, Ltd., Chicago, IL (Continued)

Construction Litigation, Commercial Litigation, Employment Law, Professional Liability, Premises Liability, Civil Rights, Insurance Coverage, Insurance Defense, Entertainment Law

Firm Profile: Cuisinier & Farahvar is a full service litigation firm located in Chicago, Illinois. It is the firm's goal to resolve all contested matters efficiently and expeditiously with a focus on ensuring that its clients are not only well represented but also well informed. We ensure aggressive representation, prompt reporting, attention to guidelines and dedication to quality service. Having years of experience in the courtroom and countless cases tried before juries, the attorneys at Cuisinier & Farahvar do not wince at the possibility of trial, when necessary.

Insurance Clients

Concert Health Plan
The Hartford
Specialty Risk Services, Inc. (SRS)
Travelers

Discover Re
Omni Insurance Group, Inc.
State Auto Insurance Companies

Non-Insurance Clients

Village of Schaumburg

Partners

Francis P. Cuisinier — 1948 — University of Wisconsin, B.A., 1970; Loyola University Chicago School of Law, J.D., 1973 — Admitted to Bar, 1973, Illinois; U.S. District Court, Central and Northern Districts of Illinois; U.S. District Court, Northern District of Indiana; U.S. District Court, Eastern District of Michigan — Member Illinois State and Chicago (Litigation Management Council) Bar Associations; Illinois Association of Defense Trial Counsel — Practice Areas: Product Liability; Construction Law; Premises Liability; Insurance Defense; Municipal Law; Toxic Torts — E-mail: pcuisinier@candflaw.net

Paul A. Farahvar — 1974 — University of Illinois, B.A., 1996; University of Illinois College of Law, J.D., 1999 — Admitted to Bar, 1999, Illinois; U.S. District Court, Northern District of Illinois — Member Chicago Bar Association — Practice Areas: Civil Rights; Health Care; Commercial Law; Construction Law; Insurance Defense; Sports and Entertainment Liability — E-mail: pfarahvar@candflaw.net

Victoria R. Benson — 1980 — Loyola University Chicago, B.A. (cum laude), 2001; University of Illinois College of Law, J.D., 2004 — Admitted to Bar, 2004, Illinois; 2005, U.S. District Court, Central and Northern Districts of Illinois — Member Illinois State and Chicago Bar Associations; Illinois Association of Defense Trial Counsel; Defense Research Institute — Practice Areas: Toxic Torts; Environmental Law; Premises Liability; Product Liability; Insurance Defense — E-mail: vbenson@candflaw.net

Dinsmore & Shohl LLP

227 West Monroe Street, Suite 3850
Chicago, Illinois 60606
  Telephone: 312-372-6060
  Fax: 312-372-6085
  www.dinsmore.com

(Cincinnati, OH Office*: 255 East Fifth Street, 45202)
  (Tel: 513-977-8200)
  (Fax: 513-977-8141)
(Lexington, KY Office*: Lexington Financial Center, 250 West Main Street, 40507)
  (Tel: 859-425-1000)
  (Fax: 859-425-1099)

Agent/Broker Liability, Bad Faith, Insurance Coverage, Insurance Defense, Insurance Litigation, Trial and Appellate Practice

Firm Member

Thomas G. Drennan — University of Illinois at Urbana-Champaign, B.A., 1998; Indiana University School of Law, J.D., 2001 — Admitted to Bar, 2001, Illinois — Member American Bar Association; Illinois Association of Defense Trial Counsel — Tel: 312-428-2728 — E-mail: tom.drennan@dinsmore.com

CHICAGO   ILLINOIS

Dinsmore & Shohl LLP, Chicago, IL   (Continued)

(See listing under Cincinnati, OH for additional information)

Doherty & Progar LLC

200 West Adams Street, Suite 2220
Chicago, Illinois 60606-5231
   Telephone: 312-630-9630
   Fax: 312-630-9001
   E-Mail: mail@doherty-progar.com
   www.doherty-progar.com

(Merrillville, IN Office: 8105 Georgia Street, 46410-6224)
   (Tel: 219-513-9000)
   (Fax: 219-513-9010)
(Milwaukee, WI Office: 250 East Wisconsin Avenue, Suite 1800, 53202-4232)
   (Tel: 414-347-9600)
   (Fax: 414-347-9611)

Established: 2001

Civil Litigation, Child Care Litigation, Class Actions, Common Carrier & Innkeeper Liability, Construction Liability, Directors and Officers Liability, Dram Shop, Employment Discrimination, Employment Practices Liability, Errors and Omissions, General Civil Trial and Appellate Practice, Insurance Coverage, Insurance Defense, Nursing Home Litigation, Municipal Law, Personal and Commercial Vehicle, Personal Injury, Premises Liability, Professional Liability, Toxic Torts, Transportation Liability, Workers' Compensation

Firm Profile: Our firm concentrates on advising and representing insurance carriers, their insureds, and businesses in all types of matters in Illinois, Indiana, and Wisconsin. We represent our clients in suits pending in state and federal courts, in claims filed with state and federal administrative agencies, and in negotiations, mediation, arbitration, and other alternative dispute resolution formats. Our attorneys are active in risk management, continuing legal education, and legal publications in the areas in which they practice.

Insurance Clients

AFLAC, Inc.
Broadspire Services, Inc.
The Cincinnati Insurance Companies
Dallas National Insurance Company
GUARD Insurance Group
Harleysville Insurance Company
Liberty Mutual Group
Mt. Hawley Insurance Company
NIE Insurance
Pekin Insurance Company
RLI Group
RSKCo
Sedgwick Claims Management Services, Inc.
United States Liability Insurance Group
Auto Club Group
Catlin Specialty Insurance Company
CNA Insurance Company
GAB Robins North America, Inc.
Gallagher Bassett Services, Inc.
Hanover Insurance Company
Indiana Insurance Guaranty Association
National Insurance Company
NovaPro Risk Solutions
Philadelphia Insurance Companies
Rockford Mutual Insurance Company
T.H.E. Insurance Company
Topa Insurance Company
VeriClaim, Inc.
Xchanging

Non-Insurance Clients

Athens Construction Co., Inc.
Cottingham & Butler Claims, Inc.
Garland Industries, Inc.
Installations Services, Inc.
MV Transportation, Inc.
Regal Ware, Inc.
Rockwell Automation, Inc.
The Select Family of Staffing Companies
Windsor Windows & Doors
ConGlobal Industries
The Garland Company, Inc.
Graphic Packaging International, Inc.
Pentair, Inc.
Reliance Relocation Services, Inc.
Schindler Elevator Corporation
TCF Bank
White Transportation

Partners

Kevin W. Doherty — The John Marshall Law School, J.D., 1981 — Admitted to Bar, 1981, Illinois

Doherty & Progar LLC, Chicago, IL   (Continued)

Michael J. Progar — DePaul University College of Law, J.D., 1981 — Admitted to Bar, 1981, Illinois; Wisconsin; Indiana
Mary Jo Greene — Loyola University School of Law, J.D., 1983 — Admitted to Bar, 1983, Illinois
Michael T. Sprengnether — Loyola University Chicago, J.D. (with honors), 1976 — Admitted to Bar, 1976, Illinois; Wisconsin
Edward D. D'Arcy, Jr. — Chicago-Kent College of Law, J.D., 1983 — Admitted to Bar, 1983, Illinois; Indiana; Wisconsin

Of Counsel

Patrick W. Martin   John W. Schmidt

Associates

Brian T. Ginley   Christopher R. Reinkall
Ryan A. Danahey   Michael M. Oberman

Fisher Kanaris, P.C.

One South Wacker Drive, 31st Floor
Chicago, Illinois 60606
   Telephone: 312-474-1400
   Fax: 312-474-1410
   www.fisherkanaris.com

Established: 1992

Architects and Engineers, Arson, Bad Faith, Business Interruption, Complex Litigation, Construction Litigation, Design Professionals, Environmental Coverage, First and Third Party Defense, Insurance Coverage, Insurance Litigation, General Liability, Policy Construction and Interpretation, Property and Casualty, Reinsurance, Subrogation, Trial and Appellate Practice

Insurance Clients

The Hartford   Zurich U.S.

Shareholders

Steven B. Fisher — Co-Managing Director — University of Illinois, B.S., 1984; Illinois Institute of Technology, Chicago-Kent College of Law, J.D., 1987 — Admitted to Bar, 1987, Illinois; U.S. District Court, Northern District of Illinois — Member Illinois State Bar Association; International Association of Arson Investigators
David E. Heiss — Director — DePauw University, B.A., 1993; The John Marshall Law School, J.D., 1997 — Phi Delta Phi — Admitted to Bar, 1997, Illinois; U.S. District Court, Northern District of Illinois — Member Illinois State and Chicago Bar Associations
Suanne P. Hirschhaut — Director — Indiana University, B.A., 1978; Illinois Institute of Technology, Chicago-Kent College of Law, J.D., 1981 — Admitted to Bar, 1981, Illinois; U.S. District Court, Northern District of Illinois; 1982, U.S. Court of Appeals, Seventh Circuit — Member Chicago Bar Association
Peter E. Kanaris — Co-Managing Director — Duke University, B.A., 1982; Washington University, J.D., 1985 — Associate Editor, Journal of Urban and Contemporary Law, 1984-1985 — Admitted to Bar, 1985, Illinois; 1992, New York; U.S. District Court, Northern District of Illinois including Trial Bar; U.S. Court of Appeals, Seventh and Tenth Circuits; 1992, U.S. District Court, Southern District of New York — Member American and Chicago Bar Associations; Association of Trial Lawyers of America
Stephen A. Whelan — Director — Boston College, B.A. (cum laude), 1989; Loyola University, J.D., 1992 — Omicron Delta Epsilon; Golden Key — Admitted to Bar, 1992, Illinois; U.S. District Court, Northern District of Illinois
Eric D. Stubenvoll — Director — University of Illinois, B.A., 1989; University of Illinois College of Law, J.D., 1992 — Admitted to Bar, 1992, Michigan; 1993, Illinois; U.S. District Court, Eastern and Western Districts of Michigan; U.S. District Court, Western District of Wisconsin; U.S. District Court, Northern District of Illinois; U.S. District Court, District of Colorado; U.S. District Court, Southern District of Indiana; U.S. Court of Appeals, Sixth and Seventh Circuits; U.S. Supreme Court
Jeffrey C. Arnold — Hope College, B.A., 1993; Illinois Institute of Technology, Chicago-Kent College of Law, J.D., 1996 — Admitted to Bar, 1997, Illinois; U.S. District Court, Northern District of Illinois

Fisher Kanaris, P.C., Chicago, IL (Continued)

Cheryl L. Mondi — DePauw University, B.A., 1997; Illinois Institute of Technology, Chicago-Kent College of Law, J.D., 2000 — Admitted to Bar, 2000, Illinois; U.S. District Court, Central and Northern Districts of Illinois

John M. Schmidt — Augustana College, B.A., 1994; The John Marshall Law School, J.D., 1998 — Admitted to Bar, 1998, Illinois; U.S. District Court, Northern District of Illinois

Jefferson Patten — 1972 — University of Illinois at Chicago, B.S., 1998; The John Marshall Law School, J.D. (cum laude), 2001 — Admitted to Bar, 2001, Illinois; U.S. District Court, District of Illinois; U.S. District Courts of Indiana; U.S. District Court, Eastern and Western Districts of Wisconsin; U.S. Court of Appeals, Second, Fifth and Seventh Circuits — United States Marine Corp

C. Zachary Ransel — 1975 — Miami University, B.S., 1997; Indiana University School of Law, J.D., 2001 — Admitted to Bar, 2001, Illinois; 2005, U.S. District Court, Northern District of Illinois; 2010, U.S. District Court, Eastern District of Michigan

John N. Rooks — 1979 — DePauw University, B.S., 2001; Loyola University College of Law, J.D., 2005 — Admitted to Bar, 2005, Illinois; U.S. District Court, Northern District of Illinois — Languages: French

(This firm is also listed in the Subrogation section of this directory)

Garofalo, Schreiber & Storm, Chartered

55 West Wacker Drive
10th Floor
Chicago, Illinois 60601
Telephone: 312-670-2000
Fax: 312-419-1336
Toll Free: 877-419-2300
www.gsslawoffice.com

Established: 1997

Insurance Defense, Workers' Compensation, Employer Liability, Trial Practice, Appellate Practice, State and Federal Courts

Insurance Clients

ACE USA
AIG Claim Services, Inc.
American Contractors Insurance Co RRG
American Family Insurance Company
Argonaut Great Central Insurance Company
Cannon Cochran Management Services, Inc.
CMI Octagon, Inc.
Crawford & Company
Creative Risk Solutions, Inc.
Frank Gates Acclaim, Inc.
GatesMcDonald
Hastings Mutual Insurance Company
Illinois Insurance Guaranty Fund
ITT Specialty Risk Services, Inc.
Meridian Mutual Insurance Company
North American Specialty Insurance Company
NovaPro Risk Solutions
Royal & SunAlliance USA
Sentry Claims Services
Travelers
United Fire & Casualty Company
Utica National Insurance Group
Ward North America, Inc.
Williams Insurance Group
Zurich American Insurance Company
Addison Insurance Company
Allstate Insurance Company
American Country Insurance Company
Amerisure Insurance Company
AmTrust Group
Broadspire
Cambridge Integrated Services
Chesterfield Services, Inc.
Church Mutual Insurance Company
CompManagement, Inc./Sedgwick James
Crum & Forster Insurance Group
Gallagher Bassett Services, Inc.
Grinnell Mutual Reinsurance Company
Illinois Compensation Trust/Hospital Association
Liberty Mutual Insurance Company
Milwaukee Insurance Company/Unitrin
Northwestern Medical Faculty Foundation
Risk Enterprise Management, Ltd.
SeaBright Insurance Company
Tar Heel Insurance Management Services
Universal Underwriters Group
Vanliner Insurance Company
West Bend Mutual Insurance Company

Non-Insurance Clients

Accenture, LLP
Advocate Health Centers
A.M. Castle & Co.
Acres Group, Inc.
Alcoa Engineered Products
American Airlines, Inc.

Garofalo, Schreiber & Storm, Chartered, Chicago, IL (Continued)

American Bottling Company
Anning Johnson Company
Army and Air Force Exchange Service
Bay Shipbuilding Co.
Bunge Edible Oil
Central Steel & Wire Company
Chicago Bridge & Iron Company
C.J. Vitner Company
CNF Transportation, Inc.
Construction Program Group
Conway Central Express
Covenant Management
Denk & Roche Builders, Inc.
Dick Corporation
G.E. Riddiford Company
Graycor, Inc.
International Decorators, Inc.
Jernberg Industries, Inc.
Kenny Construction Company
Lakeside Building Maintenance
Lutheran Social Services/P.A. Peterson
Marinette Marine Corporation
Marmon/Keystone Corporation
Meccon Industries, Inc.
Meyer Steel Drum, Inc.
National Beverage Corporation
Northwestern University
Ozinga Brothers, Inc.
Patten Tractor & Equipment Co.
Pepper Construction Company
Pickus Construction
Prairie Material Sales
Rail Terminal Services
Rockford Memorial Hospital
RUSH Oak Park Hospital
Sears, Roebuck and Co.
Septran, Inc.
Sisters of St. Francis/St. James Hospital
Spherion Corporation
SUPERVALU/Jewel
Textron, Inc.
Turano Baking Company
United Technologies Corporation
VITAS Hospice Services, L.L.C.
Wabtec Corporation
West Irving Dye Corporation
Wolseley N.A.
W.W. Grainger, Inc.
AMS Mechanical Systems, Inc.
Arch Construction
Arnold Logistics
Babcock & Wilcox Construction Co.
Cadbury Schweppes Bottling Group
Chicago Sun-Times, Inc.
Clark Construction Group, Inc.
Consolidated Freightway Corporation
Corn Products International, Inc.
CPC Logistics, Inc.
Department of Navy
Dominick's
GES Exposition Services, Inc.
Hyatt Corporation
James McHugh Construction Company
Knaack Manufacturing
Lear Corporation
The Manitowoc Company, Inc.
Marianjoy Rehabilitation/Wheaton Franciscan Services, Inc.
McNulty Brothers Construction
Medline Industries, Inc.
Naperville School District #203
New Breed, Inc.
Novak Construction Company
Panera Bread
PeopleLink Staffing Solutions
Pepsi-Cola Bottlers, Inc.
Power Maintenance & Constructors, LLC
Rehabilitation Institute of Chicago
Rockford Products
Safway Steel Products, Inc.
Select Staffing
Signal Administration, Inc.
Snap-on Tools Corporation
Southwest Airlines Company
Starwood Hotels & Resorts Worldwide, Inc.
Thatcher Engineering
Turtle Wax, Inc.
Vienna Beef, Inc.
Vitran Express, Inc.
Waste Management, Inc.
Wm. Wrigley Jr. Company
Wright Tree Service

Shareholder

Joseph A. Garofalo — 1952 — North Park College, B.A. (magna cum laude), 1974; DePaul University College of Law, J.D., 1977 — Admitted to Bar, 1977, Illinois; Illinois; U.S. District Court, Northern District of Illinois including Trial Bar; 1987, U.S. Court of Appeals, Seventh Circuit — Member Illinois State, Chicago and Will County Bar Associations; Workers' Compensation Lawyers Association; Justinian Society of Lawyers; The College of Workers' Compensation Lawyers, Inc. — Reported Cases: Johnson Outboards v. Industrial Commission, 77Ill.2d 67, 394 N.E.2d 1176, 31 Ill. Dec. 799 (1979); Auto-Trol Technology Corporation v. Industrial Commission, 189 Ill.App.3d 1065, 545 N.E.2d 939 (1989) — Chicago Bar Association Lecturer: "Trial of a Workers' Compensation Case," Spring, 1984; "Case Developments in Workers' Compensation," Spring, 1988; Arbitrator, Circuit Court of Cook County, 1990; Leading Lawyers Network-The Top Lawyers, 2004-present; Illinois Super Lawyers, 2006-present — Practice Areas: Workers' Compensation; Insurance Defense; Trial Practice — Tel: 312-670-2000 — E-mail: jgarofalo@gsslawoffice.com

Scott T. Schreiber — 1956 — Valparaiso University, B.A., 1978; J.D., 1981 — Managing Editor, Valparaiso University Law Review (1980-1981) — Admitted to Bar, 1981, Illinois — Member Workers' Compensation Lawyers Association — Author: "The Unsupervised Child: Parental Negligence or Necessity," Valparaiso University Law Review, Vol. 15, P. 167, Fall, 1980 — Leading Lawyers Network-The Top Lawyers, 2004-present; Illinois Super Lawyers, 2007-present — Practice Areas: Workers' Compensation; Insurance Defense; Trial Practice — Tel: 312-670-2000 — E-mail: sschreiber@gsslawoffice.com

Derek A. Storm — 1959 — Eastern Illinois University, B.A. (with honors), 1981; DePaul University, J.D., 1984; University of London, England, LL.M.

Garofalo, Schreiber & Storm, Chartered, Chicago, IL
(Continued)

(with merit), 1989 — Admitted to Bar, 1984, Illinois; 1987, U.S. Court of Appeals, Fourth Circuit — Member Chicago Bar Association; Workers' Compensation Lawyers Association (Board of Directors; Past President) — Leading Lawyers Network-The Top Lawyers, 2004-present — Practice Areas: Workers' Compensation; Insurance Defense; Trial Practice — Tel: 312-670-2000 — E-mail: dstorm@gsslawoffice.com

Shareholders

Philip G. Brinckerhoff — 1958 — Marquette University, A.B., 1980; Saint Louis University, J.D., 1985 — Admitted to Bar, 1985, Illinois — Member Chicago Bar Association; Illinois Association of Defense Trial Counsel — Leading Lawyers Network, The Top Lawyers (2012 - present) — Practice Areas: Civil Litigation; Insurance Defense; Employer Liability; Trial Practice; Construction Law — Tel: 312-670-2000 — E-mail: pbrinckerhoff@gsslawoffice.com

Steven R. Scarlati, Jr. — 1963 — Eastern Illinois University, B.A., 1986; Illinois Institute of Technology, Chicago-Kent College of Law, J.D., 1990 — Admitted to Bar, 1990, Illinois — Member Will County and Chicago Bar Associations; Workers' Compensation Lawyers Association — Practice Areas: Workers' Compensation; Insurance Defense; Trial Practice — Tel: 312-670-2000 — E-mail: sscarlati@gsslawoffice.com

James R. Clune — 1953 — University of Notre Dame, B.A., 1975; Stetson University College of Law, J.D., 1978 — Admitted to Bar, 1978, Florida; 1980, Illinois; 1979, U.S. Court of Appeals, Fifth Circuit; 1981, U.S. District Court, Northern District of Illinois including Trial Bar — Member Illinois State Bar Association; The Florida Bar; Workers' Compensation Lawyers Association — Author: "Illinois Continuing Legal Education-Workers Compensation Chapter 2"; "Employer-Employee Relationship" — Leading Lawyers Network, The Top Lawyers (2013 - present) — Tel: 312-670-2000 — E-mail: jclune@gsslawoffice.com

Andrew L. Rane — 1967 — University of Illinois at Urbana-Champaign, B.A., 1990; Northern Illinois University, J.D. (cum laude), 1994 — American Jurisprudence Award in Administrative Law — Admitted to Bar, 1994, Illinois; U.S. District Court, Northern District of Illinois — Member Illinois State Bar Association; Workers' Compensation Lawyers Association (Board of Directors, 2008-2010) — Practice Areas: Workers' Compensation; Insurance Defense; Trial Practice — Tel: 312-670-2000 — E-mail: arane@gsslawoffice.com

Todd E. Wegman — 1969 — Illinois State University, B.S., 1991; Illinois Institute of Technology, Chicago-Kent College of Law, J.D., 1996 — Admitted to Bar, 1996, Illinois — Member American Bar Association; Workers' Compensation Lawyers Assocation — Practice Areas: Workers' Compensation; Insurance Defense; Trial Practice — Tel: 312-670-2000 — E-mail: twegman@gsslawoffice.com

Daniel L. Grant — 1975 — Illinois State University, B.S., 1998; DePaul University, J.D., 2002 — Admitted to Bar, 2002, Illinois — Member American and Chicago (Legislative Liaison, Workers' Compensation Section, 2011-present) Bar Associations; Workers' Compensation Lawyers Association — Practice Areas: Workers' Compensation; Insurance Defense; Trial Practice; Longshore and Harbor Workers' Compensation — Tel: 312-670-2000 — E-mail: dgrant@gsslawoffice.com

Senior Associates

Craig M. Scarpelli — 1970 — University of Wisconsin, B.A. (cum laude), 1992; DePaul University, J.D., 1996 — Admitted to Bar, 1996, Illinois; U.S. District Court, Northern District of Illinois — Member Illinois State Bar Association; Workers' Compensation Lawyers Association — Practice Areas: Workers' Compensation; Insurance Defense; Trial Practice — Tel: 312-670-2000 — E-mail: cscarpelli@gsslawoffice.com

David P. Hanson — 1974 — Indiana University, B.S., 1997; DePaul University, J.D., 2000 — Admitted to Bar, 2001, Illinois; U.S. District Court, Northern District of Illinois including Trial Bar — Member American Bar Association; Workers' Compensation Lawyers Association — Languages: Japanese — Practice Areas: Workers' Compensation; Insurance Defense; Trial Practice — Tel: 312-670-2000 — E-mail: dhanson@gsslawoffice.com

Associates

Matthew J. Novak — 1978 — Buena Vista University, B.A. (magna cum laude), 2001; The University of Iowa College of Law, J.D., 2005 — Admitted to Bar, 2005, Illinois — Member Illinois State Bar Association; Workers' Compensation Lawyers Association — Practice Areas: Workers' Compensation; Insurance Defense; Trial Practice — Tel: 312-670-2000 — E-mail: mnovak@gsslawoffice.com

Garofalo, Schreiber & Storm, Chartered, Chicago, IL
(Continued)

Jason L. Cutler — 1983 — University of Wisconsin Law School, J.D., 2008 — Admitted to Bar, 2008, Illinois; Wisconsin — Member Illinois State and Chicago Bar Associations; State Bar of Wisconsin; Workers' Compensation Lawyers Association — Practice Areas: Workers' Compensation; Insurance Defense — E-mail: jcutler@gsslawoffice.com

Molly H. Nartonis — 1986 — Saint Louis University, B.A. (cum laude), 2008; DePaul University College of Law, J.D., 2011 — Admitted to Bar, 2011, Illinois — Member American Bar Association; Illinois Workers' Compensation Lawyers Association — Practice Areas: Workers' Compensation — Tel: 312-670-2000 — E-mail: mnartonis@gsslawoffice.com

Kelly E. Kamstra — 1988 — Gonzaga University, B.A. (cum laude), 2006-2010; DePaul University College of Law, J.D., 2010-2013 — Admitted to Bar, 2013, Illinois — Member Illinois State Bar — Tel: 312-670-2000 — E-mail: kkamstra@gsslawoffice.com

Of Counsel

Ralph L. Berke — Wheaton College, B.A. (with high honors), 1971; Northwestern University, J.D., 1974 — Admitted to Bar, 1974, Illinois; 1981, U.S. District Court, Northern District of Illinois; 1986, U.S. Court of Appeals, Seventh Circuit; 1989, U.S. Supreme Court; 1990, U.S. Court of Appeals for the Armed Forces — Ret. Lt. Col., U.S. Army Reserve — Practice Areas: Workers' Compensation; Insurance Defense; Litigation; Estate Planning — Tel: 312-670-2000 — E-mail: rberke@gsslawoffice.com

Norman H. Burdick — 1950 — Northeastern Illinois University, B.A. (Dean's List), 1968-1972; The John Marshall Law School in Chicago, J.D., 1972-1975 — Admitted to Bar, 1976, Illinois; 1976, U.S. District Court, Central and Northern Districts of Illinois; 1976, U.S. Court of Appeals, Seventh Circuit — Member Illinois State and Chicago Bar Associations; Workers' Compensation Lawyers Association; Coalition Against Fraud; International Association of Fraud Examiners — Practice Areas: Fraud; Criminal Law; Workers' Compensation; Insurance Fraud; Insurance Law — Tel: 312-670-2000 — E-mail: nburdick@gsslawoffice.com

Gunty & McCarthy

150 South Wacker Drive, Suite 1025
Chicago, Illinois 60606
   Telephone: 312-541-0022
   Fax: 312-541-0033
   www.guntymccarthy.com

(Edwardsville, IL Office*: 201 Hillsboro Avenue, Suite 204, 62025)
   (Tel: 618-659-3690)
   (Fax: 618-659-4630)

Established: 1991

Insurance Defense, Asbestos Litigation, Automobile, Bodily Injury, Casualty, Environmental Law, General Liability, Insurance Coverage, Product Liability, Property Damage, Medical Devices, Subrogation, Construction Accidents, Mass Tort, Wrongful Death, Toxic Torts, Federal Employer Liability Claims (FELA), Railroad Law, Transportation, Mold Litigation

Insurance Clients

Admiral Insurance Company	AIG
Alfa Insurance Company	Allianz of America, Inc.
Allstate Insurance Company	Amerisure Insurance Company
Arch Insurance Group	Arrowpoint Capital
Arthur J. Gallagher & Company	Aspen Specialty Insurance Management, Inc.
Atlantic Mutual Insurance Company	Berkshire Hathaway Specialty Insurance
Bituminous Insurance Company	
Brandywine Group of Insurance and Reinsurance Companies	Cavell America (formerly Randall America)
Chubb Group of Insurance Companies	Cincinnati Insurance Company
Commercial Union Insurance Company	CNA Insurance Companies
	Crawford & Company
	Crum & Forster
Evanston Insurance Company	Farmers Insurance Group
Fireman's Fund Insurance Company	First Nonprofit Insurance Company
	Gallagher Bassett Services, Inc.
General Accident Insurance Company	Great American Insurance Group
	Harleysville Insurance Company

Gunty & McCarthy, Chicago, IL (Continued)

The Hartford Insurance Group
Kemper Insurance Companies
Liberty Mutual Insurance Company
National Fire and Marine Insurance Company
Nationwide Insurance
Ohio Casualty Group
OneBeacon Insurance
PMA Insurance Group
Resolute Management, Inc.
Royal Insurance Company
Safeco Insurance
SEICO/Hartford Insurance Company
Sompo Japan Insurance Company of America
Travelers Insurance Companies
Hiscox USA
Lexington Insurance Company
Lumbermens Mutual Group
National Indemnity Company
National Union Fire Insurance Company
Oklahoma Farmers Union Mutual Insurance Company
QBE Regional Insurance
RiverStone Claims Management, LLC
St. Paul Fire and Marine Insurance Company
Sentry Insurance
Sumitomo Marine and Fire Insurance Company, Ltd.
Utica Mutual Insurance Company

Non-Insurance Clients

Acme Holding Company, Inc.
Apex Oil Company, Inc.
Altra Industrial Motion, Inc. f/k/a Colfax
Boylston Steam Specialty, Co.
Cooper Tire & Rubber Company
Corning Incorporated
Crane Co.
Edelbrock, LLC
Endeavor General Agency, LLC
Fluid Concepts, Inc.
General Tool Company
Industrial Kiln & Dryer Group
International American Management Company
Lydall, Inc.
Mario Tricoci Hair Salon & Day Spas, Inc.
Midland Engineering Company, Inc.
New Monarch Machine Tool, Inc.
North American Salt Company
Polyglass USA, Inc.
Prysmian Cables and Systems USA, LLC
SPX Corporation
Texas Industries, Inc.
ThyssenKrupp North America, Inc.
UHDE Corporation of America
Veolia Water North America
Whitney Automotive Group, Inc.., f/k/a J.C. Whitney & Co.
Ajax Electric
The A. Louis Supply Co.
Bearing Headquarters Company
Betts Industries, Inc.
Consolidated Edison Company
Corhart Incorporated
Corn Products International, Inc.
Dossert Corporation
Elizabeth Arden Red Door Spas
Federated Development, LLC
General Medical Corporation
The H.B. Smith Company, Incorporated
Kraft Chemical Company
LoboStar Inc.
Manhattan American Terrazzo Strip Company, Inc.
Meriden Molded Plastics, Inc.
Navistar, Inc./International Truck and Engine Corporation
Niagara Blower Company
PepsiCo, Inc.
Polysius Corporation
Santa Fe International Corporation
Sciaky, Inc.
Stainless Foundry & Engineering, Inc.
ThyssenKrupp Presta Danville, LLC
Water Application Distribution Group, Inc.

Partners

Susan Gunty — 1953 — Loyola University Chicago, B.A., 1975; M.A., 1977; J.D., 1980 — Admitted to Bar, 1980, Illinois; 1995, Missouri; 1996, Indiana; 1986, U.S. District Court, Northern District of Illinois including Trial Bar; 1990, U.S. District Court, Central District of Illinois; 1995, U.S. District Court, Eastern and Western Districts of Wisconsin; 1995, U.S. District Court, Southern District of Illinois; 1995, U.S. Court of Appeals, Seventh Circuit; 1995, U.S. Supreme Court; 2000, U.S. District Court, Northern District of Indiana; 2004, U.S. District Court, Southern District of Indiana; 2005, U.S. District Court, Western District of Michigan — Member Illinois State and Chicago Bar Associations; The Missouri Bar; Defense Research Institute; Illinois Association of Defense Trial Counsel — E-mail: susan.gunty@guntymccarthy.com

James P. McCarthy — 1959 — University of Notre Dame, B.B.A., 1981; The John Marshall Law School, J.D., 1984 — Admitted to Bar, 1984, Illinois; 1986, U.S. District Court, Northern District of Illinois; 1999, U.S. District Court, Southern District of Illinois; 2008, U.S. Court of Appeals, Eighth Circuit; 2014, U.S. District Court, Central District of Illinois — Member Illinois State, Du Page County and Chicago Bar Associations; Casualty Adjusters Association of Chicago; Western Loss Association; Blue Goose International; Workers' Compensation Claims Association; Illinois Self Insured Association; National Association of Railroad Trial Counsel (NARTC); Defense Research Institute; Illinois Association of Defense Trial Counsel — E-mail: jim.mccarthy@guntymccarthy.com

Paul Van Lysebettens — 1961 — American Conservatory of Music, B.Mus., 1983; Illinois Institute of Technology, Chicago-Kent College of Law, J.D., 1994 — Admitted to Bar, 1994, Illinois; 1994, U.S. District Court, Northern District of Illinois; 1998, U.S. Supreme Court — Member American and Illinois State Bar Associations; Defense Research Institute; Illinois Association of Defense Trial Counsel — E-mail: paul.vanlysebettens@guntymccarthy.com

James P. Kasper — 1976 — Loras College, B.A., 1999; The John Marshall Law School, J.D., 2004 — Admitted to Bar, 2004, Illinois; 2004, Indiana; 2005, U.S. District Court, Northern and Southern Districts of Indiana; 2005, U.S. District Court, Northern and Southern Districts of Indiana; 2011, U.S. District Court, Eastern District of Pennsylvania; U.S. District Court, Central and Southern Districts of Illinois — E-mail: jamie.kasper@guntymccarthy.com

Associates

Catherine L. Carlson — 1978 — Stephens College, B.A., 2000; Chicago-Kent College of Law, J.D., 2003 — Admitted to Bar, 2003, Illinois; 2004, Indiana; 2003, U.S. District Court, Northern District of Illinois; 2004, U.S. District Court, Northern and Southern Districts of Indiana; 2013, U.S. District Court, Central District of Illinois — Practice Areas: Insurance Defense — E-mail: cathie.carlson@guntymccarthy.com

Mara E. Cohen — 1974 — Indiana University, B.A., 1996; The John Marshall Law School, J.D., 2000 — Admitted to Bar, 2000, Illinois; 2000, U.S. District Court, Northern District of Illinois — Practice Areas: Insurance Defense — E-mail: mara.cohen@guntymccarthy.com

Jean M. French — University of Illinois at Urbana-Champaign, B.S., 1982; The John Marshall Law School, J.D., 1985 — Admitted to Bar, 1986, Illinois; 2010, Colorado; 1986, U.S. District Court, Northern District of Illinois — Member Illinois State, The Colorado and Chicago Bar Associations; Women's Bar Association of Illinois — Investigator, Chicago Bar Association Judicial Evaluation Committee; Arbitrator, Cook County Mandatory Arbitration; Adjunct Faculty, The John Marshall Law School, Chicago, Illinois — Practice Areas: Personal Injury; Insurance Law; Asbestos Litigation; Subrogation; Product Liability; Insurance Defense — E-mail: jean.french@guntymccarthy.com

Jeremy B. Harris — 1974 — The University of Arizona, B.A., 1997; DePaul University College of Law, J.D., 2000 — Admitted to Bar, 2001, Illinois — Practice Areas: Insurance Defense — E-mail: jeremy.harris@guntymccarthy.com

Sheryl E. Healy — 1950 — The University of Iowa, B.A., 1973; Loyola University Chicago School of Law, J.D. (with honors), 1984 — Admitted to Bar, 1985, Illinois; 1985, U.S. District Court, Northern District of Illinois — Member Association of Trial Lawyers of America — Law Degree in Alternative Dispute Resolution — Certified, Cook County Circuit Court Mediator — Practice Areas: Environmental Law; Construction Law; Toxic Torts; Insurance Defense — E-mail: sherry.healy@guntymccarthy.com

Patricia M. Kelly — 1953 — College of William & Mary, B.A., 1975; DePaul University College of Law, J.D., 1980 — Admitted to Bar, 1980, Illinois; 1980, U.S. District Court, Northern District of Illinois; 1993, U.S. District Court, Northern District of California; 2008, U.S. Court of Appeals, Eighth Circuit; U.S. Supreme Court; 2013, U.S. District Court, Southern District of Illinois — Member Illinois State and Chicago Bar Associations; Defense Research Institute; National Association of Railroad Trial Counsel — E-mail: patricia.kelly@guntymccarthy.com

Stephen K. Milott — Northeastern Illinois University, B.A., 1971; The John Marshall Law School, J.D. (with distinction), 1977 — Admitted to Bar, 1977, Illinois; 2001, Indiana; 1978, U.S. District Court, Northern District of Illinois; 1988, U.S. Court of Appeals, Seventh Circuit; 1995, U.S. Supreme Court — Member American (Former Member), Illinois State and Chicago Bar Associations — E-mail: stephen.milott@guntymccarthy.com

James A. Telthorst — Missouri University of Science and Technology, B.S. Mech. Engr., 1985; Saint Louis University School of Law, J.D., 1992 — Admitted to Bar, 1992, Illinois; 1993, Missouri; 1994, U.S. District Court, Southern District of Illinois; 1995, U.S. Court of Appeals, Seventh Circuit; 2002, U.S. Patent and Trademark Office — Member Illinois State and Madison County Bar Associations; The Missouri Bar; Bar Association of Metropolitan St. Louis — Certified Licensed Professional Engineer, Missouri — E-mail: jim.telthorst@guntymccarthy.com

James B. Walton — 1976 — Loyola University Chicago, B.A., 1998; University of Denver Sturm College of Law, J.D., 2007 — Admitted to Bar, 2008, Illinois — Practice Areas: Toxic Torts; Construction Law; Insurance Law; Coverage Issues; Subrogation; Product Liability — E-mail: james.walton@guntymccarthy.com

HeplerBroom LLC

30 North LaSalle Street, Suite 2900
Chicago, Illinois 60602
   Telephone: 312-230-9100
   Fax: 312-230-9201
   E-Mail: firm@heplerbroom.com
   www.heplerbroom.com

(Additional Offices: Edwardsville, IL*; St. Louis, MO*; Springfield, IL*)

Antitrust, Insurance Defense, Product Liability, Toxic Torts, Property and Casualty, Class Actions, Legal Malpractice, Commercial Litigation, Pharmaceutical, General Liability, Asbestos Litigation, Medical Malpractice, Workers' Compensation, Employment Litigation, Insurance Coverage, Transportation, Automobile, Trucking Law, Agent and Brokers Errors and Omissions, Personal Injury, Skilled Nursing Facilities, Construction Liability, White Collar Criminal Defense, Qui Tam/False Claims Act Litigation

Partners

Anthony J. Tunney — 1947 — The John Marshall Law School, J.D., 1977 — Admitted to Bar, 1977, Illinois — Tel: 312-205-7707 — E-mail: ajt@heplerbroom.com

Catherine C. Reiter — DePaul University College of Law, J.D., 1981 — Admitted to Bar, 1981, Illinois — Tel: 312-205-7708 — E-mail: ccr@heplerbroom.com

(See listing under Edwardsville, IL for additional information)

Heyl, Royster, Voelker & Allen
A Professional Corporation

19 South La Salle Street, Suite 1203
Chicago, Illinois 60603
   Telephone: 312-853-8700
   Fax: 312-782-0040
   E-Mail: firm@heylroyster.com
   www.heylroyster.com

(Additional Offices: Peoria, IL*; Springfield, IL*; Urbana, IL*; Rockford, IL*; Edwardsville, IL*)

Civil Trial Practice, Insurance Defense, Appellate Practice, Class Actions, Coverage Issues, Employment Law, Professional Malpractice, Self-Insured Defense, Toxic Torts, Workers' Compensation

Managing Partner

Tobin J. Taylor — Bradley University, B.S. (magna cum laude), 1993; Washington University School of Law, J.D., 1996 — Admitted to Bar, 1977, Illinois — Member American (Toxic Tort and Environmental Law and Litigation Sections), Illinois State (Past Steering Committee Member, Employment Law Section), Peoria County (Past Co-Chair, Young Lawyer Committee) and Chicago Bar Associations; Bar Association of the Central and Southern Federal Districts of Illinois; Abraham Lincoln American Inn of Court; Defense Research Institute; Illinois Association of Defense Trial Counsel

(Our lawyers are members of the American, state and local bar associations and, in many cases, are members of the local American Inn of Court chapters; leadership positions in these organizations are listed.)
(See Peoria, Rockford, Springfield and Urbana, IL Listings for additional information.)

Horvath & Weaver, P.C.

10 South LaSalle Street, Suite 1500
Chicago, Illinois 60603
   Telephone: 312-419-6600
   Fax: 312-419-6666
   Toll Free: 800-511-7710
   www.horvathlaw.org

Established: 1987

Insurance Defense, Coverage Issues, Legal Malpractice, Medical Malpractice, Professional Liability, Directors and Officers Liability, Product Liability, Environmental Law, Toxic Torts, Commercial Litigation, Transportation, Inland Marine, Governmental Liability, Fire, Arson, Fraud, Fidelity and Surety, Subrogation, Life Insurance, Accident and Health, Excess and Reinsurance, Workers' Compensation, Investigation and Adjustment, Drug and Medical Claims, Warehouse Law

Insurance Clients

Chubb Group of Insurance Companies
Hanover Insurance Group
Fireman's Fund Insurance Company
Underwriters at Lloyd's, London

Partners

John F. Horvath — DePaul University, B.S., 1968; The John Marshall Law School, J.D., 1974 — Admitted to Bar, 1974, Illinois; 1974, U.S. District Court, Northern District of Illinois; 1976, U.S. Court of Appeals, Seventh Circuit; 1980, U.S. District Court, Eastern District of Wisconsin; 1992, U.S. District Court, Eastern District of Michigan; 1996, U.S. Court of Appeals, Sixth Circuit; 2006, U.S. Court of Appeals, Eighth and Ninth Circuits — Member American, Illinois State and Chicago Bar Associations; International Association of Defense Counsel; Illinois Association of Defense Trial Counsel; Defense Research Institute — Practice Areas: Transportation; Professional Liability; Insurance Coverage; Insurance Defense; Subrogation; Product Liability; Inland Marine; Cargo; Commercial Litigation — E-mail: jhorvath@hlpc-law.com

Rosemarie J. Guadnolo — Loyola University, B.A. (with honors), 1968; Northwestern University School of Law, J.D., 1973 — Admitted to Bar, 1973, Illinois; 1973, U.S. District Court, Northern District of Illinois; 1976, U.S. Court of Appeals, Seventh Circuit; 1981, U.S. Supreme Court — Practice Areas: Commercial Litigation; Appellate Practice; Professional Liability — E-mail: rguadnolo@hlpc-law.com

Associate

Renata M. Zloza — Northwestern University, B.A., 2001; DePaul University College of Law, J.D. (magna cum laude), 2005 — Admitted to Bar, 2005, Illinois; 2005, U.S. District Court, Northern District of Illinois — Member American and Chicago Bar Associations; Polish Advocate Society — Languages: Polish — Practice Areas: Commercial Litigation; Insurance Defense — E-mail: rzloza@hlpc-law.com

(This firm is also listed in the Subrogation, Investigation and Adjustment section of this directory)

Hughes, Socol, Piers, Resnick & Dym Ltd.

Three First National Plaza
70 West Madison Street, Suite 4000
Chicago, Illinois 60602
   Telephone: 312-580-0100
   Fax: 312-580-1994
   E-Mail: jhughes@hsplegal.com
   www.hsplegal.com

Established: 1985

Insurance Defense, Self-Insured, Professional Liability, Personal Injury, Property Damage, Medical Malpractice, Architects and Engineers, Construction Defect, Legal Malpractice, Accountant Malpractice, Coverage Litigation, Commercial Casualty

ILLINOIS

Hughes, Socol, Piers, Resnick & Dym Ltd., Chicago, IL
(Continued)

Firm Profile: HSP Ltd's self insured, professional liability and commercial casualty insurance practice represents railroads, manufacturers, medical, legal, insurance and construction design professionals in litigation in Nortneast Illinois, Northwest Indiana and Southeast Wisconsin. The firm has 30 lawyers and a diversity of litigation practice.

Insurance Clients

Architects and Engineers Insurance Company, Inc., A RRG
General Star Professional Liability
ISME Illinois State Medical
Everest National Insurance Company
Great American Insurance Group
Liberty International Underwriters

Non-Insurance Clients

Perkins & Will Architects
T.Y. Lin International
Thornton Tomasetti
Vibra-Tech, Inc.

Firm Members

John K. Hughes — College of the Holy Cross, A.B. (cum laude), 1970; The University of Chicago, M.A., 1971; J.D., 1974 — Admitted to Bar, 1974, Illinois; 1986, Wisconsin; 1982, U.S. District Court, Northern District of Illinois including Trial Bar; 1980, U.S. Court of Appeals, Seventh Circuit; 1993, U.S. District Court, Eastern District of Wisconsin — Member American, Illinois State and Chicago Bar Associations; Society of Trial Lawyers; American Board of Trial Advocates; Defense Research Institute

Donna Kaner Socol — Northwestern University, B.A. (cum laude), 1973; DePaul University, J.D. (cum laude), 1976 — Admitted to Bar, 1976, Illinois; 1982, U.S. District Court, Northern District of Illinois including Trial Bar — Member American, Illinois State and Chicago Bar Associations; American Academy of Hospital Attorneys; Illinois Association of Hospital Attorneys; Defense Research Institute

Donald G. Peterson — Miami University, B.A., 1962; Northwestern University, J.D., 1991 — Admitted to Bar, 1966, Illinois; 1982, U.S. District Court, Northern District of Illinois including Trial Bar; 1983, U.S. Court of Appeals, Seventh Circuit; 1984, U.S. Supreme Court; 1999, U.S. District Court, Northern District of Indiana — Member American, Illinois State and Chicago Bar Associations; Appellate Lawyers Association of Illinois; Society of Trial Lawyers; Illinois Association of Defense Trial Counsel

J. Eric Vander Arend — University of the Arts, B.F.A., 1980; Northwestern University, J.D., 1991 — Admitted to Bar, 1991, Illinois; 1992, U.S. District Court, Northern District of Illinois; 1995, U.S. Court of Appeals, Seventh Circuit — Member Illinois State Bar Association

Robert R. Anderson, III — Boston University, B.A., 1981; Northwestern University, J.D., 1984 — Admitted to Bar, 1984, Illinois — Member Chicago Bar Association; Defense Research Institute

Daniel A. Waitzman — University of Illinois-Urbana-Champaign, B.S., 2000; Illinois Institute of Technology, Chicago-Kent College of Law, J.D. (with honors), 2006 — Admitted to Bar, 2006, Illinois; U.S. District Court, Northern District of Illinois — Member Illinois State and Chicago Bar Associations

Benjamin P. Beringer — Wabash College, B.A. (summa cum laude), 1987; Indiana University, J.D. (cum laude), 1990 — Admitted to Bar, 1990, Illinois; U.S. District Court, Northern District of Illinois — Member Illinois State and Chicago Bar Associations

Roger Littman — University of Illinois at Urbana-Champaign, B.A., 1976; University of Illinois, J.D., 1979 — Admitted to Bar, 1979, Illinois; 1984, U.S. District Court, Northern District of Illinois including Trial Bar

Christopher A. Johnson — University of Illinois at Urbana-Champaign, B.A. Political Science, 2007; DePaul University, J.D., 2010 — Admitted to Bar, 2010, Illinois; 2012, U.S. District Court, Northern District of Illinois — Member Illinois State Bar Association; Defense Research Institute

Scott Mueller — Eastern Illinois University, B.A., 1988; The John Marshall Law School, J.D., 2003 — Admitted to Bar, 2003, Illinois; U.S. District Court, Northern District of Illinois — Member Illinois State and Chicago Bar Associations

Adam Snyder — University of Illinois at Chicago, B.S., 2005; The John Marshall Law School, J.D. (magna cum laude), 2010 — Admitted to Bar, 2010, Illinois; U.S. District Court, Northern District of Illinois — Member American, Illinois State and Chicago Bar Associations; West Suburban Bar Association (Board of Governors); Illinois Association of Healthcare Attorneys; American Society for Healthcare Risk Management; Defense Research Institute; Illinois Association of Defense Trial Counsel

CHICAGO

The Hunt Law Group, LLC
20 North Wacker Drive
Suite 1711
Chicago, Illinois 60606
Telephone: 312-384-2300
Fax: 312-443-9391
E-Mail: bhunt@hunt-lawgroup.com
www.hunt-lawgroup.com

Construction Litigation, Insurance Coverage, Premises Liability, Product Liability, Professional Liability, Transportation

Insurance Clients

Cannon Cochran Management Services, Inc.
Cincinnati Specialty Underwriters
Risk Enterprise Management, Ltd.
Canopius US Insurance, Inc.
Cincinnati Insurance Company
Insurance Program Administrators

Non-Insurance Clients

Acceas Partners
Correct Construction, Inc.
Fabcon
Optimal Energy, LLC
Combined Oil Company
Electrolux
Marten Transport, Ltd.
Solid Platforms, Inc.

Principal

Brian J. Hunt — 1964 — University of Michigan, B.B.A. (with high distinction), 1986; University of Illinois, J.D. (magna cum laude), 1991 — Beta Alpha Psi — University of Illinois Law Review — Admitted to Bar, 1991, Illinois; U.S. District Court, Northern District of Illinois including Trial Bar; U.S. District Court, Central and Southern Districts of Illinois; U.S. District Court, Northern and Southern Districts of Indiana; U.S. Court of Appeals, Third and Seventh Circuits; Supreme Court of Illinois; U.S. Supreme Court — Member American and Illinois State Bar Associations; American Law Institute; Defense Research Institute; Trucking Industry Defense Association; Transportation Lawyers Association; Professional Liability Underwriting Society; Illinois Association of Defense Trial Counsel — Certified Public Accountant, Illinois, 1986; Illinois CPA Society — Practice Areas: Commercial Litigation; Professional Liability; Construction Litigation; Product Liability; Transportation; Insurance Coverage; Appellate Practice

Of Counsel

Mario R. Cusumano — 1965 — DePaul University, B.S., 1987; The John Marshall Law School, J.D., 1991 — Admitted to Bar, 1993, Illinois; U.S. District Court, Northern District of Illinois — Member National Institute of Trial Advocacy — Practice Areas: Transportation; Premises Liability; Construction Litigation; Insurance Coverage

Attorney

Brian H. Myers — 1986 — Miami University, B.A./B.S., 2008; DePaul University College of Law, J.D. (cum laude), 2011 — Admitted to Bar, 2011, Illinois; 2013, U.S. District Court, Central, Northern and Southern Districts of Illinois — Member American, Illinois State and Chicago Bar Associations — Practice Areas: Commercial Litigation; Construction Litigation; Premises Liability

Matthew J. Ennis — 1986 — Arizona State University, B.S., 2008; Loyola University Chicago School of Law, J.D., 2012 — Admitted to Bar, 2012, Illinois; 2013, U.S. District Court, Northern District of Illinois — Member American and Chicago Bar Associations — Practice Areas: Commercial Litigation; Construction Litigation; Premises Liability

Courtney E. Healy — 1985 — Michigan State University, B.A. (cum laude), 2008; DePaul University College of Law, J.D., 2011 — Admitted to Bar, 2011, Illinois; 2012, U.S. District Court, Northern District of Illinois — Member American and Illinois State Bar Association; Women's Bar Association — Practice Areas: Insurance Defense; Construction Liability; Premises Liability; Product Liability

Sarah R. Riedl — 1988 — University of Illinois at Urbana-Champaign, B.A., 2010; Wake Forest University School of Law, J.D., 2013 — Admitted to Bar, 2013, Illinois; U.S. District Court, Northern District of Illinois — Practice Areas: Premises Liability; Product Liability

Angela M. Rentz — 1985 — The Ohio State University, B.A., 2008; DePaul University College of Law, J.D., 2011 — Admitted to Bar, 2011, Illinois; U.S. District Court, Northern District of Illinois including Trial Bar; U.S. Court of Appeals, Seventh Circuit — Member American Bar Association; Women's Bar Association — Practice Areas: Premises Liability; Product Liability

CHICAGO   ILLINOIS

Jump & Associates, P.C.

1 North LaSalle Street, Suite 1820
Chicago, Illinois 60602
 Telephone: 312-629-5757
Fax: 312-629-9339
E-Mail: jumplaw@att.net

Established: 1994

Tort Litigation, Construction Litigation, Product Liability, Insurance Coverage, Personal and Commercial Vehicle, Premises Liability, Uninsured and Underinsured Motorist, Insurance Defense, Trial Practice, Appellate Practice, Arbitration, Mediation, General Civil Trial and Appellate Practice, Alternative Dispute Resolution

Firm Profile: Jump & Associates, P.C. is a small insurance defense trial firm with extensive experience in presenting complex liability and insurance coverage cases in mediations and in other forms of alternative dispute resolution.

Insurance Clients

American National Property and Casualty Company
Fireman's Fund Insurance Company
United Fire & Casualty Company
West Bend Mutual Insurance Company
Amerisure Companies
The Cincinnati Insurance Companies
Lincoln General Insurance Company
Zurich American Insurance Group

Non-Insurance Clients

Federal Building Services
TD Insurance
McNelly Services, Inc.
Temtex Industries, Inc.

Partner

R. Howard Jump — 1953 — Mercer University, B.A., 1976; Mercer University Walter F. George School of Law, J.D., 1979 — IDC President's Commendation, 1995; Chicago Volunteer Legal Services Foundation, Distinguished Service Award, 2000; IDC Meritorious Service Award, 2006; IDC Distinguished Member Award, 2008; IDC President's Commendation, 2010;IDC Certificate of Appreciation for Service to the Defense Bar, 2013; DRI Exceptional Performance Citation, 2013. — Mercer Law Review — Admitted to Bar, 1979, Georgia; 1981, Illinois; 1979, U.S. District Court, Southern District of Georgia; 1981, U.S. District Court, Northern District of Illinois; 1987, U.S. Court of Appeals, Seventh Circuit — Member American Bar Association (Litigation, Tort Trial and Insurance Practice Sections, 1979-Present); Illinois State and Chicago (Insurance, ADR and Tort Law Committees, 1981-Present) Bar Associations; State Bar of Georgia; Defense Research Institute; Association of Defense Trial Attorneys; Panel Member Chicago Volunteer Legal Services; Illinois Association of Defense Trial Counsel (IDC): Insurance Law Committee, 1990-1995; Defense Trial Tactics Spring Seminar Chairman, 1995; Spring Seminar Committee, 1987-1995; Trial Academy Faculty, 1998-1999; Board Liaison to Insurance Law Committee, 2004-2008; Planning Committee Construction Coverage Symposium, St. Louis, Mo. Fall 2007; Board of Directors, 2000-2008; Executive Committee, Secretary-Treasurer, 2008-2009, Second-Vice President, 2009, First Vice President, 2010, President Elect 2011, President, 2012. — Contributing Author: "Significant Coverage Decisions Affecting UM/UIM; Conflict of Interest; Property Damage and Occurrence; and Contractors' Insurance," IDC Monograph, IDC Quarterly, Third Quarter, 1992, Vol. 2 No. 3; "Punitive Damages and Conflict of Interest: Why Illinois Defense Lawyers Need Statutory Relief," IDC Monograph, IDC Quarterly, Fourth Quarter, 1993, Vol. 3 No. 4; "How Much Room Under the Umbrella? An Examination of Ancillary Insurance Relationships. The Primary-Excess Relationship: Equitable Subrogation v. Direct Duty," IDC Monograph, IDC Quarterly, Fourth Quarter, 1994, Vol. 4 No. 4; "Horizontal Exhaustion Trumps Selective Tender," Insurance Law Column, IDC Quarterly, Fourth Quarter, 2006, Vol. 4 No. 4; IDC "Recent Developments in Additional Insured Case Law," Insurance Law Committee Newsletter, Defense Update, 2006, Vol. 6 No. 1 — Qualified Chairperson, Cook County Mandatory Arbitration Program; Harvard Law School, Program of Instruction for Lawyers, Mediation Workshop, 2003

Jump & Associates, P.C., Chicago, IL   (Continued)

Senior Associate

Mei Chan — 1970 — Loyola University Chicago, B.A. (magna cum laude), 1992; Illinois Institute of Technology, Chicago-Kent College of Law, J.D., 1996 — Admitted to Bar, 1996, Illinois; U.S. District Court, Northern District of Illinois; 2008, U.S. District Court, Northern District of Illinois including Trial Bar — Member Illinois Association of Defense Trial Counsel — Arbitration Panelist, Circuit Court of Cook County Mandatory Arbitration Program (2001-2005); Panel Member, Chicago Volunteer Legal Services

Senior Counsel

John R. Garofalo

Kopon Airdo, LLC

Willis Tower
233 South Wacker Drive, Suite 4450
Chicago, Illinois 60606
 Telephone: 312-506-4470
Fax: 312-506-4460
E-Mail: akopon@koponairdo.com
www.koponairdo.com

Administrative Law, Business Litigation, Complex Litigation, Construction Law, Employment Law, Health Care, Insurance, Mediation, Municipal Law, Product Liability, Premises Liability, Catastrophic Litigation, Negligence General Tort, Retail Establishments Liability

Firm Profile: Kopon Airdo, LLC is dedicated to providing our clients with the highest quality, responsive legal representation. We have broad experience in successfully representing commercial businesses and not-for-profit organizations in a variety of matters that are headed toward, or are already in, litigation. Our unwavering commitment to our clients drives our work and our investment in state of the art technology and highly qualified and skilled trial attorneys.

Insurance Clients

Christian Brothers Risk Pooling Trust
Society Insurance, A Mutual Company

Members

Michael A. Airdo — DePaul University, B.A. (summa cum laude), 1993; DePaul University College of Law, J.D. (with honors), 1996 — Order of the Coif — Admitted to Bar, 1996, Illinois; U.S. District Court, Northern District of Illinois; 2002, U.S. District Court, Northern District of Indiana — Member Claims and Litigation Management Alliance; International Association of Defense Counsel; Illinois Association of Defense Trial Counsel; Defense Research Institute — Tel: 312-506-4480 — E-mail: mairdo@koponairdo.com

P. Patrick Cella — Miami University, B.A. Political Science, 1999; DePaul University College of Law, J.D. (cum laude), 2002 — Admitted to Bar, 2002, Illinois; U.S. District Court, Northern District of Illinois — Member Tooling & Manufacturing Association, Young Leaders' Committee; Illinois Association of Defense Trial Counsel — Tel: 312-506-4476 — E-mail: pcella@koponairdo.com

Andrew Kopon, Jr. — Providence College, B.A., 1976; The John Marshall Law School, J.D. (with distinction), 1980 — The John Marshall Law School Law Review — Admitted to Bar, 1980, Illinois; 1982, New Jersey; 1980, U.S. District Court, Northern District of Illinois; 1982, U.S. District Court, District of New Jersey; 1984, U.S. District Court, Northern District of Illinois including Trial Bar — Member International Association of Defense Counsel; The Foundation of the International Association of Defense Counsel, Board of Directors; National Foundation for Judicial Excellence; International Association of Defense Counsel; Illinois Association of Defense Trial Counsel; Defense Research Institute — Martindale-Hubbell® AV Preeminent Rated; Illinois Super Lawyers (2006, 2012-2013); Leading Lawyers Network — Tel: 312-506-4470 — E-mail: akopon@koponairdo.com

Mollie N. Werwas — Southern Illinois University, B.A. (summa cum laude), 2003; Southern Illinois University School of Law, J.D. (summa cum laude), 2006 — Admitted to Bar, 2006, Illinois; U.S. District Court, Northern District of Illinois — Member American and Chicago Bar Associations; Defense

Kopon Airdo, LLC, Chicago, IL (Continued)

Research Institute — Tel: 312-506-4474 — E-mail: mwerwas@koponairdo.com

Rachel E. Yarch — Michigan State University, B.A., 1998; DePaul University College of Law, J.D., 2001 — Admitted to Bar, 2001, Illinois; U.S. District Court, Northern District of Illinois; 2005, Federal Trial Bar; 2006, U.S. Court of Appeals, Seventh Circuit; 2007, U.S. District Court, Northern District of Indiana — Member National Association of College and University Attorneys; Defense Research Institute; International Association of Defense Counsel — Tel: 312-506-4471 — E-mail: ryarch@koponairdo.com

Associates

Kurt Asprooth
David Duffey
Joseph Giambrone
Kathryn B. Harvey
Jaclyn Bacallao
Christie Bolsen
Bret Franco
Ryan Greely
Eleonora P. Khazanova
Joseph Stafford

LaBarge, Campbell & Lyon L.L.C.

200 West Jackson, Suite 2050
Chicago, Illinois 60606
    Telephone: 312-580-9010
    Fax: 312-580-9011
    E-Mail: kcampbell@lcllaw.com
    www.lcllaw.com

Established: 1997

Insurance Defense, Casualty, General Liability, Automobile, Homeowners, Construction Law, Medical Malpractice, Asbestos Litigation, Commercial Litigation, Insurance Coverage, Product Liability, Trucking Law

Firm Profile: LaBarge, Campbell & Lyon, L.L.C. was founded in 1997 by Michael R. LaBarge, Kevin Campbell and Bruce W. Lyon. The firm represents individuals, corporations and insurance carriers in all aspects of civil litigation and insurance related matters. The firm is dedicated to providing the highest quality legal services in a personal and cost efficient manner.

Insurance Clients

Cincinnati Insurance Company
Grange Insurance Company
ProNational Insurance Company
Erie Insurance Group
Great West Casualty Company

Partners

Michael R. LaBarge — 1956 — University of Notre Dame, B.A., 1979; University of Illinois, J.D., 1982 — Admitted to Bar, 1982, Illinois; 1982, U.S. District Court, Northern District of Illinois including Trial Bar — Member Illinois State and Chicago Bar Associations; Defense Research Institute; Trucking Industry Defense Association — Tel: 312-580-9014 — E-mail: mlabarge@lcllaw.com

Kevin Campbell — 1956 — Denison University, B.A., 1979; Boston University, J.D., 1982 — Admitted to Bar, 1982, Illinois; 1982, U.S. District Court, Northern District of Illinois — Member Illinois State and Chicago Bar Associations; Society of Trial Lawyers; Illinois Association of Healthcare Attorneys; Council on Litigation Management; Defense Research Institute — Tel: 312-580-9017 — E-mail: kcampbell@lcllaw.com

Bruce W. Lyon — 1959 — St. Olaf College, B.A. (cum laude), 1981; DePaul University, J.D. (with honors), 1984 — Admitted to Bar, 1984, Illinois; 1984, U.S. District Court, Central, Northern and Southern Districts of Illinois; 1984, U.S. District Court, Western District of Wisconsin; 1984, U.S. District Court, Northern District of Indiana — Member Illinois State and Chicago Bar Associations; Illinois Association of Defense Trial Counsel — Tel: 312-580-9013 — E-mail: blyon@lcllaw.com

Melanie A. Strubbe — 1970 — Northwestern University, B.A., 1992; University of Houston Law Center, J.D. (cum laude), 1995 — Admitted to Bar, 1995, California; 1996, Nevada; 1997, Illinois; 1995, U.S. District Court, Southern District of California — Member Illinois State, Orange County and Chicago Bar Associations — Tel: 312-580-9021 — E-mail: mstrubbe@lcllaw.com

Angie M. Grove — 1976 — Miami University, B.A., 1998; DePaul University, J.D., 2001 — Admitted to Bar, 2001, Illinois; 2001, U.S. District Court,

LaBarge, Campbell & Lyon L.L.C., Chicago, IL (Continued)

Northern District of Illinois; 2011, U.S. Court of Appeals, Seventh Circuit — Member Chicago Bar Association — Tel: 312-580-7930 — E-mail: agrove@lcllaw.com

Associates

Camilla M. Pollock-Flynn — 1982 — University of Notre Dame, B.B.A. (cum laude), 2004; DePaul University College of Law, J.D. (cum laude), 2007 — Admitted to Bar, 2007, Illinois; U.S. District Court, Northern District of Illinois — Member Women's Bar Association of Illinois; Illinois Association of Defense Trial Counsel — Certificate in Health Law — E-mail: cpollock-flynn@lcllaw.com

Kathleen J. Scanlan — 1984 — Villanova University, B.A. (cum laude), 2007; Loyola University Chicago School of Law, J.D. (Dean's List), 2010 — Admitted to Bar, 2010, Illinois — Member American and Chicago Bar Associations — E-mail: kscanlan@lcllaw.com

Katherine Larson — 1986 — University of Illinois at Urbana-Champaign, B.A. (with distinction), 2008; DePaul University College of Law, J.D. (summa cum laude), 2011 — Admitted to Bar, 2011, Illinois — Member American, Illinois State and Chicago Bar Associations — E-mail: klarson@lcllaw.com

Marie K. Lynch — 1988 — Marquette University, B.A. (summa cum laude), 2009; Loyola University Chicago School of Law, J.D. (Dean's List), 2012 — Admitted to Bar, 2012, Illinois — E-mail: mlynch@lcllaw.com

Micki J. Kennedy — 1979 — The University of Iowa, B.A., 2002; Creighton University School of Law, J.D. (cum laude), 2005 — Admitted to Bar, 2005, Illinois; 2007, Iowa (Inactive); U.S. District Court, Northern District of Illinois — Member Chicago Bar Association — Certificate in Dispute Resolution — E-mail: mkennedy@lcllaw.com

Corinne M. Koopman — 1988 — University of Illinois at Urbana-Champaign, B.A. (cum laude), 2010; Loyola University Chicago School of Law, J.D. (Dean's List), 2013 — Admitted to Bar, 2013, Illinois; 2014, U.S. District Court, Northern District of Illinois — E-mail: ckoopman@kllaw.com

Langhenry, Gillen, Lundquist & Johnson, LLC

33 North Dearborn, Suite 1600
Chicago, Illinois 60602
    Telephone: 312-704-6700
    Fax: 312-704-6777
    E-Mail: rdeporte@lglfirm.com
    www.lglfirm.com

(Joliet, IL Office*: 18 West Cass Street, Suite 500, 60432)
    (Tel: 815-726-3600)
    (Fax: 815-726-3676)
(Wheaton, IL Office*: 311 South County Farm Road, Suite L, 60187)
    (Tel: 630-653-5775)
    (Fax: 630-653-5980)
(Rockford, IL Office*: 6785 Weaver Road, Suite 2E, 61114)
    (Tel: 815-636-1800)
    (Fax: 815-636-2860)
(Princeton, IL Office*: 605 South Main Street, 61356)
    (Tel: 815-915-8540)
    (Fax: 815-915-8581)
    (E-Mail: rdeporte@lgljfirm.com)
    (www.lgljfirm.com)

Established: 1997

Medical Malpractice, General Liability, Subrogation, Coverage Issues, Opinions, Declaratory Judgments, Automobile, Property Damage, Personal Injury, Premises Liability, Product Liability, Defense Litigation, Employment Discrimination, Class Actions, Construction Litigation

Firm Profile: Your partner from the boardroom to the courtroom. Langhenry, Gillen, Lundquist and Johnson, LLC is a litigation and business firm that combines large firm legal experience and ability, with small firm accessibility and attention.

CHICAGO

Langhenry, Gillen, Lundquist & Johnson, LLC, Chicago, IL (Continued)

Insurance Clients

ACUITY
Atlantic Mutual Insurance Company
GuideOne Insurance
ISMIE Mutual Insurance Company
PRMS, Inc. - Professional Risk Management Services, Inc.
Unitrin Property and Casualty Insurance Group
West Bend Mutual Insurance Company
Argonaut Insurance Company
Badger Mutual Insurance Company
Federated Insurance Company
HARCO Insurance
Mercury Insurance Company
Safeco Insurance
Travelers Insurance Company
Universal Underwriters Group
Universal Underwriters Insurance Company

Managing Partner

John G. Langhenry III — 1958 — University of Notre Dame, A.B., 1980; Loyola University Chicago School of Law, J.D., 1984 — Admitted to Bar, 1985, Illinois — Member Illinois State and DuPage County Bar Associations; Defense Research Institute; Illinois Association of Defense Trial Counsel — Practice Areas: Civil Litigation; Medical Malpractice Defense; General Liability; Premises Liability — E-mail: jlanghenry@lglfirm.com

Partners

William B. Weiler — 1963 — University of Notre Dame, B.A.E., 1985; The John Marshall Law School, J.D. (with high honors), 1989 — Admitted to Bar, 1989, Illinois; 2013, Indiana; 1990, U.S. District Court, Northern District of Illinois — Member American and Illinois State Bar Associations; Illinois Defense Counsel — Practice Areas: Litigation — E-mail: bweiler@lglfirm.com

Thomas R. Weiler — 1958 — University of Notre Dame, B.B.A., 1980; Loyola University Chicago School of Law, J.D., 1983 — Admitted to Bar, 1983, Illinois; 1989, U.S. District Court, Northern District of Illinois; 1995, U.S. Court of Appeals, Seventh Circuit — Member Illinois State and DuPage County Bar Associations — Practice Areas: Defense Litigation; Civil Rights; Employment Litigation — E-mail: tweiler@lglfirm.com

Melissa J. Gordon — 1969 — The University of Texas, B.S., 1991; Illinois Institute of Technology, Chicago-Kent College of Law, J.D. (with honors), 1994 — Admitted to Bar, 1994, Illinois; U.S. District Court, Northern District of Illinois — Member Illinois State and Chicago Bar Associations — Practice Areas: Medical Malpractice Defense; Nursing Home Liability; Nursing Home Litigation; Litigation Defense — E-mail: mgordon@lglfirm.com

Michael R. Radak — 1976 — University of Illinois, B.A., 1998; DePaul University College of Law, J.D., 2001 — Admitted to Bar, 2003, Illinois; U.S. District Court, Northern District of Illinois — Member Illinois State and Chicago Bar Associations — Practice Areas: Personal Injury Litigation; Construction Litigation; Dram Shop; Slip and Fall; Motor Vehicle; Commercial Insurance; Subrogation; Product Liability Defense; Medical Malpractice Defense — E-mail: mradak@lglfirm.com

(See Joliet, Rockford and Wheaton, IL listings for additional information)

(This firm is also listed in the Subrogation section of this directory)

Lipe Lyons Murphy Nahrstadt & Pontikis Ltd.

230 West Monroe Street, Suite 2260
Chicago, Illinois 60606
Telephone: 312-448-6230
Fax: 312-726-2273
E-Mail: bcn@lipelyons.com
www.lipelyons.com

Established: 2012

Commercial Litigation, Construction Law, General Liability, Insurance, Labor and Employment, Product Liability, Professional Liability, Transportation

Firm Profile: Lipe Lyons Murphy Nahrstadt & Pontikis was founded after the five name partners, with decades of experience, departed from their former firm together in order to better serve their long-standing clients. A testament to the relationships that the firm builds with each of its clients, the firm and its

ILLINOIS

Lipe Lyons Murphy Nahrstadt & Pontikis Ltd., Chicago, IL (Continued)

clients work in partnership to maximize the value afforded to each client. This dedication to client service serves as the foundation of every firm undertaking.

Allianz Global Risks U.S. Insurance Company
Goodman Manufacturing
Zurich North America
BorgWarner, Inc.
CCMSI
McWane, Inc.

Partners

Jeremy T. Burton — Loyola University, B.A. (cum laude), 1995; University of Wisconsin Law School, J.D., 2001 — Admitted to Bar, 2001, Illinois; Wisconsin; U.S. District Court, Northern District of Illinois — E-mail: jtb@lipelyons.com

Jeffrey H. Lipe — Tulane University, B.A., 1980; University of Illinois College of Law, J.D., 1983 — Admitted to Bar, 1983, Illinois; U.S. District Court, Northern District of Illinois including Trial Bar; U.S. District Court, Central District of Illinois; U.S. District Court, Northern District of Indiana — E-mail: jhl@lipelyons.com

Raymond Lyons, Jr. — Loyola University, B.S., 1973; DePaul University College of Law, J.D. (with honors), 1980 — Admitted to Bar, 1980, Illinois; U.S. District Court, Northern District of Illinois including Trial Bar; U.S. District Court, Central District of Illinois; U.S. District Court, Southern District of Indiana; U.S. District Court, Eastern District of Wisconsin — E-mail: rl@lipelyons.com

Edward J. Murphy — Illinois Institute of Technology, B.S., 1969; DePaul University College of Law, J.D. (with honors), 1980 — Admitted to Bar, 1980, Illinois; U.S. District Court, Northern District of Illinois including Trial Bar; U.S. District Court, Central District of Illinois; U.S. Court of Appeals, Seventh Circuit; Prarie Band Potawatomi Nation Tribal Court — E-mail: ejm@lipelyons.com

Bradley C. Nahrstadt — Monmouth College, B.A. (summa cum laude, with distinction), 1989; University of Illinois College of Law, J.D., 1992 — Admitted to Bar, 1992, Illinois; U.S. District Court, Northern District of Illinois including Trial Bar; U.S. District Court, Southern District of Illinois; U.S. District Court, Southern District of Indiana; U.S. District Court, Eastern District of Michigan; U.S. Court of Appeals, Seventh and Tenth Circuits — E-mail: bcn@lipelyons.com

Thomas J. Pontikis — DePaul University, B.A. (with honors), 1983; DePaul University College of Law, J.D., 1986 — Admitted to Bar, 1986, Illinois; U.S. District Court, Northern District of Illinois including Trial Bar; U.S. District Court, Central and Southern Districts of Illinois — E-mail: tjp@lipelyons.com

James H. Whalen — Indiana University, B.A., 2000; DePaul University College of Law, J.D., 2004 — Admitted to Bar, 2004, Illinois; 2014, Ohio; 2004, U.S. District Court, Northern District of Illinois — E-mail: jhw@lipelyons.com

Associates

Derek J. Crimando
Ryan A. Kelly
Lauren N. Tuckey
Edward A. DeVries
Lindsey T. Millman
Frank Tung

Locke Lord LLP

111 South Wacker Drive
Chicago, Illinois 60606-4410
Telephone: 312-443-0700
Fax: 312-443-0336
www.lockelord.com

(Atlanta, GA Office*: Terminus 200, Suite 1200, 3333 Piedmont Road NE, 30305)
(Tel: 404-870-4600)
(Fax: 404-872-5547)
(Austin, TX Office*: 600 Congress Avenue, Suite 2200, 78701-2748)
(Tel: 512-305-4700)
(Fax: 512-305-4800)

ILLINOIS / CHICAGO

Locke Lord LLP, Chicago, IL (Continued)

(Dallas, TX Office*: 2200 Ross Avenue, Suite 2200, 75201)
  (Tel: 214-740-8000)
  (Fax: 214-740-8800)
(Houston, TX Office*: 2800 JPMorgan Chase Tower, 600 Travis, 77002-3095)
  (Tel: 713-226-1200)
  (Fax: 713-223-3717)
(London, United Kingdom Office*: 201 Bishopsgate, DX 567 London/City, EC2M 3AB)
  (Tel: +44 (0) 20 7861 9000 (Int'l))
  (Tel: 011 44 207861 9000 (US))
  (Fax: +44 (0) 20 7785 6869 201 (Bishopsgate))
(Los Angeles, CA Office*: 300 South Grand Avenue, Suite 2600, 90071-3119)
  (Tel: 213-485-1500)
  (Fax: 213-485-1200)
(New Orleans, LA Office*: 601 Poydras, Suite 2660, 70130)
  (Tel: 504-558-5100)
  (Fax: 504-558-5200)
(New York, NY Office*: Three World Financial Center, Floor 20, 10281)
  (Tel: 212-415-8600)
  (Fax: 212-303-2754)
(Sacramento, CA Office: 500 Capitol Mall, Suite 1800, 95814)
  (Tel: 916-554-0240)
  (Fax: 916-554-5440)
(San Francisco, CA Office*: 44 Montgomery Street, Suite 2400, 94104)
  (Tel: 415-318-8810)
  (Fax: 415-676-5816)
(Washington, DC Office*: 701 8th Street, N.W., Suite 700, 20001)
  (Tel: 202-521-4100)
  (Fax: 202-521-4200)
(Hong Kong, China-PRC Office: 21/F Bank of China Tower, 1 Garden Road, Central)
  (Tel: +852 3465 0600)
  (Fax: +852 3014 0991)

Established: 1914

Antitrust, Arbitration, Aviation, Business Law, Class Actions, Construction Law, Corporate Law, Directors and Officers Liability, Employee Benefits, Environmental Law, Health Care, Insurance Law, Intellectual Property, Labor and Employment, Land Use, Admiralty and Maritime Law, Mergers and Acquisitions, Product Liability, Railroad Law, Regulatory and Compliance, Reinsurance, Securities, Technology, Transportation, Litigation, Appellate, Long Term Care

Firm Profile: Locke Lord's more than 70 insurance attorneys have a breadth and depth of experience that touches on every aspect of the insurance and reinsurance industries, including Regulatory & Transactional, Litigation & Counseling, Aviation and Insurance Commercial Litigation. Our insurance teams focus on a full range of insurance matters and continue a tradition of 100-plus years serving insurance clients around the United States and around the world. Locke Lord's Insurance attorneys have earned a global reputation for excellence, dependability, solid solutions and client service, and are known for helping clients meet the challenges of today while preparing for the opportunities of tomorrow.

Insurance Clients

Commercial Union Insurance Company
General Accident Insurance Company

Partners

Robert A. Badgley — 1965 — University of Illinois, B.A. (summa cum laude), 1988; The University of Chicago, J.D., 1991 — Bronze Tablet — Admitted to Bar, 1991, Illinois — Languages: French — Practice Areas: Insurance Coverage; Insurance Litigation; Reinsurance

Christopher R. Barth — 1965 — The University of Iowa, B.B.A., 1988; DePaul University College of Law, J.D., 1991 — Admitted to Bar, 1991, Illinois; U.S. District Court, Northern District of Illinois including Trial Bar; 2001, U.S. District Court, Central District of Illinois — Member Illinois State Bar Association — Practice Areas: Aviation; Insurance Coverage; Insurance Litigation

Jon Biasetti — 1962 — Boston College, B.A. (cum laude), 1984; Boston College Law School, J.D. (magna cum laude), 1987 — Admitted to Bar, 1987, Illinois — Member Chicago Bar Association — Languages: Italian, French, Spanish — Practice Areas: Mergers and Acquisitions; Insurance Law; Regulatory and Compliance

T. Patrick Byrnes — DePaul University College of Law, J.D. (Dean's List), 1999 — Admitted to Bar, 1999, Illinois

Nick J. DiGiovanni — 1955 — Southern Methodist University, B.B.A. (cum laude), 1977; University of Notre Dame, J.D. (cum laude), 1980 — Admitted to Bar, 1980, Illinois; 1980, U.S. District Court, Northern District of Illinois; 1987, U.S. Court of Appeals, Seventh, Eighth and Ninth Circuits — Member American and Chicago Bar Associations — Practice Areas: Arbitration; Insurance Law; Reinsurance

Kirk W. Dillard — 1955 — Western Illinois University, B.A. (with honors), 1977; DePaul University, J.D., 1982 — Admitted to Bar, 1983, Illinois; 1983, U.S. District Court, Northern District of Illinois; 1984, U.S. District Court, Central District of Illinois — Member American, Illinois State and Chicago Bar Associations — Practice Areas: Corporate Law; Insurance Law; Professional Liability; Product Liability

Sean C. Fifield — 1972 — University of Michigan, B.S.E. (cum laude), 1993; J.D., 1996 — Admitted to Bar, 1997, Illinois; 1997, U.S. District Court, Northern District of Illinois — Member American, Illinois State and Chicago Bar Associations — Practice Areas: Corporate Law; Regulatory and Compliance

Matthew T. Furton — University of Michigan, B.A., 1992; Indiana University Maurer School of Law, J.D. (magna cum laude), 1995 — Order of the Coif — Notes and Comments Editor, Indiana Law Review — Admitted to Bar, 1995, Illinois; U.S. District Court, Eastern District of Michigan; U.S. District Court, Northern District of Illinois including Trial Bar; U.S. Court of Appeals, Seventh, Eighth and Eleventh Circuits — Member American (Tort Trial and Insurance Practice; Intellectual Property Law; Science & Technology Law; Litigation) and Chicago Bar Associations; Lawyers Club of Chicago — Practice Areas: Business Litigation; Dispute Resolution; Insurance; Reinsurance; Copyright and Trademark Law

Laurence A. Hansen — 1950 — St. Norbert College, B.S., 1972; University of Wisconsin, J.D. (cum laude), 1975 — Admitted to Bar, 1975, Wisconsin; 1975, Illinois — Member American and Chicago Bar Associations — Practice Areas: Employee Benefits

Martin W. Jaszczuk — The John Marshall Law School, J.D. (magna cum laude), 2002 — Admitted to Bar, 2000, Manitoba; 2002, Illinois

Thomas W. Jenkins — 1950 — Western Illinois University, B.A., 1972; Illinois Institute of Technology, Chicago-Kent College of Law, J.D. (cum laude), 1977 — Admitted to Bar, 1977, Illinois; 1988, California; 1979, U.S. District Court, Northern District of California; 1988, U.S. District Court, Central District of California — Member State Bar of California — Practice Areas: Insurance Law; Corporate Law; Regulatory and Compliance

David L. Kendall — 1956 — University of Michigan, B.B.A. (with high honors), 1979; University of Illinois, J.D. (cum laude), 1984 — Harno Fellowship; American Jurisprudence Awards — Admitted to Bar, 1984, Illinois — Member American and Chicago Bar Associations — Practice Areas: Corporate Law

John F. Kloecker — Harvard University, B.A. (cum laude), 1988; Northwestern University School of Law, J.D. (cum laude), 1995 — Admitted to Bar, 1995, Illinois; U.S. District Court, Northern District of Illinois; U.S. Court of Appeals, Sixth and Seventh Circuits — Member American Bar Association — Practice Areas: Business Litigation; Dispute Resolution; Class Actions; Insurance

Kay W. McCurdy — 1950 — Bradley University, B.A. (summa cum laude), 1972; The University of Chicago, J.D., 1975 — Admitted to Bar, 1975, Illinois; 1975, U.S. District Court, Northern District of Illinois — Practice Areas: Corporate Law

Thomas J. Murnighan — 1955 — DePaul University, B.A., 1978; Northwestern University, J.D., 1981 — Admitted to Bar, 1981, Illinois; 1981, U.S. District Court, Northern District of Illinois — Member American Bar Association — Practice Areas: Insurance Law; Reinsurance

Ernesto R. Palomo — University of Illinois, B.A. (with high distinction), 1999; University of Illinois College of Law, J.D., 2002 — Phi Beta Kappa — Symposium Editor, University of Illinois Law Review — Admitted to Bar, 2002, Illinois; U.S. District Court, Northern District of Illinois — Member Chicago Bar Association; Hispanic Lawyers Association of Illinois — Languages: Spanish — Practice Areas: Business Litigation; Arbitration; Insurance Law; Reinsurance

J. Brett Pritchard — 1962 — Bates College, B.A. (with high honors), 1984; Cornell University Law School, J.D., 1990 — Admitted to Bar, 1990,

CHICAGO   ILLINOIS

Locke Lord LLP, Chicago, IL   (Continued)

Illinois — Member American Bar Association — Practice Areas: Mergers and Acquisitions

Michael K. Renetzky — 1972 — Saint Louis University, B.S.B.A. (summa cum laude), 1993; Harvard University, J.D., 1996 — Admitted to Bar, 1996, Illinois; 1996, U.S. District Court, Northern District of Illinois — Member American Bar Association — Practice Areas: Securities

Daniel I. Schlessinger — 1954 — Brandeis University, B.A., 1975; University of Illinois, J.D. (cum laude), 1978 — Admitted to Bar, 1978, Illinois; 1978, U.S. District Court, Northern District of Illinois; 1987, U.S. District Court, Eastern District of Michigan; 1987, U.S. Court of Appeals, Sixth Circuit; 1989, U.S. Court of Appeals, Seventh Circuit; 1994, U.S. District Court, Central District of Illinois — Member American and Chicago Bar Associations — Practice Areas: Business Law

Anthony B. Sherman — 1967 — University of Wisconsin-Madison, B.B.A. (with distinction), 1989; J.D. (cum laude), 1992 — Order of the Coif — Admitted to Bar, 1992, Wisconsin; Illinois; 1992, U.S. District Court, Northern District of Illinois; 1992, U.S. District Court, Western District of Wisconsin — Member American and Chicago Bar Associations — Chartered Property and Casualty Underwriter — Practice Areas: Insurance Law; Mergers and Acquisitions

Molly McGinnis Stine — 1965 — Macalester College, B.A. (cum laude), 1987; University of Michigan, J.D., 1990 — Admitted to Bar, 1990, Illinois — Member American Bar Association — Practice Areas: Insurance Law

Ann C. Taylor — 1962 — Miami University, B.A., 1983; University of Cincinnati, J.D. (magna cum laude), 1992 — Admitted to Bar, 1992, Illinois; 1992, U.S. District Court, Northern District of Illinois — Practice Areas: Aviation; Environmental Law; Insurance Law

Paige D. Waters — Miami University, B.A., 1986; Chicago-Kent College of Law, J.D., 1989 — Admitted to Bar, 1989, Illinois; U.S. District Court, Northern District of Illinois — Member International Association of Insurance Receivers (Amicus Committee); INSOL International; AIDA Reinsurance and Insurance Arbitration Society (ARIAS) — Chambers USA, Insurance: Transactional & Regulatory (2005-2013); Legal 500 Insurance: Non-Contentious (2011); Illinois Super Lawyers (2009-2012) — Practice Areas: Health Care; Insurance; Reinsurance

Gary W. Westerberg — 1945 — Cornell College, B.A., 1968; Southern Methodist University, Dedman School of Law, J.D., 1971 — Order of the Coif — Admitted to Bar, 1971, Illinois; 1971, Supreme Court of Illinois; 1972, U.S. Court of Appeals, Seventh Circuit; 1973, U.S. District Court, Northern District of Illinois; 1982, U.S. Court of Appeals, Third and Tenth Circuits; 1983, U.S. District Court, Northern District of Illinois including Trial Bar; 1997, U.S. District Court, District of Arizona — Member International and American Bar Associations; National Transportation Safety Board Bar Association; International Association of Defense Counsel; Lawyer-Pilots Bar Association — Practice Areas: Insurance Coverage; Litigation; Product Liability

Steven T. Whitmer — 1971 — Wheaton College, B.A. (magna cum laude), 1993; The University of Chicago, J.D., 1997 — Admitted to Bar, 1997, Illinois; 1997, U.S. District Court, Northern District of Illinois; 2001, U.S. Court of Appeals, First Circuit — Member American Bar Association — Practice Areas: Business Law

Julie L. Young — University of Michigan, B.A. (with distinction), 1997; University of Michigan Law School, J.D. (cum laude), 2000 — Admitted to Bar, 2000, Illinois; U.S. District Court, Northern District of Illinois — Member Chicago Bar Association; Children's Law Pro Bono Project; Midwest Immigrant & Human Rights Pro Bono Project — Practice Areas: Directors and Officers Liability; Business Law; Arbitration

Senior Counsel

Mark A. Deptula   Timothy S. Farber
Keith Gibson   Julie N. Johnston

Of Counsel

R. Dean Conlin   John Costello
Lawrence M. Friedman   Roger R. Fross
Stephanie O'Neill Marco   Maynerd I. Steinberg

Associates

Baird Allis   Katherine Heid Harris
Ryan M. Holz   Matthew J. Kalas
Ashlee Knuckey   Ben Sykes

Magnani & Buck Ltd.
321 South Plymouth Court, Suite 1700
Chicago, Illinois 60604
  Telephone: 312-294-4800
  Fax: 312-294-4815
  E-Mail: law@magnanibuck.com
  www.magnanibuck.com

Construction Liability, General Liability, Insurance Law, Product Liability, Professional Malpractice, Transportation

Firm Profile: The firm was founded in 1987 and concentrates in defense litigation. The firm's civil trial and appellate practice includes representation of both insurers and self-insurers in state and federal courts throughout Illinois.

Insurance Clients

Allstate Insurance Company   American Southern Insurance
Discover Re   Company
Encompass Insurance   General Star Indemnity Company
Progressive Casualty Insurance
  Company

Non-Insurance Clients

American Claims Service, Ltd.   Ariens Company / Gravely
Avis Budget Group, Inc.   International
Cook-Illinois Corporation   Dollar-Thrifty Automotive Group,
Enterprise Rent-A-Car Company   Inc.
GameStop   Sears Holdings Management
Sedgwick Claims Management   Corporation
  Services, Inc.   Stevens Transport, Inc.
York Claims Service, Inc.

Partners

Peter J. Magnani — 1946 — Indiana University, B.S., 1971; J.D., 1974 — Admitted to Bar, 1974, Illinois; 1974, U.S. Court of Appeals, Seventh Circuit; 1974, U.S. District Court, Northern District of Illinois — Member American, Illinois State and Chicago Bar Associations; Illinois Association of Defense Trial Counsel; Defense Research Institute

Thomas L. Buck — 1957 — Vanderbilt University, B.A., 1979; DePaul University, J.D., 1983 — Admitted to Bar, 1983, Illinois; U.S. District Court, Central, Northern and Southern Districts of Illinois; U.S. Court of Appeals, Seventh Circuit — Member Illinois State and Chicago Bar Associations

Associates

Jennifer Rawe Wagner — 1978 — University of Northern Iowa, B.A. (summa cum laude), 2000; The University of Iowa, J.D. (with distinction), 2003 — Admitted to Bar, 2003, Iowa; 2004, Illinois; 2009, U.S. District Court, Northern District of Illinois — Member Illinois State Bar Association

Matthew T. Volk — 1972 — Michigan State University, B.A. (with honors), 1998; The University of Iowa, J.D., 2002 — Admitted to Bar, 2002, Illinois; U.S. District Court, Northern District of Illinois

Allison A. Batt — 1974 — Drake University, B.A. (cum laude), 1997; DePaul University College of Law, J.D., 2000 — Admitted to Bar, 2000, Illinois; U.S. District Court, Northern District of Illinois — Member Chicago Bar Association

Matushek, Nilles & Sinars, L.L.C.
55 West Monroe Street, Suite 700
Chicago, Illinois 60603
  Telephone: 312-750-1215
  Fax: 312-750-1273
  E-Mail: ejmatushek@matushek.com
  www.matushek.com

Established: 1998

Asbestos Litigation, Toxic Torts, Aviation, Product Liability, Commercial Litigation, Health Care Liability, Construction Defect, Nursing Home Liability, Transportation

Firm Profile: Matushek, Nilles & Sinars, L.L.C. has an enviable record of defending thousands of complex mass toxic tort cases, including multi-party

Matushek, Nilles & Sinars, L.L.C., Chicago, IL
(Continued)

asbestos personal injury and wrongful death claims. The firm also defends aviation cases, as well as automotive parts, medical device, and construction defect claims. In addition to its Main Office in Chicago, the firm operates a branch office in Madison County to provide efficient service throughout the State of Illinois, and in St. Louis, Missouri. The firm of Matushek, Nilles & Sinars, L.L.C., and each of its equity partners individually, have been given the highest rating by their peers.

Insurance Clients

AIG Technical Services, Inc.
Cavell USA, Inc.
Fireman's Fund Insurance Company
Resolute Management, Inc.
Zurich North America
Avemco Insurance Company
CNA Insurance Company
Hanover Insurance Group
The Hartford
The RiverStone Group

Self-Insured Clients

U.S. Steel Corporation

Managing Partner

Edward J. Matushek III — 1954 — Illinois Wesleyan University, B.A., 1975; The John Marshall Law School, J.D., 1982 — Admitted to Bar, 1982, Illinois; 1982, U.S. District Court, Northern District of Illinois including Trial Bar; 1996, U.S. District Court, District of Arizona; 2000, U.S. District Court, Northern District of Indiana

Partners

David A. Nilles — 1962 — University of Illinois, B.S., 1985; The John Marshall Law School, J.D., 1989 — Admitted to Bar, 1989, Illinois; 1989, U.S. District Court, Northern District of Illinois; 2000, U.S. District Court, Northern District of Indiana

Douglas M. Sinars — 1968 — University of Notre Dame, B.A., 1990; DePaul University, J.D., 1993 — Admitted to Bar, 1993, Illinois; 2012, Missouri; 1994, U.S. District Court, Central District of Illinois; 1995, U.S. District Court, Northern District of Illinois; 2000, U.S. District Court, Northern District of Indiana

James T. Rollins — DePaul University, B.A., 2000; Valparaiso University School of Law, J.D., 2003 — Admitted to Bar, 2007, Illinois; U.S. District Court, Northern District of Illinois

Megan S. Slowikowski — University of Illinois at Urbana-Champaign, B.S., 2001; Chicago-Kent College of Law, J.D. (with honors), 2004 — Admitted to Bar, 2004, Illinois; 2013, Missouri; 2004, U.S. District Court, Northern District of Illinois

Randall Smith — Loyola University Chicago School of Law, J.D., 1985 — Admitted to Bar, 1985, Illinois; 1985, U.S. District Court, Northern District of Illinois

Associates

Owen Blood — University of Notre Dame, B.S., 2005; Tulane University Law School, J.D., 2008 — Admitted to Bar, 2008, Illinois

Brent Eisenberg — Indiana University, B.A., 2005; DePaul University College of Law, J.D., 2008 — Admitted to Bar, 2008, Illinois

John-Michael Porretta — University of Notre Dame, B.S.B.A., 2005; DePaul University College of Law, J.D., 2008 — Admitted to Bar, 2008, Illinois

Amy M. Callaghan — University of Michigan, B.A. Political Science, 2007; University of Illinois College of Law, J.D., 2010 — Admitted to Bar, 2010, Illinois

C. Matt Alva — University of Illinois at Urbana-Champaign, B.A., 2005; Chicago-Kent College of Law, J.D., 2011 — Admitted to Bar, 2011, Illinois

Michael D. Martinez — University of Illinois at Urbana-Champaign, B.A., 2006; Northern Illinois University College of Law, J.D. (magna cum laude), 2009 — Admitted to Bar, 2009, Illinois; 2010, Indiana; U.S. District Court, Northern District of Illinois

Jack A. Gould — University of Illinois at Urbana-Champaign, B.A. Political Science (cum laude), 2008; Chicago - Kent School of Law, J.D., 2011 — Admitted to Bar, 2011, Illinois

Thomas P. Cahill — Northwestern University, B.S., 1992; The John Marshall Law School, J.D., 1995 — Admitted to Bar, 1995, Illinois; 1995, U.S. District Court, Northern District of Illinois

Christopher Griffin — Northwestern University, B.A., 2005; Chicago-Kent College of Law, J.D. (Dean's List), 2012 — Admitted to Bar, 2012, Illinois

Matushek, Nilles & Sinars, L.L.C., Chicago, IL
(Continued)

Patrick M. Grand — Loyola University of Chicago, B.A. (Dean's Scholar), 2007; Loyola University Chicago School of Law, J.D., 2013 — Admitted to Bar, 2013, Illinois; 2014, Missouri

Gina R. Gerardi — University of Illinois at Urbana-Champaign, B.A. (with distinction), 2002; University of Miami, J.D., 2005 — Admitted to Bar, 2005, Illinois; 2007, U.S. District Court, Northern District of Illinois

Alayna S. Rush — Indiana University, B.A., 2008; The John Marshall Law School in Chicago, J.D. (cum laude, Dean's List), 2012 — Admitted to Bar, 2012, Illinois

Michael P. Murphy — University of Illinois at Urbana-Champaign, B.S., 2008; The John Marshall Law School in Chicago, J.D. (magna cum laude, Dean's List), 2011 — Admitted to Bar, 2011, Illinois

Kate E. Fosdick — Skidmore College, B.A. (cum laude), 2007; DePaul University College of Law, J.D., 2012 — Admitted to Bar, 2012, Illinois

Matthew A. Vlasman — Indiana University, B.S., 2005; University of South Carolina School of Law, J.D. (Dean's List), 2013

Jessica K. Velez — University of Illinois, B.A., 2007; Chicago-Kent College of Law, J.D., 2012 — Admitted to Bar, 2012, Illinois

McCullough, Campbell & Lane LLP

205 North Michigan Avenue, Suite 4100
Chicago, Illinois 60601
Telephone: 312-923-4000
Fax: 312-923-4329
www.mcandl.com

Established: 1987

Insurance Defense, General Liability, Product Liability, Professional Liability, Aviation, Property and Casualty, Reinsurance, Errors and Omissions, Coverage Issues

Firm Profile: McCullough, Campbell & Lane LLP was established in 1987 in Chicago. From the outset, the firm has had a national as well as a local orientation, because much of its work is performed on behalf of foreign insurance organizations with legal questions arising under the laws of jurisdictions across the country. Today, the firm continues to be engaged in a diverse national and international practice focused on Insurance Law, Litigation and Business Counseling. Our attorneys possess specialized knowledge in a broad range of specific subjects that cut across these practice areas. These include professional liability, directors and officers liability, products liability, aviation, health care, and employment law. Within these subject areas, we can, for example, defend claims, counsel insurers, draft policies and contracts or litigate coverage disputes. We believe this strengthens our capacity to assist our clients in achieving their business objectives.

Insurance Clients

A.C.E. Insurance Company, Ltd.
Allied World Assurance Company
Aspen Insurance UK Limited
Assicurazioni Generali S.p.A.
Catamount Indemnity Limited
CIGNA Property and Casualty Insurance Company
Continental Insurance Company
Endurance Specialty Insurance Ltd.
Fireman's Fund Insurance Company
Hannover Re Group
Ironshore Specialty Insurance Company
Marsh & McLennan Companies
National Union Fire Insurance Company
RLI Insurance Company
Royale Belge I.R.S.A. D'Assurances
Underwriters at Lloyd's, London
XL Insurance (Bermuda) Ltd.
Zurich Specialties London Limited
Allianz Insurance Company
American International Underwriters
Beazley Insurance Company, Inc.
Chubb Group of Insurance Companies
CNA Insurance Companies
Crum & Forster Insurance Group
Evanston Insurance Company
Gerling-Konzern AG
Global Aerospace, Inc.
Hartford Specialty Company
Lexington Insurance Company
L&F Indemnity Limited
Munich Reinsurance America, Inc.
Nautilus Insurance Company
OneBeacon Professional Partners, Inc.
St. Paul Travelers
Swiss Reinsurance Company
Wausau Insurance Companies
Zurich American Insurance Group

Non-Insurance Clients

Cessna Aircraft Company

CHICAGO
ILLINOIS

McCullough, Campbell & Lane LLP, Chicago, IL
(Continued)

Partners

John W. McCullough — Northwestern University, B.A., 1962; University of Michigan, J.D., 1965 — Member, Barristers — Admitted to Bar, 1966, Illinois; 1967, U.S. District Court, Northern District of Illinois; 1967, U.S. Court of Appeals, Seventh Circuit — Member American, Chicago and Seventh Circuit Bar Associations; The Lawyers Club of Chicago — E-mail: jmccullough@mcandl.com

F. Dennis Nelson — 1952 — University of Michigan, A.B. (with high distinction), 1974; J.D. (cum laude), 1977 — Admitted to Bar, 1978, Illinois; 1978, U.S. District Court, Northern District of Illinois; 1981, U.S. Court of Appeals, Third, Fifth, Seventh and Eleventh Circuits — Member International Bar Association (Chairman, Professional Indemnity Subcommittee of Insurance Section - 1992-1996); Seventh Circuit Bar Association; Professional Liability Underwriting Society — E-mail: fnelson@mcandl.com

Paul S. Turner — 1953 — Harvard University, A.B., 1975; J.D., 1978 — Admitted to Bar, 1978, Ohio; 1982, Illinois; 1978, U.S. District Court, Northern District of Ohio; 1982, U.S. District Court, Northern District of Illinois; 1986, U.S. Court of Appeals, Seventh Circuit — Member American and Chicago Bar Associations — E-mail: pturner@mcandl.com

Patrick M. Graber — 1950 — Purdue University, B.S.A.E., 1972; University of Notre Dame, J.D., 1979 — Admitted to Bar, 1979, Illinois; 1979, U.S. District Court, Northern and Southern Districts of Illinois including Trial Bar; 1988, U.S. Court of Appeals, Tenth Circuit; 1989, U.S. Court of Appeals, Third Circuit; 1993, U.S. Court of Appeals, Seventh Circuit — Member Defense Research Institute — E-mail: pgraber@mcandl.com

David L. Joslyn — 1948 — Northwestern University, B.A., 1970; J.D. (cum laude), 1975 — Admitted to Bar, 1975, Illinois; U.S. District Court, Northern District of Illinois; 1995, U.S. Court of Appeals, Seventh Circuit — Member American (Tort and Insurance) and Chicago Bar Associations — E-mail: djoslyn@mcandl.com

Dennis L. Frostic — 1943 — University of Michigan, B.A., 1964; J.D., 1967 — Admitted to Bar, 1969, Michigan; 1972, Illinois; 1969, U.S. District Court, Eastern District of Michigan; 1972, U.S. District Court, Northern and Southern Districts of Illinois; 1984, U.S. Court of Appeals, Ninth Circuit — Member American Bar Association; State Bar of Michigan — E-mail: dfrostic@mcandl.com

Ann P. Goodman — 1957 — Wellesley College, A.B. (cum laude), 1979; Vanderbilt University, J.D., 1984 — Admitted to Bar, 1984, Illinois; 1984, U.S. District Court, Northern District of Illinois including Trial Bar; 1989, U.S. Court of Appeals, Seventh Circuit; 1995, U.S. Supreme Court — Member American and Chicago Bar Associations — E-mail: agoodman@mcandl.com

Anne E. Sammons — 1960 — University of Illinois, B.A. (Bronze Tablet), 1982; J.D. (cum laude), 1985 — Admitted to Bar, 1985, Illinois; 1985, U.S. District Court, Northern District of Illinois — Member American and Chicago Bar Associations — E-mail: asammons@mcandl.com

Debra A. Emry — 1962 — The University of Iowa, B.A., 1984; University of Illinois, J.D., 1987 — Admitted to Bar, 1987, Illinois; 1987, U.S. District Court, Northern District of Illinois — Member American, Illinois State and Chicago Bar Associations — E-mail: demry@mcandl.com

M. Bart Rinn — 1963 — Northern Illinois University, B.S. (summa cum laude), 1985; University of Illinois, J.D. (cum laude), 1988 — Admitted to Bar, 1988, Illinois; 1989, U.S. District Court, Northern District of Illinois — E-mail: mrinn@mcandl.com

Myra J. Brown — 1950 — Drake University, B.A., 1971; DePaul University, J.D., 1974 — Admitted to Bar, 1974, Illinois; 1977, U.S. District Court, Northern District of Illinois; 1977, U.S. Court of Appeals, Seventh Circuit — Member American, Illinois State and Chicago Bar Associations — E-mail: mbrown@mcandl.com

Stephen D. Koslow — 1969 — University of Illinois at Urbana-Champaign, B.S. (with high honors), 1991; DePaul University College of Law, J.D., 1994 — Admitted to Bar, 1994, Illinois; U.S. District Court, Northern District of Illinois; 2005, U.S. District Court, Northern District of Indiana; 2006, U.S. District Court, Southern District of Illinois — Member Illinois State Bar Association — E-mail: skoslow@mcandl.com

Brian Dusek — 1972 — University of Minnesota, B.A., 1994; DePaul University College of Law, J.D., 1998 — Admitted to Bar, 1998, Illinois — Member Illinois State Bar Association — Author: "Ghost in the Machinists," 10 DePaul Bus. L.J. 103 (1997) — E-mail: bdusek@mcandl.com

Veronica Nulman — 1973 — Northwestern University, B.A., 1995; Boston University, J.D., 1998 — Admitted to Bar, 1998, Massachusetts; 1999, New York; 2000, Illinois; U.S. District Court, Northern District of Illinois; 2002,

McCullough, Campbell & Lane LLP, Chicago, IL
(Continued)

U.S. District Court, Northern District of Indiana — Member Chicago Bar Association — Languages: Russian, French — E-mail: vnulman@mcandl.com

Samuel B. Rainey — 1976 — Miami University, B.A., 1999; University of Pittsburgh School of Law, J.D., 2002 — Admitted to Bar, 2002, Illinois; U.S. District Court, Northern District of Illinois — Member American Bar Association — E-mail: srainey@mcandl.com

Of Counsel

Marvin Green — 1925 — The University of Chicago, A.B., 1948; J.D., 1950 — Admitted to Bar, 1950, Illinois; U.S. District Court, Northern District of Illinois; 1992, U.S. Court of Appeals, Seventh Circuit — Lecturer/Instructor, De Paul University, Roosevelt University and University of Chicago — E-mail: mgreen@mcandl.com

Anne Jentry-Green — 1946 — University of Illinois; Loyola University Chicago School of Law, J.D., 1976; DePaul University College of Law, LL.M. (Taxation), 1981 — Admitted to Bar, 1976, Illinois; 1976, U.S. District Court, Northern District of Illinois; 1980, U.S. Tax Court; 1992, U.S. Court of Appeals, Seventh Circuit — E-mail: ajentry@mcandl.com

Carl D. Liggio — 1943 — Georgetown University, A.B. (with distinction), 1963; New York University, J.D. (cum laude), 1967 — Admitted to Bar, 1967, New York; District of Columbia; 1982, Wisconsin; 1998, Illinois; 1967, U.S. District Court for the District of Columbia; 1967, U.S. District Court, Eastern and Southern Districts of New York; 1967, U.S. Court of Military Appeals; 1967, U.S. Court of Appeals for the District of Columbia Circuit; 1973, U.S. Court of Appeals, Tenth Circuit; 1973, U.S. Supreme Court; 1974, U.S. Court of Appeals, Second Circuit; 1978, U.S. Court of Appeals, Eighth and Ninth Circuits; 1980, U.S. Tax Court; 1980, U.S. Court of Appeals, Fourth and Fifth Circuits; 1981, U.S. Court of Appeals, Eleventh Circuit; 1984, Temporary Emergency Court of Appeals; 1991, Federal Circuit Court; 1997, U.S. District Court, District of Illinois; 2000, U.S. Court of Appeals, First Circuit — Member American, New York State and Illinois State Bar Associations; The District of Columbia Bar; State Bar of Wisconsin; American Corporate Counsel Association (Founder, 1982; Chairman, 1984); Fellow, College of Law Practice Management, 1995; American Law Institute (Life Member, 1977) — E-mail: cliggio@mcandl.com

Mark D. Siebert — 1960 — University of Illinois, A.B., 1983; J.D. (magna cum laude), 1986 — Order of the Coif — Admitted to Bar, 1986, Illinois; 1986, U.S. District Court, Northern District of Illinois — Member American Bar Association — E-mail: msiebert@mcandl.com

Associate

Joseph R. Menning — 1979 — Santa Clara University, B.S.B.A., 2001; University of Illinois College of Law, J.D., 2006 — Admitted to Bar, 2006, Maryland; 2007, Illinois — Member Maryland State and Chicago Bar Associations — E-mail: jmenning@mcandl.com

McKenna Storer

33 North LaSalle Street, 14th Floor
Chicago, Illinois 60602-2610
Telephone: 312-558-3900
Fax: 312-558-8348
E-Mail: postmaster@mckenna-law.com
www.mckenna-law.com

(Woodstock, IL Office*: 666 Russel Court, Suite 303, 60098)
(Tel: 815-334-9690)
(Fax: 815-334-9697)

Established: 1954

General Civil Trial and Appellate Practice, Insurance Defense, Insurance Coverage, Product Liability, Commercial Liability, Environmental Law, Toxic Torts, Employment Law, Professional Malpractice, Premises Liability, Litigation, Medical Malpractice, Examinations Under Oath, Mediation, Bankruptcy, Professional Errors and Omissions, Professional Liability, Professional Liability (Non-Medical) Defense, Business Law, Commercial Transactions, Franchise

Firm Profile: McKenna Storer, established in 1954, has been serving insurance companies, Fortune 500 companies, local businesses and individuals

McKenna Storer, Chicago, IL (Continued)

in Chicago and the surrounding area. The Firm focuses on cost effective business and litigation solutions.

Insurance Clients

AIU Insurance Company
Allstate Insurance Company
American Family Mutual Insurance Company
ClaimGuard Insurance Company of America, Inc.
Crum & Forster Insurance
Gallagher Bassett Services, Inc.
GuideOne Insurance
Illinois State Medical Insurance Services, Inc.
Iowa Mutual Insurance Company
National Chiropractic Mutual Insurance Company
Royal Insurance Company
TIG Holdings Group
West Bend Mutual Insurance Company
ALLIED Mutual Insurance Company
American International Group, Inc.
Ameriprise Auto & Home Insurance
CNA Insurance Companies
Fireman's Fund Insurance Company
Hartford Insurance Company
Indiana Lumbermens Mutual Insurance Company
Liberty Mutual Insurance Company
Resolute Management, Inc.
RiverStone Claims Management, LLC
The Travelers Companies, Inc.
Zurich American Insurance Company

Non-Insurance Clients

Fifth Third Bank
The Krez Group
ServiceMaster Company
FirstCity Financial Corporation
Nokia Siemens Networks

Founder

William J. McKenna — (1923-1975)

John F. White — (1929-2002)

Eugene J. Farrug — (1928-2007)

Royce G. Rowe — (1926-2011)

Partners

James P. DeNardo — DePaul University, B.A., 1964; J.D., 1967 — Admitted to Bar, 1967, Illinois; 1976, U.S. Court of Appeals, Seventh Circuit — E-mail: jdenardo@mckenna-law.com

Timothy J. Murtaugh, III — University of Notre Dame, A.B., 1958; University of Michigan, LL.B., 1961 — Admitted to Bar, 1962, Illinois — E-mail: tmurtaugh@mckenna-law.com

John W. Egan — Xavier University, A.B. (cum laude), 1969; Fordham University, M.A., 1973; Northwestern University, J.D., 1977 — Admitted to Bar, 1977, Illinois — E-mail: jegan@mckenna-law.com

Gregory L. Cochran — University of Michigan, B.A., 1977; J.D., 1980 — Admitted to Bar, 1980, Illinois; U.S. District Court, Northern District of Illinois; 2001, U.S. District Court, Northern District of Indiana — E-mail: gcochran@mckenna-law.com

Julie A. Ramson — University of Wisconsin, B.S.N., 1971; Loyola University, J.D., 1982 — Admitted to Bar, 1982, Illinois; U.S. District Court, District of Illinois — E-mail: jramson@mckenna-law.com

Sara E. Cook — The University of Iowa, B.A., 1975; Loyola University, J.D., 1980 — Admitted to Bar, 1980, Illinois; 1985, U.S. Court of Appeals, Seventh Circuit — E-mail: scook@mckenna-law.com

Bruce B. Marr — University of Virginia, B.A., 1976; M.E., 1978; DePaul University, J.D., 1981 — Admitted to Bar, 1981, Indiana; 1983, Illinois; 1981, U.S. District Court, Northern and Southern Districts of Indiana; 1984, U.S. District Court, Northern District of Illinois including Trial Bar — E-mail: bmarr@mckenna-law.com

Robert P. Pisani — University of Wisconsin-Madison, B.A., 1983; DePaul University, J.D., 1986 — Admitted to Bar, 1986, Illinois; U.S. District Court, Northern District of Illinois — E-mail: rpisani@mckenna-law.com

Dawn E. Ehrenberg — Lewis University, B.A., 1984; University of Illinois, J.D., 1987 — Admitted to Bar, 1987, Illinois; U.S. District Court, Northern District of Illinois — E-mail: dehrenberg@mckenna-law.com

Thomas F. Lucas — University of Illinois, B.A., 1975; Loyola University, J.D., 1978 — Admitted to Bar, 1978, Illinois; 1981, U.S. District Court, Central and Northern Districts of Illinois — E-mail: tlucas@mckenna-law.com

Margaret M. Foster — University of Arkansas, B.A., 1979; M.A. (with honors), 1980; J.D. (with honors), 1988 — Admitted to Bar, 1988, Illinois; U.S. District Court, Eastern and Northern Districts of Illinois — E-mail: mfoster@mckenna-law.com

McKenna Storer, Chicago, IL (Continued)

Associates

Kristin Taurus Dvorsky — The University of Iowa, B.A., 1989; DePaul University College of Law, J.D. (with honors), 1993 — Admitted to Bar, 1993, Illinois; 1994, U.S. Court of Appeals, Seventh Circuit — E-mail: ktaurus@mckenna-law.com

Thomas W. Hayes — United States Military Academy at West Point, B.S., 1978; DePaul University, J.D., 1986 — Admitted to Bar, 1986, Illinois; 2009, Missouri — E-mail: thayes@mckenna-law.com

Paul S. Steinhofer — Indiana University-Bloomington, B.S., 1988; Indiana University School of Law-Bloomington, J.D., 1993 — Admitted to Bar, 1993, Indiana; 2003, Illinois; 1993, U.S. District Court, Northern and Southern Districts of Indiana; 2003, U.S. District Court, Northern District of Illinois — E-mail: psteinhofer@mckenn-law.com

Timothy M. Hayes — Purdue University, B.A., 2004; The John Marshall Law School in Chicago, J.D., 2007 — Admitted to Bar, 2007, Illinois — E-mail: tmhayes@mckenna-law.com

Alexander Sweis — DePaul University, B.A., 2005; J.D., 2009 — Admitted to Bar, 2009, Illinois — E-mail: asweis@mckenna-law.com

Kelly E. Purkey — The University of Arizona, B.A., 1995; Southern Illinois University, J.D., 2004 — Admitted to Bar, 2004, Illinois

Of Counsel

Andrew D. Bratzel — Michigan State University, B.A., 1981; DePaul University College of Law, J.D., 1984 — Admitted to Bar, 1984, Illinois; U.S. District Court, Northern District of Illinois — E-mail: abratzel@mckenna-law.com

Jaime Dowell — Michigan State University, B.A., 1998; Benjamin N. Cardozo School of Law, Yeshiva University, J.D., 2001 — U.S. District Court, Northern District of Illinois; Illinois State Court — E-mail: jdowell@mckenna-law.com

Alison J. Harkins — The University of Arizona, B.S., 1988; The University of Arizona College of Law, J.D., 1993 — Admitted to Bar, 1993, Arizona; 1995, Illinois — E-mail: aharkins@mckenna-law.com

Momkus McCluskey, LLC

221 North LaSalle Street, Suite 2050
Chicago, Illinois 60601
Telephone: 312-345-1955
Fax: 312-419-1546
www.momlaw.com

Insurance Defense, Insurance Law, Special Investigations, Litigation, Business Law, Corporate Law, Contracts, Employment Law, Large Loss Subrogation

Firm Profile: Momkus McCluskey, LLC represents clients throughout the United States in legal matters involving liability defense, insurance defense and coverage disputes, special investigations, large loss subrogation, business and corporate law, contracts and agreements, employment law, real estate, financing and loan transactions, family law and divorce, appeals and estate planning.

(See listing under Lisle, IL for additional information)

Moore Strickland

60 West Randolph Street # 300
Chicago, Illinois 60601
Telephone: 312-578-9000
Fax: 312-578-9020
E-Mail: attorneys@moore-strickland.com
www.moore-strickland.com

Established: 1985

CHICAGO   ILLINOIS

Moore Strickland, Chicago, IL   (Continued)

Insurance Defense, Product Liability, Municipal Liability, Construction Law, Coverage Issues, Lead Paint, Toxic Torts, Alternative Dispute Resolution, Employment Practices Liability, Medical Devices, Commercial General Liability, Sexual Abuse Litigation

Firm Profile: Moore Strickland is a Chicago-based firm of experienced trial and appellate lawyers who excel at defending our clients against civil liability claims, employment litigation and insurance coverage disputes. For over 20 years, we have defended insurers, corporations, non-profits and self-insured entities. We bring a commitment to providing the highest level of legal expertise and personal attention, which helps us turn clients into long-term partners and friends.

Partners Gary Moore and Darlene Strickland have over 50 years of collective experience working in state and federal courtrooms and have tried over 75 cases to verdict. Our knowledge, experience and reputation affords us the ability to negotiate favorable settlements from a position of strength—and should a claim come to trial, few firms can match our depth of trial experience and record of results.

We have had the privilege of defending our clients in a variety of claims, and have developed a particular expertise with high profile and complex personal injury litigation involving toxic tort, construction, assault, sexual abuse and products/medical device claims. We're also adept at handling multiple claim issues and overseeing national coordination of claim defense.

Insurance Clients

AIG
Chubb Services Corporation
Empire Fire and Marine Insurance Company
Medmarc Insurance Group
The Travelers Companies, Inc.
Zurich Insurance Group
Alliance of Nonprofits for Insurance
Global Indemnity Group, Inc.
Hanover Insurance Group
National Indemnity Company
United States Fidelity and Guaranty Company

Non-Insurance Clients

Big Brothers Big Sisters of America
Gallagher Bassett & Co.
HMS Host Corporation
Chicago Housing Authority
Denny's, Inc.
Hamilton Resources Corporation
Rockville Risk Management Associates, Inc.

Partners

Gary K. Moore — 1946 — University of Illinois, B.A., 1969; M.A., 1971; Loyola University Chicago, J.D., 1974 — Admitted to Bar, 1974, Illinois; 1974, U.S. District Court, Northern District of Illinois; 1974, U.S. Court of Appeals, Seventh Circuit — Member Defense Research Institute

Darlene Strickland — 1953 — Northern Illinois University, B.A. (magna cum laude), 1977; Loyola University School of Law, J.D., 1992 — Admitted to Bar, 1992, Illinois; 1992, U.S. District Court, Northern District of Illinois; 1995, U.S. Court of Appeals, Seventh Circuit — Member American Bar Association; Defense Research Institute; Illinois Association of Defense Trial Counsel

Pretzel & Stouffer Chartered

One South Wacker Drive, Suite 2500
Chicago, Illinois 60606-4673
 Telephone: 312-346-1973
 Fax: 312-346-8242
 www.pretzel-stouffer.com

Established: 1946

Insurance Defense, Trial Practice, Fire, Casualty, Marine, Life Insurance

Firm Profile: Since 1946, our focus has been attracting and developing those lawyers with the courage, poise and passion to advocate on behalf of a client in the public forum of a courtroom, an appellate court or a regulatory commission. We have the distinction of having among our ranks many of the country's most highly regarded trial and appellate attorneys.

Pretzel & Stouffer Chartered, Chicago, IL   (Continued)

Insurance Clients

American International Group, Inc.
Auto-Owners Insurance Company
Chubb Group of Insurance Companies
Fireman's Fund Insurance Companies
ISBA Mutual Insurance Company
Ohio Casualty Group
Philadelphia Insurance Company
St. Paul Insurance Company
State Auto Insurance Company
American Physicians Assurance Corp.
CNA Insurance Companies
Electric Insurance Company
Gallagher Bassett Services, Inc.
Illinois State Medical Insurance Services, Inc.
Pekin Insurance Company
ProAssurance Corporation
Specialty Risk Services, Inc. (SRS)

Non-Insurance Clients

BP Amoco
Keeler/Dorr-Oliver

Partners

Paul W. Pretzel — (1906-1987)

David M. Bennett — 1964 — Illinois Institute of Technology, Chicago-Kent College of Law, J.D., 1989 — Admitted to Bar, 1989, Illinois

Robert Marc Chemers — 1951 — Indiana University, J.D., 1976 — Admitted to Bar, 1976, Illinois — Member American, Illinois State, Chicago and Indianapolis Bar Associations

Suzanne M. Crowley — 1961 — The John Marshall Law School, J.D., 1987 — Admitted to Bar, 1987, Illinois

Matthew J. Egan — 1957 — Loyola University, J.D., 1982 — Admitted to Bar, 1983, Illinois — Member Illinois State and Chicago Bar Associations

Donald P. Eckler — 1976 — The University of Chicago, A.B., 1998; University of Florida, J.D., 2003 — Admitted to Bar, 2004, Illinois; Florida; 2005, Indiana; 2004, U.S. District Court, Northern District of Illinois

William W. Elinski — 1961 — Lewis & Clark College, J.D., 1998 — Admitted to Bar, 1998, Illinois

Patrick F. Healy — 1961 — The John Marshall Law School, J.D., 1986 — Admitted to Bar, 1986, Illinois

Brian T. Henry — 1954 — University of Illinois College of Law, J.D., 1980 — Admitted to Bar, 1980, Illinois

Scott L. Howie — 1966 — Illinois Institute of Technology, Chicago-Kent College of Law, J.D., 1994 — Admitted to Bar, 1994, Illinois

Belle L. Katubig — 1966 — University of Illinois at Urbana-Champaign, B.S., 1988; The John Marshall Law School, J.D., 1996 — Admitted to Bar, 1997, Illinois

Richard P. Kenyon — 1968 — DePaul University, J.D., 1995 — Admitted to Bar, 1995, Illinois

James A. LaBarge — 1962 — Northern Illinois University, J.D., 1990 — Admitted to Bar, 1990, Illinois

Thomas A. Lang II — 1975 — University of Illinois at Urbana-Champaign, B.A., 1997; DePaul University, J.D., 2000 — Admitted to Bar, 2000, Illinois

Matthew J. Ligda — 1968 — Emory University, B.B.A., 1990; DePaul University, J.D., 1995 — Admitted to Bar, 1995, Illinois; U.S. District Court, Northern District of Illinois including Trial Bar

Daniel B. Mills — 1963 — Northern Illinois University, J.D., 1989 — Admitted to Bar, 1989, Illinois

Mimi Y. Moon — 1975 — Miami University, B.S., 1997; The Ohio State University Moritz College of Law, J.D., 2000 — Admitted to Bar, 2000, Michigan; 2003, Illinois

Brendan J. Nelligan — 1971 — University of Notre Dame, B.A. (with high honors), 1993; Georgetown University, J.D., 1996 — Admitted to Bar, 1996, Illinois; 2000, U.S. District Court, Northern District of Illinois

Edward H. Nielsen — 1946 — Valparaiso University, J.D., 1973 — Admitted to Bar, 1973, Illinois — Member American, Illinois State and Chicago Bar Associations

Donald J. O'Meara, Jr. — 1966 — The John Marshall Law School, J.D., 1991 — Admitted to Bar, 1991, Illinois

Howard J. Pikel — 1953 — University of Illinois at Chicago, B.A., 1977; The John Marshall Law School, J.D., 1981 — Admitted to Bar, 1981, Illinois; 1999, Indiana; 1981, U.S. District Court, Northern District of Illinois; 1987, Federal Trial Bar; 1998, U.S. District Court, Central District of Illinois; 1999, U.S. District Court, Northern and Southern Districts of Indiana

Heather E. Plunkett — 1978 — University of Illinois, B.A., 2000; Loyola University, J.D., 2004 — Admitted to Bar, 2004, Illinois

Neil K. Quinn — 1929 — DePaul University, J.D., 1957 — Admitted to Bar,

ILLINOIS   CHICAGO

Pretzel & Stouffer Chartered, Chicago, IL   (Continued)

1957, Illinois — Member American, Illinois State and Chicago Bar Associations; Society of Trial Lawyers; International Association of Defense Counsel; Illinois Defense Counsel

Charles F. Redden — 1958 — Loyola University, J.D., 1984 — Admitted to Bar, 1984, Illinois — Member American, Illinois State and Chicago Bar Associations

Brian C. Rocca — 1953 — University of Northern Iowa, B.A., 1976; The University of Iowa College of Law, J.D., 1982 — Admitted to Bar, 1982, Illinois; 1982, U.S. District Court, Northern District of Illinois — Member American, Illinois and Chicago Bar Associations; Society of Trial Lawyers; Illinois Association of Defense Trial Counsel

Edward B. Ruff III — 1954 — DePaul University, J.D., 1981 — Admitted to Bar, 1981, Illinois — Member American, Illinois State and Chicago (Young Lawyers Section) Bar Associations

Miguel A. Ruiz — 1963 — University of Illinois at Chicago, B.A., 1989; University of Wisconsin, J.D., 1992 — Admitted to Bar, 1992, Illinois; Wisconsin — Member Illinois State and Chicago Bar Associations; Hispanic Lawyers Association of Illinois

Steven W. Ryan — 1968 — Loyola University, J.D., 1993 — Admitted to Bar, 1993, Illinois

Lewis M. Schneider — 1944 — The John Marshall Law School, J.D., 1973 — Admitted to Bar, 1973, Illinois — Member Chicago Bar Association

Alan J. Schumacher — 1959 — University of Illinois, J.D., 1984 — Admitted to Bar, 1984, Illinois — Member American and Illinois State Bar Association

Robert E. Sidkey — 1974 — Valparaiso University, B.A. (magna cum laude), 1996; Chicago-Kent College of Law, J.D., 1999 — Admitted to Bar, 2000, Illinois; 2001, U.S. District Court, Northern District of Illinois

James J. Sipchen — 1968 — Indiana University-Bloomington, B.A., 1990; The John Marshall Law School, J.D., 1994 — Admitted to Bar, 1994, Illinois — Member Chicago Bar Association

John V. Smith II — 1957 — University of Notre Dame, J.D., 1982 — Admitted to Bar, 1982, Illinois — Member American Bar Association

Brian C. Sundheim — 1957 — Loyola University Chicago, B.A., 1981; The John Marshall Law School, J.D., 1986 — Admitted to Bar, 1986, Illinois; 1988, U.S. District Court, Northern District of Illinois

Amy J. Thompson — 1972 — Valparaiso University School of Law, J.D., 1997 — Admitted to Bar, 1997, Illinois

Matthew F. Tibble — 1977 — DePaul University, B.A., 1999; DePaul University College of Law, J.D., 2004 — Admitted to Bar, 2004, Illinois; 2004, U.S. District Court, Northern District of Illinois

Michael P. Turiello — 1970 — Bradley University, B.S., 1992; Villanova University School of Law, J.D., 1996 — Admitted to Bar, 1996, Illinois; U.S. District Court, Northern District of Illinois; 2001, U.S. District Court, Central District of Illinois

Stephen C. Veltman — 1954 — Loyola University, J.D., 1979 — Admitted to Bar, 1979, Illinois

John J. Walsh III — 1946 — Loyola University, J.D., 1982 — Admitted to Bar, 1982, Illinois — Member American, Illinois State and Chicago Bar Associations

Richard M. Waris — 1954 — University of Notre Dame, J.D., 1980 — Admitted to Bar, 1980, Illinois — Member American, Illinois State and Chicago Bar Associations

Timothy A. Weaver — 1948 — University of Illinois, J.D., 1974 — Admitted to Bar, 1974, Illinois — Member American, Illinois State and Chicago Bar Associations

Firm Members

Scott L. Anderson — 1974 — Cornell College, B.A. (Dean's List), 1996; Loyola University Chicago School of Law, J.D., 1999 — Phi Alpha Delta — Admitted to Bar, 1999, Illinois

Edward J. Aucoin, Jr. — 1971 — Loyola University New Orleans, B.A., 1993; Loyola University New Orleans College of Law, J.D., 1996 — Admitted to Bar, 1996, Illinois; 1999, Louisiana; 1996, U.S. District Court, Northern District of Illinois

Michael A. Barry — 1982 — St. Joseph's College, B.A./B.S. (summa cum laude), 2005; The John Marshall Law School, J.D. (cum laude), 2008 — Order of John Marshall — Admitted to Bar, 2008, Illinois

Brian Boyle — 1985 — Colorado College, B.A. (cum laude), 2007; University of Notre Dame Law School, J.D. (cum laude), 2012 — Admitted to Bar, 2012, Illinois

Pretzel & Stouffer Chartered, Chicago, IL   (Continued)

Philip Brandt — 1970 — Augustana College, A.B., 1992; The John Marshall Law School in Chicago, J.D., 2008 — Law Clerk, Justice Robert E. Gordon, Illinois Appellate Court, First District — Admitted to Bar, 2008, Illinois

Richard M. Burgland — 1979 — DePauw University, B.A., 2002; The John Marshall Law School, J.D., 2006 — Admitted to Bar, 2007, Illinois; 2009, U.S. District Court, Southern District of Indiana

Mary H. Cronin — 1978 — Marquette University, B.A., 2000; Loyola University Chicago School of Law, J.D., 2005 — Admitted to Bar, 2005, Illinois

Thomas V.P. Draths — 1985 — University of Illinois at Urbana-Champaign, B.A. (Dean's Honors), 2007; Loyola University School of Law, J.D. (Dean's Honors), 2010 — Admitted to Bar, 2010, Illinois

Eliot D. Hellman — 1982 — Amherst College, B.A., 2004; University of Illinois College of Law, J.D. (cum laude), 2012 — Admitted to Bar, 2012, Illinois

Todd Hunnewell — 1975 — Northern Illinois University, B.A. Political Science, 1997; DePaul University College of Law, J.D. (cum laude), 2000 — Order of the Coif — Admitted to Bar, 2000, Illinois; U.S. District Court, Northern District of Illinois

Kelly Kono — 1986 — Washington University in St. Louis, B.A., 2009; University of Illinois College of Law, J.D. (magna cum laude), 2013 — Admitted to Bar, 2013, Illinois

David N. Larson — 1969 — Northwestern University, 1991; California Western School of Law, J.D., 1994 — Admitted to Bar, 1994, Illinois; California

Sommer R. Luzynczyk — 1978 — University of Memphis, B.A. (magna cum laude), 2005; The John Marshall Law School, J.D. (cum laude), 2009 — Managing Editor, The John Marshall Law Review — Admitted to Bar, 2009, Illinois

Shauna M. Martin — 1984 — University of Wisconsin-Madison, B.A., 2006; Loyola University School of Law, J.D. (Dean's Scholar), 2010 — Admitted to Bar, 2010, Illinois

Michael R. O'Connell — 1982 — University of Notre Dame, B.A. (cum laude), 2006; University of Notre Dame Law School, J.D., 2009 — Admitted to Bar, 2009, Illinois

Matthew Reddy — 1985 — University of Michigan, B.A., 2007; Boston University, J.D., 2010 — Admitted to Bar, 2010, Illinois

Adrian T. Rohrer — University of Wisconsin-Oshkosh, B.A., 2001; Chicago-Kent College of Law, J.D. (with high honors), 2004 — Admitted to Bar, 2004, Illinois

Joseph Sheahan — 1985 — Marian College of Fond du Lac, B.S. (magna cum laude), 2009; The John Marshall Law School in Chicago, J.D. (magna cum laude), 2013 — Admitted to Bar, 2013, Illinois

David Stein — 1984 — Washington University in St. Louis, B.A., 2007; University of Illinois College of Law, J.D. (summa cum laude), 2011 — Admitted to Bar, 2011, Illinois

Peter G. Syregelas — 1980 — Loyola University Chicago, B.S., 2002; The John Marshall Law School, J.D. (Dean's List), 2006 — Phi Delta Phi — Admitted to Bar, 2006, Illinois; 2007, U.S. District Court, Northern District of Illinois

(Revisors of the Illinois Insurance Law Digest for this Publication)

Purcell & Wardrope, Chartered

10 South LaSalle Street, Suite 1200
Chicago, Illinois 60603
 Telephone: 312-427-3900
 Toll Free: 866-4purcel
 Fax: 312-427-3944
 E-Mail: bsp@pw-law.com
 E-Mail: tbu@pw-law.com
 www.purcellwardrope.com

Established: 1968

CHICAGO ILLINOIS

Purcell & Wardrope, Chartered, Chicago, IL (Continued)

Insurance Defense, Self-Insured Defense, Civil Litigation, Appellate Practice, Employment Law, Arbitration, Automobile Liability, Personal Liability, Commercial Liability, Environmental Coverage, Insurance Coverage, Legal Malpractice, Long-Term Care, Premises Liability, Product Liability, Professional Liability, Transportation, Tort Litigation, Toxic Torts, Uninsured and Underinsured Motorist, Dram Shop, Medical Malpractice, Construction Accidents, Municipal Liability

Insurance Clients

ACE Westchester Specialty Group
Associated Adjusters, Inc.
Broadspire, a Crawford Company
Central Insurance Companies
Claims Management, Inc.
COUNTRY Mutual Insurance Company
Fireman's Fund Insurance Company
Glencoe Group Services, Inc.
HCC Public Risk Claim Service, Inc.
Magna Carta Companies
Meadowbrook Claims Service
National Interstate Insurance Company
Sedgwick Claims Management Services, Inc.
United Fire & Casualty Group
West Bend Mutual Insurance Company
York Claims Service, Inc.
American International Group, Inc.
AXIS Professional Lines
Cambridge Integrated Services
Chubb Group
CNA
Discover Re
Everest National Insurance Company
Gallagher Bassett Services, Inc.
Great American Insurance Companies
Lexington Insurance Company
Markel Insurance Company
Medmarc Insurance Company
Professional Claims Managers, Inc.
RSUI Group, Inc.
Society Insurance
Specialty Risk Services, Inc. (SRS)
Virginia Surety Company, Inc.
Wisconsin Mutual Insurance Company

Non-Insurance Clients

Celadon Trucking Services, Inc.
The Home Depot
Payless ShoeSource
Chipotle Mexican Grill, Inc.
Labor Ready, Inc.

Partners

Bradford S. Purcell — 1962 — Valparaiso University, B.A. (summa cum laude), 1984; University of Notre Dame Law School, J.D., 1987 — Admitted to Bar, 1987, Illinois; 1988, U.S. District Court, Northern District of Illinois, Eastern Division; U.S. District Court, Central District of Illinois — Member Illinois State and Chicago Bar Associations; Illinois Association of Defense Trial Counsel; Defense Research Institute — AV-Rated® by Martindale-Hubbell; Franciscan Outreach Association-Lawyers United For the Homeless — Practice Areas: Premises Liability; Construction Transactions; Municipal Liability; Insurance Defense; Construction Accidents; Dram Shop; Commercial Transportation Litigation; Professional Liability; Product Liability; Toxic Torts; Construction Defect; Appellate Practice; Construction Litigation; Uninsured and Underinsured Motorist

Thomas B. Underwood — University of Illinois, B.A., 1974; University of Illinois College of Law, J.D., 1978 — Admitted to Bar, 1978, Illinois; U.S. District Court, Central, Northern and Southern Districts of Illinois; U.S. District Court, Northern District of Indiana; U.S. District Court, Eastern District of Wisconsin; U.S. District Court, Western District of Missouri; U.S. Court of Appeals, Seventh Circuit — Member Illinois State Bar Association; Defense Research Institute — AV-Rated® by Martindale-Hubbell — Practice Areas: Insurance Coverage; Professional Liability; Excess and Umbrella; Construction Defect; Coverage Analysis; Toxic Torts; Coverage Litigation; Employment Law; Coverage Opinions; Appellate Practice; Coverage Issues; Civil Rights

Jonathan P. Schaefer — 1957 — DePaul University, B.A., 1979; DePaul University College of Law, J.D., 1982 — Admitted to Bar, 1982, Illinois; U.S. District Court, Northern District of Illinois including Trial Bar; 1999, U.S. District Court, Eastern District of Michigan; 2000, U.S. District Court, Central District of Illinois; 2002, U.S. District Court, District of Colorado; 2004, U.S. District Court, Southern District of Illinois; 2005, U.S. District Court, Northern District of Indiana; 2009, U.S. Court of Appeals, Seventh Circuit; 2012, U.S. District Court, Eastern District of Wisconsin — Member Illinois State Bar Association; Defense Research Institute — Practice Areas: Commercial Law; Arbitration; Premises Liability; Product Liability; Commercial Vehicle; Civil Litigation; Construction Liability; Insurance Defense; Civil Defense

Michael D. Sanders — 1969 — Northeast Missouri State University, B.A. (cum laude), 1991; Chicago-Kent College of Law, J.D. (cum laude), 1995 — Admitted to Bar, 1995, Illinois; U.S. District Court, Northern District of Illinois, Eastern Division; 2002, U.S. Court of Appeals, Seventh Circuit; 2003, U.S. District Court, Central District of Illinois — Practice Areas: Insurance Coverage; Environmental Coverage; Professional Liability; Legal Malpractice; Appellate Practice; Civil Rights; Construction Defect; Comprehensive General Liability; Excess and Umbrella; Uninsured and Underinsured Motorist; Premises Liability

Jason J. Friedl — 1972 — Arizona State University, B.A., 1995; Chicago-Kent College of Law, J.D., 2000 — Admitted to Bar, 2000, Illinois; U.S. District Court, Northern District of Illinois; 2012, U.S. District Court, Eastern District of Michigan; U.S. Court of Appeals, Sixth Circuit — Practice Areas: Personal Injury; Professional Liability; Premises Liability; Commercial Vehicle; Product Liability; Consumer Law; Construction Litigation; Dram Shop Liability; Appellate Practice

Mark J. Mickiewicz — 1978 — University of Illinois, B.S., 2000; University of Illinois College of Law, J.D. (cum laude), 2003 — Admitted to Bar, 2003, Illinois; 2007, U.S. District Court, Northern District of Illinois; 2008, U.S. District Court, Northern District of Indiana; 2010, U.S. Court of Appeals, Seventh Circuit — Practice Areas: Tort Litigation; Class Actions; Premises Liability; Construction Transactions; Automobile Liability; Construction Litigation; Intentional Torts; Construction Defect; Appellate Practice; Construction Accidents; Contract Disputes; Construction Claims; Civil Rights Defense; Construction Law; Commercial Transactions; Construction Liability

Kingshuk K. Roy — 1978 — University of Illinois at Urbana-Champaign, B.S. (with honors), 2000; University of Illinois College of Law, J.D., 2003 — Admitted to Bar, 2003, Illinois; U.S. District Court, Central and Northern Districts of Illinois — Member Illinios State Bar Association; Defense Research Institute; Illinois Association of Defense Trial Counsel — AV-Rated® by Martindale-Hubbell — Practice Areas: Insurance Defense; Construction Liability; Professional Liability; Premises Liability; Construction Law; Wrongful Death; Employer Liability

Senior Associates

Richard J. VanSwol — 1981 — University of Illinois at Urbana-Champaign, B.A./B.A. (summa cum laude), 2003; M.A., 2005; Northwestern University School of Law, J.D. (cum laude), 2008 — Admitted to Bar, 2008, Illinois; 2009, U.S. District Court, Northern District of Illinois; 2010, U.S. District Court, Northern District of Indiana; 2011, U.S. District Court, Eastern District of Wisconsin; 2011, U.S. Court of Appeals, Seventh Circuit; 2012, U.S. District Court, Southern District of Illinois — Member Illinois State and Chicago Bar Associations — Practice Areas: Insurance Coverage; Insurance Defense; Appellate Practice; Professional Liability; Insurance Litigation

Emily E. Schnidt — 1983 — University of Illinois at Urbana-Champaign, B.A. Political Science (Dean's List), 2005; The John Marshall Law School, J.D. (Dean's List), 2009 — Admitted to Bar, 2009, Illinois; U.S. District Court, Northern District of Illinois — Member Illinois Defense Counsel — Chicago Volunteer Legal Services Junior Board Chair — Practice Areas: Civil Rights; Employment Law; Municipal Liability; Commercial Litigation; Insurance Defense

Associate

Mark M. Abellera — 1977 — DePaul University, B.A. (Dean's List), 1999; The John Marshall Law School, J.D. (Dean's List), 2010 — Admitted to Bar, 2010, Illinois; 2011, U.S. District Court, Northern District of Illinois — Member American and Chicago Bar Associations — Practice Areas: Commercial Litigation; Construction Liability; Professional Liability; Insurance Coverage

Shipley Law Group

Two Prudential Plaza
180 North Stetson, Suite 4525
Chicago, Illinois 60601
   Telephone: 312-566-0040
   Fax: 312-566-0041
   E-Mail: rshipley@qpwblaw.com
   www.qpwblaw.com

Construction Litigation, Medical Malpractice, Personal Injury, Product Liability, Property and Casualty, Insurance Defense, Professional Malpractice, Property Defense, Subrogation, Mediation

ILLINOIS   CHICAGO

Shipley Law Group, Chicago, IL   (Continued)

Firm Profile: The firm concentrates its practice in civil litigation and general business law with an emphasis on all aspects of insurance, commercial, construction and tort litigation and trial practice, as well as general corporate law and business counseling. We pride ourselves on providing our clients with the highest quality legal services at competitive rates and alternative billing arrangements.

The practice originally started in 1989 with the formation of Shipley & Wilner, Ltd. In 1994 the firm name changed to Shipley & Associates, Ltd. and from 1999 to 2003 the firm was known as Franklin & Shipley, Ltd.

Insurance Clients

Country Companies   ESIS

Senior Partner

Robert A. Shipley — 1953 — University of Illinois at Urbana-Champaign, B.A., 1975; Northern Illinois University College of Law, J.D., 1978 — Admitted to Bar, 1979, Illinois; U.S. District Court, Northern District of Illinois including Trial Bar — Member American, Illinois State and Chicago Bar Associations; Illinois Association of Defense Trial Counsel; Defense Research Institute — Graduate, DePaul University Center for Dispute Resolution — Certified Mediator

Traub Lieberman Straus & Shrewsberry LLP

303 West Madison, Suite 1200
Chicago, Illinois 60606
  Telephone: 312-332-3900
  Fax: 312-332-3908
  www.traublieberman.com

(Hawthorne, NY Office*: Mid-Westchester Executive Park, Seven Skyline Drive, 10532)
  (Tel: 914-347-2600)
  (Fax: 914-347-8898)
  (E-Mail: swolfe@traublieberman.com)
(Red Bank, NJ Office*: 322 Highway 35, 07701)
  (Tel: 732-985-1000)
  (Fax: 732-985-2000)
(St. Petersburg, FL Office*: 360 Central Avenue, 33701)
  (Tel: 727-898-8100)
  (Fax: 727-895-4838)
(Los Angeles, CA Office*: 626 Wilshire Boulevard, Suite 800, 90017)
  (Tel: 213-624-4500)
(London, United Kingdom Office*: Gallery 4, 12 Leadenhall Street, EC3V1LP)
  (Tel: +44 (0) 020 7816 5856)
(New York, NY Office*: 100 Park Avenue, 16th Floor, 10017)
  (Tel: 646-227-1700)

Established: 2008

Admiralty and Maritime Law, Bad Faith, Civil Rights, Commercial Liability, Construction Defect, Construction Litigation, Employment Law, Environmental Coverage, Insurance Coverage, Insurance Litigation, Product Liability, Professional Liability, Professional Negligence, Medical Malpractice

Partners

Brian C. Bassett — University of Dayton, B.A., 2002; The John Marshall Law School, J.D., 2005 — Admitted to Bar, 2005, Illinois; U.S. District Court, Central, Northern and Southern Districts of Illinois — E-mail: bbassett@traublieberman.com

James M. Eastham — University of Illinois, B.S., 1991; University of Illinois College of Law, J.D., 1994 — Admitted to Bar, 1994, Illinois — E-mail: jeastham@traublieberman.com

Michael S. Knippen — St. Norbert College, B.A., 1978; DePaul University College of Law, J.D., 1983 — Admitted to Bar, 1983, Illinois; 1993, Texas; 1995, Colorado; 1984, U.S. District Court, Northern District of Illinois; 1994, U.S. District Court, Eastern, Northern and Southern Districts of Texas; U.S.

Traub Lieberman Straus & Shrewsberry LLP, Chicago, IL   (Continued)

District Court, District of Arizona; 2001, U.S. District Court, District of Colorado; U.S. Court of Appeals, Seventh Circuit — Member Society of Trial Lawyers of Illinois; Federation of Defense and Corporate Counsel — E-mail: mknippen@traublieberman.com

Natalie M. Limber — University of California, Los Angeles, B.A., 2002; Chicago-Kent College of Law, J.D. (with honors), 2005 — Admitted to Bar, 2005, Illinois; U.S. Court of Appeals for the District of Columbia and Seventh Circuits; U.S. District Court, Northern District of Illinois — E-mail: nlimber@traublieberman.com

Kimberly H. Petrina — University of Notre Dame, B.A. (cum laude), 2001; Loyola University Chicago School of Law, J.D., 2005 — Admitted to Bar, 2005, Illinois; U.S. District Court, Northern District of Illinois — E-mail: kpetrina@traublieberman.com

Mark F. Wolfe — University of Wisconsin, B.S., 1980; Marquette University Law School, J.D., 1983 — Admitted to Bar, 1983, Illinois; Wisconsin — E-mail: mwolfe@traublieberman.com

Associates

Katherine Dempster   Katherine M. Kelleher
Kevin Lahm   Jeremy S. Macklin
Christopher J. Nadeau   David J. Rock
Swathi S. Staley   Jason Taylor

(See listing under Hawthorne, NY for additional information)

Tucker, Robin & Merker, LLC

30 North LaSalle Street, Suite 2736
Chicago, Illinois 60602
  Telephone: 312-346-4700
  Fax: 312-346-4711
  www.trmlaw.com

Established: 2001

Insurance Defense, Trial Practice, Medical Malpractice, Professional Liability, Property Liability, General Liability, Insurance Coverage, Product Liability, Workers' Compensation, Construction Litigation, Business Litigation, Commercial Litigation, Directors and Officers Liability, Professional Negligence, Transportation Liability, Employment Liability

Firm Profile: The firm of Tucker Robin & Merker, LLC was established in 2001 by founding partners who averaged more than 15 years experience. We are engaged in a diverse practice focused on insurance law and litigation. We provide both claims defense and litigation coverage disputes. The firm is dedicated to providing the highest quality legal services in a cost-efficient manner.

Insurance Clients

AAA Life Insurance Company   AAA Member Select Insurance
ACUITY   Company
AFLAC, Inc.   Allied, A Division of Nationwide
Berkley Specialty Underwriting   Broadspire
  Managers, LLC   Chubb Group of Insurance
Country-Wide Insurance Company   Companies
Erie Insurance Group   Federated Insurance Company
GMAC Insurance   Great American Custom Insurance
Hertz Claim Management   Services
Infinity Property & Casualty Group K & K Insurance Group, Inc.
Liberty Mutual Insurance Company   Midwest Insurance Company
Nationwide Insurance   OMS National Insurance Company
Travelers Insurance   VeriClaim, Inc.
Western Litigation Specialists, Inc.

Non-Insurance Clients

Founders Bank   The Habitat Company
InterPark, Inc.   National Express Corp.
Ravenswood Disposal Service, Inc.   SAIA Motor Freight Line, Inc.
Yellow Freight System

CHICAGO ILLINOIS

Tucker, Robin & Merker, LLC, Chicago, IL (Continued)

Partners

Creed T. Tucker — University of Illinois, A.B. (with distinction), 1982; Northern Illinois University, J.D., 1985 — Admitted to Bar, 1985, Illinois; 1993, U.S. District Court, Northern District of Illinois including Trial Bar — Member Illinois Association of Defense Trial Counsel — Practice Areas: Insurance Defense; Civil Trial Practice; Insurance Coverage — E-mail: ctucker@trmlaw.com

Barry A. Robin — University of Illinois, B.S. (with distinction), 1979; The John Marshall Law School, J.D., 1983 — Admitted to Bar, 1983, Illinois; 1984, U.S. District Court, Northern District of Illinois; U.S. Court of Appeals, Seventh Circuit; U.S. District Court, Central District of Illinois — Member DuPage County and Chicago Bar Associations — Arbitrator - Cook and DuPage Counties; Mentor, Moot Court Council — Practice Areas: Product Liability; Construction Litigation; Complex Litigation; Toxic Torts; Insurance Defense — E-mail: brobin@trmlaw.com

Timothy G. Merker — University of Dayton, B.A. (magna cum laude), 1981; University of Notre Dame Law School, J.D., 1984 — Admitted to Bar, 1984, Michigan; 1990, Illinois; 1984, U.S. District Court, Eastern District of Michigan; 1991, U.S. District Court, Northern District of Illinois; 1994, U.S. Court of Appeals, Seventh Circuit — Member Illinois State and Chicago Bar Associations — Practice Areas: Medical Malpractice; Professional Liability; Product Liability; Insurance Defense; Civil Litigation — E-mail: tmerker@trmlaw.com

Associates

Peter H. Rodenburg — 1963 — University of Illinois, B.B.S., 1986; Loyola University Chicago School of Law, J.D., 1998 — Admitted to Bar, 1998, Illinois; 1998, U.S. District Court, Northern District of Illinois — Member Illinois State Bar Association — Practice Areas: Construction Litigation; Insurance Defense; Insurance Coverage; Workers' Compensation; Contracts — E-mail: prodenburg@trmlaw.com

Bonnie B. Bijak — Eastern Illinois University, B.A., 1981; The John Marshall Law School in Chicago, J.D., 1987 — Admitted to Bar, 1987, Illinois; U.S. District Court, Northern District of Illinois — Member Workers' Compensation Lawyers Association — Arbitration Panelist, Circuit Court of Cook County — Practice Areas: Civil Litigation; Insurance Defense; Workers' Compensation — E-mail: bbijak@trmlaw.com

Of Counsel

Randall E. Server — Princeton University, A.B. (cum laude), 1973; Northwestern University, J.D., 1976 — Admitted to Bar, 1976, Illinois; 1977, U.S. District Court, Northern District of Illinois including Trial Bar; 1977, U.S. Court of Appeals, Seventh Circuit; 2001, U.S. District Court, Central District of Illinois — Member Illinois State and Chicago Bar Associations — Arbitration Panelist, Circuit Court of Cook County — Practice Areas: Business Law; Commercial Litigation; Class Actions; Insurance Defense — E-mail: rserver@trmlaw.com

Jessica B. Tucker — University of Michigan, B.B.A., 1981; Thomas M. Cooley Law School, J.D., 1985 — Admitted to Bar, 1985, Michigan; 1986, Illinois; 1986, Colorado; 1985, U.S. District Court, Eastern District of Michigan; 1986, U.S. District Court, Northern District of Illinois; 1993, U.S. Court of Appeals, Seventh Circuit — Member Appellate Lawyers Association of Illinois — Arbitration Panelist, Circuit Court of Cook County; Village of Winnetka (Trustee, 2004-2008; President, 2009-2013) — Practice Areas: Appeals; Civil Defense — E-mail: jtucker@trmlaw.com

Urgo & Nugent, Ltd.

2 North LaSalle Street, Suite 1800
Chicago, Illinois 60602
Telephone: 312-263-6635
Fax: 312-263-1329

(Wheaton, IL Office: 330 South Naperville Road, Suite 240, 60187)
(Tel: 630-653-0123)
(Fax: 630-653-0674)

Established: 1968

Litigation, Subrogation, Personal Injury Defense

Urgo & Nugent, Ltd., Chicago, IL (Continued)

Firm Profile: In 1968, Garretson & Santora, Ltd. established itself as a respected law firm in Chicago. Urgo & Nugent, Ltd. continues this tradition in its Chicago and Wheaton offices.

The firm's attorneys practice in Cook, Lake, DuPage, Kane, Will and Kankakee Counties in Illinois, as well as all of the various Municipal Districts located in Cook County, Illinois. The firm also practices in the United States District Court for the Northern District of Illinois and before various arbitration, administrative, and alternative dispute resolution tribunals.

Urgo & Nugent, Ltd.'s major emphasis is in the area of trial advocacy in every level of the Illinois Court system, including the Appellate Courts. Urgo & Nugent, Ltd. is a firm made up of trial lawyers committed to providing vigorous and quality representation, while attempting to reduce the economic burdens of litigation on its clients and insurance carriers.

Insurance Clients

Employers Mutual Companies   State Farm Mutual Automobile Insurance Company

Partners

Michael J. Urgo, Jr. — 1956 — Loyola University, B.A., 1978; DePaul University College of Law, J.D., 1981 — Admitted to Bar, 1981, Illinois

Richard E. Nugent — 1955 — College of St. Thomas, B.A., 1977; Loyola University School of Law, J.D., 1984 — Admitted to Bar, 1984, Illinois — Member American, Illinois State, DuPage County and Chicago Bar Associations; Casualty Adjuster Association of Chicago; Defense Research Institute; Illinois Association of Defense Trial Counsel

Associates

Philip G. Heitz — 1949 — Northwestern University, B.S.J., 1971; Loyola University School of Law, J.D., 1974 — Admitted to Bar, 1974, Illinois

Amy J. Hemmingsen — The University of Iowa, B.A., 1986; Creighton University School of Law, J.D., 1992 — Admitted to Bar, 1992, Illinois; 1993, Nebraska; 1993, U.S. District Court, Northern District of Illinois

David B. Reeves — 1973 — Northern Illinois University, B.A., 1996; Northern Illinois University College of Law, J.D., 2000 — Admitted to Bar, 2001, Illinois; U.S. District Court, Northern District of Illinois

Alfredo Alvarez — 1975 — University of Illinois, B.S., 1998; Loyola University Chicago School of Law, J.D., 2004 — Admitted to Bar, 2004, Illinois — Languages: Spanish

Aaron M. LaRue — 1981 — Anderson University, B.A., 2003; Thomas M. Cooley Law School, J.D., 2010 — Admitted to Bar, 2010, Illinois

Terence P. Naughton — 1983 — University of Illinois-Urbana-Champaign, B.A., 2005; Valparaiso University School of Law, J.D., 2009 — Admitted to Bar, 2010, Illinois; 2011, U.S. District Court, Northern District of Illinois

Ryan S. Showalter — 1983 — Indiana University, B.A., 2006; Thomas M. Cooley Law School, J.D., 2010 — Admitted to Bar, 2010, Illinois

Elizabeth S. Watson — 1984 — Northern Illinois University, B.S., 2006; University of Missouri-Kansas City School of Law, J.D., 2009 — Admitted to Bar, 2010, Illinois

Sarah E. Albrecht — The John Marshall Law School, J.D., 2008 — Admitted to Bar, 2008, Illinois; 2010, U.S. District Court, Northern District of Illinois

Michael Terranova — 1980 — Western Illinois University, B.A., 2007; Chicago-Kent College of Law, J.D., 2013 — Admitted to Bar, 2014, Illinois

Lisa M. Anderson — 1986 — Thomas M. Cooley Law School, J.D., 2012 — Admitted to Bar, 2013, Illinois

Wiedner & McAuliffe, Ltd.

One North Franklin Street, Suite 1900
Chicago, Illinois 60606
Telephone: 312-855-1105
Fax: 312-855-1792
E-Mail: rjleamy@wmlaw.com
www.wmlaw.com

Litigation, Workers' Compensation, Civil Litigation, Employment Law, Personal Injury, Insurance Coverage, Product Liability, Professional Liability, Subrogation

Wiedner & McAuliffe, Ltd., Chicago, IL (Continued)

Firm Profile: Wiedner & McAuliffe represents clients in the manufacturing, retailing, insurance, construction, transportation, food product and health care industries. For more than 30 years we have provided our clients with solutions to their litigation defense needs. Our litigation practice includes workers' compensation, employment and insurance law, insurance litigation as well as the successful defense of construction, class action, personal injury, property damage, product liability and professional liability lawsuits.

Insurance Clients

Cincinnati Insurance Company U.S. Aviation Underwriters

Non-Insurance Clients

United Airlines, Inc.

Firm Members

Richard J. Leamy, Jr. — 1952 — Western Michigan University, B.A., 1974; DePaul University, J.D., 1977 — Law Clerk, Michigan Court of Appeals, 1977-1978 — Admitted to Bar, 1978, Michigan; 1979, Illinois; U.S. District Court, Northern District of Illinois including Trial Bar — Member American Bar Association (Litigation, Insurance, Negligence and Compensation Law Sections); Illinois State and Chicago Bar Associations; Illinois Defense Counsel

Timothy D. McMahon — 1952 — John Carroll University, B.A., 1974; DePaul University, J.D. (cum laude), 1977 — Admitted to Bar, 1977, Illinois; U.S. District Court, Northern District of Illinois including Trial Bar — Member Illinois State and DuPage County Bar Associations; Chicago Bar Association (Circuit Court, Civil Litigation, Employment Litigation, Judicial Evaluation and Tort Litigation Committees); Illinois Association of Defense Trial Counsel; Defense Research Institute — Assistant State's Attorney, Cook County, Illinois, 1977-1983 — Practice Areas: Construction Accidents; Product Liability; Premises Liability; Wrongful Death; Insurance Coverage; Employment Practices Liability; Commercial Law; Appellate Practice

COLLINSVILLE   25,579 Madison Co.

McMahon Berger

400 North Bluff Road
Collinsville, Illinois 62234
Telephone: 618-345-5822
Fax: 618-345-6483
E-Mail: lawfirm@mcmahonberger.com
www.mcmahonberger.com

(St. Louis, MO Office*: 2730 North Ballas Road, Suite 200, 63131, P.O. Box 31901, 63131-0901)
(Tel: 314-567-7350)
(Fax: 314-567-5968)

Employment Law, Labor and Employment, Employment Discrimination, Administrative Law

(See listing under St. Louis, MO for additional information)

DANVILLE   † 33,027 Vermilion Co.

Dukes, Ryan, Meyer, & Freed Ltd.

146 North Vermilion Street
Danville, Illinois 61832
Telephone: 217-442-0384
Fax: 217-442-0009
E-Mail: shariellis83@yahoo.com

Established: 1968

Insurance Defense, Personal Injury, Property Damage, Automobile, Homeowners, General Practice, Criminal Law

Dukes, Ryan, Meyer, & Freed Ltd., Danville, IL (Continued)

Insurance Clients

Allstate Insurance Company
Encompass Indemnity Company
Meridian Insurance Company
State Farm Insurance Company
West Bend Mutual Insurance Company
Auto-Owners Insurance Company
Madison Mutual Insurance Company
Unitrin Specialty Insurance

Partners

David J. Ryan — 1951 — Loyola University, B.A. (magna cum laude), 1973; University of Illinois, J.D., 1976 — Admitted to Bar, 1976, Illinois; 1977, U.S. District Court, Central District of Illinois; 1983, U.S. Court of Appeals, Seventh Circuit; 1992, U.S. Supreme Court — Member Illinois State and Vermilion County Bar Associations

Christopher P. Meyer — 1954 — University of Illinois, B.S., 1976; Northern Illinois University, J.D. (magna cum laude), 1985 — Admitted to Bar, 1985, Illinois; 1985, U.S. District Court, Central District of Illinois; 1995, U.S. Court of Appeals, Seventh Circuit — Member Illinois State and Vermilion County Bar Associations

Kelly M. Freed — 1956 — Illinois State University, B.S. (with honors), 1979; Northern Illinois University, J.D. (with honors), 1994 — Admitted to Bar, 1994, Illinois; 1994, U.S. District Court, Central District of Illinois; 1998, U.S. District Court, Southern District of Illinois — Member Illinois State and Vermilion County Bar Associations

The following firms also service this area.

Craig & Craig, LLC
1807 Broadway Avenue
P.O. Box 689
Mattoon, Illinois 61938
Telephone: 217-234-6481
Fax: 217-234-6486
Fax: 217-258-8292

Automobile Liability, Casualty, Civil Rights, Dram Shop, Employment Practices Liability, Family Law, Fire, Insurance Coverage, Intellectual Property, Mediation, Product Liability, Premises Liability, Professional Liability, Surety, Uninsured and Underinsured Motorist, Workers' Compensation

SEE COMPLETE LISTING UNDER MATTOON, ILLINOIS (88 MILES)

DECATUR   † 76,122 Macon Co.

Refer To

Craig & Craig, LLC
1807 Broadway Avenue
P.O. Box 689
Mattoon, Illinois 61938
Telephone: 217-234-6481
Fax: 217-234-6486
Fax: 217-258-8292

Automobile Liability, Casualty, Civil Rights, Dram Shop, Employment Practices Liability, Family Law, Fire, Insurance Coverage, Intellectual Property, Mediation, Product Liability, Premises Liability, Professional Liability, Surety, Uninsured and Underinsured Motorist, Workers' Compensation

SEE COMPLETE LISTING UNDER MATTOON, ILLINOIS (44 MILES)

Refer To

Rammelkamp Bradney, P.C.
232 West State
Jacksonville, Illinois 62650
Telephone: 217-245-6177
Fax: 217-243-7322

Mailing Address: P.O. Box 550, Jacksonville, IL 62651-0550

Insurance Law, Fire Loss, Arson, First Party Matters, Litigation, Declaratory Judgments, Workers' Compensation, Americans with Disabilities Act, Civil Rights, Construction Litigation, Employment Practices Liability, Trial and Appellate Practice

SEE COMPLETE LISTING UNDER JACKSONVILLE, ILLINOIS (74 MILES)

EDWARDSVILLE ILLINOIS

DIXON † 15,733 Lee Co.

Refer To

Mateer Goff & Honzel LLP
401 West State Street, Suite 400
Rockford, Illinois 61101
   Telephone: 815-965-7745
   Fax: 815-965-7749

Insurance Law, Fire, Casualty Insurance Law, Defense Litigation, Trial and Appellate Practice

SEE COMPLETE LISTING UNDER ROCKFORD, ILLINOIS (44 MILES)

Refer To

Russell, English, Scoma & Beneke, P.C.
Ten Park Avenue West
Princeton, Illinois 61356
   Telephone: 815-875-4555
   Fax: 815-875-2211

Insurance Law, Trial Practice, Personal Injury, Property Damage, Tort Litigation, Coverage Issues, Litigation

SEE COMPLETE LISTING UNDER PRINCETON, ILLINOIS (33 MILES)

EDWARDSVILLE † 24,293 Madison Co.

Gunty & McCarthy

201 Hillsboro Avenue, Suite 204
Edwardsville, Illinois 62025
   Telephone: 618-659-3690
   Fax: 618-659-4630
   www.guntymccarthy.com

Insurance Defense, Asbestos Litigation, Automobile, Bodily Injury, Casualty, Environmental Law, General Liability, Insurance Coverage, Product Liability, Property Damage, Medical Devices, Subrogation, Construction Accidents, Mass Tort, Wrongful Death, Toxic Torts, Federal Employer Liability Claims (FELA), Railroad Law, Transportation, Mold Litigation

(See listing under Chicago, IL for additional information)

HeplerBroom LLC

130 North Main Street
Edwardsville, Illinois 62025
   Telephone: 618-656-0184
   Fax: 618-656-1364
   E-Mail: firm@heplerbroom.com
   www.heplerbroom.com

(St. Louis, MO Office*: 211 North Broadway, Suite 2700, 63102)
   (Tel: 314-241-6160)
   (Fax: 314-241-6116)
(Chicago, IL Office*: 30 North LaSalle Street, Suite 2900, 60602)
   (Tel: 312-230-9100)
   (Fax: 312-230-9201)
(Springfield, IL Office*: 4340 Acer Grove Drive, Suite A, 62711)
   (Tel: 217-528-3674)
   (Fax: 217-528-3964)

Established: 1894

Antitrust, Insurance Defense, Product Liability, Toxic Torts, Property and Casualty, Class Actions, Legal Malpractice, Commercial Litigation, Pharmaceutical, General Liability, Asbestos Litigation, Medical Malpractice, Workers' Compensation, Employment Litigation, Insurance Coverage, Transportation, Automobile, Trucking Law, Agent and Brokers Errors and Omissions, Personal Injury, Skilled Nursing Facilities, Construction Liability, White Collar Criminal Defense, Qui Tam/False Claims Act Litigation

HeplerBroom LLC, Edwardsville, IL (Continued)

Firm Profile: The law firm of HeplerBroom LLC has a history spanning over one hundred years. HeplerBroom is one of the top litigation and trial law firms in the U.S. and has successfully represented clients in major cases both in state and federal courts. HeplerBroom's trial lawyers handle cases in a wide variety of areas, primarily representing defendants in civil law suits including class actions, product liability, pharmaceutical, personal injury, asbestos, employment, toxic torts, transportation and trucking, legal and medical malpractice, nursing home, insurance, workers' compensation, commercial law and white collar criminal defense. The firm provides comprehensive representation for its business clients, from entity selection and formation to day-to-day management and employment issues, tax planning, contract preparation, real estate matters, succession planning and representation in mergers, acquisitions, and sales. The firm also offers sophisticated estate planning services for business owners and other individuals.

The firm serves a practice area with a primary focus throughout the states of Illinois and Missouri.

Insurance Clients

Cincinnati Insurance Company
Swiss Re/Westport Insurance Corporation
St. Paul Travelers

Non-Insurance Clients

Ameren Corporation
St. James Hospital & Health Center
Prairie Farms Dairy, Inc.

Partners

Larry E. Hepler — 1943 — Washington and Lee University, J.D. (magna cum laude), 1968 — Admitted to Bar, 1968, Missouri; 1971, Illinois — Tel: 618-307-1117 — E-mail: leh@heplerbroom.com

Jeffrey S. Hebrank — 1957 — Saint Louis University, J.D., 1982 — Admitted to Bar, 1982, Illinois; 1983, Missouri — Tel: 618-307-1129 — E-mail: jsh@heplerbroom.com

Troy A. Bozarth — 1969 — Drake University, J.D./M.B.A., 1996 — Admitted to Bar, 1996, Illinois — Tel: 618-307-1124 — E-mail: tab@heplerbroom.com

Heyl, Royster, Voelker & Allen
A Professional Corporation

Mark Twain Plaza III, Suite 100
105 West Vandalia Street
Edwardsville, Illinois 62025-1935
   Telephone: 618-656-4646
   Fax: 618-656-7940
   E-Mail: firm@heylroyster.com
   www.heylroyster.com

(Additional Offices: Peoria, IL*; Springfield, IL*; Urbana, IL*; Rockford, IL*; Chicago, IL*)

Civil Trial Practice, Insurance Defense, Appellate Practice, Class Actions, Coverage Issues, Employment Law, Professional Malpractice, Self-Insured Defense, Toxic Torts, Workers' Compensation

Managing Partner

Robert H. Shultz, Jr. — 1952 — University of Illinois, A.B., 1975; J.D., 1978 — Admitted to Bar, 1978, Illinois

(Our lawyers are members of the American, state and local bar associations and, in many cases, are members of the local American Inn of Court chapters; leadership positions in these organizations are listed.)
(See Peoria, Rockford, Springfield and Urbana, IL Listings for additional information.)

Reed Armstrong Mudge & Morrissey P.C.

115 North Buchanan Street
Edwardsville, Illinois 62025
   Telephone: 618-656-0257, 217-525-1366
   Fax: 618-692-4416, 217-525-0986
   E-Mail: dloepker@reedarmstrong.com
   www.reedarmstrong.com

Established: 1927

Product Liability, Class Actions, Insurance Defense, Insurance Coverage, Premises Liability, Construction Law, General Liability, Professional Malpractice, Workers' Compensation, Municipal Liability, Employment Practices Liability, Commercial and Business Torts, Mass Tort Liability, Vehicle Liability, Contract and Property Law, Sports and Recreational Liability, Commercial Trucking Liability, Defamation

Firm Profile: Reed Armstrong Mudge & Morrissey P.C., is a civil practice law firm with an emphasis in the defense of complex personal injury and property damage litigation. Based in Edwardsville, Illinois, the county seat of Madison County. The firm was founded in 1927, and serves the needs of clients throughout Central and Southern Illinois.

Reed, Armstrong has an established reputation as a winning civil defense trial firm in the Madison, St. Clair County and surrounding regions. Although the Firm provides an array of services, its special skill is litigation. The Firm has successfully fought for individual, business and corporate clients for over fifty years. It is the most experienced civil trail defense firm in Southern Illinois. Combined, the partners have tried over one thousand civil jury trials. Appellate Court experience is also extensive. All of the equity partners are experienced trial attorneys and associates obtain court experience. Most of them have had trial experience as the firm believes that this is essential to the development of the firm's young attorneys. Through hard work, extensive trial experience, and superior knowledge of the region and the courts, the Firm is able to provide their clients with excellent legal service, advice, and judgment.

Insurance Clients

Acceptance Insurance Company
Allstate Insurance Company
American International Group, Inc.
Chartis Insurance
Compirion Healthcare Solutions, LLC
Employers Casualty Company
General Casualty Companies
Harco National Insurance Company
Illinois Agricultural Association
Lexington Insurance Company
Millers Mutual Insurance Company
National Farmers Union Standard Insurance Company
Pekin Insurance Company
RiverStone Claims Management, LLC
State Farm Insurance Companies
Travelers
Westfield Insurance
Allied Insurance Company
American International Adjustment Company
CNA Insurance Company
COUNTRY Mutual Insurance Company
Gallagher Bassett Services, Inc.
Grinnell Mutual Reinsurance Company
IAT Specialty
Illinois Casualty Company
Millers First Insurance Companies
Mt. Hawley Insurance Company
Nationwide Insurance
Naughton Insurance, Inc.
QBE
RLI Insurance Company
Shelter Insurance Companies
TIG Insurance Company
Unitrin Property and Casualty Insurance Group

Non-Insurance Clients

Air Products and Chemicals, Inc.
Inductotherm Corporation
Fluor Corporation
United States Gypsum Company

Partners

James L. Reed — (Deceased)

Harry C. Armstrong — (Retired)

Stephen C. Mudge — 1952 — St. Ambrose College, B.A., 1974; Saint Louis University, J.D., 1977 — Admitted to Bar, 1977, Illinois; 1991, Missouri — Member Illinois State and Madison County Bar Associations; The Missouri Bar; Illinois Association of Defense Trial Counsel; American Board of Trial Advocates; American College of Trial Lawyers; Defense Research Institute — E-mail: smudge@reedarmstrong.com

Martin K. Morrissey — 1959 — University of Illinois at Urbana-Champaign, B.A., 1982; Southern Illinois University, J.D., 1985 — Admitted to Bar, 1985, Illinois — Member American, Illinois State and Madison County Bar Associations; Illinois Association of Defense Trial Counsel; American Board of Trial Advocates; American College of Trial Lawyers; Defense Research Institute — E-mail: mmorrissey@reedarmstrong.com

Michael J. Bedesky — 1966 — Loyola University, B.A., 1988; University of Illinois, J.D., 1991 — Admitted to Bar, 1991, Illinois — Member Illinois State and Madison County Bar Associations — E-mail: mbedesky@reedarmstrong.com

Bryan L. Skelton — 1960 — Mid-America Nazarene College, B.A., 1983; Saint Louis University School of Law, J.D., 1993 — Admitted to Bar, 1993, Illinois — Member The Missouri Bar; Illinois State and Madison County Bar Associations; Defense Research Institute — E-mail: bskelton@reedarmstrong.com

William B. Starnes II — 1962 — Kansas University, B.S.B.A., 1984; University of Missouri-Kansas City School of Law, J.D., 1988 — Admitted to Bar, 1995, Missouri — Member Illinois State and Madison County Bar Associations; The Missouri Bar; Defense Research Institute — E-mail: wstarnes@reedarmstrong.com

Michael C. Hobin — 1970 — Bradley University, B.S., 1992; Illinois State University, M.S., 1994; Southern Illinois University, J.D., 2000 — Admitted to Bar, 2000, Illinois — Member Illinois State and Madison County Bar Associations; Illinois Association of Defense Trial Counsel — E-mail: mhobin@reedarmstrong.com

Dominique N. Seymoure — 1976 — Southern Illinois University, B.A., 1998; J.D., 2001 — Admitted to Bar, 2001, Illinois — Member Illinois State and Madison County Bar Associations; Defense Research Institute; Illinois Association of Defense Trial Counsel — E-mail: dseymoure@reedarmstrong.com

Associates

Tori L. Walls — 1978 — Illinois College, B.A., 2000; Southern Illinois University School of Law, J.D., 2003 — Admitted to Bar, 2003, Illinois; 2004, Missouri; U.S. District Court, Southern District of Illinois — Member The Missouri Bar; Illinois State and Madison County Bar Associations; Bar Association of Metropolitan St. Louis — E-mail: twalls@reedarmstrong.com

Joshua Severit — 1985 — University of Illinois, B.A., 2007; Southern Illinois University School of Law, J.D. (cum laude), 2010 — Admitted to Bar, 2010, Illinois; U.S. District Court, Southern District of Illinois — Member Illinois State and Madison County Bar Associations — Practice Areas: Insurance Defense — E-mail: jseverit@reedarmstrong.com

Jennifer M. Wagner — Washington University in St. Louis, B.A. (Dean's List), 2003; Southern Illinois University Law School, J.D. (cum laude), 2011 — Howard Hughes Medical Institute Fellowship, Washington University in St. Louis — Admitted to Bar, 2011, Illinois; 2012, U.S. Court of Appeals, Seventh Circuit — Member Illinois State and Madison County Bar Associations

Mitchell Martin — Harding University, B.A., 2008; Southern Illinois University, J.D. (cum laude), 2013 — Admitted to Bar, 2013, Illinois; 2014, Missouri — Member Illinois State and Madison County Bar Associations — E-mail: mmartin@reedarmstrong.com

Travis Pour — Purdue University, B.S., 2010; Southern Illinois University Carbondale, J.D., 2013 — Admitted to Bar, 2013, Illinois; 2014, Missouri — Member Illinois State and Madison County Bar Associations — E-mail: tpour@reedarmstrong.com

---

The following firms also service this area.

Hoagland, Fitzgerald & Pranaitis

401 Market Street
Alton, Illinois 62002
   Telephone: 618-465-7745
   Fax: 618-465-3744
   Toll Free: 866-830-1066
Mailing Address: P.O. Box 130, Alton, IL 62002

Insurance Defense

SEE COMPLETE LISTING UNDER ALTON, ILLINOIS (16 MILES)

HARDIN

Neville, Richards & Wuller, LLC
5 Park Place Professional Centre
Illinois Street and Fullerton Road
Belleville, Illinois 62226
Telephone: 618-277-0900
Fax: 618-277-0970

Mailing Address: P.O. Box 23977, Belleville, IL 62226-0070

Insurance Defense, Professional Negligence, Product Liability, Premises Liability, Automobile, Bodily Injury, Fraud, Arson, Coverage Issues, Medical Malpractice, General Liability

SEE COMPLETE LISTING UNDER BELLEVILLE, ILLINOIS (20 MILES)

Rammelkamp Bradney, P.C.
232 West State
Jacksonville, Illinois 62650
Telephone: 217-245-6177
Fax: 217-243-7322

Mailing Address: P.O. Box 550, Jacksonville, IL 62651-0550

Insurance Law, Fire Loss, Arson, First Party Matters, Litigation, Declaratory Judgments, Workers' Compensation, Americans with Disabilities Act, Civil Rights, Construction Litigation, Employment Practices Liability, Trial and Appellate Practice

SEE COMPLETE LISTING UNDER JACKSONVILLE, ILLINOIS (74 MILES)

Williams Venker & Sanders LLC
Bank of America Tower
100 North Broadway, 21st Floor
St. Louis, Missouri 63102
Telephone: 314-345-5000
Fax: 314-345-5055

Premises Liability, Product Liability, Professional Liability, Property and Casualty

SEE COMPLETE LISTING UNDER ST. LOUIS, MISSOURI (36 MILES)

EFFINGHAM † 12,328 Effingham Co.
Refer To

Craig & Craig, LLC
1807 Broadway Avenue
P.O. Box 689
Mattoon, Illinois 61938
Telephone: 217-234-6481
Fax: 217-234-6486
Fax: 217-258-8292

Automobile Liability, Casualty, Civil Rights, Dram Shop, Employment Practices Liability, Family Law, Fire, Insurance Coverage, Intellectual Property, Mediation, Product Liability, Premises Liability, Professional Liability, Surety, Uninsured and Underinsured Motorist, Workers' Compensation

SEE COMPLETE LISTING UNDER MATTOON, ILLINOIS (24 MILES)

FAIRFIELD † 5,154 Wayne Co.
Refer To

Craig & Craig, LLC
P.O. Box 1545
Mount Vernon, Illinois 62864
Telephone: 618-244-7511
Fax: 618-244-7628

Professional Liability, Workers' Compensation, Product Liability, Civil Rights, Dram Shop, Premises Liability, Automobile Liability, Fire, Casualty, Surety, Life Insurance, Uninsured and Underinsured Motorist, Employment Law, Intellectual Property, Family Law, Criminal Defense, Mediation

SEE COMPLETE LISTING UNDER MOUNT VERNON, ILLINOIS (32 MILES)

FREEPORT † 25,638 Stephenson Co.
Refer To

Mateer Goff & Honzel LLP
401 West State Street, Suite 400
Rockford, Illinois 61101
Telephone: 815-965-7745
Fax: 815-965-7749

Insurance Law, Fire, Casualty Insurance Law, Defense Litigation, Trial and Appellate Practice

SEE COMPLETE LISTING UNDER ROCKFORD, ILLINOIS (35 MILES)

GALENA † 3,429 Jo Daviess Co.
Refer To

Mateer Goff & Honzel LLP
401 West State Street, Suite 400
Rockford, Illinois 61101
Telephone: 815-965-7745
Fax: 815-965-7749

Insurance Law, Fire, Casualty Insurance Law, Defense Litigation, Trial and Appellate Practice

SEE COMPLETE LISTING UNDER ROCKFORD, ILLINOIS (82 MILES)

GENEVA † 21,495 Kane Co.
Refer To

Mulherin, Rehfeldt & Varchetto, P.C.
211 South Wheaton Avenue, Suite 200
Wheaton, Illinois 60187
Telephone: 630-653-9300
Fax: 630-653-9316

Insurance Defense, Medical Malpractice, Coverage Issues, Automobile Liability, Commercial Liability, General Liability, Liquor Liability, Dram Shop, Premises Liability, Product Liability, Construction Accidents, Employment Law, Bodily Injury, Property Damage, Subrogation, Environmental Law, Toxic Torts, Professional Liability, Municipal Liability, Workers' Compensation

SEE COMPLETE LISTING UNDER WHEATON, ILLINOIS (12 MILES)

GREENVILLE † 7,000 Bond Co.
Refer To

Neville, Richards & Wuller, LLC
5 Park Place Professional Centre
Illinois Street and Fullerton Road
Belleville, Illinois 62226
Telephone: 618-277-0900
Fax: 618-277-0970

Mailing Address: P.O. Box 23977, Belleville, IL 62226-0070

Insurance Defense, Professional Negligence, Product Liability, Premises Liability, Automobile, Bodily Injury, Fraud, Arson, Coverage Issues, Medical Malpractice, General Liability

SEE COMPLETE LISTING UNDER BELLEVILLE, ILLINOIS (45 MILES)

HARDIN † 967 Calhoun Co.
Refer To

Rammelkamp Bradney, P.C.
232 West State
Jacksonville, Illinois 62650
Telephone: 217-245-6177
Fax: 217-243-7322

Mailing Address: P.O. Box 550, Jacksonville, IL 62651-0550

Insurance Law, Fire Loss, Arson, First Party Matters, Litigation, Declaratory Judgments, Workers' Compensation, Americans with Disabilities Act, Civil Rights, Construction Litigation, Employment Practices Liability, Trial and Appellate Practice

SEE COMPLETE LISTING UNDER JACKSONVILLE, ILLINOIS (56 MILES)

HARRISBURG † 9,017 Saline Co.

Jelliffe, Ferrell, Doerge & Phelps
108 East Walnut Street
Harrisburg, Illinois 62946
 Telephone: 618-253-7153, 618-253-7647
 Fax: 618-252-1843
 E-Mail: jfdplaw@gmail.com
 www.jfdplaw.com

Established: 1920

Insurance Law, Negligence, Personal Injury, Workers' Compensation, Product Liability, General Civil Practice, State and Federal Courts, Trial Practice, Appellate Practice, All Tort Litigation

Firm Profile: The Practice of Jelliffe, Ferrell, Doerge & Phelps in Harrisburg, Illinois, through its former partners, has been in existence since 1920. The firm serves, and is engaged in, litigation in the southern one-third of the State of Illinois. The firm is actively involved in litigation regarding all areas related to personal injury, torts, workers' compensation and insurance.

Insurance Clients

Auto-Owners Insurance Company
Midwestern Insurance Alliance
National Liability and Fire Insurance Company
PMA Insurance Group
COUNTRY Mutual Insurance Company
OccuSure Workers' Compensation Specialist
State Farm Insurance Company

Partners

Charles R. Jelliffe — (Retired)

Donald V. Ferrell — 1944 — University of Illinois, B.S., 1966; The University of Alabama, J.D., 1969 — Admitted to Bar, 1969, Illinois; 1971, U.S. District Court, Southern District of Illinois; 1978, U.S. Court of Appeals, Seventh Circuit; 1990, U.S. Court of Appeals, Eighth Circuit; 1991, U.S. District Court, Southern District of Indiana; 2000, U.S. District Court, Western District of Michigan — Member American, Illinois State and Saline County Bar Associations; American College of Trial Lawyers — Practice Areas: Insurance Coverage & Defense; Insurance Coverage Litigation; Personal Injury; Product Liability; General Civil Litigation — E-mail: dvferrell@gmail.com

Michal Doerge — 1958 — Murray State University, B.S., 1981; Southern Illinois University, J.D., 1984 — Admitted to Bar, 1984, Illinois; 1992, U.S. District Court, Southern District of Illinois; 1994, U.S. Court of Appeals, Seventh Circuit; 1995, U.S. Supreme Court — Member Illinois State and Saline County Bar Associations — Practice Areas: Personal Injury; Product Liability; Insurance Law — E-mail: michaldoerge@gmail.com

Kelly R. Phelps — 1970 — University of Illinois, B.A., 1992; Southern Illinois University, J.D., 1995 — Admitted to Bar, 1995, Illinois; 1999, U.S. Court of Appeals, Seventh Circuit; 1996, U.S. District Court, Southern District of Illinois — Member Illinois State and Saline County Bar Associations — Practice Areas: Personal Injury; Workers' Compensation; Insurance Law — E-mail: kphelps70@gmail.com

The following firms also service this area.

Craig & Craig, LLC
P.O. Box 1545
Mount Vernon, Illinois 62864
 Telephone: 618-244-7511
 Fax: 618-244-7628

Professional Liability, Workers' Compensation, Product Liability, Civil Rights, Dram Shop, Premises Liability, Automobile Liability, Fire, Casualty, Surety, Life Insurance, Uninsured and Underinsured Motorist, Employment Law, Intellectual Property, Family Law, Criminal Defense, Mediation

SEE COMPLETE LISTING UNDER MOUNT VERNON, ILLINOIS (59 MILES)

Feirich/Mager/Green/Ryan
2001 West Main Street
Carbondale, Illinois 62901
 Telephone: 618-529-3000
 Fax: 618-529-3008
Mailing Address: P.O. Box 1570, Carbondale, IL 62903-1570

Insurance Defense, Medical Negligence, Casualty, Construction Litigation, Product Liability, Workers' Compensation, Civil Rights, Trial Practice, Appellate Practice, Professional Liability, Subrogation, Coverage Issues

SEE COMPLETE LISTING UNDER CARBONDALE, ILLINOIS (38 MILES)

HAVANA † 3,301 Mason Co.

Refer To

Rammelkamp Bradney, P.C.
232 West State
Jacksonville, Illinois 62650
 Telephone: 217-245-6177
 Fax: 217-243-7322
Mailing Address: P.O. Box 550, Jacksonville, IL 62651-0550

Insurance Law, Fire Loss, Arson, First Party Matters, Litigation, Declaratory Judgments, Workers' Compensation, Americans with Disabilities Act, Civil Rights, Construction Litigation, Employment Practices Liability, Trial and Appellate Practice

SEE COMPLETE LISTING UNDER JACKSONVILLE, ILLINOIS (40 MILES)

HENNEPIN † 757 Putnam Co.

Refer To

Russell, English, Scoma & Beneke, P.C.
Ten Park Avenue West
Princeton, Illinois 61356
 Telephone: 815-875-4555
 Fax: 815-875-2211

Insurance Law, Trial Practice, Personal Injury, Property Damage, Tort Litigation, Coverage Issues, Litigation

SEE COMPLETE LISTING UNDER PRINCETON, ILLINOIS (15 MILES)

HILLSBORO † 6,207 Montgomery Co.

Refer To

Neville, Richards & Wuller, LLC
5 Park Place Professional Centre
Illinois Street and Fullerton Road
Belleville, Illinois 62226
 Telephone: 618-277-0900
 Fax: 618-277-0970
Mailing Address: P.O. Box 23977, Belleville, IL 62226-0070

Insurance Defense, Professional Negligence, Product Liability, Premises Liability, Automobile, Bodily Injury, Fraud, Arson, Coverage Issues, Medical Malpractice, General Liability

SEE COMPLETE LISTING UNDER BELLEVILLE, ILLINOIS (65 MILES)

JACKSONVILLE † 19,446 Morgan Co.

Rammelkamp Bradney, P.C.
232 West State
Jacksonville, Illinois 62650
 Telephone: 217-245-6177
 Fax: 217-243-7322
 E-Mail: info@rblawyers.net
 www.rblawyers.net

(Springfield, IL Office*: 741 South Grand Avenue West, 62704)
 (Tel: 217-522-6000)
 (Fax: 217-522-6018)
(Winchester, IL Office: 46 South Hill Street, 62694)
 (Tel: 217-742-5215)
 (Fax: 217-742-3537)

Established: 1895

JACKSONVILLE

Rammelkamp Bradney, P.C., Jacksonville, IL
(Continued)

Insurance Law, Fire Loss, Arson, First Party Matters, Litigation, Declaratory Judgments, Workers' Compensation, Americans with Disabilities Act, Civil Rights, Construction Litigation, Employment Practices Liability, Trial and Appellate Practice

Insurance Clients

CIGNA Property and Casualty Insurance Company
COUNTRY Mutual Insurance Company
Grinnell Mutual Reinsurance Company
MetLife Auto & Home
National American Insurance Company
Selective Insurance Company of America
State Farm Fire and Casualty Company
Travelers Insurance Companies
COUNTRY Life Insurance Company
Federated Insurance Company
General Casualty Company of Wisconsin
Interstate Fire & Casualty Company
Pekin Insurance Company
St. Paul Fire and Marine Insurance Company
State Auto Insurance Companies
State Farm Mutual Automobile Insurance Company

Non-Insurance Clients

EMI Manufacturing (USA)

Partners

L.O. Vaught — (1894-1955)

Carl E. Robinson — (1886-1964)

Orville N. Foreman — (1904-1972)

Albert W. Hall — (1912-1986)

Theodore C. Rammelkamp — (1919-2005)

Larry D. Kuster — 1947 — Augustana College, B.A., 1969; The University of Iowa, J.D. (with honors), 1973 — Admitted to Bar, 1973, Illinois; 1980, U.S. District Court, Central District of Illinois; 1996, U.S. District Court, Southern District of Illinois — Member Illinois State Bar Association (Civil Practice and Procedure Council, 1976-1977, 1986-1991; Workers' Compensation Section Council, 1980-1985; Secretary, 1982, Vice Chairman, 1983, Chairman, 1984); Morgan County Bar Association; Federation of Defense and Corporate Counsel; Master, Lincoln-Douglas Inn of Court (President-Elect, 2003-2004) — Practice Areas: Commercial Law; Construction Law; Insurance Defense; School Law — E-mail: lkuster@rblawyers.net

Forrest G. Keaton — 1952 — Bradley University, B.A., 1974; University of Illinois, J.D., 1977 — Admitted to Bar, 1977, Iowa; Illinois; U.S. District Court, Central District of Illinois; U.S. Court of Appeals, Seventh Circuit — Member Illinois State Bar Association (Insurance Law Section Council, 1992-1994); Iowa State and Morgan County Bar Associations; Committee on Character and Fitness (2001-2009); Master, Lincoln-Douglas American Inn of Court; Illinois Association of Defense Trial Counsel — Judge Advocate, USAF, (1977-1982); USAFR, (1982-2007) — Practice Areas: Commercial Litigation; Corporate Law; Insurance Litigation — E-mail: fkeaton@rblawyers.net

Barbara Fritsche — 1949 — Cleveland State University, 1972; DePaul University, J.D., 1977 — Admitted to Bar, 1977, Illinois; 1978, U.S. District Court, Central District of Illinois — Member Illinois State and Morgan County Bar Associations; Illinois Supreme Court Character and Fitness Committee, 1991-2000 (Chair, Fourth District, 1997-1999); Illinois Defense Counsel; Illinois Association of Defense Trial Counsel — Practice Areas: Employment Law; Insurance Defense — E-mail: bfritsche@rblawyers.net

Richard R. Freeman — 1963 — Bradley University, B.S. (magna cum laude), 1985; Washington University, J.D., 1988 — Admitted to Bar, 1988, Illinois — Member Illinois State and Morgan County Bar Associations — Practice Areas: Business Law — E-mail: rfreeman@rblawyers.net

H. Allen Yow — 1963 — Wabash College, A.B., 1986; Southern Illinois University, J.D., 1989 — Student Articles Editor, Southern Illinois University Law Journal, 1988-1989 — Admitted to Bar, 1989, Illinois; 1990, Missouri; 1992, U.S. District Court, Central District of Illinois — Member The Missouri Bar, Illinois State and Morgan County Bar Associations; Committee on Character and Fitness (2010-present) — Practice Areas: Insurance Defense; School Law; Municipal Law; Family Law — E-mail: ayow@rblawyers.net

Bradley W. Wilson — 1968 — University of Illinois, B.S. (with high honors), 1989; Illinois Institute of Technology, Chicago-Kent College of Law, J.D., 1998 — Order of the Coif — Admitted to Bar, 1998, Illinois — Member Illinois State and Morgan County Bar Associations; National Lawyers Association — Practice Areas: Corporate Law; Estate Planning — E-mail: bwilson@rblawyers.net

Gary L. Cline — 1956 — University of Illinois, B.A., 1977; J.D., 1981 — Admitted to Bar, 1981, Illinois; 1985, U.S. District Court, Central District of Illinois; U.S. Supreme Court — Member Illinois and Sangamon County Bar Associations; Illinois Trial Lawyers Association — Practice Areas: Personal Injury; Workers' Compensation — Resident Springfield, IL Office — Tel: 217-522-6000 — Fax: 217-522-6108 — E-mail: gcline@rblawyers.net

Amy L. Jackson — 1968 — Illinois Wesleyan University, B.A., 1990; Saint Louis University School of Law, J.D., 1993 — Admitted to Bar, 1993, Missouri; 1994, Illinois; 1996, U.S. District Court, Central District of Illinois — Member Illinois State and Morgan County Bar Associations; The Missouri Bar; Illinois Defense Counsel — Practice Areas: Environmental Law; Litigation; Insurance Defense; Workers' Compensation; Employment Law — E-mail: ajackson@rblawyers.net

Anthony J. DelGiorno — 1978 — Illinois College, B.A. (magna cum laude), 1999; American University, Washington College of Law, J.D., 2002 — Admitted to Bar, 2002, Illinois — Member American, Illinois State and Sangamon County Bar Associations — Practice Areas: Commercial Litigation; Insurance Defense — Resident Springfield Office — E-mail: tdelgiorno@rblawyers.net

Ryan D. Byers — 1982 — University of Illinois at Urbana-Champaign, B.A. (with high honors), 2004; Michigan State University College of Law, J.D. (magna cum laude), 2007 — Admitted to Bar, 2007, Illinois; 2011, U.S. District Court, Central District of Illinois; 2012, U.S. District Court, Northern District of Illinois including General and Trial Bars — Member American, Illinois State and Morgan County Bar Associations; Illinois Association of Defense Trial Counsel; Lincoln-Douglas Inn of Court; Defense Research Institute — Practice Areas: Litigation; Insurance Defense; Family Law — E-mail: rbyers@rblawyers.net

Associates

Aaron D. Evans — 1986 — University of Illinois, B.S., 2008; Florida Coastal School of Law, J.D. (cum laude), 2011 — Admitted to Bar, 2011, Illinois — Member American, Illinois State and Morgan County Bar Associations — Practice Areas: Estate Planning; Real Estate; Business Transactions — E-mail: aevans@rblawyers.net

Edward J. Boula III — Northern Illinois University College of Law, J.D. (magna cum laude), 2012 — Admitted to Bar, 2012, Illinois — Member American, Illinois State and Morgan County Bar Associations — Practice Areas: Litigation; Employment Law; School Law; Probate — E-mail: eboula@rblawyers.net

Zachary P. Boren — Northwestern University, B.A. (cum laude), 2004; Washington University in St. Louis School of Law, J.D. (Order of the Coif), 2006 — Admitted to Bar, 2007, Illinois — Practice Areas: Business Law; Estate Planning; Real Estate

Retired

Robert E. Bradney — Illinois College, A.B., 1947; Harvard University, J.D., 1950 — Admitted to Bar, 1950, Illinois; 1955, U.S. District Court, Central District of Illinois

---

The following firms also service this area.

Scholz, Loos, Palmer, Siebers & Duesterhaus LLP
625 Vermont Street
Quincy, Illinois 62301-3088
  Telephone: 217-223-3444
  Fax: 217-223-3450

Insurance Defense, Subrogation, Professional Liability, Public Officials Liability, Corporate Law, Commercial Liability, Product Liability, Civil Rights, Municipal Corporate and Governmental Law

SEE COMPLETE LISTING UNDER QUINCY, ILLINOIS (70 MILES)

JERSEYVILLE † 8,465 Jersey Co.

Refer To

Hoagland, Fitzgerald & Pranaitis
401 Market Street
Alton, Illinois 62002
  Telephone: 618-465-7745
  Fax: 618-465-3744
  Toll Free: 866-830-1066

Mailing Address: P.O. Box 130, Alton, IL 62002

Insurance Defense

SEE COMPLETE LISTING UNDER ALTON, ILLINOIS (21 MILES)

Refer To

Rammelkamp Bradney, P.C.
232 West State
Jacksonville, Illinois 62650
  Telephone: 217-245-6177
  Fax: 217-243-7322

Mailing Address: P.O. Box 550, Jacksonville, IL 62651-0550

Insurance Law, Fire Loss, Arson, First Party Matters, Litigation, Declaratory Judgments, Workers' Compensation, Americans with Disabilities Act, Civil Rights, Construction Litigation, Employment Practices Liability, Trial and Appellate Practice

SEE COMPLETE LISTING UNDER JACKSONVILLE, ILLINOIS (40 MILES)

JOLIET † 147,433 Will Co.

Best, Vanderlaan & Harrington
1000 Essington Road
Joliet, Illinois 60435
  Telephone: 815-740-1500
  Fax: 815-740-6304
  E-Mail: BVH@Bestfirm.com
  www.bestfirm.com

Established: 1999

Medical Malpractice, General Liability, Coverage Issues, Opinions, Declaratory Judgments, Automobile, Property Damage, Personal Injury, Premises Liability, Product Liability, Defense Litigation, Employment Discrimination, Class Actions, Construction Litigation, Professional Malpractice

Managing Partner

Alison Harrington — 1971 — The University of Iowa, B.S., 1994; Marquette University, J.D., 1997 — Admitted to Bar, 1997, Illinois; Wisconsin; U.S. District Court, Central and Northern Districts of Illinois — Member Illinois State Bar Association; Defense Research Institute — Illinois Leading Lawyer — Practice Areas: Civil Litigation; Insurance Defense; Medical Malpractice; Employment Discrimination — E-mail: aharrington@bestfirm.com

(See listing under Chicago, IL for additional information)

Langhenry, Gillen, Lundquist & Johnson, LLC
18 West Cass Street, Suite 500
Joliet, Illinois 60432
  Telephone: 815-726-3600
  Fax: 815-726-3676
  E-Mail: rdeporte@lglfirm.com
  www.lglfirm.com

Medical Malpractice, Public Officials Liability, Product Liability, General Liability, Subrogation, Property Damage, Premises Liability, Governmental Defense

Langhenry, Gillen, Lundquist & Johnson, LLC, Joliet, IL (Continued)

Firm Profile: Your partner from the boardroom to the courtroom. Langhenry, Gillen, Lundquist and Johnson, LLC is a litigation and business firm that combines large firm legal experience and ability, with small firm accessibility and attention.

Managing Partner

Troy A. Lundquist — 1967 — University of Illinois, B.A., 1989; The John Marshall Law School, J.D., 1992 — Admitted to Bar, 1992, Illinois; U.S. District Court, Northern District of Illinois — Member Illinois State, Will County and Bureau County Bar Associations; Illinois Association of Defense Trial Counsel; Defense Research Institute — Practice Areas: Medical Malpractice Defense; Construction Litigation; Product Liability Defense; Governmental Defense; Public Officials Defense — E-mail: tlundquist@lglfirm.com

Partners

Anastasia L. Hess — University of Illinois, B.A. (Dean's List), 1989; Valparaiso University School of Law, J.D. (magna cum laude), 1999 — Admitted to Bar, 1999, Illinois — Member Illinois State and Will County Bar Associations — E-mail: ahess@lglfirm.com

Mohammed A. Nofal — 1977 — University of Illinois, B.A. (with honors), 1998; Chicago-Kent College of Law, J.D. (with honors), 2001 — Admitted to Bar, 2001, Illinois; U.S. District Court, Northern District of Illinois — Member Illinois State and Will County Bar Associations — Village of Tinley Park's Economic Development Commissioner — Languages: Arabic — E-mail: mnofal@lglfirm.com

(See Chicago, Rockford and Wheaton, IL listings for additional information)

(This firm is also listed in the Subrogation section of this directory)

JONESBORO † 1,821 Union Co.

Refer To

Feirich/Mager/Green/Ryan
2001 West Main Street
Carbondale, Illinois 62901
  Telephone: 618-529-3000
  Fax: 618-529-3008

Mailing Address: P.O. Box 1570, Carbondale, IL 62903-1570

Insurance Defense, Medical Negligence, Casualty, Construction Litigation, Product Liability, Workers' Compensation, Civil Rights, Trial Practice, Appellate Practice, Professional Liability, Subrogation, Coverage Issues

SEE COMPLETE LISTING UNDER CARBONDALE, ILLINOIS (22 MILES)

Refer To

Jelliffe, Ferrell, Doerge & Phelps
108 East Walnut Street
Harrisburg, Illinois 62946
  Telephone: 618-253-7153, 618-253-7647
  Fax: 618-252-1843

Mailing Address: P.O. Box 406, Harrisburg, IL 62946

Insurance Law, Negligence, Personal Injury, Workers' Compensation, Product Liability, General Civil Practice, State and Federal Courts, Trial Practice, Appellate Practice, All Tort Litigation

SEE COMPLETE LISTING UNDER HARRISBURG, ILLINOIS (60 MILES)

LACON † 1,937 Marshall Co.

Refer To

Russell, English, Scoma & Beneke, P.C.
Ten Park Avenue West
Princeton, Illinois 61356
  Telephone: 815-875-4555
  Fax: 815-875-2211

Insurance Law, Trial Practice, Personal Injury, Property Damage, Tort Litigation, Coverage Issues, Litigation

SEE COMPLETE LISTING UNDER PRINCETON, ILLINOIS (36 MILES)

LAWRENCEVILLE † 4,348 Lawrence Co.

Refer To

Craig & Craig, LLC
P.O. Box 1545
Mount Vernon, Illinois 62864
   Telephone: 618-244-7511
   Fax: 618-244-7628

Professional Liability, Workers' Compensation, Product Liability, Civil Rights, Dram Shop, Premises Liability, Automobile Liability, Fire, Casualty, Surety, Life Insurance, Uninsured and Underinsured Motorist, Employment Law, Intellectual Property, Family Law, Criminal Defense, Mediation

SEE COMPLETE LISTING UNDER MOUNT VERNON, ILLINOIS (90 MILES)

LEWISTOWN † 2,384 Fulton Co.

Refer To

Rammelkamp Bradney, P.C.
232 West State
Jacksonville, Illinois 62650
   Telephone: 217-245-6177
   Fax: 217-243-7322

Mailing Address: P.O. Box 550, Jacksonville, IL 62651-0550

Insurance Law, Fire Loss, Arson, First Party Matters, Litigation, Declaratory Judgments, Workers' Compensation, Americans with Disabilities Act, Civil Rights, Construction Litigation, Employment Practices Liability, Trial and Appellate Practice

SEE COMPLETE LISTING UNDER JACKSONVILLE, ILLINOIS (49 MILES)

LINCOLN † 14,504 Logan Co.

Refer To

Drake, Narup & Mead, P.C.
107 East Allen Street, Suite 100
Springfield, Illinois 62704
   Telephone: 217-528-9776
   Fax: 217-528-9401

Insurance Defense, Malpractice, Casualty, Automobile, Fire Loss, Coverage Issues, Professional Liability, Construction Law, Truck Liability, Product Liability, Subrogation, Mediation

SEE COMPLETE LISTING UNDER SPRINGFIELD, ILLINOIS (40 MILES)

LISLE 22,390 DuPage Co.

Momkus McCluskey, LLC
1001 Warrenville Road, Suite 500
Lisle, Illinois 60532
   Telephone: 630-434-0400
   Fax: 630-434-0444
   E-Mail: aspyratos@momlaw.com
   www.momlaw.com

(Chicago, IL Office*: 221 North LaSalle Street, Suite 2050, 60601)
   (Tel: 312-345-1955)
   (Fax: 312-419-1546)

Insurance Defense, Insurance Law, Special Investigations, Litigation, Business Law, Corporate Law, Contracts, Employment Law, Large Loss Subrogation

Firm Profile: Momkus McCluskey, LLC represents clients throughout the United States in legal matters involving liability defense, insurance defense and coverage disputes, special investigations, large loss subrogation, business and corporate law, contracts and agreements, employment law, real estate, financing and loan transactions, family law and divorce, appeals and estate planning.

Insurance Clients

ACUITY, A Mutual Insurance Company
USAA
State Farm Mutual Automobile Insurance Company
XL Design Professional

Momkus McCluskey, LLC, Lisle, IL (Continued)

Firm Members

James P. Marsh — Eastern Illinois University, B.A., 1983; The John Marshall Law School, J.D., 1988 — Admitted to Bar, 1988, Illinois — Member Illinois State and DuPage County (Chairman, Appellate Committee) Bar Associations; Defense Research Institute; Illinois Association of Defense Trial Counsel — AVVO Rated

E. Angelo Spyratos — Elmhurst College, B.A., 1988; Valparaiso University School of Law, J.D., 1991 — Pi Gamma Mu — Admitted to Bar, 1991, Illinois — Member Illinois State, DuPage County and Hellenic Bar Associations; Hellenic Bar Association (Director); Illinois Association of Defense Trial Counsel; Defense Research Institute — AVVO Rated — Resident Lisle, IL and Chicago, IL Office

Kimberly A. Davis — Morton College, A.A., 1985; Southern Illinois University, B.S., 1987; Chicago-Kent College of Law, J.D. (with honors), 1997 — Recipient, Michael J. Angarola Scholarship for Excellence in Trial Advocacy — Admitted to Bar, 1997, Illinois — Member Illinois State Bar Association (Civil Practice Section Council, 2006-Present); DuPage County Bar Association; American Inns of Court (DuPage County Chapter, President, 2008-2009); DuPage Association of Women Lawyers (President, 2005-2006); Illinois Association of Defense Trial Counsel — AVVO Rated

LOUISVILLE † 1,139 Clay Co.

Refer To

Craig & Craig, LLC
P.O. Box 1545
Mount Vernon, Illinois 62864
   Telephone: 618-244-7511
   Fax: 618-244-7628

Professional Liability, Workers' Compensation, Product Liability, Civil Rights, Dram Shop, Premises Liability, Automobile Liability, Fire, Casualty, Surety, Life Insurance, Uninsured and Underinsured Motorist, Employment Law, Intellectual Property, Family Law, Criminal Defense, Mediation

SEE COMPLETE LISTING UNDER MOUNT VERNON, ILLINOIS (55 MILES)

MACOMB † 19,288 McDonough Co.

Refer To

Rammelkamp Bradney, P.C.
232 West State
Jacksonville, Illinois 62650
   Telephone: 217-245-6177
   Fax: 217-243-7322

Mailing Address: P.O. Box 550, Jacksonville, IL 62651-0550

Insurance Law, Fire Loss, Arson, First Party Matters, Litigation, Declaratory Judgments, Workers' Compensation, Americans with Disabilities Act, Civil Rights, Construction Litigation, Employment Practices Liability, Trial and Appellate Practice

SEE COMPLETE LISTING UNDER JACKSONVILLE, ILLINOIS (73 MILES)

Refer To

Scholz, Loos, Palmer, Siebers & Duesterhaus LLP
625 Vermont Street
Quincy, Illinois 62301-3088
   Telephone: 217-223-3444
   Fax: 217-223-3450

Insurance Defense, Subrogation, Professional Liability, Public Officials Liability, Corporate Law, Commercial Liability, Product Liability, Civil Rights, Municipal Corporate and Governmental Law

SEE COMPLETE LISTING UNDER QUINCY, ILLINOIS (64 MILES)

MARION † 17,193 Williamson Co.

Bleyer and Bleyer
601 West Jackson Street
Marion, Illinois 62959-0487
   Telephone: 618-997-1331
   Fax: 618-997-6559
   E-Mail: bleyer@bleyerlaw.com

Established: 1986

Bleyer and Bleyer, Marion, IL (Continued)

Insurance Law, Trial Practice, Insurance Defense, Tort, Workers' Compensation, Civil Rights, Municipal Liability

Insurance Clients

COUNTRY Insurance & Financial Services
Governmental Interinsurance Exchange
Pekin Insurance Company
Southern Illinois Counties Insurance Trust
Farmers Insurance Company
GEICO
Illinois Casualty Company
Madison Mutual Insurance Company

Non-Insurance Clients

Illinois Municipal League

Members

James B. Bleyer — 1928 — Southern Illinois University, B.A., 1951; University of Notre Dame, J.D., 1954 — Admitted to Bar, 1955, Illinois — Member Illinois State and Williamson County (President, 1959-1960) Bar Associations; Defense Research Institute; Fellow, American College of Trial Lawyers; Illinois Association of Defense Trial Counsel — Practice Areas: Insurance Defense; Municipal Liability; Workers' Compensation — E-mail: jbbleyer@bleyerlaw.com

Joseph A. Bleyer — 1961 — Southern Illinois University, B.S., 1983; J.D., 1986 — Admitted to Bar, 1986, Illinois; 1986, U.S. District Court, Southern District of Illinois; 2001, U.S. Court of Appeals, Seventh Circuit; 2008, U.S. Supreme Court — Member American, Illinois State and Williamson County Bar Associations; Illinois Association of Defense Trial Counsel (Board of Directors, 2009-2015); Defense Research Institute — Practice Areas: Civil Rights; Governmental Liability; Insurance Defense; Workers' Compensation — E-mail: jableyer@bleyerlaw.com

Knute Rockne Bleyer — 1953 — Southern Illinois University, B.S., 1994; J.D., 1997 — Admitted to Bar, 1997, Illinois; 1998, U.S. District Court, Southern District of Illinois — E-mail: kbleyer@bleyerlaw.com

The following firms also service this area.

Craig & Craig, LLC
P.O. Box 1545
Mount Vernon, Illinois 62864
  Telephone: 618-244-7511
  Fax: 618-244-7628

Professional Liability, Workers' Compensation, Product Liability, Civil Rights, Dram Shop, Premises Liability, Automobile Liability, Fire, Casualty, Surety, Life Insurance, Uninsured and Underinsured Motorist, Employment Law, Intellectual Property, Family Law, Criminal Defense, Mediation

SEE COMPLETE LISTING UNDER MOUNT VERNON, ILLINOIS (43 MILES)

Feirich/Mager/Green/Ryan
2001 West Main Street
Carbondale, Illinois 62901
  Telephone: 618-529-3000
  Fax: 618-529-3008

Mailing Address: P.O. Box 1570, Carbondale, IL 62903-1570

Insurance Defense, Medical Negligence, Casualty, Construction Litigation, Product Liability, Workers' Compensation, Civil Rights, Trial Practice, Appellate Practice, Professional Liability, Subrogation, Coverage Issues

SEE COMPLETE LISTING UNDER CARBONDALE, ILLINOIS (17 MILES)

Jelliffe, Ferrell, Doerge & Phelps
108 East Walnut Street
Harrisburg, Illinois 62946
  Telephone: 618-253-7153, 618-253-7647
  Fax: 618-252-1843

Mailing Address: P.O. Box 406, Harrisburg, IL 62946

Insurance Law, Negligence, Personal Injury, Workers' Compensation, Product Liability, General Civil Practice, State and Federal Courts, Trial Practice, Appellate Practice, All Tort Litigation

SEE COMPLETE LISTING UNDER HARRISBURG, ILLINOIS (24 MILES)

MARSHALL † 3,933 Clark Co.

Refer To
Craig & Craig, LLC
1807 Broadway Avenue
P.O. Box 689
Mattoon, Illinois 61938
  Telephone: 217-234-6481
  Fax: 217-234-6486
  Fax: 217-258-8292

Automobile Liability, Casualty, Civil Rights, Dram Shop, Employment Practices Liability, Family Law, Fire, Insurance Coverage, Intellectual Property, Mediation, Product Liability, Premises Liability, Professional Liability, Surety, Uninsured and Underinsured Motorist, Workers' Compensation

SEE COMPLETE LISTING UNDER MATTOON, ILLINOIS (40 MILES)

MATTOON 18,555 Coles Co.

Craig & Craig, LLC
1807 Broadway Avenue
P.O. Box 689
Mattoon, Illinois 61938
  Telephone: 217-234-6481
  Fax: 217-234-6486
  Fax: 217-258-8292
  E-Mail: mattoon@craiglaw.net
  www.craiglaw.net

(Mount Vernon, IL Office*: P.O. Box 1545, 62864)
  (Tel: 618-244-7511)
  (Fax: 618-244-7628)
  (E-Mail: mtvernon@craiglaw.net)

Established: 1868

Automobile Liability, Casualty, Civil Rights, Dram Shop, Employment Practices Liability, Family Law, Fire, Insurance Coverage, Intellectual Property, Mediation, Product Liability, Premises Liability, Professional Liability, Surety, Uninsured and Underinsured Motorist, Workers' Compensation

Firm Profile: Craig & Craig, LLC was founded in 1868, and has been practicing continuously since then at the same location in Mattoon. The Mt. Vernon office was opened in 1986. The primary areas of practice are civil litigation and especially civil defense involving personal injury. Medical malpractice and insurance coverage practice areas are a significant part of the firm's civil practice. The firm also has a significant employment law practice. Banking work, real property, trust and estate and commercial and corporate matters, both consultation and litigation, are regularly handled by the firm. Many of the members in the firm are active in the Illinois Association of Defense Trial Counsel (Ken Werts concluded his year of presidency of the organization on June 30, 2011) and many are members of the DRI and have been active in the Illinois State Bar Association. One active Member of the firm, and three retired Members, are Fellows of the American College of Trial Lawyers.

Insurance Clients

American Family Insurance Company
Capitol Indemnity Corporation
Cincinnati Insurance Company
Electric Insurance Company
Hartford Insurance Company
OneBeacon Professional Insurance
Professional Solutions Insurance Company
Specialty Risk Insurance Company
Township Officials of Illinois Risk Management Association
U.S. Liability Insurance Company
American Interstate Insurance Company
Central Insurance Companies
CNA
GEICO Insurance Companies
K & K Insurance Group, Inc.
ProAssurance Company
Rockford Mutual Insurance Company
Swiss Re
Underwriters at Lloyd's, London
United Fire Group
Wells Fargo Disability Management

Non-Insurance Clients

Agracel, Inc.
American Coal Company

MOUNT CARMEL

Craig & Craig, LLC, Mattoon, IL (Continued)

Bonutti Orthopedic Clinic, Ltd.
Carle Risk Management
Consolidated Communications
First Federal Savings and Loan Association of Mattoon, Illinois
Heartland Dental
International Paper Company
Peabody Coal Company
Pinnacle Foods Group LLC
Springfield Coal Company, LLC
Village of Greenup, Illinois
Cannon Cochran Management Services, Inc.
Deere & Company
First Mid-Illinois Bank & Trust
Freeman United Coal Mining Company
Justrite Manufacturing Company
Peabody Energy Corporation
R.R. Donnelley & Sons Company
Tri County Coal Company

Member

Robert G. Grierson — 1950 — University of Illinois, J.D., 1975 — Admitted to Bar, 1975, Illinois; 1976, U.S. District Court, Central and Southern Districts of Illinois; 1977, U.S. Court of Appeals, Seventh Circuit — Member American, Illinois State and Coles-Cumberland County Bar Associations — E-mail: rgg@craiglaw.net

Gregory C. Ray — 1952 — University of Illinois, J.D., 1976 — Admitted to Bar, 1976, Illinois — Member American, Illinois State and Coles-Cumberland County Bar Associations; Illinois Appellate Lawyers Association; Illinois Association of Defense Trial Counsel (President, 2002-2003); Defense Research Institute — E-mail: gcr@craiglaw.net

Paul R. Lynch — 1952 — University of Illinois, J.D., 1977 — Admitted to Bar, 1977, Illinois — Member Seventh Circuit, Illinois State and Jefferson County Bar Associations; Fellow, American College of Trial Lawyers; Supreme Court Committee on Illinois Evidence; Southern Illinois American Inn of Court (President, 2012-2014); Illinois Association of Defense Trial Counsel (Board of Directors, 2007-Present) — Resident Mount Vernon, IL Office — E-mail: prl@craiglaw.net

Kenneth F. Werts — 1957 — University of Illinois, B.A., 1979; Southern Illinois University, J.D., 1984 — Admitted to Bar, 1984, Illinois — Member Illinois State and Jefferson County Bar Associations; Illinois Association of Defense Trial Counsel (President, 2010-2011); Association of Defense Trial Attorneys; National Association of Railroad Trial Counsel — Resident Mount Vernon, IL Office — E-mail: kfw@craiglaw.net

John L. Barger — 1958 — Eastern Illinois University, B.A., 1980; University of Arkansas, J.D., 1983 — Admitted to Bar, 1984, Illinois — Member American, Illinois State and Coles-Cumberland County Bar Associations; Illinois Association of Defense Trial Counsel — E-mail: jlb@craiglaw.net

Julie A. Webb — 1971 — University of Illinois, B.A., 1993; Southern Illinois University, J.D., 1996 — Admitted to Bar, 1996, Illinois; 1996, U.S. District Court, Southern District of Illinois — Member American, Illinois State and Jefferson County Bar Associations; The Bar Association of the Central and Southern Federal Districts of Illinois; Illinois Association of Defense Trial Counsel — Court Approved Mediator, Second Judicial Circuit — Resident Mount Vernon, IL Office — E-mail: jaw@craiglaw.net

John F. Watson — 1967 — Bradley University, B.S.M.E., 1990; The John Marshall Law School, J.D. (cum laude), 1993 — Associate Lead Editor, The John Marshall Law Review (1992-1993) — Admitted to Bar, 1993, Illinois; 1994, U.S. Patent and Trademark Office; 1999, U.S. District Court, Central District of Illinois; 2005, U.S. District Court, Southern District of Illinois; 2006, U.S. Court of Appeals, Seventh Circuit — Member American, Illinois State and Coles-Cumberland County(President, 2013-2014; Treasurer, 2000-2003) Bar Associations; The Bar Association of the Central and Southern Federal Districts of Illinois; Illinois Association of Defense Trial Counsel (IDC Quarterly Board of Directors; Vice Chair, Amicus Committee) — Resident Mattoon, IL Office — E-mail: jfw@craiglaw.net

R. Sean Hocking — 1973 — University of Illinois, B.S., 1995; Southern Illinois University, J.D., 1999 — Admitted to Bar, 1999, Illinois; 2000, U.S. Patent and Trademark Office — Member Illinois State and Coles-Cumberland County Bar Associations; Illinois Association of Defense Trial Counsel — E-mail: rsh@craiglaw.net

Associates

J. Patrick Lee — 1974 — Eastern Illinois University, B.A., 1996; University of Illinois, J.D., 2002 — Admitted to Bar, 2002, Illinois — E-mail: jpl@craiglaw.net

Carolyn R. Bates — 1985 — Eastern Illinois University, B.A. (with honors), 2008; Southern Illinois University School of Law, J.D., 2011 — Admitted to Bar, 2011, Illinois — Member Illinois State and Coles-Cumberland County Bar Associations — E-mail: crb@craiglaw.net

Of Counsel

Stephen L. Corn — Retired — 1944 — University of Illinois, J.D., 1969 —

Craig & Craig, LLC, Mattoon, IL (Continued)

Admitted to Bar, 1969, Illinois — Member Illinois State Bar Association; Illinois Defense Counsel (President, 1991-1992); Fellow, American College of Trial Lawyers — E-mail: slc@craiglaw.net

John P. Ewart — Retired — 1936 — University of Illinois, J.D., 1960 — Admitted to Bar, 1961, Illinois — Member Coles-Cumberland County Bar Association; Illinois Defense Counsel (President, Board of Directors, 1978-1979); Illinois Appellate Lawyers Association; Fellow, American College of Trial Lawyers — E-mail: jpe@craiglaw.net

Richard F. Record, Jr. — Retired — The George Washington University, J.D., 1963 — Admitted to Bar, 1963, Illinois — Member Illinois State and Coles-Cumberland County Bar Associations; Illinois Appellate Lawyers Association (President, 1980); Illinois Defense Counsel; Fellow, American College of Trial Lawyers — E-mail: rfr@craiglaw.net

MCLEANSBORO † 2,883 Hamilton Co.

Refer To

Craig & Craig, LLC
P.O. Box 1545
Mount Vernon, Illinois 62864
Telephone: 618-244-7511
Fax: 618-244-7628

Professional Liability, Workers' Compensation, Product Liability, Civil Rights, Dram Shop, Premises Liability, Automobile Liability, Fire, Casualty, Surety, Life Insurance, Uninsured and Underinsured Motorist, Employment Law, Intellectual Property, Family Law, Criminal Defense, Mediation

SEE COMPLETE LISTING UNDER MOUNT VERNON, ILLINOIS (28 MILES)

METROPOLIS † 6,537 Massac Co.

Refer To

Jelliffe, Ferrell, Doerge & Phelps
108 East Walnut Street
Harrisburg, Illinois 62946
Telephone: 618-253-7153, 618-253-7647
Fax: 618-252-1843

Mailing Address: P.O. Box 406, Harrisburg, IL 62946

Insurance Law, Negligence, Personal Injury, Workers' Compensation, Product Liability, General Civil Practice, State and Federal Courts, Trial Practice, Appellate Practice, All Tort Litigation

SEE COMPLETE LISTING UNDER HARRISBURG, ILLINOIS (48 MILES)

MORRISON † 4,188 Whiteside Co.

Refer To

Mateer Goff & Honzel LLP
401 West State Street, Suite 400
Rockford, Illinois 61101
Telephone: 815-965-7745
Fax: 815-965-7749

Insurance Law, Fire, Casualty Insurance Law, Defense Litigation, Trial and Appellate Practice

SEE COMPLETE LISTING UNDER ROCKFORD, ILLINOIS (72 MILES)

MOUNT CARMEL † 7,284 Wabash Co.

Refer To

Kahn, Dees, Donovan & Kahn, LLP
501 Main Street, Suite 305
Evansville, Indiana 47708
Telephone: 812-423-3183
Fax: 812-423-3841

Mailing Address: P.O. Box 3646, Evansville, IN 47735-3646

Asbestos Litigation, Automobile, Construction Law, Coverage Issues, Environmental Law, Insurance Defense, General Liability, Labor and Employment, Mass Tort, Medical Malpractice, Personal Injury, Premises Liability, Product Liability, Property, Public Entities, Self-Insured, Subrogation, Workers' Compensation

SEE COMPLETE LISTING UNDER EVANSVILLE, INDIANA (40 MILES)

MOUNT CARROLL † 1,717 Carroll Co.

Refer To
Mateer Goff & Honzel LLP
401 West State Street, Suite 400
Rockford, Illinois 61101
  Telephone: 815-965-7745
  Fax: 815-965-7749

Insurance Law, Fire, Casualty Insurance Law, Defense Litigation, Trial and Appellate Practice

SEE COMPLETE LISTING UNDER ROCKFORD, ILLINOIS (60 MILES)

MOUNT PROSPECT 54,167 Cook Co.

Law Office of David J. E. Roe
1699 Wall Street, Suite 530
Mount Prospect, Illinois 60056
  Telephone: 312-948-4080
  Fax: 866-402-4532
  E-Mail: DRoe@RoeLegal.com
  www.RoeLegal.com

(Chicago, IL Office: 180 North LaSalle Street, Suite 3700, 60601)

General Liability, Automobile, Declaratory Judgments, Insurance Defense, Insurance Litigation, Professional Liability

Firm Profile: Clients select our small firm because they seek extensive large firm experience, responsive attorneys with competitive rates that focus on swift resolution and avoidance of protracted litigation if possible.

We provide aggressive, focused, and cost-efficient representation in insurance and business matters ranging from general liability, professional liability, to direct defense and more. Our extensive skill set and education provides clients with attorneys that understand legal and business issues faced by insurance companies in the corporate, manufacturing, software, internet and service industries and offer efficient solutions that may be unseen by other attorneys.

With our clients, we examine litigation matters in depth in order to determine the most efficient plan to achieve the best resolution. We achieve client goals in the most efficient manner through close client involvement in the planning stage and throughout the project. We offer alternative billing such as milestone achievement, flat fee, and performance-based billing.

Insurance Clients

Aftermath, Inc.
Greater New York Mutual Insurance Company
American Insurance Services Company

David J. E. Roe — The University of Iowa, B.A., 1989; Keller Graduate School of Management, M.B.A., 2005; Detroit College of Law, Michigan State University, J.D., 1993 — Admitted to Bar, 1993, Michigan; 1996, Illinois — Author: Thomson Reuters, "Illinois Practice Series: Illinois Vehicle Insurance Coverage," 2008-2015 Editions; Thomson Reuters, "Illinois Civil Jury Instructions Companion Handbook," 2008- 2015 Editions

MOUNT STERLING † 2,025 Brown Co.

Refer To
Rammelkamp Bradney, P.C.
232 West State
Jacksonville, Illinois 62650
  Telephone: 217-245-6177
  Fax: 217-243-7322
Mailing Address: P.O. Box 550, Jacksonville, IL 62651-0550

Insurance Law, Fire Loss, Arson, First Party Matters, Litigation, Declaratory Judgments, Workers' Compensation, Americans with Disabilities Act, Civil Rights, Construction Litigation, Employment Practices Liability, Trial and Appellate Practice

SEE COMPLETE LISTING UNDER JACKSONVILLE, ILLINOIS (36 MILES)

Refer To
Scholz, Loos, Palmer, Siebers & Duesterhaus LLP
625 Vermont Street
Quincy, Illinois 62301-3088
  Telephone: 217-223-3444
  Fax: 217-223-3450

Insurance Defense, Subrogation, Professional Liability, Public Officials Liability, Corporate Law, Commercial Liability, Product Liability, Civil Rights, Municipal Corporate and Governmental Law

SEE COMPLETE LISTING UNDER QUINCY, ILLINOIS (40 MILES)

MOUNT VERNON † 15,277 Jefferson Co.

Craig & Craig, LLC
P.O. Box 1545
Mount Vernon, Illinois 62864
  Telephone: 618-244-7511
  Fax: 618-244-7628
  E-Mail: mtvernon@craiglaw.net
  www.craiglaw.net

(Mattoon, IL Office*: 1807 Broadway Avenue, P.O. Box 689, 61938)
  (Tel: 217-234-6481)
  (Fax: 217-234-6486)
  (Fax: 217-258-8292)
  (E-Mail: mattoon@craiglaw.net)

Professional Liability, Workers' Compensation, Product Liability, Civil Rights, Dram Shop, Premises Liability, Automobile Liability, Fire, Casualty, Surety, Life Insurance, Uninsured and Underinsured Motorist, Employment Law, Intellectual Property, Family Law, Criminal Defense, Mediation

(See listing under Mattoon, IL for additional information)

MURPHYSBORO † 7,970 Jackson Co.

Refer To
Craig & Craig, LLC
P.O. Box 1545
Mount Vernon, Illinois 62864
  Telephone: 618-244-7511
  Fax: 618-244-7628

Professional Liability, Workers' Compensation, Product Liability, Civil Rights, Dram Shop, Premises Liability, Automobile Liability, Fire, Casualty, Surety, Life Insurance, Uninsured and Underinsured Motorist, Employment Law, Intellectual Property, Family Law, Criminal Defense, Mediation

SEE COMPLETE LISTING UNDER MOUNT VERNON, ILLINOIS (65 MILES)

Refer To
Feirich/Mager/Green/Ryan
2001 West Main Street
Carbondale, Illinois 62901
  Telephone: 618-529-3000
  Fax: 618-529-3008

Mailing Address: P.O. Box 1570, Carbondale, IL 62903-1570

Insurance Defense, Medical Negligence, Casualty, Construction Litigation, Product Liability, Workers' Compensation, Civil Rights, Trial Practice, Appellate Practice, Professional Liability, Subrogation, Coverage Issues

SEE COMPLETE LISTING UNDER CARBONDALE, ILLINOIS (8 MILES)

PARIS

Refer To

Jelliffe, Ferrell, Doerge & Phelps
108 East Walnut Street
Harrisburg, Illinois 62946
Telephone: 618-253-7153, 618-253-7647
Fax: 618-252-1843
Mailing Address: P.O. Box 406, Harrisburg, IL 62946

Insurance Law, Negligence, Personal Injury, Workers' Compensation, Product Liability, General Civil Practice, State and Federal Courts, Trial Practice, Appellate Practice, All Tort Litigation

SEE COMPLETE LISTING UNDER HARRISBURG, ILLINOIS (46 MILES)

NAPERVILLE 141,853 DuPage Co.

Best, Vanderlaan & Harrington
400 East Diehl Road, Suite 280
Naperville, Illinois 60563
Telephone: 630-752-8000
Fax: 630-752-8763
E-Mail: BVH@Bestfirm.com
www.bestfirm.com

Established: 1999

Medical Malpractice, General Liability, Coverage Issues, Opinions, Declaratory Judgments, Automobile, Property Damage, Personal Injury, Premises Liability, Product Liability, Defense Litigation, Employment Discrimination, Class Actions, Construction Litigation, Professional Malpractice

(See listing under Chicago, IL for additional information)

NASHVILLE † 3,258 Washington Co.

Refer To

Craig & Craig, LLC
P.O. Box 1545
Mount Vernon, Illinois 62864
Telephone: 618-244-7511
Fax: 618-244-7628

Professional Liability, Workers' Compensation, Product Liability, Civil Rights, Dram Shop, Premises Liability, Automobile Liability, Fire, Casualty, Surety, Life Insurance, Uninsured and Underinsured Motorist, Employment Law, Intellectual Property, Family Law, Criminal Defense, Mediation

SEE COMPLETE LISTING UNDER MOUNT VERNON, ILLINOIS (27 MILES)

Refer To

Neville, Richards & Wuller, LLC
5 Park Place Professional Centre
Illinois Street and Fullerton Road
Belleville, Illinois 62226
Telephone: 618-277-0900
Fax: 618-277-0970
Mailing Address: P.O. Box 23977, Belleville, IL 62226-0070

Insurance Defense, Professional Negligence, Product Liability, Premises Liability, Automobile, Bodily Injury, Fraud, Arson, Coverage Issues, Medical Malpractice, General Liability

SEE COMPLETE LISTING UNDER BELLEVILLE, ILLINOIS (35 MILES)

NEWTON † 2,849 Jasper Co.

Refer To

Craig & Craig, LLC
1807 Broadway Avenue
P.O. Box 689
Mattoon, Illinois 61938
Telephone: 217-234-6481
Fax: 217-234-6486
Fax: 217-258-8292

Automobile Liability, Casualty, Civil Rights, Dram Shop, Employment Practices Liability, Family Law, Fire, Insurance Coverage, Intellectual Property, Mediation, Product Liability, Premises Liability, Professional Liability, Surety, Uninsured and Underinsured Motorist, Workers' Compensation

SEE COMPLETE LISTING UNDER MATTOON, ILLINOIS (45 MILES)

OLNEY † 9,115 Richland Co.

Refer To

Craig & Craig, LLC
1807 Broadway Avenue
P.O. Box 689
Mattoon, Illinois 61938
Telephone: 217-234-6481
Fax: 217-234-6486
Fax: 217-258-8292

Automobile Liability, Casualty, Civil Rights, Dram Shop, Employment Practices Liability, Family Law, Fire, Insurance Coverage, Intellectual Property, Mediation, Product Liability, Premises Liability, Professional Liability, Surety, Uninsured and Underinsured Motorist, Workers' Compensation

SEE COMPLETE LISTING UNDER MATTOON, ILLINOIS (67 MILES)

OREGON † 3,721 Ogle Co.

Refer To

Mateer Goff & Honzel LLP
401 West State Street, Suite 400
Rockford, Illinois 61101
Telephone: 815-965-7745
Fax: 815-965-7749

Insurance Law, Fire, Casualty Insurance Law, Defense Litigation, Trial and Appellate Practice

SEE COMPLETE LISTING UNDER ROCKFORD, ILLINOIS (28 MILES)

OTTAWA † 18,768 La Salle Co.

Refer To

Russell, English, Scoma & Beneke, P.C.
Ten Park Avenue West
Princeton, Illinois 61356
Telephone: 815-875-4555
Fax: 815-875-2211

Insurance Law, Trial Practice, Personal Injury, Property Damage, Tort Litigation, Coverage Issues, Litigation

SEE COMPLETE LISTING UNDER PRINCETON, ILLINOIS (40 MILES)

PARIS † 8,837 Edgar Co.

Refer To

Craig & Craig, LLC
1807 Broadway Avenue
P.O. Box 689
Mattoon, Illinois 61938
Telephone: 217-234-6481
Fax: 217-234-6486
Fax: 217-258-8292

Automobile Liability, Casualty, Civil Rights, Dram Shop, Employment Practices Liability, Family Law, Fire, Insurance Coverage, Intellectual Property, Mediation, Product Liability, Premises Liability, Professional Liability, Surety, Uninsured and Underinsured Motorist, Workers' Compensation

SEE COMPLETE LISTING UNDER MATTOON, ILLINOIS (39 MILES)

ILLINOIS

Refer To
Dukes, Ryan, Meyer, & Freed Ltd.
146 North Vermilion Street
Danville, Illinois 61832
 Telephone: 217-442-0384
 Fax: 217-442-0009

Insurance Defense, Personal Injury, Property Damage, Automobile, Homeowners, General Practice, Criminal Law

SEE COMPLETE LISTING UNDER DANVILLE, ILLINOIS (37 MILES)

PEORIA † 115,007 Peoria Co.

Heyl, Royster, Voelker & Allen
A Professional Corporation

Suite 600, Chase Building
124 S.W. Adams Street
Peoria, Illinois 61602-1352
 Telephone: 309-676-0400
 Fax: 309-676-3374
 E-Mail: firm@heylroyster.com
 www.heylroyster.com

(Additional Offices: Springfield, IL*; Urbana, IL*; Rockford, IL*; Edwardsville, IL*; Chicago, IL*)

Established: 1907

Civil Trial Practice, Insurance Defense, Appellate Practice, Class Actions, Coverage Issues, Employment Law, Professional Malpractice, Self-Insured Defense, Toxic Torts, Workers' Compensation

Insurance Clients

Auto-Owners Insurance Company	Cincinnati Insurance Company
CNA Insurance Companies	Continental Western Group
COUNTRY Insurance & Financial Services	Erie Insurance Group
	General Casualty Companies
Great West Casualty Company	GuideOne Insurance
Illinois State Medical Insurance Services, Inc.	Iowa Mutual Insurance Company
	Liberty Mutual Group
The Medical Protective Company	MetLife Auto & Home
State Farm Fire and Casualty Company	Zurich North America

Non-Insurance Clients

Caterpillar Inc.
Proctor Hospital
John P. Pearl & Associates, Ltd.

Managing Partner

Gary D. Nelson — 1950 — University of Illinois, B.A., 1972; J.D., 1977 — Admitted to Bar, 1977, Illinois

Our lawyers are members of the American, state and local bar associations and, in many cases, are members of the local American Inn of Court chapters; leadership positions in these organizations are listed.

PETERSBURG † 2,260 Menard Co.

Refer To
Rammelkamp Bradney, P.C.
232 West State
Jacksonville, Illinois 62650
 Telephone: 217-245-6177
 Fax: 217-243-7322

Mailing Address: P.O. Box 550, Jacksonville, IL 62651-0550

Insurance Law, Fire Loss, Arson, First Party Matters, Litigation, Declaratory Judgments, Workers' Compensation, Americans with Disabilities Act, Civil Rights, Construction Litigation, Employment Practices Liability, Trial and Appellate Practice

SEE COMPLETE LISTING UNDER JACKSONVILLE, ILLINOIS (25 MILES)

PEORIA

PINCKNEYVILLE † 5,648 Perry Co.

Refer To
Craig & Craig, LLC
P.O. Box 1545
Mount Vernon, Illinois 62864
 Telephone: 618-244-7511
 Fax: 618-244-7628

Professional Liability, Workers' Compensation, Product Liability, Civil Rights, Dram Shop, Premises Liability, Automobile Liability, Fire, Casualty, Surety, Life Insurance, Uninsured and Underinsured Motorist, Employment Law, Intellectual Property, Family Law, Criminal Defense, Mediation

SEE COMPLETE LISTING UNDER MOUNT VERNON, ILLINOIS (42 MILES)

Refer To
Feirich/Mager/Green/Ryan
2001 West Main Street
Carbondale, Illinois 62901
 Telephone: 618-529-3000
 Fax: 618-529-3008

Mailing Address: P.O. Box 1570, Carbondale, IL 62903-1570

Insurance Defense, Medical Negligence, Casualty, Construction Litigation, Product Liability, Workers' Compensation, Civil Rights, Trial Practice, Appellate Practice, Professional Liability, Subrogation, Coverage Issues

SEE COMPLETE LISTING UNDER CARBONDALE, ILLINOIS (32 MILES)

PITTSFIELD † 4,576 Pike Co.

Refer To
Rammelkamp Bradney, P.C.
232 West State
Jacksonville, Illinois 62650
 Telephone: 217-245-6177
 Fax: 217-243-7322

Mailing Address: P.O. Box 550, Jacksonville, IL 62651-0550

Insurance Law, Fire Loss, Arson, First Party Matters, Litigation, Declaratory Judgments, Workers' Compensation, Americans with Disabilities Act, Civil Rights, Construction Litigation, Employment Practices Liability, Trial and Appellate Practice

SEE COMPLETE LISTING UNDER JACKSONVILLE, ILLINOIS (36 MILES)

PRINCETON † 7,660 Bureau Co.

Langhenry, Gillen, Lundquist & Johnson, LLC

605 South Main Street
Princeton, Illinois 61356
 Telephone: 815-915-8540
 Fax: 815-915-8581
 E-Mail: rdeporte@lgljfirm.com
 www.lgljfirm.com

Medical Malpractice, General Liability, Subrogation, Coverage Issues, Opinions, Declaratory Judgments, Automobile, Property Damage, Personal Injury, Premises Liability, Product Liability, Defense Litigation, Employment Discrimination, Class Actions, Construction Litigation

Firm Profile: Your partner from the boardroom to the courtroom. Langhenry, Gillen, Lundquist and Johnson, LLC is a litigation and business firm that combines large firm legal experience and ability, with small firm accessibility and attention.

Managing Partner

Troy A. Lundquist — 1967 — University of Illinois, B.A., 1989; The John Marshall Law School, J.D., 1992 — Admitted to Bar, 1992, Illinois; U.S. District Court, Northern District of Illinois — Member Illinois State, Will County and Bureau County Bar Associations; Illinois Association of Defense Trial Counsel; Defense Research Institute — Practice Areas: Medical Malpractice

Langhenry, Gillen, Lundquist & Johnson, LLC, Princeton, IL (Continued)

Defense; Construction Litigation; Product Liability Defense; Governmental Defense; Public Officials Defense — E-mail: tlundquist@lglfirm.com

(See listing under Chicago, IL for additional information)

(See Joliet, Rockford and Wheaton, IL listings for additional information)

(This firm is also listed in the Subrogation section of this directory)

Russell, English, Scoma & Beneke, P.C.

Ten Park Avenue West
Princeton, Illinois 61356
   Telephone: 815-875-4555
Fax: 815-875-2211
E-Mail: tenpark@theramp.net

Established: 1847

Insurance Law, Trial Practice, Personal Injury, Property Damage, Tort Litigation, Coverage Issues, Litigation

Insurance Clients

Aetna Casualty and Surety Company	American Motorists Insurance Company
American States Insurance Company	American Surety Company
The Cincinnati Insurance Companies	Auto-Owners Insurance Company
Employers Mutual Casualty Company	COUNTRY Mutual Insurance Company
Farmers Insurance Group	The Farmers Automobile Insurance Association
Great Central Insurance Company	General Casualty Company of Wisconsin
Grinnell Mutual Reinsurance Company	Hartford Accident and Indemnity Company
Inter-Insurance Exchange of Chicago Motor Club	Kemper Insurance Companies
Meridian Mutual Insurance Company	Lloyd's
Pekin Insurance Company	National Indemnity Company
State Farm Insurance Company	Ohio Casualty Insurance Company
Suburban Casualty Company	Rockford Mutual Insurance Company
Travelers Insurance Companies	Transamerica Insurance Company
	United Fire & Casualty Company

Non-Insurance Clients

National of Hartford

Partners

Daniel K. Russell — 1944 — Western Illinois University, B.A., 1966; University of Illinois College of Law, J.D., 1969 — Admitted to Bar, 1969, Illinois — Member Illinois State and Bureau County (President, 1990-1992) Bar Associations; Illinois Association of Defense Trial Counsel

Robert F. Russell — 1948 — Stanford University, A.B., 1970; University of Illinois College of Law, J.D., 1973 — Admitted to Bar, 1974, Illinois — Member Illinois State and Bureau County Bar Associations

Michael L. English — 1953 — Indiana University, B.A., 1975; University of Minnesota Law School, J.D. (cum laude), 1978 — Phi Beta Kappa — Admitted to Bar, 1978, Wisconsin; 1980, Illinois — Member American, Illinois State, Wisconsin State and Bureau County Bar Associations

Paul M. Scoma — 1952 — Northern Illinois University, B.A. (magna cum laude), 1974; Loyola University Chicago, J.D., 1982 — Omicron Delta Kappa — Admitted to Bar, 1982, Illinois — Member Illinois State and Bureau County Bar Associations; Illinois Association of Defense Trial Counsel

William S. Beneke — 1953 — Cornell College, B.A., 1975; The University of Oklahoma College of Law, J.D., 1978 — Admitted to Bar, 1979, Iowa; 1982, Illinois — Member Illinois State, Iowa State and Bureau County Bar Associations; American Agricultural Law Association

---

QUINCY † 40,633 Adams Co.

Scholz, Loos, Palmer, Siebers & Duesterhaus LLP

625 Vermont Street
Quincy, Illinois 62301-3088
   Telephone: 217-223-3444
   Fax: 217-223-3450
www.slpsd.com

Established: 1928

Insurance Defense, Subrogation, Professional Liability, Public Officials Liability, Corporate Law, Commercial Liability, Product Liability, Civil Rights, Municipal Corporate and Governmental Law

Firm Profile: Scholz, Loos, Palmer, Siebers & Duesterhaus LLP is a full-service law firm, specializing in areas in addition to insurance defense and corporate municipal liability defenses. It has departments that cover employment practice liability coverage questions as well as general litigation. Please see our website for more information.

Insurance Clients

Allied Group	American Family Insurance Company
Amerisure Insurance Company	Camp Point Mutual Insurance Company
Auto-Owners Insurance Company	Crum & Forster Insurance Group
Cincinnati Insurance Company	Farmers Mutual Hail Insurance Company of Iowa, Property and Casualty Division
CNA-RSKCo.	
Diamond Insurance Company	
Federated Insurance Company	Frank Gates Service Company
Fireman's Fund Insurance Company	Illinois Casualty Company
Gallagher Bassett Services, Inc.	Lexington Insurance Company
Indiana Farm Bureau	Municipal Insurance Cooperative Agency
Madison Mutual Insurance Company	Safeco/American States Insurance Company
Progressive Insurance Company	
St. Paul Travelers	United States Liability Insurance Company
Standard Mutual Insurance Company	Western Heritage Insurance Company
West Bend Mutual Insurance Company	

Non-Insurance Clients

Advance Physical Therapy & Sports Medicine, LLC	City of Quincy
Family Medicine Associates of Quincy, Chartered	Exchange Bank of Northeast Missouri
Heartland Bank and Trust Company	First Bankers Trust Company, N.A.
Marlboro Wire. LTD	Industrial Workforce, Ltd.
Peoples Prosperity Bank	Kohl Grocer Company
Quincy Broadcasting Company	Niemann Foods, Inc.
Quincy Newspapers, Inc.	Poepping, Stone, Bach & Associates, Inc.
Quincy Public Library	Quincy Notre Dame High School
The Salvation Army	Rinella Company
United State Bank	Sunset Home
	Wally Hutter Oil Company

Partners

Richard F. Scholz, Sr. — (1901-1975)

Delbert Loos — (1909-1993)

Charles A. Scholz — (1926-2011)

James L. Palmer — 1948 — Quincy University, B.A. (with high honors), 1970; University of Illinois, J.D., 1973 — Phi Alpha Theta — Admitted to Bar, 1973, Illinois; 1991, Missouri; 1973, U.S. District Court, Central District of Illinois; 1979, U.S. Court of Appeals, Seventh Circuit; 1979, U.S. Supreme Court; 1992, U.S. District Court, Eastern District of Missouri; 1992, U.S. Court of Appeals, Eighth Circuit — Member American, Illinois State and Adams County Bar Associations; The Missouri Bar; The Bar Association of the Central and Southern Federal Districts of Illinois; Capital Litigation Trial Bar Screening Committee for the Fourth Judicial District, Supreme Court of Illinois; Illinois Association of Healthcare Attorneys; Illinois Association of Defense Trial Counsel; Association of Defense Trial Attorneys; Illinois Trial Lawyers Association; Defense Research Institute; American Association for Justice — Member, Leading Lawyers Network

Scholz, Loos, Palmer, Siebers & Duesterhaus LLP, Quincy, IL (Continued)

Steven E. Siebers — 1954 — Western Illinois University, B.B. (with high honors), 1976; University of Illinois, J.D. (magna cum laude), 1979 — Order of the Coif — Admitted to Bar, 1979, Illinois; 1980, Missouri — Member American, Illinois State and Adams County Bar Associations; The Missouri Bar; Illinois CPA Society — Certified Public Accountant Certificate

Joseph A. Duesterhaus — 1953 — Grinnell College, B.A. (with high honors), 1980; The University of Iowa, J.D. (with honors), 1983 — Admitted to Bar, 1983, Illinois; 1991, Missouri; 1990, U.S. District Court, Central District of Illinois; 1992, U.S. District Court, Eastern District of Missouri; 2001, U.S. Court of Appeals, Seventh Circuit — Member American, Illinois State and Adams County Bar Associations; The Missouri Bar; Commercial Law League of America; Association of Defense Trial Attorneys

Christopher G. Scholz — 1957 — Western Illinois University, B.A. (with high honors), 1984; Mercer University, J.D., 1987 — Phi Kappa Phi; Phi Alpha Delta — Admitted to Bar, 1987, Illinois; 2003, Missouri; 1988, U.S. District Court, Central District of Illinois; 1992, U.S. Supreme Court — Member Illinois State and Adams County Bar Associations; The Missouri Bar

Jennifer A. Winking — 1966 — Quincy University, B.A. (summa cum laude), 1993; University of Missouri, J.D., 1996 — Phi Alpha Delta; Phi Alpha Theta; Phi Kappa Phi; Order of the Coif — Admitted to Bar, 1996, Illinois; 1997, Missouri; 1997, U.S. District Court, Central District of Illinois; 1997, U.S. District Court, Eastern District of Missouri; 1997, U.S. Court of Appeals, Seventh Circuit — Member American, Illinois State and Adams County Bar Associations; The Missouri Bar; Illinois Association of Defense Trial Counsel

William L. Siebers — 1971 — Quincy University, B.S. (cum laude), 1993; Valparaiso University School of Law, J.D. (summa cum laude), 1996 — Admitted to Bar, 1996, Illinois; 2004, Missouri; 1996, U.S. District Court, Central and Northern Districts of Illinois; U.S. Supreme Court — Member Illinois State and Adams County Bar Association; The Missouri Bar; National Academy of Elder Law Attorneys

Associate

Emily Schuering Jones — 1978 — Quincy University, B.A. (magna cum laude), 1999; Saint Louis University, J.D., 2004 — Quincy University Academic and Athletic Scholarship; Saint Louis University Academic Scholarship — Admitted to Bar, 2004, Illinois — Member Illinois State and Adams County Bar Associations

---

The following firms also service this area.

Drake, Narup & Mead, P.C.
107 East Allen Street, Suite 100
Springfield, Illinois 62704
 Telephone: 217-528-9776
 Fax: 217-528-9401

Insurance Defense, Malpractice, Casualty, Automobile, Fire Loss, Coverage Issues, Professional Liability, Construction Law, Truck Liability, Product Liability, Subrogation, Mediation

SEE COMPLETE LISTING UNDER SPRINGFIELD, ILLINOIS (115 MILES)

Rammelkamp Bradney, P.C.
232 West State
Jacksonville, Illinois 62650
 Telephone: 217-245-6177
 Fax: 217-243-7322
Mailing Address: P.O. Box 550, Jacksonville, IL 62651-0550

Insurance Law, Fire Loss, Arson, First Party Matters, Litigation, Declaratory Judgments, Workers' Compensation, Americans with Disabilities Act, Civil Rights, Construction Litigation, Employment Practices Liability, Trial and Appellate Practice

SEE COMPLETE LISTING UNDER JACKSONVILLE, ILLINOIS (70 MILES)

ROBINSON † 7,713 Crawford Co.

Refer To
Craig & Craig, LLC
1807 Broadway Avenue
P.O. Box 689
Mattoon, Illinois 61938
 Telephone: 217-234-6481
 Fax: 217-234-6486
 Fax: 217-258-8292

Automobile Liability, Casualty, Civil Rights, Dram Shop, Employment Practices Liability, Family Law, Fire, Insurance Coverage, Intellectual Property, Mediation, Product Liability, Premises Liability, Professional Liability, Surety, Uninsured and Underinsured Motorist, Workers' Compensation

SEE COMPLETE LISTING UNDER MATTOON, ILLINOIS (70 MILES)

ROCK ISLAND † 39,018 Rock Island Co.

Refer To
Mateer Goff & Honzel LLP
401 West State Street, Suite 400
Rockford, Illinois 61101
 Telephone: 815-965-7745
 Fax: 815-965-7749

Insurance Law, Fire, Casualty Insurance Law, Defense Litigation, Trial and Appellate Practice

SEE COMPLETE LISTING UNDER ROCKFORD, ILLINOIS (122 MILES)

ROCKFORD † 152,871 Winnebago Co.

Best, Vanderlaan & Harrington

129 South Phelps Avenue, Suite 800
Rockford, Illinois 61108
 Telephone: 815-964-9500
 Fax: 815-964-8778
 E-Mail: BVH@Bestfirm.com
 www.bestfirm.com

Established: 1999

Medical Malpractice, General Liability, Coverage Issues, Opinions, Declaratory Judgments, Automobile, Property Damage, Personal Injury, Premises Liability, Product Liability, Defense Litigation, Employment Discrimination, Class Actions, Construction Litigation, Professional Malpractice

(See listing under Chicago, IL for additional information)

Heyl, Royster, Voelker & Allen
A Professional Corporation

PNC Bank Building, Second Floor
120 West State Street
Rockford, Illinois 61101
 Telephone: 815-963-4454
 Fax: 815-963-0399
 E-Mail: firm@heylroyster.com
 www.heylroyster.com

(Additional Offices: Peoria, IL*; Springfield, IL*; Urbana, IL*; Edwardsville, IL*; Chicago, IL*)

Civil Trial Practice, Insurance Defense, Appellate Practice, Class Actions, Coverage Issues, Employment Law, Professional Malpractice, Self-Insured Defense, Toxic Torts, Workers' Compensation

ROCKFORD — ILLINOIS

Heyl, Royster, Voelker & Allen, A Professional Corporation, Rockford, IL (Continued)

Managing Partner

Tobin J. Taylor — Bradley University, B.S. (magna cum laude), 1993; Washington University School of Law, J.D., 1996 — Admitted to Bar, 1977, Illinois — Member American (Toxic Tort and Environmental Law and Litigation Sections), Illinois State (Past Steering Committee Member, Employment Law Section), Peoria County (Past Co-Chair, Young Lawyer Committee) and Chicago Bar Associations; Bar Association of the Central and Southern Federal Districts of Illinois; Abraham Lincoln American Inn of Court; Defense Research Institute; Illinois Association of Defense Trial Counsel

(Our lawyers are members of the American, state and local bar associations and, in many cases, are members of the local American Inn of Court chapters; leadership positions in these organizations are listed.)
(See Edwardsville, Peoria, Springfield and Urbana, IL Listings for additional information.)

Langhenry, Gillen, Lundquist & Johnson, LLC

6785 Weaver Road, Suite 2E
Rockford, Illinois 61114
Telephone: 815-636-1800
Fax: 815-636-2860
E-Mail: rdeporte@lglfirm.com
www.lglfirm.com

Medical Malpractice, General Liability, Subrogation, Coverage Issues, Opinions, Declaratory Judgments, Automobile, Property Damage, Personal Injury, Premises Liability, Product Liability, Defense Litigation, Employment Discrimination, Class Actions, Construction Litigation

Firm Profile: Your partner from the boardroom to the courtroom. Langhenry, Gillen, Lundquist and Johnson, LLC is a litigation and business firm that combines large firm legal experience and ability, with small firm accessibility and attention.

Managing Partner

Suzanne Favia Gillen — 1961 — Lake Forest College, B.A., 1984; Illinois Institute of Technology, Chicago-Kent College of Law, J.D., 1987 — Admitted to Bar, 1987, Illinois — Member Illinois State and DuPage County Bar Associations — Practice Areas: Medical Malpractice Defense; General Liability; Civil Tort; Employment Litigation — E-mail: sgillen@lglfirm.com

Troy A. Lundquist — 1967 — University of Illinois, B.A., 1989; The John Marshall Law School, J.D., 1992 — Admitted to Bar, 1992, Illinois; U.S. District Court, Northern District of Illinois — Member Illinois State, Will County and Bureau County Bar Associations; Illinois Association of Defense Trial Counsel; Defense Research Institute — Practice Areas: Medical Malpractice Defense; Construction Litigation; Product Liability Defense; Governmental Defense; Public Officials Defense — E-mail: tlundquist@lglfirm.com

(See Chicago, Joliet and Wheaton, IL listings for additional information)

(This firm is also listed in the Subrogation section of this directory)

Mateer Goff & Honzel LLP

401 West State Street, Suite 400
Rockford, Illinois 61101
Telephone: 815-965-7745
Fax: 815-965-7749
www.mateerlawfirm.com

Established: 1971

Insurance Law, Fire, Casualty Insurance Law, Defense Litigation, Trial and Appellate Practice

Mateer Goff & Honzel LLP, Rockford, IL (Continued)

Firm Profile: Mateer Goff & Honzel LLP, formerly Mateer & Associates, has been providing legal services in the Northern Illinois area for over 40 years. The attorneys are all active civil trial attorneys trying bench and jury trials in State and Federal courts.

Insurance Clients

Aegis Security Insurance Company
Amerisure Insurance Company
CNL/Insurance America, Inc.
CUNA Mutual Group
Economy Fire & Casualty Company
General Casualty Companies
Hanover Insurance Company
Indiana Insurance Company
The Infinity Group
ISBA Mutual Insurance Company
Madison Mutual Insurance Company
Preferred Risk Mutual Insurance Company
Rockford Mutual Insurance Company
Springfield Fire & Casualty Company
Time Insurance Company n.k.a. Assurant Health
Allied, A Division of Nationwide
Atlanta Casualty Company
CSE Safeguard Insurance Company
Empire Fire and Marine Insurance Company
Grange Insurance Association
Illinois Farmers Insurance Company
Iowa Mutual Insurance Company
Leader Insurance Company
NCMIC Insurance Company
North Pointe Insurance Company
Progressive Casualty Insurance Company
Safeway Insurance Company
St. Paul Insurance Company
State Farm Mutual Automobile Insurance Company
World Insurance Company
Zurich Insurance Company

Non-Insurance Clients

Commonwealth Edison Company
Group4 Consulting, Inc.
Flying J, Inc.

Partners

William M. Goff — 1956 — Western Illinois University, B.A., 1978; Drake University, J.D. (with honors), 1984 — Leading Lawyers, Illinois — Admitted to Bar, 1984, Illinois; 1984, Iowa; 1986, U.S. District Court, Northern District of Illinois — Member American, Illinois State and Winnebago County Bar Associations; Illinois Association of Defense Trial Counsel; Defense Research Institute — Arbitrator, Seventeenth Judical Circuit — E-mail: wgoff@mateerlawfirm.com

Donna R. Honzel — 1965 — Central Missouri State University, B.S. (magna cum laude, with honors), 1988; University of Illinois at Urbana-Champaign, J.D., 1991 — Phi Sigma Alpha; Phi Kappa Phi — Admitted to Bar, 1991, Illinois; 1996, U.S. District Court, Northern District of Illinois — Member American and Illinois State Bar Associations; Winnebago County Bar Association (Board of Directors, 2008-2011; Chairman, Trial and Appellate Sections, 2010-2011, 2nd Vice President, 2014); Illinois Association of Defense Trial Counsel; Defense Research Institute — Mediator and Arbitrator, Seventeenth Judicial Circuit — E-mail: dhonzel@mateerlawfirm.com

Of Counsel

Don M. Mateer — 1945 — University of Michigan, B.A., 1967; University of Illinois, J.D., 1971 — Illinois Leading Lawyer; Illinois Super Lawyer — Admitted to Bar, 1971, Illinois; 1971, U.S. District Court, Northern District of Illinois; 1974, U.S. Court of Appeals, Seventh Circuit; 1981, U.S. Supreme Court — Member American Bar Association (Vice Chairman, Trial Techniques Committee, Tort and Insurance Practice Section, 1987-1989); Illinois State Bar Association (Assembly Representative, 1988-1993, 2010; Senior Lawyers Section Council, 2009, Secretary 2010; Committee on Legal Tec; Winnebago County Bar Association (Chairman, Judicial Liaison Committee, 1986-1987; Chairman, Professional Responsibility Committee, 1997-1998); Arbitrator, American Arbitration Association; Seventeenth Judicial Circuit Court of Winnebago County; Illinois Defense Counsel; Defense Research Institute; Fellow, American College of Trial Lawyers — Mediator and Arbitrator, Winnebago County — E-mail: dmateer@mateerlawfirm.com

Gary R. Kardell — University of Illinois, B.S., 1970; J.D., 1973 — Admitted to Bar, 1973, Illinois — Illinois Leading Lawyer — Arbitrator for the 17th Judicial Circuit — E-mail: gkardell@mateerlawfirm.com

Associate

Heather M. Hoekstra — 1982 — University of Illinois at Chicago, B.A., 2005; The University of Alabama, J.D., 2008 — Admitted to Bar, 2008, Illinois — Member Illinois State and Winnebago County Bar Associations — Arbitrator, Seventeenth Judicial Circuit — E-mail: hhoekstra@mateerlawfirm.com

RUSHVILLE † 3,192 Schuyler Co.

Refer To

Rammelkamp Bradney, P.C.
232 West State
Jacksonville, Illinois 62650
   Telephone: 217-245-6177
   Fax: 217-243-7322

Mailing Address: P.O. Box 550, Jacksonville, IL 62651-0550

Insurance Law, Fire Loss, Arson, First Party Matters, Litigation, Declaratory Judgments, Workers' Compensation, Americans with Disabilities Act, Civil Rights, Construction Litigation, Employment Practices Liability, Trial and Appellate Practice

SEE COMPLETE LISTING UNDER JACKSONVILLE, ILLINOIS (34 MILES)

SALEM † 7,485 Marion Co.

Refer To

Craig & Craig, LLC
P.O. Box 1545
Mount Vernon, Illinois 62864
   Telephone: 618-244-7511
   Fax: 618-244-7628

Professional Liability, Workers' Compensation, Product Liability, Civil Rights, Dram Shop, Premises Liability, Automobile Liability, Fire, Casualty, Surety, Life Insurance, Uninsured and Underinsured Motorist, Employment Law, Intellectual Property, Family Law, Criminal Defense, Mediation

SEE COMPLETE LISTING UNDER MOUNT VERNON, ILLINOIS (22 MILES)

Refer To

Neville, Richards & Wuller, LLC
5 Park Place Professional Centre
Illinois Street and Fullerton Road
Belleville, Illinois 62226
   Telephone: 618-277-0900
   Fax: 618-277-0970

Mailing Address: P.O. Box 23977, Belleville, IL 62226-0070

Insurance Defense, Professional Negligence, Product Liability, Premises Liability, Automobile, Bodily Injury, Fraud, Arson, Coverage Issues, Medical Malpractice, General Liability

SEE COMPLETE LISTING UNDER BELLEVILLE, ILLINOIS (55 MILES)

SHAWNEETOWN † 1,239 Gallatin Co.

Refer To

Jelliffe, Ferrell, Doerge & Phelps
108 East Walnut Street
Harrisburg, Illinois 62946
   Telephone: 618-253-7153, 618-253-7647
   Fax: 618-252-1843

Mailing Address: P.O. Box 406, Harrisburg, IL 62946

Insurance Law, Negligence, Personal Injury, Workers' Compensation, Product Liability, General Civil Practice, State and Federal Courts, Trial Practice, Appellate Practice, All Tort Litigation

SEE COMPLETE LISTING UNDER HARRISBURG, ILLINOIS (20 MILES)

SHELBYVILLE † 4,700 Shelby Co.

Refer To

Craig & Craig, LLC
1807 Broadway Avenue
P.O. Box 689
Mattoon, Illinois 61938
   Telephone: 217-234-6481
   Fax: 217-234-6486
   Fax: 217-258-8292

Automobile Liability, Casualty, Civil Rights, Dram Shop, Employment Practices Liability, Family Law, Fire, Insurance Coverage, Intellectual Property, Mediation, Product Liability, Premises Liability, Professional Liability, Surety, Uninsured and Underinsured Motorist, Workers' Compensation

SEE COMPLETE LISTING UNDER MATTOON, ILLINOIS (24 MILES)

SPRINGFIELD † 116,250 Sangamon Co.

Drake, Narup & Mead, P.C.

107 East Allen Street, Suite 100
Springfield, Illinois 62704
   Telephone: 217-528-9776
   Fax: 217-528-9401
   E-Mail: mead@dnmpc.com
   www.dnmpc.com

Established: 1989

Insurance Defense, Malpractice, Casualty, Automobile, Fire Loss, Coverage Issues, Professional Liability, Construction Law, Truck Liability, Product Liability, Subrogation, Mediation

Firm Profile: The law firm of Drake, Narup & Mead, P.C. enjoys a general practice with special emphasis on insurance defense litigation. The firm's philosophy is that all steps taken in the defense of a tort claim should be done for the purpose of achieving a goal and bringing the case closer to termination.

Insurance Clients

Burlington Insurance Company
Hastings Mutual Insurance Company
Illinois State Medical Inter-Insurance Exchange
ISBA Mutual Insurance Company
Medical Protective Insurance Services
Preferred Professional Insurance Company
Shelter Mutual Insurance Company
State Farm Fire and Casualty Company
West Bend Mutual Insurance Company
Chubb Executive Risk, Inc.
Illinois Provider Trust
Illinois Risk Management Services
Indiana Farmers Mutual Insurance Company
Liberty Mutual Group
Northland Insurance Company
Preferred Physicians Medical Risk Retention Group, Inc.
Progressive Premiere Insurance Company of Illinois
State Farm Mutual Automobile Insurance Company
Zurich American Insurance Company

Non-Insurance Clients

Brandt Consolidated Inc.
CEC Entertainment, Inc.

Partners

David L. Drake — 1948 — Western Illinois University, B.A., 1970; Illinois Institute of Technology, Chicago-Kent College of Law, J.D., 1973 — Delta Theta Phi — Admitted to Bar, 1973, Illinois; 1973, U.S. District Court, Central District of Illinois; 1973, U.S. Court of Appeals, Seventh Circuit — Member Illinois State Bar Association; Master, Lincoln-Douglas Inn of Court — Adjunct Assistant Professor, Southern Illinois University School of Medicine — E-mail: drake@dnmpc.com

Richard H. Narup — 1956 — Blackburn College, B.A., 1978; Southern Illinois University, J.D., 1981 — Admitted to Bar, 1981, Illinois; 1981, U.S. District Court, Central and Southern Districts of Illinois; 1981, U.S. Court of Appeals, Seventh Circuit — Member Illinois State Bar Association — E-mail: narup@dnmpc.com

Randall A. Mead — 1956 — Western Illinois University, B.A., 1978; Southern Illinois University School of Law, J.D., 1981 — Admitted to Bar, 1981, Illinois; 1981, U.S. District Court, Central District of Illinois; 1981, U.S. Court of Appeals, Seventh Circuit — Member Illinos State Bar Association; Defense Research Institute — Adjunct Assistant Professor, Southern Illinois University School of Medicine — Practice Areas: Insurance Defense; Insurance Coverage; Trucking Litigation; Construction Litigation — E-mail: mead@dnmpc.com

Kirk W. Laudeman — 1965 — University of Illinois, B.A., 1987; The John Marshall Law School, J.D., 1990 — Admitted to Bar, 1990, Illinois; 1990, U.S. District Court, Northern District of Illinois; 1991, U.S. District Court, Central District of Illinois; 2007, U.S. District Court, Southern District of Illinois; 2008, U.S. Court of Appeals, Seventh Circuit — Member Illinois State Bar Association; Illinois Association of Defense Trial Counsel — E-mail: laudeman@dnmpc.com

Associates

Christian D. Biswell — 1971 — Southern Illinois University, B.A., 1994; M.A., 1997; J.D., 2001 — Admitted to Bar, 2001, Illinois; 2001, U.S. District

SPRINGFIELD   ILLINOIS

Drake, Narup & Mead, P.C., Springfield, IL   (Continued)

Court, Central District of Illinois; 2011, U.S. Court of Appeals, Seventh Circuit — E-mail: biswell@dnmpc.com

Steven C. Ward — 1956 — DePauw University, B.A., 1978; Illinois Institute of Technology, Chicago-Kent College of Law, J.D., 1982 — Admitted to Bar, 1983, Illinois; 1985, U.S. District Court, Northern District of Illinois; 1988, U.S. District Court, Central District of Illinois; 1989, U.S. District Court, Southern District of Illinois; 1992, U.S. Court of Appeals, Seventh Circuit — Member Illinois State Bar Association — E-mail: ward@dnmpc.com

HeplerBroom LLC

4340 Acer Grove Drive, Suite A
Springfield, Illinois 62711
Telephone: 217-528-3674
Fax: 217-528-3964
E-Mail: firm@heplerbroom.com
www.heplerbroom.com

(Additional Offices: Edwardsville, IL*; St. Louis, MO*; Chicago, IL*)

Antitrust, Insurance Defense, Product Liability, Toxic Torts, Property and Casualty, Class Actions, Legal Malpractice, Commercial Litigation, Pharmaceutical, General Liability, Asbestos Litigation, Medical Malpractice, Workers' Compensation, Employment Litigation, Insurance Coverage, Transportation, Automobile, Trucking Law, Agent and Brokers Errors and Omissions, Personal Injury, Skilled Nursing Facilities, Construction Liability, White Collar Criminal Defense, Qui Tam/False Claims Act Litigation

Partners

Stephen R. Kaufmann — 1952 — Northwestern University, J.D., 1978 — Admitted to Bar, 1978, Arizona; 1980, Illinois — Tel: 217-993-7146 — E-mail: srk@heplerbroom.com

Thomas H. Wilson — 1964 — Southern Illinois University, J.D., 1989 — Admitted to Bar, 1989, Illinois — Tel: 217-993-7144 — E-mail: thw@heplerbroom.com

Lance T. Jones — 1958 — DePaul University College of Law, J.D., 1984 — Admitted to Bar, 1984, Illinois — Tel: 217-993-7151 — E-mail: ltj@heplerbroom.com

(See listing under Edwardsville, IL for additional information)

Heyl, Royster, Voelker & Allen
A Professional Corporation

3731 Wabash Avenue
Springfield, Illinois 62711
Telephone: 217-522-8822
Fax: 217-523-3902
E-Mail: firm@heylroyster.com
www.heylroyster.com

(Additional Offices: Peoria, IL*; Urbana, IL*; Rockford, IL*; Edwardsville, IL*; Chicago, IL*)

Civil Trial Practice, Insurance Defense, Appellate Practice, Class Actions, Coverage Issues, Employment Law, Professional Malpractice, Self-Insured Defense, Toxic Torts, Workers' Compensation

Managing Partner

Gary L. Borah — 1949 — University of Illinois, B.S., 1971; The University of Toledo, J.D., 1975 — Admitted to Bar, 1975, Illinois

Partners

Gary S. Schwab — 1956 — Illinois Wesleyan University, B.A. (summa cum laude), 1978; The University of Iowa, J.D. (with distinction), 1981 — Admitted to Bar, 1981, Illinois

Heyl, Royster, Voelker & Allen, A Professional Corporation, Springfield, IL   (Continued)

Daniel R. Simmons — 1959 — Augustana College, B.A. (magna cum laude), 1981; The University of Iowa, J.D., 1984 — Admitted to Bar, 1985, Illinois — Member Lincoln-Douglas Inn of Court (President, 2000-2001)

Michael T. Kokal — University of Notre Dame, B.S., 1987; Washington University, M.L.A., 1989; University of Missouri School of Law, J.D. (Order of the Coif), 1992 — Admitted to Bar, 1992, Illinois

John O. Langfelder

Partner/Shareholder

Adrian E. Harless — 1956 — University of Illinois, B.S., 1979; Saint Louis University, J.D., 1982 — Admitted to Bar, 1982, Illinois — Member Illinois Supreme Court Committee, Past Member (Pattern Jury Instructions in Civil Cases)

Theresa M. Powell — 1969 — Eastern Illinois University, B.A. (summa cum laude), 1991; Southern Illinois University, J.D. (cum laude), 1995 — Admitted to Bar, 1995, Illinois

Associates

Douglas R. Bitner — Southern Illinois University, B.S. (cum laude), 2008; J.D. (cum laude), 2011 — Admitted to Bar, 2011, Illinois

John D. Hoelzer — Carleton College, B.A. (cum laude), 2004; Saint Louis University School of Law, J.D., 2007 — Admitted to Bar, 2008, Illinois

John T. Robinson — Southern Illinois University, B.S., 2006; Southern Illinois University School of Law, J.D., 2010 — Admitted to Bar, 2010, Illinois

Joseph N. Rupcich — University of Illinois, B.A., 2000; Southern Illinois University Law School, J.D. (cum laude), 2004 — Admitted to Bar, 2004, Illinois

Brett E. Siegel — University of Illinois, B.A. (with distinction), 2009; Chicago - Kent School of Law, J.D., 2012 — Admitted to Bar, 2012, Illinois

(Our lawyers are members of the American, state and local bar associations and, in many cases, are members of the local American Inn of Court chapters; leadership positions in these organizations are listed.)
(See Edwardsville, Peoria, Rockford and Urbana, IL Listings for additional information.)

Koepke & Hiltabrand

2341 West White Oaks Drive, Suite A
Springfield, Illinois 62704
Telephone: 217-726-8646
Fax: 217-726-8861
E-Mail: kkoepke@koepkelaw.net
kandhlawfirm.com

Established: 2004

Automobile, Commercial Law, Construction Law, Employment Law, General Liability, Homeowners, Insurance Defense, Premises Liability, Product Liability, Professional Liability, Subrogation, Workers' Compensation

Firm Profile: The law firm of Koepke & Hiltabrand is a progressive law firm specializing in all aspects of civil litigation including insurance defense, worker's compensation, employment law, general civil trial and appellate practice, professional liability defense and insurance coverage.

Insurance Clients

COUNTRY Insurance	Employers Security Insurance Company
Farmers Insurance Company	Illinois Casualty Company
Foremost Insurance Group	Kingsway America, Inc.
Illinois Insurance Guaranty Fund	Midwest Insurance Company
MetLife Insurance Company	Rockford Mutual Insurance Company
Pekin Insurance Company	21st Century Insurance Company
Safe Auto Insurance Company	Zenith Insurance Company
State Farm Insurance Company	
USAgencies Direct Insurance Company	

Non-Insurance Clients

GAB Robins North America, Inc.   Hinz Claim Management, Inc.

ILLINOIS SULLIVAN

Koepke & Hiltabrand, Springfield, IL (Continued)
Members
Kurt M. Koepke — 1961 — Western Illinois University, B.A., 1983; Southern Illinois University, J.D., 1988 — Admitted to Bar, 1988, Illinois; 2012, Wisconsin; U.S. District Court, Central District of Illinois; 1990, U.S. Court of Appeals, Seventh Circuit; 2009, U.S. Supreme Court — Member Illinois State and Sangamon County Bar Associations; Adjuster Association of Central Illinois — E-mail: kkoepke@koepkelaw.net

Lori Poppe Hiltabrand — 1969 — Illinois Wesleyan University, B.A., 1991; Southern Illinois University School of Law, J.D. (cum laude), 1997 — Admitted to Bar, 1997, Illinois; U.S. District Court, Central District of Illinois — Member Illinois State and Sangamon County Bar Associations; Adjuster Association of Central Ilinois — E-mail: lhiltabrand@koepkelaw.net

Associate
Jason G. Schutte — Western Illinois University, B.S., 2004; Southern Illinois University School of Law, J.D., 2008 — Admitted to Bar, 2008, Illinois; Missouri — Member American and Illinois State (Construction Law Council) Bar Associations; The Missouri Bar; Illinois Nursing Home Administrators Association; Illinois Home Builders Association — E-mail: jschutte@kopekelaw.net

Rammelkamp Bradney, P.C.
741 South Grand Avenue West
Springfield, Illinois 62704
   Telephone: 217-522-6000
   Fax: 217-522-6018
   www.rblawyers.net

(Jacksonville, IL Office*: 232 West State, 62650, P.O. Box 550, 62651-0550)
   (Tel: 217-245-6177)
   (Fax: 217-243-7322)
   (E-Mail: info@rblawyers.net)
(Winchester, IL Office: 46 South Hill Street, 62694)
   (Tel: 217-742-5215)
   (Fax: 217-742-3537)

Insurance Law, Fire Loss, Arson, First Party Matters, Litigation, Declaratory Judgments, Workers' Compensation, Americans with Disabilities Act, Civil Rights, Construction Litigation, Employment Practices Liability, Trial and Appellate Practice

(See listing under Jacksonville, IL for additional information)

The following firms also service this area.

Craig & Craig, LLC
1807 Broadway Avenue
P.O. Box 689
Mattoon, Illinois 61938
   Telephone: 217-234-6481
   Fax: 217-234-6486
   Fax: 217-258-8292

Automobile Liability, Casualty, Civil Rights, Dram Shop, Employment Practices Liability, Family Law, Fire, Insurance Coverage, Intellectual Property, Mediation, Product Liability, Premises Liability, Professional Liability, Surety, Uninsured and Underinsured Motorist, Workers' Compensation

SEE COMPLETE LISTING UNDER MATTOON, ILLINOIS (83 MILES)

Neville, Richards & Wuller, LLC
5 Park Place Professional Centre
Illinois Street and Fullerton Road
Belleville, Illinois 62226
   Telephone: 618-277-0900
   Fax: 618-277-0970
Mailing Address: P.O. Box 23977, Belleville, IL 62226-0070

Insurance Defense, Professional Negligence, Product Liability, Premises Liability, Automobile, Bodily Injury, Fraud, Arson, Coverage Issues, Medical Malpractice, General Liability

SEE COMPLETE LISTING UNDER BELLEVILLE, ILLINOIS (100 MILES)

Rammelkamp Bradney, P.C.
232 West State
Jacksonville, Illinois 62650
   Telephone: 217-245-6177
   Fax: 217-243-7322
Mailing Address: P.O. Box 550, Jacksonville, IL 62651-0550

Insurance Law, Fire Loss, Arson, First Party Matters, Litigation, Declaratory Judgments, Workers' Compensation, Americans with Disabilities Act, Civil Rights, Construction Litigation, Employment Practices Liability, Trial and Appellate Practice

SEE COMPLETE LISTING UNDER JACKSONVILLE, ILLINOIS (33 MILES)

SULLIVAN † 4,440 Moultrie Co.
Refer To

Craig & Craig, LLC
1807 Broadway Avenue
P.O. Box 689
Mattoon, Illinois 61938
   Telephone: 217-234-6481
   Fax: 217-234-6486
   Fax: 217-258-8292

Automobile Liability, Casualty, Civil Rights, Dram Shop, Employment Practices Liability, Family Law, Fire, Insurance Coverage, Intellectual Property, Mediation, Product Liability, Premises Liability, Professional Liability, Surety, Uninsured and Underinsured Motorist, Workers' Compensation

SEE COMPLETE LISTING UNDER MATTOON, ILLINOIS (17 MILES)

SYCAMORE † 17,519 DeKalb Co.
Refer To

Mateer Goff & Honzel LLP
401 West State Street, Suite 400
Rockford, Illinois 61101
   Telephone: 815-965-7745
   Fax: 815-965-7749

Insurance Law, Fire, Casualty Insurance Law, Defense Litigation, Trial and Appellate Practice

SEE COMPLETE LISTING UNDER ROCKFORD, ILLINOIS (40 MILES)

TAYLORVILLE † 11,246 Christian Co.
Refer To

Craig & Craig, LLC
1807 Broadway Avenue
P.O. Box 689
Mattoon, Illinois 61938
   Telephone: 217-234-6481
   Fax: 217-234-6486
   Fax: 217-258-8292

Automobile Liability, Casualty, Civil Rights, Dram Shop, Employment Practices Liability, Family Law, Fire, Insurance Coverage, Intellectual Property, Mediation, Product Liability, Premises Liability, Professional Liability, Surety, Uninsured and Underinsured Motorist, Workers' Compensation

SEE COMPLETE LISTING UNDER MATTOON, ILLINOIS (57 MILES)

TOLEDO † 1,238 Cumberland Co.
Refer To

Craig & Craig, LLC
1807 Broadway Avenue
P.O. Box 689
Mattoon, Illinois 61938
   Telephone: 217-234-6481
   Fax: 217-234-6486
   Fax: 217-258-8292

Automobile Liability, Casualty, Civil Rights, Dram Shop, Employment Practices Liability, Family Law, Fire, Insurance Coverage, Intellectual Property, Mediation, Product Liability, Premises Liability, Professional Liability, Surety, Uninsured and Underinsured Motorist, Workers' Compensation

SEE COMPLETE LISTING UNDER MATTOON, ILLINOIS (22 MILES)

VIRGINIA

TUSCOLA † 4,480 Douglas Co.

Refer To
Craig & Craig, LLC
1807 Broadway Avenue
P.O. Box 689
Mattoon, Illinois 61938
Telephone: 217-234-6481
Fax: 217-234-6486
Fax: 217-258-8292

Automobile Liability, Casualty, Civil Rights, Dram Shop, Employment Practices Liability, Family Law, Fire, Insurance Coverage, Intellectual Property, Mediation, Product Liability, Premises Liability, Professional Liability, Surety, Uninsured and Underinsured Motorist, Workers' Compensation

SEE COMPLETE LISTING UNDER MATTOON, ILLINOIS (27 MILES)

URBANA † 41,250 Champaign Co.

Heyl, Royster, Voelker & Allen
A Professional Corporation

102 East Main Street, Suite 300
Urbana, Illinois 61801
Telephone: 217-344-0060
Fax: 217-344-9295
E-Mail: firm@heylroyster.com
www.heylroyster.com

(Additional Offices: Peoria, IL*; Springfield, IL*; Rockford, IL*; Edwardsville, IL*; Chicago, IL*)

Civil Trial Practice, Insurance Defense, Appellate Practice, Class Actions, Coverage Issues, Employment Law, Professional Malpractice, Self-Insured Defense, Toxic Torts, Workers' Compensation

Managing Partner

Edward M. Wagner — 1951 — Marquette University, B.A., 1973; Creighton University, J.D. (cum laude), 1980 — Admitted to Bar, 1980, Illinois

(Our lawyers are members of the American, state and local bar associations and, in many cases, are members of the local American Inn of Court chapters; leadership positions in these organizations are listed.)
(See Edwardsville, Peoria, Rockford and Springfield, IL Listings for additional information.)

The following firms also service this area.

Craig & Craig, LLC
1807 Broadway Avenue
P.O. Box 689
Mattoon, Illinois 61938
Telephone: 217-234-6481
Fax: 217-234-6486
Fax: 217-258-8292

Automobile Liability, Casualty, Civil Rights, Dram Shop, Employment Practices Liability, Family Law, Fire, Insurance Coverage, Intellectual Property, Mediation, Product Liability, Premises Liability, Professional Liability, Surety, Uninsured and Underinsured Motorist, Workers' Compensation

SEE COMPLETE LISTING UNDER MATTOON, ILLINOIS (50 MILES)

ILLINOIS

VANDALIA † 7,042 Fayette Co.

Refer To
Craig & Craig, LLC
1807 Broadway Avenue
P.O. Box 689
Mattoon, Illinois 61938
Telephone: 217-234-6481
Fax: 217-234-6486
Fax: 217-258-8292

Automobile Liability, Casualty, Civil Rights, Dram Shop, Employment Practices Liability, Family Law, Fire, Insurance Coverage, Intellectual Property, Mediation, Product Liability, Premises Liability, Professional Liability, Surety, Uninsured and Underinsured Motorist, Workers' Compensation

SEE COMPLETE LISTING UNDER MATTOON, ILLINOIS (60 MILES)

Refer To
Neville, Richards & Wuller, LLC
5 Park Place Professional Centre
Illinois Street and Fullerton Road
Belleville, Illinois 62226
Telephone: 618-277-0900
Fax: 618-277-0970

Mailing Address: P.O. Box 23977, Belleville, IL 62226-0070

Insurance Defense, Professional Negligence, Product Liability, Premises Liability, Automobile, Bodily Injury, Fraud, Arson, Coverage Issues, Medical Malpractice, General Liability

SEE COMPLETE LISTING UNDER BELLEVILLE, ILLINOIS (60 MILES)

VIENNA † 1,434 Johnson Co.

Refer To
Feirich/Mager/Green/Ryan
2001 West Main Street
Carbondale, Illinois 62901
Telephone: 618-529-3000
Fax: 618-529-3008

Mailing Address: P.O. Box 1570, Carbondale, IL 62903-1570

Insurance Defense, Medical Negligence, Casualty, Construction Litigation, Product Liability, Workers' Compensation, Civil Rights, Trial Practice, Appellate Practice, Professional Liability, Subrogation, Coverage Issues

SEE COMPLETE LISTING UNDER CARBONDALE, ILLINOIS (36 MILES)

Refer To
Jelliffe, Ferrell, Doerge & Phelps
108 East Walnut Street
Harrisburg, Illinois 62946
Telephone: 618-253-7153, 618-253-7647
Fax: 618-252-1843

Mailing Address: P.O. Box 406, Harrisburg, IL 62946

Insurance Law, Negligence, Personal Injury, Workers' Compensation, Product Liability, General Civil Practice, State and Federal Courts, Trial Practice, Appellate Practice, All Tort Litigation

SEE COMPLETE LISTING UNDER HARRISBURG, ILLINOIS (32 MILES)

VIRGINIA † 1,611 Cass Co.

Refer To
Rammelkamp Bradney, P.C.
232 West State
Jacksonville, Illinois 62650
Telephone: 217-245-6177
Fax: 217-243-7322

Mailing Address: P.O. Box 550, Jacksonville, IL 62651-0550

Insurance Law, Fire Loss, Arson, First Party Matters, Litigation, Declaratory Judgments, Workers' Compensation, Americans with Disabilities Act, Civil Rights, Construction Litigation, Employment Practices Liability, Trial and Appellate Practice

SEE COMPLETE LISTING UNDER JACKSONVILLE, ILLINOIS (16 MILES)

ILLINOIS WATERLOO

WATERLOO † 9,811 Monroe Co.

Refer To
Neville, Richards & Wuller, LLC
5 Park Place Professional Centre
Illinois Street and Fullerton Road
Belleville, Illinois 62226
  Telephone: 618-277-0900
  Fax: 618-277-0970

Mailing Address: P.O. Box 23977, Belleville, IL 62226-0070

Insurance Defense, Professional Negligence, Product Liability, Premises Liability, Automobile, Bodily Injury, Fraud, Arson, Coverage Issues, Medical Malpractice, General Liability

SEE COMPLETE LISTING UNDER BELLEVILLE, ILLINOIS (15 MILES)

WATSEKA † 5,255 Iroquois Co.

Refer To
Dukes, Ryan, Meyer, & Freed Ltd.
146 North Vermilion Street
Danville, Illinois 61832
  Telephone: 217-442-0384
  Fax: 217-442-0009

Insurance Defense, Personal Injury, Property Damage, Automobile, Homeowners, General Practice, Criminal Law

SEE COMPLETE LISTING UNDER DANVILLE, ILLINOIS (48 MILES)

WHEATON † 52,894 Du Page Co.

Langhenry, Gillen, Lundquist & Johnson, LLC

311 South County Farm Road, Suite L
Wheaton, Illinois 60187
  Telephone: 630-653-5775
  Fax: 630-653-5980
  E-Mail: rdeporte@lglfirm.com
  www.lglfirm.com

Medical Malpractice, General Liability, Subrogation, Coverage Issues, Opinions, Declaratory Judgments, Automobile, Property Damage, Personal Injury, Premises Liability, Product Liability, Defense Litigation, Employment Discrimination, Class Actions, Construction Litigation

Firm Profile: Your partner from the boardroom to the courtroom. Langhenry, Gillen, Lundquist and Johnson, LLC is a litigation and business firm that combines large firm legal experience and ability, with small firm accessibility and attention.

Managing Partners

Suzanne Favia Gillen — 1961 — Lake Forest College, B.A., 1984; Illinois Institute of Technology, Chicago-Kent College of Law, J.D., 1987 — Admitted to Bar, 1987, Illinois — Member Illinois State and DuPage County Bar Associations — Practice Areas: Medical Malpractice Defense; General Liability; Civil Tort; Employment Litigation — E-mail: sgillen@lglfirm.com

Steven R. Johnson — 1963 — Northwestern University, B.S., 1985; The John Marshall Law School, J.D., 1992 — Admitted to Bar, 1992, Illinois; U.S. District Court, Northern District of Illinois; 1997, U.S. District Court, Central District of Illinois; 1998, U.S. District Court, Northern District of Indiana; 2000, U.S. District Court, District of Nebraska; 2002, U.S. Court of Appeals, Eighth Circuit — Member American Bar Association; National Fire Protection Association; Western Loss Association; National Association of Subrogation Professionals; Defense Research Institute — Practice Areas: Complex Commercial Litigation; Construction Litigation; Fire and Water Subrogation; Insurance Coverage & Defense; Premises Liability; Property Defense; Property Subrogation — E-mail: sjohnson@lglfirm.com

Michelle M. Paveza — 1970 — The University of Arizona, B.A., 1991; DePaul University College of Law, J.D., 1996 — Admitted to Bar, 1996, Illinois; U.S. District Court, Northern District of Illinois; 1998, U.S. District Court, Central District of Illinois — Member Illinois State and DuPage County Bar

Langhenry, Gillen, Lundquist & Johnson, LLC, Wheaton, IL (Continued)

Associations — Practice Areas: Medical Malpractice Defense; Employment Discrimination; Civil Defense — E-mail: mpaveza@lglfirm.com

(See Chicago, Joliet and Rockford, IL listings for additional information)

(This firm is also listed in the Subrogation section of this directory)

Mulherin, Rehfeldt & Varchetto, P.C.

211 South Wheaton Avenue, Suite 200
Wheaton, Illinois 60187
  Telephone: 630-653-9300
  Fax: 630-653-9316
  E-Mail: mrv@mrvlaw.com
  www.mrvlaw.com

Insurance Defense, Medical Malpractice, Coverage Issues, Automobile Liability, Commercial Liability, General Liability, Liquor Liability, Dram Shop, Premises Liability, Product Liability, Construction Accidents, Employment Law, Bodily Injury, Property Damage, Subrogation, Environmental Law, Toxic Torts, Professional Liability, Municipal Liability, Workers' Compensation

Firm Profile: Mulherin, Rehfeldt & Varchetto, P.C. was formed in 1997 as a successor to Wylie, Mulherin, Rehfeldt & Varchetto which originated in 1972. Mulherin, Rehfeldt & Varchetto, P.C. is one of the largest law firms in DuPage County, Illinois of which Wheaton is the County seat. The firm concentrates in insurance defense and subrogation litigation including appeals in Federal and State courts, but is also engaged in general civil practice. The firm services the Northern counties of Illinois concentrating on Chicago and the surrounding suburban counties.

Insurance Clients

Chartis	ISMIE Mutual Insurance Company
Nationwide Insurance	Risk Enterprise Management, Ltd.
Safe Auto Insurance Company	Scottsdale Insurance Company
State Farm Fire and Casualty Company	Travelers Insurance Companies
Zurich American Insurance Company	Willis Group

Non-Insurance Clients

Hollywood Casino   University of Illinois Hospitals

Partners

John M. Mulherin — 1942 — University of Illinois, B.A., 1964; Northwestern University School of Law, J.D., 1967 — Admitted to Bar, 1967, Illinois; 1967, U.S. District Court, Northern District of Illinois — Member Illinois State Bar Association (Corporations and Health Care); DuPage County Bar Association (Editor-Bar Brief 1985-1991) — E-mail: jmulherin@mrvlaw.com

Louis A. Varchetto — 1954 — University of Illinois at Urbana-Champaign, B.A., 1976; The John Marshall Law School, J.D. (with distinction), 1979 — Admitted to Bar, 1979, Illinois; 2002, Missouri; 1979, U.S. District Court, Northern District of Illinois; 1986, U.S. Court of Appeals, Seventh Circuit; 1986, U.S. Supreme Court; 1992, U.S. District Court, Eastern District of Wisconsin — Member Illinois State and DuPage County (Director, 1986-1989) Bar Associations; American Board of Trial Advocates — E-mail: lvarchetto@mrvlaw.com

Stephen A. Rehfeldt — 1948 — Purdue University, B.S., 1970; University of Illinois College of Law, J.D., 1974 — Admitted to Bar, 1975, Illinois; 1991, U.S. Court of Appeals, Seventh Circuit; 1996, U.S. Supreme Court — Member Illinois State and DuPage County Bar Associations; Illinois Appellate Lawyers Association — E-mail: srehfeldt@mrvlaw.com

Joseph G. Skryd — 1963 — Purdue University, B.A., 1985; The John Marshall Law School, J.D., 1988 — Admitted to Bar, 1988, Illinois; 1988, U.S. District Court, Northern District of Illinois; 2000, U.S. District Court, Central District of Illinois — Member American, Illinois State and DuPage County Bar Associations — E-mail: jskryd@mrvlaw.com

Ray H. Rittenhouse — 1953 — DePaul University, B.A. (with high honors), 1976; DePaul University College of Law, J.D., 1981 — Admitted to Bar, 1981, Illinois; 1981, U.S. District Court, Northern District of Illinois; 1994,

Mulherin, Rehfeldt & Varchetto, P.C., Wheaton, IL (Continued)

Federal Trial Bar; 1996, U.S. Court of Appeals, Seventh Circuit; 2000, U.S. District Court, Central District of Illinois; 2009, U.S. District Court, Southern District of Illinois; 2010, U.S. District Court, Western District of Michigan — Member Illinois State and Chicago Bar Associations; Illinois Association of Defense Trial Counsel; Defense Research Institute — Practice Areas: Insurance Coverage — E-mail: rhrittenhouse@mrvlaw.com

James P. Moran — 1957 — University of Notre Dame, B.B.A., 1979; Illinois Institute of Technology, Chicago-Kent College of Law, J.D. (with high honors), 1982 — Admitted to Bar, 1982, Illinois; 1982, U.S. District Court, Northern District of Illinois — Member American and Chicago Bar Associations — E-mail: jmoran@mrvlaw.com

William J. Ulrich, Jr. — 1949 — Robert Morris College, A.S.B.A., 1969; Northern Illinois University, B.S. (with honors), 1971; DePaul University, J.D., 1979 — Admitted to Bar, 1980, Illinois; 1980, U.S. District Court, Northern District of Illinois; 1980, U.S. Court of Appeals, Seventh Circuit; 1986, U.S. Supreme Court — Member Illinois State and DuPage County Bar Associations — E-mail: wulrich@mrvlaw.com

Patricia L. Argentati — 1953 — Marquette University, B.A. (cum laude), 1975; Illinois Institute of Technology, Chicago-Kent College of Law, J.D., 1982 — Admitted to Bar, 1982, Illinois; 1987, U.S. District Court, Northern District of Illinois; 1987, U.S. Court of Appeals, Seventh Circuit — Member American, Illinois State and DuPage County Bar Associations; DuPage Association of Women Lawyers; Defense Research Institute — E-mail: pargentati@mrvlaw.com

Marcelline DeFalco — 1970 — Northeastern Illinois University, B.A. (with honors), 1992; The John Marshall Law School, J.D. (cum laude), 1997 — Admitted to Bar, 1997, Illinois — Member American, Illinois State and DuPage County Bar Associations; DuPage Association of Women Lawyers — E-mail: mdefalco@mrvlaw.com

Andrew R. Poyton — 1970 — University of Colorado at Boulder, B.A., 1992; DePaul University College of Law, J.D., 1996 — Admitted to Bar, 1996, Illinois; 1996, U.S. District Court, Northern District of Illinois — Member Illinois State and DuPage County Bar Associations — E-mail: apoyton@mrvlaw.com

William R. Brodzinski — 1973 — Purdue University, B.S., 1995; Illinois Institute of Technology, Chicago-Kent College of Law, J.D. (with honors), 1999 — Admitted to Bar, 1999, Illinois; 1999, U.S. District Court, Northern District of Illinois — Member Illinois State, DuPage County and Chicago Bar Associations — E-mail: wbrodzinski@mrvlaw.com

Associates

Stephanie Lynn Smith — 1982 — Elmhurst College, B.S. (magna cum laude), 2005; The John Marshall Law School, J.D., 2008 — Admitted to Bar, 2008, Illinois — Member Illinois State, DuPage County and Chicago Bar Associations — Practice Areas: Insurance Defense — E-mail: ssmith@mrvlaw.com

James J. Temple — 1978 — Carthage College, B.A., 2001; The John Marshall Law School, J.D., 2004 — Admitted to Bar, 2004, Illinois — Member American, Illinois State and DuPage County Bar Associations — Practice Areas: Insurance Defense — E-mail: jtemple@mrvlaw.com

Shana A. O'Grady — 1979 — Cornell College, B.A. (cum laude), 2001; University of San Diego, J.D., 2004 — Admitted to Bar, 2004, Illinois; 2005, U.S. District Court, Northern District of Illinois; 2009, U.S. Court of Appeals, Seventh Circuit — Member Illinois State and Chicago Bar Associations; Defense Reserach Institute (Vice Chair, Professional Liability); Illinois Defense Counsel — Practice Areas: Legal Malpractice; Medical Malpractice — E-mail: sogrady@mrvlaw.com

Matthew R. Schreck — 1979 — Evangel University, B.S., 2001; The John Marshall Law School, J.D., 2004 — Admitted to Bar, 2004, Illinois; 2005, U.S. District Court, Northern and Southern Districts of Illinois — Member Illinois State and DuPage County Bar Associations — Practice Areas: Insurance Defense — E-mail: mschreck@mrvlaw.com

Jennifer M. Anderson — 1979 — Northwestern University, B.A., 2002; Drake University Law School, J.D., 2005 — Admitted to Bar, 2005, Illinois; 2007, U.S. District Court, Northern District of Illinois — Member American, Illinois State and DuPage County Bar Associations — Practice Areas: Insurance Defense — E-mail: janderson@mrvlaw.com

John T. White — 1977 — University of Dallas, B.A., 1999; University of Notre Dame, J.D., 2007 — Admitted to Bar, 2007, Illinois; U.S. District Court, Northern District of Illinois — Member American Bar Association — Practice Areas: Civil Litigation; Insurance Defense — E-mail: jwhite@mrvlaw.com

Kelly Johnson — 1976 — University of Illinois at Urbana-Champaign, B.A., 1998; Northern Illinois University College of Law, J.D., 2001 — Admitted to Bar, 2001, Illinois — Member Illinois State Bar Association; Workers' Compensation Lawyers Association — Practice Areas: Workers' Compensation; Insurance Defense — E-mail: kjohnson@mrvlaw.com

Jeremy L. Dershow — 1975 — Michigan State University, B.A., 1998; Chicago-Kent College of Law, J.D., 2001 — Admitted to Bar, 2002, Illinois; U.S. District Court, Northern District of Illinois — Member Illinois State and Chicago Bar Associations — Practice Areas: Construction Law; Trucking Law; Automobile; Premises Liability; Negligence — E-mail: jdershow@mrvlaw.com

Kristopher Capadona — 1981 — Lewis University, B.A., 2004; The John Marshall Law School, J.D., 2007 — Admitted to Bar, 2007, Illinois; U.S. District Court, Northern District of Illinois — Member Will County Bar Association — Practice Areas: Commercial Law; Commercial Litigation; Civil Litigation — E-mail: kcapadona@mrvlaw.com

Matthew J. Brennan — 1983 — DePaul University, B.S., 2007; The John Marshall Law School, J.D., 2010 — Admitted to Bar, 2010, Illinois — Member American, Illinois State, Northwest Suburban and Chicago Bar Associations — E-mail: mbrennan@mrvlaw.com

Bridget A. Liccardi — 1982 — Miami University, B.A., 2005; The John Marshall Law School, J.D., 2008 — Admitted to Bar, 2008, Illinois; 2009, U.S. District Court, Northern District of Illinois — Member DuPage County and Chicago Bar Associations; Women's Bar Association of Illinois; Inter-Pacific Bar Association; Defense Research Institute — Practice Areas: Legal Malpractice; Medical Malpractice; General Civil Litigation — E-mail: bliccardi@mrvlaw.com

Jessica Briney — 1983 — Elmhurst College, B.A. (cum laude), 2006; The John Marshall Law School, J.D., 2010 — Admitted to Bar, 2010, Illinois — Member American, Illinois State and Kane County Bar Associations — Practice Areas: Insurance Defense; Professional Malpractice — E-mail: jbriney@mrvlaw.com

Ryan H. Voss — 1983 — University of Illinois at Chicago, B.A. (Dean's List), 2006; The John Marshall Law School, J.D. (Dean's List), 2010 — Admitted to Bar, 2010, Illinois; 2011, U.S. District Court, Northern District of Illinois — Practice Areas: Trucking; Construction Law; Personal Injury — E-mail: rvoss@mrvlaw.com

Scott Koontz — 1985 — Illinois Wesleyan University, B.A., 2007; DePaul University College of Law, J.D., 2010 — Admitted to Bar, 2010, Illinois — Member Chicago Bar Association — E-mail: skoontz@mrvlaw.com

Kelly Bailey — 1984 — Illinois State University, B.S. (summa cum laude), 2007; Valparaiso University School of Law, J.D. (with honors), 2010 — Admitted to Bar, 2010, Illinois — Member Illinois State and DuPage County Bar Association — E-mail: kbailey@mrvlaw.com

Nicole Giulietta Demik — 1984 — DePaul University, B.S., 2007; The John Marshall Law School, J.D., 2011 — Phi Alpha Delta — Admitted to Bar, 2011, Illinois — Member DuPage County, Kane County and Chicago Bar Associations; The Justinian Society — Practice Areas: Insurance Defense — E-mail: ndemik@mrvlaw.com

Dara Marie Andrews — 1983 — Gannon University, B.S. (summa cum laude), 2004; The John Marshall Law School, J.D., 2011 — Admitted to Bar, 2011, Illinois; 2012, U.S. District Court, Northern District of Illinois — Member Chicago Bar Association — Languages: Mandarin Chinese — Practice Areas: Insurance Defense — E-mail: dandrews@mrvlaw.com

Joseph J. Lombardo — 1985 — DePaul University, B.A., 2007; The John Marshall Law School, J.D., 2011 — Admitted to Bar, 2011, Illinois; 2012, U.S. District Court, Northern District of Illinois — Member American, DuPage County and Chicago Bar Associations — Practice Areas: Insurance Defense; Commercial Litigation; Subrogation — E-mail: jlombardo@mrvlaw.com

Kelly Hejlik — 1985 — The University of Iowa, B.A. (with honors), 2008; The John Marshall Law School, J.D., 2011 — John Marshall Law Review of Intellectual Property Law — Admitted to Bar, 2011, Illinois — Member Illinois State Bar Association; Women's Bar Association of Illinois; Bohemian Lawyers Association of Chicago; Defense Research Institute — Practice Areas: Medical Malpractice Defense; Nursing Home Litigation — E-mail: khejlik@mrvlaw.com

ILLINOIS

Paulsen, Malec & Malartsik, Ltd.
1761 South Naperville Road, Suite 202
Wheaton, Illinois 60189
   Telephone: 630-871-1414
   Fax: 630-871-1755
   E-Mail: pmmlaw@paulsenmalec.net
   www.paulsenmalec.net

Established: 1982

Insurance Defense, Coverage Issues, Litigation, Automobile, Transportation, Homeowners, Commercial Law, Product Liability, Personal Injury, Residential Real Estate, Wills, Trusts & Estate Planning

Firm Profile: With over 65 years of experience as trial lawyers, we pride ourselves on bringing a case to a successful conclusion while maintaining a commitment to serving the best interests of the client. We understand civil litigation and provide our clients with the most knowledgeable advice on the law.

Insurance Clients

ACUITY	AMEX Assurance Company
Atlantic Mutual Insurance Company	General Casualty Companies
Omni Insurance Group, Inc.	Jewelers Mutual Insurance Company
Safety Insurance Company	SECURA Insurance Companies
Sentry Insurance a Mutual Company	Society Insurance
	West Bend Mutual Insurance Company

Partners

Harvey A. Paulsen — 1953 — DePaul University, B.A., 1974; Tulane University, J.D., 1977 — Admitted to Bar, 1977, Illinois; 1997, U.S. District Court, Northern District of Illinois; U.S. Court of Appeals, Seventh Circuit — Member Illinois State and DuPage County Bar Associations; Council on Litigation Management; Defense Research Institute — E-mail: hpaulsen@paulsenmalec.net

Kenneth J. Malec — 1952 — University of Illinois, B.S., 1974; The John Marshall Law School, J.D., 1982 — Admitted to Bar, 1982, Illinois; 1982, U.S. Court of Appeals, Seventh Circuit — E-mail: kmalec@paulsenmalec.net

Jon P. Malartsik — 1969 — Vanderbilt University, B.A. (cum laude), 1991; DePaul University, J.D., 1995 — Admitted to Bar, 1995, Illinois; 1995, U.S. Court of Appeals, Seventh Circuit — Member Illinois State and DuPage County Bar Associations — E-mail: jmalartsik@paulsenmalec.net

Associates

William G. Nickol — Northern Illinois University, B.S., 2005; Marquette University Law School, J.D., 2008 — Admitted to Bar, 2008, Wisconsin; 2009, Illinois — Member Illinois State Bar Association; State Bar of Wisconsin — E-mail: bnickol@paulsenmalec.net

WINCHESTER † 1,593 Scott Co.

Refer To
Rammelkamp Bradney, P.C.
232 West State
Jacksonville, Illinois 62650
   Telephone: 217-245-6177
   Fax: 217-243-7322
Mailing Address: P.O. Box 550, Jacksonville, IL 62651-0550

Insurance Law, Fire Loss, Arson, First Party Matters, Litigation, Declaratory Judgments, Workers' Compensation, Americans with Disabilities Act, Civil Rights, Construction Litigation, Employment Practices Liability, Trial and Appellate Practice

SEE COMPLETE LISTING UNDER JACKSONVILLE, ILLINOIS (14 MILES)

WOODSTOCK † 24,770 McHenry Co.

McKenna Storer
666 Russel Court, Suite 303
Woodstock, Illinois 60098
   Telephone: 815-334-9690
   Fax: 815-334-9697
   E-Mail: postmaster@mckenna-law.com
   www.mckenna-law.com

(Chicago, IL Office*: 33 North LaSalle Street, 14th Floor, 60602-2610)
   (Tel: 312-558-3900)
   (Fax: 312-558-8348)

Established: 1954

General Civil Trial and Appellate Practice, Insurance Defense, Insurance Coverage, Product Liability, Commercial Liability, Environmental Law, Toxic Torts, Employment Law, Professional Malpractice, Premises Liability, Litigation, Medical Malpractice, Examinations Under Oath, Mediation, Professional Errors and Omissions, Professional Liability (Non-Medical) Defense

Firm Profile: McKenna Storer, established in 1954, has been serving insurance companies, Fortune 500 companies, local businesses and individuals in Chicago and the surrounding area. The Firm focuses on cost effective business and litigation solutions.

(See listing under Chicago, IL for additional information)

The following firms also service this area.

Mateer Goff & Honzel LLP
401 West State Street, Suite 400
Rockford, Illinois 61101
   Telephone: 815-965-7745
   Fax: 815-965-7749

Insurance Law, Fire, Casualty Insurance Law, Defense Litigation, Trial and Appellate Practice

SEE COMPLETE LISTING UNDER ROCKFORD, ILLINOIS (55 MILES)

INDIANA

CAPITAL: INDIANAPOLIS

COUNTIES AND COUNTY SEATS

County	County Seat
Adams	Decatur
Allen	Fort Wayne
Bartholomew	Columbus
Benton	Fowler
Blackford	Hartford City
Boone	Lebanon
Brown	Nashville
Carroll	Delphi
Cass	Logansport
Clark	Jeffersonville
Clay	Brazil
Clinton	Frankfort
Crawford	English
Daviess	Washington
Dearborn	Lawrenceburg
Decatur	Greensburg
De Kalb	Auburn
Delaware	Muncie
Dubois	Jasper
Elkhart	Goshen
Fayette	Connersville
Floyd	New Albany
Fountain	Covington
Franklin	Brookville
Fulton	Rochester
Gibson	Princeton
Grant	Marion
Greene	Bloomfield
Hamilton	Noblesville
Hancock	Greenfield
Harrison	Corydon
Hendricks	Danville
Henry	New Castle
Howard	Kokomo
Huntington	Huntington
Jackson	Brownstown
Jasper	Rensselaer
Jay	Portland
Jefferson	Madison
Jennings	Vernon
Johnson	Franklin
Knox	Vincennes
Kosciusko	Warsaw
Lagrange	Lagrange
Lake	Crown Point
La Porte	La Porte
Lawrence	Bedford
Madison	Anderson
Marion	Indianapolis
Marshall	Plymouth
Martin	Shoals
Miami	Peru
Monroe	Bloomington
Montgomery	Crawfordsville
Morgan	Martinsville
Newton	Kentland
Noble	Albion
Ohio	Rising Sun
Orange	Paoli
Owen	Spencer
Parke	Rockville
Perry	Cannelton
Pike	Petersburg
Porter	Valparaiso
Posey	Mount Vernon
Pulaski	Winamac
Putnam	Greencastle
Randolph	Winchester
Ripley	Versailles
Rush	Rushville
St. Joseph	South Bend
Scott	Scottsburg
Shelby	Shelbyville
Spencer	Rockport
Starke	Knox
Steuben	Angola
Sullivan	Sullivan
Switzerland	Vevay
Tippecanoe	Lafayette
Tipton	Tipton
Union	Liberty
Vanderburgh	Evansville
Vermillion	Newport
Vigo	Terre Haute
Wabash	Wabash
Warren	Williamsport
Warrick	Boonville
Washington	Salem
Wayne	Richmond
Wells	Bluffton
White	Monticello
Whitley	Columbia City

In the text that follows "†" indicates County Seats.

Our files contain additional verified data on the firms listed herein. This additional information is available on request.

A.M. BEST COMPANY

INDIANA

BEDFORD † 13,413 Lawrence Co.

Refer To

Ferguson & Ferguson
403 East Sixth Street
Bloomington, Indiana 47408-4098
  Telephone: 812-332-2113
  Fax: 812-334-3892

Insurance Defense, School Law, Commercial Law, General Liability, Product Liability, Premises Liability, Motor Vehicle, Uninsured and Underinsured Motorist, Life, Accident and Health, General Civil Trial and Appellate Practice, Employment Issues, Including ADA, Business and Real Estate Litigation, Municipal and Governmental Entity Liability, including §1983 Actions

SEE COMPLETE LISTING UNDER BLOOMINGTON, INDIANA (25 MILES)

Refer To

Kahn, Dees, Donovan & Kahn, LLP
501 Main Street, Suite 305
Evansville, Indiana 47708
  Telephone: 812-423-3183
  Fax: 812-423-3841

Mailing Address: P.O. Box 3646, Evansville, IN 47735-3646

Asbestos Litigation, Automobile, Construction Law, Coverage Issues, Environmental Law, Insurance Defense, General Liability, Labor and Employment, Mass Tort, Medical Malpractice, Personal Injury, Premises Liability, Product Liability, Property, Public Entities, Self-Insured, Subrogation, Workers' Compensation

SEE COMPLETE LISTING UNDER EVANSVILLE, INDIANA (125 MILES)

BLOOMFIELD † 2,405 Greene Co.

Refer To

Ferguson & Ferguson
403 East Sixth Street
Bloomington, Indiana 47408-4098
  Telephone: 812-332-2113
  Fax: 812-334-3892

Insurance Defense, School Law, Commercial Law, General Liability, Product Liability, Premises Liability, Motor Vehicle, Uninsured and Underinsured Motorist, Life, Accident and Health, General Civil Trial and Appellate Practice, Employment Issues, Including ADA, Business and Real Estate Litigation, Municipal and Governmental Entity Liability, including §1983 Actions

SEE COMPLETE LISTING UNDER BLOOMINGTON, INDIANA (30 MILES)

BLOOMINGTON † 80,405 Monroe Co.

Ferguson & Ferguson

403 East Sixth Street
Bloomington, Indiana 47408-4098
  Telephone: 812-332-2113
  Fax: 812-334-3892
  Mobile: 812-219-8644
  E-Mail: DLF@ferglaw.com
  www.ferglaw.com

Established: 1953

Insurance Defense, School Law, Commercial Law, General Liability, Product Liability, Premises Liability, Motor Vehicle, Uninsured and Underinsured Motorist, Life, Accident and Health, General Civil Trial and Appellate Practice, Employment Issues, Including ADA, Business and Real Estate Litigation, Municipal and Governmental Entity Liability, including §1983 Actions

Firm Profile: For over sixty years, the firm of Ferguson & Ferguson and its predecessors have been providing quality legal services to the insurance industry including defense of individual and corporate insureds in litigation and pre-litigation stages. In building relationships with its insurance clients, Ferguson & Ferguson works on an early defense strategy with the client to quickly identify cases which could be resolved early to limit litigation costs.

Ferguson & Ferguson, Bloomington, IN   (Continued)

Ferguson & Ferguson regularly provides full-service representation in state and federal litigation and appeals to individuals and businesses, including personal injury, property damage, products liability, insurance coverage issues and disputes, and workplace harassment and discrimination claims. Ferguson & Ferguson's clients include fire departments, municipalities, construction companies, trucking companies, and school corporations around the state.

Attorneys of the firm are admitted to both the Southern and Northern Federal Districts of Indiana. Attorneys of the firm are members of the DRI and the Defense Trial Counsel of Indiana.

See our website for more information: www.ferglaw.com.

Insurance Clients

AAA Insurance Claims - Mid-Atlantic
Canal Insurance Company
Daily Underwriters of America
FCCI Insurance Company
Glatfelter Insurance Group
GoAmerica Auto Insurance
Pafco General Insurance Company
United National Insurance Company
American National Property and Casualty Company
Citizens Insurance Company of America
General Agents Insurance Company of America, Inc.
Indiana Farmers Mutual Insurance Company

Non-Insurance Clients

BASF Corporation
Fairmont Homes, Incorporated
Indiana Insurance Guaranty Association
Missouri Insurance Guaranty Association
Cook, Incorporated
Gallagher Bassett Services, Inc.
Indiana University Risk Management
VFIS Claims Management

Partners

James H. Ferguson — (1928-2001)

David L. Ferguson — Indiana University, B.S. (with distinction), 1978; J.D., 1981 — Beta Gamma Sigma — Metz Scholar, 1974-1978 — Admitted to Bar, 1981, Indiana; U.S. District Court, Northern and Southern Districts of Indiana; U.S. Court of Appeals, Seventh Circuit; U.S. Supreme Court — Member American Bar Association (Business Law, Tort & Insurance, Labor & Employment Law, Litigation, and Real Property, Trust & Estate Law Practice Sections); Indiana State and Monroe County Bar Associations; Defense Trial Counsel of Indiana (Rules, and Employment Law Committees); Defense Research Institute — E-mail: DLF@ferglaw.com

Associates

Christine L. Zook — Indiana University-Bloomington, B.A. (Dean's List), 2007; Indiana University School of Law-Bloomington, J.D., 2010 — Admitted to Bar, 2011, Indiana — Served on Federal Communications Law Journal in Law School

Megan J. Schueler — Franklin College, B.A., 1997; University of Nebraska College of Law, J.D., 2000 — Admitted to Bar, 2012, Indiana; 2003, West Virginia (Inactive); 2000, Missouri (Inactive)

Of Counsel

Stephen L. Ferguson — Chairman of the Board, Cook Group, Inc.

BOONVILLE † 6,246 Warrick Co.

Refer To

Kahn, Dees, Donovan & Kahn, LLP
501 Main Street, Suite 305
Evansville, Indiana 47708
  Telephone: 812-423-3183
  Fax: 812-423-3841

Mailing Address: P.O. Box 3646, Evansville, IN 47735-3646

Asbestos Litigation, Automobile, Construction Law, Coverage Issues, Environmental Law, Insurance Defense, General Liability, Labor and Employment, Mass Tort, Medical Malpractice, Personal Injury, Premises Liability, Product Liability, Property, Public Entities, Self-Insured, Subrogation, Workers' Compensation

SEE COMPLETE LISTING UNDER EVANSVILLE, INDIANA (19 MILES)

EAST CHICAGO INDIANA

BRAZIL † 7,912 Clay Co.
Refer To
Cox, Zwerner, Gambill & Sullivan, LLP
511 Wabash Avenue
Terre Haute, Indiana 47807
   Telephone: 812-232-6003
   Fax: 812-232-6567

Insurance Defense, Trial Practice

SEE COMPLETE LISTING UNDER TERRE HAUTE, INDIANA (16 MILES)

CARMEL 79,191 Hamilton Co.

House Reynolds & Faust, LLP

11711 N. Pennsylvania Street, Suite 190
Carmel, Indiana 46032
   Telephone: 317-564-8490
   Fax: 317-564-8499
   E-Mail: treynolds@housereynoldsfaust.com
   www.housereynoldsfaust.com

Established: 2012

Civil Litigation, Mediation, Arbitration, Commercial Litigation, Wills, Trusts, Estate Litigation, Municipal Law, Insurance, Insurance Coverage, Bad Faith, Appellate, Professional Liability, Business & Corporate Counseling, Debtor & Creditor Law

Firm Profile: We serve our client's needs with a sense of urgency; we are service oriented; and provide high quality work. We hire great people, who are also great attorneys, paralegals and assistants. We train our people so they improve and grow personally and professionally.

Insurance Clients

The Bar Plan	Celina Insurance Group
CNA	Harleysville Lake States Insurance
Occidental Wilshire Insurance	Company
Company	Zurich North America

Partners

Briane M. House — 1957 — Wabash College, B.A. (cum laude), 1979; Indiana University Robert H. McKinney School of Law, J.D., 1982 — Admitted to Bar, 1982, Indiana; U.S. District Court, Northern and Southern Districts of Indiana; 1992, U.S. Court of Appeals, Seventh Circuit; U.S. Supreme Court — Member American, Indiana State and Indianapolis Bar Associations — E-mail: bhouse@housereynoldsfaust.com

Thomas Todd Reynolds — 1954 — Indiana University, B.S., 1976; M.P.A., 1981; Indiana University School of Law-Bloomington, J.D., 1981 — Phi Alpha Alpha — Admitted to Bar, 1981, Indiana; U.S. District Court, Southern District of Indiana; 1994, U.S. District Court, Northern District of Indiana — Member Indiana State and Indianapolis (Litigation Section Chairman, 1989) Bar Associations; Indianapolis Law Club; Defense Trial Counsel of Indiana; Defense Research Institute; American Board of Trial Advocates — Federal Executive Institute - Senior Executive Education Program — E-mail: treynolds@housereynoldsfaust.com

Raymond L. Faust — 1950 — Indiana University-Bloomington, A.B. (Departmental Honors), 1973; Indiana University Maurer School of Law, J.D. (cum laude), 1976 — Admitted to Bar, 1976, Indiana; U.S. District Court, Southern District of Indiana; 1979, U.S. Supreme Court — Member American, Indiana State and Indianapolis Bar Associations; Defense Research Institute — E-mail: rfaust@housereynoldsfaust.com

Associate

R. Daniel Faust — 1983 — Wabash College, B.A. (magna cum laude), 2005; Indiana University Maurer School of Law, J.D. (cum laude), 2009 — Admitted to Bar, 2009, Indiana; U.S. District Court, Northern and Southern Districts of Indiana — Member Indiana State Bar Association — E-mail: dfaust@housereynoldsfaust.com

Of Counsel

Dorie Hertzel Maryan — 1973 — University of Illinois at Urbana-Champaign, B.A., 1995; Indiana University School of Law, J.D., 2000 — Admitted to

House Reynolds & Faust, LLP, Carmel, IN   (Continued)
Bar, 2000, Indiana; U.S. District Court, Northern and Southern Districts of Indiana — Member Indiana State Bar Association — E-mail: dmaryan@housereynoldsfaust.com

Thomas R. Haley III — 1961 — Indiana University, B.A., 1984; Indiana University School of Law-Indianapolis, J.D., 1987 — Admitted to Bar, 1987, Indiana; U.S. District Court, Northern and Southern Districts of Indiana; 1988, U.S. Court of Appeals, Seventh Circuit — E-mail: thaley@housereynoldsfaust.com

CLINTON 4,893 Vermillion Co.
Refer To
Cox, Zwerner, Gambill & Sullivan, LLP
511 Wabash Avenue
Terre Haute, Indiana 47807
   Telephone: 812-232-6003
   Fax: 812-232-6567

Insurance Defense, Trial Practice

SEE COMPLETE LISTING UNDER TERRE HAUTE, INDIANA (20 MILES)

COLUMBUS † 44,061 Bartholomew Co.
Refer To
Ferguson & Ferguson
403 East Sixth Street
Bloomington, Indiana 47408-4098
   Telephone: 812-332-2113
   Fax: 812-334-3892

Insurance Defense, School Law, Commercial Law, General Liability, Product Liability, Premises Liability, Motor Vehicle, Uninsured and Underinsured Motorist, Life, Accident and Health, General Civil Trial and Appellate Practice, Employment Issues, Including ADA, Business and Real Estate Litigation, Municipal and Governmental Entity Liability, including §1983 Actions

SEE COMPLETE LISTING UNDER BLOOMINGTON, INDIANA (37 MILES)

CROWN POINT † 27,317 Lake Co.
Refer To
Spangler, Jennings & Dougherty, P.C.
8396 Mississippi Street
Merrillville, Indiana 46410-6398
   Telephone: 219-769-2323
   Fax: 219-769-5007

Insurance Law, Fire, Property, Casualty, Surety, Life Insurance, Environmental Law, Toxic Torts, Product Liability, Professional Liability, Workers' Compensation, Coverage Issues, Appellate Practice, Subrogation, Medical Malpractice Defense, Mortgage Foreclosure

SEE COMPLETE LISTING UNDER MERRILLVILLE, INDIANA (6 MILES)

EAST CHICAGO 29,698 Lake Co.
Refer To
Spangler, Jennings & Dougherty, P.C.
8396 Mississippi Street
Merrillville, Indiana 46410-6398
   Telephone: 219-769-2323
   Fax: 219-769-5007

Insurance Law, Fire, Property, Casualty, Surety, Life Insurance, Environmental Law, Toxic Torts, Product Liability, Professional Liability, Workers' Compensation, Coverage Issues, Appellate Practice, Subrogation, Medical Malpractice Defense, Mortgage Foreclosure

SEE COMPLETE LISTING UNDER MERRILLVILLE, INDIANA (15 MILES)

INDIANA   EVANSVILLE

EVANSVILLE † 117,429 Vanderburgh Co.

Fine & Hatfield
A Professional Corporation

520 N.W. Second Street
Evansville, Indiana 47708
Telephone: 812-425-3592
Fax: 812-421-4269
E-Mail: fine@fine-hatfield.com
www.fine-hatfield.com

Insurance Defense, Commercial General Liability, Construction Litigation, Property and Casualty, Product Liability, Professional Malpractice, Workers' Compensation, Employment Practices Liability

Firm Profile: Established in 1921, Fine & Hatfield has an extensive insurance defense practice throughout the Tri-State area, which encompasses southern Indiana, southeastern Illinois and western Kentucky. The firm has heavily invested in technology and continues to lead the way in adapting to change in the legal industry. The Firm's case handling philosophy includes an emphasis on frequent communication, both with the insurance carrier and the insured, flexible fee arrangements, and the ability to produce invoices in any format required for electronic billing.

Insurance Clients

Carolina Casualty Insurance Company
CNA Insurance Company
Hartford Insurance Company
Westfield Insurance Company
Zurich American Insurance Group
The Cincinnati Insurance Companies
CUNA Mutual Group
The Medical Protective Company
Zenith Insurance Company

Non-Insurance Clients

E & O Professionals

Partners

Danny E. Glass — 1950 — Hanover College, B.A., 1973; Indiana University School of Law, J.D., 1976 — Phi Eta Sigma — Admitted to Bar, 1977, Indiana; 1994, Illinois; 1995, Kentucky; 1977, U.S. District Court, Southern District of Indiana; 1994, U.S. District Court, Southern District of Illinois; U.S. Court of Appeals, Seventh Circuit; 1995, U.S. District Court, Western District of Kentucky — Member Indiana State, Illinois State, Kentucky and Evansville Bar Associations; Fellow, American College of Trial Lawyers — E-mail: deg@fine-hatfield.com

Thomas H. Bryan — 1944 — Purdue University, B.S.M.E., 1966; Indiana University School of Law, J.D., 1969 — Admitted to Bar, 1969, Indiana; 1971, Illinois; 1969, U.S. District Court, Southern District of Indiana; 1971, U.S. District Court, Northern District of Illinois; U.S. Court of Appeals, Seventh Circuit; 1984, U.S. Supreme Court — Member Indiana State, Illinois State and Evansville Bar Associations; Fellow, American College of Trial Lawyers — E-mail: thb@fine-hatfield.com

H. Linwood "Lin" Shannon, III — 1970 — Centre College of Kentucky, B.A., 1992; Louis D. Brandeis School of Law, University of Louisville, J.D., 1995 — Admitted to Bar, 1995, Kentucky; Indiana; 1995, U.S. District Court, Northern and Southern Districts of Indiana; U.S. District Court, Western District of Kentucky — Member Indiana State, Kentucky, Evansville and Henderson Bar Associations — E-mail: hls@fine-hatfield.com

Members

John J. Kreighbaum — 1952 — State University of New York, B.S., 1989; Indiana University School of Law-Indianapolis, J.D. (cum laude), 1994 — Admitted to Bar, 1994, Indiana; 1994, U.S. District Court, Northern and Southern Districts of Indiana; 1994, U.S. Court of Appeals, Seventh Circuit — Member Indiana State and Evansville Bar Associations — U.S. Navy, 1970-1979 — E-mail: jjk@fine-hatfield.com

Adam S. Glass — 1978 — Centre College of Kentucky, B.A., 2001; Thomas M. Cooley Law School, J.D., 2007 — Admitted to Bar, 2007, Indiana; 2007, U.S. District Court, Northern and Southern Districts of Indiana — Member Indiana State and Evansville Bar Associations — E-mail: asg@fine-hatfield.com

Jeremy B. Morris — 1978 — Creighton University, B.S., 2000; Creighton University School of Law, J.D., 2003 — Admitted to Bar, 2003, Nebraska; 2004,

Fine & Hatfield, A Professional Corporation, Evansville, IN (Continued)

Iowa; 2011, Indiana; 2003, U.S. District Court, District of Nebraska; 2011, U.S. District Court, Southern District of Indiana — Member Indiana State and Evansville Bar Associations — E-mail: jbm@fine-hatfield.com

Associate

Andrew E. Skinner — 1983 — University of Southern Indiana, B.S. (cum laude), 2006; Indiana University School of Law, J.D. (magna cum laude), 2014 — Admitted to Bar, 2014, Indiana — Member Indiana State and Evansville Bar Associations — E-mail: aes@fine-hatfield.com

Kahn, Dees, Donovan & Kahn, LLP

501 Main Street, Suite 305
Evansville, Indiana 47708
Telephone: 812-423-3183
Fax: 812-423-3841
E-Mail: EvvLaw@KDDK.com
www.KDDK.com

Established: 1908

Asbestos Litigation, Automobile, Construction Law, Coverage Issues, Environmental Law, Insurance Defense, General Liability, Labor and Employment, Mass Tort, Medical Malpractice, Personal Injury, Premises Liability, Product Liability, Property, Public Entities, Self-Insured, Subrogation, Workers' Compensation

Firm Profile: Kahn, Dees, Donovan & Kahn is an experienced full-service law firm that serves the legal needs of regional, national and international clients including Fortune 500 companies, small businesses and individuals. We foster client relationships to successfully provide results-oriented legal services.

Insurance Clients

ACUITY
American International Group, Inc.
Chubb/Federal Insurance Company
COUNTRY Mutual Insurance Company
General Accident Group
Illinois Casualty Company
Mitsui Sumitomo Marine Management (USA), Inc.
St. Paul Mercury Insurance Company
State Farm Insurance Companies
Zurich American Insurance Group
Allstate Insurance Company
Chartis Insurance
Chubb Group of Insurance Companies
Farm Bureau Insurance Companies
Hanover Insurance Group
Mendota Insurance Company
St. Paul Fire and Marine Insurance Company
SECURA Insurance Companies
Shelter Insurance Companies
The Travelers Companies, Inc.

Partners

Jeffrey W. Ahlers — DePauw University, B.A., 1984; Valparaiso University School of Law, J.D., 1987 — Admitted to Bar, 1987, Indiana; U.S. District Court, Northern and Southern Districts of Indiana; U.S. District Court, Western District of Kentucky; 2002, U.S. District Court, Southern District of Illinois — Member American, Indiana State and Evansville Bar Associations; Defense Trial Counsel of Indiana; American Inns of Court — Practice Areas: Civil Litigation; Mediation; Civil Rights; Civil Tort; Commercial Litigation; Construction Litigation; Employment Litigation; Environmental Liability; Insurance Coverage; Insurance Defense; Medical Malpractice Defense; Personal Injury Litigation — E-mail: jahlers@KDDK.com

Christopher D. Lee — DePauw University, B.A., 1989; Indiana University Maurer School of Law, J.D., 1993 — Admitted to Bar, 1993, Indiana; U.S. District Court, Northern and Southern Districts of Indiana; U.S. Court of Appeals, Seventh Circuit; U.S. Supreme Court — Member Indiana State and Evansville Bar Associations; Defense Trial Counsel of Indiana; National Institute of Trial Advocacy; Defense Research Institute; American Inns of Court — AV Preeminent; Super Lawyers — U.S. Military Veteran; Bronze Star Recipient — Practice Areas: Civil Litigation; Trial Practice; Tort Litigation; Insurance Defense; Mass Tort; Medical Malpractice Defense — E-mail: clee@KDDK.com

Greg J. Freyberger — Indiana State University, B.S., 1998; Indiana University

EVANSVILLE   INDIANA

Kahn, Dees, Donovan & Kahn, LLP, Evansville, IN
(Continued)

Robert H. McKinney School of Law, J.D., 2001 — Admitted to Bar, 2001, Indiana; U.S. District Court, Northern and Southern Districts of Indiana — Member Indiana State and Evansville Bar Associations; Defense Trial Counsel of Indiana; American Inns of Court — AV Preeminent; Super Lawyers Rising Star; Best Lawyers in America — Practice Areas: Civil Litigation; Appeals; Insurance Defense; Trial Practice; Workers' Compensation; Subrogation — E-mail: gfreyberger@KDDK.com

Stephen S. Lavallo — Denison University, B.A., 1983; Washington University School of Law, J.D., 1986 — Admitted to Bar, 1987, Indiana; U.S. District Court, Southern District of Indiana; U.S. Supreme Court — Member Indiana State and Evansville Bar Associations; Defense Trial Counsel of Indiana — AV Preeminent; Best Lawyers in Indiana Worker's Compensation Law — Practice Areas: Workers' Compensation; Mediation — E-mail: slavallo@KDDK.com

Michele S. Bryant — DePauw University, B.A. Political Science, 1986; Indiana University Maurer School of Law, J.D., 1988 — Admitted to Bar, 1989, Indiana; U.S. District Court, Northern and Southern Districts of Indiana; U.S. Court of Appeals, Seventh Circuit; U.S. Supreme Court — Member Indiana State and Evansville Bar Associations; Bar Association of the Seventh Federal Circuit; American Health Lawyers Association; Defense Research Institute; Defense Trial Counsel of Indiana; International Association of Defense Counsel — AV Preeminent; Super Lawyers — Practice Areas: Medical Malpractice Defense; Health Care; Litigation — E-mail: mbryant@KDDK.com

(This firm is also listed in the Subrogation section of this directory)

Kightlinger & Gray, LLP

7220 Eagle Crest Boulevard
Evansville, Indiana 47715
 Telephone: 812-474-4400
 Fax: 812-474-4414
 E-Mail: info@k-glaw.com
 www.k-glaw.com

(Indianapolis, IN Office*: One Indiana Square, Suite 300, 211 North
 Pennsylvania Street, 46204)
 (Tel: 317-638-4521)
 (Fax: 317-636-5917)
(New Albany, IN Office*: Bonterra Building, Suite 200, 3620 Blackiston
 Boulevard, 47150)
 (Tel: 812-949-2300)
 (Fax: 812-949-8556)
(Merrillville, IN Office*: Merrillville Corporate Center, 8001 Broadway,
 Suite 100, 46410)
 (Tel: 219-769-0413)
 (Fax: 219-769-0798)
(Louisville, KY Office*: 312 South Fourth Street, Suite 700, 40202)
 (Tel: 502-442-2295)
 (Fax: 502-442-2703)

Established: 1946

Insurance Defense, Insurance Litigation, Defense Litigation, Litigation, Insurance Law, Coverage Issues, Carrier Defense, Self-Insured Defense, Comprehensive General Liability, Trial and Appellate Practice, State and Federal Courts, General Civil Trial and Appellate Practice, Casualty Defense, Product Liability, Workers' Compensation, Employment Law, Subrogation, Toxic Torts, Aviation, Surety, Administrative Law, Agent/Broker Liability, Bad Faith, Business Law, Automobile Liability, Trucking Law, Asbestos Litigation, Construction Law, Corporate Law, Complex Litigation, Construction Litigation, Coverage Analysis, First and Third Party Defense, Fire Loss, Professional Liability, Malpractice, Agency Defense, Agent and Brokers Errors and Omissions, Medical Malpractice, School Law, Transportation, Real Estate, Bankruptcy, Municipal Liability, Class Actions, Mediation, Securities Litigation and Arbitration

Kightlinger & Gray, LLP, Evansville, IN   (Continued)

Insurance Clients

American International Group, Inc.	Auto-Owners Insurance Company
Chubb Group of Insurance Companies	Grange Mutual Insurance Company
Liberty Mutual Insurance	Grinnell Mutual Reinsurance Company
State Farm Fire and Casualty Company	State Farm Mutual Automobile Insurance Company

Non-Insurance Clients

Aon Technical Insurance Services	Claims Management, Inc.
Continental Loss Adjusting Services	Jeff Ellis & Associates, Inc.
	Western General Management, Inc.

Partners

Sacha L. Armstrong — University of Maryland, B.A., 1999; Louis D. Brandeis School of Law, University of Louisville, J.D., 2003 — Admitted to Bar, 2003, Kentucky; 2004, Indiana; U.S. District Court, Western District of Kentucky; U.S. District Court, Northern and Southern Districts of Indiana — Tel: 812-474-4400 ext. 6319 — E-mail: sarmstrong@k-glaw.com

Brent R. Weil — Purdue University, B.S., 1982; Valparaiso University School of Law, J.D., 1985 — Admitted to Bar, 1985, Indiana; Michigan; U.S. District Court, Northern and Southern Districts of Indiana; U.S. Court of Appeals, Seventh Circuit; U.S. Supreme Court — Tel: 812-474-4400 ext. 6321 — E-mail: bweil@k-glaw.com

Associates

Adam S. Ira — Indiana University, B.A., 2011; Indiana University Robert H. McKinney School of Law, J.D., 2014 — Admitted to Bar, 2014, Indiana; U.S. District Court, Southern District of Indiana — Tel: 812-474-4400 ext. 6313 — E-mail: aira@k-glaw.com

Krystal M. Lechner — Indiana University, B.A., 2008; Indiana University School of Law, J.D., 2011 — Admitted to Bar, 2011, Indiana; U.S. District Court, Northern and Southern Districts of Indiana — Tel: 812-474-4400 ext. 6317 — E-mail: klechner@k-glaw.com

(This firm is also listed in the Subrogation section of this directory)

Statham Allega and Jessen, LLP

915 Main Street, Suite 400
Evansville, Indiana 47708
 Telephone: 812-425-5223
 Fax: 812-421-4238
 E-Mail: saj@statham-aj.com

Insurance Defense

Insurance Clients

American Family Mutual Insurance Company	American States Insurance Company
Bituminous Insurance Companies	CNA Insurance Companies
Colonial Penn Insurance Company	Commercial Union Insurance Company
Companion Insurance Company	Federated Mutual Insurance Company
Farm Bureau Insurance Company	
Fremont Casualty Insurance Company	Globe Indemnity Company
Grain Dealers Mutual Insurance Company	Great Central Insurance Company
	Gulf Insurance Company
Hartford Accident and Indemnity Company	Kentucky Farm Bureau Mutual Insurance Company
Lloyd's	The Medical Protective Company
Meridian Mutual Insurance Company	Monroe Guaranty Insurance Company
National Indemnity Company	Northland Insurance Company
Ohio Casualty Insurance Company	Preferred Risk Group
Royal Globe Insurance Company	St. Paul Insurance Company
Shelter Insurance Companies	Standard Mutual Insurance Company
State Auto Insurance Companies	
Statesman Insurance Company	U.S. Insurance Group

Firm Members

William Statham — 1932 — University of Evansville, B.A., 1952; Indiana University, J.D. (with distinction), 1956 — Admitted to Bar, 1956, Indiana — Member American, Indiana State and Evansville Bar Associations; American Board of Trial Advocates

INDIANA FORT WAYNE

Statham Allega and Jessen, LLP, Evansville, IN
(Continued)

Gerald F. Allega — 1953 — Indiana State University, B.S. (magna cum laude), 1974; Indiana University, J.D. (magna cum laude), 1977 — Admitted to Bar, 1977, Indiana — Member Indiana State and Evansville Bar Associations; Defense Trial Counsel of Indiana; American Board of Trial Advocates

Douglas V. Jessen — 1946 — Iowa State University, B.S., 1969; Indiana University, J.D. (cum laude), 1980 — Admitted to Bar, 1981, Indiana — Member Indiana State and Evansville Bar Associations

FORT WAYNE † 253,691 Allen Co.

Barrett & McNagny LLP

215 East Berry Street
Fort Wayne, Indiana 46802
Telephone: 260-423-9551
Fax: 260-423-8920
www.barrettlaw.com
E-Mail: info@barrettlaw.com

Accident, Alternative Dispute Resolution, Appellate Practice, Business Litigation, Civil Rights, Complex Commercial Litigation, Construction Litigation, Copyright and Trademark Law, Employment Law, Environmental Law, ERISA, General Practice, Insurance Coverage, Insurance Defense, Intellectual Property, Litigation, Mediation, Medical Malpractice, Motor Vehicle, Nursing Home Litigation, Patents, Product Liability, Premises Liability, Transportation, Workers' Compensation

Firm Profile: Founded in 1876, Barrett & McNagny LLP is among the largest northeastern Indiana law firms and one of the oldest law partnerships in the state. The firm represents insurance carriers and self insureds throughout Northern Indiana and the tri-state region. The firm's client base is a cross-section of the Fort Wayne business community including banks, utilities, insurance companies, health care providers, manufacturers, and media companies, as well as many family-owned and closely held businesses.

Insurance Clients

ACE Westchester Specialty Group
Aetna Insurance Company
Allied Group Insurance
American Home Insurance Company
Celina Group
Chicago Motor Club Insurance Company
Citizens Insurance Company of America
EMC Insurance Company
Erie Insurance Company
Farm Bureau Insurance Company
Farmers Insurance Group
Fireman's Fund Insurance Company
GEICO
Government Employees Insurance Company
The Hartford Insurance Group
Hastings Mutual Insurance Company
Indiana Lumbermens Mutual Insurance Company
Interstate Assurance Company
Lancer Insurance Company
Lincoln National Life Insurance Company
Markel Southwest
MetLife Auto & Home
National Interstate Insurance Company
OHIC Insurance Company
Pekin Insurance Company
Progressive Casualty Insurance Company
Prudential Property and Casualty Insurance Company
Admiral Insurance Company
Aetna Life and Casualty Company
Allstate Insurance Company
Auto-Owners Insurance Company
Canal Insurance Company
Central Mutual Insurance Company
Church Mutual Insurance Company
Cincinnati Insurance Company
CNA Insurance Company
Disability Reinsurance Management Services, Inc.
Everest National Insurance Company
Federated Insurance Company
Foremost Insurance Company
Frankenmuth Mutual Insurance Company
GRE Insurance Group
Harco National Insurance Company
Indiana Farm Bureau
Indiana Insurance Company
Interinsurance Exchange of the Automobile Club
K & K Insurance Group, Inc.
Liberty Mutual Insurance
Madison National Life Insurance Company, Inc.
The Medical Protective Company
Metropolitan Insurance Company
Nationwide Insurance
Nautilus Insurance Company
Pafco General Insurance Company
Philadelphia Insurance Companies
Prudential Insurance Company of America
Reliant American Insurance Company

Barrett & McNagny LLP, Fort Wayne, IN (Continued)

Sagamore Insurance Company
Sentry Insurance a Mutual Company
Standard Security Life Insurance Company of New York
State Farm Insurance Company
Travelers Insurance Companies
United National Group
Westfield Companies
Zurich Insurance Company
Selective Insurance Company of America
Shelter Mutual Insurance Company
State Auto Insurance Company
State Farm Fire and Casualty Company
Trident Insurance
Unitrin Property and Casualty Insurance Group

Lead Counsel for

Brotherhood Mutual Insurance Company

Representative Non Insurance Clients

BF Goodrich Company
Extendicare Health Services, Inc.
K & K Insurance Agency
Lake City Bank
Overnite Transportation Company
Do it Best Corp.
Indiana Insurance Guaranty Association
OmniSource Corp.
Steel Dynamics, Inc.

Litigation Partners

Thomas M. Kimbrough — 1954 — Indiana University, B.A., 1977; Indiana University School of Law, J.D. (magna cum laude), 1980 — Admitted to Bar, 1980, Indiana; U.S. District Court, Northern and Southern Districts of Indiana; U.S. Court of Appeals, Seventh and Eleventh Circuits; U.S. District Court, Northern District of Ohio; U.S. District Court, Middle District of Florida; U.S. District Court, District of New Jersey; U.S. District Court, District of Connecticut; U.S. Court of Appeals, Sixth Circuit — Member Defense Trial Counsel of Indiana; American College of Trial Lawyers — Practice Areas: Labor and Employment; Insurance Defense; Business Litigation — E-mail: tmk@barrettlaw.com

Thomas A. Herr — 1956 — Simpson College, B.A. (cum laude), 1978; Drake University Law School, J.D., 1981 — Admitted to Bar, 1982, Iowa; 1984, Indiana; 1985, U.S. District Court, Northern and Southern Districts of Indiana; 1982, U.S. District Court, Northern and Southern Districts of Iowa; 1999, U.S. District Court, Southern District of Ohio; U.S. District Court, Western District of Missouri; 1999, U.S. District Court, Western District of Michigan — Practice Areas: Professional Negligence; Copyright and Trademark Law; Business Litigation; Complex Litigation; Construction Litigation — E-mail: tah@barrettlaw.com

Robert T. Keen, Jr. — 1957 — University of Notre Dame, B.A. (cum laude), 1979; University of Notre Dame Law School, J.D., 1982 — Admitted to Bar, 1982, Indiana; U.S. District Court, Northern and Southern Districts of Indiana; U.S. Court of Appeals, Seventh Circuit; U.S. Supreme Court — Member American College of Trial Lawyers; Defense Trial Counsel of Indiana; Federation of Defense and Corporate Counsel; Defense Research Institute — Practice Areas: Civil Litigation; Civil Rights; Commercial Litigation; Employment Litigation; Governmental Liability; Insurance Defense; Premises Liability; Product Liability — E-mail: rtk@barrettlaw.com

Anthony M. Stites — 1963 — The University of Toledo, B.B.A., 1985; University of Notre Dame, J.D., 1988 — Admitted to Bar, 1988, Indiana; 1989, Ohio; 1988, U.S. District Court, Northern and Southern Districts of Indiana; U.S. Court of Appeals, Seventh Circuit; 1989, U.S. District Court, Northern District of Ohio; 2010, U.S. District Court, Eastern District of Michigan — Practice Areas: Labor and Employment; Litigation; Transportation; Alternative Dispute Resolution; Insurance Defense; Mediation — E-mail: ams@barrettlaw.com

Kevin K. Fitzharris — 1965 — Purdue University, B.A., 1987; University of Notre Dame, J.D., 1990 — Phi Beta Kappa — Admitted to Bar, 1990, Indiana; U.S. District Court, Northern and Southern Districts of Indiana — Member Defense Trial Counsel of Indiana; Defense Research Institute — Practice Areas: Civil Litigation; Business Litigation; Alternative Dispute Resolution; Workers' Compensation; Insurance Defense — E-mail: kkf@barrettlaw.com

Cathleen M. Shrader — 1969 — Indiana University, B.S. (cum laude), 1990; Duke University, J.D., 1994 — Admitted to Bar, 1994, Indiana; U.S. District Court, Northern and Southern Districts of Indiana; U.S. Court of Appeals, Seventh and Eleventh Circuits; U.S. Supreme Court; U.S. District Court, Western District of Michigan — Practice Areas: Appellate Practice; Business Litigation; Complex Commercial Litigation — E-mail: cms@barrettlaw.com

H. Joseph Cohen — 1970 — Indiana University-Bloomington, B.S., 1993; Indiana University-Indianapolis, J.D., 1996 — Admitted to Bar, 1996, Indiana; U.S. District Court, Northern and Southern Districts of Indiana; 1997, U.S. Court of Appeals, Sixth and Seventh Circuits — Member Defense Trial

Barrett & McNagny LLP, Fort Wayne, IN (Continued)

Counsel of Indiana; Defense Research Institute — Practice Areas: Employment Law; Labor and Employment; Litigation; Health Care — E-mail: hjc@barrettlaw.com

Patrick G. Murphy — 1970 — Indiana University-Fort Wayne, B.S., 1993; Indiana University School of Law, J.D., 1996 — Admitted to Bar, 1996, Indiana; U.S. District Court, Northern and Southern Districts of Indiana — Member Defense Trial Counsel of Indiana; Defense Research Institute — Practice Areas: Business Litigation; Insurance Defense — E-mail: pat@barrettlaw.com

Michael H. Michmerhuizen — 1973 — Grand Valley State University, B.B.A. (magna cum laude), 1995; University of Michigan Law School, J.D. (cum laude), 1999 — Admitted to Bar, 2000, Indiana; 2014, Michigan; U.S. District Court, Northern and Southern Districts of Indiana; U.S. District Court, Eastern District of Michigan; U.S. Court of Appeals, Seventh Circuit — Practice Areas: Appellate Practice; Commercial Litigation; Insurance Defense — E-mail: mhm@barrettlaw.com

James J. O'Connor, Jr. — 1975 — Emory University, B.A., 1997; Loyola University New Orleans College of Law, J.D., 2001 — Admitted to Bar, 2001, Indiana; U.S. District Court, Northern and Southern Districts of Indiana — Civil Mediator — Practice Areas: Litigation; Insurance Defense; Mediation; Workers' Compensation — E-mail: jjo@barrettlaw.com

Charles Christopher Dubes — 1977 — DePauw University, B.A., 2000; Indiana University School of Law-Indianapolis, J.D., 2003 — Admitted to Bar, 2003, Indiana; U.S. District Court, Northern and Southern Districts of Indiana — Member Defense Research Institute; Defense Trial Counsel of Indiana — Practice Areas: Medical Malpractice; Litigation; Insurance Defense; Nursing Home Liability; Health Care — E-mail: ccd@barrettlaw.com

Jeremy N. Gayed — 1978 — Wheaton College, B.S., 2001; University of Notre Dame Law School, J.D., 2004 — Admitted to Bar, 2004, Illinois; 2008, Indiana; 2009, U.S. Patent — Practice Areas: Patents; Patent Infringement Litigation; Litigation; Intellectual Property — E-mail: jng@barrettlaw.com

Litigation Associates

Hillary L. Knipstein — 1983 — Valparaiso University, B.S., 2005; Indiana University School of Law-Indianapolis, J.D./M.B.A., 2009 — Admitted to Bar, 2009, Indiana; U.S. District Court, Northern and Southern Districts of Indiana — Practice Areas: Litigation; Insurance Defense; Employment Law — E-mail: hlk@barrettlaw.com

Mark H. Bains — 1983 — Wabash College, B.A. (cum laude), 2006; Indiana University School of Law-Bloomington, J.D. (cum laude), 2010 — Admitted to Bar, 2010, Indiana; U.S. District Court, Northern and Southern Districts of Indiana — Practice Areas: Litigation; Insurance Defense; Business Litigation — E-mail: mhb@barrettlaw.com

Partners

N. Thomas Horton, II
Thomas M. Fink
Craig R. Finlayson
Thomas P. Yoder
Thomas J. Markle
Thomas M. Niezer
John C. Barce
Samuel J. Talarico, Jr.
Henry P. Najdeski
Renee L. Riecke
Joshua C. Neal
Patrick G. Michaels
Richard E. Fox
John P. Martin
Ronald J. Ehinger
Michael P. O'Hara
David R. Steiner
Dawn Snow Mattox
Trisha J. Paul
Anne E. Simerman
Jeffrey M. Woenker
Zachary E. Klutz

Senior Counsel

Robert S. Walters
William D. Swift

Counsel

Stephen L. Chapman
Emily S. Szaferski

Associates

Philip A. Wagler
Robert G. Westfall

Hunt Suedhoff Kalamaros LLP

803 South Calhoun Street, 9th Floor
Fort Wayne, Indiana 46802
Telephone: 260-423-1311
Fax: 260-424-5396
Toll Free: 800-215-8258
www.hsk-law.com

(South Bend, IN Office*: 205 West Jefferson Boulevard, Suite 300, 46601, P.O. Box 4156, 46634-4156)
  (Tel: 574-232-4801)
  (Fax: 574-232-9736)
(Indianapolis, IN Office*: 6323 South East Street, 46227)
  (Tel: 317-784-4966)
  (Fax: 317-784-5566)
(St. Joseph, MI Office*: 301 State Street, 2nd Floor, P.O. Box 46, 49085-0046)
  (Tel: 269-983-4405)
  (Fax: 269-983-5645)

Established: 1950

Insurance Defense, Automobile, Commercial Law, Product Liability, Professional Liability, Property and Casualty, Medical Malpractice, Workers' Compensation, Public Entities, Self-Insured, Health Care, Toxic Torts, Environmental Law, Coverage Issues, Mediation, Arbitration

Firm Profile: The firm offers a variety of legal services in the commercial and corporate areas, estate planning and probate, and the healthcare industry.

Representative Clients

Allied Group
Amerisure Companies
Auto-Owners Insurance Company
Cincinnati Insurance Company
CNA Insurance Companies
The Doctors Company
Employers Reinsurance Corporation
Fireman's Fund Insurance Company
Frankenmuth Mutual Insurance Company
Indiana Farmers Mutual Insurance Company
Liberty Mutual Insurance Company
National General Insurance Company
Pekin Insurance
Scottsdale Insurance Company
Sedgwick CMS
South Bend Medical Foundation
Travelers Property Casualty Corporation
Zurich American Insurance Group
American Family Insurance Company
Chubb Group of Insurance Companies
CSAA Insurance Group
EMC Insurance Company
Erie Insurance Company
FCCI Insurance Company
First Acceptance Insurance Company, Inc.
Gallagher Bassett Insurance Company
Indiana Insurance Company
Indiana University Health
Motorists Insurance Company
Nationwide Group
OneBeacon Insurance
Safeco/American States Insurance Company
Sentry Insurance a Mutual Company
United Farm Bureau Mutual Insurance Company

Partners

Scott L. Bunnell — 1954 — Michigan State University, B.A., 1979; J.D., 1983 — Admitted to Bar, 1983, Indiana — E-mail: sbunnell@hsk-law.com

Kathleen A. Kilar — 1962 — University of Michigan, B.A., 1984; University of Detroit, J.D., 1987 — Admitted to Bar, 1987, Illinois; 1990, Indiana — E-mail: kkilar@hsk-law.com

Branch R. Lew — 1957 — Indiana University, B.A. (with highest distinction), 1979; J.D. (cum laude), 1982 — Admitted to Bar, 1982, Indiana — E-mail: blew@hsk-law.com

N. Jean Schendel — 1956 — Purdue University, B.S.N., 1990; Valparaiso University, J.D. (magna cum laude), 1994 — Sigma Theta Tau Nursing Honor Society — Admitted to Bar, 1995, Indiana — E-mail: njschendel@hsk-law.com

James J. Shea — 1959 — King's College, B.A., 1981; Valparaiso University, J.D., 1984 — Admitted to Bar, 1984, Indiana — E-mail: jshea@hsk-law.com

Timothy W. DeGroote — 1969 — Marquette University, B.A., 1991; Valparaiso University, J.D., 1995 — Admitted to Bar, 1995, Indiana — E-mail: tdegroote@hsk-law.com

INDIANA

Hunt Suedhoff Kalamaros LLP, Fort Wayne, IN (Continued)

Stephen E. Dever — 1967 — Indiana University-Purdue University Indianapolis, B.S., 1989; Indiana University School of Law, J.D., 1995 — Admitted to Bar, 1995, Indiana — E-mail: sdever@hsk-law.com

Linda A. Polley — 1959 — Indiana University, B.A., 1982; University of Dayton, J.D., 1985 — Admitted to Bar, 1986, Indiana — E-mail: lpolley@hsk-law.com

Daniel J. Palmer — 1966 — Butler University, B.S. (cum laude), 1988; Indiana University School of Law, J.D. (cum laude), 1991 — Admitted to Bar, 1991, Indiana

Andrew S. Williams — 1974 — Ball State University, B.S. (cum laude), 1995; Baylor Law School, J.D., 2001 — Admitted to Bar, 2002, Texas; 2002, Indiana

Eric M. Wilkins — 1978 — Indiana University, B.S., 2001; University of Dayton School of Law, J.D. (cum laude), 2005 — Admitted to Bar, 2005, Indiana — E-mail: ewilkins@hsk-law.com

Associates

Codie J. Ross — 1977 — Purdue University, B.A., 1999; Thomas M. Cooley Law School, J.D. (with distinction), 2007 — Admitted to Bar, 2008, Indiana — E-mail: cross@hsk-law.com

Michelle K. Floyd — 1979 — Indiana University-Bloomington, B.A., 2002; Valparaiso University School of Law, J.D. (cum laude), 2010 — Admitted to Bar, 2010, Indiana — E-mail: mfloyd@hsk-law.com

Angela N. Aneiros — 1984 — Michigan State University, B.A. (cum laude), 2006; Indiana University School of Law, J.D., 2009 — Admitted to Bar, 2009, Illinois; 2012, Indiana — E-mail: aaneiros@hsk-law.com

Dustin J. Tirpak — 1982 — Indiana University-Bloomington, B.S., 2004; Indiana University Robert H. McKinney School of Law, J.D., 2011 — Admitted to Bar, 2011, Indiana — E-mail: dtirpak@hsk-law.com

Jeremy D. Lemon — 1987 — Liberty University, B.S., 2009; Liberty University School of Law, J.D. (magna cum laude), 2012 — Admitted to Bar, 2012, Indiana — E-mail: jlemon@hsk-law.com

Joshua A. Atkinson — 1987 — Manchester College, B.A., 2010; Valparaiso University School of Law, J.D., 2013 — Admitted to Bar, 2013, Indiana — E-mail: jatkinson@hsk-law.com

GARY 80,294 Lake Co.

Refer To

Spangler, Jennings & Dougherty, P.C.
8396 Mississippi Street
Merrillville, Indiana 46410-6398
   Telephone: 219-769-2323
   Fax: 219-769-5007

Insurance Law, Fire, Property, Casualty, Surety, Life Insurance, Environmental Law, Toxic Torts, Product Liability, Professional Liability, Workers' Compensation, Coverage Issues, Appellate Practice, Subrogation, Medical Malpractice Defense, Mortgage Foreclosure

SEE COMPLETE LISTING UNDER MERRILLVILLE, INDIANA (8 MILES)

GREENWOOD 49,791 Johnson Co.

Refer To

Ferguson & Ferguson
403 East Sixth Street
Bloomington, Indiana 47408-4098
   Telephone: 812-332-2113
   Fax: 812-334-3892

Insurance Defense, School Law, Commercial Law, General Liability, Product Liability, Premises Liability, Motor Vehicle, Uninsured and Underinsured Motorist, Life, Accident and Health, General Civil Trial and Appellate Practice, Employment Issues, Including ADA, Business and Real Estate Litigation, Municipal and Governmental Entity Liability, including §1983 Actions

SEE COMPLETE LISTING UNDER BLOOMINGTON, INDIANA (46 MILES)

GARY

HAMMOND 80,830 Lake Co.

Refer To

Spangler, Jennings & Dougherty, P.C.
8396 Mississippi Street
Merrillville, Indiana 46410-6398
   Telephone: 219-769-2323
   Fax: 219-769-5007

Insurance Law, Fire, Property, Casualty, Surety, Life Insurance, Environmental Law, Toxic Torts, Product Liability, Professional Liability, Workers' Compensation, Coverage Issues, Appellate Practice, Subrogation, Medical Malpractice Defense, Mortgage Foreclosure

SEE COMPLETE LISTING UNDER MERRILLVILLE, INDIANA (18 MILES)

INDIANAPOLIS † 820,445 Marion Co.

Allen, Kopet & Associates, PLLC
3905 Vincennes Road, Suite 303
Indianapolis, Indiana 46268
   Telephone: 317-522-0644
   Fax: 317-602-5887

(See listing under Chattanooga, TN for additional information)

Law Offices of Collier-Magar, P.C.
211 South Ritter Avenue, Suite C
Indianapolis, Indiana 46219
   Telephone: 317-261-1885
   Fax: 317-261-1887
   www.cmrlawfirm.com

Established: 1995

Insurance Defense, Municipal Liability, Public Entities, Civil Rights, School Law, Property and Casualty, Tort, Employment Law, First and Third Party Defense, Insurance Coverage, Coverage Issues, Americans with Disabilities Act, Equal Employment Opportunity Commission, Premises Liability, Bodily Injury, Jail/Prison Defense

Corporate Clients

Barcelona Indy, LLC	The Cure Baseball, Inc.
Indiana Buddhist Center	

Insurance Clients

Erie Insurance Group	Hallmark Insurance Company
Indiana Municipal Insurance Program	OneBeacon Insurance
Trident Insurance Services	Travelers Insurance

Principal Shareholder

Kenneth Collier-Magar — 1948 — Saint Vincent College, B.A. (magna cum laude), 1970; University of Pittsburgh School of Law, J.D., 1973 — Admitted to Bar, 1973, Pennsylvania (Inactive); 1984, Indiana; 1987, Tennessee (Inactive); 1981, U.S. Court of Appeals, Third Circuit; 1984, U.S. Court of Appeals, Seventh Circuit; 1987, U.S. Court of Appeals, Sixth Circuit; 1987, U.S. Supreme Court — Member American and Indiana State (Ethics and Federal Judiciary Committees) Bar Associations; Indianapolis Bar Association (Professional Responsibility Committee); Defense Research Institute — Reported Cases: Chenoweth v. Estate of Wilson, 827 N.E.2d 44 (Ind. Ct. App. 2005); Holt v. Quality Motor Sales, Inc., 776 N.E.2d 361 (Ind. Ct. App. 2002); Gerbers, Ltd. v. Wells County Drainage Bd., 608 N.E.2d 997 (Ind. Ct. App. 1993); Mauller v. City of Columbus, 552 N.E.2d 500 (Ind. Ct. App. 1990); Trobaugh v. Hellman, 564 N.E.2d 285 (Ind. Ct. App. 1990); U.S. v. Church, 970 F.2d 401 (7th Cir. 1992); Pounds v. Griepenstroh, 970 F.2d 338 (7th Cir. 1992); Tapia v. City of Greenwood, 965 F.2d 336 (7th Cir. 1992); Hilligoss v. Hovious, 1993 WL 8707 (S.D. Ind. 1993); Dunlap v. Refuse Dept. Sanitary Dist., Slip Copy, 2006 WL 1707268 (2006); City of Marion v. Howard, 832 N.E.2d 528 (Ind. Ct. App. 2005); Daugherty v. Dearborn County, 827 N.E.2d 34 (Ind. Ct. App. 2005); Tuffendsam v. Dearborn County Bd. of Health, 385 F.3d 1124 (7th Cir. 2004); Foley v. City of Lafayette, Ind., 359 F.3d 925 (7th

INDIANAPOLIS INDIANA

Law Offices of Collier-Magar, P.C., Indianapolis, IN (Continued)

Cir. 2004); Kline v. Hughes, 131 F.3d 708 (7th Cir. 1997); Brown v. Alexander, 876 N.E.2D 376 (Ind Ct. App 2008) — Certified Mediator (1994)

Of Counsel

Larry Furnas — Indiana State University, B.S., 1971; Indiana University School of Law, J.D., 1976 — Admitted to Bar, 1976, Indiana; U.S. District Court, Northern and Southern Districts of Indiana; U.S. Court of Appeals, Seventh Circuit; 1980, U.S. Supreme Court — Indiana State Police Officer (1964-1989); Superintendent of The Indiana State Police (1986-1989)

Hill Fulwider, P.C.

One Indiana Square, Suite 2400
Indianapolis, Indiana 46204-2013
  Telephone: 317-488-2000
  Fax: 317-630-2768
  E-Mail: info@hillfulwider.com
  www.hillfulwider.com

Established: 1981

Appellate, Asbestos Litigation, Business Law, Commercial Litigation, Estate Planning, Family Law, General Civil Litigation, Insurance Coverage, Insurance Defense, Medical Malpractice Defense, Product Liability Defense, Subrogation, Toxic Torts, Workers' Compensation, Mediation and Arbitration, Medical Review Panel Chair

Firm Profile: Founded in 1981, Hill Fulwider serves individuals, small businesses, and large corporations in a full range of legal practice areas. For more than thirty years, the firm has taken pride in carefully and thoughtfully representing the legal interests of its clients.

Insurance Clients

Accident Fund Insurance Company of America
COUNTRY Mutual Insurance Company
Great American Insurance Company
Travelers Property Casualty Insurance Company
Chubb Group of Insurance Companies
Eastern Alliance Insurance Company
Society Insurance
Travelers Indemnity Company

Non-Insurance Clients

Clarian Health Partners
Southern Indiana Gas & Electric Company
Sears, Roebuck and Co.

Founder

Douglas J. Hill — 1933 — University of Michigan, B.B.A., 1955; LL.B., 1960 — Admitted to Bar, 1960, Indiana; U.S. District Court, Southern District of Indiana — Member American, Indiana State and Indianapolis Bar Associations; Defense Trial Counsel of Indiana — Practice Areas: Alternative Dispute Resolution; Arbitration; Mediation — E-mail: doug@hillfulwider.com

Managing Director

Elizabeth H. Knotts — 1964 — Indiana University, B.A., 1986; Indiana University-Indianapolis, J.D. (cum laude), 1991 — Admitted to Bar, 1991, Indiana; U.S. District Court, Northern and Southern Districts of Indiana — Member Indiana State and Indianapolis Bar Associations — Practice Areas: Medical Malpractice Defense; General Civil Litigation — E-mail: beth@hillfulwider.com

Directors/Shareholders

Rori L. Goldman — 1970 — Indiana University-Bloomington, B.A., 1992; Hofstra University, J.D., 1995 — Admitted to Bar, 1996, New York; 1997, Indiana; U.S. District Court, Northern and Southern Districts of Indiana; 2012, U.S. Court of Appeals, Seventh Circuit — Member Indiana State and Indianapolis Bar Associations; Defense Research Institute; Defense Trial Counsel of Indiana — Practice Areas: Appellate; Employment; Insurance Coverage; Insurance Defense; Workers' Compensation; Medical Malpractice Defense; Professional Liability — E-mail: rori@hillfulwider.com

Ty M. Craver — 1972 — Indiana University, B.S., 1994; Indiana University School of Law-Indianapolis, J.D., 1998 — Admitted to Bar, 1998, Indiana;

Hill Fulwider, P.C., Indianapolis, IN (Continued)

U.S. District Court, Northern and Southern Districts of Indiana; 2012, U.S. Court of Appeals, Seventh Circuit — Member Indiana State and Indianapolis Bar Associations; Defense Trial Counsel of Indiana — Practice Areas: Workers' Compensation; Subrogation; Product Liability; Insurance Defense; Professional Liability; Mediation; Insurance Coverage; Commercial Litigation; Employment — E-mail: ty@hillfulwider.com

Keith J. Hays — 1972 — Wittenberg University, B.S., 1994; Indiana University-Indianapolis, J.D., 1998 — Admitted to Bar, 1998, Indiana; 2009, Illinois; 1998, U.S. District Court, Northern and Southern Districts of Indiana; 2009, U.S. District Court, Northern and Southern Districts of Illinois — Member Indiana State and Indianapolis Bar Associations; Defense Research Institute; Defense Trial Counsel of Indiana — Practice Areas: Toxic Torts; Asbestos Litigation; Product Liability; Premises Liability; Commercial Litigation; Insurance Coverage; Insurance Defense; Subrogation — E-mail: khays@hillfulwider.com

Christopher N. Wahl — 1978 — Augsburg College, B.A., 2000; Indiana University-Indianapolis, J.D., 2003 — Admitted to Bar, 2003, Indiana; U.S. District Court, Northern and Southern Districts of Indiana — Member Indiana State and Indianapolis Bar Associations; Defense Research Institute; Defense Trial Counsel of Indiana — Practice Areas: Asbestos Litigation; Product Liability Defense; Insurance Coverage; Insurance Defense; Toxic Torts — E-mail: chris@hillfulwider.com

Kye J. Steffey — 1973 — Hanover College, B.A., 1995; Purdue University, M.S., 1996; Indiana University-Indianapolis, J.D., 2003 — Admitted to Bar, 2003, Indiana; 2006, Florida; 2003, U.S. District Court, Northern and Southern Districts of Indiana; Supreme Court of Indiana; 2006, Supreme Court of Florida — Member Indiana State and Indianapolis Bar Associations; The Florida Bar — Practice Areas: Wills; Trusts; Business Formation; Business Law; Franchise Law; Mergers and Acquisitions; Estate Planning; Estate Administration; Guardian and Conservatorships; Contracts; Real Estate — E-mail: kye@hillfulwider.com

Associates

Elizabeth A. Trachtman — 1986 — Indiana University, B.A., 2007; Indiana University-Indianapolis, J.D., 2010 — Admitted to Bar, 2010, Indiana; U.S. District Court, Northern and Southern Districts of Indiana — Member Indiana State and Indianapolis Bar Associations; Defense Trial Counsel of Indiana — Practice Areas: Medical Malpractice Defense; Insurance Defense; Product Liability; Subrogation; Workers' Compensation — E-mail: elizabeth@hillfulwider.com

David J. Saferight — 1986 — Indiana University, B.S., 2009; Valparaiso University, J.D. (summa cum laude), 2012 — Admitted to Bar, 2012, Indiana; U.S. District Court, Northern and Southern Districts of Indiana — Member Indiana State and Indianapolis Bar Associations; Defense Trial Counsel of Indiana — Practice Areas: Asbestos Litigation; Toxic Torts; Subrogation; Insurance Defense; Product Liability; Workers' Compensation — E-mail: david@hillfulwider.com

Justin O. Sorrell — 1984 — Indiana University-Bloomington, B.M., 2006; M.M., 2009; Indiana University, J.D., 2012 — Admitted to Bar, 2012, Indiana; 2013, U.S. District Court, Northern District of Indiana; 2014, U.S. District Court, Southern District of Indiana — Member Indiana State and Indianapolis Bar Associations; Defense Trial Counsel of Indiana — Practice Areas: Professional Liability; Workers' Compensation; Premises Liability; Commercial Litigation; Employment; Insurance Coverage; Insurance Defense — E-mail: jsorrell@hillfulwider.com

Christopher D. Simpkins — 1982 — Ohio University, B.A. Political Science, 2005; Indiana University-Indianapolis, J.D., 2009 — Admitted to Bar, 2009, Indiana; U.S. District Court, Northern and Southern Districts of Indiana — Member Indiana State and Indianapolis Bar Associations; Defense Research Institute; Defense Trial Counsel of Indiana — Practice Areas: Insurance Defense; Insurance Coverage; Medical Malpractice Defense; Professional Liability; Workers' Compensation; Subrogation; Product Liability; Appellate — E-mail: csimpkins@hillfulwider.com

Of Counsel

Kevin A. Hoover — 1958 — Ball State University, B.S. (summa cum laude), 1981; Indiana University-Indianapolis, J.D., 1984 — Admitted to Bar, 1984, Indiana; U.S. District Court, Northern and Southern Districts of Indiana; Supreme Court of Indiana — Member Indiana State, Indianapolis and Johnson County Bar Associations — Practice Areas: Family Law; Mediation; Estate Planning; Commercial Litigation — E-mail: kevin@hillfulwider.com

Douglas W. Meagher — 1957 — Indiana State University, B.S., 1980; M.P.A., 1987; Indiana University, J.D., 1997 — Admitted to Bar, 1997, Indiana; U.S.

INDIANA | INDIANAPOLIS

Hill Fulwider, P.C., Indianapolis, IN (Continued)

District Court, Northern and Southern Districts of Indiana — Member Indiana State Bar Association — Practice Areas: Workers' Compensation; Mediation — E-mail: dmeagher@hillfulwider.com

Hume Smith Geddes Green & Simmons, LLP

54 Monument Circle, Fourth Floor
Indianapolis, Indiana 46204-2996
Telephone: 317-632-4402
Fax: 317-632-5595
E-Mail: (first initial) (last name) @humesmith.com
www.humesmith.com

Established: 1951

Insurance Defense, Arbitration, Commercial Liability, Employment Law, First and Third Party Defense, Bad Faith, Personal Injury, Product Liability, Professional Liability, Property and Casualty, Toxic Torts, Insurance Coverage, Workers' Compensation, Construction Litigation

Firm Profile: Hume Smith Geddes Green & Simmons, LLP is a law partnership founded in 1951. The firm provides legal counsel to insurance companies and their insureds in all areas of first and third party litigation. With its central location in Indianapolis, the firm represents clients throughout Indiana in both State and Federal Courts.

Insurance Clients

ACE USA
ALLIED Property and Casualty Insurance Company
Carolina Casualty Insurance Company
CNA Insurance Company
Essex Insurance Company
Fireman's Fund Specialty Group
Freedom Specialty Insurance Company
Horace Mann Insurance Company
Illinois Casualty Company
Markel Southwest
Metropolitan Property and Casualty Insurance Company
Progressive Insurance Company
Sagamore Insurance Company
State Farm Fire and Casualty Company
XL Insurance
Admiral Insurance Company
Berkley Specialty Underwriting Managers, LLC
Catlin Specialty Insurance Company
Colony Insurance Company
Farmland Mutual Insurance Company
Fulcrum Insurance Company
General Casualty Insurance Company
Indiana Farmers Mutual Insurance Company
Nationwide Insurance
Nautilus Insurance Company
QBE Regional Insurance
Scottsdale Insurance Company
Titan Indemnity Company
Western Heritage Insurance Company

Non-Insurance Clients

Associated Claims Enterprises, Inc.
Cavell USA, Inc.
ELCO Administrative Services
Gallagher Bassett Services, Inc.
Protective Adjustment Company
Securitas Security Services USA, Inc.
Western Continent Claims Association
Cambridge Integrated Services
Crawford & Company
GAB Robins North America, Inc.
Indiana Life and Health Insurance Guaranty Association
Sedgwick Claims Management Services, Inc.
Xchanging

Firm Members

Gordon Smith — (1933-2010)

John T. Hume, III — 1933 — Indiana University, B.S., 1955; J.D., 1958 — Delta Theta Phi — Admitted to Bar, 1958, Indiana; U.S. District Court, Southern District of Indiana; 1970, U.S. Court of Appeals, Seventh Circuit; 1975, U.S. Supreme Court — Member American, Indiana State and Indianapolis Bar Associations; Defense Trial Counsel of Indiana (President, 1991-); Christian Legal Society; Fellow, American College of Trial Lawyers; Federation of Defense and Corporate Counsel — Practice Areas: Insurance Coverage; Insurance Defense; Civil Litigation — E-mail: jhume@humesmith.com

Robert W. Geddes — 1929 — Indiana University, B.S., 1956; J.D., 1962 — Phi Delta Phi — Admitted to Bar, 1962, Indiana; U.S. District Court, Southern District of Indiana; 1971, U.S. Supreme Court — Member Indiana State and Indianapolis Bar Associations — Former Assistant U.S. Attorney, 1962-1965; U.S. Commissioner, U.S. District Court for the Southern District

Hume Smith Geddes Green & Simmons, LLP, Indianapolis, IN (Continued)

of Indiana, 1966-1971; U.S. Magistrate, 1971-1973 — Practice Areas: Litigation; Mediation; Arbitration — E-mail: rgeddes@humesmith.com

John C. Green — 1942 — Indiana University, B.S., 1965; J.D., 1969 — Phi Delta Phi — Admitted to Bar, 1969, Indiana; U.S. District Court, Southern District of Indiana; 1980, U.S. Court of Appeals, Seventh Circuit; 1981, U.S. Supreme Court; 2002, U.S. District Court, Northern District of Indiana — Member Indiana State and Indianapolis Bar Associations; Indiana Trial Lawyers Association; Association of American Trial Lawyers — Practice Areas: Personal Injury; Litigation; Mediation — E-mail: jgreen@humesmith.com

Michael E. Simmons — 1954 — Indiana University, B.S., 1976; J.D. (magna cum laude), 1979 — Phi Delta Phi — Admitted to Bar, 1979, Indiana; U.S. District Court, Northern and Southern Districts of Indiana; U.S. Supreme Court; 1984, U.S. Court of Appeals, Seventh Circuit — Member Indiana State and Indianapolis Bar Associations; Indiana Trial Lawyers Association; Defense Trial Counsel of Indiana; American Association for Justice; Defense Research Institute — Practice Areas: Insurance Defense; Personal Injury; Litigation; Arbitration; Mediation; Insurance Coverage; Trucking Law — E-mail: msimmons@humesmith.com

Andrew P. Wirick — 1961 — DePauw University, B.A., 1983; Indiana University, J.D., 1986 — Admitted to Bar, 1986, Indiana; U.S. Court of Appeals, Seventh Circuit — Member Federal, Indiana State and Indianapolis Bar Associations; Indiana Municipal Lawyers Association; Indiana Association of Cities and Towns; Indiana Association of Counties; Defense Research Institute — Practice Areas: Insurance Defense; Employment Law; Governmental Liability; Personal Injury — E-mail: awirick@humesmith.com

Edward F. Harney, Jr. — 1967 — Purdue University, B.A., 1990; Valparaiso University, J.D. (magna cum laude), 1993 — Admitted to Bar, 1993, Indiana; Illinois; U.S. District Court, Northern and Southern Districts of Indiana; 2002, U.S. District Court, Central and Northern Districts of Illinois — Member Indiana State and Indianapolis Bar Associations; Defense Trial Counsel of Indiana; Defense Research Institute — Practice Areas: Insurance Defense; First and Third Party Defense; Bad Faith; Toxic Torts — E-mail: eharney@humesmith.com

Theodore J. Blanford — 1949 — Indiana University, B.S., 1977; J.D., 1984 — Admitted to Bar, 1984, Indiana; U.S. District Court, Northern and Southern Districts of Indiana; 2004, U.S. Court of Appeals, Seventh Circuit — Member Indiana State and Indianapolis Bar Associations; Defense Trial Counsel of Indiana; Defense Research Institute — Indiana National Guard (Retired) — Practice Areas: Insurance Defense; Legal Malpractice; Environmental Law — E-mail: tblanford@humesmith.com

Michael R. Bain — 1968 — Indiana University-Bloomington, B.A., 1991; Indiana University-Indianapolis, J.D., 1994 — Admitted to Bar, 1994, Indiana; U.S. District Court, Northern and Southern Districts of Indiana; 2002, U.S. Supreme Court — Member Indiana State and Indianapolis Bar Associations; Defense Trial Counsel of Indiana; Defense Research Institute — Practice Areas: Civil Litigation; Construction Litigation; Insurance Defense; Bad Faith — E-mail: mbain@humesmith.com

Christopher D. Cody — 1978 — Wake Forest University, B.A., 2000; Indiana University, J.D., 2003 — Order of the Barristers — Admitted to Bar, 2003, Indiana; U.S. District Court, Northern and Southern Districts of Indiana — Member Indianapolis Bar Association — Practice Areas: Civil Litigation; Premises Liability; Employment Law; Civil Rights — E-mail: ccody@humesmith.com

Christopher A. Pearcy — 1978 — Indiana University-Bloomington, B.S. (with distinction), 2000; J.D., 2003 — Admitted to Bar, 2004, Indiana; 2005, Illinois; U.S. District Court, Southern District of Indiana — Member American, Indiana State and Hamilton County Bar Associations — Practice Areas: Insurance Defense; Civil Litigation; Business Law; Personal Injury — E-mail: cpearcy@humesmith.com

Seth R. Wilson — 1980 — Taylor University, B.A., 2003; Regent University, J.D., 2006 — Admitted to Bar, 2006, Indiana; U.S. District Court, Northern and Southern Districts of Indiana — Member American, Indiana State and Indianapolis Bar Associations; Christian Legal Society — Practice Areas: Insurance Defense; Workers' Compensation; Mass Tort — E-mail: swilson@humesmith.com

Mark M. Holdridge — 1977 — Colgate University, B.A., 1999; Thomas M. Cooley Law School, J.D., 2006 — Admitted to Bar, 2006, Indiana; U.S. District Court, Northern and Southern Districts of Indiana — Member Indiana State and Indianapolis Bar Associations; Defense Trial Counsel of Indiana — Practice Areas: Insurance Defense — E-mail: mholdridge@humesmith.com

Beth A. Barnes — 1982 — Ball State University, B.S. (cum laude), 2003; Indiana University-Indianapolis, J.D. (with honors), 2009 — Admitted to Bar, 2010, Indiana; U.S. District Court, Northern and Southern Districts of

Hume Smith Geddes Green & Simmons, LLP, Indianapolis, IN (Continued)

Indiana — Member American, Indiana State and Indianapolis Bar Associations; Defense Trial Counsel of Indiana; Defense Research Institute — Practice Areas: Insurance Defense; Personal Injury; Collections — E-mail: bbarnes@humesmith.com

William D. Beyers — 1983 — Indiana University, B.A., 2005; Indiana University-Indianapolis, J.D., 2009 — Admitted to Bar, 2009, Indiana; U.S. District Court, Northern District of Indiana; 2011, U.S. District Court, Southern District of Indiana — Member American Bar Association; Defense Trial Counsel of Indiana — E-mail: bbeyers@humesmith.com

Hunt Suedhoff Kalamaros LLP

6323 South East Street
Indianapolis, Indiana 46227
   Telephone: 317-784-4966
   Fax: 317-784-5566
   www.hsk-law.com

(Fort Wayne, IN Office*: 803 South Calhoun Street, 9th Floor, 46802, P.O. Box 11489, 46858-1489)
   (Tel: 260-423-1311)
   (Fax: 260-424-5396)
   (Toll Free: 800-215-8258)
(South Bend, IN Office*: 205 West Jefferson Boulevard, Suite 300, 46601, P.O. Box 4156, 46634-4156)
   (Tel: 574-232-4801)
   (Fax: 574-232-9736)
(St. Joseph, MI Office*: 301 State Street, 2nd Floor, P.O. Box 46, 49085-0046)
   (Tel: 269-983-4405)
   (Fax: 269-983-5645)

Insurance Defense, Trial and Appellate Practice, Automobile, Product Liability, Professional Liability, Property and Casualty, Medical Malpractice, Workers' Compensation, Public Entities, Self-Insured, Health Care, Toxic Torts, Environmental Law, Coverage Issues, Mediation, Arbitration

Partner

Brian L. England — 1966 — Indiana University, B.A., 1989; J.D. (magna cum laude), 1992 — Admitted to Bar, 1992, Indiana — Member Indiana State Bar Association; Indiana Workers' Compensation Institute; Defense Trial Counsel of Indiana; Defense Research Institute — Practice Areas: Workers' Compensation; Insurance Litigation; Employment Law; Appeals — E-mail: bengland@hsk-law.com

Associate

Ryan J. Guillory — 1981 — Tulane University, B.A./B.S., 2003; M.A., 2005; Indiana University-Bloomington, J.D., 2008 — Admitted to Bar, 2008, Indiana — Member Indiana State and Indianapolis Bar Associations; Defense Trial Counsel of Indiana; Defense Research Institute — Practice Areas: Insurance Litigation; Workers' Compensation — E-mail: rguillory@hsk-law.com

(See listing under Fort Wayne, IN for additional information)

Kightlinger & Gray, LLP

One Indiana Square, Suite 300
211 North Pennsylvania Street
Indianapolis, Indiana 46204
   Telephone: 317-638-4521
   Fax: 317-636-5917
   E-Mail: info@k-glaw.com
   www.k-glaw.com

(Evansville, IN Office*: 7220 Eagle Crest Boulevard, 47715)
   (Tel: 812-474-4400)
   (Fax: 812-474-4414)

Kightlinger & Gray, LLP, Indianapolis, IN (Continued)

(New Albany, IN Office*: Bonterra Building, Suite 200, 3620 Blackiston Boulevard, 47150)
   (Tel: 812-949-2300)
   (Fax: 812-949-8556)
(Merrillville, IN Office*: Merrillville Corporate Center, 8001 Broadway, Suite 100, 46410)
   (Tel: 219-769-0413)
   (Fax: 219-769-0798)
(Louisville, KY Office*: 312 South Fourth Street, Suite 700, 40202)
   (Tel: 502-442-2295)
   (Fax: 502-442-2703)

Established: 1946

Insurance Defense, Insurance Litigation, Defense Litigation, Litigation, Insurance Law, Coverage Issues, Carrier Defense, Self-Insured Defense, Comprehensive General Liability, Trial and Appellate Practice, State and Federal Courts, General Civil Trial and Appellate Practice, Casualty Defense, Product Liability, Workers' Compensation, Employment Law, Subrogation, Toxic Torts, Aviation, Surety, Administrative Law, Agent/Broker Liability, Bad Faith, Business Law, Automobile Liability, Trucking Law, Asbestos Litigation, Construction Law, Corporate Law, Complex Litigation, Construction Litigation, Coverage Analysis, First and Third Party Defense, Fire Loss, Professional Liability, Malpractice, Agency Defense, Agent and Brokers Errors and Omissions, Medical Malpractice, School Law, Transportation, Real Estate, Bankruptcy, Municipal Liability, Class Actions, Mediation, Securities Litigation and Arbitration

Insurance Clients

American International Group, Inc.	Auto-Owners Insurance Company
Chubb Group of Insurance Companies	Grange Mutual Insurance Company
Liberty Mutual Group	Grinnell Mutual Reinsurance Company
Scottsdale Insurance Company	State Farm Fire and Casualty Company
State Farm Mutual Automobile Insurance Company	

Non-Insurance Clients

Aon Technical Insurance Services	Consolidated Freightway Corporation
GAB Robins North America, Inc.	
Jeff Ellis & Associates, Inc.	

Partners

Michael E. Brown — Indiana University, B.A., 1974; M.B.A., 1978; Indiana University School of Law, J.D., 1978 — Admitted to Bar, 1978, Indiana; U.S. District Court, Northern and Southern Districts of Indiana; U.S. Court of Appeals, Seventh and Eighth Circuits; U.S. Supreme Court — Tel: 317-968-8119 — E-mail: mbrown@k-glaw.com

Matthew D. Bruno — Purdue University, B.A., 2004; Indiana University School of Law, J.D., 2007 — Admitted to Bar, 2007, Indiana; U.S. District Court, Northern and Southern Districts of Indiana — Tel: 317-968-8183 — E-mail: mbruno@k-glaw.com

Pfenne P. Cantrell — Wabash College, B.A., 1992; Indiana University School of Law-Indianapolis, J.D., 1995 — Admitted to Bar, 1995, Indiana; U.S. District Court, Northern and Southern Districts of Indiana; U.S. Court of Appeals, Seventh Circuit — Tel: 317-968-8181 — E-mail: pcantrell@k-glaw.com

Kristen M. Carroll — Samford University, B.S., 1995; Indiana University School of Law-Indianapolis, J.D., 2001 — Admitted to Bar, 2001, Indiana; U.S. District Court, Northern and Southern Districts of Indiana; U.S. Court of Appeals, Seventh Circuit; U.S. Supreme Court — Tel: 317-968-8188 — E-mail: kcarroll@k-glaw.com

Erin A. Clancy — Purdue University, B.S., 1995; Indiana University School of Law, J.D., 1998 — Admitted to Bar, 1998, Massachusetts; 2000, Indiana; U.S. District Court, Northern and Southern Districts of Indiana; U.S. Court of Appeals, Sixth and Seventh Circuits — Tel: 317-968-8148 — E-mail: eclancy@k-glaw.com

Melissa F. Danielson — Harvard University, A.B., 1999; University of Virginia School of Law, J.D., 2003 — Admitted to Bar, 2003, California; 2005, Indiana; U.S. District Court, Northern and Southern Districts of Indiana; U.S.

Kightlinger & Gray, LLP, Indianapolis, IN (Continued)

District Court, Central District of California — Tel: 317-968-8174 — E-mail: mdanielson@k-glaw.com

John B. Drummy — Creighton University, B.S.B.A., 1982; Indiana University School of Law-Indianapolis, J.D., 1985 — Admitted to Bar, 1985, Indiana; U.S. District Court, Northern and Southern Districts of Indiana; U.S. Court of Appeals, Sixth and Seventh Circuits; U.S. Supreme Court — Tel: 317-968-8142 — E-mail: jdrummy@k-glaw.com

Mark D. Gerth — Indiana University, B.A., 1974; Indiana University School of Law, J.D., 1977 — Admitted to Bar, 1977, Indiana; U.S. District Court, Northern and Southern Districts of Indiana; U.S. Court of Appeals, Seventh Circuit — Tel: 317-968-8129 — E-mail: mgerth@k-glaw.com

Jeffrey D. Hawkins — Indiana University, B.A., 1993; The John Marshall Law School, J.D., 1996 — Admitted to Bar, 1996, Indiana; U.S. District Court, Northern and Southern Districts of Indiana — Tel: 317-968-8156 — E-mail: jhawkins@k-glaw.com

Thomas J. Jarzyniecki, Jr. — State University of New York at Buffalo, B.A., 1982; Valparaiso University School of Law, J.D., 1985 — Admitted to Bar, 1985, Indiana; Illinois; U.S. District Court, Northern and Southern Districts of Indiana — Tel: 317-968-8163 — E-mail: tjarzyniecki@k-glaw.com

Robert M. Kelso — Indiana University, B.S., 1977; Indiana University School of Law-Indianapolis, J.D., 1981 — Admitted to Bar, 1981, Indiana; U.S. District Court, Northern and Southern Districts of Indiana; U.S. Court of Appeals, Seventh Circuit — Chartered Property Casualty Underwriter, 1996 — Tel: 317-968-8154 — E-mail: rkelso@k-glaw.com

Nicholas W. Levi — Indiana University, B.A., 2000; Indiana University School of Law, J.D., 2003 — Admitted to Bar, 2003, Indiana; U.S. District Court, Northern and Southern Districts of Indiana — Tel: 317-968-8122 — E-mail: nlevi@k-glaw.com

Libby Valos Moss — Ball State University, B.S., 1995; Indiana University School of Law, J.D., 1999 — Admitted to Bar, 1999, Indiana; U.S. District Court, Northern and Southern Districts of Indiana — Tel: 317-968-8175 — E-mail: lmoss@k-glaw.com

Aubrey Kuchar Noltemeyer — Centre College of Kentucky, B.A., 2001; Valparaiso University School of Law, J.D., 2004 — Admitted to Bar, 2004, Indiana; U.S. District Court, Northern and Southern Districts of Indiana — Tel: 317-968-8147 — E-mail: anoltemeyer@k-glaw.com

Ginny L. Peterson — Purdue University, B.A., 1977; Indiana University School of Law, J.D., 1997 — Admitted to Bar, 1997, Indiana; U.S. District Court, Northern and Southern Districts of Indiana — Chartered Property Casualty Underwriter, 1987 — Tel: 317-968-8182 — E-mail: gpeterson@k-glaw.com

James W. Roehrdanz — Indiana University, B.S., 1975; Valparaiso University School of Law, J.D., 1978 — Admitted to Bar, 1978, Indiana; U.S. District Court, Northern and Southern Districts of Indiana; U.S. Court of Appeals, Seventh Circuit — Registered Civil Mediator — Tel: 317-968-8124 — E-mail: jroehrdanz@k-glaw.com

Steven E. Springer — Purdue University, B.S., 1971; Indiana University School of Law-Indianapolis, J.D., 1979 — Admitted to Bar, 1979, Indiana; U.S. District Court, Northern and Southern Districts of Indiana; U.S. Court of Appeals, Seventh Circuit — Chartered Property Casualty Underwriter, 1994 — Tel: 317-968-8130 — E-mail: sspringer@k-glaw.com

Casey R. Stafford — Butler University, B.A., 2004; Indiana University School of Law-Indianapolis, J.D., 2007 — Admitted to Bar, 2007, Indiana; U.S. District Court, Northern and Southern Districts of Indiana — Tel: 317-968-8118 — E-mail: cstafford@k-glaw.com

Peter A. Velde — Purdue University, B.A., 1971; Albany Law School, J.D., 1975 — Admitted to Bar, 1976, Indiana; U.S. District Court, Northern and Southern Districts of Indiana; U.S. Court of Appeals, Seventh Circuit — Tel: 317-968-8131 — E-mail: pvelde@k-glaw.com

Michael Wroblewski — Indiana University of Pennsylvania, B.A., 1999; Valparaiso University School of Law, J.D., 2002 — Admitted to Bar, 2002, Illinois; 2005, Indiana; U.S. District Court, Northern District of Illinois; U.S. District Court, Northern and Southern Districts of Indiana — Tel: 317-968-8136 — E-mail: mwroblewski@k-glaw.com

Richard A. Young — Ball State University, B.S., 1973; Indiana University School of Law-Indianapolis, J.D. (cum laude), 1976 — Admitted to Bar, 1976, Indiana; U.S. District Court, Northern and Southern Districts of Indiana — Tel: 317-968-8161 — E-mail: ryoung@k-glaw.com

D. Bryce Zoeller — Indiana University, B.A., 1991; Indiana University School of Law, J.D., 1995 — Admitted to Bar, 1995, Illinois; 1997, Indiana; U.S. District Court, Northern District of Illinois; U.S. District Court, Northern and Southern Districts of Indiana — Tel: 317-968-8155 — E-mail: bzoeller@k-glaw.com

Kightlinger & Gray, LLP, Indianapolis, IN (Continued)

Staff Attorney

Marcia A. Mahony — University of Oregon, B.S., 1984; Indiana University School of Law, J.D., 1995 — Admitted to Bar, 1995, Indiana; U.S. District Court, Northern and Southern Districts of Indiana; U.S. Court of Appeals, Seventh Circuit — Tel: 317-968-8162 — E-mail: mmahony@k-glaw.com

Associates

Louis J. Britton — Indiana University, B.S., 2004; Indiana University School of Law-Indianapolis, J.D., 2008 — Admitted to Bar, 2008, Indiana; U.S. District Court, Northern and Southern Districts of Indiana — Tel: 317-968-8120 — E-mail: lbritton@k-glaw.com

Ashley A. Butz — Indiana University, B.A., 2006; Indiana University Robert H. McKinney School of Law, J.D., 2010 — Admitted to Bar, 2010, Indiana; U.S. District Court, Northern and Southern Districts of Indiana — Tel: 317-968-8187 — E-mail: abutz@k-glaw.com

Cristina A. Costa — Purdue University, B.A., 2010; Indiana University Maurer School of Law, J.D., 2013 — Admitted to Bar, 2013, Indiana; U.S. District Court, Northern and Southern Districts of Indiana — Tel: 317-968-8126 — E-mail: CCosta@k-glaw.com

William J. Horvath — Valparaiso University, B.A., 2008; Valparaiso University School of Law, J.D., 2011 — Admitted to Bar, 2011, Indiana; U.S. District Court, Northern and Southern Districts of Indiana — Tel: 317-968-8173 — E-mail: whorvath@k-glaw.com

Marie Alexander Kuck — Indiana University, B.A., 2006; Indiana University School of Law-Indianapolis, J.D., 2010 — Admitted to Bar, 2010, Indiana; U.S. District Court, Northern and Southern Districts of Indiana — Tel: 317-968-8923 — E-mail: malexander@k-glaw.com

Matthew K. Phillips — University of Evansville, B.A., 2006; Indiana University School of Law-Indianapolis, J.D., 2009 — Admitted to Bar, 2009, Indiana; U.S. District Court, Northern and Southern Districts of Indiana — Tel: 317-968-8117 — E-mail: mphillips@k-glaw.com

Eric Sanders — Indiana University, B.A., 2006; University of Dayton School of Law, J.D., 2009 — Admitted to Bar, 2009, Ohio (Inactive); 2012, Indiana; U.S. District Court, Southern District of Indiana; U.S. District Court, Southern District of Ohio — Tel: 317-968-8145 — E-mail: esanders@k-glaw.com

Keenan D. Wilson — Ball State University, B.A., 2009; Indiana University Robert H. McKinney School of Law, J.D., 2013 — Admitted to Bar, 2013, Indiana; U.S. District Court, Northern and Southern Districts of Indiana — Tel: 317-968-8127 — E-mail: kwilson@k-glaw.com

Of Counsel

Donald L. Dawson — Indiana University, B.A., 1966; Indiana University School of Law-Indianapolis, J.D., 1969 — Admitted to Bar, 1970, Indiana; U.S. District Court, Northern and Southern Districts of Indiana; U.S. Court of Appeals, Seventh Circuit; U.S. Supreme Court — Tel: 317-968-8133 — E-mail: ddawson@k-glaw.com

(This firm is also listed in the Subrogation section of this directory)

Lewis Wagner, LLP

501 Indiana Avenue, Suite 200
Indianapolis, Indiana 46202-6150
Telephone: 317-237-0500
Toll Free: 800-237-0505
Fax: 317-630-2790
E-Mail: info@lewiswagner.com
www.lewiswagner.com

Established: 1955

Insurance Defense, Insurance Coverage, Bad Faith, Administrative Law, Appellate Practice, Automobile, Business Law, Class Actions, Commercial General Liability, Commercial Law, Complex Litigation, Construction Litigation, Contracts, Corporate Law, Employment Law, Family Law, Legal Malpractice, Medical Devices, Medical Malpractice, Premises Liability, Product Liability, Professional Liability, Real Estate, Subrogation, Trucking, Toxic Torts, Agriculture, Environmental Law, Estate Planning, Collaborative Law, Transportation Law, Administration & Probate

INDIANAPOLIS
INDIANA

Lewis Wagner, LLP, Indianapolis, IN (Continued)

Firm Profile: Since 1955, the attorneys of Lewis Wagner have provided pro-active counsel for individuals, small businesses and Fortune 500 companies. Our unique approach inspires imaginative and practical solutions for clients and utilizes traits all too rare today-common sense and accountability.

Our success is based on our ability to help clients meet their legal and business goals in a timely and cost-effective manner. We have never forgotten that the legal industry is a client-service business, and our success is measured by exceeding the expectations of our clients.

Many insurance claims require a prompt and objective review of coverage issues. The critical factor in any coverage claim is the interpretation of the applicable policy. The attorneys at Lewis Wagner can assist you in interpreting that policy and analyzing the validity of first and third party insurance coverage issues.

Our attorneys provide practical solutions to complex insurance disputes involving self-insured parties, businesses and insurance companies. Our team of attorneys has advised individuals and businesses about insurance coverage issues including insurance policy coverage opinions, declaratory judgments on policy coverage and defense of insurers against breach of contract and bad faith claims.

We handle insurance coverage disputes and defend declaratory judgment and bad faith actions with respect to: commercial and construction liability insurance; personal and commercial auto insurance; homeowner insurance; life, health, and disability insurance; environmental insurance; "claims made" and professional liability insurance; duties to additional insureds and certificate holders; property insurance; product liability insurance; business interruption insurance; legal malpractice; medical malpractice.

Insurance Clients

ACE USA/ESIS, Inc.
Affirmative Insurance Company
Brotherhood Mutual Insurance Company
Environmental Claims Administrators, Inc.
General Star
Great American Insurance Company
Indiana Department of Insurance
Indiana Farm Bureau
Indiana Insurance Institute
Liberty Mutual Insurance Company
Medmarc Mutual Insurance Company
M-J Insurance, Inc.
Pharmacists Mutual Insurance Company
Travelers Insurance
Zurich American Insurance Group
Acuity Insurance Company
Bituminous Insurance Companies
Chubb & Son, a division of Federal Insurance Company
Erie Insurance Group
Everett Cash Mutual Insurance Company
Hanover Insurance Group
Hortica Insurance and Employer Benefits
Indiana Farmers Mutual Insurance Company
Meadowbrook Insurance Group
Minnesota Lawyers Mutual Insurance Company
Nationwide Insurance
SECURA Insurance Companies
Titan Indemnity Company
Western Reserve Group

Non-Insurance Clients

Hillenbrand Industries
Pacers Sports & Entertainment
Marsh Supermarkets
Simon Property Group, Inc.

In Memoriam

Edward D. Lewis — (1922-1996)
Judith T. Kirtland — (1947-1990)
Mark E. Walker — (1969-2000)

Founding Partner

Robert F. Wagner — 1935 — Indiana University Robert H. McKinney School of Law, J.D., 1967 — Admitted to Bar, 1967, Indiana

Managing Partner

John C. Trimble — 1955 — Indiana University Robert H. McKinney School of Law, J.D. (magna cum laude), 1981 — Admitted to Bar, 1981, Indiana

Partners

Thomas C. Hays — 1951 — Woodrow Wilson College of Law, J.D., 1977 — Admitted to Bar, 1977, Georgia; 1979, Indiana
Jarrell B. Hammond — 1955 — Indiana University Robert H. McKinney School of Law, J.D., 1982 — Admitted to Bar, 1982, Indiana

Lewis Wagner, LLP, Indianapolis, IN (Continued)

Mary Foley Panszi — Indiana University Robert H. McKinney School of Law, J.D., 1988 — Admitted to Bar, 1988, Indiana
Daun A. Weliever — 1964 — Indiana University Robert H. McKinney School of Law, J.D., 1990 — Admitted to Bar, 1990, Indiana
Richard K. Shoultz — 1965 — Indiana University Robert H. McKinney School of Law, J.D., 1990 — Admitted to Bar, 1990, Indiana
Susan E. Cline — 1961 — Indiana University Robert H. McKinney School of Law, J.D., 1990 — Admitted to Bar, 1990, Indiana
Dina M. Cox — 1969 — Indiana University Robert H. McKinney School of Law, J.D. (cum laude), 1995 — Admitted to Bar, 1995, Indiana
Anthony M. Eleftheri — 1971 — Indiana University Robert H. McKinney School of Law, J.D., 1996 — Admitted to Bar, 1996, Indiana
A. Richard M. Blaiklock — 1968 — Indiana University Robert H. McKinney School of Law, J.D. (summa cum laude), 1997 — Admitted to Bar, 1997, Indiana
Robert R. Foos, Jr. — 1970 — The John Marshall Law School, J.D., 1997 — Admitted to Bar, 1997, Illinois; 1998, Indiana
Kyle A. Lansberry — 1972 — Indiana University Robert H. McKinney School of Law, J.D., 1998 — Admitted to Bar, 1998, Indiana
Stefanie Crawford — 1971 — Indiana University Robert H. McKinney School of Law, J.D., 1999 — Admitted to Bar, 1999, Indiana
Stephanie L. Cassman — 1974 — Indiana University Robert H. McKinney School of Law, J.D., 2000 — Admitted to Bar, 2000, Indiana
Robert M. Baker IV — 1979 — Indiana University Robert H. McKinney School of Law, J.D. (summa cum laude), 2005 — Admitted to Bar, 2005, Indiana
Lewis S. Wooton — 1980 — Indiana University Maurer School of Law, J.D., 2006 — Admitted to Bar, 2006, Indiana
Brett Y. Hoy — 1981 — Indiana University Robert H. McKinney School of Law, J.D., 2006 — Admitted to Bar, 2006, Indiana
Jason M. Lee — 1979 — Indiana University Robert H. McKinney School of Law, J.D., 2006 — Admitted to Bar, 2006, Indiana

Senior Counsel

Thomas A. Withrow — 1942 — Indiana University Robert H. McKinney School of Law, J.D., 1969 — Admitted to Bar, 1969, Indiana; 1998, Colorado

Counsel

Neal Bowling — 1968 Indiana University Maurer School of Law, J.D., 1995 — Admitted to Bar, 1996, Indiana
Charles R. Whybrew — 1972 — Indiana University Robert H. McKinney School of Law, J.D., 1998 — Admitted to Bar, 1998, Indiana
Eric C. McNamar — 1970 — Valparaiso School of Law, J.D., 2000 — Admitted to Bar, 2000, Indiana; 2005, New York

Of Counsel

Lisa M. Dillman — 1969 — Indiana University Robert H. McKinney School of Law, J.D., 1995 — Admitted to Bar, 1995, Indiana

Associates

Wandini B. Riggins — 1979 — Valparaiso University School of Law, J.D., 2005 — Admitted to Bar, 2006, Indiana
Lesley A. Pfleging — 1980 — Indiana University Robert H. McKinney School of Law, J.D., 2006 — Admitted to Bar, 2007, Indiana
Edward J. Fujawa — 1981 — Thomas M. Cooley Law School, J.D., 2007 — Admitted to Bar, 2007, Indiana
Theresa R. Parish — Indiana University Robert H. McKinney School of Law, J.D., 2008 — Admitted to Bar, 2008, Indiana
Ryan J. Vershay — 1983 — University of Notre Dame Law School, J.D. (cum laude), 2008 — Admitted to Bar, 2008, Indiana
Edward D. Thomas — 1974 — Indiana University Robert H. McKinney School of Law, J.D., 2009 — Admitted to Bar, 2010, Indiana
Brandon W. Ehrie — 1984 — Michigan State University College of Law, J.D. (cum laude), 2010 — Admitted to Bar, 2010, Indiana
Neha M. Matta — 1984 — University of Cincinnati College of Law, J.D. (Dean's List), 2010 — Admitted to Bar, 2010, Indiana
Katherine S. Strawbridge — 1986 — Indiana University Robert H. McKinney School of Law, J.D., 2011 — Admitted to Bar, 2011, Indiana
Janelle P. Kilies — 1984 — Indiana University Robert H. McKinney School of Law, J.D., 2012 — Admitted to Bar, 2012, Indiana

Lewis Wagner, LLP, Indianapolis, IN (Continued)

Keenan M. Jones — 1987 — University of Denver Sturm College of Law, J.D., 2012 — Admitted to Bar, 2012, Colorado; 2013, Indiana

Nabeela Virjee — 1986 — Indiana University Robert H. McKinney School of Law, J.D., 2013 — Admitted to Bar, 2013, Indiana

Michael R. Giordano — 1988 — Indiana University Maurer School of Law, J.D., 2013 — Admitted to Bar, 2013, Indiana

Jonathan W. Padish — 1988 — University of Illinois College of Law, J.D. (magna cum laude), 2014 — Admitted to Bar, 2014, Indiana

Barath S. Raman — 1987 — Indiana University Robert H. McKinney School of Law, J.D. (cum laude), 2014 — Admitted to Bar, 2014, Indiana

Kristen J. Davee — 1988 — Indiana University Maurer School of Law, J.D. (cum laude), 2014 — Admitted to Bar, 2014, Indiana

(This firm is also listed in the Subrogation section of this directory)

Pollack Law Firm, P.C.
10333 North Meridian Street, Suite 111
Indianapolis, Indiana 46290
  Telephone: 317-660-4880
  Fax: 317-660-4888
  E-Mail: cpollack@pollacklawpc.com
  www.pollacklawpc.com

Established: 2009

Insurance Defense, Personal Injury, Civil Rights, Wrongful Death, Municipal Torts, School Liability, Employment, Probate, Guardianships, Trusts and Minors' Compromises

Firm Profile: Pollack Law Firm, P.C., a certified woman-owned business, concentrates its practice in the area of insurance defense litigation, including personal injury, civil rights, property & casualty, school liability and employment law. The firm was founded in 2009 by Caren Pollack, a litigation attorney with over 27 years' experience.

Practicing with Ms. Pollack is Lana Swingler. Swingler has been practicing in the area of insurance defense law for over thirty years.

Insurance Clients

Crum & Forster Insurance
First Mercury Insurance Company
OneBeacon Government Risks
Selective Insurance Company
Summit Risk Services, Inc.
Engle Martin & Associates
JWF Specialty Company, Inc.
ProSight Specialty Insurance Company

Non-Insurance Clients

Fraternal Order of Police - (FOP)
Metropolitan School District of Pike Township
Indianapolis Public Schools
PORAC Legal Defense Fund

Principal

Caren L. Pollack — Washington University in St. Louis, B.S., 1982; University of North Carolina at Chapel Hill School of Law, J.D., 1987 — Admitted to Bar, 1987, Indiana; U.S. District Courts of Indiana — Member Federal and Indiana State Bar Associations; Defense Research Institute — Reported Cases: *Hupp v. Hill*, 578 N.E. 2d 1320 (Ind. App. 1991); *Tapia v. City of Greenwood*, 965 F. 2d 336 (7th Circuit 1992); *Ritchhart v. Indianapolis Public Schools*, 822 N.E. 2nd 982 (Ind. App. 2004), transfer denied; *Pettigrew v. Board of Commissioners of Indianapolis Public Schools*, 851 N.E. 2d 326 (Ind. App. 2006), transfer denied

Of Counsel

Lana R. Swingler — Ball State University, B.S. (magna cum laude), 1979; Indiana University, J.D., 1982 — Associate Editor, Indiana Law Review — Admitted to Bar, 1982, Indiana; U.S. District Court, Southern District of Indiana — Member Indiana State and Indianapolis Bar Associations

Reminger Co., L.P.A.
3925 River Crossing Parkway, Suite 280
Indianapolis, Indiana 46240
  Telephone: 317-663-8570
  Fax: 317-663-8580
  www.reminger.com

(Cleveland, OH Office*: 101 West Prospect Avenue, Suite 1400, 44115-1093)
  (Tel: 216-687-1311)
  (Fax: 216-687-1841)
(Cincinnati, OH Office*: 525 Vine Street, Suite 1700, 45202)
  (Tel: 513-721-1311)
  (Fax: 513-721-2553)
(Columbus, OH Office*: Capitol Square Office Building, 65 East State Street, 4th Floor, 43215)
  (Tel: 614-228-1311)
  (Fax: 614-232-2410)

Trial Practice, State and Federal Courts, Insurance Law, Malpractice, Self-Insured, Risk Management, Transportation, Product Liability, Errors and Omissions, Civil Rights, Investigation and Adjustment

Firm Members

Ronald A. Mingus — John Carroll University, B.S.B.A. (cum laude), 1987; Case Western Reserve University School of Law, J.D. (magna cum laude, Order of the Coif), 1990 — Admitted to Bar, 1990, Ohio; 2013, Indiana — E-mail: rmingus@reminger.com

(See listing under Cleveland, OH for additional information)

Rocap Musser LLP
10401 North Meridian Street, Suite 120
Indianapolis, Indiana 46290-1090
  Telephone: 317-846-0700
  Fax: 317-846-0973
  E-Mail: jam@rocap-law.com
  E-Mail: rar@rocap-law.com
  E-Mail: sdas@rocap-law.com
  www.rocap-law.com

Established: 1904

Automobile, Premises Liability, Product Liability, Trucking Law, Professional Liability, Commercial Litigation, General Practice, Insurance Defense, Litigation, Motor Carriers, Mediation, Coverage Disputes, Worker's Compensation Defense

Firm Profile: Rocap Musser LLP and its predecessors have been an integral part of the Indiana legal community for over 100 years. Our attorneys are focused on solving your problems and serving your needs in the most efficient and economical manner possible. Our experience and history give us a unique perspective on the legal needs of our clients and allow us to search for creative and cost-effective ways to meet those needs. Rocap Musser LLP has dedicated itself to meeting the needs of the insurance industry. Our staff is knowledgeable and experienced in helping insurance professionals perform. Let us help you.

Insurance Clients

Alfa Vision Insurance Corp.
Bituminous Insurance Company
Mendota Insurance Company
RLI Insurance Company
Travelers Casualty Company
American Modern Home Insurance Company
Motorists Mutual Insurance Company
Zurich Insurance Company

Representative Clients

Kenan Advantage Group
Monarch Beverage

INDIANAPOLIS

INDIANA

Rocap Musser LLP, Indianapolis, IN (Continued)

Self-Insured Clients

Arkansas Best Corporation
United Water

Third Party Administrators

Constitution State Service Company
Gallagher Bassett Services, Inc.
Sedgwick Claims Management Services, Inc.

James E. Rocap, Jr. — (1917-2006)

Partners

Richard A. Rocap — 1955 — University of Notre Dame, B.B.A., 1977; Indiana University, J.D., 1980 — Admitted to Bar, 1980, Indiana — Member Indiana State and Indianapolis Bar Associations; Defense Trial Counsel of Indiana

Jeffrey A. Musser — 1959 — University of Cincinnati, B.U.P. (cum laude), 1989; Indiana University, J.D., 1996 — Admitted to Bar, 1996, Indiana; U.S. District Court, Northern and Southern Districts of Indiana — Member Indiana State and Indianapolis Bar Associations; Defense Trial Counsel of Indiana

Sonia Das — 1975 — Indiana University-Bloomington, B.A., 1996; Indiana University, J.D., 2000 — Admitted to Bar, 2000, Indiana; U.S. District Court, Northern and Southern Districts of Indiana — Member Indiana State (Vice Chair, Diversity Committee) and Indianapolis Bar Associations; Defense Trial Counsel of Indiana; Defense Research Institute

Retired

James D. Witchger

Associate

Kristen M. Moorehead — 1985 — Purdue University, B.A. (Dean's List), 2007; Indiana University-Indianapolis, J.D., 2010 — Hon. Jane Magnus Stinson, US District Court, Southern District of Indiana (Externship) — Admitted to Bar, 2011, Indiana — Member American, Indiana State and Indianapolis Bar Associations

Smith Fisher Maas & Howard, P.C.

7209 North Shadeland Avenue
Indianapolis, Indiana 46250
Telephone: 317-578-1900
Fax: 317-578-1330
E-Mail: defenselaw@smithfisher.com
www.smithfisher.com

Established: 1993

Insurance Defense, First and Third Party Defense, General Liability, Coverage Issues, Property Damage, Bad Faith, Product Liability, Arson, Fraud, Mediation, Appellate Practice, Automobile Liability, Builders Risk, Casualty Insurance Law, Catastrophic Injury, Civil Rights, Commercial and Personal Lines, Commercial Vehicle, Comprehensive General Liability, Construction Liability, Declaratory Judgments, Environmental Coverage, Environmental Litigation, Examinations Under Oath, Governmental Entity Defense, Police Liability Defense, Premises Liability, Punitive Damages, Self-Insured Defense, Slip and Fall, Trucking Litigation, Uninsured and Underinsured Motorist, Wrongful Death, Civil Appeals

Firm Profile: Established in 1993, the law firm of Smith Fisher Maas & Howard, P.C. offers legal services throughout the state of Indiana. The firm is a state-certified woman owned business and member of the National Association of Minority & Women Owned Law Firms and the National Association of Women Business Owners. The firm's defense trial practice covers most areas of tort and contract law.

Counsel For

American Family Insurance
ATT Corp.
Celina Group
Erie Insurance Group
Amerisure Companies
Bituminous Insurance Company
Columbia Insurance Group
Esurance

Smith Fisher Maas & Howard, P.C., Indianapolis, IN (Continued)

Fireman's Fund Insurance Companies
Hastings Mutual Insurance Company
Last Chance Wrecker & Sales, Inc.
Marathon Petroleum Company, LLC
Meridian Security/State Auto Insurance
Nationwide Mutual Fire Insurance Company
Progressive Insurance
Standard Mutual Insurance Company
United Fire Group
West Bend Mutual Insurance Company
General Casualty Company
Hanover Professionals
Indiana Farmers Mutual Insurance Company
Lincoln General Insurance Company
Mennonite Mutual Insurance Company
Motorists Insurance Group
Ohio Mutual Insurance Group
Pekin Insurance Company
Selective Insurance Company of America
State Farm Insurance Company
United National Group
Western Reserve Group
Westfield Companies

Partners

Mark R. Smith, CPCU — 1959 — Hanover College, B.A. (magna cum laude), 1981; Insurance Institute of America, C.P.C.U., 1991; Indiana University, J.D. (magna cum laude), 1984 — Admitted to Bar, 1984, Indiana; U.S. District Court, Northern and Southern Districts of Indiana; 1993, U.S. Court of Appeals, Seventh Circuit — Member Indiana State and Indianapolis Bar Associations; Society of Chartered Property and Casualty Underwriters; Defense Trial Counsel of Indiana; Defense Research Institute — Chartered Property Casualty Underwriter — Practice Areas: Insurance Coverage; Bad Faith; Appellate Practice — E-mail: msmith@smithfisher.com

Donna H. Fisher — 1947 — Susquehanna University, B.A., 1969; Indiana University, J.D. (cum laude), 1983 — Admitted to Bar, 1984, Indiana; U.S. District Court, Northern and Southern Districts of Indiana; 1991, U.S. Court of Appeals, Seventh Circuit — Member Indiana State and Indianapolis Bar Associations; Defense Research Institute; Defense Trial Counsel of Indiana — Certified Civil Mediator — Practice Areas: Environmental Coverage; Environmental Law; First and Third Party Defense; Bad Faith; Insurance Fraud; Property Defense; Arbitration; Mediation — E-mail: dfisher@smithfisher.com

Rebecca J. Maas — 1961 — Taylor University, B.A., 1983; Indiana University, J.D., 1988 — Admitted to Bar, 1988, Indiana; U.S. District Court, Northern and Southern Districts of Indiana; U.S. Court of Appeals, Seventh Circuit — Member Indiana State and Indianapolis Bar Associations; Defense Research Institute; Defense Trial Counsel of Indiana — Practice Areas: Insurance Defense; First and Third Party Defense; Personal Injury; Premises Liability; Negligence; Construction Litigation; Environmental Law; Construction Law — E-mail: rmaas@smithfisher.com

Kimberly E. Howard — 1966 — Indiana University, B.A., 1988; J.D., 1991 — Admitted to Bar, 1991, Indiana; U.S. District Court, Northern and Southern Districts of Indiana — Member Indiana State and Indianapolis Bar Associations; Defense Research Institute; Defense Trial Counsel of Indiana — Practice Areas: Litigation; First and Third Party Defense; Business Law; Truck Liability; Construction Law — E-mail: khoward@smithfisher.com

Marcum J. Lloyd — 1973 — Valparaiso University, B.S. (magna cum laude), 1995; J.D. (with honors), 1999 — Admitted to Bar, 1999, Indiana; U.S. District Court, Northern and Southern Districts of Indiana — Member Indiana State and Indianapolis Bar Associations; Defense Research Institute; Defense Trial Counsel of Indiana — Practice Areas: Insurance Defense; First and Third Party Defense; Construction Accidents; Workers' Compensation — E-mail: mlloyd@smithfisher.com

Associates

Freedom D. Villa — 1978 — Ball State University, B.S., 2000; Indiana University School of Law-Indianapolis, J.D., 2006 — Admitted to Bar, 2006, Indiana; U.S. District Court, Northern and Southern Districts of Indiana — Member Indiana State and Indianapolis Bar Associations; Defense Research Institute; Defense Trial Counsel of Indiana — Certified Civil Mediator — Practice Areas: Insurance Defense; Environmental Law; Insurance Coverage — E-mail: fvilla@smithfisher.com

Aimee Rivera Cole — 1976 — Indiana University, B.S., 1998; Valparaiso University School of Law, J.D., 2003 — Admitted to Bar, 2004, Indiana; U.S. District Court, Northern and Southern Districts of Indiana; U.S. Court of Appeals, Seventh Circuit — Member Indiana State and Indianapolis Bar Associations; Defense Research Institute; Defense Trial Counsel of Indiana — Languages: French, Spanish — Practice Areas: Insurance Defense; First and Third Party Defense; Employment Law; Governmental Liability; Government Affairs; Railroad Law; Federal Employer Liability Claims (FELA) — E-mail: arivera@smithfisher.com

INDIANA — INDIANAPOLIS

Smith Fisher Maas & Howard, P.C., Indianapolis, IN (Continued)

Dirk E. Wallsmith — 1954 — Ball State University, B.S., 1977; Indiana University School of Law-Indianapolis, J.D. (cum laude), 1987 — Admitted to Bar, 1987, Indiana; U.S. District Court, Northern and Southern Districts of Indiana — Member Indiana State and Indianapolis Bar Associations; Defense Research Institute; Defense Trial Counsel of Indiana — Practice Areas: Insurance Defense; Third Party — E-mail: dwallsmith@smithfisher.com

Spangler, Jennings & Dougherty, P.C.

8425 Keystone Crossing, Suite 114
Indianapolis, Indiana 46240
  Telephone: 317-571-7690
  Fax: 317-571-7686
  www.sjdlaw.com

(Merrillville, IN Office*: 8396 Mississippi Street, 46410-6398)
  (Tel: 219-769-2323)
  (Fax: 219-769-5007)

Established: 1952

Insurance Law, Fire, Casualty, Surety, Life Insurance, Environmental Law, Toxic Torts, Product Liability, Professional Liability, Workers' Compensation, Coverage Issues, Appellate Practice, Subrogation

Resident Associate

Gregory A. Purvis — 1951 — Ball State University, B.S., 1974; Indiana University, J.D., 1977 — Admitted to Bar, 1997, Indiana — Member Indiana State Bar Association

(See Merrillville, IN Listing for additional information)

Threlkeld & Associates

50 South Meridian Street, Suite 400
Indianapolis, Indiana 46204-3539
  Telephone: 317-655-5200
  Fax: 317-655-3150
  E-Mail: debbie@threlkeld-legal.com
  www.threlkeld-legal.com

Established: 2000

Insurance Defense, Property and Casualty, General Liability, Construction Law, Automobile, Professional Liability, Product Liability, Insurance Fraud, Arson, Workers' Compensation

Insurance Clients

American Family Insurance Company
Penn-America Insurance Company
Shelter Mutual Insurance Company
State Farm Mutual Automobile Insurance Company
Ameriprise Insurance Company
Gateway Insurance Company
The St. Paul/Travelers Companies, Inc.

Partner

W. Brent Threlkeld — 1946 — Indiana State University, B.S., 1968; Indiana University, J.D., 1971 — Phi Alpha Delta — Admitted to Bar, 1972, Indiana; 1972, U.S. District Court, Southern District of Indiana; U.S. Court of Appeals, Seventh Circuit; U.S. Supreme Court; U.S. Court of Military Appeals — Member Indiana State and Indianapolis Bar Associations; Defense Trial Counsel of Indiana; Defense Research Institute; Association of Trial Lawyers of America; American Board of Trial Advocates — Captain, U.S. Marine Corps, 1972-1975; Judge Advocate, Military Judge, 1974-1975 — Practice Areas: Insurance Defense; Trial Practice — E-mail: brent@threlkeld-legal.com

Associates

Benjamin G. Stevenson — 1978 — Indiana University-Bloomington, J.D., 2003 — Admitted to Bar, 2003, Indiana — Member Indiana State, Hamilton

Threlkeld & Associates, Indianapolis, IN (Continued)

County and Indianapolis Bar Associations — E-mail: bstevenson@threlkeld-legal.com

Melanie A. Smith — 1980 — Indiana University, B.S. (with honors), 2002; Indiana University Maurer School of Law, J.D., 2005 — Admitted to Bar, 2005, Indiana; 2009, Arizona (Inactive) — Member Indianapolis Bar Association — E-mail: masmith@threlkeld-legal.com

Kelly A. Roth — 1981 — University of Florida, B.S., 2003; Indiana University School of Law-Indianapolis, J.D., 2006 — Admitted to Bar, 2006, Indiana; U.S. District Court, Northern and Southern Districts of Indiana — Member Defense Trial Counsel of Indiana — E-mail: kroth@threlkeld-legal.com

Paul A. Jansen — 1982 — Wabash College, B.A., 2005; Indiana University Robert H. McKinney School of Law, J.D., 2011 — Admitted to Bar, 2011, Indiana; U.S. District Court, Central and Southern Districts of Indiana; U.S. District Court, Eastern District of Michigan; U.S. District Court, Eastern District of Wisconsin — Member Federal, American, Indiana State, Hamilton County, Allen County and Indianapolis Bar Associations — E-mail: pjansen@threlkeld-legal.com

The Tyra Law Firm, P.C.

355 Indiana Avenue, Suite 150
Indianapolis, Indiana 46204
  Telephone: 317-636-1304
  Fax: 317-636-1343
  E-Mail: kevin.tyra@tyralaw.net
  www.tyralaw.net

Established: 2007

General Liability, Insurance Coverage, Insurance Defense, Insurance Fraud, Medical Malpractice, Nursing Home Liability, Workers' Compensation, Contract Disputes, Intellectual Property, Construction Defect Liability and Litigation

Firm Profile: The Tyra Law Firm, P.C. is a law firm serving clients throughout Indiana from its office in Indianapolis, with an emphasis on serving the insurance defense and coverage needs of carriers.

Insurance Clients

Amica Mutual Insurance Company
IFG Companies
MetLife Auto & Home
Western Reserve Group
Brotherhood Mutual Insurance Company
State Farm Insurance Companies
Zurich North America

Non-Insurance Clients

Australian Gold
Avis Budget Car Rental, LLC

Firm Member

Kevin C. Tyra — 1956 — Purdue University, B.A. (cum laude), 1978; Vanderbilt University Law School, J.D., 1981 — Phi Beta Kappa — Admitted to Bar, 1981, Tennessee; 1987, Indiana; 1986, U.S. Court of Military Appeals; 1987, U.S. District Court, Southern District of Indiana; 1996, U.S. District Court, Northern District of Indiana; U.S. Court of Appeals, Seventh Circuit — Member Defense Trial Counsel of Indiana (Chair, Insurance Coverage Section, 2008-2009; Board of Directors, 2010-present); National Society of Professional Insurance Investigators (Indiana Board of Directors, 2010-present); Defense Research Institute — Co-Author: "Mediation Confidentiality: Myth and Misnomer?" 3 Ind. Civ. Lit. Review, Spring 2006; Author: "What Would Jesus Do? A Gospel-Based Approach To Defending The Catholic Church Against Allegations of Abuse," 5 Ind. Civ. Lit. Review, Summer 2008 — Reported Cases: Kelly v. Bennett, 732 N.E. 2d 859 (Ind. App. 2000); In the Matter of the Paternity of T.P., 920 N.E. 2d 726 (Ind. App. 2010); BMIC v. Michiana Contracting, Inc., 971 N.E. 2d 127 (Ind. App 2012); Hammerstone v. Indiana Ins. Co., 986 N.E. 2d 841, (Ind. App. 2013) — Registered Civil and Family Mediator — LT., JAGC, USNR, active duty, 1981-1987 — Practice Areas: General Liability; Insurance Litigation; Insurance Coverage; Insurance Fraud; Medical Malpractice; Litigation; Contract Disputes — E-mail: kevin.tyra@tyralaw.net

Associates

Jerry M. Padgett — 1976 — University of Indianapolis, B.A., 1998; Indiana University School of Law-Indianapolis, J.D., 2007 — Admitted to Bar, 2007, Indiana; U.S. District Court, Northern and Southern Districts of Indiana; U.S.

The Tyra Law Firm, P.C., Indianapolis, IN (Continued)

Court of Appeals, Seventh Circuit — Member Indiana State Bar Association; Brownsburg Chamber of Commerce; Defense Trial Counsel of Indiana; Defense Research Institute — Co-Author: "Causation as a Case Dispositive Issue," The Indiana Lawyer, October 14, 2009 — Reported Cases: In the Matter of the Paternity of T.P., 920 N.E. 2d 726 (Ind. App. 2010); Hammerstone v. Indiana Ins. Co., 986 N.E. 2d 841, (Ind. App. 2013) — Practice Areas: General Liability; Insurance Litigation; Insurance Coverage; Insurance Fraud; Medical Malpractice; Litigation; Contract Disputes; Commercial Litigation — E-mail: jerry.padgett@tyralaw.net

Elizabeth Steele — 1987 — DePauw University, B.A. (magna cum laude), 2008; Indiana University School of Law-Bloomington, J.D., 2011 — Admitted to Bar, 2011, Indiana; U.S. District Court, Northern and Southern Districts of Indiana — Member Indiana State Bar Association; Defense Trial Counsel of Indiana; Defense Research Institute — Practice Areas: Insurance Litigation; Insurance Coverage; General Liability; Litigation; Intellectual Property — E-mail: elizabeth.steele@tyralaw.net

Zeigler Cohen & Koch

9465 Counselors Row, Suite 104
Indianapolis, Indiana 46240
 Telephone: 317-844-5200
 Fax: 317-844-7200
 www.zcklaw.com

Insurance Defense, Automobile, Casualty Defense, General Liability, Homeowners, Coverage Issues, Medical Malpractice

Insurance Clients

American Physicians Assurance Corp.
Medical Protective Insurance Services
ProAssurance Group
Shelter Insurance Companies
Indiana Residual Malpractice Insurance Authority
OneBeacon Professional Insurance
Preferred Professional Insurance Company

Non-Insurance Clients

Ascension Health
Community Health Systems, Inc.
Caronia Corporation
Western Litigation Specialists, Inc.

Partners

Robert G. Zeigler — 1950 — Illinois College, B.A., 1970; University of Illinois, M.A., 1971; J.D., 1980 — Phi Beta Kappa — Admitted to Bar, 1980, Indiana; U.S. District Court, Southern District of Indiana; 1984, U.S. Court of Appeals, Seventh Circuit; 1985, U.S. District Court, Northern District of Indiana — Member American and Indiana State Bar Associations

Steven J. Cohen — 1952 — Northwestern University, B.S., 1974; Indiana University, J.D., 1980 — Admitted to Bar, 1980, Indiana; U.S. District Court, Southern District of Indiana; 1985, U.S. District Court, Northern District of Indiana; 1989, U.S. Court of Appeals, Seventh Circuit — Member Indiana State and Indianapolis Bar Associations

Edna M. Koch — 1951 — St. Anthony Hospital School of Nursing, 1972; Indiana State University, B.S.N. (cum laude), 1977; Indiana University, J.D. (cum laude), 1980 — Admitted to Bar, 1980, Indiana; U.S. District Court, Southern District of Indiana — Member American, Indiana State and Indianapolis Bar Associations; American Society of Law Medicine and Ethics

David D. Becsey — 1953 — Duke University, B.H.S. (magna cum laude), 1984; Indiana University, J.D., 1991 — Admitted to Bar, 1991, Indiana; U.S. District Court, Northern and Southern Districts of Indiana — Member American, Indiana State and Indianapolis Bar Associations

Roger K. Kanne — 1957 — Indiana University, B.A., 1979; University of San Diego, J.D., 1982 — Phi Delta Phi — Admitted to Bar, 1983, California; 1993, Indiana; 1986, U.S. District Court, Central District of California; 1990, U.S. District Court, Southern District of California; 1991, U.S. District Court, Eastern District of California; 1993, U.S. District Court, Southern District of Indiana — Member American and Indiana State Bar Associations; State Bar of California; Los Angeles and Burbank Bar Associations

Joseph D. McPike, II — 1966 — Auburn University, B.S., 1990; Indiana University, J.D. (cum laude), 1993 — Admitted to Bar, 1993, Indiana; U.S. District Court, Northern and Southern Districts of Indiana

Zeigler Cohen & Koch, Indianapolis, IN (Continued)

Associates

Marilyn A. Young — 1960 — Purdue University, B.S., 1983; Indiana University, J.D. (cum laude), 1989 — Admitted to Bar, 1989, Indiana — Member Indiana State Bar Association (Healthcare and Litigation Sections); Indianapolis Bar Association (Healthcare and Litigation Sections)

Jennifer A. Padgett — 1976 — Northwestern University, B.A., 1998; Indiana University-Bloomington, J.D. (cum laude), 2001 — Admitted to Bar, 2001, Indiana; U.S. District Court, Southern District of Indiana

Bobby J. Avery-Seagrave — 1976 — Indiana State University, B.S. (magna cum laude), 1998; Indiana University-Indianapolis, J.D./M.H.A. (magna cum laude), 2001 — Admitted to Bar, 2002, Indiana; U.S. District Court, Northern and Southern Districts of Indiana — Member American and Indiana State Bar Associations — Languages: German

Karen L. Withers — 1976 — University of Evansville, B.S., 1998; University of Miami, J.D. (cum laude), 2005 — Admitted to Bar, 2005, Indiana; U.S. District Court, Northern and Southern Districts of Indiana

Philip J. List — 1982 — Indiana University, B.A./B.A., 2004; University of Dayton, J.D., 2009 — Admitted to Bar, 2009, Indiana; U.S. District Court, Southern District of Indiana

---

The following firms also service this area.

Ferguson & Ferguson

403 East Sixth Street
Bloomington, Indiana 47408-4098
 Telephone: 812-332-2113
 Fax: 812-334-3892

Insurance Defense, School Law, Commercial Law, General Liability, Product Liability, Premises Liability, Motor Vehicle, Uninsured and Underinsured Motorist, Life, Accident and Health, General Civil Trial and Appellate Practice, Employment Issues, Including ADA, Business and Real Estate Litigation, Municipal and Governmental Entity Liability, including §1983 Actions

SEE COMPLETE LISTING UNDER BLOOMINGTON, INDIANA (49 MILES)

Kahn, Dees, Donovan & Kahn, LLP

501 Main Street, Suite 305
Evansville, Indiana 47708
 Telephone: 812-423-3183
 Fax: 812-423-3841
Mailing Address: P.O. Box 3646, Evansville, IN 47735-3646

Asbestos Litigation, Automobile, Construction Law, Coverage Issues, Environmental Law, Insurance Defense, General Liability, Labor and Employment, Mass Tort, Medical Malpractice, Personal Injury, Premises Liability, Product Liability, Property, Public Entities, Self-Insured, Subrogation, Workers' Compensation

SEE COMPLETE LISTING UNDER EVANSVILLE, INDIANA (184 MILES)

JASPER † 15,038 Dubois Co.

Refer To

Kahn, Dees, Donovan & Kahn, LLP

501 Main Street, Suite 305
Evansville, Indiana 47708
 Telephone: 812-423-3183
 Fax: 812-423-3841

Mailing Address: P.O. Box 3646, Evansville, IN 47735-3646

Asbestos Litigation, Automobile, Construction Law, Coverage Issues, Environmental Law, Insurance Defense, General Liability, Labor and Employment, Mass Tort, Medical Malpractice, Personal Injury, Premises Liability, Product Liability, Property, Public Entities, Self-Insured, Subrogation, Workers' Compensation

SEE COMPLETE LISTING UNDER EVANSVILLE, INDIANA (60 MILES)

JEFFERSONVILLE † 44,953 Clark Co.

Refer To

Kahn, Dees, Donovan & Kahn, LLP
501 Main Street, Suite 305
Evansville, Indiana 47708
   Telephone: 812-423-3183
   Fax: 812-423-3841

Mailing Address: P.O. Box 3646, Evansville, IN 47735-3646

Asbestos Litigation, Automobile, Construction Law, Coverage Issues, Environmental Law, Insurance Defense, General Liability, Labor and Employment, Mass Tort, Medical Malpractice, Personal Injury, Premises Liability, Product Liability, Property, Public Entities, Self-Insured, Subrogation, Workers' Compensation

SEE COMPLETE LISTING UNDER EVANSVILLE, INDIANA (123 MILES)

Refer To

Kightlinger & Gray, LLP
Bonterra Building, Suite 200
3620 Blackiston Boulevard
New Albany, Indiana 47150
   Telephone: 812-949-2300
   Fax: 812-949-8556

Insurance Defense, Insurance Litigation, Defense Litigation, Litigation, Insurance Law, Coverage Issues, Carrier Defense, Self-Insured Defense, Comprehensive General Liability, Trial and Appellate Practice, State and Federal Courts, General Civil Trial and Appellate Practice, Casualty Defense, Product Liability, Workers' Compensation, Employment Law, Subrogation, Toxic Torts, Aviation, Surety, Administrative Law, Agent/Broker Liability, Bad Faith, Business Law, Automobile Liability, Trucking Law, Asbestos Litigation, Construction Law, Corporate Law, Complex Litigation, Construction Litigation, Coverage Analysis, First and Third Party Defense, Fire Loss, Professional Liability, Malpractice, Agency Defense, Agent and Brokers Errors and Omissions, Medical Malpractice, School Law, Transportation, Real Estate, Bankruptcy, Municipal Liability, Class Actions, Mediation, Securities Litigation and Arbitration

SEE COMPLETE LISTING UNDER NEW ALBANY, INDIANA (5 MILES)

KENTLAND † 1,748 Newton Co.

Refer To

Spangler, Jennings & Dougherty, P.C.
8396 Mississippi Street
Merrillville, Indiana 46410-6398
   Telephone: 219-769-2323
   Fax: 219-769-5007

Insurance Law, Fire, Property, Casualty, Surety, Life Insurance, Environmental Law, Toxic Torts, Product Liability, Professional Liability, Workers' Compensation, Coverage Issues, Appellate Practice, Subrogation, Medical Malpractice Defense, Mortgage Foreclosure

SEE COMPLETE LISTING UNDER MERRILLVILLE, INDIANA (61 MILES)

LA PORTE † 22,053 La Porte Co.

Refer To

Spangler, Jennings & Dougherty, P.C.
8396 Mississippi Street
Merrillville, Indiana 46410-6398
   Telephone: 219-769-2323
   Fax: 219-769-5007

Insurance Law, Fire, Property, Casualty, Surety, Life Insurance, Environmental Law, Toxic Torts, Product Liability, Professional Liability, Workers' Compensation, Coverage Issues, Appellate Practice, Subrogation, Medical Malpractice Defense, Mortgage Foreclosure

SEE COMPLETE LISTING UNDER MERRILLVILLE, INDIANA (39 MILES)

LAFAYETTE † 67,140 Tippecanoe Co.

Hoffman, Luhman & Masson, PC

200 Ferry Street, Suite C
Lafayette, Indiana 47901
   Telephone: 765-423-5404
   Fax: 765-742-6448
   E-Mail: hlb@hlblaw.com
   www.hlblaw.com

Established: 1957

Fire, Casualty Insurance Law, Product Liability, Personal Injury, Subrogation

Corporate Clients

Archer Daniels Midland Company

Insurance Clients

Farm Bureau Insurance Company
Nautilus Insurance Group
State Farm Insurance Companies
Hastings Mutual Insurance Company
West Bend Mutual Insurance Company

Self-Insured Clients

Tippecanoe County, Indiana

Partners

David W. Luhman — Purdue University, B.S., 1973; Indiana University, J.D. (cum laude), 1977 — Admitted to Bar, 1977, Indiana — Member American, Indiana State and Tippecanoe County Bar Associations; Bar Association of Seventh Federal Circuit; Defense Research Institute — Tippecanoe County Attorney, 1995-Present

Douglas J. Masson — 1971 — Miami University, B.A., 1993; Indiana University, J.D. (cum laude), 1996 — Admitted to Bar, 1996, Indiana — Member American, Indiana State and Tippecanoe County Bar Associations

Founder

J. Frederick Hoffman — (1922-2003)

Associate

Matthew A. Salsbery — 1979 — Indiana University School of Law-Indianapolis, J.D. (cum laude), 2007 — Admitted to Bar, 2007, Missouri; 2010, Indiana

(This firm is also listed in the Subrogation section of this directory)

MARTINSVILLE † 11,828 Morgan Co.

Refer To

Ferguson & Ferguson
403 East Sixth Street
Bloomington, Indiana 47408-4098
   Telephone: 812-332-2113
   Fax: 812-334-3892

Insurance Defense, School Law, Commercial Law, General Liability, Product Liability, Premises Liability, Motor Vehicle, Uninsured and Underinsured Motorist, Life, Accident and Health, General Civil Trial and Appellate Practice, Employment Issues, Including ADA, Business and Real Estate Litigation, Municipal and Governmental Entity Liability, including §1983 Actions

SEE COMPLETE LISTING UNDER BLOOMINGTON, INDIANA (19 MILES)

MERRILLVILLE 35,246 Lake Co.

Garan Lucow Miller, P.C.

8401 Virginia Street
Merrillville, Indiana 46410
   Telephone: 219-756-7901
   Fax: 219-756-7902
   Toll Free: 877-804-2801

MERRILLVILLE   INDIANA

Garan Lucow Miller, P.C., Merrillville, IN   (Continued)

(Additional Offices: Detroit, MI*; Ann Arbor, MI*; Grand Blanc, MI*(See Flint listing); Grand Rapids, MI*; Lansing, MI*; Marquette, MI*; Port Huron, MI*; Traverse City, MI*; Troy, MI*)

Business Law, Employment Law, Insurance Defense, Municipal Liability, No-Fault, Workers' Compensation

(See listing under Detroit, MI for additional information)

Kightlinger & Gray, LLP

Merrillville Corporate Center
8001 Broadway, Suite 100
Merrillville, Indiana 46410
  Telephone: 219-769-0413
  Fax: 219-769-0798
  E-Mail: info@k-glaw.com
  www.k-glaw.com

(Indianapolis, IN Office*: One Indiana Square, Suite 300, 211 North Pennsylvania Street, 46204)
  (Tel: 317-638-4521)
  (Fax: 317-636-5917)
(Evansville, IN Office*: 7220 Eagle Crest Boulevard, 47715)
  (Tel: 812-474-4400)
  (Fax: 812-474-4414)
(New Albany, IN Office*: Bonterra Building, Suite 200, 3620 Blackiston Boulevard, 47150)
  (Tel: 812-949-2300)
  (Fax: 812-949-8556)
(Louisville, KY Office*: 312 South Fourth Street, Suite 700, 40202)
  (Tel: 502-442-2295)
  (Fax: 502-442-2703)

Established: 1946

Insurance Defense, Insurance Litigation, Defense Litigation, Litigation, Insurance Law, Coverage Issues, Carrier Defense, Self-Insured Defense, Comprehensive General Liability, Trial and Appellate Practice, State and Federal Courts, General Civil Trial and Appellate Practice, Casualty Defense, Product Liability, Workers' Compensation, Employment Law, Subrogation, Toxic Torts, Aviation, Surety, Administrative Law, Agent/Broker Liability, Bad Faith, Business Law, Automobile Liability, Trucking Law, Asbestos Litigation, Construction Law, Corporate Law, Complex Litigation, Construction Litigation, Coverage Analysis, First and Third Party Defense, Fire Loss, Professional Liability, Malpractice, Agency Defense, Agent and Brokers Errors and Omissions, Medical Malpractice, School Law, Transportation, Real Estate, Bankruptcy, Municipal Liability, Class Actions, Mediation, Securities Litigation and Arbitration

Partners

Galen A. Bradley — Eastern Illinois University, B.A., 1988; Valparaiso University School of Law, J.D., 1995 — Admitted to Bar, 1995, Indiana; Illinois; U.S. District Court, Northern District of Illinois; U.S. District Court, Northern and Southern Districts of Indiana — Tel: 219-769-0413 ext.7107 — E-mail: gbradley@k-glaw.com

John H. Halstead — Brigham Young University, B.A. (cum laude), 1999; Indiana University Maurer School of Law, J.D. (magna cum laude), 2002 — Admitted to Bar, 2002, Indiana; U.S. District Court, Northern and Southern Districts of Indiana — Tel: 219-769-0413 ext.7103 — E-mail: jhalstead@k-glaw.com

Associates

Laura J. Gard — Purdue University, B.A., 2006; Seton Hall University School of Law, J.D., 2009 — Admitted to Bar, 2009, Illinois; 2010, Indiana; U.S. District Court, Northern and Southern Districts of Indiana — Tel: (219) 769-0413 ext. 7106 — E-mail: lsims@k-glaw.com

Kightlinger & Gray, LLP, Merrillville, IN   (Continued)

Mark J. Schocke — Purdue University, B.A., 2007; Indiana University Robert H. McKinney School of Law, J.D., 2010 — Admitted to Bar, 2011, Indiana; Illinois; U.S. District Court, Northern and Southern Districts of Indiana; U.S. Supreme Court — Tel: 219-769-0413 ext. 7104 — E-mail: mschocke@k-glaw.com

(This firm is also listed in the Subrogation section of this directory)

Spangler, Jennings & Dougherty, P.C.

8396 Mississippi Street
Merrillville, Indiana 46410-6398
  Telephone: 219-769-2323
  Fax: 219-769-5007
  www.sjdlaw.com

(Indianapolis, IN Office*: 8425 Keystone Crossing, Suite 114, 46240)
  (Tel: 317-571-7690)
  (Fax: 317-571-7686)

Established: 1952

Insurance Law, Fire, Property, Casualty, Surety, Life Insurance, Environmental Law, Toxic Torts, Product Liability, Professional Liability, Workers' Compensation, Coverage Issues, Appellate Practice, Subrogation, Medical Malpractice Defense, Mortgage Foreclosure

Insurance Clients

AIG Risk Management, Inc.	Allstate Insurance Company
American International Group, Inc.	Amica Mutual Insurance Company
Auto-Owners Insurance Company	Capitol Indemnity Corporation
Farm Bureau Mutual Insurance Company	Farmers Insurance Group
	Foremost Insurance Company
Great West Casualty Company	Hawkeye-Security Insurance Company
Indiana Residual Malpractice Insurance Authority	Medical Assurance of Indiana
Meridian Mutual Insurance Company	Metropolitan Insurance Company
	National Union Fire Insurance Company
ProNational Insurance Company	The St. Paul Companies
Safeco Insurance Company of America	State Farm Insurance Companies
TIG Insurance Company	Wausau Insurance Companies
Western Casualty Insurance Company	Zurich American Insurance Group

Non-Insurance Clients

Ancilla Systems, Inc.

Firm Members

Samuel J. Furlin — (1935-1997)
Joseph E. McDonald — (1941-1997)
David J. Hanson — (1941-2001)
Allen B. Zaremba — (1943-2004)
James T. McNiece — (1948-2004)
Richard A. Mayer — (1934-2008)
Robert D. Hawk, Sr. — 1938 — Indiana University, B.S., 1963; J.D., 1967 — Admitted to Bar, 1967, Indiana — Member Indiana State Bar Association
James D. McQuillan — 1950 — Wabash College, B.A., 1972; The University of Iowa, J.D., 1975 — Admitted to Bar, 1975, Indiana — Member Indiana State Bar Association
Lawrence A. Kalina — 1951 — Villanova University, B.A., 1973; University of Miami, J.D., 1977; DePaul University, LL.M., 1981 — Admitted to Bar, 1977, Indiana — Member American and Indiana State Bar Associations
Gregory J. Tonner — 1957 — Indiana University, B.S., 1979; The University of Tulsa, J.D., 1982 — Admitted to Bar, 1982, Indiana — Member American, Indiana State and Oklahoma Bar Associations
Kathleen M. Maicher — 1949 — Indiana State University, B.A., 1971; Purdue University, M.A., 1974; Loyola University, J.D., 1983 — Admitted to Bar, 1983, Indiana — Member American, Illinois State and Indiana State Bar Associations

Spangler, Jennings & Dougherty, P.C., Merrillville, IN (Continued)

James M. Portelli — 1968 — University of Michigan, B.A. (with distinction), 1990; Indiana University, J.D., 1993 — Admitted to Bar, 1993, Indiana — Member American, Indiana State and Lake County Bar Associations

Robert D. Hawk, Jr. — 1968 — Knox College, B.A., 1990; Drake University, J.D. (cum laude), 1995 — Admitted to Bar, 1995, Indiana — Member Indiana State Bar Association

Ricardo A. Hall — 1964 — Virginia Union University, B.A. (cum laude), 1986; Howard University, M.M.E. (magna cum laude), 1988; Indiana University, J.D., 1995 — Admitted to Bar, 1996, Indiana — Member American and Indiana State Bar Associations

James L. Hough — 1971 — Grand Rapids Baptist College, B.A. (magna cum laude), 1994; Valparaiso University School of Law, J.D. (summa cum laude), 1998 — Admitted to Bar, 1998, Indiana — Member Indiana State Bar Association

Jon S. Diston — 1967 — Eastern College, B.A. (cum laude), 1990; Valparaiso University, J.D., 1999 — Admitted to Bar, 2000, Indiana

Caleb S. Johnson — 1977 — Purdue University, B.A., 1999; Valparaiso University School of Law, J.D., 2002 — Admitted to Bar, 2003, Indiana; 2005, Illinois

Adam J. Moore — 1974 — Valparaiso University, B.A., 1996; Valparaiso University School of Law, J.D., 1999 — Admitted to Bar, 2000, Indiana

(This firm is also listed in the Subrogation section of this directory)

MICHIGAN CITY 31,479 La Porte Co.

Huelat Mack & Kreppein P.C.

450 Saint John Road, Suite 204
Michigan City, Indiana 46360
Telephone: 219-879-3253
Fax: 219-879-3090
E-Mail: jhuelat@hmkattorneys.com
www.hmkattorneys.com

Insurance Defense, Civil Trial Practice, Automobile Liability, Commercial Liability, Construction Law, Fire, Arson, Fraud, Insurance Law, Personal Injury, Product Liability, Subrogation, Truck Liability, Civil Rights Defense, Insurance Coverage Issues

Firm Profile: Huelat Mack & Kreppein P.C. concentrates its practice in civil insurance defense litigation, which encompasses trial and appellate practice in state and federal courts; insurance coverage issues and disputes; wrongful death claims; construction law; motor vehicle and trucking litigation; products liability, including warranty issues and unsafe products; fraud; premises liability, including slip and falls; fire loss and arson; civil rights and employment law defense, including defense of discrimination, sexual harassment and wrongful termination claims; sexual abuse claims defense; libel and slander defense; commercial liability; and complex commercial litigation. Our staff is proficient with many electronic billing systems and coding for same. The firm's goal is to provide its clients with the highest quality legal representation in a timely and efficient manner.

Insurance Clients

ACUITY	American Freedom Insurance Company
Amerisure Insurance Company	
Auto-Owners Insurance Company	Brotherhood Mutual Insurance Company
Cincinnati Insurance Company	
Hastings Mutual Insurance Company	Indiana Farmers Mutual Insurance Company
Maxum Specialty Insurance Group	Specialty Risk of America
State Auto Insurance Companies	Tokio Marine and Fire Insurance Company, Ltd.

Non-Insurance Clients

Simon Property Group, Inc.

Partners

Jerry E. Huelat — 1953 — The Pennsylvania State University, B.A., 1977; Northern Illinois University, J.D., 1981 — Admitted to Bar, 1981, Indiana; 1981, U.S. District Court, Northern and Southern Districts of Indiana; 1981,

Huelat Mack & Kreppein P.C., Michigan City, IN (Continued)

U.S. Court of Appeals, Seventh Circuit; 2012, U.S. Supreme Court — Member Indiana State and LaPorte County Bar Associations; Defense Trial Counsel of Indiana (Immediate Past President, Board of Directors); Defense Research Institute

Beverly J. Mack — 1961 — Eastern Illinois University, B.A., 1983; University of Illinois, J.D., 1989 — Admitted to Bar, 1989, Illinois; 1996, Indiana; 1990, U.S. District Court, Central District of Illinois; 1991, U.S. District Court, Southern District of Illinois; 1995, U.S. Court of Appeals, Seventh Circuit; 1998, U.S. District Court, Northern District of Indiana — Member Illinois State, Indiana State and LaPorte County Bar Associations; Women Lawyers Association; Defense Trial Counsel of Indiana; Defense Research Institute

Michael A. Kreppein — 1971 — University of Illinois at Chicago, B.A., 1994; Valparaiso University, J.D., 2000 — Admitted to Bar, 2000, Indiana; 2000, U.S. District Court, Northern and Southern Districts of Indiana; 2004, U.S. Court of Appeals, Seventh Circuit — Member Indiana State (Litigation Section, Chair; Young Lawyers Section, District Representative, 2004-2008) and LaPorte County (Liaison to ISBA) Bar Associations; Defense Trial Counsel of Indiana; Defense Research Institute — Trial Lawyers Mock Trial Team, Member/President, Student Association, 1998-2000

Jaime M. Oss — 1978 — Indiana University-Purdue University Indianapolis, B.A., 2000; Valparaiso University, J.D., 2003 — Phi Alpha Delta — Admitted to Bar, 2003, Indiana; U.S. District Court, Northern and Southern Districts of Indiana; 2012, U.S. Supreme Court — Member Indiana State (Section: Litigation (District 2 Representative) Committees: Legal Ethics, Improvements in the Judicial System, and Community Service, Chair) and LaPorte County (Immediate Past President and Board of Governors) Bar Associations; Women Lawyers Association; Defense Trial Counsel of Indiana (Board of Directors); Defense Research Institute — 2012 Indiana State Bar Association Leadership Development Academy

Associates

David A. Mack — 1965 — Indiana University-Bloomington, B.S., 1988; Indiana University, J.D., 1991 — Admitted to Bar, 1991, Illinois (Inactive); 1994, Indiana; U.S. District Court, Northern and Southern Districts of Indiana

Robert J. Penney — 1971 — University of Illinois, B.A. Political Science (magna cum laude), 1993; University of California, Los Angeles, M.A., 1997; Indiana University, J.D., 2001 — Phi Beta Kappa — Admitted to Bar, 2001, Indiana; 2003, Ohio (Inactive); 2013, Illinois; 2002, U.S. District Court, Northern and Southern Districts of Indiana

---

The following firms also service this area.

Spangler, Jennings & Dougherty, P.C.
8396 Mississippi Street
Merrillville, Indiana 46410-6398
Telephone: 219-769-2323
Fax: 219-769-5007

Insurance Law, Fire, Property, Casualty, Surety, Life Insurance, Environmental Law, Toxic Torts, Product Liability, Professional Liability, Workers' Compensation, Coverage Issues, Appellate Practice, Subrogation, Medical Malpractice Defense, Mortgage Foreclosure

SEE COMPLETE LISTING UNDER MERRILLVILLE, INDIANA (31 MILES)

MOUNT VERNON † 6,687 Posey Co.

Refer To

Kahn, Dees, Donovan & Kahn, LLP
501 Main Street, Suite 305
Evansville, Indiana 47708
Telephone: 812-423-3183
Fax: 812-423-3841

Mailing Address: P.O. Box 3646, Evansville, IN 47735-3646

Asbestos Litigation, Automobile, Construction Law, Coverage Issues, Environmental Law, Insurance Defense, General Liability, Labor and Employment, Mass Tort, Medical Malpractice, Personal Injury, Premises Liability, Product Liability, Property, Public Entities, Self-Insured, Subrogation, Workers' Compensation

SEE COMPLETE LISTING UNDER EVANSVILLE, INDIANA (19 MILES)

NASHVILLE † 803 Brown Co.

Refer To

Ferguson & Ferguson
403 East Sixth Street
Bloomington, Indiana 47408-4098
  Telephone: 812-332-2113
  Fax: 812-334-3892

Insurance Defense, School Law, Commercial Law, General Liability, Product Liability, Premises Liability, Motor Vehicle, Uninsured and Underinsured Motorist, Life, Accident and Health, General Civil Trial and Appellate Practice, Employment Issues, Including ADA, Business and Real Estate Litigation, Municipal and Governmental Entity Liability, including §1983 Actions

SEE COMPLETE LISTING UNDER BLOOMINGTON, INDIANA (20 MILES)

NEW ALBANY † 36,372 Floyd Co.

Kightlinger & Gray, LLP

Bonterra Building, Suite 200
3620 Blackiston Boulevard
New Albany, Indiana 47150
  Telephone: 812-949-2300
  Fax: 812-949-8556
  E-Mail: info@k-glaw.com
  www.k-glaw.com

(Indianapolis, IN Office*: One Indiana Square, Suite 300, 211 North Pennsylvania Street, 46204)
  (Tel: 317-638-4521)
  (Fax: 317-636-5917)
(Evansville, IN Office*: 7220 Eagle Crest Boulevard, 47715)
  (Tel: 812-474-4400)
  (Fax: 812-474-4414)
(Merrillville, IN Office*: Merrillville Corporate Center, 8001 Broadway, Suite 100, 46410)
  (Tel: 219-769-0413)
  (Fax: 219-769-0798)
(Louisville, KY Office*: 312 South Fourth Street, Suite 700, 40202)
  (Tel: 502-442-2295)
  (Fax: 502-442-2703)

Established: 1946

Insurance Defense, Insurance Litigation, Defense Litigation, Litigation, Insurance Law, Coverage Issues, Carrier Defense, Self-Insured Defense, Comprehensive General Liability, Trial and Appellate Practice, State and Federal Courts, General Civil Trial and Appellate Practice, Casualty Defense, Product Liability, Workers' Compensation, Employment Law, Subrogation, Toxic Torts, Aviation, Surety, Administrative Law, Agent/Broker Liability, Bad Faith, Business Law, Automobile Liability, Trucking Law, Asbestos Litigation, Construction Law, Corporate Law, Complex Litigation, Construction Litigation, Coverage Analysis, First and Third Party Defense, Fire Loss, Professional Liability, Malpractice, Agency Defense, Agent and Brokers Errors and Omissions, Medical Malpractice, School Law, Transportation, Real Estate, Bankruptcy, Municipal Liability, Class Actions, Mediation, Securities Litigation and Arbitration

Insurance Clients

American International Group, Inc.
Chubb Group of Insurance Companies
Liberty Mutual Insurance
Scottsdale Insurance Company
State Farm Mutual Automobile Insurance Company
Auto-Owners Insurance Company
Grange Mutual Insurance Company
Grinnell Mutual Reinsurance Company
State Farm Fire and Casualty Company

Non-Insurance Clients

Aon Technical Insurance Services
Jeff Ellis & Associates, Inc.
GAB Robins North America, Inc.

Kightlinger & Gray, LLP, New Albany, IN (Continued)

Partners

Laurie Goetz Kemp — Miami University, B.S., 1992; Louis D. Brandeis School of Law, University of Louisville, J.D., 1996 — Admitted to Bar, 1996, Indiana; Kentucky; U.S. District Court, Northern and Southern Districts of Indiana; U.S. District Court, Eastern and Western Districts of Kentucky; U.S. Court of Appeals, Sixth and Seventh Circuits — Tel: 812-949-2300 ext. 5136 — E-mail: lkemp@k-glaw.com

R. Jeffrey Lowe — The University of North Carolina, B.A., 1994; Louis D. Brandeis School of Law, University of Louisville, J.D., 1998 — Admitted to Bar, 1998, Kentucky; 1999, Indiana; U.S. District Court, Southern District of Indiana; U.S. District Court, Western District of Kentucky; U.S. Court of Appeals, Seventh Circuit — Tel: 812-949-2300 ext. 5132 — E-mail: jlowe@k-glaw.com

Richard T. Mullineaux — Indiana University, B.S., 1974; George Mason University, J.D., 1978 — Admitted to Bar, 1978, Virginia; 1980, Indiana; U.S. District Court, Southern District of Indiana; U.S. District Court, Eastern District of Virginia; U.S. Court of Appeals, Seventh Circuit — Tel: 812-949-2300 ext. 5129 — E-mail: rmullineaux@k-glaw.com

Steven K. Palmquist — Cornell College, B.A., 1976; University of Cincinnati College of Law, J.D., 1979 — Admitted to Bar, 1979, Indiana; 1980, Kentucky; U.S. District Court, Southern District of Indiana; U.S. District Court, Eastern and Western Districts of Kentucky — Tel: 812-949-2300 ext. 5113 — E-mail: spalmquist@k-glaw.com

Crystal G. Rowe — Indiana University, B.A., 1997; Indiana University School of Law, J.D., 2000 — Admitted to Bar, 2000, Indiana; 2006, Kentucky; U.S. District Court, Northern and Southern Districts of Indiana; U.S. District Court, Eastern and Western Districts of Kentucky; U.S. Court of Appeals, Sixth and Seventh Circuits — Tel: 812-949-2300 ext. 5122 — E-mail: crowe@k-glaw.com

William E. Smith, III — Franklin College, B.A., 1976; University of Dayton School of Law, J.D., 1979 — Admitted to Bar, 1979, Indiana; 1980, Kentucky; U.S. District Court, Southern District of Indiana; U.S. District Court, Eastern and Western Districts of Kentucky; U.S. Court of Appeals, Sixth Circuit — Tel: 812-949-2300 ext.5141 — E-mail: wsmith@k-glaw.com

J. Todd Spurgeon — Wabash College, B.A., 1996; Indiana University, J.D., 1999 — Admitted to Bar, 1999, Indiana; U.S. District Court, Southern District of Indiana — Tel: 812-949-2300 ext. 5130 — E-mail: tspurgeon@k-glaw.com

Kasé L. Stiefvater — Northwestern University, B.S., 2002; William Mitchell College of Law, J.D., 2005 — Admitted to Bar, 2005, Indiana; U.S. District Court, Southern District of Indiana — Tel: 812-474-4400 ext. 6305 — E-mail: kstiefvater@k-glaw.com

Van T. Willis — University of Kentucky, B.A., 1983; University of Kentucky College of Law, J.D., 1988 — Admitted to Bar, 1988, Kentucky; 1990, Indiana; U.S. District Court, Southern District of Indiana; U.S. District Court, Eastern and Western Districts of Kentucky; U.S. Court of Appeals, Seventh Circuit — Tel: 812-949-2300 ext. 5127 — E-mail: vwillis@k-glaw.com

Associates

Ashley Gillenwater Eade — Indiana University, B.S., 2007; Louis D. Brandeis School of Law, University of Louisville, J.D., 2010 — Admitted to Bar, 2010, Kentucky; 2011, Indiana; U.S. District Court, Southern District of Indiana; U.S. District Court, Eastern and Western Districts of Kentucky — Tel: 812-949-2300 ext.5131 — E-mail: aeade@k-glaw.com

William F. English — University of Kentucky, B.A., 2006; Indiana University School of Law, J.D., 2009 — Admitted to Bar, 2010, Indiana; Kentucky; 2011, Virginia; U.S. District Court, Southern District of Indiana; U.S. District Court, Western District of Kentucky — Tel: 812-949-2300 ext. 5143 — E-mail: wenglish@k-glaw.com

Dustin L. Howard — Marian College, B.S., 1995; Salmon P. Chase College of Law, J.D., 2006 — Admitted to Bar, 2006, Indiana; U.S. District Court, Northern and Southern Districts of Indiana — Tel: 812-949-2300 ext. 5117 — E-mail: dhoward@k-glaw.com

Kathryn L. Swany — The University of Georgia, B.A., 2010; University of Kentucky College of Law, J.D., 2014 — Admitted to Bar, 2014, Indiana; U.S. District Court, Northern and Southern Districts of Indiana — Tel: 812-949-2300 ext. 5121 — E-mail: kswany@k-glaw.com

(See Evansville and Indianapolis, IN listings for additional information)

(This firm is also listed in the Subrogation section of this directory)

INDIANA

The following firms also service this area.

Kahn, Dees, Donovan & Kahn, LLP
501 Main Street, Suite 305
Evansville, Indiana 47708
   Telephone: 812-423-3183
   Fax: 812-423-3841

Mailing Address: P.O. Box 3646, Evansville, IN 47735-3646

Asbestos Litigation, Automobile, Construction Law, Coverage Issues, Environmental Law, Insurance Defense, General Liability, Labor and Employment, Mass Tort, Medical Malpractice, Personal Injury, Premises Liability, Product Liability, Property, Public Entities, Self-Insured, Subrogation, Workers' Compensation

SEE COMPLETE LISTING UNDER EVANSVILLE, INDIANA (115 MILES)

PRINCETON   † 8,644 Gibson Co.

Refer To

Kahn, Dees, Donovan & Kahn, LLP
501 Main Street, Suite 305
Evansville, Indiana 47708
   Telephone: 812-423-3183
   Fax: 812-423-3841

Mailing Address: P.O. Box 3646, Evansville, IN 47735-3646

Asbestos Litigation, Automobile, Construction Law, Coverage Issues, Environmental Law, Insurance Defense, General Liability, Labor and Employment, Mass Tort, Medical Malpractice, Personal Injury, Premises Liability, Product Liability, Property, Public Entities, Self-Insured, Subrogation, Workers' Compensation

SEE COMPLETE LISTING UNDER EVANSVILLE, INDIANA (29 MILES)

Refer To

Kightlinger & Gray, LLP
7220 Eagle Crest Boulevard
Evansville, Indiana 47715
   Telephone: 812-474-4400
   Fax: 812-474-4414

Insurance Defense, Insurance Litigation, Defense Litigation, Litigation, Insurance Law, Coverage Issues, Carrier Defense, Self-Insured Defense, Comprehensive General Liability, Trial and Appellate Practice, State and Federal Courts, General Civil Trial and Appellate Practice, Casualty Defense, Product Liability, Workers' Compensation, Employment Law, Subrogation, Toxic Torts, Aviation, Surety, Administrative Law, Agent/Broker Liability, Bad Faith, Business Law, Automobile Liability, Trucking Law, Asbestos Litigation, Construction Law, Corporate Law, Complex Litigation, Construction Litigation, Coverage Analysis, First and Third Party Defense, Fire Loss, Professional Liability, Malpractice, Agency Defense, Agent and Brokers Errors and Omissions, Medical Malpractice, School Law, Transportation, Real Estate, Bankruptcy, Municipal Liability, Class Actions, Mediation, Securities Litigation and Arbitration

SEE COMPLETE LISTING UNDER EVANSVILLE, INDIANA (31 MILES)

RENSSELAER   † 5,859 Jasper Co.

Refer To

Spangler, Jennings & Dougherty, P.C.
8396 Mississippi Street
Merrillville, Indiana 46410-6398
   Telephone: 219-769-2323
   Fax: 219-769-5007

Insurance Law, Fire, Property, Casualty, Surety, Life Insurance, Environmental Law, Toxic Torts, Product Liability, Professional Liability, Workers' Compensation, Coverage Issues, Appellate Practice, Subrogation, Medical Malpractice Defense, Mortgage Foreclosure

SEE COMPLETE LISTING UNDER MERRILLVILLE, INDIANA (43 MILES)

PRINCETON

ROCKVILLE   † 2,607 Parke Co.

Refer To

Cox, Zwerner, Gambill & Sullivan, LLP
511 Wabash Avenue
Terre Haute, Indiana 47807
   Telephone: 812-232-6003
   Fax: 812-232-6567

Insurance Defense, Trial Practice

SEE COMPLETE LISTING UNDER TERRE HAUTE, INDIANA (24 MILES)

SOUTH BEND   † 101,168 St. Joseph Co.

Hunt Suedhoff Kalamaros LLP

205 West Jefferson Boulevard, Suite 300
South Bend, Indiana 46601
   Telephone: 574-232-4801
   Fax: 574-232-9736
   www.hsk-law.com

(Fort Wayne, IN Office*: 803 South Calhoun Street, 9th Floor, 46802, P.O. Box 11489, 46858-1489)
   (Tel: 260-423-1311)
   (Fax: 260-424-5396)
   (Toll Free: 800-215-8258)
(Indianapolis, IN Office*: 6323 South East Street, 46227)
   (Tel: 317-784-4966)
   (Fax: 317-784-5566)
(St. Joseph, MI Office*: 301 State Street, 2nd Floor, P.O. Box 46, 49085-0046)
   (Tel: 269-983-4405)
   (Fax: 269-983-5645)

Insurance Defense, Trial and Appellate Practice, Automobile, Product Liability, Professional Liability, Property and Casualty, Medical Malpractice, Workers' Compensation, Public Entities, Self-Insured, Health Care, Toxic Torts, Environmental Law, Coverage Issues, Mediation, Arbitration

Representative Clients

AAA California
American Family Insurance Company
Chubb Group of Insurance Companies
CNA Insurance Companies
EMC Insurance Company
Erie Insurance Company
FCCI Insurance Company
Fireman's Fund Insurance Company
Frankenmuth Mutual Insurance Company
Indiana Farmers Mutual Insurance Company
Liberty Mutual Insurance Company
National General Insurance Company
Pekin Insurance
Scottsdale Insurance Company
Sedgwick CMS
South Bend Medical Foundation
Travelers Property Casualty Corporation
Zurich American Insurance Group

Allied Group
Amerisure Companies
Auto-Owners Insurance Company
Chubb Services Corporation
Cincinnati Insurance Company
The Doctors Company
Employers Reinsurance Corporation
FCCI Insurance Group
First Acceptance Insurance Company, Inc.
Gallagher Bassett Insurance Company
Indiana Insurance Company
Indiana University Health
Motorists Insurance Company
Nationwide Group
OneBeacon Insurance
Safeco/American States Insurance Company
Sentry Insurance a Mutual Company
United Farm Bureau Mutual Insurance Company

Partners

Thomas F. Cohen — 1953 — University of Notre Dame, A.B., 1975; Indiana University, J.D., 1978 — Admitted to Bar, 1978, Indiana — E-mail: tcohen@hsk-law.com

Kevin W. Kearney — 1961 — University of Notre Dame, B.A., 1983; Seton Hall University School of Law, J.D., 1986 — Admitted to Bar, 1986, New Jersey; 1993, Indiana — E-mail: kkearney@hsk-law.com

Hunt Suedhoff Kalamaros LLP, South Bend, IN (Continued)

Lyle R. Hardman — 1966 — DePauw University, B.A. (cum laude), 1988; Indiana University School of Law, J.D., 1991 — Admitted to Bar, 1991, Indiana; 2006, Michigan — E-mail: lhardman@hsk-law.com

Keith C. Doi — 1963 — Indiana University, B.A., 1985; Indiana University School of Law, J.D., 1988 — Admitted to Bar, 1990, Indiana — E-mail: kdoi@hsk-law.com

Philip E. Kalamaros — University of Notre Dame, B.B.A., 1984; University of Notre Dame Law School, J.D., 1987 — Admitted to Bar, 1987, Indiana — E-mail: pkalamaros@hsk-law.com

Associates

Peter J. Bagiackas — 1961 — University of Notre Dame, B.A., 1983; Indiana University, J.D., 1994 — Admitted to Bar, 1994, Indiana — E-mail: pbagiackas@hsk-law.com

Charles H. Bassford — 1955 — Bryan College, B.S., 1978; Tennessee Technological University, M.B.A., 1979; University of Memphis, J.D., 1983 — Admitted to Bar, 1984, Tennessee; 1994, Indiana — E-mail: cbassford@hsk-law.com

Dinah H. Sampson — 1978 — DePauw University, B.A., 2000; University of Notre Dame, J.D. (cum laude), 2003 — Admitted to Bar, 2003, Indiana — E-mail: dsampson@hsk-law.com

Jennifer L. Butnaru — 1979 — Valparaiso University, B.S.B.A. (summa cum laude), 2002; J.D. (magna cum laude), 2007 — Admitted to Bar, 2007, Indiana — E-mail: jworth@hsk-law.com

Patricia A. Mastagh — 1954 — Indiana University, A.G.S. (with distinction), 2000; B.G.S., 2002; Valparaiso University, J.D., 2007 — Admitted to Bar, 2007, Indiana — E-mail: pmastagh@hsk-law.com

Luke N. Reilander — 1979 — Thomas Aquinas College, B.A., 2002; Ave Maria School of Law, J.D. (magna cum laude), 2005 — Admitted to Bar, 2006, Michigan; 2008, California (Inactive); 2012, Indiana — E-mail: lreilander@hsk-law.com

(See listing under Fort Wayne, IN for additional information)

Tuesley Hall Konopa, LLP

212 East LaSalle Avenue, Suite 100
South Bend, Indiana 46617
  Telephone: 574-232-3538
  Fax: 574-232-3790
  E-Mail: rkonopa@thklaw.com
  www.thklaw.com

(Cassopolis, MI Office: 21550 Shore Acres Road, 49031)
(Tel: 269-445-1818)

Established: 1993

Insurance Defense, Automobile, General Liability, Product Liability, Property and Casualty, Alternative Dispute Resolution, Bad Faith, Contract Disputes, Breach of Contract, Fire Loss, Arson, Insurance Litigation, Premises Liability, Employment Disputes

Insurance Clients

AFLAC - American Family Life Assurance Company of Columbus
Auto-Owners Insurance Company
West Bend Mutual Insurance Company
Allstate Insurance Company
Assurant Insurance Group
Cherokee Insurance Company

Partners

Robert J. Konopa — 1941 — University of Notre Dame, A.B., 1963; M.A., 1964; J.D., 1967 — Admitted to Bar, 1967, Indiana; U.S. District Court, Northern and Southern Districts of Indiana; U.S. District Court, Western District of Michigan; U.S. Court of Appeals, Seventh Circuit — Member National Lawyers, Indiana State, (Member, Board of Managers, 1988-1990), St. Joseph County and Seventh Circuit Bar Associations; Fellow, Indiana Bar Foundation; Master Emeritus, Robert A. Grant Inn of Court (President, 1998-1999); Defense Research Institute (Diplomat); Fellow, Litigation Counsel of America; Indiana Trial Lawyers Association; Fellow, American College of Trial Lawyers; Defense Trial Counsel of Indiana; American Association for Justice; American Trial Lawyers Association — Certified Mediator — Practice Areas: Insurance Defense; Automobile; General Liability; Product Liability; Property and Casualty; Alternative Dispute Resolution; Bad Faith; Contract Disputes; Breach of Contract; Fire Loss; Arson; Insurance Litigation; Premises Liability — E-mail: rkonopa@thklaw.com

Eric W. Von Deck — 1971 — Stetson University, B.A., 1993; University of Notre Dame, J.D. (magna cum laude), 1999 — Admitted to Bar, 2006, Indiana; U.S. District Court, Northern District of Indiana — Member American, Indiana State and St. Joseph County Bar Associations — Practice Areas: Insurance Defense; Commercial Litigation; Real Estate; Personal Injury — E-mail: evondeck@thklaw.com

Associate

Mark D. Kundmueller — 1973 — Flagler College, B.A. (summa cum laude), 1995; University of Notre Dame, J.D. (cum laude), 2003 — Admitted to Bar, 2003, Michigan; 2006, Illinois; 2009, Indiana; 2003, U.S. District Court, Western District of Michigan; 2009, U.S. District Court, Northern District of Illinois; U.S. District Court, Northern District of Indiana — Member Indiana State, Chicago and St. Joseph County Bar Associations; State Bar of Michigan — Practice Areas: Litigation; Insurance Defense; Insurance Coverage; Bad Faith — E-mail: mkundmueller@thklaw.com

The following firms also service this area.

Spangler, Jennings & Dougherty, P.C.
8396 Mississippi Street
Merrillville, Indiana 46410-6398
  Telephone: 219-769-2323
  Fax: 219-769-5007

Insurance Law, Fire, Property, Casualty, Surety, Life Insurance, Environmental Law, Toxic Torts, Product Liability, Professional Liability, Workers' Compensation, Coverage Issues, Appellate Practice, Subrogation, Medical Malpractice Defense, Mortgage Foreclosure

SEE COMPLETE LISTING UNDER MERRILLVILLE, INDIANA (65 MILES)

SPENCER † 2,217 Owen Co.

Refer To

Ferguson & Ferguson
403 East Sixth Street
Bloomington, Indiana 47408-4098
  Telephone: 812-332-2113
  Fax: 812-334-3892

Insurance Defense, School Law, Commercial Law, General Liability, Product Liability, Premises Liability, Motor Vehicle, Uninsured and Underinsured Motorist, Life, Accident and Health, General Civil Trial and Appellate Practice, Employment Issues, Including ADA, Business and Real Estate Litigation, Municipal and Governmental Entity Liability, including §1983 Actions

SEE COMPLETE LISTING UNDER BLOOMINGTON, INDIANA (20 MILES)

SULLIVAN † 4,249 Sullivan Co.

Refer To

Cox, Zwerner, Gambill & Sullivan, LLP
511 Wabash Avenue
Terre Haute, Indiana 47807
  Telephone: 812-232-6003
  Fax: 812-232-6567

Insurance Defense, Trial Practice

SEE COMPLETE LISTING UNDER TERRE HAUTE, INDIANA (25 MILES)

INDIANA

TELL CITY

TELL CITY † 7,272 Perry Co.
Refer To

Kahn, Dees, Donovan & Kahn, LLP
501 Main Street, Suite 305
Evansville, Indiana 47708
Telephone: 812-423-3183
Fax: 812-423-3841

Mailing Address: P.O. Box 3646, Evansville, IN 47735-3646

Asbestos Litigation, Automobile, Construction Law, Coverage Issues, Environmental Law, Insurance Defense, General Liability, Labor and Employment, Mass Tort, Medical Malpractice, Personal Injury, Premises Liability, Product Liability, Property, Public Entities, Self-Insured, Subrogation, Workers' Compensation

SEE COMPLETE LISTING UNDER EVANSVILLE, INDIANA (53 MILES)

TERRE HAUTE † 60,785 Vigo Co.

Cox, Zwerner, Gambill & Sullivan, LLP
511 Wabash Avenue
Terre Haute, Indiana 47807
Telephone: 812-232-6003
Fax: 812-232-6567
www.coxlaw.net

Insurance Defense, Trial Practice

Firm Profile: Cox, Zwerner, Gambill & Sullivan was established prior to 1900 and is one of the oldest law firms in West Central Indiana. The firm's eight lawyers provide a broad range of legal services to individuals as well as business and industry. The firm's clients include banks, newspapers, colleges and universities, real estate developers, contractors, insurance companies, manufacturers, auto dealers, medical professionals, small business owners, retailers, and service providers. The firm strives to serve its clients by providing quality legal services in an efficient manner.

Insurance Clients

American Ambassador Casualty Company
Amerisure Companies
Colonial Insurance Company of California
Farmers Insurance Group
Federated Insurance Company
Fireman's Fund Insurance Company
Grange Insurance Company
Grinnell Mutual Reinsurance Company
Hamilton Mutual Insurance Company
Leader Insurance Company
Metropolitan Life Insurance Company
Pafco General Insurance Company
Selective Insurance Group, Inc.
Travelers Property Casualty Corporation
Unitrin Specialty Insurance
Utica Mutual Insurance Company
American Modern Home Insurance Company
Atlanta Casualty Company
Commercial Union Group
The Equitable Life Assurance Society of the United States
Fidelity National Insurance Company
General Accident Insurance Company
Guaranty National Insurance Company
Hanover Insurance Company
The Hartford Insurance Group
Meridian Mutual Insurance Company
Milwaukee Insurance Company
Pekin Insurance Company
State Farm Mutual Automobile Insurance Company
United Services Automobile Association (USAA)
Viking Insurance Company of Wisconsin

Non-Insurance Clients

City of Clinton
Indiana State University
Pfizer, Inc.
Sears, Roebuck and Co.
Sisters of Providence
Tribune-Star Publishing Company
First Financial Bank, NA
Montezuma Town Council
Rose-Hulman Institute of Technology
Terre Haute Sanitary District
Vigo County Public Library

Firm Members

Ernest J. Zwerner — (1918-1980)

Benjamin G. Cox — (1915-1988)

Gilbert W. Gambill, Jr. — (1921-2001)

Cox, Zwerner, Gambill & Sullivan, LLP, Terre Haute, IN (Continued)

James E. Sullivan — 1919 — University of Notre Dame, B.S.C., 1955; LL.B., 1957 — Admitted to Bar, 1957, Indiana; U.S. District Court, Southern District of Indiana; U.S. Court of Appeals, Seventh Circuit; U.S. Supreme Court; U.S. Claims Court — Member American, Indiana State and Terre Haute Bar Associations; The Florida Bar; Indiana Defense Lawyers Association

Benjamin Guille Cox, Jr. — 1946 — Massachusetts Institute of Technology, B.S., 1968; Harvard Law School, J.D., 1971 — Admitted to Bar, 1971, Indiana; U.S. Court of Appeals, Seventh Circuit — Member American, Indiana State and Terre Haute Bar Associations

David W. Sullivan — 1948 — University of Notre Dame, B.B.A., 1970; Indiana University, J.D. (cum laude), 1973 — Admitted to Bar, 1973, Indiana; U.S. District Court, Southern District of Indiana; U.S. Court of Appeals, Seventh Circuit — Member American, Indiana State and Terre Haute Bar Associations; Defense Research Institute; Defense Trial Counsel of Indiana — E-mail: dsullivan@coxlaw.net

Louis F. Britton — 1953 — Indiana University, B.S., 1974; J.D. (magna cum laude), 1977 — Admitted to Bar, 1977, Indiana — Member American, Indiana State and Terre Haute Bar Associations — E-mail: lbritton@coxlaw.net

Scott Craig — 1971 — Wabash College, B.A. (magna cum laude), 1994; Indiana University School of Law-Bloomington, J.D. (magna cum laude), 1997 — Admitted to Bar, 1997, Indiana; U.S. District Court, Northern and Southern Districts of Indiana — Member American, Indiana State and Terre Haute Bar Associations — E-mail: scraig@coxlaw.net

Donald J. Bonomo — 1975 — Indiana State University, B.S. (cum laude), 1997; Indiana University, J.D., 2000 — Admitted to Bar, 2000, Indiana; U.S. District Court, Northern and Southern Districts of Indiana — Member Indiana State and Terre Haute Bar Associations — E-mail: dbonomo@coxlaw.net

Lakshmi Reddy — 1970 — Vanderbilt University, B.S., 1992; Indiana University, J.D. (cum laude), 1997 — Admitted to Bar, 1997, Indiana; U.S. District Court, Northern and Southern Districts of Indiana; U.S. Court of Appeals, Seventh Circuit — Member American, Indiana State, Terre Haute and Indianapolis Bar Associations

Traci M. Lawson — 1974 — Indiana University, B.S. (with distinction), 1997; University of California, Los Angeles, J.D. (with distinction), 2000 — Admitted to Bar, 2000, California; 2006, Indiana; U.S. District Court, Central, Eastern, Northern and Southern Districts of California; U.S. Court of Appeals, Seventh and Ninth Circuits; U.S. District Court, Northern and Southern Districts of Indiana — Member American, Indiana State and Clay County Bar Associations — E-mail: tlawson@coxlaw.net

The following firms also service this area.

Ferguson & Ferguson
403 East Sixth Street
Bloomington, Indiana 47408-4098
Telephone: 812-332-2113
Fax: 812-334-3892

Insurance Defense, School Law, Commercial Law, General Liability, Product Liability, Premises Liability, Motor Vehicle, Uninsured and Underinsured Motorist, Life, Accident and Health, General Civil Trial and Appellate Practice, Employment Issues, Including ADA, Business and Real Estate Litigation, Municipal and Governmental Entity Liability, including §1983 Actions

SEE COMPLETE LISTING UNDER BLOOMINGTON, INDIANA (59 MILES)

Kahn, Dees, Donovan & Kahn, LLP
501 Main Street, Suite 305
Evansville, Indiana 47708
Telephone: 812-423-3183
Fax: 812-423-3841

Mailing Address: P.O. Box 3646, Evansville, IN 47735-3646

Asbestos Litigation, Automobile, Construction Law, Coverage Issues, Environmental Law, Insurance Defense, General Liability, Labor and Employment, Mass Tort, Medical Malpractice, Personal Injury, Premises Liability, Product Liability, Property, Public Entities, Self-Insured, Subrogation, Workers' Compensation

SEE COMPLETE LISTING UNDER EVANSVILLE, INDIANA (111 MILES)

WASHINGTON

VINCENNES † 18,423 Knox Co.

Refer To

Kahn, Dees, Donovan & Kahn, LLP
501 Main Street, Suite 305
Evansville, Indiana 47708
   Telephone: 812-423-3183
   Fax: 812-423-3841

Mailing Address: P.O. Box 3646, Evansville, IN 47735-3646

Asbestos Litigation, Automobile, Construction Law, Coverage Issues, Environmental Law, Insurance Defense, General Liability, Labor and Employment, Mass Tort, Medical Malpractice, Personal Injury, Premises Liability, Product Liability, Property, Public Entities, Self-Insured, Subrogation, Workers' Compensation

SEE COMPLETE LISTING UNDER EVANSVILLE, INDIANA (53 MILES)

Refer To

Kightlinger & Gray, LLP
7220 Eagle Crest Boulevard
Evansville, Indiana 47715
   Telephone: 812-474-4400
   Fax: 812-474-4414

Insurance Defense, Insurance Litigation, Defense Litigation, Litigation, Insurance Law, Coverage Issues, Carrier Defense, Self-Insured Defense, Comprehensive General Liability, Trial and Appellate Practice, State and Federal Courts, General Civil Trial and Appellate Practice, Casualty Defense, Product Liability, Workers' Compensation, Employment Law, Subrogation, Toxic Torts, Aviation, Surety, Administrative Law, Agent/Broker Liability, Bad Faith, Business Law, Automobile Liability, Trucking Law, Asbestos Litigation, Construction Law, Corporate Law, Complex Litigation, Construction Litigation, Coverage Analysis, First and Third Party Defense, Fire Loss, Professional Liability, Malpractice, Agency Defense, Agent and Brokers Errors and Omissions, Medical Malpractice, School Law, Transportation, Real Estate, Bankruptcy, Municipal Liability, Class Actions, Mediation, Securities Litigation and Arbitration

SEE COMPLETE LISTING UNDER EVANSVILLE, INDIANA (50 MILES)

WASHINGTON † 11,509 Daviess Co.

Refer To

Kahn, Dees, Donovan & Kahn, LLP
501 Main Street, Suite 305
Evansville, Indiana 47708
   Telephone: 812-423-3183
   Fax: 812-423-3841

Mailing Address: P.O. Box 3646, Evansville, IN 47735-3646

Asbestos Litigation, Automobile, Construction Law, Coverage Issues, Environmental Law, Insurance Defense, General Liability, Labor and Employment, Mass Tort, Medical Malpractice, Personal Injury, Premises Liability, Product Liability, Property, Public Entities, Self-Insured, Subrogation, Workers' Compensation

SEE COMPLETE LISTING UNDER EVANSVILLE, INDIANA (61 MILES)

IOWA

CAPITAL: DES MOINES

COUNTIES AND COUNTY SEATS

County	County Seat
Adair	Greenfield
Adams	Corning
Allamakee	Waukon
Appanoose	Centerville
Audubon	Audubon
Benton	Vinton
Black Hawk	Waterloo
Boone	Boone
Bremer	Waverly
Buchanan	Independence
Buena Vista	Storm Lake
Butler	Allison
Calhoun	Rockwell City
Carroll	Carroll
Cass	Atlantic
Cedar	Tipton
Cerro Gordo	Mason City
Cherokee	Cherokee
Chickasaw	New Hampton
Clarke	Osceola
Clay	Spencer
Clayton	Elkader
Clinton	Clinton
Crawford	Denison
Dallas	Adel
Davis	Bloomfield
Decatur	Leon
Delaware	Manchester
Des Moines	Burlington
Dickinson	Spirit Lake
Dubuque	Dubuque
Emmet	Estherville
Fayette	West Union
Floyd	Charles City
Franklin	Hampton
Fremont	Sidney
Greene	Jefferson
Grundy	Grundy Center
Guthrie	Guthrie Center
Hamilton	Webster City
Hancock	Garner
Hardin	Eldora
Harrison	Logan
Henry	Mount Pleasant
Howard	Cresco
Humboldt	Dakota City
Ida	Ida Grove
Iowa	Marengo
Jackson	Maquoketa
Jasper	Newton
Jefferson	Fairfield
Johnson	Iowa City
Jones	Anamosa
Keokuk	Sigourney
Kossuth	Algona
Lee	Fort Madison
Linn	Cedar Rapids
Louisa	Wapello
Lucas	Chariton
Lyon	Rock Rapids
Madison	Winterset
Mahaska	Oskaloosa
Marion	Knoxville
Marshall	Marshalltown
Mills	Glenwood
Mitchell	Osage
Monona	Onawa
Monroe	Albia
Montgomery	Red Oak
Muscatine	Muscatine
O'Brien	Primghar
Osceola	Sibley
Page	Clarinda
Palo Alto	Emmetsburg
Plymouth	Le Mars
Pocahontas	Pocahontas
Polk	Des Moines
Pottawattamie	Council Bluffs
Poweshiek	Montezuma
Ringgold	Mount Ayr
Sac	Sac City
Scott	Davenport
Shelby	Harlan
Sioux	Orange City
Story	Nevada
Tama	Toledo
Taylor	Bedford
Union	Creston
Van Buren	Keosauqua
Wapello	Ottumwa
Warren	Indianola
Washington	Washington
Wayne	Corydon
Webster	Fort Dodge
Winnebago	Forest City
Winneshiek	Decorah
Woodbury	Sioux City
Worth	Northwood
Wright	Clarion

In the text that follows "†" indicates County Seats.

Our files contain additional verified data on the firms listed herein. This additional information is available on request.

A.M. BEST COMPANY

IOWA

ALGONA † 5,560 Kossuth Co.

Fenchel, Doster & Buck, P.L.C.
107 North Harlan Street
Algona, Iowa 50511
   Telephone: 515-295-9361
   Fax: 515-295-9372
   E-Mail: algonalawoffice@lawfdb.com

(Britt, IA Office: 95 Main Avenue South, 50423)
   (Tel: 641-843-3873)
   (Fax: 641-843-4914)
   (E-Mail: brittlawoffice@lawfdb.com)

Established: 1997

Insurance Defense, Workers' Compensation, Subrogation

Insurance Clients

Farm Bureau Mutual Insurance Company
IMT Insurance Company
Pekin Insurance Company
Sentry Insurance a Mutual Company
Farmers Casualty Insurance Company
Milwaukee Insurance Company
Pharmacists Mutual Insurance Company
United Fire & Casualty Company

Partners

David L. Fenchel — 1955 — The University of Iowa, B.A. (with honors and high distinction), 1977; J.D., 1980 — Admitted to Bar, 1980, Iowa — Member Iowa State and Kossuth County Bar Associations; Iowa Defense Counsel Association; Defense Research Institute — E-mail: DFenchel@lawfdb.com

Paul R. Doster — 1954 — Morningside College, B.A. (summa cum laude), 1976; The University of Iowa, J.D., 1979 — Admitted to Bar, 1979, Iowa — Member Iowa State and Kossuth County Bar Associations

John E. Buck — (1950-2009)

Associate

Benjamin J. Ennen — Drake University, B.S./B.A. (cum laude), 2008; M.Acc., 2011; J.D. (with honors), 2011 — Admitted to Bar, 2011, Iowa; Minnesota — Member Iowa State, Minnesota State and Kossuth County Bar Associations — E-mail: Bennen@lawfdb.com

ALLISON † 1,029 Butler Co.

Refer To

Clark, Butler, Walsh & Hamann
315 East 5th Street
Waterloo, Iowa 50701
   Telephone: 319-234-5701
   Fax: 319-232-9579
   Toll Free: 800-825-2971

Mailing Address: P.O. Box 596, Waterloo, IA 50704

Automobile, Product Liability, Malpractice, Subrogation, Life and Health, Workers' Compensation, Surety, Insurance Defense, Investigation and Adjustment

SEE COMPLETE LISTING UNDER WATERLOO, IOWA (43 MILES)

BURLINGTON † 25,663 Des Moines Co.

Aspelmeier, Fisch, Power, Engberg & Helling, P.L.C.
321 North Third Street
Burlington, Iowa 52601
   Telephone: 319-754-6587
   Fax: 319-754-7514
   www.seialaw.com

Established: 1877

Aspelmeier, Fisch, Power, Engberg & Helling, P.L.C., Burlington, IA (Continued)

Insurance Law

Insurance Clients

ACUITY
EMC Insurance Companies
GEICO Direct
Hawkeye-Security Insurance Company
MetLife Auto & Home Group
Nobel Insurance Company
SGI Canada
Tri-State Insurance Company of Minnesota
Auto-Owners Insurance Company
Farm Bureau Mutual Insurance Company
Heritage Insurance Group
Lee County Mutual Insurance Association
Saskatchewan Government Insurance
United Fire & Casualty Company

Firm Members

Robert A. Engberg — 1946 — The University of Iowa, B.B.A., 1968; J.D. (with distinction), 1973 — Admitted to Bar, 1973, Iowa; 1978, U.S. District Court, Southern District of Iowa; U.S. Supreme Court — Member American, Iowa State (Litigation Section) and Des Moines County (President, 1987-1988) Bar Associations; Iowa Defense Counsel Association (Board of Directors, 1988-; President, 1996-1997); State Judicial Nominating Commission, (1987-1993); Defense Research Institute — Des Moines County Magistrate (1973-1974)

Brian J. Helling — 1964 — The University of Iowa, B.A., 1986; J.D. (with distinction), 1989 — Admitted to Bar, 1989, Iowa; Illinois — Member Iowa State and Des Moines County Bar Associations

William R. Jahn, Jr. — 1969 — Grinnell College, B.A. (with honors), 1991; The University of Iowa, J.D. (with distinction), 1994 — Admitted to Bar, 1994, Iowa; 1997, U.S. District Court, Southern District of Iowa — Member Iowa State and Des Moines County Bar Associations

Brent R. Ruther — 1968 — The University of Iowa, B.A., 1990; University of Denver, J.D., 1993 — Admitted to Bar, 1993, Colorado; 1999, Iowa; 1995, U.S. District Court, District of Colorado; 1997, U.S. Court of Appeals, Tenth Circuit; 1999, U.S. District Court, Southern District of Iowa; 2000, U.S. Court of Appeals, Eighth Circuit — Member Iowa State and Des Moines County Bar Associations; The Colorado Bar Association; Iowa Defense Counsel Association (Board of Directors, 2001-2007; Chairman, Tort & Workers' Compensation Committee, 2012-Present; Board of Editors, *Defense Update*, 2009-Present); Defense Research Institute

Sara L. Haas — 1977 — Loras College, B.A., 2000; Syracuse University, J.D., 2003 — Admitted to Bar, 2003, Iowa; 2007, Nevada; 2008, Illinois; 2007, U.S. District Court, District of Nevada — Member Iowa State, Illinois State and Des Moines County Bar Associations

Of Counsel

William Scott Power — 1945 — The University of Iowa, B.A. (with honors), 1967; J.D. (with distinction), 1971 — Phi Beta Kappa — Admitted to Bar, 1971, Iowa; U.S. District Court, Southern District of Iowa; 1981, U.S. Court of Appeals, Eighth Circuit — Member Iowa State and Des Moines County Bar Associations

Associates

Matthew D. Bessine — 1976 — The University of Iowa, B.A., 1998; J.D., 2001 — Admitted to Bar, 2001, Iowa; 2002, Missouri; 2001, U.S. District Court, Southern District of Iowa; 2002, U.S. District Court, Western District of Missouri — Member Iowa State and Des Moines County Bar Associations; The Missouri Bar

Clay W. Baker — 1987 — The University of Iowa, B.A. (with highest distinction), 2009; J.D. (with highest distinction), 2013 — Order of the Coif — Admitted to Bar, 2013, Iowa — Member Iowa State and Des Moines County Bar Associations; Iowa Defense Counsel Association (Board of Editors, *Defense Update*, 2014-Present); Iowa State Bar Review School (Board of Directors, 2014-Present); Defense Research Institute

CEDAR RAPIDS † 126,326 Linn Co.

Bradley & Riley PC
2007 First Avenue Southeast
Cedar Rapids, Iowa 52402
 Telephone: 319-363-0101
 Fax: 319-363-9824
 E-Mail: thill@bradleyriley.com
 www.bradleyriley.com

(Iowa City, IA Office: Tower Place, One South Gilbert Street, 52240)

Business Transactions, Construction Law, Labor and Employment, Litigation, Real Estate, Health Law

Firm Profile: The 26 attorneys of Bradley & Riley PC provide the highest quality legal services to clients throughout Iowa and beyond. We offer a full range of insurance services from both coverage and defense consulting and litigation for insurers, to coverage evaluations, consulting and litigation, including defense, for insureds. The firm has twenty-plus years of experience providing insurance coverage and defense representation and frequently leads seminars on a wide range of coverage topics.

Insurance Clients

Chubb Insurance Company
MMA Insurance Company
United Fire & Casualty Company
Federated Life Insurance Company
Specialty Global Insurance
United Life Insurance Company

Non-Insurance Clients

Berthel Fisher & Company
Infinity Contact
ITC Midwest, LLC
Lil' Drug Store Products, Inc.
Mercy Hospital Iowa City
Stine Seed Company
East Central Iowa Council of Governments
Knutson Construction Services Midwest, Inc.
Miron Construction Co., Inc.

Insurance Litigation Attorneys

Kelly R. Baier — 1953 — Iowa State University, B.A. (with distinction), 1975; The University of Iowa, M.A., 1979; The University of Iowa College of Law, J.D. (with high distinction), 1978 — Admitted to Bar, 1979, Iowa; District of Columbia; 1982, U.S. District Court for the District of Columbia; 1983, U.S. District Court, Northern and Southern Districts of Iowa; U.S. Court of Appeals for the District of Columbia Circuit; 1993, U.S. Court of Appeals, Eighth Circuit — Practice Areas: Discrimination; Civil Rights; Labor and Employment; Civil Trial Practice

Paul D. Burns — 1967 — University of Northern Iowa, B.A., 1989; The University of Iowa College of Law, J.D. (with high distinction), 1993 — Order of the Coif — Law Clerk, Hon. Harold D. Vietor, U.S. District Judge, Southern District of Iowa (1993-1995) — Articles Editor, Iowa Law Review, Vol. 78 (1992-1993) — Admitted to Bar, 1993, Iowa; 1995, U.S. District Court, Northern and Southern Districts of Iowa; U.S. Court of Appeals, Eighth Circuit — Practice Areas: Commercial Litigation; Construction Litigation; Employment Law

Timothy J. Hill — 1966 — The University of Iowa, B.A. (summa cum laude), 1988; University of Virginia School of Law, J.D., 1991 — Phi Beta Kappa — Admitted to Bar, 1991, Illinois; 1992, Iowa; 1991, U.S. District Court, Northern District of Illinois; 1997, U.S. District Court, Eastern District of Michigan; 1998, U.S. District Court, Northern and Southern Districts of Iowa; U.S. District Court, Central District of Illinois; 2003, U.S. Court of Appeals, Eighth Circuit — "Bad Faith Insurance Claims in Iowa," National Business Institute (Spring 2007, Fall 2009); "Insurance Coverage Litigation," National Business Institute (Fall 2006); "Evaluating and Litigating Iowa Insurance Coverage Disputes," National Business Institute (Winter 2005) — Practice Areas: Commercial Litigation; Insurance Law

Vernon P. Squires — 1964 — Institute for European Studies, Vienna, Austria, 1984; Williams College, B.A., 1986; University of Minnesota Law School, J.D. (cum laude), 1993 — Admitted to Bar, 1993, Illinois; 1995, Iowa; 1993, U.S. District Court, Northern District of Illinois; 1995, U.S. District Court, Northern and Southern Districts of Iowa; U.S. District Court, Eastern and Western Districts of Michigan; 1998, U.S. Court of Appeals, Seventh and Eighth Circuits — Practice Areas: Labor and Employment; Commercial Litigation; Intellectual Property

Bradley & Riley PC, Cedar Rapids, IA (Continued)

Donald G. Thompson — 1949 — University of Nebraska, B.A., 1971; University of Nebraska College of Law, J.D. (with distinction), 1976 — Order of the Coif — Admitted to Bar, 1976, Nebraska; 1983, Iowa; 1976, U.S. District Court, District of Nebraska; U.S. Court of Appeals, Eighth Circuit; 1983, U.S. District Court, Northern and Southern Districts of Iowa; 1990, U.S. Supreme Court; 1992, U.S. District Court, Central District of Illinois; 1993, U.S. Court of Appeals, Seventh Circuit; U.S. Tax Court — Practice Areas: Construction Litigation; Commercial Litigation; Civil Trial Practice; Appeals; Mediation; Arbitration

(This firm is also listed in the Investigation and Adjustment section of this directory)

Johnson & Legislador, PLC
Northridge Professional Park
1636 42nd Street, NE
Cedar Rapids, Iowa 52402-3002
 Telephone: 319-395-0700
 Fax: 319-395-9192
 E-Mail: rlegislador@jllawplc.com
 www.jllawplc.com

Insurance Law, Workers' Compensation, Personal Injury, Wrongful Death, Nursing Home Liability, Employment Law

Firm Profile: At Johnson & Legislador we are committed to serving our clients in their time of need by providing the highest quality legal services in an aggressive, prompt, yet cost-effective manner. Our attorneys and staff work together to focus their decades of legal experience to achieve results and strive to provide each client with timely, personalized service of the highest professional standard.

Insurance Clients

The Cincinnati Companies
United Fire & Casualty Company

Firm Members

J. Richard Johnson — 1952 — Marietta College, B.A., 1974; The University of Iowa, J.D., 1978 — Admitted to Bar, 1978, Iowa; U.S. District Court, Northern and Southern Districts of Iowa; U.S. Court of Appeals, Eighth Circuit — Member Iowa State and Linn County Bar Associations; Iowa Defense Counsel Association; Iowa Association of Workers' Compensation Lawyers — E-mail: rjohnson@jllawplc.com

Robert J. Legislador — 1972 — The University of Iowa, B.S., 1996; Drake University, J.D., 2000 — Admitted to Bar, 2000, Iowa; U.S. District Court, Northern District of Iowa; 2001, U.S. District Court, Southern District of Iowa; U.S. Court of Appeals, Eighth Circuit — Member American, Iowa State and Linn County Bar Associations, Iowa Association of Workers' Compensation Lawyers; American, Iowa State and Linn County Bar Associations; Iowa Association of Workers' Compensation Lawyers — E-mail: rlegislador@jllawplc.com

Lederer Weston Craig, P.L.C.
118-3rd Avenue SE, Suite 700
Cedar Rapids, Iowa 52401
 Telephone: 319-365-1184
 Fax: 319-365-1186
 E-Mail: mweston@lwclawyers.com
 www.lwclawyers.com

(West Des Moines, IA Office*: 4401 Weston Parkway, Suite 310, 50266)
 (Tel: 515-224-3911)
 (Fax: 515-224-2698)

Established: 2007

Civil Litigation, Insurance Defense, Commercial Litigation, Motor Vehicle, Municipal Law, Premises Liability, Product Liability, Professional Liability, Professional Negligence, Tort

Lederer Weston Craig, P.L.C., Cedar Rapids, IA
(Continued)

Firm Profile: The attorneys of Lederer Weston Craig, PLC are trial lawyers who have tried hundreds of cases to verdict. Its lawyers routinely appear in state and federal courts throughout Iowa and the Midwest, and serves as regional trial counsel for various clients. In addition, our lawyers have been privileged to serve as leaders and board members of defense, general bar and business organizations at the international, national, state and local levels. Its lawyers have served as officers of IADC, DRI and LCJ. The firm maintains a Martindale AV rating and is listed in Chambers USA Leading Lawyers for Business.

Insurance Clients

American Family Insurance Group
Crawford & Company
Integrity Insurance Company
Maxum Specialty Insurance Group
Pharmacists Mutual Insurance Company
State Farm Fire and Casualty Company
United Fire Group
Westfield Insurance Company
Colony Insurance Company
Hastings Mutual Insurance Company
Minnesota Lawyers Mutual Insurance Company
Society Insurance
State Farm Mutual Automobile Insurance Company
West Bend Mutual Insurance Company

Non-Insurance Clients

Crown Equipment Corporation
Firmenich, Inc.
Kaiser Gypsum Company, Inc.
Merck & Company, Inc.
Wal-Mart Stores, Inc.
Dynacraft BSC, Inc.
Home Depot USA, Inc.
Medtronic, Inc.
Nibco, Inc.
Wilbur-Ellis Company

Firm Members

Gregory M. Lederer — 1951 — University of Nebraska, B.A., 1973; Drake University, J.D., 1977 — Admitted to Bar, 1977, Iowa — Member Iowa State Bar Association (Litigation Section, 1990-; Litigation Section Council, 1994-1997; Committee on Administrative Law, 1980-1986); Linn County Bar Association; Iowa Defense Counsel Association (Board of Directors, 1991-Present; Secretary, 1992-1993; President-Elect, 1993-1994; President, 1994-1995; Civil Jury Instructions Task Force); International Association of Defense Counsel (Executive Committee, 2001-2007; Chair, General Convention, 2001; President, 2005-2006; Past Chair, Legal Malpractice Committee; Product Liability Committee; Faculty Member, 1995 Trial Academy); Defense Research Institute (Board of Directors, 2001-2007; State Representative, 1997-2001); Advocate, American Board of Trial Advocates; Fellow, Iowa Academy of Trial Lawyers — Commissioner, Iowa State Judicial Nominating Commission, 1993-1999; Chair, U.S. District Court Magistrate Judge Merit Selection Panel, Northern District of Iowa, 1995, 1996, 2003, 2006; Federal Practice Committee, Northern District of Iowa, 2002-; President-Elect, Lawyers for Civil Justice, 2007- — E-mail: Glederer@lwclawyers.com

J. Michael Weston — 1955 — The University of Iowa, B.A., 1977; J.D., 1980 — Omicron Delta Kappa — Editor, Moot Court Board, 1980 — Admitted to Bar, 1980, Iowa; U.S. District Court, Northern and Southern Districts of Iowa; U.S. District Court, Northern District of Illinois; U.S. Court of Appeals, Eighth Circuit; U.S. Supreme Court — Member American Bar Association (Litigation, Tort and Insurance Practice Sections); Iowa State Bar Association (Litigation Section; Board of Governors, 2000-2004); Linn County Bar Association (Chair, Fee Arbitration Committee, 1988-1992; Chair, Ethics and Grievance Committee, 1992-1998; Board of Governors, 1996-2001; President, 1999-2000); Iowa Defense Counsel Association (Board of Directors, 1995-2007; Chairman, Jury Instruction Committee, 1996-1997; Chairman, Legislative Committee, 1997-2002; Secretary, 2000-2001; President Elect, 2001-2002; President, 2002-2003; Membership Chair, 2004-2007); International Association of Defense Counsel (Trial Tactics, Product Liability and Insurance Committees; Faculty Member, IADC Trial Academy, 2003; Masters in Advocacy, 2004; Plains Region and Iowa Membership Chair, 2008-Present); DRI - The Voice of the Defense Bar (President Elect, 2012-Present; Product Liability, Insurance and Diversity Committees; Iowa State Representative; Long Range Planning Committee, 2005-2007; Chair, Annual Meeting, 2008; National Board Director, 2007-2010; Chair, Public Policy Committee, 2009-2010); Life Fellow, Iowa State Bar Association Foundation; Lawyers for Civil Justice (Board of Directors, 2012-Present; Associate Member); National Foundation for Judicial Excellence (Board of Directors, 2013-Present); Association of Defense Trial Attorneys; American Board of Trial Advocates; Fellow, American Bar Foundation — Adjunct Professor, Mount Mercy College, 1981-1987; Board Chair, 2004-2005, Cedar Rapids Area Chamber of Commerce; Iowa Super Lawyer; Rated in Chambers USA-Lawyers for Business (Civil Litigation-Defense; Product Liability; Insurance) — E-mail: Mweston@lwclawyers.com

James P. Craig — 1956 — The University of Iowa, B.A., 1979; M.A.P.A., 1981; J.D. (with distinction), 1983 — Admitted to Bar, 1983, Iowa; U.S. District Court, Northern and Southern Districts of Iowa; U.S. Court of Appeals, Eighth Circuit — Member Iowa State Bar Association (Member, Board of Governors, 2004-2008; Committees: Judicial Independence, Judicial Administration, Citizenship, and Jury Instructions; Litigation Section Council; Task Force for Enhanced Delivery of Legal Services, 2009-2010); Linn County Bar Association (Member, Board of Governors, 1999-2004; President, 2002-2003); Iowa Defense Counsel Association (Board of Directors, 2009-Present; Secretary, 2011-2012; President Elect, 2012-2013; President, 2013-2014); Defense Research Institute (Litigation Committee); International Association of Defense Counsel (Faculty Member 2009 Trial Academy); Iowa Academy of Trial Lawyers; Fellow, American Board of Trial Advocates; Association of Defense Trial Attorneys (State Membership Chair, 2012-Present; Marketing Committee Chair, 2012-Present); Association of Defense Trial Attorneys — Iowa Supreme Court Task Force on Civil Justice Reform (2010-2011); City of Cedar Rapids Charter Review Commission (2011); Ohnward Bank & Trust, Board of Directors (2006-Present) — E-mail: Jcraig@lwclawyers.com

Brenda K. Wallrichs — 1970 — Drake University, B.A. (cum laude), 1992; The University of Iowa, J.D. (with distinction), 1995 — Articles Editor, Iowa Law Review, Vol. 80, 1994-1995 — Admitted to Bar, 1995, Iowa; U.S. District Court, Northern and Southern Districts of Iowa; 2000, U.S. Court of Appeals, Eighth Circuit — Member American Bar Association (Tort and Insurance Practice Sections); Iowa State and Linn County Bar Associations; Defense Research Institute (Insurance Law Committee, Social Media Chair, *For the Defense* Editor, Steering Committee); Iowa Defense Counsel Association — City of Cedar Rapids Risk Management Committee (2011-Present); Judicial Nominating Committee, Sixth Judicial District of Iowa (2010-Present); Variety The Children's Charity Board Member (2000-2006) — E-mail: Bwallrichs@lwclawyers.com

Kimberly K. Hardeman — 1970 — St. Cloud State University, B.S. (summa cum laude), 1992; Drake University, J.D., 1995 — Admitted to Bar, 1996, Iowa; U.S. District Court, Northern and Southern Districts of Iowa — Member American, Iowa State, Iowa County (President, 1996-1997) and Linn County Bar Associations; Jasper County Legal Aid Internship for Drake University Legal Clinic, 1994-1995; Defense Research Institute (Vice-Chair Women in the Law Committee Membership); International Association of Defense Counsel (Trial Academy Facility, 2013); Litigation Counsel of America; Iowa Defense Counsel Association; Iowa Trial Lawyers Association; American Board of Trial Advocates; Iowa Academy of Trial Lawyers — Great Plains Super Lawyer, 2012; Adjunct Faculty Member, Kirkwood Community College 2002-2005; American Red Cross, Board Member, 2005-Present — E-mail: Khardeman@lwclawyers.com

Mark J. Parmenter — 1963 — University of Missouri-Kansas City, B.A., 1993; Drake University Law School, J.D., 2003 — Executive Editor, Drake Law Review, 2003- — Admitted to Bar, 2003, Iowa; U.S. District Court, Northern and Southern Districts of Iowa — Member Iowa State and Linn County Bar Associations (Member, Board of Governors, 2012-Present); Iowa Defense Counsel Association; Defense Research Institute — E-mail: Mparmenter@lwclawyers.com

Benjamin M. Weston — 1982 — The University of Iowa, B.S., 2005; Creighton University School of Law, J.D., 2008 — Admitted to Bar, 2008, Iowa; U.S. District Court, Northern and Southern Districts of Iowa — Member Iowa State and Linn County Bar Associations; Defense Research Institute; Iowa Defense Counsel Association — E-mail: bweston@lwclawyers.com

Megan R. Dimitt — 1983 — Grinnell College, B.A., 2006; The University of Iowa College of Law, J.D., 2010 — Admitted to Bar, 2010, Iowa; U.S. District Court, Northern and Southern Districts of Iowa — Member Iowa State and Linn County Bar Associations; Iowa Municipal Attorneys Association; Defense Research Institute; Iowa Defense Counsel Association — E-mail: mdimitt@lwclawyers.com

DES MOINES   IOWA

The following firms also service this area.

Clark, Butler, Walsh & Hamann
315 East 5th Street
Waterloo, Iowa 50701
  Telephone: 319-234-5701
  Fax: 319-232-9579
  Toll Free: 800-825-2971

Mailing Address: P.O. Box 596, Waterloo, IA 50704

Automobile, Product Liability, Malpractice, Subrogation, Life and Health, Workers' Compensation, Surety, Insurance Defense, Investigation and Adjustment

SEE COMPLETE LISTING UNDER WATERLOO, IOWA (58 MILES)

CHARLES CITY † 7,652 Floyd Co.

Refer To

Clark, Butler, Walsh & Hamann
315 East 5th Street
Waterloo, Iowa 50701
  Telephone: 319-234-5701
  Fax: 319-232-9579
  Toll Free: 800-825-2971

Mailing Address: P.O. Box 596, Waterloo, IA 50704

Automobile, Product Liability, Malpractice, Subrogation, Life and Health, Workers' Compensation, Surety, Insurance Defense, Investigation and Adjustment

SEE COMPLETE LISTING UNDER WATERLOO, IOWA (50 MILES)

DAVENPORT † 99,685 Scott Co.

Refer To

Lederer Weston Craig, P.L.C.
118-3rd Avenue SE, Suite 700
Cedar Rapids, Iowa 52401
  Telephone: 319-365-1184
  Fax: 319-365-1186

Mailing Address: P.O. Box 1927, Cedar Rapids, IA 52406-1927

Civil Litigation, Insurance Defense, Commercial Litigation, Motor Vehicle, Municipal Law, Premises Liability, Product Liability, Professional Liability, Professional Negligence, Tort

SEE COMPLETE LISTING UNDER CEDAR RAPIDS, IOWA (76 MILES)

DECORAH † 8,127 Winneshiek Co.

Refer To

Clark, Butler, Walsh & Hamann
315 East 5th Street
Waterloo, Iowa 50701
  Telephone: 319-234-5701
  Fax: 319-232-9579
  Toll Free: 800-825-2971

Mailing Address: P.O. Box 596, Waterloo, IA 50704

Automobile, Product Liability, Malpractice, Subrogation, Life and Health, Workers' Compensation, Surety, Insurance Defense, Investigation and Adjustment

SEE COMPLETE LISTING UNDER WATERLOO, IOWA (79 MILES)

DES MOINES † 203,433 Polk Co.

Ahlers & Cooney, P.C.

100 Court Avenue, Suite 600
Des Moines, Iowa 50309
  Telephone: 515-243-7611
  Fax: 515-243-2149
  515-246-0325
  E-Mail: dluginbill@ahlerslaw.com
  www.ahlerslaw.com

Established: 1887

Ahlers & Cooney, P.C., Des Moines, IA   (Continued)

Aviation, Commercial Litigation, Complex Litigation, Construction Litigation, Copyright and Trademark Law, Design Professionals, Directors and Officers Liability, Employment Practices Liability, Fire Loss, Insurance Defense, Insurance Coverage, Labor and Employment, Legal Malpractice, Mass Tort, Medical Devices, Mold and Mildew Claims, Municipal Liability, Product Liability, Professional Liability, Restaurant Liability, School Law, Toxic Torts, Truck Liability, Workers' Compensation, Wrongful Termination, Accountants and Attorneys Liability

Firm Profile: Ahlers & Cooney, a Professional Corporation, and its predecessor partnerships have been practicing law in Des Moines, Iowa, since 1887. The firm provides a wide range of legal services to Iowa, national and international clients. In addition to general insurance defense litigation, the firm also practices in the areas of business law and litigation, public finance, employment law and litigation, environmental law and local government law and litigation. Each practice group has members experienced in litigation. Interested persons may visit the firm's website at www.ahlerslaw.com

Insurance Clients

Admiral Insurance Company
Colorado Western Insurance Company
Employers Mutual Insurance Company
GuideOne Insurance
Liberty Mutual Group
Summit Risk Services, Inc.
United States Aviation Underwriters, Inc.

Cambridge Integrated Services
Crawford & Company
DPIC Companies, Inc.
Federated Insurance Company
GMAC Insurance Group
Jevco Insurance Company
Northbridge Insurance
Travelers Insurance Companies
XL Design Professional

Non-Insurance Clients

Cunningham Lindsey U.S., Inc.
Hardyston Management Company
Monsanto Company

Des Moines University
Kraft Foods, Inc.
Volvo GM Heavy Truck Corporation

Litigation Members

David H. Luginbill — 1951 — The University of Iowa, B.A., 1973; Drake University Law School, J.D. (with honors), 1976 — Order of the Coif; National Order of the Barristers; National Moot Court Team — Case Notes Editor, Drake University Law Review, 1975-1976 — Admitted to Bar, 1976, Iowa; U.S. District Court, Northern and Southern Districts of Iowa; U.S. Court of Appeals, Eighth Circuit — Member American, Iowa State and Polk County Bar Associations; Iowa Defense Counsel Association (Board of Directors); Defense Research Institute; American Board of Trial Advocates; International Association of Defense Counsel — E-mail: dluginbill@ahlerslaw.com

Edward W. Remsburg — 1948 — The University of Iowa, B.B.A. (with highest distinction), 1970; The University of Iowa College of Law, J.D. (with honors), 1973 — Phi Delta Phi — Beta Gamma Sigma; Phi Eta Sigma; Order of the Coif — Law Clerk, Judge Roy L. Stephenson, U.S. Court of Appeals, Eighth Circuit, 1976-1978 — Board of Editors, Iowa Law Review, 1972 — Admitted to Bar, 1973, Iowa; U.S. District Court, Northern and Southern Districts of Iowa; U.S. Court of Appeals, Eighth Circuit — Member American, Iowa State and Polk County Bar Associations — Lt. JAGC, U.S. Navy, 1973-1976 — E-mail: eremsburg@ahlerslaw.com

Randall H. Stefani — 1956 — The University of Iowa, B.B.A., 1978; The University of Iowa College of Law, J.D. (with distinction), 1981 — Admitted to Bar, 1981, Iowa; U.S. District Court, Northern and Southern Districts of Iowa; U.S. Court of Appeals, Eighth Circuit — Member American, Iowa State and Polk County Bar Associations; Iowa Trial Lawyers Association (Board of Governors, 1998-2000) — Certified Public Accountant — E-mail: rstefani@ahlerslaw.com

James R. Wainwright — 1970 — Boston College, B.A., 1992; Drake University Law School, J.D. (with honors), 1999 — Law Clerk to the Honorable Scott D. Rosenberg, Polk County District Court — Admitted to Bar, 1999, Iowa; U.S. District Court, Northern and Southern Districts of Iowa — Member American, Iowa State and Polk County Bar Associations; Iowa Municipal Attorneys Association; Iowa Defense Counsel Association — E-mail: jwainwright@ahlerslaw.com

Nathan J. Overberg — Central College, B.A. (summa cum laude), 1994; The University of Iowa College of Law, J.D. (with highest distinction), 1997 — National Moot Court Team; Order of the Coif — Law Clerk, Hon. Harold D. Vietor, Senior U.S. District Judge, Southern District of Iowa (1997-1999) —

IOWA | DES MOINES

Ahlers & Cooney, P.C., Des Moines, IA (Continued)

Associate Editor, Iowa Law Review — Admitted to Bar, 1997, Iowa; U.S. District Court, Northern and Southern Districts of Iowa; U.S. Court of Appeals, Eighth Circuit — Member American and Polk County Bar Associations; Iowa State Bar Association (Federal Practice Committee; Labor and Employment Law Section Council; Professionalism Committee; Bench/Bar Conference Committee) — Practice Areas: Litigation; Employment Law — E-mail: noverberg@ahlerslaw.com

Andrew T. Tice — Iowa State University, B.A., 1998; University of Illinois College of Law, J.D. (cum laude), 2001 — Admitted to Bar, 2001, Iowa; U.S. District Court, Northern and Southern Districts of Iowa; U.S. Court of Appeals, Eighth Circuit — Member American, Iowa and Polk County Bar Associations; Iowa Defense Counsel Association; Defense Research Institute — Associate Editor, Elder Law Journal — E-mail: atice@ahlerslaw.com

Amanda G. Jansen — The University of Iowa, B.A., 2001; Drake University Law School, J.D. (with highest honors), 2004 — Order of the Coif — Law Clerk, Hon. Mark S. Cady, Iowa Supreme Court Justice (2004-2006) — Projects Editor, Drake Law Review — Admitted to Bar, 2004, Iowa; 2006, U.S. District Court, Northern and Southern Districts of Iowa; U.S. Court of Appeals, Eighth Circuit — Member American, Iowa State and Polk County Bar Associations; Iowa Defense Counsel Association — Intern, Hon. James E. Gritzner, U.S. District Court, Southern District of Iowa — E-mail: ajansen@ahlerslaw.com

Jason M. Craig — The University of Iowa, B.A. (Dean's List), 2000; The University of Iowa College of Law, J.D. (with highest distinction), 2004 — Order of the Coif — Admitted to Bar, 2004, Iowa; U.S. District Court, Northern and Southern Districts of Iowa; U.S. Court of Appeals, Eighth Circuit — Member American, Iowa State and Polk County Bar Associations; Iowa Defense Counsel Association — E-mail: jcraig@ahlerslaw.com

Michael J. Streit — The University of Iowa, B.A., 1972; University of San Diego School of Law, J.D., 1975 — Admitted to Bar, 1975, Iowa; Nebraska; California; U.S. District Court, Northern and Southern Districts of Iowa; U.S. Tax Court; Nebraska Supreme Court; Supreme Court of California; Supreme Court of Iowa — Member Blackstone Inn of Court — Profiles in Courage Award, May 2012, John F. Kennedy Foundation; Distinguished Alumni Award, University of San Diego — E-mail: mstreit@ahlerslaw.com

Litigation Associate

Nicholas J. Pellegrin — Denison University, B.A. (cum laude), 2006; Drake University Law School, J.D. (with highest honors), 2011 — Drake Law Review — Admitted to Bar, 2011, Iowa — Member American, Iowa State and Polk County Bar Associations — E-mail: npellegrin@ahlerslaw.com

Lindsay A. Vaught — Miami University, B.A. Economics, 2006; University of Denver College of Law, J.D. (summa cum laude), 2010 — Law Clerk to the Honorable Ronald E. Longstaff and the Honorable Celeste F. Bremer, United States District Court, Southern District of Iowa — Admitted to Bar, 2013, Iowa — Member American, Iowa State and Polk County Bar Associations — E-mail: lvaught@ahlerslaw.com

Attorneys with other Specialties

Patricia A. Martin	Mark W. Beerman
John D. Hintze	Jane B. McAllister
William J. Noth	R. Mark Cory
Elizabeth A. Grob	J. Eric Boehlert
Elizabeth Gregg Kennedy	Ivan T. Webber
James C. Hanks	Ronald L. Peeler
Andrew J. Bracken	Steven M. Nadel
Jennifer A. Clendenin	Danielle Jess Haindfield
John H. Bunz	Michael M. Galloway
Kristy M. Latta	Miriam D. Van Heukelem
Rocky J. Robbins	Kristin B. Cooper
Katherine A. Beenken	

Elverson Vasey

700 Second Avenue
Des Moines, Iowa 50309
Telephone: 515-243-1914
Fax: 515-243-2235
E-Mail: jon.vasey@elversonlaw.com
www.evpllp.com

Established: 1989

Elverson Vasey, Des Moines, IA (Continued)

Insurance Defense, First and Third Party Defense, Bodily Injury, Automobile, Homeowners, Commercial Law, Property, Casualty, Product Liability, Subrogation, Coverage Opinions and Litigation

Firm Profile: Established in 1989, we provide all types of insurance representation including liability and coverage issues. Our representation is tailored to each client's individual philosophy with regard to handling files, reporting requirements and billing procedures.

Our goal is to provide efficient, cost effective representation for our clients and believe that legal expenses should be limited to those necessary to fully protect our clients' interest.

Insurance Clients

AAA Insurance	Allstate Insurance Company
Brotherhood Mutual Insurance Company	COUNTRY Insurance & Financial Services
COUNTRY Mutual Insurance Company	Encompass Insurance Company
State Farm Fire and Casualty Company	State Auto Insurance Company
	State Farm Mutual Automobile Insurance Company
Universal Casualty Company	West Bend Mutual Insurance Company

Partners

Todd A. Elverson — 1956 — Drake University, B.F.A. (with honors), 1978; J.D., 1981 — Admitted to Bar, 1981, Iowa; 1981, U.S. District Court, Southern District of Iowa — Member Iowa State Bar Association (Section on Corporation and Business Law); Polk County Bar Association (Title Standards Committee, 1989-1991)

Jon A. Vasey — 1957 — The University of Iowa, B.B.A., 1980; Drake University, J.D., 1983 — Delta Theta Phi (Dean, 1982-1983) — Admitted to Bar, 1983, Iowa; 1984, U.S. District Court, Northern and Southern Districts of Iowa — Member Iowa State Bar Association (Insurance Committee, 1989-1993); Polk County Bar Association (Unauthorized Practice Committee); Iowa Defense Counsel Association; Defense Research and Trial Lawyers Association

Allison R. Abbott — 1973 — Arizona State University, B.A., 1994; Drake University, J.D. (with honors), 1999 — Delta Theta Phi — Admitted to Bar, 1999, Iowa — Member Iowa State and Polk County Bar Associations; Defense Research Institute; Iowa Defense Counsel Association

Associates

W. Adam Buckley — 1978 — Knox College, B.A., 2001; Drake University Law School, J.D. (with high honors), 2007 — Admitted to Bar, 2007, Iowa — Member Iowa State and Polk County Bar Associations

Susan Ekstrom — Drake University, B.A., 1973; Drake University Law School, J.D., 1976 — Admitted to Bar, 1976, Iowa — Member Iowa State (Board of Governers, 2008-2012) and Polk County (President, 2007) Bar Associations; Lincoln Inn of Court

Max Burkey — University of Northern Iowa, B.A., 1973; Drake University Law School, J.D., 1976 — Admitted to Bar, 1976, Iowa; U.S. District Court, Northern and Southern Districts of Iowa — Member Iowa State and Polk County Bar Associations — U.S. Army

Nathan A. Russell — 1983 — Iowa State University, B.A., 2007; University of Dayton, J.D., 2010 — Admitted to Bar, 2011, Iowa

Finley, Alt, Smith, Scharnberg, Craig, Hilmes & Gaffney P.C.

699 Walnut Street, Suite 1900
Des Moines, Iowa 50309
Telephone: 515-288-0145
Fax: 515-288-2724
www.finleylaw.com

Established: 1924

Insurance Defense, Workers' Compensation, Property Damage, Casualty, General Liability, Product Liability, Medical Liability, Dental Malpractice, Legal Malpractice, Architects and Engineers, Directors and Officers Liability, Accountant Malpractice, Subrogation

DES MOINES   IOWA

Finley, Alt, Smith, Scharnberg, Craig, Hilmes & Gaffney P.C., Des Moines, IA (Continued)

Insurance Clients

Capitol Indemnity Corporation
Great West Casualty Company
Minnesota Lawyers Mutual Insurance Company
CNA Insurance Company
Midwest Medical Insurance Company
Travelers - Architects and Engineers

Non-Insurance Clients

Catholic Health Corporation
UnityPoint Health
Mercy Medical Center

Firm Members

Thomas A. Finley — 1940 — State University of Iowa, B.A., 1965; LL.B., 1966 — Admitted to Bar, 1966, Iowa; U.S. District Court, Northern and Southern Districts of Iowa — Member Iowa State and Polk County Bar Associations; Iowa Trial Lawyers Association; Iowa Defense Counsel Association; Defense Research Institute — E-mail: tfinley@finleylaw.com

Jerry P. Alt — 1940 — The University of Iowa, B.A., 1963; Drake University Law School, J.D., 1968 — Admitted to Bar, 1968, Iowa — Member Iowa State and Polk County Bar Associations — E-mail: jalt@finleylaw.com

Glenn L. Smith — 1944 — Drake University, B.A., 1965; Drake University Law School, J.D., 1968 — Admitted to Bar, 1968, Iowa; 1969, U.S. District Court, Southern District of Iowa; 1970, U.S. District Court, Northern District of Iowa — Member American, Iowa State and Polk County Bar Associations — E-mail: gsmith@finleylaw.com

Steven K. Scharnberg — 1949 — The University of Iowa, B.A., 1971; The University of Iowa College of Law, J.D., 1974 — Admitted to Bar, 1974, Iowa; U.S. District Court, Northern and Southern Districts of Iowa — Member Iowa State and Polk County Bar Associations; Iowa Defense Counsel Association; Iowa Academy of Trial Lawyers; American College of Trial Lawyers — E-mail: sscharnberg@finleylaw.com

David C. Craig — 1947 — Regis College, B.S., 1969; The University of Iowa College of Law, J.D., 1975 — Admitted to Bar, 1975, Iowa; U.S. District Court, Southern District of Iowa; 1976, U.S. District Court, Northern District of Iowa — Member Iowa State and Polk County Bar Associations — E-mail: dcraig@finleylaw.com

Jack Hilmes — 1954 — University of Northern Colorado, B.A., 1976; Drake University Law School, J.D., 1979 — Admitted to Bar, 1979, Iowa; U.S. District Court, Southern District of Iowa; 1980, U.S. District Court, Northern District of Iowa — Member Iowa State and Polk County Bar Associations; Iowa Defense Counsel Association; American College of Trial Lawyers; Iowa Academy of Trial Lawyers — E-mail: jhilmes@finleylaw.com

R. Todd Gaffney — 1953 — Drake University, B.S.B.A., 1976; Drake University Law School, J.D., 1979 — Admitted to Bar, 1979, Iowa; 1994, Missouri; 1979, U.S. District Court, Northern and Southern Districts of Iowa — Member Iowa State and Polk County Bar Associations; Iowa Trial Lawyers Association; National Association of Railroad Trial Counsel — E-mail: tgaffney@finleylaw.com

Kermit B. Anderson — 1950 — The University of Iowa, B.B.A., 1972; The University of Iowa College of Law, J.D., 1975 — Admitted to Bar, 1975, Iowa; U.S. District Court, Southern District of Iowa; 1994, U.S. District Court, Northern District of Iowa — Member Iowa State and Polk County Bar Associations; Iowa Defense Counsel Association — E-mail: kanderson@finleylaw.com

Kevin J. Driscoll — 1960 — Loras College, B.A., 1982; Drake University Law School, J.D., 1987 — Admitted to Bar, 1988, Missouri; 1998, Iowa; 1999, Minnesota; 1988, U.S. District Court, Western District of Missouri; 1999, U.S. District Court, Southern District of Iowa; 2003, U.S. District Court, Northern District of Iowa — Member American, Iowa State, Minnesota State and Polk County Bar Associations; The Missouri Bar; Iowa Academy of Trial Lawyers; Defense Research Institute — E-mail: kdriscoll@finleylaw.com

Connie L. Diekema — 1961 — Morningside College, B.S., 1983; Drake University Law School, J.D., 1987 — Admitted to Bar, 1988, Iowa; U.S. District Court, Northern and Southern Districts of Iowa — Member American, Iowa State and Polk County Bar Associations; Iowa Defense Counsel Association; Iowa Trial Lawyers Association; American College of Trial Lawyers — E-mail: cdiekema@finleylaw.com

Frederick T. Harris — 1964 — Loras College, B.A., 1987; Drake University, M.B.A., 1989; Creighton University School of Law, J.D., 1993 — Admitted to Bar, 1994, Iowa; Nebraska; U.S. District Court, District of Nebraska; U.S. District Court, Northern and Southern Districts of Iowa — Member American, Iowa State and Nebraska State Bar Associations; Iowa Defense Counsel Association — E-mail: rharris@finleylaw.com

Finley, Alt, Smith, Scharnberg, Craig, Hilmes & Gaffney P.C., Des Moines, IA (Continued)

Stacie M. Codr — 1976 — The University of Iowa, B.A., 1998; The University of Iowa College of Law, J.D., 2002 — Admitted to Bar, 2002, Iowa; U.S. District Court, Northern and Southern Districts of Iowa — Member American, Iowa State and Polk County Bar Associations; Defense Research Institute — E-mail: scodr@finleylaw.com

Robert L. Johnson — 1960 — The University of Iowa, B.A., 1982; University of San Diego School of Law, J.D., 1986 — Admitted to Bar, 2004, Iowa — Member American, Iowa State and Polk County Bar Associations — E-mail: rjohnson@finleylaw.com

Eric G. Hoch — 1974 — The University of Iowa, B.A., 1997; The University of Iowa College of Law, J.D., 2004 — Admitted to Bar, 2004, Iowa; U.S. District Court, Northern and Southern Districts of Iowa — Member American, Iowa State and Polk County Bar Associations — U.S. Air Force Captain, 1997-2001 — E-mail: ehoch@finleylaw.com

Erik P. Bergeland — 1982 — Iowa State University, B.A., 2004; The University of Iowa College of Law, J.D., 2008 — Admitted to Bar, 2008, Iowa — Member American, Iowa State and Polk County Bar Associations — E-mail: ebergeland@finleylaw.com

James S. Blackburn — 1954 — University of Colorado, B.S., 1976; Drake University Law School, J.D., 1979 — Admitted to Bar, 1979, Iowa — Member Iowa State and Polk County Bar Associations — E-mail: jblackburn@finleylaw.com

Megan Kennedy Marty — 1983 — Iowa State University, B.S. (summa cum laude), 2004; The University of Iowa, M.Acc., 2005; The University of Iowa College of Law, J.D., 2008 — Admitted to Bar, 2008, Minnesota; 2010, Iowa; 2011, Montana — Member American, Iowa State and Polk County Bar Associations — E-mail: mmarty@finleylaw.com

Jeffrey A. Craig — 1985 — Marquette University, B.A., 2008; The University of Iowa College of Law, J.D., 2011 — Admitted to Bar, 2011, Iowa; U.S. District Court, Northern and Southern Districts of Iowa — Member American, Iowa State and Polk County Bar Associations — E-mail: jcraig@finleylaw.com

Kellen B. Bubach — 1985 — Jamestown College, B.A., 2008; The University of Iowa College of Law, J.D., 2011 — Admitted to Bar, 2011, Iowa — Member American, Iowa State and Polk County Bar Associations — E-mail: kbubach@finleylaw.com

Andrew T. Patton — 1986 — University of Missouri, B.S./B.A., 2008; Drake University Law School, J.D., 2012 — Admitted to Bar, 2013, Iowa — Member American, Iowa State and Polk County Bar Associations — E-mail: apatton@finleylaw.com

Patterson Law Firm, L.L.P.

505 Fifth Avenue, Suite 729
Des Moines, Iowa 50309-2390
Telephone: 515-283-2147
Fax: 515-283-1002
www.pattersonfirm.com

Established: 1965

Civil Trial Practice, General Civil Practice, Insurance Defense, Personal Injury, Product Liability, Professional Liability, Workers' Compensation

Insurance Clients

ACE USA
Chubb Indemnity Insurance Company
MetLife Insurance Company
SECURA Insurance Companies
Shelter Insurance Companies
Bituminous Insurance Company
Farmers Insurance Company
Grinnell Mutual Insurance Company
Sedgwick James
Specialty Risk Services

Members

Gary D. Ordway — 1942 — Drake University, B.S., 1964; J.D., 1966 — Delta Theta Phi — Admitted to Bar, 1966, Iowa — Member Iowa State and Polk County Bar Associations

Robin L. Hermann — 1943 — United States Military Academy at West Point; The University of Iowa, LL.B., 1968 — Phi Delta Phi — Admitted to Bar, 1968, Iowa — Member Iowa State and Polk County Bar Associations

Harry Perkins, III — 1947 — Creighton University, B.S.B.A., 1970; Drake University, J.D., 1973 — Admitted to Bar, 1973, Iowa — Member American,

Patterson Law Firm, L.L.P., Des Moines, IA (Continued)

Iowa State and Polk County Bar Associations; Federation of Defense and Corporate Counsel; Defense Research Institute; Iowa Academy of Trial Lawyers; Iowa Defense Counsel Association

Jeffrey A. Boehlert — 1953 — Syracuse University, B.S. (magna cum laude), 1975; Drake University, J.D., 1978 — Admitted to Bar, 1978, Iowa; 1987, Nebraska — Member Iowa State and Polk County Bar Associations

Douglas A. Haag — 1952 — Mankato State College, B.S. (summa cum laude), 1975; Drake University, J.D., 1979 — Admitted to Bar, 1979, Iowa — Member Iowa State and Polk County Bar Associations; Defense Research Institute

Patrick V. Waldron — 1969 — Marycrest College, B.A. (magna cum laude), 1992; Drake University, J.D. (with honors), 1995 — Admitted to Bar, 1995, Iowa — Member American, Iowa State and Polk County Bar Associations; Iowa Association of Workers' Compensation Lawyers

Michael S. Jones — 1962 — The University of Iowa, B.B.A., 1985; University of Denver; Drake University, J.D. (with honors), 1995 — Admitted to Bar, 1995, Iowa — Member Iowa State and Polk County Bar Associations; Society of CPCU; Defense Research Institute; Iowa Defense Counsel Association — Chartered Property and Casualty Underwriter (CPCU)

Gregory A. Witke — 1961 — Iowa State University, B.S. (with distinction), 1984; The University of Iowa College of Law, J.D. (with distinction), 1987 — Admitted to Bar, 1987, Iowa — Member American, Iowa State and Polk County Bar Associations

Ryan M. Clark — 1973 — Arizona State University, B.A., 1995; Drake University, J.D. (with honors), 1999 — Admitted to Bar, 1999, Iowa — Member Iowa State and Polk County Bar Associations; Iowa Association of Workers' Compensation Lawyers

Mark A. King — 1973 — Creighton University, B.S., 1997; Drake University, J.D. (with honors), 2001 — Admitted to Bar, 2001, Iowa — Member Iowa State and Polk County Bar Associations; Iowa Association of Workers' Compensation Lawyers

Cory D. Abbas — 1973 — Drake University, B.S.B.A. (magna cum laude), 1994; J.D. (with high honors), 2004 — Admitted to Bar, 2004, Iowa — Member American, Iowa State and Polk County Bar Associations

Jason W. Miller — 1977 — St. Ambrose University, B.A. (summa cum laude), 1999; The University of Iowa, J.D. (with distinction), 2002 — Admitted to Bar, 2002, Iowa — Member American, Iowa State and Polk County Bar Associations

Michael J. Miller — 1976 — The University of Iowa, B.A. (with honors and highest distinction), 1998; J.D. (with high distinction), 2002 — Admitted to Bar, 2002, Iowa — Member American, Iowa State and Polk County Bar Associations

Benjamin R. Merrill — 1982 — St. John's University, B.A., 2005; Drake University, J.D. (with honors), 2008 — Admitted to Bar, 2008, Iowa — Member American, Iowa State and Polk County Bar Associations

Julie C. Gray — 1984 — University of Northern Iowa, B.A. (summa cum laude), 2007; Drake University, J.D. (with high honors), 2010 — Admitted to Bar, 2010, Iowa — Member American, Iowa and Polk County Bar Associations

DUBUQUE † 57,637 Dubuque Co.

Fuerste, Carew, Juergens & Sudmeier, P.C.

200 Security Building
151 West 8th Street
Dubuque, Iowa 52001-6832
Telephone: 563-556-4011
Fax: 563-556-7134
E-Mail: mail@fuerstelaw.com
www.fuerstelaw.com

Established: 1965

Corporate Law, Commercial Law, Construction Law, Contracts, Litigation, Personal Injury, Professional Liability, Workers' Compensation, Family Law, Education Law, Insurance, Labor Law, Employment Law

Insurance Clients

CNA Insurance Company   EMC Insurance Companies

Fuerste, Carew, Juergens & Sudmeier, P.C., Dubuque, IA (Continued)

Farmers Mutual Hail Insurance
General Casualty Insurance Company
Rice Insurance Services Company, LLC
State Farm Mutual Automobile Insurance Company
Gallagher Bassett Services, Inc.
Harleysville Insurance Company
Partners Mutual Insurance Company
State Farm Fire and Casualty Company

Members

William C. Fuerste — (Deceased)

Allan J. Carew — (Retired)

Stephen J. Juergens — 1947 — Loras College, B.A. (with honors), 1969; The University of Iowa, J.D. (with high distinction), 1973 — Phi Alpha Theta, Phi Alpha Delta — Admitted to Bar, 1973, Iowa; 1974, U.S. District Court, Northern District of Iowa; 1975, U.S. District Court, Southern District of Iowa; U.S. Court of Appeals, Eighth Circuit — Member American, Iowa State (Board of Governers, 1998-2005) and Dubuque County (President, 1997-1998); Iowa Municipal Attorneys Association; Iowa Council of School Board Attorneys; National Association of Ski Defense Attorneys — E-mail: sjuergens@fuerstelaw.com

Robert L. Sudmeier — 1948 — The University of Iowa, B.B.A. (with high distinction), 1970; J.D. (with distinction), 1973 — Beta Gamma Sigma, Phi Alpha Delta — Admitted to Bar, 1973, Iowa; 1984, Wisconsin; 1974, U.S. District Court, Northern District of Iowa; 1975, U.S. District Court, Southern District of Iowa; 1984, U.S. District Court, Western District of Wisconsin — Member American, Iowa State and Dubuque County (President, 2002-2003) Bar Associations; State Bar of Wisconsin; Fellow, Iowa Academy of Trial Lawyers; Iowa Municipal Attorneys Association; Iowa Defense Counsel Association — E-mail: rsudmeier@fuerstelaw.com

Douglas M. Henry — 1952 — The University of Iowa, B.A., 1973; J.D. (with honors), 1977 — Admitted to Bar, 1977, Iowa; U.S. District Court, Southern District of Iowa; 1978, U.S. District Court, Northern District of Iowa; U.S. Court of Appeals, Eighth Circuit — Member American, Iowa State and Dubuque County Bar Associations; Fellow, Iowa Academy of Trial Lawyers; American Association for Justice (Associate Member); Iowa Municipal Attorneys Association; Iowa Defense Counsel Association; Association of Trial Lawyers of America; Association of Defense Trial Attorneys — Certified Mediator — E-mail: dhenry@fuerstelaw.com

Mark J. Willging — 1953 — Loras College, B.A. (magna cum laude), 1975; The University of Iowa, J.D. (with honors), 1978 — Admitted to Bar, 1978, Iowa; 1990, U.S. District Court, Northern District of Iowa; U.S. Tax Court — Member American, Iowa State and Dubuque County Bar Associations; Iowa Trust Association; Iowa Academy of Trust and Estate Counsel — E-mail: mwillging@fuerstelaw.com

A. Theodore Huinker — 1973 — Loras College, B.A. (magna cum laude), 1995; The University of Iowa, J.D., 1998 — Phi Delta Phi — Admitted to Bar, 1998, Iowa — Member American, Iowa State and Dubuque County Bar Associations; Iowa Municipal Attorneys Association; Iowa Association of School Board Attorneys — E-mail: thuinker@fuerstelaw.com

Danita L. Grant — 1975 — University of Wisconsin, B.A. (magna cum laude), 1997; Drake University, J.D. (with honors), 2000 — Delta Theta Phi — Admitted to Bar, 2000, Iowa; 2008, Wisconsin — Member American, Iowa State (District Representative, Young Lawyers Division, 2002-2006) and Dubuque County Bar Associations; State Bar of Wisconsin; Iowa Association of Workers' Compensation Lawyers, Inc.; Association of Ski Defense Attorneys; National Organization of Social Security Claimant Representatives (N.O.S.S.C.R.); Association of Defense Trial Attorneys — Certified Mediator — E-mail: dgrant@fuerstelaw.com

Jenny L. Weiss — 1980 — The University of Iowa, B.A., 2003; J.D., 2007 — Admitted to Bar, 2007, Iowa; 2008, Illinois — Member American, Iowa State, Illinois State and Dubuque County Bar Associations; Iowa Municipal Attorneys Association; Attorney Registration & Disciplinary Commission — E-mail: jweiss@fuerstelaw.com

Associates

Nicholas C. Thompson — 1981 — The University of Iowa, B.A., 2004; DePaul University College of Law, J.D., 2011 — Admitted to Bar, 2011, Illinois; 2013, Iowa — Member American, Illinois State, Iowa State and Dubuque County Bar Associations — E-mail: nthompson@fuerstelaw.com

Richard W. Kirkendall — 1982 — The University of Iowa, B.S. (with distinction), 2000; Northwestern University, J.D. (cum laude), 2008 — Admitted to Bar, 2008, Iowa — Member American, Iowa State and Dubuque County Bar Associations — E-mail: rkirkendall@fuerstelaw.com

FORT DODGE † 25,206 Webster Co.

Kersten Brownlee Hendricks L.L.P.
Seventh Floor, Snell Building
805 Central Avenue
Fort Dodge, Iowa 50501
 Telephone: 515-576-4127
 Fax: 515-576-6340
 E-Mail: stevekersten@kbhlaw.net
 www.kerstenbrownleehendricks.com

Established: 1955

Insurance Defense, General Liability, Automobile, Product Liability, Professional Liability, Coverage Issues, Bad Faith

Firm Profile: Kersten Brownlee Hendricks L.L.P. has practiced extensively in the area of insurance defense litigation for over 40 years throughout north-central and northwest Iowa in state and federal courts. The firm strives to provide high quality legal services at a reasonable cost while keeping its clients appropriately advised of file activity.

Insurance Clients

American Family Insurance Company
Chubb Group of Insurance Companies
Cornhusker Casualty Company
Deep South Insurance Services
Farm Bureau Mutual Insurance Company
Illinois Casualty Company
Kemper Insurance Company
Nationwide Insurance
North American Risk Services
Zurich American Insurance Company
Auto-Owners Insurance Company
Brotherhood Mutual Insurance Company
Continental Western Insurance Company
Employers Mutual Casualty Company
GMAC Insurance
Integrity Insurance Company
Midlands Claim Administrators, Inc.
North Pointe Insurance Company

Litigation Partners

Stephen G. Kersten — 1953 — Georgetown University, B.S., 1975; The University of Iowa, M.S., 1977; Drake University, J.D., 1980 — Admitted to Bar, 1980, Iowa; 1980, U.S. District Court, Northern and Southern Districts of Iowa — Member Iowa State and Webster County Bar Associations; Iowa Defense Counsel Association; Iowa Academy of Trial Lawyers — E-mail: stevekersten@frontiernet.net

Mark S. Brownlee — 1954 — Washington and Lee University, 1972-1974; Iowa State University, B.S., 1976; The University of Iowa, J.D., 1979 — Admitted to Bar, 1979, Iowa; 1979, U.S. District Court, Northern and Southern Districts of Iowa — Member Iowa State (Litigation Section) and Webster County Bar Associations; Iowa Defense Counsel Association (Past President); Defense Research Institute; Iowa Academy of Trial Lawyers; Association of Defense Trial Attorneys — E-mail: brownlee@frontiernet.net

FORT MADISON † 11,051 Lee Co.

Refer To
Aspelmeier, Fisch, Power, Engberg & Helling, P.L.C.
321 North Third Street
Burlington, Iowa 52601
 Telephone: 319-754-6587
 Fax: 319-754-7514
Mailing Address: P.O. Box 1046, Burlington, IA 52601-1046

Insurance Law

SEE COMPLETE LISTING UNDER BURLINGTON, IOWA (20 MILES)

INDEPENDENCE † 5,966 Buchanan Co.

Refer To
Clark, Butler, Walsh & Hamann
315 East 5th Street
Waterloo, Iowa 50701
 Telephone: 319-234-5701
 Fax: 319-232-9579
 Toll Free: 800-825-2971
Mailing Address: P.O. Box 596, Waterloo, IA 50704

Automobile, Product Liability, Malpractice, Subrogation, Life and Health, Workers' Compensation, Surety, Insurance Defense, Investigation and Adjustment

SEE COMPLETE LISTING UNDER WATERLOO, IOWA (29 MILES)

IOWA CITY † 67,862 Johnson Co.

Refer To
Lederer Weston Craig, P.L.C.
118-3rd Avenue SE, Suite 700
Cedar Rapids, Iowa 52401
 Telephone: 319-365-1184
 Fax: 319-365-1186
Mailing Address: P.O. Box 1927, Cedar Rapids, IA 52406-1927

Civil Litigation, Insurance Defense, Commercial Litigation, Motor Vehicle, Municipal Law, Premises Liability, Product Liability, Professional Liability, Professional Negligence, Tort

SEE COMPLETE LISTING UNDER CEDAR RAPIDS, IOWA (26 MILES)

KEOKUK † 10,780 Lee Co.

Refer To
Aspelmeier, Fisch, Power, Engberg & Helling, P.L.C.
321 North Third Street
Burlington, Iowa 52601
 Telephone: 319-754-6587
 Fax: 319-754-7514
Mailing Address: P.O. Box 1046, Burlington, IA 52601-1046

Insurance Law

SEE COMPLETE LISTING UNDER BURLINGTON, IOWA (44 MILES)

MANCHESTER † 5,179 Delaware Co.

Refer To
Clark, Butler, Walsh & Hamann
315 East 5th Street
Waterloo, Iowa 50701
 Telephone: 319-234-5701
 Fax: 319-232-9579
 Toll Free: 800-825-2971
Mailing Address: P.O. Box 596, Waterloo, IA 50704

Automobile, Product Liability, Malpractice, Subrogation, Life and Health, Workers' Compensation, Surety, Insurance Defense, Investigation and Adjustment

SEE COMPLETE LISTING UNDER WATERLOO, IOWA (52 MILES)

MARSHALLTOWN † 27,552 Marshall Co.

Refer To
Clark, Butler, Walsh & Hamann
315 East 5th Street
Waterloo, Iowa 50701
 Telephone: 319-234-5701
 Fax: 319-232-9579
 Toll Free: 800-825-2971
Mailing Address: P.O. Box 596, Waterloo, IA 50704

Automobile, Product Liability, Malpractice, Subrogation, Life and Health, Workers' Compensation, Surety, Insurance Defense, Investigation and Adjustment

SEE COMPLETE LISTING UNDER WATERLOO, IOWA (56 MILES)

MASON CITY † 28,079 Cerro Gordo Co.
Refer To
Clark, Butler, Walsh & Hamann
315 East 5th Street
Waterloo, Iowa 50701
   Telephone: 319-234-5701
   Fax: 319-232-9579
   Toll Free: 800-825-2971

Mailing Address: P.O. Box 596, Waterloo, IA 50704

Automobile, Product Liability, Malpractice, Subrogation, Life and Health, Workers' Compensation, Surety, Insurance Defense, Investigation and Adjustment

SEE COMPLETE LISTING UNDER WATERLOO, IOWA (81 MILES)

MOUNT PLEASANT † 8,668 Henry Co.
Refer To
Aspelmeier, Fisch, Power, Engberg & Helling, P.L.C.
321 North Third Street
Burlington, Iowa 52601
   Telephone: 319-754-6587
   Fax: 319-754-7514

Mailing Address: P.O. Box 1046, Burlington, IA 52601-1046

Insurance Law

SEE COMPLETE LISTING UNDER BURLINGTON, IOWA (26 MILES)

NEW HAMPTON † 3,571 Chickasaw Co.
Refer To
Clark, Butler, Walsh & Hamann
315 East 5th Street
Waterloo, Iowa 50701
   Telephone: 319-234-5701
   Fax: 319-232-9579
   Toll Free: 800-825-2971

Mailing Address: P.O. Box 596, Waterloo, IA 50704

Automobile, Product Liability, Malpractice, Subrogation, Life and Health, Workers' Compensation, Surety, Insurance Defense, Investigation and Adjustment

SEE COMPLETE LISTING UNDER WATERLOO, IOWA (41 MILES)

ORANGE CITY † 6,004 Sioux Co.
Refer To
DeKoter, Thole & Dawson, P.L.C.
315 Ninth Street
Sibley, Iowa 51249
   Telephone: 712-754-4601
   Fax: 712-754-2301

Mailing Address: P.O. Box 253, Sibley, IA 51249-0253

Insurance Law, Trial Practice, Casualty, Automobile, Product Liability, Personal Injury, Commercial Liability, Subrogation, Investigation and Adjustment

SEE COMPLETE LISTING UNDER SIBLEY, IOWA (30 MILES)

ROCK RAPIDS † 2,549 Lyon Co.
Refer To
DeKoter, Thole & Dawson, P.L.C.
315 Ninth Street
Sibley, Iowa 51249
   Telephone: 712-754-4601
   Fax: 712-754-2301

Mailing Address: P.O. Box 253, Sibley, IA 51249-0253

Insurance Law, Trial Practice, Casualty, Automobile, Product Liability, Personal Injury, Commercial Liability, Subrogation, Investigation and Adjustment

SEE COMPLETE LISTING UNDER SIBLEY, IOWA (24 MILES)

SIBLEY † 2,798 Osceola Co.

DeKoter, Thole & Dawson, P.L.C.
315 Ninth Street
Sibley, Iowa 51249
   Telephone: 712-754-4601
   Fax: 712-754-2301
   www.sibleylaw.com

Established: 1936

Insurance Law, Trial Practice, Casualty, Automobile, Product Liability, Personal Injury, Commercial Liability, Subrogation, Investigation and Adjustment

Insurance Clients

Capitol Indemnity Corporation
Farmers Mutual Insurance Company
Sentry Claims Services
Society Insurance
West Bend Mutual Insurance Company
Crawford & Company
Jarden Risk Management
North Star Mutual Insurance Company
United States Liability Insurance Company

Non-Insurance Clients

Canadian Pacific Railroad
Dethmers Manufacturing Company
Diversified Technologies, Inc.
Dakota, Minnesota & Eastern Railroad
Sudenga Industries, Inc.

Partners

Richard D. Zito — (1944-1994)

Daniel E. DeKoter — 1955 — Northwestern College; Calvin College, B.A., 1977; The University of Iowa, J.D. (with high honors), 1980 — Admitted to Bar, 1980, Iowa; 1982, U.S. District Court, Northern District of Iowa; 1989, U.S. Court of Appeals, Eighth Circuit — Member Iowa State and Osceola County Bar Associations; Defense Research Institute; National Association of Railroad Trial Counsel; Iowa Defense Counsel Association — E-mail: dandekoter@sibleylaw.com

Michael E. Thole — 1952 — Southwest State University; The University of Iowa, B.B.A., 1974; Creighton University, J.D., 1979 — Admitted to Bar, 1979, Nebraska; 1980, Iowa; 1980, U.S. District Court, Northern District of Iowa — Member Iowa State and Osceola County Bar Associations — E-mail: mthole@sibleylaw.com

Harold D. Dawson — 1955 — Arizona State University, B.S., 1978; The University of Iowa, J.D. (with distinction), 1984 — Admitted to Bar, 1984, Iowa; 1984, U.S. District Court, Northern District of Iowa — Member Iowa State and Osceola County Bar Associations; Northwest Iowa Collaborative Law Professionals — E-mail: hdawson@sibleylaw.com

Associate

Nathan J. Rockman — 1986 — Iowa State University, B.A. Political Science, 2009; Creighton University, J.D., 2013 — Admitted to Bar, 2013, Iowa; 2014, U.S. District Court, Northern District of Iowa — Member American, Iowa State and Osceola County Bar Associations — E-mail: nrockman@sibleylaw.com

SIOUX CITY † 82,684 Woodbury Co.

Heidman Law Firm, L.L.P.
1128 Historic 4th Street
Sioux City, Iowa 51101
   Telephone: 712-255-8838
   Fax: 712-258-6714
   E-Mail: mail@heidmanlaw.com
   www.heidmanlaw.com

Established: 1891

STORM LAKE IOWA

Heidman Law Firm, L.L.P., Sioux City, IA (Continued)

Automobile, Automobile Liability, Bodily Injury, Coverage Issues, Fraud, General Liability, Insurance Defense, Personal Injury, Slip and Fall, Workers' Compensation

Firm Profile: Heidman Law Firm in Sioux City serves IA, MN, NE and SD and has a strong history of representing companies who provide liability, worker's comp, professional liability, health, and life insurance. Practice areas also include business, employment, real estate, estate planning, health and litigation.

Insurance Clients

ACUITY
Allstate Insurance Company
Applied Risk Services, Inc.
Brotherhood Mutual Insurance Company
Catholic Mutual Group
Creative Risk Solutions, Inc.
Federated Mutual Insurance Company
Hartford Insurance Company
IMT Insurance Company
Metropolitan Property and Casualty Insurance Company
MMIC Group
North Pointe Insurance Company
QBE Insurance Group
Sedgwick Claims Management Services, Inc.
State Farm Insurance Companies
Travelers Property Casualty
United Heartland Inc
West Bend Mutual Insurance Company
Allied Group Insurance
Amica Mutual Insurance Company
Auto-Owners Insurance Company
Cannon Cochran Management Services, Inc.
CorVel Corporation
ESIS
Great West Casualty Company
Grinnell Mutual Reinsurance Company
Iowa Mutual Insurance Company
Minnesota Lawyers Mutual Insurance Company
National Indemnity Company
Progressive Insurance Company
St. Paul Travelers
Sentry Insurance Company
Specialty Risk Services, Inc. (SRS)
Swiss Re
United Fire & Casualty Company
Unitrin, Inc.
Zurich U.S.

Partners

James W. Redmond — 1947 — Briar Cliff College, B.A., 1971; Marquette University, J.D., 1973 — Admitted to Bar, 1973, Wisconsin; 1974, Iowa; 1989, Nebraska; 2004, South Dakota — E-mail: jim.redmond@heidmanlaw.com

Daniel D. Dykstra — 1955 — Dordt College, B.A., 1977; The University of Iowa, J.D. (with distinction), 1980 — Admitted to Bar, 1980, Iowa; 2004, South Dakota — E-mail: daniel.dykstra@heidmanlaw.com

Lance D. Ehmcke — 1950 — Iowa State University, B.S., 1972; Drake University, J.D., 1980 — Admitted to Bar, 1980, Iowa; 1981, Nebraska — E-mail: lance.ehmcke@heidmanlaw.com

Cynthia C. Moser — 1952 — Northwestern College, B.A., 1974; The University of Iowa, J.D. (with honors), 1977 — Admitted to Bar, 1977, Iowa; 2005, South Dakota; U.S. District Court, Southern District of Iowa; 1979, U.S. District Court, Northern District of Iowa — E-mail: cynthia.moser@heidmanlaw.com

John C. Gray — 1955 — The University of Iowa, B.A., 1978; J.D., 1981 — Admitted to Bar, 1981, Iowa; 1989, Nebraska; 2004, South Dakota — E-mail: john.gray@heidmanlaw.com

Patrick L. Sealey — 1970 — University of Nebraska, B.A. (with high distinction), 1992; The University of Iowa, J.D. (with distinction), 1995 — Admitted to Bar, 1995, Iowa; South Dakota; Nebraska — E-mail: patrick.sealey@heidmanlaw.com

Jeff W. Wright — 1973 — Northwestern College, B.A. (cum laude), 1995; The University of Iowa, J.D. (with distinction), 1998 — Admitted to Bar, 1998, Iowa; 1999, Nebraska; 2007, South Dakota; 2012, Minnesota; U.S. District Court, Northern District of Iowa; U.S. District Court, District of Nebraska — E-mail: jeff.wright@heidmanlaw.com

Rosalynd J. Koob — 1975 — Briar Cliff College, B.A. (magna cum laude), 1998; Creighton University, J.D. (with distinction), 2001 — Admitted to Bar, 2001, Iowa; 2002, Nebraska; Winnebago Tribal Court; U.S. District Court, Northern and Southern Districts of Iowa; Omaha Tribal Court; Crow Creek Sioux Tribal Court — E-mail: roz.koob@heidmanlaw.com

Joel D. Vos — 1977 — Dordt College, B.A., 1999; The University of Iowa, J.D. (with highest distinction), 2002 — Admitted to Bar, 2002, Iowa; 2003, South Dakota; U.S. District Court, Northern District of Iowa — E-mail: joel.vos@heidmanlaw.com

Sarah Kuehl Kleber — 1972 — Drake University, B.A. (summa cum laude), 1995; Washington and Lee University, J.D., 1998 — Admitted to Bar, 1998,

Heidman Law Firm, L.L.P., Sioux City, IA (Continued)

Iowa; 1999, Nebraska; South Dakota; U.S. District Court, Northern and Southern Districts of Iowa — E-mail: sarah.kleber@heidmanlaw.com

Associates

Jacob B. Natwick — 1984 — University of Minnesota, B.A. (summa cum laude), 2007; The University of Iowa, J.D. (with high distinction), 2010 — Admitted to Bar, 2010, Iowa; 2011, Nebraska — E-mail: jacob.natwick@heidmanlaw.com

Heidi L. Oligmueller — 1975 — Briar Cliff University, B.S. (cum laude), 2002; University of South Dakota, J.D., 2008 — Sterling Honor Graduate — Admitted to Bar, 2008, Iowa; 2009, South Dakota; 2014, Nebraska — E-mail: heidi.oligmueller@heidmanlaw.com

Allyson C. Dirksen — 1986 — Iowa State University, B.S. (summa cum laude), 2008; Creighton University, J.D. (magna cum laude), 2011 — Admitted to Bar, 2011, Iowa; 2012, Nebraska — E-mail: allyson.dirksen@heidmanlaw.com

Jason D. Bring — 1987 — Briar Cliff University, B.A., 2010; University of Nebraska, J.D., 2013 — Admitted to Bar, 2013, Iowa; 2014, Nebraska — E-mail: Jason.Bring@heidmanlaw.com

Of Counsel

Marvin F. Heidman — (Retired)
Alan E. Fredregill — (Retired)
Thomas M. Plaza — (Retired)

(This firm is also listed in the Subrogation section of this directory)

SPENCER † 11,233 Clay Co.

Refer To
DeKoter, Thole & Dawson, P.L.C.
315 Ninth Street
Sibley, Iowa 51249
Telephone: 712-754-4601
Fax: 712-754-2301
Mailing Address: P.O. Box 253, Sibley, IA 51249-0253

Insurance Law, Trial Practice, Casualty, Automobile, Product Liability, Personal Injury, Commercial Liability, Subrogation, Investigation and Adjustment

SEE COMPLETE LISTING UNDER SIBLEY, IOWA (43 MILES)

SPIRIT LAKE † 4,840 Dickinson Co.

Refer To
DeKoter, Thole & Dawson, P.L.C.
315 Ninth Street
Sibley, Iowa 51249
Telephone: 712-754-4601
Fax: 712-754-2301
Mailing Address: P.O. Box 253, Sibley, IA 51249-0253

Insurance Law, Trial Practice, Casualty, Automobile, Product Liability, Personal Injury, Commercial Liability, Subrogation, Investigation and Adjustment

SEE COMPLETE LISTING UNDER SIBLEY, IOWA (34 MILES)

STORM LAKE † 10,600 Buena Vista Co.

Law Offices of Redenbaugh, Mohr, & Redenbaugh

111 West Sixth Street
Storm Lake, Iowa 50588
Telephone: 712-732-1873
Fax: 712-732-4274
Emer/After Hrs: 712-732-3986
Mobile: 712-299-6220
E-Mail: phil@redenlaw.com
www.iowapersonalinjurylaw.net

Established: 1975

IOWA | TAMA

Law Offices of Redenbaugh, Mohr, & Redenbaugh, Storm Lake, IA (Continued)

Insurance Defense, Automobile, Product Liability, Casualty, Subrogation, Investigation and Adjustment

Firm Profile: The Law Offices of Redenbaugh, Mohr & Redenbaugh is an Iowa law firm established by Phil Redenbaugh in 1975. Located in downtown Storm Lake the firm represents individual and business clients in the areas of insurance defense, personal injury, workers compensation, and other general areas of the law.

Attorneys in our firm are licensed to practice in Iowa and South Dakota and are also experienced legal practitioners in both the Northern and Southern Districts of Iowa's Federal District Court and the Court of Appeals.

Our lawyers seek to provide individual care and attention to each case, treating all of our clients with courtesy and professionalism.

Insurance Clients

Acceleration National Insurance Company
CUNA Mutual Group
Farmers Casualty Insurance Company
Great West Casualty Company
Hartford Insurance Company
Illinois Casualty Company
Iowa Mutual Insurance Company
Mutual Protective Insurance Company
Nationwide Group
Pafco General Insurance Company
Scottsdale Insurance Company
Union Standard Insurance Company
Washington National Insurance Company
Acceptance Insurance Company
ACUITY
Employers Mutual Companies
General Casualty Companies
Great American Insurance Company
Heritage Insurance Group
IMT Insurance Company
MSI Preferred Insurance Company
National Casualty Company
National Insurance Association
OneBeacon Insurance
Public Entity Risk Services of Iowa
Union Mutual Insurance Company
United States Liability Insurance Company
Western National Insurance Group

Non-Insurance Clients

Hy-Vee, Inc.

Founding Partner

Phil C. Redenbaugh — 1941 — Buena Vista College, B.A., 1963; Drake University, J.D., 1970 — Admitted to Bar, 1970, Iowa; U.S. District Court, Northern and Southern Districts of Iowa — Member Iowa State and Buena Vista County Bar Associations; Iowa Academy of Trial Lawyers (Board of Governors; President, 2004); Iowa Defense Counsel Association; Fellow, American College of Trial Lawyers — Practice Areas: Liability Defense; Automobile Litigation

Partners

Ryan A. Mohr — 1978 — The University of Iowa, B.A., 2002; University of South Dakota, J.D. (with honors), 2007 — Sterling Honor Society — Law Clerk, South Dakota Supreme Court — Admitted to Bar, 2008, South Dakota; Iowa — Member Iowa State Bar Association (Board of Governors, 2012-Present)

Brett C. Redenbaugh — 1980 — The University of Iowa, B.A., 2003; Drake University, J.D., 2008 — Delta Theta Phi — Admitted to Bar, 2008, Iowa — Member Iowa State, Polk County and Buena Vista County Bar Associations

TAMA 2,877 Tama Co.

Refer To

Clark, Butler, Walsh & Hamann
315 East 5th Street
Waterloo, Iowa 50701
   Telephone: 319-234-5701
   Fax: 319-232-9579
   Toll Free: 800-825-2971
Mailing Address: P.O. Box 596, Waterloo, IA 50704

Automobile, Product Liability, Malpractice, Subrogation, Life and Health, Workers' Compensation, Surety, Insurance Defense, Investigation and Adjustment

SEE COMPLETE LISTING UNDER WATERLOO, IOWA (45 MILES)

WAPELLO † 2,067 Louisa Co.

Refer To

Aspelmeier, Fisch, Power, Engberg & Helling, P.L.C.
321 North Third Street
Burlington, Iowa 52601
   Telephone: 319-754-6587
   Fax: 319-754-7514
Mailing Address: P.O. Box 1046, Burlington, IA 52601-1046

Insurance Law

SEE COMPLETE LISTING UNDER BURLINGTON, IOWA (28 MILES)

WATERLOO † 68,406 Black Hawk Co.

Clark, Butler, Walsh & Hamann
315 East 5th Street
Waterloo, Iowa 50701
   Telephone: 319-234-5701
   Fax: 319-232-9579
   Toll Free: 800-825-2971
   E-Mail: TIM.HAMANN@CBWHLAW.COM
   www.cbwh-law.com

Established: 1929

Automobile, Product Liability, Malpractice, Subrogation, Life and Health, Workers' Compensation, Surety, Insurance Defense, Investigation and Adjustment

Insurance Clients

Aetna Life and Casualty Company
American International Group, Inc.
American States Insurance Company
Atlantic Companies
AXA Global Risks US Insurance Company
Driver's Direct Insurance
Fireman's Fund Insurance Company
Government Employees Insurance Company
Illinois National Insurance Company
Minnesota Mutual Companies
Northland Insurance Company
Pekin Insurance Company
Prudential Insurance Company of America
SECURA Insurance Companies
State Farm Mutual Automobile Insurance Company
American Family Insurance Company
Amerisure Companies
Amerisure Insurance Company
Auto-Owners Insurance Company
Bituminous Insurance Companies
Continental Insurance Company
Farmers Insurance Group
Fremont Indemnity Company
Globe Indemnity Company
Great Central Insurance Company
Home Mutual Insurance Company
IMT Insurance Company
Interstate Fire & Casualty Company
Occidental Fire & Casualty Company of North Carolina
Reliance Insurance Group
Royal Globe Insurance Company
Shelter Insurance Companies
United Fire & Casualty Company

Non-Insurance Clients

General Motors Corporation
Symons International Group, Inc.

Firm Members

Fred G. Clark, Jr. — (1922-1984)

Wallace W. Butler — 1920 — The University of Iowa, B.S., 1942; J.D., 1948 — Admitted to Bar, 1948, Iowa — Member American, Iowa State, Black Hawk County and First Judicial District Bar Associations

James E. Walsh, Jr. — 1949 — University of Illinois, B.A., 1971; Loyola University, J.D., 1975 — Admitted to Bar, 1975, Illinois; 1976, Iowa — Member American, Iowa State and Black Hawk County Bar Associations; Iowa Academy of Trial Lawyers; Defense Research Institute

Timothy W. Hamann — 1954 — The University of Iowa, B.B.A., 1977; M.A. (Insurance), 1981; J.D., 1981 — Admitted to Bar, 1981, Iowa — Member American, Iowa State and Black Hawk County Bar Associations; Defense Research Institute; Iowa Trial Lawyers Association; American Board of Trial Advocates — Adjunct Professor of Insurance, University of Northern Iowa; Chartered Property and Casualty Underwriter — E-mail: tim.hamann@cbwhlaw.com

Clark, Butler, Walsh & Hamann, Waterloo, IA (Continued)

Christy R. Liss — 1966 — University of Nebraska, B.A. (magna cum laude), 1989; The University of Iowa, J.D. (with distinction), 1992 — Admitted to Bar, 1992, Iowa — Member American, Iowa State and Black Hawk County Bar Associations

Christopher S. Wendland — 1965 — Harvard College, A.B. (cum laude), 1987; The University of Iowa College of Law, J.D. (with high distinction), 1995 — Admitted to Bar, 1995, Iowa — Member American Bar Association; Iowa State Bar Association (Workers' Compensation Section, Advisory Rules Committee); Black Hawk County Bar Association

Associates

Jared Knapp — 1975 — Cornell College, B.A. (cum laude), 1998; The University of Iowa, J.D., 2001 — Admitted to Bar, 2001, Iowa — Member Iowa State Bar Association

Emily Bartekoske — 1984 — University of Northern Iowa, B.A., 2006; Drake University Law School, J.D., 2009 — Admitted to Bar, 2009, Iowa — Member Iowa State and Black Hawk County Bar Associations; Iowa Association of Mediators; International Academy of Dispute Resolution

Joshua L. Christensen — 1982 — Wartburg College, B.A. (magna cum laude), 2003; The University of Iowa, J.D., 2011; The University of Iowa College of Education, Graduate, 2012 — Admitted to Bar, 2012, Iowa — Member Iowa State Bar Association

Swisher & Cohrt, P.L.C.

528 West Fourth Street
Waterloo, Iowa 50701
Telephone: 319-232-6555
Fax: 319-232-4835
E-Mail: office@s-c-law.com
www.swishercohrt.com

Established: 1913

General Practice, Insurance Law, Casualty, Surety, Product Liability, Professional Malpractice, Life Insurance, Workers' Compensation, Investigation and Adjustment

Insurance Clients

ACUITY
American Family Insurance Group
Benton Mutual Insurance Association
Horace Mann Insurance Company
Liberty Mutual Insurance Company
ProAssurance Company
Society Insurance
United Heartland Inc
Universal Underwriters Group
Western World Insurance Company
Allied Group
Austin Mutual Insurance Company
Employers Mutual Companies
Gallagher Bassett Services, Inc.
Indiana Insurance Company
MSI Preferred Insurance Company
Sentry Insurance a Mutual Company
Unitrin, Inc.
Wausau Insurance Companies

Firm Members

Benjamin F. Swisher — (1878-1959)

Benjamin F. Swisher, Jr. — (1906-1938)

Leo J. Cohrt — (1898-1974)

Charles F. Swisher — (1919-1986)

Steven A. Weidner — 1940 — University of Notre Dame, B.A., 1962; J.D., 1965 — Admitted to Bar, 1965, Iowa; 1966, U.S. Court of Military Appeals; 1969, U.S. District Court, Northern District of Iowa; 1970, U.S. Court of Appeals, Eighth Circuit; 1983, U.S. District Court, Southern District of Iowa — Member Iowa State, Black Hawk County and First District Bar Associations — Iowa Council of School Board Attorneys; Rotary Club — JAGC, U.S. Navy, 1965-1968 — E-mail: weidner@s-c-law.com

Stephen J. Powell — 1950 — University of Northern Colorado, B.A., 1972; Drake University, J.D. (with honors), 1974 — Admitted to Bar, 1975, Iowa; 1975, U.S. District Court, Northern and Southern Districts of Iowa — Member Iowa State and Black Hawk County Bar Associations; Fellow, American College of Trial Lawyers; Iowa Defense Counsel Association; Iowa Academy of Trial Lawyers; Defense Research Institute; International Association of Defense Counsel; American Board of Trial Advocates — E-mail: powell@s-c-law.com

Swisher & Cohrt, P.L.C., Waterloo, IA (Continued)

Jim D. DeKoster — 1945 — Iowa State University, B.S., 1967; The University of Iowa, J.D. (with distinction), 1970 — Admitted to Bar, 1970, Iowa; U.S. Court of Military Appeals; 1977, U.S. District Court, Northern District of Iowa; U.S. Court of Appeals, Eighth Circuit; 1980, U.S. District Court, Southern District of Iowa; 1983, U.S. Supreme Court — Member Iowa State and Black Hawk County Bar Associations — JAGC, U.S. Navy, 1970-1976 — E-mail: dekoster@s-c-law.com

Samuel C. Anderson — 1959 — The University of Iowa, B.A., 1981; Drake University, J.D., 1984 — Admitted to Bar, 1984, Iowa; 1984, U.S. District Court, Northern and Southern Districts of Iowa — Member Iowa State and Black Hawk County Bar Associations; Iowa Council of School Board Attorneys; Iowa Defense Counsel Association; Defense Research Institute; Association of Defense Trial Attorneys; Iowa Academy of Trial Lawyers — E-mail: sanderson@s-c-law.com

Kevin R. Rogers — 1958 — The University of Iowa, B.A., 1984; Drake University, J.D. (with honors), 1987 — Admitted to Bar, 1987, Iowa; 1987, U.S. District Court, Northern and Southern Districts of Iowa — Member Iowa State and Black Hawk County Bar Associations; Iowa Council of School Board Attorneys; Iowa Defense Counsel Association; Iowa Association of Workers' Compensation Lawyers; Iowa Academy of Trial Lawyers — E-mail: rogers@s-c-law.com

Beth E. Hansen — 1951 — The University of Iowa, B.A., 1973; Creighton University, J.D. (cum laude), 1991 — Admitted to Bar, 1991, Iowa; U.S. District Court, Northern and Southern Districts of Iowa; U.S. Court of Appeals, Eighth Circuit; U.S. Supreme Court — Member Iowa State (Board of Governors) and Black Hawk County Bar Associations; Iowa Council of School Board Attorneys; Iowa Defense Counsel Association; Association of Defense Trial Attorneys; Defense Research Institute — E-mail: hansen@s-c-law.com

Mark F. Conway — 1960 — Buena Vista College, B.A., 1982; University of South Dakota, J.D., 1991 — Managing Editor, South Dakota Law Review, 1990-1991 — Admitted to Bar, 1991, Iowa; 1991, U.S. District Court, Northern and Southern Districts of Iowa; 1991, U.S. Court of Appeals, Eighth Circuit — Member American, Iowa State and Black Hawk County Bar Associations — E-mail: conway@s-c-law.com

Natalie Williams Burris — 1969 — University of Northern Iowa, B.A., 1991; The University of Iowa, J.D. (with distinction), 1994 — Admitted to Bar, 1994, Iowa; 1994, U.S. District Court, Northern and Southern Districts of Iowa — Member Iowa State and Black Hawk County Bar Associations — E-mail: burris@s-c-law.com

Lynn M. Smith — 1971 — Wartburg College, B.A. (cum laude), 1994; Drake University, J.D. (with honors), 1997 — Admitted to Bar, 1997, Iowa; 1998, Minnesota; U.S. District Court, Northern and Southern Districts of Iowa — Member Iowa State, Minnesota State and Black Hawk County Bar Associations — E-mail: smith@s-c-law.com

Henry J. Bevel III — 1959 — Kentucky State University, B.A. (magna cum laude), 1981; University of Kentucky, J.D., 1984 — Admitted to Bar, 1988, Iowa; U.S. District Court, Northern District of Iowa — Member American and Iowa State Bar Associations; Iowa Defense Counsel Association; Defense Research Institute — E-mail: bevel@s-c-law.com

Joseph G. Martin — 1981 — University of Northern Iowa, B.A., 2004; Drake University, J.D., 2007 — Admitted to Bar, 2007, Iowa; 2008, U.S. District Court, Northern District of Iowa — Member Iowa State and Black Hawk County Bar Associations — E-mail: martin@s-c-law.com

Robert M. Bembridge — 1979 — Loras College, B.A., 2001; The John Marshall Law School, J.D., 2004 — Admitted to Bar, 2004, Georgia; 2010, Iowa — Member State Bar of Georgia (Young Lawyers Division) — E-mail: bembridge@s-c-law.com

Dustin T. Zeschke — 1986 — The University of Iowa, B.A., 2008; Drake University Law School, Law Degree (J.D. equivalent) (with honors), 2011 — Admitted to Bar, 2011, Iowa — Member Black Hawk County Bar Association — E-mail: zeschke@s-c-law.com

(This firm is also listed in the Investigation and Adjustment section of this directory)

IOWA — WEST DES MOINES

The following firms also service this area.

Lederer Weston Craig, P.L.C.
118-3rd Avenue SE, Suite 700
Cedar Rapids, Iowa 52401
  Telephone: 319-365-1184
  Fax: 319-365-1186

Mailing Address: P.O. Box 1927, Cedar Rapids, IA 52406-1927

Civil Litigation, Insurance Defense, Commercial Litigation, Motor Vehicle, Municipal Law, Premises Liability, Product Liability, Professional Liability, Professional Negligence, Tort

SEE COMPLETE LISTING UNDER CEDAR RAPIDS, IOWA (66 MILES)

WEST DES MOINES   56,609 Polk Co.

Lederer Weston Craig, P.L.C.
4401 Weston Parkway, Suite 310
West Des Moines, Iowa 50266
  Telephone: 515-224-3911
  Fax: 515-224-2698
  www.lwclawyers.com

(Cedar Rapids, IA Office*: 118-3rd Avenue SE, Suite 700, 52401, P.O. Box 1927, 52406-1927)
  (Tel: 319-365-1184)
  (Fax: 319-365-1186)
  (E-Mail: mweston@lwclawyers.com)

Civil Litigation, Insurance Defense, Commercial Litigation, Motor Vehicle, Municipal Law, Premises Liability, Product Liability, Professional Liability, Professional Negligence, Tort

(See listing under Cedar Rapids, IA for additional information)

WEST UNION   † 2,486 Fayette Co.

Refer To

Clark, Butler, Walsh & Hamann
315 East 5th Street
Waterloo, Iowa 50701
  Telephone: 319-234-5701
  Fax: 319-232-9579
  Toll Free: 800-825-2971

Mailing Address: P.O. Box 596, Waterloo, IA 50704

Automobile, Product Liability, Malpractice, Subrogation, Life and Health, Workers' Compensation, Surety, Insurance Defense, Investigation and Adjustment

SEE COMPLETE LISTING UNDER WATERLOO, IOWA (60 MILES)

KANSAS

CAPITAL: TOPEKA

COUNTIES AND COUNTY SEATS

County	County Seat
Allen	Iola
Anderson	Garnett
Atchison	Atchison
Barber	Medicine Lodge
Barton	Great Bend
Bourbon	Fort Scott
Brown	Hiawatha
Butler	El Dorado
Chase	Cottonwood Falls
Chautauqua	Sedan
Cherokee	Columbus
Cheyenne	Saint Francis
Clark	Ashland
Clay	Clay Center
Cloud	Concordia
Coffey	Burlington
Comanche	Coldwater
Cowley	Winfield
Crawford	Girard
Decatur	Oberlin
Dickinson	Abilene
Doniphan	Troy
Douglas	Lawrence
Edwards	Kinsley
Elk	Howard
Ellis	Hays
Ellsworth	Ellsworth
Finney	Garden City
Ford	Dodge City
Franklin	Ottawa
Geary	Junction City
Gove	Gove
Graham	Hill City
Grant	Ulysses
Gray	Cimarron
Greeley	Tribune
Greenwood	Eureka
Hamilton	Syracuse
Harper	Anthony
Harvey	Newton
Haskell	Sublette
Hodgeman	Jetmore
Jackson	Holton
Jefferson	Oskaloosa
Jewell	Mankato
Johnson	Olathe
Kearny	Lakin
Kingman	Kingman
Kiowa	Greensburg
Labette	Oswego
Lane	Dighton
Leavenworth	Leavenworth
Lincoln	Lincoln
Linn	Mound City
Logan	Oakley
Lyon	Emporia
Marion	Marion
Marshall	Marysville
McPherson	McPherson
Meade	Meade
Miami	Paola
Mitchell	Beloit
Montgomery	Independence
Morris	Council Grove
Morton	Elkhart
Nemaha	Seneca
Neosho	Erie
Ness	Ness City
Norton	Norton
Osage	Lyndon
Osborne	Osborne
Ottawa	Minneapolis
Pawnee	Larned
Phillips	Phillipsburg
Pottawatomie	Westmoreland
Pratt	Pratt
Rawlins	Atwood
Reno	Hutchinson
Republic	Belleville
Rice	Lyons
Riley	Manhattan
Rooks	Stockton
Rush	La Crosse
Russell	Russell
Saline	Salina
Scott	Scott City
Sedgwick	Wichita
Seward	Liberal
Shawnee	Topeka
Sheridan	Hoxie
Sherman	Goodland
Smith	Smith Center
Stafford	St. John
Stanton	Johnson
Stevens	Hugoton
Sumner	Wellington
Thomas	Colby
Trego	Wakeeney
Wabaunsee	Alma
Wallace	Sharon Springs
Washington	Washington
Wichita	Leoti
Wilson	Fredonia
Woodson	Yates Center
Wyandotte	Kansas City

In the text that follows "†" indicates County Seats.

Our files contain additional verified data on the firms listed herein. This additional information is available on request.

A.M. BEST COMPANY

KANSAS

ABILENE † 6,844 Dickinson Co.

Refer To

Hampton & Royce, L.C.
United Building, Ninth Floor
119 West Iron Avenue
Salina, Kansas 67401
   Telephone: 785-827-7251
   Fax: 785-827-2815

Mailing Address: P.O. Box 1247, Salina, KS 67402-1247

Accident, Agent/Broker Liability, Errors and Omissions, Agriculture, Alternative Dispute Resolution, Appellate Practice, Arson, Automobile Liability, Banking, Bankruptcy, Bodily Injury, Business Law, Casualty Insurance Law, Civil Litigation, Class Actions, Collections, Commercial and Personal Lines, Commercial General Liability, Commercial Litigation, Commercial Transactions, Construction Liability, Construction Litigation, Contract Disputes, Contractors Liability, Contracts, Corporate Law, Coverage Analysis, Directors and Officers Liability, Employer Liability, Employment Discrimination, Employment Law, Employment Practices Liability, Environmental Law, Estate Planning, General Civil Practice, Health Care, Insurance Coverage, Insurance Fraud, Insurance Litigation, Intentional Torts, Labor and Employment, Legal Malpractice, Lender Liability Defense, Mediation, Medical Liability, Medical Malpractice, Mergers and Acquisitions, Negligence, Nursing Home Liability, Personal Injury, Policy Construction and Interpretation, Premises Liability, Probate, Product Liability, Professional Negligence, Sexual Harassment, Slip and Fall, Subrogation, Tort Liability, Tort Litigation, Uninsured and Underinsured Motorist, Workers' Compensation, Wrongful Death, Wrongful Termination, Life and Health Insurance Claims and Litigation, Accountant Liability and Malpractice, , Contract Litigation, Coverage Disputes, Domestic, Excess and Umbrella Coverage and Litigation, Family Law and Litigation, First and Third Party Claims, Foreclosures, Health Insurance Litigation, Homeowners Liability, Pensions, Property and Casualty Losses, Real Estate Contracts, Real Estate Disputes and Litigation, Receiverships, Shareholders Claims, Trusts and Trust Litigation

SEE COMPLETE LISTING UNDER SALINA, KANSAS (27 MILES)

ATCHISON † 11,021 Atchison Co.

Refer To

Logan Logan & Watson, L.C.
8340 Mission Road
Prairie Village, Kansas 66206
   Telephone: 913-381-1121
   Fax: 913-381-6546

Insurance Law, Trial and Appellate Practice, Commercial Law, General Liability, Professional Liability, Property, Legal Malpractice, Medical Malpractice, Product Liability, Coverage Issues, Automobile

SEE COMPLETE LISTING UNDER PRAIRIE VILLAGE, KANSAS (55 MILES)

COLBY † 5,387 Thomas Co.

Refer To

Hampton & Royce, L.C.
United Building, Ninth Floor
119 West Iron Avenue
Salina, Kansas 67401
   Telephone: 785-827-7251
   Fax: 785-827-2815

Mailing Address: P.O. Box 1247, Salina, KS 67402-1247

Accident, Agent/Broker Liability, Errors and Omissions, Agriculture, Alternative Dispute Resolution, Appellate Practice, Arson, Automobile Liability, Banking, Bankruptcy, Bodily Injury, Business Law, Casualty Insurance Law, Civil Litigation, Class Actions, Collections, Commercial and Personal Lines, Commercial General Liability, Commercial Litigation, Commercial Transactions, Construction Liability, Construction Litigation, Contract Disputes, Contractors Liability, Contracts, Corporate Law, Coverage Analysis, Directors and Officers Liability, Employer Liability, Employment Discrimination, Employment Law, Employment Practices Liability, Environmental Law, Estate Planning, General Civil Practice, Health Care, Insurance Coverage, Insurance Fraud, Insurance Litigation, Intentional Torts, Labor and Employment, Legal Malpractice, Lender Liability Defense, Mediation, Medical Liability, Medical Malpractice, Mergers and Acquisitions, Negligence, Nursing Home Liability, Personal Injury, Policy Construction and Interpretation, Premises Liability, Probate, Product Liability, Professional Negligence, Sexual Harassment, Slip and Fall, Subrogation, Tort Liability, Tort Litigation, Uninsured and Underinsured Motorist, Workers' Compensation, Wrongful Death, Wrongful Termination, Life and Health Insurance Claims and Litigation, Accountant Liability and Malpractice, , Contract Litigation, Coverage Disputes, Domestic, Excess and Umbrella Coverage and Litigation, Family Law and Litigation, First and Third Party Claims, Foreclosures, Health Insurance Litigation, Homeowners Liability, Pensions, Property and Casualty Losses, Real Estate Contracts, Real Estate Disputes and Litigation, Receiverships, Shareholders Claims, Trusts and Trust Litigation

SEE COMPLETE LISTING UNDER SALINA, KANSAS (204 MILES)

CONCORDIA † 5,395 Cloud Co.

Refer To

Clark, Mize & Linville, Chartered
129 South 8th Street
Salina, Kansas 67401
   Telephone: 785-823-6325
   Fax: 785-823-1868

Mailing Address: P.O. Box 380, Salina, KS 67402-0380

Automobile, Workers' Compensation, Defense Litigation, Employment Discrimination, Public Entities, Medical Malpractice, Professional Malpractice

SEE COMPLETE LISTING UNDER SALINA, KANSAS (55 MILES)

KANSAS CITY

Refer To

Hampton & Royce, L.C.
United Building, Ninth Floor
119 West Iron Avenue
Salina, Kansas 67401
   Telephone: 785-827-7251
   Fax: 785-827-2815

Mailing Address: P.O. Box 1247, Salina, KS 67402-1247

Accident, Agent/Broker Liability, Errors and Omissions, Agriculture, Alternative Dispute Resolution, Appellate Practice, Arson, Automobile Liability, Banking, Bankruptcy, Bodily Injury, Business Law, Casualty Insurance Law, Civil Litigation, Class Actions, Collections, Commercial and Personal Lines, Commercial General Liability, Commercial Litigation, Commercial Transactions, Construction Liability, Construction Litigation, Contract Disputes, Contractors Liability, Contracts, Corporate Law, Coverage Analysis, Directors and Officers Liability, Employer Liability, Employment Discrimination, Employment Law, Employment Practices Liability, Environmental Law, Estate Planning, General Civil Practice, Health Care, Insurance Coverage, Insurance Fraud, Insurance Litigation, Intentional Torts, Labor and Employment, Legal Malpractice, Lender Liability Defense, Mediation, Medical Liability, Medical Malpractice, Mergers and Acquisitions, Negligence, Nursing Home Liability, Personal Injury, Policy Construction and Interpretation, Premises Liability, Probate, Product Liability, Professional Negligence, Sexual Harassment, Slip and Fall, Subrogation, Tort Liability, Tort Litigation, Uninsured and Underinsured Motorist, Workers' Compensation, Wrongful Death, Wrongful Termination, Life and Health Insurance Claims and Litigation, Accountant Liability and Malpractice, , Contract Litigation, Coverage Disputes, Domestic, Excess and Umbrella Coverage and Litigation, Family Law and Litigation, First and Third Party Claims, Foreclosures, Health Insurance Litigation, Homeowners Liability, Pensions, Property and Casualty Losses, Real Estate Contracts, Real Estate Disputes and Litigation, Receiverships, Shareholders Claims, Trusts and Trust Litigation

SEE COMPLETE LISTING UNDER SALINA, KANSAS (53 MILES)

GARDEN CITY † 26,658 Finney Co.

Refer To

Hampton & Royce, L.C.
United Building, Ninth Floor
119 West Iron Avenue
Salina, Kansas 67401
   Telephone: 785-827-7251
   Fax: 785-827-2815

Mailing Address: P.O. Box 1247, Salina, KS 67402-1247

Accident, Agent/Broker Liability, Errors and Omissions, Agriculture, Alternative Dispute Resolution, Appellate Practice, Arson, Automobile Liability, Banking, Bankruptcy, Bodily Injury, Business Law, Casualty Insurance Law, Civil Litigation, Class Actions, Collections, Commercial and Personal Lines, Commercial General Liability, Commercial Litigation, Commercial Transactions, Construction Liability, Construction Litigation, Contract Disputes, Contractors Liability, Contracts, Corporate Law, Coverage Analysis, Directors and Officers Liability, Employer Liability, Employment Discrimination, Employment Law, Employment Practices Liability, Environmental Law, Estate Planning, General Civil Practice, Health Care, Insurance Coverage, Insurance Fraud, Insurance Litigation, Intentional Torts, Labor and Employment, Legal Malpractice, Lender Liability Defense, Mediation, Medical Liability, Medical Malpractice, Mergers and Acquisitions, Negligence, Nursing Home Liability, Personal Injury, Policy Construction and Interpretation, Premises Liability, Probate, Product Liability, Professional Negligence, Sexual Harassment, Slip and Fall, Subrogation, Tort Liability, Tort Litigation, Uninsured and Underinsured Motorist, Workers' Compensation, Wrongful Death, Wrongful Termination, Life and Health Insurance Claims and Litigation, Accountant Liability and Malpractice, , Contract Litigation, Coverage Disputes, Domestic, Excess and Umbrella Coverage and Litigation, Family Law and Litigation, First and Third Party Claims, Foreclosures, Health Insurance Litigation, Homeowners Liability, Pensions, Property and Casualty Losses, Real Estate Contracts, Real Estate Disputes and Litigation, Receiverships, Shareholders Claims, Trusts and Trust Litigation

SEE COMPLETE LISTING UNDER SALINA, KANSAS (219 MILES)

HAYS † 20,510 Ellis Co.

Refer To

Clark, Mize & Linville, Chartered
129 South 8th Street
Salina, Kansas 67401
   Telephone: 785-823-6325
   Fax: 785-823-1868

Mailing Address: P.O. Box 380, Salina, KS 67402-0380

Automobile, Workers' Compensation, Defense Litigation, Employment Discrimination, Public Entities, Medical Malpractice, Professional Malpractice

SEE COMPLETE LISTING UNDER SALINA, KANSAS (98 MILES)

Refer To

Hampton & Royce, L.C.
United Building, Ninth Floor
119 West Iron Avenue
Salina, Kansas 67401
   Telephone: 785-827-7251
   Fax: 785-827-2815

Mailing Address: P.O. Box 1247, Salina, KS 67402-1247

Accident, Agent/Broker Liability, Errors and Omissions, Agriculture, Alternative Dispute Resolution, Appellate Practice, Arson, Automobile Liability, Banking, Bankruptcy, Bodily Injury, Business Law, Casualty Insurance Law, Civil Litigation, Class Actions, Collections, Commercial and Personal Lines, Commercial General Liability, Commercial Litigation, Commercial Transactions, Construction Liability, Construction Litigation, Contract Disputes, Contractors Liability, Contracts, Corporate Law, Coverage Analysis, Directors and Officers Liability, Employer Liability, Employment Discrimination, Employment Law, Employment Practices Liability, Environmental Law, Estate Planning, General Civil Practice, Health Care, Insurance Coverage, Insurance Fraud, Insurance Litigation, Intentional Torts, Labor and Employment, Legal Malpractice, Lender Liability Defense, Mediation, Medical Liability, Medical Malpractice, Mergers and Acquisitions, Negligence, Nursing Home Liability, Personal Injury, Policy Construction and Interpretation, Premises Liability, Probate, Product Liability, Professional Negligence, Sexual Harassment, Slip and Fall, Subrogation, Tort Liability, Tort Litigation, Uninsured and Underinsured Motorist, Workers' Compensation, Wrongful Death, Wrongful Termination, Life and Health Insurance Claims and Litigation, Accountant Liability and Malpractice, , Contract Litigation, Coverage Disputes, Domestic, Excess and Umbrella Coverage and Litigation, Family Law and Litigation, First and Third Party Claims, Foreclosures, Health Insurance Litigation, Homeowners Liability, Pensions, Property and Casualty Losses, Real Estate Contracts, Real Estate Disputes and Litigation, Receiverships, Shareholders Claims, Trusts and Trust Litigation

SEE COMPLETE LISTING UNDER SALINA, KANSAS (98 MILES)

KANSAS CITY † 145,786 Wyandotte Co.

McAnany, Van Cleave & Phillips, P.A.

10 East Cambridge Circle Drive, Suite 300
Kansas City, Kansas 66103
   Telephone: 913-371-3838
   Fax: 913-371-4722
   www.mvplaw.com

(McAnany, Van Cleave & Phillips, P.C.*: 505 North 7th Street, Suite 2100, St. Louis, MO, 63101)
   (Tel: 314-621-1133)
   (Fax: 314-621-4405)
(McAnany, Van Cleave & Phillips, P.C.*: 4650 South National Avenue, Suite D-2, Springfield, MO, 65810)
   (Tel: 417-865-0007)
   (Fax: 417-865-0008)
(McAnany, Van Cleave & Phillips, P.C.*: 10665 Bedford Avenue, Suite 101, Omaha, NE, 68134)
   (Tel: 402-408-1340)
   (Fax: 402-493-0860)
(McAnany, Van Cleave & Phillips, P.C.*: 2021 South Lewis, Suite 225, Tulsa, OK, 74104)
   (Tel: 918-771-4465)

Established: 1901

McAnany, Van Cleave & Phillips, P.A., Kansas City, KS (Continued)

Administrative Law, Antitrust, Bankruptcy, Business Law, Construction Law, Corporate Law, Creditor Rights, Directors and Officers Liability, Insurance Law, Labor and Employment, Land Use, Litigation, Municipal Law, Personal Injury, Product Liability, Professional Liability, Public Entities, Railroad Law, Real Estate, School Law, Transportation, Trial and Appellate Practice, Workers' Compensation

Firm Profile: McAnany, Van Cleave & Phillips is a full-service law firm with offices strategically located to serve Kansas, Missouri, Illinois, Arkansas, Oklahoma, Nebraska, and Iowa. Our Firm is focused on service with results, ethics with integrity, and creativity with solutions to advance our clients' interests.

Insurance Clients

Accident Fund Insurance Company of America
Kansas Association of School Boards
Travelers Insurance Companies
ACE USA/ESIS, Inc.
Argonaut Insurance Company
Liberty Mutual Insurance Company
Missouri Employers Mutual Insurance Company

Non-Insurance Clients

Kansas City, KS Public Schools
YRC Enterprise Services, Inc.
Unified Government of Wyandotte County/Kansas City, Kansas

Partners/Shareholders

Charles A. Getto — 1950 — University of California, Berkeley, B.A., 1973; University of California, Los Angeles, J.D., 1976 — Admitted to Bar, 1976, California; 1978, Kansas; U.S. District Court, District of Kansas; U.S. District Court, Western District of Missouri; U.S. District Court, Central District of California; U.S. Court of Appeals, Eighth and Tenth Circuits — E-mail: cgetto@mvplaw.com

Frederick J. Greenbaum — 1952 — Kansas State University, B.S., 1974; Washburn University, J.D., 1980 — Admitted to Bar, 1980, Kansas; 1987, Missouri; U.S. District Court, District of Kansas; U.S. District Court, Western District of Missouri — E-mail: fgreenbaum@mvplaw.com

Lawrence D. Greenbaum — 1955 — The University of Kansas, B.S., 1977; J.D., 1984 — Admitted to Bar, 1984, Kansas; 1989, Missouri; U.S. District Court, Western District of Missouri; U.S. District Court, District of Kansas — E-mail: lgreenbaum@mvplaw.com

John David Jurcyk — 1959 — Creighton University, B.A., 1981; Washburn University, J.D., 1984 — Admitted to Bar, 1984, Kansas; 1989, Missouri; U.S. District Court, District of Kansas; U.S. Court of Appeals, Tenth Circuit — E-mail: jjurcyk@mvplaw.com

Douglas M. Greenwald — 1959 — Washington University, B.A., 1981; The University of Kansas, J.D., 1984 — Admitted to Bar, 1984, Kansas; 1985, Missouri; U.S. District Court, Eastern and Western Districts of Missouri; U.S. District Court, District of Kansas; U.S. Court of Appeals, Eighth and Tenth Circuits — E-mail: dgreenwald@mvplaw.com

Anton C. Andersen — 1960 — The University of Kansas, B.S., 1983; Washburn University, J.D., 1986 — Admitted to Bar, 1986, Kansas; 1993, Missouri; U.S. District Court, District of Kansas — E-mail: aandersen@mvplaw.com

Gregory D. Worth — 1960 — University of Nebraska-Lincoln, B.S., 1982; J.D., 1986 — Admitted to Bar, 1987, Kansas; 2007, Missouri; Nebraska — E-mail: gworth@mvplaw.com

Deryl W. Wynn — 1961 — Emporia State University, B.S., 1983; B.F.A., 1983; Washburn University, J.D., 1986; U.S. Army Judge Advocate General's School, 1986 — Admitted to Bar, 1986, Kansas; 2006, Missouri; U.S. Court of Military Appeals; U.S. District Court, District of Kansas; U.S. District Court, Western District of Missouri; U.S. Court of Appeals, Fourth and Tenth Circuits — E-mail: dwynn@mvplaw.com

Clifford K. Stubbs — 1965 — The University of Kansas, B.A., 1988; J.D., 1991 — Admitted to Bar, 1991, Kansas; 1992, Missouri; U.S. District Court, District of Kansas; U.S. District Court, Western District of Missouri — E-mail: cstubbs@mvplaw.com

Carl A. Gallagher — 1953 — The University of Kansas, B.A., 1974; Washburn University, J.D., 1981 — Admitted to Bar, 1981, Kansas; 2012, Missouri; 1981, U.S. District Court, District of Kansas; U.S. District Court, Western District of Missouri; U.S. Court of Appeals, Eighth and Tenth Circuits — E-mail: cgallagher@mvplaw.com

Eric T. Lanham — 1960 — University of Missouri-Columbia, B.S., 1987; University of Missouri-Kansas City, J.D., 1992 — Admitted to Bar, 1993, Missouri; Kansas; Iowa — E-mail: elanham@mvplaw.com

Gregory P. Goheen — 1968 — The University of Kansas, B.A., 1990; Southern Methodist University, J.D., 1993 — Admitted to Bar, 1993, Kansas; 2006, Missouri; U.S. District Court, Eastern and Western Districts of Missouri; U.S. District Court, District of Kansas; U.S. Court of Appeals, Tenth Circuit; U.S. Supreme Court — E-mail: ggoheen@mvplaw.com

David F. Menghini — 1967 — The University of Kansas, B.S., 1991; University of Missouri-Kansas City, J.D., 1996 — Admitted to Bar, 1996, Kansas; 1997, Missouri; U.S. District Court, District of Kansas — E-mail: dmenghini@mvplaw.com

Joseph W. Hemberger — 1962 — Creighton University, B.S., 1985; Tulane University of Louisiana, J.D., 1988 — Admitted to Bar, 1988, Kansas; 1989, Missouri; U.S. District Court, District of Kansas; U.S. District Court, Western District of Missouri — E-mail: jhemberger@mvplaw.com

Ryan B. Denk — 1973 — The University of Kansas, B.A., 1995; J.D., 1998 — Admitted to Bar, 1998, Kansas; 1999, Missouri; U.S. District Court, District of Kansas; U.S. District Court, Western District of Missouri; U.S. Court of Appeals, Tenth Circuit — E-mail: rdenk@mvplaw.com

John R. Emerson — 1971 — The University of Kansas, B.A., 1993; J.D., 1996 — Admitted to Bar, 1996, Kansas; 2000, Missouri — E-mail: jemerson@mvplaw.com

George D. Halper — 1958 — University of Colorado, B.S., 1979; The University of Kansas, J.D., 1984 — Admitted to Bar, 1984, Missouri; 1990, Kansas; U.S. District Court, District of Kansas; U.S. District Court, Western District of Missouri; U.S. Tax Court — E-mail: ghalper@mvplaw.com

Thomas J. Walsh — 1970 — The University of Iowa, B.B.A., 1994; University of Missouri-Kansas City, J.D., 1997 — Admitted to Bar, 1997, Missouri; 1998, Kansas — E-mail: twalsh@mvplaw.com

Elizabeth Reid Dotson — 1974 — The University of New Mexico, B.A., 1996; Washburn University, J.D., 2000 — Admitted to Bar, 2001, Kansas; 2002, Missouri; U.S. District Court, District of Kansas; U.S. District Court, Western District of Missouri — E-mail: edotson@mvplaw.com

Robert J. Wonnell — 1976 — Phillips University, B.S., 1998; The University of Kansas, J.D., 2001 — Admitted to Bar, 2002, Missouri; Kansas; 2008, Nebraska; U.S. District Court, Western District of Missouri; U.S. District Court, District of Kansas — E-mail: rwonnell@mvplaw.com

Samantha N. Benjamin-House — 1974 — University of Central Oklahoma, B.S., 1996; M.S., 1997; The University of Oklahoma, J.D., 1999 — Admitted to Bar, 2000, Missouri; Kansas; 2007, Oklahoma; U.S. District Court, District of Kansas — E-mail: sbenjamin@mvplaw.com

James P. Wolf — 1976 — Kansas State University, B.S., 1998; M.A., 1999; The University of Kansas, J.D., 2002 — Admitted to Bar, 2003, Kansas; Missouri — E-mail: jwolf@mvplaw.com

Katie M. Black — 1977 — Northern Arizona University, B.S., 1999; University of Missouri-Kansas City, J.D., 2006 — Admitted to Bar, 2006, Missouri; 2007, Kansas — E-mail: kblack@mvplaw.com

Jodi J. Fox — 1973 — Luther College, B.A., 1995; The University of Tulsa, J.D./M.A., 1998 — Admitted to Bar, 1999, Oklahoma; 2001, Missouri; 2004, Kansas; U.S. District Court, Northern District of Oklahoma — E-mail: jfox@mvplaw.com

Byron A. Bowles, Jr. — 1968 — Southwest Missouri State University, B.A., 1991; The University of Kansas, J.D., 1994 — Admitted to Bar, 1994, Kansas; 1995, Missouri; 2008, Illinois; U.S. District Court, Eastern and Western Districts of Missouri; U.S. District Court, Southern District of Illinois; U.S. Court of Appeals, Seventh, Eighth and Tenth Circuits; U.S. Supreme Court — E-mail: bbowles@mvplaw.com

Joseph F. Reardon — 1968 — Rockhurst College, B.A. (summa cum laude), 1990; The University of Kansas, J.D., 1994 — Admitted to Bar, 1994, Kansas — E-mail: jreardon@mvplaw.com

Karl L. Wenger — 1980 — University of Central Missouri, B.S., 2002; Washburn University, J.D., 2008 — Admitted to Bar, 2008, Kansas; 2009, Missouri — E-mail: kwenger@mvplaw.com

Of Counsel

John J. Jurcyk — Creighton University, B.A., 1981; Washburn University, J.D., 1984 — Admitted to Bar, 1984, Kansas; 1985, Missouri; U.S. District Court, District of Kansas; U.S. Court of Appeals, Tenth Circuit — E-mail: jjurcyk@mvplaw.com

Robert D. Benham — Retired — 1932 — The University of Kansas, B.A., 1956; LL.B., 1958 — Admitted to Bar, 1958, Kansas; 1993, Missouri

LAWRENCE

McAnany, Van Cleave & Phillips, P.A., Kansas City, KS (Continued)

Associates

Brent M. Johnston — 1980 — Arizona State University, B.S., 2006; Washburn University, J.D., 2009 — Admitted to Bar, 2009, Missouri; 2010, Kansas — E-mail: bjohnston@mvplaw.com

Kendra M. Oakes — 1982 — University of Nevada, B.S., 2006; The University of Kansas, J.D. (Order of the Coif), 2010 — Admitted to Bar, 2010, Missouri; 2011, Kansas — E-mail: koakes@mvplaw.com

Teresa A. Mata — 1983 — Kansas University, B.A., 2006; Washburn University, J.D., 2010 — Admitted to Bar, 2010, Kansas; 2012, Missouri — E-mail: tmata@mvplaw.com

Kristina D. Schlake — 1985 — Saint Louis University, B.A., 2006; Arizona State University, M.S., 2009; University of Missouri-Kansas City School of Law, J.D. (magna cum laude), 2013 — Admitted to Bar, 2013, Missouri; 2014, Kansas — E-mail: kschlake@mvplaw.com

Robert M. Smith — 1988 — St. Olaf College, B.A., History, 2010; University of Missouri-Kansas City, J.D. (summa cum laude), 2013 — Admitted to Bar, 2013, Missouri; 2014, Kansas — E-mail: rsmith@mvplaw.com

Rachel E. Nelson — 1988 — The University of Kansas, B.S./B.A., 2010; The University of Kansas School of Law, J.D., 2013 — Admitted to Bar, 2013, Missouri; 2014, Kansas — E-mail: rnelson@mvplaw.com

Kelsy E. Allison — Drury University, B.S., 2010; Washburn University School of Law, J.D., 2013 — Admitted to Bar, 2014, Missouri — E-mail: kallison@mvplaw.com

(Revisors of the Kansas Insurance Law Digest for this Publication)

The following firms also service this area.

Clark, Mize & Linville, Chartered
129 South 8th Street
Salina, Kansas 67401
   Telephone: 785-823-6325
   Fax: 785-823-1868
Mailing Address: P.O. Box 380, Salina, KS 67402-0380

Automobile, Workers' Compensation, Defense Litigation, Employment Discrimination, Public Entities, Medical Malpractice, Professional Malpractice

SEE COMPLETE LISTING UNDER SALINA, KANSAS (180 MILES)

Hampton & Royce, L.C.
United Building, Ninth Floor
119 West Iron Avenue
Salina, Kansas 67401
   Telephone: 785-827-7251
   Fax: 785-827-2815
Mailing Address: P.O. Box 1247, Salina, KS 67402-1247

Accident, Agent/Broker Liability, Errors and Omissions, Agriculture, Alternative Dispute Resolution, Appellate Practice, Arson, Automobile Liability, Banking, Bankruptcy, Bodily Injury, Business Law, Casualty Insurance Law, Civil Litigation, Class Actions, Collections, Commercial and Personal Lines, Commercial General Liability, Commercial Litigation, Commercial Transactions, Construction Litigation, Construction Litigation, Contract Disputes, Contractors Liability, Contracts, Corporate Law, Coverage Analysis, Directors and Officers Liability, Employer Liability, Employment Discrimination, Employment Law, Employment Practices Liability, Environmental Law, Estate Planning, General Civil Practice, Health Care, Insurance Coverage, Insurance Fraud, Insurance Litigation, Intentional Torts, Labor and Employment, Legal Malpractice, Lender Liability Defense, Mediation, Medical Liability, Medical Malpractice, Mergers and Acquisitions, Negligence, Nursing Home Liability, Personal Injury, Policy Construction and Interpretation, Premises Liability, Probate, Product Liability, Professional Negligence, Sexual Harassment, Slip and Fall, Subrogation, Tort Liability, Tort Litigation, Uninsured and Underinsured Motorist, Workers' Compensation, Wrongful Death, Wrongful Termination, Life and Health Insurance Claims and Litigation, Accountant Liability and Malpractice, , Contract Litigation, Coverage Disputes, Domestic, Excess and Umbrella Coverage and Litigation, Family Law and Litigation, First and Third Party Claims, Foreclosures, Health Insurance Litigation, Homeowners Liability, Pensions, Property and Casualty Losses, Real Estate Contracts, Real Estate Disputes and Litigation, Receiverships, Shareholders Claims, Trusts and Trust Litigation

SEE COMPLETE LISTING UNDER SALINA, KANSAS (173 MILES)

KANSAS

Logan Logan & Watson, L.C.
8340 Mission Road
Prairie Village, Kansas 66206
   Telephone: 913-381-1121
   Fax: 913-381-6546

Insurance Law, Trial and Appellate Practice, Commercial Law, General Liability, Professional Liability, Property, Legal Malpractice, Medical Malpractice, Product Liability, Coverage Issues, Automobile

SEE COMPLETE LISTING UNDER PRAIRIE VILLAGE, KANSAS (10 MILES)

Payne & Jones, Chartered
11000 King
Overland Park, Kansas 66210-1233
   Telephone: 913-469-4100
   Fax: 913-469-8182
   Toll Free: 800-875-4101
Mailing Address: P.O. Box 25625, Overland Park, KS 66225

Insurance Defense, Trial Practice, Personal Injury, Workers' Compensation, Professional Negligence, Environmental Law, Business Law, Commercial Law, Coverage Issues, Employer Liability, General Liability, Product Liability, Property Liability, Wrongful Termination, Employment Practices Liability, Homeowners Liability, Property Damage Liability, Automobile (All-Lines)

SEE COMPLETE LISTING UNDER OVERLAND PARK, KANSAS (10 MILES)

Sanders Warren & Russell LLP
40 Corporate Woods
9401 Indian Creen Parkway, Suite 1250
Overland Park, Kansas 66210
   Telephone: 913-234-6100
   Fax: 913-234-6199

Insurance Defense, Business Law, Automobile, Property, Homeowners, Life Insurance, Commercial Law, Professional Liability, Municipal Law, Employment Law, Workers' Compensation, Comprehensive General Liability, Alternative Dispute Resolution, Appellate Practice, Bad Faith, Construction Litigation, Governmental Liability, Insurance Coverage, Medical Malpractice, Premises Liability, Product Liability, Truck Liability

SEE COMPLETE LISTING UNDER OVERLAND PARK, KANSAS (13 MILES)

LAWRENCE † 87,643 Douglas Co.

Refer To
Logan Logan & Watson, L.C.
8340 Mission Road
Prairie Village, Kansas 66206
   Telephone: 913-381-1121
   Fax: 913-381-6546

Insurance Law, Trial and Appellate Practice, Commercial Law, General Liability, Professional Liability, Property, Legal Malpractice, Medical Malpractice, Product Liability, Coverage Issues, Automobile

SEE COMPLETE LISTING UNDER PRAIRIE VILLAGE, KANSAS (40 MILES)

Refer To
Sanders Warren & Russell LLP
40 Corporate Woods
9401 Indian Creen Parkway, Suite 1250
Overland Park, Kansas 66210
   Telephone: 913-234-6100
   Fax: 913-234-6199

Insurance Defense, Business Law, Automobile, Property, Homeowners, Life Insurance, Commercial Law, Professional Liability, Municipal Law, Employment Law, Workers' Compensation, Comprehensive General Liability, Alternative Dispute Resolution, Appellate Practice, Bad Faith, Construction Litigation, Governmental Liability, Insurance Coverage, Medical Malpractice, Premises Liability, Product Liability, Truck Liability

SEE COMPLETE LISTING UNDER OVERLAND PARK, KANSAS (42 MILES)

KANSAS

LEAVENWORTH † 35,251 Leavenworth Co.

Refer To

Logan Logan & Watson, L.C.
8340 Mission Road
Prairie Village, Kansas 66206
Telephone: 913-381-1121
Fax: 913-381-6546

Insurance Law, Trial and Appellate Practice, Commercial Law, General Liability, Professional Liability, Property, Legal Malpractice, Medical Malpractice, Product Liability, Coverage Issues, Automobile

SEE COMPLETE LISTING UNDER PRAIRIE VILLAGE, KANSAS (25 MILES)

Refer To

Sanders Warren & Russell LLP
40 Corporate Woods
9401 Indian Creen Parkway, Suite 1250
Overland Park, Kansas 66210
Telephone: 913-234-6100
Fax: 913-234-6199

Insurance Defense, Business Law, Automobile, Property, Homeowners, Life Insurance, Commercial Law, Professional Liability, Municipal Law, Employment Law, Workers' Compensation, Comprehensive General Liability, Alternative Dispute Resolution, Appellate Practice, Bad Faith, Construction Litigation, Governmental Liability, Insurance Coverage, Medical Malpractice, Premises Liability, Product Liability, Truck Liability

SEE COMPLETE LISTING UNDER OVERLAND PARK, KANSAS (36 MILES)

LEAWOOD 31,867 Johnson Co.

Bottaro, Morefield, Kubin & Yocum, P.C.

11300 Tomahawk Creek Parkway, Suite 190
Leawood, Kansas 66211
Telephone: 913-948-8200
Fax: 816-948-8228
E-Mail: info@kc-lawyers.com

Established: 1996

Insurance Defense, Trial and Appellate Practice, Casualty, Workers' Compensation, Product Liability, Fidelity and Surety, Reinsurance, Property, Excess, Business Law, Native American Law, Coverage Questions

Insurance Clients

American Centennial Insurance Company
Century Surety Company
Connecticut Specialty Insurance Company
EBI Companies
The Fire and Casualty Insurance Company of Connecticut
GAB Robins North America, Inc.
Glatfelter Claims Management, Inc.
The Infinity Group
Insurance Company of the State of Pennsylvania
Mead Reinsurance Corporation
Millers Insurance Group
National Union Fire Insurance Company
Northwestern National Insurance Company
Star Insurance Company
Argonaut Insurance Group
Balboa Life Insurance Company
The Connecticut Indemnity Company
CUNA Mutual Group
Economical Mutual Insurance Company
First State Insurance Company
Gallagher Bassett Services, Inc.
GRE Insurance Group
Haul Risk Management Services, Inc.
Liberty Mutual Insurance Company
Meadowbrook Insurance Group
Milirisk Insurance Services
National Insurance Association
Northland Insurance Company
North River Insurance Company
Ohio Casualty Group
Old Republic Insurance Company
Transportation Insurance Company

Non-Insurance Clients

Alexsis, Inc.
Helmsman Management Services, Inc.
KWELM
Leaseway Logistics
Moore Group, Inc.
Penske Truck Leasing
Canteen Corporation
Highway Carrier Company
International Cinema Equipment Company, Inc.
Missouri Gas Energy
Penske Corporation
XS Lighting

Bottaro, Morefield, Kubin & Yocum, P.C., Leawood, KS (Continued)

Firm Members

Patrick F. Bottaro — 1959 — Creighton University, B.A. (summa cum laude), 1982; The University of Iowa, J.D. (with distinction), 1985 — Moot Court Team; Selected as a Kansas and Missouri SuperLawyer (2006-2007) — Admitted to Bar, 1985, Missouri; U.S. District Court, Eastern and Western Districts of Missouri; U.S. Court of Appeals, Eighth Circuit; 2001, U.S. District Court, District of Kansas — Member American and Kansas City Metropolitan Bar Associations; The Missouri Bar; The Lawyers Association of Kansas City (Board of Directors, 1987-1993; Young Lawyers Section, President, 1992-1993) — Practice Areas: Civil Litigation; Personal Injury; Workers' Compensation — E-mail: pfb@kc-lawyers.com

Richard W. Morefield, Jr. — 1961 — Rice University, B.A., 1983; The University of Kansas, J.D., 1986 — Rice Scholar, 1983-1986; National Moot Court Team; Selected as a Kansas and Missouri SuperLawyer, 2006-2007 — Admitted to Bar, 1986, Missouri; 1987, Kansas; U.S. District Court, Western District of Missouri; U.S. District Court, District of Kansas; 1990, U.S. Supreme Court — Member American Bar Association (Sections: Litigation, Tort, Trial and Insurance Practice; Council, 2007-2010; Editorial Board, 2002-2005; Task Force on Young Lawyers, 2002-2005; Law Practice Management; Young Lawyers Division, Assembly Speaker, 1996-1997; Officer, 1995-1997); The Missouri Bar (Young Lawyers Section Executive Committee, 1991-1997; Outstanding Service Award, 1997); Lawyers Association of Kansas City (President, 2004-2005; Board of Directors, 1994-1995; 2001-2005; President, Young Lawyers Section, 1994-1995) — Author: "The Federal Tort Claims Act", University of Missouri/Columbia Lawyers Association of Kansas City CLE, 1994; Editor in Chief, "The Brief", 2006-2008 — Reported Cases: Downey v. McKee, 218 S.W.3d 492 (Mo.Ct.App. 2007) — E-mail: rwm@kc-lawyers.com

Kip A. Kubin — The University of Kansas, B.A., 1980; J.D., 1983 — Selected as a Kansas and Missouri SuperLawyer, 2006-2007 — Admitted to Bar, 1983, Kansas; 1990, Missouri; 1983, U.S. District Court, District of Kansas; 1984, U.S. Court of Appeals, Tenth Circuit — Member Kansas Bar Association (Board of Governors, 2005-present); The Missouri Bar; Johnson County Bar Association (President, 1993-1994) — E-mail: kak@kc-lawyers.com

Rebecca S. Yocum — Missouri Southern State College, B.S./B.S.B.A. (summa cum laude), 1979; University of Missouri-Kansas City School of Law, J.D. (Dean's List), 1983 — Admitted to Bar, 1983, Missouri; 1989, Kansas; U.S. District Court, District of Kansas; U.S. District Court, Western District of Missouri; U.S. Court of Appeals for the Federal, Eighth and Tenth Circuits — Member American, Kansas and Kansas City Metropolitan Bar Associations; The Missouri Bar; Lawyers Association of Kansas City — Practice Areas: Real Estate; Construction Litigation; Business Law; Employment Law — E-mail: rsy@kc-lawyers.com

Senior Associate

Andrew L. Speicher — 1976 — MidAmerica Nazarene University, B.A. (magna cum laude), 1998; Drake University Law School, J.D. (with honors), 2001 — Admitted to Bar, 2001, Missouri; 2002, Kansas; U.S. District Court, Western District of Missouri; U.S. District Court, District of Kansas; Missouri State Court — Member American, Kansas and Kansas City Metropolitan Bar Associations; The Missouri Bar — Practice Areas: Civil Litigation; Personal Injury; Workers' Compensation — E-mail: als@kc-lawyers.com

Associate

Kasey A. Klenda — 1986 — Benedictine College, B.S. (magna cum laude), 2009; Washburn University School of Law, J.D., 2012 — Admitted to Bar, 2012, Kansas; Missouri; Missouri State Court — E-mail: kak@kc-lawyers.com

MANHATTAN † 52,281 Riley Co.

Refer To

Hampton & Royce, L.C.
United Building, Ninth Floor
119 West Iron Avenue
Salina, Kansas 67401
  Telephone: 785-827-7251
  Fax: 785-827-2815

Mailing Address: P.O. Box 1247, Salina, KS 67402-1247

Accident, Agent/Broker Liability, Errors and Omissions, Agriculture, Alternative Dispute Resolution, Appellate Practice, Arson, Automobile Liability, Banking, Bankruptcy, Bodily Injury, Business Law, Casualty Insurance Law, Civil Litigation, Class Actions, Collections, Commercial and Personal Lines, Commercial General Liability, Commercial Litigation, Commercial Transactions, Construction Liability, Construction Litigation, Contract Disputes, Contractors Liability, Contracts, Corporate Law, Coverage Analysis, Directors and Officers Liability, Employer Liability, Employment Discrimination, Employment Law, Employment Practices Liability, Environmental Law, Estate Planning, General Civil Practice, Health Care, Insurance Coverage, Insurance Fraud, Insurance Litigation, Intentional Torts, Labor and Employment, Legal Malpractice, Lender Liability Defense, Mediation, Medical Liability, Medical Malpractice, Mergers and Acquisitions, Negligence, Nursing Home Liability, Personal Injury, Policy Construction and Interpretation, Premises Liability, Probate, Product Liability, Professional Negligence, Sexual Harassment, Slip and Fall, Subrogation, Tort Liability, Tort Litigation, Uninsured and Underinsured Motorist, Workers' Compensation, Wrongful Death, Wrongful Termination, Life and Health Insurance Claims and Litigation, Accountant Liability and Malpractice, , Contract Litigation, Coverage Disputes, Domestic, Excess and Umbrella Coverage and Litigation, Family Law and Litigation, First and Third Party Claims, Foreclosures, Health Insurance Litigation, Homeowners Liability, Pensions, Property and Casualty Losses, Real Estate Contracts, Real Estate Disputes and Litigation, Receiverships, Shareholders Claims, Trusts and Trust Litigation

SEE COMPLETE LISTING UNDER SALINA, KANSAS (71 MILES)

MCPHERSON † 13,155 McPherson Co.

Refer To

Hampton & Royce, L.C.
United Building, Ninth Floor
119 West Iron Avenue
Salina, Kansas 67401
  Telephone: 785-827-7251
  Fax: 785-827-2815

Mailing Address: P.O. Box 1247, Salina, KS 67402-1247

Accident, Agent/Broker Liability, Errors and Omissions, Agriculture, Alternative Dispute Resolution, Appellate Practice, Arson, Automobile Liability, Banking, Bankruptcy, Bodily Injury, Business Law, Casualty Insurance Law, Civil Litigation, Class Actions, Collections, Commercial and Personal Lines, Commercial General Liability, Commercial Litigation, Commercial Transactions, Construction Liability, Construction Litigation, Contract Disputes, Contractors Liability, Contracts, Corporate Law, Coverage Analysis, Directors and Officers Liability, Employer Liability, Employment Discrimination, Employment Law, Employment Practices Liability, Environmental Law, Estate Planning, General Civil Practice, Health Care, Insurance Coverage, Insurance Fraud, Insurance Litigation, Intentional Torts, Labor and Employment, Legal Malpractice, Lender Liability Defense, Mediation, Medical Liability, Medical Malpractice, Mergers and Acquisitions, Negligence, Nursing Home Liability, Personal Injury, Policy Construction and Interpretation, Premises Liability, Probate, Product Liability, Professional Negligence, Sexual Harassment, Slip and Fall, Subrogation, Tort Liability, Tort Litigation, Uninsured and Underinsured Motorist, Workers' Compensation, Wrongful Death, Wrongful Termination, Life and Health Insurance Claims and Litigation, Accountant Liability and Malpractice, , Contract Litigation, Coverage Disputes, Domestic, Excess and Umbrella Coverage and Litigation, Family Law and Litigation, First and Third Party Claims, Foreclosures, Health Insurance Litigation, Homeowners Liability, Pensions, Property and Casualty Losses, Real Estate Contracts, Real Estate Disputes and Litigation, Receiverships, Shareholders Claims, Trusts and Trust Litigation

SEE COMPLETE LISTING UNDER SALINA, KANSAS (38 MILES)

NEWTON † 19,132 Harvey Co.

Refer To

Hampton & Royce, L.C.
United Building, Ninth Floor
119 West Iron Avenue
Salina, Kansas 67401
  Telephone: 785-827-7251
  Fax: 785-827-2815

Mailing Address: P.O. Box 1247, Salina, KS 67402-1247

Accident, Agent/Broker Liability, Errors and Omissions, Agriculture, Alternative Dispute Resolution, Appellate Practice, Arson, Automobile Liability, Banking, Bankruptcy, Bodily Injury, Business Law, Casualty Insurance Law, Civil Litigation, Class Actions, Collections, Commercial and Personal Lines, Commercial General Liability, Commercial Litigation, Commercial Transactions, Construction Liability, Construction Litigation, Contract Disputes, Contractors Liability, Contracts, Corporate Law, Coverage Analysis, Directors and Officers Liability, Employer Liability, Employment Discrimination, Employment Law, Employment Practices Liability, Environmental Law, Estate Planning, General Civil Practice, Health Care, Insurance Coverage, Insurance Fraud, Insurance Litigation, Intentional Torts, Labor and Employment, Legal Malpractice, Lender Liability Defense, Mediation, Medical Liability, Medical Malpractice, Mergers and Acquisitions, Negligence, Nursing Home Liability, Personal Injury, Policy Construction and Interpretation, Premises Liability, Probate, Product Liability, Professional Negligence, Sexual Harassment, Slip and Fall, Subrogation, Tort Liability, Tort Litigation, Uninsured and Underinsured Motorist, Workers' Compensation, Wrongful Death, Wrongful Termination, Life and Health Insurance Claims and Litigation, Accountant Liability and Malpractice, , Contract Litigation, Coverage Disputes, Domestic, Excess and Umbrella Coverage and Litigation, Family Law and Litigation, First and Third Party Claims, Foreclosures, Health Insurance Litigation, Homeowners Liability, Pensions, Property and Casualty Losses, Real Estate Contracts, Real Estate Disputes and Litigation, Receiverships, Shareholders Claims, Trusts and Trust Litigation

SEE COMPLETE LISTING UNDER SALINA, KANSAS (64 MILES)

OLATHE † 125,872 Johnson Co.

Refer To

Case Linden P.C.
2600 Grand Boulevard, Suite 300
Kansas City, Missouri 64108
  Telephone: 816-979-1500
  Fax: 816-979-1501

Appellate Practice, Bodily Injury, Civil Trial Practice, Class Actions, Commercial Litigation, Discrimination, Errors and Omissions, Insurance Defense, Labor and Employment, Legal Malpractice, Medical Malpractice, Premises Liability, Product Liability, Professional Liability, Regulatory and Compliance, Tort, Workers' Compensation

SEE COMPLETE LISTING UNDER KANSAS CITY, MISSOURI (19 MILES)

Refer To

Logan Logan & Watson, L.C.
8340 Mission Road
Prairie Village, Kansas 66206
  Telephone: 913-381-1121
  Fax: 913-381-6546

Insurance Law, Trial and Appellate Practice, Commercial Law, General Liability, Professional Liability, Property, Legal Malpractice, Medical Malpractice, Product Liability, Coverage Issues, Automobile

SEE COMPLETE LISTING UNDER PRAIRIE VILLAGE, KANSAS (17 MILES)

Refer To

Payne & Jones, Chartered
11000 King
Overland Park, Kansas 66210-1233
  Telephone: 913-469-4100
  Fax: 913-469-8182
  Toll Free: 800-875-4101

Mailing Address: P.O. Box 25625, Overland Park, KS 66225

Insurance Defense, Trial Practice, Personal Injury, Workers' Compensation, Professional Negligence, Environmental Law, Business Law, Commercial Law, Coverage Issues, Employer Liability, General Liability, Product Liability, Property Liability, Wrongful Termination, Employment Practices Liability, Homeowners Liability, Property Damage Liability, Automobile (All-Lines)

SEE COMPLETE LISTING UNDER OVERLAND PARK, KANSAS (11 MILES)

KANSAS

Refer To
Sanders Warren & Russell LLP
40 Corporate Woods
9401 Indian Creen Parkway, Suite 1250
Overland Park, Kansas 66210
   Telephone: 913-234-6100
   Fax: 913-234-6199

Insurance Defense, Business Law, Automobile, Property, Homeowners, Life Insurance, Commercial Law, Professional Liability, Municipal Law, Employment Law, Workers' Compensation, Comprehensive General Liability, Alternative Dispute Resolution, Appellate Practice, Bad Faith, Construction Litigation, Governmental Liability, Insurance Coverage, Medical Malpractice, Premises Liability, Product Liability, Truck Liability

SEE COMPLETE LISTING UNDER OVERLAND PARK, KANSAS (12 MILES)

OVERLAND PARK   173,372 Johnson Co.

Payne & Jones, Chartered
11000 King
Overland Park, Kansas 66210-1233
   Telephone: 913-469-4100
   Fax: 913-469-8182
   Toll Free: 800-875-4101
   E-Mail: jcramer@paynejones.com
   E-Mail: mlowe@paynejones.com
   www.paynejones.com

Established: 1926

Insurance Defense, Trial Practice, Personal Injury, Workers' Compensation, Professional Negligence, Environmental Law, Business Law, Commercial Law, Coverage Issues, Employer Liability, General Liability, Product Liability, Property Liability, Wrongful Termination, Employment Practices Liability, Homeowners Liability, Property Damage Liability, Automobile (All-Lines)

Insurance Clients

California Casualty Insurance Company	CNA Insurance Companies
Shelter Insurance Companies	Liberty Mutual Insurance Company
Tokio Marine and Fire Insurance Company, Ltd.	TIG Insurance Company
	Travelers Property Casualty Corporation
Utica Mutual Insurance Company	Wausau General Insurance Company

Partners

James J. Cramer — 1962 — Kansas University, B.S. (with honors), 1984; Southern Methodist University, J.D. (with honors), 1987 — Admitted to Bar, 1987, Kansas; 1988, Missouri; 1987, U.S. District Court, District of Kansas; 1988, U.S. Court of Appeals, Eighth and Tenth Circuits; 1988, U.S. District Court, Western District of Missouri — Member American, Kansas and Johnson County Bar Associations; Kansas Association of Defense Counsel — Practice Areas: Insurance Defense; Employment Practices Liability — E-mail: jcramer@paynejones.com

Michael B. Lowe — 1964 — University of Michigan, B.A. (with honors), 1987; The University of Kansas School of Law, J.D., 1990 — Admitted to Bar, 1990, Kansas; 1991, Missouri; 1990, U.S. District Court, District of Kansas; 1991, U.S. District Court, Western District of Missouri — Member American, Kansas and Johnson County Bar Associations; The Missouri Bar — Practice Areas: Commercial Litigation; Litigation; Insurance Defense; Medical Malpractice

Tyler Peters — 1965 — The University of Kansas, B.S., 1988; University of Missouri-Kansas City, J.D., 1991 — Admitted to Bar, 1991, Kansas; 1992, Missouri; 1992, U.S. District Court, District of Kansas; 1996, U.S. District Court, Western District of Missouri — Member American, Kansas and Johnson County Bar Associations; The Missouri Bar — Practice Areas: Commercial Litigation; Litigation; Insurance Defense; Medical Malpractice

Christopher J. Sherman — 1972 — Wichita State University, B.G.S. (with honors), 1995; The University of Kansas, J.D., 2001 — Order of the Coif — Admitted to Bar, 2001, Kansas; 2002, Missouri; 2001, U.S. District Court, District of Kansas; 2002, U.S. District Court, Western District of Missouri — Member Kansas and Johnson County Bar Associations; The Missouri Bar —

OVERLAND PARK

Payne & Jones, Chartered, Overland Park, KS
(Continued)

Practice Areas: Commercial Litigation; Insurance Defense; Trial Practice; General Liability — E-mail: csherman@paynejones.com

Sanders Warren & Russell LLP
40 Corporate Woods
9401 Indian Creen Parkway, Suite 1250
Overland Park, Kansas 66210
   Telephone: 913-234-6100
   Fax: 913-234-6199
   E-Mail: b.sanders@swrllp.com
   E-Mail: r.warren@swrllp.com
   E-Mail: b.russell@swrllp.com
   www.swrllp.com

(Kansas City, MO Office*: 420 Nichols Road, Suite 200, 64112)
   (Tel: 913-234-6100)
   (Fax: 913-234-6199)
(Springfield, MO Office*: American National Center 2-102, 1949 East Sunshine, 65804)
   (Tel: 417-281-5100)
   (Fax: 417-281-5199)

Established: 1999

Insurance Defense, Business Law, Automobile, Property, Homeowners, Life Insurance, Commercial Law, Professional Liability, Municipal Law, Employment Law, Workers' Compensation, Comprehensive General Liability, Alternative Dispute Resolution, Appellate Practice, Bad Faith, Construction Litigation, Governmental Liability, Insurance Coverage, Medical Malpractice, Premises Liability, Product Liability, Truck Liability

Firm Profile: Sanders Warren & Russell LLP is a full service civil practice and insurance defense firm handling suits throughout western Missouri and eastern Kansas. Our goal is to successfully defend lawsuits on a cost effective basis.

Insurance Clients

AAO Services, Inc.	ALLIED Mutual Insurance Company
Allstate Insurance Company	Atlantic Mutual Insurance Company
American Family Insurance Company	Berkley Risk Administrators Company, LLC
Bar Plan Group	Brotherhood Mutual Insurance Company
Berkshire Hathaway Homestate Companies	Chartis Insurance
Carolina Casualty Insurance Company	Clarendon National Insurance Company
Church Insurance Company	Empire Fire and Marine Insurance Company
Cornerstone National Insurance Company	Fireman's Fund Insurance Company
Employers Mutual Companies	Gallagher Bassett Services, Inc.
Essex Insurance Company	Great American Insurance Companies
First Mercury Insurance Company	The Hartford Insurance Group
Founders Insurance Company	Hertz Claim Management
GAN North America Group	Kansas Medical Mutual Insurance Company (KaMMCO)
Great West Casualty Company	Medmarc Insurance Company
Harco National Insurance Company	Mid-Continent Assurance Company
Housing Authority Insurance, Inc.	National Indemnity Company
Lexington Insurance Company	Nationwide Insurance
Markel Southwest Underwriters, Inc.	NCMIC Insurance Company
National American Insurance Company	North American Risk Services
National Security Fire and Casualty Company	Oak River Insurance Company
North American Insurance Company	Shand Morahan & Company, Inc.
Scottsdale Insurance Company	Specialty Risk Services, Inc. (SRS)
SISCO Self Insured Services Company	Travelers Insurance Company
United Fire & Casualty Company	Unitrin Specialty Insurance
U.S. Risk Insurance Group, Inc.	Utica Mutual Insurance Company
Vesta Insurance Group, Inc.	Western Litigation Specialists, Inc.

Sanders Warren & Russell LLP, Overland Park, KS
(Continued)

Non-Insurance Clients

Avis Corporation
Commerce Bank
Metcalf Bank
Payless ShoeSource
Rack Room Shoes, Inc.
Walton Construction Company, LLC
CertainTeed Corporation
Harmon Construction Company
Off Broadway Shoes
Phoenix Building Group, Inc.
Wal-Mart Stores, Inc.

Contact Attorneys

William H. Sanders, Jr. — 1952 — Washington and Lee University, B.A. (cum laude), 1974; The University of Kansas, J.D., 1977 — Admitted to Bar, 1977, Missouri; 2006, Kansas; 1977, U.S. District Court, Western District of Missouri — Member Kansas Bar Association; The Missouri Bar; Missouri Organization of Defense Lawyers — Practice Areas: Insurance Law; Litigation; Alternative Dispute Resolution — E-mail: b.sanders@swrllp.com

Roger W. Warren — 1951 — Kansas State University, B.S., 1973; Washburn University, J.D. (with honors), 1988 — Admitted to Bar, 1988, Missouri; 1989, Kansas; 1988, U.S. District Court, Western District of Missouri; 1989, U.S. District Court, District of Kansas — Member Kansas Bar Association; The Missouri Bar; Trucking Industry Defense Association — Practice Areas: Insurance Law; Litigation; Professional Liability; Construction Law — E-mail: r.warren@swrllp.com

Bradley S. Russell — 1963 — Kansas State University, B.S. (with honors), 1985; The University of Kansas, J.D., 1988 — Admitted to Bar, 1988, Kansas; 1989, Missouri; 1988, U.S. District Court, District of Kansas; 1989, U.S. District Court, Western District of Missouri — Member Kansas Bar Association; The Missouri Bar — Practice Areas: Insurance Law; Litigation — E-mail: b.russell@swrllp.com

Partners

Jana V. Richards — 1965 — The University of Kansas, B.A., 1987; J.D., 1990 — Admitted to Bar, 1990, Kansas; 1990, Missouri; U.S. District Court, Western District of Missouri; U.S. District Court, District of Kansas — Member American and Kansas Bar Associations; The Missouri Bar — Practice Areas: Employment Law; Insurance Law; Litigation; Product Liability — E-mail: j.richards@swrllp.com

Daniel L. Doyle — 1956 — Benedictine College, B.A., 1978; Washburn University, J.D., 1981 — Admitted to Bar, 1982, Kansas; 1982, Illinois; 1988, Missouri; U.S. District Court, Western District of Missouri — Member Kansas and Wyandotte County Bar Associations — Practice Areas: Insurance Law; Litigation; Workers' Compensation — E-mail: d.doyle@swrllp.com

Michael C. Kirkham — 1969 — University of Missouri-Columbia, B.A., 1991; J.D., 1994 — Admitted to Bar, 1994, Missouri; 2001, Kansas; 1994, U.S. District Court, Western District of Missouri — Member The Missouri Bar — Practice Areas: Insurance Law; Litigation; Workers' Compensation — E-mail: m.kirkham@swrllp.com

John E. Bordeau — 1968 — Sacred Heart University, B.S., 1990; The University of Kansas, J.D., 1996 — Admitted to Bar, 1996, Kansas; 1997, Missouri; 1996, U.S. District Court, District of Kansas; 1997, U.S. District Court, Western District of Missouri — Member Kansas and Johnson County Bar Associations; The Missouri Bar — Practice Areas: Insurance Law; Litigation; Product Liability; Professional Liability — E-mail: j.bordeau@swrllp.com

Curtis O. Roggow — 1953 — Augustana College, B.A., 1975; Drake University, J.D., 1991 — Order of the Coif — Drake Law Review — Admitted to Bar, 1991, Kansas; 1992, Missouri; 1991, U.S. District Court, District of Kansas; 1992, U.S. District Court, Western District of Missouri; 1997, U.S. Court of Appeals, Tenth Circuit; 2001, U.S. Court of Appeals, Eighth Circuit; 2012, U.S. Supreme Court — Member Kansas Bar Association; The Missouri Bar — Practice Areas: Insurance Law; Litigation — E-mail: c.roggow@swrllp.com

Jeffrey C. Baker — 1972 — The University of Kansas, B.A., 1994; University of Missouri-Kansas City, J.D., 1998 — Admitted to Bar, 1998, Missouri; 1999, Kansas; 1998, U.S. District Court, Western District of Missouri; 1999, U.S. District Court, District of Kansas — Member Kansas Bar Association; The Missouri Bar — Practice Areas: Insurance Law; Litigation — E-mail: jc.baker@swrllp.com

Sean P. Edwards — 1971 — MidAmerica Nazarene University, B.A. (with honors), 1993; The University of Oklahoma, J.D., 2000 — Admitted to Bar, 2000, Missouri; 2001, Kansas; 2000, U.S. District Court, Western District of Missouri; 2001, U.S. District Court, District of Kansas — Member Kansas Bar Association; The Missouri Bar — Practice Areas: Insurance Law; Litigation; Product Liability — E-mail: s.edwards@swrllp.com

Sanders Warren & Russell LLP, Overland Park, KS
(Continued)

William P. Denning — 1974 — Pittsburg State University, B.S., 1999; University of Missouri-Kansas City, J.D., 2003 — Admitted to Bar, 2003, Missouri; 2004, Kansas; 2003, U.S. District Court, Western District of Missouri; 2004, U.S. District Court, District of Kansas — Member Kansas, Johnson County and Kansas City Metropolitan Bar Associations; The Missouri Bar — Practice Areas: Insurance Law — E-mail: w.denning@swrllp.com

Sean M. Sturdivan — 1977 — Baker University, B.S., 1999; University of Oregon, J.D., 2002 — Admitted to Bar, 2002, California; 2003, Kansas; 2004, Missouri; 2002, U.S. District Court, Eastern District of California; 2005, U.S. District Court, District of Kansas; 2005, U.S. District Court, Western District of Missouri — Member American, Kansas, Johnson County and Kansas City Metropolitan Bar Associations; The Missouri Bar — Practice Areas: Civil Litigation; Construction Litigation; Personal Injury — E-mail: s.sturdivan@swllrp.com

Randy P. Scheer — 1959 — The University of Kansas, B.A. (cum laude), 1982; Washburn University School of Law, J.D. (with honors), 1987 — Admitted to Bar, 1987, Missouri; 1988, Kansas; 1996, Nebraska — Member Nebraska State, Kansas and Springfield Metropolitan Bar Associations; The Missouri Bar; Missouri Organization of Defense Lawyers — Practice Areas: Product Liability; Toxic Torts; Medical Liability; Professional Liability; Trucking; Insurance Coverage; Insurance Defense; Construction Litigation; Business Litigation — E-mail: r.scheer@swrllp.com

Christopher J. Carpenter — 1968 — Southwest Baptist University, B.S., 1990; University of Missouri-Kansas City School of Law, J.D., 1993 — Admitted to Bar, 1993, Missouri; 1994, Kansas; 2009, Illinois; U.S. District Court, Western District of Missouri; U.S. District Court, District of Kansas; U.S. Court of Appeals, Eighth Circuit — Member Kansas and Illinois State Bar Associations; The Missouri Bar; Missouri Organization of Defense Lawyers — Practice Areas: Insurance Coverage; Insurance Litigation; Insurance Defense; Professional Negligence — E-mail: cj.carpenter@swrllp.com

Brian L. Burge — 1974 — Rockhurst College, B.A., 2000; The University of Kansas, J.D., 2003 — Admitted to Bar, 2003, Missouri; 2004, Kansas; 2004, U.S. District Court, Western District of Missouri; 2004, U.S. District Court, District of Kansas — Practice Areas: Insurance Defense; Personal Injury; Professional Malpractice; Tort; Family Law — E-mail: b.burge@swrllp.com

S. Jacob Sappington — 1977 — University of Missouri-Columbia, B.A. (magna cum laude), 1999; University of Missouri-Columbia School of Law, J.D., 2002 — Admitted to Bar, 2002, Missouri; U.S. District Court, Western District of Missouri — Member The Missouri Bar — Practice Areas: Product Liability; Business Litigation; Insurance Litigation; Tort Litigation — E-mail: j.sappington@swrllp.com

Associates

Tracy M. Hayes — 1980 — Florida State University, B.S. (magna cum laude), 2003; University of Missouri-Columbia School of Law, J.D., 2006 — Admitted to Bar, 2006, Missouri; 2007, Kansas; 2006, U.S. District Court, Western District of Missouri; 2007, U.S. District Court, District of Kansas — Member American and Kansas City Metropolitan Bar Associations; The Missouri Bar; Association of Women Lawyers of Kansas City — Practice Areas: Insurance Defense; Commercial Litigation; Construction Litigation — E-mail: t.hayes@swrllp.com

Kenneth A. Sprenger — 1979 — Harding University, B.A., 2002; University of Arkansas, Fayetteville, J.D., 2005 — Admitted to Bar, 2005, Missouri; U.S. District Court, Western District of Missouri — Member The Missouri Bar; Springfield Metropolitan Bar Association — Practice Areas: Business Litigation; Insurance Defense; Trucking; Transportation; Commercial Litigation; Construction Litigation; Product Liability; Medical Malpractice — E-mail: k.sprenger@swrllp.com

Douglas P. Hill — 1984 — Southern Methodist University, B.A. (with honors), 2007; Southern Methodist University, Dedman School of Law, J.D., 2010 — Admitted to Bar, 2010, Missouri; 2011, Kansas; 2010, U.S. District Court, Western District of Missouri; 2011, U.S. District Court, District of Kansas; 2012, U.S. District Court, Eastern District of Missouri — Member American Bar Association; The Missouri Bar — Practice Areas: Civil Litigation; Insurance Defense — E-mail: dp.hill@swrllp.com

Joshua D. Scott — 1978 — University of Missouri, B.A., 2000; University of Missouri School of Law, J.D. (cum laude), 2011 — Admitted to Bar, 2011, Missouri; 2012, U.S. District Court, Western District of Missouri — Member American Bar Association; The Missouri Bar — Practice Areas: Business Litigation; Construction Law; Product Liability; Insurance Defense; Insurance Coverage Litigation — E-mail: j.scott@swrllp.com

Ryan R. Cox — 1972 — Ripon College, B.A., 1995; Drake University Law School, J.D., 1998 — Admitted to Bar, 2004, Missouri; 2004, Kansas; 2004, U.S. District Court, Western District of Missouri; 2004, U.S. District Court,

KANSAS

Sanders Warren & Russell LLP, Overland Park, KS (Continued)

District of Kansas — Member Kansas, Johnson County and Kansas City Metropolitan Bar Associations; The Missouri Bar — Practice Areas: Civil Litigation; Insurance Defense; Professional Liability; Employment Law; Employment Litigation; Personal Injury — E-mail: r.cox@swrllp.com

Tyler C. Hibler — 1983 — Baker University, B.A., 2005; The University of Kansas, J.D., 2008 — Admitted to Bar, 2008, Kansas; 2009, Missouri; 2008, U.S. District Court, District of Kansas; 2009, U.S. District Court, Western District of Missouri — Member American, Kansas, Johnson County and Kansas City Metropolitan Bar Associations; The Missouri Bar — Practice Areas: Insurance Defense; Commercial Litigation; Construction Litigation; Personal Injury; Employment Law; Employment Litigation; Professional Liability — E-mail: t.hibler@swrllp.com

Nathan P. Dayani — 1980 — University of Kansas School of Journalism, B.A., 2003; The University of Kansas School of Law, J.D., 2011 — Admitted to Bar, 2011, Kansas; 2012, Missouri — Practice Areas: Insurance Defense; Construction Law; Commercial Litigation — E-mail: n.dayani@swrllp.com

Matthew D. Quandt — 1986 — Baker University, B.S., 2009; Washburn University, J.D., 2012 — Admitted to Bar, 2012, Missouri; 2012, U.S. District Court, Western District of Missouri — Practice Areas: Insurance Defense; Civil Litigation — E-mail: m.quandt@swrllp.com

Tucker L. Poling — The University of Kansas, B.A., 2002; J.D., 2007 — Admitted to Bar, 2007, Kansas; 2010, Missouri; 2007, U.S. District Court, District of Kansas; U.S. District Court, Western District of Missouri — Member Kansas, Kansas City Metropolitan and Johnson County Bar Associations; The Missouri Bar — Practice Areas: Professional Negligence; Personal Injury Defense; Business Litigation; Construction Litigation; Employment Litigation — E-mail: t.poling@swrllp.com

Kaitlin M. Marsh-Blake — Washburn University, B.A., 2010; J.D., 2013 — Admitted to Bar, 2013, Missouri — Member The Missouri Bar; Kansas City Metropolitan Bar Association — Practice Areas: General Civil Litigation; Insurance Defense — E-mail: k.marsh-blake@swrllp.com

Jordon T. Stanley — University of Missouri-Columbia, B.A., 1998; University of Missouri-Kansas City, J.D., 2004 — Admitted to Bar, 2004, Missouri — Member The Missouri Bar; Kansas City Metropolitan Bar Association — Practice Areas: Litigation; Employment Litigation; Construction Litigation; Premises Liability; Personal Injury — E-mail: j.stanley@swrllp.com

Erin K. DeKoster — Iowa State University, B.S., 2007; The University of Kansas, J.D., 2011 — Admitted to Bar, 2011, Kansas; U.S. District Court, District of Kansas — Member American and Kansas Bar Associations; Kansas Association for Defense Counsel; Defense Research Institute — Practice Areas: Professional Negligence; Personal Injury — E-mail: e.dekoster@swrllp.com

Of Counsel

William F. High — University of Missouri, B.S., 1984; The University of Kansas, J.D., 1988 — Admitted to Bar, 1988, Missouri; 1989, Kansas; 1988, U.S. District Court, Western District of Missouri; 1989, U.S. District Court, District of Kansas; 1989, U.S. Court of Appeals, Tenth Circuit — Member Kansas and Kansas City Metropolitan Bar Associations; The Missouri Bar — Practice Areas: Litigation — E-mail: w.high@servantchristian.com

Terri Z. Austenfeld — 1958 — The University of Kansas, B.S., 1981; Washburn University, J.D., 1985 — Admitted to Bar, 1986, Kansas; 1986, Missouri — Member Kansas and Johnson County (Past Chair, Workers' Compensation Committee) Bar Associations; Association of Women Lawyers — Practice Areas: Litigation; Insurance Law; Workers' Compensation — E-mail: t.austenfeld@swrllp.com

Gregg C. Yowell — 1955 — University of Wisconsin-La Crosse, B.S., 1977; The University of Kansas, M.B.A., 1996; University of Wisconsin Law School, J.D., 1981 — Admitted to Bar, 1981, Kansas; 1982, Wisconsin; 2008, Missouri; 1981, U.S. District Court, District of Kansas — Member Kansas and Kansas City Metropolitan Bar Associations — E-mail: g.yowell@swrllp.com

Michael L. Hughes — 1968 — Baker University, B.S.M., 1998; University of Missouri-Kansas City, J.D., 2002 — Admitted to Bar, 2002, Missouri; 2003, Kansas — Member Kansas Bar Association; The Missouri Bar — Practice Areas: Personal Injury; Commercial Litigation; Insurance Defense — E-mail: m.hughes@swrllp.com

PAOLA

The following firms also service this area.

Hampton & Royce, L.C.
United Building, Ninth Floor
119 West Iron Avenue
Salina, Kansas 67401
   Telephone: 785-827-7251
   Fax: 785-827-2815
Mailing Address: P.O. Box 1247, Salina, KS 67402-1247

Accident, Agent/Broker Liability, Errors and Omissions, Agriculture, Alternative Dispute Resolution, Appellate Practice, Arson, Automobile Liability, Banking, Bankruptcy, Bodily Injury, Business Law, Casualty Insurance Law, Civil Litigation, Class Actions, Collections, Commercial and Personal Lines, Commercial General Liability, Commercial Litigation, Commercial Transactions, Construction Liability, Construction Litigation, Contract Disputes, Contractors Liability, Contracts, Corporate Law, Coverage Analysis, Directors and Officers Liability, Employer Liability, Employment Discrimination, Employment Law, Employment Practices Liability, Environmental Law, Estate Planning, General Civil Practice, Health Care, Insurance Coverage, Insurance Fraud, Insurance Litigation, Intentional Torts, Labor and Employment, Legal Malpractice, Lender Liability Defense, Mediation, Medical Liability, Medical Malpractice, Mergers and Acquisitions, Negligence, Nursing Home Liability, Personal Injury, Policy Construction and Interpretation, Premises Liability, Probate, Product Liability, Professional Negligence, Sexual Harassment, Slip and Fall, Subrogation, Tort Liability, Tort Litigation, Uninsured and Underinsured Motorist, Workers' Compensation, Wrongful Death, Wrongful Termination, Life and Health Insurance Claims and Litigation, Accountant Liability and Malpractice, , Contract Litigation, Coverage Disputes, Domestic, Excess and Umbrella Coverage and Litigation, Family Law and Litigation, First and Third Party Claims, Foreclosures, Health Insurance Litigation, Homeowners Liability, Pensions, Property and Casualty Losses, Real Estate Contracts, Real Estate Disputes and Litigation, Receiverships, Shareholders Claims, Trusts and Trust Litigation

SEE COMPLETE LISTING UNDER SALINA, KANSAS (177 MILES)

McAnany, Van Cleave & Phillips, P.A.
10 East Cambridge Circle Drive, Suite 300
Kansas City, Kansas 66103
   Telephone: 913-371-3838
   Fax: 913-371-4722

Administrative Law, Antitrust, Bankruptcy, Business Law, Construction Law, Corporate Law, Creditor Rights, Directors and Officers Liability, Insurance Law, Labor and Employment, Land Use, Litigation, Municipal Law, Personal Injury, Product Liability, Professional Liability, Public Entities, Railroad Law, Real Estate, School Law, Transportation, Trial and Appellate Practice, Workers' Compensation

SEE COMPLETE LISTING UNDER KANSAS CITY, KANSAS (7 MILES)

Waldeck & Patterson, P.A.
5000 West 95th Street, Suite 350
Prairie Village, Kansas 66207
   Telephone: 913-749-0300
   Fax: 913-749-0301

Civil Litigation, Insurance Defense, Commercial Litigation, Appellate Practice, Employment Law, Contract Disputes, Premises Liability, Professional Liability, Dram Shop, Product Liability, Tort Liability, Coverage Issues, Reinsurance, Business Litigation

SEE COMPLETE LISTING UNDER PRAIRIE VILLAGE, KANSAS (7 MILES)

PAOLA † 5,602 Miami Co.

Refer To

Logan Logan & Watson, L.C.
8340 Mission Road
Prairie Village, Kansas 66206
   Telephone: 913-381-1121
   Fax: 913-381-6546

Insurance Law, Trial and Appellate Practice, Commercial Law, General Liability, Professional Liability, Property, Legal Malpractice, Medical Malpractice, Product Liability, Coverage Issues, Automobile

SEE COMPLETE LISTING UNDER PRAIRIE VILLAGE, KANSAS (40 MILES)

PRAIRIE VILLAGE 21,447 Johnson Co.

Logan Logan & Watson, L.C.
8340 Mission Road
Prairie Village, Kansas 66206
  Telephone: 913-381-1121
  Fax: 913-381-6546
  E-Mail: slogan@loganlaw.com
  www.loganlaw.com

Established: 1978

Insurance Law, Trial and Appellate Practice, Commercial Law, General Liability, Professional Liability, Property, Legal Malpractice, Medical Malpractice, Product Liability, Coverage Issues, Automobile

Insurance Clients

HealthCap	HealthSouth Corporation
Kansas Health Care Provider Insurance Availibility Plan	Kansas Health Care Stabilization Fund
Kansas Medical Mutual Insurance Company (KaMMCO)	Medical Protective Insurance Services
Missouri Medical Malpractice Joint Underwriting Association	Missouri Professionals Mutual Ophthalmic Mutual Insurance Company
Preferred Physicians Medical Risk Retention Group, Inc.	Shawnee Mission Physicians Group
Sisters of Charity of Leavenworth Health System	

Non-Insurance Clients

Medicalodges, Inc.	The Tutera Group

Partners

Fred J. Logan, Jr. — 1952 — Indiana University, B.A. (with distinction), 1974; J.D. (cum laude), 1977 — Admitted to Bar, 1977, Kansas; 1990, Missouri; 1977, U.S. District Court, District of Kansas; 1990, U.S. Supreme Court; 1994, U.S. District Court, Western District of Missouri — Member American, Kansas and Johnson County Bar Associations; The Missouri Bar; Earl E. O'Connor Inn of Court (Master of the Bench)

Scott K. Logan — 1955 — William Jewell College, B.A. (cum laude), 1977; Washburn University, J.D., 1980 — Admitted to Bar, 1980, Kansas; 1990, Missouri; 1980, U.S. District Court, District of Kansas; 1990, U.S. District Court, Western District of Missouri — Member American, Kansas, Johnson County and Wyandotte County Bar Associations; Kansas City Metropolitan Bar Association; Kansas Association of Defense Counsel; American College of Trial Lawyers

M. Bradley Watson — 1958 — Wichita State University; The University of Kansas, B.A., 1980; J.D., 1984 — Admitted to Bar, 1984, Kansas; 1995, Missouri; 1987, U.S. District Court, District of Kansas — Member Kansas and Johnson County Bar Associations; The Missouri Bar; Kansas City Metropolitan Bar Association; American Trial Lawyers Association

Jeff K. Brown — 1969 — Wichita State University, B.S. (cum laude), 1992; The University of Kansas, J.D., 1996 — Admitted to Bar, 1996, Kansas; 2005, Missouri; 1996, U.S. Court of Appeals, Tenth Circuit — Member Kansas and Johnson County Bar Associations; The Missouri Bar; Kansas City Metropolitan Bar Association; Kansas Association of Defense Counsel; LTC Risk Legal Forum; Defense Research Institute; Missouri Organization of Defense Lawyers

Associates

Christopher H. Logan — Indiana University, B.A., 2005; American University, J.D., 2011 — Admitted to Bar, 2012, Kansas; Missouri; U.S. District Court, District of Kansas — Member American, Kansas and Johnson County Bar Associations; The Missouri Bar; Kansas City Metropolitan Bar Association

David M. Tyrrell — Southern Methodist University, B.S./B.B.A., 2003; University of Missouri-Kansas City School of Law, J.D., 2006 — Admitted to Bar, 2006, Kansas; 2007, Missouri — Member Kansas and Johnson County Bar Associations; The Missouri Bar; Kansas City Metropolitan Bar Association

Waldeck & Patterson, P.A.
5000 West 95th Street, Suite 350
Prairie Village, Kansas 66207
  Telephone: 913-749-0300
  Fax: 913-749-0301
  E-Mail: JohnW@waldeckpatterson.com
  www.waldeckpatterson.com

(Kansas City, MO Office*: Two Pershing Square, 2300 Main Street, Ninth Floor, 64108)
(Tel: 816-448-3770)

Civil Litigation, Insurance Defense, Commercial Litigation, Appellate Practice, Employment Law, Contract Disputes, Premises Liability, Professional Liability, Dram Shop, Product Liability, Tort Liability, Coverage Issues, Reinsurance, Business Litigation

Insurance Clients

Berkley Risk Administrators Company, LLC	Berkley Specialty Underwriting Managers, LLC
Gallagher Bassett Services, Inc.	St. Paul Travelers
Scottsdale Insurance Company	Stratford Insurance Company
Tudor Insurance Company	United States Liability Insurance Group
Western World Insurance Group	

Partner/Shareholder

John M. Waldeck — 1968 — Emporia State University, B.S.B., 1990; Thomas M. Cooley Law School, J.D. (with distinction), 1996 — Admitted to Bar, 1996, Missouri; 1997, Kansas

Meagan L. Pop Patterson — 1975 — Bellarmine University, B.A., 2000; University of Kentucky College of Law, J.D., 2004 — Admitted to Bar, 2004, Kentucky; 2006, Missouri; 2006, Kansas

Associates

Kelly M. Cochran — 1985 — The University of Kansas, B.S./B.A., 2008; The University of Kansas School of Law, M.A./J.D., 2011 — Admitted to Bar, 2011, Kansas; 2012, Missouri

Matthew E. Terry — 1979 — The University of North Carolina at Chapel Hill, B.A., 2002; University of Missouri School of Law, J.D., 2010 — Admitted to Bar, 2010, Missouri

RUSSELL † 4,506 Russell Co.

Refer To
Hampton & Royce, L.C.
United Building, Ninth Floor
119 West Iron Avenue
Salina, Kansas 67401
  Telephone: 785-827-7251
  Fax: 785-827-2815

Mailing Address: P.O. Box 1247, Salina, KS 67402-1247

Accident, Agent/Broker Liability, Errors and Omissions, Agriculture, Alternative Dispute Resolution, Appellate Practice, Arson, Automobile Liability, Banking, Bankruptcy, Bodily Injury, Business Law, Casualty Insurance Law, Civil Litigation, Class Actions, Collections, Commercial and Personal Lines, Commercial General Liability, Commercial Litigation, Commercial Transactions, Construction Liability, Construction Litigation, Contract Disputes, Contractors Liability, Contracts, Corporate Law, Coverage Analysis, Directors and Officers Liability, Employer Liability, Employment Discrimination, Employment Law, Employment Practices Liability, Environmental Law, Estate Planning, General Civil Practice, Health Care, Insurance Coverage, Insurance Fraud, Insurance Litigation, Intentional Torts, Labor and Employment, Legal Malpractice, Lender Liability Defense, Mediation, Medical Liability, Medical Malpractice, Mergers and Acquisitions, Negligence, Nursing Home Liability, Personal Injury, Policy Construction and Interpretation, Premises Liability, Probate, Product Liability, Professional Negligence, Sexual Harassment, Slip and Fall, Subrogation, Tort Liability, Tort Litigation, Uninsured and Underinsured Motorist, Workers' Compensation, Wrongful Death, Wrongful Termination, Life and Health Insurance Claims and Litigation, Accountant Liability and Malpractice, , Contract Litigation, Coverage Disputes, Domestic, Excess and Umbrella Coverage and Litigation, Family Law and Litigation, First and Third Party Claims, Foreclosures, Health Insurance Litigation, Homeowners Liability, Pensions, Property and Casualty Losses, Real Estate Contracts, Real Estate Disputes and Litigation, Receiverships, Shareholders Claims, Trusts and Trust Litigation

SEE COMPLETE LISTING UNDER SALINA, KANSAS (73 MILES)

SALINA † 47,707 Saline Co.

Clark, Mize & Linville, Chartered
129 South 8th Street
Salina, Kansas 67401
  Telephone: 785-823-6325
  Fax: 785-823-1868
  www.cml-law.com

(Lindsborg, KS Office: 128 North Main, 67456)
  (Tel: 785-227-2010)
  (Fax: 785-823-1868)

Established: 1946

Automobile, Workers' Compensation, Defense Litigation, Employment Discrimination, Public Entities, Medical Malpractice, Professional Malpractice

Insurance Clients

Church Insurance Company
CNA Insurance Companies
The Hartford
Kansas Health Care Stabilization Fund
Kansas Workers Risk Cooperative for Counties
National Fire and Marine Insurance Company
Zurich U.S.
CIGNA Group
Columbia Insurance Group
Kansas County Association Multiline Pool (KCAMP)
Kansas Medical Mutual Insurance Company (KaMMCO)
Mitsui Sumitomo Insurance Group
TRISTAR Risk Management
United Fire Group

Third Party Administrators

Berkley Administrators
Insurance Management Association
Sedgwick Claims Management Services, Inc.
Gallagher Bassett Services, Inc.
Kansas Health Service Corporation

Attorneys

Peter L. Peterson — 1946 — The University of Kansas, J.D. (with highest distinction), 1971 — Admitted to Bar, 1971, Kansas

John W. Mize — 1950 — Southern Methodist University, J.D., 1975 — Admitted to Bar, 1975, Kansas

Greg A. Bengtson — 1954 — The University of Kansas, J.D., 1979 — Admitted to Bar, 1980, Kansas

Mickey W. Mosier — 1944 — Wichita State University, B.B.A., 1967; M.A., 1968; University of San Diego, J.D., 1974 — Admitted to Bar, 1975, Kansas; 1975, U.S. District Court, District of Kansas; 1987, U.S. Court of Appeals, Tenth Circuit; 2006, U.S. Supreme Court — Member Kansas and Saline-Ottawa Counties (President - 1990) Bar Associations; Kansas Association of Defense Counsel; Association of Defense Trial Attorneys — Assistant Saline County Attorney, 1977-1985; Saline County Attorney, 1985-1988; Member, District Judicial Nomination Commission, 28th Judicial District, 1996-2000 — E-mail: mwmosier@cml-law.com

Paula J. Wright — 1945 — The University of Oklahoma, Ph.D., 1976; The University of Kansas, J.D., 1986 — Admitted to Bar, 1986, Kansas; 1986, U.S. District Court, District of Kansas; 1987, U.S. Court of Appeals, Tenth Circuit; 2006, U.S. Supreme Court — Member American, Kansas and Saline-Ottawa Counties (President, 2004) Bar Associations; Kansas Association of Defense Counsel; National Association of School Boards Council of School Attorneys; Defense Research Institute — E-mail: pjwright@cml-law.com

Eric N. Anderson — 1963 — The University of Kansas, J.D., 1988 — Admitted to Bar, 1988, Kansas

Dustin J. Denning — 1973 — The University of Kansas, B.A., 1995; J.D., 1999 — Admitted to Bar, 1999, Kansas; 1999, U.S. District Court, District of Kansas — Member Kansas and Saline-Ottawa Counties Bar Associations; Kansas Association of Defense Counsel (Past President); Kansas Association of Hospital Attorneys; Defense Research Institute; Association of Defense Trial Attorneys — E-mail: djdenning@cml-law.com

Peter S. Johnston — 1971 — The University of Kansas, B.A. (with honors), 1994; The University of Kansas School of Law, J.D., 1997 — Admitted to Bar, 1997, Kansas; 1998, Missouri; 1997, U.S. District Court, District of Kansas; 1998, U.S. Court of Appeals, Tenth Circuit; 1998, U.S. District Court, Western District of Missouri — Member American, Kansas and Saline-Ottawa Counties Bar Associations; The Missouri Bar; Kansas Association of Hospital Attorneys; Kansas Association of Defense Counsel; American Health Lawyers Association; Defense Research Institute — E-mail: psjohnston@cml-law.com

Jared T. Hiatt — 1980 — The University of Kansas, B.A., 2004; The University of Kansas School of Law, J.D., 2007 — Admitted to Bar, 2008, Kansas; 2008, U.S. District Court, District of Kansas — Member Kansas and Saline-Ottawa Counties Bar Associations; Kansas Association of Defense Counsel; Association of Defense Trial Attorneys; Defense Research Institute — E-mail: jthiatt@cml-law.com

Joshua C. Howard — 1983 — University of Nebraska College of Law, J.D. (with highest distinction), 2009 — Admitted to Bar, 2009, Kansas; 2010, Nebraska; U.S. District Court, District of Kansas

Aaron O. Martin — 1983 — Washburn University School of Law, J.D. (magna cum laude), 2009 — Admitted to Bar, 2009, Kansas; U.S. District Court, District of Kansas

Jacob E. Peterson — 1988 — Washburn University, B.A. (summa cum laude), 2009; Washington University in St. Louis, J.D. (cum laude), 2012 — Admitted to Bar, 2012, Kansas; U.S. District Court, District of Kansas — Member Kansas and Saline-Ottawa Counties Bar Association; American Health Lawyers Association; Defense Research Institute — E-mail: jepeterson@cml-law.com

Hampton & Royce, L.C.
United Building, Ninth Floor
119 West Iron Avenue
Salina, Kansas 67401
  Telephone: 785-827-7251
  Fax: 785-827-2815
  www.hamptonlaw.com

Established: 1885

Accident, Agent/Broker Liability, Errors and Omissions, Agriculture, Alternative Dispute Resolution, Appellate Practice, Arson, Automobile Liability, Banking, Bankruptcy, Bodily Injury, Business Law, Casualty Insurance Law, Civil Litigation, Class Actions, Collections, Commercial and Personal Lines, Commercial General Liability, Commercial Litigation, Commercial Transactions, Construction Liability, Construction Litigation, Contract Disputes, Contractors Liability, Contracts, Corporate Law, Coverage Analysis, Directors and Officers Liability, Employer Liability, Employment Discrimination, Employment Law, Employment Practices Liability, Environmental Law, Estate Planning, General Civil Practice, Health Care, Insurance Coverage, Insurance Fraud, Insurance Litigation, Intentional Torts, Labor and Employment, Legal Malpractice, Lender Liability Defense, Mediation, Medical Liability, Medical Malpractice, Mergers and Acquisitions, Negligence, Nursing Home Liability, Personal Injury, Policy Construction and Interpretation, Premises Liability, Probate, Product Liability, Professional Negligence, Sexual Harassment, Slip and Fall, Subrogation, Tort Liability, Tort Litigation, Uninsured and Underinsured Motorist, Workers' Compensation, Wrongful Death, Wrongful Termination, Life and Health Insurance Claims and Litigation, Accountant Liability and Malpractice, , Contract Litigation, Coverage Disputes, Domestic, Excess and Umbrella Coverage and Litigation, Family Law and Litigation, First and Third Party Claims, Foreclosures, Health Insurance Litigation, Homeowners Liability, Pensions, Property and Casualty Losses, Real Estate Contracts, Real Estate Disputes and Litigation, Receiverships, Shareholders Claims, Trusts and Trust Litigation

Firm Profile: Established in 1885, the law firm of Hampton & Royce, L.C. has been serving the people of Kansas for well over one hundred twenty-five years. Located in Salina, the firm extends service to the entire state. As the oldest law firm in Salina, the firm's experience affords their clients proven, quality legal representation that reflects their high standards.

TOPEKA   KANSAS

Hampton & Royce, L.C., Salina, KS   (Continued)

Insurance Clients

Allied Insurance Company
Attorneys Liability Protection Society
Farm Bureau Insurance Company
Farmland Insurance Company
Great West Casualty Company
State Farm Group
American Family Insurance Group
Buckeye State Mutual Insurance Company
Farmers Insurance Group
Federated Mutual Insurance Company
Western Agricultural Insurance Company

Non-Insurance Clients

Kansas Health Care Stabilization Fund

Members

N. Royce Nelson — 1947 — The University of Kansas, B.S., 1969; J.D., 1972 — Beta Gamma Sigma; Order of the Coif; Recipient, Wall Street Journal Student Achievement Award — Kansas Law Review, 1971-1972 — Admitted to Bar, 1972, Kansas — Member American Bar Association; Kansas Bar Association (Executive Committee Tax Law Section, 1987-Present; President, 1989); Saline-Ottawa Counties Bar Association — E-mail: nroyce@hamptonlaw.com

Sidney A. Reitz — 1950 — Kansas State University, B.S., 1971; Washburn University of Topeka, J.D., 1975 — Phi Alpha Delta — Admitted to Bar, 1976, Kansas — Member American, Kansas and Saline-Ottawa Counties Bar Associations — E-mail: sidney@hamptonlaw.com

David (Dusty) D. Moshier — 1948 — Kansas State University, B.S., 1974; Washburn University of Topeka, J.D., 1976 — Admitted to Bar, 1977, Kansas — Member American and Saline-Ottawa Counties Bar Associations — E-mail: mopg@hamptonlaw.com

Debra Egli James — 1959 — Iowa State University, B.A., 1981; Drake University, J.D. (with honors), 1984 — Order of the Barristers — Law Clerk to Hon. J.L. Larson, Iowa Supreme Court, 1984-1985 — Admitted to Bar, 1984, Iowa; 1985, Nebraska; 1987, Kansas; U.S. District Court, District of Kansas; U.S. Court of Appeals, Tenth Circuit; U.S. Supreme Court — Member American, Iowa State, Nebraska State and Saline-Ottawa Counties Bar Associations; Kansas Bar Association (Board of Governors, 1997-2003; President, Litigation Section, 2007-2008; Ethics and Grievance Committee); Kansas Board for Discipline of Attorneys; Kansas Association of Defense Council (Board of Governors, 1996-2002); International Association of Defense Counsel; American Trial Lawyers Association — Practice Areas: Appellate Practice; General Civil Litigation; Trial Practice; Insurance Law — E-mail: debjames@hamptonlaw.com

Jeffrey E. King — 1955 — Washburn University, B.B.A., 1978; J.D., 1980 — Admitted to Bar, 1981, Kansas — Member Kansas (President, Litigation Section, 1989-1990) and Saline-Ottawa Counties Bar Associations; Kansas Association of Defense Counsel (Board of Directors, 1988-1996; President, 1995) — Co-Editor, Kansas Workers' Compensation Manual (1991-Present) — E-mail: jeking@hamptonlaw.com

Brian W. Wood — 1968 — The University of Kansas, B.A., 1990; J.D., 1993 — Kansas Law Review, 1992-1993; Kansas Journal of Law and Public Policy, 1991-1992 — Admitted to Bar, 1993, Kansas — Member Kansas and Saline-Ottawa Counties Bar Associations — E-mail: bwwood@hamptonlaw.com

Tisha S. Morrical — 1967 — Bethany College, B.A., 1990; The University of Kansas, J.D./M.S.W., 1996 — KU Native American Law Student, 1993-1996 (President, 1996) — Admitted to Bar, 1996, Kansas — Member American, Kansas (President, Family Law Section, 2011), Saline-Ottawa Counties Bar Associations; 28th Judicial District Bench-Bar Committee (Chairperson, 2011-2012) — E-mail: tish.morrical@hamptonlaw.com

Todd W. Davidson — 1974 — The University of Kansas, B.S., 1995; University of San Diego, J.D./M.B.A., 1998 — Admitted to Bar, 1998, Kansas; 2005, Colorado; 2010, Iowa — Member Kansas and Saline-Ottawa Counties Bar Associations — E-mail: davidson@hamptonlaw.com

Russel B. Prophet — 1974 — Pittsburg State University, B.B.A. (magna cum laude), 1997; Washington and Lee University, J.D., 2000 — Law Clerk, Chief Staff Attorney's Office for the Supreme Court of Virginia, 2000-2002 — Admitted to Bar, 2002, Kansas; U.S. District Court, District of Kansas; U.S. Bankruptcy Court, District of Kansas — Member Kansas and Saline-Ottawa Counties Bar Associations — E-mail: rprophet@hamptonlaw.com

Nathanael W. Berg — 1979 — Southwest Baptist University, B.S., 2002; University of Nebraska, J.D., 2005 — Admitted to Bar, 2005, Kansas — Member American Bar Association — E-mail: nberg@hamptonlaw.com

Hampton & Royce, L.C., Salina, KS   (Continued)

Associate

Lee Legleiter — 1986 — Kansas State University, B.S. (magna cum laude), 2008; The University of Kansas, J.D., 2011 — Admitted to Bar, 2011, Kansas; U.S. District Court, District of Kansas — Member Kansas Bar Association — E-mail: lee.legleiter@hamptonlaw.com

Of Counsel

C. Stanley Nelson — 1925 — The University of Kansas, A.B., 1951; LL.B., 1951 — Admitted to Bar, 1951, Kansas — Member Kansas and Saline-Ottawa Counties (President, 1970) Bar Associations; Kansas Association of Defense Counsel; Fellow, American College of Trial Lawyers — E-mail: olddog@hamptonlaw.com

TOPEKA † 127,473 Shawnee Co.

Goodell, Stratton, Edmonds & Palmer, L.L.P.

515 South Kansas Avenue
Topeka, Kansas 66603-3999
Telephone: 785-233-0593
Toll Free: 800-332-0248
Fax: 785-233-8870
E-Mail: gsep@gseplaw.com
www.gseplaw.com

Established: 1881

General Practice, Subrogation, Bankruptcy, Business Law, Civil Litigation, Insurance Defense, Labor and Employment, Real Estate, Medical Malpractice, Workers' Compensation

Firm Profile: The attorneys and staff of Goodell, Stratton, Edmonds & Palmer, L.L.P. have the knowledge, experience and dedication to provide our clients with the highest level of personal and legal services. Our team stands ready to help you solve your legal challenges.

Insurance Clients

American Home Life Insurance Company
Fireman's Fund Insurance Company
The Hartford Insurance Group
Health Care Stabilization Fund
Massachusetts Mutual Life Insurance Company
National Farmers Union Property & Casualty Company
CNA Insurance Company
Farm Bureau Mutual Insurance Company
Hanover Insurance Group
Health Care Indemnity, Inc.
Kansas Medical Mutual Insurance Company (KaMMCO)
Monitor Liability Managers, LLC
Zurich Insurance Company

Partners

Arthur E. Palmer — 1938 — Washburn University, B.B.A., 1960; J.D., 1963 — Admitted to Bar, 1963, Kansas; U.S. District Court, District of Kansas; U.S. District Court, Western District of Missouri; U.S. Court of Appeals, Tenth Circuit; U.S. Supreme Court — Member Kansas (President, Employment Law Section, 1984) and Topeka (President, 1987-1988) Bar Associations; Kansas Association of Defense Counsel; Kansas Bar Foundation (President, 2001-2002); American Bar Foundation; Defense Research Institute — Practice Areas: Business Law; Health Care; Litigation; Labor and Employment; Real Estate — E-mail: apalmer@gseplaw.com

H. Philip Elwood — 1946 — Wichita State University, B.S., 1968; Washburn University, J.D., 1971 — Admitted to Bar, 1971, Kansas; 1971, U.S. District Court, District of Kansas — Member American, Kansas and Topeka Bar Associations; Kansas Association of Hospital Attorneys; American Health Lawyers Association — Practice Areas: Business Law; Corporate Law; Securities; Health Care — E-mail: pelwood@gseplaw.com

Patrick M. Salsbury — 1946 — Washburn University, B.B.A., 1971; J.D., 1974 — Admitted to Bar, 1974, Kansas; 1974, U.S. District Court, District of Kansas; U.S. Court of Appeals, Tenth Circuit — Member Kansas and Topeka (President, 2006-2007) Bar Associations; Kansas Association of Defense Counsel; Defense Research Institute — Practice Areas: Civil Trial Practice; Insurance Defense; Workers' Compensation; Mediation — E-mail: psalsbury@gseplaw.com

KANSAS / TOPEKA

Goodell, Stratton, Edmonds & Palmer, L.L.P., Topeka, KS (Continued)

John H. Stauffer, Jr. — 1954 — Washburn University, B.B.A., 1976; The University of Kansas, J.D., 1979 — Admitted to Bar, 1979, Kansas; 1979, U.S. District Court, District of Kansas; 1979, U.S. Court of Appeals, Tenth Circuit — Member American, Kansas and Topeka Bar Associations — Practice Areas: Securities

N. Larry Bork — 1955 — Midland Lutheran College, B.A. (cum laude), 1978; Creighton University, J.D., 1983 — Admitted to Bar, 1983, Kansas; 1984, Nebraska; 2008, Missouri; 2013, Oklahoma; 1983, U.S. District Court, District of Kansas; 1984, U.S. District Court, District of Nebraska; 1985, U.S. Court of Appeals for the Federal, Eighth and Tenth Circuits; 1991, U.S. Supreme Court; 1998, U.S. District Court, Western District of Missouri; 2008, U.S. District Court, Eastern District of Missouri — Member Kansas, Nebraska State and Topeka Bar Associations; Kansas Association of Defense Counsel; Defense Research Institute — Practice Areas: Civil Trial Practice; Environmental Law; Insurance Defense; Subrogation — E-mail: lbork@gseplaw.com

Nathan D. Leadstrom — 1976 — Pittsburg State University, B.A., 1998; Washburn University, J.D., 2001 — Phi Delta Phi — Admitted to Bar, 2001, Kansas; 2003, Missouri; 2001, U.S. District Court, District of Kansas; U.S. Court of Appeals, Tenth Circuit; 2002, U.S. District Court, Western District of Missouri — Member Kansas and Topeka Bar Associations; Sam A. Crow American Inn of Court; Kansas Association of Defense Counsel; Kansas Association of Hosptial Attorneys; American Health Lawyers Association; Defense Research Institute — Practice Areas: Civil Trial Practice; Copyright and Trademark Law; Health Care; Hospitals; Insurance Defense; Medical Malpractice — E-mail: nleadstrom@gseplaw.com

Miranda K. Carmona — 1978 — Kansas State University, B.S., 2000; M.Acc., 2001; The University of Kansas, J.D., 2004 — Admitted to Bar, 2004, Kansas; 2004, U.S. District Court, District of Kansas — Member American, Kansas and Topeka Bar Associations; Sam A. Crow American Inns of Court; Kansas Women Attorneys Association; Women Attorney Association of Topeka — Practice Areas: Estate Planning; Probate; Wills — E-mail: mcarmona@gseplaw.com

Mary E. Christopher — 1958 — Kansas State University, B.A., 1982; Washburn University, J.D., 2001 — Admitted to Bar, 2001, Kansas; U.S. District Court, District of Kansas — Member Kansas and Topeka Bar Associations; Kansas Women Attorney Association; Women Attorney Association of Topeka; Kansas Association of Defense Counsel; American Health Lawyers Association — Practice Areas: Civil Litigation; Insurance Defense; Health Care; Business Law; Appellate Practice; Medical Malpractice — E-mail: mchristopher@gseplaw.com

Associates

Richard J. Raimond — 1976 — University of Bristol, England, B.A. (with honors), 1999; The University of Kansas, J.D., 2006 — Admitted to Bar, 2006, Kansas; U.S. District Court, District of Kansas; U.S. District Court, Western District of Missouri; U.S. Court of Appeals, Tenth Circuit — Member Kansas and Topeka Bar Associations; Kansas Association of Hospital Attorneys; Sam A. Crow American Inn of Court — Practice Areas: Litigation; Bankruptcy; Collections; Health Care; Insurance Defense — E-mail: rraimond@gseplaw.com

Alison J. St. Clair — 1985 — Kansas State University, B.S. (summa cum laude), 2008; Washburn University, J.D. (summa cum laude), 2012 — Admitted to Bar, 2012, Kansas; U.S. District Court, District of Kansas — Member Kansas and Topeka Bar Associations; Kansas Women Attorney Association; Women Attorney Association of Topeka; Sam A. Crow American Inn of Court — Practice Areas: Bankruptcy; Collections; Transactional Law; Civil Litigation — E-mail: astclair@gseplaw.com

Of Counsel

Gerald J. Letourneau — 1937 — Benedictine College, B.S. (summa cum laude), 1959; Washburn University, J.D. (cum laude), 1962; New York University, LL.M., 1965 — Admitted to Bar, 1962, Kansas; U.S. District Court, District of Kansas; 1969, U.S. Court of Appeals, Tenth Circuit — Member American, Kansas and Topeka Bar Associations — Practice Areas: Estate Planning; Probate; Wills — E-mail: jletourneau@gseplaw.com

Harold S. Youngentob — 1945 — Hunter College, A.B., 1966; State University of New York, J.D., 1969 — Admitted to Bar, 1970, New York; 1972, Kansas; 1998, Missouri; 1972, U.S. District Court, District of Kansas; 1972, U.S. Court of Appeals, Tenth Circuit; U.S. District Court, Western District of Missouri — Member Kansas Trial Lawyers Association; Kansas Association of Defense Counsel; Association of Trial Lawyers of America; Defense Research Institute — Practice Areas: Civil Trial Practice; Insurance Defense; Labor and Employment; Health Care — E-mail: hyoungentob@gseplaw.com

Goodell, Stratton, Edmonds & Palmer, L.L.P., Topeka, KS (Continued)

(This firm is also listed in the Subrogation section of this directory)

Larson & Blumreich, Chartered

5601 Southwest Barrington Court South
Topeka, Kansas 66614
Telephone: 785-273-7722
Fax: 785-273-8560

Established: 1962

General Defense

Insurance Clients

- Allied Group
- American Insurance Group
- Brotherhood Mutual Insurance Company
- Depositors Insurance Company
- Farm Bureau Financial Services
- Farmers Alliance Mutual Insurance Company
- Farmers Insurance Group
- Great American Insurance Company
- Kansas Building Industry Workers' Compensation Fund
- Nationwide Insurance
- The Patrons Group
- The Principal Financial Group
- Sedgwick Claims Management Services, Inc.
- State Farm Mutual Automobile Insurance Company
- Traders Insurance Company
- West American Insurance Company
- America First Insurance
- Broadspire
- Chartis Insurance
- Columbia Insurance Group
- Employers Reinsurance Corporation
- Farmers Casualty Insurance Company
- Farmers Mutual Insurance Company of Nebraska
- John Deere Insurance Company
- Liberty Mutual Insurance
- National Indemnity Company
- Ohio Casualty Insurance Company
- Pharmacists Mutual Insurance Company
- Shelter Insurance Companies
- State Farm Fire and Casualty Company
- Swiss Re
- Travelers Insurance Companies
- Westport Insurance

Non-Insurance Clients

- Advantage Claim Services, Inc.
- American International Adjustment Company
- City of Topeka
- GAB Robins North America, Inc.
- Kansas Association of Insurance Agents
- Kohl's Department Stores, Inc.
- Richard & Associates, Inc.
- York Insurance Services Group, Inc.
- Alexsis Risk Management Services, Inc.
- Atlantic Companies
- Crawford & Company
- Gallagher Bassett Services, Inc.
- Kansas Workers' Compensation Fund
- NPC International, Inc. dba Pizza Hut

Firm Members

William A. Larson — 1948 — Kansas State University, B.S., 1970; Washburn University of Topeka, J.D. (magna cum laude), 1977 — Admitted to Bar, 1977, Kansas; 1977, U.S. District Court, District of Kansas; 1977, U.S. Court of Appeals, Tenth Circuit; 1977, U.S. Supreme Court — Member Kansas and Topeka Bar Associations; Kansas Association of Defense Counsel

Craig C. Blumreich — 1954 — Washburn University of Topeka, B.B.A. (summa cum laude), 1976; J.D. (cum laude), 1979 — Phi Delta Phi; Phi Kappa Phi — Associate Comments Editor, Washburn Law Journal, 1978-1979 — Admitted to Bar, 1979, Kansas; 1979, U.S. District Court, District of Kansas; 1979, U.S. Court of Appeals, Tenth Circuit — Member American, Kansas and Topeka Bar Associations; Kansas Association of Defense Counsel; American Inns of Court, 1981-1996; Defense Research Institute; International Association of Arson Investigators; American Board of Trial Advocates — Adjunct Professor of Business Law, Washburn University

Matthew S. Crowley — 1961 — Oklahoma Panhandle State University, B.B.A., 1984; Washburn University of Topeka, J.D., 1989 — Admitted to Bar, 1989, Kansas; 1989, U.S. Court of Appeals, Tenth Circuit — Member Kansas and Topeka Bar Associations

Associates

Joel W. Riggs — 1967 — The University of Kansas, B.S.B.A. (with distinction), 1990; J.D., 1993 — Admitted to Bar, 1993, Kansas; 1993, U.S. District Court, District of Kansas — Member Kansas, Topeka and Wichita Bar

WICHITA   KANSAS

Larson & Blumreich, Chartered, Topeka, KS (Continued)

Associations; Kansas Association of Defense Counsel — Practice Areas: Litigation; Insurance Coverage

Alan E. Streit — 1975 — Kansas State University, B.S., 1997; The University of Kansas School of Law, J.D., 2000 — Admitted to Bar, 2000, Kansas; 2000, U.S. District Court, District of Kansas — Member Kansas (Bench/Bar Committee) and Topeka Bar Associations — Municipal Court Judge — Practice Areas: Civil Litigation; Insurance Coverage; Real Estate

---

The following firms also service this area.

Case Linden P.C.
2600 Grand Boulevard, Suite 300
Kansas City, Missouri 64108
Telephone: 816-979-1500
Fax: 816-979-1501

Appellate Practice, Bodily Injury, Civil Trial Practice, Class Actions, Commercial Litigation, Discrimination, Errors and Omissions, Insurance Defense, Labor and Employment, Legal Malpractice, Medical Malpractice, Premises Liability, Product Liability, Professional Liability, Regulatory and Compliance, Tort, Workers' Compensation

SEE COMPLETE LISTING UNDER KANSAS CITY, MISSOURI (60 MILES)

Clark, Mize & Linville, Chartered
129 South 8th Street
Salina, Kansas 67401
Telephone: 785-823-6275
Fax: 785-823-1868

Mailing Address: P.O. Box 380, Salina, KS 67402-0380

Automobile, Workers' Compensation, Defense Litigation, Employment Discrimination, Public Entities, Medical Malpractice, Professional Malpractice

SEE COMPLETE LISTING UNDER SALINA, KANSAS (112 MILES)

Sanders Warren & Russell LLP
40 Corporate Woods
9401 Indian Creen Parkway, Suite 1250
Overland Park, Kansas 66210
Telephone: 913-234-6100
Fax: 913-234-6199

Insurance Defense, Business Law, Automobile, Property, Homeowners, Life Insurance, Commercial Law, Professional Liability, Municipal Law, Employment Law, Workers' Compensation, Comprehensive General Liability, Alternative Dispute Resolution, Appellate Practice, Bad Faith, Construction Litigation, Governmental Liability, Insurance Coverage, Medical Malpractice, Premises Liability, Product Liability, Truck Liability

SEE COMPLETE LISTING UNDER OVERLAND PARK, KANSAS (65 MILES)

WICHITA † 382,368 Sedgwick Co.

Foulston Siefkin LLP
1551 North Waterfront Parkway, Suite 100
Wichita, Kansas 67203
Telephone: 316-291-9784
Fax: 866-347-3143
E-Mail: cwest@foulston.com
www.foulston.com

(Topeka, KS Office: Bank of America Tower, Suite 1400, 534 South Kansas Avenue, 66603)
(Tel: 785-233-3600)
(Fax: 785-233-1610)
(Overland Park, KS Office: 32 Corporate Woods, Suite 600, 9225 Indian Creek Parkway, 66210)
(Tel: 913-498-2100)
(Fax: 913-498-2101)

Established: 1919

Foulston Siefkin LLP, Wichita, KS (Continued)

Insurance Defense, Comprehensive General Liability, Errors and Omissions, Premises Liability, Product Liability, Professional Liability, Coverage Analysis, Uninsured and Underinsured Motorist, Wrongful Termination, Workers' Compensation, Employment Law, Bad Faith and Coverage, Commercial and Complex Litigation

Firm Profile: Foulston Siefkin, the largest law firm in Kansas, with offices in Wichita, Topeka and Kansas City, offers a full range of practice areas including insurance defense, product liability, professional malpractice, commercial and complex litigation, employment law and insurance regulatory law.

Insurance Clients

American Modern Insurance Group, Inc.	CNA Insurance Company
Great West Casualty Company	Farmland Mutual Insurance Company
Nationwide Mutual Insurance Company	Shelter Insurance Companies
Utica National Insurance Company	State Auto Insurance Company

Craig W. West — 1961 — Kansas State University, B.S., 1984; Washburn University School of Law, J.D. (magna cum laude), 1987 — Editor-Washburn Law Journal — Admitted to Bar, 1987, Kansas — Member Kansas Association of Defense Counsel; Fellow: Kansas Bar Foundation; International Association of Defense Counsel; Fellow, American College of Trial Lawyers — Practice Areas: Defense Litigation — E-mail: cwest@foulston.com

McDonald, Tinker, Skaer, Quinn & Herrington
R.H. Garvey Building
300 West Douglas Avenue, Suite 500
Wichita, Kansas 67202
Telephone: 316-263-5851
Fax: 316-263-4677
E-Mail: mtsqh@mcdonaldtinker.com
www.mcdonaldtinker.com

Established: 1905

Workers' Compensation, Civil Litigation, Insurance Law, Medical Malpractice, Legal Malpractice, Appellate Practice, Business Law, Civil Rights, Civil Trial Practice, Construction Law, Employment Law, Environmental Law, Health Care, Labor and Employment, Product Liability, Estate Planning, Probate, Bankruptcy, Elder Law, Real Property, Aeronautics, Law Enforcement, Partnerships, Personal Injury Defense, Professional Liability Defense, Social Security

Firm Profile: For over a century, McDonald, Tinker, Skaer, Quinn & Herrington, P.A. has maintained a reputation as one of Kansas' leading litigation firms.

Insurance Clients

ALLIED Insurance	Allstate Insurance Company
American Family Insurance Company	Chubb Insurance Company
ESIS/ACE USA Group	EMC Insurance Companies
The Hartford Insurance Group	Federated Insurance Company
Progressive Insurance Company	Kansas Restaurant & Hospitality Association
Royal & SunAlliance Insurance Companies	Scottsdale Insurance Company
State Farm Fire and Casualty Company	Shelter Insurance Companies
Zurich Insurance Company	Travelers Property Casualty Insurance Company

Of Counsel

Kevin M. McMaster — 1958 — The University of Kansas, B.S., 1981; J.D., 1984 — Admitted to Bar, 1984, Kansas — Practice Areas: Civil Litigation; Insurance Defense; Product Liability; Professional Liability; Business Law; Commercial Law — E-mail: kmcmaster@mcdonaldtinker.com

McDonald, Tinker, Skaer, Quinn & Herrington, Wichita, KS (Continued)

Paul F. Good — The University of Kansas, B.S., 1982; Washburn University of Topeka, J.D. (with honors), 1985 — Admitted to Bar, 1985, Kansas — Practice Areas: Business Law; Trusts; Corporate Law; Real Estate; Mergers and Acquisitions; Business Formation — E-mail: pfgood@mcdonaldtinker.com

Members

Vincent A. Burnett — 1963 — Wichita State University, B.S. (cum laude), 1985; Washburn University of Topeka, J.D., 1987 — Admitted to Bar, 1988, Kansas — Practice Areas: Workers' Compensation — E-mail: vburnett@mcdonaldtinker.com

P. Kelly Donley — 1960 — Cloud County Community College, A.A., 1980; The University of Kansas, B.S., 1982; Washburn University of Topeka, J.D. (with honors), 1989 — Admitted to Bar, 1989, Kansas — Practice Areas: Workers' Compensation — E-mail: kdonley@mcdonaldtinker.com

Edward L. Keeley — 1953 — Washburn University of Topeka, B.A. (magna cum laude), 1975; Arizona State University, J.D. (magna cum laude), 1978 — Admitted to Bar, 1978, Arizona; 1979, Kansas — Practice Areas: Civil Rights; Personal Injury; Commercial Law; Construction Law; Employment Discrimination; Wrongful Termination; Breach of Contract; Medical Malpractice — E-mail: ekeeley@mcdonaldtinker.com

Scott E. Sanders — 1973 — Kansas State University, B.S. (cum laude), 1995; Washburn University of Topeka, J.D. (with honors), 1998 — Admitted to Bar, 1998, Kansas — Practice Areas: Insurance Litigation; Business Law; Civil Litigation; Insurance Defense; Personal Injury; Product Liability; Premises Liability — E-mail: ssanders@mcdonaldtinker.com

Matthew J. Schaefer — 1974 — Wichita State University, B.B.A. (magna cum laude), 1996; Washburn University of Topeka, J.D. (with honors), 2000 — Admitted to Bar, 2000, Kansas — Practice Areas: Workers' Compensation — E-mail: mschaefer@mcdonaldtinker.com

Jennifer M. Hill — 1978 — University of Notre Dame, B.A., 2000; Washburn University, J.D., 2003 — Admitted to Bar, 2003, Kansas — Member American, Kansas and Wichita (President-Elect, 2013, President, 2014) Bar Associations; Wichita Young Lawyers Association; Wichita Women Attorneys Association — Kansas Bar Association Outstanding Young Lawyer (2008); Wichita Business Journal 40 under 40 (2007) — Practice Areas: Personal Injury; Employment Law; Insurance Coverage — E-mail: jhill@mcdonaldtinker.com

Dallas L. Rakestraw — 1980 — The University of Kansas, B.A., 2003; J.D., 2006 — Admitted to Bar, 2006, Kansas — Practice Areas: Workers' Compensation — E-mail: drakestraw@mcdonaldtinker.com

Associates

Katy E. Tompkins   Erin S. Good

Withers, Gough, Pike, Pfaff & Peterson, LLC

O.W. Garvey Building
200 West Douglas, Suite 1010
Wichita, Kansas 67202
Telephone: 316-267-1562
Fax: 316-303-1018
www.withersgough.com

Established: 2002

Insurance Defense, Personal Injury, Automobile, Product Liability, Drug, Medical Devices, Surety, Construction Law, Accident, Life and Health, Commercial Law, Professional Liability, Arson, Fraud, First Party Matters, Directors and Officers Liability, Securities and Shareholders' Claims, Employment Practices Liability, Environmental Law, Insurance Coverage, Agent and Brokers Errors and Omissions, Subrogation, Oil and Gas, Architects and Engineers, Bonds, Accountant Malpractice, Legal Malpractice

Insurance Clients

American Farmers & Ranchers Insurance Company
Burlington Insurance Company
Columbia Insurance Group
Bar Plan Group
Brotherhood Mutual Insurance Company
Deep South of Tennessee, Inc.

Withers, Gough, Pike, Pfaff & Peterson, LLC, Wichita, KS (Continued)

Fidelity National Insurance Company
James River Insurance Company
State Farm Mutual Automobile Insurance Company
Goodville Mutual Casualty Company
Mid-Continent Casualty Company
United Fire & Casualty Company
Wilshire Insurance Company

Partners

Larry A. Withers — (1942-2004)

Steven D. Gough — 1951 — The University of Kansas, B.A. (with highest distinction), 1973; J.D., 1976 — Order of the Coif; Phi Beta Kappa — Kansas Law Review 1975-1976 — Admitted to Bar, 1976, Kansas; 1976, U.S. District Court, District of Kansas; 1976, U.S. Court of Appeals, Tenth Circuit; 1986, U.S. Supreme Court — Member American, Kansas and Wichita Bar Associations — Practice Areas: Business Law; Corporate Law; Environmental Law; Oil and Gas; Personal Injury; Professional Liability; Insurance Defense; Product Liability — E-mail: sgough@withersgough.com

John G. Pike — 1952 — The University of Kansas, B.S., 1975; J.D., 1978 — Admitted to Bar, 1978, Kansas; 1978, U.S. District Court, District of Kansas — Member Kansas and Wichita Bar Associations; Kansas Independent Oil and Gas Association — Practice Areas: Administrative Law; Oil and Gas — E-mail: jpike@withersgough.com

Alan R. Pfaff — 1962 — Emporia State University, B.S., 1983; The University of Kansas, J.D., 1986 — Admitted to Bar, 1986, Kansas; 1986, U.S. District Court, District of Kansas; 1986, U.S. Court of Appeals, Tenth Circuit — Member Kansas and Wichita Bar Associations — Practice Areas: Insurance Defense; Arson; Fraud; Insurance Coverage; Subrogation; Employment Law — E-mail: apfaff@withersgough.com

Donald N. Peterson, II — 1963 — Wichita State University, B.A., 1985; The University of Kansas, J.D./M.A., 1988 — Judicial Clerk, Kansas Court of Appeals, 1988-1990 — Admitted to Bar, 1988, Kansas; U.S. District Court, District of Kansas; U.S. Court of Appeals, Tenth Circuit — Member American, Kansas and Wichita Bar Associations — Co-Author: Chapter on 42 U.S.C. 1983 in Kansas Employment Law, 2d. Published by the Kansas Bar Association (2001) — Practice Areas: Employment Law; Product Liability; Insurance Coverage; Insurance Defense — E-mail: dpeterson@withersgough.com

Associates

Sean M. McGivern — 1980 — Kansas State University, B.A., 2004; The University of Kansas, J.D., 2006 — Admitted to Bar, 2007, Kansas; U.S. Court of Appeals, Tenth Circuit — Member American, Kansas and Wichita Bar Associations — Practice Areas: Insurance Defense; Employment Law; Business Law — E-mail: smcgivern@withersgough.com

Nathan R. Elliott — 1981 — Fort Hays State University, B.B.A., 2007; The University of Kansas, J.D., 2010 — Admitted to Bar, 2010, Kansas; U.S. District Court, District of Kansas — Member Kansas and Wichita Bar Associations — Practice Areas: Insurance Defense; Legal Malpractice; Probate; Business Law — E-mail: nelliott@withersgough.com

---

The following firms also service this area.

Clark, Mize & Linville, Chartered
129 South 8th Street
Salina, Kansas 67401
Telephone: 785-823-6325
Fax: 785-823-1868

Mailing Address: P.O. Box 380, Salina, KS 67402-0380

Automobile, Workers' Compensation, Defense Litigation, Employment Discrimination, Public Entities, Medical Malpractice, Professional Malpractice

SEE COMPLETE LISTING UNDER SALINA, KANSAS (90 MILES)

WICHITA

KANSAS

Hampton & Royce, L.C.
United Building, Ninth Floor
119 West Iron Avenue
Salina, Kansas 67401
    Telephone: 785-827-7251
    Fax: 785-827-2815
Mailing Address: P.O. Box 1247, Salina, KS 67402-1247

Accident, Agent/Broker Liability, Errors and Omissions, Agriculture, Alternative Dispute Resolution, Appellate Practice, Arson, Automobile Liability, Banking, Bankruptcy, Bodily Injury, Business Law, Casualty Insurance Law, Civil Litigation, Class Actions, Collections, Commercial and Personal Lines, Commercial General Liability, Commercial Litigation, Commercial Transactions, Construction Liability, Construction Litigation, Contract Disputes, Contractors Liability, Contracts, Corporate Law, Coverage Analysis, Directors and Officers Liability, Employer Liability, Employment Discrimination, Employment Law, Employment Practices Liability, Environmental Law, Estate Planning, General Civil Practice, Health Care, Insurance Coverage, Insurance Fraud, Insurance Litigation, Intentional Torts, Labor and Employment, Legal Malpractice, Lender Liability Defense, Mediation, Medical Liability, Medical Malpractice, Mergers and Acquisitions, Negligence, Nursing Home Liability, Personal Injury, Policy Construction and Interpretation, Premises Liability, Probate, Product Liability, Professional Negligence, Sexual Harassment, Slip and Fall, Subrogation, Tort Liability, Tort Litigation, Uninsured and Underinsured Motorist, Workers' Compensation, Wrongful Death, Wrongful Termination, Life and Health Insurance Claims and Litigation, Accountant Liability and Malpractice, , Contract Litigation, Coverage Disputes, Domestic, Excess and Umbrella Coverage and Litigation, Family Law and Litigation, First and Third Party Claims, Foreclosures, Health Insurance Litigation, Homeowners Liability, Pensions, Property and Casualty Losses, Real Estate Contracts, Real Estate Disputes and Litigation, Receiverships, Shareholders Claims, Trusts and Trust Litigation

SEE COMPLETE LISTING UNDER SALINA, KANSAS (90 MILES)

KENTUCKY

CAPITAL: FRANKFORT

COUNTIES AND COUNTY SEATS

County	County Seat	County	County Seat	County	County Seat
Adair	Columbia	Grant	Williamstown	McLean	Calhoun
Allen	Scottsville	Graves	Mayfield	Meade	Brandenburg
Anderson	Lawrenceburg	Grayson	Leitchfield	Menifee	Frenchburg
Ballard	Wickliffe	Green	Greensburg	Mercer	Harrodsburg
Barren	Glasgow	Greenup	Greenup	Metcalfe	Edmonton
Bath	Owingsville	Hancock	Hawesville	Monroe	Tompkinsville
Bell	Pineville	Hardin	Elizabethtown	Montgomery	Mount Sterling
Boone	Burlington	Harlan	Harlan	Morgan	West Liberty
Bourbon	Paris	Harrison	Cynthiana	Muhlenberg	Greenville
Boyd	Catlettsburg	Hart	Munfordville	Nelson	Bardstown
Boyle	Danville	Henderson	Henderson	Nicholas	Carlisle
Bracken	Brooksville	Henry	New Castle	Ohio	Hartford
Breathitt	Jackson	Hickman	Clinton	Oldham	La Grange
Breckinridge	Hardinsburg	Hopkins	Madisonville	Owen	Owenton
Bullitt	Shepherdsville	Jackson	McKee	Owsley	Booneville
Butler	Morgantown	Jefferson	Louisville	Pendleton	Falmouth
Caldwell	Priceton	Jessamine	Nicholasville	Perry	Hazard
Calloway	Murray	Johnson	Paintsville	Pike	Pikeville
Campbell	Alexandria	Kenton	Independence	Powell	Stanton
Carlisle	Bardwell	Knott	Hindman	Pulaski	Somerset
Carroll	Carrollton	Knox	Barbourville	Robertson	Mount Olivet
Carter	Grayson	Larue	Hodgenville	Rockcastle	Mount Vernon
Casey	Liberty	Laurel	London	Rowan	Morehead
Christian	Hopkinsville	Lawrence	Louisa	Russell	Jamestown
Clark	Winchester	Lee	Beattyville	Scott	Georgetown
Clay	Manchester	Leslie	Hyden	Shelby	Shelbyville
Clinton	Albany	Letcher	Whitesburg	Simpson	Franklin
Crittenden	Marion	Lewis	Vanceburg	Spencer	Taylorsville
Cumberland	Burkesville	Lincoln	Stanford	Taylor	Campbellsville
Daviess	Owensboro	Livingston	Smithland	Todd	Elkton
Edmonson	Brownsville	Logan	Russellville	Trigg	Cadiz
Elliott	Sandy Hook	Lyon	Eddyville	Trimble	Bedford
Estill	Irvine	Madison	Richmond	Union	Morganfield
Fayette	Lexington	Magoffin	Salyersville	Warren	Bowling Green
Fleming	Flemingsburg	Marion	Lebanon	Washington	Springfield
Floyd	Prestonsburg	Marshall	Benton	Wayne	Monticello
Franklin	Frankfort	Martin	Inez	Webster	Dixon
Fulton	Hickman	Mason	Maysville	Whitley	Williamsburg
Gallatin	Warsaw	McCracken	Paducah	Wolfe	Campton
Garrard	Lancaster	McCreary	Whitley City	Woodford	Versailles

In the text that follows "†" indicates County Seats.

Our files contain additional verified data on the firms listed herein. This additional information is available on request.

A.M. BEST COMPANY

KENTUCKY   ASHLAND

ASHLAND 21,684 Boyd Co.

Refer To

Coleman Lochmiller & Bond
2907 Ring Road
Elizabethtown, Kentucky 42701
 Telephone: 270-737-0600
 Fax: 270-737-0488

Mailing Address: P.O. Box 1177, Elizabethtown, KY 42702-1177

Insurance Defense, Automobile, Commercial Law, Product Liability, Professional Liability, Property and Casualty, Medical Malpractice, Litigation, General

SEE COMPLETE LISTING UNDER ELIZABETHTOWN, KENTUCKY (223 MILES)

Refer To

Jenkins Fenstermaker, PLLC
325 8th Street
Huntington, West Virginia 25701
 Telephone: 304-523-2100
 Fax: 304-523-2347, 304-523-9279
 Toll Free: 800-982-3476

Mailing Address: P.O. Box 2688, Huntington, WV 25726

Civil Litigation, State and Federal Courts, Mediation, Arbitration, Trial Practice, Appellate Practice, Commercial Litigation, Personal Injury, Product Liability, Medical Malpractice, Professional Malpractice, Toxic Torts, Construction Litigation, Insurance Defense, Insurance Coverage, ERISA, Workers' Compensation, Employment Law, Administrative Law, Labor and Employment Law, Automobile Warranty, Labor Negotiations, Counseling, Warranty Litigation

SEE COMPLETE LISTING UNDER HUNTINGTON, WEST VIRGINIA (15 MILES)

BARBOURVILLE † 3,165 Knox Co.

Refer To

Taylor, Keller & Oswald, PLLC
1306 West 5th Street, Suite 100
London, Kentucky 40741
 Telephone: 606-878-8844
 Fax: 606-878-8850

Mailing Address: P.O. Box 3440, London, KY 40743-3440

Trial Practice, Automobile Liability, Property, Insurance Coverage, Product Liability, Premises Liability, Subrogation, Insurance Fraud, Bad Faith, Governmental Liability, General Insurance and Corporate Defense

SEE COMPLETE LISTING UNDER LONDON, KENTUCKY (26 MILES)

BARDSTOWN † 11,700 Nelson Co.

Refer To

Coleman Lochmiller & Bond
2907 Ring Road
Elizabethtown, Kentucky 42701
 Telephone: 270-737-0600
 Fax: 270-737-0488

Mailing Address: P.O. Box 1177, Elizabethtown, KY 42702-1177

Insurance Defense, Automobile, Commercial Law, Product Liability, Professional Liability, Property and Casualty, Medical Malpractice, Litigation, General

SEE COMPLETE LISTING UNDER ELIZABETHTOWN, KENTUCKY (25 MILES)

Refer To

Kerrick Bachert PSC
2413 Ring Road, Suite 117
Elizabethtown, Kentucky 42701
 Telephone: 270-737-9088
 Fax: 270-769-2905

Product Liability, Malpractice, Automobile, Workers' Compensation, Accident and Health, General Liability, Subrogation, Commercial Law, Intellectual Property, Copyright and Trademark Law, Health Care, Employment Law, Insurance Law, Real Estate, Banking Law

SEE COMPLETE LISTING UNDER ELIZABETHTOWN, KENTUCKY (25 MILES)

BOWLING GREEN † 58,067 Warren Co.

Cole & Moore P.S.C.

921 College Street - Phoenix Place
Bowling Green, Kentucky 42101
 Telephone: 270-782-6666
 Fax: 270-782-8666
 E-Mail: cm@coleandmoore.com
 www.coleandmoore.com

Established: 1974

Insurance Defense, Trial Practice, Product Liability, Casualty, Workers' Compensation, Medical Malpractice, Toxic Torts, Fidelity and Surety

Counsel For

Clark Beverage Group
Graves Gilbert Clinic
Scott Murphy & Daniel, LLC
Scott & Murphy, Inc.
Scottsville-Allen County Planning Commission
Warren County Codes Enforcement Board

Clark Distributing Company, Inc.
Planning Commission of Bowling Green/Warren County
Scott & Ritter, Inc.
Scotty's Contracting and Stone Company
Warren County Water District
Western Kentucky Coca-Cola Bottling Company

Insurance Clients

Acuity Insurance Company
Berkley Risk Administrators Company, LLC
CIGNA Insurance Company
CNA Insurance Companies
Everest National Insurance Company
Gallagher Bassett Services, Inc.
Go America Auto Insurance
Hanover Insurance Company
Indiana Lumbermens Mutual Insurance Company
Monroe Guaranty Insurance Company
Penn National Insurance
ProAssurance Company
Ranger Insurance Company
Royal Insurance Company
The Seibels Bruce Group, Inc.
State Volunteer Mutual Insurance Company
United States Aviation Underwriters, Inc.
Zurich American Insurance Company

American Claims Service, Inc.
Burlington Insurance Group
Carolina Casualty Insurance Company
Electric Mutual Liability Insurance Company
Fireman's Fund Insurance Company
Guaranty National Insurance Company
Liberty Mutual Insurance Company
Lincoln General Insurance Company
Ohio Casualty Company
Permanent General Assurance Corporation
Reliance Insurance Company
St. Paul Fire and Marine Insurance Company
TIG Insurance Company
Travelers Insurance Companies
Wausau Insurance Companies
XL Insurance

Local Counsel For

General Growth Management, Inc.
Rite Aid of Kentucky, Inc.

Non-Insurance Clients

American Home Products, Inc.
Coca-Cola Bottlers Association
Golden Foods/Golden Brands

Budget Rent-A-Car Corporation
Crane Co.
Ryder System, Inc.

Partners

John David Cole, Sr. — 1938 — University of Kentucky, B.S., 1962; LL.B., 1964 — Phi Delta Phi — Admitted to Bar, 1964, Kentucky; U.S. District Court, Eastern and Western Districts of Kentucky; U.S. Court of Appeals, Sixth Circuit; 1968, U.S. Supreme Court — Member American, Kentucky, Bowling Green/Warren County (Past President) and Louisville Bar Associations; Kentucky Bar Foundation; Sixth Circuit Judicial Conference (Life Member); International Association of Defense Counsel; Federation of Defense and Corporate Counsel — Western Kentucky University (Board of Regents, Chairman, 1977-1983); Kentucky Board of Bar Examiners (1996-Present); listed in The Best Lawyers in America — E-mail: dcole@coleandmoore.com

Frank Hampton Moore, Jr. — 1952 — Western Kentucky University, B.S., 1975; Salmon P. Chase College of Law, J.D., 1979 — Admitted to Bar, 1979,

BOWLING GREEN   **KENTUCKY**

Cole & Moore P.S.C., Bowling Green, KY   (Continued)

Kentucky; U.S. District Court, Eastern and Western Districts of Kentucky; U.S. Court of Appeals, Sixth Circuit; U.S. Supreme Court — Member American, Kentucky and Bowling Green/Warren County (President) Bar Associations; Fellow, Kentucky Bar Foundaction (Board Member); American Planning Association; International Association of Defense Counsel; Defense Research Institute — E-mail: hmoore@coleandmoore.com

Stefan Richard Hughes — 1968 — Transylvania University, B.A. (summa cum laude), 1990; University of Kentucky College of Law, J.D., 1993 — Admitted to Bar, 1994, Kentucky; U.S. District Court, Eastern and Western Districts of Kentucky; U.S. Court of Appeals, Sixth Circuit; U.S. Supreme Court — Member Kentucky and Bowling Green/Warren County Bar Associations — Author, Comment: "Cumberland Reclamation Co. v. United States: Defining Coal Dredging as Surface Mining Under SMCRA," 8 Journal of National Resources & Environmental Law — Languages: German — E-mail: rhughes@coleandmoore.com

Matthew P. Cook — 1971 — The University of North Carolina at Chapel Hill, B.A. (with honors), 1994; Louis D. Brandeis School of Law, University of Louisville, J.D. (cum laude), 1998 — Admitted to Bar, 1998, Kentucky; U.S. District Court, Eastern and Western Districts of Kentucky; U.S. Court of Appeals, Sixth Circuit; U.S. Supreme Court — Member Federal, American, Kentucky, Bowling Green/Warren County (Past President) and Louisville Bar Associations; Six Circuit Judicial Conference (Life Member); Life Fellow, Kentucky Bar Foundation — Co-Author, Chapter "Closing Arguments," Kentucky Civil Practice at Trial, 2nd & 3rd Eds., University of Kentucky Continuing Legal Education Series — E-mail: mcook@coleandmoore.com

Associate

Frank Hampton Moore, III — 1983 — Transylvania University, B.A., 2005; Appalachian School of Law, J.D., 2009 — Admitted to Bar, 2009, Kentucky; 2011, U.S. District Court, Eastern and Western Districts of Kentucky; U.S. Court of Appeals, Sixth Circuit — Member Kentucky and Bowling Green/Warren County Bar Associations — E-mail: mooreiii@coleandmoore.com

Kerrick Bachert PSC

1025 State Street
Bowling Green, Kentucky 42101
   Telephone: 270-782-8160
   Fax: 270-782-5856
   E-Mail: Kerrickbachertlaw@kerricklaw.com
   www.kerrickbachertlaw.com

(Elizabethtown, KY Office*: 2413 Ring Road, Suite 117, 42701)
   (Tel: 270-737-9088)
   (Fax: 270-769-2905)
   (E-Mail: thulsey@kerrickfirm.com)

Established: 1984

Product Liability, Malpractice, Automobile, Workers' Compensation, Accident and Health, General Liability, Subrogation, Commercial Law, Intellectual Property, Copyright and Trademark Law, Health Care, Employment Law, Real Estate, Insurance Defense

Firm Profile: Kerrick Bachert PSC is a full-service law firm founded on strength in litigation and advocacy, and focused on our clients' best interests.

We routinely represent clients in state and federal courts throughout Kentucky and offer a wide range of legal services to meet your needs. Our attorneys have over 150 years of combined experience and have achieved an AV rating from Martindale-Hubbell as well as been named Super Lawyers, The Best Lawyers in America, Super Lawyers of Kentucky and ATLA Top 100 Trial Lawyers. KB attorneys monitor recent legal developments and business trends, helping their clients seek new opportunities and minimize risk. Superior client service is what KB strives for - providing creative, practical solutions and proven results.

Counsel For

Western Kentucky University

Kerrick Bachert PSC, Bowling Green, KY   (Continued)

Insurance Clients

Aetna Life and Casualty Company
Anthem Insurance Companies, Inc.
Century Surety Group
Cincinnati Insurance Company
Employers Reinsurance
  Corporation
Fireman's Fund Insurance
  Company
Grange Mutual Casualty Company
The Hartford Insurance Group
Health Care Indemnity, Inc.
Kentucky League of Cities
Kentucky National Insurance
  Company
Nationwide Insurance
Occidental Fire & Casualty
  Company of North Carolina
Western Surety Company
American Family Insurance Group
Century American Insurance
  Company
Crawford & Company
Executive Risk Specialty Insurance
  Company
Generali - US Branch
Golden Rule Insurance Company
Hamilton Mutual Insurance
  Company
Kemper National Insurance
  Companies
National American Insurance
  Company
Northland Insurance Company
Scottsdale Insurance Company
Travelers Insurance Companies
Zurich North America

Non-Insurance Clients

Coverage Option Associates

Equity Partners

Thomas N. Kerrick — 1955 — University of Kentucky, B.S., 1977; J.D., 1980 — Admitted to Bar, 1980, Kentucky; 1980, U.S. District Court, Western District of Kentucky; 1986, U.S. District Court, Eastern District of Kentucky; 1986, U.S. Court of Appeals, Sixth Circuit — Member American, Kentucky and Bowling Green/Warren County Bar Associations; Kentucky Academy of Trial Attorneys; Association of Trial Lawyers of America; American Board of Trial Advocates; Kentucky Defense Counsel — Certified Mediator — Practice Areas: Insurance Defense; Trial Practice; Personal Injury; Product Liability; Construction Law; Medical Malpractice — E-mail: tkerrick@ksclawfirm.com

Laura M. Hagan — 1964 — University of Kentucky, B.H.S., 1987; J.D., 1993 — Admitted to Bar, 1993, Kentucky; U.S. Patent and Trademark Office — Member Kentucky and Bowling Green/Warren County Bar Associations; American Society of Medical Technologists (1987-1993); American Intellectual Property Law Association; Association of University Technology Managers — Registered to practice before U.S. Patent and Trademark Offices — E-mail: lhagan@ksclawfirm.com

Shawn Rosso Alcott — 1967 — Vanderbilt University, B.A., 1990; University of Kentucky, J.D., 1993 — Admitted to Bar, 1993, Kentucky; 1996, U.S. District Court, Eastern and Western Districts of Kentucky — Member Kentucky and Bowling Green/Warren County County Bar Associations; Kentucky Academy of Hospital Attorneys — Adjunct Professor, Environmental Law, Geology Department, Western Kentucky University — E-mail: salcott@ksclawfirm.com

Non-Equity Partner

Scott D. Laufenberg — 1973 — University of Wisconsin-Platteville, B.S., 1996; Drake University, M.P.A., 1999; J.D., 1999 — Delta Theta Phi — Law Clerk, Kentucky Court of Appeals, 1999-2000 — Admitted to Bar, 2000, Kentucky; U.S. District Court, Western District of Kentucky; U.S. Court of Appeals, Sixth Circuit; 2005, U.S. Supreme Court — Member American (Fellow), Kentucky and Bowling Green-Warren County Bar Associations — Adjunct Professor, Management, Western Kentucky University — E-mail: slaufenberg@ksclawfirm.com

Of Counsel

D. Michael Coyle — 1940 — University of Kentucky, B.S., 1962; J.D., 1965 — Admitted to Bar, 1965, Kentucky; U.S. District Court, Eastern and Western Districts of Kentucky; U.S. Supreme Court — Member Kentucky and Hardin County Bar Associations — Master Commisioner and Domestic Relations Commissioner for Hardin Circuit Court, 1996-2002 — Certified Mediator, Contracts and Commercial Disputes; Certified Public Accountant — E-mail: dmcoyle@ksclawfirm.com

Jeffrey R. Ogrody — 1946 — Vanderbilt University, B.A., 1968; University of Kentucky, J.D., 1971 — Admitted to Bar, 1971, Kentucky; 1971, U.S. District Court, Eastern and Western Districts of Kentucky — Member The Florida Bar; Kentucky Bar Association

S. Frank Smith, Jr. — 1940 — Vanderbilt University, B.A., 1963; Memphis State University, J.D., 1973 — Admitted to Bar, 1973, Kentucky; U.S. District Court, Western District of Kentucky — Member Kentucky and Bowling Green/Warren County Bar Associations — E-mail: fsmith@ksclawfirm.com

KENTUCKY

Kerrick Bachert PSC, Bowling Green, KY (Continued)

Karl N. Crandall — 1942 — University of Kentucky, B.A., 1964; J.D., 1967 — Admitted to Bar, 1967, Kentucky; U.S. District Court, Eastern and Western Districts of Kentucky — Member Kentucky and Bowling Green/Warren County Bar Associations

James D. Harris, Jr — 1943 — The University of Alabama, B.A., 1965; The University of Alabama School of Law, J.D., 1967 — Admitted to Bar, 1967, Alabama; 1983, Kentucky; 1971, U.S. Supreme Court; 1983, U.S. District Court, Western District of Kentucky; 1987, U.S. Court of Appeals, Sixth Circuit; 1997, U.S. District Court, Eastern District of Kentucky — Member American, Kentucky, and Bowling Green-Warren County Bar Associations; Alabama State Bar; Transportation Lawyers Association; Defense Research Institute; Association of Defense Trial Attorneys; Kentucky Defense Counsel — Kentucky Super Lawyers, 2007; Special Justice for the Supreme Court of Kentucky — Ret. Col., US Army Reserves; Decorated Vietnam War Veteran — Practice Areas: General Civil Litigation; Product Liability; Commercial Litigation; Construction Litigation; Contracts; Insurance Defense; Negligence — E-mail: jharris@ksclawfirm.com

Associates

Andrea P. Anderson — 1981 — Western Kentucky University, B.A., 2003; University of Kentucky, J.D., 2006 — Admitted to Bar, 2006, Kentucky; U.S. District Court, Eastern and Western Districts of Kentucky — Member Kentucky and Bowling Green/Warren County Bar Associations; Trial Advocacy Board — E-mail: aanderson@ksclawfirm.com

Lucas A. Davidson — 1982 — Western Kentucky University, B.A., 2005; University of Louisville, J.D., 2009 — Admitted to Bar, 2009, Kentucky; 2011, Tennessee; U.S. District Court, Eastern and Western Districts of Kentucky — Member Kentucky, Tennessee and Bowling Green-Warren County Bar Associations — Practice Areas: Personal Injury; Construction Litigation; Commercial Litigation; Business Law; Real Estate — E-mail: ldavidson@ksclawfirm.com

Lee Cassie Clagett — 1980 — Saint Mary's College, B.B.A., 2002; Thomas M. Cooley Law School, J.D., 2005 — Admitted to Bar, 2005, Illinois; 2006, Minnesota; District of Columbia; 2007, Kentucky; 2005, U.S. District Court, Northern and Southern Districts of Illinois; 2007, U.S. District Court, District of Minnesota; 2009, U.S. District Court, Eastern and Western Districts of Kentucky — Member American, Kentucky and Hardin County Bar Associations — E-mail: lglagett@ksclawfirm.com

Lauren E. Marley — 1986 — Transylvania University, B.A., 2008; Salmon P. Chase College of Law, J.D., 2011 — Admitted to Bar, 2011, Kentucky; U.S. District Court, Western District of Kentucky — Member Kentucky and Bowling Green-Warren County Bar Associations; Kentucky Justice Association; American Association for Justice — E-mail: thulsey@ksclawfirm.com

(This firm is also listed in the Subrogation section of this directory)

The following firms also service this area.

Coleman Lochmiller & Bond
2907 Ring Road
Elizabethtown, Kentucky 42701
   Telephone: 270-737-0600
   Fax: 270-737-0488

Mailing Address: P.O. Box 1177, Elizabethtown, KY 42702-1177

Insurance Defense, Automobile, Commercial Law, Product Liability, Professional Liability, Property and Casualty, Medical Malpractice, Litigation, General

SEE COMPLETE LISTING UNDER ELIZABETHTOWN, KENTUCKY (71 MILES)

Kahn, Dees, Donovan & Kahn, LLP
501 Main Street, Suite 305
Evansville, Indiana 47708
   Telephone: 812-423-3183
   Fax: 812-423-3841

Mailing Address: P.O. Box 3646, Evansville, IN 47735-3646

Asbestos Litigation, Automobile, Construction Law, Coverage Issues, Environmental Law, Insurance Defense, General Liability, Labor and Employment, Mass Tort, Medical Malpractice, Personal Injury, Premises Liability, Product Liability, Property, Public Entities, Self-Insured, Subrogation, Workers' Compensation

SEE COMPLETE LISTING UNDER EVANSVILLE, INDIANA (110 MILES)

BRANDENBURG

King, Deep & Branaman
127 North Main Street
Henderson, Kentucky 42420
   Telephone: 270-827-1852
   Fax: 270-826-7729

Mailing Address: P.O. Box 43, Henderson, KY 42419-0043

Insurance Defense, Product Liability, Malpractice, Workers' Compensation, Bad Faith, Coverage

SEE COMPLETE LISTING UNDER HENDERSON, KENTUCKY (101 MILES)

BRANDENBURG † 2,643 Meade Co.

Refer To

Coleman Lochmiller & Bond
2907 Ring Road
Elizabethtown, Kentucky 42701
   Telephone: 270-737-0600
   Fax: 270-737-0488

Mailing Address: P.O. Box 1177, Elizabethtown, KY 42702-1177

Insurance Defense, Automobile, Commercial Law, Product Liability, Professional Liability, Property and Casualty, Medical Malpractice, Litigation, General

SEE COMPLETE LISTING UNDER ELIZABETHTOWN, KENTUCKY (34 MILES)

Refer To

Kerrick Bachert PSC
2413 Ring Road, Suite 117
Elizabethtown, Kentucky 42701
   Telephone: 270-737-9088
   Fax: 270-769-2905

Product Liability, Malpractice, Automobile, Workers' Compensation, Accident and Health, General Liability, Subrogation, Commercial Law, Intellectual Property, Copyright and Trademark Law, Health Care, Employment Law, Insurance Law, Real Estate, Banking Law

SEE COMPLETE LISTING UNDER ELIZABETHTOWN, KENTUCKY (34 MILES)

BROWNSVILLE † 836 Edmonson Co.

Refer To

Kerrick Bachert PSC
1025 State Street
Bowling Green, Kentucky 42101
   Telephone: 270-782-8160
   Fax: 270-782-5856

Mailing Address: P.O. Box 9547, Bowling Green, KY 42102-9547

Product Liability, Malpractice, Automobile, Workers' Compensation, Accident and Health, General Liability, Subrogation, Commercial Law, Intellectual Property, Copyright and Trademark Law, Health Care, Employment Law, Real Estate, Insurance Defense

SEE COMPLETE LISTING UNDER BOWLING GREEN, KENTUCKY (25 MILES)

CALHOUN † 763 McLean Co.

Refer To

Al Miller
Attorney at Law
428 North Second Street
Central City, Kentucky 42330-1124
   Telephone: 270-754-5502
   Fax: 270-754-5503

Insurance Defense, Automobile Liability, Property Damage, Fire, Trial Practice, Appellate Practice, Investigations, Slip and Fall, Wrongful Death, Bad Faith, Liquor Liability, Legal Malpractice, Medical Malpractice, Coverage Issues, State and Federal Courts, Unfair Claims Practices

SEE COMPLETE LISTING UNDER CENTRAL CITY, KENTUCKY (23 MILES)

COVINGTON   KENTUCKY

CAMPBELLSVILLE † 9,108 Taylor Co.

Refer To

Kerrick Bachert PSC
2413 Ring Road, Suite 117
Elizabethtown, Kentucky 42701
   Telephone: 270-737-9088
   Fax: 270-769-2905

Product Liability, Malpractice, Automobile, Workers' Compensation, Accident and Health, General Liability, Subrogation, Commercial Law, Intellectual Property, Copyright and Trademark Law, Health Care, Employment Law, Insurance Law, Real Estate, Banking Law

SEE COMPLETE LISTING UNDER ELIZABETHTOWN, KENTUCKY (71 MILES)

CENTRAL CITY   5,978 Muhlenberg Co.

Al Miller
Attorney at Law

428 North Second Street
Central City, Kentucky 42330-1124
   Telephone: 270-754-5502
   Fax: 270-754-5503
   E-Mail: al_millerlaw@yahoo.com

Established: 1974

Insurance Defense, Automobile Liability, Property Damage, Fire, Trial Practice, Appellate Practice, Investigations, Slip and Fall, Wrongful Death, Bad Faith, Liquor Liability, Legal Malpractice, Medical Malpractice, Coverage Issues, State and Federal Courts, Unfair Claims Practices

Insurance Clients

Indiana Farm Bureau
Ohio Casualty Group
Westfield Companies

Kentucky Farm Bureau Mutual Insurance Company

Partners and Associates

Al Miller — 1947 — Murray State University, B.S., 1969; University of Louisville, J.D., 1973 — Admitted to Bar, 1974, Kentucky; U.S. District Court, Western District of Kentucky; U.S. Court of Appeals, Sixth Circuit — Member Kentucky and Muhlenberg County Bar Associations — Reported Cases: Ohio Cas. Ins. Co. v. Atherton, 656 S.W.2d 724 (Ky. 1983); FB Ins. Co. v. Jones, Ky App., 864 S.W.2d 926; True v. Raines, Ky., 99 S.W.3d 439 — U.S. Army Reserves, 1969-1971, First Lieutenant Vietnam Bronze Star

Karen E. Miller — 1979 — Murray State University, B.A. (cum laude), 2001; Louis D. Brandeis School of Law, University of Louisville, J.D., 2004 — Admitted to Bar, 2004, Kentucky; U.S. District Court, Western District of Kentucky — KATA Brandeis School of Law Champion and State Finalist Closing Argument Competition, 2003

The following firms also service this area.

Franklin, Gordon & Hobgood
24 Court Street
Madisonville, Kentucky 42431
   Telephone: 270-821-7252
   Fax: 270-821-2360
Mailing Address: P.O. Box 547, Madisonville, KY 42431

Insurance Defense, Litigation, Professional Liability, Product Liability, Medical Malpractice, Civil Rights, General Liability

SEE COMPLETE LISTING UNDER MADISONVILLE, KENTUCKY (24 MILES)

Kerrick Bachert PSC
1025 State Street
Bowling Green, Kentucky 42101
   Telephone: 270-782-8160
   Fax: 270-782-5856
Mailing Address: P.O. Box 9547, Bowling Green, KY 42102-9547

Product Liability, Malpractice, Automobile, Workers' Compensation, Accident and Health, General Liability, Subrogation, Commercial Law, Intellectual Property, Copyright and Trademark Law, Health Care, Employment Law, Real Estate, Insurance Defense

SEE COMPLETE LISTING UNDER BOWLING GREEN, KENTUCKY (56 MILES)

COLUMBIA † 4,452 Adair Co.

Refer To

Kerrick Bachert PSC
1025 State Street
Bowling Green, Kentucky 42101
   Telephone: 270-782-8160
   Fax: 270-782-5856
Mailing Address: P.O. Box 9547, Bowling Green, KY 42102-9547

Product Liability, Malpractice, Automobile, Workers' Compensation, Accident and Health, General Liability, Subrogation, Commercial Law, Intellectual Property, Copyright and Trademark Law, Health Care, Employment Law, Real Estate, Insurance Defense

SEE COMPLETE LISTING UNDER BOWLING GREEN, KENTUCKY (72 MILES)

COVINGTON † 40,640 Kenton Co.

Adams, Stepner, Woltermann & Dusing, P.L.L.C.

40 West Pike Street
Covington, Kentucky 41011
   Telephone: 859-394-6200
   Fax: 859-291-7902, 859-392-7200

(Florence, KY Office*: 8100 Burlington Pike, Suite 342, 41042, P.O. Box 576, 41022-0576)
(Tel: 859-371-7276)
(Fax: 859-371-7370)

Carrier Defense, Automobile, General Liability, Product Liability, Workers' Compensation, Governmental Liability, Insurance Law, Surety, Life and Health, Disability, Accident, Litigation, Appellate Practice, Civil Rights, Employment Law, Construction Litigation, Construction Law, Condemnation, Eminent Domain, Domestic Relations

Insurance Clients

American General Group
American States Insurance Company
Canadian Universal Insurance Company
Colonial Insurance Company
Erie Insurance Company
Federated Insurance Company
Golden Rule Insurance Company
The Hartford Insurance Group
Home Insurance Company
Housing Authority Risk Retention Group, Inc.
J. C. Penney Casualty Insurance Company
Kentucky National Insurance Company
Manchester Insurance Group
Metropolitan Life Insurance Company
Occidental Life Insurance Company of North Carolina
Protective Life Insurance Company
Providian Financial Corporation
Puritan Insurance Company

American Specialist Claims Service, Inc.
American Universal Insurance Company
Catholic Mutual Group
The Equitable Life Assurance Society of the United States
Forum Insurance Company
Grange Mutual Insurance Company
Hartford Specialty Risk Services, Inc.
Imperial Casualty and Indemnity Company
Kentucky All Lines Fund
Kentucky Municipal Risk Management Association
Life of the South Service Company
Meridian Mutual Insurance Company
National Casualty Company
Ohio Casualty Group
Phoenix Life Insurance Company
Providence Washington Insurance Company
Reliance Insurance Group

KENTUCKY

Adams, Stepner, Woltermann & Dusing, P.L.L.C., Covington, KY (Continued)

Scottsdale Insurance Company
State Automobile Mutual Insurance Company
Summit Risk Services, Inc.
Tennessee Farmers Mutual Insurance Company
Vernon Fire & Casualty Insurance Company
Sentry Insurance a Mutual Company
Statesman Insurance Company
Sun Life Assurance Company of Canada
Underwriters Safety and Claims
Western and Southern Life Insurance Company

Non-Insurance Clients

Alternative Service Concepts, LLC
Moore Group, Inc.
Tenco Services, Inc.
Monumental Agency Group, Inc.
Sears, Roebuck and Co.

Members of the Firm

Donald L. Stepner — 1939 — Wentworth Institute of Technology, A.A., 1958; Kentucky Wesleyan College, B.A., 1963; University of Kentucky, J.D., 1966 — Admitted to Bar, 1966, Kentucky; 1993, Ohio; 1966, U.S. District Court, Eastern District of Kentucky; 1966, U.S. Court of Appeals, Sixth Circuit; 1971, U.S. Supreme Court — Member American Bar Association; Kentucky Bar Association (Board of Governors, 1990-1996; Vice President, 1997-1998; President-Elect, 1998-1999; President, 1999-2000); Northern Kentucky, Ohio, Cincinnati and Kenton County (President, 1973) Bar Associations; Kentucky Defense Counsel Association; Kentucky Bar Foundation; Defense Research Institute; Fellow, American College of Trial Lawyers — City Attorney, City of Union, 1978; Kentucky Delegate, House of Representatives, American Bar Association; Lecturer, Kentucky Bar Association, Northern Kentucky University, Continuing Legal Education — Practice Areas: Construction Law; Product Liability; Business Law; Litigation; Malpractice

Jeffrey C. Mando — 1959 — Thomas More College, B.A., 1980; Northern Kentucky University, Salmon P. Chase College of Law, J.D., 1983 — Admitted to Bar, 1983, Kentucky; 1990, Ohio; 1983, U.S. District Court, Eastern District of Kentucky; 1986, U.S. Court of Appeals, Sixth Circuit; 1998, U.S. Supreme Court — Member American Bar Association (Tort and Insurance Practice Section); Ohio State, Kentucky and Northern Kentucky (Board of Directors, 1988-1990) Bar Associations; Defense Research Institute

Stacey L. Graus — 1965 — Northern Kentucky University, B.A., 1988; University of Kentucky, J.D. (with distinction), 1991 — Admitted to Bar, 1991, Kentucky; 1992, Ohio; 1992, U.S. District Court, Eastern District of Kentucky; 1993, U.S. Court of Appeals, Sixth Circuit; 2000, U.S. District Court, Southern District of Ohio — Member American Bar Association; Kentucky Bar Association (House of Delegates, 2000-2005); Northern Kentucky and Cincinnati Bar Associations — Lecturer-Continuing Legal Education (Workers' Compensation; Ethics; Personal Injury; Subrogation) — Tel: 859-394-6200 — Fax: 859-392-7253 — E-mail: sgraus@aswdlaw.com

Mary Ann Stewart — 1963 — Thomas More College, B.A. (magna cum laude), 1985; University of Cincinnati College of Law, J.D., 1988 — Phi Alpha Delta — Admitted to Bar, 1988, Kentucky; 1989, Ohio; 1988, U.S. District Court, Eastern District of Kentucky; 1989, U.S. District Court, Southern District of Ohio; 1991, U.S. Court of Appeals, Sixth Circuit — Member Kentucky Bar Association (House of Delegates, 1994-2000); Northern Kentucky Bar Association (Board of Directors, 1995-1999); Cincinnati Bar Association — Practice Areas: School Law; Civil Rights; Litigation; Municipal Law; Personal Injury; Public Entities; State and Federal Courts

Scott M. Guenther — 1967 — University of Kentucky, B.B.A., 1989; University of Kentucky College of Law, J.D., 1993 — Admitted to Bar, 1993, Kentucky; 1997, U.S. District Court, Eastern District of Kentucky; 1998, U.S. Court of Appeals, Sixth Circuit — Member Kentucky, Northern Kentucky and Cincinnati Bar Associations; American Trial Lawyers Association — Practice Areas: Construction Litigation; Defense Litigation; Personal Injury; Workers' Compensation

Jeffrey Adam Stepner — 1972 — Miami University, B.A., 1994; University of Kentucky College of Law, J.D., 1997 — Admitted to Bar, 1997, Ohio; 1998, Kentucky; 1997, U.S. District Court, Southern District of Ohio; 1998, U.S. District Court, Eastern District of Kentucky; 1998, U.S. Court of Appeals, Sixth Circuit — Member Kentucky, Northern Kentucky and Cincinnati Bar Associations — Practice Areas: Defense Litigation; Insurance Defense; Personal Injury; Contracts

Jason C. Kuhlman — 1976 — University of Kentucky, B.A. (summa cum laude), 1998; University of Kentucky College of Law, J.D. (cum laude), 2001 — Admitted to Bar, 2001, Ohio; 2002, Kentucky; 2002, U.S. District Court, Eastern District of Kentucky — Member American, Ohio State, Kentucky, Northern Kentucky and Cincinnati Bar Associations — Practice Areas: Commercial Litigation; Employment Law; Insurance Defense

Adams, Stepner, Woltermann & Dusing, P.L.L.C., Covington, KY (Continued)

Gerald F. Dusing — 1949 — Thomas More College, B.A., 1971; University of Kentucky College of Law, J.D., 1974 — Admitted to Bar, 1974, Kentucky; 1974, U.S. District Court, Eastern District of Kentucky; 1974, U.S. Court of Appeals, Sixth Circuit; 1986, U.S. Supreme Court — Practice Areas: Litigation; Commercial Law; Personal Injury; Administrative Law; Trial and Appellate Practice

Daniel E. Linneman — 1975 — Ohio University, B.A. (cum laude), 1999; University of Cincinnati College of Law, J.D. (with honors), 2004 — Admitted to Bar, 2004, Ohio; 2006, U.S. District Court, Southern District of Ohio — Member Northern Kentucky, Ohio State and Cincinnati Bar Associations — Practice Areas: Commercial Litigation; Malpractice; Insurance Defense

Matthew T. Lockaby — 1977 — Centre College of Kentucky, B.A., 2000; Salmon P. Chase College of Law, J.D. (cum laude), 2006 — Admitted to Bar, 2006, Ohio; 2007, U.S. District Court, Southern District of Florida; U.S. District Court, Eastern and Western Districts of Kentucky; U.S. Court of Appeals, Sixth Circuit — Member American, Ohio State and Cincinnati Bar Associations — Practice Areas: Municipal Law; Governmental Liability; Civil Rights; School Law; Appellate Practice

---

The following firms also service this area.

Coleman Lochmiller & Bond
2907 Ring Road
Elizabethtown, Kentucky 42701
Telephone: 270-737-0600
Fax: 270-737-0488
Mailing Address: P.O. Box 1177, Elizabethtown, KY 42702-1177

Insurance Defense, Automobile, Commercial Law, Product Liability, Professional Liability, Property and Casualty, Medical Malpractice, Litigation, General

SEE COMPLETE LISTING UNDER ELIZABETHTOWN, KENTUCKY (140 MILES)

DIXON † 786 Webster Co.

Refer To

Franklin, Gordon & Hobgood
24 Court Street
Madisonville, Kentucky 42431
Telephone: 270-821-7252
Fax: 270-821-2360
Mailing Address: P.O. Box 547, Madisonville, KY 42431

Insurance Defense, Litigation, Professional Liability, Product Liability, Medical Malpractice, Civil Rights, General Liability

SEE COMPLETE LISTING UNDER MADISONVILLE, KENTUCKY (20 MILES)

EDMONTON † 1,595 Metcalfe Co.

Refer To

Kerrick Bachert PSC
1025 State Street
Bowling Green, Kentucky 42101
Telephone: 270-782-8160
Fax: 270-782-5856
Mailing Address: P.O. Box 9547, Bowling Green, KY 42102-9547

Product Liability, Malpractice, Automobile, Workers' Compensation, Accident and Health, General Liability, Subrogation, Commercial Law, Intellectual Property, Copyright and Trademark Law, Health Care, Employment Law, Real Estate, Insurance Defense

SEE COMPLETE LISTING UNDER BOWLING GREEN, KENTUCKY (49 MILES)

ELIZABETHTOWN † 28,531 Hardin Co.

Coleman Lochmiller & Bond
2907 Ring Road
Elizabethtown, Kentucky 42701
Telephone: 270-737-0600
Fax: 270-737-0488
E-Mail: clb@clblegal.com
http://clblegal.com

FORT MITCHELL   KENTUCKY

Coleman Lochmiller & Bond, Elizabethtown, KY
(Continued)

Established: 1988

Insurance Defense, Automobile, Commercial Law, Product Liability, Professional Liability, Property and Casualty, Medical Malpractice, Litigation, General

Firm Profile: Coleman Lochmiller & Bond is a full service litigation firm established in 1988. Since its founding, the firm has served the entire state of Kentucky, both at the trial court and appellate court level. The vast majority of its clients are major insurance carriers, self-insured groups, and self-insured companies. As such, the firm handles a wide range of insurance litigation including claims related to automobile accidents, bad faith, products liability, premises liability, municipal liability, state and federal discrimination, fidelity and surety, medical and legal malpractice, contracts, and insurance coverage disputes.

Insurance Clients

American National Property and Casualty Company
Gallagher Bassett Services, Inc.
The Hartford Insurance Group
Lawyers Mutual Insurance Company of Kentucky
SECURA Insurance Companies
State Auto Insurance Company
Universal Underwriters Insurance Company
Auto-Owners Insurance Company
Fireman's Fund Insurance Company
Kentucky Farm Bureau Mutual Insurance Company
Rice Insurance Services Company, LLC
United Services Automobile Association (State Counsel)

Non-Insurance Clients

CFS Insurance Management Services
Kentucky Association of Counties
Kentucky Association of Counties All Lines Fund

Partners

Reford H. Coleman — 1938 — University of Kentucky, B.S., 1960; J.D., 1963 — Admitted to Bar, 1963, Kentucky; 1974, U.S. Supreme Court; 1981, U.S. District Court, Western District of Kentucky; 1986, U.S. Court of Appeals, Sixth Circuit; 1996, U.S. District Court, Eastern District of Kentucky — Member Kentucky and Hardin County (President, 1974-1975) Bar Associations; Kentucky Bar Foundation (Board of Directors, 1988-1992); Kentucky Defense Counsel (Secretary-Treasurer and Board of Directors, 1980-1983); Fellow, American College of Trial Lawyers; Defense Research Institute — Special Justice, Kentucky Supreme Court, 1998

Beth A. Lochmiller — 1968 — Bucknell University, B.S., 1990; University of Pittsburgh, J.D., 1994 — Admitted to Bar, 1994, Kentucky; 1995, Pennsylvania; 1999, U.S. District Court, Western District of Kentucky; 2000, U.S. District Court, Eastern District of Kentucky; U.S. Court of Appeals, Sixth Circuit; U.S. Supreme Court; Supreme Court of Kentucky — Member Kentucky and Hardin County Bar Associations; Kentucky Defense Counsel (Board Member, 2008-2011; Mass Tort Litigation Committee, 2007-2010) — Practice Areas: Insurance Litigation

R. Keith Bond — 1954 — University of Louisville, B.S., 1975; J.D., 1978 — Admitted to Bar, 1979, Kentucky; U.S. District Court, Western District of Kentucky; U.S. Court of Appeals, Sixth Circuit; 2007, U.S. District Court, Eastern District of Kentucky — Member Kentucky and Hardin County Bar Associations; Kentucky Defense Counsel; Defense Research Institute

Eric A. Hamilton — 1974 — University of Kentucky, B.A., 1997; Salmon P. Chase College of Law, J.D., 2000 — Northern Kentucky Law Review — Admitted to Bar, 2000, Kentucky; 2001, U.S. District Court, Western District of Kentucky; 2005, U.S. District Court, Eastern District of Kentucky; U.S. Court of Appeals, Sixth Circuit; 2006, U.S. Supreme Court — Member Kentucky and Hardin County Bar Associations; Kentucky Defense Counsel — Practice Areas: Insurance Litigation

Associate

Brandon T. Lally — 1985 — Centre College, B.A./B.A., 2007; University of Kentucky, J.D., 2011 — Admitted to Bar, 2011, Kentucky — Member American and Kentucky Bar Associations; American Association for Justice; Kentucky Defense Counsel

Kerrick Bachert PSC

2413 Ring Road, Suite 117
Elizabethtown, Kentucky 42701
Telephone: 270-737-9088
Fax: 270-769-2905
E-Mail: thulsey@kerrickfirm.com
www.kerrickbachertlaw.com

(Bowling Green, KY Office*: 1025 State Street, 42101, P.O. Box 9547, 42102-9547)
  (Tel: 270-782-8160)
  (Fax: 270-782-5856)
  (E-Mail: Kerrickbachertlaw@kerricklaw.com)

Product Liability, Malpractice, Automobile, Workers' Compensation, Accident and Health, General Liability, Subrogation, Commercial Law, Intellectual Property, Copyright and Trademark Law, Health Care, Employment Law, Insurance Law, Real Estate, Banking Law

Firm Profile: Kerrick Stivers Coyle, PLLC has a general practice of law with its foundation and strength in litigation. Over the years, the firm has handled cases in state courts across Kentucky and in federal courts represented a roster of distinguished and diverse clients. Kerrick Stivers Coyle, PLLC strives to provide quality legal services on a cost-efficient basis. Our best asset is the quality of our lawyers, who have strong academic credentials, work hard and prepare well. Our attorneys are involved in various civic affairs and professional associations and are participants and lecturers in continuing legal education seminars.

(See listing under Bowling Green, KY for additional information)

(This firm is also listed in the Subrogation section of this directory)

FLORENCE 29,951 Boone Co.

Adams, Stepner, Woltermann & Dusing, P.L.L.C.

8100 Burlington Pike, Suite 342
Florence, Kentucky 41042
Telephone: 859-371-7276
Fax: 859-371-7370

(Covington, KY Office*: 40 West Pike Street, 41011, P.O. Box 861, 41012-0861)
  (Tel: 859-394-6200)
  (Fax: 859-291-7902, 859-392-7200)

Carrier Defense, Admiralty and Maritime Law, Automobile, Medical Malpractice, General Liability, Product Liability, Workers' Compensation, Surety, Life and Health, Accident, Litigation, Appellate Practice, Civil Rights, Employment Law, Condemnation, Eminent Domain

(See listing under Covington, KY for additional information)

FORT MITCHELL 8,207 Kenton Co.

Freund, Freeze & Arnold, A Legal Professional Association

Chamber Office Park
2400 Chamber Center Drive, Suite 200
Ft Mitchell, Kentucky 41017
Telephone: 859-292-2088
Toll Free: 877-FFA-1LAW
E-Mail: ffalawky@ffalaw.com
www.ffalawky.com

KENTUCKY   FRANKFORT

Freund, Freeze & Arnold, A Legal Professional Association, Fort Mitchell, KY (Continued)

Established: 1984

Product Liability, Professional Malpractice, Life and Health, Automobile, Bodily Injury, Errors and Omissions, Property Damage, Bad Faith, Insurance Coverage

FRANKFORT † 25,527 Franklin Co.

McBrayer, McGinnis, Leslie & Kirkland, PLLC

300 Whitaker Bank Building
305 Ann Street
Frankfort, Kentucky 40602-1100
  Telephone: 502-223-1200
  Fax: 502-227-7385
  E-Mail: kirkland@mmlklaw.com
  www.mmlklaw.com

(Greenup, KY Office: Main and Harrison Streets, P.O. Box 280, 41144-0280)
  (Tel: 606-473-7303)
  (Fax: 606-473-9003)
(Louisville, KY Office: 9300 Shelbyville Road, Suite 210, 40222)
  (Tel: 502-327-5400)
  (Fax: 502-327-5444)
(Lexington, KY Office: 201 East Main Street, Suite 900, 40507)
  (Tel: 859-231-8780)
  (Fax: 859-231-6518)

Established: 1963

Insurance Law, Personal Injury, Casualty Defense, Subrogation, Investigation and Adjustment, Administrative Law, General Litigation

Firm Profile: Founded in 1963 by W. Terry McBrayer in Greenup, Kentucky, McBrayer, McGinnis, Leslie and Kirkland has grown to a full-service firm with a state-wide and regional practice. The firm has 55 attorneys with offices in Greenup, Lexington, Frankfort and Louisville, Kentucky. The Frankfort office opened in the early 1980's. The firm has a very broad range of clientele, including Fortune 500 companies and national financial institutions, together with local businesses throughout Kentucky. Although the experience of each office is diverse, the Frankfort office practices extensively in the areas of insurance defense, administrative law and creditors' rights. The Frankfort office also has a full-time Governmental Relations department to effectively represent the interests of clients before the General Assembly and state agencies. The firm is Kentucky's exclusive representative in the State Capital Law Firm Group, a consortium of fifty law firms, each with an office in its state capital. Member firms of the State Capital Law Firm Group practice independently and not in a relationship for the joint practice of law.

Insurance Clients

Alfa Vision Insurance Corp.
American Family Insurance Company
American Specialty Insurance Company
Atlantic American Corp.
Clarendon National Insurance Company
Globe American Casualty Company
GoAmerica Auto Insurance
Grocers Insurance Company
Home Insurance Company
Kemper Insurance Companies
Lincoln National Health & Casualty Insurance Company
American Bankers Life Assurance Company of Florida
American Republic Insurance Company
American United Life Insurance Company
CNA Insurance Company
Equity Insurance Company
Globe Life and Accident Insurance Company
Great West Casualty Company
Hamilton Mutual Insurance Company
Kentucky National Insurance Company
Lloyd's

McBrayer, McGinnis, Leslie & Kirkland, PLLC, Frankfort, KY (Continued)

Madison Mutual Insurance Company
Phoenix Life and Annuity Company
Republic Insurance Company
Republic Western Insurance Company
Sentry Insurance Group
United American Insurance Company
MetLife Auto & Home Group
Midwest Family Mutual Insurance Company
Reliance Standard Life Insurance Company
Safeway Insurance Company of Alabama
21st Century Insurance Company
Western Surety Company

Non-Insurance Clients

Baine Clark Company, Inc.
Ernst and Young, LLP
Green Tree Servicing, LLC
Trailer Marketing, Inc.
Vanderbilt Mortgage and Finance, Inc.
Branch Banking and Trust Company
Kenvirons, Inc.
21st Mortgage Corporation
Varsity Spirit Corporation

Firm Members

Watson Clay — (1908-1985)

W. Terry McBrayer — 1937 — Morehead State University, B.S., 1959; University of Louisville, LL.B., 1962 — Admitted to Bar, 1962, Kentucky — Member American, Kentucky, Fayette County and Greenup County Bar Associations — Kentucky House of Representatives, 1966-1975; Speaker, Pro Tem, 1968-1969; Majority Leader, 1970-1971 — Practice Areas: Insurance Defense; Litigation

William D. Kirkland — 1942 — Centre College of Kentucky, B.A., 1964; Vanderbilt University, J.D., 1967 — Admitted to Bar, 1967, Kentucky; 1969, U.S. District Court, Eastern District of Kentucky; 1970, U.S. Court of Appeals, Sixth Circuit; 1976, U.S. District Court, Western District of Kentucky; 1979, U.S. Supreme Court — Member American, Kentucky and Franklin County Bar Associations; Sixth Circuit Judicial Conference (Life Member); Kentucky Board of Elections (2002-2010); Kentucky Defense Counsel; Defense Research Institute; American Board of Trial Advocates — Attorney for Commonwealth of Kentucky, 1967-1970; Assistant U.S. Attorney, 1970-1976 — Practice Areas: Insurance Defense; Litigation

Kembra Sexton Taylor — 1956 — Centre College of Kentucky, B.A., 1978; University of Kentucky, J.D., 1981 — Omicron Delta Kappa; Phi Alpha Theta — Admitted to Bar, 1981, Kentucky; 1985, U.S. District Court, Eastern and Western Districts of Kentucky; 1992, U.S. Court of Appeals, Sixth Circuit — Member American, Kentucky and Franklin County Bar Associations — Retired, General Counsel, Kentucky Labor Cabinet — Languages: German — Practice Areas: Administrative Law; Appellate Practice

Associates

G. Michael Cain, II — 1971 — Morehead State University, B.B.A. (magna cum laude), 1993; University of Dayton, J.D., 1997 — Admitted to Bar, 1998, Kentucky; 2004, U.S. District Court, Eastern and Western Districts of Kentucky — Member American, Kentucky and Franklin County Bar Associations — Practice Areas: Litigation; Insurance Defense; Commercial Law

Zachary A. Horn — 1982 — Transylvania University, B.A. (cum laude), 2008; University of Kentucky, J.D., 2011 — Admitted to Bar, 2011, Kentucky; 2012, U.S. District Court, Eastern District of Kentucky; U.S. Bankruptcy Court, Eastern District of Kentucky — Member Kentucky Bar Association — Languages: German — Practice Areas: Creditor's Rights; Banking; Litigation; Insurance Defense; Bankruptcy

(This firm is also listed in the Investigation and Adjustment, Regulatory and Compliance section of this directory)

FRANKLIN † 8,408 Simpson Co.

Refer To

Kerrick Bachert PSC

1025 State Street
Bowling Green, Kentucky 42101
  Telephone: 270-782-8160
  Fax: 270-782-5856

Mailing Address: P.O. Box 9547, Bowling Green, KY 42102-9547

Product Liability, Malpractice, Automobile, Workers' Compensation, Accident and Health, General Liability, Subrogation, Commercial Law, Intellectual Property, Copyright and Trademark Law, Health Care, Employment Law, Real Estate, Insurance Defense

SEE COMPLETE LISTING UNDER BOWLING GREEN, KENTUCKY (21 MILES)

GLASGOW † 14,028 Barren Co.
Refer To
Kerrick Bachert PSC
1025 State Street
Bowling Green, Kentucky 42101
Telephone: 270-782-8160
Fax: 270-782-5856

Mailing Address: P.O. Box 9547, Bowling Green, KY 42102-9547

Product Liability, Malpractice, Automobile, Workers' Compensation, Accident and Health, General Liability, Subrogation, Commercial Law, Intellectual Property, Copyright and Trademark Law, Health Care, Employment Law, Real Estate, Insurance Defense

SEE COMPLETE LISTING UNDER BOWLING GREEN, KENTUCKY (32 MILES)

GREENSBURG † 2,163 Green Co.
Refer To
Kerrick Bachert PSC
2413 Ring Road, Suite 117
Elizabethtown, Kentucky 42701
Telephone: 270-737-9088
Fax: 270-769-2905

Product Liability, Malpractice, Automobile, Workers' Compensation, Accident and Health, General Liability, Subrogation, Commercial Law, Intellectual Property, Copyright and Trademark Law, Health Care, Employment Law, Insurance Law, Real Estate, Banking Law

SEE COMPLETE LISTING UNDER ELIZABETHTOWN, KENTUCKY (82 MILES)

GREENUP † 1,188 Greenup Co.
Refer To
Jenkins Fenstermaker, PLLC
325 8th Street
Huntington, West Virginia 25701
Telephone: 304-523-2100
Fax: 304-523-2347, 304-523-9279
Toll Free: 800-982-3476

Mailing Address: P.O. Box 2688, Huntington, WV 25726

Civil Litigation, State and Federal Courts, Mediation, Arbitration, Trial Practice, Appellate Practice, Commercial Litigation, Personal Injury, Product Liability, Medical Malpractice, Professional Malpractice, Toxic Torts, Construction Litigation, Insurance Defense, Insurance Coverage, ERISA, Workers' Compensation, Employment Law, Administrative Law, Labor and Employment Law, Automobile Warranty, Labor Negotiations, Counseling, Warranty Litigation

SEE COMPLETE LISTING UNDER HUNTINGTON, WEST VIRGINIA (25 MILES)

GREENVILLE † 4,312 Muhlenberg Co.
Refer To
Franklin, Gordon & Hobgood
24 Court Street
Madisonville, Kentucky 42431
Telephone: 270-821-7252
Fax: 270-821-2360

Mailing Address: P.O. Box 547, Madisonville, KY 42431

Insurance Defense, Litigation, Professional Liability, Product Liability, Medical Malpractice, Civil Rights, General Liability

SEE COMPLETE LISTING UNDER MADISONVILLE, KENTUCKY (28 MILES)

Refer To
Al Miller
Attorney at Law
428 North Second Street
Central City, Kentucky 42330-1124
Telephone: 270-754-5502
Fax: 270-754-5503

Insurance Defense, Automobile Liability, Property Damage, Fire, Trial Practice, Appellate Practice, Investigations, Slip and Fall, Wrongful Death, Bad Faith, Liquor Liability, Legal Malpractice, Medical Malpractice, Coverage Issues, State and Federal Courts, Unfair Claims Practices

SEE COMPLETE LISTING UNDER CENTRAL CITY, KENTUCKY (7 MILES)

HARDINSBURG † 2,343 Breckinridge Co.
Refer To
Coleman Lochmiller & Bond
2907 Ring Road
Elizabethtown, Kentucky 42701
Telephone: 270-737-0600
Fax: 270-737-0488

Mailing Address: P.O. Box 1177, Elizabethtown, KY 42702-1177

Insurance Defense, Automobile, Commercial Law, Product Liability, Professional Liability, Property and Casualty, Medical Malpractice, Litigation, General

SEE COMPLETE LISTING UNDER ELIZABETHTOWN, KENTUCKY (55 MILES)

Refer To
Kerrick Bachert PSC
2413 Ring Road, Suite 117
Elizabethtown, Kentucky 42701
Telephone: 270-737-9088
Fax: 270-769-2905

Product Liability, Malpractice, Automobile, Workers' Compensation, Accident and Health, General Liability, Subrogation, Commercial Law, Intellectual Property, Copyright and Trademark Law, Health Care, Employment Law, Insurance Law, Real Estate, Banking Law

SEE COMPLETE LISTING UNDER ELIZABETHTOWN, KENTUCKY (55 MILES)

HARLAN † 1,745 Harlan Co.
Refer To
Taylor, Keller & Oswald, PLLC
1306 West 5th Street, Suite 100
London, Kentucky 40741
Telephone: 606-878-8844
Fax: 606-878-8850

Mailing Address: P.O. Box 3440, London, KY 40743-3440

Trial Practice, Automobile Liability, Property, Insurance Coverage, Product Liability, Premises Liability, Subrogation, Insurance Fraud, Bad Faith, Governmental Liability, General Insurance and Corporate Defense

SEE COMPLETE LISTING UNDER LONDON, KENTUCKY (75 MILES)

HARTFORD † 2,672 Ohio Co.
Refer To
Kerrick Bachert PSC
1025 State Street
Bowling Green, Kentucky 42101
Telephone: 270-782-8160
Fax: 270-782-5856

Mailing Address: P.O. Box 9547, Bowling Green, KY 42102-9547

Product Liability, Malpractice, Automobile, Workers' Compensation, Accident and Health, General Liability, Subrogation, Commercial Law, Intellectual Property, Copyright and Trademark Law, Health Care, Employment Law, Real Estate, Insurance Defense

SEE COMPLETE LISTING UNDER BOWLING GREEN, KENTUCKY (45 MILES)

Refer To
Al Miller
Attorney at Law
428 North Second Street
Central City, Kentucky 42330-1124
Telephone: 270-754-5502
Fax: 270-754-5503

Insurance Defense, Automobile Liability, Property Damage, Fire, Trial Practice, Appellate Practice, Investigations, Slip and Fall, Wrongful Death, Bad Faith, Liquor Liability, Legal Malpractice, Medical Malpractice, Coverage Issues, State and Federal Courts, Unfair Claims Practices

SEE COMPLETE LISTING UNDER CENTRAL CITY, KENTUCKY (30 MILES)

KENTUCKY

HAZARD † 4,456 Perry Co.

Barret, Haynes, May & Carter P.S.C.
113 Lovern Street
Hazard, Kentucky 41701
   Telephone: 606-436-2165
   Fax: 606-439-1450

Insurance Law, Civil Litigation, Workers' Compensation, Environmental Law, Product Liability

Firm Profile: Since the firm was founded, it has been dedicated to servicing the people of Eastern Kentucky, and surrounding areas, primarily in the field of civil defense work. Based in Hazard, Kentucky, the firm extends quality legal services to all of Eastern Kentucky. The firm specializes in the areas of general civil practice, insurance, products liability, environmental law, utility law and employment law. The firm is committed to providing quality, cost-efficient representation reflecting the highest standards of diligence and integrity. All members have extensive trial experience.

Insurance Clients

AIG Technical Services, Inc.
Bituminous Insurance Companies
Commercial Union Insurance Company
GAINSCO, Inc.
Great American Insurance Company
Heritage Insurance Company
Kentucky Central Insurance Company
Nationwide Insurance
Nobel Insurance Company
Penn-America Insurance Company
Ranger Insurance Company
St. Paul Insurance Company
Transport Insurance Company
Underwriters at Lloyd's, London
Underwriters Safety and Claims
Western Surety Company
Zurich American Insurance Group
American Hardware Mutual Insurance Company
ESIS
Federated Insurance Company
GEICO General Insurance Company
Guaranty National Group
Home Insurance Company
Legion Insurance Company
Motorists Mutual Insurance Company
Old Republic Insurance Company
Prestige Claims
St. Paul Fire and Marine Group
Shelter Insurance Companies
Travelers Property Casualty Corporation
Wausau Insurance Companies
Willis Administrative Services Corporation

Non-Insurance Clients

A.K.P. Coal Company
Bledsoe Coal Corporation
Blue Diamond Mining Company
East Kentucky Beverage Company
Equitable Resources, Inc.
Kentucky Power Company
Miller Brothers Coal Company
Appalachian Regional Manufacturing
Cardinal Chevrolet Cadillac Geo, Inc.
KACO Claims
Kycoga Company
Perry County Coal Corporation

Firm Members

Maxwell P. Barret — (1918-1988)

Hoover Haynes — **(Emeritus)** — (Retired)

Randall Scott May — 1950 — University of Kentucky, B.A.; Northern Kentucky University, Salmon P. Chase College of Law, J.D., 1978 — Northern Kentucky Law Review and Co-author of a Comment — Admitted to Bar, 1978, Kentucky; U.S. District Court, Eastern District of Kentucky — Member Kentucky Bar Association (Board of Governors, 1989-1991 and 1993-1999; Chair, Rules Committee); Perry County Bar Association; Board of Directors, Kentucky Defense Counsel (1990-1992); Fellow, American College of Trial Lawyers; International Association of Defense Counsel — Supreme Court of Kentucky Civil Rules Committee

Ralph D. Carter — 1949 — Eastern Kentucky University, B.S., 1972; Northern Kentucky University, Salmon P. Chase College of Law, J.D. — Admitted to Bar, 1978, Kentucky — Member Kentucky and Perry County Bar Associations

---

The following firms also service this area.

Taylor, Keller & Oswald, PLLC
1306 West 5th Street, Suite 100
London, Kentucky 40741
   Telephone: 606-878-8844
   Fax: 606-878-8850

Mailing Address: P.O. Box 3440, London, KY 40743-3440

Trial Practice, Automobile Liability, Property, Insurance Coverage, Product Liability, Premises Liability, Subrogation, Insurance Fraud, Bad Faith, Governmental Liability, General Insurance and Corporate Defense

SEE COMPLETE LISTING UNDER LONDON, KENTUCKY (59 MILES)

HENDERSON † 28,757 Henderson Co.

King, Deep & Branaman
127 North Main Street
Henderson, Kentucky 42420
   Telephone: 270-827-1852
   Fax: 270-826-7729
   E-Mail: kdb@kdblaw.com

Insurance Defense, Product Liability, Malpractice, Workers' Compensation, Bad Faith, Coverage

Insurance Clients

Allstate Insurance Company
Indiana Insurance Company
Nationwide Insurance
State Auto Insurance Company
Chubb Insurance Company
Liberty Mutual Insurance Company
Progressive Insurance Company

Non-Insurance Clients

Methodist Hospital
Old National Bank

Partners

Harry L. Mathison, Jr. — University of Notre Dame, B.A. (cum laude), 1974; University of Kentucky, J.D., 1976 — Admitted to Bar, 1977, Kentucky; 1989, Indiana

W. Mitchell Deep — Western Kentucky University, B.A. (cum laude), 1976; Louis D. Brandeis School of Law, University of Louisville, J.D., 1979 — Admitted to Bar, 1979, Kentucky — Member Kentucky Defense Counsel

H. Randall Redding — University of Kentucky, B.S., 1979; J.D., 1982 — Admitted to Bar, 1982, Kentucky — Member Kentucky Defense Counsel

Associates

Leslie M. Newman
Eric Shappell
C. Donald Thompson, Jr.
Jennifer Anderson

The following firms also service this area.

Kahn, Dees, Donovan & Kahn, LLP
501 Main Street, Suite 305
Evansville, Indiana 47708
   Telephone: 812-423-3183
   Fax: 812-423-3841

Mailing Address: P.O. Box 3646, Evansville, IN 47735-3646

Asbestos Litigation, Automobile, Construction Law, Coverage Issues, Environmental Law, Insurance Defense, General Liability, Labor and Employment, Mass Tort, Medical Malpractice, Personal Injury, Premises Liability, Product Liability, Property, Public Entities, Self-Insured, Subrogation, Workers' Compensation

SEE COMPLETE LISTING UNDER EVANSVILLE, INDIANA (11 MILES)

LEXINGTON   KENTUCKY

Refer To
Al Miller
Attorney at Law
428 North Second Street
Central City, Kentucky 42330-1124
   Telephone: 270-754-5502
   Fax: 270-754-5503

Insurance Defense, Automobile Liability, Property Damage, Fire, Trial Practice, Appellate Practice, Investigations, Slip and Fall, Wrongful Death, Bad Faith, Liquor Liability, Legal Malpractice, Medical Malpractice, Coverage Issues, State and Federal Courts, Unfair Claims Practices

SEE COMPLETE LISTING UNDER CENTRAL CITY, KENTUCKY (67 MILES)

HODGENVILLE † 3,206 Larue Co.

Refer To
Coleman Lochmiller & Bond
2907 Ring Road
Elizabethtown, Kentucky 42701
   Telephone: 270-737-0600
   Fax: 270-737-0488

Mailing Address: P.O. Box 1177, Elizabethtown, KY 42702-1177

Insurance Defense, Automobile, Commercial Law, Product Liability, Professional Liability, Property and Casualty, Medical Malpractice, Litigation, General

SEE COMPLETE LISTING UNDER ELIZABETHTOWN, KENTUCKY (12 MILES)

Refer To
Kerrick Bachert PSC
2413 Ring Road, Suite 117
Elizabethtown, Kentucky 42701
   Telephone: 270-737-9088
   Fax: 270-769-2905

Product Liability, Malpractice, Automobile, Workers' Compensation, Accident and Health, General Liability, Subrogation, Commercial Law, Intellectual Property, Copyright and Trademark Law, Health Care, Employment Law, Insurance Law, Real Estate, Banking Law

SEE COMPLETE LISTING UNDER ELIZABETHTOWN, KENTUCKY (11 MILES)

HOPKINSVILLE † 31,577 Christian Co.

Refer To
Franklin, Gordon & Hobgood
24 Court Street
Madisonville, Kentucky 42431
   Telephone: 270-821-7252
   Fax: 270-821-2360

Mailing Address: P.O. Box 547, Madisonville, KY 42431

Insurance Defense, Litigation, Professional Liability, Product Liability, Medical Malpractice, Civil Rights, General Liability

SEE COMPLETE LISTING UNDER MADISONVILLE, KENTUCKY (40 MILES)

Refer To
Kerrick Bachert PSC
1025 State Street
Bowling Green, Kentucky 42101
   Telephone: 270-782-8160
   Fax: 270-782-5856

Mailing Address: P.O. Box 9547, Bowling Green, KY 42102-9547

Product Liability, Malpractice, Automobile, Workers' Compensation, Accident and Health, General Liability, Subrogation, Commercial Law, Intellectual Property, Copyright and Trademark Law, Health Care, Employment Law, Real Estate, Insurance Defense

SEE COMPLETE LISTING UNDER BOWLING GREEN, KENTUCKY (60 MILES)

Refer To
King, Deep & Branaman
127 North Main Street
Henderson, Kentucky 42420
   Telephone: 270-827-1852
   Fax: 270-826-7729

Mailing Address: P.O. Box 43, Henderson, KY 42419-0043

Insurance Defense, Product Liability, Malpractice, Workers' Compensation, Bad Faith, Coverage

SEE COMPLETE LISTING UNDER HENDERSON, KENTUCKY (73 MILES)

Refer To
Al Miller
Attorney at Law
428 North Second Street
Central City, Kentucky 42330-1124
   Telephone: 270-754-5502
   Fax: 270-754-5503

Insurance Defense, Automobile Liability, Property Damage, Fire, Trial Practice, Appellate Practice, Investigations, Slip and Fall, Wrongful Death, Bad Faith, Liquor Liability, Legal Malpractice, Medical Malpractice, Coverage Issues, State and Federal Courts, Unfair Claims Practices

SEE COMPLETE LISTING UNDER CENTRAL CITY, KENTUCKY (48 MILES)

LEBANON † 5,539 Marion Co.

Refer To
Kerrick Bachert PSC
2413 Ring Road, Suite 117
Elizabethtown, Kentucky 42701
   Telephone: 270-737-9088
   Fax: 270-769-2905

Product Liability, Malpractice, Automobile, Workers' Compensation, Accident and Health, General Liability, Subrogation, Commercial Law, Intellectual Property, Copyright and Trademark Law, Health Care, Employment Law, Insurance Law, Real Estate, Banking Law

SEE COMPLETE LISTING UNDER ELIZABETHTOWN, KENTUCKY (51 MILES)

LEITCHFIELD † 6,699 Grayson Co.

Refer To
Coleman Lochmiller & Bond
2907 Ring Road
Elizabethtown, Kentucky 42701
   Telephone: 270-737-0600
   Fax: 270-737-0488

Mailing Address: P.O. Box 1177, Elizabethtown, KY 42702-1177

Insurance Defense, Automobile, Commercial Law, Product Liability, Professional Liability, Property and Casualty, Medical Malpractice, Litigation, General

SEE COMPLETE LISTING UNDER ELIZABETHTOWN, KENTUCKY (32 MILES)

Refer To
Kerrick Bachert PSC
2413 Ring Road, Suite 117
Elizabethtown, Kentucky 42701
   Telephone: 270-737-9088
   Fax: 270-769-2905

Product Liability, Malpractice, Automobile, Workers' Compensation, Accident and Health, General Liability, Subrogation, Commercial Law, Intellectual Property, Copyright and Trademark Law, Health Care, Employment Law, Insurance Law, Real Estate, Banking Law

SEE COMPLETE LISTING UNDER ELIZABETHTOWN, KENTUCKY (32 MILES)

LEXINGTON † 225,366 Fayette Co.

Allen, Kopet & Associates, PLLC
301 East Main Street, Suite 400
Lexington, Kentucky 40507
   Telephone: 859-281-1301
   Fax: 859-281-1210

(See listing under Chattanooga, TN for additional information)

Boehl Stopher & Graves, LLP
444 West Second Street
Lexington, Kentucky 40507
   Telephone: 859-252-6721
   Fax: 859-253-1445
   www.bsg-law.com

KENTUCKY   LEXINGTON

Boehl Stopher & Graves, LLP, Lexington, KY (Continued)

(Louisville, KY Office*: 400 West Market Street, Suite 2300, 40202-3354)
  (Tel: 502-589-5980)
  (Fax: 502-561-9400)
  (E-Mail: louisville@bsg-law.com)
(New Albany, IN Office: Elsby East, 400 Pearl Street, Suite 204, 47150)
  (Tel: 812-948-5053)
(Paducah, KY Office*: 410 Broadway Street, 42001)
  (Tel: 270-442-4369)
  (Fax: 270-442-4689)
(Pikeville, KY Office*: 137 Main Street, Suite 2, 41501, P.O. Box 1132, 41502)
  (Tel: 606-432-9670)

Insurance Litigation, Casualty, Surety, Workers' Compensation, Product Liability, Medical Malpractice, Professional Malpractice

Insurance Clients

Amerisure Companies	Argonaut Insurance Company
Associated Aviation Underwriters	Bituminous Casualty Corporation
CIGNA Property and Casualty Insurance Company	CNA Insurance Company
	Continental Insurance Company
Great American Insurance Company	Gulf Insurance Company
	Hartford Insurance Company
McLarens Toplis North America, Inc.	Monroe Guaranty Insurance Company
Old Republic Insurance Company	Prudential Property and Casualty Insurance Company
Reserve Life Insurance Company	
St. Paul Fire and Marine Insurance Company	United States Aviation Underwriters, Inc.
Utica Mutual Insurance Company	Zurich American Insurance Company

(See listing under Louisville, KY for additional information)

Bowles Rice LLP

333 West Vine Street, Suite 1700
Lexington, Kentucky 40507
  Telephone: 859-252-2202
  Fax: 859-259-2927

Insurance Defense, Product Liability, Construction Litigation, Employment Law (Management Side), Extra-Contractual Litigation, Real Estate

Partners

J. Stan Lee	Spencer D. Noe
Donald M. Wakefield	Timothy C. Wills

(See listing under Charleston, WV for additional information)

Dinsmore & Shohl LLP

Lexington Financial Center
250 West Main Street
Lexington, Kentucky 40507
  Telephone: 859-425-1000
  Fax: 859-425-1099
  www.dinsmore.com

(Cincinnati, OH Office*: 255 East Fifth Street, 45202)
  (Tel: 513-977-8200)
  (Fax: 513-977-8141)
(Chicago, IL Office*: 227 West Monroe Street, Suite 3850, 60606)
  (Tel: 312-372-6060)
  (Fax: 312-372-6085)

Agent/Broker Liability, Bad Faith, Insurance Coverage, Insurance Defense, Insurance Litigation, Trial and Appellate Practice

Dinsmore & Shohl LLP, Lexington, KY (Continued)
Partner

Mindy G. Barfield — 1963 — Transylvania University, B.A., 1985; The George Washington University, M.A., 1988; University of Kentucky, J.D., 1993 — Admitted to Bar, 1993, Kentucky; U.S. District Court, Eastern and Western Districts of Kentucky; U.S. Court of Appeals, Sixth Circuit — Member Kentucky and Fayette County Bar Assocations — Tel: 859-425-1025 — E-mail: barfield@dinsmore.com

(See listing under Cincinnati, OH for additional information)

Fowler Bell PLLC

300 West Vine Street, Suite 600
Lexington, Kentucky 40507-1751
  Telephone: 859-252-6700
  Fax: 859-255-3735
  www.FowlerLaw.com

Established: 1959

Insurance Defense, Personal Injury, Professional Liability, Product Liability, Property and Casualty, Subrogation, Trial and Appellate Practice, Uninsured and Underinsured Motorist, Environmental Law, Coverage Issues, Architects and Engineers, Arson, Automobile, Bad Faith, Business Law, Carrier Defense, Commercial Litigation, School Law

Insurers and Clients

American Family Mutual Insurance Company	American International Group, Inc.
	Auto-Owners Insurance Company
Burlington/First Financial Insurance Company	CNA Insurance Company
	Encompass Insurance Company
Fireman's Fund Insurance Company	GMAC Insurance
	Kentucky Farm Bureau Mutual Insurance Company
Lawyers Mutual Insurance Company of Kentucky	Nationwide Life Insurance Company
Nautilus Insurance Company	
Prudential Insurance Company of America	State Automobile Mutual Insurance Company

Members

Guy R. Colson — 1947 — Eastern Kentucky University, B.A., 1970; University of Kentucky College of Law, J.D., 1974 — Admitted to Bar, 1974, Kentucky; U.S. District Court, Eastern and Western Districts of Kentucky; U.S. Court of Appeals, Sixth Circuit; U.S. Supreme Court — Member Fayette County Bar Association (Board of Governors, 1980-1982); Kentucky Defense Counsel (Board, 1993-1997; President, 1998-1999); Kentucky Counsel of School Board Attorneys; Kentucky Character and Fitness Committee (Associate Member, 1985-1986); Defense Research Institute — Martindale Hubbell, AV Preeminent Rated, 2014; Kentucky Super Lawyers 2007-Present; Fayette County Bar Association Citizen Lawyer Award, 2009 — Practice Areas: School Law; Insurance Coverage & Defense; Legal Malpractice; Insurance Agent Errors & Omissions; Bad Faith — E-mail: GColson@FowlerLaw.com

Barry M. Miller — 1959 — Eastern Kentucky University, B.A., 1981; University of Kentucky College of Law, J.D., 1988 — Admitted to Bar, 1988, Kentucky; U.S. District Court, Eastern and Western Districts of Kentucky; U.S. Court of Appeals, Sixth Circuit — Member Fayette County Bar Association; National Society of Professional Insurance Investigators; Primerus Coverage and Bad Faith Committee; Defense Research Institute — Martindale Hubbell, AV Preeminent Rated, 2014; Kentucky Super Lawyer, 2013 — Practice Areas: Bad Faith; Insurance Coverage & Defense; Fraud; Arson — E-mail: BMiller@FowlerLaw.com

Casey C. Stansbury — 1974 — Louisiana State University, B.A., 1998; Ohio Northern University, Pettit College of Law, J.D., 2001 — Admitted to Bar, 2001, Kentucky; U.S. District Court, Eastern and Western Districts of Kentucky; U.S. Court of Appeals, Sixth Circuit — Member Fayette County Bar Association; The Claims and Litigation Management Alliance; Kentucky Defense Counsel (President Elect, 2013-2014); Defense Research Institute (Civil Rights and Governmental Liability Program Chair, 2014) — Kentucky Rising Stars, 2013 — Practice Areas: Agent and Brokers Errors and Omissions; Coverage Issues; Civil Rights; Governmental Liability; Insurance Coverage & Defense — E-mail: CStansbury@FowlerLaw.com

Fowler Bell PLLC, Lexington, KY (Continued)

Matthew D. Ellison — 1978 — University of Kentucky, B.A., 2000; University of Kentucky College of Law, J.D., 2005 — Admitted to Bar, 2005, Kentucky; U.S. District Court, Eastern and Western Districts of Kentucky; U.S. Bankruptcy Court, Eastern District of Kentucky — Member Fayette County Bar Association (Young Lawyers Section) — Practice Areas: Employment Law; Workers' Compensation; Insurance Coverage & Defense; Bankruptcy; Alternative Dispute Resolution — E-mail: MEllison@FowlerLaw.com

Associates

Christina L. Vessels — 1978 — Western Kentucky University, B.A., 2001; University of Kentucky College of Law, J.D., 2004 — Admitted to Bar, 2004, Kentucky; U.S. District Court, Eastern and Western Districts of Kentucky; U.S. Court of Appeals, Sixth Circuit — Member Fayette County Bar Association (Young Lawyers Section and Women's Law Association); Defense Research Institute; Kentucky Defense Counsel — Kentucky Rising Stars, 2013 — Practice Areas: Bad Faith; Insurance Coverage & Defense; Governmental Liability; Civil Rights; Insurance Agent Errors & Omissions; School Law — E-mail: CVessels@FowlerLaw.com

Christopher G. Colson — 1984 — Transylvania University, B.A., 2006; University of Kentucky College of Law, J.D., 2009 — Admitted to Bar, 2009, Kentucky; U.S. District Court, Eastern and Western Districts of Kentucky; U.S. Bankruptcy Court, Eastern District of Kentucky; U.S. Court of Appeals, Sixth Circuit — Member Fayette County Bar Association (Board of Governors, 2014) — Practice Areas: Bankruptcy; Commercial Litigation; Insurance Coverage & Defense; Subrogation — E-mail: CGColson@FowlerLaw.com

Tia J. Combs — 1986 — Thomas More College, B.A., 2008; University of Kentucky College of Law, J.D., 2011 — Kentucky Law Journal — Admitted to Bar, 2011, Kentucky; U.S. District Court, Eastern and Western Districts of Kentucky; U.S. Court of Appeals, Sixth Circuit — Member Fayette County Bar Association (Young Lawyers Section and Women's Law Association); Kentucky Defense Counsel (Young Lawyers' Committee, 2013-2014); Defense Research Institute — Practice Areas: Insurance Coverage & Defense; Insurance Agent Errors & Omissions; Bad Faith; School Law; Insurance Fraud; Subrogation — E-mail: TCombs@FowlerLaw.com

Laura E. Salzman — 1986 — Northern Kentucky University, B.A., 2009; University of Kentucky College of Law, J.D., 2012 — Admitted to Bar, 2012, Kentucky; U.S. District Court, Eastern and Western Districts of Kentucky; U.S. Court of Appeals, Sixth Circuit — Member Fayette County (Young Lawyers Section and Women's Law Association) and Louisville Bar Associations; Defense Research Institute (Young Lawyers Section Marketing Sub-Committee Member); Kentucky Defense Counsel — Practice Areas: Insurance Defense; Civil Litigation; Subrogation; Employment Law; Medical Malpractice — E-mail: LSalzman@FowlerLaw.com

Curt M. Graham — 1986 — University of Kentucky, B.A., 2008; University of Kentucky College of Law, J.D., 2012 — Admitted to Bar, 2012, Colorado (Inactive); Kentucky; U.S. District Court, Eastern and Western Districts of Kentucky; U.S. Court of Appeals, Sixth Circuit — Member Fayette County Bar Association (Young Lawyers' Section) — Practice Areas: Insurance Coverage & Defense; Subrogation; Civil Rights; Governmental Liability; Collections — E-mail: CGraham@FowlerLaw.com

Of Counsel

Robert C. Welleford — 1966 — University of Kentucky, B.S.B.E., Economics, 1988; University of Kentucky College of Law, J.D., 1991 — Admitted to Bar, 1991, Kentucky; U.S. District Court, Eastern and Western Districts of Kentucky — Member Fayette County Bar Association; Kentucky Defense Counsel — Practice Areas: Medical Malpractice; Civil Litigation; Insurance Defense — E-mail: RWelleford@FowlerLaw.com

Golden and Walters, PLLC

771 Corporate Drive, Suite 905
Lexington, Kentucky 40503
Telephone: 859-219-9090
Toll Free: 877-221-4299
Fax: 859-219-9292
E-Mail: regina@goldenandwalters.com
www.goldenandwalters.com

Insurance Defense, Civil Rights, School Law, Construction Law, Employment Law, Workers' Compensation, Product Liability, Class Actions

Golden and Walters, PLLC, Lexington, KY (Continued)

Firm Profile: After years of successful litigation, our legal team understands the complexities of trial preparation and the dynamics of courtroom communication. We focus on all aspects of litigation, including discovery, motion practice, alternative dispute resolution and trial.

Insurance Clients

Alfa Vision Insurance Corp.
Nationwide Insurance
Westfield Insurance Company
Motorists Mutual Insurance Company

Firm Members

John W. Walters — Transylvania University, B.A. (cum laude), 1990; University of Kentucky, M.B.A. (with distinction), 1995; University of Kentucky College of Law, J.D. (magna cum laude), 1995 — Admitted to Bar, 1995, Kentucky; U.S. District Court, Eastern and Western Districts of Kentucky; U.S. Court of Appeals, Fourth and Sixth Circuits; 2007, Supreme Court of Kentucky — Member Kentucky and Fayette County Bar Associations — E-mail: john@goldenandwalters.com

Green Chesnut & Hughes PLLC

201 East Main Street, Suite 1250
Lexington, Kentucky 40507
Telephone: 859-475-1471
Fax: 859-455-3332
E-Mail: rgreen@gcandh.com
www.gcandh.com

Established: 2010

Professional Liability, Medical Malpractice, Product Liability, Employment Law, General Liability, Bad Faith, Personal Injury, Automobile Liability, Truck Liability, Governmental Liability, Appellate Practice, Family Law, Aviation Liability Defense, Insurance Coverage Analysis and Litigation

Firm Profile: Green Chesnut & Hughes PLLC is a civil litigation and insurance defense firm. The three named principals have a combined 84 years experience representing businesses, professionals, insurance companies and those who are insured in personal injury, professional liability, employment and civil rights cases. We offer large firm experience with small firm personal service, which we believe to be the best of both worlds. The firm supports and is a member of the Insurance Institute of Kentucky.

Insurance Clients

Acuity Insurance Company
Amerisure Insurance Company
Cincinnati Insurance Company
Gateway Insurance Company
Monitor Liability Managers, Inc.
Selective Insurance Company
United States Aircraft Insurance Group
Admiral Insurance Company
Bituminous Casualty Corporation
Fireman's Fund Insurance Company
Riverport Insurance Company
Swiss Re

Non-Insurance Clients

Delta Air Lines, Inc.
Kaz, Inc
Mereworth Farm, LLC, The Susan S. Donaldson Foundation, Inc.
84 Lumber Company
Mary Breckinridge Hospital
Res-Care, Inc.

Firm Members

Ronald L. Green — 1955 — Murray State University, B.S. (cum laude), 1978; University of Kentucky, J.D., 1980 — International Moot Court — Kentucky Law Journal — Admitted to Bar, 1981, Kentucky; 1985, U.S. District Court, Eastern and Western Districts of Kentucky; U.S. Court of Appeals, Fifth and Sixth Circuits; 1986, U.S. Supreme Court — Member Kentucky and Fayette County Bar Associations; Claims and Litigation Management Alliance; National Association of Forensic Economics; Professional Liability Defense Federation; Kentucky Executive Branch Ethics Commission (2007-2011); Defense Research Institute; Kentucky Defense Counsel — Special Justice, Kentucky Supreme Court (2006) — Practice Areas: Aviation; Professional Liability; Product Liability; Bad Faith — E-mail: rgreen@gcandh.com

Pamela Adams Chesnut — 1959 — University of Kentucky, B.A. (Phi Beta Kappa), 1980; University of Kentucky College of Law, J.D., 1984 —

Green Chesnut & Hughes PLLC, Lexington, KY
(Continued)

Admitted to Bar, 1984, Kentucky; 1986, U.S. District Court, Eastern District of Kentucky; U.S. Court of Appeals, Sixth Circuit; 1996, U.S. District Court, Western District of Kentucky — Member Kentucky and Fayette County Bar Associations; Claims and Litigation Management Alliance; Professional Liability Defense Federation; Kentucky Defense Counsel; Defense Research Institute — Practice Areas: Coverage Analysis; Coverage Litigation; Medical Malpractice; Construction Liability; Automobile Liability; Truck Liability; Governmental Liability; Civil Rights; Bad Faith; Product Liability — E-mail: pchesnut@gcandh.com

Elizabeth S. Hughes — 1966 — Vanderbilt University, B.A. (magna cum laude), 1988; University of Kentucky College of Law, J.D. (with distinction), 1991 — Associate Editor, Kentucky Law Journal — Admitted to Bar, 1991, Kentucky; U.S. District Court, Eastern and Western Districts of Kentucky; 1993, U.S. Court of Appeals, Sixth Circuit — Member Kentucky (Board of Bar Examiners, 2002-2009) and Fayette County (Director, 1998-2006, President, 2004-2005) Bar Associations; Life Fellow, Kentucky Bar Foundation; Founding Fellow, Fayette County Bar Foundation; Litigation Council of America; Fellow, American Bar Foundation; Defense Research Institute — Practice Areas: Employment Law; Civil Rights; Civil Litigation; Criminal Defense; Family Law — E-mail: ehughes@gcandh.com

Nora A. Koffman — University of Kentucky, B.B.A. (magna cum laude), 1998; The University of Tennessee, J.D. (cum laude), 2001 — University of Tennessee Moot Court Board; Constitutional Law Moot Court Team — Admitted to Bar, 2001, Kentucky; 2002, U.S. District Court, Eastern and Western Districts of Kentucky; 2014, U.S. Court of Appeals, Sixth Circuit — Member Kentucky and Fayette County Bar Associations; Claims and Litigation Management Alliance; Central Kentucky American Inn of Court — AV Martindale Rating; Super Lawyers Rising Star, 2014, 2015 — Practice Areas: Insurance Defense; Employment Law; Civil Litigation; Family Law — E-mail: nkoffman@gcandh.com

James M. Inman — 1977 — Centre College, B.S., 2000; University of Kentucky College of Law, J.D., 2008 — Judicial Law Clerk to the Honorable Joseph M. Hood, U.S. District Court for Eastern District of Kentucky (2008-2009) — Articles Editor, Kentucky Law Journal — Admitted to Bar, 2008, Kentucky; 2009, U.S. District Court, Eastern and Western Districts of Kentucky; U.S. Court of Appeals, Sixth Circuit — Member Kentucky and Fayette County Bar Associations; Kentucky Defense Counsel; Defense Research Institute — Captain, U.S. Army (2000-2004) — Practice Areas: Insurance Defense; Employment Law; Public Entities; Civil Rights; Automobile Liability; Premises Liability — E-mail: jinman@gcandh.com

Kriz, Jenkins, Prewitt & Jones, P.S.C.

200 West Vine Street, Suite 710
Lexington, Kentucky 40507-1620
Telephone: 859-255-6885
Fax: 859-253-9709
www.kjpjlaw.com

Insurance Defense, Personal Injury, Automobile, Bad Faith, General Liability, Product Liability, Property Damage, Workers' Compensation, Medical Malpractice, Civil Rights, Employment Law, Environmental Law

Firm Profile: The law firm of Kriz, Jenkins, Prewitt & Jones, P.S.C. provides its clients with high quality, cost effective, results oriented legal services. The focus of our practice is litigation and from our central location in Lexington, the heart of Bluegrass country, we represent clients in state and federal courts and administrative tribunals throughout the Commonwealth of Kentucky. We are small enough to offer individualized service to our clients, yet large enough to handle the most complex legal matters. We invite you to learn more about our attorneys and our areas of practice.

Insurance Clients

AIG Personal Lines Claims	American States Insurance Company
Bituminous Insurance Companies	General Reinsurance Corporation
General Casualty Companies	Great West Casualty Company
Georgia Casualty & Surety Company	Indiana Insurance Company

Kriz, Jenkins, Prewitt & Jones, P.S.C., Lexington, KY
(Continued)

Liberty Mutual Insurance Company	Lumbermen's Underwriting Alliance
Motorists Mutual Insurance Company	Northbrook Property and Casualty Insurance Company
State Farm Mutual Automobile Insurance Company	Wausau General Insurance Company
Westfield Companies	

Non-Insurance Clients

American Specialty Claims Service	Blackmoor Group, Inc.
Broadspire	Corporate Services, Inc.
Crawford & Company	Cunningham Lindsey Claims Management, Inc.
DHL Worldwide Express	
Gallagher Bassett Services, Inc.	Kentucky Employers Safety Association/KESA
Lexington-Fayette Urban County Government	Thomas Howell Group
University of Kentucky Chandler Medical Center	

Firm Members

Barbara A. Kriz — 1959 — University of Kentucky, B.A., 1981; J.D., 1984 — Phi Beta Kappa — Admitted to Bar, 1984, Illinois; 1985, Kentucky; 1986, U.S. District Court, Eastern District of Kentucky; 1986, U.S. Court of Appeals, Sixth Circuit; 2000, U.S. District Court, Western District of Kentucky — Member American, Kentucky and Fayette County Bar Associations; Kentucky Trial Lawyers Association; Association of Trial Lawyers of America

Christopher R. Jenkins — 1961 — Indiana University, B.A., 1983; University of Kentucky, J.D., 1988 — Admitted to Bar, 1988, Kentucky; 1989, U.S. District Court, Eastern District of Kentucky; 1990, U.S. Court of Appeals, Sixth Circuit; 1994, U.S. District Court, Western District of Kentucky — Member American, Kentucky and Fayette County Bar Associations; American Immigration Lawyers Association

H. Caywood Prewitt, Jr. — 1962 — University of Kentucky, B.A., 1986; M.A., 1989; J.D., 1993 — Admitted to Bar, 1993, Kentucky; 1993, U.S. District Court, Eastern and Western Districts of Kentucky — Member American, Kentucky and Fayette County Bar Associations

David C. Jones — 1959 — Georgetown College, B.A. (cum laude), 1983; University of Louisville, J.D., 1988 — Admitted to Bar, 1988, Kentucky; 1989, U.S. District Court, Western District of Kentucky; 1993, U.S. District Court, Eastern District of Kentucky — Member American, Kentucky, Fayette County and Louisville Bar Associations; Kentucky Academy of Trial Attorneys

Associates

Christopher S. Turner — 1976 — Hanover College, B.A., 1998; University of Kentucky College of Law, J.D., 2001 — Admitted to Bar, 2001, Kentucky; 2002, U.S. District Court, Eastern District of Kentucky

Megan Smyth Horne — 1983 — Transylvania University, B.A., 2005; University of Kentucky College of Law, J.D., 2008 — Best Oral Argument, First Year Legal Writing Club — Admitted to Bar, 2008, Kentucky — Member Kentucky and Fayette County Bar Associations

Landrum & Shouse LLP

106 West Vine Street, Suite 800
Lexington, Kentucky 40507
Telephone: 859-255-2424
Fax: 859-233-0308
www.landrumshouse.com

(Louisville, KY Office*: 220 West Main Street, Suite 1900, 40202)
 (Tel: 502-589-7616)
 (Fax: 502-589-2119)

Established: 1986

LEXINGTON   KENTUCKY

Landrum & Shouse LLP, Lexington, KY   (Continued)

General Civil Practice, Trial and Appellate Practice, Alternative Dispute Resolution, Fire, Casualty, Life Insurance, Employment Law, Product Liability, Medical Malpractice, Workers' Compensation, Environmental Law, Railroad Law, Aviation, Administrative Law, Employee Benefits, ERISA, Municipal Law, Bad Faith, Insurance Defense, Business Law, Criminal Defense, Education Law, Employment Defense, Estate Planning, Product Liability Defense, Trucking Industry Defense, Workers' Compensation Subrogation, Wills, Family Law Mediation, Legal Liability, Taxation

Insurance Clients

Cincinnati Insurance Company
Great American Insurance Company
National Indemnity Company
Ohio Casualty Group
Safeco Insurance Companies
Scottsdale Insurance Company
Wausau Insurance Companies
Crawford & Company
Indiana Insurance Company
Liberty Mutual
Northland Insurance Company
Penn-America Insurance Company
Safeco Select Markets
State Farm Insurance Companies

Non-Insurance Clients

Illinois Central Gulf Railroad Company
Schneider National, Inc.

Founders

Charles Landrum, Jr. — (1917-1990)
Weldon Shouse — (1915-2004)

Resident Partners

William C. Shouse — 1948 — Louis D. Brandeis School of Law, University of Louisville, J.D., 1978 — Admitted to Bar, 1973, Kentucky — Member Kentucky and Fayette County Bar Associations

Pierce W. Hamblin — 1951 — University of Kentucky, J.D., 1977 — Admitted to Bar, 1977, Kentucky — Member American, Kentucky and Fayette County Bar Associations; Kentucky Academy of Trial Lawyers; Kentucky Defense Attorneys Association — Certified Mediator

Mark L. Moseley — 1949 — University of Kentucky, J.D., 1974 — Admitted to Bar, 1974, Kentucky — Member American, Kentucky and Fayette County Bar Associations; National Association of Railroad Trial Counsel

Leslie Patterson Vose — 1953 — University of Kentucky, J.D., 1978 — Admitted to Bar, 1978, Kentucky — Member American, Kentucky and Fayette County Bar Associations — Certified Civil Trial Specialist, National Board of Trial Advocacy (1991-Present)

Larry C. Deener — 1950 — Salmon P. Chase College of Law, J.D., 1979 — Admitted to Bar, 1979, Kentucky — Member American, Kentucky and Fayette County Bar Associations; National Association of Railroad Trial Counsel

Mark J. Hinkel — 1957 — University of Kentucky, J.D., 1983 — Admitted to Bar, 1983, Kentucky — Member American, Kentucky and Fayette County Bar Associations

John G. McNeill — 1958 — University of Kentucky, J.D., 1982 — Admitted to Bar, 1982, Kentucky — Member American, Kentucky and Fayette County Bar Associations

Douglas L. Hoots — 1961 — University of Kentucky, J.D., 1985 — Admitted to Bar, 1985, Kentucky — Member American, Kentucky and Fayette County Bar Associations; Kentucky Academy of Trial Attorneys — Chartered Property and Casualty Underwriters

Daniel E. Murner — 1963 — University of Kentucky, J.D., 1988 — Admitted to Bar, 1988, Kentucky — Member American, Kentucky and Fayette County Bar Associations

Estill D. Banks II — 1962 — Thomas M. Cooley Law School, J.D., 1991 — Admitted to Bar, 1991, Kentucky — Member Kentucky and Fayette County Bar Associations

Bradley C. Hooks — 1970 — University of Kentucky, J.D., 1997 — Admitted to Bar, 1998, Kentucky — Member Kentucky and Fayette County Bar Associations

Jeffrey A. Taylor — 1969 — The John Marshall Law School, J.D., 1996 — Admitted to Bar, 1996, Kentucky — Member American, Kentucky and Fayette County Bar Associations

Michael E. Hammond — 1975 — University of Kentucky, J.D., 2000 — Admitted to Bar, 2000, Kentucky — Member American, Kentucky and Fayette County Bar Associations; Trucking Industry Defense Association

Landrum & Shouse LLP, Lexington, KY   (Continued)

Evan B. Jones — 1970 — University of Kentucky, J.D., 1997 — Admitted to Bar, 1998, Kentucky — Member Kentucky Bar Association

Elizabeth A. Deener — 1979 — University of Kentucky, J.D., 2004 — Admitted to Bar, 2004, Kentucky; U.S. District Court, Eastern and Western Districts of Kentucky; U.S. Court of Appeals, Fourth and Sixth Circuits; U.S. Patent and Trademark Office — Member American and Kentucky Bar Associations; American Intellectual Property Law Association

Resident Associates

Bennett E. Bayer — 1953 — University of Kentucky, J.D., 1982 — Admitted to Bar, 1982, Kentucky — Member American, Kentucky and Fayette County Bar Associations

Erin C. Sammons — 1978 — University of Kentucky College of Law, J.D., 2005 — Admitted to Bar, 2005, Kentucky — Member American, Kentucky and Fayette County Bar Associations

Elizabeth J. Winchell — 1981 — University of Kentucky College of Law, J.D., 2007 — Admitted to Bar, 2007, Kentucky — Member Kentucky and Fayette County Bar Associations

Kyle W. Ray — 1980 — University of Kentucky College of Law, J.D., 2007 — Admitted to Bar, 2007, Kentucky — Member Kentucky and Fayette County Bar Associations

J. Lacey Fiorella — 1980 — University of Kentucky, J.D., 2007 — Admitted to Bar, 2007, Kentucky; 2008, U.S. District Court, Eastern and Western Districts of Kentucky — Member Kentucky and Fayette County Bar Associations

Hilary M. Jarvis — 1983 — University of Kentucky College of Law, J.D., 2008 — Admitted to Bar, 2008, Kentucky — Member Kentucky and Fayette County Bar Associations

Todd G. Allen — 1984 — University of Kentucky College of Law, J.D., 2010 — Admitted to Bar, 2010, Georgia; 2011, Kentucky — Member Kentucky and Fayette County Bar Associations

Carson W. Smith — 1982 — University of Dayton School of Law, J.D., 2008 — Admitted to Bar, 2009, Kentucky — Member Kentucky and Fayette County Bar Associations

David G. Noble — 1985 — University of Kentucky College of Law, J.D., 2012 — Admitted to Bar, 2012, Kentucky — Member American, Kentucky and Fayette County Bar Associations

Gregory M. Funfsinn — 1980 — Chicago-Kent College of Law, J.D., 2007 — Admitted to Bar, 2008, Illinois; 2012, Kentucky — Member Kentucky and Fayette County Bar Associations

Gregory A. Jackson — 1988 — University of Kentucky College of Law, J.D., 2014 — Admitted to Bar, 2014, Kentucky — Member Kentucky and Fayette County Bar Associations

Of Counsel

Thomas M. Cooper — 1939 — University of Kentucky, J.D., 1974 — Admitted to Bar, 1974, Kentucky — Member American, Kentucky and Fayette County Bar Associations

John H. Burrus — 1944 — (Retired)

(See Louisville, KY Listing for additional information)
(Revisors of the Kentucky Insurance Law Digest for this Publication)

McBrayer, McGinnis, Leslie & Kirkland, PLLC

201 East Main Street, Suite 900
Lexington, Kentucky 40507
  Telephone: 859-231-8780
  Fax: 859-231-6518
  E-Mail: mhall@mmlk.com
  www.mmlk.com

(Frankfort, KY Office: 300 Whitaker Bank Building, 40602, P.O. Box 1100, 40602-1100)
  (Tel: 502-223-1200)
  (Fax: 502-227-7385)

KENTUCKY   LEXINGTON

McBrayer, McGinnis, Leslie & Kirkland, PLLC,
Lexington, KY   **(Continued)**

(Greenup, KY Office: Main and Harrison Streets, 41144, P.O. Box 280, 41144-0280)
  (Tel: 606-473-7303)
  (Fax: 606-473-9003)
(Louisville, KY Office: 9300 Shelbyville Road, Suite 210, 40222)
  (Tel: 502-327-5400)
  (Fax: 502-327-5444)
(Washington, DC Office*: 1341 G Street, N.W., Suite 700, 20005-3131)
  (Tel: 202-730-9531)

Established: 1963

Casualty Defense, Insurance Law, Insurance Defense, Personal Injury, Coverage Analysis, Civil Rights

Firm Profile: Since our foundation in 1963, our firm has successfully handled a wide range of complex legal problems for businesses and professionals. Our clients are consistently impressed with our immediacy in dealing with the substance of their legal problems, not to mention the positive results we provide.

Insurance Clients

Acuity Insurance Company	American Modern Insurance Group, Inc.
Auto-Owners Insurance Company	Everest National Insurance Company
EMC Insurance Company	
FCCI Insurance Group	GuideOne Insurance
Great American Insurance Group	Nationwide Insurance Company of America
Kentucky National Insurance Company	
Old Republic Insurance Company	Safeco Insurance Companies
Travelers Insurance Companies	Zurich North America

Non-Insurance Clients

Kentucky Association of Counties All Lines Fund Trust   Republic Services, Inc.

Members

Stephen G. Amato — 1965 — Transylvania University, B.A., 1987; University of Kentucky College of Law, J.D., 1990 — Admitted to Bar, 1990, Kentucky; 1990, U.S. District Court, Eastern and Western Districts of Kentucky; 1993, U.S. Court of Appeals, Sixth Circuit — Member Amercian, Kentucky and Fayette County Bar Associations; Defense Research Institute (Government Liability Section) — Practice Areas: Litigation; Casualty Defense; Insurance Defense; Insurance Coverage; Employment Law; Mediation; Arbitration; Administrative Law; Estate Planning — E-mail: samato@mmlk.com

Jaron P. Blandford — 1972 — Western Kentucky University, B.A. (magna cum laude), 1995; University of Kentucky College of Law, J.D., 1998 — Admitted to Bar, 1998, Kentucky; 2009, Tennessee; 1998, U.S. District Court, Eastern and Western Districts of Kentucky; 1998, U.S. Court of Appeals, Sixth Circuit; 2007, U.S. Supreme Court — Member Federal, Kentucky and Fayette County Bar Associations; Defense Research Institute — Practice Areas: Insurance Defense; Litigation; Insurance Law; Employment Law; Business Litigation — E-mail: jblandford@mmlk.com

David J. Guarnieri — 1971 — Centre College, B.A., 1993; University of Kentucky College of Law, J.D., 1996 — Admitted to Bar, 1996, Kentucky; 1996, U.S. District Court, Eastern and Western Districts of Kentucky; 1996, U.S. Court of Appeals, Sixth Circuit; 1999, U.S. Supreme Court — Member Federal, American, Kentucky and Franklin Bar Associations; Kentucky Justice Association; Kentucky Academy of Trial Lawyers; National Association of Criminal Defense Lawyers; American Association for Justice — Practice Areas: Insurance Defense; Civil Litigation; Administrative Law; Family Law; Probate — E-mail: dguarnieri@mmlk.com

Robert E. Maclin, III — 1955 — University of Kentucky, B.S., 1977; M.S., 1979; University of Kentucky College of Law, J.D., 1984 — Admitted to Bar, 1984, Kentucky; 2002, Texas; 1985, U.S. District Court, Eastern District of Kentucky; 1988, U.S. Court of Appeals, Sixth Circuit; 1991, U.S. District Court, Western District of Kentucky; 2003, U.S. District Court, Central District of Illinois; 2003, U.S. District Court, Southern District of Texas — Member American, Kentucky and Fayette County (Business Law Section) Bar Associations; State Bar of Texas; Trade Association — Practice Areas: Insurance Defense; Litigation; Coverage Analysis; Insurance Law; Commercial Litigation; Commercial Transactions; Corporate Law; Equine Law — E-mail: remaclin@mmlk.com

McBrayer, McGinnis, Leslie & Kirkland, PLLC,
Lexington, KY   **(Continued)**

Robert T. Watson — 1965 — Transylvania University, B.A., 1987; University of Kentucky College of Law, J.D., 1990 — Admitted to Bar, 1990, Kentucky; 1991, U.S. District Court, Eastern and Western Districts of Kentucky; 1992, U.S. Court of Appeals, Sixth Circuit; 1994, U.S. Supreme Court; 2000, U.S. District Court, Southern District of Indiana; 2000, U.S. Court of Appeals, Seventh Circuit — Member American, Kentucky, Fayette County and Louisville Bar Associations; Defense Research Institute (Governmental Liability Section) — Practice Areas: Insurance Defense; Civil Rights; Municipal Law; Civil Litigation; Real Estate; Corporate Law — Resident Louisville, KY Office — E-mail: rwatson@mmlk.com

Associates

Chris J. Gadansky — 1975 — Bellarmine University, B.A. (cum laude), 1997; Stetson University College of Law, J.D. (cum laude), 2001 — Admitted to Bar, 2002, Kentucky; 2003, U.S. District Court, Eastern and Western Districts of Kentucky; 2003, U.S. Court of Appeals, Sixth Circuit; 2004, U.S. District Court, Southern District of Indiana; 2005, U.S. Supreme Court — Member Kentucky and Louisville Bar Associations; Defense Research Institute — Practice Areas: Insurance Defense; Civil Rights; Municipal Law — Resident Louisville, KY Office — E-mail: cgadansky@mmlk.com

Jason S. Morgan — 1976 — University of Kentucky, B.S. (cum laude), 1998; M.B.A. (cum laude), 2000; Salmon P. Chase College of Law, J.D. (cum laude), 2004 — Admitted to Bar, 2005, Ohio; 2006, Kentucky; 2007, U.S. District Court, Eastern District of Kentucky; U.S. District Court, Southern District of Ohio; U.S. Court of Appeals, Sixth Circuit — Member Kentucky, Northern Kentucky, Ohio, and Cincinnati Bar Associations; Ohio Association of Civil Trial Attorneys — Practice Areas: Business Litigation; Insurance Defense; Construction Law; Real Estate; Criminal Defense; Family Law — E-mail: jmorgan@mmlk.com

Benjamin Riddle — 1977 — Indiana University, B.A., 2000; Indiana University School of Law, J.D., 2003 — Admitted to Bar, 2003, Illinois; 2006, Kentucky; 2003, U.S. District Court, Northern District of Illinois; 2006, U.S. District Court, Eastern and Western Districts of Kentucky — Member Illinois State, Kentucky, Fayette County, Chicago and Louisville Bar Associations; Defense Research Institute — Practice Areas: Insurance Defense; Litigation; Insurance Law; Employment Law — Resident Louisville, KY Office — E-mail: briddle@mmlk.com

Luke A. Wingfield — 1975 — Western Kentucky University, B.A. (summa cum laude), 1997; University of Kentucky College of Law, J.D., 2000 — Admitted to Bar, 2000, Kentucky; 2002, U.S. District Court, Eastern District of Kentucky; 2003, U.S. District Court, Western District of Kentucky; 2008, U.S. Court of Appeals, Sixth Circuit — Member Kentucky and Fayette County Bar Associations — Practice Areas: Insurance Law; Litigation; Employment Law; Administrative Law — E-mail: lwingfield@mmlk.com

Of Counsel

Amy D. Cubbage — 1972 — Georgetown College, B.A. (summa cum laude), 1994; University of Kentucky College of Law, J.D. (summa cum laude), 1997 — Admitted to Bar, 1997, Kentucky; 1997, U.S. District Court, Western District of Kentucky; 1998, U.S. District Court, Eastern District of Kentucky; 1998, U.S. Court of Appeals, Sixth Circuit; 2002, U.S. Court of Appeals, Fourth Circuit; 2006, U.S. Court of Appeals, Ninth Circuit; 2008, U.S. Supreme Court — Member American, Kentucky, and Louisville Bar Associations — Practice Areas: Insurance Defense; Commercial Litigation; Energy; Government Affairs — Resident Louisville, KY Office — E-mail: acubbage@mmlk.com

Robinson and Havens, PSC

101 Prosperous Place, Suite 100
Lexington, Kentucky 40509
Telephone: 859-559-4533
Fax: 859-264-0444
E-Mail: crobinson@robinsonhavens.com
www.robinsonhavens.com

Established: 2008

Insurance Defense, Medical Malpractice, Professional Liability, Hospital Liability Defense

Firm Profile: Robinson and Havens, PSC is a seven lawyer litigation firm in Lexington, Kentucky. Our practice is focused on the defense of physicians,

LEXINGTON KENTUCKY

Robinson and Havens, PSC, Lexington, KY (Continued)

hospitals and health care professionals in all courts, both state and federal, in the Commonwealth of Kentucky. We also defend healthcare professionals before the Kentucky boards of professional licensure.

Insurance Clients

Healthcare Underwriters Group of Kentucky
University of Kentucky Chandler Medical Center
The Medical Protective Company
State Volunteer Mutual Insurance Company

Firm Members

Clayton L. Robinson — 1963 — Kent State University, B.S., 1985; The University of Akron, J.D., 1988 — National and Regional Moot Court (1987-1988) — Admitted to Bar, 1988, Ohio; 1994, Kentucky; U.S. District Court, Eastern and Western Districts of Kentucky; U.S. District Court, Northern District of Ohio; U.S. Court of Appeals, Sixth Circuit; U.S. Supreme Court — Member Kentucky and Fayette County Bar Associations; Kentucky Defense Counsel; Defense Research Institute

Adam W. Havens — 1977 — University of Kentucky, B.B.A., 2000; J.D., 2003 — Admitted to Bar, 2003, Kentucky — Member Kentucky and Fayette County Bar Associations

Shannon M. Naish — 1959 — University of Kentucky, J.D., 1997 — Admitted to Bar, 1997, Kentucky; U.S. District Court, Eastern and Western Districts of Kentucky; U.S. Court of Appeals, Sixth Circuit — Member Kentucky and Fayette County Bar Associations

Barbra S. McGuire — 1977 — University of Kentucky, B.A., 1999; J.D., 2004 — Law Clerk, Judge Thomas Clark, Fayette Circuit Court (2004) — Admitted to Bar, 2004, Kentucky; 2010, Texas; 2005, Supreme Court of Kentucky

Devin M. Hendricks — 1986 — University of Kentucky, B.A., 2008; Salmon P. Chase College of Law, J.D., 2011 — Admitted to Bar, 2011, Kentucky — Member Kentucky and Fayette County Bar Associations

Nicholas W. Edwards — University of Kentucky, B.A., 2008; University of Dayton School of Law, J.D., 2013 — Admitted to Bar, 2013, Kentucky — Member Kentucky and Fayette County Bar Associations

Juliette B. Symons — University of Virginia, B.A., 2009; Vermont Law School, J.D., 2013 — Admitted to Bar, 2013, Kentucky — Member Kentucky and Fayette County Bar Associations

Roland Legal PLLC

P.O. Box 910454
Lexington, Kentucky 40511
Telephone: 859-402-2671
Fax: 859-422-4944
E-Mail: mroland@rolandlegal.com
rolandlegal.com

Established: 2007

Workers' Compensation, General Practice

Firm Profile: Marcus A. Roland has practice experience in multiple areas of the law but has spent the largest part of his career handling workers' compensation claims. Marc has represented workers' compensation clients, appeared before workers' compensation Administrative Law Judges and presented arguments to the Kentucky Workers' Compensation Board, the Kentucky Court of Appeals and the Kentucky Supreme Court in over 1,000 workers' compensation matters.

Representative Clients

CBOCS, Inc.
Collins and Company, Inc.
Lexington-Fayette Urban County Government
Thomas & King
CCMSI
Gallagher Bassett Services, Inc.
Risk Management Services, Inc.
Strategic Comp

Marcus A. Roland — Union College, B.A.; University of Cincinnati, M.A.; University of Kentucky College of Law, J.D. — Admitted to Bar, 1994, Kentucky; 1995, U.S. District Court, Eastern District of Kentucky — Member American Bar Association; Kentucky Bar Association (KBA Workers' Compensation Section); Fayette County Bar Association — Contributing Writer:

Roland Legal PLLC, Lexington, KY (Continued)

"The Complete Guide to Medicare Secondary Payer Compliance," published by LexisNexis — Certified Medicare Set-Aside Consultant (MSCC) by the International Commission on Healthcare Certification (ICHC) — E-mail: mroland@rolandlegal.com

Steptoe & Johnson PLLC

One Paragon Centre
2525 Harrodsburg Road, Suite 300
Lexington, Kentucky 40504
Telephone: 859-255-7080
Fax: 859-255-6903
E-Mail: jeff.phillips@steptoe-johnson.com
www.steptoe-johnson.com

Established: 1913

Professional Malpractice, Toxic Torts, Employment Practices Liability, Commercial Litigation, Insurance First Party/Bad Faith/Coverage/Fraud, General Civil Litigation Defense

Resident Partner

Jeffrey K. Phillips

(See listing under Bridgeport, WV for additional information)

(This firm is also listed in the Investigation and Adjustment section of this directory)

Sturgill, Turner, Barker & Moloney, PLLC

333 West Vine Street, Suite 1400
Lexington, Kentucky 40507
Telephone: 859-255-8581
Fax: 859-231-0851
E-Mail: LParsons@sturgillturner.com
www.sturgillturner.com

Casualty, Automobile, Bad Faith, Extra-Contractual Law, Product Liability, Medical Malpractice, Long-Term Care, Employment, Education Law, Civil Rights, General Insurance and Trial Practice, Insurance Coverage Analysis, Municipality & Public Entity

Firm Profile: Serving Our Clients with Integrity

For almost 60 years, Sturgill Turner has been committed to providing our clients with quality legal services in a timely, efficient and economical manner. Our attention to client service began in April 1957 when Don Sturgill, Roy Moreland and Gardner Turner started practicing law together in Lexington as Sturgill, Moreland & Turner. Their dedication, hard work and integrity created a solid foundation that has allowed us to grow into a premier law firm representing local, regional and national clients. In addition to providing exemplary legal service, we guarantee that we will be prompt, professional and passionate in our representation.

Insurance Clients

Allstate Insurance Company
Encompass Insurance Company
Southern States Insurance Exchange
State Volunteer Mutual Insurance Company
United Educators
EMC Insurance Companies
Kentucky League of Cities
State Farm Automobile Insurance Co.
Travelers Insurance Companies
Trident Insurance Services

Non-Insurance Clients

Dollar General Corporation

Members

Stephen L. Barker — University of Kentucky College of Law, J.D., 1975 — Admitted to Bar, 1975, Kentucky — E-mail: sbarker@sturgillturner.com

Sturgill, Turner, Barker & Moloney, PLLC, Lexington, KY (Continued)

Donald P. Moloney, II — University of Kentucky College of Law, J.D., 1973 — Admitted to Bar, 1973, Kentucky — E-mail: patmoloney@sturgillturner.com

Phillip M. Moloney — University of Kentucky College of Law, J.D., 1982 — Admitted to Bar, 1982, Kentucky — E-mail: pmoloney@sturgillturner.com

Kevin G. Henry — University of Kentucky College of Law, J.D., 1978 — Admitted to Bar, 1978, Kentucky — E-mail: khenry@sturgillturner.com

Ernest H. Jones, II — University of Kentucky College of Law, J.D., 1973 — Admitted to Bar, 1974, Kentucky — E-mail: hjones@sturgillturner.com

E. Douglas Stephan — University of Kentucky College of Law, J.D., 1980 — Admitted to Bar, 1980, Kentucky — E-mail: dstephan@sturgillturner.com

Kevin W. Weaver — University of Kentucky College of Law, J.D., 1994 — Admitted to Bar, 1995, Kentucky — E-mail: kweaver@sturgillturner.com

Charles D. Cole — University of Kentucky College of Law, J.D., 1997 — Admitted to Bar, 1997, Kentucky — E-mail: ccole@sturgillturner.com

Bryan H. Beauman — University of Kentucky College of Law, J.D., 1997 — Admitted to Bar, 1997, Kentucky — E-mail: bbeauman@sturgillturner.com

R. Douglas Martin — University of Kentucky College of Law, J.D., 1989 — Admitted to Bar, 1989, Kentucky — E-mail: dmartin@sturgillturner.com

Andrew D. DeSimone — University of Kentucky College of Law, J.D., 2000 — Admitted to Bar, 2000, Kentucky — E-mail: adesimone@sturgillturner.com

Joshua M. Salsburey — University of Kentucky College of Law, J.D., 2001 — Admitted to Bar, 2001, Kentucky — E-mail: jsalsburey@sturgillturner.com

Of Counsel

Katherine M. Coleman — University of Kentucky College of Law, J.D., 1991 — Admitted to Bar, 1991, Kentucky — E-mail: kcoleman@sturgillturner.com

Associates

Patsey E. Jacobs
Derrick T. Wright
Stephanie M. Wurdock
M. Todd Osterloh
Jamie Wilhite Dittert
Jason P. Woodall

Taylor, Keller & Oswald, PLLC

Hamburg Place Office Park
1795 Alysheba Way, Suite 2201
Lexington, Kentucky 40509
Telephone: 859-543-1613
Fax: 859-543-1654
www.tkolegal.com

(London, KY Office*: 1306 West 5th Street, Suite 100, 40741, P.O. Box 3440, 40743-3440)
(Tel: 606-878-8844)
(Fax: 606-878-8850)

Trial Practice, Automobile Liability, Property, Insurance Coverage, Product Liability, Premises Liability, Subrogation, Insurance Fraud, Bad Faith, Governmental Liability, General Insurance and Corporate Defense

Firm Profile: The firm of Taylor, Keller & Oswald, PLLC, has an extensive civil practice throughout the Commonwealth of Kentucky with an emphasis on all types of insurance and corporate defense, subrogation, insurance fraud and business litigation. The firm strives to provide high-quality legal services to its clients and relies on an excellent legal support staff and the most modern information technology to achieve this goal.

Insurance Clients

AIG
Allstate Insurance Company
American Claims Service
American General Life Insurance Company
American National Property and Casualty Company
Cincinnati Insurance Company
EMC/Hamilton Mutual Insurance Company
Frankenmuth Insurance Company
Atlantic Casualty Insurance Company
American Fellowship Mutual Insurance Company
American Indemnity Group/United Fire Group
Argo Group
Direct General Insurance Company
Encompass Insurance Company
Federated Rural Electric Insurance Exchange
Gallagher Bassett Insurance Services, Inc.
The Hartford Insurance Group
Kentucky Farm Bureau Insurance Companies
McLarens Young International
Motor Transport Underwriters, Inc.
National Claims Management
Northland Insurance Company
Pennsylvania Lumbermens Mutual Insurance Company
Sentry Insurance
State Farm Fire and Casualty Company
Transportation Claims, Inc.
United Services Automobile Association (USAA)
GuideOne Insurance
Hanover Insurance Company
Kemper Auto and Home
Liberty Mutual Insurance Company
Markel Insurance Company
Motorists Insurance Company
Murdock Claim Management Company
Ohio Casualty Insurance Company
Safeco Insurance
St. Paul Insurance Company
State Auto Insurance Company
State Farm Mutual Automobile Insurance Company
Travelers Insurance Companies
Unitrin Direct Insurance Company

Non-Insurance Clients

Appalachian Research and Defense Fund
Kentucky Mountain Housing Development Corp., Inc.
Cooper Industries, Inc.
Jackson Energy Cooperative
Kentucky Propane Plus, LLC
NTA, Inc.

Partners

Boyd F. Taylor — (1924-2012)

J. Warren Keller — 1954 — Rider College, B.A. (with honors), 1976; College of William & Mary, J.D., 1979 — Phi Alpha Delta — Admitted to Bar, 1979, Kentucky; 1984, U.S. Court of Appeals, Sixth Circuit; 1988, U.S. District Court, Eastern and Western Districts of Kentucky; 2003, U.S. Supreme Court — Member American Bar Association (Tort Trial and Insurance Practice Section; Property Insurance Law Committee, Vice-Chair, 1992-1997); Kentucky Bar Association (Board of Governors, 1996-2002); Laurel County Bar Association (President, 1992-1993); National Society of Professional Insurance Investigators (Kentucky Chapter President, 1998-2000; National Board Member, 2000-2001; National President, 2003-2004); Kentucky Bar Foundation (President, 2006-2007); Kentucky Interest on Lawyers Trust Accounts (IOLTA) (Trustee, 2012-2015); Florida Advisory Committee on Arson Prevention; Kentucky Defense Counsel — E-mail: wkeller@tkolegal.com

Clayton O. Oswald — 1976 — Eastern Kentucky University, B.A. (cum laude), 1997; University of Kentucky, J.D. (cum laude), 2004 — Admitted to Bar, 2004, Kentucky; U.S. District Court, Eastern District of Kentucky; 2008, U.S. District Court, Western District of Kentucky; 2009, U.S. Court of Appeals, Sixth Circuit; 2010, U.S. Supreme Court — Member Federal, American, Kentucky and Laurel County Bar Associations; National Society of Professional Insurance Investigators; Bluegrass Claims Association; Electric Cooperative Bar Association; Kentucky Defense Counsel (Board Member, 2014-Present); Defense Research Institute — E-mail: coswald@tkolegal.com

Associates

Bradley S. Harn — 1986 — Eastern Kentucky University, B.A. Political Science (summa cum laude), 2009; University of Kentucky, J.D., 2012 — Admitted to Bar, 2012, Kentucky; U.S. District Court, Eastern and Western Districts of Kentucky — E-mail: bharn@tkolegal.com

Mary Katherine Bing — 1985 — University of Kentucky, B.A. Political Science (magna cum laude), 2008; J.D., 2013 — Former Law Clerk, Kentucky Supreme Court — Special Features Editor, Kentucky Law Journal, Vol. 101 — Admitted to Bar, 2013, Kentucky — Member Kentucky Bar Association (At-Large Respresentative,, Young Lawyers Division) — E-mail: kbing@tkolegal.com

(See listing under London, KY for additional information)

Ward, Hocker & Thornton, PLLC

Bluegrass Corporate Center
333 West Vine Street, Suite 1100
Lexington, Kentucky 40507
Telephone: 859-422-6000
Fax: 859-422-6001
www.whtlaw.com

LEXINGTON   KENTUCKY

Ward, Hocker & Thornton, PLLC, Lexington, KY
(Continued)

(Louisville, KY Office: Hurstbourne Place, 9300 Shelbyville Road, Suite 700, 40222)
(Tel: 502-583-7012)
(Fax: 502-583-7018)

Established: 1984

Appellate Practice, Construction Law, Commercial Litigation, Business Litigation, Extra-Contractual Litigation, Coverage Issues, Fidelity and Surety, Fire, Casualty, Governmental Liability, Insurance Defense, Product Liability, Premises Liability, Trucking Litigation, Transportation, Workers' Compensation, Automobile/Motor Vehicle Litigation, Healthcare Professional Liability, Large Loss Subrogation

Firm Profile: WHT is an "insurance defense" litigation firm that routinely represents individuals, businesses and corporations through their respective insurance policies throughout the state of Kentucky and neighboring states. We also directly represent insurance carriers and self-insured corporations, many of which are Fortune 500 companies. WHT has earned the reputation as having some of the most competent and well-respected lawyers in the region. Our team of 30+ attorneys has tremendous litigation experience and has collectively handled thousands of cases encompassing several different service areas. Our goal is to provide you and your business with result-oriented legal services in an effective, cost-efficient manner.

Insurance Clients

Auto-Owners Insurance Company
Clarendon Insurance Group
Erie Insurance Group
Great American Insurance Company
Progressive Insurance Company
SECURA Insurance Companies
Specialty Risk Services, Inc. (SRS)
Underwriters Safety and Claims
USAA
Chubb Insurance Company
CNA Insurance Company
Grange Mutual Insurance Company
The Hartford Insurance Group
Mitsui Sumitomo Insurance Group
St. Paul Fire and Marine Insurance Company
Travelers Property Casualty Corporation
Zurich American Insurance Group

Non-Insurance Clients

Armstrong Wood Products, Inc.
Barton Brands, Ltd.
Broadspire Services, Inc.
Cracker Barrel Old Country Stores
Flynn Enterprises, Inc.
The Gap, Inc.
Hi-View Construction
Mountain Enterprises, Inc.
Northern Kentucky University
Old Navy, Inc.
Sedgwick CMS
Tractor Supply Co.
Transfreight, Inc.
University of Kentucky
UPS Freight f/k/a Overnite Transportation Co.
ATS Construction
Bizzack, Inc.
Chesterfield Services, Inc.
Dana Corporation
Gallagher Bassett Services, Inc.
Harley-Davidson, Inc.
Houchens Industries/Save-A-Lot
NationsBuilders Insurance Services, Inc.
Sears/KMart
Target Stores, Division of Dayton Hudson Corporation
Tyson Foods, Inc.
University of Kentucky Chandler Medical Center
White Lodging Services

Members

Walter A. Ward — 1948 — Western Kentucky University, B.A., 1970; University of Kentucky College of Law, J.D., 1973 — Omicron Delta Kappa; Delta Sigma Rho; Tau Kappa Alpha; Best Lawyers: 2012 Workers Compensation Law-Employers, Lexington — Admitted to Bar, 1973, Kentucky; 1975, U.S. District Court, Eastern District of Kentucky — Member American, Kentucky and Fayette County Bar Associations — Practice Areas: Workers' Compensation; Insurance Defense; Civil Litigation — E-mail: wward@whtlaw.com

George B. Hocker — 1959 — University of Kentucky, B.S., 1981; University of Kentucky College of Law, J.D., 1985 — Law Clerk to Kentucky Court of Appeals Judge Anthony M. Wilhoit (1985-1986) — Admitted to Bar, 1985, Kentucky; 1994, Ohio; 1986, U.S. District Court, Eastern District of Kentucky; 1988, U.S. District Court, Western District of Kentucky; 1989, U.S. Court of Appeals, Sixth Circuit — Member American, Kentucky and Fayette County Bar Associations; Defense Research Institute; Kentucky Defense Counsel — Practice Areas: Fidelity and Surety; Insurance Defense; Civil Litigation; Product Liability; Construction Law; Municipal Liability — E-mail: ghocker@whtlaw.com

Gregg E. Thornton — 1963 — University of Kentucky, B.S., 1985; Northern Kentucky University, Salmon P. Chase College of Law, J.D., 1988 — Admitted to Bar, 1988, Kentucky; 1993, Ohio; 1988, U.S. District Court, Eastern

Ward, Hocker & Thornton, PLLC, Lexington, KY
(Continued)

and Western Districts of Kentucky; U.S. Court of Appeals, Sixth Circuit; 2009, U.S. Supreme Court — Member Kentucky and Fayette County Bar Associations; Kentucky Academy of Trial Attorneys; Association of Trial Lawyers of America; Kentucky Defense Counsel; Defense Research Institute — Practice Areas: Insurance Defense; Civil Litigation; Municipal Liability; Product Liability; Medical Malpractice — E-mail: gthornton@whtlaw.com

Thomas L. Travis — 1961 — Western Kentucky University, 1981; University of Kentucky, B.A., 1984; University of Kentucky College of Law, J.D., 1987 — Admitted to Bar, 1987, Kentucky; U.S. District Court, Eastern and Western Districts of Kentucky — Member American, Kentucky and Barren County Bar Associations — Practice Areas: Civil Litigation; Insurance Defense — E-mail: ttravis@whtlaw.com

Brian H. Stephenson — 1974 — Birmingham-Southern College, B.S., 1995; University of Kentucky College of Law, J.D., 1998 — Admitted to Bar, 1998, Kentucky; U.S. District Court, Eastern and Western Districts of Kentucky; U.S. Court of Appeals, Sixth Circuit — Member American, Kentucky and Fayette County Bar Associations; Kentucky Academy of Trial Attorneys — Practice Areas: Insurance Defense; Civil Litigation — E-mail: bstephenson@whtlaw.com

Gene F. Zipperle, Jr. — University of Louisville, B.S., 1980; M.S., 1984; Louis D. Brandeis School of Law, University of Louisville, J.D., 1988 — Admitted to Bar, 1988, Kentucky; 1989, Indiana; U.S. District Court, Northern and Southern Districts of Indiana; U.S. District Court, Eastern and Western Districts of Kentucky; 1996, U.S. Court of Appeals, Sixth Circuit; U.S. District Court, Middle District of North Carolina; 2005, U.S. District Court, Middle District of Florida; U.S. Court of Appeals, Fourth Circuit — Member Kentucky, Indiana State and Louisville Bar Associations; Defense Research Institute; Kentucky Defense Counsel; Trucking Industry Defense Association — Practice Areas: Trucking Litigation; Transportation; Insurance Coverage; Fidelity and Surety; Insurance Defense; Automobile; Motor Vehicle — E-mail: gzipperle@whtlaw.com

Licha H. Farah, Jr. — 1969 — University of Kentucky, B.B.A., 1991; University of Kentucky College of Law, J.D., 1994 — Admitted to Bar, 1994, Kentucky; 1996, U.S. District Court, Western District of Kentucky; 1999, U.S. District Court, Eastern District of Kentucky; 2002, U.S. Court of Appeals, Sixth Circuit — Member Kentucky and Fayette County Bar Associations — Practice Areas: Insurance Defense; Civil Litigation; Workers' Compensation; Fidelity and Surety; Construction Law — E-mail: lfarah@whtlaw.com

William H. Partin, Jr. — 1964 — University of Kentucky, B.A., 1986; University of Kentucky College of Law, J.D., 1989 — Admitted to Bar, 1989, Kentucky; 1993, Tennessee; 1990, U.S. District Court, Eastern and Western Districts of Kentucky; 1994, U.S. District Court, Middle District of Tennessee — Member Kentucky and Tennessee Bar Associations; Kentucky Academy of Trial Lawyers; Tennessee Trial Lawyers Association — Practice Areas: Insurance Defense; Civil Litigation; Workers' Compensation; Product Liability — E-mail: wpartin@whtlaw.com

Melissa A. Wilson — 1954 — University of Kentucky, B.S.N., 1976; M.S.N., 1981; B.A., 1992; University of Kentucky College of Law, J.D., 1996 — Admitted to Bar, 1996, Kentucky; 1999, U.S. District Court, Eastern District of Kentucky — Member Kentucky and Fayette County (Chair, Steering Committee for the Women's Section) Bar Associations — Practice Areas: Insurance Defense; Civil Litigation; Medical Malpractice; Product Liability; Municipal Liability — E-mail: mwilson@whtlaw.com

Donald C. Walton, III — 1965 — United States Military Academy at West Point, B.S., 1987; University of Kentucky College of Law, J.D., 1998 — Admitted to Bar, 1998, Kentucky — Member Kentucky Bar Association — U.S. Army [1987-1995]; Major, U.S. Army Reserves [1995-Current] — Practice Areas: Insurance Defense; Civil Litigation; Workers' Compensation — E-mail: dwalton@whtlaw.com

Associates

Scott C. Wilhoit — 1963 — University of Kentucky, B.A., 1985; University of Kentucky College of Law, J.D., 1989 — Admitted to Bar, 1989, Kentucky; U.S. District Court, Eastern and Western Districts of Kentucky; 1992, U.S. Court of Appeals, Sixth Circuit; 1998, U.S. District Court, Northern and Southern Districts of Indiana — Member American and Kentucky Bar Associations; Kentucky Defense Counsel; Association of Trial Lawyers of America — Practice Areas: Workers' Compensation; Insurance Defense; Civil Litigation; Civil Rights — E-mail: swilhoit@whtlaw.com

Chadwick A. Wells — 1974 — Transylvania University, B.A. (with honors), 1997; University of Kentucky College of Law, J.D., 2000 — Admitted to Bar, 2000, Kentucky; 2001, U.S. District Court, Eastern District of Kentucky — Member Kentucky and Fayette County Bar Associations — Practice Areas: Insurance Defense; Civil Litigation — E-mail: cwells@whtlaw.com

Ward, Hocker & Thornton, PLLC, Lexington, KY (Continued)

John O. Hollon — 1968 — Vanderbilt University, B.A. Political Science, 1991; University of Kent, Canterbury, J.D., 1994 — Admitted to Bar, 1994, Kentucky; 1997, Florida; 2011, Virginia; 1995, U.S. District Court, Eastern and Western Districts of Kentucky; 1997, U.S. Court of Appeals, Sixth Circuit; 1998, U.S. District Court, Middle District of Florida; 1999, U.S. Court of Appeals, Eleventh Circuit — Member Kentucky, Virginia and Fayette County Bar Associations; The Florida Bar — Practice Areas: Civil Litigation; Insurance Defense; Accident — E-mail: John.Hollon@whtlaw.com

James E. Skaggs — 1974 — Murray State University, B.S., 1998; University of Kentucky, J.D., 2001 — Admitted to Bar, 2001, Kentucky; U.S. District Court, Western District of Kentucky — Member Kentucky, Christian County and 56th Judicial Circuit Bar Associations — E-mail: jskaggs@whtlaw.com

Brian M. Gudalis — 1973 — Asbury College, B.S., 1995; Regent University, J.D., 2002 — Admitted to Bar, 2002, Kentucky; U.S. District Court, Eastern District of Kentucky; 2007, U.S. District Court, Western District of Kentucky; U.S. Court of Appeals, Sixth Circuit — Member Kentucky and Fayette County Bar Associations — Practice Areas: Civil Litigation; Personal Injury; Professional Malpractice; Product Liability — E-mail: Brian.Gudalis@whtlaw.com

R. Johnson Powell — 1970 — Transylvania University, B.A., 1992; University of Kentucky, M.S., 1994; J.D., 2001 — Admitted to Bar, 2001, Kentucky; 2004, U.S. District Court, Eastern and Western Districts of Kentucky; U.S. Court of Appeals, Sixth Circuit — Member Kentucky Bar Association — Practice Areas: Workers' Compensation; Administrative Law; Civil Litigation; Insurance Defense — E-mail: jpowell@whtlaw.com

Noelle J. Bailey — 1980 — Transylvania University, B.A., 2003; University of Kentucky, J.D., 2007 — Admitted to Bar, 2007, Kentucky; 2007, U.S. District Court, Eastern and Western Districts of Kentucky; 2008, U.S. District Court, Northern and Southern Districts of Indiana — Member American, Kentucky, Indiana State and Louisville Bar Associations — Practice Areas: Insurance Defense; Automobile; Fire; Premises Liability — E-mail: nbailey@whtlaw.com

James M. Bricken IV — 1983 — Asbury College, B.A., 2005; University of Kentucky, J.D., 2008 — Admitted to Bar, 2008, Kentucky — Member Kentucky and Fayette County Bar Associaitons — Practice Areas: Personal Injury; Premises Liability; Product Liability — E-mail: jbricken@whtlaw.com

Ashley K. Brown — 1983 — University of Kentucky, B.A. (cum laude), 2005; J.D., 2008 — Admitted to Bar, 2008, Kentucky — Member Kentucky and Fayette County Bar Associations — Languages: Spanish — Practice Areas: Civil Litigation; Insurance Defense — E-mail: abrown@whtlaw.com

Jennifer L. Fell — 1981 — Centre College, B.A., 2004; University of Louisville, J.D., 2010 — Admitted to Bar, 2010, Kentucky — Member Kentucky and Louisville Bar Associations — Practice Areas: Automobile; Fire; Insurance Defense; Premises Liability — E-mail: JFell@whtlaw.com

Benjamin A. Bellamy — 1981 — University of Kentucky, B.S., 2005; University of Louisville, J.D., 2008 — Admitted to Bar, 2008, Kentucky; 2011, U.S. District Court, Western District of Kentucky — Member Kentucky and Louisville Bar Associations — Practice Areas: Commercial Litigation; Insurance Defense; Premises Liability — E-mail: BBellamy@whtlaw.com

Allison Helsinger — 1985 — Eastern Kentucky University, B.A. Political Science, 2007; University of Kentucky, J.D., 2010 — Admitted to Bar, 2011, Kentucky; U.S. District Court, Eastern District of Kentucky — Member Kentucky and Fayette County Bar Associations — Practice Areas: Motor Vehicle; Insurance Defense; Premises Liability; Product Liability — E-mail: AHelsinger@whtlaw.com

Elisabeth M. Lyons — 1985 — University of Kentucky, B.A., 2007; J.D., 2011 — Admitted to Bar, 2011, Kentucky; U.S. District Court, Eastern District of Kentucky — Member Kentucky and Fayette County Bar Associations — Practice Areas: Automobile; Insurance Defense; Premises Liability; Product Liability — E-mail: MLyons@whtlaw.com

Jillian M. Dove — 1985 — Centre College, B.A., 2008; University of Kentucky, J.D., 2011 — Admitted to Bar, 2011, Kentucky; 2012, U.S. District Court, Eastern District of Kentucky — Member Kentucky and Fayette County Bar Associations — Practice Areas: Insurance Defense — E-mail: Jillian.Dove@whtlaw.com

Scott E. Burroughs — 1986 — The Ohio State University, B.A., 2008; University of Kentucky, J.D., 2011 — Admitted to Bar, 2011, Kentucky; 2012, U.S. District Court, Western District of Kentucky — Member American, Kentucky and Louisville Bar Associations — E-mail: Scott.Burroughs@whtlaw.com

Emily H. Brooks — 1983 — Centre College, B.A., 2005; Northern Kentucky University, J.D., 2011 — Admitted to Bar, 2011, Kentucky; 2012, U.S. District Court, Eastern and Western Districts of Kentucky; U.S. Bankruptcy Court — Member American and Kentucky Bar Associations — Practice Areas: Insurance Defense; Surety — E-mail: Emily.Brooks@whtlaw.com

Donald J. Niehaus — 1984 — University of Louisville, B.S., 2007; J.D., 2010 — Admitted to Bar, 2010, Kentucky; 2011, U.S. District Court, Western District of Kentucky — Member Kentucky Bar Association — Practice Areas: Workers' Compensation — E-mail: Donnie.Niehaus@whtlaw.com

Leslie N. Obrzut — 1983 — University of Kentucky, B.A., 2005; West Virginia University, J.D., 2008 — Admitted to Bar, 2009, West Virginia; 2011, Kentucky; 2009, U.S. District Court, Southern District of West Virginia — Member Kentucky Bar Association; West Virginia State Bar — E-mail: LObrzut@whtlaw.com

Blake A. Vogt — 1982 — University of Kentucky, B.S., 2005; Northern Kentucky University, J.D., 2009 — Admitted to Bar, 2009, Ohio; 2010, Kentucky; 2010, U.S. District Court, Southern District of Ohio; 2011, U.S. District Court, Eastern District of Kentucky — Member Kentucky and Fayette County Bar Associations — Practice Areas: Automobile; Insurance Defense; Premises Liability — E-mail: Blake.Vogt@whtlaw.com

Katherine M. Adams — 1985 — Transylvania University, B.A., 2008; Northern Kentucky University, J.D., 2011 — Admitted to Bar, 2012, Kentucky — E-mail: Katherine.Adams@whtlaw.com

The following firms also service this area.

Coleman Lochmiller & Bond
2907 Ring Road
Elizabethtown, Kentucky 42701
Telephone: 270-737-0600
Fax: 270-737-0488
Mailing Address: P.O. Box 1177, Elizabethtown, KY 42702-1177

Insurance Defense, Automobile, Commercial Law, Product Liability, Professional Liability, Property and Casualty, Medical Malpractice, Litigation, General

SEE COMPLETE LISTING UNDER ELIZABETHTOWN, KENTUCKY (86 MILES)

McNabb, Bragorgos & Burgess, PLLC
81 Monroe Avenue, Sixth Floor
Memphis, Tennessee 38103-5402
Telephone: 901-624-0640
Toll Free: 888-251-8000
Fax: 901-624-0650

Insurance Defense, Trucking Litigation, Fire, Casualty, Malpractice, Fraud, Litigation, Marine, Product Liability, Workers' Compensation, Automobile, Mass Tort, Personal Injury, Commercial Law, Premises Liability, Subrogation, Construction Law, Nursing Home Defense

SEE COMPLETE LISTING UNDER MEMPHIS, TENNESSEE (431 MILES)

LONDON † 7,993 Laurel Co.

Taylor, Keller & Oswald, PLLC

1306 West 5th Street, Suite 100
London, Kentucky 40741
Telephone: 606-878-8844
Fax: 606-878-8850
www.tkolegal.com

(Lexington, KY Office*: Hamburg Place Office Park, 1795 Alysheba Way, Suite 2201, 40509)
(Tel: 859-543-1613)
(Fax: 859-543-1654)

Trial Practice, Automobile Liability, Property, Insurance Coverage, Product Liability, Premises Liability, Subrogation, Insurance Fraud, Bad Faith, Governmental Liability, General Insurance and Corporate Defense

Firm Profile: The firm of Taylor, Keller & Oswald, PLLC, has an extensive civil practice throughout the Commonwealth of Kentucky with an emphasis on all types of insurance and corporate defense, subrogation, insurance fraud and business litigation. The firm strives to provide high-quality legal services to its

LONDON   KENTUCKY

Taylor, Keller & Oswald, PLLC, London, KY (Continued)

clients and relies on an excellent legal support staff and the most modern information technology to achieve this goal.

Insurance Clients

AIG	Allstate Insurance Company
American Claims Service	American Fellowship Mutual Insurance Company
American General Life Insurance Company	American Indemnity Group/United Fire Group
American National Property and Casualty Company	Argo Group
Atlantic Casualty Insurance Company	Cincinnati Insurance Company
	Direct General Insurance Company
EMC/Hamilton Mutual Insurance Company	Encompass Insurance Company
Frankenmuth Insurance Company	Federated Rural Electric Insurance Exchange
Gallagher Bassett Insurance Services, Inc.	GuideOne Insurance
	Hanover Insurance Company
The Hartford Insurance Group	Kemper Auto and Home
Kentucky Farm Bureau Insurance Companies	Liberty Mutual Insurance Company
	Markel Insurance Company
McLarens Young International	Motorists Insurance Company
Motor Transport Underwriters, Inc.	Murdock Claim Management Company
National Claims Management	
Northland Insurance Company	Ohio Casualty Insurance Company
Pennsylvania Lumbermens Mutual Insurance Company	Safeco Insurance
	St. Paul Insurance Company
Sentry Insurance	State Auto Insurance Company
State Farm Fire and Casualty Company	State Farm Mutual Automobile Insurance Company
Transportation Claims, Inc.	Travelers Insurance Companies
United Services Automobile Association (USAA)	Unitrin Direct Insurance Company

Non-Insurance Clients

Appalachian Research and Defense Fund	Cooper Industries, Inc.
	Jackson Energy Cooperative
Kentucky Mountain Housing Development Corp., Inc.	Kentucky Propane Plus, LLC
	NTA, Inc.

Partners

Boyd F. Taylor — (1924-2012)

J. Warren Keller — 1954 — Rider College, B.A. (with honors), 1976; College of William & Mary, J.D., 1979 — Phi Alpha Delta — Admitted to Bar, 1979, Kentucky; 1984, U.S. Court of Appeals, Sixth Circuit; 1988, U.S. District Court, Eastern and Western Districts of Kentucky; 2003, U.S. Supreme Court — Member American Bar Association (Tort Trial and Insurance Practice Section; Property Insurance Law Committee, Vice-Chair, 1992-1997); Kentucky Bar Association (Board of Governors, 1996-2002); Laurel County Bar Association (President, 1992-1993); National Society of Professional Insurance Investigators (Kentucky Chapter President, 1998-2000; National Board Member, 2000-2001; National President, 2003-2004); Kentucky Bar Foundation (President, 2006-2007); Kentucky Interest on Lawyers Trust Accounts (IOLTA) (Trustee, 2012-2015); Florida Advisory Committee on Arson Prevention; Kentucky Defense Counsel — E-mail: wkeller@tkolegal.com

Clayton O. Oswald — 1976 — Eastern Kentucky University, B.A. (cum laude), 1997; University of Kentucky, J.D. (cum laude), 2004 — Admitted to Bar, 2004, Kentucky; U.S. District Court, Eastern District of Kentucky; 2008, U.S. District Court, Western District of Kentucky; 2009, U.S. Court of Appeals, Sixth Circuit; 2010, U.S. Supreme Court — Member Federal, American, Kentucky and Laurel County Bar Associations; National Society of Professional Insurance Investigators; Bluegrass Claims Association; Electric Cooperative Bar Association; Kentucky Defense Counsel (Board Member, 2014-Present); Defense Research Institute — E-mail: coswald@tkolegal.com

Associates

Bradley S. Harn — 1986 — Eastern Kentucky University, B.A. Political Science (summa cum laude), 2009; University of Kentucky, J.D., 2012 — Admitted to Bar, 2012, Kentucky; U.S. District Court, Eastern and Western Districts of Kentucky — E-mail: bharn@tkolegal.com

Mary Katherine Bing — 1985 — University of Kentucky, B.A. Political Science (magna cum laude), 2008; J.D., 2013 — Former Law Clerk, Kentucky Supreme Court — Special Features Editor, Kentucky Law Journal, Vol. 101 — Admitted to Bar, 2013, Kentucky — Member Kentucky Bar Association (At-Large Respresentative,, Young Lawyers Division) — E-mail: kbing@tkolegal.com

Tooms & Dunaway, PLLC

1306 West 5th Street, Suite 200
London, Kentucky 40741
   Telephone: 606-864-4145
   Fax: 606-878-5547
   Emer/After Hrs: 606-864-8746
   E-Mail: bdunaway@toomsdunaway.com
   www.toomsdunaway.com

Established: 1948

Trial Practice, Automobile Liability, Property, Insurance Coverage, Product Liability, Premises Liability, Insurance Fraud, Bad Faith, Governmental Liability, General Insurance and Corporate Defense, Condemnation and Eminent Domain

Firm Profile: The firm of Tooms & Dunaway, PLLC, has an extensive civil practice primarily in Southeastern, Southern and Central Kentucky with an emphasis on insurance and corporate defense, insurance coverage, insurance fraud, business and government litigation, and condemnation and eminent domain.

Insurance Clients

Adriatic Insurance Company	American National Property and Casualty Company
Auto-Owners Insurance Company	Grocers Insurance Company
Canal Insurance Company	Lawyers Mutual Insurance Company of Kentucky
Kentucky Farm Bureau Mutual Insurance Company	National Union Fire Insurance Company
Motor Transport Underwriters, Inc.	State Farm Insurance Company
Northland Insurance Company	Tennessee Farmers Mutual Insurance Company
Pennsylvania Lumbermens Mutual Insurance Company	United States Liability Insurance Group
Travelers Insurance Companies	
United Farm Family Mutual Insurance Company	

Non-Insurance Clients

Beall's, Inc.	Commonwealth of Kentucky
Georgia Gulf Sulfur Corporation	IFC Credit Corporation
Kentucky League of Cities Insurance Trust	National Claims Management
	Transportation Claims, Inc.

Partners

R. William Tooms — 1945 — University of Kentucky, B.A., 1967; J.D. (with distinction), 1974 — Admitted to Bar, 1974, Kentucky; 1974, U.S. District Court, Eastern District of Kentucky; 1974, U.S. Court of Appeals, Sixth Circuit; 1995, U.S. District Court, Western District of Kentucky; 2000, U.S. Supreme Court — Member American and Kentucky Bar Associations; Kentucky Defense Counsel (Board of Directors, 1981-1985 and 1988-1994; President, 1992-1993); Defense Research Institute (Board of Directors, 1997-2000; State Representative, 1995-1997; State Chair, 1993-1995); Federation of Defense and Corporate Counsel (State Representative, 2002-2006; Admissions Committee, 2004-2010; Chair, Foundation Committee, 2010-2012); Association of Defense Trial Attorneys; American Board of Trial Advocates; Kentucky Bar Foundation (Board of Directors, 1986-1997; President 1995-1996) — U.S. Navy, 1968-1972 — E-mail: btooms@toomsdunaway.com

Bridget L. Dunaway, CPCU — 1962 — Eastern Kentucky University, B.A. (summa cum laude), 1984; University of Kentucky, J.D., 1989 — Admitted to Bar, 1989, Kentucky; 1989, U.S. Court of Appeals, Sixth Circuit; 1990, U.S. District Court, Eastern District of Kentucky; 1996, U.S. District Court, Western District of Kentucky; 2002, U.S. Supreme Court — Member Kentucky and Laurel County (President, 1997) Bar Associations; Kentucky Defense Counsel (Board of Directors, 1995-1999; 2009-2013); National Association Insurance Women; CPCU Society; Defense Research Institute; Association of Defense Trial Attorneys — E-mail: bdunaway@toomsdunaway.com

Associate

John Michael Carter — 1986 — Western Kentucky University, B.A. (summa cum laude), 2008; University of Kentucky, J.D., 2012 — Admitted to Bar, 2012, Kentucky — Member American and Kentucky Bar Associations; Defense Research Institute; Kentucky Defense Counsel — E-mail: jcarter@toomsdunaway.com

KENTUCKY

LOUISA † 2,467 Lawrence Co.

Refer To

Jenkins Fenstermaker, PLLC
325 8th Street
Huntington, West Virginia 25701
  Telephone: 304-523-2100
  Fax: 304-523-2347, 304-523-9279
  Toll Free: 800-982-3476
Mailing Address: P.O. Box 2688, Huntington, WV 25726

Civil Litigation, State and Federal Courts, Mediation, Arbitration, Trial Practice, Appellate Practice, Commercial Litigation, Personal Injury, Product Liability, Medical Malpractice, Professional Malpractice, Toxic Torts, Construction Litigation, Insurance Defense, Insurance Coverage, ERISA, Workers' Compensation, Employment Law, Administrative Law, Labor and Employment Law, Automobile Warranty, Labor Negotiations, Counseling, Warranty Litigation

SEE COMPLETE LISTING UNDER HUNTINGTON, WEST VIRGINIA (35 MILES)

LOUISVILLE † 256,231 Jefferson Co.

Alber Crafton, PSC

9418 Norton Commons Boulevard, Suite 200
Prospect, Kentucky 40059
  Telephone: 502-815-5000
  Fax: 502-815-5005
  E-Mail: lhutchens@albercrafton.com
  www.albercrafton.com

(Troy, MI Office*: 2301 West Big Beaver Road, Suite 300, 48084)
  (Tel: 248-822-6190)
  (Fax: 248-822-6191)
(Westerville, OH Office*: 501 West Schrock Road, Suite 104, 43081-3360)
  (Tel: 614-890-5632)
  (Fax: 614-890-5638)
(Oklahoma: P.O. Box 14517, Tulsa, OK, 74159)
  (Tel: 918-935-3459)

Fidelity and Surety, Insurance Defense, Investigations, Defense Litigation, Policy Litigation, Construction Law, Appellate Law

Firm Profile: Alber Crafton, PSC is a regional surety, fidelity, construction law, policy litigation, probate litigation, and commercial litigation firm that is the product of relationships forged by years of trust and confidence between its attorneys and clients.

Today our firm represents the product of 30 years of successful client representation and thrives on the solid relationships that have developed through years of trust.

To serve the interests of our clients effectively, our attorneys hold licenses to practice in Arkansas, Kansas, Kentucky, Michigan, Missouri and Ohio. Furthermore, by partnering with local counsel, we have been able to expand our geographic boundaries to represent our clients in Alabama, Colorado, Florida, Indiana, Minnesota, North Carolina, Pennsylvania, South Carolina, Tennessee, Texas, Virginia, Washington D.C., and West Virginia.

Our goal is to reach an expeditious and fair resolution of our clients' matters. However, if other methods to resolve the issues are not successful, our experienced trial lawyers are proficient at successfully prosecuting or defending a claim through trial.

Surety and Insurance Clients

American Contractors Indemnity Company
Argonaut Insurance Company
AXIS Insurance Company
Chubb & Son, Inc.
CNA Surety Corporation
Employers Mutual Casualty Company
Great American Insurance Companies
Hanover Insurance Group
American International Group, Inc.
AmTrust Group
Auto-Owners Insurance Company
CapSpecialty
Cincinnati Insurance Company
CUNA Mutual Group
Erie Insurance Company
FCCI Insurance Company
The Guarantee Company of North America
Hartford Fire Insurance Company

Alber Crafton, PSC, Louisville, KY   (Continued)

ICW Group
Landmark Companies
Liberty Mutual Insurance Company
NAS Insurance Company
Old Republic Surety Company
RLI Insurance Company
State Automobile Mutual Insurance Company
Travelers Insurance Companies
Universal Surety of America
Western Surety Company
Westfield Insurance Company
International Fidelity Insurance Company
Merchants Bonding Company
Ohio Casualty Group
Philadelphia Insurance Company
Selective Insurance Company
State Farm Fire and Casualty Company
United Fire & Casualty Company
Washington International Insurance Company
Zurich North America

Partners

Phillip G. Alber — 1948 — University of Michigan, B.A. (cum laude), 1971; Wayne State University, J.D. (cum laude), 1974 — Admitted to Bar, 1975, Michigan; U.S. District Court, Eastern and Western Districts of Michigan; U.S. Court of Appeals, Sixth Circuit; 1990, U.S. District Court, District of Arizona; 1991, U.S. District Court, Northern District of Indiana; 2006, U.S. Court of Federal Claims — Member American (Sections: Torts, Insurance Practice; Fidelity and Surety Law Committee; Forum Committee on Construction Law), Macomb County and Oakland County Bar Associations; State Bar of Michigan; Surety Claims Institute; National Bond Claims Association; International Association of Defense Counsel — Practice Areas: Fidelity and Surety; Construction Law; Construction Litigation — Resident Troy, MI Office

Thomas E. Crafton — 1949 — Western Kentucky University, B.S., 1972; Indiana University, J.D., 1985 — Admitted to Bar, 1991, Kentucky; Ohio; U.S. District Court, Eastern and Western Districts of Kentucky; U.S. District Court, Northern District of Florida; U.S. District Court, Southern District of Ohio; U.S. Court of Appeals, Sixth Circuit — Member American, Kentucky and Louisville Bar Associations; National Bond Claims Association; Surety Claims Institute; Northeast Surety Fidelity Claims conference — Practice Areas: Fidelity and Surety; Construction Litigation; Commercial Litigation — Resident Louisville, KY Office

Jeffrey M. Frank — 1967 — University of Michigan, B.A. (cum laude), 1989; Boston University, J.D., 1992 — Admitted to Bar, 1992, Michigan; U.S. District Court, Eastern District of Michigan; 1998, U.S. District Court, Western District of Michigan; 2007, U.S. Court of Appeals, Sixth Circuit — Member American Bar Association (Torts and Insurance Practice Section; Fidelity and Surety Law Committee; Co-Chair, Young Professionals Division, 2001-2003; Member, Miscellaneous Bonds Sub-Committee and Forum Committee on Construction Law); State Bar of Michigan; Oakland County Bar Association; National Bond Claims Association; Defense Research Institute (Fidelity, and Surety Steering Committee); West Bloomfield School District Educational Foundation (Board of Directors 2007-2010); Wayne County Probate Bar Association (Board of Directors, 2007-Present); Northeast Surety Fidelity Claims conference — Practice Areas: Fidelity and Surety; Construction Litigation; Commercial Litigation; Probate — Resident Troy, MI Office

Omar J. Harb — 1969 — Cornell University, B.A., 1991; University of Michigan, J.D. (cum laude), 1994 — Admitted to Bar, 1994, Michigan; U.S. District Court, Eastern District of Michigan; 1999, U.S. District Court, Western District of Michigan — Member American Bar Association (Torts and Insurance Practice Section; Fidelity and Surety Law Committee; Co-Chair, Young Professionals Division, 2005-2007; Technology Chair, 2006-2012; Co-Editor-in-Chief, Fidelity and Surety Law Committee Newsletter, 2012-present; State Bar of Michigan; Northeast Surety Fidelity Claims conference — Practice Areas: Fidelity and Surety; Construction Law; Commercial Litigation; Probate — Resident Troy, MI Office

Lee M. Brewer — 1954 — The University of Tennessee, B.S. Accounting, 1978; Capital University, M.B.A., 1982; J.D. (cum laude), 1989 — Admitted to Bar, 1989, Ohio; U.S. District Court, Southern District of Ohio; 2003, U.S. District Court, Northern District of Ohio, 2011, U.S. Court of Appeals, Sixth Circuit; 2013, U.S. District Court, Eastern District of Michigan — Member American Bar Association (Torts and Insurance Practice Section; Vice-Chair, Surety and Fidelity Law Committee; former Co-Chair, Women's Development Subcommittee; Forum Committee on Construction Law); Ohio State and Columbus Bar Associations; Surety and Fidelity Claim Institute; Northeast Surety Fidelity Claims conference — Practice Areas: Fidelity and Surety; Commercial Litigation; Construction Law — Resident Westerville, OH Office

Associates

Wendell L. Jones — 1963 — University of North Carolina Wilmington, B.A., 1990; University of Louisville, J.D., 1994 — Admitted to Bar, 1994, Kentucky; 1995, U.S. District Court, Eastern and Western Districts of Kentucky;

LOUISVILLE KENTUCKY

Alber Crafton, PSC, Louisville, KY (Continued)

U.S. Court of Appeals, Sixth Circuit; 2002, U.S. District Court, Southern District of Indiana; 2009, U.S. District Court, Northern District of Florida — Member American, Kentucky and Louisville Bar Associations — Practice Areas: Surety; Construction Law; Commercial Litigation — Resident Louisville, KY Office

Maureen P. Taylor — 1942 — University of Michigan - Flint, B.A. (Phi Kappa Phi, magna cum laude), 1963; Michigan State University, M.A., 1964; Western Michigan University, Ed.D., 1978; University of Michigan, J.D. (cum laude), 1989 — Executive Editor, Michigan Law Review — Admitted to Bar, 1989, Kentucky; 1997, Ohio; 1989, U.S. District Court, Eastern District of Kentucky; 1990, U.S. District Court, Western District of Kentucky; U.S. Court of Appeals, Sixth Circuit; 1997, U.S. District Court, Southern District of Ohio — Member American, Kentucky, Ohio State and Louisville Bar Associations — Practice Areas: Fidelity and Surety; Construction Law; Appeals — Resident Louisville, KY Office

Jessica L. Wynn — 1985 — Central Michigan University, B.S. (cum laude, with honors), 2007; Thomas M. Cooley Law School, J.D. (cum laude), 2011 — Admitted to Bar, 2011, Michigan; 2013, U.S. District Court, Eastern District of Michigan — Member American and Oakland County Bar Associations; Wayne County Probate Bar Association; Women Lawyers Association of Michigan — Resident Troy, MI Office

Of Counsel

W. Brant Warrick — 1970 — University of Arkansas, B.A. (cum laude), 1993; J.D., 1996 — Admitted to Bar, 1996, Arkansas; 2005, Kentucky; Missouri; Oklahoma; 2003, U.S. District Court, Eastern and Western Districts of Arkansas; 2005, U.S. District Court, Western District of Kentucky; 2007, U.S. District Court, Eastern District of Kentucky; U.S. District Court, Western District of Oklahoma — Member American Bar Association (Tort, Trial and Insurance Practice Section; Fidelity and Surety Law Committee); Kentucky (Civil Litigation Section and Construction Section), Arkansas (Construction Law Section, Civil Litigation Section and Debtor/Creditor Section), Oklahoma (Litigation Section, Financial Institutions Section and Commercial Law Section) and Tulsa County Bar Associations; The Missouri Bar; Defense Research Institute (Surety Committee); Oklahoma Surety Underwriters Association — Practice Areas: Fidelity and Surety; Construction Litigation; Commercial Litigation — Resident Tulsa, OK Office

Boehl Stopher & Graves, LLP

400 West Market Street, Suite 2300
Louisville, Kentucky 40202-3354
  Telephone: 502-589-5980
  Fax: 502-561-9400
  E-Mail: louisville@bsg-law.com
  www.bsg-law.com

(New Albany, IN Office: Elsby East, 400 Pearl Street, Suite 204, 47150)
  (Tel: 812-948-5053)
(Lexington, KY Office*: 444 West Second Street, 40507)
  (Tel: 859-252-6721)
  (Fax: 859-253-1445)
(Paducah, KY Office*: 410 Broadway Street, 42001)
  (Tel: 270-442-4369)
  (Fax: 270-442-4689)
(Pikeville, KY Office*: 137 Main Street, Suite 2, 41501, P.O. Box 1132, 41502)
  (Tel: 606-432-9670)

Established: 1950

Insurance Litigation, Casualty, Surety, Admiralty and Maritime Law, Workers' Compensation, Product Liability, Medical Malpractice, Professional Malpractice

Firm Profile: Attorneys at Boehl Stopher & Graves, LLP have over one hundred years of experience and are the eighth largest law firm in Kentucky. They have carried an "AV" rating in Martindale Hubbell for over 45 years.

Insurance Clients

Amerisure Companies
Associated Aviation Underwriters
Bituminous Casualty Corporation
Argonaut Insurance Company
Bankers Multiple Line Insurance Company
CIGNA Property and Casualty Insurance Company
Great American Insurance Company
Kemper Insurance Companies
Metropolitan Property and Casualty Insurance Company
Old Republic Group
St. Paul Fire and Marine Insurance Company
Utica Mutual Insurance Company
Wausau Insurance Companies
Continental Insurance Company
Fireman's Fund Insurance Company
The Hartford Insurance Group
Liberty Mutual Insurance Company
Motorists Mutual Insurance Company
Prudential Property and Casualty Insurance Company
State Farm Mutual Automobile Insurance Company

Partners

Herbert F. Boehl — (1894-1986)
Arthur J. Deindoefer — (1907-1990)
Raymond O. Harmon — (1918-1990)
James M. Graves — (1912-1994)
William M. Newman, Jr. — (1949-1995)
Joseph E. Stopher — (1914-2006)
Larry J. Johnson — (1940-2010)
Edward H. Stopher — 1943 — University of Virginia, J.D., 1968 — Admitted to Bar, 1968, Kentucky — Member American and Kentucky Bar Associations; Life Member, Sixth Circuit Judicial Conference — E-mail: estopher@bsg-law.com
Nolan Carter, Jr. — 1938 — University of Kentucky, J.D., 1962 — Admitted to Bar, 1962, Kentucky — Member Kentucky and Fayette County Bar Associations — Resident Lexington, KY Office — E-mail: ncarter@bsglex.com
Philip J. Reverman, Jr. — 1946 — University of Louisville, J.D., 1975 — Admitted to Bar, 1975, Kentucky — Member American and Kentucky Bar Associations — E-mail: preverman@bsg-law.com
Robert E. Stopher — 1952 — University of Virginia, J.D., 1977 — Admitted to Bar, 1977, Kentucky — Member American, Kentucky and Louisville Bar Associations — E-mail: rstopher@bsg-law.com
Peter J. Glauber — 1946 — University of Kentucky, J.D., 1973 — Admitted to Bar, 1974, Kentucky — Member Kentucky Bar Association — E-mail: pglauber@bsg-law.com
Raymond G. Smith — 1951 — Southern Methodist University, J.D., 1977 — Admitted to Bar, 1977, Kentucky — E-mail: rsmith@bsg-law.com
Walter E. Harding — 1952 — University of Louisville, J.D., 1978 — Admitted to Bar, 1979, Kentucky — E-mail: wharding@bsg-law.com
Richard L. Walter — 1955 — University of Kentucky, J.D., 1980 — Admitted to Bar, 1980, Kentucky — Resident Paducah, KY Office — E-mail: rwalter@bsgpad.com
Guillermo A. Carlos — 1956 — University of Kentucky, J.D., 1982 — Admitted to Bar, 1982, Kentucky — Member Kentucky Bar Association — Resident Lexington, KY Office — E-mail: gcarlos@bsglex.com
Jeffrey L. Hansford — 1953 — University of Louisville, J.D., 1987 — Admitted to Bar, 1987, Kentucky — Resident New Albany, IN Office — E-mail: jhansford@bsg-in.com
Matthew Hunter Jones — 1961 — University of Louisville, J.D., 1987 — Admitted to Bar, 1987, Kentucky — Member American, Indiana State and Floyd County Bar Associations; National Association of Life Underwriters — Resident New Albany, IN Office — E-mail: mjones@bsg-in.com
Richard W. Edwards — 1961 — University of Kentucky, J.D., 1988 — Admitted to Bar, 1988, Kentucky — Member Kentucky and Louisville Bar Associations — E-mail: redwards@bsg-law.com
David T. Klapheke — 1964 — Indiana University, B.A. (with distinction), 1985; Vanderbilt University, J.D., 1988 — Admitted to Bar, 1988, Minnesota; 1995, Kentucky; 1989, U.S. District Court, Eastern District of Wisconsin; 1990, U.S. District Court, District of Minnesota — Member American, Minnesota State and Kentucky Bar Associations — E-mail: dklapheke@bsg-law.com
C. Tom Anderson — 1952 — University of Kentucky, B.B.A. (with honors), 1975; Northern Kentucky University, Salmon P. Chase College of Law, J.D., 1978 — Admitted to Bar, 1978, Kentucky — Member Kentucky and Pike County Bar Associations — Resident Pikeville, KY Office — E-mail: tanderson@bsgeast.com
James L. Fischer — 1963 — University of Louisville, J.D., 1989 — Admitted to Bar, 1998, Kentucky — Member Indiana State Bar Association — Resident New Albany, IN Office — E-mail: jfischer@bsg-in.com

KENTUCKY | LOUISVILLE

Boehl Stopher & Graves, LLP, Louisville, KY (Continued)

Rod D. Payne — 1967 — Western Kentucky University, B.A., 1994; University of Louisville, J.D., 1997 — Admitted to Bar, 1997, Kentucky — Member Louisville Bar Association — E-mail: rpayne@bsg-law.com

Scott A. Davidson — 1970 — University of Kentucky, J.D., 1994 — Admitted to Bar, 1994, Kentucky — Member Kentucky and Louisville Bar Associations — E-mail: sdavidson@bsg-law.com

Tiara B. Shoter — 1971 — Barnard College, B.A., 1993; Brooklyn Law School, J.D., 1996 — Admitted to Bar, 1996, New Jersey; 1997, New York; 1998, Kentucky — E-mail: tshoter@bsg-law.com

Earl L. Martin — 1973 — University of Virginia, B.A., 1996; Emory University, J.D., 1999 — Admitted to Bar, 2000, Kentucky — Member Louisville Bar Association — E-mail: emartin@bsg-law.com

David E. Crittenden — 1971 — Virginia Polytechnic Institute and State University, B.S., 1992; University of Louisville, J.D., 1995 — Admitted to Bar, 1996, Kentucky — E-mail: dcrittenden@bsg-law.com

Darryl S. Lavery — 1975 — The Catholic University of America, B.A., 1998; Indiana University School of Law, J.D., 2001 — Admitted to Bar, 2001, Kentucky — E-mail: dlavery@bsg-law.com

Matthew B. Gay — 1973 — University of Kentucky, B.A., 1995; University of Louisville, J.D., 1998 — Admitted to Bar, 1998, Kentucky — E-mail: mgay@bsg-law.com

Bradley E. Moore — 1968 — University of Kentucky, B.A., 1994; J.D., 1998 — Admitted to Bar, 1998, Kentucky — Resident Lexington, KY Office — E-mail: bmoore@bsglex.com

Edwin A. Jones — 1964 — Evangel University, B.A., 1987; University of Kentucky, J.D., 1990 — Admitted to Bar, 1990, Kentucky; U.S. District Court, Western District of Kentucky — Member Kentucky and McCracken Bar Associations — Resident Paducah, KY Office — E-mail: ejones@bsgpad.com

Michael S. Jackson — 1969 — University of South Carolina, B.A., 1991; University of Louisville, J.D., 1994 — Admitted to Bar, 1994, Kentucky — E-mail: mjackson@bsg-law.com

Curtis P. Moutardier — 1974 — Indiana University, B.A. (with distinction), 1996; J.D. (magna cum laude), 2002 — Admitted to Bar, 2002, Indiana — Resident New Albany, IN Office — E-mail: cmoutardier@bsg-in.com

Associates

Robert M. Brooks — 1956 — University of Kentucky, J.D., 1981 — Admitted to Bar, 1981, Kentucky — E-mail: rbrooks@bsg-law.com

Charles D. Walter — 1961 — Southern Illinois University, J.D., 1986 — Admitted to Bar, 1986, Illinois; 1988, Kentucky — Member American, Illinois State, Kentucky and McCracken County Bar Associations — Resident Paducah, KY Office — E-mail: cwalter@bsgpad.com

Bayard V. Collier — 1953 — Eastern Kentucky University, A.B. (with high distinction), 1976; University of Kentucky, J.D., 1979 — Admitted to Bar, 1979, Kentucky — Member Kentucky, Pike County and Floyd County Bar Associations — Resident Pikesville, KY Office — E-mail: bcollier@bsgeast.com

Robert D. Bobrow — 1960 — University of Louisville, B.A., 1983; J.D., 1995 — Admitted to Bar, 1995, Kentucky — Member Louisville Bar Association — E-mail: rbobrow@bsg-law.com

Julie A. Sharp — 1977 — Pikeville College, B.B.A., 2000; Northern Kentucky University, Salmon P. Chase College of Law, J.D., 2003 — Admitted to Bar, 2004, Kentucky; 2004, U.S. District Court, Eastern District of Kentucky — Member American, Kentucky and Pike County Women's Bar Associations — Resident Pikeville, KY Office — E-mail: jsharp@bsgeast.com

Elsabe Meyer — 1978 — Indiana University, B.S., 2000; DePaul University, J.D., 2003 — Admitted to Bar, 2004, Kentucky; U.S. District Court, Eastern and Western Districts of Kentucky — Member American, Kentucky and Louisville Bar Associations — E-mail: emeyer@bsg-law.com

Amanda L. Tomlin — 1978 — The University of Iowa, B.S., 2000; Ohio Northern University, Pettit College of Law, J.D., 2003 — Admitted to Bar, 2003, Kentucky — Member Kentucky Bar Association — Resident Lexington, KY Office — E-mail: abrockmann@bsglex.com

Charles H. Stopher — 1979 — University of Virginia, B.A., 2001; University of Virginia School of Law, J.D., 2005 — Admitted to Bar, 2005, Kentucky; U.S. District Court, Western District of Kentucky — Member Louisville Bar Association — E-mail: cstopher@bsg-law.com

Michelle Duncan — University of Kentucky, B.B.A., 2004; University of Kentucky College of Law, J.D., 2008 — Admitted to Bar, 2008, Kentucky; U.S. District Court, Eastern and Western Districts of Kentucky; U.S. Court of Appeals, Sixth Circuit — Member American, Kentucky and Louisville Bar Associations; Kentucky Women's Lawyers Association — E-mail: mduncan@bsg-law.com

Boehl Stopher & Graves, LLP, Louisville, KY (Continued)

Julie Ann Tennyson — 1974 — East Tennessee State University, B.S. (magna cum laude), 1996; The University of Georgia, M.S.W., 1999; The University of Tennessee College of Law, J.D. (magna cum laude), 2003 — Order of the Coif — Admitted to Bar, 2003, Georgia; Tennessee; 2009, Kentucky; 2007, U.S. District Court, Northern District of Georgia; 2008, U.S. District Court, Middle District of Georgia; 2009, U.S. District Court, Western District of Kentucky; 2011, U.S. District Court, Western District of Tennessee — Member McCracken County Bar Association — Resident Paducah, KY Office — E-mail: jtennyson@bsgpad.com

William Lucas McCall — 1979 — Murray State University, B.S., 2001; Southern Illinois University Law School, J.D. (magna cum laude), 2010 — Admitted to Bar, 2011, Kentucky — Member Kentucky and McCracken County Bar Associations — Resident Paducah, KY Office — E-mail: lmccall@bsgpad.com

Todd P. Greer — 1982 — University of Kentucky, B.A./B.A. (with honors), 2004; Louis D. Brandeis School of Law, University of Louisville, J.D. (cum laude), 2008 — Admitted to Bar, 2008, Kentucky; 2011, U.S. District Court, Western District of Kentucky; 2012, U.S. Court of Appeals, Sixth Circuit — E-mail: tgreer@bsg-law.com

M. Jake Bliss — 1983 — Transylvania University, B.A., 2005; University of Kentucky College of Law, J.D., 2008 — Admitted to Bar, 2008, Kentucky; 2009, U.S. District Court, Eastern and Western Districts of Kentucky — Resident Lexington, KY Office — E-mail: jbliss@bsglex.com

E. Michael Ooley — Indiana University, B.A., 1986; Louis D. Brandeis School of Law, University of Louisville, J.D., 1993 — Admitted to Bar, 1993, Indiana; U.S. District Court, Northern and Southern Districts of Indiana — Resident New Albany, IN Office — E-mail: Mikeooley@bsg-in.com

Randall T. Starnes — 1979 — University of Kentucky, B.A. (cum laude), 2001; University of Kentucky College of Law, J.D., 2006 — Admitted to Bar, 2006, Kentucky; 2009, U.S. District Court, Eastern District of Kentucky — Member Kentucky, Fayette County and Madison County Bar Associations — E-mail: tstarnes@bsglex.com

Chastity R. Beyl — 1975 — Western Kentucky University, B.A., 1998; Louis D. Brandeis School of Law, University of Louisville, J.D. (cum laude), 2001 — Admitted to Bar, 2001, Kentucky; 2012, U.S. District Court, Eastern and Western Districts of Kentucky — Member Kentucky and Louisville Bar Associations — E-mail: cbeyl@bsg-law.com

Kristin Logan-Mischel — 1976 — University of Kentucky, B.A., 1998; Louis D. Brandeis School of Law, University of Louisville, J.D., 2001 — Admitted to Bar, 2001, Kentucky; 2005, U.S. District Court, Eastern and Western Districts of Kentucky; 2011, U.S. District Court, Southern District of Indiana — Member Kentucky and Louisville Bar Associations — E-mail: klogan@bsg-law.com

Fogle Keller Purdy, PLLC

333 Guthrie Green, Suite 203
Louisville, Kentucky 40202
Telephone: 502-582-1381
Fax: 502-581-9887
E-Mail: info@fkplaw.com
www.fkplaw.com

(Lexington, KY Office: 300 East Main Street, Suite 400, 40507)
(Tel: 859-253-4700)
(Fax: 859-253-4702)
(Bowling Green, KY Office: 1830 Destiny Court, Suite 113, 42104)
(Tel: 270-796-2050)
(Fax: 270-796-2066)
(Florence, KY Office: 1655 Burlington Pike, Suite 50, 41042)
(Tel: 859-980-1573)
(Fax: 859-980-1574)
(Charleston, WV Office: 1018 Kanawha Boulevard East, Suite 300, 25301)
(Tel: 304-720-3759)
(Fax: 304-720-3761)

Insurance Defense, Workers' Compensation, Subrogation, General Liability, Automobile Liability, Americans with Disabilities Act, Premises Liability, Municipal Liability, Governmental Liability, Coverage Issues, Medical Malpractice, Legal Malpractice, Mediation, Arbitration, Employment Law (Management Side), Property and Casualty

LOUISVILLE   KENTUCKY

Fogle Keller Purdy, PLLC, Louisville, KY   (Continued)

Firm Profile: Workers' Compensation defense continues to be the major concentration of this practice. With offices staffed with experienced counsel, strategically located throughout the State, the firm provides: Efficient and time sensitive communications with insureds and their carriers; Uniform approaches on the handling and disposition of a claim; Cost-Effective and in-depth analysis on issues affecting company decisions; Value Added professional advice to resolve claim controversies; Aggressive Defense in representing the best of the insured.

We currently possess over 300 years of combined experience with workers' compensation claims. We have represented insureds in over 20,000 cases at every level, up to the state's highest court. Thomas L. Ferreri and James G. Fogle have assisted past Governors and Legislative task force committees in drafting workers' compensation legislation and regulations and have served as speakers on all aspects of workers' compensation to the business community, attorneys, physicians and legislators.

Insurance Clients

Amerisure Mutual Insurance Company
Bituminous Insurance Companies
Chartis Insurance
EMC Insurance Company
GAB Robins North America, Inc.
Gallagher Bassett Services, Inc.
GEICO General Insurance Company
Indiana Insurance Company
Kentucky Employers' Mutual Insurance - KEMI
Kentucky School Boards Insurance Trust
Liberty Mutual Insurance Company
Selective Insurance Company of America
Travelers Insurance Companies
Underwriters Safety and Claims
Wausau General Insurance Company
Zenith Insurance Company

Non-Insurance Clients

Alliance Coal, LLC
Averitt Express, Inc.
City of Louisville
City of Owensboro
Commonwealth of Kentucky
Food Lion, LLC
James River Coal Company
Kentucky Employers Safety Association/KESA
Kentucky Retail Federation
Kohl's Department Stores, Inc.
Lexington-Fayette Urban County Government
Louisville Gas and Electric Energy Corporation
Louisville Water Company
Macy's
Walgreen Co.

Members

James G. Fogle — 1953 — Morehead State University, B.A., 1975; Salmon P. Chase College of Law, J.D., 1978 — Admitted to Bar, 1978, Kentucky; 1982, U.S. District Court, Eastern District of Kentucky; 1986, U.S. Court of Appeals, Sixth Circuit; 1987, U.S. District Court, Western District of Kentucky — Member Kentucky Bar Association (Workers' Compensation Section, Treasurer, 1987; President-Elect, 1988; President, 1989) — Author, "Prehearings and Hearings," Workers' Compensation in Kentucky, 1991; "Benefits and Calculations," Workers' Compensation in Kentucky, 1995

Sherri P. Keller — 1967 — Murray State University, B.S. (cum laude), 1989; Louis D. Brandeis School of Law, University of Louisville, J.D., 1992 — Phi Alpha Delta (President) — University of Louisville Law Review — Admitted to Bar, 1992, Kentucky; 1996, U.S. District Court, Eastern District of Kentucky — Member Kentucky Bar Association (Workers' Compensation Section)

H. Brett Stonecipher — 1961 — Marquette University, B.S., 1984; University of Kentucky, J.D., 1993 — Admitted to Bar, 1993, Kentucky — Journal of Natural Resources and Environmental Law

Denis S. Kline — 1948 — Western Kentucky University, B.S., 1970; Louis D. Brandeis School of Law, University of Louisville, J.D., 1975 — Admitted to Bar, 1976, Kentucky; 1976, U.S. District Court, Eastern and Western Districts of Kentucky — Member Kentucky Bar Association — Department of Workers' Claims Administrative Law Judge, 1991-1999

Kamp Townsend Purdy — 1974 — Michigan State University, B.S., 1996; University of Kentucky College of Law, J.D., 1999 — Admitted to Bar, 1999, Michigan; 2000, Kentucky — Member Kentucky Bar Association

Anthony K. Finaldi — 1970 — State University of New York at Buffalo, B.A. (cum laude), 1992; University of Louisville, J.D., 1995 — Admitted to Bar, 1995, Indiana; 1996, Kentucky; U.S. District Court, Northern and Southern Districts of Indiana; U.S. District Court, Western District of Kentucky — Member American, Kentucky, Indiana State and Lousville Bar Associations

Gregory Little — 1969 — Salmon P. Chase College of Law, J.D. (magna cum laude), 2000 — Admitted to Bar, Kentucky — Member American and Kentucky Bar Associations

Fogle Keller Purdy, PLLC, Louisville, KY   (Continued)

Timothy J. Walker — 1958 — University of Kentucky College of Law, J.D., 1985 — Admitted to Bar, Kentucky; U.S. District Court, Eastern and Western Districts of Kentucky; U.S. Court of Appeals for the District of Columbia Circuit; U.S. Supreme Court — Member Kentucky Bar Association

Scott M. Brown — 1972 — University of Kentucky, B.A. (with distinction), 1994; J.D., 1998 — Admitted to Bar, 1998, Kentucky — Member Kentucky Bar Association

Johanna F. Ellison — 1979 — University of Kentucky, B.A. (summa cum laude), 2001; J.D., 2005 — Admitted to Bar, 2005, Kentucky — Member Kentucky and Fayette County Bar Associations

Stephanie D. Ross — 1970 — University of Kentucky, B.A. (with distinction), 1992; University of Kentucky College of Law, J.D., 1995 — Admitted to Bar, 1996, Kentucky — Member Kentucky Bar Association

Associates

John "Ward" E. Ballerstedt Jr — 1981 — University of Kentucky, B.B.A., 2002; University of Louisville, J.D., 2006 — Admitted to Bar, 2006, Kentucky — Member Kentucky Bar Association

John W. Spies — 1970 — Indiana University, B.A., 2001; Salmon P. Chase College of Law, J.D., 2004 — Admitted to Bar, 2004, Kentucky — Member Kentucky Bar Association

James R. Wagoner — 1947 — Bellarmine College, B.A., 1972; University of Louisville, J.D., 1975 — Admitted to Bar, 1976, Kentucky — Member Kentucky Bar Association

Matthew Zanetti — 1979 — Indiana University, B.A., 2001; Vanderbilt University Law School, J.D., 2005 — Admitted to Bar, 2005, Kentucky; 2007, U.S. District Court, Eastern and Western Districts of Kentucky — Member Kentucky Bar Association

Pierre J. Coolen — 1979 — University of Kentucky, B.S., 2002; University of Kentucky College of Law, J.D., 2006 — Admitted to Bar, 2007, Kentucky — Member Kentucky Bar Association

Daniel J. Urbon — 1975 — Michigan State University, B.A., 1999; Michigan State University College of Law, J.D., 2002 — Michigan State University Alumni Scholarship — Admitted to Bar, 2002, Michigan; 2006, Kentucky — Member American (Young Lawyers Section) and Kentucky Bar Associations; State Bar of Michigan

Daniel G. Murdock — 1967 — State University of New York at Binghamton, B.A., 1990; Washington and Lee University School of Law, J.D., 2001 — Admitted to Bar, 2002, West Virginia; U.S. District Court, Southern District of West Virginia; 2003, U.S. District Court, Northern District of West Virginia

Tighe A. Estes — 1981 — Georgetown College, B.A./B.A., 2003; University of Kentucky College of Law, J.D., 2006 — Moot Court Board — Admitted to Bar, 2006, Kentucky; 2007, U.S. District Court, Eastern and Western Districts of Kentucky; U.S. Court of Appeals, Sixth Circuit

Of Counsel

William P. Emrick — 1953 — University of Kentucky, B.A. (with high distinction), 1975; University of Kentucky College of Law, J.D., 1978 — Admitted to Bar, 1978, Kentucky; 1979, U.S. District Court, Eastern District of Kentucky; 1989, U.S. Court of Appeals, Sixth Circuit; 2002, U.S. District Court, Western District of Kentucky — Member Kentucky Bar Association; International Association of Industrial Accident Boards

(This firm is also listed in the Subrogation section of this directory)

Goldberg Simpson LLC

9301 Dayflower Street
Norton Commons
Prospect, Kentucky 40059
  Telephone: 502-589-4440
  Fax: 502-581-1344
  Toll Free: 1-800-928-4440
  www.goldbergsimpson.com

Established: 1981

KENTUCKY — LOUISVILLE

Goldberg Simpson LLC, Louisville, KY (Continued)

Accident, Automobile, Automobile Liability, Automobile Tort, Bad Faith, Bodily Injury, Carrier Defense, Casualty Defense, Civil Litigation, Civil Trial Practice, Commercial General Liability, Commercial Liability, Commercial Litigation, Commercial Vehicle, Commercial and Personal Lines, Common Carrier, Comprehensive General Liability, Construction Law, Construction Litigation, Defense Litigation, First Party Matters, First and Third Party Defense, General Civil Practice, General Defense, Insurance Defense, Insurance Law, General Liability, General Practice, Insurance Litigation, Litigation, Mediation, Motor Carriers, Motor Vehicle, Negligence, No-Fault, Personal Injury, Personal Liability, Personal Lines, Personal and Commercial Vehicle, Premises Liability, Product Liability, Property, Property Damage, Property Defense, Property Liability, Property Loss, Property and Casualty, Self-Insured, Self-Insured Defense, Slip and Fall, State and Federal Courts, Tort, Tort Liability, Tort Litigation, Transportation, Trial Practice, Truck Liability, Trucking Law, Trucks/Heavy Equipment, Uninsured and Underinsured Motorist, Wrongful Death

Firm Profile: Most successful business law firms are either boutiques, organized around a single, narrowly defined industry or area of practice, or they strive for the full-service model, trying to provide every conceivable type of legal service a large corporate client could need. Goldberg & Simpson is neither. Our firm is not organized around a single practice area, nor do we try to be all things to all people.

Instead, our firm has grown as an assemblage of practices that we can run efficiently and that provide needed services to the Louisville community. Law firm management types love to talk about "synergy" between practice groups. We're more interested in finding the synergy between our abilities and our clients' goals. We're together as a firm less because of what we do than because of how we do it.

What we have in common is a passionate love of what we do, a long-standing commitment to the Louisville community, and a never-flagging desire to stay ever on the move on behalf of our clients.

Insurance Clients

Chubb Group
Indiana Insurance Company
Liberty Mutual Group
Safeco Insurance
Zurich North America
Colorado Casualty Insurance Company
Ohio Casualty Co.
Wausau General Insurance Company

Firm Members

Charles H. Cassis — 1965 — Southern Methodist University, B.A., 1987; University of Kentucky, J.D., 1990 — Admitted to Bar, 1991, Kentucky; 1991, U.S. District Court, Eastern and Western Districts of Kentucky; 1991, U.S. Court of Appeals for the Federal and Sixth Circuits; 2007, U.S. Supreme Court; 2010, U.S. District Court, Southern District of Indiana; 2011, U.S. Court of Appeals, Seventh Circuit — Member American, Kentucky and Louisville Bar Associations — E-mail: ccassis@goldbergsimpson.com

Jonathan D. Goldberg
Stephen E. Smith
K. Gail Russell
Stephanie L. Morgan-White
Aaron J. Silletto
Troy D. DeMuth
John H. Helmers, Jr.
Mitchell A. Charney
Jan M. West
David B. Gray
Stephen R. Solomon
Mark J. Sandlin
Callie E. Walton
Kelli E. Brown

Associates

Richard T. Frank
Allison Russell
Megan P. Keane
Caroline L. Kaufmann
Megan M. Cleveland
Kevin P. Weis
Kelley M. Rule
Jarad N. Key
S. Carlos Wood

Goldberg Simpson LLC, Louisville, KY (Continued)

Of Counsel

Ronald V. Simpson
Charles D. Greenwell

Harville Law Offices PLLC

Anchorage Office Plaza
2527 Nelson Miller Parkway, Suite 102
Louisville, Kentucky 40223
Telephone: 502-245-2333
Fax: 502-245-2399
E-Mail: BDH@Harvillelaw.com
www.Harvillelaw.com

Automobile, Trucking Law, Premises Liability, Product Liability, General Civil Litigation, Cargo

Firm Profile: Harville Law Offices PLLC represents insurers, insureds, businesses and individuals in civil litigation matters including car and truck accidents, cargo claims, workers' compensation, products liability, personal injury, and commercial disputes. Mr. Harville is also admitted to practice in Indiana.

Insurance Clients

Celina Insurance Group
Vanliner Insurance Company
Hanover Insurance Company

Non-Insurance Clients

Allied Van Lines
Transportation Claims, Inc.

Firm Member

Bradley D. Harville — University of Kentucky, B.A., 1982; University of Kentucky College of Law, J.D., 1985 — Admitted to Bar, 1985, Kentucky; 1992, Indiana; U.S. District Court, Eastern and Western Districts of Kentucky; U.S. District Court, Southern District of Indiana; U.S. Court of Appeals, Sixth Circuit; Supreme Court of Kentucky — Member Kentucky and Louisville Bar Associations — Speaker, Louisville Bar Association Continuing Legal Education Programs — Practice Areas: Insurance Defense; Civil Litigation; Trial Practice — E-mail: bdh@harvillelaw.com

Associate

Dana Taylor Skaggs — Bellarmine University, B.A. (with honors), 1994; Louis D. Brandeis School of Law, University of Louisville, J.D., 1998 — Admitted to Bar, 1999, Kentucky — Member Kentucky and Louisville Bar Associations — Practice Areas: Civil Litigation; Workers' Compensation; Real Property — E-mail: dts@harvillelaw.com

Of Counsel

Scott A. Hite

Kightlinger & Gray, LLP

312 South Fourth Street, Suite 700
Louisville, Kentucky 40202
Telephone: 502-442-2295
Fax: 502-442-2703
E-Mail: info@k-glaw.com
www.k-glaw.com

(Indianapolis, IN Office*: One Indiana Square, Suite 300, 211 North Pennsylvania Street, 46204)
(Tel: 317-638-4521)
(Fax: 317-636-5917)
(Evansville, IN Office*: 7220 Eagle Crest Boulevard, 47715)
(Tel: 812-474-4400)
(Fax: 812-474-4414)
(New Albany, IN Office*: Bonterra Building, Suite 200, 3620 Blackiston Boulevard, 47150)
(Tel: 812-949-2300)
(Fax: 812-949-8556)

LOUISVILLE   KENTUCKY

Kightlinger & Gray, LLP, Louisville, KY   (Continued)

(Merrillville, IN Office*: Merrillville Corporate Center, 8001 Broadway, Suite 100, 46410)
 (Tel: 219-769-0413)
 (Fax: 219-769-0798)

Established: 1946

Insurance Defense, Insurance Litigation, Defense Litigation, Litigation, Insurance Law, Coverage Issues, Carrier Defense, Self-Insured Defense, Comprehensive General Liability, Trial and Appellate Practice, State and Federal Courts, General Civil Trial and Appellate Practice, Casualty Defense, Product Liability, Workers' Compensation, Employment Law, Subrogation, Toxic Torts, Aviation, Surety, Administrative Law, Agent/Broker Liability, Bad Faith, Business Law, Automobile Liability, Trucking Law, Asbestos Litigation, Construction Law, Corporate Law, Complex Litigation, Construction Litigation, Coverage Analysis, First and Third Party Defense, Fire Loss, Professional Liability, Malpractice, Agency Defense, Agent and Brokers Errors and Omissions, Medical Malpractice, School Law, Transportation, Real Estate, Bankruptcy, Municipal Liability, Class Actions, Mediation, Securities Litigation and Arbitration

Partners

Sacha L. Armstrong — University of Maryland, B.A., 1999; Louis D. Brandeis School of Law, University of Louisville, J.D., 2003 — Admitted to Bar, 2003, Kentucky; 2004, Indiana; U.S. District Court, Western District of Kentucky; U.S. District Court, Northern and Southern Districts of Indiana — Tel: 812-474-4400 ext. 6319 — E-mail: sarmstrong@k-glaw.com

Laurie Goetz Kemp — Miami University, B.S., 1992; Louis D. Brandeis School of Law, University of Louisville, J.D., 1996 — Admitted to Bar, 1996, Indiana; Kentucky; U.S. District Court, Northern and Southern Districts of Indiana; U.S. District Court, Eastern and Western Districts of Kentucky; U.S. Court of Appeals, Sixth and Seventh Circuits — Tel: 812-949-2300 ext. 5136 — E-mail: lkemp@k-glaw.com

R. Jeffrey Lowe — The University of North Carolina, B.A., 1994; Louis D. Brandeis School of Law, University of Louisville, J.D., 1998 — Admitted to Bar, 1998, Kentucky; 1999, Indiana; U.S. District Court, Southern District of Indiana; U.S. District Court, Western District of Kentucky; U.S. Court of Appeals, Seventh Circuit — Tel: 812-949-2300 ext. 5132 — E-mail: jlowe@k-glaw.com

Steven K. Palmquist — Cornell College, B.A., 1976; University of Cincinnati College of Law, J.D., 1979 — Admitted to Bar, 1979, Indiana; 1980, Kentucky; U.S. District Court, Southern District of Indiana; U.S. District Court, Eastern and Western Districts of Kentucky — Tel: 812-949-2300 ext. 5113 — E-mail: spalmquist@k-glaw.com

Crystal G. Rowe — Indiana University, B.A., 1997; Indiana University School of Law, J.D., 2000 — Admitted to Bar, 2000, Indiana; 2006, Kentucky; U.S. District Court, Northern and Southern Districts of Indiana; U.S. District Court, Eastern and Western Districts of Kentucky; U.S. Court of Appeals, Sixth and Seventh Circuits — Tel: 812-949-2300 ext. 5122 — E-mail: crowe@k-glaw.com

William E. Smith, III — Franklin College, B.A., 1976; University of Dayton School of Law, J.D., 1979 — Admitted to Bar, 1979, Indiana; 1980, Kentucky; U.S. District Court, Southern District of Indiana; U.S. District Court, Eastern and Western Districts of Kentucky; U.S. Court of Appeals, Sixth Circuit — Tel: 812-949-2300 ext.5141 — E-mail: wsmith@k-glaw.com

Van T. Willis — University of Kentucky, B.A., 1983; University of Kentucky College of Law, J.D., 1988 — Admitted to Bar, 1988, Kentucky; 1990, Indiana; U.S. District Court, Southern District of Indiana; U.S. District Court, Eastern and Western Districts of Kentucky; U.S. Court of Appeals, Seventh Circuit — Tel: 812-949-2300 ext. 5127 — E-mail: vwillis@k-glaw.com

Associates

Ashley Gillenwater Eade — Indiana University, B.S., 2007; Louis D. Brandeis School of Law, University of Louisville, J.D., 2010 — Admitted to Bar, 2010, Kentucky; 2011, Indiana; U.S. District Court, Southern District of Indiana; U.S. District Court, Eastern and Western Districts of Kentucky — Tel: 812-949-2300 ext.5131 — E-mail: aeade@k-glaw.com

William F. English — University of Kentucky, B.A., 2006; Indiana University School of Law, J.D., 2009 — Admitted to Bar, 2010, Indiana; Kentucky; 2011, Virginia; U.S. District Court, Southern District of Indiana; U.S. District

Kightlinger & Gray, LLP, Louisville, KY   (Continued)

Court, Western District of Kentucky — Tel: 812-949-2300 ext. 5143 — E-mail: wenglish@k-glaw.com

(This firm is also listed in the Subrogation section of this directory)

Landrum & Shouse LLP

220 West Main Street, Suite 1900
Louisville, Kentucky 40202
 Telephone: 502-589-7616
 Fax: 502-589-2119
 www.landrumshouse.com

(Lexington, KY Office*: 106 West Vine Street, Suite 800, 40507, P.O. Box 951, 40588-0951)
 (Tel: 859-255-2424)
 (Fax: 859-233-0308)

Established: 1986

General Civil Practice, Trial and Appellate Practice, Fire, Casualty, Life Insurance, Product Liability, Medical Malpractice, Workers' Compensation, Construction Law, Fidelity and Surety, Environmental Law, Railroad Law, Aviation, Administrative Law, Intellectual Property, Employee Benefits, ERISA, Legal Liability

Resident Partners

John R. Martin, Jr. — 1953 — University of Kentucky, J.D., 1979 — Admitted to Bar, 1979, Kentucky — Member American, Kentucky and Louisville Bar Associations; Kentucky Academy of Trial Attorneys — Certified Civil Trial Advocate, National Board of Trial Advocacy

R. Kent Westberry — Centre College of Kentucky, B.A., 1977; Salmon P. Chase College of Law, J.D., 1980 — Sigma Chi — Admitted to Bar, 1981, Kentucky — Member American Bar Association; Kentucky Bar Association (Board of Governors, 1992-2000; President, 2004-2005; Chairman, Mentoring Committee, 2006-Present); National Association of Criminal Defense Attorneys; U.S. Sixth Circuit Judicial Conference (Life Member); Federal Defenders Corporation, Western District of Kentucky (Board of Directors, 2001-Present); Kentucky Registry of Election Finance (Vice Chairman, 1995-1999); U.S. District Court Magistrate Judge Merit Selection Panel, Western District of Kentucky (Chairman, 2011); American Board of Trial Advocates; Defense Research Institute — Classes/Seminars Taught: The Criminal Trial: Voir Dire to Closing, National Business Institute, 2009-2011; Election Laws in Kentucky, Louisville Bar Association, 1998-Present; White Collar Crime, Louisville Bar Association, 1997-Present; Preparing Witnesses to Testify in a Criminal Case, Louisville Bar Association, 1997-Present; Ethics in Kentucky, Ethics in Kentucky, 1997-Present; Litigation Ethics (Pretrail Investigation and Rule 11), Louisville Bar Association, 1990-Present; Criminal RICO Seminar, Louisville Bar Association, 1986-Present; Comprehensive Crime Control Act, Salmon P. Chase, College of Law, 1986-Present

Jennifer A. Peterson — 1972 — University of Louisville, J.D., 1997 — Admitted to Bar, 1998, Kentucky — Member Louisville Bar Association

Resident Associates

Michael K. Nisbet — 1964 — Louis D. Brandeis School of Law, University of Louisville, J.D., 1999 — Admitted to Bar, 1999, Kentucky; 2000, Indiana

Ashley Smith Lant — 1984 — Capital University Law School, J.D., 2007-2010 — Admitted to Bar, 2010, Ohio; 2011, Kentucky — Member Kentucky and Louisville Bar Associations

Of Counsel

Bridget M. Bush — 1961 — Harvard Law School, J.D., 1985-1988 — Admitted to Bar, 1989, Pennsylvania; 1990, District of Columbia; 2007, Kentucky — Member Kentucky and Louisville Bar Associations

(See Lexington, KY Listing for additional information)
(Revisors of the Kentucky Insurance Law Digest for this Publication)

KENTUCKY   LOUISVILLE

Lynch, Cox, Gilman & Goodman P.S.C.

500 West Jefferson Street, Suite 2100
Louisville, Kentucky 40202
    Telephone: 502-589-4215
    Fax: 502-589-4994
    E-Mail: atty@lcgandm.com
    www.lynchcoxlaw.com

Trial Practice, Workers' Compensation, Surety, Asbestos Litigation, Toxic Torts, Product Liability, Professional Liability, Insurance Coverage, Coverage, General Civil Litigation, Insurance Defense Litigation

Insurance Clients

American Safety Insurance Company
Carolina Casualty Insurance Company
Great West Casualty Company
Hanover Insurance Company
Leader Insurance Company
Motorists Insurance Group
Ohio Farmers Insurance Company
StarNet Insurance Company
Travelers Insurance Companies
United America Indemnity Group
Vanguard Insurance Company
Auto-Owners Insurance Company
Bituminous Insurance Company
Fireman's Fund Insurance Company
GuideOne Insurance
The Hartford
Meridian Mutual Insurance Company
Protective Insurance Company
State Auto Insurance Company
Underwriters Safety and Claims
Unitrin Insurance Company

Non-Insurance Clients

ArvinMeritor, Inc.
Cardinal Industrial Insulation Company, Inc.
FedEx Custom Critical
FedEx Ground Package System, Inc.
Kentucky Employers Safety Association/KESA
Berkley Risk Administrators Company, LLC
Constitution State Service Company
FedEx Home Delivery
Gallagher Bassett Services, Inc.
Rockwell Automation, Inc.

Firm Members

Scott D. Spiegel — 1955 — Miami University, J.D., 1980 — Admitted to Bar, 1980, Kentucky; U.S. District Court, Eastern and Western Districts of Kentucky; U.S. Court of Appeals, Fourth, Sixth and Seventh Circuits; U.S. Court of Appeals for the Federal Circuit — Member American, Kentucky and Louisville Bar Associations

Joseph P. Hummel — 1971 — University of Kentucky, J.D., 1996 — Admitted to Bar, 1996, Kentucky — Member Kentucky and Louisville Bar Associations

Richard G. Segal — 1937 — Franklin & Marshall College, A.B., 1959; University of Pennsylvania, J.D., 1962 — Admitted to Bar, 1962, Pennsylvania; 1968, Kentucky; 1982, Indiana; U.S. Court of Appeals, Sixth and Seventh Circuits — Member American, Kentucky, Indiana State and Louisville Bar Associations; Kentucky Defense Counsel; Defense Research Institute

Associate

William Thomas Rump, IV — 1969 — Spalding University, B.A. (magna cum laude), 1998; Louis D. Brandeis School of Law, University of Louisville, J.D., 2001 — Admitted to Bar, 2001, Kentucky; U.S. District Court, Eastern and Western Districts of Kentucky; 2004, U.S. Court of Appeals, Sixth Circuit — Member Kentucky and Louisville Bar Associations

Of Counsel

Berlin Tsai — 1967 — University of Louisville, J.D., 1993 — Admitted to Bar, 1994, Kentucky; 1996, U.S. District Court, Western District of Kentucky; 2001, U.S. District Court, Southern District of Indiana

Napier Gault Schupbach & Moore, PLC

730 West Main Street, Suite 400
Louisville, Kentucky 40202
    Telephone: 502-855-3800
    Fax: 502-855-3838
    E-Mail: tnapier@napiergaultlaw.com
    www.napiergaultlaw.com

Napier Gault Schupbach & Moore, PLC, Louisville, KY (Continued)

General Liability, Medical Malpractice, Product Liability, Premises Liability, Professional Liability, Mass Tort, Toxic Torts, Special Liability, Media Law

Firm Profile: Napier Gault Schupbach & Moore is an insurance defense firm that focuses primarily on medical malpractice defense (hospital and physician), special liability defense (mass tort, toxic tort and products liability), premises liability and general civil litigation. Feel free to visit our website for more information.

Insurance Clients

Kentuckiana Medical Reciprocal Risk Retention Group
Travelers, Special Liability Group

Partners

Timothy H. Napier — Louis D. Brandeis School of Law, University of Louisville, J.D., 1993 — Admitted to Bar, 1994, Kentucky — Practice Areas: Medical Malpractice; Insurance Defense — E-mail: tnapier@napiergaultlaw.com
Patrick W. Gault
John B. Moore
Rebecca F. Schupbach

Counsel

Victoria E. Boggs

Associate

Willis S. Taylor

O'Bryan, Brown & Toner, PLLC

1500 Starks Building
455 South Fourth Street
Louisville, Kentucky 40202
    Telephone: 502-585-4700
    Fax: 502-585-4703
    www.obtlaw.com
    E-Mail: obt@obtlaw.com

(Indianapolis, IN Office: 3003 East 98th Street, Suite 131, 46280) (Tel: 317-669-0087)

Established: 1991

Insurance Defense, Litigation, Medical Malpractice, Automobile, Bodily Injury, Errors and Omissions, General Liability, Homeowners, Dental Malpractice, Legal Malpractice, Product Liability, Property and Casualty, Workers' Compensation, Insurance Coverage Questions and Policy Interpretation

Firm Profile: O'Bryan, Brown & Toner, PLLC was founded in 1991. We practice in both the State and Federal Courts throughout Kentucky and Indiana. We have offices in both Kentucky and Indiana.

If there is a distinction (as we often hear) between a litigator and a trial lawyer, we are trial lawyers, dedicated to the defense of tort claims. Our practice includes but is not limited to the following types of claims: Medical Malpractice, Professional Negligence, Product Liability, Premises Liability, Motor Vehicle Negligence, Workers' Compensation, Professional License Defense and Federal and State Appeals.

Insurance Clients

ACUITY
APCapital
Baptist Health
Colony Insurance Company
Forcht Group of Kentucky
Kentuckiana Medical Reciprocal Risk Retention Group
Lawyers Mutual Insurance Company
National General Insurance Company
American Healthcare Indemnity Company
Catholic Mutual Group
The Doctors Company
Hudson Insurance Group
Kentucky Employers Safety Association/KESA
Markel Corporation
The Medical Protective Company
OHIC Insurance Company
OneBeacon Insurance

O'Bryan, Brown & Toner, PLLC, Louisville, KY
(Continued)

ProAssurance Company
State Volunteer Mutual Insurance Company
U.S. Liability Insurance Company
Rice Insurance Services Company, LLC
Travelers Insurance Company

Non-Insurance Clients

KHA Solutions Group (formerly Coverage Options Associates)
Starbucks Corporation
Louisville Metro Government
McDonalds
Unity Physician Group, P.C.

Joseph C. O'Bryan — (1932-2012)

Partners

Donald K. Brown, Jr. — University of Kentucky, B.A., 1972; The University of Tennessee, J.D., 1979 — Admitted to Bar, 1980, Kentucky; Tennessee

Christopher P. O'Bryan — University of Louisville, B.S., 1982; J.D., 1985 — Admitted to Bar, 1985, Kentucky

Gerald R. Toner — Harvard University, A.B., 1972; Vanderbilt University, J.D., 1975 — Admitted to Bar, 1975, Kentucky

James P. Grohmann — DePauw University, B.A., 1986; University of Kentucky, J.D., 1990 — Admitted to Bar, 1990, Kentucky

David S. Strite — Virginia Polytechnic Institute and State University, B.A., 1988; University of Louisville, J.D., 1991 — Admitted to Bar, 1991, Kentucky; Indiana

Tracy S. Prewitt — University of Louisville, B.S., 1986; J.D., 1990 — Admitted to Bar, 1990, Kentucky; Indiana

Clay A. Edwards — University of Kentucky, B.A., 1991; University of Louisville, J.D., 1995 — Admitted to Bar, 1995, Kentucky; Indiana

Michael B. Dailey — University of Kentucky, B.A., 1996; Louis D. Brandeis School of Law, University of Louisville, J.D., 1999 — Admitted to Bar, 1999, Kentucky

Mark E. Hammond — Centre College of Kentucky, B.S., 1997; University of Kentucky College of Law, J.D., 2000 — Admitted to Bar, 2000, Kentucky; 2001, Indiana

Andie B. Camden — University of Kentucky, B.B.A., 1996; University of Kentucky College of Law, J.D., 2000 — Admitted to Bar, 2000, Kentucky

Joseph C. Klausing — Centre College of Kentucky, B.A., 2001; University of Louisville, J.D., 2004 — Admitted to Bar, 2004, Kentucky; 2005, Indiana

Michael P. Reilly — University of Kentucky, B.A., 1995; University of Dayton School of Law, J.D., 2001 — Admitted to Bar, 2001, Kentucky; 2004, Indiana

Joshua W. Davis — Centre College of Kentucky, B.A., 2001; University of Louisville, J.D., 2004 — Admitted to Bar, 2004, Kentucky; 2006, Indiana

Katherine K. Vesely — Mercer University at Macon, B.A., 1995; Vanderbilt University, M.A., 1997; University of Louisville, J.D., 2006 — Admitted to Bar, 2006, Kentucky; 2007, Indiana

Associate Attorneys

Benjamin J. Weigel
Andrew D. Pellino
Brent E. Dye
Holly S. Barger
Colleen C. Hartley
Whitney R. Kramer
Krista A. Willike
Robert C. Veldman
Brittany Perrin Asher
Stephanie L. Caldwell
Mary Elizabeth O'Bryan
Andolyn R. Johnson
Chad J. Bradford
Christopher J. Leopold
Brant W. Sloan
Cecilia F. Weihe

Phillips Parker Orberson & Arnett, P.L.C.

716 West Main Street, Suite 300
Louisville, Kentucky 40202
Telephone: 502-583-9900
Fax: 502-587-1927
E-Mail: worberson@ppoalaw.com
www.ppoalaw.com

(Lexington, KY Office: 163 East Main Street, Suite 130, 40507)
(Tel: 859-559-4457)
(Fax: 859-425-4099)

Phillips Parker Orberson & Arnett, P.L.C., Louisville, KY
(Continued)

(Key West, FL Office: 624 Whitehead Street, 33040)
(Tel: 305-292-4020)

Established: 1999

General Liability, Automobile, Professional Liability, Construction Law, Coverage Issues, Medical Malpractice, Hospital Malpractice, Nursing Home Liability, Workers' Compensation

Firm Profile: The law firm of Phillips Parker Orberson & Arnett, P.L.C. was founded in July, 1999. There are currently 10 partners, 7 associates and 4 of counsel.

The emphasis of our practice is the defense of insurance, automobile, medical/hospital, corporate and municipal litigation. We routinely represent defendants in State and Federal courts throughout Kentucky and in Southern Indiana.

Our attorneys have developed considerable expertise in areas including medical negligence, products liability, automobile negligence, bad faith, construction negligence, insurance coverage, premises liability, professional liability, wrongful discharge, toxic tort litigation, workers' compensation and small business matters. We also have a staff of experienced paralegals and nurse paralegals who provide significant assistance and support with all aspects of our practice.

The firm's reported cases include *Degener v. Hall Contracting*, 27 S.W.3rd 775 (2000); *Brisco v. Amazing Products*, 23 S.W.3rd 228; *Liggons v. House & Associates*, 3 S.W.3rd 363.

Insurance Clients

ACUITY
Amerisure Insurance Company
CNA Commercial Insurance Company
FCCI Insurance Company
Kentuckiana Medical Reciprocal Risk Retention Group
The Medical Protective Company
PICA Group
Shelter Insurance Companies
American Commerce Insurance Company
Encompass Insurance
Farmers Insurance Company
Hallmark Insurance Company
Kentucky Hospital Insurance Company
Motorists Mutual Insurance Company
Zurich U.S.

Non-Insurance Clients

Baptist Health Care System, Inc.
Community Health Systems, Inc.
Davita, Inc.
LifePoint Hospitals, Inc.
Norton Healthcare, Inc.
Papa John's International, Inc.
Churchill Downs, Inc.
Cracker Barrel Old Country Stores
Kentucky League of Cities
Louisville Metro Housing Authority
Steak 'n Shake, Inc.

Partners

John W. Phillips — 1956 — University of Kentucky, B.A. (with high distinction), 1977; J.D., 1981; Exeter College, Oxford University — Phi Beta Kappa — Kentucky Law Journal, 1979-1981 — Admitted to Bar, 1981, Kentucky; 1981, U.S. District Court, Eastern and Western Districts of Kentucky; 1981, U.S. Court of Appeals, Sixth Circuit; 1981, U.S. Supreme Court — Member American, Kentucky and Louisville Bar Associations; Kentucky Association of Trial Attorneys; Defense Research Institute; Kentucky Defense Counsel — E-mail: jphillips@ppoalaw.com

Susan D. Phillips — 1956 — University of Kentucky, B.A., 1978; J.D., 1981 — Omicron Delta Kappa; Kappa Delta Pi — Kentucky Law Journal, 1979-1981 — Admitted to Bar, 1981, Kentucky; 1982, U.S. District Court, Eastern District of Kentucky; 1984, U.S. District Court, Western District of Kentucky; 1985, U.S. Court of Appeals, Sixth Circuit — Member American, Kentucky (Trial Commissioner) and Louisville Bar Associations; Louisville Bar Foundation (Board of Directors); American College of Trial Lawyers; Defense Research Institute; Kentucky Defense Counsel — E-mail: sphillips@ppoalaw.com

John F. Parker, Jr. — 1962 — University of Kentucky, B.S., 1984; University of Louisville, J.D., 1987 — Admitted to Bar, 1987, Kentucky; 1987, U.S. District Court, Western District of Kentucky; 1988, U.S. District Court, Eastern District of Kentucky — Member American, Kentucky and Louisville Bar Associations; Kentucky Academy of Trial Lawyers; Defense Research Institute; Kentucky Defense Counsel — E-mail: jparker@ppoalaw.com

Phillips Parker Orberson & Arnett, P.L.C., Louisville, KY (Continued)

William B. Orberson — 1962 — Bellarmine University, B.A. (magna cum laude), 1983; University of Louisville, J.D. (cum laude), 1986 — Admitted to Bar, 1986, Kentucky; 1986, U.S. District Court, Eastern and Western Districts of Kentucky; 1986, Supreme Court of Kentucky — Member American Bar Association (Member, Tort and Insurance Practice Section); Kentucky and Louisville Bar Associations; Defense Research Institute; Kentucky Defense Counsel — Member, Brandeis Society; Recipient, John C. Jayes Award; Former Member, Adjunct Faculty, University of Louisville School of Law — E-mail: worberson@ppoalaw.com

Martin A. Arnett — 1956 — The University of Tennessee, B.S., 1979; University of Louisville, J.D., 1982 — Admitted to Bar, 1983, Kentucky; 1983, U.S. District Court, Eastern and Western Districts of Kentucky — Member American, Kentucky and Louisville Bar Associations; Kentucky Academy of Trial Attorneys; Kentucky Society for Healthcare Risk Management; Kentucky Academy of Hospital Attorneys; American Academy of Hospital Attorneys; The Association of Trial Attorneys; Defense Research Institute — E-mail: marnett@ppoalaw.com

Paul J. Bishop — 1967 — University of Kentucky, B.A., 1990; M.S., 1992; University of Louisville, J.D., 1996 — Psi Chi — Articles Editor and Member, University of Louisville Journal — Admitted to Bar, 1996, Kentucky; 1997, Indiana; 1997, U.S. District Court, Eastern and Western Districts of Kentucky; 1997, U.S. District Court, Southern District of Indiana; 1997, U.S. Court of Appeals, Sixth Circuit — Member American, Kentucky, Indiana and Louisville Bar Associations; Kentucky Academy of Trial Lawyers; Kentucky Defense Counsel; Defense Research Institute — E-mail: pbishop@ppoalaw.com

Joseph M. Effinger — 1972 — University of Dayton, B.A., 1994; University of Louisville, J.D., 1998 — Admitted to Bar, 1998, Kentucky; 1998, U.S. District Court, Western District of Kentucky; 2001, U.S. District Court, Eastern District of Kentucky — Member American, Kentucky and Louisville Bar Associations — E-mail: jeffinger@ppoalaw.com

D. Sean Ragland — 1966 — Western Kentucky University, B.A. (cum laude), 1988; University of Louisville, J.D. (cum laude), 1992 — Brandeis Honor Society — Admitted to Bar, 1992, Kentucky; 1992, U.S. District Court, Eastern and Western Districts of Kentucky — Practice Areas: Insurance Defense; Medical Malpractice; Product Liability; Civil Rights; Employment Law — E-mail: sragland@ppoalaw.com

Patricia C. Le Meur — 1969 — Bryn Mawr College, A.B., 1994; University of Louisville, M.S., 1996; J.D., 2001 — Admitted to Bar, 2001, Kentucky — Member American, Kentucky and Louisville Bar Associations — E-mail: plemeur@ppoalaw.com

M. David Thompson — 1976 — University of Louisville, B.A., 1998; University of Kentucky, J.D., 2001 — Admitted to Bar, 2001, Virginia; 2008, Kentucky; U.S. District Court, Eastern and Western Districts of Kentucky — Member Kentucky and Louisville Bar Associations; Virginia State Bar — E-mail: dthompson@ppoalaw.com

Associates

Tera M. Rehmel — 1972 — Milligan College, B.A. (cum laude), 1993; The University of Tennessee, J.D., 1996 — Admitted to Bar, 1996, Kentucky; 1999, U.S. District Court, Eastern and Western Districts of Kentucky — Member American, Kentucky and Louisville Bar Associations — E-mail: trehmel@ppoalaw.com

Christopher M. Mayer — 1978 — University of Kentucky, B.S. (summa cum laude), 2001; J.D. (cum laude), 2004 — Admitted to Bar, 2004, Kentucky — Member American, Kentucky and Louisville Bar Associations; American Trial Lawyers Association; Defense Research Institute — Practice Areas: Insurance Defense — E-mail: cmayer@ppoalaw.com

Megan P. O'Reilly — 1979 — University of Dayton, B.A. Political Science, 2001; University of Louisville, J.D., 2004 — Admitted to Bar, 2005, Illinois; 2012, Kentucky — Member Kentucky and Louisville Bar Associations; Illinois Women's Bar Association — E-mail: moreilly@ppoalaw.com

Nicholas R. Hart — 1981 — Colorado College, B.A., 2004; University of Kentucky, J.D., 2007 — Admitted to Bar, 2007, Kentucky; 2008, Indiana; 2007, U.S. District Court, Eastern and Western Districts of Kentucky; 2008, U.S. District Court, Southern District of Indiana — Member Kentucky, Indiana State and Louisville Bar Associations — E-mail: nhart@ppoalaw.com

Katherine T. Watts — 1984 — Union College, B.A./B.S.B.A., 2006; Louis D. Brandeis School of Law, University of Louisville, J.D., 2009 — Admitted to Bar, 2009, Kentucky; 2009, U.S. District Court, Western District of Kentucky; 2010, U.S. Court of Appeals, Sixth Circuit — Member American, Kentucky and Louisville Bar Associations — E-mail: kwatts@ppoalaw.com

Phillips Parker Orberson & Arnett, P.L.C., Louisville, KY (Continued)

Matthew A. Piekarski — 1983 — Marquette University, B.A., 2006; Louis D. Brandeis School of Law, University of Louisville, J.D., 2009 — Admitted to Bar, 2009, Kentucky; 2010, U.S. District Court, Western District of Kentucky — Member Kentucky and Louisville Bar Associations — E-mail: mpiekarski@ppoalaw.com

Gregory E. Mayes, Jr. — 1987 — Georgetown College, B.A., 2009; Louis D. Brandeis School of Law, University of Louisville, J.D., 2012 — Admitted to Bar, 2012, Kentucky; 2013, U.S. District Court, Eastern and Western Districts of Kentucky; U.S. District Court, Southern District of Indiana — Member Kentucky and Louisville Bar Associations — E-mail: gmayes@ppoalaw.com

Of Counsel

William P. Swain — 1937 — Centre College of Kentucky, A.B., 1959; Vanderbilt University, LL.B., 1961 — Staff Member, Vanderbilt Law Review, Vanderbilt University, 1960-1961 — Admitted to Bar, 1961, Kentucky; 1961, U.S. District Court, Eastern and Western Districts of Kentucky; 1961, U.S. Court of Appeals, Sixth and Seventh Circuits; 1961, U.S. Supreme Court — Member American, Kentucky and Louisville Bar Associations — E-mail: wswain@ppoalaw.com

R. David Clark — 1947 — Western Kentucky University, B.S., 1967; Florida State University, M.S., 1968; University of Kentucky, J.D., 1972 — Admitted to Bar, 1973, Kentucky; U.S. District Court, Eastern and Western Districts of Kentucky; U.S. Court of Appeals, Sixth Circuit — Member American, Kentucky and Fayette County Bar Associations; Defense Research Institute — E-mail: dclark@ppoalaw.com

Edward (Ted) H. Bartenstein — 1961 — University of Kentucky, B.A., 1985; Louis D. Brandeis School of Law, University of Louisville, J.D., 1988 — Admitted to Bar, 1988, Kentucky; 1989, Indiana; U.S. Court of Appeals for the Federal and Sixth Circuits; U.S. District Court, Eastern and Western Districts of Kentucky; U.S. District Court, Northern and Southern Districts of Indiana — Member American and Louisville Bar Associations — E-mail: tbartenstein@ppoalaw.com

James C. Wade — 1971 — Bellarmine University, B.A., 1993; Louis D. Brandeis School of Law, University of Louisville, J.D., 1998 — Admitted to Bar, 1998, Kentucky; 2002, Indiana; 1999, U.S. District Court, Eastern and Western Districts of Kentucky; 2002, U.S. District Court, Southern District of Indiana — Member Kentucky and Louisville Bar Associations — E-mail: jwade@ppoalaw.com

Schiller Osbourn Barnes & Maloney, PLLC

One Riverfront Plaza, Suite 1600
401 West Main Street
Louisville, Kentucky 40202
Telephone: 502-583-4777
Fax: 502-583-4780
E-Mail: acoots@sobmlegal.com
www.sobmlegal.com

Employment Law, Environmental Litigation, Extra-Contractual Liability, Insurance Coverage, Motor Vehicle, Municipal Liability, Premises Liability, Professional Negligence, Product Liability, Transportation, Builders & Contractors, Fire, Explosion & Fraud, Mining & Blasting Litigation

Firm Profile: Schiller Osbourn Barnes & Maloney, PLLC carries Martindale-Hubbell's highest "AV" rating. The firm was formed in 1986 and is now among the leading civil defense firms in Kentucky. For nearly thirty years, the firm's steady growth has been measured to ensure the internal development of experienced litigators. Each of our attorneys has a unique concentration to his or her practice, which provides our clients with the requisite knowledge, resources, and experience to handle even the most complex cases. Each attorney is licensed to practice before all courts in the Commonwealth, including Kentucky's federal courts. We also have attorneys licensed to practice in other states and before the United States Sixth Circuit Court of Appeals and the United States Supreme Court.

Our firm's lawyers are committed to efficient representation of our clients. We work closely with our clients to identify their goals and expectations, and to implement a plan of action that best fits their needs on a case by case basis. We do not forget that we earn the privilege of representing our clients with every single assignment. The firm's original commitment to hard work has

LOUISVILLE   KENTUCKY

Schiller Osbourn Barnes & Maloney, PLLC, Louisville, KY (Continued)

never diminished. For further details on the firm and the areas of practice of our attorneys, please visit us at www.sobmlegal.com.

Insurance Clients

Auto-Owners Insurance Company
Grange Mutual Casualty Company
ProAssurance Company
Travelers Indemnity Company
Deep South/QBE Insurance
The Medical Protective Company
SECURA Insurance Companies

Partners

Richard P. Schiller — Hanover College, B.A., 1978; Louis D. Brandeis School of Law, University of Louisville, J.D., 1981 — Admitted to Bar, 1981, Kentucky

Mark A. Osbourn — Eastern Kentucky University, B.A., 1982; Louis D. Brandeis School of Law, University of Louisville, J.D., 1985 — Admitted to Bar, 1985, Kentucky

David K. Barnes — Alma College, B.A., 1983; University of Kentucky College of Law, J.D., 1986 — Admitted to Bar, 1986, Kentucky

Michael S. Maloney — University of Kentucky, B.A., 1990; Louis D. Brandeis School of Law, University of Louisville, J.D., 1993 — Admitted to Bar, 1993, Kentucky

Deanna M. Marzian Tucker — University of Louisville, B.A. (cum laude), 1995; University of Dayton School of Law, J.D., 1998 — Admitted to Bar, 1998, Kentucky; 1999, Indiana

Carol Schureck Petitt — University of Kentucky, B.A. (magna cum laude), 1992; Louis D. Brandeis School of Law, University of Louisville, J.D., 1997 — Admitted to Bar, 1998, Kentucky

James R. Chadward Kessinger — Centre College, B.S., 1996; University of Kentucky College of Law, J.D., 1999 — Admitted to Bar, 1999, Kentucky

Terri E. Kirkpatrick — West Virginia University, B.S. (summa cum laude), 1988; Louis D. Brandeis School of Law, University of Louisville, J.D. (cum laude), 1995 — Admitted to Bar, 1995, Kentucky

Stephen C. Keller — University of Kentucky, B.S./M.A., 1995; Louis D. Brandeis School of Law, University of Louisville, J.D., 1999 — Admitted to Bar, 1999, Kentucky

Associates

Katherine S. Dozier — University of Maryland, College Park, B.A. (cum laude), 1999; University of Kentucky College of Law, J.D., 2002 — Admitted to Bar, 2002, Kentucky

Noel R. Halpin — University College Dublin, B.A. (with high honors), 1995; Graduate (with high honors), 1996; The University of Tennessee College of Law, J.D., 2007 — Admitted to Bar, 2008, Kentucky

Adam E. Fuller — Murray State University, B.S., 2004; Louis D. Brandeis School of Law, University of Louisville, J.D., 2008 — Admitted to Bar, 2008, Kentucky

Christine D. Campbell — Bellarmine University, B.A. (cum laude), 1995; Louis D. Brandeis School of Law, University of Louisville, J.D., 2000 — Admitted to Bar, 2000, Kentucky; 2002, Indiana

Justin M. Schaefer — University of Kentucky, B.B.A. (summa cum laude, with honors), 2003; University of Kentucky College of Law, J.D., 2006 — Admitted to Bar, 2006, Kentucky

Kyle M. Vaughn — University of Louisville, B.S., 2004; Louis D. Brandeis School of Law, University of Louisville, J.D., 2009 — Admitted to Bar, 2009, Kentucky

Blake V. Edwards — University of Kentucky, B.S. (summa cum laude), 2007; University of Kentucky College of Law, J.D., 2010 — Admitted to Bar, 2010, Kentucky

Deron M. Schulten — Bellarmine University, B.A., 1996; Louis D. Brandeis School of Law, University of Louisville, J.D., 2011 — Admitted to Bar, 2011, Kentucky

Christopher E. Hutchison — Miami University, B.A., 1991; Louis D. Brandeis School of Law, University of Louisville, J.D., 1994 — Admitted to Bar, 1994, Kentucky

Gregory L. Finch — Transylvania University, B.A., 2011; Louis D. Brandeis School of Law, University of Louisville, J.D., 2014 — Admitted to Bar, 2014, Kentucky

Sewell, O'Brien & Neal, PLLC

220 West Main Street, Suite 1800
Louisville, Kentucky 40202
 Telephone: 502-582-2030
 Fax: 502-561-0766
 E-Mail: psewell@sonlegal.com
 www.sonlegal.com

Established: 1995

Automobile Accidents, Construction Accidents, Construction Defect, Insurance Coverage, Premises Liability, Product Liability, Workers' Compensation, Truck Accidents

Firm Profile: Sewell, O'Brien & Neal, PLLC defends individuals and businesses in wrongful death, products liability, personal injury, workers' compensation and insurance coverage litigation. We provide the highest quality legal services for individuals, companies and insurers with impeccable integrity.

Insurance Clients

Auto-Owners Insurance Company
Gallagher Bassett Services, Inc.
Penn National Insurance Company
Capitol Insurance Company
OneBeacon Insurance
Travelers Insurance Company

Non-Insurance Clients

The David Joseph Company

Partners

Peter J. Sewell — University of Kentucky, B.A., 1976; J.D., 1980 — Admitted to Bar, 1980, Kentucky; 1981, Indiana; U.S. District Court, Eastern and Western Districts of Kentucky; U.S. District Court, Southern District of Indiana — Member American, Kentucky and Louisville Bar Associations; Defense Research Institute — E-mail: psewell@sonlegal.com

Kenneth P. O'Brien — University of Louisville, B.A., 1989; J.D., 1992 — Admitted to Bar, 1992, Kentucky; 1993, U.S. District Court, Eastern and Western Districts of Kentucky; U.S. Court of Appeals, Sixth Circuit — Member American, Kentucky and Louisville Bar Associations; Association for Conflict Resolution; Kentucky Defense Counsel; Defense Research Institute — E-mail: kobrien@sonlegal.com

Michael P. Neal — Western Kentucky University, B.S. (cum laude), 1986; University of Kentucky, J.D., 1990 — Admitted to Bar, 1990, Kentucky; 1997, Indiana; 1990, U.S. District Court, Western District of Kentucky; 1995, U.S. District Court, Eastern District of Kentucky — Member American, Kentucky and Louisville Bar Associations — Lt., U.S. Navy, 1990-1994 — E-mail: mneal@sonlegal.com

Associates

Cathy M. Sewell — University of Kentucky, J.D., 1980 — Admitted to Bar, 1980, Kentucky

Michael D. DeFilippo — Northern Kentucky University, Salmon P. Chase College of Law, J.D., 2004 — Admitted to Bar, 2004, Kentucky

Thomas N. Peters — University of Kentucky, J.D., 2002 — Admitted to Bar, 2002, Kentucky

Erin C. Farnham — University of Louisville, J.D., 2003 — Admitted to Bar, 2003, Kentucky

Charles A. Walker — University of Louisville, J.D., 2008 — Admitted to Bar, 2008, Kentucky

---

The following firms also service this area.

Coleman Lochmiller & Bond
2907 Ring Road
Elizabethtown, Kentucky 42701
 Telephone: 270-737-0600
 Fax: 270-737-0488

Mailing Address: P.O. Box 1177, Elizabethtown, KY 42702-1177

Insurance Defense, Automobile, Commercial Law, Product Liability, Professional Liability, Property and Casualty, Medical Malpractice, Litigation, General

SEE COMPLETE LISTING UNDER ELIZABETHTOWN, KENTUCKY (45 MILES)

KENTUCKY

King, Deep & Branaman
127 North Main Street
Henderson, Kentucky 42420
  Telephone: 270-827-1852
  Fax: 270-826-7729

Mailing Address: P.O. Box 43, Henderson, KY 42419-0043

Insurance Defense, Product Liability, Malpractice, Workers' Compensation, Bad Faith, Coverage

SEE COMPLETE LISTING UNDER HENDERSON, KENTUCKY (127 MILES)

McNabb, Bragorgos & Burgess, PLLC
81 Monroe Avenue, Sixth Floor
Memphis, Tennessee 38103-5402
  Telephone: 901-624-0640
  Toll Free: 888-251-8000
  Fax: 901-624-0650

Insurance Defense, Trucking Litigation, Fire, Casualty, Malpractice, Fraud, Litigation, Marine, Product Liability, Workers' Compensation, Automobile, Mass Tort, Personal Injury, Commercial Law, Premises Liability, Subrogation, Construction Law, Nursing Home Defense

SEE COMPLETE LISTING UNDER MEMPHIS, TENNESSEE (392 MILES)

MADISONVILLE † 19,591 Hopkins Co.

Franklin, Gordon & Hobgood
24 Court Street
Madisonville, Kentucky 42431
  Telephone: 270-821-7252
  Fax: 270-821-2360
  E-Mail: fghlaw@bellsouth.net

Established: 1960

Insurance Defense, Litigation, Professional Liability, Product Liability, Medical Malpractice, Civil Rights, General Liability

Firm Profile: We concentrate on defending medical care providers and hospitals. We have successfully done so since 1977. We also provide defense on all general liability claims in Federal and State courts. Mr. Hobgood was certified by the old St. Paul Company on c.p. cases and Charles Franklin was on heart related cases. We are trial attorneys. Our firm enjoys an "AV" rating from Martindale-Hubbell.

Insurance Clients

Aetna Insurance Company
American International Adjustment Company
Assurance Insurance Company
Audubon Insurance Company
Central Insurance Companies
Central States Health & Life Company of Omaha
CIGNA Group
Cincinnati Insurance Company
Columbia Insurance Reserves
Crawford & Company
Economy Fire & Casualty Company
Farmland Mutual Insurance Company
GAB Robins North America, Inc.
Hamilton Mutual Insurance Company
Healthcare Underwriters Group of Florida
Jefferson Insurance Group
Kentucky Insurance Guarantee Fund
Liberty Mutual Insurance Company
Metropolitan Property and Casualty Insurance Company
Mill Mutuals Insurance Company
Milwaukee Insurance Company
National Continental Insurance Company
AIG Claim Services, Inc.
Amerisure Companies
Anthem Insurance Companies, Inc.
Atlanta Casualty Company
Cambridge Integrated Services
Central Mutual Insurance Company
Chrysler Insurance Company
Chubb Group of Insurance Companies
Collins and Company, Inc.
COUNTRY Mutual Insurance Company
EMC Insurance Companies
Farmers Insurance Group
Federated Mutual Insurance Company
Guaranty National Group
Harco National Insurance Company
Indiana Insurance Company
Insurance Company of North America
Lawyers Mutual Insurance Company
Meridian Mutual Insurance Company
The Midwestern Indemnity Company
Morrison Assurance Company
National Transportation Adjusters, Inc.

MADISONVILLE

Franklin, Gordon & Hobgood, Madisonville, KY
(Continued)

New Hampshire Insurance Company
Progressive Casualty Insurance Company
Seneca Insurance Company, Inc.
Southern General Insurance Company
Steadfast Insurance Company
Tennessee Farmers Mutual Insurance Company
21st Century Claims Service
Universal Underwriters Group
Woodmen of the World Life Insurance Society
The Professionals Insurance Company
Scottish & York International Insurance Group
Shelter Insurance Companies
State Volunteer Mutual Insurance Company
SUA Insurance Company
Time Insurance Company n.k.a. Assurant Health
United National Group
Western Surety Company
Zurich Insurance Company

Non-Insurance Clients

Alexsis, Inc.
Calhoun Feed Service, LLC
Cates Oldsmobile-Cadillac, Inc.
CSX Corporation
Dyno Nobel, Inc.
IHDS Corporation
Joy Technologies Inc.
The Northern Group
Baptist Health Madisonville Inc.
Cambridge Transportation (NTA)
Colonial Farms, LLC
Daughters of Charity National Health Care System
Jennie Stuart Medical Center
Kmart Corporation
Spectrum Emergency Care, Inc.

Partners

Byron Lee Hobgood — 1947 — Western Kentucky University, B.A. (with honors, magna cum laude), 1969; University of Kentucky, J.D., 1972 — Admitted to Bar, 1972, Kentucky; U.S. District Court, Western District of Kentucky; 1979, U.S. Court of Appeals, Sixth Circuit — Member Federal, American, Kentucky (Former Member, House of Delagates) and Hopkins County (Former President) Bar Associations; Kentucky Defense Counsel Association (Former Board of Directors Member); National Association of Railroad Trial Counsel; Defense Research Institute — Member, Governors Task Force on Corrections (1979); Special Kentucky Supreme Court Justice on two cases by Governor's appointment; City Attorney for Madisonville, KY (1975-1990); Kentucky Bar Association Ethics Committee Member; Kentucky Bar Association Ethics Hotline Subcommittee for 1st Supreme Court District — Practice Areas: Medical Malpractice Defense; General Liability; Motor Vehicle; Civil Rights; Professional Liability

Charles G. Franklin II — 1952 — Western Kentucky University, B.A., 1976; Salmon P. Chase College of Law, J.D., 1981 — Admitted to Bar, 1982, Kentucky; U.S. District Court, District of Kentucky; U.S. Court of Appeals, Sixth Circuit; U.S. District Court, Western District of Kentucky — Member American, Kentucky and Hopkins County (President, 2012-2013) Bar Associations; Kentucky Defense Counsel (Board Member); Defense Research Institute — Practice Areas: Medical Malpractice Defense; Professional Liability; Product Liability; Motor Vehicle

Associates

Randall L. Hardesty — 1958 — University of Kentucky, B.A. (with distinction), 1980; J.D., 1984 — Admitted to Bar, 1984, Kentucky; U.S. District Court, Eastern and Western Districts of Kentucky; U.S. Court of Appeals, Sixth Circuit — Member American, Kentucky and Hopkins County (Former President) Bar Associations — Practice Areas: General Liability; Motor Vehicle; Civil Rights

Hannah E. Kington — 1987 — Western Kentucky University, B.A. (magna cum laude), 2009; Salmon P. Chase College of Law, J.D., 2012 — Admitted to Bar, 2012, Kentucky; 2013, U.S. District Court, Western District of Kentucky; U.S. Court of Appeals, Sixth Circuit — Member American, Kentucky and Hopkins County Bar Associations — Practice Areas: Medical Malpractice Defense

---

The following firms also service this area.

King, Deep & Branaman
127 North Main Street
Henderson, Kentucky 42420
  Telephone: 270-827-1852
  Fax: 270-826-7729

Mailing Address: P.O. Box 43, Henderson, KY 42419-0043

Insurance Defense, Product Liability, Malpractice, Workers' Compensation, Bad Faith, Coverage

SEE COMPLETE LISTING UNDER HENDERSON, KENTUCKY (39 MILES)

PADUCAH   KENTUCKY

Al Miller
Attorney at Law
428 North Second Street
Central City, Kentucky 42330-1124
   Telephone: 270-754-5502
   Fax: 270-754-5503

Insurance Defense, Automobile Liability, Property Damage, Fire, Trial Practice, Appellate Practice, Investigations, Slip and Fall, Wrongful Death, Bad Faith, Liquor Liability, Legal Malpractice, Medical Malpractice, Coverage Issues, State and Federal Courts, Unfair Claims Practices

SEE COMPLETE LISTING UNDER CENTRAL CITY, KENTUCKY (31 MILES)

MORGANFIELD † 3,285 Union Co.

Refer To
Franklin, Gordon & Hobgood
24 Court Street
Madisonville, Kentucky 42431
   Telephone: 270-821-7252
   Fax: 270-821-2360

Mailing Address: P.O. Box 547, Madisonville, KY 42431

Insurance Defense, Litigation, Professional Liability, Product Liability, Medical Malpractice, Civil Rights, General Liability

SEE COMPLETE LISTING UNDER MADISONVILLE, KENTUCKY (47 MILES)

MORGANTOWN † 2,394 Butler Co.

Refer To
Kerrick Bachert PSC
1025 State Street
Bowling Green, Kentucky 42101
   Telephone: 270-782-8160
   Fax: 270-782-5856

Mailing Address: P.O. Box 9547, Bowling Green, KY 42102-9547

Product Liability, Malpractice, Automobile, Workers' Compensation, Accident and Health, General Liability, Subrogation, Commercial Law, Intellectual Property, Copyright and Trademark Law, Health Care, Employment Law, Real Estate, Insurance Defense

SEE COMPLETE LISTING UNDER BOWLING GREEN, KENTUCKY (24 MILES)

MUNFORDVILLE † 1,615 Hart Co.

Refer To
Coleman Lochmiller & Bond
2907 Ring Road
Elizabethtown, Kentucky 42701
   Telephone: 270-737-0600
   Fax: 270-737-0488

Mailing Address: P.O. Box 1177, Elizabethtown, KY 42702-1177

Insurance Defense, Automobile, Commercial Law, Product Liability, Professional Liability, Property and Casualty, Medical Malpractice, Litigation, General

SEE COMPLETE LISTING UNDER ELIZABETHTOWN, KENTUCKY (31 MILES)

Refer To
Kerrick Bachert PSC
1025 State Street
Bowling Green, Kentucky 42101
   Telephone: 270-782-8160
   Fax: 270-782-5856

Mailing Address: P.O. Box 9547, Bowling Green, KY 42102-9547

Product Liability, Malpractice, Automobile, Workers' Compensation, Accident and Health, General Liability, Subrogation, Commercial Law, Intellectual Property, Copyright and Trademark Law, Health Care, Employment Law, Real Estate, Insurance Defense

SEE COMPLETE LISTING UNDER BOWLING GREEN, KENTUCKY (42 MILES)

OWENSBORO † 57,265 Daviess Co.

Refer To
Coleman Lochmiller & Bond
2907 Ring Road
Elizabethtown, Kentucky 42701
   Telephone: 270-737-0600
   Fax: 270-737-0488

Mailing Address: P.O. Box 1177, Elizabethtown, KY 42702-1177

Insurance Defense, Automobile, Commercial Law, Product Liability, Professional Liability, Property and Casualty, Medical Malpractice, Litigation, General

SEE COMPLETE LISTING UNDER ELIZABETHTOWN, KENTUCKY (94 MILES)

Refer To
Franklin, Gordon & Hobgood
24 Court Street
Madisonville, Kentucky 42431
   Telephone: 270-821-7252
   Fax: 270-821-2360

Mailing Address: P.O. Box 547, Madisonville, KY 42431

Insurance Defense, Litigation, Professional Liability, Product Liability, Medical Malpractice, Civil Rights, General Liability

SEE COMPLETE LISTING UNDER MADISONVILLE, KENTUCKY (64 MILES)

Refer To
Kahn, Dees, Donovan & Kahn, LLP
501 Main Street, Suite 305
Evansville, Indiana 47708
   Telephone: 812-423-3183
   Fax: 812-423-3841

Mailing Address: P.O. Box 3646, Evansville, IN 47735-3646

Asbestos Litigation, Automobile, Construction Law, Coverage Issues, Environmental Law, Insurance Defense, General Liability, Labor and Employment, Mass Tort, Medical Malpractice, Personal Injury, Premises Liability, Product Liability, Property, Public Entities, Self-Insured, Subrogation, Workers' Compensation

SEE COMPLETE LISTING UNDER EVANSVILLE, INDIANA (38 MILES)

Refer To
King, Deep & Branaman
127 North Main Street
Henderson, Kentucky 42420
   Telephone: 270-827-1852
   Fax: 270-826-7729

Mailing Address: P.O. Box 43, Henderson, KY 42419-0043

Insurance Defense, Product Liability, Malpractice, Workers' Compensation, Bad Faith, Coverage

SEE COMPLETE LISTING UNDER HENDERSON, KENTUCKY (31 MILES)

Refer To
Al Miller
Attorney at Law
428 North Second Street
Central City, Kentucky 42330-1124
   Telephone: 270-754-5502
   Fax: 270-754-5503

Insurance Defense, Automobile Liability, Property Damage, Fire, Trial Practice, Appellate Practice, Investigations, Slip and Fall, Wrongful Death, Bad Faith, Liquor Liability, Legal Malpractice, Medical Malpractice, Coverage Issues, State and Federal Courts, Unfair Claims Practices

SEE COMPLETE LISTING UNDER CENTRAL CITY, KENTUCKY (35 MILES)

PADUCAH † 25,024 McCracken Co.

Boehl Stopher & Graves, LLP
410 Broadway Street
Paducah, Kentucky 42001
   Telephone: 270-442-4369
   Fax: 270-442-4689
   www.bsg-law.com

Boehl Stopher & Graves, LLP, Paducah, KY (Continued)

(Louisville, KY Office*: 400 West Market Street, Suite 2300, 40202-3354)
  (Tel: 502-589-5980)
  (Fax: 502-561-9400)
  (E-Mail: louisville@bsg-law.com)
(New Albany, IN Office: Elsby East, 400 Pearl Street, Suite 204, 47150)
  (Tel: 812-948-5053)
(Lexington, KY Office*: 444 West Second Street, 40507)
  (Tel: 859-252-6721)
  (Fax: 859-253-1445)
(Pikeville, KY Office*: 137 Main Street, Suite 2, 41501, P.O. Box 1132, 41502)
  (Tel: 606-432-9670)

Insurance Law, Casualty, Surety, Workers' Compensation, Product Liability, Medical Malpractice, Professional Malpractice

Insurance Clients

Amerisure Companies
Bituminous Casualty Corporation
Fireman's Fund Insurance Company
Hartford Accident and Indemnity Company
Ohio Casualty Group
Prudential Property and Casualty Insurance Company
Utica Mutual Insurance Company
Argonaut Insurance Company
CIGNA Property and Casualty Insurance Company
Great American Insurance Company
Kemper Insurance Companies
Old Republic Insurance Company
St. Paul Fire and Marine Insurance Company

(See listing under Louisville, KY for additional information)

Denton & Keuler, LLP

Paducah Bank Building
555 Jefferson Street, Suite 301
Paducah, Kentucky 42001
  Telephone: 270-443-8253
  Fax: 270-442-6000
  E-Mail: dk@dklaw.com
  www.dklaw.com

Established: 1979

Insurance Defense, Automobile, Workers' Compensation, Admiralty and Maritime Law, Personal Injury, Subrogation, Trust and Estate Litigation, Banking, Business and Real Estate Transactions, Business Law, Commercial Real Estate Law, Commercial Law, Elder Law, Employment Law, Estate Administration, Property and Casualty, Construction Law, Estate and Tax Planning, General Civil Litigation, Guardian and Conservatorships, Governmental Entity Defense

Insurance Clients

Allied Insurance Company
Clarendon National Insurance Company
Employers Reinsurance Corporation
Great American Insurance Group
Kentucky League of Cities f/k/a Kentucky Municipal Risk Management Association
Ohio Casualty Group
Sentry Insurance
VELA Insurance Services (A Berkley Company)
Zurich North America
Cincinnati Insurance Company
CNA Insurance Company
Countryway Insurance Company
Federated Rural Electric Insurance Exchange
Hanover Insurance Group
Madison Mutual Insurance Company
Michigan Millers Mutual Insurance Company
Trident Insurance Services
W.R. Berkley (Union Standard Insurance Group)

Non-Insurance Clients

City of Paducah
James Marine, Inc.
Kentucky Association of Counties All Lines Fund
Jackson Purchase Energy Corporation
Lourdes Hospital, Inc.

Denton & Keuler, LLP, Paducah, KY (Continued)

Managing Partner

David L. Kelly — 1965 — Kentucky Wesleyan College, B.A. (magna cum laude), 1987; University of Kentucky, J.D., 1990 — Admitted to Bar, 1990, Kentucky — Member Kentucky and McCracken County Bar Associations

Partners

W. David Denton — 1941 — Murray State University, B.S., 1964; University of Kentucky, J.D., 1969 — Admitted to Bar, 1969, Kentucky; 1969, U.S. District Court, Western District of Kentucky — Member Federal, American, Kentucky and McCracken County Bar Associations

Thomas J. Keuler — 1950 — University of Wisconsin, B.S. (magna cum laude), 1972; University of Louisville, J.D., 1976 — Admitted to Bar, 1976, Kentucky; 1976, U.S. District Court, Western District of Kentucky — Member Kentucky and McCracken County Bar Associations

William E. Pinkston — 1953 — University of Kentucky, B.S., 1975; J.D., 1979 — Admitted to Bar, 1979, Kentucky; 1979, U.S. District Court, Western District of Kentucky — Member American, Kentucky and McCracken County Bar Associations

Glenn D. Denton — 1969 — Centre College of Kentucky, B.A., 1992; Salmon P. Chase College of Law, J.D., 1995 — Admitted to Bar, 1995, Kentucky; 1996, Illinois; 1996, U.S. District Court, Western District of Kentucky — Member American, Kentucky, Illinois State and McCracken County Bar Associations

Stacey A. Blankenship — 1970 — Murray State University, B.S. (cum laude), 1991; Southern Illinois University, J.D. (magna cum laude), 1995 — Admitted to Bar, 1995, Kentucky; 1998, U.S. District Court, Western District of Kentucky; 1998, U.S. Court of Appeals, Sixth Circuit — Member Kentucky and McCracken County Bar Associations

---

The following firms also service this area.

Coleman Lochmiller & Bond
2907 Ring Road
Elizabethtown, Kentucky 42701
  Telephone: 270-737-0600
  Fax: 270-737-0488

Mailing Address: P.O. Box 1177, Elizabethtown, KY 42702-1177

Insurance Defense, Automobile, Commercial Law, Product Liability, Professional Liability, Property and Casualty, Medical Malpractice, Litigation, General

SEE COMPLETE LISTING UNDER ELIZABETHTOWN, KENTUCKY (172 MILES)

Franklin, Gordon & Hobgood
24 Court Street
Madisonville, Kentucky 42431
  Telephone: 270-821-7252
  Fax: 270-821-2360

Mailing Address: P.O. Box 547, Madisonville, KY 42431

Insurance Defense, Litigation, Professional Liability, Product Liability, Medical Malpractice, Civil Rights, General Liability

SEE COMPLETE LISTING UNDER MADISONVILLE, KENTUCKY (81 MILES)

King, Deep & Branaman
127 North Main Street
Henderson, Kentucky 42420
  Telephone: 270-827-1852
  Fax: 270-826-7729

Mailing Address: P.O. Box 43, Henderson, KY 42419-0043

Insurance Defense, Product Liability, Malpractice, Workers' Compensation, Bad Faith, Coverage

SEE COMPLETE LISTING UNDER HENDERSON, KENTUCKY (96 MILES)

PIKEVILLE   KENTUCKY

McNabb, Bragorgos & Burgess, PLLC
81 Monroe Avenue, Sixth Floor
Memphis, Tennessee 38103-5402
  Telephone: 901-624-0640
  Toll Free: 888-251-8000
  Fax: 901-624-0650

Insurance Defense, Trucking Litigation, Fire, Casualty, Malpractice, Fraud, Litigation, Marine, Product Liability, Workers' Compensation, Automobile, Mass Tort, Personal Injury, Commercial Law, Premises Liability, Subrogation, Construction Law, Nursing Home Defense

SEE COMPLETE LISTING UNDER MEMPHIS, TENNESSEE (198 MILES)

PIKEVILLE † 6,903 Pike Co.

Boehl Stopher & Graves, LLP
137 Main Street, Suite 2
Pikeville, Kentucky 41501
  Telephone: 606-432-9670
  www.bsg-law.com

(Louisville, KY Office*: 400 West Market Street, Suite 2300, 40202-3354)
  (Tel: 502-589-5980)
  (Fax: 502-561-9400)
  (E-Mail: louisville@bsg-law.com)
(New Albany, IN Office: Elsby East, 400 Pearl Street, Suite 204, 47150)
  (Tel: 812-948-5053)
(Lexington, KY Office*: 444 West Second Street, 40507)
  (Tel: 859-252-6721)
  (Fax: 859-253-1445)
(Paducah, KY Office*: 410 Broadway Street, 42001)
  (Tel: 270-442-4369)
  (Fax: 270-442-4689)

Insurance Litigation, Casualty, Surety, Workers' Compensation, Product Liability

Insurance Clients

Argonaut Insurance Company
Atlantic Mutual Insurance Company
CNA Insurance Company
Continental Insurance Company
Great American Insurance Company
Hartford Insurance Company
Liberty Mutual Insurance Company
Maryland Casualty Company
Monroe Guaranty Insurance Company
Old Republic Insurance Company
Reserve Life Insurance Company
St. Paul Fire and Marine Insurance Company
United States Aviation Underwriters, Inc.
Associated Aviation Underwriters
Bituminous Casualty Corporation
CIGNA Property and Casualty Insurance Company
Coregis Insurance Company
GRE Insurance Group
Gulf Insurance Company
Home Insurance Company
Lloyd's
McLarens Toplis North America, Inc.
National Indemnity Company
Prudential Property and Casualty Insurance Company
State Farm Mutual Automobile Insurance Company
Utica Mutual Insurance Company
Zurich American Insurance Company

(See listing under Louisville, KY for additional information)

Stratton Law Firm, P.S.C.
111 Pike Street
Pikeville, Kentucky 41501
  Telephone: 606-437-7800
  Fax: 606-437-7569
  E-Mail: strattonlaw@setel.com
  www.strattonlawfirm.net

Established: 1898

Stratton Law Firm, P.S.C., Pikeville, KY   (Continued)

Insurance Defense, Automobile Liability, Casualty, General Liability, Life Insurance, Disability, Coverage Issues, Employment Law, Breach of Contract, Subrogation, Product Liability

Firm Profile: Stratton Law Firm was founded in 1898 by P. B. Stratton, who had various partners during his 55 years in practice. His son, Henry D. Stratton, joined the firm in 1950, and built a statewide reputation for legal excellence. He served as president of the KBA, and was recognized as Kentucky's Outstanding Attorney in 1989. David C. Stratton and Daniel P. Stratton, Henry's sons, now lead the firm, seeking to carry on the family's commitment to legal excellence and professionalism.

Insurance Clients

Anthem Blue Cross and Blue Shield
Colony Insurance Company
Dairyland Insurance Company
Electric Insurance Company
First Mercury Insurance Company
Homesite Insurance Company
Integon General Insurance Corporation
John Deere Insurance Company
Maxum Specialty Insurance Group
Monumental Life Insurance Company
Sagamore Insurance Company
The Seibels Bruce Group, Inc.
Shenandoah Life Insurance Company
The Vision Insurance Group
Assurity Life Insurance Company
Cambridge Integrated Services
Crawford & Co./YMCA Insurance Claims Service
Federated Insurance Company
Guaranty National Insurance Company
Investors Underwriting Managers, Inc.
Kentucky Association of Counties All Lines Fund
Motor Transport Underwriters, Inc.
Providian Financial Corporation
Scottsdale Insurance Company
Sentry Claims Services
United Ohio Insurance Company
Veterans Life Insurance Company

Non-Insurance Clients

Indiana Mills and Manfacturing, Incorporated
Sony Electronics Inc.
Virginia Drilling Co., LLC
Kellogg Company
Marathon Realty Corporation
TransUnion Settlement Solutions, Inc.

Partners

David C. Stratton — 1953 — Eastern Kentucky University, B.A., 1975; Northern Kentucky University, Salmon P. Chase College of Law, J.D., 1978 — Phi Alpha Delta — Admitted to Bar, 1979, Kentucky; 1979, U.S. District Court, Eastern District of Kentucky; 1979, U.S. Court of Appeals, Sixth Circuit; 1989, U.S. Supreme Court — Member Kentucky Bar Association (Board of Governors, 1989-1991 and 1996-2002; Chairman, Kentucky House of Delegates, 1990-1991); Pike County Bar Association; Kentucky Bar Foundation; Kentucky Defense Counsel; Defense Research Institute — E-mail: dcstratton@setel.com

Daniel P. Stratton — 1953 — Eastern Kentucky University, B.A. (with distinction), 1975; Northern Kentucky University, Salmon P. Chase College of Law, J.D., 1978 — Phi Alpha Delta — Admitted to Bar, 1978, Kentucky; 1979, U.S. District Court, Eastern District of Kentucky; 2002, U.S. Court of Appeals, Sixth Circuit; 2002, U.S. Supreme Court — Member Kentucky Bar Association (Board of Governors, 1985-1986); Pike County Bar Association (President, 1980-1981); Kentucky Bar Foundation (Director, 1985-1991; President, 1989-1990) — Lawyers Mutual Insurance Company of Kentucky (Secretary-Treasurer, 1987-1993; Treasurer, 2000-) (Director, 1987-1993 and 1999-present) — E-mail: dpstratton@setel.com

Associate

Brandt M. Spears — 1987 — Pikeville College, B.A. (magna cum laude), 2009; Thomas M. Cooley Law School, J.D. (cum laude), 2013 — Admitted to Bar, 2013, Kentucky — Member Kentucky Bar Association (Young Lawyers Division) — E-mail: bmspears@setel.com

KENTUCKY

PRESTONSBURG † 3,255 Floyd Co.
Refer To
Stratton Law Firm, P.S.C.
111 Pike Street
Pikeville, Kentucky 41501
   Telephone: 606-437-7800
   Fax: 606-437-7569

Mailing Address: P.O. Box 1530, Pikeville, KY 41502

Insurance Defense, Automobile Liability, Casualty, General Liability, Life Insurance, Disability, Coverage Issues, Employment Law, Breach of Contract, Subrogation, Product Liability

SEE COMPLETE LISTING UNDER PIKEVILLE, KENTUCKY (26 MILES)

PRINCETON † 6,329 Caldwell Co.
Refer To
Al Miller
Attorney at Law
428 North Second Street
Central City, Kentucky 42330-1124
   Telephone: 270-754-5502
   Fax: 270-754-5503

Insurance Defense, Automobile Liability, Property Damage, Fire, Trial Practice, Appellate Practice, Investigations, Slip and Fall, Wrongful Death, Bad Faith, Liquor Liability, Legal Malpractice, Medical Malpractice, Coverage Issues, State and Federal Courts, Unfair Claims Practices

SEE COMPLETE LISTING UNDER CENTRAL CITY, KENTUCKY (48 MILES)

RUSSELLVILLE † 6,960 Logan Co.
Refer To
Kerrick Bachert PSC
1025 State Street
Bowling Green, Kentucky 42101
   Telephone: 270-782-8160
   Fax: 270-782-5856

Mailing Address: P.O. Box 9547, Bowling Green, KY 42102-9547

Product Liability, Malpractice, Automobile, Workers' Compensation, Accident and Health, General Liability, Subrogation, Commercial Law, Intellectual Property, Copyright and Trademark Law, Health Care, Employment Law, Real Estate, Insurance Defense

SEE COMPLETE LISTING UNDER BOWLING GREEN, KENTUCKY (28 MILES)

SCOTTSVILLE † 4,226 Allen Co.
Refer To
Kerrick Bachert PSC
1025 State Street
Bowling Green, Kentucky 42101
   Telephone: 270-782-8160
   Fax: 270-782-5856

Mailing Address: P.O. Box 9547, Bowling Green, KY 42102-9547

Product Liability, Malpractice, Automobile, Workers' Compensation, Accident and Health, General Liability, Subrogation, Commercial Law, Intellectual Property, Copyright and Trademark Law, Health Care, Employment Law, Real Estate, Insurance Defense

SEE COMPLETE LISTING UNDER BOWLING GREEN, KENTUCKY (25 MILES)

SHEPHERDSVILLE † 11,222 Bullitt Co.
Refer To
Coleman Lochmiller & Bond
2907 Ring Road
Elizabethtown, Kentucky 42701
   Telephone: 270-737-0600
   Fax: 270-737-0488

Mailing Address: P.O. Box 1177, Elizabethtown, KY 42702-1177

Insurance Defense, Automobile, Commercial Law, Product Liability, Professional Liability, Property and Casualty, Medical Malpractice, Litigation, General

SEE COMPLETE LISTING UNDER ELIZABETHTOWN, KENTUCKY (25 MILES)

SOMERSET † 11,196 Pulaski Co.
Refer To
Taylor, Keller & Oswald, PLLC
1306 West 5th Street, Suite 100
London, Kentucky 40741
   Telephone: 606-878-8844
   Fax: 606-878-8850

Mailing Address: P.O. Box 3440, London, KY 40743-3440

Trial Practice, Automobile Liability, Property, Insurance Coverage, Product Liability, Premises Liability, Subrogation, Insurance Fraud, Bad Faith, Governmental Liability, General Insurance and Corporate Defense

SEE COMPLETE LISTING UNDER LONDON, KENTUCKY (33 MILES)

TOMPKINSVILLE † 2,402 Monroe Co.
Refer To
Kerrick Bachert PSC
1025 State Street
Bowling Green, Kentucky 42101
   Telephone: 270-782-8160
   Fax: 270-782-5856

Mailing Address: P.O. Box 9547, Bowling Green, KY 42102-9547

Product Liability, Malpractice, Automobile, Workers' Compensation, Accident and Health, General Liability, Subrogation, Commercial Law, Intellectual Property, Copyright and Trademark Law, Health Care, Employment Law, Real Estate, Insurance Defense

SEE COMPLETE LISTING UNDER BOWLING GREEN, KENTUCKY (62 MILES)

WHITESBURG † 2,139 Letcher Co.
Refer To
Stratton Law Firm, P.S.C.
111 Pike Street
Pikeville, Kentucky 41501
   Telephone: 606-437-7800
   Fax: 606-437-7569

Mailing Address: P.O. Box 1530, Pikeville, KY 41502

Insurance Defense, Automobile Liability, Casualty, General Liability, Life Insurance, Disability, Coverage Issues, Employment Law, Breach of Contract, Subrogation, Product Liability

SEE COMPLETE LISTING UNDER PIKEVILLE, KENTUCKY (45 MILES)

WILLIAMSBURG † 5,245 Whitley Co.
Refer To
Taylor, Keller & Oswald, PLLC
1306 West 5th Street, Suite 100
London, Kentucky 40741
   Telephone: 606-878-8844
   Fax: 606-878-8850

Mailing Address: P.O. Box 3440, London, KY 40743-3440

Trial Practice, Automobile Liability, Property, Insurance Coverage, Product Liability, Premises Liability, Subrogation, Insurance Fraud, Bad Faith, Governmental Liability, General Insurance and Corporate Defense

SEE COMPLETE LISTING UNDER LONDON, KENTUCKY (30 MILES)

LOUISIANA

CAPITAL: BATON ROUGE

PARISHES AND PARISH SEATS

Parish	Parish Seat	Parish	Parish Seat	Parish	Parish Seat
Acadia	Crowley	Iberia	New Iberia	St. Charles	Hahnville
Allen	Oberlin	Iberville	Plaquemine	St. Helena	Greensburg
Ascension	Donaldsonville	Jackson	Jonesboro	St. James	Convent
Assumption	Napoleonville	Jefferson	Gretna	St. John The Baptist	La Place
Avoyelles	Marksville	Jefferson Davis	Jennings	St. Landry	Opelousas
Beauregard	De Ridder	Lafayette	Lafayette	St. Martin	St. Martinville
Bienville	Arcadia	Lafourche	Thibodaux	St. Mary	Franklin
Bossier	Benton	La Salle	Jena	St. Tammany	Covington
Caddo	Shreveport	Lincoln	Ruston	Tangipahoa	Amite
Calcasieu	Lake Charles	Livingston	Livingston	Tensas	St. Joseph
Caldwell	Columbia	Madison	Tallulah	Terrebonne	Houma
Cameron	Cameron	Morehouse	Bastrop	Union	Farmerville
Catahoula	Harrisonburg	Natchitoches	Natchitoches	Vermilion	Abbeville
Claiborne	Homer	Orleans	New Orleans	Vernon	Leesville
Concordia	Vidalia	Ouachita	Monroe	Washington	Franklinton
De Soto	Mansfield	Plaquemines	Pointe a la Hache	Webster	Minden
East Baton Rouge	Baton Rouge	Pointe Coupee	New Roads	West Baton Rouge	Port Allen
East Carroll	Lake Providence	Rapides	Alexandria	West Carroll	Oak Grove
East Feliciana	Clinton	Red River	Coushatta	West Feliciana	St. Francisville
Evangeline	Ville Platte	Richland	Rayville	Winn	Winnfield
Franklin	Winnsboro	Sabine	Many		
Grant	Colfax	St. Bernard	Chalmette		

In the text that follows "†" indicates Parish Seats.

Our files contain additional verified data on the firms listed herein. This additional information is available on request.

A.M. BEST COMPANY

LOUISIANA — ALEXANDRIA

ALEXANDRIA † 47,723 Rapides Par.

Bolen, Parker, Brenner & Lee, Ltd.
A Professional Law Corporation

709 Versailles Boulevard
Alexandria, Louisiana 71303
   Telephone: 318-445-8236
   Fax: 318-443-1770
   E-Mail: belaw@bolenlaw.com
   www.bolenlaw.com

Established: 1972

General Defense, Casualty, Fire, Surety, Life Insurance, Workers' Compensation, Product Liability, Professional Liability, Automobile and Hospitalization Insurance Law

Insurance Clients

Allstate Insurance Company
Central Mutual Insurance Company
Chicago Insurance Company
Fireman's Fund Insurance Company
Gulf Insurance Company
Indiana Lumbermens Mutual Insurance Company
Trinity Universal Insurance Company
American Centennial Insurance Company
CIGNA Insurance Company
First American Insurance Agency, Inc.
Horace Mann Insurance Company
Liberty Mutual Insurance Company
The Medical Protective Company
Zurich American Insurance Company

Non-Insurance Clients

Chevron U.S.A., Inc.
E.I. du Pont de Nemours and Company, Inc.
Procter & Gamble Company
Clark Equipment Company
INTERUNFALL
Petrolane, Inc.
Riley Mobile Homes

Firm Members

James A. Bolen, Jr. — 1937 — Louisiana State University, B.A., 1961; LL.B., 1965 — Admitted to Bar, 1965, Louisiana — Member American Bar Association (Sections: Litigation and Insurance, Negligence and Compensation); Louisiana State Bar Association (House of Delegates, 1972-1974); Alexandria Bar Association; American Inn of Court Crossroads; Louisiana Association of Defense Counsel; Defense Research Institute; International Association of Defense Counsel — E-mail: jbolen@bolenlaw.com

L. Lyle Parker — 1957 — Louisiana Tech University, B.S. (summa cum laude), 1978; Louisiana State University, J.D., 1985 — Admitted to Bar, 1986, Louisiana — Member American, State and Alexandria Bar Associations — E-mail: lparker@bolenlaw.com

Daniel G. Brenner — 1960 — Louisiana Tech University, B.A., 1983; Louisiana State University, J.D., 1987 — Admitted to Bar, 1987, Louisiana — Member American, Louisiana State and Alexandria Bar Associations — E-mail: dbrenner@bolenlaw.com

Madeline J. Lee — 1961 — Louisiana State University, B.S., 1987; J.D., 1990 — Admitted to Bar, 1990, Louisiana — Member American, Louisiana State and Alexandria Bar Associations; Central Louisiana Association of Women Attorneys; Louisiana Association of Defense Counsel — E-mail: mjlee@bolenlaw.com

Gregory Engelsman — 1967 — Louisiana State University, B.A., 1989; J.D., 1992 — Admitted to Bar, 1992, Louisiana — Member Louisiana State and Alexandria (Executive Committee, 2008) Bar Associations — E-mail: gengelsman@bolenlaw.com

Eric J. Miller — 1966 — Louisiana State University, B.A., 1989; J.D., 1992 — Admitted to Bar, 1993, Louisiana — Member Louisiana Association of Defense Counsel; American Inns of Court — Languages: Spanish — E-mail: ejmiller@bolenlaw.com

Christina Slay — 1981 — Louisiana College, B.A., 2003; Regent University, J.D., 2006 — Admitted to Bar, 2006, Louisiana; U.S. District Court, Western District of Louisiana — E-mail: cslay@bolenlaw.com

Richard P. Mansour Jr. — 1980 — Louisiana State University at Baton Rouge, B.A., 2003; Loyola University New Orleans College of Law, J.D., 2007 — Admitted to Bar, 2008, Louisiana — E-mail: pmansour@bolenlaw.com

Bolen, Parker, Brenner & Lee, Ltd., A Professional Law Corporation, Alexandria, LA (Continued)

Patricia K. Penny — 1983 — Louisiana State University, B.A. (magna cum laude), 2005; Paul M Hebert Law School at Louisiana State University, J.D./B.C.L., 2008 — Admitted to Bar, 2008, Louisiana; 2010, U.S. District Court, Western District of Louisiana — Member Louisiana State and Alexandria Bar Associations — Languages: Spanish — E-mail: kpenny@bolenlaw.com

Bussey & Lauve, LLC

3640 Bayou Rapides Road
Alexandria, Louisiana 71303-3653
   Telephone: 318-449-1937
   Fax: 318-487-6032
   E-Mail: BusLav@aol.com
   www.blclawgroup.com

Established: 1996

Insurance Defense, Automobile, Workers' Compensation, Bodily Injury, General Liability, Medical Malpractice, Personal Injury, Employment Discrimination, Nursing Home Liability, Product Liability

Firm Profile: Old fashioned, conservative values are the trademark of Bussey & Lauve, L.L.C., Attorneys at Law. We make it our business to keep our clients informed during each stage of litigation. Our approach creates a team atmosphere, and results in equitable, cost effective case results.

We concentrate on insurance defense litigation, which includes personal injury, property damage, workers' compensation, medical malpractice, product liability, automobile liability defense, environmental defense, nursing home liability, and employment discrimination. We are also active in estate planning, various business transactions and in numerous real estate transactions.

Reported Cases involving members of this firm include *Caskey v. Merrick Const. Co., Inc.,* 949 So.2d 560 (La. App. 2 Cir. 2007); *International Paper, Inc. v. Hilton,* 950 So.2d 1 (La. App. 3 Cir. 2006); *Armand v. Lachney,* 921 So.2d 1196 (La. App. 3 Cir. 2006).

Insurance Clients

American Equity Insurance Company
Boston Old Colony Insurance Company
Glatfelter Insurance Group
GuideOne Insurance
Insurance Corporation of America
Louisiana Commerce and Trade Association
Mor-Tem Risk Management Services, Inc.
Phoenix Indemnity Insurance Company
Risk Management Services, L.L.C.
Self-Insurers Service Bureau, Inc.
Underwriters at Lloyd's, London
Zurich American Insurance Company
American Home Shield
Audubon Insurance Company
Executive Risk Consultants, Inc.
First Nonprofit Insurance Company
Gray Insurance Company
Hallmark Insurance Company
Lincoln General Insurance Company
Louisiana Insurance Guaranty Association
New Hampshire Insurance Company
RISCORP National Insurance Company
Transamerica Group/AEGON USA, Inc.

Non-Insurance Clients

Acadian Ambulance Service, Inc.
State of Louisiana
Patients Compensation Fund

Firm Members

Robert L. Bussey — 1950 — The University of Texas, B.A., 1973; Northern Illinois University, M.S., 1980; Louisiana State University, J.D., 1985 — Admitted to Bar, 1985, Louisiana; 1986, U.S. District Court, Western District of Louisiana; 1986, U.S. Court of Appeals, Fifth Circuit — Member American and Louisiana State (House of Delegates) Bar Associations; Louisiana Association of Business and Industry; Louisiana Association of Defense Counsel; Defense Research Institute — E-mail: rlb@blclawgroup.com

Lewis O. Lauve, Jr. — 1958 — Louisiana State University, B.S., 1980; J.D., 1991 — Admitted to Bar, 1991, Louisiana; 1992, U.S. District Court, Eastern

ALEXANDRIA LOUISIANA

Bussey & Lauve, LLC, Alexandria, LA (Continued)

and Western Districts of Louisiana; 1992, U.S. Court of Appeals, Fifth Circuit — Member American, Louisiana State and Alexandria Bar Associations; Louisiana Association of Defense Counsel

Associate

Kimmie B. Leyser — 1961 — Louisiana State University at Shreveport, B.S., 1986; Louisiana State University, J.D., 1990 — Admitted to Bar, 1991, Louisiana; 1991, U.S. District Court, Western District of Louisiana; 1991, U.S. Court of Appeals, Fifth Circuit — Member Louisiana State and Alexandria Bar Associations

Faircloth, Melton & Keiser, LLC

105 Yorktown Drive
Alexandria, Louisiana 71303
Telephone: 318-619-7755
Fax: 318-619-7744
E-Mail: rkeiser@fairclothlaw.com
www.fairclothlaw.com

(Additional Offices: Baton Rouge, LA*)

Insurance Defense, Workers' Compensation, Municipal Liability, Governmental Liability, Property, Casualty, Life Insurance, Automobile, Health Care, Professional Liability, Product Liability, Bad Faith, Civil Rights, Subrogation, Arbitration, Mediation, Commercial Law, Class Actions, Nursing Home Liability, Government Affairs, Commercial Litigation, Mergers and Acquisitions, Contract Disputes, Environmental Law, Oil and Gas, Pharmacy, Medical and Allied Health Malpractice, Police Liability

Firm Profile: Faircloth, Melton & Keiser, LLC provides the high quality and broad range of legal representation associated with large firms, but the personal service and efficiency of a small one. The firm has developed a reputation for handling difficult and novel legal issues in a variety of practice areas.

Insurance Clients

Colony Insurance Company	Economy Preferred Insurance Company
First State Management Group, Inc.	GAB Robins, Inc.
GuideOne Insurance	Hochheim Prairie Casualty Insurance Company
Kemper Insurance Company	Pharmacists Mutual Insurance Company
Louisiana Insurance Guaranty Association	RLI/Mt. Hawley Insurance Company
Risk Management, Inc.	State Farm Insurance Companies
Scottsdale Insurance Company	Trinity Universal Insurance Company
State Auto Insurance Companies	Universal Casualty Company
State National Insurance Company, Inc.	
Unitrin, Inc.	

Non-Insurance Clients

JWF Specialty Company, Inc. (CNA)	Keenan & Associates
	RISC (CNA)

Firm Members

Jimmy R. Faircloth, Jr. — Louisiana Tech University, B.S., 1987; Georgia State University, J.D., 1990; Emory University, LL.M., 1991 — Admitted to Bar, 1990, Georgia; 1991, Louisiana; 1990, Supreme Court of Georgia; 1991, U.S. District Court, Middle and Western Districts of Louisiana; 1997, U.S. District Court, Northern District of Georgia; U.S. Court of Appeals, Fifth Circuit; U.S. Court of Federal Claims — Member American, Louisiana State, Fifth Federal Circuit and Alexandria Bar Associations; State Bar of Georgia; Crossroads American Inns of Court, Alexandria-Pineville (Executive Board, 2002-2004; Chairman, Mentoring Committee, 2003-2004) — Author: "Prosecutorial Misconduct in Closing Argument," Criminal Law Section, State Bar of Georgia, Summer 1990 — Board Certified Trial Advocacy Specialist by the National Board of Trial Advocacy — Resident Alexandria, LA and Baton Rouge, LA Office — E-mail: jfaircloth@fairclothlaw.com

Randall B. Keiser — Northeast Louisiana University, B.S., 1984; Louisiana State University and A & M College, J.D., 1991 — Admitted to Bar, 1991, Louisiana; 1991, Texas (Inactive); 1991, U.S. District Court, Western District of Louisiana; 1992, U.S. District Court, Eastern District of Texas; 1994, U.S.

Faircloth, Melton & Keiser, LLC, Alexandria, LA (Continued)

Court of Appeals, Fifth Circuit; 1995, U.S. Supreme Court; 1998, U.S. District Court, Middle District of Louisiana — Member American, Louisiana State, Alexandria and Fifth Federal Circuit Bar Associations; State Bar of Texas; Defense Research Institute (Governmental Liability Committee); Fellow, American Society for Pharmacy Law; Louisiana Pharmacists Association; Crossroads American Inn of Court; Louisiana Association of Defense Counsel (Board of Directors, 2009-2011); American Health Lawyers Association — Author: Comment, "Does This Hurt?" - Constitutional Challenges of Damage Caps and the Review Panel Process in Medical Malpractice Actions in Louisiana," 51 La. L. Rev. 1233 (1991); "Déjà Vu All Over Again?: The National Childhood Vaccine Injury Compensation Act of 1986," 47 Food and Drug L.J.15 (1992); Lecturer, "Topics in Pharmacy Law," University of Texas College of Pharmacy, Option-II Masters Degree Program, Austin, Texas (1992); — Lecturer, "Topics in Pharmacy Law," University of Texas College of Pharmacy, Option-II Masters Degree Program, Austin, Texas (1992); Mediator and Arbitrator Training, American Arbitration Association (1994) — Registered Pharmacist (1985) — E-mail: rkeiser@fairclothlaw.com

Barbara Bell Melton — University of Louisiana at Lafayette, B.A., 1998; Loyola University School of Law, J.D. (cum laude), 2002 — Admitted to Bar, 2002, Louisiana; U.S. District Court, Eastern, Middle and Western Districts of Louisiana; U.S. Court of Appeals, Fifth Circuit — Member American (Council Member), Louisiana State and Alexandria Bar Associations; Central Louisiana Young Lawyers Association (Treasurer); Louisiana State Young Lawyers Council (Council Member); Central Louisiana Pro Bono Project (Vice President) — E-mail: bmelton@fairclothlaw.com

Associates

Lauren Stokes Laborde — Northwestern State University, B.S., 2005; Louisiana State University, Paul M. Hebert Law Center, J.D., 2008 — Admitted to Bar, 2009, Louisiana — Member Louisiana State and Alexandria Bar Associations; Crossroads American Inns of Court — E-mail: llaborde@fairclothlaw.com

Matthew L. Nowlin — Texas A. & M. University, B.A., 2007; Louisiana State University, Paul M. Hebert Law Center, J.D., 2011 — Admitted to Bar, 2011, Louisiana — Member Louisiana State, Baton Rouge and Alexandria Bar Associations; Crossroads American Inns of Court — E-mail: mnowlin@fairclothlaw.com

Amanda Westergard — Louisiana State University, B.A., 2009; Elon University, J.D., 2013 — Admitted to Bar, 2014, Louisiana — Member American Bar Association (Young Lawyers Division; Government and Public Sector Lawyers Division; Sections: Real Property, Trust and Estate Law, Criminal Justice, Family Law); Louisiana State Bar Association (Young Lawyers Division, 2013-present) — E-mail: awestergard@fairclothlaw.com

Christie C. Wood — Louisiana Tech University, B.A. (magna cum laude), 1999; Louisiana State University, Paul M. Hebert Law Center, J.D./B.C.L., 2008 — Admitted to Bar, 2008, Louisiana; U.S. District Court, Western District of Louisiana; 2009, U.S. District Court, Eastern and Middle Districts of Louisiana; U.S. Court of Appeals, Fifth Circuit — Member Louisiana State and Alexandria Bar Associations — E-mail: cwood@fairclothlaw.com

Gold, Weems, Bruser, Sues & Rundell
A Professional Law Corporation

2001 MacArthur Drive
Alexandria, Louisiana 71301
Telephone: 318-445-6471
Fax: 318-445-6476
www.goldweems.com

Established: 1950

Alternative Dispute Resolution, Business Law, Corporate Law, Health Care, Insurance Defense, Labor and Employment, Medical Malpractice, Product Liability, Public Liability, Construction Law, Contracts, Indian Law, Real Estate, Employment Litigation

Firm Profile: Since 1950 the Gold Firm has molded solutions for the businesses and the people of the Central South. Vision, strong relationships and commitment to excellence are our hallmarks. As one of the state's largest and most diversified law firms outside New Orleans, Gold Weems has achieved and maintained its preeminent position in the Louisiana legal community through the quality and dedication of its members and staff.

LOUISIANA / ALEXANDRIA

Gold, Weems, Bruser, Sues & Rundell, A Professional Law Corporation, Alexandria, LA (Continued)

Uncompromising standards are reflected in the ability and integrity of these professionals. The approach of the Gold Firm to the practice of law seeks to ensure that each client is served not by a single lawyer, but by firm-wide resources and expertise. The availability of counsel with training and experience in areas of specialization, each committed to analyzing a problem from the client's perspective, assures the efficient achievement of that objective.

Local Counsel For

American International Group, Inc.
Chubb Group
Danube Insurance, Limited
The Goodyear Tire & Rubber Company
Kelsey Hayes Company
The Rapides Foundation
Rapides Regional Medical Center
RoyOMartin Lumber Company, Inc.
Shelter Mutual Insurance Company
American National Property and Casualty Company
Design Professionals Insurance Company
Gulf Insurance Company
Louisiana Medical Mutual Insurance Company
Red River Waterway Commission
St. Paul Fire and Marine Insurance Company

Firm Members

Charles S. Weems, III — 1943 — Louisiana State University and A & M College, B.S., 1965; J.D., 1969 — Phi Alpha Delta; Omicron Delta Kappa; Phi Eta Sigma; Phi Kappa Phi; Order of the Coif — Editor-In-Chief: Louisiana Law Review — Admitted to Bar, 1969, Louisiana; 1969, U.S. District Court, Eastern, Middle and Western Districts of Louisiana; 1969, U.S. Court of Appeals for the Federal, Fifth and Eleventh Circuits; 1969, U.S. Supreme Court; 1969, Supreme Court of Louisiana — Member American Bar Association (Business Law Section); Louisiana State Bar Association (Chair, 1976-1977; President, 1996-1997; Board of Governors, 1990-1992, 1995-1998); Alexandria Bar Association; American Society of Hospital Attorneys of the American Hospital Association; Louisiana Bankers Association (Bank Counsel Section); Louisiana Bar Foundation (Board of Directors, 1995-1998); Louisiana State Law Institute (Council); Secretary of State's Commission on Corporations (Advisory Committee); National Conference of Bar Presidents; Louisiana Bankers Association (Bank Counsel Section); Southern Conference of Bar Presidents; Louisiana State University and A. & M. College (Board of Supervisors; Member 1991-; Chairman, 1998-2000); Crossroads-American Inn of Court of Alexandria-Pineville (Master of the Bench); National Health Lawyers Association; Fellow, American Bar Foundation — Lecturer: Expropriation (1983), Commercial Litigation (1987), Evidence (1991), Director and Officer Liability (1991-1992), Business Organizations for the Committee on Continuing Legal Education (1993, 1996) — Board Certified Tax Attorney, Louisiana Board of Legal Specialization — Practice Areas: Commercial Law — E-mail: cweems@goldweems.com

Henry B. Bruser, III — 1942 — Louisiana State University and A & M College, B.S., 1965; J.D., 1969 — Winner, 1966-1967, Robert Lee Tullis Moot Court Competition — Law Clerk to E. Gordon West, Chief Judge, U.S. District Court for the Eastern District of Louisiana, 1968-1969 — Admitted to Bar, 1969, Louisiana; 1969, Supreme Court of Louisiana; 1969, U.S. District Court, Eastern, Middle and Western Districts of Louisiana; 1969, U.S. Court of Appeals, Fifth Circuit; 1969, U.S. Supreme Court — Member American Bar Association (Sections: Litigation, Tort and Insurance Law); Louisiana State Bar Association (Sections: Insurance, Negligence, Compensation and Admiralty Law, Civil Law, Litigation; Environmental Law; Fidelity, Surety and Construction Law); Alexandria (President, 1983-1984) and Fifth Federal Circuit Bar Associations; Louisiana Bar Foundation; Louisiana Association of Defense Counsel (Board of Directors, 1986-1988, 1990-1998); President, 1997, Faculty, Trial Academy, 1989, 1991, 1996, 1997); Louisiana City Attorneys Association; Fellow, American Bar Foundation; Louisiana Bar Foundation; Crossroads-American Inn of Court of Alexandria-Pineville (President, 1993-1994; Master of the Bench); Federation of Defense and Corporate Counsel — Faculty, National Institute for Trial Advocacy, Gulf South Region, 1991-1997; Adjunct Instructor in Trial Advocacy, Louisiana State University Law Center, 1991-1997; Lecturer, "Effective Civil Jury Trial Techniques for the Defense," 1977-1978, & "Judges & Lawyers Cooperating & Coping," 1988; Program Chair, "Insurance Hot Spots," 1996; "Trying a Case in Louisiana and All That Jazz - Demonstrations Cross-Examination of Plaintiff's Doctor," for the Committee on Continuing Legal Education, 1998; Lecturer, Loyola School of Law, Continuing Legal Education, "Evidence: The Concepts of Relevancy and Foundation and How to Establish Them," 1991, and "The Law of Automobile Accident Reconstruction in the 1990's," 1990; Lecture/Demonstration, Louisiana State University Law Center, Continuing Legal Education, "Cross-Examination of Plaintiff's Neurosurgeon and Economist in a Personal Injury Case," 1989 — Practice

Gold, Weems, Bruser, Sues & Rundell, A Professional Law Corporation, Alexandria, LA (Continued)

Areas: Arbitration; Commercial Litigation; Product Liability — E-mail: hbruser@goldweems.com

Eugene J. Sues — 1944 — Louisiana State University and A & M College, B.S., 1966; J.D., 1970 — Law Clerk, Court of Appeal of Louisiana, Second Circuit, 1970-1971 — Admitted to Bar, 1970, Louisiana; 1970, Supreme Court of Louisiana; 1970, U.S. District Court, Eastern and Western Districts of Louisiana; 1970, U.S. Court of Appeals, Fifth Circuit — Member American, Louisiana State (Sections: Insurance, Negligence, Compensation and Admiralty Law) and Alexandria Bar Associations; Louisiana Society of Hospital Attorneys of the Louisiana Hospital Association; Fellow, Louisiana Bar Foundation; Master of the Bench, Crossroads-American Inn of Court of Alexandria-Pineville; Louisiana Association of Defense Counsel; International Association of Defense Counsel; Defense Research Institute — Lecturer, "Workers' Compensation: Plaintiff and Defense Viewpoints," 1991, for the Committee on Continuing Legal Education — Capt. JAGC, U.S. Army, 1970-1974 — Practice Areas: Insurance Defense; Medical Malpractice — E-mail: gsues@goldweems.com

Edward E. Rundell — 1944 — Louisiana College; Louisiana Tech University, B.A., 1965; M.A., 1966; The University of Texas, Ph.D., 1973; J.D., 1970 — Admitted to Bar, 1970, Texas; 1974, Louisiana; 1970, Supreme Court of Texas; 1974, Supreme Court of Louisiana; 1974, U.S. District Court, Eastern, Middle and Western Districts of Louisiana; 1974, U.S. Court of Appeals, Fifth Circuit — Member Federal and American (Sections: Tort and Insurance Practice, Litigation) Bar Associations; State Bar of Texas (College of the State Bar of Texas, 1994-1996); Louisiana State Bar Association (Sections on: Insurance Negligence, Compensation and Admiralty Law; Civil Law and Litigation); Fifth Federal Circuit and Alexandria Bar Associations; Louisiana Association of Defense Counsel (Faculty, Trial Academy, 1991); The Defense Research Institute, Inc. (Product Liability Advisory Counsel); National Institute for Trial Advocacy (Faculty, Gulf Coast, New Orleans, 1992-2002); Crossroads-American Inn of Court of Alexandria-Pineville (Master of the Bench); American Board of Trial Advocates — Contributing Author: "Opening Statement and Closing Argument," Louisiana Association of Defense Counsel Product Liability Trial Notebook, 1991 — Lecturer, "The Use of Documentary Evidence at Trial," Tulane University School of Law, Mastering the Evidence, 4th Trial by Masters, Tulane University School of Law, 1991, 1992; "Recent Developments in Insurance Law," Summer School for Lawyers, Issues and Trends in Insurance Law, 1992; "Using the Evidence in Opening Statement," Loyola University School of Law, Seventh Annual Evidence Law Conference, 1992-1995; "Opening Statement and Closing Argument," "Back to the Future: A New Look at the Old Principles of Persuasion," LSBA Young Lawyers Section, CLE in Grand Cayman, 1992; "The Use of Deposition at Trial," National Institute for Trial Advocacy, 1992; "Persuasive Speaking," LSBA Young Lawyers Section, Walkin' to New Orleans Delta Conference, 1993; "Persuasive Speaking," Young Lawyers Division Southern Regional Affiliate Meeting, 1993; "Preparation of the Client for a Discovery Deposition," Crossroads American Inn of Court, 1993; "Armed and Dangerous: Preparing Yourself and Your Client for the Deposition," Depositions from A-Z, LSBA, 1994; "How to Win Friends and Influence People: The Closing Argument in a Jury Trial," Louisiana Department of Justice, Litigation Division B.R., Fall Trial Tactics Seminar, 1995; "Life on the High Wire - The Duty to Defend in LA," LADC N.O., 1995; "Life on the High Wire-the Duty to Defend in LA," 1995; "Don't Gamble on Opening Statement and Closing Argument," Young Lawyers Section, The Central LA Pro Bono Project, 1995 — Practice Areas: Product Liability; Medical Malpractice; Architects and Engineers; Insurance Defense — E-mail: erundell@goldweems.com

Robert G. Nida — 1947 — Northwestern State University, B.S., 1969; Louisiana State University and A & M College, J.D., 1978 — Phi Kappa Phi — Louisiana Law Review — Admitted to Bar, 1978, Louisiana; 1978, Supreme Court of Louisiana; 1978, U.S. District Court, Eastern and Western Districts of Louisiana; 1978, U.S. Court of Appeals, Fifth Circuit; 1978, U.S. Supreme Court — Member American Bar Association (Sections: General Practice, Real Property Probate and Trust Law, Litigation); Louisiana State and Alexandria Bar Associations; Louisiana Bankers Association (Bank Counsel Section) — Practice Areas: Commercial Law — E-mail: rnida@goldweems.com

Sam N. Poole, Jr. — 1954 — Louisiana Tech University, B.A., 1976; Louisiana State University and A & M College, J.D., 1979 — Omicron Delta Kappa; Phi Kappa Phi — Louisiana Law Review — Admitted to Bar, 1979, Louisiana; 1979, Supreme Court of Louisiana; 1979, U.S. District Court, Western District of Louisiana — Member American, Louisiana State and Alexandria Bar Associations; Louisiana Association of Defense Counsel; Defense Research Institute — Practice Areas: Insurance Defense; Labor and Employment — E-mail: spoole@goldweems.com

Gold, Weems, Bruser, Sues & Rundell, A Professional Law Corporation, Alexandria, LA (Continued)

Peggy D. St. John — 1953 — Louisiana College, B.A. (magna cum laude), 1974; Louisiana State University and A & M College, J.D., 1983 — Admitted to Bar, 1983, Louisiana; 2002, Maryland; 1983, Supreme Court of Louisiana; 1983, U.S. District Court, Middle and Western Districts of Louisiana; 1983, U.S. Court of Appeals, Fifth Circuit; 2002, U.S. Court of Appeals, Fourth Circuit — Member American and Alexandria Bar Associations; Louisiana State (Board of Governors, 1984-1986; Special Committee on Judicial Electoral Process, 1991-1992); Louisiana Association of Defense Counsel (Board of Directors, 2002-); Crossroads-American Inn of Court of Alexandria-Pineville (President, 1995-1996; Master of the Bench) — Advisory Group for the United States District Court, District of Louisiana, Appointed Under the Civil Justice Reform Act of 1990) — Practice Areas: Employment Law; Insurance Defense; Workers' Compensation — E-mail: pstjohn@goldweems.com

Randall L. Wilmore — 1961 — Centenary College, B.S., 1984; Louisiana State University and A & M College, J.D., 1987 — Associate Editor, Louisiana Law Review — Admitted to Bar, 1987, Louisiana; 1987, Supreme Court of Louisiana; 1987, U.S. District Court, Western District of Louisiana — Member American Bar Association; Louisiana State Bar Association (Sections: Civil Law and Litigation; Corporation and Business Law; Trusts, Estate, Probate and Immovable Property Law; Consumer Protection, Lender Liability, and Bankruptcy Law); Alexandria Bar Association; Crossroads-American Inn of Court of Alexandria-Pineville (Barrister) — Author: "The Right of Passage for the Benefit of an Enclosed Estate," 47 Louisiana Law Review 199, 1986 — Practice Areas: Corporate Law — E-mail: rwilmore@goldweems.com

Dorrell J. Brister — 1940 — Louisiana State University and A & M College, B.S., 1972; M.S., 1977; J.D., 1987 — Order of the Coif; Phi Kappa Phi; Co-Winner, Robert Lee Tullis Moot Court Competition — Admitted to Bar, 1987, Louisiana; 1988, Texas; 1987, Supreme Court of Louisiana; 1988, Supreme Court of Texas; 1988, U.S. District Court, Eastern, Middle and Western Districts of Louisiana; 1988, U.S. Court of Appeals, Fifth Circuit — Member Federal and American Bar Associations; State Bar of Texas (Sections: Real Estate, Probate and Trust, and Taxation Law); Louisiana State (Sections: Corporation and Business Law; Taxation; Trusts, Estate, Probate and Immovable Property Law); Alexandria Bar Association (Chair, 1989-1990; Young Lawyers Section Bench Bar Conference Committee; Continuing Legal Education Committee, 1990-1991; Nominating Committee, 1991-1992; Treasurer, 1994-1996; Vice-President, 1999-2000; President, 2000-2001); Louisiana State Law Institute; Louisiana Commercial Law Committee; American Association of Attorney-Certified Public Accountants; Alexandria Society of Certified Public Accountants; Louisiana Society of Public Accountants; American Institute of Certified Public Accountants; Crossroads-American Inn of Court of Alexandria-Pineville (Barrister) — Lecturer, "Selected Areas of Finance Under Chapter 9 of the Uniform Commercial Code," Louisiana State University Law Center, Continuing Legal Education, 1991; "General Information Scope and Nature of Secured Transactions," 1989; "Agricultural and Timber Financing," Southern University Law Center, Continuing Legal Education, 1990 — Board Certified Tax Attorney, Louisiana Board of Legal Specialization; Board Certified Estate Planning and Administration Specialist, Louisiana Board of Legal Specialization; Certified Public Accountant — Practice Areas: Commercial Law — E-mail: dbrister@goldweems.com

Gregory B. Upton — 1960 — Tulane University, B.A. (summa cum laude), 1982; J.D. (cum laude), 1985; The George Washington University, LL.M., 1991 — Phi Beta Kappa — Law Clerk to Judge F.A. Little, Jr., U.S. District Court, Western District of Louisiana, 1985-1986 — Admitted to Bar, 1985, Louisiana; 1985, Supreme Court of Louisiana; 1985, U.S. District Court, Middle and Western Districts of Louisiana; 1985, U.S. Court of Appeals, Fifth Circuit; 1985, U.S. Supreme Court; 1985, U.S. Court of Military Appeals; 1985, U.S. Army Court of Military Review — Member American, Louisiana State and Alexandria Bar Associations — Capt., JAGC, U.S. Army, 1986-1991 — Practice Areas: Corporate Law — E-mail: gupton@goldweems.com

Randall M. Seeser — 1964 — Louisiana State University and A & M College, B.S., 1987; J.D., 1990 — Law Clerk to Justice James L. Dennis, Louisiana Supreme Court, 1990-1991 — Admitted to Bar, 1990, Louisiana; 1990, Supreme Court of Louisiana; 1990, U.S. District Court, Middle and Western Districts of Louisiana; 1990, U.S. Court of Appeals, Fifth Circuit — Member American Bar Association; Louisiana State Bar Association (High School Essay Contest Committee, 1991-1993; Sections: Civil Law and Litigation, Insurance, Negligence, Compensation and Admiralty Law); Alexandria Bar Association; Fellow, Louisiana Bar Foundation; Louisiana Association of Defense Counsel — Practice Areas: Insurance Defense; Medical Malpractice — E-mail: rseeser@goldweems.com

Gold, Weems, Bruser, Sues & Rundell, A Professional Law Corporation, Alexandria, LA (Continued)

Michael J. O'Shee — 1954 — Louisiana State University, B.A., 1976; J.D., 1979 — Admitted to Bar, 1980, Louisiana; 1980, U.S. District Court, Eastern, Middle and Western Districts of Louisiana; 1980, U.S. Court of Appeals, Fifth and Eleventh Circuits; 1980, U.S. Supreme Court; 1980, Supreme Court of Louisiana; 1980, U.S. Court of Federal Claims — Member American Bar Association; Louisiana State Bar Association (Sections: Civil Law and Litigation; Insurance, Negligence, Compensation and Admiralty Law); Alexandria Bar Association; Crossroads-American Inn of Court of Alexandria-Pineville (Master of the Bench) — Practice Areas: Commercial Litigation; Insurance Defense — E-mail: mo'shee@goldweems.com

Brandon A. Sues — 1972 — Louisiana State University, B.S., 1994; J.D., 1997 — Admitted to Bar, 1998, Louisiana; 1998, Supreme Court of Louisiana; 1998, U.S. District Court, Eastern, Middle and Western Districts of Louisiana; 1998, U.S. Court of Appeals, Fifth Circuit — Member American and Louisiana State Bar Associations; Alexandria Bar Association (Young Lawyers Council, 1999-2001; Treasurer, 2000-2001; Chair-Elect, 2001-2002); Crossroads-American Inn of Court of Alexandria-Pineville (Associate); Louisiana Association of Defense Counsel — Practice Areas: Commercial Litigation; Health Care; Insurance Defense — E-mail: bsues@goldweems.com

Lottie L. Bash — 1974 — Millsaps College, B.A., 1996; Mercer University Walter F. George School of Law, J.D., 1999 — Phi Beta Kappa; Omicron Kappa Delta — Articles Editor, Mercer Law Review, 1998-1999; Member 1997-1998 — Admitted to Bar, 1999, Louisiana; 2000, Georgia; 1999, U.S. District Court, Middle and Western Districts of Louisiana; 1999, U.S. Court of Appeals, Fifth Circuit — Member Louisiana State Bar Association; State Bar of Georgia; Crossroads-American Inn of Court of Alexandria-Pineville (Associate) — Practice Areas: Business Law; Insurance Defense — E-mail: lbash@goldweems.com

Trevor S. Fry — 1974 — Auburn University, B.A. (summa cum laude), 1996; Louisiana State University and A & M College, J.D., 2000 — Admitted to Bar, 2000, Louisiana; 2000, Supreme Court of Louisiana — Member Louisiana State Bar Association (Labor and Employment Law Section); Crossroads-American Inn of Court of Alexandria-Pineville (Associate); Society for Human Resource Management; Louisiana Association of Defense Counsel — Practice Areas: Labor and Employment — E-mail: tfry@goldweems.com

Bradley L. Drell — 1971 — Sewanee, The University of the South, B.A., 1993; Louisiana State University, J.D., 1996 — Admitted to Bar, 1996, Louisiana; 1996, U.S. District Court, Middle and Western Districts of Louisiana; 1996, U.S. Court of Appeals, Fifth Circuit — Member Louisiana State and Alexandria Bar Associations; Crossroads-American Inn of Court — Practice Areas: Litigation — E-mail: bdrell@goldweems.com

Steven M. Oxenhandler — 1954 — University of Cincinnati, B.S. (cum laude), 1977; Florida Atlantic University, M.P.A. (magna cum laude), 1985; University of Miami, J.D. (magna cum laude), 2001 — Admitted to Bar, 2002, Florida; 2003, Louisiana; 2003, U.S. District Court, Eastern, Middle and Western Districts of Louisiana; 2003, U.S. Court of Appeals, Fifth Circuit — Member Louisiana State and Alexandria Bar Associations — Languages: Hebrew, Spanish — Practice Areas: Product Liability; Public Liability; Employment Law; Employment Litigation — E-mail: soxenhandler@goldweems.com

Stephen A. LaFleur — 1953 — Louisiana State University, B.S., 1975; J.D., 2003 — Admitted to Bar, 2003, Louisiana; U.S. District Court, Middle and Western Districts of Louisiana; U.S. Court of Appeals, Fifth Circuit — Member Louisiana State and Alexandria Bar Associations — Practice Areas: Corporate Law — E-mail: slafleur@goldweems.com

Heather M. Mathews — 1979 — Louisiana College, B.A. (summa cum laude), 2002; Tulane University, J.D., 2005 — Admitted to Bar, 2005, Louisiana; 2005, U.S. District Court, Eastern, Middle and Western Districts of Louisiana; 2005, U.S. Court of Appeals, Fifth Circuit; 2005, Supreme Court of Louisiana — Member Louisiana State and Alexandria Bar Associations — Practice Areas: Commercial Litigation; Medical Malpractice; Product Liability — E-mail: hmathews@goldweems.com

Associates

Joseph H. L. Perez-Montes — Louisiana College, B.A. (summa cum laude), 2004; Tulane University Law School, J.D. (summa cum laude), 2009 — Recipient, CALI Excellence for the Future Awards in Torts, Civil Law Property II, Administrative Law, Family Law and Constitutional Law: First Amendment — Law Clerk to Hon. Dee D. Drell, Judge, U.S. District Court, Western District of Louisiana (2009-2010) — Managing Editor, Tulane Law Review; Senior Legal Research and Writing Fellow; Research Assistant to Professor A.N. Yiannopoulos — Admitted to Bar, 2010, Louisiana; U.S. District Court, Eastern, Middle and Western Districts of Louisiana; U.S. Court of Appeals, Fifth Circuit; Supreme Court of Louisiana — Member American, Louisiana

Gold, Weems, Bruser, Sues & Rundell, A Professional Law Corporation, Alexandria, LA (Continued)

State and Alexandria Bar Associations; Crossroads-American Inn of Court of Alexandria-Pineville — Author: "Justiciability in Modern War Zones: Is the Political Question Doctrine a Viable Bar to Tort Claims Against Private Military Contractors?," 83 Tul. L. Rev. 219 (2008) — Practice Areas: Employment Litigation; Employment Law; Labor and Employment — E-mail: jperez-montes@goldweems.com

Christopher K. Kinnison — Auburn University, B.A., 2001; Golden Gate College, M.A., 2007; Paul M Hebert Law School at Louisiana State University, J.D. (cum laude), 2010 — Recipient of the Law Excellence Award in Environmental Law Seminar — Admitted to Bar, 2010, Louisiana; Supreme Court of Louisiana — Member Louisiana State Bar Association — Languages: Thai, Khmer — Practice Areas: Insurance Defense; Public Liability — E-mail: ckinnison@goldweems.com

B. Gene Taylor, III — Louisiana College, B.A., 2007; Mississippi College, J.D. (summa cum laude), 2010 — Best Oralist Award at the 2009 Pace National Environmental Competition; Recipient of American Jurisprudence Awards in Commercial Paper, Domestic Relations, Judicial Administration, Capital Puunishment, Federal Indian Law and Ethics; Awarded the 2009 Litigation Section of the Mississippi Bar Scholarship — Associate Editor, Mississippi College Law Review — Admitted to Bar, 2010, Louisiana; U.S. District Court, Eastern, Middle and Western Districts of Louisiana; U.S. Court of Appeals, Fifth Circuit; Supreme Court of Louisiana — Member Louisiana State and Alexandria Bar Associations; Crossroads-American Inn of Court of Alexandria-Pineville — Civil Procedure Teaching Assistant to Professor Jeffrey J. Jackson — Practice Areas: Bankruptcy; Creditor Rights; Commercial Litigation; Insurance Defense; Public Liability — E-mail: gtaylor@goldweems.com

Sarah Spruill Couvillon — 1979 — Louisiana College, B.S., 2001; Louisiana State University, J.D., 2005 — Admitted to Bar, 2005, Louisiana; 2005, U.S. District Court, Eastern, Middle and Western Districts of Louisiana; 2005, U.S. Court of Appeals, Fifth Circuit; 2005, Supreme Court of Louisiana — Member Louisiana State and Alexandria Bar Associations; American Immigration Lawyers Association; Legal Association of Women; American Intellectual Property Law Association; American Health Law Association — Practice Areas: Insurance Defense; Medical Malpractice; Product Liability — E-mail: scouvillon@goldweems.com

Gregory B. Odom, II — Louisiana State University at Baton Rouge, B.S.E., 2006; Baylor Law School, J.D. (Dean's List), 2010 — Admitted to Bar, 2010, Louisiana; U.S. District Court, Middle District of Louisiana; U.S. District Court, Eastern and Western Districts of Louisiana; U.S. District Court, Eastern District of Texas; U.S. Court of Appeals, Fifth Circuit; Supreme Court of Louisiana

Jonathan D. Stokes — Louisiana College, B.A., 1998; Washington University School of Law, J.D. (magna cum laude), 2010 — Recipient, 2009 GNIP/GNOP Excellence in Legal Writing Award for Best Comment — Editor-in-Chief, Washburn Law Journal — Admitted to Bar, 2011, Louisiana; Kansas; 2010, U.S. District Court, District of Kansas; U.S. District Court, Eastern, Middle and Western Districts of Louisiana; Supreme Court of Kansas; 2011, Supreme Court of Louisiana; U.S. Court of Appeals, Fifth and Tenth Circuits

Leslie E. Halle — Louisiana State University, B.S.A., 2007; Paul M Hebert Law School at Louisiana State University, J.D./G.D.C.L., 2010 — Law Clerk to Hon. Mary L. Doggett, Judge, Ninth Judicial District Court, State of Louisiana (2010-2011) — Admitted to Bar, 2010, Louisiana; U.S. District Court, Eastern, Middle and Western Districts of Louisiana; U.S. Court of Appeals, Fifth Circuit; Supreme Court of Louisiana

Leisa B. Lawson — Rice University, B.A., 2008; Paul M Hebert Law School at Louisiana State University, J.D./G.D.C.L., 2011 — Chancellor's List (TwoTimes); Recipient, CALI Excellence for the Future Awards in Legal Professions; Served as an LSU Law Ambassador (2009-2011) — Admitted to Bar, 2011, Louisiana; U.S. District Court, Eastern, Middle and Western Districts of Louisiana; U.S. Court of Appeals, Fifth Circuit — Legal Association of Women and Black Law Students Association (Former Member)

Provosty, Sadler, deLaunay, Fiorenza & Sobel
A Professional Corporation

Capital One Bank Building
934 Third Street, 8th Floor
Alexandria, Louisiana 71301
Telephone: 318-445-3631
Fax: 318-445-9377
E-Mail: attys@provosty.com
www.provosty.com

(Marksville, LA Office: 237 South Washington Street, 71351)
(Tel: 318-253-4435)
(Fax: 318-253-6626)

Established: 1945

Civil Trial Practice, Corporate Law, Insurance Law, Medical Malpractice, Legal Malpractice, Admiralty and Maritime Law, Product Liability, Health Care, Mediation, Oil and Gas, Environmental Law, Employment Law, Business Transactions

Firm Profile: Provosty, Sadler, deLaunay, Fiorenza & Sobel, A Professional Corporation, founded in 1945, is the oldest business and defense oriented firm in Central Louisiana, serving local, statewide and national clients. The firm handles cases in all Louisiana state and federal courts and the U.S. Supreme Court. Three of its members have served as President of the Louisiana State Bar Association. Our firm has extensive experience representing insurance clients in a wide variety of legal matters.

Insurance Clients

American Indemnity Group   Louisiana Medical Mutual
                                  Insurance Company

President

David R. Sobel — Tulane University, J.D., 1986 — Admitted to Bar, 1986, Louisiana; 1988, Texas — E-mail: dsobel@provosty.com

Stafford, Stewart & Potter

3112 Jackson Street
Alexandria, Louisiana 71301
Telephone: 318-487-4910
Fax: 318-487-9417
E-Mail: rpotter@ssplaw.com

Established: 1976

General Civil Practice, Insurance Defense, Tort, Workers' Compensation, Product Liability, Trial Practice, Civil Trials

Insurance Clients

American Alternative Insurance Corporation	American Modern Home Insurance Company
Amerisure Insurance Company	AmTrust North America
Atlantic Casualty Insurance Company	CNA Insurance Companies
	Colonial Penn Insurance Company
Employers Reinsurance Corporation	The Equitable Life Assurance Society of the United States
GAB Robins North America, Inc.	Government Employees Insurance Company
Harco National Insurance Company	JWF Specialty Company, Inc.
Lafayette Insurance Company	Maryland Insurance Company
Metropolitan Insurance Company	Metropolitan Property and Casualty Insurance Company
National Security Fire and Casualty Company	National Union Fire Insurance Company
North Carolina Farm Bureau Mutual Insurance Company	Northland Casualty Company
Northwestern National Casualty Company	Producers Agriculture Insurance Company
Prudential Property and Casualty Insurance Company	Sentry Select Insurance Company
	Shelter Mutual Insurance Company
Southern Farm Bureau Life Insurance Company	Trinity Universal Insurance Company

BATON ROUGE   LOUISIANA

Stafford, Stewart & Potter, Alexandria, LA   (Continued)

United Fire Group
Winterthur Swiss Insurance Company
United States Fidelity and Guaranty Company

Non-Insurance Clients

Alexandria Daily Town Talk
Arkansas Freightways, Inc.
BancorpSouth
Borden, Inc.
Circle K Stores, Inc., a division of Tosco Corp.
General Electric Company
Greyhound Lines, Inc.
John Deere Company
Phillips Petroleum Company
Ryder Truck Rental, Inc.
Allied Van Lines
AT&T Telecommunications, Inc.
Boise Cascade, L.L.C.
Budget Rent-A-Car Corporation
Deere & Company
Federal Express
The Goodyear Tire & Rubber Company
Lycoming Engines, A Division of AVCO Corporation
Stevens Forestry Service, Inc.

Partners

Russell L. Potter — 1951 — Louisiana State University and A & M College, B.A., 1973; J.D., 1976 — Admitted to Bar, 1976, Louisiana; 1976, U.S. District Court, Middle and Western Districts of Louisiana; 1976, U.S. Court of Appeals, Fifth Circuit; 1976, Supreme Court of Louisiana — Member Louisiana State and Alexandria Bar Associations; Louisiana Association of Defense Counsel

Andrew P. Texada — 1960 — Louisiana State University, B.S., 1982; J.D., 1986 — Admitted to Bar, 1986, Louisiana; 1986, U.S. District Court, Eastern and Western Districts of Louisiana; 1986, U.S. Court of Appeals, Fifth Circuit — Member Louisiana State and Alexandria Bar Associations; Louisiana Association of Defense Counsel (Director, 2003-2004)

Associates

Paul M. Lafleur — 1967 — Louisiana State University Law Center, J.D., 1992 — Admitted to Bar, 1993, Louisiana — Member Louisiana State and Alexandria Bar Associations; Crossroads Inns of Court; Louisiana Association of Defense Counsel — Practice Areas: Insurance Defense — E-mail: plafleur@ssplaw.com

Penny H. Tullos — 1985 — Louisiana State University, J.D./Graduate Diploma in Civil Law, 2010 — Admitted to Bar, 2011, Louisiana — Member Louisiana State Bar Association — E-mail: ptullos@ssplaw.com

Of Counsel

Grove Stafford, Jr. — 1928 — Louisiana State University, A.B., 1951; Tulane University, LL.B., 1954 — Admitted to Bar, 1954, Louisiana; 1954, U.S. District Court, Eastern, Middle and Western Districts of Louisiana; 1954, U.S. Court of Appeals, Fifth Circuit — Member Louisiana State and Alexandria Bar Associations; International Association of Defense Counsel; Federation of Defense and Corporate Counsel; Louisiana Association of Defense Counsel

Larry A. Stewart — 1949 — Louisiana State University and A & M College, B.S., 1971; J.D., 1976 — Admitted to Bar, 1976, Louisiana; 1976, U.S. District Court, Eastern, Middle and Western Districts of Louisiana; 1976, U.S. Court of Appeals, Fifth Circuit; 1976, Supreme Court of Louisiana — Member Louisiana State and Alexandria (President, 1988-89) Bar Associations; Louisiana Association of Defense Counsel

---

The following firms also service this area.

Hailey, McNamara, Hall, Larmann & Papale, L.L.P.

One Galleria Boulevard, Suite 1400
Metairie, Louisiana 70001
 Telephone: 504-836-6500
 Fax: 504-836-6565
Mailing Address: P.O. Box 8288, Metairie, LA 70011-8288

Admiralty and Maritime Law, Commercial Litigation, Construction Litigation, Employment Practices Liability, Insurance Litigation, Product Liability, Professional Malpractice, Toxic Torts, Casualty, Insurance Coverage, Intellectual Property, Premises Liability, Transportation, Mass Tort, Property, Workers' Compensation, Automobile Liability, Appellate, Environmental

SEE COMPLETE LISTING UNDER METAIRIE, LOUISIANA (214 MILES)

Perkins & Associates, L.L.C.

401 Market Street, Suite 900
Shreveport, Louisiana 71101
 Telephone: 318-222-2426
 Fax: 318-222-0458

Commercial Litigation, Trucking Litigation, Estate Planning, Insurance Defense, Commercial Vehicle, Trucking Law, Professional Malpractice, Employment Law, Workers' Compensation, Bodily Injury, Product Liability, Errors and Omissions, General Liability, Subrogation

SEE COMPLETE LISTING UNDER SHREVEPORT, LOUISIANA (125 MILES)

BATON ROUGE   † 229,493 East Baton Rouge Par.

Boyer, Hebert, Abels & Angelle, LLC

1280 Del Este Avenue
Denham Springs, Louisiana 70726
 Telephone: 225-664-4335
 Fax: 225-664-4490
 E-Mail: babels@bhaalaw.com
 www.bhaalaw.com

(Breaux Bridge, LA Office: 401 East Mills Avenue, 70517)
 (Tel: 337-332-0616)
 (Fax: 337-332-0633)

Established: 2005

Automobile, Business Litigation, General Liability, Insurance Defense, Oil and Gas, Product Liability, Real Estate, Workers' Compensation

Firm Profile: We learned our trade by starting in firms with fast paced litigation practices. It is that experience, along with a desire to build and sustain a practice embedded with the character, integrity, and zeal of its members, that gives us confidence as we represent our clients throughout Louisiana.

Insurance Clients

Broadspire
XL Specialty Insurance Company
Kemper Insurance Company

Partners

Mark D. Boyer — Louisiana Tech University, B.S. (with honors), 1996; Loyola University New Orleans College of Law, J.D. (with honors), 1999 — Admitted to Bar, 1999, Louisiana; U.S. District Court, Eastern, Middle and Western Districts of Louisiana; U.S. Court of Appeals, Fifth Circuit; 2008, U.S. Supreme Court — Member Louisiana State, Livingston Parish and Baton Rouge Bar Associations

Bart J. Hebert — University of Southwestern Louisiana, B.S. (magna cum laude), 1999; Louisiana State University Law Center, J.D., 2002 — Admitted to Bar, 2002, Louisiana; U.S. District Court, Eastern, Middle and Western Districts of Louisiana; U.S. Court of Appeals, Fifth Circuit — Member American and Louisiana State Bar Associations; Louisiana Land Title Association; Inn of the Teche — Resident Breaux Bridge, LA Office

Brian K. Abels — Louisiana State University at Baton Rouge, B.C.J., 1992; Louisiana State University Law Center, J.D., 1997 — Admitted to Bar, 1997, Louisiana; U.S. District Court, Eastern, Middle and Western Districts of Louisiana; U.S. Court of Appeals, Fifth Circuit; 2008, U.S. Supreme Court — Member American, Louisiana State, Twenty-First Judicial District and Baton Rouge Bar Associations; Louisiana City Attorneys Association

Randy P. Angelle — University of Southwestern Louisiana, B.A., 1974; Loyola University New Orleans College of Law, J.D., 1977 — Admitted to Bar, 1977, Louisiana; U.S. District Court, Eastern, Middle and Western Districts of Louisiana; U.S. Court of Appeals, Fifth Circuit; U.S. Supreme Court — Member Louisiana State, Lafayette Parish and St. Martin Parish Bar Associations; Inn of the Teche; Louisiana City Court Judge's Association; Louisiana Council of Juvenile and Family Court Judges

Associates

Christi R. Hemphill
Maryanna B. Haynes
Meaghan L. Young
René D. Guidry
Scott H. Nettles
Gordon Van Greig

LOUISIANA   BATON ROUGE

Breazeale, Sachse & Wilson, L.L.P.

One American Place, Suite 2300
301 Main Street
Baton Rouge, Louisiana 70801
 Telephone: 225-387-4000
 Fax: 225-387-5397
 E-Mail: info@bswllp.com
 www.bswllp.com

(Covington, LA Office: St. Tammany Business Center, 506 East Rutland Street, 70433-3219)
 (Tel: 985-871-7992)
 (Fax: 985-871-7996)
(New Orleans, LA Office: LL & E Tower, Suite 1500, 909 Poydras Street, 70112-4004)
 (Tel: 504- 619-1800)
 (Fax: 504- 584-5452)

Established: 1928

General Civil Trial and Appellate Practice, Business Law, Energy, Environmental Law, Product Liability, Real Estate, Medical Malpractice, Municipal Law, Workers' Compensation, Class Actions, Energy, Oil & Gas, Healthcare, Construction, Corporate, Insurance, Labor, Insurance Regulatory Law

Firm Profile: Breazeale, Sachse & Wilson, L.L.P. is one of the diversified and most respected law firms in Louisiana. With 70 attorneys and offices in Baton Rouge, New Orleans and Covington, we provide innovative, effective legal representation across a wide range of industries and practice areas. Our clients include individuals and start-up companies, Fortune 500 corporations, government entities and not-for-profit institutions. And every client gets our best - including a highly skilled, well-organized support staff and attorney teams structured to meet very specific objectives.

Insurance Clients

Clarendon America Insurance Company
LUBA Workers' Comp
National Interstate Insurance Company
Crawford & Company
Imperial Fire and Casualty Insurance Company
Republic Insurance Company

Non-Insurance Clients

Illinois Central Railroad Company
Quanta Services, Inc.

Partners

Van R. Mayhall, Jr. — 1946 — Louisiana State University, Paul M. Hebert Law Center, J.D. (with honors), 1971; Georgetown University, M.L.T., 1979 — Admitted to Bar, 1971, Louisiana; U.S. Supreme Court; U.S. Tax Court — Member American and Lousiana State Bar Associations; Federation of Regulatory Counsel — Board Certified Tax Attorney — Practice Areas: Regulatory and Compliance; Litigation — E-mail: VRM@bswllp.com

Van R. Mayhall III — 1974 — Louisiana Tech University, B.A. (cum laude), 1995; Louisiana State University, M.B.A., 2005; J.D., 2001 — Admitted to Bar, 2001, Louisiana — Member American (Insurance Regulation Committee, Tort, Trial and Insurance Practice Section) and Louisiana State Bar Associations; Federation of Regulatory Counsel — Practice Areas: Regulatory and Compliance; Corporate Law — E-mail: VM@bswllp.com

Degan, Blanchard & Nash

6421 Perkins Road, Building C, Suite B
Baton Rouge, Louisiana 70808
 Telephone: 225-610-1110
 Fax: 225-610-1220
 E-Mail: SDegan@Degan.com

Degan, Blanchard & Nash, Baton Rouge, LA (Continued)

(New Orleans, LA Office*: Texaco Center, Suite 2600, 400 Poydras Street, 70130)
 (Tel: 504-529-3333)
 (Fax: 504-529-3337)
 (www.degan.com)

Insurance Defense, Commercial Law, General Liability, Bodily Injury, Property Damage, Insurance Coverage, Admiralty and Maritime Law, Environmental Law, Energy, Toxic Torts, Professional Liability, Workers' Compensation, Pharmaceutical, Medical Products Litigation, Subrogation, Casualty, Commercial Litigation, Construction Defect, Medical Malpractice, Product Liability, Trucking, Commercial Vehicle, Appeals, Arbitration, Class Actions, Collections, First Amendment, Media Law, Longshore and Harbor Workers' Compensation, Municipal Law, Civil Rights Defense, Exposure, Insurance Bad Faith, Employment Practices Exposures, Trials in All Courts, Defense Base Act

Partners

Sidney W. Degan, III — 1954 — The University of New Orleans, B.A. (with distinction), 1977; Tulane University, J.D., 1980 — Admitted to Bar, 1981, Louisiana; U.S. District Court, Eastern, Middle and Western Districts of Louisiana; 1990, U.S. District Court, Eastern District of Texas; U.S. Court of Appeals, Fifth and Eleventh Circuits — Member Federal, Louisiana State and New Orleans Bar Associations; Proctor, Maritime Law Association of the United States; International Society of Primerus Law Firms; Professional Liability Defense Institute; National Workers' Compensation Defense Network; The Maritime Law Association of the United States; Louisiana Association of Defense Counsel; Defense Research Institute — E-mail: SDegan@Degan.com

Brian W. Harrell — 1975 — Tulane University Law School, J.D., 2001 — Law Clerk to the Hon. Douglas M. Gonzales, Louisiana First Circuit Court of Appeals — Admitted to Bar, 2003, Louisiana — Practice Areas: Civil Litigation — E-mail: BHarrell@Degan.com

Associates

Eric D. Burt — 1970 — Nova Southeastern University, B.A., 1999; Paul M Hebert Law School at Louisiana State University, J.D., 2005 — Associate Justice, Moot Court Board, 2005 — Admitted to Bar, 2005, Louisiana — Member American and Louisiana State Bar Associations; Louisiana Association of Defense Counsel — E-mail: EBurt@Degan.com

John W. Strange — 1979 — Louisiana State University, B.S.B.A., 2003; Mississippi College School of Law, J.D., 2006 — Law School Fellowship — Admitted to Bar, 2007, Louisiana — Member American and Louisiana State Bar Associations — E-mail: JStrange@Degan.com

Micah A. Gautreaux — 1977 — Louisiana State University, B.A., 2000; Louisiana State University, Paul M. Hebert Law Center, J.D./B.C.L., 2006 — Admitted to Bar, 2006, Louisiana — E-mail: MGautreaux@Degan.com

(See listing under New Orleans, LA for additional information)

Faircloth, Melton & Keiser, LLC

One American Drive
301 Main Street, Suite 920
Baton Rouge, Louisiana 70825
 Telephone: 225-343-9535
 Fax: 225-343-9538
 www.fairclothlaw.com

(Alexandria, LA Office*: 105 Yorktown Drive, 71303)
 (Tel: 318-619-7755)
 (Fax: 318-619-7744)
 (E-Mail: rkeiser@fairclothlaw.com)

BATON ROUGE   LOUISIANA

Faircloth, Melton & Keiser, LLC, Baton Rouge, LA
(Continued)

Insurance Defense, Workers' Compensation, Municipal Liability, Governmental Liability, Property, Casualty, Life Insurance, Automobile, Health Care, Professional Liability, Product Liability, Bad Faith, Civil Rights, Subrogation, Arbitration, Mediation, Commercial Law, Class Actions, Nursing Home Liability, Government Affairs, Commercial Litigation, Mergers and Acquisitions, Contract Disputes, Environmental Law, Oil and Gas, Pharmacy, Medical and Allied Health Malpractice, Police Liability, Governmental Liability, Health Care

Firm Profile: Faircloth, Melton & Keiser, LLC provides the high quality and broad range of legal representation associated with large firms, but the personal service and efficiency of a small one. The firm has developed a reputation for handling difficult and novel legal issues in a variety of practice areas.

Associates

Jonathan Ringo — Louisiana State University, B.S., 2003; Louisiana State University, Paul M. Hebert Law Center, J.D., 2009 — Admitted to Bar, 2009, Louisiana — E-mail: jringo@faircothlaw.com

Brook Landry Thibodeaux — Louisiana State University, B.S., 2005; Louisiana State University, Paul M. Hebert Law Center, J.D., 2008 — Admitted to Bar, 2008, Louisiana — E-mail: bthibodeaux@faircothlaw.com

(See listing under Alexandria, LA for additional information)

Forrester & Clark

4981 Bluebonnet Boulevard
Baton Rouge, Louisiana 70809
  Telephone: 225-928-5400
  Fax: 225-928-7733
  E-Mail: meg@forresterclark.com
  www.forresterclark.com

Established: 1994

Admiralty and Maritime Law, Arbitration, Automobile, Bad Faith, Business Law, Casualty Defense, Class Actions, Commercial Litigation, Construction Law, Federal Employer Liability Claims (FELA), Fraud, Indian Law, Insurance Coverage, Insurance Defense, Labor and Employment, Mediation, Motor Carriers, Premises Liability, Product Liability, Railroad Law, Subrogation, Tort, Trial and Appellate Practice, Toxic Torts, Insurance Fraud, Arson, Constitutional Law, Workers' Compensation Defense

Insurance Clients

Allstate Insurance Company
Travelers Insurance Companies
Louisiana Farm Bureau Mutual Insurance Company

Founding Member

Shelly D. Dick

Partners

David C. Forrester — Randolph-Macon College, B.A., 1972; Louisiana State University, J.D., 1977 — Admitted to Bar, 1977, Louisiana; 1979, U.S. District Court, Eastern District of Louisiana; 1984, U.S. District Court, Middle District of Louisiana; 1987, U.S. Court of Appeals, Fifth Circuit — Member American, Louisiana State and Baton Rouge Bar Associations; International Association of Arson Investigators — Research Assistant, Impeachment Inquiry Staff, Committee on the Judiciary, U.S. House of Representatives (1973-1974); Assistant to the Insurance Commissioner and State Treasurer, State of Florida (1977-1979); Assistant Attorney General, Medicaid Fraud Control Unit, Louisiana Attorney General's Office (1979-1983); Governor's Insurance Anti-Fraud Advisory Board; Super Lawyer (2013)

Amanda Giering Clark — Louisiana State University, B.A., 1993; J.D., 1996 — Admitted to Bar, 1996, Louisiana; 1997, U.S. District Court, Eastern, Middle and Western Districts of Louisiana — Member Louisiana State and Baton

Forrester & Clark, Baton Rouge, LA (Continued)

Rouge Bar Associations; Louisiana Association of Defense Counsel — Practice Areas: Labor and Employment; Civil Rights; Litigation; Trial and Appellate Practice; Tribal Law; Workers' Compensation

Associates

Erica M. Schirling — Louisiana State University, Paul M. Hebert Law Center, J.D., 2012 — Law Clerk to Hon. Judge Mary Ann Vial Lemmon, U.S. District Court, Eastern District of Louisiana — Admitted to Bar, 2012, Louisiana; U.S. District Court, Eastern, Middle and Western Districts of Louisiana — Member Federal, Louisiana State and Baton Rouge Bar Associations

Mason C. Johnson — Georgetown University, A.B., 2005; Mississippi College Jackson School of Law, J.D., 2008 — Phi Alpha Delta — Law Clerk to Hon. Frank J. Polozola, U.S. District Court, Middle District of Louisiana — Admitted to Bar, 2009, Louisiana; U.S. District Court, Eastern, Middle and Western Districts of Louisiana; U.S. Court of Appeals, Fifth Circuit — Member Louisiana State and Baton Rouge Bar Associations — Attorney, First Circuit Court of Appeals; Intern, United States Senate, Senator John Breaux — Practice Areas: Insurance Defense; Personal Injury Defense; Workers' Compensation

Gaudry, Ranson, Higgins & Gremillion, L.L.C.

2223 Quail Run Drive, Suite C-2
Baton Rouge, Louisiana 70808
  Telephone: 225-663-6101
  Fax: 225-663-6102
  www.grhg.net

(Gretna, LA Office*: Oakwood Corporate Center, 401 Whitney Avenue, Suite 500, 70056, P.O. Box 1910, 70054-1910)
  (Tel: 504-362-2466)
  (Fax: 504-362-5938)

Insurance Defense, Automobile, Premises Liability, Product Liability, Medical Malpractice, Hospital Malpractice, State and Federal Workers' Compensation

(See listing under Gretna, LA for additional information)

Guglielmo, Marks, Schutte, Terhoeve & Love, L.L.P.

320 Somerulos Street
Baton Rouge, Louisiana 70802
  Telephone: 225-387-6966
  Fax: 225-387-8338
  www.gmstl.com

Established: 1995

Americans with Disabilities Act, Arson, Casualty Defense, Bad Faith, Civil Rights, Class Actions, Commercial General Liability, Contractors Liability, Coverage Issues, Directors and Officers Liability, Dispute Resolution, ERISA, Environmental Liability, Employment Discrimination, Extra-Contractual Litigation, Fraud, Health Care, Insurance Agents, Insurance Coverage, Insurance Defense, Intellectual Property, Life and Health, Medical Malpractice, Motor Carriers, Premises Liability, Product Liability, Special Investigative Unit Claims, Subrogation, Title Insurance, Workers' Compensation, Fidelity and Surety Bonds, Accountants and Attorneys Professional Liability, Architects and Engineers Professional Liability, Nursing Home and Medical Malpractice

Insurance Clients

America First/One Beacon Insurance Company
Kemper Insurance Companies
Louisiana Insurance Guaranty Association
Farm Bureau Insurance Companies
GEICO Insurance Companies
Liberty Mutual Insurance Company
Lumbermen's Underwriting Alliance

Guglielmo, Marks, Schutte, Terhoeve & Love, L.L.P., Baton Rouge, LA (Continued)

Metropolitan Property and Casualty Insurance Company
Safeco Insurance Companies
State Farm Insurance Companies
United Services Automobile Association (USAA)
Progressive Security Insurance Company
Sentry Insurance Group
Travelers Insurance Company
Unitrin Auto & Home Insurance Company

Non-Insurance Clients

Federal Express
General Motors Acceptance Corporation

Partners

Carey J. Guglielmo — 1938 — Louisiana State University, B.A., 1960; J.D., 1963 — Admitted to Bar, 1963, Louisiana; 1963, U.S. District Court, Eastern, Middle and Western Districts of Louisiana

Charles A. Schutte, Jr. — 1952 — The University of New Orleans, B.S., 1974; Louisiana State University, J.D., 1977 — Admitted to Bar, 1978, Louisiana; U.S. District Court, Eastern, Middle and Western Districts of Louisiana

Henry G. Terhoeve — 1959 — Louisiana State University, B.S., 1981; J.D., 1984 — Admitted to Bar, 1984, Louisiana; Texas; U.S. District Court, Eastern, Southern and Western Districts of Louisiana

Glen Scott Love — 1958 — Louisiana State University, B.S., 1980; J.D., 1984 — Admitted to Bar, 1984, Louisiana; U.S. District Court, Eastern, Middle and Western Districts of Louisiana — Certified Public Accountant; Chartered Property Casualty Underwriter; Mediation

Keith L. Richardson — 1967 — Louisiana State University, B.A., 1989; The George Washington University, J.D., 1992 — Admitted to Bar, 1992, Georgia; Louisiana; U.S. District Court, Eastern, Middle and Western Districts of Louisiana; U.S. District Court, Middle, Northern and Southern Districts of Georgia; U.S. Court of Appeals, Fifth Circuit — Judge Advocate, U.S. Marine Corps 1989-1996

Andrew W. Eversberg — 1969 — Millsaps College, B.B.A., 1992; The University of Mississippi, J.D., 1995 — Admitted to Bar, 1995, Mississippi; 1999, Louisiana; 1995, U.S. District Court, Northern and Southern Districts of Mississippi; U.S. Court of Appeals, Fifth Circuit; 1999, U.S. District Court, Eastern, Middle and Western Districts of Louisiana

Stephen D. Cronin — 1968 — Louisiana State University, B.A., 1990; University of Delaware, M.A., 1992; Louisiana State University, J.D., 2001 — Admitted to Bar, 2001, Louisiana; U.S. District Court, Eastern, Middle and Western Districts of Louisiana; U.S. Court of Appeals, Fifth Circuit

Valerie A. Judice — 1962 — Louisiana State University, B.S. (summa cum laude), 1984; Southeastern Louisiana University, B.S.N., 1987; Louisiana State University, J.D./B.C.L., 2004 — Admitted to Bar, 2004, Louisiana; U.S. District Court, Eastern, Middle and Western Districts of Louisiana; U.S. Court of Appeals, Fifth Circuit

Brad M. Boudreaux — 1981 — Louisiana State University, B.S., 2003; Louisiana State University Law Center, B.C.L./J.D., 2006 — Admitted to Bar, 2006, Louisiana; U.S. District Court, Eastern, Middle and Western Districts of Louisiana; U.S. Court of Appeals, Fifth Circuit

Associate

Morgan E. Levy — 1982 — Louisiana State University at Baton Rouge, B.A. Political Science, 2005; Tulane University Law School, J.D., 2012 — Admitted to Bar, 2012, Louisiana; U.S. District Court, Eastern, Middle and Western Districts of Louisiana; U.S. Court of Appeals, Fifth Circuit

Of Counsel

John David Ziober — 1954 — Louisiana State University at Baton Rouge, J.D. — Admitted to Bar, 1978, Louisiana; 1979, U.S. District Court, Eastern and Western Districts of Louisiana; 1981, U.S. Court of Appeals, Fifth and Eleventh Circuits; 1983, U.S. District Court, Middle District of Louisiana; 1985, U.S. Supreme Court

Jones Walker LLP

Four United Plaza
8555 United Plaza Boulevard
Baton Rouge, Louisiana 70809
Telephone: 225-248-2000
Fax: 225-248-2010
E-Mail: info@joneswalker.com
www.joneswalker.com

Jones Walker LLP, Baton Rouge, LA (Continued)

(New Orleans, LA Office*: 201 St. Charles Avenue, 70170-5100)
  (Tel: 504-582-8000)
  (Fax: 504-582-8583)
(Mobile, AL Office*: RSA Battle House Tower, 11 North Water Street, Suite 1200, 36602, P.O. Box 46, 36601)
  (Tel: 251-432-1414)
  (Fax: 251-433-4106)
(Lafayette, LA Office*: 600 Jefferson Street, Suite 1600, 70501)
  (Tel: 337-593-7600)
  (Fax: 337-593-7601)
(Birmingham, AL Office*: One Federal Place, 1819 5th Avenue North, Suite 1100, 35203)
  (Tel: 205-244-5200)
  (Fax: 205-244-5400)
(Jackson, MS Office*: 190 East Capitol Street, Suite 800, 39201, P.O. Box 427, 39205-0427)
  (Tel: 601-949-4900)
  (Fax: 601-949-4804)
(Olive Branch, MS Office*: 6897 Crumpler Boulevard, Suite 100, 38654)
  (Tel: 662-895-2996)
  (Fax: 662-895-5480)

Accountants, Admiralty and Maritime Law, Agent/Broker Liability, Antitrust, Appellate Practice, Asbestos Litigation, Aviation, Bankruptcy, Cargo, Class Actions, Commercial Litigation, Complex Litigation, Construction Law, Contracts, Directors and Officers Liability, Disability, Employment Law, Energy, Entertainment Law, Environmental Law, ERISA, Errors and Omissions, Health Care, Insurance Coverage, Insurance Defense, Intellectual Property, International Law, Labor and Employment, Life Insurance, Medical Malpractice, Mergers and Acquisitions, Motor Carriers, Oil and Gas, Personal Injury, Product Liability, Professional Liability, Regulatory and Compliance, Toxic Torts, Workers' Compensation

Firm Profile: Since 1937, Jones Walker LLP has grown to become one of the largest law firms in the southeastern U.S. We serve local, regional, national, and international business interests in a wide range of markets and industries. Today, we have more than 375 attorneys in 19 offices.

Jones Walker is committed to providing proactive legal services to major multinational, public, and private corporations; *Fortune 500®* companies; money center banks and worldwide insurers; and family and emerging businesses located in the United States and abroad.

Firm Members

Kevin O. Ainsworth — Louisiana State University, B.S., 1996; Louisiana State University, Paul M. Hebert Law Center, J.D., 2000 — Admitted to Bar, 2000, Louisiana; 2010, Texas; 2001, U.S. District Court, Middle and Western Districts of Louisiana; U.S. Court of Appeals, Fifth Circuit; 2006, U.S. Supreme Court; 2007, U.S. District Court, Eastern District of Louisiana — Member Louisiana State and Baton Rouge Bar Associations; Defense Research Institute; Louisiana Association of Defense Counsel — E-mail: kainsworth@joneswalker.com

William L. Schuette, Jr. — Louisiana State University, B.S., 1980; J.D., 1983 — Admitted to Bar, 1983, Louisiana; U.S. District Court, Eastern, Middle and Western Districts of Louisiana; U.S. Court of Appeals, Fifth Circuit — Member American, Louisiana State, Fifth Federal Circuit and Baton Rouge Bar Associations; Defense Research Institute; Louisiana Association of Defense Counsel — E-mail: wschuette@joneswalker.com

(See Listing under New Orleans, LA for a List of Firm Clients and Additional Information)

Kantrow, Spaht, Weaver & Blitzer
A Professional Law Corporation

Suite 300, City Plaza
445 North Boulevard
Baton Rouge, Louisiana 70802
  Telephone: 225-383-4703
  Fax: 225-343-0630, 225-343-0637

BATON ROUGE   **LOUISIANA**

Kantrow, Spaht, Weaver & Blitzer, A Professional Law Corporation, Baton Rouge, LA   (Continued)

Casualty, Life Insurance, Surety, Workers' Compensation, Product Liability, Professional Malpractice, Medical Malpractice

Insurance Clients

CNA
St. Paul Travelers
Starmount Life Insurance Company
FCCI Insurance Group/Brierfield Insurance Company

Firm Members

Byron R. Kantrow — (1909-1997)

Carlos G. Spaht — (1906-2001)

Geraldine B. Weaver — (Retired)

Sidney M. Blitzer, Jr. — 1944 — Duke University, A.B., 1966; Louisiana State University, J.D., 1969 — Admitted to Bar, 1969, Louisiana — Member American, Louisiana State and Baton Rouge Bar Associations

Paul H. Spaht — 1946 — Rhodes College; Louisiana State University, B.A. (magna cum laude), 1968; J.D., 1971 — Admitted to Bar, 1971, Louisiana — Member American, Louisiana State and Baton Rouge Bar Associations; American Judicature Society

Lee C. Kantrow — 1945 — Tulane University of Louisiana, B.A. (cum laude), 1967; Harvard Law School, J.D. (cum laude), 1971 — Admitted to Bar, 1971, Louisiana — Member American, Louisiana State, Baton Rouge and New Orleans Bar Associations

John C. Miller — 1946 — Louisiana State University, B.A., 1969; J.D., 1972 — Admitted to Bar, 1972, Louisiana — Member American, Louisiana State and Baton Rouge Bar Associations; Louisiana Association of Defense Counsel

David S. Rubin — 1952 — Louisiana State University, B.S., 1974; J.D., 1978 — Admitted to Bar, 1978, Louisiana — Member American, Louisiana State and Baton Rouge Bar Associations

Diane L. Crochet — 1954 — Louisiana State University, B.S. (summa cum laude), 1976; J.D., 1978 — Admitted to Bar, 1978, Louisiana — Member American, Louisiana State and Baton Rouge Bar Associations

Richard F. Zimmerman, Jr. — 1955 — Louisiana State University, B.S. (magna cum laude), 1978; J.D., 1981 — Admitted to Bar, 1981, Louisiana — Member American, Louisiana State and Baton Rouge Bar Associations; Defense Research Institute; Louisiana Association of Defense Counsel

Bob D. Tucker — 1951 — Louisiana State University, B.S., 1974; M.B.A., 1977; Tulane University, J.D. (magna cum laude), 1984 — Admitted to Bar, 1984, Louisiana — Member Louisiana State and Baton Rouge Bar Associations

Connell L. Archey — 1961 — Louisiana State University, B.M.E. (magna cum laude), 1985; J.D., 1990 — Admitted to Bar, 1990, Louisiana — Member American, Louisiana State and Baton Rouge Bar Associations

Randal J. Robert — 1962 — Louisiana State University, B.S., 1984; J.D., 1992 — Admitted to Bar, 1992, Louisiana — Member American, Louisiana State and Baton Rouge Bar Associations

W. Scott Keaty — 1969 — University of Notre Dame, B.B.A., 1991; University of Notre Dame Law School, J.D. (cum laude), 1994 — Admitted to Bar, 1994, Louisiana — Member American, Louisiana State and Baton Rouge Bar Associations

Jennifer Aaron Hataway — 1974 — Louisiana State University, B.A., 1996; J.D., 1999 — Order of the Coif — Louisiana Law Review — Admitted to Bar, 1999, Louisiana — Member Louisiana State and Baton Rouge Bar Associations

Julie M. McCall — 1980 — Louisiana Tech University, B.A. (summa cum laude), 1998-2001; Louisiana State University, Paul M. Hebert Law Center, J.D./B.C.L. (Order of the Coif), 2005 — Admitted to Bar, 2005, Louisiana — Member American, Louisiana State and Baton Rouge Bar Associations

Associates

Jacob M. Kantrow
W. Carlos Spaht
Benjamin J. Nelson
Lucie R. Kantrow
Keith J. Fernandez

Keogh, Cox & Wilson, Ltd.

701 Main Street
Baton Rouge, Louisiana 70802
Telephone: 225-383-3796
Fax: 225-343-9612
E-Mail: kcwlaw@kcwlaw.com
www.kcwlaw.com

Established: 1969

Casualty, Fire, Surety, Architects and Engineers, Engineers, Dental Malpractice, Legal Malpractice, Workers' Compensation, Product Liability, Coverage Analysis, Errors and Omissions, Legislative Law, Regulatory and Compliance, Subrogation, Mediation, Admiralty and Maritime Law, Labor and Employment, Accountants and Attorneys Liability, Advertising Injury, Agent and Brokers Errors and Omissions, Alternative Dispute Resolution, Americans with Disabilities Act, Appellate Practice, Arbitration, Automobile Liability, Bad Faith, Casualty Insurance Law, Commercial General Liability, Commercial Litigation, Complex Litigation, Construction Accidents, Construction Defect, Contractors Liability, Defense Litigation, Design Professionals, Directors and Officers Liability, Disability, Discrimination, Employment Discrimination, Employment Law, Employment Practices Liability, Engineering and Construction, Environmental Law, Environmental Coverage, Excess and Umbrella, Extra-Contractual Litigation, First Party Matters, First and Third Party Defense, Homeowners, Hospital Malpractice, Insurance Agents, Insurance Coverage, Insurance Defense, Jones Act, Mass Tort, Medical Devices, Medical Liability, Medical Negligence, Mold and Mildew Claims, Municipal Law, Personal Injury, Policy Construction and Interpretation, Premises Liability, Primary and Excess Insurance, Professional Errors and Omissions, Professional Liability (Non-Medical) Defense, Professional Malpractice, Property and Casualty, Protection and Indemnity, Public Officials Liability, Sexual Harassment, Slip and Fall, State and Federal Courts, Toxic Torts, Trial and Appellate Practice, Trial Practice, Truck Liability, Trucks/Heavy Equipment, Uninsured and Underinsured Motorist, Wrongful Death, Wrongful Termination, Class Actions, Nursing Home Liability, Premium Dispute, Business Formation and Litigation, Life Sciences, Chinese Drywall

Firm Profile: Keogh, Cox & Wilson, Ltd has proudly represented insurance industry clients in Louisiana for more than 40 years. We strive to provide the highest quality legal services in a timely and cost effective manner. With our offices centrally located in Baton Rouge, our experienced trial and appellate lawyers handle matters in all state, federal and administrative venues.

Insurance Clients

ACE USA
Amica Mutual Insurance Company
Chubb Group of Insurance Companies
ESIS
Federated Mutual Insurance Company
The Hartford Financial Services Group, Inc.
HealthSmart Benefit Solutions
Louisiana Construction and Industry Self-Insurers Fund
Medmarc Insurance Group
Mercury Insurance Company
Nationwide Insurance and Affiliates
Sentry Insurance a Mutual Company
Trover Solutions, Inc.
Admiral Insurance Company
AXIS Insurance Company
CNA Insurance Companies
Employers Mutual Casualty Company
Gallagher Bassett Services, Inc.
Gray Insurance Company
HDI-Gerling America Insurance Company
Indiana Lumbermens Mutual Insurance Company
Medmarc Casualty Insurance Company
Midwest Employers Casualty Company
Scottsdale Insurance Company
T.H.E. Insurance Company
TRISTAR Risk Management
Zurich U.S.

Non-Insurance Clients

Albertson's LLC
Atlantic Scaffolding, LLC
Allen & LeBlanc
Basic Industries, Inc.

LOUISIANA — BATON ROUGE

Keogh, Cox & Wilson, Ltd., Baton Rouge, LA (Continued)

Brock Services, LLC
Dick Corporation
Dollar General Corporation
Outback Steakhouse, Inc.
RaceTrac Petroleum, Inc.
S & B Engineers and Contractors, Ltd.
United Scaffolding, Inc.
Circle K Stores, Inc., a division of Tosco Corp.
Jacobs Engineering Group, Inc.
Pilot Corporation
Rheem Manufacturing Company
State of Louisiana
Taylor International Services, Inc.
Wells Fargo Armored Services

Partners

Stephen R. Wilson — (1950-2010)

John E. Cox — (1923-2010)

John P. Wolff, III — 1959 — University of Southwestern Louisiana, B.A. (cum laude), 1981; Louisiana State University, J.D., 1984 — Phi Delta Phi — Admitted to Bar, 1984, Louisiana; 1995, Texas; 1984, U.S. District Court, Middle and Western Districts of Louisiana; U.S. Court of Appeals, Fifth Circuit; 1985, U.S. District Court, Eastern District of Louisiana; 2013, U.S. District Court, Southern District of Texas; U.S. Supreme Court — Member American, Lafayette Parish and East Baton Rouge Parish Bar Associations; Louisiana State Bar Association (Bench and Bar Section; Ad Hoc Judiciary Committee); State Bar of Texas; Claims and Litigation Management Alliance; Louisiana Association of Defense Counsel; Defense Research Institute — Practice Areas: Admiralty and Maritime Law; Class Actions; Complex Litigation; Environmental Law; Excess; General Liability; Insurance Coverage; Product Liability; Professional Liability; Medical Devices; Bad Faith; Insurance Litigation — E-mail: jwolff@kcwlaw.com

Steven C. Judice — 1956 — University of Southwestern Louisiana, B.S., 1978; North Texas State University, M.S., 1979; Louisiana State University, J.D., 1983 — Delta Theta Phi — Admitted to Bar, 1983, Louisiana; 1983, U.S. Court of Appeals, Fifth Circuit; 1985, U.S. District Court, Eastern, Middle and Western Districts of Louisiana; U.S. Tax Court — Member Louisiana State and East Baton Rouge Parish (Judicial Liaison Committee 1987-1988) Bar Associations; Louisiana Association of Defense Counsel (Board of Governors); Defense of Medical Professional Liability and Land Based Casualty Claims — Practice Areas: Insurance Defense; Mediation; Professional Liability; Accident; Business Law; Casualty; Medical Malpractice; Product Liability — E-mail: sjudice@kcwlaw.com

Andrew Blanchfield — 1959 — University of Wisconsin, B.A., 1981; Louisiana State University, J.D., 1985 — Admitted to Bar, 1985, Louisiana; 1987, U.S. District Court, Eastern, Middle and Western Districts of Louisiana; 1988, U.S. Court of Appeals, Fifth Circuit — Member Louisiana State, Baton Rouge and New Orleans Bar Associations — Practice Areas: Professional Liability; General Liability; Business Law; Medical Malpractice; Nursing Home Liability — E-mail: ablanchfield@kcwlaw.com

Edward F. Stauss, III — 1961 — Tulane University, B.A., 1983; Louisiana State University, J.D., 1986 — Admitted to Bar, 1986, Louisiana; U.S. District Court, Eastern, Middle and Western Districts of Louisiana; U.S. Court of Appeals, Fifth Circuit — Member Louisiana State and Baton Rouge Bar Associations — Practice Areas: Workers' Compensation; Subrogation; Automobile Liability; Premises Liability; Insurance Defense — E-mail: estauss@kcwlaw.com

Kirk L. Landry — 1966 — Louisiana State University, B.S., 1987; M.A.H., 1997; J.D., 1990 — Admitted to Bar, 1991, Louisiana; 1996, Texas; 1991, U.S. District Court, Middle District of Louisiana; 1992, U.S. District Court, Eastern and Western Districts of Louisiana; 2004, U.S. Court of Appeals, Fifth Circuit; 2010, U.S. Supreme Court — Member Louisiana State and Baton Rouge Bar Associations; State Bar of Texas; Louisiana Association of Business and Industry; Louisiana Claims Association; Louisiana Association of Self Insured Employers; Louisiana Association of Defense Counsel; Defense Research Institute — Practice Areas: Workers' Compensation; Subrogation; Business Litigation — E-mail: klandry@kcwlaw.com

Gracella Simmons — 1947 — Louisiana State University, B.A., 1971; J.D., 1976 — Admitted to Bar, 1977, Louisiana; U.S. District Court, Eastern, Middle and Western Districts of Louisiana; 1981, U.S. Supreme Court — Member Louisiana State and Baton Rouge Bar Associations; American Board of Trial Advocates (Past-National Board Member, Past-President-Louisiana Chapter and Louisiana Chapter Executive Committee); Louisiana Association of Defense Counsel — Practice Areas: General Liability; Legal Malpractice; Medical Malpractice; Insurance Defense; Product Liability; Commercial Liability — E-mail: gracella@kcwlaw.com

Nancy B. Gilbert — 1955 — Earlham College, B.A., 1977; Louisiana State University, J.D., 1994 — Order of the Coif — Admitted to Bar, 1994, Louisiana; U.S. District Court, Eastern, Middle and Western Districts of Louisiana; 1995, U.S. Court of Appeals, Fifth Circuit; 2014, U.S. Supreme Court — Member Louisiana State and Baton Rouge Bar Associations; Defense Research Institute — Practice Areas: Appellate Practice; General Liability; Insurance Defense; Product Liability; Professional Liability; Complex Litigation; Toxic Torts — E-mail: ngilbert@kcwlaw.com

Collin J. LeBlanc — 1970 — Louisiana State University, B.A. (magna cum laude), 1993; J.D. (with honors), 1996 — Order of the Coif — Admitted to Bar, 1996, Louisiana; 1997, U.S. District Court, Eastern, Middle and Western Districts of Louisiana — Member Louisiana State and Baton Rouge Bar Associations — Practice Areas: Appellate Practice; Commercial Litigation; General Liability; Insurance Defense; Product Liability; Subrogation; Legal Malpractice — E-mail: cleblanc@kcwlaw.com

Chad A. Sullivan — 1974 — McNeese State University, B.S.N. (cum laude), 1997; Louisiana State University, J.D., 2001 — Admitted to Bar, 2001, Louisiana; U.S. District Court, Eastern, Middle and Western Districts of Louisiana; U.S. Court of Appeals, Fifth Circuit — Member Federal, Louisiana State and Baton Rouge Bar Associations; The American Association of Nurse Attorneys; Health Care Compliance Association — Serves as Attorney Chair in Medical Malpractice Cases — Registered Nurse; Health Care Compliance by HCCA — Practice Areas: Litigation; Medical Malpractice; General Liability; Medical Devices; Product Liability; Professional Liability; Personal Injury; Nursing Home Defense — E-mail: csullivan@kcwlaw.com

Christopher K. Jones — 1977 — Tulane University, B.S., 1998; Louisiana State University, Paul M. Hebert Law Center, J.D., 2002 — Admitted to Bar, 2002, Louisiana; U.S. District Court, Eastern, Middle and Western Districts of Louisiana; U.S. Court of Appeals, Fifth Circuit — Member Federal, Louisiana State and Baton Rouge Bar Associations — Practice Areas: Insurance Defense; Class Actions; Complex Litigation; Litigation — E-mail: cjones@kcwlaw.com

Mary Anne Wolf — 1961 — Louisiana State University, B.S.E.E., 1983; Louisiana State University, Paul M. Hebert Law Center, J.D., 1999 — Louisiana Law Review — Admitted to Bar, 1999, Louisiana; 2005, U.S. District Court, Eastern, Middle and Western Districts of Louisiana — Member American (Construction Industry Forum), Louisiana State and Baton Rouge Bar Associations; Louisiana Engineering Society; Louisiana Association of Defense Counsel — Presenter, Seminars on Construction Law Topics — Licensed Engineer — Practice Areas: Construction Law; Professional Liability; Product Liability — E-mail: mwolf@kcwlaw.com

Martin E. Golden — 1959 — Louisiana State University, B.A., 1981; J.D., 1984 — Order of the Coif — Law Clerk to Hon. Justice James L. Dennis, Louisiana Supreme Court, 1984-1985 — Associate Editor, Louisiana Law Review, 1984 — Admitted to Bar, 1984, Louisiana; U.S. District Court, Eastern, Middle and Western Districts of Louisiana; 1985, U.S. District Court, Middle District of Louisiana; 1995, U.S. Court of Appeals, Fifth Circuit — Member American, Louisiana State and Baton Rouge Bar Associations; Louisiana Association of Defense Counsel; Defense Research Institute — Practice Areas: General Liability; Product Liability; Class Actions; Employer Liability; Automobile Liability; Insurance Coverage; Workers' Compensation; Subrogation — E-mail: mgolden@kcwlaw.com

Brian T. Butler — 1961 — Louisiana State University, B.S.B.A., 1983; Louisiana State University Law Center, J.D., 1986 — Admitted to Bar, 1986, Louisiana; Supreme Court of Louisiana — Practice Areas: Complex Litigation; Wrongful Death; Product Liability; Fire — E-mail: bbutler@kcwlaw.com

Tori S. Bowling — 1980 — Louisiana State University, B.A., 2002; Louisiana State University, Paul M. Hebert Law Center, J.D./B.C.L., 2005 — Admitted to Bar, 2005, Louisiana; U.S. District Court, Eastern, Middle and Western Districts of Louisiana; U.S. Court of Appeals, Fifth Circuit — Member Louisiana State and Baton Rouge Bar Associations — Practice Areas: Maritime Law; Employment Law; Commercial Litigation; Premises Liability; Personal Injury; Construction Law — E-mail: tbowling@kcwlaw.com

Virginia J. McLin — 1982 — Louisiana State University, B.S. (summa cum laude), 2004; Louisiana State University, Paul M. Hebert Law Center, J.D., 2007 — Admitted to Bar, 2007, Louisiana; U.S. District Court, Eastern, Middle and Western Districts of Louisiana; U.S. Court of Appeals, Fifth Circuit — Member Louisiana State and Baton Rouge Bar Associations — Practice Areas: Litigation; Workers' Compensation; Insurance Defense; Class Actions; Commercial Litigation; Business Formation; Appellate Advocacy — E-mail: jmclin@kcwlaw.com

Associates

C. Reynolds LeBlanc — 1981 — Louisiana State University, B.A. (magna cum laude, Dean's List), 2003; Louisiana State University Law Center, J.D. (with honors), 2011 — Admitted to Bar, 2011, Louisiana; U.S. Court of Appeals, Fifth Circuit; U.S. District Court, Eastern, Middle and Western Districts of Louisiana; U.S. Court of Appeals, Fifth Circuit — Member Federal, Louisiana State and Baton Rouge Bar Associations — Practice Areas: Appellate

Keogh, Cox & Wilson, Ltd., Baton Rouge, LA (Continued)

Advocacy; Insurance Defense; Litigation; Commercial Litigation — E-mail: rleblanc@kcwlaw.com

Richard W. Wolff — 1984 — Louisiana State University, B.A. Political Science, 2009; Loyola University New Orleans College of Law, J.D., 2012 — Admitted to Bar, 2012, Louisiana; U.S. District Court, Eastern, Middle and Western Districts of Louisiana; U.S. Court of Appeals, Fifth Circuit — Practice Areas: Litigation; Personal Injury; Insurance Defense; Complex Litigation; Commercial Litigation; Premises Liability — E-mail: rwolff@kcwlaw.com

Brent J. Cobb — 1985 — Louisiana State University, B.A., History, 2008; Louisiana State University, Paul M. Hebert Law Center, D.C.L./J.D. (cum laude), 2012 — Admitted to Bar, 2012, Louisiana; U.S. District Court, Eastern, Middle and Southern Districts of Louisiana; U.S. Court of Appeals, Fifth Circuit — Member Louisiana State and Baton Rouge Bar Associations — Practice Areas: General Civil Litigation — E-mail: bcobb@kcwlaw.com

Mark T. Assad — Louisiana State University, B.A. (cum laude), 2010; Louisiana State University, Paul M. Hebert Law Center, J.D. (cum laude), 2013 — Phi Beta Kappa — Chancellor's List; Paul M. Hebert Scholar; National Energy & Sustainability Moot Court Competition — Senior Notes and Comments Editior, LSU Journal of Energy Law and Resources — Admitted to Bar, 2013, Louisiana

Special Counsel

Andrew J. Hodges, IV — 1968 — Louisiana State University, B.A., 1991; Southern University Law Center, J.D., 1995 — Admitted to Bar, 1996, Louisiana; U.S. District Court, Eastern and Middle Districts of Louisiana — Member Federal, Louisiana State and Baton Rouge Bar Associations; Louisiana Association of Criminal Defense Lawyers — Baton Rouge City Court Judge Pro Tempore — Practice Areas: Litigation — E-mail: ajhodges@kcwlaw.com

Of Counsel

John R. Keogh — 1944 — Louisiana State University, J.D., 1969 — Admitted to Bar, 1969, Louisiana; U.S. District Court, Eastern, Middle and Western Districts of Louisiana; U.S. Court of Military Appeals — Lt. Col., JAGC (Retired) — Practice Areas: Insurance Defense; Product Liability; Professional Malpractice — E-mail: jkeogh@kcwlaw.com

Perry, Atkinson, Balhoff, Mengis & Burns, L.L.C.

2141 Quail Run Drive
Baton Rouge, Louisiana 70808
Telephone: 225-767-7730
Fax: 225-767-7967
E-Mail: atkinson@pabmb.com
www.pabmb.com

Established: 1995

First and Third Party Defense, General Liability, Insurance Defense, Casualty Defense, Environmental Law, Civil Trial Practice, Mediation, Subrogation

Firm Profile: Firm founded in 1995 from partners originally with the defense firm of Mathews, Atkinson, Guglielmo, Marks & Day. The firm has extensive experience in civil trial and appellate areas. Additionally, the firm is well known for providing quality alternative dispute resolution services (mediations/arbitrations).

Insurance Clients

Catholic Mutual Group Hartford Insurance Company
Liberty Mutual Insurance OneBeacon Insurance
St. Paul Insurance Company

Members of the Firm

John W. Perry, Jr. — 1954 — Nicholls State University, B.A., 1976; Louisiana State University, J.D., 1978 — Admitted to Bar, 1979, Louisiana — Member American, Louisiana State and Baton Rouge Bar Associations; Louisiana Trial Lawyers Association; Louisiana Association of Defense Counsel; American College of Trial Lawyers — E-mail: perry@pabmb.com

Daniel R. Atkinson, Jr. — 1961 — Louisiana State University, B.S.M.E., 1983; J.D., 1987 — Admitted to Bar, 1987, Louisiana — Member Louisiana State and Baton Rouge Bar Associations; American Society of Mechanical Engineers; Louisiana Association of Defense Counsel; Defense Research Institute — E-mail: atkinson@pabmb.com

Daniel J. Balhoff — 1963 — Louisiana State University, B.S.Ch.E., 1985; J.D., 1988 — Admitted to Bar, 1988, Louisiana — Member Federal, Louisiana State and Baton Rouge Bar Associations — E-mail: balhoff@pabmb.com

Joseph W. Mengis — 1966 — Louisiana State University, B.S., 1989; J.D., 1992 — Admitted to Bar, 1992, Louisiana — Member Louisiana State and Baton Rouge Bar Associations; Louisiana Association of Defense Counsel — E-mail: mengis@pabmb.com

Robert J. Burns, Jr. — 1966 — Louisiana State University, B.A., 1988; J.D., 1991 — Admitted to Bar, 1991, Louisiana — Member American, Louisiana State and Baton Rouge Bar Associations; Defense Research Institute; Louisiana Association of Defense Counsel — E-mail: burns@pabmb.com

Randi Simoneaux Ellis — Louisiana State University, B.A., 1994; J.D., 1997 — Admitted to Bar, 1997, Louisiana — Member Louisiana State and Baton Rouge Bar Associations; Dean Henry George McMahon Inn of Court — E-mail: ellis@pabmb.com

Attorney

John W. Perry III — 1984 — Louisiana State University Law Center, J.D., 2010 — Admitted to Bar, 2010, Louisiana — E-mail: jonathon@pabmb.com

Of Counsel

Daniel R. Atkinson Sr. — 1935 — Spring Hill College, B.S., 1957; Louisiana State University, J.D., 1962 — Admitted to Bar, 1962, Louisiana — Member Federal, American, Louisiana State and Baton Rouge Bar Associations; Louisiana Association of Defense Counsel; American College of Trial Lawyers

Phelps Dunbar LLP

II City Plaza
400 Convention Street, Suite 1100
Baton Rouge, Louisiana 70802-5618
Telephone: 225-346-0285
Fax: 225-381-9197
E-Mail: info@phelps.com
www.phelpsdunbar.com

(New Orleans, LA Office*: Canal Place, 365 Canal Street, Suite 2000, 70130-6534)
  (Tel: 504-566-1311)
  (Fax: 504-568-9130)
(Jackson, MS Office*: 4270 I-55 North, 39211-6391, P.O. Box 16114, 39236-6114)
  (Tel: 601-352-2300)
  (Fax: 601-360-9777)
(Tupelo, MS Office*: One Mississippi Plaza, 201 South Spring Street, Seventh Floor, 38804, P.O. Box 1220, 38802-1220)
  (Tel: 662-842-7907)
  (Fax: 662-842-3873)
(Gulfport, MS Office*: NorthCourt One, 2304 19th Street, Suite 300, 39501)
  (Tel: 228-679-1130)
  (Fax: 228-679-1131)
(Houston, TX Office*: One Allen Center, 500 Dallas Street, Suite 1300, 77002)
  (Tel: 713-626-1386)
  (Fax: 713-626-1388)
(Tampa, FL Office*: 100 South Ashley Drive, Suite 1900, 33602-5311)
  (Tel: 813-472-7550)
  (Fax: 813-472-7570)
(Mobile, AL Office*: 2 North Royal Street, 36602, P.O. Box 2727, 36652-2727)
  (Tel: 251-432-4481)
  (Fax: 251-433-1820)
(London, United Kingdom Office*: Lloyd's, Suite 725, Level 7, 1 Lime Street, EC3M 7DQ)
  (Tel: 011-44-207-929-4765)
  (Fax: 011-44-207-929-0046)
(Raleigh, NC Office*: 4140 Parklake Avenue, Suite 100, 27612-3723)
  (Tel: 919-789-5300)
  (Fax: 919-789-5301)

LOUISIANA — BATON ROUGE

Phelps Dunbar LLP, Baton Rouge, LA (Continued)

(Southlake, TX Office*(See Dallas listing): 115 Grand Avenue, Suite 222, 76092)
(Tel: 817-488-3134)
(Fax: 817-488-3214)

Insurance Law

Insurance Clients

- Acceptance Casualty Insurance Company
- Aegis Janson Green Insurance Services Inc.
- AIG
- Alabama Municipal Insurance Corporation
- AmTrust Underwriters, Inc.
- Arch Insurance Company (Europe) Ltd.
- Aspen Insurance UK Limited
- Associated Aviation Underwriters
- Bankers Insurance Group
- Berkley Select, LLC
- Bluebonnet Life Insurance Company
- Britannia Steam Ship Insurance Association Ltd.
- CNA
- Commercial Union Insurance Company
- Companion Property and Casualty Group
- ELCO Administrative Services
- Endurance Services, Ltd.
- Erie Insurance Company
- Evanston Insurance Company
- Fidelity National Financial
- First Premium Insurance Group, Inc.
- GE Insurance Solutions
- General & Cologne Life Reinsurance of America
- General Star Indemnity Company
- Glencoe Group
- Global Special Risks, Inc.
- Great American Insurance Companies
- Gulf Insurance Group
- The Hartford Insurance Group
- Homesite Group, Inc.
- ICAT Boulder Claims
- Infinity Insurance Company
- Lexington Insurance Company
- Liberty Mutual Group
- Louisiana Farm Bureau Mutual Insurance Company
- Louisiana Workers' Compensation Corporation
- Markel
- MetLife Auto & Home
- NAS Insurance Group
- Nautilus Insurance Company
- Old American Insurance Company
- Pharmacists Mutual Insurance Company
- RenaissanceRe
- RLI Insurance Company
- Royal & SunAlliance
- SCOR Global P&C
- Sedgwick Claims Management Services, Inc.
- SR International Business Insurance Company, Ltd.
- Steamship Mutual Underwriting Association Limited
- Torus
- Underwriters at Lloyd's, London
- Unitrin Business Insurance
- Vesta Eiendom AS
- Western Heritage Insurance Company
- Westport Insurance Corporation
- XL Insurance Group
- ACE Group of Insurance and Reinsurance Companies
- Aetna Insurance Company
- AFLAC - American Family Life Assurance Company of Columbus
- Allstate Insurance Company
- American Family Life Assurance Company of Columbus
- Argonaut Insurance Company
- Aspen Insurance
- Aspen Re
- AXIS Insurance
- Beazley
- Bituminous Insurance Company
- Blue Cross & Blue Shield of Mississippi
- Chartis Insurance
- Chubb Group of Insurance Companies
- Commonwealth Insurance Company
- Cotton States Insurance
- Criterion Claim Solutions
- Employers Reinsurance Corporation
- Esurance Insurance Company
- Farmers Insurance Group
- Fireman's Fund Insurance Company
- Foremost Insurance Company
- General American Life Insurance Company
- General Reinsurance Corporation
- General Star Management Company
- Golden Rule Insurance Company
- Great Southern Life Insurance Company
- Hanover Insurance Group
- Hermitage Insurance Company
- Houston Casualty Company
- Indian Harbor Insurance Company
- Ironshore Insurance, Ltd.
- Liberty International Underwriters
- Life Insurance Company of Alabama
- Louisiana Health Insurance Association
- Lyndon Property Insurance Company
- Munich-American Risk Partners
- Nationwide Insurance
- The Navigators Group, Inc.
- OneBeacon Insurance Group
- Prime Syndicate
- QBE
- Republic Western Insurance Company
- St. Paul Travelers
- Scottsdale Insurance Company
- Sentry Insurance
- Southern Farm Bureau Casualty Insurance Company
- State National Insurance Company, Inc.
- Terra Nova Insurance Company Limited
- United States Fidelity and Guaranty Company
- Victoria Insurance Group
- West of England Ship Owners Mutual Insurance Association (Luxembourg)
- Zurich

Phelps Dunbar LLP, Baton Rouge, LA (Continued)

Members of the Firm

Shelton Dennis Blunt — University of Louisiana at Monroe, B.A. (cum laude), 1988; Southern University Law Center, J.D. (cum laude), 1991; Emory University School of Law, LL.M., 1992 — Admitted to Bar, 1992, Louisiana; U.S. District Court, Eastern, Middle and Western Districts of Louisiana; U.S. Court of Appeals, Fifth and Ninth Circuits — Member National, American, Louisiana State and Baton Rouge Bar Associations; Defense Research Institute; Louisiana Association of Defense Counsel

Allen D. Darden — Louisiana State University, B.S., 1977; Louisiana State University, Paul M. Hebert Law Center, J.D. (Order of the Coif), 1984 — Admitted to Bar, 1985, Louisiana; U.S. District Court, Eastern, Middle and Western Districts of Louisiana; U.S. Court of Appeals, Fifth Circuit; U.S. Patent and Trademark Office — Member Louisiana State, New Orleans and Baton Rouge Bar Associations; American Intellectual Property Law Association — Licensed Patent Attorney

Virginia Y. Dodd — Louisiana State University, B.S., 1993; J.D. (Order of the Coif), 1997 — Admitted to Bar, 1997, Louisiana — Member Louisiana State and Baton Rouge Bar Associations; Defense Research Institute — Resident Baton Rouge, LA and London, United Kingdom Office

Heather Duplantis — University of Southwestern Louisiana, B.A. (summa cum laude), 1997; The University of Texas School of Law, J.D. (with high honors), 2000 — Admitted to Bar, 2000, Louisiana; Texas; U.S. District Court, Eastern, Middle and Western Districts of Louisiana; U.S. District Court, Western District of Texas; U.S. Court of Appeals, Fifth Circuit — Member Louisiana State and Baton Rouge Bar Associations; State Bar of Texas

Kelsey Kornick Funes — Louisiana State University, B.A. (Phi Beta Kappa), 1994; Louisiana State University, Paul M. Hebert Law Center, J.D. (Order of the Coif), 1997 — Admitted to Bar, 1997, Louisiana; U.S. District Court, Eastern, Middle and Western Districts of Louisiana; U.S. Court of Appeals, Fifth Circuit — Member Federal, American, Louisiana State and Baton Rouge Bar Associations; Louisiana State Law Institute

Susan W. Furr — Louisiana State University, B.A. (cum laude), 1986; Louisiana State University, Paul M. Hebert Law Center, J.D., 1989 — Admitted to Bar, 1989, Louisiana; U.S. District Court, Eastern, Middle and Western Districts of Louisiana; U.S. Court of Appeals, Fifth and Ninth Circuits — Member Federal, American, Louisiana State and Baton Rouge Bar Associations; Fellow, Litigation Counsel of America; National Association of Women Lawyers; Louisiana Association of Defense Counsel

Karleen J. Green — Louisiana State University, B.S., 1994; Louisiana State University, Paul M. Hebert Law Center, J.D., 1997 — Admitted to Bar, 1997, Louisiana; U.S. District Court, Eastern, Middle and Western Districts of Louisiana; U.S. Court of Appeals, Fifth Circuit — Member Federal, American, Louisiana State and Baton Rouge Bar Associations; Southwest Benefits Association

J. Alan Harrell — Louisiana State University, B.A., 1994; Louisiana State University, Paul M. Hebert Law Center, J.D., 1997 — Admitted to Bar, 1997, Louisiana; U.S. District Court, Eastern, Middle and Western Districts of Louisiana; U.S. Court of Appeals, Fifth Circuit — Member American, Louisiana State and Baton Rouge Bar Associations

Michael D. Hunt — Louisiana State University, B.A., 1974; Louisiana State University, Paul M. Hebert Law Center, J.D., 1977 — Admitted to Bar, 1977, Louisiana; U.S. District Court, Eastern, Middle and Western Districts of Louisiana; U.S. Court of Appeals, Fifth and Eleventh Circuits; U.S. Supreme Court — Member American, Fifth Circuit, Louisiana State and Baton Rouge Bar Associations

H. Alston Johnson, III — Georgetown University, A.B. (cum laude), 1967; Louisiana State University, Paul M. Hebert Law Center, J.D. (Order of the Coif), 1970 — Admitted to Bar, 1970, Louisiana — Member American and Louisiana State Bar Associations; American Law Institute; Louisiana Association of Defense Counsel

Thomas H. Kiggans — Louisiana Tech University, B.A. (magna cum laude), 1981; Louisiana State University, Paul M. Hebert Law Center, J.D., 1984 — Admitted to Bar, 1984, Louisiana; 1985, Texas; U.S. District Court, Eastern, Northern, Southern and Western Districts of Texas; U.S. District Court, Eastern, Middle and Western Districts of Louisiana; U.S. Court of Appeals, Fifth, Ninth and Eleventh Circuits; U.S. Supreme Court — Member American, Louisiana State and Baton Rouge Bar Associations; State Bar of Texas — Board Certified in Labor and Employment Law, Texas Board of Legal Specialization

Steven J. Levine — University of Maryland, B.S., 1974; Louisiana State University, M.S., 1977; Louisiana State University, Paul M. Hebert Law Center, J.D., 1984 — Admitted to Bar, 1984, Louisiana — Member American, Louisiana State and Baton Rouge Bar Associations

Phelps Dunbar LLP, Baton Rouge, LA (Continued)

Marshall M. Redmon — Rhodes College, B.A., 1984; Louisiana State University, Paul M. Hebert Law Center, J.D. (Order of the Coif), 1987 — Admitted to Bar, 1987, Louisiana; U.S. District Court, Eastern, Middle and Western Districts of Louisiana; U.S. Court of Appeals, Fifth Circuit — Member Federal, American, Louisiana State, Baton Rouge and Fifth Federal Circuit Bar Associations; Louisiana Association of Defense Counsel; International Association of Defense Counsel; Professional Liability Underwriting Society — Resident Baton Rouge, LA and London, United Kingdom Office

Counsel

Jane R. Goldsmith — Louisiana State University, B.S., 1982; Louisiana State University, Paul M. Hebert Law Center, J.D. (Order of the Coif), 1988 — Admitted to Bar, 1988, Louisiana — Member Federal, Louisiana State and Baton Rouge Bar Associations

A. Paul LeBlanc, Jr. — Louisiana State University, B.A., 1988; Louisiana State University, Paul M. Hebert Law Center, J.D. (Order of the Coif), 1994 — Admitted to Bar, 1994, Louisiana; 1997, Texas — Member Louisiana State Bar Association; State Bar of Texas

Patrick O'Hara — College of William & Mary, B.A., 1974; Louisiana State University, M.A., 1976; Louisiana State University Law Center, J.D., 1992 — Admitted to Bar, 1992, Louisiana — Member American, Louisiana State, and Baton Rouge Bar Associations

John B. Shortess — Vanderbilt University, B.A., 1991; Tulane University Law School, J.D. (cum laude), 1999 — Admitted to Bar, 1999, Louisiana; U.S. District Court, Eastern, Middle and Western Districts of Louisiana; U.S. Court of Appeals, Fifth Circuit — Member Federal, American, Louisiana State and Baton Rouge Bar Associations

(See listing under New Orleans, LA for additional information)

Powers, Sellers & Chapoton, L.L.P.

7967 Office Park Boulevard
Baton Rouge, Louisiana 70809
Telephone: 225-928-1951
Fax: 225-929-9834
E-Mail: dpowers@powersfirm.com
www.powersfirm.com

Established: 1983

General Practice, Trial Practice, Insurance Law, Subrogation, Workers' Compensation, Carrier Defense, Real Estate, Environmental

Insurance Clients

American International Group, Inc.
Audubon Insurance Company
Mount Vernon Fire Insurance Company
Prudential Insurance Company of America
Utica Mutual Insurance Company
Audubon Indemnity Company
Hertz Claim Management
New Hampshire Insurance Company
Sentry Insurance a Mutual Company
Yosemite Insurance Company

Non-Insurance Clients

American International Recovery, Inc.

Partners

John Dale Powers — 1936 — Louisiana State University, B.S., 1958; J.D., 1960 — Phi Delta Phi — Admitted to Bar, 1960, Louisiana; U.S. District Court, Eastern, Middle and Western Districts of Louisiana; U.S. Court of Appeals, Fifth Circuit; U.S. Supreme Court — Member American, Louisiana State (President 1990-1991; House of Delegates, 1964-1975; Board of Governors, 1989-1992) and Baton Rouge Bar Associations; Louisiana Association of Defense Counsel

Andrew P. Sellers, Jr. — 1970 — Louisiana State University, B.A., 1992; Loyola University, J.D., 1996 — Admitted to Bar, 1997, Louisiana; 1999, U.S. District Court, Middle District of Louisiana — Member Louisiana State and Baton Rouge Bar Associations

Douglas M. Chapoton — 1972 — Louisiana State University, B.A., 1995; J.D., 1998 — Admitted to Bar, 1998, Louisiana; 1998, U.S. District Court, Eastern, Middle and Western Districts of Louisiana — Member American, Louisiana

Powers, Sellers & Chapoton, L.L.P., Baton Rouge, LA (Continued)

State and Baton Rouge Bar Associations; Louisiana Association of Defense Counsel

Associate

Steven H. Watterson — 1968 — The University of Georgia, B.B.A., 1991; Louisiana State University, J.D., 2000 — Admitted to Bar, 2000, Louisiana — Member American, Louisiana State and Baton Rouge Bar Associations

Watson, Blanche, Wilson & Posner
Registered Limited Liability Partnership

505 North Boulevard
Baton Rouge, Louisiana 70802
Telephone: 225-387-5511
Fax: 225-387-5972

Established: 1945

Insurance Defense, Health Care, Product Liability, Medical Malpractice, General Liability, Workers' Compensation, Employee Benefits

Insurance Clients

American International Group, Inc.
Bituminous Fire & Marine Insurance Company
Mid-Continent Group
Safety National Casualty Corporation
Bituminous Casualty Corporation
CNA HealthPro
Michigan Mutual Insurance Company
Travelers Insurance Companies

Non-Insurance Clients

Louisiana Hospital Association Trust Funds
Louisiana Nursing Home Association Trust Fund

Warren O. Watson — (1893-1973)

Fred A. Blanche — (1898-1977)

Charles W. Wilson — (1910-1981)

Harvey H. Posner — (1919-2003)

Peter T. Dazzio — 1941 — Louisiana State University, B.S., 1963; J.D., 1966 — Phi Delta Phi — Law Clerk to E. Gordon West, U.S. District Judge, Middle District of Louisiana 1966-1967 — Admitted to Bar, 1966, Louisiana; 1966, U.S. District Court, Eastern, Middle and Western Districts of Louisiana; 1966, U.S. Court of Appeals, Fifth Circuit — Member Federal Bar Association (President, Baton Rouge Chapter 1971-1972); Louisiana State Bar Association (House of Delegates 1978-1979 and 1980-1981; Disciplinary Hearing Committee, First Circuit, 1990-1994; Disciplinary Board, 1999-2005); Louisiana Association of Defense Counsel (Board of Directors 1981-1983); Louisiana Association of Hospital Attorneys; American Inns of Court; Defense Research Institute — Adjunct Assistant Professor, Louisiana State University Law School (1981-1985)

William E. Scott, III — 1955 — Louisiana State University, B.S., 1977; J.D., 1981 — Moot Court Board 1979-1980 — Admitted to Bar, 1982, Louisiana — Member Louisiana State and Baton Rouge Bar Associations; Louisiana Association of Defense Counsel; Defense Research Institute

Michael M. Remson — 1960 — Louisiana State University, B.A., 1982; J.D., 1985 — Admitted to Bar, 1985, Louisiana — Member American, Louisiana State (Board of Governors, 1998-) and Baton Rouge Bar Associations; State Bar of Texas; Louisiana Association of Hospital Attorneys; Louisiana Association of Defense Counsel; Defense Research Institute

Randall L. Champagne — 1957 — Louisiana State University, B.A., 1978; J.D., 1982 — Phi Delta Phi — Moot Court Board — Law Clerk to Hon. G. Bradford Ware, District Judge, 19th Judicial District Court, Louisiana 1982-1983 — Admitted to Bar, 1982, Louisiana — Member Federal, Louisiana State and Baton Rouge Bar Associations; Louisiana Association of Defense Counsel

Rene J. Pfefferle — 1957 — Louisiana State University, B.S., 1980; Loyola University, J.D., 1987 — Phi Delta Phi — Admitted to Bar, 1987, Louisiana — Member Federal, American, Louisiana State and Baton Rouge Bar Associations; Louisiana Association of Defense Counsel

Watson, Blanche, Wilson & Posner, Registered Limited Liability Partnership, Baton Rouge, LA (Continued)

Chris J. LeBlanc — 1970 — Lamar University, B.B.A. (summa cum laude), 1991; Louisiana State University and A & M College, J.D., 1995 — Admitted to Bar, 1995, Louisiana — Member Louisiana State and Baton Rouge Bar Associations

Robert W. Robison, Jr. — 1963 — Louisiana State University, B.S./M.S., 1986; J.D., 1996 — Admitted to Bar, 1996, Louisiana — Member Federal, Louisiana State and Baton Rouge Bar Associations

Thomas H. Wartelle — 1978 — Louisiana State University Law Center, J.D., 2003 — Admitted to Bar, 2003, Louisiana — Member Louisiana Association of Defense Counsel — Languages: French — Practice Areas: Insurance Defense; Medical Malpractice

Adrien G. Busekist — 1978 — Louisiana State University Law Center, B.C.L./J.D., 2003 — Admitted to Bar, 2003, Louisiana; 2005, New York — Languages: Spanish

Robert L. Roland

The following firms also service this area.

Hailey, McNamara, Hall, Larmann & Papale, L.L.P.
One Galleria Boulevard, Suite 1400
Metairie, Louisiana 70001
  Telephone: 504-836-6500
  Fax: 504-836-6565

Mailing Address: P.O. Box 8288, Metairie, LA 70011-8288

Admiralty and Maritime Law, Commercial Litigation, Construction Litigation, Employment Practices Liability, Insurance Litigation, Product Liability, Professional Malpractice, Toxic Torts, Casualty, Insurance Coverage, Intellectual Property, Premises Liability, Transportation, Mass Tort, Property, Workers' Compensation, Automobile Liability, Appellate, Environmental

SEE COMPLETE LISTING UNDER METAIRIE, LOUISIANA (72 MILES)

Law Office of Eric J. Halverson, Jr.
3925 North I-10 Service Road West, Suite 123
Metairie, Louisiana 70002
  Telephone: 504-885-0105
  Fax: 504-885-2001

Mailing Address: P.O. Box 8761, Metairie, LA 70011-8761

Insurance Defense, Admiralty and Maritime Law, Jones Act, Workers' Compensation, Errors and Omissions, Medical Malpractice, General Liability, Product Liability, Automobile, Truck Liability, Collision and P & I, Longshore

SEE COMPLETE LISTING UNDER METAIRIE, LOUISIANA (72 MILES)

Juge, Napolitano, Guilbeau, Ruli & Frieman
3320 West Esplanade Avenue North
Metairie, Louisiana 70002
  Telephone: 504-831-7270
  Fax: 504-831-7284

Insurance Defense, Workers' Compensation, Employer Liability, Subrogation, Jones Act, Premises Liability, General Liability, Automobile Liability, Longshore & Harbor Workers' Compensation Act, General Maritime Law

SEE COMPLETE LISTING UNDER METAIRIE, LOUISIANA (72 MILES)

Lugenbuhl, Wheaton, Peck, Rankin & Hubbard
Pan American Life Center, Suite 2775
601 Poydras Street
New Orleans, Louisiana 70130
  Telephone: 504-568-1990
  Fax: 504-310-9195

Insurance Coverage, Insurance Defense, Insurance Litigation, Admiralty and Maritime Law, Personal Injury, Jones Act, Environmental Law, Automobile, General Liability, Product Liability, Protection and Indemnity, Subrogation, Comprehensive

SEE COMPLETE LISTING UNDER NEW ORLEANS, LOUISIANA (80 MILES)

Swetman Baxter Massenburg, LLC
650 Poydras Street, Suite 2400
New Orleans, Louisiana 70130
  Telephone: 504-799-0500
  Fax: 504-799-0501

Asbestos Litigation, Bad Faith, Construction Claims, Construction Law, Contractors Liability, Declaratory Judgments, Drug, Environmental Law, Hazardous Waste, Insurance Defense, Intellectual Property, Mold and Mildew Claims, Municipal Liability, Premises Liability, Product Liability, Trucking Liability, Trucking Litigation, Toxic Torts, Uninsured and Underinsured Motorist, Workers' Compensation, Wrongful Death

SEE COMPLETE LISTING UNDER NEW ORLEANS, LOUISIANA (80 MILES)

Ungarino & Eckert, L.L.C.
3850 North Causeway Boulevard, Suite 1280
Metairie, Louisiana 70002
  Telephone: 504-836-7555
  Fax: 504-836-7566

Litigation, Appellate Practice, State and Federal Courts, Class Actions, Insurance Coverage, Premises Liability, Professional Liability, Directors and Officers Liability, Insurance Defense, Construction Law, Toxic Torts, Personal Injury, Arson, Insurance Fraud, Admiralty and Maritime Law, Extra-Contractual Litigation, Bad Faith, Product Liability, Alternative Dispute Resolution, Civil Rights, Workers' Compensation, Environmental Law, Employment Law, Automobile, Truck Liability, Errors and Omissions, Common Carrier, Medical Malpractice, Construction Defect, Constitutional Law, Department of Insurance Complaints, ERISA Claims, Government Relations, Complex Casualty, Consumer Defense, Creditor Rights, Debt Collections, Discrimination Claims, Electric Utility Liability, Engineering Malpractice, Family Law (Divorce, Custody, Support, Adoption), Fraud, General Liability, Governmental Entity Liability, Insurance Subrogation, Landlord Liability, Medical Device Liability, Property Ownership, State and Municipality Litigation, Successions, Warranty/Redhibition Actions

SEE COMPLETE LISTING UNDER METAIRIE, LOUISIANA (72 MILES)

CAMERON † 406 Cameron Par.

Refer To

Woodley, Williams Law Firm, L.L.C.
One Lakeshore Drive, Suite 1750
Lake Charles, Louisiana 70629
  Telephone: 337-433-6328
  Fax: 337-433-7513

Mailing Address: P.O. Box 3731, Lake Charles, LA 70602-3731

Admiralty and Maritime Law, Arson, Dram Shop, Construction Law, Employment Discrimination, Fraud, Health Care, Hospitals, Investigations, Liquor Liability, Medical Liability, Oil and Gas, Premises Liability, Product Liability, Subrogation, Toxic Torts, Trial Practice, Workers' Compensation, Wrongful Termination, Reinsurance, Medical Malpractice, Asbestosis, Silicosis and Hazardous Waste Litigation, Legal and Insurance Broker Malpractice Law, Civil Practice

SEE COMPLETE LISTING UNDER LAKE CHARLES, LOUISIANA (50 MILES)

CHALMETTE † 16,751 St. Bernard Par.

Refer To

Evans & Clesi, PLC
336 Lafayette Street, Suite 200
New Orleans, Louisiana 70130
  Telephone: 504-523-8523
  Fax: 504-523-8522

Insurance Defense, Automobile Liability, Personal Injury, Premises Liability, Business Interruption, Construction Law, Workers' Compensation, Medical Malpractice, Employment Discrimination, Admiralty and Maritime Law

SEE COMPLETE LISTING UNDER NEW ORLEANS, LOUISIANA (10 MILES)

Refer To

Gaudry, Ranson, Higgins & Gremillion, L.L.C.
Oakwood Corporate Center
401 Whitney Avenue, Suite 500
Gretna, Louisiana 70056
  Telephone: 504-362-2466
  Fax: 504-362-5938

Mailing Address: P.O. Box 1910, Gretna, LA 70054-1910

Insurance Defense, Automobile, Premises Liability, Product Liability, Medical Malpractice, Hospital Malpractice, State and Federal Workers' Compensation

SEE COMPLETE LISTING UNDER GRETNA, LOUISIANA (5 MILES)

COVINGTON — LOUISIANA

Refer To
Hailey, McNamara, Hall, Larmann & Papale, L.L.P.
One Galleria Boulevard, Suite 1400
Metairie, Louisiana 70001
   Telephone: 504-836-6500
   Fax: 504-836-6565
Mailing Address: P.O. Box 8288, Metairie, LA 70011-8288

Admiralty and Maritime Law, Commercial Litigation, Construction Litigation, Employment Practices Liability, Insurance Litigation, Product Liability, Professional Malpractice, Toxic Torts, Casualty, Insurance Coverage, Intellectual Property, Premises Liability, Transportation, Mass Tort, Property, Workers' Compensation, Automobile Liability, Appellate, Environmental

SEE COMPLETE LISTING UNDER METAIRIE, LOUISIANA (14 MILES)

COVINGTON † 8,765 St. Tammany Par.

The Truitt Law Firm

149 North New Hampshire Street
Covington, Louisiana 70433-3235
   Telephone: 985-327-5266
   Fax: 985-327-5252
   Mobile: 985-778-1973
   E-Mail: mail@truittlaw.com
   www.truittlaw.com

(Metairie, LA Office: 433 Metairie Road, Suite 209, 70005)
   (Tel: 504-831-3393)

Civil Litigation, Appellate Practice, Insurance Defense, Premises Liability, Automobile, Legal Malpractice, Longshore and Harbor Workers' Compensation, Pharmaceutical, Admiralty and Maritime Law, Automobile Liability, Casualty Defense, Construction Litigation, Malpractice, Personal Injury Litigation, Product Liability Defense, Professional Errors and Omissions, Workers' Compensation, Trial and Appellate Practice, Professional Malpractice, Maritime Law, Business Litigation, Pharmaceutical Liability, Domestic Litigation, Louisiana and Federal Workers' Compensation

Firm Profile: We are trial attorneys. We do not subscribe to the stereotype of most lawyers who simply work a file, then settle it on the steps of the courthouse. Our record of "zero verdicts" in over five hundred trials evidences our commitment to representing our clients effectively. Moreover, our published cases demonstrate that we are equally effective on the appellate level.

Insurance Clients

AIG Personal Lines Group
Fairmont Specialty Insurance Company
Crum & Forster
Farmers Insurance Group

Non-Insurance Clients

Belk, Inc.
Kmart Corporation
Tonti Properties
Family Dollar Stores, Inc.
Southern Cleaning Services, Inc.

Managing Partner

Jack E. "Bobby" Truitt — 1962 — Louisiana State University, B.S., 1984; Loyola University, J.D., 1987 — 2011 Leadership in Law Class (Member); 2012 Super Lawyer — Admitted to Bar, 1987, Louisiana; 1994, Texas; 1987, U.S. District Court, Eastern, Middle and Western Districts of Louisiana; 1987, U.S. Court of Appeals, Fifth Circuit; 1995, U.S. Supreme Court — Member American and Louisiana State Bar Associations; State Bar of Texas; NRRDA; Louisiana Association of Defense Counsel; Defense Research Institute — Reported Cases: Perez v. Wal-Mart Stores, Inc., 608 So.2d 1006 (La. 11/30/92); Verret v. Tonti Management Corp., 662 So.2d 480 (La. App. 5th Cir. 6/28/95); Bungart v. K-mart Corp., 668 So.2d 1335 (La. App. 1st Cir. 2/23/96); Fisher v. Walgreen Louisiana Corp., Inc., 746 So.2d 161 (La. App. 5th Cir. 10/13/99); Wainwright v. Fontenot, 774 So.2d 70 (La. 10/17/00); Griffin v. K-Mart Corp., 776 So.2d 1226 (La. App. 5th Cir. 11/28/00);

The Truitt Law Firm, Covington, LA *(Continued)*

Dodson v. Kmart Corp., 891 So.2d 789 (La. App. 3rd Cir. 12/22/04); Bailey v. Walgreen Co., 891 So.2d 1268 (La. 1/20/05)

Associate Attorneys

Pamela S. Chehardy — 1968 — Louisiana State University at Baton Rouge, B.A., 1990; Loyola University New Orleans, J.D., 1994 — Admitted to Bar, 1995, Louisiana — Member American, Louisiana State and Covington Bar Associations

Ryan D. Kelley — 1984 — Rice University, B.A. Arts and Culture, 2006; Tulane University Law School, J.D., 2009 — Admitted to Bar, 2009, Louisiana — Member Louisiana State Bar Association

Alexandra J. Schultz — 1986 — The George Washington University, B.A. (magna cum laude), 2008; Tulane University Law School, J.D., 2013 — Admitted to Bar, 2013, Louisiana — Member Louisiana State Bar Association

Of Counsel

Arthur J. Brewster — 1962 — The University of New Orleans, B.A., 1984; Loyola University, J.D., 1987 — Phi Delta Phi — Admitted to Bar, 1987, Louisiana; U.S. District Court, Eastern District of Louisiana; 1988, U.S. District Court, Middle District of Louisiana; U.S. Court of Appeals, Fifth Circuit — Member American and Louisiana State Bar Associations; Association of Trial Lawyers of America; Louisiana Association of Defense Counsel

---

The following firms also service this area.

Gaudry, Ranson, Higgins & Gremillion, L.L.C.
Oakwood Corporate Center
401 Whitney Avenue, Suite 500
Gretna, Louisiana 70056
   Telephone: 504-362-2466
   Fax: 504-362-5938
Mailing Address: P.O. Box 1910, Gretna, LA 70054-1910

Insurance Defense, Automobile, Premises Liability, Product Liability, Medical Malpractice, Hospital Malpractice, State and Federal Workers' Compensation

SEE COMPLETE LISTING UNDER GRETNA, LOUISIANA (35 MILES)

Hailey, McNamara, Hall, Larmann & Papale, L.L.P.
One Galleria Boulevard, Suite 1400
Metairie, Louisiana 70001
   Telephone: 504-836-6500
   Fax: 504-836-6565
Mailing Address: P.O. Box 8288, Metairie, LA 70011-8288

Admiralty and Maritime Law, Commercial Litigation, Construction Litigation, Employment Practices Liability, Insurance Litigation, Product Liability, Professional Malpractice, Toxic Torts, Casualty, Insurance Coverage, Intellectual Property, Premises Liability, Transportation, Mass Tort, Property, Workers' Compensation, Automobile Liability, Appellate, Environmental

SEE COMPLETE LISTING UNDER METAIRIE, LOUISIANA (35 MILES)

Law Office of Eric J. Halverson, Jr.
3925 North I-10 Service Road West, Suite 123
Metairie, Louisiana 70002
   Telephone: 504-885-0105
   Fax: 504-885-2001
Mailing Address: P.O. Box 8761, Metairie, LA 70011-8761

Insurance Defense, Admiralty and Maritime Law, Jones Act, Workers' Compensation, Errors and Omissions, Medical Malpractice, General Liability, Product Liability, Automobile, Truck Liability, Collision and P & I, Longshore

SEE COMPLETE LISTING UNDER METAIRIE, LOUISIANA (35 MILES)

Schafer & Schafer
328 Lafayette Street
New Orleans, Louisiana 70130
   Telephone: 504-522-0011
   Fax: 504-523-2795

Insurance Defense, Automobile, Premises Liability, Product Liability, Employer Liability, Medical Malpractice, Coverage Issues, Employment Law, Bad Faith, Comprehensive General Liability, Complex Litigation, Civil Trial Practice, Excess and Umbrella, Fire Loss, Homeowners, Uninsured and Underinsured Motorist, Wrongful Death

SEE COMPLETE LISTING UNDER NEW ORLEANS, LOUISIANA (45 MILES)

LOUISIANA

DE RIDDER † 9,808 Beauregard Par.

Refer To

Plauché, Smith & Nieset, LLC
1123 Pithon Street
Lake Charles, Louisiana 70601
  Telephone: 337-436-0522
  Fax: 337-436-9637

Mailing Address: P.O. Drawer 1705, Lake Charles, LA 70602

Automobile Liability, Fire, Arson, Inland Marine, Casualty, Workers' Compensation, Admiralty and Maritime Law, Product Liability, Professional Malpractice, Environmental Law, Toxic Torts, Subrogation, Surety Bonds, Construction Law, Directors and Officers Liability, Employment Law

SEE COMPLETE LISTING UNDER LAKE CHARLES, LOUISIANA (45 MILES)

EDGARD † 2,441 St. John The Baptist Par.

Refer To

Gaudry, Ranson, Higgins & Gremillion, L.L.C.
Oakwood Corporate Center
401 Whitney Avenue, Suite 500
Gretna, Louisiana 70056
  Telephone: 504-362-2466
  Fax: 504-362-5938

Mailing Address: P.O. Box 1910, Gretna, LA 70054-1910

Insurance Defense, Automobile, Premises Liability, Product Liability, Medical Malpractice, Hospital Malpractice, State and Federal Workers' Compensation

SEE COMPLETE LISTING UNDER GRETNA, LOUISIANA (30 MILES)

GRETNA † 17,736 Jefferson Par.

Gaudry, Ranson, Higgins & Gremillion, L.L.C.

Oakwood Corporate Center
401 Whitney Avenue, Suite 500
Gretna, Louisiana 70056
  Telephone: 504-362-2466
  Fax: 504-362-5938
  www.grhg.net

(Baton Rouge, LA Office*: 2223 Quail Run Drive, Suite C-2, 70808)
  (Tel: 225-663-6101)
  (Fax: 225-663-6102)

Established: 1975

Insurance Defense, Automobile, Premises Liability, Product Liability, Medical Malpractice, Hospital Malpractice, State and Federal Workers' Compensation

Firm Profile: The law firm of Gaudry, Ranson, Higgins & Gremillion is strategically located in the New Orleans metro area at 401 Whitney Avenue, Ste. 500, Gretna, La in Jefferson Parish across the Mississippi River from downtown New Orleans. The firm has served insurance, industry and individual clients for over 40 years and enjoys an AV rating from Martindale-Hubbell - the highest possible peer review rating from the leading source of information on the legal profession.

In recent years, the firm has established a Baton Rouge office to better serve the needs of its clients throughout south and central Louisiana.

Our litigation section attorneys are experienced in handling a variety of casualty litigation. This section has represented clients in lawsuits involving such diverse areas as industrial casualties, automobile and UM liability, premises liability, property damage claims, products liability, environmental law, construction litigation, maritime and Jones Act claims, municipal law, medical malpractice, state and federal workers' compensation claims, class actions and trucking liability.

The attorneys in the firm also have extensive experience in insurance coverage disputes.

Gaudry, Ranson, Higgins & Gremillion, L.L.C., Gretna, LA (Continued)

The commercial litigation and transactions section of the firm provide a wide array of services to clients. The attorneys in this section have represented individual and corporate clients in the formation of business entities, commercial litigation, real estate transactions, construction law, contracts, contractual litigation, hospital and health care law, and secured transactions.

We are committed to providing exceptional representation and responsiveness to our clients' specific needs. We focus on providing superior service and results and pride ourselves on the experience and expertise we can offer our clients. After all, we would not be here if not for the relationships we have established with our clients and their trust in us.

Insurance Clients

Adventist Risk Management, Inc.
Crawford & Company
Harleysville Mutual Insurance Company
National Automotive Insurance Company
Risk Management, Inc.
Zurich American Insurance Group
Catholic Mutual Group
F.A. Richard & Associates, Inc.
Hartford Life Insurance Company
Louisiana Automotive Dealers Association Self-Insurers Fund
Nautilus Insurance Group
Safeco Insurance Company of America

Non-Insurance Clients

Archdiocese of New Orleans
BellSouth Telecommunications, Inc.
Ladder Management Services
Mid South Controls Lines, Inc.
Mothe Funeral Homes, Inc.
Ruelco, Inc.
Sysco Food Service of New Orleans, LLC
Barriere Construction Company, LLC
Federated Department Stores, Inc.
Louisiana United Businesses Association Self-Insurers Fund
The Parish of Jefferson
Securitas, Inc.
Tenet Healthcare Corporation
Touro Infirmary

Partners

Thomas L. Gaudry, Jr. — 1947 — The University of New Orleans, B.S., 1969; Loyola University, J.D., 1974 — Admitted to Bar, 1974, Louisiana; 1976, U.S. District Court, Eastern District of Louisiana; 1981, U.S. District Court, Middle District of Louisiana — Member Louisiana State, Jefferson and New Orleans Bar Associations; Louisiana Association of Defense Counsel; Defense Research Institute — E-mail: tgaudry@grhg.net

Daniel A. Ranson — 1954 — The University of New Orleans, B.S., 1976; Loyola University, J.D., 1979 — Admitted to Bar, 1979, Louisiana — Member Louisiana State Bar Association; Louisiana Association of Defense Counsel

Daryl A. Higgins — 1952 — University of Southwestern Louisiana, B.S., 1974; Loyola University, J.D., 1977 — Admitted to Bar, 1977, Louisiana — Member American, Louisiana State and Jefferson Bar Associations

Gregory G. Gremillion — 1953 — The University of New Orleans, B.S., 1976; Loyola University, J.D., 1980 — Admitted to Bar, 1980, Louisiana — Member Louisiana State and Jefferson Bar Associations; Louisiana Association of Defense Counsel

Wade A. Langlois, III — 1961 — Louisiana State University, B.S., 1983; Loyola University, J.D., 1986 — Admitted to Bar, 1986, Louisiana — Member American, Louisiana State and New Orleans Bar Associations; Louisiana Association of Defense Counsel

Michael D. Peytavin — 1958 — Nicholls State University, B.A., 1981; Loyola University, J.D., 1984 — Admitted to Bar, 1984, Louisiana — Member Louisiana State Bar Association

Special Partners

Steven D. Oliver — 1961 — Louisiana State University, B.A., 1983; Loyola University, J.D., 1987 — Admitted to Bar, 1987, Louisiana — Member American and Louisiana State Bar Associations; Louisiana Association of Defense Counsel

Thomas W. Darling — 1959 — Louisiana State University, B.S., 1983; Loyola University, J.D., 1994 — Admitted to Bar, 1994, Louisiana — Member Federal, Louisiana State and Young Lawyers Bar Associations

Associates

William H. Voigt — 1945 — Loyola University, B.A., 1967; J.D., 1972 — Admitted to Bar, 1972, Louisiana; 1974, U.S. District Court, Eastern District of Louisiana; 1996, U.S. District Court, Western District of Louisiana

Alan M. Flake — Louisiana State University, B.S., 1984; Loyola University, J.D., 1987 — Admitted to Bar, 1987, Louisiana; 2005, Texas; U.S. District

Gaudry, Ranson, Higgins & Gremillion, L.L.C., Gretna, LA (Continued)

Court, Eastern, Middle and Western Districts of Louisiana; U.S. District Court, Eastern, Northern, Southern and Western Districts of Texas; U.S. Court of Appeals, Fifth Circuit

Jairo F. Sanchez — 1974 — The University of New Orleans, B.S., 2001; Loyola University New Orleans, J.D., 2008 — Admitted to Bar, 2008, Louisiana — Languages: Spanish

Ryan C. Higgins — 1985 — Louisiana State University, B.A., 2007; Loyola University New Orleans, J.D., 2010 — Admitted to Bar, 2010, Louisiana

Elizabeth A. Liuzza — 1986 — Louisiana State University, B.A., 2008; Loyola University, J.D., 2012 — Admitted to Bar, 2012, Louisiana

John J. Danna Jr. — 1976 — Our Lady of Holy Cross College, B.A., 1998; Loyola University, J.D., 2003 — Admitted to Bar, 2004, Louisiana

Jonathan L. Brehm — 1981 — Tulane University, B.A., 2003; Louisiana State University, J.D., 2012 — Admitted to Bar, 2013, Louisiana

Of Counsel

Stacie E. Petersen — 1978 — Louisiana State University, B.A. (Dean's List), 2000; Loyola University New Orleans College of Law, J.D., 2003 — Admitted to Bar, 2004, Louisiana — Member Louisiana State and New Orleans (Young Lawyers Division) Bar Associations; Judge John C. Boutall American Inn of Court (Associate Member)

The following firms also service this area.

Evans & Clesi, PLC
336 Lafayette Street, Suite 200
New Orleans, Louisiana 70130
   Telephone: 504-523-8523
   Fax: 504-523-8522

Insurance Defense, Automobile Liability, Personal Injury, Premises Liability, Business Interruption, Construction Law, Workers' Compensation, Medical Malpractice, Employment Discrimination, Admiralty and Maritime Law

SEE COMPLETE LISTING UNDER NEW ORLEANS, LOUISIANA (7 MILES)

Hailey, McNamara, Hall, Larmann & Papale, L.L.P.
One Galleria Boulevard, Suite 1400
Metairie, Louisiana 70001
   Telephone: 504-836-6500
   Fax: 504-836-6565

Mailing Address: P.O. Box 8288, Metairie, LA 70011-8288

Admiralty and Maritime Law, Commercial Litigation, Construction Litigation, Employment Practices Liability, Insurance Litigation, Product Liability, Professional Malpractice, Toxic Torts, Casualty, Insurance Coverage, Intellectual Property, Premises Liability, Transportation, Mass Tort, Property, Workers' Compensation, Automobile Liability, Appellate, Environmental

SEE COMPLETE LISTING UNDER METAIRIE, LOUISIANA (7 MILES)

Schafer & Schafer
328 Lafayette Street
New Orleans, Louisiana 70130
   Telephone: 504-522-0011
   Fax: 504-523-2795

Insurance Defense, Automobile, Premises Liability, Product Liability, Employer Liability, Medical Malpractice, Coverage Issues, Employment Law, Bad Faith, Comprehensive General Liability, Complex Litigation, Civil Trial Practice, Excess and Umbrella, Fire Loss, Homeowners, Uninsured and Underinsured Motorist, Wrongful Death

SEE COMPLETE LISTING UNDER NEW ORLEANS, LOUISIANA (7 MILES)

HAHNVILLE † 3,344 St. Charles Par.

Refer To
Evans & Clesi, PLC
336 Lafayette Street, Suite 200
New Orleans, Louisiana 70130
   Telephone: 504-523-8523
   Fax: 504-523-8522

Insurance Defense, Automobile Liability, Personal Injury, Premises Liability, Business Interruption, Construction Law, Workers' Compensation, Medical Malpractice, Employment Discrimination, Admiralty and Maritime Law

SEE COMPLETE LISTING UNDER NEW ORLEANS, LOUISIANA (40 MILES)

Refer To
Gaudry, Ranson, Higgins & Gremillion, L.L.C.
Oakwood Corporate Center
401 Whitney Avenue, Suite 500
Gretna, Louisiana 70056
   Telephone: 504-362-2466
   Fax: 504-362-5938

Mailing Address: P.O. Box 1910, Gretna, LA 70054-1910

Insurance Defense, Automobile, Premises Liability, Product Liability, Medical Malpractice, Hospital Malpractice, State and Federal Workers' Compensation

SEE COMPLETE LISTING UNDER GRETNA, LOUISIANA (25 MILES)

HOUMA † 33,727 Terrebonne Par.

Refer To
Gaudry, Ranson, Higgins & Gremillion, L.L.C.
Oakwood Corporate Center
401 Whitney Avenue, Suite 500
Gretna, Louisiana 70056
   Telephone: 504-362-2466
   Fax: 504-362-5938

Mailing Address: P.O. Box 1910, Gretna, LA 70054-1910

Insurance Defense, Automobile, Premises Liability, Product Liability, Medical Malpractice, Hospital Malpractice, State and Federal Workers' Compensation

SEE COMPLETE LISTING UNDER GRETNA, LOUISIANA (50 MILES)

Refer To
Lugenbuhl, Wheaton, Peck, Rankin & Hubbard
Pan American Life Center, Suite 2775
601 Poydras Street
New Orleans, Louisiana 70130
   Telephone: 504-568-1990
   Fax: 504-310-9195

Insurance Coverage, Insurance Defense, Insurance Litigation, Admiralty and Maritime Law, Personal Injury, Jones Act, Environmental Law, Automobile, General Liability, Product Liability, Protection and Indemnity, Subrogation, Comprehensive

SEE COMPLETE LISTING UNDER NEW ORLEANS, LOUISIANA (60 MILES)

JENNINGS † 10,383 Jefferson Davis Par.

Refer To
Plauché, Smith & Nieset, LLC
1123 Pithon Street
Lake Charles, Louisiana 70601
   Telephone: 337-436-0522
   Fax: 337-436-9637

Mailing Address: P.O. Drawer 1705, Lake Charles, LA 70602

Automobile Liability, Fire, Arson, Inland Marine, Casualty, Workers' Compensation, Admiralty and Maritime Law, Product Liability, Professional Malpractice, Environmental Law, Toxic Torts, Subrogation, Surety Bonds, Construction Law, Directors and Officers Liability, Employment Law

SEE COMPLETE LISTING UNDER LAKE CHARLES, LOUISIANA (30 MILES)

Refer To
Woodley, Williams Law Firm, L.L.C.
One Lakeshore Drive, Suite 1750
Lake Charles, Louisiana 70629
   Telephone: 337-433-6328
   Fax: 337-433-7513

Mailing Address: P.O. Box 3731, Lake Charles, LA 70602-3731

Admiralty and Maritime Law, Arson, Dram Shop, Construction Law, Employment Discrimination, Fraud, Health Care, Hospitals, Investigations, Liquor Liability, Medical Liability, Oil and Gas, Premises Liability, Product Liability, Subrogation, Toxic Torts, Trial Practice, Workers' Compensation, Wrongful Termination, Reinsurance, Medical Malpractice, Asbestosis, Silicosis and Hazardous Waste Litigation, Legal and Insurance Broker Malpractice Law, Civil Practice

SEE COMPLETE LISTING UNDER LAKE CHARLES, LOUISIANA (30 MILES)

LAFAYETTE † 120,623 Lafayette Par.

Breaud & Meyers, P.L.C.
600 Jefferson Street, Suite 1101
Lafayette, Louisiana 70501
Telephone: 337-266-2200
Fax: 337-266-2204

Established: 1993

Insurance Defense, Admiralty and Maritime Law, Coverage Issues, Personal Injury, Professional Liability, Malpractice, Business Litigation, Labor and Employment, Civil Litigation, Product Liability

Firm Profile: Breaud & Meyers, P.L.C. was founded in 1993 on the principle of providing specialized litigation services to a select group of clients. Breaud & Meyers continues to build upon the foundation of strong personal relationships with their clients to provide the quality service and personal attention necessary to meet their client's goals. The firm serves clients throughout the state of Louisiana.

Insurance Clients

AIG Claim Services, Inc.
CGU Insurance Company
CNA/U.S. Marine Claims
Osprey Underwriting Agency Ltd.
Sagamore Insurance Company
Travelers Insurance Companies
American National Property and Casualty Company
Louisiana Medical Mutual Insurance Company
Specialty Risk Services

Non-Insurance Clients

American Pollution Control Corporation
BE & K Construction Company
Deep South Surplus, Inc.
Estis Well Service, LLC
Key Energy Services, Inc.
The Lemoine Company
Performance Wellhead and Frac Components, Inc.
Stabiltec Downhole Tools, LLC
T3 Energy Services
AMPOL
Averitt Express, Inc.
Brookshire Grocery Company
Ensco PLC
Kergan Brothers, Inc.
Koch Industries, Inc.
Omega Protein, Inc.
REM
Siemens Corporation
Tools International Corporation

Partners

Alan K. Breaud — 1953 — Louisiana Tech University; Louisiana State University, B.A., 1975; Loyola University, J.D., 1979 — Admitted to Bar, 1979, Louisiana; 1979, U.S. District Court, Eastern, Middle and Western Districts of Louisiana; 1979, U.S. District Court, Southern District of Mississippi; 1979, U.S. Court of Appeals, Fifth Circuit; 1984, U.S. Supreme Court — Member American and Louisiana State Bar Associations; The Maritime Law Association of the United States; Louisiana Association of Defense Counsel; Southeastern Admiralty Law Institute; Defense Research Institute

Andrew H. Meyers — 1958 — Louisiana State University, B.S., 1980; J.D., 1984 — Admitted to Bar, 1984, Louisiana; 1984, U.S. District Court, Eastern, Middle and Western Districts of Louisiana; 1984, U.S. District Court, Eastern District of Texas; 1984, U.S. Court of Appeals, Fifth Circuit — Member Louisiana State, Lafayette Parish and Fifteenth Judicial District Bar Associations; Louisiana Association of Defense Counsel

Timothy W. Basden — 1966 — Louisiana State University, B.A. (with honors), 1988; J.D., 1992 — Admitted to Bar, 1992, Louisiana; 1995, U.S. District Court, Eastern, Middle and Western Districts of Louisiana; 1995, U.S. Court of Appeals, Fifth Circuit — Member Federal, Louisiana State and Lafayette Parish Bar Associations; Louisiana Association of Defense Counsel

Associate

Jade A. Forouzanfar — 1987 — Louisiana State University at Baton Rouge, B.S. (summa cum laude), 2008; J.D., 2012 — Admitted to Bar, 2013, Louisiana; 2014, U.S. District Court, Eastern District of Louisiana

Galloway, Johnson, Tompkins, Burr & Smith
328 Settler's Trace Boulevard
Lafayette, Louisiana 70508
Telephone: 337-735-1760
Fax: 337-993-0933
E-Mail: info@gallowayjohnson.com
www.gallowayjohnson.com

(Additional Offices: New Orleans, LA*; Pensacola, FL*; St. Louis, MO*; Houston, TX*; Mandeville, LA*; Gulfport, MS*; Tampa, FL*; Mobile, AL*; Atlanta, GA*)

Maritime, Automobile Liability, Bad Faith, Class Actions, Construction, Energy, Employment, Insurance Coverage, Insurance Defense, Product Liability, Professional Liability, Property, Transportation, General Casualty, Title Resolution, Environmental

(See listing under New Orleans, LA for additional information)

Hill & Beyer
A Professional Law Corporation
101 La Rue France, Suite #502
Lafayette, Louisiana 70508
Telephone: 337-232-9733
Fax: 337-237-2566
E-Mail: hb@hillandbeyer.com
www.hillandbeyer.com

Established: 1988

Insurance Defense, Automobile, Product Liability, Workers' Compensation, Admiralty and Maritime Law, Commercial Law, Construction Law, Professional Liability, Insurance Coverage

Firm Profile: The firm Hill & Beyer was established in 1988 by John K. Hill, Jr. and Bret C. Beyer, Sr. The firm consists of two partners and one associate attorney as well as four paralegals and three support staff. The firm services the entire State of Louisiana for some clients, and otherwise concentrates its practice in the Acadiana area (the approximately eight Cajun Country Parishes—counties—of South Central and Southwest Louisiana) and Baton Rouge Areas. In addition to insurance defense issues, the firm also concentrates its practice in the defense of large, self-insured companies and insurance coverage matters.

Insurance Clients

ACE American Insurance Company
Capital City Insurance Company, Inc.
Specialty Risk Services, Inc. (SRS)
American Modern Home Insurance Company
F.A. Richard & Associates, Inc.
Gallagher Bassett Services, Inc.
Zurich Insurance Company

Non-Insurance Clients

Baker Hughes, Incorporated
Philip Services Corporation
Republic Services, Inc.
Keith Lawyer Management Company

Partners

John K. Hill, Jr. — (1944-1996)

Eugene P. Matherne — (1962-1996)

Bret C. Beyer, Sr. — 1962 — The University of Texas at Austin, B.B.A. (magna cum laude), 1984; Louisiana State University, J.D., 1987 — Order of the Coif; Honored Member of Who's Who in Practicing Attorneys for 1990, Louisiana State University Hall of Fame — Senior Editor of the Louisiana Law Review, Vol. 47 — Admitted to Bar, 1987, Louisiana; 1987, U.S. District Court, Eastern, Middle and Western Districts of Louisiana; 1987, U.S. Court of Appeals, Fifth Circuit; 1996, U.S. Supreme Court — Member American, Louisiana State and Lafayette Parish Bar Associations; Louisiana Association of Defense Counsel

LAFAYETTE   LOUISIANA

Hill & Beyer, A Professional Law Corporation, Lafayette, LA (Continued)

Erin Sherburne Beyer — 1967 — Louisiana State University, B.A., 1989; J.D., 1992 — Admitted to Bar, 1992, Louisiana; 1992, U.S. District Court, Eastern, Middle and Western Districts of Louisiana — Member Federal, American, Louisiana State and Lafayette Parish Bar Associations

Associate

Marianna Broussard — 1943 — University of Southwestern Louisiana, B.A., 1965; Loyola University, J.D., 1995 — Admitted to Bar, 1996, Louisiana; 1996, U.S. District Court, Eastern, Middle and Western Districts of Louisiana — Member American, Louisiana State and Lafayette Parish Bar Associations

Hurlburt, Monrose & Ernest

700 St. John Street, Suite 200
Lafayette, Louisiana 70501
Telephone: 337-237-0261
Fax: 337-237-9117
www.lawyers.com/hpm-plc

Established: 1977

Insurance Defense, Automobile Liability, Transportation, Property Damage, Workers' Compensation, General Liability, Product Liability, Bodily Injury, Personal Injury, Admiralty and Maritime Law, Arson, Fraud, Indian Law

Firm Profile: The firm practices statewide in State and Federal Courts with emphasis on insurance litigation, including automobile, general liability, all workers' compensation, products liability, admiralty/maritime personal injury, premises liability, police/municipality liability and property claims in the particular area of arson and fraud.

Insurance Clients

American Family Mutual Insurance Company
Central Mutual Insurance Company
GAB Robins North America, Inc.
Guaranty National Insurance Company
Lexington Insurance Company
Manitoba Public Insurance Corporation
Tribal First Insurance Company
Westchester Fire Insurance Company
Associated International Insurance Company
Fireman's Fund Insurance Company
Hanover Insurance Company
Hudson Insurance Company
Louisiana Insurance Guaranty Association
North American Specialty Insurance Company
Zurich American Insurance Company

Non-Insurance Clients

AT&T
Chitimacha Tribe of Louisiana
Edward D. Jones & Co., L.P.
The Home Depot
Pepsi Beverages Company
Royal Associates Management, Inc.
Strategic Comp
Walgreen Company
Candy Fleet, LLC
Cypress Bayou Casino
Federal Express Corporation
Marriott International, Inc.
Rowan Companies, Inc.
Safway Services, LLC
Sedgwick CMS
Veolia ES Special Services

Firm Members

David A. Hurlburt — 1950 — Augustana College, B.A., 1974; Louisiana State University, J.D., 1977 — Order of the Coif — Admitted to Bar, 1977, Louisiana; 1977, U.S. District Court, Eastern, Middle and Western Districts of Louisiana; 1977, U.S. Court of Appeals, Fifth Circuit; 1984, U.S. Supreme Court; 1993, Chitimacha Tribal Court — Member Louisiana State, Lafayette Parish and 15th Judicial District Bar Associations — E-mail: david.hurlburt@hpmatty.com

M. Blake Monrose — 1956 — Louisiana State University, B.A., 1978; J.D., 1982 — Admitted to Bar, 1982, Louisiana; 1982, U.S. District Court, Eastern, Middle and Western Districts of Louisiana — Member American, Louisiana State, Lafayette Parish and 15th Judicial District Bar Associations — E-mail: blake.monrose@hpmatty.com

George D. Ernest III — 1960 — Louisiana State University, B.S., 1982; J.D., 1985 — Admitted to Bar, 1985, Louisiana; 1985, U.S. District Court, Eastern, Middle and Western Districts of Louisiana; 1985, U.S. District Court, Eastern and Southern Districts of Texas; 1985, U.S. Court of Appeals, Fifth Circuit;

Hurlburt, Monrose & Ernest, Lafayette, LA (Continued)

1985, U.S. Supreme Court — Member Federal, Louisiana State and Lafayette Parish Bar Associations; State Bar of Texas; Acadiana Legal Services Corporation — E-mail: dave.ernest@hpmatty.com

Associate

Matthew D. Fontenot — 1980 — Louisiana State University, J.D./B.C.L., 2005 — Admitted to Bar, 2005, Louisiana — Member Louisiana State and Lafayette Bar Associations — E-mail: matthew.fontenot@hpmatty.com

Jeansonne & Remondet, L.L.C.

200 West Congress Street, Suite 1100
Lafayette, Louisiana 70501
Telephone: 337-237-4370
Fax: 337-235-2011
Toll Free: 800-446-2745
www.jeanrem.com

(New Orleans, LA Office: One Canal Place, 365 Canal Street, Suite 1660, 70130)
(Tel: 504-524-7333)
(Fax: 504-524-3339)

Admiralty and Maritime Law, Asbestos, Automobile, Complex Litigation, Construction Law, Coverage Issues, Governmental Defense, Mass Tort, Premises Liability, Subrogation, Toxic Torts, Workers' Compensation

Firm Profile: Jeansonne & Remondet, L.L.C. is made up of 8 seasoned attorneys who are licensed in multiple states, each of whom offer expertise and knowledge in various areas of the law, including a broad range of legal experiences throughout Louisiana and Eastern Texas.

Insurance Clients

CIGNA Insurance Company
Lincoln General Insurance Company
TIG Insurance Group
K & K Claims Service
Republic Western Insurance Company

Non-Insurance Clients

Louisiana Transportation, Inc.

John A. Jeansonne, Jr. — Tulane University, J.D., 1968 — Admitted to Bar, 1968, Louisiana; 1999, Texas

Michael J. Remondet, Jr. — Louisiana State University at Baton Rouge, J.D., 1991 — Admitted to Bar, 1991, Louisiana; 2001, Texas

Jones Walker LLP

600 Jefferson Street, Suite 1600
Lafayette, Louisiana 70501
Telephone: 337-593-7600
Fax: 337-593-7601
E-Mail: info@joneswalker.com
www.joneswalker.com

(New Orleans, LA Office*: 201 St. Charles Avenue, 70170-5100)
(Tel: 504-582-8000)
(Fax: 504-582-8583)
(Mobile, AL Office*: RSA Battle House Tower, 11 North Water Street, Suite 1200, 36602, P.O. Box 46, 36601)
(Tel: 251-432-1414)
(Fax: 251-433-4106)
(Baton Rouge, LA Office*: Four United Plaza, 8555 United Plaza Boulevard, 70809)
(Tel: 225-248-2000)
(Fax: 225-248-2010)
(Birmingham, AL Office*: One Federal Place, 1819 5th Avenue North, Suite 1100, 35203)
(Tel: 205-244-5200)
(Fax: 205-244-5400)

LOUISIANA — LAFAYETTE

Jones Walker LLP, Lafayette, LA (Continued)

(Jackson, MS Office*: 190 East Capitol Street, Suite 800, 39201, P.O. Box 427, 39205-0427)
 (Tel: 601-949-4900)
 (Fax: 601-949-4804)
(Olive Branch, MS Office*: 6897 Crumpler Boulevard, Suite 100, 38654)
 (Tel: 662-895-2996)
 (Fax: 662-895-5480)

Accountants, Admiralty and Maritime Law, Agent/Broker Liability, Antitrust, Appellate Practice, Asbestos Litigation, Aviation, Bankruptcy, Cargo, Class Actions, Commercial Litigation, Complex Litigation, Construction Law, Contracts, Directors and Officers Liability, Disability, Employment Law, Energy, Entertainment Law, Environmental Law, ERISA, Errors and Omissions, Health Care, Insurance Coverage, Insurance Defense, Intellectual Property, International Law, Labor and Employment, Life Insurance, Medical Malpractice, Mergers and Acquisitions, Motor Carriers, Oil and Gas, Personal Injury, Product Liability, Professional Liability, Regulatory and Compliance, Toxic Torts, Workers' Compensation

Firm Profile: Since 1937, Jones Walker LLP has grown to become one of the largest law firms in the southeastern U.S. We serve local, regional, national, and international business interests in a wide range of markets and industries. Today, we have more than 375 attorneys in 19 offices.

Jones Walker is committed to providing proactive legal services to major multinational, public, and private corporations; *Fortune* 500® companies; money center banks and worldwide insurers; and family and emerging businesses located in the United States and abroad.

Firm Members

Michael G. Lemoine — Louisiana State University, B.A. (with honors), 1977; Louisiana State University, Paul M. Hebert Law Center, J.D., 1981 — Admitted to Bar, 1981, Louisiana — Member Louisiana State and Lafayette Parish Bar Associations; Louisiana Association of Defense Counsel — E-mail: mlemoine@joneswalker.com

Douglas C. Longman, Jr. — Tulane University, B.A., 1975; Louisiana State University, J.D., 1978 — Admitted to Bar, 1978, Louisiana; 1992, Texas — Member Louisiana State and Lafayette Parish Bar Associations; Bar Association of the Fifth Federal Circuit; State Bar of Texas; Southwest Association of Defense Counsel; Texas Association of Defense Counsel — E-mail: dlongman@joneswalker.com

Ian A. Macdonald — The University of Utah, B.S., 1982; Louisiana State University, Paul M. Hebert Law Center, J.D., 1986 — Admitted to Bar, 1986, Louisiana — Member American Bar Association; Louisiana State Bar Association (Labor and Employment Law Section); Lafayette Parish Bar Association (Past Member, Board of Directors); Lafayette Young Lawyers Association (Past President); Louisiana Society of Hospital Attorneys; Defense Research Institute; Louisiana Association of Defense Counsel — E-mail: imacdonald@joneswalker.com

Gary J. Russo — Louisiana State University, B.A., 1976; J.D., 1979 — Admitted to Bar, 1979, Louisiana; 1992, Texas; U.S. District Court, Eastern, Middle and Western Districts of Louisiana; U.S. Court of Appeals, Fifth and Eleventh Circuits — Member American, Louisiana State and Lafayette Bar Associations; Bar Association of the Fifth Federal Circuit; State Bar of Texas; Louisiana Association of Defense Counsel (Certified Mediator); Texas Association of Defense Counsel — Practice Areas: Business Litigation; Commercial Litigation; Class Actions; Energy; Oil and Gas; Environmental Law; Toxic Torts; Insurance Coverage Litigation — E-mail: grusso@joneswalker.com

(See Listing under New Orleans, LA for a List of Firm Clients and Additional Information)

Juneau David
A Professional Law Corporation

The Harding Center
1018 Harding Street, Suite 202
Lafayette, Louisiana 70503
 Telephone: 337-269-0052
 Fax: 337-269-0061
 E-Mail: mjj@juneaudavid.com
 www.juneaudavid.com

Established: 1993

Insurance Coverage, Errors and Omissions, Accountants, Architects and Engineers, Legal, Insurance Agents, Directors and Officers Liability, Automobile, Admiralty and Maritime Law, Aviation, Contracts, Environmental Law, Toxic Torts, Marine, Personal Injury, Negligence, Employment Law, Product Liability, Commercial Litigation, Construction Law, Labor and Employment, Discrimination, Wrongful Death, Automobile General Casualty, Truck Accidents

Insurance Clients

- ACE USA
- Allianz Insurance Company
- American Re-Insurance Company
- Arch Insurance Group
- Aspen Specialty Insurance Company
- Everest National Insurance Company
- Hiscox USA
- Jewelers Mutual Insurance Company
- Mid-Continent Group
- New Hampshire Insurance Company
- Travelers
- York Claims Service, Inc.
- Zurich Insurance Group
- ACE Westchester Specialty Group
- American International Group, Inc. (AIG)
- Argo Group
- Catlin, Inc.
- Colony Insurance Company
- Gallagher Bassett Services, Inc.
- The Hartford Insurance Group
- Ironshore Insurance, Ltd.
- Lexington Insurance Company
- Meadowbrook Insurance Group
- National Union Fire Insurance Company
- Star Insurance Company
- XL Group
- York Risk Services Group, Inc.

Non-Insurance Clients

- Bombardier, Inc.
- Browning and Winchester Firearms
- Chase Investment Services Corp.
- Coca Cola Bottling Company United, Inc.
- Dynamic Energy Services International Holdings LLC
- Greenfield Energy Services, Inc.
- Huntsman Corporation
- OMNI Energy Services Corp.
- PlayPower, Inc.
- The Schumacher Group
- Bristol-Myers Squibb Company
- Cardiovascular Institute of the South
- Cunningham Lindsey U.S., Inc.
- Dupré Logistics, LLC
- Ensco PLC
- General Parts International, Inc.
- Home Furniture Company
- Manchester Tank and Equipment Company
- Rotorcraft Leasing Company, LLC
- Weatherby, Inc.

Firm Members

Patrick A. Juneau — 1937 — Louisiana State University, B.A., 1960; J.D., 1965 — Admitted to Bar, 1965, Louisiana; 1965, U.S. Court of Appeals, Fifth, Eighth and Eleventh Circuits; 1965, U.S. Supreme Court — Member American and Louisiana State Bar Associations; Louisiana Defense Counsel Association (Past President); Products Liability Advisory Counsel; Fellow, Louisiana Bar Foundation; Federation of Insurance Counsel; Fellow, American College of Trial Lawyers; Fellow, International Academy of Trial Lawyers — E-mail: paj@juneaudavid.com

Michael J. Juneau — 1962 — Louisiana State University, B.S. (magna cum laude), 1984; Harvard University, J.D. (cum laude), 1987 — Admitted to Bar, 1987, Louisiana; 1987, U.S. District Court, Eastern, Middle and Western Districts of Louisiana; 1987, U.S. Court of Appeals, Fifth Circuit; 1987, Supreme Court of Louisiana; 2001, U.S. Supreme Court — Member American, Louisiana State (House of Delegates) and Lafayette Bar Associations; Christian Legal Society; Fellow, Louisiana Bar Foundation; Louisiana Association of Defense Counsel; Defense Research Institute — E-mail: mjj@juneaudavid.com

Thomas R. Juneau, Sr. — 1969 — Louisiana State University, B.G.S., 1991; Tulane University, J.D., 1994 — Justice, Moot Court Board; Best Advocate, Domenick L. Gabrielli National Moot Court Competition in Albany, N.Y.; Winner Tulane Interschool Moot Court Competition; Member, Tulane Civil

LAFAYETTE   LOUISIANA

Juneau David, A Professional Law Corporation, Lafayette, LA (Continued)

Litigation Clinic — Admitted to Bar, 1994, Louisiana; 2000, Texas; District of Columbia; 1994, U.S. District Court, Eastern, Middle and Western Districts of Louisiana; U.S. Court of Appeals, Fifth Circuit; 2000, U.S. District Court, Eastern and Southern Districts of Texas; U.S. Supreme Court — Member Louisiana State and Lafayette Bar Associations; College of Master Advocates and Barristers; Product Liability Advisory Council; Academy of Court-Appointed Masters; National Academy of Distinguished Neutrals; Louisiana Association of Defense Counsel; Defense Research Institute; Federation of Defense and Corporate Counsel — Martindale-Hubbell AV Rated; Louisiana Super Lawyer — E-mail: trj@juneaudavid.com

Robert J. David, Jr. — 1967 — Cornell University, B.S., 1989; Louisiana State University, J.D., 1992 — Chancellor's List; Moot Court Board — Admitted to Bar, 1992, Louisiana; U.S. District Court, Eastern, Middle and Western Districts of Louisiana; U.S. District Court, Eastern District of Texas; U.S. Court of Appeals, Fifth, Sixth and Eleventh Circuits — Member Federal, American and Louisiana State Bar Associations; Defense Research Institute; Professional Liability Underwriting Society — Director of Accommodations, Supreme Court of Louisiana (Bar Admissions Committee); The Best Lawyers in America (Labor and Employment/Personal Injury); Martindale-Hubbell AV Rated — E-mail: rjd@juneaudavid.com

Marc D. Moroux — 1962 — University of Louisiana at Lafayette, B.A. (cum laude), 1984; Louisiana State University Law Center, J.D., 1988 — Admitted to Bar, 1988, Louisiana; 2002, Texas; 1988, U.S. Court of Appeals, Fifth Circuit; 1997, U.S. Supreme Court; U.S. District Court, Eastern and Southern Districts of Texas; 1998, U.S. District Court, Eastern, Middle and Western Districts of Louisiana — Member Louisiana State and Lafayette Bar Associations; State Bar of Texas

Joshua K. Trahan — 1977 — Louisiana State University and A & M College, B.S., 1999; Southern Methodist University, Dedman School of Law, J.D., 2003 — Phi Beta Kappa — International Law Review. — Admitted to Bar, 2003, Texas; 2006, Louisiana — Member American, Louisiana State and Lafayette Bar Associations; State Bar of Texas; Lafayette Young Lawyers Association — E-mail: jkt@juneaudavid.com

Alyse S. Richard — Louisiana State University, B.S., 2004; Louisiana State University, Paul M. Hebert Law Center, J.D./B.C.L., 2008 — Admitted to Bar, 2008, Louisiana; U.S. District Court, Eastern, Middle and Western Districts of Louisiana; U.S. Court of Appeals, Fifth Circuit — Member Louisiana State and Lafayette Bar Associations — E-mail: asr@juneaudavid.com

Kyle N. Choate — 1983 — University of Louisiana at Lafayette, B.S., 2006; Loyola University New Orleans College of Law, J.D., 2010 — Admitted to Bar, 2010, Louisiana; U.S. District Court, Eastern, Middle and Western Districts of Louisiana; U.S. Court of Appeals, Fifth Circuit — Member Louisiana State and Lafayette Bar Associations; Lafayette Young Lawyers Association — E-mail: knc@juneaudavid.com

Eva D. Conner — 1989 — Louisiana State University, B.A., History (summa cum laude), 2010; Paul M Hebert Law School at Louisiana State University, J.D./B.C.L. (magna cum laude, Order of the Coif), 2013 — Admitted to Bar, 2013, Louisiana — Member American, Louisiana State and Lafayette Bar Associations — E-mail: edc@juneaudavid.com

Preis PLC

Versailles Centre, Suite 400
102 Versailles Boulevard
Lafayette, Louisiana 70501
 Telephone: 337-237-6062
 Fax: 337-237-9129
 E-Mail: preisplc@preisplc.com
 www.preisplc.com

(New Orleans, LA Office*: Pan American Life Center, Suite 1700, 601 Poydras Street, 70130)
 (Tel: 504-581-6062)
 (Fax: 504-522-9129)

(Houston, TX Office*: Weslayan Tower, Suite 2050, 24 Greenway Plaza, 77046)
 (Tel: 713-355-6062)
 (Fax: 713-572-9129)

Established: 1980

Litigation

Preis PLC, Lafayette, LA (Continued)

Firm Profile: Preis PLC is a regional defense law firm with offices in Lafayette, New Orleans and Houston which provide legal representation along the entire Gulf Coast. We have built a reputation over the past 30 years of aggressively defending both domestic and international clients through trial and appellate proceedings.

Insurance Clients

The ACE Group
AIG
Alaska National Insurance Company
Arch Insurance Group
Aspen Insurance
Berkley Public Entity Managers, LLC
Catlin, Inc.
Evanston Insurance Company
GAB Robins North America, Inc.
HDI-Gerling Industrie Versicherung AG
James River Insurance Company
Markel American Insurance Company
OneBeacon Insurance Group
Ramsgate Managing Insurance
St. Paul Fire and Marine Insurance Company
Steamship Mutual Underwriting Association Limited
Underwriters at Lloyd's, London
Western World Insurance Group

AGCS - Allianz Global Corporate & Specialty/Fireman's Fund Insurance
American Steamship Owners Mutual Protection and Indemnity Association, Inc.
Berkshire Hathaway Specialty Insurance
CV Starr / Starr Adjustment Services, Inc.
Gallagher Bassett Insurance Services, Inc.
Ironshore, Inc.
Lexington Insurance Company
Markel Insurance Company
Navigators Insurance Company
Pennsylvania Lumbermens Mutual Insurance Company
Sedgwick Caronia
Signal Mutual Indemnity Association
Terra Nova Insurance Company Limited

Non-Insurance Clients

Accutrans, Inc.
Badger Oil Corporation
Calypso Exploration, LLC/Stephens Production Company
Clayton Williams Energy, Inc.
Crescent Towing & Salvage Co., Inc.
Gilchrist Construction Company
Lafayette Parish Sheriff's Department
Mitchell Lift Boats LLC
Orion Marine Group, Inc.
Riceland Petroleum Company
Seamar Divers International
Smith Production Company
Walgreens

American Club
Buzzi Unicem USA
CB&I Energy Services, LLC
CB&I Offshore Services, Inc.
CDI Corporation
Cooper/T. Smith Mooring Co., Inc.
Eagle Consulting, LLC
Fluid Crane & Construction, Inc.
G & M Marine, Inc.
Lone Star Industries, Inc.
Madere & Sons Towing, Inc.
Noble Drilling Corporation
Petroleum Engineers, Inc.
River Cement Company
Settoon Towing, LLC
Transocean, Inc.
WHC, Inc.

Firm Members

Edwin G. Preis, Jr. — 1947 — University of Southwestern Louisiana, B.A. (with distinction), 1969; Louisiana State University, J.D., 1972 — Admitted to Bar, 1972, Louisiana; 2001, Texas

Robert M. Kallam — 1965 — Louisiana State University, B.S., 1987; J.D., 1990 — Admitted to Bar, 1990, Louisiana; 2002, Texas

Frank A. Piccolo — 1956 — The University of New Orleans, B.S., 1980; Loyola University School of Law, J.D., 1983 — Admitted to Bar, 1983, Louisiana; 2001, Texas — Resident Houston, TX Office

John M. Ribarits — 1960 — State University of New York at Buffalo, B.A. (cum laude), 1982; Tulane University, J.D., 1985 — Admitted to Bar, 1985, Louisiana; 1995, Texas — Resident Houston, TX Office

Catherine M. Landry — 1973 — Tulane University, B.A. (cum laude), 1995; Louisiana State University, J.D., 1998 — Admitted to Bar, 1998, Louisiana; 2004, Texas

James A. Lochridge, Jr. — 1963 — Spring Hill College, B.S., 1985; Loyola University, J.D., 1989 — Admitted to Bar, 1990, Louisiana

Charles J. Boudreaux, Jr. — 1954 — Louisiana State University, B.S., 1976; J.D., 1979 — Admitted to Bar, 1980, Louisiana

David L. Pybus — 1961 — The University of Texas at Austin, B.B.A. (with high honors), 1982; J.D. (with honors), 1986 — Admitted to Bar, 1986, Texas — Resident Houston, TX Office

David M. Flotte — 1956 — Louisiana State University, B.S., 1978; J.D., 1982 — Admitted to Bar, 1982, Louisiana; 1995, Texas — Resident New Orleans, LA Office

Preis PLC, Lafayette, LA (Continued)

Leah Nunn Engelhardt — 1965 — Auburn University, B.S., 1988; Louisiana State University, J.D., 1994 — Admitted to Bar, 1994, Louisiana; 1995, Georgia — Resident New Orleans, LA Office

Edward F. Kohnke IV — 1946 — Loyola University, B.A., 1969; Tulane University Law School, J.D., 1973 — Admitted to Bar, 1973, Louisiana — Resident New Orleans, LA Office

Jennifer A. Wells — 1971 — The University of North Carolina at Charlotte, B.S.C.J., 1995; Louisiana State University, J.D., 1999 — Admitted to Bar, 1999, Louisiana

Jonathan L. Woods — 1978 — Louisiana State University, B.A., 2000; J.D., 2003 — Admitted to Bar, 2003, Louisiana

M. Benjamin Alexander — 1979 — Louisiana State University, B.S. (magna cum laude), 2001; J.D./B.C.L., 2004 — Admitted to Bar, 2004, Louisiana; 2013, Texas

Kevin T. Dossett — 1966 — Nicholls State University, B.A. (magna cum laude), 1992; The University of Mississippi School of Law, J.D., 1996; Tulane University Law School, LL.M., 1997 — Admitted to Bar, 1998, Texas — Resident Houston, TX Office

Kenneth H. Tribuch — 1967 — The University of Texas at Austin, B.B.A., 1989; University of Miami, J.D., 1993 — Admitted to Bar, 1993, Florida; 2003, Texas — Resident Houston, TX Office

Marjorie C. Nicol — 1965 — The University of Texas at Austin, B.A. (with highest honors), 1988; Georgetown University Law Center, J.D., 1992 — Admitted to Bar, 1992, Texas — Resident Houston, TX Office

Matthew S. Green — 1979 — University of Richmond, B.A. (cum laude), 2001; Suffolk University Law School, J.D. (cum laude), 2005 — Admitted to Bar, 2005, Massachusetts; 2005, Rhode Island; 2009, Louisiana

Jean Ann Billeaud — 1962 — The University of Texas, B.S. (with honors), 1984; South Texas College of Law, J.D., 1996 — Admitted to Bar, 1996, Texas; 1997, Louisiana

John F. Colowich — 1952 — Georgetown University, B.A. (cum laude), 1974; The George Washington University, M.A., 1976; Loyola University, J.D., 1979 — Admitted to Bar, 1979, Louisiana; 1993, Florida

John L. Robert III — 1978 — Louisiana State University, B.S. (cum laude), 2000; Tulane University, J.D. (cum laude), 2004 — Admitted to Bar, 2004, Louisiana; 2011, Texas

William W. Fitzgerald — 1966 — University of Houston-Clear Lake, B.S., 1999; South Texas College of Law, J.D., 2002 — Admitted to Bar, 2003, Texas — Resident Houston, TX Office

Daryl J. Daigle — 1962 — Louisiana State University, B.S., 1984; J.D., 1988 — Admitted to Bar, 1988, Louisiana; 1994, Texas; 2010, Mississippi — Resident New Orleans, LA Office

Caroline T. Webb — 1974 — Baylor University, B.A., 1996; South Texas College of Law, J.D. (cum laude), 2005 — Admitted to Bar, 2005, Texas — Resident Houston, TX Office

Mandy A. Simon — 1982 — University of Louisiana at Lafayette, B.A. (magna cum laude), 2004; Loyola University, J.D. (magna cum laude), 2010 — Admitted to Bar, 2010, Louisiana

Thomas H. Prince — 1982 — Rhodes College, B.A. (cum laude), 2004; The University of Mississippi, J.D. (cum laude), 2006; The George Washington University, LL.M., 2008 — Admitted to Bar, 2009, Louisiana — Resident New Orleans, LA Office

Rachal D. Chance — 1981 — Baylor University, B.S., 2003; Louisiana State University, J.D./B.C.L., 2007 — Admitted to Bar, 2007, Louisiana — Resident New Orleans, LA Office

Craig R. Bordelon II — 1986 — Louisiana State University, B.A., 2009; Loyola College, J.D. (cum laude), 2012 — Admitted to Bar, 2012, Louisiana

Jared O. Brinlee — 1985 — Louisiana State University, B.S., 2008; D.C.L./J.D. (magna cum laude, Order of the Coif), 2012 — Admitted to Bar, 2012, Louisiana

Kellye Rosenzweig Grinton — 1987 — Louisiana State University, B.A., 2009; Loyola College, J.D., 2012 — Admitted to Bar, 2012, Louisiana

Nina D. Dargin — 1987 — University of Louisiana at Lafayette, B.S. (summa cum laude), 2008; M.B.A., 2009; Southern University Law Center, J.D. (magna cum laude), 2014 — Admitted to Bar, 2014, Louisiana

Rabalais & Hebert

701 Robley Drive, Suite 210
Lafayette, Louisiana 70503-5200
Telephone: 337-981-0309
Fax: 337-981-0905
www.rabalaishebert.com

Established: 1994

Insurance Defense, Automobile Liability, Admiralty and Maritime Law, Employer Liability, Workers' Compensation, Longshore and Harbor Workers' Compensation, Premises Liability, Product Liability, Toxic Torts, Life Insurance, Transportation, Trucking, Insurance Coverage, Construction Defect

Insurance Clients

Admiral Insurance Company
AIG Environmental
American Interstate Insurance Company
American Management Equity Corporation
Atlanta Casualty Company
Cherokee National Life Insurance Company
Clarendon Insurance Company
Clearwater Insurance Company
Colony Insurance Company
Deep South Surplus, Inc.
ESIS
First Financial Insurance Company
The Hartford
Highlands Insurance Company
Liberty Mutual Insurance Company
Metropolitan Property and Casualty Insurance Company
National Fire and Marine Insurance Company
Scottsdale Insurance Company
Sentry Select Insurance Company
Southern Insurance Company
Specialty Claims, Incorporated
Travelers Insurance Companies
Underwriters Reinsurance Company
VFIS Claims Management
AIG/American International Group
American Contractors Insurance Group
American Longshore Mutual Association Ltd./American Underwriters, Inc.
Atrium Underwriters Limited at Lloyd's of London
The Cincinnati Insurance Companies
CNA Insurance Company
The Connecticut Indemnity Company
First Assurance Life of America
Hallmark Specialty Insurance Company
Hudson Insurance Group
Lumbermen's Underwriting Alliance
Mid-Continent Casualty Company
Royal & SunAlliance Insurance Company
Self Insurance Administrators, Inc.
Southern Heritage Insurance Company
Travelers Indemnity Company
Underwriters at Lloyd's, London
United America Insurance Group
U.S. Liability Insurance Company
Zurich North America

Non-Insurance Clients

American Discovery Energy
Consolidated Companies, Inc.
Fischbach and Moore, Incorporated
Harvest Petroleum, Inc.
Hercules Transport, Inc.
HLSI
Kemper Services
Lone Star Industries, Inc.
National Dairy Holdings L.P.
Roclan Services, Inc.
Stallion Oilfield Services, Inc.
Tradition Resources Operating, LLC
Bayou Food Stores, Inc.
Dupré Logistics, LLC
Global X-Ray & Testing Corporation
The Hertz Corporation
International Oilfield Services/RNA
The NACHER Corporation
O'Nealgas, Inc.
Smith International, Inc.
Supervisory Services

Partners

Steven B. Rabalais — 1960 — Louisiana State University, B.A. (summa cum laude), 1982; J.D., 1985 — Admitted to Bar, 1985, Louisiana; 1985, U.S. District Court, Eastern, Middle and Western Districts of Louisiana; 1985, U.S. Court of Appeals, Fifth Circuit — Member Louisiana State and Lafayette Parish Bar Associations; Trucking Industry Defense Association (TIDA); Louisiana Motor Transport Association; Louisiana Association of Defense Counsel; Transportation Lawyers Association — Practice Areas: Insurance Defense; Transportation; Trucking; Insurance Coverage; Construction Defect; Premises Liability — E-mail: srabalais@rhhnet.com

Christopher H. Hebert — 1965 — Louisiana State University, B.S. (summa cum laude), 1987; Tulane University, J.D. (cum laude), 1990 — Notes and Comments Editor, Tulane Maritime Law Journal — Admitted to Bar, 1990, Louisiana; 1990, U.S. District Court, Eastern, Middle and Western Districts

LAKE CHARLES — LOUISIANA

Rabalais & Hebert, Lafayette, LA (Continued)

of Louisiana; 1992, U.S. Court of Appeals, Fifth Circuit — Member Louisiana State, Lafayette Parish and Fifth Federal Circuit Bar Associations; Louisiana Association of Defense Counsel — E-mail: chebert@rhhnet.com

Of Counsel

Fred W. Davis — 1955 — Duquesne University, B.A. (cum laude), 1980; Loyola University New Orleans, J.D., 1983 — Admitted to Bar, 1983, Louisiana; 1983, U.S. District Court, Western District of Louisiana — Member Louisiana State and Lafayette Parish Bar Associations — E-mail: fdavis@rhhnet.com

Melvin A. Eiden — 1949 — State University of New York at New Paltz, B.S. (with honors), 1973; Russell Sage University, M.P.A., 1978; Pace University School of Law, J.D. (magna cum laude), 1989 — Admitted to Bar, 1989, New York; 1989, Louisiana; 1990, U.S. District Court, Eastern, Middle and Western Districts of Louisiana; 1994, U.S. Court of Appeals, Fifth Circuit; 2004, U.S. Supreme Court — Member Louisiana State and Lafayette Parish Bar Associations — Practice Areas: Insurance Defense — E-mail: meiden@rhhnet.com

(This firm is also listed in the Subrogation section of this directory)

The following firms also service this area.

Boyer, Hebert, Abels & Angelle, LLC
1280 Del Este Avenue
Denham Springs, Louisiana 70726
Telephone: 225-664-4335
Fax: 225-664-4490

Automobile, Business Litigation, General Liability, Insurance Defense, Oil and Gas, Product Liability, Real Estate, Workers' Compensation

SEE COMPLETE LISTING UNDER BATON ROUGE, LOUISIANA (55 MILES)

Hailey, McNamara, Hall, Larmann & Papale, L.L.P.
One Galleria Boulevard, Suite 1400
Metairie, Louisiana 70001
Telephone: 504-836-6500
Fax: 504-836-6565

Mailing Address: P.O. Box 8288, Metairie, LA 70011-8288

Admiralty and Maritime Law, Commercial Litigation, Construction Litigation, Employment Practices Liability, Insurance Litigation, Product Liability, Professional Malpractice, Toxic Torts, Casualty, Insurance Coverage, Intellectual Property, Premises Liability, Transportation, Mass Tort, Property, Workers' Compensation, Automobile Liability, Appellate, Environmental

SEE COMPLETE LISTING UNDER METAIRIE, LOUISIANA (130 MILES)

Lugenbuhl, Wheaton, Peck, Rankin & Hubbard
Pan American Life Center, Suite 2775
601 Poydras Street
New Orleans, Louisiana 70130
Telephone: 504-568-1990
Fax: 504-310-9195

Insurance Coverage, Insurance Defense, Insurance Litigation, Admiralty and Maritime Law, Personal Injury, Jones Act, Environmental Law, Automobile, General Liability, Product Liability, Protection and Indemnity, Subrogation, Comprehensive

SEE COMPLETE LISTING UNDER NEW ORLEANS, LOUISIANA (100 MILES)

Ungarino & Eckert, L.L.C.
3850 North Causeway Boulevard, Suite 1280
Metairie, Louisiana 70002
Telephone: 504-836-7555
Fax: 504-836-7566

Litigation, Appellate Practice, State and Federal Courts, Class Actions, Insurance Coverage, Premises Liability, Professional Liability, Directors and Officers Liability, Insurance Defense, Construction Law, Toxic Torts, Personal Injury, Arson, Insurance Fraud, Admiralty and Maritime Law, Extra-Contractual Litigation, Bad Faith, Product Liability, Alternative Dispute Resolution, Civil Rights, Workers' Compensation, Environmental Law, Employment Law, Automobile, Truck Liability, Errors and Omissions, Common Carrier, Medical Malpractice, Construction Defect, Constitutional Law, Department of Insurance Complaints, ERISA Claims, Government Relations, Complex Casualty, Consumer Defense, Creditor Rights, Debt Collections, Discrimination Claims, Electric Utility Liability, Engineering Malpractice, Family Law (Divorce, Custody, Support, Adoption), Fraud, General Liability, Governmental Entity Liability, Insurance Subrogation, Landlord Liability, Medical Device Liability, Property Ownership, State and Municipality Litigation, Successions, Warranty/Redhibition Actions

SEE COMPLETE LISTING UNDER METAIRIE, LOUISIANA (130 MILES)

LAKE CHARLES † 71,993 Calcasieu Par.

Plauché, Smith & Nieset, LLC

1123 Pithon Street
Lake Charles, Louisiana 70601
Telephone: 337-436-0522
Fax: 337-436-9637
www.psnlaw.com

Automobile Liability, Fire, Arson, Inland Marine, Casualty, Workers' Compensation, Admiralty and Maritime Law, Product Liability, Professional Malpractice, Environmental Law, Toxic Torts, Subrogation, Surety Bonds, Construction Law, Directors and Officers Liability, Employment Law

Insurance Clients

AIG Insurance Company
American National Property and Casualty Company
Argonaut Insurance Company
Bituminous Insurance Companies
Cambridge Integrated Services
Chartis Insurance
Clarendon National Insurance Company
Colony Insurance Company
Farm Bureau Insurance Companies
Federated Mutual Insurance Company
Gallagher Bassett Services, Inc.
Great West Casualty Company
Highlands Insurance Company
Liberty Mutual Insurance Company
Metropolitan Property and Casualty Insurance Company
Safeco Insurance
Shelter Insurance Companies
Specialty Risk Services, Inc. (SRS)
State Farm Insurance Companies
State Farm Mutual Automobile Insurance Company
Zurich Group Companies
America First Insurance
American Premier Underwriters, Inc.
Atlantic Casualty Insurance Company
Canal Insurance Company
Clarendon America Insurance Company
CNA Insurance Companies
ESIS
Farmers Insurance Group
First Mercury Insurance Company
Foremost Insurance Company
GMAC Insurance
Hanover Insurance Group
Horace Mann Insurance Company
Louisiana Insurance Guaranty Association
Progressive Insurance Company
Sedgwick Claims Management Services, Inc.
State Farm Fire and Casualty Company
Texas Mutual Insurance Company
Travelers Insurance Companies

Non-Insurance Clients

Acadia Parish School Board
Alfred Palma Inc. Construction Company
Beauregard Parish School Board
Boise Cascade, L.L.C.
Calcasieu Parish Police Jury
Calcasieu Parish Sheriff's Office
Cameron Parish School Board
Champion Enterprises, Inc.
City of Lake Charles
Deer Valley Home Builders, Inc.
Harrah's Entertainment, Inc.
Acme Truck Line, Inc.
Allen Parish School Board
AT&T
BellSouth Telecommunications, Inc.
Calcasieu Parish School Board Risk Program
Cavalier Homes, Inc.
Cintas Corporation
City of Sulphur
GREX, Inc.
The Kroger Co.

Plauché, Smith & Nieset, LLC, Lake Charles, LA
(Continued)

Lake Charles Harbor and Terminal
Lake Charles Pilots
Martin De Porres Nursing Home
Polaris Engineering, Inc.
Rapid Response Restoration, Inc.
Transportation Claims, Inc.
Lake Charles Memorial Hospital
Market Basket Stores, Inc
Noble Energy, Inc.
Port of Lake Charles
Stine Lumber Company

Partners

S. W. Plauche — (1889-1952)

S. W. Plauche, Jr. — (1915-1966)

A. Lane Plauche — (1919-2006)

Allen L. Smith, Jr. — 1936 — Louisiana State University, B.A., 1959; J.D., 1964 — Recipient, Louisiana Bar Association Boisfontaine Trial Advocacy Award (2004); President's Award for Outstanding Contribution (1990) — Admitted to Bar, 1964, Louisiana — Member American Bar Association; Louisiana State Bar Association (House of Delegates, 1974-78); Southwest Louisiana Bar Association (President, 1977-78); Advocate, American Board of Trial Advocates; Fellow, American College of Trial Lawyers; Louisiana Association of Defense Counsel, (President, 1987-88); The Maritime Law Association of the United States — E-mail: asmith@psnlaw.com

James R. Nieset — **(Of Counsel)** — 1942 — Tulane University of Louisiana, J.D., 1967 — Admitted to Bar, 1967, Louisiana — Member American Bar Association; Louisiana State Bar Association (Board of Governors, 2004-2006; Treasurer, 2006-2008); Southwest Louisiana Bar Association (Secretary-Treasurer, 1971-1972, 2006-2008; President, 1992-1993); Louisiana and Southwest Louisiana Associations of Defense Counsel; Maritime Law Institute; Tulane Admiralty Law Institute; The Maritime Law Association of the United States; Defense Research Institute — E-mail: jrnieset@psnlaw.com

Frank M. Walker, Jr. — 1951 — The University of the South, B.S., 1973; Louisiana State University, J.D., 1976 — Admitted to Bar, 1976, Louisiana — Member American, Louisiana State and Southwest Louisiana Bar Associations; Litigation Counsel of America; Louisiana Association of Defense Counsel — Super Lawyers; Best Lawyers in America — E-mail: fmwalkerjr@psnlaw.com

Michael J. McNulty, III — 1951 — Tulane University, B.A. (cum laude), 1973; J.D., 1976 — Admitted to Bar, 1976, Louisiana — Member American, Louisiana State, Southwest Lousiana and St. Mary's Parish (President, 1979-1980) Bar Associations; Louisiana Association of Defense Counsel (Director); Southwest Louisiana Association of Defense Counsel; The Best Lawyers In America; American Board of Trial Advocates; Defense Research Institute — Practice Areas: Automobile; Construction Law; Premises Liability; Product Liability — E-mail: mmcnulty@psnlaw.com

Jeffrey M. Cole — 1954 — Louisiana State University, B.A., 1976; J.D., 1979 — Admitted to Bar, 1980, Louisiana — Member Louisiana State and Southwest Louisiana (President, 2005) Bar Associations; Louisiana Association of Defense Counsel (Former Board Member); Louisiana Supreme Court MCLE Committee; Southwest Louisiana Bar Foundation (Board Member) — E-mail: jcole@psnlaw.com

Charles V. Musso, Jr. — 1955 — Louisiana State University, B.S., 1979; Louisiana State University Law Center, J.D., 1984 — Admitted to Bar, 1984, Louisiana — Member American, Louisiana State and Southwest Louisiana Bar Associations; Louisiana Association of Defense Counsel; Defense Research Institute — E-mail: cvmusso@psnlaw.com

Christopher P. Ieyoub — 1960 — McNeese State University, B.S., 1982; Tulane University of Louisiana, J.D., 1985 — Admitted to Bar, 1985, Louisiana — Member American, Louisiana State and Southwest Louisiana Bar Associations; Southwest Louisiana Association of Defense Counsel; Louisiana Association of Defense Counsel (District Director) — E-mail: cieyoub@psnlaw.com

H. David Vaughan II — 1961 — McNeese State University, B.A. (magna cum laude), 1982; Louisiana State University, J.D., 1988 — Admitted to Bar, 1988, Louisiana — Member Louisiana State and Southwest Louisiana Bar Associations; Southwest Association of Defense Counsel; Louisiana Association of Defense Counsel — E-mail: dvaughan@psnlaw.com

Joseph R. Pousson, Jr. — 1962 — McNeese State University, B.S., 1985; Louisiana State University, J.D., 1993 — Admitted to Bar, 1993, Louisiana — Member American, Louisiana State and Southwest Louisiana Bar Associations; Southwest Louisiana Association of Defense Counsel; Louisiana Association of Defense Counsel — E-mail: jrpousson@psnlaw.com

V. Ed McGuire, III — 1969 — McNeese State University, B.S. (cum laude), 1992; Louisiana State University, J.D., 1995 — Admitted to Bar, 1995, Louisiana — Member American, Louisiana State and Southwest Louisiana Bar Associations; Southwest Louisiana Association of Defense Counsel

Plauché, Smith & Nieset, LLC, Lake Charles, LA
(Continued)

Eric W. Roan — 1967 — Louisiana State University, B.S., 1989; J.D., 1993 — Admitted to Bar, 1993, Louisiana — Member American, Louisiana State and Southwest Louisiana Bar Associations; Louisiana Association of Defense Counsel — E-mail: eroan@psnlaw.com

Samuel B. Gabb — 1968 — The University of New Orleans, B.A., 1990; Tulane University Law School, J.D., 1993 — Admitted to Bar, 1993, Louisiana — Member Louisiana State and Southwest Louisiana Bar Associations; Southwest Louisiana Association of Defense Counsel — E-mail: sgabb@psnlaw.com

Kendrick J. Guidry — 1968 — McNeese State University, B.A., 1990; Louisiana State University, J.D., 2000 — Admitted to Bar, 2000, Louisiana — Member Louisiana State and Southwest Louisiana (President, 2008) Bar Associations; Southwest Louisiana Association of Defense Counsel; Defense Research Institute; Louisiana Association of Defense Counsel — E-mail: kjguidry@psnlaw.com

Michael J. Williamson — 1980 — Louisiana State University, B.A., 2002; J.D., 2006 — Admitted to Bar, 2007, Louisiana — Member American, Louisiana State and Southwest Louisiana Bar Associations; Louisiana Association of Defense Counsel — E-mail: mwilliamson@psnlaw.com

Associate

Wes A. Romero — 1984 — Louisiana State University, B.S., 2007; J.D./D.C.L., 2010 — Admitted to Bar, 2010, Louisiana — Member Louisiana State and Southwest Louisiana (Young Lawyers Executive Committee 2012-2014) Bar Associations; Louisiana Association of Defense Counsel; Defense Research Institute — E-mail: wromero@psnlaw.com

(This firm is also listed in the Subrogation section of this directory)

Raggio, Cappel, Chozen & Berniard

Magnolia Life Building, Suite 500
1011 Lakeshore Drive
Lake Charles, Louisiana 70601
  Telephone: 337-436-9481
  Fax: 337-436-9499

Insurance Law

Insurance Clients

Aetna Insurance Company of Connecticut
American Health and Life Insurance Company
Bridgefield Casualty Insurance Company
Criterion Casualty Company
Government Employees Insurance Company
The Medical Protective Company
Minnesota Life Insurance Company
Pioneer Mutual Life Insurance Company
Provident Life and Accident Insurance Company
St. Paul Fire and Marine Insurance Company
United American Insurance Company
Allstate Insurance Company
American Family Life Assurance Company of New York
Bankers Life and Casualty Company
Consolidated National Life Insurance Company
The Hartford Insurance Group
Liberty Life Insurance Company
Metropolitan Life Insurance Company
Pan-American Life Insurance Company
Preferred Professional Insurance Company
Republic National Life Insurance Company
Standard Life Insurance Company
Washington National Insurance Company

Partners

Thomas Louis Raggio — (1917-2000)

Richard A. Chozen — (1939-2003)

Richard B. Cappel — (Retired)

Frederick L. Cappel — (Retired)

Stephen A. Berniard, Jr. — 1942 — Vanderbilt University, B.A., 1963; Louisiana State University, J.D., 1967 — Admitted to Bar, 1967, Louisiana; 1970, Canal Zone — Member American, Louisiana State and Southwest Louisiana Bar Associations; Southwest Louisiana Defense Counsel Association; Louisiana Association of Defense Counsel

Christopher Mark Trahan — 1951 — McNeese State University, B.A., 1973; Louisiana State University, J.D., 1975 — Admitted to Bar, 1975,

LAKE CHARLES   LOUISIANA

Raggio, Cappel, Chozen & Berniard, Lake Charles, LA (Continued)

Louisiana — Member American, Louisiana State, Southwest Louisiana and Lawyer-Pilots Bar Associations; Southwest Louisiana Defense Counsel Association; Louisiana Association of Defense Counsel; Defense Research Institute

L. Paul Foreman — 1954 — University of Houston, B.B.A., 1979; Louisiana State University, J.D., 1982 — Admitted to Bar, 1982, Louisiana — Member American, Louisiana State and Southwest Louisiana Bar Associations; Southwest Louisiana Defense Counsel Association; Louisiana Association of Defense Counsel; Defense Research Institute

Kevin Joseph Koenig — 1965 — Louisiana State University, B.C.J., 1988; J.D., 1991 — Phi Delta Phi — Admitted to Bar, 1991, Louisiana — Member American, Louisiana State, Southwest Louisiana and Baton Rouge Bar Associations

Associate

Amanda K. Gammon — 1986 — Louisiana State University, B.A./B.A., 2009; LL.B., 2013 — Phi Alpha Delta — Admitted to Bar, 2013, Louisiana — Member American Bar Association; Southwest Louisiana Defense Counsel Association; Louisiana Association of Defense Counsel

Woodley, Williams Law Firm, L.L.C.

One Lakeshore Drive, Suite 1750
Lake Charles, Louisiana 70629
   Telephone: 337-433-6328
   Fax: 337-433-7513
   E-Mail: woodley@woodleywilliams.com

Admiralty and Maritime Law, Arson, Dram Shop, Construction Law, Employment Discrimination, Fraud, Health Care, Hospitals, Investigations, Liquor Liability, Medical Liability, Oil and Gas, Premises Liability, Product Liability, Subrogation, Toxic Torts, Trial Practice, Workers' Compensation, Wrongful Termination, Reinsurance, Medical Malpractice, Asbestosis, Silicosis and Hazardous Waste Litigation, Legal and Insurance Broker Malpractice Law, Civil Practice

Insurance Clients

Alfa Insurance Company	American Claims Service
American Re-Insurance Company	Atlantic Risk Management, Inc.
Audubon Insurance Company	CIGNA Claims Service
The Cincinnati Companies	CNA Insurance Company
The Colony Group	El Paso Insurance Company, Ltd.
Employers Casualty Corporation	Employers Insurance Company of Texas Group
Employers Mutual Casualty Company	Employers National Insurance Company
Employers Reinsurance Corporation	F.A. Richard & Associates, Inc.
Florida Insurance Guaranty Association	Guaranty National Insurance Company
Humana Insurance Company	James River Insurance Company
Jeff Davis Insurance Agency	Lafayette Insurance Company
LEMIC Insurance Company	Lexington Insurance Company
Liberty Mutual Insurance Company	Louisiana Insurance Guaranty Association
Louisiana Workers' Compensation Corporation	National Security Fire and Casualty
North American Specialty Insurance Company	Progressive American Insurance Company
Progressive Insurance Company	RLI Insurance Company
Sentry Claims Services	Sentry Insurance a Mutual Company
Travelers Indemnity Company	United States Fire Insurance Company
Travelers Insurance Companies	
Zurich American Insurance Group	

Non-Insurance Clients

Agency Management Corporation	American Management, Inc.
BP America, Inc.	Calcasieu Parish School Board Risk Program
Calcasieu Parish Sheriff's Office	City of Lake Charles
Cameron Offshore Boats, Inc.	Dan-Gulf Shipping, Inc.
Crawford & Company	Devillier Truck Sales, Inc.
Degussa Corporation	Dunham Price Group, LLC
Dimmick Supply Company, Inc.	Goldsmith Farms, LLC
Fuel Stop 36, Inc.	Lake Charles American Press
Jefferson Davis Police Jury	LNG Terminal Services
L'Auberge du Lac Casino Resort	

Woodley, Williams Law Firm, L.L.C., Lake Charles, LA (Continued)

Louisiana Commerce and Trade Association	Louisiana Patient's Compensation Fund
LUBA Workers Compensation Fund	Matheson Tri-Gas
SAIA Motor Freight Line, Inc.	Polymer Components, Inc.
Southwest Louisiana Legal Services Society, Inc.	Southwest Beverage Company, Inc.
Stewart Relocation Services	State of Louisiana, Office of Risk Management
TMS International, Inc.	Texas Timberjack, Inc.
Union Carbide Corporation	Town of Vinton
Westchester Specialty Group Companies	Vinton Public Power Authority (VPPA)

Edmund E. Woodley — (1925-1989)

Paul E. Palmer — (1929-2004)

Robert J. Boudreau — (1930-2010)

James E. Williams — (1939-2011)

James A. Leithead — (1915-2013)

Donald C. Brown — 1947 — Louisiana Tech University, B.A., 1969; Louisiana State University, J.D., 1972 — Admitted to Bar, 1972, Louisiana; 1993, Texas; 1973, U.S. District Court, Western District of Louisiana; 1973, U.S. Court of Appeals, Fifth Circuit; 1977, U.S. Supreme Court; 1984, U.S. District Court, Eastern District of Texas; 1985, U.S. District Court, Middle District of Louisiana; 1992, U.S. District Court, Southern District of Texas — Member American, Louisiana State and Southwest Louisiana Bar Associations; State Bar of Texas; Maritime Lawyers Association; Louisiana Association of Defense Counsel — E-mail: dcbrown@woodleywilliams.com

Thomas J. Solari — 1963 — McNeese State University, B.S., 1985; Loyola University, J.D., 1988 — Admitted to Bar, 1988, Louisiana; 1988, U.S. District Court, Eastern, Middle and Western Districts of Louisiana — Member Louisiana State and Southwest Louisiana Bar Associations; Southwest Louisiana Association of Defense Counsel (Secretary-Treasurer 1990-1991; President, 1991-1992); Louisiana Association of Defense Counsel — Practice Areas: Automobile; Complex Litigation; Insurance Defense; Marine Insurance; Premises Liability; Workers' Compensation — E-mail: tsolari@woodleywilliams.com

Darrell W. Alston — 1955 — McNeese State University, B.S., 1977; Loyola University, J.D., 1989 — Admitted to Bar, 1989, Louisiana; 1991, U.S. District Court, Western District of Louisiana — Member Louisiana State Bar Association; Southwest Louisiana Bar Association — E-mail: dalston@woodleywilliams.com

Michael D. Carleton — 1957 — Louisiana State University, B.A., 1979; J.D., 1982 — Pi Sigma Alpha — Law Clerk, Louisiana Third Circuit Court of Appeals, 1982-1983 — Admitted to Bar, 1982, Louisiana; 1989, U.S. District Court, Western District of Louisiana — Member American Bar Association (Sections: Real Property, Probate and Trust Law); Louisiana State Bar Association (Uniform Title Standards Committee; Sections: Real Property, Probate and Trust Law); Southwest Louisiana Bar Association (Executive Counsel, 2012-2014; Chairman, Technology Committee, 1998; Past-Member, Professionalism Committee); American College of Mortgage Attorneys (Louisiana State Chairman, 2010-); Southwest Louisiana Title Attorneys Roundtable (Chairman, 1999 and 2006) — Author: "Avoiding Title Problems in Probate", Trust and Estate Law Report, Vol. 2 No. 1 — Instructor, McNeese State University, Paralegal Program-Real Property Course (1992-1994); Guest Lecturer, Gulf South Real Estate Institute (1992-1998); Real Estate Attorney for Calcasieu Parish School Board — Certified Real Estate Instructor by the Louisiana Real Estate Commission (1991-2007) — Practice Areas: Real Estate; Commercial Law; Probate — E-mail: mcarleton@woodleywilliams.com

Lance B. Vinson — Houston Baptist University, B.A., 1990; Louisiana State University, J.D., 2002 — Admitted to Bar, 2002, Louisiana; U.S. District Court, Eastern, Middle and Western Districts of Louisiana — Practice Areas: General Liability; Insurance Defense; Workers' Compensation; Construction Defect; Premises Liability — E-mail: lbvinson@woodleywilliams.com

LOUISIANA

The following firms also service this area.

Hailey, McNamara, Hall, Larmann & Papale, L.L.P.
One Galleria Boulevard, Suite 1400
Metairie, Louisiana 70001
   Telephone: 504-836-6500
   Fax: 504-836-6565

Mailing Address: P.O. Box 8288, Metairie, LA 70011-8288

Admiralty and Maritime Law, Commercial Litigation, Construction Litigation, Employment Practices Liability, Insurance Litigation, Product Liability, Professional Malpractice, Toxic Torts, Casualty, Insurance Coverage, Intellectual Property, Premises Liability, Transportation, Mass Tort, Property, Workers' Compensation, Automobile Liability, Appellate, Environmental

SEE COMPLETE LISTING UNDER METAIRIE, LOUISIANA (201 MILES)

LEESVILLE † 6,612 Vernon Par.

Refer To
Plauché, Smith & Nieset, LLC
1123 Pithon Street
Lake Charles, Louisiana 70601
   Telephone: 337-436-0522
   Fax: 337-436-9637

Mailing Address: P.O. Drawer 1705, Lake Charles, LA 70602

Automobile Liability, Fire, Arson, Inland Marine, Casualty, Workers' Compensation, Admiralty and Maritime Law, Product Liability, Professional Malpractice, Environmental Law, Toxic Torts, Subrogation, Surety Bonds, Construction Law, Directors and Officers Liability, Employment Law

SEE COMPLETE LISTING UNDER LAKE CHARLES, LOUISIANA (60 MILES)

Refer To
Woodley, Williams Law Firm, L.L.C.
One Lakeshore Drive, Suite 1750
Lake Charles, Louisiana 70629
   Telephone: 337-433-6328
   Fax: 337-433-7513

Mailing Address: P.O. Box 3731, Lake Charles, LA 70602-3731

Admiralty and Maritime Law, Arson, Dram Shop, Construction Law, Employment Discrimination, Fraud, Health Care, Hospitals, Investigations, Liquor Liability, Medical Liability, Oil and Gas, Premises Liability, Product Liability, Subrogation, Toxic Torts, Trial Practice, Workers' Compensation, Wrongful Termination, Reinsurance, Medical Malpractice, Asbestosis, Silicosis and Hazardous Waste Litigation, Legal and Insurance Broker Malpractice Law, Civil Practice

SEE COMPLETE LISTING UNDER LAKE CHARLES, LOUISIANA (60 MILES)

MANDEVILLE 11,560 St. Tammany Par.

Galloway, Johnson, Tompkins, Burr & Smith

#3 Sanctuary Boulevard, Third Floor
Mandeville, Louisiana 70471
   Telephone: 985-674-6680
   Fax: 985-674-6681
   E-Mail: thassinger@gallowayjohnson.com
   www.gallowayjohnson.com

(Additional Offices: New Orleans, LA*; Lafayette, LA*; Pensacola, FL*; St. Louis, MO*; Houston, TX*; Gulfport, MS*; Tampa, FL*; Mobile, AL*; Atlanta, GA*)

Maritime, Automobile Liability, Bad Faith, Class Actions, Construction, Energy, Employment, Insurance Coverage, Insurance Defense, Product Liability, Professional Liability, Property, Transportation, General Casualty, Title Resolution, Environmental

(See listing under New Orleans, LA for additional information)

LEESVILLE

Pajares & Schexnaydre, L.L.C.

68031 Capital Trace Row
Mandeville, Louisiana 70471
   Telephone: 985-231-1791
   Fax: 985-292-2001
   Toll Free: 888-339-0696
   E-Mail: info@pajares-schexnaydre.com
   www.pajares-schexnaydre.com

Established: 2003

Insurance Defense, General Liability, Commercial Litigation, Automobile Liability, Personal Injury, Product Liability, Medical Malpractice, Trucking Law, Transportation, Insurance Coverage, Toxic Torts, Class Actions, Veterinary Malpractice

Firm Profile: Pajares & Schexnaydre aggressively and efficiently serves clients in greater New Orleans, statewide, nationally and internationally for a wide variety of negotiated and litigated issues - from maritime law to trucking and transportation, from products liability to commercial litigation.

Insurance Clients

ABM Insurance Services
Atlantic Mutual Insurance
  Company
Centennial Insurance Company
District of Columbia Insurance
  Guaranty Association
Fulcrum Insurance Company
General Reinsurance Corporation
The Hartford Financial Services
  Group, Inc.
Louisiana Insurance Guaranty
  Association
Occidental Fire & Casualty
  Company
Progressive Security Insurance
  Company
St. Paul Fire and Marine Insurance
  Company
Travelers, Special Liability Group
Zurich American Insurance
  Company

Alabama Insurance Guaranty
  Association
Caliber One Indemnity Company
The Colony Group
Electric Insurance Company
The Fire and Casualty Insurance
  Company of Connecticut
General Star Indemnity Company
Liberty International Underwriters
Liberty Surplus Insurance
  Corporation
National Union Fire Insurance
  Company
Progressive Insurance Company
Prudential Property and Casualty
  Insurance Company
Texas Property and Casualty
  Insurance Guaranty Association
United National Insurance
  Company

Non-Insurance Clients

The Artis Group
ThyssenKrupp Elevator
  Corporation

Christian Brothers Risk Pooling
  Trust

Partners and Members

Raymond J. Pajares — The University of New Orleans, B.A., 1978; Loyola University, J.D., 1985 — Admitted to Bar, 1986, Louisiana; 1986, U.S. District Court, Eastern, Middle and Western Districts of Louisiana; 1987, U.S. Court of Appeals, Fifth Circuit — Member Federal, American, Louisiana State, Fifth Federal Circuit and New Orleans Bar Associations; Louisiana Association of Defense Counsel; Defense Research Institute

David J. Schexnaydre — The University of New Orleans, B.S., 1987; Tulane University, J.D. (cum laude), 1991 — Admitted to Bar, 1991, Louisiana; 1991, U.S. District Court, Eastern, Middle and Western Districts of Louisiana; 1991, U.S. Court of Appeals, Fifth Circuit; 1997, U.S. Supreme Court — Member Louisiana State, New Orleans and Covington Bar Associations; Louisiana Association of Business and Industry (Liability Task Force); Louisiana Association of Defense Counsel; Defense Research Institute

Of Counsel

Mark A. Myers

Associates

Mary B. Lord
Beth Rambin
Diana Tonagel

Kristi U. Louque
Susan Bowers

METAIRIE — LOUISIANA

The following firms also service this area.

Law Office of Eric J. Halverson, Jr.
3925 North I-10 Service Road West, Suite 123
Metairie, Louisiana 70002
  Telephone: 504-885-0105
  Fax: 504-885-2001
Mailing Address: P.O. Box 8761, Metairie, LA 70011-8761

Insurance Defense, Admiralty and Maritime Law, Jones Act, Workers' Compensation, Errors and Omissions, Medical Malpractice, General Liability, Product Liability, Automobile, Truck Liability, Collision and P & I, Longshore

SEE COMPLETE LISTING UNDER METAIRIE, LOUISIANA (29 MILES)

METAIRIE 138,481 Jefferson Par.

Hailey, McNamara, Hall, Larmann & Papale, L.L.P.

One Galleria Boulevard, Suite 1400
Metairie, Louisiana 70001
  Telephone: 504-836-6500
  Fax: 504-836-6565
  www.haileymcnamara.com

(Baton Rouge, LA Office: 10771 Perkins Road, Suite 100, 70810)
  (Tel: 225-766-5567)
  (Fax: 225-766-5548)
(New Orleans, LA Office: 1100 Poydras Street, Suite 2900, 70183)
  (Tel: 504-799-2271)
  (Fax: 504-836-6565)
(Gulfport, MS Office*: 302 Courthouse Road, Suite A, 39507)
  (Tel: 228-896-1144)
  (Fax: 228-896-1177)

Established: 1976

Admiralty and Maritime Law, Commercial Litigation, Construction Litigation, Employment Practices Liability, Insurance Litigation, Product Liability, Professional Malpractice, Toxic Torts, Casualty, Insurance Coverage, Intellectual Property, Premises Liability, Transportation, Mass Tort, Property, Workers' Compensation, Automobile Liability, Appellate, Environmental

Firm Profile: Hailey McNamara provides aggressive, experienced and innovative representation to all of its clients, including corporations, insurers, manufacturers and professionals, which face complex lawsuits that demand the most rigorous defense.

Insurance Clients

Accessible Insurance Agency, Inc.
Admiral Insurance Company
AIG/American International Group
AIX Group/NOVA Casualty Company
American National Property and Casualty Company
American Vehicle Insurance Company
ANPAC
Argo Select
Assurance Company of America
AWAC Services Company
AXA Insurance Company
Bankers Insurance Group
Berkley Insurance Company
Broadspire
Burlington Insurance Group
Chartis Insurance
Chubb Group of Insurance Companies
CNA
Commerce and Industry Insurance Company
Crum & Forster Insurance Group
Accident Insurance Company, Inc./Appalachian Underwriters, Inc.
American Claims Services, Inc.
American Equity Underwriters, Inc. - VT Halter Marine, Inc.
American Standard Insurance Company
AmRisc, LP
Arch Insurance Company
Arrowpoint Capital Corporation
Avizent Risk Management Solutions
Baldwin & Lyons, Inc.
Benfield Syndicate - Lloyd's
Berkley Specialty Underwriting Managers, LLC
Century Surety/Meadowbrook Insurance Company
Clarendon National Insurance Company
Colony Insurance Company
Countrywide Insurance Group
Croft ClaimWorks, L.C.
CSSI

Hailey, McNamara, Hall, Larmann & Papale, L.L.P., Metairie, LA (Continued)

Cunningham Lindsey Claims Management, Inc.
Delos Insurance
Discover Property and Casualty Insurance Company
Edgewood Partners Insurance Center
Empire Insurance Group
Employers Mutual Casualty Company
Federal Insurance Company
Fireman's Fund Insurance Companies
First Mercury Insurance Company
GAB Business Services, Inc.
Gallagher Bassett Services, Inc.
Global Hawk Insurance Company
Great American Insurance Company
The Hartford
Huey T. Littleton Claim Service
The Infinity Group
K & K Insurance Group, Inc.
Liberty Mutual Group
Louisiana Citizens Property Insurance Corporation
Louisiana Insurance Guaranty Association
Madison Insurance Group
Maryland Casualty Company
MetLife Auto & Home Group
Metropolitan Direct Property & Casualty Insurance Company
Motor Transport Underwriters, Inc.
Mountain States Mutual Casualty Company
North American Specialty Insurance Company
Northland Insurance Company
Old Republic International Corporation
Plaza Insurance Company
Praetorian Financial Group
Prudential Property and Casualty Insurance Company
QBE the Americas
Rental Insurance Services
RiverStone Claims Management, LLC
Sedgwick Claims Management Services, Inc.
Sentry Insurance Group
SPARTA Insurance
State Farm Fire and Casualty Company
Sterling National Insurance Agency
Swiss Re Group
TIG Insurance Company
TM Claims Service, Inc.
Trinity Universal Insurance Company
United Automobile Insurance Group
US Administrator Claims
U.S. Specialty Insurance Company
Vanliner Insurance Company
Vesta Insurance Group, Inc.
XL Insurance Group
York Risk Services Group, Inc.
Zurich American Insurance Group
Custard Insurance Adjusters, Inc.
Darwin National Assurance Company
Discover Re
Economy Premier Assurance Company
Empire Fire and Marine Insurance Company
Farmers Mutual Insurance Company
Fidelity and Deposit Company of Maryland
First Financial Insurance Company
First Premium Insurance Group, Inc.
General Casualty Insurance Company
Great West Casualty Company
Hanover Insurance Group
Hudson Insurance Company
IAT Reinsurance Company
Ironshore Insurance, Ltd.
Lexington Insurance Company
Lighthouse Property Insurance Corporation
Louisiana Farm Bureau Insurance Companies
Louisiana Medical Mutual Insurance Company
Merchants and Business Men's Mutual Insurance Company
Mid-Continent Casualty Company
Mississippi Insurance Guaranty Association
New England Insurance Company
North American Risk Services
Northern Insurance Company of New York
Oklahoma Property and Casualty Insurance Guaranty Association
Pennsylvania Lumbermens Mutual Insurance Company
Protective Insurance Company
QBE FIRST Insurance Agency, Inc.
Quanta U.S. Holdings Inc.
The Republic Group
RLI Insurance Company
RSUI Group, Inc.
Selective Insurance Company of the Southeast
Society Insurance
Standard Mutual Insurance Company
State Farm Mutual Automobile Insurance Company
Terra Nova Insurance Company Limited
The Travelers Companies, Inc.
Underwriters at Lloyd's, London
Union Standard Insurance Group
Unitrin Specialty Insurance
USAA Group
USAgencies Casualty Insurance Company, Inc.
Vela Insurance Services, LLC
Westport Insurance Corporation
York Claims Service, Inc.
York STB, Inc.

Non-Insurance Clients

ABM Industries, Inc.
Alamo Rent-A-Car, LLC
AMC Construction
American Express Companies
Anderson Trucking Service
The Bank of New York Mellon Corporation
Berryland Motors
Brookdale Senior Living
Burger King Corporation
Burnette Enterprises, Inc.
Cambridge Integrated Services
ACE Group
Alco Manufacturing Company
AMEC Construction Company
American Homestar Corporation
Andover Capital Group, LLC
Barton Protective Services, Inc.
Bay Plastering, Inc.
Big Lots Stores, Inc.
Bunch CareSolutions, A Xerox Company
Cajun Lodging, LLC
Capital One, N.A.

Hailey, McNamara, Hall, Larmann & Papale, L.L.P., Metairie, LA (Continued)

Carlisle Syntec Systems, Inc.
Certified Security Systems, Inc.
CEVA Logistics
Chiquita Fresh, LLC
Conservation Technologies, LLC
Cott Corporation
Crete Carrier Corporation
Curves International, Inc.
Destrehan Drugs, Inc.
DHL
Diamond Offshore Drilling, Inc.
Dillard University
Dyna-Play, LLC
The Ellis Company
Epicor Software Corporation
Fancrease Industries, Inc.
The Freeman Companies
Gallo Winery
G.N. Rouse Syndicate
G&P Trucking Company c/o Gallagher Bassett Services, Inc.
Haynes Motor Lines, Inc.
HealthPort Technologies, LLC
Hertz Investment Group
Homelite
Insituform, Inc.
InvestTerra, LLC
J & J Worldwide Services
KEL Construction Company, Inc.
KLLM, Inc.
Lawyer's Protector Plan
Linde, LLC
Lodgian Program
Louisiana Restaurant Association
Lowe's Companies, Inc.
Marten Transport, Ltd.
Martin Transportation Systems, Inc.
Matrix Service Company
Metropolitan Electronics, Inc.
Mississippi Auto Auction, Inc.
Mississippi Coast Foreign Trade Zone, Inc.
National Car Rental
Navico, Inc.
New Orleans Aviation Board
Northwest National Administration Corporation
O'Reilly Auto Parts
Pellerin Milnor Corporation
Performance Tire & Wheel, Inc.
Piccadilly Cafeterias, Inc.
Progressive Waste Services, Inc.
The Redwoods Group
Results Unlimited of New Orleans, Inc.
River Parish Disposal, Inc.
Robinwood Forest Utilities, Inc.
SAIA Motor Freight Line, Inc.
Saks Fifth Avenue
Satterfield & Pontikes Construction, Inc.
Securitas Security Services USA, Inc.
Slay Transportation Company
Sonesta International Hotels Corporation
Standard Crane & Hoist, LLC
STC Julia, LLC
Suntory Water Group
Tambrands, Inc.
Temple-Inland Inc.
Textron, Inc.
Tidewater Marine, L.L.C.
TMC Transportation
Trail King Industries, Inc.
Transportation Claims, Inc.
Union Pump Company
Verizon Wireless
The Warranty Group, Inc.
Wendy's International, Inc.
Western Consolidated Premium Properties/EMA
WillStaff Worldwide
Celebration Station/Whitco Industries, Inc.
Charter Communications, Inc. c/o Broadspire
Constar, Inc.
Crawford & Company
Cross Road Centers
CVS Pharmacy, Inc.
Dexter Axle Company
Diamondhead Country Club & Property Owners Association
Dollar General Corporation
ECHO, Inc.
Empire Truck Lines, Inc.
Estes Express Lines
Fleet Car Carriers, Inc.
Frontier Stall & Tent Rental, Inc.
Gates Corporation
Godfrey Conveyor Company, Inc.
Grand Isle Rotary Club
Gulf Regional Planning Commission
Henkels & McCoy, Inc.
Hilton Hotels Corporation
H2O Salon & Spa
Integra Medical Management
Jim Walter Homes, Inc.
John Deere Consumer Products, Inc.
Knight Transportation Company
Limited Brands, Inc.
Lockheed Martin Corporation
Louisiana Horsemen's Benevolent and Protective Association
Maintenance Enterprises Incorporated c/o Gallagher Bassett Services, Inc.
MasRam Mechanical, LP
MEK Construction, Ltd.
Minas de Oro Nacional, S.A. de C.V.
Mitsubishi Caterpillar Forklift America Inc.
National Safety Consultants, Inc.
NCA Group, Inc.
Nissan North America, Inc.
Novak Construction Company
Omnicell, Inc.
Parish of Jefferson, LA
Pep Boys, Inc.
Petco Animal Supplies, Inc.
Precision America
Purvis Marine Limited
Regal-Beloit Corporation
R.G.I.S., LLC
Rite Aid Corporation
Roadway Express, Inc.
Rodco Worldwide, Inc.
St. Cyr, Inc.
Sara Lee Corporation
Saxon Mortgage Services, Inc.
Schindler Elevator Corporation
The Shaw Group, Inc.
Signature Homes, Inc.
S&M Transportation, Inc.
SouthGroup Insurance and Financial Services, LLC
State of Louisiana
Stericycle, Inc.
Taco Bell Corporation
Taylor Seidenbach, Inc.
Texas Star Express
Thomson Consumer Electronics
Titan Transfer, Inc.
Tour Truck Lines
Trans America, LLC
Transwood, Inc.
USA Logistics Carriers, LLC
The Waggoners Trucking
Wells Fargo Risk and Insurance Management
Western International Gas & Cylinders, Inc.
Wilson Warehouse Company, Inc.

Hailey, McNamara, Hall, Larmann & Papale, L.L.P., Metairie, LA (Continued)

Winn-Dixie Stores, Inc.
Wolf Industries d/b/a Grace Healthcare

Members

Richard Terrell Simmons, Jr. — Managing Partner — 1945 — Louisiana State University and A & M College, B.A., 1967; J.D., 1970; The George Washington University, LL.M., 1974 — Moot Court Finalist, Louisiana State University; Publication in Law Review; Director's Award for "Brilab" Racketeering Prosecution Department of Justice (1982) — Admitted to Bar, 1970, Louisiana; U.S. District Court, Eastern, Middle and Western Districts of Louisiana — Member Federal, American and Louisiana State Bar Associations — Reported Cases: Contributing writer to Louisiana Environmental Handbook, Criminal Defense Counsel in U.S. vs. Gov. Edwin Edwards (1985-1986); Criminal Defense Counsel in U.S. vs. D.A. Harry Connick (1990); United States vs. Senator Mike O'Keefe (1996); Attorney Generals' Investigation, Dr. Anna Pou/Memorial Hospital, Post Katrina (2006); Representation of Executive Officer of BP Marine Board Investigation of BP Oil Spill (2010) — Assistant U.S. District Attorney, Eastern District of Louisiana (1978-1982), Chief of Civil Division (1978-1979); Chief of Trials (1982); Assistant, Federal Public Defenders (1974-1978); Instructor, Trial Advocacy, Tulane University (1981); Lecturer, American Bar Association, White Collar Crime and Qui Tam Lawsuits; Consultant, Japan Federation Bar Association; Listed in Best Lawyers; Super Lawyers (2007-2012) — Lt. Col. JAG Corp, U.S. Army Reserves (Retired); Legion of Merit Award — Practice Areas: Criminal Law; Trial Practice; Commercial Litigation; Health Care; Professional Liability — E-mail: rsimmons@hmhlp.com

Dominic J. Ovella — Managing Partner — 1956 — The University of New Orleans, B.S., 1980; Loyola University, J.D., 1984 — Law Clerk to Hon. A. J. McNamara, U.S. District Court, Eastern District of Louisiana, 1984 — Admitted to Bar, 1985, Louisiana; 2004, Mississippi; 2004, Texas; U.S. District Court, Districts of Louisiana, Mississippi and Texas; U.S. Court of Appeals, Fifth Circuit; U.S. Supreme Court — Member Federal, American, Louisiana State, Harrison County, Jefferson Parish, Houston and New Orleans Bar Associations; The Mississippi Bar; State Bar of Texas; Louisiana Association of Business & Industry (Sections: Task Force; Corporate; Environmental; Insurance; Products Liability; Mass Tort; Construction); Mississippi, Texas and Lousiana Association of Defense Counsel; International Association of Defense Counsel; Defense Research Institute — Practice Areas: Environmental Law; Insurance Defense; Product Liability; Toxic Torts; Automobile Liability; General Liability; Construction Law; Premises Liability; Professional Liability; Trucking; Extra-Contractual Law — E-mail: novella@hmhlp.com

C. Kelly Lightfoot — Managing Partner — 1958 — University of Florida, B.S.B.A., 1981; Loyola University, J.D., 1985 — Admitted to Bar, 1985, Louisiana; U.S. District Court, Eastern, Middle and Western Districts of Louisiana; U.S. Court of Appeals, Fifth Circuit; 1989, U.S. Supreme Court — Member American, Louisiana State, New Orleans and Jefferson Parish Bar Associations; Louisiana Association of Business and Industry Task Force for Workers' Compensation; Louisiana Association of Defense Counsel; Defense Research Institute — Practice Areas: Environmental Law; Toxic Torts; Workers' Compensation; Insurance Defense; Casualty Defense — E-mail: klightfoot@hmhlp.com

W. Evan Plauché — Managing Partner — 1957 — Tulane University, B.S.M.E., 1979; Loyola University, J.D., 1991 — Pi Tau Sigma Honorary Engineering Society; Phi Delta Phi Legal Fraternity — Admitted to Bar, 1991, Louisiana; 2005, Mississippi; 1991, U.S. District Court, Eastern, Middle and Western Districts of Louisiana; 1992, U.S. Court of Appeals, Fifth Circuit; 2005, U.S. District Court, Northern and Southern Districts of Mississippi — Member Federal, American, Louisiana State and New Orleans Bar Associations; The Mississippi Bar; American Society of Mechanical Engineers; American Society of Automotive Engineers (Honorary Member); Association for Transportation Law, Logistics and Policy; Federation of Defense and Corporate Counsel; Counsel of Litigation Management; Defense Research Institute; Louisiana Association of Defense Counsel; Trucking Industry Defense Association — Super Lawyer by Law and Politics (2007,2011,2013) — Practice Areas: Trial Practice; Product Liability; Toxic Torts; Environmental Law; Transportation; Construction Law; Professional Liability; Maritime Law; Intellectual Property; Premises Liability; Casualty; Mass Tort; Property — E-mail: eplauche@hmhlp.com

Michael J. Vondenstein — Managing Partner — 1957 — The University of New Orleans, B.S., 1979; Loyola University, J.D., 1982 — Law Clerk to Honorable A. J. McNamara, U.S. District Court, Eastern District of Louisiana, 1982 — Admitted to Bar, 1982, Louisiana; 1983, U.S. District Court, Eastern District of Louisiana; 1984, U.S. District Court, Middle District of Louisiana; U.S. Court of Appeals, Fifth Circuit; 1991, U.S. District Court, Western District of Louisiana — Member Federal, American and Louisiana

Hailey, McNamara, Hall, Larmann & Papale, L.L.P., Metairie, LA (Continued)

State Bar Associations; International Association of Insurance Counsel Trial Academy; Defense Research Institute; Louisiana Association of Defense Counsel; Southeastern Admiralty Law Institute; The Maritime Law Association of the United States — Practice Areas: Admiralty and Maritime Law; Product Liability; Insurance Defense — E-mail: mvondenstein@hmhlp.com

David K. Persons — Managing Partner — 1957 — Louisiana State University and A & M College, B.A., 1980; Loyola University, J.D., 1983 — Admitted to Bar, 1983, Louisiana; U.S. District Court, Eastern District of Louisiana; 1993, U.S. District Court, Middle District of Louisiana; 2005, U.S. District Court, Western District of Louisiana — Member Federal, American, Louisiana State and New Orleans Bar Associations; Louisiana Association of Business and Industry (Liability Task Force, Workers' Compensation Task Force, and Employee Relations Council); Louisiana Association of Defense Counsel; Defense Research Institute — Practice Areas: Insurance Defense; Civil Litigation; Product Liability — E-mail: dpersons@hmhlp.com

Caroline D. Ibos — 1963 — Louisiana State University Dental School, B.S./R.D.H., 1985; Louisiana State University, J.D., 1991 — Admitted to Bar, 1992, Louisiana; 1992, U.S. District Court, Eastern, Middle and Western Districts of Louisiana — Member Louisiana Association of Defense Counsel; Defense Research Institute — Practice Areas: Automobile Liability; Commercial General Liability; Extra-Contractual Litigation; Premises Liability; Insurance Fraud; Insurance Coverage — E-mail: cibos@hmhlp.com

Joseph L. Spilman III — 1958 — Duke University, B.A., 1980; University of Miami, M.A., 1983; Tulane University, J.D./M.B.A., 1985 — Beta Gamma Sigma — Admitted to Bar, 1985, Maryland; 1986, Louisiana; 1986, District of Columbia; 1997, Alabama; 1986, U.S. District Court, Eastern District of Louisiana; 1986, U.S. Court of Appeals, Fifth Circuit; 1987, U.S. District Court, Middle and Western Districts of Louisiana; 1990, U.S. Supreme Court; 1997, U.S. District Court, Middle District of Alabama — Member Louisiana State and Maryland State Bar Associations; Alabama State Bar; District of Columbia Bar — Practice Areas: Insurance Coverage; Litigation; Insurance Fraud; Professional Liability; Complex Litigation; Class Actions; Product Liability; Contracts — E-mail: jspilman@hmhlp.com

Kevin O. Larmann — 1968 — Loyola University, B.A., 1991; J.D., 1996 — Admitted to Bar, 1996, Louisiana; U.S. District Court, Eastern, Middle and Western Districts of Louisiana — Member American, Jefferson Parish and New Orleans Bar Associations; Louisiana State Bar Association (House of Delegates, 2005-2006); Inn of Court; Louisiana Association of Defense Counsel; Defense Research Institute — Practice Areas: Casualty Defense; Construction Law; Premises Liability; Automobile; Trucking Law — E-mail: klarmann@hmhlp.com

Darren A. Patin — 1969 — Fairfield University, B.A., 1991; The George Washington University, J.D., 1994 — Admitted to Bar, 1994, Louisiana; 1995, U.S. District Court, Eastern District of Louisiana; 1998, U.S. District Court, Western District of Louisiana; 1999, U.S. District Court, Middle District of Louisiana; U.S. Court of Appeals, Fifth Circuit — Member Federal, Louisiana State and New Orleans Bar Associations; Louis Martinet Legal Society; Defense Research Institute; Louisiana Association of Defense Counsel — Practice Areas: Employment Practices Liability — E-mail: dpatin@hmhlp.com

Anne E. Medo — 1971 — University of Virginia, B.A., 1993; Louisiana State University, J.D., 1996 — Admitted to Bar, 1996, Louisiana; 2009, Texas; 1997, U.S. District Court, Eastern and Western Districts of Louisiana; 1998, U.S. District Court, Middle District of Louisiana; 2007, U.S. Court of Appeals, Fifth Circuit; 2009, U.S. District Court, Southern District of Texas — Member Federal, American, Louisiana State and New Orleans Bar Associations; State Bar of Texas; National Retail and Restaurant Defense Association; Louisiana Association of Defense Counsel; Defense Research Institute — Practice Areas: Tort Litigation; Premises Liability; Product Liability; Medical Malpractice; Toxic Torts; Class Actions — E-mail: amedo@hmhlp.com

Sean P. Mount — 1975 — Louisiana State University, B.A. (with honors), 1998; J.D., 2001 — Admitted to Bar, 2001, Louisiana; 2004, Mississippi; 2009, Texas; 2001, U.S. District Court, Eastern, Middle and Western Districts of Louisiana; U.S. Court of Appeals, Fifth Circuit; 2004, U.S. District Court, Northern and Southern Districts of Mississippi; U.S. District Court, Southern District of Texas; U.S. Supreme Court — Member Federal, American, Louisiana State and New Orleans Bar Associations; The Mississippi Bar; State Bar of Texas; Council on Litigation Management; Association of Builders and Contractors; Texas Defense Lawyers Association; Louisiana Association of Defense Counsel; Defense Research Institute; Mississippi Defense Lawyers Association — Practice Areas: Civil Litigation; Class Actions; Toxic Torts; Premises Liability; Product Liability; Inland Marine; Professional Liability; Lender Liability Defense; Coverage Analysis; Commercial Litigation; Construction Litigation; Trucking Litigation — E-mail: smount@hmhlp.com

Gabriel J. Veninata — 1965 — Baruch College, City University of New York, B.B.A., 1989; Loyola University, J.D., 1994 — Admitted to Bar, 1995, Louisiana; U.S. District Court, Eastern District of Louisiana; 2001, U.S. District Court, Middle and Western Districts of Louisiana — Member American and Louisiana State Bar Associations; Louisiana Association of Defense Counsel — Practice Areas: Casualty Defense; Workers' Compensation; Insurance Litigation; Mass Tort; Preferred Provider Organization Litigation; Commercial Litigation — E-mail: gveninata@hmhlp.com

Justin E. Alsterberg — 1982 — University of Michigan - Ann Arbor, B.A. (with honors), 2004; Tulane University Law School, J.D., 2007 — Admitted to Bar, 2007, Louisiana; U.S. District Court, Eastern, Middle and Western Districts of Louisiana; U.S. Court of Appeals, Fifth Circuit — Member Federal, American, Louisiana State and New Orleans Bar Associations; Defense Research Institute — Practice Areas: Construction Litigation; Construction Law; Insurance Coverage; Insurance Litigation; Intellectual Property; Casualty Defense — E-mail: jalsterberg@hmhlp.com

Jason M. Baer — 1983 — Louisiana State University, B.S., 2005; Loyola University New Orleans College of Law, J.D., 2008 — Admitted to Bar, 2008, Louisiana; U.S. District Court, Eastern, Middle and Western Districts of Louisiana; U.S. Court of Appeals, Fifth Circuit — Member Federal, American and Louisiana State Bar Associations; Defense Research Institute; Louisiana Association of Defense Counsel — Practice Areas: Premises Liability; Casualty Defense; Insurance Coverage; Construction Law; Commercial Litigation — E-mail: jbaer@hmhlp.com

Of Counsel

John E. Unsworth, Jr. — 1941 — Loyola University, B.S., 1965; J.D., 1968 — Admitted to Bar, 1968, Louisiana; 1969, U.S. District Court, Eastern District of Louisiana; 1994, U.S. Court of Appeals, Fifth Circuit; 2000, U.S. District Court, Middle District of Louisiana — Member Louisiana State Bar Association; Louisiana Association of Defense Counsel; Defense Research Institute — Certified Mediator — Practice Areas: General Civil Litigation; Insurance Law; Insurance Coverage; Premises Liability — E-mail: junsworth@hmhlp.com

Alayne R. Corcoran — 1964 — Louisiana Tech University, B.A., 1986; The University of North Dakota, J.D., 1994 — Admitted to Bar, 1995, Louisiana; U.S. Court of Appeals for the Federal and Fifth Circuits; U.S. Supreme Court — Member Louisiana State Bar Association — Practice Areas: Appellate Practice — E-mail: acorcoran@hmhlp.com

Lauren E. Brisbi — 1979 — Louisiana State University, B.A., 2001; Loyola University New Orleans, J.D., 2005 — Admitted to Bar, 2005, Louisiana; U.S. District Court, Eastern District of Louisiana; U.S. Court of Appeals, Fifth Circuit — Member Federal and Louisiana State Bar Associations; Louisiana Association of Defense Counsel; Defense Research Institute — Practice Areas: Insurance Defense; Premises Liability; Toxic Torts — E-mail: lbrisbi@hmhlp.com

James D. Garvey, Jr. — 1964 — Loyola University, B.B.A., 1987; J.D./M.B.A., 1991 — Admitted to Bar, 1992, Louisiana; 2006, U.S. District Court, Eastern, Middle and Western Districts of Louisiana — Member American, Louisiana State and New Orleans Bar Associations — Certified Public Accountant (Louisiana, 1994; inactive status) — Practice Areas: Insurance Law — E-mail: jgarvey@hmhlp.com

Retired

James W. Hailey, Jr. — 1928 — Louisiana State University, B.S., 1950; Tulane University, LL.B., 1960 — Admitted to Bar, 1960, Louisiana — Member Federal, American, Louisiana State, New Orleans and Jefferson Parish Bar Associations; Louisiana Association of Defense Counsel (Member, Board of Directors, 1972-74); International Association of Defense Counsel; The Maritime Law Association of the United States — Practice Areas: Toxic Torts; Product Liability; Automobile Liability

W. Marvin Hall — 1940 — Louisiana State University, B.S., 1962; Loyola University, J.D., 1969 — Admitted to Bar, 1969, Louisiana — Member American, Louisiana State and New Orleans Bar Associations; Association of Transportation Practitioners; Defense Research Institute; Louisiana Association of Defense Counsel — Practice Areas: Premises Liability; Bad Faith; Extra-Contractual Litigation

Laurence E. Larmann — 1941 — Loyola University, B.B.A., 1963; J.D., 1967 — Admitted to Bar, 1967, Louisiana — Member Louisiana State and Jefferson Parish Bar Associations; Louisiana Association of Defense Counsel; Defense Research Institute — Practice Areas: Legal Malpractice; Product Liability; Automobile — E-mail: llarmann@hmhlp.com

LOUISIANA — METAIRIE

Hailey, McNamara, Hall, Larmann & Papale, L.L.P., Metairie, LA (Continued)

Antonio E. Papale, Jr. — 1942 — Loyola University, A.B., 1963; J.D., 1966 — Admitted to Bar, 1966, Louisiana; U.S. District Court, Eastern, Middle and Western Districts of Louisiana; U.S. Court of Appeals, Fifth Circuit; U.S. Supreme Court — Member Federal and Louisiana State Bar Associations; Defense Research Institute — Practice Areas: Admiralty and Maritime Law; Insurance Defense; Medical Malpractice — E-mail: apapale@hmhlp.com

Claude A. Greco — 1938 — Tulane University, B.S.M.E., 1963; Loyola University, J.D., 1988 — Admitted to Bar, 1988, Louisiana; U.S. District Court, Eastern, Middle and Western Districts of Louisiana; U.S. Court of Appeals, Fifth Circuit — Member Federal, Louisiana State and Jefferson Parish Bar Associations; Louisiana Association of Defense Counsel; Defense Research Institute — Practice Areas: Toxic Torts — E-mail: cgreco@hmhlp.com

Special Counsel

Barbara Bourdonnay O'Donnell — 1961 — The University of New Orleans, B.A., 1982; Tulane University, J.D., 1986 — Admitted to Bar, 1988, Louisiana; U.S. District Court, Eastern, Middle and Western Districts of Louisiana; U.S. Court of Appeals, Fifth Circuit — Member Louisiana State and New Orleans Bar Associations; Defense Research Institute; Louisiana Association of Defense Counsel — Practice Areas: Environmental Law; Insurance Defense; Toxic Torts; Automobile Liability; General Liability; Class Actions; Complex Litigation — E-mail: bodonnell@hmhlp.com

Associate Counsel

William R. Seay, Jr. — 1954 — The University of New Orleans, B.A., 1976; Loyola University, J.D., 1980 — Admitted to Bar, 1980, Louisiana; U.S. District Court, Eastern District of Louisiana — Member Louisiana State Bar Association; Defense Research Institute; Louisiana Association of Defense Counsel — Manager of Information Systems — Practice Areas: Casualty Defense; Commercial Litigation; Intellectual Property — E-mail: rseay@hmhlp.com

Stephen C. Kogos, Jr. — 1974 — Loyola University, B.A. (cum laude), 1996; University of Southern Mississippi, Ph.D. (cum laude), 2002; Loyola University, J.D., 2008 — Admitted to Bar, 2008, Louisiana; U.S. District Court, Eastern, Middle and Western Districts of Louisiana; U.S. Court of Appeals, Fifth Circuit — Member Federal and Louisiana State Bar Associations; Inn of Court; Association of Builders and Contractors; Louisiana Association of Defense Counsel; Defense Research Institute — Practice Areas: Premises Liability; Casualty Defense; Insurance Coverage; Maritime Law; Construction Law; Medical Malpractice — E-mail: skogos@hmhlp.com

Richard J. Garvey, Jr. — 1958 — Tulane University, School of Science and Engineering, B.S.E.E., 1980; Loyola University Law School, J.D., 1991 — Admitted to Bar, 1991, Louisiana; U.S. District Court, Eastern, Middle and Western Districts of Louisiana; U.S. Court of Appeals, Third, Fifth and Eleventh Circuits — Member Louisiana State Bar Association; Louisiana Association of Defense Counsel; Defense Research Institute — Practice Areas: Toxic Torts — E-mail: rgarvey@hmhlp.com

Philip D. Lorio IV — 1986 — Vanderbilt University, B.A., 2009; Loyola University New Orleans College of Law, J.D., 2012 — Moot Court — Admitted to Bar, 2012, Louisiana; U.S. District Court, Eastern, Middle and Western Districts of Louisiana — Member Federal, Louisiana State and Jefferson (Young Lawyers Division) Bar Associations; St. Thomas Moore Inn of Court (Board Member) — Practice Areas: Premises Liability; Casualty Defense; Asbestos Litigation — E-mail: plorio@hmhlp.com

Matthew D. Moghis — 1986 — University of North Carolina Wilmington, B.A., 2008; Loyola University New Orleans College of Law, J.D., 2011 — Admitted to Bar, 2011, Louisiana — Member Louisiana State and Jefferson Bar Associations — Research Assistant, Scholarly Journal of Public Interest Law — Practice Areas: Commercial Litigation; Insurance Litigation; Product Liability; Insurance Coverage; Premises Liability; Workers' Compensation; Automobile Liability — E-mail: mmoghis@hmhlp.com

Edward J. Lassus, Jr. — 1952 — The University of New Orleans, B.A., 1974; Loyola University, J.D., 1977 — Admitted to Bar, 1977, Louisiana; U.S. District Court, Eastern, Middle and Western Districts of Louisiana; U.S. Court of Appeals, Fifth Circuit — E-mail: elassus@hmhlp.com

Eiland S. Ponder — 1981 — Centenary College of Louisiana, B.A./B.A., 2003; Louisiana State University, Paul M. Hebert Law Center, J.D./B.C.L., 2006 — Admitted to Bar, 2006, Louisiana; 2007, U.S. District Court, Eastern, Middle and Western Districts of Louisiana; U.S. Court of Appeals, Fifth Circuit — Member Louisiana State and Baton Rouge Bar Associations — E-mail: sponder@hmhlp.com

Law Office of Eric J. Halverson, Jr.

3925 North I-10 Service Road West, Suite 123
Metairie, Louisiana 70002
  Telephone: 504-885-0105
  Fax: 504-885-2001
  E-Mail: insdfnse@bellsouth.net

Insurance Defense, Admiralty and Maritime Law, Jones Act, Workers' Compensation, Errors and Omissions, Medical Malpractice, General Liability, Product Liability, Automobile, Truck Liability, Collision and P & I, Longshore

Insurance Clients

Argonaut Great Central Insurance Company	Argonaut Insurance Company
FCCI Insurance Group	Claim Indemnity Services, Inc.
Transamerica Insurance Company	Petrosurance Casualty Company

Non-Insurance Clients

Haul Risk Management/Allied Systems	LQ Management, L.L.C. dba LaQuinta Inns, Inc.
Ryder System, Inc.	Wyndham International

Eric J. Halverson, Jr., P.C. — 1948 — The University of New Orleans, B.G.S., 1978; Loyola University of the South, J.D., 1983; Tulane University of Louisiana, LL.M., 1989 — Admitted to Bar, 1984, Louisiana; 1986, U.S. District Court, Eastern District of Louisiana; 1987, U.S. District Court, Middle District of Louisiana; 1988, U.S. District Court, Western District of Louisiana; 1988, U.S. Court of Appeals, Fifth Circuit — Member American Bar Association (Tort and Insurance Practice; Admiralty); Louisiana State Bar Association; Mariners Club of the Port of New Orleans; The Maritime Law Association of the United States

Hebbler & Giordano, L.L.C.

3501 North Causeway Boulevard, Suite 400
Metairie, Louisiana 70002
  Telephone: 504-833-8007
  Fax: 504-833-2866
  www.hebblergiordano.com

Insurance Defense, Insurance Coverage, Asbestos Litigation, Automobile, Civil Litigation, Medical Malpractice, Casualty, Product Liability, Premises Liability, Toxic Torts, Workers' Compensation, Business Litigation

Firm Profile: Hebbler & Giordano, L.L.C. is a law firm whose members specialize in the defense of civil litigation. Our clients include national and international insurance companies, corporations and individuals.

Insurance Clients

AAA Insurance	Argonaut Group, Inc./Grocers Insurance
Arrowpoint Capital Corporation	Bernard Claim Service
Auto Club Family Insurance Company	Canal Indemnity Company
Catlin Specialty Insurance Company	Chubb Services Corporation
Everest National Insurance Company	The Colony Group
Lancer Insurance Company	The Hartford Insurance Group
Landmark American Insurance Company	Jewelers Mutual Insurance Company
Nautilus Insurance Company	MetLife Auto & Home
Permanent General Assurance Corporation	National Continental Insurance Company
RSUI Indemnity Company	Progressive Casualty Insurance Company
Zurich American Insurance Group	Sagamore Insurance Company

Non-Insurance Clients

Avis Budget Car Rental, LLC	Boyd Gaming Corporation
Budget Truck Rentals, Inc.	Cardinal Health, Inc.
The Hertz Corporation	Rapid American Corp.
R. F. Mattei & Associates, Inc.	Werner Enterprises, Inc.

METAIRIE   LOUISIANA

Hebbler & Giordano, L.L.C., Metairie, LA (Continued)

Members

Charles V. Giordano — Louisiana State University, B.A., 1990; Loyola University, J.D., 1993 — Admitted to Bar, 1993, Louisiana; U.S. District Court, Eastern, Middle and Western Districts of Louisiana — Member American, Louisiana State and Jefferson Bar Associations; Louisiana Association of Defense Counsel; Trucking Industry Defense Association

George P. Hebbler, Jr. — The University of New Orleans, B.S., 1973; Loyola University, J.D., 1977 — Admitted to Bar, 1977, Louisiana; U.S. District Court, Eastern, Middle and Western Districts of Louisiana; U.S. Court of Appeals for the Federal and Fifth Circuits; U.S. Court of Federal Claims — Member American, Louisiana State, Fifth Federal Circuit and Jefferson Bar Associations; Louisiana Association of Defense Counsel; Trucking Industry Defense Association; Defense Research Institute

Partners

Thomas M. Young — Louisiana State University at New Orleans, B.S., 1967; Loyola University, J.D., 1969 — Admitted to Bar, 1969, Louisiana; U.S. District Court, Eastern and Western Districts of Louisiana; U.S. Court of Appeals, Fifth Circuit; U.S. Supreme Court — Member Louisiana State Bar Association; Defense Research Institute; Louisiana Association of Defense Counsel

Anthony J. Milazzo, Jr. — Louisiana State University at New Orleans, B.S., 1972; Loyola University School of Law, J.D., 1975 — Admitted to Bar, 1975, Louisiana; U.S. District Court, Eastern District of Louisiana; 1979, U.S. Court of Appeals, Fifth Circuit; 1982, U.S. District Court, Middle District of Louisiana; 1999, U.S. District Court, Western District of Louisiana — Member Louisiana State and Jefferson Bar Associations; Commercial Law League of America

Tasha Warino Hebert — Loyola University, B.A. (summa cum laude), 1995; J.D., 1998 — Admitted to Bar, 1998, Louisiana; U.S. District Court, Eastern, Middle and Western Districts of Louisiana; U.S. Court of Appeals, Fifth Circuit — Member Louisiana State and Jefferson Parish Bar Associations; Louisiana Association of Defense Counsel

Associates

Michael E. Escudier — Tulane University, B.S.M., 1996; Loyola University, J.D., 1999 — Admitted to Bar, 2000, Louisiana; U.S. District Court, Eastern District of Louisiana; U.S. Court of Appeals, Fifth Circuit — Member Louisiana State and Jefferson Bar Associations; Judge John C. Boutall American Inn of Court

Thomas H. Cook — Louisiana State University, B.S., 2008; Loyola University New Orleans College of Law, J.D., 2011 — Admitted to Bar, 2011, Louisiana — Member Louisiana State Bar Association

Devin J. Barnett — Tulane University, B.A., 2007; Tulane University Law School, J.D., 2010; University of Miami School of Law, LL.M., 2011 — Admitted to Bar, 2010, Louisiana; 2011, Florida — Member Louisiana State Bar Association

Michael Rodrigue Jr. — A. B. Freeman School of Business, Tulane University, B.S. (magna cum laude), 2004; Loyola University New Orleans College of Law, J.D., 2007 — Admitted to Bar, 2007, Louisiana — Member Federal, American, Louisiana State and New Orleans Bar Associations

Frances I. McGinnis — The University of New Orleans, J.D., 2000 — Admitted to Bar, 2000, Louisiana — Member Louisiana State Bar Association

Special Counsel

Frank A. Romeu, Jr. — Southeastern Louisiana University, B.S., 1983; Louisiana State University, J.D., 1987 — Admitted to Bar, 1987, Louisiana; 1988, California; 2006, Texas; U.S. District Court, Eastern, Middle and Western Districts of Louisiana; U.S. District Court, Central District of California — Member Louisiana State Bar Association; State Bar of California; State Bar of Texas

Juge, Napolitano, Guilbeau, Ruli & Frieman

3320 West Esplanade Avenue North
Metairie, Louisiana 70002
Telephone: 504-831-7270
Fax: 504-831-7284
E-Mail: djuge@wcdefense.com
www.wcdefense.com

Juge, Napolitano, Guilbeau, Ruli & Frieman, Metairie, LA (Continued)

(Covington, LA Office: 330 North New Hampshire Street, 70433)

Established: 1983

Insurance Defense, Workers' Compensation, Employer Liability, Subrogation, Jones Act, Premises Liability, General Liability, Automobile Liability, Longshore & Harbor Workers' Compensation Act, General Maritime Law

Insurance Clients

ACE USA Group
American International Group, Inc.
Bituminous Insurance Companies
Chubb Group of Insurance Companies
Hartford Insurance Company
Louisiana Retailers Mutual Insurance Company
Sedgwick Claims Management Services, Inc.
AIG
Amerisure Insurance Company
Bridgefield Casualty Insurance Company
Crawford & Company
Louisiana Commerce and Trade Association
LUBA Mutual Holding Company
Travelers Insurance Companies
Zurich American Insurance Group

Non-Insurance Clients

American Airlines, Inc.
Barriere Construction Company, LLC
Halliburton Energy Services Corporation
Shell Oil Company
AT&T
Bed Bath & Beyond, Inc.
Coca-Cola Enterprises Inc.
Michaels Stores, Inc.
RaceTrac Petroleum, Inc.

Directors

Denis Paul Juge — 1947 — The University of New Orleans, B.A., 1970; M.A., 1972; Loyola University, J.D., 1976 — Admitted to Bar, 1976, Louisiana; 2004, Mississippi; 1976, U.S. District Court, Eastern District of Louisiana; 2004, U.S. District Court, Northern and Southern Districts of Mississippi — Member Louisiana State Bar Association; Louisiana Association of Business and Industry (Workers' Compensation Task Force); Southern Association of Workers' Compensation Administrators; Defense Research Institute (Past National Chairman, Workers' Compensation Committee, 1989-1992); Louisiana Association of Defense Counsel; International Association of Defense Counsel — Co-Author: "LABI/Workers' Compensation Desk Book," Published by the Louisiana Association of Business and Industry; Author: "Louisiana Workers' Compensation," a treatise, Lexis Law Publishing; "A Medical-Legal Analysis of Cardiovascular Claims in Workers' Compensation," Article, Vol. 2, Defense Research Institute, 1987; "The Proper Use of Surveillance," Article, For the Defense, The Defense Research Institute, June 1990; "Cardiovascular Claims in Workers' Compensation. The Evolving Laws," Article, 32 Loyola Law Review, 895; "Marking Out Boundaries; The Relationship Between Work and Psychological Disorders, a Legal and Medical Analysis," Article, 30 Loyola Law Review, 249; "Cumulative Trauma Disorder - 'The Disease of the 90's'," Article, 55 Louisiana Law Review Issue Number 5, May 1995 — Adjunct Faculty, State Workers' Compensation and Insurance Law, Loyola University (1982-2005)

Jeffrey C. Napolitano — 1960 — Louisiana State University, B.S. (cum laude), 1982; Loyola University, J.D., 1985 — Loyola Law Review — Admitted to Bar, 1985, Louisiana; 1986, U.S. District Court, Eastern District of Louisiana — Member Louisiana State Bar Association; Defense Research Institute (Past National Chairman, Workers' Compensation Committee 2002-2003); Governor's Workers' Compensation Pharmacy Taskforce (2012); Fellow, The College of Workers' Compensation Lawyers; Workers' Compensation Defense Institute — Author: "The Question of Qualifications," Public Risk, September 1992; "Out of Network/Attorney Directed and Physician Directed Pharmacies," LexisNexis Communities, Workers' Compensation Law Blog, June 15, 2011

Joseph B. Guilbeau — 1954 — University of Southwestern Louisiana, B.S., 1976; Loyola University, J.D., 1984 — Admitted to Bar, 1984, Louisiana; 1984, U.S. District Court, Eastern District of Louisiana; 1985, U.S. District Court, Middle and Western Districts of Louisiana — Member Louisiana State Bar Association; Louisiana Association of Defense Counsel; Defense Research Institute — Author: "A Look at the Longshore and Harbor Workers' Compensation Act," The Risk Report, Article, Volume VII, No. 7, 1985

Thomas M. Ruli — 1964 — Loyola University, B.S., 1986; J.D., 1989 — Admitted to Bar, 1989, Louisiana; 1989, U.S. District Court, Eastern, Middle and Western Districts of Louisiana — Member American and Louisiana State Bar Associations; Louisiana Association of Defense Counsel; Defense Research Institute

Juge, Napolitano, Guilbeau, Ruli & Frieman, Metairie, LA (Continued)

Lawrence B. Frieman — 1961 — Louisiana State University Medical Center, B.S., 1985; Loyola University, J.D., 1992 — Admitted to Bar, 1992, Louisiana; 1995, U.S. District Court, Western District of Louisiana — Member American and Louisiana State Bar Associations; Louisiana Association of Defense Counsel — Licensed Physical Therapist and Athletic Trainer, State of Louisiana

Matthew M. Putfark — 1972 — Louisiana State University, B.A., 1994; J.D., 1998 — Admitted to Bar, 1998, Louisiana

Jeffrey I. Mandel — 1962 — University of Cincinnati, B.A. (cum laude), 1984; The Ohio State University, M.L.H.R., 1985; Loyola University, J.D., 1991 — Loyola Law Review — Admitted to Bar, 1991, Louisiana; 1992, Ohio; U.S. District Court, Eastern, Middle and Western Districts of Louisiana; U.S. Court of Appeals, Fifth Circuit; U.S. Supreme Court — Member American and Louisiana State Bar Associations; Society for Human Resource Management

Keith E. Pittman — 1971 — The University of New Orleans, B.A., 1994; Loyola University New Orleans, J.D., 1998 — Admitted to Bar, 1998, Louisiana — Member Federal and Louisiana State Bar Associations

Associates

Bradley P. Naccari — 1971 — Louisiana State University, B.A., 1992; Loyola University New Orleans, J.D., 1996 — Admitted to Bar, 1996, Louisiana — Member Louisiana State Bar Association

John V. Quaglino — 1968 — Loyola University, B.A., 1990; Louisiana State University, J.D., 1993 — Admitted to Bar, 1993, Louisiana; 1993, U.S. District Court, Eastern, Middle and Western Districts of Louisiana — Member Louisiana State Bar Association

Denise M. Ledet — 1964 — Our Lady of Holy Cross College, B.S., 1989; Loyola University School of Law, J.D., 1995 — Admitted to Bar, 1995, Louisiana; 2008, Mississippi; 1995, U.S. District Court, Eastern and Middle Districts of Louisiana; 2008, U.S. District Court, Northern and Southern Districts of Mississippi — Member Louisiana State Bar Association; The Mississippi Bar

Jennifer M. Sullivan Lambert — 1980 — Louisiana State University at Baton Rouge, B.S., 2002; Loyola University New Orleans College of Law, J.D., 2005 — Admitted to Bar, 2005, Louisiana; U.S. District Court, Eastern District of Louisiana — Member Federal, American, Louisiana State and Jefferson Parish Bar Associations

Donald C. Douglas, Jr. — 1966 — The University of New Orleans, B.A., 1990; Louisiana State University, J.D., 1993 — Admitted to Bar, 1993, Louisiana; U.S. District Court, Middle and Western Districts of Louisiana; 2000, U.S. Court of Appeals, Fifth Circuit; U.S. Supreme Court — Member Louisiana State and Greater Covington Bar Associations

Kathleen W. Will — Louisiana State University, B.S., 1982; J.D., 1985 — Admitted to Bar, 1985, Louisiana; U.S. District Court, Eastern District of Louisiana; U.S. Court of Appeals, Fifth Circuit

Elizabeth L. Finch — 1981 — Mississippi State University, B.A., 2004; Loyola University New Orleans College of Law, J.D., 2012 — Admitted to Bar, 2012, Louisiana; U.S. District Court, Eastern, Middle and Western Districts of Louisiana; U.S. Court of Appeals, Fifth Circuit — Member Federal, American and Louisiana State Bar Associations

Larzelere Picou Wells Simpson Lonero, LLC

Two Lakeway Center, Suite 1100
3850 North Causeway Boulevard
Metairie, Louisiana 70002
 Telephone: 504-834-6500
 Fax: 504-834-6565
 Telex: 402325 (LLP NLN)
 www.lpwsl.com

Established: 1989

Insurance Law, Trucking Law, Transportation, Toxic Torts, Marine, Energy, Recoveries, Pollution, General Casualty

Insurance Clients

American National Property and Casualty Company
AXA Marine & Aviation Insurance (UK) Ltd.

Larzelere Picou Wells Simpson Lonero, LLC, Metairie, LA (Continued)

Crum & Forster Insurance
Interstate Insurance Underwriters, Inc.
MOAC - A CNA Maritime Division
Ranger Insurance Company
The RiverStone Group
Terra Nova Insurance Company Limited
Zurich Insurance Company
The Hartford Insurance Group
Lexington Insurance Company
Mid-Continent Group
Navigators Insurance Company
Northland Insurance Company
The Republic Group
St. Paul Surplus Lines Insurance Company
Underwriters at Lloyd's, London

Partners

J. Daniel Picou — 1956 — Tulane University, B.A., 1978; J.D., 1981 — Admitted to Bar, 1981, Louisiana; 2001, Texas; 1982, U.S. District Court, Eastern, Middle and Western Districts of Louisiana; 1982, U.S. Court of Appeals, Fifth Circuit; 1988, U.S. District Court, Southern District of Texas; 1989, U.S. Supreme Court — Member Federal and American (Tort and Insurance Practice, Litigation and Natural Resources, Energy and Environmental Sections); Louisiana State Bar Association (Insurance, Negligence, Compensation, Admiralty, and Environmental Law Sections); Defense Research Institute (Admiralty Law Committee); The Maritime Law Association of the United States; Louisiana Association of Defense Counsel; Southeastern Admiralty Law Institute

Morgan J. Wells, Jr. — 1962 — Southeastern Louisiana University, B.S. (cum laude), 1984; Loyola University, J.D., 1987 — Admitted to Bar, 1987, Louisiana; 1988, U.S. District Court, Eastern, Middle and Western Districts of Louisiana — Member Federal, American and Louisiana State Bar Associations; The Maritime Law Association of the United States

T. Justin Simpson — 1957 — University of Michigan, B.S. (magna cum laude), 1979; Loyola University, J.D., 1987 — Admitted to Bar, 1993, Texas; 1987, Louisiana; 1987, U.S. District Court, Eastern, Middle and Western Districts of Louisiana; 1991, U.S. Court of Appeals, Fifth Circuit; 1991, U.S. Supreme Court; 1991, U.S. District Court, Central District of Illinois; 1993, U.S. District Court, Southern District of Texas — Member Federal, American and Louisiana State Bar Associations; Defense Research Institute; The Maritime Law Association of the United States

Jay M. Lonero — 1965 — Louisiana State University, B.A., 1987; Louisiana State University, Paul M. Hebert Law Center, J.D., 1990 — Law Clerk to U.S. District Judge, Marcel Livaudais, Jr., Eastern District of Louisiana (1990-1991) — Admitted to Bar, 1991, Louisiana; 2001, Texas; 1991, U.S. District Court, Eastern, Middle and Western Districts of Louisiana; 1991, U.S. Court of Appeals, Fifth Circuit; 2001, U.S. District Court, Southern District of Texas; 2014, U.S. Supreme Court — Member Federal, American and Louisiana State Bar Associations; State Bar of Texas; Louisiana Association of Defense Counsel; The Maritime Law Association of the United States; Federation of Defense and Corporate Counsel

Stephen M. Larzelere — 1969 — Florida State University, B.S. (cum laude), 1991; Louisiana State University, Paul M. Hebert Law Center, J.D., 1994 — Law Clerk to Attorney General Richard P. Ieyoub, 1992-1994 — Admitted to Bar, 1994, Louisiana — Member Louisiana State Bar Association

Christopher R. Pennison — 1968 — Loyola University, B.B.A., 1990; Louisiana State University, J.D., 1993 — Admitted to Bar, 1993, Louisiana; 1996, Arizona; 1994, U.S. District Court, Eastern District of Louisiana; 1996, U.S. District Court, District of Arizona — Member Louisiana State Bar Association; State Bar of Arizona

Angie Arceneaux Akers — 1975 — Spring Hill College, B.S. (summa cum laude), 1997; Tulane University, J.D., 2000 — Admitted to Bar, 2000, Louisiana — Member American and Louisiana State Bar Associations

Wilson L. Maloz, III — 1973 — Louisiana State University, B.A. (magna cum laude), 1996; Tulane University Law School, J.D., 1999 — Admitted to Bar, 1999, Louisiana; 1999, U.S. District Court, Eastern, Middle and Western Districts of Louisiana; 1999, U.S. Court of Appeals, Fifth Circuit — Member Federal and American Bar Associations; Defense Research Institute; Louisiana Association of Defense Counsel — Louisiana Army National Guard (1993-2003)

Benjamin Ward — 1965 — Millsaps College, B.A., 1987; Loyola Law School, J.D., 1990 — Admitted to Bar, 1990, Louisiana — Member Louisiana State Bar Association

Associates

Mary Kerrigan Dennard — 1962 — University of Virginia, B.A., 1984; Tulane University, J.D. (cum laude), 1987 — Admitted to Bar, 1987, Louisiana; 1988, U.S. District Court, Eastern and Middle Districts of Louisiana; 1989, U.S. District Court, Western District of Louisiana; 1993, U.S. District

METAIRIE   LOUISIANA

Larzelere Picou Wells Simpson Lonero, LLC, Metairie, LA (Continued)

Court, Southern District of Texas — Member Louisiana State and New Orleans Bar Associations

Lee M. Peacocke — 1959 — Carleton College, B.A., 1982; The University of Mississippi, J.D., 1986 — Admitted to Bar, 1982, Louisiana; 1986, Mississippi; 1986, U.S. District Court, Northern and Southern Districts of Mississippi; 1987, U.S. District Court, Eastern, Middle and Western Districts of Louisiana; 1988, U.S. District Court, Southern District of Texas; U.S. District Court, Southern District of Alabama — Member Louisiana State Bar Association; The Mississippi Bar

Jennifer R. Kretschmann — 1978 — College of William & Mary, B.A. (cum laude), 2000; Tulane University, J.D. (cum laude), 2003 — Articles Editor, Tulane Law Review, 2002-2003 — Admitted to Bar, 2003, Louisiana — Member Louisiana State and New Orleans Bar Associations

Mary E. Lorenz — 1979 — Louisiana State University, B.A., 2001; Loyola University New Orleans College of Law, J.D., 2004 — Admitted to Bar, 2004, Louisiana; 2006, U.S. District Court, Eastern and Middle Districts of Louisiana — Member Federal, American, Louisiana State and New Orleans Bar Associations; Womens Energy Network

Evan J. Godofsky — 1984 — Louisiana State University, B.A., 2006; Loyola University New Orleans College of Law, J.D., 2009 — Articles Editor, Loyola Journal of Public Interest Law, 2008-2009 — Admitted to Bar, 2009, Louisiana — Member Federal, American and Louisiana State Bar Associations

Cory T. Stuart — 1982 — Louisiana State University at Baton Rouge, B.A., 2004; Loyola University New Orleans College of Law, J.D., 2010 — Admitted to Bar, 2010, Louisiana; U.S. District Court, Eastern, Middle and Western Districts of Louisiana — Member Federal and Louisiana State Bar Associations — "The Wake of Discovery - A Primer on Legal, Historical, and Practical Shipwreck Salvage Dynamics," Loyola Maritime Law Journal, 2011 - Volume 9

Thomas Peyton — Loyola University New Orleans College of Law, J.D., 2009 — Louisiana State Bar Association Leadership Class Member (2013-2014); Louisiana State Bar Association Century Club Award (2013); Pro Bono Project Distinguished Service Awards (2011-2013) — Admitted to Bar, 2009, Louisiana; U.S. District Court, Eastern and Middle Districts of Louisiana; 2013, U.S. Court of Appeals, Fifth Circuit — Member Federal, Louisiana State and New Orleans Bar Associations — Note, State v. Kennedy, 9 Loy.J.Pub.Int.L. 87 (2007) — CASA of Jefferson (Board of Directors)

Shelly Gilbreath Wells — 1963 — Southeastern Louisiana University, B.A. (magna cum laude), 1985; Loyola University, J.D., 1988 — Admitted to Bar, 1988, Louisiana; U.S. District Court, Eastern, Middle and Western Districts of Louisiana — Member Louisiana State Bar Association

Staines & Eppling

3500 North Causeway Boulevard, Suite 820
Metairie, Louisiana 70002
  Telephone: 504-838-0019
  Fax: 504-838-0043
  E-Mail: SE@staines-eppling.com
  www.staines-eppling.com

Established: 1992

Insurance Defense, Admiralty and Maritime Law, Casualty, Workers' Compensation, Labor and Employment, Inland and Ocean Marine, Cargo, Automobile, Transportation, Premises Liability, Toxic Torts, Energy, Construction Law, Coverage Issues, Product Liability, Asbestos Litigation

Insurance Clients

AIG
Argenta Syndicate Management Ltd.
Brit Insurance Limited
Catlin Insurance Company, Inc.
Condon Claims Management, Inc.
FARA Insurance Services
Gray Insurance Company
Houston Casualty Company
Liberty Mutual Group
Louisiana Insurance Guaranty Association
Allianz Global Corporate & Specialty
Bowen Miclette & Britt of Louisiana
CNA Insurance Company
Ellsworth Corporation
Fidelis Marine
Gulf Coast Marine, Inc.
IMU/OneBeacon Insurance
Lockton Companies
McGriff, Seibels & Williams, Inc.
Navigators Insurance Company

Staines & Eppling, Metairie, LA (Continued)

Newman, Martin and Buchan, Ltd.
Paul's Agency LLC
R K Harrison Group Limited
Samsung Fire & Marine Insurance Company, Ltd.
Starr Marine Agency
Trident Marine Managers, Inc.
USI Southwest
Willis Limited
XL Insurance Company, Ltd.
Osprey Underwriting Agency Ltd.
Price Forbes, Ltd.
St. Paul Travelers
Sedgwick Claims Management Services, Inc.
Travelers Property Casualty Corporation
VeriClaim, Inc.
Wright & Percy Insurance

Non-Insurance Clients

AAA Platinum
American Cargo Assurance, LLC
Aqueos Corporation
Ashton Marine, LLC
Boat Services of Galveston, Inc.
Circle K Stores, Inc., a division of Tosco Corp.
Community Coffee
DIRECTV, LLC
Ergon, Inc.
Glazers, Inc.
Hiller Investments, Inc.
Jefferson Marine Towing, Inc.
K & K Offshore LLC
Louisiana Coca-Cola Bottling Co., LLC
Low Land Construction Company, Inc.
Max Welders, Inc.
M & M Wireline & Offshore Services, LLC
Premiere Offshore Catering
Sailboat Bay Apartments, LLC
Shore Construction, LLC
Specialty Offshore
Superior Derrick Services LLC
VT Halter Marine, Inc.
W.W. Grainger, Inc.
Accutrans, Inc.
Amicus, Inc.
Ashland Services LLC
Bayou Fleet, Inc.
Carpenter & Paterson, Inc.
Coastal Catering, LLC
The Coca-Cola Company
Couvillion Group LLC
DS Water
Florida Marine Transporters, Inc.
Great Southern Dredging, Inc
Inland Dredging Company LLC
Kentwood Spring Water
Lin-Bar Marine, Inc.
Louisiana Machinery, LLC
Louisiana Safety Association of Timbermen
Magnolia Marine Transport Company
Offshore Services of Acadiana
Olympic Marine Company
SAIA Motor Freight Line, Inc.
Scope Logistical Specialist, Inc.
Southern Towing Company
Sunburst Media-Louisiana, LLC
T & D Towing, LLC
Weber Marine, Inc.
Y & S Marine, Inc.

Partners

Anthony J. Staines — 1955 — The University of New Orleans, B.S., 1976; Louisiana State University, J.D., 1980 — Law Clerk to Hon. Frank J. Polozola, U.S. District Judge, Middle District of Louisiana, 1980-1981 — Admitted to Bar, 1980, Louisiana; 1981, U.S. District Court, Eastern, Middle and Western Districts of Louisiana; U.S. Court of Appeals, Fifth and Eleventh Circuits; 1996, U.S. Supreme Court — Practice Areas: Admiralty and Maritime Law; Asbestos Litigation; Employment Law; Toxic Torts; Insurance Litigation — E-mail: tony@staines-eppling.com

Thomas J. Eppling — 1957 — Louisiana State University, B.Eng., 1979; Loyola University, J.D., 1984 — Admitted to Bar, 1984, Louisiana; U.S. District Court, Eastern, Middle and Western Districts of Louisiana; 1985, U.S. Court of Appeals, Fifth Circuit; 1996, U.S. Supreme Court — Registered Professional Engineer, State of Louisiana

Lance E. Harwell — 1962 — University of Louisiana at Lafayette, B.S., 1984; Loyola University, J.D., 1992 — Admitted to Bar, 1992, Louisiana; U.S. District Court, Eastern, Middle and Western Districts of Louisiana; U.S. Court of Appeals, Fifth Circuit

Julie Steed Kammer — 1970 — Centenary College of Louisiana, B.S., 1993; Louisiana State University, J.D., 1996 — Admitted to Bar, 1996, Louisiana; 1997, U.S. District Court, Eastern, Middle and Western Districts of Louisiana; U.S. Court of Appeals, Fifth Circuit — Practice Areas: Appellate Practice; ERISA; Labor and Employment; Wage and Hour Law; Transportation; Insurance Defense; Insurance Coverage Claims; Contract Litigation

Craig W. Brewer — 1969 — Rhodes College, B.A., 1991; Tulane University, J.D., 1995 — Admitted to Bar, 1995, Louisiana; U.S. District Court, Eastern, Middle and Western Districts of Louisiana; U.S. Court of Appeals, Fifth Circuit — Seminar Presenter, "Emerging Issues in Louisiana Mold & Mildew Litigation", 2003 — Practice Areas: Admiralty and Maritime Law; Construction Law; Insurance Coverage

Associates

Sara P. Scurlock — 1980 — University of Southern Mississippi, B.A. (magna cum laude), 2001; Tulane University Law School, J.D., 2005 — Admitted to Bar, 2005, Louisiana; 2006, U.S. District Court, Eastern, Middle and Western Districts of Louisiana; U.S. Court of Appeals, Fifth Circuit

Jason R. Kenney — 1980 — Louisiana State University, B.S., 2002; Tulane University, J.D., 2005 — Admitted to Bar, 2005, Louisiana; U.S. District

LOUISIANA   MONROE

Staines & Eppling, Metairie, LA   (Continued)

Court, Eastern and Middle Districts of Louisiana; U.S. Court of Appeals, Fifth Circuit

Corey P. Parenton — 1984 — Louisiana State University, B.A., 2005; Loyola University New Orleans College of Law, J.D., 2009 — Admitted to Bar, 2010, Louisiana; U.S. District Court, Eastern, Middle and Western Districts of Louisiana; U.S. Court of Appeals, Fifth Circuit — Practice Areas: Admiralty and Maritime Law; Construction Law; Insurance Coverage

Jeff D. Peuler — 1980 — Louisiana State University, B.A., 2002; Loyola Law School, J.D., 2005 — Admitted to Bar, 2005, Louisiana; U.S. District Court, Eastern, Middle and Western Districts of Louisiana — Practice Areas: Energy; Construction Law; Class Actions; Maritime Law; Automobile; Insurance Coverage

Of Counsel

Ashley Boyd — 1983 — University of North Texas, B.A. (summa cum laude), 2006; Tulane University Law School, J.D., 2009 — Admitted to Bar, 2009, Louisiana; U.S. District Court, Eastern, Middle and Western Districts of Louisiana

Ungarino & Eckert, L.L.C.

3850 North Causeway Boulevard, Suite 1280
Metairie, Louisiana 70002
Telephone: 504-836-7555
Fax: 504-836-7566
E-Mail: mungarino@ungarino-eckert.com
www.ungarino-eckert.com

(Baton Rouge, LA Office: 3909 Plaza Tower Drive, 70816)
  (Tel: 225-292-2000)
  (Fax: 225-208-1132)
(Shreveport, LA Office: 910 Pierremont Road, Suite 103, 71106)
  (Tel: 318-866-9599)
  (Fax: 318-866-9836)
(Lafayette, LA Office: 200 West Congress Street, Suite 1010, 70501)
  (Tel: 337-235-5656)
  (Fax: 337-205-8679)
(Ridgeland, MS Office: 800 Woodlands Parkway, Suite 209, 39157)
  (Tel: 601-932-3544)
  (Fax: 601-510-9108)
(Gulfport, MS Office: 1323 28th Avenue, Suite A, 39501)
  (Tel: 228-868-7666)
  (Fax: 601-510-9108)

Established: 1994

Litigation, Appellate Practice, State and Federal Courts, Class Actions, Insurance Coverage, Premises Liability, Professional Liability, Directors and Officers Liability, Insurance Defense, Construction Law, Toxic Torts, Personal Injury, Arson, Insurance Fraud, Admiralty and Maritime Law, Extra-Contractual Litigation, Bad Faith, Product Liability, Alternative Dispute Resolution, Civil Rights, Workers' Compensation, Environmental Law, Employment Law, Automobile, Truck Liability, Errors and Omissions, Common Carrier, Medical Malpractice, Construction Defect, Constitutional Law, Department of Insurance Complaints, ERISA Claims, Government Relations, Complex Casualty, Consumer Defense, Creditor Rights, Debt Collections, Discrimination Claims, Electric Utility Liability, Engineering Malpractice, Family Law (Divorce, Custody, Support, Adoption), Fraud, General Liability, Governmental Entity Liability, Insurance Subrogation, Landlord Liability, Medical Device Liability, Property Ownership, State and Municipality Litigation, Successions, Warranty/Redhibition Actions

Firm Profile: The law firm of Ungarino & Eckert was co-founded in 1994 by Matthew Ungarino and Bill Eckert based upon a shared commitment to providing an exceptional level of client service. Since that time, the firm has steadily grown from a single office in the Greater New Orleans Area to six offices strategically located throughout Louisiana and Mississippi through which we are able to efficiently and effectively represent our diverse range of clients. Through our continued commitment to providing exceptional client service, we expect this steady growth pattern to continue into the future.

Ungarino & Eckert, L.L.C., Metairie, LA   (Continued)

Insurance Clients

Assurant Insurance Group
Burlington Insurance Company
Church Mutual Insurance Company
CNA
GuideOne Insurance
Hanover Insurance Company
Montpelier US Insurance Company
Penn-America Insurance Company
RLI Corp.
Safeco Insurance
Swiss Re
York Claims Service, Inc.

Bankers Insurance Group
Catlin Specialty Insurance Company
First Financial Insurance Company
Hallmark Insurance Company
Liberty International Underwriters
Nationwide Insurance
Republic Western Insurance Company
Scottsdale Insurance Company
Tower Group Companies

Non-Insurance Clients

Albertsons, Inc.
Dollar-Thrifty Automotive Group, Inc.
Genuine Parts Company
The Kroger Co.

CHRISTUS Health Risk Management
Federated Electric
Health Care Indemnity, Inc.
Stein Mart, Inc.

Senior Partners

Matthew J. Ungarino — 1959 — Tulane University, B.S.M., 1981; Loyola University, J.D./M.B.A., 1984 — Admitted to Bar, 1984, New York; 1985, Louisiana; 1985, U.S. District Court, Eastern, Middle and Western Districts of Louisiana; 1985, U.S. Court of Appeals, Fifth Circuit; 1985, U.S. Supreme Court — Member Louisiana State Bar Association; Louisiana Association of Defense Counsel — E-mail: mungarino@ungarino-eckert.com

William H. Eckert — 1961 — Tulane University, B.A., 1983; Loyola University, J.D., 1987 — Admitted to Bar, 1987, Louisiana — Member Louisiana State Bar Association — E-mail: beckert@ungarino-eckert.com

Wayne R. Maldonado
Brian D. Smith

Emile A. Bagneris, III
Michael J. Tarleton

Partners

David I. Bordelon
James M. Benson
Philip E. Roberts

Imelda T. Fruge, R.N.
J. Michael Nash

Associates

Kelly O. Thibeaux

Daniel G. Collarini

Special Counsel

Rhonda J. Thomas, R.N.

Arthur Garitty

The following firms also service this area.

Schafer & Schafer
328 Lafayette Street
New Orleans, Louisiana 70130
  Telephone: 504-522-0011
  Fax: 504-523-2795

Insurance Defense, Automobile, Premises Liability, Product Liability, Employer Liability, Medical Malpractice, Coverage Issues, Employment Law, Bad Faith, Comprehensive General Liability, Complex Litigation, Civil Trial Practice, Excess and Umbrella, Fire Loss, Homeowners, Uninsured and Underinsured Motorist, Wrongful Death

SEE COMPLETE LISTING UNDER NEW ORLEANS, LOUISIANA (5 MILES)

MONROE † 48,815 Ouachita Par.

Davenport, Files & Kelly

1509 Lamy Lane
Monroe, Louisiana 71201
  Telephone: 318-387-6453
  Fax: 318-323-6533
  Emer/After Hrs: 318-387-6456, 318-325-3344
  E-Mail: dfk@dfklaw.com
  www.dfklaw.com

Established: 1951

MONROE   LOUISIANA

Davenport, Files & Kelly, Monroe, LA   (Continued)

Administrative Law, Agriculture, Automobile Liability, Aviation, Civil Rights, Commercial Litigation, Construction Law, Contracts, Employment Law, Environmental Law, Insurance Defense, Litigation, Mass Tort, Medical Malpractice, Nursing Home Liability, Personal Injury, Premises Liability, Product Liability, Professional Malpractice, School Law, Truck Liability, Workers' Compensation

Insurance Clients

Acceptance Insurance Company
American International Group, Inc.
American National Property and Casualty Company
Chubb Group of Insurance Companies
Crum & Forster Insurance Group
Employers Insurance Company of Wausau
Essex Insurance Company
Farmland Mutual Insurance Company
GMAC Insurance
Great West Casualty Company
Gulf Insurance Company
Houston Casualty Company
James River Insurance Company
Lafayette Insurance Company
Metropolitan Property and Casualty Insurance Company
Midland Risk Insurance Company
Motors Insurance Corporation
National Fire and Marine Insurance Company
OneBeacon Insurance
Security National Insurance Company
Underwriters at Lloyd's, London
United Fire & Casualty Company
United States Aircraft Insurance Group
Western Heritage Insurance Company
American Home Assurance Company
Carolina Casualty Insurance Company
Clarendon America Insurance Company
Electric Mutual Liability Insurance Company
Employers Mutual Casualty Company
Federated Mutual Insurance Company
Government Employees Insurance Company
Highlands Insurance Company
Indiana Lumbermens Mutual Insurance Company
Louisiana Insurance Guaranty Association
Michigan Millers Mutual Insurance Company
MSI Preferred Insurance Company
National Indemnity Company
Nationwide Mutual Insurance Company
Shelter Mutual Insurance Company
State Farm Mutual Automobile Insurance Company
United National Insurance Company
United States Fidelity and Guaranty Company
Zurich American Insurance Group

Non-Insurance Clients

Delta Air Lines, Inc.
James Construction Group
Yellow Freight System
Federal Express
NPC International

Partners

Mike C. Sanders — 1953 — Northeast Louisiana University, B.A., 1978; Louisiana State University, J.D., 1981 — Admitted to Bar, 1981, Louisiana; 1982, U.S. District Court, Middle and Western Districts of Louisiana; 1985, U.S. Court of Appeals, Fifth Circuit — Member National, Louisiana State and Fourth Judicial District Bar Associations; Louisiana Association of Defense Counsel; Defense Research Institute

M. Shane Craighead — 1967 — Northeast Louisiana University, B.A. (summa cum laude), 1988; Louisiana State University, J.D., 1992 — Order of the Coif — Senior Editor, Louisiana Law Review, 1991-1992 — Admitted to Bar, 1992, Louisiana — Member Louisiana State and Fourth Judicial District (President, Young Lawyers Section, 1996-1997) Bar Associations; Louisiana Association of Defense Counsel (Director, 2003-2004)

W. David Hammett — 1968 — Northeast Louisiana University, B.B.A., 1991; Loyola University, J.D., 1994 — Moot Court Board — Loyola Law Review — Admitted to Bar, 1994, Louisiana; 1994, U.S. District Court, Eastern, Middle and Western Districts of Louisiana; 1994, U.S. Court of Appeals, Fifth Circuit — Member Louisiana State and Fourth Judicial District Bar Associations; Louisiana Association of Defense Counsel

Carey B. Underwood — 1966 — Northeast Louisiana University, B.A. (cum laude), 1988; Louisiana State University, J.D., 1992 — Order of the Coif; Moot Court Board — Admitted to Bar, 1992, Louisiana; 1992, U.S. District Court, Middle District of Louisiana; 1993, U.S. District Court, Western District of Louisiana; U.S. District Court, Eastern District of Louisiana; U.S. Court of Appeals, Fifth Circuit — Member American, Louisiana State and Fourth Judicial District Bar Associations; Louisiana Association of Defense Counsel

Davenport, Files & Kelly, Monroe, LA   (Continued)

Associates

Lara A. Lane — 1970 — Northeast Louisiana University, B.A., 1999; Louisiana State University, J.D., 2002 — Admitted to Bar, 2002, Louisiana — Member Federal, Louisiana State and Fourth Judicial District Bar Associations; Louisiana Association of Defense Counsel

Ethan A. Hunt — 1979 — Louisiana Tech University, B.S., 2001; Louisiana State University, J.D./B.C.L., 2006 — Admitted to Bar, 2006, Louisiana; U.S. District Court, Eastern, Middle and Western Districts of Louisiana; U.S. Court of Appeals, Fifth Circuit — Member Louisiana State and Fourth Judicial District (Young Lawyers Section) Bar Associations; Defense Research Institute; Louisiana Association of Defense Counsel

John Heath Sullivan — 1985 — University of Louisiana at Monroe, B.B.A. (magna cum laude, with honors), 2010; Mississippi College School of Law, J.D. (magna cum laude, with honors), 2012 — Admitted to Bar, 2012, Louisiana

Of Counsel

Thomas W. Davenport — (1909-1962)

Thomas W. Davenport, Jr. — 1941 — Louisiana State University, J.D., 1965 — Admitted to Bar, 1965, Louisiana

William G. Kelly, Jr. — 1930 — Louisiana State University, J.D., 1954 — Admitted to Bar, 1954, Louisiana

Jack B. Files — 1931 — Louisiana State University, B.S., 1955; J.D., 1957 — Admitted to Bar, 1957, Louisiana

Hayes, Harkey, Smith & Cascio, L.L.P.

2811 Kilpatrick Boulevard
Monroe, Louisiana 71201
  Telephone: 318-387-2422
  Fax: 318-388-5809
  www.hhsclaw.com

(New Orleans, LA Office*: 201 St. Charles Avenue, Suite 2500, 70170)
  (Tel: 504-754-6969)
  (Fax: 504-524-7979)

Accountants, Architects and Engineers, Automobile, Civil Litigation, Commercial Litigation, Construction Liability, Employment Law, Insurance Coverage, Medical Malpractice, Nursing Home Liability, Premises Liability, Product Liability, Professional Liability, Transportation, Trucking Law, Uninsured and Underinsured Motorist, Workers' Compensation

Firm Profile: For over 60 years, Hayes Harkey has been devoted to providing unprecedented service to its clients. The firm has extensive experience defending claims against insurance companies in state and federal courts. Because of this, we have the proven skills to handle your insurance defense litigation.

Insurance Clients

ACE USA
Canal Insurance Company
CNA HealthPro
CNA Insurance Companies
Empire Fire and Marine Insurance Company
State Farm Fire and Casualty Company
Stonington Insurance Company
Western Surety Company
Burlington Insurance Group
Carolina Casualty Insurance Company
Colony Insurance Company
Hanover Insurance Company
Rain & Hail, L.L.C.
State Farm Mutual Automobile Insurance Company
Travelers Insurance Companies
Westport Insurance Corporation

Non-Insurance Clients

ABF Freight System, Inc.
IASIS Healthcare Corporation
P&S Surgical Hospital
Ryder Truck Rental, Inc.
St. Francis Medical Center
T.X.I., Inc.
Glenwood Resolution Authority
Ouachita Community Hospital
Riverwood International Corporation
Swift Transportation Company, Inc.

Partners

Thomas M. Hayes, III — Sewanee, The University of the South, B.A. (with honors), 1974; Louisiana State University, J.D., 1977 — Admitted to Bar,

LOUISIANA   MONROE

Hayes, Harkey, Smith & Cascio, L.L.P., Monroe, LA
(Continued)

1977, Louisiana; U.S. District Court, Middle and Western Districts of Louisiana; U.S. Court of Appeals, Fifth Circuit — Member American, Louisiana State and Fourth Judicial District Bar Associations; Louisiana Law Institute; Louisiana Association of Defense Counsel; Federation of Defense and Corporate Counsel; Association of Insurance Attorneys; Fellow, American Bar Foundation; Fellow, American College of Trial Lawyers

Thomas M. Hayes, IV — University of Richmond, B.A., 2000; Louisiana State University, J.D., 2003 — Admitted to Bar, 2003, Louisiana; U.S. District Court, Eastern, Middle and Western Districts of Louisiana; U.S. Court of Appeals, Fifth Circuit — Member Louisiana State and Fourth Judicial District Bar Associations; Inns of Court; Louisiana Association of Defense Counsel

Bruce McKamy Mintz — Vanderbilt University, B.A., 1973; The University of Mississippi, J.D., 1976 — Admitted to Bar, 1981, Louisiana — Member American and Louisiana State Bar Associations; Louisiana Hospital Attorneys Association; Louisiana Association of Defense Counsel; American Health Lawyers Association

Harry M. Moffett, IV — Tulane University, B.A., 1990; J.D., 1995 — Admitted to Bar, 1995, Louisiana; U.S. District Court, Eastern, Middle and Western Districts of Louisiana; U.S. Court of Appeals, Fifth Circuit — Member American, Louisiana State and Fourth Judicial District Bar Associations; Louisiana Society of Hospital Attorneys; Louisiana Hospital Association; Louisiana Association of Defense Counsel; Defense Research Institute

John C. Roa — Kent State University, B.A. (cum laude), 1980; Mississippi College School of Law, J.D. (summa cum laude), 2000 — Admitted to Bar, 2000, Louisiana — Member Federal, American and Louisiana State Bar Associations; American Inns of Court

C. Joseph Roberts III — Louisiana State University, B.A., 1972; J.D., 1975 — Admitted to Bar, 1975, Louisiana — Member American, Louisiana State and Fourth Judicial District Bar Associations; Louisiana Association of Defense Counsel; American Inns of Court

John B. Saye — Millsaps College, B.A., 1986; Louisiana State University, J.D., 1989 — Admitted to Bar, 1989, Louisiana — Member American, Louisiana State and Fourth Judicial District Bar Associations; Louisiana Association of Defense Counsel; International Association of Defense Counsel

Associates

Laura S. Achord
Paul F. Lensing
Brandon W. Creekbaum

Clint R. Hanchey
Fred Scott Franklin, Jr.

Hudson, Potts & Bernstein L.L.P.

1800 Hudson Lane, Suite 300
Monroe, Louisiana 71201
Telephone: 318-388-4400
Fax: 318-388-2758
www.hpblaw.com

General Liability, Insurance Coverage, Insurance Defense, Medical Malpractice, Product Liability, Professional Liability, Subrogation, Toxic Torts, Transportation, Workers' Compensation, Employment

Firm Profile: Hudson, Potts & Bernstein is the oldest and largest law firm in northeast Louisiana. Our rich history, strong knowledge of Louisiana courts and laws, and trusted client relationships are hallmarks of our business.

Insurance Clients

Allstate Insurance Company
American Resources Insurance Company, Inc.
Church Mutual Insurance Company
Liberty Mutual Insurance Company
Markel International, Ltd.
Professional Claims Service
Risk Management Services, L.L.C.
USAgencies Casualty Insurance Company, Inc.

American Century Casualty Company
Blue Cross of Louisiana
Direct Adjusting Company, Inc.
Louisiana Workers' Compensation Corporation
Risk Management, Inc.
Shelter Mutual Insurance Company

Partners

Gordon L. James — Northeast Louisiana University, B.A., 1976; Louisiana State University, J.D., 1979 — Omicron Delta Kappa, Phi Eta Sigma, Phi Alpha Theta, Order of the Coif — Louisiana Law Review, 1978-1979 — Admitted to Bar, 1979, Louisiana — Member Louisiana State Bar Association;

Hudson, Potts & Bernstein L.L.P., Monroe, LA
(Continued)

Defense Research Institute; Louisiana Association of Defense Counsel — E-mail: gjames@hpblaw.com

Robert M. Baldwin — Louisiana Tech University, B.A., 1979; Louisiana State University and A & M College, J.D., 1982 — Moot Court Board — Admitted to Bar, 1982, Louisiana — Member Louisiana State Bar Association; Louisiana Trial Lawyers Association; Association of Trial Lawyers of America; Defense Research Institute; Louisiana Association of Defense Counsel — E-mail: rbaldwin@hpblaw.com

Charles W. Herold, III — University of Louisiana at Monroe, B.B.A., 1983; The University of Mississippi, J.D., 1986 — Admitted to Bar, 1986, Louisiana — Member Louisiana State Bar Asssociation; Fred J. Fudickar American Inn of Court; Louisiana Association of Defense Counsel — Assistant Bar Examiner — E-mail: cherold@hpblaw.com

Jay P. Adams — Louisiana State University, B.S., 1985; J.D., 1988 — Delta Theta Phi — Admitted to Bar, 1988, Louisiana — Member Louisiana State Bar Association; Defense Research Institute; Louisiana Association of Defense Counsel — E-mail: jadams@hpblaw.com

Brian P. Bowes — Southeastern Louisiana University, B.A. (cum laude), 1987; Tulane University Law School, J.D., 1990 — Omicron Delta Epsilon, Phi Alpha Delta — Admitted to Bar, 1990, Louisiana — Member Louisiana State Bar Association; Fred J. Fudickar American Inn of Court (Master of the Bench); Louisiana Association of Self Insured Employers; Louisiana Nursing Home Association; Louisiana Association of Business and Industry; Louisiana Association of Defense Counsel — E-mail: bbowes@hpblaw.com

Jan Peter Christiansen — Louisiana Tech University, B.S., 1987; Tulane University Law School, J.D., 1990 — Admitted to Bar, 1990, Louisiana — Member Louisiana State Bar Association (House of Delegates, 1998-2000); Louisiana Association of Defense Counsel; Defense Research Institute — E-mail: jpchris@hpblaw.com

Nelson Zentner Sartor and Snellings, LLC

1507 Royal Avenue
Monroe, Louisiana 71201
Telephone: 318-388-4454
Fax: 318-388-4447
E-Mail: nzss@nzsslaw.com
www.nzsslaw.com

Commercial Litigation, Insurance Defense, Professional Liability, Collections

Insurance Clients

America First/One Beacon Insurance Company
Colonial Insurance Company
EMC Insurance Companies
GE Insurance Company
Kemper/Unitrin
Louisiana Farm Bureau Insurance Companies
Louisiana Medical Mutual Insurance Company
Progressive Insurance Company
The Republic Group
StoneTrust Commercial Insurance Company

Arch Insurance Group
Chartis Insurance
Crawford & Company
Farmers Insurance Group
Hartford Insurance Company
Liberty Mutual Insurance Company
Louisiana Insurance Guaranty Association
Maxum Insurance Company
Metropolitan Property and Casualty Insurance Company
State Farm Mutual Automobile Insurance Company

Non-Insurance Clients

Brookshire Grocery Company
Jackson Parish Hospital
J.D. Byrider Systems, Inc.
Marlin Firearms Company
Ouachita Parish Policy Jury
Republic Financial Services, Inc.
St. Francis Medical Center
Trenton Loans

House of Raeford Farms, Inc. of Louisiana
Lincoln Parish Police Jury
Morehouse General Hospital
Remington Arms Company
Ride Time, Inc.
State of Louisiana

Members

David H. Nelson — 1955 — Louisiana Tech University, B.S., 1977; Louisiana State University, J.D., 1981 — Admitted to Bar, 1981, Louisiana — Member Louisiana State Bar Association (District Seven Representative, 1986-1987;

Nelson Zentner Sartor and Snellings, LLC, Monroe, LA (Continued)

Chairman, Young Lawyers Section, 1989); Defense Research Institute; International Association of Defense Counsel; Louisiana Association of Defense Counsel

Thomas G. Zentner, Jr. — 1957 — Centenary College, B.A., 1979; Louisiana State University and A & M College, J.D., 1982 — Admitted to Bar, 1982, Louisiana — Member American Bar Association; Louisiana State Bar Association (District Seven Representative, Young Lawyers Section, 1988-1990; House of Delegates Representative, 1991-1993; District Seven Representative, Board of Governors, 1994-1997); Defense Research Institute; Louisiana Association of Defense Counsel

F. Williams Sartor, Jr. — 1961 — Northeast Louisiana University, B.B.A., 1985; Loyola Law School, J.D., 1988 — Admitted to Bar, 1988, Louisiana — Member Federal, American, Louisiana State and Fourth Judicial District Bar Associations; Louisiana Association of Defense Counsel; Defense Research Institute

George M. Snellings, IV — 1966 — Louisiana State University and A & M College, B.S., 1988; Mississippi College School of Law, J.D., 1993 — Admitted to Bar, 1994, Louisiana; Mississippi — Member Federal, American, Louisiana State and Fourth Judicial District Bar Associations; The Mississippi Bar; Louisiana Association of Defense Counsel

Associates

Allison McCain Jarrell — 1975 — Northeast Louisiana University, B.B.A., 1997; Mississippi College School of Law, J.D., 2001 — Admitted to Bar, 2001, Louisiana — Member Federal, American, Louisiana State and Fourth Judicial District (President, Young Lawyers Section) Bar Associations

Charlen Trascher Campbell — 1974 — Louisiana State University, B.A. (cum laude), 1996; J.D., 1999 — Admitted to Bar, 1999, Louisiana — Member Louisiana State and Fourth Judicial District Bar Associations; Fred Fudickar American Inns of Court — Qualified Family Law Mediator and General Civil Mediator, Louisiana Mediation Act — Practice Areas: Family Law; Bankruptcy; Collections; Insurance Defense

The following firms also service this area.

Hailey, McNamara, Hall, Larmann & Papale, L.L.P.
One Galleria Boulevard, Suite 1400
Metairie, Louisiana 70001
   Telephone: 504-836-6500
   Fax: 504-836-6565
Mailing Address: P.O. Box 8288, Metairie, LA 70011-8288

Admiralty and Maritime Law, Commercial Litigation, Construction Litigation, Employment Practices Liability, Insurance Litigation, Product Liability, Professional Malpractice, Toxic Torts, Casualty, Insurance Coverage, Intellectual Property, Premises Liability, Transportation, Mass Tort, Property, Workers' Compensation, Automobile Liability, Appellate, Environmental

SEE COMPLETE LISTING UNDER METAIRIE, LOUISIANA (278 MILES)

Perkins & Associates, L.L.C.
401 Market Street, Suite 900
Shreveport, Louisiana 71101
   Telephone: 318-222-2426
   Fax: 318-222-0458

Commercial Litigation, Trucking Litigation, Estate Planning, Insurance Defense, Commercial Vehicle, Trucking Law, Professional Malpractice, Employment Law, Workers' Compensation, Bodily Injury, Product Liability, Errors and Omissions, General Liability, Subrogation

SEE COMPLETE LISTING UNDER SHREVEPORT, LOUISIANA (98 MILES)

NATCHITOCHES † 18,323 Natchitoches Par.

Refer To

Perkins & Associates, L.L.C.
401 Market Street, Suite 900
Shreveport, Louisiana 71101
   Telephone: 318-222-2426
   Fax: 318-222-0458

Commercial Litigation, Trucking Litigation, Estate Planning, Insurance Defense, Commercial Vehicle, Trucking Law, Professional Malpractice, Employment Law, Workers' Compensation, Bodily Injury, Product Liability, Errors and Omissions, General Liability, Subrogation

SEE COMPLETE LISTING UNDER SHREVEPORT, LOUISIANA (77 MILES)

NEW ORLEANS † 343,829 Orleans Par.

Adams Hoefer Holwadel, LLC
400 Poydras Street, Suite 2450
New Orleans, Louisiana 70130
   Telephone: 504-581-2606
   Fax: 504-525-1488
   E-Mail: tsd@ahhelaw.com
   www.ahhelaw.com

Established: 1987

Insurance Defense, Coverage Issues, Coverage Analysis, Automobile, Uninsured and Underinsured Motorist, Product Liability, General Liability, Professional Liability, Workers' Compensation, Personal Injury, Property Damage, Errors and Omissions, Marine Liability

Insurance Clients

American International Specialty Lines Insurance
Commercial Underwriters Insurance Company
Homeport Insurance Company
Liberty Mutual Insurance Company
Mercury Insurance Group
Progressive Insurance Company
St. Paul Reinsurance Company Limited
York Claims Service, Inc.
Arch Insurance Company
Certain Underwriters at Lloyd's
Farmers Insurance Group
Fulcrum Insurance Company
Interstate Insurance Group
Lloyd's Market Insurance Companies
Royal & Sun Alliance Insurance
Trinity Universal Insurance Company

Non-Insurance Clients

Beech Aircraft Corporation
Burlington Resources, Inc.
El Paso Energy Corporation
International Gaming Technologies
Nexen Petroleum USA, Inc.
Phoenix Aviation Managers, Inc.
Stevedoring Services of America (SSA Marine, Inc.)
Bell Helicopter Textron Inc.
ChevronTexaco
ExxonMobil Corporation
Michelin North America, Inc.
Penske Truck Leasing
Sears, Roebuck and Co.

Firm Members

Bruce R. Hoefer, Jr. — 1954 — Louisiana State University, B.S., 1976; J.D., 1980 — Admitted to Bar, 1980, Louisiana; 1992, Texas; 1980, U.S. District Court, Eastern District of Louisiana; 1981, U.S. District Court, Middle and Western Districts of Louisiana; 1981, U.S. Court of Appeals, Fifth Circuit; 1986, U.S. Supreme Court — Member Federal, American and Louisiana State Bar Associations; Houston Mariners Club; The Maritime Law Association of the United States; Louisiana Association of Defense Counsel

D. Russell Holwadel — 1959 — The University of Mississippi, B.B.A., 1981; J.D., 1984 — Admitted to Bar, 1984, Mississippi; 1985, Louisiana — Member Louisiana State and New Orleans Bar Associations; The Mississippi Bar; Louisiana Association of Defense Counsel

Associates

Ira J. Rosenzweig — 1960 — Tulane University, B.A., 1982; Loyola University, J.D., 1985 — Clerk to Hon. Chief Justice John Dixon, Louisiana Supreme Court — Editor-in-Chief, Loyola Law Review — Admitted to Bar, 1985, Louisiana; 1985, U.S. District Court, Eastern District of Louisiana; 1987, U.S. District Court, Western District of Louisiana; 1988, U.S. Court of Appeals, Fifth Circuit; 1991, U.S. Supreme Court; 1994, U.S. Court of Appeals for the District of Columbia Circuit; 1997, U.S. District Court, Middle District of Louisiana — Member Louisiana State and New Orleans Bar Associations; DOL-Joint Bar Association; International Association of Gaming Attorneys — Practice Areas: Longshore and Harbor Workers' Compensation; Insurance Law; Energy; Gaming Law

Phillip J. Rew — Georgetown University, B.A., 1991; Case Western Reserve University, J.D., 1998 — Admitted to Bar, 1998, Louisiana; 2001, U.S. District Court, Eastern District of Louisiana; 2003, U.S. District Court, Middle and Western Districts of Louisiana — Member Louisiana State and New Orleans Bar Associations; Louisiana Association of Defense Counsel — Languages: Spanish — Practice Areas: Insurance Defense

Heather England Reznik — 1978 — University of Michigan, B.A., 2000; University of Colorado Law School, J.D., 2004 — Admitted to Bar, 2004, Louisiana; 2006, Colorado; 2007, U.S. District Court, Eastern District of

LOUISIANA

Adams Hoefer Holwadel, LLC, New Orleans, LA (Continued)

Louisiana — Member Louisiana State and New Orleans Bar Associations; Louisiana Association of Defense Counsel — Practice Areas: Insurance Litigation; Casualty

Gregory O. Currier — 1957 — The University of New Orleans, B.A., 1982; Tulane University Law School, J.D., 1985 — Admitted to Bar, 1985, Louisiana; 1991, Mississippi; U.S. District Court, Eastern, Middle and Western Districts of Louisiana; U.S. District Court, Northern and Southern Districts of Mississippi — Member Louisiana State and New Orleans Bar Associations; The Mississippi Bar; Louisiana Association of Defense Counsel — Practice Areas: Insurance Defense; Product Liability; Oil and Gas

Of Counsel

Robert M. Johnston — 1941 — University of Notre Dame, B.A., 1963; Tulane University Law School, J.D., 1966 — Tulane Moot Court Board — Admitted to Bar, 1966, Louisiana — Member Louisiana State and New Orleans Bar Associations; Louisiana Association of Defense Counsel; International Association of Defense Counsel; Defense Research Institute — Certified Mediator

Jesse R. Adams, Jr. — 1941 — The University of Mississippi, J.D., 1967 — Admitted to Bar, 1967, Mississippi; 1969, Louisiana; 1993, Texas — Member New Orleans Bar Association

Beirne, Maynard & Parsons, LLP

Pan-American Life Center
601 Poydras Street, Suite 2200
New Orleans, Louisiana 70130
   Telephone: 504-586-1241
   Fax: 504-584-9142
   E-Mail: info@bmpllp.com
   www.bmpllp.com

(Houston, TX Office*: 1300 Post Oak Boulevard, Suite 2500, 77056)
   (Tel: 713-623-0887)
   (Fax: 713-960-1527)
(Dallas, TX Office*: 1700 Pacific Avenue, Suite 4400, 75201)
   (Tel: 214-237-4300)
   (Fax: 214-237-4340)
(San Antonio, TX Office*: Weston Centre, 112 East Pecan Street, Suite 2750, 78205)
   (Tel: 210-582-0220)
   (Fax: 210-582-0231)
(Austin, TX Office: 401 West 15th Street, Suite 845, 78701)
   (Tel: 512-623-6700)
   (Fax: 512-623-6701)

Insurance Defense, Product Liability, Commercial Litigation, Mass Tort, Environmental, Maritime

Partner

Hal C. Welch — Louisiana State University, B.A., 1974; Louisiana State University Law Center, J.D. (Order of the Coif), 1977 — Admitted to Bar, 1977, Louisiana; 2007, Texas — Member Louisiana State Bar Association; State Bar of Texas; Louisiana Association of Defense Counsel; The Maritime Law Association of the United States

Marne A. Jones — University of Missouri, B.A. (cum laude), 2004; Tulane University Law School, J.D. (magna cum laude), 2007 — Admitted to Bar, 2007, Arizona; 2009, Louisiana

(See listing under Houston, TX for additional information)

Bienvenu, Foster, Ryan & O'Bannon, LLC

1010 Common Street, Suite 2200
New Orleans, Louisiana 70112
   Telephone: 504-310-1500, 504-581-2146
   Fax: 504-310-1501, 504-522-7859
   www.bienvenufoster.com

NEW ORLEANS

Bienvenu, Foster, Ryan & O'Bannon, LLC, New Orleans, LA (Continued)

Established: 1952

Insurance Law, Trial Practice, Subrogation

Representative Clients

Boh Bros. Construction Company, L.L.C.
GAB Robins North America, Inc.
J. Caldarera & Co., Inc.
Landis Construction Co., LLC
NOLA Restaurant Group, LLC
NOLA Ventures, LLC
Caillouet Land Corporation
Critical Mass Holdings, LLC
GAF-Elk Corporation
Lafourche Realty Company, Inc.
New Orleans Private Patrol Services, Inc.

Representative Insurance Clients

Audubon Insurance Company
Central Mutual Insurance Company
Chartis-Global Recovery Services
CNA Insurance Company
Crum & Forster Insurance Group
Hanover Insurance Company
Industrial Risk Insurers
Markel American Insurance Company
New Hampshire Insurance Company
RLI Insurance Company
Safeco Insurance
TransGuard Insurance Company of America, Inc.
Western World Insurance Group
York Risk Services Group, Inc.
Berkley Risk Administrators Company, LLC
Chubb Group of Insurance Companies
Fireman's Fund Insurance Companies
Louisiana Citizens Property Insurance Corporation
National Chiropractic Mutual Insurance Company
Property Insurance Association of Louisiana
Swett & Crawford Group
Travelers Insurance Companies
United Services Automobile Association (USAA)
Zurich American Insurance Group

Founding Partners

P. A. Bienvenu — (1911-1984)

John M. Culver — (1910-1974)

Robert N. Ryan — (1931-2002)

H. F. Foster, III — (1925-2013)

In Memoriam

Hugh M. Glenn, Jr. — (1932-2010)

Michael F. Bollman — (1959-2012)

Members of the Firm

P. Albert Bienvenu, Jr. — 1948 — Louisiana State University, J.D., 1973 — Admitted to Bar, 1973, Louisiana — Member American, Louisiana State and New Orleans Bar Associations — E-mail: ABienvenu@bfrob.com

Gregory J. McDonald — 1958 — Georgetown University, J.D., 1983 — Admitted to Bar, 1983, Louisiana; 1991, Florida — Member American and Louisiana State Bar Associations; The Florida Bar; Federation of Defense and Corporate Counsel; Defense Research Institute — E-mail: GMcDonald@bfrob.com

John W. Waters, Jr. — 1950 — Louisiana State University, J.D., 1975 — Admitted to Bar, 1975, Louisiana — Member American, Louisiana State and New Orleans Bar Associations; Fellow, American College of Trial Lawyers; International Association of Defense Counsel; Defense Research Institute — E-mail: JWaters@bfrob.com

Special Counsel

Ernest L. O'Bannon — 1934 — Tulane University, LL.B., 1960 — Admitted to Bar, 1960, Louisiana — Member Federal, American, Louisiana State and New Orleans Bar Associations; Federation of Defense and Corporate Counsel; Fellow, American College of Trial Lawyers — E-mail: EObannon@bfrob.com

Leonard A. Young — 1941 — The University of Mississippi, J.D., 1965 — Admitted to Bar, 1965, Mississippi; 1966, Louisiana — Member American and Louisiana State Bar Associations; Mississippi State Bar — E-mail: LYoung@bfrob.com

Of Counsel

David E. Walle — 1947 — Louisiana State University, J.D., 1973 — Admitted to Bar, 1973, Louisiana — Member Louisiana State Bar Association; Louisiana Association of Defense Counsel — E-mail: DWalle@bfrob.com

NEW ORLEANS   LOUISIANA

Bienvenu, Foster, Ryan & O'Bannon, LLC, New Orleans, LA (Continued)

Associates

Peter E. Castaing
Robin C. O'Bannon

Kristin G. Mosely Jones

Brown Sims, P.C.

Poydras Center, Suite 2200
650 Poydras Street
New Orleans, Louisiana 70130-7239
  Telephone: 504-569-1007
  Fax: 504-569-9255

(Houston, TX Office*: Tenth Floor, 1177 West Loop South, 77027-9030)
  (Tel: 713-629-1580)
  (Fax: 713-629-5027)
  (E-Mail: firm@brownsims.com)
  (www.brownsims.com)
(Miami, FL Office*: 9130 South Dadeland Boulevard, Suite 1600, 33156-7851)
  (Tel: 305-274-5507)
  (Fax: 305-274-5517)
(Gulfport, MS Office*: 2304 19th Street, Suite 101, 39501)
  (Tel: 228-867-8711)
  (Fax: 228-867-8712)

Insurance Defense, Trial and Appellate Practice, Admiralty and Maritime Law, Insurance Coverage, Construction Litigation, Product Liability, Premises Liability, Negligence, Employment Law, Casualty Defense, Professional Liability, Toxic Torts, Environmental Law, Workers' Compensation, Longshore and Harbor Workers' Compensation

(See listing under Houston, TX for additional information)

Kevin Christensen & Associates, LLC

Pan American Life Center
601 Poydras Street, Suite 2335
New Orleans, Louisiana 70130
  Telephone: 504-528-8878
  Fax: 866-524-5076
  E-Mail: kjc@kevinchristensen.net
  www.kcalaw.net

Admiralty and Maritime Law, Construction Defect, Professional Liability, Product Liability, Employment Law (Management Side), Defense Litigation, Insurance Defense

Insurance Clients

CNA Global Resource Managers
State Auto Insurance Company
Zurich American Insurance Group

National Automotive Insurance Company

Non-Insurance Clients

J. C. Penney Company, Inc.

Managing Shareholder

Kevin J. Christensen — 1958 — University of Michigan, B.G.S., 1982; Tulane University Law School, J.D., 1995; LL.M., 2002 — Phi Delta Phi — Senior Editor, Tulane Journal of International and Comparative Law, 1994-1995 — Admitted to Bar, 1995, Louisiana; 2006, Tennessee; 2009, Florida; 2013, Texas; 1995, U.S. District Court, Eastern, Middle and Western Districts of Louisiana; U.S. Court of Appeals, Fifth and Eleventh Circuits; 2001, U.S. Supreme Court; 2002, U.S. District Court, Eastern and Northern Districts of Texas; 2004, U.S. District Court, Northern District of Florida; 2006, U.S. District Court, Western District of Tennessee; U.S. District Court, Middle District of Florida — Member Federal, American, Louisiana State, Tennessee, Fifth Federal Circuit and New Orleans Bar Associations; Inn of Court; Defense Research Institute; Louisiana Association of Defense Counsel;

Kevin Christensen & Associates, LLC, New Orleans, LA (Continued)

Southeastern Admiralty Law Institute; The Maritime Law Association of the United States — Author: "Of Comity: Aerospatiale As Lex Maritima", 2 Loy. Mar. L.J. 1 (2003).

Degan, Blanchard & Nash

Texaco Center, Suite 2600
400 Poydras Street
New Orleans, Louisiana 70130
  Telephone: 504-529-3333
  Fax: 504-529-3337
  E-Mail: SDegan@Degan.com
  www.degan.com

(Baton Rouge, LA Office*: 6421 Perkins Road, Building C, Suite B, 70808)
  (Tel: 225-610-1110)
  (Fax: 225-610-1220)

Established: 1991

Insurance Defense, Commercial Law, General Liability, Bodily Injury, Property Damage, Insurance Coverage, Admiralty and Maritime Law, Environmental Law, Energy, Toxic Torts, Professional Liability, Workers' Compensation, Subrogation, Casualty, Commercial Litigation, Construction Defect, Medical Malpractice, Product Liability, Pharmaceutical, Medical Products Litigation, Trucking, Commercial Vehicle, Appeals, Arbitration, Class Actions, Collections, First Amendment, Media Law, Longshore and Harbor Workers' Compensation, Municipal Law, Civil Rights Defense, Exposure, Insurance Bad Faith, Employment Practices Exposures, Trials in All Courts, Defense Base Act

Firm Profile: Degan, Blanchard & Nash is a dynamic, full service, client-oriented firm actively engaged in a diverse litigation practice. Degan, Blanchard & Nash is dedicated to and focused on providing each client with the highest level of legal services rendered in the most efficient and cost-effective manner and takes pride in its responsiveness to the needs of its clients. Our attorneys and staff are a dedicated, hard-working and skilled team of professionals whose collective goal is serving our clients. The firm's size and practice has grown over the years due to its ability to adapt to the ever changing needs of its clients and to provide high quality legal representation.

Insurance Clients

American International Group, Inc.
Empire Fire and Marine Insurance Company
First Financial Insurance Company
Great Central Insurance Company
Lloyd's

Chubb Group of Insurance Companies
Fireman's Fund Insurance Company
Homestead Insurance Company
William H. McGee & Company, Inc.

Partners

Sidney W. Degan, III — 1954 — The University of New Orleans, B.A. (with distinction), 1977; Tulane University, J.D., 1980 — Admitted to Bar, 1981, Louisiana; U.S. District Court, Eastern, Middle and Western Districts of Louisiana; 1990, U.S. District Court, Eastern District of Texas; U.S. Court of Appeals, Fifth and Eleventh Circuits — Member Federal, Louisiana State and New Orleans Bar Associations; Proctor, Maritime Law Association of the United States; International Society of Primerus Law Firms; Professional Liability Defense Institute; National Workers' Compensation Defense Network; The Maritime Law Association of the United States; Louisiana Association of Defense Counsel; Defense Research Institute — E-mail: SDegan@Degan.com

R. Edward Blanchard — 1950 — Louisiana State University and A & M College, B.S., 1972; J.D., 1981 — Admitted to Bar, 1981, Louisiana; U.S. District Court, Eastern, Middle and Western Districts of Louisiana; U.S. Court of Appeals, Fifth and Eleventh Circuits — Member Federal, American, Louisiana State and New Orleans Bar Associations; Louisiana Association of Defense Counsel; The Maritime Law Association of the United States

Foster P. Nash, III — 1963 — Louisiana State University, B.A., 1985; Loyola University, J.D., 1988 — Admitted to Bar, 1988, Louisiana; U.S. District

Degan, Blanchard & Nash, New Orleans, LA (Continued)

Court, Eastern, Middle and Western Districts of Louisiana; U.S. Court of Appeals, Fifth Circuit — Member Louisiana State and New Orleans Bar Associations; Louisiana Association of Defense Counsel; The Maritime Law Association of the United States — E-mail: FNash@Degan.com

James A. Rowell — 1951 — University of Southern Mississippi, B.S., 1974; University of California, J.D., 1988 — Admitted to Bar, 1988, California; 1992, Louisiana; U.S. District Court, Eastern, Middle and Western Districts of Louisiana; U.S. District Court, Central, Northern and Southern Districts of California; U.S. Court of Appeals, Ninth Circuit — Member American and Louisiana State Bar Associations; State Bar of California

Julia A. Dietz — 1958 — Georgetown University, A.B., 1980; J.D., 1988 — Admitted to Bar, 1988, Louisiana; U.S. District Court, Eastern, Middle and Western Districts of Louisiana; 1991, U.S. Court of Appeals, Fifth Circuit; 1993, U.S. Court of Appeals, Fourth and Eighth Circuits — Member Louisiana State Bar Association

Jeffrey C. Brennan — 1971 — Tulane University, B.A., 1993; Loyola University, J.D., 1998 — Admitted to Bar, 1998, Louisiana; U.S. District Court, Eastern, Middle and Western Districts of Louisiana; U.S. District Court, Eastern and Southern Districts of Texas; U.S. District Court, Southern District of Mississippi; U.S. Court of Appeals, Fifth Circuit — Member New Orleans Bar Association — E-mail: JBrennan@Degan.com

Brian W. Harrell — 1975 — Tulane University Law School, J.D., 2001 — Law Clerk to the Hon. Douglas M. Gonzales, Louisiana First Circuit Court of Appeals — Admitted to Bar, 2003, Louisiana; 2012, Texas — Practice Areas: Civil Litigation — Tel: 225-610-1110 — Fax: 225-610-1220 — E-mail: BHarrell@Degan.com

Of Counsel

Travis L. Bourgeois — 1966 — Tulane University, B.A., 1989; Katholieke Universiteit Leuven, Belgium, M.A. (with honors), 1991; Tulane University Law School, J.D., 1994 — Admitted to Bar, 1994, Louisiana; U.S. District Court, Eastern, Middle and Western Districts of Louisiana; U.S. Court of Appeals, Fifth Circuit; U.S. Court of Appeals, Sixth Circuit; U.S. Supreme Court — E-mail: TBourgeois@Degan.com

Keith A. Kornman — 1969 — Duke University, B.A., 1991; Tulane University Law School, J.D. (cum laude), 1994 — Admitted to Bar, 1994, Louisiana; 2001, Texas — Member Federal Bar Association

Jena W. Smith — 1971 — Louisiana State University, B.A. (with honors), 1993; Tulane University Law School, J.D. (Order of the Coif), 1997 — Admitted to Bar, 1997, Louisiana; U.S. District Court, Eastern, Middle and Western Districts of Louisiana; U.S. Court of Appeals, Fifth and Eleventh Circuits — E-mail: JSmith@Degan.com

Karl H. Schmid — 1966 — Cornell University, B.S., 1988; Loyola University New Orleans, M.A./J.D., 1997; The University of North Carolina at Chapel Hill, Ph.D., 2001 — Law Clerk to Hon. Judge DeMoss, U.S. District Court of Appeals for the Fifth Circuit; Hon. Judge Lemmon, U.S. District Court for the Eastern District of Louisiana — Admitted to Bar, 1997, Louisiana; 2003, Texas; U.S. District Court, Eastern and Western Districts of Louisiana; U.S. District Court, Northern and Southern Districts of Texas; U.S. Court of Appeals, Fifth Circuit — E-mail: KSchmid@Degan.com

Renee F. Smith — 1968 — Loyola University New Orleans, B.A., 1990; Loyola University New Orleans College of Law, J.D./M.A., 1994 — Honoree, New Orleans City Business Leadership in Law Award (2008) — Admitted to Bar, 1995, Louisiana; 2001, Texas; 2001, U.S. District Court, Eastern, Middle and Western Districts of Louisiana; 2008, U.S. District Court, Southern District of Texas; U.S. Court of Appeals, Fifth Circuit — Member Louisiana State Bar Association; State Bar of Texas; Louisiana Association of Defense Counsel; New Orleans Association of Defense Counsel — AV Rated by Mardindale-Hubble — E-mail: RSmith@Degan.com

Associates

Richard C. Badeaux — 1958 — Tulane School of Public Health and Tropical Medicine; Loyola University, J.D., 1992 — Admitted to Bar, 1992, Louisiana; U.S. District Court, Eastern, Middle and Western Districts of Louisiana — Member Louisiana State Bar Association — E-mail: RBadeaux@Degan.com

Eric D. Burt — 1970 — Southeastern Louisiana University, B.A., 1999; Paul M Hebert Law School at Louisiana State University, J.D., 2005 — Associate Justice, Moot Court Board, 2005 — Admitted to Bar, 2005, Louisiana — Member American and Louisiana State Bar Associations; Louisiana Association of Defense Counsel — Resident Baton Rouge Office — Tel: 225-610-1110 — Fax: 225-610-1220 — E-mail: EBurt@Degan.com

John W. Strange — 1979 — Louisiana State University, B.S.B.A., 2003;

Degan, Blanchard & Nash, New Orleans, LA (Continued)

Mississippi College School of Law, J.D., 2006 — Law School Fellowship — Admitted to Bar, 2007, Louisiana — Member American and Louisiana State Bar Associations — E-mail: JStrange@Degan.com

Maryann G. Hoskins — 1966 — Newcomb College, Tulane University, B.A., 1988; Tulane University Law School, J.D., 1991 — Admitted to Bar, 1991, Louisiana; U.S. District Court, Eastern and Middle Districts of Louisiana — E-mail: MHoskins@Degan.com

Stephanie L. Cheralla — 1978 — The University of New Orleans, B.A., 2000; Loyola University New Orleans, J.D., 2007 — Advocate on National Championship Team at ABA National Criminal Trial Competition (2007) — Admitted to Bar, 2008, Louisiana; U.S. District Court, Eastern, Middle and Western Districts of Louisiana; U.S. Court of Appeals, Fifth Circuit — Member American and Louisiana State Bar Associations — Super Lawyers Rising Star in General Litigation (2012) — Common Law — E-mail: SCheralla@Degan.com

Carolyn C. Kolbe — 1981 — University of Florida, B.S., 2002; Loyola University, J.D., 2007 — Admitted to Bar, 2008, Louisiana — Practice Areas: Insurance Litigation — E-mail: CKolbe@Degan.com

Emily R. Adler — 1982 — The University of Georgia, B.B.A., 2005; Loyola University New Orleans College of Law, J.D., 2008 — Admitted to Bar, 2008, Louisiana; 2009, U.S. District Court, Eastern, Middle and Western Districts of Louisiana — Member American and Louisiana State Bar Associations — Practice Areas: Insurance Litigation — E-mail: EAdler@Degan.com

Mary K. Cryar — 1970 — Louisiana State University, B.A., 1992; J.D., 1995; DePaul University, M.B.A., 2008 — Admitted to Bar, 1996, Louisiana; 2003, Illinois — E-mail: MCryar@Degan.com

Micah A. Gautreaux — 1977 — Louisiana State University, B.A., 2000; Louisiana State University, Paul M. Hebert Law Center, J.D./B.C.L., 2006 — Admitted to Bar, 2006, Louisiana — E-mail: MGautreaux@Degan.com

Jill R. Menard — Loyola University New Orleans, B.A. (magna cum laude), 2005; Loyola University New Orleans College of Law, J.D., 2010 — Phi Alpha Delta Legal Fraternity — Admitted to Bar, 2011, Louisiana; 2012, U.S. District Court, Eastern District of Louisiana — Member American, Louisiana State and New Orleans Bar Associations; Association for Women Attorneys — E-mail: jmenard@degan.com

Nicholas J. Cenac — University of Washington, B.A. (magna cum laude), 2009; Tulane University Law School, J.D. (magna cum laude), 2012 — Maritime Law Certificate; Order of Barristers (Honorary 2013) — Admitted to Bar, 2012, Louisiana; 2013, U.S. District Court, Eastern, Middle and Western Districts of Louisiana; U.S. Court of Appeals, Fifth Circuit — Member Federal and Louisiana State (Legal Services for Persons with Disabilities Committee) Bar Associations — Practice Areas: Insurance Defense; Admiralty and Maritime Law — E-mail: ncenac@degan.com

Catherine N. Thigpen — 1978 — Louisiana State University, B.A., 2001; Loyola University New Orleans College of Law, J.D. (cum laude), 2005 — Admitted to Bar, 2005, Louisiana; U.S. District Court, Eastern, Middle and Western Districts of Louisiana — Member American, Louisiana State and New Orleans Bar Associations — Practice Areas: Insurance Coverage; Insurance Defense — E-mail: cthigpen@degan.com

Ashley E. Gilbert — Louisiana State University, B.A., 2000; Louisiana State University, Paul M. Hebert Law Center, J.D./B.C.L., 2004 — Admitted to Bar, 2004, Louisiana; U.S. District Court, Eastern, Middle and Western Districts of Louisiana; U.S. Court of Appeals, Fifth Circuit — Member Louisiana State Bar Association; Louisiana Association of Defense Counsel — Practice Areas: Casualty; Product Liability; Insurance Coverage; Commercial Litigation; Professional Liability — E-mail: egilbert@degan.com

DeRouen Law Firm

Poydras Center, Suite 2230
650 Poydras Street
New Orleans, Louisiana 70115
  Telephone: 504-274-3660
  Fax: 504-274-3664
  E-Mail: pderouen@derouenlaw.com
  www.derouenlaw.com

Established: 2009

NEW ORLEANS   **LOUISIANA**

DeRouen Law Firm, New Orleans, LA   (Continued)

Transportation, Truck Liability, Motor Carriers, Commercial Litigation, Fraud, Automobile, Excess and Reinsurance, Extra-Contractual Litigation, Fire, First and Third Party Defense, General Liability, Insurance Coverage, Business Interruption, Property and Casualty, Self-Insured, Uninsured and Underinsured Motorist, Arbitration, Insurance Defense, Arson, Casualty, Civil Litigation, Personal Injury, Premises Liability, Governmental Liability, Insurance Bad Faith, Construction, Katrina Work

Firm Profile: DeRouen Law Firm is a New Orleans-based litigation firm represents local, national and international insurers and businesses with interests in Louisiana. Our lawyers routinely practice in all state and federal courts throughout Louisiana. We deliver exceptional legal services with a combination of energy, integrity, ingenuity, insight and determination.

Insurance Clients

Allstate Insurance Company
Canal Insurance Company
OneBeacon Insurance
Pelican General Agency/Gemini Insurance Company
Armed Forces Insurance Exchange
Carolina Casualty Insurance Company
State Farm Fire and Casualty Company

Non-Insurance Clients

St. Bernard Parish Government

Owner

Patrick D. DeRouen — Loyola University, B.B.A., 1985; M.B.A., 1990; Tulane University, J.D. (cum laude), 1990 — Member Federal, American (Sections: TIPS, Commercial Transportation Committee), Louisiana State and New Orleans Bar Associations — E-mail: pderouen@derouenlaw.com

Associate

Laurie L. DeArmound — Colgate University, B.A., 1996; Loyola University Law School, J.D., 1999; University of San Diego, LL.M., 2000 — Member American and Louisiana State Bar Associations — E-mail: ldearmound@derouenlaw.com

Evans & Clesi, PLC
336 Lafayette Street, Suite 200
New Orleans, Louisiana 70130
  Telephone: 504-523-8523
  Fax: 504-523-8522
  E-Mail: info@evansandclesi.com
  www.evansandclesi.com

Established: 1994

Insurance Defense, Automobile Liability, Personal Injury, Premises Liability, Business Interruption, Construction Law, Workers' Compensation, Medical Malpractice, Employment Discrimination, Admiralty and Maritime Law

Insurance Clients

Pioneer State Mutual Insurance Company
State Farm Mutual Automobile Insurance Company
State Farm Fire and Casualty Company
21st Century Insurance and Financial Services

Non-Insurance Clients

Elevating Boats, Inc.
Flying J, Inc.

Partners

K. Randall Evans — 1960 — Georgetown University, B.S.F.S., 1982; Louisiana State University, J.D., 1985 — Admitted to Bar, 1985, Louisiana; 1986, U.S. District Court, Eastern District of Louisiana; 1989, U.S. District Court, Middle District of Louisiana; 1994, U.S. Court of Appeals, Fifth Circuit — Member American, Louisiana State and New Orleans Bar Associations; Louisiana Association of Defense Counsel; American Judicature Society; Defense Research Institute — E-mail: krevans@evansandclesi.com

Evans & Clesi, PLC, New Orleans, LA   (Continued)

H. James Parker — 1964 — Drury College, B.A., 1986; Loyola University, J.D., 1993 — Admitted to Bar, 1994, Louisiana; 1994, U.S. District Court, Eastern, Middle and Western Districts of Louisiana; 2000, U.S. Court of Appeals, Fifth Circuit — Member Federal, American, Louisiana State, Jefferson Parish and New Orleans Bar Associations; Louisiana Association of Defense Counsel — E-mail: hjparker@evansandclesi.com

Associates

Randy J. Boudreaux — 1969 — Tulane University of Louisiana, B.S., 1991; Tulane University Law School, J.D., 1995 — Admitted to Bar, 1996, Louisiana — Member Louisiana State Bar Association

Jaimie A. Tuchman — 1985 — Tulane University, School of Science and Engineering, B.A., 2007; Tulane University Law School, J.D., 2010 — Admitted to Bar, 2010, Louisiana — Member Louisiana State Bar Association

Of Counsel

Anthony J. Clesi, Jr. — 1932 — Tulane University of Louisiana, B.A., 1952; LL.B., 1954 — Admitted to Bar, 1954, Louisiana; 1954, U.S. District Court, Eastern and Middle Districts of Louisiana; 1954, U.S. Court of Appeals, Fifth Circuit; 1954, U.S. Supreme Court — Member Louisiana State, Baton Rouge and New Orleans Bar Associations; Fellow, Louisiana Bar Foundation; Louisiana Association of Defense Counsel; International Association of Defense Counsel; Defense Research Institute — E-mail: ajclesi@evansandclesi.com

Jeanne L. Billings — 1964 — H. Sophie Newcomb Memorial College, Tulane University, B.S., 1984; Tulane University, J.D., 1987 — Admitted to Bar, 1987, Louisiana — Member Louisiana State Bar Association

Evans & Co.
629 Cherokee Street
New Orleans, Louisiana 70118
  Telephone: 504-522-1400
  Fax: 877-585-1401
  Toll Free: 800-EVANSCO
  E-Mail: revans@evanslawfirm.com
  www.evanslawfirm.com

(Additional Offices: Durango, CO*; Greensboro, NC*; Katy, TX*(See Houston listing); Farmington, NM*; Jackson, WY*)

Established: 1983

Admiralty and Maritime Law, Aviation, Comprehensive General Liability, Construction Law, Directors and Officers Liability, Employment Practices Liability, Energy, Environmental Law, Excess and Umbrella, Insurance Coverage, Insurance Defense, Motor Carriers, Oil and Gas, Product Liability, Professional Liability, Property and Casualty, Railroad Law, Toxic Torts

Insurance Clients

Accident Insurance Company
AequiCap Claims Services
All Risk Claims Service, Inc.
American Family Insurance Company
American Hallmark Insurance Services, Inc.
American National Property and Casualty Company
Assicurazioni Generali S.p.A.
Atlantic Casualty Insurance Company
Bituminous Casualty Corporation
Canal Indemnity Company
Claims Management Corporation
CNA Insurance Company
Construction Insurance Company
COUNTRY Financial
Employers Insurance Company of Wausau
Erie Insurance Group
Farm Family Insurance Companies
General Security Insurance Company
H & W Insurance Services, Inc.
Liberty Insurance Services, Inc.
ACE Westchester Specialty Group
Allianz Insurance Company
American Ambassador Casualty Company
American Fidelity Insurance Company
American Interstate Insurance Company
Anchor General Insurance Company
Atlantic Mutual Companies
Atlas Insurance Company
Boat/U.S. Marine Insurance
The Cincinnati Insurance Companies
Colony Insurance Group
Continental Western Group
Deep South Surplus, Inc.
Employers Mutual Casualty Company
Essex Insurance Company
First Financial Insurance Company
Greenwich Insurance Company
GuideOne Insurance
Kiln Group
Markel Insurance Company

2015 BEST'S DIRECTORIES OF RECOMMENDED INSURANCE ATTORNEYS AND ADJUSTERS — *For Current Listings access www.ambest.com/directories* — **689**

LOUISIANA NEW ORLEANS

Evans & Co., New Orleans, LA (Continued)

Meadowbrook Insurance Group
National Farmers Union Property & Casualty Company
Occidental Fire & Casualty Company of North Carolina
Penn National Insurance
Phoenix Indemnity Insurance Company
Professional Insurance Underwriters, Inc.
Shelter Insurance Companies
State National Companies, Inc.
Texas Select Lloyds Insurance Company
Transportation Casualty Insurance Company
Underwriters Indemnity Company
United Educators Insurance
United Fire & Casualty Company
United Specialty Insurance Company
Unitrin Property and Casualty Insurance Group
Virginia Mutual Insurance Company
XL Insurance
Mountain States Insurance Group
National Grange Mutual Insurance Company
Ocean Marine Indemnity Insurance Company
Phoenix Aviation Managers, Inc.
Preferred Contractors Insurance Company
St. Paul Fire and Marine Insurance Company
Southern Insurance Company
Texas All Risk General Agency, Inc.
T.H.E. Insurance Company
Transportation Claims, Inc.
Underwriters at Lloyd's, London
Underwriters Service Company, Inc.
United National Insurance Company
United States Liability Insurance Company
Universal Underwriters Insurance Company
Wilshire Insurance Company
Zurich North America

Non-Insurance Clients

High Country Transportation, Inc.
SAIA Motor Freight Line, Inc.
Jones Motor Group
United States Postal Service

Attorneys

Robert C. Evans — 1954 — Columbia University, B.A., 1975; University of Maryland, J.D. (with honors), 1980 — Admitted to Bar, 1980, Louisiana; Maryland; 1999, Colorado; 1980, U.S. District Court, Eastern, Middle and Western Districts of Louisiana; U.S. District Court, District of Maryland; U.S. Court of Appeals, Fifth Circuit; 1991, U.S. Court of Appeals, Eleventh Circuit — Member Louisiana State, Maryland State and New Orleans Bar Associations; The Colorado Bar Association; New Orleans Association of Defense Counsel; Louisiana Association of Defense Counsel; Lawyer-Pilots Bar Association; The Maritime Law Association of the United States; Defense Research Institute

Karen M. Worthington — 1959 — Louisiana State University, B.A. (cum laude), 1981; J.D. (with honors), 1984 — Admitted to Bar, 1984, Louisiana; U.S. District Court, Eastern, Middle and Western Districts of Louisiana; U.S. Court of Appeals, Fifth Circuit — Member Louisiana State Bar Association

Mark Fierro — 1962 — The University of Texas at El Paso, B.B.A., 1983; J.D., 1985 — Admitted to Bar, 1986, Texas; 1987, Louisiana — Member State Bar of Texas

John Grimes — West Virginia University, B.A., 2006; Loyola University New Orleans College of Law, J.D., 2009 — Admitted to Bar, 2009, Louisiana — Member Louisiana State Bar Association

Amanda Hogue — Florida State University, B.S./B.S., 2006; Loyola University New Orleans College of Law, J.D., 2009; The George Washington University Law School, LL.M., 2010 — Admitted to Bar, 2009, Louisiana; 2010, U.S. District Court, Eastern and Middle Districts of Louisiana; 2010, U.S. Bankruptcy Court, Eastern District of Louisiana; U.S. Bankruptcy Court, Eastern District of Louisiana

Katherine Weatherly Trotter — The University of Tennessee Knoxville, B.A., 2005; Loyola University New Orleans College of Law, J.D., 2010 — Admitted to Bar, 2010, Louisiana — Member American, Louisiana State and New Orleans Bar Associations

Galloway, Johnson, Tompkins, Burr & Smith

701 Poydras Street, 40th Floor
New Orleans, Louisiana 70139
    Telephone: 504-525-6802
    Fax: 504-525-2456
    E-Mail: info@gallowayjohnson.com
    www.gallowayjohnson.com

Galloway, Johnson, Tompkins, Burr & Smith, New Orleans, LA (Continued)

(Additional Offices: Lafayette, LA*; Pensacola, FL*; St. Louis, MO*; Houston, TX*; Mandeville, LA*; Gulfport, MS*; Tampa, FL*; Mobile, AL*; Atlanta, GA*)

Established: 1987

Maritime, Automobile Liability, Bad Faith, Class Actions, Construction, Energy, Employment, Insurance Coverage, Insurance Defense, Product Liability, Professional Liability, Property, Transportation, General Casualty, Title Resolution, Environmental

Insurance Clients

Arch Insurance Group

Non-Insurance Clients

BBC Chartering and Logistic GmbH & Co. KG

Managing Director

Jason P. Waguespack — Louisiana State University, B.A., 1988; Tulane University, J.D., 1991 — Admitted to Bar, 1991, Louisiana; U.S. District Court, Eastern, Middle and Western Districts of Louisiana; U.S. Court of Appeals, Fifth Circuit; 1995, U.S. District Court, Eastern, Northern, Southern and Western Districts of Texas; U.S. Court of Appeals, Second Circuit; U.S. Supreme Court — Member Federal, Louisiana State and New Orleans Bar Associations; Southeastern Admiralty Law Institute; The Maritime Law Association of the United States — E-mail: jwaguespack@gallowayjohnson.com

Gieger, Laborde & Laperouse, L.L.C.

One Shell Square
701 Poydras Street, Suite 4800
New Orleans, Louisiana 70139
    Telephone: 504-561-0400
    Fax: 504-561-1011
    E-Mail: info@glllaw.com
    www.glllaw.com

(Houston, TX Office*: 1177 West Loop South, Suite 750, 77027)
    (Tel: 832-255-6000)
    (Fax: 832-255-6001)

Established: 2002

Administrative Law, Insurance Defense, Product Liability, Environmental Law, Aviation, Admiralty and Maritime Law, Drug, Medical Devices, Toxic Torts, Professional Liability, Property, Insurance Coverage Disputes

Insurance Clients

ACE USA
AIG Companies
Allianz Aviation Managers, LLC
American Alternative Insurance Corporation
American International Specialty Lines Insurance
Aspen Specialty Insurance Company
Berkley Aviation, LLC
Chartis Specialty Insurance Company
CTC Services Aviation
Electric Insurance Company
Gallagher Bassett Services, Inc.
Granite State Insurance Company
Great Lakes Reinsurance (U.K.) PLC
Illinois National Insurance Company
Ironshore Holdings (US) Inc.
Lexington Insurance Company
AIG Aerospace
AIG Property Casualty
Allied World Assurance Company
American Empire Group
American Home Assurance Company
Arch Insurance Company
Audubon Insurance Company
Aviation LS
Berkshire Hathaway Specialty Insurance
Commerce and Industry Insurance Company
ESIS
Global Aerospace, Inc.
Great American Insurance Company
Hartford Insurance Company
The Insurance Company of the State of Pennsylvania
Landmark Insurance Company
Munich Reinsurance America, Inc.

NEW ORLEANS   LOUISIANA

Gieger, Laborde & Laperouse, L.L.C., New Orleans, LA
(Continued)

National Union Fire Insurance Company of Pittsburgh, PA
New Hampshire Insurance Company
RSUI Indemnity Company
Stonington Insurance Company
TIG Insurance Company
XL Insurance
York Risk Services Group, Inc.
National Union Fire Insurance Company of LA
OneBeacon Professional Insurance
Resolute Management, Inc.
St. Paul Fire and Marine Insurance Company
United States Aircraft Insurance Group
Zurich North America

Non-Insurance Clients

A. O. Smith Corporation
Dialysis Clinic, Inc.
Environmental Chemical Corporation
Fleming & Hall Administrators, Inc.
Industrial Helicopters, Inc.
Kimberly-Clark Corporation
National Dairy Holdings L.P.
NES Rentals, L.P.
Parker-Hannifin Corporation
Pioneer Natural Resources Company
SDS Petroleum Consultants, LLC
Werner Company, Inc.
Apache Corporation
Energy XXI GOM, LLC
Era Helicopters, LLC
Fieldwood Energy, LLC
Forest River, Inc.
General Electric Company
Ingersoll-Rand Company
LLOG Exploration Company, L.L.C.
Newfield Exploration Company
Petrodome Energy, LLC
Porsche Cars North America, Inc.
Sanchez Oil & Gas Corporation
Thomas & Betts Corporation
Yuma Exploration and Production Company

Partners

Ernest P. Gieger, Jr. — 1951 — Louisiana State University, B.S., 1973; J.D., 1976 — Admitted to Bar, 1976, Louisiana; 2006, Texas; 1977, U.S. District Court, Eastern District of Louisiana; 1979, U.S. District Court, Middle District of Louisiana; 1980, U.S. District Court, Western District of Louisiana; 1981, U.S. Court of Appeals, Fifth Circuit; 2004, U.S. District Court, Eastern and Western Districts of Arkansas; 2009, U.S. District Court, Southern District of Texas; 2010, U.S. District Court, Eastern District of Texas; 2011, U.S. District Court, Northern District of Texas; 2012, U.S. District Court, District of Arizona — Member American Bar Association (Tort and Insurance Practice; Toxic Tort and Environmental Sections); Louisiana State Bar Association (Insurance and Negligence Sections); Product Liability Advisory Council; Louisiana Association of Defense Counsel; Defense Research Institute; International Association of Defense Counsel — Admitted to Practice Pro Hac Vice in State Court in the States of Arizona, Arkansas, Kentucky, Mississippi and Ohio and in Federal Court in the States of Florida, Hawaii and Washington — Practice Areas: Civil Litigation; Environmental Law; Insurance Defense; Personal Injury; Product Liability; Toxic Torts — E-mail: egieger@glllaw.com

Kenneth H. Laborde — 1953 — Louisiana State University, B.S., 1975; Loyola University, J.D., 1979 — Phi Delta Phi — Admitted to Bar, 1979, Louisiana; 1990, Texas; 1979, U.S. District Court, Eastern and Western Districts of Louisiana; U.S. Court of Appeals, Fifth Circuit; 1980, U.S. District Court, Middle District of Louisiana; 1981, U.S. Court of Appeals, Eleventh Circuit; 1988, U.S. Supreme Court; 1990, U.S. District Court, Eastern and Southern Districts of Texas; 1999, U.S. District Court, Northern District of Texas; 2001, U.S. District Court, Western District of Texas; 2004, U.S. Court of Appeals, Sixth Circuit — Member American and Louisiana State Bar Associations; State Bar of Texas (Aviation Section); American College of Trial Lawyers; Defense Research Institute (Chairman of Aerospace Committee, 1989-1993); Louisiana Association of Defense Counsel; Texas Association of Defense Counsel; Federation of Defense and Corporate Counsel — Practice Areas: Admiralty and Maritime Law; Aviation; Environmental Law; Insurance Defense; Product Liability; Transportation — E-mail: klaborde@glllaw.com

Lambert M. Laperouse — 1953 — Louisiana State University, B.S., 1975; Loyola University, J.D., 1979 — Phi Delta Phi — Admitted to Bar, 1979, Louisiana; 2012, Texas; 1979, U.S. District Court, Eastern and Western Districts of Louisiana; U.S. Court of Appeals, Fifth Circuit; 1980, U.S. District Court, Middle District of Louisiana — Member American, Louisiana State and New Orleans Bar Associations — Lecturer, Loyola University School of Law (Mineral Law) 1979-2007 — Practice Areas: Oil and Gas — E-mail: laperouse@glllaw.com

Robert I. Siegel — 1954 — University of Illinois; State University of New York at Binghamton, B.A., 1976; Loyola University, J.D., 1979 — Admitted to Bar, 1979, Louisiana; 2006, Texas; 1979, U.S. District Court, Eastern, Middle and Western Districts of Louisiana; 1981, U.S. Court of Appeals, Fifth and Eleventh Circuits; 1994, U.S. Supreme Court — Member American and Louisiana State Bar Associations; Defense Research Institute — Practice Areas: Insurance Coverage; Property; Bad Faith; Admiralty and Maritime Law; Medical Malpractice; Negligence; Product Liability; Professional Liability — E-mail: rsiegel@glllaw.com

Andrew A. Braun — 1955 — Drexel University, B.S., 1977; Tulane University, J.D. (cum laude), 1981 — Admitted to Bar, 1981, Louisiana; 2008, Texas; 1981, U.S. District Court, Eastern and Middle Districts of Louisiana; U.S. Court of Appeals, Fifth Circuit; 1986, U.S. District Court, Western District of Louisiana — Member American, Louisiana State and New Orleans Bar Associations; Commercial Law League of America; Louisiana Association of Defense Counsel; Defense Research Institute — Practice Areas: Insurance Defense; Product Liability; Construction Law; Commercial Litigation; Bankruptcy; Creditor Rights — E-mail: abraun@glllaw.com

Leo R. McAloon, III — 1961 — United States Merchant Marine Academy, B.S., 1983; Tulane University, J.D. (cum laude), 1988 — Admitted to Bar, 1988, Louisiana; 1994, Texas; 1994, U.S. District Court, Eastern, Middle and Western Districts of Louisiana; U.S. Court of Appeals, Fifth Circuit — Member Louisiana State Bar Association; State Bar of Texas — Practice Areas: Aviation; Insurance Defense; Admiralty and Maritime Law; Oil and Gas; Contracts; Contract Disputes — E-mail: lmcaloon@glllaw.com

John E. W. Baay II — 1962 — Tulane University, B.S., 1984; The University of New Orleans, M.B.A., 1989; Louisiana State University, J.D., 1994 — Admitted to Bar, 1994, Louisiana; 1997, Texas; 2004, Mississippi; 1994, U.S. District Court, Eastern, Middle and Western Districts of Louisiana; U.S. Court of Appeals, Fifth Circuit; 1997, U.S. District Court, Southern District of Texas — Member American and Louisiana State Bar Associations; State Bar of Texas; Fellow, Louisiana Bar Foundation; Defense Research Institute; Louisiana Association of Defense Counsel — Reported Cases: Moll vs. ABB 218 F.3d 472 (5th Cir. 2000) — Practice Areas: Class Actions; Commercial Litigation; Admiralty and Maritime Law; ERISA; Insurance Coverage; Insurance Defense — E-mail: jbaay@glllaw.com

Daniel G. Rauh — 1969 — University of Colorado, B.A., 1992; Tulane University, J.D. (cum laude), 2000 — Admitted to Bar, 2001, Louisiana; U.S. District Court, Eastern, Middle and Western Districts of Louisiana; U.S. Court of Appeals, Fifth Circuit — Practice Areas: Commercial Litigation; Product Liability; Entertainment Law; Toxic Torts; Complex Litigation; Class Actions; Oil and Gas; Contract Disputes; Appellate Practice — E-mail: drauh@glllaw.com

Rachel G. Webre — 1975 — The University of New Orleans, B.A., 1997; Tulane University, J.D. (cum laude), 2000 — Admitted to Bar, 2000, Louisiana; U.S. District Court, Eastern, Middle and Western Districts of Louisiana; U.S. Court of Appeals, Fifth Circuit — Member Federal and Louisiana State Bar Associations — Practice Areas: Health Care; Insurance Defense; Medical Malpractice; Product Liability; Civil Litigation; Insurance Coverage — E-mail: rwebre@glllaw.com

Christopher R. Teske — 1975 — Macalester College, B.A. (cum laude), 1997; Tulane University, J.D. (cum laude), 2000 — Admitted to Bar, 2000, Louisiana; 2012, Texas; 2000, U.S. District Court, Eastern, Middle and Western Districts of Louisiana; 2010, U.S. District Court, Northern and Southern Districts of Texas — Practice Areas: Insurance Coverage; Insurance Litigation; First Party Matters; Defense Litigation — E-mail: cteske@glllaw.com

William A. Barousse — 1979 — Tulane University, B.A. (cum laude), 2002; Georgetown University; Louisiana State University, J.D./B.C.L., 2005 — Admitted to Bar, 2005, Louisiana; 2006, U.S. District Court, Eastern, Middle and Western Districts of Louisiana; U.S. Court of Appeals, Fifth Circuit — Member Federal and Louisiana State (New Orleans Chapter) Bar Associations — Languages: French — Practice Areas: Insurance Defense; Civil Litigation; Product Liability; Toxic Torts — E-mail: wbarousse@glllaw.com

Michael E. Hill — 1972 — West Virginia University, B.S. (magna cum laude), 1994; Tulane University, J.D., 1998 — Admitted to Bar, 1998, Louisiana; 2011, Texas; 2004, U.S. District Court, Eastern, Middle and Western Districts of Louisiana; 2011, U.S. District Court, Northern and Southern Districts of Texas — Practice Areas: Insurance Defense; Product Liability; Construction Law; Commercial Litigation; Bankruptcy; Creditor Rights — E-mail: mhill@glllaw.com

Associates

Michael D. Cangelosi — 1980 — Louisiana State University, B.A., 2002; Paul M Hebert Law School at Louisiana State University, J.D., 2006 — Admitted to Bar, 2006, Louisiana; U.S. District Court, Eastern, Middle and Western Districts of Louisiana; U.S. Court of Appeals, Fifth Circuit — Member Louisiana State Bar Association — Practice Areas: Civil Litigation; Insurance Defense; Product Liability — E-mail: mcangelosi@glllaw.com

Gieger, Laborde & Laperouse, L.L.C., New Orleans, LA (Continued)

Tara E. Clement — 1970 — Louisiana Tech University, B.S., 1992; Paul M Hebert Law School at Louisiana State University, J.D., 2001 — Admitted to Bar, 2001, Louisiana; 2009, Texas; U.S. Court of Appeals, Fifth Circuit; U.S. District Court, Eastern, Middle and Western Districts of Louisiana; 2007, U.S. Court of Appeals, Eleventh Circuit — Member Federal, Louisiana State and New Orleans Bar Associations — Practice Areas: Insurance Defense; Insurance Coverage; Commercial Litigation; Corporate Law; Business Law; Municipal Law; Land Use — E-mail: tclement@glllaw.com

Elizabeth A. Chickering — 1981 — Duke University, B.A., 2003; Tulane University Law School, J.D. (magna cum laude), 2007 — Admitted to Bar, 2007, Louisiana; U.S. District Court, Eastern, Middle and Western Districts of Louisiana; U.S. Court of Appeals, Fifth Circuit— Member Federal and Louisiana State Bar Associations — Practice Areas: Litigation — E-mail: echickering@glllaw.com

Eric C. Walton — 1971 — Towson University, B.S., 1993; Tulane University Law School, J.D., 2004 — Admitted to Bar, 2004, Louisiana; 2007, U.S. District Court, Eastern District of Louisiana — Member Louisiana State Bar Association — Captain, U.S. Army, Armor 1993-1999 — Practice Areas: Insurance Defense; Personal Injury; Admiralty and Maritime Law; Construction Defect; Product Liability; Complex Litigation — E-mail: ewalton@glllaw.com

Jameson M. Taylor — 1981 — University of Florida, B.S., 2004; Louisiana State University, J.D., 2009 — Admitted to Bar, 2009, Louisiana; U.S. District Court, Eastern, Middle and Western Districts of Louisiana; U.S. Court of Appeals, Fifth Circuit — E-mail: jtaylor@glllaw.com

Matthew F. Morgan — 1976 — Loyola University New Orleans, B.A. (summa cum laude), 1998; Ohio University, M.F.A., 2001; Loyola University New Orleans College of Law, J.D. (summa cum laude), 2009 — Admitted to Bar, 2010, Louisiana; U.S. District Court, Eastern, Southern and Western Districts of Louisiana; U.S. Court of Appeals, Fifth Circuit — Practice Areas: Civil Litigation; Appellate Practice; Personal Injury; Premises Liability; Admiralty and Maritime Law; Environmental Liability; Insurance Defense — E-mail: mmorgan@glllaw.com

A. Simone Manuel — 1979 — University of Louisiana at Lafayette, B.A., 2001; Loyola University New Orleans College of Law, J.D. (cum laude), 2006 — Admitted to Bar, 2006, Louisiana; U.S. District Court, Eastern, Middle and Western Districts of Louisiana; U.S. Court of Appeals, Fifth Circuit — Member Federal, American, Louisiana State and New Orleans Bar Associations — Practice Areas: Commercial Litigation; Insurance Coverage; Insurance Defense — E-mail: smanuel@glllaw.com

Emily E. Eagan — 1977 — Davidson College, B.A., 1999; Tulane University Law School, J.D. (magna cum laude), 2004 — Admitted to Bar, 2004, Louisiana; U.S. District Court, Eastern, Middle and Western Districts of Louisiana; U.S. Court of Appeals, Fifth Circuit — Member Federal, American, Louisiana State and New Orleans Bar Associations — Practice Areas: Litigation — E-mail: eeagan@glllaw.com

Victoria E. Emmerling — 1984 — Louisiana State University, B.S., 2007; Paul M Hebert Law School at Louisiana State University, J.D. (cum laude), 2010 — Admitted to Bar, 2010, Louisiana; U.S. District Court, Eastern, Middle and Western Districts of Louisiana; U.S. Court of Appeals, Fifth Circuit — Member Federal, American and Louisiana State Bar Associations — Practice Areas: Commercial Litigation; Insurance Coverage; Insurance Defense; Toxic Torts; Complex Litigation; Product Liability — E-mail: temmerling@glllaw.com

Megan Cambre — 1986 — Louisiana State University, B.S., 2008; Loyola University New Orleans, J.D. (cum laude), 2011 — Admitted to Bar, 2011, Louisiana; U.S. District Court, Eastern, Middle and Western Districts of Louisiana; U.S. Court of Appeals, Fifth Circuit — Practice Areas: Insurance Defense; Toxic Torts; Civil Litigation — E-mail: mcambre@glllaw.com

Eric S. Charleston — 1980 — Syracuse University, B.F.A. (Dean's List), 2002; Georgetown University Law Center, J.D., 2008 — Law Clerk to Hon. James E. Boasberg, D.C., Superior Court (2008-2009) and Hon. F. Weisberg, D.C., Superior Court (2010-2011) — Admitted to Bar, 2009, New York; 2010, District of Columbia; 2012, Louisiana; 2010, U.S. District Court, Southern District of New York; U.S. District Court, Eastern and Southern Districts of New York; 2012, U.S. District Court, Eastern, Middle and Western Districts of Louisiana; U.S. Court of Appeals, Fifth Circuit — Languages: Spanish — Practice Areas: Civil Litigation; Toxic Torts; Environmental Law; Insurance Defense — E-mail: echarleston@glllaw.com

Caitlin Hill — 1985 — Louisiana State University, B.A. (cum laude), 2007; Tulane University Law School, J.D. (cum laude), 2010 — Admitted to Bar, 2010, Mississippi; 2012, Louisiana — E-mail: chill@glllaw.com

Jonathan S. Ord — 1981 — The Evergreen State College, B.S., 2003; The University of New Orleans, Ph.D., 2010; Tulane University Law School, J.D.

Gieger, Laborde & Laperouse, L.L.C., New Orleans, LA (Continued)

(magna cum laude), 2013 — Admitted to Bar, 2013, Louisiana; U.S. District Court, Eastern, Middle and Western Districts of Louisiana; U.S. Court of Appeals, Fifth Circuit — Practice Areas: Insurance Defense; Insurance Coverage; Commercial Litigation; Toxic Torts; Maritime Law — E-mail: jord@glllaw.com

Bradley J. Schwab — 1987 — Louisiana State University, B.S. Biology (magna cum laude), 2009; The University of New Orleans, M.S. HCM (summa cum laude), 2010; Tulane University Law School, J.D. (magna cum laude), 2013 — Admitted to Bar, 2013, Louisiana — E-mail: bschwab@glllaw.com

Of Counsel

Gina S. Montgomery — 1964 — The University of New Orleans, B.A., 1986; Loyola University, J.D. (cum laude), 1989 — Admitted to Bar, 1989, Louisiana; 1991, U.S. District Court, Eastern District of Louisiana — Member American and Louisiana State Bar Associations — Practice Areas: Environmental Law; Admiralty and Maritime Law; Aviation; Insurance Defense; Product Liability; Transportation — E-mail: gmontgomery@glllaw.com

Janet H. Aschaffenburg — 1957 — Louisiana State University, B.S., 1979; Tulane University, J.D., 1990 — Admitted to Bar, 1993, Louisiana — Member Louisiana State Bar Association; Professional Landmen's Association of New Orleans; Association of Professional Landmen — Practice Areas: Contracts; Oil and Gas — E-mail: jaschaffenburg@glllaw.com

J. Mike DiGiglia — 1955 — Utah State University, B.S., 1980; McNeese State University, M.S., 1986; Louisiana State University, J.D. (Order of the Coif), 1996 — Admitted to Bar, 1996, Louisiana; 1999, Colorado; U.S. District Court, Eastern, Middle and Western Districts of Louisiana; U.S. District Court, District of Colorado; U.S. Court of Appeals, Fifth and Tenth Circuits — Member American Bar Association (Environmental, Energy and Resources Committees: Air Quality, Environmental Enforcement and Crimes, Environmental Litigation and Toxic Torts, Oil and Gas, Superfund and Natural Resources Damages Litigation, Waste and Resource Recovery, Water Quality and Wetlands and Water Resources; Louisiana State (Environmental Law Committee), The Colorado (Environmental Committee) and El Paso County (Colorado) Bar Associations; Professional Landmen's Society of New Orleans; Louisiana Criminal Defense Lawyers Association; Environmental Law Institute; Defense Research Institute — Registered Environmental Manager; Environmental Auditor; Hazardous Materials Manager (Master Level); Hazard Control Manager (Master Level) — Practice Areas: Environmental Law; Administrative Law; Toxic Torts; Class Actions; Complex Litigation

Alistair M. Ward — 1970 — Dartmouth College, A.B., 1992; Tulane University, J.D. (Order of the Coif), 1996 — Admitted to Bar, 1996, Louisiana; U.S. District Court, Eastern, Middle and Western Districts of Louisiana — Practice Areas: Commercial Litigation; Insurance Coverage — E-mail: award@glllaw.com

(Revisors of the Louisiana Insurance Law Digest for this Publication)

Gordon Arata McCollam Duplantis & Eagan, LLC

201 St. Charles Avenue, Suite 4000
New Orleans, Louisiana 70170-4000
Telephone: 504-582-1111
Fax: 504-582-1121
www.gordonarata.com

(Lafayette, LA Office: 400 East Kaliste Saloom Road, Suite 4200, 70508-8517)
 (Tel: 337-237-0132)
 (Fax: 337-237-3451)
(Baton Rouge, LA Office: 301 Main Street, Suite 1600, 70801-1916)
 (Tel: 225-381-9643)
 (Fax: 225-336-9763)
(Houston, TX Office: 1980 Post Oak Boulevard, Suite 1800, 77056)
 (Tel: 713-333-5500)
 (Fax: 713-333-5501)

Established: 1970

NEW ORLEANS

LOUISIANA

Gordon Arata McCollam Duplantis & Eagan, LLC, New Orleans, LA (Continued)

Insurance Defense, Life and Health, Medical Malpractice, Commercial Litigation, Reinsurance, Class Actions, Employment Law, Energy, Oil and Gas, Antitrust

Firm Profile: Gordon Arata has attorneys in one Texas and three Louisiana offices. We are fiercely committed to winning, which to us means achieving the best possible results for our clients, whether we're in the courtroom or at the negotiating table. We thoroughly understand business and industry, and are skilled problem solvers for our clients.

Insurance Clients

Admiral Insurance Company
First Capital Life Insurance Company of Louisiana
Liberty Mutual Insurance Company
Liberty Surplus Insurance Corporation
Progressive Insurance Group
Safeco Insurance Company of America
State Mutual Life Assurance Company

First American Title Insurance Company
Great-West Life and Annuity Insurance Company
Life Insurance Company of Georgia
Rockhill Insurance Company
St. Paul Fire and Marine Insurance Company
Swiss Re Life & Health America, Inc.

Non-Insurance Clients

Universal Health Services, Inc.

Members

B. J. Duplantis — Louisiana State University, B.S., 1961; Loyola University, J.D., 1966 — Admitted to Bar, 1966, Louisiana — Practice Areas: Oil and Gas; Energy — Tel: 337-237-0132 — E-mail: bduplantis@gordonarata.com

Steven W. Copley — University of Illinois at Springfield, B.A., 1976; Loyola University New Orleans College of Law, J.D., 1985 — Admitted to Bar, 1985, Louisiana; 2006, Texas — Practice Areas: Antitrust; Bankruptcy; Class Actions; Commercial Litigation; Corporate Law; Insurance; Product Liability — Tel: 504-569-1648 — E-mail: scopley@gordonarata.com

Martin E. Landrieu — Louisiana State University, B.S., 1985; Loyola University New Orleans College of Law, J.D., 1988 — Admitted to Bar, 1988, Louisiana — Practice Areas: Commercial Litigation; Insurance; Real Estate; Class Actions — Tel: 504-582-1832 — E-mail: mlandrieu@gordonarata.com

A. Gregory Grimsal — Tulane University of Louisiana, B.A. (cum laude), 1972; J.D., 1979; Cambridge University, LL.B., 1981 — Admitted to Bar, 1979, Louisiana — Practice Areas: Banking; Employment Law; Product Liability Defense; Commercial Litigation; Insurance; Real Estate; Antitrust; Class Actions — Tel: 504-569-1834 — E-mail: ggrimsal@gordonarata.com

Tina C. White — Loyola University, B.B.A. (cum laude), 1986; Tulane University Law School, J.D. (magna cum laude), 1994 — Admitted to Bar, 1994, Louisiana — Practice Areas: Construction Law; Commercial Litigation; Antitrust; Corporate Law; Class Actions; Product Liability Defense; Appellate — Tel: 504-569-1895 — E-mail: twhite@gordonarata.com

Terrence K. Knister — The University of Mississippi, B.P.A., 1978; J.D., 1981 — Admitted to Bar, 1981, Mississippi; Louisiana — Practice Areas: Environmental Law; Admiralty and Maritime Law; Employment Law; Product Liability Defense; Commercial Litigation; Insurance; Oil and Gas; Energy; Class Actions — Tel: 504-569-1865 — E-mail: tknister@gordonarata.com

Fernand L. Laudumiey IV — Loyola University, B.A. (magna cum laude), 1992; Louisiana State University, Paul M. Hebert Law Center, J.D., 1996 — Admitted to Bar, 1996, Louisiana — Practice Areas: Oil and Gas; Energy; Bankruptcy — Tel: 504-569-1660 — E-mail: flaudumiey@gordonarata.com

Michael E. Botnick — The University of New Orleans, B.A., 1972; Tulane University, J.D., 1975 — Admitted to Bar, 1975, Louisiana — Practice Areas: Commercial Litigation; Corporate Law; Real Estate; Trust and Estate Litigation; Construction Law — Tel: 504-679-9814 — E-mail: mbotnick@gordonarata.com

Phillip J. Antis — James Madison University, B.M., 1997; Tulane University, J.D. (cum laude), 2004 — Admitted to Bar, 2004, Louisiana — Practice Areas: Commercial Litigation; Class Actions; Construction Law; Insurance; Labor and Employment; Appellate — Tel: 504-569-1864 — E-mail: pantis@gordonarata.com

Hayes, Harkey, Smith & Cascio, L.L.P.

201 St. Charles Avenue, Suite 2500
New Orleans, Louisiana 70170
  Telephone: 504-754-6969
  Fax: 504-524-7979
  www.hhsclaw.com

(Monroe, LA Office*: 2811 Kilpatrick Boulevard, 71201, P.O. Box 8032, 71211-8032)
  (Tel: 318-387-2422)
  (Fax: 318-388-5809)

Accountants, Architects and Engineers, Automobile, Civil Litigation, Commercial Litigation, Construction Liability, Employment Law, Insurance Coverage, Medical Malpractice, Nursing Home Liability, Premises Liability, Product Liability, Professional Liability, Transportation, Trucking Law, Uninsured and Underinsured Motorist, Workers' Compensation

(See listing under Monroe, LA for additional information)

The Javier Law Firm, LLC

1100 Poydras Street, Suite 2010
New Orleans, Louisiana 70163
  Telephone: 504-599-8570
  Fax: 504-599-8579
  E-Mail: rogerj@javierlawfirm.com
  www.javierlawfirm.com

Premises Liability, Restaurant Liability, Workers' Compensation, Corporate Law, Employment Law, Litigation

Insurance Clients

American Modern Insurance Group, Inc.
Imperial Casualty and Indemnity Company

Colony Insurance Company
Gallagher Bassett Services, Inc.
The Travelers Companies, Inc.

Non-Insurance Clients

Coca-Cola Bottling Company
Manpower, Inc.
OfficeMax Incorporated
Whole Foods Market, Inc.
Yum! Brands

Macy's
Marriott International, Inc.
Starwood Hotels & Resorts Worldwide, Inc.

Founder & Senior Managing Partner

Roger A. Javier — 1971 — Emory University, B.B.A., 1993; Loyola University, J.D., 1998 — Admitted to Bar, 1999, Louisiana — Member Federal, American, Louisiana State, Fifth Federal Circuit and Jefferson Parish Bar Associations — Languages: Spanish

Johnson, Yacoubian & Paysse, APLC

One Shell Square
701 Poydras Street, Suite 4700
New Orleans, Louisiana 70139-7708
  Telephone: 504-528-3001
  Fax: 504-528-3030
  Toll Free: 800-649-3454
  E-Mail: info@jyplawfirm.com
  www.jyplawfirm.com

Established: 1991

Insurance Defense, Automobile, Casualty, Workers' Compensation, Admiralty and Maritime Law, Property Damage, Coverage Issues, General Liability, Personal Injury, Subrogation, Toxic Torts, Medical Malpractice

Johnson, Yacoubian & Paysse, APLC, New Orleans, LA (Continued)

Insurance Clients

Louisiana Restaurant Association Underwriters at Lloyd's, London

Partners

Edward S. Johnson — 1954 — Louisiana State University, 1976; J.D., 1979 — Admitted to Bar, 1979, Louisiana; 1992, Texas; 1980, U.S. District Court, Eastern, Middle and Western Districts of Louisiana; 1979, U.S. Court of Appeals, Fifth and Eleventh Circuits; 1992, U.S. District Court, Southern District of Texas; 1999, U.S. Supreme Court — Member American, Louisiana State and New Orleans Bar Associations; State Bar of Texas; The Maritime Law Association of the United States; Southeastern Admiralty Law Institute — Louisiana Super Lawyers — E-mail: ejohnson@jyplawfirm.com

Alan J. Yacoubian — 1960 — Tulane University, B.A. (cum laude), 1982; J.D. (cum laude), 1985 — Admitted to Bar, 1985, Louisiana; U.S. District Court, Eastern, Middle and Western Districts of Louisiana; U.S. Court of Appeals, Fifth Circuit; U.S. Supreme Court — Member Federal Bar Association (Sections: General Practice, Litigation, Tort and Insurance Practice; Committees: Insurance Coverage Litigation, Self-Insurers and Risk Managers, Workers Compensation and Employers' Liability Law); American Bar Association (Sections: General Practice, Litigation, Tort and Insurance Practice; Committees: Insurance Coverage Litigation, Self-Insurers and Risk Managers, Workers Compensation and Employers' Liability Law); Louisiana State Bar Association (Co-Chairman, Workers' Compensation Committee, 1992; Sections: Negligence, Compensation and Admiralty Law, Civil Law and Litigation, Labor and Employment Law, Fidelity, Surety & Construction Law, Insurance, Negligence, Compensation and Admiralty Law, and Sole Practitioners and Small Firms); New Orleans Bar Association; Bureau of Governmental Research (Board of Directors and Nominating Committee); Goodwill Industries of Southeastern Louisiana, Inc. (Board of Directors and General Counsel 2006-Present); Louisiana Association of Self Insurance Employers; Louisiana Association of Business and Industry (Liability Task Force, Labor Management Relations Council and Employee Relations Council); Louisiana Bar Foundation; Louisiana Organization for Judicial Excellence (Board of Directors); Louisiana Restaurant Association, Inc. (General Counsel, 2007-Present); New Orleans Chamber of Commerce; New Orleans Claims Association; Risk and Insurance Management Society, Inc.; Louisiana Association of Defense Counsel; International Association of Defense Counsel; Defense Research Institute; American Judicature Society — E-mail: ajy@jyplawfirm.com

Rene S. Paysse, Jr. — 1961 — Tulane University, B.A., 1983; Loyola University, J.D., 1991 — Admitted to Bar, 1992, Louisiana; U.S. District Court, Eastern, Middle and Western Districts of Louisiana; U.S. Court of Appeals, Fifth Circuit — Member Federal, American, Louisiana State and New Orleans Bar Associations; Louisiana Association of Defense Counsel — E-mail: rspaysse@jyplawfirm.com

Neal J. Favret — 1965 — The University of New Orleans, B.Ed., 1990; Loyola Law School, J.D. (cum laude), 1996 — Loyola Law Review — Admitted to Bar, 1996, Louisiana; U.S. District Court, Eastern, Middle and Western Districts of Louisiana; U.S. Court of Appeals, Fifth Circuit; 2010, U.S. Supreme Court — Member American, Louisiana State and New Orleans Bar Associations; Louisiana Association of Defense Counsel; Defense Research Institute

Special Counsel

Julianne T. Echols — 1963 — Tulane University, B.S.M., 1985; Loyola University, J.D., 1992 — Admitted to Bar, 1993, Louisiana — Member Federal and Louisiana State Bar Associations

Maurice C. Ruffin — 1977 — The University of New Orleans, B.A.E. (Dean's List), 2000; Loyola University New Orleans College of Law, J.D., 2003 — Loyola Law Review — Admitted to Bar, 2003, Louisiana; U.S. District Court, Eastern, Middle and Western Districts of Louisiana — Member American, Louisiana State and New Orleans Bar Associations

Robert B. Acomb — 1954 — Tulane University, B.A., 1976; Tulane University Law School, J.D., 1979 — Admitted to Bar, 1979, Louisiana; U.S. District Court, Eastern, Middle and Western Districts of Louisiana — Member Louisiana State and New Orleans Bar Associations; U.S. Fifth Circuit Bar Association; Maritime Law Association; Louisiana Association of Defense Counsel

Christopher M. G'sell — 1974 — Yale University, B.A., 1996; J.D., 1999 — Admitted to Bar, 1999, Louisiana — Member Federal, Louisiana State, New Orleans and Jefferson Bar Associations; Defense Research Institute; Louisiana Association of Defense Counsel

Johnson, Yacoubian & Paysse, APLC, New Orleans, LA (Continued)

Associates

Genevieve K. Jacques — 1971 — Louisiana State University, B.A., 1994; Loyola University School of Law, J.D., 2001 — Admitted to Bar, 2002, Louisiana; U.S. District Court, Eastern and Middle Districts of Louisiana — Member Louisiana State Bar Association

Cyril G. Lowe, Jr — 1961 — Tulane University, B.S.M., 1983; Loyola University, J.D., 1986 — Admitted to Bar, 1986, Louisiana; U.S. District Court, Eastern and Middle Districts of Louisiana — Member Louisiana State Bar Association; Louisiana Association of Defense Counsel

Rachel Riser McMahon — 1983 — Christian Brothers University, B.S. (summa cum laude), 2005; Loyola University School of Law, J.D., 2008 — Admitted to Bar, 2008, Louisiana; U.S. District Court, Eastern District of Louisiana — Member Louisiana State and New Orleans Bar Associations

Jennifer D. Le Carpentier — 1979 — The University of Mississippi, B.A. Political Science, 2001; Paul M Hebert Law School at Louisiana State University, J.D., 2004 — Admitted to Bar, 2004, Louisiana — Member New Orleans Bar Association; Louisiana Association of Defense Counsel; New Orleans Association of Defense Counsel

Dylan K. Knoll — 1983 — University of Melbourne, Australia, B.A. Political Science, 2006; St. Thomas School of Law, J.D. (Dean's Scholar), 2013 — Admitted to Bar, 2014, Louisiana; Texas — Member Federal, American, Louisiana State and New Orleans Bar Associations; State Bar of Texas

Jason M. Freas — 1985 — Loyola University, 2014 — Admitted to Bar, 2014, Louisiana — Member Louisiana State Bar

Christopher L. Williams — 1984 — The University of Georgia, B. Mus, Psychology, 2008; Tulane University Law School, J.D., 2014 — Admitted to Bar, 2014, Louisiana — Member Louisiana State Bar

Jones Walker LLP

201 St. Charles Avenue
New Orleans, Louisiana 70170-5100
Telephone: 504-582-8000
Fax: 504-582-8583
E-Mail: info@joneswalker.com
www.joneswalker.com

(Mobile, AL Office*: RSA Battle House Tower, 11 North Water Street, Suite 1200, 36602, P.O. Box 46, 36601)
  (Tel: 251-432-1414)
  (Fax: 251-433-4106)
(Baton Rouge, LA Office*: Four United Plaza, 8555 United Plaza Boulevard, 70809)
  (Tel: 225-248-2000)
  (Fax: 225-248-2010)
(Lafayette, LA Office*: 600 Jefferson Street, Suite 1600, 70501)
  (Tel: 337-593-7600)
  (Fax: 337-593-7601)
(Birmingham, AL Office*: One Federal Place, 1819 5th Avenue North, Suite 1100, 35203)
  (Tel: 205-244-5200)
  (Fax: 205-244-5400)
(Jackson, MS Office*: 190 East Capitol Street, Suite 800, 39201, P.O. Box 427, 39205-0427)
  (Tel: 601-949-4900)
  (Fax: 601-949-4804)
(Olive Branch, MS Office*: 6897 Crumpler Boulevard, Suite 100, 38654)
  (Tel: 662-895-2996)
  (Fax: 662-895-5480)

Established: 1937

NEW ORLEANS   **LOUISIANA**

Jones Walker LLP, New Orleans, LA (Continued)

Accountants, Admiralty and Maritime Law, Agent/Broker Liability, Antitrust, Appellate Practice, Asbestos Litigation, Aviation, Bankruptcy, Cargo, Class Actions, Commercial Litigation, Complex Litigation, Construction Law, Contracts, Directors and Officers Liability, Disability, Employment Law, Energy, Entertainment Law, Environmental Law, ERISA, Errors and Omissions, Health Care, Insurance Coverage, Insurance Defense, Intellectual Property, International Law, Labor and Employment, Life Insurance, Medical Malpractice, Mergers and Acquisitions, Motor Carriers, Oil and Gas, Personal Injury, Product Liability, Professional Liability, Regulatory and Compliance, Toxic Torts, Workers' Compensation

Firm Profile: Since 1937, Jones Walker LLP has grown to become one of the largest law firms in the southeastern U.S. We serve local, regional, national, and international business interests in a wide range of markets and industries. Today, we have more than 375 attorneys in 19 offices.

Jones Walker is committed to providing proactive legal services to major multinational, public, and private corporations; *Fortune* 500® companies; money center banks and worldwide insurers; and family and emerging businesses located in the United States and abroad.

Insurance Clients

- ACE Insurance Company
- AEGON USA, LLC
- AIPSO
- Alabama Municipal Insurance Corporation
- AMEX Life Assurance Company
- Bankers Life Insurance Company
- Berkley Oil & Gas Specialty Services, LLC
- Canal Insurance Company
- Carolina Casualty Insurance Company
- CNA Insurance Companies
- Continental Casualty Company
- Farm Bureau Insurance Company
- Farmers Insurance Group
- Fred Loya Insurance
- GEICO
- Great West Casualty Company
- Guaranty National Insurance Company
- HealthMarkets, Inc.
- Infinity Property & Casualty Group
- International Marine Underwriters
- John Deere Insurance Company
- Liberty Mutual Insurance Company
- Lincoln National Life Insurance Company
- Markel Rhulen Underwriters and Brokers
- MGA Insurance Company, Inc.
- Mid-West National Life Insurance Company of Tennessee
- Northbrook Property and Casualty Insurance Company
- Nutmeg Insurance Company
- Phoenix Life Insurance Company
- Providence Washington Insurance Company
- Reassure America Life Insurance Company
- South Carolina Farm Bureau Mutual Insurance Company
- Texas Farm Bureau Mutual Insurance Group
- The Travelers Companies, Inc.
- Travelers Property Casualty Corporation
- Wausau General Insurance Company
- Western and Southern Life Insurance Company
- Zurich American Insurance Group
- ACE USA
- Aetna Casualty and Surety Company
- American General Life Companies
- Amerisafe Insurance Group
- AssuranceAmerica Insurance Company
- Bituminous Casualty Corporation
- Blue Cross and Blue Shield of Louisiana
- Cincinnati Insurance Company
- Clarendon National Insurance Company
- Continental Insurance Company
- Farmers Insurance Exchange
- Fireman's Fund Insurance Company
- Georgia Casualty & Surety Company
- Gulf Insurance Company
- The Hartford
- Imperial Fire and Casualty Insurance Company
- Interstate Insurance Group
- Kemper Insurance Companies
- Lincoln National Health & Casualty Insurance Company
- Lumbermen's Underwriting Alliance
- The MEGA Life and Health Insurance Company
- Monumental Life Insurance Company
- North Carolina Farm Bureau Insurance Group
- Penn National Insurance
- Progressive Security Insurance Company
- Prudential Insurance Company of America
- Safeco Insurance Company of America
- Stonebridge Life Insurance Company
- Transamerica Life Insurance Company
- USAgencies Casualty Insurance Company, Inc.
- Western Heritage Insurance Company
- XL Insurance Company, Ltd.
- Zurich American Insurance Company

Jones Walker LLP, New Orleans, LA (Continued)

Firm Members

H. Mark Adams — Mississippi State University, B.A., 1976; The University of Mississippi, J.D., 1981 — Admitted to Bar, 1981, Louisiana; Mississippi — Member American (Sections: Labor and Employment Law, Litigation) and Louisiana State Bar Associations; The Mississippi Bar — Practice Areas: Labor and Employment; Insurance Coverage Litigation — E-mail: madams@joneswalker.com

L. Etienne Balart — The University of New Orleans, B.A., 1994; Louisiana State University, J.D., 1997 — Admitted to Bar, 1997, Louisiana; 1998, U.S. District Court, Eastern, Middle and Western Districts of Louisiana; U.S. Court of Appeals, Fifth Circuit — Member Federal, Louisiana State and New Orleans Bar Associations; The Maritime Law Association of the United States; Southeastern Admiralty Law Institute — E-mail: ebalart@joneswalker.com

Robert B. Bieck, Jr. — Rensselaer Polytechnic Institute; University of Nebraska, B.A., 1974; Texas Tech University, J.D. (with high honors), 1977 — Admitted to Bar, 1977, Louisiana; Texas; 1992, District of Columbia — Member American Bar Association (Litigation Section Committees: Directors and Officers, Insurance Liability, Broker-Dealer Litigation, Public Offering Litigation, Business Law; Federal Regulation of Securities; Civil Litigation and Enforcement Matters Subcommittee, Business and Corporate Litigation and Criminal Laws); State Bar of Texas; The District of Columbia Bar; Louisiana Bankers Association (Bank Counsel Section); Securities Industry Association (Legal and Compliance Division); National Association of Compliance Professionals — Languages: French, Spanish, Turkish — E-mail: rbieck@joneswalker.com

Madeleine Fischer — Harvard College, A.B., 1972; Tulane University, J.D., 1975 — Admitted to Bar, 1975, Louisiana; 1992, Texas — Member American Bar Association (Vice Chair, Insurance Coverage Litigation Committee Tort Trial and Insurance Practice Section); Louisiana State and New Orleans (Chair, Insurance Law Committee) Bar Associations; State Bar of Texas; New Orleans Association of Defense Counsel (Past President); Louisiana Association of Defense Counsel (Past Board Member) — Editorial Board Member, CGL Reporter (Publication of the Insurance Risk Management Institute) — Board Certified in Civil Trial Advocacy by the National Board of Trial Advocacy — E-mail: mfischer@joneswalker.com

Covert J. Geary — Washington and Lee University, B.S. (cum laude), 1980; Louisiana State University, J.D., 1984 — Admitted to Bar, 1984, Louisiana; 1991, District of Columbia — Member American Bar Association (Sections on Litigation: Torts and Insurance and Natural Resources Law; Past Chair, Life Insurance Law Committee); Louisiana State Bar Association; Defense Research Institute (Life, Health and Disability Insurance Committee); Rocky Mountain Mineral Law Institute — E-mail: cgeary@joneswalker.com

John G. Gomila Jr. — The University of New Orleans, B.S., 1973; Loyola University, J.D., 1976 — Admitted to Bar, 1976, Louisiana; 1981, U.S. Court of Appeals, Fifth Circuit; U.S. Supreme Court — Member Federation of Defense and Corporate Counsel; Louisiana Association of Defense Counsel; Defense Research Institute — U.S. Army — E-mail: jgomila@joneswalker.com

Glenn G. Goodier — Loyola University, B.B.A., 1970; J.D., 1971 — Admitted to Bar, 1971, Louisiana — Member Federal, American and New Orleans Bar Associations; The Maritime Law Association of the United States (Board of Directors, 2002-2005); Association of Average Adjusters of the United States; Southeastern Admiralty Law Institute; International Association of Defense Counsel — E-mail: ggoodier@joneswalker.com

Marc C. Hebert — Tulane University, B.A., 1991; Loyola University School of Law, J.D., 1994; The George Washington University, LL.M., 1996 — Admitted to Bar, 1994, Louisiana; 1996, Virginia; 1997, District of Columbia; U.S. District Court, Eastern, Middle and Western Districts of Louisiana; U.S. District Court, Southern District of Texas; U.S. Court of Appeals for the Federal, Fourth and Fifth Circuits; U.S. Court of International Trade — Member Louisiana State Bar Association; The District of Columbia Bar; Virginia State Bar — E-mail: mhebert@joneswalker.com

Cornelius R. Heusel — Loyola University, B.B.A./J.D., 1967 — Admitted to Bar, 1967, Louisiana; U.S. District Court, Eastern, Middle and Western Districts of Louisiana; U.S. District Court, Eastern, Northern and Western Districts of Texas; U.S. District Court, Eastern and Western Districts of Arkansas; U.S. District Court, District of Colorado; U.S. Court of Appeals, Fourth, Fifth, Sixth, Eighth and Eleventh Circuits; U.S. Supreme Court — Member American, Louisiana State and New Orleans Bar Associations — E-mail: nheusel@joneswalker.com

Thomas P. Hubert — Trinity University, B.S., 1986; Louisiana State University, J.D., 1989 — Admitted to Bar, 1989, Louisiana — Member Federal, American and New Orleans Bar Associations — E-mail: thubert@joneswalker.com

Jones Walker LLP, New Orleans, LA (Continued)

William J. Joyce — St. Francis College, B.A., 1966; University of West Florida, B.A., 1981; Loyola University, J.D., 1988 — Admitted to Bar, 1988, Louisiana; 1995, Florida; 2006, Texas — Member The Florida Bar (Aviation Law Certification Committee); National Transportation Safety Board Bar Association; Lawyer-Pilots Bar Association — Board Certified Aviation Law Specialist by the Florida Bar — Practice Areas: Aviation; Insurance Defense — E-mail: bjoyce@joneswalker.com

Edward J. Koehl, Jr. — Louisiana State University, B.S., 1968; Loyola University, J.D., 1971 — Admitted to Bar, 1971, Louisiana — Member American, Louisiana State, and New Orleans Bar Associations; Bar Association of the Fifth Federal Circuit; The Maritime Law Association of the United States — E-mail: ekoehl@joneswalker.com

Robert T. Lemon, II — United States Merchant Marine Academy, B.S., 1975; Tulane University, J.D. (cum laude), 1980; University of London, University College Faculty of Laws, LL.M. (cum laude), 1981; Hague Academy of International Law, The Hague, Netherlands, 1984 — Admitted to Bar, 1980, Louisiana; 2004, Texas — Member Federal, American, Louisiana State and New Orleans Bar Associations; State Bar of Texas; American Society of International Law; Average Adjusters Association of the United States; The Maritime Law Association of the United States; Southeastern Admiralty Law Institute — E-mail: blemon@joneswalker.com

Joseph J. Lowenthal, Jr. — The George Washington University, B.A. (cum laude), 1976; Tulane University, J.D., 1979 — Admitted to Bar, 1980, Louisiana — Member New Orleans Association of Defense Counsel (President, 1989-1990); National Association of College and University Attorneys; Defense Research Institute; American Health Lawyers Association — E-mail: jlowenthal@joneswalker.com

Christopher S. Mann — Emory University, B.A., 1994; Tulane University of Louisiana, J.D. (magna cum laude), 1999 — Admitted to Bar, 1999, Louisiana; 2008, Texas; 1999, U.S. District Court, Eastern, Middle and Western Districts of Louisiana; U.S. Court of Appeals, Fifth Circuit; 2007, U.S. District Court, Eastern and Western Districts of Arkansas; 2008, U.S. District Court, Southern District of Texas — Member Federal, Louisiana State and New Orleans Bar Associations; State Bar of Texas; The Maritime Law Association of the United States — E-mail: cmann@joneswalker.com

David G. Radlauer — The University of New Orleans, B.A. (magna cum laude), 1975; Georgetown University, J.D., 1978 — Admitted to Bar, 1978, Louisiana; 1999, Colorado — Member American and Louisiana State Bar Associations — E-mail: dradlauer@joneswalker.com

Jefferson R. Tillery — Louisiana State University, B.S., 1983; J.D., 1986 — Order of the Coif — Admitted to Bar, 1986, Louisiana — Member Federal and Louisiana State Bar Associations; The Maritime Law Association of the United States — E-mail: jtillery@joneswalker.com

Jarred G. Trauth — Louisiana State University, B.S., 1996; Loyola University, J.D., 2000 — Admitted to Bar, 2001, Louisiana — Member Louisiana State Bar Association — E-mail: jtrauth@joneswalker.com

Richard J. Tyler — Georgetown University, A.B., 1978; J.D., 1981; Harvard Law School, Mediation Workshop, 2008 — Admitted to Bar, 1981, District of Columbia; 1983, Louisiana; 2004, Texas — Member American Bar Association (Forum on the Construction Industry, Governing Committee, 2009; Chair Division 3 Design Steering Committee, 2006-2008); Litigation Section (Program Co-Chair, Construction Litigation Committee, 2001-2009); Louisiana State Bar Association; State Bar of Texas; American Arbitration Association National Roster of Neutrals; Fellow, Litigation Counsel of America; International Association of Defense Counsel; Defense Research Institute — E-mail: rtyler@joneswalker.com

Robert L. Walsh — Spring Hill College, B.A./B.S. (summa cum laude), 1982; Loyola University New Orleans College of Law, J.D. (magna cum laude), 1986 — Admitted to Bar, 1986, Louisiana; U.S. District Court, Eastern, Middle and Western Districts of Louisiana — Member Louisiana State (Medical/Legal Interprofessional Committee) and New Orleans Bar Associations; New Orleans Association of Defense Counsel (Past President); Louisiana Association of Defense Counsel; Defense Research Institute — E-mail: rwalsh@joneswalker.com

Edward Dirk Wegmann — Louisiana State University, B.A., 1977; J.D., 1979 — Admitted to Bar, 1980, Louisiana; U.S. District Court, Eastern, Middle and Western Districts of Louisiana; U.S. Court of Appeals, Fifth Circuit; U.S. Supreme Court; U.S. Tax Court; U.S. Claims Court — Member Federal and American Bar Associations; Louisiana State Bar Association (Sections: Litigation, Tort and Insurance Practice; Construction; Patent, Trademark and Copyright Law); New Orleans Bar Association; American Academy of Hospital Attorneys; Louisiana Association of Defense Counsel — E-mail: dwegmann@joneswalker.com

Scott T. Zander — University of Aberdeen, Scotland; Claremont McKenna College, B.A., 1986; The University of North Carolina at Chapel Hill, J.D., 1989 — Admitted to Bar, 1990, Louisiana — Member Federal, American, Louisiana State and New Orleans Bar Associations — E-mail: szander@joneswalker.com

Wayne G. Zeringue Jr. — 1961 — Louisiana State University at Baton Rouge, B.S., 1983; Louisiana State University Law Center, J.D., 1987 — Admitted to Bar, 1987, Louisiana; U.S. District Court, Eastern, Middle and Western Districts of Louisiana — Member American, Louisiana State and New Orleans Bar Associations — Navy League — Practice Areas: Maritime Law; Construction Law; Oil and Gas

Lobman, Carnahan, Batt, Angelle & Nader

400 Poydras Street, Suite 2300
New Orleans, Louisiana 70130
Telephone: 504-586-9292
Fax: 504-586-1290
www.lcba-law.com

Established: 1979

Insurance Defense, Product Liability, General Liability, Bodily Injury, Casualty, Workers' Compensation, Admiralty and Maritime Law, Insurance Fraud, Insurance Coverage, Environmental Law

Insurance Clients

American International Group, Inc.
Aspen Specialty Insurance Company
Crum & Forster Insurance Group
Hanover Insurance Company
The Hartford Insurance Group
State Farm Mutual Automobile Insurance Company
American National Property and Casualty Company
Chubb Services Group
Government Employees Insurance Company
Horace Mann Insurance Company

Non-Insurance Clients

IMO Industries, Inc.

Firm Members

Edward P. Lobman — (1941-2004)

Burt K. Carnahan — **(Retired)** — 1945 — Washington and Lee University, B.A., 1966; Louisiana State University, J.D., 1972 — Admitted to Bar, 1972, Louisiana — Member American and Louisiana State Bar Associations; Defense Research Institute; Louisiana Association of Defense Counsel

David V. Batt — 1952 — Tulane University, B.A., 1974; J.D., 1977 — Admitted to Bar, 1977, Louisiana — Member Federal, American and Louisiana State Bar Associations; Defense Research Institute; Louisiana Association of Defense Counsel — E-mail: dvb@lcba-law.com

Sidney J. Angelle — 1956 — Louisiana State University, B.S., 1979; J.D., 1982 — Admitted to Bar, 1983, Louisiana — Member Louisiana State Bar Association; Defense Research Institute; Louisiana Association of Defense Counsel — E-mail: sja@lcba-law.com

James P. Nader — 1958 — Assumption College, B.A., 1981; Loyola University, J.D., 1984 — Admitted to Bar, 1984, Louisiana; Oklahoma — Member Federal, American and Louisiana State Bar Associations; Louisiana Trial Lawyers Association; Association of Trial Lawyers of America; Defense Research Institute; Louisiana Association of Defense Counsel — E-mail: jpn@lcba-law.com

Joseph M. Messina — 1959 — Tulane University, B.A. (cum laude), 1981; Louisiana State University, J.D., 1984 — Admitted to Bar, 1984, Louisiana — Member Louisiana State Bar Association; Louisiana Association of Defense Counsel; Defense Research Institute — E-mail: jmm@lcba-law.com

Brant J. Cacamo — 1973 — Louisiana State University, B.S., 1995; Louisiana State University Law Center, J.D., 1999 — Admitted to Bar, 1999, Louisiana — Member Louisiana State Bar Association — E-mail: bjc@lcba-law.com

Pamela K. Richard — 1954 — Nicholls State University, B.A. (magna cum laude), 1994; Louisiana State University, J.D., 1997 — Admitted to Bar, 1997, Louisiana — Member Louisiana State and New Orleans Bar Associations; Louisiana Association of Defense Counsel — E-mail: pkr@lcba-law.com

Eric B. Berger — 1974 — The University of Texas at Austin, B.A., 1995; Tulane University Law School, J.D. (magna cum laude), 1999 — Admitted to Bar, 1999, Louisiana — E-mail: ebb@lcba-law.com

Lobman, Carnahan, Batt, Angelle & Nader, New Orleans, LA (Continued)

James J. Young IV — 1971 — The University of New Orleans, B.A., 1994; Louisiana State University, Paul M. Hebert Law Center, J.D., 1998 — Admitted to Bar, 1998, Louisiana — E-mail: jjy@lcba-law.com

Locke Lord LLP

601 Poydras, Suite 2660
New Orleans, Louisiana 70130
   Telephone: 504-558-5100
   Fax: 504-558-5200
   www.lockelord.com

(Chicago, IL Office*: 111 South Wacker Drive, 60606-4410)
   (Tel: 312-443-0700)
   (Fax: 312-443-0336)
(Atlanta, GA Office*: Terminus 200, Suite 1200, 3333 Piedmont Road NE, 30305)
   (Tel: 404-870-4600)
   (Fax: 404-872-5547)
(Austin, TX Office*: 600 Congress Avenue, Suite 2200, 78701-2748)
   (Tel: 512-305-4700)
   (Fax: 512-305-4800)
(Dallas, TX Office*: 2200 Ross Avenue, Suite 2200, 75201)
   (Tel: 214-740-8000)
   (Fax: 214-740-8800)
(Houston, TX Office*: 2800 JPMorgan Chase Tower, 600 Travis, 77002-3095)
   (Tel: 713-226-1200)
   (Fax: 713-223-3717)
(London, United Kingdom Office*: 201 Bishopsgate, DX 567 London/City, EC2M 3AB)
   (Tel: +44 (0) 20 7861 9000 (Int'l))
   (Tel: 011 44 207861 9000 (US))
   (Fax: +44 (0) 20 7785 6869 201 (Bishopsgate))
(Los Angeles, CA Office*: 300 South Grand Avenue, Suite 2600, 90071-3119)
   (Tel: 213-485-1500)
   (Fax: 213-485-1200)
(New York, NY Office*: Three World Financial Center, Floor 20, 10281)
   (Tel: 212-415-8600)
   (Fax: 212-303-2754)
(Sacramento, CA Office*: 500 Capitol Mall, Suite 1800, 95814)
   (Tel: 916-554-0240)
   (Fax: 916-554-5440)
(San Francisco, CA Office*: 44 Montgomery Street, Suite 2400, 94104)
   (Tel: 415-318-8810)
   (Fax: 415-676-5816)
(Washington, DC Office*: 701 8th Street, N.W., Suite 700, 20001)
   (Tel: 202-521-4100)
   (Fax: 202-521-4200)
(Hong Kong, China-PRC Office: 21/F Bank of China Tower, 1 Garden Road, Central)
   (Tel: +852 3465 0600)
   (Fax: +852 3014 0991)

Antitrust, Arbitration, Aviation, Business Law, Class Actions, Construction Law, Corporate Law, Directors and Officers Liability, Employee Benefits, Environmental Law, Health Care, Insurance Law, Intellectual Property, Labor and Employment, Land Use, Admiralty and Maritime Law, Mergers and Acquisitions, Product Liability, Railroad Law, Regulatory and Compliance, Reinsurance, Securities, Technology, Transportation, Litigation, Appellate, Long Term Care

Partner

Monique Lafontaine — Texas Woman's University, B.A. (cum laude), 1991; Loyola University School of Law, J.D., 1996 — Admitted to Bar, 1996, Louisiana; U.S. District Court, Eastern, Middle and Western Districts of Louisiana; U.S. Court of Appeals, Fifth Circuit — Member American and Louisiana State Bar Associations; Louisiana Bar Foundation; Thomas More Inn of

Locke Lord LLP, New Orleans, LA (Continued)

Court (1997-Present) — Practice Areas: Business Litigation; Dispute Resolution; Insurance; Product Liability

(See listing under Chicago, IL for additional information)

Lugenbuhl, Wheaton, Peck, Rankin & Hubbard

Pan American Life Center, Suite 2775
601 Poydras Street
New Orleans, Louisiana 70130
   Telephone: 504-568-1990
   Fax: 504-310-9195
   www.lawla.com

(Houston, TX Office*: 815 Walker Street, Suite 1447, 77002)
   (Tel: 713-222-1990)
   (Fax: 713-222-1996)

Established: 1986

Insurance Coverage, Insurance Defense, Insurance Litigation, Admiralty and Maritime Law, Personal Injury, Jones Act, Environmental Law, Automobile, General Liability, Product Liability, Protection and Indemnity, Subrogation, Comprehensive

Insurance Clients

Century Surety Company
Covenant Claims Service, LLC
First Financial Insurance Company
Great American Insurance Company
Liberty Mutual Insurance Company
Prudential Insurance Company of America
TIG Specialty Insurance Company
Travelers Life and Annuity Company
Zurich American Insurance Company
Continental Underwriters, Ltd.
Fidelis Group Holdings LLC
Gray & Company
The Hanover Insurance Group
The Hartford
PRMS, Inc. - Professional Risk Management Services, Inc.
SPARTA Insurance
The Travelers Companies
Westchester Specialty Insurance Services, Inc.

Non-Insurance Clients

Avis Budget Group, Inc.
Diversified Group, Inc.
Reagan Equipment Company
Regions Financial Corporation
Conmaco/Rector, LP
Gulf Coast Marine, Inc.
Regions Bank
Superior Energy Services, Inc.

Shareholders

Scott R. Wheaton, Jr. — 1950 — Stanford University, B.A., 1972; Columbia University, M.B.A., 1977; Vanderbilt University, J.D., 1977 — Admitted to Bar, 1977, Louisiana; 1980, New York — Member International, Inter-American, American, Louisiana State and New York State Bar Associations; The Maritime Law Association of the United States; New Orleans Association of Defense Counsel; Louisiana Association of Defense Counsel; Defense Research Institute

Stewart F. Peck — 1952 — Kenyon College, A.B. (magna cum laude), 1974; Case Western Reserve University, 1975; Tulane University of Louisiana, J.D., 1977 — Phi Beta Kappa — Admitted to Bar, 1977, Louisiana — Member American and Louisiana State Bar Associations; Louisiana Association of Defense Counsel

Ralph S. Hubbard III — 1949 — Louisiana State University, B.A., 1972; M.A., 1974; Tulane University of Louisiana, J.D., 1977 — Order of the Coif — Admitted to Bar, 1977, Louisiana — Member American, Louisiana State and New Orleans Bar Associations; Louisiana Association of Defense Counsel; International Association of Defense Counsel

Stanley J. Cohn — 1955 — Tulane University of Louisiana, B.A. (cum laude), 1978; J.D., 1981 — Omicron Delta Kappa — Admitted to Bar, 1981, Louisiana — Member Federal, American, Louisiana State and New Orleans Bar Associations; Louisiana Association of Defense Counsel; The Maritime Law Association of the United States — Practice Areas: Business Law; Civil Litigation; Admiralty and Maritime Law

Kristopher M. Redmann — 1957 — The University of New Orleans, B.A., 1981; Loyola University, J.D., 1986 — Admitted to Bar, 1987, Louisiana —

LOUISIANA   NEW ORLEANS

Lugenbuhl, Wheaton, Peck, Rankin & Hubbard, New Orleans, LA (Continued)

Member Federal, American and Louisiana State Bar Associations; Louisiana Association of Defense Counsel

David B. Sharpe — 1963 — Tulane University, B.S.E.E., 1985; The George Washington University Law School, J.D. (with honors), 1990 — Admitted to Bar, 1990, Louisiana — Member American Bar Association; The Maritime Law Association of the United States

Simeon Bernard Reimonenq, Jr. — 1962 — The University of New Orleans, B.S.M.E., 1984; Loyola University, J.D., 1989 — Admitted to Bar, 1989, Louisiana; 1990, Connecticut

Celeste D. Elliott — 1969 — University of Virginia, B.A., 1991; Tulane University, J.D. (magna cum laude), 1994 — Order of the Coif — Admitted to Bar, 1994, Virginia; 1995, Maryland; 1996, Louisiana — Member American and Louisiana State Bar Associations; Defense Research Institute — Practice Areas: Insurance Coverage; Insurance Litigation

Kristopher T. Wilson — 1969 — Louisiana State University, B.S., 1991; J.D., 1995 — Admitted to Bar, 1995, Louisiana

Joseph P. Guichet — 1971 — Loyola University New Orleans, B.A. (cum laude), 1993; Tulane University, J.D. (cum laude), 1996 — Admitted to Bar, 1996, Louisiana — Member American Bar Association

Seth A. Schmeeckle — 1975 — Louisiana State University, B.S., 1997; J.D., 2000 — Admitted to Bar, 2000, Louisiana

Elia Diaz-Yaeger — University of Southwestern Louisiana, B.A./B.S. (cum laude), 1987; M.S. (cum laude), 1989; Loyola University Law School, J.D., 1994 — Admitted to Bar, 1995, Louisiana — Practice Areas: Litigation

Tina Kappen — 1978 — Stephens College, B.A./B.A. (magna cum laude), 2000; Tulane University Law School, J.D. (magna cum laude), 2003 — Admitted to Bar, 2004, New York; 2005, Louisiana — Member Louisiana State and New York State Bar Associations

Miles C. Thomas — Clemson University, B.A., 2000; The University of Tennessee College of Law, J.D., 2004 — Admitted to Bar, 2004, South Carolina; 2007, Louisiana

Attorneys

LaDonna G. Schexnyder — Northeast Louisiana University, B.A. (magna cum laude), 1989; Loyola Law School, J.D., 2003 — Admitted to Bar, 2003, Louisiana — Practice Areas: Litigation

Anne E. Briard — Cornell University, B.A., 2000; Tulane University Law School, J.D. (magna cum laude), 2004 — Admitted to Bar, 2004, Louisiana; 2008, New Mexico — Practice Areas: Litigation

Heather Sharp — Louisiana State University, B.S. (cum laude), 2001; J.D., 2005 — Admitted to Bar, 2005, Louisiana — Practice Areas: Litigation

(This firm is also listed in the Subrogation section of this directory)

Mouledoux, Bland, Legrand & Brackett, L.L.C.

701 Poydras Street, Suite 4250
New Orleans, Louisiana 70139-6001
 Telephone: 504-595-3000
 Fax: 504-522-2121
 E-Mail: info@mblb.com
 www.mblb.com
 www.navwaters.com

(Lafayette, LA Office: One Lafayette Square, 345 Doucet Road, Suite 200H, 70503)
 (Tel: 337-993-8897)
 (Fax: 337-988-0393)
 (E-Mail: dhoerner@mblb.com)

Established: 1997

Insurance Defense, Coverage Analysis, Opinions, Product Liability, Medical Malpractice, General Liability, Automobile, Admiralty and Maritime Law, Jones Act, Personal Injury, Third Party, Investigation and Adjustment, Subrogation, Longshore and Harbor Workers' Compensation, Policy Construction and Interpretation, Defense Base Act, War Hazard Compensation Act

Mouledoux, Bland, Legrand & Brackett, L.L.C., New Orleans, LA (Continued)

Firm Profile: At Mouledoux, Bland, Legrand & Brackett, our primary focus is to customize our services in meeting each client's needs.

State-of-the-Art research and communications tools provide our clients with the most up-to-date information and resources regarding all areas of law and industry. Our commitment to continuing education is reflected in programs that benefit both clients and attorneys. These programs include newsletters designed to illuminate current legal issues and seminars programmed to particular client interests. Our well-trained, versatile attorneys are also encouraged to maintain an active presence in the community and in local charities.

With a broad range of knowledge and experience, the attorneys of Mouledoux, Bland, Legrand & Brackett are able to afford our clients full legal services in all phases of trial and appellate practice in Louisiana, Mississippi, Texas and other areas of the United States.

Insurance Clients

ACE American Insurance Company
American Equity Insurance Company
American Longshore Mutual Association, Ltd.
Everest Indemnity Insurance Company
FCCI Insurance Company
National Union Fire Insurance Company
RLI Insurance Company
Union Standard Insurance Group

Allianz Global Corporate & Specialty
American Home Assurance Company
Chartis Marine Adjusters, Inc.
CNA
Everest National Insurance Company
Global Indemnity Group, Inc.
OneBeacon Insurance
Optimum Claim Services, Inc.
St. Paul Travelers

Non-Insurance Clients

American Electric Power
B & J Martin, Inc.
Cooper/T. Smith Stevedoring Company
Ingram Barge Company
LOOP L.L.C.
M/G Transport Services, Inc.
Pine Bluff Sand and Gravel Company
Shaw Environmental & Infrastructure Group

Archer Daniels Midland Company
C.F. Bean L.L.C.
G & M Marine, Inc.
Iberia Marine Service, LLC
ITT Corporation
May Trucking Company
Millennium Healthcare Management, LLC
Ports America, Inc.

Members

André J. Mouledoux — 1951 — Loyola University New Orleans, B.A., 1972; Loyola University New Orleans College of Law, J.D., 1977 — Admitted to Bar, 1977, Louisiana; U.S. District Court, Eastern, Middle and Western Districts of Louisiana; U.S. Court of Appeals, Fifth and Sixth Circuits; U.S. Supreme Court — Member Louisiana State Bar Association (House of Delegates); New Orleans Board of Trade; Claims and Litigation Management Alliance; Louisiana Association of Defense Counsel; The Maritime Law Association of the United States; Defense Research Institute — E-mail: amouledoux@mblb.com

Wilton E. Bland, III — 1950 — Tulane University, B.A., 1973; J.D., 1975 — Admitted to Bar, 1975, Louisiana; U.S. District Court, Eastern, Middle and Western Districts of Louisiana; U.S. Court of Appeals, Fifth Circuit; U.S. Supreme Court — Member Louisiana State Bar Association; The Maritime Law Association of the United States; Louisiana Association of Defense Counsel — E-mail: wbland@mblb.com

Georges M. Legrand — 1954 — The University of New Orleans, B.S., 1976; Loyola University, J.D., 1979 — Admitted to Bar, 1979, Louisiana; U.S. District Court, Eastern, Middle and Western Districts of Louisiana; U.S. District Court, Eastern and Southern Districts of Texas; U.S. Court of Appeals, Fifth Circuit; U.S. Supreme Court — Member Federal, American and Louisiana State Bar Associations; Louisiana Association of Defense Counsel; The Maritime Law Association of the United States — E-mail: glegrand@mblb.com

Alan G. Brackett — 1960 — Tulane University, B.A., 1982; J.D., 1984 — Admitted to Bar, 1984, Louisiana; U.S. District Court, Eastern, Middle and Western Districts of Louisiana; U.S. Court of Appeals, Fifth, Ninth and Eleventh Circuits; U.S. Supreme Court — Member American (Sections: Tort and Insurance Practice, Business Law), Louisiana State and New Orleans Bar Associations; The Maritime Law Association of the United States (Proctor); College of Workers' Compensation Lawyers; Louisiana Association of Defense Counsel; New Orleans Association of Defense Counsel; Southeastern

Mouledoux, Bland, Legrand & Brackett, L.L.C., New Orleans, LA (Continued)

Admiralty Law Institute; Defense Research Institute — Practice Areas: Admiralty and Maritime Law; Workers' Compensation — E-mail: abrackett@mblb.com

Patrick E. Costello — 1974 — University of Kentucky, B.A., 1996; Loyola University New Orleans College of Law, J.D., 1999 — Admitted to Bar, 2000, Louisiana; U.S. District Court, Eastern, Middle and Western Districts of Louisiana — Member American and Louisiana State Bar Associations; Louisiana Association of Defense Counsel; Defense Research Institute — E-mail: pcostello@mblb.com

C. William Emory — 1963 — Louisiana State University, B.S., 1985; Louisiana State University, Paul M. Hebert Law Center, J.D., 1990 — Admitted to Bar, 1990, Louisiana; U.S. District Court, Eastern, Middle and Western Districts of Louisiana; U.S. Court of Appeals, Fifth Circuit; U.S. Supreme Court — Member American and Louisiana State Bar Associations; Louisiana Association of Defense Counsel — E-mail: bemory@mblb.com

Daniel J. Hoerner — 1964 — The University of New Orleans, B.A., 1989; Loyola University New Orleans College of Law, J.D., 1992 — Admitted to Bar, 1992, Louisiana; U.S. District Court, Eastern, Middle and Western Districts of Louisiana; U.S. Court of Appeals, Fifth Circuit; U.S. Supreme Court — Member American, Louisiana State and Lafayette Bar Associations; American Inn of Court of Acadiana; Louisiana Association of Defense Counsel — Resident Lafayette, LA Office — E-mail: dhoerner@mblb.com

Jon B. Robinson — 1979 — Louisiana State University, B.A., 2002; Loyola University New Orleans College of Law, J.D., 2006 — Admitted to Bar, 2006, Louisiana; U.S. District Court, Eastern, Middle and Western Districts of Louisiana; U.S. Court of Appeals, Fifth and Ninth Circuits — Member American and Louisiana State Bar Associations; DOL-Joint Bar Association; Louisiana Association of Defense Counsel — E-mail: jrobinson@mblb.com

Robert N. Popich — 1977 — University of Louisiana at Lafayette, B.A., 2000; Loyola University New Orleans College of Law, J.D., 2004 — Admitted to Bar, 2004, Louisiana; U.S. District Court, Eastern, Middle and Western Districts of Louisiana; U.S. Court of Appeals, Fifth Circuit — Member Federal, American and Louisiana State Bar Associations; Louisiana Bar Foundation; Louisiana Association of Defense Counsel — E-mail: rpopich@mblb.com

Patrick J. Babin — 1983 — Tulane University, B.A., 2005; Loyola University New Orleans College of Law, J.D., 2008 — Admitted to Bar, 2008, Louisiana; U.S. District Court, Eastern, Middle and Western Districts of Louisiana; U.S. Court of Appeals, Fifth Circuit — Member American, Louisiana State and New Orleans Bar Associations; Louisiana Bar Foundation; DOL-Joint Bar Association; Louisiana Association of Defense Counsel — E-mail: pbabin@mblb.com

Associates

Adam P. Sanderson — 1982 — Louisiana State University, B.A., 2004; Loyola University School of Law, J.D., 2007 — Admitted to Bar, 2007, Louisiana; U.S. District Court, Eastern, Middle and Western Districts of Louisiana; U.S. District Court, Southern District of Mississippi; U.S. District Court, Southern District of Texas; U.S. Court of Appeals, Fifth Circuit — Member Federal, American, Louisiana State and New Orleans Bar Associations; Fellow, Louisiana Bar Foundation; Louisiana Association of Defense Counsel — E-mail: asanderson@mblb.com

Beth S. Bernstein — 1982 — Newcomb College, Tulane University, B.A., 2003; Tulane University Graduate School, M.A., 2004; Tulane University Law School, J.D., 2007 — Admitted to Bar, 2008, Louisiana; U.S. District Court, Eastern, Middle and Western Districts of Louisiana; U.S. Court of Appeals, Fifth Circuit — Member Federal, American, Louisiana State and New Orleans Bar Associations; DOL-Joint Bar Association; Women's International Shipping and Trade Association; New Orleans Association of Defense Counsel; Louisiana Association of Defense Counsel; Southeastern Admiralty Law Institute — E-mail: bbernstein@mblb.com

Wilton E. Bland, IV — 1981 — The University of the South, B.A., 2004; Louisiana State University, Paul M. Hebert Law Center, J.D., 2010 — Admitted to Bar, 2010, Louisiana; U.S. District Court, Eastern, Middle and Western Districts of Louisiana; U.S. Court of Appeals, Fifth Circuit — Member Federal and Louisiana State Bar Associations; Louisiana Association of Defense Counsel; The Maritime Law Association of the United States; Defense Research Institute — E-mail: wblandiv@mblb.com

Trevor M. Cutaiar — 1984 — St. Bonaventure University, B.A., 2006; Loyola University New Orleans College of Law, J.D., 2010 — Admitted to Bar, 2010, Louisiana; U.S. District Court, Eastern, Middle and Western Districts of Louisiana; U.S. Court of Appeals, Fifth Circuit — Member Federal, American, Louisiana State and New Orleans Bar Associations; The Maritime Law Association of the United States; Louisiana Association of Defense Counsel; Defense Research Institute — E-mail: tcutaiar@mblb.com

Mouledoux, Bland, Legrand & Brackett, L.L.C., New Orleans, LA (Continued)

Mark E. Hanna — 1963 — Creighton University, B.A., 1985; Tulane University Law School, J.D., 1988 — Admitted to Bar, 1989, Louisiana; U.S. District Court, Eastern, Middle and Western Districts of Louisiana; U.S. Court of Appeals, Fifth Circuit — Member Louisiana State, New Orleans and Jefferson Bar Associations; Claims and Litigation Management Alliance; Louisiana Bar Foundation; Defense Research Institute; Louisiana Association of Defense Counsel — E-mail: mhanna@mblb.com

Kirby P. Blanchard — 1975 — Embry-Riddle Aeronautical University, B.S., 2002; Paul M Hebert Law School at Louisiana State University, J.D., 2006 — Admitted to Bar, 2006, Louisiana; U.S. District Court, Eastern, Middle and Western Districts of Louisiana — Member Federal, Louisiana State and Terrebonne Parish Bar Associations — E-mail: kblanchard@mblb.com

Cassie E. Preston — 1985 — Louisiana State University, B.S., 2007; Loyola University School of Law, J.D., 2010 — Admitted to Bar, 2010, Louisiana; U.S. District Court, Eastern, Middle and Western Districts of Louisiana; U.S. Court of Appeals, Fifth Circuit — Member Federal, American, Louisiana State and New Orleans Bar Associations; DOL-Joint Bar Association; St. Thomas More Inn of Courts; Women's International Shipping and Trading Association; Louisiana Association of Defense Counsel — E-mail: cpreston@mblb.com

Simone H. Yoder — 1981 — Rhodes College, B.A., 2003; Loyola University New Orleans College of Law, J.D., 2008 — Admitted to Bar, 2008, Louisiana; U.S. District Court, Eastern, Middle and Western Districts of Louisiana; U.S. Court of Appeals, Fifth Circuit — Member American, Louisiana State and New Orleans Bar Association; DOL-Joint Bar Association; Women's International Shipping and Trading Association; Louisiana Association of Defense Counsel — E-mail: syoder@mblb.com

Caitlin R. Byars — 1985 — Louisiana State University, B.S., 2007; Loyola University School of Law, J.D., 2011 — Admitted to Bar, 2011, Louisiana; U.S. District Court, Eastern, Middle and Western Districts of Louisiana; U.S. Court of Appeals, Fifth Circuit — Member Federal, Louisiana State, Fifth Federal Circuit and New Orleans Bar Associations; DOL-Joint Bar Association; Association of Women Attorneys; St. Thomas More Inn of Court; Women's International Shipping and Trade Association; Louisiana Association of Defense Counsel; Southeastern Admiralty Law Institute — E-mail: cbyars@mblb.com

(This firm is also listed in the Subrogation section of this directory)

O'Bryon & Schnabel, PLC

1010 Common Street, Suite 1950
New Orleans, Louisiana 70112
Telephone: 504-799-4200
Fax: 504-799-4211
E-Mail: kob@obryonlaw.com
www.obryonlaw.com

Insurance Defense, Automobile, Coverage Issues, Asbestos Litigation, Professional Liability

Insurance Clients

Century Surety Company	CNA Global Specialty Lines
Commercial Casualty Insurance Company	COUNTRY Mutual Insurance Company
Evanston Insurance Company	GEICO
Louisiana Restaurant Association Self Insurer's Fund	Markel Underwriting Managers, Inc.
Metropolitan Property and Casualty Insurance Company	Mt. Morris Mutual Insurance Company
Nationwide Insurance	RiverStone Claims Management, LLC
Sedgwick Claims Management Services, Inc.	TRISTAR Risk Management
Wausau Insurance Companies	Westport Insurance Corporation
Zurich North America	

Non-Insurance Clients

Doctor's Associates, Inc./Subway	Hancock/Whitney National Bank
Hoffinger Industries, Inc.	Montgomery KONE, Inc.
Northern Telecom, Inc.	

O'Bryon & Schnabel, PLC, New Orleans, LA (Continued)

Partners

Kevin O'Bryon — 1955 — Tulane University, B.S., 1977; J.D., 1981 — Admitted to Bar, 1982, Louisiana; U.S. District Court, Eastern, Middle and Western Districts of Louisiana; U.S. Court of Appeals, Fifth Circuit; U.S. Supreme Court — Member Louisiana State, New Orleans and Jefferson Parish Bar Associations; New Orleans Association of Defense Counsel; Federation of Defense and Corporate Counsel; Defense Research Institute — Practice Areas: Insurance Defense; Excess; Coverage Issues; Professional Liability

Marta-Ann Schnabel — 1957 — Memorial University of Newfoundland, B.A. (with honors), 1978; Loyola University College of Law, J.D., 1981 — Admitted to Bar, 1981, Louisiana; U.S. District Court, Eastern, Middle and Western Districts of Louisiana — Member American, Louisiana State (Past President) and New Orleans (Past President) Bar Associations; Louisiana Association of Defense Counsel (President); Louisiana Bar Foundation; New Orleans Association of Defense Counsel — Practice Areas: Insurance Defense; Excess; Coverage Issues; Professional Liability

Special Partner

Sherry A. Watters — 1957 — The University of Iowa, B.S., 1979; Loyola University College of Law, J.D., 1982 — Admitted to Bar, 1982, Louisiana; U.S. Supreme Court — Member Louisiana State and New Orleans Bar Associations; Louisiana Bar Foundation; Louisiana Association of Defense Counsel — Practice Areas: Insurance Defense; Appellate Advocacy; Coverage Issues

Of Counsel

Jean Melancon — Tulane University, B.S., 1976; University of Virginia; Tulane University Law School, J.D., 1980 — Admitted to Bar, 1980, Louisiana; 1987, Guam — Member Guam and Louisiana State Bar Associations; The Maritime Law Association of the United States

Ostendorf Tate Barnett, LLP

The Poydras Center
650 Poydras Street, Suite 1460
New Orleans, Louisiana 70130
    Telephone: 504-527-0700
    Fax: 504-527-5111
    Emer/After Hrs: 504-415-5514
    Mobile: 504-415-5514
    E-Mail: lanceostendorf@otbtlaw.com

(Bellaire, TX Office: 6300 West Loop South, Suite 340, 77401)
    (Tel: 281-271-7107)
    (Fax: 832-324-7773)
(Laguna Hills, CA Office: 23041 Mill Creek Drive, 92653)
    (Tel: 949-246-7688)
    (Fax: 949-380-1128)

Coverage Issues, Insurance Defense, Personal Injury, Premises Liability, Product Liability, Truck Liability, Workers' Compensation, Class Actions, Admiralty and Maritime Law, Retail Liability, Toxic Torts, Longshore Act

Firm Profile: The firm focusses its representation on the protection of the interest of corporations and insurance companies in personal injury, property damage, contract and insurance coverage cases.

Insurance Clients

AIG Insurance Company   Hudson Insurance Company
Zurich Insurance Company

Non-Insurance Clients

SAIA Motor Freight Line, Inc.

Members of the Firm

Lance S. Ostendorf — 1957 — Loyola University, B.B.A. (summa cum laude), 1976; J.D., 1980 — Admitted to Bar, 1980, Louisiana; U.S. District Court, Eastern District of Louisiana; U.S. Court of Appeals, Fifth Circuit; U.S. Supreme Court — Member Federal, American, International, Louisiana State, Jefferson Parish and New Orleans Bar Associations; American Institute of Average Adjusters; Association in Transportation Law, Logistics and Policy; Defense Research Institute; Louisiana Association of Defense Counsel; The Maritime Law Association of the United States; Transportation Lawyers Association; Trucking Industry Defense Association — Practice Areas: Corporate Law; Insurance Defense — E-mail: lanceostendorf@otbtlaw.com

Wayne P. Tate — 1957 — Nicholls State University, B.S. (dean's list, President's List), 1981; Loyola University, J.D., 1986 — Admitted to Bar, 1986, Louisiana; 1988, California; 1990, U.S. District Court, Central District of California — Member Louisiana State and Orange County Bar Associations; State Bar of California (Workers' Compensation Section) — Practice Areas: Defense Litigation; Retail Liability; Business Litigation — E-mail: waynetate@otbtlaw.com

David L. Barnett — 1953 — Southern Methodist University, B.S., 1975; University of Houston, J.D., 1983 — Admitted to Bar, 1984, Texas; 1985, Louisiana; 1985, U.S. District Court, Eastern and Middle Districts of Louisiana; U.S. Court of Appeals, Fifth Circuit; 1987, U.S. District Court, Western District of Louisiana; 1990, Supreme Court of the United States; 1995, U.S. District Court, Eastern and Northern Districts of Texas; 2009, U.S. District Court, Southern District of Texas — Member Louisiana State, Fifth Federal Circuit, New Orleans, Houston and Dallas Bar Associations; State Bar of Texas; U.S. Naval Institute; Southeastern Admiralty Law Institute; The Maritime Law Association of the United States; Texas Association of Defense Counsel — Practice Areas: Admiralty and Maritime Law; Insurance Coverage — E-mail: davidbarnett@otbtlaw.com

Windi Brown   John G. Alsobrook
Alejandro J. Rodriguez

Perrier & Lacoste, LLC

One Canal Place
365 Canal Street, Suite 2550
New Orleans, Louisiana 70130-1137
    Telephone: 504-212-8820
    Fax: 504-212-8825
    E-Mail: gperrier@perrierlacoste.com
    www.perrierlacoste.com

(Gulfport, MS Office: Toggery Building, 2501 14th Street, Suite 205, 39501)
    (Tel: 228-214-1250)
    (Fax: 504-212-8825)

Transportation, Insurance Defense, Insurance Coverage, Civil Litigation, Premises Liability, Product Liability, Business Litigation, Commercial Litigation, Workers' Compensation, Admiralty and Maritime

Firm Profile: Perrier & Lacoste, LLC is a law firm comprised of 16 attorneys who maintain an active civil defense practice. The firm also handles first party claims, represents insurers on coverage disputes, and litigates bad faith and extra-contractual claims throughout Louisiana and Mississippi.

Insurance Clients

Arch Insurance Company   Crum & Forster Insurance
Vanliner Insurance Company

Non-Insurance Clients

Federal Express   McLane Company, Inc.
Penske Truck Leasing Company

Contact Attorneys

Guy D. Perrier — 1964 — Louisiana State University, B.S., 1987; Tulane University of Louisiana, J.D., 1990 — Admitted to Bar, 1990, Louisiana; U.S. District Court, Eastern, Middle and Western Districts of Louisiana — Member Federal, Louisiana State and New Orleans (Board of Directors, 1996-2001; Third Vice President, 2000; Chair, Young Lawyers Section, 1996) Bar Associations; Council on Litigation Management; Louisiana Motor Transport Association; American Trucking Association; Louis A. Martinet Foundation; Louisiana Bar Foundation; New Orleans Bar Foundation; Themis Advocates Group; Defense Research Institute; Louisiana Association of Defense Counsel; New Orleans Association of Defense Counsel; Trucking Industry Defense Association; Transportation Lawyers Association

Rodney J. Lacoste, Jr. — 1963 — Loyola University, B.B.A., 1986; M.B.A., 1989; J.D., 1989 — Admitted to Bar, 1990, Louisiana; 1990, U.S. District

NEW ORLEANS   **LOUISIANA**

Perrier & Lacoste, LLC, New Orleans, LA (Continued)

Court, Eastern, Middle and Western Districts of Louisiana — Member Louisiana State and New Orleans Bar Associations; Louisiana Bar Foundation; Louisiana Motor Transport Association; New Orleans Association of Defense Counsel (Board of Directors, 2003-present; President, 2010); Themis Advocates Group; Defense Research Institute; Louisiana Association of Defense Counsel; Transportation Lawyers Association — Certified Public Accountant (inactive status)

Phelps Dunbar LLP

Canal Place
365 Canal Street, Suite 2000
New Orleans, Louisiana 70130-6534
   Telephone: 504-566-1311
   Fax: 504-568-9130
   E-Mail: info@phelps.com
   www.phelpsdunbar.com

(Baton Rouge, LA Office*: II City Plaza, 400 Convention Street, Suite 1100, 70802-5618, P.O. Box 4412, 70821-4412)
   (Tel: 225-346-0285)
   (Fax: 225-381-9197)
(Jackson, MS Office*: 4270 I-55 North, 39211-6391, P.O. Box 16114, 39236-6114)
   (Tel: 601-352-2300)
   (Fax: 601-360-9777)
(Tupelo, MS Office*: One Mississippi Plaza, 201 South Spring Street, Seventh Floor, 38804, P.O. Box 1220, 38802-1220)
   (Tel: 662-842-7907)
   (Fax: 662-842-3873)
(Gulfport, MS Office*: NorthCourt One, 2304 19th Street, Suite 300, 39501)
   (Tel: 228-679-1130)
   (Fax: 228-679-1131)
(Houston, TX Office*: One Allen Center, 500 Dallas Street, Suite 1300, 77002)
   (Tel: 713-626-1386)
   (Fax: 713-626-1388)
(Tampa, FL Office*: 100 South Ashley Drive, Suite 1900, 33602-5311)
   (Tel: 813-472-7550)
   (Fax: 813-472-7570)
(Mobile, AL Office*: 2 North Royal Street, 36602, P.O. Box 2727, 36652-2727)
   (Tel: 251-432-4481)
   (Fax: 251-433-1820)
(London, United Kingdom Office*: Lloyd's, Suite 725, Level 7, 1 Lime Street, EC3M 7DQ)
   (Tel: 011-44-207-929-4765)
   (Fax: 011-44-207-929-0046)
(Raleigh, NC Office*: 4140 Parklake Avenue, Suite 100, 27612-3723)
   (Tel: 919-789-5300)
   (Fax: 919-789-5301)
(Southlake, TX Office*(See Dallas listing): 115 Grand Avenue, Suite 222, 76092)
   (Tel: 817-488-3134)
   (Fax: 817-488-3214)

Established: 1853

Insurance Law

Insurance Clients

Acceptance Casualty Insurance Company
Aegis Janson Green Insurance Services Inc.
AIG Columbus
Alabama Municipal Insurance Corporation
AmTrust Underwriters, Inc.
Arch Insurance Company (Europe) Ltd.
Aspen Insurance UK Limited
Associated Aviation Underwriters
ACE Group of Insurance and Reinsurance Companies
Aetna Insurance Company
AFLAC - American Family Life Assurance Company of Columbus
Allstate Insurance Company
American Family Life Assurance Company of Columbus
Argonaut Insurance Company
Aspen Insurance
Aspen Re
AXIS Insurance

Phelps Dunbar LLP, New Orleans, LA (Continued)

Bankers Insurance Group
Berkley Select, LLC
Bluebonnet Life Insurance Company
Britannia Steam Ship Insurance Association Ltd.
CNA
Commercial Union Insurance Company
Companion Property and Casualty Group
ELCO Administrative Services
Endurance Services, Ltd.
Erie Insurance Company
Evanston Insurance Company
Fidelity National Financial
First Premium Insurance Group, Inc.
GE Insurance Solutions
General & Cologne Life Reinsurance of America
General Star Indemnity Company
Glencoe Group
Global Special Risks, Inc.
Great American Insurance Companies
Gulf Insurance Group
The Hartford Insurance Group
Homesite Group, Inc.
ICAT Boulder Claims
Infinity Insurance Company
Lexington Insurance Company
Liberty Mutual Group
Louisiana Farm Bureau Mutual Insurance Company
Louisiana Workers' Compensation Corporation
Markel
MetLife Auto & Home
NAS Insurance Group
Nautilus Insurance Company
Old American Insurance Company
Pharmacists Mutual Insurance Company
RenaissanceRe
RLI Insurance Company
Royal & SunAlliance
SCOR Global P&C
Sedgwick Claims Management Services, Inc.
SR International Business Insurance Company, Ltd.
Steamship Mutual Underwriting Association Limited
Torus
Underwriters at Lloyd's, London
Unitrin Business Insurance
Vesta Eiendom AS
Western Heritage Insurance Company
Westport Insurance Corporation
XL Insurance Group
Beazley
Bituminous Insurance Company
Blue Cross & Blue Shield of Mississippi
Chartis Insurance
Chubb Group of Insurance Companies
Commonwealth Insurance Company
Cotton States Insurance
Criterion Claim Solutions
Employers Reinsurance Corporation
Esurance Insurance Company
Farmers Insurance Group
Fireman's Fund Insurance Company
Foremost Insurance Company
General American Life Insurance Company
General Reinsurance Corporation
General Star Management Company
Golden Rule Insurance Company
Great Southern Life Insurance Company
Hanover Insurance Group
Hermitage Insurance Company
Houston Casualty Company
Indian Harbor Insurance Company
Ironshore Insurance, Ltd.
Liberty International Underwriters
Life Insurance Company of Alabama
Louisiana Health Insurance Association
Lyndon Property Insurance Company
Munich-American Risk Partners
Nationwide Insurance
The Navigators Group, Inc.
OneBeacon Insurance Group
Prime Syndicate
QBE
Republic Western Insurance Company
St. Paul Travelers
Scottsdale Insurance Company
Sentry Insurance
Southern Farm Bureau Casualty Insurance Company
State National Insurance Company, Inc.
Terra Nova Insurance Company Limited
United States Fidelity and Guaranty Company
Victoria Insurance Group
West of England Ship Owners Mutual Insurance Association (Luxembourg)
Zurich

Members of the Firm

M. Nan Alessandra — The University of New Orleans, B.A., 1982; Loyola University New Orleans College of Law, J.D. (cum laude), 1985 — Admitted to Bar, 1985, Louisiana; 1993, Texas — Member Federal, American, Louisiana State, Jefferson, New Orleans and Fifth Federal Circuit Bar Associations; State Bar of Texas; American Arbitration Association; Fellow, American Bar Foundation

Jane E. Armstrong — San Diego State University, B.A. (with distinction), 1974; Tulane University Law School; Vanderbilt University Law School, J.D. (Order of the Coif), 1979 — Admitted to Bar, 1980, New York; 1982, Louisiana — Member American and Louisiana State Bar Associations — Board Certified Tax Attorney

Barbara L. Arras — Northwestern University, B.A., 1971; Loyola University Chicago School of Law, J.D., 1977 — Admitted to Bar, 1978, Illinois; 1987, Louisiana; 1997, Texas; U.S. District Court, Eastern, Middle and Western Districts of Louisiana; U.S. Court of Appeals, Fifth Circuit — Member Louisiana State Bar Association; Defense Research Institute; Louisiana Association of Defense Counsel; International Association of Defense Counsel

Phelps Dunbar LLP, New Orleans, LA (Continued)

Robert J. Barbier — Louisiana State University, B.S., 1968; Loyola University New Orleans College of Law, J.D., 1972 — Admitted to Bar, 1972, Louisiana; U.S. District Court, Eastern, Middle and Western Districts of Louisiana; U.S. Court of Appeals, Fifth and Eleventh Circuits — Member Louisiana State and New Orleans Bar Associations; Southeastern Admiralty Law Institute; The Maritime Law Association of the United States

Kim M. Boyle — Princeton University, A.B., 1984; University of Virginia, J.D., 1987 — Admitted to Bar, 1987, Louisiana; U.S. District Court, Eastern, Middle and Western Districts of Louisiana; U.S. Court of Appeals, Fifth Circuit; U.S. Supreme Court — Member Federal, National, American, Louisiana State and New Orleans Bar Associations

Michael M. Butterworth — California Maritime Academy, B.S., 1980; Tulane University Law School, J.D., 1989 — Admitted to Bar, 1989, Washington; 1992, Louisiana; 1989, U.S. District Court, Eastern and Western Districts of Washington; 1992, U.S. District Court, Eastern, Middle and Western Districts of Louisiana; U.S. Court of Appeals, Fifth and Ninth Circuits; U.S. Supreme Court — Member Louisiana State and Washington State Bar Associations; Association of Average Adjusters of the United States; Southeastern Admiralty Law Institute; The Maritime Law Association of the United States — Registered Civil Mediator, Louisiana State Bar Association; Master, 1600 Tons, Oceans Radar Enforcement, STCW Certified

Brandon E. Davis — Loyola University New Orleans, B.B.A. (magna cum laude), 2001; Tulane University Law School, J.D., 2005 — Admitted to Bar, 2005, Louisiana; Texas — Member Federal, American, National, Louisiana State and New Orleans Bar Associations; American Immigration Lawyers Association; Defense Research Institute; Louisiana Association of Defense Counsel

Richard N. Dicharry — Loyola University, B.A. (magna cum laude), 1972; Loyola University New Orleans College of Law, J.D., 1975; Boston University, LL.M., 1978 — Admitted to Bar, 1975, Louisiana; U.S. District Court, Eastern, Middle and Western Districts of Louisiana; U.S. Court of Appeals, Fifth Circuit — Member American and Louisiana State Bar Associations; International Association of Claim Professionals (Adjunct Member); American College of Coverage and Extracontractual Counsel; The Maritime Law Association of the United States — Resident New Orleans, LA and London, United Kingdom Office

Mark C. Dodart — The University of New Orleans, B.A. (with honors), 1983; Louisiana State University, Paul M. Hebert Law Center, J.D. (Order of the Coif), 1986 — Admitted to Bar, 1986, Louisiana; Texas — Member Federal, Louisiana State and Fifth Federal Circuit Bar Associations; Defense Research Institute

Pablo Gonzalez — Sewanee, The University of the South, B.A. (Order of Gownsmen), 2000; Loyola University New Orleans College of Law, J.D. (cum laude), 2004 — Admitted to Bar, 2004, Louisiana; U.S. District Court, Eastern, Middle and Western Districts of Louisiana; U.S. Court of Appeals, Fifth Circuit; U.S. Supreme Court — Member American, Louisiana State and New Orleans Bar Associations

George B. Hall, Jr. — Tulane University, B.A., 1970; The University of Tennessee, M.S.P., 1973; Tulane University Law School, J.D., 1977 — Admitted to Bar, 1977, Louisiana; 1992, Texas — Member Louisiana State, Houston and New Orleans Bar Associations; State Bar of Texas; Defense Research Institute — Resident New Orleans, LA and Houston, TX Office

Stephen P. Hall — Tulane University, B.A., 1980; Tulane University Law School, J.D. (magna cum laude, Order of the Coif), 1983 — Admitted to Bar, 1983, Louisiana; Texas — Member Federal, American and Louisiana State Bar Associations; State Bar of Texas; Louisiana Association of Defense Counsel; Defense Research Institute — Registered Civil Mediator, Louisiana State Bar Association — Resident New Orleans, LA and London, United Kingdom Office

Gary A. Hemphill — Harvard University, B.A., 1978; Tulane University Law School, J.D. (magna cum laude), 1981 — Admitted to Bar, 1981, Louisiana — Member American, Louisiana State and New Orleans Bar Associations; Louisiana Association of Defense Counsel; Southeastern Admiralty Law Institute; The Maritime Law Association of the United States — Resident New Orleans, LA and London, United Kingdom Office

David M. Korn — Tulane University, B.A., 1989; Tulane University Law School, J.D. (cum laude), 1992 — Admitted to Bar, 1992, Louisiana; Texas; U.S. District Court, Eastern, Middle and Western Districts of Louisiana; U.S. District Court, Southern District of Texas; U.S. Court of Appeals, Fifth, Eighth and Tenth Circuits; U.S. Supreme Court — Member American and Louisiana State Bar Associations; State Bar of Texas; National Association of College and University Attorneys; Defense Research Institute

Kevin J. LaVie — Louisiana State University, B.A., 1981; Louisiana State University, Paul M. Hebert Law Center, J.D., 1984 — Admitted to Bar, 1984, Louisiana; U.S. District Court, Eastern, Middle and Western Districts of Louisiana; U.S. Court of Appeals, Fifth Circuit; U.S. Supreme Court — Member Louisiana State and New Orleans Bar Associations; The Maritime Law Association of the United States

David B. Lawton — Brown University, A.B., 1973; Vanderbilt University, J.D., 1977 — Admitted to Bar, 1977, Louisiana — Member Federal, Louisiana State and New Orleans Bar Associations; Southeastern Admiralty Law Institute; The Maritime Law Association of the United States

John P. Manard, Jr. — Tulane University, 1966-1968; Tulane University Law School, J.D., 1971; LL.M., 1999 — Admitted to Bar, 1971, Louisiana — Member American and Louisiana State Bar Associations; Defense Research Institute; New Orleans Association of Defense Counsel; International Association of Defense Counsel; Louisiana Association of Defense Counsel

Robert P. McCleskey, Jr. — Louisiana State University, Paul M. Hebert Law Center, J.D., 1979 — Admitted to Bar, 1979, Louisiana; 1992, Texas; U.S. District Court, Eastern, Middle and Western Districts of Louisiana; U.S. District Court, Southern District of Texas; U.S. Court of Appeals, Fifth Circuit; U.S. Supreme Court — Member Louisiana State and Fifth Federal Circuit Bar Associations; State Bar of Texas; U.S. Supreme Court Bar Association; Tulane Admiralty Law Institute; Offshore Marine Service Association; National Ocean Industries Association; Southeastern Admiralty Law Institute; The Maritime Law Association of the United States; Defense Research Institute

Evans Martin McLeod — The University of Mississippi, B.Accy, 1991; Loyola University New Orleans College of Law, J.D., 1996 — Admitted to Bar, 1997, Louisiana; 1998, Mississippi; U.S. District Court, Eastern, Middle and Western Districts of Louisiana; U.S. District Court, Northern and Southern Districts of Mississippi; U.S. Court of Appeals, Fifth Circuit; U.S. Supreme Court — Member Louisiana State and New Orleans Bar Associations; The Mississippi Bar; Southeastern Admiralty Law Institute — Licensed by the Securities and Exchange Commission Series 8 — Resident New Orleans, LA and London, United Kingdom Office

Allen C. Miller — Xavier University, B.A., 1995; Southern University Law Center, J.D. (cum laude), 1999 — Admitted to Bar, 1999, Louisiana — Member Federal, American, National, Louisiana State and New Orleans Bar Associations; National Institute of Trial Advocacy; Council on Litigation Management; Louisiana Association of Defense Counsel; International Association of Defense Counsel; National Institute of Trial Advocacy

Thomas Kent Morrison — The University of Georgia, B.S., 1995; Tulane University Law School, J.D. (cum laude), 1998 — Admitted to Bar, 1998, Louisiana — Member Federal and Louisiana State Bar Associations; Southeastern Admiralty Law Institute; The Maritime Law Association of the United States

David L. Patrón — Princeton University, A.B. (magna cum laude) 1990; Stanford Law School, J.D., 1993 — Admitted to Bar, 1993, Louisiana; U.S. District Court, Eastern, Middle and Western Districts of Louisiana; U.S. Court of Appeals, Fifth Circuit — Member Federal, Louisiana State and New Orleans Bar Associations

Katherine Karam Quirk — Louisiana State University, B.A. (cum laude), 1991; Tulane University Law School, J.D. (cum laude), 1994 — Admitted to Bar, 1994, Louisiana — Member American, Louisiana State and New Orleans Bar Associations; Defense Research Institute — Resident New Orleans, LA and London, United Kingdom Office

Christopher K. Ralston — College of William & Mary, B.A., 1992; Tulane University Law School, J.D., 1999 — Admitted to Bar, 2000, Louisiana; U.S. District Court, Eastern, Middle and Western Districts of Louisiana; U.S. Court of Appeals, Fifth Circuit; U.S. Supreme Court — Member Federal, American, Louisiana State, Fifth Federal Circuit and New Orleans Bar Associations; Former Federal Law Clerks Association

William J. Riviere — Nicholls State University, B.S. (summa cum laude), 1987; Georgetown University Law Center, J.D. (magna cum laude), 1990 — Admitted to Bar, 1991, Louisiana; U.S. District Court, Eastern and Middle Districts of Louisiana; U.S. Court of Appeals, Fifth Circuit; U.S. Supreme Court — Member Louisiana State and New Orleans Bar Associations; The Maritime Law Association of the United States; Southeastern Admiralty Law Institute — Resident New Orleans, LA and London, United Kingdom Office

Harry Rosenberg — Case Western Reserve University, B.A., 1969; Tulane University Law School, J.D., 1972 — Admitted to Bar, 1972, Louisiana; U.S. District Court, Eastern, Middle and Western Districts of Louisiana; U.S. District Court, Northern District of Texas; U.S. Court of Appeals, Fifth Circuit; U.S. Supreme Court — Member Federal, American, Louisiana State and New Orleans Bar Associations; American Counsel Association; Former United States Attorneys Association; National Association of Criminal Defense Lawyers

Mary Ellen Roy — University of Louisiana at Lafayette, B.A. (summa cum laude), 1981; Harvard Law School, J.D. (cum laude), 1984 — Admitted to

Phelps Dunbar LLP, New Orleans, LA (Continued)

Bar, 1984, Louisiana; U.S. District Court, Eastern, Middle and Western Districts of Louisiana; U.S. Court of Appeals, Fifth Circuit — Member American and Louisiana State Bar Associations; Media Law Resource Center (Defense Counsel Section)

Bruce V. Schewe — Louisiana State University, B.S. (magna cum laude), 1978; Louisiana State University, Paul M. Hebert Law Center, J.D. (Order of the Coif), 1981 — Admitted to Bar, 1981, Louisiana — Member Federal, American, Louisiana State, Fifth Federal Circuit and New Orleans Bar Associations; Louisiana Bankers Association — Abritrator, FINRA Dispute Resolution

Jay Russell Sever — University of Maryland, B.S., 1986; Tulane University Law School, J.D., 1991 — Admitted to Bar, 1993, California; 1995, Louisiana; U.S. District Court, Eastern, Middle and Western Districts of Louisiana; U.S. District Court, Central, Eastern, Northern and Southern Districts of California; U.S. District Court, Western District of Tennessee; U.S. Court of Appeals, Fourth, Fifth and Ninth Circuits; U.S. Supreme Court — Member Federal, American, Louisiana State and Fifth Federal Circuit Bar Associations; State Bar of California; American College of Coverage and Extracontractual Counsel; Defense Research Institute; Federation of Defense and Corporate Counsel — Resident New Orleans, LA and London, United Kingdom Office

Patrick A. Talley, Jr. — Armstrong State College, B.A., 1976; Louisiana State University Law Center, J.D., 1982; Tulane University Law School, LL.M., 1993 — Admitted to Bar, 1982, Louisiana; Texas; U.S. District Court, Eastern, Middle and Western Districts of Louisiana; U.S. Court of Appeals, Fifth Circuit — Member Federal, American, Louisiana State, Fifth Federal Circuit, New Orleans and Baton Rouge Bar Associations; State Bar of Texas; National Association of Railroad Trial Counsel; The Maritime Law Association of the United States; Southeastern Admiralty Law Institute; Defense Research Institute

Brian D. Wallace — St. Mary's University, B.S. (magna cum laude), 1980; Dalhousie University, LL.B., 1984; Tulane University Law School, LL.M. (with distinction), 1985 — Admitted to Bar, 1985, Louisiana — Member American and Louisiana State Bar Associations; Maritime Law Association of Canada; International Association of Gaming Attorneys; Canadian Maritime Law Association; The Maritime Law Association of the United States

Counsel

P. Christopher Bynog — Centenary College of Louisiana, B.A., 1991; Louisiana State University, Paul M. Hebert Law Center, J.D., 1996 — Admitted to Bar, 1996, Louisiana; 1998, Texas — Member American, Louisiana State and New Orleans Bar Associations; State Bar of Texas

Thear J. Lemoine — Loyola University, B.A., 1995; Louisiana State University, J.D., 1999 — Admitted to Bar, 1999, Louisiana; 2000, Mississippi — Member American and Louisiana State Bar Associations; The Mississippi Bar

Pamela G. Michiels — Tulane University, B.A., 1985; Tulane University Law School, J.D. (cum laude), 1990 — Admitted to Bar, 1990, Louisiana; U.S. District Court, Eastern, Middle and Western Districts of Louisiana — Member American, Louisiana State and New Orleans Bar Associations

Charlotte Jane Sawyer — Sewanee, The University of the South, B.A. (cum laude), 1999; Tulane University Law School, J.D., 2003 — Admitted to Bar, Louisiana — Member Federal, Louisiana State and New Orleans Bar Associations; Association for Women Attorneys; New Orleans Association of Defense Counsel

Of Counsel

John A. Bolles
Harry S. Redmon, Jr.

G. Edward Merritt
Hugh Ramsay Straub

Plauché Maselli Parkerson L.L.P.
Attorneys at Law

701 Poydras Street, Suite 3800
New Orleans, Louisiana 70139
  Telephone: 504-582-1142
  Fax: 504-582-1172
  www.pmpllp.com

Established: 1981

Plauché Maselli Parkerson L.L.P., Attorneys at Law, New Orleans, LA (Continued)

General Liability, Automobile Liability, Product Liability, Premises Liability, Insurance and Corporate Defense Litigation, Environmental Exposure Liability, Natural Gas Litigation, Excess Liability, Coverage Opinions, Management of Multi-Party/Industrywide Litigation, Defense of First Party Property Matters, Defense of Extra-Contractual Claims

Insurance Clients

AEGIS Insurance Services, Inc.
Chubb Group of Insurance Companies
Farm Bureau Insurance Companies
Houston Casualty Company
Meadowbrook Insurance Group
RiverStone Claims Management, LLC

AmTrust Group
Crum & Forster
Electric Insurance Company
First Mercury Insurance Company
Kemper Services
Regional Insurance Services Company, LLC
Scottsdale Insurance Company

Non-Insurance Clients

Advance Publications
Atmos Energy Corporation
Dean Foods
ExxonMobil Corporation
Hancock Bank
Hill-Rom Company
John Crane, Inc.
Lamons Gasket Company
Tri-Mas Corporation
Wendy's International, Inc.

Alcoa, Inc.
Cequent Trailer Products
Energy Transfer Partners, L.P.
Frito-Lay, Inc.
Hillenbrand Industries
Hilton Worldwide
Johnson & Johnson
Standard Parking Corporation
Tulane University
Whitney National Bank

Partners

Andrew L. Plauché, Jr. — Tulane University, B.A., 1969; J.D., 1972 — Board of Student Editors, Tulane Law Review, 1970-1972 — Admitted to Bar, 1972, Louisiana; U.S. District Court, Eastern, Middle and Western Districts of Louisiana; U.S. Court of Appeals, Fifth Circuit; U.S. Supreme Court — Member American and Louisiana State Bar Associations; Louisiana Association of Defense Counsel; New Orleans Association of Defense Counsel; International Association of Defense Counsel; Defense Research Institute — Practice Areas: Insurance Coverage Litigation; Product Liability; Automobile Liability; Premises Liability — E-mail: aplauche@pmpllp.com

Joseph Maselli, Jr. — Tulane University, B.A., 1969; J.D., 1974 — Admitted to Bar, 1974, Louisiana; U.S. District Court, Eastern, Middle and Western Districts of Louisiana; U.S. Court of Appeals, Fifth Circuit; U.S. Supreme Court — Member American, Louisiana State and New Orleans Bar Associations; Louisiana Association of Defense Counsel (Director, 2002-); New Orleans Association of Defense Counsel; Defense Research Institute — Practice Areas: Premises Liability; Product Liability; Automobile Liability; Extra-Contractual Litigation; Commercial Litigation; First Party Matters — E-mail: jmaselli@pmpllp.com

G. Bruce Parkerson — Southern Methodist University, B.B.A., 1979; J.D., 1982 — Moot Court Board — Admitted to Bar, 1983, Louisiana; 1994, North Carolina; 1995, Texas; 1983, U.S. District Court, Eastern, Middle and Western Districts of Louisiana; U.S. Court of Appeals, Fifth Circuit — Member Louisiana and North Carolina Bar Associations; State Bar of Texas; Fellow, American College of Trial Lawyers; Louisiana Association of Defense Counsel; Federation of Defense and Corporate Counsel; Defense Research Institute; Transportation Lawyers Association — Practice Areas: Premises Liability; Product Liability; Commercial Litigation; Automobile Liability; Oil and Gas — E-mail: bparkerson@pmpllp.com

Mark E. Young — Louisiana State University, B.A., 1987; J.D., 1990 — Moot Court Board — Admitted to Bar, 1990, Louisiana; 2007, Texas; 1990, U.S. District Court, Eastern, Middle and Western Districts of Louisiana; U.S. Court of Appeals, Fifth Circuit — Member Louisiana State Bar Association; State Bar of Texas; Louisiana Association of Defense Counsel; Transportation Lawyers Association; Defense Research Institute — Practice Areas: Product Liability; Premises Liability; Transportation; Trucking Liability; Construction Defect — E-mail: myoung@pmpllp.com

Kenan S. Rand, Jr. — Middlebury College, B.A., 1988; Tulane University, J.D. (cum laude), 1994 — Admitted to Bar, 1994, Louisiana; 1994, U.S. District Court, Eastern, Middle and Western Districts of Louisiana; 1995, U.S. Court of Appeals, Fifth Circuit; U.S. Supreme Court — Member Louisiana State Bar Association; Defense Research Institute — Languages: German — Practice Areas: Premises Liability; Product Liability; Toxic Torts; Class Actions — E-mail: krand@pmpllp.com

LOUISIANA — NEW ORLEANS

Plauché Maselli Parkerson L.L.P., Attorneys at Law, New Orleans, LA (Continued)

James K. Ordeneaux — Tulane University, B.A., 1999; Louisiana State University, J.D., 2002 — Admitted to Bar, 2002, Louisiana; U.S. District Court, Eastern, Middle and Western Districts of Louisiana — Member Louisiana State Bar Association; International Association of Defense Counsel; Defense Research Institute; Louisiana Association of Defense Counsel — Practice Areas: Automobile Litigation; Insurance Coverage Litigation; Trucking — E-mail: jordeneaux@pmpllp.com

George C. Drennan — Sewanee, The University of the South, B.S., 1998; Louisiana State University, J.D./B.C.L., 2002 — Admitted to Bar, 2002, Louisiana; 2002, U.S. District Court, Eastern, Middle and Western Districts of Louisiana; U.S. Court of Appeals, Fifth Circuit — Member Federal, American, Louisiana State and New Orleans Bar Associations; Louisiana Association of Defense Counsel — Practice Areas: Automobile Liability; Premises Liability; Product Liability; Workers' Compensation; Construction Defect; Employment Law — E-mail: gdrennan@pmpllp.com

Senior Counsel

Scott H. Mason — The University of New Orleans, B.A., 2001; Loyola University School of Law, J.D., 2004 — Admitted to Bar, 2004, Louisiana; U.S. District Court, Eastern, Middle and Western Districts of Louisiana; U.S. Court of Appeals, Fifth Circuit — Member Louisiana State and New Orleans Bar Associations — Practice Areas: Insurance Litigation; Premises Liability; Product Liability; Toxic Torts; Commercial Litigation; Construction Defect — E-mail: smason@pmpllp.com

Attie Carville — The University of Texas, B.A., 1998; Louisiana State University, J.D./B.C.L., 2002 — Admitted to Bar, 2002, Louisiana; U.S. District Court, Eastern, Middle and Western Districts of Louisiana; U.S. Court of Appeals, Fifth Circuit — Practice Areas: Insurance Coverage Litigation; Product Liability; Environmental Litigation; Commercial Litigation — E-mail: acarville@pmpllp.com

Associates

Lauren Baylor Dietzen — Southern Methodist University, B.B.A., 2002; Stetson University College of Law, J.D., 2006 — Moot Court Board, 2006 — Admitted to Bar, 2006, Florida; 2008, Louisiana — Practice Areas: Product Liability; Premises Liability; Excess; Automobile Liability — E-mail: ldietzen@pmpllp.com

Lacey E. Sarver — Louisiana State University, B.S. (cum laude), 2007; Louisiana State University Law Center, J.D. (cum laude), 2010 — Admitted to Bar, 2010, Louisiana; 2013, U.S. District Court, Eastern, Middle and Western Districts of Louisiana; U.S. Court of Appeals, Fifth Circuit — Member Louisiana State and New Orleans Bar Associations; Louisiana Association of Defense Counsel — Practice Areas: Premises Liability; Product Liability; Commercial Litigation; Automobile Liability — E-mail: lsarver@pmpllp.com

Peter Gahagan — Tulane University, B.A. (cum laude), 2007; Loyola University Law School, J.D., 2010 — Admitted to Bar, 2010, Louisiana; U.S. District Court, Eastern, Middle and Western Districts of Louisiana — Member Louisiana State Bar Association; Louisiana Association of Defense Counsel — Practice Areas: Automobile; Trucking; Premises Liability; Insurance Coverage — E-mail: pgahagan@pmpllp.com

Jessica Savoie — Missouri State University, B.A. (summa cum laude), 2007; University of Notre Dame Law School, J.D., 2010 — Admitted to Bar, 2010, Louisiana; U.S. District Court, Eastern, Middle and Western Districts of Louisiana; U.S. Court of Appeals, Fifth Circuit — Member Louisiana State and New Orleans Bar Associations; Louisiana Association of Defense Counsel — Practice Areas: Automobile; Trucking; Premises Liability; Product Liability — E-mail: jsavoie@pmpllp.com

Conrad Rolling — Southeastern Louisiana University, B.S., 2006; Loyola University New Orleans College of Law, J.D., 2010 — Admitted to Bar, 2010, Louisiana — Member Louisiana State Bar Association; Louisiana Association of Defense Counsel; Defense Research Institute — Practice Areas: Product Liability; Medical Devices; Premises Liability; Automobile; Trucking; Transportation; First and Third Party Defense; Commercial Litigation; Employment Litigation — E-mail: crolling@pmpllp.com

Katelyn Wear Harrell — The University of Mississippi, B.A., 2009; The University of Mississippi School of Law, J.D., 2013 — Admitted to Bar, 2013, Louisiana — Member Louisiana State Bar Association — Practice Areas: Premises Liability; Product Liability; Automobile; Trucking; Transportation — E-mail: kharrell@pmpllp.com

---

Porteous, Hainkel and Johnson, L.L.P.

704 Carondelet Street
New Orleans, Louisiana 70130-3774
  Telephone: 504-581-3838
  Fax: 504-581-4069
  www.phjlaw.com

(Covington, LA Office: 408 North Columbia Street, 70433-2920)
  (Tel: 985-893-4790)
  (Fax: 985-893-1392)
(Thibodaux, LA Office: 211 West Fifth Street, 70301-3199)
  (Tel: 985-446-8451)
  (Fax: 985-447-3004)
(Baton Rouge, LA Office: 343 Third Street, Suite 202, 70801-1309)
  (Tel: 225-383-8900)
  (Fax: 225-383-7900)

Established: 1928

Insurance Defense, Coverage Issues, Admiralty and Maritime Law, Special Investigative Unit Claims, Toxic Torts, Bad Faith

Firm Profile: Porteous, Hainkel & Johnson is a Louisiana insurance defense firm. For 85 years, the firm has defended insurers in all types of cases. Fortune Magazine recently recognized the firm in a group of one-half of 1% of all law firms achieving a superior AV Martindale-Hubbell rating. The firm has offices in New Orleans, Thibodaux, Covington and Baton Rouge.

Insurance Clients

Allstate Insurance Company
ANPAC
Endurance Specialty Insurance Ltd.
Farm Bureau Mutual Insurance Company
Nationwide Insurance
Southern Farm Bureau Casualty Insurance Company
State Farm Mutual Automobile Insurance Company
USAA
American Family Insurance Group
Chubb Group of Insurance Companies
Farmers Insurance Group
Lafayette Insurance Company
Scottsdale Insurance Company
State Farm Fire and Casualty Company
Travelers
Underwriters at Lloyd's, London

Non-Insurance Clients

L & M BoTruc Rentals, Inc.
U-Haul

Partners

William A. Porteous, Jr. — (1899-1969)

F. Carter Johnson, Jr. — (1905-1964)

John J. Hainkel, Jr. — (1938-2005)

William A. Porteous, III — (1937-2006)

C. Gordon Johnson, Jr. — (Retired)

James S. Thompson — 1950 — Tulane University, B.A., 1972; J.D., 1975 — Admitted to Bar, 1975, Louisiana — Practice Areas: Insurance Defense — E-mail: jthompson@phjlaw.com

Ralph R. Alexis, III — 1949 — Tulane University, B.A., 1971; J.D., 1973; The George Washington University, LL.M., 1976 — Admitted to Bar, 1973, Louisiana; 1977, District of Columbia; 1975, U.S. Court of Federal Claims; 1977, U.S. Tax Court; 1977, U.S. Supreme Court — Practice Areas: Civil Rights; Litigation; Wills; Estate Planning; Trusts; General Civil Practice; Professional Liability (Non-Medical) Defense; Employment Law — E-mail: ralexis@phjlaw.com

Adrianne Landry Baumgartner — 1953 — H. Sophie Newcomb Memorial College, B.A. (cum laude), 1975; Louisiana State University and A & M College; Tulane University, J.D., 1978 — Order of the Coif — Admitted to Bar, 1978, Louisiana; 2007, U.S. Supreme Court — Resident Covington, LA Office — E-mail: abaumgartner@phjlaw.com

James R. Carter — 1953 — University of Richmond, B.S.B.A. (summa cum laude), 1975; Tulane University, J.D., 1978 — Order of the Coif — Admitted to Bar, 1978, Louisiana — E-mail: jcarter@phjlaw.com

Glenn B. Adams — 1953 — Louisiana State University, B.A., 1975; J.D., 1978 — Admitted to Bar, 1978, Louisiana — E-mail: gadams@phjlaw.com

Fred M. Trowbridge, Jr. — 1953 — St. Mary's Dominican College, B.S. (cum laude), 1980; Loyola University, J.D., 1984 — Admitted to Bar, 1985, Louisiana — E-mail: ftrowbridge@phjlaw.com

NEW ORLEANS

Porteous, Hainkel and Johnson, L.L.P., New Orleans, LA (Continued)

William C. Lozes — 1955 — University of Southwestern Louisiana, B.S., 1981; Loyola University, J.D., 1987 — Admitted to Bar, 1987, Louisiana — E-mail: wlozes@phjlaw.com

Charles L. Chassaignac, IV — 1965 — Louisiana State University, B.S., 1988; J.D., 1991 — Admitted to Bar, 1991, Louisiana — E-mail: cchassaignac@phjlaw.com

Michael G. Gee — 1964 — Tulane University, B.A., 1987; Louisiana State University, J.D., 1990 — Admitted to Bar, 1990, Louisiana — E-mail: mgee@phjlaw.com

Dan Richard Dorsey — 1962 — Louisiana State University, B.A., 1984; Loyola University, J.D., 1987 — Admitted to Bar, 1987, Louisiana — E-mail: ddorsey@phjlaw.com

James R. Nieset, Jr. — 1968 — Tulane University, B.A., 1991; J.D., 1996 — Admitted to Bar, 1997, Louisiana — E-mail: jnieset@phjlaw.com

J. Eric Johnson — 1966 — University of Southwestern Louisiana, B.S.M.E., 1990; University of Colorado, J.D., 1995 — Admitted to Bar, 1995, Louisiana — E-mail: ejohnson@phjlaw.com

Chauntis T. Jenkins — 1973 — Loyola University New Orleans, B.A., 1995; Southern University Law Center, J.D., 1998 — Admitted to Bar, 1999, Louisiana — E-mail: cjenkins@phjlaw.com

Kathleen E. Simon — 1961 — Newcomb College, Tulane University, B.A., 1983; Loyola University, J.D., 1986 — Admitted to Bar, 1986, Louisiana — E-mail: ksimon@phjlaw.com

Nicholas C. Gristina — 1977 — Millsaps College, B.A. (cum laude), 1999; Paul M Hebert Law School at Louisiana State University, J.D./B.C.L., 2002 — Admitted to Bar, 2002, Louisiana — E-mail: ngristina@phjlaw.com

Bryan J. Haydel, Jr. — 1975 — Louisiana State University, B.A., 1997; Louisiana State University, Paul M. Hebert Law Center, J.D., 2001 — Admitted to Bar, 2001, Louisiana — E-mail: bhaydel@phjlaw.com

Managing Partner

William Ryan Acomb — 1960 — Tulane University, B.A., 1982; J.D., 1985 — Admitted to Bar, 1985, Louisiana — Practice Areas: Insurance Defense; Admiralty and Maritime Law — E-mail: racomb@phjlaw.com

Associates

Patricia P. Barattini — 1956 — University of Louisiana at Lafayette, B.A. (summa cum laude), 1978; Loyola University, J.D., 1981 — Admitted to Bar, 1981, Louisiana — E-mail: pbarattini@phjlaw.com

Nancy Lee Cromartie — 1963 — University of Virginia, B.A. (with distinction), 1985; J.D., 1988 — Admitted to Bar, 1988, Louisiana — E-mail: ncromartie@phjlaw.com

Emily Stickney Morrison — 1959 — Trinity University, B.A., 1981; Loyola University New Orleans, J.D., 1987 — Admitted to Bar, 1987, Louisiana — E-mail: emorrison@phjlaw.com

Michele L. Trowbridge — 1976 — Louisiana State University, B.S., 1998; Loyola University New Orleans College of Law, J.D., 2006 — Admitted to Bar, 2007, Louisiana — E-mail: mtrowbridge@phjlaw.com

Ralph J. Aucoin — 1982 — Belmont Abbey College, B.A. (cum laude), 2004; Loyola University New Orleans College of Law, J.D., 2007 — Admitted to Bar, 2007, Louisiana — E-mail: raucoin@phjlaw.com

Matthew L. Mann — 1981 — Louisiana State University, Paul M. Hebert Law Center, J.D./B.C.L., 2008 — Admitted to Bar, 2008, Louisiana — E-mail: mmann@phjlaw.com

Darrin M. O'Connor — 1971 — Admitted to Bar, 1996, Louisiana — Tel: 985-893-4790 — E-mail: doconnor@phjlaw.com

Eleanor W. Wall — 1970 — Admitted to Bar, 2001, Texas; 2005, Louisiana — Tel: 225-383-8900 — E-mail: ewall@phjlaw.com

Lloyd T. Bourgeois Jr. — 1968 — Southern University, J.D., 1997 — Admitted to Bar, 1997, Louisiana — E-mail: tbourgeois@phjlaw.com

Gordon P. Guthrie III — 1985 — Paul M Hebert Law School at Louisiana State University, J.D./G.D.C.L., 2012 — Admitted to Bar, 2012, Louisiana — E-mail: GGuthrie@phjlaw.com

Rylee Area — Louisiana State University, B.S.F., 2008; Louisiana State University, Paul M. Hebert Law Center, J.D./G.D.C.L., 2012 — Admitted to Bar, 2012, Louisiana

Sam P. Baumgartner — 1983 — The University of Mississippi, B.A., 2007; Loyola University New Orleans College of Law, J.D., 2014 — Admitted to Bar, 2014, Louisiana

Kelly R. Englert — 1986 — Louisiana State University and A & M College,

Porteous, Hainkel and Johnson, L.L.P., New Orleans, LA (Continued)

B.S. (Dean's List), 2008; Paul M Hebert Law School at Louisiana State University, J.D./G.D.C.L., 2012 — Admitted to Bar, 2012, Louisiana — Resident Baton Rouge, LA Office

Michelle D. Brooks — 1979 — University of Louisiana at Lafayette, B.S. (Dean's List), 2001; Paul M Hebert Law School at Louisiana State University, J.D./B.C.L., 2004 — Admitted to Bar, 2004, Louisiana — Languages: French — Resident Thibodaux, LA Office

Preis PLC

Pan American Life Center, Suite 1700
601 Poydras Street
New Orleans, Louisiana 70130
   Telephone: 504-581-6062
   Fax: 504-522-9129
   E-Mail: preisplc@preisplc.com
   www.preisplc.com

(Lafayette, LA Office*: Versailles Centre, Suite 400, 102 Versailles Boulevard, 70501, P.O. Drawer 94-C, 70509)
   (Tel: 337-237-6062)
   (Fax: 337-237-9129)
(Houston, TX Office*: Weslayan Tower, Suite 2050, 24 Greenway Plaza, 77046)
   (Tel: 713-355-6062)
   (Fax: 713-572-9129)

Litigation

(See listing under Lafayette, LA for additional information)

Provosty & Gankendorff, L.L.C.

650 Poydras Street, Suite 2700
New Orleans, Louisiana 70130
   Telephone: 504-410-2795
   Fax: 504-410-2796
   E-Mail: attorneys@provostylaw.com
   www.provostylaw.com

General Civil Practice, Insurance Defense, Insurance Coverage, Insurance Litigation, Casualty Defense, Product Liability, Personal Injury, Admiralty and Maritime Law, Environmental Law, Toxic Torts, Oil and Gas, Complex Litigation, Class Actions, Antitrust, Corporate Law, International Law, Construction Law, Commercial Litigation, Business Litigation, Bankruptcy, Sports Law, Copyright and Trademark Law, Intellectual Property, Public Entities, Medical Malpractice, Legal Malpractice, Professional Liability, Health Care, Nursing Home Liability, Mediation, Business Transactions, Road Hazard Defense, Merchant Liability, Multi-District Litigation, Corporate Governance, Government Contacts, International, Local and Interstate Transactional Litigation, Expropriation, Entertainment and Media Law, Healthcare Professional Liability, Healthcare Licensing, Healthcare and Medical Malpractice Liability, Federal and State Employment Practices and Law, State Constitutional Law, Domestic and International Arbitration

Firm Profile: Based in New Orleans, Louisiana, Provosty & Gankendorff, L.L.C. is a full service law firm that represents foreign and domestic businesses, entertainers and athletes, insurance companies, and medical and legal professionals in a number of highly specialized areas of the law.

Corporate Clients

Heerema Marine Contractors Nederland SE	Raven Energy, L.L.C.
Wright Enrichment, Inc.	Solomon Group Entertainment, L.L.C.

Provosty & Gankendorff, L.L.C., New Orleans, LA (Continued)

Insurance Clients

AIG
Berkley Life Sciences, L.L.C.
Canopius Managing Agents Limited
Fleming & Hall, LTD
QBE European Operations
Westfield Insurance Company
Alterra Specialty Insurance Company / Markel
Cathedral Underwriting, Ltd.
Certain Underwriters at Lloyd's, London
State of Louisiana, Office of Risk Management

Third Party Administrators

Affirmative Risk Management, Inc.
Burns & Wilcox Ltd.
American Claims Services, Inc.
SyNerGy Adjusting Corporation

Partners

Henry St. Paul Provosty — University of Oregon, B.S., 1980; Tulane University Law School, J.D., 1983 — Admitted to Bar, 1983, Louisiana; U.S. District Court, Eastern, Middle and Western Districts of Louisiana; U.S. Court of Appeals, Fifth Circuit; U.S. Supreme Court — Member Louisiana State and New Orleans Bar Associations; New Orleans Mariners Club (President, 1997-1998); Houston Mariners Club; National Association of Professional Surplus Lines Offices; Louisiana Surplus Line Association; Louisiana Claims Association; New Orleans Claims Association; International Association of Defense Counsel; Defense Research Institute; Louisiana Association of Defense Counsel — E-mail: hprovosty@provostylaw.com

Edgar D. Gankendorff — Tulane University, B.A., 1987; Tulane University Law School, J.D., 1990 — Phi Sigma Alpha — Admitted to Bar, 1991, Louisiana; U.S. District Court, Eastern, Middle and Western Districts of Louisiana; U.S. Court of Appeals, Fifth Circuit; U.S. Supreme Court — Member American, Louisiana State and New Orleans Bar Associations; New Orleans Mariners Club — E-mail: egankendorff@provostylaw.com

Christophe B. Szapary — Duke University, B.A., 1991; Tulane University Law School, J.D. (cum laude), 1998; M.A., 2001 — Admitted to Bar, 1998, Louisiana; U.S. District Court, Eastern, Middle and Western Districts of Louisiana; U.S. Court of Appeals, Fifth Circuit — Member Louisiana State and New Orleans Bar Associations; World Trade Center of New Orleans — Languages: French — E-mail: cszapary@provostylaw.com

Eric R. G. Belin — Université Jean Moulin Faculté de Droit, LL.M., 1990; Tulane University Law School, J.D., 1996 — Admitted to Bar, 2001, Louisiana; U.S. District Court, Eastern, Middle and Western Districts of Louisiana; U.S. Court of Appeals, Fifth Circuit — Member American, Louisiana State and New Orleans Bar Associations; French-American Chamber of Commerce — Languages: French, German — E-mail: ebelin@provostylaw.com

Associates

Lena D. Giangrosso — Rutgers University, Douglass College, B.A. (with honors), 2002; Tulane University Law School, J.D., 2008 — Admitted to Bar, 2008, Louisiana; 2009, Texas; U.S. District Court, Eastern, Middle and Western Districts of Louisiana; U.S. Court of Appeals, Fifth Circuit; U.S. Supreme Court — Member American, Louisiana State and New Orleans Bar Associations; State Bar of Texas — E-mail: lgiangrosso@provostylaw.com

Keelie M. Broom — Millsaps College, B.A. (magna cum laude), 2007; Tulane University Law School, J.D., 2010 — Admitted to Bar, 2010, Louisiana; U.S. District Court, Eastern, Middle and Western Districts of Louisiana; U.S. Court of Appeals, Fifth Circuit — Member American, Louisiana State and New Orleans Bar Associations — E-mail: kbroom@provostylaw.com

Jason P. Franco — Louisiana State University at Baton Rouge, B.A., 2002; Loyola University New Orleans College of Law, J.D., 2005 — Admitted to Bar, 2005, Louisiana; U.S. District Court, Eastern, Middle and Western Districts of Louisiana; U.S. Court of Appeals, Fifth Circuit — Member American, Louisiana State and New Orleans Bar Associations — E-mail: jfranco@provostylaw.com

Schafer & Schafer

328 Lafayette Street
New Orleans, Louisiana 70130
Telephone: 504-522-0011
Fax: 504-523-2795
E-Mail: gschafer@schafer-law.com
www.schafer-law.com

Schafer & Schafer, New Orleans, LA (Continued)

(Covington, LA Office: 410 East Lockwood Avenue, 70433-2916)
(Tel: 985-893-3331)
(Fax: 985-249-2705)

Established: 1974

Insurance Defense, Automobile, Premises Liability, Product Liability, Employer Liability, Medical Malpractice, Coverage Issues, Employment Law, Bad Faith, Comprehensive General Liability, Complex Litigation, Civil Trial Practice, Excess and Umbrella, Fire Loss, Homeowners, Uninsured and Underinsured Motorist, Wrongful Death

Insurance Clients

AAA Auto Club South Insurance Company
AIG
American National Property & Casualty
California Casualty Indemnity
Founders Insurance Company
Government Employees Insurance Company
Volunteer Fireman's Insurance Service
Accordia Life and Annuity Insurance Company
American Alternative Insurance Corporation
Bituminous Insurance Companies
Erie Insurance Company
Glatfelter Insurance Group
Lexington Insurance Company
United Services Automobile Association (USAA)

Non-Insurance Clients

Forethought Capital Funding, Inc.
The Redwoods Group

Partners

Timothy G. Schafer — 1939 — Loyola University, B.B.A., 1961; LL.B., 1963 — Admitted to Bar, 1963, Louisiana; U.S. District Court, Eastern, Middle and Western Districts of Louisiana; U.S. Court of Appeals, Fifth Circuit; U.S. Supreme Court — Member American, Louisiana State and New Orleans Bar Associations; American Board of Trial Advocates (Diplomate); Louisiana Association of Defense Counsel; International Association of Defense Counsel; Defense Research Institute — Practice Areas: Appellate Practice; Civil Litigation; Insurance Defense — E-mail: tschafer@schafer-law.com

T. Gregory Schafer — 1970 — University of Colorado at Boulder, B.A. (Phi Beta Kappa), 1993; Tulane University of Louisiana, J.D. (cum laude), 1996 — Admitted to Bar, 1996, Louisiana; U.S. District Court, Eastern, Middle and Western Districts of Louisiana; U.S. Court of Appeals, Fifth Circuit — Member American, Louisiana State and New Orleans Bar Associations; Louisiana Association of Defense Counsel; American Board of Trial Advocates; Defense Research Institute — Practice Areas: Civil Litigation; Insurance Defense; Appellate Practice — E-mail: gschafer@schafer-law.com

Rachel S. Kellogg — 1978 — Louisiana State University, B.S., 1999; Louisiana State University Law Center, J.D., 2002; B.C.L., 2002 — Admitted to Bar, 2002, Louisiana; 2003, U.S. District Court, Eastern District of Louisiana; 2005, U.S. District Court, Middle and Western Districts of Louisiana; 2010, U.S. Court of Appeals, Fifth Circuit — Member Federal and Louisiana State Bar Associations; Louisiana Association of Defense Counsel; Defense Research Institute — Practice Areas: Appellate Practice; Complex Litigation; Employment Law; Insurance Defense; Coverage Issues — E-mail: rkellogg@schafer-law.com

Roy L. Schroeder — 1981 — Louisiana State University, B.A., 2003; Tulane University, J.D., 2006 — Certificate in Admiralty and Maritime Law — Admitted to Bar, 2006, Louisiana; U.S. District Court, Eastern and Western Districts of Louisiana — Member Louisiana State Bar Association; Louisiana Association of Defense Counsel — Practice Areas: Civil Litigation; Insurance Defense; Personal Injury; Admiralty and Maritime Law — E-mail: rschroeder@schafer-law.com

Associates

Rachel L. Flarity — 1985 — Louisiana State University, B.A., 2007; Louisiana State University, Paul M. Hebert Law Center, J.D./B.C.L., 2010 — Admitted to Bar, 2010, Louisiana; U.S. District Court, Eastern, Middle and Western Districts of Louisiana; U.S. Court of Appeals, Fifth Circuit — Member Federal, American and Louisiana State Bar Associations; Louisiana Association of Defense Counsel — Practice Areas: Civil Litigation; Insurance Defense; Transactional Law; Appellate Practice — E-mail: rflarity@schafer-law.com

Kathryn E. Fernandez — 1985 — Tulane University, B.A. (summa cum laude), 2007; University of California, Berkeley Boalt Hall School of Law, J.D., 2011 — Admitted to Bar, 2011, Louisiana — E-mail: kfernandez@schafer-law.com

Schafer & Schafer, New Orleans, LA (Continued)

Laurent J. Demosthenidy — 1979 — University of California, Santa Barbara, B.A., 2002; Tulane University Law School, J.D., 2006 — Admitted to Bar, 2006, Louisiana; 2007, Mississippi; U.S. District Court, Eastern, Middle and Western Districts of Louisiana; U.S. District Court, Northern and Southern Districts of Mississippi; U.S. Court of Appeals, Fifth Circuit — Member Louisiana State and New Orleans Bar Associations; The Mississippi Bar; Defense Research Institute — Practice Areas: Civil Litigation; Appellate Practice; Insurance Defense; Bad Faith; Admiralty and Maritime Law; Personal Injury; Product Liability; Life Insurance; Commercial Litigation — E-mail: ljd@schafer-law.com

Law Offices of Gordon P. Serou, Jr., L.L.C.

Poydras Center, Suite 1002
650 Poydras Street
New Orleans, Louisiana 70130
   Telephone: 504-299-3421
   Fax: 504-799-2525
   E-Mail: gps@seroulaw.com
   www.seroulaw.com

Legal Malpractice, Agent/Broker Liability, Church Law, Property Damage, Defamation, Complex Scientific and Medical Claims

Firm Profile: Legal counsel and trial attorneys licensed in Louisiana and Texas. We cultivate long term client relationships based on understanding our clients' businesses and their goals for litigation.

Insurance Clients

Assurant, Inc.	HomeFirst Agency, Inc.

Gordon P. Serou, Jr. — The University of New Orleans, B.A., 1981; Tulane University Law School, J.D., 1984 — Admitted to Bar, 1984, Louisiana; 1992, Texas — Member Louisiana State Bar Association; State Bar of Texas; The Maritime Law Association of the United States; Louisiana Association of Defense Counsel

Shields | Mott L.L.P.

650 Poydras Street, Suite 2600
New Orleans, Louisiana 70130
   Telephone: 504-581-4445
   Fax: 504-581-4440
   E-Mail: LNS@shieldsmott.com
   www.shieldsmott.com

Established: 1995

Construction Law, Insurance Defense, Product Liability, Surety Defense

Firm Profile: Shields | Mott L.L.P. specializes in litigation and business transactions. The firm has an extensive practice including construction industry, surety and insurance defense, labor and employment law, products liability, general commercial litigation, bankruptcy, real estate and zoning law, communications systems regulation, general corporate matters and intellectual property matters.

The firm prides itself in vigorously and aggressively representing its clients in the courtroom, at the negotiating table, and in the halls of government. Moreover, our size enables us to respond quickly and cost effectively to the needs of every client. Shields | Mott is a progressive law firm designed to handle sophisticated business transactions and litigation while developing and maintaining close working relationships with our clients.

State-of-the-art computer and communications systems provide the firm with the ability to quickly respond to a client's most complex legal and business requirements. The firm uses the latest case management, legal research and litigation support software, including computerized document handling for large-scale litigation. The lawyers of Shields | Mott are dedicated to

Shields | Mott L.L.P., New Orleans, LA (Continued)

excellence, regardless of the size of the matter at hand. More detailed information about our services is available upon request. We encourage you to find out more about our lawyers and our track record in servicing business and individual clients.

Firm Affiliations: American Arbitration Association; American Bar Association; Associated Builders and Contractors; Associated General Contractors; Defense Research Institute; Louisiana Association of Defense Counsel; Surety Association of Louisiana; National Bond Claims Association; Surety Claims Institute; Construction Financial Management Association; Pearlman Association

Insurance Clients

CGU Surety Company	Employers Mutual Casualty Company
Great American Insurance Company	HCC Surety Group
Insurance Company of the State of Pennsylvania	Liberty Mutual Insurance Company
RLI Insurance Company	Ohio Casualty Insurance Company

Members

Lloyd N. Shields — 1951 — Tulane University, B.Arch., 1974; M.Arch., 2004; J.D., 1977 — Admitted to Bar, 1977, Louisiana — Member American and Louisiana State Bar Associations — E-mail: LNS@shieldsmott.com

Norman A. Mott, III — 1950 — Princeton University, A.B., 1972; The University of Mississippi, J.D., 1976 — Admitted to Bar, 1976, Mississippi; 1977, Louisiana; 1992, Texas — Member American, Louisiana State and New Orleans Bar Associations; The Mississippi Bar — E-mail: MofoMotz@aol.com

Elizabeth L. Gordon — Tulane University, B.S., 1986; Loyola University, J.D., 1992 — Admitted to Bar, 1992, Louisiana — E-mail: ELGordon@shieldsmott.com

Andrew G. Vicknair — Louisiana Tech University, B.S., 1997; Loyola University, J.D., 2002 — Admitted to Bar, 2003, Louisiana; 2003, Texas; 2009, New York; U.S. Patent and Trademark Office — E-mail: AGVicknair@shieldsmott.com

Adrian A. D'Arcy — University College Dublin, B.A., 1990; Loyola University, J.D., 2004 — Admitted to Bar, 2004, Louisiana — E-mail: AADarcy@shieldsmott.com

Associates

Jeffrey K. Prattini — Louisiana State University and A & M College, B.A., 1996; Loyola University School of Law, J.D., 2006 — Admitted to Bar, 2006, Louisiana — E-mail: JKPrattini@shieldsmott.com

Ashley B. Robinson — Louisiana State University, B.S., 2004; Louisiana State University, Paul M. Hebert Law Center, J.D., 2007 — Admitted to Bar, 2007, Louisiana — E-mail: ABRobinson@shieldsmott.com

Jessica R. Derenbecker — Louisiana State University at Baton Rouge, B.A. (summa cum laude), 2006; Tulane University Law School, J.D., 2009 — Admitted to Bar, 2009, Louisiana — E-mail: JRDerenbecker@shieldsmott.com

Michael S. Blackwell — University of South Alabama, B.A., 2005; Loyola University New Orleans College of Law, J.D. (magna cum laude), 2009 — Admitted to Bar, 2009, Louisiana — E-mail: MSBlackwell@shieldsmott.com

Adrienne C. May — Tulane University, B.A. (magna cum laude), 2010; Tulane University Law School, J.D., 2013 — Admitted to Bar, 2013, Louisiana — E-mail: ACMay@shieldsmott.com

Eric A. Mund — Texas State University, B.A. (summa cum laude), 2005; Loyola University New Orleans College of Law, J.D./M.B.A. (magna cum laude), 2010 — Admitted to Bar, 2010, Louisiana — E-mail: EAMund@shieldsmott.com

Swetman Baxter Massenburg, LLC

650 Poydras Street, Suite 2400
New Orleans, Louisiana 70130
   Telephone: 504-799-0500
   Fax: 504-799-0501
   E-Mail: mswetman@sbm-legal.com
   www.sbm-legal.com

LOUISIANA

Swetman Baxter Massenburg, LLC, New Orleans, LA (Continued)

(Hattiesburg, MS Office*: 1700 South 28th Avenue, Suite D, 39402)
 (Tel: 601-255-0259)
 (Fax: 601-255-0260)
 (E-Mail: cmassenburg@sbm-legal.com)

Asbestos Litigation, Bad Faith, Construction Claims, Construction Law, Contractors Liability, Declaratory Judgments, Drug, Environmental Law, Hazardous Waste, Insurance Defense, Intellectual Property, Mold and Mildew Claims, Municipal Liability, Premises Liability, Product Liability, Trucking Liability, Trucking Litigation, Toxic Torts, Uninsured and Underinsured Motorist, Workers' Compensation, Wrongful Death

Firm Profile: Swetman Baxter Massenburg, LLC is AV rated by Martindale-Hubbell.

Insurance Clients

Allstate Insurance Company
CNA
The Hartford
Nationwide Indemnity Company
RiverStone Claims Management, LLC
TIG Insurance Company
Travelers Special Liability Group
Chartis Insurance
First State Insurance Company
Liberty Mutual
Resolute Management, Inc.
Sentry Insurance
St. Paul Travelers Insurance Company

Partners

Max Swetman — 1967 — Louisiana State University, B.A., 1989; Tulane School of Public Health, M.P.H.; Louisiana State University, J.D., 1992 — New Orleans City Business 2011 Leadership in Law Honoree — Admitted to Bar, 1992, Louisiana; 1993, Mississippi; 2007, Texas; 1992, U.S. District Court, Eastern and Middle Districts of Louisiana; 1993, U.S. District Court, Northern and Southern Districts of Mississippi; 1993, U.S. Court of Appeals, Fifth Circuit — Member Federal, Louisiana State and New Orleans Bar Associations; The Mississippi Bar; State Bar of Texas; International Society for Environmental Epidemiology (Air Quality, Water Quality and Hazardous Wastes Sections); American Public Health Association (Epidemiology Section); American Statistical Association (Statistics in Epidemiology, Statistics and the Environmental and Risk Analysis Sections); Defense Research Institute; Louisiana Association of Defense Counsel; New Orleans Association of Defense Counsel — Languages: Spanish — Practice Areas: Real Property; Complex Litigation; Environmental Law; Toxic Substances; Toxic Torts; Product Liability; Asbestos Litigation; Pollution; Defense Litigation; Construction Law; Civil Trial Practice; Regulatory and Compliance; Mold Litigation — E-mail: mswetman@sbm-legal.com

Kay Baxter — University of Arkansas at Little Rock, B.A. (magna cum laude), 1991; Loyola University School of Law, J.D., 1994 — New Orleans City Business 2011 Leadership in Law Honoree — Admitted to Bar, 1994, Louisiana; 1995, Arkansas; 1997, Mississippi; 2006, Texas; 1994, U.S. District Court, Middle District of Louisiana; 1994, U.S. Court of Appeals, Fifth Circuit; 1997, U.S. District Court, Northern and Southern Districts of Mississippi — Member Louisiana State, Arkansas, Baton Rouge and New Orleans Bar Associations; The Mississippi Bar; State Bar of Texas; National Association of Women Lawyers; Defense Research Institute; Association of Trial Lawyers of America; Louisiana Association of Defense Counsel — Practice Areas: Insurance Defense; Toxic Torts; Product Liability; Premises Liability; Construction Law; Civil Trial Practice; Environmental Law — E-mail: kbaxter@sbm-legal.com

Christopher Massenburg — 1975 — Loyola University, B.B.A., 1997; Tulane University, J.D., 2000 — Super Lawyers 2010 Mid-South Rising Stars — Admitted to Bar, 2000, Louisiana; 2001, Mississippi; 2007, Texas; 2010, Tennessee; 2001, U.S. District Court, Northern and Southern Districts of Mississippi; 2001, U.S. Court of Appeals, Fifth Circuit; 2005, U.S. Supreme Court — Member Louisiana State, Tennessee and South Central Mississippi Bar Associations; The Mississippi Bar; State Bar of Texas; Hattiesburg Area Young Lawyers Association; Mississippi Tort Claims Board; Defense Research Institute — Practice Areas: Admiralty and Maritime Law; Environmental Law; Insurance Defense; Civil Litigation; Complex Litigation; Asbestos Litigation; Mold Litigation; Toxic Torts; Product Liability; Premises Liability; Intellectual Property; Truck Liability; Construction Law — Tel: 601-255-0259 — Fax: 601-255-0260 — E-mail: cmassenburg@sbm-legal.com

NEW ORLEANS

Swetman Baxter Massenburg, LLC, New Orleans, LA (Continued)

Associates

Margaret Adams Casey — Louisiana State University, B.S., 1986; The University of New Orleans, Paralegal Studies, 1991; Loyola University School of Law, J.D., 1994 — Admitted to Bar, 1994, Louisiana; 1994, U.S. District Court, Eastern, Middle and Western Districts of Louisiana

Adam Hays — University of Southern Mississippi, B.A., 2001; Louisiana State University Law Center, J.D./B.C.L., 2004 — Admitted to Bar, 2004, Mississippi; 2006, Louisiana; 2010, Alabama; 2004, U.S. District Court, Northern and Southern Districts of Mississippi

Brandie L. Thibodeaux — Louisiana State University, B.S., 2000; Tulane University Law School, J.D., 2004 — Admitted to Bar, 2004, Louisiana; 2006, U.S. District Court, Middle and Western Districts of Louisiana — Member American, Louisiana State and New Orleans Bar Associations; Trial Advocacy Honors Designation; Appointment to Interviewing and Appointments Committee

Kristen R. Stanley — Louisiana State University, B.A., 2002; Paul M Hebert Law School at Louisiana State University, J.D./B.C.L., 2005 — Admitted to Bar, 2005, Louisiana — Member Louisiana State Bar Association; East St. Tammany Chamber of Commerce Emerging Young Professionals (Founding President, 2010-2012; Secretary, 2012-present; Board Member of the Year, 2011); East St. Tammany Chamber of Commerce (Member of the Month, 2011)

The Waltz Law Group

1100 Poydras Street, Suite 2621
New Orleans, Louisiana 70163
 Telephone: 504-264-5260
 Fax: 504-264-5487
 E-Mail: jeff@waltzlawgroup.com
 www.waltzlawgroup.com

Established: 2013

Admiralty and Maritime Law, Bad Faith, Class Actions, Collections, Commercial Litigation, Commercial Vehicle, Construction Law, Insurance Coverage, Insurance Defense, Longshore and Harbor Workers' Compensation, Jones Act, Oil and Gas, Product Liability, Premises Liability, Property and Casualty, Toxic Torts, Trucking, Workers' Compensation

Firm Profile: The Waltz Law Group brings large firm experience to clients on a more personal level, resulting in a close, cost-effective relationship that provides for a better overall experience. We consult directly with our clients to formulate a decisive plan that combines our expertise and innovation to meet their expectations and deliver strong results. Our goal is to create a personal relationship that helps our clients achieve their ultimate goals.

Insurance Clients

Gray Insurance Company
LCI Workers' Compensation

Non-Insurance Clients

FRSTeam
Rapiere Resources Company

Partners

Jill Waltz — University of Memphis, B.A., 1999; Paul M Hebert Law School at Louisiana State University, J.D., 2002 — Admitted to Bar, 2002, Louisiana; U.S. District Court, Eastern, Middle and Western Districts of Louisiana; U.S. Court of Appeals, Fifth Circuit; Louisiana State Courts — Member Louisiana State and New Orleans Bar Associations; Louisiana Claims Association; Claims & Litigation Management Alliance (CLM)

Jeff Waltz — Louisiana State University, B.A. (magna cum laude), 1999; Loyola University New Orleans, J.D., 2003 — Admitted to Bar, 2003, Louisiana; U.S. District Court, Eastern, Middle and Western Districts of Louisiana; U.S. Court of Appeals, Fifth Circuit — Member Louisiana State, Fifth Federal Circuit and New Orleans Bar Associations; Louisiana Claims Association

OPELOUSAS

The following firms also service this area.

Gaudry, Ranson, Higgins & Gremillion, L.L.C.
Oakwood Corporate Center
401 Whitney Avenue, Suite 500
Gretna, Louisiana 70056
    Telephone: 504-362-2466
    Fax: 504-362-5938

Mailing Address: P.O. Box 1910, Gretna, LA 70054-1910

Insurance Defense, Automobile, Premises Liability, Product Liability, Medical Malpractice, Hospital Malpractice, State and Federal Workers' Compensation

SEE COMPLETE LISTING UNDER GRETNA, LOUISIANA (5 MILES)

Hailey, McNamara, Hall, Larmann & Papale, L.L.P.
One Galleria Boulevard, Suite 1400
Metairie, Louisiana 70001
    Telephone: 504-836-6500
    Fax: 504-836-6565

Mailing Address: P.O. Box 8288, Metairie, LA 70011-8288

Admiralty and Maritime Law, Commercial Litigation, Construction Litigation, Employment Practices Liability, Insurance Litigation, Product Liability, Professional Malpractice, Toxic Torts, Casualty, Insurance Coverage, Intellectual Property, Premises Liability, Transportation, Mass Tort, Property, Workers' Compensation, Automobile Liability, Appellate, Environmental

SEE COMPLETE LISTING UNDER METAIRIE, LOUISIANA (5 MILES)

Law Office of Eric J. Halverson, Jr.
3925 North I-10 Service Road West, Suite 123
Metairie, Louisiana 70002
    Telephone: 504-885-0105
    Fax: 504-885-2001

Mailing Address: P.O. Box 8761, Metairie, LA 70011-8761

Insurance Defense, Admiralty and Maritime Law, Jones Act, Workers' Compensation, Errors and Omissions, Medical Malpractice, General Liability, Product Liability, Automobile, Truck Liability, Collision and P & I, Longshore

SEE COMPLETE LISTING UNDER METAIRIE, LOUISIANA (5 MILES)

Juge, Napolitano, Guilbeau, Ruli & Frieman
3320 West Esplanade Avenue North
Metairie, Louisiana 70002
    Telephone: 504-831-7270
    Fax: 504-831-7284

Insurance Defense, Workers' Compensation, Employer Liability, Subrogation, Jones Act, Premises Liability, General Liability, Automobile Liability, Longshore & Harbor Workers' Compensation Act, General Maritime Law

SEE COMPLETE LISTING UNDER METAIRIE, LOUISIANA (5 MILES)

Larzelere Picou Wells Simpson Lonero, LLC
Two Lakeway Center, Suite 1100
3850 North Causeway Boulevard
Metairie, Louisiana 70002
    Telephone: 504-834-6500
    Fax: 504-834-6565

Insurance Law, Trucking Law, Transportation, Toxic Torts, Marine, Energy, Recoveries, Pollution, General Casualty

SEE COMPLETE LISTING UNDER METAIRIE, LOUISIANA

Staines & Eppling
3500 North Causeway Boulevard, Suite 820
Metairie, Louisiana 70002
    Telephone: 504-838-0019
    Fax: 504-838-0043

Insurance Defense, Admiralty and Maritime Law, Casualty, Workers' Compensation, Labor and Employment, Inland and Ocean Marine, Cargo, Automobile, Transportation, Premises Liability, Toxic Torts, Energy, Construction Law, Coverage Issues, Product Liability, Asbestos Litigation

SEE COMPLETE LISTING UNDER METAIRIE, LOUISIANA (5 MILES)

Ungarino & Eckert, L.L.C.
3850 North Causeway Boulevard, Suite 1280
Metairie, Louisiana 70002
    Telephone: 504-836-7555
    Fax: 504-836-7566

Litigation, Appellate Practice, State and Federal Courts, Class Actions, Insurance Coverage, Premises Liability, Professional Liability, Directors and Officers Liability, Insurance Defense, Construction Law, Toxic Torts, Personal Injury, Arson, Insurance Fraud, Admiralty and Maritime Law, Extra-Contractual Litigation, Bad Faith, Product Liability, Alternative Dispute Resolution, Civil Rights, Workers' Compensation, Environmental Law, Employment Law, Automobile, Truck Liability, Errors and Omissions, Common Carrier, Medical Malpractice, Construction Defect, Constitutional Law, Department of Insurance Complaints, ERISA Claims, Government Relations, Complex Casualty, Consumer Defense, Creditor Rights, Debt Collections, Discrimination Claims, Electric Utility Liability, Engineering Malpractice, Family Law (Divorce, Custody, Support, Adoption), Fraud, General Liability, Governmental Entity Liability, Insurance Subrogation, Landlord Liability, Medical Device Liability, Property Ownership, State and Municipality Litigation, Successions, Warranty/Redhibition Actions

SEE COMPLETE LISTING UNDER METAIRIE, LOUISIANA (5 MILES)

OBERLIN † 1,770 Allen Par.

Refer To

Plauché, Smith & Nieset, LLC
1123 Pithon Street
Lake Charles, Louisiana 70601
    Telephone: 337-436-0522
    Fax: 337-436-9637

Mailing Address: P.O. Drawer 1705, Lake Charles, LA 70602

Automobile Liability, Fire, Arson, Inland Marine, Casualty, Workers' Compensation, Admiralty and Maritime Law, Product Liability, Professional Malpractice, Environmental Law, Toxic Torts, Subrogation, Surety Bonds, Construction Law, Directors and Officers Liability, Employment Law

SEE COMPLETE LISTING UNDER LAKE CHARLES, LOUISIANA (40 MILES)

Refer To

Woodley, Williams Law Firm, L.L.C.
One Lakeshore Drive, Suite 1750
Lake Charles, Louisiana 70629
    Telephone: 337-433-6328
    Fax: 337-433-7513

Mailing Address: P.O. Box 3731, Lake Charles, LA 70602-3731

Admiralty and Maritime Law, Arson, Dram Shop, Construction Law, Employment Discrimination, Fraud, Health Care, Hospitals, Investigations, Liquor Liability, Medical Liability, Oil and Gas, Premises Liability, Product Liability, Subrogation, Toxic Torts, Trial Practice, Workers' Compensation, Wrongful Termination, Reinsurance, Medical Malpractice, Asbestosis, Silicosis and Hazardous Waste Litigation, Legal and Insurance Broker Malpractice Law, Civil Practice

SEE COMPLETE LISTING UNDER LAKE CHARLES, LOUISIANA (40 MILES)

OPELOUSAS † 16,634 St. Landry Par.

Refer To

Woodley, Williams Law Firm, L.L.C.
One Lakeshore Drive, Suite 1750
Lake Charles, Louisiana 70629
    Telephone: 337-433-6328
    Fax: 337-433-7513

Mailing Address: P.O. Box 3731, Lake Charles, LA 70602-3731

Admiralty and Maritime Law, Arson, Dram Shop, Construction Law, Employment Discrimination, Fraud, Health Care, Hospitals, Investigations, Liquor Liability, Medical Liability, Oil and Gas, Premises Liability, Product Liability, Subrogation, Toxic Torts, Trial Practice, Workers' Compensation, Wrongful Termination, Reinsurance, Medical Malpractice, Asbestosis, Silicosis and Hazardous Waste Litigation, Legal and Insurance Broker Malpractice Law, Civil Practice

SEE COMPLETE LISTING UNDER LAKE CHARLES, LOUISIANA (87 MILES)

LOUISIANA

POINTE A LA HACHE † 187 Plaquemines Par.

Refer To
Gaudry, Ranson, Higgins & Gremillion, L.L.C.
Oakwood Corporate Center
401 Whitney Avenue, Suite 500
Gretna, Louisiana 70056
   Telephone: 504-362-2466
   Fax: 504-362-5938
Mailing Address: P.O. Box 1910, Gretna, LA 70054-1910

Insurance Defense, Automobile, Premises Liability, Product Liability, Medical Malpractice, Hospital Malpractice, State and Federal Workers' Compensation

SEE COMPLETE LISTING UNDER GRETNA, LOUISIANA (45 MILES)

SHREVEPORT † 199,311 Caddo Par.

Abrams & Lafargue, L.L.C.
330 Marshall Street, Suite 1020
Shreveport, Louisiana 71101
   Telephone: 318-222-9100
   Fax: 318-222-9191

Established: 1995

Insurance Defense, Commercial Vehicle, Tort Liability, Medical Malpractice, Appellate Practice, Health Care, Municipal Law, Product Liability, School Law

Firm Profile: Abrams & Lafargue, L.L.C., formed June of 1995, by Reginald W. Abrams and Julie Mobley Lafargue, is a law firm emphasizing in the defense of insurance companies and their insureds, school law, as well as the defense of lawsuits against municipalities, parishes, and police juries, particularly those involving flooding.

Their combined experience includes the successful representation of the City of Shreveport, Caddo Parish, the State of Louisiana, the Caddo Parish School Board, several national insurance companies, and a major drug store chain. Their practice areas include civil litigation, school law, insurance defense, medical malpractice defense, defense of municipalities, defense of medical products and pharmaceutical claims and products liability defense.

Insurance Clients

AIG Aerospace Adjustment Services, Inc.
Atlantic Casualty Insurance Company
The California Casualty Indemnity Exchange
First Financial Insurance Company
Guaranty National Group
Lloyd's
MGA Insurance Company, Inc.
St. Paul Travelers Insurance Companies
Allstate Insurance Company
American Equity Insurance Company
Auto-Owners Insurance Company
Chubb Executive Risk, Inc.
Fireman's Fund Insurance Company
Indiana Farm Bureau
The Medical Protective Company
St. Paul Fire and Marine Insurance Company
Travelers Insurance Companies

Non-Insurance Clients

Baxter Healthcare Corporation
City of Shreveport
Crinco Investments
David Raines Community Health Center
GESPIA Fasteners
Griggs Enterprises, LLC d/b/a McDonalds
Louisiana Department of Transportation and Development
Norman Reitman Company, Inc.
Parish of Caddo
Southern Industrial Contractors
Tetra Technologies, Inc.
United-Bilt Homes
Whirlpool Corporation
Caddo Parish School Board
Communications One
CVS Pharmacy, Inc.
DeSoto Parish Library Board
Dixie Weld Fab
Grambling State University
Harrah's-Horseshoe Entertainment
The Limited, Inc.
McDuffy Enterprises, LLC d/b/a McDonalds
O'NAL, LLC d/b/a McDonalds
Penske Truck Leasing Company
State of Louisiana
Twin State Trucks, Inc.
Walden Hill Properties
Wirekraft Industries, Inc.

Abrams & Lafargue, L.L.C., Shreveport, LA (Continued)

Partners

Reginald W. Abrams — 1956 — Louisiana State University, 1976; Northeast Louisiana University, B.S., 1978; Louisiana State University, J.D., 1987 — Admitted to Bar, 1987, Louisiana; 2001, Texas; 1989, U.S. District Court, Western District of Louisiana — Member Federal, American, Louisiana State and Shreveport Bar Associations; Shreveport Black Lawyers Association; Louisiana Pharmacist Association; Louisiana Association of Defense Counsel — E-mail: rabrams@abramslafargue.com

Julie Mobley Lafargue — 1956 — Louisiana Tech University, B.S. (summa cum laude), 1978; Louisiana State University, J.D., 1981 — Admitted to Bar, 1981, Louisiana; 1995, Texas; 1983, U.S. District Court, Western District of Louisiana; 1983, U.S. Court of Appeals, Fifth Circuit — Member Federal, American, Louisiana State and Shreveport Bar Associations; Louisiana Association of Defense Counsel; American Board of Trial Advocates; Defense Research Institute — E-mail: jlafargue@abramslafargue.com

Perkins & Associates, L.L.C.
401 Market Street, Suite 900
Shreveport, Louisiana 71101
   Telephone: 318-222-2426
   Fax: 318-222-0458
   Mobile: 318-272-2500
   E-Mail: perkins@perkinsfirm.com
   www.perkinsfirm.com

Established: 1998

Commercial Litigation, Trucking Litigation, Estate Planning, Insurance Defense, Commercial Vehicle, Trucking Law, Professional Malpractice, Employment Law, Workers' Compensation, Bodily Injury, Product Liability, Errors and Omissions, General Liability, Subrogation

Firm Profile: Organized to meet the specific legal needs of a select group of insurance companies and insured clients, Perkins & Associates, L.L.C. consists of highly experienced lawyers with a well-trained support staff. Our goal is to meet the needs of a select group of clients at a competitive rate. In addition to general insurance defense, the firm also practices professional liability, corporate and employment defense.

Insurance Clients

Agricultural Workers Mutual Auto Insurance Company
Captive Resources, LLC
Clarendon National Insurance Company
Criterion Claim Solutions
First Mercury Insurance Company
First State Management Group, Inc.
Great American Insurance Companies
Hudson Insurance Group
Liberty Bell Insurance Company
Markel Insurance Company of Canada
Motor Transport Underwriters, Inc.
North American Risk Services
Protective Insurance Company
Rice Insurance Services Company, LLC
RLI Transportation
TIG Specialty Insurance Company
Truck Claims, Inc.
Baldwin & Lyons, Inc.
Broadspire
Carolina Casualty Insurance Company
CNA Insurance Companies
Fireman's Fund Insurance Company
Gateway Insurance Company
General Casualty Insurance Company
Great West Casualty Company
K & K Insurance Group, Inc.
Maiden Reinsurance Company
Midway Insurance Management International
National Transportation Adjusters, Inc.
Republic Western Insurance Company
Risk Management Services, Inc.
State Auto Insurance Company
Transportation Claims, Inc.
Zurich North America Insurance Group

Non-Insurance Clients

AAA Cooper Transportation
American Van Lines
Annett Holdings, Inc.
B & W Cartage
Crete Carrier Corporation
Greatwide Logistics Services, LLC
McLane Company, Inc.
AB Transport
Anderson Trucking Service
Averitt Express, Inc.
Cambridge Transportation (NTA)
Dart Transit Company, Inc.
Louisiana College
Old Dominion Freight Line, Inc.

SHREVEPORT   LOUISIANA

Perkins & Associates, L.L.C., Shreveport, LA (Continued)

Pacer International, Inc.
Southern RV Supercenter
Wal-Mart Transportation
Southeastern Freight Lines
USA Truck, Inc.
Western Petroleum, Inc.

Partner

Mark A. Perkins — 1962 — Northeast Louisiana University, B.A. (magna cum laude), 1983; Louisiana State University, Paul M. Hebert Law Center, J.D., 1987 — Admitted to Bar, 1987, Louisiana; 2009, Texas; 1987, U.S. District Court, Western District of Louisiana; U.S. Court of Appeals, Fifth Circuit; 2002, U.S. District Court, Middle District of Louisiana; U.S. Supreme Court — Member American (Sections: Employment, Litigation), Louisiana State and Shreveport Bar Associations; State Bar of Texas; Lousiana Association of Business and Industry; Christian Legal Society; Louisiana Motor Transport Association; Louisiana Association of Defense Counsel; Trucking Industry Defense Association; American Arbitration Association; Defense Research Institute; Transportation Lawyers Association — Practice Areas: Commercial Litigation; Employment Practices Liability; Transportation; Truck Liability; Trucks/Heavy Equipment — E-mail: perkins@perkinsfirm.com

Associates

Tara J. Hoffmann — 1987 — Louisiana Tech University, B.A. Psychology and English (summa cum laude), 2008; Louisiana State University Law Center, J.D., 2011 — Admitted to Bar, 2012, Louisiana — Member Louisiana State and Shreveport Bar Associations

Kyle S. McGuire — 1983 — Louisiana State University at Shreveport, B.A., 2006; Louisiana State University Law Center, J.D., 2012 — Admitted to Bar, 2012, Louisiana; 2013, U.S. District Court, Middle and Western Districts of Louisiana — Member Louisiana State and Shreveport Bar Associations — Practice Areas: Commercial Litigation; Trucking Litigation; Estate Planning — E-mail: mcguire@perkinsfirm.com

Of Counsel

Christopher T. Baker — 1975 — Regent University, B.A., 2000; Regent University School of Law, J.D., 2009 — Admitted to Bar, 2009, Louisiana; U.S. District Court, Western District of Louisiana — Member Louisiana State and Shreveport Bar Associations — Practice Areas: Commercial Litigation; Insurance Defense; Trucking Law; Trucking Liability; Trucking Litigation — E-mail: baker@perkinsfirm.com

Wilkinson, Carmody & Gilliam

400 Travis Street, Suite 1700
Shreveport, Louisiana 71101
   Telephone: 318-221-4196
   Fax: 318-221-3705
   E-Mail: administrator@wcglawfirm.com
   www.wilkinsoncarmodyandgilliam.com

Established: 1895

Insurance Law, Trial Practice, Appellate Practice

Firm Profile: Wilkinson, Carmody & Gilliam traces its origins to January 1, 1895. For over one hundred years the firm has maintained a broad civil practice, including the representation of insurance, utility, railway, financial institutions, and other corporate and individual clients with state and national interests. Its attorneys practice in a broad scope of legal areas with an emphasis on litigation. It is proud of the legal abilities and personal qualities of its attorneys, who, among past and present attorneys, include an Associate Justice of the Louisiana Supreme Court, a Justice of the Second Circuit Court of Appeals, a member of the Louisiana House of Representatives, a founder of the Federal Power Bar Association and a chairman of the governing boards of several educational institutions.

Insurance Clients

American General Group
Connecticut General Life Insurance
   Company
Farmers Insurance Group
The Hartford Insurance Group
Massachusetts Mutual Life
   Insurance Company
Colonial Life and Accident
   Insurance Company
Continental Life & Accident
   Company
Lexington Insurance Company
New England Insurance Company
OneBeacon Professional Insurance

Wilkinson, Carmody & Gilliam, Shreveport, LA (Continued)

Puritan Insurance Company
UNUM Provident Life and
   Accident Insurance Company
Republic National Life Insurance
   Company

Non-Insurance Clients

American Electric Power
Kansas City Southern Railway
   Company
Gamble Guest Care Group
Southwestern Electric Power
   Company

Partners

Bobby S. Gilliam — 1953 — Ouachita Baptist University, B.A. (cum laude), 1975; Louisiana State University, J.D., 1978 — Admitted to Bar, Louisiana; U.S. District Court, Eastern, Middle and Western Districts of Louisiana; U.S. Court of Appeals, Fifth Circuit — Member Federal, Louisiana State and Shreveport Bar Associations; National Association of Railroad Trial Counsel; International Association of Defense Counsel; Defense Research Institute; Louisiana Association of Defense Counsel — E-mail: bgilliam@wcglawfirm.com

Mark E. Gilliam — 1956 — University of Arkansas, B.S., 1978; Louisiana State University, J.D., 1981 — Admitted to Bar, 1981, Louisiana; U.S. District Court, Eastern, Middle and Western Districts of Louisiana; U.S. Court of Appeals, Fifth Circuit — Member Federal, Louisiana State and Shreveport Bar Associations; American Institute of Certified Public Accountants; Society of Louisiana Certified Public Accountants; National Association of Railroad Trial Counsel; Defense Research Institute; American Inns of Court; Louisiana Association of Defense Counsel — Certfied Public Accountant (1984) — E-mail: mgilliam@wcglawfirm.com

Associates

Jonathan P. McCartney — 1980 — The University of Texas at Austin, B.A., 2002; Louisiana State University, Paul M. Hebert Law Center, J.D./B.C.L., 2007 — Admitted to Bar, 2008, Louisiana; U.S. District Court, Western District of Louisiana; U.S. Court of Appeals, Fifth Circuit — Member Federal, Louisiana State and Shreveport Bar Associations; National Association of Railroad Trial Counsel; American Inns of Court; Louisiana Association of Defense Counsel — E-mail: jmccartney@wcglawfirm.com

David L. Bruce — 1985 — Louisiana State University at Baton Rouge, B.A.S. (cum laude), 2008; Louisiana State University, Paul M. Hebert Law Center, J.D., 2011 — Admitted to Bar, 2011, Louisiana; U.S. District Court, Middle and Western Districts of Louisiana — Member Federal, Louisiana State and Shreveport Bar Associations; National Association of Railroad Trial Counsel; Louisiana Association of Defense Counsel

Elizabeth A. Aycock — 1987 — Louisiana State University at Baton Rouge, B.S. (magna cum laude), 2009; Louisiana State University Law Center, J.D., 2012 — Admitted to Bar, 2012, Louisiana; U.S. District Court, Western District of Louisiana; U.S. Court of Appeals, Fifth Circuit — Member Louisiana State and Shreveport Bar Associations; Louisiana Association of Defense Counsel

Of Counsel

Arthur R. Carmody, Jr. — 1928 — Fordham University, B.A., 1949; Louisiana State University, LL.B., 1952 — Admitted to Bar, 1952, Louisiana; U.S. District Court, Eastern, Middle and Western Districts of Louisiana; U.S. Court of Appeals, Fifth Circuit — Member Federal, Louisiana State and Shreveport Bar Associations; National Association of Railroad Trial Counsel; Defense Research Institute; Fellow, American College of Trial Lawyers — E-mail: acarmody@wcglawfirm.com

John Dallas Wilkinson — (1867-1929)
W. Scott Wilkinson — (1895-1985)

LOUISIANA — SLIDELL

The following firms also service this area.

Hailey, McNamara, Hall, Larmann & Papale, L.L.P.
One Galleria Boulevard, Suite 1400
Metairie, Louisiana 70001
   Telephone: 504-836-6500
   Fax: 504-836-6565

Mailing Address: P.O. Box 8288, Metairie, LA 70011-8288

Admiralty and Maritime Law, Commercial Litigation, Construction Litigation, Employment Practices Liability, Insurance Litigation, Product Liability, Professional Malpractice, Toxic Torts, Casualty, Insurance Coverage, Intellectual Property, Premises Liability, Transportation, Mass Tort, Property, Workers' Compensation, Automobile Liability, Appellate, Environmental

SEE COMPLETE LISTING UNDER METAIRIE, LOUISIANA (337 MILES)

Ungarino & Eckert, L.L.C.
3850 North Causeway Boulevard, Suite 1280
Metairie, Louisiana 70002
   Telephone: 504-836-7555
   Fax: 504-836-7566

Litigation, Appellate Practice, State and Federal Courts, Class Actions, Insurance Coverage, Premises Liability, Professional Liability, Directors and Officers Liability, Insurance Defense, Construction Law, Toxic Torts, Personal Injury, Arson, Insurance Fraud, Admiralty and Maritime Law, Extra-Contractual Litigation, Bad Faith, Product Liability, Alternative Dispute Resolution, Civil Rights, Workers' Compensation, Environmental Law, Employment Law, Automobile, Truck Liability, Errors and Omissions, Common Carrier, Medical Malpractice, Construction Defect, Constitutional Law, Department of Insurance Complaints, ERISA Claims, Government Relations, Complex Casualty, Consumer Defense, Creditor Rights, Debt Collections, Discrimination Claims, Electric Utility Liability, Engineering Malpractice, Family Law (Divorce, Custody, Support, Adoption), Fraud, General Liability, Governmental Entity Liability, Insurance Subrogation, Landlord Liability, Medical Device Liability, Property Ownership, State and Municipality Litigation, Successions, Warranty/Redhibition Actions

SEE COMPLETE LISTING UNDER METAIRIE, LOUISIANA (337 MILES)

SLIDELL 27,068 St. Tammany Par.
Refer To

Law Office of Eric J. Halverson, Jr.
3925 North I-10 Service Road West, Suite 123
Metairie, Louisiana 70002
   Telephone: 504-885-0105
   Fax: 504-885-2001

Mailing Address: P.O. Box 8761, Metairie, LA 70011-8761

Insurance Defense, Admiralty and Maritime Law, Jones Act, Workers' Compensation, Errors and Omissions, Medical Malpractice, General Liability, Product Liability, Automobile, Truck Liability, Collision and P & I, Longshore

SEE COMPLETE LISTING UNDER METAIRIE, LOUISIANA (36 MILES)

VILLE PLATTE † 7,430 Evangeline Par.
Refer To

Woodley, Williams Law Firm, L.L.C.
One Lakeshore Drive, Suite 1750
Lake Charles, Louisiana 70629
   Telephone: 337-433-6328
   Fax: 337-433-7513

Mailing Address: P.O. Box 3731, Lake Charles, LA 70602-3731

Admiralty and Maritime Law, Arson, Dram Shop, Construction Law, Employment Discrimination, Fraud, Health Care, Hospitals, Investigations, Liquor Liability, Medical Liability, Oil and Gas, Premises Liability, Product Liability, Subrogation, Toxic Torts, Trial Practice, Workers' Compensation, Wrongful Termination, Reinsurance, Medical Malpractice, Asbestos, Silicosis and Hazardous Waste Litigation, Legal and Insurance Broker Malpractice Law, Civil Practice

SEE COMPLETE LISTING UNDER LAKE CHARLES, LOUISIANA (84 MILES)

712 — For Current Listings access www.ambest.com/directories — 2015 BEST'S DIRECTORIES OF RECOMMENDED INSURANCE ATTORNEYS AND ADJUSTERS

MAINE

CAPITAL: AUGUSTA

COUNTIES AND COUNTY SEATS

County	County Seat
Androscoggin	Auburn
Aroostook	Houlton
Cumberland	Portland
Franklin	Farmington
Hancock	Ellsworth
Kennebec	Augusta

County	County Seat
Knox	Rockland
Lincoln	Wiscasset
Oxford	South Paris
Penobscot	Bangor
Piscataquis	Dover-Foxcroft
Sagadahoc	Bath

County	County Seat
Somerset	Skowhegan
Waldo	Belfast
Washington	Machias
York	Alfred

In the text that follows "†" indicates County Seats.

Our files contain additional verified data on the firms listed herein. This additional information is available on request.

A.M. BEST COMPANY

MAINE — AUBURN

AUBURN † 23,055 Androscoggin Co.

Skelton, Taintor & Abbott

95 Main Street
Auburn, Maine 04210
   Telephone: 207-784-3200
   Fax: 207-784-3345
   Toll Free: 800-639-7026
   www.STA-Law.com

Aviation, General Defense, Insurance Coverage, First and Third Party Defense, Product Liability, Professional Liability, Uninsured and Underinsured Motorist

Firm Profile: Skelton, Taintor & Abbott is accessible, affordable and small enough to offer a personal touch without compromising quality.

Insurance Clients

Metropolitan Life Insurance Company
OMSNIC
Westport Insurance Corporation
National Interstate Insurance Company
Utica Mutual Insurance Company

Attorneys

James E. Belleau — Bowdoin College, A.B. (magna cum laude), 1993; The University of Maine, J.D. (cum laude), 1996 — Admitted to Bar, 1996, Maine

John B. Cole — Bowdoin College, A.B., 1970; Syracuse University, J.D., 1974 — Admitted to Bar, 1974, Maine

Bryan M. Dench — Harvard University, A.B. (cum laude), 1972; The University of Maine, J.D. (cum laude), 1975 — Admitted to Bar, 1975, Maine

Marc N. Frenette — Duke University, A.B. (magna cum laude), 1998; University of Maine School of Law, J.D. (summa cum laude), 2001 — Admitted to Bar, 2001, Maine

Michael R. Poulin — Rensselaer Polytechnic Institute, B.S., 1973; The University of Maine, J.D. (cum laude), 1982 — Admitted to Bar, 1982, Maine — Practice Areas: Employment Defense; Employment Discrimination; Employment Law (Management Side); Employment Practices; Hospital Law; Hospitals

Alan G. Stone — Boston University, B.S. (magna cum laude), 1972; Washington University, J.D., 1975 — Admitted to Bar, 1975, Maine

Stephen B. Wade — University of New Hampshire, B.S. (cum laude), 1976; Thomas M. Cooley Law School, J.D. (cum laude), 1980 — Admitted to Bar, 1980, Maine; 1981, Michigan

(This firm is also listed in the Subrogation section of this directory)

AUGUSTA † 19,136 Kennebec Co.

Johnson & Webbert, L.L.P.

160 Capitol Street
Augusta, Maine 04330
   Telephone: 207-623-5110
   Fax: 207-622-4160
   www.johnsonwebbert.com

(Portland, ME Office: 97 India Street, 04101)
   (Tel: 207-772-2060)
(Camden, ME Office: 39 Mechanic Street, Suite 320, 04843)
   (Tel: 207-236-2390)

Established: 1992

Aviation, Comprehensive General Liability, Employment Discrimination, Environmental Law, Insurance Coverage, Product Liability, Professional Malpractice, Legal Malpractice, Medical Malpractice

---

Johnson & Webbert, L.L.P., Augusta, ME (Continued)

Insurance Clients

AIG Aviation, Inc.
Avemco Insurance Company
Houston Casualty Company
Universal Loss Management, Inc.
U.S. Aviation Underwriters
American Equity Insurance Company
Providence Washington Insurance Company
Zurich North America

Non-Insurance Clients

Central Maine Power Company
Energy East
Cives Steel Corporation
Union Water Power Company

Firm Members

Phillip E. Johnson — 1950 — Miami University, B.A., 1972; Case Western Reserve University, J.D., 1975 — Admitted to Bar, 1975, Ohio; 1977, Maine; 1975, U.S. District Court, Northern District of Ohio; 1977, U.S. District Court, District of Maine — Member American, Maine State and Kennebec County Bar Associations; Maine Professional Ethics Commission; Defense Research Institute; Lawyer-Pilots Bar Association

David G. Webbert — 1961 — Yale University, B.A. (magna cum laude), 1982; Harvard University, J.D. (magna cum laude), 1985 — Admitted to Bar, 1986, Maryland; 1989, District of Columbia; 1991, Maine — Member American and Maine State Bar Associations; Maine Employment Lawyers Association; American Judicature Society; Association of Trial Lawyers of America

Matthew S. Keegan — 1966 — Duke University, A.B., 1989; Harvard University, M.Ed., 1994; The University of Maine, J.D. (magna cum laude), 1999 — Admitted to Bar, 1999, Maine; 2001, U.S. District Court, District of Maine — Member American, Maine State and Kennebec County Bar Associations; Maine Trial Lawyers Association

---

The following firms also service this area.

Wheeler & Arey, P.A.

27 Temple Street
Waterville, Maine 04901
   Telephone: 207-873-7771
   Fax: 207-877-9454
   Toll Free: 888-451-8400 (In State)
Mailing Address: P.O. Box 376, Waterville, ME 04903-0376

Insurance Law, Subrogation

SEE COMPLETE LISTING UNDER WATERVILLE, MAINE (19 MILES)

BANGOR † 33,039 Penobscot Co.

Gross, Minsky & Mogul, P.A.

23 Water Street, Suite 400
Bangor, Maine 04401
   Telephone: 207-942-4644
   Fax: 207-942-3699
   E-Mail: law@grossminsky.com
   www.grossminsky.com

Established: 1938

Insurance Defense, Health Care, Medical Malpractice, Coverage Issues, Employment Law, Product Liability, Professional Liability, Legal Malpractice

Firm Profile: Our reputation is built by our clients. We are a law firm of distinction offering a broad array of legal services to individuals and businesses throughout Maine and beyond for over 75 years.

Insurance Clients

Arbella Mutual Insurance Company
The Doctors Company
Chubb Executive Risk, Inc.
Coverys
Executive Risk, Inc.

Gross, Minsky & Mogul, P.A., Bangor, ME (Continued)

The HUM Division of MLMIC
Medical Mutual Insurance Company of Maine
North American Specialty Insurance Company
The Travelers Companies, Inc.
Imperial Casualty and Indemnity Company
National Chiropractic Mutual Insurance Company
Ophthalmic Mutual Insurance Company

Firm Members

John F. Logan — 1940 — Boston College, A.B., 1963; Willamette University College of Law, J.D., 1966 — Admitted to Bar, 1969, Maine; 1969, U.S. District Court, District of Maine — Member Maine State and Penobscot County Bar Associations — E-mail: jflogan@grossminsky.com

George W. Kurr, Jr. — 1944 — Rutgers College, A.B., 1966; University of Kentucky, J.D., 1969 — Admitted to Bar, 1971, Maine; 1971, U.S. District Court, District of Maine — Member Maine State and Penobscot County Bar Associations — E-mail: gwkurr@grossminsky.com

Edward W. Gould — 1957 — Brown University, A.B., 1979; Boston University, J.D. (cum laude), 1982 — Admitted to Bar, 1982, Maine; 1985, U.S. Court of Appeals, First Circuit — Member Maine State and Penobscot County Bar Associatons — E-mail: ewgould@grossminsky.com

Steven J. Mogul — 1957 — University of Pennsylvania, B.A., 1980; University of Miami School of Law, J.D., 1983 — Admitted to Bar, 1984, Maine; 2000, U.S. District Court, District of Maine; 2000, U.S. Court of Appeals, First Circuit — Member Maine State and Penobscot County Bar Associations — E-mail: smogul@grossminsky.com

Sandra L. Rothera — 1950 — EMMC School of Nursing, R.N., 1973; The University of Maine, B.A. (cum laude), 1989; Franklin Pierce Law Center, J.D., 1993 — Admitted to Bar, 1994, Maine; 1994, U.S. District Court, District of Maine — Member Maine State and Penobscot County Bar Associations — E-mail: srothera@grossminsky.com

James S. Nixon — 1965 — The University of Maine, B.A., 1988; The Catholic University of America, Columbus School of Law, J.D., 1994 — Admitted to Bar, 1995, Maine; 1995, U.S. District Court, District of Maine; 2000, U.S. Court of Appeals, First Circuit — Member Maine State and Penobscot County Bar Associations — E-mail: jnixon@grossminsky.com

Firm Member

Joseph M. Bethony — 1977 — University of Maine School of Law, J.D. (magna cum laude), 2005 — Law Clerk to Associate Justice Warren M. Silver, Maine Supreme Judicial Court, 2005-2006 — Admitted to Bar, 2005, Maine; 2006, U.S. District Court, District of Maine; 2010, U.S. Court of Appeals, First Circuit — Member Maine State and Penobscot County Bar Associations; American Inns of Court — E-mail: jmbethony@grossminsky.com

Associates

Mariann Zampano Malay — 1955 — Boston University, B.S., 1977; J.D., 1981 — Admitted to Bar, 1981, Massachusetts; 2006, Maine; 1982, U.S. Court of Appeals, First Circuit; 2008, U.S. District Court, District of Maine — Member Maine State and Penobscot County Bar Associations — E-mail: mzmalay@grossminsky.com

Joy A. Trueworthy — 1983 — Smith College, B.A., 2006; Rutgers University School of Law, J.D., 2009 — Law Clerk, Justice Andrew M. Mead, Maine Supreme Court, 2009-2010 — Admitted to Bar, 2009, Maine; 2010, U.S. District Court, District of Maine — E-mail: jatrueworthy@grossminsky.com

Of Counsel

Norman Minsky — 1930 — Boston University, B.S., 1951; LL.B., 1953 — Admitted to Bar, 1953, Maine — Member Maine State and Penobscot County Bar Associations

Brent R. Slater — 1947 — The University of Maine, B.S., 1969; University of Maine School of Law, J.D., 1973 — Admitted to Bar, 1974, Maine — Member Maine State and Penobscot County Bar Associations

Joseph L. Ferris — 1944 — The University of Maine, B.S., 1967; University of Maine School of Law, J.D., 1970 — Admitted to Bar, 1970, Maine

Richardson, Whitman, Large & Badger

1 Merchants Plaza, Suite 603
Bangor, Maine 04401
   Telephone: 207-945-5900
   Fax: 207-945-0758
   www.rwlb.com

Richardson, Whitman, Large & Badger, Bangor, ME (Continued)

(Portland, ME Office*: 465 Congress Street, 04101, P.O. Box 9545, 04112-9545)
   (Tel: 207-774-7474)
   (Fax: 207-774-1343)

Civil Litigation, Construction Law, Contract Disputes, Declaratory Judgments, Employment Law, Insurance Law, Medical Malpractice, Personal Injury, Premises Liability, Product Liability, Professional Liability, Property and Casualty, Retail Liability, Transportation, Workers' Compensation

Firm Profile: Richardson, Whitman, Large & Badger have taken hundreds of cases to trial. We believe our success rate in the courtroom is unmatched, but winning trials is only half the story. Our goal is to work with you to manage your litigation, or pre-litigation dispute, in the most effective manner possible.

(See listing under Portland, ME for additional information)

(Revisors of the Maine Insurance Law Digest for this Publication)

Tucker Law Group

One Cumberland Place, Suite 308
Bangor, Maine 04401
   Telephone: 207-945-4720
   Fax: 207-945-4719
   Toll Free: 800-585-4720
   E-Mail: win@tuckerlawmaine.com
   www.tuckerlawmaine.com

(Portland, ME Office: 75 Pearl Street, 04101)
   (Tel: 800-585-4720)
   (Fax: 207-945-4719)
(Caribou, ME Office: 43 Hatch Drive, Suite 305, 04736)
   (Tel: 800-585-4720)
   (Fax: 207-945-4719)

Established: 1993

Insurance Defense, General Liability, Workers' Compensation, Coverage Issues, Employment Law, Administrative Law

Firm Profile: The attorneys at Tucker Law Group have a practice firmly committed to the vigorous and successful defense of insurers, self-insurers, major industrial companies and other employers throughout the State of Maine with statewide offices in Bangor, Portland and Caribou.

Insurance Clients

CNA Insurance Companies
Hanover Insurance Company
Maine Employers' Mutual Insurance Company
Travelers Insurance Company
Cross Insurance TPA, Inc.
The Hartford Insurance Group
Sedgwick Claims Management Services, Inc.

Non-Insurance Clients

FairPoint Communications, Inc.
Louisiana-Pacific Corporation
Pepsi Beverage Company
Georgia-Pacific LLC
NewPage Corporation
University of Maine System

Partners

Richard D. Tucker — 1957 — Saint Anselm College, A.B. (magna cum laude), 1979; Saint Louis University, J.D./M.H.A., 1983 — Admitted to Bar, 1983, Illinois; 1986, Maine; 1983, U.S. District Court, Northern District of Illinois; 1991, U.S. District Court, District of Maine; 2011, U.S. Court of Appeals, First Circuit — Member American, Maine State and Penobscot County Bar Associations; Tri-State Defense Lawyers Association; Defense Research Institute (State Representative) — E-mail: RDT@tuckerlawmaine.com

Tucker Law Group, Bangor, ME (Continued)

Joshua E. Birocco — 1973 — Indiana University of Pennsylvania, B.A., 1996; New England School of Law, J.D., 1999 — Admitted to Bar, 2000, Maine; 2001, U.S. District Court, District of Maine — Member Maine State and Penobscot County Bar Associations; Tri-State Defense Lawyers Association; Defense Research Institute (Chair, Workers' Compensation Webcast Subcommittee) — E-mail: JEB@tuckerlawmaine.com

Travis C. Rackliffe — 1972 — St. Joseph's College, B.A. (magna cum laude), 1995; DePaul University College of Law, J.D., 1998 — Admitted to Bar, 2004, Maine; 2004, U.S. District Court, District of Maine — Member American, Maine State and Penobscot County Bar Associations; Tri-State Defense Lawyers Association; Defense Research Institute (Vice-Chair, Workers' Compensation Publications Subcommittee) — E-mail: TCR@tuckerlawmaine.com

Associate Attorneys

Michael Tadenev — Williams College, B.A., 2003; The George Washington University Law School, J.D., 2006 — Admitted to Bar, 2006, Maryland; 2009, District of Columbia; 2010, Maine; 2008, U.S. District Court, District of Maryland — Member Maine State and Hancock County Bar Associations; Tri-State Defense Lawyers Association; Defense Research Institute — E-mail: MT@tuckerlawmaine.com

Matthew T. Dubois — 1985 — State University of New York at Geneseo, B.A., 2009; State University of New York at Buffalo Law School, J.D. (cum laude), 2013 — Admitted to Bar, 2013, Maine — Member American and Maine State Bar Associations; Tri-State Defense Lawyers Association; Defense Research Institute — E-mail: MTD@tuckerlawmaine.com

Weatherbee Law Office, P.A.

51 Haymarket Square
Bangor, Maine 04401
   Telephone: 207-942-9900
   Fax: 207-942-6999

Established: 1991

Automobile Liability, Casualty, Coverage Issues, General Liability, Homeowners, Insurance Defense, Personal Injury, Product Liability, Property Damage, Workers' Compensation

Insurance Clients

Acadia Insurance Company
Cross Insurance TPA, Inc.
ESIS
OneBeacon Insurance
Cannon Cochran Management Services, Inc.
Gallagher Bassett Services, Inc.
Sedgwick Claims Management Services, Inc.

Non-Insurance Clients

Bowater, Inc.
Dexter Shoe Company
Verso Paper Company
Columbia Forest Products
SAPPI Fine Paper

Attorney

Peter M. Weatherbee — 1943 — Bates College, A.B., 1965; The University of Maine, LL.B., 1968 — Admitted to Bar, 1968, Maine; 1968, U.S. District Court, District of Maine — Member Maine State and Penobscot County Bar Associations; Defense Research Institute — Practice Areas: Workers' Compensation; General Liability; Insurance Defense — E-mail: peter@weatherbeelaw.com

BATH † 8,514 Sagadahoc Co.

Refer To
Petruccelli, Martin & Haddow, LLP
2 Monument Square, Suite 900
Portland, Maine 04101
   Telephone: 207-775-0200
   Fax: 207-775-2360
Mailing Address: P.O. Box 17555, Portland, ME 04112-8555

General Civil Practice, Trial and Appellate Practice, Business Law, Commercial Law, Construction Law, Corporate Law, Environmental Law, Insurance Law, Intellectual Property, Mediation, Arbitration, Medical Malpractice, Municipal Law, Product Liability, Fire, Casualty, General Liability, Professional Liability, Hospitals, Accountants, Engineers, Surety, Administrative Law, Elder Law, Physicians, Lawyers

SEE COMPLETE LISTING UNDER PORTLAND, MAINE (32 MILES)

Refer To
Wheeler & Arey, P.A.
27 Temple Street
Waterville, Maine 04901
   Telephone: 207-873-7771
   Fax: 207-877-9454
   Toll Free: 888-451-8400 (In State)
Mailing Address: P.O. Box 376, Waterville, ME 04903-0376

Insurance Law, Subrogation

SEE COMPLETE LISTING UNDER WATERVILLE, MAINE (53 MILES)

BELFAST † 6,668 Waldo Co.

Refer To
Johnson & Webbert, L.L.P.
160 Capitol Street
Augusta, Maine 04330
   Telephone: 207-623-5110
   Fax: 207-622-4160
Mailing Address: P.O. Box 79, Augusta, ME 04332-0079

Aviation, Comprehensive General Liability, Employment Discrimination, Environmental Law, Insurance Coverage, Product Liability, Professional Malpractice, Legal Malpractice, Medical Malpractice

SEE COMPLETE LISTING UNDER AUGUSTA, MAINE (45 MILES)

Refer To
Wheeler & Arey, P.A.
27 Temple Street
Waterville, Maine 04901
   Telephone: 207-873-7771
   Fax: 207-877-9454
   Toll Free: 888-451-8400 (In State)
Mailing Address: P.O. Box 376, Waterville, ME 04903-0376

Insurance Law, Subrogation

SEE COMPLETE LISTING UNDER WATERVILLE, MAINE (38 MILES)

CAMDEN 3,570 Knox Co.

Refer To
Wheeler & Arey, P.A.
27 Temple Street
Waterville, Maine 04901
   Telephone: 207-873-7771
   Fax: 207-877-9454
   Toll Free: 888-451-8400 (In State)
Mailing Address: P.O. Box 376, Waterville, ME 04903-0376

Insurance Law, Subrogation

SEE COMPLETE LISTING UNDER WATERVILLE, MAINE (60 MILES)

PORTLAND — MAINE

DOVER-FOXCROFT † 2,528 Piscataquis Co.

Refer To

Wheeler & Arey, P.A.
27 Temple Street
Waterville, Maine 04901
  Telephone: 207-873-7771
  Fax: 207-877-9454
  Toll Free: 888-451-8400 (In State)
  Mailing Address: P.O. Box 376, Waterville, ME 04903-0376

Insurance Law, Subrogation

SEE COMPLETE LISTING UNDER WATERVILLE, MAINE (60 MILES)

FARMINGTON † 4,288 Franklin Co.

Refer To

Wheeler & Arey, P.A.
27 Temple Street
Waterville, Maine 04901
  Telephone: 207-873-7771
  Fax: 207-877-9454
  Toll Free: 888-451-8400 (In State)
  Mailing Address: P.O. Box 376, Waterville, ME 04903-0376

Insurance Law, Subrogation

SEE COMPLETE LISTING UNDER WATERVILLE, MAINE (34 MILES)

PORTLAND † 66,194 Cumberland Co.

Lambert Coffin

477 Congress Street
Portland, Maine 04101
  Telephone: 207-874-4000
  Fax: 207-874-4040
  Toll Free: 800-841-1238
  E-Mail: info@lambertcoffin.com
  www.lambertcoffin.com

(Blue Hill, ME Office: Eastlight Building, One West Lane, P.O. Box 1198, 04614)
  (Tel: 207-374-5833)
  (Fax: 207-374-5889)

Established: 1986

Coverage Issues, Insurance Defense, Automobile, Employee Benefits, Construction Law, Disability, Dram Shop, Employment Law, Environmental Law, Errors and Omissions, Fidelity, Fire, First Party Matters, General Liability, Law Enforcement Liability, Product Liability, Professional Liability, Dental Malpractice, Legal, Malpractice, Surety, Workers' Compensation, Title Insurance

Firm Profile: Lambert Coffin provides legal services that empower businesses and individuals to achieve their goals through strategic counsel, imaginative approaches to preventing and solving problems, and an unwavering commitment to responsive client service. First formed in 1986, the firm has grown steadily ever since. It represents a diverse group—including individuals, entrepreneurs and Maine-based and national corporations and insurance companies—in a broad spectrum of legal matters.

Insurance Clients

Acadia Insurance Company
Colonial Penn Insurance Company
Essex Insurance Company
Liberty Mutual Insurance Company
Medical Mutual Insurance Company of Maine
National Casualty Company
Cincinnati Insurance Company
Coverys
Great Falls Insurance Company
Markel Insurance Company
MiddleOak
Middlesex Mutual Assurance Company

Lambert Coffin, Portland, ME (Continued)

National Grange Mutual Insurance Company
Safeco/American States Insurance Company
Travelers Insurance
United America Indemnity Group
Westco Claims Management Services, Inc.
Zurich Insurance Group
Penn-America Insurance Company
Preferred Professional Insurance Company
TIG Specialty Insurance Solutions
Tudor Insurance Company
U.S. Liability Insurance Company
Western World Insurance Company

Non-Insurance Clients

CHG Companies, Inc.
Mercy Hospital
Eastern Maine Healthcare
Synchrony

Shareholders

John F. Lambert, Jr. — 1954 — Middlebury College, A.B. (cum laude), 1976; The George Washington University, J.D. (cum laude), 1981 — Admitted to Bar, 1981, Maine; 1981, U.S. District Court, District of Maine; 1981, U.S. Court of Appeals, First Circuit — Member Maine State and Cumberland County Bar Associations; Maine Trial Lawyers Association; Defense Research Institute — Practice Areas: Labor and Employment; Agriculture; Government Affairs — E-mail: jlambert@lambertcoffin.com

Philip M. Coffin III — 1955 — The University of Maine, B.A. (summa cum laude), 1978; University of Maine School of Law, J.D. (cum laude), 1981 — Admitted to Bar, 1981, Maine; 1981, U.S. District Court, District of Maine; 1981, U.S. Court of Appeals, First Circuit — Member Maine State and Cumberland County Bar Associations; American Board of Trial Advocates; Defense Research Institute; International Society of Barristers — Practice Areas: Medical Malpractice Defense; Professional Liability; Product Liability Defense — E-mail: pcoffin@lambertcoffin.com

Samuel K. Rudman — 1956 — Wesleyan University, B.A., 1979; The George Washington University, J.D., 1983 — Admitted to Bar, 1983, Maine; 1983, U.S. District Court, District of Maine — Member Maine State and Cumberland County Bar Associations; Maine Trial Lawyers Association; American Trial Lawyers Association — Practice Areas: Personal Injury; Workers' Compensation; Labor and Employment — E-mail: srudman@lambertcoffin.com

H. Peter Del Bianco, Jr. — 1958 — University of Maryland, B.A., 1984; Boston University, J.D. (cum laude), 1987 — Admitted to Bar, 1988, Maine; 1988, U.S. District Court, District of Maine; 1988, U.S. Court of Appeals, First Circuit — Member Maine State and Cumberland County Bar Associations; Maine Trial Lawyers Association — Practice Areas: Insurance Defense; Insurance Coverage; Construction Litigation; Class Actions — E-mail: pdelbianco@lambertcoffin.com

Jonathan T. Harris — Vassar College, B.A. (with honors), 1973; Harvard University, M.Ed., 1986; Northeastern University, J.D., 1990 — Admitted to Bar, 1990, Massachusetts; 1991, Maine; 1992, U.S. District Court, District of Maine; 1996, U.S. District Court, District of Massachusetts — Member Maine State and Cumberland County Bar Associations — Practice Areas: Estate Planning; Real Estate; Corporate Law — E-mail: jharris@lambertcoffin.com

Robyn G. March — 1955 — University of Michigan, B.A., 1985; University of Maine School of Law, J.D., 1996 — Admitted to Bar, 1996, Maine; 1997, Massachusetts; U.S. Court of Appeals for the Federal Circuit — Member Maine State and Cumberland County Bar Associations — Practice Areas: Labor and Employment; Immigration Law — E-mail: rmarch@lambertcoffin.com

Teresa M. Cloutier — 1970 — Yale University, B.A., 1993; University of Maine School of Law, J.D. (cum laude), 1996 — Admitted to Bar, 1996, Maine; 1998, U.S. District Court, District of Maine; 2000, U.S. Court of Appeals, First Circuit; 2002, U.S. Supreme Court — Member Maine State and Cumberland County Bar Associations; Maine Trial Lawyers Association; Defense Research Institute — Practice Areas: Insurance Coverage; Insurance Defense; Commercial Litigation — E-mail: tcloutier@lambertcoffin.com

Elizabeth A. Boepple — University of Vermont, B.A., 1980; Vermont Law School, J.D., 1997 — Admitted to Bar, 1997, Vermont; 2009, Maine; 2012, New Hampshire; 1998, U.S. District Court, District of Vermont — Member Maine State, New Hampshire, Vermont, Cumberland County and Hancock County Bar Associations — Practice Areas: Commercial Transactions; Real Estate; Land Use; Environmental Law — E-mail: eboepple@lambertcoffin.com

Associates

Jeffrey D. Russell
Abigail C. Varga
Maureen M. Sturtevant

MAINE — PORTLAND

Lambert Coffin, Portland, ME (Continued)

(This firm is also listed in the Investigation and Adjustment section of this directory)

Perkins Thompson, P.A.

One Canal Plaza
Portland, Maine 04101
Telephone: 207-774-2635
Fax: 207-871-8026
E-Mail: dmcconnell@perkinsthompson.com
www.perkinsthompson.com

Established: 1871

Insurance Defense, Personal Injury, Coverage Issues, Asbestos Litigation, Environmental Law, Product Liability

Firm Profile: Perkins Thompson has provided legal services to businesses, institutions and individuals since 1871. We strive to give our clients, whether local, regional, national or international, excellent, innovative and cost-effective representation. We pride ourselves on providing successful solutions to the most challenging tasks.

Insurance Clients

AIAC/National Union Insurance Companies
Commercial Union Insurance Companies
Design Professionals Insurance Company
Great American Insurance Company
Maine Insurance Guaranty Association
Petroleum Casualty Company
Prudential Insurance Company of America
Security Mutual Life Insurance Company of New York
Allstate Insurance Company
American Mutual Insurance Company
The Connecticut Indemnity Company
Exxon Risk Management Services, Inc.
Liberty Mutual Group
Mutual Marine Office, Inc.
Northbrook Excess & Surplus Insurance Company
Security Insurance Company of Hartford

Non-Insurance Clients

Massachusetts Insurers Insolvency Fund

Insurance Counsel

David B. McConnell — 1966 — Dartmouth College, B.A. (cum laude), 1988; University of Virginia, J.D. (with distinction), 1995 — Dana H. Rowe Memorial Scholarship — Virginia Environmental Law Journal — Admitted to Bar, 1995, Maine; U.S. District Court, District of Maine; U.S. Court of Appeals, First Circuit — Member American and Maine State Bar Associations; TIPS — Author: "Surgeon Demographic and Medical Malpractice in Adult Reconstruction," published November 7, 2008, in Clinical Orthopaedics and Related Research; "The Sevin Made Me Do It: Mental Non-Responsibility and the Neurotoxic Damage Defense", 14 Virginia Environmental Law Journal 151, 1995. Reprinted in MacArthur Foundation Law & Neuroscience Project Bibliography, 2010

John A. Hobson — 1953 — Hampshire College; University of Massachusetts, B.A., 1977; The University of Maine, J.D., 1983 — Admitted to Bar, 1983, Maine

Thomas Schulten — 1936 — University of New Hampshire, B.A., 1957; Harvard University, LL.B., 1964 — Admitted to Bar, 1964, Maine

Petruccelli, Martin & Haddow, LLP

2 Monument Square, Suite 900
Portland, Maine 04101
Telephone: 207-775-0200
Fax: 207-775-2360
E-Mail: info@pmhlegal.com
www.pmhlegal.com

Established: 1980

Petruccelli, Martin & Haddow, LLP, Portland, ME (Continued)

General Civil Practice, Trial and Appellate Practice, Business Law, Commercial Law, Construction Law, Corporate Law, Environmental Law, Insurance Law, Intellectual Property, Mediation, Arbitration, Medical Malpractice, Municipal Law, Product Liability, Fire, Casualty, General Liability, Professional Liability, Hospitals, Accountants, Engineers, Surety, Administrative Law, Elder Law, Physicians, Lawyers

Firm Profile: Since its inception in 1980, the firm has represented a wide range of individual and institutional clients in diverse, complex, and often ground-breaking cases. The firm offers comprehensive legal services, from preventing disputes by planning drafting to resolving them through alternate dispute resolution, trial and appellate advocacy. Partners and associates involve themselves in legal scholarship, service to the court, professional organizations and community volunteer programs.

Insurance Clients

Great American Insurance Company
Norfolk and Dedham Mutual Fire Insurance Company
Penn-America Insurance Company
Philadelphia Insurance Company
Stewart Title Guaranty Company
Union Mutual Fire Insurance Company
New England Guaranty Insurance Company, Inc.
Old Republic Insurance Company
Peerless Insurance Company
Phenix Mutual Fire Insurance Company
Ticor Title Insurance Company
United Educators Insurance

Firm Members

Gerald F. Petruccelli — 1943 — Boston College, A.B., 1964; Boston College Law School, LL.B., 1967 — Admitted to Bar, 1967, Massachusetts; 1969, Maine — E-mail: gpetruccelli@pmhlegal.com

Michael K. Martin — 1957 — University of Southern Maine, B.A.S. (summa cum laude), 1985; The University of Maine, J.D. (cum laude), 1989 — Admitted to Bar, 1989, Maine — E-mail: mmartin@pmhlegal.com

James B. Haddow — 1959 — Colby College, A.B., 1982; The University of Maine, J.D., 1986 — Admitted to Bar, 1986, Maine — E-mail: jhaddow@pmhlegal.com

Bruce A. McGlauflin — 1951 — Bucknell University, B.S., 1973; The University of Maine, M.P.S.C.D., 1977; J.D. (magna cum laude), 1996 — Admitted to Bar, 1996, Maine — E-mail: bmcglauflin@pmhlegal.com

Bradford A. Pattershall — 1972 — Colby College, B.A., 1994; The University of Maine, J.D., 1999 — Admitted to Bar, 1999, Maine — Languages: French — E-mail: bpattershall@pmhlegal.com

Associate

Jisel E. Lopez — 1978 — Colby College, B.A. (summa cum laude), 2001; University of Maine School of Law, J.D. (cum laude), 2005 — Admitted to Bar, 2005, Maine — Languages: French, Spanish — E-mail: jlopez@pmhlegal.com

Preti, Flaherty, Beliveau & Pachios, LLP

One City Center
Portland, Maine 04101
Telephone: 207-791-3000
Fax: 207-791-3111
E-Mail: info@preti.com
www.preti.com

(Augusta, ME Office: 45 Memorial Circle, P. O. Box 1058, 04332-1058)
(Tel: 207-623-5300)
(Fax: 207-623-2914)
(Concord, NH Office: 57 North Main Street, 03301-4934, P.O. Box 1318, 03302-1318)
(Tel: 603-410-1500)
(Fax: 603-410-1501)
(Boston, MA Office: Ten Post Office Square, 02109)
(Tel: 617-226-3800)
(Fax: 617-226-3801)

Established: 1971

PORTLAND   MAINE

Preti, Flaherty, Beliveau & Pachios, LLP, Portland, ME (Continued)

Fire, Casualty, Surety, Life Insurance, Trial Practice, Professional Liability, Workers' Compensation, Medical Malpractice, Legal Malpractice, Agent/Broker Liability, Errors and Omissions, Dental Malpractice, Toxic Torts, General Liability

Firm Profile: Preti Flaherty is one of northern New England's largest law firms. Headquartered in Portland, ME, the firm also has offices in Augusta, ME; Concord, NH; Boston and Washington, D.C. With more than 100 attorneys, the firm counsels clients in the areas of business law, energy, environmental, estate planning, health care, intellectual property, labor and employment, legislative and regulatory, litigation, technology and telecommunications. More information about the firm is available at www.preti.com.

Insurance Clients

Chubb Group of Insurance Companies
Crum & Forster Insurance Group
Granite State Insurance Company
Hartford Fire Insurance Company
Holyoke Mutual Insurance Company in Salem
Metropolitan Property and Casualty Insurance Company
Norfolk and Dedham Mutual Fire Insurance Company
Quincy Mutual Fire Insurance Company
The St. Paul/Travelers Companies, Inc.
Texas Medical Liability Trust
Vermont Mutual Insurance Company
Westport Insurance Corporation

CIGNA Group
Continental Insurance Companies
The Doctors Company
Hanover Mutual Fire Insurance Company
James River Insurance Company
Medical Mutual Insurance Company of Maine
New Hampshire Insurance Company
ProMutual Group
Reliance Insurance Company
St. Paul Fire and Marine Insurance Company
Sumitomo Marine and Fire Insurance Company, Ltd.
West Newbury Mutual Fire Insurance Company

Non-Insurance Clients

Willis of Northern New England, Inc.

Members

Jonathan S. Piper — 1950 — Bowdoin College, A.B. (magna cum laude), 1972; University of Maine School of Law, J.D., 1976 — Admitted to Bar, 1976, Maine; 1976, U.S. District Court, District of Maine; 1976, U.S. Court of Appeals, First Circuit — Member Maine State and Cumberland County Bar Associations; Libel Defense Resource Center (Defense Counsel Section)

Daniel Rapaport — 1953 — Colby College, B.A., 1974; Cornell University Law School, J.D., 1978 — Admitted to Bar, 1978, Massachusetts; 1978, U.S. District Court, District of Massachusetts; 1978, U.S. District Court, District of Maine — Member American and Cumberland County Bar Associations; Maine Trial Lawyers Association

Bruce C. Gerrity — 1953 — The University of Maine, B.A., 1976; College of William & Mary, J.D., 1979 — Admitted to Bar, 1979, Maine; 1979, U.S. District Court, District of Maine; 1979, U.S. Court of Appeals for the District of Columbia Circuit; 1979, U.S. Supreme Court — Member American and Maine State Bar Associations; American Trial Lawyers Association

Jeffrey T. Edwards — 1949 — Colby College, A.B. (cum laude), 1971; University of Southern Maine, M.B.A., 1985; Syracuse University, J.D., 1974 — Admitted to Bar, 1974, Maine — Member Maine State Bar Association

Randall B. Weill — 1947 — Washington and Lee University, B.S., 1969; University of Virginia, J.D., 1977 — Admitted to Bar, 1977, Virginia; 1978, District of Columbia; 1983, Maine; 1979, U.S. District Court for the District of Columbia; 1982, U.S. Court of Appeals for the Federal Circuit; 1982, U.S. Court of Federal Claims; 1983, U.S. District Court, District of Maine — Member American, Maine State and Cumberland County Bar Associations

Evan M. Hansen — 1954 — University of Southern Maine, B.A. (summa cum laude), 1981; University of Maine School of Law, J.D. (cum laude), 1984 — Phi Kappa Phi — Admitted to Bar, 1984, Maine; 1984, U.S. District Court, District of Maine; 1984, U.S. Court of Appeals, First Circuit — Member Maine State Bar Association; Maine Trial Lawyers Association; Association of Ski Defense Attorneys

Michael Kaplan — 1949 — Massachusetts Institute of Technology; The University of New Orleans, B.G.S., 1982; Tulane University, J.D. (magna cum laude), 1985 — Admitted to Bar, 1986, Maine; 1986, U.S. District Court,

Preti, Flaherty, Beliveau & Pachios, LLP, Portland, ME (Continued)

District of Maine; 1987, U.S. Court of Appeals, First Circuit — Member American and Maine State Bar Associations; Propeller Club of the United States; The Maritime Law Association of the United States

Stephen E.F. Langsdorf — 1960 — Texas A&M University, B.A., 1983; The University of Texas, J.D., 1986 — Admitted to Bar, 1986, Texas; 1987, Maine; 1987, U.S. District Court, District of Maine — Member American, Maine State and Kennebec County Bar Associations; State Bar of Texas

Nelson J Larkins — 1961 — Allegheny College, B.A., 1983; The Ohio State University Moritz College of Law, J.D., 1986 — Admitted to Bar, 1986, Maine — Member American, Maine State and Cumberland County Bar Associations

Timothy J. Bryant — 1966 — University of Massachusetts, B.B.A., 1988; Villanova University, J.D., 1993 — Admitted to Bar, 1993, Maine; 1993, U.S. District Court, District of Maine

Gregory P. Hansel — 1960 — Harvard University, B.A., 1992; Aristotle University, Thessaloniki, Greece, 1982-1983; University of Virginia, J.D., 1986 — Admitted to Bar, 1986, Florida; 1988, District of Columbia; 1997, Maine; 1986, U.S. Court of Appeals, Eleventh Circuit; 1987, U.S. District Court, Middle District of Florida; 1992, U.S. Supreme Court — Member American and Maine State Bar Associations; The Florida Bar

Matthew J. LaMourie — 1961 — Michigan State University, B.A., 1983; University of Delaware, M.M.S., 1985; Northeastern University, J.D., 1995 — Admitted to Bar, 1996, Massachusetts; Maine; 1996, U.S. District Court, District of Maine — Member Maine State and Cumberland County Bar Associations; Maine Trial Lawyers Association

Richardson, Whitman, Large & Badger

465 Congress Street
Portland, Maine 04101
Telephone: 207-774-7474
Fax: 207-774-1343
www.rwlb.com

(Bangor, ME Office*: 1 Merchants Plaza, Suite 603, 04401, P.O. Box 2429, 04402-2429)
(Tel: 207-945-5900)
(Fax: 207-945-0758)

Civil Litigation, Construction Law, Contract Disputes, Declaratory Judgments, Employment Law, Insurance Law, Medical Malpractice, Personal Injury, Premises Liability, Product Liability, Professional Liability, Property and Casualty, Retail Liability, Transportation, Workers' Compensation

Firm Profile: Richardson, Whitman, Large & Badger have taken hundreds of cases to trial. We believe our success rate in the courtroom is unmatched, but winning trials is only half the story. Our goal is to work with you to manage your litigation, or pre-litigation dispute, in the most effective manner possible.

Insurance Clients

Acadia Insurance Company
Atlantic Mutual Companies
CNA Insurance Company
The Concord Group Insurance Companies
Great American Insurance Company
Middlesex Mutual Assurance Company
Patrons Oxford Insurance Company
United Services Automobile Association (USAA)

ACE USA
Attorneys Liability Protection Society (ALPS)
Fireman's Fund Insurance Companies
Liberty Mutual Insurance Company
Medical Mutual Insurance Company
OneBeacon Insurance
Progressive Insurance Company
St. Paul Travelers

Shareholders

John S. Whitman — Harvard College, B.A., 1967; Harvard Law School, J.D., 1972 — Admitted to Bar, 1973, California; 1976, Maine — Member Maine Trial Lawyers Association

Wendell G. Large — The University of North Carolina, A.B., 1975; University of Virginia, J.D., 1978 — Admitted to Bar, 1978, Maine — Member Maine

2015 BEST'S DIRECTORIES OF RECOMMENDED INSURANCE ATTORNEYS AND ADJUSTERS — For Current Listings access www.ambest.com/directories — 719

MAINE   PORTLAND

Richardson, Whitman, Large & Badger, Portland, ME (Continued)

State Bar Association (Board of Governors); Maine Trial Lawyers Association (Advisory Board); Defense Research Institute; American Board of Trial Advocates; American College of Trial Lawyers

Frederick J. Badger, Jr. — Kent State University, B.A., 1965; The Ohio State University, J.D., 1968 — Admitted to Bar, 1969, Ohio; 1972, Maine — Member Maine Trial Lawyers Association; American Trial Lawyers Association; Defense Research Institute — Resident Bangor Office

Elizabeth G. Stouder — Middlebury College, B.A. (cum laude), 1979; Temple University, J.D. (cum laude), 1983 — Admitted to Bar, 1983, Maine — Member Gignoux Inns of Court

Barri Lynn Bloom — Cornell University, B.S., 1977; Boston University, J.D., 1980 — Admitted to Bar, 1981, New York; 1985, Maine

Frederick F. Costlow — Shenandoah Conservatory, B.M.E., 1974; Vermont Law School, J.D./M.S.L. (cum laude), 1988 — Admitted to Bar, 1988, Maine — Resident Bangor Office

Thomas R. McKeon — Colby College, B.A., 1982; Columbia University, M.A., 1986; Boston College, J.D. (cum laude), 1992 — Admitted to Bar, 1992, Maine — Member Gignoux Inns of Court

Associates

Carol I. Eisenberg
Joseph L. Cahoon Jr.
Heidi J. Hart
Joshua A. Randlett

Of Counsel

Gerard O. Fournier

(Revisors of the Maine Insurance Law Digest for this Publication)

Robinson, Kriger & McCallum

Twelve Portland Pier
Portland, Maine 04101-4713
Telephone: 207-772-6565
Fax: 207-773-5001
E-Mail: attorneys@rkmlegal.com
www.rkmlegal.com

Established: 1978

Insurance Defense, Commercial Law, Workers' Compensation, Administrative Law

Firm Profile: The firm of Robinson, Kriger & McCallum (RK&M) is a professional team of attorneys, paralegals and staff providing legal services to businesses, insurers and individuals in the areas of litigation and workers' compensation law, business and corporate law, general practice, estate planning, elder law, family law, criminal law, (environmental, land use) administrative law, municipal law, and appellate practice. Our attorneys appear before all the courts of the State of Maine, the Workers' Compensation Commission, the federal district courts of Maine and the First Circuit Court of Appeals.

Insurance Clients

Acadia Insurance Company
Cambridge Integrated Services
Crawford & Company
ESIS New England
Gallagher Bassett Services, Inc.
Liberty Mutual Insurance Company
OneBeacon Insurance
Sedgwick Group
Utica Mutual Insurance Company
AIG Claim Services, Inc.
CNA Insurance Companies
Electric Insurance Company
GAB Robins North America, Inc.
GUARD Insurance Group
Lumber Mutual Insurance Company
Travelers Insurance Companies
Zurich U.S.

Non-Insurance Clients

Arrow Hart
Cooper Industries, Inc.
Roman Catholic Diocese of Portland
Bath Iron Works Corporation
PalletOne, Inc.
Time Warner Cable
Willis of Northern New England, Inc.

Robinson, Kriger & McCallum, Portland, ME (Continued)

Firm Members

John M. McCallum* — 1949 — Colby College, B.A., 1971; Loyola College, Montreal, Quebec; University of Maine School of Law, J.D., 1975 — Admitted to Bar, 1975, Maine — Member Maine State Bar Association (Former Chairperson, Workers' Compensation Section); American and Cumberland County Bar Associations — Assistant District Attorney, York County, Maine (1975-1977) — E-mail: jmccallum@rkmlegal.com

James C. Hunt — 1942 — Hamilton College, A.B., 1964; Harvard University, Ph.D., 1970; The University of Maine, J.D., 1985 — Phi Beta Kappa — Clerk, Maine Supreme Judicial Court (1985-1986) — Admitted to Bar, 1985, Maine; 1986, U.S. District Court, District of Maine — Member Maine State Bar Associations; Maine Trial Lawyers Association; Maine Historical Society — Author: "Group Homes for the Mentally Retarded in Maine: Legislative Intent & Administrative Process," Maine Law Review, Vol. 37, No. 1., 1985 — E-mail: jhunt@rkmlegal.com

Thomas Quartararo* — 1963 — State University of New York at Oswego, B.A., 1985; Western New England College School of Law, J.D., 1990 — Admitted to Bar, 1990, Maine; 1991, U.S. District Court, District of Maine — Member American and Maine State Bar Associations — E-mail: tquartararo@rkmlegal.com

Thomas R. Kelly — 1958 — Haverford College, B.A., 1980; The University of Maine, J.D., 1992 — Admitted to Bar, 1992, Maine; Massachusetts; 1993, U.S. District Court, District of Maine — Member Maine State Bar Association — E-mail: tkelly@rkmlegal.com

Douglas J. Alofs* — 1963 — Hamilton College, B.A., 1985; University of New Hampshire School of Law, J.D., 1991 — Admitted to Bar, 1992, Maine — Member Maine State Bar Association; Maine Trial Lawyers Association — E-mail: dalofs@rkmlegal.com

Marianna M. Fenton Hibbard — University of Southern Maine, B.A. (summa cum laude), 1993; University of Maine School of Law, J.D., 1996 — Admitted to Bar, 1997, Maine — Member Maine State Bar Association — E-mail: mhibbard@rkmlegal.com

Richard D. Bayer* — University of Rhode Island, B.A. (with high distinction), 1990; University of Maine School of Law, J.D., 1996 — Admitted to Bar, 1996, Maine — Member Maine State Bar Association — Practice Areas: Workers' Compensation — E-mail: rbayer@rkmlegal.com

Humphrey H. Johnson — 1963 — American University, B.A. (summa cum laude), 1990; University of Maine School of Law, J.D. (cum laude), 1997 — Admitted to Bar, 1997, Maine; 2011, New Hampshire — Member Maine State Bar Association; New Hampshire Bar Association; Tri State Defense Lawyers Association; Defense Research Institute — Practice Areas: Insurance Defense; Civil Litigation; Fire Loss; Construction Defect; Product Liability — E-mail: hjohnson@rkmlegal.com

Cara L. Biddings* — 1978 — Simmons College, B.A. (cum laude), 2001; University of Maine School of Law, J.D., 2004 — Admitted to Bar, 2005, Maine — Practice Areas: Workers' Compensation; Personal Injury — E-mail: cbiddings@rkmlegal.com

Jeffrey B. Wilson* — 1981 — University of Massachusetts Amherst, B.A. (summa cum laude), 2004; Boston College Law School, J.D., 2007 — Admitted to Bar, 2007, Massachusetts (Inactive); 2007, Vermont (Inactive); 2011, Maine; 2009, U.S. District Court, District of Vermont — Practice Areas: Workers' Compensation; Civil Litigation — E-mail: jwilson@rkmlegal.com

Kaitlin G. Roy — Saint Michael's College, B.A. (cum laude), 2003; University of Maine School of Law, J.D. (cum laude), 2011 — Admitted to Bar, 2011, Maine; 2011, Massachusetts — E-mail: kroy@rkmlegal.com

Alan R. Nye — 1955 — The University of Maine, B.A. (Dean's List), 1977; New England School of Law, J.D. (cum laude), 1980 — Admitted to Bar, 1980, Maine; U.S. District Court, District of Maine — Member American and Maine State Bar Associations — "How to Stop Paying High Property Taxes in Maine" — Practice Areas: Family Law; Corporate Law; Real Estate — E-mail: anye@rkmlegal.com

(* Denotes Workers' Compensation Attorneys.)

Thompson & Bowie, LLP

Three Canal Plaza
Portland, Maine 04101
Telephone: 207-774-2500
Fax: 207-774-3591
www.thompsonbowie.com

PORTLAND   MAINE

Thompson & Bowie, LLP, Portland, ME   (Continued)

Established: 1978

Admiralty and Maritime Law, Alternative Dispute Resolution, Civil Rights, Commercial Litigation, Employment Law, Insurance, Municipal Liability, Product Liability, Professional Liability, Property and Casualty, Transportation, Workers' Compensation

Insurance Clients

Acadia Insurance Company
Arch Insurance Group
Argonaut Insurance Company
Canal Insurance Company
Cannon Cochran Management Services, Inc.
CIGNA Property and Casualty Insurance Company
CNA Insurance Companies
Fitchburg Mutual Insurance Company
Great American Insurance Company
Maine Municipal Association
Patriot Insurance Company
Pawtucket Insurance Company
Philadelphia Insurance Companies
Sedgwick Group
United States Liability Insurance Group
XL Insurance Company, Ltd.
American Commerce Insurance Company
Automobile Club Insurance Company
Chubb Group of Insurance Companies
Clarendon National Insurance Company
Crum & Forster Insurance Group
GEICO Insurance Companies
General Star Indemnity Company
Hanover Insurance Group
The Hartford Insurance Group
Norfolk & Dedham Group
Patrons Oxford Insurance Company
St. Paul Travelers
Synernet
Western Litigation, Inc.
W.R. Berkley Corporation

Non-Insurance Clients

Avis Budget Group, Inc.
City of Portland
J.B. Hunt Transport, Inc.
Portland School Department
Schneider National, Inc.
Wal-Mart Stores, Inc.
Avis Rent-A-Car System, LLC
The Hertz Corporation
National Food Processors Association
Shaw's Supermarkets

Partners

Edward R. Benjamin, Jr. — University of New Hampshire, B.A. (cum laude), 1981; University of Maine School of Law, J.D., 1984 — University of Maine Law Review — Admitted to Bar, 1984, Maine; U.S. District Court, District of Maine; 1988, U.S. Court of Appeals, First Circuit; 1993, Passamaquoddy Tribal Court; 1999, U.S. Supreme Court — Member Maine State and Cumberland County Bar Associations; Defense Research Institute — E-6, U.S. Navy, 1973-1979 — Practice Areas: Civil Rights; Employment Law; Municipal Liability — E-mail: ebenjamin@thompsonbowie.com

James M. Bowie — Managing Partner — Bowdoin College, A.B. (cum laude), 1974; The University of Maine, J.D. (cum laude), 1977 — Admitted to Bar, 1977, Maine; U.S. District Court, District of Maine; 1982, U.S. Court of Appeals, First Circuit; 1987, U.S. Supreme Court — Member American, Maine State and Cumberland County Bar Associations; Center for Professional Responsibility; Maine Trial Lawyers Association; Tri-State Defense Lawyers Association; Professional Ethics Commission of the Board of Overseers of the Bar; National Academy of Distinguished Neutrals; Defense Research Institute — Mediation Arbitration and Early Neutral Evaluation Panels Maintained by CADRES for the Maine Superior Court — Practice Areas: Alternative Dispute Resolution; Commercial Litigation; Insurance; Professional Liability — E-mail: jbowie@thompsonbowie.com

Paul C. Catsos — Cornell University, B.A., 1982; Suffolk University, J.D. (cum laude), 1989 — Admitted to Bar, 1989, Maine; 2009, New Hampshire; 1989, U.S. District Court, District of Maine; 2000, U.S. Supreme Court; 2009, U.S. Court of Appeals, First Circuit; 2011, U.S. District Court, District of New Hampshire — Member Maine State, New Hampshire, Massachusetts and Cumberland County Bar Associations; Claims and Litigation Management Alliance; Southern Maine Claims Association; Tri-State Defense Lawyers Association; Professional Liability Defense Federation; Defense Research Institute — Practice Areas: Alternative Dispute Resolution; Commercial Litigation; Product Liability; Professional Liability; Property and Casualty; Transportation; Workers' Compensation — E-mail: pcatsos@thompsonbowie.com

Rebecca H. Farnum — Colby College, B.A., 1973; The University of Maine, J.D., 1977 — Admitted to Bar, 1977, Maine; U.S. District Court, District of Maine — Member American (Construction Forum), Maine State and Cumberland County Bar Associations; Tri-State Defense Lawyers Association; Defense Research Institute — Practice Areas: Alternative Dispute Resolution; Professional Liability — E-mail: rfarnum@thompsonbowie.com

Thompson & Bowie, LLP, Portland, ME   (Continued)

Mark V. Franco — Bowdoin College, B.A., 1981; University of New Hampshire School of Law, J.D., 1984 — Admitted to Bar, 1984, Maine; 2008, New Hampshire; 1984, U.S. District Court, District of Maine; 1998, U.S. Court of Appeals, First Circuit; 2008, U.S. District Court, District of New Hampshire — Member American, Maine State, New Hampshire and Cumberland County Bar Associations; Maine Trial Lawyers Association; Tri-State Defense Lawyers Association; Defense Research Institute; Association of Defense Trial Attorneys; Trucking Industry Defense Association; Transportation Lawyers Association — Practice Areas: Alternative Dispute Resolution; Civil Rights; Commercial Litigation; Employment Law; Municipal Liability; Professional Liability; Property and Casualty; Transportation; Workers' Compensation — E-mail: mfranco@thompsonbowie.com

Dale L. Gavin — Colby College, A.B. (magna cum laude), 1977; Stanford University, M.A., 1979; University of Maine School of Law, J.D., 1983 — Admitted to Bar, 1983, Maine; Massachusetts; 2013, New Hampshire; 1983, U.S. District Court, District of Maine — Member Maine State and New Hampshire Bar Associations; Tri-State Defense Lawyers Association; Defense Research Institute — Practice Areas: Employment Law; Workers' Compensation — E-mail: dgavin@thompsonbowie.com

Robert C. Hatch — Hamilton College, A.B., 1995; Oxford University, England; Georgetown University; University of Maine School of Law, J.D., 2000 — Law Clerk to the Hon. Donald G. Alexander, Maine Supreme Judicial Court — University of Maine Law Review, 1998-2000 — Admitted to Bar, 2001, Maine; U.S. District Court, District of Maine; 2002, U.S. Court of Appeals, First Circuit — Member American, Maine State and Cumberland County Bar Associations; Maine Trial Lawyers Association; Tri-State Defense Lawyers Association; Defense Research Institute — Practice Areas: Alternative Dispute Resolution; Commercial Litigation; Insurance; Product Liability; Professional Liability; Property and Casualty — E-mail: rhatch@thompsonbowie.com

Daniel R. Mawhinney — The University of Maine, B.A. (cum laude), 1974; Boston College Graduate School, 1975; Saint Louis University, J.D., 1978 — Admitted to Bar, 1978, Missouri; 1979, Maine; 1979, U.S. District Court, District of Maine; 1982, U.S. Court of Appeals, First Circuit; 2004, U.S. Supreme Court — Member American, Maine State and Cumberland County Bar Associations; Tri-State Defense Lawyers Association; Federation of Defense and Corporate Counsel — Practice Areas: Commercial Litigation; Insurance; Product Liability; Property and Casualty — E-mail: dmawhinney@thompsonbowie.com

Cathy S. Roberts — University of Rhode Island, B.S., 1978; New England School of Law, J.D., 1985 — Admitted to Bar, 1985, Massachusetts; 1989, Maine; 2013, New Hampshire; 1985, U.S. District Court, District of Massachusetts; 1989, U.S. District Court, District of Maine — Member American, Maine State, Massachusetts and New Hampshire Bar Associations; Maine Trial Lawyers Association; Tri-State Defense Lawyers Association; Maritime and Admiralty Law Committee; Propeller Club; Defense Research Institute; The Maritime Law Association of the United States — LT, JAGC, U.S. Navy Reserves, Active Duty, 1985-1989 — Practice Areas: Admiralty and Maritime Law; Commercial Litigation; Product Liability; Property and Casualty; Transportation; Workers' Compensation — E-mail: croberts@thompsonbowie.com

Michael E. Saucier — Boston College, A.B. (cum laude), 1975; The University of Maine, J.D., 1978 — University of Maine Law Review — Admitted to Bar, 1978, Maine; 2011, New Hampshire; 1978, U.S. District Court, District of Maine; 1979, U.S. Court of Appeals, First Circuit; 2012, U.S. District Court, District of New Hampshire — Member American, Maine State, New Hampshire and Cumberland County Bar Associations; Claims Litigation Management Alliance; Tri-State Defense Lawyers Association; Cleaves Law Library (Board of Directors); Gignoux Inn of Court; Maine Supreme Judicial Court Rules of Evidence Advisory Committee; Defense Research Institute — Co-Author: "Commentary to Maine Juvenile Code," Published by West Publishing Company, Vol. 8, Maine Revised Statutes Annotated, 1980 — Assistant Attorney General, State of Maine (1979-1982); Assistant District Attorney, Prosecutorial District #1, Alfred, Maine (1982-1984); Chairman, Committee to Monitor Implementation of the Juvenile Code (1981-1989); Criminal Law Advisory Commission (1983-1989; Chair 1987-1989); Maine Juvenile Justice Advisory Group (1985-2000; Chair, 1990-1997) — Practice Areas: Civil Rights; Commercial Litigation; Employment; Municipal Liability; Product Liability; Professional Liability; Property and Casualty — E-mail: msaucier@thompsonbowie.com

Associates

Hillary J. Bouchard — Colby College, B.A. (summa cum laude), 2002; University of Maine School of Law, J.D. (cum laude), 2006 — Admitted to Bar, 2006, Maine; 2007, Massachusetts; 2007, U.S. District Court, District of Maine; 2013, U.S. Court of Appeals, First Circuit — Member American,

MAINE

Thompson & Bowie, LLP, Portland, ME (Continued)

Maine State and Cumberland County Bar Associations; Maine Trial Lawyers Association; Defense Research Institute — Practice Areas: Commercial Litigation; Insurance; Professional Liability; Property and Casualty; Transportation — E-mail: hbouchard@thompsonbowie.com

Twain Braden — Hobart College, B.A., 1996; University of Aberdeen, Scotland; Charleston School of Law, J.A. (cum laude), 2007 — Admitted to Bar, 2009, New Hampshire; 2012, Maine; 2013, U.S. District Court, District of Maine — Member Maine State and New Hampshire Bar Associations; Propeller Club; The Maritime Law Association of the United States — Practice Areas: Admiralty and Maritime Law; Commercial Litigation — E-mail: tbraden@thompsonbowie.com

Jason P. Donovan — Loyola College, B.A. (cum laude), 1992; University of Maine School of Law, J.D. (cum laude), 2006 — Admitted to Bar, 2007, Maine; U.S. District Court, District of Maine; 2010, U.S. Court of Appeals, First Circuit; U.S. Supreme Court — Member Maine State and Cumberland County Bar Associations; Tri-State Defense Lawyers Association — Practice Areas: Civil Rights; Commercial Litigation; Insurance; Municipal Liability; Professional Liability — E-mail: jdonovan@thompsonbowie.com

Sarah Y. Gayer — Bowdoin College, B.A. (cum laude), 2005; University of Maine School of Law, J.D., 2008 — Admitted to Bar, 2009, Maine; U.S. District Court, District of Maine — Member American, Maine State and Cumberland County Bar Associations; Maine Trial Lawyers Association; Tri-State Defense Lawyers Association; Gignoux Inn of Court; The Propeller Club; The Maritime Law Association of the United States — Languages: Russian — Practice Areas: Admiralty and Maritime Law; Professional Liability — E-mail: sgayer@thompsonbowie.com

Rosie M. Williams — University of Vermont, B.A. (magna cum laude), 2001; University of Maine School of Law, J.D., 2006 — Admitted to Bar, 2006, Maine; U.S. District Court, District of Maine; 2007, U.S. Court of Appeals, First Circuit — Member American and Maine State Bar Associations; Maine Trial Lawyers Association; Gignoux Inn of Court; Defense Research Institute — Practice Areas: Civil Rights; Municipal Liability; Property and Casualty; Transportation — E-mail: rwilliams@thompsonbowie.com

Of Counsel

Leonard W. Langer — Colgate University, B.A. (cum laude), 1973; University of Maine School of Law, J.D. (cum laude), 1978 — Editor, Maine Law Review, 1977-1978 — Admitted to Bar, 1979, Maine; U.S. District Court, District of Maine; 1987, U.S. Court of Appeals, First Circuit; 2003, U.S. Court of Appeals, Third Circuit; 2004, U.S. Supreme Court — Member American, Maine State and Cumberland County Bar Associations; Tri-State Defense Lawyers Association; Gignoux Inn of Court; Propeller Club; Defense Research Institute; The Maritime Law Association of the United States — Author, Comment: "The Validity of the Restrictions on the Modern Advisory Opinion," 29 Maine Law Review 305 (1978) — U.S. District Court, District of Maine (Chairman, Local Rules Advisory Committee); State of Maine (ex officio, Civil Rules Committee) — Practice Areas: Admiralty and Maritime Law; Commercial Litigation; Property and Casualty — E-mail: lwlanger@thompsonbowie.com

Elizabeth K. Peck — Mount Holyoke College, A.B., 1983; The University of Maine, J.D., 1988 — Editorial Board, Maine Law Review, 1987-1988 — Admitted to Bar, 1988, Maine; U.S. District Court, District of Maine; 1991, U.S. Court of Appeals, First Circuit — Member Maine State Bar Association; Tri-State Defense Lawyers Association — Practice Areas: Commercial Litigation; Employment Law; Insurance; Product Liability; Property and Casualty — E-mail: epeck@thompsonbowie.com

Roy E. Thompson, Jr. — Yale University, B.A., 1967; Boston College, J.D., 1973 — Admitted to Bar, 1973, Maine; U.S. District Court, District of Maine; U.S. Court of Appeals, First Circuit — Member Maine State and Aroostook County Bar Associations; Tri-State Defense Lawyers Association — Lieut., U.S. Naval Reserve, active duty, 1967-1970 — Practice Areas: Commercial Litigation; Professional Liability — E-mail: rthompson@thompsonbowie.com

Wright & Associates, P.A.

The Congress Building
615 Congress Street, 2nd Floor
Portland, Maine 04101
　Telephone: 207-775-7722
　Fax: 207-775-7727
　E-Mail: law@legalwrights.com
　www.legalwrights.com

ROCKLAND

Wright & Associates, P.A., Portland, ME (Continued)

Established: 1992

Asbestos Litigation, Environmental Law, Hazardous Waste, Insurance Coverage, Premises Liability, Product Liability, Toxic Torts

Firm Profile: Wright & Associates, P.A. provides comprehensive national, regional and local legal services to a variety of corporate, insurance, and individual clients. The firm blends local pragmatism with national experience at the trial and appellate levels in both federal and state courts, and works closely with and appears before administrative and regulatory agencies.

Insurance Clients

Liberty Mutual Insurance Company
Special Claims Services, Inc.
Resolute Management, Inc.
Travelers Property Casualty Group

Non-Insurance Clients

Aurora Pump Company
Foster Wheeler
Gorman-Rupp Company
IMO Industries, Inc.
I.U. North America, Inc.
Robertson-Ceco Corporation
Warren Pumps LLC
DeZurik
Georgia-Pacific LLC
Hopeman Brothers Marine Interiors, LLC
Patterson Pump Company
Taco, Inc.

Managing Shareholder

Steven Wright — 1948 — The University of Maine, B.A., 1970; University of New Hampshire School of Law, J.D., 1976 — Admitted to Bar, 1976, Maine; 1993, District of Columbia; 1977, U.S. District Court, District of Maine; 1985, U.S. Court of Appeals, First Circuit; 1986, U.S. Supreme Court; 1988, U.S. Court of Federal Claims; 1988, U.S. Court of Appeals for the Federal Circuit; 1991, U.S. Court of Appeals, Second Circuit — Member American, Maine State and Cumberland County Bar Associations; Defense Research Institute — Assistant Attorney General, 1976-1981

ROCKLAND † 7,297 Knox Co.

Refer To

Johnson & Webbert, L.L.P.
160 Capitol Street
Augusta, Maine 04330
　Telephone: 207-623-5110
　Fax: 207-622-4160
Mailing Address: P.O. Box 79, Augusta, ME 04332-0079

Aviation, Comprehensive General Liability, Employment Discrimination, Environmental Law, Insurance Coverage, Product Liability, Professional Malpractice, Legal Malpractice, Medical Malpractice

SEE COMPLETE LISTING UNDER AUGUSTA, MAINE (42 MILES)

Refer To

Wheeler & Arey, P.A.
27 Temple Street
Waterville, Maine 04901
　Telephone: 207-873-7771
　Fax: 207-877-9454
　Toll Free: 888-451-8400 (In State)
Mailing Address: P.O. Box 376, Waterville, ME 04903-0376

Insurance Law, Subrogation

SEE COMPLETE LISTING UNDER WATERVILLE, MAINE (60 MILES)

SKOWHEGAN † 6,297 Somerset Co.

Refer To

Wheeler & Arey, P.A.
27 Temple Street
Waterville, Maine 04901
　Telephone: 207-873-7771
　Fax: 207-877-9454
　Toll Free: 888-451-8400 (In State)
Mailing Address: P.O. Box 376, Waterville, ME 04903-0376

Insurance Law, Subrogation

SEE COMPLETE LISTING UNDER WATERVILLE, MAINE (18 MILES)

WATERVILLE   MAINE

WATERVILLE 15,722 Kennebec Co.

Wheeler & Arey, P.A.
27 Temple Street
Waterville, Maine 04901
　Telephone: 207-873-7771
　Fax: 207-877-9454
　Toll Free: 888-451-8400 (In State)
　E-Mail: ducharme@wheelerlegal.com
　www.wheelerlegal.com

Established: 1971

Insurance Law, Subrogation

Insurance Clients

American International Adjustment Company
Colonial Penn Insurance Company
Dairyland Insurance Company
Hanover Insurance Company
Hermitage Insurance Company
Lexington Insurance Company
MGA Insurance Services
Middlesex Insurance Company
New England Guaranty Insurance Company, Inc.
Patrons Oxford Insurance Company
Scottsdale Insurance Company
United States Fidelity and Guaranty Company
York Insurance Company
CIGNA Property and Casualty Insurance Company
Commercial Union Insurance Company
The Hartford Insurance Group
Home Insurance Company
Maine Mutual Fire Insurance Company
Mutual Fire Insurance Company
New Hampshire Insurance Company
Public Service Mutual Insurance Company
Sentry Claims Services
Vanliner Insurance Company
Vermont Mutual Insurance Company

Non-Insurance Clients

Morse, Payson & Noyes
Northern Securities
Northern General Services

Partners

Ronald A. Ducharme — 1959 — University of Notre Dame, B.A., 1981; California Western School of Law, J.D., 1985 — Admitted to Bar, 1985, Maine — Member American, Maine State, Kennebec County and Waterville Bar Associations — E-mail: ducharme@wheelerlegal.com

Peter T. Marchesi — 1962 — Colby College, B.A., 1986; Vermont Law School, J.D., 1989 — Admitted to Bar, 1989, Maine; 1990, U.S. District Court, District of Maine — Member American and Maine State Bar Associations — E-mail: pbear@wheelerlegal.com

Associate

Cassandra S. Shaffer — 1977 — Brown University, B.A., 1999; Roger Williams University School of Law, J.D., 2004 — Admitted to Bar, 2004, Maine; 2005, U.S. District Court, District of Maine — Member American and Maine State Bar Associations — E-mail: cshaffer@wheelerlegal.com

MARYLAND

CAPITAL: ANNAPOLIS

COUNTIES AND COUNTY SEATS

County	County Seat
Allegany	Cumberland
Anne Arundel	Annapolis
Baltimore	Towson
Calvert	Prince Frederick
Caroline	Denton
Carroll	Westminster
Cecil	Elkton
Charles	La Plata
Dorchester	Cambridge
Frederick	Frederick
Garrett	Oakland
Harford	Bel Air
Howard	Ellicott City
Kent	Chestertown
Montgomery	Rockville
Prince Georges	Upper Marlboro
Queen Anne's	Centreville
Saint Mary's	Leonardtown
Somerset	Princess Anne
Talbot	Easton
Washington	Hagerstown
Wicomico	Salisbury
Worcester	Snow Hill

In the text that follows "†" indicates County Seats.

Our files contain additional verified data on the firms listed herein. This additional information is available on request.

A.M. BEST COMPANY

MARYLAND

ANNAPOLIS † 38,394 Anne Arundel Co.

Hyatt & Weber, P.A.
200 Westgate Circle, Suite 500
Annapolis, Maryland 21401
Telephone: 410-266-0626
Fax: 410-841-5065
E-Mail: info@hwlaw.com
www.hwlaw.com

Established: 1979

Real Estate Transactions, Commercial Law, Business Law, Banking, Land Use, Zoning, Corporate Law, Environmental Law, Insurance Coverage, Estate Planning, Medical Malpractice, Personal Injury, Professional License Defense

Firm Profile: The Hyatt & Weber, P.A. philosophy begins with a commitment to work closely with each and every client. This means applying the legal expertise and attention to detail that each matter deserves, in an efficient and effective manner. Our lawyers know that our success depends on the satisfaction of our clients.

With decades of litigation, land use, estate planning and real estate experience, extensive lobbying activities and active involvement in our communities and development industry, our unique team of professionals is able to deliver sound counsel and creative solutions to meet your land use, real estate, litigation and estate planning goals. Our attorneys stand ready to bring our experience and resources to help you achieve your objectives.

Insurance Clients

Allstate Insurance Company
High Point Safety and Insurance Management Corporation
NCMIC Insurance Company
Prudential Insurance Company of America
Westport Insurance Corporation
American Independent Insurance Company
Leader Insurance Company
Pennsylvania National Mutual Casualty Insurance Company
Transport Insurance Company

Non-Insurance Clients

Dunbar Armored, Inc.
Housing Authority of the City of Annapolis (HACA)
Housing Authority of Baltimore City (HABC)

Partners

Alan J. Hyatt — Bryant College, B.S. (summa cum laude), 1975; University of Baltimore, J.D., 1978 — Admitted to Bar, 1978, Maryland; 1979, U.S. District Court, District of Maryland — Member Maryland State and Anne Arundel County Bar Associations

Paul J. Weber — James Madison University, B.S. (cum laude), 1980; University of Baltimore, J.D., 1983 — Admitted to Bar, 1984, Maryland; 1985, U.S. District Court, District of Maryland; 1990, U.S. Court of Appeals, Fourth Circuit — Member American, Maryland State and Anne Arundel County Bar Associations; Maryland Association of Defense Trial Counsel

Gregg M. Weinberg — Tulane University, B.S.M., 1989; University of Baltimore, J.D., 1992 — Admitted to Bar, 1992, Maryland; 1995, U.S. District Court, District of Maryland — Member American, Maryland State and Anne Arundel Bar Associations

Stephen B. Stern — Cornell University School of Industrial and Labor Relations, B.S., 1993; Georgetown University Law Center, J.D., 1996 — Admitted to Bar, 1997, Maryland; 1998, District of Columbia; Virginia; U.S. District Court, District of Maryland; U.S. District Court, Eastern District of Virginia; U.S. Court of Appeals for the District of Columbia, Third and Fourth Circuits; District of Columbia Court of Appeals

Mark E. Rosasco — Loyola College, B.A., 1981; University of Baltimore School of Law, J.D., 1990 — Admitted to Bar, 1999, Maryland; District of Columbia — Member Anne Arundel County Bar Association; Maryland Association for Justice

Associates

Jonathan M. Wall — Boston University, B.A., 1985; The University of Iowa, M.F.A., 1988; University of Baltimore, J.D., 1995 — Admitted to Bar, 1995, Maryland; U.S. District Court, District of Maryland; U.S. Court of Appeals, Fourth Circuit; 1995, Maryland State Courts — Member American, Maryland State and Anne Arundel County Bar Associations

Shannon T. Waldron — 1972 — University of Florida, B.A., 1994; Penn State University, M.S., 1997; Vermont Law School, J.D., 2002 — Admitted to Bar, 2002, Maryland — Member Maryland State Bar Association

Amanda C. Sprehn — 1978 — University of Maryland, College Park, B.A., 2000; University of Baltimore, J.D., 2003 — Admitted to Bar, 2003, Maryland — Member American, Maryland State and Anne Arundel County Bar Associations

Christine E. Neiderer — Villanova University, B.A., 1998; University of Baltimore, J.D., 2005 — Admitted to Bar, 2005, Maryland — Member American, Maryland State and Anne Arundel County Bar Associations

Robert D. Miller — West Virginia University, B.S., 1975; University of Baltimore School of Law, J.D., 1985 — Admitted to Bar, 1986, Maryland

Lisa Mannisi — American University, B.S. Business Admin., 2006; University of Maryland School of Law, J.D., 2009 — Admitted to Bar, 2009, Maryland — Member Maryland State and Anne Arundel County Bar Associations; Maryland Association for Justice

Seth B. Zirkle — Wabash College, B.S., 2004; Indiana School of Law, 2008 — Admitted to Bar, 2008, Maryland; U.S. District Court, District of Maryland — Member Maryland State and Anne Arundel County Bar Associations

Andrew Kerner — University of Dallas, B.A., 2007; Saint Mary's College, J.D., 2011 — Admitted to Bar, 2011, Maryland — Member American, Maryland State and Anne Arundel County Bar Associations; Maryland Association for Justice

Adam Smith — University of South Carolina, B.A., 2009; University of Baltimore School of Law, J.D., 2012 — Admitted to Bar, 2012, Maryland — Member Maryland State and Anne Arundel County Bar Associations

Wharton, Levin, Ehrmantraut & Klein, P.A.
104 West Street
Annapolis, Maryland 21401
Telephone: 410-263-5900
Fax: 410-280-2230

Established: 1984

Insurance Defense, Medical Malpractice, Legal Malpractice, Product Liability, Toxic Torts, Asbestos Litigation, Appellate Practice

Insurance Clients

The Hartford
Ophthalmic Mutual Insurance Company
Medical Mutual Liability Insurance Society of Maryland
United States Aviation Underwriters, Inc.

Non-Insurance Clients

Bell Helicopter Textron Inc.
The Goodyear Tire & Rubber Company
Product Liability Advisory Counsel, Inc.
Bridgestone/Firestone, Inc.
Johns Hopkins Health System
Medstar Health, Inc.
Trinity Health

Shareholders

James T. Wharton — (1930-2003)

David A. Levin — 1947 — University of Maryland, B.S., 1968; J.D., 1972 — Admitted to Bar, 1972, Maryland; 1973, District of Columbia; 1972, U.S. District Court, District of Maryland; 1972, U.S. Court of Appeals, Fourth Circuit; 1973, U.S. District Court for the District of Columbia; 1973, U.S. Court of Appeals for the District of Columbia Circuit — Member American Bar Association (Sections: Litigation, Professional Liability Committee; Tort and Insurance Practice); Maryland State Bar Association (Litigation, Professional Liability Committee Section); The District of Columbia Bar; American Academy of Hospital Attorneys; Advocate, American Board of Trial Advocates; Fellow, Maryland Bar Foundation; American Inns of Court, Inn XIII; Maryland Association of Defense Trial Counsel; Defense Research Institute; International Association of Defense Counsel

Robert D. Klein — 1951 — Durham University, England, 1972; Massachusetts Institute of Technology, B.S., 1973; Columbia University, J.D., 1976 — Admitted to Bar, 1976, Maryland; 1983, District of Columbia; 1977, U.S. District Court, District of Maryland; 1978, U.S. Court of Appeals, Fourth Circuit;

Wharton, Levin, Ehrmantraut & Klein, P.A., Annapolis, MD (Continued)

1983, U.S. District Court for the District of Columbia — Member Maryland State (Co-Chair, Products Liability Committee, 1990-1994; Litigation Section) and Anne Arundel County Bar Associations; The Bar Association of Baltimore City (Standing Committee on Legislation, 1982-1987; Chairman, Special Committee on Video, 1983; Executive Council, 1984-1987; Standing Committee on Public Relations, 1984-1986; Standing Committee on Long Range Planning, 1986-1987; Chairman, Product Liability Committee, 1987-1988; Special Committee on Tort Reform, 1987); Maryland Defense Counsel (President, 1986-1987; Products Liability Committee, 1989-1991; Judicial Selections Committee, 1991-1992; Chairman, Standing Committee on Rules of Practice and Procedure, 1992-1994; Committees: Product Liability, Industrywide Litigation); Product Liability Advisory Council, Inc. (Co-Chair, Rules of Civil Procedure Action Group, 1991-1998; Executive Committee, 1997-2000); Standing Committee on the Rules of Practice and Procedure of the Court of Appeals of Maryland (1984-2012); ADR Maryland (Mediation Panel); Paralegal Studies Advisory Board, Stevenson University (flkla Villa Julie College), 1984-present; Defense Research Institute — Maryland Super Lawyer (2009 to present); Defense Research Institute Exeptional Performance Citation (1987); Biographee in Marquis Who's Who in America, Who's Who in the World, Who's Who in American Law, and Who's Who in Industry and Finance

D. Lee Rutland — 1958 — Mount St. Mary's College, B.S. (cum laude), 1980; University of Maryland, J.D., 1983 — Admitted to Bar, 1983, Maryland; 1985, District of Columbia; 1993, Virginia; 1984, U.S. District Court, District of Maryland; 1985, U.S. District Court for the District of Columbia; 1986, U.S. Court of Appeals for the District of Columbia and Fourth Circuits; 1987, U.S. Supreme Court; 1993, U.S. District Court, Eastern District of Virginia — Member American Bar Association (Sections: Litigation, Tort and Insurance Practice),; Maryland State (Litigation Section) and Anne Arundel County Bar Associations; The District of Columbia Bar; Virginia State Bar; Defense Research Institute; American Board of Trial Advocates; District of Columbia Defense Lawyers Association — Best Lawyers in America (2012); District of Columbia Defense Lawyers Association Lawyer of the Year (2012)

Michael T. Wharton — 1956 — University of Virginia, B.A. (with distinction), 1978; University of Maryland, J.D. (with honors), 1981 — Admitted to Bar, 1981, Maryland; 1982, U.S. District Court, District of Maryland; 1986, U.S. District Court for the District of Columbia; 1986, U.S. Court of Appeals, Fourth Circuit; 1986, U.S. Supreme Court; 1987, U.S. Court of Appeals for the District of Columbia Circuit — Member American Bar Association (Tort and Insurance Practice Section; Aviation and Space Law Committee); Maryland State Bar Association (Litigation Section; Product Liability Committee); Product Liability Advisory Council, Inc; Maryland Association of Defense Trial Counsel

Andrew E. Vernick — 1956 — College of William & Mary, B.A., 1978; University of Maryland, J.D., 1981 — Admitted to Bar, 1982, Maryland; 1983, District of Columbia; 2010, Delaware; 1982, U.S. District Court, District of Maryland; 1982, U.S. Court of Appeals, Fourth Circuit; 1983, U.S. District Court for the District of Columbia; 1983, U.S. Court of Appeals for the District of Columbia Circuit; 2010, U.S. District Court, District of Delaware — Member American Bar Association (Sections: Litigation, Tort and Insurance Practice; Professional Liability Committee); Maryland State (Litigation Section; Professional Liability Committee), Delaware State and Anne Arundel County Bar Associations; The District of Columbia Bar; American Academy of Hospital Attorneys; American Inns of Court, Inn XIII; Rodney Inn of Court (Delaware); Maryland Association of Defense Trial Counsel — Maryland Super Lawyers (2006-present); Super Lawyers (Business, 2010-present) — Practice Areas: Medical Malpractice; Legal Malpractice; Defense Litigation

David A. Roling — 1962 — University of Maryland, B.A. (magna cum laude), 1984; University of Baltimore, J.D. (magna cum laude), 1987 — Admitted to Bar, 1987, Maryland; 1988, District of Columbia; 1988, U.S. District Court, District of Maryland; 1990, U.S. District Court for the District of Columbia; 1991, U.S. Court of Appeals for the District of Columbia Circuit; 1994, U.S. Supreme Court; 1996, U.S. Court of Appeals, Fourth Circuit — Member Maryland State Bar Association; Maryland Association of Defense Trial Counsel; American Board of Trial Advocates

Daniel C. Costello — 1966 — University of Maryland, B.A. (cum laude), 1987; J.D. (with honors), 1990 — Admitted to Bar, 1990, Maryland; 1991, District of Columbia; 1996, Virginia; 1991, U.S. District Court, District of Maryland; 1993, U.S. District Court for the District of Columbia; 1993, U.S. Court of Appeals for the District of Columbia Circuit; 1997, U.S. Court of Appeals, Fourth Circuit; 1998, U.S. District Court, Eastern District of Virginia — Member Maryland State and Anne Arundel County Bar Associations; The District of Columbia Bar; Virginia State Bar; American Board of Trial Advocates

Wharton, Levin, Ehrmantraut & Klein, P.A., Annapolis, MD (Continued)

Michael K. Wiggins — 1967 — Saint Mary's College, B.S., 1990; University of Baltimore, J.D., 1994 — Admitted to Bar, 1994, Maryland; 1996, District of Columbia; 1995, U.S. District Court, District of Maryland; 1997, U.S. District Court for the District of Columbia; 1997, U.S. Court of Appeals, Fourth Circuit — Member The District of Columbia Bar — Maryland Super Lawyers (2007-present); Best Lawyers DC (2010); Best Lawyers in America (2009-present)

Robert J. Farley — 1960 — Loyola College, B.A., 1982; University of Baltimore, J.D., 1985 — Admitted to Bar, 1985, Maryland; 1987, Virginia; 1988, District of Columbia; 1997, West Virginia; 1986, U.S. District Court, District of Maryland; 1987, U.S. Court of Appeals, Fourth Circuit; 1988, U.S. District Court for the District of Columbia; 1998, U.S. Supreme Court — Member Maryland State, Virginia and West Virginia Bar Associations; The District of Columbia Bar; Maryland Association of Defense Trial Counsel

Lance I. Yateman — 1948 — Towson University, B.S., 1970; University of Baltimore, J.D., 1973 — Admitted to Bar, 1973, Maryland; 1975, U.S. District Court, District of Maryland; 1977, U.S. Supreme Court — Member American, Maryland State and Anne Arundel County Bar Associations

Robert S. Morter — 1964 — The University of Texas at Austin, B.A. (with honors), 1986; South Texas College of Law, J.D., 1999 — Admitted to Bar, 1999, Maryland; 2001, District of Columbia; 2001, U.S. District Court, District of Maryland — Member Maryland State Bar Association; Defense Research Institute

Gregory S. McKee — 1973 — Randolph-Macon College, B.A., 1995; University of Baltimore, J.D., 1998 — Admitted to Bar, 1998, Maryland; 1999, District of Columbia; 1999, U.S. District Court, District of Maryland; 1999, U.S. Court of Appeals for the Federal Circuit; 2004, U.S. Court of Appeals for the District of Columbia Circuit — Member Maryland State, Calvert County and Prince Georges County Bar Associations — Practice Areas: Medical Liability; Professional Liability

Michelle R. Mitchell — 1974 — United States Naval Academy; University of Maryland, B.A., 1996; M.P.M., 2001; J.D., 2001 — Law Clerk to Hon. Lynne A. Battaglia, U.S. Court of Appeals of Maryland (2001-2002) — Admitted to Bar, 2001, Maryland; 2007, District of Columbia; 2002, U.S. District Court, District of Maryland; 2002, U.S. Court of Appeals for the Armed Forces; 2006, U.S. Supreme Court — Member Maryland State and Anne Arundel County Bar Associations; The District of Columbia Bar; Standing Commission on Professionalism — Practice Areas: Medical Liability; Civil Litigation; Appellate Practice

J. Kristen Moore — 1974 — Villa Julie College, B.S. (summa cum laude), 1997; University of Baltimore, J.D. (cum laude), 2001 — Judicial Clerk to Hon. John F. Fader, III, Circuit Court for Baltimore County, 2001-2002; Judicial Clerk to Hon. Alan M. Wilner, Court of Appeals of Maryland, 2002-2003 — Staff Editor, University of Baltimore School of Law, Law Forum (2000 - 2001) — Admitted to Bar, 2001, Maryland; 2007, District of Columbia; 2006, U.S. District Court, District of Maryland; 2007, U.S. Court of Appeals for the District of Columbia Circuit — Member Maryland State Bar Association; The District of Columbia Bar — Practice Areas: Medical Malpractice; Civil Litigation; Defense Litigation; Appellate Practice

Dennis C. Weisberg — 1955 — Franklin & Marshall College, B.A., 1977; University of Maryland, J.D., 1981 — Admitted to Bar, 1981, Maryland; U.S. District Court, District of Maryland; U.S. Bankruptcy Court — Member Maryland State and Anne Arundel County Bar Assocations — Practice Areas: Corporate Law; Estate Planning; Civil Litigation

Associates

Dana K. Schultz — 1974 — San Diego State University, B.A., 1997; Southwestern University School of Law, J.D., 2000 — Admitted to Bar, 2000, California; 2004, Maryland; 2009, District of Columbia; 2000, U.S. District Court, Central District of California; 2001, U.S. District Court, Southern District of California; 2009, U.S. District Court, District of Maryland; 2010, U.S. Court of Appeals for the District of Columbia Circuit — Member Maryland State Bar Association; State Bar of California; The District of Columbia Bar — Practice Areas: Civil Litigation; Medical Malpractice

Jennifer E. Phillips — 1973 — Boston College, B.S., 1995; The Catholic University of America, Columbus School of Law, J.D., 1999 — Admitted to Bar, 1999, Maryland; 2005, District of Columbia; 2005, U.S. District Court for the District of Columbia and District of Maryland — Member Maryland State and Montgomery County Bar Associations — Practice Areas: Medical Malpractice

Tiffany D. Randolph — 1981 — University of Virginia, B.S., 2003; University of Maryland School of Law, J.D., 2007 — Admitted to Bar, 2008, Maryland; 2011, District of Columbia — Member Maryland State Bar Association; The District of Columbia Bar

MARYLAND

Wharton, Levin, Ehrmantraut & Klein, P.A., Annapolis, MD (Continued)

Joshua H. Meyeroff — 1982 — Franklin & Marshall College, B.A. (magna cum laude), 2004; Widener University, J.D. (magna cum laude), 2007 — Admitted to Bar, 2007, Delaware; 2007, New Jersey; 2008, Pennsylvania; 2007, U.S. District Court, District of New Jersey; 2008, U.S. District Court, District of Delaware; 2010, U.S. Court of Appeals, Third Circuit — Member Delaware State and Pennsylvania Bar Associations

Michael S. Rubin — 1983 — Franklin & Marshall College, B.A. (cum laude), 2006; University of Maryland School of Law, J.D. (cum laude), 2010 — Admitted to Bar, 2010, Maryland

Aubrey W. Fitch, IV — 1983 — Miami University, B.A., 2006; The George Washington University Law School, J.D. (with high honors), 2011 — Judicial Clerk to Hon. Joseph M. Quirk, Circuit Court for Montgomery County (2011); Judicial Clerk to Hon. Terrence J. McGann, Circuit Court for Montgomery County (2011-2012) — Admitted to Bar, 2012, Maryland — Member American and Maryland State Bar Associations — Practice Areas: Medical Malpractice; Defense Litigation

Timothy D. Fisher — 1980 — Loyola College in Maryland, B.A., 2002; University of Baltimore School of Law, J.D. (cum laude), 2005 — Admitted to Bar, 2005, Maryland; 2006, District of Columbia; 2006, U.S. District Court, District of Maryland; 2007, U.S. District Court for the District of Columbia — Member Maryland State and Montgomery County Bar Associations; The Bar Association of Baltimore City; District of Columbia Defense Lawyers Association

Ryan T. Keating — 1981 — Florida State University, B.S., 2004; The George Washington University Law School, J.D., 2010 — Admitted to Bar, 2010, Delaware; 2011, U.S. District Court, District of Delaware — Member Delaware State Bar Association

BALTIMORE   620,961 Independent City

Eccleston and Wolf
Professional Corporation

Baltimore Washington Law Center
7240 Parkway Drive, 4th Floor
Hanover, Maryland 21076
Telephone: 410-752-7474
Fax: 410-752-0611

(Additional Offices: Washington, DC*; Fairfax, VA*)

Insurance Defense, Premises Liability, Product Liability, Professional Malpractice, Title Insurance, Accountants, Architects and Engineers, Engineers, Medical Liability, Automobile, Aviation, Construction, Environmental, Coverage, Attorneys, Employment, Physicians, Nurses, Investment Advisors

Insurance Clients

ACE
AIG
CAMICO Mutual Insurance Company
Gallagher Bassett Services, Inc.
Lexington Insurance Company
Metropolitan Property and Casualty Insurance Company
Monitor Liability Managers, Inc.
Nationwide Insurance
Safeco Insurance
Scottsdale Insurance Company
XL Companies
Admiral Insurance Company
Arch Specialty Insurance Company
CNA Insurance Companies
Coregis/Westport Insurance Company
Liberty International Underwriters
Minnesota Lawyers Mutual Insurance Company
National Casualty Company
Philadelphia Insurance Company
The St. Paul Companies
Travelers Insurance Company
Zurich

Firm Members

Edward J. Hutchins, Jr. — **Managing Partner** — 1957 — University of Maryland, B.A. (magna cum laude), 1979; J.D. (with honors), 1982 — Admitted to Bar, 1982, Maryland; 1996, District of Columbia; 1983, U.S. District Court, District of Maryland; 1983, U.S. Court of Appeals, Fourth Circuit — E-mail: hutchins@ewmd.com

Alvin I. Frederick — 1950 — University of Maryland, B.A. (with honors), 1972; J.D. (with honors), 1976 — Admitted to Bar, 1976, Maryland; 1984, District of Columbia; 1977, U.S. District Court, District of Maryland; 1977, U.S. Court of Appeals, Fourth Circuit; 1980, U.S. Supreme Court; 1984, U.S. Court of Appeals for the District of Columbia Circuit — Member Maryland

Eccleston and Wolf, Professional Corporation, Baltimore, MD (Continued)

State Bar Association (Chairman, Professional Malpractice Committee, 1987-1994; Civil Subcommittee on Pattern Jury Instructions, 1991-; Committee on Laws, 1993; Special Sub-Committee on Tort Reform, 1993; Chairman, Ethics 2000-2002; Litigation Section: Council, 1990-; Chairman, 1997-1998); Fellow, American College of Trial Lawyers; American Board of Trial Advocates — E-mail: frederick@ewmd.com

Shirlie Norris Lake — 1944 — MacMurray College, B.A., 1966; University of Maryland, J.D. (with honors), 1980 — Admitted to Bar, 1980, Maryland; 1997, District of Columbia; 1980, U.S. District Court, District of Maryland; 1981, U.S. Court of Appeals, Fourth Circuit; 1997, U.S. District Court for the District of Columbia — E-mail: lake@ewmd.com

John S. VanderWoude — 1959 — Calvin College, B.A., 1981; University of Maryland, J.D. (with honors), 1984 — Admitted to Bar, 1985, Maryland; 2004, District of Columbia; 1985, U.S. District Court, District of Maryland; 1991, U.S. Court of Appeals, Fourth Circuit — E-mail: vanderwoude@ewmd.com

Thomas J. Althauser — 1956 — State University of New York, B.S., 1983; University of Maryland, J.D. (with honors), 1988 — Admitted to Bar, 1988, Maryland; 1989, U.S. District Court, District of Maryland; 1995, U.S. Supreme Court — U.S.N. 1975-1983 — E-mail: althauser@ewmd.com

Stacey A. Moffet — 1969 — Washington University in St. Louis, B.S. (with honors), 1991; University of Maryland, J.D., 1994 — Phi Beta Kappa — Admitted to Bar, 1994, Maryland; 2002, District of Columbia; 1995, U.S. District Court, District of Maryland; 2000, U.S. Court of Appeals, Fourth Circuit — E-mail: moffet@ewmd.com

James E. Dickerman — 1965 — Johns Hopkins University, B.A., 1987; Boston University, J.D. (cum laude), 1991 — Admitted to Bar, 1991, Maryland; 2003, District of Columbia; 1992, U.S. District Court, District of Maryland; 1993, U.S. Court of Appeals, Fourth Circuit — E-mail: dickerman@ewmd.com

Gregg E. Viola — 1970 — University of Maryland, B.S., 1992; University of Baltimore School of Law, J.D. (cum laude), 1996 — Admitted to Bar, 1996, Maryland; 1999, U.S. District Court, District of Maryland; 2005, U.S. Court of Appeals, Fourth Circuit — E-mail: viola@ewmd.com

Robert S. Krause — 1969 — Villanova University, B.A., 1990; The Catholic University of America, Columbus School of Law, J.D., 1994 — Admitted to Bar, 1994, Maryland; 1996, U.S. District Court, District of Maryland; 1998, U.S. Court of Appeals, Fourth Circuit — E-mail: krause@ewmd.com

Jeffrey W. Bredeck — 1965 — University of Maryland, B.A., 1991; University of Baltimore School of Law, J.D. (cum laude), 1994 — Admitted to Bar, 1994, Maryland; 1995, U.S. District Court, District of Maryland; 1997, U.S. Court of Appeals, Fourth Circuit — E-mail: bredeck@ewmd.com

Erin A. Risch — College of Holy Cross, B.A., 2003; University of Baltimore School of Law, J.D. (magna cum laude), 2006 — Admitted to Bar, 2006, Maryland; Maryland Court of Appeals; 2007, U.S. District Court, District of Maryland — E-mail: erisch@ewmd.com

Eric M. Rigatuso — University of Maryland, Baltimore County, B.A., 1996; University of Maryland School of Law, J.D. (with honors), 2002 — Admitted to Bar, 2002, Maryland; 2004, U.S. District Court, District of Maryland; 2013, U.S. Court of Appeals, Fourth Circuit; Maryland Court of Appeals — E-mail: rigatuso@ewmd.com

Associates

Elias G. Saboura-Polkovotsy
Daniel R. Hodges
Richard J. Berwanger
Mark P. Johnson
Stephen M. Cornelius
Lauren E. Marini
Ashley L. Marucci
Melissa E. Goldmeier
Matthew W. Fogleman
Susannah E. Smith
Jeannette L. Calomeris
Megan E. Green
Brad M. Schavio
Emily M. Patterson

Ferguson, Schetelich & Ballew, P.A.

1401 Bank of America Center
100 South Charles Street
Baltimore, Maryland 21201-2725
   Telephone: 410-837-2200
   Fax: 410-837-1188
   E-Mail: rferguson@fsb-law.com
   www.fsb-law.com

Established: 1996

Insurance Defense, General Liability, Casualty, Coverage Issues, Construction Litigation, Environmental Law, Product Liability, Professional Liability, Aviation, Marine

Firm Profile: The firm was formed on February 1, 1996 from an established litigation and insurance defense department at another Baltimore law firm. Our firm consists of six partners, six associates and three paralegals in addition to a support staff. The firm represents insurance carriers and self-insureds in litigation in Maryland, the District of Columbia and Delaware. The firm also has attorneys with extensive experience in construction law, estate planning, business law and criminal law. Our offices are conveniently located in Baltimore's Inner Harbor adjacent to the Federal Courthouse and within a short distance of the Baltimore City Courts.

Insurance Clients

Allianz Underwriters Insurance Company
Chartis Aerospace Insurance Services, Inc.
International Marine Underwriters
Investors Insurance Group
Life Investors Insurance Company of America
Nautilus Insurance Company
The Travelers Companies, Inc.
U.S. Liability Insurance Company
Bankers United Life Assurance Company
Cincinnati Insurance Company
Hortica, The Florists' Mutual Insurance Company
K & K Insurance Group, Inc.
Motorists Mutual Insurance Company
OneBeacon Insurance
United America Indemnity Group

Non-Insurance Clients

LAD Aviation, Inc.

Partners

Robert L. Ferguson, Jr. — 1945 — University of Maryland, B.S.E.E., 1968; J.D. (with honors), 1972 — Admitted to Bar, 1972, Maryland; 1985, District of Columbia; 1972, U.S. District Court, District of Maryland; 1985, U.S. District Court for the District of Columbia; 1985, U.S. Court of Appeals for the District of Columbia, Third and Fourth Circuits — Member American and Maryland State Bar Associations; The Bar Association of Baltimore City; The District of Columbia Bar; The Maritime Law Association of the United States; Maryland Association of Defense Trial Counsel; Association of Defense Trial Attorneys; International Association of Defense Counsel; Defense Research Institute; Fellow, American College of Trial Lawyers — Practice Areas: Aviation; Construction Law; Insurance Law; Admiralty and Maritime Law — E-mail: rferguson@fsb-law.com

Thomas J. Schetelich — 1955 — Kean College of New Jersey, B.A. (summa cum laude), 1977; Washington and Lee University, J.D. (magna cum laude), 1980 — Admitted to Bar, 1980, Maryland; 1980, U.S. District Court, District of Maryland; 1980, U.S. Court of Appeals for the District of Columbia and Fourth Circuits; 1999, U.S. Supreme Court — Member Maryland State Bar Association; The Bar Association of Baltimore City — Practice Areas: Business Law; Family Law; Wills; Wills and Estate Litigation — E-mail: tschetelich@fsb-law.com

Craig F. Ballew — 1959 — University of Maryland, Baltimore County, B.A., 1981; University of Maryland, J.D., 1984 — Admitted to Bar, 1985, Maryland; 1985, U.S. District Court of Maryland; 1993, U.S. Court of Appeals, Fourth Circuit — Member American and Maryland State Bar Associations; The Bar Association of Baltimore City — Practice Areas: Labor and Employment — E-mail: cballew@fsb-law.com

Peter J. Basile — 1965 — State University of New York at Albany, B.S. (cum laude), 1987; The George Washington University, J.D., 1990 — Admitted to Bar, 1990, Maryland; 1991, District of Columbia; 1992, U.S. District Court, District of Maryland; 2004, U.S. District Court for the District of Columbia; 2011, U.S. Court of Appeals, Fourth Circuit — Member Maryland State and Prince George's County Bar Associations; The District of Columbia Bar; The Bar Association of Baltimore City — E-mail: pbasile@fsb-law.com

Ferguson, Schetelich & Ballew, P.A., Baltimore, MD (Continued)

Michael K. Hourigan — 1973 — Loyola College, B.A. (Dean's List), 1995; University of Maryland, J.D., 1998 — Maryland Law Review — Admitted to Bar, 1998, Maryland; 2001, District of Columbia; 1999, U.S. District Court, District of Maryland; 2004, U.S. District Court for the District of Columbia; 2007, U.S. Court of Appeals, Fourth Circuit — Member Maryland State and Anne Arundel County Bar Associations; The Bar Association of Baltimore City — Author: "Waskiewicz v. General Motors Corp.: Failing to Construe the Workers' Compensation Act Liberally" 56 Md. Law Rev. 1019 (1997) — Practice Areas: Business Law; Business Litigation; Corporate Law; Labor and Employment; Real Estate — E-mail: mhourigan@fsb-law.com

Associates

Ann D. Ware — 1969 — University of Virginia, B.A., 1991; University of Baltimore School of Law, J.D. (cum laude), 1995 — Admitted to Bar, 1995, Maryland; 1996, U.S. District Court, District of Maryland; 1998, U.S. Court of Appeals, Fourth Circuit — Member Baltimore County Bar Association; The Bar Association of Baltimore City; Maryland Association of Defense Trial Counsel — E-mail: aware@fsb-law.com

Jocelyn S. Szymanowski — 1978 — University of Baltimore, B.S. (summa cum laude), 2000; Tulane University Law School, J.D., 2003; University of Baltimore School of Law, LL.M., 2005 — Admitted to Bar, 2003, Maryland; 2004, U.S. District Court, District of Maryland — Member Maryland State Bar Association; The Bar Association of Baltimore City — Practice Areas: Banking; Business Law; Real Estate; Estate Planning; Trusts — E-mail: jszymanowski@fsb-law.com

Jonathan D. Nelson — 1983 — Washington University in St. Louis, B.A. (with honors), 2006; University of Maryland School of Law, J.D. (magna cum laude), 2009 — Law Clerk to Hon. Pamela J. White — Admitted to Bar, 2009, Maryland — Member Maryland State Bar Association; The Bar Association of Baltimore City — Practice Areas: Civil Litigation; Insurance Defense — Tel: jnelson@fsb-law.com

Ashley M. Tavantzis — University of Richmond, B.A., 2007; University of Virginia School of Law, J.D., 2010 — Admitted to Bar, 2010, Virginia; 2011, Maryland; 2012, U.S. District Court, Eastern District of Virginia; 2013, U.S. District Court, District of Maryland — Member Maryland State Bar Association; The Bar Association of Baltimore City; Virginia State Bar; Defense Research Institute; Virginia Association of Defense Attorneys; Maryland Association of Defense Trial Counsel — Practice Areas: Civil Litigation; Insurance Defense — E-mail: atavantzis@fsb-law.com

James N. Lewis — University of Delaware, B.S., 2009; Widener University School of Law, J.D., 2012 — Editor-in-Chief, Widener Journal of Law, Economics & Race — Admitted to Bar, 2012, Maryland — Member Maryland State Bar Association; The Bar Association of Baltimore City — Practice Areas: Insurance Defense; Civil Litigation — E-mail: jlewis@fsb-law.com

Daniel S. Baurer — Penn State University, B.S. Business Admin. (with honors), 2009; University of Baltimore School of Law, J.D. (cum laude), 2012 — Admitted to Bar, 2012, Maryland — Member Maryland State Bar Association; The Bar Association of Baltimore City — Practice Areas: General Civil Litigation; Insurance Defense — E-mail: dbaurer@fsb-law.com

Gorman & Williams

36 South Charles Street, Suite 900
Baltimore, Maryland 21201-3754
   Telephone: 410-528-0600
   Fax: 410-528-0602
   E-Mail: attorneys@GandWlaw.com
   www.GandWlaw.com

(Washington, DC Office: 1020 19th Street, N.W., 7th Floor, 20036)
   (Tel: 202-628-0564)
   (Fax: 410-528-0602)

Established: 1995

Gorman & Williams, Baltimore, MD (Continued)

Insurance Defense, Comprehensive General Liability, Commercial Liability, Business Litigation, Business Law, Mergers and Acquisitions, Negligence, Product Liability, Insurance Coverage, Corporate Law, Antitrust, Arbitration, Mediation, Construction Law, Employment Law, Admiralty and Maritime Law, Estate Planning, Commercial Law, Patents, Tradmarks, Copyrights and Technology Licensing and Infringement, Real Property Law, Consumer Protection Law, International Trade, Estate Administration, Executive Liability, Maryland Insurance Administration Regulatory Representation, Securities Litigation

Firm Profile: Gorman & Williams consists of 11 attorneys, 2 law clerks/paralegals, and 5 staff personnel. The firm represents clients throughout the Maryland-Washington D.C. area. In addition to insurance matters, the firm practices corporate and commercial law, intellectual property law, maritime law, and other areas.

Reported cases: *The Provident Bank v. May,* 2012 WL 3995140 (D.Md. 2012); *Cook v. Britton,* 2012 WL 2523385 (D.Md. 2012); *Brooks v. Prestige Fin. Servs., Inc.,* 827 F. Supp. 2d 509 (D. Md. 2011); *Baney Corporation v. Agilysys NV, LLC,* 773 F. Supp.2d 593 (D.Md. 2011); *BTR Hampstead v. Source Interlink,* 194 Md. App. 415 (Md. App. 2010); *Jones v. Koons Auto, Inc.,* 752 F. Supp. 670 (D.Md. 2010); *Bi-Tech North, Inc. v. Lockheed Martin Corp.,* 2005 U.S. App. LEXIS 4026 (4th Cir.), *aff'g,* 2004 U.S. District LEXIS 27606 (D. Md.); *Zervitz v. Hollywood Pictures,* 989 F. Supp. 727 and 995 F. Supp. 596 (D. Md. 1996); *Robinson v. New Line Cinema,* 59 U.S.P.Q. 2d 1150, 211 F.3d 1265, 2000 U.S. App. LEXIS 6848 (4th Cir. 2000), *rev.,* 42 F. Supp. 2d 578 (D.Md. 1999); *John Wilkes Booth Exhumation Petition,* 110 Md. App. 383 (1996); *Dietrich v. Key Bank,* 72 F.3d 1509 (11th Cir. 1996); *Leading Edge Tech. v. Sun Automation,* 23 U.S.P.Q. 2d 1161 (1990); *O'Well Novelty Co. v. Offenbacher, Inc.,* 225 F.3d 655, 2000 WL 1055108 (4th Cir. 2000); *Carney Family Inv. Trust v. Insurance Co. of North America,* 296 F. Supp. 2d 629 (D. Md. 2004)

Insurance Clients

Allianz Global Corporate & Specialty
Eastern Insurance Holdings, Inc.
Foremost Insurance Company
Lexington Insurance Company
Maryland Casualty Company
Northern Insurance Company of New York
Selective Insurance Company of America
21st Century Insurance Company

Balboa Insurance Company
Bristol West Insurance Group
Farmers Insurance Company
Great American Insurance Company
North American Specialty Insurance Company
St. Paul Fire and Marine Insurance Company
Truck Insurance Exchange

Non-Insurance Clients

American Cruise Lines, Inc.
Chemed Corporation/Roto-Rooter

Partners

Charles L. Simmons Jr. — 1967 — Towson State University, B.S., 1992; University of Baltimore, J.D. (magna cum laude), 1996 — Admitted to Bar, 1996, Maryland; 1997, District of Columbia; 1996, U.S. District Court, District of Maryland; 1999, U.S. Court of Appeals, Fourth Circuit; 2014, U.S. District Court for the District of Columbia — Member American and Maryland State Bar Associations; The Bar Association of Baltimore City; Mid-Atlantic Mariner's Club (Past-President, Marine Insurance); Wednesday Law Club; The Maritime Law Association of the United States — Author: "Business Insurance Targets Risks Posed by New Technology," Maryland Bar Journal, Jan./Feb. 2005; "Digital Distribution of Entertainment Content...A Battle is Being Waged," Maryland Bar Journal July/August 2000 — Adjunct Professor, University of Baltimore School of Law, Admiralty and Maritime Law; Lecturer, National Business Institute

Francis J. Gorman — 1942 — Georgetown University School of Foreign Service, B.S.F.S., 1963; Georgetown University Law Center, J.D., 1969 — Law Clerk to Chief Judge Roszel C. Thomsen, U.S. District Court — Board of Editors, Geo. L. Rev. — Admitted to Bar, 1970, Maryland; 1974, District of Columbia; U.S. District Court, District of Maryland; U.S. Court of Appeals, Fourth Circuit; 1977, U.S. Supreme Court; 1985, U.S. Court of Appeals for the Federal Circuit — Member American Bar Association; Maryland State Bar Association (Board of Governors, 1984-1986; Chair, Intellectual Property Committee, 1999-2000); The Bar Association of Baltimore City; Fellow, Maryland Bar Foundation; Fellow, Baltimore Bar Foundation; American College of Trial Lawyers — Author: "Evolving Standards of Care—Technology Meets Professional Responsibility," 2005; Co-Author: "Intellectual Property 2012"; "Local Counsel—Duties and Responsibilities," 2001; "Negligent Settlement Recommendations," 2004 — Reported Cases: GWW Associates, LLC v. Flagship Atlanta Dairy, LLC et al., Court of Chancery of Delaware, Civil Action 4141-VCL (suit by minority members derivative and direct suit for breaches of fiduciary duties, subordination and/or re-characterization of debt, and redemption of preferred units (2012); Baney Corporation v. Agilysys NV, LLC, U.S. District Court for the District of Maryland, 773 F.Supp.2d 593 (2011) (suit against developer and licensor of property management software seeking recovery in tort and contract, including for alleged breach of warranty in written licensing agreement); Pizzorno v. L-Soft International, Inc. et al., U.S. District Court for the District of Maryland, 2008 WL5082105, 2008 Copr.L.Dec. P 29,665, 302Fed.Appx. 148 (4th Cir. 2008) (affirming judgment for Pizzorno after successful three week-jury trial resulting in $5.2 million verdict for copyright infringement)(related litigation against defendant's insurer). — Adjunct Faculty, University of Baltimore Law School (Maritime Law Litigation Process and Maryland Procedure); Lecturer, Judicial Institute of Maryland; Maryland Bar Association Lee Caplan Pro Bono Award (2005) — Lieutenant, U.S. Army

David McI. Williams — 1949 — Princeton University, A.B., 1971; Georgetown University, J.D., 1975 — Admitted to Bar, 1975, Maryland; 1984, District of Columbia; 1976, U.S. District Court, District of Maryland; 1982, U.S. Court of Appeals, Fourth Circuit; 1984, U.S. District Court for the District of Columbia; 1986, U.S. Court of Appeals, Third Circuit; 1988, U.S. Court of Appeals for the Federal Circuit; 1994, U.S. Court of Appeals, Eleventh Circuit — Member American Bar Association (Advisor, National Conference of Commissioners on Uniform State Laws; Drafting Committee on Uniform Certificate of Title for Vessels, 2009-2011); Maryland State Bar Association (Board of Governors, 2011-2013; Co-Chair, Business Courts Litigation Committee, 2012-present; Business Section Council, 2010-present); The Bar Association of Baltimore City (Chair, Business Law Committee, 2009-present); Fellow, Maryland Bar Foundation; Fellow, Baltimore Bar Foundation; The Maritime Law Association of the United States (Chair, Marine Financing Committee, 1992-1996) — Author: "2 Benedict on Admiralty", (Chapter 11); Moore's Federal Practice Third Edition (Admiralty Volume Chapter 5) — Practice Areas: Admiralty and Maritime Law; Business Law; Business Transactions; Civil Litigation

Martin B. King — 1964 — University of Maryland, B.S., 1986; University of Baltimore, J.D., 1993 — Admitted to Bar, 1993, Maryland — Member American and Maryland State Bar Associations; American Institute of Certified Public Accountants; Maryland Association of Certified Public Accountants

Associates

Angela D. Sheehan — 1962 — University of Dayton, B.A. (summa cum laude), 1984; Georgetown University Law Center, J.D. (cum laude), 1987 — Admitted to Bar, 1987, California; 1989, District of Columbia; 1993, Maryland; 1989, U.S. District Court for the District of Columbia; 2004, U.S. District Court, District of Maryland — Member Maryland State Bar Association

Razvan E. Miutescu — 1979 — Hiram College, B.A. (cum laude), 2002; University of Maryland, Baltimore County, M.A., 2003; University of Notre Dame Law School, J.D., 2006 — Admitted to Bar, 2006, Maryland; 2007, U.S. District Court, District of Maryland — Member American and Maryland State Bar Associations; The Bar Association of Baltimore City; US-Romanian Business Council (Executive Vice-President); Maryland Volunteer Lawyers for the Arts (Board of Directors); Global Romanian Association of Young Professionals (Project Manager) — Co-Author: "Vessel Excise Tax," Maryland Taxes 4th Ed., MICPEL 1969 — Languages: German, Romanian

Michael R. Naccarato — 1969 — University of Baltimore, Merrick School of Business, B.A., 1992; M.B.A., 1995; University of Baltimore School of Law, J.D. (cum laude), 2008 — Admitted to Bar, 2008, Maryland; 2010, District of Columbia; 2009, U.S. District Court, District of Maryland — Member Maryland State Bar Association; The Bar Association of Baltimore City — Practice Areas: Civil Litigation; Business Formation; Business Transactions; Estate Planning

Sara H. Deriu — 1980 — Gettysburg College, B.A. (cum laude), 2002; University of Maryland School of Law, J.D., 2007 — Admitted to Bar, 2007, Maryland — Member Maryland State and Baltimore County Bar Associations — Reported Cases: Grady v. Brown 408 Md. 182 (2009) — Practice Areas: Insurance Defense; Civil Litigation

James R. Jeffcoat — 1983 — Maine Maritime Academy, B.S. (cum laude), 2005; University of Baltimore School of Law, J.D. (summa cum laude), 2012 — Heuisler Honor Society — Admitted to Bar, 2012, Maryland; 2013, U.S. District Court, District of Maryland — Member Maryland State Bar Association — Maryland Real Estate Agent — Practice Areas: Admiralty and Maritime Law; Civil Litigation; Insurance Coverage & Defense

BALTIMORE   MARYLAND

Gorman & Williams, Baltimore, MD   (Continued)

Wayne H. Xu — 1984 — University of Maryland, College Park, B.S. (distinguished graduate), 2002-2005; West Virginia University College of Law, J.D., 2006-2009 — Admitted to Bar, 2010, West Virginia; 2012, Maryland — Member American, Maryland State and West Virginia Bar Associations — Languages: Taiwanese, Chinese, English — Practice Areas: Business Litigation; Business Transactions; Commercial Law; Commercial Litigation; Insurance Defense

Sonia Cho — 1974 — Binghamton University, B.S. Biology (with honors), 1997; University of Maryland School of Law, J.D. (with honors), 2002 — Fulbright Fellowship, Erlangen, Germany 1997-1998 — University of Maryland Law Review — Admitted to Bar, 2002, Maryland — Member American and Maryland State Bar Associations — Languages: German, Korean — Practice Areas: Business Litigation; Commercial Insurance; Commercial Law; Commercial Litigation; Contract Litigation; Insurance Defense

(This firm is also listed in the Subrogation section of this directory)

Karpinski, Colaresi & Karp

120 East Baltimore Street
Suite 1850
Baltimore, Maryland 21202-1605
  Telephone: 410-727-5000
  Fax: 410-727-0861
  E-Mail: bkcklaw@aol.com
  www.kcklegal.com

Established: 1989

Insurance Defense, Automobile, Coverage Issues, General Liability, Product Liability, Civil Rights, Appellate Practice, Election Law

Firm Profile: Karpinski, Colaresi & Karp, founded in 1970, provides legal services in the defense of liability claims for the insurance, business & political communities. Areas of expertise include litigation, local government defense, municipal law, product liability, premises liability, construction, employment law, torts & civil rights defense in all federal & state courts in Maryland & DC. The firm serves a client base that includes some of the nation's largest insurance carriers, business & municipal self insurance pools.

Insurance Clients

Acceptance Insurance Company	Admiral Insurance Company
GAB Robins North America, Inc.	Hallmark Insurance Company
Hiscox Inc.	Lancer Insurance Company
MAPFRE USA Insurance	National General Insurance Company
Nationwide Insurance	
Nautilus Insurance Company	Scottsdale Insurance Company
T.H.E. Insurance Company	Transit Insurance Group
Travelers Insurance	Vela Insurance Services, Inc./Gemini Insurance Company

Non-Insurance Clients

City of District Heights	City of Frederick
City of Hyattsville	Local Government Insurance Trust
Montgomery County Board of Elections	Office of Sheriff for St. Mary's County
Prince George's County	Town of Bladensburg
Town of Cheverly	Town of Landover Hills
Town of Rising Sun	Town of Snow Hill

Partners

Daniel Karp — 1950 — Duke University, B.A. (with honors), 1973; University of Maryland, J.D. (with honors), 1976 — Admitted to Bar, 1976, Maryland; 1990, District of Columbia; 1976, U.S. District Court, District of Maryland; 1990, U.S. District Court for the District of Columbia; U.S. Court of Appeals for the Federal and District of Columbia Circuits; 2002, U.S. Supreme Court — Member American and Maryland State Bar Associations; The Bar Association of Baltimore City; The District of Columbia Bar; American Judicature Society; International Association of Defense Counsel — Practice Areas: Public Officials Liability; Civil Rights; Civil Litigation; Municipal Liability; Amusements; Appellate Practice; Sexual Harassment; Employment Discrimination; Employment Litigation; Automobile Liability; Automobile Tort; Automobile; Business Litigation; Casualty Defense; Catastrophic Injury; Commercial General Liability; Common Carrier; Complex Litigation;

Karpinski, Colaresi & Karp, Baltimore, MD   (Continued)

Comprehensive General Liability; Construction Litigation; Coverage Issues; Discrimination; Examinations Under Oath; General Liability; Government Affairs; Governmental Entity Defense; Insurance Coverage; Insurance Law; Intentional Torts; Land Use; Litigation; Personal Injury; Property Damage; Property Liability; Public Liability; Automotive Products Liability; Casualty Insurance Law; Civil Trial Practice; Commercial Vehicle; Construction Accidents; Construction Law; Coverage Analysis; Declaratory Judgments; Employer Liability; Employment Law; Employment Practices Liability; Errors and Omissions; Fire Loss; General Defense; Governmental Defense; Governmental Liability; Insurance Defense; Insurance Litigation; Jail/Prison Defense; Law Enforcement Liability; Municipal Law; Negligence; Opinions; Property and Casualty; Property Loss; Accident — E-mail: brunokarp@aol.com

Kevin B. Karpinski — 1968 — Frostburg State University, B.S. (with honors), 1990; University of Baltimore School of Law, J.D., 1993 — Admitted to Bar, 1993, District of Columbia; 1994, Maryland; U.S. District Court, District of Maryland; U.S. Court of Appeals, Third and Fourth Circuits — Member American, Maryland State and Montgomery County Bar Associations; The Bar Association of Baltimore City — Practice Areas: Public Officials Liability; Civil Rights; Civil Litigation; Municipal Liability; Amusements; Appellate Practice; Sexual Harassment; Employment Discrimination; Employment Litigation; Automobile Liability; Automobile Tort; Automobile; Business Litigation; Casualty Defense; Catastrophic Injury; Commercial General Liability; Common Carrier; Complex Litigation; Comprehensive General Liability; Construction Litigation; Coverage Issues; Discrimination; Examinations Under Oath; General Liability; Government Affairs; Governmental Entity Defense; Insurance Coverage; Insurance Law; Intentional Torts; Land Use; Litigation; Personal Injury; Property Damage; Property Liability; Public Liability; Automotive Products Liability; Casualty Insurance Law; Civil Trial Practice; Commercial Vehicle; Construction Accidents; Construction Law; Coverage Analysis; Declaratory Judgments; Employer Liability; Employment Law; Employment Practices Liability; Errors and Omissions; Fire Loss; General Defense; Governmental Defense; Governmental Liability; Insurance Defense; Insurance Litigation; Jail/Prison Defense; Law Enforcement Liability; Municipal Law; Negligence; Opinions; Property and Casualty; Property Loss; Accident — E-mail: kevin@bkcklaw.com

Richard T. Colaresi — 1944 — Stonehill College, B.A. (cum laude), 1966; University of Baltimore, J.D., 1978 — Admitted to Bar, 1978, Maryland; 1980, U.S. District Court, District of Maryland; 1991, U.S. Court of Appeals, Fourth Circuit — Member International Municipal Lawyers Association — Practice Areas: Administrative Law; Civil Rights; Land Use; Contract Disputes; Eminent Domain; Employment Discrimination; Government Affairs; Municipal Law; Municipal Liability — E-mail: rcolaresi@bkcklaw.com

Victoria M. Shearer — 1968 — Villanova University, B.A., 1990; University of Baltimore, J.D., 1996 — Admitted to Bar, 1996, Maryland; 2006, District of Columbia; 2000, U.S. District Court, District of Maryland; 2001, U.S. Court of Appeals, Fourth Circuit; 2003, U.S. District Court for the District of Columbia — Member American and Maryland State Bar Associations; The District of Columbia Bar; Defense Research Institute — Practice Areas: Appellate Practice; Civil Litigation; Civil Rights Defense; Election Law; Employment Discrimination; Employment Law; Employment Litigation; Federal Anti-Discrimination Defense and Litigation; Governmental Defense; Governmental Liability; Insurance Defense; Land Use; Municipal Law; Planning and Zoning Litigation; Police Liability Defense; Police Liability Litigation; Public Officials Defense — E-mail: vshearer@bkcklaw.com

Associates

Sandra D. Lee	Michael B. Rynd
J. Michael Colliton	Ernest I. Cornbrooks, IV
Nina M. Baek	

Kramer & Connolly

465 Main Street
Reisterstown, Maryland 21136
  Telephone: 410-581-0070
  Fax: 410-581-1524
  E-Mail: law@KramersLaw.com
  www.KramersLaw.com

Casualty, Automobile, Errors and Omissions, Professional Liability, Construction Defect, Coverage/SIU

MARYLAND **BALTIMORE**

Kramer & Connolly, Baltimore, MD (Continued)

Firm Profile: Defending carriers and their insureds in state and federal courts throughout Maryland and Washington, DC. A recognized leader in Alternative Fee Arrangements, we take pride in client service, use cutting-edge technology to enhance efficiency, and recognize that our professionalism and effectiveness reflects on the quality of the carriers we serve.

Insurance Clients

Crum & Forster Insurance   Northland Insurance Company

Managing Attorney

Irwin R. Kramer — Towson University, B.A., 1984; University of Maryland, J.D., 1987; Columbia University, LL.M., 1989 — Admitted to Bar, 1987, Maryland; 1989, District of Columbia

Partner

James M. Connolly

Of Counsel

Edward J. Hiller

Niles, Barton & Wilmer, LLP

111 South Calvert Street, Suite 1400
Baltimore, Maryland 21202
  Telephone: 410-783-6300
  Fax: 410-783-6363
  E-Mail: info@nilesbarton.com
  www.nilesbarton.com

Established: 1838

Admiralty and Maritime Law, Alternative Dispute Resolution, Commercial Litigation, Construction Law, Employment Practices Liability, Insurance Coverage, Insurance Defense, Intellectual Property, Professional Liability, Property, Subrogation, Transportation, Appellate Law

Firm Profile: Niles Barton counsels insurance companies, brokers and businesses regarding property insurance, claims, coverage, and defense. Our attorneys have substantial experience investigating and litigating insurance matters, including various coverage issues, first party and third party defense, and fraud.

Insurance Clients

Atrium Underwriters Limited at Lloyd's of London
Catholic Mutual Group
Progressive Insurance Company
Southern Insurance Company of Virginia
Brethren Mutual Insurance Company
Local Government Insurance Trust Fund

Managing Partner

Craig D. Roswell — Loyola College in Maryland, B.A., 1988; University of Baltimore School of Law, J.D., 1991 — Admitted to Bar, 1991, Maryland; 1992, Virginia; District of Columbia; U.S. District Court, District of Maryland; U.S. District Court, Eastern District of Virginia; 1994, U.S. District Court for the District of Columbia; U.S. Court of Appeals, Fourth Circuit; 2000, U.S. District Court, Western District of Virginia; U.S. Bankruptcy Court, Eastern District of Virginia — Tel: 410-783-6341 — E-mail: cdroswell@nilesbarton.com

Partner

Jeffrey A. Wothers — University of Maryland, B.A., 1988; Widener University School of Law, J.D., 1991 — Admitted to Bar, 1991, Maryland; 1992, District of Columbia; 2000, Pennsylvania; 2008, West Virginia; 1992, U.S. District Court, District of Maryland; U.S. Court of Appeals, Fourth Circuit; 1994, U.S. District Court for the District of Columbia; U.S. Court of Appeals for the District of Columbia Circuit; 2000, U.S. District Court, Eastern and Middle Districts of Pennsylvania; U.S. Court of Appeals, Third Circuit; 2003, U.S.

Niles, Barton & Wilmer, LLP, Baltimore, MD (Continued)

District Court, Western District of Pennsylvania; 2008, U.S. District Court, Northern and Southern Districts of West Virginia — Tel: 410-783-6365 — E-mail: jawothers@nilesbarton.com

Pessin Katz Law, P.A.

901 Dulaney Valley Road
Suite 400
Towson, Maryland 21204
  Telephone: 410-938-8800
  Fax: 410-832-5600
  E-Mail: plambert@pklaw.com
  www.pklaw.com

(Columbia, MD Office: 10500 Little Patuxent Parkway, Suite 650, 21044)
  (Tel: 410-740-2000, 301-596-1717)
  (Fax: 410-740-2005)
(Bel Air, MD Office: 139 North Main Street, Suite 100, 21014)
  (Tel: 410-893-0100)
  (Fax: 410-893-0795)

Established: 1988

Insurance Defense, Coverage Issues, Regulatory and Compliance, Administrative Law, Agent and Brokers Errors and Omissions, Disability, Business Law, Construction Law, Class Actions

Insurance Clients

AAA Mid-Atlantic Insurance Company
Ascension Health
Assurant Insurance Group
Church Mutual Insurance Company
CUNA Mutual Group
Everett Cash Mutual Insurance Company
The Hartford
HDI-Gerling America Insurance Company
Markel Insurance Company of Canada
The Medical Protective Company
MEEMIC Insurance Company
Merastar Insurance Company
OneBeacon Insurance
Scottsdale Insurance Company
Allstate Insurance Company
Arbella Mutual Insurance Company
AXA Global Risks (UK) Ltd.
CUMIS Insurance Society, Inc.
The Doctors Company
Grange Insurance Company
Harford Mutual Insurance Companies
Kingsway General Insurance Company
Maryland Medicine Comprehensive Insurance Program
Meloche Monnex
Nationwide Mutual Insurance Company
Zurich American Insurance Company

Non-Insurance Clients

A.I. Transport
American Crane and Equipment Corporation
The ASU Group
John H. Camlin Company
Cedar Fair, LLC
Cowan Systems, LLC
DavCo Restaurants, Inc.
Foot Locker
General Mills, Inc.
GMAC-RFC
Johns Hopkins University
Media Associates, Inc.
Missouri Guaranty Association
Patient First
Quality Carriers, Inc.
REM - Supervalu, Inc.
University of Maryland Medical Systems
Weyerhaeuser Company
A.I. Transport Canada
American Golf Corporation
Apogee Enterprises, Inc.
Baxter Healthcare Corporation
Carlson Restaurants
City of Baltimore
Crawford & Company
Domino's Pizza, LLC
GatesMcDonald
Genesis HealthCare
Johns Hopkins Health System
Knight Transportation, Inc.
Mercy Health Services
PACCAR, Inc.
Performance Food Group
Randa Corporation
Sid Harvey Industries, Inc
Upper Chesapeake Health
Venator Group

Members

Barry Bach — University of Maryland, B.A., 1964; J.D., 1969 — Omicron Delta Kappa — Admitted to Bar, 1969, Maryland; U.S. District Court, District of Maryland; U.S. Court of Appeals, Fourth and Seventh Circuits — Member American, Maryland State (Former Chair, Litigation Section Council; Judicial Appointments Committee) and Baltimore County Bar Associations — Attorney Grievance Commission; Review Board of the Attorney Grievance Commission Peer Review Panel, 1986-1990; Court of Appeals

BALTIMORE   MARYLAND

Pessin Katz Law, P.A., Baltimore, MD   (Continued)

Character Committee (1995-present); Governor's Commission on Juvenile Justice; Judicial Conference of the Fourth Circuit — E-mail: bbach@pklaw.com

Patricia McHugh Lambert — The University of North Carolina, B.A., 1979; Wake Forest University, J.D. (cum laude), 1982 — Admitted to Bar, 1982, Maryland; 1983, U.S. District Court, District of Maryland; U.S. Court of Appeals, Fourth Circuit; 1990, U.S. Court of Appeals for the District of Columbia Circuit; U.S. Supreme Court — Member Maryland Automobile Insurance Fund (Former Chair); Injured Worker's Insurance Fund (Board) — E-mail: plambert@pklaw.com

Natalie C. Magdeburger — Duke University, A.B. (cum laude), 1984; University of Maryland School of Law, J.D., 1987 — Admitted to Bar, 1987, Maryland; U.S. District Court, District of Maryland — Member American and Maryland State Bar Associations; Maryland Defense Counsel; Maryland Society of Healtcare Risk Management; Defense Research Institute — E-mail: nmagdeburger@pklaw.com

Catherine W. Steiner — Tufts University, B.A., 1986; College of William & Mary, Marshall-Wythe School of Law, J.D., 1991 — Admitted to Bar, 1991, Maryland; 1992, U.S. District Court, District of Maryland; 2007, U.S. Court of Appeals, Fourth Circuit — Member American and Maryland State Bar Associations; Maryland Defense Counsel; Maryland Society for Healthcare Risk Management; Defense Research Institute; Fellow, American College of Trial Lawyers — E-mail: csteiner@pklaw.com

Mairi Pat Maguire — The Catholic University of America, B.S.N. (magna cum laude), 1983; University of Baltimore, J.D. (cum laude) 1992 — Admitted to Bar, 1992, Maryland; 1994, District of Columbia; 1992, U.S. District Court, District of Maryland — Member American and Maryland State Bar Associations; Maryland Society for Healthcare Risk Management; Maryland Defense Counsel; Defense Research Institute — E-mail: mpmaguire@pklaw.com

Robert S. Campbell — Towson University, B.A., 1994; University of Baltimore School of Law, J.D. (cum laude), 1998 — Admitted to Bar, 1998, Maryland; U.S. District Court, District of Maryland; U.S. Court of Appeals, Fourth Circuit — E-mail: rcampbell@pklaw.com

James R. Benjamin, Jr. — University of Maryland, College Park, B.A., 1994; University of Maryland, J.D., 2001 — Admitted to Bar, 2002, Maryland; 2003, U.S. District Court, District of Maryland — Member Maryland State and Baltimore County Bar Associations; The Bar Association of Baltimore City; University of Maryland School of Law Alumni Association (Board Member); Fellow, Maryland Bar Foundation — Board of Visitors of the College of Behavorial and Social Sciences at University of Maryland-College Park (Board Member); Pro Bono Resource Center of Maryland (Board Member) — E-mail: jbenjamin@pklaw.com

Elliott D. Petty — The University of Utah, B.A., 1999; Brigham Young University, J.D. (magna cum laude), 2002 — Admitted to Bar, 2002, Maryland; 2007, U.S. District Court, District of Maryland — Member Baltimore County Bar Association; Maryland State Bar Ethics Committee — E-mail: epetty@pklaw.com

Joan Cerniglia-Lowensen — St. Joseph's Hospital School of Nursing, 1979; University of Maryland School of Nursing, 1981; University of Maryland Graduate School, 1981; University of Maryland School of Law, J.D., 1992 — Sigma Theta Tau — Admitted to Bar, 1992, Maryland; 1993, District of Columbia; U.S. District Court, District of Maryland; Supreme Court of the United States — Member Women's Bar Association; American Society of Healthcare Risk Managers; Maryland Society of Healthcare Risk Managers; Association of Nurse Attorneys; Counsel on Litigation Management; American Veterinary Medical Law Association; Fellow, Litigation Counsel of America — E-mail: jclowensen@pklaw.com

Semmes, Bowen & Semmes
A Professional Corporation

25 South Charles Street, Suite 1400
Baltimore, Maryland 21201
   Telephone: 410-539-5040
   Fax: 410-539-5223
   E-Mail: semmes@semmes.com
   www.semmes.com

(Vienna, VA Office: 1577 Spring Hill Road, Suite 200, 22182)
   (Tel: 703-760-9473)
   (Fax: 703-442-7538)
(Hagerstown, MD Office: 322 East Antietam Street, Suite 102, 21221)
   (Tel: 301-739-4558)
   (Fax: 301-739-9316)

Semmes, Bowen & Semmes, A Professional Corporation, Baltimore, MD   (Continued)

(Washington, DC Office: 1025 Connecticut Avenue N.W., Suite 1000, 20036)
   (Tel: 202-822-8258)
   (Fax: 202-293-2649)
(Charles Town, WV Office: 116 West Washington Street, Suite 2E, 25414)
   (Tel: 301-739-4558)
   (Fax: 304-596-6207)
(Salisbury, MD Office: 231 West Main Street, Suite 202, 21801)
   (Tel: 410-749-1710)
   (Fax: 410-860-2856)

Established: 1887

Alternative Dispute Resolution, Business Litigation, Construction Litigation, Corporate Governance, Creditor Rights, Environmental Law, Estate Planning, Insurance Coverage, Insurance Defense, Insurance Regulation, Labor and Employment, Litigation, Lobbying, Maritime Law, Product Liability, Professional Liability, Real Estate, Self-Insured Defense, Toxic Torts, Transportation, Workers' Compensation, Small Business Investment

Insurance Clients

ACE USA	AIG
American Home Assurance Company	Broadspire
Chubb Group of Insurance Companies	Chesapeake Employers Insurance Fund
Federal Insurance Company	The Cincinnati Insurance Companies
Gallagher Bassett Services, Inc.	Great American Insurance Company - Environmental & Health Hazard Claims Department
GUARD Insurance Group	
Insurance Company of the State of Pennsylvania	
Liberty Mutual Insurance Company	Maryland Medicine Comprehensive Insurance Program
National Union Fire Insurance Company	
RCM&D Self-Insured Services Company, Inc.	St. Paul Travelers Insurance Companies
Sedgwick Claims Management Services, Inc.	Specialty Risk Services, Inc. (SRS)
Zurich American Insurance Company	UNUM Life Insurance Company of America

Principals

James W. Bartlett III — Vanderbilt University, J.D., 1975 — Admitted to Bar, 1975, Maryland — Editorial Board of the Journal of Maritime Law, Maritime Law Association — Tel: 410-576-4833 — E-mail: jbartlett@semmes.com

Barry D. Bernstein — University of Maryland School of Law, J.D., 2004 — Admitted to Bar, 2005, Maryland; 2011, District of Columbia — Tel: 410-385-3943 — E-mail: bbernstein@semmes.com

Paul N. Farquharson — University of Virginia, J.D., 1987 — Admitted to Bar, 1987, Maryland — Tel: 410-576-4742 — E-mail: pfarquharson@semmes.com

James R. Forrester — University of Baltimore School of Law, J.D. (cum laude), 1998 — Admitted to Bar, 1999, Maryland; 2000, District of Columbia — Tel: 410-576-4812 — E-mail: jforrester@semmes.com

Alan N. Gamse — University of Maryland School of Law, LL.B., 1967 — Admitted to Bar, 1967, Maryland; 1982, District of Columbia — Member International Association of Insurance Receivers — Special Deputy Insurance Commissioner of the District of Columbia for the Liquidations of Atlantic and Pacific International Assurance Co. and Capital Casualty Insurance Company — Tel: 410-576-4734 — E-mail: agamse@semmes.com

Joseph F. Giordano — William & Mary School of Law, J.D., 1983 — Admitted to Bar, 1983, Virginia; 1984, District of Columbia; 1985, Maryland — Member Association of Compensation and Insurance Attorneys — Tel: 703-288-2527 — E-mail: jgiordano@semmes.com

Thomas G. Hagerty — American University, Washington College of Law, J.D., 1978 — Admitted to Bar, 1978, District of Columbia; 1987, Maryland — Member Association of Compensation Insurance Attorneys — Tel: 703-288-2536 — E-mail: thagerty@semmes.com

Robert L. Hebb — University of Baltimore School of Law, J.D., 1993 — Admitted to Bar, 1993, Maryland; 1996, District of Columbia — Tel: 410.576.4862 — E-mail: rhebb@semmes.com

MARYLAND — BALTIMORE

Semmes, Bowen & Semmes, A Professional Corporation, Baltimore, MD (Continued)

Brett S. Lininger — University of Baltimore School of Law, J.D. (cum laude), 2005 — Admitted to Bar, 2007, Maryland — Tel: 410-576-4815 — E-mail: blininger@semmes.com

Thomas V. McCarron — University of Maryland School of Law, J.D. (with honors), 1990 — Admitted to Bar, 1990, Maryland; 2000, District of Columbia — Tel: 410-576-4854 — E-mail: tmccarron@semmes.com

Stephen S. McCloskey — University of Maryland, J.D. (summa cum laude), 1987 — Admitted to Bar, 1987, Maryland; 2000, District of Columbia — Tel: 410-576-4842 — E-mail: smccloskey@semmes.com

J. Marks Moore III — Tulane University, J.D. (cum laude), 1981 — Admitted to Bar, 1982, Maryland — Tel: 410-576-4722 — E-mail: mmoore@semmes.com

Joel E. Ogden — University of Maryland, J.D., 1998 — Admitted to Bar, 1998, Maryland; 2000, District of Columbia — Tel: 410-576-4727 — E-mail: jogden@semmes.com

Scott H. Phillips — Columbus School of Law, J.D., 1992 — Admitted to Bar, 1994, Pennsylvania; 1995, Maryland; 1997, District of Columbia — Tel: 410-576-4717 — E-mail: sphillips@semmes.com

Robert E. Rockwell — Dickinson School of Law, J.D., 1984 — Admitted to Bar, 1987, Maryland; 2008, West Virginia — Tel: 301-766-7742 — E-mail: rrockwell@semmes.com

Rudolph L. Rose — The Catholic University of America, Columbus School of Law, J.D., 1973 — Admitted to Bar, 1973, Maryland — Tel: 410-576-4721 — E-mail: rrose@semmes.com

Richard W. Scheiner — Chairman — University of Baltimore, J.D., 1981 — Admitted to Bar, 1981, Maryland — Tel: 410-576-4831 — E-mail: rscheiner@semmes.com

Robert E. Scott, Jr. — Georgetown University Law Center, J.D., 1970 — Admitted to Bar, 1970, Maryland; 1980, District of Columbia — Tel: 410-576-4725 — E-mail: rscott@semmes.com

Sean E. Smith — Widener University School of Law, J.D., 2000 — Admitted to Bar, 2000, New Jersey; 2002, New York; 2004, Maryland — Tel: 410-576-4792 — E-mail: ssmith@semmes.com

J. Snowden Stanley, Jr. — Georgetown University, J.D., 1967 — Admitted to Bar, 1967, Maryland; 1982, District of Columbia — Tel: 410-576-4811 — E-mail: jstanley@semmes.com

Joseph C. Tarpine — Dickinson School of Law, J.D., 1997 — Admitted to Bar, 1998, New Jersey; 2000, Maryland; 2000, District of Columbia — Tel: 410-576-4736 — E-mail: jtarpine@semmes.com

Scott M. Trager — University of Baltimore School of Law, J.D. (magna cum laude), 1998 — Admitted to Bar, 1988, Maryland; 1999, District of Columbia — Tel: 410-576-4846 — E-mail: strager@semmes.com

Anthony Zaccagnini — University of Baltimore School of Law, J.D., 1986 — Admitted to Bar, 1987, Maryland; 1987, District of Columbia — Tel: 410-576-4781 — E-mail: azaccagnini@semmes.com

JoAnne Zawitowski — Georgetown University Law Center, J.D., 1980 — Admitted to Bar, 1981, Maryland — Tel: 410-576-4899 — E-mail: jzawitowski@semmes.com

Andrew M. Alexander	Christina Bolmarcich
Donald F. Burke	Anthony J. D'Alessandro
James R. Forrester	Larry G. Giambelluca
Alexander M. Giles	R. Michael Haynes
Stan M. Haynes	James A. Johnson
William H. Kable	Heather H. Kraus
Stuart M. Lesser	James S. Maloney
John A. Roberts	Kenneth M. Shaffrey
Patrick E. Tedesco	Marisa A. Trasatti
Christopher R. West	Jane A. Wilson

Whiteford, Taylor & Preston L.L.P.

Seven Saint Paul Street
Baltimore, Maryland 21202-1636
  Telephone: 410-347-8700
  Toll Free: 800-987-8705
  Fax: 410-752-7092
  E-Mail: info@wtplaw.com
  www.wtplaw.com

Whiteford, Taylor & Preston L.L.P., Baltimore, MD (Continued)

(Towson, MD Office: 1 West Pennsylvania Avenue, Suite 300, 21204-5025)
  (Tel: 410-832-2000)
  (Fax: 410-832-2015)
(Columbia, MD Office: 10500 Little Patuxent Parkway, Suite 750, 21044-3585)
  (Tel: 410-884-0700)
  (Fax: 410-884-0719)
(Falls Church, VA Office: 3190 Fairview Park Drive, Suite 300, 22042-4510)
  (Tel: 703-836-5742)
  (Fax: 703-573-1287)
(Washington, DC Office*: 1025 Connecticut Avenue, N.W., 20036-5405)
  (Tel: 202-659-6800)
  (Fax: 202-331-0573)
(Wilmington, DE Office: The Renaissance Centre, Suite 500, 405 North King Street, 19801-3700)
  (Tel: 302-353-4144)
  (Fax: 302-661-7950)
(Bethesda, MD Office: 7501 Wisconsin Avenue, Suite 700W, 20814)
  (Tel: 301-804-3610)
  (Fax: 301-215-6359)
(Dearborn, MI Office: Fairlane Plaza North, 290 Town Center Drive, Suite 324, 48126)
  (Tel: 313-406-5759)
  (Fax: 313-406-5840)
(Roanoke, VA Office: 114 Market Street, Suite 210, 24011)
  (Tel: 540-759-3560)
  (Fax: 540-759-3569)
(Lexington, KY Office: 120 Prosperous Place, Suite 100, 40509)
  (Tel: 859-687-6700)
  (Fax: 859-263-3239)
(Betheny Beach, DE Office: 209 Fifth Street, Suite 200, 19930)
  (Tel: 302-829-3040)
  (Fax: 302-829-3041)

Established: 1933

General Liability, Casualty, Directors and Officers Liability, Fire, Surety, Malpractice, Product Liability, Insurance Coverage, Environmental Law, Toxic Torts, Wrongful Termination, Intellectual Property, Professional Liability

Firm Profile: We have a long history representing commercial insureds in claims arising out of general negligence, professional liability, premises liability, product liability, employment practices, environmental impairment, errors and omissions, fiduciary liability, toxic tort, workers compensation, and others.

Insurance Clients

Allstate Insurance Company	American International Group, Inc.
CNA Insurance Companies	Continental Casualty Company
Federal Insurance Company	Fidelity and Deposit Company of Maryland
General Accident Insurance Company	Great American Insurance Company
Kemper Insurance Companies	Metropolitan Property and Casualty Insurance Company
Liberty Mutual Insurance Company	Ohio Casualty Group
National American Insurance Company	Penn National Insurance
Old Republic Surety Company	TIG Insurance Company
Reliance Surety Company	
Western Surety Company	

Non-Insurance Clients

Continental Guaranty and Credit Corporation	Leizure Associates, Inc.

Partners

Steven E. Bers — 1953 — Johns Hopkins University, B.A., 1975; University of Maryland, J.D., 1978 — Admitted to Bar, 1978, Maryland — Member Federal and Maryland State (Labor Law Section) Bar Associations; The Bar Association of Baltimore City

Edward M. Buxbaum — 1958 — Tufts University, B.S., 1980; American University, Washington College of Law, J.D., 1984 — Admitted to Bar, 1985,

BALTIMORE

MARYLAND

Whiteford, Taylor & Preston L.L.P., Baltimore, MD (Continued)

Maryland; 1987, District of Columbia — Member American, Maryland State and Baltimore County Bar Associations; The District of Columbia Bar

Robert F. Carney — 1961 — Haverford College, B.A., 1983; University of Maryland, J.D., 1990 — Admitted to Bar, 1990, Maryland; 1993, District of Columbia — Member American Bar Association; The District of Columbia Bar

Adam Cizek — 1973 — Salisbury State University, B.A., 1996; University of Baltimore, J.D., 2000 — Admitted to Bar, 2000, Maryland — Member American and Maryland State Bar Associations

Jonathan E. Claiborne — 1955 — University of Maryland, B.A./B.S., 1977; Duke University, J.D., 1981 — Admitted to Bar, 1981, Maryland; 1982, District of Columbia — Member American and Maryland State Bar Associations; The District of Columbia Bar

David Daneman — 1964 — Franklin & Marshall College, B.S., 1986; University of Baltimore School of Law, J.D., 1989 — Admitted to Bar, 1989, Maryland; 2000, District of Columbia — Member Maryland State Bar Association; Bankruptcy Bar Association

Gardner M. Duvall — 1961 — Tulane University, B.A., 1983; University of Maryland, J.D., 1986 — Admitted to Bar, 1986, Maryland — Member American and Maryland State Bar Associations; The Bar Association of Baltimore City

Howard R. Feldman — 1962 — University of Maryland, B.S., 1984; J.D., 1988 — Admitted to Bar, 1988, Maryland; 1989, District of Columbia; 1993, U.S. Supreme Court — Member Maryland State Bar Association; The Bar Association of Baltimore City; The District of Columbia Bar

Michael C. Gartner — 1971 — Virginia Polytechnic Institute and State University, B.A., 1993; William Mitchell College of Law, J.D., 1997 — Admitted to Bar, 1997, Virginia; 1999, District of Columbia — Member Virginia and Fairfax County Bar Associations — Resident Falls Church, VA Office

Daniel A. Griffith — 1965 — Rutgers University, B.A., 1987; Rutgers University School of Law, J.D., 1990 — Admitted to Bar, 1990, New Jersey; 2002, Delaware — Member American, Delaware State and New Jersey State Bar Associations — Resident Wilmington, DE Office

Peter D. Guattery — 1962 — Johns Hopkins University, B.A., 1984; University of Pennsylvania, J.D., 1987 — Admitted to Bar, 1987, Maryland — Member American Bar Association

John J. Hathway — 1955 — The Catholic University of America, B.A., 1977; University of Baltimore, J.D., 1985 — Admitted to Bar, 1985, Maryland; 1988, District of Columbia — Member Maryland State Bar Association — Resident Washington, DC Office

Kenneth J. Ingram — 1945 — Amherst College, B.A., 1967; Washington University, J.D., 1970 — Admitted to Bar, 1970, Missouri; 1972, District of Columbia; 1982, Virginia; 1973, U.S. Claims Court — Member American and Virginia Bar Associations; The District of Columbia Bar — Resident Washington, DC Office

Jennifer S. Jackman — 1973 — University of Delaware, B.A., 1995; University of Baltimore, J.D., 1998 — Admitted to Bar, 1998, Maryland; 2000, District of Columbia; 2001, Virginia — Member Federal, American, Maryland State and Virginia Bar Associations; The District of Columbia Bar; District of Columbia Defense Lawyers Association — Resident Washington, DC Office

Harry S. Johnson — 1954 — University of Maryland, B.A., 1976; J.D., 1979 — Admitted to Bar, 1979, Maryland; 1993, District of Columbia — Member National, American, Maryland State and Monumental City Bar Associations; The Bar Association of Baltimore City (Elected, 1981); The District of Columbia Bar

Kevin A. Kernan — 1967 — State University of New York, B.S., 1989; Widener University, J.D., 1995 — Admitted to Bar, 1995, Pennsylvania; 1996, Maryland; 1997, District of Columbia; 1998, Virginia — Member Alexandria Bar Association; The District of Columbia Bar — Resident Washington, DC Office

Jennifer L. Lazenby — 1971 — University of Delaware, B.S., 1993; University of Baltimore, J.D., 1998 — Admitted to Bar, 1998, Maryland — Member Maryland State Bar Association — Resident Towson, MD Office

Kevin C. McCormick — 1955 — University of Notre Dame, B.A., 1976; College of William & Mary, Marshall-Wythe School of Law, J.D., 1979; Georgetown University, LL.M., 1984 — Admitted to Bar, 1979, Virginia; 1980, New York; 1985, Maryland — Member American (Labor and Employment Law Section), Maryland State, New York State and Virginia Bar Associations

Albert J. Mezzanotte, Jr. — 1956 — Western Maryland College, B.A., 1978; University of Baltimore, J.D., 1981 — Admitted to Bar, 1981, Maryland;

Whiteford, Taylor & Preston L.L.P., Baltimore, MD (Continued)

1986, District of Columbia — Member American and Maryland State Bar Associations; The District of Columbia Bar; Maryland Association of Defense Trial Counsel

Barry S. Neuman — 1949 — University of Rochester, B.A. (with high distinction), 1971; University of California, Berkeley Boalt Hall School of Law, J.D., 1974 — Admitted to Bar, 1975, District of Columbia; 2001, Maryland — Member Maryland State Bar Association; Bar Association of the District of Columbia

Gary S. Posner — 1962 — Loyola College, B.S., 1984; Emory University, J.D., 1988 — Admitted to Bar, 1988, Maryland — Member Maryland State Bar Association

Tiffany R. Releford — 1977 — University of Maryland, B.S., 1999; Howard University, J.D., 2005 — Admitted to Bar, 2005, Maryland; 2006, Virginia — Member Maryland State, Virginia and Howard County Bar Associations — Resident Washington, DC Office

Dennis M. Robinson Jr. — 1975 — Towson State University, B.A., 1997; University of Baltimore, J.D., 2002 — Admitted to Bar, 2002, Maryland — Member American and Maryland State Bar Associations; The Bar Association of Baltimore City

William F. Ryan, Jr. — 1951 — Princeton University, A.B., 1976; University of Baltimore, J.D., 1979 — Admitted to Bar, 1979, Maryland — Member American and Maryland State Bar Associations; The Bar Association of Baltimore City

Jerome C. Schaefer — 1946 — John Carroll University, B.A., 1969; The Catholic University of America, Columbus School of Law, J.D., 1972 — Admitted to Bar, 1972, Maryland; 1976, District of Columbia — Member American and Maryland State Bar Associations; The District of Columbia Bar — Resident Columbia, MD Office

Dwight W. Stone, II — 1968 — Princeton University, A.B., 1990; University of Maryland, J.D., 1993 — Admitted to Bar, 1993, Maryland — Member American and Maryland State Bar Associations; The Bar Association of Baltimore City

Ilana Subar — 1972 — McGill University, B.A., 1994; University of Maryland, J.D., 1997 — Admitted to Bar, 1997, Maryland

Andrew J. Terrell — 1962 — Saint Michael's College, B.A., 1984; George Mason University, J.D., 1989 — Admitted to Bar, 1989, Virginia; 1991, District of Columbia — Member American, Virginia and Alexandria Bar Associations; The District of Columbia Bar — Resident Falls Church, VA Office

Valerie L. Tetro — 1960 — Connecticut College, B.A., 1982; American University, Washington College of Law, J.D., 1985; Georgetown University, LL.M., 1986 — Admitted to Bar, 1987, Maryland — Member American and Maryland State Bar Associations — Resident Baltimore, MD and Washington, DC Office

Steven E. Tiller — 1966 — James Madison University, B.S., 1988; University of Kentucky, J.D., 1992 — Admitted to Bar, 1992, Maryland — Member Maryland State and Baltimore County Bar Associations; The District of Columbia Bar

Chad J. Toms — 1972 — University of Delaware, B.A., 1995; Widener University School of Law, J.D. (cum laude), 2001 — Admitted to Bar, 2001, New Jersey; Delaware — Member American and Delaware State Bar Associations — Resident Wilmington, DE Office

Warren N. Weaver — 1957 — Georgetown University, B.A., 1979; J.D., 1982 — Admitted to Bar, 1982, Maryland — Member American, National and Maryland State Bar Associations; Maryland Association of Defense Trial Counsel

Thomas J. Whiteford — 1966 — Bucknell University, B.A., 1989; University of Baltimore, J.D., 1992 — Admitted to Bar, 1992, Maryland

Thurman W. Zollicoffer, Jr. — 1962 — Towson University, B.A., 1984; University of Maryland, J.D., 1988 — Admitted to Bar, 1989, Maryland — Member National, Maryland State and Monumental Bar Associations

Associates

Christopher C. Jeffries — 1979 — Wesleyan University, B.A., 2001; The George Washington University, J.D., 2005 — Admitted to Bar, 2005, Maryland — Member Maryland State Bar Association; The Bar Association of Baltimore City

Dorothy Deng — 1980 — National Taiwan University, LL.B., 2003; The Pennsylvania State University Dickinson School of Law, J.D., 2006 — Admitted to Bar, 2007, District of Columbia — Member American Bar Association — Languages: Mandarin Chinese — Resident Washington, DC Office

MARYLAND — **BALTIMORE**

Whiteford, Taylor & Preston L.L.P., Baltimore, MD (Continued)

Emily Lashley — Towson University, B.S. (cum laude), 2001; University of Baltimore School of Law, J.D., 2005 — Admitted to Bar, 2005, Maryland — Member Maryland State Bar Association

Erin O'Brien Millar — 1979 — Wake Forest University, B.A., 2001; Villanova University, J.D., 2006 — Admitted to Bar, 2006, Maryland — Member Maryland State Bar Association

Kathleen A. Waldy — College of William & Mary, B.A., 2004; Widener University School of Law, J.D., 2007 — Admitted to Bar, 2007, Virginia — Member Virginia Bar Association

Merrilyn E. Ratliff — University of Maryland, B.S. (cum laude), 2004; University of Baltimore School of Law, J.D., 2009 — Admitted to Bar, 2009, Maryland — Member Maryland State Bar Association

Patrick McKevitt — University of Maryland, B.A., 2005; University of Baltimore School of Law, J.D. (magna cum laude), 2011 — Admitted to Bar, 2011, Maryland; 2012, District of Columbia — Member American and Maryland State Bar Associations

Senior Counsel

Dale B. Garbutt — 1947 — Norwich University, B.A., 1968; University of Maryland, J.D., 1975 — Admitted to Bar, 1975, Maryland — Member American, Maryland State and Baltimore County Bar Associations; The District of Columbia Bar

Counsel

Thomas Mugavero — 1962 — Yale University, B.A., 1985; Georgetown University, J.D., 1989 — Admitted to Bar, 1989, Maryland; Virginia; 1989, District of Columbia — Member Maryland State and Virginia Bar Associations — Resident Falls Church, VA Office

Jane Rogers — 1949 — American University, B.A., 1971; George Mason University, J.D., 1997 — Admitted to Bar, 1997, Virginia; 1998, Maryland; District of Columbia — Member American, Maryland State and Virginia Bar Associations; The District of Columbia Bar; American League of Lobbyist — Resident Washington, DC Office

Erek Barron — University of Maryland, B.A., 1996; The George Washington University Law School, J.D., 1999; Georgetown University Law Center, LL.M., 2007 — Admitted to Bar, 2003, District of Columbia — Member American and Maryland State Bar Associations — Resident Bethesda, MD Office

Scott G. Wilcox — 1969 — University of Delaware, B.A., 1991; Thomas M. Cooley Law School, J.D., 1999 — Admitted to Bar, 1999, Delaware — Member American and Delaware State Bar Associations — Resident Wilmington, DE Office

Thomas C. Beach, III — 1942 — Georgetown University; University of Maryland, B.S., 1965; LL.B., 1968 — Admitted to Bar, 1968, Maryland — Member American, Maryland State and Baltimore County Bar Associations; The Bar Association of Baltimore City

Jeffrey C. Seaman — University of Kentucky, B.A., 1988; University of Kentucky College of Law, J.D., 1992 — Admitted to Bar, 1992, District of Columbia — Member Bar Association of the District of Columbia; Montgomery County Bar Association

Wright, Constable & Skeen, L.L.P.

100 North Charles Street
16th Floor
Baltimore, Maryland 21201
   Telephone: 410-659-1300
   Fax: 410-659-1350
   Toll Free: 888-894-7602
   E-Mail: info@wcslaw.com
   www.wcslaw.com

(Towson, MD Office: 220 Bosley Avenue, 21204)
   (Tel: 410-296-1163)

Established: 1906

Wright, Constable & Skeen, L.L.P., Baltimore, MD (Continued)

Insurance Defense, Automobile, General Liability, Marine, Bodily Injury, Fire, Professional Malpractice, Alternative Dispute Resolution, Commercial Litigation, Construction Liability, Employment Practices Liability, Railroad Law, Fidelity and Surety, Coverage

Firm Profile: The law firm of Wright, Constable & Skeen has been a presence in the Maryland legal community for over 100 years. Its practice consists primarily of civil litigation, estates and trusts, commercial work and corporate work. The firm has extensive experience in the defense of general liability, professional liability, employment discrimination, maritime, construction and surety, and complex commercial matters.

In addition to major insurance companies, Wright, Constable & Skeen's litigation clients include numerous self-insureds, including a number of multi-state companies.

Our size, approximately 25 attorneys plus support staff, allows us to preserve the cost effective and client friendly aspects of service associated with smaller firms, while maintaining the capability of handling diverse and complex matters in our areas of concentration.

Insurance Clients

Acceptance Risk Managers, Inc.
AI Marine Adjusters, Inc.
American Bankers Insurance Company of Florida
CIGNA Insurance Company
DPIC Companies, Inc.
ESIS
Farmers Insurance Group
Lancer Claims Services, Inc.
Lombard Canada
Minnesota Lawyers Mutual Insurance Company
Navigators Management Company
North American Specialty Insurance Company
Platte River Insurance Company
Response Insurance Company
Safeco Insurance
St. Paul Fire and Marine Insurance Company
United States Liability Insurance Company
Wausau Insurance Companies
Zurich American Insurance Group
ACE USA
Alliance of Nonprofits for Insurance
Aon Risk Services, Inc.
CNA Insurance Company
Employers Reinsurance Corporation
Great American Insurance Companies
Marine Office of America Corporation (MOAC)
National Marine Underwriters, Inc.
North American Risk Services
NovaPro Risk Solutions
Pennsylvania National Mutual Casualty Insurance Company
Risk Administration and Management Company
Seaworthy Insurance Company
Underwriters at Lloyd's, London
United States Liability Insurance Group
Westchester Fire Insurance Company

Non-Insurance Clients

Anne Arundel County Employees Federal Credit Union
Brink's, Inc.
Comfort Systems USA
Constellation Energy Group
First Transit, Inc.
Marine M.G.A., Inc.
National Loss Management
Norfolk Southern Railway Company
Siemens Financial Services, Inc.
The Terminal Corporation
Vulcan Materials Company
Boat/U.S. - Boat Owners Association of United States
Carnival Cruise Lines, Inc.
Consolidated Rail Corporation
Energy Federal Credit Union
Liggett Group, Inc.
Marine Office of America, Inc.
Norfolk Southern Corporation
Schwan's Sales Enterprises, Inc.
Siemens Corporation
Siemens Medical Systems, Inc.
Triple Crown Services Company

Partners

Michael J. Abromaitis — 1940 — Loyola College, A.B., 1962; University of Maryland, LL.B., 1967; Georgetown University, LL.M., 1971 — Recipient, Stanley L. Seligman Award (Appellate Advocacy), 1966 — Admitted to Bar, 1967, Maryland; 1967, U.S. District Court, District of Maryland — Member American and Maryland State Bar Associations; The Bar Association of Baltimore City — Practice Areas: Business Law; Corporate Law; Estate Planning — Tel: 410-659-1316 — E-mail: mabromaitis@wcslaw.com

James W. Constable — 1942 — University of Virginia, B.A., 1965; University of Maryland, LL.B., 1968 — Best's Recommended Insurance Attorneys (2011); Top Listed in Best Lawyers; The World's Premier Guide, AV Rated for Ethical Standards and Legal Ability (2010); Maryland Super Lawyers for Business/Corporate (2009-2014) — Admitted to Bar, 1968, Maryland; 1968, U.S. District Court, District of Maryland; 1968, U.S. Court of Appeals,

BALTIMORE MARYLAND

Wright, Constable & Skeen, L.L.P., Baltimore, MD (Continued)

Fourth Circuit; 1974, U.S. Supreme Court — Member American and Maryland State Bar Associations; The Bar Association of Baltimore City; Association of Transportation Practitioners; Maryland/District of Columbia Public Utilities Association — Practice Areas: Corporate Law; Business Law; Labor and Employment; Estate Planning; Litigation; Maritime Law; Transportation; Arbitration; Mediation; Real Estate — Tel: 410-659-1315 — E-mail: jconstable@wcslaw.com

David W. Skeen — 1946 — Princeton University, A.B., 1968; University of Maryland, J.D., 1973 — Maryland Super Lawyers for Transportation & Maritime (2007-2014); Best Lawyers in America for Admiralty & Maritime Law, Alternative Dispute Resolution, Mediation, (1989-2014). — Admitted to Bar, 1973, Maryland; 1973, U.S. District Court, District of Maryland; 1973, U.S. Court of Appeals, Fourth Circuit; 1973, U.S. Supreme Court — Member American and Maryland State Bar Associations; The Bar Association of Baltimore City (Past President); The Maritime Law Association of the United States; Defense Research Institute — Practice Areas: Arbitration; Insurance Defense; Litigation; Maritime Law; Mediation; Transportation — Tel: 410-659-1305 — E-mail: dskeen@wcslaw.com

Kenneth F. Davies — 1956 — Ohio University, B.S. (cum laude), 1978; University of Maryland, J.D. (with honors), 1981 — Admitted to Bar, 1981, Maryland; 1981, U.S. District Court, District of Maryland — Member American, Maryland State and Baltimore County Bar Associations; The Bar Association of Baltimore City — Practice Areas: Bankruptcy; Creditor Rights; Estate Planning; Real Estate — Tel: 410-659-1303 — E-mail: kdavies@wcslaw.com

Stephen F. White — 1953 — The University of North Carolina at Chapel Hill, B.A., 1975; University of Maryland, J.D. (with honors), 1982 — Maryland Super Lawyers for Transportation/Maritime (2009-2014); Listed in The Best Lawyers of America for Maritime Law (2008-2014); Selected by Who's Who Legal for Inclusion in The International Who's Who of Shipping & Maritime Lawyers (2009); Selected by Who's Who Legal for inclusion in The International Who's Who of Business Lawyers (2010) — Admitted to Bar, 1982, Maryland; 1983, U.S. District Court, District of Maryland; 1987, U.S. Supreme Court; 1995, U.S. Court of Appeals, Fourth Circuit — Member American Bar Association (Torts and Insurance Practice Section); Maryland State and Howard County Bar Associations; The Bar Association of Baltimore City; Maryland Marine Trades Association; Society of Naval Architects and Marine Engineers; The Maritime Law Association of the United States; Southeastern Admiralty Law Institute — Private Pilot Certificate (SEL) with High Performance Endorsement — Commander, U.S. Naval Reserves (Ret.) — Practice Areas: Admiralty and Maritime Law; Commercial Litigation; Insurance Defense; Personal Injury; Subrogation; Workers' Compensation — Tel: 410-659-1304 — E-mail: swhite@wcslaw.com

Monte Fried — 1943 — University of Pennsylvania, B.S., 1963; University of Maryland, LL.B., 1967 — Maryland Super Lawyers for Employment & Labor, (2009-2014); Martindale-Hubbell Top Rated Lawyer in Health Care, AV Peer Review Rated, Martindale-Hubbell (2010); Martindale-Hubbell's Washington D.C. & Baltimore's Top Rated Lawyer (2014) — Admitted to Bar, 1967, Maryland; 1967, U.S. District Court, District of Maryland; 1968, U.S. Court of Appeals, Fourth Circuit; 1997, U.S. District Court for the District of Columbia; 1997, U.S. Court of Military Appeals — Member American and Maryland State Bar Associations; The Bar Association of Baltimore City; Maryland Association of Defense Trial Counsel; Defense Research Institute — Practice Areas: Health Care; Labor and Employment; Litigation — Tel: 410-659-1312 — E-mail: mfried@wcslaw.com

Frederick L. Kobb — Managing Partner — 1956 — Cornell University, B.S., 1978; J.D., 1985 — Maryland Super Lawyers for Family Law (2012-2014) — Admitted to Bar, 1985, Maryland; 1987, U.S. District Court, District of Maryland; 1993, U.S. Court of Appeals, Fourth Circuit — Member American, Maryland State and Baltimore County Bar Associations; The Bar Association of Baltimore City; National Association of Railroad Trial Counsel — Practice Areas: Insurance Defense; Transportation; Litigation; Family Law — Tel: 410-659-1348 — E-mail: fkobb@wcslaw.com

Paul F. Evelius — 1961 — Loyola College, B.A. (summa cum laude), 1983; University of Maryland, J.D., 1987 — Maryland Super Lawyers for Business & Corporate Law (2011-2013); Best Lawyers in America for Corporate Law (2013, 2014) — Admitted to Bar, 1987, Maryland; 1989, U.S. District Court, District of Maryland; 1992, U.S. Court of Appeals, Fourth Circuit; U.S. Supreme Court — Member American and Maryland State Bar Associations; The Bar Association of Baltimore City — Practice Areas: Labor and Employment; Litigation; Corporate Law; Business Law — Tel: 410-659-1302 — E-mail: pevelius@wcslaw.com

Mary Alice Smolarek — Syracuse University, A.B. (magna cum laude), 1984; Georgetown University, J.D., 1987 — Phi Beta Kappa — Maryland Super Lawyers for Estate Planning & Probate (2007-2014); Top Woman Lawyer in Northeast for Trust & Estate, Wills & Probate, Martindale-Hubbell (2011) — Admitted to Bar, 1987, Maryland; 1989, District of Columbia — Member Maryland State Bar Association; The Bar Association of the District of Columbia; The Bar Association of Baltimore City (Past-President) — Practice Areas: Estate Planning; Trusts; Wills — Tel: 410-659-1318 — E-mail: masmolarek@wcslaw.com

Robert W. Hesselbacher, Jr. — 1948 — Michigan State University, B.S., 1969; Johns Hopkins University, M.A., 1973; University of Maryland, J.D., 1977 — Maryland Super Lawyers for Business Litigation (2007-2014) — Admitted to Bar, 1977, Maryland; 1988, District of Columbia; 1992, Virginia; 1978, U.S. District Court, District of Maryland; 1978, U.S. Court of Appeals, Fourth Circuit; 1988, U.S. District Court for the District of Columbia; 1992, U.S. District Court, Eastern District of Virginia; 1993, U.S. District Court, Western District of Virginia — Member Federal, American and Maryland State Bar Associations; The Bar Association of Baltimore City; Fellow, Litigation Counsel of America; Professional Liability Defense Federation; Defense Research Institute — Practice Areas: Business Litigation; Commercial Litigation; Insurance Coverage; Insurance Defense; Litigation; Mediation — Tel: 410-659-1317 — E-mail: rhesselbacher@wcslaw.com

Howard S. Stevens — 1966 — Guilford College, B.S., 1988; University of Maryland, J.D., 1997 — Maryland Super Lawyers for Construction Litigation (2010-2014); Best Lawyers in America for Construction Law, (2013, 2014); Named Top 100 for 2012 and 2014 Maryland Super Lawyers — Admitted to Bar, 1998, Maryland; 1999, U.S. District Court, District of Maryland; 2000, U.S. Court of Appeals for the District of Columbia and Fourth Circuits; 2003, U.S. District Court for the District of Columbia; U.S. District Court, Northern District of Illinois — Member American and Maryland State Bar Associations; The Bar Association of Baltimore City — Practice Areas: Construction Law; Mechanics Liens; Civil Litigation; Business Law; Corporate Law — Tel: 410-659-1309 — E-mail: hstevens@wcslaw.com

Louis J. Kozlakowski, Jr. — 1948 — University of Baltimore, B.S. (cum laude), 1970; J.D., 1974 — Maryland Super Lawyers for Construction and Surety (2007-2014) — Admitted to Bar, 1974, Maryland; 1974, U.S. District Court, District of Maryland; 1974, U.S. Court of Appeals, Fourth Circuit — Member American and Maryland State Bar Associations — Practice Areas: Construction Law; Contracts; Commercial Litigation; Surety — Tel: 410-659-1314 — E-mail: lkozlakowski@wcslaw.com

Michael A. Stanley — 1970 — Florida State University, B.S., 1992; University of Baltimore, J.D. (cum laude), 1997 — Maryland Super Lawyers Rising Stars — Admitted to Bar, 1997, Maryland; 2003, U.S. District Court, District of Maryland — Member Maryland State Bar Association; The Bar Association of Baltimore City — Practice Areas: Commercial Litigation; Commercial Transactions; Estate Planning; Real Estate; Trucking Litigation; Trusts — Tel: 410-659-1374 — E-mail: mstanley@wcslaw.com

Michael I. Gordon — 1936 — University of Baltimore, A.A., 1956; University of Baltimore School of Law, J.D., 1959 — Maryland Super Lawyers for Estate Planning & Probate (2007-2014); Presidential Award by the Bar Association of Baltimore City (1995) — Admitted to Bar, 1959, Maryland; 1960, U.S. District Court, District of Maryland; 1973, U.S. Court of Appeals, Fourth Circuit; 2000, U.S. Supreme Court — Member American, Maryland State (Board of Governors, 1996-1998, 2003-2004) and Baltimore County Bar Associations; The Bar Association of Baltimore City (Executive Council, 1987-Present; Secretary, 2000-2001); Baltimore Bar Foundation (Secretary, 2000-2001); Bar Associations Insurance Trust (Secretary, 1998-Present) — Practice Areas: Construction Law; Corporate Law; Estate Planning; Real Estate; Mediation; Arbitration — Tel: 410-659-1306 — E-mail: mgordon@wcslaw.com

Michael A. Stover — 1964 — University of Maryland, B.S., 1987; University of Maryland School of Law, J.D. (with honors), 1991 — Best Lawyers in America for Construction Law (2013, 2014) — Admitted to Bar, 1991, Maryland; U.S. District Court, District of Maryland; U.S. Court of Appeals, Third and Fourth Circuits; U.S. Court of Federal Claims — Member Federal, American (TIPS, Fidelity & Surety Law Committee; Forum on the Construction Industry) and Anne Arundel County Bar Associations; Maryland State Bar Association (Former Member, Board of Governors and Chair, Young Lawyers Section); Surety Claims Institute — Practice Areas: Construction Law; Fidelity and Surety; Insurance Defense; Government Contracts — Tel: 410-659-1321 — E-mail: mstover@wcslaw.com

George J. Bachrach — 1948 — Harvard University, B.A. (cum laude), 1971; Georgetown University Law Center, J.D., 1974 — Recipient, Martin J. Andrew Award for Lifetime Achievement in Fidelity & Surety Law from the ABA/TIPS, Fidelity & Surety Law Committee (May 2009); AV Peer Review Rated, Martinedale-Hubbell (2010); Listed in The Best Lawyers in America for Construction Law and Insurance Law (2007-2014); Maryland Super Lawyers for Construction Law (2007) — Admitted to Bar, 1974, Maryland —

MARYLAND

BEL AIR

Wright, Constable & Skeen, L.L.P., Baltimore, MD (Continued)

Member American and Maryland State Bar Associations — Practice Areas: Surety; Bankruptcy; Construction Law — Tel: 410-659-1300 — Fax: 410-659-1350 — E-mail: gbachrach@wcslaw.com

Gerard P. Sunderland — 1946 — Tulane University, B.A., 1968; University of Maryland School of Law, J.D. (Order of the Coif), 1973 — AV Peer Review Rated: Martindale-Hubbell; Maryland Super Lawyers for Construction/Surety (2007, 2010-2014); Best Lawyers in America for Insurance Law (2013, 2014) — Admitted to Bar, 1973, Maryland; 1980, District of Columbia — Member American and Maryland State Bar Associations; The District of Columbia Bar; Defense Research Institute — Practice Areas: Fidelity and Surety; Construction Law; Insurance Coverage — Tel: 410-659-1300 — Fax: 410-659-1350 — E-mail: gsunderland@wcslaw.com

Cynthia E. Rodgers-Waire — 1967 — University of Virginia, B.A., 1989; University of Maryland School of Law, J.D. (with honors), 1992 — Best Lawyers in America for Construction Law and Construction Litigation (2011-2014) — Admitted to Bar, 1992, Maryland — Member American Bar Association — Practice Areas: Construction Law; Fidelity and Surety; Bankruptcy; Litigation; Mediation; Arbitration — Tel: 410-659-1310 — E-mail: crodgers-waire@wcslaw.com

Associates

Mollie G. Caplis — 1979 — Brandeis University, B.A. (cum laude), 2001; University of Baltimore School of Law, J.D. (cum laude), 2004 — Admitted to Bar, 2004, Maryland; 2006, District of Columbia; 2005, U.S. District Court, District of Maryland — Member Maryland State Bar Association; The Bar Association of Baltimore City (Chair, Young Lawyers Division) — Practice Areas: Family Law; Estate Planning; Litigation; Trusts — Tel: 410-659-1325 — E-mail: mshuman@wcslaw.com

Jason R. Potter — 1970 — The Ohio State University, B.A., 1995; University of Baltimore School of Law, J.D., 2005 — Clinical Excellency Award, 2004-2005; Maryland Super Lawyers Rising Stars (2011-2014) — Law Clerk to Hon. Thomas E. Marshall, Harford County Circuit Court, 2005-2006 — Admitted to Bar, 2005, Maryland — Member American and Maryland State Bar Associations; The Bar Association of Baltimore City — Languages: Spanish — Practice Areas: Civil Litigation; Construction Law; Surety; Immigration Law — Tel: 410-659-1340 — E-mail: jpotter@wcslaw.com

Meighan Griffin Burton — 1980 — University of Maryland, B.A., 2002; J.D. (with honors), 2005 — Maryland Super Lawyers, List of Rising Stars (2009-2014) — Admitted to Bar, 2005, Maryland; 2006, U.S. District Court, District of Maryland — Member Federal, American and Maryland State (Board of Governors, 2010) Bar Associations; The Bar Association of Baltimore City (Young Lawyers Division; Chair-Elect) — Practice Areas: Business Law; Construction Law; Corporate Law; Insurance Defense; Litigation; Maritime Law; Transportation — Tel: 410-659-1324 — E-mail: mburton@wcslaw.com

Marc A. Campsen — 1977 — James Madison University, B.S., 1999; University of Baltimore School of Law, J.D., 2008 — Admitted to Bar, 2008, Maryland; New York; District of Columbia — Member American and Maryland State Bar Associations — Practice Areas: Litigation — Tel: 410-659-1343 — E-mail: mcampsen@wcslaw.com

Lisa D. Sparks — 1984 — University of Baltimore, B.A. (summa cum laude), 2005; University of Baltimore School of Law, J.D. (summa cum laude), 2007 — Maryland SuperLawyers Rising Star, 2013 Maryland SuperLawyers, Super Lawyer, 2014 — Admitted to Bar, 2007, Maryland; District of Columbia; Virginia; U.S. District Court, District of Maryland; U.S. District Court, Eastern and Western Districts of Virginia; U.S. Tax Court — Member Maryland State and Baltimore County Bar Associations — Maryland Defense Force Captain, Judge Advocate Unit — Practice Areas: Insurance Defense; Litigation; Mediation; Arbitration; Fidelity and Surety — Tel: 410-659-1322 — E-mail: lsparks@wcslaw.com

Allyson B. Goldscher — University of Delaware, B.S., 2006; University of Baltimore School of Law, J.D., 2009 — Maryland Super Lawyer Rising Star (2013, 2014) — Judicial Law Clerk to Hon. William M. Dunn, Domestic Relations Master, Circuit Court for Baltimore City — Admitted to Bar, 2009, Maryland — Member American (Family Law Section) and Maryland State (Family and Juvenile Law Section) Bar Associations; The Bar Association of Baltimore City (Co-Chair, Family Law Committee) — Volunteer Settlement Officer, Baltimore City Circuit Court, Family Division; Volunteer Attorney, Maryland Volunteer Lawyers Service — Court-Appointed Attorney for Children in Custody and Access Disputes; Designated Mediator; Qualified Court Designated Mediator in Child Custody & Access Disputes — Practice Areas: Family Law; Litigation; Mediation — Tel: 410-659-1359

(Revisors of the Maryland Insurance Law Digest for this Publication)

The following firms also service this area.

Carr Maloney P.C.
2000 L Street, NW, Suite 450
Washington, District of Columbia 20036
Telephone: 202-310-5500
Fax: 202-310-5555

Appellate Practice, Civil Rights, Commercial Litigation, Complex Litigation, Construction Law, Directors and Officers Liability, General Liability, Government Investigations and Enforcement, Health Care, Immigration Law, Insurance Coverage, Labor and Employment, Product Liability, Professional Liability, Religious Institutions, Retailers and Chain Restaurant Litigation, Risk Management, Toxic Torts, Mass Tort, Trust and Estate Litigation

SEE COMPLETE LISTING UNDER WASHINGTON, DISTRICT OF COLUMBIA (39 MILES)

BEL AIR † 10,080 Harford Co.

Refer To
Pessin Katz Law, P.A.
901 Dulaney Valley Road
Suite 400
Towson, Maryland 21204
Telephone: 410-938-8800
Fax: 410-832-5600

Insurance Defense, Coverage Issues, Regulatory and Compliance, Administrative Law, Agent and Brokers Errors and Omissions, Disability, Business Law, Construction Law, Class Actions

SEE COMPLETE LISTING UNDER BALTIMORE, MARYLAND (20 MILES)

BETHESDA 60,858 Montgomery Co.

Budow and Noble, P.C.

7315 Wisconsin Avenue, Suite 500 West
Bethesda, Maryland 20814
Telephone: 301-654-0896
Fax: 301-907-9591
E-Mail: info@budownoble.com
www.budownoble.com

Established: 1981

Insurance Defense, Automobile, Property Liability, General Liability, Arson, Fraud, Casualty, Medical Malpractice, Workers' Compensation

Firm Profile: Budow and Noble, P.C. provides quality representation in a wide variety of civil and commercial litigation matters, serving insurance companies, businesses, local governments, and individuals alike. Founded in 1981, the firm is well recognized in Maryland as a leader in the insurance law arena.

Insurance Clients

Allstate Insurance Company	Erie Insurance Group
Fireman's Fund Insurance Company	GEICO General Insurance Company
Hartford Insurance Company	Metropolitan Property and Casualty Insurance Company
Nationwide Insurance	
State Farm Fire and Casualty Company	State Farm Mutual Automobile Insurance Company
United Services Automobile Association (USAA)	

Non-Insurance Clients

Howard County Public School System

Marriott International, Inc.

Partners

Michael J. Budow — 1946 — University of Wisconsin, B.A. (with honors), 1968; The George Washington University, J.D. (with honors), 1972 — Law Clerk to Judge Irving A. Levine, U.S. Court of Appeals, Fourth Circuit, 1972-1973 — Admitted to Bar, 1972, Maryland; 1975, District of Columbia;

CENTREVILLE | MARYLAND

Budow and Noble, P.C., Bethesda, MD (Continued)

1975, U.S. District Court, District of Maryland — Member American, Maryland State and Montgomery County Bar Associations; The District of Columbia Bar; The Bar Association of the District of Columbia; Maryland Arson Control Association; Association of Trial Lawyers of America — E-mail: mbudow@budownoble.com

Allan A. Noble — 1944 — Alfred University, B.A., 1966; American University, J.D., 1972 — Admitted to Bar, 1972, Maryland; 1973, District of Columbia; 1973, U.S. District Court for the District of Columbia; 1973, U.S. Court of Appeals for the District of Columbia Circuit; 1975, U.S. District Court, District of Maryland; 1975, U.S. Court of Appeals, Fourth Circuit; 1976, U.S. Supreme Court — Member American, Maryland State and Montgomery County Bar Associations; The Bar Association of the District of Columbia — Captain, U.S. Army (1966-1968) — E-mail: anoble@budownoble.com

Richard E. Schimel — 1954 — Princeton University, A.B. (cum laude), 1975; The George Washington University, J.D. (with honors), 1978 — Law Clerk to Hon. William H. McCullough, Administrative and Associate Judge, Circuit Court, Prince George County, State of Maryland, 1978-1979 — Admitted to Bar, 1978, Maryland; 1979, District of Columbia; 1979, U.S. District Court for the District of Columbia; 1979, U.S. Court of Appeals for the District of Columbia Circuit; 1979, U.S. District Court, District of Maryland — Member Maryland State, Montgomery County and Prince George's County Bar Associations; The Bar Association of the District of Columbia — E-mail: rschimel@budownoble.com

Walter E. Gillcrist, Jr. — 1959 — Villanova University, B.S., 1981; The Catholic University of America, J.D., 1984 — Law Clerk, Senior Judges for the District of Columbia Court of Appeals, 1984-1986; Hon. Frank Q. Nebeker, Associate Judge for the District of Columbia Court of Appeals, 1986-1987 — Catholic University Law Review, 1983-1984 — Admitted to Bar, 1985, Maryland; 1986, District of Columbia — Member American and Maryland State Bar Associations — E-mail: wgillcrist@budownoble.com

Anne Kelley Howard — 1959 — Boston College, B.A. (magna cum laude), 1981; University of Maryland, J.D. (with honors), 1987 — Editor-in-Chief: Maryland Journal of International Law, 1986-1987 — Admitted to Bar, 1987, Maryland; 1988, District of Columbia — Member Maryland State Bar Association — E-mail: ahoward@budownoble.com

J. Charles Szczesny — 1964 — University of Maryland, B.A., 1986; University of Baltimore, J.D., 1991 — Admitted to Bar, 1991, Maryland; 2001, District of Columbia; 1992, U.S. District Court, District of Maryland — Member Maryland State Bar Association — E-mail: jcszczesny@budownoble.com

Laura Basem Jacobs — 1969 — University of Delaware, B.A., 1991; The George Washington University, J.D., 1994 — Law Clerk to Hon. Gregory E. Mize, Superior Court for the District of Columbia — Law Review — Admitted to Bar, 1994, Maryland; 1996, District of Columbia; 1997, U.S. District Court, District of Maryland — Member American and Maryland State Bar Associations; The District of Columbia Bar — E-mail: ljacobs@budownoble.com

Melissa D. McNair — 1973 — University of Maryland, College Park, B.S. (with honors), 1996; University of Baltimore, J.D. (magna cum laude), 2002 — Admitted to Bar, 2002, Maryland; 2010, District of Columbia — Member Maryland State Bar Association — E-mail: mmcnair@budownoble.com

Howard Meinster — 1969 — University of Maryland, B.A., 1999; J.D., 2003 — Admitted to Bar, 2003, Maryland; 2008, District of Columbia; 2004, U.S. District Court, District of Maryland — Member American and Maryland State Bar Associations — E-mail: hmeinster@budownoble.com

Associates

Matthew M. Davey — 1976 — The Catholic University of America, B.A., 1999; The Catholic University of America, Columbus School of Law, J.D., 2002 — Admitted to Bar, 2002, Maryland; 2004, District of Columbia; U.S. District Court, District of Maryland — E-mail: mdavey@budownoble.com

G. Calvin Awkward, III — 1984 — Washington and Lee University, B.A., 2006; Washington and Lee University School of Law, J.D., 2009 — Admitted to Bar, 2009, Virginia; 2010, Maryland — E-mail: cawkward@budownoble.com

Robyn A. McQuillen — 1983 — The University of Oklahoma, B.A. Psychology and English (summa cum laude), 2005; University of Baltimore School of Law, J.D. (cum laude), 2011 — Admitted to Bar, 2011, Maryland — Member Maryland State Bar Association — E-mail: rmcquillen@budownoble.com

Marie-Therese P. Goff — 1985 — Loyola College in Maryland, B.A. (summa cum laude, Phi Beta Kappa), 2008; University of Baltimore School of Law, J.D. (cum laude), 2011 — Judicial Law Clerk to the Hon. Ruth Jakubowski, Circuit Court for Baltimore County, 2011-2013 — Admitted to Bar, 2011, Maryland; 2013, District of Columbia — Member American and Maryland

Budow and Noble, P.C., Bethesda, MD (Continued)

State Bar Associations; Women's Bar Association of Maryland — E-mail: mgoff@budownoble.com

Veronica K. Yu — 1988 — Boston College, B.A., 2010; American University, Washington College of Law, J.D., 2013 — Admitted to Bar, 2013, Maryland — Member Maryland State Bar Association — E-mail: vyu@budownoble.com

Charles J. Coughlin — 1987 — University of Maryland, College Park, B.A., 2009; Georgetown University Law Center, J.D., 2012 — Admitted to Bar, 2012, Maryland; 2013, District of Columbia — Member Maryland State Bar Association; Bar Association of the District of Columbia — E-mail: ccoughlin@budownoble.com

CAMBRIDGE † 12,326 Dorchester Co.

Refer To

Seidel, Baker & Tilghman, P.A.
Masonic Building
110 North Division Street
Salisbury, Maryland 21801
  Telephone: 410-742-8176
  Fax: 410-742-3117

Casualty, Fire, Surety, Workers' Compensation, Product Liability, Insurance Defense, Personal Injury, Subrogation

SEE COMPLETE LISTING UNDER SALISBURY, MARYLAND (32 MILES)

Refer To

Webb, Burnett, Cornbrooks, Wilber, Vorhis, Douse & Mason, L.L.P.
115 Broad Street
Salisbury, Maryland 21801
  Telephone: 410-742-3176
  Fax: 410-742-0438
Mailing Address: P.O. Box 910, Salisbury, MD 21803-0910

Insurance Defense, Automobile, General Liability, Personal Injury, Property Damage, Workers' Compensation, Subrogation

SEE COMPLETE LISTING UNDER SALISBURY, MARYLAND (32 MILES)

CENTREVILLE † 4,285 Queen Anne's Co.

Refer To

Seidel, Baker & Tilghman, P.A.
Masonic Building
110 North Division Street
Salisbury, Maryland 21801
  Telephone: 410-742-8176
  Fax: 410-742-3117

Casualty, Fire, Surety, Workers' Compensation, Product Liability, Insurance Defense, Personal Injury, Subrogation

SEE COMPLETE LISTING UNDER SALISBURY, MARYLAND (67 MILES)

Refer To

Webb, Burnett, Cornbrooks, Wilber, Vorhis, Douse & Mason, L.L.P.
115 Broad Street
Salisbury, Maryland 21801
  Telephone: 410-742-3176
  Fax: 410-742-0438
Mailing Address: P.O. Box 910, Salisbury, MD 21803-0910

Insurance Defense, Automobile, General Liability, Personal Injury, Property Damage, Workers' Compensation, Subrogation

SEE COMPLETE LISTING UNDER SALISBURY, MARYLAND (67 MILES)

MARYLAND

CHESTERTOWN † 5,252 Kent Co.
Refer To

Seidel, Baker & Tilghman, P.A.
Masonic Building
110 North Division Street
Salisbury, Maryland 21801
Telephone: 410-742-8176
Fax: 410-742-3117

Casualty, Fire, Surety, Workers' Compensation, Product Liability, Insurance Defense, Personal Injury, Subrogation

SEE COMPLETE LISTING UNDER SALISBURY, MARYLAND (85 MILES)

Refer To

Webb, Burnett, Cornbrooks, Wilber, Vorhis, Douse & Mason, L.L.P.
115 Broad Street
Salisbury, Maryland 21801
Telephone: 410-742-3176
Fax: 410-742-0438
Mailing Address: P.O. Box 910, Salisbury, MD 21803-0910

Insurance Defense, Automobile, General Liability, Personal Injury, Property Damage, Workers' Compensation, Subrogation

SEE COMPLETE LISTING UNDER SALISBURY, MARYLAND (85 MILES)

COLUMBIA 99,615 Howard Co.
Refer To

Pessin Katz Law, P.A.
901 Dulaney Valley Road
Suite 400
Towson, Maryland 21204
Telephone: 410-938-8800
Fax: 410-832-5600

Insurance Defense, Coverage Issues, Regulatory and Compliance, Administrative Law, Agent and Brokers Errors and Omissions, Disability, Business Law, Construction Law, Class Actions

SEE COMPLETE LISTING UNDER BALTIMORE, MARYLAND (18 MILES)

DENTON † 4,418 Caroline Co.
Refer To

Seidel, Baker & Tilghman, P.A.
Masonic Building
110 North Division Street
Salisbury, Maryland 21801
Telephone: 410-742-8176
Fax: 410-742-3117

Casualty, Fire, Surety, Workers' Compensation, Product Liability, Insurance Defense, Personal Injury, Subrogation

SEE COMPLETE LISTING UNDER SALISBURY, MARYLAND (50 MILES)

Refer To

Webb, Burnett, Cornbrooks, Wilber, Vorhis, Douse & Mason, L.L.P.
115 Broad Street
Salisbury, Maryland 21801
Telephone: 410-742-3176
Fax: 410-742-0438
Mailing Address: P.O. Box 910, Salisbury, MD 21803-0910

Insurance Defense, Automobile, General Liability, Personal Injury, Property Damage, Workers' Compensation, Subrogation

SEE COMPLETE LISTING UNDER SALISBURY, MARYLAND (50 MILES)

EASTON † 15,945 Talbot Co.
Refer To

Seidel, Baker & Tilghman, P.A.
Masonic Building
110 North Division Street
Salisbury, Maryland 21801
Telephone: 410-742-8176
Fax: 410-742-3117

Casualty, Fire, Surety, Workers' Compensation, Product Liability, Insurance Defense, Personal Injury, Subrogation

SEE COMPLETE LISTING UNDER SALISBURY, MARYLAND (47 MILES)

Refer To

Webb, Burnett, Cornbrooks, Wilber, Vorhis, Douse & Mason, L.L.P.
115 Broad Street
Salisbury, Maryland 21801
Telephone: 410-742-3176
Fax: 410-742-0438
Mailing Address: P.O. Box 910, Salisbury, MD 21803-0910

Insurance Defense, Automobile, General Liability, Personal Injury, Property Damage, Workers' Compensation, Subrogation

SEE COMPLETE LISTING UNDER SALISBURY, MARYLAND (47 MILES)

GREENBELT 23,068 Prince George's Co.

Bacon, Thornton, Palmer, L.L.P.
6411 Ivy Lane
Suite 500
Greenbelt, Maryland 20770-1411
Telephone: 301-345-7001
Fax: 301-345-7075
www.lawbtp.com

Established: 1999

Insurance Defense, General Liability, Casualty, Construction Defect, Product Liability, Employment Law, Retail Liability, Premises Liability, Environmental Law, Asbestos Litigation, Lead Paint, Mold and Mildew Claims

Firm Profile: Bacon, Thornton & Palmer, L.L.P., is a law firm of experienced civil litigation attorneys practicing in the greater Baltimore-Washington region. The firm is conveniently located within the Baltimore-Washington corridor, providing efficient access to all major court systems throughout the region.

The firm's practice includes serving as regional trial counsel for various insurance and self-insured companies. Members of the firm have participated as counsel in numerous appellate decisions, involving such issues as the standard for recovery of punitive damages for various torts; insurance coverage; application and interpretation of wrongful death statutes; interrelationship and interpretation of workers' compensation and third-party liability laws; employment law (including ERISA); construction defect litigation; premises liability; and various additional issues within the firm's areas of practice.

Insurance Clients

Harford Mutual Insurance Company
Sedgwick Group of Illinois, Inc.
Travelers Property Casualty Group
The Hartford
St. Paul Fire and Marine Insurance Company
United National Insurance Company

Non-Insurance Clients

The May Department Stores Company

Founder & Senior Managing Partner

Edward C. Bacon — 1953 — University of Maryland, B.A., 1975; J.D., 1978 — Admitted to Bar, 1978, Maryland; 1979, District of Columbia; 1979, U.S.

ROCKVILLE   MARYLAND

Bacon, Thornton, Palmer, L.L.P., Greenbelt, MD
(Continued)

District Court, District of Maryland; 1981, U.S. District Court for the District of Columbia — Member American, Maryland State and Prince George's County Bar Associations; District of Columbia Defense Lawyers Association — E-mail: ebacon@lawbtp.com

Founding Partners

Patricia M. Thornton — 1953 — McGill University, B.A., 1976; The Catholic University of America, J.D., 1980 — Admitted to Bar, 1981, Maryland — Member Maryland State Bar Association; The Bar Association of the District of Columbia; Maryland Defense Trial Lawyers Association; District of Columbia Defense Lawyers Association — E-mail: pthornton@lawbtp.com

Mark D. Palmer — 1958 — Ohio Wesleyan University, B.A., 1980; The Catholic University of America, Columbus School of Law, J.D., 1984 — Admitted to Bar, 1985, Maryland — Member Maryland State and Prince George's County Bar Associations; The District of Columbia Bar; Maryland Defense Trial Lawyers Association; Association of Defense Trial Attorneys — E-mail: mpalmer@lawbtp.com

Partner

R. Brent Fuller — 1973 — St. Francis University, B.S. (cum laude), 1995; University of Maryland, J.D. (with honors), 2004 — Admitted to Bar, 2004, Maryland; 2005, U.S. District Court, District of Maryland — Member Anne Arundel County Bar Association — Practice Areas: Civil Litigation; Commercial Litigation; Insurance Defense — E-mail: rbfuller@lawbtp.com

Associates

Sean V. Werner — 1977 — Colgate University, B.A., 1999; American University, J.D., 2003 — Admitted to Bar, 2003, Maryland; 2004, District of Columbia; 2004, U.S. District Court, District of Maryland — Practice Areas: Asbestos Litigation; Insurance Defense; Personal Injury — E-mail: swerner@lawbtp.com

Sha'Donna M. Osborne — E-mail: sosborne@lawbtp.com

Claire J. Kim — E-mail: ckim@lawbtp.com

Patrick J. Flores — E-mail: pflores@lawbtp.com

Omar K. Barakat — E-mail: obarakat@lawbtp.com

HANOVER   7,907 Anne Arundel Co.

Refer To

Eccleston and Wolf
Professional Corporation
Baltimore Washington Law Center
7240 Parkway Drive, 4th Floor
Hanover, Maryland 21076
  Telephone: 410-752-7474
  Fax: 410-752-0611

Insurance Defense, Premises Liability, Product Liability, Professional Malpractice, Title Insurance, Accountants, Architects and Engineers, Engineers, Medical Liability, Automobile, Aviation, Construction, Environmental, Coverage, Attorneys, Employment, Physicians, Nurses, Investment Advisors

SEE COMPLETE LISTING UNDER BALTIMORE, MARYLAND (11 MILES)

OCEAN CITY   7,102 Worcester Co.

Refer To

Seidel, Baker & Tilghman, P.A.
Masonic Building
110 North Division Street
Salisbury, Maryland 21801
  Telephone: 410-742-8176
  Fax: 410-742-3117

Casualty, Fire, Surety, Workers' Compensation, Product Liability, Insurance Defense, Personal Injury, Subrogation

SEE COMPLETE LISTING UNDER SALISBURY, MARYLAND (28 MILES)

PRINCESS ANNE † 3,290 Somerset Co.

Refer To

Seidel, Baker & Tilghman, P.A.
Masonic Building
110 North Division Street
Salisbury, Maryland 21801
  Telephone: 410-742-8176
  Fax: 410-742-3117

Casualty, Fire, Surety, Workers' Compensation, Product Liability, Insurance Defense, Personal Injury, Subrogation

SEE COMPLETE LISTING UNDER SALISBURY, MARYLAND (13 MILES)

Refer To

Webb, Burnett, Cornbrooks, Wilber, Vorhis, Douse & Mason, L.L.P.
115 Broad Street
Salisbury, Maryland 21801
  Telephone: 410-742-3176
  Fax: 410-742-0438

Mailing Address: P.O. Box 910, Salisbury, MD 21803-0910

Insurance Defense, Automobile, General Liability, Personal Injury, Property Damage, Workers' Compensation, Subrogation

SEE COMPLETE LISTING UNDER SALISBURY, MARYLAND (13 MILES)

ROCKVILLE † 61,209 Montgomery Co.

Brault Graham, LLC
101 South Washington Street
Rockville, Maryland 20850
  Telephone: 301-424-1060
  Fax: 301-424-7991
  E-Mail: BG@braultgraham.com
  www.braultgrahamlaw.com

Established: 1952

Alternative Dispute Resolution, Automobile Liability, Automobile Tort, Bad Faith, Breach of Contract, Business Law, Carrier Defense, Civil Litigation, Civil Trial Practice, Construction Accidents, Coverage Issues, Defense Litigation, Dental Malpractice, First and Third Party Defense, General Civil Trial and Appellate Practice, Insurance Law, Trial Practice, Hospital Malpractice, Hospitals, Insurance Coverage, Insurance Defense, Insurance Litigation, Intentional Torts, Legal Malpractice, Litigation, Malpractice, Medical Malpractice, Medical Negligence, Motor Vehicle, Negligence, Personal Injury, Premises Liability, Product Liability, Professional Errors and Omissions, Professional Liability (Non-Medical) Defense, Professional Malpractice, Professional Negligence, Slip and Fall, Tort, Tort Liability, Tort Litigation, Trial and Appellate Practice, Uninsured and Underinsured Motorist, Wrongful Death

Firm Profile: Brault Graham, LLC was founded over fifty years ago as a general civil litigation firm and has experienced a measured growth to its present size of some nine lawyers. The firm maintains its principal office in Rockville, Maryland. It has the capacity to litigate in state and federal courts throughout the State of Maryland, Washington, D.C. and Northern Virginia. It will litigate in any jurisdiction required by its clients where its particular talents and expertise are needed.

The firm practices all aspects of insurance law, including policy interpretation, declaratory judgments, direct defense of insurers, excess insurance and general insurance defense litigation with special emphasis on medical and professional malpractice defense. In addition the firm practices extensively in the fields of commercial, corporate and estate litigation. Members of the firm also conduct civil mediations and arbitrations.

It has a wealth of experience in general litigation and in the defense of claims involving allegations of legal malpractice, medical malpractice, commercial, premises, products and automobile accident liability. Brault Graham, LLC also

Brault Graham, LLC, Rockville, MD (Continued)

regularly serves as counsel for numerous corporate clients, and as defense counsel for other corporate and business entities who are self-insured.

Since the firm's founding four members have been inducted as Fellows of the American College of Trial Lawyers and two have been elected to serve on the Board of Regents. Members of the firm have served as officers of local and state bar associations, have taught trial techniques, and have participated in numerous seminars involving the insurance industry, risk management and professional liability.

Insurance Clients

American Inter-Insurance Exchange	Andover Companies
CNA Insurance Company	Bituminous Casualty Corporation
Criterion Casualty Company	Colonial Penn Insurance Company
Fireman's Fund Insurance Companies	Crum & Forster Insurance Group
	Government Employees Insurance Company
The Hartford Insurance Group	Home Insurance Companies
Kemper Insurance Companies	Medical Mutual Liability Insurance Society of Maryland
National Indemnity Company	
Reliance Insurance Group	Safeco Insurance Companies
Transport Indemnity Company	United States Fire Insurance Company
USAA Insurance Company	
Utica Mutual Insurance Company	Virginia Farm Bureau Mutual Insurance Company

Non-Insurance Clients

C & P Telephone Company   Medlantic Healthcare Group

Resident Partners

Albert E. Brault — (Deceased)

Albert D. Brault — Georgetown University, B.S., 1955; J.D., 1958 — Admitted to Bar, 1958, District of Columbia; Maryland; U.S. District Court, District of Maryland; U.S. District Court for the District of Columbia; U.S. Court of Appeals, Fourth Circuit; U.S. Court of Appeals for the District of Columbia Circuit; U.S. Supreme Court; Superior Court for the District of Columbia — Member American and District of Columbia Bar Associations; Maryland State Bar Association (Past Member, Board of Governors and Executive Committee); Montgomery County Bar Association (Past-President); District of Columbia Defense Lawyers' Association; Standing Committee on Rules of Practice and Procedure of the Court of Appeals of Maryland; Maryland Bar Foundation; American Bar Foundation; American College of Trial Lawyers (Regent and Past Chairman for Maryland and District of Columbia); Master of the Bench, J. Dudley Digges and Montgomery Inns of Court; American Board of Trial Advocates; Defense Research Institute; Maryland Association of Defense Trial Counsel — Past Chairman, Qualifications Committee for Admission to the U.S. District Court, District of Maryland; Acting Chairman, Trial Court's Judicial Nominating Commission for the Sixth Judicial Circuit; Past Chairman, Appointed First Term by Governor Schaefer and Second Term by Governor Glendening, Maryland Appellate Judicial Nominating Commission; Lifetime Member, Fourth Circuit Judicial Conference; Devitt Commission on Lawyer Competency before the Federal Courts; District Advisory Board, Public Defender (1972-1984); Montgomery-Prince George's Continuing Education Institute (President, 1986-1988) — Practice Areas: Commercial Litigation; Professional Malpractice — E-mail: adb@braultgraham.com

James S. Wilson — Washington and Lee University, B.A., 1969; J.D. (cum laude), 1973 — Admitted to Bar, 1974, Maryland; 1976, District of Columbia; U.S. District Court, District of Maryland; U.S. Court of Appeals for the District of Columbia Circuit; U.S. Court of Appeals for the Federal Circuit; U.S. Court of Appeals, Fourth Circuit; U.S. Supreme Court — Member American, Maryland State and Montgomery County (Judicial Selections Committees) Bar Associations; Bar Association for the District of Columbia; Fellow, Maryland Bar Foundation; Defense Research Institute; Maryland Association of Defense Trial Counsel; Fellow, American College of Trial Lawyers — Appointed by Governor Ehrlich, Judicial Nominating Commission for District Eleven — Practice Areas: Arbitration; Litigation; Insurance Law; Mediation; Personal Injury; Professional Malpractice — E-mail: jsw@braultgraham.com

Daniel L. Shea — University of Florida, B.S., 1975; Potomac School of Law, J.D. (cum laude), 1979 — Admitted to Bar, 1979, Georgia; Maryland; 1986, District of Columbia; U.S. District Court for the District of Columbia; U.S. District Court, District of Maryland; U.S. Court of Appeals for the District of Columbia Circuit; U.S. Court of Appeals, Fourth Circuit; U.S. Supreme Court; Supreme Court of Georgia — Member American, District of Columbia, Maryland State and Montgomery County (Past Chairman, Insurance Committee) Bar Associations; State Bar of Georgia; Past Chairman, Ethics Committee; Past Panel Member, Attorney Grievance Commission of Maryland (1994-1996); Maryland Association of Defense Trial Counsel — Practice Areas: Commercial Law; Litigation; Insurance Law; Product Liability; Professional Malpractice — E-mail: dls@braultgraham.com

David Mulquin — College of the Holy Cross, A.B., 1981; The Catholic University of America, Columbus School of Law, J.D., 1984 — Admitted to Bar, 1985, Maryland; U.S. District Court, District of Maryland; U.S. Court of Appeals, Fourth Circuit — Member American, Maryland State and Montgomery County Bar Associations; Montgomery County Bar Foundation (The Speakers Bureau, School Division Committee); Alternative Dispute Resolution Committee — Mediator, District Court Mediation Program — Practice Areas: Civil Litigation; Insurance Law; Personal Injury; Product Liability; Professional Malpractice — E-mail: dmulquin@braultgraham.com

James M. Brault — 1960 — Furman University, B.A., 1982; University of Baltimore, J.D., 1986 — Admitted to Bar, 1986, Maryland; 1988, District of Columbia; U.S. District Court, District of Maryland; U.S. District Court for the District of Columbia; U.S. Court of Appeals, Fourth Circuit; U.S. Court of Appeals for the District of Columbia Circuit — Member American and District of Columbia Bar Associations; Maryland State Bar Association (Board of Governors, 2002-2004); Montgomery County Bar Association (Executive Committee, 1998-1999; Treasurer, 2000-2001); Barrister, Montgomery Inn of Court (1989-1991); Montgomery County Bar Foundation (Treasurer, 2001-2002); Maryland Board of Law Examiners (Character Committee, 1991-2000); Maryland Association of Defense Trial Counsel — Practice Areas: Civil Litigation; Commercial Law; Insurance Law; Professional Malpractice — E-mail: jmbrault@braultgraham.com

Stuart N. Herschfeld — University of New Hampshire, B.A., 1983; The George Washington University, M.A., 1987; American University, J.D., 1991 — Admitted to Bar, 1991, Maryland; District of Columbia; 1991, U.S. District Court, District of Maryland; 1991, U.S. District Court for the District of Columbia — Member American, District of Columbia, Maryland State and Montgomery County Bar Associations — Practice Areas: Civil Litigation; Drug; Medical Devices; Medical Liability; Professional Liability — E-mail: snh@braultgraham.com

David Franklin Ryder — American University, J.D., 1986 — Admitted to Bar, 1986, Maryland; 1988, District of Columbia — Member Montgomery County Bar Association; Bar Association of the District of Columbia — E-mail: dryder@braultgraham.com

O'Connell & O'Connell, LLC

401 East Jefferson Street, Suite 204
Rockville, Maryland 20850
  Telephone: 301-424-2300
  Fax: 301-424-2394
  www.oconnelllaw.com

(Fairfax, VA Office: 11130 Fairfax Boulevard, Suite 310, 22030)
  (Tel: 703-591-0698)
(Washington, DC Office: 1707 L Street NW, Suite 500, 20036-4202)

Established: 1992

Insurance Defense, Automobile, General Liability, Workers' Compensation, Employment Law, Coverage Issues, Personal Injury, Premises Liability, Subrogation, Education Law, Elevators/Escalators

Firm Profile: O'Connell & O'Connell, LLC's list of corporate, insurance, self-insured and public sector clients reflects the success of our litigation approach. We listen carefully to our clients and we strive to serve as advisors and problem solvers and to immediately and effectively respond to emergencies.

Insurance Clients

Arch Insurance Company	Automobile Club Inter-Insurance Exchange
Brotherhood Mutual Insurance Company	Brownyard Claims Management, Inc.
Chubb Group of Insurance Companies	Companion Property and Casualty Insurance Company
Gallagher Bassett Services, Inc.	
The Harleysville Insurance	The Hartford Insurance Company
Kemper Insurance Companies	Liberty Mutual Insurance Company
MiddleOak	Millers Mutual Group
Motorists Insurance Group	OneBeacon Insurance

SALISBURY   MARYLAND

O'Connell & O'Connell, LLC, Rockville, MD (Continued)

Non-Insurance Clients

Avis Budget Group, Inc.
Coach USA
Crawford & Company
Enterprise Leasing Company
Inova Health System
Potomac Electric Power Company
Safeway Stores, Inc.
Tractor Supply Co.
Cambridge Integrated Services Group, Inc.
Dollar Rent A Car Systems, Inc.
Hertz Claim Management
Miller & Long Concrete Construction
ThyssenKrupp Elevator Corporation

Firm Members

Kevin J. O'Connell — 1950 — Villanova University, B.A., 1972; Georgetown University, J.D., 1978 — Admitted to Bar, 1978, District of Columbia; 1982, Maryland; 1991, Virginia; 1979, U.S. District Court for the District of Columbia; U.S. Court of Appeals for the District of Columbia Circuit; 1988, U.S. Supreme Court; 1991, U.S. District Court, Eastern District of Virginia; U.S. Court of Appeals, Fourth Circuit; 1994, U.S. District Court, District of Maryland — Member Maryland State Bar Association; The District of Columbia Bar; Association of Compensation Insurance Attorneys; District of Columbia Defense Lawyers Association; Defense Research Institute — Practice Areas: Civil Litigation; Workers' Compensation — E-mail: kevin@oconnelllaw.com

Terence J. O'Connell — 1956 — The Catholic University of America, B.A., 1978; J.D., 1982 — Admitted to Bar, 1982, District of Columbia; 1983, Maryland; U.S. District Court of Maryland; U.S. District Court for the District of Columbia; 1996, U.S. Court of Appeals for the District of Columbia Circuit; 2001, U.S. Supreme Court — Member Maryland State and Montgomery County Bar Associations; The District of Columbia Bar; Maryland Defense Lawyers Association; Claims and Litigation Management Alliance; District of Columbia Defense Lawyers Association; Defense Research Institute — Practice Areas: Civil Litigation; Insurance Defense — E-mail: toconnell@oconnelllaw.com

William T. Kennard — 1957 — Hofstra University, B.A., 1981; St. Johns University School of Law, J.D., 1985 — Admitted to Bar, 1986, New York; 1994, District of Columbia; 1995, Virginia; 1991, U.S. District Court, Eastern and Southern Districts of New York; 1996, U.S. District Court, Eastern District of Virginia; 2000, U.S. District Court, Western District of Virginia — Member Virginia Bar Association; The District of Columbia Bar — E-mail: bkennard@oconnelllaw.com

Associate Attorneys

Nathalie Johnson-Noon — 1977 — College of William & Mary, B.A., 1999; The Pennsylvania State University Dickinson School of Law, J.D., 2002 — Admitted to Bar, 2002, Maryland; 2003, District of Columbia; 2004, Virginia — E-mail: njohnson-noon@oconnelllaw.com

Shawn M. Nolen — 1974 — University of Notre Dame, B.A., 1997; Rutgers University School of Law, J.D., 2002 — Admitted to Bar, 2003, Indiana; 2009, District of Columbia; 2011, Maryland; U.S. District Court, Northern and Southern Districts of Indiana — E-mail: shawn@oconnelllaw.com

Danielle E. Banducci — 1986 — The Pennsylvania State University, B.A., 2007; The University of Chicago Law School, J.D., 2010 — Admitted to Bar, 2010, Pennsylvania; 2012, Virginia — E-mail: danielle@oconnelllaw.com

Bryan J. McDermott — 1984 — College of William & Mary, B.A., 2007; The Catholic University of America, Columbus School of Law, J.D., 2012 — Admitted to Bar, 2012, Alabama; New Jersey

Jennifer K. Buell — East Carolina University, B.S., 2001; M.S., 2003; University of Baltimore, J.D., 2006 — Admitted to Bar, 2006, Maryland — E-mail: jbuell@oconnelllaw.com

---

The following firms also service this area.

Carr Maloney P.C.
2000 L Street, NW, Suite 450
Washington, District of Columbia 20036
   Telephone: 202-310-5500
   Fax: 202-310-5555

Appellate Practice, Civil Rights, Commercial Litigation, Complex Litigation, Construction Law, Directors and Officers Liability, General Liability, Government Investigations and Enforcement, Health Care, Immigration Law, Insurance Coverage, Labor and Employment, Product Liability, Professional Liability, Religious Institutions, Retailers and Chain Restaurant Litigation, Risk Management, Toxic Torts, Mass Tort, Trust and Estate Litigation

SEE COMPLETE LISTING UNDER WASHINGTON, DISTRICT OF COLUMBIA (20 MILES)

Law Offices of Joseph F. Cunningham & Associates, PLC
1600 Wilson Boulevard, Suite 1008
Arlington, Virginia 22209
   Telephone: 703-294-6500
   Fax: 703-294-4885

Insurance Defense, Professional Liability, Workers' Compensation, Alternative Dispute Resolution, Coverage Issues, Litigation, Appeals, Arbitration, Condo Disputes, Health Law, Construction Disputes, Trucking Defense, Litigation, Aviation Law

SEE COMPLETE LISTING UNDER ARLINGTON, VIRGINIA (28 MILES)

SALISBURY † 30,343 Wicomico Co.

Seidel, Baker & Tilghman, P.A.

Masonic Building
110 North Division Street
Salisbury, Maryland 21801
   Telephone: 410-742-8176
   Fax: 410-742-3117
   E-Mail: SeidelBakerandTilghman@gmail.com
   www.sbtlawfirm.com

Established: 1932

Casualty, Fire, Surety, Workers' Compensation, Product Liability, Insurance Defense, Personal Injury, Subrogation

Insurance Clients

Alfa Vision Insurance Corp.
Colonial Penn Insurance Company
Empire Insurance Company
Kemper Insurance Companies
Maryland Automobile Insurance Fund
New York Central Mutual Fire Insurance Company
State Farm Mutual Automobile Insurance Company
Utica Mutual Insurance Company
Canal Insurance Company
Continental Insurance Company
GEICO-Government Employees Insurance Company
National Indemnity Company
Nationwide Insurance
The Peninsula Insurance Company
Penn National Insurance
United Services Automobile Association (USAA)

Non-Insurance Clients

Beth Israel Congregation
Town of Berlin Planning Commission
Tri-County Council for the Lower Eastern Shore of Maryland
Pocomoke City, Maryland
Town of Princess Anne, Maryland
Town of Vienna, Maryland

Sheldon B. Seidel — (1925-2001)

S. Mark Tilghman — 1959 — University of Maryland (with honors), 1980; University of Baltimore, J.D., 1984 — Admitted to Bar, 1985, Maryland; 2001, U.S. District Court, District of Maryland; U.S. Court of Appeals, Fourth Circuit — Member Maryland State and Wicomico County Bar Associations

Susan Seidel Tilghman — 1959 — Goucher College, B.A., 1980; University of Baltimore School of Law, J.D., 1983 — Admitted to Bar, 1983, Maryland — Member Maryland State and Wicomico County Bar Associations

Peter J. Golba — 1970 — Southern Illinois University Carbondale, B.S., 1991; Widener University School of Law, J.D., 1996 — Admitted to Bar, 1997, Maryland; Delaware — Member Delaware State and Wicomico County Bar Associations

Webb, Burnett, Cornbrooks, Wilber, Vorhis, Douse & Mason, L.L.P.

115 Broad Street
Salisbury, Maryland 21801
   Telephone: 410-742-3176
   Fax: 410-742-0438
   E-Mail: ecornbrooks@webbnetlaw.com
   www.webbburnett.com

MARYLAND

Webb, Burnett, Cornbrooks, Wilber, Vorhis, Douse & Mason, L.L.P., Salisbury, MD (Continued)

(Ocean City, MD Office: Ocean Creek Plaza, 12216 Ocean Gateway, Suite 500, 21842)
(Tel: 443-664-2630)
(Fax: 443-664-2689)

Established: 1913

Insurance Defense, Automobile, General Liability, Personal Injury, Property Damage, Workers' Compensation, Subrogation

Insurance Clients

Allstate Insurance Company
Donegal Mutual Insurance Company
Liberty Mutual Insurance Company
Ohio Casualty Group
Selective Insurance Company of America
Brethren Mutual Insurance Company
GEICO-Government Employees Insurance Company
The Peninsula Insurance Company

Firm Members

John W. T. Webb — (1918-1990)

Ernest I. Cornbrooks, III — 1945 — Washington and Lee University, A.B., 1967; University of Maryland, J.D., 1970 — Admitted to Bar, 1970, Maryland; 1970, U.S. District Court, District of Maryland; 1970, U.S. Court of Appeals, Fourth Circuit; 1970, U.S. Supreme Court — Member American Bar Association (Sections on Litigation and Tort and Insurance Practice); Maryland State and Wicomico County Bar Associations; Selden Society; The Federalist Society for Law and Public Policy Studies; Fellow, Maryland State Bar Foundation; Defense Research Institute; Maryland Association of Defense Trial Counsel — Practice Areas: Litigation; Insurance Law; Negligence

Paul D. Wilber — 1949 — Washington and Lee University, B.A., 1971; J.D., 1974 — Admitted to Bar, 1974, Maryland; 1974, U.S. District Court, District of Maryland — Member American, Maryland State and Wicomico County Bar Associations; Fellow, Maryland State Bar Foundation

David A. Vorhis — 1952 — Swarthmore College, B.A., 1974; University of Virginia, J.D., 1977 — Admitted to Bar, 1977, Maryland; 1977, U.S. District Court, District of Maryland — Member American, Maryland State and Wicomico County Bar Associations

David B. Douse — 1955 — University of Virginia, B.A., 1977; J.D., 1980 — Admitted to Bar, 1980, Maryland; 1982, U.S. District Court, District of Maryland — Member American, Maryland State and Wicomico County Bar Associations — Practice Areas: Litigation

Chris Schiller Mason — 1968 — Salisbury State University, B.A., 1990; University of Baltimore, J.D., 1993 — Admitted to Bar, 1993, Maryland; 1993, U.S. District Court, District of Maryland — Member Maryland State and Wicomico County Bar Associations — Practice Areas: Litigation

Roscoe R. Leslie — 1978 — University of Delaware, B.A., 2000; Washington and Lee University School of Law, J.D., 2006 — Admitted to Bar, 2006, Maryland; 2008, District of Columbia; 2007, U.S. District Court, District of Maryland; 2010, U.S. Court of Appeals, Fourth Circuit — Member American Bar Association — Practice Areas: Civil Litigation; Construction Litigation; Real Estate

Of Counsel

K. King Burnett — 1935 — University of Virginia, B.A., 1957; LL.B., 1960 — Admitted to Bar, 1960, Virginia; 1961, Maryland; 1963, New York; 1963, U.S. District Court, District of Maryland; 1963, U.S. Court of Appeals, Fourth Circuit; 1963, U.S. Supreme Court — Member American, Maryland State, New York State and Wicomico County Bar Associations; Virginia State Bar; The Association of the Bar of the City of New York; Fellow, American College of Trial Lawyers — Languages: French

SILVER SPRING

SILVER SPRING 71,452 Montgomery Co.

Saunders & Schmieler, P.C.

The Montgomery Center, Suite 1202
8630 Fenton Street
Silver Spring, Maryland 20910-3808
Telephone: 301-588-7717
Fax: 301-588-5073
E-Mail: schmielerj@sslawfirm.com
www.sslawfirm.com

Advertising Injury, Animal Law, Appellate Practice, Civil Rights, Class Actions, Contracts, Construction Liability, Corporate Law, Directors and Officers Liability, Environmental Law, Errors and Omissions, Insurance Coverage, Risk Management, Intellectual Property, Labor and Employment, Mass Tort, Medical Malpractice, Personal Injury, Premises Liability, Product Liability, Professional Malpractice, Sports Law, Real Estate, Self-Insured Defense, Toxic Torts, Workers' Compensation, Wrongful Death

Firm Profile: Saunders & Schmieler, P.C. is a full service law firm engaged in the practice of law in all state and federal courts in Maryland, Washington, D.C. and Virginia. The firm has represented the interests of a wide spectrum of individual, corporate and insurance clients. Our attorneys emphasize the importance of providing sound legal advice and affording personal representation of the highest quality in order to meet the goals of our clients.

Insurance Clients

Broadspire
Chubb Group of Insurance Companies

Founding Member

Jeffrey R. Schmieler — Duquesne University School of Law; University of Maryland School of Law, J.D., 1967 — Phoenix Award for Scholastic Achievement, 1964; Clarence Darrow Scholarship for Outstanding Scholastic Achievement, 1967 — Admitted to Bar, 1967, Maryland; 1969, District of Columbia; 1991, Virginia; 1967, U.S. Court of Appeals, Fourth Circuit; 1968, U.S. District Court, District of Maryland; 1969, U.S. District Court for the District of Columbia; 1969, U.S. Court of Appeals for the District of Columbia Circuit; 1969, U.S. Court of Appeals for the Armed Forces; 1969, U.S. Tax Court; 1970, U.S. Court of Federal Claims; 1971, U.S. Supreme Court; 1991, U.S. District Court, Eastern District of Virginia — Member American, Maryland State and Montgomery County Bar Associations; The District of Columbia Bar; Virginia State Bar; Governor's Executive Advisory Counsel; Select Panel on Insurance Fraud; Washington Claim Association; National Council of Self-Insurers; Defense Research Institute

Principal

Brian E. Hoffman — American University, Washington College of Law, J.D. (magna cum laude), 2000 — Moot Court; Environmental Law Society; International Law Society — Admitted to Bar, 2000, Maryland; 2001, District of Columbia; 2001, U.S. District Court for the District of Columbia; 2001, U.S. District Court, District of Maryland; 2005, U.S. Court of Appeals, Fourth Circuit; 2007, U.S. Court of Appeals for the District of Columbia Circuit — Member American and Maryland State Bar Associations; The District of Columbia Bar

Senior Associate

Alan B. Neurick — University of Baltimore School of Law, J.D., 1999 — Moot Court Board; Constitutional Law Achievement Scholar; Intellectual Property Law Journal — Admitted to Bar, 1999, Maryland; 2002, District of Columbia; 2000, U.S. District Court, District of Maryland; 2004, U.S. Court of Appeals, Fourth Circuit; 2006, U.S. District Court for the District of Columbia; 2011, U.S. Court of Appeals for the District of Columbia Circuit — Member The District of Columbia Bar; Maryland State Bar Association

Associates

Samuel T. Wolf
Lisa N. Walters
Connie M. Ng
Brian P. McIlhargie
Nathan J. Bresee

TOWSON MARYLAND

SNOW HILL † 2,103 Worcester Co.

Refer To
Seidel, Baker & Tilghman, P.A.
Masonic Building
110 North Division Street
Salisbury, Maryland 21801
    Telephone: 410-742-8176
    Fax: 410-742-3117

Casualty, Fire, Surety, Workers' Compensation, Product Liability, Insurance Defense, Personal Injury, Subrogation

SEE COMPLETE LISTING UNDER SALISBURY, MARYLAND (18 MILES)

Refer To
Webb, Burnett, Cornbrooks, Wilber, Vorhis, Douse & Mason, L.L.P.
115 Broad Street
Salisbury, Maryland 21801
    Telephone: 410-742-3176
    Fax: 410-742-0438

Mailing Address: P.O. Box 910, Salisbury, MD 21803-0910

Insurance Defense, Automobile, General Liability, Personal Injury, Property Damage, Workers' Compensation, Subrogation

SEE COMPLETE LISTING UNDER SALISBURY, MARYLAND (18 MILES)

TOWSON † 55,197 Baltimore Co.

Refer To
Pessin Katz Law, P.A.
901 Dulaney Valley Road
Suite 400
Towson, Maryland 21204
    Telephone: 410-938-8800
    Fax: 410-832-5600

Insurance Defense, Coverage Issues, Regulatory and Compliance, Administrative Law, Agent and Brokers Errors and Omissions, Disability, Business Law, Construction Law, Class Actions

SEE COMPLETE LISTING UNDER BALTIMORE, MARYLAND (10 MILES)

Refer To
Tighe & Cottrell, P.A.
One Customs House
704 King Street, Suite 500
Wilmington, Delaware 19801
    Telephone: 302-658-6400
    Fax: 302-658-9836

Mailing Address: P.O. Box 1031, Wilmington, DE 19899-1031

General Liability, Professional Liability, Construction Law, Coverage Issues, Litigation, Surety Bonds, Subrogation, Malpractice

SEE COMPLETE LISTING UNDER WILMINGTON, DELAWARE (70 MILES)

MASSACHUSETTS

CAPITAL: BOSTON

COUNTIES AND COUNTY SEATS

County	County Seat	County	County Seat	County	County Seat
Barnstable	Barnstable	Franklin	Greenfield	Norfolk	Dedham
Berkshire	Pittsfield	Hampden	Springfield	Plymouth	Plymouth
Bristol	Taunton	Hampshire	Northampton	Suffolk	Boston
Dukes	Edgartown	Middlesex	Cambridge	Worcester	Worcester
Essex	Salem	Nantucket	Nantucket		

In the text that follows "†" indicates County Seats.

Our files contain additional verified data on the firms listed herein. This additional information is available on request.

A.M. BEST COMPANY

MASSACHUSETTS

BARNSTABLE † 2,790 Barnstable Co.

Refer To

Rubin, Rudman, Chamberlain and Marsh
Cape Cod Office of Rubin and Rudman LLP
99 Willow Street
Yarmouth Port, Massachusetts 02675
 Telephone: 508-362-6262
 Fax: 508-362-6060

Mailing Address: P.O. Box 40, Yarmouth Port, MA 02675

Insurance Defense, Automobile, General Liability, Product Liability, Medical Malpractice, Civil Litigation

SEE COMPLETE LISTING UNDER YARMOUTH PORT, MASSACHUSETTS (3 MILES)

Refer To

Zizik, Powers, O'Connell, Spaulding & Lamontagne, P.C.
690 Canton Street, Suite 306
Westwood, Massachusetts 02090
 Telephone: 781-320-5400
 Fax: 781-320-5444

Insurance Defense, Automobile, Construction Law, Coverage Issues, Disability, Environmental Law, General Liability, Hazardous Waste, Life Insurance, Liquor Liability, Personal Injury, Premises Liability, Product Liability, Toxic Torts, Alternative Dispute Resolution, Antitrust, Employment Law, Commercial Litigation, Fire Loss, Trucking Litigation

SEE COMPLETE LISTING UNDER WESTWOOD, MASSACHUSETTS (73 MILES)

BELMONT   24,729 Middlesex Co.

Refer To

Avery Dooley & Noone, LLP
3 Brighton Street
Belmont, Massachusetts 02478
 Telephone: 617-489-5300
 Fax: 617-489-0085

Insurance Defense, Trial Practice, Automobile, Homeowners, Casualty, Fire, Fraud, Subrogation, Comprehensive General Liability, Environmental Law, General Liability, Accident and Health, Life Insurance, Coverage Issues, Product Liability, Professional Liability, Workers' Compensation, Employment Law, Employment Practices Liability, Toxic Torts, Liquor Liability, Litigation, Arbitration, Mediation, Alternative Dispute Resolution, Bad Faith, Federal Employment Law

SEE COMPLETE LISTING UNDER BOSTON, MASSACHUSETTS (10 MILES)

BOSTON † 617,594 Suffolk Co.

Adler, Cohen, Harvey, Wakeman & Guekguezian LLP

75 Federal Street, 10th Floor
Boston, Massachusetts 02110
 Telephone: 617-423-6674
 Fax: 617-423-7152
 E-Mail: adlercohen@adlercohen.com
 www.adlercohen.com

(Providence, RI Office: 170 Westminster Street, 02903)
 (Tel: 401-521-6100)
 (Fax: 401-521-1001)

Established: 1995

Administrative Law, Appellate Practice, Asbestos Litigation, Bodily Injury, Casualty Defense, Civil Litigation, Civil Trial Practice, Commercial Litigation, Complex Litigation, Construction Litigation, Dental Malpractice, Employment Law, Hospital Malpractice, Insurance Defense, Insurance Law, Legal Malpractice, Medical Devices, Medical Liability, Medical Malpractice, Mold and Mildew Claims, Personal Injury, Pharmaceutical, Premises Liability, Product Liability, Professional Liability, Slip and Fall, State and Federal Courts, Tort, Toxic Torts, Wrongful Death

---

Adler, Cohen, Harvey, Wakeman & Guekguezian LLP, Boston, MA (Continued)

Insurance Clients

Allied Professionals Insurance Company
CMIC Group
CNA HealthPro
Coverys
Electric Insurance Company
The Hartford
Lifespan Risk Services, Inc.
The Medical Protective Company
MedPro Claims
NCMIC Group - Professional Solutions Insurance Company
OMS National Insurance Company
Utica Mutual Insurance Company
CHG Healthcare Services, Inc.
Chubb Group of Insurance Companies
CNE Risk Management
CRICO/RMF
Fortress Insurance Company
Liberty Mutual Insurance Group
Medical Malpractice Joint Underwriting Association of Rhode Island
NCMIC Insurance Company
Northeast Health System
St. Paul Travelers
Western Litigation, Inc.

Non-Insurance Clients

Boston Medical Center
Feld Entertainment
Lahey Clinic
Massachusetts Medical Society
Tufts Medical Center
Federal Signal Corporation
Ingersoll-Rand Company
Leach Company
The 3M Company

Partners

Ellen Epstein Cohen — 1959 — State University of New York at Binghamton, B.A. (with honors), 1980; Boston University School of Law, J.D., 1983 — Admitted to Bar, 1983, Massachusetts — E-mail: ecohen@adlercohen.com

Alexandra B. Harvey — 1958 — University of Colorado, B.A. (magna cum laude), 1983; Boston University School of Law, J.D. (cum laude), 1986 — Admitted to Bar, 1986, Massachusetts — E-mail: aharvey@adlercohen.com

George E. Wakeman, Jr. — 1956 — Princeton University, B.A. (cum laude), 1978; Suffolk University, J.D., 1981 — Admitted to Bar, 1981, Massachusetts; 1994, Rhode Island — E-mail: gwakeman@adlercohen.com

A. Bernard Guekguezian — 1964 — Harvard University, B.A., 1986; Vanderbilt University, J.D., 1991 — Admitted to Bar, 1991, Massachusetts — E-mail: bguekguezian@adlercohen.com

Jennifer Boyd Herlihy — 1971 — Boston University, B.S. (cum laude), 1993; Suffolk University Law School, J.D. (cum laude), 1997 — Admitted to Bar, 1997, Massachusetts; 2003, Rhode Island — E-mail: jherlihy@adlercohen.com

Michael B. Barkley — 1978 — Tufts University, B.A., 2000; Boston University School of Law, J.D. (cum laude), 2003 — Admitted to Bar, 2003, Massachusetts — E-mail: mbarkley@adlercohen.com

Gabriel W. Bell — 1973 — Macalester College, B.A. (cum laude), 1996; University of Connecticut School of Law, J.D. (with honors), 2003 — Admitted to Bar, 2004, Massachusetts — E-mail: gbell@adlercohen.com

Associates

Brooks L. Glahn — 1973 — Union College, B.A., 1995; Northeastern University School of Law, J.D., 2000 — Admitted to Bar, 2001, Massachusetts — E-mail: bglahn@adlercohen.com

Megan M. Grew — 1976 — Saint Anselm College, H.B.A. (with honors), 1999; Suffolk University Law School, J.D. (cum laude), 2002 — Admitted to Bar, 2002, Massachusetts — E-mail: mgrew@adlercohen.com

E. Amy LaBrecque — 1979 — College of the Holy Cross, B.A., 2001; University of Connecticut School of Law, J.D., 2004 — Admitted to Bar, 2004, Massachusetts; 2006, Connecticut — E-mail: alabrecque@adlercohen.com

Timothy M. Zabbo — 1980 — Providence College, B.A. (magna cum laude), 2002; Suffolk University Law School, J.D. (cum laude), 2005 — Admitted to Bar, 2005, Massachusetts; 2005, Rhode Island; 2012, Connecticut — E-mail: tzabbo@adlercohen.com

Deirdre Kirby Lydon — 1980 — Hamilton College, B.A., 2002; Suffolk University Law School, J.D., 2007 — Admitted to Bar, 2007, Massachusetts — E-mail: dlydon@adlercohen.com

Kara L. Lisavich — 1981 — Colgate University, B.A. (Dean's List), 2004; Suffolk University Law School, J.D., 2009 — Admitted to Bar, 2009, Massachusetts; 2009, Rhode Island — E-mail: klisavich@adlercohen.com

Brent W. Gilbert — 1985 — Providence College, B.A., 2007; Suffolk University Law School, J.D., 2010 — Admitted to Bar, 2010, Massachusetts; 2010, Rhode Island — E-mail: bgilbert@adlercohen.com

Cassandra L. Feeney — 1987 — University of Rhode Island, B.A. (summa cum laude), 2007; New England School of Law, J.D. (magna cum laude),

BOSTON   MASSACHUSETTS

Adler, Cohen, Harvey, Wakeman & Guekguezian LLP, Boston, MA (Continued)

2011 — Admitted to Bar, 2011, Rhode Island; 2011, Massachusetts — E-mail: cfeeney@adlercohen.com

Rachael E. Gramet — 1985 — Tufts University, B.A. (cum laude), 2008; Northeastern University School of Law, J.D., 2011 — Admitted to Bar, 2011, Massachusetts — Member Women's Bar Association of Massachusetts — E-mail: rgramet@adlercohen.com

Thaddeus M. Lenkiewicz — 1984 — University of Notre Dame, B.A., 2007; Vanderbilt University Law School, J.D., 2011 — Admitted to Bar, 2012, Massachusetts; 2012, New York — E-mail: tlenkiewicz@adlercohen.com

Michelle L. McClafferty — 1987 — Syracuse University, B.A. (magna cum laude), 2009; Boston College Law School, J.D., 2012 — Admitted to Bar, 2012, Massachusetts — E-mail: mmcclafferty@adlercohen.com

Alexander E. Terry — 1988 — Boston College, B.A., 2010; Suffolk University Law School, J.D., 2013 — Admitted to Bar, 2013, Massachusetts; 2013, Rhode Island — E-mail: aterry@adlercohen.com

Adler Pollock & Sheehan P.C.

175 Federal Street, 10th Floor
Boston, Massachusetts 02110-2210
Telephone: 617-482-0600
Fax: 617-482-0604
www.apslaw.com

(Providence, RI Office*: One Citizens Plaza, 8th Floor, 02903-1345)
(Tel: 401-274-7200)
(Fax: 401-751-0604)
(Newport, RI Office: 49 Bellevue Avenue, 02840)
(Tel: 401-847-1919)

Insurance Defense, General Liability, Property and Casualty, Fidelity and Surety, Coverage Issues, Workers' Compensation, Subrogation

Firm Profile: With offices in Providence, RI, Newport RI, Boston, MA and Manchester, NH, Adler Pollock & Sheehan P.C. is a full service law firm offering a wide variety of practice areas ready to handle all the legal needs of clients.

Insurance Clients

Acadia Insurance Company
Admiral Insurance Company
Burlington Insurance Company
Chartis Insurance
Church Insurance Company
CNA Insurance Companies
CNA Surety Corporation
Connecticut Underwriters, Inc.
Eagle Insurance Company
Electric Mutual Liability Insurance Company
Fidelity and Deposit Company of Maryland
Gallagher Bassett Services, Inc.
Great Oaks Casualty Insurance Company
Gulf Insurance Group
Highlands Insurance Group
Imperial Casualty and Indemnity Company
Lexington Insurance Company
Lloyd's Underwriters
Maxum Specialty Insurance Group
MiddleOak
New London County Mutual Insurance Company
OneBeacon Insurance
Providence Washington Insurance Company
The St. Paul/Travelers Companies, Inc.
TIG Insurance Company
Travelers Casualty and Surety Company
United Educators Insurance
United States Liability Insurance Group
ACE/USA Insurance Company
Arrowpoint Capital Corporation
Caliber One Indemnity Company
Chubb Group of Insurance Companies
CNA PRO
Commerce Insurance Company
Crum & Forster Insurance
Eastern Dentists Insurance Company
Essex Insurance Company
First Financial Insurance Company
First Mercury Insurance Company
General Star Management Company
Guilford Specialty Group, Inc.
HDI-Gerling America Insurance Company
Investors Underwriting Managers, Inc.
Liberty Mutual Insurance Company
Markel Corporation
Merchants Insurance Group
Nautilus Insurance Group
The Northwestern Mutual Life Insurance Company
The Patrons Group
Royal Surplus Assurance
Safeco Insurance
Scottsdale Insurance Company
Secure Insurance Company
Transcontinental Insurance Company
Trust Insurance Company
United States Fire Insurance Company
USF Insurance Company

Adler Pollock & Sheehan P.C., Boston, MA (Continued)

Wawanesa Mutual Insurance Company
York Risk Services Group, Inc.
Winterthur Group
W.R. Berkley Corporation

Non-Insurance Clients

Aegis Protection Group, Inc.
Carolina Door Controls, Inc
Elliott Company
Home Depot USA, Inc.
Merrill Lynch, Pierce, Fenner & Smith, Inc.
Nuttall Gear, LLC
Transportation Program Administrators
American International Adjustment Company
The Glynn Hospitality Group, Inc.
K. MacDonald and Associates, Inc.
National Association of Securities Dealers, Inc.
On Target Utility Services

Firm Members

John A. Tarantino — Dartmouth College, A.B. (magna cum laude), 1976; Boston College, J.D. (magna cum laude), 1981 — Admitted to Bar, 1981, Rhode Island; Massachusetts; 1982, U.S. District Court, District of Rhode Island; 1984, U.S. District Court, District of Massachusetts; U.S. District Court, District of Connecticut; U.S. Court of Appeals, First Circuit; 1986, U.S. Supreme Court; 1989, U.S. Court of Appeals, Ninth Circuit; 1997, U.S. District Court, District of Arizona — Member American (Tort and Insurance Practice Section), Rhode Island (President, 1997-1998), Massachusetts and New England (President, 2002-2003) Bar Associations; Defense Research Institute; Fellow, American College of Trial Lawyers; American Board of Trial Advocates; Fellow, American Bar Foundation — "Personal Injury Forms," James Publishing 2d. Ed. (1996); "Trial Evidence Foundations," James Publishing 2d. Ed. (1996); "Litigating Neck and Back Injuries," James Publishing (1987); "Environmental Liability Transaction Guide," Wiley Law (1992); "Strategic Use of Scientific Evidence," Wiley Law (1988); Co-Author: "Estimating and Proving Personal Injury Damages," James Publishing (1988); "Personal Injury Trial Handbook," Wiley Law (1989); "Premises Security, Law and Practice," Wiley Law (1990); "Commercial remises Liability," Wiley Law (1991) — E-mail: jtarantino@apslaw.com

Richard R. Beretta, Jr. — College of the Holy Cross, A.B., 1982; Tufts University School of Dental Medicine, D.M.D., 1986; Northeastern University, J.D., 1989 — Admitted to Bar, 1989, Massachusetts; 1990, Rhode Island; 1989, U.S. District Court, District of Massachusetts; 1990, U.S. District Court, District of Rhode Island — Member American (Insurance and Health Sections), Massachusetts, and Rhode Island Bar Associations; Defense Research Institute — E-mail: rberetta@apslaw.com

Michael D. Riseberg — University of Massachusetts Amherst, B.A. (summa cum laude), 1991; Boston College, J.D., 1994 — Admitted to Bar, 1994, Massachusetts; 1995, U.S. District Court, District of Massachusetts; 2005, U.S. Court of Appeals, First Circuit — Member Massachusetts Defense Lawyers Association (Vice President, Director, Past Chair; Insurance and Bad Faith Law Committee); Defense Research Institute — E-mail: mriseberg@apslaw.com

(See listing under Providence, RI for additional information)

Avery Dooley & Noone, LLP

3 Brighton Street
Belmont, Massachusetts 02478
Telephone: 617-489-5300
Fax: 617-489-0085
E-Mail: info@averydooley.com
www.averydooley.com

Established: 1921

Insurance Defense, Trial Practice, Automobile, Homeowners, Casualty, Fire, Fraud, Subrogation, Comprehensive General Liability, Environmental Law, General Liability, Accident and Health, Life Insurance, Coverage Issues, Product Liability, Professional Liability, Workers' Compensation, Employment Law, Employment Practices Liability, Toxic Torts, Liquor Liability, Litigation, Arbitration, Mediation, Alternative Dispute Resolution, Bad Faith, Federal Employment Law

Firm Profile: Established in 1921, Avery Dooley & Noone, LLP is a versatile, multi-disciplinary law firm that specializes in insurance defense and

Avery Dooley & Noone, LLP, Boston, MA (Continued)

federal and state employment litigation. Our practice also includes the representation of businesses and individuals concerning their closely held and family based entities, real estate matters, and personal legal issues.

Insurance Clients

Acceptance Insurance Company
American Bankers Insurance Company of Florida
Auto-Owners Insurance Company
California Casualty Insurance Company
Canadian Indemnity Company
Central Mutual Insurance Company
Cincinnati Insurance Company
Civil Service Employees Insurance Company
Connecticut Security Insurance Company
Country-Wide Insurance Company
Dairyland Insurance Company
Eagle Star Insurance Company, Ltd.
Employers Casualty Company
Employers National Insurance Company
Farmers Insurance Group
Financial Indemnity Company
General Mutual Insurance Company
Guardian Insurance Company of Canada
Harleysville Mutual Insurance Company
Industrial Indemnity Company
International Service Insurance Company
Iowa National Mutual Insurance Company
Meridian Mutual Insurance Company
Motor Club of America Group
Motorists Mutual Insurance Company
National Casualty Company
National Insurance Underwriters
New Jersey Manufacturers Insurance Company
Ocean Accident Insurance Company
Ohio Farmers Insurance Company
Penn National Insurance
Pennsylvania Manufacturers' Association Insurance Company
Protective Insurance Company
Prudential Property and Casualty Insurance Company
State Farm Insurance Companies
State Farm Mutual Automobile Insurance Company
United States Casualty Company
Universal Underwriters Insurance Company
ACUITY, A Mutual Insurance Company
American Specialty Insurance & Risk Services, Inc.
Canadian General Insurance Company
Carriers Insurance Company
Chubb Group of Insurance Companies
Commercial Standard Insurance Company
Cooperative Insurance Service
COUNTRY Mutual Insurance Company
Detroit Automobile Inter-Insurance Exchange
Educator and Executive Insurance Company
Farm Bureau Mutual Insurance Company
Federal Services Underwriters
Florists' Insurance Company
Great Lakes Mutual Insurance Company
GuideOne Mutual Insurance Company
Indiana Insurance Company
Indiana Lumbermens Mutual Insurance Company
Investors Underwriting Managers, Inc.
Main Insurance Company
Markel Investors Underwriting Managers, Inc.
Merit Insurance Company of Canada
Mutual Service Casualty Insurance Company
National Indemnity Company
National Union Fire Insurance Company
Northwestern National Insurance Company
Ohio Casualty Insurance Company
Pawtucket Insurance Company
Pennsylvania Lumbermens Mutual Insurance Company
Progressive County Mutual Insurance Company
Reserve Insurance Company
Southern Farm Bureau Casualty Group
Unigard Insurance Company
United Farm Bureau Mutual Insurance Company

Non-Insurance Clients

Alamo Rent-A-Car, LLC
AutoNation Incorporated
Carolina Freight Carriers Corporation
ENSR International
Intex Recreation Corp
Missouri Auto Club
Republic Industries Waste Management
Automobile Legal Association
Canadian Freight Carrier's Corporation
CarTemps USA
ING Western Union
Jones Motor Group
National Car Rental
Tenet Healthcare Corporation

Self-Insured Clients

Boston Red Sox Baseball Club

Partners

Joseph M. Noone — 1965 — College of the Holy Cross, B.A., 1988; Suffolk University, J.D., 1991 — Admitted to Bar, 1991, Massachusetts; U.S. District Court, District of Massachusetts; U.S. Court of Appeals, First Circuit —

Avery Dooley & Noone, LLP, Boston, MA (Continued)

Member American, Massachusetts, Middlesex County and Cambridge-Arlington-Belmont Bar Associations; Real Estate Bar Association for Massachusetts; Defense Research Institute; Massachusetts Defense Lawyers Association — Practice Areas: Bad Faith; Civil Litigation; Insurance Defense; Complex Litigation; Comprehensive General Liability; Real Estate; Estate Planning — E-mail: jnoone@averydooley.com

Peter H. Noone — 1969 — Princeton University, B.A., 1992; Suffolk University, J.D., 1995 — Admitted to Bar, 1995, Massachusetts; U.S. District Court, District of Massachusetts; U.S. Court of Appeals for the Federal and Ninth Circuits; U.S. Supreme Court; Supreme Judicial Court of Massachusetts — Member American, Massachusetts and Cambridge-Belmont Bar Associations; Defense Research Institute — Practice Areas: Insurance Defense; Comprehensive General Liability; Complex Litigation; Employment Discrimination; Employment Law — E-mail: pnoone@averydooley.com

Associates

Julie M. Brady — 1966 — Tufts University, B.A., 1989; Suffolk University Law School, J.D., 1995 — Admitted to Bar, 1995, Massachusetts; 1996, U.S. District Court, District of Massachusetts — Member Massachusetts and Cambridge-Belmont Bar Associations — Practice Areas: Civil Litigation; Insurance Defense; Employment Law; Employment Discrimination — E-mail: jbrady@averydooley.com

Brien P. Connolly — 1967 — Assumption College, B.A. (magna cum laude), 1989; New England School of Law, J.D., 1992 — Admitted to Bar, 1992, Massachusetts; 1993, U.S. District Court, District of Massachusetts; U.S. Court of Appeals, First Circuit — Member Massachusetts and Cambridge-Arlington-Belmont Bar Associations — Practice Areas: Employment Law; Insurance Defense; Real Estate; Estate Planning; Probate — E-mail: bconnolly@averydooley.com

Robert J. Fedder — 1968 — Princeton University, A.B., 1991; Washington and Lee University School of Law, J.D., 1996 — Law Clerk to Hon. John A. MacKenzie, U.S. District Court Judge, Eastern District of Virginia — Admitted to Bar, 1996, North Carolina; 1996, Virginia — Member American Bar Association — Practice Areas: Employment Litigation; Insurance Defense; Real Estate — E-mail: rfedder@averydooley.com

Ngai Otieno — Amherst College, B.A., 2006; Suffolk University Law School, J.D., 2009 — Admitted to Bar, 2009, Massachusetts — Member Massachusetts and Boston Bar Associations — Practice Areas: Employment Litigation; Insurance Defense; Probate — E-mail: notieno@averydooley.com

Danielle Marie Gifford — Boston College, B.A. (Dean's List), 2002-2006; University of Maryland School of Law, J.D., 2006-2009 — Associate Editor, Journal of Health Care Law & Policy, 2008-2009 — Admitted to Bar, 2009, Massachusetts — Member Boston Bar Association; Massachusetts Association of Hispanic Attorneys — Certified Mediator in Maryland — Practice Areas: Employment Law; Insurance Defense; Real Estate; Business Law; Corporate Law — E-mail: dgifford@averydooley.com

Sean M. Foley — University of Connecticut, B.A., 2008; Suffolk University Law School, J.D., 2012 — Transnational Law Review, Chief Production Editor, 2011-2012 — Admitted to Bar, 2012, Massachusetts; Connecticut — Member Massachusetts Bar Association; Boston Bar Association; Connecticut Bar Association — Practice Areas: Environmental Litigation; Insurance Defense — E-mail: sfoley@averydooley.com

Patricia M. Ballard — Boston College, B.A., 1990; New England School of Law, J.D. (Dean's List), 1997 — Admitted to Bar, 1997, Massachusetts — Member Massachusetts Bar Association; Women's Bar Association of Massachusetts — Practice Areas: Employment Law; Insurance Defense; Business Law; Corporate Law; Real Estate — E-mail: pballard@averydooley.com

Byrne & Anderson, LLP

50 Redfield Street
Boston, Massachusetts 02122
Telephone: 617-265-3900
Fax: 617-265-3627
E-Mail: firm@byrneanderson.com
www.byrneanderson.com

Insurance Defense, General Liability, Professional Malpractice, Product Liability, Coverage Issues, Automobile, Homeowners, Bodily Injury, Liquor Liability

BOSTON MASSACHUSETTS

Byrne & Anderson, LLP, Boston, MA (Continued)

Insurance Clients

Arbella Mutual Insurance Company
Liberty Mutual Group
Quincy Mutual Fire Insurance Company
Commerce Insurance Company
Hospitality Mutual Insurance Company f/k/a Liquor Liability JUA

Non-Insurance Clients

Boston Police Patrolmen's Association, Inc.
Massachusetts Coalition of Police
Middlesex Sheriff's Office

Partners

James E. Byrne — 1954 — Harvard University, B.A. (cum laude), 1976; Suffolk University, J.D., 1980 — Admitted to Bar, 1980, Massachusetts; 1981, U.S. District Court, District of Massachusetts; 1981, U.S. Court of Appeals, First Circuit — Member Massachusetts and Boston Bar Associations

Kenneth H. Anderson — 1964 — Suffolk University Law School, J.D., 1990 — Admitted to Bar, 1990, Massachusetts; 1991, U.S. District Court, District of Massachusetts; 2000, U.S. Court of Appeals, First Circuit; 2001, U.S. Supreme Court

Campbell Campbell Edwards & Conroy

One Constitution Center, 3rd Floor
Boston, Massachusetts 02129
Telephone: 617-241-3000
Fax: 617-241-5115
E-Mail: jmcampbell@campbell-trial-lawyers.com
www.campbell-trial-lawyers.com

(Additional Offices: Berwyn, PA; Philadelphia, PA; Mount Laurel, NJ; Portland, ME; Bedford, NH; Providence, RI; Hartford, CT)

Appellate Practice, Asbestos, Automotive Products Liability, Aviation, Business Litigation, Class Actions, Commercial Litigation, Construction Litigation, Directors and Officers Liability, Employment Litigation, Environmental Litigation, Hospitality, Insurance Coverage, Intellectual Property, Legal Malpractice, Mass Tort, Medical Devices, Medical Malpractice, Personal Injury, Pharmaceutical, Premises Liability, Product Liability, Professional Liability, Retail Liability, Toxic Torts, Transportation, Trucking

Firm Profile: Matched by only a select group of firms, Campbell Campbell Edwards & Conroy have successfully tried hundreds of large-value, high-exposure, technically complex cases to verdict on a national and regional level. With unrelenting courtroom representation, we can try virtually any case, anywhere, anytime.

Insurance Clients

The ACE Group
Chartis Insurance

Non-Insurance Clients

Caterpillar Inc.
Ford Motor Company

Shareholders

James M. Campbell — Boston College, B.A. (magna cum laude), 1980; University of Virginia School of Law, J.D., 1983 — Leading Individual in Chambers USA for Product Liability and Mass Torts (Nationwide); Star Individual in Chambers USA for Product Liability (Automotive); Recognized by The Legal 500 as one of 9 Leading Lawyers Nationwide (2014); Top 10 Most Highly Regarded Individuals in Products Liability Defence in the Who's Who Legal; Listed as one of the World's Leading Product Liability Lawyers in the Euromoney Expert Guides; Listed as a Litigation Star by Benchmark Litigation; Among Best Lawyers in America in Products Liability Litigation (Defendants) — Admitted to Bar, 1983, Massachusetts; Florida; Maine; New Hampshire; U.S. District Court, District of Massachusetts; U.S. District Court, Middle District of Florida; U.S. District Court, District of New Hampshire; U.S. District Court, District of Connecticut; U.S. District Court, District of Maine; U.S. District Court, District of Vermont; U.S. Court of Appeals, First and Eleventh Circuits; U.S. Supreme Court — Member Federal, American, New Hampshire and Boston Bar Associations; The Florida Bar; Massachusetts Bar Foundation; American College of Trial Lawyers; American Board of Trial Advocates; International Association of Defense Counsel;

Campbell Campbell Edwards & Conroy, Boston, MA (Continued)

Massachusetts Defense Lawyers Association; Defense Research Institute; Association of Defense Trial Attorneys; Federation of Defense and Corporate Counsel — Practice Areas: Product Liability Defense; Pharmaceutical Litigation; Medical Devices; Medical Product Liability; Civil Litigation; Toxic Torts; Mass Tort; Medical Litigation; Professional Liability; Professional Liability (Non-Medical) Defense; Premises Liability; Automobile Litigation; Automobile Tort; Automotive Products Liability; Catastrophic Injury

Richard P. Campbell — University of Massachusetts, B.A., 1970; Boston College Law School, J.D. (cum laude), 1974 — Listed in Who's Who Legal in Product Liability Defense; Listed as Litigation Star by Benchmark Litigation; Best Lawyers in America for Products Liability Litigation (Defendants and Personal Injury Litigation); Boston 2012 Best Lawyers Lawyer of the Year for Personal Injury Litigation (Defendants) — Admitted to Bar, 1974, Massachusetts; New Jersey; Rhode Island; Florida; Maine; New Hampshire; U.S. District Court, District of New Jersey; U.S. District Court, District of Massachusetts; U.S. District Court, District of Rhode Island; U.S. District Court, District of Maine; U.S. District Court, District of Connecticut; U.S. District Court, District of Vermont; U.S. District Court, District of New Hampshire; U.S. District Court, Eastern District of Michigan; U.S. District Court, Eastern, Northern and Southern Districts of New York; U.S. Court of Appeals for the District of Columbia and First Circuits; U.S. Supreme Court — Member Federal, American, Massachusetts and Boston Bar Associations; Massachusetts Bar Foundation; American College of Trial Lawyers; International Association of Defense Counsel; Defense Research Institute; American Board of Trial Advocates — University of Massachusetts (Board of Trustees); University of Massachusetts Building Authority; Founding Member, Boston College Law School Board of Overseers — Practice Areas: Aviation; Asbestos Litigation; Automobile Litigation; Business Litigation; Commercial Litigation; Employment Litigation; Class Actions; Mass Tort; Toxic Torts; Product Liability; Product Liability Defense; Environmental Litigation

William J. Conroy — Lycoming College, B.A. (cum laude), 1978; Temple University School of Law, J.D., 1982 — Leading Individual in Chambers USA for Product Liability and Mass Torts (Nationwide); Listed in Who's Who Legal for Product Liability Defense; Best Lawyers in America for Products Liability Litigation (Defendants) — Admitted to Bar, 1982, Pennsylvania; New Jersey; U.S. District Court, District of New Jersey; U.S. District Court, Eastern and Middle Districts of Pennsylvania; U.S. Court of Appeals, Third Circuit; U.S. Supreme Court — Member American College of Trial Lawyers; International Association of Defense Counsel; Defense Research Institute; Pennsylvania Defense Institute; Federation of Defense and Corporate Counsel; Philadelphia Association of Defense Counsel — Faculty Member, International Association of Defense Counsel 35th Annual Trial Academy, Stanford Law School (2007) — Practice Areas: Product Liability Defense; Product Liability; Catastrophic Injury — Resident Berwyn, PA Office

Choate, Hall & Stewart LLP

Two International Place
Boston, Massachusetts 02110
Telephone: 617-248-5000
Fax: 617-248-4000
E-Mail: info@choate.com
www.choate.com

Established: 1899

Insurance Coverage, Reinsurance

Firm Profile: One of the nation's premier law firms for well over 100 years, Choate has an increasingly unique model: Approximately 175 lawyers, under one roof, focused on areas where we practice at the top of the market and represent sophisticated clients across and outside the US.

Reported Cases: *Polaroid Corp. v. Travelers Indem. Co.,* 414 Mass. 747 (1993); *Compagnie de Reassurance d'ile de France v. New England Reinsurance Corp.,* 57 F.3d 56 (1st Cir. 1995); *Parker v. D'Avolio,* 40 Mass. App. Ct. 394 (1996); *Dryden Oil Co. of New England, Inc. v. Travelers Indem. Co.,* 91 F.3d 278 (1st Cir. 1996); *Odyssey Re (London Ltd. v. Stirling Cooke Brown Holdings Limited,)* 99 Civ. 2326 (S.D.N.Y. 2000), *aff'd,* 00-7356 (2d Cir. 2001); *Commercial Union Co. v. Swiss Reinsurance America Corp.,* Civil Action No. 00 CV 12267 (DPW) (D.Mass. March 31, 2003); *American Employers Ins. Co. v. Swiss Reinsurance America Corp.,* Civil Action No. 00CV12266 (JLT) (D.Mass August 5, 2003).

MASSACHUSETTS   BOSTON

Choate, Hall & Stewart LLP, Boston, MA   (Continued)

Insurance Clients

The Hartford
Travelers Insurance
Swiss Reinsurance America Corporation

Partners

David A. Attisani — 1964 — Williams College, B.A. (magna cum laude), 1987; Harvard Law School, J.D. (cum laude), 1991 — Admitted to Bar, 1991, Colorado; 1993, Massachusetts; 2011, New York; 1992, U.S. District Court, District of Colorado; 1992, U.S. Court of Appeals, First Circuit; 1993, U.S. District Court, District of Massachusetts; 2000, U.S. Court of Appeals, Second Circuit — Member American Bar Association (Co-Chairman, Reinsurance Subcommittee, Insurance Litigation Section, 2002-2008); ARIAS-U.S. (Education Committee, 2012); Fellow, American College of Coverage and Extracontractual Counsel — Editor, Appleman Reinsurance Treatise, 2012

Mark D. Cahill — 1958 — Rutgers University, A.B., 1980; Drake University Law School, J.D. (with honors), 1984 — Admitted to Bar, 1985, Massachusetts; 1985, U.S. District Court, District of Massachusetts; 1985, U.S. Court of Appeals, First Circuit — Member Boston Bar Association

Robert A. Kole — 1971 — Lafayette College, B.A. (cum laude), 1993; University of Virginia School of Law, J.D., 1996 — Admitted to Bar, 1996, Massachusetts; 1996, U.S. District Court, District of Massachusetts; 1996, U.S. Court of Appeals, First Circuit — Member Massachusetts and Boston Bar Associations; ARIAS-U.S. (Law Committee, 2006-2007)

John A. Nadas — Managing Partner — 1951 — Swarthmore College, B.A. (with high honors), 1973; Cornell University Law School, J.D., 1976 — Admitted to Bar, 1977, Massachusetts; 1977, U.S. District Court, District of Massachusetts — Member Massachusetts and Boston Bar Associations; American Law Institute

A. Hugh Scott — 1947 — Williams College, B.A. (cum laude), 1968; Columbia Law School, J.D., 1974 — Admitted to Bar, 1974, Massachusetts; 1975, U.S. District Court, District of Massachusetts; 1975, U.S. Court of Appeals, First Circuit; 1982, U.S. Supreme Court; 1988, U.S. Court of Appeals for the Federal Circuit; 1995, U.S. Court of Federal Claims; 2006, U.S. Court of Appeals, Ninth Circuit — Member American, Massachusetts and Boston Bar Associations; Fellow, American College of Coverage and Extracontractual Counsel

Cornell & Gollub

75 Federal Street
Boston, Massachusetts 02110
    Telephone: 617-482-8100
    Fax: 617-482-3917
    E-Mail: cgmail@cornellgollub.com
    www.cornellgollub.com

Established: 1964

Product Liability, Medical Malpractice, Insurance Law, Commercial Litigation, General Civil Trial and Appellate Practice, Tort Liability, Toxic Torts

Insurance Clients

The Hartford Insurance Group
Tokio Marine Management, Inc.
Lloyd's

Non-Insurance Clients

American Honda Motor Company, Inc.
Bayerische Motoren Werke AG
Chrysler Group LLC
Emerson Electric Company
Genmar Holdings, Inc.
Kawasaki Motors Corporation, U.S.A.
Makita USA, Inc.
Mitsubishi Motors Corporation
Rheem Manufacturing Company
Scaffolding Industry Association Insurance Company
Tracker Marine L.P.
Yamaha Motor Company, Ltd.
Yamaha Motor Corporation, U.S.A.
American Suzuki Motor Corporation
BMW of North America, Inc.
Easton Sports, Inc.
Fichtel & Sachs Industries, Inc.
Kawasaki Heavy Industries, Ltd.
Larson Boats
Lynn Ladder & Scaffolding Company, Inc.
Mori Seiki Company, Ltd.
Samsung Display Devices Company, Ltd.
Toyota Motor Sales, U.S.A., Inc.
Wellcraft Manufacturing A Division of Genmar Corporation

Cornell & Gollub, Boston, MA   (Continued)

Firm Members

Robert W. Cornell — (1910-1987)

Karl L. Gollub — (1934-1985)

Peter M. Durney — 1954 — Suffolk University, J.D., 1980 — Admitted to Bar, 1980, Massachusetts; 1990, New Hampshire; 1990, Maine — E-mail: pdurney@cornellgollub.com

Marie E. Chafe — 1965 — The George Washington University, J.D., 1990 — Admitted to Bar, 1990, Massachusetts; 1991, Connecticut — E-mail: mchafe@cornellgollub.com

Senior Counsel

James P. Kerr — Boston College, J.D., 1993 — Admitted to Bar, 1993, Massachusetts; 2005, Connecticut; 2005, U.S. District Court, District of Connecticut — E-mail: jkerr@cornellgollub.com

Patricia A. Hartnett — Rutgers University, J.D. (cum laude), 1993 — Admitted to Bar, 1994, Massachusetts; 1995, Rhode Island — E-mail: phartnett@cornellgollub.com

Associates

Justin J. Shireman — Roger Williams University School of Law, J.D. (magna cum laude), 2007 — Admitted to Bar, 2007, Massachusetts; Rhode Island — E-mail: jshireman@cornellgollub.com

Christopher P. Fitzgerald — Suffolk University Law School, J.D. (summa cum laude), 2012 — Admitted to Bar, 2012, Massachusetts — Member Massachusetts and Boston Bar Associations — E-mail: cfitzgerald@cornellgollub.com

Coughlin Betke LLP

175 Federal Street
Boston, Massachusetts 02110
    Telephone: 617-988-8050
    Fax: 617-988-8005
    E-Mail: cbetke@coughlinbetke.com
    www.coughlinbetke.com

(Nashua, NH Office: 20 Trafalgar Square, 03063)
    (Tel: 603-589-4025)
(Providence, RI Office: 10 Dorrance Street, Suite 700, 02903)
    (Tel: 401-519-3637)

Architects and Engineers, Casualty, Civil Rights, Construction Law, Contract Disputes, Creditor Rights, Employment Law, Environmental Law, Fire, Fraud, Insurance Coverage, Legal Malpractice, Personal Injury, Premises Liability, Product Liability, Professional Liability, Property Damage, Real Estate, Tort Litigation, Transportation

Insurance Clients

ACE USA

Non-Insurance Clients

Carl Warren & Company
Costco Wholesale Corporation

Partners

Emily G. Coughlin — Brown University, B.A. (cum laude), 1984; Suffolk University Law School, J.D. (cum laude), 1989 — Admitted to Bar, 1989, Massachusetts; U.S. District Court, District of Massachusetts — Member American and Massachusetts Bar Associations; Mass. Joint Bar Committee on Judicial Appointments (2010-2013); MBA Task Force on the Future of Preemptory Challenges (2009-2011); MBA Task Force on Plain English Jury Instructions (2009-2010); Mass. Defense Lawyers Association (President, 2009-2010; Board of Directors and Officers, 2002-Present); Defense Research Institute (Mass. State Representative, 2010-2013); State & Local Bar Relationship Committee); International Association of Defense Counsel

Christopher G. Betke — University at Albany, Nelson Rockefeller School of Public Affairs and Policy, B.A. (cum laude), 1985; Boston College Law School, J.D. (cum laude), 1988 — Admitted to Bar, 1988, Massachusetts; New York; New Hampshire; U.S. District Court, District of Massachusetts; U.S. District Court, Northern and Southern Districts of New York; U.S. Supreme Court — Member Massachusetts Bar Association; Defense Research

BOSTON   MASSACHUSETTS

Coughlin Betke LLP, Boston, MA   (Continued)

Institute (Professional Liability Steering Committee); Claims & Litigation Management Alliance; Massachusetts Defense Lawyers Association

Andrew R. Ferguson — Colgate University, B.A., 1991; Albany Law School of Union University, J.D. (with honors), 1994 — Admitted to Bar, 1995, New York; Massachusetts; Rhode Island; U.S. District Court, Northern District of New York; U.S. District Court, District of Massachusetts — Member American, Massachusetts, Rhode Island and New York State Bar Associations; Defense Research Institute; Massachusetts Defense Lawyers Association

Of Counsel

Kevin J. O'Leary

Associates

Matthew J. Lynch, Jr.   Lauren E. Chanatry

Cummings, King & MacDonald

One Gateway Center, Suite 351
Newton, Massachusetts 02458
Telephone: 617-630-5100
Fax: 617-630-0816
E-Mail: mroberts@ckmlaw.net
www.ckmlaw.net

Established: 1976

Fire, Automobile, Product Liability, Mediation, Medical Liability, Slip and Fall

Firm Profile: Full service insurance defense firm specializing in all aspects of liability defense and coverage issues including premises liability, motor vehicle accident, product liability, educator, employer and civil rights liability claims.

Insurance Clients

Avis Budget Group, Inc.	Cambridge Mutual Fire Insurance Company
Horace Mann Insurance Company	MiddleOak
Merrimack Mutual Fire Insurance Company	Preferred Mutual Insurance Company

Managing Partner

Bradley A. MacDonald — 1950 — Suffolk University Law School, J.D., 1978 — Admitted to Bar, 1978, Massachusetts; 1978, U.S. District Court, District of Massachusetts; 2000, U.S. Court of Appeals for the Federal and First Circuits — Member Massachusetts and Norfolk County Bar Associations; Massachusetts Defense Lawyers Association — E-mail: bmacdonald@ckmlaw.net

Founding Partner

Paul L. Cummings — 1938 — Suffolk University Law School, J.D., 1962 — Admitted to Bar, 1962, Massachusetts — Member Massachusetts and Norfolk County Bar Associations; Massachusetts Academy of Trial Attorneys; Massachusetts Defense Lawyers Association

Senior Associate

Cheryl Mancuso — 1970 — University of Dayton, B.S. (magna cum laude), 1992; University of Cincinnati, M.S., 1993; New England School of Law, J.D. (cum laude), 2001 — Admitted to Bar, 2002, Massachusetts; U.S. District Court, District of Massachusetts — Member American and Massachusetts Bar Associations — E-mail: cmancuso@ckmlaw.net

Emeritus

Richard P. King — (1927-1999)

Gold, Albanese & Barletti

50 Congress Street, Suite 225
Boston, Massachusetts 02109
Telephone: 617-723-5118
Fax: 617-367-8840
www.goldandalbanese.com

Gold, Albanese & Barletti, Boston, MA   (Continued)

(Morristown, NJ Office*: 48 South Street, 07960-4136)
 (Tel: 973-326-9099)
 (Fax: 973-326-9841)
 (E-Mail: main@goldandalbanese.com)
(Red Bank, NJ Office*: 58 Maple Avenue, 07701)
 (Tel: 732-936-9901)
 (Fax: 732-936-9904)
(Massapequa, NY Office: 544 Broadway, Suite 200, 11758)
 (Tel: 516-541-0021)
 (Fax: 516-541-1964)

Automobile, Civil Rights, Comprehensive General Liability, Construction Litigation, Employment Discrimination, Environmental Law, Insurance Coverage, Intellectual Property, Medical Malpractice, Personal Injury, Pharmaceutical, Premises Liability, Product Liability, Professional Liability, Property Damage, Wrongful Death, Occupational Exposure, Insurance Fraud Investigation and Litigation, Commercial Trucking Litigation, Public Entity Tort Litigation

(See listing under Morristown, NJ for additional information)

Governo Law Firm LLC

Two International Place
Boston, Massachusetts 02110
Telephone: 617-737-9045
Fax: 617-737-9046
E-Mail: info@governo.com
www.governo.com

Established: 1995

Civil Litigation, Construction Defect, Environmental Law, Mass Tort, Insurance Coverage, Toxic Torts, Product Liability, Asbestos Litigation, Complex Litigation, Mold and Mildew Claims, Risk Management, Builders Risk, Construction Accidents, Lead Paint, Premises Liability, Commercial Litigation, Contracts, Pollution, Trial Practice, Indoor Air Quality

Firm Profile: Founded in 1995, Governo Law Firm has earned an outstanding reputation as an elite law firm with the talent, determination, and resources to deliver superior results. We specialize in the defense of cases involving complex technical, scientific, medical, and legal issues. This specialty brings us clients in a variety of areas: toxic tort, environmental, pollution, construction, real estate, products liability, premises liability, cyber liability, data privacy, and mass disasters. Our team includes attorneys with diverse backgrounds, outstanding experience, and achievements. We are united by a bold and creative spirit and are committed to serving our clients. What sets Governo Law Firm apart is two-fold: (1) how well we understand each client's needs, and (2) what we actually do with this information to accomplish our client's goals. We assess the key factual, legal, and political implications to identify and recommend the ideal strategy to achieve optimal results. Our comprehensive risk management counseling is based on a thorough, nuanced, multi-dimensional approach rooted in sophisticated legal analysis and practical problem-solving.

In addition to defending individuals and companies in our home state of Massachusetts, we represent clients throughout the northeast and nationally. Our attorneys are licensed to practice in states throughout New England, as well as in New York, Tennessee, and Washington, DC. We are part of a network of veteran trial attorneys located throughout the country who routinely share information regarding new discovery strategies, top experts, and emerging scientific and medical studies. Access to this intelligence enables us to stay current with national trends and use this advantage to maximize our clients' results.

Governo Law Firm LLC, Boston, MA (Continued)

Our commitment to staying on the cutting edge of legal, medical, technical, scientific, political, business, and even social developments is unparalleled and is evidenced by the many continuing education programs taught by our attorneys. We regularly publish articles and give national and local presentations on the topics most important to our clients. To stay current with insurance-related developments, we are a member of the Insurance Library Association of Boston. We have attained Martindale-Hubbell's highest rating (AV), and many of our attorneys have received the prestigious honor of being selected as New England Super Lawyers and Rising Stars.

Simply put, Governo Law Firm's philosophy is straightforward: each client deserves the best result and we deliver it.

Insurance Clients

Admiral Insurance Company	Allstate Insurance Company
American Family Insurance Group	American Safety Insurance Company
Arrowpoint Capital Corporation	
Atlantic Mutual Insurance Company	AXA Insurance Company
	Chubb Group of Insurance Companies
Colony Insurance Group	
Crum & Forster	Fireman's Fund Insurance Company
General Casualty Company	
Great American Insurance Group	The Hartford Insurance Group
Liberty Mutual Insurance Company	Nationwide Insurance
Ohio Casualty Group	OneBeacon Insurance
Resolute Management, Inc.	RiverStone Claims Management, LLC
Safeco Insurance Companies	
St. Paul Travelers	Travelers Insurance Companies
Unigard Insurance Group	Utica National Insurance Group

Partners

David M. Governo — 1956 — Providence College, B.A. (magna cum laude), 1978; Northeastern University, J.D., 1981 — Admitted to Bar, 1981, Massachusetts; 1982, U.S. District Court, District of Massachusetts; 1982, U.S. Court of Appeals, First Circuit — Member American, Massachusetts and Boston Bar Associations; Lawyers for Civil Justice; International Association of Privacy Professionals; Fellow, American Bar Association; Defense Research Institute; Federation of Defense and Corporate Counsel — Co-Author: Toxic Mold Litigation, Second Edition (2009) Lawyers and Judges Publishing Co.; Co-Author: "Successful Trial Tactics in Toxic Tort Cases", 60 FDCC Quarterly No. 2 (2010); Co-Author: "Speaking from the Grave - The Admissibility of a Decedent's Testimony," FDCC Quarterly (2012); Co-Author: "Staying Compliant Amid Escalating Cyber Threats," Claims Magazine (2012); Co-Author: "The Generation X and Y Factors," For the Defense (2013); Co-Author: "Size v. Substance: Consumer Expectations and Nanomaterials in Products", Claims (June 2014) — Practice Areas: Civil Litigation; Asbestos Litigation; Builders Risk; Complex Litigation; Construction Accidents; Construction Defect; Environmental Law; Insurance Coverage; Lead Paint; Mass Tort; Mold and Mildew Claims; Premises Liability; Product Liability; Risk Management; Toxic Torts; Architects and Engineers; Business Law; Commercial General Liability; Construction Law; Contractors Liability; Engineering and Construction; General Civil Practice; Hazardous Waste; Litigation; Professional Liability; Property Loss; Trial and Appellate Practice; Trial Practice — Tel: 617-737-9047 — E-mail: dgoverno@governo.com

Jeniffer A.P. Carson — 1974 — Suffolk University, B.S., 1996; Suffolk University Law School, J.D., 1999 — Admitted to Bar, 1999, Massachusetts; 2003, U.S. District Court, District of Massachusetts; 2005, U.S. Court of Appeals, First Circuit — Member Massachusetts and Boston Bar Associations — Practice Areas: Asbestos Litigation; Toxic Torts; Civil Litigation; Mass Tort — Tel: 617-737-9265 — E-mail: jcarson@governo.com

Bryna Rosen Misiura — 1965 — Allegheny College, B.A., 1987; University of Virginia, J.D., 1992 — Admitted to Bar, 1992, Massachusetts; 1995, District of Columbia; 1993, U.S. District Court, District of Massachusetts; 2007, U.S. District Court, District of Connecticut — Co-Author: "Social Media: Understanding and Controlling Your Liability," Cleaning & Restoration (2011); Co-Author: "Asbestos Liability in the Cleaning and Restoration Industry," Cleaning & Restoration (2007) — Practice Areas: Insurance Defense; Asbestos Litigation; Toxic Torts; Civil Litigation; Insurance Coverage; Mass Tort — Tel: 617-737-9266 — E-mail: bmisiura@governo.com

David A. Goldman — 1965 — University of Michigan - Ann Arbor, B.A. (cum laude), 1987; Suffolk University Law School, J.D. (cum laude), 1993 — Admitted to Bar, 1993, Massachusetts; 2004, Rhode Island; 1994, U.S. District Court, District of Massachusetts; 2009, U.S. District Court, District of Rhode Island — Practice Areas: Civil Litigation; Asbestos Litigation; Toxic Torts — Tel: 617-737-9267 — E-mail: dgoldman@governo.com

Governo Law Firm LLC, Boston, MA (Continued)

Nancy Kelly — 1959 — Brandeis University, B.A. (Dean's List), 1981; Boston University School of Law, J.D., 1984 — Admitted to Bar, 1985, Massachusetts; 1991, Maine; 2001, Rhode Island; 1985, U.S. District Court, District of Massachusetts; 1993, U.S. District Court, District of Connecticut — Member Law Society of England and Wales — Author: "Insurance Coverage Issues in Mold-Related Claims," National Business Institute, 2003; "The Present State of Mold Litigation," The Mold Muddle (MCLE, Inc. 2004) — Reported Cases: In re New York City Asbestos Litigation, Brooklyn Navy Yard — Qualified Solicitor in England and Wales — Languages: French — Practice Areas: Insurance Coverage; Reinsurance; Toxic Torts; Litigation — Tel: 617-532-9214 — E-mail: nkelly@governo.com

John P. Gardella — 1977 — Vanderbilt University, B.A. (magna cum laude), 2000; Vanderbilt University Law School, J.D., 2003 — Admitted to Bar, 2003, Tennessee; 2005, Massachusetts; 2008, U.S. District Court, District of Massachusetts — Member Massachusetts and Boston Bar Associations — Co-Author: "Asbestos Liability in the Cleaning and Restoration Industry," Cleaning & Restoration (2007) — Languages: Japanese — Practice Areas: Asbestos Litigation; Complex Litigation; Environmental Law; Product Liability; Toxic Torts; Lead Paint — E-mail: jgardella@governo.com

Associates

Brendan J. Gaughan — 1974 — Boston College, B.S., 1996; Suffolk University Law School, J.D., 2000 — Admitted to Bar, 2001, Massachusetts; 2002, U.S. District Court, District of Massachusetts — Co-Author: "Successful Trial Tactics in Toxic Tort Cases", 60 FDCC Quarterly No. 2 (2010) — Practice Areas: Asbestos Litigation; Complex Litigation; Construction Accidents; Construction Defect; Environmental Law; Automobile; Litigation; Product Liability; Toxic Torts; Civil Litigation; Property and Casualty — E-mail: bgaughan@governo.com

Michael D. Simons — 1968 — Brown University, A.B., 1990; University of Florida College of Law, J.D., 1993 — Admitted to Bar, 1993, Massachusetts; 1997, New York; 1996, U.S. District Court, District of Massachusetts; 2002, U.S. District Court, Southern District of New York; 2009, U.S. District Court, District of Connecticut — Practice Areas: Asbestos Litigation; Complex Litigation; Product Liability; Contracts; Construction Defect; Toxic Torts; Appellate Practice; Builders Risk; Environmental Law; Insurance Coverage; Litigation; Risk Management; Mold and Mildew Claims — E-mail: msimons@governo.com

Sarah E. O'Leary — 1970 — Northeastern University, B.S.B.A. (cum laude), 1992; Northeastern University School of Law, J.D., 1996 — Admitted to Bar, 1996, Massachusetts; 1997, New Hampshire; 1997, U.S. District Court, District of Massachusetts; 1997, U.S. District Court, District of New Hampshire — Co-Author: "Legal Developments in Health & Safety," Restoration & Remediation (2010); Co-Author: "Size v. Substance: Consumer Expectations and Nanomaterials in Products," (2014) — Practice Areas: Asbestos Litigation; Toxic Torts; Product Liability; Personal Injury; Construction Accidents; Construction Defect; Civil Litigation; Complex Litigation; Regulatory and Compliance — E-mail: soleary@governo.com

Kendra A. Bergeron — 1980 — The George Washington University, B.A. (cum laude), 2002; New England School of Law, J.D. (cum laude), 2006 — Admitted to Bar, 2006, Massachusetts; 2006, Rhode Island; 2007, Connecticut — Practice Areas: Asbestos Litigation; Civil Litigation; Insurance Defense; Product Liability; Construction Liability; Premises Liability — E-mail: kbergeron@governo.com

Alan Wong — 1988 — University of Illinois at Urbana-Champaign, B.A., 2010; Northeastern University, J.D., 2013 — Admitted to Bar, 2013, Massachusetts; 2013, Rhode Island; 2014, U.S. District Court, District of Rhode Island — Practice Areas: Insurance Defense; Product Liability; Toxic Torts — Tel: 617-737-9217 — E-mail: awong@governo.com

Colin Holmes — 1981 — University of Pennsylvania, B.A., 2002; University of Connecticut School of Law, J.D., 2006 — Admitted to Bar, 2007, New York; 2013, Massachusetts; 2009, U.S. District Court, Southern District of New York — Member Boston Bar Association — Practice Areas: Toxic Torts; Class Actions — Tel: 617-737-9930 — E-mail: cholmes@governo.com

Christopher van Tienhoven — 1984 — Denison University, B.A., 2006; South Texas College of Law, J.D., 2009 — Admitted to Bar, 2009, Massachusetts; 2009, Rhode Island; 2010, Connecticut; 2010, U.S. District Court, District of Rhode Island — Practice Areas: Litigation — E-mail: cvantienhoven@governo.com

BOSTON   MASSACHUSETTS

Governo Law Firm LLC, Boston, MA   (Continued)

Mark J. Hoover — 1965 — Marietta College, B.A. (cum laude), 1987; Boston College Law School, J.D., 1993 — Admitted to Bar, 1993, Massachusetts; 1995, Connecticut; 1997, Maine; 1994, U.S. District Court, District of Massachusetts; 1996, U.S. District Court, District of Connecticut; U.S. District Court, District of Vermont; 1997, U.S. District Court, District of Maine; 2002, U.S. Supreme Court — Member American and Massachusetts Bar Associations; Defense Research Institute; Massachusetts Defense Lawyers Association; Connecticut Trial Lawyers Association — Practice Areas: Insurance Defense; Product Liability; Toxic Torts — Tel: 617-532-9217 — E-mail: mhoover@governo.com

Alexander T. Green — 1983 — The George Washington University, B.A., 2005; Northeastern University School of Law, J.D., 2010 — Admitted to Bar, 2010, Massachusetts; 2013, New York — Practice Areas: Toxic Torts; Product Liability — E-mail: agreen@governo.com

Jan M. Kendrick — 1976 — Louisiana State University, B.A., 2001; M.S.W., 2003; Suffolk University Law School, J.D. (magna cum laude), 2010 — Admitted to Bar, 2010, Massachusetts; 2012, U.S. District Court, District of Massachusetts — Member American and Boston Bar Associations — Army National Guard — Practice Areas: Toxic Torts; Product Liability — E-mail: jkendrick@governo.com

Marisa K. Howe — 1983 — University of Minnesota Twin Cities, B.I.S., 2005; Suffolk University Law School, J.D., 2010 — Admitted to Bar, 2010, Massachusetts — Practice Areas: Toxic Torts; Insurance Defense — E-mail: mhowe@governo.com

Michaela E. Bradley — 1982 — Villanova University, B.A. (cum laude), 2004; Brooklyn Law School, J.D., 2007 — Admitted to Bar, 2008, New York; 2012, Massachusetts — E-mail: mbradley@governo.com

Of Counsel

Timothy J. Dodd — 1959 — Georgetown University, B.A. (magna cum laude), 1981; Suffolk University, J.D., 1984 — Admitted to Bar, 1984, Massachusetts; 1994, Rhode Island; 1994, U.S. District Court, District of Rhode Island

(This firm is also listed in the Regulatory and Compliance section of this directory)

Hassett & Donnelly, P.C.

125 Summer Street, 16th Floor
Boston, Massachusetts 02110
    Telephone: 617-892-6080
    Fax: 617-345-6796
    www.hassettanddonnelly.com

(Additional Offices: Worcester, MA*; Hartford, CT*)

Insurance Defense, Defense Litigation, Construction Litigation, Coverage Analysis, Declaratory Judgments, Bad Faith, Professional Liability, Product Liability, Premises Liability, Municipal Liability, Workers' Compensation, Civil Litigation, Commercial General Liability, Employment Law, Motor Vehicle, Negligence, Toxic Torts, Wrongful Death, Breach of Contract, Property Defense, Environmental Litigation, Business Litigation, Fire, Homeowners, First and Third Party Defense, Property and Casualty, Reinsurance, Self-Insured Defense, Uninsured and Underinsured Motorist, Employment Law (Management Side), Trial and Appellate Practice

Partners

David F. Hassett — **Managing Partner** — 1959 — College of the Holy Cross, B.A. (cum laude), 1981; Boston College Law School, J.D., 1984 — Admitted to Bar, 1985, Massachusetts; 1988, U.S. District Court, District of Massachusetts; 1992, U.S. Court of Appeals, First Circuit; 2011, U.S. Court of Appeals, Fifth Circuit — Member Massachusetts and Worcester County Bar Associations; Defense Research Institute; American Board of Trial Advocates; International Association of Defense Counsel; Massachusetts Defense Lawyers Association — Assistant District Attorney (1985-1987); Massachusetts Super Lawyers (2006-2013); Boston's Top Rated Lawyers (2012); Best Lawyers in America (2012) — E-mail: dhassett@hassettanddonnelly.com

Gerard T. Donnelly — 1953 — Worcester State College, 1976; Western New England College, J.D., 1988 — Admitted to Bar, 1989, Massachusetts; 1989, U.S. District Court, District of Massachusetts — Member Massachusetts and

Hassett & Donnelly, P.C., Boston, MA   (Continued)

Worcester County Bar Associations; Defense Research Institute — E-mail: gdonnelly@hassettanddonnelly.com

Associates

Tara E. Lynch — 1984 — Fairfield University, B.A. (with honors and high distinction), 2006; Syracuse University, J.D. (magna cum laude), 2009 — Admitted to Bar, 2010, New York; Massachusetts

Margarita Warren — 1982 — Brown University, B.A. (with honors), 2004; The University of Chicago, M.A.; Suffolk University Law School, J.D. (cum laude), 2011 — Admitted to Bar, 2011, Massachusetts — Languages: Spanish — E-mail: mwarren@hassettanddonnelly.com

(See listing under Worcester, MA for additional information)

Lyne, Woodworth & Evarts LLP

12 Post Office Square
Boston, Massachusetts 02109
    Telephone: 617-523-6655
    Fax: 617-248-9877
    E-Mail: info@lwelaw.com
    www.lwelaw.com

Established: 1919

General Practice, Life Insurance, Health, Disability, Administrative Law, Employment Law

Insurance Clients

All American Life Agency Services, Inc.
Berkshire Life Insurance Company
Federal Kemper Life Assurance Company
Fidelity Security Life Insurance Company
General American Life Insurance Company
IDS Life Insurance Company
John Hancock Financial Services Group
Minnesota Life Insurance Company
New York Life Insurance Company
North American Life & Casualty Company
Omaha Property and Casualty Insurance Company
PFL Life Insurance Company
Phoenix Life Insurance Company
Provident Mutual Life Insurance Company
Teachers Insurance and Annuity Association of America
Union Bankers Insurance Company
United of Omaha Life Insurance Company
USLIFE Credit Life Insurance Company
Allianz Life Insurance Company of North America
Federal Home Life Insurance Company
Fidelity Mutual Life Insurance Company
Fortis Benefits Insurance Company
Gerber Life Insurance Company
The Guardian Life Insurance Company of America
Massachusetts Mutual Life Insurance Company
MONY Group, Inc.
Mutual of Omaha Insurance Company
NN Life Insurance Company of Canada
The Northwestern Mutual Life Insurance Company
Penn Mutual Life Insurance Company
Provident Life and Accident Insurance Company
ReliaStar Life Insurance Company
UNICARE Life & Health Insurance Company
The Union Central Life Insurance Company
U.S. Financial Life Insurance Company

Partners

Joseph F. Ryan — Boston College Law School, J.D., 1966 — Admitted to Bar, 1966, Massachusetts

Edward P. McPartlin — Boston College Law School, J.D., 1966 — Admitted to Bar, 1966, Massachusetts

Frances X. Hogan — Boston College Law School, J.D., 1970 — Admitted to Bar, 1970, Massachusetts

Norman C. Sabbey — Boston College Law School, J.D., 1970 — Admitted to Bar, 1970, Massachusetts

Domenic P. Aiello — New England School of Law, J.D., 1981 — Admitted to Bar, 1981, Massachusetts

Lyne, Woodworth & Evarts LLP, Boston, MA (Continued)

Associate

E. Kate Buyuk — University of Maryland, J.D., 1999 — Admitted to Bar, 1999, Massachusetts

Of Counsel

Edmund Polubinski Jr. — College of William & Mary, J.D., 1976 — Admitted to Bar, 1976, Massachusetts

(Revisors of the Massachusetts Insurance Law Digest for this Publication)

Manion Gaynor & Manning LLP

21 Custom House Street
Boston, Massachusetts 02110
 Telephone: 617-670-8800
 Fax: 617-670-8801
 E-Mail: info@mgmlaw.com
 www.mgmlaw.com

(Providence, RI Office: One Center Place, 02903)
 (Tel: 401-427-0391)
 (Fax: 401-223-6407)
(Wilmington, DE Office: 1007 North Orange Street, 10th Floor, 19801)
 (Tel: 302-657-2100)
 (Fax: 302-657-2104)
(San Francisco, CA Office: 201 Spear Street, 18th Floor, 94105)
 (Tel: 415-512-4381)
 (Fax: 415-512-6791)
(Los Angeles, CA Office: 444 South Flower Street, Suite 2150, 90071)
 (Tel: 213-622-7300)
 (Fax: 213-622-7313)

Established: 1984

Product Liability, Complex Tort Litigation, Mass Tort, Commercial Litigation, Asbestos Litigation, Premises Liability, Environmental Litigation, Professional Liability, Employment Litigation, Food-Borne Illness, Toxic Tort Litigation, White Collar & Government Investigation

Firm Profile: Manion Gaynor & Manning LLP (MG&M) is a national litigation firm focused on Products Liability and Complex Tort, and Commercial and Business Disputes with fully integrated offices in Boston, Los Angeles, Providence, San Francisco and Wilmington. Our focus on providing strategic, responsive legal counsel in each of our core practices has made us the law firm of choice for clients facing high-stakes litigation. Clients value our guidance on sophisticated matters ranging from complex commercial and business disputes, toxic tort and products liability, intellectual property, real estate, employment, to white collar and regulatory matters. Our unwavering commitment to excellence is premised on the concept that there is an optimal resolution for every case-whether through voluntary dismissal, summary judgment, reasonable settlement or trial. We rapidly assess and efficiently achieve our clients' desired outcome with a streamlined, efficient operating model and a thorough understanding of their specific industry and goals. We deliver practical insight on our clients' most important matters and ensure a successful partnership through a culture of close collaboration. Our firm and, therefore, our clients' defense, are truly integrated. Across offices-across the country-we work as a unified team actively developing collective knowledge and providing optimal service. MG&M leverages the unique experience and skills of our lawyers to their best and highest use, protecting and advancing the interests of our clients wherever they do business.

Non-Insurance Clients

Amsted Industries
Flowserve Corporation
The Boeing Company
Georgia-Pacific LLC

Partners

John B. Manning — Harvard University, B.A. (cum laude), 1988; Suffolk University, J.D. (cum laude), 1991 — Admitted to Bar, 1991, Massachusetts; 2003, Rhode Island; 1992, U.S. District Court, District of Massachusetts; 1993, U.S. Court of Appeals, First Circuit; 2006, U.S. District Court, District of Rhode Island — Member American, Massachusetts and Rhode Island Bar Associations; Fellow, Litigation Counsel of America — Best Lawyers In America (Mass Tort Litigation and Class Actions for Defendants 2013, 2014, 2015); Martindale-Hubbell AV Rated Attorney; Massachusetts Super Lawyer — Practice Areas: Product Liability; Complex Tort Litigation

John T. Hugo — University of Massachusetts, B.A. (cum laude), 1991; Suffolk University, J.D. (cum laude), 1994 — Admitted to Bar, 1994, Massachusetts; 2007, Rhode Island; 2010, California; 1996, U.S. District Court, District of Massachusetts; 2010, U.S. District Court, Eastern District of California; 2011, U.S. District Court, Central District of California; 2011, U.S. Court of Appeals, First Circuit — Member American Bar Association (Vice-Chair, Products General Liability and Consumer Law Committee); Massachusetts, California and Rhode Island Bar Associations — Massachusetts Super Lawyers, Rising Star — Practice Areas: Product Liability; Complex Tort Litigation

Brian D. Gross — University of Maryland, B.S., 1991; Northeastern University, J.D., 1997 — Admitted to Bar, 1997, Massachusetts; 2003, Rhode Island; 2005, New Hampshire; 1998, U.S. District Court, District of Massachusetts; 1998, U.S. Court of Appeals, First Circuit; 2005, U.S. District Court, District of New Hampshire; 2006, U.S. District Court, District of Rhode Island — Member American Bar Association (Vice-Chair; Toxic Tort and Environmental Litigation Committee); Massachusetts, Rhode Island and New Hampshire Bar Associations — Co-Author: "Toxic Tort Case Management," Toxic Torts 11, Massachusetts Continuing Legal Education, Inc. (1999); "The Death of Federal Mass Tort Class Actions," 1 IADC Class Actions and Multi-Party Litigation Committee Newsletters 1 (1997); "Emerging Toxic Torts: Latex Glove Litigation," 106 Products Liability Advisor 12 (1997); "Crashing into Court: Litigation Facing the In-Line Skate Industry, Safety in Ice Hockey: Third Volume," ASTM STP1341, American Society of Tests & Measures (1997) — Martindale-Hubbell Preeminent AV Rating; Massachusetts Super Lawyers, Rising Star — Practice Areas: Product Liability; Complex Tort Litigation

Jonathan F. Tabasky — Skidmore College, B.A. (cum laude), 1992; Suffolk University, J.D. (cum laude), 1995 — Admitted to Bar, 1995, Massachusetts; 2003, Connecticut; 2003, Rhode Island; 2009, Maine; 1996, U.S. District Court, District of Massachusetts; 2005, U.S. District Court, District of Connecticut; 2009, U.S. District Court, District of Maine; 2011, U.S. District Court, District of Rhode Island — Member American and Massachusetts Bar Associations; Defense Research Institute — AV Rated by Martindale-Hubbell; Massachusetts Rising Stars, Super Lawyers Edition of Boston Magazine, 2010; Massachusetts Super Lawyers, 2014 — Practice Areas: Product Liability; Complex Tort Litigation

Jason A. Cincilla — Virginia Military Institute, B.A., 1994; Pennsylvania State University-Dickinson School of Law, J.D. (magna cum laude), 2002 — Admitted to Bar, 2002, Delaware; 2005, U.S. Court of Appeals, Third Circuit — Member Federal, American and Delaware State Bar Associations; Defense Research Institute — Martindale-Hubbell Preeminent AV Rated — Practice Areas: Product Liability; Complex Tort Litigation — Resident Wilmington, DE Office — Tel: 302-657-2100

Daniel P. McCarthy — University of Massachusetts Amherst, B.A., 1998; Suffolk University Law School, J.D. (cum laude), 2001 — Admitted to Bar, 2002, Massachusetts; 2002, U.S. District Court, District of Massachusetts — Member Massachusetts and Boston Bar Associations — Practice Areas: Product Liability; Complex Tort Litigation

Rosie Badgett — The University of Mississippi, B.P.A. (cum laude), 1991; Saint Louis University School of Law, J.D., 1999 — Admitted to Bar, 1999, Illinois; 1999, Missouri; 2006, California; 2008, U.S. District Court, Central and Northern Districts of California; 2010, U.S. District Court, Eastern District of Pennsylvania — Member Illinois State Bar Association; The Missouri Bar — Practice Areas: Product Liability; Complex Tort Litigation — Resident Los Angeles, CA Office

Amaryah K. Bocchino — University of Delaware, B.A. (magna cum laude), 2003; Tulane University, J.D. (summa cum laude), 2006 — Admitted to Bar, 2006, Delaware; 2006, U.S. District Court, District of Delaware — Member American and Delaware Bar Associations — Practice Areas: Product Liability; Complex Tort Litigation — Resident Wilmington, DE Office — Tel: 302-504-6802

Brent M. Karren — The University of Texas at Austin, B.B.A., 1988; Washington University in St. Louis, J.D., 1992 — Admitted to Bar, 1992, Texas; 2013, California; 2002, U.S. District Court, Northern District of Texas — Member American Bar Association; Texas Bar Association; Defense Research Institute — AV Rated by Martindale-Hubbell — Practice Areas: Product Liability; Complex Tort Litigation — Tel: 415-512-4381

Manion Gaynor & Manning LLP, Boston, MA (Continued)

Howard P. Skebe — University of California, Santa Barbara, B.A. (cum laude), 1991; University of California, Hastings College of the Law, J.D., 1997 — American Jurisprudence Award for Trial Advocacy, Hastings College of Law — Admitted to Bar, 1997, California; 2012, U.S. District Court, Central, Eastern, Northern and Southern Districts of California; U.S. District Court, Eastern District of Pennsylvania — Practice Areas: Product Liability; Complex Tort Litigation — Resident San Francisco, CA Office — Tel: 415-512-4381

Eric V. Skelly — Roger Williams University, B.S., 1999; Suffolk University, J.D., 2003 — Admitted to Bar, 2003, Massachusetts; 2009, Maine; 2013, Illinois; 2004, U.S. District Court, District of Massachusetts; 2013, U.S. District Court, District of Maine — Member Massachusetts, Maine State and Boston Bar Associations; Massachusetts Defense Lawyers Association — Practice Areas: Product Liability; Complex Tort Litigation

Of Counsel

Anthony S. Miller
Marc J. Phillips

Associates

Nathan D. Barillo
Amanda Biggerstaff
Kenneth R. Costa
Whitney L. Frame
Kevin W. Hadfield
Jeremiah J. Harvey
Tracy A. R. Jolly
William B. Larson Jr.
April M. Luna
Brendan D. O'Brien
Jessica L. Reno
Andrew J. Shriro
Bryan P. Smith
Lindsay Weiss
Dustin C. Beckley
Ryan W. Browning
David Davidson
Javier F. Flores
Nicole A. Harrison
Stephen Jenkins
Meghan D. Landry
Carrie S. Lin
Elizabeth A. Moore
Matthew R. Pierce
Carolyn E. Riggs
Stephanie Smiertka
Brian C. Spring

Melick & Porter

1 Liberty Square
Boston, Massachusetts 02109
Telephone: 617-523-6200
Fax: 617-523-8130
E-Mail: rpowers@melicklaw.com
www.melicklaw.com

(Providence, RI Office: 49 Weybossett Street, 02903)
(Tel: 401-941-0909)
(Fax: 401-941-6269)
(Waterbury, CT Office: 76 Center Street, 06702)
(Tel: 203-596-0500)
(Fax: 203-721-8532)
(Plymouth, MA Office: 4 Court Street, Suite 209, 02360)
(Tel: 508-746-2282)
(Fax: 508-746-2259)
(Portsmouth, NH Office: 2 International Drive, Suite 110, 03801)
(Tel: 603-627-0010)
(Fax: 603-627-0460)
(New York, NY Office: 830 Third Avenue, 5th Floor, 10022)
(Tel: 212-541-7236)
(Fax: 212-840-8560)

Established: 1983

Melick & Porter, Boston, MA (Continued)

Accountants, Administrative Law, Advertising Injury, Agent/Broker Liability, Appellate Practice, Architects and Engineers, Asbestos, Automobile, Bad Faith, Commercial Litigation, Complex Litigation, Construction Litigation, Dental Malpractice, Directors and Officers Liability, Employment Practices, Environmental Law, Fire, General Liability, Health Care, Hospitality, Insurance Coverage, Insurance Defense, Lead Paint, Legal Malpractice, Life Insurance, Liquor Liability, Medical Devices, Pharmaceutical, Pollution, Premises Liability, Product Liability, Professional Liability, Property and Casualty, Public Entities, Real Estate Agents & Brokers Liability, Restaurant Liability, State and Federal Courts, Toxic Torts, Transportation, Trucking, Workers' Compensation

Firm Profile: Melick & Porter is a firm of trial and appellate attorneys. We represent clients in New England and nationally. Founded in 1983, the firm has a widely recognized insurance defense practice, which includes representation of insurance carriers and their clients, self-insured corporations, hospitals, municipalities, professionals and individuals. Our clients value the aggressive and cost-effective legal representation provided by our experienced and innovative attorneys.

Insurance Clients

ACE Group
Arch Insurance Group
Chubb & Son, Inc.
Nationwide Insurance
Risk Management Foundation
AIG
Berkshire Hathaway Specialty Insurance
Navigators Insurance Company
Swiss Reinsurance America Corporation

Non-Insurance Clients

Academy Express, LLC
CVS Caremark
Harvard University
Stop & Shop, Inc./PeaPod
Watts Water Technologies, Inc.
Boy Scouts of America
Family Dollar Stores, Inc.
Insperity
Tufts University

Members of the Firm

Robert P. Powers — Boston College, A.B. (magna cum laude), 1981; The Catholic University of America, J.D., 1984 — Admitted to Bar, 1985, Massachusetts; U.S. District Court, District of Massachusetts; U.S. Court of Appeals, First Circuit; 1992, U.S. Supreme Court — Member Massachusetts and Boston Bar Associations; Defense Research Institute (DRI); Massachusetts Defense Lawyers Association — Practice Areas: Insurance Litigation; Commercial Litigation; Civil Trial Practice; Appellate Practice; Professional Liability; Employment Practices; Insurance Coverage; Bad Faith; Life Sciences; Cyber Liability — E-mail: rpowers@melicklaw.com

John F. Rooney, III — Suffolk University, B.S. (summa cum laude), 1979; New England School of Law, J.D., 1983 — Admitted to Bar, 1983, Massachusetts; Connecticut; District of Columbia; New Hampshire; New York; Pennsylvania; U.S. District Court, District of Massachusetts; U.S. District Court, District of Connecticut; U.S. District Court, District of New Hampshire; U.S. Court of Appeals, First and Second Circuits — Member Massachusetts, New Hampshire and Connecticut Bar Associations; Bar Association of the District of Columbia; Defense Research Institute (DRI) — Practice Areas: Toxic Torts; Product Liability; Construction Litigation; Premises Liability; Criminal Law — E-mail: jrooney@melicklaw.com

William D. Chapman — University of Massachusetts Amherst, B.A. (cum laude), 1983; Suffolk University, J.D., 1987 — Admitted to Bar, 1987, Massachusetts; U.S. District Court, District of Massachusetts; U.S. Court of Appeals, First Circuit — Member Massachusetts Bar Association; Professional Liability Defense Association; Massachusetts Defense Lawyers Association (Board of Directors) — Practice Areas: Insurance Defense; Civil Trial Practice; Property and Casualty; Professional Liability; Directors and Officers Liability; Complex Litigation; Construction Litigation; Architects and Engineers; Hospitality — E-mail: wchapman@melicklaw.com

Michael J. Mazurczak — Marquette University, B.A., 1986; J.D., 1989 — Admitted to Bar, 1989, Massachusetts; New York; Wisconsin; U.S. District Court, District of Massachusetts; U.S. District Court, Eastern and Western Districts of Wisconsin; U.S. Court of Appeals, First Circuit — Member American and Massachusetts Bar Associations; State Bar of Wisconsin; Defense Research Institute (DRI) (Employement and Labor Law Committee); Association of Professional Responsibility Lawyers — Practice Areas: Employment Practices; Professional Liability; Insurance Coverage; Complex Litigation; Cyber Liability — E-mail: maz@melicklaw.com

Melick & Porter, Boston, MA (Continued)

Partners

Erin J. M. Alarcon
John A. Caletri
Adam M. Guttin
Robert S. Ludlum
Jeremy I. Stein
T. Dos Urbanski
Mark S. Bodner
Shannon McQueeney Doherty
William L. Keville, Jr.
Andre A. Sansoucy
Robert T. Treat
Matthew C. Welnicki

Associates

Allison B. Cherundolo
Kathleen A. Federico
Jared B. Giroux
Donald P. Healy
Carolyn M. Miller
Kathryn T. Rogers
Eva M. Zelnick
Brian C. Davis
Christopher D. George
Jean M. Hamer
Eric N. Losey
Renè M. Pickett
John G. Wheatley

Of Counsel

Greta T. Hutton
John A. Sakakeeny

Mitchell & DeSimone

101 Arch Street
Boston, Massachusetts 02110
Telephone: 617-737-8300
Fax: 617-737-8390
www.mitchelldesimone.com

(Worcester, MA Office*: 255 Park Avenue, Suite 1000, 01608)
(Tel: 508-756-8310)

Insurance Defense, Premises Liability, Contractors Liability, Employment Law, Discrimination, Environmental Law, Automobile, Tort, General Liability, Liquor Liability, Product Liability, Coverage Issues, Subrogation, Directors and Officers Liability, Professional Liability

Firm Profile: With offices in Boston and Worcester, MA, Mitchell & DeSimone attorneys practice in all counties of the Commonwealth. The firm has developed a national presence, handling matters throughout the United States, and is often retained for representation to corporations in complex litigation matters.

Insurance Clients

American States Insurance Company
Liberty Mutual Insurance Company
Progressive Insurance Companies
Safeco Insurance Companies
Travelers Insurance
United States Liability Insurance Company
General Accident Insurance Company
Massachusetts Insurers Insolvency Fund
State Farm Insurance Company
United National Group

Partners

John C. DeSimone — 1961 — Bates College, B.A. (with honors), 1983; Suffolk University, J.D. (with honors), 1987 — Admitted to Bar, 1987, Massachusetts; 1988, U.S. District Court, District of Massachusetts; 1991, U.S. Court of Appeals, First Circuit — Member Massachusetts and Worcester County (Committees: Insurance Defense; Labor and Employment Law) Bar Associations; Massachusetts Defense Lawyers Association

Paul E. Mitchell — 1961 — Ohio Wesleyan University, B.A., 1984; Suffolk University, J.D., 1987 — Admitted to Bar, 1987, Massachusetts; 1988, U.S. District Court, District of Massachusetts — Member Massachusetts and Boston Bar Associations; Insurance Advisory Association; Massachusetts Defense Lawyers Association; American Arbitration Association; Defense Research Institute — Arbitrator, American Arbitration Association

John DiSciullo — 1971 — Fairfield University, B.A., 1993; Suffolk University, J.D. (cum laude), 1996 — Admitted to Bar, 1996, Massachusetts; U.S. District Court, District of Massachusetts — Member Massachusetts Bar Association (Committees: Litigation, General Practice Solo, Small Firms

Mitchell & DeSimone, Boston, MA (Continued)

Associates

Janine H. McNulty — Bates College, B.A., 1993; Suffolk University Law School, J.D. (cum laude), 2003 — Admitted to Bar, 2003, Massachusetts

Samara Bell — Colgate University, B.A., 2002; Suffolk University Law School, J.D., 2006 — Admitted to Bar, 2006, Massachusetts; 2008, New Jersey; 2009, New York; 2008, U.S. District Court, District of Massachusetts; U.S. District Court, District of New Jersey

Kathryn H. Petit — University of Rhode Island, B.A. (cum laude), 2005; Roger Williams University, J.D. (magna cum laude), 2009 — Law Clerk, Rhode Island Superior Court (2009-2011) — Admitted to Bar, 2009, Rhode Island; 2010, Massachusetts

Caitlin A. Romasco — Bryn Mawr College, B.A. (cum laude), 2009; Suffolk University Law School, J.D. (magna cum laude), 2012 — Admitted to Bar, 2012, Massachusetts

(This firm is also listed in the Subrogation section of this directory)

Monahan & Associates, P.C.

113 Union Wharf East
Boston, Massachusetts 02109
Telephone: 617-227-1500
Fax: 617-227-6700
E-Mail: wmonahan@monahanlaw.net

Fire, Marine Insurance, Casualty Insurance Law, Trial Practice, Defense Litigation, Law-Trial-Subrogation-Defense and Adjustment Insurance Laws

Insurance Clients

Adjustment Services, Inc.
Allstate Insurance Company
American Hardware Mutual Insurance Company
American Motorists Insurance Company
American Southern Insurance Company
Barnstable County Mutual Insurance Company
Brownstone Agency
Brownyard Claims Management, Inc.
Commerce Insurance Company
Crawford & Company
Eastern Adjustment Company
Factory Mutual Insurance Company
FM Global Group
General Security Insurance Company
Great American Custom Insurance Services
Indian Harbor Insurance Company
Insurance Claims Services, Inc.
LMG Property
Manufacturers and Merchants Mutual Insurance Company
Max Specialty Insurance Company
Metropolitan Property and Casualty Insurance Company
Nautilus Insurance Company
Norfolk and Dedham Mutual Fire Insurance Company
NOVA Casualty Company
The Providence Mutual Fire Insurance Company
Recreational Coverage Association
Travelers Property Casualty Insurance Company
Union Mutual Fire Insurance Company
U.S. Adjustment Corporation
U.S. Liability Insurance Company
XL Insurance Global Risk
Affiliated FM Insurance Company
American Empire Group
American International Adjustment Company
American Reliable Insurance Company
Andover Companies
Armed Forces Insurance Exchange
Bell & Clements Limited
Berkley Risk Administrators Company, LLC
Central Mutual Insurance Company
Claim Professionals Liability Insurance Company, A RRG
East Coast Claims Service, Inc.
Essex Insurance Company
Fitchburg Mutual Insurance Company
Friedline, Carter & Barrow Adjustment
General Star Management Company
Gulf Insurance Company
The Infinity Group
Lloyd's
Maine Mutual Fire Insurance Company
Massachusetts Property Insurance Underwriting Association
Narragansett Bay Insurance Company
New York Central Mutual Fire Insurance Company
North American Risk Services
Penn Millers Insurance Company
Providence Washington Insurance Company
Safety Insurance Company
Underwriters at Lloyd's, London
Underwriting Management Inc.
United Services Automobile Association (USAA)
USA Inc.
Vermont Mutual Insurance Company

BOSTON   MASSACHUSETTS

Monahan & Associates, P.C., Boston, MA   (Continued)

Principal

William O. Monahan — 1956 — Northeastern University, B.S., 1980; Suffolk University Law School, J.D., 1984 — Admitted to Bar, 1984, Massachusetts; 1986, Rhode Island; 1984, U.S. District Court, District of Massachusetts; 1993, U.S. Supreme Court — Member American, Massachusetts and Rhode Island Bar Associations; Defense Research Institute — Assistant District Attorney, Suffolk County, 1984-1985 — E-mail: wmonahan@monahanlaw.net

Senior Associate

Matthew Mahoney — 1958 — College of the Holy Cross, A.B., 1980; Boston College, J.D., 1986 — Admitted to Bar, 1986, Massachusetts; 1989, U.S. District Court, District of Massachusetts — Member Massachusetts Bar Association; Massachusetts Defense Lawyers Association — E-mail: mmahoney@monahanlaw.net

Associates

William F. Walsh — 1979 — Holy Cross College, B.S., 2001; Suffolk University, J.D., 2006 — Admitted to Bar, 2006, Massachusetts — E-mail: wwalsh@monahanlaw.net

Christopher J. Greeley — 1976 — Suffolk University Law School, J.D., 2007 — Admitted to Bar, 2007, Massachusetts — Unrestricted MACS Construction Supervisor's License; OSHA Safety Certification — Practice Areas: Insurance Coverage; Insurance Defense; Subrogation — E-mail: cgreeley@monahanlaw.net

Edward A. Bopp — 1974 — The College of New Jersey, B.S., 1996; Southern Methodist University, Dedman School of Law, J.D., 2008 — Admitted to Bar, 2008, Massachusetts; Rhode Island; 2009, U.S. District Court, District of Massachusetts — Member Massachusetts and Boston Bar Associations — E-mail: ebopp@monahanlaw.com

Bryan R. Wieland — 1985 — Wesleyan University, B.A., 2009; Suffolk University Law School, J.D. (Dean's List), 2012 — Admitted to Bar, 2012, Massachusetts — E-mail: bwieland@monahanlaw.com

(This firm is also listed in the Subrogation section of this directory)

Murphy & Riley, P.C.
101 Summer Street
Boston, Massachusetts 02110
   Telephone: 617-423-3700
   Fax: 617-423-1010
   E-Mail: EMail@MurphyRiley.com
   www.MurphyRiley.com

Established: 1993

Appeals, Automobile, Bad Faith, Construction Litigation, Employment Law, Environmental Law, Health Care Professional Licensure Defense, Insurance Coverage, Lead Paint, Legal Malpractice, Medical Malpractice, Mold and Mildew Claims, Nursing Home Liability, Product Liability, Professional Liability, Property Damage, Restaurant Liability, Trucking Law, Professional Licensure

Firm Profile: Murphy & Riley is a leading civil litigation firm, concentrating on the defense of insureds, self insureds, and insurers in all state and federal courts in the Commonwealth. The firm's experienced and talented trial attorneys possess the expertise and state of the art resources to identify and analyze promptly and efficiently the issues facing our clients. We counsel our clients through the litigation process, navigating them clear of litigation altogether where appropriate, all in a cost effective manner. Murphy & Riley has built a reputation as a smart, aggressive firm that works closely and proactively with its clients to bring about the best possible result in every matter commited to our care.

Insurance Clients

AIG Claim Services, Inc.
American Hardware Mutual Insurance Company
Endurance Services, Ltd.
First Mercury Insurance Company
Homesite Group, Inc.
Lancer Insurance Company
Alterra Specialty
Argo Group US
Controlled Risk Insurance Company
Hartford Financial Products
Hudson Insurance Group
Lexington Insurance Company

Murphy & Riley, P.C., Boston, MA   (Continued)

Mercury Insurance Group
Motorists Mutual Insurance Company
Penn-America Insurance Company
Pennsylvania Lumbermens Mutual Insurance Company
Stonecreek Insurance Company of America
Vermont Mutual Insurance Company
MiddleOak
Nautilus Insurance Company
New Jersey Manufacturers Insurance Company
Philadelphia Insurance Companies
Rockville Risk Management Associates, Inc.
United National Insurance Company

Non-Insurance Clients

Boston Medical Center
Budget Rent-A-Car System, Inc.
Harvard University
Milwaukee Electric Tool Corporation
Tyson Foods, Inc.
Boston Scientific Corporation
Cumberland Farms, Inc.
J.B. Hunt Transport, Inc.
New England Motor Freight, Inc.
Steward Health Care
Werner Enterprises, Inc.

Firm Members

Walter G. Murphy — (1925-2000)

Robert J. Murphy — College of the Holy Cross, B.A., 1977; Suffolk University, J.D., 1980 — Admitted to Bar, 1980, Massachusetts; 1980, U.S. District Court, District of Massachusetts; 2006, U.S. Court of Appeals, First Circuit — Member American Bar Association; Providers Council; Claims & Litigation Management Alliance; Federation of Defense and Corporate Counsel; Defense Research Institute; Massachusetts Defense Lawyers Association — Practice Areas: Professional Liability; Insurance Coverage; Not for Profit/Social Service Agencies; Trucking and Land Transport — E-mail: RMurphy@MurphyRiley.com

Richard J. Riley — Harvard University, B.A. (cum laude), 1979; Boston College, J.D. (cum laude), 1982 — Admitted to Bar, 1982, Massachusetts; 1983, U.S. District Court, District of Massachusetts; 1984, U.S. Court of Appeals, First Circuit — Member Defense Research Institute; Massachusetts Defense Lawyers Association — Practice Areas: Construction Litigation; Tort Litigation; Insurance Defense; Professional Liability-Medical and Legal — E-mail: RRiley@MurphyRiley.com

Susan Donnelly Murphy — University of Vermont, B.A., 1980; Suffolk University, J.D. (cum laude), 1983 — Admitted to Bar, 1983, Massachusetts; 1984, U.S. District Court, District of Massachusetts; 1993, U.S. Court of Appeals, First Circuit — Member Massachusetts Defense Lawyers Association (President, 2007-2008; Board of Directors, 2000-2010); International Association of Defense Counsel; Defense Research Institute — Practice Areas: Medical Malpractice; Not for Profit/Social Service Agencies; Professional Licensing and Regulatory — E-mail: SDonnellyMurphy@MurphyRiley.com

Joseph A. King — Bates College, B.A., 1987; Northeastern University, J.D., 1990 — Admitted to Bar, 1991, Massachusetts; 1991, U.S. District Court, District of Massachusetts; 2005, U.S. Court of Appeals, First Circuit — Member Massachusetts Defense Lawyers Association (Board of Directors 2007-2011); Frank J. Murray Inn of Court (Board of Directors 2012-Present, Secretary 2014-Present) — Practice Areas: Insurance Defense; Insurance Coverage — E-mail: JKing@MurphyRiley.com

John P. Coakley — Providence College, B.A. (magna cum laude), 1988; Villanova University, J.D. (magna cum laude), 1991 — Admitted to Bar, 1991, Massachusetts; 1997, U.S. District Court, District of Massachusetts; 2002, U.S. Court of Appeals, First Circuit — Lt. Colonel, U.S. Army Reserves, JAGC — Practice Areas: Civil Litigation; Insurance Coverage; Product Liability; Premises Liability; Employment Litigation; Professional Malpractice; Automobile and Land Transport; Civil Rights Litigation — E-mail: JCoakley@MurphyRiley.com

Kevin M. Sullivan — Brown University, B.A., 1989; Tulane University Law School, J.D. (cum laude), 1994 — Admitted to Bar, 1994, Massachusetts; 2012, New Hampshire; 1997, U.S. Court of Appeals for the Armed Forces; 2000, U.S. District Court, District of Massachusetts; 2000, U.S. Court of Appeals, First Circuit; 2013, U.S. District Court, District of New Hampshire — Lt., U.S. Navy, JAGC (1995-1999) — Practice Areas: Medical Malpractice; Professional Malpractice; Construction Accidents; Product Liability; Premises Liability; Business Litigation; Bad Faith; Motor Vehicle, Trucking and Land Transport Liability; Summary Process — E-mail: KSullivan@MurphyRiley.com

Frank L. DePasquale — Providence College, B.A. (cum laude), 1993; American University, J.D., 1997 — Admitted to Bar, 1998, New York; 2003, Massachusetts; 2005, U.S. District Court, Southern District of New York; U.S. District Court, District of Massachusetts — Practice Areas: Personal Injury Defense; Contract Disputes; Domestic Relations — E-mail: FDepasquale@MurphyRiley.com

Murphy & Riley, P.C., Boston, MA (Continued)

Associates

Christopher G. Long
Susan E. Devlin
Lauren J. Birnbaum
Lisa Oliver White
Brian R. Charville
Chesley H. Davis
Elizabeth J. Riley
Joan F. Renehan
William P. Mekrut
Melissa Arnold
Richard A. Christine
Stephen D. Coppolo
David R. Greco

Of Counsel

Peter C. Kober — University of Denver, B.A. (cum laude), 1973; Boston University School of Law, J.D., 1976 — Admitted to Bar, 1977, Massachusetts; 1981, New York; 1977, U.S. District Court, District of Massachusetts; 1978, U.S. Court of Appeals, First Circuit; 1981, U.S. Court of Appeals, Second Circuit; U.S. Supreme Court; 1982, U.S. District Court, Southern District of New York — E-mail: PKober@MurphyRiley.com

Joel D. Hillygus

W. Paul Needham, P.C.

10 Liberty Square, Suite 600
Boston, Massachusetts 02109
Telephone: 617-482-0500
Fax: 617-482-0456

Established: 1980

Insurance Law, Product Liability

Insurance Clients

Fitchburg Mutual Insurance Company
Hingham Mutual Fire Insurance Company
Lincoln Insurance Group
The Providence Mutual Fire Insurance Company
General Reinsurance Corporation
Great American Insurance Company
Interstate National Corporation
Markel Insurance Company

W. Paul Needham — 1944 — Boston University, B.A., 1967; Harvard University; University of Miami School of Law, J.D., 1974 — Admitted to Bar, 1974, Massachusetts — Member Boston Bar Association; Defense Research Institute

Associate

Mark A. Johnson — 1976 — The University of North Carolina at Chapel Hill, B.A., 1998; University of Maryland School of Law, J.D., 2001 — Admitted to Bar, 2002, Massachusetts — Member American and Massachusetts Bar Associations

Peabody & Arnold LLP

Federal Reserve Plaza
600 Atlantic Avenue
Boston, Massachusetts 02210
Telephone: 617-951-2100
Fax: 617-951-2125
www.peabodyarnold.com

(Providence, RI Office: 40 Westminster Street, Suite 201, 02903)
(Tel: 401-521-3742)
(Fax: 617-951-2125)

Established: 1899

Peabody & Arnold LLP, Boston, MA (Continued)

Antitrust Litigation, Aviation Law, Bank and Credit Union Litigation, Bankruptcy and Creditors' Rights Litigation, Business Litigation, Construction Litigation, Corporate, Real Estate, Trusts and Estates, Directors, Officers, Professional, and Corporate Liability Coverage, Drug and Medical Device Litigation, Employment Law, Environmental Law, Estate and Probate Litigation, FDCPA/FCRA Litigation, Fidelity and Surety Litigation, Healthcare Litigation, Insurance Coverage Litigation, Intellectual Property and Trade Secrets Protection, Personal Injury Litigation, Premises Liability Litigation, Products Liability Litigation, Professional Liability Litigation, Property and Fire Loss Litigation, Real Estate Litigation, Toxic Torts Litigation

Firm Profile: Established in 1899, Peabody & Arnold is one of Boston's oldest law firms. It has offices in Boston, MA and Providence, RI. The firm is a general practice firm with a concentraton in litigation and insurance law. See below for a partial list of clients:

Insurance Clients

AIU North America, Inc.
Aspen Insurance
CGU Insurance Companies
Chubb Executive Risk, Inc.
CRICO/RMF
CUMIS Insurance Society, Inc.
Fidelity and Deposit Company of Maryland
Fireman's Fund Risk Management Services, Inc.
GAB Robins North America, Inc.
Great American Insurance Company
Hanover Insurance Company
Hartford Specialty Company
Industrial Underwriters Insurance Company
Kemper Insurance Companies
Liberty Bond Services
National Union Fire Insurance Company of Pittsburgh, PA
Northland Insurance Company
Pacific Insurance Company
Risk Enterprise Management, Ltd.
RSKCo
Swiss Re/Westport Insurance Corporation
Travelers Indemnity Company
Trumbull Insurance Company
Tudor Insurance Company
United States Liability Insurance Group
Western World Insurance Company
Zurich North America
American Home Assurance Company CAB
Chartis
CNA Insurance Company
Crum & Forster Insurance Group
Federal Deposit Insurance Corporation
Fireman's Fund Insurance Company
First State Insurance Company
General Insurance Company of America
Gulf Insurance Company
Hartford Insurance Company
Hudson Insurance Company
International Fidelity Insurance Company
Lexington Insurance Company
Mount Vernon Fire Insurance Company
New England Insurance Company
Nutmeg Insurance Company
PRMS, Inc. - Professional Risk Management Services, Inc.
Stratford Insurance Company
Travelers Casualty and Surety Company
Travelers Property Casualty Corporation
Twin City Fire Insurance Company
Westchester Fire Insurance Company
XL Specialty Insurance Company
Zurich American Insurance Group

Partners

George A. Berman — Harvard College, B.A. (magna cum laude), 1975; Harvard Law School, J.D. (cum laude), 1979 — Admitted to Bar, 1979, Massachusetts

Jennifer E. Burke — University of Virginia, B.A. (with honors), 1986; Harvard Law School, J.D., 1989 — Admitted to Bar, 1989, Massachusetts

Susan E. Cohen — 1961 — University of Massachusetts Amherst, B.A. (cum laude), 1983; Boston University School of Law, J.D., 1988 — Admitted to Bar, 1988, Massachusetts

Frederick E. Connelly, Jr. — 1958 — St. Lawrence University, B.A. (cum laude), 1980; Suffolk University, J.D. (cum laude), 1984 — Admitted to Bar, 1985, Massachusetts

Philip M. Cronin — 1932 — Harvard University, A.B. (cum laude), 1953; J.D., 1956 — Admitted to Bar, 1956, Massachusetts

Allen N. David — **Managing Partner** — 1952 — University of Massachusetts, B.A. (magna cum laude), 1974; Boston University, J.D. (cum laude), 1977 — Admitted to Bar, 1977, Massachusetts

Michael P. Duffy — 1957 — University of Rhode Island, B.A. (with highest honors), 1979; Harvard University, J.D. (cum laude), 1982 — Admitted to Bar, 1982, Massachusetts; 1992, Rhode Island

Peabody & Arnold LLP, Boston, MA (Continued)

Timothy O. Egan — College of the Holy Cross, B.A., 1994; University of Notre Dame Law School, J.D., 1997 — Admitted to Bar, 1997, Massachusetts

Matthew J. Griffin — College of Holy Cross, B.A., 1995; Suffolk University Law School, J.D., 1998 — Admitted to Bar, 1998, Massachusetts

Michael J. Griffin — 1961 — St. Lawrence University, B.S., 1984; Albany Law School, J.D., 1987 — Admitted to Bar, 1987, New York; 1987, Massachusetts

Colleen M. Hennessey — 1966 — Colby College, B.A. (magna cum laude), 1988; Suffolk University, J.D. (cum laude), 1991 — Admitted to Bar, 1991, Massachusetts

Elizabeth Houlding — Queen's University, B.A. (with honors), 1983; Columbia University, M.A., 1987; Ph.D., 1991; Northeastern University School of Law, J.D., 2000 — Admitted to Bar, 2000, Massachusetts

Katherine Kenney — Tufts University, B.A., 1992; Suffolk University Law School, J.D. (cum laude), 1997 — Admitted to Bar, 1997, Massachusetts

Jennifer L. Markowski — University of Massachusetts Amherst, B.A., 1997; Suffolk University Law School, J.D. (cum laude), 2002 — Admitted to Bar, 2002, Massachusetts

Robert A. McCall — 1961 — Harvard University, A.B. (cum laude), 1983; Northeastern University, J.D., 1988 — Admitted to Bar, 1988, Massachusetts

Richard L. Nahigian — 1961 — Columbia University, A.B., 1983; Boston University School of Law, J.D., 1986 — Admitted to Bar, 1986, Massachusetts

David G. O'Brien — Northeastern University, B.S. (cum laude), 1989; New England School of Law, J.D. (cum laude), 1996 — Admitted to Bar, 1996, Massachusetts; 1997, New York

John J. O'Connor — 1960 — American International College, B.A. (summa cum laude), 1984; The Catholic University of America, Columbus School of Law, J.D., 1989 — Admitted to Bar, 1989, Massachusetts

E. Joseph O'Neil — 1964 — Washington University, B.A., 1986; University of Oregon, J.D., 1991 — Admitted to Bar, 1991, Massachusetts

Christopher A. Parady — Tufts University, B.A., 1990; Boston University School of Law, J.D., 1993 — Admitted to Bar, 1993, Massachusetts

Tamara Smith Holtslag — University of New Hampshire, B.A. (cum laude), 1993; Suffolk University Law School, J.D., 1996 — Admitted to Bar, 1996, Massachusetts; 2011, New Hampshire

Michael J. Stone — 1947 — Columbia University, B.S., 1968; M.S., 1970; Northeastern University, J.D., 1976 — Admitted to Bar, 1977, Massachusetts

Harvey Weiner — 1942 — Harvard University, A.B. (cum laude), 1964; Columbia University, J.D., 1967; The London School of Economics and Political Science, LL.M., 1968 — Admitted to Bar, 1968, Massachusetts

Rebecca J. Wilson — 1953 — Trinity College, B.A. (summa cum laude), 1975; Boston College, J.D. (cum laude), 1979 — Admitted to Bar, 1979, Massachusetts

Of Counsel

Kathleen M. Colbert
Kerri E. Duffell
Kathleen A. Papadeas
James J. Duane III
Sherry Y. Mulloy
Allan E. Taylor

Senior Counsel

Jason M. Cotton

Associates

Kiley M. Belliveau
Michael R. Brown
Sarah-Elizabeth Cloutier
William R. Covino
Ian J. Gemmell
Cortney M. Godin
Jane A. Horne
Kristyn Dery Kaupas
Michael A. Kippins
Timothy M. Pomarole
Jennifer L. Rousseau
Jill Brannelly
Barton E. Centauro
Christopher Conroy
Sharon Fry
Lindsey A. Gil
Michael H. Greene
Stephanie Kao
Catherine B. Kelleher
Daniel R. Lentz
Scarlett M. Rajbanshi
Courtney C. Shea

Regan & Kiely LLP

88 Black Falcon Avenue, Suite 330
Boston, Massachusetts 02210
Telephone: 617-723-0901
Fax: 617-723-0977
E-Mail: rek@regankiely.com
www.regankiely.com

Admiralty and Maritime Law, Employment Law, Product Liability, Premises Liability, Liquor Liability, Lead Paint, Automobile Liability, Construction Law, Medical Malpractice, Dental Malpractice, Commercial Litigation, Subrogation, Insurance Law

Firm Profile: Regan & Kiely, LLP represents insurance companies, large institutions, smaller self-insured businesses and individuals, as well as in arbitrations and mediations. The firm has built its' reputation on outstanding results, personal attention and communication with clients at each step of their case.

Insurance Clients

Sunderland Marine Mutual Insurance Company Limited
Travelers Insurance Companies

Non-Insurance Clients

Knowledge Learning Corporation

Members of the Firm

Joseph A. Regan — 1954 — Suffolk University, B.A. (magna cum laude), 1976; J.D., 1979 — Admitted to Bar, 1980, Massachusetts; 1980, U.S. District Court, District of Massachusetts; 1980, U.S. Court of Appeals, First Circuit — Member American Bar Association (Sections: Tort and Insurance Practice; Litigation); Massachusetts Bar Association; The Maritime Law Association of the United States (Proctor Member); Massachusetts Defense Lawyers Association; Defense Research Institute — Captain, U.S. Marine Corps, Judge Advocate, 1979-1983

Robert E. Kiely — 1965 — Fairfield University, B.A., 1987; Suffolk University, J.D. (cum laude), 1990 — Articles Editor, Suffolk Transnational Law Journal, 1989-1990 — Admitted to Bar, 1990, Massachusetts; U.S. District Court, District of Massachusetts; U.S. Court of Appeals, First Circuit — Member Massachusetts Bar Association; Massachusetts Defense Lawyers Association; The Maritime Law Association of the United States; International Association of Defense Counsel; Defense Research Institute

Associates

Sean P. Scanlon — 1975 — Northeastern University, B.S. (magna cum laude), 1999; Suffolk University School of Management, M.P.A., 2003; Suffolk University Law School, J.D., 2003 — Admitted to Bar, 2003, Massachusetts; 2006, U.S. District Court, District of Massachusetts — Member Massachusetts Bar Association

Jeffrey W. Ward — 1976 — James Madison University, B.A., 1999; Roger Williams University School of Law, J.D. (cum laude), 2006 — Admitted to Bar, 2006, Rhode Island; 2007, Massachusetts; U.S. District Court, District of Rhode Island; 2008, U.S. District Court, District of Massachusetts; 2009, U.S. Court of Appeals, First Circuit

Ropers, Majeski, Kohn & Bentley
A Professional Corporation

Ten Post Office Square, 8th Floor South
Boston, Massachusetts 02109
Telephone: 617-850-9087
Fax: 617-850-9088
www.rmkb.com

(Redwood City, CA Office*: 1001 Marshall Street, Suite 500, 94063)
 (Tel: 650-364-8200)
 (Fax: 650-780-1701)
(Los Angeles, CA Office*: 515 South Flower Street, Suite 1100, 90071)
 (Tel: 213-312-2000)
 (Fax: 213-312-2001)

MASSACHUSETTS   BOSTON

Ropers, Majeski, Kohn & Bentley, A Professional Corporation, Boston, MA (Continued)

(San Francisco, CA Office*: 150 Spear Street, Suite 850, 94105)
   (Tel: 415-543-4800)
   (Fax: 415-972-6301)
(San Jose, CA Office*: 50 West San Fernando Street, Suite 1400, 95113)
   (Tel: 408-287-6262)
   (Fax: 408-918-4501)
(New York, NY Office*: 750 Third Avenue, 25th Floor, 10017)
   (Tel: 212-668-5927)
   (Fax: 212-668-5929)

Established: 1950

Antitrust, Appellate Practice, Business Litigation, Commercial Litigation, Civil Rights, Class Actions, Complex Litigation, Construction Law, Corporate Law, Elder Abuse, Employment Law, Entertainment Law, Environmental Law, ERISA, Estate Planning, Governmental Entity Defense, Health Care, Intellectual Property, International Law, Mergers and Acquisitions, Personal Injury, Premises Liability, Product Liability, Professional Liability, Real Estate, Toxic Torts, Asset Protection, Banking/Consumer Credit, Catastrophic Injury, Cost Control, Elder Rights, Fee Disputes, Insurance Services, IT and Business Process Outsourcing, Litigation Management, Non-Profit, Proposition 65, Special Education Law, Taxation, Wealth Management

Partners

Lita M. Verrier — 1964 — The Wharton School of the University of Pennsylvania, B.S., 1991; Pepperdine University School of Law, J.D. (magna cum laude), 1995 — Admitted to Bar, 1995, California; Massachusetts; U.S. District Court, Eastern, Northern and Southern Districts of California — Member State Bar of California; Massachusetts and Santa Clara County Bar Associations; Women's Bar Association — Languages: Spanish — Practice Areas: Business Litigation; Commercial Litigation; Intellectual Property; Professional Liability; Directors and Officers Liability; Corporate Law; Real Estate

(See listing under Redwood City, CA for additional information)

Sloane and Walsh

3 Center Plaza, 8th Floor
Boston, Massachusetts 02108
   Telephone: 617-523-6010
   Fax: 617-227-0927
   www.sloanewalsh.com

Insurance Defense, Complex Litigation, State and Federal Courts, Professional Liability, Medical Liability, Accountants, Directors and Officers Liability, Architects and Engineers, Insurance Agents, Agent/Broker Liability, Environmental Liability, Hazardous Waste, Asbestos Litigation, Pollution, Employer Liability, Product Liability, General Liability, Automobile, Fire, Marine, Casualty, Property and Casualty, Construction Law, Insurance Coverage, Bad Faith, Insurance Fraud, Lead Paint, Health Care Providers, Lawyers, Environmental Consultants, Indoor Air Pollution, Latent Injuries, Toxic Tort and Sick Building Torts

Insurance Clients

Aetna Casualty and Surety Company
Amerisure Companies
Amica Mutual Insurance Company
Fireman's Fund Insurance Companies
GAB Robins North America, Inc.
The Hartford Insurance Group
John Hancock Property and Casualty Insurance Company
American International Group, Inc.
American Modern Home Insurance Company
CRICO Insurance Company
First State Insurance Company
First State Management Group, Inc.
Jefferson Insurance Company
Lexington Insurance Company
Lifespan Risk Services, Inc.

Sloane and Walsh, Boston, MA (Continued)

Maryland Casualty Company
Medical Professional Mutual Insurance Company
Republic Claims Service
Royal & SunAlliance Insurance Company
Massachusetts Property Insurance Underwriting Association
North American Specialty Insurance Company
Travelers Insurance Companies
Universal Underwriters Group

Non-Insurance Clients

Carlisle Syntec Systems, Inc.
Murray Products, Inc.
Mack Trucks, Inc.

Partners

William J. Dailey, Jr. — 1938 — Boston College, B.A., 1960; Georgetown University Law Center, LL.B., 1963 — Admitted to Bar, 1963, Massachusetts — Member Massachusetts, Middlesex and Central Middlesex (Past-President) Bar Associations; Massachusetts Academy of Trial Lawyers (Governor); Defense Research Institute; Fellow, American College of Trial Lawyers

John P. Ryan — Boston College, A.B., 1971; Suffolk University Law School, J.D., 1974 — Admitted to Bar, 1974, Massachusetts — Member American, Massachusetts, Boston and Norfolk Bar Associations; Massachusetts Defense Lawyers Association (Board of Directors); Defense Research Institute; Fellow, American College of Trial Lawyers

Robert H. Gaynor — Tufts University, B.A., 1973; Suffolk University Law School, J.D., 1977 — Admitted to Bar, 1977, Massachusetts — Member Massachusetts Bar Association; Massachusetts Defense Lawyers Association; Defense Research Institute

Edward T. Hinchey — Occidental College, B.A., 1977; Boston College, J.D., 1981 — Admitted to Bar, 1981, Massachusetts — Member Massachusetts and Norfolk Bar Associations; Massachusetts Trial Lawyers Association (Officer); American Trial Lawyers Association; Massachusetts Defense Lawyers Association; Defense Research Institute; Fellow, American College of Trial Lawyers

Lawrence J. Kenney, Jr. — Boston College, B.A., 1969; Suffolk University Law School, J.D., 1980 — Admitted to Bar, 1980, Massachusetts — Member Massachusetts and Central Middlesex Bar Associations; Massachusetts Academy of Trial Attorneys; Massachusetts Defense Lawyers Association; Defense Research Institute

Myles W. McDonough — Harvard University, A.B., 1980; Suffolk University, J.D., 1985 — Admitted to Bar, 1985, Massachusetts; 1985, U.S. District Court, District of Massachusetts — Member Massachusetts Bar Association; Massachusetts Defense Lawyers Association

Marcia K. Divoll — Mary Fletcher School of Nursing; Emmanuel College, B.S., 1976; Boston University, M.P.H., 1985; J.D., 1984 — Admitted to Bar, 1984, Massachusetts — Member American and Massachusetts Bar Associations; American Society of Clinical Pharmacology and Therapeutics (1979-1984) — Assistant Professor of Psychiatry, Tufts University School of Medicine, 1985-1989; Instructor, Massachusetts College of Pharmacy and Applied Health, 1986-1988 — Registered Nurse

Ross A. Kimball — Bowdoin College, B.A., 1974; The University of Maine, J.D., 1978 — Admitted to Bar, 1978, Massachusetts; 1978, U.S. District Court, District of Massachusetts — Member Massachusetts and Essex County Bar Associations

William J. Dailey, III — Boston College, B.S., 1988; Georgetown University, J.D., 1991 — Admitted to Bar, 1991, Massachusetts; 1991, U.S. District Court, District of Massachusetts — Member American, Massachusetts and Boston Bar Associations

Anthony J. Antonellis — Wesleyan University, B.A., 1986; Suffolk University, J.D., 1991 — Admitted to Bar, 1991, Massachusetts; 1991, U.S. District Court, District of Massachusetts — Member American, Massachusetts and Boston Bar Associations — Adjunct Professor of Environmental Law, Suffolk University Law School, Department of Justice Environmental Law Instructor

Laura Meyer Gregory — 1967 — Grinnell College, B.A., 1989; The University of Iowa, J.D. (with distinction), 1992 — Admitted to Bar, 1993, Massachusetts; 1994, U.S. District Court, District of Massachusetts; 1994, U.S. Court of Appeals, First Circuit — Member American, Massachusetts and Boston (Chair, Insurance Law Committee, 1997-1999) Bar Associations; Frank J. Murray Inn of Court; Chartered Property and Casualty Underwriting Society; Defense Research Institute — Chartered Property and Casualty Underwriter (CPCU)

Michael P. Guagenty — University of Massachusetts, B.A., 1987; New England School of Law, J.D., 1994 — Admitted to Bar, 1994, Massachusetts; 1994, U.S. District Court, District of Massachusetts — Member Massachusetts Bar Association

BOSTON   MASSACHUSETTS

Sloane and Walsh, Boston, MA   (Continued)

John A. Donovan, III — Kenyon College, B.A., 1992; Suffolk University, J.D., 1995 — Admitted to Bar, 1995, Massachusetts — Member Massachusetts Bar Association

Brian H. Sullivan — 1966 — The University of Maine, B.A., 1992; Boston College Law School, J.D., 1995 — Admitted to Bar, 1995, Massachusetts — Member American and Massachusetts Bar Associations — Lt. Commander, U.S. Navy, 1995-Courts-Martial of the Armed Forces

John McCormack — 1961 — Stonehill College, A.B., 1984; New England School of Law, J.D., 1992 — Admitted to Bar, 1992, Massachusetts; 1994, U.S. District Court, District of Massachusetts; 1994, U.S. Court of Appeals, First Circuit — Member Massachusetts Bar Association; Defense Research Institute; Massachusetts Defense Lawyers Association

Michael J. Kerrigan — Boston College, B.A., 1995; Boston College Law School, J.D., 2003 — Admitted to Bar, 2003, Massachusetts — Member Massachusetts Bar Association

Tanya K. Oldenhoff — Boston College, B.A., 1995; Suffolk University Law School, J.D., 2000 — Admitted to Bar, 2001, Massachusetts — Member Massachusetts and Boston Bar Associations

Associates

Harry A. Pierce — 1946 — Syracuse University, B.A., 1970; Boston College Law School, J.D., 1973 — Admitted to Bar, 1976, Massachusetts; 1978, U.S. District Court, District of Massachusetts — Member Massachusetts Bar Association

David Hartigan — 1950 — Boston College, B.A. (magna cum laude), 1971; Northeastern University School of Law, J.D., 1976 — Admitted to Bar, 1977, Massachusetts; 1977, U.S. District Court, District of Massachusetts; 1977, U.S. Court of Appeals, First Circuit — Member Boston Bar Association

Robert T. Norton — University of Rhode Island, B.A., 1992; Boston University School of Law, J.D., 1995 — Admitted to Bar, 1995, Massachusetts — Member Massachusetts Bar Association

Nichole J. Todesco — Boston University, B.A., 2001; The Catholic University of America, Columbus School of Law, J.D., 2004 — Admitted to Bar, 2004, Massachusetts; Rhode Island; 2006, Connecticut — Member Massachusetts, Rhode Island and Newport Bar Associations

Lisa A. Bombardieri — University of Vermont, B.A., 1999; Pepperdine University School of Law, J.D., 2006 — Admitted to Bar, 2006, Massachusetts — Member Massachusetts Bar Association

Harry A. Pierce — Syracuse University, B.A., 1970; Boston College Law School, J.D., 1973 — Admitted to Bar, 1973, Massachusetts — Member Massachusetts Bar Association

Tierney M. Chadwick — Dickinson College, B.A., 1998; Suffolk University Law School, J.D., 2003 — Admitted to Bar, 2003, Massachusetts — Member Massachusetts and Boston Bar Associations

Timothy Sweetland — State University of New York at Albany, B.A., 2002; New England School of Law, J.D., 2005 — Admitted to Bar, 2005, Massachusetts — Member Massachusetts Bar Association

Christopher M. Reilly — Duke University, B.A., 2003; Boston College Law School, J.D., 2008 — Admitted to Bar, 2008, Massachusetts — Member Massachusetts Bar Association

Tyson C. Roy — Colorado College, B.A., 2003; Suffolk University Law School, J.D., 2008 — Admitted to Bar, 2008, Massachusetts — Member Massachusetts Bar Association

Charles F. Rourke, II — Wheaton College, B.A., 2001; Suffolk University, J.D., 2009 — Admitted to Bar, 2009, Massachusetts; U.S. District Court, District of Massachusetts; U.S. Court of Appeals, First Circuit — Member Massachusetts Bar Association

Matthew D. Rush — Boston College, B.S., 2001; Duke University, M.E.M., 2003; Vermont Law School, J.D., 2007 — Admitted to Bar, 2007, Massachusetts — Member Massachusetts Bar Association

Gail M. Ryan — Boston College, B.A., 2005; Suffolk University Law School, J.D., 2009 — Admitted to Bar, 2009, Massachusetts; 2010, Rhode Island — Member Massachusetts, Rhode Island and Women's Bar Associations

(This firm is also listed in the Subrogation section of this directory)

Smith Duggan Buell & Rufo LLP

Three Center Plaza, Suite 800
Boston, Massachusetts 02108-2011
Telephone: 617-228-4400
Fax: 617-248-9320
E-Mail: SDBR@smithduggan.com
www.smithduggan.com

(Lincoln, MA Office: 55 Old Bedford Road, Lincoln North, Suite 300, 01773)
(Tel: 617-228-4400)
(Fax: 781-259-1112)

Administrative Law, Appellate Practice, Aviation, Business Litigation, Construction Defect, Employment Law, Estate Planning, Family Law, Fire & Explosion, Health Care, Insurance Coverage & Defense, Medical Malpractice Defense, Premises Liability, Probate, Product Liability, Professional Liability, Real Estate, Trusts, Workers' Compensation

Firm Profile: Smith Duggan offers exceptional legal advice and a responsive, individualized approach to their clients. At the outset of our representation, we work closely with clients to identify their specific goals. Our collegial and friendly spirit encourages attentive, helpful and creative legal solutions.

Insurance Clients

AIG Aerospace
Electric Insurance Company
Ironshore Environmental
The Medical Protective Company
United States Aircraft Insurance Group

Atrium Risk Management Services (Washington) Ltd.
McLarens Young International
Travelers Property Casualty Insurance Company
United States Aviation Underwriters, Inc.

Non-Insurance Clients

Broan-NuTone LLC
CEC Entertainment Concepts, L.P.
Lowe's Companies, Inc.
Nortek, Inc.
Stanley Black & Decker, Inc.
Vanguard Health Systems, Inc.

Brown University
Emcare/AMR
Massachusetts Port Authority
Partners HealthCare System, Inc.
Tenet Healthcare Corporation

Partners

Barbara Hayes Buell — Brandeis University, B.A., 1964; Northeastern University, J.D., 1971; Boston University School of Medicine and Public Health, M.P.H., 1994 — Admitted to Bar, 1971, Massachusetts; Rhode Island; U.S. District Court, District of Massachusetts; U.S. Court of Appeals, First Circuit; U.S. Supreme Court — Member Massachusetts and Rhode Island Bar Associations; Massachusetts Defense Lawyers Association (Board of Directors, 1993); Alumni Association Northeastern University School of Law (Past President, 1984-1986); Defense Research Institute — Practice Areas: Administrative Law; Health Care; Medical Malpractice; Litigation

Gerard A. Butler, Jr. — Boston College, B.S., 1987; Boston University School of Law, J.D., 1990 — Admitted to Bar, 1990, Massachusetts; 1997, U.S. District Court, District of Massachusetts — Practice Areas: Business Litigation; Contracts; Family Law; Health Care; Medical Malpractice; Product Liability

Thomas G. Cooper — Rensselaer Polytechnic Institute, B.S., 1972; Harvard Law School, J.D. (cum laude), 1983 — Admitted to Bar, 1983, Massachusetts; 1984, U.S. District Court, District of Massachusetts — Member Defense Research Institute; Massachusetts Defense Lawyers Association — Practice Areas: Fire & Explosion; Litigation; Product Liability

Christopher A. Duggan — Boston College, B.A. (summa cum laude), 1981; University of Virginia School of Law, J.D., 1984 — Admitted to Bar, 1985, Massachusetts; U.S. District Court, District of Massachusetts; U.S. Court of Appeals, First Circuit; U.S. Supreme Court — Member Boston Bar Association; American Board of Trial Advocates (Diplomate Member and President, Massachusetts Chapter, 2007-); Massachusetts Defense Lawyers Association (President, 1999-2000; President Elect, 1998-1999; First Vice President, 1997-1998; Board of Directors, 1991-2001); Faculty, National Institute of Trial Advocacy; Defense Research Institute; International Association of Defense Counsel — Practice Areas: Aviation; Fire & Explosion; Insurance Coverage; Product Liability; Professional Liability

MASSACHUSETTS

Smith Duggan Buell & Rufo LLP, Boston, MA
(Continued)

Tamara L. Ricciardone — Johns Hopkins University, B.A. (cum laude), 1989; Boston College Law School, J.D. (cum laude), 1992 — Admitted to Bar, 1992, Massachusetts; 1993, U.S. District Court, District of Massachusetts — Practice Areas: Commercial Litigation; Product Liability; Workers' Compensation

John B. Savoca — Harvard University, A.B. (summa cum laude, Phi Beta Kappa), 1979; J.D., 1982 — Admitted to Bar, 1982, Massachusetts; U.S. District Court, District of Massachusetts — Member Massachusetts Bar Association — Practice Areas: Fire & Explosion; Litigation; Product Liability

Christina Schenk-Hargrove — Massachusetts College of Art and Design, B.F.A., 1990; Boston College Law School, J.D. (magna cum laude), 1999 — Admitted to Bar, 1999, Massachusetts; 2001, U.S. District Court, District of Massachusetts; 2006, U.S. Court of Appeals, First Circuit — Member Massachusetts Womens Bar Association (Womens Leadership Initiative) — Languages: German — Practice Areas: Workers' Compensation; Employment; Contracts; Premises Liability

Matthew J. Walko — Dartmouth College, A.B., 1989; Albany Law School, J.D. (magna cum laude), 1992 — Admitted to Bar, 1992, Massachusetts; 1994, New York; 1996, U.S. District Court, District of Massachusetts; U.S. Court of Appeals, First Circuit — Member Massachusetts and New York State Bar Associations; Massachusetts Defense Lawyers Association; Defense Research Institute — Practice Areas: Appellate Practice; Commercial Litigation; Construction Law; Insurance Coverage; Insurance Defense; Premises Liability; Product Liability; Professional Liability

Kenneth M. Wright — Colgate University, A.B., 1980; Suffolk University Law School, J.D. (cum laude), 1985 — Suffolk University Law School Law Review — Admitted to Bar, 1985, Massachusetts; 1986, U.S. District Court, District of Massachusetts; 1991, U.S. Court of Appeals, First Circuit — Member Frank Murray American Inn of Court; NACE International; Legus International Network of Law Firms; Society for Protective Coatings; Massachusetts Collaborative Law Council; Defense Research Institute — NACE International CIP Level 1 — Practice Areas: Product Liability; Business Litigation; Construction Litigation; Fire & Explosion; Premises Liability; Probate

Associates

Kara Bettigole
Pauline Jauquet
Andrew D. Black
Dallin Wilson

Weston - Patrick, P.A.

84 State Street
Boston, Massachusetts 02109
Telephone: 617-742-9310
Fax: 617-742-5734
E-Mail: reh@westonpatrick.com

Established: 1897

Insurance Law, Casualty, Fire, Life Insurance, Automobile, Aviation, Product Liability, Professional Liability, Errors and Omissions, Environmental Law

Insurance Clients

Chubb Group of Insurance Companies
Colonial Penn Franklin Insurance Company
Criterion Casualty Company
Farmers Insurance Company
The Fidelity and Casualty Company of New York
Government Employees Insurance Company
Great Southwest Fire Insurance Company
National Casualty Company
Nationwide Mutual Insurance Company
St. Paul Fire and Marine Insurance Company
Southeastern Aviation Underwriters
CNA Insurance Company
Colonial Insurance Company of California
The Concord Group Insurance Companies
Federated Mutual Insurance Company
Gallagher Bassett Services, Inc.
Great American Insurance Company
Harbor Insurance Company
J. C. Penney Casualty Insurance Company
Northland Insurance Company
Pacific Indemnity Insurance Company
Security Insurance Group
Transport Indemnity Company
Transport Insurance Company

BRAINTREE

Weston - Patrick, P.A., Boston, MA (Continued)

Truck Insurance Exchange
Western Employers Insurance Company
United Services Automobile Association (USAA)

Non-Insurance Clients

Amoco Oil Company
North American Van Lines
Crawford & Company

Ronald E. Harding — 1950 — State University of New York at Albany, B.A. (cum laude), 1972; New England School of Law, J.D. (cum laude), 1975 — Admitted to Bar, 1975, Massachusetts

Allison K. Gurley — Suffolk University Law School, J.D. (magna cum laude), 2000 — Admitted to Bar, 2001, Massachusetts

Edward K. Law — University of Maine School of Law, J.D. (Dean's List), 1998 — Admitted to Bar, 1998, Massachusetts

Elizabeth Caiazzi — University of Maine School of Law, J.D. (cum laude), 1994 — Admitted to Bar, 1994, Massachusetts

Marissa A. Varnadore — New England School of Law, J.D., 2011 — Admitted to Bar, 2011, Massachusetts; Connecticut

BRAINTREE 33,698 Norfolk Co.

Curley & Curley, P.C.

35 Braintree Hill Office Park, Suite 103
Braintree, Massachusetts 02184
Telephone: 617-523-2990
Fax: 617-523-7602
E-Mail: rac@curleylaw.com

Insurance Defense, General Liability, Automobile, Product Liability, Coverage Issues, Tort, Casualty, Bodily Injury, Construction Defect, Asbestos Litigation, Toxic Torts

Firm Profile: Curley & Curley P.C. is a general practice law firm with offices at 35 Braintree Hill Office Park in Braintree MA. The major emphasis of the firm's practice is civil litigation, and the roots of this practice extend back over the course of five decades.

Curley & Curley P.C. represents its clients in all trial and appellate Courts of the Commonwealth of Massachusetts, the U.S. District Court for the District of Massachusetts, the U.S. Appeals Court for the First Circuit, the U.S. Supreme Court, the Massachusetts Commission Against Discrimination, and many other State and Federal Administrative agencies. From time to time, we also appear in the State and Federal Courts of New Hampshire.

Curley & Curley P.C. commits itself to quality, cost-effective representation of its clients. As a general rule, one attorney has the primary responsibility for each client matter but, where necessary and appropriate, has the support of the diverse talents and resources of the firm.

Curley & Curley P.C. is proud of its history and the service which it has provided to its clients and to the community. We believe we have compiled an outstanding record of success in representing our clients before trial, at trial, and on appeal. The firm looks forward to providing dedicated and quality representation to its clients in the years to come.

Insurance Clients

ACE Property & Casualty Insurance Company
Guaranty Fund Management Services
Peerless Insurance Company
Quincy Mutual Fire Insurance Company
Tower Group Companies
Electric Insurance Company
Great American Insurance Company
Liberty Mutual Insurance Company
Preferred Mutual Insurance Company
Resurgens Specialty Underwriting, Inc.

Shareholders

Robert A. Curley, Jr. — 1949 — Harvard University, A.B. (cum laude), 1971; Cornell University, J.D., 1974 — Admitted to Bar, 1974, Massachusetts; 1974, U.S. District Court, District of Massachusetts; 1975, U.S. Court of Appeals, First Circuit — Member American and Massachusetts Bar Associations; International Association of Defense Counsel; Massachusetts Defense

CAMBRIDGE   MASSACHUSETTS

Curley & Curley, P.C., Braintree, MA   (Continued)

Lawyers Association; Defense Research Institute; Fellow, American College of Trial Lawyers — Practice Areas: Insurance Coverage; Product Liability; Catastrophic Injury

Eugene F. Nowell — 1948 — College of the Holy Cross, B.A., 1970; Boston College, J.D., 1973 — Admitted to Bar, 1973, Massachusetts; 1973, U.S. District Court, District of Massachusetts — Practice Areas: Construction Defect; Personal Injury; Product Liability

David D. Dowd — 1953 — College of the Holy Cross, B.A. (cum laude), 1975; Boston College Law School, J.D. (cum laude), 1979 — Admitted to Bar, 1979, Massachusetts; 1980, U.S. District Court, District of Massachusetts; 1981, U.S. Court of Appeals, First Circuit — Practice Areas: Civil Litigation; Insurance Coverage

Martin J. Rooney — 1957 — University of New Hampshire, B.A. (summa cum laude), 1979; Boston College Law School, J.D. (magna cum laude), 1982 — Admitted to Bar, 1982, Massachusetts; 1983, New Hampshire; U.S. District Court, District of Massachusetts; U.S. District Court, District of New Hampshire; U.S. Court of Appeals, First Circuit; 1998, U.S. Supreme Court — Member Massachusetts and New Hampshire Bar Associations; Massachusetts Defense Lawyers Association (Board Member); Defense Research Institute; International Association of Defense Counsel — Practice Areas: Civil Rights; Insurance Defense; Employment Law

Lisabeth Ryan Kundert — 1959 — Brown University, A.B., 1981; Boston College Law School, J.D. (cum laude), 1986 — Admitted to Bar, 1986, Massachusetts; 1987, U.S. District Court, District of Massachusetts; 1987, U.S. Court of Appeals, First Circuit; 1993, U.S. Supreme Court — Practice Areas: Civil Litigation; Insurance Defense; Product Liability

Attorneys

James C. Wood — 1980 — Penn State University, B.A., 2002; University of Connecticut School of Law, J.D., 2006 — Admitted to Bar, 2006, Massachusetts; 2008, U.S. District Court, District of Massachusetts; U.S. Court of Appeals, First Circuit — Member Massachusetts Bar Association; Massachusetts Defense Lawyers Association; Defense Research Institute — Practice Areas: Civil Litigation; Insurance Defense; Product Liability

Joseph P. Evans — 1957 — Boston College, B.A., 1985; Suffolk University, J.D., 1988 — Admitted to Bar, 1988, Massachusetts

BROCKTON † 93,810 Plymouth Co.

Refer To

Mitchell & DeSimone
101 Arch Street
Boston, Massachusetts 02110
  Telephone: 617-737-8300
  Fax: 617-737-8390

Insurance Defense, Premises Liability, Contractors Liability, Employment Law, Discrimination, Environmental Law, Automobile, Tort, General Liability, Liquor Liability, Product Liability, Coverage Issues, Subrogation, Directors and Officers Liability, Professional Liability

SEE COMPLETE LISTING UNDER BOSTON, MASSACHUSETTS (15 MILES)

CAMBRIDGE † 105,162 Middlesex Co.

Clark, Hunt, Ahern & Embry

150 Cambridgepark Drive, Suite 9
Cambridge, Massachusetts 02140-2328
  Telephone: 617-494-1920
  Fax: 617-494-1921
  E-Mail: info@chelaw.com
  www.chelaw.com

Established: 1986

Insurance Defense, Coverage Issues, General Liability, Personal Injury, Property Damage, Slip and Fall, Automobile, Subrogation

Firm Profile: Clark, Hunt, Ahern & Embry has been representing national and international insurers for over 25 years. Our wealth of experience enables us to provide the insurance industry with a full spectrum of legal services. The size of our firm and the quality of our attorneys allow us to provide these services at the highest level. Many of our attorneys were trained in the insurance industry, and some have attained the Chartered Property and

Clark, Hunt, Ahern & Embry, Cambridge, MA (Continued)

Casualty Underwriter (C.P.C.U.) designation. Because of our unique background, training, and experience, we provide sophisticated coverage analysis, opinions, and advice to our insurer clients. We fully appreciate the collaborative effort needed to successfully defend a claim. By keeping our insurers apprised of all developments in our cases, we eliminate the element of surprise. Through communication we are able to arrive at the most effective means to obtain our litigation goals.

Our highly skilled trial lawyers litigate cases in all of the state and federal courts of Massachusetts and Rhode Island. We have also been specially admitted to practice in other states. Although we handle simple tort claims aggressively, efficiently, and cost effectively, we specialize in complex, sophisticated, and high-exposure cases in the product liability, construction, and premises liability areas. For many insurers, we are the defense firm of last resort. Because of our expertise in both insurance coverage and contract law, we identify and zealously pursue risk transfer at every opportunity.

Insurance Clients

AXA Global Risks US Insurance Company	Barnstable County Mutual Insurance Company
Cambridge Mutual Fire Insurance Company	Commonwealth Mutual Insurance Company
Empire Insurance Company	Everest National Insurance Company
Farm Family Insurance Companies	
Merrimack Mutual Fire Insurance Company	Metropolitan Property and Casualty Insurance Company
RLI Insurance Company	St. Paul Fire and Marine Insurance Company
Shelby Insurance Company	
Travelers Indemnity Company	Travelers Property Casualty Insurance Company
Vermont Mutual Insurance Company	

Non-Insurance Clients

American Hospitality Concepts, Inc.   H. P. Hood, Inc.

Members of the Firm

William J. Hunt — 1951 — Dickinson College, B.A. (cum laude), 1973; Suffolk University, J.D., 1976 — Admitted to Bar, 1976, Pennsylvania; 1978, Massachusetts; 1982, New Jersey; 1990, Rhode Island; 1979, U.S. District Court, Eastern District of Pennsylvania; 1979, U.S. Court of Appeals, Third Circuit; 1982, U.S. District Court, District of New Jersey; 1986, U.S. District Court, District of Massachusetts; 1986, U.S. Court of Appeals, First Circuit; 1991, U.S. District Court, District of Rhode Island — Member Massachusetts and Rhode Island Bar Associations; Boston Inn of Court — Faculty, National Institute for Trial Advocacy, Emory Law School, Hofstra Law School, and University of San Francisco — Chartered Property and Casualty Underwriter — E-mail: whunt@chelaw.com

Bruce J. Embry — 1949 — Tufts University, B.A. (magna cum laude), 1971; Boston University, J.D., 1976 — Admitted to Bar, 1977, Massachusetts — Member American and Massachusetts Bar Associations — E-mail: bembry@chelaw.com

William F. Ahern, Jr. — 1956 — Wesleyan University, B.A., 1978; University of Connecticut, J.D., 1982 — Admitted to Bar, 1982, Massachusetts; 1983, Connecticut; 1995, Rhode Island; 1983, U.S. District Court, District of Connecticut; 1983, U.S. District Court, District of Massachusetts; 1983, U.S. Court of Appeals, First Circuit — Member Rhode Island Bar Association — Reported Cases: Rhode v. Beacon Sales, 416 Mass. 14 (1993) — E-mail: wahern@chelaw.com

Henry W. Clark — 1945 — Harvard Divinity School, B.D., 1971; Boston College, Ph.D., 1984; Suffolk University, J.D. (cum laude), 1989 — Admitted to Bar, 1989, Massachusetts; 1989, U.S. District Court, District of Massachusetts — Member Massachusetts Bar Association — E-mail: hclark@chelaw.com

Diane Swierczynski — 1959 — Mount Holyoke College, B.A., 1981; Suffolk University, J.D., 1984 — Admitted to Bar, 1985, Massachusetts; 1999, Rhode Island; 1985, U.S. District Court, District of Massachusetts; 1985, U.S. Court of Appeals, First Circuit — Member Rhode Island and Essex County Bar Associations — Reported Cases: McDonald v. Lavery, 27 Mass. App. Ct. 1108 (1989); Sawash v. Suburban Welders, 407 Mass. 311 (1990); Callahan v. First Congregational, 441 Mass. 699 (2004) — E-mail: dianes@chelaw.com

Joshua D. Krell — 1967 — Bates College, B.A., 1989; The University of Maine, J.D., 1992 — Admitted to Bar, 1992, Maine; Massachusetts — Member Massachusetts Bar Association; Boston Inn of Court — E-mail: jkrell@chelaw.com

MASSACHUSETTS

Clark, Hunt, Ahern & Embry, Cambridge, MA (Continued)

Janine Brown-Smith — 1961 — University of Massachusetts, B.A., 2002; New England School of Law, J.D., 2005 — Admitted to Bar, 2005, Massachusetts — E-mail: jbrown-smith@chelaw.com

David G. Hanson — 1952 — University of Massachusetts, B.S. (cum laude), 1980; New England School of Law, J.D., 1985 — Admitted to Bar, 1987, Massachusetts — E-mail: dhanson@chelaw.com

Associates

Marisa S. Gregg — 1973 — Boston University, B.A., 1995; Suffolk University, J.D., 2000 — Admitted to Bar, 2002, Massachusetts — Member Womens Bar Association; Real Estate Bar of Massachusetts — E-mail: mgregg@chelaw.com

Jeremy Y. Weltman — 1979 — University of Denver, B.A., 2001; Northeastern University School of Law, J.D., 2004 — Admitted to Bar, 2005, Massachusetts — Member Massachusetts and Boston Bar Associations — E-mail: jweltman@chelaw.com

Katherine M. Felluca — 1982 — University at Albany, B.A. (summa cum laude), 2003; Boston University School of Law, J.D., 2007 — Admitted to Bar, 2007, Massachusetts — Member American, Massachusetts and Boston Bar Associations; Women's Bar Association of Massachusetts — E-mail: kfelluca@chelaw.com

Michael J. Rossi — 1979 — Johns Hopkins University, B.A., 2001; Suffolk University Law School, J.D. (cum laude), 2006 — Admitted to Bar, 2006, Massachusetts; U.S. District Court, District of Massachusetts — Member Massachusetts Bar Association — E-mail: mrossi@chelaw.com

(This firm is also listed in the Subrogation section of this directory)

The following firms also service this area.

Zizik, Powers, O'Connell, Spaulding & Lamontagne, P.C.
690 Canton Street, Suite 306
Westwood, Massachusetts 02090
   Telephone: 781-320-5400
   Fax: 781-320-5444

Insurance Defense, Automobile, Construction Law, Coverage Issues, Disability, Environmental Law, General Liability, Hazardous Waste, Life Insurance, Liquor Liability, Personal Injury, Premises Liability, Product Liability, Toxic Torts, Alternative Dispute Resolution, Antitrust, Employment Law, Commercial Litigation, Fire Loss, Trucking Litigation

SEE COMPLETE LISTING UNDER WESTWOOD, MASSACHUSETTS (21 MILES)

FALL RIVER † 88,857 Bristol Co.

Refer To

Hassett & Donnelly, P.C.
446 Main Street, 12th Floor
Worcester, Massachusetts 01608
   Telephone: 508-791-6287
   Fax: 508-791-2652

Insurance Defense, Defense Litigation, Construction Litigation, Coverage Analysis, Declaratory Judgments, Bad Faith, Professional Liability, Product Liability, Premises Liability, Municipal Liability, Workers' Compensation, Civil Litigation, Commercial General Liability, Employment Law, Motor Vehicle, Negligence, Toxic Torts, Wrongful Death, Breach of Contract, Property Defense, Environmental Litigation, Business Litigation, Fire, Homeowners, First and Third Party Defense, Property and Casualty, Self-Insured Defense, Uninsured and Underinsured Motorist, Employment Law (Management Side), Trial and Appellate Practice

SEE COMPLETE LISTING UNDER WORCESTER, MASSACHUSETTS (40 MILES)

Refer To

Mitchell & DeSimone
101 Arch Street
Boston, Massachusetts 02110
   Telephone: 617-737-8300
   Fax: 617-737-8390

Insurance Defense, Premises Liability, Contractors Liability, Employment Law, Discrimination, Environmental Law, Automobile, Tort, General Liability, Liquor Liability, Product Liability, Coverage Issues, Subrogation, Directors and Officers Liability, Professional Liability

SEE COMPLETE LISTING UNDER BOSTON, MASSACHUSETTS (40 MILES)

Refer To

Zizik, Powers, O'Connell, Spaulding & Lamontagne, P.C.
40 Westminster Street, Suite 201
Providence, Rhode Island 02903
   Telephone: 401-421-7110
   Fax: 401-421-7111

Insurance Defense, Automobile, Construction Law, Coverage Issues, Disability, Environmental Law, General Liability, Hazardous Waste, Life Insurance, Liquor Liability, Personal Injury, Premises Liability, Product Liability, Toxic Torts, Antitrust, Commercial Law, Employment Litigation, Trucking Litigation

SEE COMPLETE LISTING UNDER PROVIDENCE, RHODE ISLAND (16 MILES)

FITCHBURG † 40,318 Worcester Co.

Refer To

Hassett & Donnelly, P.C.
446 Main Street, 12th Floor
Worcester, Massachusetts 01608
   Telephone: 508-791-6287
   Fax: 508-791-2652

Insurance Defense, Defense Litigation, Construction Litigation, Coverage Analysis, Declaratory Judgments, Bad Faith, Professional Liability, Product Liability, Premises Liability, Municipal Liability, Workers' Compensation, Civil Litigation, Commercial General Liability, Employment Law, Motor Vehicle, Negligence, Toxic Torts, Wrongful Death, Breach of Contract, Property Defense, Environmental Litigation, Business Litigation, Fire, Homeowners, First and Third Party Defense, Property and Casualty, Self-Insured Defense, Uninsured and Underinsured Motorist, Employment Law (Management Side), Trial and Appellate Practice

SEE COMPLETE LISTING UNDER WORCESTER, MASSACHUSETTS (25 MILES)

GREAT BARRINGTON 2,231 Berkshire Co.

Refer To

Campoli & Monteleone
27 Willis Street
Pittsfield, Massachusetts 01201
   Telephone: 413-443-6485
   Fax: 413-448-6233

Mailing Address: P.O. Box 1384, Pittsfield, MA 01202

Insurance Law

SEE COMPLETE LISTING UNDER PITTSFIELD, MASSACHUSETTS (20 MILES)

GREENFIELD † 13,716 Franklin Co.

Refer To

Doherty, Wallace, Pillsbury & Murphy, P.C.
One Monarch Place, Suite 1900
Springfield, Massachusetts 01144-1900
   Telephone: 413-733-3111
   Fax: 413-734-3910
   Toll Free: 888-680-3111

Insurance Defense, Premises Liability, Product Liability, General Liability, Homeowners, Automobile Liability, Liquor Liability, Medical Malpractice, Legal Malpractice, Toxic Torts, Commercial Law, Bad Faith, Coverage Issues, Opinions, Litigation, Lead Paint, Environmental Law, Intellectual Property, Employment Law

SEE COMPLETE LISTING UNDER SPRINGFIELD, MASSACHUSETTS (40 MILES)

Refer To

Hassett & Donnelly, P.C.
446 Main Street, 12th Floor
Worcester, Massachusetts 01608
   Telephone: 508-791-6287
   Fax: 508-791-2652

Insurance Defense, Defense Litigation, Construction Litigation, Coverage Analysis, Declaratory Judgments, Bad Faith, Professional Liability, Product Liability, Premises Liability, Municipal Liability, Workers' Compensation, Civil Litigation, Commercial General Liability, Employment Law, Motor Vehicle, Negligence, Toxic Torts, Wrongful Death, Breach of Contract, Property Defense, Environmental Litigation, Business Litigation, Fire, Homeowners, First and Third Party Defense, Property and Casualty, Self-Insured Defense, Uninsured and Underinsured Motorist, Employment Law (Management Side), Trial and Appellate Practice

SEE COMPLETE LISTING UNDER WORCESTER, MASSACHUSETTS (62 MILES)

HYANNIS 14,543 Barnstable Co.

Zizik, Powers, O'Connell, Spaulding & Lamontagne, P.C.

540 Main Street
Hyannis, Massachusetts 02601
   Telephone: 781-320-5400
   Fax: 781-320-5444
   E-Mail: dzizik@zizikpowers.com
   www.zizikpowers.com

(Westwood, MA Office*: 690 Canton Street, Suite 306, 02090)
   (Tel: 781-320-5400)
   (Fax: 781-320-5444)
(Providence, RI Office*: 40 Westminster Street, Suite 201, 02903)
   (Tel: 401-421-7110)
   (Fax: 401-421-7111)

Insurance Defense, Automobile, Construction Law, Coverage Issues, Disability, Environmental Law, General Liability, Hazardous Waste, Life Insurance, Liquor Liability, Personal Injury, Premises Liability, Product Liability, Professional Liability, Toxic Torts

(See listing under Westwood, MA for additional information)

LYNN 90,329 Essex Co.

Bradley Moore Primason Cuffe & Weber, LLP

85 Exchange Street
Lynn, Massachusetts 01901
   Telephone: 781-595-2050
   Fax: 781-599-5160
   E-Mail: counsel@bradleymoorelaw.com
   www.bradleymoorelaw.com

First and Third Party Defense, Insurance Coverage

Insurance Clients

Essex Insurance Company
Markel Insurance Company
Farmers Insurance Group

Non-Insurance Clients

The Salvation Army

Of Counsel

Ethan Warren — Princeton University, A.B., 1976; Suffolk University, J.D. (cum laude), 1980 — Admitted to Bar, 1980, Massachusetts; 1981, U.S. District Court, District of Massachusetts; 1983, U.S. Court of Appeals, First Circuit

NATICK 30,432 Middlesex Co.

Refer To
Hassett & Donnelly, P.C.
446 Main Street, 12th Floor
Worcester, Massachusetts 01608
   Telephone: 508-791-6287
   Fax: 508-791-2652

Insurance Defense, Defense Litigation, Construction Litigation, Coverage Analysis, Declaratory Judgments, Bad Faith, Professional Liability, Product Liability, Premises Liability, Municipal Liability, Workers' Compensation, Civil Litigation, Commercial General Liability, Employment Law, Motor Vehicle, Negligence, Toxic Torts, Wrongful Death, Breach of Contract, Property Defense, Environmental Litigation, Business Litigation, Fire, Homeowners, First and Third Party Defense, Property and Casualty, Self-Insured Defense, Uninsured and Underinsured Motorist, Employment Law (Management Side), Trial and Appellate Practice

SEE COMPLETE LISTING UNDER WORCESTER, MASSACHUSETTS (30 MILES)

NEEDHAM 28,886 Norfolk Co.

Heifetz Rose, LLP

175 Highland Avenue, Suite 407
Needham, Massachusetts 02494
   Telephone: 617-986-6210
   Fax: 617-725-0533
   www.heifetzrose.com

Insurance Defense, Transportation, Product Liability, Personal Injury, Premises Liability, Liquor Liability, Commercial Law, Coverage Issues, Environmental Coverage, Environmental Law, Errors and Omissions, Labor and Employment, Property Damage, Workers' Compensation

Firm Profile: Heifetz Rose LLP, an AV-rated law firm, proudly opened its doors for business on January 1, 2013. This marks the thirty-fifth year of practicing law for the firm's founder and managing partner, Richard E. Heifetz. The firm is comprised of seven civil trial attorneys, each of whom previously practiced in the Boston firm of Tucker, Heifetz & Saltzman, LLP.

The firm handles cases in all state and federal courts in the Commonwealth of Massachusetts, as well as our neighboring states of New Hampshire, Rhode Island, and Connecticut.

Insurance Clients

Arch Insurance Company
General Star Management Company
Lumber Mutual Insurance Company
Utica Mutual Insurance Company
Farm Family Casualty Insurance Company
Hudson Insurance Group
Old Republic Insurance Company
Safeco Select Markets

Non-Insurance Clients

Bovis Lend Lease Holdings, Inc.
Constitution State Service Company
Polka Dog Designs, LLC
Tresca Brothers Sand & Gravel, Inc.
Brand Energy and Infrastructure Services, LLC
New England Water Heater Company

Partners

Richard E. Heifetz — University of New Hampshire, B.A. (cum laude), 1972; New England School of Law, J.D. (cum laude), 1978 — Admitted to Bar, 1978, Massachusetts; 2005, New Hampshire; 1978, U.S. District Court, District of Massachusetts; 2010, U.S. District Court, District of New Hampshire — Member American (Torts and Insurance Practice Section), New Hampshire and Massachusetts Bar Associations; Defense Research Institute; American Board of Trial Advocates — Rated AV Preeminent by Martindale-Hubbell; 2013 Top Rated Lawyer in Insurance Law — E-mail: rheifetz@heifetzrose.com

William P. Rose — University of Massachusetts Amherst, B.A., 1977; Suffolk University, J.D. (cum laude), 1990 — Admitted to Bar, 1990, Massachusetts;

MASSACHUSETTS

Heifetz Rose, LLP, Needham, MA (Continued)

1991, U.S. District Court, District of Massachusetts; U.S. Court of Appeals, First Circuit — Reported Cases: Coombes v. Florio; LeBlanc v. Hilton Hotels — Practice Areas: Insurance Coverage; Asbestos; Agent and Brokers Errors and Omissions — E-mail: wrose@heifetzrose.com

James T. Scamby — Boston College, B.S., 1992; New England School of Law, J.D., 1995 — Admitted to Bar, 1995, Massachusetts; 1997, Pennsylvania; New Jersey; 1996, U.S. District Court, District of Massachusetts; U.S. Court of Appeals, First Circuit — Member American Bar Association; Defense Research Institute; Massachusetts Academy of Trial Attorneys; Massachusetts Defense Lawyers Association — Co-Author: Errors & Omissions "Hotspots" and How to Address Them, The John Liner Review, Summer 2011 — E-mail: scamby@heifetzrose.com

Associates

J. Nathan Cole — Bates College, B.A., 1997; Boston College Law School, J.D., 2003 — Admitted to Bar, 2003, Massachusetts; 2006, U.S. District Court, District of Massachusetts — Member Massachusetts Bar Association — Massachusetts Super Lawyers Rising Stars (2013) — E-mail: jncole@heifetzrose.com

Syd A. Saloman — University of Massachusetts Dartmouth, B.S. (cum laude), 1996; Suffolk University Law School, J.D. (cum laude), 1999 — Admitted to Bar, 1999, Massachusetts; 2002, Rhode Island; 2000, U.S. District Court, District of Massachusetts; U.S. Court of Appeals, First Circuit — Member Massachusetts Bar Association — E-mail: ssaloman@heifetzrose.com

Darian Butcher — Randolph-Macon Woman's College, B.A. (magna cum laude), 2009; Boston University School of Law, J.D., 2012 — Admitted to Bar, 2012, Massachusetts — Member American Bar Association; Women's Bar Association of Massachusetts; Massachusetts Black Lawyers Association; The Association of Latino Professionals in Finance and Accounting — E-mail: dbutcher@heifetzrose.com

NEW BEDFORD † 95,072 Bristol Co.

Refer To

Mitchell & DeSimone
101 Arch Street
Boston, Massachusetts 02110
Telephone: 617-737-8300
Fax: 617-737-8390

Insurance Defense, Premises Liability, Contractors Liability, Employment Law, Discrimination, Environmental Law, Automobile, Tort, General Liability, Liquor Liability, Product Liability, Coverage Issues, Subrogation, Directors and Officers Liability, Professional Liability

SEE COMPLETE LISTING UNDER BOSTON, MASSACHUSETTS (73 MILES)

NORTH ADAMS 13,708 Berkshire Co.

Campoli & Monteleone

40 Main Street
North Adams, Massachusetts 01247
Telephone: 413-663-9501
Fax: 413-663-9564
www.campolilaw.com

(Pittsfield, MA Office*: 27 Willis Street, 01201, P.O. Box 1384, 01202)
(Tel: 413-443-6485)
(Fax: 413-448-6233)

Insurance Law

(See listing under Pittsfield, MA for additional information)

NEW BEDFORD

The following firms also service this area.

Campoli & Monteleone
27 Willis Street
Pittsfield, Massachusetts 01201
Telephone: 413-443-6485
Fax: 413-448-6233
Mailing Address: P.O. Box 1384, Pittsfield, MA 01202

Insurance Law

SEE COMPLETE LISTING UNDER PITTSFIELD, MASSACHUSETTS (22 MILES)

NORTHAMPTON † 28,549 Hampshire Co.

Refer To

Doherty, Wallace, Pillsbury & Murphy, P.C.
One Monarch Place, Suite 1900
Springfield, Massachusetts 01144-1900
Telephone: 413-733-3111
Fax: 413-734-3910
Toll Free: 888-680-3111

Insurance Defense, Premises Liability, Product Liability, General Liability, Homeowners, Automobile Liability, Liquor Liability, Medical Malpractice, Legal Malpractice, Toxic Torts, Commercial Law, Bad Faith, Coverage Issues, Opinions, Litigation, Lead Paint, Environmental Law, Intellectual Property, Employment Law

SEE COMPLETE LISTING UNDER SPRINGFIELD, MASSACHUSETTS (20 MILES)

PITTSFIELD † 44,737 Berkshire Co.

Campoli & Monteleone

27 Willis Street
Pittsfield, Massachusetts 01201
Telephone: 413-443-6485
Fax: 413-448-6233
www.campolilaw.com

(North Adams, MA Office*: 40 Main Street, 01247)
(Tel: 413-663-9501)
(Fax: 413-663-9564)

Insurance Law

Insurance Clients

AIG Risk Management, Inc.	American Fidelity Group
American International Adjustment Company	Atlantic Casualty Insurance Company
Continental Insurance Company	Continental Loss Adjusting Services
Crawford Risk Management Services	Essex Insurance Company
GAB Robins North America, Inc.	Hanover Insurance Company
Hartford Accident and Indemnity Company	Jefferson Insurance Company
	Lexington Insurance Company
Mutual Insurance Company of Burlington	National Grange Mutual Insurance Company
National Union Fire Insurance Company	New Hampshire Insurance Company
New York Central Mutual Fire Insurance Company	Northeastern Fire Insurance Company
North East Insurance Company	Penn-America Insurance Company
Philadelphia Insurance Company	Preferred Mutual Insurance Company
Transamerica Insurance Company	
Underwriters Adjusting Company	Underwriters at Lloyd's, London
Union Standard Insurance Company	United Community Insurance Company
Utica Mutual Insurance Company	Zurich American Insurance Company

Non-Insurance Clients

BF Services, Inc.	International Transport, Inc.

Thomas L. Campoli — 1956 — University of Vermont, B.A., 1978; Suffolk University Law School, J.D., 1981 — Admitted to Bar, 1981, Massachusetts;

PLYMOUTH — MASSACHUSETTS

Campoli & Monteleone, Pittsfield, MA (Continued)

1982, U.S. District Court, District of Massachusetts — Member Massachusetts Bar Association — Regional Governor, Massachusetts Academy of Trial Attorneys

J. Peri Campoli — 1959 — University of Massachusetts, B.A., 1981; Thomas M. Cooley Law School, J.D., 1986 — Admitted to Bar, 1986, Massachusetts; 1986, U.S. District Court, District of Massachusetts — Member Massachusetts and Berkshire County Bar Associations; Massachusetts Conveyancers Association

Robert A. Monteleone, Jr. — 1961 — Harvard University, A.B., 1983; Suffolk University Law School, J.D. (cum laude), 1991 — Admitted to Bar, 1991, Massachusetts; 1992, U.S. District Court, District of Massachusetts — Member American, Massachusetts and Berkshire County Bar Associations

Scott W. Ellis — 1969 — Holy Cross College, B.A., 1991; St. John's University, J.D. (Dean's List), 1994 — Admitted to Bar, 1994, Massachusetts; 1999, Connecticut; 2000, U.S. District Court, District of Massachusetts; 2000, U.S. Court of Appeals, First Circuit — Member Berkshire County Bar Association

Matthew Mozian — 1976 — State University of New York at Geneseo, B.A., 1998; Albany Law School of Union University, J.D. (cum laude), 2001 — Admitted to Bar, 2002, New York; 2007, Massachusetts — Member Berkshire County and Albany County Bar Associations

Of Counsel

Andrew T. Campoli — 1924 — Tufts University, B.S., 1948; Boston University Law School, LL.B., 1951 — Admitted to Bar, 1951, Massachusetts — Member Massachusetts and Berkshire County Bar Associations; Massachusetts Trial Lawyers Association — Public Defender, Berkshire County, 1960-1986

Flournoy & Galvagni, P.C.

75 North Street, Suite 310
Pittsfield, Massachusetts 01201-5150
  Telephone: 413-499-0500
  Fax: 413-445-7403
  E-Mail: ldf@flournoylaw.com
  www.lawyers.com/flournoy

Civil Litigation, Commercial Law, Employment Law, Insurance Defense

Firm Profile: Flournoy & Galvagni, P.C. offer quick and personal client response and effective litigation throughout Western Massachusetts, tailored to business and individual client's situations and strategies. The firm concentrates its defense work in medical malpractice, automobile and general liability claims and does significant commercial and employment cases.

Insurance Clients

Gulf Insurance Company   ProMutual Group

Non-Insurance Clients

Berkshire Concrete Corp.   Berkshire Housing Services, Inc.
Dion Money Management, Inc.   Enterprise Rent-A-Car Company

Members

Lee D. Flournoy — 1950 — Wellesley College, B.A. (with honors), 1971; Northeastern University, J.D., 1974 — Admitted to Bar, 1975, Massachusetts; 1976, U.S. District Court, District of Massachusetts — Member Massachusetts Bar Association (Criminal Justice Section Council, 2002-2004); Berkshire Bar Association (Chair, Bench Bar Appellate Committee); Massachusetts Collaborative Law Council — Assistant District Attorney, Berkshire District (1979-1989) — E-mail: ldf@flournoylaw.com

Jennifer L. Galvagni — 1980 — University of Massachusetts, B.A. (cum laude), 2002; University of Maine School of Law, J.D., 2005 — Admitted to Bar, 2005, Massachusetts — E-mail: jlg@flournoylaw.com

Beth S. Stomberg — 1959 — University of Massachusetts, B.A. (magna cum laude), 1985; Georgetown University, J.D., 1988 — Admitted to Bar, 1989, Massachusetts; 1990, U.S. District Court, District of Massachusetts — E-mail: bss@flournoylaw.com

---

The following firms also service this area.

Doherty, Wallace, Pillsbury & Murphy, P.C.

One Monarch Place, Suite 1900
Springfield, Massachusetts 01144-1900
  Telephone: 413-733-3111
  Fax: 413-734-3910
  Toll Free: 888-680-3111

Insurance Defense, Premises Liability, Product Liability, General Liability, Homeowners, Automobile Liability, Liquor Liability, Medical Malpractice, Legal Malpractice, Toxic Torts, Commercial Law, Bad Faith, Coverage Issues, Opinions, Litigation, Lead Paint, Environmental Law, Intellectual Property, Employment Law

SEE COMPLETE LISTING UNDER SPRINGFIELD, MASSACHUSETTS (50 MILES)

Hassett & Donnelly, P.C.

446 Main Street, 12th Floor
Worcester, Massachusetts 01608
  Telephone: 508-791-6287
  Fax: 508-791-2652

Insurance Defense, Defense Litigation, Construction Litigation, Coverage Analysis, Declaratory Judgments, Bad Faith, Professional Liability, Product Liability, Premises Liability, Municipal Liability, Workers' Compensation, Civil Litigation, Commercial General Liability, Employment Law, Motor Vehicle, Negligence, Toxic Torts, Wrongful Death, Breach of Contract, Property Defense, Environmental Litigation, Business Litigation, Fire, Homeowners, First and Third Party Defense, Property and Casualty, Self-Insured Defense, Uninsured and Underinsured Motorist, Employment Law (Management Side), Trial and Appellate Practice

SEE COMPLETE LISTING UNDER WORCESTER, MASSACHUSETTS (65 MILES)

PLYMOUTH † 7,494 Plymouth Co.

Refer To

Melick & Porter

1 Liberty Square
Boston, Massachusetts 02109
  Telephone: 617-523-6200
  Fax: 617-523-8130

Accountants, Administrative Law, Advertising Injury, Agent/Broker Liability, Appellate Practice, Architects and Engineers, Asbestos, Automobile, Bad Faith, Commercial Litigation, Complex Litigation, Construction Litigation, Dental Malpractice, Directors and Officers Liability, Employment Practices, Environmental Law, Fire, General Liability, Health Care, Hospitality, Insurance Coverage, Insurance Defense, Lead Paint, Legal Malpractice, Life Insurance, Liquor Liability, Medical Devices, Pharmaceutical, Pollution, Premises Liability, Product Liability, Professional Liability, Property and Casualty, Public Entities, Real Estate Agents & Brokers Liability, Restaurant Liability, State and Federal Courts, Toxic Torts, Transportation, Trucking, Workers' Compensation

SEE COMPLETE LISTING UNDER BOSTON, MASSACHUSETTS (42 MILES)

Refer To

Mitchell & DeSimone

101 Arch Street
Boston, Massachusetts 02110
  Telephone: 617-737-8300
  Fax: 617-737-8390

Insurance Defense, Premises Liability, Contractors Liability, Employment Law, Discrimination, Environmental Law, Automobile, Tort, General Liability, Liquor Liability, Product Liability, Coverage Issues, Subrogation, Directors and Officers Liability, Professional Liability

SEE COMPLETE LISTING UNDER BOSTON, MASSACHUSETTS (40 MILES)

Refer To

Zizik, Powers, O'Connell, Spaulding & Lamontagne, P.C.

540 Main Street
Hyannis, Massachusetts 02601
  Telephone: 781-320-5400
  Fax: 781-320-5444

Insurance Defense, Automobile, Construction Law, Coverage Issues, Disability, Environmental Law, General Liability, Hazardous Waste, Life Insurance, Liquor Liability, Personal Injury, Premises Liability, Product Liability, Professional Liability, Toxic Torts

SEE COMPLETE LISTING UNDER HYANNIS, MASSACHUSETTS (33 MILES)

MASSACHUSETTS

SALEM † 41,340 Essex Co.

Refer To

Clark, Hunt, Ahern & Embry
150 Cambridgepark Drive, Suite 9
Cambridge, Massachusetts 02140-2328
  Telephone: 617-494-1920
  Fax: 617-494-1921

Insurance Defense, Coverage Issues, General Liability, Personal Injury, Property Damage, Slip and Fall, Automobile, Subrogation

SEE COMPLETE LISTING UNDER CAMBRIDGE, MASSACHUSETTS (24 MILES)

Refer To

Zizik, Powers, O'Connell, Spaulding & Lamontagne, P.C.
690 Canton Street, Suite 306
Westwood, Massachusetts 02090
  Telephone: 781-320-5400
  Fax: 781-320-5444

Insurance Defense, Automobile, Construction Law, Coverage Issues, Disability, Environmental Law, General Liability, Hazardous Waste, Life Insurance, Liquor Liability, Personal Injury, Premises Liability, Product Liability, Toxic Torts, Alternative Dispute Resolution, Antitrust, Employment Law, Commercial Litigation, Fire Loss, Trucking Litigation

SEE COMPLETE LISTING UNDER WESTWOOD, MASSACHUSETTS (42 MILES)

SPRINGFIELD † 153,060 Hampden Co.

Doherty, Wallace, Pillsbury & Murphy, P.C.

One Monarch Place, Suite 1900
Springfield, Massachusetts 01144-1900
  Telephone: 413-733-3111
  Fax: 413-734-3910
  Toll Free: 888-680-3111
  E-Mail: dwpm@dwpm.com
  www.dwpm.com

(Northampton, MA Office: 60 State Street, 01060)
  (Tel: 413-584-1500)
  (Fax: 413-584-1670)

Established: 1967

Insurance Defense, Premises Liability, Product Liability, General Liability, Homeowners, Automobile Liability, Liquor Liability, Medical Malpractice, Legal Malpractice, Toxic Torts, Commercial Law, Bad Faith, Coverage Issues, Opinions, Litigation, Lead Paint, Environmental Law, Intellectual Property, Employment Law

Firm Profile: Doherty, Wallace, Pillsbury and Murphy is a full-service law firm located in Springfield, Massachusetts. Respected state-wide, it is one of the largest law firms in Western Massachusetts, offering capabilities in virtually every area of the law, including a broad litigation practice, extensive corporate, real estate, and intellectual property practices, and sophisticated estate and probate practices. The firm is large enough to meet the diverse legal needs of a wide variety of clients yet small enough to allow prompt referrals to the most appropriate attorney.

Insurance Clients

AIG Technical Services, Inc.
Andover Companies
The Cincinnati Insurance Companies
Darwin National Assurance Company
Gallagher Bassett Services, Inc.
General Casualty Insurance Company
Hertz Claim Management
Metropolitan Property and Casualty Insurance Company
New London County Mutual Insurance Company
Alterra USA
Arbella Mutual Insurance Company
The Concord Group Insurance Companies
Electric Insurance Company
GEICO
Greater New York Mutual Insurance Company
Liberty Mutual Insurance Company
MiddleOak
Montgomery Insurance
Penn Millers Insurance Company
Pilgrim Insurance Company
Progressive Insurance Company
Risk Enterprise Management, Ltd.
Safeco/American States Insurance Company
Specialty Risk Services, Inc. (SRS)
Union Mutual Fire Insurance Company
Utica Mutual Insurance Company
XL Environmental, Inc.
York Risk Services Group, Inc.
Quincy Mutual Fire Insurance Company
Safety Insurance Company
Sedgwick Claims Management Services, Inc.
United States Liability Insurance Company
Vermont Mutual Insurance Company

Non-Insurance Clients

National Food Processors Association
Pioneer Valley Transit Authority

Firm Members

Dudley B. Wallace — (1900-1987)

Frederick S. Pillsbury — (1919-1996)

Robert E. Murphy — (1919-2003)

Samuel A. Marsella — (1931-2004)

Paul S. Doherty — 1934 — Bowdoin College, B.A., 1956; Harvard University, LL.B., 1960; Boston University, LL.M., 1967 — Admitted to Bar, 1960, Massachusetts — Member American, Massachusetts and Hampden County Bar Associations — E-mail: pdoherty@dwpm.com

Philip J. Callan, Jr. — 1939 — Boston College, A.B., 1961; LL.B., 1964 — Admitted to Bar, 1964, Massachusetts; 1965, U.S. Court of Military Appeals — Member Massachusetts and Hampden County (President, 1995-1996) Bar Associations; American College of Trial Lawyers (State Chair, 2001-2002); Fellow, American College of Trial Lawyers; International Association of Defense Counsel; Massachusetts Defense Lawyers Association — E-mail: pcallan@dwpm.com

Gary P. Shannon — 1948 — Bates College, B.A., 1970; Washington and Lee University, J.D., 1973 — Admitted to Bar, 1973, Massachusetts — Member Massachusetts and Hampden County Bar Associations — E-mail: gshannon@dwpm.com

Robert L. Leonard — 1947 — College of the Holy Cross, A.B., 1969; Boston College, J.D., 1972 — Admitted to Bar, 1972, Massachusetts; 1972, U.S. District Court, District of Massachusetts; 1972, U.S. Court of Appeals, First Circuit; 1972, U.S. Supreme Court; 1972, U.S. Court of Military Appeals — Member Massachusetts and Hampden County Bar Associations — E-mail: rleonard@dwpm.com

A. Craig Brown — 1952 — Dartmouth College, A.B., 1974; Georgetown University Law Center, J.D., 1977 — Admitted to Bar, 1977, Massachusetts — Member American, Massachusetts and Hampden County Bar Associations — E-mail: cbrown@dwpm.com

L. Jeffrey Meehan — 1950 — Bowdoin College, A.B., 1972; Suffolk University, J.D., 1975 — Admitted to Bar, 1975, Massachusetts; 1975, U.S. District Court, District of Massachusetts; 1979, U.S. Supreme Court — Member Massachusetts and Hampden County Bar Associations; Fellow, Massachusetts Bar Foundation; Massachusetts Academy of Trial Attorneys; Fellow, American College of Trial Lawyers — E-mail: lmeehan@dwpm.com

David J. Martel — 1943 — College of the Holy Cross, A.B., 1965; The Catholic University of America, J.D., 1972 — Admitted to Bar, 1973, New York; 1974, Massachusetts; 1974, U.S. District Court, District of Massachusetts — Member American, Massachusetts and Hampden County Bar Associations — E-mail: dmartel@dwpm.com

John J. McCarthy — 1948 — Mount St. Mary's College, B.S., 1970; Western New England College School of Law, J.D., 1980 — Admitted to Bar, 1980, Massachusetts; 1981, U.S. District Court, District of Massachusetts — Member Massachusetts, Hampden County and Chicopee Bar Associations; Association of Trial Lawyers of America; Massachusetts Academy of Trial Attorneys — E-mail: jmccarthy@dwpm.com

Barry M. Ryan — 1958 — Dartmouth College, A.B., 1980; Georgetown University, J.D., 1985 — Admitted to Bar, 1985, Massachusetts; 1986, U.S. District Court, District of Massachusetts — Member Massachusetts and Hampden County Bar Associations — E-mail: bryan@dwpm.com

Deborah A. Basile — 1960 — Albertus Magnus College, B.A., 1982; California Western School of Law, J.D., 1986 — Admitted to Bar, 1986, Massachusetts; 1986, U.S. District Court, District of Massachusetts — Member American, Massachusetts and Hampden County Bar Associations — E-mail: dbasile@dwpm.com

Paul M. Maleck — 1957 — St. Lawrence University, B.A. (cum laude), 1980; Western New England College, J.D., 1984 — Admitted to Bar, 1985, Massachusetts; 1985, U.S. District Court, District of Massachusetts — Member

WAKEFIELD   MASSACHUSETTS

Doherty, Wallace, Pillsbury & Murphy, P.C., Springfield, MA (Continued)

American, Massachusetts and Hampden County Bar Associations — E-mail: pmaleck@dwpm.com

W. Garth Janes — 1958 — Tufts University, B.A. (magna cum laude), 1980; Harvard University, M.P.A., 1985; Cornell University, J.D. (cum laude), 1983 — Admitted to Bar, 1983, Massachusetts; 1985, District of Columbia; 1986, U.S. District Court for the District of Columbia; U.S. Court of Appeals for the Federal Circuit; U.S. Court of International Trade; 1987, U.S. District Court, District of Massachusetts; 1988, U.S. Claims Court — Member American Bar Association (Vice Chairman, Ad Hoc Committee on Export Assistance, Section of International Law and Practice); Hampden County Bar Association; The Bar Association of the District of Columbia — E-mail: wjanes@dwpm.com

Gregory A. Schmidt — 1948 — University of Massachusetts Amherst, B.A., 1971; Western New England College, J.D. (with honors), 1977 — Admitted to Bar, 1977, Massachusetts; 1977, U.S. District Court, District of Massachusetts; 1979, U.S. Court of Appeals, First Circuit — Member American, Massachusetts and Hampden County Bar Associations — E-mail: gschmidt@dwpm.com

Michael K. Callan — 1966 — Boston College, B.A. (magna cum laude), 1988; J.D., 1991 — Admitted to Bar, 1991, Massachusetts; 1993, Connecticut; 1993, U.S. District Court, District of Massachusetts — Member Massachusetts and Hampden County Bar Associations — E-mail: mcallan@dwpm.com

Michael D. Sweet — 1970 — Brown University, B.A., 1992; Boston University, J.D., 1995 — Admitted to Bar, 1996, Connecticut; 1997, Massachusetts; 1999, New York — Member American, Massachusetts and Hampden County Bar Associations — E-mail: msweet@dwpm.com

Michele A. Rooke — 1963 — Springfield College, M.Ed., 1992; Western New England College, J.D., 1999 — Admitted to Bar, 1999, Massachusetts — Member Massachusetts and Hampden County Bar Associations — E-mail: mrooke@dwpm.com

Thomas M. Growhoski — 1939 — University of Massachusetts, B.A., 1961; Suffolk University, LL.B., 1965 — Admitted to Bar, 1965, Massachusetts — Member Massachusetts and Hampshire County Bar Associations; Massachusetts Bar Foundation — Practice Areas: Real Estate — E-mail: tgrowhoski@dwpm.com

Brenda S. Doherty — 1962 — Brown University, B.A. (magna cum laude), 1984; Harvard University, J.D., 1987 — Admitted to Bar, 1987, Massachusetts — Member Massachusetts and Hampden County Bar Associations — E-mail: bdoherty@dwpm.com

Karen K. Chadwell — 1971 — Loyola University Chicago, B.S. (cum laude), 1993; The Ohio State University, Ph.D., 1996; Loyola University Chicago, J.D., 2001 — Admitted to Bar, 2001, Connecticut; 2002, Massachusetts; 2001, U.S. Patent and Trademark Office — Member American, Connecticut and Massachusetts Bar Associations — E-mail: kchadwell@dwpm.com

Gregory M. Schmidt — 1979 — Boston College, B.A., 2002; Suffolk University Law School, J.D., 2005 — Admitted to Bar, 2005, Massachusetts — Member Massachusetts and Hampden County Bar Associations — E-mail: gmschmidt@dwpm.com

Rebecca L. Bouchard — 1964 — Dartmouth College, B.A., 1987; Harvard University, M.Ed., 1992; Western New England College School of Law, J.D. (cum laude), 2003 — Admitted to Bar, 2003, Massachusetts; Connecticut — Member Massachusetts and Hampden County Bar Associations — E-mail: rbouchard@dwpm.com

Michael S. Schneider — 1975 — Dickinson College, B.A., 1997; Arizona State University, M.A., 2002; Suffolk University Law School, J.D., 2007 — Admitted to Bar, 2007, Massachusetts; 2008, Connecticut — E-mail: mschneider@dwpm.com

Jesse Belcher-Timme — 1979 — New York University, B.A., 2001; New England School of Law, J.D., 2004 — Admitted to Bar, 2004, Massachusetts — E-mail: jtimme@dwpm.com

Jose A. Aguiar — 1975 — American International College, B.A., 1998; Western New England College School of Law, J.D., 2001 — Admitted to Bar, 2002, Massachusetts; Connecticut — Member Massachusetts, Connecticut and Hampden County Bar Associations — Languages: Portuguese — E-mail: jaguiar@dwpm.com

Rebecca M. Thibault — 1979 — Trinity College, B.S., 2001; Washington University in St. Louis School of Law, J.D., 2011 — Admitted to Bar, 2011, Massachusetts — E-mail: rthibault@dwpm.com

Angelina P. Stafford — 1986 — University of Michigan, B.A. (with distinction), 2008; Western New England College School of Law, J.D. (summa cum laude), 2012 — Admitted to Bar, 2012, Massachusetts; 2012, Connecticut — E-mail: apargoffstafford@dwpm.com

Doherty, Wallace, Pillsbury & Murphy, P.C., Springfield, MA (Continued)

Counsel

William M. Bennett — 1947 — Fordham University, B.A., 1969; Suffolk University Law School, J.D., 1974 — Admitted to Bar, 1974, Massachusetts — Member Massachusetts and Hampden County Bar Associations — Hampden County District Attorney (1991-2010)

Rosemary Crowley — 1964 — Dartmouth College, A.B., 1986; Boston College Law School, J.D., 1991 — Admitted to Bar, 1991, Massachusetts; 1997, South Carolina

The following firms also service this area.

Hassett & Donnelly, P.C.
446 Main Street, 12th Floor
Worcester, Massachusetts 01608
Telephone: 508-791-6287
Fax: 508-791-2652

Insurance Defense, Defense Litigation, Construction Litigation, Coverage Analysis, Declaratory Judgments, Bad Faith, Professional Liability, Product Liability, Premises Liability, Municipal Liability, Workers' Compensation, Civil Litigation, Commercial General Liability, Employment Law, Motor Vehicle, Negligence, Toxic Torts, Wrongful Death, Breach of Contract, Property Defense, Environmental Litigation, Business Litigation, Fire, Homeowners, First and Third Party Defense, Property and Casualty, Self-Insured Defense, Uninsured and Underinsured Motorist, Employment Law (Management Side), Trial and Appellate Practice

SEE COMPLETE LISTING UNDER WORCESTER, MASSACHUSETTS (50 MILES)

Wolf, Horowitz & Etlinger, L.L.C.
99 Pratt Street, Fourth Floor
Hartford, Connecticut 06103
Telephone: 860-724-6667
Fax: 860-293-1979

Insurance Defense, Litigation, Toxic Torts, Product Liability, Insurance Coverage, Malpractice, Surety, Fidelity, Construction Law, Subrogation

SEE COMPLETE LISTING UNDER HARTFORD, CONNECTICUT (26 MILES)

Zizik, Powers, O'Connell, Spaulding & Lamontagne, P.C.
690 Canton Street, Suite 306
Westwood, Massachusetts 02090
Telephone: 781-320-5400
Fax: 781-320-5444

Insurance Defense, Automobile, Construction Law, Coverage Issues, Disability, Environmental Law, General Liability, Hazardous Waste, Life Insurance, Liquor Liability, Personal Injury, Premises Liability, Product Liability, Toxic Torts, Alternative Dispute Resolution, Antitrust, Employment Law, Commercial Litigation, Fire Loss, Trucking Litigation

SEE COMPLETE LISTING UNDER WESTWOOD, MASSACHUSETTS (90 MILES)

WAKEFIELD   24,932 Middlesex Co.

Moriarty & Associates, P.C.
Edgewater Office Park
301 Edgewater Place, Suite 300
Wakefield, Massachusetts 01880
Telephone: 781-246-8000
Fax: 781-246-8080
www.moriartywc.com

(Worcester, MA Office*: 340 Main Street, Suite 307, 01608)
(Tel: 781-246-8000)
(Fax: 508-791-7548)

Established: 2002

Insurance Defense, Workers' Compensation

Firm Profile: Moriarty & Associates, P.C. concentrates exclusively in experienced legal representation and advice to national, regional, and Massachusetts insurers, self-insurers, third party administrators, and self-insurance groups.

MASSACHUSETTS   WATERTOWN

Moriarty & Associates, P.C., Wakefield, MA   (Continued)

Insurance Clients

Acadia Insurance Company
Chubb Group of Insurance Companies
AIG Insurance Company
Chubb Services Corporation
GUARD Insurance Group

Non-Insurance Clients

FutureComp

Partners

James L. O'Brien — (1949-2003)

Edward M. Moriarty, Jr. — 1953 — Northeastern University, B.A. (magna cum laude), 1976; Temple University, J.D., 1979 — Phi Kappa Phi; Pi Sigma Alpha — Executive Editor of The Jurist, 1978-1979 — Admitted to Bar, 1979, Massachusetts; U.S. District Court, District of Massachusetts — Member Massachusetts Bar Association; Massachusetts Academy of Trial Attorneys; Massachusetts Defense Lawyers Association; Defense Research Institute — Author: "Prosecuting the System: An Interview with F. Lee Bailey," 16 Criminal Law Bulletin 1, 1980

David G. Shay — 1956 — Suffolk University, B.S. (cum laude), 1979; Northeastern University, J.D., 1983; Suffolk University, J.D., 1989 — Admitted to Bar, 1989, Massachusetts; 1991, U.S. District Court, District of Massachusetts; 1993, U.S. Supreme Court — Member Massachusetts Bar Association — U.S. Army, 1974-1977

Director

Joseph R. Conte — 1962 — College of the Holy Cross, B.A., 1985; Southern New England School of Law, J.D., 1993 — Admitted to Bar, 1995, Massachusetts; U.S. District Court, District of Massachusetts — Member Massachusetts and Worcester County Bar Associations

Associates

Thomas F. Finn — 1963 — Suffolk University, B.S. (cum laude), 1985; Suffolk University Law School, J.D. (cum laude), 1988 — Admitted to Bar, 1989, Massachusetts; U.S. District Court, District of Massachusetts — Member Massachusetts Bar Association — U.S. Army, 1990-1996; U.S. Army Reserves, 1996-Present

Joseph M. Spinale — 1967 — Norwich University, B.A., 1989; Franklin Pierce Law Center, J.D., 1997 — Admitted to Bar, 1997, Massachusetts — Member American and Massachusetts Bar Associations

Of Counsel

Sheila S. Cunningham — 1958 — University of Scranton, B.S. (cum laude), 1980; Suffolk University Law School, J.D., 1983 — Admitted to Bar, 1983, Massachusetts

Gregory M. Iudice — 1975 — Fordham University, B.A., 1997; Suffolk University Law School, J.D. (cum laude), 2002 — Admitted to Bar, 2002, Massachusetts

Ellen Harrington Sullivan — 1942 — Emmanuel College, B.A., 1964; Massachusetts School of Law, J.D., 1996 — Admitted to Bar, 1996, Massachusetts; U.S. District Court, District of Massachusetts — Member American and Massachusetts Bar Associations

WATERTOWN   32,986 Middlesex Co.

Loughran & Corbett, Attorneys, Inc.

75 North Beacon Street
Watertown, Massachusetts 02472
   Telephone: 617-926-4466
   Fax: 617-923-1123
   E-Mail: bloughran@lawlc.com
   www.loughrancorbett.com

Casualty Insurance Law, Workers' Compensation

Insurance Clients

Gallagher Bassett Services, Inc.
National Grange Mutual Insurance Company

Loughran & Corbett, Attorneys, Inc., Watertown, MA (Continued)

Firm Members

Bernard T. Loughran — 1924 — Boston College, B.S.B.A., 1945; Harvard Law School, J.D., 1948 — Admitted to Bar, 1948, Massachusetts — Member Massachusetts and Middlesex County Bar Associations

Bernard T. Loughran, Jr. — 1960 — Providence College, B.A., 1982; Boston College Law School, J.D., 1985 — Admitted to Bar, 1985, Massachusetts — Member American and Massachusetts Bar Associations

Alicia M. DelSignore — Boston College, B.A., 1993; New England School of Law, J.D., 1996 — Admitted to Bar, 1996, Massachusetts — Member Massachusetts Bar Association

WELLESLEY   27,982 Norfolk Co.

Davids & Cohen, P.C.

40 Washington Street
Suite 20
Wellesley, Massachusetts 02481
   Telephone: 781-416-5055
   Fax: 781-416-4344
   E-Mail: rdavids@davids-cohen.com
   www.davids-cohen.com

Established: 1998

Civil Litigation, Commercial Litigation, Contract Disputes, Employment Discrimination, Employment Practices Liability, Insurance Coverage, Insurance Defense, Intellectual Property, Malpractice, Personal Injury, Premises Liability, Product Liability, Sexual Harassment, Wrongful Termination

Firm Profile: Davids & Cohen strives to handle every matter as if it were the highest priority and works hard to provide creative, efficient and excellent results. The firm focuses on the overriding objective in every matter, large or small, to bring about the best result in the most efficient manner.

Insurance Clients

AIG Claim Services, Inc.
CNA Claim Plus
Holyoke Mutual Insurance Company in Salem
Patrons Mutual Insurance Company of Connecticut
Sedgwick Claims Management Services, Inc.
Vermont Mutual Insurance Company
AmTrust North America
The Hartford Insurance Company
MiddleOak
Middlesex Mutual Assurance Company
RSKCo
Specialty Risk Services, Inc. (SRS)
State Auto Insurance Companies

Non-Insurance Clients

Automotive Profit Builders, Inc.
DocuServe, Inc.
Legal Sea Foods, LLC
Metropolitan Moving & Storage
R.K. Associates
Samuels & Associates
Softscape, Inc.
Staples, Inc.
BJ's Wholesale Club, Inc.
Impact Performance Group
Massachusetts Port Authority
New England Development, Inc.
Safety-Kleen Corporation
Simon Property Group, Inc.
S.R. Weiner & Associates, Inc.
Stop & Shop Supermarket Company, LLC

Partners

Ronald M. Davids — 1956 — Colby College, B.A. (with high honors), 1978; Boston University School of Law, J.D., 1981 — Recipient, American Jurisprudence Book Award for Torts — Admitted to Bar, 1981, Massachusetts; 1985, Florida; 1987, Maine; 1981, U.S. District Court, District of Massachusetts; 1982, U.S. Court of Appeals, First Circuit; 1985, U.S. District Court, Middle District of Florida; 1985, U.S. Court of Appeals, Eleventh Circuit — Member American Bar Association (Tort Practice Section); Maine State and Boston (Former Chairman, Business Litigation Committee) Bar Associations; The Florida Bar; Greater Boston Legal Services (Board of Directors; Former Member, Executive Committee); Claims & Litigation Management Alliance; American Board of Trial Advocates (ABOTA) — Martindale-Hubbell AV Rating; Massachusetts Super Lawyer (2005-present)

Davids & Cohen, P.C., Wellesley, MA (Continued)

Adam G. Cohen — 1966 — Clark University, B.A. (cum laude), 1988; Suffolk University Law School, J.D., 1991 — Admitted to Bar, 1991, Massachusetts; 2005, New Hampshire; 1993, U.S. District Court, District of Massachusetts; 1997, U.S. Court of Appeals, First Circuit; 2005, U.S. District Court, District of New Hampshire; 2011, U.S. Supreme Court — Member American and New Hampshire Bar Associations; Boston Association of Claims Executive; Claims & Litigation Management Alliance; Defense Research Institute

Associates

Lana Sullivan — Brown University, B.A. (with honors), 1996; University of Connecticut School of Law, J.D. (with honors), 1999 — Admitted to Bar, 1999, Connecticut; 2000, New York; 2001, Massachusetts; 2000, U.S. District Court, District of Connecticut; 2001, U.S. District Court, District of Massachusetts; 2002, U.S. Court of Appeals, First Circuit

Young B. Han — 1980 — Tufts University, B.A., 2002; Boston University School of Law, J.D., 2005 — Admitted to Bar, 2005, Massachusetts; 2013, Connecticut; 2006, U.S. District Court, District of Massachusetts; 2010, U.S. Court of Appeals, First Circuit; U.S. Bankruptcy Court, District of Massachusetts; 2014, U.S. District Court, District of Connecticut

Gino Spinelli — 1978 — Dartmouth College, B.A., 2000; Suffolk University Law School, J.D., 2006 — Admitted to Bar, 2006, Massachusetts; 2007, U.S. District Court, District of Massachusetts — Member Associated Builders & Contractors (Massachusetts Chapter); United States Green Building Council (Massachusetts Chapter); Dartmouth Lawyers Association

Michael J. St. Andre — Michigan State University, B.A., 1992; Suffolk University Law School, J.D. (cum laude), 1995 — Suffolk Law Review — Admitted to Bar, 1996, Massachusetts; 1996, Connecticut; 1998, U.S. District Court, District of Massachusetts; 2014, U.S. District Court, District of Connecticut — Member American (Litigation and Torts Section), Massachusetts, and Boston Bar Associations; Metrowest Chamber of Commerce; Christopher Columbus Club; Massachusetts Defense Lawyers Association — 2010 Super Lawyers Rising Star

Etie-Lee Schaub — Macalester College, B.A., 2008; Benjamin N. Cardozo School of Law, J.D. (cum laude), 2012 — Admitted to Bar, 2012, Massachusetts; Rhode Island; 2013, U.S. District Court, District of Massachusetts; U.S. District Court, District of Rhode Island — Member Rhode Island Bar Association

Lash & Associates, P.C.

27 Mica Lane, Suite 101
Wellesley, Massachusetts 02481-1741
  Telephone: 617-357-8200
  Fax: 617-357-8201
  E-Mail: slash@lashlaw.com

Established: 2003

Casualty, Construction Liability, Coverage Issues, Employment Law, Environmental Law, Fire, Insurance Defense, General Liability, Governmental Liability, Liquor Liability, Motor Vehicle, Premises Liability, Product Liability, Professional Liability, Property Liability, Subrogation

Insurance Clients

ABM Insurance Services	Acadia Insurance Company
American International Group	CNA Insurance Companies
Holyoke Mutual Insurance Company	ING/Halifax Insurance Company
Manufacturers and Merchants Mutual Insurance Company	Lexington Insurance Company
Middlesex Mutual Assurance Company	Metropolitan Property and Casualty Insurance Company
Patriot Insurance Company	Motorists Insurance Group
Phoenix Indemnity Insurance Company	OneBeacon Insurance Group
Sedgwick Claims Management Services, Inc.	Phenix Mutual Fire Insurance Company
West Bend Mutual Insurance Company	Royal Arcanum
	Shield Insurance Services, Inc.
	Tower Group Companies
	York Claims Service, Inc.

Non-Insurance Clients

Kohler Company	Marsh USA, Inc.

Lash & Associates, P.C., Wellesley, MA (Continued)

Principal

Stephen H. Lash — 1954 — University of Vermont, B.A., 1975; Suffolk University, J.D., 1978; Boston University, LL.M., 1981 — Admitted to Bar, 1978, Massachusetts; 1979, U.S. District Court, District of Massachusetts; U.S. Court of Appeals, First Circuit; 2011, U.S. Court of Appeals, Second Circuit — Member American and Massachusetts Bar Associations; Defense Research Institute — Author: "Arbitration of Medical Malpractice Disputes," Insurance Law Journal, 1979 — E-mail: slash@lashlaw.com

Associates

Richard F. McCarthy, Jr. — 1974 — The University of Chicago, B.A., 1998; Washington and Lee University, J.D. (cum laude), 2004 — Admitted to Bar, 2004, Massachusetts — Member American and Massachusetts Bar Associations — Case Note Writer for Race and Ethnic Ancestry Law Journal — E-mail: rmccarthy@lashlaw.com

Stephen T. Connolly — 1982 — Providence College, B.A. (cum laude), 2005; Villanova University School of Law, J.D., 2009 — Admitted to Bar, 2009, Massachusetts; Rhode Island; 2010, U.S. District Court, District of Massachusetts — Member Massachusetts Bar Association — E-mail: sconnolly@lashlaw.com

(This firm is also listed in the Subrogation section of this directory)

WESTWOOD   14,117 Norfolk Co.

Zizik, Powers, O'Connell, Spaulding & Lamontagne, P.C.

690 Canton Street, Suite 306
Westwood, Massachusetts 02090
  Telephone: 781-320-5400
  Fax: 781-320-5444
  E-Mail: dzizik@zizikpowers.com
  www.zizikpowers.com

(Hyannis, MA Office*: 540 Main Street, 02601)
  (Tel: 781-320-5400)
  (Fax: 781-320-5444)
(Providence, RI Office*: 40 Westminster Street, Suite 201, 02903)
  (Tel: 401-421-7110)
  (Fax: 401-421-7111)

Established: 1989

Insurance Defense, Automobile, Construction Law, Coverage Issues, Disability, Environmental Law, General Liability, Hazardous Waste, Life Insurance, Liquor Liability, Personal Injury, Premises Liability, Product Liability, Toxic Torts, Alternative Dispute Resolution, Antitrust, Employment Law, Commercial Litigation, Fire Loss, Trucking Litigation

Insurance Clients

Acadia Insurance Company	Admiral Insurance Company
Aetna Casualty and Surety Company	AIG Life Insurance Company
ASU Risk Management Services, Ltd.	Allied Adjustment Service
Boston Mutual Life Insurance Company	AXA Global Risks US Insurance Company
Exxon Risk Management Services, Inc.	CGU Insurance Company
The Harleysville Insurance	CNA Insurance Companies
Lumber Insurance Companies	Gallagher Bassett Services, Inc.
National Grange Mutual Insurance Company	Grinnell Mutual Group
Nautilus Insurance Company	Kemper Insurance Companies
Old Republic Insurance Company	Metropolitan Property and Casualty Insurance Company
Orion Specialty Group, Inc.	Naughton Insurance, Inc.
Sun Life Assurance Company of Canada	New York Casualty Insurance Company
United Services Automobile Association (USAA)	Penn-America Insurance Company
Worcester Insurance Company	Travelers Property Casualty Insurance Company
	Utica National Insurance Group
	Vermont Mutual Insurance Company

MASSACHUSETTS WORCESTER

Zizik, Powers, O'Connell, Spaulding & Lamontagne, P.C., Westwood, MA (Continued)

Non-Insurance Clients

Atlantic Richfield Company
Borg-Warner Protective Services Corporation
Colonial Gas Company
Cumberland Farms, Inc.
Drug, Cosmetic and Beauty Trades Service, Inc.
Fresenius Medical Care - North America
Shell Oil Company
Wells Fargo Alarm Services, Inc.
Black & Decker
Butterworth & O'Toole, Inc.
CNG Transmission Corporation
Conair Corporation
Dean Foods
Eastman Kodak Company
Equiva Services LLC/Motiva
Frito-Lay, Inc.
Liberty International Canada
Warren Petroleum Company, Limited Partnership

Shareholders

David W. Zizik — 1954 — Boston College, A.B. (magna cum laude), 1976; J.D. (magna cum laude) 1979 — Admitted to Bar, 1979, Massachusetts; 1980, Rhode Island; 1980, U.S. District Court, District of Massachusetts — Member Massachusetts Bar Association (Liaison, Standing Committee on ADR, Litigation Section, 1993-1994); Rhode Island Bar Association (Superior Court Bench/Bar and ADR Committees); Boston Bar Association (Civil Procedure Committee, 1985-); Panel of Arbitrators, American Arbitration Association; Minority Counsel to the Rhode Island Senate (1981) — Tel: 781-320-5401 — E-mail: dzizik@zizikpowers.com

Brian A. O'Connell — 1962 — Boston College, A.B. (magna cum laude), 1984; J.D. (cum laude), 1987 — Admitted to Bar, 1987, Massachusetts; 1994, Rhode Island; 1988, U.S. District Court, District of Massachusetts — Member Massachusetts (Committees: Litigation and Tort) and Rhode Island Bar Associations — Tel: 781-320-5402 — E-mail: boconnell@zizikpowers.com

Cathryn Spaulding — 1961 — Northeastern University, B.S. (cum laude), 1983; New England School of Law, J.D., 1993 — Admitted to Bar, 1993, Massachusetts; 1994, Rhode Island; 1994, U.S. District Court, District of Massachusetts; 1996, U.S. District Court, District of Rhode Island — Member Massachusetts and Rhode Island Bar Associations — Tel: 781-320-5429 — E-mail: cspaulding@zizikpowers.com

Donna M. Lamontagne — 1968 — College of the Holy Cross, A.B. (cum laude), 1990; Boston College, J.D. (cum laude), 1993 — Admitted to Bar, 1993, Massachusetts; 1994, Rhode Island; 1993, U.S. District Court, District of Massachusetts; 1995, U.S. District Court, District of Rhode Island — Member Massachusetts and Rhode Island Bar Associations — Tel: 401-421-3681 — E-mail: dlamontagne@zizikpowers.com

Members

Steven T. Hayes — 1971 — Boston College, B.A., 1993; Roger Williams University, J.D., 1998 — Admitted to Bar, 1998, Rhode Island; U.S. District Court, District of Rhode Island — Member Rhode Island Bar Association — Tel: 401-454-3043 — E-mail: shayes@zizikpowers.com

William J. Fidurko — 1969 — University of Massachusetts, B.A., 1991; Boston College Law School, J.D., 1994 — Admitted to Bar, 1994, Massachusetts; 1996, U.S. District Court, District of Massachusetts — Member Massachusetts Bar Association — Tel: 781-320-5461 — E-mail: wfidurko@zizikpowers.com

Partner

Kevin C. Cain — 1962 — Boston College, B.S., 1984; Boston College Law School, J.D. (cum laude), 1987 — Admitted to Bar, 1987, Massachusetts; 1988, Rhode Island; 1998, California; 1988, U.S. District Court, District of Massachusetts; U.S. Court of Appeals, First Circuit; 1989, U.S. District Court, District of Rhode Island; 1996, U.S. District Court, Northern District of New York; 2002, U.S. Patent and Trademark Office; 2005, U.S. Court of Appeal for the Federal Circuit — Member American, Massachusetts and Rhode Island Bar Associations; State Bar of California; Aircraft Owners and Pilot Association; American Intellectual Property Law Association; American Arbitration Association; Lawyer-Pilots Bar Association — Tel: 781-320-5441 — E-mail: kcain@zizikpowers.com

Associate

Louise Saunders — Mount Holyoke College, B.A. Political Science, 2003; University of Illinois at Chicago, M.A., 2006; New England School of Law, J.D., 2010 — Admitted to Bar, 2010, Massachusetts — Member Massachusetts and Boston Bar Associations — Tel: 781-320-5480

Retired

Richard E. Powers — 1953 — Boston College, A.B. (summa cum laude), 1975; J.D. (cum laude), 1978 — Admitted to Bar, 1978, Massachusetts; 1979,

Zizik, Powers, O'Connell, Spaulding & Lamontagne, P.C., Westwood, MA (Continued)

U.S. District Court, District of Massachusetts; 1979, U.S. Court of Appeals, First Circuit; 1985, U.S. Supreme Court — Member Federal Bar Association (Vice-President, Massachusetts Chapter, 1991-1993); American Bar Association (Sections: Tort and Insurance Practice, Litigation, Natural Resources, Energy and Environmental Law, Alternative Dispute Resolution); Massachusetts Bar Association (Committees: Litigation, and Alternative Dispute Resolution); Boston Bar Association (Committees: Tort, Insurance and Litigation); Massachusetts Defense Lawyers Association (Legislation Committee); American Arbitration Association (National Panel of Arbitrators); Defense Research Institute — Instructor, Boston University Law School, 1983-1986; Adjunct Professor, Boston College, 2000-

WORCESTER † 181,045 Worcester Co.

Hassett & Donnelly, P.C.

446 Main Street, 12th Floor
Worcester, Massachusetts 01608
 Telephone: 508-791-6287
 Fax: 508-791-2652
 E-Mail: dhassett@hassettanddonnelly.com
 www.hassettanddonnelly.com

(Hartford, CT Office*: 100 Pearl Street, 11th Floor, 06103)
 (Tel: 860-247-0644)
 (Fax: 860-247-0653)
(Boston, MA Office*: 125 Summer Street, 16th Floor, 02110)
 (Tel: 617-892-6080)
 (Fax: 617-345-6796)

Established: 1974

Insurance Defense, Defense Litigation, Construction Litigation, Coverage Analysis, Declaratory Judgments, Bad Faith, Professional Liability, Product Liability, Premises Liability, Municipal Liability, Workers' Compensation, Civil Litigation, Commercial General Liability, Employment Law, Motor Vehicle, Negligence, Toxic Torts, Wrongful Death, Breach of Contract, Property Defense, Environmental Litigation, Business Litigation, Fire, Homeowners, First and Third Party Defense, Property and Casualty, Self-Insured Defense, Uninsured and Underinsured Motorist, Employment Law (Management Side), Trial and Appellate Practice

Firm Profile: Founded in 1974, Hassett & Donnelly, P.C. (f/k/a Healy & Rocheleau, P.C.) is committed to providing high quality legal and litigation services that exceed each client's specific needs and expectations.

With offices located in Massachusetts and Connecticut, Hassett & Donnelly affords convenient access to federal and state courts and administrative agencies throughout both states. Our firm organization and structure promotes collaboration and sharing of ideas and experiences among our attorneys, resulting in more effective service for our clients.

Insurance Clients

Acadia Insurance Company
Adventist Risk Management, Inc.
American International Group, Inc.
Atlantic Casualty Insurance Company
Community Association Underwriters of America, Inc.
Cunningham Lindsey Claims Management, Inc.
Guilford Specialty Group, Inc.
Harleysville Worcester Insurance Company
IFG Companies
Lumber Insurance Companies
MIIA/Cabot Risk Strategies, LLC
National Grange Mutual Insurance Company
Norfolk & Dedham Group
The Patrons Group
ACE USA/ESIS, Inc.
Allied World Assurance Company
Amica Mutual Insurance Company
Bunker Hill Insurance Company
Chartis Insurance
The Concord Group Insurance Companies
Gallagher Bassett Services, Inc.
Grange Insurance Company
Hanover Insurance Company
Housing Authority Risk Retention Group, Inc.
Lexington Insurance Company
Massachusetts Interlocal Insurance Association
Nationwide Insurance
NLC Mutual Insurance Company
OneBeacon Insurance
Pilgrim Insurance Company

WORCESTER   MASSACHUSETTS

Hassett & Donnelly, P.C., Worcester, MA   (Continued)

Preferred Mutual Insurance Company
Riverport Insurance Company
Sedgwick CMS
Summit Risk Services, Inc.
Vermont Mutual Insurance Company
Progressive Insurance Company
Quincy Mutual Fire Insurance Company
State Auto Insurance Company
United States Liability Insurance Group

Non-Insurance Clients

Department of Housing and Community Development
Massachusetts Port Authority

Partners

David F. Hassett — Managing Partner — 1959 — College of the Holy Cross, B.A. (cum laude), 1981; Boston College Law School, J.D., 1984 — Admitted to Bar, 1985, Massachusetts; 1988, U.S. District Court, District of Massachusetts; 1992, U.S. Court of Appeals, First Circuit; 2011, U.S. Court of Appeals, Fifth Circuit — Member Massachusetts and Worcester County Bar Associations; Defense Research Institute; American Board of Trial Advocates; International Association of Defense Counsel; Massachusetts Defense Lawyers Association — Assistant District Attorney (1985-1987); Massachusetts Super Lawyers (2006-2013); Boston's Top Rated Lawyers (2012); Best Lawyers in America (2012) — E-mail: dhassett@hassettanddonnelly.com

Gerard T. Donnelly — 1953 — Worcester State College, 1976; Western New England College, J.D., 1988 — Admitted to Bar, 1989, Massachusetts; 1989, U.S. District Court, District of Massachusetts — Member Massachusetts and Worcester County Bar Associations; Defense Research Institute — E-mail: gdonnelly@hassettanddonnelly.com

Sarah B. Christie — 1969 — University of Massachusetts, B.B.A. (cum laude), 1991; Georgetown University, J.D., 1994 — Admitted to Bar, 1994, Massachusetts; 1998, Connecticut; 1996, U.S. District Court, District of Massachusetts — E-mail: schristie@hassettanddonnelly.com

Scott T. Ober — 1969 — Villanova University, B.S., 1991; Vermont Law School, J.D. (cum laude), 1994 — Admitted to Bar, 1994, Massachusetts; 1995, New Hampshire; 1998, Connecticut; 2014, Vermont; 1995, U.S. District Court, District of Massachusetts; 2001, U.S. District Court, District of New Hampshire; 2007, U.S. District Court, District of Connecticut; U.S. Court of Appeals, First Circuit — E-mail: sober@hassettanddonnelly.com

Paul S. Rainville — 1965 — Providence College, B.A. (cum laude), 1988; New England School of Law, J.D., 1992 — Admitted to Bar, 1992, Massachusetts; 1993, Connecticut; 1993, U.S. District Court, District of Massachusetts — E-mail: prainville@hassettanddonnelly.com

Associates

Matthew G. Lindberg — 1970 — Boston University, B.A. (magna cum laude), 1992; M.A., 1996; J.D., 1996 — Admitted to Bar, 1996, Massachusetts; 2001, U.S. District Court, District of Massachusetts — E-mail: mlindberg@hassettanddonnelly.com

John M. Dealy — 1975 — Boston College, B.S. (magna cum laude), 1997; J.D., 2000 — Admitted to Bar, 2000, Massachusetts; 2001, U.S. District Court, District of Massachusetts — E-mail: jdealy@hassettanddonnelly.com

John A. Girouard — 1969 — Plymouth State College, B.A. (with honors), 1991; Franklin Pierce Law Center, J.D., 1997 — Admitted to Bar, 1997, Massachusetts — E-mail: jgirouard@hassettanddonnelly.com

Courtney E. Mayo — 1978 — Regis College, B.A., 2000; Suffolk University, J.D., 2003 — Admitted to Bar, 2003, Massachusetts; 2004, U.S. District Court, District of Massachusetts — E-mail: cmayo@hassettanddonnelly.com

Peter G. Barrett — 1965 — University of Hartford, B.S.B.A., 1988; Texas Southern University, J.D., 1993 — Admitted to Bar, 1994, Massachusetts; 1995, Connecticut; 1995, U.S. District Court, District of Connecticut; 1996, U.S. Bankruptcy Court — E-mail: pbarrett@hassettanddonnelly.com

Kelly A. O'Brien — 1984 — University of New Haven, B.A. (magna cum laude), 2007; Quinnipiac College School of Law, J.D. (cum laude), 2010 — Admitted to Bar, 2011, Connecticut; New York — E-mail: kobrien@hassettanddonnelly.com

Tara E. Lynch — 1984 — Fairfield University, B.A. (with honors and high distinction), 2006; Syracuse University, J.D. (magna cum laude), 2009 — Admitted to Bar, 2010, New York; Massachusetts

Margarita Warren — 1982 — Brown University, B.A. (with honors), 2004; The University of Chicago, M.A.; Suffolk University Law School, J.D. (cum laude), 2011 — Admitted to Bar, 2011, Massachusetts — Languages: Spanish — E-mail: mwarren@hassettanddonnelly.com

Michael S. Melville — Clark University, B.A. Economics (Phi Beta Kappa), 2008; Boston College Law School, J.D. (magna cum laude, Order of the Coif), 2011 — Admitted to Bar, 2011, Massachusetts; 2011, Pennsylvania; 2014, U.S. District Court, District of Massachusetts

Timothy A. Smith — 1982 — University of Connecticut, B.A. Political Science (magna cum laude), 2004; Quinnipiac College School of Law, J.D. (magna cum laude), 2009 — Admitted to Bar, 2009, Connecticut; 2010, New York — E-mail: tsmith@hassettanddonnelly.com

John G. Miller — 1977 — Skidmore College, B.A., 1999; New York Law School, J.D., 2003 — Admitted to Bar, 2003, Connecticut; 2004, New York; Massachusetts; 2007, U.S. District Court, District of Connecticut; U.S. District Court, District of Massachusetts — E-mail: jmiller@hassettanddonnelly.com

Milton, Laurence & Dixon, L.L.P.

33 Waldo Street, Fourth Floor East
Worcester, Massachusetts 01608
Telephone: 508-791-6386
Fax: 508-799-4879
www.mldlaw.com

Established: 1894

Automobile Tort, Civil Litigation, Insurance Defense, Insurance Litigation, Medical Malpractice Defense, Premises Liability, Trial and Appellate Practice, Wrongful Death

Firm Profile: The Firm has served as trial counsel throughout Massachusetts for over 120 years.

Insurance Clients

Allstate Insurance Company
Encompass Insurance
Quincy Mutual Fire Insurance Company
Coverys
Liberty Mutual Insurance Company
Vermont Mutual Insurance Company

Senior Partner

Gerard R. Laurence — Georgetown University, J.D., 1964 — Admitted to Bar, 1964, Massachusetts — Member Fellow, American College of Trial Lawyers — E-mail: glaurence@mldlaw.com

Partners

Paul P. O'Connor — Loyola University, J.D., 1976 — Admitted to Bar, 1977, Massachusetts — Member Fellow, American College of Trial Lawyers — E-mail: poconnor@mldlaw.com

Jennifer DeFronzo — Northeastern University School of Law, J.D., 2002 — Admitted to Bar, 2002, Massachusetts — E-mail: jdefronzo@mldlaw.com

Associate

Jason E. Wadman — Suffolk University Law School, J.D., 2010 — Admitted to Bar, 2010, Massachusetts — E-mail: jwadman@mldlaw.com

Mitchell & DeSimone

255 Park Avenue, Suite 1000
Worcester, Massachusetts 01608
Telephone: 508-756-8310
www.mitchelldesimone.com

(Boston, MA Office*: 101 Arch Street, 02110)
 (Tel: 617-737-8300)
 (Fax: 617-737-8390)

Insurance Defense, Premises Liability, Contractors Liability, Employment Law, Discrimination, Environmental Law, Automobile, Tort, General Liability, Liquor Liability, Product Liability, Workers' Compensation, Coverage Issues, Subrogation

(See listing under Boston, MA for additional information)

(This firm is also listed in the Subrogation section of this directory)

MASSACHUSETTS   YARMOUTH PORT

Moriarty & Associates, P.C.

340 Main Street, Suite 307
Worcester, Massachusetts 01608
   Telephone: 781-246-8000
   Fax: 508-791-7548
   www.moriartywc.com

(Wakefield, MA Office*: Edgewater Office Park, 301 Edgewater Place,
  Suite 300, 01880)
   (Tel: 781-246-8000)
   (Fax: 781-246-8080)

Insurance Defense, Workers' Compensation

(See listing under Wakefield, MA for additional information)

The following firms also service this area.

Zizik, Powers, O'Connell, Spaulding & Lamontagne, P.C.
690 Canton Street, Suite 306
Westwood, Massachusetts 02090
   Telephone: 781-320-5400
   Fax: 781-320-5444

Insurance Defense, Automobile, Construction Law, Coverage Issues, Disability, Environmental Law, General Liability, Hazardous Waste, Life Insurance, Liquor Liability, Personal Injury, Premises Liability, Product Liability, Toxic Torts, Alternative Dispute Resolution, Antitrust, Employment Law, Commercial Litigation, Fire Loss, Trucking Litigation

SEE COMPLETE LISTING UNDER WESTWOOD, MASSACHUSETTS (45 MILES)

YARMOUTH PORT 5,320 Barnstable Co.

Rubin, Rudman, Chamberlain and Marsh
Cape Cod Office of Rubin and Rudman LLP

99 Willow Street
Yarmouth Port, Massachusetts 02675
   Telephone: 508-362-6262
   Fax: 508-362-6060

(Rubin and Rudman LLP (Main Office): 50 Rowes Wharf, Boston, MA,
  02110)
   (Tel: 617-330-7000)

Established: 1989

Insurance Defense, Automobile, General Liability, Product Liability, Medical Malpractice, Civil Litigation

Insurance Clients

American International Group, Inc.
Barnstable County Mutual
  Insurance Company
Motorists Mutual Insurance
  Company
Quincy Mutual Fire Insurance
  Company

Barnstable County Insurance
  Company
Lexington Insurance Company
Providence Washington Insurance
  Company

Non-Insurance Clients

Cape Cod Hospital

Cape Cod Regional Transit
  Authority

Partners

Robert C. Chamberlain — 1956 — Duke University, B.A. (cum laude), 1978; Boston College Law School, J.D. (cum laude), 1981 — Admitted to Bar, 1981, Massachusetts; 1982, U.S. District Court, District of Massachusetts; 1982, U.S. Court of Appeals, First Circuit — Member American, Massachusetts and Barnstable County Bar Associations; Fellow, Massachusetts Bar Foundation

Pamela B. Marsh — 1950 — Middlebury College, B.A. (cum laude), 1972;

Rubin, Rudman, Chamberlain and Marsh, Cape Cod Office of Rubin and Rudman LLP, Yarmouth Port, MA (Continued)

Boston College Law School, J.D., 1975 — Admitted to Bar, 1975, Massachusetts; 1976, U.S. District Court, District of Massachusetts — Member Massachusetts and Barnstable County Bar Associations; Fellow and Prior Member, Board of Trustees (2004-2008); Massachusetts Bar Foundation; Defense Research Institute

Associates

Thomas J. Perrino — 1964 — Fitchburg State College, B.S. (cum laude), 1986; Suffolk University Law School, J.D., 1989 — Admitted to Bar, 1989, Massachusetts; 1990, U.S. District Court, District of Massachusetts — Member American, Massachusetts and Barnstable County Bar Associations

Jennifer N. Lucas — 1970 — Boston College, B.A., 1992; Roger Williams University, J.D., 1999 — Admitted to Bar, 2000, Massachusetts; 2000, Supreme Judicial Court of Massachusetts — Member American, Massachusetts and Barnstable County Bar Associations

Of Counsel

Todd M. Machnik   Bruce P. Gilmore

MICHIGAN

CAPITAL: LANSING

COUNTIES AND COUNTY SEATS

County	County Seat
Alcona	Harrisville
Alger	Munising
Allegan	Allegan
Alpena	Alpena
Antrim	Bellaire
Arenac	Standish
Baraga	L'Anse
Barry	Hastings
Bay	Bay City
Benzie	Beulah
Berrien	St. Joseph
Branch	Coldwater
Calhoun	Marshall
Cass	Cassopolis
Charlevoix	Charlevoix
Cheboygan	Cheboygan
Chippewa	Sault Ste. Marie
Clare	Harrison
Clinton	St. Johns
Crawford	Grayling
Delta	Escanaba
Dickinson	Iron Mountain
Eaton	Charlotte
Emmet	Petoskey
Genesee	Flint
Gladwin	Gladwin
Gogebic	Bessemer
Grand Traverse	Traverse City
Gratiot	Ithaca
Hillsdale	Hillsdale
Houghton	Houghton
Huron	Bad Axe
Ingham	Mason
Ionia	Ionia
Iosco	Tawas City
Iron	Crystal Falls
Isabella	Mt. Pleasant
Jackson	Jackson
Kalamazoo	Kalamazoo
Kalkaska	Kalkaska
Kent	Grand Rapids
Keweenaw	Eagle River
Lake	Baldwin
Lapeer	Lapeer
Leelanau	Leland
Lenawee	Adrian
Livingston	Howell
Luce	Newberry
Mackinac	St. Ignace
Macomb	Mt. Clemens
Manistee	Manistee
Marquette	Marquette
Mason	Ludington
Mecosta	Big Rapids
Menominee	Menominee
Midland	Midland
Missaukee	Lake City
Monroe	Monroe
Montcalm	Stanton
Montmorency	Atlanta
Muskegon	Muskegon
Newaygo	White Cloud
Oakland	Pontiac
Oceana	Hart
Ogemaw	West Branch
Ontonagon	Ontonagon
Osceola	Reed City
Oscoda	Mio
Otsego	Gaylord
Ottawa	Grand Haven
Presque Isle	Rogers City
Roscommon	Roscommon
Saginaw	Saginaw
St. Clair	Port Huron
St. Joseph	Centreville
Sanilac	Sandusky
Schoolcraft	Manistique
Shiawassee	Corunna
Tuscola	Caro
Van Buren	Paw Paw
Washtenaw	Ann Arbor
Wayne	Detroit
Wexford	Cadillac

In the text that follows "†" indicates County Seats.

Our files contain additional verified data on the firms listed herein. This additional information is available on request.

A.M. BEST COMPANY

ADRIAN † 21,133 Lenawee Co.

Refer To

Conlin, McKenney & Philbrick, P.C.
350 South Main Street, Suite 400
Ann Arbor, Michigan 48104-2131
   Telephone: 734-761-9000
   Fax: 734-761-9001

Insurance Defense, Construction Litigation, Automobile, Commercial Law, General Liability, Product Liability, Casualty, Professional Malpractice, Litigation, Construction Liability, Premises Liability, Highway Design, Coverage Questions

SEE COMPLETE LISTING UNDER ANN ARBOR, MICHIGAN (40 MILES)

ALPENA † 10,483 Alpena Co.

White and Wojda

313 N. Second Avenue
Alpena, Michigan 49707
   Telephone: 989-354-4104
   Fax: 989-356-0747
   E-Mail: dwwhite@dwwhitelaw.com

Established: 1898

Casualty Defense, First and Third Party Defense, Insurance Defense, Legal Malpractice, Opinions, Personal Lines, Special Investigative Unit Claims, All Lines, Municipal Defense

Insurance Clients

Auto Club Insurance Association
Hartford Insurance Company
HCC Public Risk Claim Service, Inc.
Fremont Insurance Company
Hastings Mutual Insurance Company
Pioneer State Mutual Insurance Company

Firm Members

Daniel W. White — 1951 — Dartmouth College, A.B. (cum laude), 1974; Case Western Reserve University, J.D., 1977 — Admitted to Bar, 1977, Michigan; 1980, U.S. District Court, Eastern District of Michigan; 2006, U.S. District Court, Western District of Michigan; 2006, U.S. Court of Appeals, Sixth Circuit — Member State Bar of Michigan; Defense Research Institute; Michigan Defense Trial Counsel — Practice Areas: Civil Litigation; Insurance Defense — E-mail: dwwhite@dwwhitelaw.com

Matthew J. Wojda — 1983 — Adrian College, B.A. (magna cum laude), 2005; Ave Maria School of Law, J.D., 2008 — Admitted to Bar, 2009, Michigan — Member State Bar of Michigan — Practice Areas: Insurance Defense; Civil Litigation — E-mail: mjwojda@dwwhitelaw.com

---

The following firms also service this area.

Bensinger, Cotant & Menkes, P.C.
308 West Main Street
Gaylord, Michigan 49735
   Telephone: 989-732-7536
   Fax: 989-732-4922

General Defense, Automobile Liability, Fire Loss, Professional Liability, Product Liability, Workers' Compensation, Subrogation, Medical Malpractice, Liquor Liability

SEE COMPLETE LISTING UNDER GAYLORD, MICHIGAN (72 MILES)

ANN ARBOR † 113,934 Washtenaw Co.

Conlin, McKenney & Philbrick, P.C.

350 South Main Street, Suite 400
Ann Arbor, Michigan 48104-2131
   Telephone: 734-761-9000
   Fax: 734-761-9001
   www.cmplaw.com

Conlin, McKenney & Philbrick, P.C., Ann Arbor, MI (Continued)

Established: 1937

Insurance Defense, Construction Litigation, Automobile, Commercial Law, General Liability, Product Liability, Casualty, Professional Malpractice, Litigation, Construction Liability, Premises Liability, Highway Design, Coverage Questions

Insurance Clients

Acceptance Risk Managers, Inc.
Auto-Owners Insurance Company
Citizens Insurance Company of America
Michigan County Road Association Self-Insurance Pool
PMA Insurance Group
State Farm Mutual Automobile Insurance Company
Auto Club Group Insurance Company
Farm Bureau Insurance Company
Hastings Mutual Insurance Company
Michigan Millers Mutual Insurance Company
Titan Insurance Company
Wolverine Mutual Insurance Company

Non-Insurance Clients

Crawford & Company
Washtenaw County Road Commission
Domino's Pizza, Inc.

Firm Members

Allen J. Philbrick — 1944 — Michigan State University, B.A., 1966; University of Michigan, J.D., 1969 — Admitted to Bar, 1970, Illinois; 1971, Michigan; 1971, U.S. District Court, Eastern District of Michigan; 1998, U.S. Court of Appeals, Sixth Circuit — Member American and Washtenaw County Bar Associations; State Bar of Michigan (Negligence Section); Defense Research Institute; Michigan Defense Trial Counsel — Arbitrator, American Arbitration Association — E-mail: philbrick@cmplaw.com

Neil J. Juliar — 1946 — Dartmouth College, B.A., 1968; University of Michigan, J.D., 1972 — Admitted to Bar, 1973, Michigan; 1973, U.S. District Court, Eastern District of Michigan; 1983, U.S. Court of Appeals, Sixth Circuit — Member American and Washtenaw County Bar Associations; State Bar of Michigan — E-mail: juliar@cmplaw.com

Bradley J. McLampy — 1956 — Indiana University, B.A., 1979; J.D., 1982 — Phi Beta Kappa — Admitted to Bar, 1982, Michigan; 1982, U.S. District Court, Western District of Michigan; 1987, U.S. District Court, Eastern District of Michigan — Member American and Grand Rapids Bar Associations; State Bar of Michigan — E-mail: melampy@cmplaw.com

Joseph W. Phillips — 1948 — Oakland University, B.A., 1970; Wayne State University, J.D., 1982 — Admitted to Bar, 1982, Michigan; 1982, U.S. District Court, Eastern District of Michigan — Member American and Washtenaw County Bar Associations; State Bar of Michigan — E-mail: phillips@cmplaw.com

William M. Sweet — 1950 — Michigan State University, B.S., 1972; Detroit College of Law, J.D., 1978 — Admitted to Bar, 1978, Michigan; 1978, U.S. District Court, Eastern District of Michigan — Member American, Ingham County and Washtenaw County Bar Associations; State Bar of Michigan; Michigan Defense Trial Counsel; Defense Research Institute — E-mail: sweet@cmplaw.com

Richard P. Peterson, II — 1964 — University of Michigan, B.A., 1987; The University of Toledo, J.D., 1993 — Admitted to Bar, 1993, Michigan; 1999, U.S. District Court, Eastern District of Michigan — Member American and Washtenaw County Bar Associations; State Bar of Michigan — E-mail: peterson@cmplaw.com

W. Daniel Troyka — 1968 — Princeton University, B.A. (cum laude), 1990; Boston University Law School, J.D. (magna cum laude), 1994 — Admitted to Bar, 1995, Massachusetts; 2003, Michigan; 1997, U.S. District Court, District of Massachusetts; 2003, U.S. District Court, Eastern District of Michigan — Member American and Massachusetts Bar Associations; State Bar of Michigan — E-mail: troyka@cmplaw.com

Andrew D. Sugerman — 1963 — James Madison College at Michigan State University, B.A., 1985; American University, Washington College of Law, J.D., 1988 — Admitted to Bar, 1989, New York; 1991, District of Columbia; 1992, Michigan; U.S. District Court, Eastern District of New York; 2000, U.S. District Court, Eastern District of Michigan — Member American and Washtenaw County Bar Associations; State Bar of Michigan — E-mail: sugerman@cmplaw.com

Erik Duenas — 1968 — University of Michigan - Dearborn, B.A., 1996; University of Detroit Mercy School of Law, J.D., 1999 — Admitted to Bar, 1999,

BATTLE CREEK   MICHIGAN

Conlin, McKenney & Philbrick, P.C., Ann Arbor, MI (Continued)

Michigan; U.S. District Court, Eastern District of Michigan — U.S. Army Reserve, 1992-2000 — E-mail: duenas@cmplaw.com

Matthew C. Rettig — University of Michigan, B.A., 2001; Michigan State University College of Law, J.D. (summa cum laude), 2004 — Admitted to Bar, 2004, Michigan; 2005, U.S. District Court, Western District of Michigan; 2008, U.S. District Court, Eastern District of Michigan — Member American and Washtenaw County Bar Associations; State Bar of Michigan — E-mail: rettig@cmplaw.com

Dickinson Wright PLLC

350 South Main Street, Suite 300
Ann Arbor, Michigan 48104
   Telephone: 734-623-7075
   Fax: 734-623-1625
   E-Mail: Fortiz@dickinsonwright.com
   www.dickinson-wright.com

(Detroit, MI Office*: 500 Woodward Avenue, Suite 4000, 48226-3425)
   (Tel: 313-223-3500)
   (Fax: 313-223-3598)
   (www.dickinsonwright.com)
(Lansing, MI Office*: 215 South Washington Square, Suite 200, 48933-1816)
   (Tel: 517-371-1730)
   (Fax: 517-487-4700)
(Nashville, TN Office*: 424 Church Street, Suite 1401, 37219)
   (Tel: 615-244-6538)
   (Fax: 615-256-8386)
(Phoenix, AZ Office*: 1850 North Central Avenue, Suite 1400, 85004)
   (Tel: 602-285-5000)
   (Fax: 602-285-5100)
(Troy, MI Office*: 2600 West Big Beaver Road, Suite 300, 48084-3312)
   (Tel: 248-433-7200)
   (Fax: 248-433-7274)

Disability, Life Insurance, Medical Malpractice, Health Care, Coverage Issues, Personal Injury, Commercial Litigation, Employment Litigation, ERISA, Accountant Malpractice, Construction Litigation, Directors and Officers Liability

Firm Profile: Dickinson Wright has long been a preferred provider of sophisticated, cost-effective legal services to insurers in the life, health, disability, property, casualty, and alternative insurance (self-insured programs, risk pools, and captives) fields. Our insurance team also represents governmental entities, captive insurers and assigned-risk pools.

Firm Member

Michael G. Vartanian — University of Michigan Law School, J.D., 1973 — Admitted to Bar, 1973, Michigan; U.S. District Court, Southern District of Florida; U.S. District Court, Eastern and Western Districts of Michigan; U.S. Court of Appeals, Sixth Circuit — Practice Areas: Commercial Issues; Commercial Litigation; Life Insurance — Tel: 734-623-1690 — E-mail: mvartanian@dickinsonwright.com

(See listing under Detroit, MI for additional information)

Garan Lucow Miller, P.C.

101 North Main Street, Suite 460
Ann Arbor, Michigan 48104-5507
   Telephone: 734-930-5600
   Fax: 734-930-0043
   Toll Free: 800-878-5600
   24 Hour Toll Free: 888-332-0540
   www.garanlucow.com

Garan Lucow Miller, P.C., Ann Arbor, MI (Continued)

(Additional Offices: Detroit, MI*; Grand Blanc, MI*(See Flint listing); Grand Rapids, MI*; Lansing, MI*; Marquette, MI*; Port Huron, MI*; Traverse City, MI*; Troy, MI*; Merrillville, IN*)

Business Law, Employment Law, Insurance Defense, Municipal Liability, No-Fault, Workers' Compensation

(See listing under Detroit, MI for additional information)

The following firms also service this area.

Maddin, Hauser, Roth & Heller, P.C.
28400 Northwestern Highway, Second Floor
Southfield, Michigan 48034
   Telephone: 248-354-4030
   Fax: 248-359-6149
Mailing Address: P.O. Box 215, Southfield, MI 48037

Insurance Defense, Professional Liability (Non-Medical) Defense, Insurance Coverage, Legal Malpractice, Accountant Malpractice, Insurance Agents, Errors and Omissions, Directors and Officers Liability, Employment Practices Liability, Complex Litigation, Appellate Practice, Securities Litigation

SEE COMPLETE LISTING UNDER SOUTHFIELD, MICHIGAN (35 MILES)

Siemion Huckabay, P.C.
One Towne Square, Suite 1400
Southfield, Michigan 48076
   Telephone: 248-357-1400
   Fax: 248-357-3343
Mailing Address: P.O. Box 5068, Southfield, MI 48086-5068

Insurance Defense, Automobile, General Liability, Legal Malpractice, Medical Malpractice, Product Liability, Errors and Omissions, Trial Practice, Appellate Practice, Asbestos Litigation, Aviation, Workers' Compensation, Securities Litigation

SEE COMPLETE LISTING UNDER SOUTHFIELD, MICHIGAN (35 MILES)

Law Offices of Ward, Anderson, Porritt & Bryant, PLC
4190 Telegraph Road, Suite 2300
Bloomfield Hills, Michigan 48302
   Telephone: 248-593-1440
   Fax: 248-593-7920

Insurance Defense, Property and Casualty, Arson, Transportation, Liquor Liability, General Liability, Professional Malpractice, Errors and Omissions, Automobile, Product Liability, Discrimination, Coverage Issues, Truck Liability, Trucking Law

SEE COMPLETE LISTING UNDER BLOOMFIELD HILLS, MICHIGAN (50 MILES)

BATTLE CREEK   52,347 Calhoun Co.

Refer To

Lennon, Miller, O'Connor & Bartosiewicz, PLC
900 Comerica Building
151 South Rose Street
Kalamazoo, Michigan 49007
   Telephone: 269-381-8844
   Fax: 269-381-8822

Civil Trial Practice, State and Federal Courts, Insurance Defense, Reinsurance, Personal Injury, Real Property, Product Liability, Professional Liability, Environmental Law, Fidelity and Surety, Municipal Liability, Workers' Compensation, Coverage Opinions, Sports and Spectator Liability, Utility Liability, First and Third Party Auto Liability

SEE COMPLETE LISTING UNDER KALAMAZOO, MICHIGAN (24 MILES)

BESSEMER † 1,905 Gogebic Co.

Refer To
Bensinger, Cotant & Menkes, P.C.
122 West Bluff Street
Marquette, Michigan 49855
Telephone: 906-225-1000
Fax: 906-225-0818

General Defense, Automobile Liability, Fire Loss, Professional Liability, Product Liability, Workers' Compensation, Subrogation, Medical Malpractice, Liquor Liability

SEE COMPLETE LISTING UNDER MARQUETTE, MICHIGAN (150 MILES)

BINGHAM FARMS 1,111 Oakland Co.

Provizer & Phillips, P.C.
30200 Telegraph Road, Suite 200
Bingham Farms, Michigan 48025
Telephone: 248-642-0444
Fax: 248-642-6661
Toll Free: 800-288-9080
E-Mail: rphillips@p-ppc.com
www.provizer-phillips.com

Accountant Malpractice, Architects and Engineers, Arson, Automobile Liability, Bad Faith, Class Actions, Commercial Litigation, Complex Litigation, Construction Defect, Directors and Officers Liability, Discrimination, Drug, Employment Law, Environmental Law, Errors and Omissions, Excess and Surplus Lines, First Party Matters, Fraud, Litigation, Governmental Liability, Insurance Law, Insurance Agents, Intellectual Property, Legal Malpractice, Mass Tort, Medical Malpractice, Municipal Liability, Premises Liability, Product Liability, Professional Liability, Property and Casualty, Reinsurance, Sexual Harassment, Subrogation, Toxic Torts, Truck Liability

Firm Profile: Provizer & Phillips, P.C., is a full-service law firm dedicated to meeting the legal needs of its nationwide clientele. The experience, expertise and professionalism of each member of their team assure its clients the most effective representation available.

Insurance Clients

Hudson Insurance Company	Royal & Sun Alliance Insurance
Utica Mutual Insurance Company	XL Insurance

Members

Randall E. Phillips — Managing Partner — University of Michigan, B.A., 1972; University of Michigan Law School, J.D., 1975 — Admitted to Bar, 1975, Michigan; 1976, Florida; 1990, U.S. District Court, Eastern and Western Districts of Michigan; U.S. Court of Appeals, Sixth Circuit; 2004, U.S. Supreme Court — Member American (Insurance Section), Oakland County and Detroit Bar Associations; State Bar of Michigan; Michigan Defense Trial Lawyers Association; PLUS; American Arbitration Association; Defense Research Institute

Marilyn A. Madorsky — University of Michigan, B.A. (with high distinction), 1975; University of Michigan Law School, J.D., 1977 — Admitted to Bar, 1978, Michigan; Wisconsin — Member State Bar of Michigan; Oakland County Bar Association; Women Lawyers Association; Defense Research Institute

Associates

Mark S. Baumkel — Oakland University, B.A. (cum laude), 1973; Wayne State University, J.D. (cum laude), 1977 — Admitted to Bar, 1977, Michigan; 1985, U.S. District Court, Eastern District of Michigan; U.S. Court of Appeals, Sixth Circuit — Member State Bar of Michigan; Oakland County Bar Association — Arbitrator, American Arbitration Association; Mediator, Wayne, Oakland Michigan

Donald Parthum, Jr. — Central Michigan University, B.S.B.A., 1984; Detroit College of Law, J.D. (cum laude), 1993 — Admitted to Bar, 1993, Michigan — Member State Bar of Michigan (Sections: Natural Resource and Environmental Law, Young Lawyers, Probate and Estate Planning)

BLOOMFIELD HILLS 3,869 Oakland Co.

Anselmi & Mierzejewski, P.C.
1750 South Telegraph Road, Suite 306
Bloomfield Hills, Michigan 48302
Telephone: 248-338-2290
Fax: 248-338-4451
www.a-mlaw.com

Established: 1988

Insurance Defense, Automobile, Commercial Law, General Liability, Medical Malpractice, Personal Injury, Dram Shop, Product Liability, Premises Liability, Amusements

Firm Profile: As a premier insurance defense firm handling claims throughout the state of Michigan, Anselmi & Mierzejewski, P.C., has helped clients contain costs for more than two decades.

Insurance Clients

AAA Michigan	Agricultural Excess and Surplus Insurance Company
AIG Claim Services, Inc.	American Specialty Insurance Company
American International Group, Inc.	Citizens Insurance Company of America
AMEX Assurance Company	
Auto-Owners Insurance Company	Evanston Insurance Company
Conifer Insurance Company	Farmers Insurance Company
Crawford & Company	GAB Robins North America, Inc.
Farm Bureau Mutual Insurance Company	Michigan Insurance Company
Haas & Wilkerson Risk Management	Pioneer State Mutual Insurance Company
Prime Syndicate	T.H.E. Insurance Company
Royal Specialty Underwriting, Inc.	Titan Insurance Company
TIG Insurance Company	
Utah Home Fire Insurance Company	

Non-Insurance Clients

TNT Canada

Firm Members

Kurt A. Anselmi — 1954 — University of Michigan, B.A., 1976; Detroit College of Law, J.D., 1981 — Admitted to Bar, 1981, Michigan; 1984, Ohio; 1995, Colorado — Member State Bar of Michigan; Oakland County Bar Association

Joseph S. Mierzejewski — 1950 — Eastern Michigan University, B.S., 1974; Detroit College of Law, J.D., 1981 — Admitted to Bar, 1981, Michigan; 1995, Colorado — Member State Bar of Michigan; Oakland County Bar Association

John D. Ruth — 1967 — Michigan State University, B.A., 1991; Detroit College of Law, J.D., 1994 — Admitted to Bar, 1994, Michigan; 1995, Illinois; 1997, Colorado — Member American, Colorado, Illinois State, Oakland County and Chicago Bar Associations; State Bar of Michigan

Mark D. Sowle — 1978 — Michigan State University, B.A., 2001; Wayne State University, J.D., 2004 — Admitted to Bar, 2004, Michigan — Member State Bar of Michigan; Oakland County Bar Association

Associates

Julie A. Brainer — 1981 — Michigan State University, B.A., 2003; Michigan State University College of Law, J.D., 2006 — Admitted to Bar, 2006, Michigan; 2010, Florida — Member State Bar of Michigan; The Florida Bar; Oakland County Bar Association

Matthew L. Frizzo — 1986 — Ohio Wesleyan University, B.A., 2009; The University of Toledo College of Law, J.D., 2012 — Admitted to Bar, 2012, Michigan — Member State Bar of Michigan; Oakland County Bar Association

Ruth A. Goldner — 1985 — University of Michigan - Dearborn, B.A., 2007; Wayne State University Law School, J.D. (cum laude), 2011 — Admitted to Bar, 2011, Michigan — Member State Bar of Michigan; Oakland County Bar Association

Casey R. Krause — 1972 — Michigan State University, B.A., 1994; Wake Forest University, J.D., 1997 — Admitted to Bar, 1997, Michigan — Member State Bar of Michigan; Oakland County Bar Association

CLARE   MICHIGAN

Anselmi & Mierzejewski, P.C., Bloomfield Hills, MI
(Continued)

Christopher A. Lawicki — 1981 — Wayne State University, B.A., 2006; Thomas M. Cooley Law School, J.D., 2011 — Admitted to Bar, 2011, Michigan — Member State Bar of Michigan; Oakland County Bar Association

Marcy E. Mierzejewski — 1981 — Central Michigan University, B.S., 2003; University of Detroit Mercy School of Law, J.D., 2007 — Admitted to Bar, 2007, Michigan — Member State Bar of Michigan; Oakland County Bar Association

Lawrence J. Pochron, Jr. — 1975 — Oakland University, B.A., 1998; Wayne State University, J.D., 2001 — Admitted to Bar, 2001, Michigan — Member State Bar of Michigan; Oakland County Bar Association

Michael D. Phillips — 1983 — Michigan State University, B.A., 2006; Michigan State University College of Law, J.D., 2009 — Admitted to Bar, 2009, Michigan — Member State Bar of Michigan; Oakland County Bar Association

Stephen M. Smolenski — 1982 — University of Michigan, B.A., 2005; Indiana University Maurer School of Law-Bloomington, J.D., 2009 — Admitted to Bar, 2009, Michigan — Member State Bar of Michigan; Oakland County Bar Association

Kevin P. Wirth — 1984 — Michigan State University, B.S., 2006; Michigan State University College of Law, J.D., 2009 — Admitted to Bar, 2009, Michigan — Member State Bar of Michigan; Oakland County Bar Association

Law Offices of Ward, Anderson, Porritt & Bryant, PLC

4190 Telegraph Road, Suite 2300
Bloomfield Hills, Michigan 48302
   Telephone: 248-593-1440
   Fax: 248-593-7920
   E-Mail: firm@wardanderson.com
   www.wardanderson.com

(Toledo, OH Office*: 5757 Park Center Court, 43615)
   (Tel: 419-841-7211)
   (Fax: 419-843-9850)
   (E-Mail: ohio@wardanderson.com)

Established: 1994

Insurance Defense, Property and Casualty, Arson, Transportation, Liquor Liability, General Liability, Professional Malpractice, Errors and Omissions, Automobile, Product Liability, Discrimination, Coverage Issues, Truck Liability, Trucking Law

Insurance Clients

American Claim Systems	Auto-Owners Group
Carolina Casualty Insurance Company	Colony Insurance Group
Gallagher Bassett Services, Inc.	Empire Fire and Marine Insurance Company
Horace Mann Educators Corporation	IFG Companies
Western World Insurance Company	State Automobile Mutual Insurance Company

Non-Insurance Clients

Budget Rent-A-Car Corporation

Partners

David S. Anderson — 1953 — Michigan State University, B.A., 1975; Detroit College of Law, J.D., 1980 — Admitted to Bar, 1980, Michigan — Member Federal and Oakland County Bar Associations; State Bar of Michigan — Mediator, Oakland County Circuit Court — E-mail: danderson@wardanderson.com

Russell W. Porritt II — 1954 — Michigan State University, B.A. (with honors), 1976; Thomas M. Cooley Law School, J.D., 1981 — Admitted to Bar, 1982, Texas; 1986, Michigan; 1994, Ohio — Member State Bar of Michigan; Oakland County and Dallas Bar Associations — E-mail: rporritt@wardanderson.com

Michael D. Bryant — 1961 — Central Michigan University, 1983; University of Detroit School of Law, 1986 — Admitted to Bar, 1986, Michigan — Member State Bar of Michigan — E-mail: mbryant@wardanderson.com

Law Offices of Ward, Anderson, Porritt & Bryant, PLC, Bloomfield Hills, MI
(Continued)

Of Counsel

L. Graham Ward — 1946 — Western Michigan University, B.S., 1968; Wayne State University, J.D., 1972 — Admitted to Bar, 1972, Michigan — Member State Bar of Michigan (Negligence and Workers' Compensation Sections); Detroit and Oakland County Bar Associations — E-mail: lward@wardanderson.com — (Retired)

CADILLAC † 10,355 Wexford Co.

Refer To

Bensinger, Cotant & Menkes, P.C.
308 West Main Street
Gaylord, Michigan 49735
   Telephone: 989-732-7536
   Fax: 989-732-4922

General Defense, Automobile Liability, Fire Loss, Professional Liability, Product Liability, Workers' Compensation, Subrogation, Medical Malpractice, Liquor Liability

SEE COMPLETE LISTING UNDER GAYLORD, MICHIGAN (80 MILES)

CHARLEVOIX † 2,513 Charlevoix Co.

Refer To

Bensinger, Cotant & Menkes, P.C.
308 West Main Street
Gaylord, Michigan 49735
   Telephone: 989-732-7536
   Fax: 989-732-4922

General Defense, Automobile Liability, Fire Loss, Professional Liability, Product Liability, Workers' Compensation, Subrogation, Medical Malpractice, Liquor Liability

SEE COMPLETE LISTING UNDER GAYLORD, MICHIGAN (45 MILES)

CHEBOYGAN † 4,867 Cheboygan Co.

Refer To

Bensinger, Cotant & Menkes, P.C.
308 West Main Street
Gaylord, Michigan 49735
   Telephone: 989-732-7536
   Fax: 989-732-4922

General Defense, Automobile Liability, Fire Loss, Professional Liability, Product Liability, Workers' Compensation, Subrogation, Medical Malpractice, Liquor Liability

SEE COMPLETE LISTING UNDER GAYLORD, MICHIGAN (49 MILES)

Refer To

White and Wojda
313 N. Second Avenue
Alpena, Michigan 49707
   Telephone: 989-354-4104
   Fax: 989-356-0747

Casualty Defense, First and Third Party Defense, Insurance Defense, Legal Malpractice, Opinions, Personal Lines, Special Investigative Unit Claims, All Lines, Municipal Defense

SEE COMPLETE LISTING UNDER ALPENA, MICHIGAN (79 MILES)

CLARE 3,118 Clare Co.

Refer To

Bensinger, Cotant & Menkes, P.C.
308 West Main Street
Gaylord, Michigan 49735
   Telephone: 989-732-7536
   Fax: 989-732-4922

General Defense, Automobile Liability, Fire Loss, Professional Liability, Product Liability, Workers' Compensation, Subrogation, Medical Malpractice, Liquor Liability

SEE COMPLETE LISTING UNDER GAYLORD, MICHIGAN (87 MILES)

MICHIGAN

CRYSTAL FALLS † 1,469 Iron Co.

Refer To

Bensinger, Cotant & Menkes, P.C.
122 West Bluff Street
Marquette, Michigan 49855
   Telephone: 906-225-1000
   Fax: 906-225-0818

General Defense, Automobile Liability, Fire Loss, Professional Liability, Product Liability, Workers' Compensation, Subrogation, Medical Malpractice, Liquor Liability

SEE COMPLETE LISTING UNDER MARQUETTE, MICHIGAN (75 MILES)

DETROIT † 713,777 Wayne Co.

Alexander & Angelas, P.C.

30200 Telegraph Road, Suite 400
Bingham Farms, Michigan 48025-4502
   Telephone: 248-290-5600
   Fax: 248-290-5800
   Toll Free: 800-219-0007
   Mobile: 248-330-5584
   E-Mail: peter@alexanderANDangelas.com
   www.alexanderANDangelas.com

Established: 1992

Insurance Defense, Workers' Compensation, Bodily Injury, Truck Liability, No-Fault, Construction Defect

Insurance Clients

Accident Fund Insurance Company of America
Harco National Insurance Company
Great American Insurance Company
State Auto Insurance Company

Non-Insurance Clients

FedEx Freight
Sysco Corporation

Partners

John T. Alexander — 1961 — University of Michigan - Dearborn, A.B., 1983; University of Detroit, J.D., 1990 — Admitted to Bar, 1990, Michigan

Peter A. Angelas — 1963 — University of Michigan, B.A., 1985; University of Detroit, J.D., 1988 — Admitted to Bar, 1988, Michigan; 2010, Ohio

Blake, Kirchner, Symonds, Larson, Kennedy & Smith, P.C.

535 Griswold, Suite 1400
Detroit, Michigan 48226
   Telephone: 313-961-7321
   Fax: 313-961-5972
   E-Mail: bks@blakekirchner.com
   www.blakekirchner.com

Established: 1990

Insurance Defense, Product Liability, Premises Liability, Toxic Torts, Environmental Law, Asbestos Litigation, Medical Malpractice, Dental Malpractice, Workers' Compensation, Employer Liability, Automobile Liability, Commercial Litigation, Contracts, Contract Disputes, Corporate Law, Directors and Officers Liability, Mergers and Acquisitions, Alternative Dispute Resolution, Real Estate

Firm Profile: The firm offers professional legal services in several important areas of law. We are committed to providing all of our clients, whether individuals, businesses, insurers, or major corporations, with innovative and dynamic legal representation, without unreasonably high legal fees.

Blake, Kirchner, Symonds, Larson, Kennedy & Smith, P.C., Detroit, MI (Continued)

Insurance Clients

Bituminous Insurance Companies
Chartis
Continental Insurance Company
Electric Mutual Liability Insurance Company
FirstComp Insurance Company
The Hartford
ProAssurance Group
Risk Enterprise Management, Ltd.
CCMSI
Chubb Group of Insurance Companies
Fireman's Fund Insurance Company
Gallagher Bassett Services, Inc.
Liberty Mutual Insurance Company
Professional Indemnity Agency

Non-Insurance Clients

Allen Electric Supply Company
Cooper Industries, Inc.
Detroit Edison Company
General Electric Company
Republic Waste Services, Inc.
Sanit-Air
SmithGroup Companies, Inc.
Strobl Construction Company
Wayne Metropolitan Community Action Agency
Ascension Health
Dana Companies, LLC
Fabricon Products, Inc.
Progressive Associates, Inc.
St. John Hospital and Medical Center
Standard Electric Company
Waste Management, Inc.

Partners

F. Peter Blake — 1948 — John Carroll University, B.S., 1970; University of Detroit, M.B.A., 1973; Detroit College of Law, J.D., 1976 — Delta Theta Phi — Admitted to Bar, 1976, Michigan; 1976, U.S. District Court, Eastern and Western Districts of Michigan; 1984, U.S. Court of Appeals, Sixth Circuit — Member State Bar of Michigan; Macomb County and Detroit Bar Associations; International Association of Defense Counsel (Product Liability Committee); Michigan Defense Trial Counsel; Association of Defense Trial Counsel; American Board of Trial Advocates; Defense Research Institute

Arthur G. Kirchner III — 1947 — Wayne State University, B.A., 1970; Detroit College of Law, J.D., 1976 — Admitted to Bar, 1976, Michigan; 1976, U.S. District Court, Eastern District of Michigan — Member State Bar of Michigan (Workers' Compensation Section); Defense Research Institute

Kevin T. Kennedy — 1962 — Western Michigan University, B.B.A., 1984; Detroit College of Law, J.D. (cum laude), 1987 — Admitted to Bar, 1987, Michigan; U.S. District Court, Eastern District of Michigan — Member American and Oakland County Bar Associations; State Bar of Michigan (Negligence Section); Defense Research Institute

Richard P. Smith — 1959 — Wayne State University, B.A. (with distinction), 1981; Detroit College of Law, J.D. (cum laude), 1984 — Delta Theta Phi — Admitted to Bar, 1984, Michigan; U.S. District Court, Eastern District of Michigan — Member American, Macomb County and Detroit Bar Associations; State Bar of Michigan; National Employment Lawyers Association; Defense Research Institute — Special Assistant Attorney General for the State of Michigan

Jane Price Garrett — 1950 — Middle Tennessee State University, 1967-1968; Michigan State University, B.A. (with honors), 1971; University of Detroit, J.D., 1980 — Phi Beta Kappa — Admitted to Bar, 1980, Michigan; 1980, U.S. District Court, Eastern District of Michigan; 1982, U.S. Court of Appeals, Sixth Circuit — Member American and Detroit Bar Associations; State Bar of Michigan; Association of Defense Trial Counsel; Defense Research Institute

David B. Klein — 1964 — Michigan State University, B.A. (with distinction), 1987; University of Detroit, J.D., 1990 — Admitted to Bar, 1990, Michigan; 1990, U.S. District Court, Eastern District of Michigan — Member American and Detroit Bar Associations; State Bar of Michigan (Environmental Law Section); Defense Research Institute

John A. O'Brien — 1964 — University of Detroit, J.D., 1989 — Admitted to Bar, 1989, Michigan — Member Macomb County Bar Association; Michigan Self-Insurer's Association

Rebecca S. Austin — 1969 — University of Michigan - Dearborn, A.B. (with distinction), 1992; Wayne State University, J.D., 1995 — Admitted to Bar, 1995, Michigan; 1996, U.S. District Court, Eastern District of Michigan — Member State Bar of Michigan; Detroit Bar Association; Women Lawyers Association of Michigan

Associates

Andrew F. Smith — 1977 — University of Michigan, B.A., 1999; University of Detroit Mercy School of Law, J.D., 2002 — Admitted to Bar, 2002, Michigan; 2002, U.S. District Court, Eastern District of Michigan — Member American Bar Association; Association of Trial Lawyers of America

DETROIT   MICHIGAN

Blake, Kirchner, Symonds, Larson, Kennedy & Smith, P.C., Detroit, MI   (Continued)

Karen M. Melcher — 1976 — Michigan State University, B.A., 1998; University of Detroit Mercy School of Law, J.D., 2001 — Admitted to Bar, 2001, Michigan; 2001, U.S. District Court, Eastern District of Michigan — Member State Bar of Michigan

Michael L. Ossy — 1984 — Wayne State University Law School, J.D., 2009 — Admitted to Bar, 2009, Michigan

Dickinson Wright PLLC

500 Woodward Avenue, Suite 4000
Detroit, Michigan 48226-3425
　Telephone: 313-223-3500
　Fax: 313-223-3598
　E-Mail: Fortiz@dickinsonwright.com
　www.dickinsonwright.com

(Ann Arbor, MI Office*: 350 South Main Street, Suite 300, 48104)
　(Tel: 734-623-7075)
　(Fax: 734-623-1625)
　(www.dickinson-wright.com)
(Lansing, MI Office*: 215 South Washington Square, Suite 200, 48933-1816)
　(Tel: 517-371-1730)
　(Fax: 517-487-4700)
　(www.dickinson-wright.com)
(Nashville, TN Office*: 424 Church Street, Suite 1401, 37219)
　(Tel: 615-244-6538)
　(Fax: 615-256-8386)
　(www.dickinson-wright.com)
(Phoenix, AZ Office*: 1850 North Central Avenue, Suite 1400, 85004)
　(Tel: 602-285-5000)
　(Fax: 602-285-5100)
　(www.dickinson-wright.com)
(Troy, MI Office*: 2600 West Big Beaver Road, Suite 300, 48084-3312)
　(Tel: 248-433-7200)
　(Fax: 248-433-7274)
　(www.dickinson-wright.com)

Disability, Life Insurance, Medical Malpractice, Health Care, Coverage Issues, Personal Injury, Commercial Litigation, Employment Litigation, ERISA, Accountant Malpractice, Construction Litigation, Directors and Officers Liability

Firm Profile: Dickinson Wright has long been a preferred provider of sophisticated, cost-effective legal services to insurers in the life, health, disability, property, casualty, and alternative insurance (self-insured programs, risk pools, and captives) fields. Our insurance team also represents governmental entities, captive insurers and assigned-risk pools.

Insurance Clients

Amerisure Insurance Company
Blue Cross Blue Shield of South
　Carolina
Federated Rural Electric Insurance
　Exchange
Travelers
Unum Group

Blue Cross Blue Shield of
　Michigan
Church Mutual Insurance Company
The Hanover Insurance Group
John Hancock Property and
　Casualty Insurance Company
York Pro, Inc.

Firm Members

Francis R. Ortiz — **Practice Department Manager** — Harvard Law School, J.D., 1980 — Admitted to Bar, 1980, Michigan; U.S. District Court, Eastern and Western Districts of Michigan; U.S. Court of Appeals, Sixth Circuit; U.S. Supreme Court — Practice Areas: Life Insurance; ERISA; Commercial Litigation — Tel: 313-223-3690 — E-mail: fortiz@dickinsonwright.com

K. Scott Hamilton — Wayne State University Law School, J.D., 1989 — Admitted to Bar, 1990, Michigan; U.S. District Court, Northern District of Illinois; U.S. District Court, Eastern and Western Districts of Michigan; U.S. District Court, Western District of Pennsylvania; U.S. District Court, District of Utah; U.S. District Court, Western District of Oklahoma; U.S. Court of

Dickinson Wright PLLC, Detroit, MI   (Continued)

Appeals, Second, Sixth and Tenth Circuits — Practice Areas: ERISA; Disability; Commercial Litigation — Tel: 313-223-3041 — E-mail: khamilton@dickinsonwright.com

Feikens, Stevens, Kennedy & Galbraith, P.C.

660 Woodward Avenue, Suite 1975
Detroit, Michigan 48226-3577
　Telephone: 313-962-5909
　Fax: 313-962-3125
　E-Mail: nealkennedy@feikenspc.com
　www.feikenspc.com

Civil Litigation, Commercial Law, Common Carrier, Construction Law, Contracts, Employment Law, Errors and Omissions, Health Care, Insurance Law, Managed Care Liability, Medical Malpractice, Professional Liability, Product Liability, Transportation

Firm Profile: Since our beginning, we have made a commitment to keep Feikens, Stevens, Kennedy & Galbraith, P.C., as a medium-sized law firm, believing that, as such, we can maintain better control over the quality of the services that we provide as well as sustain close, effective communications with our clients. We are proud of our strong client relationships.

Professionalism, client service, and success on behalf of our clients are our most important goals—ones that we take very seriously and do our best to achieve every day.

Insurance Clients

American Physicians Assurance
　Corp.
Health Alliance Plan
Medilink Insurance Company, Ltd.
Travelers Insurance

Clarendon National Insurance
　Company
Henry Ford Health System
SelectCare HMO, Inc.

Non-Insurance Clients

Garden City Hospital
Greyhound Lines, Inc.
Western Litigation Specialists, Inc.

GLI Corporate Risk Solutions
Michigan Community Blood
　Centers

Partners

Jon Feikens — 1943 — Calvin College, B.A., 1964; University of Michigan Law School, J.D., 1967 — Order of the Coif — Assistant Editor, Michigan Law Review, 1966-1967 — Admitted to Bar, 1968, Michigan; U.S. District Court, Eastern District of Michigan; U.S. District Court, Northern District of Ohio; U.S. Court of Appeals, Sixth Circuit; U.S. Supreme Court — Member American, Oakland County and Detroit Bar Associations; State Bar of Michigan; Michigan State Bar Foundation; American Board of Trial Advocates (Advocate); Sixth Circuit Judicial Conferences (Life Member); Fellow, American College of Trial Lawyers — Languages: French

L. Neal Kennedy — 1947 — Wayne State University, B.A., 1970; Detroit College of Law, J.D., 1976 — Admitted to Bar, 1976, Michigan; 1999, Ohio; 1976, U.S. District Court, Eastern and Western Districts of Michigan; U.S. Court of Appeals, Sixth Circuit; 1999, U.S. District Court, Northern District of Ohio — Member American, Oakland County, Macomb County, Detroit and Toledo Bar Associations; State Bar of Michigan; Defense Research Institute

Lee A. Stevens — 1952 — Albion College, A.B. (cum laude), 1974; University of Detroit, J.D. (cum laude), 1978 — Admitted to Bar, 1978, Michigan; U.S. District Court, Eastern District of Michigan; U.S. Court of Appeals, Sixth Circuit — Member Federal and Detroit Bar Associations; State Bar of Michigan

Linda Meza Galbraith — 1953 — Michigan State University, B.A., 1974; Detroit College of Law, J.D., 1979 — Admitted to Bar, 1979, Michigan; U.S. District Court, Eastern District of Michigan; U.S. Court of Appeals, Sixth Circuit — Member Oakland County, Macomb County and Detroit Bar Associations; State Bar of Michigan (Past Chair, Negligence Section); Michigan State Bar Foundation; American Board of Trial Advocates (Associate); Michigan Defense Trial Counsel

MICHIGAN   DETROIT

Feikens, Stevens, Kennedy & Galbraith, P.C., Detroit, MI (Continued)

Associates

Jeffrey Feikens — 1964 — Calvin College, A.B. (with honors), 1986; University of Michigan, J.D. (cum laude), 1989 — Executive Editor, Michigan Journal of International Law, 1988-1989 — Admitted to Bar, 1989, Michigan; 1990, U.S. District Court, Eastern District of Michigan — Member State Bar of Michigan

Barbara A. Roulo — 1953 — University of Notre Dame, A.B., 1975; University of Detroit, J.D., 1978 — Admitted to Bar, 1978, Michigan; U.S. District Court, Eastern District of Michigan — Member State Bar of Michigan

Foster, Meadows & Ballard, P.C.

Shelby Congress Building
607 Shelby Street, Seventh Floor
Detroit, Michigan 48226
  Telephone: 313-961-3234
  Fax: 313-961-6184
  E-Mail: FosterMeadows@FosterMeadows.com
  www.fostermeadows.com

Established: 1940

Insurance Defense, Personal Injury, Premises Liability, Admiralty and Maritime Law, Jones Act, Railroad Law, Trucking Law, Transportation, Cargo, Aviation, Agent/Broker Liability, Errors and Omissions, Product Liability, Asbestos Litigation, Coverage Analysis, Subrogation, Commercial General Liability, Professional Liability, Trial and Appellate Practice

Firm Profile: Foster, Meadows & Ballard, P.C. has been in existence for more than 70 years and has specialized in litigation defense. Founded in 1940, the firm spent its early years primarily engaged in the representation of domestic and foreign ship-owners and their underwriters, including the principal English, Japanese and Scandinavian Protection and Indemnity Associations worldwide. Over the years of its existence, the firm has greatly expanded its practice beyond the transportation industry, providing litigation defense services in a wide range of practice areas.

Insurance Clients

ACE USA
Assurant Specialty Property
Chartis Marine Adjusters, Inc.
Church Insurance Company
Citizens Insurance Company of America
Eagle Underwriting Group, Inc.
Fremont Insurance Company
Great American Insurance Company
International Marine Underwriters
Nationwide Insurance
Underwriters Marine Services, Inc.
York Claims Service, Inc.
Aon Reed Stenhouse, Inc.
Auto-Owners Insurance Company
Chubb Group of Insurance Companies
Claim Professionals Liability Insurance Company, A RRG
Farmers Insurance Group
Great American Custom Insurance Services
Hanover Insurance Group
Metropolitan Property and Casualty Insurance Company
Utica Mutual Insurance Company

Non-Insurance Clients

Alaska Tanker Co., LLC
BNSF Railway Company
Federal Express
Grand Trunk Western Railroad Co. (CN)
Marina Operator Association of America
Professional Indemnity Agency
Union Pacific Railroad Company
American Steamship Co.
Champion's Auto Ferry, Inc.
GATX Corporation
Laken Shipping, LLC
Maersk, Inc.
Matson Navigation Company
Phoenix Aviation Managers, Inc.
SMT(USA), Inc.
United States Steel Corporation

Sparkman D. Foster — (1897-1967)

Charles D. Meadows — (1916-2011)

Raymond A. Ballard — (1921-1996)

Richard A. Dietz — 1954 — University of Michigan, A.B. (with distinction), 1977; University of Detroit, J.D. (cum laude), 1980 — Admitted to Bar, 1980, Michigan; 1992, Ohio — Member American and Ohio State Bar Associations; State Bar of Michigan; National Association of Railroad Trial Counsel;

Foster, Meadows & Ballard, P.C., Detroit, MI (Continued)

The Maritime Law Association of the United States — E-mail: rdietz@fostermeadows.com

Camille A. Raffa-Dietz — 1954 — Wayne State University, B.S. (with honors), 1982; University of Michigan, J.D., 1985 — Admitted to Bar, 1985, Michigan — Member American Bar Association; State Bar of Michigan — E-mail: craffadietz@fostermeadows.com

Michael J. Liddane — 1960 — University of Dayton, B.A., 1982; Detroit College of Law, J.D., 1985 — Admitted to Bar, 1986, Michigan — Member American Bar Association; State Bar of Michigan; Association of Transportation Law, Logistics and Policy; The Maritime Law Association of the United States; National Association of Railroad Trial Counsel — E-mail: mliddane@fostermeadows.com

(This firm is also listed in the Subrogation section of this directory)

Galbraith, Delie & James, P.C.

660 Woodward Avenue, Suite 1975
Detroit, Michigan 48226-3577
  Telephone: 248-357-3910
  Fax: 248-357-2665
  Mobile: 248-217-4710
  E-Mail: office@galbraithpc.com
  www.galbraithpc.com

Established: 1982

Insurance Defense, Workers' Compensation, Property and Casualty, Automobile, General Liability, Product Liability, Coverage Issues, Malpractice, Professional Errors and Omissions

Insurance Clients

Allstate Insurance Company
Amerisure Companies
Brotherhood Mutual Insurance Company
Founders Insurance Company
General Star Management Company
GuideOne Insurance
Lancer Claims Services, Inc.
Maxum Specialty Insurance Group
MEEMIC Insurance Company
OneBeacon Professional Insurance
Republic Western Insurance Company
American Empire Surplus Lines Insurance Company
Fireman's Fund Insurance Company
Fremont Insurance Company
Great American Insurance Company
Gulf Insurance Group
Lincoln Heritage Life Insurance Company
Northland Insurance Company
Oxford Life Insurance Company
St. Paul Travelers
United Life Insurance Company

Partners/Shareholders

Steven B. Galbraith — 1950 — Michigan State University, B.A., 1972; Detroit College of Law, J.D., 1977 — Moot Court — Admitted to Bar, 1977, Michigan; U.S. District Court, Eastern and Western Districts of Michigan; U.S. Court of Appeals, Sixth Circuit — Member American, Oakland County and Detroit Bar Associations; State Bar of Michigan (Negligence Council - Chair, 2013-2014); American Board of Trial Advocates (ABOTA); American Inns of Court (Emeritus); Michigan Defense Trial Counsel (Excellence in Defense Award, 2013); Michigan Association for Justice (Respected Advocate Award, 2013) — E-mail: sgalbraith@galbraithpc.com

David L. Delie Jr — 1959 — University of Michigan, B.A., 1981; Detroit College of Law, J.D., 1985 — Admitted to Bar, 1985, Michigan; 1989, Florida (Inactive); 1986, U.S. District Court, Eastern and Western Districts of Michigan — Member State Bar of Michigan; Oakland County Bar Association — E-mail: ddelie@galbraithpc.com

Laura A. James — 1969 — Central Michigan University, B.A. (cum laude), 1991; University of Detroit School of Law, J.D. (Valedictorian), 1994 — Admitted to Bar, 1994, Michigan; U.S. District Court, Eastern and Western Districts of Michigan — Member Federal and Oakland County Bar Associations; State Bar of Michigan — Practice Areas: Personal Injury; Premises Liability; Product Liability; Insurance Coverage — E-mail: ljames@galbraithpc.com

Of Counsel

Thomas M. Jinks — Michigan State University, B.A., 1967; Detroit College of Law, J.D., 1973 — Admitted to Bar, 1973, Michigan; U.S. District Court,

DETROIT   **MICHIGAN**

Galbraith, Delie & James, P.C., Detroit, MI (Continued)

Eastern and Western Districts of Michigan; U.S. Court of Appeals, Sixth Circuit — Member Oakland County Bar Association; State Bar of Michigan — Chartered Property Casualty Underwriter (CPCU)

Garan Lucow Miller, P.C.

Woodbridge Place
1000 Woodbridge Street
Detroit, Michigan 48207-3192
   Telephone: 313-446-1530
   Fax: 313-259-0450
   Toll Free: 800-875-1530
   24 Hour Toll Free: 888-332-0540
   www.garanlucow.com

(Additional Offices: Ann Arbor, MI*; Grand Blanc, MI*(See Flint listing); Grand Rapids, MI*; Lansing, MI*; Marquette, MI*; Port Huron, MI*; Traverse City, MI*; Troy, MI*; Merrillville, IN*)

Established: 1948

Business Law, Employment Law, Insurance Defense, Municipal Liability, No-Fault, Workers' Compensation

Insurance Clients

American Country Insurance Company	Auto-Owners Insurance Company
Citizens Insurance Company of America	Cincinnati Insurance Company
Farm Bureau Mutual Insurance Company	Crawford & Company
Frankenmuth Mutual Insurance Company	Employers Mutual Insurance Company
The Hartford	Farmers Insurance Group
Meadowbrook Claims Service	GMAC Insurance
Progressive Insurance Company	Great West Casualty Company
State Farm Insurance Company	Liberty Mutual Insurance Company
Zurich North America	North Pointe Insurance Company
	Safeco Insurance
	USAA

Non-Insurance Clients

The Detroit Medical Center	Dow Corning Corporation
MGM Grand Detroit Casino	MotorCity Casino
Oakwood Healthcare Service Corp.	

Managing Attorney

John J. Gillooly — Chairman, Executive Committee — University of Detroit School of Law, J.D., 1988 — Admitted to Bar, 1988, Michigan — Super Lawyer (2011-2013)

Giarmarco, Mullins & Horton, P.C.

1001 Woodward Avenue, Suite 1000
Detroit, Michigan 48226
   Telephone: 248-457-7000
   Fax: 248-457-7001
   www.gmhlaw.com

(Troy, MI Office*: Tenth Floor Columbia Center, 101 West Big Beaver Road, 48084-5280)
   (Tel: 248-457-7000)
   (Fax: 248-457-7001)

General Defense, Property and Casualty, Workers' Compensation, Civil Rights, Product Liability, Medical Malpractice, Dental Malpractice, Dram Shop, Civil Litigation, Trial and Appellate Practice, Employment

(See listing under Troy, MI for additional information)

Kaufman, Payton & Chapa

40 1/2 East Ferry Street
Detroit, Michigan 48202-3802
   Telephone: 248-626-5000
   Fax: 248-626-6361
   Emer/After Hrs: 248-437-4249
   Mobile: 248-437-4249
   E-Mail: ajkaufman@kaufmanlaw.com
   www.kaufmanlaw.com

(Farmington Hills, MI Office*: 200 Kaufman Financial Center, 30833 Northwestern Highway, 48334-2551)
   (Tel: 248-626-5000)
   (Fax: 248-626-6361)
   (Emer/After Hrs: 248-974-6048)
   (Mobile: 248-974-6048)
(Grand Rapids, MI Office*: 161 Ottawa Avenue, N.W., Suite 205C, 49503)
   (Tel: 616-459-4200)
   (Fax: 248-626-6361)
   (Emer/After Hrs: 248-437-4249)
   (Mobile: 248-437-4249)

Insurance Law, Premises Liability, Medical Malpractice, Professional Liability, Product Liability, Employment Law, Regulatory

(See listing under Farmington Hills, MI for additional information)

Kitch Drutchas Wagner Valitutti & Sherbrook

One Woodward Avenue
Suite 2400
Detroit, Michigan 48226-5485
   Telephone: 313-965-7900
   Fax: 313-965-7403
   www.kitch.com

(Okemos, MI Office: 2379 Woodlake Drive, Suite 400, 48864)
   (Tel: 517-381-4426)
   (Fax: 517-381-4427)
(Marquette, MI Office: Old City Hall, 220 West Washington, Suite 500, 49855-4344)
   (Tel: 906-228-0001)
   (Fax: 906-228-0003)
(Mount Clemens, MI Office: Town Square Development, 10 South Main Street, Suite 200, 48043-7903)
   (Tel: 586-463-9770)
   (Fax: 586-463-8994)
(Toledo, OH Office: 405 Madison Avenue, Suite 1500, 43604-1235)
   (Tel: 419-243-4006)
   (Fax: 419-243-7333)
(Chicago, IL Office: 70 West Madison, Suite 2080, 60602-4252)
   (Tel: 312-332-7901)
   (Fax: 312-332-7903)

Established: 1969

MICHIGAN DETROIT

Kitch Drutchas Wagner Valitutti & Sherbrook, Detroit, MI (Continued)

Alternative Dispute Resolution, Appeals, Asbestos Litigation, Banking, Business Transactions, Civil Rights, Collections, Commercial Litigation, Complex Litigation, Construction Law, Construction Litigation, Corporate Law, Creditor Rights, Dental Malpractice, Elder Law, Employee Benefits, Employment Litigation, Energy, Environmental Law, Equine Law, Family Law, Insurance Agents, Insurance Coverage, Intellectual Property, Labor and Employment, Land Use, Landlord and Tenant Law, Legal Malpractice, Long-Term Care, Managed Care Liability, Mass Tort, Medical Malpractice, Mergers and Acquisitions, Premises Liability, Product Liability, Professional Liability, Real Estate, Skilled Nursing Facilities, Title Insurance, Toxic Torts, Tribal Law, Trucking, Transportation, Wills, Workers' Compensation, Accounting Malpractice, Alternative Risk Financing, Antitrust/Unfair Competition, Appellate, Architectural Malpractice, Assisted Living, Auto-Michigan No-Fault, Auto-Ohio Litigation, Bar Exam Appeals, birth Trauma, Business/Personal Tax, Catastrophic Damage Control, Commercial Issues, Commercial Real Estate, Communication and Media, Complex Settlements, Computer Contracts, Condominiums, Construction Contracts, Construction Disputes, Business Structure, Defamation/Business Torts, Employment Consultation and Drafting, EMTALA Compliance, Estate Administration, Estate Taxation, General Litigation, Government, Government Administration, Government Affairs and Negotiation, Government Litigation, HIPAA/Confidentiality, Healthcare Business/Regulation, Healthcare Fraud Enforcement, Healthcare Payment Issues, Healthcare Regulation, Healthcare Transactions, Home Health Services, Hospital Operations, Insurance, Labor Relations, Long Term Care Litigation, Medical Marijuana, Medical Staff, Medical Staff Bylaws, Medical Staff Hearings and Litigation, Medical Staff Peer Review, Medical-Legal Issues, Mental Health Law, Pharmacy Malpractice, Planning and Land Use, Psychiatric Malpractice, RAC Audits, Real Estate Litigation, Regulatory Law, Residential Real Estate, Securities Disputes, Securities Fraud Litigation, Tax Litigation, Telecommunications and Cable, Title Litigation, Tort Reform, Trusts and Estates, Zoning

Firm Profile: The Kitch firm is dedicated to offering highly effective representation at a reasonable cost. With over 100 attorneys and five offices in Michigan, Ohio and Illinois, the Kitch firm works to combine superior knowledge with exceptional service to effectively meet its clients' needs.

Since its founding over 45 years ago, the Kitch firm has worked with local and national clients, with a particular emphasis on healthcare liability, insurance coverage and product liability. The firm's experience ranges from evaluation insurance and risk management issues to assisting with construction and performance bonds to managing high-exposure birth trauma and mass tort cases, such as those involving asbestos products, locally, regionally and nationwide for leading insurers and some of America's largest companies. With its successful history and its client-directed approach to business, the Kitch firm has earned its status as a strong regionally based firm with services provided nationwide.

Insurance Clients

The ACE Group	ACUITY
AIG	Carolina Casualty Insurance Company
CNA Insurance Companies	
Coverys/MHA Insurance Company	Coverys/OHA Insurance Solutions, Inc.
Farbman Group	
Great West Casualty Company	Manufacturing Technology Mutual Insurance Company
Michigan Municipal Risk Management Authority	ProAssurance Corporation
Sedgwick Claims Management Services, Inc.	Sentry Insurance Company
	State Farm Insurance Companies
U.S. Liability Insurance Company	Utica Mutual Insurance Company

Non-Insurance Clients

Allegiance Health Services	Ascension Health
Biotronic NeuroNetwork	Burger King Corporation
Central Michigan University	Central Refrigerated Service, Inc.
Ciena Healthcare Management, Inc.	Comcar Industries, Inc.
	County of Macomb
Covenant Medical Center, Inc.	CVS Pharmacy, Inc.
Detroit Board of Education	The Detroit Medical Center
Edward W. Sparrow Hospital Association	HCR Manor Care, Inc.
	Henry Ford Health System
Hurley Medical Center	International Hearing Society
Johnson & Johnson	Mackinaw Administrators
McLaren Health Care Corporation	Michigan Municipal League
Motor City Electric Co.	Nexcare Health Systems LLC
Oakwood Healthcare, Inc.	Owner Operator Independent Driver Association
ProMedica Health System, Inc.	
PROTEC	St. John Providence Health
Trinity Health	War Memorial Hospital
Wayne State University	Wayne Westland Community Schools
Wyoming Medical Center	

Principals

Richard A. Kitch — 1930 — Wayne State University Law School, LL.B. (with honors), 1954 — Admitted to Bar, 1955, Michigan — Member State Bar of Michigan (Chairman, Panel #19 Attorney Discipline Board, 1983-; Negligence and Healthcare Law Sections)

Gregory G. Drutchas — 1949 — University of Michigan, A.B., 1970; Duke Law School, J.D., 1973 — Admitted to Bar, 1973, Michigan; 1974, U.S. District Court, Eastern District of Michigan; 1977, U.S. Court of Appeals, Sixth Circuit; 1985, U.S. District Court, Western District of Michigan; 1985, U.S. Supreme Court — Member State Bar of Michigan (Former Chairperson, Committee on Insurance Law; Health Law Section); Michigan Society of Healthcare Attorneys; Arbitrator, American Arbitration Association; American Health Lawyers Association

Ronald E. Wagner — 1944 — Western Michigan University, B.A., 1966; M.A., 1969; Detroit College of Law, J.D., 1975 — Admitted to Bar, 1975, Michigan; 1975, U.S. District Court, Eastern and Western Districts of Michigan; 1978, U.S. Court of Appeals, Sixth Circuit — Member State Bar of Michigan; Michigan Defense Trial Counsel; Defense Research Institute

Ralph F. Valitutti, Jr. — 1950 — Babson College, B.S.B.A., 1972; Detroit College of Law, J.D., 1976 — Admitted to Bar, 1976, Michigan; 1976, U.S. District Court, Eastern District of Michigan; 1977, U.S. Court of Appeals, Sixth Circuit; 1979, U.S. District Court, Western District of Michigan — Member State Bar of Michigan (Former Chairperson, Medical/Legal Committee); Michigan Society of Hospital Attorneys; Catholic Lawyers Society; American Society of Law and Medicine; Defense Research Institute; Association of Defense Trial Counsel; Michigan Defense Trial Counsel

Harry J. Sherbrook — 1951 — University of Michigan, B.G.S. (with distinction), 1974; Detroit College of Law, J.D. (cum laude), 1977 — Admitted to Bar, 1977, Michigan — Member State Bar of Michigan

Charles W. Fisher — 1950 — University of Michigan, B.A. (with high distinction), 1973; Detroit College of Law, J.D., 1979 — Admitted to Bar, 1979, Michigan; 1995, Ohio — Member State Bar of Michigan

Victor J. Abela — 1946 — Wayne State University, B.A., 1970; Detroit College of Law, J.D., 1975 — Admitted to Bar, 1975, Michigan; 1975, U.S. District Court, Western District of Michigan — Member State Bar of Michigan; Oakland County Bar Association; Michigan Self-Insurers Association (Workers Disability Compensation, 1975-) — Languages: Maltese

John P. Ryan — 1953 — University of Michigan, B.A./B.G.S. (with distinction), 1976; Thomas M. Cooley Law School, J.D. (cum laude), 1981 — Admitted to Bar, 1981, Michigan — Member American Bar Association; State Bar of Michigan (Negligence Section)

William D. Chaklos — 1956 — Michigan State University, B.A. (with high honors), 1978; Thomas M. Cooley Law School, J.D. (cum laude), 1981 — Admitted to Bar, 1981, Michigan — Member State Bar of Michigan; Association of Trial Lawyers of America

Susan H. Zitterman — 1956 — University of Michigan, B.A. (with distinction), 1978; Wayne State University, J.D., 1981 — Admitted to Bar, 1981, Michigan; 1991, Ohio; 1981, U.S. District Court, Eastern District of Michigan; 1985, U.S. Court of Appeals, Sixth Circuit; 1986, U.S. Supreme Court — Member State Bar of Michigan (Chairman, Standing Committee on Appellate Court Administration, 1987-1993; Bench Bar Foundation Conference, 1995 and 1998; Co-Chairman, Michigan Cover Practice Committee, 1997-2004; Council Member, Appellate Section, 1998-2004); Incorporated Society of Irish-American Lawyers

John S. Wasung — 1958 — University of Michigan, B.A., 1981; Wayne State University, J.D., 1984 — Admitted to Bar, 1984, Michigan; 1991, Ohio; 1984, U.S. District Court, Eastern District of Michigan; 1990, U.S. District Court, Northern District of Ohio — Member American (Torts and Insurance Practice Section), Ohio State and Toledo Bar Associations; State Bar of Michigan (Environmental Law and Negligence Law Sections); Society of

DETROIT   MICHIGAN

Kitch Drutchas Wagner Valitutti & Sherbrook, Detroit, MI (Continued)

Ohio Hospital Attorneys; Association of Defense Trial Counsel; Ohio Association of Civil Trial Attorneys; Defense Research Institute

John Paul Hessburg — 1961 — St. John's University, B.S., 1983; The Catholic University of America, J.D., 1986 — Admitted to Bar, 1986, Michigan; 1989, District of Columbia; 1986, U.S. District Court, Eastern District of Michigan — Member Bar Association of the District of Columbia; State Bar of Michigan; Healthcare Association of Michigan; Michigan Home Health Association; Michigan Center for Assisted Living; American Health Lawyers Association; Defense Research Institute

Karen Bernard Berkery — 1959 — Rutgers University, Douglass College, B.A. (with honors), 1981; State University of New York at Buffalo, J.D. (cum laude), 1984 — Admitted to Bar, 1985, Michigan; New York; 1988, U.S. District Court, Eastern District of Michigan; 1989, U.S. Court of Appeals, Sixth Circuit; 1990, U.S. District Court, Western District of Michigan — Member New York State Bar Association; State Bar of Michigan; Michigan Society of Hospital Attorneys

Daniel R. Shirey — 1960 — Michigan State University, B.A. (with honors), 1982; University of Illinois, J.D., 1986 — Admitted to Bar, 1986, Michigan; 1988, Florida; 1986, U.S. District Court, Eastern District of Michigan — Member State Bar of Michigan; The Florida Bar

John M. Sier — 1961 — Loyola University, A.B., 1983; Drake University, M.A./J.D., 1986 — Admitted to Bar, 1986, Iowa; Michigan; 1986, U.S. District Court, Eastern District of Michigan; 1991, U.S. District Court, Western District of Michigan; 1996, U.S. Court of Appeals, Sixth Circuit; 2003, U.S. District Court, Northern District of Ohio — Member State Bar of Michigan; Catholic Lawyers Society (President, 1999-2001; Emeritus Director, 2002-); Building Owners and Managers Association of Metropolitan Detroit (Secretary and Board Member, 2002-)

Stephen R. Brzezinski — 1963 — University of Michigan, A.B., 1985; University of Detroit, J.D., 1988 — Admitted to Bar, 1988, Michigan — Member State Bar of Michigan; Oakland County Bar Association

Michael J. Watza — 1956 — Michigan State University, B.A., 1978; Detroit College of Law, J.D., 1986 — Admitted to Bar, 1986, Michigan; 1987, U.S. District Court, Eastern District of Michigan; 1987, U.S. Court of Appeals, Sixth Circuit — Member State Bar of Michigan

Thomas R. Shimmel — 1962 — Albion College, B.A., 1984; Wayne State University, J.D., 1987 — Admitted to Bar, 1988, Michigan; 1988, U.S. District Court, Eastern District of Michigan — Member State Bar of Michigan

Mark A. Wisniewski — 1965 — University of Michigan, A.B., 1987; University of Detroit, J.D., 1990 — Admitted to Bar, 1990, Michigan; 1991, Illinois — Member Illinois State Bar Association; State Bar of Michigan; Wayne County Asbestos Steering Committee

Barbara A. Martin — 1958 — Albion College, B.A. (with honors), 1980; University of Detroit, J.D., 1990 — Admitted to Bar, 1990, Michigan; 1990, U.S. District Court, Eastern District of Michigan — Member State Bar of Michigan; Oakland County Bar Association; Michigan Society of Healthcare Risk Management

Julia Kelly McNelis — 1961 — University of Michigan, B.S.N., 1983; Wayne State University, J.D., 1990 — Admitted to Bar, 1990, Michigan — Member State Bar of Michigan; Macomb County Bar Association

Richard J. Suhrheinrich — 1966 — Vanderbilt University, B.A., 1988; Indiana University, J.D./M.B.A. (cum laude), 1992 — Admitted to Bar, 1992, Michigan; U.S. District Court, Western District of Michigan; 1993, U.S. Court of Appeals, Sixth Circuit; 1996, U.S. District Court, Eastern District of Michigan

Laura L. Witty — 1968 — University of Michigan, A.B., 1990; University of Detroit, J.D., 1993 — Admitted to Bar, 1994, Michigan — Member State Bar of Michigan

Donald B. Lenderman — 1963 — Northwestern University, B.A., 1985; DePaul University College of Law, J.D., 1989 — Admitted to Bar, 1989, Illinois; 1998, Michigan; 1989, U.S. District Court, Northern District of Illinois; 1992, U.S. District Court, Central District of Illinois

Timothy S. Groustra — 1968 — Clark University, B.A., 1990; University of Detroit, J.D., 1993 — Admitted to Bar, 1993, Michigan; 1997, Arkansas; U.S. Court of Appeals, Sixth Circuit — Member Arkansas Bar Association; State Bar of Michigan; Transportation Lawyers Association — Languages: Spanish

Lisa Panah — 1966 — University of Michigan, B.A., 1988; Wayne State University, J.D., 1991; DePaul University College of Law, LL.M., 1996 — Admitted to Bar, 1992, Michigan; Illinois; U.S. District Court, Eastern District of Michigan — Member Illinois State Bar Association; State Bar of Michigan; Michigan Society of Healthcare Attorneys; Healthcare Financial Management Association; American Health Lawyers Association

Kitch Drutchas Wagner Valitutti & Sherbrook, Detroit, MI (Continued)

Susan Douglas MacGregor — 1960 — Ferris State University, B.S., 1981; Valparaiso University, J.D., 1988 — Admitted to Bar, 1988, Michigan — Member Society for Human Resource Management; Defense Research Institute; Michigan Defense Trial Counsel

Adam B. Kutinsky — 1975 — James Madison College at Michigan State University, B.A., 1997; Wayne State University, J.D., 2000 — Admitted to Bar, 2000, Michigan; U.S. District Court, Eastern District of Michigan — Member State Bar of Michigan; Oakland County Bar Association; Michigan Land Title Association

Steve N. Cheolas — 1955 — Hillsdale College, B.L.S., 1977; Wake Forest University, J.D., 1980 — Admitted to Bar, 1980, Michigan — Member State Bar of Michigan; Macomb County Bar Association

R. Michael O'Boyle — 1957 — Western Michigan University, B.A., 1979; University of Detroit, J.D., 1983 — Admitted to Bar, 1983, Michigan; U.S. District Court, Eastern District of Michigan — Member State Bar of Michigan; Oakland County Bar Association

Richard J. Joppich — 1959 — Bowling Green State University, B.S., 1982; Detroit College of Law, J.D., 1988 — Admitted to Bar, 1988, Michigan; U.S. District Court, Eastern District of Michigan; 1989, U.S. District Court, Western District of Michigan; U.S. Court of Appeals, Sixth Circuit; 1995, U.S. Supreme Court — Member State Bar of Michigan; Washtenaw County Bar Association; Michigan Society of Hospital Risk Managers; Michigan Rural Health Association

Dean A. Etsios — 1964 — University of Michigan, B.A., 1986; Indiana University School of Law-Bloomington, J.D., 1990 — Admitted to Bar, 1990, Michigan — Member Hellenic and Washtenaw County Bar Associations; State Bar of Michigan; Michigan Society of Health Care Risk Management

Cheryl A. Cardelli — 1949 — Central Michigan University, A.B. (cum laude), 1970; M.A., 1972; Detroit College of Law, J.D. (cum laude), 1983 — Admitted to Bar, 1983, Michigan — Member State Bar of Michigan; Defense Research Institute

Mary Catherine Storen — 1968 — Michigan State University, B.A. (with honors), 1990; University of Detroit, J.D., 1993 — Admitted to Bar, 1994, Michigan — Member State Bar of Michigan; Women's Economic Club of Detroit

R. Scott Glover — 1974 — Western Michigan University, B.A., 1996; Wayne State University, J.D., 1999 — Admitted to Bar, 1999, Michigan — Member State Bar of Michigan

David C. Wiegel — 1965 — Michigan State University, B.S., 1988; University of Detroit Mercy School of Law, J.D. (cum laude), 1997 — Admitted to Bar, 1997, Michigan; U.S. District Court, Eastern District of Michigan — Member American Bar Association; State Bar of Michigan; Catholic Lawyers Society

Margaret A. Chamberlain — 1966 — Knox College, B.A., 1988; Thomas M. Cooley Law School, J.D. (cum laude), 1997 — Admitted to Bar, 1998, Michigan — Member State Bar of Michigan; Healthcare Association of Michigan; American Health Lawyers Association

Jenna P. Wright — 1975 — University of Michigan, B.S. (cum laude), 1997; Thomas M. Cooley Law School, J.D. (cum laude), 2000 — Admitted to Bar, 2000, Michigan — Member American Bar Association; State Bar of Michigan

Christina R. Ginter — 1971 — University of Michigan, B.A., 1993; J.D. (cum laude), 1995 — Admitted to Bar, 1996, Michigan; U.S. District Court, Eastern District of Michigan; 1998, U.S. Court of Appeals, Sixth Circuit — Member State Bar of Michigan (State Bar Appellate Practice Court Liaison/Rules Comment Committee; Appellate Practice Section Counsel, 2005-)

Kimberly K. Pendrick — 1967 — University of Michigan, B.G.S., 1996; Wayne State University, J.D., 1999 — Admitted to Bar, 1999, Michigan; U.S. District Court, Eastern and Western Districts of Michigan — Member State Bar of Michigan

Michael J. St. John — 1975 — University of Michigan - Ann Arbor, B.A., 1997; Western Illinois University, M.A., 1999; University of Michigan - Ann Arbor, J.D., 2001 — Admitted to Bar, 2002, Michigan; U.S. District Court, Eastern District of Michigan — Member State Bar of Michigan (Governing Council, Student Section, 1991-2001; Healthcare Law and Litigation Sections) — Languages: German

Mark M. Sesi — 1976 — Michigan State University, B.A., 1998; J.D., 2001 — Admitted to Bar, 2001, Michigan — Member American Bar Association; State Bar of Michigan — Languages: Chaldean

Ryan D. Ewles — 1976 — University of Michigan, B.A., 1999; DePaul University College of Law, J.D., 2002 — Admitted to Bar, 2002, Michigan; U.S. District Court, Eastern District of Michigan — Member State Bar of Michigan; Macomb County Bar Association (Law Day Committee)

Kitch Drutchas Wagner Valitutti & Sherbrook, Detroit, MI (Continued)

Michael T. Walsh — St. John's University, Collegeville, B.S., 1988; The John Marshall Law School, J.D., 1991 — Admitted to Bar, 1991, Illinois; U.S. District Court, Northern District of Illinois; U.S. Court of Appeals, Fifth Circuit — Member American, Illinois State and Chicago Bar Associations

Marcy A. Tayler — 1963 — University of Michigan, B.A., 1985; Wayne State University, J.D., 1988 — Admitted to Bar, 1988, Michigan; U.S. District Court, Eastern District of Michigan — Member State Bar of Michigan (Treasurer, Litigation Section)

Terence P. Durkin — 1972 — Millikin University, B.A., 1995; Thomas M. Cooley Law School, J.D., 2001 — Admitted to Bar, 2001, Michigan; 2003, U.S. District Court, Eastern District of Michigan — Member State Bar of Michigan; Michigan Defense Trial Counsel (Chair, Professional Liability and Health Care Section)

Christina A. Doyle — 1980 — Michigan State University, B.A., 2002; University of Michigan, J.D., 2005 — Admitted to Bar, 2005, Michigan; U.S. District Court, Eastern District of Michigan — Member State Bar of Michigan

Genevieve E. Delonis — 1979 — University of Michigan, B.A., 2001; Pennsylvania State University-Dickinson School of Law, J.D., 2004 — Admitted to Bar, 2004, Michigan; 2007, U.S. District Court, Eastern District of Michigan — Member State Bar of Michigan (Negligence and Litigation Section); Women Lawyers Association of Michigan

Patrick M. Fishman — University of Michigan, B.B.A., 1985; University of Detroit School of Law, J.D., 1988 — Admitted to Bar, 1988, Michigan; U.S. District Court, Eastern District of Michigan — Member State Bar of Michigan; Oakland County and Detroit Metropolitan Bar Associations

Andrew M. Harris — 1977 — University of Michigan, B.A., 2000; Wayne State University, J.D., 2003; LL.M. Taxation, 2010 — Admitted to Bar, 2003, Michigan; 2005, U.S. District Court, Eastern District of Michigan — Member American and Oakland County Bar Associations; State Bar of Michigan (Sections: Taxation; Real Property and Business)

Associate Principals

Robert M. Birach
Joyce A. Reynolds
Steven P. McCauslin
Patrick B. Cavanaugh
Michael E. Geraghty
Brett J. Miller
Lindsay C. Kelley-Bliven
Thomas P. Sullivan
Ryan M. Dempsey
Keith F. Wright

Dina M. Ferrari
Beth A. Wittmann
Anne M. Brossia
David T. Henderson
Amy L. Carriveau
Rick J. Wittmer
Kimberly M. Babcock
A. Gabe Sybesma
Robert A. Welch Jr.
Shereen L. Silver

Senior Associates

Matthew A. Brooks
Sylvia R. Wiegel
Jennifer M. Jenkins
Kally Goodwin
Rachel M. Enoch

Kristen Cook
Joslyn Muller
Margaret M. Philpot
Batoul Makki

Associates

Kaitlin V. Brown
Andrea M. Symbal
Kimberly A. Elwell
Amanda S. Kakos
Lindsay Rose
Jeffrey S. Segal

Nicole L. Coleman
Rachel S. Croke
Catherine M. Hart
Shant R. Sagherian
Charles Kowalski

Of Counsel

William D. Hodgman
Stuart Trager

Abraham Singer
Suzanne D. Nolan

Morrison & Morrison

3164 Penobscot Building
645 Griswold Street, Suite 3164
Detroit, Michigan 48226
   Telephone: 313-393-1000
   Fax: 313-964-2273
   E-Mail: ken.morrison@morrisonmorrison.com

Established: 1978

Morrison & Morrison, Detroit, MI (Continued)

Insurance Defense, Liquor Liability, Personal Injury, Product Liability, Coverage Issues, Subrogation, Investigation and Adjustment, Accountant Malpractice, Advertising Injury, Agent and Brokers Errors and Omissions, Amusements, Bad Faith, Carrier Defense, Commercial Vehicle, Commercial and Personal Lines, Complex Litigation, Construction Liability, Declaratory Judgments, Environmental Coverage, Examinations Under Oath, Excess and Surplus Lines, Fire Loss, First Party Matters, Homeowners, Insurance Agents, Insurance Regulation, Mold and Mildew Claims, No-Fault, Policy Construction and Interpretation, Premises Liability, Restaurant Liability, Toxic Torts, Truck Liability, Uninsured and Underinsured Motorist

Insurance Clients

American Equity Insurance Company
Jefferson Insurance Company
Scottsdale Insurance Company
Western Heritage Insurance Company

Burlington Insurance Company
Calvert Insurance Company
Nautilus Insurance Company
Underwriters at Lloyd's, London

Non-Insurance Clients

Firestone Agency Corporation
Michigan Licensed Beverage Association

McCrory Corporation

Kenneth W. Morrison — 1944 — Michigan State University, B.A., 1965; Detroit College of Law, J.D., 1968 — Admitted to Bar, 1968, Michigan; 1968, U.S. District Court, Eastern District of Michigan; 1990, U.S. Court of Appeals, Sixth Circuit — Member State Bar of Michigan (Sections: Negligence Law and Probate Law)

Rutledge, Manion, Rabaut, Terry & Thomas, P.C.

333 West Fort Street, Suite 1600
Detroit, Michigan 48226
   Telephone: 313-965-6100
   Fax: 313-965-6558
   www.rmrtt.com

Alternative Dispute Resolution, Toxic Torts, Real Estate, Commercial Litigation, Civil Rights, Construction Liability, Errors and Omissions, General Civil Litigation, Governmental Liability, Insurance Coverage, Premises Liability, Product Liability, Professional Liability, Property and Casualty, Real Estate Agents & Brokers Liability, Airline Liability, Appellate Issues, Appraiser Liability, Asbestos, Automobile First and Third Party Claims, Commercial Contract Disputes, Employer/Employee Relations, Insurance Broker Liability, Medical/Dental/Pharmacy Malpractice

Insurance Clients

Admiral Insurance Company
Amerisure Companies
Arch Insurance Company
AZOA Resolution Services
Chubb Group of Insurance Companies
Continental Western Insurance Company
The Hartford
Housing Authority Insurance Group
Liberty Mutual
The Medical Protective Company
OMS National Insurance Company
ProAssurance Group
Sedgwick Group
Steadfast Insurance Company
US Health and Life Insurance Company

American Safety Insurance Company
Argo Pro
Catlin Underwriting Agency U.S., Inc.
CNA Insurance Company
Essex Insurance Company
General Star Management Company
Intercare Insurance Services, Inc.
Lexington Insurance Company
Liberty Mutual Insurance Company
Nobel Insurance Company
Pinnacle Risk Management Services
Specialty Risk Services
United American Insurance Company
Westport Insurance Company

DETROIT   MICHIGAN

Rutledge, Manion, Rabaut, Terry & Thomas, P.C., Detroit, MI (Continued)

Zurich American Insurance Group

Non-Insurance Clients

Arctic Cat, Inc.
Davita, Inc.
Genuine Parts Company
Kennametal, Inc.
Oakland Regional Hospital
Rex Roto Corporation
Rite Aid Corporation
Western Litigation, Inc.
Berkley Risk Administrators Company, LLC
Hamilton Sundstrand
Michigan Surgery Specialists, P.C.
Positive Safety Manufacturing Company
Triumph Hospital Detroit

Senior Partners

Alvin A. Rutledge — 1942 — John Carroll University, A.B., 1964; University of Detroit, J.D., 1967 — Admitted to Bar, 1967, Michigan — Member State Bar of Michigan (Quality of Professional Life Committee); Michigan Association of Defense Trial Counsel (Charter Member); Incorporated Society of Irish American Lawyers (Founder and Past President); Eagle International Associates (Past Chairman, Board of Directors); Fellow, Michigan State Bar Foundation; Fellow, Federation of Defense and Corporate Counsel; Fellow, State Bar of Michigan; Association of Defense Trial Counsel — E-mail: arutledge@rmrtt.com

Paul J. Manion — 1947 — College of the Holy Cross, B.A., 1969; Detroit College of Law, J.D., 1972 — Admitted to Bar, 1972, Michigan — Member American Bar Association; State Bar of Michigan (Fellow); Association of Defense Trial Counsel (Board Member); Catholic Lawyers Society (Board Member); Catholic Youth Organization (Past Board Member); Incorporated Society of Irish American Lawyers (Founding and Past Board Member); American Constitution Society; Fellow, Michigan State Bar Foundation; Fellow, Detroit Metropolitan Bar Association; Fellow, Litigation Counsel of America; State Bar District H Character and Fitness Committee; Defense Research Institute; Michigan Defense Trial Counsel; American Board of Trial Advocates; Fellow, American College of Trial Lawyers — E-mail: pmanion@rmrtt.com

Vincent C. Rabaut, Jr. — 1946 — University of Detroit, B.S., 1969; J.D., 1974 — Admitted to Bar, 1974, Michigan — Member American, Macomb County and Detroit Metropolitan Bar Associations; State Bar of Michigan; Michigan Association of Defense Trial Counsel; Wayne County Case Evaluation Tribunal; Association of Defense Trial Counsel; Defense Research Institute — E-mail: vrabaut@rmrtt.com

Christopher L. Terry — 1947 — University of Michigan, B.A., 1969; Wayne State University, J.D., 1972 — Admitted to Bar, 1972, Michigan — Member American Bar Association (Sections: Tort and Insurance Practice, Litigation); State Bar of Michigan; Michigan Association of Defense Trial Counsel; Association of Defense Trial Counsel; Defense Research Institute — E-mail: cterry@rmrtt.com

David M. Thomas — 1952 — Michigan State University, B.A., 1976; Michigan State University College of Law, J.D., 1981 — Admitted to Bar, 1981, Michigan — Member American (Tort and Insurance Practice Sections) and Macomb County (Volunteer Lawyers Committee) Bar Associations; State Bar of Michigan; Association of Defense Trial Counsel (Past President); Wayne County Mediation Tribunal (Board of Directors); Medical-Legal Society; Defense Research Institute; Michigan Defense Trial Counsel — E-mail: dthomas@rmrtt.com

Partners

Anthony J. Calati — 1953 — Western Michigan University, B.S., 1978; Michigan State University College of Law, J.D., 1983 — Admitted to Bar, 1983, Michigan — Member American Bar Association (Law Practice Management, Litigation, Tort Trial and Insurance Practice Sections); State Bar of Michigan (Negligence and Public Corporation Sections); Italian-American, Macomb County and Detroit Metropolitan Bar Associations; National Counsel in Asbestos Litigation; Association of Defense Trial Counsel; Defense Research Institute — E-mail: acalati@rmrtt.com

Matthew A. Brauer — 1967 — Central Michigan University, B.S., 1990; Detroit College of Law, J.D. (cum laude), 1994 — Admitted to Bar, 1994, Michigan; U.S. District Court, Eastern District of Michigan, 1999, U.S. District Court, Western District of Michigan, 2003, U.S. Court of Appeals, Sixth Circuit, 2005, U.S. Supreme Court — Member American Bar Association; State Bar of Michigan; Association of Defense Trial Counsel — E-mail: mbrauer@rmrtt.com

Dora A. Brantley — 1968 — University of Michigan, B.A., 1990; Wayne State University, J.D., 1993 — Admitted to Bar, 1993, Michigan — Member National and Wolverine Bar Associations; State Bar of Michigan; Federation of Defense & Corporate Counsel (FDCC); Michigan Defense Trial Counsel — E-mail: dbrantley@rmrtt.com

Joseph J. Wright — 1962 — Michigan State University, B.A., 1984; Michigan State University College of Law, J.D., 1987 — Admitted to Bar, 1988, Michigan — Member State Bar of Michigan (Negligence Section); Association of Defense Trial Counsel; Defense Research Institute; Michigan Defense Trial Counsel — E-mail: jwright@rmrtt.com

Madeleine R. Szymanski — 1952 — Wayne State University, B.A., 1990; University of Detroit Mercy School of Law, J.D., 1996 — Admitted to Bar, 1996, Michigan — Member American Bar Association; State Bar of Michigan; Michigan Association of Justice; Michigan Trial Lawyers Association; American Trial Lawyers Association; Association of Defense Trial Counsel — E-mail: mszymanski@rmrtt.com

Amy E. Schlotterer — 1973 — University of Detroit Mercy School of Law, B.A. (magna cum laude), 1995; Wayne State University, J.D., 1998 — Admitted to Bar, 1999, Michigan — Member American Bar Association; State Bar of Michigan; Association of Defense Trial Counsel — E-mail: aschlotterer@rmrtt.com

Dale A. Robinson — 1967 — University of Windsor, B.A., 1989; Detroit College of Law, Michigan State University, J.D., 1996 — Admitted to Bar, 1996, Michigan; 2011, Ohio; 2005, U.S. District Court, Eastern District of Michigan; U.S. Court of Appeals, Sixth Circuit; 2007, U.S. Supreme Court; 2008, U.S. District Court, Western District of Michigan — Member American and Detroit Metropolitan Bar Associations; State Bar of Michigan; Society of Automotive Engineers (2000-2005); Michigan Trial Lawyers Association (1997-2004); Association of Defense Trial Counsel — E-mail: drobinson@rmrtt.com

Matthew J. Thomas — 1974 — University of Detroit Mercy School of Law, B.A. (magna cum laude), 1996; Wayne State University, J.D., 1999 — Admitted to Bar, 1999, Michigan — Member State Bar of Michigan (Negligence Section); Michigan Defense Trial Counsel; Association of Defense Trial Counsel — E-mail: mthomas@rmrtt.com

---

The following firms also service this area.

Bowen, Radabaugh & Milton, P.C.
4967 Crooks Road, Suite 150
Troy, Michigan 48098
Telephone: 248-641-8000
Fax: 248-641-8219

Defense Litigation, Trial and Appellate Practice, State and Federal Courts, Declaratory Judgments, Arbitration, Examinations Under Oath, Opinions, Employment Law, Americans with Disabilities Act, Discrimination, Wrongful Termination, Equal Employment Opportunity Commission, Civil Rights, Sexual Harassment, Employee Benefits, Coverage Analysis, Policy Construction and Interpretation, Tort Litigation, Product Liability, Property Loss, Property Damage, Arson, Premises Liability, Intentional Torts, Insurance Fraud, Wrongful Death, Personal Injury, Automobile, No-Fault, First and Third Party Defense, Uninsured and Underinsured Motorist, Theft, Bodily Injury, Deceptive Trade Practices, Life Insurance, Accident and Health, Homeowners, Disability, Self-Insured Defense, Aviation, Corporate Law, Real Estate, Estate Planning, Probate, Mergers and Acquisitions, Counseling, Credit Insurance, Warranty Litigation, Consumer Law, Vendor Contracts

SEE COMPLETE LISTING UNDER TROY, MICHIGAN (18 MILES)

Harvey Kruse, P.C.
1050 Wilshire Drive, Suite 320
Troy, Michigan 48084-1526
Telephone: 248-649-7800
Fax: 248-649-2316

Trial and Appellate Practice, State and Federal Courts, Asbestos Litigation, Automobile Liability, Aviation, Casualty, Civil Rights, Commercial Litigation, Construction Liability, Dental Malpractice, Employment Discrimination, Environmental Law, Errors and Omissions, Fidelity and Surety, Fraud, General Liability, Hospital Malpractice, Insurance Defense, Malpractice, Insurance Coverage, Medical Malpractice, No-Fault, Premises Liability, Product Liability, Subrogation, Toxic Torts, Property Damage, Uninsured and Underinsured Motorist

SEE COMPLETE LISTING UNDER TROY, MICHIGAN (18 MILES)

MICHIGAN

Maddin, Hauser, Roth & Heller, P.C.
28400 Northwestern Highway, Second Floor
Southfield, Michigan 48034
   Telephone: 248-354-4030
   Fax: 248-359-6149
Mailing Address: P.O. Box 215, Southfield, MI 48037

Insurance Defense, Professional Liability (Non-Medical) Defense, Insurance Coverage, Legal Malpractice, Accountant Malpractice, Insurance Agents, Errors and Omissions, Directors and Officers Liability, Employment Practices Liability, Complex Litigation, Appellate Practice, Securities Litigation

SEE COMPLETE LISTING UNDER SOUTHFIELD, MICHIGAN (5 MILES)

Law Offices of Ward, Anderson, Porritt & Bryant, PLC
4190 Telegraph Road, Suite 2300
Bloomfield Hills, Michigan 48302
   Telephone: 248-593-1440
   Fax: 248-593-7920

Insurance Defense, Property and Casualty, Arson, Transportation, Liquor Liability, General Liability, Professional Malpractice, Errors and Omissions, Automobile, Product Liability, Discrimination, Coverage Issues, Truck Liability, Trucking Law

SEE COMPLETE LISTING UNDER BLOOMFIELD HILLS, MICHIGAN (20 MILES)

EAST LANSING 48,579 Ingham Co.

Hackney Grover Hoover & Bean

1715 Abbey Road, Suite A
East Lansing, Michigan 48823
   Telephone: 517-333-0306
   Fax: 517-333-0319
   E-Mail: rhackney@hghblaw.com
   www.hghblaw.com

Established: 1999

Insurance Defense, Medical Malpractice, Professional Malpractice, General Liability, Commercial Litigation, Complex Litigation

Firm Profile: Our firm recognizes that each client's situation is unique and prides ourselves in providing personalized solutions. Our team of attorneys and paralegals provide a cost-effective, innovative response to each client's individual needs. We are committed to meet and exceed our clients' expectations.

Insurance Clients

National Liability Management, Inc.
NCMIC Group - Professional Solutions Insurance Company

Partner

Randy J. Hackney — 1953 — University of Michigan, B.B.A., 1975; University of Detroit School of Law, J.D., 1978 — Admitted to Bar, 1978, Michigan; 1984, U.S. District Court, Eastern District of Michigan; 1989, U.S. District Court, Western District of Michigan; 1991, U.S. Court of Appeals, Sixth Circuit — Member American and Ingham County Bar Associations; State Bar of Michigan; Michigan Association of the Professions; American Board of Trial Advocates; Michigan Defense Trial Counsel; Defense Research Institute — Practice Areas: Professional Negligence

ESCANABA † 12,616 Delta Co.

Refer To
Bensinger, Cotant & Menkes, P.C.
122 West Bluff Street
Marquette, Michigan 49855
   Telephone: 906-225-1000
   Fax: 906-225-0818

General Defense, Automobile Liability, Fire Loss, Professional Liability, Product Liability, Workers' Compensation, Subrogation, Medical Malpractice, Liquor Liability

SEE COMPLETE LISTING UNDER MARQUETTE, MICHIGAN (75 MILES)

EAST LANSING

FARMINGTON HILLS 79,740 Oakland Co.

Kaufman, Payton & Chapa

200 Kaufman Financial Center
30833 Northwestern Highway
Farmington Hills, Michigan 48334-2551
   Telephone: 248-626-5000
   Fax: 248-626-6361
   Emer/After Hrs: 248-974-6048
   Mobile: 248-974-6048
   E-Mail: ajkaufman@kaufmanlaw.com
   www.kaufmanlaw.com

(Grand Rapids, MI Office*: 161 Ottawa Avenue, N.W., Suite 205C, 49503)
   (Tel: 616-459-4200)
   (Fax: 248-626-6361)
   (Emer/After Hrs: 248-437-4249)
   (Mobile: 248-437-4249)
(Detroit, MI Office*: 40 1/2 East Ferry Street, 48202-3802)
   (Tel: 248-626-5000)
   (Fax: 248-626-6361)
   (Emer/After Hrs: 248-437-4249)
   (Mobile: 248-437-4249)

Established: 1975

Insurance Law, Trial and Appellate Practice, Professional Liability, Premises Liability, Product Liability, Medical Malpractice, Employment Law, Directors and Officers Liability, Municipal Law, Public Officials Liability, Reinsurance, Excess, Environmental Law, Regulatory

Firm Profile: Kaufman, Payton & Chapa serves both as legal advocates and counselors for a distinguished roster of clients that includes local, national, and international companies in insurance, health care, manufacturing, finance, real estate, government, retail, and recreation.

Insurance Clients

Alterra Specialty
Atain Insurance Companies
Burns & Wilcox Ltd.
CNA Insurance Company
Employers Reinsurance Corporation
First Mercury Insurance Company
Lexington Insurance Company
Nationwide Insurance
Scottsdale Insurance Company
Underwriters at Lloyd's, London
Vela Insurance Services, LLC
American International Group, Inc.
Atain Specialty Insurance Company
Colony Insurance Company
Essex Insurance Company
Evanston Insurance Company
Interstate Insurance Group
Markel Insurance Company
Pioneer State Mutual Insurance Company
U.S. Liability Insurance Company

Non-Insurance Clients

Lasko Products, Inc.

Representative Insurance Clients

Berkley Risk Administrators Company, LLC

Self-Insured Clients

Skechers USA, Inc.

Third Party Administrators

Crawford Technical Services
Media Professionals
RiverStone Claims Management, LLC
Fleming & Hall, LTD
RC Services
Sedgwick Claims Management Services, Inc.

Partners

Alan Jay Kaufman — 1948 — Michigan State University, B.A., 1970; University of Notre Dame, J.D., 1973 — Admitted to Bar, 1973, Michigan — Mediation Panels Wayne and Oakland County-Arbitrator — Tel: 248-626-5000 Ext. 2255

FLINT   MICHIGAN

Kaufman, Payton & Chapa, Farmington Hills, MI
(Continued)

Donald L. Payton — 1949 — Michigan State University, B.A., 1971; Detroit College of Law, J.D., 1977 — Admitted to Bar, 1977, Michigan — Mediator

Ralph C. Chapa, Jr. — 1961 — Michigan State University, B.A., 1984; Wayne State University, J.D., 1987 — Admitted to Bar, 1987, Michigan; 1988, Florida

Lawrence C. Atorthy — 1962 — Rutgers University School of Law, J.D., 1988 — Admitted to Bar, 1989, California; 1991, Michigan

Associate Litigators

Frank A. Misuraca
Howard S. Weingarden
Daniel J. Kaufman
Sue Singer Kaufman
Jennifer M. Levine
Brian A. Catrinar

FLINT † 102,434 Genesee Co.

Garan Lucow Miller, P.C.

8332 Office Park Drive
Grand Blanc, Michigan 48439-2035
  Telephone: 810-695-3700
  Fax: 810-695-6488
  Toll Free: 800-875-3700
  www.garanlucow.com
  24 Hour Toll Free: 888-332-0540

(Additional Offices: Detroit, MI*; Ann Arbor, MI*; Grand Rapids, MI*; Lansing, MI*; Marquette, MI*; Port Huron, MI*; Traverse City, MI*; Troy, MI*; Merrillville, IN*)

Business Law, Employment Law, Insurance Defense, Municipal Liability, No-Fault, Workers' Compensation

(See listing under Detroit, MI for additional information)

Harvey Kruse, P.C.

5206 Gateway Centre Drive, Suite 200
Flint, Michigan 48507
  Telephone: 810-230-1000
  Fax: 810-230-0844
  www.HarveyKruse.com

(Troy, MI Office*: 1050 Wilshire Drive, Suite 320, 48084-1526)
  (Tel: 248-649-7800)
  (Fax: 248-649-2316)
(Grand Rapids, MI Office*: 60 Monroe Center NW, Suite 500B, 49503-2926)
  (Tel: 616-771-0050)
  (Fax: 616-776-3646)

Established: 1969

Trial and Appellate Practice, State and Federal Courts, Asbestos Litigation, Automobile Liability, Aviation, Casualty, Civil Rights, Commercial Litigation, Construction Liability, Dental Malpractice, Employment Discrimination, Environmental Law, Errors and Omissions, Fidelity and Surety, Fraud, General Liability, Hospital Malpractice, Insurance Defense, Malpractice, Insurance Coverage, Medical Malpractice, No-Fault, Premises Liability, Product Liability, Subrogation, Toxic Torts, Property Damage, Uninsured and Underinsured Motorist

(See listing under Troy, MI for additional information)

Morrissey, Bove & Ebbott

221 West Fifth Street
Flint, Michigan 48502
  Telephone: 810-238-0455
  Fax: 810-238-0458
  E-Mail: mbebbott@sbcglobal.net

Insurance Defense, Civil Trial Practice, Tort, Wrongful Death, Premises Liability, Motor Vehicle

Firm Profile: Our firm has been in existence for 50 years. We have always practiced insurance defense work as a major portion of our practice.

Insurance Clients

Pioneer State Mutual Insurance Company

Non-Insurance Clients

Bisbee Car Company, Inc.
Executive Property Development, LLC
Executive Auto Brokers, LLC

Partners

Richard H. Ebbott — 1941 — University of Wisconsin, B.S., 1964; University of Wisconsin Law School, J.D., 1967 — Admitted to Bar, 1967, Wisconsin; 1971, Michigan; U.S. District Court, Eastern District of Michigan; 1999, U.S. Supreme Court — Member State Bar of Michigan; State Bar of Wisconsin; Genesee County Bar Association

Christopher J. Ebbott — 1968 — Michigan State University, B.A., 1991; Detroit College of Law, J.D. (cum laude), 1995 — Admitted to Bar, 1995, Michigan; 1996, U.S. District Court, Eastern District of Michigan; 1999, U.S. Supreme Court — Member State Bar of Michigan; Genesee County Bar Association

---

The following firms also service this area.

Maddin, Hauser, Roth & Heller, P.C.
28400 Northwestern Highway, Second Floor
Southfield, Michigan 48034
  Telephone: 248-354-4030
  Fax: 248-359-6149
Mailing Address: P.O. Box 215, Southfield, MI 48037

Insurance Defense, Professional Liability (Non-Medical) Defense, Insurance Coverage, Legal Malpractice, Accountant Malpractice, Insurance Agents, Errors and Omissions, Directors and Officers Liability, Employment Practices Liability, Complex Litigation, Appellate Practice, Securities Litigation

SEE COMPLETE LISTING UNDER SOUTHFIELD, MICHIGAN (45 MILES)

Siemion Huckabay, P.C.
One Towne Square, Suite 1400
Southfield, Michigan 48076
  Telephone: 248-357-1400
  Fax: 248-357-3343
Mailing Address: P.O. Box 5068, Southfield, MI 48086-5068

Insurance Defense, Automobile, General Liability, Legal Malpractice, Medical Malpractice, Product Liability, Errors and Omissions, Trial Practice, Appellate Practice, Asbestos Litigation, Aviation, Workers' Compensation, Securities Litigation

SEE COMPLETE LISTING UNDER SOUTHFIELD, MICHIGAN (45 MILES)

Law Offices of Ward, Anderson, Porritt & Bryant, PLC
4190 Telegraph Road, Suite 2300
Bloomfield Hills, Michigan 48302
  Telephone: 248-593-1440
  Fax: 248-593-7920

Insurance Defense, Property and Casualty, Arson, Transportation, Liquor Liability, General Liability, Professional Malpractice, Errors and Omissions, Automobile, Product Liability, Discrimination, Coverage Issues, Truck Liability, Trucking Law

SEE COMPLETE LISTING UNDER BLOOMFIELD HILLS, MICHIGAN (35 MILES)

MICHIGAN

GAYLORD † 3,645 Otsego Co.

Bensinger, Cotant & Menkes, P.C.
308 West Main Street
Gaylord, Michigan 49735
Telephone: 989-732-7536
Fax: 989-732-4922
www.bcma.net

(Marquette, MI Office*: 122 West Bluff Street, 49855)
(Tel: 906-225-1000)
(Fax: 906-225-0818)

Established: 1978

General Defense, Automobile Liability, Fire Loss, Professional Liability, Product Liability, Workers' Compensation, Subrogation, Medical Malpractice, Liquor Liability

Firm Profile: Bensinger, Cotant & Menkes, P.C. is a Michigan law firm with offices in Gaylord & Marquette. We are a full service defense team, with extensive experience in the following areas: medical malpractice, auto negligence, product liability, premises liability, patent law, dram shop, and estate planning.

Insurance Clients

ACUITY
APCapital
Badger Mutual Insurance Company
Creative Risk Management
Employers Mutual Casualty Company
Farm Bureau Mutual Insurance Company
Federated Insurance Company
Frankenmuth Mutual Insurance Company
Great Lakes Casualty Insurance Company
The Medical Protective Company
MEEMIC Insurance Company
Michigan Insurance Company
Michigan Millers Mutual Insurance Company
Michigan Property and Casualty Guaranty Association
OMS National Insurance Company
Pioneer Insurance Company
Professionals Direct Insurance Company
ProNational Insurance Company
Royal & SunAlliance Insurance Company
State Farm Mutual Automobile Insurance Company
TIG Insurance Company
United National Insurance Company
Zurich American Insurance Company

Allstate Insurance Company
Auto-Owners Insurance Company
Capitol Indemnity Corporation
The Doctors Company
Employers Reinsurance Corporation
Farmers and Merchants Insurance Company
Fireman's Fund Insurance Company
Fremont Insurance Company
Great Midwest Insurance Company
Hastings Mutual Insurance Company
Michigan Basic Property Insurance Association
Michigan Mutual Insurance Company
Midwest Claims Service
North Pointe Insurance Company
Partners Mutual Insurance Company
Progressive Casualty Insurance Company
R.C.A. Insurance Group
SECURA Insurance Companies
State Farm Fire and Casualty Company
State Mutual Insurance Company
Titan Insurance Company
Ward North America, Inc.
Westport Insurance Company

Lead Counsel for

Great Lakes Mutual Insurance Company

Northern Mutual Insurance Company

Non-Insurance Clients

Baraga County Memorial Hospital
Michigan Licensed Beverage Association
Tendercare, Inc. (MI)

Michigan Hospital Association
Otsego Memorial Hospital
PGI Commercial

Firm Members

Michael E. Menkes — President — 1953 — Indiana University, B.A., 1979; Valparaiso University School of Law, J.D., 1979 — Admitted to Bar, 1980, Michigan — Member American and Otsego County Bar Associations; State Bar of Michigan; Defense Research Institute — AV Rated by Martindale Hubbell; Listed in the Bar Register of Preeminent Lawyers — Practice Areas: Premises Liability; Product Liability — E-mail: mmenkes@bcma.net

Patrick J. Michaels — Vice-President — 1953 — University of Michigan, B.A., 1975; University of Detroit, J.D., 1981 — Admitted to Bar, 1981, Michigan — Member State Bar of Michigan; Otsego County Bar Association; Defense Research Institute — Listed in the Bar Register of Preeminent Lawyers — Practice Areas: Dram Shop; Premises Liability — E-mail: pmichaels@bcma.net

Gregory A. Elzinga — 1952 — Central Michigan University, B.S., 1975; Thomas M. Cooley Law School, J.D., 1979 — Admitted to Bar, 1979, Michigan — Member American and Marquette County Bar Associations; State Bar of Michigan; Michigan Defense Trial Counsel Northern Representative; Blue Goose Insurance Organization (U.P. Puddle); Michigan Trial Lawyers Association; Defense Research Institute — Listed in the Bar Register of Preeminent Lawyers — Practice Areas: Medical Malpractice; Premises Liability — Resident Marquette, MI Office — Tel: 906-225-1000 — E-mail: gelzinga@bcma.net

William J. Maynard — 1961 — Central Michigan University, B.S. (magna cum laude), 1983; The University of Toledo College of Law, J.D., 1986 — Admitted to Bar, 1986, Michigan — Member American and Marquette County Bar Associations; State Bar of Michigan; Blue Goose Insurance Organization (U.P. Puddle); Michigan Defense Trial Counsel; International Association of Arson Investigators; Defense Research Institute — Listed in the Bar Register of Preeminent Lawyers — Practice Areas: Premises Liability; Product Liability — Resident Marquette, MI Office — Tel: 906-225-1000 — E-mail: wmaynard@bcma.net

Glenn W. Smith — 1956 — Michigan Technological University, B.S., 1978; Pepperdine University, 1982; Loyola University of Los Angeles, J.D., 1989 — Admitted to Bar, 1989, Michigan — Member American and Marquette County Bar Associations; State Bar of Michigan; American Society of Mechanical Engineers — Listed in the Bar Register of Preeminent Lawyers — Practice Areas: Product Liability — Resident Marquette, MI Office — Tel: 906-225-1000 — E-mail: gws@bcma.net

Roger W. Zappa — 1959 — Michigan Technological University, B.S. (summa cum laude), 1981; University of Michigan, J.D., 1984 — Admitted to Bar, 1984, Michigan — Member State Bar of Michigan; Marquette County Bar Association; Bar of the 6th Circuit Court of Appeals — Listed in the Bar Register of Preeminent Lawyers — Practice Areas: Premises Liability; Estate Planning — Resident Marquette, MI Office — Tel: 906-225-1000 — E-mail: rzappa@bcma.net

Bradley S. Bensinger — 1974 — Albion College, B.A., 1996; Detroit College of Law, Michigan State University, J.D. (magna cum laude), 1999 — Admitted to Bar, 2000, Michigan — Member American and Otsego County Bar Associations; State Bar of Michigan; Defense Research Institute — Listed in the Bar Register of Preeminent Lawyers — Practice Areas: Premises Liability; Product Liability — E-mail: bbensinger@bcma.net

The following firms also service this area.

White and Wojda
313 N. Second Avenue
Alpena, Michigan 49707
Telephone: 989-354-4104
Fax: 989-356-0747

Casualty Defense, First and Third Party Defense, Insurance Defense, Legal Malpractice, Opinions, Personal Lines, Special Investigative Unit Claims, All Lines, Municipal Defense

SEE COMPLETE LISTING UNDER ALPENA, MICHIGAN (72 MILES)

GRAND RAPIDS † 188,040 Kent Co.

Bosch Killman VanderWal, P.C.
f/k/a Strain, Murphy & VanderWal, P.C.

2900 East Beltline Avenue, N.E.
Grand Rapids, Michigan 49525
Telephone: 616-364-2900
Fax: 616-364-2901
www.bkvpc.com

Established: 1912

Bosch Killman VanderWal, P.C., f/k/a Strain, Murphy & VanderWal, P.C., Grand Rapids, MI (Continued)

Insurance Law, Trial and Appellate Practice, Negligence, Medical Malpractice, Environmental Law, Product Liability, Premises Liability, Fire, Subrogation, Workers' Compensation, No-Fault, Casualty

Insurance Clients

American International Group, Inc.
Farmland Mutual Insurance Company
Pioneer State Mutual Insurance Company
State Farm Mutual Automobile Insurance Company
Auto-Owners Insurance Company
Fremont Insurance Company
Michigan Millers Mutual Insurance Company
State Farm Fire and Casualty Company

Firm Members

Dale M. Strain — (Retired)

Larry D. VanderWal — 1948 — Valparaiso University, J.D., 1973 — Admitted to Bar, 1973, Michigan — Member State Bar of Michigan; Grand Rapids Bar Association — E-mail: lvanderwal@bkvpc.com

Joseph P. VanderVeen — 1955 — Detroit College of Law, J.D., 1981 — Admitted to Bar, 1981, Michigan — Member State Bar of Michigan; Grand Rapids Bar Association — E-mail: jvanderveen@bkvpc.com

Peter D. Bosch — 1958 — University of Michigan, B.A., 1980; University of Detroit School of Law, J.D. (cum laude), 1983 — Admitted to Bar, 1983, Michigan; U.S. District Court, Eastern and Western Districts of Michigan; U.S. Court of Appeals, Sixth Circuit; U.S. Court of Claims — Member State Bar of Michigan; Grand Rapids Bar Association — Practice Areas: Automobile Liability; Construction Law; Business Litigation; Insurance Defense; Insurance Litigation; Subrogation; Real Property; Personal Injury — E-mail: pbosch@bkvpc.com

Kurt R. Killman — 1962 — Thomas M. Cooley Law School, J.D., 1987 — Admitted to Bar, 1987, Michigan — Member Grand Rapids Bar Association — E-mail: kkillman@bkvpc.com

Steven L. Birn — 1978 — Michigan State University, B.A., 2000; Case Western Reserve University, J.D., 2003 — Admitted to Bar, 2004, Michigan; 2004, U.S. District Court, Western District of Michigan — Member State Bar of Michigan; Grand Rapids Bar Association — E-mail: sbirn@bkvpc.com

Stephen L. Elkins — 1955 — Michigan State University, B.A. (with honors), 1978; M.I.L.R., 1980; Thomas M. Cooley Law School, J.D., 1982 — Admitted to Bar, 1982, Michigan — Member State Bar of Michigan; Grand Rapids Bar Association — Practice Areas: Corporate Law; Estate Planning; Probate; Real Estate — E-mail: selkins@bkvpc.com

Robert M. Brownley — 1963 — Wittenberg University, B.A., 1985; The University of Toledo College of Law, J.D., 1988 — Admitted to Bar, 1988, Michigan; 1988, U.S. District Court, Western District of Michigan — Member American and Grand Rapids Bar Associations; State Bar of Michigan — Practice Areas: Construction Law; Insurance Defense; Personal Injury; Subrogation; Toxic Torts — E-mail: rbrownley@bkvpc.com

Jennifer Van Horn-Pfeiffelman — 1970 — Michigan State University, B.A., 1992; Wayne State University, J.D. (cum laude), 1995 — Admitted to Bar, 1995, Michigan; U.S. District Court, Eastern and Western Districts of Michigan — Member Van Buren County Bar Association; State Bar of Michigan; Grand Rapids Bar Association — Practice Areas: Family Law; Civil Litigation — E-mail: jvanhorn@bkvpc.com

John C. Worsfold — 1977 — University of Michigan - Ann Arbor, B.S., 1999; The University of Montana School of Law, J.D., 2005 — Admitted to Bar, 2005, Montana; 2008, California; 2014, Michigan — Practice Areas: Criminal Defense; Business Litigation; Insurance Defense; Personal Injury Litigation — E-mail: jworsfold@bkvpc.com

(This firm is also listed in the Subrogation section of this directory)

Garan Lucow Miller, P.C.

300 Ottawa Avenue, N.W., 8th Floor
Grand Rapids, Michigan 49503-3003
 Telephone: 616-742-5500
 Fax: 616-742-5566
 Toll Free: 800-494-6312
 24 Hour Toll Free: 888-332-0540
 www.garanlucow.com

(Additional Offices: Detroit, MI*; Ann Arbor, MI*; Grand Blanc, MI*(See Flint listing); Lansing, MI*; Marquette, MI*; Port Huron, MI*; Traverse City, MI*; Troy, MI*; Merrillville, IN*)

Business Law, Employment Law, Insurance Defense, Municipal Liability, No-Fault, Workers' Compensation

(See listing under Detroit, MI for additional information)

Harvey Kruse, P.C.

60 Monroe Center NW, Suite 500B
Grand Rapids, Michigan 49503-2926
 Telephone: 616-771-0050
 Fax: 616-776-3646
 www.HarveyKruse.com

(Troy, MI Office*: 1050 Wilshire Drive, Suite 320, 48084-1526)
 (Tel: 248-649-7800)
 (Fax: 248-649-2316)
(Flint, MI Office*: 5206 Gateway Centre Drive, Suite 200, 48507)
 (Tel: 810-230-1000)
 (Fax: 810-230-0844)

Established: 1969

Trial and Appellate Practice, State and Federal Courts, Asbestos Litigation, Automobile Liability, Aviation, Casualty, Civil Rights, Commercial Litigation, Construction Liability, Dental Malpractice, Employment Discrimination, Environmental Law, Errors and Omissions, Fidelity and Surety, Fraud, General Liability, Hospital Malpractice, Insurance Defense, Malpractice, Insurance Coverage, Medical Malpractice, No-Fault, Premises Liability, Product Liability, Subrogation, Toxic Torts, Property Damage, Uninsured and Underinsured Motorist

(See listing under Troy, MI for additional information)

Kaufman, Payton & Chapa

161 Ottawa Avenue, N.W., Suite 205C
Grand Rapids, Michigan 49503
 Telephone: 616-459-4200
 Fax: 248-626-6361
 Emer/After Hrs: 248-437-4249
 Mobile: 248-437-4249
 E-Mail: ajkaufman@kaufmanlaw.com
 www.kaufmanlaw.com

(Farmington Hills, MI Office*: 200 Kaufman Financial Center, 30833 Northwestern Highway, 48334-2551)
 (Tel: 248-626-5000)
 (Fax: 248-626-6361)
 (Emer/After Hrs: 248-974-6048)
 (Mobile: 248-974-6048)
(Detroit, MI Office*: 40 1/2 East Ferry Street, 48202-3802)
 (Tel: 248-626-5000)
 (Fax: 248-626-6361)
 (Emer/After Hrs: 248-437-4249)
 (Mobile: 248-437-4249)

MICHIGAN   GRAND RAPIDS

Kaufman, Payton & Chapa, Grand Rapids, MI
(Continued)

Insurance Law, Premises Liability, Medical Malpractice, Professional Liability, Product Liability, Employment Law, Liquor Liability, Regulatory

(See listing under Farmington Hills, MI for additional information)

Kluczynski, Girtz & Vogelzang

5005 Cascade Road SE, Suite A
Grand Rapids, Michigan 49546
   Telephone: 616-459-0556
   Fax: 616-459-5829
   www.kgvlaw.com

(Southfield, MI Office: 18530 West 10 Mile, 48075)
   (Tel: 248-559-3830)
   (Fax: 248-559-5018)

Established: 1981

Insurance Defense, Automobile, Fire, Casualty, General Liability, Product Liability, Workers' Compensation, Subrogation, Environmental Law, Occupational Disease

Firm Profile: Kluczynski, Girtz & Vogelzang is an established and respected general practice law firm located in Grand Rapids, Michigan.

The law firm was founded in 1978 by Gilbert A. Girtz. His objective was the establishment of a "client driven" law firm to provide cost effective litigation defense service to the insurance industry. Since those early years, the firm has grown in size to fourteen attorneys. Additional areas of legal expertise now include corporate law, employment law and family law.

Kluczynski, Girtz & Vogelzang has one of the largest workers' compensation practices in the state. It represents insurance clients in all agency locations within the State of Michigan. Non-insurance businesses and clients are serviced in all federal, state and local courts and administrative agencies. Areas of general practice expertise include contract interpretation and enforcement, commercial litigation, corporate organization/re-organization, valuation and buy/sell negotiations, employment practices, including harassment, discrimination, discharge and unfair labor practices, estate planning and probate, family law, government immunity involving State of Michigan agencies, school districts and municipalities, professional liability, property and casualty issues.

Insurance Clients

Accident Fund Insurance Company of America
Amerisafe Insurance Group
Amerisure Insurance Company
Arrowpoint Capital Corporation
ASU Risk Management Services, Ltd.
Chartis
Citizens Insurance Company of America
Coverys
Crum & Forster Insurance
Electric Insurance Company
Everest National Insurance Company
Fireman's Fund Insurance Company
Great Midwest Insurance Company
Great West Casualty Company
Liberty Mutual
Meadowbrook Insurance Group
Michigan Insurance Company
Mitsui Sumitomo Insurance Group
PMA Companies, Inc.
Sentry Insurance
SET-SEG (School Employers' Trust-School Employers' Group)
State Auto Insurance Company
Tower Group Companies
ACUITY
American Modern Home Insurance Company
Argonaut Insurance Company of Michigan
Broadspire
CCMSI
Cincinnati Insurance Company
CMI, A York Risk Service Co.
CNA Insurance Company
Crawford & Company
Eagle Claims Management
ESIS Group
Farm Bureau Insurance Companies
FCCI Insurance Group
Gallagher Bassett Services, Inc.
Great American Insurance Company
Hastings Mutual Insurance Company
Michigan Commercial Insurance Mutual
MLBA Mutual Insurance Company
Sedgwick Claims Management Services, Inc.
Sompo Japan Insurance Company of America
TIG Specialty Insurance Solutions
The Travelers Companies, Inc.

Kluczynski, Girtz & Vogelzang, Grand Rapids, MI
(Continued)

Tribal First/Alliant Specialty Insurance Services, Inc.
Zurich Insurance Company
West Bend Mutual Insurance Company

Non-Insurance Clients

Alternative Service Concepts, LLC
CompOne Administrators, Inc.
DENSO Manufacturing
Mackinaw Administrators
Matrix Absence Management, Inc.
Meijer, GLLP
Michigan Municipal League
SPX Corporation
Alticor/Amway
Comprehensive Risk Management Services
Magna Corporation
Maxcis, Inc.
Michigan Automotive Compressor
Schwan's Sales Enterprises, Inc.
Trinity Health

Partners

Gilbert A. Girtz — 1940 — University of Minnesota, B.S., 1967; Detroit College of Law, J.D., 1973 — Admitted to Bar, 1973, Michigan — Member State Bar of Michigan — Practice Areas: Workers' Compensation — E-mail: ggirtz@kgvlaw.com

William Vogelzang, Jr. — 1947 — Calvin College, B.A., 1969; Valparaiso University, J.D., 1978 — Admitted to Bar, 1978, Michigan — Member State Bar of Michigan; Grand Rapids Bar Association — Practice Areas: Bodily Injury; General Liability; Product Liability; Subrogation — E-mail: wvogelzang@kgvlaw.com

Duncan A. McMillan — 1953 — University of Michigan, B.A., 1974; J.D., 1978 — Admitted to Bar, 1978, Michigan — Member State Bar of Michigan; Grand Rapids Bar Association — Practice Areas: Workers' Compensation — E-mail: dmcmillan@kgvlaw.com

Gregory J. Rapp — 1951 — Grand Valley State College, B.A., 1972; Wayne State University, J.D., 1975 — Admitted to Bar, 1975, Michigan — Member State Bar of Michigan — Practice Areas: Workers' Compensation — E-mail: grapp@kgvlaw.com

Richard Radke, Jr. — 1953 — Michigan State University, B.A., 1975; University of Detroit, J.D. (cum laude), 1978 — Admitted to Bar, 1978, Michigan — Member State Bar of Michigan; Grand Rapids Bar Association; Michigan Trial Lawyers Association — Practice Areas: Automobile Liability; General Liability; Premises Liability; Product Liability — E-mail: rradke@kgvlaw.com

Robert W. Steelman — 1950 — Michigan State University, B.A., 1972; Thomas M. Cooley Law School, J.D. (magna cum laude), 1985 — Admitted to Bar, 1985, Michigan — Member State Bar of Michigan — Practice Areas: Workers' Compensation — E-mail: rsteelman@kgvlaw.com

Allen J. Geurink — 1950 — Michigan State University, B.S., 1972; Thomas M. Cooley Law School, J.D. (cum laude), 1985 — Admitted to Bar, 1985, Michigan — Member State Bar of Michigan; Grand Rapids Bar Association — Practice Areas: Workers' Compensation — E-mail: ageurink@kgvlaw.com

James E. Stark, Jr. — 1955 — Grand Valley State College, B.S., 1979; Thomas M. Cooley Law School, J.D. (magna cum laude), 1987 — Admitted to Bar, 1988, Michigan — Member State Bar of Michigan — Practice Areas: Workers' Compensation — E-mail: jstark@kgvlaw.com

Michael J. Kosta — 1968 — Purdue University, B.A., 1991; Valparaiso University, J.D., 1994 — Admitted to Bar, 1994, Michigan — Practice Areas: Workers' Compensation — E-mail: mkosta@kgvlaw.com

Associates

Dennis P. Flynn — 1966 — University of Michigan, B.G.S., 1990; Detroit College of Law, J.D., 1994 — Admitted to Bar, 1994, Michigan — Member State Bar of Michigan; Grand Rapids Bar Association — Practice Areas: Workers' Compensation — E-mail: dflynn@kgvlaw.com

Mark T. Ostrowski — 1960 — Michigan State University, B.A., 1989; DePaul University College of Law, J.D., 1992 — Admitted to Bar, 1992, Illinois; 1994, Michigan — Practice Areas: Civil Litigation; Commercial Law — E-mail: mostrowski@kgvlaw.com

Kara T. Rozin — 1982 — Purdue University, B.S., 2004; Thomas M. Cooley Law School, J.D. (with honors), 2008 — Admitted to Bar, 2008, Michigan — Member State Bar of Michigan; Grand Rapids Bar Association; Young Lawyers Association; Women Lawyers Association of Michigan — Practice Areas: Civil Litigation; Commercial Law; Bodily Injury; General Liability; Product Liability; Subrogation — E-mail: krozin@kgvlaw.com

Stephen B. Wieber — 1966 — Embry-Riddle Aeronautical University, B.S. (magna cum laude), 1991; M.A.S., 1993; Thomas M. Cooley Law School, J.D. (cum laude), 2001 — Admitted to Bar, 2002, Michigan — Member American Bar Association; State Bar of Michigan — Staff Sgt., U.S. Air

HARRISVILLE   MICHIGAN

Kluczynski, Girtz & Vogelzang, Grand Rapids, MI *(Continued)*

Force, 1986-1993 — Practice Areas: Workers' Compensation — E-mail: swieber@kgvlaw.com

Secrest, Wardle, Lynch, Hampton, Truex and Morley, P.C.

2025 East Beltline SE, Suite 600
Grand Rapids, Michigan 49546
   Telephone: 616-285-0143
   Fax: 616-285-0145
   E-Mail: hemrich@secrestwardle.com
   www.secrestwardle.com

Appellate Practice, Commercial Law, Construction Law, Environmental Law, Fire, Property and Casualty, No-Fault, General Liability, Insurance Coverage, Premises Liability, Professional Liability, Employment, Governmental Litigation, Intellectual Property/Advertising Injury Malpractice, Municipal

Resident Partner

Henry S. Emrich

(See listing under Troy, MI for additional information)

Wheeler Upham
A Professional Corporation

Calder Plaza Building
250 Monroe Avenue N.W., Suite 100
Grand Rapids, Michigan 49503
   Telephone: 616-459-7100
   Fax: 616-459-6366
   www.wuattorneys.com

Established: 1883

First and Third Party Defense, Self-Insured Defense, Litigation, Insurance Law, Product Liability, Personal Injury Protection (PIP), No-Fault, Primary and Excess Insurance, Motor Vehicle, Trucking Law, Aviation, Railroad Law, Business Law, Contracts, Construction Law, Commercial Litigation, Premises Liability, Employment Law, Alternative Dispute Resolution, Agent and Brokers Errors and Omissions, Life Insurance, Appellate Practice, Environmental Liability

Insurance Clients

ACE USA/ESIS, Inc.	American Premier Underwriters, Inc.
Auto-Owners Insurance Company	
Bristol West Insurance Group	Canal Insurance Company
COUNTRY Insurance & Financial Services	Farm Bureau Insurance Company
	Farmers Insurance Group
Foremost Insurance Company	Great West Casualty Company
Metropolitan Life Insurance Company	Old Republic Insurance Company
	Penn-America Insurance Company
Progressive Michigan Insurance Company	Protective Insurance Company
	Prudential Insurance Company of America
Travelers Insurance Companies	
United America Indemnity Group	

Firm Members

John M. Roels — 1950 — University of Michigan Law School, J.D., 1975 — Admitted to Bar, 1976, Michigan — Member State Bar of Michigan; Grand Rapids Bar Association — E-mail: roels@wheelerupham.com

Gary A. Maximiuk — 1951 — University of Michigan - Ann Arbor, A.B., 1972; Wayne State University Law School, J.D., 1976 — Admitted to Bar, 1976, Michigan — Member State Bar of Michigan; Grand Rapids Bar Association; American Board of Trial Advocates — Contributing Author: "Michigan Insurance Law and Practice"; Co-Editor and Contributing Author: "A

Wheeler Upham, A Professional Corporation, Grand Rapids, MI *(Continued)*

Practical Guide to Depositions in Michigan" (1st and 2nd ed.) — E-mail: maximiuk@wheelerupham.com

James M. Shade — 1949 — University of Michigan, J.D. (cum laude), 1981 — Admitted to Bar, 1982, Michigan — Member State Bar of Michigan; Grand Rapids Bar Association — E-mail: shade@wheelerupham.com

Glenn L. Smith — 1963 — University of Michigan, B.A., 1985; J.D., 1989 — Admitted to Bar, 1989, Michigan — E-mail: smith@wheelerupham.com

Kenneth E. Tiews — 1948 — University of Michigan Law School, J.D., 1973 — Admitted to Bar, 1976, Michigan — Member American and Grand Rapids Bar Associations; State Bar of Michigan — E-mail: tiews@wheelerupham.com

Michael J. TerBeek — 1974 — University of Minnesota Law School, J.D. (cum laude), 2005 — Admitted to Bar, 2005, Michigan — Member State Bar of Michigan; Grand Rapids Bar Association

Jon J. Schrotenboer — 1956 — Hope College, B.A., 1979; Thomas M. Cooley Law School, J.D., 1982 — Admitted to Bar, 1982, Michigan

Catherine M. Sullivan — 1962 — The University of Toledo College of Law, J.D., 1987 — Admitted to Bar, 1987, Michigan — Member State Bar of Michigan; Grand Rapids Bar Association — E-mail: sullivan@wheelerupham.com

Kevin M. Keenan — 1967 — Thomas M. Cooley Law School, J.D., 2008 — Admitted to Bar, 2008, Michigan — Member American and Grand Rapids Bar Associations

Jonathan A. Fennell — 1973 — Calvin College, B.A., 1998; University of Notre Dame Law School, J.D., 2005 — Admitted to Bar, 2005, Michigan

The following firms also service this area.

Law Offices of Ward, Anderson, Porritt & Bryant, PLC
4190 Telegraph Road, Suite 2300
Bloomfield Hills, Michigan 48302
   Telephone: 248-593-1440
   Fax: 248-593-7920

Insurance Defense, Property and Casualty, Arson, Transportation, Liquor Liability, General Liability, Professional Malpractice, Errors and Omissions, Automobile, Product Liability, Discrimination, Coverage Issues, Truck Liability, Trucking Law

SEE COMPLETE LISTING UNDER BLOOMFIELD HILLS, MICHIGAN (148 MILES)

GRAYLING † 1,884 Crawford Co.

Refer To

Bensinger, Cotant & Menkes, P.C.
308 West Main Street
Gaylord, Michigan 49735
   Telephone: 989-732-7536
   Fax: 989-732-4922

General Defense, Automobile Liability, Fire Loss, Professional Liability, Product Liability, Workers' Compensation, Subrogation, Medical Malpractice, Liquor Liability

SEE COMPLETE LISTING UNDER GAYLORD, MICHIGAN (25 MILES)

HARRISVILLE † 493 Alcona Co.

Refer To

White and Wojda
313 N. Second Avenue
Alpena, Michigan 49707
   Telephone: 989-354-4104
   Fax: 989-356-0747

Casualty Defense, First and Third Party Defense, Insurance Defense, Legal Malpractice, Opinions, Personal Lines, Special Investigative Unit Claims, All Lines, Municipal Defense

SEE COMPLETE LISTING UNDER ALPENA, MICHIGAN (30 MILES)

MICHIGAN

HOUGHTON † 7,708 Houghton Co.

Refer To

Bensinger, Cotant & Menkes, P.C.
122 West Bluff Street
Marquette, Michigan 49855
  Telephone: 906-225-1000
  Fax: 906-225-0818

General Defense, Automobile Liability, Fire Loss, Professional Liability, Product Liability, Workers' Compensation, Subrogation, Medical Malpractice, Liquor Liability

SEE COMPLETE LISTING UNDER MARQUETTE, MICHIGAN (101 MILES)

HOWELL † 9,489 Livingston Co.

Refer To

Conlin, McKenney & Philbrick, P.C.
350 South Main Street, Suite 400
Ann Arbor, Michigan 48104-2131
  Telephone: 734-761-9000
  Fax: 734-761-9001

Insurance Defense, Construction Litigation, Automobile, Commercial Law, General Liability, Product Liability, Casualty, Professional Malpractice, Litigation, Construction Liability, Premises Liability, Highway Design, Coverage Questions

SEE COMPLETE LISTING UNDER ANN ARBOR, MICHIGAN (30 MILES)

IRON MOUNTAIN † 7,624 Dickinson Co.

Refer To

Bensinger, Cotant & Menkes, P.C.
122 West Bluff Street
Marquette, Michigan 49855
  Telephone: 906-225-1000
  Fax: 906-225-0818

General Defense, Automobile Liability, Fire Loss, Professional Liability, Product Liability, Workers' Compensation, Subrogation, Medical Malpractice, Liquor Liability

SEE COMPLETE LISTING UNDER MARQUETTE, MICHIGAN (81 MILES)

JACKSON † 33,534 Jackson Co.

Refer To

Conlin, McKenney & Philbrick, P.C.
350 South Main Street, Suite 400
Ann Arbor, Michigan 48104-2131
  Telephone: 734-761-9000
  Fax: 734-761-9001

Insurance Defense, Construction Litigation, Automobile, Commercial Law, General Liability, Product Liability, Casualty, Professional Malpractice, Litigation, Construction Liability, Premises Liability, Highway Design, Coverage Questions

SEE COMPLETE LISTING UNDER ANN ARBOR, MICHIGAN (35 MILES)

Refer To

Maddin, Hauser, Roth & Heller, P.C.
28400 Northwestern Highway, Second Floor
Southfield, Michigan 48034
  Telephone: 248-354-4030
  Fax: 248-359-6149

Mailing Address: P.O. Box 215, Southfield, MI 48037

Insurance Defense, Professional Liability (Non-Medical) Defense, Insurance Coverage, Legal Malpractice, Accountant Malpractice, Insurance Agents, Errors and Omissions, Directors and Officers Liability, Employment Practices Liability, Complex Litigation, Appellate Practice, Securities Litigation

SEE COMPLETE LISTING UNDER SOUTHFIELD, MICHIGAN (70 MILES)

KALAMAZOO † 74,262 Kalamazoo Co.

James, Dark & Brill

850 Comerica Building
151 South Rose Street
Kalamazoo, Michigan 49007-4777
  Telephone: 269-343-1338
  Fax: 269-343-3685

Insurance Defense, Casualty, Workers' Compensation, Fire, Trial Practice, Automobile Liability, No-Fault, Product Liability, Civil Rights, Liquor Liability

Insurance Clients

Auto Club Insurance Association
Farmers Insurance Group
Great American Insurance Company
Horace Mann Insurance Company
K & K Insurance Group, Inc.
MEEMIC Insurance Company
State Farm Fire and Casualty Company
United Fire & Casualty Company
Farm Bureau Insurance Company
Fireman's Fund Insurance Company
Hastings Mutual Insurance Company
League General Insurance Company
State Farm Insurance Company
Titan Insurance Company
Wolverine Mutual Insurance Company

Non-Insurance Clients

Marathon Oil Corporation
Ryder Truck Rental, Inc.
MLBA Limited Liability Pool
Speedway SuperAmerica, LLC

Partners

Richard M. James — (1915-1979)

J. William Dark — (1928-1991)

Arthur W. Brill — 1945 — Michigan State University, B.A., 1966; University of Wisconsin, J.D., 1969 — Admitted to Bar, 1969, Michigan — Member American and Kalamazoo County Bar Associations; State Bar of Michigan; Michigan Defense Trial Counsel — E-mail: awb@jdbrill.com

John C. Fish — 1953 — Michigan State University, B.A., 1975; Thomas M. Cooley Law School, J.D., 1978 — Admitted to Bar, 1978, Michigan — Member American and Kalamazoo County Bar Associations; State Bar of Michigan; Michigan Defense Trial Counsel — E-mail: jcf@jdbrill.com

David M. Dark — 1955 — Western Michigan University, B.B.A., 1979; Wayne State University, J.D., 1983 — Admitted to Bar, 1983, Michigan — Member American and Kalamazoo County Bar Associations; State Bar of Michigan — E-mail: dmd@jdbrill.com

Associates

Christopher N. Rork — 1969 — Western Michigan University, B.A., 1991; The University of Montana, J.D., 1998 — Admitted to Bar, 1998, Montana; 2003, Michigan; 1998, U.S. District Court, District of Montana; 2003, U.S. District Court, Western District of Michigan; 2003, U.S. Court of Appeals, Ninth Circuit — Member Kalamazoo County Bar Association; State Bar of Michigan; State Bar of Montana; Michigan Defense Trial Counsel — E-mail: cnr@jdbrill.com

Matthew L. Cooper — 1981 — Hope College, B.A. (cum laude), 2004; University of Detroit Mercy School of Law, J.D., 2008 — Admitted to Bar, 2008, Illinois; 2013, Michigan; U.S. District Court, Northern District of Illinois; 2014, U.S. District Court, Eastern and Western Districts of Michigan — Member Illinois State and Kalamazoo County Bar Associations; State Bar of Michigan — E-mail: mlc@jdbrill.com

Lennon, Miller, O'Connor & Bartosiewicz, PLC

900 Comerica Building
151 South Rose Street
Kalamazoo, Michigan 49007
  Telephone: 269-381-8844
  Fax: 269-381-8822
  E-Mail: gbartosiewicz@lennonmiller.com
  www.lennonmiller.com

Lennon, Miller, O'Connor & Bartosiewicz, PLC, Kalamazoo, MI (Continued)

Civil Trial Practice, State and Federal Courts, Insurance Defense, Reinsurance, Personal Injury, Real Property, Product Liability, Professional Liability, Environmental Law, Fidelity and Surety, Municipal Liability, Workers' Compensation, Coverage Opinions, Sports and Spectator Liability, Utility Liability, First and Third Party Auto Liability

Insurance Clients

Allied Insurance Company
Amerisure Insurance Company
Arch Insurance Group
Auto-Owners Insurance Company
The Cincinnati Insurance Companies
Employers Mutual Insurance Company
Federated Rural Electric Insurance Exchange
Great American Custom Insurance Services
Great West Casualty Company
Indiana Insurance Company
Kemper Insurance Companies
Lancer Claims Services, Inc.
Markel Insurance Company
The Medical Protective Company
Michigan Insurance Company
Michigan Millers Mutual Insurance Company
Pioneer State Mutual Insurance Company
Royal Specialty Underwriting, Inc.
Southern Michigan Insurance Company
Swiss Re
Tokio Marine & Nichido Fire Insurance Co., Ltd
U.S. Liability Insurance Company
Volunteer Adjustment Inc.
XL Select Professional
Zurich American Insurance Company
American Capitol Insurance Company
The ASU Group
Capitol Indemnity Corporation
Eagle Claims Management
Empire Fire and Marine Insurance Company
Farm Bureau Insurance Company
Fireman's Fund Insurance Company
Great Lakes Casualty Insurance Company
Hastings Mutual Insurance Company
K & K Insurance Group, Inc.
Liberty Mutual Insurance Company
Meadowbrook Claims Service
Michigan Basic Property Insurance Association
National Indemnity Company
Partners Mutual Insurance Company
Progressive Insurance Company
SECURA Insurance, A Mutual Company
State Farm Insurance Company
TIG Insurance Company
Travelers Insurance Companies
United Capitol Insurance Company
Utica Mutual Insurance Company
West Bend Mutual Insurance Company

Non-Insurance Clients

Crawford & Company
PFS - Premium Finance Corporation
Kalamazoo Metro Transit (KMetro)

Firm Members

Vincent T. Early — (1922-2001)

Gary P. Bartosiewicz — 1952 — University of Detroit; Western Michigan University, B.A., 1975; Wayne State University, J.D., 1978 — Admitted to Bar, 1978, Michigan; 1979, U.S. District Court, Eastern and Western Districts of Michigan; 1982, U.S. Court of Appeals, Sixth Circuit; 1982, U.S. Supreme Court — Member American (Litigation and Insurance Section) and Kalamazoo County (Past President) Bar Associations; State Bar of Michigan (Sections: Insurance and Indemnity Law, Labor and Employment Law, Alternative Dispute Resolution, Environmental Law and Litigation Law) — E-mail: gbartosiewicz@lennonmiller.com

Ron W. Kimbrel — 1954 — Western Michigan University, B.A., 1977; Thomas M. Cooley Law School, J.D., 1981 — Admitted to Bar, 1981, Michigan — Member American (Tort and Insurance Practice Section) and Kalamazoo County Bar Associations; State Bar of Michigan (Negligence Law Section) — E-mail: rkimbrel@lennonmiller.com

Christopher D. Morris — 1957 — Kalamazoo College, B.A., 1979; Thomas M. Cooley Law School, J.D., 1983 — Admitted to Bar, 1984, Michigan; 2004, Indiana — Member American, Indiana State and Kalamazoo County Bar Associations; State Bar of Michigan (Workers' Compensation Section); Association of Defense Trial Counsel — Special Assistant to the Attorney General — E-mail: cmorris@lennonmiller.com

Tyren R. Cudney — 1957 — Western Michigan University, B.B.A., 1988; Thomas M. Cooley Law School, J.D. (cum laude), 1991 — Admitted to Bar, 1991, Michigan — Member American (General Practice, Solo and Small Firm Sections) and Kalamazoo County Bar Associations; State Bar of Michigan (General Practice Section); Michigan Defense Trial Counsel — E-mail: tcudney@lennonmiller.com

Lennon, Miller, O'Connor & Bartosiewicz, PLC, Kalamazoo, MI (Continued)

William R. Bates — 1962 — Spring Arbor College, B.A. (with high honors), 1985; Valparaiso University School of Law, J.D., 1988 — Admitted to Bar, 1988, Indiana; 1990, Michigan; 1988, U.S. District Court, Northern and Southern Districts of Indiana; 1990, U.S. District Court, Western District of Michigan — Member American and Kalamazoo County Bar Associations; State Bar of Michigan — E-mail: wbates@lennonmiller.com

Ryan M. Opria — 1972 — Yale University, B.A., 1994; University of Michigan Law School, J.D., 1997 — Admitted to Bar, 1997, Illinois; 2006, Connecticut; 2007, Michigan; 1997, U.S. District Court, Northern District of Illinois; 2001, U.S. Court of Appeals, Ninth Circuit; 2007, U.S. District Court, Western District of Michigan — Member Illinois State and Kalamazoo County Bar Associations — E-mail: ropria@lennonmiller.com

Zachary M. Zurek — 1986 — Michigan State University, B.A., 2009; University of Michigan Law School, J.D., 2012 — Admitted to Bar, 2013, Michigan; U.S. District Court, Western District of Michigan — Member State Bar of Michigan; Kalamazoo County Bar Association — Practice Areas: Insurance Defense — E-mail: zzurek@lennonmiller.com

George H. Lennon, III
Andrew J. Vorbrich
Robert M. Taylor
Michael D. O'Connor
Gordon C. Miller
Gail M. Towne

Of Counsel

David S. York — 1939 — Wayne State University, B.S., 1962; J.D., 1969 — Admitted to Bar, 1969, Michigan; 1972, U.S. District Court, Western District of Michigan; 1993, U.S. Court of Appeals, Sixth Circuit — Member State Bar of Michigan; Kalamazoo County Bar Association; Greater Kalamazoo Insurance Agents Association; Michigan Defense Trial Counsel — E-mail: dyork@lennonmiller.com

Harold E. Fischer, Jr.
John T. Peters, Jr.

The following firms also service this area.

Kluczynski, Girtz & Vogelzang
5005 Cascade Road SE, Suite A
Grand Rapids, Michigan 49546
Telephone: 616-459-0556
Fax: 616-459-5829

Insurance Defense, Automobile, Fire, Casualty, General Liability, Product Liability, Workers' Compensation, Subrogation, Environmental Law, Occupational Disease

SEE COMPLETE LISTING UNDER GRAND RAPIDS, MICHIGAN (55 MILES)

KALKASKA † 2,020 Kalkaska Co.

Refer To

Bensinger, Cotant & Menkes, P.C.
308 West Main Street
Gaylord, Michigan 49735
Telephone: 989-732-7536
Fax: 989-732-4922

General Defense, Automobile Liability, Fire Loss, Professional Liability, Product Liability, Workers' Compensation, Subrogation, Medical Malpractice, Liquor Liability

SEE COMPLETE LISTING UNDER GAYLORD, MICHIGAN (40 MILES)

L'ANSE † 2,107 Baraga Co.

Refer To

Bensinger, Cotant & Menkes, P.C.
122 West Bluff Street
Marquette, Michigan 49855
Telephone: 906-225-1000
Fax: 906-225-0818

General Defense, Automobile Liability, Fire Loss, Professional Liability, Product Liability, Workers' Compensation, Subrogation, Medical Malpractice, Liquor Liability

SEE COMPLETE LISTING UNDER MARQUETTE, MICHIGAN (68 MILES)

MICHIGAN

LANSING 114,297 Ingham Co.

Dickinson Wright PLLC

215 South Washington Square, Suite 200
Lansing, Michigan 48933-1816
  Telephone: 517-371-1730
  Fax: 517-487-4700
  E-Mail: Fortiz@dickinsonwright.com
  www.dickinson-wright.com

(Detroit, MI Office*: 500 Woodward Avenue, Suite 4000, 48226-3425)
  (Tel: 313-223-3500)
  (Fax: 313-223-3598)
  (www.dickinsonwright.com)
(Ann Arbor, MI Office*: 350 South Main Street, Suite 300, 48104)
  (Tel: 734-623-7075)
  (Fax: 734-623-1625)
(Nashville, TN Office*: 424 Church Street, Suite 1401, 37219)
  (Tel: 615-244-6538)
  (Fax: 615-256-8386)
(Phoenix, AZ Office*: 1850 North Central Avenue, Suite 1400, 85004)
  (Tel: 602-285-5000)
  (Fax: 602-285-5100)
(Troy, MI Office*: 2600 West Big Beaver Road, Suite 300, 48084-3312)
  (Tel: 248-433-7200)
  (Fax: 248-433-7274)

Disability, Life Insurance, Medical Malpractice, Health Care, Coverage Issues, Personal Injury, Commercial Litigation, Employment Litigation, ERISA, Accountant Malpractice, Construction Litigation, Directors and Officers Liability

Firm Profile: Dickinson Wright has long been a preferred provider of sophisticated, cost-effective legal services to insurers in the life, health, disability, property, casualty, and alternative insurance (self-insured programs, risk pools, and captives) fields. Our insurance team also represents governmental entities, captive insurers and assigned-risk pools.

Firm Members

James E. Lozier — Fordham Law School, J.D., 1975 — Admitted to Bar, 1975, Michigan; U.S. District Court, Central District of Illinois; U.S. District Court, Eastern and Western Districts of Michigan; U.S. District Court, Northern and Southern Districts of Iowa; U.S. Court of Appeals, Sixth Circuit — Practice Areas: Coverage Issues; Commercial Litigation; Board of Directors Liability — Tel: 517-487-4775 — E-mail: jlozier@dickinsonwright.com

Scott R. Knapp — Temple University School of Law, J.D., 1995 — Admitted to Bar, 2000, Michigan; U.S. District Court, Eastern and Western Districts of Michigan; U.S. District Court, Eastern District of Pennsylvania; U.S. District Court, Northern District of Illinois; U.S. District Court, District of New Jersey — Practice Areas: Coverage; Commercial Litigation; Disability — Tel: 517-487-4762 — E-mail: sknapp@dickinsonwright.com

(See listing under Detroit, MI for additional information)

Foster Swift Collins & Smith, P.C.

313 South Washington Square
Lansing, Michigan 48933
  Telephone: 517-371-8100
  Fax: 517-371-8200
  E-Mail: info@fosterswift.com
  www.fosterswift.com

(Farmington Hills, MI Office: 32300 Northwestern Highway, Suite 230, 48334)
  (Tel: 248-539-9900)
  (Fax: 248-851-7504)

LANSING

Foster Swift Collins & Smith, P.C., Lansing, MI
(Continued)

(Grand Rapids, MI Office: 1700 East Beltline, N.E., Suite 200, 49525-2076)
  (Tel: 616-726-2200)
  (Fax: 616-726-2299)
(Detroit, MI Office: 333 West Fort Street, 48226)
  (Tel: 248-539-9900)
  (Fax: 248-851-7504)

Established: 1902

Administrative Law, Alternative Dispute Resolution, Appellate Practice, Class Actions, Commercial Litigation, Construction Litigation, Corporate Law, Employee Benefits, Energy, Governmental Liability, Health Care, Insurance Defense, Insurance Regulation, Intellectual Property, Labor and Employment, Litigation, Mass Tort, Medical Malpractice, Mergers and Acquisitions, Municipal Law, Oil and Gas, Subrogation, Transportation, Workers' Compensation, Construction, Environmental

Firm Profile: Foster Swift's reputation is built on ageless values including ethics, integrity and exemplary attention to client service. That reputation speaks for itself and is valued by clients and attorneys in other firms who use the depth, experience, and resources of Foster Swift to enhance their own service to clients. We are often selected as local counsel or Michigan counsel for national and international clients, as well as businesses and individuals throughout Michigan needing representation.

Insurance Clients

Farm Bureau Insurance Company
Jackson National Life Insurance Company
Midwest Claims Service
SECURA Insurance Companies
Gallagher Bassett Insurance Company
Michigan Millers Mutual Insurance Company

Members

Scott L. Mandel — Michigan State University, B.A. (with high honors), 1978; Wayne State University, J.D. (cum laude), 1981 — Admitted to Bar, 1981, Michigan; U.S. District Court, Eastern and Western Districts of Michigan; U.S. Court of Appeals, Sixth Circuit

Thomas R. Meagher — Michigan State University, B.A. (with high honors), 1978; American Graduate School of International Management, M.I.M., 1989; Wayne State University, J.D. (magna cum laude), 1981 — Admitted to Bar, 1981, Michigan; U.S. District Court, Eastern and Western Districts of Michigan; U.S. Court of Appeals, Sixth Circuit — Member American Judicature Society; Michigan Defense Trial Counsel

Paul J. Millenbach — Northern Michigan University, B.S., 1984; Thomas M. Cooley Law School, J.D., 1989 — Admitted to Bar, 1989, Michigan; U.S. District Court, Eastern District of Michigan — Member State Bar of Michigan (Negligence Section); Transportation Lawyers Association — Resident Farmington Hills, MI Office

John P. Nicolucci — Purdue University, B.S., 1986; Indiana University School of Law, J.D., 1993 — Admitted to Bar, 1993, Michigan; U.S. District Court, Eastern and Western Districts of Michigan; U.S. Court of Appeals, Sixth Circuit — Member Ingham County Bar Association (Chair, Litigation Section, 1999-2000)

Michael D. Sanders — University of Illinois, B.A. (magna cum laude), 1980; J.D., 1983 — Admitted to Bar, 1983, Michigan; Illinois; U.S. District Court, Eastern and Western Districts of Michigan

Webb A. Smith — Michigan State University, B.A., 1960; University of Michigan, LL.B., 1963 — Admitted to Bar, 1963, Michigan; U.S. District Court, Eastern and Western Districts of Michigan; U.S. Court of Appeals, Sixth Circuit; U.S. Supreme Court — Member Michigan Defense Trial Counsel (Director, 1985-1989); Fellow, Michigan State Bar Foundation; Association of Insurance Attorneys; Defense Research Institute; Fellow, American Bar Foundation — Steering Committee and Faculty, U.S. District Court, Western District of Michigan, Hillman Advocacy Institute, 1988-2001

Scott A. Storey — University of Michigan, B.G.S. (with honors), 1976; Washington and Lee University, J.D., 1979 — Executive Editor, Washington and Lee University Law Review — Admitted to Bar, 1979, Michigan; U.S. District Court, Eastern and Western Districts of Michigan; U.S. Court of Appeals, Sixth Circuit; U.S. Supreme Court; U.S. Bankruptcy Court, Western District of Arkansas — Member Ingham County Bar Association (Board of

Foster Swift Collins & Smith, P.C., Lansing, MI (Continued)

Directors, 1998-2001); Defense Research Institute — Representative Assembly, State Bar of Michigan (1986-1993)

Julie I. Fershtman — Emory University, B.A., 1983; Emory University School of Law, J.D., 1986 — Admitted to Bar, 1986, Michigan; U.S. District Court, Eastern and Western Districts of Michigan; U.S. District Court, Northern District of Illinois; U.S. District Court, Western District of Missouri; U.S. Court of Appeals, Sixth Circuit — Member American and Oakland County Bar Associations; State Bar of Michigan; Fellow, American Bar Foundation; Michigan Defense Trial Counsel — Resident Farmington Hills, MI Office

Bruce A. Vande Vusse — Calvin College, B.A., 1970; University of Detroit, J.D., 1977 — Admitted to Bar, 1978, Michigan — Member American Bar Association; State Bar of Michigan; Association of Defense Trial Counsel — Resident Farmington Hills, MI Office

Pamela C. Dausman — Michigan State University, B.A. (with high honors), 1999; Detroit College of Law, Michigan State University, J.D. (magna cum laude), 2002 — Admitted to Bar, 2002, Michigan; U.S. District Court, Western District of Michigan; U.S. Court of Appeals, Sixth Circuit — Member American and Ingham County Bar Associations; State Bar of Michigan

Thomas R. TerMaat — Hope College, B.A. (cum laude), 1990; Indiana University School of Law-Bloomington, J.D., 1994 — Admitted to Bar, 1994, Michigan; U.S. District Court, Western District of Michigan; U.S. District Court, Northern District of Indiana — Member State Bar of Michigan; Grand Rapids Bar Association — Resident Grand Rapids, MI Office

Mark J. Colon — University of Notre Dame, B.A., 1985; Valparaiso University, J.D., 1988 — Admitted to Bar, 1988, Michigan; U.S. District Court, Eastern and Western Districts of Michigan — Member Federal, American and Grand Rapids Bar Associations; State Bar of Michigan — Resident Grand Rapids, MI Office

Joseph E. Kozely, Jr. — University of Detroit, B.A. (cum laude), 1968; Wayne State University Law School, J.D. (cum laude), 1981 — Admitted to Bar, 1981, Michigan — Member American and Oakland County Bar Associations; State Bar of Michigan — Resident Farmington Hills, MI Office

Garan Lucow Miller, P.C.

Office Park West
504 South Creyts Road, Suite A
Lansing, Michigan 48917-8265
　Telephone: 517-327-0300
　Fax: 517-327-0309
　Toll Free: 888-910-0300
　24 Hour Toll Free: 888-332-0540
　www.garanlucow.com

(Additional Offices: Detroit, MI*; Ann Arbor, MI*; Grand Blanc, MI*(See Flint listing); Grand Rapids, MI*; Marquette, MI*; Port Huron, MI*; Traverse City, MI*; Troy, MI*; Merrillville, IN*)

Business Law, Construction Litigation, Employment Law, Municipal Liability, No-Fault, Workers' Compensation, Insurance Defense

(See listing under Detroit, MI for additional information)

Murphy & Spagnuolo, P.C.

4572 South Hagadorn Road, Suite 1A
East Lansing, Michigan 48823
　Telephone: 517-351-2020
　Fax: 517-351-4420
　E-Mail: kmaddox@mbspclaw.com
　www.mbspclaw.com

Accident, Casualty, Premises Liability, Product Liability, Liquor Liability, Coverage

Firm Profile: Murphy & Spagnuolo, P.C. represents leading insurance companies, third party administrators and self-insured corporations throughout Michigan in all areas of insurance litigation. We provide quality results in mediations, trials and appeals for clients requiring experience, superior credentials and commitment to claim completion.

Murphy & Spagnuolo, P.C., Lansing, MI (Continued)

Insurance Clients

American International Group, Inc.
Capitol Indemnity Corporation
Employers Casualty Company
Employers Mutual Casualty Company
Michigan Transit Insurance Pool
Sentry Insurance a Mutual Company
Auto-Owners Insurance Company
CIGNA Group
Employers Insurance Company of Wausau
The Hartford Insurance Group
Prudential Insurance Company of America
Zurich American Insurance Company

Non-Insurance Clients

American Home Products, Inc.
FASCO, DC Motors Division
Armour Swift-Eckrich
Michigan Education Association

Partners

Alphonsus C. Murphy — University of Michigan, A.B., 1951; M.B.A., 1952; University of Wisconsin, LL.B., 1961 — Admitted to Bar, 1961, Wisconsin; 1969, Michigan; 1974, U.S. Court of Appeals for the District of Columbia Circuit; U.S. Supreme Court — Member State Bar of Michigan; State Bar of Wisconsin — Practice Areas: Insurance Defense

Vincent P. Spagnuolo — Michigan State University, B.A. (with high honors), 1976; Thomas M. Cooley Law School, J.D., 1979 — Admitted to Bar, 1979, Michigan; 1980, U.S. District Court, Western District of Michigan; 1983, U.S. District Court, Eastern District of Michigan; U.S. Supreme Court — Member American Bar Association (Insurance Practice Section); State Bar of Michigan (Negligence Section); Ingham County Bar Association (Negligence and Tort Sections); Defense Research Institute — Practice Areas: Insurance Defense

Senior Attorneys

Gary L. Bender — Central Michigan University, B.S., 1975; Thomas M. Cooley Law School, J.D., 1980 — Admitted to Bar, 1980, Michigan; 1993, District of Columbia — Member State Bar of Michigan; District of Columbia Bar — Practice Areas: Copyright and Trademark Law; Corporate Law; Litigation

Richard A. Cascarilla — Grand Valley State College, B.S., 1976; Thomas M. Cooley Law School, J.D., 1980 — Admitted to Bar, 1982, Michigan; 1981, U.S. District Court, Eastern and Western Districts of Michigan; 1984, U.S. Court of Appeals, Sixth Circuit; 1988, Supreme Court of Michigan — Member State Bar of Michigan — Circuit Court Mediator, 1997 — Practice Areas: Corporate Law; Liquor Liability; Litigation

Associate

Lindsay N. Dangl

Secrest, Wardle, Lynch, Hampton, Truex and Morley, P.C.

6639 Centurion Drive, Suite 100
Lansing, Michigan 48917
　Telephone: 517-886-1224
　Fax: 517-886-9284
　E-Mail: jbradley@secrestwardle.com
　www.secrestwardle.com

Appellate Practice, Commercial Law, Construction Law, Environmental Law, Fire, Property and Casualty, No-Fault, General Liability, Insurance Coverage, Premises Liability, Professional Liability, Employment, Governmental Litigation, Intellectual Property/Advertising Injury Malpractice, Municipal

Resident Partner

James R. Bradley

(See listing under Troy, MI for additional information)

MICHIGAN

The following firms also service this area.

Kluczynski, Girtz & Vogelzang
5005 Cascade Road SE, Suite A
Grand Rapids, Michigan 49546
Telephone: 616-459-0556
Fax: 616-459-5829

Insurance Defense, Automobile, Fire, Casualty, General Liability, Product Liability, Workers' Compensation, Subrogation, Environmental Law, Occupational Disease

SEE COMPLETE LISTING UNDER GRAND RAPIDS, MICHIGAN (65 MILES)

Maddin, Hauser, Roth & Heller, P.C.
28400 Northwestern Highway, Second Floor
Southfield, Michigan 48034
Telephone: 248-354-4030
Fax: 248-359-6149
Mailing Address: P.O. Box 215, Southfield, MI 48037

Insurance Defense, Professional Liability (Non-Medical) Defense, Insurance Coverage, Legal Malpractice, Accountant Malpractice, Insurance Agents, Errors and Omissions, Directors and Officers Liability, Employment Practices Liability, Complex Litigation, Appellate Practice, Securities Litigation

SEE COMPLETE LISTING UNDER SOUTHFIELD, MICHIGAN (71 MILES)

Law Offices of Ward, Anderson, Porritt & Bryant, PLC
4190 Telegraph Road, Suite 2300
Bloomfield Hills, Michigan 48302
Telephone: 248-593-1440
Fax: 248-593-7920

Insurance Defense, Property and Casualty, Arson, Transportation, Liquor Liability, General Liability, Professional Malpractice, Errors and Omissions, Automobile, Product Liability, Discrimination, Coverage Issues, Truck Liability, Trucking Law

SEE COMPLETE LISTING UNDER BLOOMFIELD HILLS, MICHIGAN (81 MILES)

MARQUETTE † 21,355 Marquette Co.

Bensinger, Cotant & Menkes, P.C.
122 West Bluff Street
Marquette, Michigan 49855
Telephone: 906-225-1000
Fax: 906-225-0818
www.bcma.net

(Gaylord, MI Office*: 308 West Main Street, 49735)
(Tel: 989-732-7536)
(Fax: 989-732-4922)

General Defense, Automobile Liability, Fire Loss, Professional Liability, Product Liability, Workers' Compensation, Subrogation, Medical Malpractice, Liquor Liability

Firm Members

Gregory A. Elzinga — 1952 — Central Michigan University, B.S., 1975; Thomas M. Cooley Law School, J.D., 1979 — Admitted to Bar, 1979, Michigan — Member American and Marquette County Bar Associations; State Bar of Michigan; Michigan Defense Trial Counsel Northern Representative; Blue Goose Insurance Organization (U.P. Puddle); Michigan Trial Lawyers Association; Defense Research Institute — Listed in the Bar Register of Preeminent Lawyers — Practice Areas: Medical Malpractice; Premises Liability — E-mail: gelzinga@bcma.net

William J. Maynard — 1961 — Central Michigan University, B.S. (magna cum laude), 1983; The University of Toledo College of Law, J.D., 1986 — Admitted to Bar, 1986, Michigan — Member American and Marquette County Bar Associations; State Bar of Michigan; Blue Goose Insurance Organization (U.P. Puddle); Michigan Defense Trial Counsel; International Association of Arson Investigators; Defense Research Institute — Listed in the Bar Register of Preeminent Lawyers — Practice Areas: Premises Liability; Product Liability — E-mail: wmaynard@bcma.net

Glenn W. Smith — 1956 — Michigan Technological University, B.S., 1978; Pepperdine University, 1982; Loyola University of Los Angeles, J.D.,

MARQUETTE

Bensinger, Cotant & Menkes, P.C., Marquette, MI
(Continued)

1989 — Admitted to Bar, 1989, Michigan — Member American and Marquette County Bar Associations; State Bar of Michigan; American Society of Mechanical Engineers — Listed in the Bar Register of Preeminent Lawyers — Practice Areas: Product Liability — E-mail: gws@bcma.net

Roger W. Zappa — 1959 — Michigan Technological University, B.S. (summa cum laude), 1981; University of Michigan, J.D., 1984 — Admitted to Bar, 1984, Michigan — Member State Bar of Michigan; Marquette County Bar Association; Bar of the 6th Circuit Court of Appeals — Listed in the Bar Register of Preeminent Lawyers — Practice Areas: Premises Liability; Estate Planning — E-mail: rzappa@bcma.net

(See listing under Gaylord, MI for additional information)

Garan Lucow Miller, P.C.
1440 West Ridge Street
Marquette, Michigan 49855-3199
Telephone: 906-226-2524
Fax: 906-226-3068
Toll Free: 888-841-7772
www.garanlucow.com
24 Hour Toll Free: 888-332-0540

(Additional Offices: Detroit, MI*; Ann Arbor, MI*; Grand Blanc, MI*(See Flint listing); Grand Rapids, MI*; Lansing, MI*; Port Huron, MI*; Traverse City, MI*; Troy, MI*; Merrillville, IN*)

Business Law, Employment Law, Insurance Defense, Municipal Liability, No-Fault, Workers' Compensation

(See listing under Detroit, MI for additional information)

MENOMINEE † 8,599 Menominee Co.

Refer To
Bensinger, Cotant & Menkes, P.C.
122 West Bluff Street
Marquette, Michigan 49855
Telephone: 906-225-1000
Fax: 906-225-0818

General Defense, Automobile Liability, Fire Loss, Professional Liability, Product Liability, Workers' Compensation, Subrogation, Medical Malpractice, Liquor Liability

SEE COMPLETE LISTING UNDER MARQUETTE, MICHIGAN (119 MILES)

MONROE † 20,733 Monroe Co.

Refer To
Conlin, McKenney & Philbrick, P.C.
350 South Main Street, Suite 400
Ann Arbor, Michigan 48104-2131
Telephone: 734-761-9000
Fax: 734-761-9001

Insurance Defense, Construction Litigation, Automobile, Commercial Law, General Liability, Product Liability, Casualty, Professional Malpractice, Litigation, Construction Liability, Premises Liability, Highway Design, Coverage Questions

SEE COMPLETE LISTING UNDER ANN ARBOR, MICHIGAN (40 MILES)

Refer To
Law Offices of Ward, Anderson, Porritt & Bryant, PLC
4190 Telegraph Road, Suite 2300
Bloomfield Hills, Michigan 48302
Telephone: 248-593-1440
Fax: 248-593-7920

Insurance Defense, Property and Casualty, Arson, Transportation, Liquor Liability, General Liability, Professional Malpractice, Errors and Omissions, Automobile, Product Liability, Discrimination, Coverage Issues, Truck Liability, Trucking Law

SEE COMPLETE LISTING UNDER BLOOMFIELD HILLS, MICHIGAN (45 MILES)

PONTIAC   MICHIGAN

MOUNT CLEMENS † 16,314 Macomb Co.

Refer To

Maddin, Hauser, Roth & Heller, P.C.
28400 Northwestern Highway, Second Floor
Southfield, Michigan 48034
   Telephone: 248-354-4030
   Fax: 248-359-6149

Mailing Address: P.O. Box 215, Southfield, MI 48037

Insurance Defense, Professional Liability (Non-Medical) Defense, Insurance Coverage, Legal Malpractice, Accountant Malpractice, Insurance Agents, Errors and Omissions, Directors and Officers Liability, Employment Practices Liability, Complex Litigation, Appellate Practice, Securities Litigation

SEE COMPLETE LISTING UNDER SOUTHFIELD, MICHIGAN (28 MILES)

Refer To

Siemion Huckabay, P.C.
One Towne Square, Suite 1400
Southfield, Michigan 48076
   Telephone: 248-357-1400
   Fax: 248-357-3343

Mailing Address: P.O. Box 5068, Southfield, MI 48086-5068

Insurance Defense, Automobile, General Liability, Legal Malpractice, Medical Malpractice, Product Liability, Errors and Omissions, Trial Practice, Appellate Practice, Asbestos Litigation, Aviation, Workers' Compensation, Securities Litigation

SEE COMPLETE LISTING UNDER SOUTHFIELD, MICHIGAN (28 MILES)

Refer To

Law Offices of Ward, Anderson, Porritt & Bryant, PLC
4190 Telegraph Road, Suite 2300
Bloomfield Hills, Michigan 48302
   Telephone: 248-593-1440
   Fax: 248-593-7920

Insurance Defense, Property and Casualty, Arson, Transportation, Liquor Liability, General Liability, Professional Malpractice, Errors and Omissions, Automobile, Product Liability, Discrimination, Coverage Issues, Truck Liability, Trucking Law

SEE COMPLETE LISTING UNDER BLOOMFIELD HILLS, MICHIGAN (20 MILES)

MUSKEGON † 38,401 Muskegon Co.

Refer To

Kluczynski, Girtz & Vogelzang
5005 Cascade Road SE, Suite A
Grand Rapids, Michigan 49546
   Telephone: 616-459-0556
   Fax: 616-459-5829

Insurance Defense, Automobile, Fire, Casualty, General Liability, Product Liability, Workers' Compensation, Subrogation, Environmental Law, Occupational Disease

SEE COMPLETE LISTING UNDER GRAND RAPIDS, MICHIGAN (45 MILES)

NEWBERRY † 1,519 Luce Co.

Refer To

Bensinger, Cotant & Menkes, P.C.
122 West Bluff Street
Marquette, Michigan 49855
   Telephone: 906-225-1000
   Fax: 906-225-0818

General Defense, Automobile Liability, Fire Loss, Professional Liability, Product Liability, Workers' Compensation, Subrogation, Medical Malpractice, Liquor Liability

SEE COMPLETE LISTING UNDER MARQUETTE, MICHIGAN (108 MILES)

ONTONAGON † 1,494 Ontonagon Co.

Refer To

Bensinger, Cotant & Menkes, P.C.
122 West Bluff Street
Marquette, Michigan 49855
   Telephone: 906-225-1000
   Fax: 906-225-0818

General Defense, Automobile Liability, Fire Loss, Professional Liability, Product Liability, Workers' Compensation, Subrogation, Medical Malpractice, Liquor Liability

SEE COMPLETE LISTING UNDER MARQUETTE, MICHIGAN (115 MILES)

PETOSKEY † 5,670 Emmet Co.

Refer To

Bensinger, Cotant & Menkes, P.C.
308 West Main Street
Gaylord, Michigan 49735
   Telephone: 989-732-7536
   Fax: 989-732-4922

General Defense, Automobile Liability, Fire Loss, Professional Liability, Product Liability, Workers' Compensation, Subrogation, Medical Malpractice, Liquor Liability

SEE COMPLETE LISTING UNDER GAYLORD, MICHIGAN (35 MILES)

PONTIAC † 59,515 Oakland Co.

Refer To

Maddin, Hauser, Roth & Heller, P.C.
28400 Northwestern Highway, Second Floor
Southfield, Michigan 48034
   Telephone: 248-354-4030
   Fax: 248-359-6149

Mailing Address: P.O. Box 215, Southfield, MI 48037

Insurance Defense, Professional Liability (Non-Medical) Defense, Insurance Coverage, Legal Malpractice, Accountant Malpractice, Insurance Agents, Errors and Omissions, Directors and Officers Liability, Employment Practices Liability, Complex Litigation, Appellate Practice, Securities Litigation

SEE COMPLETE LISTING UNDER SOUTHFIELD, MICHIGAN (12 MILES)

Refer To

Siemion Huckabay, P.C.
One Towne Square, Suite 1400
Southfield, Michigan 48076
   Telephone: 248-357-1400
   Fax: 248-357-3343

Mailing Address: P.O. Box 5068, Southfield, MI 48086-5068

Insurance Defense, Automobile, General Liability, Legal Malpractice, Medical Malpractice, Product Liability, Errors and Omissions, Trial Practice, Appellate Practice, Asbestos Litigation, Aviation, Workers' Compensation, Securities Litigation

SEE COMPLETE LISTING UNDER SOUTHFIELD, MICHIGAN (12 MILES)

Refer To

Law Offices of Ward, Anderson, Porritt & Bryant, PLC
4190 Telegraph Road, Suite 2300
Bloomfield Hills, Michigan 48302
   Telephone: 248-593-1440
   Fax: 248-593-7920

Insurance Defense, Property and Casualty, Arson, Transportation, Liquor Liability, General Liability, Professional Malpractice, Errors and Omissions, Automobile, Product Liability, Discrimination, Coverage Issues, Truck Liability, Trucking Law

SEE COMPLETE LISTING UNDER BLOOMFIELD HILLS, MICHIGAN (5 MILES)

MICHIGAN   PORT HURON

PORT HURON † 30,184 St. Clair Co.

Garan Lucow Miller, P.C.
Port Huron Office Center
511 Fort Street, Suite 505
Port Huron, Michigan 48060-3922
    Telephone: 810-985-4400
    Fax: 810-985-4107
    Toll Free: 800-875-4400
    24 Hour Toll Free: 888-332-0540
    www.garanlucow.com

(Additional Offices: Detroit, MI*; Ann Arbor, MI*; Grand Blanc, MI*(See Flint listing); Grand Rapids, MI*; Lansing, MI*; Marquette, MI*; Traverse City, MI*; Troy, MI*; Merrillville, IN*)

Business Law, Employment Law, ERISA, Insurance Defense, Municipal Liability, No-Fault, Workers' Compensation

(See listing under Detroit, MI for additional information)

The following firms also service this area.

Law Offices of Ward, Anderson, Porritt & Bryant, PLC
4190 Telegraph Road, Suite 2300
Bloomfield Hills, Michigan 48302
    Telephone: 248-593-1440
    Fax: 248-593-7920

Insurance Defense, Property and Casualty, Arson, Transportation, Liquor Liability, General Liability, Professional Malpractice, Errors and Omissions, Automobile, Product Liability, Discrimination, Coverage Issues, Truck Liability, Trucking Law

SEE COMPLETE LISTING UNDER BLOOMFIELD HILLS, MICHIGAN (61 MILES)

ROGERS CITY † 2,827 Presque Isle Co.

Refer To
Bensinger, Cotant & Menkes, P.C.
308 West Main Street
Gaylord, Michigan 49735
    Telephone: 989-732-7536
    Fax: 989-732-4922

General Defense, Automobile Liability, Fire Loss, Professional Liability, Product Liability, Workers' Compensation, Subrogation, Medical Malpractice, Liquor Liability

SEE COMPLETE LISTING UNDER GAYLORD, MICHIGAN (65 MILES)

Refer To
White and Wojda
313 N. Second Avenue
Alpena, Michigan 49707
    Telephone: 989-354-4104
    Fax: 989-356-0747

Casualty Defense, First and Third Party Defense, Insurance Defense, Legal Malpractice, Opinions, Personal Lines, Special Investigative Unit Claims, All Lines, Municipal Defense

SEE COMPLETE LISTING UNDER ALPENA, MICHIGAN (35 MILES)

ROSCOMMON † 1,075 Roscommon Co.

Refer To
Bensinger, Cotant & Menkes, P.C.
308 West Main Street
Gaylord, Michigan 49735
    Telephone: 989-732-7536
    Fax: 989-732-4922

General Defense, Automobile Liability, Fire Loss, Professional Liability, Product Liability, Workers' Compensation, Subrogation, Medical Malpractice, Liquor Liability

SEE COMPLETE LISTING UNDER GAYLORD, MICHIGAN (40 MILES)

SAULT STE. MARIE † 14,144 Chippewa Co.

Refer To
Bensinger, Cotant & Menkes, P.C.
308 West Main Street
Gaylord, Michigan 49735
    Telephone: 989-732-7536
    Fax: 989-732-4922

General Defense, Automobile Liability, Fire Loss, Professional Liability, Product Liability, Workers' Compensation, Subrogation, Medical Malpractice, Liquor Liability

SEE COMPLETE LISTING UNDER GAYLORD, MICHIGAN (115 MILES)

Refer To
White and Wojda
313 N. Second Avenue
Alpena, Michigan 49707
    Telephone: 989-354-4104
    Fax: 989-356-0747

Casualty Defense, First and Third Party Defense, Insurance Defense, Legal Malpractice, Opinions, Personal Lines, Special Investigative Unit Claims, All Lines, Municipal Defense

SEE COMPLETE LISTING UNDER ALPENA, MICHIGAN (152 MILES)

SOUTHFIELD 71,739 Oakland Co.

Collins Einhorn Farrell PC
4000 Town Center, Suite 909
Southfield, Michigan 48075
    Telephone: 248-355-4141
    Fax: 248-355-2277
    E-Mail: collins.einhorn@ceflawyers.com
    www.ceflawyers.com

Appellate Practice, Asbestos, Employment Law, General Liability, Insurance Coverage, Professional Liability

Firm Profile: Collins Einhorn Farrell leads the way in defense litigation and expert legal representation in a wide variety of industries throughout the Midwest. Learn more about how our 42 lawyer firm can assist you with effective, practical, and well-reasoned legal solutions by visiting www.ceflawyers.com.

Representative Insurance Clients

Fireman's Fund Insurance Company   Liberty Mutual Insurance Company

Firm Member

Michael J. Sullivan — University of Notre Dame, B.A., 1980; University of Detroit, J.D., 1983 — Admitted to Bar, 1983, Michigan — Member American and Oakland County Bar Associations; State Bar of Michigan; Fellow, Michigan State County Bar Foundation; Association of Defense Trial Counsel

Maddin, Hauser, Roth & Heller, P.C.
28400 Northwestern Highway, Second Floor
Southfield, Michigan 48034
    Telephone: 248-354-4030
    Fax: 248-359-6149
    E-Mail: hheller@maddinhauser.com
    www.maddinhauser.com

Established: 1982

Insurance Defense, Professional Liability (Non-Medical) Defense, Insurance Coverage, Legal Malpractice, Accountant Malpractice, Insurance Agents, Errors and Omissions, Directors and Officers Liability, Employment Practices Liability, Complex Litigation, Appellate Practice, Securities Litigation

Maddin, Hauser, Roth & Heller, P.C., Southfield, MI
(Continued)

Firm Profile: Maddin, Hauser, Roth & Heller, P.C. is an established multi-specialty law firm. A strong component of the firm's practice is in the area of civil litigation/defense. The firm maintains a special expertise in non-medical professional liability including the defense of claims against attorneys, accountants, appraisers, architects and engineers, employers, agents and brokers, as well as directors, officers, and financial advisors. In addition, the firm is involved in the direct representation of insurance companies rendering coverage opinions and acting as counsel in coverage litigation. Substantial defense work is also done in the areas of FDCPA, rental housing, discrimination and all other forms of ADA. The firm has developed a quality team of professionals who realize that quality, cost-efficient legal representation includes both technical expertise and effective communication. Harvey R. Heller is the shareholder in charge of our defense practice and insurance coverage group.

Insurance Clients

ACE USA
AIG
AmTrust North America
Aon Technical Insurance Services
Aspen Insurance
BCS Insurance Company
Beazley Group
Catlin, Inc.
Chubb Group of Insurance Companies
Darwin National Assurance Company
Fireman's Fund Insurance Company
General Star Management Company
Great West Casualty Company
Hanover Insurance Group
The Hartford
Ironshore Insurance, Ltd.
Liberty Insurance Underwriters, Inc.
LVL Claims Services, LLC
Media Professionals
Navigators Pro
North Pointe Insurance Company
Philadelphia Insurance Company
ProNational Insurance Company
Republic Western Insurance Company
Swiss Re/Westport Insurance Corporation
Underwriters at Lloyd's, London
Zurich North America
ACE Westchester Specialty Group
Allied World National Assurance Company
Arch Insurance Group
AXIS Specialty Insurance Company
Burlington Insurance Company
Chicago Insurance Company
CNA Insurance Companies
Colony Specialty Insurance Company
Endurance U.S. Insurance Operations
Freedom Specialty Insurance Company
Great American Insurance Company
Hanover Professionals
HUB International Northeast, Ltd.
ISBA Mutual Insurance Company
Lumbermens Mutual Casualty Company
Markel
Minnesota Lawyers Mutual Insurance Company
OneBeacon Professional Partners, Inc.
ProSight Specialty Insurance
St. Paul Travelers
Specialty National Insurance Company
Torus
Virginia Surety Company, Inc.

Third Party Administrators

Custard Insurance Adjusters, Inc.
Gallagher Bassett Services, Inc.
Lancer Claims Services, Inc.
Midlands Claim Administrators, Inc.
RiverStone Claims Management, LLC
York Risk Services Group, Inc.
Engle Martin Claims Administrative Services (EMCAS, Inc.)
NAS Insurance Services, Inc.
The Plus Companies, Inc.
TIG Insurance Company
Xchanging

Shareholders

Harvey R. Heller — Michigan State University, B.A. (with honors), 1973; Detroit College of Law, J.D. (cum laude), 1977 — Admitted to Bar, 1977, Michigan; U.S. District Court, Eastern and Western Districts of Michigan — Member American and Oakland County Bar Associations; State Bar of Michigan (Lawyers Professional Liability Insurance Committee); International Association of Defense Counsel — Tel: 248-827-1899

Julie Chenot Mayer — University of Michigan, B.A., 1983; Detroit College of Law, J.D. (cum laude), 1986 — Admitted to Bar, 1986, Michigan; U.S. District Court, Eastern District of Michigan — Member American Bar Association; State Bar of Michigan

Steven M. Wolock — University of California, Santa Cruz, B.S., 1977; University of Michigan, J.D., 1985 — Admitted to Bar, 1985, Michigan; U.S. District Court, Eastern District of Michigan, 1986, U.S. District Court, Western District of Michigan; U.S. Court of Appeals, Sixth Circuit — Member American and Oakland County Bar Associations; State Bar of Michigan

Maddin, Hauser, Roth & Heller, P.C., Southfield, MI
(Continued)

David M. Saperstein — University of California, Berkeley, B.A. (with high distinction), 1989; University of Michigan, J.D., 1993 — Admitted to Bar, 1993, Michigan; 1994, California; 1999, Ohio — Member Ohio State Bar Association; State Bar of Michigan; State Bar of California (inactive); Michigan Defense Trial Counsel

Richard M. Mitchell — University of Michigan, B.A., 1988; Indiana University, J.D., 1991 — Admitted to Bar, 1991, Michigan; 1994, U.S. District Court, Eastern District of Michigan; 1996, U.S. District Court, Western District of Michigan; U.S. Court of Appeals, Sixth Circuit — Member State Bar of Michigan; Oakland County Bar Association; American Society for CPLV

Kathleen H. Klaus — The University of Iowa, B.A. (with distinction), 1987; University of Michigan Law School, J.D., 1992 — Admitted to Bar, 1992, Illinois; 1992, U.S. District Court, Northern District of Illinois; 1993, U.S. Court of Appeals, Seventh Circuit; 1997, U.S. Court of Appeals, Fifth Circuit; 2001, U.S. Supreme Court — Member Illinois State Bar Association; State Bar of Michigan; United States Supreme Court Bar

Associates

Karen L. Ludden — University of Michigan - Ann Arbor, B.A. (magna cum laude), 1990; University of Michigan Law School, J.D., 1993 — Admitted to Bar, 1993, Michigan; U.S. District Court, Eastern and Western Districts of Michigan; U.S. Court of Appeals, Sixth Circuit — Member Federal, American and Oakland County Bar Associations; State Bar of Michigan

Thomas W. Werner — Eastern Michigan University, B.S. (with honors), 1999; Indiana University School of Law-Bloomington, J.D. (cum laude), 2004 — Admitted to Bar, 2004, Michigan; U.S. District Court, Western District of Pennsylvania; U.S. District Court, Eastern District of Michigan; U.S. District Court, Northern District of Indiana — Member American and Oakland County Bar Associations; State Bar of Michigan

Siemion Huckabay, P.C.

One Towne Square, Suite 1400
Southfield, Michigan 48076
Telephone: 248-357-1400
Fax: 248-357-3343
www.siemion-huckabay.com

Established: 1981

Insurance Defense, Automobile, General Liability, Legal Malpractice, Medical Malpractice, Product Liability, Errors and Omissions, Trial Practice, Appellate Practice, Asbestos Litigation, Aviation, Workers' Compensation, Securities Litigation

Insurance Clients

American Equity Insurance Company
American Physicians Assurance Corp.
Clarendon National Insurance Company
GMAC Insurance Group
Gulf Insurance Company
Meadowbrook Insurance Group
Northland Insurance Company
Progressive Michigan Insurance Company
American Modern Home Insurance Company
Amerisure Insurance Company
APCapital
CNA Insurance Company
Esurance Insurance Company
Great West Casualty Company
Lexington Insurance Company
MIC General Insurance Corporation
ProNational Insurance Company
St. Paul Travelers Insurance Companies

Non-Insurance Clients

Cambridge Integrated Services
Emergency Physicians Medical Group, P.C.
Midwest Health Center
Oakwood Health Care System
St. Mary Hospital
Thrifty Rent-A-Car Systems, Inc.
ELCO Administrative Services
Marsh USA, Inc.
Michigan Brain and Spine Institute
Northland Family Planning
St. John Hospital and Medical Center
Trinity Health

Firm Members

Robert P. Siemion — 1949 — University of Detroit, B.S., 1971; J.D., 1974 — Admitted to Bar, 1974, Michigan — Member American and Oakland County

MICHIGAN   **SOUTHFIELD**

Siemion Huckabay, P.C., Southfield, MI (Continued)

Bar Associations; State Bar of Michigan; American Board of Trial Advocates; Association of Defense Trial Counsel; Michigan Trial Lawyers Association

Raymond W. Morganti — 1951 — Michigan State University, B.A., 1973; University of Detroit, J.D., 1976 — Admitted to Bar, 1976, Michigan — Member State Bar of Michigan; Michigan Defense Trial Counsel

Cathy R. Bowerman — 1953 — The University of North Carolina, B.A., 1973; University of Michigan, M.Ph., 1977; Wayne State University, J.D., 1976 — Admitted to Bar, 1976, Michigan — Member American Bar Association; State Bar of Michigan; American Public Health Association; American Society of Law and Medicine; Michigan Defense Trial Counsel

Mark A. Roberts — 1950 — Western Michigan University, B.A., 1972; Wayne State University, J.D., 1976 — Admitted to Bar, 1976, Michigan — Member Federal and Oakland County Bar Associations; State Bar of Michigan; Michigan Defense Trial Counsel

Steven B. Sinkoff — 1950 — Oakland University, B.A., 1972; Wayne State University, M.A., 1973; J.D., 1978 — Admitted to Bar, 1978, Michigan — Member State Bar of Michigan; Oakland County Bar Association; Association of Defense Trial Counsel; Association of Defense Trial Counsel; Michigan Defense Trial Counsel

Eugene Kelly Cullen — 1956 — Manhattan College, B.A., 1978; Detroit College of Law, J.D., 1985 — Admitted to Bar, 1985, Michigan — Member State Bar of Michigan; Defense Research Institute

Karen M. Faett — 1961 — Gannon University, B.S. (magna cum laude), 1983; Wayne State University, J.D. (cum laude), 1988 — Admitted to Bar, 1988, Michigan — Member State Bar of Michigan; Michigan Defense Trial Counsel; Defense Research Institute

Thomas M. Caplis — 1960 — Eastern Michigan University, B.S., 1983; Detroit College of Law, J.D., 1986 — Admitted to Bar, 1986, Michigan; 1986, U.S. District Court, Eastern District of Michigan — Member State Bar of Michigan

Susan J. Zbikowski — 1958 — Kalamazoo College, B.A. (with honors), 1980; Michigan State University, M.A., 1982; Detroit College of Law, J.D. (summa cum laude), 1987 — Admitted to Bar, 1987, Michigan; 1987, U.S. District Court, Eastern District of Michigan; 1987, U.S. Court of Appeals, Sixth Circuit — Member State Bar of Michigan; Wayne County Mediation Tribunal; Michigan Defense Trial Counsel

Associate

Jeffrey G. Jelinski — 1981 — University of Michigan, B.S., 2003; University of Detroit Mercy School of Law, J.D., 2006 — Admitted to Bar, 2006, Michigan

Sullivan, Ward, Asher & Patton, P.C.

1000 Maccabees Center
25800 Northwestern Highway, Suite 1000
Southfield, Michigan 48075-8412
   Telephone: 248-746-0700
   Fax: 248-746-2760
   E-Mail: swappc@swappc.com
   www.swappc.com

Established: 1951

Casualty, Workers' Compensation, Accident and Health, Trial and Appellate Practice, Negligence, Admiralty and Maritime Law, Railroad Law, Medical Malpractice, Hospital Malpractice, Architects and Engineers, Malpractice, Aviation, Property, Subrogation, Construction Liability, Surety and Indemnity Bonds, Auto and Truck Accident Litigation, ADA Litigation, Warranty

Firm Profile: Sullivan, Ward, Asher & Patton, P.C. was founded in 1951 and has grown to its present size of approximately forty-nine attorneys over the past sixty-three years. Originally formed by former claims managers and insurance personnel who are still firm partners, the firm naturally specialized as defense trial attorneys in various tort litigation in the field of medical and hospital malpractice, design professionals as well as accountants, attorneys, engineers, insurance agents and litigation and hearings before legislative and regulatory bodies.

The attorneys at Sullivan, Ward, Asher & Patton have successfully handled matters from the trial level to the U.S. Supreme Court. Our litigation practice

Sullivan, Ward, Asher & Patton, P.C., Southfield, MI (Continued)

includes medical and hospital malpractice, insurance contract litigation, contract liability, general negligence, construction litigation, insurance law, manufacturers liability, municipal liability, labor matters, auto and truck accident litigation and ADA litigation.

Some years ago the firm expanded and added specialists in the disciplines of various practices to form a complete and full service Firm and now maintains departments for corporate law, tax and estate planning and the handling of personal concerns of clients such as family law and financial planning.

Insurance Clients

Argo Select
Broadspire
CIGNA Group
CNA Insurance Companies
ESIS
GAB Robins North America, Inc.
The Hartford Insurance Group
Hudson Insurance Group
Lexington Insurance Company
The Medical Protective Company
MetLife Auto & Home
Nautilus Insurance Company
Podiatry Insurance Company of America (PICA)
Professional Solutions Insurance Company
St. Paul Fire and Marine Insurance Company
Specialty Claims, Incorporated
State Farm Insurance Companies
Utica Mutual Insurance Company
XL Design Professional
Berkley Risk Administrators Company, LLC
Clearwater Insurance Company
Crawford & Company
Farm Bureau Insurance Companies
Hanover Professionals
Hastings Mutual Insurance Company
Liberty Mutual Insurance Company
MEEMIC Insurance Company
Nationwide Mutual Insurance Company
ProAssurance/ProNational Insurance Company
Propel Insurance
Republic Insurance Company
Scottsdale Insurance Company
Shelter Insurance Companies
State Auto Insurance Companies
Travelers Insurance Companies
Western Surety Company
Zurich Insurance Company

Non-Insurance Clients

AIMCO Risk Management
CMS Energy
Disability Management Services, Inc.
Marks Management Corporation
Swift Transportation Corporation
Vanguard Health Systems
Williams-Sonoma, Inc.
Yamaha Motor Corporation, U.S.A.
Alexsis, Inc.
Con-Way Truckload, Inc.
General Growth Properties, Inc.
Gymboree
Milacron, Inc.
The Taubman Company
William Beaumont Hospital
Wilson, Elser, Moskowitz, Edelman & Dicker LLP

Managing Partners

Anthony A. Asher — 1936 — University of Detroit, B.S., 1961; J.D., 1965 — Admitted to Bar, 1966, Michigan; 2000, New York; 1966, U.S. District Court, Eastern and Western Districts of Michigan; U.S. Court of Appeals, Second and Sixth Circuits; U.S. Supreme Court — Member American and Oakland County Bar Associations; State Bar of Michigan — Practice Areas: Antitrust; Labor and Employment — E-mail: aasher@swappc.com

A. Stuart Tompkins — 1946 — Eastern Michigan University, B.A., 1970; University of Detroit, J.D. (magna cum laude), 1973 — Admitted to Bar, 1973, Michigan; U.S. District Court, Eastern District of Michigan; 1975, U.S. District Court, Western District of Michigan; U.S. Court of Appeals, Sixth Circuit — Member American, Southfield and Oakland County Bar Associations; State Bar of Michigan — Practice Areas: Commercial Litigation; Mergers and Acquisitions; Corporate Law — E-mail: stompkins@swappc.com

Lee C. Patton — 1949 — Eastern Michigan University, B.A., 1972; The University of Toledo, J.D., 1975 — Admitted to Bar, 1976, Michigan; 2007, Illinois; U.S. District Court, Eastern and Western Districts of Michigan; 1982, U.S. Court of Appeals, Sixth Circuit — Member American and Oakland County Bar Associations; State Bar of Michigan; International Association of Defense Counsel; Michigan Defense Trial Counsel — Practice Areas: Automobile; Construction Law; Negligence; Professional Negligence; Trial Practice — Tel: 248-746-2730 — Fax: 248-746-2837 — E-mail: lpatton@swappc.com

Scott D. Feringa — 1953 — Calvin College, B.A., 1975; University of Detroit, J.D., 1978 — Admitted to Bar, 1978, Michigan; U.S. District Court, Eastern and Western Districts of Michigan — Member American, Oakland County and Detroit Bar Associations; State Bar of Michigan; Michigan Society of Hospital Attorneys; Association of Ski Defense Attorneys (Board of Directors) — Practice Areas: Aviation; Litigation; Medical Devices; Medical Malpractice; Oil and Gas; Product Liability — Tel: 248-746-2727 — Fax: 248-746-2815 — E-mail: sferinga@swappc.com

Sullivan, Ward, Asher & Patton, P.C., Southfield, MI (Continued)

Kevin J. Gleeson — 1951 — Oakland University, B.A., 1973; Thomas M. Cooley Law School, J.D., 1979 — Admitted to Bar, 1979, Michigan; U.S. District Court, Eastern and Western Districts of Michigan — Member Federal, American, Kalamazoo County, Kent County, Oakland County and Detroit Bar Associations; State Bar of Michigan; Court of Claims Bar Association; American Arbitration Association Large Case Panel (Advisory Committee) — Practice Areas: Architects and Engineers; Contracts; Accountant Malpractice; Legal Malpractice; Construction Litigation; Environmental Law — E-mail: kgleeson@swappc.com

Shareholders

Gerard J. Andree — 1950 — National University of Ireland, Dublin; University College Dublin; University of Detroit, A.B. (summa cum laude), 1972; J.D., 1975 — Admitted to Bar, 1975, Michigan; U.S. District Court, Eastern District of Michigan; 2004, U.S. Supreme Court — Member State Bar of Michigan; Michigan Defense Trial Counsel; Association of Defense Trial Counsel; Defense Research Institute; American Society of Law and Medicine; International Association of Defense Counsel — Practice Areas: Medical Malpractice; Product Liability; Professional Liability — Tel: 248-746-2731 — E-mail: gandree@swappc.com

John M. Simmerer — 1949 — University of Dayton, B.S., 1973; Detroit College of Law, J.D., 1979 — Admitted to Bar, 1979, Michigan; U.S. District Court, Eastern District of Michigan — Member American and Macomb County Bar Associations; State Bar of Michigan; Incorporated Society of Irish American Laywers; Michigan Defense Trial Counsel — Practice Areas: Agent and Brokers Errors and Omissions; Automobile Liability; Insurance Defense; Premises Liability; Architects and Engineers; Construction Liability; Professional Liability — E-mail: jsimmerer@swappc.com

Jeffry G. Powers — 1946 — Michigan State University, B.S., 1969; Wayne State University, J.D., 1972 — Admitted to Bar, 1973, Michigan; 2001, Ohio; 1973, U.S. District Court, Eastern and Western Districts of Michigan; U.S. Court of Appeals, Sixth Circuit — Member Ohio State and Oakland County Bar Associations; State Bar of Michigan; Michigan Trucking Association; Defense Research Institute; Michigan Defense Trial Counsel — Practice Areas: Personal Injury — Tel: 248-746-2718 — E-mail: jpowers@swappc.com

Ronald S. Lederman — University of Detroit, J.D. (cum laude), 1985 — Admitted to Bar, 1985, Michigan; U.S. District Court, Eastern and Western Districts of Michigan; U.S. Court of Appeals, Second, Sixth and Eleventh Circuits — E-mail: rlederman@swappc.com

Sheri B. Cataldo — 1961 — University of Michigan, B.A. (with high distinction), 1983; Wayne State University, J.D., 1986 — Admitted to Bar, 1986, Michigan; U.S. District Court, Eastern and Western Districts of Michigan; U.S. Court of Appeals, Sixth Circuit; 2003, U.S. Court of Appeals, Seventh Circuit — Member American and Womens Bar Associations; State Bar of Michigan — Practice Areas: Business Law; Commercial Litigation; Contract Disputes; Employment Law — E-mail: scataldo@swappc.com

Cornelius C. Hare, Jr. — 1962 — Western Michigan University, B.S., 1984; Wayne State University, J.D., 1989 — Admitted to Bar, 1989, Michigan; 1991, Illinois; 1989, U.S. District Court, Eastern and Western Districts of Michigan; U.S. Court of Appeals, Sixth Circuit — Practice Areas: Employment Law; Personal Injury — E-mail: chare@swappc.com

Jonathan M. Jaffa — Wayne State University, B.A., 1970; Detroit College of Law, J.D., 1974 — Admitted to Bar, 1974, Michigan; 2002, Ohio; 1974, U.S. District Court, Eastern District of Michigan; U.S. Court of Appeals, Sixth Circuit; U.S. Supreme Court — Member State Bar of Michigan; Oakland County Bar Association; Michigan Defense Trial Counsel — Practice Areas: Automobile Liability; Construction Litigation; Negligence; Malpractice; Medical Liability; Nursing Home Liability; Premises Liability; Product Liability — E-mail: jjaffa@swappc.com

Craig S. Thompson — Albion College, B.A., 1990; University of Detroit, J.D., 1993 — Admitted to Bar, 1993, Michigan; U.S. District Court, Eastern District of Michigan — Member American and Oakland County Bar Associations; American Arbitration Association Advisory Council; Michigan Defense Trial Counsel — Practice Areas: Construction Litigation — Tel: 248-746-2776 — E-mail: cthompson@swappc.com

Nicole Krentler Nugent — Wayne State University, B.S. (summa cum laude), 1995; J.D., 1999 — Admitted to Bar, 1999, Michigan; 2000, U.S. District Court, Eastern District of Michigan — Member American Bar Association; State Bar of Michigan — Practice Areas: Medical Malpractice; Product Liability — E-mail: nnugent@swappc.com

Maria Lourdes Meldrum — California Polytechnic State University, B.S.C.E., 1983; University of California, Los Angeles, M.B.A., 1987; Detroit College of Law, J.D., 1997 — Admitted to Bar, 1997, Michigan; 2007, California; 1998, U.S. Court of Appeals, Sixth Circuit — Member American and Oakland County Bar Associations; State Bar of Michigan — Practice Areas: Complex Litigation; Construction Litigation; Contract Disputes; Professional Malpractice — E-mail: mmeldrum@swappc.com

Jennifer R. Moran — 1977 — University of Michigan - Dearborn, B.S., 1999; University of Detroit Mercy School of Law, J.D., 2002 — Admitted to Bar, 2002, Michigan; U.S. District Court, Eastern District of Michigan — Member State Bar of Michigan; Detroit Bar Association — Practice Areas: Appellate Practice — E-mail: jmoran@swappc.com

Bryan L. Patton — 1983 — Albion College, B.A. (cum laude), 2006; University of Notre Dame Law School, J.D., 2009 — Admitted to Bar, 2009, Michigan; U.S. District Court, Eastern District of Michigan — Member American Bar Association; State Bar of Michigan — Practice Areas: Insurance Defense; Premises Liability — E-mail: bpatton@swappc.com

Keith P. Felty — Michigan State University, B.A. (with honors), 1989; Wayne State University, J.D., 1992 — Admitted to Bar, 1992, Michigan — Tel: 248-746-2726 — Fax: 248-746-2784 — E-mail: kfelty@swappc.com

Christopher B. McMahon — 1971 — Western Michigan University, B.B.A./M.B.A. (with honors), 1993; University of Detroit, J.D., 1997 — Admitted to Bar, 1997, Michigan; 2005, Maryland; 2006, Washington; 2008, Illinois; 1998, U.S. District Court, Eastern District of Michigan; 1999, U.S. District Court, Western District of Michigan — Member American and Oakland County Bar Associations — Practice Areas: Architects and Engineers; Construction Law; Construction Accidents; Contracts; Litigation; Personal Injury; Professional Malpractice — Tel: 248-746-2772 — E-mail: cmcmahon@swappc.com

John M. Toth — 1956 — University of Michigan, B.A. (with high distinction), 1977; Villanova University, J.D. (with high distinction), 1981 — Admitted to Bar, 1982, Michigan; 1991, Ohio — Member State Bar of Michigan; Oakland County, Livingston County and Detroit Bar Associations; Michigan Defense Trial Counsel — Tel: 248-746-2715

Senior Attorneys

Alan S. Helmore — 1943 — Western Michigan University, B.B.A., 1965; Detroit College of Law, J.D., 1972 — Admitted to Bar, 1972, Michigan; U.S. District Court, Eastern District of Michigan; 1983, U.S. Court of Appeals, Sixth Circuit; U.S. Supreme Court — Member American Bar Association; State Bar of Michigan — Practice Areas: Personal Injury — E-mail: ahelmore@swappc.com

Charles E. Randau — 1938 — Wayne State University, B.S., 1962; J.D., 1965 — Admitted to Bar, 1966, Michigan; U.S. District Court, Eastern District of Michigan — Member State Bar of Michigan; Oakland County and Detroit Bar Associations; Michigan Defense Trial Counsel — Practice Areas: Arbitration; Automobile Liability; Casualty Defense; Civil Litigation; Defense Litigation; Hospital Malpractice; Medical Liability; Motor Carriers; Premises Liability; State and Federal Courts — E-mail: crandau@swappc.com

Associate Attorneys

Miranda J. Welbourne Eleázar — University of Michigan - Ann Arbor, B.A. (with distinction), 2004; J.D. (cum laude), 2007 — Admitted to Bar, 2007, Michigan; 2010, New York — Tel: 248-746-2758 — E-mail: mwelbourne@swappc.com

Jill H. Vandercook — Western Michigan University, B.B.A. (cum laude), 2000; Wayne State University, J.D., 2004 — Admitted to Bar, 2004, Michigan — Tel: 248-746-2724 — E-mail: jvandercook@swappc.com

Robert J. Hoard — 1982 — James Madison College at Michigan State University, B.A., 2004; The University of Toledo College of Law, J.D., 2009 — Admitted to Bar, 2009, Michigan — Tel: 248-228-1164

Breanne M. Patton — 1984 — Albion College, B.A. (magna cum laude), 2006; University of Notre Dame, J.D., 2009 — Admitted to Bar, 2011, Michigan — Tel: 248-746-2757

Eric T. Ramar — 1987 — University of Toledo School of Law, J.D. (Dean's List), 2013 — Admitted to Bar, 2013, Michigan; U.S. District Court, Eastern District of Michigan — Member State Bar of Michigan — Tel: 248-746-2768

A. Adam Post — 1983 — University of Detroit Mercy School of Law, J.D. (magna cum laude), 2011 — Admitted to Bar, 2011, Michigan; 2012, U.S. District Court, Eastern District of Michigan; 2013, U.S. District Court, Western District of Michigan — Tel: 248-746-2732

Ashley C. Quackenbush — 1987 — University of Michigan - Ann Arbor, B.A. (with honors), 2009; Wayne State University Law School, J.D., 2012 — Admitted to Bar, 2012, Michigan; 2013, U.S. District Court, Eastern District of Michigan; 2014, U.S. District Court, Western District of Michigan — Tel: 248-746-2710

MICHIGAN

Thomas, DeGrood & Witenoff, P.C.
400 Galleria Officentre, Suite 550
Southfield, Michigan 48034
　Telephone: 248-353-4450
　Fax: 248-353-4451
　E-Mail: gthomas@thomasdegrood.com
　www.thomasdegrood.com

Established: 1988

Construction Litigation, Errors and Omissions, Negligence, Municipal Liability, Personal Injury, Professional Liability, Disability, ERISA

Insurance Clients

American Specialty Insurance Services, Inc.	AXIS Insurance
Colonial Life and Accident Insurance Company	Clarendon National Insurance Company
Endurance Services Limited	Coregis Insurance Company
First Specialty Insurance Corporation	Engle Martin Claims Administrative Services (EMCAS, Inc.)
Great American Custom Insurance Services	Gulf Insurance Company
K & K Insurance Group, Inc.	Hudson Insurance Group
Markel American Insurance Company	Lawyer's Protector Plan
Monarch Life Insurance Company	Michigan Municipal League Liability & Property Pool
Swiss Re Insurance	St. Paul Travelers Insurance Companies
Unum Group	U.S. Financial Life Insurance Company
Westport Insurance Company	Zurich Insurance Company
XL Design Professional	

Non-Insurance Clients

Integrated Disability Resources, Inc.

Partners

Gregory I. Thomas — 1955 — Michigan State University, B.A., 1977; University of Detroit, J.D. (cum laude), 1980 — Admitted to Bar, 1981, Michigan; 1981, U.S. District Court, Eastern and Western Districts of Michigan; 1981, U.S. Court of Appeals, Sixth Circuit — Member American and Oakland County Bar Associations; State Bar of Michigan; Association of Defense Counsel

George M. DeGrood, III — 1954 — University of Michigan, B.S., 1976; Detroit College of Law, J.D., 1982 — Admitted to Bar, 1982, Michigan; 1982, U.S. District Court, Eastern and Western Districts of Michigan; 1982, U.S. Court of Appeals, Sixth Circuit — Member American Bar Association; State Bar of Michigan (Tort, Insurance Sections)

Stephen L. Witenoff — 1951 — Wayne State University, B.A., 1974; Detroit College of Law, J.D. (cum laude), 1979 — Admitted to Bar, 1979, Michigan; 1979, U.S. District Court, Eastern and Western Districts of Michigan; 1979, U.S. Court of Appeals, Sixth Circuit — Member Defense Research Institute (Life, Health, Disability and ERISA Section)

Associate

Michael F. Healy — 1953 — Southern Illinois University, B.A. (with honors), 1975; DePaul University, J.D., 1978; LL.M., 1999 — Admitted to Bar, 1978, Illinois; 2001, Michigan; 1978, U.S. District Court, Northern District of Illinois; 1998, U.S. District Court, Northern and Southern Districts of Indiana; 2001, U.S. District Court, Eastern and Western Districts of Michigan — Member Oakland County Bar Association; State Bar of Michigan

---

The following firms also service this area.

Galbraith, Delie & James, P.C.
660 Woodward Avenue, Suite 1975
Detroit, Michigan 48226-3577
　Telephone: 248-357-3910
　Fax: 248-357-2665

Insurance Defense, Workers' Compensation, Property and Casualty, Automobile, General Liability, Product Liability, Coverage Issues, Malpractice, Professional Errors and Omissions

SEE COMPLETE LISTING UNDER DETROIT, MICHIGAN (5 MILES)

ST. IGNACE

ST. IGNACE † 2,452 Mackinac Co.

Refer To
Bensinger, Cotant & Menkes, P.C.
308 West Main Street
Gaylord, Michigan 49735
　Telephone: 989-732-7536
　Fax: 989-732-4922

General Defense, Automobile Liability, Fire Loss, Professional Liability, Product Liability, Workers' Compensation, Subrogation, Medical Malpractice, Liquor Liability

SEE COMPLETE LISTING UNDER GAYLORD, MICHIGAN (60 MILES)

ST. JOSEPH † 8,365 Berrien Co.

Hunt Suedhoff Kalamaros LLP
301 State Street, 2nd Floor
St. Joseph, Michigan 49085-0046
　Telephone: 269-983-4405
　Fax: 269-983-5645
　www.hsk-law.com

(Fort Wayne, IN Office*: 803 South Calhoun Street, 9th Floor, 46802, P.O. Box 11489, 46858-1489)
　(Tel: 260-423-1311)
　(Fax: 260-424-5396)
　(Toll Free: 800-215-8258)
(South Bend, IN Office*: 205 West Jefferson Boulevard, Suite 300, 46601, P.O. Box 4156, 46634-4156)
　(Tel: 574-232-4801)
　(Fax: 574-232-9736)
(Indianapolis, IN Office*: 6323 South East Street, 46227)
　(Tel: 317-784-4966)
　(Fax: 317-784-5566)

Insurance Defense, Trial and Appellate Practice, Automobile, Product Liability, Professional Liability, Property and Casualty, Medical Malpractice, Workers' Compensation, Public Entities, Self-Insured, Health Care, Toxic Torts, Environmental Law, Coverage Issues, Mediation, Arbitration

Representative Clients

AAA California	Allied Group
American Family Insurance Company	American International Group, Inc.
Auto-Owners Insurance Company	Amerisure Companies
Chubb Services Corporation	Chubb Group of Insurance Companies
Cincinnati Insurance Company	CNA Insurance Companies
The Doctors Company	EMC Insurance Company
Employers Reinsurance Corporation	Erie Insurance Company
Fireman's Fund Insurance Company	FCCI Insurance Company
Frankenmuth Mutual Insurance Company	First Acceptance Insurance Company, Inc.
Indiana Farmers Mutual Insurance Company	Gallagher Bassett Insurance Company
Liberty Mutual Insurance Company	Indiana Insurance Company
National General Insurance Company	Indiana University Health
Pekin Insurance	Motorists Insurance Company
Scottsdale Insurance Company	Nationwide Group
Sedgwick CMS	OneBeacon Insurance
South Bend Medical Foundation	Safeco/American States Insurance Company
Travelers Property Casualty Corporation	Sentry Insurance a Mutual Company
Zurich American Insurance Group	United Farm Bureau Mutual Insurance Company

Partners

Philip E. Kalamaros — University of Notre Dame, B.B.A., 1984; University of Notre Dame Law School, J.D., 1987 — Admitted to Bar, 1987, Indiana — E-mail: pkalamaros@hsk-law.com

TROY
MICHIGAN

Hunt Suedhoff Kalamaros LLP, St. Joseph, MI
(Continued)

Michael G. Getty — 1962 — University of Michigan, B.A., 1984; Southern Illinois University School of Law, J.D., 1987 — Admitted to Bar, 1987, Illinois; 1993, Indiana — E-mail: mgetty@hsk-law.com

Associates

Brad R. Pero — 1984 — Western Michigan University, B.A. (magna cum laude), 2007; Michigan State University School of Law, J.D. (cum laude), 2011 — Admitted to Bar, 2011, Michigan — E-mail: bpero@hsk-law.com

Karol Ann ("Karrie") Schwartz — 1970 — Emory University, B.A., 1992; Georgia State University College of Law, 2001; Chicago-Kent College of Law, J.D., 2003 — Admitted to Bar, 2004, Indiana — E-mail: kschwartz@hsk-law.com

Amanda N. Zaluckyj — 1986 — Grand Valley State University, B.S., 2008; Michigan State University College of Law, J.D. (summa cum laude), 2012 — Admitted to Bar, 2012, Michigan — E-mail: azaluckyj@hsk-law.com

(See listing under Fort Wayne, IN for additional information)

The following firms also service this area.

Lennon, Miller, O'Connor & Bartosiewicz, PLC
900 Comerica Building
151 South Rose Street
Kalamazoo, Michigan 49007
   Telephone: 269-381-8844
   Fax: 269-381-8822

Civil Trial Practice, State and Federal Courts, Insurance Defense, Reinsurance, Personal Injury, Real Property, Product Liability, Professional Liability, Environmental Law, Fidelity and Surety, Municipal Liability, Workers' Compensation, Coverage Opinions, Sports and Spectator Liability, Utility Liability, First and Third Party Auto Liability

SEE COMPLETE LISTING UNDER KALAMAZOO, MICHIGAN (50 MILES)

TAWAS CITY † 1,827 Iosco Co.

Refer To
White and Wojda
313 N. Second Avenue
Alpena, Michigan 49707
   Telephone: 989-354-4104
   Fax: 989-356-0747

Casualty Defense, First and Third Party Defense, Insurance Defense, Legal Malpractice, Opinions, Personal Lines, Special Investigative Unit Claims, All Lines, Municipal Defense

SEE COMPLETE LISTING UNDER ALPENA, MICHIGAN (64 MILES)

TRAVERSE CITY † 14,674 Grand Traverse Co.

Garan Lucow Miller, P.C.

1131 East Eighth Street
Traverse City, Michigan 49685-3150
   Telephone: 231-941-1611
   Fax: 231-941-4420
   Toll Free: 888-923-1611
   24 Hour Toll Free: 888-332-0540
   www.garanlucow.com

(Additional Offices: Detroit, MI*; Ann Arbor, MI*; Grand Blanc, MI*(See Flint listing); Grand Rapids, MI*; Lansing, MI*; Marquette, MI*; Port Huron, MI*; Troy, MI*; Merrillville, IN*)

Business Law, Employment Law, Insurance Defense, Municipal Liability, No-Fault, Workers' Compensation

(See listing under Detroit, MI for additional information)

The following firms also service this area.

Bensinger, Cotant & Menkes, P.C.
308 West Main Street
Gaylord, Michigan 49735
   Telephone: 989-732-7536
   Fax: 989-732-4922

General Defense, Automobile Liability, Fire Loss, Professional Liability, Product Liability, Workers' Compensation, Subrogation, Medical Malpractice, Liquor Liability

SEE COMPLETE LISTING UNDER GAYLORD, MICHIGAN (65 MILES)

Kluczynski, Girtz & Vogelzang
5005 Cascade Road SE, Suite A
Grand Rapids, Michigan 49546
   Telephone: 616-459-0556
   Fax: 616-459-5829

Insurance Defense, Automobile, Fire, Casualty, General Liability, Product Liability, Workers' Compensation, Subrogation, Environmental Law, Occupational Disease

SEE COMPLETE LISTING UNDER GRAND RAPIDS, MICHIGAN (150 MILES)

White and Wojda
313 N. Second Avenue
Alpena, Michigan 49707
   Telephone: 989-354-4104
   Fax: 989-356-0747

Casualty Defense, First and Third Party Defense, Insurance Defense, Legal Malpractice, Opinions, Personal Lines, Special Investigative Unit Claims, All Lines, Municipal Defense

SEE COMPLETE LISTING UNDER ALPENA, MICHIGAN (135 MILES)

TROY 80,980 Oakland Co.

Alber Crafton, PSC

2301 West Big Beaver Road, Suite 300
Troy, Michigan 48084
   Telephone: 248-822-6190
   Fax: 248-822-6191
   www.albercrafton.com

(Prospect, KY Office*(See Louisville listing): 9418 Norton Commons Boulevard, Suite 200, 40059)
   (Tel: 502-815-5000)
   (Fax: 502-815-5005)
   (E-Mail: lhutchens@albercrafton.com)
(Westerville, OH Office*: 501 West Schrock Road, Suite 104, 43081-3360)
   (Tel: 614-890-5632)
   (Fax: 614-890-5638)
(Oklahoma: P.O. Box 14517, Tulsa, OK, 74159)
   (Tel: 918-935-3459)

Fidelity and Surety, Construction Law

(See listing under Louisville, KY for additional information)

Bowen, Radabaugh & Milton, P.C.

4967 Crooks Road, Suite 150
Troy, Michigan 48098
   Telephone: 248-641-8000
   Fax: 248-641-8219
   E-Mail: trbowen@brmattorneys.com
   www.brmattorneys.com

Bowen, Radabaugh & Milton, P.C., Troy, MI (Continued)

(Additional Offices: Toledo, OH)

Established: 1995

Defense Litigation, Trial and Appellate Practice, State and Federal Courts, Declaratory Judgments, Arbitration, Examinations Under Oath, Opinions, Employment Law, Americans with Disabilities Act, Discrimination, Wrongful Termination, Equal Employment Opportunity Commission, Civil Rights, Sexual Harassment, Employee Benefits, Coverage Analysis, Policy Construction and Interpretation, Tort Litigation, Product Liability, Property Loss, Property Damage, Arson, Premises Liability, Intentional Torts, Insurance Fraud, Wrongful Death, Personal Injury, Automobile, No-Fault, First and Third Party Defense, Uninsured and Underinsured Motorist, Theft, Bodily Injury, Deceptive Trade Practices, Life Insurance, Accident and Health, Homeowners, Disability, Self-Insured Defense, Aviation, Corporate Law, Real Estate, Estate Planning, Probate, Mergers and Acquisitions, Counseling, Credit Insurance, Warranty Litigation, Consumer Law, Vendor Contracts

Firm Profile: The mission of Bowen, Radabaugh & Milton, P.C., is to assist our clients in managing their legal and business relationships in an exceedingly complex world. Our members enjoy reputations for aggressive and creative approaches to problem-solving for our clients. We strive to provide our clients with updates regarding current trends in the law and provide presentations to our clients in legal areas which are of concern to them. We are committed to efficiently and economically handle all matters through the application of cost-saving technology.

Insurance Clients

Acuity Insurance Company
CUMIS Insurance Society, Inc.
CUNA Mutual Life Insurance Company
Intercargo Insurance Company
Progressive Insurance Company
Citizens Insurance Company of America
Farm Bureau Insurance Company
General Casualty Companies
North American Specialty Insurance Company

Non-Insurance Clients

Black & Decker (U.S.), Inc.
CKGP/PW & Associates, Inc.
Credit Union One
Family Dollar Stores of Michigan, Inc.
Gordon Food Service, Inc.
Intier Automotive
Michigan Credit Union League
National Loan Investors, LP
Pontiac Flight Service, Inc.
Riddell, Inc.
Terex Corporation
Waterford Aviation, Inc.
Bombardier Recreational Products Inc.
DFCU Financial Credit Union
Gala & Associates, Inc.
Genisys Credit Union
HMS Mfg. Co.
Meijer, Inc.
Motown Automotive Distributing
Oakland University
Pro-Motion Technology Group, LLC
Wanigas Credit Union
Western General Management, Inc.

Partners

Thomas R. Bowen — 1952 — Michigan State University, B.A., 1974; Detroit College of Law, J.D. (cum laude), 1977 — Named Michigan Super Lawyer (2007-2014) — Admitted to Bar, 1977, Michigan; 1977, U.S. District Court, Eastern and Western Districts of Michigan; 1978, U.S. Court of Appeals, Sixth Circuit — Member State Bar of Michigan; Oakland County Bar Association; Michigan State Bar Foundation; Association of Defense Trial Counsel — Practice Areas: Defense Litigation; Trial and Appellate Practice; State and Federal Courts; Declaratory Judgments; Arbitration; Employment Law; Americans with Disabilities Act; Discrimination; Wrongful Termination; Equal Employment Opportunity Commission; Civil Rights; Sexual Harassment; Tort Litigation; Product Liability; Homeowners; Premises Liability; Intentional Torts; Automobile; No-Fault; Self-Insured Defense — Tel: 248-641-0611 (Direct Dial) — E-mail: TRBowen@brmattorneys.com

James M. Radabaugh — 1952 — Western Michigan University, B.S. (summa cum laude), 1974; Wayne State University, J.D., 1977; LL.M. Taxation, 1989 — DBusiness, Southeast Michigan Journal for Business, Top Lawyers (2009) — Admitted to Bar, 1977, Michigan; 1977, U.S. District Court, Eastern District of Michigan; 1980, U.S. Court of Appeals, Sixth Circuit; 1981, U.S. Supreme Court — Member State Bar of Michigan (Sections: Business Law, Real Property, Probate and Estate Planning, International Law) — Delegate, LawPact, An International Association of Business Law Firms — Practice Areas: Corporate Law; Mergers and Acquisitions; Real Estate; Probate; Estate Planning — Tel: 248-641-9663 (Direct Dial) — E-mail: JMRadabaugh@brmattorneys.com

Lisa T. Milton — 1959 — Michigan State University, B.A., 1981; Detroit College of Law, J.D., 1985 — Admitted to Bar, 1985, Michigan; 2010, Ohio; 1987, U.S. District Court, Eastern District of Michigan; 1987, U.S. Court of Appeals, Sixth Circuit; 1990, U.S. District Court, Western District of Michigan — Member State Bar of Michigan; Oakland County and Toledo Bar Associations — Practice Areas: Commercial Litigation; Defense Litigation; Trial and Appellate Practice; State and Federal Courts; Declaratory Judgments; Arbitration; Opinions; Employment Law; Americans with Disabilities Act; Discrimination; Wrongful Termination; Equal Employment Opportunity Commission; Civil Rights; Sexual Harassment; Tort Litigation; Premises Liability; Intentional Torts; Insurance Fraud; Personal Injury; Deceptive Trade Practices; Life Insurance; Accident and Health; Homeowners; Disability; Self-Insured Defense; Business Law; Employer Liability; Shareholder Disputes — Tel: 248-641-8486 (Direct Dial) — E-mail: LTMilton@brmattorneys.com

Geoffrey D. Marshall — 1969 — Michigan State University, B.A., 1992; Michigan State University College of Law, J.D., 1995 — Named "2008 Michigan Super Lawyers Rising Star" — Admitted to Bar, 1995, Michigan; 1995, U.S. District Court, Eastern District of Michigan; 2000, U.S. Court of Appeals, Sixth Circuit; 2013, U.S. District Court, Western District of Michigan — Member State Bar of Michigan; Oakland County Bar Association — Practice Areas: Commercial Litigation; Corporate Law; Defense Litigation; Trial and Appellate Practice; State and Federal Courts; Declaratory Judgments; Arbitration; Opinions; Employment Law; Coverage Analysis; Policy Construction and Interpretation; Tort Litigation; Product Liability; Property Loss; Arson; Premises Liability; Intentional Torts; Insurance Fraud; Wrongful Death; Personal Injury; Automobile; No-Fault; First and Third Party Defense; Uninsured and Underinsured Motorist; Life Insurance; Accident and Health; Homeowners; Disability — Tel: 248-641-8992 (Direct Dial) — E-mail: GDMarshall@brmattorneys.com

Michael D.P. Burwell — 1956 — University of Michigan, B.A., 1978; Thomas M. Cooley Law School, J.D., 1981 — Admitted to Bar, 1981, Michigan; 2009, Ohio; 1981, U.S. District Court, Eastern District of Michigan; 1986, U.S. Court of Appeals, Sixth Circuit — Member State Bar of Michigan; Oakland County, NTSB and Toledo Bar Associations; Lawyer-Pilots Bar Association — Practice Areas: Automobile Liability; Business Law; Commercial Litigation; Banking; Corporate Law; Mergers and Acquisitions; Real Estate; Defense Litigation; Employment Law; Negligence; Premises Liability; Probate; Aviation; Estate Planning; State and Federal Courts; Tort Litigation; Trial and Appellate Practice — Tel: 248-641-8099 (Direct Dial) — E-mail: MDBurwell@brmattorneys.com

David T. Bowen — 1980 — Miami University, B.A., 2003; Michigan State University College of Law, J.D. (summa cum laude), 2006 — Admitted to Bar, 2006, Michigan; 2012, U.S. District Court, Eastern District of Michigan; 2013, U.S. Court of Appeals, Sixth Circuit — Member State Bar of Michigan; Oakland County Bar Association — Practice Areas: Defense Litigation; Employment Law; Tort Litigation; Product Liability; Premises Liability; Insurance Defense; Automobile Liability; No-Fault — Tel: 248-641-7594 (Direct Dial) — E-mail: DTBowen@brmattorneys.com

Associate

Marc T. Bowen — 1983 — Michigan State University, B.A., 2006; Michigan State University College of Law, J.D. (cum laude), 2009 — Admitted to Bar, 2009, Michigan; 2012, U.S. District Court, Eastern District of Michigan — Member State Bar of Michigan — Practice Areas: Insurance Defense; No-Fault; Personal Injury; Premises Liability; Employment Law; Product Liability — Tel: 248-641-8799 (Direct Dial) — E-mail: MTBowen@brmattorneys.com

Of Counsel

Mary Rourke Benedetto — 1959 — University of Michigan, B.A., 1981; Wayne State University, J.D., 1984 — Admitted to Bar, 1984, Michigan; U.S. District Court, Eastern and Western Districts of Michigan; U.S. Court of Appeals, Sixth Circuit — Member State Bar of Michigan — Practice Areas: Employment Law; Insurance Defense; Personal Injury; No-Fault; First and Third Party Defense; Uninsured and Underinsured Motorist; Premises Liability; Automobile Liability; Negligence; Contracts; Insurance Coverage — E-mail: MRBenedetto@brmattorneys.com

TROY   MICHIGAN

Dickinson Wright PLLC

2600 West Big Beaver Road, Suite 300
Troy, Michigan 48084-3312
   Telephone: 248-433-7200
   Fax: 248-433-7274
   E-Mail: Fortiz@dickinsonwright.com
   www.dickinson-wright.com

(Detroit, MI Office*: 500 Woodward Avenue, Suite 4000, 48226-3425)
   (Tel: 313-223-3500)
   (Fax: 313-223-3598)
   (www.dickinsonwright.com)
(Ann Arbor, MI Office*: 350 South Main Street, Suite 300, 48104)
   (Tel: 734-623-7075)
   (Fax: 734-623-1625)
(Lansing, MI Office*: 215 South Washington Square, Suite 200, 48933-1816)
   (Tel: 517-371-1730)
   (Fax: 517-487-4700)
(Nashville, TN Office*: 424 Church Street, Suite 1401, 37219)
   (Tel: 615-244-6538)
   (Fax: 615-256-8280)
(Phoenix, AZ Office*: 1850 North Central Avenue, Suite 1400, 85004)
   (Tel: 602-285-5000)
   (Fax: 602-285-5100)

Disability, Life Insurance, Medical Malpractice, Health Care, Coverage Issues, Personal Injury, Commercial Litigation, Employment Litigation, ERISA, Accountant Malpractice, Construction Litigation, Directors and Officers Liability

Firm Profile: Dickinson Wright has long been a preferred provider of sophisticated, cost-effective legal services to insurers in the life, health, disability, property, casualty, and alternative insurance (self-insured programs, risk pools, and captives) fields. Our insurance team also represents governmental entities, captive insurers and assigned-risk pools.

Firm Member

Kimberly J. Ruppel — Benjamin N. Cardozo School of Law, Yeshiva University, J.D., 1988 — Admitted to Bar, 2001, Michigan; U.S. District Court, Eastern and Western Districts of Michigan; U.S. Court of Appeals, Sixth Circuit — Practice Areas: Disability Insurance; Life Insurance; ERISA — Tel: 248-433-7291 — E-mail: kruppel@dickinsonwright.com

(See listing under Detroit, MI for additional information)

Garan Lucow Miller, P.C.

1111 West Long Lake Road, Suite 300
Troy, Michigan 48098-6333
   Telephone: 248-641-7600
   Fax: 248-641-0222
   Toll Free: 800-875-7600
   24 Hour Toll Free: 888-332-0540
   www.garanlucow.com

(Additional Offices: Detroit, MI*; Ann Arbor, MI*; Grand Blanc, MI*(See Flint listing); Grand Rapids, MI*; Lansing, MI*; Marquette, MI*; Port Huron, MI*; Traverse City, MI*; Merrillville, IN*)

Business Law, Employment Law, Insurance Defense, Municipal Liability, No-Fault, Workers' Compensation

(See listing under Detroit, MI for additional information)

Giarmarco, Mullins & Horton, P.C.

Tenth Floor Columbia Center
101 West Big Beaver Road
Troy, Michigan 48084-5280
   Telephone: 248-457-7000
   Fax: 248-457-7001
   www.gmhlaw.com

(Detroit, MI Office*: 1001 Woodward Avenue, Suite 1000, 48226)
   (Tel: 248-457-7000)
   (Fax: 248-457-7001)

Established: 1970

General Defense, Property and Casualty, Workers' Compensation, Civil Rights, Product Liability, Medical Malpractice, Dental Malpractice, Dram Shop, Civil Litigation, Trial and Appellate Practice, Employment

Firm Profile: The law firm of Giarmarco, Mullins & Horton consists of 71 attorneys dedicated to high quality, personalized service to help our clients meet their objectives. Controlling the cost of services is an important concern at Giarmarco, Mullins & Horton. Our size allows for specialization and back up not available at smaller firms and avoids bureaucratic inefficiencies of larger firms. Our exceptional legal expertise, together with cost consciousness and service motivation, results in outstanding value.

Giarmarco, Mullins & Horton is an acknowledged leader in the area of litigation, with extensive experience in insurance defense and workers' compensation, representing insurance carriers, employers in conjunction with their third party administrators, corporations and self-insured funds. The firm also practices in the areas of business and tax law, health care, labor and employment, estate planning, real estate, employee benefits and government law.

Insurance Clients

Accident Fund Insurance Company of America	ASU Risk Management Services, Ltd.
Broadspire	CCMSI - Cannon Claims Management Services, Inc.
Citizens Insurance Company of America	The Doctors Company
EBI Indemnity Company	Gallagher Bassett Services, Inc.
General Casualty Company of Wisconsin	Great American Insurance Company
The Hartford Insurance Group	Lancet Indemnity Risk Retention Group
McLaren Corporate Insurance and Risk	Michigan Health and Hospital Association
Michigan Mutual Insurance Company	Mitsui Sumitomo Insurance Company
Ophthalmic Mutual Insurance Company	

Non-Insurance Clients

Port Huron Hospital	William Beaumont Hospital

Attorney Contacts

Andrew T. Baran — Harvard University, A.B. (cum laude), 1977; Wayne State University, J.D. (cum laude), 1980 — Admitted to Bar, 1980, Michigan; 1982, U.S. Court of Appeals, Sixth Circuit

Bruce E. Bigler — Michigan State University, B.S., 1970; Wayne State University, J.D., 1973 — Admitted to Bar, 1973, Michigan; U.S. District Court, Eastern and Western Districts of Michigan

Michael Bosnic — Michigan State University, B.A., 1992; University of Notre Dame Law School, J.D., 1995 — Admitted to Bar, 1995, Michigan; U.S. District Court, Eastern District of Michigan; U.S. Court of Appeals, Sixth Circuit

Kenneth Chapie — Michigan State University, B.A., 2000; University of Detroit Mercy School of Law, J.D. (cum laude), 2003 — Admitted to Bar, 2003, Michigan; U.S. District Court, Eastern District of Michigan; U.S. Court of Appeals, Sixth Circuit

John Clark — Michigan State University, B.A., 1990; University of Detroit, J.D., 1994 — Admitted to Bar, 1994, Michigan — American Arbitration Association (Certified)

Jennifer Englehardt — University of Michigan, B.A., 1995; Wayne State University, J.D., 2002 — Admitted to Bar, 2002, Michigan

Giarmarco, Mullins & Horton, P.C., Troy, MI (Continued)

Daniel J. Kelly — Western Michigan University, B.S., 1984; University of Detroit Mercy School of Law, J.D., 1987 — Admitted to Bar, 1988, Michigan; U.S. District Court, Eastern District of Michigan; U.S. Court of Appeals, Sixth Circuit; Supreme Court of Michigan

Stephen J. Hitchcock — University of Michigan; Western Michigan University, B.A., 1970; Detroit College of Law, J.D., 1973 — Admitted to Bar, 1973, Michigan; Florida; Supreme Court of Michigan; U.S. Court of Appeals, Sixth Circuit; U.S. Supreme Court

Anne E. Lawter — University of Michigan - Flint, B.A., 1989; Thomas M. Cooley Law School, J.D., 1996 — Admitted to Bar, 1996, Michigan; 1997, U.S. District Court, Western District of Michigan; 2000, U.S. District Court, Eastern District of Michigan

Tori S. Lehman — University of Michigan, B.A. (with high distinction), 2004; Wayne State University, J.D. (cum laude), 2008 — Admitted to Bar, 2008, Michigan; U.S. District Court, Eastern District of Michigan — Languages: Spanish

Adam Levitsky — University of Michigan, B.A., 1987; University of Wisconsin Law School, J.D., 1990 — Admitted to Bar, 1990, Minnesota; Wisconsin; 1997, Michigan; 1990, U.S. District Court, District of Minnesota; U.S. District Court, Western District of Wisconsin; 1997, U.S. District Court, Eastern and Western Districts of Michigan

Katharine McCarthy — The College of Wooster, B.A. (cum laude), 2009; Wayne State University Law School, J.D. (cum laude), 2013 — Admitted to Bar, 2013, Michigan

J. Travis Mihelick — James Madison College at Michigan State University, B.A., 2006; Ave Maria School of Law, J.D., 2009 — Admitted to Bar, 2009, Michigan; 2010, Ohio; 2009, U.S. District Court, Eastern District of Michigan; 2010, U.S. District Court, Western District of Michigan

John Miller — Northern Michigan University, B.A. (cum laude), 2005; M.P.A. (summa cum laude); Michigan State University College of Law, J.D. (summa cum laude), 2008 — Admitted to Bar, 2008, Michigan; 2009, U.S. District Court, Eastern District of Michigan; U.S. Court of Appeals, Sixth Circuit

Timothy J. Mullins — Wayne State University, B.A. (with distinction), 1974; Detroit College of Law, J.D., 1977 — Admitted to Bar, 1977, Michigan; 1993, U.S. District Court, Eastern and Western Districts of Michigan; U.S. Court of Appeals, Sixth Circuit; U.S. Supreme Court

Christopher Ryan — Western Michigan University, B.B.A. (cum laude), 2007; Michigan State University College of Law, J.D. (cum laude), 2010 — Admitted to Bar, 2010, Michigan; U.S. District Court, Western District of Michigan; 2012, U.S. District Court, Eastern District of Michigan

Jared Trust — Florida State University, B.S. (with honors), 2005; University of Detroit Mercy School of Law, J.D. (with honors), 2009 — Admitted to Bar, 2009, Michigan; U.S. District Court, Eastern District of Michigan

Katherine Trust — Hope College, B.S. (cum laude), 2006; University of Detroit Mercy School of Law, J.D. (cum laude), 2009 — Admitted to Bar, 2009, Michigan

Donald Warwick — Wayne State University, B.A., 1986; Detroit College of Law, Michigan State University, J.D., 1991 — Admitted to Bar, 1991, Michigan

Marsha Woods — University of Michigan; Michigan State University, B.A. (cum laude), 1972; Detroit College of Law, J.D., 1975 — Admitted to Bar, 1975, Michigan

Leroy H. Wulfmeier, III — Wayne State University; Michigan State University College of Law, J.D., 1970 — Admitted to Bar, 1970, Michigan; U.S. District Court, Eastern District of Michigan

Gregory and Meyer, P.C.

340 East Big Beaver, Suite 520
Troy, Michigan 48083
Telephone: 248-689-3920
Fax: 248-689-4560
E-Mail: tjarvis@gregorylaw.com
www.gregorylaw.com

Established: 1978

Gregory and Meyer, P.C., Troy, MI (Continued)

Insurance Defense, Commercial Law, Personal Lines, Special Investigative Unit Claims, State and Federal Courts, Trial and Appellate Practice, Examinations Under Oath, Subrogation, First and Third Party Defense, Arson, Automobile, Breach of Contract, Casualty, Common Carrier, Coverage Analysis, Declaratory Judgments, Environmental Law, Fire, Fraud, No-Fault, Personal Injury, Premises Liability, Product Liability, Property, Theft

Firm Profile: The firm of Gregory and Meyer, P.C. was incorporated in 1978. Our attorneys have focused on insurance defense matters throughout their legal careers. We actively sponsor and participate in educational programs and seminars for the benefit of the insurance industry. We are committed to developing enduring client relationships through professionalism, communication, cost-effective litigation management strategies and the application of modern technology.

Insurance Clients

Auto-Owners Insurance Company
Church Mutual Insurance Company
The Cincinnati Insurance Companies
CNA Insurance Companies
Encompass Insurance
Great American Insurance Company
Harleysville Insurance Company
IFG Companies/Wholesale Insurance Group
Lloyd's
Nationwide Insurance
St. Paul Travelers
State Auto Insurance Companies

Chubb Group of Insurance Companies
Citizens Insurance Company of America
Community Association Underwriters of America, Inc.
Great Lakes Reinsurance (U.K.) PLC
Hastings Mutual Insurance Company
Indiana Lumbermens Mutual Insurance Company
PrimeOne Insurance Company
Seneca Insurance Company, Inc.
Westfield Group

Non-Insurance Clients

Middle Cities Risk Management Trust

SET-SEG (School Employers' Trust-School Employers' Group)

Partners

Alan G. Gregory — 1952 — Michigan State University, B.A., 1974; Detroit College of Law, J.D., 1978 — Admitted to Bar, 1978, Michigan; U.S. District Court, Eastern and Western Districts of Michigan; U.S. District Court, District of South Dakota; U.S. District Court, Southern District of Ohio; 1994, U.S. Court of Appeals, Sixth and Seventh Circuits — Member American Bar Association (Property Insurance Law Committee); National Society of Professional Insurance Investigators; International Association of Arson Investigators; Defense Research Institute — E-mail: agregory@gregorylaw.com

Kurt D. Meyer — 1957 — Oakland University, B.A., 1981; Wayne State University, J.D., 1985 — Admitted to Bar, 1985, Michigan; 2011, Ohio; 1987, U.S. District Court, Eastern and Western Districts of Michigan; U.S. Court of Appeals, Sixth Circuit; Supreme Court of Michigan — Member Michigan Chapter of National Society of Professional Insurance Investigators (Past President) — Presenter, International Association of Special Investigation Units Regional Seminars; Presenter, National Society of Professional Insurance Investigators National Conference; Presenter, Property Loss Research Bureau, National Conference — E-mail: kmeyer@gregorylaw.com

Glen Howard Pickover — 1960 — Central Michigan University, B.S., 1982; Detroit College of Law, J.D., 1990 — Admitted to Bar, 1990, Michigan; 2009, Wisconsin; 1990, U.S. District Court, Eastern and Western Districts of Michigan; U.S. Court of Appeals, Sixth Circuit; 2010, U.S. District Court, Eastern District of Wisconsin; 2013, U.S. District Court, District of Colorado — Member Oakland County Bar Association; National Society of Professional Insurance Investigators (Past-President, Michigan Chapter); Defense Research Institute — Presenter, NSPII Michigan Chapter and National Conferences — E-mail: gpickover@gregorylaw.com

Michele A. Chapnick — 1968 — Northwestern University, B.S., 1990; Loyola University Chicago School of Law, J.D., 1993 — Admitted to Bar, 1993, Michigan; 2008, Ohio; U.S. District Court, Eastern and Western Districts of Michigan; U.S. District Court, Northern District of Ohio — Member American and Oakland County Bar Associations; State Bar of Michigan; Defense Research Institute — Author: "Michigan Chapter on the Uniform Trade Practices Act", Defense Research Institute, 2005 — Presenter, NASP Michigan Chapter, May 2007; Presenter, Property Loss Research Bureau, National Conference — E-mail: mchapnick@gregorylaw.com

Gregory and Meyer, P.C., Troy, MI (Continued)

Associates

Corinne F. Shoop — 1960 — Michigan State University, B.A., 1981; University of Detroit School of Law, J.D., 1985 — Admitted to Bar, 1985, Michigan; U.S. District Court, Eastern District of Michigan — Member Association of Defense Trial Counsel — Co-Author with Frank Ortiz: "Applicability of Michigan's Comparative - Fault Statutes to Probate Litigation", Michigan Bar Journal, 2011 — Presenter, NSP II Michigan Chapter and National Conference — Practice Areas: Insurance Law; No-Fault; Personal Injury; Product Liability; Professional Malpractice — E-mail: cshoop@gregorylaw.com

Paul J. Ellison — 1957 — University of Michigan, B.A., 1984; Antioch School of Law, Univeristy of the District of Columbia, J.D., 1987 — Admitted to Bar, 1989, Michigan; U.S. District Court, Eastern and Western Districts of Michigan; U.S. District Court, District of South Dakota; U.S. District Court, Southern District of Ohio; U.S. Court of Appeals for the Federal and Sixth Circuits — Member Federal and Oakland County Bar Associations; State Bar of Michigan; Michigan Defense Trial Association — E-mail: pellison@gregorylaw.com

Sarah J. Brutman — 1973 — University of Detroit Mercy, B.S. (summa cum laude), 2000; Wayne State University Law School, J.D. (cum laude), 2003 — Admitted to Bar, 2004, Michigan; U.S. District Court, Eastern District of Michigan — E-mail: sbrutman@gregorylaw.com

Judith M. Carson — University of Michigan - Ann Arbor, B.A., 1983; University of Detroit School of Law, J.D., 1986 — Admitted to Bar, 1986, Michigan; U.S. District Court, Eastern District of Michigan; 1992, U.S. Court of Appeals, Sixth Circuit — E-mail: jcarson@gregorylaw.com

(This firm is also listed in the Subrogation section of this directory)

Harvey Kruse, P.C.

1050 Wilshire Drive, Suite 320
Troy, Michigan 48084-1526
Telephone: 248-649-7800
Fax: 248-649-2316
www.HarveyKruse.com

(Flint, MI Office*: 5206 Gateway Centre Drive, Suite 200, 48507)
(Tel: 810-230-1000)
(Fax: 810-230-0844)
(Grand Rapids, MI Office*: 60 Monroe Center NW, Suite 500B, 49503-2926)
(Tel: 616-771-0050)
(Fax: 616-776-3646)

Established: 1969

Trial and Appellate Practice, State and Federal Courts, Asbestos Litigation, Automobile Liability, Aviation, Casualty, Civil Rights, Commercial Litigation, Construction Liability, Dental Malpractice, Employment Discrimination, Environmental Law, Errors and Omissions, Fidelity and Surety, Fraud, General Liability, Hospital Malpractice, Insurance Defense, Malpractice, Insurance Coverage, Medical Malpractice, No-Fault, Premises Liability, Product Liability, Subrogation, Toxic Torts, Property Damage, Uninsured and Underinsured Motorist

Firm Profile: Many Areas of Expertise, One Overriding Goal: Getting Results for Our Clients As Efficiently As Possible

Insurance Clients

AAA Insurance
ACE USA
ACUITY
American Fellowship Mutual Insurance Company
Auto-Owners Insurance Company
Bituminous Insurance Company
Century Surety Company
Colony Insurance Company
Co-operators General Insurance Company
GMAC/MIC Insurance
Accident Fund Insurance Company of America
Allied Insurance Company
Amerisure Companies
Argonaut Specialty Insurance
Badger Mutual Insurance Company
Caliber One Insurance
Citizens Insurance Company of America
Crawford & Company
ESIS
Gulf Insurance Company

Harvey Kruse, P.C., Troy, MI (Continued)

The Hartford Insurance Group
HDI-Gerling America Insurance Company
Indiana Insurance Company
Maxum Specialty Insurance Group
Nationwide Insurance
Pioneer State Mutual Insurance Company
Sedgwick Claims Management Services, Inc.
Titan Insurance Company
Travelers Insurance Companies
Wausau Insurance Companies
Western Heritage Insurance
Zurich North America
The Hartford Steam Boiler Inspection and Insurance Company
Liberty Mutual Insurance Company
MEEMIC Insurance Company
Northland Insurance Company
RLI Transportation
Scottsdale Insurance Company
Sompo Japan Insurance Company of America
Tower Group Companies
Victoria Insurance Company
West Bend Mutual Insurance Company

Non-Insurance Clients

Amchem
ASEA Brown Boveri, Inc.
BASF Corporation
CBOCS, Inc.
Crane Co.
Emerson Electric Company
Hyundai Motor America
Kennametal, Inc.
Kia Motors America, Inc.
The Manitowoc Company, Inc.
MTD Products, Inc.
Rockwell Automation, Inc.
United Parcel Service, Inc.
Apogent Technologies
Ashland, Inc.
Bendix Corporation
Comcast Cable Telecommunications, Inc.
Honeywell International, Inc.
J.H. France Refractories
Key Plastics L.L.C.
Kohler Company
Meijer Great Lakes, LLP
Quick-Sav Food Stores
TRQSS, Inc.

Firm Members

John A. Kruse — 1926 — University of Detroit, J.D. (cum laude), 1952 — Admitted to Bar, 1952, Michigan — Member State Bar of Michigan; Detroit Bar Association; Product Liability Advisory Council; International Association of Defense Counsel; Defense Research Institute; Association of Defense Trial Counsel — E-mail: jakruse@harveykruse.com

Dennis M. Goebel — 1947 — Wayne State University, J.D. (cum laude), 1973 — Admitted to Bar, 1973, Michigan — Member American and Detroit Bar Associations; State Bar of Michigan; International Association of Defense Counsel; Defense Research Institute — E-mail: dgoebel@harveykruse.com

Michael F. Schmidt — 1949 — University of Detroit, B.S. (summa cum laude), 1971; J.D. (magna cum laude), 1975 — Alpha Sigma Nu, Beta Gamma Sigma — Associate Editor, Journal of Urban Law, 1974-1975 — Admitted to Bar, 1975, Michigan — Member State Bar of Michigan; Oakland County Bar Association; Defense Research Institute; Association of Defense Trial Counsel — E-mail: mschmidt@harveykruse.com

Francis H. Porretta — 1952 — University of Notre Dame, B.B.A., 1974; University of Detroit, J.D. (cum laude), 1977 — Gamma Eta Gamma — Admitted to Bar, 1977, Michigan — Member State Bar of Michigan (Negligence Law Section); Detroit Bar Association; Defense Research Institute — E-mail: fporretta@harveykruse.com

George W. Steel — 1946 — University of Michigan, B.B.A., 1967; University of Detroit, J.D. (cum laude), 1977 — Associate Editor, Journal of Urban Law, 1977 — Admitted to Bar, 1977, Michigan — Member State Bar of Michigan; Genesee County Bar Association; Defense Research Institute — E-mail: gsteel@harveykruse.com — (Retired)

James E. Sukkar — 1952 — Detroit College of Law, J.D. (cum laude), 1978 — Admitted to Bar, 1978, Michigan — Member American Bar Association; State Bar of Michigan; Defense Research Institute — E-mail: jsukkar@harveykruse.com

Larry W. Davidson — 1951 — Western Michigan University, B.A., 1973; Detroit College of Law, J.D., 1976 — Admitted to Bar, 1976, Michigan — Member State Bar of Michigan (Negligence Law Section); Oakland County Bar Association; Defense Research Institute — E-mail: ldavidson@harveykruse.com

Dale R. Burmeister — 1953 — Western Michigan University, B.A. (magna cum laude), 1975; University of Detroit School of Law, J.D. (magna cum laude), 1978 — Admitted to Bar, 1978, Michigan — Member American and Detroit Bar Associations; State Bar of Michigan; Defense Research Institute — E-mail: dburmeister@harveykruse.com

Gary L. Stec — 1954 — University of Michigan, B.S.A., 1977; University of Detroit, J.D. (cum laude), 1980 — Order of Barristers — Admitted to Bar, 1980, Michigan — Member American and Grand Rapids Bar Associations; State Bar of Michigan; Defense Research Institute — E-mail: gstec@harveykruse.com

Harvey Kruse, P.C., Troy, MI (Continued)

William F. Rivard — 1957 — Michigan State University, B.S., 1979; Detroit College of Law, J.D. (cum laude), 1984 — Note and Comment Editor, Detroit College Law Review, 1983 — Admitted to Bar, 1984, Michigan — Member State Bar of Michigan — E-mail: wrivard@harveykruse.com

Michael J. Guss — 1964 — University of Michigan - Dearborn, B.A. (with distinction), 1986; Detroit College of Law, J.D. (cum laude), 1989 — Admitted to Bar, 1989, Michigan; 1989, U.S. District Court, Eastern District of Michigan — Member American and Genesee County Bar Associations; State Bar of Michigan — E-mail: mguss@harveykruse.com

J. Kenneth Wainwright, Jr. — 1948 — Boston College, A.B. (summa cum laude), 1970; J.D. (cum laude), 1975 — Admitted to Bar, 1975, Michigan; 1978, New Jersey — Member American and New Jersey State Bar Associations; State Bar of Michigan; American Corporate Counsel; Defense Research Institute — E-mail: jkwainwright@msn.com

John R. Prew — 1962 — Michigan State University, B.A., 1985; Detroit College of Law, J.D. (cum laude), 1988 — Admitted to Bar, 1988, Michigan — Member American Bar Association; State Bar of Michigan — E-mail: jprew@harveykruse.com

Jason R. Mathers — 1974 — Wayne State University, B.S., 1999; Wayne State University Law School, J.D. (cum laude), 2003 — Admitted to Bar, 2003, Michigan; 2003, U.S. District Court, Eastern District of Michigan — Member American Bar Association; State Bar of Michigan — E-mail: jmathers@harveykruse.com

Anne V. McArdle — 1972 — Michigan State University, B.S.B.A., 1995; University of Detroit Mercy School of Law, J.D., 2000 — Admitted to Bar, 2000, Michigan — Member Federal Bar Association; State Bar of Michigan — Resident Flint Office — E-mail: amcardle@harveykruse.com

Dahlia N. Dallo — 1978 — James Madison College at Michigan State University, B.A., 2000; University of Detroit Mercy School of Law, J.D., 2003 — Admitted to Bar, 2003, Michigan — Member State Bar of Michigan; Oakland County and Chaldean Bar Associations — E-mail: ddallo@harveykruse.com

Associates

Lanae L. Monera — 1971 — Grand Valley State University, B.A. (magna cum laude), 1993; Wayne State University, J.D. (cum laude), 1996 — Admitted to Bar, 1996, Michigan — Member State Bar of Michigan — E-mail: lmonera@harveykruse.com

Kimberly A. Kardasz — 1974 — University of Michigan, B.A., 1997; Michigan State University, Detroit College of Law, J.D. (magna cum laude), 2000 — Admitted to Bar, 2000, Michigan; U.S. District Court, Eastern and Western Districts of Michigan; U.S. Court of Appeals, Sixth Circuit

Nathan G. Peplinski — 1977 — Quincy University, B.A. (summa cum laude), 2000; Wayne State University Law School, J.D. (cum laude), 2003 — Admitted to Bar, 2003, Michigan — Member State Bar of Michigan — E-mail: npeplinski@harveykruse.com

Anthony J. Sukkar — 1982 — Michigan State University, B.A. (cum laude), 2004; Wayne State University Law School, J.D., 2007 — Admitted to Bar, 2007, Michigan; 2008, U.S. District Court, Eastern District of Michigan — Member State Bar of Michigan — E-mail: asukkar@harveykruse.com

Michael D. Cummings — 1966 — The University of Utah, B.A., 1991; Gonzaga University School of Law, J.D., 1995 — Admitted to Bar, 2002, Michigan; New York; U.S. District Court, Eastern District of Michigan; U.S. District Court, Eastern District of New York — Member State Bar of Michigan — E-mail: mcummings@harveykruse.com

Daniel J. James — 1980 — Hope College, B.A. (magna cum laude), 2003; Wayne State University Law School, J.D., 2007 — Admitted to Bar, 2007, Illinois; 2011, Michigan — Member State Bar of Michigan — E-mail: djames@harveykruse.com

Eric T. Ketelhut — 1984 — Wayne State University, B.S., 2007; University of Detroit Mercy School of Law, J.D. (magna cum laude), 2011 — Admitted to Bar, 2011, Michigan; U.S. District Court, Eastern District of Michigan — Member State Bar of Michigan — E-mail: eketelhut@harveykruse.com

David C. Moll — 1971 — University of Michigan - Dearborn, B.A., 1994; Wayne State University Law School, J.D. (cum laude), 2000 — Admitted to Bar, 2002, Michigan — Member State Bar of Michigan — E-mail: dmoll@harveykruse.com

Gregory P. LaVoy — 1983 — Kalamazoo College, B.A., 2006; Ave Maria School of Law, J.D. (magna cum laude), 2009 — Admitted to Bar, 2009, Michigan

Harvey Kruse, P.C., Troy, MI (Continued)

Of Counsel

Denise P. Hickey — 1969 — University of Michigan, A.B., 1991; University of Detroit, J.D., 1995 — Admitted to Bar, 1995, Michigan — Member American Bar Association; State Bar of Michigan

Michael T. Small — 1955 — Michigan State University, B.A., 1978; Wayne State University Law School, J.D. (cum laude), 1981 — Admitted to Bar, 1981, Michigan — Member State Bar of Michigan; Grand Rapids Bar Association — E-mail: msmall@harveykruse.com

(This firm is also listed in the Subrogation section of this directory)

Secrest, Wardle, Lynch, Hampton, Truex and Morley, P.C.

2600 Troy Center Drive
Troy, Michigan 48084
   Telephone: 248-851-9500
   Fax: 248-538-1223
   E-Mail: info@secrestwardle.com
   www.secrestwardle.com

(Grand Rapids, MI Office*: 2025 East Beltline SE, Suite 600, 49546)
   (Tel: 616-285-0143)
   (Fax: 616-285-0145)
   (E-Mail: hemrich@secrestwardle.com)
(Lansing, MI Office*: 6639 Centurion Drive, Suite 100, 48917)
   (Tel: 517-886-1224)
   (Fax: 517-886-9284)
   (E-Mail: jbradley@secrestwardle.com)

Established: 1912

Appellate Practice, Alternative Dispute Resolution, Commercial Law, Construction Law, Environmental Law, Liquor Liability, No-Fault, General Liability, Insurance Coverage, Premises Liability, Toxic Torts, Class Actions, Agent and Brokers Errors and Omissions, Asbestos Litigation, Automobile Liability, Complex Litigation, Copyright and Trademark Law, Employment Law, Insurance Agents, Intellectual Property, Legal Malpractice, Mass Tort, Mold and Mildew Claims, Municipal Liability, Nursing Home Liability, Pharmaceutical, Probate, Estate Planning, Product Liability, Professional Liability, Truck Liability, Fire, Property and Casualty

Firm Profile: Secrest Wardle is committed to getting results. Our entire approach to litigation and counsel is explicitly structured to meet our clients' needs. Whether defending in litigation or helping to identify, manage, and eliminate legal risks, we seek the most direct solution possible, minimizing costs and time expended.

Insurance Clients

AIG	Auto Club Group
Auto-Owners Insurance Company	Citizens Insurance Company of America
CNA	
Employers Mutual Insurance Company	Frankenmuth Mutual Insurance Company
GEICO	The Hartford
Hastings Mutual Insurance Company	Horace Mann Insurance Company
	Innovative Risk Management, Inc.
Michigan Insurance Company	Michigan Municipal Risk
Progressive Insurance Company	Management Authority
QBE	Zurich North America

Non-Insurance Clients

AT&T	Barton Malow Company
Bloomfield Township	BP Amoco
City of Auburn Hills	City of Bloomfield Hills
Eaton Corporation	Wyeth Laboratories

Secrest, Wardle, Lynch, Hampton, Truex and Morley, P.C., Troy, MI (Continued)

Senior Partners

Bruce A. Truex — Western Michigan University, B.B.A. (cum laude), 1970; Wayne State University, J.D. (cum laude), 1975 — Admitted to Bar, 1976, Michigan

Mark E. Morley — Alma College, B.A., 1969; University of Notre Dame, J.D., 1972 — Admitted to Bar, 1972, Michigan

Daniel P. Makarski — Wayne State University, Ph.B., 1968; M.Ed., 1971; J.D., 1972 — Admitted to Bar, 1972, Michigan

Nathan J. Edmonds — University of Detroit, B.A. (cum laude), 1991; Detroit College of Law, J.D. (magna cum laude), 1994 — Admitted to Bar, 1994, Michigan

Thomas J. Azoni — University of Michigan, B.A., 1974; Detroit College of Law, J.D. (cum laude), 1977 — Admitted to Bar, 1977, Michigan

Mark F. Masters — Wayne State University, B.A., 1992; J.D., 1995 — Admitted to Bar, 1995, Michigan

Executive Partners

Robert G. Chaklos, Jr.
Terry S. Welch
James R. Bradley
Timothy J. Batton
Caroline A. Grech-Clapper
Margaret A. Scott
John G. Mitchell
Henry S. Emrich
Derk W. Beckerleg
Tara Hanley Bratton
Lisa Sabon Anstess

Partners

Robert B. Holt, Jr.
John L. Weston
Rebecca H. Filiatraut
Anthony A. Randazzo
Justin L. Cole
Terri L. Antisdale
Dennis R. Pollard
Kellie C. Joyce
Mark S. Roberts
Jane Kent Mills
Brian J. Casey
Renee T. Townsend
Javon L. Williams
Elizabeta Misovska
Amanda B. Fopma
Nancy Cooper Green
Sante S. Fratarcangeli
William D. Shailor
Steven L. Kreuger
Brian E. Fischer
James P. Molloy
Drew W. Broaddus
Sidney A. Klingler
Douglas D. Moseley
Daniel T. Rizzo
Vahan C. Vanerian
C. Grant VanderVeer
Krystal D. Hermiz
Chase M. Kubica
Mark C. Vanneste
Leah M. Rayfield
Alison M. Quinn
Devon R. Glass
Sarah L. Walburn

Associates

Jason R. Church
Craig O. Pavlock
Jennifer C. Hill
Kristen M. Buter
Justin A. Grimske
Ashley S. Zaleski
David M. Givskud
Lauren A. Frederick
Matthew J. Consolo
Alexander R. Baum
Meghan K. Connolly
Jarett M. Smith
Erin A. Sedmak
Jeffrey R. Bozell

Of Counsel

John R. Secrest
William P. Hampton
Roger F. Wardle

WEST BRANCH † 2,139 Ogemaw Co.

Refer To

Bensinger, Cotant & Menkes, P.C.
308 West Main Street
Gaylord, Michigan 49735
  Telephone: 989-732-7536
  Fax: 989-732-4922

General Defense, Automobile Liability, Fire Loss, Professional Liability, Product Liability, Workers' Compensation, Subrogation, Medical Malpractice, Liquor Liability

SEE COMPLETE LISTING UNDER GAYLORD, MICHIGAN (60 MILES)

MINNESOTA

CAPITAL: ST. PAUL

COUNTIES AND COUNTY SEATS

County	County Seat
Aitkin	Aitkin
Anoka	Anoka
Becker	Detroit Lakes
Beltrami	Bemidji
Benton	Foley
Big Stone	Ortonville
Blue Earth	Mankato
Brown	New Ulm
Carlton	Carlton
Carver	Chaska
Cass	Walker
Chippewa	Montevideo
Chisago	Center City
Clay	Moorhead
Clearwater	Bagley
Cook	Grand Marais
Cottonwood	Windom
Crow Wing	Brainerd
Dakota	Hastings
Dodge	Mantorville
Douglas	Alexandria
Faribault	Blue Earth
Fillmore	Preston
Freeborn	Albert Lea
Goodhue	Red Wing
Grant	Elbow Lake
Hennepin	Minneapolis
Houston	Caledonia
Hubbard	Park Rapids
Isanti	Cambridge
Itasca	Grand Rapids
Jackson	Jackson
Kanabec	Mora
Kandiyohi	Willmar
Kittson	Hallock
Koochiching	International Falls
Lac qui Parle	Madison
Lake	Two Harbors
Lake of the Woods	Baudette
Le Sueur	Le Center
Lincoln	Ivanhoe
Lyon	Marshall
Mahnomen	Mahnomen
Marshall	Warren
Martin	Fairmont
McLeod	Glencoe
Meeker	Litchfield
Mille Lacs	Milaca
Morrison	Little Falls
Mower	Austin
Murray	Slayton
Nicollet	St. Peter
Nobles	Worthington
Norman	Ada
Olmsted	Rochester
Otter Tail	Fergus Falls
Pennington	Thief River Falls
Pine	Pine City
Pipestone	Pipestone
Polk	Crookston
Pope	Glenwood
Ramsey	St. Paul
Red Lake	Red Lake Falls
Redwood	Redwood Falls
Renville	Olivia
Rice	Faribault
Rock	Luverne
Roseau	Roseau
St. Louis	Duluth
Scott	Shakopee
Sherburne	Elk River
Sibley	Gaylord
Stearns	St. Cloud
Steele	Owatonna
Stevens	Morris
Swift	Benson
Todd	Long Prairie
Traverse	Wheaton
Wabasha	Wabasha
Wadena	Wadena
Waseca	Waseca
Washington	Stillwater
Watonwan	St. James
Wilkin	Breckenridge
Winona	Winona
Wright	Buffalo
Yellow Medicine	Granite Falls

In the text that follows "†" indicates County Seats.

Our files contain additional verified data on the firms listed herein. This additional information is available on request.

A.M. BEST COMPANY

APPLE VALLEY 49,084 Dakota Co.

Tentinger Law Firm, P.A.
15000 Garrett Avenue
Apple Valley, Minnesota 55124
   Telephone: 952-953-3330
   Fax: 952-953-3331
   E-Mail: jay@tentingerlawfirm.com
   www.tentingerlawfirm.com

Established: 1997

Agriculture, Arbitration, General Liability, Insurance Coverage, Mediation, Motor Vehicle, No-Fault, Premises Liability, Product Liability, Subrogation, Construction, Farm Accidents, Motorcycles, Trucks and Farm Equipment

Firm Profile: Jay A. Tentinger has extensive litigation experience in defending automobile and motorcycle general liability and farm accidents claims. A background in farming has provided him with specialized knowledge and expertise to handle agricultural accidents. His dedication is the foundation for long-standing relationships with clients. Former Assistant Attorney General and Public Defender.

Anna M. Yakle started her career as a Paralegal. She has five years of litigation experience and has a wealth of knowledge and experience in general litigation.

Insurance Clients

American Claim Service, Inc.	Auto-Owners Insurance Company
EMC Insurance Companies	Ohio Casualty Group

Jay A. Tentinger — Westmar College, B.S., 1971; Northern Illinois University, M.B.A., 1973; Hamline University, J.D., 1976 — Admitted to Bar, 1980, Iowa; 1982, Nebraska; 1987, Minnesota — Member Minnesota State, Iowa State and Nebraska State Bar Associations; Minnesota Defense Lawyers Association

Associate

Anna M. Yakle — Winona State University, B.S., 2004; Hamline University, J.D., 2008 — Admitted to Bar, 2008, Minnesota; 2010, U.S. District Court, District of Minnesota — Member Minnesota State Bar Association

BEMIDJI † 13,431 Beltrami Co.

Refer To
Swanson & Warcup, Ltd.
1397 Library Circle, Suite 202
Grand Forks, North Dakota 58201
   Telephone: 701-772-3407
   Fax: 701-772-3833
Mailing Address: P.O. Box 12909, Grand Forks, ND 58208-2909

Insurance Defense, Casualty, Fire, Automobile, Product Liability, Professional Liability, Negligence, Governmental Liability, Coverage Issues, Insurance Litigation, Dram Shop, Construction Law

SEE COMPLETE LISTING UNDER GRAND FORKS, NORTH DAKOTA (120 MILES)

CALEDONIA † 2,868 Houston Co.

Refer To
Johns, Flaherty & Collins, S.C.
205 Fifth Avenue South, Suite 600
La Crosse, Wisconsin 54601
   Telephone: 608-784-5678
   Fax: 608-784-0557
Mailing Address: P.O. Box 1626, La Crosse, WI 54602

Insurance Defense, Trial Practice, Workers' Compensation, Medical Malpractice, Product Liability, Automobile, Bodily Injury, Coverage Issues, Professional Liability

SEE COMPLETE LISTING UNDER LA CROSSE, WISCONSIN (24 MILES)

Refer To
Moen Sheehan Meyer, Ltd.
201 Main Street, Suite 700
La Crosse, Wisconsin 54601
   Telephone: 608-784-8310
   Fax: 608-782-6611
   Toll Free: 800-346-3457
Mailing Address: P.O. Box 786, La Crosse, WI 54602-0786

Insurance Defense, Trial Practice, Automobile, Product Liability, Medical Malpractice, Professional Liability, Premises Liability, Coverage Issues, Bodily Injury

SEE COMPLETE LISTING UNDER LA CROSSE, WISCONSIN (24 MILES)

CROOKSTON † 7,891 Polk Co.

Refer To
Swanson & Warcup, Ltd.
1397 Library Circle, Suite 202
Grand Forks, North Dakota 58201
   Telephone: 701-772-3407
   Fax: 701-772-3833
Mailing Address: P.O. Box 12909, Grand Forks, ND 58208-2909

Insurance Defense, Casualty, Fire, Automobile, Product Liability, Professional Liability, Negligence, Governmental Liability, Coverage Issues, Insurance Litigation, Dram Shop, Construction Law

SEE COMPLETE LISTING UNDER GRAND FORKS, NORTH DAKOTA (25 MILES)

DETROIT LAKES † 8,569 Becker Co.

Refer To
Flom Law Office, P.A.
1703 32nd Avenue South
Fargo, North Dakota 58103-5936
   Telephone: 701-280-2300
   Fax: 701-280-1880

Insurance Defense, Trial and Appellate Practice, State and Federal Courts, Medical Malpractice, Professional Malpractice, Civil Rights, Construction Law, Product Liability, Casualty, Fire, Automobile Liability, Asbestos Litigation, Toxic Substances, Pollution, No-Fault, Coverage Issues, Liquor Liability, Automobile, Premises Liability, Commercial Litigation, Subrogation, Environmental Law, Employment Law, Governmental Liability, Municipal Liability, Errors and Omissions, Health

SEE COMPLETE LISTING UNDER FARGO, NORTH DAKOTA (45 MILES)

DULUTH † 86,265 St. Louis Co.

Hanft Fride, P.A.
130 West Superior Street, Suite 1000
Duluth, Minnesota 55802
   Telephone: 218-722-4766
   Fax: 218-529-2401
   E-Mail: firm@hanftlaw.com
   www.hanftlaw.com

Established: 1899

Insurance Law, Trial Practice, Business Law, Intellectual Property, Professional Malpractice, Employment Practices Liability, Product Liability, Environmental Law, Tort Litigation, Workers' Compensation

Firm Profile: Established in 1899, Hanft Fride has broad transactional and litigation practices. Our active trial practice encompasses professional liability, environmental, employment, workers' compensation construction law, intellectual property, commercial, products liability and personal injury matters.

Insurance Clients

American Family Insurance Group	Auto Club Group Insurance Company
Auto-Owners Insurance Company	
Chartis	Church Mutual Insurance Company

DULUTH MINNESOTA

Hanft Fride, P.A., Duluth, MN (Continued)

Continental Western Insurance Group
General Casualty Companies
Great West Casualty Company
Integrity Mutual Insurance Company
Nationwide Insurance
RiverStone Claims Management, LLC
Travelers Insurance Companies
Wausau Insurance Companies
Zurich North America
EMC Insurance Companies
GEICO
Great American Insurance Company
MetLife
Minnesota Lawyers Mutual Insurance Company
Sedgwick CMS
Sentry Insurance
Utica Mutual Insurance Company
Western National Mutual Insurance Company

Shareholders

Gilbert W. Harries — 1932 — University of Minnesota, B.S.L., 1953; LL.B., 1955 — Admitted to Bar, 1955, Minnesota; 1984, Wisconsin — Member American Bar Association; Minnesota State Bar Association (Board of Governors, 1987-1989); Eleventh Judicial District Bar Association (President, 1986-1987); State Bar of Wisconsin — E-mail: gwh@hanftlaw.com

William M. Burns — 1943 — University of Michigan, B.A. (with honors), 1965; J.D. (magna cum laude), 1968 — Admitted to Bar, 1968, Minnesota; 1968, U.S. District Court, District of Minnesota — Member American, Minnesota State and Eleventh Judicial District Bar Associations — E-mail: wmb@hanftlaw.com

John D. Kelly — 1946 — Harvard University, B.A., 1968; University of Minnesota, J.D. (cum laude), 1974 — Admitted to Bar, 1974, Minnesota; 1986, Wisconsin; 1974, U.S. District Court, District of Minnesota; 1984, U.S. Court of Appeals, Eighth Circuit — Member American, Minnesota State and Eleventh Judicial District Bar Associations; State Bar of Wisconsin; Minnesota Defense Lawyers Association; International Association of Defense Counsel; American Board of Trial Advocates; American College of Trial Lawyers — Tel: 218-529-2437 — Fax: 218-529-2401 — E-mail: jdk@hanftlaw.com

Frederick A. Dudderar, Jr. — 1954 — Indiana University, B.A., 1976; Valparaiso University, J.D., 1979 — Admitted to Bar, 1979, Indiana; 1981, Minnesota; 1982, U.S. District Court, District of Minnesota — Member American, Minnesota State and Eleventh Judicial District Bar Associations — E-mail: fad@hanftlaw.com

Tim A. Strom — 1956 — University of Minnesota, B.A. (magna cum laude), 1981; William Mitchell College of Law, J.D. (cum laude), 1985 — Admitted to Bar, 1985, Minnesota; 1998, Wisconsin; 1988, U.S. District Court, District of Minnesota; 1996, U.S. Court of Appeals, Eighth Circuit — Member American, Minnesota State and Eleventh Judicial District Bar Associations; Minnesota Defense Lawyers Association; Defense Research Institute — E-mail: tas@hanftlaw.com

R. Thomas Torgerson — 1958 — University of Wisconsin, B.A. (with distinction), 1981; J.D. (cum laude), 1985 — Admitted to Bar, 1985, Minnesota; Wisconsin; 1985, U.S. District Court, District of Minnesota; 1992, U.S. Court of Appeals, Eighth Circuit; 1999, U.S. District Court, Western District of Wisconsin — Member American, Minnesota State and Eleventh Judicial District Bar Associations; State Bar of Wisconsin; Minnesota Defense Lawyers Association; Defense Research Institute — E-mail: rtt@hanftlaw.com

Cheryl M. Prince — 1963 — University of Wisconsin, B.S. (magna cum laude), 1985; J.D. (cum laude), 1988 — Admitted to Bar, 1988, Wisconsin; 1988, U.S. District Court, Western District of Wisconsin; 1989, U.S. District Court, District of Minnesota — Member American, Minnesota State and Eleventh Judicial District Bar Associations; State Bar of Wisconsin — E-mail: cmp@hanftlaw.com

Robin C. Merritt — 1963 — Carleton College, B.A. (cum laude), 1985; University of Minnesota, J.D. (cum laude), 1988 — Admitted to Bar, 1988, Minnesota; 1995, Wisconsin; 1990, U.S. District Court, District of Minnesota; 1991, U.S. Court of Appeals, Eighth Circuit; 2002, U.S. District Court, Western District of Wisconsin — Member American, Minnesota State and Eleventh Judicial District Bar Associations; State Bar of Wisconsin; Minnesota Defense Lawyers Association; Defense Research Institute — E-mail: rcm@hanftlaw.com

Jennifer L. Carey — 1965 — University of Wisconsin, B.A. (with distinction), 1988; J.D., 1991 — Admitted to Bar, 1991, Wisconsin; Minnesota; 1991, U.S. District Court, District of Minnesota; U.S. District Court, Western District of Wisconsin — Member American, Minnesota State, Eleventh Judicial District and Douglas County Bar Associations; State Bar of Wisconsin; American College of Real Estate Lawyers — E-mail: jlc@hanftlaw.com

Mark D. Pilon — 1968 — Hamline University, B.A. (magna cum laude), 1990; University of Minnesota, J.D. (cum laude), 1993 — Admitted to Bar, 1993, Minnesota; 1994, Wisconsin; 1993, U.S. District Court, District of

Hanft Fride, P.A., Duluth, MN (Continued)

Minnesota — Member American, Minnesota State and Eleventh Judicial Bar Associations; State Bar of Wisconsin; Defense Research Institute — E-mail: mdp@hanftlaw.com

Jacob J. Baker — 1975 — St. John's University, B.A., 1997; William Mitchell College of Law, J.D., 2000 — Admitted to Bar, 2000, Minnesota; 2006, Wisconsin; 2000, U.S. District Court, District of Minnesota — Member American, Minnesota State, Eleventh Judicial District and Second Judicial District Bar Associations — E-mail: jjb@hanftlaw.com

Kenneth A. Kimber — 1976 — Colgate University, B.A., 1998; Washington University School of Law, J.D., 2002 — Admitted to Bar, 2002, Minnesota; 2008, Wisconsin; 2002, U.S. District Court, District of Minnesota; 2003, U.S. District Court, Western District of Wisconsin — Member American and Minnesota State Bar Associations; Defense Research Institute; Minnesota Defense Lawyers Association — E-mail: kak@hanftlaw.com

Scott A. Witty — 1981 — Gustavus Adolphus College, B.A. (magna cum laude), 2003; Hamline University School of Law, J.D. (cum laude), 2006 — Admitted to Bar, 2006, Minnesota; 2008, U.S. District Court, District of Minnesota — Member American, Minnesota State and Eleventh Judicial District Bar Associations; Defense Research Institute; Minnesota Defense Lawyers Association — E-mail: saw@hanftlaw.com

David L. Tilden — 1979 — University of Minnesota Duluth, B.A. (cum laude), 2004; University of Miami, J.D. (magna cum laude), 2007 — Admitted to Bar, 2007, North Dakota; 2008, Minnesota; 2007, U.S. District Court, District of North Dakota; 2008, U.S. District Court, District of Minnesota — Member American and Minnesota State Bar Associations; Minnesota Defense Lawyers Association — E-mail: dlt@hanftlaw.com

Associates

Kimberly E. Brzezinski — 1982 — University of Wisconsin-Superior, B.A., 2004; William Mitchell College of Law, J.D., 2008 — Admitted to Bar, 2008, Minnesota; U.S. District Court, District of Minnesota — Real Property Law Specialist — E-mail: keb@hanftlaw.com

Holly LaBoone-Haller — 1988 — Yale University, B.A., 2010; William Mitchell College of Law, J.D. (summa cum laude), 2013 — Admitted to Bar, 2013, Minnesota; 2014, U.S. District Court, District of Minnesota — E-mail: hlh@hanftlaw.com

Of Counsel

Richard R. Burns — 1946 — University of Michigan, B.A. (with honors), 1968; J.D. (magna cum laude), 1971 — Admitted to Bar, 1972, California; 1976, Minnesota; 1983, Wisconsin; 1979, U.S. District Court, District of Minnesota; 1983, U.S. Tax Court — Member American and Minnesota State Bar Associations; Eleventh Judicial District Bar Association (Past President and Past Chairman, Ethics Committee); State Bar of California; State Bar of Wisconsin; American College of Trust & Estate Counsel (Minnesota State Chair) — Tel: 218-529-2433 — Fax: 218-529-2401 — E-mail: rrb@hanftlaw.com

Charles "Huck" Andresen — 1941 — University of Minnesota Duluth, B.A. (magna cum laude), 1963; University of Minnesota Twin Cities, J.D., 1966 — Admitted to Bar, 1966, Minnesota; U.S. District Court, District of Minnesota — E-mail: cha@hanftlaw.com

Thibodeau, Johnson & Feriancek, PLLP

800 Lonsdale Building
302 West Superior Street
Duluth, Minnesota 55802
Telephone: 218-722-0073
Fax: 218-722-0390
Toll Free: 800-279-1910
E-Mail: jdf@trialgroupnorth.com
www.trialgroupnorth.com

Insurance Defense, General Liability, Bodily Injury, Property Damage, Commercial Law, Trucking Law, Asbestos Litigation, Coverage Issues, Workers' Compensation

Insurance Clients

AIG Technical Services, Inc.
Auto-Owners Insurance Company
Carolina Casualty Insurance Company
Austin Mutual Insurance Company
Burlington Insurance Company
Chubb & Son, Inc.
CNA

MINNESOTA

Thibodeau, Johnson & Feriancek, PLLP, Duluth, MN
(Continued)

Coregis Insurance Company
First Financial Insurance Company
General Casualty Insurance Company
Hartford Insurance Company
Metropolitan Insurance Company
RCA Insurance Group
SECURA Insurance, A Mutual Company
Travelers Insurance Companies
Unitrin, Inc.
Fireman's Fund Insurance Companies
Great American Insurance Company
Meridian Mutual Insurance Company
St. Paul Fire and Marine Insurance Company
Sentry Insurance a Mutual Company
Zurich North America

Non-Insurance Clients

Azcon Corporation
J.B. Hunt Transport Services, Inc.
Moose International, Inc.
Pneumo-Abex Corporation
Walgreen Co.
Honeywell, Inc.
Lorillard Tobacco Company
North American Refractories Company

Partners

Thomas R. Thibodeau — University of St. Thomas, B.A. (cum laude), 1964; University of Minnesota, J.D., 1967 — Admitted to Bar, 1967, Minnesota; 1983, Wisconsin; 1996, England; 1996, Wales; 2000, North Dakota; 1983, U.S. District Court, Eastern and Western Districts of Wisconsin; 1983, U.S. District Court, District of Minnesota; 1983, U.S. Court of Appeals, Seventh and Eighth Circuits; 1983, U.S. Supreme Court — Member Minnesota State, England, Wales and Eleventh District Bar Associations; Fellow, International Society of Barristers; Diplomate, American Board of Trial Advocates; International Association of Defense Counsel; Minnesota Defense Lawyers Association; Fellow, American College of Trial Lawyers; Association of Defense Trial Attorneys; Defense Research Institute — Certified Civil Trial Advocate, National Board of Trial Advocacy; Certified Civil Trial Specialist, Minnesota State Bar Association

David M. Johnson — 1966 — The University of North Dakota, B.B.A., 1989; University of Minnesota, J.D., 1992 — Admitted to Bar, 1992, Minnesota; 1998, Wisconsin; 1992, U.S. District Court, District of Minnesota — Member Minnesota State and Eleventh District Bar Associations; Minnesota Defense Lawyers Association; Defense Research Institute; American Board of Trial Advocates — Co-Author: "Taking the Offensive; How Summary Judgement Practice Can Lead Your File Preparation," Minnesota Defense, Spring 1994; "Cross Examination of Medical Experts," Defense Research Institute Magazine, For the Defense, February 1997; "Ethical Considerations in Settlements," Minnesota Defense Lawyers Association Release Deskbook, Fourth Edition, 1998 — Certified Civil Trial Specialist

Jerome D. Feriancek — 1967 — Hamline University, B.A., 1989; William Mitchell College of Law, J.D. (cum laude), 1993 — Admitted to Bar, 1993, Minnesota; 1999, Wisconsin; 1993, U.S. District Court, District of Minnesota; 1996, U.S. District Court, Eastern and Western Districts of Wisconsin — Member Minnesota State and Eleventh District Bar Associations; Minnesota Defense Lawyers Association; Defense Research Institute — Certified Civil Trial Specialist

Matthew R. Thibodeau — 1971 — University of St. Thomas, B.A., 1993; University of Minnesota, J.D., 1997 — Admitted to Bar, 1997, Minnesota; 1997, U.S. District Court, District of Minnesota — Member Minnesota State Bar Association; International Association of Defense Counsel Trial Academy; Minnesota Defense Lawyers Association — Languages: Spanish, Aymara, Quechua

Associates

Gabriel D. Johnson — 1979 — University of Minnesota Duluth, B.A., 2002; California Western School of Law, J.D., 2005 — Admitted to Bar, 2005, Minnesota; 2006, U.S. District Court, District of Minnesota; 2007, U.S. Court of Appeals, Eighth Circuit — Member Minnesota State and Eleventh District Bar Associations; Minnesota Defense Lawyers Association — Practice Areas: Litigation; Workers' Compensation

Christopher S. Davis, Jr. — 1984 — College of St. Scholastica, B.A., 2006; University of La Verne, M.B.A., 2011; University of La Verne College of Law, J.D., 2011 — Admitted to Bar, 2011, California; 2012, Minnesota; 2013, U.S. District Court, District of Minnesota — Member Minnesota State and Eleventh District (New Lawyers Section) Bar Associations; State Bar of California; Minnesota Defense Lawyers Association — Co-Author: "Hold Your Fire: The Injustice of NCAA Sanctions on Innocent Student Athletes," Virginia Sports and Entertainment Law Journal, Vol. 11, Issue 2, Spring 2012, 423-459; The Myth of the "Full Ride": Cheating Our Collegiate Athletes and the Need for Additional NCAA Scholarship-Limit Reform, Oklahoma Law Review, Vol. 65, No. 4, Summer 2013, 605-643 — Practice Areas: Litigation; Product Liability; Wrongful Death; Personal Injury; Construction Law; Asbestos Litigation; Contracts; Employment Law; Insurance Defense; Sports Law; Contract Disputes; Commercial Law

Ryan C. Stutzman — 1975 — University of Illinois at Chicago, B.A., 1998; Hamline University School of Law, J.D., 2009 — Admitted to Bar, 2010, Minnesota; 2013, U.S. District Court, District of Minnesota — Member Minnesota State and Eleventh District Bar Associations; Minnesota Defense Lawyers Association — Practice Areas: Asbestos Litigation; Contracts; Employment Law; Insurance Defense; Personal Injury; Product Liability; Toxic Torts; Wrongful Death

Christopher R. Sall — 1986 — University of St. Thomas, B.A., 2009; William Mitchell College of Law, J.D., 2013 — Admitted to Bar, 2013, Minnesota; U.S. District Court, District of Minnesota — Member Minnesota State and Eleventh District Bar Associations; The Pro Se Project; Minnesota Defense Lawyers Association — Practice Areas: Contracts; Insurance Defense; Personal Injury; Workers' Compensation

EAST GRAND FORKS 8,601 Polk Co.

Refer To

Swanson & Warcup, Ltd.
1397 Library Circle, Suite 202
Grand Forks, North Dakota 58201
Telephone: 701-772-3407
Fax: 701-772-3833

Mailing Address: P.O. Box 12909, Grand Forks, ND 58208-2909

Insurance Defense, Casualty, Fire, Automobile, Product Liability, Professional Liability, Negligence, Governmental Liability, Coverage Issues, Insurance Litigation, Dram Shop, Construction Law

SEE COMPLETE LISTING UNDER GRAND FORKS, NORTH DAKOTA (1 MILES)

FERGUS FALLS † 13,138 Otter Tail Co.

Refer To

Flom Law Office, P.A.
1703 32nd Avenue South
Fargo, North Dakota 58103-5936
Telephone: 701-280-2300
Fax: 701-280-1880

Insurance Defense, Trial and Appellate Practice, State and Federal Courts, Medical Malpractice, Professional Malpractice, Civil Rights, Construction Law, Product Liability, Casualty, Fire, Automobile Liability, Asbestos Litigation, Toxic Substances, Pollution, No-Fault, Coverage Issues, Liquor Liability, Automobile, Premises Liability, Commercial Litigation, Subrogation, Environmental Law, Employment Law, Governmental Liability, Municipal Liability, Errors and Omissions, Health

SEE COMPLETE LISTING UNDER FARGO, NORTH DAKOTA (56 MILES)

MINNEAPOLIS † 382,578 Hennepin Co.

Briggs and Morgan
2200 IDS Center
80 South 8th Street
Minneapolis, Minnesota 55402
Telephone: 612-977-8400
Fax: 612-977-8650
www.briggs.com

(St. Paul, MN Office: W2200 First National Bank Building, 332 Minnesota Street, 55101)
(Tel: 651-808-6600)
(Fax: 651-808-6450)

Established: 1882

Professional Liability, Alternative Dispute Resolution, Appellate Practice, Bankruptcy, Class Actions, Construction Litigation, Employee Benefits, Energy, Environmental Liability, ERISA, Health Care, Intellectual Property, Labor and Employment, Mergers and Acquisitions, Product Liability, Transportation, Privacy and Data Security

Briggs and Morgan, Minneapolis, MN (Continued)

Firm Profile: Briggs and Morgan, P.A. is a trusted name in business law and litigation services with a rich 130-year history. One of Minnesota's largest law firms, Briggs is known for finding creative and efficient solutions to help clients resolve their most complex legal issues. Briggs's more than 160 lawyers are committed to providing responsive, superior client services and sound legal counsel. We offer a broad range of legal services and diversified backgrounds to regional, national and international clients including Fortune 500 corporations, middle market companies, startups, nonprofit and charitable institutions, utilities, public bodies and individuals.

Insurance Clients

The Dentists Insurance Company - TDIC
Federated Insurance Company
Illinois Farmers Insurance Company

Non-Insurance Clients

Gold'n Plump Poultry, Inc.

Shareholders

Lauren E. Lonergan — Macalester College, B.A., 1979; University of Minnesota, J.D., 1982 — Admitted to Bar, 1982, Minnesota; U.S. District Court, District of Minnesota; U.S. Court of Appeals, Eighth Circuit — Practice Areas: Insurance Coverage; Regulatory and Compliance; Third Party; Business Litigation

Frank A. Taylor — The University of Iowa, B.A., 1974; J.D., 1977 — Admitted to Bar, 1977, Iowa; Nebraska; New York; Minnesota; U.S. District Court, District of Nebraska; U.S. District Court, District of Minnesota; U.S. District Court, District of Arizona; U.S. District Court, Southern District of New York; U.S. Court of Appeals, Sixth, Eighth, Tenth and Eleventh Circuits; U.S. Supreme Court; Supreme Court of Minnesota; U.S. Court of Federal Claims; U.S. Tax Court — Practice Areas: Insurance Defense; Alternative Dispute Resolution; Class Actions; Antitrust; Complex Litigation; Regulatory and Compliance; Arbitration

Timothy R. Thornton — Carleton College, B.A., 1971; Florida State University, J.D., 1974 — Admitted to Bar, 1975, Minnesota; Florida; Wisconsin — Practice Areas: Alternative Dispute Resolution; Class Actions; Complex Litigation; Contracts; Insurance Coverage; Mass Tort; Product Liability; Business Litigation; Corporate Law

Gregory J. Stenmoe — University of Minnesota, B.A., 1977; M.B.A., 1992; William Mitchell College of Law, J.D., 1981 — Admitted to Bar, 1981, Minnesota; U.S. District Court, District of Minnesota; U.S. Court of Appeals, Eighth Circuit; U.S. Supreme Court — Practice Areas: Investigations; Employment Law; Sexual Harassment; Litigation and Counseling

John M. Degnan — University of Minnesota, B.A., 1970; William Mitchell College of Law, J.D., 1976 — Admitted to Bar, 1976, Minnesota; U.S. District Court, District of Minnesota; U.S. Court of Appeals, Eighth Circuit; U.S. Supreme Court — Practice Areas: Insurance Defense; Medical Malpractice; Professional Liability; Commercial Litigation; Business Litigation; Directors and Officers Liability; Personal Injury

Thomas J. Basting, Jr. — Cornell University, B.A., 1985; Vermont Law School, J.D., 1992 — Admitted to Bar, 1992, Wisconsin; Minnesota; U.S. District Court, Eastern and Western Districts of Wisconsin; U.S. District Court, District of Minnesota; U.S. Court of Appeals, Eighth Circuit — Practice Areas: First Party Matters; Investigations; Business Litigation; Personal Injury; Product Liability; Property Damage

David A. Schooler — St. Olaf College, B.A., 1987; William Mitchell College of Law, J.D., 1992 — Admitted to Bar, 1992, Minnesota; North Dakota; U.S. District Court, District of Minnesota; U.S. District Court, Central District of Illinois — Practice Areas: Professional Liability; Business Litigation; Employment Litigation; Product Liability; Class Actions

Brownson & Ballou PLLP

225 South Sixth Street, Suite 4800
Minneapolis, Minnesota 55402
Telephone: 612-332-4020
Fax: 612-332-4025
E-Mail: info@brownsonballou.com
www.brownsonballou.com

Established: 2001

Brownson & Ballou PLLP, Minneapolis, MN (Continued)

Asbestos Litigation, Employment Discrimination, Environmental Law, General Liability, Premises Liability, Product Liability, Professional Liability, Toxic Torts, Commercial Litigation, Insurance Coverage, Insurance Defense, Trade Secrets, Employment, Workers' Compensation Defense, Unfair Competition

Firm Profile: Brownson & Ballou, PLLP is a firm with a litigation practice before state and federal trial and appellate courts, and administrative agencies. The firm practices in the areas of commercial and insurance defense and coverage litigation with a focus on environmental, toxic tort, insurance coverage, premises liability, product liability, employment, construction and surety, and workers' compensation defense work.

Insurance Clients

Arrowood Indemnity Company
Broadspire
CNA Insurance Company
Employers Mutual Casualty Company
Gallagher Bassett Services, Inc.
Houston Casualty Company
Navigators Insurance Company
Sedgwick CMS
Selective Insurance Company of South Carolina
Western Pacific Mutual Insurance Company
Berkley Administrators
Chartis Insurance
EMC Insurance Company
Fireman's Fund Insurance Company
HCC Insurance Holdings Group
Integrity Administrators
Professional Indemnity Agency
Selective Insurance Company of America
Unitrin, Inc.

Non-Insurance Clients

Leucadia National Corporation

Partners

Robert D. Brownson — 1953 — St. Olaf College, B.A. (cum laude), 1975; William Mitchell College of Law, J.D., 1979 — Admitted to Bar, 1979, Minnesota — Member Minnesota State and Hennepin County Bar Associations; Minnesota Defense Lawyers Association (Chairman, Litigation Committee, Environmental Law Section, 1980-1990); American Board of Trial Advocates (ABOTA); Defense Research Institute — Practice Areas: Toxic Torts; Asbestos; Environmental Law; Insurance Coverage; Product Liability

Thomas J. Linnihan — 1954 — College of St. Thomas, B.A., 1976; Hamline University, J.D., 1980 — Admitted to Bar, 1980, Minnesota — Member American, Minnesota State and Hennepin County Bar Associations

Kristi K. Brownson — 1969 — Concordia College, B.A. (summa cum laude), 1991; University of Minnesota, J.D. (cum laude), 1995 — Admitted to Bar, 1995, Minnesota; 2004, North Dakota — Member Minnesota State and Hennepin County Bar Associations; Claims & Litigation Management Alliance (CLM); American Arbitration Association (Neutral, Panel of Arbitrators); Defense Research Institute; Minnesota Defense Lawyers Association — Adjunct Professor, University of Minnesota Law School (1998-2014) — Practice Areas: Toxic Torts; Asbestos; Environmental Law; Trade Secrets; Employment; Sexual Harassment; Wage and Hour Law; Insurance

Patrick M. Biren — 1974 — St. John's University, B.A., 1996; William Mitchell College of Law, J.D., 2002 — Admitted to Bar, 2002, Minnesota

Associates

Shannon N.L. Cooper — University of Minnesota Morris, B.A. (with highest distinction), 2002; University of Minnesota Law School, J.D. (cum laude), 2005 — Admitted to Bar, 2005, Minnesota — Member Minnesota State and Hennepin County Bar Associations; Minnesota Defense Lawyers Association

Kristine L. Cook — State University of New York at Plattsburgh, B.A. (magna cum laude), 2006; Hofstra University School of Law, J.D. (magna cum laude), 2009 — Admitted to Bar, 2012, Minnesota — Member Minnesota State and Hennepin County Bar Associations; Minnesota Defense Lawyers Association

Sarah A. Wall — University of Minnesota, B.A., 2010; University of Minnesota Law School, J.D., 2013 — Admitted to Bar, 2013, Minnesota — Member Minnesota State and Hennepin County Bar Associations; Minnesota Defense Lawyers Association

MINNESOTA   MINNEAPOLIS

Cousineau McGuire Chartered

1550 Utica Avenue South, Suite 600
Minneapolis, Minnesota 55416-5318
   Telephone: 952-546-8400
   Fax: 952-546-0628
   E-Mail: cmc@cousineaulaw.com
   www.cousineaulaw.com

(Ironwood, MI Office: 1439 East Cloverland Drive, 49938)
   (Tel: 800-877-8661)
   (Fax: 906-932-1688)
   (E-Mail: lfk@cousineaulaw.net)

Established: 1948

Civil Litigation, Insurance Defense, Workers' Compensation, Insurance Coverage, Subrogation, Commercial Trucking and Transportation

Firm Profile: Please visit our website at www.cousineaulaw.com for complete biographies of our attorneys. To register for our Case Summary Series newsletter or to receive a list of representative clients, send an email to cmc@cousineaulaw.com.

Members of our firm have been selected as fellows of prestigious organizations such as Claims & Litigation Management and Litigation Council of America and several are MSBA Board Certified Civil Trial Specialists. Cousineau attorneys are regularly acknowledged by *Super Lawyers* and *Leading American Attorneys*.

Practice: For more than sixty-five years, Cousineau McGuire has vigorously represented insurers, businesses and professionals in the Upper Midwest. Cousineau McGuire represents insurers, third party administrators, self-insured entities, businesses and professionals with a concentration of practices in areas such as: workers' compensation, insurance coverage and defense, professional liability, commercial trucking and transportation, construction, negligence, products and premises liability, automobile and transportation liability, employment law, appellate advocacy and subrogation.

Memberships: DRI, MDLA, American Board of Trial Advocates, Larson's National Workers' Compensation Advisory Board, Trucking Industry Defense Association, Minnesota Trucking Association and Care Providers of Minnesota, and the exclusive Minnesota member of National Workers' Compensation Defense Network.

Insurance Clients

Austin Mutual Insurance Company	Auto-Owners Insurance Company
Chubb Group of Insurance Companies	CNA Insurance Companies
	ESIS Insurance Services
Gallagher Bassett Insurance Services, Inc.	General Casualty Insurance Company
Great West Casualty Company	Horace Mann Insurance Group
Kemper Insurance Companies	Lumbermen's Underwriting Alliance
Philadelphia Insurance Companies	
SECURA Insurance Companies	Sedgwick Claims Management Services, Inc.
Travelers	
United Fire & Casualty Company	Westfield Companies
Zurich American Insurance Company	

Non-Insurance Clients

ARAMARK Corporation	Center Point Energy Minnegasco
ConAgra, Inc.	Domino's Pizza, Inc.
Holiday Companies	Minnesota Vikings Football Club, Inc.
RTW Corporation	

Firm Members

Peter G. Van Bergen — William Mitchell College of Law, J.D. (cum laude), 1974 — Admitted to Bar, 1974, Minnesota — Practice Areas: Civil Litigation — E-mail: pvb@cousineaulaw.com

Civil Litigation

James L. Haigh	Michael W. McNee
Susan D. Thurmer	Michael D. Barrett
Andrea E. Reisbord	Dawn L. Gagne
Christopher P. Malone	Tamara L. Novotny

Cousineau McGuire Chartered, Minneapolis, MN
(Continued)

Jessica J. Theisen	Meaghan C. Bryan
Mark L. Pfister	David A. Wikoff
Robyn K. Johnson	Kimberly Fleming
Michael D. Sharkey	Stephanie N. Swanson
Rachel E. Bendtsen	

Workers' Compensation

James R. Waldhauser	Thomas P. Kieselbach
John T. Thul	Mark A. Kleinschmidt
Thomas F. Coleman	Richard W. Schmidt
Lisa F. Kinney	Jennifer M. Fitzgerald
Craig A. Larsen	Whitney L. Teel
Natalie K. Lund	Thomas W. Atchison
Zachary T. Chalgren	Michael Johnson
Elizabeth Cox	

Fitch, Johnson, Larson & Held, P.A.

2021 East Hennepin Avenue, Suite 100
Minneapolis, Minnesota 55413-1769
   Telephone: 612-332-1023
   Fax: 612-332-3173
   E-Mail: jhupp@fitchjohnson.com
   www.fitchjohnson.com

Established: 1968

Insurance Law, Workers' Compensation, Product Liability, Subrogation, Employment Law

Insurance Clients

ACE USA/ESIS, Inc.	Auto-Owners Insurance Company
CNA Insurance Company	Continental Western Insurance Company
Employers Insurance Company of Wausau	Federated Insurance Company
Gallagher Bassett Insurance Company	General Casualty Companies
	Great American Insurance Company
Great Central Insurance Company	Indiana Insurance Company
Highlands Insurance Group	Motorists Group-American Hardware/Iowa Mutual
Minnesota Counties Insurance Trust	
MSIG Claims	Ohio Casualty Insurance Company/Liberty Mutual
Providence Property and Casualty Insurance Company	RAM Mutual Insurance Company
Reliamax Insurance Company	Risk Enterprise Management, Ltd.
Safeco/American States Insurance Company	Sedgwick Group of Minnesota, Inc.
Western National Mutual Insurance Company	Travelers Property Casualty Insurance Company
	Zurich American Insurance Company

Non-Insurance Clients

Constitution State Service Company	Frank Gates Service Company

Firm Members

Victor C. Johnson — University of Minnesota, J.D., 1964 — Admitted to Bar, 1964, Minnesota — Member Minnesota State and Hennepin County Bar Associations

David N. Larson — William Mitchell College of Law, J.D., 1976 — Admitted to Bar, 1976, Minnesota; 1982, Wisconsin — Member Minnesota State and Hennepin County Bar Associations; State Bar of Wisconsin

Howard Y. Held — William Mitchell College of Law, J.D., 1983 — Admitted to Bar, 1983, Minnesota; 1988, Wisconsin; 2010, Nebraska; 2012, Oklahoma — Member Minnesota State and Hennepin County Bar Associations; State Bar of Wisconsin

David O. Nirenstein — Washington University, J.D., 1993 — Admitted to Bar, 1993, Minnesota; 1995, U.S. District Court, District of Minnesota — Member Minnesota State and Hennepin County Bar Associations

Ryan J. Courtney — William Mitchell College of Law, J.D., 2004 — Admitted to Bar, 2004, Minnesota; Wisconsin; 2004, U.S. District Court, District of Minnesota — Member Minnesota State and Hennepin County Bar Associations; State Bar of Wisconsin

Fitch, Johnson, Larson & Held, P.A., Minneapolis, MN
(Continued)

Karen R. Swanton — William Mitchell College of Law, J.D., 1986 — Admitted to Bar, 1986, Minnesota — Member Minnesota State and Hennepin County Bar Associations; Minnesota Defense Lawyers Association

Teresa R. Flack — William Mitchell College of Law, J.D., 2004 — Admitted to Bar, 2004, Minnesota; 2004, U.S. District Court, District of Minnesota — Member Minnesota State and Hennepin County Bar Associations

Melissa S. Hareid — William Mitchell College of Law, J.D., 2006 — Admitted to Bar, 2006, Minnesota; 2007, Wisconsin — Member Minnesota State and Hennepin County Bar Associations; State Bar of Wisconsin

Kelly P. Falsani — William Mitchell College of Law, J.D., 2009 — Admitted to Bar, 2009, Minnesota; 2010, Wisconsin — Member Minnesota State and Hennepin County Bar Associations; Minnesota Defense Lawyers Association

Sarah A. Bennett — University of Michigan - Ann Arbor, J.D. (cum laude), 2010 — Admitted to Bar, 2010, Minnesota — Member Minnesota State and Hennepin County Bar Associations

Patricia M. Koth — University of Minnesota Law School, J.D. (magna cum laude), 2012 — Admitted to Bar, 2012, Wisconsin; 2013, Minnesota — Member Minnesota State and Hennepin County Bar Associations; State Bar of Wisconsin

William R. Moody — University of Minnesota Law School, J.D. (magna cum laude), 2011 — Admitted to Bar, 2011, Minnesota — Member Minnesota State and Hennepin County Bar Associations

Goetz & Eckland PA
43 Main Street SE, Suite 505
Minneapolis, Minnesota 55414
Telephone: 612-874-1552
Fax: 612-331-2473
E-Mail: deckland@goetzeckland.com
www.goetzeckland.com

Established: 2002

Construction Law, Insurance Defense, Premises Liability, Product Liability, Insurance Coverage, Daycare Defense

Insurance Clients

Auto-Owners Insurance Company	Westfield Insurance Company

Partners

Deborah Causey Eckland — University of Southern Mississippi, B.S. (with honors), 1985; Paul M Hebert Law School at Louisiana State University, J.D., 1988 — Phi Alpha Delta — Admitted to Bar, 1988, Louisiana; 1989, Minnesota; U.S. District Court, District of Minnesota — Member Amdahl Inn of Court; American Board of Trial Advocates; Minnesota Defense Lawyers Association — E-mail: deckland@goetzeckland.com

Dan Singel — University of Minnesota Law School, J.D. (cum laude), 2005 — Admitted to Bar, 2005, Minnesota; 2010, Wisconsin; 2005, U.S. District Court, District of Minnesota — Member Minnesota Defense Lawyers Association — E-mail: dsingel@goetzeckland.com

Alan P. King — William Mitchell College of Law, J.D., 2004 — Admitted to Bar, 2005, Minnesota; Wisconsin; U.S. District Court, District of Minnesota — Member Minnesota State Bar Association — E-mail: aking@goetzeckland.com

Associates

Rachel Osdoba — University of Minnesota Law School, J.D. (cum laude), 2013 — Admitted to Bar, 2013, Minnesota — Member Minnesota State Bar Association — E-mail: rosdoba@goetzeckland.com

Scott R. Johnson — University of Minnesota Law School, J.D., 2008 — Admitted to Bar, 2008, Minnesota — Member Minnesota State Bar Association — E-mail: sjohnson@goetzeckland.com

Hanson Lulic & Krall, LLC
700 Northstar East
608 Second Avenue South
Minneapolis, Minnesota 55402
Telephone: 612-333-2530
Fax: 612-392-3675
www.hlk.com

Established: 1986

Insurance Defense, Property and Casualty, Arson, Fraud, Marine, General Liability, Product Liability, Civil Litigation, Bad Faith, Construction Litigation, Coverage Litigation, Coverage Opinions, Fidelity

Insurance Clients

ACUITY	Allied Group
Allstate Insurance Group	American Family Insurance Company
Austin Mutual Insurance Company	California Casualty Insurance Company
Auto-Owners Insurance Company	Continental Western Insurance Company
Chubb Group of Insurance Companies	General Casualty Insurance Company
EMC Insurance Companies	Metropolitan Property and Casualty Insurance Company
Farmers Insurance Group	National Farmers Union Casualty Group
Great American Insurance Company	West Bend Mutual Insurance Company
Minnesota Counties Insurance Trust	
Penn-America Insurance Company	
United Fire & Casualty Company	
Western National Insurance Group	
Westfield Insurance Company	

Founding Partner

Jon A. Hanson — University of Minnesota, B.A., 1969; University of Nebraska, J.D., 1972 — Admitted to Bar, 1972, Minnesota; Nebraska; 1985, Wisconsin — Member Nebraska State, Minnesota State and Hennepin County Bar Associations; State Bar of Wisconsin; International Association of Arson Investigators; Defense Research Institute; Minnesota Defense Lawyers Association

Partners

Joseph F. Lulic — University of Minnesota, B.A., 1975; Hamline University, J.D., 1978 — Admitted to Bar, 1978, Minnesota; 1985, Wisconsin; 1978, U.S. District Court, District of Minnesota — Member Minnesota State and Hennepin County Bar Associations; State Bar of Wisconsin

Tony R. Krall — University of Wisconsin-La Crosse, B.S. (with honors), 1981; Hamline University, J.D. (cum laude), 1984 — Admitted to Bar, 1984, Minnesota; 1984, U.S. District Court, District of Minnesota; 1989, U.S. Court of Appeals, Eighth Circuit — Member Minnesota State and Ramsey County Bar Associations; International Association of Arson Investigators (Minnesota Chapter)

Timothy S. Poeschl — University of Minnesota Duluth, B.A., 1998; William Mitchell College of Law, J.D., 2001 — Admitted to Bar, 2001, Minnesota; 2007, Wisconsin; 2012, Iowa — Member American, Minnesota State and Hennepin County Bar Associations; State Bar Wisconsin

Associate Attorneys

Joshua K. Sandey — William Mitchell College of Law, J.D. (cum laude), 2010 — Admitted to Bar, 2010, Minnesota — Member Minnesota State Bar Association

Lucas C. Laakso — Hamline University School of Law, J.D., 2005 — Admitted to Bar, 2005, Minnesota — Member Minnesota State Bar Association; Hennepin County Bar Association

Bradley K. Hammond — Southern Illinois University Carbondale, J.D., 2010 — Admitted to Bar, 2010, Minnesota; 2011, Wisconsin; Illinois (Inactive) — Member Minnesota State Bar Association

Wade T. Johnson — University of South Dakota School of Law, J.D., 2007 — Admitted to Bar, 2007, Minnesota — Member Minnesota State Bar Association

Leah A. Indrelie — William Mitchell College of Law, J.D., 2009 — Admitted to Bar, 2009, Minnesota

Finn S. Jacobsen — University of Minnesota Law School, J.D., 2013 — Admitted to Bar, 2013, Minnesota

MINNESOTA / MINNEAPOLIS

Hanson Lulic & Krall, LLC, Minneapolis, MN (Continued)

Stephanie R. Losching — Hamline University School of Law, J.D., 2013 — Admitted to Bar, 2013, Minnesota — Member Minnesota State and Hennepin County Bar Associations

(This firm is also listed in the Subrogation section of this directory)

Johnson & Lindberg, P.A.

780 Northland Plaza
3800 American Boulevard West
Minneapolis, Minnesota 55431-4459
 Telephone: 952-851-0700
 Fax: 952-851-0900

Insurance Law, Defense Litigation, Coverage Issues, Subrogation

Insurance Clients

- Admiral Insurance Company
- AIG Aviation, Inc.
- Allianz Aviation Managers, LLC
- American Modern Home Insurance Company
- Associated Claims Enterprises, Inc.
- Avemco Insurance Company
- Chartis Aerospace
- CIGNA Property and Casualty Insurance Company
- Farmers Alliance Mutual Insurance Company
- First State Insurance Company
- Foremost Insurance Company
- GEICO General Insurance Company
- K & K Insurance Group, Inc.
- Medmarc Insurance Group
- Republic Western Insurance Company
- United Fire & Casualty Company
- Aerospace Claims Management Group
- American Family Insurance Company
- American Specialty Insurance Services, Inc.
- Berkley Specialty Underwriting Managers, LLC
- Criterion Casualty Company
- Environmental Claims Administrators, Inc.
- Fireman's Fund Insurance Company
- Gallagher Bassett Services, Inc.
- Global Aerospace, Inc.
- Gulf Insurance Company
- Meadowbrook Insurance Group
- Minnesota Counties Insurance Trust
- Transport Insurance Company
- United States Aviation Underwriters, Inc.

Non-Insurance Clients

- Allied Van Lines
- Phoenix Aviation Managers, Inc.
- State of Minnesota
- Citicorp National Services, Inc.
- Republic Financial Services, Inc.
- U-Haul International, Inc.

Michael C. Lindberg — 1951 — Carleton College, B.A. (cum laude), 1973; University of Minnesota, J.D. (cum laude), 1976 — Admitted to Bar, 1976, Minnesota; 1977, U.S. District Court, District of Minnesota; U.S. District Court, Eastern and Western Districts of Wisconsin; U.S. Court of Appeals, Seventh and Eighth Circuits — Member American Bar Association (Tort and Insurance Practice Section: Self-Insurance Committee; Property Insurance Committee; Litigation Section: Insurance Coverage Committee); Minnesota State and Hennepin County Bar Associations; Minnesota Defense Lawyers Association (Governmental Liability Committee) — Certified Civil Trial Specialist

John R. Crawford — 1955 — Middlebury College, B.A. (cum laude), 1978; William Mitchell College of Law, J.D. (cum laude), 1984 — Admitted to Bar, 1984, Minnesota — Member Minnesota State and Hennepin County Bar Associations; Minnesota Defense Lawyers Association — Certified Civil Trial Specialist

Mark J. Peschel — 1954 — St. John's University, B.A., 1976; University of Minnesota, J.D., 1984 — Admitted to Bar, 1984, Minnesota; 1990, North Dakota; 1993, Wisconsin — Member American, Minnesota State and Hennepin County Bar Associations; State Bar Association of North Dakota; State Bar of Wisconsin; Minnesota Defense Lawyers Association (Law Improvement Committee)

Jason M. Hill — 1973 — The University of North Dakota, B.A. (summa cum laude), 1996; University of Minnesota, J.D. (cum laude), 1999 — Admitted to Bar, 1999, Minnesota

Benjamin A. Johnson — Carleton College, B.A. (cum laude), 1998; University of Wisconsin Law School, J.D. (cum laude), 2007 — Admitted to Bar, 2002, Minnesota

Johnson & Lindberg, P.A., Minneapolis, MN (Continued)

Peter M. Lindberg — St. Olaf College, B.A. (magna cum laude), 2005; William Mitchell College of Law, J.D. (cum laude), 2010 — Admitted to Bar, 2010, Minnesota

Of Counsel

Daniel E. Hintz — 1970 — Hamline University, B.A. (cum laude), 1992; The University of Iowa, M.A., 1994; University of Minnesota, J.D. (cum laude), 1999 — Admitted to Bar, 1999, Minnesota

(This firm is also listed in the Subrogation section of this directory)

McCollum, Crowley, Moschet, Miller & Laak, Ltd.

700 Wells Fargo Plaza
7900 Xerxes Avenue South
Minneapolis, Minnesota 55431
 Telephone: 952-831-4980
 Fax: 952-831-2942
 www.mccollumlaw.com

(Rice Lake, WI Office: 315 East South Street, Suite B, 54868)
 (Tel: 715-234-2656)
 (Fax: 715-234-1491)
(Denver, CO Office: 1400 16th Street, Suite 400, 80202)
 (Tel: 303-415-2068)
 (Fax: 303-785-8340)

Established: 1986

Environmental Law, Construction Law, Automobile, Property, Product Liability, Workers' Compensation, Subrogation, Business Law, Civil Litigation, Commercial Law, Personal Injury, Coverage, Employment, Clergy Misconduct, Health Professional License and Discipline, Litigation Management

Insurance Clients

- Adjusting Services Unlimited
- American Family Insurance Company
- American International Group, Inc.
- American States Insurance Company
- Berkley Risk Services, LLC
- Employers Mutual Companies
- ESIS
- Farmers Insurance Company
- Farmland Mutual Insurance Company
- First State Management Group, Inc.
- GuideOne Insurance
- Hartford Insurance Company
- Kemper Insurance Companies
- Liberty Mutual Insurance Company
- Meadowbrook Insurance Group
- Meridian Mutual Insurance Company
- Minnesota Counties Insurance Trust
- Minnesota Insurance Guaranty Association
- National Farmers Union Casualty Group
- Risk Enterprise Management, Ltd.
- RTW, Inc.
- Safeco Insurance
- Security Insurance Company of Hartford
- State Farm Insurance Companies
- USAA Insurance Company
- Westfield Companies
- Zurich Insurance Company
- American Compensation Insurance Company
- American Insurance Company
- American Interstate Insurance Company
- Argonaut Insurance Company
- CNA Insurance Company
- Equity Adjustment Company
- Farm Bureau Mutual Insurance Company
- Fireman's Fund Insurance Company
- Gallagher Bassett Services, Inc.
- General Casualty Companies
- The Harleysville Insurance
- Indiana Lumbermens Mutual Insurance Company
- Lumbermen's Underwriting Alliance
- MetLife Auto & Home Group
- MICOA Group
- Minnesota Fire and Casualty Company
- Monroe Guaranty Insurance Company
- Pharmacists Mutual Insurance Company
- RSKCo
- Rural Mutual Insurance Company
- The St. Paul Companies
- Sedgwick Group
- SFM Mutual Insurance Company
- Travelers Insurance Companies
- Wausau General Insurance Company

Non-Insurance Clients

- American Crystal Sugar
- Cambridge Integrated Services

MINNEAPOLIS / MINNESOTA

McCollum, Crowley, Moschet, Miller & Laak, Ltd., Minneapolis, MN (Continued)

Christian Brothers Risk Pooling Trust
Federal Express
GatesMcDonald
Kraft Foods, Inc.
Marriott Casualty Claims
New Mech Companies
Preferred Works, Inc.
Crawford & Company
Dakota County
Frank Gates Service Company
Kmart Corporation
Kraus-Anderson Construction
Minnesota Department of Employee Relations
Ryder System, Inc.

Shareholders

Robert L. McCollum — University of Minnesota, B.A., 1972; William Mitchell College of Law, J.D. (cum laude), 1976 — Admitted to Bar, 1976, Minnesota; 1994, Wisconsin; 2005, Colorado; 1976, U.S. District Court, District of Minnesota; 2002, U.S. Court of Appeals, Eighth Circuit — Member American Bar Association (Tort and Insurance Section); Minnesota State and Hennepin County Bar Associations; State Bar of Wisconsin; Minnesota Defense Lawyers Association; Defense Research Institute — Practice Areas: Civil Litigation; Employment Law; Environmental Law; Insurance Coverage; Malpractice; Personal Injury; Product Liability; Construction Law; Toxic Torts — Tel: 952-345-9700 — E-mail: rlm@mccollumlaw.com

Deborah L. Crowley — Augsburg College, B.A. (cum laude), 1976; William Mitchell College of Law, J.D., 1982 — Admitted to Bar, 1982, Minnesota; 1983, U.S. District Court, District of Minnesota — Member American, Minnesota State and Hennepin County Bar Associations; Minnesota Defense Lawyers Association — Practice Areas: Workers' Compensation; Arbitration — Tel: 952-345-9716 — E-mail: dlc@mccollumlaw.com

Robyn N. Moschet — Concordia College, B.A. (magna cum laude), 1972; University of Minnesota, J.D., 1975 — Admitted to Bar, 1975, Minnesota; 2010, Colorado; 1979, U.S. District Court, District of Minnesota; 2011, U.S. Supreme Court — Member American, Minnesota State and Hennepin County Bar Associations; Minnesota Defense Lawyers Association; Defense Research Institute — Practice Areas: Insurance Coverage; Product Liability; Construction Defect; Civil Litigation; Arbitration; Mediation; Toxic Torts; Personal Injury — Tel: 952-345-9746 — E-mail: rnm@mccollumlaw.com

Michael D. Miller — University of Minnesota, B.A., 1975; Hamline University, J.D., 1982 — Admitted to Bar, 1983, Minnesota; 1991, Wisconsin; 1984, U.S. District Court, District of Minnesota — Member American and Minnesota State Bar Associations; Minnesota Defense Lawyers Association — Practice Areas: Workers' Compensation; Business Law; Commercial Law; Contracts; Motor Vehicle; Property and Casualty; Personal Injury — Tel: 952-345-9748 — E-mail: mdm@mccollumlaw.com

William G. Laak — Mankato State University, B.S., 1986; William Mitchell College of Law, J.D., 1992 — Admitted to Bar, 1992, Minnesota — Member Minnesota State and Hennepin County Bar Associations — Practice Areas: Workers' Compensation — Tel: 952-345-9730 — E-mail: wgl@mccollumlaw.com

Cynthia K. Thurston — University of St. Thomas, B.A. (magna cum laude), 1990; William Mitchell College of Law, J.D. (cum laude), 1995 — Admitted to Bar, 1995, Minnesota; 1996, Wisconsin; 1999, U.S. District Court, District of Minnesota; 1999, U.S. District Court, Western District of Wisconsin — Member Minnesota State Bar Association; State Bar of Wisconsin — Practice Areas: Civil Litigation; Workers' Compensation — Resident Rice Lake, WI Office — Tel: 715-234-2656 — E-mail: ckt@mccollumlaw.com

Richard P. Wright — St. Thomas College, B.A., 1972; Hamline University, J.D., 1977 — Admitted to Bar, 1977, Minnesota; 1977, U.S. District Court, District of Minnesota; 2005, U.S. District Court, Eastern and Western Districts of Wisconsin — Member Minnesota State and Hennepin County Bar Associations — Practice Areas: Personal Injury; Product Liability; Construction Defect; Contracts — Tel: 952-345-9774 — E-mail: rpw@mccollumlaw.com

Timothy J. Fetterly — Lewis & Clark College, B.A., 1985; Vermont Law School, J.D. (cum laude), 1990 — Admitted to Bar, 1990, Minnesota; 2006, Colorado; 1990, U.S. District Court, District of Minnesota — Member Minnesota State and Hennepin County Bar Associations — Practice Areas: Civil Litigation; Construction Defect; Fire; Complex Litigation; Product Liability; Pharmaceutical; Transportation — Tel: 952-345-9740 — E-mail: tjf@mccollumlaw.com

Cheryl Hood Langel — Loras College, B.A. (maxima cum laude), 1987; University of Minnesota, J.D. (cum laude), 1991 — Admitted to Bar, 1991, Minnesota; 1991, U.S. District Court, District of Minnesota; 1991, U.S. Court of Appeals, Eighth Circuit — Member Minnesota State Bar Association — Practice Areas: Litigation; Personal Injury; Civil Litigation; Appellate Practice; Insurance Coverage — Tel: 952-345-9780 — E-mail: chl@mccollumlaw.com

McCollum, Crowley, Moschet, Miller & Laak, Ltd., Minneapolis, MN (Continued)

Thomas J. Peterson — The University of Iowa, B.S., 1974; J.D. (with distinction), 1977 — Admitted to Bar, 1978, Iowa (Inactive); 1981, Minnesota — Member Minnesota State and Hennepin County Bar Associations; Minnesota Defense Lawyers Association — Practice Areas: Insurance Defense; Workers' Compensation — Tel: 952-345-9712 — E-mail: tjp@mccollumlaw.com

M. Shannon Peterson — University of Minnesota, B.A., 1979; J.D., 1982 — Admitted to Bar, 1982, Minnesota; 2002, Wisconsin — Member Minnesota State and Hennepin County Bar Associations; State Bar of Wisconsin; Minnesota Women Lawyers Association — Practice Areas: Workers' Compensation — Tel: 952-345-9792 — E-mail: msp@mccollumlaw.com

Brett R. Parnes — University of California, Berkeley, B.A., 1994; University of Florida College of Journalism and Communications, M.A., 1999; University of Florida College of Law, J.D., 1999 — Admitted to Bar, 1999, Colorado; 2010, Arizona — Member The Colorado Bar Association; State Bar of Arizona — Practice Areas: Workers' Compensation — Resident Denver, CO Office — Tel: 303-415-2068 — E-mail: brp@mccollumlaw.com

Senior Associate

Stephen D. Garrison — University of Minnesota, B.S., 1978; Hamline University School of Law, J.D., 1982 — Admitted to Bar, 1982, Minnesota; U.S. District Court, District of Minnesota — Member Minnesota State and Hennepin County Bar Associations — Practice Areas: Civil Litigation; Insurance Defense; Personal Injury; Motor Vehicle; No-Fault; Property and Casualty; Construction Defect — Tel: 952-345-9794 — E-mail: sdg@mccollumlaw.com

Attorneys

Scott A. Stoneking — Gustavus Adolphus College, B.A., 1996; Michigan State University, M.S., 1998; Hamline University School of Law, J.D., 2008 — Admitted to Bar, 2009, Minnesota — Member Minnesota State and Hennepin County Bar Associations; Minnesota Defense Lawyers Association — Practice Areas: Workers' Compensation — Tel: 952-345-9859 — E-mail: sas@mccollumlaw.com

Michael J. Conway — University of Minnesota Twin Cities, B.A., 2009; William Mitchell College of Law, J.D. (Dean's List), 2013 — Admitted to Bar, 2013, Minnesota — Member Minnesota State and Hennepin County Bar Associations; Minnesota Defense Lawyers Association — Practice Areas: Workers' Compensation; Civil Litigation; Construction Law; Insurance Law — Tel: 952-345-9818 — E-mail: mjc@mccollumlaw.com

Of Counsel

Gary J. Gordon — Brooklyn College, B.A., 1967; University of Minnesota Law School, J.D., 1972 — Admitted to Bar, 1977, Minnesota; 1986, Wisconsin; 2010, Colorado — Member American, Minnesota State and Hennepin County Bar Associations; State Bar of Wisconsin; American Board of Trial Advocates; International Association of Defense Counsel; American Board of Professional Liability Attorneys; Mississippi Defense Lawyers Association — Practice Areas: Complex Litigation; Product Liability; Class Actions; Mass Tort; Professional Negligence; Commercial Litigation; Personal Injury; Fire — Tel: 952-345-9822 — E-mail: gjg@mccollumlaw.com

O'Meara, Leer, Wagner & Kohl, P.A.

7401 Metro Boulevard, Suite 600
Minneapolis, Minnesota 55439-3034
Telephone: 952-831-6544
Fax: 952-831-1869
Toll Free: 800-869-1035
E-Mail: spomeara@olwklaw.com
www.olwklaw.com

Established: 1973

Insurance Defense, Asbestos Litigation, Construction Law, Employer Liability, Environmental Law, General Civil Trial and Appellate Practice, Liquor Liability, No-Fault, Product Liability, School Law, Subrogation, Toxic Torts, Workers' Compensation, Insurance Coverage, Transportation, Trucking, Premises Liability, Professional Liability, Governmental Liability, Employment Law (Management Side), Employment Litigation, Medicare Compliance

O'Meara, Leer, Wagner & Kohl, P.A., Minneapolis, MN
(Continued)

Firm Profile: We have been guiding clients to effective decisions for over 40 years. Our AV-rated attorneys achieve client success based on a commitment to create relationships, provide reliable advice and deliver results through exceptional client service and superior work product. Because we know our clients well, our strategies are more effective, our work is more efficient, and our clients obtain the best possible results.

We serve leading Fortune 500 businesses and insurers, accomplished individuals, and public entities. Our collective experience promotes our ability to manage legal issues of any scale, and collaborate with clients to craft innovative solutions to successfully navigate the uncertainty of litigation. Our attorneys are seasoned litigators and advisors, and have shaped the law in key areas affecting our client's rights. Our firm is a member of Primerus, an international society of law firms.

Our transactional practice includes construction and commercial contracting, employment law, real estate, insurance coverage, business planning and public entity policy development.

Insurance Clients

Accident Fund
Allied World National Assurance Company
American Interstate Insurance Company
Austin Mutual Insurance Company
Cambridge Integrated Services
Farmers Insurance
Great American Insurance Company
Hartford Insurance Company
Interstate Insurance Group
Lexington Insurance Company
Liberty Mutual Insurance
Lumbermen's Underwriting Alliance
Midwest Insurance Company
Minnesota Counties Insurance Trust
Minnesota School Boards Association Insurance Trust
OneBeacon Insurance
Optum
Pharmacists Mutual Insurance Company
PMA Companies, Inc.
RLI Insurance Company
Riverport Insurance Company
RTW, Inc.
Specialty Global Insurance
State Farm Group
Strategic Comp
Travelers Insurance
United Heartland Life Insurance Company
Western National Mutual Insurance Company
Wilson Mutual Insurance Company
Wright Risk Management
Zenith Insurance Company

Third Party Administrators

AIG Claim Services, Inc.
Berkley Risk Administrators Company, LLC
Broadspire
Cottingham and Butler, Inc.
Crawford & Company
Gallagher Bassett Services, Inc.
Meadowbrook Insurance Group
Sedgwick Group of Minnesota, Inc.
York Risk Services Group, Inc.

Managing Partner

Shamus P. O'Meara — 1961 — University of Minnesota, B.A., 1988; William Mitchell College of Law, J.D., 1991 — Admitted to Bar, 1991, Minnesota; 1992, U.S. District Court, District of Minnesota; 2002, U.S. Court of Appeals, Eighth Circuit — Member American Bar Association; Minnesota State and Hennepin County Bar Associations; American Arbitration Association (Construction and Commercial Arbitrator); Minnesota Construction Association; Associated General Contractors of Minnesota; Minnesota Defense Lawyers Association; National Council of School Attorneys; Minnesota Association of School Business Officials; Minnesota Employers Workers Compensation Alliance; Minnesota Governor's Council on Developmental Disabilities; Defense Research Institute; Primerus Defense Institute — United States Civil Rights Commission State Advisory Committee — Practice Areas: Construction Law; Commercial Litigation; Education Law; Governmental Liability; Workers' Compensation Subrogation; Employer Liability; Property Subrogation; Product Liability; Civil Rights; Arbitration; Mediation — E-mail: spomeara@olwklaw.com

Shareholders

Christopher E. Celichowski — 1962 — University of Wisconsin-Stevens Point, B.S. (magna cum laude), 1984; University of Minnesota, J.D., 1988 — Admitted to Bar, 1989, Minnesota; 1990, U.S. District Court, District of Minnesota — Member Minnesota State and Hennepin County Bar Associations; Minnesota Defense Lawyers Association — Practice Areas: Subrogation; Dram Shop; Employment Law; Workers' Compensation — E-mail: cecelichowski@olwklaw.com

Timothy J. Leer — 1954 — University of Minnesota, B.A., 1977; William Mitchell College of Law, J.D., 1982 — Admitted to Bar, 1982, Minnesota; 1995, Wisconsin; 1982, U.S. District Court, District of Minnesota — Member Minnesota State Bar Association; State Bar of Wisconsin — E-mail: tjleer@olwklaw.com

Mark A. Wagner — 1963 — Gustavus Adolphus College, B.A. (cum laude), 1985; Hamline University School of Law, J.D. (cum laude), 1988 — Admitted to Bar, 1988, Minnesota — Member Minnesota State and Hennepin County Bar Associations; Minnesota Defense Lawyers Association — Practice Areas: Workers' Compensation — E-mail: mawagner@olwklaw.com

Dale O. Thornsjo — 1957 — University of Minnesota, B.A., 1981; William Mitchell College of Law, J.D. (cum laude), 1984 — Admitted to Bar, 1984, Minnesota; 1984, U.S. District Court, District of Minnesota; 1987, U.S. Court of Appeals, Eighth Circuit; 1991, U.S. District Court, Western District of Wisconsin; 1994, U.S. District Court, Eastern District of Michigan; 2008, U.S. District Court, Eastern District of Wisconsin; 2009, U.S. District Court, District of North Dakota — Member Federal, Minnesota State and Hennepin County Bar Associations; The Association of the Bar of the United States Court of Appeals for the Eighth Circuit; Primerus Defense Institute; Defense Research Institute; Minnesota Defense Lawyers Association — Practice Areas: Insurance Coverage Litigation; Construction Law; Product Liability — E-mail: dothornsjo@olwklaw.com

Mary E. Kohl — University of Minnesota, B.S. (with distinction), 1980; William Mitchell College of Law, J.D. (magna cum laude), 1990 — Admitted to Bar, 1991, Minnesota; 1998, Wisconsin; 1992, U.S. District Court, District of Minnesota; 1993, U.S. District Court, Western District of Wisconsin — Member Minnesota State Bar Associations; Fellow, Litigation Counsel of America; Minnesota Defense Lawyers Association — Practice Areas: Workers' Compensation — E-mail: mekohl@olwklaw.com

Jeremy D. Rosenberg — 1969 — University of California, Berkeley, B.A., 1991; William Mitchell College of Law, J.D., 1997 — Admitted to Bar, 1997, Minnesota; U.S. District Court, District of Minnesota; 1999, U.S. Court of Appeals, Eighth Circuit — Practice Areas: Workers' Compensation — E-mail: jdrosenberg@olwklaw.com

Kristen Anderson Ryan — 1972 — DePauw University, B.A. (Dean's List), 1994; Hamline University, J.D. (Dean's List), 1997 — Admitted to Bar, 1997, Minnesota; 1998, U.S. District Court, District of Minnesota — Member Minnesota State and Hennepin County Bar Associations; Minnesota Defense Lawyers Association — Practice Areas: Workers' Compensation — E-mail: karyan@olwklaw.com

Morgan A. Godfrey — 1958 — University of Wisconsin, B.A. (with distinction), 1986; William Mitchell College of Law, J.D., 1990 — Associate Editor Law Review — Admitted to Bar, 1990, Minnesota; 2006, Wisconsin; U.S. District Court, District of Minnesota; U.S. District Court, Eastern and Western Districts of Wisconsin; U.S. Court of Appeals, Seventh and Eighth Circuits — Practice Areas: Governmental Liability; Employment; Insurance Coverage; Construction Litigation; Police Liability Litigation — E-mail: magodfrey@olwklaw.com

Timothy P. Eclov — 1959 — University of Minnesota, B.A., 1982; Hamline University, J.D., 1988 — Admitted to Bar, 1988, Minnesota; 1990, U.S. District Court, District of Minnesota — Member Minnesota State and Hennepin County Bar Associations; American Inns of Court — Practice Areas: Workers' Compensation — E-mail: tpeclov@olwklaw.com

Michael M. Skram — 1974 — St. John's University, B.S., 1997; William Mitchell College of Law, J.D. (cum laude), 2004 — Admitted to Bar, 2004, Minnesota; U.S. District Court, District of Minnesota; U.S. Court of Appeals, Eighth Circuit; 2010, Supreme Court of Iowa — Member Minnesota State and Hennepin County Bar Associations; Minnesota Defense Lawyers Association (Board of Directors); Defense Research Institute — Practice Areas: Motor Vehicle; Uninsured and Underinsured Motorist; Premises Liability; Professional Liability; Toxic Torts; Transportation — E-mail: mmskram@olwklaw.com

Senior Counsel

Elizabeth B. Powell — 1966 — University of Wisconsin-Madison, B.A. (with honors), 1988; William Mitchell College of Law, J.D., 1991 — Admitted to Bar, 1991, Minnesota; 1992, U.S. District Court, District of Minnesota — Member Minnesota State and Hennepin County Bar Associations; Minnesota Defense Lawyers Association — E-mail: ebpowell@olwklaw.com

Mark R. Azman — 1967 — College of the Holy Cross, B.A., 1989; William Mitchell College of Law, J.D. (cum laude), 1993 — William Mitchell Law Review — Admitted to Bar, 1993, Minnesota; 1995, U.S. District Court, District of Minnesota; 1996, U.S. District Court, Western District of Wisconsin; 1997, U.S. Court of Appeals, Seventh Circuit; 2000, U.S. Court of Appeals, Eighth Circuit; 2003, U.S. District Court, Eastern District of Wisconsin — Member Federal, Minnesota State, Hennepin County and Eighth Circuit Bar

O'Meara, Leer, Wagner & Kohl, P.A., Minneapolis, MN
(Continued)

Associations; Council of School Attorneys; Primerus Defense Institute; Minnesota and National School Boards Associations; Minnesota Defense Lawyers Association; Defense Research Institute — Practice Areas: Insurance Coverage; School Law; Construction Law; Subrogation; Commercial Litigation; Governmental Liability — E-mail: mrazman@olwklaw.com

Associates

Sarah E. Foulkes — 1972 — College of St. Benedict, B.S. (magna cum laude), 1995; William Mitchell College of Law, J.D. (cum laude), 1999 — Admitted to Bar, 1999, Minnesota — Member Minnesota State Bar Association — Practice Areas: Workers' Compensation — E-mail: sefoulkes@olwklaw.com

Sarah Groskreutz — 1977 — Hamline University, B.A., 1999; William Mitchell College of Law, J.D., 2002 — Admitted to Bar, 2003, Minnesota — Member Minnesota State Bar Association — Practice Areas: Workers' Compensation — E-mail: segroskreutz@olwklaw.com

Brian P. Thompson — 1972 — St. Olaf College, B.A., 1995; William Mitchell College of Law, J.D., 2002 — Admitted to Bar, 2002, Minnesota — Member Minnesota State Bar Association — Practice Areas: Workers' Compensation — E-mail: bpthompson@olwklaw.com

Allison R. Haley — University of Nebraska, B.S. (with distinction), 2003; University of Minnesota Law School, J.D. (cum laude), 2006 — Admitted to Bar, 2006, Minnesota — Member Federal and Minnesota State Bar Associations; MSP Task Force; National Alliance of Medicare Set-Aside Professionals (Board of Directors); Defense Research Institute — Certified Medicare Set-Aside Consultant — Practice Areas: Health; Litigation; Workers' Compensation — E-mail: arhaley@olwklaw.com

Brian M. McSherry — 1973 — University of Minnesota, B.A., 2003; University of St. Thomas School of Law, J.D. (cum laude), 2007 — Admitted to Bar, 2007, Minnesota — Member Defense Research Institute; Minnesota Defense Lawyers Association — Practice Areas: Insurance Defense; Trucking; Trucking Industry Defense; Trucking Litigation — E-mail: bmmcsherry@olwklaw.com

Sarah M. Hunter — 1982 — College of St. Scholastica, B.A. (cum laude), 2004; Hamline University School of Law, J.D., 2007 — Admitted to Bar, 2007, Minnesota — Member Minnesota State (Board of Directors) and Hennepin County Bar Associations; Minnesota Defense Lawyers Association — 2014 LINC (Leaders Impacting the Nonprofit Community) Program Graduate — Practice Areas: Workers' Compensation — E-mail: smhunter@olwklaw.com

Annie M. Davidson — 1983 — University of Minnesota, B.A. Political Science, 2005; William Mitchell College of Law, J.D. (cum laude), 2011 — Admitted to Bar, 2011, Minnesota — Member American, Minnesota State and Hennepin County Bar Associations; Defense Research Institute; Minnesota Women Lawyers Association; Minnesota Defense Lawyers Association — Certified Medicare Secondary Payer Professional — Practice Areas: Workers' Compensation — E-mail: amdavidson@olwklaw.com

Lance D. Meyer — 1986 — Concordia University, B.A. (magna cum laude), 2009; William Mitchell College of Law, J.D. (summa cum laude), 2012 — Law Clerk, Minnesota Court of Appeals — Admitted to Bar, 2012, Minnesota; 2013, U.S. District Court, District of Minnesota; U.S. Court of Appeals, Eighth Circuit; 2014, U.S. District Court, Western District of Wisconsin — Member American, Minnesota State and Hennepin County Bar Associations; Minnesota Defense Lawyers Association; Defense Research Institute — Practice Areas: Construction Law; Product Liability; Appeals; Insurance Coverage — E-mail: ldmeyer@olwklaw.com

Stephanie L. Chandler — 1987 — University of Wisconsin-Eau Claire, B.A. (summa cum laude), 2010; William Mitchell College of Law, J.D. (summa cum laude), 2013 — Admitted to Bar, 2013, Minnesota; 2014, U.S. District Court, District of Minnesota — Member American and Minnesota State Bar Associations; Minnesota Women Lawyers Association — Practice Areas: General Liability — E-mail: slchandler@olwklaw.com

Lauren E. Clausen — 1988 — Gustavus Adolphus College, B.A., 2010; William Mitchell College of Law, J.D., 2013 — Admitted to Bar, 2013, Minnesota — Member Minnesota State Bar Association — Practice Areas: Workers' Compensation — E-mail: leclausen@olwklaw.com

(Revisors of the Minnesota Insurance Law Digest for this Publication)

(This firm is also listed in the Subrogation section of this directory)

Waldeck Law Firm P.A.
1400 TCF Tower
121 South Eighth Street
Minneapolis, Minnesota 55402
 Telephone: 612-375-1550
 Fax: 612-375-0647
 www.waldeckpa.com

Trials and Appeals for the Defense in Minnesota and Wisconsin in the Areas of Commercial Liability, General Liability, Premises Liability, Product Liability, D & O, E & O, Professional Liability (Accountants, Appraisers, Churches, Day Care Centers, Drug Rehabilitation, Engineers, Foster Homes, Health Care Providers, Insurance Agents, Lawyers, Medical and Dental Personnel, Nursing Homes, Real Estate Agent and Brokers), and Automobile and Trucking Liability, Construction Defect, Liquor Liability and Coverage Opinions and Declaratory Judgment Actions

Insurance Clients

Alterra USA
Argonaut Insurance Group
Argonaut Specialty Insurance
Assicurazioni Generali S.p.A.
Brotherhood Mutual Insurance Company
Church Mutual Insurance Company
Colony Specialty Insurance Company
EMC Insurance Companies
First Mercury Insurance Company
First Specialty Insurance Corporation
GuideOne Insurance
Hanover Insurance Group
The Hartford Financial Services Group, Inc.
IPC International Corporation
Maxum Specialty Insurance Group
NovaPro Risk Solutions
Occidental Fire & Casualty Company of North Carolina
Pinnacle Risk Management Services
SECURA Insurance Companies
Specialty Risk Services
Swiss Reinsurance Company
Underwriters at Lloyd's, London
United Fire Group
Verus Underwriting Managers, LLC
WESTCAP Insurance Services
Western National Insurance Group
Westport Insurance Company
World Wide Claims Management
York Risk Services Group, Inc.
American Insurance Adjustment Agency
Argo Pro
AXA Reinsurance Company
Catlin Group Limited
Christensen Group IRI
Cincinnati Insurance Company
The Concord Group Insurance Companies
Employers Reinsurance Corporation
Gallagher Bassett Services, Inc.
General Star Management Company
Harco National Insurance Company
IFG Companies
Markel Corporation
North American Risk Services
NSI a Division of West Bend Mutual Insurance Company
Penn-America Group, Inc.
RSUI Group, Inc.
Scottsdale Insurance Company
Selective Insurance Company of America
Travelers
United America Indemnity Group
United National Group
West Bend Mutual Insurance Company
Western Heritage Insurance Company
Westwood Professional Services
Wright Risk Management

Non-Insurance Clients

American Professional Agency
Gibson & Associates
Ruby Tuesday, Inc.
Cunningham Lindsey U.S., Inc.
Rite Aid Corporation
VeriClaim, Inc.

Firm Members

Timothy W. Waldeck — 1947 — Bradley University, B.S., 1970; Drake University, J.D., 1972 — Admitted to Bar, 1973, Minnesota; 1985, Wisconsin — Member Minnesota State and Hennepin County Bar Associations; State Bar of Wisconsin; Twin Cities Claims Association; Eagle International Associates, Inc.; Claims and Litigation Management Alliance; National Retail and Restaurant Association; Minnesota Defense Lawyers Association — E-mail: twaldeck@waldeckpa.com

Peter M. Waldeck — 1975 — Drake University, B.A., 1997; The John Marshall Law School, J.D., 2000 — Admitted to Bar, 2000, Minnesota; 2006, Wisconsin — Member Minnesota State and Hennepin County Bar Associations; State Bar of Wisconsin; Twin Cities Claims Association; Claims and Litigation Management Alliance; Minnesota Defense Lawyers Association — E-mail: pwaldeck@waldeckpa.com

MINNESOTA   MOORHEAD

Waldeck Law Firm P.A., Minneapolis, MN   (Continued)

Theodore J. Waldeck — 1982 — Creighton University, B.A., 2004; University of St. Thomas School of Law, J.D., 2008 — Admitted to Bar, 2008, Minnesota; 2009, Wisconsin — Member Minnesota State and Hennepin County Bar Associations; State Bar of Wisconsin; Twin Cities Claims Association; Claims and Litigation Management Alliance; Minnesota Defense Lawyers Association — E-mail: tjwaldeck@waldeckpa.com

Lindsey J. Woodrow — 1981 — Gustavus Adolphus College, B.A., 2004; Hamline University School of Law, J.D., 2008 — Admitted to Bar, 2008, Minnesota — Member Minnesota State and Hennepin County Bar Associations; Twin Cities Claims Association; Claims and Litigation Management Alliance; Minnesota Defense Lawyers Association — E-mail: lwoodrow@waldeckpa.com

Jason M. Stoffel — 1984 — St. John's University, B.A., 2006; University of Minnesota Law School, J.D., 2010 — Admitted to Bar, 2010, Minnesota — Member Minnesota State and Hennepin County Bar Associations; Minnesota Hispanic Bar Association; Twin Cities Claims Association — E-mail: jstoffel@waldeckpa.com

(This firm is also listed in the Subrogation section of this directory)

Winthrop & Weinstine, P.A.

Capella Tower, Suite 3500
225 South Sixth Street
Minneapolis, Minnesota 55402-4629
   Telephone: 612-604-6400
   Fax: 612-604-6800
   www.winthrop.com

Commercial Litigation, Insurance Law, Insurance Regulation, Legislative Law, Health, Construction Law, Labor and Employment, Employee Benefits, Real Estate, Intellectual Property, Alternative Dispute Resolution, Appeals, Corporate Law

Firm Profile: Winthrop & Weinstine, P.A., is a full-service law firm that provides legal services to a wide range of public and private business corporations. The firm's practice encompasses a broad spectrum of litigation and corporate transactions, positioning the firm well to advise on almost any issue that may arise.

The firm is dedicated to advancing the best interests of its clients and community through the timely delivery of legal services that are of exceptional quality, innovative character, and unsurpassed value.

Insurance Clients

AIG Property Casualty	American Insurance Association
Fidelity National Financial	(AIA)

Shareholders

David M. Aafedt — William Mitchell College of Law, J.D. (magna cum laude), 1997 — Admitted to Bar, 1997, Minnesota — Practice Areas: Commercial Litigation; Insurance; Health; Legislative Law; Energy

Jeffrey R. Ansel — University of Minnesota Law School, J.D. (cum laude), 1985 — Admitted to Bar, 1985, Minnesota; 1992, Wisconsin — Practice Areas: Commercial Litigation; Real Estate; Construction Law; Bankruptcy; Insurance; Alternative Dispute Resolution

Thomas H. Boyd — The University of Iowa College of Law, J.D., 1987 — Admitted to Bar, 1987, Iowa; 1987, Illinois; 1988, Missouri; 1989, Minnesota; 1996, Wisconsin — Practice Areas: Appellate Practice; Eminent Domain; Commercial Litigation; Environmental Law; Land Use; Trusts; Intellectual Property; Insurance

Aimée D. Dayhoff — William Mitchell College of Law, J.D. (magna cum laude), 2002 — Admitted to Bar, 2002, Minnesota — Practice Areas: Commercial Litigation; Employment Law; Insurance; Bankruptcy; Construction Law

Christianna L. Finnern — The University of Iowa College of Law, J.D., 2001 — Admitted to Bar, 2001, Minnesota; 2003, Iowa (Inactive) — Practice Areas: Commercial Litigation; Construction Law; Insurance; Bankruptcy; Health

John C. Holper — Hamline University School of Law, J.D., 1992 — Admitted to Bar, 1992, Minnesota — Practice Areas: Commercial Litigation; Construction Law; Insurance; Bankruptcy; Real Estate

Winthrop & Weinstine, P.A., Minneapolis, MN
(Continued)

John A. Knapp — The University of Iowa College of Law, J.D. (with distinction), 1974 — Admitted to Bar, 1974, Minnesota; 1974, Iowa (Inactive) — Practice Areas: Insurance; Legislative Law; Energy; Environmental Law; Land Use

David P. Pearson — Northwestern University School of Law, J.D., 1976 — Admitted to Bar, 1976, Minnesota — Practice Areas: Insurance; Commercial Litigation; Intellectual Property; Employment Law; Securities

(This firm is also listed in the Regulatory and Compliance section of this directory)

The following firms also service this area.

Tentinger Law Firm, P.A.
15000 Garrett Avenue
Apple Valley, Minnesota 55124
   Telephone: 952-953-3330
   Fax: 952-953-3331

Agriculture, Arbitration, General Liability, Insurance Coverage, Mediation, Motor Vehicle, No-Fault, Premises Liability, Product Liability, Subrogation, Construction, Farm Accidents, Motorcycles, Trucks and Farm Equipment

SEE COMPLETE LISTING UNDER APPLE VALLEY, MINNESOTA (18 MILES)

MOORHEAD   † 38,065 Clay Co.

Oppegard & Quinton

2901 South Frontage Road
Moorhead, Minnesota 56560-2572
   Telephone: 218-233-8105
   Fax: 218-233-8620
   Toll Free: 877-233-2336
   E-Mail: poppegard@owqlaw.com
   www.owqlaw.com

(Fargo, ND Office: 2309 Rose Creek Boulevard S., 58104)
   (Tel: 218-233-8105)
   (Fax: 218-233-8620)

Established: 1994

Insurance Defense, Personal Injury, Property Damage, Asbestos Litigation, Environmental Law, Toxic Torts, Insurance Coverage, Professional Malpractice, Automobile, Product Liability, Bodily Injury, General Liability, Homeowners, Casualty, Subrogation

Firm Profile: The law firm of Oppegard & Quinton has over 50 years experience in representing insurance companies, large corporations, and individual plaintiffs in civil litigation matters. The firm prides itself on its continued relationships with numerous respected clients. Oppegard & Quinton has had extensive experience in civil litigation and trying cases in courtrooms before juries.

With offices in Moorhead, MN, and Fargo, ND, the Oppegard & Quinton firm provides efficient legal services to clients throughout ND and MN.

Insurance Clients

ACE USA	Admiral Insurance Company
AIG/American International Group	Allied Group
Alpha Property & Casualty Insurance Company	Arrowpoint Capital Corporation
	Austin Mutual Insurance Company
CGU Insurance Company	Chubb Group of Insurance Companies
Cincinnati Insurance Company	
Continental Western Insurance Company	Great West Casualty Company
	Grinnell Mutual Reinsurance Company
The Harleysville Insurance	
Liberty Mutual Group	Milbank/State Auto Insurance Company
Nationwide Insurance	
North Dakota Insurance Reserve Fund	Ohio Casualty Group
	St. Paul Travelers Insurance Companies
Sentry Insurance	

WINONA MINNESOTA

Oppegard & Quinton, Moorhead, MN (Continued)

Westfield Insurance Company
Zurich American Insurance Company

Non-Insurance Clients

Cavell America
Cooper Industries, Inc.
Graybar Electric Company, Inc
Tyco International, Ltd.
Uniroyal Holding, Inc.
Chicago-Wilcox Mfg. Co., Inc.
Deere & Company
Starwood Hotels & Resorts Worldwide, Inc.

Partner

Paul R. Oppegard — 1954 — Concordia College, B.A. (summa cum laude), 1976; William Mitchell College of Law, J.D., 1980 — Admitted to Bar, 1980, Minnesota; North Dakota; 1980, U.S. District Court, District of Minnesota; 1980, U.S. District Court, District of North Dakota; 1980, U.S. Court of Appeals, Eighth Circuit; 1980, U.S. Supreme Court — Member American, Minnesota State, Cass County and Clay County Bar Associations; State Bar Association of North Dakota; Blue Goose International; Minnesota Defense Lawyers Association; North Dakota Defense Lawyers Association; Defense Research Institute — Certified Civil Trial Specialist, Civil Litigation Section, Minnesota State Bar Association; Certified Civil Trial Advocate, National Board of Trial Advocacy

Member

Corey J. Quinton — 1969 — Northern State College, B.S., 1992; The University of North Dakota, J.D. (with distinction), 1995 — Admitted to Bar, 1995, Minnesota; North Dakota; 1995, U.S. District Court, District of North Dakota — Member Minnesota State, Cass County and Clay County Bar Associations; State Bar Association of North Dakota

---

The following firms also service this area.

Flom Law Office, P.A.
1703 32nd Avenue South
Fargo, North Dakota 58103-5936
Telephone: 701-280-2300
Fax: 701-280-1880

Insurance Defense, Trial and Appellate Practice, State and Federal Courts, Medical Malpractice, Professional Malpractice, Civil Rights, Construction Law, Product Liability, Casualty, Fire, Automobile Liability, Asbestos Litigation, Toxic Substances, Pollution, No-Fault, Coverage Issues, Liquor Liability, Automobile, Premises Liability, Commercial Litigation, Subrogation, Environmental Law, Employment Law, Governmental Liability, Municipal Liability, Errors and Omissions, Health

SEE COMPLETE LISTING UNDER FARGO, NORTH DAKOTA (1 MILES)

Nilles Law Firm
201 North Fifth Street
Fargo, North Dakota 58102
Telephone: 701-237-5544
Fax: 701-280-0762

Mailing Address: P.O. Box 2626, Fargo, ND 58108-2626

Fire, Casualty, Surety, Life and Health, Investigation and Adjustment

SEE COMPLETE LISTING UNDER FARGO, NORTH DAKOTA (1 MILES)

Swanson & Warcup, Ltd.
1397 Library Circle, Suite 202
Grand Forks, North Dakota 58201
Telephone: 701-772-3407
Fax: 701-772-3833

Mailing Address: P.O. Box 12909, Grand Forks, ND 58208-2909

Insurance Defense, Casualty, Fire, Automobile, Product Liability, Professional Liability, Negligence, Governmental Liability, Coverage Issues, Insurance Litigation, Dram Shop, Construction Law

SEE COMPLETE LISTING UNDER GRAND FORKS, NORTH DAKOTA (85 MILES)

ROSEAU † 2,633 Roseau Co.

Refer To

Swanson & Warcup, Ltd.
1397 Library Circle, Suite 202
Grand Forks, North Dakota 58201
Telephone: 701-772-3407
Fax: 701-772-3833

Mailing Address: P.O. Box 12909, Grand Forks, ND 58208-2909

Insurance Defense, Casualty, Fire, Automobile, Product Liability, Professional Liability, Negligence, Governmental Liability, Coverage Issues, Insurance Litigation, Dram Shop, Construction Law

SEE COMPLETE LISTING UNDER GRAND FORKS, NORTH DAKOTA (130 MILES)

ST. PAUL † 285,068 Ramsey Co.

Refer To

Tentinger Law Firm, P.A.
15000 Garrett Avenue
Apple Valley, Minnesota 55124
Telephone: 952-953-3330
Fax: 952-953-3331

Agriculture, Arbitration, General Liability, Insurance Coverage, Mediation, Motor Vehicle, No-Fault, Premises Liability, Product Liability, Subrogation, Construction, Farm Accidents, Motorcycles, Trucks and Farm Equipment

SEE COMPLETE LISTING UNDER APPLE VALLEY, MINNESOTA (18 MILES)

THIEF RIVER FALLS † 8,573 Pennington Co.

Refer To

Swanson & Warcup, Ltd.
1397 Library Circle, Suite 202
Grand Forks, North Dakota 58201
Telephone: 701-772-3407
Fax: 701-772-3833

Mailing Address: P.O. Box 12909, Grand Forks, ND 58208-2909

Insurance Defense, Casualty, Fire, Automobile, Product Liability, Professional Liability, Negligence, Governmental Liability, Coverage Issues, Insurance Litigation, Dram Shop, Construction Law

SEE COMPLETE LISTING UNDER GRAND FORKS, NORTH DAKOTA (60 MILES)

WINONA † 27,592 Winona Co.

Refer To

Johns, Flaherty & Collins, S.C.
205 Fifth Avenue South, Suite 600
La Crosse, Wisconsin 54601
Telephone: 608-784-5678
Fax: 608-784-0557

Mailing Address: P.O. Box 1626, La Crosse, WI 54602

Insurance Defense, Trial Practice, Workers' Compensation, Medical Malpractice, Product Liability, Automobile, Bodily Injury, Coverage Issues, Professional Liability

SEE COMPLETE LISTING UNDER LA CROSSE, WISCONSIN (30 MILES)

Refer To

Moen Sheehan Meyer, Ltd.
201 Main Street, Suite 700
La Crosse, Wisconsin 54601
Telephone: 608-784-8310
Fax: 608-782-6611
Toll Free: 800-346-3457

Mailing Address: P.O. Box 786, La Crosse, WI 54602-0786

Insurance Defense, Trial Practice, Automobile, Product Liability, Medical Malpractice, Professional Liability, Premises Liability, Coverage Issues, Bodily Injury

SEE COMPLETE LISTING UNDER LA CROSSE, WISCONSIN (30 MILES)

MISSISSIPPI

CAPITAL: JACKSON

COUNTIES AND COUNTY SEATS

County	County Seat
Adams	Natchez
Alcorn	Corinth
Amite	Liberty
Attala	Kosciusko
Benton	Ashland
Bolivar	Cleveland & Rosedale
Calhoun	Pittsboro
Carroll	Carrollton & Vaiden
Chickasaw	Houston & Okolona
Choctaw	Ackerman
Claiborne	Port Gibson
Clarke	Quitman
Clay	West Point
Coahoma	Clarksdale
Copiah	Hazelhurst
Covington	Collins
DeSoto	Hernando
Forrest	Hattiesburg
Franklin	Meadville
George	Lucedale
Greene	Leakesville
Grenada	Grenada
Hancock	Bay Saint Louis
Harrison	Biloxi & Gulfport
Hinds	Jackson & Raymond
Holmes	Lexington
Humphreys	Belzoni
Issaquena	Mayersville
Itawamba	Fulton
Jackson	Pascagoula
Jasper	Bay Springs & Paulding
Jefferson	Fayette
Jefferson Davis	Prentiss
Jones	Ellisville & Laurel
Kemper	De Kalb
Lafayette	Oxford
Lamar	Purvis
Lauderdale	Meridian
Lawrence	Monticello
Leake	Carthage
Lee	Tupelo
Leflore	Greenwood
Lincoln	Brookhaven
Lowndes	Columbus
Madison	Canton
Marion	Columbia
Marshall	Holly Springs
Monroe	Aberdeen
Montgomery	Winona
Neshoba	Philadelphia
Newton	Decatur
Noxubee	Macon
Oktibbeha	Starkville
Panola	Batesville & Sardis
Pearl River	Poplarville
Perry	New Augusta
Pike	Magnolia
Pontotoc	Pontotoc
Prentiss	Booneville
Quitman	Marks
Rankin	Brandon
Scott	Forest
Sharkey	Rolling Fork
Simpson	Mendenhall
Smith	Raleigh
Stone	Wiggins
Sunflower	Indianola
Tallahatchie	Charleston & Sumner
Tate	Senatobia
Tippah	Ripley
Tishomingo	Iuka
Tunica	Tunica
Union	New Albany
Walthall	Tylertown
Warren	Vicksburg
Washington	Greenville
Wayne	Waynesboro
Webster	Walthall
Wilkinson	Woodville
Winston	Louisville
Yalobusha	Coffeeville & Water Valley
Yazoo	Yazoo City

In the text that follows "†" indicates County Seats.

Our files contain additional verified data on the firms listed herein. This additional information is available on request.

A.M. BEST COMPANY

MISSISSIPPI

ABERDEEN † 5,612 Monroe Co.

Refer To

Hicks & Smith, PLLC
Regions Bank, 2nd Floor
710 Main Street
Columbus, Mississippi 39701
 Telephone: 662-243-7300
 Fax: 662-327-1485

Mailing Address: P.O. Box 1111, Columbus, MS 39703-1111

Bad Faith, Automobile, Premises Liability, Workers' Compensation, Casualty, Product Liability, Medical Malpractice, Subrogation, Class Actions, Commercial Litigation, Employment Law, Extra-Contractual Litigation, Professional Negligence, Truck Liability, Governmental Liability, Public Entities, Civil Rights, Insurance Sales Practice Litigation, Constitutional, General Insurance Defense, Admiralty, Construction, Business Litigation, Environmental Litigation

SEE COMPLETE LISTING UNDER COLUMBUS, MISSISSIPPI (27 MILES)

Refer To

Webb Sanders & Williams PLLC
363 North Broadway
Tupelo, Mississippi 38804
 Telephone: 662-844-2137
 Fax: 662-842-3863

Mailing Address: P.O. Box 496, Tupelo, MS 38802-0496

Insurance Defense, Insurance Coverage, Automobile, Property, Fire, Arson, Fraud, First Party Matters, Bad Faith, Special Investigations, Product Liability, Automobile Liability, Uninsured and Underinsured Motorist, Professional Malpractice, Medical Malpractice, Workers' Compensation, General Liability, Premises Liability, Defense Litigation, Corporate Law, Commercial Law, Commercial Litigation, Real Estate, Transportation, Environmental Law, Toxic Torts, Bankruptcy, Creditor Rights, Labor and Employment, ERISA, Construction Litigation, Fidelity and Surety, Insurance Fraud, General Civil Practice, Trial Practice, Appellate Practice, Employment Discrimination, Coverage Analysis, Coverage Issues

SEE COMPLETE LISTING UNDER TUPELO, MISSISSIPPI (35 MILES)

BATESVILLE † 7,463 Panola Co.

Refer To

Webb Sanders & Williams PLLC
363 North Broadway
Tupelo, Mississippi 38804
 Telephone: 662-844-2137
 Fax: 662-842-3863

Mailing Address: P.O. Box 496, Tupelo, MS 38802-0496

Insurance Defense, Insurance Coverage, Automobile, Property, Fire, Arson, Fraud, First Party Matters, Bad Faith, Special Investigations, Product Liability, Automobile Liability, Uninsured and Underinsured Motorist, Professional Malpractice, Medical Malpractice, Workers' Compensation, General Liability, Premises Liability, Defense Litigation, Corporate Law, Commercial Law, Commercial Litigation, Real Estate, Transportation, Environmental Law, Toxic Torts, Bankruptcy, Creditor Rights, Labor and Employment, ERISA, Construction Litigation, Fidelity and Surety, Insurance Fraud, General Civil Practice, Trial Practice, Appellate Practice, Employment Discrimination, Coverage Analysis, Coverage Issues

SEE COMPLETE LISTING UNDER TUPELO, MISSISSIPPI (75 MILES)

BAY ST. LOUIS † 9,260 Hancock Co.

Refer To

Franke & Salloum, PLLC
10071 Lorraine Road
Gulfport, Mississippi 39503
 Telephone: 228-868-7070
 Fax: 228-868-7090

Mailing Address: P.O. Drawer 460, Gulfport, MS 39502

Insurance Defense, Medical Malpractice, General Liability, Workers' Compensation, Admiralty and Maritime Law, Product Liability, Bad Faith, Subrogation

SEE COMPLETE LISTING UNDER GULFPORT, MISSISSIPPI (20 MILES)

Refer To

Hailey, McNamara, Hall, Larmann & Papale, L.L.P.
302 Courthouse Road, Suite A
Gulfport, Mississippi 39507
 Telephone: 228-896-1144
 Fax: 228-896-1177

Admiralty and Maritime Law, Commercial Litigation, Construction Litigation, Employment Practices Liability, Insurance Litigation, Product Liability, Professional Malpractice, Toxic Torts, Casualty, Insurance Coverage, Intellectual Property, Premises Liability, Transportation, Appellate, Mass Tort, Property, Workers' Compensation, Automobile Liability, Environmental

SEE COMPLETE LISTING UNDER GULFPORT, MISSISSIPPI (20 MILES)

BILOXI † 44,054 Harrison Co.

Currie Johnson Griffin & Myers, P.A.

925 Tommy Munro Drive, Suite H
Biloxi, Mississippi 39352
 Telephone: 228-385-1010
 Fax: 228-385-1011
 www.curriejohnson.com

(Jackson, MS Office*: 1044 River Oaks Drive, 39232, P.O. Box 750, 39205-0750)
 (Tel: 601-969-1010)
 (Fax: 601-969-5120)

Insurance Defense, General Liability, Product Liability, Automobile, Uninsured and Underinsured Motorist, Coverage Issues, Fire, Arson, Commercial Litigation, Medical Malpractice, Professional Liability, Fraud, Special Investigative Unit Claims, Premises Liability, Bad Faith, Utility Law

Shareholders

Peter C. Abide — 1959 — Louisiana State University, B.S., 1981; The University of Mississippi, J.D., 1986 — Phi Delta Phi — Law Clerk to Former Chief Justice Armis Hawkins, Mississippi Supreme Court, 1986-1987 — Research Editor and Casenote Editor, Mississippi Law Journal, 1985-1986 — Admitted to Bar, 1986, Mississippi; U.S. District Court, Southern District of Mississippi; U.S. Court of Appeals, Fifth Circuit; U.S. Supreme Court — Member American (Litigation Section) and Harrison County Bar Associations; The Mississippi Bar; American Inns of Court; Defense Research Institute; Mississippi Defense Lawyers Association — Note, "Demand Futility and the Business Judgement Rule," 55:1 Mississippi Law Journal, 1985; "Supreme Court Review - Contracts, Corporations and Commercial Law," 55:1 Mississippi Law Journal, 1985 — Named to Mid-South Super Lawyers, Personal Injury General: Defense, 2014 — E-mail: pabide@curriejohnson.com

Amanda B. Seymour — 1977 — The University of Mississippi, B.A. (magna cum laude), 1999; J.D., 2002 — Phi Kappa Phi — Recipient, James Oliver Eastland Scholarship — National Security Law Journal — Admitted to Bar, 2002, Mississippi — Member American Bar Association; The Mississippi Bar — E-mail: aseymour@curriejohnson.com

(See listing under Jackson, MS for additional information)

Page, Mannino, Peresich & McDermott, P.L.L.C.

759 Vieux Marche Mall
Biloxi, Mississippi 39530
 Telephone: 228-374-2100
 Fax: 228-432-5539
 E-Mail: Stephen.Peresich@pmp.org
 www.pmp.org

(Jackson, MS Office*: 460 Briarwood Drive, Suite 415, 39206, P.O. Box 16450, 39236-6450)
 (Tel: 601-896-0114)
 (Fax: 601-896-0145)

CARTHAGE — MISSISSIPPI

Page, Mannino, Peresich & McDermott, P.L.L.C., Biloxi, MS (Continued)

(Gulfport, MS Office*: 2408 14th Street, 39501-2019, P.O. Box 7618, 39506-7618)
  (Tel: 228-868-8999)
  (Fax: 228-868-8940)

Established: 1972

Insurance Defense, Banking, Bankruptcy, Business Law, Commercial Litigation, Construction Law, Environmental Litigation, Government Affairs, Governmental Entity Defense, Health Care, Hospital Law, Labor and Employment, Medical Malpractice, Municipal Law, Personal Injury, Product Liability, Professional Malpractice, Real Estate, Toxic Torts

Firm Profile: Page, Mannino, Peresich & McDermott is one of the oldest and most respected law firms in Mississippi. We are a full service law firm, offering a variety of services for business, insurance, governmental agencies and individual clients. Please contact us for a complete list of clients.

Representative Clients

State Farm Insurance Company   Travelers Insurance

Members of the Firm

Stephen G. Peresich — The University of Mississippi, J.D., 1981 — The Best Lawyers in America 2012 Recognition in Insurance Law and Medical Malpractice Defense — Admitted to Bar, 1981, Mississippi — Member American and Harrison County Bar Associations; The Mississippi Bar; Mississippi Defense Lawyers Association; Defense Research Institute

---

The following firms also service this area.

Franke & Salloum, PLLC
10071 Lorraine Road
Gulfport, Mississippi 39503
  Telephone: 228-868-7070
  Fax: 228-868-7090

Mailing Address: P.O. Drawer 460, Gulfport, MS 39502

Insurance Defense, Medical Malpractice, General Liability, Workers' Compensation, Admiralty and Maritime Law, Product Liability, Bad Faith, Subrogation
  SEE COMPLETE LISTING UNDER GULFPORT, MISSISSIPPI (15 MILES)

Hailey, McNamara, Hall, Larmann & Papale, L.L.P.
302 Courthouse Road, Suite A
Gulfport, Mississippi 39507
  Telephone: 228-896-1144
  Fax: 228-896-1177

Admiralty and Maritime Law, Commercial Litigation, Construction Litigation, Employment Practices Liability, Insurance Litigation, Product Liability, Professional Malpractice, Toxic Torts, Casualty, Insurance Coverage, Intellectual Property, Premises Liability, Transportation, Appellate, Mass Tort, Property, Workers' Compensation, Automobile Liability, Environmental
  SEE COMPLETE LISTING UNDER GULFPORT, MISSISSIPPI (15 MILES)

BRANDON † 21,705 Rankin Co.

Refer To

Bennett, Lotterhos, Sulser & Wilson, P.A.
188 East Capitol Street, Suite 1400
Jackson, Mississippi 39201
  Telephone: 601-944-0466
  Fax: 601-944-0467

Mailing Address: P.O. Box 98, Jackson, MS 39205-0098

Insurance Defense, Environmental Law
  SEE COMPLETE LISTING UNDER JACKSON, MISSISSIPPI (14 MILES)

Refer To

Markow Walker, P.A.
599 Highland Colony Parkway, Suite 100
Ridgeland, Mississippi 39157
  Telephone: 601-853-1911
  Fax: 601-853-8284

Mailing Address: P.O. Box 13669, Jackson, MS 39236-3669

Insurance Defense, Product Liability, Bodily Injury, Toxic Torts, Medical Malpractice, Workers' Compensation
  SEE COMPLETE LISTING UNDER JACKSON, MISSISSIPPI (14 MILES)

Refer To

Obert Law Group, P.A.
599 B Steed Road, Suite 100
Ridgeland, Mississippi 39157
  Telephone: 601-856-9690
  Fax: 601-856-9686

Mailing Address: P.O. Box 2081, Madison, MS 39130-2081

Insurance Defense, Automobile, Product Liability, General Liability, Property and Casualty, Agent and Brokers Errors and Omissions, Coverage Issues, Premises Liability, Workers' Compensation, Subrogation
  SEE COMPLETE LISTING UNDER JACKSON, MISSISSIPPI (14 MILES)

CANTON † 13,189 Madison Co.

Refer To

Bennett, Lotterhos, Sulser & Wilson, P.A.
188 East Capitol Street, Suite 1400
Jackson, Mississippi 39201
  Telephone: 601-944-0466
  Fax: 601-944-0467

Mailing Address: P.O. Box 98, Jackson, MS 39205-0098

Insurance Defense, Environmental Law
  SEE COMPLETE LISTING UNDER JACKSON, MISSISSIPPI (27 MILES)

Refer To

Markow Walker, P.A.
599 Highland Colony Parkway, Suite 100
Ridgeland, Mississippi 39157
  Telephone: 601-853-1911
  Fax: 601-853-8284

Mailing Address: P.O. Box 13669, Jackson, MS 39236-3669

Insurance Defense, Product Liability, Bodily Injury, Toxic Torts, Medical Malpractice, Workers' Compensation
  SEE COMPLETE LISTING UNDER JACKSON, MISSISSIPPI (27 MILES)

Refer To

Obert Law Group, P.A.
599 B Steed Road, Suite 100
Ridgeland, Mississippi 39157
  Telephone: 601-856-9690
  Fax: 601-856-9686

Mailing Address: P.O. Box 2081, Madison, MS 39130-2081

Insurance Defense, Automobile, Product Liability, General Liability, Property and Casualty, Agent and Brokers Errors and Omissions, Coverage Issues, Premises Liability, Workers' Compensation, Subrogation
  SEE COMPLETE LISTING UNDER JACKSON, MISSISSIPPI (27 MILES)

CARTHAGE † 5,075 Leake Co.

Refer To

Markow Walker, P.A.
599 Highland Colony Parkway, Suite 100
Ridgeland, Mississippi 39157
  Telephone: 601-853-1911
  Fax: 601-853-8284

Mailing Address: P.O. Box 13669, Jackson, MS 39236-3669

Insurance Defense, Product Liability, Bodily Injury, Toxic Torts, Medical Malpractice, Workers' Compensation
  SEE COMPLETE LISTING UNDER JACKSON, MISSISSIPPI (45 MILES)

MISSISSIPPI — CLARKSDALE

CLARKSDALE † 17,962 Coahoma Co.

Refer To

Webb Sanders & Williams PLLC
363 North Broadway
Tupelo, Mississippi 38804
 Telephone: 662-844-2137
 Fax: 662-842-3863

Mailing Address: P.O. Box 496, Tupelo, MS 38802-0496

Insurance Defense, Insurance Coverage, Automobile, Property, Fire, Arson, Fraud, First Party Matters, Bad Faith, Special Investigations, Product Liability, Automobile Liability, Uninsured and Underinsured Motorist, Professional Malpractice, Medical Malpractice, Workers' Compensation, General Liability, Premises Liability, Defense Litigation, Corporate Law, Commercial Law, Commercial Litigation, Real Estate, Transportation, Environmental Law, Toxic Torts, Bankruptcy, Creditor Rights, Labor and Employment, ERISA, Construction Litigation, Fidelity and Surety, Insurance Fraud, General Civil Practice, Trial Practice, Appellate Practice, Employment Discrimination, Coverage Analysis, Coverage Issues

SEE COMPLETE LISTING UNDER TUPELO, MISSISSIPPI (111 MILES)

CLEVELAND † 12,334 Bolivar Co.

Refer To

Webb Sanders & Williams PLLC
363 North Broadway
Tupelo, Mississippi 38804
 Telephone: 662-844-2137
 Fax: 662-842-3863

Mailing Address: P.O. Box 496, Tupelo, MS 38802-0496

Insurance Defense, Insurance Coverage, Automobile, Property, Fire, Arson, Fraud, First Party Matters, Bad Faith, Special Investigations, Product Liability, Automobile Liability, Uninsured and Underinsured Motorist, Professional Malpractice, Medical Malpractice, Workers' Compensation, General Liability, Premises Liability, Defense Litigation, Corporate Law, Commercial Law, Commercial Litigation, Real Estate, Transportation, Environmental Law, Toxic Torts, Bankruptcy, Creditor Rights, Labor and Employment, ERISA, Construction Litigation, Fidelity and Surety, Insurance Fraud, General Civil Practice, Trial Practice, Appellate Practice, Employment Discrimination, Coverage Analysis, Coverage Issues

SEE COMPLETE LISTING UNDER TUPELO, MISSISSIPPI (148 MILES)

COLUMBUS † 23,640 Lowndes Co.

Hicks & Smith, PLLC

Regions Bank, 2nd Floor
710 Main Street
Columbus, Mississippi 39701
 Telephone: 662-243-7300
 Fax: 662-327-1485
 E-Mail: nsmith@ghs-law.com
 E-Mail: dhicks@ghs-law.com

Established: 2007

Bad Faith, Automobile, Premises Liability, Workers' Compensation, Casualty, Product Liability, Medical Malpractice, Subrogation, Class Actions, Commercial Litigation, Employment Law, Extra-Contractual Litigation, Professional Negligence, Truck Liability, Governmental Liability, Public Entities, Civil Rights, Insurance Sales Practice Litigation, Constitutional, General Insurance Defense, Admiralty, Construction, Business Litigation, Environmental Litigation

Firm Profile: Hick & Smith, PLLC is dedicated to providing quality legal representation to its clients. The firm represents national and regional concerns as well as individuals. With a broad general practice built on decades of insurance defense, and a diverse list of specialized practice areas with an emphasis on litigation in both state and federal courts, the firm's clients include banks, businesses, insurance companies, governmental entities, public officials, and individuals.

Insurance Clients

Admiral Insurance Company
Alfa Insurance Company

Hicks & Smith, PLLC, Columbus, MS (Continued)

American Fidelity Insurance Company
Great American Insurance Company
Phillips & Associates
Prudential Insurance Company of America
The St. Paul Companies
St. Paul Fire and Marine Insurance Company
Southwestern Life Insurance Company
Trinity Insurance Company
Union Standard Insurance Company
Utica Mutual Insurance Company
Woodmen of the World
American Indemnity Group
American States Insurance Company
MetLife Insurance Company
Preferred Risk Mutual Insurance Company
Reliance National Insurance Company
Sedgwick James, Inc.
Shelter Insurance Companies
State Farm Insurance Companies
Travelers Insurance Companies
Union National Life Insurance Company
Universal Underwriters Insurance Company
Zurich North America

Non-Insurance Clients

Adjustco, Inc.
American Freightways, Inc.
Baldor Electric Company
Cash Distributing Company
Columbus Brick Company
Dutch Oil Company, Inc.
Golden Triangle Regional Airport Authority
Impressions Solutions, Inc.
Lewis Brothers Lumber Company
Mississippi Municipal Service Company
Monroe-Tufline Manufacturing Company
Office Management Systems
Synergetics Diversified Computer Services, Inc.
Tenn-Tom Tank, Inc.
Trustmark National Bank
Airline Manufacturing Company
APAC, Inc.
Cadence Bank, N.A.
Ceco Building Systems
Columbus Marble Works
Georgia Gulf Chemicals and Vinyls, LLC
Hydro-Vac Industrial Services, Inc.
Institutions of Higher Learning Board
Mississippi State University
Mississippi Tort Claims Board
Morrison Assurance Company
Ocean Bio-Chem, Inc.
Penn General Service Corporation
Tennessee Tombigbee Waterway Development Authority
Tom Soya Grain Company
Weyerhaeuser Company

Partners

Dewitt T. Hicks, Jr. — 1933 — Mississippi State University, B.S., 1954; The University of Mississippi, J.D., 1959 — Admitted to Bar, 1959, Mississippi; U.S. District Court, Northern and Southern Districts of Mississippi — Member American and Lowndes County Bar Associations; The Mississippi Bar; American Arbitration Association (Arbitrator); International Association of Defense Counsel; Mississippi Defense Lawyers Association; Defense Research Institute — Practice Areas: Commercial Litigation; General Practice; Insurance Defense; Construction Litigation; Public Entities; Bad Faith — Tel: 662-243-7307 — E-mail: dhicks@ghs-law.com

P. Nelson Smith, Jr. — 1964 — The University of Mississippi, B.A., 1986; J.D., 1990 — Admitted to Bar, 1990, Mississippi; U.S. District Court, Northern and Southern Districts of Mississippi; U.S. Court of Appeals, Fifth Circuit — Member The Mississippi Bar; Lowndes County Bar Association; Mississippi Defense Lawyers Association; Defense Research Institute — Practice Areas: Civil Litigation; Construction Litigation; Insurance Defense; Bad Faith; Product Liability; Commercial Litigation — Tel: 662-243-7311 — E-mail: nsmith@ghs-law.com

Kerby Law Firm, L.L.C.

722 College Street
Columbus, Mississippi 39701
 Telephone: 662-889-8247
 Fax: 662-328-9553
 E-Mail: ksearcyk@bellsouth.net
 www.kerbylaw.com

Civil Litigation, Public Entities, Employment Law, Civil Rights

Non-Insurance Clients

Mississippi Institutions of Higher Learning
Mississippi Tort Claims Board

Katherine S. Kerby — 1957 — The University of Mississippi, B.A., 1979; J.D., 1982 — Admitted to Bar, 1982, Mississippi; 1982, U.S. District Court, Northern and Southern Districts of Mississippi; 1982, U.S. Court of Appeals, Fifth Circuit; 1992, U.S. Supreme Court; 2006, Choctaw Tribal Court —

GREENWOOD | MISSISSIPPI

Kerby Law Firm, L.L.C., Columbus, MS (Continued)

Member Federal, American, Lowndes County and Magnolia Bar Associations; The Mississippi Bar; Mississippi Defense Lawyers Association (Past President); Defense Research Institute (Mississippi State Representative, 2004-2007); Mississippi Expert Evidence Action Team; Mississippi Woman Lawyers Association; International Association of Defense Counsel — AV-Rated, Martindale Hubble

---

The following firms also service this area.

Webb Sanders & Williams PLLC
363 North Broadway
Tupelo, Mississippi 38804
   Telephone: 662-844-2137
   Fax: 662-842-3863

Mailing Address: P.O. Box 496, Tupelo, MS 38802-0496

Insurance Defense, Insurance Coverage, Automobile, Property, Fire, Arson, Fraud, First Party Matters, Bad Faith, Special Investigations, Product Liability, Automobile Liability, Uninsured and Underinsured Motorist, Professional Malpractice, Medical Malpractice, Workers' Compensation, General Liability, Premises Liability, Defense Litigation, Corporate Law, Commercial Law, Commercial Litigation, Real Estate, Transportation, Environmental Law, Toxic Torts, Bankruptcy, Creditor Rights, Labor and Employment, ERISA, Construction Litigation, Fidelity and Surety, Insurance Fraud, General Civil Practice, Trial Practice, Appellate Practice, Employment Discrimination, Coverage Analysis, Coverage Issues

SEE COMPLETE LISTING UNDER TUPELO, MISSISSIPPI (61 MILES)

CORINTH † 14,573 Alcorn Co.

Refer To

Webb Sanders & Williams PLLC
363 North Broadway
Tupelo, Mississippi 38804
   Telephone: 662-844-2137
   Fax: 662-842-3863

Mailing Address: P.O. Box 496, Tupelo, MS 38802-0496

Insurance Defense, Insurance Coverage, Automobile, Property, Fire, Arson, Fraud, First Party Matters, Bad Faith, Special Investigations, Product Liability, Automobile Liability, Uninsured and Underinsured Motorist, Professional Malpractice, Medical Malpractice, Workers' Compensation, General Liability, Premises Liability, Defense Litigation, Corporate Law, Commercial Law, Commercial Litigation, Real Estate, Transportation, Environmental Law, Toxic Torts, Bankruptcy, Creditor Rights, Labor and Employment, ERISA, Construction Litigation, Fidelity and Surety, Insurance Fraud, General Civil Practice, Trial Practice, Appellate Practice, Employment Discrimination, Coverage Analysis, Coverage Issues

SEE COMPLETE LISTING UNDER TUPELO, MISSISSIPPI (53 MILES)

FOREST † 5,684 Scott Co.

Refer To

Markow Walker, P.A.
599 Highland Colony Parkway, Suite 100
Ridgeland, Mississippi 39157
   Telephone: 601-853-1911
   Fax: 601-853-8284

Mailing Address: P.O. Box 13669, Jackson, MS 39236-3669

Insurance Defense, Product Liability, Bodily Injury, Toxic Torts, Medical Malpractice, Workers' Compensation

SEE COMPLETE LISTING UNDER JACKSON, MISSISSIPPI (45 MILES)

FULTON † 3,961 Itawamba Co.

Refer To

Webb Sanders & Williams PLLC
363 North Broadway
Tupelo, Mississippi 38804
   Telephone: 662-844-2137
   Fax: 662-842-3863

Mailing Address: P.O. Box 496, Tupelo, MS 38802-0496

Insurance Defense, Insurance Coverage, Automobile, Property, Fire, Arson, Fraud, First Party Matters, Bad Faith, Special Investigations, Product Liability, Automobile Liability, Uninsured and Underinsured Motorist, Professional Malpractice, Medical Malpractice, Workers' Compensation, General Liability, Premises Liability, Defense Litigation, Corporate Law, Commercial Law, Commercial Litigation, Real Estate, Transportation, Environmental Law, Toxic Torts, Bankruptcy, Creditor Rights, Labor and Employment, ERISA, Construction Litigation, Fidelity and Surety, Insurance Fraud, General Civil Practice, Trial Practice, Appellate Practice, Employment Discrimination, Coverage Analysis, Coverage Issues

SEE COMPLETE LISTING UNDER TUPELO, MISSISSIPPI (24 MILES)

GREENVILLE † 34,400 Washington Co.

Refer To

Webb Sanders & Williams PLLC
363 North Broadway
Tupelo, Mississippi 38804
   Telephone: 662-844-2137
   Fax: 662-842-3863

Mailing Address: P.O. Box 496, Tupelo, MS 38802-0496

Insurance Defense, Insurance Coverage, Automobile, Property, Fire, Arson, Fraud, First Party Matters, Bad Faith, Special Investigations, Product Liability, Automobile Liability, Uninsured and Underinsured Motorist, Professional Malpractice, Medical Malpractice, Workers' Compensation, General Liability, Premises Liability, Defense Litigation, Corporate Law, Commercial Law, Commercial Litigation, Real Estate, Transportation, Environmental Law, Toxic Torts, Bankruptcy, Creditor Rights, Labor and Employment, ERISA, Construction Litigation, Fidelity and Surety, Insurance Fraud, General Civil Practice, Trial Practice, Appellate Practice, Employment Discrimination, Coverage Analysis, Coverage Issues

SEE COMPLETE LISTING UNDER TUPELO, MISSISSIPPI (150 MILES)

GREENWOOD † 15,205 Leflore Co.

Upshaw, Williams, Biggers & Beckham, L.L.P.
309 Fulton Street
Greenwood, Mississippi 38930
   Telephone: 662-455-1613
   Fax: 662-453-9245
   Toll Free: 800-748-8720
   www.upshawwilliams.com

(Ridgeland, MS Office*: 713 South Pear Orchard Road, Suite 102, 39157, P.O. Box 3080, 39158-3080)
   (Tel: 601-978-1996)
   (Fax: 601-978-1949)
   (Toll Free: 800-422-1379)
(Hernando, MS Office*: 2446 Caffey Street, 38632, P.O. Drawer 8230, 38935-8230)
   (Tel: 662-426-5890)
   (Fax: 662-429-5920)
   (Toll Free: 800-748-8720)

Established: 1971

MISSISSIPPI   GREENWOOD

Upshaw, Williams, Biggers & Beckham, L.L.P., Greenwood, MS (Continued)

General Civil Practice, State and Federal Courts, Administrative Law, Appellate Practice, Arson, Aviation, Bad Faith, Casualty, Civil Trial Practice, Commercial Law, Construction Law, Contracts, Corporate Law, Environmental Law, Federal Employer Liability Claims (FELA), Fidelity, Fraud, Insurance Defense, Insurance Coverage, Legal Malpractice, General Liability, Litigation, Mass Tort, Medical Malpractice, Negligence, Oil and Gas, Personal Injury, Product Liability, Professional Liability, Property, Railroad Law, Self-Insured, Surety, Tort, Transportation, Uninsured and Underinsured Motorist, Workers' Compensation, Real Estate, Probate, Agriculture

Firm Profile: Upshaw, Williams, Biggers & Beckham LLP is a thriving midsize, Mississippi law firm founded on a commitment to innovative and entrepreneurial service. We provide the balance of size, reach and responsiveness that many clients consider ideal. With our team orientation and commitment to personal and individualized attention, the firm provides the service capabilities of a very large firm with the efficiency of a small one. That's one reason why we can readily advise you on your legal matters.

Whether our clients come from the financial, high-tech, real estate, media, securities, insurance industries or small town business and concerns, they value our creative spirit, solution-oriented approach and unwavering commitment to the highest professional standards. They have helped build our reputation for insightful counseling, timely advice and constructive contributions to their legal business.

Representative Clients

Advocate, MD
Allianz Aviation Managers, LLC
AmFed Companies, L.L.C.
Avizent
Berkley Specialty Underwriting Managers, LLC
Canadian National
Cannon Cochran Management Services, Inc.
CNA Insurance Companies
Deep South Surplus, Inc.
The Doctors Company
Foremost Insurance Company
GEICO
Grain Dealers Mutual Insurance Company
LEMIC Insurance Company
Liberty Mutual Insurance Company
Medical Assurance Company of Mississippi Inc.
Mississippi Manufacturers Association Workers' Compensation Group
National Builders and Contractors
NL Industries, Inc.
Professional Claims Management
Safeco Insurance
State Auto Insurance Company
Summit Risk Services, Inc.
The Travelers Companies, Inc.
United Airlines, Inc.
Western Heritage Insurance
Zurich American Insurance Company

Alexsis, Inc.
American States Insurance Company
Berkley Insurance Company
Boyd Mississippi, Inc.
Bridgefield Casualty Insurance Company
Capital City Insurance Company, Inc.
Corrections Corporation of America
Farmers Insurance Exchange
Fred's Stores of Tennessee
General Casualty Insurance Company
Infinity Insurance Company
Liberty International
Lorillard Tobacco Company
Mississippi Hospitality & Restaurant Workers' Compensation Trust
Mississippi Tort Claims Board
MS Truck, Food, & Fuel
Nationwide Insurance
Phoenix Aviation Managers, Inc.
Progressive Insurance Company
Shelter Insurance Companies
State Volunteer Mutual Insurance Company
Union Standard Insurance Group
United States Aviation Underwriters, Inc.

Attorneys

Tommie G. Williams — 1953 — Mississippi State University, B.S., 1975; The University of Mississippi, J.D., 1978 — Admitted to Bar, 1978, Mississippi; 1978, U.S. District Court, Northern and Southern Districts of Mississippi; 1978, U.S. Court of Appeals, Fifth Circuit — Member American College of Trial Lawyers — The Best Lawyers in America; Mid South Super Lawyers

Marc A. Biggers — 1950 — Mississippi State University, B.S., 1972; The University of Mississippi, J.D., 1976 — Admitted to Bar, 1976, Mississippi; 1976, U.S. District Court, Northern and Southern Districts of Mississippi; 1980, U.S. Court of Appeals, Fifth Circuit — Member The Mississippi Bar; Leflore County Bar Association; Mississippi Defense Lawyers Association; National Association of Railroad Trial Counsel

Glenn F. Beckham — 1955 — Mississippi State University, B.A., 1977; The University of Mississippi, J.D., 1981 — Admitted to Bar, 1981, Mississippi;

Upshaw, Williams, Biggers & Beckham, L.L.P., Greenwood, MS (Continued)

2006, Tennessee; 1981, U.S. District Court, Northern and Southern Districts of Mississippi; 1985, U.S. Court of Appeals, Fifth Circuit — Member The Mississippi Bar; Leflore County Bar Association; Mississippi Defense Lawyers Association; National Association of Railroad Trial Counsel

F. Ewin Henson III — 1950 — Mississippi State University, B.A., 1972; The University of Mississippi, J.D. (with distinction), 1974 — Admitted to Bar, 1974, Mississippi; 1974, U.S. District Court, Northern District of Mississippi; 1977, U.S. Court of Appeals, Fifth Circuit; 1981, U.S. Court of Appeals, Eleventh Circuit — Member The Mississippi Bar; Fifth Federal Circuit Bar Association; Mississippi Claims Association; Mississippi Defense Lawyers Association (President, 2011); Defense Research Institute

Lonnie D. Bailey — 1951 — The University of Mississippi, B.A., 1973; Mississippi College, J.D. (with special distinction), 1982 — Admitted to Bar, 1982, Mississippi; 1982, U.S. District Court, Southern District of Mississippi; 1985, U.S. District Court, Northern District of Mississippi; 1986, U.S. Court of Appeals, Fifth Circuit; 1995, U.S. Supreme Court — Member The Mississippi Bar; Leflore County and Fifth Federal Circuit Bar Associations; Mississippi Defense Lawyers Association; Defense Research Institute

Robert S. Upshaw — 1955 — Mississippi State University, B.A., 1981; The University of Mississippi, J.D., 1984 — Admitted to Bar, 1985, Mississippi; 1985, U.S. District Court, Northern and Southern Districts of Mississippi; 1986, U.S. Court of Appeals, Fifth Circuit — Member The Mississippi Bar; Leflore County Bar Association; William C. Keady American Inn of Court (Barrister); National Association of Railroad Trial Counsel; Mississippi Defense Lawyers Association — U.S. Navy (1976-1980) — Practice Areas: Workers' Compensation

Clinton M. Guenther — 1955 — The University of Mississippi, B.A. (summa cum laude), 1977; Mississippi College, J.D. (with distinction), 1981 — Admitted to Bar, 1981, Mississippi; 1985, U.S. District Court, Northern and Southern Districts of Mississippi; 1985, U.S. Court of Appeals, Fifth Circuit — Member The Mississippi Bar; Leflore County Bar Association; Mississippi Defense Lawyers Association (Director, 1992-1995; President, 2001); Defense Research Institute (State Representative, 2009-2012)

Richard L. Kimmel — 1961 — Mississippi State University, B.S., 1983; Mississippi College School of Law, J.D., 1986 — Admitted to Bar, 1987, Mississippi; 1987, U.S. District Court, Northern and Southern Districts of Mississippi; 1987, U.S. Court of Appeals, Fifth Circuit — Member The Mississippi Bar; Leflore County Bar Association; Mississippi Defense Lawyers Association; Lawyer-Pilots Bar Association — Practice Areas: Insurance Defense; Aviation

James L. Wilson, IV — 1971 — The University of Mississippi, B.B.A., 1993; J.D., 1997 — Admitted to Bar, 1997, Mississippi; 1997, U.S. District Court, Northern and Southern Districts of Mississippi; 1997, U.S. Court of Appeals, Fifth Circuit — Member The Mississippi Bar; Leflore County Bar Association

Steven C. Cookston — 1968 — Arizona State University, B.A., 1991; Mississippi College School of Law, J.D., 1996 — Admitted to Bar, 1996, Nevada; 1996, U.S. District Court, District of Nevada; 1996, U.S. Court of Appeals, Ninth Circuit; 1998, U.S. District Court, Northern and Southern Districts of Mississippi; 1998, U.S. Court of Appeals, Fifth Circuit — Member The Mississippi Bar; State Bar of Nevada; Leflore County and Fifth Federal Circuit Bar Associations; Mississippi Defense Lawyers Association (Board of Directors, 2010-2012); Defense Research Institute

Harris F. Powers, III — 1975 — Sewanee, The University of the South, B.A., 1997; The University of Mississippi, J.D., 2001 — Admitted to Bar, 2001, Mississippi; 2001, Tennessee; U.S. District Court, Northern and Southern Districts of Mississippi; U.S. District Court, Western District of Tennessee — Member The Mississippi Bar; Leflore County Bar Association

Charles C. "Cam" Auerswald — 1975 — Delta State University, B.S., 2000; The University of Mississippi, J.D., 2003 — Admitted to Bar, 2003, Mississippi; 2003, U.S. District Court, Northern and Southern Districts of Mississippi; 2003, U.S. Court of Appeals, Fifth Circuit — Member The Mississippi Bar; Leflore County Bar Association; Mississippi Defense Lawyers Association

Tommie G. Williams, Jr. — 1982 — Mississippi State University, B.A., 2004; The University of Mississippi, J.D., 2007 — Admitted to Bar, 2007, Mississippi; U.S. District Court, Northern and Southern Districts of Mississippi; U.S. Court of Appeals, Fifth Circuit; Supreme Court of Mississippi — Member The Mississippi Bar; Leflore County Bar Association; Mississippi Defense Lawyers Association; Defense Research Institute

Brooke U. Bullard — Wichita State University, B.A., 2007; The University of Mississippi, J.D., 2011 — Admitted to Bar, 2011, Mississippi; 2011, Tennessee; U.S. District Court, Northern and Southern Districts of Mississippi; U.S. Court of Appeals, Fifth Circuit; Supreme Court of Mississippi — Member

GULFPORT   MISSISSIPPI

Upshaw, Williams, Biggers & Beckham, L.L.P., Greenwood, MS   (Continued)

The Mississippi Bar; Tennessee and Leflore County Bar Associations; Mississippi Women Lawyers Association; National Association of Legal Professionals (Greenwood Chapter); Christian Legal Society; Mississippi Defense Lawyers Association — E-mail: bbullard@upshawwilliams.com

The following firms also service this area.

Webb Sanders & Williams PLLC
363 North Broadway
Tupelo, Mississippi 38804
  Telephone: 662-844-2137
  Fax: 662-842-3863

Mailing Address: P.O. Box 496, Tupelo, MS 38802-0496

Insurance Defense, Insurance Coverage, Automobile, Property, Fire, Arson, Fraud, First Party Matters, Bad Faith, Special Investigations, Product Liability, Automobile Liability, Uninsured and Underinsured Motorist, Professional Malpractice, Medical Malpractice, Workers' Compensation, General Liability, Premises Liability, Defense Litigation, Corporate Law, Commercial Law, Commercial Litigation, Real Estate, Transportation, Environmental Law, Toxic Torts, Bankruptcy, Creditor Rights, Labor and Employment, ERISA, Construction Litigation, Fidelity and Surety, Insurance Fraud, General Civil Practice, Trial Practice, Appellate Practice, Employment Discrimination, Coverage Analysis, Coverage Issues

SEE COMPLETE LISTING UNDER TUPELO, MISSISSIPPI (156 MILES)

GRENADA † 13,092 Grenada Co.

Refer To

Webb Sanders & Williams PLLC
363 North Broadway
Tupelo, Mississippi 38804
  Telephone: 662-844-2137
  Fax: 662-842-3863

Mailing Address: P.O. Box 496, Tupelo, MS 38802-0496

Insurance Defense, Insurance Coverage, Automobile, Property, Fire, Arson, Fraud, First Party Matters, Bad Faith, Special Investigations, Product Liability, Automobile Liability, Uninsured and Underinsured Motorist, Professional Malpractice, Medical Malpractice, Workers' Compensation, General Liability, Premises Liability, Defense Litigation, Corporate Law, Commercial Law, Commercial Litigation, Real Estate, Transportation, Environmental Law, Toxic Torts, Bankruptcy, Creditor Rights, Labor and Employment, ERISA, Construction Litigation, Fidelity and Surety, Insurance Fraud, General Civil Practice, Trial Practice, Appellate Practice, Employment Discrimination, Coverage Analysis, Coverage Issues

SEE COMPLETE LISTING UNDER TUPELO, MISSISSIPPI (112 MILES)

GULFPORT † 67,793 Harrison Co.

Aultman Law Firm, Ltd.

1901 21st Avenue
Gulfport, Mississippi 39501
  Telephone: 228-863-6913
  Fax: 228-868-8505
  E-Mail: DeeAultman@aultmanlaw.com

(Hattiesburg, MS Office*: 315 Hemphill Street, 39401, P.O. Drawer 750, 39403-0750)
  (Tel: 601-583-2671)
  (Fax: 601-583-2677)
  (E-Mail: da@aultmanlaw.com)

Established: 1918

General Civil Practice, Insurance Law, Fire, Casualty, Surety, Life Insurance, Workers' Compensation, Trial Practice, Admiralty and Maritime Law, Subrogation, Environmental Law, Toxic Torts

Resident Partner

Dorrance "Dee" Aultman, Jr. — 1962 — University of Southern Mississippi, B.S., 1984; The University of Mississippi, J.D., 1986 — Admitted to Bar,

Aultman Law Firm, Ltd., Gulfport, MS   (Continued)

1987, Mississippi; 1987, U.S. District Court, Northern and Southern Districts of Mississippi; 1987, U.S. Court of Appeals, Fifth Circuit — Member The Mississippi Bar — Captain, USAR JAGC — Practice Areas: Civil Litigation; Medical Malpractice; Insurance Law; Commercial Litigation; Professional Liability — E-mail: deeaultman@bellsouth.net

(See listing under Hattiesburg, MS for additional information)

Brown Sims, P.C.

2304 19th Street, Suite 101
Gulfport, Mississippi 39501
  Telephone: 228-867-8711
  Fax: 228-867-8712

Insurance Defense, Trial and Appellate Practice, Admiralty and Maritime Law, Insurance Coverage, Construction Litigation, Product Liability, Premises Liability, Negligence, Employment Law, Casualty Defense, Professional Liability, Toxic Torts, Environmental Law, Workers' Compensation, Longshore and Harbor Workers' Compensation

(See listing under Houston, TX for additional information)

Franke & Salloum, PLLC

10071 Lorraine Road
Gulfport, Mississippi 39503
  Telephone: 228-868-7070
  Fax: 228-868-7090
  E-Mail: info@frslaw.com
  www.frankesalloum.com

Established: 1981

Insurance Defense, Medical Malpractice, General Liability, Workers' Compensation, Admiralty and Maritime Law, Product Liability, Bad Faith, Subrogation

Firm Profile: After practicing together for several years in another defense firm, Paul M. Franke, Jr., William M. Rainey and Richard P. Salloum founded a new firm in 1981. Mr. Rainey retired from the practice in 2006 and the firm name was changed to Franke & Salloum, PLLC. The firm engages in all facets of state and federal civil, trial and appellate practice including state and federal workers' compensation. The firm services clients on a statewide and regional basis.

Insurance Clients

CNA Insurance Company	Dallas National Insurance Company
Government Employees Insurance Company	Gray Insurance Company
Homeport Insurance Company	LEMIC Insurance Company
Lumbermen's Underwriting Alliance	Medical Assurance Company of Mississippi Inc.
Mississippi Insurance Guaranty Association	Strategic Comp
	Summit Consulting, Inc.

Non-Insurance Clients

Diamond M Company	Huntington Ingalls Incorporated
Stevedoring Services of America (SSA Marine, Inc.)	

Partners

Richard P. Salloum — 1948 — University of Notre Dame; The University of Mississippi, B.B.A., 1969; The University of Texas; Tulane University, J.D., 1972 — Admitted to Bar, 1972, Mississippi; 1972, U.S. Court of Appeals, Fourth, Fifth and Eleventh Circuits; 1972, U.S. Supreme Court — Member Federal, American and Harrison County Bar Associations; The Mississippi Bar; Fellow, Mississippi Bar Foundation; Mississippi Claims Association; Mississippi Defense Lawyers Association; Defense Research Institute; The

Franke & Salloum, PLLC, Gulfport, MS (Continued)

Maritime Law Association of the United States; Southeastern Admiralty Law Institute; American Inns of Court — E-mail: rps@frslaw.com

Paul B. Howell — 1957 — The University of Mississippi, B.A., 1979; J.D., 1981 — Admitted to Bar, 1981, Mississippi; 1981, U.S. District Court, Northern and Southern Districts of Mississippi; 1988, U.S. Court of Appeals, Fifth Circuit; 1996, U.S. Supreme Court — Member American and Harrison County Bar Associations; The Mississippi Bar; Mississippi Claims Association; Benefits Review Board, Advisory Board; Mississippi Defense Lawyers Association; Defense Research Institute; American Inns of Court — E-mail: pbh@frslaw.com

Fredrick B. Feeney II — 1958 — University of Southern Mississippi, B.S., 1980; Mississippi College School of Law, J.D. (with distinction), 1983 — Admitted to Bar, 1983, Mississippi; 1986, U.S. District Court, Southern District of Mississippi; 1986, U.S. Court of Appeals, Fifth Circuit; 1993, U.S. Supreme Court — Member Federal, American, Fifth Circuit and Harrison County Bar Associations; The Mississippi Bar; Mississippi Defense Lawyers Association; Defense Research Institute; American Inns of Court — E-mail: fbf@frslaw.com

Traci M. Castille — 1961 — University of Southwestern Louisiana, B.A., 1982; Tulane University, J.D., 1985 — Admitted to Bar, 1985, Louisiana; 1989, Mississippi; 1985, U.S. District Court, Eastern District of Louisiana; 1985, U.S. Court of Appeals, Fifth Circuit; 1989, U.S. District Court, Northern and Southern Districts of Mississippi — Member American, Louisiana State, Harrison County and Fifth Federal Circuit Bar Associations; The Mississippi Bar; Harrison County Young Lawyers Association; Defense Research Institute; American Inns of Court — E-mail: tmc@frslaw.com

Donald P. Moore — 1966 — Southeastern Louisiana University, B.A. (cum laude), 1988; Tulane University, J.D. (cum laude), 1991 — Admitted to Bar, 1991, Louisiana; 1993, Mississippi; 1991, U.S. District Court, Eastern District of Louisiana; 1993, U.S. District Court, Southern District of Mississippi; 1993, U.S. Court of Appeals, Fifth Circuit — Member American, Louisiana State and Harrison County Bar Associations; The Mississippi Bar; American Inns of Court; Mississippi Defense Lawyers Association; Defense Research Institute — E-mail: dpm@frslaw.com

Susan F. Bruhnke — 1972 — University of South Alabama, B.A. (magna cum laude), 1994; The University of Mississippi, J.D. (cum laude), 1999 — Admitted to Bar, 1999, Mississippi; 2000, U.S. District Court, Northern and Southern Districts of Mississippi; U.S. Court of Appeals, Fifth Circuit — Member The Mississippi Bar; Defense Research Institute; Mississippi Defense Lawyers Association; American Inns of Court — Languages: German — E-mail: sfs@frslaw.com

Associates

Shellye V. McDonald — 1960 — The University of Mississippi, B.S., 1982; J.D., 1985 — Admitted to Bar, 1985, Mississippi; 1985, U.S. District Court, Northern and Southern Districts of Mississippi; 1985, U.S. Court of Appeals, Fifth Circuit — Member Harrison County Bar Association; The Mississippi Bar; Risk and Insurance Management Society; Mississippi Defense Lawyers Association; American Inns of Court — E-mail: svm@frslaw.com

Nathan L. Burrow — 1981 — The University of Mississippi, B.A. (cum laude), 2004; The University of Mississippi School of Law, J.D. (magna cum laude), 2008 — Admitted to Bar, 2008, Mississippi; 2014, Alabama — Member The Mississippi Bar; Alabama State Bar; Mississippi Defense Lawyers Association; American Inns of Court — E-mail: nlb@frslaw.com

Of Counsel

Paul M. Franke Jr — 1937 — The University of Mississippi; University of Southern Mississippi, B.S., 1961; The University of Mississippi School of Law; Mississippi College School of Law, LL.B., 1966 — Sigma Delta Kappa — Admitted to Bar, 1966, Mississippi — Member Federal, American, Harrison County and Fifth Federal Circuit Bar Associations; The Mississippi Bar (Chairman, Workers' Compensation Committee, 1978 and 1988); Mississippi Defense Lawyers Association (Vice President, 1987); Fellow, Mississippi Bar Foundation; Mississippi Claims Association; The Maritime Law Association of the United States; Southeastern Admiralty Law Institute; Defense Research Institute; American Inns of Court — Administrative Judge, 1966-1969; Mississippi Workers' Compensation Commission (Commissioner, 1969); Mississippi State Port Authority (Member, 1975-Present; President, 1979 and 1984); Commission to Revise Mississippi Constitution (1985); Mississippi Development (Bond) Bank (Chairman, 1986) — E-mail: pmf@frslaw.com

Galloway, Johnson, Tompkins, Burr & Smith

2510 14th Street, Suite 910
Gulfport, Mississippi 39501
Telephone: 228-214-4250
Fax: 228-214-9650
E-Mail: dbobadilla@gallowayjohnson.com
www.gallowayjohnson.com

(Additional Offices: New Orleans, LA*; Lafayette, LA*; Pensacola, FL*; St. Louis, MO*; Houston, TX*; Mandeville, LA*; Tampa, FL*; Mobile, AL*; Atlanta, GA*)

Maritime, Automobile Liability, Bad Faith, Class Actions, Construction, Energy, Employment, Insurance Coverage, Insurance Defense, Product Liability, Professional Liability, Property, Transportation, General Casualty, Title Resolution, Environmental

(See listing under New Orleans, LA for additional information)

Hailey, McNamara, Hall, Larmann & Papale, L.L.P.

302 Courthouse Road, Suite A
Gulfport, Mississippi 39507
Telephone: 228-896-1144
Fax: 228-896-1177
www.haileymcnamara.com

(Metairie, LA Office*: One Galleria Boulevard, Suite 1400, 70001, P.O. Box 8288, 70011-8288)
 (Tel: 504-836-6500)
 (Fax: 504-836-6565)
(Baton Rouge, LA Office: 10771 Perkins Road, Suite 100, 70810)
 (Tel: 225-766-5567)
 (Fax: 225-766-5548)
(New Orleans, LA Office: 1100 Poydras Street, Suite 2900, 70183)
 (Tel: 504-799-2271)
 (Fax: 504-836-6565)

Admiralty and Maritime Law, Commercial Litigation, Construction Litigation, Employment Practices Liability, Insurance Litigation, Product Liability, Professional Malpractice, Toxic Torts, Casualty, Insurance Coverage, Intellectual Property, Premises Liability, Transportation, Appellate, Mass Tort, Property, Workers' Compensation, Automobile Liability, Environmental

Members

Dominic J. Ovella — Managing Partner — 1956 — The University of New Orleans, B.S., 1980; Loyola University, J.D., 1984 — Law Clerk to Hon. A. J. McNamara, U.S. District Court, Eastern District of Louisiana, 1984 — Admitted to Bar, 1985, Louisiana; 2004, Mississippi; 2004, Texas; U.S. District Court, Districts of Louisiana, Mississippi and Texas; U.S. Court of Appeals, Fifth Circuit; U.S. Supreme Court — Member Federal, American, Louisiana State, Harrison County, Jefferson Parish, Houston and New Orleans Bar Associations; The Mississippi Bar; State Bar of Texas; Louisiana Association of Business & Industry (Sections: Task Force; Corporate; Environmental; Insurance; Products Liability; Mass Tort; Construction); Mississippi, Texas and Louisiana Association of Defense Counsel; International Association of Defense Counsel; Defense Research Institute — Practice Areas: Environmental Law; Insurance Defense; Product Liability; Toxic Torts; Automobile Liability; General Liability; Construction Law; Premises Liability; Professional Liability; Trucking; Extra-Contractual Law — E-mail: novella@hmhlp.com

W. Evan Plauché — Managing Partner — 1957 — Tulane University, B.S.M.E., 1979; Loyola University, J.D., 1991 — Pi Tau Sigma Honorary Engineering Society; Phi Delta Phi Legal Fraternity — Admitted to Bar, 1991, Louisiana; 2005, Mississippi; 1991, U.S. District Court, Eastern, Middle and Western Districts of Louisiana; 1992, U.S. Court of Appeals, Fifth Circuit; 2005, U.S. District Court, Northern and Southern Districts of Mississippi — Member Federal, American, Louisiana State and New Orleans Bar

Hailey, McNamara, Hall, Larmann & Papale, L.L.P., Gulfport, MS (Continued)

Associations; The Mississippi Bar; American Society of Mechanical Engineers; American Society of Automotive Engineers (Honorary Member); Association for Transportation Law, Logistics and Policy; Defense Research Institute; Louisiana Association of Defense Counsel; Trucking Industry Defense Association; Federation of Defense and Corporate Counsel — Super Lawyer by Law and Politics (2007,2011, 2013) — Practice Areas: Trial Practice; Product Liability; Toxic Torts; Environmental Law; Transportation; Construction Law; Professional Liability; Maritime Law; Intellectual Property; Premises Liability; Casualty; Mass Tort; Property — E-mail: eplauche@hmhlp.com

Sean P. Mount — Equity Partner — 1975 — Louisiana State University, B.A. (with honors), 1998; J.D., 2001 — Admitted to Bar, 2001, Louisiana; 2004, Mississippi; 2009, Texas; 2001, U.S. District Court, Eastern, Middle and Western Districts of Louisiana; U.S. Court of Appeals, Fifth Circuit; 2004, U.S. District Court, Northern and Southern Districts of Mississippi; U.S. Supreme Court; 2009, U.S. District Court, Southern District of Texas — Member Federal, American, Louisiana State and New Orleans Bar Associations; The Mississippi Bar; State Bar of Texas; Council on Litigation Management; Association of Builders and Contractors; Texas Defense Lawyers Association; Louisiana Association of Defense Counsel; Defense Research Institute; Mississippi Defense Lawyers Association — Practice Areas: Civil Litigation; Class Actions; Toxic Torts; Premises Liability; Product Liability; Inland Marine; Professional Liability; Lender Liability Defense; Coverage Analysis; Commercial Litigation; Construction Litigation; Trucking Litigation — E-mail: smount@hmhlp.com

Special Counsel

Richard B. Tubertini — 1960 — Mississippi State University, B.A., 1982; The University of Mississippi, J.D., 1984 — Admitted to Bar, 1985, Mississippi; U.S. District Court, Northern and Southern Districts of Mississippi; U.S. Court of Appeals, Fifth Circuit — Member Harrison County and Fifth Federal Circuit Bar Associations; The Mississippi Bar; Defense Research Institute (Commercial Litigation and Insurance Law Committees); Mississippi Defense Lawyers Association — E-mail: rtubertini@hmhlp.com

Of Counsel

H. John Gutierrez — 1965 — Brown University, A.B., 1988; University of California, Berkeley, M.L.S., 1991; Georgetown University Law Center, J.D., 1999 — Admitted to Bar, 2000, Mississippi; 2005, California; 2008, Texas; 2000, U.S. District Court, Northern and Southern Districts of Mississippi; 2002, U.S. Court of Appeals, Fifth Circuit; 2005, U.S. District Court, Central, Eastern and Northern Districts of California — Member The Mississippi Bar (Public Information Committee) — E-mail: jgutierrez@hmhlp.com

Stephen A. Anderson — 1954 — University of Southern Mississippi, B.S., 1975; The University of Mississippi, J.D., 1978 — Admitted to Bar, 1978, Mississippi; U.S. District Court, Northern and Southern Districts of Mississippi — Member The Mississippi Bar; Harrison County Bar Association; Defense Research Institute — E-mail: sanderson@hmhlp.com

(See complete listing under Metairie, LA for additional clients & information)

Page, Mannino, Peresich & McDermott, P.L.L.C.

2408 14th Street
Gulfport, Mississippi 39501-2019
   Telephone: 228-868-8999
   Fax: 228-868-8940
   E-Mail: Stephen.Peresich@pmp.org
   www.pmp.org

Insurance Defense, Banking, Bankruptcy, Business Law, Commercial Litigation, Construction Law, Environmental Litigation, Government Affairs, Governmental Entity Defense, Health Care, Hospital Law, Labor and Employment, Medical Malpractice, Municipal Law, Personal Injury, Product Liability, Professional Malpractice, Real Estate, Toxic Torts

(See listing under Biloxi, MS for additional information)

Phelps Dunbar LLP

NorthCourt One
2304 19th Street, Suite 300
Gulfport, Mississippi 39501
   Telephone: 228-679-1130
   Fax: 228-679-1131
   E-Mail: info@phelps.com
   www.phelpsdunbar.com

(New Orleans, LA Office*: Canal Place, 365 Canal Street, Suite 2000, 70130-6534)
   (Tel: 504-566-1311)
   (Fax: 504-568-9130)
(Baton Rouge, LA Office*: II City Plaza, 400 Convention Street, Suite 1100, 70802-5618, P.O. Box 4412, 70821-4412)
   (Tel: 225-346-0285)
   (Fax: 225-381-9197)
(Jackson, MS Office*: 4270 I-55 North, 39211-6391, P.O. Box 16114, 39236-6114)
   (Tel: 601-352-2300)
   (Fax: 601-360-9777)
(Tupelo, MS Office*: One Mississippi Plaza, 201 South Spring Street, Seventh Floor, 38804, P.O. Box 1220, 38802-1220)
   (Tel: 662-842-7907)
   (Fax: 662-842-3873)
(Houston, TX Office*: One Allen Center, 500 Dallas Street, Suite 1300, 77002)
   (Tel: 713-626-1386)
   (Fax: 713-626-1388)
(Tampa, FL Office*: 100 South Ashley Drive, Suite 1900, 33602-5311)
   (Tel: 813-472-7550)
   (Fax: 813-472-7570)
(Mobile, AL Office*: 2 North Royal Street, 36602, P.O. Box 2727, 36652-2727)
   (Tel: 251-432-4481)
   (Fax: 251-433-1820)
(London, United Kingdom Office*: Lloyd's, Suite 725, Level 7, 1 Lime Street, EC3M 7DQ)
   (Tel: 011-44-207-929-4765)
   (Fax: 011-44-207-929-0046)
(Raleigh, NC Office*: 4140 Parklake Avenue, Suite 100, 27612-3723)
   (Tel: 919-789-5300)
   (Fax: 919-789-5301)
(Southlake, TX Office*(See Dallas listing): 115 Grand Avenue, Suite 222, 76092)
   (Tel: 817-488-3134)
   (Fax: 817-488-3214)

Insurance Law

Insurance Clients

Acceptance Casualty Insurance Company	ACE Group of Insurance and Reinsurance Companies
Aegis Janson Green Insurance Services Inc.	Aetna Insurance Company
AIG	AFLAC - American Family Life Assurance Company of Columbus
Alabama Municipal Insurance Corporation	Allstate Insurance Company
AmTrust Underwriters, Inc.	American Family Life Assurance Company of Columbus
Arch Insurance Company (Europe) Ltd.	Argonaut Insurance Company
Aspen Insurance UK Limited	Aspen Insurance
Associated Aviation Underwriters	Aspen Re
Bankers Insurance Group	AXIS Insurance
Berkley Select, LLC	Beazley
Bluebonnet Life Insurance Company	Bituminous Insurance Company
Britannia Steam Ship Insurance Association Ltd.	Blue Cross & Blue Shield of Mississippi
CNA	Chartis Insurance
Commercial Union Insurance Company	Chubb Group of Insurance Companies
Companion Property and Casualty Group	Commonwealth Insurance Company
ELCO Administrative Services	Cotton States Insurance
Endurance Services, Ltd.	Criterion Claim Solutions
	Employers Reinsurance Corporation

MISSISSIPPI / GULFPORT

Phelps Dunbar LLP, Gulfport, MS   (Continued)

Erie Insurance Company
Esurance Insurance Company
Evanston Insurance Company
Farmers Insurance Group
Fidelity National Financial
Fireman's Fund Insurance Company
First Premium Insurance Group, Inc.
Foremost Insurance Company
GE Insurance Solutions
General American Life Insurance Company
General & Cologne Life Reinsurance of America
General Reinsurance Corporation
General Star Indemnity Company
General Star Management Company
Glencoe Group
Golden Rule Insurance Company
Global Special Risks, Inc.
Great Southern Life Insurance Company
Great American Insurance Companies
Gulf Insurance Group
Hanover Insurance Group
The Hartford Insurance Group
Hermitage Insurance Company
Homesite Group, Inc.
Houston Casualty Company
ICAT Boulder Claims
Indian Harbor Insurance Company
Infinity Insurance Company
Ironshore Insurance, Ltd.
Lexington Insurance Company
Liberty International Underwriters
Liberty Mutual Group
Life Insurance Company of Alabama
Louisiana Farm Bureau Mutual Insurance Company
Louisiana Health Insurance Association
Louisiana Workers' Compensation Corporation
Lyndon Property Insurance Company
Markel
Munich-American Risk Partners
MetLife Auto & Home
NAS Insurance Group
Nationwide Insurance
Nautilus Insurance Company
The Navigators Group, Inc.
Old American Insurance Company
OneBeacon Insurance Group
Pharmacists Mutual Insurance Company
Prime Syndicate
QBE
RenaissanceRe
Republic Western Insurance Company
RLI Insurance Company
Royal & SunAlliance
St. Paul Travelers
SCOR Global P&C
Scottsdale Insurance Company
Sedgwick Claims Management Services, Inc.
Sentry Insurance
Southern Farm Bureau Casualty Insurance Company
SR International Business Insurance Company, Ltd.
State National Insurance Company, Inc.
Steamship Mutual Underwriting Association Limited
Terra Nova Insurance Company Limited
Torus
United States Fidelity and Guaranty Company
Underwriters at Lloyd's, London
Unitrin Business Insurance
Victoria Insurance Group
Vesta Eiendom AS
West of England Ship Owners Mutual Insurance Association (Luxembourg)
Western Heritage Insurance Company
Westport Insurance Corporation
Zurich
XL Insurance Group

Members of the Firm

Scott Ellzey — The University of Mississippi, B.B.A., 1993; The University of Mississippi School of Law, J.D. (cum laude), 1996 — Admitted to Bar, 1996, Mississippi; U.S. District Court, Northern and Southern Districts of Mississippi; U.S. Court of Appeals, Fifth Circuit; Mississippi Band of Choctaw Indians Tribal Court — Member Harrison County Bar Association; The Mississippi Bar; Mississippi Claims Association; Defense Research Institute; Mississippi Defense Lawyers Association

Kyle S. Moran — Mississippi State University, B.B.A., 1994; The University of Mississippi School of Law, J.D., 1997 — Admitted to Bar, 1997, Mississippi; Louisiana; U.S. District Court, Northern and Southern Districts of Mississippi; U.S. District Court, Eastern, Middle and Western Districts of Louisiana; U.S. Court of Appeals, Fifth Circuit — Member Louisiana State and Harrison County Bar Associations; The Mississippi Bar — Resident Gulfport, MS and London, United Kingdom Office

James G. Wyly, III — Louisiana State University, B.S., 1975; Mississippi College School of Law, J.D., 1980 — Admitted to Bar, 1980, Mississippi; 1981, Louisiana; U.S. District Court, Eastern and Western Districts of Louisiana; U.S. District Court, Southern District of Mississippi; U.S. Court of Appeals, Fifth Circuit — Member Louisiana State and Harrison County Bar Associations; The Mississippi Bar; Louisiana Association of Defense Counsel — Certified Arbitrator and Mediator

(See listing under New Orleans, LA for additional information)

Vernis & Bowling of Southern Mississippi, PLLC

2501 14th Street, Suite 207
Gulfport, Mississippi 39501
  Telephone: 225-539-0021
  Fax: 228-539-0022

(Vernis & Bowling of Palm Beach, P.A.*: 884 U.S. Highway #1, North Palm Beach, FL, 33408-5408)
  (Tel: 561-775-9822)
  (Fax: 561-775-9821)
  (E-Mail: gjvernis@florida-law.com)
  (www.national-law.com)
(Vernis & Bowling of Southern Alabama, LLC*: 61 St. Joseph Street, 11th Floor, Mobile, AL, 36602)
  (Tel: 251-432-0337)
  (Fax: 251-432-0244)
  (E-Mail: info@law-alabama.com)
  (www.law-alabama.com)
(Vernis & Bowling of Broward, P.A.*(See Fort Lauderdale listing): 5821 Hollywood Boulevard, First Floor, Hollywood, FL, 33021)
  (Tel: 954-927-5330)
  (Fax: 954-927-5320)
  (E-Mail: info@florida-law.com)
  (www.national-law.com)
(Vernis & Bowling of Northwest Florida, P.A.*: 315 South Palafox Street, Pensacola, FL, 32502)
  (Tel: 850-433-5461)
  (Fax: 850-432-0166)
  (E-Mail: info@florida-law.com)
  (www.national-law.com)

Established: 1970

Civil Litigation, Insurance Law, Workers' Compensation, Premises Liability, Labor and Employment, Civil Rights, Commercial Litigation, Complex Litigation, Product Liability, Directors and Officers Liability, Errors and Omissions, Construction Law, Construction Defect, Environmental Liability, Personal and Commercial Vehicle, Appellate Practice, Admiralty and Maritime Law, Real Estate, Family Law, Elder Law, Liability Defense, SIU/Fraud Litigation, Education Law (ESE/IDEA), Property and Casualty (Commercial and Personal Lines), Long-Haul Trucking Liability, Government Law, Public Law, Criminal, White Collar, Business Litigation

Firm Profile: VERNIS & BOWLING represents individuals, businesses, insurance carriers and self-insureds. With 115 offices located in Florida, Georgia, Alabama, North Carolina & Mississippi, we provide cost effective, full service legal representation that consistently exceeds the expectations of our clients.

Insurance Clients

AAA Michigan
AutoNation Incorporated
Auto-Owners Insurance Company
Burlington Insurance Company
Chrysler Insurance Company
Chubb Group of Insurance Companies
CNA Insurance Companies
Crum & Forster Insurance Group
Florida Insurance Guaranty Association
Lexington Insurance Company
Lowe's Home Centers, Inc.
National General Insurance Company
National Service Industries, Inc.
State of Florida
United Automobile Insurance Group

Firm Members & Associates

Christopher B. Estes — Spring Hill College, B.S. (cum laude), 1995; The University of Alabama School of Law, J.D. (cum laude), 1998 — Admitted to Bar, 1998, Alabama; Mississippi — E-mail: cestes@national-law.com

(See listing under North Palm Beach, FL for additional information)

Webb Sanders & Williams PLLC

45 Hardy Court, Suite 164
Gulfport, Mississippi 39507
   Telephone: 228-822-2137
   Fax: 228-822-2139
   www.webbsanders.com

(Tupelo, MS Office*: 363 North Broadway, 38804, P.O. Box 496, 38802-0496)
   (Tel: 662-844-2137)
   (Fax: 662-842-3863)
   (E-Mail: info@webbsanders.com)

Insurance Defense, Insurance Coverage, Automobile, Property, Fire, Arson, Fraud, First Party Matters, Bad Faith, Special Investigations, Product Liability, Automobile Liability, Uninsured and Underinsured Motorist, General Liability, Premises Liability, Defense Litigation, Corporate Law, Commercial Law, Commercial Litigation, Toxic Torts, ERISA, Construction Litigation

(See listing under Tupelo, MS for additional information)

The following firms also service this area.

Hicks Law Firm, PLLC
211 South 29th Avenue, Suite 201
Hattiesburg, Mississippi 39401
   Telephone: 601-544-6770
   Fax: 601-544-6775
Mailing Address: P.O. Box 18350, Hattiesburg, MS 39404-8350

Insurance Defense, General Liability, Automobile, Bodily Injury, Casualty, Product Liability, Premises Liability, Commercial Litigation, Bad Faith, Trucking Law, Construction Litigation, Commercial Vehicle, Professional Liability, Commercial and Personal Lines

SEE COMPLETE LISTING UNDER HATTIESBURG, MISSISSIPPI (70 MILES)

Swetman Baxter Massenburg, LLC
1700 South 28th Avenue, Suite D
Hattiesburg, Mississippi 39402
   Telephone: 601-255-0259
   Fax: 601-255-0260

Asbestos Litigation, Bad Faith, Construction Claims, Construction Law, Contractors Liability, Declaratory Judgments, Drug, Environmental Law, Hazardous Waste, Insurance Defense, Intellectual Property, Mold and Mildew Claims, Municipal Liability, Premises Liability, Product Liability, Toxic Torts, Trucking Liability, Trucking Litigation, Uninsured and Underinsured Motorist, Workers' Compensation, Wrongful Death

SEE COMPLETE LISTING UNDER HATTIESBURG, MISSISSIPPI (70 MILES)

Ungarino & Eckert, L.L.C.
3850 North Causeway Boulevard, Suite 1280
Metairie, Louisiana 70002
   Telephone: 504-836-7555
   Fax: 504-836-7566

Litigation, Appellate Practice, State and Federal Courts, Class Actions, Insurance Coverage, Premises Liability, Professional Liability, Directors and Officers Liability, Insurance Defense, Construction Law, Toxic Torts, Personal Injury, Arson, Insurance Fraud, Admiralty and Maritime Law, Extra-Contractual Litigation, Bad Faith, Product Liability, Alternative Dispute Resolution, Civil Rights, Workers' Compensation, Environmental Law, Employment Law, Automobile, Truck Liability, Errors and Omissions, Common Carrier, Medical Malpractice, Construction Defect, Constitutional Law, Department of Insurance Complaints, ERISA Claims, Government Relations, Complex Casualty, Consumer Defense, Creditor Rights, Debt Collections, Discrimination Claims, Electric Utility Liability, Engineering Malpractice, Family Law (Divorce, Custody, Support, Adoption), Fraud, General Liability, Governmental Entity Liability, Insurance Subrogation, Landlord Liability, Medical Device Liability, Property Ownership, State and Municipality Litigation, Successions, Warranty/Redhibition Actions

SEE COMPLETE LISTING UNDER METAIRIE, LOUISIANA (82 MILES)

HATTIESBURG † 45,989 Forrest Co.

Aultman Law Firm, Ltd.
315 Hemphill Street
Hattiesburg, Mississippi 39401
   Telephone: 601-583-2671
   Fax: 601-583-2677
   E-Mail: da@aultmanlaw.com

(Gulfport, MS Office*: 1901 21st Avenue, 39501, P.O. Box 607, 39502-0607)
   (Tel: 228-863-6913)
   (Fax: 228-868-8505)
   (E-Mail: DeeAultman@aultmanlaw.com)

Established: 1918

General Civil Practice, Insurance Law, Fire, Casualty, Surety, Life Insurance, Workers' Compensation, Trial Practice, Admiralty and Maritime Law, Subrogation, Environmental Law, Toxic Torts

Firm Profile: Aultman Law Firm, Ltd. is a civil law firm that focuses on defense litigation. Established in 1918, Aultman Law combines its long-standing presence in the Southeast with a forward thinking approach to providing legal solutions. We pride ourselves on legal excellence, forceful advocacy, and ethical integrity.

Insurance Clients

American National Property and Casualty Company	Georgia Casualty & Surety Company
The Hartford Insurance Group	Kingsway America, Inc.
Liberty Mutual Insurance Company	Nationwide Insurance
Norcal Mutual Insurance Company	North Carolina Mutual Life Insurance Company
Safeco Insurance	
Scottsdale Insurance Company	South Carolina Insurance Company
Transamerica Group/AEGON USA, Inc.	Westport Insurance Corporation
	Zurich American Insurance Company

Resident Partner

Dorrance Aultman — 1933 — University of Southern Mississippi, B.S., 1954; The University of Mississippi, LL.B., 1956; William Carey College, LL.D., 2008 — Phi Alpha Delta — Doctor of Law, William Carey University (2008) — Admitted to Bar, 1956, Mississippi; 1956, U.S. District Court, Northern and Southern Districts of Mississippi; 1956, U.S. Court of Appeals, Fifth and Eleventh Circuits — Member American and South Central Mississippi Bar Associations; The Mississippi Bar; Mississippi Board of Bar Admissions by Appointment of Supreme Court, 1979-1982; Mississippi Defense Lawyers Association; American Board of Trial Advocates — BG. State Staff Judge Advocate, MSANG, 1970-1986 (Retired) — Practice Areas: Civil Litigation; Medical Malpractice; Insurance Law; Commercial Litigation; Professional Liability — E-mail: da@aultmanlaw.com

S. Wayne Easterling
120 South Tenth Avenue
Hattiesburg, Mississippi 39401
   Telephone: 601-544-8900

Insurance Defense, Automobile, General Liability, Workers' Compensation, Casualty, Truck Liability

Insurance Clients

American General Life and Accident Insurance Company	Government Employees Insurance Company
Nationwide Insurance	St. Paul Insurance Company

Non-Insurance Clients

Comcar Industries, Inc.

MISSISSIPPI — HATTIESBURG

S. Wayne Easterling, Hattiesburg, MS (Continued)

Shareholder

S. Wayne Easterling — 1944 — University of Southern Mississippi, B.S., 1965; The University of Mississippi, J.D., 1968 — Admitted to Bar, 1968, Mississippi; 1968, U.S. District Court, Northern and Southern Districts of Mississippi — Member South Central Mississippi Bar Association; The Mississippi Bar

Hicks Law Firm, PLLC

211 South 29th Avenue, Suite 201
Hattiesburg, Mississippi 39401
Telephone: 601-544-6770
Fax: 601-544-6775
E-Mail: clark@hicksattorneys.com
www.hicksattorneys.com

Established: 1984

Insurance Defense, General Liability, Automobile, Bodily Injury, Casualty, Product Liability, Premises Liability, Commercial Litigation, Bad Faith, Trucking Law, Construction Litigation, Commercial Vehicle, Professional Liability, Commercial and Personal Lines

Firm Profile: Hicks Law Firm, PLLC, is a civil litigation law firm with a significant portion of the law practice directly related to insurance defense, bad faith, and coverage litigation. The firm handles cases in all state and federal courts in Mississippi.

Representative Insurance Clients

Bituminous Insurance Companies
FCCI Insurance Group
Liberty Mutual
Ohio Casualty Insurance Company
Economy Premier Assurance Company
MetLife Auto & Home
XL Specialty Insurance Company

Representative Non Insurance Clients

Bell Contractors, Inc.
Coburn Supply Company, Inc.
ERMC II, L.P.
Food Giant Supermarkets, Inc.
Hotel of Laurel, LLC
Pierce Construction and Maintenance Co., Inc.
Rite Aid Corporation
Blendco, Inc.
Delphi Oil, Inc.
Evergreen Lumber & Truss, Inc.
Hattiesburg Housing Authority
Mississippi Municipal Liability Plan
Regions Bank
Servpro Industries, Inc.

Third Party Administrators

Pinnacle Risk Management Services
Statewide Claims Service

Firm Member

L. Clark Hicks, Jr. — 1966 — The University of Mississippi, J.D. (cum laude), 1991 — Admitted to Bar, 1991, Mississippi

Associates

R. Lane Dossett — 1982 — Appalachian School of Law, J.D. (summa cum laude), 2008 — Admitted to Bar, 2008, Mississippi

John Knox — 1981 — The University of Mississippi, J.D., 2013 — Admitted to Bar, 2013, Mississippi

Swetman Baxter Massenburg, LLC

1700 South 28th Avenue, Suite D
Hattiesburg, Mississippi 39402
Telephone: 601-255-0259
Fax: 601-255-0260
E-Mail: cmassenburg@sbm-legal.com
www.sbm-legal.com

(New Orleans, LA Office*: 650 Poydras Street, Suite 2400, 70130)
(Tel: 504-799-0500)
(Fax: 504-799-0501)
(E-Mail: mswetman@sbm-legal.com)

Swetman Baxter Massenburg, LLC, Hattiesburg, MS (Continued)

Asbestos Litigation, Bad Faith, Construction Claims, Construction Law, Contractors Liability, Declaratory Judgments, Drug, Environmental Law, Hazardous Waste, Insurance Defense, Intellectual Property, Mold and Mildew Claims, Municipal Liability, Premises Liability, Product Liability, Toxic Torts, Trucking Liability, Trucking Litigation, Uninsured and Underinsured Motorist, Workers' Compensation, Wrongful Death

Partner

Christopher Massenburg — 1975 — Loyola University, B.B.A., 1997; Tulane University, J.D., 2000 — Super Lawyers 2010 Mid-South Rising Stars — Admitted to Bar, 2000, Louisiana; 2001, Mississippi; 2007, Texas; 2010, Tennessee; 2001, U.S. District Court, Northern and Southern Districts of Mississippi; 2001, U.S. Court of Appeals, Fifth Circuit; 2005, U.S. Supreme Court — Member Louisiana State, Tennessee and South Central Mississippi Bar Associations; The Mississippi Bar; State Bar of Texas; Hattiesburg Area Young Lawyers Association; Mississippi Tort Claims Board; Defense Research Institute — Practice Areas: Admiralty and Maritime Law; Environmental Law; Insurance Defense; Civil Litigation; Complex Litigation; Asbestos Litigation; Mold Litigation; Toxic Torts; Product Liability; Premises Liability; Intellectual Property; Truck Liability; Construction Law — E-mail: cmassenburg@sbm-legal.com

Associate

Adam Hays — University of Southern Mississippi, B.A., 2001; Louisiana State University Law Center, J.D./B.C.L., 2004 — Admitted to Bar, 2004, Mississippi; 2006, Louisiana; 2010, Alabama; 2004, U.S. District Court, Northern and Southern Districts of Mississippi — Member American, Louisiana State and South Central Mississippi Bar Associations; The Mississippi Bar; Hattiesburg Area Young Lawyers Association

(See listing under New Orleans, LA for additional information)

The following firms also service this area.

Hailey, McNamara, Hall, Larmann & Papale, L.L.P.
302 Courthouse Road, Suite A
Gulfport, Mississippi 39507
Telephone: 228-896-1144
Fax: 228-896-1177

Admiralty and Maritime Law, Commercial Litigation, Construction Litigation, Employment Practices Liability, Insurance Litigation, Product Liability, Professional Malpractice, Toxic Torts, Casualty, Insurance Coverage, Intellectual Property, Premises Liability, Transportation, Appellate, Mass Tort, Property, Workers' Compensation, Automobile Liability, Environmental

SEE COMPLETE LISTING UNDER GULFPORT, MISSISSIPPI (69 MILES)

Webb Sanders & Williams PLLC
363 North Broadway
Tupelo, Mississippi 38804
Telephone: 662-844-2137
Fax: 662-842-3863

Mailing Address: P.O. Box 496, Tupelo, MS 38802-0496

Insurance Defense, Insurance Coverage, Automobile, Property, Fire, Arson, Fraud, First Party Matters, Bad Faith, Special Investigations, Product Liability, Automobile Liability, Uninsured and Underinsured Motorist, Professional Malpractice, Medical Malpractice, Workers' Compensation, General Liability, Premises Liability, Defense Litigation, Corporate Law, Commercial Law, Commercial Litigation, Real Estate, Transportation, Environmental Law, Toxic Torts, Bankruptcy, Creditor Rights, Labor and Employment, ERISA, Construction Litigation, Fidelity and Surety, Insurance Fraud, General Civil Practice, Trial Practice, Appellate Practice, Employment Discrimination, Coverage Analysis, Coverage Issues

SEE COMPLETE LISTING UNDER TUPELO, MISSISSIPPI (69 MILES)

HERNANDO
MISSISSIPPI

HAZLEHURST † 4,009 Copiah Co.

Refer To

Bennett, Lotterhos, Sulser & Wilson, P.A.
188 East Capitol Street, Suite 1400
Jackson, Mississippi 39201
   Telephone: 601-944-0466
   Fax: 601-944-0467
Mailing Address: P.O. Box 98, Jackson, MS 39205-0098

Insurance Defense, Environmental Law

SEE COMPLETE LISTING UNDER JACKSON, MISSISSIPPI (35 MILES)

Refer To

Markow Walker, P.A.
599 Highland Colony Parkway, Suite 100
Ridgeland, Mississippi 39157
   Telephone: 601-853-1911
   Fax: 601-853-8284
Mailing Address: P.O. Box 13669, Jackson, MS 39236-3669

Insurance Defense, Product Liability, Bodily Injury, Toxic Torts, Medical Malpractice, Workers' Compensation

SEE COMPLETE LISTING UNDER JACKSON, MISSISSIPPI (35 MILES)

HERNANDO † 14,090 Desoto Co.

Upshaw, Williams, Biggers & Beckham, L.L.P.

2446 Caffey Street
Hernando, Mississippi 38632
   Telephone: 662-426-5890
   Fax: 662-429-5920
   Toll Free: 800-748-8720
   www.upshawwilliams.com

(Greenwood, MS Office*: 309 Fulton Street, 38930, P.O. Drawer 8230, 38935-8230)
   (Tel: 662-455-1613)
   (Fax: 662-453-9245)
   (Toll Free: 800-748-8720)
(Ridgeland, MS Office*: 713 South Pear Orchard Road, Suite 102, 39157, P.O. Box 3080, 39158-3080)
   (Tel: 601-978-1996)
   (Fax: 601-978-1949)
   (Toll Free: 800-422-1379)

Established: 2012

General Civil Practice, State and Federal Courts, Administrative Law, Appellate Practice, Arson, Aviation, Bad Faith, Casualty, Civil Trial Practice, Commercial Law, Construction Law, Contracts, Corporate Law, Environmental Law, Federal Employer Liability Claims (FELA), Fidelity, Fraud, Insurance Defense, Insurance Coverage, Legal Malpractice, General Liability, Litigation, Mass Tort, Medical Malpractice, Negligence, Oil and Gas, Personal Injury, Product Liability, Professional Liability, Property, Railroad Law, Self-Insured, Surety, Tort, Transportation, Uninsured and Underinsured Motorist, Workers' Compensation, Real Estate, Probate, Agriculture

Firm Profile: Upshaw, Williams, Biggers & Beckham LLP is a thriving midsize, Mississippi law firm founded on a commitment to innovative and entrepreneurial service. We provide the balance of size, reach and responsiveness that many clients consider ideal. With our team orientation and commitment to personal and individualized attention, the firm provides the service capabilities of a very large firm with the efficiency of a small one. That's one reason why we can readily advise you on your legal matters.

Whether our clients come from the financial, high-tech, real estate, media, securities, insurance industries or small town business and concerns, they value our creative spirit, solution-oriented approach and unwavering commitment to the highest professional standards. They have helped build our

Upshaw, Williams, Biggers & Beckham, L.L.P., Hernando, MS   (Continued)

reputation for insightful counseling, timely advice and constructive contributions to their legal business.

Representative Clients

Advocate, MD
Allianz Aviation Managers, LLC
AmFed Companies, L.L.C.
Avizent
Berkley Specialty Underwriting Managers, LLC
Canadian National
Cannon Cochran Management Services, Inc.
CNA Insurance Companies
Deep South Surplus, Inc.
The Doctors Company
Foremost Insurance Company
GEICO
Grain Dealers Mutual Insurance Company
LEMIC Insurance Company
Liberty Mutual Insurance Company
Medical Assurance Company of Mississippi Inc.
Mississippi Manufacturers Association Workers' Compensation Group
National Builders and Contractors
NL Industries, Inc.
Professional Claims Management
Safeco Insurance
State Auto Insurance Company
Summit Risk Services, Inc.
The Travelers Companies, Inc.
United Airlines, Inc.
Western Heritage Insurance
Zurich American Insurance Company
Alexsis, Inc.
American States Insurance Company
Berkley Insurance Company
Boyd Mississippi, Inc.
Bridgefield Casualty Insurance Company
Capital City Insurance Company, Inc.
Corrections Corporation of America
Farmers Insurance Exchange
Fred's Stores of Tennessee
General Casualty Insurance Company
Infinity Insurance Company
Liberty International
Lorillard Tobacco Company
Mississippi Hospitality & Restaurant Workers' Compensation Trust
Mississippi Tort Claims Board
MS Truck, Food, & Fuel
Nationwide Insurance
Phoenix Aviation Managers, Inc.
Progressive Insurance Company
Shelter Insurance Companies
State Volunteer Mutual Insurance Company
Union Standard Insurance Group
United States Aviation Underwriters, Inc.

Attorneys

Tommie G. Williams — 1953 — Mississippi State University, B.S., 1975; The University of Mississippi, J.D., 1978 — Admitted to Bar, 1978, Mississippi; 1978, U.S. District Court, Northern and Southern Districts of Mississippi; 1978, U.S. Court of Appeals, Fifth Circuit — Member American College of Trial Lawyers — The Best Lawyers in America; Mid South Super Lawyers — Resident Greenwood, MS Office

Marc A. Biggers — 1950 — Mississippi State University, B.S., 1972; The University of Mississippi, J.D., 1976 — Admitted to Bar, 1976, Mississippi; 1976, U.S. District Court, Northern and Southern Districts of Mississippi; 1980, U.S. Court of Appeals, Fifth Circuit — Member The Mississippi Bar; Leflore County Bar Association; Mississippi Defense Lawyers Association; National Association of Railroad Trial Counsel — Resident Greenwood, MS Office — E-mail: mbiggers@upshawwilliams.com

F. Ewin Henson III — 1950 — Mississippi State University, B.A., 1972; The University of Mississippi, J.D. (with distinction), 1974 — Admitted to Bar, 1974, Mississippi; 1974, U.S. District Court, Northern District of Mississippi; 1977, U.S. Court of Appeals, Fifth Circuit; 1981, U.S. Court of Appeals, Eleventh Circuit — Member The Mississippi Bar; Fifth Federal Circuit Bar Association; Mississippi Claims Association; Mississippi Defense Lawyers Association (President, 2011); Defense Research Institute — Resident Greenwood, MS Office — E-mail: ehenson@upshawwilliams.com

Richard L. Kimmel — 1961 — Mississippi State University, B.S., 1983; Mississippi College School of Law, J.D., 1986 — Admitted to Bar, 1987, Mississippi; 1987, U.S. District Court, Northern and Southern Districts of Mississippi; 1987, U.S. Court of Appeals, Fifth Circuit — Member The Mississippi Bar; Leflore County Bar Association; Mississippi Defense Lawyers Association; Lawyer-Pilots Bar Association — Practice Areas: Insurance Defense; Aviation — Resident Greenwood, MS Office — E-mail: rkimmel@upshawwilliams.com

Patrick M. Tatum — 1969 — Auburn University, B.S., 1991; The University of Mississippi, J.D., 1994 — Admitted to Bar, 1994, Mississippi; 1994, U.S. District Court, Northern and Southern Districts of Mississippi; 1994, U.S. Court of Appeals, Fifth Circuit — Member The Mississippi Bar; Hinds County Bar Association; Jackson Young Lawyers Association; Mississippi Defense Lawyers Association — E-mail: ptatum@upshawwilliams.com

James L. Wilson, IV — 1971 — The University of Mississippi, B.B.A., 1993; J.D., 1997 — Admitted to Bar, 1997, Mississippi; 1997, U.S. District Court,

Upshaw, Williams, Biggers & Beckham, L.L.P., Hernando, MS (Continued)

Northern and Southern Districts of Mississippi; 1997, U.S. Court of Appeals, Fifth Circuit — Member The Mississippi Bar; Leflore County Bar Association — Resident Greenwood, MS Office — E-mail: jwilson@upshawwilliams.com

Steven C. Cookston — 1968 — Arizona State University, B.A., 1991; Mississippi College School of Law, J.D., 1996 — Admitted to Bar, 1996, Nevada; 1996, U.S. District Court, District of Nevada; 1996, U.S. Court of Appeals, Ninth Circuit; 1998, U.S. District Court, Northern and Southern Districts of Mississippi; 1998, U.S. Court of Appeals, Fifth Circuit — Member The Mississippi Bar; State Bar of Nevada; Leflore County and Fifth Federal Circuit Bar Associations; Mississippi Defense Lawyers Association (Board of Directors, 2010-2012); Defense Research Institute — Resident Greenwood, MS Office — E-mail: scookston@upshawwilliams.com

Brooke U. Bullard — Wichita State University, B.A., 2007; The University of Mississippi, J.D., 2011 — Admitted to Bar, 2011, Mississippi; 2011, Tennessee; U.S. District Court, Northern and Southern Districts of Mississippi; U.S. Court of Appeals, Fifth Circuit; Supreme Court of Mississippi — Member The Mississippi Bar; Tennessee and Leflore County Bar Associations; Mississippi Women Lawyers Association; National Association of Legal Professionals (Greenwood Chapter); Christian Legal Society; Mississippi Defense Lawyers Association — Resident Greenwood, MS Office — E-mail: bbullard@upshawwilliams.com

(See listing under Greenwood, MS for additional information)

Walker, Brown & Brown, P.A.

2540 Highway 51 South
Hernando, Mississippi 38632
Telephone: 662-429-5277
Telephone: 901-521-9292
Fax: 662-429-5280
E-Mail: bbrown@wbblaw.us
www.wbblaw.us

Established: 1982

Insurance Defense, Commercial General Liability, Self-Insured Defense, Product Liability, Mediation, Arbitration, General Civil Practice

Insurance Clients

Brotherhood Mutual Insurance Company
Northland Insurance Company
Zurich U.S.

CGU Insurance Company
Infinity Insurance Company
Tower Group, Inc.

Non-Insurance Clients

BancorpSouth Bank
First Tennessee Bank, N.A.
Trustmark National Bank

Community Bank
Southern Bancorp

Partners

William A. Brown — 1957 — The University of Mississippi, B.B.A. (magna cum laude), 1978; J.D., 1981 — Admitted to Bar, 1981, Mississippi; U.S. District Court, Northern District of Mississippi — Member The Mississippi Bar (Commissioner, 2002-2005); DeSoto County Bar Association (President, 1996-1998); Mississippi Defense Lawyers Association; Defense Research Institute — E-mail: bbrown@wbblaw.us

Mary Lee Walker Brown

The following firms also service this area.

Webb Sanders & Williams PLLC
363 North Broadway
Tupelo, Mississippi 38804
  Telephone: 662-844-2137
  Fax: 662-842-3863
Mailing Address: P.O. Box 496, Tupelo, MS 38802-0496

Insurance Defense, Insurance Coverage, Automobile, Property, Fire, Arson, Fraud, First Party Matters, Bad Faith, Special Investigations, Product Liability, Automobile Liability, Uninsured and Underinsured Motorist, Professional Malpractice, Medical Malpractice, Workers' Compensation, General Liability, Premises Liability, Defense Litigation, Corporate Law, Commercial Law, Commercial Litigation, Real Estate, Transportation, Environmental Law, Toxic Torts, Bankruptcy, Creditor Rights, Labor and Employment, ERISA, Construction Litigation, Fidelity and Surety, Insurance Fraud, General Civil Practice, Trial Practice, Appellate Practice, Employment Discrimination, Coverage Analysis, Coverage Issues

SEE COMPLETE LISTING UNDER TUPELO, MISSISSIPPI (114 MILES)

HOLLY SPRINGS † 7,699 Marshall Co.

Refer To

Webb Sanders & Williams PLLC
363 North Broadway
Tupelo, Mississippi 38804
  Telephone: 662-844-2137
  Fax: 662-842-3863
Mailing Address: P.O. Box 496, Tupelo, MS 38802-0496

Insurance Defense, Insurance Coverage, Automobile, Property, Fire, Arson, Fraud, First Party Matters, Bad Faith, Special Investigations, Product Liability, Automobile Liability, Uninsured and Underinsured Motorist, Professional Malpractice, Medical Malpractice, Workers' Compensation, General Liability, Premises Liability, Defense Litigation, Corporate Law, Commercial Law, Commercial Litigation, Real Estate, Transportation, Environmental Law, Toxic Torts, Bankruptcy, Creditor Rights, Labor and Employment, ERISA, Construction Litigation, Fidelity and Surety, Insurance Fraud, General Civil Practice, Trial Practice, Appellate Practice, Employment Discrimination, Coverage Analysis, Coverage Issues

SEE COMPLETE LISTING UNDER TUPELO, MISSISSIPPI (60 MILES)

HOUSTON † 3,623 Chickasaw Co.

Refer To

Webb Sanders & Williams PLLC
363 North Broadway
Tupelo, Mississippi 38804
  Telephone: 662-844-2137
  Fax: 662-842-3863
Mailing Address: P.O. Box 496, Tupelo, MS 38802-0496

Insurance Defense, Insurance Coverage, Automobile, Property, Fire, Arson, Fraud, First Party Matters, Bad Faith, Special Investigations, Product Liability, Automobile Liability, Uninsured and Underinsured Motorist, Professional Malpractice, Medical Malpractice, Workers' Compensation, General Liability, Premises Liability, Defense Litigation, Corporate Law, Commercial Law, Commercial Litigation, Real Estate, Transportation, Environmental Law, Toxic Torts, Bankruptcy, Creditor Rights, Labor and Employment, ERISA, Construction Litigation, Fidelity and Surety, Insurance Fraud, General Civil Practice, Trial Practice, Appellate Practice, Employment Discrimination, Coverage Analysis, Coverage Issues

SEE COMPLETE LISTING UNDER TUPELO, MISSISSIPPI (30 MILES)

JACKSON † 173,514 Hinds Co.

Allen, Kopet & Associates, PLLC

745 Avignon Drive, Suite C
Ridgeland, Mississippi 39157
  Telephone: 601-321-1994
  Fax: 601-321-1995

(See listing under Chattanooga, TN for additional information)

Anderson Crawley & Burke, pllc

P.O. Box 2540
Ridgeland, Mississippi 39158-2540
   Telephone: 601-707-8800
   Fax: 601-707-8801
   www.acblaw.com

Employment Law, Insurance Regulation, Personal Injury, Product Liability, Transportation, Workers' Compensation

Firm Profile: Anderson Crawley & Burke, pllc is a Mississippi law firm headquartered in the Jackson, Mississippi metropolitan area with an additional office in North Mississippi (Oxford). ACB represents businesses, the insurance community, and governmental entities throughout Mississippi in a broad spectrum of practice areas.

Insurance Clients

Liberty Mutual Insurance Company

Non-Insurance Clients

The Home Depot

James M. Anderson — University of Southern Mississippi, B.S. (with honors), 1971; Mississippi College School of Law, J.D. (cum laude), 1978 — Admitted to Bar, 1978, Mississippi — Practice Areas: Workers' Compensation; Insurance Regulation; Mediation — E-mail: janderson@acblaw.com

Bennett, Lotterhos, Sulser & Wilson, P.A.

188 East Capitol Street, Suite 1400
Jackson, Mississippi 39201
   Telephone: 601-944-0466
   Fax: 601-944-0467
   www.blswlaw.com

Established: 1980

Insurance Defense, Environmental Law

Insurance Clients

Aetna Life and Casualty Company	American National Property and Casualty Company
Brotherhood Mutual Insurance Company	Gulf Insurance Company
Hartford Insurance Company	Home Insurance Company
Insurance Corporation of America	Shand Morahan & Company, Inc.
Time Insurance Company n.k.a. Assurant Health	Utica Mutual Insurance Company
	Wausau General Insurance Company

Non-Insurance Clients

Agrilease Corporation	American Air Filter Company, Inc.
Consolidated Pipe Company	Lennox Industries, Inc.
Masonite Corporation	National Car Rental
Royster Company, Inc.	

Firm Members

Richard T. Bennett — 1939 — Mississippi College, B.A., 1961; M.A., 1962; The University of Mississippi, J.D., 1965 — Admitted to Bar, 1965, Mississippi — Member Federal and Hinds County (President, 1982-1983) Bar Associations; The Mississippi Bar; Fellow, Mississippi Bar Foundation; Mississippi Defense Lawyers Association

Joseph E. Lotterhos — 1944 — The University of Mississippi, B.B.A., 1966; J.D., 1972 — Admitted to Bar, 1972, Mississippi; 1972, U.S. District Court, Northern and Southern Districts of Mississippi; 1972, U.S. Court of Appeals, Fifth Circuit; 1972, U.S. Court of Military Appeals; 1972, U.S. Supreme Court — Member Federal and Hinds County Bar Associations; The Mississippi Bar; Mississippi Defense Lawyers Association

Marcus M. Wilson — 1953 — The University of North Carolina, B.A., 1977; Mississippi College of Law, J.D., 1980 — Admitted to Bar, 1980, Mississippi — Member The Mississippi Bar; Hinds County Bar Association (Secretary/Treasurer 1993-1994)

Bennett, Lotterhos, Sulser & Wilson, P.A., Jackson, MS
(Continued)

Charles F. F. Barbour — 1972 — The University of Mississippi, B.A., 1996; J.D., 1999 — Admitted to Bar, 1999, Mississippi — Member Federal and Hinds County Bar Associations; The Mississippi Bar; Charles Clark Inns of Court; Jackson Young Lawyers Association — Law Clerk, U.S. District Court, Northern District of Mississippi, 1999-2000

Of Counsel

Floyd M. Sulser, Jr. — 1946 — The University of Mississippi, B.B.A., 1968; J.D., 1971 — Admitted to Bar, 1971, Mississippi; 1971, U.S. Court of Military Appeals — Member The Mississippi Bar; Hinds County Bar Association

Biggs, Ingram & Solop, PLLC

111 East Capitol Street, Suite 101
Jackson, Mississippi 39201
   Telephone: 601-713-1192
   Fax: 601-713-2049
   E-Mail: info@bislawyers.com
   www.bislawyers.com

Established: 2006

Commercial Law, General Defense, Insurance Defense, General Liability, Medical Malpractice, Premises Liability, Product Liability, Health Care, Oil and Gas, Insurance Law, Real Estate Litigation, Transportation, Professional Liability, Employment Law, Alternative Dispute Resolution, Workers' Compensation, Government Procurement Contracts, Hospital Defense, Construction and Surety Law, Public Contract Law

Firm Profile: Biggs, Ingram & Solop, PLLC comprises successful, experienced transactional and litigation attorneys who approach each matter with our firm philosophy: provide business-minded, innovative, solution-driven counsel. We are proud to have garnered numerous recognitions for our expertise, ethics, and standing in the legal industry. BIS is listed as a Preeminent Firm by Martindale-Hubbell, and our attorneys have earned prestigious peer-review distinctions, including Best Lawyers in America, Chambers USA, AV Preeminent Ratings by Martindale-Hubbell, and Mid-South Super Lawyers.

Insurance Clients

Bituminous Insurance Company	CNA PRO
Combined Insurance Company of America	Crum & Forster
Farmers Insurance Group	Employers Mutual Companies
State Auto Insurance Company	Markel Shand, Inc.
XL Specialty Insurance Company	Utica National Insurance Group

Members

Robert A. Biggs, III — 1951 — The University of Mississippi, B.S., 1973; J.D., 1976 — Former Law Clerk to Chief Judge, Fifth Circuit Court of Appeals, Association of Former Federal Law Clerks — Admitted to Bar, 1976, Mississippi — Member Federal, American and Hinds County Capitol Area Bar Associations; The Mississippi Bar (Chair, Litigation and General Practice Section, 1998; Board of Bar Commissioners, 1992-1996); Mississippi Defense Lawyers Association (Board of Directors, 1997-99; President, 2003); Fellow and Trustee, Mississippi Bar Foundation; Defense Research Institute; Federation of Defense and Corporate Counsel — E-mail: bbiggs@bislawyers.com

Stan T. Ingram — 1951 — The University of Mississippi, B.P.A., 1973; Mississippi College School of Law, J.D. (cum laude), 1977 — Admitted to Bar, 1977, Mississippi — Member The Mississippi Bar; Hinds County Capitol Area Bar Association; Mississippi Oil and Gas Lawyers Association (Vice President, 1997; President, 1998-99); American Association of Petroleum Landmen; American Association of Dental Examiners; Mississippi Association of Petroleum Landmen (Board of Directors, 2005); Federation of State Medical Boards — E-mail: singram@bislawyers.com

Christopher Solop — 1955 — Arizona State University, B.S., 1977; The University of Mississippi, J.D. (cum laude), 1987 — Admitted to Bar, 1987, Mississippi; 2005, Tennessee; U.S. Court of Appeals for the Federal Circuit; U.S. Court of Federal Claims — Member American (Public Contract Law Section) and Hinds County Capitol Area Bar Associations; The Mississippi Bar;

Biggs, Ingram & Solop, PLLC, Jackson, MS (Continued)

American Arbitration Association Construction Panel; Mississippi Associated General Contractors (General Counsel); Associated Builders and Contractors of Mississippi; Defense Research Institute — E-mail: csolop@bislawyers.com

Lynn Patton Thompson — 1966 — Emory University, B.A. (summa cum laude), 1988; J.D., 1992 — Admitted to Bar, 1992, Georgia; 1994, Virginia; 1996, Mississippi — Member American (Forum on Construction Industry and Public Contract Law) and Hinds County Capitol Area Bar Associations; The Mississippi Bar; Mississippi Associated General Contractors — E-mail: lynn.thompson@bislawyers.com

Travis J. Conner — Indiana University-Purdue University Indianapolis, B.A., 1999; Mississippi College Jackson School of Law, J.D., 2005 — Admitted to Bar, 2005, Mississippi; 2010, Alabama; U.S. District Court, Northern and Southern Districts of Mississippi — Member Mississippi Oil and Gas Lawyers Association; Mississippi Association of Petroleum Landmen — E-mail: tconner@bislawyers.com

Of Counsel

Edward Otis Johnson, Jr. — 1930 — The University of Mississippi, B.B.A., 1952; LL.B., 1956; J.D., 1968 — Admitted to Bar, 1956, Mississippi — Member The Mississippi Bar; Hinds County Capitol Area Bar Association; Mississippi Oil and Gas Lawyers Association (Past President); U.S. Oil and Gas Association (Former Director); Fellow, Mississippi Bar Foundation — E-mail: ojohnson@bislawyers.com

Richard M. Edmonson — 1938 — The University of Mississippi, B.A., 1960; LL.B., 1963 — Admitted to Bar, 1963, Mississippi — Member American and Hinds County Capitol Area (President, 1986-87) Bar Associations; The Mississippi Bar (Commissioner, Seventh District, 1988-91); Mississippi Defense Lawyers Association (President, 1980); Defense Research Institute (State Chairman, 1977-80); International Association of Insurance Counsel; Federation of Insurance and Corporate Counsel; Fellow, Mississippi Bar Foundation — E-mail: redmonson@bislawyers.com

Brenda T. Redfern — 1958 — The University of Mississippi, B.B.A. (cum laude), 1979; J.D. (magna cum laude), 1987 — Admitted to Bar, 1987, Mississippi — Member The Mississippi Bar; American Institute of Certified Public Accountants; Mississippi Society of Certified Public Accountants — Certified Public Accountant (1982); Certified Public Manager (2002) — E-mail: bredfern@bislawyers.com

Associates

Kimberly B. Taft — The University of Alabama, B.A. (cum laude), 2009; The University of Mississippi School of Law, J.D., 2012 — Admitted to Bar, 2012, Mississippi; Alabama; U.S. District Court, Northern and Southern Districts of Mississippi — Member The Mississippi Bar; Jackson Young Lawyers Association — For Love of the Game, 1 Miss. Sports L. Rev 179 (2011), Inaugural Issue, The Mississippi Sports Law Review — E-mail: ktaft@bislawyers.com

Brian T. Alexander — 1987 — The University of Mississippi, B.Bus.Admin., 2010; The University of Mississippi School of Law, J.D., 2014 — Admitted to Bar, 2014, Mississippi — E-mail: balexander@bislawyers.com

Brunini, Grantham, Grower & Hewes, PLLC

190 East Capitol Street, Suite 100
Jackson, Mississippi 39201
Telephone: 601-948-3101
Fax: 601-960-6902, 601-960-6927
www.brunini.com

(Biloxi, MS Office: 727 Howard Avenue, Suite 401, 39530)
(Tel: 228-435-1198)
(Fax: 228-435-0639)
(Columbus, MS Office: 410 Main Street, 39701)
(Tel: 662-240-9744)
(Fax: 662-240-4127)

Alternative Dispute Resolution, Appellate Practice, Bankruptcy, Construction Law, Environmental Law, Health Care, Intellectual Property, Labor and Employment, Mass Tort, Mergers and Acquisitions, Oil and Gas, Personal Injury, Premises Liability, Product Liability, Regulatory and Compliance, Surety, Governmental Relations

Brunini, Grantham, Grower & Hewes, PLLC, Jackson, MS (Continued)

Insurance Clients

American Modern Insurance Group, Inc.	Auto-Owners Insurance Company
Darwin National Assurance Company, member of Allied World Assurance Group	Catholic Mutual Group
	Liberty Mutual Insurance Company
	Lumbermen's Underwriting Alliance
Mitsui Sumitomo Marine Management (USA), Inc.	Park Avenue Property and Casualty Insurance Company
Westport Insurance	Zurich North America

Firm Members

Stephen J. Carmody — University of Southern Mississippi, B.S.B.A. (cum laude), 1984; Southern Methodist University, J.D., 1987 — Admitted to Bar, 1987, Georgia; Mississippi; U.S. District Court, Northern District of Georgia; U.S. District Court, Northern and Southern Districts of Mississippi; U.S. Court of Appeals, Fifth Circuit; Supreme Court of Mississippi

Cheri D. Green — The University of Mississippi, B.P.A. (summa cum laude), 1983; J.D. (cum laude), 1986 — Admitted to Bar, 1986, Mississippi; Tennessee; U.S. District Court, Northern and Southern Districts of Mississippi; U.S. District Court, Middle and Western Districts of Tennessee; U.S. Court of Appeals, Fifth Circuit

William Trey Jones III — Mississippi College, B.S. (summa cum laude), 1995; J.D. (summa cum laude), 1998 — Admitted to Bar, 1998, Mississippi; U.S. District Court, Northern and Southern Districts of Mississippi; U.S. Court of Appeals, Fifth Circuit; U.S. Supreme Court

R. David Kaufman — The University of Mississippi, B.A., 1975; J.D., 1978 — Admitted to Bar, 1978, Mississippi; U.S. District Court, Northern and Southern Districts of Mississippi; U.S. Court of Appeals, Fifth and Eleventh Circuits; U.S. Supreme Court — Member American Board of Trial Advocates; Fellow, American College of Trial Lawyers

Claire W. Ketner — Millsaps College, B.A., 1996; Mississippi College School of Law, J.D., 1999 — Admitted to Bar, 1999, Mississippi; U.S. District Court, Northern and Southern Districts of Mississippi; 2003, U.S. Court of Appeals for the Federal and Fifth Circuits

John E. Wade, Jr. — The University of Mississippi, B.B.A., 1980; J.D., 1983 — Admitted to Bar, 1983, Mississippi; U.S. District Court, Northern and Southern Districts of Mississippi; U.S. Court of Appeals, Fifth Circuit; U.S. Supreme Court — Member American Board of Trial Advocates

Matt Allen	Lawrence E. Allison Jr.
Sheldon G. Alston	P. David Andress
Benje Bailey	Leonard Blackwell
R. Richard Cirilli, Jr.	Matthew Dowd
J. Gordon Flowers	John M. Flynt
Christopher R. Fontan	Louis G. Fuller
Lynne K. Green	James L. Halford
Curt Hebert	Karen Howell
Samuel C. Kelly	James A. McCullough II
M. Patrick McDowell	John E. Milner
William C. Penick IV	Ken Rogers
Joseph A. Sclafani	Scott Singley
Granville Tate, Jr.	Watts Ueltschey
Leonard D. Van Slyke, Jr.	Joseph E. Varner III
Gene Wasson	Walter S. Weems
Jonathan R. Werne	Ron A. Yarbrough

Carroll Warren & Parker PLLC

188 East Capitol Street, Suite 1200
Jackson, Mississippi 39201
Telephone: 601-592-1010
Fax: 601-592-6060
E-Mail: rdukes@cwplaw.com
www.cwplaw.com

(Houston, TX Office*: 3040 Post Oak Boulevard, #1010, 77056-6529)
(Tel: 713-863-9029)
(Fax: 713-583-6531)

JACKSON   MISSISSIPPI

Carroll Warren & Parker PLLC, Jackson, MS (Continued)

Administrative Law, Civil Litigation, Commercial Litigation, Insurance Coverage, Bad Faith, Construction Defect, Employment Law, Premises Liability, Product Liability, Professional Liability, Personal Injury, Transportation, Regulatory and Compliance, Eminent Domain, Subrogation, Arbitration, Mediation

Firm Profile: Wisdom, courage, and uncompromising work ethic are prerequisites to success in the world of dispute resolution. Carroll Warren & Parker thrives in this demanding environment. The firm has a confidence, tenacity, and success rate in handling disputes and litigation that few can claim.

Insurance Clients

AEGIS	Allianz
Arch Insurance Group	AXIS
Chartis	Commonwealth Insurance
Liberty International Underwriters	Company
Munich Re Group	Navigators
SCOR	Swiss Re
Travelers	XL Insurance America, Inc.
Zurich	

Senior Counsel

James L. Carroll — Millsaps College, B.A., 1967; The University of Mississippi, J.D., 1972 — Admitted to Bar, 1972, Mississippi; U.S. District Court, Northern and Southern Districts of Mississippi; U.S. Court of Appeals, First, Third, Fifth, Sixth and Eleventh Circuits — Member American, Capital Area and Fifth Federal Circuit Bar Associations; The Mississippi Bar; Mississippi Bar Foundation; AIDA Reinsurance and Insurance Arbitration Society (ARIAS-US); Barrister, American Inns of Court; Mississippi Defense Lawyers Association; International Association of Defense Counsel; American Board of Trial Advocates; Defense Research Institute

Members

James L. Warren, III — University of Southern Mississippi, B.S., 1984; The University of Mississippi, J.D., 1987 — Admitted to Bar, 1987, Mississippi; U.S. District Court, Northern and Southern Districts of Mississippi; U.S. District Court, Eastern and Southern Districts of Texas; U.S. District Court, Middle, Northern and Southern Districts of Florida; U.S. District Court, District of Puerto Rico; U.S. District Court, District of the Virgin Islands; U.S. Court of Appeals, Third, Fifth and Eleventh Circuits; U.S. Supreme Court; Superior Court of the U.S. Virgin Islands — Member American, Virgin Islands, Capital Area and Fifth Federal Circuit Bar Associations; The Mississippi Bar (Co-Chair, Arbitration Committee and Unauthorized Practice of Law Committee); National Association of Criminal Defense Attorneys; AIDA Reinsurance and Insurance Arbitration Society (ARIAS-US); Chartered Institute of Arbitrators; Million Dollar Advocates Forum

Myles A. Parker — Northwestern State University, B.S., 1987; The University of Mississippi, J.D. (with honors), 1990 — Admitted to Bar, 1990, Mississippi; 2006, Texas; U.S. District Court, Northern and Southern Districts of Mississippi; U.S. District Court, Eastern, Northern, Southern and Western Districts of Texas; U.S. Court of Appeals, Fifth Circuit; U.S. District Court, District of Puerto Rico; U.S. Supreme Court — Member Federal, American, Capital Area and Fifth Circuit Bar Associations; The Mississippi Bar; State Bar of Texas; AIDA Reinsurance and Insurance Arbitration Society (ARIAS-US); Barrister, American Inns of Court; Litigation Counsel of America; Million Dollar Advocates Forum; International Association of Defense Counsel; American Association for Justice

J. Chadwick Mask — The University of Mississippi, B.A., 1992; M.B.A., 1994; J.D. (with honors), 1997 — Admitted to Bar, 1997, Mississippi; U.S. District Court, Northern and Southern Districts of Mississippi; U.S. Court of Appeals, Fifth Circuit — Member American and Capital Area Bar Associations; The Mississippi Bar; Mississippi Municipal League; American Association for Justice (Business Torts Section)

R. Douglas Morgan — James Madison University, B.A., 1994; The University of Mississippi, J.D., 2000 — Admitted to Bar, 2000, Mississippi; U.S. District Court, Northern and Southern Districts of Mississippi; U.S. Court of Appeals, Fifth Circuit — Member American (Insurance Coverage Litigation Committee; Trial and Practice Section) and Capital Area Bar Associations; The Mississippi Bar; American Association for Justice

Lee Ann C. Thigpen — The University of Mississippi, B.A. (magna cum laude), 1998; J.D., 2000 — Admitted to Bar, 2001, Mississippi; 2008, Texas; U.S. District Court, Northern and Southern Districts of Mississippi; U.S. District Court, Eastern and Southern Districts of Texas; U.S. Court of Appeals,

Carroll Warren & Parker PLLC, Jackson, MS (Continued)

Fifth Circuit — Member American and Capital Area Bar Associations; The Mississippi Bar; AIDA Reinsurance and Insurance Arbitration Society (ARIAS-US)

Alexandra F. Markov — The University of Mississippi, B.A. (magna cum laude), 1997; J.D. (magna cum laude), 2001 — Admitted to Bar, 2001, Mississippi; 2009, Texas; 2011, New York; U.S. District Court, Northern and Southern Districts of Mississippi; U.S. District Court, Eastern and Southern Districts of Texas; U.S. Court of Appeals, Fifth Circuit — Member American and Capital Area Bar Associations; The Mississippi Bar; Mississippi Women Lawyers Association; AIDA Reinsurance and Insurance Arbitration Society (ARIAS-US); Jackson Young Lawyers Association — Languages: French

Counsel

Dustin L. DuBose — Mississippi College, B.S., 2001; Southwestern Law School, J.D., 2004 — Admitted to Bar, 2004, Florida; 2007, Mississippi; 2011, Texas; U.S. District Court, Northern and Southern Districts of Mississippi; U.S. District Court, Southern District of Texas; U.S. Court of Appeals, Fifth Circuit — Member American and Houston Bar Associations; State Bar of Texas

Stacey P. Stracener — Millsaps College, B.A. (cum laude), 1992; The University of Mississippi, J.D., 1996 — Admitted to Bar, 1996, Mississippi; U.S. District Court, Northern and Southern Districts of Mississippi; U.S. Court of Appeals, Fifth Circuit — Member American and Capital Area Bar Associations; The Mississippi Bar; Mississippi Women Lawyers Association

Associates

Christopher H. Coleman	Jacob T. E. Stutzman
Clifton M. Decker	D. Scott Murray
Nicholas J. Greene	Lauren M. McCarty
Erin Guyton	Trey Gunn
Josh Daniel	

(This firm is also listed in the Subrogation section of this directory)

Cosmich Simmons & Brown, PLLC

101 South Congress Street
Jackson, Mississippi 39201
Telephone: 601-863-2100
Fax: 601-863-0078
E-Mail: mike@cs-law.com
www.cs-law.com

Established: 2002

Automobile, Bad Faith, Business Law, Commercial Litigation, Construction Law, Coverage Issues, Employment Litigation, Environmental Coverage, First and Third Party Defense, Mass Tort, Premises Liability, Product Liability, Property and Casualty, Real Estate, Retail Liability, Transportation

Firm Profile: Cosmich Simmons & Brown, PLLC is within walking distance of the Mississippi State Capitol Building, state government offices, and the Mississippi Supreme Court and state trial courts. The firm is dedicated to zealously representing clients, and has built their practice on the highest standards.

Insurance Clients

Champion Property & Casualty Group (FARA)	Chubb Group of Insurance Companies
Merchants Insurance Group	

Non-Insurance Clients

Lloyd's London, Chaucer Syndicates Ltd.	Lloyd's of London, Cathedral Group

Firm Members

John D. Cosmich — The University of Mississippi, B.A. Accounting (cum laude), 1985; J.D., 1988 — Phi Kappa Phi — Recipient, J.O. Eastland Scholarship in Law — Admitted to Bar, 1988, Mississippi — Member The Mississippi Bar — Faculty Member, National Institute of Trial Advocacy Trial School — Practice Areas: Mass Tort; Toxic Torts; Commercial Litigation

MISSISSIPPI

Cosmich Simmons & Brown, PLLC, Jackson, MS
(Continued)

Michael D. Simmons, Sr. — The University of Georgia, B.A., 1988; Mississippi College School of Law, J.D. (with special distinction), 1994 — Recipient, Hearin-Hess Scholarship and Alumni Association Scholarship — Admitted to Bar, 1994, Mississippi — Member The Mississippi Bar — Author: "Section 1983 Litigation: History and Policy Spell the Demise of Qualified Immunity for Private Defendants," 14 Miss. C. L. Rev.127 (1993); Contributing Author: Encyclopedia of Mississippi Law, (West Group, 2001) — U.S. Marine Corps Reserve, 1987-1993 — Practice Areas: Mass Tort; Commercial Litigation; Tort Litigation; Insurance Litigation; Employment Law; Appellate Practice

Richard A. Brown — Louisiana Tech University, B.A., 1992; Loyola University, M.B.A., 1994; Mississippi College School of Law, J.D., 1999 — Admitted to Bar, 1999, Mississippi — Member American Bar Association; The Mississippi Bar — Practice Areas: Mass Tort; Toxic Torts

LaKeysha Greer Isaac — Millsaps College, B.A., 1997; Emory University School of Law, J.D., 2000 — Omicron Delta Kappa; Recipient, Distinguished Student Scholarship; Bergamark Scholarship — Admitted to Bar, 2000, Mississippi — Member American, Hinds County and Magnolia Bar Associations; The Mississippi Bar — Practice Areas: Mass Tort; Toxic Torts; Tort Litigation; Insurance Litigation

Donna M. Meehan — University of Memphis, B.S. (cum laude), 1998; Mississippi College School of Law, J.D. (cum laude), 2002 — Moot Court; Fellowship at the University of Michigan School of Law — Admitted to Bar, 2002, Mississippi — Member The Mississippi Bar; Defense Research Institute; Mississippi Defense Lawyers Association

Associates

M. James Dempsey — Millsaps College, B.S., 1991; Mississippi College School of Law, J.D., 2002 — Vice Chairman, Moot Court Board — Admitted to Bar, 2003, Mississippi; Louisiana — Member Louisiana State Bar Association; The Mississippi Bar — Practice Areas: Mass Tort; Toxic Torts; Insurance Litigation

Kathleen S. Cook — Belhaven College, B.A./B.A., 1992; Mississippi College School of Law, J.D., 2006 — Admitted to Bar, 2006, Mississippi — Practice Areas: Tort; Insurance Litigation; Mass Tort; Toxic Torts; Commercial Litigation

---

Currie Johnson Griffin & Myers, P.A.

1044 River Oaks Drive
Jackson, Mississippi 39232
Telephone: 601-969-1010
Fax: 601-969-5120
www.curriejohnson.com

(Biloxi, MS Office*: 925 Tommy Munro Drive, Suite H, 39352)
(Tel: 228-385-1010)
(Fax: 228-385-1011)

Established: 1994

Insurance Defense, General Liability, Product Liability, Automobile, Uninsured and Underinsured Motorist, Coverage Issues, Fire, Arson, Commercial Litigation, Medical Malpractice, Professional Liability, Fraud, Special Investigative Unit Claims, Premises Liability, Bad Faith, Utility Law

Firm Profile: The attorneys of Currie Johnson Griffin & Myers, P.A., handle a variety of cases in state and federal courts throughout the State of Mississippi. The firm regularly defends cases involving personal injury, property, casualty, premises liability, products liability, medical malpractice, matters pertaining to health care facilities, as well as matters involving insurance coverage and bad faith claims. The firm also represents clients in employment and discrimination cases.

The firm was named as a Top 500 Go To Law Firm for 2013 & 2014. The firm was named as 2013 Law Firm of the Year in Insurance Law for Mississippi by International Law Global Experts. The firm was named 2010-2013 as a Best Law Firm by Best Lawyers, Top Tier in the fields of personal injury defense, medical malpractice-defense and insurance law. The firm has been listed for over 10 years by A.M Best as a recommended insurance law firm.

Currie Johnson Griffin & Myers, P.A., Jackson, MS
(Continued)

The firm with 20 lawyers is listed in the top ten firms in the state with the most pending cases in state and federal courts. The firm is almost exclusively an insurance defense firm with vast trial experience in all areas of casualty throughout the State. Also given the firm's heavy involvement in the defense of medical cases, it's lawyers have the expertise and the contacts necessary to defend complex medical causation issues even when the liability issues are adverse to our clients. The firm lawyers have been awarded many honors over their careers. Additionally, the firm has a reputation for its willingness to try cases.

Insurance Clients

AIG Insurance Group
Alteris Insurance Services, Inc.
Brierfield Insurance Company
Catlin Insurance Group
The Doctors Company
Esurance Insurance Services, Inc.
Fairmont Specialty Insurance Company
Hudson Insurance Group
JWF Specialty Company, Inc. (CNA)
Medicus Insurance Company
Mississippi Insurance Managers, Inc.
Nationwide Mutual Insurance Company
PRMS, Inc. - Professional Risk Management Services, Inc.
Universal Health Services, Inc.
Allstate Insurance Company
Applied Medico-Legal Solutions Risk Retention Group, Inc.
CNA Insurance Company
EMC Insurance Companies
Everest National Insurance Company
Farmers Insurance Exchange
Infinity Insurance Company
Lloyd's
Medical Assurance Company of Mississippi Inc.
Nationwide Mutual Fire Insurance Company
Old Republic Insurance Company
ProAssurance Corporation
Safeway Insurance Company
Shelter Insurance Companies
Zurich North America Insurance Group

Non-Insurance Clients

American Freightways, Inc.
Atlas Financial
Brookshire Grocery Company
Hartford Environmental Facility
American Transportation Corporation
Community Health Systems, Inc.
University of Mississippi Medical Center

Shareholders

Edward J. Currie, Jr. — 1951 — The University of Mississippi, B.A., 1973; J.D., 1976 — Phi Delta Phi — Admitted to Bar, 1976, Mississippi; 1976, U.S. District Court, Northern and Southern Districts of Mississippi; 1978, U.S. Court of Appeals, Fifth Circuit; 1979, U.S. Supreme Court — Member Federal (President, Mississippi Chapter, 1988-1989) and Capital Area Bar Associations; The Mississippi Bar Association (Board of Directors, Young Lawyers Section, 1981-1982; Chairman, General Practice and Litigation Section, 1982; Board of Bar Commissioners, 1999-2000); Mississippi Defense Lawyers Association (President, 2005; Board of Directors, 2000-2004); Jackson Young Lawyers Association (Board of Directors, 1980-1981); Mississippi Supreme Court Advisory Committee on the Mississippi Rules of Civil Procedure; Mississippi Bar Foundation; International Association of Defense Counsel (Faculty, Trial Academy, 1992); Mississippi Judicial Council (Model Civil Jury Instruction Committee, 1991-1992); American Inns of Court (1998-2000); National Lawyers Association (Chairman, Insurance Section 1997-1999); National Lawyers Association Foundation (Board of Directors); Fellow, Litigation Counsel of America; American College of Coverage (Founding Member and Secretary/Treasurer); Council On Litigation Management; Federation of Defense and Corporate Counsel (Co-Chair, Trial Masters Program) — Adjunct Professor, Mississippi College School of Law (1977-1981); Listed in Best Lawyers, 2005-2013; Lawyer of the Year, 2012 in Insurance Law, Jackson, Mississippi, Personal Injury Defense; Named Product Liability Lawyer of the Year in Mississippi by International Global Law Experts; Named Super Lawyer in Personal Injury Defense, 2006-2014; The American Lawyer & Martindale-Hubbell 2013 Top Rated Lawyer in Insurance Law — E-mail: ecurrie@curriejohnson.com

Whitman B. Johnson III — 1954 — The University of Mississippi, B.A., 1976; J.D. (with honors), 1979 — Admitted to Bar, 1979, Mississippi; 1979, U.S. District Court, Northern and Southern Districts of Mississippi; 1981, U.S. Court of Appeals, Fifth Circuit; 1990, U.S. Supreme Court — Member The Mississippi Bar; Capital Area and Rankin County Bar Associations; Mississippi Defense Lawyers Association — Listed in Best Lawyers, 2007-2014; Best Lawyers in Medical Malpractice Defense, 2011-2014; Lawyer of the Year in Medical Malpractice Defense 2011 and 2014 — Practice Areas: Medical Malpractice Defense; Medical Litigation; Medical Negligence — E-mail: wjohnson@curriejohnson.com

Currie Johnson Griffin & Myers, P.A., Jackson, MS
(Continued)

William C. Griffin — 1954 — Vanderbilt University; Millsaps College, B.S., 1980; The University of Mississippi, J.D. (cum laude), 1983 — Phi Delta Phi — Moot Court Board (Trial Division Chairman, 1983) — Admitted to Bar, 1983, Mississippi; 1983, U.S. District Court, Northern and Southern Districts of Mississippi; 1984, U.S. Court of Appeals, Fifth Circuit; 2005, U.S. Supreme Court — Member Federal, Capital Area, Rankin County and Fifth Federal Circuit Bar Associations; The Mississippi Bar; Mississippi Defense Lawyers Association — Best Lawyers in America in Personal Injury Defense and Insurance Law, 2008-2013 — E-mail: bgriffin@curriejohnson.com

Michael F. Myers — 1962 — The University of Mississippi, B.S., 1985; J.D., 1988 — Moot Court Board — Research Editor, Mississippi Law Journal, 1987-1988 — Admitted to Bar, 1988, Mississippi; 1988, U.S. District Court, Northern and Southern Districts of Mississippi; 1988, U.S. Court of Appeals, Fifth Circuit — Member Federal, Capital Area and Rankin County Bar Associations; The Mississippi Bar; Mississippi Defense Lawyers Association; Defense Research Institute — E-mail: mmyers@curriejohnson.com

Frances R. Shields — 1949 — Millsaps College, B.A., 1970; Delta State University, M.Ed., 1982; The University of Mississippi, J.D., 1989 — Phi Alpha Delta, Chi Omega, Chi Delta, — Recipient, American Jurisprudence Award in Local Government Law — Admitted to Bar, 1989, Mississippi; 1989, U.S. District Court, Northern and Southern Districts of Mississippi; 1989, U.S. Court of Appeals, Fifth Circuit — Member American, Capital Area and Rankin County Bar Associations; The Mississippi Bar; Mississippi Defense Lawyers Association (Sections: Insurance Law, Trial Practice and Procedure); Federation of Defense and Corporate Counsel — E-mail: fshields@curriejohnson.com

William H. Creel, Jr. — 1965 — University of Southern Mississippi, B.S., 1987; Mississippi College School of Law, J.D., 1990 — Phi Delta Phi — Admitted to Bar, 1990, Mississippi; 1990, U.S. District Court, Northern and Southern Districts of Mississippi; 1990, U.S. Court of Appeals, Fifth Circuit — Member Federal, Capital Area, Rankin County and Fifth Federal Circuit Bar Associations; The Mississippi Bar; Mississippi Defense Lawyers Association; Defense Research Institute; International Association of Defense Counsel — Listed in Best Lawyers in Insurance Law since 2013 — E-mail: bcreel@curriejohnson.com

Lisa Williams McKay — 1968 — The University of Mississippi, B.A. Accounting (magna cum laude), 1990; J.D. (cum laude), 1993 — Phi Kappa Phi; Omicron Delta Kappa — Moot Court Board — Casenote Editor, Mississippi Law Journal — Admitted to Bar, 1993, Mississippi; 1993, U.S. District Court, Northern and Southern Districts of Mississippi; 1993, U.S. Court of Appeals, Fifth Circuit — Member The Mississippi Bar; Capitol Area Bar Association; Jackson Young Lawyers Association (Chair, Mock Trial Committee, 1998; Director, 1999-2001); Mississippi Defense Lawyers Association (Vice President, 2013); Defense Research Institute — Listed in Best Lawyers in Medical Malpractice Defense, 2010-2014; Named by Mid-South Super Lawyers as one of The Top 50 Women Lawyers in the Mid South, 2012; Named in Super Lawyers for Personal Injury Defense, 2009-2013 — E-mail: lmckay@curriejohnson.com

William W. McKinley, Jr. — 1963 — Millsaps College, B.A., 1985; The University of Mississippi, J.D. (cum laude), 1994 — Recipient, Mississippi Bar Foundation Scholarship; Moot Court Board — Law Clerk to Hon. Leslie H. Southwick, Mississippi Court of Appeals; Hon. Armis E. Hawkins and Hon. Michael P. Mills, Supreme Court of Mississippi — Associate Editor, Mississippi Cases, Mississippi Law Journal (1984) — Admitted to Bar, 1995, Mississippi; 1995, U.S. District Court, Northern and Southern Districts of Mississippi; 1995, U.S. Court of Appeals, Fifth Circuit — Member The Mississippi Bar; Capital Area Bar Association; Mississippi Defense Lawyers Association — E-mail: wmckinley@curriejohnson.com

Rebecca Barge Cowan — 1955 — William Jennings Bryan University, B.S. (cum laude), 1976; University of South Alabama, M.S., 1979; The University of Mississippi, J.D., 1982 — Phi Alpha Delta — Admitted to Bar, 1982, Mississippi; U.S. District Court, Northern District of Mississippi; Supreme Court of Mississippi; 1983, U.S. Court of Appeals, Fifth Circuit; 1984, U.S. District Court, Southern District of Mississippi — Member Federal, Capital Area and Fifth Federal Circuit Bar Associations; The Mississippi Bar — E-mail: bcowan@curriejohnson.com

Lorraine W. Boykin — 1978 — Mississippi State University, B.A. (cum laude), 2000; The University of Mississippi, J.D., 2003 — Phi Kappa Phi; Omicron Delta Kappa; Lamba Sigma — Receipient, Robert C. Khayat Scholarship and Leonard B. Melvin Scholarship; Moot Court Board — Judicial Law Clerk to the Hon. Charles W. Pickering, Sr., Fifth Circuit Court of Appeals — Executive Editor, Mississippi Law Journal, 2002-2003 — Admitted to Bar, 2003, Mississippi; U.S. District Court, Northern and Southern Districts of Mississippi; U.S. Court of Appeals, Fifth Circuit; Supreme Court of Mississippi — Member The Mississippi Bar; Capital Area Bar Association;

Currie Johnson Griffin & Myers, P.A., Jackson, MS
(Continued)

Mississippi Defense Lawyers Association; American Inns of Court — Named a Rising Star by Super Lawyers in Healthcare, 2013 — E-mail: lboykin@curriejohnson.com

Jeremy T. Hutto — 1979 — Mississippi State University, B.B.A. (cum laude), 2001; The University of Mississippi School of Law, J.D., 2004 — Omicron Delta Kappa, Alpha Theta Chi, Phi Delta Phi — Admitted to Bar, 2005, Mississippi; Tennessee; U.S. District Court, Northern and Southern Districts of Mississippi; U.S. Court of Appeals, Fifth Circuit; Supreme Court of Mississippi — Member The Mississippi Bar; Capital Area Bar Association; Defense Research Institute; Mississippi Defense Lawyers Association — Author: "What is Everybody Else Doing About It? A Foreign Jurisdictional Analysis of Internet Gaming Regulation," Gaming Law Review, Feb. 2005, Vol. 9, No. 1: 26-34, Available at 9 GAMLR 26; "Mississippi Torts Claims Act Update," The MDLA Quarterly, Summer 2007; "First-Served v. Last-Served Defendant Rule: Whether the First Served Rule Has Been Weakened in Lieu of Murphy Bros. V. Michetti Pipe"; "The Judicial Improvement Act," The MDLA Quarterly, Fall 2006 — Named as Mid-South Rising Star by Mid-South Super Lawyers in Personal Injury Defense, 2012-2014 — E-mail: jhutto@curriejohnson.com

G. Spencer Beard, Jr. — 1973 — The University of North Carolina at Chapel Hill, B.A., 1996; The University of Mississippi, J.D. (cum laude), 2005 — Phi Delta Phi — Moot Court Board — Admitted to Bar, 2005, Mississippi; U.S. District Court, Northern and Southern Districts of Mississippi; U.S. Court of Appeals, Fifth Circuit; Supreme Court of Mississippi — Member American Bar Association; The Mississippi Bar — E-mail: sbeard@curriejohnson.com

Katrina S. Brown — 1980 — University of Southern Mississippi, B.A. (with honors), 2003; The University of Mississippi, J.D., 2005 — Phi Kappa Phi; Omicron Delta Kappa — American Jurisprudence Award in Alternative Dispute Resolution; Moot Court Board; Editor, Journal of Space Law — Admitted to Bar, 2006, Mississippi; U.S. District Court, Northern and Southern Districts of Mississippi; U.S. Court of Appeals, Fifth Circuit; Supreme Court of Mississippi — Member American, National, Capital Area and Magnolia Bar Associations; Jackson Young Lawyers Association; Mississippi Defense Lawyers Association; Defense Research Institute — Named to Lawyers of Color "First Annual Hot List" (2013); Graduate of Leadership Greater Jackson, Class of 2013-14; Named as One of the Top 40 Under 40 Outstanding Business Leaders by the MS Business Journal (2014) — E-mail: kbrown@curriejohnson.com

Associates

Joseph W. Gill — 1981 — Mississippi College, B.S. (summa cum laude), 2004; The University of Mississippi, J.D. (summa cum laude), 2007 — Phi Delta Phi; Christian Legal Society — Moot Court Board (Vice-Chairman); Mississippi Bar Foundation Scholarship; American Jurisprudence Awards in Torts I, Torts II, Evidence, Family Law — Associate Editor, Mississippi Law Journal — Admitted to Bar, 2007, Mississippi; U.S. District Court, Northern and Southern Districts of Mississippi; U.S. Court of Appeals, Fifth Circuit; Supreme Court of Mississippi — Member The Mississippi Bar; Capital Area Bar Association — Named a Rising Star by Super Lawyers in Insurance Coverage, 2012-2013 — E-mail: jgill@curriejohnson.com

Lilli Evans Bass — 1984 — Tougaloo College, B.A. (summa cum laude), 2005; The University of Mississippi School of Law, J.D. (cum laude), 2008 — Phi Delta Phi — American Jurisprudence Award for Alternative Dispute Resolution; American Jurisprudence Award for Pretrial Practice — Intern to Hon. S. Allan Alexander, Magistrate Judge, U.S. District Court, Northern District of Mississippi; Judicial Law Clerk to Hon. George C. Carlson, Jr., Presiding Justice, Mississippi Supreme Court — Admitted to Bar, 2008, Mississippi; U.S. District Court, Northern and Southern Districts of Mississippi; U.S. Court of Appeals, Fifth Circuit; Supreme Court of Mississippi — Member American, National and Capital Bar Associations; The Mississippi Bar — E-mail: lbass@curriejohnson.com

Ben C. Lewis — 1986 — Mississippi State University, B.A., 2009; The University of Mississippi, J.D., 2013 — Moot Court Board; Gibbons National Criminal Procedure Competition; Dean's Leadership Counsel; Criminal Appeals Clinic — Legal Extern to Hon. George C. Carlson, Jr., Presiding Justice, Mississippi Supreme Court — Admitted to Bar, 2013, Mississippi; U.S. District Court, Northern and Southern Districts of Mississippi; U.S. Court of Appeals, Fifth Circuit; Supreme Court of Mississippi — Member American and Capital Area Bar Associations; The Mississippi Bar; Healthcare Law Association; Mississippi Defense Lawyers Association (Law Student Division); Jackson Young Lawyers Association — Former Policy and PAC Manager, Hardwood Federation, a national hardwood products advocacy group based in Washington, DC — E-mail: blewis@curriejohnson.com

MISSISSIPPI

Currie Johnson Griffin & Myers, P.A., Jackson, MS
(Continued)

James D. Boone — 1979 — Brigham Young University, Idaho, B.A., 2003; Mississippi College School of Law, J.D., 2006 — Admitted to Bar, 2006, Mississippi; U.S. District Court, Northern and Southern Districts of Mississippi; U.S. Court of Appeals, Fifth Circuit; Supreme Court of Mississippi — Member The Mississippi Bar; Capital Area Bar Association — Author: "A Brief Guide to the Duty to Defend Post-Moeller", The MDLA Quarterly, Vol. 34, No. 3, Fall 2010; "Federal Court Predicts Mississippi Supreme Court Would Adopt a "Continuous Trigger" Theory in Context of Damage Caused by Faulty Construction Work", The MDLA Quarterly, Vol. 31, No. 2, Summer 2007 — Reported Cases: Employers Mutual Casualty Company vs. Charlie Raddin, et al.; 506 Fed. Appx. 312 (5th Cir. 2013) (unpublished); United Servs. Auto. Ass'n v. Lisanby, 47 So. 3d 1172 (Miss. 2010); Bituminous Cas. Corp. v. Buckley, 348 Fed. Appx. 23 (5th Cir. Miss. 2009) — E-mail: jboone@curriejohnson.com

Justin P. Warren — 1987 — Mississippi College, B.S. (summa cum laude), 2010; Mississippi College School of Law, J.D. (summa cum laude), 2013 — Moot Court Board (Vice-Chairman) — Executive Editor, Mississippi Law Review — Admitted to Bar, 2013, Mississippi; U.S. District Court, Northern and Southern Districts of Mississippi; U.S. Court of Appeals, Fifth Circuit; Supreme Court of Mississippi — Member The Mississippi Bar; Capital Area Bar Association — E-mail: jwarren@curriejohnson.com

Jones Walker LLP

190 East Capitol Street, Suite 800
Jackson, Mississippi 39201
   Telephone: 601-949-4900
   Fax: 601-949-4804
   E-Mail: info@joneswalker.com
   www.joneswalker.com

(New Orleans, LA Office*: 201 St. Charles Avenue, 70170-5100)
   (Tel: 504-582-8000)
   (Fax: 504-582-8583)
(Mobile, AL Office*: RSA Battle House Tower, 11 North Water Street, Suite 1200, 36602, P.O. Box 46, 36601)
   (Tel: 251-432-1414)
   (Fax: 251-433-4106)
(Baton Rouge, LA Office*: Four United Plaza, 8555 United Plaza Boulevard, 70809)
   (Tel: 225-248-2000)
   (Fax: 225-248-2010)
(Lafayette, LA Office*: 600 Jefferson Street, Suite 1600, 70501)
   (Tel: 337-593-7600)
   (Fax: 337-593-7601)
(Birmingham, AL Office*: One Federal Place, 1819 5th Avenue North, Suite 1100, 35203)
   (Tel: 205-244-5200)
   (Fax: 205-244-5400)
(Olive Branch, MS Office*: 6897 Crumpler Boulevard, Suite 100, 38654)
   (Tel: 662-895-2996)
   (Fax: 662-895-5480)

Accountants, Admiralty and Maritime Law, Agent/Broker Liability, Antitrust, Appellate Practice, Asbestos Litigation, Aviation, Bankruptcy, Cargo, Class Actions, Commercial Litigation, Complex Litigation, Construction Law, Contracts, Directors and Officers Liability, Disability, Employment Law, Energy, Entertainment Law, Environmental Law, ERISA, Errors and Omissions, Health Care, Insurance Coverage, Insurance Defense, Intellectual Property, International Law, Labor and Employment, Life Insurance, Medical Malpractice, Mergers and Acquisitions, Motor Carriers, Oil and Gas, Personal Injury, Product Liability, Professional Liability, Regulatory and Compliance, Toxic Torts, Workers' Compensation

Firm Profile: Since 1937, Jones Walker LLP has grown to become one of the largest law firms in the southeastern U.S. We serve local, regional, national, and international business interests in a wide range of markets and industries. Today, we have more than 375 attorneys in 19 offices.

Jones Walker is committed to providing proactive legal services to major multinational, public, and private corporations; *Fortune* 500® companies;

Jones Walker LLP, Jackson, MS (Continued)

money center banks and worldwide insurers; and family and emerging businesses located in the United States and abroad.

Insurance Clients

American Fidelity Assurance Company	Comprehensive Health Insurance Risk Pool Association
Fidelity National Financial	Life Insurance Company of Alabama
Magna Insurance Company	
The Medical Protective Company	The MEGA Life and Health Insurance Company
Mississippi Life and Health Insurance Guaranty Association	OneBeacon Insurance
Progressive Insurance Group	Property Casualty Insurers Association of America
Ross & Yerger Insurance Agency	
Versant Life Insurance Company	

Firm Members

George (Pete) F. Bloss — The University of Mississippi, B.P.A., 1972; The University of Mississippi School of Law, J.D., 1974 — Admitted to Bar, 1974, Mississippi; U.S. District Court, Northern and Southern Districts of Mississippi; 1977, U.S. Court of Appeals, Fifth Circuit; 1984, U.S. Supreme Court — Member Federal, American (Sections: Health Law, Torts and Insurance) and Harrison County Bar Associations; The Mississippi Bar (Health Law Section); International Association of Defense Counsel (Member by Invitation); Mississippi Defense Lawyers Association (Former Officer and Director); Mississippi Supreme Court Advisory Committee on Rules by Supreme Court Appointment (1999-present) — E-mail: pbloss@joneswalker.com

Neville H. Boschert — The University of Mississippi, B.A., 1978; The University of Mississippi School of Law, J.D. (cum laude), 1981 — Admitted to Bar, 1981, Mississippi; U.S. District Court, Northern and Southern Districts of Mississippi; U.S. Court of Appeals, Fifth, Ninth and Eleventh Circuits; 1998, U.S. Supreme Court; 2000, U.S. District Court for the District of Columbia — Member Federal and American (Co-Chairman, Litigation Section, Medical Device Subcommittee of the Products Liability Committee, 2008-present) Bar Associations; Captiol Area Bar Association; The Mississippi Bar; Defense Research Institute (Drug & Medical Device Committee); International Association of Defense Counsel — E-mail: nboschert@joneswalker.com

H. Mitchell (Micky) Cowan — University of Southern Mississippi, B.S., 1980; M.S., 1981; The University of Mississippi School of Law, J.D. (cum laude), 1984 — Admitted to Bar, 1984, Mississippi — Member American Bar Association; The Mississippi Bar; Defense Research Institute; Mississippi Defense Lawyers Association — E-mail: mcowan@joneswalker.com

Mark D. Herbert — Millsaps College, B.A. (cum laude), 1975; The University of Mississippi School of Law, J.D., 1978 — Admitted to Bar, 1979, Mississippi; U.S. District Court, Northern and Southern Districts of Mississippi; U.S. Court of Appeals, Fifth Circuit — Member American (Sections: Construction Industy, Torts and Insurance, Fidelity and Surety Law; Forum Committee) and Capitol Area Bar Associations; The Mississippi Bar; American Arbitration Association (National Panel of Commercial and Construction Arbitrators and Mediators); Mississippi Bar Foundation (Fellow; Board of Trustees, Past-Member; President, 19950-1996); International Association of Defense Counsel — E-mail: mherbert@joneswalker.com

Robert (Bobby) B. House — The University of Mississippi, B.Accy, 1984; The University of Mississippi School of Law, J.D., 1988 — Admitted to Bar, 1988, Mississippi; U.S. District Court, Northern and Southern Districts of Mississippi — Member American Bar Association (Sections: Business Law, Tort Trial and Insurance Practice; Past Chair, Insurance Regulation Committee); Capitol Area Bar Association; The Mississippi Bar (Business Law Section; Past Chairman, Group Insurance Committee); Mississippi Society of Certified Public Accountants; Federation of Regulatory Counsel; American Health Lawyers Association — E-mail: rhouse@joneswalker.com

David L. Martin — Millsaps College, B.A., 1969; University of Virginia School of Law, J.D., 1976 — Admitted to Bar, 1976, Mississippi; U.S. District Court, Southern District of Mississippi — Member American Bar Association (Business Law Section; Committees: Securities Law , Insurance Regulation, Tort Trial and Insurance Practice); Capitol Area Bar Association; The Mississippi Bar (Past Chair and Executive Committee, Business Law Section; Past Chair, Group Insurance Committee); Federation of Regulatory Counsel — E-mail: davidmartin@joneswalker.com

Keith R. Raulston — The University of Tennessee at Chattanooga, B.A. (magna cum laude), 1976; University of Cincinnati College of Law, J.D. (Order of the Coif), 1979 — Admitted to Bar, 1980, Mississippi; U.S. District Court, Southern District of Mississippi; U.S. Court of Appeals, Fifth Circuit; 1991, U.S. District Court, Northern District of Mississippi; 2002, U.S. Supreme Court — Member Federal, American (Sections: Litigation, Tort and Insurance Practice) and Capitol Area Bar Associations; The Mississippi Bar;

JACKSON   MISSISSIPPI

Jones Walker LLP, Jackson, MS (Continued)

American Inns of Court (Past Barrister, Charles Clark Chapter); Fellow, Litigation Counsel of America; Mississippi Law Institute (Past Chairman; Past Editor-in-Chief); Mississippi Claims Association; Defense Research Institute; Mississippi Defense Lawyers Association — E-mail: kraulston@joneswalker.com

Bradford (Brad) C. Ray — Mississippi College, B.A. (cum laude), 2000; Mississippi College School of Law, J.D., 2003 — Admitted to Bar, 2003, Mississippi; 2009, Tennessee; U.S. District Court, Northern and Southern Districts of Mississippi; 2003, U.S. District Court, Northern and Southern Districts of Mississippi; U.S. Court of Appeals, Fifth Circuit; U.S. Court of Appeals, Fifth Circuit; 2010, U.S. District Court, Western District of Tennessee; 2010, U.S. District Court, Western District of Tennessee — Member The Mississippi Bar — E-mail: bray@joneswalker.com

Christopher R. Shaw — The University of Mississippi, B.A. (cum laude), 1997; The University of Mississippi School of Law, J.D., 2001 — Admitted to Bar, 2001, Mississippi; U.S. District Court, Northern and Southern Districts of Mississippi; U.S. Court of Appeals, Fifth Circuit — Member American (Tort, Trial and Insurance Practice Section) and Capitol Area Bar Associations; The Mississippi Bar; Defense Research Institute — E-mail: cshaw@joneswalker.com

Adam Stone — Loyola University, B.A., 1993; The University of Mississippi School of Law, J.D., 1996 — Admitted to Bar, 1996, Mississippi; U.S. District Court, Northern and Southern Districts of Mississippi; U.S. Court of Appeals, Fifth Circuit — Member American Bar Association; The Mississippi Bar; Aircraft Owners and Pilots Association; Mississippi Surety Association — E-mail: astone@joneswalker.com

(See Listing under New Orleans, LA for a List of Firm Clients and Additional Information)

Markow Walker, P.A.

599 Highland Colony Parkway, Suite 100
Ridgeland, Mississippi 39157
   Telephone: 601-853-1911
   Fax: 601-853-8284
   www.markowwalker.com

(Oxford, MS Office*: 265 North Lamar Boulevard, Suite 1, 38655, P.O. Drawer 50, 38655-0050)
   (Tel: 662-234-9899)
   (Fax: 662-234-9762)

(Ocean Springs, MS Office*: Building M, 2113 Government Street, 39564)
   (Tel: 228-872-1923)
   (Fax: 228-872-1973)

Insurance Defense, Product Liability, Bodily Injury, Toxic Torts, Medical Malpractice, Workers' Compensation

Insurance Clients

Aetna Casualty and Surety Company
American Bankers Insurance Group
American International Group, Inc.
American States Insurance Company
Crum & Forster Insurance
GAB Robins North America, Inc.
Georgia Casualty & Surety Company
Home Insurance Company
John Deere Insurance Company
Kemper Insurance Companies
Lumbermen's Underwriting Alliance
Mississippi Casualty Insurance Program
Mutual Service Insurance Companies
National Union Fire Insurance Company
Northwestern National Insurance Company
Progressive Insurance Group
Alfa Insurance Group
Allied American Life Insurance Company
American Federated Insurance Company
CIGNA Insurance Company
Continental Insurance Company
Fireman's Fund Insurance Companies
Granite State Insurance Company
Hartford Accident and Indemnity Company
Kanawha Insurance Company
Liberty Mutual Insurance Company
Medical Assurance Company of Mississippi Inc.
Mississippi Insurance Guaranty Association
National Farmers Union Property & Casualty Company
Nationwide Group
New Hampshire Indemnity Company, Inc.
Omni Insurance Group, Inc.
Sedgwick Group

Markow Walker, P.A., Jackson, MS (Continued)

Transamerica Group/AEGON USA, Inc.
United States Fidelity and Guaranty Company
The Virginia Insurance Reciprocal
United Southern Assurance Company
U.S. Security Insurance Company, Inc.
Wausau Insurance Companies

Non-Insurance Clients

Abbott Laboratories
B.C. Rogers, Inc.
Bryan Foods, Inc.
GatesMcDonald
Ladder Management Services
MMI Companies Group
PECO Foods of Mississippi, Inc.
Associated General Contractors of Mississippi, Inc.
Executive Risk Consultants, Inc.
Graward General Companies
Mississippi Attorney General's Office

Shareholders

Christopher J. Walker — 1951 — Millsaps College, B.A., 1973; The University of Mississippi, J.D., 1976 — Admitted to Bar, 1977, Mississippi — Member Federal, American (Sections: Litigation, Tort and Insurance Practice) and Hinds County Bar Associations; The Mississippi Bar; International Association of Defense Counsel; Federation of Defense and Corporate Counsel; Defense Research Institute; Mississippi Defense Lawyers Association — Lamar Order

Richard M. Edmonson, Jr. — 1963 — The University of Mississippi, B.B.A., 1985; J.D., 1988 — Phi Delta Phi — Admitted to Bar, 1988, Mississippi; 1988, U.S. District Court, Northern and Southern Districts of Mississippi; 1988, U.S. Court of Appeals, Fifth Circuit — Member American (Litigation, Tort and Insurance Law Sections) and Hinds County Bar Associations; The Mississippi Bar; Mississippi Claims Association; Jackson Young Lawyers Association; Mississippi Defense Lawyers Association

Peter J. Markow, Jr. — 1952 — The University of Mississippi, B.B.A., 1975; J.D., 1977 — Admitted to Bar, 1977, Mississippi; 1977, U.S. District Court, Northern District of Mississippi — Member The Mississippi Bar; Hinds County Bar Association

Hubert Wesley Williams, III — 1967 — Rhodes College, B.A., 1989; Mississippi College School of Law, J.D., 1992 — Admitted to Bar, 1992, Mississippi; 1993, Louisiana; Arkansas; Tennessee; District of Columbia; 1992, U.S. District Court, Northern and Southern Districts of Mississippi; 1992, U.S. Court of Appeals, Fifth Circuit; 1993, U.S. District Court, Western District of Tennessee — Member American Bar Association (Tort and Insurance Practice Section); Louisiana State, Arkansas, Tennessee and Hinds County Bar Associations; The Mississippi Bar; The District of Columbia Bar; Jackson Young Lawyers Association

L. Pepper Cossar — 1963 — The University of Mississippi, B.A., 1985; J.D., 1989 — Admitted to Bar, 1989, Alabama; 1991, Mississippi; 1991, U.S. District Court, Northern and Southern Districts of Mississippi; 1991, U.S. Court of Appeals, Fifth Circuit — Member Alabama State and Hinds County Bar Associations; The Mississippi Bar; Jackson Young Lawyers Association

T. G. Bolen, Jr. — 1963 — Tulane University, B.S.M., 1986; The University of Mississippi, J.D., 1989 — Admitted to Bar, 1990, Mississippi; Illinois; 1990, U.S. District Court, Northern and Southern Districts of Mississippi; 1990, U.S. Court of Appeals, Fifth Circuit — Member American, Illinois and Hinds County Bar Associations; The Mississippi Bar

Michael D. Young — 1970 — Mississippi College, B.A., 1993; J.D., 1997 — Admitted to Bar, 1997, Mississippi; 1997, U.S. District Court, Northern and Southern Districts of Mississippi — Member American and Hinds County Bar Associations; The Mississippi Bar

Bryan Bridges — 1977 — Mississippi State University, B.S.B.A., 2000; The University of Mississippi, J.D., 2003 — Admitted to Bar, 2003, Mississippi; 2003, U.S. District Court, Northern and Southern Districts of Mississippi

Amy L. Topik — 1973 — Mississippi University for Women, B.A., 1995; Mississippi College, J.D., 1998 — Admitted to Bar, 1998, Mississippi

Associates

David L. Carney — 1979 — The University of Mississippi, B.A. (cum laude), 2001; J.D., 2004 — Admitted to Bar, 2005, Mississippi; U.S. District Court, Northern and Southern Districts of Mississippi; U.S. Court of Appeals, Fifth Circuit; Mississippi Band of Choctaw Indians Tribal Bar — Member American Bar Association; The Mississippi Bar

Courtney Titus — 1985 — The University of Mississippi, B.A. (magna cum laude), 2006; J.D. (cum laude), 2009 — Admitted to Bar, 2009, Mississippi

Nick Saucier — 1977 — Mississippi State University, B.B.A. (cum laude), 1999; The University of Mississippi, J.D., 2006 — Admitted to Bar, 2006,

Markow Walker, P.A., Jackson, MS (Continued)

Mississippi; U.S. District Court, Northern and Southern Districts of Mississippi; U.S. Court of Appeals, Fifth Circuit — Member American and Capital Area Bar Associations — Captain, MS National Guard

Jared Hawkins — 1985 — The University of Mississippi, B.A., 2008; Mississippi College School of Law, J.D., 2010 — Admitted to Bar, 2011, Mississippi; U.S. District Court, Northern and Southern Districts of Mississippi — Member Madison County Bar Association

Brittney Pinkham Thompson — 1984 — The University of Mississippi, B.S. (magna cum laude), 2008; Mississippi College School of Law, J.D. (cum laude), 2011 — Admitted to Bar, 2011, Mississippi; U.S. District Court, Northern and Southern Districts of Mississippi

J. Andrew Faggert — 1988 — The University of Mississippi, B.A., 2010; Mississippi College School of Law, J.D., 2013 — Admitted to Bar, 2013, Mississippi; U.S. District Court, Northern and Southern Districts of Mississippi — Member Federal, American and Capital Area Bar Associations

Of Counsel

Michael Garner Berry — 1979 — The University of Mississippi, B.A./B.A. (cum laude), 1999; The University of Mississippi School of Law, J.D., 2002 — Admitted to Bar, 2003, Mississippi; U.S. District Court, Northern and Southern Districts of Mississippi — Member American, Madison County and Fifth Federal Circuit Bar Associations

Massey, Higginbotham, Vise & Phillips, P.A.

3003 Lakeland Cove, Suite E
Jackson, Mississippi 39232
Telephone: 601-420-2200
Fax: 601-420-2202
E-Mail: mmassey@mhvplaw.com
www.mhvplaw.com

Established: 1999

Insurance Defense, Insurance Coverage, Bad Faith, Medical Malpractice, Professional Liability, Premises Liability, Commercial Litigation, Product Liability, Automobile, Trial Practice, Nursing Home Liability, Environmental Law, State and Federal

Insurance Clients

Cannon Cochran Management Services, Inc.
GEICO Insurance Companies
Mississippi Builders & Contractors Insurance Company
Ross & Yerger Insurance, Inc.
United of Omaha Life Insurance Company
Central United Life Insurance Company
Medical Assurance Company of Mississippi Inc.
Progressive Commercial Auto Group
Zurich North America

Non-Insurance Clients

BancorpSouth Bank
Higginbotham Automobiles, LLC
National Textile and Apparel, Inc.
Temple-Inland Forest Products Corporation
Car Care Clinic, Inc.
Mississippi Tort Claims Board
New South Equipment Mats, LLC

Partners

G. Michael Massey — 1964 — Mississippi State University, B.P.A., 1986; The University of Mississippi, J.D. (cum laude), 1992 — Casenote Editor, Mississippi Law Journal — Admitted to Bar, 1992, Mississippi; U.S. District Court, Northern and Southern Districts of Mississippi; U.S. Court of Appeals, Fifth Circuit — Member American and Capital Area Bar Associations; The Mississippi Bar (President, Business Law Section, 2006-2007); American Institute of Certified Public Accountants; Mississippi Society of Certified Public Accountants — E-mail: mmassey@mhvplaw.com

Robert T. Higginbotham, Jr. — 1966 — The University of Mississippi, B.S. (cum laude), 1989; J.D., 1992 — Research Editor, Mississippi Law Journal — Admitted to Bar, 1992, Mississippi; 1992, U.S. District Court, Northern and Southern Districts of Mississippi; 1992, U.S. Court of Appeals, Fifth Circuit — Member American and Capital Area Bar Associations; The Mississippi Bar (Commissioner, 2001-2004); Mississippi Young Lawyers

Massey, Higginbotham, Vise & Phillips, P.A., Jackson, MS (Continued)

Association (President, 2002; Fellow) — Mid-South Super Lawyer; Graduate, National Institute for Trial Advocacy — E-mail: bhigginbotham@mhvplaw.com

J. Wilbourn Vise — 1967 — Southern Methodist University, B.S., 1990; Texas A&M University, M.S., 1992; Tulane University, J.D. (cum laude), 1995 — Tulane Environmental Law Journal — Admitted to Bar, 1995, Mississippi; 1995, U.S. District Court, Northern and Southern Districts of Mississippi; 1995, U.S. Court of Appeals, Fifth Circuit — Member American and Capital Area Bar Associations; The Mississippi Bar — Certificate in Environmental Law; Environmental Law Clinic — E-mail: willvise@mhvplaw.com

Of Counsel

C. Alton Phillips — 1943 — The University of Mississippi, B.B.A., 1965; Washington and Lee University, J.D., 1968 — Law Clerk to Chief Judge, U.S. District Court, Western District of Virginia — Washington and Lee Law Review — Admitted to Bar, 1968, Mississippi; 1968, U.S. District Court, Northern and Southern Districts of Mississippi; 1968, U.S. Court of Appeals, Fifth Circuit — Capt., Judge Advocate General's Corps, U.S. Air Force — E-mail: alton@mhvplaw.com

Obert Law Group, P.A.

599 B Steed Road, Suite 100
Ridgeland, Mississippi 39157
Telephone: 601-856-9690
Fax: 601-856-9686
E-Mail: obertlaw@bellsouth.net

Established: 1997

Insurance Defense, Automobile, Product Liability, General Liability, Property and Casualty, Agent and Brokers Errors and Omissions, Coverage Issues, Premises Liability, Workers' Compensation, Subrogation

Insurance Clients

ACE USA
Auto-Owners Insurance Company
Dixie Specialty Insurance, Inc.
Hanover Insurance Company
Infinity Insurance Group
Lloyd's
MS Casualty Insurance Company
Shelby Insurance Company
ACUITY
Chubb Group
General Star Management Company
John Deere Insurance Group
Mississippi Farm Bureau Casualty Insurance Company
Southern United Fire Insurance Company

Non-Insurance Clients

AutoZone, Inc.
The Gap, Inc.
Redland Transportation
Barnes & Noble, Inc.
Playcore, Inc.
Toys "R" Us, Inc.

Keith D. Obert — 1962 — The University of Alabama, B.S., 1984; The University of Mississippi, J.D., 1988 — Moot Court Board; Order of Barristers — Admitted to Bar, 1988, Mississippi; Tennessee; 1989, Alabama; 1988, U.S. District Court, Northern and Southern Districts of Mississippi; 1988, U.S. District Court, Western District of Tennessee; 1988, U.S. Court of Appeals, Fifth Circuit; 1990, U.S. District Court, Northern and Southern Districts of Alabama; 2000, U.S. District Court, Middle District of Alabama — Member American Bar Association (Sections: Litigation, Torts and Insurance Practice; Automobile Law Committee); Tennessee, Hinds County (Director, 1995-1997) and Fifth Federal Circuit Bar Associations; The Mississippi Bar (Director, Young Lawyers Division, 1996-1997; Chair, Membership Services, 1997-1998; Chair, Public Relations Committee, 1999-2000; Business Law Section, 1999-2000; Fellow, Young Lawyers Division, 2002-; Chair, Public Information Committee, 2002-2003); Alabama State Bar; Jackson Young Lawyers Association (Treasurer, 1994-1995; Vice President, 1995-1996; President, 1996-1997); Mississippi Claims Association; Mississippi Defense Lawyers Association; Defense Research and Trial Lawyers Association — E-mail: obert@bellsouth.net

JACKSON   MISSISSIPPI

Obert Law Group, P.A., Jackson, MS (Continued)
Of Counsel

William F. Brown — 1964 — Millsaps College, B.A., 1986; The University of Mississippi, J.D., 1990 — Admitted to Bar, 1991, Mississippi; 1991, U.S. District Court, Northern and Southern Districts of Mississippi — Member Hinds County Bar Association; The Mississippi Bar

Page, Mannino, Peresich & McDermott, P.L.L.C.

460 Briarwood Drive, Suite 415
Jackson, Mississippi 39206
    Telephone: 601-896-0114
    Fax: 601-896-0145
    E-Mail: Stephen.Peresich@pmp.org
    www.pmp.org

Insurance Defense, Banking, Bankruptcy, Business Law, Commercial Litigation, Construction Law, Environmental Litigation, Government Affairs, Governmental Entity Defense, Health Care, Hospital Law, Labor and Employment, Medical Malpractice, Municipal Law, Personal Injury, Product Liability, Professional Malpractice, Real Estate, Toxic Torts

(See listing under Biloxi, MS for additional information)

Phelps Dunbar LLP

4270 I-55 North
Jackson, Mississippi 39211-6391
    Telephone: 601-352-2300
    Fax: 601-360-9777
    E-Mail: info@phelps.com
    www.phelpsdunbar.com

(New Orleans, LA Office*: Canal Place, 365 Canal Street, Suite 2000, 70130-6534)
    (Tel: 504-566-1311)
    (Fax: 504-568-9130)
(Baton Rouge, LA Office*: II City Plaza, 400 Convention Street, Suite 1100, 70802-5618, P.O. Box 4412, 70821-4412)
    (Tel: 225-346-0285)
    (Fax: 225-381-9197)
(Tupelo, MS Office*: One Mississippi Plaza, 201 South Spring Street, Seventh Floor, 38804, P.O. Box 1220, 38802-1220)
    (Tel: 662-842-7907)
    (Fax: 662-842-3873)
(Gulfport, MS Office*: NorthCourt One, 2304 19th Street, Suite 300, 39501)
    (Tel: 228-679-1130)
    (Fax: 228-679-1131)
(Houston, TX Office*: One Allen Center, 500 Dallas Street, Suite 1300, 77002)
    (Tel: 713-626-1386)
    (Fax: 713-626-1388)
(Tampa, FL Office*: 100 South Ashley Drive, Suite 1900, 33602-5311)
    (Tel: 813-472-7550)
    (Fax: 813-472-7570)
(Mobile, AL Office*: 2 North Royal Street, 36602, P.O. Box 2727, 36652-2727)
    (Tel: 251-432-4481)
    (Fax: 251-433-1820)
(London, United Kingdom Office*: Lloyd's, Suite 725, Level 7, 1 Lime Street, EC3M 7DQ)
    (Tel: 011-44-207-929-4765)
    (Fax: 011-44-207-929-0046)
(Raleigh, NC Office*: 4140 Parklake Avenue, Suite 100, 27612-3723)
    (Tel: 919-789-5300)
    (Fax: 919-789-5301)

Phelps Dunbar LLP, Jackson, MS (Continued)
(Southlake, TX Office*(See Dallas listing): 115 Grand Avenue, Suite 222, 76092)
    (Tel: 817-488-3134)
    (Fax: 817-488-3214)

Insurance Law

Insurance Clients

Acceptance Casualty Insurance Company
Aegis Janson Green Insurance Services Inc.
AIG
Alabama Municipal Insurance Corporation
AmTrust Underwriters, Inc.
Arch Insurance Company (Europe) Ltd.
Aspen Insurance UK Limited
Associated Aviation Underwriters
Bankers Insurance Group
Berkley Select, LLC
Bluebonnet Life Insurance Company
Britannia Steam Ship Insurance Association Ltd.
CNA
Commercial Union Insurance Company
Companion Property and Casualty Group
ELCO Administrative Services
Endurance Services, Ltd.
Erie Insurance Company
Evanston Insurance Company
Fidelity National Financial
First Premium Insurance Group, Inc.
GE Insurance Solutions
General & Cologne Life Reinsurance of America
General Star Indemnity Company
Glencoe Group
Global Special Risks, Inc.
Great American Insurance Companies
Gulf Insurance Group
The Hartford Insurance Group
Homesite Group, Inc.
ICAT Boulder Claims
Infinity Insurance Company
Lexington Insurance Company
Liberty Mutual Group
Louisiana Farm Bureau Mutual Insurance Company
Louisiana Workers' Compensation Corporation
Markel
MetLife Auto & Home
NAS Insurance Group
Nautilus Insurance Company
Old American Insurance Company
Pharmacists Mutual Insurance Company
RenaissanceRe
RLI Insurance Company
Royal & SunAlliance
SCOR Global P&C
Sedgwick Claims Management Services, Inc.
SR International Business Insurance Company, Ltd.
Steamship Mutual Underwriting Association Limited
Torus
Underwriters at Lloyd's, London
Unitrin Business Insurance
Vesta Eiendom AS
Western Heritage Insurance Company
Westport Insurance Corporation
XL Insurance Group

ACE Group of Insurance and Reinsurance Companies
Aetna Insurance Company
AFLAC - American Family Life Assurance Company of Columbus
Allstate Insurance Company
American Family Life Assurance Company of Columbus
Argonaut Insurance Company
Aspen Insurance
Aspen Re
AXIS Insurance
Beazley
Bituminous Insurance Company
Blue Cross & Blue Shield of Mississippi
Chartis Insurance
Chubb Group of Insurance Companies
Commonwealth Insurance Company
Cotton States Insurance
Criterion Claim Solutions
Employers Reinsurance Corporation
Esurance Insurance Company
Farmers Insurance Group
Fireman's Fund Insurance Company
Foremost Insurance Company
General American Life Insurance Company
General Reinsurance Corporation
General Star Management Company
Golden Rule Insurance Company
Great Southern Life Insurance Company
Hanover Insurance Group
Hermitage Insurance Company
Houston Casualty Company
Indian Harbor Insurance Company
Ironshore Insurance, Ltd.
Liberty International Underwriters
Life Insurance Company of Alabama
Louisiana Health Insurance Association
Lyndon Property Insurance Company
Munich-American Risk Partners
Nationwide Insurance
The Navigators Group, Inc.
OneBeacon Insurance Group
Prime Syndicate
QBE
Republic Western Insurance Company
St. Paul Travelers
Scottsdale Insurance Company
Sentry Insurance
Southern Farm Bureau Casualty Insurance Company
State National Insurance Company, Inc.
Terra Nova Insurance Company Limited
United States Fidelity and Guaranty Company
Victoria Insurance Group
West of England Ship Owners Mutual Insurance Association (Luxembourg)
Zurich

Phelps Dunbar LLP, Jackson, MS (Continued)

Members of the Firm

Reuben V. Anderson — Tougaloo College, B.A., 1964; The University of Mississippi School of Law, J.D., 1967 — Admitted to Bar, 1967, Mississippi; 1968, U.S. Court of Appeals, Fifth Circuit; 1971, U.S. Supreme Court — Member National, Hinds County, Fifth Federal Circuit and Magnolia Bar Associations; The Mississippi Bar; U.S. Supreme Court Bar Association

Fred L. Banks, Jr. — Howard University, B.A., 1965; Howard University School of Law, J.D. (cum laude), 1968 — Admitted to Bar, 1968, Mississippi; 1969, District of Columbia — Member National, American and Magnolia Bar Associations; The Mississippi Bar; The District of Columbia Bar; American Law Institute

Ross F. Bass, Jr. — Vanderbilt University, B.A., 1970; The University of Mississippi School of Law, J.D. (with honors), 1973 — Admitted to Bar, 1973, Mississippi; 1973, Georgia; 1977, U.S. Supreme Court — Member American Bar Association; The Mississippi Bar; State Bar of Georgia

Gary E. Friedman — Georgia Institute of Technology, B.S.I.E., 1971; The University of Mississippi School of Law, J.D. (with distinction), 1982 — Admitted to Bar, 1982, Mississippi; U.S. District Court, Northern and Southern Districts of Mississippi; U.S. Court of Appeals, Fifth Circuit; U.S. Supreme Court — Member Federal and Capital Area Bar Associations; The Mississippi Bar; Defense Research Institute; Federation of Defense and Corporate Counsel

LaToya C. Merritt — Grambling State University, B.A. (magna cum laude), 1997; North Carolina Central University School of Law, J.D. (cum laude), 2000 — Admitted to Bar, 2000, Mississippi; U.S. District Court, Northern and Southern Districts of Mississippi; U.S. Court of Appeals, Fifth Circuit — Member American Bar Association; The Mississippi Bar; Mississippi Women's Law Association

Seale Pylate — Hendrix College, B.A. (with honors), 1996; Boston College Law School, J.D., 1999 — Admitted to Bar, 1999, Mississippi; 2000, Arkansas — Member American and Arkansas Bar Associations; The Mississippi Bar; National Association of Stock Plan Professionals

James W. Shelson — Michigan State University, B.A., 1984; The Pennsylvania State University, J.D., 1993 — Admitted to Bar, 1993, Mississippi; 1996, Alabama; U.S. District Court, Northern and Southern Districts of Mississippi; U.S. Court of Appeals, Fifth Circuit — Member American, Capital Area and Fifth Federal Circuit Bar Associations; The Mississippi Bar; Alabama State Bar; International Association of Defense Counsel

W. Thomas Siler, Jr. — Millsaps College, B.B.A., 1979; The University of Mississippi School of Law, J.D. (with distinction), 1983 — Admitted to Bar, 1983, Mississippi — Member American and Capital Area Bar Associations; The Mississippi Bar; Mississippi Defense Lawyers Association; Defense Research Institute; International Association of Defense Counsel

Frank W. Trapp — The University of Mississippi, B.A., 1969; The University of Mississippi School of Law, J.D., 1972 — Admitted to Bar, 1972, Mississippi; 1979, Georgia; 1980, District of Columbia; 1982, Florida; U.S. District Court, Northern and Southern Districts of Mississippi; U.S. District Court, Middle and Southern Districts of Florida; U.S. Court of Appeals, Fifth and Eleventh Circuits — Member American Bar Association; The District of Columbia Bar; The Florida Bar; The Mississippi Bar; State Bar of Georgia; Mississippi Trial Lawyers Association; American Trial Lawyers Association

Counsel

Mark Fijman — Emerson College, B.S., 1983; Mississippi College School of Law, J.D., 1998 — Admitted to Bar, 1998, Mississippi; U.S. District Court, Northern and Southern Districts of Mississippi; U.S. Court of Appeals, Fifth Circuit — Member Federal Bar Association

(See listing under New Orleans, LA for additional information)

Scott, Sullivan, Streetman & Fox, P.C.

725 Avignon Drive
Ridgeland, Mississippi 39157-5109
Telephone: 601-607-4800
Fax: 601-607-4801

Insurance Defense, Litigation, Product Liability, Medical Malpractice, Professional Malpractice, Workers' Compensation, Trial Practice, State and Federal Courts

Scott, Sullivan, Streetman & Fox, P.C., Jackson, MS (Continued)

Insurance Clients

AAOMS National Insurance Company
Canal Insurance Company
Crum & Forster Insurance
Fireman's Fund Insurance Company
Gallagher Bassett Services, Inc.
Guaranty National Insurance Company
Hamlin & Burton Liability Management
Legion Insurance Company
Medmarc Mutual Insurance Company
Ohio Casualty Group
Philadelphia Insurance Companies
Progressive Insurance Company
Royal & SunAlliance Group
Safety National Casualty Corporation
Southern Heritage Insurance Company
USAA Casualty Insurance Company
Affirmative Insurance Company
Alfa Insurance Corporation
Coastal Insurance Enterprises, Inc.
Evans/Giordano Insurance Companies
GAINSCO, Inc.
Great American Insurance Companies
GuideOne Insurance
The Hartford
Insura Property and Casualty Insurance Company, Inc.
National Home Insurance Company
Patterson Insurance Company
Professional Claims Managers, Inc.
The Reciprocal Alliance (Risk Retention Group)
Shelby Insurance Company
Southern Guaranty Insurance Company
Southern Risk Services, Inc.

Non-Insurance Clients

American Medical Electronics, Inc.
Applied Silicone Company
Becton Dickinson and Company
City of Ridgeland, Mississippi
Dollar General Corporation
J.B. Hunt Transport Services, Inc.
MCH Transportation Company
Mississippi Forest Related Workers' Compensation Group
Mississippi Tort Claims Board
NuSil Silicone Technology
Pfizer, Inc.
Sunrise Medical, Inc.
University of Mississippi Medical Center
American Medical Systems, Inc.
Badger Meter, Inc.
Boston Scientific Corporation
Consolidated Freightway Corporation
Mallinckrodt, Inc.
Mississippi Administrative Services, Inc.
Mississippi Municipal Service Company
Parke-Davis
Pro-Tech Respirators
Tiffin Motor Homes, Inc.
Walgreen Co.
Warner-Lambert Company

Firm Members

William A. Scott, Jr. — 1943 — The University of Alabama, B.S., 1965; Cumberland School of Law of Samford University, J.D., 1968 — Admitted to Bar, 1968, Alabama; 1987, Tennessee; 1970, U.S. District Court, Middle, Northern and Southern Districts of Alabama; U.S. Court of Appeals, Eleventh Circuit — Member American, Tennessee, Jefferson County, Shelby County and Birmingham Bar Associations; Alabama State Bar; Alabama Defense Lawyers Association; Association of Trial Lawyers of America; Defense Research Institute; International Association of Defense Counsel — Resident Birmingham, AL Office

Carroll H. Sullivan — 1950 — Auburn University, B.S., 1972; Cumberland School of Law of Samford University, J.D. (cum laude), 1975 — Admitted to Bar, 1975, Alabama — Member American and Mobile Bar Associations; Alabama State Bar; International Association of Defense Counsel; Alabama Defense Lawyers Association; Defense Research Institute — Resident Mobile, AL Office

James P. Streetman, III — 1953 — Auburn University, B.S., 1976; Mississippi College School of Law, J.D., 1979 — Admitted to Bar, 1979, Mississippi; 2001, Mississippi Band of Choctaw Indians Tribal Bar; 1979, U.S. Court of Appeals, Fifth Circuit; 1980, U.S. District Court, Northern and Southern Districts of Mississippi; 1989, U.S. Supreme Court — Member American and Hinds County Bar Association; The Mississippi Bar; Mississippi Claims Association; Mississippi Defense Lawyers Association; Defense Research Institute; Federation of Defense and Corporate Counsel — E-mail: jstreetman@sssf-ms.com

Anthony N. Fox — 1958 — Maryville College, B.A., 1980; Cumberland School of Law of Samford University, J.D. (cum laude), 1983 — Admitted to Bar, 1983, Alabama; 1983, U.S. District Court, Middle and Northern Districts of Alabama; U.S. Court of Appeals, Eleventh Circuit — Member Alabama State Bar (Workers' Compensation Section); Alabama Claims Association; Alabama Defense Lawyers Association; Alabama Workers' Compensation Claims Association — Resident Birmingham, AL Office

Wade G. Manor — 1969 — Auburn University, B.S., 1991; Mississippi College School of Law, J.D., 1995 — Admitted to Bar, 1996, Mississippi; 2001,

Scott, Sullivan, Streetman & Fox, P.C., Jackson, MS (Continued)

Mississippi Band of Choctaw Indians Tribal Bar; 1995, U.S. District Court, Northern and Southern Districts of Mississippi; 1995, U.S. Court of Appeals, Fifth Circuit — Member American Bar Association; The Mississippi Bar; Defense Research Institute — E-mail: wmanor@sssf-ms.com

- **C. Paige Herring** — 1970 — University of Southern Mississippi, B.A., 1992; Mississippi State University, M.A., 1994; Cumberland School of Law of Samford University, J.D., 1997 — Admitted to Bar, 1997, Mississippi; 1999, Georgia; 2001, Mississippi Band of Choctaw Indians Tribal Bar; 1997, U.S. District Court, Southern District of Mississippi; 1997, U.S. Court of Appeals, Fifth Circuit — Member American Bar Association; The Mississippi Bar; State Bar of Georgia — E-mail: pherring@sssf-ms.com
- **J. Scott Rogers** — 1969 — University of Southern Mississippi; William Carey College, B.S., 1997; Mississippi College School of Law, J.D., 2000 — Admitted to Bar, 2000, Mississippi; 2001, Mississippi Band of Choctaw Indians Tribal Bar; 2000, U.S. District Court, Northern and Southern Districts of Mississippi; 2000, U.S. Court of Appeals, Fifth Circuit — Member American Bar Association; The Mississippi Bar — E-mail: srogers@sssf-ms.com
- **Jeremy D. Hawk** — University of South Alabama, B.A., 2000; Mississippi College School of Law, J.D., 2003 — Admitted to Bar, 2003, Mississippi; 2003, U.S. District Court, Northern and Southern Districts of Mississippi; 2003, U.S. Court of Appeals, Fifth Circuit — Member American Bar Association; The Mississippi Bar — E-mail: jhawk@sssf-ms.com
- **Leah N. Ledford** — Mississippi State University, B.A., 2000; The University of Mississippi School of Law, J.D., 2004 — Admitted to Bar, 2004, Mississippi; 2004, U.S. District Court, Northern and Southern Districts of Mississippi; 2004, U.S. Court of Appeals, Fifth Circuit — Member American Bar Association; The Mississippi Bar — E-mail: lledford@sssf-ms.com
- **James L. "Jake" Banks, IV** — College of Charleston, B.A. (magna cum laude), 2002; The University of Mississippi School of Law, J.D. (magna cum laude), 2006 — Admitted to Bar, 2006, Mississippi; U.S. District Court, Southern District of Mississippi; U.S. Court of Appeals, Fifth Circuit — Member American Bar Association; The Mississippi Bar — E-mail: jbanks@sssf-ms.com
- **Andy J. Clark** — Delta State University, B.S., 1997; Mississippi College, J.D., 2008 — Admitted to Bar, 2008, Mississippi; Tennessee; U.S. District Court, Northern and Southern Districts of Mississippi; U.S. Court of Appeals, Fifth Circuit; Mississippi Band of Choctaw Indians Tribal Bar — Member American and Tennessee Bar Associations; The Mississippi Bar; Mississippi Defense Lawyers Association; Jackson Young Lawyers Association — E-mail: aclark@sssf-ms.com

---

The following firms also service this area.

Hailey, McNamara, Hall, Larmann & Papale, L.L.P.
302 Courthouse Road, Suite A
Gulfport, Mississippi 39507
   Telephone: 228-896-1144
   Fax: 228-896-1177

Admiralty and Maritime Law, Commercial Litigation, Construction Litigation, Employment Practices Liability, Insurance Litigation, Product Liability, Professional Malpractice, Toxic Torts, Casualty, Insurance Coverage, Intellectual Property, Premises Liability, Transportation, Appellate, Mass Tort, Property, Workers' Compensation, Automobile Liability, Environmental

SEE COMPLETE LISTING UNDER GULFPORT, MISSISSIPPI (181 MILES)

McNabb, Bragorgos & Burgess, PLLC
81 Monroe Avenue, Sixth Floor
Memphis, Tennessee 38103-5402
   Telephone: 901-624-0640
   Toll Free: 888-251-8000
   Fax: 901-624-0650

Insurance Defense, Trucking Litigation, Fire, Casualty, Malpractice, Fraud, Litigation, Marine, Product Liability, Workers' Compensation, Automobile, Mass Tort, Personal Injury, Commercial Law, Premises Liability, Subrogation, Construction Law, Nursing Home Defense

SEE COMPLETE LISTING UNDER MEMPHIS, TENNESSEE (217 MILES)

Ungarino & Eckert, L.L.C.
3850 North Causeway Boulevard, Suite 1280
Metairie, Louisiana 70002
   Telephone: 504-836-7555
   Fax: 504-836-7566

Litigation, Appellate Practice, State and Federal Courts, Class Actions, Insurance Coverage, Premises Liability, Professional Liability, Directors and Officers Liability, Insurance Defense, Construction Law, Toxic Torts, Personal Injury, Arson, Insurance Fraud, Admiralty and Maritime Law, Extra-Contractual Litigation, Bad Faith, Product Liability, Alternative Dispute Resolution, Civil Rights, Workers' Compensation, Environmental Law, Employment Law, Automobile, Truck Liability, Errors and Omissions, Common Carrier, Medical Malpractice, Construction Defect, Constitutional Law, Department of Insurance Complaints, ERISA Claims, Government Relations, Complex Casualty, Consumer Defense, Creditor Rights, Debt Collections, Discrimination Claims, Electric Utility Liability, Engineering Malpractice, Family Law (Divorce, Custody, Support, Adoption), Fraud, General Liability, Governmental Entity Liability, Insurance Subrogation, Landlord Liability, Medical Device Liability, Property Ownership, State and Municipality Litigation, Successions, Warranty/Redhibition Actions

SEE COMPLETE LISTING UNDER METAIRIE, LOUISIANA (181 MILES)

Webb Sanders & Williams PLLC
363 North Broadway
Tupelo, Mississippi 38804
   Telephone: 662-844-2137
   Fax: 662-842-3863

Mailing Address: P.O. Box 496, Tupelo, MS 38802-0496

Insurance Defense, Insurance Coverage, Automobile, Property, Fire, Arson, Fraud, First Party Matters, Bad Faith, Special Investigations, Product Liability, Automobile Liability, Uninsured and Underinsured Motorist, Professional Malpractice, Medical Malpractice, Workers' Compensation, General Liability, Premises Liability, Defense Litigation, Corporate Law, Commercial Law, Commercial Litigation, Real Estate, Transportation, Environmental Law, Toxic Torts, Bankruptcy, Creditor Rights, Labor and Employment, ERISA, Construction Litigation, Fidelity and Surety, Insurance Fraud, General Civil Practice, Trial Practice, Appellate Practice, Employment Discrimination, Coverage Analysis, Coverage Issues

SEE COMPLETE LISTING UNDER TUPELO, MISSISSIPPI (150 MILES)

KOSCIUSKO † 7,402 Attala Co.

Refer To

Webb Sanders & Williams PLLC
363 North Broadway
Tupelo, Mississippi 38804
   Telephone: 662-844-2137
   Fax: 662-842-3863

Mailing Address: P.O. Box 496, Tupelo, MS 38802-0496

Insurance Defense, Insurance Coverage, Automobile, Property, Fire, Arson, Fraud, First Party Matters, Bad Faith, Special Investigations, Product Liability, Automobile Liability, Uninsured and Underinsured Motorist, Professional Malpractice, Medical Malpractice, Workers' Compensation, General Liability, Premises Liability, Defense Litigation, Corporate Law, Commercial Law, Commercial Litigation, Real Estate, Transportation, Environmental Law, Toxic Torts, Bankruptcy, Creditor Rights, Labor and Employment, ERISA, Construction Litigation, Fidelity and Surety, Insurance Fraud, General Civil Practice, Trial Practice, Appellate Practice, Employment Discrimination, Coverage Analysis, Coverage Issues

SEE COMPLETE LISTING UNDER TUPELO, MISSISSIPPI (104 MILES)

MISSISSIPPI — LAUREL

LAUREL † 18,540 Jones Co.
Refer To
Hicks Law Firm, PLLC
211 South 29th Avenue, Suite 201
Hattiesburg, Mississippi 39401
   Telephone: 601-544-6770
   Fax: 601-544-6775

Mailing Address: P.O. Box 18350, Hattiesburg, MS 39404-8350

Insurance Defense, General Liability, Automobile, Bodily Injury, Casualty, Product Liability, Premises Liability, Commercial Litigation, Bad Faith, Trucking Law, Construction Litigation, Commercial Vehicle, Professional Liability, Commercial and Personal Lines

SEE COMPLETE LISTING UNDER HATTIESBURG, MISSISSIPPI (33 MILES)

LEAKESVILLE † 898 Greene Co.
Refer To
Bryan, Nelson, Schroeder, Castigliola & Banahan, PLLC
1103 Jackson Avenue
Pascagoula, Mississippi 39567
   Telephone: 228-762-6631
   Fax: 228-769-6392

Mailing Address: Post Office Drawer 1529, Pascagoula, MS 39568-1529

Insurance Defense, General Liability, Product Liability, Professional Liability, Accident and Health, Casualty, Fire, Marine, Workers' Compensation, Medical Malpractice

SEE COMPLETE LISTING UNDER PASCAGOULA, MISSISSIPPI (55 MILES)

LUCEDALE † 2,923 George Co.
Refer To
Bryan, Nelson, Schroeder, Castigliola & Banahan, PLLC
1103 Jackson Avenue
Pascagoula, Mississippi 39567
   Telephone: 228-762-6631
   Fax: 228-769-6392

Mailing Address: Post Office Drawer 1529, Pascagoula, MS 39568-1529

Insurance Defense, General Liability, Product Liability, Professional Liability, Accident and Health, Casualty, Fire, Marine, Workers' Compensation, Medical Malpractice

SEE COMPLETE LISTING UNDER PASCAGOULA, MISSISSIPPI (40 MILES)

MACON † 2,768 Noxubee Co.
Refer To
Hicks & Smith, PLLC
Regions Bank, 2nd Floor
710 Main Street
Columbus, Mississippi 39701
   Telephone: 662-243-7300
   Fax: 662-327-1485

Mailing Address: P.O. Box 1111, Columbus, MS 39703-1111

Bad Faith, Automobile, Premises Liability, Workers' Compensation, Casualty, Product Liability, Medical Malpractice, Subrogation, Class Actions, Commercial Litigation, Employment Law, Extra-Contractual Litigation, Professional Negligence, Truck Liability, Governmental Liability, Public Entities, Civil Rights, Insurance Sales Practice Litigation, Constitutional, General Insurance Defense, Admiralty, Construction, Business Litigation, Environmental Litigation

SEE COMPLETE LISTING UNDER COLUMBUS, MISSISSIPPI (31 MILES)

Refer To
Webb Sanders & Williams PLLC
363 North Broadway
Tupelo, Mississippi 38804
   Telephone: 662-844-2137
   Fax: 662-842-3863

Mailing Address: P.O. Box 496, Tupelo, MS 38802-0496

Insurance Defense, Insurance Coverage, Automobile, Property, Fire, Arson, Fraud, First Party Matters, Bad Faith, Special Investigations, Product Liability, Automobile Liability, Uninsured and Underinsured Motorist, Professional Malpractice, Medical Malpractice, Workers' Compensation, General Liability, Premises Liability, Defense Litigation, Corporate Law, Commercial Law, Commercial Litigation, Real Estate, Transportation, Environmental Law, Toxic Torts, Bankruptcy, Creditor Rights, Labor and Employment, ERISA, Construction Litigation, Fidelity and Surety, Insurance Fraud, General Civil Practice, Trial Practice, Appellate Practice, Employment Discrimination, Coverage Analysis, Coverage Issues

SEE COMPLETE LISTING UNDER TUPELO, MISSISSIPPI (85 MILES)

MADISON 24,149 Madison Co.
Refer To
Obert Law Group, P.A.
599 B Steed Road, Suite 100
Ridgeland, Mississippi 39157
   Telephone: 601-856-9690
   Fax: 601-856-9686

Mailing Address: P.O. Box 2081, Madison, MS 39130-2081

Insurance Defense, Automobile, Product Liability, General Liability, Property and Casualty, Agent and Brokers Errors and Omissions, Coverage Issues, Premises Liability, Workers' Compensation, Subrogation

SEE COMPLETE LISTING UNDER JACKSON, MISSISSIPPI (13 MILES)

MAGEE 4,408 Simpson Co.
Refer To
Markow Walker, P.A.
599 Highland Colony Parkway, Suite 100
Ridgeland, Mississippi 39157
   Telephone: 601-853-1911
   Fax: 601-853-8284

Mailing Address: P.O. Box 13669, Jackson, MS 39236-3669

Insurance Defense, Product Liability, Bodily Injury, Toxic Torts, Medical Malpractice, Workers' Compensation

SEE COMPLETE LISTING UNDER JACKSON, MISSISSIPPI (35 MILES)

MAGNOLIA † 2,420 Pike Co.
Refer To
Markow Walker, P.A.
599 Highland Colony Parkway, Suite 100
Ridgeland, Mississippi 39157
   Telephone: 601-853-1911
   Fax: 601-853-8284

Mailing Address: P.O. Box 13669, Jackson, MS 39236-3669

Insurance Defense, Product Liability, Bodily Injury, Toxic Torts, Medical Malpractice, Workers' Compensation

SEE COMPLETE LISTING UNDER JACKSON, MISSISSIPPI (75 MILES)

MCCOMB 12,790 Pike Co.
Refer To
Hicks Law Firm, PLLC
211 South 29th Avenue, Suite 201
Hattiesburg, Mississippi 39401
   Telephone: 601-544-6770
   Fax: 601-544-6775

Mailing Address: P.O. Box 18350, Hattiesburg, MS 39404-8350

Insurance Defense, General Liability, Automobile, Bodily Injury, Casualty, Product Liability, Premises Liability, Commercial Litigation, Bad Faith, Trucking Law, Construction Litigation, Commercial Vehicle, Professional Liability, Commercial and Personal Lines

SEE COMPLETE LISTING UNDER HATTIESBURG, MISSISSIPPI (75 MILES)

OCEAN SPRINGS
MISSISSIPPI

Refer To
Markow Walker, P.A.
599 Highland Colony Parkway, Suite 100
Ridgeland, Mississippi 39157
   Telephone: 601-853-1911
   Fax: 601-853-8284

Mailing Address: P.O. Box 13669, Jackson, MS 39236-3669

Insurance Defense, Product Liability, Bodily Injury, Toxic Torts, Medical Malpractice, Workers' Compensation

SEE COMPLETE LISTING UNDER JACKSON, MISSISSIPPI (70 MILES)

MENDENHALL † 2,504 Simpson Co.

Refer To
Bennett, Lotterhos, Sulser & Wilson, P.A.
188 East Capitol Street, Suite 1400
Jackson, Mississippi 39201
   Telephone: 601-944-0466
   Fax: 601-944-0467

Mailing Address: P.O. Box 98, Jackson, MS 39205-0098

Insurance Defense, Environmental Law

SEE COMPLETE LISTING UNDER JACKSON, MISSISSIPPI (30 MILES)

Refer To
Markow Walker, P.A.
599 Highland Colony Parkway, Suite 100
Ridgeland, Mississippi 39157
   Telephone: 601-853-1911
   Fax: 601-853-8284

Mailing Address: P.O. Box 13669, Jackson, MS 39236-3669

Insurance Defense, Product Liability, Bodily Injury, Toxic Torts, Medical Malpractice, Workers' Compensation

SEE COMPLETE LISTING UNDER JACKSON, MISSISSIPPI (30 MILES)

MERIDIAN † 41,148 Lauderdale Co.

Refer To
Hicks Law Firm, PLLC
211 South 29th Avenue, Suite 201
Hattiesburg, Mississippi 39401
   Telephone: 601-544-6770
   Fax: 601-544-6775

Mailing Address: P.O. Box 18350, Hattiesburg, MS 39404-8350

Insurance Defense, General Liability, Automobile, Bodily Injury, Casualty, Product Liability, Premises Liability, Commercial Litigation, Bad Faith, Trucking Law, Construction Litigation, Commercial Vehicle, Professional Liability, Commercial and Personal Lines

SEE COMPLETE LISTING UNDER HATTIESBURG, MISSISSIPPI (90 MILES)

Refer To
Hicks & Smith, PLLC
Regions Bank, 2nd Floor
710 Main Street
Columbus, Mississippi 39701
   Telephone: 662-243-7300
   Fax: 662-327-1485

Mailing Address: P.O. Box 1111, Columbus, MS 39703-1111

Bad Faith, Automobile, Premises Liability, Workers' Compensation, Casualty, Product Liability, Medical Malpractice, Subrogation, Class Actions, Commercial Litigation, Employment Law, Extra-Contractual Litigation, Professional Negligence, Truck Liability, Governmental Liability, Public Entities, Civil Rights, Insurance Sales Practice Litigation, Constitutional, General Insurance Defense, Admiralty, Construction, Business Litigation, Environmental Litigation

SEE COMPLETE LISTING UNDER COLUMBUS, MISSISSIPPI (119 MILES)

Refer To
Webb Sanders & Williams PLLC
363 North Broadway
Tupelo, Mississippi 38804
   Telephone: 662-844-2137
   Fax: 662-842-3863

Mailing Address: P.O. Box 496, Tupelo, MS 38802-0496

Insurance Defense, Insurance Coverage, Automobile, Property, Fire, Arson, Fraud, First Party Matters, Bad Faith, Special Investigations, Product Liability, Automobile Liability, Uninsured and Underinsured Motorist, Professional Malpractice, Medical Malpractice, Workers' Compensation, General Liability, Premises Liability, Defense Litigation, Corporate Law, Commercial Law, Commercial Litigation, Real Estate, Transportation, Environmental Law, Toxic Torts, Bankruptcy, Creditor Rights, Labor and Employment, ERISA, Construction Litigation, Fidelity and Surety, Insurance Fraud, General Civil Practice, Trial Practice, Appellate Practice, Employment Discrimination, Coverage Analysis, Coverage Issues

SEE COMPLETE LISTING UNDER TUPELO, MISSISSIPPI (145 MILES)

NATCHEZ † 15,792 Adams Co.

Refer To
Hicks Law Firm, PLLC
211 South 29th Avenue, Suite 201
Hattiesburg, Mississippi 39401
   Telephone: 601-544-6770
   Fax: 601-544-6775

Mailing Address: P.O. Box 18350, Hattiesburg, MS 39404-8350

Insurance Defense, General Liability, Automobile, Bodily Injury, Casualty, Product Liability, Premises Liability, Commercial Litigation, Bad Faith, Trucking Law, Construction Litigation, Commercial Vehicle, Professional Liability, Commercial and Personal Lines

SEE COMPLETE LISTING UNDER HATTIESBURG, MISSISSIPPI (144 MILES)

Refer To
Markow Walker, P.A.
599 Highland Colony Parkway, Suite 100
Ridgeland, Mississippi 39157
   Telephone: 601-853-1911
   Fax: 601-853-8284

Mailing Address: P.O. Box 13669, Jackson, MS 39236-3669

Insurance Defense, Product Liability, Bodily Injury, Toxic Torts, Medical Malpractice, Workers' Compensation

SEE COMPLETE LISTING UNDER JACKSON, MISSISSIPPI (102 MILES)

Refer To
Varner, Parker & Sessums, P.A.
1110 Jackson Street
Vicksburg, Mississippi 39180
   Telephone: 601-638-8741
   Fax: 601-638-8666
   Toll Free: 800-634-0442

Mailing Address: P.O. Box 1237, Vicksburg, MS 39181-1237

Insurance Defense, Trial Practice, State and Federal Courts, Medical Malpractice, Product Liability, Commercial and Personal Lines

SEE COMPLETE LISTING UNDER VICKSBURG, MISSISSIPPI (60 MILES)

OCEAN SPRINGS 17,442 Jackson Co.

Markow Walker, P.A.
Building M
2113 Government Street
Ocean Springs, Mississippi 39564
   Telephone: 228-872-1923
   Fax: 228-872-1973
   www.markowwalker.com

(Ridgeland, MS Office*(See Jackson listing): 599 Highland Colony Parkway, Suite 100, 39157, P.O. Box 13669, 39236-3669)
   (Tel: 601-853-1911)
   (Fax: 601-853-8284)

MISSISSIPPI   OLIVE BRANCH

Markow Walker, P.A., Ocean Springs, MS   (Continued)

(Oxford, MS Office*: 265 North Lamar Boulevard, Suite 1, 38655, P.O. Drawer 50, 38655-0050)
  (Tel: 662-234-9899)
  (Fax: 662-234-9762)

Insurance Defense, Product Liability, Bodily Injury, Toxic Torts, Medical Malpractice, Workers' Compensation

Shareholder

Jeffrey Moffett — 1975 — Southeastern Louisiana University, B.A., 1998; The University of Mississippi, J.D., 2001 — Admitted to Bar, 2001, Mississippi

Associate

Jeremy T. England — 1982 — Mississippi State University, B.A. (magna cum laude), 2005; The University of Mississippi School of Law, J.D., 2008 — Admitted to Bar, 2008, Mississippi; 2010, Alabama; 2008, U.S. District Court, Northern and Southern Districts of Mississippi; U.S. Court of Appeals, FifthCircuit — Member American and Harrison County Bar Associations; The Mississippi Bar; Mississippi Defense Lawyers Association

(See listing under Jackson, MS for additional information)

OLIVE BRANCH   33,484 DeSoto Co.

Jones Walker LLP

6897 Crumpler Boulevard, Suite 100
Olive Branch, Mississippi 38654
  Telephone: 662-895-2996
  Fax: 662-895-5480
  E-Mail: info@joneswalker.com
  www.joneswalker.com

(New Orleans, LA Office*: 201 St. Charles Avenue, 70170-5100)
  (Tel: 504-582-8000)
  (Fax: 504-582-8583)
(Mobile, AL Office*: RSA Battle House Tower, 11 North Water Street, Suite 1200, 36602, P.O. Box 46, 36601)
  (Tel: 251-432-1414)
  (Fax: 251-433-4106)
(Baton Rouge, LA Office*: Four United Plaza, 8555 United Plaza Boulevard, 70809)
  (Tel: 225-248-2000)
  (Fax: 225-248-2010)
(Lafayette, LA Office*: 600 Jefferson Street, Suite 1600, 70501)
  (Tel: 337-593-7600)
  (Fax: 337-593-7601)
(Birmingham, AL Office*: One Federal Place, 1819 5th Avenue North, Suite 1100, 35203)
  (Tel: 205-244-5200)
  (Fax: 205-244-5400)
(Jackson, MS Office*: 190 East Capitol Street, Suite 800, 39201, P.O. Box 427, 39205-0427)
  (Tel: 601-949-4900)
  (Fax: 601-949-4804)

Accountants, Admiralty and Maritime Law, Agent/Broker Liability, Antitrust, Appellate Practice, Asbestos Litigation, Aviation, Bankruptcy, Cargo, Class Actions, Commercial Litigation, Complex Litigation, Construction Law, Contracts, Directors and Officers Liability, Disability, Employment Law, Energy, Entertainment Law, Environmental Law, ERISA, Errors and Omissions, Health Care, Insurance Coverage, Insurance Defense, Intellectual Property, International Law, Labor and Employment, Life Insurance, Medical Malpractice, Mergers and Acquisitions, Motor Carriers, Oil and Gas, Personal Injury, Product Liability, Professional Liability, Regulatory and Compliance, Toxic Torts, Workers' Compensation

Firm Profile: Since 1937, Jones Walker LLP has grown to become one of the largest law firms in the southeastern U.S. We serve local, regional, national, and international business interests in a wide range of markets and industries. Today, we have more than 375 attorneys in 19 offices.

Jones Walker is committed to providing proactive legal services to major multinational, public, and private corporations; *Fortune* 500® companies; money center banks and worldwide insurers; and family and emerging businesses located in the United States and abroad.

Firm Member

Scott B. Hollis — Mississippi State University, B.A., 1995; The University of Mississippi School of Law, J.D., 1997 — Admitted to Bar, 1998, Mississippi; U.S. Court of Appeals, Fifth Circuit — Member American Bar Association; The Mississippi Bar (Executive Committee; Gaming Law Section); Defense Research Institute; Mississippi Defense Lawyers Association — Practice Areas: Business Litigation; Commercial Litigation — E-mail: shollis@joneswalker.com

(See Listing under New Orleans, LA for a List of Firm Clients and Additional Information)

The following firms also service this area.

Webb Sanders & Williams PLLC
363 North Broadway
Tupelo, Mississippi 38804
  Telephone: 662-844-2137
  Fax: 662-842-3863
Mailing Address: P.O. Box 496, Tupelo, MS 38802-0496

Insurance Defense, Insurance Coverage, Automobile, Property, Fire, Arson, Fraud, First Party Matters, Bad Faith, Special Investigations, Product Liability, Automobile Liability, Uninsured and Underinsured Motorist, Professional Malpractice, Medical Malpractice, Workers' Compensation, General Liability, Premises Liability, Defense Litigation, Corporate Law, Commercial Law, Commercial Litigation, Real Estate, Transportation, Environmental Law, Toxic Torts, Bankruptcy, Creditor Rights, Labor and Employment, ERISA, Construction Litigation, Fidelity and Surety, Insurance Fraud, General Civil Practice, Trial Practice, Appellate Practice, Employment Discrimination, Coverage Analysis, Coverage Issues

SEE COMPLETE LISTING UNDER TUPELO, MISSISSIPPI (87 MILES)

OXFORD   † 18,916 Lafayette Co.

Griffith Law Firm

P.O. Box 2248
Oxford, Mississippi 38655
  Telephone: 662-238-7727
  Fax: 662-238-7727
  E-Mail: ben@glawms.com
  www.glawms.com

Civil Rights, Governmental Liability, Law Enforcement Liability, Public Entities, Public Officials Liability, Administrative Law, Appellate Practice, Carrier Defense, Casualty Defense, Civil Trial Practice, Comprehensive General Liability, Construction Defect, Employment Discrimination, Environmental Law, Excess and Umbrella, Insurance Coverage, Insurance Defense, Municipal Law, Municipal Liability, Premises Liability, Primary and Excess Insurance, School Law, Self-Insured Defense, Sexual Harassment, ADEA Defense, ADA Defense, Water Resource Management, Water Quality and Permitting

Firm Profile: Benjamin E. Griffith, PLLC, is the principal of Griffith Law Firm. Our practice centers on civil litigation in state and federal courts. We represent public sector insurers and insureds, defend state and local governments and officials in the areas of election law, civil rights, constitutional challenges, employment discrimination, public sector insurance coverage, and environmental law.

PASCAGOULA   MISSISSIPPI

Griffith Law Firm, Oxford, MS   (Continued)

Insurance Clients

Alabama Municipal Insurance Corporation
GE Capital Services Group
Meadowbrook Insurance Group
Trident Insurance Services
Argonaut Insurance Company
First Specialty Insurance Corporation
Swiss Re America Group
Westport Insurance Company

Non-Insurance Clients

Mississippi Tort Claims Board
YMD Joint Water Management District

Principal

Benjamin E. Griffith — The University of Mississippi, B.A., 1973; J.D., 1975 — Admitted to Bar, 1975, Mississippi; U.S. Court of Appeals, Fourth, Fifth and Eleventh Circuits; U.S. Supreme Court — Member Federal, American (Chair, Standing Committee on Election Law, 2010-13; Chair, State and Local Government Law Section, 2007-2008; House of Delegates, 2008-), Bolivar County and Fifth Federal Circuit Bar Associations; The Mississippi Bar (Chair, Government Law Section, 1990-1991); Mississippi Association of County Board Attorneys (President, 1989-1990); National Association of County Civil Attorneys (President, 1992-1993); International Municipal Lawyers Association (Chair, International Steering Committee); Defense Research Institute; Mississippi Defense Lawyers Association — Board Attorney, Yazoo-Mississippi Delta Joint Water Management District (1989-) — Board Certified in Civil Trial Advocacy by the National Board of Trial Advocacy; Board Certified in Civil Pretrial Advocacy by the National Board of Trial Advocacy — Languages: German — Practice Areas: Election Law; Civil Rights Defense; Insurance Coverage; Environmental Law; Public Sector Insurance Coverage — Tel: 662-238-7727 — Fax: 662-238-7727 — E-mail: ben@glawms.com

Markow Walker, P.A.

265 North Lamar Boulevard, Suite 1
Oxford, Mississippi 38655
   Telephone: 662-234-9899
   Fax: 662-234-9762
   www.markowwalker.com

(Ridgeland, MS Office*(See Jackson listing): 599 Highland Colony Parkway, Suite 100, 39157, P.O. Box 13669, 39236-3669)
   (Tel: 601-853-1911)
   (Fax: 601-853-8284)
(Ocean Springs, MS Office*: Building M, 2113 Government Street, 39564)
   (Tel: 228-872-1923)
   (Fax: 228-872-1973)

Insurance Defense, Product Liability, Bodily Injury, Toxic Torts, Medical Malpractice, Workers' Compensation

Shareholders

Phillip Embry — 1975 — The University of Mississippi, B.A., 1998; J.D., 2001 — Admitted to Bar, 2001, Mississippi

John Hinkle, IV — 1975 — The University of Mississippi, B.A., 1997; J.D., 2001 — Admitted to Bar, 2001, Mississippi

Associates

Courtney McAlexander — 1985 — The University of Mississippi, B.A., 2007; The University of Mississippi School of Law, J.D. (cum laude), 2010 — Phi Beta Kappa, Phi Kappa Phi — Admitted to Bar, 2010, Mississippi

Ryan M. Hall — 1984 — The University of Mississippi, B.A., 2007; Mississippi College School of Law, J.D., 2009 — Admitted to Bar, 2010, Mississippi

(See listing under Jackson, MS for additional information)

Wells Marble & Hurst, PLLC

2091 Old Taylor Road, Suite 101
Oxford, Mississippi 38655
   Telephone: 662-236-1500
   Fax: 662-236-2374
   http://wellsmarble.com

(Ridgeland, MS Office*: 300 Concourse Boulevard, Suite 200, 39157, P.O. Box 131, 39205-0131)
   (Tel: 601-605-6900)
   (Fax: 601-605-6901)
   (E-Mail: kmansfield@wellsmarble.com)

Insurance Defense, Complex Litigation, ERISA, Transportation, Casualty, Life Insurance

(See listing under Ridgeland, MS for additional information)

(Revisors of the Mississippi Insurance Law Digest for this Publication)

The following firms also service this area.

Hicks & Smith, PLLC

Regions Bank, 2nd Floor
710 Main Street
Columbus, Mississippi 39701
   Telephone: 662-243-7300
   Fax: 662-327-1485

Mailing Address: P.O. Box 1111, Columbus, MS 39703-1111

Bad Faith, Automobile, Premises Liability, Workers' Compensation, Casualty, Product Liability, Medical Malpractice, Subrogation, Class Actions, Commercial Litigation, Employment Law, Extra-Contractual Litigation, Professional Negligence, Truck Liability, Governmental Liability, Public Entities, Civil Rights, Insurance Sales Practice Litigation, Constitutional, General Insurance Defense, Admiralty, Construction, Business Litigation, Environmental Litigation

SEE COMPLETE LISTING UNDER COLUMBUS, MISSISSIPPI (113 MILES)

Webb Sanders & Williams PLLC

363 North Broadway
Tupelo, Mississippi 38804
   Telephone: 662-844-2137
   Fax: 662-842-3863

Mailing Address: P.O. Box 496, Tupelo, MS 38802-0496

Insurance Defense, Insurance Coverage, Automobile, Property, Fire, Arson, Fraud, First Party Matters, Bad Faith, Special Investigations, Product Liability, Automobile Liability, Uninsured and Underinsured Motorist, Professional Malpractice, Medical Malpractice, Workers' Compensation, General Liability, Premises Liability, Defense Litigation, Corporate Law, Commercial Law, Commercial Litigation, Real Estate, Transportation, Environmental Law, Toxic Torts, Bankruptcy, Creditor Rights, Labor and Employment, ERISA, Construction Litigation, Fidelity and Surety, Insurance Fraud, General Civil Practice, Trial Practice, Appellate Practice, Employment Discrimination, Coverage Analysis, Coverage Issues

SEE COMPLETE LISTING UNDER TUPELO, MISSISSIPPI (48 MILES)

PASCAGOULA † 22,392 Jackson Co.

Bryan, Nelson, Schroeder, Castigliola & Banahan, PLLC

1103 Jackson Avenue
Pascagoula, Mississippi 39567
   Telephone: 228-762-6631
   Fax: 228-769-6392
   E-Mail: john@bnscb.com
   bnscblaw.com

Established: 1964

MISSISSIPPI

Bryan, Nelson, Schroeder, Castigliola & Banahan, PLLC, Pascagoula, MS (Continued)

Insurance Defense, General Liability, Product Liability, Professional Liability, Accident and Health, Casualty, Fire, Marine, Workers' Compensation, Medical Malpractice

Firm Profile: Bryan, Nelson, Schroeder, Castigliola & Banahan, PLLC is a civil litigation law firm located on Mississippi's Gulf of Mexico. For over 40 years, we have been serving clients with high quality and effective representation.

Insurance Clients

American National Property and Casualty Company
Farmers Insurance Group
Gulf Insurance Company
The Medical Protective Company
Mississippi Farm Bureau Mutual Insurance Company
OMS National Insurance Company
Southern Farm Bureau Group
State Farm Fire and Casualty Company
CNA Global Specialty Lines
The Doctors Company
Fortress Insurance Company
Medical Assurance Company of Mississippi Inc.
Occidental Fire & Casualty Company of North Carolina
PRMS, Inc. - Professional Risk Management Services, Inc.
State Farm Mutual Automobile Insurance Company

Non-Insurance Clients

Brown & Williamson Tobacco Company
Colle Towing Company
General Manufacturing Housing, Inc.
Jackson County Board of Supervisors
Patterson Truck Lines
Roadway Services, Inc.
Singing River Radiology Group
The Williams Companies, Inc.
Clark Seafood Company, Inc.
Coastal Trauma Care Region
Emergency Room Group, LTD
International Longshoremen's Association
Merchants and Marine Bank
Pascagoula Bar Pilots Association
Petroleum Service Corporation
SAIA Motor Freight Line, Inc.
South Mississippi Surgeons

Partners

Vincent J. Castigliola, Jr. — 1949 — The University of Mississippi, B.A., 1971; J.D., 1974 — Admitted to Bar, 1974, Mississippi; U.S. District Court, Northern and Southern Districts of Mississippi; U.S. Court of Appeals, Fifth Circuit; U.S. Supreme Court; Mississippi State Courts; Supreme Court of Mississippi — Member The Mississippi Bar; Jackson County Bar Association; The Maritime Law Association of the United States; Southeastern Admiralty Law Institute; Mississippi Defense Lawyers Association; Defense Research Institute; American Trial Lawyers Association — Practice Areas: Admiralty and Maritime Law; Automobile; Insurance Defense; Workers' Compensation — E-mail: Vincent@bnscb.com

John A. Banahan — 1957 — Mississippi State University, B.A., 1978; The University of Mississippi, J.D., 1981 — Admitted to Bar, 1981, Mississippi; U.S. District Court, Northern and Southern Districts of Mississippi; U.S. Court of Appeals, Fifth Circuit; U.S. Supreme Court; Supreme Court of Mississippi; Mississippi State Courts — Member The Mississippi Bar; Jackson County Bar Association; American Inns of Court; American Board of Trial Advocates; Federation of Defense and Corporate Counsel; International Association of Defense Counsel; Defense Research Institute; Mississippi Defense Lawyers Association — Practice Areas: Insurance Defense; Medical Malpractice; Complex Litigation — E-mail: John@bnscb.com

H. Benjamin Mullen — 1966 — University of Southern Mississippi, B.S.B.A., 1988; The University of Mississippi, J.D., 1991 — Admitted to Bar, 1991, Mississippi; 1992, Alabama; U.S. Court of Appeals, Fifth and Eleventh Circuits; Mississippi State Courts; Supreme Court of Mississippi — Member American, Fifth Federal Circuit and Jackson County Bar Associations; The Mississippi Bar; Alabama State Bar; Mississippi Defense Lawyers Association; Defense Research Institute — Practice Areas: Insurance Defense; Litigation — E-mail: Ben@bnscb.com

Matthew E. Perkins — 1980 — The University of Mississippi, B.B.A., 2002; J.D., 2006 — Admitted to Bar, 2006, Mississippi; U.S. Court of Appeals, Fifth Circuit — Member American and Jackson County Bar Associations; The Mississippi Bar; Jackson County Young Lawyers Association; Mississippi Defense Lawyers Association; Defense Research Institute — Practice Areas: Insurance Defense; Medical Malpractice — E-mail: Perkins@bnscb.com

POPLARVILLE

Bryan, Nelson, Schroeder, Castigliola & Banahan, PLLC, Pascagoula, MS (Continued)

Jessica B. McNeel — 1982 — The University of Mississippi, B.A. (magna cum laude), 2004; The University of Mississippi School of Law, J.D. (cum laude), 2007 — Admitted to Bar, 2007, Mississippi; U.S. District Court, Northern and Southern Districts of Mississippi; U.S. Court of Appeals, Fifth Circuit — Member The Mississippi Bar (Young Lawyers Section); Jackson County Bar Association; Mississippi Women Lawyers Association; Mississippi Defense Lawyers Association — Practice Areas: Insurance Litigation; Medical Malpractice; Personal Injury — E-mail: Jessica@bnscb.com

Associates

Betty C. Castigliola — 1986 — The University of Mississippi School of Law, J.D., 2012 — Admitted to Bar, 2012, Mississippi

Calen J. Wills — 1985 — The University of Mississippi School of Law, J.D., 2012 — Admitted to Bar, 2012, Mississippi

Of Counsel

Ernest R. Schroeder — 1938 — Mississippi State University, B.A., 1960; The University of Mississippi, LL.B., 1963 — Admitted to Bar, 1963, Mississippi — Member The Mississippi Bar; Jackson County Bar Association; Mississippi Defense Lawyers Association; Defense Research Institute — Pascagula City Attorney, 1969-1973 — E-mail: Ernie@bnscb.com

The following firms also service this area.

Franke & Salloum, PLLC
10071 Lorraine Road
Gulfport, Mississippi 39503
Telephone: 228-868-7070
Fax: 228-868-7090

Mailing Address: P.O. Drawer 460, Gulfport, MS 39502

Insurance Defense, Medical Malpractice, General Liability, Workers' Compensation, Admiralty and Maritime Law, Product Liability, Bad Faith, Subrogation

SEE COMPLETE LISTING UNDER GULFPORT, MISSISSIPPI (32 MILES)

POPLARVILLE † 2,894 Pearl River Co.

Refer To

Franke & Salloum, PLLC
10071 Lorraine Road
Gulfport, Mississippi 39503
Telephone: 228-868-7070
Fax: 228-868-7090

Mailing Address: P.O. Drawer 460, Gulfport, MS 39502

Insurance Defense, Medical Malpractice, General Liability, Workers' Compensation, Admiralty and Maritime Law, Product Liability, Bad Faith, Subrogation

SEE COMPLETE LISTING UNDER GULFPORT, MISSISSIPPI (45 MILES)

PORT GIBSON † 1,567 Claiborne Co.

Refer To

Markow Walker, P.A.
599 Highland Colony Parkway, Suite 100
Ridgeland, Mississippi 39157
Telephone: 601-853-1911
Fax: 601-853-8284

Mailing Address: P.O. Box 13669, Jackson, MS 39236-3669

Insurance Defense, Product Liability, Bodily Injury, Toxic Torts, Medical Malpractice, Workers' Compensation

SEE COMPLETE LISTING UNDER JACKSON, MISSISSIPPI (79 MILES)

RIDGELAND   MISSISSIPPI

Refer To

Varner, Parker & Sessums, P.A.
1110 Jackson Street
Vicksburg, Mississippi 39180
   Telephone: 601-638-8741
   Fax: 601-638-8666
   Toll Free: 800-634-0442

Mailing Address: P.O. Box 1237, Vicksburg, MS 39181-1237

Insurance Defense, Trial Practice, State and Federal Courts, Medical Malpractice, Product Liability, Commercial and Personal Lines

SEE COMPLETE LISTING UNDER VICKSBURG, MISSISSIPPI (30 MILES)

RALEIGH † 1,462 Smith Co.

Refer To

Markow Walker, P.A.
599 Highland Colony Parkway, Suite 100
Ridgeland, Mississippi 39157
   Telephone: 601-853-1911
   Fax: 601-853-8284

Mailing Address: P.O. Box 13669, Jackson, MS 39236-3669

Insurance Defense, Product Liability, Bodily Injury, Toxic Torts, Medical Malpractice, Workers' Compensation

SEE COMPLETE LISTING UNDER JACKSON, MISSISSIPPI (45 MILES)

RAYMOND † 1,933 Hinds Co.

Refer To

Bennett, Lotterhos, Sulser & Wilson, P.A.
188 East Capitol Street, Suite 1400
Jackson, Mississippi 39201
   Telephone: 601-944-0466
   Fax: 601-944-0467

Mailing Address: P.O. Box 98, Jackson, MS 39205-0098

Insurance Defense, Environmental Law

SEE COMPLETE LISTING UNDER JACKSON, MISSISSIPPI (14 MILES)

RIDGELAND 24,047 Madison Co.

Butler, Snow, O'Mara, Stevens & Cannada, PLLC

1020 Highland Colony Parkway, Suite 1400
Ridgeland, Mississippi 39157
   Telephone: 601-948-5711
   Fax: 601-985-4500
   E-Mail: info@butlersnow.com
   www.butlersnow.com

(Memphis, TN Office: Crescent Center, 6075 Poplar Avenue, Suite 500, 38119)
   (Tel: 901-680-7200)
   (Fax: 901-680-7201)
(Gulfport, MS Office: 1300 Twenty Fifth Avenue, Suite 204, 39501)
   (Tel: 228-864-1170)
   (Fax: 228-868-1531)
(Oxford, MS Office: 1200 Jefferson Ave, Suite 205, P.O. Box 1138, 38655)
   (Tel: 662-513-8000)
   (Fax: 662-513-8001)
(New Orleans, LA Office: 201 St. Charles Avenue, Suite 3310, 70170-3310)
   (Tel: 504-299-7700)
   (Fax: 504-299-7701)
(Nashville, TN Office: The Pinnacle at Symphony Place, 150 3rd Avenue South, Suite 1600, 37201)
   (Tel: 615-651-6700)
   (Fax: 615-651-6701)

**Butler, Snow, O'Mara, Stevens & Cannada, PLLC,
Ridgeland, MS   (Continued)**

(Baton Rouge, LA Office: City Plaza, 445 North Boulevard, Suite 810, 70802)
   (Tel: 225-325-8700)
   (Fax: 225-325-8800)
(Bethlehem, PA Office: 1414 Millard, 18018)
   (Tel: 610-691-8507)
   (Fax: 610-691-8507)
(Bay St. Louis, MS Office: 833 Highway 90, Suite 1, 39520)
   (Tel: 228-467-5426)
(Fort Washington, PA Office: 500 Office Center Drive, Suite 400, 19034)
   (Tel: 267-513-1885)
(Birmingham, AL Office: Colonial Plaza, 6th Avenue North, Suite 1125, 35203)
   (Tel: 205-297-2201)
(Montgomery, AL Office: 250 Commerce Street, Suite 203, 36104)
   (Tel: 334-832-2900)
(Atlanta, GA Office: Regus Suites, 400 Galleria Parkway, Suite 1500, 30339)
   (Tel: 678-385-6500)
   (Fax: 678-385-6501)

Established: 1954

Casualty, Surety, Life Insurance, Professional Liability, Product Liability, Directors and Officers Liability, Workers' Compensation, Property, Employment

Firm Profile: Some law firms promise client service. We deliver on that promise. Surveys by respected national consultants consistently rank Butler Snow among the best nationwide in service - in anticipating needs, in a commitment to help, in providing value, in client satisfaction.

Our clients' success is our success. With that principle guiding us, Butler Snow has emerged from being primarily a regional firm to one with national scope. We have built a team of talented legal professionals who share a commitment to serve clients - from Fortune 100 companies to emerging-technology start-ups.

Butler Snow has been recognized repeatedly for our teamwork and our clients' successes, across a variety of service areas. In 2009, Law360 ranked the firm as "One of the Top Ten Busiest Product Liability Practices" in its Law360 2009 Litigation Almanac. Butler Snow was named in Best's Review as one of 69 law firms "Standing the Test of Time," the firm having been recommended for decades by the insurance companies we have represented. Also in 2009, National Law Journal named Butler Snow to its Midsize Hot List, making the firm one of only 20 nationwide named for demonstrating creative, innovative strategies; developing practice areas; and recruiting and retaining top legal talent.

Our team approach allows us to utilize resources across the firm to match legal experience with client needs. As a result, clients benefit from our strategic counsel, efficient execution and innovative solutions to complex challenges.

Butler Snow's practice areas include the full range of business law and litigation services. We offer the depth to represent a broad spectrum of national and regional clients in a variety of legal areas. Our team approach allows us to utilize resources across the firm to match legal experience with client needs. As a result, clients benefit from our strategic counsel, efficient execution and innovative solutions to complex challenges.

In an increasingly sophisticated business environment, clients need law firms that have the experience and depth to handle significant matters. Our attorneys offer diverse legal, business and governmental backgrounds, bringing vast experience and practical knowledge to each client they represent. Our practice areas are focused on specific legal disciplines, but we also have teams that are equipped to address the needs of particular industries, including healthcare, banking and finance, gaming, environmental, manufacturing, governmental, pharmaceutical, telecommunications, and insurance.

We have represented clients in all 50 states and in the District of Columbia, as well as internationally in more than 20 countries, including Australia, Canada, China, Colombia, Kuwait, Mexico, Saudi Arabia and the United Kingdom.

MISSISSIPPI — RIDGELAND

Butler, Snow, O'Mara, Stevens & Cannada, PLLC, Ridgeland, MS (Continued)

Chambers USA-America's Leading Lawyers for Business describes Butler Snow as having "enormous power and presence" with a team of attorneys who have achieved national prominence because of "sheer, unambiguous quality." According to Chambers, our clients refer to the firm as "well-known for being successful" and our attorneys as "real deal-makers." Chambers also noted the firm's ability to deliver to the client "the whole package - intelligence, presence and trial experience."

The attorneys of Butler Snow are ready to meet your legal needs - whether in multi-million-dollar appeals where vital interests are at stake or in more routine business and corporate matters. At Butler Snow, our clients' interests are paramount, and we focus on exceeding expectations.

Insurance Clients

- AAA Insurance
- AEGON Insurance Group
- American Empire Group
- American Hardware Mutual Insurance Company
- Associates Insurance Company
- Burlington Insurance Company
- Chubb Group of Insurance Companies
- Clarendon National Insurance Company
- Columbia Insurance Company
- Employers Reinsurance Corporation
- Farmers Insurance Group
- Fireman's Fund Insurance Companies
- Great American Insurance Company
- Gulf Guaranty Life Insurance Company
- Merit Life Insurance Company
- Montpelier US Insurance Company
- Mt. Hawley Insurance Company
- The Navigators Group, Inc.
- Protective Insurance Company
- Response Insurance Company
- RLI Insurance Company
- Security Life and Trust Insurance Company
- State Farm Fire and Casualty Company
- TransGuard Insurance Company of America, Inc.
- Universal Underwriters Insurance Company
- Valley Forge Insurance Company
- Western Heritage Insurance Company
- Yosemite Insurance Company
- ACE USA Claims
- American Bankers Insurance Group
- American Home Assurance Company
- Bristol West Insurance Company
- Chartis Insurance Group
- Church Mutual Insurance Company
- CIGNA Group
- CNA Insurance Companies
- Coast National Insurance Company
- Continental Casualty Company
- Executive Risk Specialty Insurance Company
- Federal Insurance Company
- Genesis Insurance Company
- Globe Life and Accident Insurance Company
- Great West Casualty Company
- Infinity Insurance Company
- Kemper Insurance Companies
- Mitsui Sumitomo Fire Insurance Company, Ltd.
- National American Insurance Company
- Providian Life and Health Insurance Company
- RLI Transportation
- Select Insurance Company
- Seneca Insurance Company, Inc.
- Transcontinental Insurance Company
- Transportation Insurance Company
- United America Indemnity Group
- U.S. Risk Insurance Company
- Utica Mutual Insurance Company
- Westchester Fire Insurance Company
- XL Insurance

Firm Members & Associates

Phil B. Abernethy — The University of Mississippi, J.D. (cum laude), 1979 — Tel: 601-985-4536 — E-mail: phil.abernethy@butlersnow.com

Angela T. Baker — Faulkner University, Thomas Goode Jones School of Law, J.D., 2000 — Tel: 334-832-2906 — E-mail: angela.baker@butlersnow.com

Kevin C. Baltz — The University of Tennessee, J.D., 2003 — Tel: 615-503-9114 — E-mail: kevin.baltz@butlersnow.com

Amanda B. Barbour — The George Washington University Law School, J.D., 1997 — Tel: 601-985-4585 — E-mail: amanda.barbour@butlersnow.com

Kenneth W. Barton — The University of Mississippi, J.D. (with honors), 1972 — Tel: 601-985-4515 — E-mail: ken.barton@butlersnow.com

P. Ryan Beckett — The University of Mississippi, J.D. (magna cum laude), 1999 — Tel: 601-985-4557 — E-mail: ryan.beckett@butlersnow.com

Michael B. Beers — Cumberland University School of Law, J.D., 1977 — Tel: 334-832-2905 — E-mail: michael.beers@butlersnow.com

Patrick T. Bergin — Florida State University, J.D. (with honors), 1988 — Tel: 228-575-3040 — E-mail: patrick.bergin@butlersnow.com

John A. Crawford, Jr. — The University of Mississippi, J.D. (summa cum laude), 1996 — Tel: 601-985-4532 — E-mail: jack.crawford@butlersnow.com

Ashonti T. Davis — The University of Tennessee, J.D., 2009 — Tel: 615-503-9141 — E-mail: ashonti.davis@butlersnow.com

Paul N. Davis — Baylor University, J.D. (cum laude), 1979 — Tel: 601-985-4503 — E-mail: paul.davis@butlersnow.com

Richard M. Dye — The University of Mississippi, J.D. (cum laude), 1998 — Tel: 601-985-4513 — E-mail: rick.dye@butlersnow.com

Shannon F. Favre — The University of Tennessee College of Law, J.D., 1999 — Tel: 228-575-3026 — E-mail: shannon.favre@butlersnow.com

A. David Fawal — Cumberland University School of Law, J.D., 1990 — Tel: 205-297-2205 — E-mail: david.fawal@butlersnow.com

Robert M. Frey — Vanderbilt University Law School, J.D., 1984 — Tel: 601-985-4524 — E-mail: bob.frey@butlersnow.com

William M. Gage — The University of Mississippi, J.D. (cum laude), 1990 — Tel: 601-985-4561 — E-mail: william.gage@butlersnow.com

Robert C. Galloway — The University of Mississippi, J.D., 1967 — Tel: 228-575-3019 — E-mail: bob.galloway@butlersnow.com

Charles C. Harrell — The University of Mississippi, B.P.A., 1973; J.D., 1977 — Tel: 901-680-7327 — E-mail: chuck.harrell@butlersnow.com

John C. Henegan — The University of Mississippi, J.D. (with honors), 1976 — Tel: 601-985-4530

Frank M. Holbrook — The University of Georgia, J.D. (cum laude), 1979 — Tel: 901-680-7312 — E-mail: frank.holbrook@butlersnow.com

Eric E. Hudson — Vermont Law School, J.D. (magna cum laude), 1998 — Tel: 901-680-7309 — E-mail: eric.hudson@butlersnow.com

Christy D. Jones — University of Arkansas, J.D. (with high honors), 1977 — Tel: 601-985-4523 — E-mail: christy.jones@butlersnow.com

Sepideh C. Khansari — Washington and Lee University, J.D., 2009 — Tel: 615-503-9137 — E-mail: sepideh.khansari@butlersnow.com

B. Hart Knight — Vermont Law School, J.D., 2006 — Tel: 615-503-9136 — E-mail: hart.knight@butlersnow.com

Erin P. Lane — Harvard Law School, J.D., 2000 — Tel: 601-985-4526 — E-mail: erin.lane@butlersnow.com

Robert B. Littleton — The University of Tennessee, J.D., 1971 — Tel: 615-503-9109 — E-mail: bob.littleton@butlersnow.com

Taylor B. Mayes — The University of Tennessee, J.D., 1998 — Tel: 615-503-9110 — E-mail: taylor.mayes@butlersnow.com

Melody McAnally — Mississippi College, J.D., 2003 — Tel: 901-680-7322 — E-mail: melody.mcanally@butlersnow.com

Robert A. Miller — The University of Mississippi, J.D. (cum laude), 1981 — Tel: 601-985-4575 — E-mail: bobby.miller@butlersnow.com

Meade W. Mitchell — The University of Mississippi, J.D. (cum laude), 1993 — Tel: 601-985-4560 — E-mail: meade.mitchell@butlersnow.com

Paul S. Murphy — Thomas M. Cooley Law School, J.D., 1997 — Tel: 228-575-3033 — E-mail: paul.murphy@butlersnow.com

Randall D. Noel — The University of Mississippi, J.D., 1978 — Tel: 901-680-7346 — E-mail: randy.noel@butlersnow.com

William R. O'Bryan, Jr. — Vanderbilt University, J.D., 1977 — Tel: 615-503-9124 — E-mail: bill.obryan@butlersnow.com

Junaid A. Odubeko — Vanderbilt University, J.D., 2004 — Tel: 615-503-9132 — E-mail: junaid.odubeko@butlersnow.com

Donald P. Paul — Vanderbilt University, J.D., 1973 — Tel: 615-503-9123 — E-mail: don.paul@butlersnow.com

Amy M. Pepke — Vanderbilt University Law School, J.D., 1996 — Tel: 901-680-7324 — E-mail: amy.pepke@butlersnow.com

Katherine T. Powell — Cumberland University School of Law, J.D., 2007 — Tel: 205-297-2206 — E-mail: katie.powell@butlersnow.com

J. Stevenson Ray — The University of Mississippi, J.D. (cum laude), 1985 — Tel: 601-985-4520 — E-mail: steve.ray@butlersnow.com

E. Barney Robinson III — The University of Mississippi, J.D. (magna cum laude), 1991 — Tel: 601-985-4525 — E-mail: barney.robinson@butlersnow.com

Richard W. Sliman — The University of Mississippi School of Law, J.D., 1991 — Tel: 228-575-3034 — E-mail: richard.sliman@butlersnow.com

Arthur D. Spratlin, Jr. — The University of Mississippi, J.D. (cum laude), 1991 — Tel: 601-985-4568 — E-mail: art.spratlin@butlersnow.com

Lee Davis Thames — The University of Mississippi, J.D. (with honors), 1960 — Tel: 601-985-4517 — E-mail: lee.davis@butlersnow.com

Timothy M. Threadgill — The University of Alabama, J.D., 1990 — Tel: 601-985-4594 — E-mail: tim.threadgill@butlersnow.com

James B. Tucker — The University of Mississippi, J.D., 1966 — Tel: 601-985-4544 — E-mail: james.tucker@butlersnow.com

RIDGELAND *MISSISSIPPI*

Butler, Snow, O'Mara, Stevens & Cannada, PLLC, Ridgeland, MS (Continued)

J. Kennedy Turner III — The University of Mississippi, J.D. (with honors), 1977 — Tel: 601-985-4417 — E-mail: ken.tucker@butlersnow.com

Danny W. Van Horn — Vanderbilt University Law School, J.D., 1997 — Tel: 901-680-7331 — E-mail: danny.vanhorn@butlersnow.com

William S. Walton — The University of Tennessee, J.D., 1984 — Tel: 615-503-9117 — E-mail: bill.walton@butlersnow.com

Benjamin M. Watson — The University of Mississippi School of Law, J.D. (magna cum laude), 2000 — Tel: 601-985-4551 — E-mail: ben.watson@butlersnow.com

Joshua J. Wiener — The University of Mississippi, J.D. (magna cum laude), 1981 — Tel: 601-985-4501 — E-mail: josh.wiener@butlersnow.com

Thomas E. Williams — The University of Mississippi, J.D. (with honors), 1980 — Tel: 601-985-4519 — E-mail: tommy.williams@butlersnow.com

Upshaw, Williams, Biggers & Beckham, L.L.P.

713 South Pear Orchard Road, Suite 102
Ridgeland, Mississippi 39157
   Telephone: 601-978-1996
   Fax: 601-978-1949
   Toll Free: 800-422-1379
   www.upshawwilliams.com
(Greenwood, MS Office*: 309 Fulton Street, 38930, P.O. Drawer 8230, 38935-8230)
   (Tel: 662-455-1613)
   (Fax: 662-453-9245)
   (Toll Free: 800-748-8720)
(Hernando, MS Office*: 2446 Caffey Street, 38632, P.O. Drawer 8230, 38935-8230)
   (Tel: 662-426-5890)
   (Fax: 662-429-5920)
   (Toll Free: 800-748-8720)

Established: 1996

General Civil Practice, State and Federal Courts, Administrative Law, Appellate Practice, Arson, Aviation, Bad Faith, Casualty, Civil Trial Practice, Commercial Law, Construction Law, Contracts, Corporate Law, Environmental Law, Federal Employer Liability Claims (FELA), Fidelity, Fraud, Insurance Defense, Insurance Coverage, Legal Malpractice, General Liability, Litigation, Mass Tort, Medical Malpractice, Negligence, Oil and Gas, Personal Injury, Product Liability, Professional Liability, Property, Railroad Law, Self-Insured, Surety, Tort, Transportation, Uninsured and Underinsured Motorist, Workers' Compensation, Real Estate, Probate, Agriculture

Firm Profile: Upshaw, Williams, Biggers & Beckham LLP is a thriving midsize, Mississippi law firm founded on a commitment to innovative and entrepreneurial service. We provide the balance of size, reach and responsiveness that many clients consider ideal. With our team orientation and commitment to personal and individualized attention, the firm provides the service capabilities of a very large firm with the efficiency of a small one. That's one reason why we can readily advise you on your legal matters.

Whether our clients come from the financial, high-tech, real estate, media, securities, insurance industries or small town business and concerns, they value our creative spirit, solution-oriented approach and unwavering commitment to the highest professional standards. They have helped build our reputation for insightful counseling, timely advice and constructive contributions to their legal business.

Representative Clients

Advocate, MD
Allianz Aviation Managers, LLC
AmFed Companies, L.L.C.
Avizent
Berkley Specialty Underwriting Managers, LLC
Canadian National
Cannon Cochran Management Services, Inc.
Alexsis, Inc.
American States Insurance Company
Berkley Insurance Company
Boyd Mississippi, Inc.
Bridgefield Casualty Insurance Company
Capital City Insurance Company, Inc.

Upshaw, Williams, Biggers & Beckham, L.L.P., Ridgeland, MS (Continued)

CNA Insurance Companies
Corrections Corporation of America
Farmers Insurance Exchange
Fred's Stores of Tennessee
General Casualty Insurance Company
Infinity Insurance Company
Liberty International
Lorillard Tobacco Company
Mississippi Hospitality & Restaurant Workers' Compensation Trust
Mississippi Tort Claims Board
MS Truck, Food, & Fuel
Nationwide Insurance
Phoenix Aviation Managers, Inc.
Progressive Insurance Company
Shelter Insurance Companies
State Volunteer Mutual Insurance Company
Union Standard Insurance Group
United States Aviation Underwriters, Inc.
CNA Insurance Company
Deep South Surplus, Inc.
The Doctors Company
Foremost Insurance Company
GEICO
Grain Dealers Mutual Insurance Company
LEMIC Insurance Company
Liberty Mutual Insurance Company
Medical Assurance Company of Mississippi Inc.
Mississippi Manufacturers Association Workers' Compensation Group
National Builders and Contractors
NL Industries, Inc.
Professional Claims Managers, Inc.
Safeco Insurance
State Auto Insurance Company
Summit Risk Services, Inc.
The Travelers Companies, Inc.
United Airlines, Inc.
Western Heritage Insurance
Zurich American Insurance Company

Attorneys

Richard C. Williams, Jr. — 1946 — Virginia Military Institute; The University of Mississippi, B.B.A., 1970; J.D., 1976 — Admitted to Bar, 1976, Mississippi; 1976, U.S. District Court, Northern and Southern Districts of Mississippi; U.S. Court of Appeals, Fifth Circuit — Member The Mississippi Bar; Mississippi Defense Lawyers Association — U.S. Navy (1970-1973) — E-mail: cwilliams@upshawwilliams.com

William H. Gillon, IV — 1965 — Mississippi State University, B.A., 1988; The University of Mississippi, J.D., 1991 — Moot Court Board; Phi Delta Phi — Admitted to Bar, 1991, Mississippi; 1991, U.S. District Court, Northern and Southern Districts of Mississippi; 1991, U.S. Court of Appeals, Fifth Circuit — Member The Mississippi Bar; Jackson Young Lawyers Association — E-mail: hgillon@upshawwilliams.com

Patrick M. Tatum — 1969 — Auburn University, B.S., 1991; The University of Mississippi, J.D., 1994 — Admitted to Bar, 1994, Mississippi; 1994, U.S. District Court, Northern and Southern Districts of Mississippi; 1994, U.S. Court of Appeals, Fifth Circuit — Member The Mississippi Bar; Hinds County Bar Association; Jackson Young Lawyers Association; Mississippi Defense Lawyers Association — E-mail: ptatum@upshawwilliams.com

Peter L. Corson — 1957 — Mansfield University of Pennsylvania, B.A., 1979; Mississippi College School of Law, J.D., 1985 — Admitted to Bar, 1985, Mississippi; 1985, U.S. District Court, Northern and Southern Districts of Mississippi — E-mail: pcorson@upshawwilliams.com

William L. Morton, III — Mississippi College, B.A., 2003; Mississippi College School of Law, J.D., 2006 — Admitted to Bar, 2006, Mississippi; U.S. District Court, Northern and Southern Districts of Mississippi; U.S. Court of Appeals, Fifth Circuit — Member The Mississippi Bar — E-mail: wmorton@upshawwilliams.com

(See listing under Greenwood, MS for additional information)

Wells Marble & Hurst, PLLC

300 Concourse Boulevard, Suite 200
Ridgeland, Mississippi 39157
   Telephone: 601-605-6900
   Fax: 601-605-6901
   E-Mail: kmansfield@wellsmarble.com
   http://wellsmarble.com

(Oxford, MS Office*: 2091 Old Taylor Road, Suite 101, 38655)
   (Tel: 662-236-1500)
   (Fax: 662-236-2374)

Established: 1871

Insurance Defense, Complex Litigation, ERISA, Transportation, Casualty, Life Insurance

MISSISSIPPI   **RIPLEY**

Wells Marble & Hurst, PLLC, Ridgeland, MS (Continued)

Firm Profile: Our firm's ability to provide a full range of legal services for over a century has led to long-standing relationships with our clients. A tradition of personal attention to legal issues allows us to guide our clients through an increasingly complex legal environment and to effectively address clients' needs in, virtually, any business, corporate or personal setting.

Insurance Clients

Metropolitan Life Insurance Company   Pacific Life Insurance Company

Managing Member

Kenna L. Mansfield Jr. — The University of Mississippi, J.D., 1982 — Admitted to Bar, 1982, Mississippi — E-mail: kmansfield@wellsmarble.com

(Revisors of the Mississippi Insurance Law Digest for this Publication)

Wright & Martin, L.L.P.
742D Magnolia Street
Madison, Mississippi 39110
   Telephone: 601-856-0000
   Fax: 601-856-5767
   E-Mail: swright@wrightmartin.com

Established: 1997

Civil Litigation, State and Federal Courts, Insurance Defense, General Liability, Automobile, Subrogation

Firm Profile: The firm of Wright & Martin was established in 1997 by J. Stephen Wright, who had previously provided defense representation while a partner in other law firms. Our goal is to provide the best legal representation at the most affordable rates.

Reported Cases: *Sandra Cockrell v. Pearl River Valley Water Supply District*, 865 So. 2d 357 (Miss. 2004); *Willow Creek Exploration, et al. v. Tadlock Pipe & Equipment, Inc., et al.*, 186 F. Supp. 2d 675 (S.D. Miss. 2002); *Dowdle Butane Gas Co. v. Walter Moore*, 831 So. 2d 1124 (Miss. 2002); *L.T. ex rel. Hollins v. City of Jackson*, 145 F. Supp. 2d 750 (2000); *Warren v. Pallets, Inc.*, 747 So. 2d 875 (Miss. Ct. App. 1999); *Body Support Systems, Inc. v. Blue Ridge Tables, Inc.*, 934 F. Supp. 749 (ND Miss 1996); *Walton v. Alexander*, 44 F.3d 1297 (5th Cir. 1995) [panel decision]; *Hosford v. Ray*, 806 F. Supp. 1297 (S.D. Miss. 1992); *Alexander v. Board of Trustees of Mississippi School for the Deaf*, 599 So. 2d 930 (Miss. 1992); *In re Barrier*, 776 F.2d 1298 (5th Cir. 1985); *Alexander v. Allain*, 441 So. 2d 1329 (Miss. 1983); *ACLU of Mississippi v. Finch*, 638 F. 2d 1336 (5th Cir. 1981); *Anderson v. Winter*, 631 F.2d 1238 (5th Cir. 1980); *State ex rel. Summer v. Denton*, 382 So. 2d 461, 11 A.L.R. 4th 813 (Miss. 1980); *Collilns v. Van Zant*, 375 So. 2d 404 (Miss. 1979); *Magnolia Venture Capital Corp. v. Prudential Securities, Inc. and Mississippi Dept. of Economics and Community Development*, 151 F. 3d 439 (5th Cir. 1998), cert. denied, 119 5 Ct. 115 (1999); *Horton v. Public Employees Retirement System*, 711 So. 2d 896 (Miss. 1998); *W.H. Thames v. Jackson Production Credit Association*, 600 So. 2d 208 (Miss. 1992); *McCarthage Bank v. Kirkland*, 121 B.R. 496 (S.D. Miss. 1990).

Insurance Clients

Allstate Insurance Company
Bituminous Insurance Companies
COUNTRY Insurance & Financial Services
Hanover Insurance Company
Liberty Mutual Insurance Company
Louisiana Insurance Guaranty Association
National Interstate Insurance Company
Pacific Specialty Insurance Company
Reliance Insurance Company
Tennessee Insurance Guaranty Association
United Automobile Insurance Company

Atain Insurance Companies
Cincinnati Insurance Company
Fidelity National Insurance Company
Jamestown Mutual Insurance Company
Mississippi Insurance Guaranty Association
National Security Fire and Casualty Company
Pharmacists Mutual Insurance Company
Scottsdale Insurance Company
Union Standard Insurance Company
United Coastal Insurance Company
U.S. Liability Insurance Company

Wright & Martin, L.L.P., Ridgeland, MS (Continued)

Non-Insurance Clients

AmeriGas Propane Parts and Service Inc.
Crawford & Company
Ward North America, Inc.

Burns & Wilcox Ltd.
Cambridge Integrated Services
Mississippi Tort Claims Board

Partners

J. Stephen Wright — 1950 — Florida State University, B.A., 1972; The University of Mississippi, J.D., 1975 — Admitted to Bar, 1975, Mississippi; 1975, U.S. District Court, Northern District of Mississippi; 1975, U.S. Court of Appeals, Fifth Circuit; 1977, U.S. District Court, Southern District of Mississippi; 1980, U.S. Court of Appeals, Eleventh Circuit — Member American and Hinds County Bar Associations; The Mississippi Bar; Propane Gas Defense Association; National Fire Protection Association; Jackson Young Lawyers Association; Mississippi Defense Lawyers Association — Certified Arbitrator and Mediator, American Arbitration Association — E-mail: swright@wrightmartin.com

James C. Martin — 1959 — Mississippi College, B.S.B.A., 1981; Baylor University, J.D., 1984 — Admitted to Bar, 1984, Texas; 1985, Mississippi; 1985, U.S. District Court, Northern and Southern Districts of Mississippi; 1985, U.S. Court of Appeals, Fifth Circuit — Member American and Hinds County Bar Associations; The Mississippi Bar; State Bar of Texas — E-mail: jmartin@wrightmartin.com

---

RIPLEY   † 5,395 Tippah Co.

Refer To

Webb Sanders & Williams PLLC
363 North Broadway
Tupelo, Mississippi 38804
   Telephone: 662-844-2137
   Fax: 662-842-3863
Mailing Address: P.O. Box 496, Tupelo, MS 38802-0496

Insurance Defense, Insurance Coverage, Automobile, Property, Fire, Arson, Fraud, First Party Matters, Bad Faith, Special Investigations, Product Liability, Automobile Liability, Uninsured and Underinsured Motorist, Professional Malpractice, Medical Malpractice, Workers' Compensation, General Liability, Premises Liability, Defense Litigation, Corporate Law, Commercial Law, Commercial Litigation, Real Estate, Transportation, Environmental Law, Toxic Torts, Bankruptcy, Creditor Rights, Labor and Employment, ERISA, Construction Litigation, Fidelity and Surety, Insurance Fraud, General Civil Practice, Trial Practice, Appellate Practice, Employment Discrimination, Coverage Analysis, Coverage Issues

SEE COMPLETE LISTING UNDER TUPELO, MISSISSIPPI (47 MILES)

SENATOBIA   † 8,165 Tate Co.

Refer To

Webb Sanders & Williams PLLC
363 North Broadway
Tupelo, Mississippi 38804
   Telephone: 662-844-2137
   Fax: 662-842-3863
Mailing Address: P.O. Box 496, Tupelo, MS 38802-0496

Insurance Defense, Insurance Coverage, Automobile, Property, Fire, Arson, Fraud, First Party Matters, Bad Faith, Special Investigations, Product Liability, Automobile Liability, Uninsured and Underinsured Motorist, Professional Malpractice, Medical Malpractice, Workers' Compensation, General Liability, Premises Liability, Defense Litigation, Corporate Law, Commercial Law, Commercial Litigation, Real Estate, Transportation, Environmental Law, Toxic Torts, Bankruptcy, Creditor Rights, Labor and Employment, ERISA, Construction Litigation, Fidelity and Surety, Insurance Fraud, General Civil Practice, Trial Practice, Appellate Practice, Employment Discrimination, Coverage Analysis, Coverage Issues

SEE COMPLETE LISTING UNDER TUPELO, MISSISSIPPI (98 MILES)

SOUTHAVEN 48,982 DeSoto Co.

Refer To

Webb Sanders & Williams PLLC
363 North Broadway
Tupelo, Mississippi 38804
   Telephone: 662-844-2137
   Fax: 662-842-3863

Mailing Address: P.O. Box 496, Tupelo, MS 38802-0496

Insurance Defense, Insurance Coverage, Automobile, Property, Fire, Arson, Fraud, First Party Matters, Bad Faith, Special Investigations, Product Liability, Automobile Liability, Uninsured and Underinsured Motorist, Professional Malpractice, Medical Malpractice, Workers' Compensation, General Liability, Premises Liability, Defense Litigation, Corporate Law, Commercial Law, Commercial Litigation, Real Estate, Transportation, Environmental Law, Toxic Torts, Bankruptcy, Creditor Rights, Labor and Employment, ERISA, Construction Litigation, Fidelity and Surety, Insurance Fraud, General Civil Practice, Trial Practice, Appellate Practice, Employment Discrimination, Coverage Analysis, Coverage Issues

SEE COMPLETE LISTING UNDER TUPELO, MISSISSIPPI (99 MILES)

STARKVILLE † 23,888 Oktibbeha Co.

Refer To

Hicks & Smith, PLLC
Regions Bank, 2nd Floor
710 Main Street
Columbus, Mississippi 39701
   Telephone: 662-243-7300
   Fax: 662-327-1485

Mailing Address: P.O. Box 1111, Columbus, MS 39703-1111

Bad Faith, Automobile, Premises Liability, Workers' Compensation, Casualty, Product Liability, Medical Malpractice, Subrogation, Class Actions, Commercial Litigation, Employment Law, Extra-Contractual Litigation, Professional Negligence, Truck Liability, Governmental Liability, Public Entities, Civil Rights, Insurance Sales Practice Litigation, Constitutional, General Insurance Defense, Admiralty, Construction, Business Litigation, Environmental Litigation

SEE COMPLETE LISTING UNDER COLUMBUS, MISSISSIPPI (25 MILES)

Refer To

Webb Sanders & Williams PLLC
363 North Broadway
Tupelo, Mississippi 38804
   Telephone: 662-844-2137
   Fax: 662-842-3863

Mailing Address: P.O. Box 496, Tupelo, MS 38802-0496

Insurance Defense, Insurance Coverage, Automobile, Property, Fire, Arson, Fraud, First Party Matters, Bad Faith, Special Investigations, Product Liability, Automobile Liability, Uninsured and Underinsured Motorist, Professional Malpractice, Medical Malpractice, Workers' Compensation, General Liability, Premises Liability, Defense Litigation, Corporate Law, Commercial Law, Commercial Litigation, Real Estate, Transportation, Environmental Law, Toxic Torts, Bankruptcy, Creditor Rights, Labor and Employment, ERISA, Construction Litigation, Fidelity and Surety, Insurance Fraud, General Civil Practice, Trial Practice, Appellate Practice, Employment Discrimination, Coverage Analysis, Coverage Issues

SEE COMPLETE LISTING UNDER TUPELO, MISSISSIPPI (67 MILES)

TUNICA † 1,030 Tunica Co.

Refer To

Webb Sanders & Williams PLLC
363 North Broadway
Tupelo, Mississippi 38804
   Telephone: 662-844-2137
   Fax: 662-842-3863

Mailing Address: P.O. Box 496, Tupelo, MS 38802-0496

Insurance Defense, Insurance Coverage, Automobile, Property, Fire, Arson, Fraud, First Party Matters, Bad Faith, Special Investigations, Product Liability, Automobile Liability, Uninsured and Underinsured Motorist, Professional Malpractice, Medical Malpractice, Workers' Compensation, General Liability, Premises Liability, Defense Litigation, Corporate Law, Commercial Law, Commercial Litigation, Real Estate, Transportation, Environmental Law, Toxic Torts, Bankruptcy, Creditor Rights, Labor and Employment, ERISA, Construction Litigation, Fidelity and Surety, Insurance Fraud, General Civil Practice, Trial Practice, Appellate Practice, Employment Discrimination, Coverage Analysis, Coverage Issues

SEE COMPLETE LISTING UNDER TUPELO, MISSISSIPPI (130 MILES)

TUPELO † 34,546 Lee Co.

Phelps Dunbar LLP

One Mississippi Plaza
201 South Spring Street, Seventh Floor
Tupelo, Mississippi 38804
   Telephone: 662-842-7907
   Fax: 662-842-3873
   E-Mail: info@phelps.com
   www.phelpsdunbar.com

(New Orleans, LA Office*: Canal Place, 365 Canal Street, Suite 2000, 70130-6534)
   (Tel: 504-566-1311)
   (Fax: 504-568-9130)
(Baton Rouge, LA Office*: II City Plaza, 400 Convention Street, Suite 1100, 70802-5618, P.O. Box 4412, 70821-4412)
   (Tel: 225-346-0285)
   (Fax: 225-381-9197)
(Jackson, MS Office*: 4270 I-55 North, 39211-6391, P.O. Box 16114, 39236-6114)
   (Tel: 601-352-2300)
   (Fax: 601-360-9777)
(Gulfport, MS Office*: NorthCourt One, 2304 19th Street, Suite 300, 39501)
   (Tel: 228-679-1130)
   (Fax: 228-679-1131)
(Houston, TX Office*: One Allen Center, 500 Dallas Street, Suite 1300, 77002)
   (Tel: 713-626-1386)
   (Fax: 713-626-1388)
(Tampa, FL Office*: 100 South Ashley Drive, Suite 1900, 33602-5311)
   (Tel: 813-472-7550)
   (Fax: 813-472-7570)
(Mobile, AL Office*: 2 North Royal Street, 36602, P.O. Box 2727, 36652-2727)
   (Tel: 251-432-4481)
   (Fax: 251-433-1820)
(London, United Kingdom Office*: Lloyd's, Suite 725, Level 7, 1 Lime Street, EC3M 7DQ)
   (Tel: 011-44-207-929-4765)
   (Fax: 011-44-207-929-0046)
(Raleigh, NC Office*: 4140 Parklake Avenue, Suite 100, 27612-3723)
   (Tel: 919-789-5300)
   (Fax: 919-789-5301)
(Southlake, TX Office*(See Dallas listing): 115 Grand Avenue, Suite 222, 76092)
   (Tel: 817-488-3134)
   (Fax: 817-488-3214)

Insurance Law

MISSISSIPPI **TUPELO**

Phelps Dunbar LLP, Tupelo, MS (Continued)

Insurance Clients

Acceptance Casualty Insurance Company
Aegis Janson Green Insurance Services Inc.
AIG
Alabama Municipal Insurance Corporation
AmTrust Underwriters, Inc.
Arch Insurance Company (Europe) Ltd.
Aspen Insurance UK Limited
Associated Aviation Underwriters
Bankers Insurance Group
Berkley Select, LLC
Bluebonnet Life Insurance Company
Britannia Steam Ship Insurance Association Ltd.
CNA
Commercial Union Insurance Company
Companion Property and Casualty Group
ELCO Administrative Services
Endurance Services, Ltd.
Erie Insurance Company
Evanston Insurance Company
Fidelity National Financial
First Premium Insurance Group, Inc.
GE Insurance Solutions
General & Cologne Life Reinsurance of America
General Star Indemnity Company
Glencoe Group
Global Special Risks, Inc.
Great American Insurance Companies
Gulf Insurance Group
The Hartford Insurance Group
Homesite Group, Inc.
ICAT Boulder Claims
Infinity Insurance Company
Lexington Insurance Company
Liberty Mutual Group
Louisiana Farm Bureau Mutual Insurance Company
Louisiana Workers' Compensation Corporation
Markel
MetLife Auto & Home
NAS Insurance Group
Nautilus Insurance Company
Old American Insurance Company
Pharmacists Mutual Insurance Company
RenaissanceRe
RLI Insurance Company
Royal & SunAlliance
SCOR Global P&C
Sedgwick Claims Management Services, Inc.
SR International Business Insurance Company, Ltd.
Steamship Mutual Underwriting Association Limited
Torus
Underwriters at Lloyd's, London
Unitrin Business Insurance
Vesta Eiendom AS
Western Heritage Insurance Company
Westport Insurance Corporation
XL Insurance Group
ACE Group of Insurance and Reinsurance Companies
Aetna Insurance Company
AFLAC - American Family Life Assurance Company of Columbus
Allstate Insurance Company
American Family Life Assurance Company of Columbus
Argonaut Insurance Company
Aspen Insurance
Aspen Re
AXIS Insurance
Beazley
Bituminous Insurance Company
Blue Cross & Blue Shield of Mississippi
Chartis Insurance
Chubb Group of Insurance Companies
Commonwealth Insurance Company
Cotton States Insurance
Criterion Claim Solutions
Employers Reinsurance Corporation
Esurance Insurance Company
Farmers Insurance Group
Fireman's Fund Insurance Company
Foremost Insurance Company
General American Life Insurance Company
General Reinsurance Corporation
General Star Management Company
Golden Rule Insurance Company
Great Southern Life Insurance Company
Hanover Insurance Group
Hermitage Insurance Company
Houston Casualty Company
Indian Harbor Insurance Company
Ironshore Insurance, Ltd.
Liberty International Underwriters
Life Insurance Company of Alabama
Louisiana Health Insurance Association
Lyndon Property Insurance Company
Munich-American Risk Partners
Nationwide Insurance
The Navigators Group, Inc.
OneBeacon Insurance Group
Prime Syndicate
QBE
Republic Western Insurance Company
St. Paul Travelers
Scottsdale Insurance Company
Sentry Insurance
Southern Farm Bureau Casualty Insurance Company
State National Insurance Company, Inc.
Terra Nova Insurance Company Limited
United States Fidelity and Guaranty Company
Victoria Insurance Group
West of England Ship Owners Mutual Insurance Association (Luxembourg)
Zurich

Member of the Firm

William M. Beasley, Sr. — The University of Mississippi, B.B.A., 1973; The University of Mississippi School of Law, J.D., 1975 — Admitted to Bar, 1975, Mississippi — Member The Mississippi Bar; Lee County Bar Association

(See listing under New Orleans, LA for additional information)

Webb Sanders & Williams PLLC

363 North Broadway
Tupelo, Mississippi 38804
Telephone: 662-844-2137
Fax: 662-842-3863
E-Mail: info@webbsanders.com
www.webbsanders.com

(Gulfport, MS Office*: 45 Hardy Court, Suite 164, 39507)
(Tel: 228-822-2137)
(Fax: 228-822-2139)

Established: 1986

Insurance Defense, Insurance Coverage, Automobile, Property, Fire, Arson, Fraud, First Party Matters, Bad Faith, Special Investigations, Product Liability, Automobile Liability, Uninsured and Underinsured Motorist, Professional Malpractice, Medical Malpractice, Workers' Compensation, General Liability, Premises Liability, Defense Litigation, Corporate Law, Commercial Law, Commercial Litigation, Real Estate, Transportation, Environmental Law, Toxic Torts, Bankruptcy, Creditor Rights, Labor and Employment, ERISA, Construction Litigation, Fidelity and Surety, Insurance Fraud, General Civil Practice, Trial Practice, Appellate Practice, Employment Discrimination, Coverage Analysis, Coverage Issues

Firm Profile: Webb Sanders & Williams PLLC, is rated AV Pre-Eminent by Martindale-Hubbell and provides counsel to businesses, individuals and insurers throughout Mississippi and the Southeast United States. With attorneys also admitted in Oklahoma, Tennessee and Alabama, we represent our clients in multiple venues.

We provide representation and advice on insurance coverage, analysis and litigation, assistance in special investigations, including arson and fraud, and commercial and financial transactions. We are also active in tort litigation of all types from premises liability to complex products liability, as well as employment cases. We handle workers compensation matters at all levels from hearings to appeals. Our attorneys are supported with highly trained and educated personnel as well as the most current technological resources and tools.

Our goal is to provide our clients, individual and corporate, with the expertise, information and personal attention necessary to fully evaluate each situation and to recommend the course of action which will produce the best result. We try cases.

Insurance Clients

Allstate Insurance Company
Brotherhood Mutual Insurance Company
Farmers Insurance Group
Foremost Insurance Company
GEICO
General Casualty Insurance Company
Global Indemnity Group, Inc.
Infinity Property & Casualty Group
MetLife Auto & Home
Mid-Continent Group
National Security Fire and Casualty Company
The Republic Group
Southern Pioneer Property and Casualty Insurance Company
State Farm Mutual Automobile Insurance Company
Vanliner Insurance Company
Auto-Owners Insurance Company
EMC Insurance Companies
Farm Bureau Insurance Company
Fidelity National Insurance Company
Gemini Insurance Company
Glatfelter Claims Management, Inc.
Harleysville Insurance Company
Liberty National Life Insurance Company
Montpelier US Insurance Company
Pennsylvania Lumbermens Mutual Insurance Company
Safeco Insurance Companies
State Auto Insurance Companies
State Farm Fire and Casualty Company
Travelers Property Casualty Corporation

Non-Insurance Clients

The Cadle Company
Ryder Truck Rental, Inc.
Tupelo Country Club
Whitaker Sales, Inc.
Montgomery Enterprises, Inc.
Safe-Guard Products International, LLC

VICKSBURG   MISSISSIPPI

Webb Sanders & Williams PLLC, Tupelo, MS (Continued)

Benjamin H. Sanders — (1942-1999)

Dan W. Webb — 1949 — University of Southern Mississippi, B.S., 1971; University of Southern California, M.S.Ed., 1974; The University of Mississippi School of Law, J.D. (Valedictorian, with distinction), 1976 — Admitted to Bar, 1977, Mississippi; U.S. District Court, Northern and Southern Districts of Mississippi; U.S. District Court, Western District of Tennessee; U.S. District Court, Eastern District of Michigan; U.S. Court of Appeals, Fifth and Eleventh Circuits; U.S. Supreme Court — Member The Mississippi Bar (Delegate, Judicial Conference of Fifth Circuit, 1984-1986); Claims and Litigation Management Alliance (CLM); Mississippi Defense Lawyers Association (President, 2000; President-Elect, 1999; Secretary/Treasurer, 1998; Chair, Northeast MS Regional Committee, 1989, 1991-1992); Association of Defense Trial Attorneys; Atlanta Claims Association; International Association of Arson Investigators; Defense Research Institute — University of MS Risk Mgmt. and Ins. Advisory Board (2000-2014; Outstanding Supporter, 2008; Chair-Elect, 2003, Chair, 2004-2005); Symposium Chairman (2005); Distinguished Service Award 2005; Outstanding Lawyers of America; Mid-South "Super Lawyer" in Insurance Coverage (2007-2014); Top Rated Lawyer In Insurance Law (2014); CLM Insurance Fraud Committee (2010-2014), Founding Co-Chair (2010); CLM Insurance Bad Faith Committee (2010-2014), Co-Chair for Region 5 MS and LA (2010-2012); ABA Advisory Panel (2008-2009); MDLA Quarterly (Editor, 1998-1999; Director, 1994-1998) — Certified Civil Trial Advocate by the National Board of Trial Advocacy — U.S. Air Force, 1971-1974 (active duty) — Practice Areas: Insurance Defense; Product Liability; Bad Faith; Insurance Coverage; Fraud; Arson; Automobile Liability; Special Investigations; Corporate Litigation; Labor and Employment; Toxic Torts; Mediation; Uninsured and Underinsured Motorist; Workers' Compensation; Commercial Litigation; Agent and Brokers Errors and Omissions — E-mail: dwebb@webbsanders.com

B. Wayne Williams — 1968 — University of Miami, B.M., 1990; The University of Mississippi, J.D., 1993 — Phi Delta Phi; Moot Court Board — Admitted to Bar, 1994, Mississippi; 1994, U.S. District Court, Northern and Southern Districts of Mississippi; 1994, U.S. Court of Appeals, Fifth Circuit — Member Mississippi Claims Association; Claims and Litigation Management Alliance (CLM) (Committees: Products Liability, 2011-2012; Premises Liability, 2011-2012; Automotive/Recreational Vehicle Subcommittee, 2011-2012); Association of Defense Trial Attorneys; Mississippi Defense Lawyers Association — Mid-South "Super Lawyer" (2011, 2013-2014) — Practice Areas: Insurance Coverage; Insurance Defense; Bad Faith; Automobile Liability; Construction Law; Product Liability; Uninsured and Underinsured Motorist; Construction Litigation; Personal Injury Defense; Alternative Dispute Resolution — E-mail: wwilliams@webbsanders.com

Roechelle R. Morgan — 1972 — The University of Mississippi, B.A., 1993; The University of Tulsa, J.D., 1998 — Phi Delta Phi; Environmental Law Journal, Staff (1996-1997) — Admitted to Bar, 1998, Oklahoma; 2002, Mississippi; 2011, Tennessee; U.S. District Court, Northern and Southern Districts of Mississippi; U.S. District Court, Eastern and Northern Districts of Oklahoma; U.S. District Court, Eastern District of Michigan; U.S. District Court, Western District of Tennessee; U.S. Court of Appeals, Fifth Circuit — Member Claims and Litigation Management Alliance (CLM) (Committees: Professional Liability, 2010; Employment Practices, 2010); Defense Research Institute; Mississippi Defense Lawyers Association — Mid-South "Rising Star" in Insurance Coverage (2010-2012); Mid-South "Super Lawyer" (2010) — Practice Areas: First Party Matters; Insurance Coverage; Professional Liability; Labor and Employment; Premises Liability; Construction Law; Environmental Law; Product Liability; Tort Litigation; Automobile Liability; Product Liability Defense; Commercial Litigation — E-mail: rmorgan@webbsanders.com

Paul N. Jenkins, Jr. — 1971 — The University of Mississippi, B.B.A., 1997; J.D., 2000 — Admitted to Bar, 2000, Mississippi; 2000, U.S. District Court, Northern and Southern Districts of Mississippi; 2000, U.S. Court of Appeals, Fifth Circuit — U.S. Marine Corp, 1989-1994 — Practice Areas: Insurance Defense; Arson; Fraud; Insurance Coverage; Bad Faith; Premises Liability; Tort Litigation; Civil Litigation — E-mail: pjenkins@webbsanders.com

Reagan D. Wise — 1975 — Mississippi State University, B.A. (magna cum laude), 1997; The University of Mississippi, J.D., 2000 — Admitted to Bar, 2000, Alabama; 2001, Mississippi; 2000, U.S. District Court, Middle, Northern and Southern Districts of Alabama; 2001, U.S. District Court, Northern and Southern Districts of Mississippi; 2001, U.S. Court of Appeals, Fifth Circuit — Practice Areas: Workers' Compensation; First and Third Party Defense; Construction Litigation; Product Liability; Uninsured and Underinsured Motorist; Bad Faith; Automobile Liability; Mediation — E-mail: rwise@webbsanders.com

Norma C. Ruff — 1958 — Mississippi State University, B.A., 1980; The University of Mississippi School of Law, J.D., 1982 — Pi Sigma Alpha —

Webb Sanders & Williams PLLC, Tupelo, MS (Continued)

Admitted to Bar, 1982, Mississippi; U.S. District Court, Northern District of Mississippi; U.S. Court of Appeals, Fifth Circuit; 2006, U.S. District Court, Southern District of Mississippi; U.S. Bankruptcy Court, Northern and Southern Districts of Mississippi — Practice Areas: Insurance Coverage; Insurance Defense; Commercial Transactions; Commercial Litigation; Business Transactions; Corporate Governance — E-mail: nruff@webbsanders.com

J. Wayne Doss, Jr. — 1976 — The University of Mississippi, B.B.A. (magna cum laude), 1998; University of Florida, J.D. (with honors), 2001 — Admitted to Bar, 2002, Mississippi; U.S. District Court, Northern and Southern Districts of Mississippi; U.S. Court of Appeals, Fifth Circuit — Member Lee County Bar Association (Past President); Lee County Young Lawyers Association (Past President) — Practice Areas: Arson; Special Investigative Unit Claims; First and Third Party Defense; Commercial Litigation; Construction Law; Premises Liability; Environmental Law; Probate — E-mail: wdoss@webbsanders.com

Catherine C. Servati — 1987 — The University of Mississippi, B.A. (magna cum laude), 2009; The University of Mississippi School of Law, J.D. (magna cum laude), 2013 — Admitted to Bar, 2013, Mississippi; U.S. District Court, Northern and Southern Districts of Mississippi — Practice Areas: Insurance Coverage & Defense; Bad Faith; Commercial Litigation; Premises Liability — E-mail: cservati@webbsanders.com

The following firms also service this area.

Hicks & Smith, PLLC
Regions Bank, 2nd Floor
710 Main Street
Columbus, Mississippi 39701
Telephone: 662-243-7300
Fax: 662-327-1485
Mailing Address: P.O. Box 1111, Columbus, MS 39703-1111

Bad Faith, Automobile, Premises Liability, Workers' Compensation, Casualty, Product Liability, Medical Malpractice, Subrogation, Class Actions, Commercial Litigation, Employment Law, Extra-Contractual Litigation, Professional Negligence, Truck Liability, Governmental Liability, Public Entities, Civil Rights, Insurance Sales Practice Litigation, Constitutional, General Insurance Defense, Admiralty, Construction, Business Litigation, Environmental Litigation

SEE COMPLETE LISTING UNDER COLUMBUS, MISSISSIPPI (63 MILES)

McNabb, Bragorgos & Burgess, PLLC
81 Monroe Avenue, Sixth Floor
Memphis, Tennessee 38103-5402
Telephone: 901-624-0640
Toll Free: 888-251-8000
Fax: 901-624-0650

Insurance Defense, Trucking Litigation, Fire, Casualty, Malpractice, Fraud, Litigation, Marine, Product Liability, Workers' Compensation, Automobile, Mass Tort, Personal Injury, Commercial Law, Premises Liability, Subrogation, Construction Law, Nursing Home Defense

SEE COMPLETE LISTING UNDER MEMPHIS, TENNESSEE (109 MILES)

VICKSBURG † 23,856 Warren Co.

Dabney and Dabney
1515 Walnut Street
Vicksburg, Mississippi 39180-3535
Telephone: 601-636-6532
Fax: 601-636-1212
Emer/After Hrs: 601-636-3887
E-Mail: dabneylaw@att.net

Established: 1794

Fire, Casualty, Surety, Life Insurance

Firm Profile: This firm was established in 1794 at Gloucester, Virginia. The firm was moved to Mississippi in 1835 and it continues to provide quality legal services in both State and Federal courts with a concentration in insurance defense, credit litigation and both Federal and State regulatory law affecting the insurance and business communities.

Dabney and Dabney, Vicksburg, MS (Continued)

Insurance Clients

Allstate Insurance Company
North American Company for Life and Health Insurance
Zurich Insurance Company
Audubon Insurance Company
Ohio Casualty Group
Southern Guaranty Insurance Company

Non-Insurance Clients

Wright General Agency

Lucius B. Dabney, Jr. — 1925 — Virginia Military Institute; The University of Mississippi, LL.B., 1949 — Admitted to Bar, 1949, Mississippi; 1949, U.S. District Court, Southern District of Mississippi; 1950, U.S. Court of Appeals, Fifth Circuit; 1971, U.S. Supreme Court — Member The Mississippi Bar (Bar Commissioner 1975-1977); Warren County Bar Association (President, 1976-77) — Corporal, Signal Corps, WWII ETO; First Lieutenant, Corps of Engineers, Korean War, 24 Infantry Division in Korea

Varner, Parker & Sessums, P.A.

1110 Jackson Street
Vicksburg, Mississippi 39180
　Telephone: 601-638-8741
　Fax: 601-638-8666
　Toll Free: 800-634-0442
　E-Mail: rep@vpslaw.com
　www.vpslaw.com

Established: 1975

Insurance Defense, Trial Practice, State and Federal Courts, Medical Malpractice, Product Liability, Commercial and Personal Lines

Firm Profile: The predecessor of the present law firm, Varner & Parker, was founded in 1976 and presently has three partners, two associates, three paralegals and a highly skilled support staff of eight secretaries. Utilizing the best technology available, the law firm is a leading trial firm in a multi-county, two-state area in Mississippi and Louisiana, specializing in insurance defense, including medical malpractice (for both physicians and health care providers), commercial and personal lines and personal injury. The firm is also capable of handling toxic tort and similar cases in a cost efficient manner. The firm has sub-specialized its members so that there is a substantial devotion of time to the areas of trials, insurance defense, estates, personal injury, corporate, banking, real estate, creditor's rights in bankruptcy and family law.

Insurance Clients

Acceptance Insurance Companies
The Doctors Company
Fireman's Fund Insurance Company
Kemper Insurance Companies
MetLife Insurance Company
Mississippi Insurance Guaranty Association
North American Reinsurance Corporation
Ranger Insurance Company
St. Paul Travelers
Union Standard Insurance Company
Brierfield Insurance Company
English & American Insurance Company Ltd.
GAB Robins North America, Inc.
Medical Assurance Company of Mississippi Inc.
National Lloyds Insurance Company
Occidental Fire & Casualty Company of North Carolina
Reliance Insurance Company
State Auto Insurance Companies

Non-Insurance Clients

Caronia Corporation
Werner Enterprises, Inc.
River Region Medical Corporation

Firm Members

J. Mack Varner — 1944 — Millsaps College, B.A., 1967; The University of Mississippi, J.D., 1970 — Admitted to Bar, 1970, Mississippi; 1970, U.S. District Court, Northern and Southern Districts of Mississippi; 1972, U.S. Court of Appeals, Fifth Circuit — Member American Bar Association; The Mississippi Bar

R. E. Parker, Jr. — 1945 — Mississippi College, B.A., 1967; The University of Mississippi, J.D., 1970 — Admitted to Bar, 1970, Mississippi; 1970, U.S. District Court, Northern and Southern Districts of Mississippi; 1972, U.S. Court of Appeals, Fifth Circuit; 1975, U.S. Supreme Court — Member

Varner, Parker & Sessums, P.A., Vicksburg, MS (Continued)

American Bar Association; The Mississippi Bar; Mississippi Defense Lawyers Association (Past Vice President); Defense Research Institute; International Association of Defense Counsel — Special Mississippi Supreme Court Judge (2006-2007); Federal District Court of Mississippi (Rules Committee); Best Lawyers in America (Medical Malpractice Defense)

David M. Sessums — 1953 — University of Southern Mississippi, B.S. (with honors), 1975; Mississippi College School of Law, J.D. (with special distinction), 1978 — Admitted to Bar, 1979, Mississippi; 1983, U.S. Court of Appeals, Fifth Circuit — Member The Mississippi Bar; Warren County Bar Association (Past President); Mississippi Board of Bar Admissions (Past Member; Character and Fitness Committee)

Clifford C. Whitney III — 1947 — The University of Texas at Austin; The George Washington University, J.D. (with honors), 1981 — Admitted to Bar, 1981, Maryland; 1996, Mississippi; 1981, U.S. District Court, District of Maryland; 1981, U.S. Court of Appeals, Fourth Circuit; 1996, U.S. District Court, Northern and Southern Districts of Mississippi; 1996, U.S. Court of Appeals, Fifth Circuit — Member The Mississippi Bar

Penny B. Lawson — 1964 — Wichita State University, B.A. (Dean's Honor Roll), 1996; Mississippi College School of Law, J.D., 2009 — Admitted to Bar, 2010, Mississippi; U.S. District Court, Northern and Southern Districts of Mississippi — Member The Mississippi Bar; Warren County Bar Association (Secretary)

The following firms also service this area.

Markow Walker, P.A.
599 Highland Colony Parkway, Suite 100
Ridgeland, Mississippi 39157
　Telephone: 601-853-1911
　Fax: 601-853-8284
Mailing Address: P.O. Box 13669, Jackson, MS 39236-3669

Insurance Defense, Product Liability, Bodily Injury, Toxic Torts, Medical Malpractice, Workers' Compensation

SEE COMPLETE LISTING UNDER JACKSON, MISSISSIPPI (45 MILES)

Webb Sanders & Williams PLLC
363 North Broadway
Tupelo, Mississippi 38804
　Telephone: 662-844-2137
　Fax: 662-842-3863
Mailing Address: P.O. Box 496, Tupelo, MS 38802-0496

Insurance Defense, Insurance Coverage, Automobile, Property, Fire, Arson, Fraud, First Party Matters, Bad Faith, Special Investigations, Product Liability, Automobile Liability, Uninsured and Underinsured Motorist, Professional Malpractice, Medical Malpractice, Workers' Compensation, General Liability, Premises Liability, Defense Litigation, Corporate Law, Commercial Law, Commercial Litigation, Real Estate, Transportation, Environmental Law, Toxic Torts, Bankruptcy, Creditor Rights, Labor and Employment, ERISA, Construction Litigation, Fidelity and Surety, Insurance Fraud, General Civil Practice, Trial Practice, Appellate Practice, Employment Discrimination, Coverage Analysis, Coverage Issues

SEE COMPLETE LISTING UNDER TUPELO, MISSISSIPPI (203 MILES)

WEST POINT † 11,307 Clay Co.

Refer To
Hicks & Smith, PLLC
Regions Bank, 2nd Floor
710 Main Street
Columbus, Mississippi 39701
　Telephone: 662-243-7300
　Fax: 662-327-1485
Mailing Address: P.O. Box 1111, Columbus, MS 39703-1111

Bad Faith, Automobile, Premises Liability, Workers' Compensation, Casualty, Product Liability, Medical Malpractice, Subrogation, Class Actions, Commercial Litigation, Employment Litigation, Extra-Contractual Litigation, Professional Negligence, Truck Liability, Governmental Liability, Public Entities, Civil Rights, Insurance Sales Practice Litigation, Constitutional, General Insurance Defense, Admiralty, Construction, Business Litigation, Environmental Litigation

SEE COMPLETE LISTING UNDER COLUMBUS, MISSISSIPPI (23 MILES)

WIGGINS † 4,390 Stone Co.
Refer To
Franke & Salloum, PLLC
10071 Lorraine Road
Gulfport, Mississippi 39503
   Telephone: 228-868-7070
   Fax: 228-868-7090
Mailing Address: P.O. Drawer 460, Gulfport, MS 39502

Insurance Defense, Medical Malpractice, General Liability, Workers' Compensation, Admiralty and Maritime Law, Product Liability, Bad Faith, Subrogation
   SEE COMPLETE LISTING UNDER GULFPORT, MISSISSIPPI (30 MILES)

YAZOO CITY † 11,403 Yazoo Co.
Refer To
Markow Walker, P.A.
599 Highland Colony Parkway, Suite 100
Ridgeland, Mississippi 39157
   Telephone: 601-853-1911
   Fax: 601-853-8284
Mailing Address: P.O. Box 13669, Jackson, MS 39236-3669

Insurance Defense, Product Liability, Bodily Injury, Toxic Torts, Medical Malpractice, Workers' Compensation
   SEE COMPLETE LISTING UNDER JACKSON, MISSISSIPPI (44 MILES)

MISSOURI

CAPITAL: JEFFERSON CITY

COUNTIES AND COUNTY SEATS

County	County Seat
Adair	Kirksville
Andrew	Savannah
Atchison	Rock Port
Audrain	Mexico
Barry	Cassville
Barton	Lamar
Bates	Butler
Benton	Warsaw
Bollinger	Marble Hill
Boone	Columbia
Buchanan	St. Joseph
Butler	Poplar Bluff
Caldwell	Kingston
Callaway	Fulton
Camden	Camdenton
Cape Girardeau	Jackson
Carroll	Carrollton
Carter	Van Buren
Cass	Harrisonville
Cedar	Stockton
Chariton	Keytesville
Christian	Ozark
Clark	Kahoka
Clay	Liberty
Clinton	Plattsburg
Cole	Jefferson City
Cooper	Boonville
Crawford	Steelville
Dade	Greenfield
Dallas	Buffalo
Daviess	Gallatin
De Kalb	Maysville
Dent	Salem
Douglas	Ava
Dunklin	Kennett
Franklin	Union
Gasconade	Hermann
Gentry	Albany
Greene	Springfield
Grundy	Trenton
Harrison	Bethany
Henry	Clinton
Hickory	Hermitage
Holt	Oregon
Howard	Fayette
Howell	West Plains
Iron	Ironton
Jackson	Independence
Jasper	Carthage
Jefferson	Hillsboro
Johnson	Warrensburg
Knox	Edina
Laclede	Lebanon
Lafayette	Lexington
Lawrence	Mount Vernon
Lewis	Monticello
Lincoln	Troy
Linn	Linneus
Livingston	Chillicothe
Macon	Macon
Madison	Fredericktown
Maries	Vienna
Marion	Palmyra
McDonald	Pineville
Mercer	Princeton
Miller	Tuscumbia
Mississippi	Charleston
Moniteau	California
Monroe	Paris
Montgomery	Montgomery City
Morgan	Versailles
New Madrid	New Madrid
Newton	Neosho
Nodaway	Maryville
Oregon	Alton
Osage	Linn
Ozark	Gainesville
Pemiscot	Caruthersville
Perry	Perryville
Pettis	Sedalia
Phelps	Rolla
Pike	Bowling Green
Platte	Platte City
Polk	Bolivar
Pulaski	Waynesville
Putnam	Unionville
Ralls	New London
Randolph	Huntsville
Ray	Richmond
Reynolds	Centerville
Ripley	Doniphan
St. Charles	St. Charles
St. Clair	Osceola
St. Francois	Farmington
Ste. Genevieve	Ste. Genevieve
St. Louis	Clayton
Saline	Marshall
Schuyler	Lancaster
Scotland	Memphis
Scott	Benton
Shannon	Eminence
Shelby	Shelbyville
Stoddard	Bloomfield
Stone	Galena
Sullivan	Milan
Taney	Forsyth
Texas	Houston
Vernon	Nevada
Warren	Warrenton
Washington	Potosi
Wayne	Greenville
Webster	Marshfield
Worth	Grant City
Wright	Hartville

In the text that follows "†" indicates County Seats.

Our files contain additional verified data on the firms listed herein. This additional information is available on request.

A.M. BEST COMPANY

MISSOURI

BOONVILLE † 8,319 Cooper Co.

Refer To

Ford, Parshall & Baker
3210 Bluff Creek Drive
Columbia, Missouri 65201-3525
 Telephone: 573-449-2613
 Fax: 573-875-8154

Casualty, Workers' Compensation, Product Liability, Life Insurance, Employment Law, Governmental Liability, Legal Malpractice, Medical Malpractice, Premises Liability

SEE COMPLETE LISTING UNDER COLUMBIA, MISSOURI (25 MILES)

CARTHAGE † 14,378 Jasper Co.

Flanigan, Lasley & Moore, LLP
130 West Fourth Street
Carthage, Missouri 64836
 Telephone: 417-358-2127
 Fax: 417-358-5335
 E-Mail: flmlaw@sbcglobal.net
 www.flaniganfirm.com

Established: 1877

Insurance Defense, Insurance Coverage, Automobile, General Civil Trial and Appellate Practice, Personal Injury, Product Liability, Truck Liability, Probate, Estate Planning, Commercial, Estate and Real Estate Litigation, Mediation Services

Firm Profile: Providing quality legal services in SW Missouri since 1877, the members of this firm are active in the community and well acquainted with the judges, court staff and the community values which influence most potential jurors. We offer services comparable to large firms without sacrificing the individualized attention provided by a country law office. The Firm has recently expanded its services to include mediation.

Insurance Clients

ACE USA	Chicago Title Insurance Company
Employers Mutual Casualty Company	Farmers Insurance Group
	Germania Select Insurance
Lincoln General Insurance Company	State Farm Mutual Automobile Insurance Company
United Fire & Casualty Company	

Partners

Laurence H. Flanigan — 1923 — University of Missouri, LL.B., 1948 — Order of the Coif — Admitted to Bar, 1948, Missouri — Member Fellow, American College of Trial Lawyers — (Retired)

William J. Lasley — 1946 — University of Missouri-Kansas City, J.D., 1971 — Law Review — Admitted to Bar, 1971, Missouri; 1971, U.S. District Court, Western District of Missouri; 1997, U.S. Court of Appeals, Eighth Circuit — Member The Missouri Bar (Board of Governors, 2004-2009); Jasper County Bar Association; Fellow, American College of Trial Lawyers

Judy C. Moore — 1960 — Missouri State University, B.S. (cum laude, with honors), 1982; The University of Texas, J.D., 1990 — Texas International Law Journal — Admitted to Bar, 1990, New Mexico; 1997, Missouri; 1991, U.S. Court of Appeals, Tenth Circuit; 1997, U.S. District Court, Western District of Missouri; 1997, U.S. Tax Court — Member Jasper County Bar Association (President, 2012-2013); Defense Research Institute; Missouri Organization of Defense Lawyers

Peter J. Lasley — 1972 — University of Missouri-Kansas City, J.D., 1998 — Law Review — Admitted to Bar, 1998, Missouri; 1998, U.S. District Court, Western District of Missouri — Member Jasper County Bar Association

Jeremy S. Workman — 1979 — Missouri Southern State University, B.S., 2001; The University of Tulsa, J.D. (with honors), 2004 — Energy Law Journal — Admitted to Bar, 2004, Missouri; 2004, U.S. District Court, Western District of Missouri — Member Jasper County Bar Association

CLAYTON † 15,939 St. Louis Co.

Refer To

Hoagland, Fitzgerald & Pranaitis
401 Market Street
Alton, Illinois 62002
 Telephone: 618-465-7745
 Fax: 618-465-3744
 Toll Free: 866-830-1066
Mailing Address: P.O. Box 130, Alton, IL 62002

Insurance Defense

SEE COMPLETE LISTING UNDER ALTON, ILLINOIS (21 MILES)

Refer To

Neville, Richards & Wuller, LLC
5 Park Place Professional Centre
Illinois Street and Fullerton Road
Belleville, Illinois 62226
 Telephone: 618-277-0900
 Fax: 618-277-0970
Mailing Address: P.O. Box 23977, Belleville, IL 62226-0070

Insurance Defense, Professional Negligence, Product Liability, Premises Liability, Automobile, Bodily Injury, Fraud, Arson, Coverage Issues, Medical Malpractice, General Liability

SEE COMPLETE LISTING UNDER BELLEVILLE, ILLINOIS (25 MILES)

COLUMBIA † 108,500 Boone Co.

Atwill & Montgomery, Attorneys at Law, LLC
28 North 8th Street, Suite 200
Columbia, Missouri 65201
 Telephone: 573-442-3000
 Fax: 573-449-1094
 E-Mail: dka@lawam.com
 www.atwillmontgomerylaw.com

Established: 2000

Automobile, Business Law, Civil Litigation, Construction Law, Disability, General Liability, Governmental Liability, Insurance Law, Labor and Employment, Medical Malpractice, Personal Injury, Premises Liability, Product Liability, Public Law, Real Estate, Trial and Appellate Practice, Workers' Compensation

Firm Profile: The law firm of Atwill & Montgomery offers broad experience serving the needs of our clients. From the simplest to the most complex cases, we provide legal services for individuals, companies, and governmental entities. We represent our clients' best interests in all forms of dispute resolution, while understanding the importance of cost containment for services provided.

Insurance Clients

ACE Property & Casualty Insurance Company	AIG Claim Services, Inc.
	Alternative Risk Services
Broadspire	Cannon Cochran Management Services, Inc.
Corporate Claims Management, Inc.	ESIS
5-Star Administrators	Gallagher Bassett Services, Inc.
Great West Casualty Company	The Hartford
Helmsman Management Services, Inc.	Liberty Mutual Insurance
	MADA Services Corporation
Michigan Millers Mutual Insurance Company	Missouri Nursing Home Insurance Trust
Missouri Petroleum Storage Tank Insurance Trust	Sedgwick CMS
	Specialty Risk Services
State Farm Insurance Company	Thomas McGee Risk Management Services
Travelers Casualty and Surety Company	

Non-Insurance Clients

A. B. Chance Company	Callaway Carriers, Inc.
Capital Region Medical Center	Cerro Flow Products, Inc.

COLUMBIA   MISSOURI

Atwill & Montgomery, Attorneys at Law, LLC, Columbia, MO (Continued)

City of Columbia, Missouri
Environmental Dynamics, Inc.
Gates Corporation
Hubbell Power Systems, Inc.
Kraft Foods, Inc.
Missouri Association of Counties
Missouri State Highway Patrol
Tyson Foods, Inc.
Columbia Public Schools
Ferrellgas
Hollister Incorporated
Killark Electric Manufacturing Company
Missouri Highway & Transportation Commission
University of Missouri

Partners

Daniel K. Atwill — University of Missouri, A.B., 1969; J.D., 1971 — Admitted to Bar, 1972, Missouri; U.S. Court of Appeals, Eighth Circuit; U.S. Court of Military Appeals — Capt., USAF, JAGC, 1972-1976

Richard L. Montgomery, Jr. — University of Missouri, B.S.B.A., 1990; University of Missouri School of Law, J.D., 1993 — Admitted to Bar, 1993, Missouri; U.S. District Court, Western District of Missouri

Associates

Alex L. Wulff — Drury University, B.A., 2008; Washburn University School of Law, J.D., 2010 — Admitted to Bar, 2011, Missouri

Henry T. Herschel — Marquette University, B.A. (with honors), 1975; Washington University in St. Louis School of Law, J.D., 1980 — Admitted to Bar, 1980, Missouri; Missouri Courts of Appeals; 1987, U.S. Supreme Court

Amanda M. Sterchi — University of Missouri-Columbia, B.S., 2009; University of Missouri-Columbia School of Law, J.D., 2012 — Admitted to Bar, 2012, Missouri

Of Counsel

Kirsten Atwill Craver — University of Missouri, B.S.B.A., 1997; University of Richmond, J.D., 2001 — Admitted to Bar, 2001, Missouri; U.S. District Court, Western District of Missouri

Ford, Parshall & Baker

3210 Bluff Creek Drive
Columbia, Missouri 65201-3525
Telephone: 573-449-2613
Fax: 573-875-8154
www.fpb-law.com

Established: 1976

Casualty, Workers' Compensation, Product Liability, Life Insurance, Employment Law, Governmental Liability, Legal Malpractice, Medical Malpractice, Premises Liability

Insurance Clients

American Family Insurance Company
Automobile Club Inter-Insurance Exchange
Cameron Mutual Insurance Company
CNA HealthPro
Corporate Claims Management, Inc.
Farmers Insurance Group
GAB Robins North America, Inc.
Gateway Insurance Company
GEICO Insurance Companies
Kemper Insurance Companies
National Chiropractic Mutual Insurance Company
Progressive Insurance Company
Safeco Insurance
Scottsdale Insurance Company
State Farm Mutual Automobile Insurance Company
United Fire & Casualty Company
American Medical International, Inc.
Bar Plan Mutual Insurance Company
CGU Hawkeye-Security Insurance Company
CNA Insurance Company
Crawford & Company
Druggists Mutual Insurance Company
Gallagher Bassett Services, Inc.
Gay & Taylor, Inc.
The Hartford Insurance Group
Millers Mutual Insurance Company
OneBeacon Insurance
Pharmacists Mutual Insurance Company
St. Paul Travelers
State Farm Fire and Casualty Company
Underwriters Adjusting Company

Lead Counsel for

Columbia Insurance Group
Columbia Mutual Insurance Company

Ford, Parshall & Baker, Columbia, MO (Continued)

Non-Insurance Clients

General Growth Properties, Inc.
Medical Defense Associates
Thomas McGee, L.C.
MCM Consultants, Inc.
Phoenix Aviation Managers, Inc.
University of Missouri Self-Insurance Plan

Firm Members

Hamp Ford — 1936 — University of Missouri, B.S., 1958; J.D., 1964 — Admitted to Bar, 1964, Missouri — Member American and Boone County Bar Associations; The Missouri Bar; Missouri Society of Hospital Attorneys; Fellow, American College of Trial Lawyers; Advocate, American Board of Trial Advocates — E-mail: hford@fpb-law.com

Jeffrey O. Parshall — 1949 — University of Missouri, B.A., 1971; J.D., 1976 — Admitted to Bar, 1976, Missouri; U.S. District Court, Western District of Missouri; 1991, U.S. Court of Appeals, Eighth Circuit; 1995, U.S. Supreme Court — Member American and Boone County Bar Associations; The Missouri Bar; Missouri Organization of Defense Lawyers (Board of Directors, 1990-1999; President, 1998-1999); Advocate, American Board of Trial Advocates; Defense Research Institute; Fellow, American College of Trial Lawyers — E-mail: jparshall@fpb-law.com

Michael R. Baker — 1955 — Southeast Missouri State University, B.S., 1976; University of Missouri, J.D., 1980 — Admitted to Bar, 1980, Missouri — Member American and Boone County Bar Associations; The Missouri Bar; Association of Trial Lawyers of America; Missouri Organization of Defense Lawyers; Defense Research Institute — E-mail: mbaker@fpb-law.com

David W. Walker — 1964 — University of Missouri-Columbia, A.B., 1986; J.D., 1989 — Admitted to Bar, 1989, Missouri; U.S. District Court, Western District of Missouri — Member American and Boone County Bar Associations; The Missouri Bar — E-mail: dwalker@fpb-law.com

Jeffrey H. Blaylock — 1961 — University of Missouri-Columbia, B.S.B.A., 1983; J.D., 1986 — Admitted to Bar, 1986, Missouri; U.S. District Court, Western District of Missouri — Member American (Tort and Insurance Section) and Boone County Bar Associations; The Missouri Bar (School Law Committee); Missouri Organization of Defense Lawyers — E-mail: jblaylock@fpb-law.com

Emily Little — 1975 — Rhodes College, B.A., 1997; The University of Tennessee Knoxville, J.D., 2000 — Admitted to Bar, 2000, Missouri; U.S. District Court, Western District of Missouri — Member The Missouri Bar; Boone County Bar Association; Missouri Organization of Defense Lawyers — E-mail: elittle@fpb-law.com

Associates

Jill Jackson — 1969 — Columbia College, B.S., 1992; University of Missouri, J.D., 1995 — Admitted to Bar, 1995, Missouri — E-mail: jjackson@fpb-law.com

Michael P. Robertson — 1970 — Oberlin College, B.A., 1992; The University of Chicago, M.A., 1994; The University of Texas, J.D., 2009 — Admitted to Bar, 2010, Missouri — Member The Missouri Bar; Boone County Bar Association; Missouri Organization of Defense Lawyers — E-mail: mrobertson@fpb-law.com

Joshua C. Devine — 1981 — Truman State University, B.S., 2003; University of Missouri, J.D., 2007 — Admitted to Bar, 2007, Missouri; Illinois — Member Illinois State and Boone County Bar Associations; The Missouri Bar; Missouri Organization of Defense Lawyers — E-mail: jdevine@fpb-law.com

Clayton L. Thompson — 1986 — University of Missouri, B.A., 2009; J.D., 2012 — Admitted to Bar, 2012, Missouri; U.S. District Court, Eastern and Western Districts of Missouri — Member The Missouri Bar; Boone County Bar Association; Missouri Organization of Defense Lawyers — E-mail: cthompson@fpb-law.com

Ryan Redmon — 1974 — University of Indianapolis, B.A., 1996; University of Notre Dame Law School, J.D., 2001 — Admitted to Bar, 2001, Indiana; 2008, Arizona; 2013, Missouri — Member The Missouri Bar; Boone County Bar Association; Missouri Organization of Defense Lawyers — E-mail: rredmon@fpb-law.com

MISSOURI

The following firms also service this area.

Gibbs Pool and Turner, P.C.
3225 Emerald Lane, Suite A
Jefferson City, Missouri 65109-6864
  Telephone: 573-636-2614
  Fax: 573-636-6541

Civil Litigation, Insurance Defense, Medical Malpractice, Workers' Compensation, Administrative Law, Government Affairs, Professional Liability, Directors and Officers Liability, Employer Liability, Construction Law, Mechanics Liens, Estate Planning, Health Law, Construction Contracts, Trusts and Estates, Mergers, Acquisitions, Divestitures, Employee Rights and Employee Litigation

SEE COMPLETE LISTING UNDER JEFFERSON CITY, MISSOURI (32 MILES)

Sanders Warren & Russell LLP
420 Nichols Road, Suite 200
Kansas City, Missouri 64112
  Telephone: 913-234-6100
  Fax: 913-234-6199

Insurance Defense, Business Law, Automobile, Property, Homeowners, Life Insurance, Commercial Law, Professional Liability, Municipal Law, Employment Law, Workers' Compensation, Comprehensive General Liability, Alternative Dispute Resolution, Appellate Practice, Bad Faith, Construction Litigation, Governmental Liability, Insurance Coverage, Medical Malpractice, Premises Liability, Product Liability, Truck Liability

SEE COMPLETE LISTING UNDER KANSAS CITY, MISSOURI (124 MILES)

FULTON † 12,790 Callaway Co.

Refer To
Ford, Parshall & Baker
3210 Bluff Creek Drive
Columbia, Missouri 65201-3525
  Telephone: 573-449-2613
  Fax: 573-875-8154

Casualty, Workers' Compensation, Product Liability, Life Insurance, Employment Law, Governmental Liability, Legal Malpractice, Medical Malpractice, Premises Liability

SEE COMPLETE LISTING UNDER COLUMBIA, MISSOURI (30 MILES)

HOUSTON † 2,081 Texas Co.

Refer To
Williams, Robinson, Rigler & Buschjost, P.C.
901 North Pine Street, Fourth Floor
Rolla, Missouri 65401
  Telephone: 573-341-2266
  Fax: 573-341-5864
Mailing Address: P.O. Box 47, Rolla, MO 65402

Insurance Defense, Insurance Litigation, Automobile, Premises Liability, Product Liability, Insurance Coverage, Professional Negligence, Agriculture, Appellate Practice, Business Law, Civil Litigation, Corporate Law, Commercial Law, Employment Law, Environmental Law, Health Care, Medical Malpractice, Municipal Law, Personal Injury, Trial Practice, Truck Liability, Wrongful Death

SEE COMPLETE LISTING UNDER ROLLA, MISSOURI (48 MILES)

INDEPENDENCE † 116,830 Jackson Co.

Refer To
Logan Logan & Watson, L.C.
8340 Mission Road
Prairie Village, Kansas 66206
  Telephone: 913-381-1121
  Fax: 913-381-6546

Insurance Law, Trial and Appellate Practice, Commercial Law, General Liability, Professional Liability, Property, Legal Malpractice, Medical Malpractice, Product Liability, Coverage Issues, Automobile

SEE COMPLETE LISTING UNDER PRAIRIE VILLAGE, KANSAS (20 MILES)

FULTON

JEFFERSON CITY † 43,079 Cole Co.

Armstrong Teasdale LLP

3405 West Truman Boulevard, Suite 210
Jefferson City, Missouri 65109-5713
  Telephone: 573-636-8394
  Fax: 573-636-8457
  Toll Free: 800-243-5070
  E-Mail: armstrongteasdale@armstrongteasdale.com
  www.armstrongteasdale.com

(Additional Offices: St. Louis, MO*; Kansas City, MO*; Las Vegas, NV; Shanghai, China-PRC)

Established: 1901

Accident, Disability, Health, Life Insurance, Bad Faith, Class Actions, Directors and Officers Liability, ERISA, Errors and Omissions, Excess and Reinsurance, Extra-Contractual Litigation, Fraud, Insurance Coverage, Medical Malpractice, Property and Casualty, Asbestos Litigation, Business Law, Construction Litigation, Coverage Analysis, Deceptive Trade Practices, Environmental Law, Intellectual Property, Product Liability, Securities and Investments

Attorney Contacts

Sherry L. Doctorian — Truman State University, B.A. (cum laude), 1982; University of Missouri-Columbia School of Law, J.D., 1988 — Admitted to Bar, 1988, Missouri — Practice Areas: Health Care; Insurance Coverage; Insurance Litigation; Litigation — E-mail: sdoctorian@armstrongteasdale.com

J. Kent Lowry — Westminster College, B.A. (cum laude), 1974; University of Missouri-Columbia, J.D., 1977 — Admitted to Bar, 1977, Missouri — Practice Areas: Tort; Business Litigation; Health Care; Alternative Dispute Resolution — E-mail: klowry@armstrongteasdale.com

(See listing under St. Louis and Kansas City, MO for additional information)

Gibbs Pool and Turner, P.C.

3225 Emerald Lane, Suite A
Jefferson City, Missouri 65109-6864
  Telephone: 573-636-2614
  Fax: 573-636-6541
  www.gibbspoolturner.com

(Columbia, MO Office: 1603 Chapel Hill Road, Suite 201, 65203)

Civil Litigation, Insurance Defense, Medical Malpractice, Workers' Compensation, Administrative Law, Government Affairs, Professional Liability, Directors and Officers Liability, Employer Liability, Construction Law, Mechanics Liens, Estate Planning, Health Law, Construction Contracts, Trusts and Estates, Mergers, Acquisitions, Divestitures, Employee Rights and Employee Litigation

Firm Profile: Gibbs Pool and Turner, P.C. is an established law firm specializing in civil litigation, business law and estate planning. Gibbs Pool and Turner, P.C. is committed to providing outstanding legal representation. Located in Jefferson City and Columbia, Missouri it serves not only the Mid-Missouri area but also represents clients throughout the entire state of Missouri.

Our representative clients and results are a testament to the firm's commitment to high quality representation. Martindale-Hubbell® has provided a rating of "AV" Preeminent, the highest rating possible, to Scott Pool in the categories of Litigation, Medical Malpractice, Professional Liability, Legal Ability, and Ethical Standards.

JEFFERSON CITY

MISSOURI

Gibbs Pool and Turner, P.C., Jefferson City, MO (Continued)

Insurance Clients

Accident Fund Insurance Company of America
Amerisure Insurance Company
Capson Physicians Insurance Company
Continental Western Insurance Company
GAB Robins North America, Inc.
Intermed Insurance Company
Missouri Automobile Dealers Association Self Insured Workers' Compensation Trust
Missouri Professionals Mutual Professional Liability Insurance Company of America
Alternative Risk Services
American Family Insurance Group
Benchmark Insurance Company
CNA Insurance Company
Columbia Insurance Group
The Doctors Company
Federated Mutual Insurance Company
Medicus Insurance Company
Missouri Employers Mutual Insurance Company
Missouri Intergovernmental Risk Management Association (MIRMA)
Western Litigation, Inc.

Non-Insurance Clients

Missouri Highway & Transportation Commission

Partners

Hallie H. Gibbs II — 1961 — Southern Methodist University, B.B.A., 1984; University of Missouri-Columbia, J.D., 1987 — Admitted to Bar, 1987, Missouri; U.S. District Court, Western District of Missouri — Member The Missouri Bar; Cole County Bar Association; American Health Lawyers Association — E-mail: hgibbs@gptlaw.net

Scott R. Pool — 1968 — Southwest Missouri State University, B.S., 1990; University of Arkansas, J.D., 1993 — Admitted to Bar, 1993, Missouri; U.S. District Court, Eastern and Western Districts of Missouri — Member The Missouri Bar; Cole County Bar Association (President, 2009) — Rated AV (highest rating possible) by Martindale-Hubbell® — E-mail: pool@gptlaw.net

Susan M. Turner — 1946 — St. Luke's Hospital School of Nursing, Diploma, 1969; Lincoln University, B.A., 1983; University of Missouri-Columbia, J.D., 1989 — Admitted to Bar, 1989, Missouri; U.S. District Court, Western District of Missouri — Member The Missouri Bar; Cole County Bar Association — E-mail: turner@gptlaw.net

Associates

Michael J. Henderson — 1983 — Denison University, B.A., 2006; University of Missouri-Columbia School of Law, J.D., 2010 — Admitted to Bar, 2010, Missouri; U.S. District Court, Western District of Missouri — Member The Missouri Bar; Cole County Bar Association

Zachary J. Kluesner — 1987 — University of Missouri-Columbia, B.S.B.A. (magna cum laude), 2010; J.D., 2013 — Admitted to Bar, 2013, Missouri; U.S. District Court, Western District of Missouri — Member The Missouri Bar; Cole County Bar Association — E-mail: zkluesner@gptlaw.net

Nicholas P. Meriage — 1983 — University of Missouri-Columbia, B.S., 2005; J.D., 2013 — Admitted to Bar, 2013, Missouri; U.S. District Court, Eastern and Western Districts of Missouri — Member The Missouri Bar; Cole County Bar Association — E-mail: nmeriage@gptlaw.net

Inglish & Monaco, P.C.

237 East High Street
Jefferson City, Missouri 65101
Telephone: 573-634-2522
Fax: 573-634-4526
E-Mail: inglishmonaco@inglishmonaco.com

Established: 1962

Insurance Defense, Regulatory and Compliance, Property and Casualty, Health, General Liability, Automobile Liability, Workers' Compensation, Investigation and Adjustment

Insurance Clients

ACE USA Companies
Allegheny Casualty Company
American Community Mutual Insurance Company
Affirmative Insurance Company
Allstate Life Insurance Company
American Fidelity and Liberty Insurance Company

Inglish & Monaco, P.C., Jefferson City, MO (Continued)

American Investors Insurance Company
American Modern Home Insurance Company
Automobile Club Inter-Insurance Exchange
Blue Cross Blue Shield of Illinois
Capital Reserve Life Insurance Company
Central Security Life Insurance Company
CNA Insurance Companies
Commonwealth Land Title Insurance Company
Farmers Mutual Hail Insurance Company of Iowa
Fidelity National Title Insurance Company
Fireman's Fund Insurance Company
Funeral Directors Life Insurance Company
Golden Rule Insurance Company
Grain Dealers Mutual Insurance Company
The Hartford Insurance Group
Investors Insurance Company, Inc.
John Hancock Financial Services
Lawyers Title Insurance Corporation
Marsh & McLennan Companies
Maxum Casualty Insurance Company
Midwest Employers Casualty Company
National Alliance Insurance Company
National Guardian Life Insurance Company
Pacific Indemnity Company
The Principal Financial Group
Providence Property and Casualty Insurance Company
Reserve National Insurance Company
Scottish Re Life Corporation
State-Wide Insurance Company
Transamerica Assurance Company
Union Labor Life Insurance Company
Vanliner Insurance Company
Vision Service Plan Insurance Company
Westport Insurance Corporation
American Life and Health Insurance Company
Arch Insurance Company
Associated Insurance Group
Bankers United Life Assurance Company
Bristol West Insurance Group
Caterpillar Insurance Company
Caterpillar Life Insurance Company
Citizens Insurance Company of America
Continental General Insurance Company
Farmers New World Life Insurance Company
Financial Benefit Life Insurance Company
First Marine Insurance Company
Forethought Life Insurance Company
General Casualty Company of Wisconsin
Great West Casualty Company
Great Western Insurance Company
Homesteaders Life Company
Jackson National Life Insurance Company
Lyndon Property Insurance Company
Massachusetts Mutual Life Insurance Company
Medicus Insurance Company
Monumental Life Insurance Company
National Aviation Underwriters
National General Insurance Company
Naught-Naught Insurance Agency
Pekin Life Insurance Company
Protective Life Insurance Company
Providers Fidelity Life Insurance Company
Savers Property and Casualty Insurance Company
Security National Life Insurance Company
Trinity Universal Insurance Company
United Fire & Casualty Company
Vesta Insurance Group, Inc.
WellCare Health Plans, Inc.
Western Surety Company
Zenith Insurance Company

Non-Insurance Clients

Caterpillar Inc.
Caterpillar Product Services Corporation
Deutsche Bank AG
Surplus Lines Association of Missouri
West Corporation
Caterpillar Insurance Services Corporation
Central Crop Insurance Services
Service Corporation International (SCI, Inc.)
UBS Investment Bank

Firm Members

John W. Inglish — (1921-2008)

William Barton — (1906-2004)

Charles P. Dribben — (1929-1991)

Andrew Jackson Higgins — (Deceased)

Nicholas M. Monaco — 1930 — University of Missouri, A.B., 1952; J.D., 1958 — Order of the Barristers Award, University of Missouri at Columbia, 1984 — Admitted to Bar, 1958, Missouri; 1958, U.S. Supreme Court — Member American (Insurance Negligence and Compensation Law Section) and Cole County Bar Associations; The Missour Bar (Chairman, Insurance Law Committee, 1977-1979); Federation of Regulatory Counsel (Founder, Sec-Treas.); National Alliance of Life Companies (Board Member); Missouri Division of Insurance (Legal Staff Member, 1958-1960; Counsel, 1960-1962) — Author: "Missouri Suicide Statute: St. Louis Bar Journel, 1960; "Life Insurance Company Litigation, "National Underwriter, 1985; "Regulation of Insurance in Missouri, "Missouri Bar-Missouri Insurance Practice Manual 1977, Update 1991; Editor, Missouri Insurance Practice

MISSOURI

Inglish & Monaco, P.C., Jefferson City, MO (Continued)

Manual, 1976 — Lecturer, Missouri Bar Insurance Law, Continuing Legal Education, (1986-Present); Missouri Judicial College Instructor (1995)

Ann Monaco Warren — 1959 — Saint Mary's College, B.A., 1982; St. Mary's University, J.D., 1985 — Law Clerk to U.S. Bankruptcy Judge, Eastern District of Texas, 1988-1991 — Admitted to Bar, 1985, Texas; 1992, Oklahoma; Missouri; 1986, U.S. District Court, Eastern District of Texas; 1992, U.S. District Court, Western District of Oklahoma; 1992, U.S. District Court, Western District of Missouri — Member The Missouri Bar (Chair, Missouri Insurance Law Committee, 2002-2004); Oklahoma and Cole County (President, 2000) Bar Associations; State Bar of Texas; Mid-Missouri Claim Association (President, 1995); Federation of Regulatory Counsel — Author: Missouri Bar Insurance Practice Manual

Mark G. R. Warren — 1958 — The University of Texas at Tyler, B.S., 1990; Oklahoma City University, J.D., 1993 — Moot Court Board — Law Review — Admitted to Bar, 1993, Missouri; 1993, U.S. District Court, Western District of Missouri — Member Co-Author: Missouri Bar Insurance Practice Manual; Federation of Regulatory Counsel — City Attorney, New Bloomfield, Missouri, City of Eldon, Missouri

Associate

Todd E. Irelan — 1973 — University of Missouri-Kansas City, J.D., 2007 — Admitted to Bar, 2008, Missouri

---

The following firms also service this area.

Ford, Parshall & Baker
3210 Bluff Creek Drive
Columbia, Missouri 65201-3525
Telephone: 573-449-2613
Fax: 573-875-8154

Casualty, Workers' Compensation, Product Liability, Life Insurance, Employment Law, Governmental Liability, Legal Malpractice, Medical Malpractice, Premises Liability

SEE COMPLETE LISTING UNDER COLUMBIA, MISSOURI (30 MILES)

JOPLIN 50,150 Jasper Co.

Refer To

Baird Lightner Millsap, P.C.
1901-C South Ventura Avenue
Springfield, Missouri 65804
Telephone: 417-887-0133
Fax: 417-887-8740

Automobile, Banking, Business Formation, Civil Defense, Commercial Litigation, Corporate Governance, Employment Law, Estate Planning, Government Affairs, Insurance Law, Intellectual Property, Mergers and Acquisitions, Municipal Law, Personal Injury, Professional Liability, Property and Casualty, Real Estate, School Law, Trusts, Nonprofit Organizations

SEE COMPLETE LISTING UNDER SPRINGFIELD, MISSOURI (70 MILES)

Refer To

Flanigan, Lasley & Moore, LLP
130 West Fourth Street
Carthage, Missouri 64836
Telephone: 417-358-2127
Fax: 417-358-5335

Mailing Address: P.O. Box 272, Carthage, MO 64836

Insurance Defense, Insurance Coverage, Automobile, General Civil Trial and Appellate Practice, Personal Injury, Product Liability, Truck Liability, Probate, Estate Planning, Commercial, Estate and Real Estate Litigation, Mediation Services

SEE COMPLETE LISTING UNDER CARTHAGE, MISSOURI (18 MILES)

JOPLIN

KANSAS CITY † 459,787 Jackson Co.

Armstrong Teasdale LLP
2345 Grand Boulevard, Suite 1500
Kansas City, Missouri 64108-2617
Telephone: 816-221-3420
Fax: 816-221-0786
Toll Free: 800-243-5070
E-Mail: armstrongteasdale@armstrongteasdale.com
www.armstrongteasdale.com

(Additional Offices: St. Louis, MO*; Jefferson City, MO*; Las Vegas, NV; Shanghai, China-PRC)

Established: 1883

Accident, Disability, Health, Life Insurance, Bad Faith, Class Actions, Directors and Officers Liability, ERISA, Errors and Omissions, Excess and Reinsurance, Extra-Contractual Litigation, Fraud, Insurance Coverage, Medical Malpractice, Property and Casualty, Asbestos Litigation, Business Law, Construction Litigation, Coverage Analysis, Deceptive Trade Practices, Environmental Law, Intellectual Property, Product Liability, Securities and Investments

Contact

Gerald A. King — Rockhurst College, B.S.B.A. (cum laude), 1987; University of Missouri-Kansas City, J.D., 1990 — Admitted to Bar, 1990, Missouri; 1991, Kansas — E-mail: gking@armstrongteasdale.com

(See listing under St. Louis and Jefferson City, MO for additional information)

Baty, Holm, Numrich & Otto, P.C.
4600 Madison Avenue, Suite 210
Kansas City, Missouri 64112
Telephone: 816-531-7200
Fax: 816-531-7201
E-Mail: lbaty@batyholm.com
www.batyholm.com

Personal Injury, Product Liability, Wrongful Death, Premises Liability, Transportation, Business Litigation, Construction Litigation, Employment Litigation, Insurance Coverage, Automobile, Bad Faith, Nursing Home Liability, Asbestos, Medical Malpractice, Workers' Compensation

Firm Profile: Baty, Holm, Numrich & Otto, P.C. has been approved by many national insurers to represent their policy holders in a variety of litigation matters throughout the Midwest. With decades of experience, we guide our clients through the claims process: Investigating, Defending and Providing counsel.

Insurance Clients

CNA Insurance Company	The Hartford
Lexington Insurance Company/AIG	Scottsdale Insurance Company
	Sedgwick Group
State Auto Insurance Companies	Travelers
Western World Insurance Company	Zurich North America

Managing Partner

Lee M. Baty — University of Notre Dame, B.A., 1978; University of Missouri-Columbia School of Law, J.D., 1981 — Admitted to Bar, 1981, Missouri; 2010, Kansas; 1981, U.S. District Court, Districts of Missouri and Kansas — Member The Missouri Bar; Kansas Bar Association; Kansas City Metropolitan Bar Association; Missouri Organization of Defense Lawyers; Defense Research Institute — AV Preeminent, Martindale-Hubbel; Best

KANSAS CITY											MISSOURI

Baty, Holm, Numrich & Otto, P.C., Kansas City, MO (Continued)

Lawyers in America; Missouri/Kansas Super Lawyer — Practice Areas: Personal Injury; Insurance Coverage; Construction Litigation; Business Litigation; Transportation; Nursing Home/Medical Malpractice — E-mail: lbaty@batyholm.com

Shareholders

Theresa A. Otto — Rockhurst College, B.A. Political Science (magna cum laude), 1989; University of Notre Dame Law School, J.D., 1992 — Thomas J. White Scholar — Admitted to Bar, 1992, Missouri; 1995, Kansas; 1992, U.S. District Court, District of Missouri; 1995, U.S. District Court, District of Kansas — Member The Missouri Bar; Kansas Bar Association; Kansas City Metropolitan Bar Association; Missouri Organization of Defense Lawyers; Association for Women Lawyers; Fellow, Litigation Counsel of America — AV Preeminent, Martindale-Hubbel; Missouri/Kansas Super Lawyer; Women's Justice Award, Missouri Lawyers Weekly; Best of the Bar, Kansas City Business Journal; Influential Woman Award, Kansas City Business Magazine; 40 under 40, Ingram's Magazine — Practice Areas: Personal Injury; Transportation; Employment Litigation; Construction Defect — E-mail: totto@batyholm.com

John J. Gates — Vanderbilt University, B.A., 1997; The University of Kansas School of Law, J.D., 2000 — Admitted to Bar, 2000, Missouri; 2001, Kansas; 2000, U.S. District Court, Western District of Missouri; 2001, U.S. District Court, District of Kansas — Member Risk and Insurance Management Society (RIMS); Greater Kansas City Claims Association; Missouri Organization of Defense Lawyers — AV Preeminent, Martindale-Hubbel; Best of the Bar, Kansas City Business Journal; Rising Star, Thomson Reuters — Practice Areas: Personal Injury; Insurance Coverage; Business Law; Business Litigation; Construction Defect; Transportation; Nursing Home Liability — E-mail: jgates@batyholm.com

Brown & Ruprecht, PC

911 Main Street, Suite 2300
Kansas City, Missouri 64105-5319
Telephone: 816-292-7000
Fax: 816-292-7050
www.brlawkc.com

Established: 1975

Declaratory Judgments, Agent and Brokers Errors and Omissions, Architects and Engineers, Bad Faith, Civil Litigation, Construction Law, Fidelity and Surety, Insurance Defense, General Liability, Medical Malpractice, Product Liability, Professional Liability, Property and Casualty, Reinsurance, Toxic Torts, Mediation, Alternative Dispute Resolution, Trial Practice, Aging Services Defense, Coverage Analysis, Coverage Litigation, Transactional/Business, Long Term Care Defense

Insurance Clients

Arrowpoint Capital Group
CNA HealthPro
Fireman's Fund Insurance Company
Ohio Casualty Insurance Company
RiverStone Claims Management, LLC
St. Paul Travelers
Chubb Executive Risk, Inc.
Employers Mutual Casualty Company
Navigators Insurance Company
Ophthalmic Mutual Insurance Company
RSUI Indemnity Company

Shareholders

Stephen S. Brown — 1946 — University of Missouri, B.S.B.A., 1968; University of Missouri-Kansas City, J.D., 1971 — Recipient, Lon O. Hocker Memorial Trial Lawyers Award of the Missouri Bar Foundation (1981); Best of the Bar, Business Journal Award (2003-2013) — Staff Member, University of Missouri at Kansas City Law Review — Admitted to Bar, 1971, Missouri; U.S. District Court, Western District of Missouri; U.S. Court of Appeals, Tenth Circuit; U.S. Court of Appeals, Eighth Circuit; U.S. District Court, District of Kansas — Member American and Kansas City Metropolitan Bar Associations; Kansas City Society of Health Care Attorneys; Association of Missouri Mediators; Missouri Organization of Defense Lawyers — Named Super Lawyer (2005-2014) — Certified Mediator — Practice Areas: Professional Liability; Civil Litigation; Mediation — E-mail: sbrown@brlawkc.com

Brown & Ruprecht, PC, Kansas City, MO (Continued)

John L. Hayob — 1950 — Rockhurst College, A.B., 1972; University of Missouri-Kansas City, J.D., 1975 — Admitted to Bar, 1975, Missouri; U.S. District Court, Western District of Missouri; 1997, U.S. Court of Appeals, Tenth Circuit; 1998, U.S. District Court, District of Kansas; 1999, U.S. Court of Appeals, Eighth Circuit; 2000, U.S. District Court, Eastern District of Missouri — Member American and Kansas City Metropolitan Bar Associations; The Missouri Bar; Defense Research Institute; Missouri Organization of Defense Lawyers — Named Super Lawyer (Law and Politics, 2008-2013) — Practice Areas: Civil Litigation; Insurance Coverage; Insurance Litigation; Mediation; Alternative Dispute Resolution — E-mail: jhayob@brlawkc.com

Matthew M. Merrill — 1974 — The University of Kansas, B.G.S., 1996; J.D., 1998 — Best of the Bar, Kansas City Business Journal (2010, 2012) — Admitted to Bar, 1999, Kansas; 2000, Missouri; 1999, U.S. District Court, District of Kansas; 2000, U.S. District Court, Western District of Missouri; 2003, U.S. Court of Appeals, Tenth Circuit — Member Kansas City Metropolitan Bar Association; Kansas Association of Defense Council; Missouri Organization of Defense Lawyers; Defense Research Institute — Top 50 Attorneys in Kansas City as published in KC Magazine, 2012; Missouri and Kansas Super Lawyers (2009-2014) — Practice Areas: Civil Litigation; Medical Malpractice Defense; Aging Services Defense; Personal Injury Litigation; Commercial Litigation — E-mail: mmerrill@brlawkc.com

Case Linden P.C.

2600 Grand Boulevard, Suite 300
Kansas City, Missouri 64108
Telephone: 816-979-1500
Fax: 816-979-1501
E-Mail: kevin.case@caselinden.com
www.caselinden.com

(St. Louis, MO Office*: Two City Place Drive, 2nd Floor, 63141)
(Tel: 314-812-4750)
(Fax: 314-812-4755)

Appellate Practice, Bodily Injury, Civil Trial Practice, Class Actions, Commercial Litigation, Discrimination, Errors and Omissions, Insurance Defense, Labor and Employment, Legal Malpractice, Medical Malpractice, Premises Liability, Product Liability, Professional Liability, Regulatory and Compliance, Tort, Workers' Compensation

Firm Profile: Case Linden P.C. is a firm of experienced trial attorneys engaged in the prosecution and defense of civil cases in state and federal courts throughout Kansas and Missouri.

The firm maintains an active trial practice in Columbia, Jefferson City, Hays, Kansas City, Olathe, Springfield, St. Louis, Topeka and Wichita.

Insurance Clients

American Specialty Insurance & Risk Services, Inc.
Colony Insurance Group
Gallagher Bassett Services, Inc.
Harco National Insurance Company
Kansas County Association Multiline Pool (KCAMP)
Metropolitan Life Insurance Company
Philadelphia Insurance Companies
TIG Insurance Company
Universal Underwriters Insurance Company
Arch Insurance Company
Chicago Insurance Company
Fireman's Fund Insurance Companies
Interstate Fire & Casualty Company
Lancer Claims Services, Inc.
Metropolitan Group Property & Casualty Insurance Company
National Surety Corporation
Steadfast Insurance Company
Travelers Property Casualty Company of America
Zurich North America

Shareholders

Kevin D. Case — Baylor University, B.A., 1984; M.A., 1987; The University of Kansas, J.D., 1990 — Admitted to Bar, 1990, Kansas; 1991, Missouri; U.S. District Court, District of Kansas; U.S. District Court, Eastern and Western Districts of Missouri; U.S. Court of Appeals, Eighth and Tenth Circuits; U.S. Supreme Court — Member Kansas and Kansas City Metropolitan Bar Associations; National Association of Dealers Counsel; Universal Underwriters Insurance Company Defense Counsel Advisory Council (2003-2007); Zurich N.A. Defense Counsel Advisory Council (2009-); Defense Research Institute

MISSOURI — KANSAS CITY

Case Linden P.C., Kansas City, MO (Continued)

Patric S. Linden — Kansas State University, B.A., 1994; The University of Kansas, J.D., 1997 — Admitted to Bar, 1997, Kansas; 1998, Missouri; U.S. District Court, District of Kansas; U.S. District Court, Western District of Missouri; U.S. Court of Appeals, Eighth and Tenth Circuits; U.S. Supreme Court — Member Defense Research Institute

Randi L. Tangney — The Pennsylvania State University, B.A., 2004; Saint Louis University School of Law, J.D., 2007 — Admitted to Bar, 2008, Missouri; 2010, Kansas; U.S. District Court, Eastern and Western Districts of Missouri; U.S. District Court, District of Kansas; U.S. Court of Appeals, Eighth Circuit; 2011, Cherokee Nation Tribal Courts

David V. Cascio — Marquette University, B.A., 2007; The University of Kansas School of Law, J.D., 2010 — Admitted to Bar, 2010, Missouri; 2011, Kansas; 2012, Illinois; U.S. District Court, Eastern and Western Districts of Missouri; U.S. District Court, District of Kansas

Associates

Michael C. Skidgel — The University of Kansas, B.S., 2006; University of California, Hastings College of the Law, J.D., 2009 — Admitted to Bar, 2009, Missouri; 2010, Kansas; U.S. District Court, Western District of Missouri; U.S. District Court, District of Kansas; U.S. Court of Appeals, Eighth and Tenth Circuits

Ryan S. VanFleet — Wichita State University, B.S., 2006; University of Missouri-Kansas City School of Law, J.D., 2011 — Admitted to Bar, 2011, Missouri; 2012, Kansas; U.S. District Court, Eastern and Western Districts of Missouri; U.S. District Court, District of Kansas

Kyle S. Belew — University of Central Arkansas, B.A. (magna cum laude), 2006; University of Missouri-Kansas City School of Law, J.D., 2009 — Admitted to Bar, 2009, Missouri; 2010, Kansas

Samantha J. Horner — The University of Kansas, B.S./B.A., 2005; The University of Kansas School of Law, J.D., 2012 — Admitted to Bar, 2013, Missouri; Kansas; U.S. District Court, District of Kansas; U.S. District Court, Eastern and Western Districts of Missouri

Ryan J. Loehr — Wichita State University, B.S., 1997; Washburn University School of Law, J.D. (with honors), 2012 — Admitted to Bar, 2012, Kansas; 2014, Missouri

Lori A. Fluegel — William Woods College, B.B., 1987; University of Missouri-Kansas City School of Law, J.D., 1990 — Admitted to Bar, 1991, Missouri

Jacob L. Kurtz — Missouri State University, B.A., 2011; University of Missouri-Kansas City School of Law, J.D., 2014 — Admitted to Bar, 2014, Missouri

Coronado Katz LLC

14 West Third Street, Suite 200
Kansas City, Missouri 64105
Telephone: 816-410-6600
Fax: 816-337-3892
E-Mail: steve@coronadokatz.com
www.coronadokatz.com

Bad Faith, Construction Defect, Employment Discrimination, Governmental Liability, Personal Injury, Product Liability

Firm Profile: Insurance companies and their insureds turn to Coronado Katz LLC for trusted advice, guidance and advocacy in a broad range of legal areas. With more than a century of combined trial experience and a long history of success, we are thoroughly prepared to represent our clients' interests in court when necessary.

Insurance Clients

GuideOne Insurance
OneBeacon Insurance
Sompo Japan Insurance Company of America
Missouri Public Entity Risk Management Fund (MOPERM)

Members

Steven F. Coronado — University of Missouri-Kansas City, B.A., 1980; University of Missouri-Kansas City School of Law, J.D., 1989 — Admitted to Bar, 1989, Missouri; 1990, Kansas; 1989, U.S. District Court, Western District of Missouri; 1990, U.S. District Court, District of Kansas; 1993, U.S. Court of Appeals, Tenth Circuit; 1996, U.S. Court of Appeals, Eighth Circuit;

Coronado Katz LLC, Kansas City, MO (Continued)

2008, U.S. Supreme Court; 2010, U.S. Court of Appeals for the Federal Circuit — Languages: Spanish

Mark D. Katz — State University of New York at Binghamton, B.A., 1982; University at Buffalo Law School, J.D., 1985 — Admitted to Bar, 1986, Missouri; 1987, Kansas; 1986, U.S. District Court, Western District of Missouri; 1987, U.S. District Court, District of Kansas; 1997, U.S. Court of Appeals, Tenth Circuit; 2000, U.S. Court of Appeals, Eighth Circuit; 2001, U.S. Supreme Court; 2010, U.S. Court of Appeals for the Federal Circuit

Deacy and Deacy, LLP

Ten Main Center
920 Main Street, Suite 1900
Kansas City, Missouri 64105-2010
Telephone: 816-421-4000
Fax: 816-421-7880
E-Mail: dlb@deacylaw.com
www.deacylaw.com

Insurance Defense, Legal Malpractice, General Liability

Insurance Clients

Bar Plan Mutual Insurance Company
Great American Insurance Company
State Farm Mutual Automobile Insurance Company
Columbia Insurance Group
Dairyland Insurance Company
State Farm Fire and Casualty Company
Travelers Insurance Group

Partners

Thomas E. Deacy — (1894-1967)

Thomas E. Deacy, Jr. — 1918 — The University of Chicago, M.B.A., 1949; University of Missouri-Columbia, LL.B., 1940 — Admitted to Bar, 1940, Missouri; 1946, Illinois — Member American Bar Association (Commission on Standards of Judicial Administration, 1972-1974; Standing Committee on Federal Judiciary, 1974-1980); Illinois State, Kansas City Metropolitan and Chicago Bar Associations; The Missouri Bar; Legal Club of Chicago; Lawyers Association of Kansas City; Fellow, American College of Trial Lawyers (Regent, 1968-1972, 1974; President, 1975-1976); American Law Institute; American Bar Foundation

Spencer J. Brown — 1940 — Rockhurst College, B.S.B.A., 1961; Saint Louis University, LL.B., 1964 — Admitted to Bar, 1964, Missouri — Member Kansas City Metropolitan Bar Association; The Missouri Bar (Chairman, Civil Practice and Procedure Committee, 1976, 1977; Advisory Committee on Administration, 1977-1984; Civil Rules Committee, 1977-present); Lawyers Association of Kansas City; Fellow, American College of Trial Lawyers (Regent, 1995-present); American Bar Foundation

Dale L. Beckerman — 1949 — Amherst College, B.A., 1971; The George Washington University, J.D. (with honors), 1975 — Admitted to Bar, 1976, District of Columbia; Missouri; 1993, Kansas — Member American and Kansas City Metropolitan Bar Associations; The Missouri Bar; Lawyers Association of Kansas City; International Association of Defense Counsel (Chair, Casualty Insurance Committee, 2000-2002); Defense Research Institute

Russell C. Ashley — 1953 — University of Missouri, B.S., 1975; The George Washington University, J.D. (with honors), 1979 — Admitted to Bar, 1979, Missouri — Member Kansas City Metropolitan Bar Association; The Missouri Bar

Daniel E. Hamann — 1954 — University of Missouri-Columbia, B.S., 1975; J.D., 1979 — Admitted to Bar, 1979, Missouri — Member American and Kansas City Metropolitan Bar Associations; The Missouri Bar

Thomas M. Deacy — 1954 — St. Lawrence University; Pitzer College, B.A., 1978; The University of Kansas, J.D., 1981 — Admitted to Bar, 1982, Missouri — Member American and Kansas City Metropolitan Bar Associations; The Missouri Bar; Lawyers Association of Kansas City

Mimi E. Doherty — 1960 — Stanford University, B.A., 1982; Creighton University School of Law; University of California, Hastings College of the Law, J.D., 1985 — Admitted to Bar, 1985, Missouri; 1992, Kansas — Member Kansas and Kansas City Metropolitan Bar Associations; The Missouri Bar; Lawyers Association of Kansas City

KANSAS CITY   MISSOURI

Deacy and Deacy, LLP, Kansas City, MO   (Continued)

Associates

Meghan E. Lewis — 1984 — University of Missouri-Columbia, B.A., 2006; University of Missouri School of Law, J.D., 2009 — Admitted to Bar, 2009, Missouri; 2010, Kansas — Member American and Kansas City Metropolitan Bar Associations; Association of Women Lawyers of Greater Kansas City

Tanya M. Redecker Wendt — 1980 — University of Nebraska-Lincoln, B.A. (with distinction), 2002; The University of Kansas School of Law, J.D., 2005 — Admitted to Bar, 2005, Missouri; 2006, Kansas — Member Kansas and Kansas City Metropolitan Bar Associations; The Missouri Bar; Association of Women Lawyers

Ensz & Jester, P.C.

2121 City Center Square
1100 Main Street
Kansas City, Missouri 64105
  Telephone: 816-474-8010
  Fax: 816-471-7910
  www.enszjester.com

Established: 1982

Insurance Defense, Property Damage, Professional Liability, Bodily Injury, Automobile, General Liability, Workers' Compensation, Governmental Liability, Agriculture, Employer Liability, Employment Defense

Insurance Clients

ACUITY
Harco National Insurance
  Company
Missouri Public Entity Risk
  Management Fund (MOPERM)
Traders Insurance Company
Chubb Group of Insurance
  Companies
Lititz Mutual Insurance Company
MPR-Midwest Public Risk
Philadelphia Insurance Companies

Non-Insurance Clients

Mechanical Breakdown Protection,
  Inc.

Partners

James H. Ensz — 1944 — University of Nebraska-Lincoln, B.S., 1966; J.D., 1969 — Phi Delta Phi — Admitted to Bar, 1969, Nebraska; 1972, Missouri; 1990, Kansas; 2002, U.S. District Court, Western District of Missouri; 2004, U.S. District Court, District of Kansas — Member The Missouri Bar; Kansas City Metropolitan Bar Association — E-mail: jensz@enszjester.com

Robert O. Jester — 1946 — Southwest Baptist College, A.A., 1966; Drury College, B.A., 1968; University of Missouri-Kansas City, J.D., 1973 — Phi Alpha Delta — Admitted to Bar, 1974, Missouri; 1999, U.S. District Court, Western District of Missouri; 2003, U.S. District Court, District of Kansas — Member American and Kansas City Metropolitan Bar Associations; The Missouri Bar; Defense Research Institute — E-mail: rjester@enszjester.com

Brandon D. Mizner — 1966 — University of Nebraska, B.S.B.A., 1988; Pepperdine University, J.D. (cum laude), 1992 — Admitted to Bar, 1992, California; 1995, Missouri; Nebraska; 1997, Kansas; 2001, U.S. District Court, Western District of Missouri; 2003, U.S. District Court, District of Kansas — Member American and Kansas City Metropolitan Bar Associations; The Missouri Bar — E-mail: bmizner@enszjester.com

Matthew J. Gist — 1975 — The University of Kansas, B.G.S., 1998; J.D., 2002 — Admitted to Bar, 2002, Kansas; Missouri; 2002, U.S. District Court, Western District of Missouri; 2002, U.S. District Court, District of Kansas — Member American, Kansas and Kansas City Metropolitan Bar Associations; The Missouri Bar — E-mail: mgist@enszjester.com

Wesley J. Carrillo — 1982 — Missouri Southern State University, B.A., 2005; University of Missouri-Kansas City School of Law, J.D., 2008 — Admitted to Bar, 2008, Missouri; 2009, Kansas — E-mail: wcarrillo@enszjester.com

Associates

Benjamin A. Stelter-Embry — 1973 — Bates College, B.A., 1995; Kansas University, M.S., 2001; University of Missouri-Kansas City School of Law, J.D., 2012 — Admitted to Bar, 2012, Missouri; 2013, Kansas — E-mail: bstelter-embry@enszjester.com

Ensz & Jester, P.C., Kansas City, MO   (Continued)

Remington Smith — 1982 — Truman State University, B.S., 2005; University of Missouri-Columbia School of Law, J.D., 2008 — Admitted to Bar, 2008, Missouri — E-mail: rsmith@enszjester.com

Franke Schultz & Mullen, P.C.

8900 Ward Parkway
Kansas City, Missouri 64114
  Telephone: 816-421-7100
  Fax: 816-421-7915
  E-Mail: fsm@fsmlawfirm.com
  www.fsmlawfirm.com

(Springfield, MO Office*: 5000 South Highland Springs Boulevard, 65809)
  (Tel: 417-863-0040)
  (Fax: 417-863-6286)
  (E-Mail: info@fsmlawfirm.com)
(St. Louis, MO Office: Two City Place, Second Floor, 64131)
  (Tel: 314-812-4780)
  (Fax: 816-421-7915)

Established: 1992

Insurance Defense, Automobile, Homeowners, Truck Liability, Property and Casualty, Personal Injury, Commercial Casualty

Firm Profile: Franke Schultz & Mullen offers an aggressive, practical and cost-efficient approach to our clients' matters. We are committed to providing exceptional legal services in all facets of civil litigation, but what sets us apart is the fact that our lawyers are dedicated to resolving cases through jury trials. The partners in the firm have collectively tried over 500 jury trials.

While the lawyers in our firm are committed to taking cases to trial, we recognize that the vast majority of cases settle prior to trial. To that end, at the outset of each case, we develop a case specific litigation plan that outlines the key issues and factual disputes and identifies the most cost-efficient and effective strategy for resolving the case.

Our partners do not merely manage the work of others, but are pro-actively involved in every case.

Insurance Clients

Allmark Services, Inc.
American National Property and
  Casualty Company
Billings Mutual Insurance
  Company
Fireman's Fund Insurance
  Company
GuideOne Insurance
The Hartford/Omni Insurance
  Group
Meadowbrook Insurance Company
Metropolitan Property and Casualty
  Insurance Company
Northland Insurance Company
Progressive Insurance Group
Reinsurance Underwriters
Royal & SunAlliance
Safeco Insurance
SECURA Insurance, A Mutual
  Company
Traders Insurance Company
United Fire & Casualty Group
American Family Mutual Insurance
  Company
Benchmark Insurance Company
Capitol Indemnity Corporation
Chubb Group
Gallagher Bassett Services, Inc.
Gateway Insurance Company
Gulf Insurance Company
Home Insurance Company
The Insurance Group
Meridian Insurance Company
Midwest Mutual Insurance
  Company
Ohio Casualty Insurance Company
Redland Insurance Company
Republic Western Insurance
  Company
Sagamore Insurance Company
Sentry Claims Services
State Auto Insurance Companies
Trustgard Insurance Company

Non-Insurance Clients

Associated Wholesale Grocers
Marriott International, Inc.
Equiva Services, LLC

Partners

John E. Franke — 1962 — University of Missouri-Columbia, B.A., 1984; University of Missouri-Kansas City, J.D., 1987 — Admitted to Bar, 1987, Missouri; 1988, Kansas; 1987, U.S. District Court, Western District of Missouri; 1988, U.S. District Court, District of Kansas — Member American and Kansas City Metropolitan Bar Associations; Kansas City Claims Association; Missouri Organization of Defense Lawyers

MISSOURI
KANSAS CITY

Franke Schultz & Mullen, P.C., Kansas City, MO
(Continued)

John L. Mullen — 1966 — Southwest Missouri State University, B.S., 1988; Loyola University, J.D., 1991 — Admitted to Bar, 1991, Missouri; 1991, U.S. District Court, Western District of Missouri; 1991, U.S. Court of Appeals, Eighth and Tenth Circuits — Member American, Kansas City Metropolitan and Springfield Metropolitan Bar Associations; The Missouri Bar; Kansas City and Springfield Claims Associations; Missouri Organization of Defense Lawyers

John G. Schultz — 1962 — Central Michigan University; University of Missouri-Columbia, B.A., 1983; J.D., 1987 — Law Clerk to U.S. Magistrate Robert D. Kingsland, 1987-1988 — Admitted to Bar, 1987, Missouri; 1987, U.S. District Court, Eastern and Western Districts of Missouri — Member American Bar Association; The Missouri Bar; Kansas City Claims Association; Missouri Organization of Defense Lawyers

Ryan E. Karaim — 1961 — The University of North Dakota, B.B.A., 1984; Washburn University, J.D., 1987 — Admitted to Bar, 1987, Missouri; 1988, Kansas; 1987, U.S. District Court, Western District of Missouri; 1988, U.S. District Court, District of Kansas; 1988, U.S. Court of Appeals, Eighth and Tenth Circuits — Member American, Kansas and Kansas City Bar Associations; The Missouri Bar; Kansas City Claims Association; Missouri Organization of Defense Lawyers

Jill Frost-Smith — 1963 — Kansas State University, B.S., 1984; The University of Tulsa, J.D., 1988 — Admitted to Bar, 1988, Missouri — Member American and Kansas City Metropolitan Bar Associations; Kansas City Claims Association; Missouri Organization of Defense Lawyers

Bradley C. Nielsen — 1964 — The University of Iowa, B.A., 1986; J.D., 1989 — Admitted to Bar, 1989, Missouri; 1989, U.S. District Court, Eastern and Western Districts of Missouri; 1989, U.S. Court of Appeals, Eighth Circuit — Member American and Kansas City Bar Associations; The Missouri Bar; Kansas City Claims Association; Missouri Organization of Defense Lawyers

Keith A. Cary — 1953 — University of Missouri-Columbia, B.A., 1975; The University of Chicago, M.A., 1976; University of Missouri-Columbia, J.D., 1985 — Admitted to Bar, 1985, Missouri; 1998, Kansas; 1985, U.S. District Court, Western District of Missouri; 1998, U.S. Court of Appeals, Eighth Circuit — Member The Missouri Bar; Kansas City Metropolitan Bar Association; Missouri Organization of Defense Lawyers

Michael J. Tubbesing — 1964 — University of Notre Dame, B.A., 1986; University of Missouri-Kansas City, J.D., 1994 — Admitted to Bar, 1994, Missouri — Member American, Kansas and Kansas City Metropolitan Bar Associations

Nikki Cannezzaro — The University of Kansas, B.A., 1997; University of Missouri-Kansas City, J.D., 2000 — Admitted to Bar, 2000, Missouri; 2001, Kansas — Member Kansas and Kansas City Metropolitan Bar Associations; Lawyers Association of Kansas City; Association for Women Lawyers

Pamela Welch — 1978 — Kansas State University, B.A. (cum laude), 2000; University of Missouri-Kansas City, J.D., 2003 — Admitted to Bar, 2003, Missouri; 2004, Kansas — Member Kansas City Metropolitan Bar Association; Association of Women Lawyers; Missouri Organization of Defense Lawyers

Suzanne R. Bruss — 1972 — Iowa State University, B.A., 1994; Drake University Law School, J.D., 1997 — Admitted to Bar, 1997, Missouri; Kansas — Member Kansas and Kansas City Metropolitan Bar Associations; The Missouri Bar; State Bar of Arizona; Defense Research Institute

Nick P. Hillyard — 1978 — University of Missouri-Kansas City, J.D., 2000 — Admitted to Bar, 2005, Missouri; 2006, Kansas — Member The Missouri Bar; Kansas City Bar Association

Derek J. Johannsen — 1981 — Saint Louis University, B.S., 2003; University of Missouri-Kansas City School of Law, J.D., 2005 — Admitted to Bar, 2006, Kansas; 2007, Missouri; 2006, U.S. District Court, District of Kansas; 2006, U.S. District Court, Eastern and Western Districts of Missouri

Rachel D. Stahle — The University of Iowa, B.S./B.A., 2004; The University of Kansas, J.D., 2009 — Admitted to Bar, 2009, Kansas; Missouri; U.S. District Court, District of Kansas; U.S. District Court, Western District of Missouri — Member American and Kansas City Bar Associations; Association of Women Lawyers; Ross T. Roberts Inn of Court — Graduate, KC MBA Bar Leadership Academy

Associate

Christopher A. Brackman — University of Missouri-Columbia, B.S., 2001; University of Missouri-Kansas City School of Law, J.D., 2004 — Admitted to Bar, 2004, Missouri; 2005, Kansas; U.S. District Court, District of Kansas; U.S. District Court, Eastern and Western Districts of Missouri — Member Kansas and Kansas City Metropolitan Bar Associations; The Missouri Bar;

Franke Schultz & Mullen, P.C., Kansas City, MO
(Continued)

Ross T. Roberts Inn of Court — Graduate, KC MBA Bar Leadership Academy

Manz Swanson Hall Willson Fogarty & Gellis, P.C.

1000 Walnut Street, Suite 800
Kansas City, Missouri 64106
Telephone: 816-472-5310
Fax: 816-472-5320
www.mslawkc.com

Established: 2005

General Civil Trial and Appellate Practice, Civil Litigation, Insurance Defense, Insurance Law, Insurance Coverage, Personal Injury, Property Loss, Product Liability, Professional Liability, Architects and Engineers, Construction Litigation, Builders Risk, Automobile Liability, Truck Liability, Arson, Fraud, Business Interruption, Workers' Compensation, Construction Liability, Fire, Casualty, Commercial and Industrial, Homeowners Property Losses

Firm Profile: Manz Swanson Hall Fogarty & Gellis, P.C. - Our only business is trying lawsuits. With real and substantial trial experience honed by decades of practice, our attorneys will work with you to develop an appropriate case management plan and budget.

Insurance Clients

Allstate Insurance Company
CNA Insurance Companies
Nationwide Insurance
State Farm Insurance Company
American Family Insurance Company
Shelter Insurance Companies

Shareholders

Stephen D. Manz — University of Central Missouri, B.S., 1967; University of Missouri-Kansas City, J.D., 1970 — Admitted to Bar, 1970, Missouri; U.S. District Court, Western District of Missouri; U.S. Court of Appeals, Eighth and Tenth Circuits; U.S. Supreme Court — Member Kansas City Metropolitan Bar Association; Professional Fire and Fraud Investigators Assoc. of MO; Kansas City Arson Task Force; Missouri Advisory Committee on Arson Prevention; Kansas City Metropolitan Insurance Fraud Task Force; Council on Litigation Management; International Association of Arson Investigators — E-mail: Smanz@msmlawkc.com

Eric T. Swanson — Tulane University, B.S., 1972; Ohio Northern University, J.D., 1975 — Admitted to Bar, 1975, Missouri; U.S. District Court, Western District of Missouri; U.S. District Court, District of Kansas; U.S. Court of Appeals, Eighth and Tenth Circuits — Member Kansas City Metropolitan Bar Association — E-mail: Eswanson@mslawkc.com

Theresa Shean Hall — Stephens College, B.A./B.F.A., 1975; University of Missouri-Kansas City, J.D., 1980 — Admitted to Bar, 1980, Missouri; U.S. District Court, Western District of Missouri; U.S. District Court, District of Kansas; U.S. Court of Appeals, Eighth and Tenth Circuits — Member Kansas City Metropolitan Bar Association — E-mail: Thall@mslawkc.com

John J. Fogarty III — University of Missouri-Columbia, B.S./B.A., 2002; University of Missouri-Kansas City School of Law, J.D., 2005 — Admitted to Bar, 2005, Missouri; 2006, Kansas — Member The Missouri Bar (Insurance Law Committee; Tort Law Committee); Kansas City Metropolitan Bar Association; Missouri Organization of Defense Lawyers — E-mail: Jfogarty@mslawkc.com

David A. Gellis — University of South Carolina, B.S.C.J., 1998; Stetson University College of Law, J.D. (summa cum laude), 2003 — Admitted to Bar, 2003, Florida; 2006, Missouri; U.S. District Court, Western District of Missouri; U.S. District Court, District of Kansas — Member Kansas City Metropolitan Bar Association; Missouri Organization of Defense Lawyers — E-mail: Dgellis@mslawkc.com

Of Counsel

Desarae G. Harrah — The University of Kansas, B.A./B.S., 2002; University of Missouri-Kansas City School of Law, J.D., 2005 — Law Clerk to Hon. Vernon E. Scoville, III — Admitted to Bar, 2005, Missouri; 2007, Kansas; 2005, U.S. District Court, Eastern and Western Districts of Missouri; 2005, U.S. Court of Appeals, Eighth and Tenth Circuits; 2007, U.S. District Court,

KANSAS CITY   MISSOURI

Manz Swanson Hall Willson Fogarty & Gellis, P.C., Kansas City, MO (Continued)

District of Kansas — Member American Bar Association — E-mail: Dharrah@mslawkc.com

Associate Attorney

Sheila D. Verduzco — University of Missouri-Kansas City, B.A., 2001; University of Missouri-Kansas City School of Law, J.D., 2004 — Admitted to Bar, 2004, Missouri; 2005, Kansas; 2008, U.S. District Court, Western District of Missouri; 2008, U.S. District Court, District of Kansas; 2013, U.S. Court of Appeals, Tenth Circuit — Member Kansas City Metropolitan Bar Association; Association of Women Lawyers of Greater Kansas City — E-mail: Sverduzco@mslawkc.com

Morrow Willnauer Klosterman Church, LLC

10401 Holmes Road, Suite 300
Kansas City, Missouri 64131
Telephone: 816-382-1382
Fax: 816-382-1383
http://mwklaw.com

(St. Louis, MO Office*: 500 North Broadway, Suite 1420, 63102)
(Tel: 314-561-7300)
(Fax: 314-875-9215)
(E-Mail: kweston@mwklaw.com)
(mwklaw.com)
(Omaha, NE Office*: 1299 Farnam Street, Suite 250, 68102)
(Tel: 402-934-0100)
(Fax: 402-330-1425)
(E-Mail: kweston@mwklaw.com)

Construction Liability, Coverage Analysis, Employment Law, Personal Injury, Premises Liability, Product Liability, Professional Liability, Public Entities, Transportation, Trucking Liability, Workers' Compensation

Firm Profile: At Morrow Willnauer Klosterman Church, LLC, the client relationship comes first. MWKC serves commercial, government, and individual clients' in civil litigation, workers' compensation and corporate law.

Insurance Clients

Farmers Insurance Company   Federated Mutual Insurance Company

Members

James C. Morrow — University of Missouri-Columbia, B.S./B.A., 1980; J.D., 1983 — Note and Comment Editor, Missouri Law Review (1982 and 1983) — Admitted to Bar, 1983, Missouri; 1988, Kansas; 2003, Nebraska; U.S. District Court, District of Kansas; U.S. District Court, Eastern and Western Districts of Missouri; U.S. Court of Appeals, Eighth and Tenth Circuits; U.S. Supreme Court — Member The Missouri Bar; Kansas Bar Association; Nebraska State Bar Association; Kansas City Metropolitan Bar Association; Missouri Organization of Defense Lawyers (Board of Directors, 2004-2012); Council on Litigation Management; Missouri Association of Trial Attorneys; International Order of Barristers; Defense Research Institute; American College of Trial Lawyers; American Board of Trial Advocates; International Association of Defense Counsel — Author: "Perjured Alibi Testimony: The Defense Attorney's Conflicting Duties," 48 Missouri Law Review 257, 1983 — Best Lawyers in America 2015

Gary J. Willnauer — Park College, B.A. (summa cum laude), 1984; University of Missouri-Kansas City, J.D., 1988 — Order of Barristers; Recipient of the Terry Thomas Trial Practice Achievement Award; UMKC National Trial Competition Team; Urban Lawyers Contributor — Admitted to Bar, 1988, Missouri; 1989, Connecticut; 1990, Kansas; U.S. District Court, District of Kansas; U.S. District Court, District of Connecticut; U.S. District Court, Eastern and Western Districts of Missouri; U.S. Court of Appeals, Eighth and Tenth Circuits — Member American Bar Association; The Missouri Bar; Connecticut Bar Association; Kansas Bar Association; Kansas City Metropolitan Bar Association; Missouri Organization of Defense Lawyers (Board of Directors, 2012-Present)

M. Joan Klosterman — Avila College, B.A., 1973; M.S., 1983; University of Missouri-Kansas City, J.D., 1988 — Admitted to Bar, 1988, Missouri; 1989,

Morrow Willnauer Klosterman Church, LLC, Kansas City, MO (Continued)

Kansas; 2003, Nebraska — Member The Missouri Bar; Nebraska State Bar Association; Kansas Bar Association; Kansas City Metropolitan Bar Association; Missouri Self-Insured Association; Defense Research Institute; Missouri Organization of Defense Lawyers

Daniel F. Church — The University of Kansas, B.S., 1976; Washburn University School of Law, J.D., 1984 — Admitted to Bar, 1984, Kansas; 1985, Missouri; 2011, Nebraska; U.S. District Court, District of Kansas; U.S. District Court, Eastern and Western Districts of Missouri; U.S. Court of Appeals, Eighth and Tenth Circuits; U.S. Supreme Court — Member The Missouri Bar; Kansas Bar Association; Johnson County Bar Association; Kansas City Metropolitan Bar Association; Lawyers Association of Kansas City; American Society of Association Executives; National Association of Railroad Trial Counsel

Michael T. Moulder — University of Missouri, B.S./B.A., 1992; J.D., 1995 — Admitted to Bar, 1995, Missouri; 1996, Kansas — Member The Missouri Bar; Kansas Bar Association; Kansas City Metropolitan Bar Association; Missouri Association of Trial Attorneys; Missouri Organization of Defense Lawyers

Thomas G. Munsell — University of Missouri-Columbia, B.S./B.A., 1991; J.D., 1994 — Admitted to Bar, 1994, Missouri; 1995, Kansas; 1994, U.S. District Court, Western District of Missouri; 1995, U.S. District Court, District of Kansas; 2004, U.S. District Court, Eastern District of Missouri — Member The Missouri Bar; Kansas Bar Association; Kansas City Metropolitan Bar Association; Missouri Organization of Defense Lawyers

Randall W. Schroer — University of Missouri-Columbia, B.A., 1981; Washburn University School of Law, J.D., 1986 — Admitted to Bar, 1986, Kansas; 1987, Missouri; 2009, Iowa — Member The Missouri Bar; Kansas Bar Association; Iowa State Bar Association; Kansas City Metropolitan Bar Association

Peggy A. Wilson — Avila College, B.A., 1990; University of Missouri-Kansas City, J.D., 1998 — Admitted to Bar, 1998, Missouri; 1999, Kansas; U.S. District Court, Western District of Missouri; U.S. District Court, District of Kansas — Member The Missouri Bar; Kansas Bar Association; Johnson County Bar Association; Kansas City Metropolitan Bar Association

Associates

Patrick J. Allegri   Alisa R. Ashlock
John R. Barber   Jaudon R. Godsey
Hillary Hyde   Michael J. Kelly
Carolyn M. McCarthy   Deborah F. O'Connor
Laura A. Rhea   Terra Tecchio
Marshall Woody

Of Counsel

Stanley B. Gillespie   Julie Jorgensen
Claudio E. Molteni

Sanders Warren & Russell LLP

420 Nichols Road, Suite 200
Kansas City, Missouri 64112
Telephone: 913-234-6100
Fax: 913-234-6199
www.swrllp.com

(Overland Park, KS Office*: 40 Corporate Woods, 9401 Indian Creen Parkway, Suite 1250, 66210)
(Tel: 913-234-6100)
(Fax: 913-234-6199)
(E-Mail: b.sanders@swrllp.com)
(E-Mail: r.warren@swrllp.com)
(E-Mail: b.russell@swrllp.com)
(Springfield, MO Office*: American National Center 2-102, 1949 East Sunshine, 65804)
(Tel: 417-281-5100)
(Fax: 417-281-5199)

Established: 1999

MISSOURI KANSAS CITY

Sanders Warren & Russell LLP, Kansas City, MO (Continued)

Insurance Defense, Business Law, Automobile, Property, Homeowners, Life Insurance, Commercial Law, Professional Liability, Municipal Law, Employment Law, Workers' Compensation, Comprehensive General Liability, Alternative Dispute Resolution, Appellate Practice, Bad Faith, Construction Litigation, Governmental Liability, Insurance Coverage, Medical Malpractice, Premises Liability, Product Liability, Truck Liability

(See listing under Overland Park, KS for additional information)

Wagstaff & Cartmell, LLP

4740 Grand Avenue, Suite 300
Kansas City, Missouri 64112-2255
Telephone: 816-701-1100
Fax: 816-531-2372
www.wagstaffcartmell.com

Established: 1997

Insurance Defense, Medical Malpractice, General Liability, Professional Liability, Product Liability

Insurance Clients

ACE USA
Health Care Indemnity, Inc.
Intermed Insurance Company
Beazley, USA
Healthcare Services Group
The Medical Protective Company

Non-Insurance Clients

CBS News, Inc. / CBS Broadcasting, Inc.
Dairy Farmers of America
St. Luke's Hospital of Kansas City
Watco Companies, LLC
Children's Mercy Hospital
Curran Paint & Varnish
John Knox Village
The State of Kansas

Partners

Thomas W. Wagstaff — 1946 — Williams College, A.B., 1968; The University of Kansas, J.D., 1972 — Admitted to Bar, 1972, Missouri; 2006, Kansas — Member American and Kansas City Metropolitan Bar Associations; The Missouri Bar; Lawyers Association of Kansas City; Missouri Organization of Defense Lawyers — E-mail: twwagstaff@wcllp.com

Thomas P. Cartmell — 1968 — The University of Kansas, B.S., 1989; J.D., 1994 — Admitted to Bar, 1994, Missouri; 1995, Kansas — Member The Missouri Bar; Kansas, Johnson County and Kansas City Metropolitan Bar Associations; Missouri Organization of Defense Lawyers — E-mail: tcartmell@wcllp.com

Marc K. Erickson — 1969 — Miami University, B.A. (magna cum laude), 1991; The University of Kansas, J.D., 1994 — Admitted to Bar, 1994, Missouri; 1995, Kansas — Member The Missouri Bar; Kansas, Johnson County and Kansas City Metropolitan Bar Associations; Missouri Organization of Defense Lawyers — E-mail: merickson@wcllp.com

Jonathan P. Kieffer — 1964 — University of Missouri-Kansas City, B.A., 1990; The University of Kansas, J.D., 1997 — Admitted to Bar, 1997, Missouri; 1998, Kansas — Member The Missouri Bar; Kansas City Metropolitan Bar Association — E-mail: jpkieffer@wcllp.com

Thomas L. Wagstaff — 1973 — DePauw University, B.A., 1995; The University of Kansas, J.D., 1998 — Admitted to Bar, 1999, Missouri; 2000, Kansas — Member The Missouri Bar; Kansas City Metropolitan Bar Association — E-mail: t.l.wagstaff@wcllp.com

Eric D. Barton — 1969 — Kansas State University, B.S. (magna cum laude), 1990; The University of Kansas, J.D., 1993 — Admitted to Bar, 1993, Utah; 1994, Kansas; 2002, Missouri — Member Kansas City Metropolitan Bar Association; Missouri Organization of Defense Lawyers — E-mail: ebarton@wcllp.com

Brian J. Madden — 1966 — Rockhurst University, B.A. (summa cum laude), 1989; University of Missouri-Kansas City, J.D., 1992 — Admitted to Bar, 1992, Missouri; 1993, Kansas — Member American and Kansas City Metropolitan Bar Associations; The Missouri Bar — E-mail: bmadden@wcllp.com

Jeffrey M. Kuntz — 1974 — The University of Kansas, B.A., 1996; J.D., 2000 — Admitted to Bar, 2000, Missouri; 2001, Kansas — Member American Bar Association; Kansas City Metropolitan Bar Association — E-mail: jkuntz@wcllp.com

Thomas J. Preuss — 1978 — Rockhurst University, B.S. (cum laude), 2000; University of Missouri-Kansas City, J.D., 2003 — Admitted to Bar, 2003, Missouri; 2004, Kansas — Member Kansas City Metropolitan Bar Association — E-mail: tjpreuss@wcllp.com

Thomas A. Rottinghaus — 1972 — The University of Kansas, B.A., 1995; J.D., 1998 — Admitted to Bar, 1998, Missouri; 1999, Kansas — Member The Missouri Bar; Kansas, Wyandotte County and Kansas City Metropolitan Bar Associations; Missouri Organization of Defense Lawyers — E-mail: trottinghaus@wcllp.com

Brandon D. Henry — 1977 — Washburn University of Topeka, B.A., 2000; Kansas University, J.D., 2003 — Admitted to Bar, 2004, Missouri; Kansas — Member American, Kansas and Kansas City Metropolitan Bar Associations — E-mail: bhenry@wcllp.com

Tyler W. Hudson — 1976 — Baker University, B.S., 1998; Kansas University, J.D., 2001 — Admitted to Bar, 2001, Kansas; 2002, Missouri; 2004, District of Columbia — E-mail: thudso@wcllp.com

Diane K. Watkins — 1975 — Kansas State University, B.S., 1997; The University of Kansas, J.D., 2000 — Admitted to Bar, 2001, Colorado; 2003, Kansas; 2005, Missouri — Member The Missouri Bar; Kansas Bar Association — E-mail: dwatkins@wcllp.com

Sarah B. Ruane — 1981 — Wake Forest University, B.A., 2003; Kansas University, J.D., 2006 — Admitted to Bar, 2006, Missouri; 2007, Kansas — Member The Missouri Bar; Kansas City Metropolitan Bar Association — E-mail: sruane@wcllp.com

Christopher L. Schnieders — 1979 — Boston College, B.A. (with honors), 2002; Kansas University, J.D., 2005 — Admitted to Bar, 2005, Missouri; 2006, Kansas; Illinois — E-mail: cschnieders@wcllp.com

Counsel

Diana L. Beckman — 1981 — Miami University, B.A., 2002; The University of Kansas School of Law, J.D., 2005 — Admitted to Bar, 2005, Missouri; 2006, Kansas — Member American and Kansas City Metropolitan Bar Associations — E-mail: dbeckman@wcllp.com

Associates

Vanessa H. Gross — 1983 — University of Florida, B.A., 2005; Vanderbilt University Law School, J.D., 2008 — Admitted to Bar, 2008, Missouri; 2009, Kansas — Member The Missouri Bar; Kansas City Metropolitan Bar Associaton — E-mail: vgross@wcllp.com

Adam S. Davis — 1973 — The University of North Carolina, B.A., 1996; The University of Kansas, J.D., 2008 — Admitted to Bar, 2008, Missouri; 2009, Kansas — Member American, Kansas and Kansas City Metropolitan Bar Associations; The Missouri Bar — E-mail: adavis@wcllp.com

Jack T. Hyde — 1986 — Drury University, B.A., 2008; University of Missouri-Kansas City School of Law, J.D., 2011 — Admitted to Bar, 2011, Missouri; 2012, Kansas

David M. McMaster — 1978 — Arizona State University, B.A., 2003; The University of Kansas School of Law, J.D., 2011 — Admitted to Bar, 2011, Kansas; 2012, Missouri

Attorneys

Joan D. Toomey — 1959 — Southeast Missouri State University, B.A., 1981; University of Missouri-Kansas City, J.D., 1991 — Admitted to Bar, 1991, Missouri; 1992, Kansas — Member The Missouri Bar; Kansas Bar Association — E-mail: jtoomey@wcllp.com

Andrew N. Faes — 1978 — Western Illinois University, B.Bus.Admin., 2000; University of Missouri-Kansas City School of Law, J.D., 2007 — Admitted to Bar, 2007, Missouri

Ashley D. Dopita — 1985 — Fort Hays State University, B.A., 2008; Washburn University School of Law, J.D., 2011 — Admitted to Bar, 2011, Kansas; 2013, Missouri — Member Kansas and Kansas City Metropolitan Bar Associations; The Missouri Bar

Nathaniel M. Jones — 1982 — University of Missouri, B.A., 2005; University of Missouri-Kansas City School of Law, J.D., 2008 — Admitted to Bar, 2009, Missouri — Member The Missouri Bar — E-mail: njones@wcllp.com

Of Counsel

Scott M. Crockett — 1959 — Washburn University, B.A., 1981; The University of Kansas, J.D., 1984 — Phi Kappa Phi — Admitted to Bar, 1984, Kansas; 1985, Missouri — Member American and Kansas Bar Associations; The

MOBERLY   MISSOURI

Wagstaff & Cartmell, LLP, Kansas City, MO (Continued)

Missouri Bar; Association of Trial Lawyers of America; Federation of Defense and Corporate Counsel — E-mail: scrockett@wcllp.com

Phillip P. Ashley — 1964 — University of Missouri-Kansas City, B.A., 1986; J.D., 1988 — Admitted to Bar, 1988, Kansas — Member Kansas and Johnson County Bar Associations — E-mail: pashley@wcllp.com

Daryl J. Douglas — 1963 — William Jewell College, B.A. (summa cum laude), 1986; University of Virginia School of Law, J.D., 1989 — Admitted to Bar, 1989, Missouri — Member The Missouri Bar; Kansas City Metropolitan Bar Association — E-mail: ddouglas@wcllp.com

Waldeck & Patterson, P.A.

Two Pershing Square
2300 Main Street, Ninth Floor
Kansas City, Missouri 64108
   Telephone: 816-448-3770
   E-Mail: JohnW@waldeckpatterson.com
   www.waldeckpatterson.com

(Prairie Village, KS Office*: 5000 West 95th Street, Suite 350, 66207)
  (Tel: 913-749-0300)
  (Fax: 913-749-0301)

Civil Litigation, Insurance Defense, Commercial Litigation, Appellate Practice, Employment Law, Contract Disputes, Premises Liability, Professional Liability, Dram Shop, Product Liability, Tort Liability, Coverage Issues, Reinsurance, Business Litigation

(See listing under Prairie Village, KS for additional information)

The following firms also service this area.

Logan Logan & Watson, L.C.
8340 Mission Road
Prairie Village, Kansas 66206
   Telephone: 913-381-1121
   Fax: 913-381-6546

Insurance Law, Trial and Appellate Practice, Commercial Law, General Liability, Professional Liability, Property, Legal Malpractice, Medical Malpractice, Product Liability, Coverage Issues, Automobile

SEE COMPLETE LISTING UNDER PRAIRIE VILLAGE, KANSAS (10 MILES)

McAnany, Van Cleave & Phillips, P.A.
10 East Cambridge Circle Drive, Suite 300
Kansas City, Kansas 66103
   Telephone: 913-371-3838
   Fax: 913-371-4722

Administrative Law, Antitrust, Bankruptcy, Business Law, Construction Law, Corporate Law, Creditor Rights, Directors and Officers Liability, Insurance Law, Labor and Employment, Land Use, Litigation, Municipal Law, Personal Injury, Product Liability, Professional Liability, Public Entities, Railroad Law, Real Estate, School Law, Transportation, Trial and Appellate Practice, Workers' Compensation

SEE COMPLETE LISTING UNDER KANSAS CITY, KANSAS (5 MILES)

Payne & Jones, Chartered
11000 King
Overland Park, Kansas 66210-1233
   Telephone: 913-469-4100
   Fax: 913-469-8182
   Toll Free: 800-875-4101
Mailing Address: P.O. Box 25625, Overland Park, KS 66225

Insurance Defense, Trial Practice, Personal Injury, Workers' Compensation, Professional Negligence, Environmental Law, Business Law, Commercial Law, Coverage Issues, Employer Liability, General Liability, Product Liability, Property Liability, Wrongful Termination, Employment Practices Liability, Homeowners Liability, Property Damage Liability, Automobile (All-Lines)

SEE COMPLETE LISTING UNDER OVERLAND PARK, KANSAS (11 MILES)

LAMAR   † 4,532 Barton Co.
Refer To

Flanigan, Lasley & Moore, LLP
130 West Fourth Street
Carthage, Missouri 64836
   Telephone: 417-358-2127
   Fax: 417-358-5335
Mailing Address: P.O. Box 272, Carthage, MO 64836

Insurance Defense, Insurance Coverage, Automobile, General Civil Trial and Appellate Practice, Personal Injury, Product Liability, Truck Liability, Probate, Estate Planning, Commercial, Estate and Real Estate Litigation, Mediation Services

SEE COMPLETE LISTING UNDER CARTHAGE, MISSOURI (24 MILES)

LIBERTY   † 29,149 Clay Co.
Refer To

Sanders Warren & Russell LLP
420 Nichols Road, Suite 200
Kansas City, Missouri 64112
   Telephone: 913-234-6100
   Fax: 913-234-6199

Insurance Defense, Business Law, Automobile, Property, Homeowners, Life Insurance, Commercial Law, Professional Liability, Municipal Law, Employment Law, Workers' Compensation, Comprehensive General Liability, Alternative Dispute Resolution, Appellate Practice, Bad Faith, Construction Litigation, Governmental Liability, Insurance Coverage, Medical Malpractice, Premises Liability, Product Liability, Truck Liability

SEE COMPLETE LISTING UNDER KANSAS CITY, MISSOURI (16 MILES)

MACON   † 5,471 Macon Co.
Refer To

Ford, Parshall & Baker
3210 Bluff Creek Drive
Columbia, Missouri 65201-3525
   Telephone: 573-449-2613
   Fax: 573-875-8154

Casualty, Workers' Compensation, Product Liability, Life Insurance, Employment Law, Governmental Liability, Legal Malpractice, Medical Malpractice, Premises Liability

SEE COMPLETE LISTING UNDER COLUMBIA, MISSOURI (50 MILES)

MEXICO   † 11,543 Audrain Co.
Refer To

Ford, Parshall & Baker
3210 Bluff Creek Drive
Columbia, Missouri 65201-3525
   Telephone: 573-449-2613
   Fax: 573-875-8154

Casualty, Workers' Compensation, Product Liability, Life Insurance, Employment Law, Governmental Liability, Legal Malpractice, Medical Malpractice, Premises Liability

SEE COMPLETE LISTING UNDER COLUMBIA, MISSOURI (30 MILES)

MOBERLY   13,974 Randolph Co.
Refer To

Ford, Parshall & Baker
3210 Bluff Creek Drive
Columbia, Missouri 65201-3525
   Telephone: 573-449-2613
   Fax: 573-875-8154

Casualty, Workers' Compensation, Product Liability, Life Insurance, Employment Law, Governmental Liability, Legal Malpractice, Medical Malpractice, Premises Liability

SEE COMPLETE LISTING UNDER COLUMBIA, MISSOURI (36 MILES)

NEOSHO † 11,835 Newton Co.

Refer To

Flanigan, Lasley & Moore, LLP
130 West Fourth Street
Carthage, Missouri 64836
  Telephone: 417-358-2127
  Fax: 417-358-5335

Mailing Address: P.O. Box 272, Carthage, MO 64836

Insurance Defense, Insurance Coverage, Automobile, General Civil Trial and Appellate Practice, Personal Injury, Product Liability, Truck Liability, Probate, Estate Planning, Commercial, Estate and Real Estate Litigation, Mediation Services

SEE COMPLETE LISTING UNDER CARTHAGE, MISSOURI (24 MILES)

ROLLA † 19,559 Phelps Co.

Williams, Robinson, Rigler & Buschjost, P.C.

901 North Pine Street, Fourth Floor
Rolla, Missouri 65401
  Telephone: 573-341-2266
  Fax: 573-341-5864
  E-Mail: mail@teamlex.com
  www.teamlex.com

Insurance Defense, Insurance Litigation, Automobile, Premises Liability, Product Liability, Insurance Coverage, Professional Negligence, Agriculture, Appellate Practice, Business Law, Civil Litigation, Corporate Law, Commercial Law, Employment Law, Environmental Law, Health Care, Medical Malpractice, Municipal Law, Personal Injury, Trial Practice, Truck Liability, Wrongful Death

Firm Profile: Williams, Robinson, Rigler & Buschjost, P.C. serves the south-central Missouri area. Founded in 1930, we are one of rural Missouri's largest, full-service law firms. We provide a complete range of quality legal services, but are still small enough to value our clients as neighbors and friends.

Insurance Clients

American Family Insurance Company
Universal Underwriters Life Insurance Company
Farm Bureau Insurance Company
Shelter Insurance Companies

Attorneys

John Z. Williams — (1941-2009)

J. Kent Robinson — 1954 — University of Illinois at Springfield, B.A., 1976; University of Illinois at Urbana-Champaign, J.D., 1979 — Admitted to Bar, 1979, Illinois; 1980, Missouri — Member American Bar Association; The Missouri Bar; Academy of Family Mediators; Missouri Association of Trial Attorneys — Practice Areas: Commercial Law; Corporate Law; Contracts; Business Law; Intellectual Property; Real Estate; Alternative Dispute Resolution — E-mail: krobinson@teamlex.com

Joseph W. Rigler — 1958 — Central Missouri State University, B.S., 1980; University of Missouri-Kansas City School of Law, J.D., 1983 — Admitted to Bar, 1983, Missouri — Member American Bar Association; The Missouri Bar; American Criminal Justice Association — Adjunct Professor University of Missouri-Rolla (1984-1989); Specialist Instructor, Department of Public Safety; Assistant Prosecutor 1983-1987; Special Prosecutor (by assignment) — Practice Areas: Insurance Defense; Insurance Litigation; Insurance Coverage; Personal Injury; Automobile Tort; Truck Liability; Product Liability; Premises Liability; Professional Negligence; Wrongful Death — E-mail: jrigler@teamlex.com

Carolyn G. Buschjost — 1969 — The University of New Mexico, B.A., 1991; Saint Louis University, J.D., 1994 — Admitted to Bar, 1994, Missouri; 1995, Illinois — Member Illinois State Bar Association; The Missouri Bar — Assistant Prosecuting Attorney, Adair County, Missouri (1995-1997), Phelps County, Missouri (1997-1999) — Practice Areas: Family Law — E-mail: cbuschjost@teamlex.com

Williams, Robinson, Rigler & Buschjost, P.C., Rolla, MO (Continued)

Cary L. Hansen — 1963 — University of Missouri-Columbia, B.S., 1985; University of Missouri-Kansas City, J.D., 1989 — Admitted to Bar, 1989, Missouri — Member The Missouri Bar (Local Government Law Committee); Missouri Municipal Attorneys Association — Practice Areas: Probate; Real Estate; Corporate Law; Commercial Law; Municipal Law — E-mail: chansen@teamlex.com

Lance B. Thurman — 1974 — Truman State University, B.S., 1998; University of Missouri-Columbia School of Law, J.D., 2001 — Admitted to Bar, 2001, Missouri — Assistant Prosecuting Attorney, Phelps County, Missouri (2003-2007); Special Prosecutor (by assignment) — Practice Areas: Defense Litigation; General Civil Litigation — E-mail: lthurman@teamlex.com

Megan K. Seufert — 1979 — University of Missouri-Columbia, B.S., 2001; University of Missouri-Columbia School of Law, J.D., 2005 — Admitted to Bar, 2005, Missouri — Member The Missouri Bar — Practice Areas: Family Law; General Civil Practice — E-mail: mseufert@teamlex.com

SALEM † 4,950 Dent Co.

Refer To

Williams, Robinson, Rigler & Buschjost, P.C.
901 North Pine Street, Fourth Floor
Rolla, Missouri 65401
  Telephone: 573-341-2266
  Fax: 573-341-5864

Mailing Address: P.O. Box 47, Rolla, MO 65402

Insurance Defense, Insurance Litigation, Automobile, Premises Liability, Product Liability, Insurance Coverage, Professional Negligence, Agriculture, Appellate Practice, Business Law, Civil Litigation, Corporate Law, Commercial Law, Employment Law, Environmental Law, Health Care, Medical Malpractice, Municipal Law, Personal Injury, Trial Practice, Truck Liability, Wrongful Death

SEE COMPLETE LISTING UNDER ROLLA, MISSOURI (29 MILES)

SEDALIA † 21,387 Pettis Co.

Refer To

Ford, Parshall & Baker
3210 Bluff Creek Drive
Columbia, Missouri 65201-3525
  Telephone: 573-449-2613
  Fax: 573-875-8154

Casualty, Workers' Compensation, Product Liability, Life Insurance, Employment Law, Governmental Liability, Legal Malpractice, Medical Malpractice, Premises Liability

SEE COMPLETE LISTING UNDER COLUMBIA, MISSOURI (60 MILES)

Refer To

Payne & Jones, Chartered
11000 King
Overland Park, Kansas 66210-1233
  Telephone: 913-469-4100
  Fax: 913-469-8182
  Toll Free: 800-875-4101

Mailing Address: P.O. Box 25625, Overland Park, KS 66225

Insurance Defense, Trial Practice, Personal Injury, Workers' Compensation, Professional Negligence, Environmental Law, Business Law, Commercial Law, Coverage Issues, Employer Liability, General Liability, Product Liability, Property Liability, Wrongful Termination, Employment Practices Liability, Homeowners Liability, Property Damage Liability, Automobile (All-Lines)

SEE COMPLETE LISTING UNDER OVERLAND PARK, KANSAS (91 MILES)

Refer To

Sanders Warren & Russell LLP
420 Nichols Road, Suite 200
Kansas City, Missouri 64112
  Telephone: 913-234-6100
  Fax: 913-234-6199

Insurance Defense, Business Law, Automobile, Property, Homeowners, Life Insurance, Commercial Law, Professional Liability, Municipal Law, Employment Law, Workers' Compensation, Comprehensive General Liability, Alternative Dispute Resolution, Appellate Practice, Bad Faith, Construction Litigation, Governmental Liability, Insurance Coverage, Medical Malpractice, Premises Liability, Product Liability, Truck Liability

SEE COMPLETE LISTING UNDER KANSAS CITY, MISSOURI (96 MILES)

SPRINGFIELD † 159,498 Greene Co.

Baird Lightner Millsap, P.C.
1901-C South Ventura Avenue
Springfield, Missouri 65804
Telephone: 417-887-0133
Fax: 417-887-8740
E-Mail: rbaird@blmlawyers.com
www.blmlawyers.com

Established: 1983

Automobile, Banking, Business Formation, Civil Defense, Commercial Litigation, Corporate Governance, Employment Law, Estate Planning, Government Affairs, Insurance Law, Intellectual Property, Mergers and Acquisitions, Municipal Law, Personal Injury, Professional Liability, Property and Casualty, Real Estate, School Law, Trusts, Nonprofit Organizations

Firm Profile: Founded over 25 years ago our firm has grown largely through referrals by clients and colleagues whose trust we have earned. Our business sensibilities are firmly grounded in Midwestern values and our approach to your legal needs is professional, accessible and offered at a fair price.

All BLM partners are members of the Missouri Bar and Springfield Metropolitan Bar Associations.

Insurance Clients

Meadowbrook Insurance Group	Missouri Public Entity Risk Management Fund (MOPERM)
Savers Property and Casualty Insurance Company	Shelter Insurance Companies
Star Insurance Company	Trident Insurance Company

Non-Insurance Clients

City of Springfield	O'Reilly Auto Parts

Partners

C. Ronald Baird — Washington University, B.A., 1967; University of Missouri-Columbia, J.D., 1974 — Admitted to Bar, 1974, Missouri; 1975, U.S. District Court, Western District of Missouri — Member American Bar Association; American Academy of Matrimonial Lawyers

John R. Lightner — Drury College, B.S. (summa cum laude), 1979; University of Missouri-Columbia, J.D., 1982 — Admitted to Bar, 1982, Missouri; U.S. District Court, Western District of Missouri; 1991, U.S. Court of Appeals, Eighth Circuit — Member Missouri Association of Trial Attorneys

Mark J. Millsap — University of Missouri, B.S. (summa cum laude), 1982; J.D. (with distinction), 1985 — University Scholar Award, University of Missouri, 1981 — Admitted to Bar, 1985, Missouri — Member Missouri Organization of Defense Lawyers

Brett Roubal — Creighton University, B.S., 1996; J.D., 1999 — Creighton Law Review, 1997-1999 — Admitted to Bar, 1999, Missouri; 2000, Kansas

J. Matthew Miller — University of Missouri, B.A., 1998; University of Missouri-Columbia, J.D., 2001 — Admitted to Bar, 2001, Missouri; 2003, U.S. District Court, Western District of Missouri

Paul Link — Missouri State University, B.S., 1993; University of Missouri-Kansas City, J.D., 1996 — Admitted to Bar, 1996, Missouri; 1997, Kansas; 1996, U.S. District Court, Western District of Missouri; U.S. Court of Appeals, Eighth Circuit — Member Missouri Municipal Attorneys Association; International Municipal Lawyers Association; Claims and Litigation Management Alliance

Associates

Tina G. Fowler	Jennifer A. Mueller
Rachel A. Riso	Patrick R. Baird
Emily L. Shook	Brandon Howard
Philip R. Quinn	Katherine A. O'Dell
Alex W. Davis	

Law Office of Dale L. Davis
1111 South Glenstone, Suite 2-200
Springfield, Missouri 65804
Telephone: 417-863-0100
Fax: 417-863-6156
E-Mail: DLALaw@SBCglobal.net

Established: 1990

Insurance Defense, Fire, Fraud, Trial Practice, Casualty, Errors and Omissions, Product Liability

Insurance Clients

American National Property and Casualty Company	California Casualty Insurance Company
Cornerstone National Insurance Company	Farmers Mutual Insurance Company of Dade County
Farmers Mutual Insurance Company of Hickory County	Kemper Speciality/Unitrin Specialty
Lititz Mutual Insurance Company	Scottsdale Insurance Company
Underwriters at Lloyd's, London	Workmen's Auto Insurance Company

Dale L. Davis — 1953 — Southwest Missouri State University, B.S., 1974; University of Missouri-Columbia, J.D., 1979 — Admitted to Bar, 1979, Missouri; 1979, U.S. District Court, Western District of Missouri; 1988, U.S. Court of Appeals, Eighth Circuit — Member Springfield Metropolitan Bar Association; The Missouri Bar — E-mail: DLALaw@SBCglobal.net

Franke Schultz & Mullen, P.C.
5000 South Highland Springs Boulevard
Springfield, Missouri 65809
Telephone: 417-863-0040
Fax: 417-863-6286
E-Mail: info@fsmlawfirm.com
www.fsmlawfirm.com

(Kansas City, MO Office*: 8900 Ward Parkway, 64114)
  (Tel: 816-421-7100)
  (Fax: 816-421-7915)
  (E-Mail: fsm@fsmlawfirm.com)
(St. Louis, MO Office: Two City Place, Second Floor, 64131)
  (Tel: 314-812-4780)
  (Fax: 816-421-7915)

Insurance Defense, Automobile, Homeowners, Truck Liability, Property and Casualty, Personal Injury, Commercial Casualty

(See listing under Kansas City, MO for additional information)

Lowther Johnson Attorneys at Law, L.L.C.
901 East St. Louis Street, 20th Floor
Springfield, Missouri 65806
Telephone: 417-866-7777
Fax: 417-866-1752
E-Mail: kory@lowtherjohnson.com
www.lowtherjohnson.com

Appellate Practice, Civil Litigation, Construction Law, Commercial Law, Insurance Defense, Insurance Coverage, Bad Faith, Corporate Law, Creditor Rights, Landlord and Tenant Law

Firm Profile: For over 35 years, Lowther Johnson has been proud to serve as legal advisers to companies, organizations and individuals. A longtime resident of Springfield, Kory D. Stubblefield provides a wide range of services to clients, and also has extensive experience handling cases through the appeals process.

MISSOURI   SPRINGFIELD

Lowther Johnson Attorneys at Law, L.L.C., Springfield, MO (Continued)

Insurance Clients

Electric Insurance Company   Sentry Insurance Company

Member

Kory D. Stubblefield — Missouri State University, B.S. (summa cum laude), 2003; University of Missouri School of Law, J.D. (with first in class honors, Order of the Coif), 2006 — Note and Comment Editor, University of Missouri Law Review (2005-2006; Associate Member, 2004-2005) — Admitted to Bar, 2006, Missouri; U.S. District Court, Western District of Missouri — Member American and Springfield Metropolitan Bar Associations; Missouri Organization of Defense Lawyers; Trial Attorneys of America

McAnany, Van Cleave & Phillips, P.C.

4650 South National Avenue, Suite D-2
Springfield, Missouri 65810
   Telephone: 417-865-0007
   Fax: 417-865-0008
   www.mvplaw.com

(McAnany, Van Cleave & Phillips, P.A.*: 10 East Cambridge Circle Drive, Suite 300, Kansas City, KS, 66103)
   (Tel: 913-371-3838)
   (Fax: 913-371-4722)
(St. Louis, MO Office*: 505 North 7th Street, Suite 2100, 63101)
   (Tel: 314-621-1133)
   (Fax: 314-621-4405)
(Omaha, NE Office*: 10665 Bedford Avenue, Suite 101, 68134)
   (Tel: 402-408-1340)
   (Fax: 402-493-0860)
(Tulsa, OK Office*: 2021 South Lewis, Suite 225, 74104)
   (Tel: 918-771-4465)

Established: 1901

Administrative Law, Antitrust, Bankruptcy, Business Law, Construction Law, Corporate Law, Creditor Rights, Directors and Officers Liability, Insurance Law, Labor and Employment, Land Use, Litigation, Municipal Law, Personal Injury, Product Liability, Professional Liability, Public Entities, Railroad Law, Real Estate, School Law, Transportation, Trial and Appellate Practice, Workers' Compensation

(See listing under Kansas City, KS for additional information)

Sanders Warren & Russell LLP

American National Center 2-102
1949 East Sunshine
Springfield, Missouri 65804
   Telephone: 417-281-5100
   Fax: 417-281-5199
   www.swrllp.com

(Overland Park, KS Office*: 40 Corporate Woods, 9401 Indian Creen Parkway, Suite 1250, 66210)
   (Tel: 913-234-6100)
   (Fax: 913-234-6199)
   (E-Mail: b.sanders@swrllp.com)
   (E-Mail: r.warren@swrllp.com)
   (E-Mail: b.russell@swrllp.com)
(Kansas City, MO Office*: 420 Nichols Road, Suite 200, 64112)
   (Tel: 913-234-6100)
   (Fax: 913-234-6199)

Sanders Warren & Russell LLP, Springfield, MO (Continued)

Insurance Defense, Business Law, Automobile, Property, Homeowners, Life Insurance, Commercial Law, Professional Liability, Municipal Law, Employment Law, Workers' Compensation, Comprehensive General Liability, Alternative Dispute Resolution, Appellate Practice, Bad Faith, Construction Litigation, Governmental Liability, Insurance Coverage, Medical Malpractice, Premises Liability, Product Liability, Truck Liability

(See listing under Overland Park, KS for additional information)

Taylor, Stafford, Clithero, FitzGerald & Harris, LLP

3315 East Ridgeview, Suite 1000
Springfield, Missouri 65804
   Telephone: 417-887-2020
   Fax: 417-887-8431
   Toll Free: 800-749-0004
   www.taylorstafford.com

Established: 1974

Insurance Defense, Automobile, Commercial Law, General Liability, Product Liability, Trucking Law, Fire, Casualty, Workers' Compensation, Arbitration, Bodily Injury, Construction Law, Mediation, Medical Malpractice, Medical Negligence, Contractual Liability, Business Owners

Insurance Clients

American Farmers & Ranchers Insurance Company
American National Property and Casualty Company
Anthem Casualty Insurance Group
Cameron Mutual Insurance Company
Canal Insurance Company
Catholic Mutual Group
Central States Health & Life Company of Omaha
Columbia Insurance Group
Farm Bureau Town and Country Insurance Company of Missouri
Gallagher Bassett Services, Inc.
National General Insurance Company
Northwestern National Insurance Company
Progressive Insurance Companies
Shand Morahan & Company, Inc.
State Farm Fire and Casualty Company
State Farm Mutual Automobile Insurance Company
TIG Insurance Company
Time Insurance Company n.k.a. Assurant Health
Transport Insurance Company
United Fire & Casualty Company
West Bend Mutual Insurance Company

Non-Insurance Clients

A.I. Transport
Catholic Charities of Southwest Missouri
Cox South Hospital
Hartford Livestock
New Prime, Inc.
Roman Catholic Diocese of Springfield-Cape Girardeau
Werner Enterprises, Inc.

Partners

Monte P. Clithero — 1953 — Culver-Stockton College, B.A., 1975; University of Missouri-Columbia, J.D., 1978 — Admitted to Bar, 1978, Missouri; U.S. District Court, Eastern and Western Districts of Missouri; 1992, U.S. Court of Appeals, Eighth Circuit — Member American and Springfield Metropolitan Bar Associations; The Missouri Bar; Fellow, American College of Trial Lawyers; Fellow, Litigation Counsel of America; International Association of Defense Counsel; Defense Research Institute; Missouri Organization of Defense Lawyers — E-mail: mclithero@taylorstafford.com

Kevin M. FitzGerald — 1956 — The University of Texas at Arlington, B.B.A., 1981; University of Arkansas, J.D., 1985 — Admitted to Bar, 1985, Missouri; U.S. District Court, Western District of Missouri; U.S. Court of Appeals, Eighth Circuit — Member The Missouri Bar; Springfield Metropolitan Bar Association (Secretary 1997); National Diocesan Attorneys Association; Missouri Organization of Defense Lawyers — Legal Aid of Southwest Missouri (Board of Directors, 1993-1996); Neutral, U.S. District Court, Western District of Missouri — E-mail: kfitzgerald@taylorstafford.com

ST. CHARLES   MISSOURI

Taylor, Stafford, Clithero, FitzGerald & Harris, LLP, Springfield, MO (Continued)

Warren E. Harris — 1966 — Central Missouri State University, B.S.B.A. (summa cum laude), 1989; University of Missouri-Columbia, J.D., 1992 — Admitted to Bar, 1992, Missouri; U.S. District Court, Eastern and Western Districts of Missouri; U.S. Court of Appeals, Eighth Circuit — Member The Missouri Bar; Springfield Metropolitan Bar Association; Missouri Organization of Defense Lawyers; Defense Research Institute — Member Thirty-First Circuit Judicial Evaluation Committee (2010 to present) — E-mail: wharris@taylorstafford.com

Lance A. Roskens — 1979 — South Dakota State University, B.S./B.S. (with highest honors), 2002; University of Missouri-Columbia School of Law, J.D. (Dean's List), 2006 — Law Clerk, Missouri Court of Appeals, Southern District — University of Missouri-Columbia School of Law Law Review — Admitted to Bar, 2007, Missouri; Missouri State Court; 2009, U.S. District Court, Western District of Missouri; U.S. Court of Appeals, Eighth Circuit — Member The Missouri Bar; Springfield Metropolitan Bar Association — The Pro-Arbitration Policy: Is This What the Parties Really Intended?, 2005 Journal of Dispute Resolution 511 — Missouri Super Lawyers, Rising Star, 2013 — E-mail: lroskens@taylorstafford.com

Associate

Nathan Taylor — Missouri State University, B.S., 2004; The University of Tulsa College of Law, J.D., 2010 — Admitted to Bar, 2010, Missouri — Member The Missouri Bar; Springfield Metropolitan Bar Association

Turner, Reid, Duncan, Loomer & Patton, P.C.

1355 East Bradford Parkway, Suite A
Springfield, Missouri 65804
    Telephone: 417-883-2102
    Fax: 417-883-5024
    Toll Free: 800-842-2102
    www.turnerreid.com

Established: 1953

Civil Litigation, Trial and Appellate Practice, Product Liability, Medical Malpractice

Insurance Clients

CIGNA Insurance Company
The Doctors Company
Farm Bureau Town and Country Insurance Company of Missouri
St. Paul Fire and Marine Insurance Company
Shelter Insurance Companies
Zurich American Insurance Group
Continental Western Insurance Company
GEICO
Preferred Professional Insurance Company
Sentry Insurance a Mutual Company

Non-Insurance Clients

Bass Pro Shops, Inc.
Ford Motor Company
Harley-Davidson Motor Company, Inc.
U-Haul International, Inc.
Cox Health Systems
General Motors Corporation
Iovate Health Services, Inc.
Mercy Health Systems

Principals

Meredith B. Turner — (1913-1993)

Kenneth H. Reid — (Retired)

Rodney E. Loomer — 1949 — University of Missouri-Columbia, J.D., 1974 — Admitted to Bar, 1974, Missouri — Member American and Springfield Metropolitan (President, 2001) Bar Associations; The Missouri Bar (Board of Governors, 1985-1993); Defense Research Institute; Fellow, American College of Trial Lawyers; American Bar Foundation

Michael J. Patton — 1954 — University of Missouri-Columbia, J.D., 1980 — Admitted to Bar, 1980, Missouri; 1980, U.S. District Court, Western District of Missouri — Member American and Springfield Metropolitan Bar Associations; The Missouri Bar; International Association of Defense Counsel; Defense Research Institute; Missouri Organization of Defense Lawyers; American Board of Trial Advocates

Sherry A. Rozell — 1960 — Washington University, J.D., 1986 — Order of the

Turner, Reid, Duncan, Loomer & Patton, P.C., Springfield, MO (Continued)

Coif; American Jurisprudence Awards (Contracts, Constitutional Law, Corporations) — Admitted to Bar, 1986, Missouri — Member American and Springfield Metropolitan Bar Associations; The Missouri Bar; Defense Research Institute

Steven E. Ward — 1965 — Southwest Missouri State University, B.S.Ed., 1987; University of Missouri-Kansas City, J.D., 1994 — Admitted to Bar, 1994, Missouri; 1995, Kansas — Member The Missouri Bar; Springfield Metropolitan Bar Association; Defense Research Institute; Missouri Organization of Defense Lawyers

Jeffrey T. Davis — 1969 — Drury University, B.A. (magna cum laude), 1992; University of Missouri-Columbia, J.D., 1995 — Admitted to Bar, 1995, Missouri; 1996, Kansas — Member Kansas and Springfield Metropolitan Bar Associations; The Missouri Bar; Defense Research Institute; Missouri Organization of Defense Lawyers

Scott E. Bellm — 1970 — Southwest Missouri State University, B.S., 1992; University of Arkansas, J.D., 1995 — Recipient, David J. Dixon Appellate Advocacy Award (2004); Order of Barristers — Arkansas Law Review (1995) — Admitted to Bar, 1995, Arkansas; 1996, Missouri; 1999, U.S. District Court, Western District of Missouri; 2009, U.S. Court of Appeals, Eighth Circuit — Member The Missouri Bar; Arkansas Bar Association; Springfield Metropolitan Bar Association; Fellow, Missouri Bar Foundation; Missouri Organization of Defense Lawyers; Defense Research Institute — Practice Areas: Automobile Tort; Medical Malpractice Defense; Insurance Bad Faith; Insurance Litigation

George (Jake) W. Reinbold, IV — 1979 — University of Missouri-Columbia, B.S.B.A., 2001; J.D., 2004 — Admitted to Bar, 2004, Missouri; 2004, U.S. District Court, Western District of Missouri — Member The Missouri Bar; Springfield Metropolitan Bar Association; Missouri Organization of Defense Lawyers

Associates

Bethany G. Parsons — 1981 — Southern Methodist University, B.A., 2004; New England School of Law, J.D., 2009 — Admitted to Bar, 2009, Missouri; U.S. District Court, Western District of Missouri — Member The Missouri Bar; Springfield Metropolitan Bar Association; Missouri Organization of Defense Lawyers; Defense Research Institute

Ty Z. Harden — 1978 — Washington State University, B.A. (cum laude), 2001; University of Missouri School of Law, J.D. (Dean's List), 2011 — Admitted to Bar, 2011, Missouri — Member The Missouri Bar

Brad E. Miller — 1987 — Missouri State University, B.S. (magna cum laude), 2008; University of Missouri School of Law, J.D. (magna cum laude, Order of the Coif), 2012 — Admitted to Bar, 2012, Missouri; U.S. District Court, Western District of Missouri — Member The Missouri Bar

Kristen M. O'Neal — 1987 — Southwest Baptist University, B.S. (summa cum laude), 2009; University of Missouri-Kansas City School of Law, J.D. (summa cum laude), 2012 — Admitted to Bar, 2012, Missouri; U.S. District Court, Western District of Missouri — Member The Missouri Bar

Valerie L. Dixon — 1986 — University of Missouri-Columbia, B.A./B.S. (magna cum laude), 2008; M.B.A., 2010; University of Missouri School of Law, J.D. (Dean's List), 2013 — Admitted to Bar, 2013, Missouri; 2013, U.S. District Court, Western District of Missouri — Member The Missouri Bar

Of Counsel

Donald R. Duncan — 1935 — Washington University, J.D., 1964 — Washington University Law Review — Admitted to Bar, 1964, Missouri — Member American and Springfield Metropolitan Bar Associations; The Missouri Bar

Ben K. Upp — 1948 — Southwest Missouri State University, B.A., 1971; University of Missouri, J.D., 1974 — Admitted to Bar, 1974, Missouri — Member The Missouri Bar; Springfield Metropolitan Bar Association

ST. CHARLES † 65,794 St. Charles Co.

Niedner, Bodeux, Carmichael, Huff, Lenox, Pashos and Simpson, L.L.P.

131 Jefferson Street
St. Charles, Missouri 63301
    Telephone: 636-949-9300
    Fax: 636-949-3141
    E-Mail: jlenox@niednerlaw.com
    www.niednerlaw.com

MISSOURI

Niedner, Bodeux, Carmichael, Huff, Lenox, Pashos and Simpson, L.L.P., St. Charles, MO (Continued)

Established: 1937

Insurance Defense, Automobile, Product Liability, Homeowners, Casualty, Premises Liability

Firm Profile: The Niedner Law Firm is the oldest firm in St. Charles County, established in 1937.

Insurance Clients

American Family Insurance Company
Federated Rural Electric Insurance Exchange
SECURA Insurance Companies
Calvert Insurance Company
Cameron Mutual Insurance Company
Gryphon Insurance Group
Shelter Insurance Companies

Non-Insurance Clients

August Busch, III
Bropfs Mobile Homes
City of Flint Hill
Critical Connections, Inc.
Fuqua Homes
Lake St. Louis Community Association
St. Charles School District
T.R. Hughes
Bob Schultz Honda
City of Cottleville
City of Foristell
Cuivre River Electric Cooperative
King Arthur's Court
Missouri Builders
Oak Leaf Mobile Home Park
St. Mary's Institute

Partners

Robert F. Niedner — (1913-1988)

Paul F. Niedner — (1915-2011)

Reginald P. Bodeux — (Retired)

Jayson B. Lenox — 1964 — Central Missouri State University, B.A., 1988; University of Missouri-Columbia, J.D., 1991 — Admitted to Bar, 1991, Missouri; 1992, Illinois; 1991, U.S. District Court, Eastern District of Missouri; 2001, U.S. District Court, Southern District of Illinois; 2005, U.S. District Court, Western District of Missouri — Member American, Illinois State and St. Charles County Bar Associations; The Missouri Bar; Missouri Organization of Defense Lawyers — Assistant Prosecuting Attorney for the City of St. Peters (1994-1995); City Attorney for the City of Foristell (1998-2005)

James E. Carmichael — 1954

Timothy R. Huff — 1964

Theodore G. Pashos — 1957

Scott E. Simpson — 1981

Associates

Yvonne M. Yarnell — 1974

Bradley R. Bodeux — 1977

Jeffrey D. Gamber — 1979

The following firms also service this area.

Case Linden P.C.
Two City Place Drive, 2nd Floor
St. Louis, Missouri 63141
 Telephone: 314-812-4750
 Fax: 314-812-4755

Appellate Practice, Bodily Injury, Civil Trial Practice, Class Actions, Commercial Litigation, Discrimination, Errors and Omissions, Insurance Defense, Labor and Employment, Legal Malpractice, Medical Malpractice, Premises Liability, Product Liability, Professional Liability, Regulatory and Compliance, Tort, Workers' Compensation

SEE COMPLETE LISTING UNDER ST. LOUIS, MISSOURI (24 MILES)

ST. JOSEPH

ST. JOSEPH † 76,780 Buchanan Co.

Refer To
Logan Logan & Watson, L.C.
8340 Mission Road
Prairie Village, Kansas 66206
 Telephone: 913-381-1121
 Fax: 913-381-6546

Insurance Law, Trial and Appellate Practice, Commercial Law, General Liability, Professional Liability, Property, Legal Malpractice, Medical Malpractice, Product Liability, Coverage Issues, Automobile

SEE COMPLETE LISTING UNDER PRAIRIE VILLAGE, KANSAS (55 MILES)

Refer To
Payne & Jones, Chartered
11000 King
Overland Park, Kansas 66210-1233
 Telephone: 913-469-4100
 Fax: 913-469-8182
 Toll Free: 800-875-4101
Mailing Address: P.O. Box 25625, Overland Park, KS 66225

Insurance Defense, Trial Practice, Personal Injury, Workers' Compensation, Professional Negligence, Environmental Law, Business Law, Commercial Law, Coverage Issues, Employer Liability, General Liability, Product Liability, Property Liability, Wrongful Termination, Employment Practices Liability, Homeowners Liability, Property Damage Liability, Automobile (All-Lines)

SEE COMPLETE LISTING UNDER OVERLAND PARK, KANSAS (65 MILES)

Refer To
Sanders Warren & Russell LLP
420 Nichols Road, Suite 200
Kansas City, Missouri 64112
 Telephone: 913-234-6100
 Fax: 913-234-6199

Insurance Defense, Business Law, Automobile, Property, Homeowners, Life Insurance, Commercial Law, Professional Liability, Municipal Law, Employment Law, Workers' Compensation, Comprehensive General Liability, Alternative Dispute Resolution, Appellate Practice, Bad Faith, Construction Litigation, Governmental Liability, Insurance Coverage, Medical Malpractice, Premises Liability, Product Liability, Truck Liability

SEE COMPLETE LISTING UNDER KANSAS CITY, MISSOURI (60 MILES)

ST. LOUIS † 319,294 Independent City

Allen, Kopet & Associates, PLLC
8056 Davis Drive
Clayton, Missouri 63105
 Telephone: 314-256-9433
 Fax: 877-349-2970

(See listing under Chattanooga, TN for additional information)

Anderson & Gilbert, L.C.
515 Olive Street, Suite 704
St. Louis, Missouri 63101-1800
 Telephone: 314-721-2777
 Fax: 314-721-3515
 Toll Free: 800-721-2858
 E-Mail: info@anderson-gilbert.com
 www.anderson-gilbert.com

Insurance Defense, Trial and Appellate Practice, Medical Malpractice, Product Liability, Asbestos Litigation, Coverage Issues, State and Federal Courts, Toxic Torts, Truck Liability, Latex and Drug Product Liability

Firm Profile: Anderson & Gilbert, L.C. established in 1906, has for many years specialized in insurance defense. Our practice covers both state and federal courts in Missouri and Illinois, at trial and appellate levels.

ST. LOUIS   MISSOURI

Anderson & Gilbert, L.C., St. Louis, MO   (Continued)

Insurance Clients

American Claims Services, Inc.
CNA Insurance Companies
Fireman's Fund Insurance Company
Insurance Corporation of America
Liberty Mutual Group
St. Paul Insurance Company
Wausau Insurance Companies
Chubb Group of Insurance Companies
The Hartford Insurance Group
INS Insurance, Inc.
Intermed Insurance Company
Nationwide Indemnity Company
United States Fidelity and Guaranty Company

Partners

Roscoe Anderson — (1884-1951)

William Gilbert — (1886-1963)

Francis X. Duda — 1942 — The George Washington University; Xavier University, B.S., 1964; Saint Louis University, J.D., 1967 — Admitted to Bar, 1967, Missouri; 1980, Illinois; 1969, U.S. District Court, Eastern District of Missouri; 1980, U.S. District Court, Northern and Southern Districts of Illinois — Member Illinois State Bar Association; The Missouri Bar — E-mail: fxduda@anderson-gilbert.com

Fortis M. Lawder — 1927 — Saint Louis University, B.S.C., 1949; J.D., 1951 — Admitted to Bar, 1951, Missouri; Illinois — Member The Missouri Bar; The Bar Association of Metropolitan St. Louis — E-mail: fmlawder@anderson-gilbert.com

D. Paul Myre — 1960 — William Jewell College, B.A., 1982; University of Missouri-Kansas City, J.D., 1985 — Admitted to Bar, 1985, Missouri; 2002, Illinois; 1986, U.S. District Court, Eastern District of Missouri — Member American and St. Louis County Bar Associations; The Missouri Bar; The Bar Association of Metropolitan St. Louis — E-mail: dpmyre@anderson-gilbert.com

Mariano V. Favazza — Saint Louis University, B.A., 1987; M.A.; Saint Louis University School of Law, J.D. (cum laude), 1990 — Admitted to Bar, 1990, Illinois; 1991, Missouri — E-mail: mvfavazza@anderson-gilbert.com

Associates

Josephine Sangiorgio Hirth — State University of New York at Stony Brook, B.A., 2004; Thomas M. Cooley Law School, J.D., 2007 — Admitted to Bar, 2007, New York; 2008, Missouri; 2014, Illinois — Member The Association of the Bar of the City of New York; The Bar Association of Metropolitan St. Louis; The Missouri Bar — E-mail: jshirth@anderson-gilbert.com

Jordan L. Pauluhn — Westminster College, B.A. (summa cum laude), 2010; Washington University School of Law, J.D. (cum laude), 2013 — Admitted to Bar, 2013, Missouri; U.S. District Court, Eastern and Western Districts of Missouri — E-mail: jlpauluhn@anderson-gilbert.com

Armstrong Teasdale LLP
A Partnership Including Professional Corporations

7700 Forsyth Boulevard, Suite 1800
St. Louis, Missouri 63105
 Telephone: 314-621-5070
 Fax: 314-621-5065
 Toll Free: 800-243-5070
 E-Mail: at@armstrongteasdale.com
 www.armstrongteasdale.com

(Additional Offices: Kansas City, MO*; Jefferson City, MO*; Las Vegas, NV; Shanghai, China-PRC)

Established: 1901

Accident, Disability, Health, Life Insurance, Bad Faith, Class Actions, Directors and Officers Liability, ERISA, Errors and Omissions, Excess and Reinsurance, Extra-Contractual Litigation, Fraud, Insurance Coverage, Medical Malpractice, Property and Casualty, Asbestos Litigation, Business Law, Construction Litigation, Coverage Analysis, Deceptive Trade Practices, Environmental Law, Intellectual Property, Product Liability, Securities and Investments

Armstrong Teasdale LLP, A Partnership Including Professional Corporations, St. Louis, MO   (Continued)

Firm Profile: Insurance Defense and Litigation. When disputes arise between insurance companies or insurance companies and their policyholders or third party claimants, Armstrong Teasdale offers experienced attorneys who provide prompt and cost-effective resolutions to insurance claim disputes.

Insurance Clients

AIG Environmental
American Fidelity Group
American International Group
American Modern Insurance Group, Inc.
Athene Annuity & Life Assurance Group
AXIS Specialty Insurance Company
Central United Life Insurance Company
Fidelity and Guaranty Life Insurance Company
Hartford Life and Accident Insurance Company
Lexington Insurance Company/AIG
Lincoln National Life Insurance Company
Mutual of Omaha Group
National Life Group
North American Company for Life and Health Insurance
The Ohio National Life Insurance Company
Scottsdale Insurance Company
Stonebridge Life Insurance Company
Symetra Life Insurance Company
Thrivent Financial for Lutherans
The Travelers Companies
Trustmark Insurance Company
Western-Southern Life Assurance Company
Xchanging
Allstate Life Insurance Company
American General Life Insurance Company
Arch Insurance Group
Arthur J. Gallagher & Company
Aviva Life and Annuity Company
AXA Equitable Life Insurance Company
Celtic Insurance Company
Combined Insurance Company of America
Hartford Casualty Insurance Company
HealthMarkets, Inc.
John Hancock Life Insurance Company
Liberty Mutual Insurance Company
Meadowbrook Insurance Group
Monumental Life Insurance Company
New York Life Insurance Company
The Northwestern Mutual Life Insurance Company
Old Mutual Financial Network
Stonebridge Casualty Insurance Company
Swiss Re America Holding Corporation
Transamerica Life Insurance Company
United of Omaha Life Insurance Company
Wilton Re Services, Inc.

Attorney Contacts

Clark H. Cole — Louisiana State University, B.A., 1977; University of Missouri-Columbia, J.D. (Order of the Coif), 1980 — Admitted to Bar, 1980, Missouri; 1981, Illinois — E-mail: ccole@armstrongteasdale.com

Patrick J. Kenny — University of Missouri-Columbia, B.S.B.A., 1987; University of Missouri School of Law, J.D., 1990 — Admitted to Bar, 1990, Missouri; 1992, District of Columbia; 1994, Illinois; 1997, Kansas — E-mail: pkenny@armstrongteasdale.com

James L. Stockberger — Saint Louis University, B.A. (cum laude), 1981; Saint Louis University School of Law, J.D. (cum laude), 1988 — Admitted to Bar, 1988, Missouri; 1989, Illinois; Kansas — E-mail: jstockberger@armstrongteasdale.com

Matthew Shorey — University of Missouri-Columbia, B.A. (magna cum laude), 1995; Saint Louis University School of Law, J.D. (cum laude), 1998 — Admitted to Bar, 1998, Missouri; 1999, Illinois — E-mail: mshorey@armstrongteasdale.com

Thomas Weaver — Duke University, B.A. (magna cum laude), 1974; Saint Louis University School of Law, J.D. (magna cum laude), 1978 — Admitted to Bar, 1978, Missouri; 1979, Illinois — E-mail: tweaver@armstrongteasdale.com

Wil Tomlinson — University of Missouri-Saint Louis, B.S., 1976; University of Missouri-Columbia School of Law, J.D. (Order of the Coif), 1979; University of Missouri-Saint Louis, M.A., 2002 — Admitted to Bar, 1979, Missouri; 1991, Illinois — E-mail: wtomlinson@armstrongteasdale.com

(See listing under Kansas City and Jefferson City, MO for additional information)

MISSOURI

ST. LOUIS

Bauman Law Firm, P.C.

16100 Chesterfield Parkway, Suite 305
Chesterfield, Missouri 63017
Telephone: 636-537-3307
Fax: 636-537-5403
E-Mail: randyb@baumanlaw.com
www.baumanlaw.com

Medical Malpractice, Business Law, Civil Litigation, Coverage Issues, Contract Disputes, Wrongful Death, Employment Law

Firm Profile: The firm's founding member, Randall A. Bauman, has guided the firm's practice towards civil litigation, business law and medical malpractice defense.

The firm has a working knowledge of the medical profession, and is able to distill complicated medical and legal issues for presentation to a jury. The firm also offers comprehensive asset protection/estate planning and business consulting services.

Insurance Clients

Missouri Doctors Mutual Insurance Company
Robert Martin, Ltd.

Non-Insurance Clients

Aurora Hand Therapy, Inc.
Delta Distributing, Inc.
SourceLink World Trade, Inc.
AVG Global, LLC
Medical Liability Specialists, LLC

Attorneys

Randall A. Bauman — University of Missouri-Columbia, B.A., 1991; University of Missouri-Kansas City, J.D., 1994 — Admitted to Bar, 1994, Missouri; 1996, U.S. District Court, Eastern District of Missouri; 1997, U.S. Court of Appeals, Eighth Circuit; 2010, U.S. District Court, Western District of Missouri

Daniel K. Mannion — Indiana University-Bloomington, B.A., 1995; University of Missouri-Columbia, J.D., 2000 — Admitted to Bar, 2000, Missouri; 2007, U.S. District Court, Eastern District of Missouri

Boggs, Avellino, Lach & Boggs, LLC

7912 Bonhomme, Suite 400
St. Louis, Missouri 63105
Telephone: 314-726-2310
Fax: 314-726-2360
Toll Free: 888-942-2310
www.balblawyers.com

(Belleville, IL Office: 23 South First Street, 62220)
(Lee's Summit, MO Office: 200 NE Missouri Drive, 64086)
(Glen Carbon, IL Office: 200 West Main, 62034)
(Murphysboro, IL Office: 1400 North Wood Road, 62966)
(Columbia, MO Office: 3610 Buttonwood Drive, Suite 200, 65201)

Established: 1999

Insurance Defense, Automobile, Product Liability, Professional Negligence, Medical Malpractice, Errors and Omissions, Workers' Compensation, Personal Injury, Property Damage, Tort Litigation, Defense Litigation, Employment Law, Subrogation, Premises Liability, Construction Liability, Transportation

Firm Profile: Our firm specializes in civil defense and workers compensation defense throughout Missouri and Illinois. We represent insurance companies, their insureds, and self-insured corporations. We pride ourselves on quickly and effectively evaluating matters to obtain favorable results for our clients. The firm is WBENC certified and is a member of NAMWOLF.

Insurance Clients

American Family Mutual Insurance Company
Cincinnati Insurance Company
Founders Insurance Company
Atlantic Mutual Insurance Company
Federated Insurance Company
GMAC Insurance

Boggs, Avellino, Lach & Boggs, LLC, St. Louis, MO
(Continued)

Non-Insurance Clients

BCA Administrators
Kinder-Care

Partners

Beth Clemens Boggs — 1967 — Governors State University, B.A. (with honors), 1987; Southern Illinois University, J.D. (magna cum laude), 1991 — Admitted to Bar, 1991, Illinois; 1992, Missouri; 1991, U.S. District Court, Southern District of Illinois; 1992, U.S. District Court, Eastern District of Missouri; 1996, U.S. District Court, Central District of Illinois; 1997, U.S. District Court, Western District of Missouri; 2003, U.S. District Court, Northern District of Illinois; 2009, U.S. District Court, District of Kansas — Member American, Illinois State and St. Clair County Bar Associations; The Missouri Bar; The Bar Association of Metropolitan St. Louis; Lawyers Association of St. Louis; Women Lawyers Association; Greater St. Louis Claims Association (Sponsor); Missouri Organization of Defense Lawyers; Defense Research Institute — Practice Areas: Premises Liability; Coverage Analysis; Employment Law; Medical Malpractice; Construction Liability — E-mail: bboggs@balblawyers.com

T. Darin Boggs — 1964 — University of Illinois, B.S., 1987; Southern Illinois University Carbondale, J.D., 1990 — Admitted to Bar, 1990, Illinois; 1991, Missouri; 1991, U.S. District Court, Eastern District of Missouri; 1995, U.S. District Court, Southern District of Illinois — E-mail: tboggs@balblawyers.com

Victor T. Avellino — 1963 — Lindenwood College, B.A. (magna cum laude), 1985; Saint Louis University School of Law, J.D., 1988 — Admitted to Bar, 1989, Missouri; 2000, Illinois; 1998, U.S. District Court, Eastern District of Missouri; 2004, U.S. District Court, Southern District of Illinois — Member American Bar Association — E-mail: vavellino@balblawyers.com

Michael J. Lach — 1963 — Illinois State University, B.S., 1986; Southern Illinois University, J.D., 1989; Georgetown University, LL.M., 1994 — Admitted to Bar, 1989, Missouri; 1990, Illinois; 1990, U.S. District Court, Eastern District of Missouri; 1991, U.S. District Court, Southern District of Illinois; 1998, U.S. Supreme Court — Member American, Illinois State and St. Clair County Bar Associations; The Missouri Bar — E-mail: mlach@balblawyers.com

Kevin P. Clark — 1976 — Southeast Missouri State University, B.S.B.A., 1999; Southern Illinois University, J.D., 2002 — Admitted to Bar, 2002, Missouri; 2003, Illinois — E-mail: kclark@balblawyers.com

Robert K. Kerr — 1961 — Washington University, B.S.B.A., 1984; J.D., 1987 — Admitted to Bar, 1988, Missouri; Illinois — E-mail: rkerr@balblawyers.com

Douglas B. Keane — 1979 — Western Illinois University, B.S., 2002; Southern Illinois University, J.D., 2005 — Admitted to Bar, 2005, Missouri; 2006, Illinois; U.S. District Court, Eastern and Western Districts of Missouri; U.S. District Court, Southern District of Illinois — E-mail: dkeane@balblawyers.com

Lisa A. Reynolds — 1979 — University of Missouri, B.A., 2002; Saint Louis University School of Law, J.D., 2006 — Admitted to Bar, 2006, Missouri; 2007, Illinois — Member American and Illinois State Bar Associations; The Missouri Bar; The Bar Association of Metropolitan St. Louis — Languages: French — E-mail: lreynolds@balblawyers.com

Associates

H. Edward Ryals — 1967 — Lincoln University, B.S., 1991; University of Missouri-Columbia, J.D., 1999 — Admitted to Bar, 1999, Missouri; 2000, Illinois; 1999, U.S. District Court, Eastern District of Missouri; 2000, U.S. District Court, Central and Southern Districts of Illinois — Member American and Illinois State Bar Associations; The Missouri Bar; St. Louis Lawyers Association — E-mail: eryals@balblawyers.com

James P. McCune, III — 1969 — Washington & Jefferson College, B.A., 1991; Oklahoma City University School of Law, J.D., 1994 — Admitted to Bar, 1994, Pennsylvania; 2003, Missouri; 2004, Illinois; 1994, U.S. District Court, Western District of Pennsylvania; 1997, U.S. Court of Appeals, Third Circuit; U.S. District Court, Central and Southern Districts of Illinois; U.S. District Court, Eastern and Western Districts of Missouri — E-mail: jmccune@balblawyers.com

Brent L. Salsbury — 1981 — Illinois State University, B.S. (magna cum laude), 2002; Southern Illinois University, J.D., 2005 — Admitted to Bar, 2005, Illinois; 2006, Missouri; U.S. District Court, Southern District of Illinois; U.S. District Court, Eastern District of Missouri — Member Illinois State Bar Association; The Missouri Bar — E-mail: bsalsbury@balblawyers.com

Ryan P. Kovacs — 1978 — University of Missouri, B.S.B.A., 2000; J.D.,

Boggs, Avellino, Lach & Boggs, LLC, St. Louis, MO (Continued)

2006 — Admitted to Bar, 2006, Missouri; 2007, Illinois; U.S. District Court, Eastern District of Missouri; U.S. District Court, Southern District of Illinois — Member American Bar Association; The Missouri Bar; The Bar Association of Metropolitan St. Louis — E-mail: rkovacs@balblawyers.com

Lee J. Karge — 1971 — Washburn University, B.A., 1994; Drake University, J.D., 1997 — Admitted to Bar, 1999, Illinois; 2004, Missouri; U.S. District Court, Central and Southern Districts of Illinois; U.S. District Court, Eastern and Western Districts of Missouri — E-mail: lkarge@balblawyers.com

Justin C. Moore — Truman State University, B.S. (cum laude), 2008; Saint Louis University School of Law, J.D., 2012 — Admitted to Bar, 2012, Missouri; 2013, Illinois — E-mail: JMoore@balblawyers.com

Andrew C. Chipperfield — 1984 — University of Denver, B.A., 2007; Saint Louis University, J.D., 2011 — Admitted to Bar, 2012, Missouri; 2013, Illinois; 2012, U.S. District Court, Eastern and Western Districts of Missouri — Member Illinois State Bar Association; The Bar Association of Metropolitan St. Louis; The Missouri Bar — E-mail: achipperfield@balblawyers.com

Tyler J. Merkel — 1987 — Saint Louis University, B.A. (cum laude), 2009; J.D., 2012 — Admitted to Bar, 2012, Missouri; 2013, Illinois — Member Illinois State Bar Association; The Bar Association of Metropolitan St. Louis; The Missouri Bar — E-mail: tmerkel@balblawyers.com

Allison E. Lee — 1983 — Bradley University, B.S. (cum laude), 2006; Washington University School of Law, J.D. (cum laude), 2009 — Admitted to Bar, 2009, Missouri; 2011, Illinois; 2011, U.S. District Court, Central District of Illinois; 2013, U.S. District Court, Eastern District of Missouri — E-mail: alee@balblawyers.com

Anna K. Newell — 1987 — Indiana University, B.A. (with honors), 2010; Southern Illinois University School of Law, J.D. (Dean's List), 2013 — Admitted to Bar, 2013, Illinois; 2014, Missouri — Member Illinois State Bar Association; The Bar Association of Metropolitan St. Louis; Women Lawyers Association of Greater St. Louis — E-mail: anewell@balblawyers.com

Andrew Laquet — University of Louisville, B.S., 2009; Southern Illinois University School of Law, J.D. (Dean's List), 2013 — Admitted to Bar, 2013, Missouri; 2014, Illinois — E-mail: alaquet@balblawyers.com

Mark R. Senda — 1987 — Saint Louis University, B.A. (cum laude), 2010; Saint Louis University School of Law, J.D. (cum laude), 2013 — Admitted to Bar, 2013, Missouri; 2014, Illinois; 2013, U.S. District Court, Eastern District of Missouri — E-mail: msenda@balblawyers.com

Brooke Hurst — 1987 — University of Illinois at Urbana-Champaign, B.S., 2009; Southern Illinois University, J.D., 2012 — Admitted to Bar, 2013, Missouri — E-mail: bhurst@balblawyers.com

Of Counsel

Andrew S. Malloy — 1975 — University of Missouri, B.S., 2000; J.D., 2003 — Admitted to Bar, 2003, Missouri; 2004, Illinois

(This firm is also listed in the Subrogation section of this directory)

Buckley & Buckley, L.L.C.

1139 Olive Street, Suite 800
St. Louis, Missouri 63101-1928
 Telephone: 314-621-3434
 Fax: 314-621-3485
 E-Mail: mbuckley@buckleylawllc.com
 www.buckleylawllc.com

Established: 1996

Insurance Defense, First and Third Party Defense, General Liability, Automobile, Public Entities, Environmental Law, Medical Malpractice, Premises Liability, Product Liability, Employment Law

Firm Profile: Buckley & Buckley, L.L.C. specializes in the defense of civil jury trials in the greater St. Louis area and throughout the eastern half of Missouri. We represent insurers and self-insured corporations in matters such as products liability, professional malpractice, civil rights, employment, insurance coverage, premises liability, environmental law and automobile/trucking cases. We also handle appeals before all appellate courts in Missouri.

Buckley & Buckley, L.L.C., St. Louis, MO (Continued)

Insurance Clients

Bituminous Insurance Companies
Electric Insurance Company
Liberty Mutual Insurance Company
St. Paul Fire and Marine Insurance Company
Columbia Insurance Group
Gallagher Bassett Services, Inc.
Missouri Professionals Mutual
State Farm Fire and Casualty Company

Non-Insurance Clients

Union Pacific Railroad Company

Partners

Martin J. Buckley — 1962 — Saint Louis University, A.B. (summa cum laude), 1984; J.D. (cum laude), 1987 — Recipient, Lon O. Hocker Memorial Trial Lawyer Award 1998 — Admitted to Bar, 1987, Missouri; 1988, Illinois; 1988, U.S. District Court, Eastern District of Missouri; 1995, U.S. Court of Appeals, Eighth Circuit — Member The Missouri Bar; The Bar Association of Metropolitan St. Louis; Law Library Association of St. Louis; Missouri Organization of Defense Lawyers; Defense Research Institute — Practice Areas: Product Liability; Insurance Coverage; Premises Liability

Stephen M. Buckley — 1960 — Saint Louis University, B.A. (cum laude), 1982; J.D., 1985 — Admitted to Bar, 1985, Missouri; 1986, Illinois; 1986, U.S. District Court, Eastern District of Missouri; 1986, U.S. Court of Appeals, Eighth Circuit — Member Illinois State Bar Association; The Missouri Bar; The Bar Association of Metropolitan St. Louis; National Association of Railroad Trial Counsel — Practice Areas: Premises Liability; Product Liability; Railroad Law

Ann E. Buckley — 1954 — Saint Louis University, A.B. (summa cum laude), 1975; J.D. (cum laude), 1978 — Admitted to Bar, 1978, Missouri; 1979, Illinois; U.S. District Court, Eastern District of Missouri; 1980, U.S. Court of Appeals, Eighth Circuit; 1986, U.S. Supreme Court; 1989, U.S. District Court, Southern District of Illinois; 2005, U.S. District Court, Western District of Missouri; 2006, U.S. Court of Appeals, Tenth Circuit; 2007, U.S. District Court, District of Kansas — Member The Missouri Bar; The Bar Association of Metropolitan St. Louis; National Lawyers Association; Sub Committee, Model Civil Jury Instructions Eighth Circuit; Missouri Supreme Court Appellate Practice Committee; Missouri Organization of Defense Lawyers; Defense Research Institute — Practice Areas: ERISA; Appellate Practice

Adrian P. Sulser   Joshua J. Engelbart

Associates

Josephine P. Abshire   Tiffany L. Lightle
Monica M. Eday   Daniel J. Sullivan
John E. Gibbons

Of Counsel

Eugene K. Buckley

Case Linden P.C.

Two City Place Drive, 2nd Floor
St. Louis, Missouri 63141
 Telephone: 314-812-4750
 Fax: 314-812-4755
 www.caselinden.com

(Kansas City, MO Office*: 2600 Grand Boulevard, Suite 300, 64108)
 (Tel: 816-979-1500)
 (Fax: 816-979-1501)
 (E-Mail: kevin.case@caselinden.com)

Appellate Practice, Bodily Injury, Civil Trial Practice, Class Actions, Commercial Litigation, Discrimination, Errors and Omissions, Insurance Defense, Labor and Employment, Legal Malpractice, Medical Malpractice, Premises Liability, Product Liability, Professional Liability, Regulatory and Compliance, Tort, Workers' Compensation

(See listing under Kansas City, MO for additional information)

Eckenrode - Maupin
Attorneys At Law

8000 Maryland Avenue, Suite 1300
St. Louis, Missouri 63105
 Telephone: 314-726-6670
 Fax: 314-726-2106
 E-Mail: lawyers@eckenrode-law.com
 www.eckenrode-law.com

Established: 1998

Insurance Defense, Medical Negligence, Professional Liability, Automobile, Product Liability, Premises Liability, Tort, Civil Litigation, Construction Law, Municipal Law, Real Estate, Labor and Employment, Estate Planning, Bankruptcy, Mechanics Liens, Corporate Law

Firm Profile: Our mission is to provide cost-effective representation to our clients and to promptly identify areas of concern while vigorously defending meritless claims through trial.

Insurance Clients

American Family Insurance Company
The Doctors Company
Farmers Insurance Company
Galen Insurance Company
Healthcare Services Group
Intermed Insurance Company
Keystone Mutual Insurance Company
Missouri Doctors Mutual Insurance Company
National Lloyds Insurance Company
ProAssurance Group
Western Litigation, Inc.
Corizon
Correctional Medical Services, Inc.
Essex Insurance Company
Fireman's Fund Insurance Company
Hudson Insurance Group
Interstate Insurance Group
Lincoln Insurance Company
Medical Assurance of Missouri
Missouri Property & Casualty Insurance Guaranty Association
Oceanus Insurance Company
PHICO Insurance Company
Professional Underwriters Liability Insurance Company

Non-Insurance Clients

Market Finders Group
Morgan's Foods

Self-Insured Clients

Esse Healthcare

Partner

J. Thaddeus Eckenrode — 1958 — Siena College, B.B.A. (cum laude), 1980; Washington University, J.D., 1983 — Admitted to Bar, 1983, Missouri; 1987, Illinois; 1987, U.S. District Court, Eastern District of Missouri; 1987, U.S. Court of Appeals, Eighth Circuit; 2010, U.S. District Court, Western District of Missouri — Member American and Illinois State Bar Associations; The Missouri Bar; The Bar Association of Metropolitan St. Louis; Claims and Litigation Management Alliance; Missouri Organization of Defense Lawyers; American Society of Law and Medicine; Defense Research Institute — Reported Cases: Weiss v. Rojanasathit, 975 S.W. 2d 113 (MO 1998) — Practice Areas: Insurance Law; Medical Malpractice; Personal Injury; Premises Liability; Product Liability; Tort — E-mail: JTE@eckenrode-law.com

Senior Attorneys

John W. Maupin — 1950 — University of Missouri, B.A., 1972; J.D., 1975 — Admitted to Bar, 1975, Missouri; 1995, U.S. District Court, Western District of Missouri — Member The Missouri Bar; The Bar Association of Metropolitan St. Louis; Claims and Litigation Management Alliance; Missouri Organization of Defense Lawyers — Practice Areas: Construction Law; Medical Malpractice; Municipal Law — E-mail: JWM@eckenrode-law.com

Richard J. Magee — 1953 — Columbia University, B.A., 1975; Washington University School of Law, J.D., 1979 — Admitted to Bar, 1980, Missouri; 1984, U.S. District Court, Eastern District of Missouri; 2001, U.S. District Court, Western District of Missouri — Member The Bar Association of Metropolitan St. Louis; Community Associations Institute — Author: "Recent Developments Which Impact the Use and Management of E-Mail,"

Eckenrode - Maupin, Attorneys At Law, St. Louis, MO
(Continued)

Kirkwood/Des Peres Chamber Advantage Newsletter, October 2007; "New Developments in Employment Law," Kirkwood/Des Peres Chamber Advantage Newsletter, April 2007; "Formulating an Approach to In-Fill Development, The Missouri Municipal Review, June 2004; A series of three columns, "Business and the Law," Kirkwood/Des Peres Chamber Advantage newsletters, 2003-2004; "Section 301 Preemption of State Tort Claims," St. Louis Lawyer, April 4, 2001; "Recent Cases Involving Independent Residential Inspections," The Missouri Bar Journal, July/August, 1998; "Land Surveyors' Liability to Third Parties," Missouri Surveyor, March, 1994; "The Dilemma of the 'Full Payment' Check," St. Louis Countian and St.Louis Daily Record, April 19, 1989 — Reported Cases: Henty Construction Co., Inc. vs. Hall 783 S.W. 2d 412 (Mo. App. E.D. 1989); Griffith v. Sam Ogle Chrysler Plymouth, Inc. 769 S.W. 2d 796 (Supreme Court of Missouri, En Banc 1989); Umphres v. J.R. Mayer Enterprises, Inc. 889 S.W. 2d 86 (Mo. App. E.D. 1994); Vaughn v. Missouri Department of Social Services, Division of Family Services, 161 S.W. 3d 883 (Mo. App. E.D. 2005); Farmers Insurance Company, Inc. v. Pierrousakas, 255 F. 3d 639 (8th Circuit 2001) — Mayor, City of Glendale (2005-Present) — Practice Areas: Real Estate; Municipal Law; Mechanics Liens; Construction Law; Labor and Employment; Estate Planning; Bankruptcy; Corporate Law — E-mail: RJM@eckenrode-law.com

Attorneys

Lisa H. Howe — 1971 — Southwest Missouri State University, B.S., 1993; Saint Louis University, J.D., 1996 — Admitted to Bar, 1996, Missouri; 2003, Illinois; 2003, U.S. District Court, Eastern District of Missouri — Member The Missouri Bar; Missouri Organization of Defense Lawyers — Practice Areas: Medical Malpractice; Workers' Compensation — E-mail: LHH@eckenrode-law.com

Dwight A. Vermette — 1955 — Western Illinois University, B.A., 1985; University of Missouri, J.D., 1988 — Admitted to Bar, 1989, Missouri — Member The Missouri Bar; The Bar Association of Metropolitan St. Louis; Missouri Organization of Defense Lawyers; The Federalist Society — U.S. Navy, 1975-1984 — Practice Areas: Bankruptcy; Automobile; Insurance Defense; Medical Malpractice; Personal Injury — E-mail: DAV@eckenrode-law.com

Galloway, Johnson, Tompkins, Burr & Smith

7710 Carondelet Avenue, Suite 217
St. Louis, Missouri 63105
 Telephone: 314-725-0525
 Fax: 314-725-7150
 E-Mail: smoore@gallowayjohnson.com
 www.gallowayjohnson.com

(Additional Offices: New Orleans, LA*; Lafayette, LA*; Pensacola, FL*; Houston, TX*; Mandeville, LA*; Gulfport, MS*; Tampa, FL*; Mobile, AL*; Atlanta, GA*)

Maritime, Automobile Liability, Bad Faith, Class Actions, Construction, Energy, Employment, Insurance Coverage, Insurance Defense, Product Liability, Professional Liability, Property, Transportation, General Casualty, Title Resolution, Environmental

(See listing under New Orleans, LA for additional information)

Goffstein, Raskas, Pomerantz, Kraus & Sherman, L.L.C.

7701 Clayton Road
St. Louis, Missouri 63117
 Telephone: 314-721-7171
 Fax: 314-721-7765
 www.goffsteinraskas.com

Established: 1960

Goffstein, Raskas, Pomerantz, Kraus & Sherman, L.L.C., St. Louis, MO (Continued)

Casualty, Fire, Life Insurance, Medical Malpractice, Agent and Brokers Errors and Omissions, Product Liability, Accountant Malpractice, Employment Discrimination, Fidelity and Surety, Professional Malpractice, Truck Liability, Contractors Liability, Public Entity Liability, Marina Liability, Appraisers Liability, Fraternity Liability

Firm Profile: As one of the leading insurance defense firms in Missouri, our firm provides aggressive representation to insurance brokers, real estate appraisers, real estate agents, lawyers, accountants, and health care providers. We are prepared to handle cases from initial evaluation through trial in Missouri and southern and central Illinois.

Insurance Clients

Accredited Surety & Casualty Company, Inc.
Columbia Insurance Group
E & O Professionals
Fidelity National Title Insurance Company
GAB Robins North America, Inc.
James River Insurance Company
Philadelphia Insurance Companies
Western Litigation Specialists, Inc.
XL Insurance Select Professional
Adriatic Insurance Company
American Safety Insurance Company
EquiTrust Life Insurance Company
First Specialty Insurance Corporation
The Hartford
Media Professionals
Swiss Reinsurance Company
Westport Insurance Corporation

Non-Insurance Clients

Brown Smith Wallace, LLC
Electric Power Systems, Inc.
Hardee's Food Systems, Inc.
National Emergency Services, Inc.
Burns & Wilcox Ltd.
Gaglione, Dolan and Kaplan, P.C.
Investors Title Company
Zeta Phi Chapter of Pi Kappa Alpha Fraternity

Firm Members

Sanford Goffstein — 1936 — Washington University, B.S., 1959; B.A., 1959; J.D., 1960 — Admitted to Bar, 1960, Missouri — Member American Bar Association; The Missouri Bar — Adjunct Professor of Trial Advocacy, Washington University School of Law (2006-present) — Practice Areas: Accountants and Attorneys Liability; Agent and Brokers Errors and Omissions; Architects and Engineers; Commercial Litigation; Coverage Disputes; Defense Litigation; Insurance Coverage Litigation; Product Liability Defense; Real Estate Agents & Brokers Liability; Medical Malpractice Defense — E-mail: sgoffstein@grlawstl.com

Jerome F. Raskas — 1933 — Washington University, A.B., 1958; J.D., 1959 — Admitted to Bar, 1959, Missouri — Member American Bar Association; The Missouri Bar — Adjunct Professor, Washington University, (1980-Present) — E-mail: jraskas@grlawstl.com

Sanford E. Pomerantz — 1940 — Cincinnati University; Washington University, B.S.B.A., 1963; J.D., 1965 — Admitted to Bar, 1965, Missouri — Member The Missouri Bar — E-mail: spomerantz@grlawstl.com

Jerome S. Kraus — 1939 — Washington University, A.B., 1961; J.D., 1963 — Admitted to Bar, 1963, Missouri — Member The Missouri Bar — E-mail: jkraus@grlawstl.com

Don R. Sherman — 1945 — Washington University, A.B., 1967; J.D., 1971 — Order of the Coif — Admitted to Bar, 1971, Missouri — Member The Missouri Bar — E-mail: dsherman@grlawstl.com

Robert M. Susman — 1951 — Indiana University, B.A., 1973; Saint Louis University, J.D., 1976 — Admitted to Bar, 1976, Missouri; 2001, Illinois — Member Illinois State Bar Association; The Missouri Bar — Practice Areas: Accountants and Attorneys Liability; Architects and Engineers; Defense Litigation; Employment Litigation; Insurance Agent Errors & Omissions; Real Estate Errors and Omissions — E-mail: rsusman@grlawstl.com

Edward L. Adelman — 1953 — Saint Louis University; Washington University, A.B., 1975; J.D., 1979 — Admitted to Bar, 1979, California; 1981, Missouri; 1982, Illinois — Member Illinois State Bar Association; State Bar of California; The Missouri Bar — Practice Areas: Accountants and Attorneys Liability; Defense Litigation; Insurance Agent Errors & Omissions; Real Estate Errors and Omissions; Property Defense — E-mail: eadelman@grlawstl.com

Lori R. Koch — 1959 — University of Missouri-Saint Louis, B.S., 1981; Washington University, J.D., 1985 — Admitted to Bar, 1985, Missouri; 1986, Illinois — Member Illinois State Bar Association; The Missouri Bar; Defense Research Institute — Practice Areas: Accountants and Attorneys Liability; Architects and Engineers; Commercial Litigation; Coverage Litigation; Insurance Coverage & Defense; Real Estate Errors and Omissions; Medical Malpractice Defense — E-mail: lkoch@grlawstl.com

Robert E. Tucker — 1953 — University of Missouri-Columbia, B.J., 1975; Saint Louis University, J.D., 1985 — Admitted to Bar, 1986, Missouri; 1992, Florida; 2002, Illinois — Member Illinois State Bar Association; The Missouri Bar; The Florida Bar; St. Louis Lawyers Association — Practice Areas: Architects and Engineers; Defense Litigation; Insurance Agent Errors & Omissions; Medical Malpractice Defense; Real Estate Errors and Omissions — E-mail: rtucker@grlawstl.com

Peter H. Love — 1964 — Hobart College, B.A. (with honors), 1986; Washington University, J.D., 1989 — Admitted to Bar, 1989, Missouri; 1990, Illinois — Member Illinois State Bar Association; The Missouri Bar — E-mail: plove@grlawstl.com

Associates

Ellen Kersch Siegel — 1960 — University of Michigan, B.A. (with distinction), 1982; J.D., 1991 — Admitted to Bar, 1992, Michigan; 1994, Missouri — Member State Bar of Michigan; The Missouri Bar — E-mail: esiegel@grlawstl.com

Jeffrey L. Wax — 1979 — Miami University, B.A., 2000; Washington University, J.D. (Order of the Coif), 2004 — Admitted to Bar, 2004, Missouri; 2005, Illinois — Member The Missouri Bar; Illinois State Bar Association — E-mail: jwax@grlawstl.com

Of Counsel

Mark D. Sadow — 1950 — Washington University, A.B., 1972; Columbia University, M.P.H., 1975; Washington University, J.D., 1980; LL.M., 1992 — Admitted to Bar, 1980, Missouri — Member The Missouri Bar — E-mail: msadow@grlawstl.com

Andrew A. Rimmel — Emory University, B.A., 1974; The University of North Carolina, J.D., 1977; Washington University, LL.M., 1981 — Admitted to Bar, 1977, Missouri — Member The Missouri Bar; Estate Planning Council of St. Louis — E-mail: arimmel@grlawstl.com

Gonnerman Reinert, LLC

222 South Central Avenue, Suite 500
St. Louis, Missouri 63105
Telephone: 314-880-8060
Fax: 314-880-8059
E-Mail: mag@grstllaw.com
www.grstllaw.com

Established: 2009

Civil Litigation, Medical Liability, Product Liability, Personal Injury, Workers' Compensation, Health Care

Firm Profile: Gonnerman Reinert, LLC's attorneys are well-recognized in their fields and lecture regularly on topics related to their specialties. In addition, they have been selected to serve as leaders of numerous bar and community associations. We invite you to let us put our experience to work for you.

Insurance Clients

Cincinnati Insurance Company
MPM Insurance Company of Kansas
Missouri Professionals Mutual
Shelter Insurance Companies
Travelers

Members

Mark A. Gonnerman — University of Missouri, B.S. (cum laude), 1973; The University of Georgia, J.D. (cum laude), 1976 — Admitted to Bar, 1976, Georgia; 1998, Missouri; 1999, Illinois; U.S. District Court, Eastern District of Missouri; U.S. District Court, Southern District of Illinois; U.S. District Court, Middle District of Georgia; U.S. Court of Appeals, Eleventh Circuit; U.S. Supreme Court — Member The Missouri Bar; Illinois State Bar Association; State Bar of Georgia; International Association of Defense Counsel; Defense Research Institute; Missouri Organization of Defense Lawyers; Association of Defense Trial Attorneys — Practice Areas: Medical Malpractice; Personal Injury; Product Liability; Workers' Compensation

MISSOURI / ST. LOUIS

Gonnerman Reinert, LLC, St. Louis, MO (Continued)

James P. Reinert — University of Scranton, B.S. (cum laude), 1980; Saint Louis University, J.D., 1986 — Admitted to Bar, 1986, Missouri; 1986, Illinois; U.S. District Court, Eastern District of Missouri; U.S. Court of Appeals, Eighth Circuit — Member Missouri Organization of Defense Lawyers — Practice Areas: Medical Malpractice; Construction Law; Personal Injury; Professional Liability

Jeffrey E. Atkinson — Albion College, B.A. (cum laude), 1995; Washington University School of Law, J.D., 1998 — Admitted to Bar, 1998, Missouri; U.S. District Court, Eastern District of Missouri — Member The Missouri Bar; The Bar Association of Metropolitan St. Louis — Practice Areas: Civil Litigation; Real Estate Litigation; Workers' Compensation; Medical Malpractice

William J. Magrath — Upsala College, B.A. (magna cum laude), 1987; Saint Louis University School of Law, J.D., 1992 — Admitted to Bar, 1992, Missouri; 1993, Illinois; U.S. District Court, Eastern District of Missouri; U.S. Court of Appeals, Eighth Circuit — Member The Missouri Bar; Illinois State Bar Association; The Bar Association of Metropolitan St. Louis — Practice Areas: Medical Malpractice; Product Liability; Personal Injury

Associate

Timothy F. McCurdy — Morningside College, B.A. (magna cum laude), 1998; University of Notre Dame Law School, J.D. (cum laude), 2002 — Admitted to Bar, 2002, Missouri; 2003, Illinois; U.S. District Court, Eastern District of Missouri; U.S. District Court, Southern District of Illinois; U.S. Court of Appeals, Seventh Circuit — Member The Missouri Bar; Illinois State Bar Association; National Association of Subrogation Professionals — Practice Areas: Civil Litigation; Medical Malpractice; Personal Injury; Subrogation

HeplerBroom LLC

211 North Broadway, Suite 2700
St. Louis, Missouri 63102
   Telephone: 314-241-6160
   Fax: 314-241-6116
   E-Mail: firm@heplerbroom.com
   www.heplerbroom.com

(Additional Offices: Edwardsville, IL*; Chicago, IL*; Springfield, IL*)

Antitrust, Insurance Defense, Product Liability, Toxic Torts, Property and Casualty, Class Actions, Legal Malpractice, Commercial Litigation, Pharmaceutical, General Liability, Asbestos Litigation, Medical Malpractice, Workers' Compensation, Employment Litigation, Insurance Coverage, Transportation, Automobile, Trucking Law, Agent and Brokers Errors and Omissions, Personal Injury, Skilled Nursing Facilities, Construction Liability, White Collar Criminal Defense, Qui Tam/False Claims Act Litigation

Partners

Gerard T. Noce — 1951 — University of Missouri-Columbia, J.D., 1979 — Admitted to Bar, 1979, Missouri; 1980, Illinois — Tel: 314-480-4160 — E-mail: gtn@heplerbroom.com

Theodore J. MacDonald, Jr. — 1951 — Saint Louis University, J.D., 1977 — Admitted to Bar, 1978, New York; 1978, Missouri; 1979, Illinois — Tel: 314-480-4155 — E-mail: tjm@heplerbroom.com

Michael L. Young — 1976 — Saint Louis University School of Law, J.D., 2002 — Admitted to Bar, 2002, Illinois; 2003, Missouri — Tel: 314-480-4152 — E-mail: mly@heplerbroom.com

(See listing under Edwardsville, IL for additional information)

Leritz Plunkert & Bruning, P.C.

555 Washington Avenue, Suite 600
St. Louis, Missouri 63101
   Telephone: 314-231-9600
   Fax: 314-231-9480
   E-Mail: kpadgitt@leritzlaw.com
   www.leritzlaw.com

Leritz Plunkert & Bruning, P.C., St. Louis, MO (Continued)

Alternative Dispute Resolution, Business Interruption, Construction Litigation, Contract Disputes, Directors and Officers Liability, Errors and Omissions, Fire, Insurance Coverage, Legal Malpractice, Medical Malpractice, Nursing Home Liability, Personal Injury, Subrogation, Workers' Compensation

Firm Profile: For over 80 years the members of Leritz Plunkert & Bruning, P.C. have been among the most active litigation and trial attorneys in St. Louis. We represent clients through mediation, arbitration and litigation in federal and state courts, and argue appeals at all levels before the Missouri and Illinois Appellate Courts.

Insurance Clients

ACUITY
The Bar Plan
Bituminous Insurance Companies
Discover Re
General Casualty Insurance Company
Indemnity Insurance Corporation
Indiana Lumbermens Mutual Insurance Company
Missouri Property Insurance Placement Facility (FAIR Plan)
Nationwide Insurance
North American Risk Services
Pennsylvania Lumbermens Mutual Insurance Company
Specialty Risk Services
State Auto Insurance Company
Travelers Insurance
West Bend Mutual Insurance Company

American National Property and Casualty Company
Capitol Insurance Companies
ESIS
Global Indemnity Group, Inc.
Hortica Insurance & Employee Benefits
Lititz Mutual Insurance Company
Madison Mutual Insurance Company
National Lloyds Insurance Company
NSI
QBE the Americas
SECURA Insurance Companies
Starr Indemnity & Liability Company
Unitrin Services Group

Non-Insurance Clients

Baldwin & Lyons, Inc.
Clayton Homes, Inc.

Carrier Corporation/UTC
Otis Elevator Company

Partners

Joseph L. Leritz — Saint Louis University, J.D., 1952 — Admitted to Bar, 1952, Missouri — Member The Missouri Bar; The Bar Association of Metropolitan St. Louis; Association of Defense Counsel (President, 1969-1970); Defense Research Institute

Thomas J. Plunkert — Florida Institute of Technology, B.S. (cum laude), 1974; Saint Louis University, J.D. (cum laude), 1977 — Admitted to Bar, 1977, Missouri; 1978, Illinois — Member Illinois State Bar Association; The Missouri Bar (Board of Governors, 1982-1986, 1987-1994; Vice Chairman, Young Lawyers Section Council, 1982-1986); The Bar Association of Metropolitan St. Louis; Lawyers Association of St. Louis

Anthony S. Bruning — University of Missouri, B.A., 1977; Saint Louis University, J.D., 1980 — Admitted to Bar, 1980, Missouri; 1981, Illinois — Member The Missouri Bar (Young Lawyers Section Council, 1982-1987; Executive Committee, 1984-1986); The Bar Association of Metropolitan St. Louis; Lawyers Association of St. Louis; Million Dollar Advocate Forum; Missouri Association of Trial Attorneys; Association of Trial Lawyers of America

James C. Leritz — University of Missouri, J.D., 1986 — Admitted to Bar, 1986, Missouri; 1994, Illinois — Member The Missouri Bar; The Bar Association of Metropolitan St. Louis; Lawyers Association of St. Louis

Christopher P. Leritz — Saint Louis University, B.A. (magna cum laude), 1985; J.D., 1990 — Admitted to Bar, 1990, Missouri — Member The Missouri Bar; The Bar Association of Metropolitan St. Louis

Peter N. Leritz — Saint Louis University, B.A., 1988; J.D. (cum laude), 1993 — Admitted to Bar, 1993, Missouri; 1994, Illinois — Member The Missouri Bar; Illinois State Bar Association; The Bar Association of Metropolitan St. Louis

Associate

Anthony S. Bruning Jr. — 1981 — University of Missouri-Columbia, B.S. Business Admin., 2004; Saint Louis University School of Law, J.D., 2007 — Admitted to Bar, 2007, Missouri; 2008, Illinois

ST. LOUIS   MISSOURI

McAnany, Van Cleave & Phillips, P.C.

505 North 7th Street, Suite 2100
St. Louis, Missouri 63101
   Telephone: 314-621-1133
   Fax: 314-621-4405
   www.mvplaw.com

(McAnany, Van Cleave & Phillips, P.A.*: 10 East Cambridge Circle Drive, Suite 300, Kansas City, KS, 66103)
   (Tel: 913-371-3838)
   (Fax: 913-371-4722)
(Springfield, MO Office*: 4650 South National Avenue, Suite D-2, 65810)
   (Tel: 417-865-0007)
   (Fax: 417-865-0008)
(Omaha, NE Office*: 10665 Bedford Avenue, Suite 101, 68134)
   (Tel: 402-408-1340)
   (Fax: 402-493-0860)
(Tulsa, OK Office*: 2021 South Lewis, Suite 225, 74104)
   (Tel: 918-771-4465)

Established: 1901

Administrative Law, Antitrust, Bankruptcy, Business Law, Construction Law, Corporate Law, Creditor Rights, Directors and Officers Liability, Insurance Law, Labor and Employment, Land Use, Litigation, Municipal Law, Personal Injury, Product Liability, Professional Liability, Public Entities, Railroad Law, Real Estate, School Law, Transportation, Trial and Appellate Practice, Workers' Compensation

(See Kansas City, KS listing for additional information)

McMahon Berger

2730 North Ballas Road, Suite 200
St. Louis, Missouri 63131
   Telephone: 314-567-7350
   Fax: 314-567-5968
   E-Mail: lawfirm@mcmahonberger.com
   www.mcmahonberger.com

(Collinsville, IL Office*: 400 North Bluff Road, 62234)
   (Tel: 618-345-5822)
   (Fax: 618-345-6483)

Established: 1955

Employment Law, Labor and Employment, Employment Discrimination, Administrative Law

Insurance Clients

AIG Technical Services, Inc.
The Cincinnati Companies
Great American Insurance Company
Hudson Insurance Company
Nationwide Insurance
Royal & SunAlliance
Scottsdale Insurance Company
U.S. Specialty Insurance Company
Western General Insurance Company
Chubb Group
Fireman's Fund Insurance Company
Houston Casualty Company
National Casualty Company
Northland Insurance Company
St. Paul Travelers
Travelers Property Casualty Insurance Company
Western Heritage Insurance Company

Non-Insurance Clients

AUSCO

Partners

Alan I. Berger — (1933-1999)

Thomas O. McCarthy — 1947 — University of Missouri, B.S.E.E. (cum laude), 1970; J.D., 1972 — Admitted to Bar, 1973, Missouri — Member American Bar Association; The Missouri Bar; The Bar Association of Metropolitan St. Louis (Co-Chairman, Labor Arbitrator Development Program,

McMahon Berger, St. Louis, MO   (Continued)

1984-1985; Chairman, Labor Law Section, 1985-1986) — Practice Areas: Labor and Employment

James N. Foster, Jr. — 1954 — Saint Louis University, B.A. (magna cum laude), 1976; J.D. (cum laude), 1978 — Admitted to Bar, 1979, Missouri — Member American Bar Association; The Missouri Bar; The Bar Association of Metropolitan St. Louis (Chairman, Labor and Employment Law Section, 1990-1991) — Practice Areas: Labor and Employment

Patricia M. McFall — 1951 — Saint Louis University, A.B., 1973; J.D., 1980 — Admitted to Bar, 1981, Missouri — Member American Bar Association; The Missouri Bar; The Bar Association of Metropolitan St. Louis — Practice Areas: Labor and Employment

Kevin J. Lorenz — 1955 — Saint Louis University, B.A., 1977; J.D., 1981 — Admitted to Bar, 1982, Missouri — Member American and Illinois State Bar Associations; The Missouri Bar; The Bar Association of Metropolitan St. Louis — Practice Areas: Labor and Employment

Geoffrey M. Gilbert, Jr. — 1966 — University of Colorado, B.A., 1988; Saint Louis University, J.D., 1992 — Admitted to Bar, 1992, Missouri — Member The Missouri Bar — Practice Areas: Labor and Employment

Michelle M. Cain — 1958 — University of Illinois, B.A., 1981; The John Marshall Law School, J.D. (with highest distinction), 1988 — Admitted to Bar, 1988, Illinois; 1994, Missouri — Member American and Illinois State Bar Associations; The Missouri Bar; The Bar Association of Metropolitan St. Louis — Practice Areas: Labor and Employment

Robert D. Younger — 1965 — University of Missouri, B.S.B.A., 1989; Saint Louis University, J.D. (cum laude), 1992 — Admitted to Bar, 1992, Missouri — Member The Missouri Bar; The Bar Association of Metropolitan St. Louis; Missouri Organization of Defense Lawyers — Region X Judicial Bar Disciplinary Committee — Practice Areas: Labor and Employment

Stephen B. Maule — 1970 — University of California, Davis, B.A., 1992; University of Missouri-Columbia, J.D., 1995 — Admitted to Bar, 1995, Missouri — Member American Bar Association; The Missouri Bar; The Bar Association of Metropolitan St. Louis — Practice Areas: Labor and Employment

Bryan D. LeMoine — 1974 — Wheaton College, B.A. (cum laude), 1995; University of Missouri, J.D., 2000; Wheaton College, M.A., 2001 — Admitted to Bar, 2000, Missouri; 2001, Illinois — Member American and Illinois State Bar Associations; The Missouri Bar; The Bar Association of Metropolitan St. Louis — Practice Areas: Labor and Employment

Joshua E. Richardson — 1975 — Illinois Wesleyan University, B.A. (magna cum laude), 1997; Washington University School of Law, J.D., 2000; University of Florida, Levin College of Law, LL.M. Taxation, 2001 — Admitted to Bar, 2000, Missouri; U.S. Tax Court — Member American Bar Association (Employee Benefits Committee, Tax Section); The Missouri Bar; The Bar Association of Metropolitan St. Louis (Chairperson, Employee Benefits Section) — Lecturer, Department of Business Administration, Fontbonne University; Member Tax Advisory Board, Thompson West Publishing — Practice Areas: Employee Benefits

Daniel G. Fritz — Truman State University, B.S., 2000; Saint Louis University, J.D., 2004 — Admitted to Bar, 2004, Missouri; U.S. District Court, Eastern and Western Districts of Missouri — Member The Missouri Bar — Practice Areas: Labor and Employment

Brian C. Hey — 1976 — Truman State University, B.A., 1999; University of Missouri-Columbia, J.D., 2002 — Admitted to Bar, 2002, Missouri — Member American Bar Association (Employment and Labor Law Litigation Section); The Bar Association of Metropolitan St. Louis; The Missouri Bar; Society of Human Resource Management — Practice Areas: Labor and Employment

Associates

Brian M. O'Neal
John J. Marino
Christina M. Sondermann
Michael S. Powers
Gina Moshiri
Dean Kpere-Daibo
Rex P. Fennessey

Of Counsel

Ralph E. Kennedy
Richard R. Ross
Theodore W. Browne, II
Thomas M. Hanna
David F. Yates
John B. Renick

MISSOURI   ST. LOUIS

Morrow Willnauer Klosterman Church, LLC

500 North Broadway, Suite 1420
St. Louis, Missouri 63102
  Telephone: 314-561-7300
  Fax: 314-875-9215
  E-Mail: kweston@mwklaw.com
  mwklaw.com

(Kansas City, MO Office*: 10401 Holmes Road, Suite 300, 64131)
  (Tel: 816-382-1382)
  (Fax: 816-382-1383)
  (http://mwklaw.com)
(Omaha, NE Office*: 1299 Farnam Street, Suite 250, 68102)
  (Tel: 402-934-0100)
  (Fax: 402-330-1425)
  (http://mwklaw.com)

Automobile, Construction Liability, Coverage Analysis, Employment Law, Personal Injury, Premises Liability, Product Liability, Professional Liability, Public Entities, Transportation, Trucking Liability, Workers' Compensation

Firm Profile: At Morrow Willnauer Klosterman Church, LLC, the client relationship comes first. MWKC serves commercial, government, and individual clients' in civil litigation, workers' compensation and corporate law.

(See listing under Kansas City, MO for additional information)

Paule, Camazine & Blumenthal
A Professional Corporation

165 North Meramec Avenue, Suite 110
St. Louis, Missouri 63105
  Telephone: 314-727-2266
  Fax: 314-727-2101
  E-Mail: pcb@pcblawfirm.com

(St. Charles, MO Office: 800 Friedens Road, Suite 203, 63303)
  (Tel: 636-443-2050)
  (Fax: 314-727-2101)

Established: 1994

Insurance Defense, General Liability, Commercial Law, Municipal Liability, Law Enforcement Liability, Personal Injury, Automobile, Employment Law, Professional Liability, Medical Malpractice, Product Liability

Insurance Clients

Savers Property and Casualty   Star Insurance Company
  Insurance Company   Travelers Indemnity Company

Insurance Practice Members

D. Keith Henson — 1957 — Southeast Missouri State University, B.S. (cum laude), 1979; University of Missouri-Kansas City, J.D. (with distinction), 1984 — University of Missouri-Kansas City Law Review — Admitted to Bar, 1984, Missouri; 1994, Illinois; 1984, U.S. District Court, Eastern and Western Districts of Missouri; 1984, U.S. Supreme Court — Member Illinois State Bar Association; The Missouri Bar; The Bar Association of Metropolitan St. Louis — Practice Areas: Insurance Defense; Insurance Coverage; Defense Litigation; Municipal Law; Municipal Liability; Premises Liability; Product Liability; Employment Law; Law Enforcement Liability — Tel: 314-244-3628 — E-mail: khenson@pcblawfirm.com

Associate

Bradley J. Sylwester — 1973 — Missouri State University, B.S. (cum laude), 1996; University of Missouri-Columbia School of Law, J.D., 1999 — Missouri Law Review — Admitted to Bar, 1999, Missouri; 2000, Illinois; U.S. District Court, Eastern and Western Districts of Missouri; U.S. District Court,

Paule, Camazine & Blumenthal, A Professional Corporation, St. Louis, MO **(Continued)**

Central and Southern Districts of Illinois; U.S. Court of Appeals, Eighth Circuit — Member The Missouri Bar — Practice Areas: Insurance Defense; Insurance Coverage; Defense Litigation; Municipal Law; Municipal Liability; Premises Liability — Tel: 314-244-3660 — E-mail: bsylwester@pcblawfirm.com

Of Counsel

Michael E. Bub — 1962 — Saint Louis University, B.A., 1984; Saint Louis University School of Law, J.D., 1987 — Missouri-Kansas Super Lawyers in Civil Litigation (2005, 2006, 2007, 2008, 2009, 2010, 2011, 2012); Number Three in the Missouri Lawyers Weekly Top Defense Verdicts of 2007, Kline v. General Motors — Articles Editor, St. Louis University Law Journal, 1985-1987 — Admitted to Bar, 1987, Missouri; 1990, Illinois — Member The Missouri Bar; Defense Research Institute; Missouri Organization of Defense Lawyers — Practice Areas: Insurance Defense; Transportation; Civil Litigation; Product Liability — Tel: 314-244-3626 — E-mail: mbub@pcblawfirm.com

Rynearson, Suess, Schnurbusch & Champion, L.L.C.

500 North Broadway, Suite 1550
St. Louis, Missouri 63102
  Telephone: 314-421-4430
  Fax: 314-421-4431
  E-Mail: jkemppainen@rssclaw.com
  www.rssclaw.com

Established: 2000

Insurance Defense, Automobile Liability, Insurance Coverage, Premises Liability, Product Liability

Insurance Clients

Employers Mutual Companies   Liberty Mutual Insurance Company
St. Paul Travelers

Non-Insurance Clients

Missouri Department of
  Transportation

Members

Jeffrey K. Suess — 1960 — Washington University, B.A., 1982; J.D., 1985 — Admitted to Bar, 1985, Missouri; 1986, Illinois — Member American and Illinois State Bar Associations; The Missouri Bar; The Bar Association of Metropolitan St. Louis; Defense Research Institute; Missouri Organization of Defense Lawyers — E-mail: jsuess@rssclaw.com

Kevin P. Schnurbusch — 1959 — University of Missouri-Columbia, B.A., 1982; J.D., 1985 — Admitted to Bar, 1985, Missouri; 1986, Illinois — Member American Bar Association; The Missouri Bar; The Bar Association of Metropolitan St. Louis; Missouri Organization of Defense Lawyers — E-mail: kschnurbusch@rssclaw.com

Debbie S. Champion — 1961 — Murray State University, B.S. (cum laude), 1983; Washington University, J.D., 1988 — Admitted to Bar, 1988, Missouri; 1989, Illinois; 1988, U.S. District Court, Eastern and Western Districts of Missouri; 2001, U.S. District Court, Southern District of Illinois — Member American and Illinois State Bar Associations; The Missouri Bar; The Bar Association of Metropolitan St. Louis; Volunteer Lawyers Association; Lawyers Association of St. Louis; Women Lawyers Association; Defense Research Institute; Missouri Organization of Defense Lawyers — E-mail: dchampion@rssclaw.com

John P. Kemppainen, Jr. — 1967 — Tulane University of Louisiana, B.A., 1989; Saint Louis University, J.D., 1993 — Admitted to Bar, 1993, Missouri; 2004, Illinois; 1993, U.S. District Court, Eastern District of Missouri; 1993, U.S. Court of Appeals, Eighth Circuit — Member American and Illinois State Bar Associations; The Missouri Bar; The Bar Association of Metropolitan St. Louis; National Retail & Restaurant Defense Association (NRRDA) (Board Member); Council on Litigation Management (CLM); Missouri Organization of Defense Lawyers — Languages: Spanish — Practice Areas: Premises Liability; Product Liability; Transportation; Retail and Restaurant Defense — E-mail: jkemppainen@rssclaw.com

ST. LOUIS | MISSOURI

Rynearson, Suess, Schnurbusch & Champion, L.L.C., St. Louis, MO (Continued)

Partners

Sam P. Rynearson
Susan M. Herold
Maureen A. McMullan
Michael C. Margherio
Heather J. Hays

Associates

Victor H. Essen
Kenneth J. Mallin Jr
Sarah K. Taylor
Jennifer L. Woulfe
Hopey A. Gardner
David P. Renovitch
Ryan C. Turnage

Of Counsel

Ellen J. Brooke
R B. Regan
Margaret Smith
Patricia B. Frank
Katherine M. Smith
Dean Stark

Sandberg Phoenix & von Gontard P.C.

600 Washington Avenue
15th Floor
St. Louis, Missouri 63101-1313
 Telephone: 314-231-3332
 Toll Free: 800-225-5529
 www.sandbergphoenix.com

(Alton, IL Office: 2410 State Street, 62002)
 (Tel: 618-467-1500)
(Carbondale, IL Office: 2015 West Main, Suite 111, 62901)
 (Tel: 618-351-7200)
(St. Louis, MO Office: 120 South Central Avenue, Suite 1420, 63105)
 (Tel: 314-725-9100)
(Edwardsville, IL Office: 101 West Vandalia Street, 3rd Floor, 62025)
 (Tel: 618-659-9861)
(O'Fallon, IL Office: 475 Regency Park, Suite 175, 62269)
 (Tel: 618-397-2721)
(Overland Park, KS Office: 7450 West 130th Street, Suite 140, 66213)
 (Tel: 913-851-8484)

Established: 1979

Accountants and Attorneys Liability, Appellate Practice, Asbestos Litigation, Automotive Products Liability, Bad Faith, Banking, Business and Real Estate Transactions, Business Law, Business Litigation, Business Transactions, Class Actions, Construction Law, Consumer Litigation, Copyright and Trademark Law, Creditor's Rights, Employment Law, Employment Litigation, Estate Administration, Estate and Tax Planning, Estate Litigation, Estate Planning, Family Law, Health Care, Health Care Liability, Homeowners, Hospital Malpractice, Hospitals, Hospitality, Insurance Coverage, Insurance Coverage Litigation, Labor and Employment, Legal Malpractice, Long-Term Care, Mass Tort, Mechanics Liens, Medical Devices, Medical Malpractice Defense, Premises Liability, Product Liability, Professional Liability, Real Estate, Toxic Torts, Trucking Industry Defense, Health Law

Firm Profile: Sandberg Phoenix's more than 100 attorneys practice in the areas of Business Law, Business Litigation, Health Law and Products Liability. Bringing with them diverse experiences and a broad knowledge of their respective industries, our attorneys are equipped to handle nearly any case you or your business encounter.

Insurance Clients

AIG
The Doctors Company
Liberty International
Lloyd's
CNA Insurance Companies
Illinois State Medical Insurance Services, Inc.

Sandberg Phoenix & von Gontard P.C., St. Louis, MO (Continued)

Non-Insurance Clients

American Honda Motor Company, Inc.
Honda North America, Inc.
Six Flags Theme Parks, Inc.
Toyota Motor Sales, U.S.A., Inc.
Beverly Enterprises, Inc.
BJC Healthcare
St. Louis Children's Hospital
Tenet HealthSystem
United Rentals, Inc.

Founding Members

John S. Sandberg — University of Missouri-Columbia, B.S., 1970; J.D., 1972 — Admitted to Bar, 1972, Missouri; 1973, Illinois — Member American and Mound City Bar Associations; The Bar Association of Metropolitan St. Louis; Lawyers Association of St. Louis; Lawyer-Pilots Bar Association; American Board of Trial Advocates — Practice Areas: Business Litigation; Insurance Coverage; Bad Faith; Product Liability; Tort Liability; Construction Litigation — Tel: 314-446-4214

G. Keith Phoenix — Southern Illinois University Carbondale, B.S. (Dean's List), 1968; Saint Louis University, J.D. (cum laude), 1973 — Admitted to Bar, 1974, Missouri; Illinois — Member Illinois State and St. Clair County Bar Associations; Lawyer's Association of Metropolitan St. Louis (President, 1986-1987); American Board of Trial Advocates (President, Missouri-Southern Illinois Chapter 1993-1994); Network of Trial Law Firms (Executive Committee, 1995-2000); American Board of Trial Advocates — Practice Areas: Personal Injury; Tort

Peter von Gontard — 1948 — Saint Louis University School of Law, J.D., 1973 — Admitted to Bar, 1973, Missouri; 1974, Illinois — Member The Florida Bar; The Missouri Bar; Illinois State, St. Clair County, Madison County, East St. Louis and Alton-Woodriver-Jerseyville Bar Associations; The Bar Association of Metropolitan St. Louis; Lawyers Association of Greater St. Louis; Illinois Association of Defense Trial Counsel; Missouri Organization of Defense Lawyers; Defense Research Institute — Practice Areas: Personal Injury; Product Liability; Tort Liability

Partners/Shareholders

Jennifer Miller-Louw
Timothy O'Leary
David Neiers
Timm Schowalter
Kenneth W. Bean
Warren W. Davis
Kathleen L. Pine
Scott Greenberg
Rodney M. Sharp
Lyndon P. Sommer
Anthony L. Martin
Anthony Soukenik
Martin L. Daesch
Thomas E. Berry, Jr.
Timothy P. Dugan
Russell L. Makepeace
Todd C. Stanton
Bobbie J. Moon
Bhavik R. Patel
A. Courtney Cox
Lorraine Cavataio
Douglas Whitlock
Phil Graham
Ronald Marney
Jonathan Ries
Reed W. Sugg
Mary Anne Mellow
Kevin P. Krueger
Andrew R. Kasnetz
Stephen M. Strum
Teresa D. Bartosiak
Keith D. Price
Diane S. Robben
Michael W. Forster
Jonathan T. Barton
Jeffrey L. Dunn
Mark A. Prost
Philip J. Lading
Andrew D. Ryan
Aaron D. French
Tim Sansone
David Hoffman

Counsel

David Jones
Jonathan McCrary
Joel Green
Tom Long
Laurie Wright
John Gilbert
David Helfrey
Nick Van Deven
Sue Schultz
Richard Stockenberg
Amanda McNelley

MISSOURI ST. LOUIS

Williams Venker & Sanders LLC

Bank of America Tower
100 North Broadway, 21st Floor
St. Louis, Missouri 63102
  Telephone: 314-345-5000
  Fax: 314-345-5055
  E-Mail: twilliams@wvslaw.com
  www.wvslaw.com

(Belleville, IL Office: 23 Public Square, Suite 415, 62220)
  (Tel: 618-257-9200)
(Edwardsville, IL Office: 101 West Vandalia Street, Suite 305-C, 62025)
  (Tel: 618-659-9100)
  (Fax: 618-659-9125)

Established: 2001

Premises Liability, Product Liability, Professional Liability, Property and Casualty

Firm Profile: Williams Venker & Sanders is a trial law firm committed to timely service and the aggressive defense of clients, both inside and outside the courtroom.

Insurance Clients

AIG - Chartis
CNA Insurance Companies
EMC Insurance Company
Intact Insurance Company
Safety National Insurance Company
Cherokee Insurance Company
Electric Insurance Company
HARCO Insurance
Lexington Insurance Company
Travelers Insurance Companies
Zurich American Insurance Company

Non-Insurance Clients

Cottingham & Butler

Partners

Theodore J. Williams, Jr. — 1947 — University of Tulsa College of Law, J.D., 1974 — Admitted to Bar, 1975, Illinois; 1978, Missouri; 1982, District of Columbia; 1996, Colorado; 2006, Kansas; Oklahoma; 2007, Wisconsin; 2010, Washington; U.S. District Court, Eastern and Western Districts of Missouri; U.S. District Court, Central, Northern and Southern Districts of Illinois; U.S. District Court, Northern District of Indiana; U.S. District Court, District of Kansas; U.S. District Court, Eastern, Northern and Western Districts of Oklahoma; U.S. District Court, Eastern and Western Districts of Wisconsin; U.S. Court of Appeals, Seventh, Eighth and Tenth Circuits; U.S. Supreme Court; U.S. Court of Military Appeals — Lt. Col., U.S. Army, (Retired) — Practice Areas: Insurance Defense; Personal Injury; Product Liability; Railroad Law — Tel: 314-345-5009 — E-mail: twilliams@wvslaw.com

Paul N. Venker — 1955 — University of Missouri-Columbia School of Law, J.D., 1980 — Admitted to Bar, 1980, Missouri; 1981, Illinois; U.S. District Court, Eastern and Western Districts of Missouri; U.S. District Court, Central and Southern Districts of Illinois; U.S. Court of Appeals, Seventh, Eighth and Tenth Circuits; U.S. Supreme Court — Practice Areas: Medical Malpractice; Product Liability; Employment Discrimination; Health Care — Tel: 314-345-5001 — E-mail: pvenker@wvslaw.com

Steven P. Sanders — 1950 — Indiana University School of Law, J.D., 1975 — Admitted to Bar, 1975, Indiana; 1977, Missouri; 1978, Illinois; U.S. District Court, Eastern and Western Districts of Missouri; U.S. District Court, Northern and Southern Districts of Illinois; U.S. District Court, Southern District of Indiana; U.S. District Court, Eastern and Western Districts of Michigan; U.S. District Court, District of Nebraska; U.S. District Court, Western District of Wisconsin; U.S. Court of Appeals, Seventh, Eighth and Ninth Circuits — Practice Areas: Commercial Litigation; Product Liability; Personal Injury; Toxic Torts — Tel: 314-345-5002 — E-mail: ssanders@wvslaw.com

Thomas L. Orris — 1955 — Washington University School of Law, J.D., 1988 — Admitted to Bar, 1988, Missouri; 1989, Illinois; Kansas; U.S. District Court, Eastern District of Missouri; U.S. District Court, Central and Southern Districts of Illinois — Practice Areas: Toxic Torts; Personal Injury; Product Liability — Tel: 314-345-5003 — E-mail: torris@wvslaw.com

Michael R. Barth — 1974 — Saint Louis University School of Law, J.D.,

Williams Venker & Sanders LLC, St. Louis, MO
(Continued)

1999 — Admitted to Bar, 1999, Missouri; 2000, Illinois; U.S. District Court, Eastern District of Missouri; U.S. District Court, Southern District of Illinois — Practice Areas: Medical Malpractice; Product Liability; Health; Hospitals — Tel: 314-345-5018 — E-mail: mbarth@wvslaw.com

Robert J. Bassett — 1961 — Washington University School of Law, J.D., 1986 — Admitted to Bar, 1986, Illinois; 1992, Missouri; 1986, U.S. District Court, Central and Southern Districts of Illinois; U.S. District Court, Eastern District of Missouri; U.S. Court of Appeals, Seventh Circuit — Practice Areas: Product Liability; Transportation; Workers' Compensation — Tel: 314-345-5034 — E-mail: rbassett@wvslaw.com

Patrick I. Chavez — 1973 — Washington University School of Law, J.D., 1998 — Admitted to Bar, 1998, Missouri; 2001, Illinois; U.S. District Court, Eastern and Western Districts of Missouri; U.S. District Court, Central, Northern and Southern Districts of Illinois; U.S. Court of Appeals, Seventh and Eighth Circuits — Practice Areas: Commercial Litigation; Health Care; Product Liability; E-Discovery — Tel: 314-345-5072 — E-mail: pchavez@wvslaw.com

Michael B. Hunter — 1971 — University of Missouri-Columbia School of Law, J.D., 1996 — Admitted to Bar, 1996, Missouri; 1997, Illinois; U.S. District Court, Eastern and Western Districts of Missouri; U.S. District Court, Central and Southern Districts of Illinois; U.S. District Court, District of Kansas; U.S. Court of Appeals, Eighth Circuit; U.S. Supreme Court — Practice Areas: Insurance Defense; Product Liability; Railroad Law; Insurance Coverage; Commercial Litigation — Tel: 314-345-5012 — E-mail: mhunter@wvslaw.com

Lisa A. Larkin — 1970 — University of Illinois College of Law, J.D., 1995 — Admitted to Bar, 1995, Missouri; 1996, Illinois; U.S. District Court, Eastern District of Missouri; U.S. District Court, Southern District of Illinois; U.S. Court of Appeals, Seventh and Eighth Circuits — Practice Areas: Appellate Practice; Commercial Litigation; Product Liability — Tel: 314-345-5014 — E-mail: llarkin@wvslaw.com

John P. Lord — 1952 — University of Colorado Law School, J.D., 1977 — Admitted to Bar, 1977, Missouri; 2008, Illinois; U.S. District Court, Eastern District of Missouri; U.S. District Court, Eastern and Western Districts of Arkansas; U.S. Court of Appeals, Eighth Circuit — Practice Areas: Insurance Litigation; Personal Injury; Product Liability; Railroad Law — Tel: 314-345-5011 — E-mail: jlord@wvslaw.com

John F. Mahon, Jr. — Saint Louis University School of Law, J.D., 2004 — Admitted to Bar, 2005, Missouri; Illinois; U.S. District Court, Eastern and Western Districts of Missouri; U.S. District Court, Southern District of Illinois — Practice Areas: Medical Negligence; Business Litigation; Commercial Litigation; Personal Injury; Product Liability; Premises Liability; Toxic Torts; Insurance Litigation — Tel: 314-345-5094 — E-mail: jmahon@wvslaw.com

Matthew E. Pelikan — The University of Tulsa College of Law, J.D., 2005 — Admitted to Bar, 2006, Missouri; Illinois; U.S. District Court, Eastern District of Missouri; U.S. District Court, Southern District of Illinois — Practice Areas: Toxic Torts; Asbestos; Labor and Employment; Workers' Compensation; Product Liability; Premises Liability — Tel: 314-345-5039 — E-mail: mpelikan@wvslaw.com

Mary D. Rychnovsky — 1966 — Saint Louis University School of Law, J.D., 1993 — Admitted to Bar, 1993, Missouri; 2007, Illinois; U.S. District Court, Eastern District of Missouri; U.S. Court of Appeals, Eighth Circuit — Practice Areas: Asbestos Litigation; Commercial Litigation; Insurance Defense; Legal Malpractice — Tel: 314-345-5058 — E-mail: mrychnovsky@wvslaw.com

Lucy T. Unger — 1964 — Washington University School of Law, J.D., 1989 — Admitted to Bar, 1989, Missouri; 1990, Illinois; U.S. District Court, Eastern and Western Districts of Missouri; U.S. District Court, Central and Southern Districts of Illinois; U.S. Court of Appeals, Eighth Circuit — Practice Areas: Commercial Litigation; Product Liability — Tel: 314-345-5013 — E-mail: lunger@wvslaw.com

Steven S. Wasserman — 1965 — Creighton University School of Law, J.D., 1990 — Admitted to Bar, 1990, Missouri; 1992, Illinois; U.S. District Court, Eastern District of Missouri; U.S. District Court, Central and Southern Districts of Illinois — Practice Areas: Medical Malpractice; Personal Injury — Tel: 314-345-5008 — E-mail: swasserman@wvslaw.com

Of Counsel

Mark T. Bobak — 1959 — Saint Louis University School of Law, J.D., 1984 — Admitted to Bar, 1984, Missouri — Tel: 314-345-5023 — E-mail: mbobak@wvslaw.com

WAYNESVILLE   MISSOURI

The following firms also service this area.

Hoagland, Fitzgerald & Pranaitis
401 Market Street
Alton, Illinois 62002
   Telephone: 618-465-7745
   Fax: 618-465-3744
   Toll Free: 866-830-1066
Mailing Address: P.O. Box 130, Alton, IL 62002

Insurance Defense

SEE COMPLETE LISTING UNDER ALTON, ILLINOIS (25 MILES)

Neville, Richards & Wuller, LLC
5 Park Place Professional Centre
Illinois Street and Fullerton Road
Belleville, Illinois 62226
   Telephone: 618-277-0900
   Fax: 618-277-0970
Mailing Address: P.O. Box 23977, Belleville, IL 62226-0070

Insurance Defense, Professional Negligence, Product Liability, Premises Liability, Automobile, Bodily Injury, Fraud, Arson, Coverage Issues, Medical Malpractice, General Liability

SEE COMPLETE LISTING UNDER BELLEVILLE, ILLINOIS (17 MILES)

STEELVILLE † 1,642 Crawford Co.
Refer To

Williams, Robinson, Rigler & Buschjost, P.C.
901 North Pine Street, Fourth Floor
Rolla, Missouri 65401
   Telephone: 573-341-2266
   Fax: 573-341-5864
Mailing Address: P.O. Box 47, Rolla, MO 65402

Insurance Defense, Insurance Litigation, Automobile, Premises Liability, Product Liability, Insurance Coverage, Professional Negligence, Agriculture, Appellate Practice, Business Law, Civil Litigation, Corporate Law, Commercial Law, Employment Law, Environmental Law, Health Care, Medical Malpractice, Municipal Law, Personal Injury, Trial Practice, Truck Liability, Wrongful Death

SEE COMPLETE LISTING UNDER ROLLA, MISSOURI (28 MILES)

TROY † 10,540 Lincoln Co.
Refer To

Niedner, Bodeux, Carmichael, Huff, Lenox, Pashos and Simpson, L.L.P.
131 Jefferson Street
St. Charles, Missouri 63301
   Telephone: 636-949-9300
   Fax: 636-949-3141

Insurance Defense, Automobile, Product Liability, Homeowners, Casualty, Premises Liability

SEE COMPLETE LISTING UNDER ST. CHARLES, MISSOURI (25 MILES)

VIENNA † 610 Maries Co.
Refer To

Williams, Robinson, Rigler & Buschjost, P.C.
901 North Pine Street, Fourth Floor
Rolla, Missouri 65401
   Telephone: 573-341-2266
   Fax: 573-341-5864
Mailing Address: P.O. Box 47, Rolla, MO 65402

Insurance Defense, Insurance Litigation, Automobile, Premises Liability, Product Liability, Insurance Coverage, Professional Negligence, Agriculture, Appellate Practice, Business Law, Civil Litigation, Corporate Law, Commercial Law, Employment Law, Environmental Law, Health Care, Medical Malpractice, Municipal Law, Personal Injury, Trial Practice, Truck Liability, Wrongful Death

SEE COMPLETE LISTING UNDER ROLLA, MISSOURI (26 MILES)

WARRENTON † 7,880 Warren Co.
Refer To

Niedner, Bodeux, Carmichael, Huff, Lenox, Pashos and Simpson, L.L.P.
131 Jefferson Street
St. Charles, Missouri 63301
   Telephone: 636-949-9300
   Fax: 636-949-3141

Insurance Defense, Automobile, Product Liability, Homeowners, Casualty, Premises Liability

SEE COMPLETE LISTING UNDER ST. CHARLES, MISSOURI (30 MILES)

WAYNESVILLE † 4,830 Pulaski Co.
Refer To

Williams, Robinson, Rigler & Buschjost, P.C.
901 North Pine Street, Fourth Floor
Rolla, Missouri 65401
   Telephone: 573-341-2266
   Fax: 573-341-5864
Mailing Address: P.O. Box 47, Rolla, MO 65402

Insurance Defense, Insurance Litigation, Automobile, Premises Liability, Product Liability, Insurance Coverage, Professional Negligence, Agriculture, Appellate Practice, Business Law, Civil Litigation, Corporate Law, Commercial Law, Employment Law, Environmental Law, Health Care, Medical Malpractice, Municipal Law, Personal Injury, Trial Practice, Truck Liability, Wrongful Death

SEE COMPLETE LISTING UNDER ROLLA, MISSOURI (28 MILES)

MONTANA

CAPITAL: HELENA

COUNTIES AND COUNTY SEATS

County	County Seat	County	County Seat	County	County Seat
Beaverhead	Dillon	Granite	Philipsburg	Powell	Deer Lodge
Big Horn	Hardin	Hill	Havre	Prairie	Terry
Blaine	Chinook	Jefferson	Boulder	Ravalli	Hamilton
Broadwater	Townsend	Judith Basin	Stanford	Richland	Sidney
Carbon	Red Lodge	Lake	Polson	Roosevelt	Wolf Point
Carter	Ekalaka	Lewis and Clark	Helena	Rosebud	Forsyth
Cascade	Great Falls	Liberty	Chester	Sanders	Thompson Falls
Chouteau	Fort Benton	Lincoln	Libby	Sheridan	Plentywood
Custer	Miles City	Madison	Virginia City	Silver Bow	Butte
Daniels	Scobey	McCone	Circle	Stillwater	Columbus
Dawson	Glendive	Meagher	White Sulphur Springs	Sweet Grass	Big Timber
Deer Lodge	Anaconda	Mineral	Superior	Teton	Choteau
Fallon	Baker	Missoula	Missoula	Toole	Shelby
Fergus	Lewistown	Musselshell	Roundup	Treasure	Hysham
Flathead	Kalispell	Park	Livingston	Valley	Glasgow
Gallatin	Bozeman	Petroleum	Winnett	Wheatland	Harlowton
Garfield	Jordan	Phillips	Malta	Wibaux	Wibaux
Glacier	Cut Bank	Pondera	Conrad	Yellowstone	Billings
Golden Valley	Ryegate	Powder River	Broadus		

In the text that follows "†" indicates County Seats.

Our files contain additional verified data on the firms listed herein. This additional information is available on request.

A.M. BEST COMPANY

MONTANA   BIG SKY

BIG SKY   2,308 Madison Co.

Refer To

Moore, O'Connell & Refling, P.C.
Life of Montana Building, Suite 10
601 Haggerty Lane
Bozeman, Montana 59715
   Telephone: 406-587-5511
   Fax: 406-587-9079

Mailing Address: P.O. Box 1288, Bozeman, MT 59771-1288

General Defense, Insurance Law, Subrogation, Investigation and Adjustment

SEE COMPLETE LISTING UNDER BOZEMAN, MONTANA (41 MILES)

BIG TIMBER   † 1,641 Sweet Grass Co.

Refer To

Moulton Bellingham PC
Crowne Plaza, Suite 1900
27 North 27th Street
Billings, Montana 59101
   Telephone: 406-248-7731
   Fax: 406-248-7889

Mailing Address: P.O. Box 2559, Billings, MT 59103

Trial Practice, State and Federal Courts, Insurance Law, Workers' Compensation, Fire, Casualty Insurance Law, Professional Liability, Oil and Gas, Product Liability

SEE COMPLETE LISTING UNDER BILLINGS, MONTANA (80 MILES)

BILLINGS   † 104,170 Yellowstone Co.

Brown Law Firm, P.C.

315 North 24th Street
Billings, Montana 59101
   Telephone: 406-248-2611
   Fax: 406-248-3128
   www.brownfirm.com

(Missoula, MT Office*: 210 East Pine Street, Suite 200, 59802)
   (Tel: 406-830-3248)

Established: 1911

Defense of Complex Civil Litigation, Defense of Catastrophic Personal Injury and Wrongful Death Claims, Insurance Law Including Coverage and Defense of Bad Faith Claims, Product Liability Defense, Defense of Medical and Dental Malpractice Claims, Labor and Employee Relations, Minerals, Oil and Gas, Banking, Workers' Compensation, Real Estate, Construction Defect, Appellate Law

Firm Profile: Brown Law Firm takes great pride in its long-standing roots in Montana as a defense firm which is rated AV by Martindale-Hubbell. We continue our tradition, which began in 1911, of providing expert legal services to clients throughout Montana. The commitment and values of the firm remain the same, to offer a wide range of legal services by top quality defense counsel.

Insurance Clients

ACUITY
American National Property & Casualty
Attorneys Liability Protection Society
Chubb Group of Insurance Companies
CUNA Mutual Group
Empire Fire and Marine Insurance Company
Farmland Mutual Insurance Company
Grocers Insurance Company
Kemper/NATLSCO, Inc.
Markel Insurance Company
ALLIED Property and Casualty Insurance Company
Amerisure Insurance Company
Austin Mutual Insurance Company
BancInsure, Inc.
Cincinnati Insurance Company
Crum & Forster
The Doctors Company
Farmers Union Mutual Insurance Company (MT)
General Casualty Insurance Company
John Deere Insurance Company
Liberty Mutual Insurance Company
Nationwide Insurance

Brown Law Firm, P.C., Billings, MT   **(Continued)**

Royal & SunAlliance Group
Travelers Insurance Companies
United National Group
Universal Underwriters Insurance Company
XL Insurance Global Risk
Sentry Insurance a Mutual Company
Unitrin Property and Casualty Insurance Group
Utah Medical Insurance Association

Non-Insurance Clients

PPL Montana, LLC   Western Litigation Specialists, Inc.

Shareholders

John J. Russell — 1953 — The University of Montana, B.S., 1976; J.D., 1982 — Admitted to Bar, 1982, Montana — Member Yellowstone Area Bar Association; Montana Defense Trial Lawyers Association; Defense Research Institute — Practice Areas: Medical Malpractice; Medical Liability; Medical Negligence; Civil Trial Practice

Guy W. Rogers — 1959 — The University of Montana, B.A., 1981; J.D., 1985 — Admitted to Bar, 1986, Montana — Member Yellowstone Area Bar Association; Defense Research Institute; Montana Defense Trial Lawyers Association — Practice Areas: Civil Trial Practice; Insurance Coverage; Bad Faith; Personal Injury; Mediation

Scott G. Gratton — 1960 — The University of Montana, B.A. (with honors), 1983; J.D., 1987 — Admitted to Bar, 1987, Montana — Member Yellowstone Area Bar Association; Montana Defense Trial Lawyers Association; National Association of Railroad Trial Counsel — Practice Areas: Civil Trial Practice; Personal Injury; Property and Casualty; Product Liability; Insurance Coverage; Insurance Defense

Kelly J. Gallinger — 1975 — Montana State University, B.A., 1997; The University of Montana School of Law, J.D., 2001 — Admitted to Bar, 2001, Montana — Member Yellowstone Area Bar Association; Montana Defense Trial Lawyers Association; Defense Research Institute — Practice Areas: Insurance Defense; Insurance Coverage; Bad Faith; Product Liability; Environmental Law

Michael P. Heringer — **Managing Shareholder** — 1958 — Gonzaga University, B.B.A., 1981; The University of Montana, J.D., 1985 — Admitted to Bar, 1985, Montana — Member Yellowstone Area Bar Association; Montana Defense Trial Lawyers Association — Practice Areas: Civil Trial Practice; Personal Injury; Product Liability; Workers' Compensation; Employment Law; Oil and Gas

Jon A. Wilson — 1979 — Montana State University, B.A., 2002; The University of Montana, J.D., 2005 — Law Clerk to Justice John Warner, Montana Supreme Court, 2005-2006 — Admitted to Bar, 2005, Montana — Member Yellowstone Area Bar Association; Montana Defense Trial Lawyers Association; Defense Research Institute — Practice Areas: Civil Litigation; Insurance Defense; Insurance Coverage

Associate Attorneys

Jeffrey T. McAllister — 1957 — Montana State University, B.A. (with honors), 1979; The University of Montana School of Law, J.D., 1982 — Admitted to Bar, 1982, Montana — Member Yellowstone Area Bar Association — Practice Areas: Insurance Defense

Seth Cunningham — 1977 — United States Air Force Academy, B.S., 2000; The University of Montana, J.D., 2009 — Admitted to Bar, 2009, Montana — Member American and Yellowstone Area Bar Associations

Shane MacIntyre — 1982 — The University of Montana, B.S., 2006; The University of Montana School of Law, J.D., 2010 — Admitted to Bar, 2010, Montana — Member Montana Defense Trial Lawyers Association — Practice Areas: Insurance Defense

Thomas R. Martin — 1985 — The University of Montana, B.S., 2008; J.D., 2012 — Admitted to Bar, 2012, Montana — Member Yellowstone Area Bar Association; Montana Defense Trial Lawyers Association — Practice Areas: Civil Litigation; Workers' Compensation; Employment Law

Andrew J. Miller — 1985 — The University of Montana, B.A. (with high honors), 2007; J.D., 2012 — Admitted to Bar, 2012, Montana — Member Yellowstone Area Bar Association; Montana Defense Trial Lawyers Association — Practice Areas: Civil Defense; Insurance Coverage

Adam M. Shaw — 1983 — Arizona State University, B.A., 2006; The University of Montana, J.D., 2010 — Admitted to Bar, 2010, Montana — Practice Areas: Civil Defense; Civil Litigation

Christine M. Cole — 1988 — University of Washington, B.A. (Departmental Honors), 2010; The University of Montana School of Law, J.D., 2013 — Admitted to Bar, 2013, Montana — Languages: Italian — Practice Areas: Insurance Coverage & Defense; Personal Injury Defense; Product Liability Defense; Property Defense

Brown Law Firm, P.C., Billings, MT (Continued)
Retired

Rockwood Brown — 1928 — The University of Montana, B.A., 1950; J.D., 1952 — Admitted to Bar, 1952, Montana — Practice Areas: Civil Litigation; Mediation

John Walker Ross — 1944 — The University of Montana, B.A. (with honors), 1966; J.D., 1969 — Admitted to Bar, 1969, Montana — Member Yellowstone Area Bar Association — Practice Areas: Administrative Law; Civil Litigation; Labor and Employment; Environmental Coverage; Environmental Liability; Environmental Law; Mediation; Arbitration

Margy Bonner — 1951 — Pacific University, B.A., 1973; Portland State University, M.S., 1975; The University of Montana, J.D., 1980 — Admitted to Bar, 1980, Montana; North Dakota — Member Yellowstone Area Bar Association — Practice Areas: Insurance Defense; Professional Malpractice; Civil Trial Practice; Oil and Gas

Crowley Fleck PLLP

500 Transwestern Plaza II
490 North 31st Street
Billings, Montana 59101-1288
   Telephone: 406-252-3441
   Fax: 406-256-8526, 406-259-4159, 406-256-0277
   E-Mail: jkresslein@crowleyfleck.com
   www.crowleyfleck.com

(Bozeman, MT Office*: 45 Discovery Drive, 59718-6957)
   (Tel: 406-556-1430)
   (Fax: 406-556-1433)
(Butte, MT Office*: Thornton Building, 65 East Broadway, Suite 503, 59701)
   (Tel: 406-533-6892)
   (Fax: 406-533-6830)
(Helena, MT Office*: 900 North Last Chance Gulch, Suite 200, 59601)
   (Tel: 406-449-4165)
   (Fax: 406-449-5149)
(Kalispell, MT Office*: 1667 Whitefish Stage Road, Suite 101, 59901-4835)
   (Tel: 406-752-6644)
   (Fax: 406-752-5108)
(Missoula, MT Office*: 305 South 4th Street East, Suite 100, 59801-2701)
   (Tel: 406-523-3600)
   (Fax: 406-523-3636)
(Bismarck, ND Office*: 100 West Broadway, Suite 250, 58501, P.O. Box 2798, 58502-2798)
   (Tel: 701-223-6585)
   (Fax: 701-222-4853)
(Williston, ND Office*: 1331 9th Avenue NW, 2nd Floor, 58801, P.O. Box 1206, 58802-1206)
   (Tel: 701-572-2200)
   (Fax: 701-572-7072)
(Casper, WY Office*: 152 North Durbin Street, Suite 220, 82601)
   (Tel: 307-265-2279)
   (Fax: 307-265-2307)
(Cheyenne, WY Office*: 237 Storey Boulevard, Suite 110, 82009)
   (Tel: 307-426-4100)
   (Fax: 307-426-4099)
(Sheridan, WY Office*: 101 West Brundage Street, 82801)
   (Tel: 307-673-3000)
   (Fax: 307-672-1732)

Established: 1895

Civil Litigation, Trial and Appellate Practice, Product Liability, Personal Injury, Construction Law, Design Professionals, Malpractice, Wrongful Termination, Employer Liability, Medical Negligence, Legal, Professional Negligence, Insurance Coverage, Bad Faith, Agent/Broker Liability, Workers' Compensation, Oil and Gas, Environmental Law

Insurance Clients

Aetna Insurance Company
Allstate Insurance Company

Crowley Fleck PLLP, Billings, MT (Continued)

American West Insurance Company
Chartis Insurance
Cincinnati Insurance Company
Colony Insurance Company
Co-operators General Insurance Company
The Doctors Company
Employers Casualty Company
Essex Insurance Company
Farmers Alliance Mutual Insurance Company
GAB Robins North America, Inc.
Great Northwest Insurance Company
Horace Mann Insurance Group
Liberty Mutual Insurance Company
Metropolitan Life Insurance Company
Mountain West Farm Bureau Mutual Insurance Company
Northland Insurance Company
Penn-America Insurance Company
Prudential Insurance Company of America
Time Insurance Company
Wausau Insurance Companies
Zurich American Insurance Group
Blue Cross and Blue Shield of Montana
Chubb Group of Insurance Companies
Connecticut Mutual Life Insurance Company
CUNA Mutual Group
EBI Companies
The Equitable Life Assurance Society of the United States
Farmers Insurance Group
Federated Insurance Company
Great American Insurance Company
The Hartford Insurance Group
Kemper Insurance Companies
Media/Professional Insurance
Millers First Insurance Companies
MONY Life Insurance Company
New York Life Insurance Company
Old Republic Insurance Company
Philadelphia Insurance Company
Risk Enterprise Management, Ltd.
The St. Paul Companies
Unitrin Property and Casualty Insurance Group

Non-Insurance Clients

MDU Resource Group
PPL Montana, LLC

Litigation Partners

Alan C. Bryan — University of Wyoming College of Law, J.D., 1996 — Admitted to Bar, 1996, Wyoming; 1997, Montana

Paul C. Collins — 1966 — Wake Forest University, J.D. (cum laude), 1993 — Admitted to Bar, 1993, New Mexico; 2003, Montana

Renee L. Coppock — University of Illinois, J.D. (with high honors), 1987 — Admitted to Bar, 1987, Montana; U.S. Court of Appeals, Ninth Circuit; U.S. Supreme Court; Northern Cheyenne Tribal Court; Crow Tribal Court; Fort Belknap Tribal Court; Rocky Boy Tribal Court; Salish Kootenai Tribal Court

Jon T. Dyre — 1959 — University of Wyoming, J.D. (with honors), 1985 — Admitted to Bar, 1985, Montana; 1986, Wyoming

Robert C. Griffin — 1955 — University of Miami, J.D. (magna cum laude), 1993 — Admitted to Bar, 1993, Florida; 1995, Montana

Peter F. Habein — 1956 — The University of Montana, J.D. (with honors), 1983 — Admitted to Bar, 1983, Montana; U.S. District Court, District of Montana — Member Defense Research Institute

Steven W. Jennings — The University of Montana School of Law, J.D., 2003 — Admitted to Bar, 2003, Montana; U.S. District Court, District of Montana — Major, U.S. Marine Corps Reserves (1983-)

Jared M. Le Fevre — University of Idaho College of Law, J.D., 2001 — Admitted to Bar, 2001, Montana; 2002, Idaho; 2003, Crow Tribal Court; Northern Cheyenne Tribal Court

Steven J. Lehman — 1950 — University of Wisconsin, J.D. (cum laude), 1978 — Admitted to Bar, 1978, Wisconsin; Montana — Member American Judicature Society

William J. Mattix — 1956 — The University of Montana, J.D. (with honors), 1983 — Admitted to Bar, 1983, Montana — Member Association of Trial Lawyers of America

Joe C. Maynard, Jr. — 1959 — The University of Montana, J.D. (with highest honors), 1987 — Admitted to Bar, 1987, Montana

Steven R. Milch — 1957 — University of Idaho, J.D. (cum laude), 1987 — Admitted to Bar, 1987, Idaho; 1990, Montana

Jeffery J. Oven — 1972 — University of Wyoming, J.D., 1999 — Admitted to Bar, 1999, Wyoming; 2000, Montana

Leonard H. Smith — 1964 — Washington University, J.D., 1990 — Admitted to Bar, 1990, Montana; U.S. District Court, District of Montana; U.S. Court of Appeals, Ninth Circuit

Christopher C. Voigt — 1973 — University of Wyoming College of Law, J.D. (with honors), 1999 — Admitted to Bar, 1999, Wyoming; 2001, Montana

Monique P. Voigt — 1981 — The University of Montana School of Law, J.D., 2007 — Admitted to Bar, 2007, Montana; 2010, Wyoming; 2013, North Dakota; 2007, U.S. District Court, District of Montana; 2010, U.S. District Court, District of Wyoming; 2012, U.S. Court of Appeals, Ninth Circuit

MONTANA | BILLINGS

Crowley Fleck PLLP, Billings, MT (Continued)

Partners

Colby L. Branch
Ashley Burleson
Bruce F. Fain
Lance Hoskins
William D. Lamdin, III
Denise D. Linford
Adam M. Olschlager
Steven Ruffatto
Richard Brekke
Michael S. Dockery
Kevin P. Heaney
Stewart T. Kirkpatrick
John R. Lee
Robert G. Michelotti, Jr.
Daniela Pavuk
Christopher C. Stoneback

Senior Counsel

Gary M. Connelley

Of Counsel

Gary G. Broeder
David L. Johnson
Christopher Mangen, Jr.
Herbert I. Pierce, III
David L. Charles
Arthur F. Lamey, Jr.
Louis R. Moore
James P. Sites

Associates

Patrick Beddow
G. Trenton Hooper
Megan McCrae
Eric Peterson
Christine Prill
Elizabeth Varela
Josh Cook
Vincent Kalafat
Eli Patten
Uriah Price
Michael Tennant
Dave P. Whisenand

(Firm Members Belong to American and Yellowstone County Bar Associations and State Bar of Montana; Montana Defense Trial Lawyers Association and Montana Trial Lawyers Association)

Felt, Martin, Frazier & Weldon, P.C.

313 Hart-Albin Building
208 North Broadway
Billings, Montana 59101
Telephone: 406-248-7646
Fax: 406-248-5485
E-Mail: feltmartin@feltmartinlaw.com
www.feltmartinlaw.com

Established: 1980

Insurance Defense, Bodily Injury, Property Damage, Coverage Issues, General Liability, Workers' Compensation, Subrogation, Public Entity Defense including School Districts, Cities, and Counties, Defense of Complex Civil Litigation, Defense of Employment Practices Litigation, Professional Liability Defense, Products Liability Defense, Defense of Administrative Claims, Bankruptcy Litigation, Defense of Civil Rights Litigation, Defense of Banking Claims & Commercial Transactions, Defense of Construction Claims

Firm Profile: Since James R. Felt began practicing law in Billings in the late 1940's, this firm has established a diverse and sophisticated practice with expertise in representing a variety of businesses and institutions. Due to its size, the firm is able to give personal, efficient and cost effective service. The firm is guided by a concern for quality, thoroughness, integrity and a genuine sensitivity to the unique needs of each client. The firm prides itself on its long-standing relationships with many of its clients.

The members of this firm have represented its clients and their insurers in all phases of litigation, and their excellent reputation in the courts and administrative agencies gives their clients an edge in bringing about the best results possible. The depth of knowledge and early comprehensive planning and advice successfully prevent litigation.

In addition to its commitment to providing the highest caliber of legal services, the members of the firm are active in community affairs and serve as leaders in civil and charitable organizations and local and state bar associations.

Felt, Martin, Frazier & Weldon, P.C., Billings, MT (Continued)

Insurance Clients

AIG
Atlanta Casualty Company
Auto-Owners Insurance Company
CNA Insurance Company
Gallagher Bassett Services, Inc.
Markel Service, Incorporated
Sedgwick Claims Management Services, Inc.
American Hallmark Insurance Company of Texas
Chubb Specialty Insurance
EMC Insurance Companies
Kempes Insurance
Safeco Insurance
Western States Insurance Agency
Zurich North America

Partners

Laurence R. Martin — 1940 — Harvard College, A.B., 1962; Harvard Law School, J.D., 1965 — Admitted to Bar, 1972, Montana; 1965, New York; 1968, U.S. District Court, Southern District of New York; 1981, U.S. District Court, District of Montana; 1988, U.S. Court of Appeals, Ninth Circuit; 1995, U.S. Supreme Court — Member American Bar Association (Section: Labor & Employment Law); State Bar of Montana; Yellowstone Area Bar Association; The Association of the Bar of the City of New York; Montana Association of School District Attorneys; Montana Defense Trial Lawyers Association — Practice Areas: General Civil Practice; School Law; Labor and Employment; Insurance Defense; Negligence; Commercial Litigation; Agriculture; Construction Law; Appellate Practice

Kenneth S. Frazier — 1953 — Michigan State University, B.S., 1974; Thomas M. Cooley Law School, J.D., 1979 — Admitted to Bar, 1980, Montana; 1980, U.S. District Court, District of Montana; 1991, U.S. Court of Appeals, Ninth Circuit — Member American Bar Association; Yellowstone Area Bar Association; State Bar of Montana; American Health Lawyers Association — Practice Areas: Banking; Health Care; Real Estate; Business Transactions; Insurance Defense; Employment Law; Construction Law; Corporate Law

Jeffrey A. Weldon — 1963 — The University of Montana, B.A., 1986; M.P.A., 1994; J.D., 1996 — Admitted to Bar, 1997, Montana; U.S. District Court, District of Montana; Blackfeet Tribal Court; Flathead Tribal Court; Crow Tribal Court; Fort Belknap Tribal Court; Northern Cheyenne Tribal Court — Member State Bar of Montana; Yellowstone Area Bar Association; Montana Association of School District Attorneys — Practice Areas: School Law; Labor and Employment; Real Estate; Administrative Law; Probate; Indian Law; Civil Litigation

Of Counsel

Randolph Jacobs, Jr. — 1944 — Whitman College, B.A., 1966; The University of Montana, J.D., 1969 — Admitted to Bar, 1969, Montana; U.S. District Court, District of Montana — Member Yellowstone Area Bar Association

Associates

Mary E. Duncan — 1961 — University of Wyoming, B.A., 1983; The University of Montana, J.D., 1987 — Outstanding Law Student (1987); American Judicature Service Award (1987) — Admitted to Bar, 1987, Montana; U.S. District Court, District of Montana; U.S. Court of Appeals, Ninth Circuit — Member American Bar Association (Sections: Tort and Insurance Practice, State & Local Government, Litigation); State Bar of Montana (Sections: Ethics Committee and School Law); Yellowstone Area Bar Association; Montana Association of School District Attorneys — Adjunct Professor, Rocky Mountain College Masters Program — Practice Areas: Civil Trial Practice; Insurance Defense; Personal Injury; School Law; Employment Practices; Labor and Employment; Professional Liability; Bad Faith; Civil Rights Defense

Martin S. Smith — 1973 — Brigham Young University, B.S., 2001; The University of Utah, M.B.A. (with honors), 2003; J.D., 2006 — Admitted to Bar, 2007, Montana — Member American Bar Association; State Bar of Montana; Yellowstone Area Bar Association — Languages: Spanish — Practice Areas: Corporate Law; Commercial Transactions; Banking; Collections; Bankruptcy; Energy; Commercial and Personal Lines

Burt N. Hurwitz — 1981 — Rocky Mountain College, B.A., 2004; The University of Montana, J.D., 2007 — Outstanding Law Student Award (2007); Dean's Award in Recognition of Outstanding Student Leadership; The Carol Mitchell Award; International Academy of Trial Lawyers Student Advocacy Award — Admitted to Bar, 2007, Montana — Member American Bar Association; State Bar of Montana; Yellowstone Area Bar Association; Rural Advocacy League — Practice Areas: Agriculture; Labor and Employment; Corporate Law; Commercial Transactions; Banking; Construction Litigation; Commercial and Personal Lines; Civil Litigation; Estate Litigation

Ryan P. Browne — 1984 — Regis University, B.S./B.A., 2007; The University of Montana School of Law, J.D., 2010 — Law Clerk to Hon. Susan P. Watters, District Court Judge for Montana's 13th Judicial District,

Felt, Martin, Frazier & Weldon, P.C., Billings, MT (Continued)

2010-2011 — Admitted to Bar, 2010, Montana; U.S. District Court, District of Montana; Montana Supreme Court — Member State Bar of Montana; Yellowstone Area Bar Association — Practice Areas: Civil Litigation; Education Law; School Law; Business Law; Personal Injury Litigation

Hall & Evans, L.L.C.

401 North 31st Street, Suite 1650
Billings, Montana 59101
   Telephone: 406-969-5227
Fax: 406-969-5233

Administrative Law, Appellate Practice, Commercial Litigation, Complex Litigation, Construction Law, Coverage Issues, Employee Benefits, Employment Law, Environmental Law, ERISA, General Liability, Health Care, Insurance Law, Insurance Litigation, Intellectual Property, Legislative Law, Life Insurance, Accident and Health, Product Liability, Professional Liability, Public Entities, Regulatory and Compliance, Reinsurance, Transportation, Workers' Compensation, Coverage Law and Litigation

(See listing under Denver, CO for additional information)

Halverson & Mahlen, P.C.

Creekside Suite 301
1001 South 24th Street West
Billings, Montana 59108
   Telephone: 406-652-1011
   Fax: 406-652-8102
   E-Mail: tmahlen@hglaw.net
   www.hglaw.net

Established: 2005

Insurance Law, Insurance Coverage, Fraud, Arson, Product Liability, Construction Law, Toxic Torts, Personal Injury, Errors and Omissions, Automobile

Insurance Clients

American International Group, Inc.	Continental Western Group
Farmers Union Mutual Insurance Company (MT)	GAB Robins Risk Management Services, Inc.
Liberty Mutual Insurance Company	Motorists Insurance Group
National Farmers Union Property & Casualty Company	Nautilus Insurance Company
Zurich American Insurance Company	York Insurance Services Group, Inc.

Non-Insurance Clients

Republic Services, Inc.

Partners/Shareholders

James R. Halverson — 1957 — Montana State University, B.A. (with honors), 1980; The University of Montana, J.D., 1983 — Admitted to Bar, 1983, Montana; U.S. District Court, District of Montana; 1985, U.S. Court of Appeals, Ninth Circuit; U.S. Supreme Court — Member American and Yellowstone Area Bar Associations; State Bar of Montana; Council on Litigation Management; Defense Research Institute; Montana Defense Trial Lawyers Association — E-mail: jhalverson@hglaw.net

Thomas L. Mahlen Jr. — 1982 — University of Wisconsin-Superior, B.A., 2004; The University of North Dakota School of Law, J.D. (with distinction), 2007 — Admitted to Bar, 2007, Montana; U.S. District Court, District of Montana — Member American and Yellowstone Area Bar Associations; State Bar of Montana; Defense Research Institute; Montana Defense Trial Lawyers Association — E-mail: tmahlen@hglaw.net

Associate

John L. Wright — 1985 — University of South Carolina, B.A., 2008; The

Halverson & Mahlen, P.C., Billings, MT (Continued)

University of Montana, J.D., 2012 — Publication Editor, Public Land and Resources Law Review — Admitted to Bar, 2012, Montana; 2013, North Carolina; 2013, U.S. District Court, District of Montana — E-mail: jwright@hglaw.net

Moulton Bellingham PC

Crowne Plaza, Suite 1900
27 North 27th Street
Billings, Montana 59101
   Telephone: 406-248-7731
   Fax: 406-248-7889

Trial Practice, State and Federal Courts, Insurance Law, Workers' Compensation, Fire, Casualty Insurance Law, Professional Liability, Oil and Gas, Product Liability

Insurance Clients

Attorneys Liability Protection Society	Farmers Insurance Group
Montana Municipal Interlocal Authority	Fireman's Fund Insurance Company
	State Farm Fire and Casualty Company

Of Counsel

Brent Reed Cromley — 1941 — The University of Montana, J.D., 1968 — Admitted to Bar, 1968, Montana

Gerald B. Murphy — 1945 — The University of Montana, J.D., 1974 — Admitted to Bar, 1974, Montana

K. Kent Koolen — 1943 — The University of Montana, J.D., 1975 — Admitted to Bar, 1975, Montana

Shareholders

W. Anderson Forsythe — 1953 — The University of Montana, J.D., 1979 — Admitted to Bar, 1979, Montana

Doug James — 1957 — The University of Montana, J.D., 1982 — Admitted to Bar, 1982, Montana

Thomas E. Smith — 1959 — Gonzaga University, J.D., 1984 — Admitted to Bar, 1984, Montana

John T. Jones — 1956 — University of Puget Sound, J.D., 1983; Boston University, LL.M., 1985 — Admitted to Bar, 1983, Montana

Duncan A. Peete — 1966 — The University of Montana, J.D., 1991; University of Florida, LL.M., 1992 — Admitted to Bar, 1991, Montana

Gerry P. Fagan — 1959 — The University of Montana, J.D., 1998 — Admitted to Bar, 1998, Montana

Michele L. Braukmann — 1977 — University of Notre Dame, J.D., 2001 — Admitted to Bar, 2001, Montana

Michael E. Begley — 1970 — The University of Montana, J.D., 2002 — Admitted to Bar, 2002, Montana; Wyoming

Jeff G. Sorenson — 1976 — The University of Montana, J.D. (with honors), 2003; New York University, LL.M. (with honors), 2004 — Admitted to Bar, 2004, Montana

Kathryn J. Maehl — 1979 — The University of Montana, J.D., 2005; New York University, LL.M., 2006 — Admitted to Bar, 2005, Montana

Associate Attorneys

Christopher T. Sweeney — 1980 — The University of Montana School of Law, J.D., 2008 — Admitted to Bar, 2008, Montana; 2010, North Dakota; 2011, Wyoming

Jessica Fehr — 1979 — The University of Montana School of Law, J.D., 2004 — Admitted to Bar, 2004, Montana

Brandon Hoskins — 1985 — The University of Montana School of Law, J.D., 2010 — Admitted to Bar, 2010, Montana

Afton Ball — 1984 — Washington University in St. Louis School of Law, J.D., 2011 — Admitted to Bar, 2011, Montana

George Kimmet — 1984 — University of Pennsylvania Law School, J.D., 2009 — Admitted to Bar, 2010, New York; 2011, Montana; 2012, Wyoming

Adam Tunning — 1987 — University of Nebraska College of Law, J.D., 2012 — Admitted to Bar, 2013, Montana; Wyoming

Adam Warren — 1988 — University of Wyoming College of Law, J.D., 2013 — Admitted to Bar, 2013, Montana

MONTANA   BOZEMAN

Moulton Bellingham PC, Billings, MT   (Continued)

(All Firm Members Belong to American & Yellowstone County Bar Associations & The State Bar of Montana.)

Parker, Heitz & Cosgrove, PLLC
401 North 31st Street, Suite 805
Billings, Montana 59101
   Telephone: 406-245-9991
   Fax: 406-245-0971
   E-Mail: parkerlaw@parker-law.com

Established: 1986

Insurance Defense, Bad Faith, Personal Injury, Agent/Broker Liability, Breach of Contract, Carrier Defense

Firm Profile: Parker Law Firm was initially established in 1986 and has handled a variety of matters for insurance carriers since that time.

Insurance Clients

Ameriprise Insurance Company	Farmers Insurance Exchange
Fire Insurance Exchange	Foremost Insurance Company
Hallmark Insurance Company	Hartford Insurance Company
Liberty Mutual	Montana Insurance Guaranty Association (MIGA)
Montana Municipal Interlocal Authority	Philadelphia Insurance Company
21st Century	

Partners

Mark D. Parker — 1955 — The University of Montana, B.A. (with honors), 1977; University of San Diego, J.D. (cum laude), 1980 — Admitted to Bar, 1980, Montana; 2003, Nevada; 2010, California — Member American and Yellowstone Area Bar Associations; State Bar of Montana; State Bar of Nevada — E-mail: markdparker@parker-law.com

Casey Heitz — 1971 — The University of Montana, B.S. (with honors), 1993; J.D., 1996 — Admitted to Bar, 1996, Montana — Member American and Yellowstone Area Bar Associations; State Bar of Montana — E-mail: caseyheitz@parker-law.com

Shawn P. Cosgrove — 1965 — Montana State University, B.S., 1989; Seattle University School of Law, J.D., 1995 — Admitted to Bar, 1995, Montana — Member American and Yellowstone Area Bar Associations; State Bar of Montana — E-mail: shawncosgrove@parker-law.com

Associate Attorney

Brian M. Murphy — 1982 — University of Notre Dame, B.A., 2005; The University of Montana, J.D. (with honors), 2010 — Law Clerk to Hon. Donald W. Molloy, U.S. District Court (2010-2011) and Hon. Charles Wilson, U.S. Court of Appeals, 11th Circuit (2011-2012) — Co-Editor-in-Chief, Montana Law Review — Admitted to Bar, 2010, Montana — Member State Bar of Montana — E-mail: brianmurphy@parker-law.com

---

The following firms also service this area.

Axilon Law Group, PLLC
895 Technology Drive
Bozeman, Montana 59718
   Telephone: 866-294-9466
   Fax: 406-294-9468

Asbestos Litigation, Automobile Liability, Commercial Liability, Construction Liability, Coverage Issues, Directors and Officers Liability, Employment Litigation, Extra-Contractual Litigation, Intellectual Property, Medical Devices, Product Liability, Professional Liability, Self-Insured Defense, Toxic Torts, Trucks/Heavy Equipment

SEE COMPLETE LISTING UNDER BOZEMAN, MONTANA

Browning, Kaleczyc, Berry & Hoven, P.C.
800 North Last Chance Gulch, Suite 101
Helena, Montana 59601
   Telephone: 406-443-6820
   Fax: 406-443-6883
Mailing Address: P.O. Box 1697, Helena, MT 59624

Insurance Law, State and Federal Courts, Environmental Law, Insurance Coverage, Health, Medical Negligence, Professional Negligence, Personal Injury, Product Liability, Property Damage, Surety, Workers' Compensation, Wrongful Termination, Employer Liability, Automobile, Commercial Liability, Employment Discrimination, Federal Employer Liability Claims (FELA), Oil and Gas, Banking

SEE COMPLETE LISTING UNDER HELENA, MONTANA (240 MILES)

BOZEMAN † 37,280 Gallatin Co.

Axilon Law Group, PLLC
895 Technology Drive
Bozeman, Montana 59718
   Telephone: 866-294-9466
   Fax: 406-294-9468
   www.axilonlaw.com

Established: 2005

Asbestos Litigation, Automobile Liability, Commercial Liability, Construction Liability, Coverage Issues, Directors and Officers Liability, Employment Litigation, Extra-Contractual Litigation, Intellectual Property, Medical Devices, Product Liability, Professional Liability, Self-Insured Defense, Toxic Torts, Trucks/Heavy Equipment

Firm Profile: Axilon Law Group, LLC provides intelligent, cost-effective legal counsel across the state of Montana from its offices in Billings, Bozeman, and Missoula. The firm was founded by attorneys whose peers have been selected as "Super Lawyers," "Best Lawyers in America," Fellows of Litigation Counsel of America, and Martindale-Hubbell's "AV" rating for legal ability and ethics, the highest possible rating awarded by this nationally recognized, peer-reviewed rating system.

Insurance Clients

AXA Pacific Insurance Company	EMC Insurance Companies
Tokio Marine Claims Service, Inc.	U.S. Liability Insurance Company

Non-Insurance Clients

Bechtel Corporation	FedEx
Greene Tweed & Co.	Hydraco, Inc.
I-Flow Corporation	Rite-Hite Corporation
Sanjel (USA), Inc.	Toyota Motor Sales, U.S.A., Inc.
USF Reddaway	Walgreen Co.
Western Transport Inc.	

Members of the Firm

Frederick P. Landers — The University of Georgia School of Law, J.D., 1997 — Admitted to Bar, 1997, Georgia; 2006, Montana — Tel: 406-922-4777

Michael J. Johnson — The University of Montana School of Law, J.D. (cum laude), 1999 — Admitted to Bar, 1999, Montana — Resident Billings, MT Office

Jill M. Gerdrum — The University of Montana School of Law, J.D. (with high honors), 2006 — Admitted to Bar, 2006, Montana — Resident Missoula, MT Office

Gary D. Hermann — Northwestern University, J.D., 1971 — Admitted to Bar, 1971, Ohio; 2005, Montana — Member Federation of Defense and Corporate Counsel

Browning, Kaleczyc, Berry & Hoven, P.C.

801 West Main, Suite 2A
Bozeman, Montana 59715
    Telephone: 406-585-0888
    Fax: 406-587-0165
    www.bkbh.com

(Helena, MT Office*: 800 North Last Chance Gulch, Suite 101, 59601, P.O. Box 1697, 59624)
    (Tel: 406-443-6820)
    (Fax: 406-443-6883)
    (E-Mail: bkbh@bkbh.com)
(Missoula, MT Office*: 201 West Railroad Street, Suite 300, 59802-4252)
    (Tel: 406-728-1694)
    (Fax: 406-728-5475)
(Great Falls, MT Office*: Liberty Center, Suite 302, 9 Third Street North, 59401)
    (Tel: 406-403-0041)
    (Fax: 406-453-1634)

Insurance Law, State and Federal Courts, Environmental Law, Insurance Coverage, Health, Medical Negligence, Professional Negligence, Personal Injury, Product Liability, Property Damage, Surety, Workers' Compensation, Wrongful Termination, Employer Liability, Automobile, Commercial Liability, Employment Discrimination, Federal Employer Liability Claims (FELA), Oil and Gas, Banking

(See listing under Helena, MT for additional information)

Crowley Fleck PLLP

45 Discovery Drive
Bozeman, Montana 59718-6957
    Telephone: 406-556-1430
    Fax: 406-556-1433
    www.crowleyfleck.com

(Billings, MT Office*: 500 Transwestern Plaza II, 490 North 31st Street, 59101-1288)
    (Tel: 406-252-3441)
    (Fax: 406-256-8526, 406-259-4159, 406-256-0277)
    (E-Mail: jkresslein@crowleyfleck.com)
(Butte, MT Office*: Thornton Building, 65 East Broadway, Suite 503, 59701)
    (Tel: 406-533-6892)
    (Fax: 406-533-6830)
(Helena, MT Office*: 900 North Last Chance Gulch, Suite 200, 59601)
    (Tel: 406-449-4165)
    (Fax: 406-449-5149)
(Kalispell, MT Office*: 1667 Whitefish Stage Road, Suite 101, 59901-4835)
    (Tel: 406-752-6644)
    (Fax: 406-752-5108)
(Missoula, MT Office*: 305 South 4th Street East, Suite 100, 59801-2701)
    (Tel: 406-523-3600)
    (Fax: 406-523-3636)
(Bismarck, ND Office*: 100 West Broadway, Suite 250, 58501, P.O. Box 2798, 58502-2798)
    (Tel: 701-223-6585)
    (Fax: 701-222-4853)
(Williston, ND Office*: 1331 9th Avenue NW, 2nd Floor, 58801, P.O. Box 1206, 58802-1206)
    (Tel: 701-572-2200)
    (Fax: 701-572-7072)
(Casper, WY Office*: 152 North Durbin Street, Suite 220, 82601)
    (Tel: 307-265-2279)
    (Fax: 307-265-2307)
(Cheyenne, WY Office*: 237 Storey Boulevard, Suite 110, 82009)
    (Tel: 307-426-4100)
    (Fax: 307-426-4099)

Crowley Fleck PLLP, Bozeman, MT (Continued)

(Sheridan, WY Office*: 101 West Brundage Street, 82801)
    (Tel: 307-673-3000)
    (Fax: 307-672-1732)

Civil Litigation, Trial and Appellate Practice, Product Liability, Personal Injury, Construction Law, Design Professionals, Malpractice, Wrongful Termination, Employer Liability, Medical Negligence, Legal, Professional Negligence, Insurance Coverage, Bad Faith, Agent/Broker Liability, Workers' Compensation, Oil and Gas, Environmental Law

Litigation Partner

Neil G. Westesen — 1966 — University of Colorado, J.D. (with highest honors), 1990 — Admitted to Bar, 1990, Montana; U.S. District Court, District of Montana; U.S. Court of Appeals, Ninth Circuit; U.S. Supreme Court

Partners

Kristy L. Buckley	Julie A. Lichte
Molly A. Litzen	Ian McIntosh
Matthew F. McLean	Gina S. Sherman
David M. Wagner	

Associates

Darci Bentson	Brad J. Brown
Kelsey E. Bunkers	Nate J. Good
Matthew Hibbs	Whitney Kolivas

Of Counsel

Stephen M. Barrett	Larry A. Holle

(See listing under Billings, MT for additional information)

Landoe, Brown, Planalp & Reida, P.C.

27 North Tracy
Bozeman, Montana 59715
    Telephone: 406-586-4351
    Fax: 406-586-7877
    E-Mail: steve@landoelaw.com
    www.landoelaw.com

Established: 1939

Insurance Defense, Automobile, Professional Liability, General Liability, Property Damage, Personal Injury, Medical Malpractice, Legal Malpractice, Product Liability

Firm Profile: The firm has a 70 year history in Bozeman and southwest Montana. Firm members have longstanding relationships with local bankers, realtors, insurance agents and adjusters, health care providers, and construction and design professionals. With substantial jury trial experience, the firm offers efficient and cost effective litigation services.

Insurance Clients

Allstate Insurance Company	Auto-Owners Insurance Company
Capitol Indemnity Corporation	CNA Insurance Company
Continental Casualty Company	Employers Reinsurance Corporation
Great West Casualty Company	Montana Municipal Interlocal Authority
The Hartford Insurance Group	
National Chiropractic Mutual Insurance Company	QBE Insurance Company
RLI Insurance Company	St. Paul Travelers

Non-Insurance Clients

American Land Title Company	Big Sky Western Bank
ConAgra Group	Three Forks City

Firm Members

J. Robert Planalp — 1949 — Creighton University, B.S.B.A., 1971; J.D., 1973 — Admitted to Bar, 1974, Nebraska; Montana; 1974, U.S. District Court,

MONTANA — BUTTE

Landoe, Brown, Planalp & Reida, P.C., Bozeman, MT (Continued)

District of Montana — Member American Bar Association; State Bar of Montana — Practice Areas: Banking; Insurance Defense; Real Estate

Steven W. Reida — 1959 — University of Nebraska, B.A., 1982; J.D., 1985 — Admitted to Bar, 1986, Montana; 1987, U.S. District Court, District of Montana; 1988, U.S. Court of Appeals, Ninth Circuit — Member State Bar of Montana; Montana Defense Trial Lawyers Association (Past President, 2010) — Practice Areas: Insurance Defense; Insurance Coverage; Medical Malpractice; Product Liability

Associates

Patrick C. Riley — 1985 — California Polytechnic State University, B.S., 2007; Loyola Law School Los Angeles, J.D., 2011 — Admitted to Bar, 2011, California; 2012, Montana; U.S. District Court, District of Montana — Practice Areas: General Defense

Alexander L. Roots — 1973 — Duke University, A.B., 1996; Wake Forest University, J.D., 1999 — Admitted to Bar, 1999, Montana; 1999, U.S. District Court, District of Montana — Member State Bar of Montana; Gallatin County Bar Association — Practice Areas: Insurance Defense

Moore, O'Connell & Refling, P.C.

Life of Montana Building, Suite 10
601 Haggerty Lane
Bozeman, Montana 59715
  Telephone: 406-587-5511
  Fax: 406-587-9079
  E-Mail: morlaw@qwestoffice.net
  www.morlawfirm.com

Established: 1975

General Defense, Insurance Law, Subrogation, Investigation and Adjustment

Firm Profile: Experienced in the following areas of litigation: automobile, automobile and CGL, coverage and bad faith, professional liability, governmental liability, construction, employment and civil rights.

Insurance Clients

American Family Insurance	American Farmers & Ranchers Mutual Insurance Company
American International Group	Aspen Specialty Insurance
American National Property and Casualty Company	Fireman's Fund Insurance Company
Attorneys Liability Protection Society (ALPS)	Mid-Continent Group
Hartford Insurance Company	Westchester Surplus Lines Insurance Company
Philadelphia Insurance Company	
Zurich North America	

Directors/Shareholders

Allan H. Baris — 1947 — Stanford University, B.S. (with honors), 1969; University of Washington, J.D. (Order of the Coif), 1979 — Admitted to Bar, 1979, Washington; 1996, Montana; 1979, U.S. District Court, Western District of Washington; 1986, U.S. Court of Appeals, Ninth Circuit; 1991, U.S. District Court, Eastern District of Washington; 1997, U.S. District Court, District of Montana — Member American, Washington State and Gallatin County Bar Associations; State Bar of Montana; Montana Defense Trial Lawyers Association — Reported Cases: State Farm vs. Fryer, 2010 MT 191, 357 Mont. 329, 239 P3d 143; State Farm vs. Bush Hog LLC, 2009 MT 349, 353 Mont. 173, 219 P3d 1249; Lee vs. Great Divide Ins. Co., 2008 MT 80, 342 Mont. 147, 182 P3d 41; Richards vs. Knuchel, 2005 MT 133, 327 Mont. 249, 115 P3d 189 (2005) — AV Rated by Martindale Hubbell

Elizabeth W. Lund — 1981 — Colby College, B.A. (cum laude), 2004; Suffolk University Law School, J.D. (magna cum laude), 2009 — Admitted to Bar, 2009, Montana; U.S. District Court, District of Montana — Member American and Gallatin County Bar Associations; State Bar of Montana — E-mail: lund@qwestoffice.net

---

The following firms also service this area.

Brown Law Firm, P.C.
315 North 24th Street
Billings, Montana 59101
  Telephone: 406-248-2611
  Fax: 406-248-3128

Mailing Address: P.O. Drawer 849, Billings, MT 59103-0849

Defense of Complex Civil Litigation, Defense of Catastrophic Personal Injury and Wrongful Death Claims, Insurance Law Including Coverage and Defense of Bad Faith Claims, Product Liability Defense, Defense of Medical and Dental Malpractice Claims, Labor and Employee Relations, Minerals, Oil and Gas, Banking, Workers' Compensation, Real Estate, Construction Defect, Appellate Law

SEE COMPLETE LISTING UNDER BILLINGS, MONTANA (140 MILES)

Corette Black Carlson & Mickelson
Mayer Building
129 West Park Street, Suite 301
Butte, Montana 59701
  Telephone: 406-782-5800
  Fax: 406-723-8919

Mailing Address: P.O. Box 509, Butte, MT 59703

Trial Practice, Corporate Law, Insurance Law, Product Liability, Personal Injury, Casualty, Banking, Water Law, Mining, Probate Law

SEE COMPLETE LISTING UNDER BUTTE, MONTANA (80 MILES)

Gough, Shanahan, Johnson & Waterman, PLLP
33 South Last Chance Gulch
Helena, Montana 59601
  Telephone: 406-442-8560
  Fax: 406-442-8783

Mailing Address: P.O. Box 1715, Helena, MT 59624

Insurance Defense, Bodily Injury, Property Damage, Commercial Law, Surety Bonds, Litigation, Subrogation, Copyright and Trademark Law, Environmental Law, ERISA, Employment Law, Business Law, School Law

SEE COMPLETE LISTING UNDER HELENA, MONTANA (90 MILES)

Moulton Bellingham PC
Crowne Plaza, Suite 1900
27 North 27th Street
Billings, Montana 59101
  Telephone: 406-248-7731
  Fax: 406-248-7889

Mailing Address: P.O. Box 2559, Billings, MT 59103

Trial Practice, State and Federal Courts, Insurance Law, Workers' Compensation, Fire, Casualty Insurance Law, Professional Liability, Oil and Gas, Product Liability

SEE COMPLETE LISTING UNDER BILLINGS, MONTANA (140 MILES)

BUTTE   † 33,336 Silver Bow Co.

Corette Black Carlson & Mickelson

Mayer Building
129 West Park Street, Suite 301
Butte, Montana 59701
  Telephone: 406-782-5800
  Fax: 406-723-8919
  E-Mail: corette@montana.com

Established: 1907

Trial Practice, Corporate Law, Insurance Law, Product Liability, Personal Injury, Casualty, Banking, Water Law, Mining, Probate Law

Insurance Clients

Allstate Insurance Company	Fireman's Fund Insurance Companies
Great West Casualty Company	
St. Paul Travelers	Swiss Re
United American Insurance Company	USAA

Corette Black Carlson & Mickelson, Butte, MT
(Continued)

Gregory C. Black — 1952 — Whitman College, A.B., 1974; The George Washington University; The University of Montana, J.D., 1979 — Admitted to Bar, 1979, Montana — E-mail: gcblack@cpklawmt.com

Robert M. Carlson — 1954 — The University of Montana, B.A. (with honors), 1976; J.D., 1979 — Admitted to Bar, 1979, Montana — E-mail: bcarlson@cpklawmt.com

Marshal L. Mickelson — 1960 — Eastern Montana College, B.A., 1982; The University of Montana, J.D., 1985 — Admitted to Bar, 1985, Montana — E-mail: mmick@cpklawmt.com

C. Kathleen McBride — 1952 — University of Redlands, B.S. (with distinction), 1974; The University of Montana, M.S., 1977; J.D., 1985 — Admitted to Bar, 1985, Montana — E-mail: mcbrideck@cpklawmt.com

William M. Kebe, Jr. — 1942 — Waynesburg College, B.S., 1964; The University of Montana, J.D., 1973; Boston University, LL.M., 1974 — Admitted to Bar, 1973, Montana — E-mail: kebew@aol.com

Marie Kagie-Shutey — 1978 — Carroll College, B.A. (distinguished graduate), 2001; Gonzaga University School of Law, J.D. (magna cum laude), 2005 — Admitted to Bar, 2005, Arizona; 2008, Washington; 2011, Montana — E-mail: mshutey@cpklawmt.com

Annie N. Harris — 1982 — The University of Montana, B.A. (with high honors), 2006; University of Colorado, J.D., 2011 — Admitted to Bar, 2011, Montana — E-mail: aharris@cpklawmt.com

Angela K. Hasquet — 1985 — The University of Montana School of Law, J.D., 2012; University of Washington School of Law, LL.M. Taxation, 2013 — Admitted to Bar, 2012, Montana — E-mail: ahasquet@cpklawmt.com

(Revisors of the Montana Insurance Law Digest for this Publication)

Crowley Fleck PLLP
Thornton Building
65 East Broadway, Suite 503
Butte, Montana 59701
   Telephone: 406-533-6892
   Fax: 406-533-6830
   www.crowleyfleck.com

(Billings, MT Office*: 500 Transwestern Plaza II, 490 North 31st Street, 59101-1288)
   (Tel: 406-252-3441)
   (Fax: 406-256-8526, 406-259-4159, 406-256-0277)
   (E-Mail: jkresslein@crowleyfleck.com)
(Bozeman, MT Office*: 45 Discovery Drive, 59718-6957)
   (Tel: 406-556-1430)
   (Fax: 406-556-1433)
(Helena, MT Office*: 900 North Last Chance Gulch, Suite 200, 59601)
   (Tel: 406-449-4165)
   (Fax: 406-449-5149)
(Kalispell, MT Office*: 1667 Whitefish Stage Road, Suite 101, 59901-4835)
   (Tel: 406-752-6644)
   (Fax: 406-752-5108)
(Missoula, MT Office*: 305 South 4th Street East, Suite 100, 59801-2701)
   (Tel: 406-523-3600)
   (Fax: 406-523-3636)
(Bismarck, ND Office*: 100 West Broadway, Suite 250, 58501, P.O. Box 2798, 58502-2798)
   (Tel: 701-223-6585)
   (Fax: 701-222-4853)
(Williston, ND Office*: 1331 9th Avenue NW, 2nd Floor, 58801, P.O. Box 1206, 58802-1206)
   (Tel: 701-572-2200)
   (Fax: 701-572-7072)
(Casper, WY Office*: 152 North Durbin Street, Suite 220, 82601)
   (Tel: 307-265-2279)
   (Fax: 307-265-2307)
(Cheyenne, WY Office*: 237 Storey Boulevard, Suite 110, 82009)
   (Tel: 307-426-4100)
   (Fax: 307-426-4099)

Crowley Fleck PLLP, Butte, MT (Continued)
(Sheridan, WY Office*: 101 West Brundage Street, 82801)
   (Tel: 307-673-3000)
   (Fax: 307-672-1732)

Civil Litigation, Trial and Appellate Practice, Product Liability, Personal Injury, Construction Law, Design Professionals, Malpractice, Wrongful Termination, Employer Liability, Medical Negligence, Legal, Professional Negligence, Insurance Coverage, Bad Faith, Agent/Broker Liability, Workers' Compensation, Oil and Gas, Environmental Law

Litigation Partner

Brian Holland — 1956 — Carroll College, B.A., 1978; The University of Montana School of Law, J.D., 1982 — Admitted to Bar, 1982, Montana; 1988, Washington

(See listing under Billings, MT for additional information)

The following firms also service this area.

Browning, Kaleczyc, Berry & Hoven, P.C.
800 North Last Chance Gulch, Suite 101
Helena, Montana 59601
   Telephone: 406-443-6820
   Fax: 406-443-6883
Mailing Address: P.O. Box 1697, Helena, MT 59624

Insurance Law, State and Federal Courts, Environmental Law, Insurance Coverage, Health, Medical Negligence, Professional Negligence, Personal Injury, Product Liability, Property Damage, Surety, Workers' Compensation, Wrongful Termination, Employer Liability, Automobile, Commercial Liability, Employment Discrimination, Federal Employer Liability Claims (FELA), Oil and Gas, Banking

SEE COMPLETE LISTING UNDER HELENA, MONTANA (60 MILES)

Gough, Shanahan, Johnson & Waterman, PLLP
33 South Last Chance Gulch
Helena, Montana 59601
   Telephone: 406-442-8560
   Fax: 406-442-8783
Mailing Address: P.O. Box 1715, Helena, MT 59624

Insurance Defense, Bodily Injury, Property Damage, Commercial Law, Surety Bonds, Litigation, Subrogation, Copyright and Trademark Law, Environmental Law, ERISA, Employment Law, Business Law, School Law

SEE COMPLETE LISTING UNDER HELENA, MONTANA (60 MILES)

Johnson, Berg & Saxby, PLLP
221 First Avenue East
Kalispell, Montana 59901
   Telephone: 406-755-5535
   Fax: 406-756-9436
Mailing Address: P.O. Box 3038, Kalispell, MT 59903-3038

Bankruptcy, Business Law, Civil Litigation, Commercial Law, Entertainment Law, Insurance Defense, Personal Injury, Professional Liability, Real Estate, Workers' Compensation

SEE COMPLETE LISTING UNDER KALISPELL, MONTANA (238 MILES)

CHINOOK † 1,203 Blaine Co.
Refer To
Smith, Walsh, Clarke & Gregoire, PLLP
Galleria Building, Suite 401
104 2nd Street South
Great Falls, Montana 59401
   Telephone: 406-727-4100
   Fax: 406-727-9228
Mailing Address: P.O. Box 2227, Great Falls, MT 59403-2227

Insurance Law, Product Liability, Medical Malpractice, Workers' Compensation, Casualty, Negligence, Personal Injury, Aviation, Commercial Litigation, Construction Law, Premises Liability, Indian Law

SEE COMPLETE LISTING UNDER GREAT FALLS, MONTANA (136 MILES)

MONTANA

CHOTEAU † 1,684 Teton Co.

Refer To

Smith, Walsh, Clarke & Gregoire, PLLP
Galleria Building, Suite 401
104 2nd Street South
Great Falls, Montana 59401
   Telephone: 406-727-4100
   Fax: 406-727-9228

Mailing Address: P.O. Box 2227, Great Falls, MT 59403-2227

Insurance Law, Product Liability, Medical Malpractice, Workers' Compensation, Casualty, Negligence, Personal Injury, Aviation, Commercial Litigation, Construction Law, Premises Liability, Indian Law

SEE COMPLETE LISTING UNDER GREAT FALLS, MONTANA (50 MILES)

COLSTRIP 2,214 Rosebud Co.

Refer To

Moulton Bellingham PC
Crowne Plaza, Suite 1900
27 North 27th Street
Billings, Montana 59101
   Telephone: 406-248-7731
   Fax: 406-248-7889

Mailing Address: P.O. Box 2559, Billings, MT 59103

Trial Practice, State and Federal Courts, Insurance Law, Workers' Compensation, Fire, Casualty Insurance Law, Professional Liability, Oil and Gas, Product Liability

SEE COMPLETE LISTING UNDER BILLINGS, MONTANA (120 MILES)

CONRAD † 2,570 Pondera Co.

Refer To

Smith, Walsh, Clarke & Gregoire, PLLP
Galleria Building, Suite 401
104 2nd Street South
Great Falls, Montana 59401
   Telephone: 406-727-4100
   Fax: 406-727-9228

Mailing Address: P.O. Box 2227, Great Falls, MT 59403-2227

Insurance Law, Product Liability, Medical Malpractice, Workers' Compensation, Casualty, Negligence, Personal Injury, Aviation, Commercial Litigation, Construction Law, Premises Liability, Indian Law

SEE COMPLETE LISTING UNDER GREAT FALLS, MONTANA (60 MILES)

CUT BANK † 2,869 Glacier Co.

Refer To

Smith, Walsh, Clarke & Gregoire, PLLP
Galleria Building, Suite 401
104 2nd Street South
Great Falls, Montana 59401
   Telephone: 406-727-4100
   Fax: 406-727-9228

Mailing Address: P.O. Box 2227, Great Falls, MT 59403-2227

Insurance Law, Product Liability, Medical Malpractice, Workers' Compensation, Casualty, Negligence, Personal Injury, Aviation, Commercial Litigation, Construction Law, Premises Liability, Indian Law

SEE COMPLETE LISTING UNDER GREAT FALLS, MONTANA (110 MILES)

FORSYTH † 1,777 Rosebud Co.

Refer To

Moulton Bellingham PC
Crowne Plaza, Suite 1900
27 North 27th Street
Billings, Montana 59101
   Telephone: 406-248-7731
   Fax: 406-248-7889

Mailing Address: P.O. Box 2559, Billings, MT 59103

Trial Practice, State and Federal Courts, Insurance Law, Workers' Compensation, Fire, Casualty Insurance Law, Professional Liability, Oil and Gas, Product Liability

SEE COMPLETE LISTING UNDER BILLINGS, MONTANA (108 MILES)

FORT BENTON † 1,464 Chouteau Co.

Refer To

Smith, Walsh, Clarke & Gregoire, PLLP
Galleria Building, Suite 401
104 2nd Street South
Great Falls, Montana 59401
   Telephone: 406-727-4100
   Fax: 406-727-9228

Mailing Address: P.O. Box 2227, Great Falls, MT 59403-2227

Insurance Law, Product Liability, Medical Malpractice, Workers' Compensation, Casualty, Negligence, Personal Injury, Aviation, Commercial Litigation, Construction Law, Premises Liability, Indian Law

SEE COMPLETE LISTING UNDER GREAT FALLS, MONTANA (45 MILES)

GLASGOW † 3,250 Valley Co.

Refer To

Smith, Walsh, Clarke & Gregoire, PLLP
Galleria Building, Suite 401
104 2nd Street South
Great Falls, Montana 59401
   Telephone: 406-727-4100
   Fax: 406-727-9228

Mailing Address: P.O. Box 2227, Great Falls, MT 59403-2227

Insurance Law, Product Liability, Medical Malpractice, Workers' Compensation, Casualty, Negligence, Personal Injury, Aviation, Commercial Litigation, Construction Law, Premises Liability, Indian Law

SEE COMPLETE LISTING UNDER GREAT FALLS, MONTANA (276 MILES)

GLENDIVE † 4,935 Dawson Co.

Refer To

Moulton Bellingham PC
Crowne Plaza, Suite 1900
27 North 27th Street
Billings, Montana 59101
   Telephone: 406-248-7731
   Fax: 406-248-7889

Mailing Address: P.O. Box 2559, Billings, MT 59103

Trial Practice, State and Federal Courts, Insurance Law, Workers' Compensation, Fire, Casualty Insurance Law, Professional Liability, Oil and Gas, Product Liability

SEE COMPLETE LISTING UNDER BILLINGS, MONTANA (190 MILES)

GREAT FALLS † 58,505 Cascade Co.

Browning, Kaleczyc, Berry & Hoven, P.C.
Liberty Center, Suite 302
9 Third Street North
Great Falls, Montana 59401
   Telephone: 406-403-0041
   Fax: 406-453-1634
   www.bkbh.com

Browning, Kaleczyc, Berry & Hoven, P.C., Great Falls, MT (Continued)

(Helena, MT Office*: 800 North Last Chance Gulch, Suite 101, 59601, P.O. Box 1697, 59624)
  (Tel: 406-443-6820)
  (Fax: 406-443-6883)
  (E-Mail: bkbh@bkbh.com)
(Missoula, MT Office*: 201 West Railroad Street, Suite 300, 59802-4252)
  (Tel: 406-728-1694)
  (Fax: 406-728-5475)
(Bozeman, MT Office*: 801 West Main, Suite 2A, 59715)
  (Tel: 406-585-0888)
  (Fax: 406-587-0165)

Insurance Law, State and Federal Courts, Environmental Law, Insurance Coverage, Health, Medical Negligence, Professional Negligence, Personal Injury, Product Liability, Property Damage, Surety, Workers' Compensation, Wrongful Termination, Employer Liability, Automobile, Commercial Liability, Employment Discrimination, Federal Employer Liability Claims (FELA), Oil and Gas, Banking

(See listing under Helena, MT for additional information)

Davis Hatley Haffeman & Tighe, P.C.

The Milwaukee Station, 3rd Floor
101 River Drive North
Great Falls, Montana 59401
  Telephone: 406-761-5243
  Fax: 406-761-4126
  www.dhhtlaw.com

Established: 1912

Insurance Defense, Automobile, Product Liability, Professional Liability, Bodily Injury, Property Damage

Insurance Clients

Allstate Insurance Company
Cascade Farmers Mutual Insurance Company
Continental Western Insurance Company
Farmers Insurance Group
Federated Insurance Company
Liberty Mutual Insurance Company
Montana Municipal Interlocal Authority
St. Paul Fire and Marine Insurance Company
State of Montana, Risk Management and Tort Claims Division
American West Insurance Company
CNA
Contractors Bonding and Insurance Company (CBIC), an RLI Company
Federated Rural Electric Insurance Exchange
Nationwide Insurance
Reliance Insurance Company
Specialty Claims, Incorporated
State Farm Insurance Company
United Fire Group

Firm Members

Maxon R. Davis — 1950 — University of California, Berkeley, A.B., 1972; The University of Montana, J.D. (with high honors), 1976 — Admitted to Bar, 1976, Montana — Member American and Cascade County Bar Associations; State Bar of Montana; Montana Association of Defense Counsel; American Academy of Hospital Attorneys; National Health Lawyers Association; Montana Defense Trial Lawyers Association; Defense Research Institute

Gregory J. Hatley — 1953 — Carroll College, B.A., 1975; Gonzaga University School of Law, J.D., 1980 — Admitted to Bar, 1980, Montana — Member American and Cascade County Bar Associations; State Bar of Montana; Montana Defense Trial Lawyers Association; Defense Research Institute

Paul R. Haffeman — 1959 — Montana State University, B.A., 1985; The University of Montana, J.D. (with honors), 1988 — Admitted to Bar, 1988, Montana — Member American and Cascade County Bar Associations; State Bar of Montana; Montana Defense Trial Lawyers Association

James A. Donahue — 1965 — Stanford University, B.S.E.E., 1987; University of Minnesota, J.D., 1993 — Admitted to Bar, 1993, Minnesota; 1994, Montana — Member State Bar of Montana; Cascade County Bar Association

Davis Hatley Haffeman & Tighe, P.C., Great Falls, MT (Continued)

Jeffry M. Foster — 1981 — The University of Montana - Western, B.A. (with honors), 2005; The University of Montana School of Law, J.D., 2008 — Admitted to Bar, 2008, Montana; U.S. District Court, District of Montana; U.S. Court of Appeals, Ninth Circuit — Member American and Cascade County Bar Associations; State Bar of Montana; Criminal Justice Act Panel

Derek J. Oestreicher — University of California, Davis, B.A., 2010; The University of Montana, J.D., 2013 — Admitted to Bar, 2013, Montana; U.S. District Court, District of Montana — Member American and Cascade County Bar Associations; State Bar of Montana

Dennis Tighe — (Retired)

Faure Holden Attorneys at Law, P.C.

1314 Central Avenue
Great Falls, Montana 59401
  Telephone: 406-452-6500
  Fax: 406-452-6503
  www.faureholden.com

Labor and Employment, Civil Litigation, Insurance Coverage, Insurance Defense, Trial Practice, Directors and Officers Liability

Firm Profile: Experienced. Effective. Responsive.

Insurance Clients

Affirmative Risk Management, Inc.
Chubb Insurance Company
CUNA Mutual Insurance
Great American Insurance Company
Zurich Insurance Company
AIG - Chartis
The Cincinnati Insurance Companies
Philadelphia Insurance Companies
Travelers Bond & Financial Products

Senior Litigation Partners

Jean E. Faure — The University of Montana, J.D. (with high honors), 1986 — Admitted to Bar, 1987, Montana

Jason T. Holden — The University of Montana, J.D. (with honors), 2001 — Admitted to Bar, 2001, Montana

Senior Associate

Dana A. Henkel — Southern Methodist University Law School, J.D., 2012 — Admitted to Bar, 2012, Montana

Marra, Evenson & Bell, P.C.

2 Railroad Square, Suite C
Great Falls, Montana 59401
  Telephone: 406-268-1000
  Fax: 406-761-2610
  E-Mail: email@marralawfirm.com
  www.marralawfirm.com

Established: 1951

Insurance Defense, Trial Practice, Personal Injury, Professional Malpractice, Health Care, Workers' Compensation, Commercial Litigation, Business Law, Construction Law, Product Liability, Employment Law, Environmental Law, Hazardous Waste, Pollution, Contracts, Insurance Coverage, Surety, Civil Rights, Transportation, Automobile, Fire, Tort Litigation, Casualty, Inland Marine, Property, Subrogation, Investigation and Adjustment, Alternative Dispute Resolution, Natural Resources, Governmental Entities, Discrimination Law

Firm Profile: Marra, Evenson & Bell, P.C., has achieved and maintained the highest rating for legal ability and ethical conduct. The firm is a full service business and litigation law firm which prides itself on stability, continuity of service, and breadth of practice areas. Our firm provides business counseling and legal services in a multitude of practice areas.

Marra, Evenson & Bell, P.C., Great Falls, MT (Continued)

Insurance Clients

Acceptance Insurance Company
American National Property and Casualty Company
Chicago Title Insurance Company
Church Mutual Insurance Company
Electric Insurance Company
Empire Fire and Marine Insurance Company
GMAC Insurance Group
Great American Insurance Company
Leo P. McMeel Insurance, Inc.
Mountain West Farm Bureau Mutual Insurance Company
National Interstate Insurance Company
Philadelphia Insurance Companies
Utica Mutual Insurance Company
American Family Insurance Group
American West Insurance Company
Chubb Insurance Company
Continental General Insurance Company
Essex Insurance Company
Farmland Mutual Insurance Company
Gulf Insurance Company
Interstate Insurance Group
Mid-Continent Insurance Company
National General Insurance Company
Nationwide Agribusiness Insurance Company
Safety Insurance Company
Zurich North America

Non-Insurance Clients

Allegra Printing
Central Montana Outfitters, Inc.
Cooper Valley Landowners' Association
Easter Seals-Goodwill Northern Rocky Mountain, Inc.
Junkermier, Clark, Campanella, Stevens P.C.
Montana Resource Services, Inc.
Montana Trout Unlimited, Inc.
Owens-Illinois, Inc.
Target Corporation
Trout Montana, LLC
Big Fish Marketing, Inc.
Constitution State Service Company
Davidson Companies
Gold Medal Products Co.
Highgate Senior Living
Missouri River Trout Shop
Montana Farmers Union
Montana Specialty Mills, L.L.C.
Mountain View Co-op
Planet Earth
Town & Country Supply Association

Partners

Thomas A. Marra — 1955 — Gonzaga University, J.D., 1981 — Admitted to Bar, 1981, Montana; 1981, U.S. District Court, District of Montana; 1990, U.S. Court of Appeals, Ninth Circuit; 1992, U.S. Supreme Court; 1999, U.S. District Court, District of Minnesota; 1999, U.S. Court of Federal Claims; 2000, U.S. Court of Appeals, Eighth Circuit — Member State Bar of Montana; Cascade County Bar Association — Practice Areas: Insurance — E-mail: tmarra@marralawfirm.com

Kirk D. Evenson — 1957 — The University of Montana, J.D. (magna cum laude), 1989 — Admitted to Bar, 1989, Montana; U.S. District Court, District of Montana; 1996, U.S. Court of Appeals, Ninth Circuit; 2000, U.S. Court of Appeals, Eighth Circuit; 1996, Blackfeet Tribal Court; 1997, Chippewa-Cree Tribal Court; 1997, Salish Kootenai Tribal Court — Member State Bar of Montana; Cascade County Bar Association — Practice Areas: Commercial Litigation; Insurance — E-mail: kevenson@marralawfirm.com

Barbara E. Bell — 1948 — University of Michigan, B.A., 1970; Wayne State University, J.D., 1973 — Admitted to Bar, 1977, Montana; 1977, U.S. District Court, District of Montana; 1988, U.S. Court of Appeals, Ninth Circuit; 1992, U.S. Supreme Court — Member American Bar Association; State Bar of Montana (Character and Fitness Committee)

Antonia Marra — 1956 — Gonzaga University, B.A., 1978; J.D., 1981 — Admitted to Bar, 1981, Montana; 1981, U.S. District Court, District of Montana; 1989, U.S. Court of Appeals, Ninth Circuit; 1992, U.S. Supreme Court; 2001, U.S. Tax Court — Member State Bar of Montana (ADR Committee) — Former Prosecutor — Practice Areas: Employment; Civil Rights; Administrative Law; Appeals

Joseph R. Marra — 1924 — The University of Montana, J.D., 1951 — Admitted to Bar, 1951, Montana; 1951, U.S. District Court, District of Montana; 1951, U.S. Court of Appeals, Ninth Circuit; 1951, U.S. Supreme Court — Member American and Cascade County Bar Associations; State Bar of Montana; Association of Trial Lawyers of America — Languages: Italian

Associate

C. Nicholas Hash — 1987 — Carroll College, B.A., 2010; The University of Montana, J.D., 2013 — Admitted to Bar, 2013, Montana — Member State Bar of Montana; Cascade County Bar Association

Smith, Walsh, Clarke & Gregoire, PLLP

Galleria Building, Suite 401
104 2nd Street South
Great Falls, Montana 59401
Telephone: 406-727-4100
Fax: 406-727-9228
www.swcgfirm.com

Insurance Law, Product Liability, Medical Malpractice, Workers' Compensation, Casualty, Negligence, Personal Injury, Aviation, Commercial Litigation, Construction Law, Premises Liability, Indian Law

Firm Profile: General defense firm with experience in a number of areas including medical malpractice, E & O, products liability, work place injuries, commercial litigation, negligence, premises liability, and construction defect.

Insurance Clients

The Cincinnati Companies
Farmers Alliance Mutual Insurance Company
Fireman's Fund Insurance Company
Mountain West Farm Bureau Mutual Insurance Company
The St. Paul/Travelers Companies, Inc.
Continental Western Group
Farmers Insurance Group
Farmers Union Mutual Insurance Company (MT)
Mid-Continent Group
QBE/National Farmers Union Property & Casualty Company
Scottsdale Insurance Company
Zurich American Insurance Group

Non-Insurance Clients

Montana Rail Link
Wells Fargo & Company
Town Pump, Inc.

Founding Partner

Marvin J. Smith — (1922-2010)

Partners

Dennis P. Clarke — 1947 — University of Oregon, B.A., 1970; The University of Montana, J.D., 1974 — Admitted to Bar, 1974, Montana — Member American and Cascade County Bar Associations; State Bar of Montana

William J. Gregoire — 1947 — Eastern Montana College, B.A., 1971; Gonzaga University, J.D., 1977 — Admitted to Bar, 1977, Washington; Montana — Member American, Washington State and Cascade County Bar Associations; State Bar of Montana

Stephanie A. Hollar — 1969 — Montana State University, B.S. (with honors), 1991; The University of Montana, J.D. (with honors), 1994 — Admitted to Bar, 1994, Montana; 1994, U.S. District Court, District of Montana; Blackfeet Tribal Court; Fort Peck Tribal Court; Chippewa-Cree Tribal Court; Northern Cheyenne Tribal Court; Confederated Salish and Kootenai Tribal Court — Member State Bar of Montana; Cascade County Bar Association; Montana Defense Trial Lawyers Association; Defense Research Institute

Michael L. Rausch — 1969 — Concordia College, B.A. (summa cum laude), 1991; The University of Montana, J.D., 1994 — Admitted to Bar, 1994, Montana — Member State Bar of Montana; Cascade County Bar Association — Languages: French

Steven J. Fitzpatrick — 1978 — Montana State University, B.S., 2001; Arizona State University, J.D., 2004 — Admitted to Bar, 2004, Montana; 2005, Arizona — Member State Bar of Montana; State Bar of Arizona; Cascade County Bar Association

Associate

Dean Koffler — The University of Montana-Missoula, B.A. (with honors, Dean's List), 2009; The University of Montana School of Law, J.D., 2012 — Admitted to Bar, 2012, Montana

Retired

Robert J. Vermillion — 1939 — University of Idaho, B.A., 1961; M.A., 1963; The University of Montana, J.D., 1976 — Admitted to Bar, 1976, Montana — Member American and Washington State Bar Associations; State Bar of Montana

James R. Walsh — 1944 — Georgetown University, 1965; The University of Montana, J.D., 1968 — Admitted to Bar, 1968, Montana — Member American and Cascade County Bar Associations; State Bar of Montana; Defense Research Institute; American Judicature Society — Certified Civil Trial Specialist

(The Firm is a Member of the Montana Defense Trial Lawyers Association)

HELENA   MONTANA

The following firms also service this area.

Brown Law Firm, P.C.
315 North 24th Street
Billings, Montana 59101
  Telephone: 406-248-2611
  Fax: 406-248-3128

Mailing Address: P.O. Drawer 849, Billings, MT 59103-0849

Defense of Complex Civil Litigation, Defense of Catastrophic Personal Injury and Wrongful Death Claims, Insurance Law Including Coverage and Defense of Bad Faith Claims, Product Liability Defense, Defense of Medical and Dental Malpractice Claims, Labor and Employee Relations, Minerals, Oil and Gas, Banking, Workers' Compensation, Real Estate, Construction Defect, Appellate Law

SEE COMPLETE LISTING UNDER BILLINGS, MONTANA (219 MILES)

Gough, Shanahan, Johnson & Waterman, PLLP
33 South Last Chance Gulch
Helena, Montana 59601
  Telephone: 406-442-8560
  Fax: 406-442-8783

Mailing Address: P.O. Box 1715, Helena, MT 59624

Insurance Defense, Bodily Injury, Property Damage, Commercial Law, Surety Bonds, Litigation, Subrogation, Copyright and Trademark Law, Environmental Law, ERISA, Employment Law, Business Law, School Law

SEE COMPLETE LISTING UNDER HELENA, MONTANA (90 MILES)

Johnson, Berg & Saxby, PLLP
221 First Avenue East
Kalispell, Montana 59901
  Telephone: 406-755-5535
  Fax: 406-756-9436

Mailing Address: P.O. Box 3038, Kalispell, MT 59903-3038

Bankruptcy, Business Law, Civil Litigation, Commercial Law, Entertainment Law, Insurance Defense, Personal Injury, Professional Liability, Real Estate, Workers' Compensation

SEE COMPLETE LISTING UNDER KALISPELL, MONTANA (243 MILES)

HARDIN † 3,505 Big Horn Co.

Refer To

Moulton Bellingham PC
Crowne Plaza, Suite 1900
27 North 27th Street
Billings, Montana 59101
  Telephone: 406-248-7731
  Fax: 406-248-7889

Mailing Address: P.O. Box 2559, Billings, MT 59103

Trial Practice, State and Federal Courts, Insurance Law, Workers' Compensation, Fire, Casualty Insurance Law, Professional Liability, Oil and Gas, Product Liability

SEE COMPLETE LISTING UNDER BILLINGS, MONTANA (62 MILES)

HARLOWTON † 997 Wheatland Co.

Refer To

Smith, Walsh, Clarke & Gregoire, PLLP
Galleria Building, Suite 401
104 2nd Street South
Great Falls, Montana 59401
  Telephone: 406-727-4100
  Fax: 406-727-9228

Mailing Address: P.O. Box 2227, Great Falls, MT 59403-2227

Insurance Law, Product Liability, Medical Malpractice, Workers' Compensation, Casualty, Negligence, Personal Injury, Aviation, Commercial Litigation, Construction Law, Premises Liability, Indian Law

SEE COMPLETE LISTING UNDER GREAT FALLS, MONTANA (130 MILES)

HAVRE † 9,310 Hill Co.

Refer To

Browning, Kaleczyc, Berry & Hoven, P.C.
800 North Last Chance Gulch, Suite 101
Helena, Montana 59601
  Telephone: 406-443-6820
  Fax: 406-443-6883

Mailing Address: P.O. Box 1697, Helena, MT 59624

Insurance Law, State and Federal Courts, Environmental Law, Insurance Coverage, Health, Medical Negligence, Professional Negligence, Personal Injury, Product Liability, Property Damage, Surety, Workers' Compensation, Wrongful Termination, Employer Liability, Automobile, Commercial Liability, Employment Discrimination, Federal Employer Liability Claims (FELA), Oil and Gas, Banking

SEE COMPLETE LISTING UNDER HELENA, MONTANA (204 MILES)

Refer To

Davis Hatley Haffeman & Tighe, P.C.
The Milwaukee Station, 3rd Floor
101 River Drive North
Great Falls, Montana 59401
  Telephone: 406-761-5243
  Fax: 406-761-4126

Mailing Address: P.O. Box 2103, Great Falls, MT 59403-2103

Insurance Defense, Automobile, Product Liability, Professional Liability, Bodily Injury, Property Damage

SEE COMPLETE LISTING UNDER GREAT FALLS, MONTANA (110 MILES)

Refer To

Smith, Walsh, Clarke & Gregoire, PLLP
Galleria Building, Suite 401
104 2nd Street South
Great Falls, Montana 59401
  Telephone: 406-727-4100
  Fax: 406-727-9228

Mailing Address: P.O. Box 2227, Great Falls, MT 59403-2227

Insurance Law, Product Liability, Medical Malpractice, Workers' Compensation, Casualty, Negligence, Personal Injury, Aviation, Commercial Litigation, Construction Law, Premises Liability, Indian Law

SEE COMPLETE LISTING UNDER GREAT FALLS, MONTANA (110 MILES)

HELENA † 28,190 Lewis And Clark Co.

Browning, Kaleczyc, Berry & Hoven, P.C.
800 North Last Chance Gulch, Suite 101
Helena, Montana 59601
  Telephone: 406-443-6820
  Fax: 406-443-6883
  E-Mail: bkbh@bkbh.com
  www.bkbh.com

(Missoula, MT Office*: 201 West Railroad Street, Suite 300, 59802-4252)
  (Tel: 406-728-1694)
  (Fax: 406-728-5475)
(Bozeman, MT Office*: 801 West Main, Suite 2A, 59715)
  (Tel: 406-585-0888)
  (Fax: 406-587-0165)
(Great Falls, MT Office*: Liberty Center, Suite 302, 9 Third Street North, 59401)
  (Tel: 406-403-0041)
  (Fax: 406-453-1634)

Established: 1982

Insurance Law, State and Federal Courts, Environmental Law, Insurance Coverage, Health, Medical Negligence, Professional Negligence, Personal Injury, Product Liability, Property Damage, Surety, Workers' Compensation, Wrongful Termination, Employer Liability, Automobile, Commercial Liability, Employment Discrimination, Federal Employer Liability Claims (FELA), Oil and Gas, Banking

MONTANA | HELENA

Browning, Kaleczyc, Berry & Hoven, P.C., Helena, MT (Continued)

Firm Profile: The firm has offices in Helena, Bozeman, Great Falls and Missoula. Insurance defense litigation and risk management form the foundation of our firm's operations. We welcome the opportunity to serve insurers with their legal challenges in Montana. For additional information on BKBH, please consult our website at www.bkbh.com.

Insurance Clients

ACE USA
Amerind Risk Management Corporation
Berkley Surety Group
California Casualty Indemnity
Colony Insurance Company
First Choice Health
Great American Insurance Group
The Hartford
The Horace Mann Companies
Liberty Northwest Insurance Corporation
Montana Hospital Association Workers' Compensation Reciprocal
New West Health Services
North American Specialty Insurance Company
Travelers Indemnity Company
USAA Insurance Company
Utah Medical Insurance Association
Yellowstone Insurance Exchange, RRG
AIG Property Casualty
Amerisafe Insurance Group
Attorneys Liability Protection Society
CNA Surety Corporation
The Doctors Company
Great American Insurance Company
HCC Surety Group
Insco Dico Group
Markel Insurance Company
The Medical Protective Company
Montana Municipal Interlocal Authority
Montana Schools Group Insurance Authority
State Farm Fire and Casualty Company
United States Liability Insurance Group
Western Litigation, Inc.
Westfield Group

Non-Insurance Clients

Bank of America, N.A.
Bennett International Group, LLC
BNSF Railway Company
Community Medical Center
Deloitte Consulting, LLC
Energy Laboratories
Great Northern Properties, LP
International Paper Company
Material - Aviation - Technologies - Navigation (MATN)
Phillips 66
St. Peter's Hospital
Union Pacific Railroad Company
Benefis Health System
Bennett Motor Express, LLC
CenturyLink, Inc.
Corrections Corporation of America
Energy West Inc.
Health Care Service Corporation
Invensys Systems, Inc.
NorthWestern Corporation
Omimex Canada, Ltd.
Sears Holdings Management Corporation

Shareholders

J. Daniel Hoven — 1948 — Lincoln University, J.D., 1977 — Admitted to Bar, 1978, Montana — E-mail: dan@bkbh.com

Oliver H. Goe — 1955 — University of Santa Clara, J.D., 1980 — Admitted to Bar, 1986, Montana — E-mail: oliver@bkbh.com

Leo S. Ward — 1956 — The University of Montana, J.D. (with high honors), 1987 — Admitted to Bar, 1987, Montana — E-mail: leow@bkbh.com

Catherine A. Laughner — 1956 — Oklahoma City University, J.D., 1989 — Admitted to Bar, 1990, Montana — Resident Bozeman, MT Office — E-mail: cathyl@bkbh.com

Mark D. Etchart — 1960 — The Catholic University of America, Columbus School of Law, J.D., 1990 — Admitted to Bar, 1990, Montana — E-mail: mark@bkbh.com

G. Andrew Adamek — 1966 — Mercer University Walter F. George School of Law, J.D., 1992 — Admitted to Bar, 1998, Montana — E-mail: andy@bkbh.com

Stanley T. Kaleczyc — 1948 — The George Washington University, J.D. (with honors), 1973 — Admitted to Bar, 1982, Montana — E-mail: stan@bkbh.com

Kimberly A. Beatty — 1968 — The University of Montana, J.D., 1994 — Admitted to Bar, 1994, Montana — E-mail: kim@bkbh.com

Steven T. Wade — 1970 — The University of Montana, J.D., 1996 — Admitted to Bar, 1996, Montana; 2000, Arizona — E-mail: stevew@bkbh.com

David M. McLean — 1971 — The University of Montana, J.D., 1997 — Admitted to Bar, 1997, Montana — Resident Missoula, MT Office — E-mail: dave@bkbh.com

Sara S. Berg — 1975 — The University of Montana, J.D., 2000 — Admitted to Bar, 2000, Montana — E-mail: sara@bkbh.com

Browning, Kaleczyc, Berry & Hoven, P.C., Helena, MT (Continued)

W. John Tietz — 1962 — Seattle University School of Law, J.D., 2004 — Admitted to Bar, 2004, Montana — E-mail: john@bkbh.com

Chad E. Adams — 1973 — Baylor University, J.D., 2002 — Admitted to Bar, 2003, Montana — E-mail: chad@bkbh.com

Carlo Canty — 1964 — University of San Francisco, J.D., 1989 — Admitted to Bar, 1990, Montana — E-mail: carlo@bkbh.com

Ryan C. Willmore — 1980 — The University of Montana, J.D., 2005 — Admitted to Bar, 2005, Montana — Resident Missoula, MT Office — E-mail: ryan@bkbh.com

Daniel J. Auerbach — 1979 — University of Oregon School of Law, J.D., 2005 — Admitted to Bar, 2005, Montana — Resident Missoula, MT Office — E-mail: daniel@bkbh.com

Associates

Christy Surr McCann — 1971 — University of Colorado Law School, J.D., 2005 — Admitted to Bar, 2009, Montana — Resident Missoula, MT Office — E-mail: christy@bkbh.com

Morgan M. Weber — 1981 — Valparaiso University School of Law, J.D., 2007 — Admitted to Bar, 2007, California; 2009, Montana — E-mail: morgan@bkbh.com

Evan M. Thompson — 1982 — The University of Montana School of Law, J.D., 2011 — Admitted to Bar, 2011, Montana — E-mail: evan@bkbh.com

Kimberly P. Dudik — 1974 — The University of Montana, J.D., 2003 — Admitted to Bar, 2003, Montana — E-mail: kimd@bkbh.com

Crowley Fleck PLLP

900 North Last Chance Gulch, Suite 200
Helena, Montana 59601
  Telephone: 406-449-4165
  Fax: 406-449-5149
  www.crowleyfleck.com

(Billings, MT Office*: 500 Transwestern Plaza II, 490 North 31st Street, 59101-1288)
  (Tel: 406-252-3441)
  (Fax: 406-256-8526, 406-259-4159, 406-256-0277)
  (E-Mail: jkresslein@crowleyfleck.com)
(Bozeman, MT Office*: 45 Discovery Drive, 59718-6957)
  (Tel: 406-556-1430)
  (Fax: 406-556-1433)
(Butte, MT Office*: Thornton Building, 65 East Broadway, Suite 503, 59701)
  (Tel: 406-533-6892)
  (Fax: 406-533-6830)
(Kalispell, MT Office*: 1667 Whitefish Stage Road, Suite 101, 59901-4835)
  (Tel: 406-752-6644)
  (Fax: 406-752-5108)
(Missoula, MT Office*: 305 South 4th Street East, Suite 100, 59801-2701)
  (Tel: 406-523-3600)
  (Fax: 406-523-3636)
(Bismarck, ND Office*: 100 West Broadway, Suite 250, 58501, P.O. Box 2798, 58502-2798)
  (Tel: 701-223-6585)
  (Fax: 701-222-4853)
(Williston, ND Office*: 1331 9th Avenue NW, 2nd Floor, 58801, P.O. Box 1206, 58802-1206)
  (Tel: 701-572-2200)
  (Fax: 701-572-7072)
(Casper, WY Office*: 152 North Durbin Street, Suite 220, 82601)
  (Tel: 307-265-2279)
  (Fax: 307-265-2307)
(Cheyenne, WY Office*: 237 Storey Boulevard, Suite 110, 82009)
  (Tel: 307-426-4100)
  (Fax: 307-426-4099)
(Sheridan, WY Office*: 101 West Brundage Street, 82801)
  (Tel: 307-673-3000)
  (Fax: 307-672-1732)

HELENA   MONTANA

Crowley Fleck PLLP, Helena, MT   (Continued)

Civil Litigation, Trial and Appellate Practice, Product Liability, Personal Injury, Construction Law, Design Professionals, Malpractice, Wrongful Termination, Employer Liability, Medical Negligence, Legal, Professional Negligence, Insurance Coverage, Bad Faith, Agent/Broker Liability, Workers' Compensation, Oil and Gas, Environmental Law

Litigation Partners

Marcia J. Davenport — 1961 — Montana State University, B.S. (with honors), 1983; The University of Montana, J.D. (with honors), 1989 — Admitted to Bar, 1989, Montana

Michael W. Green — 1972 — Montana State University, B.A. (with honors), 1996; The University of Montana School of Law, J.D. (with honors), 1999 — Admitted to Bar, 1999, Montana

Kiely Keane — Carroll College, B.A., 1996; The University of Montana School of Law, J.D., 2000 — Admitted to Bar, 2000, Montana

John H. Maynard — 1951 — The University of Montana, B.A., 1973; J.D., 1978 — Admitted to Bar, 1978, Montana

Partners

Aimee M. Grmoljez   Kenneth K. Lay
Jason Loble   Sarah A. Loble
Daniel N. McLean

Associates

Daniel Wiley Barker   Alissa Chambers
Brett P. Clark   Heidi R. Goettel
Jill O. Laslovich   Christopher K. Oliveira

(See listing under Billings, MT for additional information)

Gough, Shanahan, Johnson & Waterman, PLLP

33 South Last Chance Gulch
Helena, Montana 59601
   Telephone: 406-442-8560
   Fax: 406-442-8783
   E-Mail: goughlaw@gsjw.com
   www.gsjw.com

(Billings, MT Office: 301 North 27th Street, Suite 300, 59101)
   (Tel: 406-248-3214)
(Missoula, MT Office: 280 East Front Street, Suite B, 59802)
   (Tel: 406-728-2770)
(Bozeman, MT Office: 682 Ferguson, Suite 4, 59718)
   (Tel: 406-585-3295)

Established: 1864

Insurance Defense, Bodily Injury, Property Damage, Commercial Law, Surety Bonds, Litigation, Subrogation, Copyright and Trademark Law, Environmental Law, ERISA, Employment Law, Business Law, School Law

Firm Profile: Gough, Shanahan, Johnson & Waterman, PLLP is one of the oldest law firms in Montana. Headquartered in the state's capital, we are familiar with the workings of the state and federal government at all levels. This experience enables us to consider a full range of possible administrative, judicial and legislative solutions to our clients' problems and assist them in selecting those which will be most expeditious, cost-effective and lasting.

Gough, Shanahan represents a broad range of individual, insurance, and other corporate clients. In addition to the general practice of law, the firm practice emphasizes insurance defense and insurance coverage law, health, safety and employment counseling and litigation. The firm has well-established specialty practices in employment, mining, water quality, water rights, endangered species, public school districts, and state, local and estate taxation. The firm can assist clients with regulatory permitting, compliance and enforcement

Gough, Shanahan, Johnson & Waterman, PLLP, Helena, MT   (Continued)

issues, governmental relations and experienced representation before agencies and courts on a variety of state, local and federal matters.

Insurance Clients

Cincinnati Insurance Company   EMC Insurance Companies
Farmers Insurance Group   Great American Insurance
Hartford Life Insurance Company   Company
Liberty Northwest Insurance   Markel Corporation
   Corporation   Western States Insurance Company

Non-Insurance Clients

Advanced Silicon Materials, Inc.

Partners

Ward A. Shanahan — 1931 — The University of Montana, B.A., 1953; J.D., 1958 — Phi Delta Phi — Admitted to Bar, 1958, Montana; U.S. District Court, District of Montana; 1965, Montana Supreme Court; 1968, U.S. Supreme Court; U.S. Court of Appeals, Ninth Circuit — Member State Bar of Montana (President 1982-1983); Montana Justice Foundation (President 1984-1988); Fellow, American Bar Foundation — National Judge Advocate, Navy League of the United States (1994-present) — Practice Areas: Administrative Law; Environmental Law; Lobbying — E-mail: was@gsjw.com

Ronald F. Waterman — 1944 — The University of Montana, B.A., 1966; J.D., 1969 — Admitted to Bar, 1969, Montana; 1969, U.S. District Court, District of Montana; Montana Supreme Court; 1972, U.S. Court of Appeals, Ninth Circuit; 1976, U.S. Supreme Court — Member American Judicature Society (Board Member 1979-1983); American Bar Foundation (State President 1987); Fellow, American Law Institute — Practice Areas: Construction Litigation; Insurance Defense; Litigation; Toxic Torts; Civil Rights — E-mail: rfw@gsjw.com

Jock O. Anderson — 1948 — The University of Montana, B.S., 1970; J.D., 1975 — Admitted to Bar, 1975, Montana; U.S. District Court, District of Montana; 1976, U.S. Court of Appeals, Ninth Circuit; 1978, U.S. Claims Court — Member American Bar Association; State Bar of Montana — Practice Areas: Administrative Law; Commercial Law; Real Estate; Estate Planning — E-mail: joa@gsjw.com

Thomas E. Hattersley, III — 1953 — Loyola University of Los Angeles, B.A. (cum laude), 1976; J.D., 1981 — Admitted to Bar, 1981, California; 1984, Montana; 1981, U.S. District Court, Central District of California; 1984, U.S. District Court, District of Montana; U.S. Court of Appeals for the District of Columbia and Ninth Circuits; U.S. Supreme Court; Montana Supreme Court; Supreme Court of California — Member American Bar Association; State Bar of Montana; State Bar of California — Practice Areas: Labor and Employment; Litigation; Insurance Coverage & Defense — E-mail: teh@gsjw.com

William L. MacBride, Jr. — 1951 — Colorado School of Mines, B.S., 1974; University of Houston, M.B.A., 1979; University of Denver, J.D., 1984 — Admitted to Bar, 1985, Colorado; 1994, Montana; 1985, U.S. District Court, District of Colorado; U.S. District Court, District of Montana; 1994, Supreme Court of Colorado; U.S. Court of Appeals for the Federal Circuit; U.S. Court of Appeals, Ninth and Tenth Circuits; U.S. Patent and Trademark Office — Member Colorado Bar Associations; Montana Bar Associations; American Bar Associations; Rocky Mountain Mineral Law Foundation — Practice Areas: Copyright and Trademark Law; Patents; Business Organizations; Real Property; Intellectual Property; International Law — E-mail: wlm@gsjw.com

David C. Dalthorp — 1958 — Montana State University, B.S., 1984; Eastern Montana College, B.S.Ed., 1988; The University of Montana, J.D., 1992 — Admitted to Bar, 1992, Montana; U.S. District Court, District of Montana; U.S. Court of Appeals, Ninth Circuit; Montana Supreme Court — Member State Bar of Montana — Practice Areas: Civil Litigation; Employment Law; Insurance Coverage; Civil Rights — E-mail: dcd@gsjw.com

Teri A. Walter — 1968 — Eastern New Mexico University, B.S. (summa cum laude), 1990; California Western School of Law, J.D., 1994 — Admitted to Bar, 1994, Montana; 1995, U.S. District Court, District of Montana; U.S. Court of Appeals, Ninth Circuit; Montana Supreme Court — Member American Bar Association (Sections: Tort and Insurance Practice, Labor and Employment Law, Litigation); State Bar of Montana; First Judicial District Bar Association; Montana Defense Trial Lawyers Association — Practice Areas: Civil Litigation; Insurance Defense; Labor and Employment — E-mail: taw@gsjw.com

Robert Cameron — 1957 — Ohio University, B.S.Ed. (cum laude), 1980; The University of Montana, J.D., 1993 — Admitted to Bar, 1993, Montana; 1994,

MONTANA

Gough, Shanahan, Johnson & Waterman, PLLP, Helena, MT (Continued)

U.S. District Court, District of Montana; U.S. Court of Appeals, Ninth Circuit; Montana Supreme Court — Member State Bar of Montana; First Judicial District Bar Association — Practice Areas: Administrative Law; Civil Litigation; Construction Litigation — E-mail: rtc@gsjw.com

Dana Lynn Hupp — 1974 — Miami University, B.A., 1997; Northwestern School of Law of Lewis & Clark College, J.D., 2000 — Admitted to Bar, 2001, Montana; 2003, U.S. District Court, District of Montana; U.S. Court of Appeals, Ninth and Tenth Circuits; Montana Supreme Court — Member American Bar Association — Practice Areas: Civil Litigation; Environmental Law; Insurance Defense; Insurance Coverage — E-mail: dlh@gsjw.com

Kevin D. Feeback — 1952 — The University of Montana, B.A., 1981; J.D., 2002 — Admitted to Bar, 2002, Montana; U.S. District Court, District of Montana; U.S. Court of Appeals, Ninth Circuit — Member American Bar Association; State Bar of Montana (Montana and Federal Member) — Practice Areas: Environmental Law; Property; Water Law — E-mail: kdf@gsjw.com

Peter G. Scott — University of Massachusetts Amherst, B.S., 1991; Northwestern School of Law of Lewis & Clark College, J.D. (with high honors), 1999 — Admitted to Bar, 2000, Idaho; 2001, Washington; 2007, Montana; U.S. District Court, Eastern District of Washington; U.S. District Court, District of Idaho; Montana Supreme Court; Oregon Supreme Court; Oregon Circuit Courts; Idaho Supreme Court; Supreme Court of Washington — Member American Bar Association — Practice Areas: Administrative Law; Land Use; Water Law — E-mail: pgs@gsjw.com

Murry Warhank — Carroll College, B.A. (maxima cum laude), 2004; S.J. Quinney College of Law, The University of Utah, J.D. (with high honors), 2007 — Admitted to Bar, 2010, Montana; 2007, Utah; 2007, U.S. District Court, District of Utah; 2010, U.S. District Court, District of Montana — Member State Bar of Montana — Practice Areas: Construction Law; Insurance Defense; Product Liability; Tax Litigation — E-mail: mw@gsjw.com

Associates

Hanna Warhank — Carroll College, B.S., 2006; The University of Montana School of Law, J.D., 2009 — Admitted to Bar, 2009, Montana; U.S. District Court, District of Montana — Member State Bar of Montana — Practice Areas: Business Formation; Estate Planning; Real Property; Trusts; Wills — E-mail: hw@gsjw.com

Nathan Bilyeu — The University of Montana, B.A. (with high honors), 2009; M.A., 2010; The George Washington University Law School, J.D. (with honors), 2013 — Admitted to Bar, 2013, Montana; U.S. District Court, District of Montana; Montana Supreme Court — Member State Bar of Montana — Practice Areas: Insurance Coverage & Defense; Construction Law; Employment Law; Litigation — E-mail: nb@gsjw.com

Jamie M. Iguchi — University of California, Santa Barbara, B.A. (with honors), Phi Beta Kappa), 2006; University of California Davis School of Law, J.D., 2010 — Admitted to Bar, 2010, California; 2011, Montana; 2013, New York; U.S. District Court, District of Montana — Member State Bar of Montana — E-mail: jmi@gsjw.com

Burt W. Ward — University of Wyoming, B.S. (Dean's List), 2005; The University of Montana School of Law, J.D. (with honors), 2014 — Admitted to Bar, 2014, Montana — E-mail: bww@gsjw.com

Of Counsel

Francis J. Raucci — 1936 — Saint Joseph's University, A.B., 1958; Georgetown University, J.D., 1965; University of Pennsylvania, 1978 — Admitted to Bar, 1965, Montana; 1976, Pennsylvania; U.S. District Court, District of Montana; U.S. Court of Appeals, Third and Ninth Circuits; U.S. Supreme Court — Member State Bar of Montana; Pennsylvania Bar Association; Bar Association of the District of Columbia; Fellow, Academy of Court Appointed Masters; American Arbitration Association — Mediator and Arbitrator — Practice Areas: Labor and Employment; Arbitration; Mediation; Business Law — E-mail: fjssraucci@aol.com

Terry B. Cosgrove — 1947 — University of Great Falls, B.A., 1969; The University of Montana, J.D., 1972 — Admitted to Bar, 1972, Montana; U.S. District Court, District of Montana; U.S. Supreme Court — Member State Bar of Montana — Practice Areas: Business Law; Health — E-mail: tbc@gsjw.com

---

The following firms also service this area.

Brown Law Firm, P.C.
315 North 24th Street
Billings, Montana 59101
  Telephone: 406-248-2611
  Fax: 406-248-3128

Mailing Address: P.O. Drawer 849, Billings, MT 59103-0849

Defense of Complex Civil Litigation, Defense of Catastrophic Personal Injury and Wrongful Death Claims, Insurance Law Including Coverage and Defense of Bad Faith Claims, Product Liability Defense, Defense of Medical and Dental Malpractice Claims, Labor and Employee Relations, Minerals, Oil and Gas, Banking, Workers' Compensation, Real Estate, Construction Defect, Appellate Law

SEE COMPLETE LISTING UNDER BILLINGS, MONTANA (241 MILES)

Corette Black Carlson & Mickelson
Mayer Building
129 West Park Street, Suite 301
Butte, Montana 59701
  Telephone: 406-782-5800
  Fax: 406-723-8919

Mailing Address: P.O. Box 509, Butte, MT 59703

Trial Practice, Corporate Law, Insurance Law, Product Liability, Personal Injury, Casualty, Banking, Water Law, Mining, Probate Law

SEE COMPLETE LISTING UNDER BUTTE, MONTANA (65 MILES)

Johnson, Berg & Saxby, PLLP
221 First Avenue East
Kalispell, Montana 59901
  Telephone: 406-755-5535
  Fax: 406-756-9436

Mailing Address: P.O. Box 3038, Kalispell, MT 59903-3038

Bankruptcy, Business Law, Civil Litigation, Commercial Law, Entertainment Law, Insurance Defense, Personal Injury, Professional Liability, Real Estate, Workers' Compensation

SEE COMPLETE LISTING UNDER KALISPELL, MONTANA (193 MILES)

KALISPELL † 19,927 Flathead Co.

Conradi Anderson, PLLC
307 Spokane Avenue, Suite 102
Whitefish, Montana 59937
  Telephone: 406-863-9681
  Fax: 406-863-9684
  E-Mail: janderson@conradianderson.com
  www.conradianderson.com

Established: 2013

Business Law, Civil Litigation, Commercial Litigation, Construction Law, Contracts, Coverage Issues, Employment Law, Environmental Law, Government Affairs, Insurance Law, Intellectual Property, Mergers and Acquisitions, Real Estate, Securities, Technology, Transactional Law, Water Law, Telecommunications

Insurance Clients

Contractors Bonding and Insurance Company (CBIC), an RLI Company

EMC Insurance Companies

Partners

Diane Conradi — University of South Carolina Honors College, B.A., 1987; University of Oregon, J.D., 1991 — Admitted to Bar, 1992, Oregon; 1995, Montana

Johnathan W. Anderson — Beloit College, B.S., 1990; The University of Montana, J.D., 1996 — Admitted to Bar, 1996, Montana; 1998, Texas

Crowley Fleck PLLP

1667 Whitefish Stage Road, Suite 101
Kalispell, Montana 59901-4835
  Telephone: 406-752-6644
  Fax: 406-752-5108
  www.crowleyfleck.com

(Billings, MT Office*: 500 Transwestern Plaza II, 490 North 31st Street, 59101-1288)
  (Tel: 406-252-3441)
  (Fax: 406-256-8526, 406-259-4159, 406-256-0277)
  (E-Mail: jkresslein@crowleyfleck.com)
(Bozeman, MT Office*: 45 Discovery Drive, 59718-6957)
  (Tel: 406-556-1430)
  (Fax: 406-556-1433)
(Butte, MT Office*: Thornton Building, 65 East Broadway, Suite 503, 59701)
  (Tel: 406-533-6892)
  (Fax: 406-533-6830)
(Helena, MT Office*: 900 North Last Chance Gulch, Suite 200, 59601)
  (Tel: 406-449-4165)
  (Fax: 406-449-5149)
(Missoula, MT Office*: 305 South 4th Street East, Suite 100, 59801-2701)
  (Tel: 406-523-3600)
  (Fax: 406-523-3636)
(Bismarck, ND Office*: 100 West Broadway, Suite 250, 58501, P.O. Box 2798, 58502-2798)
  (Tel: 701-223-6585)
  (Fax: 701-222-4853)
(Williston, ND Office*: 1331 9th Avenue NW, 2nd Floor, 58801, P.O. Box 1206, 58802-1206)
  (Tel: 701-572-2200)
  (Fax: 701-572-7072)
(Casper, WY Office*: 152 North Durbin Street, Suite 220, 82601)
  (Tel: 307-265-2279)
  (Fax: 307-265-2307)
(Cheyenne, WY Office*: 237 Storey Boulevard, Suite 110, 82009)
  (Tel: 307-426-4100)
  (Fax: 307-426-4099)
(Sheridan, WY Office*: 101 West Brundage Street, 82801)
  (Tel: 307-673-3000)
  (Fax: 307-672-1732)

Civil Litigation, Trial and Appellate Practice, Product Liability, Personal Injury, Construction Law, Design Professionals, Malpractice, Wrongful Termination, Employer Liability, Medical Negligence, Legal, Professional Negligence, Insurance Coverage, Bad Faith, Agent/Broker Liability, Workers' Compensation, Oil and Gas, Environmental Law

Litigation Partners

Scott D. Hagel — 1957 — The University of Montana, B.A. (with honors), 1981; University of Wyoming, J.D. (with honors), 2002 — Admitted to Bar, 2002, Montana; U.S. District Court, District of Montana

Daniel D. Johns — 1946 — St. Olaf College, B.A., 1968; Indiana University, M.B.A., 1973; J.D. (cum laude), 1973 — Admitted to Bar, 1973, Indiana; 1979, Montana

Kimberly S. More — Carroll College, B.A. (maxima cum laude), 1998; Gonzaga University, J.D. (summa cum laude), 2001 — Admitted to Bar, 2001, Montana; Washington; U.S. District Court, District of Montana

Partners

Danielle A. Coffman   Mark A. Sletto

Associates

Ashley A. Di Lorenzo   Grant Snell

(See listing under Billings, MT for additional information)

Johnson, Berg & Saxby, PLLP

221 First Avenue East
Kalispell, Montana 59901
  Telephone: 406-755-5535
  Fax: 406-756-9436
  E-Mail: jbmb@centurytel.net
  http://johnsonbergandsaxbylaw.com

Established: 1891

Bankruptcy, Business Law, Civil Litigation, Commercial Law, Entertainment Law, Insurance Defense, Personal Injury, Professional Liability, Real Estate, Workers' Compensation

Firm Profile: Johnson, Berg & Saxby, PLLP is Northwestern Montana's oldest law firm, with a practice encompassing much of Western Montana and parts of Eastern Montana.

Insurance Clients

Arch Insurance Group   Atain Insurance Companies
CNA Insurance Company   EMC Insurance Companies
Northland Insurance   Scottsdale Insurance Company

Non-Insurance Clients

Peak Development   Sandry Construction Company, Inc.

Members

Kent P. Saxby — 1955 — Walla Walla College, B.S.B.A. (cum laude), 1977; The University of Montana, J.D., 1981 — Admitted to Bar, 1981, Montana; U.S. Tax Court — Certified Public Accountant

Paul A. Sandry — 1964 — The University of Montana, B.A., 1987; J.D. (with high honors), 1990; University of Florida, LL.M., 1991 — Admitted to Bar, 1991, Montana; U.S. District Court, District of Montana; U.S. Court of Appeals, Ninth Circuit; 1992, U.S. Tax Court

Thane P. Johnson — 1967 — The University of Montana, B.A. (with high honors), 1990; University of Minnesota, J.D. (cum laude), 1993 — Admitted to Bar, 1993, Montana; U.S. District Court, District of Montana; U.S. Court of Appeals, Ninth Circuit; U.S. Supreme Court — Member Blackfeet Tribal, Salish Kootenai Crow, Northern Cheyenne, Chippewa Cree and Rocky Boy Bar Associations

Sarah D. Simkins — 1983 — Montana State University, B.A. (with honors), 2005; The University of Montana, J.D., 2009 — Admitted to Bar, 2009, Montana; U.S. District Court, District of Montana — Member State Bar of Montana

Associates

Colleen P. Donohoe — 1963 — Eastern Washington University, B.A. (summa cum laude), 2004; Gonzaga University, J.D. (magna cum laude), 2007 — Admitted to Bar, 2007, Washington; 2008, Montana — Member Washington State and Northwest Montana Bar Associations; State Bar of Montana

Kai Groenke — 1979 — Montana State University, B.A., 2001; The University of Montana School of Law, J.D., 2006 — Admitted to Bar, 2006, Montana — Member Northwest Montana (Executive Committee), Blackfeet and Salish Kootenai Tribal Bar Associations; State Bar of Montana

Of Counsel

James W. Johnson — 1941 — Stanford University, A.B., 1963; The University of Montana, J.D., 1966 — Phi Delta Phi — Admitted to Bar, 1966, Montana; U.S. District Court, District of Montana — Member American and Northwest Montana Bar Associations; State Bar of Montana (President, 1992; Trustee, 1982-1991); Fellow, American College of Trust and Estate Counsel

Stephen C. Berg — 1944 — University of Notre Dame; University of Minnesota, B.A., 1966; J.D., 1969 — Admitted to Bar, 1969, Minnesota; 1972, California; 1977, Montana — Member State Bar of Montana (Trustee, 2002-2005) — Lt. Col., USMCR, Active Duty, 1969-

Bruce McEvoy — 1953 — The University of Montana, B.A., 1975; J.D., 1979 — Admitted to Bar, 1979, Montana — Special Assistant Attorney General for Montana (1979-1981)

MONTANA   LEWISTOWN

The following firms also service this area.

Browning, Kaleczyc, Berry & Hoven, P.C.
800 North Last Chance Gulch, Suite 101
Helena, Montana 59601
  Telephone: 406-443-6820
  Fax: 406-443-6883

Mailing Address: P.O. Box 1697, Helena, MT 59624

Insurance Law, State and Federal Courts, Environmental Law, Insurance Coverage, Health, Medical Negligence, Professional Negligence, Personal Injury, Product Liability, Property Damage, Surety, Workers' Compensation, Wrongful Termination, Employer Liability, Automobile, Commercial Liability, Employment Discrimination, Federal Employer Liability Claims (FELA), Oil and Gas, Banking

SEE COMPLETE LISTING UNDER HELENA, MONTANA (229 MILES)

LEWISTOWN † 5,901 Fergus Co.

Refer To

Davis Hatley Haffeman & Tighe, P.C.
The Milwaukee Station, 3rd Floor
101 River Drive North
Great Falls, Montana 59401
  Telephone: 406-761-5243
  Fax: 406-761-4126

Mailing Address: P.O. Box 2103, Great Falls, MT 59403-2103

Insurance Defense, Automobile, Product Liability, Professional Liability, Bodily Injury, Property Damage

SEE COMPLETE LISTING UNDER GREAT FALLS, MONTANA (106 MILES)

Refer To

Moulton Bellingham PC
Crowne Plaza, Suite 1900
27 North 27th Street
Billings, Montana 59101
  Telephone: 406-248-7731
  Fax: 406-248-7889

Mailing Address: P.O. Box 2559, Billings, MT 59103

Trial Practice, State and Federal Courts, Insurance Law, Workers' Compensation, Fire, Casualty Insurance Law, Professional Liability, Oil and Gas, Product Liability

SEE COMPLETE LISTING UNDER BILLINGS, MONTANA (126 MILES)

Refer To

Smith, Walsh, Clarke & Gregoire, PLLP
Galleria Building, Suite 401
104 2nd Street South
Great Falls, Montana 59401
  Telephone: 406-727-4100
  Fax: 406-727-9228

Mailing Address: P.O. Box 2227, Great Falls, MT 59403-2227

Insurance Law, Product Liability, Medical Malpractice, Workers' Compensation, Casualty, Negligence, Personal Injury, Aviation, Commercial Litigation, Construction Law, Premises Liability, Indian Law

SEE COMPLETE LISTING UNDER GREAT FALLS, MONTANA (106 MILES)

LIVINGSTON † 7,044 Park Co.

Refer To

Moore, O'Connell & Refling, P.C.
Life of Montana Building, Suite 10
601 Haggerty Lane
Bozeman, Montana 59715
  Telephone: 406-587-5511
  Fax: 406-587-9079

Mailing Address: P.O. Box 1288, Bozeman, MT 59771-1288

General Defense, Insurance Law, Subrogation, Investigation and Adjustment

SEE COMPLETE LISTING UNDER BOZEMAN, MONTANA (26 MILES)

Refer To

Moulton Bellingham PC
Crowne Plaza, Suite 1900
27 North 27th Street
Billings, Montana 59101
  Telephone: 406-248-7731
  Fax: 406-248-7889

Mailing Address: P.O. Box 2559, Billings, MT 59103

Trial Practice, State and Federal Courts, Insurance Law, Workers' Compensation, Fire, Casualty Insurance Law, Professional Liability, Oil and Gas, Product Liability

SEE COMPLETE LISTING UNDER BILLINGS, MONTANA (110 MILES)

MILES CITY † 8,410 Custer Co.

Refer To

Moulton Bellingham PC
Crowne Plaza, Suite 1900
27 North 27th Street
Billings, Montana 59101
  Telephone: 406-248-7731
  Fax: 406-248-7889

Mailing Address: P.O. Box 2559, Billings, MT 59103

Trial Practice, State and Federal Courts, Insurance Law, Workers' Compensation, Fire, Casualty Insurance Law, Professional Liability, Oil and Gas, Product Liability

SEE COMPLETE LISTING UNDER BILLINGS, MONTANA (140 MILES)

MISSOULA † 66,788 Missoula Co.

Browning, Kaleczyc, Berry & Hoven, P.C.

201 West Railroad Street, Suite 300
Missoula, Montana 59802-4252
  Telephone: 406-728-1694
  Fax: 406-728-5475
  www.bkbh.com

(Helena, MT Office*: 800 North Last Chance Gulch, Suite 101, 59601,
  P.O. Box 1697, 59624)
  (Tel: 406-443-6820)
  (Fax: 406-443-6883)
  (E-Mail: bkbh@bkbh.com)
(Bozeman, MT Office*: 801 West Main, Suite 2A, 59715)
  (Tel: 406-585-0888)
  (Fax: 406-587-0165)
(Great Falls, MT Office*: Liberty Center, Suite 302, 9 Third Street North, 59401)
  (Tel: 406-403-0041)
  (Fax: 406-453-1634)

Insurance Law, State and Federal Courts, Environmental Law, Insurance Coverage, Health, Medical Negligence, Professional Negligence, Personal Injury, Product Liability, Property Damage, Surety, Workers' Compensation, Wrongful Termination, Employer Liability, Automobile, Commercial Liability, Employment Discrimination, Federal Employer Liability Claims (FELA), Oil and Gas, Banking

(See listing under Helena, MT for additional information)

Brown Law Firm, P.C.

210 East Pine Street, Suite 200
Missoula, Montana 59802
  Telephone: 406-830-3248
  www.brownfirm.com

Brown Law Firm, P.C., Missoula, MT (Continued)

(Billings, MT Office*: 315 North 24th Street, 59101, P.O. Drawer 849, 59103-0849)
 (Tel: 406-248-2611)
 (Fax: 406-248-3128)

Established: 1911

Defense of Complex Civil Litigation, Defense of Catastrophic Personal Injury and Wrongful Death Claims, Insurance Law Including Coverage and Defense of Bad Faith Claims, Product Liability Defense, Defense of Medical and Dental Malpractice Claims, Labor and Employee Relations, Minerals, Oil and Gas, Banking, Workers' Compensation, Bankruptcy (Debtor Claims), Real Estate, Construction Defect, Appellate Law

(See listing under Billings, MT for additional information)

Crowley Fleck PLLP

305 South 4th Street East, Suite 100
Missoula, Montana 59801-2701
 Telephone: 406-523-3600
 Fax: 406-523-3636
 www.crowleyfleck.com

(Billings, MT Office*: 500 Transwestern Plaza II, 490 North 31st Street, 59101-1288)
 (Tel: 406-252-3441)
 (Fax: 406-256-8526, 406-259-4159, 406-256-0277)
 (E-Mail: jkresslein@crowleyfleck.com)
(Bozeman, MT Office*: 45 Discovery Drive, 59718-6957)
 (Tel: 406-556-1430)
 (Fax: 406-556-1433)
(Butte, MT Office*: Thornton Building, 65 East Broadway, Suite 503, 59701)
 (Tel: 406-533-6892)
 (Fax: 406-533-6830)
(Helena, MT Office*: 900 North Last Chance Gulch, Suite 200, 59601)
 (Tel: 406-449-4165)
 (Fax: 406-449-5149)
(Kalispell, MT Office*: 1667 Whitefish Stage Road, Suite 101, 59901-4835)
 (Tel: 406-752-6644)
 (Fax: 406-752-5108)
(Bismarck, ND Office*: 100 West Broadway, Suite 250, 58501, P.O. Box 2798, 58502-2798)
 (Tel: 701-223-6585)
 (Fax: 701-222-4853)
(Williston, ND Office*: 1331 9th Avenue NW, 2nd Floor, 58801, P.O. Box 1206, 58802-1206)
 (Tel: 701-572-2200)
 (Fax: 701-572-7072)
(Casper, WY Office*: 152 North Durbin Street, Suite 220, 82601)
 (Tel: 307-265-2279)
 (Fax: 307-265-2307)
(Cheyenne, WY Office*: 237 Storey Boulevard, Suite 110, 82009)
 (Tel: 307-426-4100)
 (Fax: 307-426-4099)
(Sheridan, WY Office*: 101 West Brundage Street, 82801)
 (Tel: 307-673-3000)
 (Fax: 307-672-1732)

Civil Litigation, Trial and Appellate Practice, Product Liability, Personal Injury, Construction Law, Design Professionals, Malpractice, Wrongful Termination, Employer Liability, Medical Negligence, Legal, Professional Negligence, Insurance Coverage, Bad Faith, Agent/Broker Liability, Workers' Compensation, Oil and Gas, Environmental Law

Partners

Benjamin T. Cory Benjamin P. Hursh

Crowley Fleck PLLP, Missoula, MT (Continued)

Joel L. Kaleva Mark Stermitz

Senior Counsel

Dirk A. Williams

Associates

Matthew Baldassin Jeffrey R. Kuchel

(See listing under Billings, MT for additional information)

Garlington, Lohn & Robinson, PLLP

350 Ryman Street
Missoula, Montana 59802
 Telephone: 406-523-2500
 Fax: 406-523-2595
 E-Mail: info@garlington.com
 www.garlington.com

Established: 1955

Bad Faith, Tort Litigation, Opinions, Workers' Compensation, Professional Malpractice, Uninsured and Underinsured Motorist, Business Law, Arbitration, Mediation, Real Estate, Intellectual Property, Health Care, Medical Malpractice, Labor and Employment, Product Liability, Transportation, Class Actions

Firm Profile: Garlington, Lohn & Robinson, PLLP has years of experience with the insurance industry and direct involvement in some of the more critical insurance cases before the Montana courts. We provide counsel to insurance companies, agencies, and adjusters on a wide range of defense issues.

Insurance Clients

ACE American Insurance Company	Allied World Assurance Company
American Hallmark Insurance Company of Texas	Allstate Insurance Company
	Chubb Group of Insurance Companies
CNA Insurance Companies	Hudson Insurance Company
Kemper Insurance Company	Liberty Mutual Insurance Company
The Medical Protective Company	ProSight Specialty Insurance
UMIA Insurance	Zurich

Insurance Law Group Partners

Randall J. Colbert — Rocky Mountain College, B.S., 1990; The University of Montana, J.D., 2003 — Admitted to Bar, 2003, Montana; U.S. District Court, District of Montana — Member Federal, American and Western Montana Bar Associations; State Bar of Montana; CPCU Society; Montana Defense Trial Lawyers Association — Practice Areas: Insurance Defense; Indian Law; Bad Faith; Litigation

Kathleen L. DeSoto — Santa Clara University, B.A., 1989; The University of Montana, J.D. (with high honors), 1999 — Admitted to Bar, 1999, Montana; U.S. Court of Appeals, Ninth Circuit — Member Federal, American and Western Montana Bar Associations; State Bar of Montana; Montana Defense Trial Lawyers Association — Practice Areas: School Law; Insurance Defense; Negligence; Product Liability; Insurance Coverage; Bad Faith

Elizabeth Lowrance Hausbeck — Montana State University, B.S. (with honors), 2002 — Admitted to Bar, 2007, Montana; U.S. District Court, District of Montana — Practice Areas: General Liability; Medical Malpractice Defense; Personal Injury

Bradley J. Luck — The University of Montana, B.A. (cum laude), 1974; The University of Montana School of Law, J.D. (cum laude), 1977 — Admitted to Bar, 1977, Montana — Member American and Western Montana Bar Associations; State Bar of Montana; Defense Research Institute (State Chair, 1993-1994); Montana Defense Trial Lawyers Association (Board of Directors, 1982-1993; Vice-President, 1989; President, 1990); Federation of Defense and Corporate Counsel — Practice Areas: Bad Faith; Negligence; Workers' Compensation; Legal Malpractice; Arbitration; Mediation; Appellate Practice; Insurance Coverage

Robert C. Lukes — University of Southern California, B.A., 1984; The University of Montana School of Law, J.D. (with high honors), 1996 — Admitted to Bar, 1996, Montana — Member Federal and American (Sections: Intellectual

Garlington, Lohn & Robinson, PLLP, Missoula, MT (Continued)

Property; Litigation) Bar Associations; State Bar of Montana; Montana Defense Trial Lawyers Association — Practice Areas: Commercial Litigation; Copyright and Trademark Law; Trade Secrets; Class Actions; Employment Law; Real Estate

Kathryn S. Mahe — The University of Montana, B.A. (with high honors), 2003; J.D. (with honors), 2006 — Admitted to Bar, 2006, Montana; U.S. District Court, District of Montana — Member State Bar of Montana — Practice Areas: Insurance Defense; Employment Law; Employment Litigation; Labor Law

Charles E. McNeil — Montana State University, B.S. (cum laude), 1981; The University of Montana School of Law, J.D. (cum laude), 1984 — Admitted to Bar, 1984, Montana — Member Federal, American and Western Montana Bar Associations; State Bar of Montana; Montana Defense Trial Lawyers Association — Practice Areas: Product Liability; Insurance; Indian Law; Bad Faith; Workers' Compensation

Larry E. Riley — The University of Montana, B.A., 1963; J.D., 1966 — Admitted to Bar, 1966, Montana — Member American and Western Montana Bar Associations; State Bar of Montana; Defense Research Institute; Montana Defense Trial Lawyers Association — Practice Areas: Medical Malpractice Defense

Jeffrey Roth — United States Naval Academy, B.S., 1991; The University of Montana School of Law, J.D., 2005 — Admitted to Bar, 2005, Montana; U.S. District Court, District of Montana — Practice Areas: Civil Litigation; Insurance Defense; Commercial Litigation

Robert E. Sheridan — University of Notre Dame, B.B.A. (cum laude), 1964; The University of Montana School of Law, J.D., 1967 — Admitted to Bar, 1967, Montana — Member Federal, American and Western Montana Bar Associations; State Bar of Montana; Montana Defense Trial Lawyers Association (Past President); American Board of Trial Advocates; National Association of Railroad Trial Counsel — Practice Areas: Negligence; Governmental Liability; Product Liability; Railroad Law; Workers' Compensation; Mediation

Brian J. Smith — Carroll College, B.A., 1977; The University of Montana, J.D., 1982 — Admitted to Bar, 1982, Montana; U.S. District Court, District of Montana; U.S. Court of Appeals, Ninth Circuit; U.S. Supreme Court; Confederated Salish and Kootenai Tribal Court — Member American Bar Association; State Bar of Montana; Association of Trial Lawyers of America; Transportation Lawyers Association — Practice Areas: Commercial Law; Transportation; Civil Litigation

Peter J. Stokstad — University of Washington, B.A., 1985; Willamette University, J.D., 1989 — Admitted to Bar, 1990, Washington; 1996, Montana; U.S. District Court, District of Montana — Member American, Washington State, Western Montana and King County Bar Associations; State Bar of Montana; Montana Defense Trial Lawyers Association — Languages: Norwegian — Practice Areas: Medical Malpractice

Kevin A. Twidwell — The University of Montana, B.A., 1987; J.D. (with honors), 1994 — Admitted to Bar, 1994, Montana; 1998, Washington; U.S. District Court, District of Montana — Member Federal, American and Washington State Bar Associations; State Bar of Montana; Montana Defense Trial Lawyers Association — Practice Areas: Litigation; Media Law; Medical Malpractice

Insurance Law Group Associates

Jeffrey B. Smith   Isaac M. Kantor

Phillips Haffey PC

River Front Place
283 West Front, Suite 301
Missoula, Montana 59802
    Telephone: 406-721-7880
    Fax: 406-721-0058
    E-Mail: Phillips@phillipsmontana.com
    www.phillipsmontana.com

Established: 1984

Phillips Haffey PC, Missoula, MT (Continued)

Insurance Defense, Commercial Law, Personal Injury, Automobile Liability, Coverage Issues, Homeowners, Casualty, Inland Marine, Property Damage, Bad Faith, General Liability, Product Liability, Professional Liability, Truck Liability, Railroad Law, Construction Litigation, Title Insurance, Intellectual Property, Patent and Trademark, Surety

Firm Profile: Phillips Haffey PC practices primarily in the areas of insurance law - defense, coverage, unfair claims practices, and general civil litigation, representing individuals, businesses and institutions across a broad spectrum of legal concerns. Recognized as a leading insurance defense practice, we have earned the respect of colleagues and courts throughout Montana.

The firm maintains qualified, experienced support and administrative staff, dedicated to providing personal attention as well as professional high quality service, to each and every client.

Insurance Clients

Allianz	AmTrust North America
Farmers Insurance Group	Farmers Union Mutual Insurance Company
Fireman's Fund Insurance Company	First American Title Insurance Company
Lloyd's	
Montana Municipal Interlocal Authority	Nationwide Insurance Enterprise
RLI	Progressive Insurance Companies
	Travelers

Non-Insurance Clients

BNSF Railway Company	The Home Depot
Swift Transportation Company, Inc.	

Shareholders

Robert J. Phillips — 1952 — The University of Montana, B.A., 1975; The University of Montana School of Law, J.D., 1978 — Admitted to Bar, 1978, Montana; U.S. District Court, District of Montana; 1982, U.S. Court of Appeals, Ninth Circuit; 1983, U.S. Court of Federal Claims; Salish Kootenai Tribal Court; 1988, U.S. Supreme Court; 2005, U.S. Court of Appeals for the Federal Circuit — Member American and Western Montana (President, 1986-1987) Bar Associations; State Bar of Montana (Chair, Board of Trustees, 1986-1994; President, 1994-1995); American Board of Trial Advocates (President, Montana Chapter, 2005-2007; National Board Member); Chairman, Community Medical Center Board of Directors (2004-2009); Montana Defense Trial Lawyers Association; National Association of Railroad Trial Counsel; International Association of Defense Counsel; Defense Research Institute — Practice Areas: Construction Law; Insurance Coverage; Insurance Defense; Product Liability; Toxic Torts; Professional Malpractice; Bad Faith; Railroad Law; Trucking Litigation

John F. Haffey — 1972 — Montana Tech, B.S.E.S. (with honors), 1994; The University of Montana School of Law, J.D., 1998 — Admitted to Bar, 1998, Montana; 1999, U.S. District Court, District of Montana; U.S. Court of Appeals, Ninth Circuit; 2000, U.S. Patent and Trademark Office; 2002, U.S. Court of Appeals, Ninth Circuit; 2005, U.S. Court of Appeals for the Federal Circuit — Member American and Western Montana (President, 2009-2010) Bar Associations; State Bar of Montana; Defense Research Institute — Practice Areas: Insurance Coverage; Insurance Defense; Product Liability; Construction Litigation; Trucking Law; Intellectual Property; Tort Litigation

Carey B. Schmidt — 1976 — Willamette University, B.S., 1998; The University of Montana School of Law, J.D., 2005 — Admitted to Bar, 2005, Montana; U.S. District Court, District of Montana — Member American and Western Montana Bar Associations; State Bar of Montana; Defense Research Institute — Practice Areas: Insurance Defense; Civil Litigation; Construction Litigation

Mitch J. Vap — 1975 — Wartburg College, B.A./B.S. (Dean's List), 1998; Creighton University, DPT (summa cum laude), 2001; The University of Montana School of Law, J.D., 2009 — Admitted to Bar, 2009, Montana; 2013, U.S. Patent and Trademark Office; U.S. District Court, District of Montana — Member American and Western Montana Bar Associations; State Bar of Montana — Practice Areas: Insurance Defense; Intellectual Property; Personal Injury

Associates

Amy O. Duerk — 1971 — University of Michigan, B.A./B.S., 1994; University of Michigan Law School, J.D., 1998 — Admitted to Bar, 1999, California;

Phillips Haffey PC, Missoula, MT (Continued)

2001, Montana; U.S. District Court, District of Montana; U.S. Court of Appeals, Ninth Circuit — Member American and Western Montana Bar Associations; State Bar of Montana; State Bar of California — Practice Areas: Insurance Coverage; Insurance Defense; Insurance Law; Business Litigation; Personal Injury; Product Liability

Michael W. De Witt — 1967 — California Polytechnic State University, B.A., 1991; The University of Montana, M.B.A., 1996; The University of Montana School of Law, J.D., 2001 — Admitted to Bar, 2002, Montana; U.S. District Court, District of Montana — Member American and Western Montana Bar Associations; State Bar of Montana — Practice Areas: Insurance Defense; Civil Litigation; Construction Liability

Chris V. Fagan — University of Nevada, Reno, B.A., 2000; The University of Montana School of Law, J.D., 2004 — Admitted to Bar, 2004, Montana; U.S. District Court, District of Montana — Member American and Western Montana Bar Associations; State Bar of Montana

Mark M. Handelman — Rhodes College, B.A., 2011; The University of Montana School of Law, J.D., 2014 — Admitted to Bar, 2014, Montana

Spoon Gordon Ballew PC

800 South Third Street West
Missoula, Montana 59801
Telephone: 406-541-2200
Fax: 406-541-2202
E-Mail: firm@sgbmtlaw.com
E-Mail: info@sgbmtlaw.com
www.spoongordonballew.com

Established: 1989

Insurance Defense, Life and Health, Professional Liability, Legal Malpractice, Aviation, General Liability, Personal Injury, Automobile, Property Damage, Product Liability, Subrogation, Railroad Law, Medical Malpractice, Recreational

Firm Profile: The principals who formed the firm of Spoon Gordon Ballew PLLP in 1989 had separately practiced with larger litigation-based firms. Their objective is to provide quality legal services with the efficiency and economy of a small but progressive firm. Services provided include coverage and the defense of insureds for numerous insurance carriers in many areas including errors and omissions, arson, aviation, automobile liability, casualty, construction, environmental and toxic torts, employment, liquor liability, personal, professional, and products liability, commercial litigation, and subrogation recovery. Civil litigation includes all state and federal trial and appellate courts.

Insurance Clients

All Nation Insurance Company
Big Sky Underwriters
Capitol Indemnity Corporation
Contractors Bonding and Insurance Company (CBIC), an RLI Company
Houston General Insurance Company
United States Liability Insurance Group
U.S. Risk Managers, Inc.
American Commerce Insurance Company
Chubb Group of Insurance Companies
Crusader Insurance Company
Federated Insurance Company
St. Paul Travelers
Travelers Insurance
Unitrin Multi-Lines Insurance Company

Shareholders

Dan L. Spoon — 1951 — The University of Montana, B.S. (with honors), 1977; J.D., 1981 — Admitted to Bar, 1981, Montana; U.S. District Court, District of Montana; 1994, U.S. Court of Appeals, Ninth Circuit; 2011, Northern Cheyenne Tribal Court — Member American Bar Association; State Bar of Montana; Montana Defense Trial Lawyers Association — E-mail: dan.spoon@sgbmtlaw.com

William V. Ballew III — 1957 — Williams College, B.A., 1980; University of Houston, J.D., 1984 — Research Editor, Houston Law Review (1983-1984) — Admitted to Bar, 1984, Texas; 1999, New Mexico; 2005, Montana; 1985, U.S. District Court, Western District of Texas; 1990, U.S. Court of Appeals, Fifth Circuit — Member American Bar Association; State Bar of Montana; State Bar of Texas; State Bar of New Mexico; Montana Defense Trial Lawyers Association; National Association of Railroad Trial Counsel; Texas Association of Defense Counsel — Board Certified, Personal Injury Trial Law,

Spoon Gordon Ballew PC, Missoula, MT (Continued)

Texas Board of Legal Specialization (1996-2005) — E-mail: will.ballew@sgbmtlaw.com

Bryan L. Spoon — 1984 — Vanderbilt University, B.A. (with honors), 2007; The University of Montana, J.D., 2010 — Executive Editor, Montana Law Review, 2010 — Admitted to Bar, 2011, Montana; U.S. District Court, District of Montana; U.S. Court of Appeals, Ninth Circuit — Member American Bar Association; State Bar of Montana; Montana Defense Trial Lawyers Association; American Association for Justice — E-mail: bryan.spoon@sgbmtlaw.com

The following firms also service this area.

Axilon Law Group, PLLC
895 Technology Drive
Bozeman, Montana 59718
Telephone: 866-294-9466
Fax: 406-294-9468

Asbestos Litigation, Automobile Liability, Commercial Liability, Construction Liability, Coverage Issues, Directors and Officers Liability, Employment Litigation, Extra-Contractual Litigation, Intellectual Property, Medical Devices, Product Liability, Professional Liability, Self-Insured Defense, Toxic Torts, Trucks/Heavy Equipment

SEE COMPLETE LISTING UNDER BOZEMAN, MONTANA

RED LODGE † 2,125 Carbon Co.

Refer To

Moulton Bellingham PC
Crowne Plaza, Suite 1900
27 North 27th Street
Billings, Montana 59101
Telephone: 406-248-7731
Fax: 406-248-7889

Mailing Address: P.O. Box 2559, Billings, MT 59103

Trial Practice, State and Federal Courts, Insurance Law, Workers' Compensation, Fire, Casualty Insurance Law, Professional Liability, Oil and Gas, Product Liability

SEE COMPLETE LISTING UNDER BILLINGS, MONTANA (60 MILES)

ROUNDUP † 1,788 Musselshell Co.

Refer To

Moulton Bellingham PC
Crowne Plaza, Suite 1900
27 North 27th Street
Billings, Montana 59101
Telephone: 406-248-7731
Fax: 406-248-7889

Mailing Address: P.O. Box 2559, Billings, MT 59103

Trial Practice, State and Federal Courts, Insurance Law, Workers' Compensation, Fire, Casualty Insurance Law, Professional Liability, Oil and Gas, Product Liability

SEE COMPLETE LISTING UNDER BILLINGS, MONTANA (53 MILES)

SHELBY † 3,376 Toole Co.

Refer To

Smith, Walsh, Clarke & Gregoire, PLLP
Galleria Building, Suite 401
104 2nd Street South
Great Falls, Montana 59401
Telephone: 406-727-4100
Fax: 406-727-9228

Mailing Address: P.O. Box 2227, Great Falls, MT 59403-2227

Insurance Law, Product Liability, Medical Malpractice, Workers' Compensation, Casualty, Negligence, Personal Injury, Aviation, Commercial Litigation, Construction Law, Premises Liability, Indian Law

SEE COMPLETE LISTING UNDER GREAT FALLS, MONTANA (89 MILES)

MONTANA   SIDNEY

SIDNEY † 5,191 Richland Co.

Refer To

Brown Law Firm, P.C.
315 North 24th Street
Billings, Montana 59101
   Telephone: 406-248-2611
   Fax: 406-248-3128

Mailing Address: P.O. Drawer 849, Billings, MT 59103-0849

Defense of Complex Civil Litigation, Defense of Catastrophic Personal Injury and Wrongful Death Claims, Insurance Law Including Coverage and Defense of Bad Faith Claims, Product Liability Defense, Defense of Medical and Dental Malpractice Claims, Labor and Employee Relations, Minerals, Oil and Gas, Banking, Workers' Compensation, Real Estate, Construction Defect, Appellate Law

SEE COMPLETE LISTING UNDER BILLINGS, MONTANA (271 MILES)

Refer To

Moulton Bellingham PC
Crowne Plaza, Suite 1900
27 North 27th Street
Billings, Montana 59101
   Telephone: 406-248-7731
   Fax: 406-248-7889

Mailing Address: P.O. Box 2559, Billings, MT 59103

Trial Practice, State and Federal Courts, Insurance Law, Workers' Compensation, Fire, Casualty Insurance Law, Professional Liability, Oil and Gas, Product Liability

SEE COMPLETE LISTING UNDER BILLINGS, MONTANA (271 MILES)

WHITE SULPHUR SPRINGS † 939 Meagher Co.

Refer To

Smith, Walsh, Clarke & Gregoire, PLLP
Galleria Building, Suite 401
104 2nd Street South
Great Falls, Montana 59401
   Telephone: 406-727-4100
   Fax: 406-727-9228

Mailing Address: P.O. Box 2227, Great Falls, MT 59403-2227

Insurance Law, Product Liability, Medical Malpractice, Workers' Compensation, Casualty, Negligence, Personal Injury, Aviation, Commercial Litigation, Construction Law, Premises Liability, Indian Law

SEE COMPLETE LISTING UNDER GREAT FALLS, MONTANA (90 MILES)

WOLF POINT † 2,621 Roosevelt Co.

Refer To

Smith, Walsh, Clarke & Gregoire, PLLP
Galleria Building, Suite 401
104 2nd Street South
Great Falls, Montana 59401
   Telephone: 406-727-4100
   Fax: 406-727-9228

Mailing Address: P.O. Box 2227, Great Falls, MT 59403-2227

Insurance Law, Product Liability, Medical Malpractice, Workers' Compensation, Casualty, Negligence, Personal Injury, Aviation, Commercial Litigation, Construction Law, Premises Liability, Indian Law

SEE COMPLETE LISTING UNDER GREAT FALLS, MONTANA (325 MILES)

NEBRASKA

CAPITAL: LINCOLN

COUNTIES AND COUNTY SEATS

County	County Seat	County	County Seat	County	County Seat
Adams	Hastings	Frontier	Stockville	Nance	Fullerton
Antelope	Neligh	Furnas	Beaver City	Nemaha	Auburn
Arthur	Arthur	Gage	Beatrice	Nuckolls	Nelson
Banner	Harrisburg	Garden	Oshkosh	Otoe	Nebraska City
Blaine	Brewster	Garfield	Burwell	Pawnee	Pawnee City
Boone	Albion	Gosper	Elwood	Perkins	Grant
Box Butte	Alliance	Grant	Hyannis	Phelps	Holdrege
Boyd	Butte	Greeley	Greeley	Pierce	Pierce
Brown	Ainsworth	Hall	Grand Island	Platte	Columbus
Buffalo	Kearney	Hamilton	Aurora	Polk	Osceola
Burt	Tekamah	Harlan	Alma	Red Willow	McCook
Butler	David City	Hayes	Hayes Center	Richardson	Falls City
Cass	Plattsmouth	Hitchcock	Trenton	Rock	Bassett
Cedar	Hartington	Holt	O'Neill	Saline	Wilber
Chase	Imperial	Hooker	Mullen	Sarpy	Papillion
Cherry	Valentine	Howard	St. Paul	Saunders	Wahoo
Cheyenne	Sidney	Jefferson	Fairbury	Scotts Bluff	Gering
Clay	Clay Center	Johnson	Tecumseh	Seward	Seward
Colfax	Schuyler	Kearney	Minden	Sheridan	Rushville
Cuming	West Point	Keith	Ogallala	Sherman	Loup City
Custer	Broken Bow	Keya Paha	Springview	Sioux	Harrison
Dakota	Dakota City	Kimball	Kimball	Stanton	Stanton
Dawes	Chadron	Knox	Center	Thayer	Hebron
Dawson	Lexington	Lancaster	Lincoln	Thomas	Thedford
Deuel	Chappell	Lincoln	North Platte	Thurston	Pender
Dixon	Ponca	Logan	Stapleton	Valley	Ord
Dodge	Fremont	Loup	Taylor	Washington	Blair
Douglas	Omaha	Madison	Madison	Wayne	Wayne
Dundy	Benkelman	McPherson	Tryon	Webster	Red Cloud
Fillmore	Geneva	Merrick	Central City	Wheeler	Bartlett
Franklin	Franklin	Morrill	Bridgeport	York	York

In the text that follows "†" indicates County Seats.

Our files contain additional verified data on the firms listed herein. This additional information is available on request.

A.M. BEST COMPANY

NEBRASKA

AURORA † 4,479 Hamilton Co.

Cline Williams
Wright Johnson & Oldfather, L.L.P.

1207 M Street
Aurora, Nebraska 68818
 Telephone: 402-694-6314
 Fax: 402-694-6315

(Lincoln, NE Office*: 233 South 13th Street, 1900 US Bank Building, 68508)
 (Tel: 402-474-6900)
 (Fax: 402-474-5393)
 (www.clinewilliams.com)
(Omaha, NE Office*: One Pacific Place, Suite 600, 1125 South 103rd Street, 68124)
 (Tel: 402-397-1700)
 (Fax: 402-397-1806)
(Scottsbluff, NE Office*: 416 Valley View Drive, Suite 304, 69361)
 (Tel: 308-635-1020)
 (Fax: 308-635-7010)
(Fort Collins, CO Office*: 330 South College Avenue, Suite 300, 80524)
 (Tel: 970-221-2637)
 (Fax: 970-221-2638)

Casualty, Surety, Life Insurance, General Liability, Professional Liability, Property and Casualty, Medical Malpractice, Dental Malpractice

Insurance Practice Associate

Kara J. Ronnau — 1984 — University of Nebraska, B.A., 2007; J.D. (with distinction), 2011 — Admitted to Bar, 2011, Nebraska — E-mail: kronnau@clinewilliams.com

(See listing under Lincoln, NE for additional information)

CENTRAL CITY † 2,934 Merrick Co.

Refer To
Leininger, Smith, Johnson, Baack, Placzek & Allen
104 North Wheeler Street
Grand Island, Nebraska 68801
 Telephone: 308-382-1930
 Fax: 308-382-5521
Mailing Address: P.O. Box 790, Grand Island, NE 68802

Insurance Defense, Automobile, Product Liability, Workers' Compensation, Employment Practices Liability, Professional Malpractice, Fire, Premises Liability, Accident, Insurance Law, General Liability, Personal Injury, Professional Liability, Property and Casualty, Commercial and Personal Lines, Insurance Coverage Litigation, Trucking, Construction Defect, Automobile Liability, Commercial General Liability, Complex Litigation, Employment Law, Employment Litigation, Estate Litigation, Appellate

SEE COMPLETE LISTING UNDER GRAND ISLAND, NEBRASKA (22 MILES)

FULLERTON † 1,307 Nance Co.

Refer To
Leininger, Smith, Johnson, Baack, Placzek & Allen
104 North Wheeler Street
Grand Island, Nebraska 68801
 Telephone: 308-382-1930
 Fax: 308-382-5521
Mailing Address: P.O. Box 790, Grand Island, NE 68802

Insurance Defense, Automobile, Product Liability, Workers' Compensation, Employment Practices Liability, Professional Malpractice, Fire, Premises Liability, Accident, Insurance Law, General Liability, Personal Injury, Professional Liability, Property and Casualty, Commercial and Personal Lines, Insurance Coverage Litigation, Trucking, Construction Defect, Automobile Liability, Commercial General Liability, Complex Litigation, Employment Law, Employment Litigation, Estate Litigation, Appellate

SEE COMPLETE LISTING UNDER GRAND ISLAND, NEBRASKA (40 MILES)

GENEVA † 2,217 Fillmore Co.

Refer To
Leininger, Smith, Johnson, Baack, Placzek & Allen
104 North Wheeler Street
Grand Island, Nebraska 68801
 Telephone: 308-382-1930
 Fax: 308-382-5521
Mailing Address: P.O. Box 790, Grand Island, NE 68802

Insurance Defense, Automobile, Product Liability, Workers' Compensation, Employment Practices Liability, Professional Malpractice, Fire, Premises Liability, Accident, Insurance Law, General Liability, Personal Injury, Professional Liability, Property and Casualty, Commercial and Personal Lines, Insurance Coverage Litigation, Trucking, Construction Defect, Automobile Liability, Commercial General Liability, Complex Litigation, Employment Law, Employment Litigation, Estate Litigation, Appellate

SEE COMPLETE LISTING UNDER GRAND ISLAND, NEBRASKA (68 MILES)

GRAND ISLAND † 48,520 Hall Co.

Leininger, Smith, Johnson, Baack, Placzek & Allen

104 North Wheeler Street
Grand Island, Nebraska 68801
 Telephone: 308-382-1930
 Fax: 308-382-5521
 E-Mail: dplaczek@gilawfirm.com
 www.gilawfirm.com

Established: 1929

Insurance Defense, Automobile, Product Liability, Workers' Compensation, Employment Practices Liability, Professional Malpractice, Fire, Premises Liability, Accident, Insurance Law, General Liability, Personal Injury, Professional Liability, Property and Casualty, Commercial and Personal Lines, Insurance Coverage Litigation, Trucking, Construction Defect, Automobile Liability, Commercial General Liability, Complex Litigation, Employment Law, Employment Litigation, Estate Litigation, Appellate

Firm Profile: The insurance defense arena is served by Dan Placzek and Tanya Hansen and by associate Andrew Hanquist.

Insurance Clients

The Cincinnati Insurance Companies	Farm Bureau Financial Services
Farmers Mutual Insurance Company of Nebraska	Farmers Mutual Hail Insurance Company of Iowa
ILM Group	Grinnell Mutual Reinsurance Company
Protective Insurance Company	St. Paul Travelers
State Farm Insurance Companies	United Fire & Casualty Company

Senior Partners

Daniel M. Placzek — 1955 — University of Nebraska College of Law, J.D. (with distinction), 1981 — Admitted to Bar, 1981, Nebraska — Member Fellow, International Society of Barristers; Fellow, American College of Trial Lawyers; Defense Counsel Association of Nebraska; American Board of Trial Advocates — Practice Areas: Complex Litigation; Fire; Construction Defect; Trucking Litigation — E-mail: dplaczek@gilawfirm.com

Cathleen H. Allen — 1963 — University of Nebraska College of Law, J.D. (with high distinction), 1989 — Admitted to Bar, 1989, Nebraska — Practice Areas: Wrongful Death; Trusts; Estate Planning; Estate Administration; Probate — E-mail: callen@gilawfirm.com

Junior Partner

Tanya J. Hansen — 1977 — The University of Iowa College of Law, J.D. (with distinction), 2005 — Admitted to Bar, 2006, Nebraska — Member American and Nebraska State Bar Associations; Defense Research Institute; Nebraska Association of Trial Attorneys; Nebraska Defense Counsel Association — Practice Areas: Workers' Compensation; Employment Practices Liability; Wrongful Termination; Automobile Liability; Accident; Commercial Lines; First and Third Party Defense; Homeowners; Insurance Litigation; Personal

Leininger, Smith, Johnson, Baack, Placzek & Allen, Grand Island, NE (Continued)

Lines; Premises Liability; Third Party; Slip and Fall; Defense Litigation; Employment Defense; Employment Discrimination; E-Discovery; Employment; Employment Law; Employment Law (Management Side); Employment Litigation; Employment Practices; General Civil Trial and Appellate Practice; Construction Liability; Americans with Disabilities Act; Appellate Advocacy; Appellate Practice — E-mail: thansen@gilawfirm.com

Associate Attorney

Andrew D. Hanquist — 1985 — University of Nebraska College of Law, J.D., 2013 — Admitted to Bar, 2013, Nebraska — Member American and Nebraska State Bar Associations; Defense Research Institute; Defense Counsel Association of Nebraska — Practice Areas: General Defense; Negligence; Personal and Commercial Vehicle; Restaurant Liability — E-mail: ahanquist@gilawfirm.com

HASTINGS † 24,907 Adams Co.

Refer To

Leininger, Smith, Johnson, Baack, Placzek & Allen
104 North Wheeler Street
Grand Island, Nebraska 68801
 Telephone: 308-382-1930
 Fax: 308-382-5521

Mailing Address: P.O. Box 790, Grand Island, NE 68802

Insurance Defense, Automobile, Product Liability, Workers' Compensation, Employment Practices Liability, Professional Malpractice, Fire, Premises Liability, Accident, Insurance Law, General Liability, Personal Injury, Professional Liability, Property and Casualty, Commercial and Personal Lines, Insurance Coverage Litigation, Trucking, Construction Defect, Automobile Liability, Commercial General Liability, Complex Litigation, Employment Law, Employment Litigation, Estate Litigation, Appellate

SEE COMPLETE LISTING UNDER GRAND ISLAND, NEBRASKA (25 MILES)

HEBRON † 1,579 Thayer Co.

Refer To

Leininger, Smith, Johnson, Baack, Placzek & Allen
104 North Wheeler Street
Grand Island, Nebraska 68801
 Telephone: 308-382-1930
 Fax: 308-382-5521

Mailing Address: P.O. Box 790, Grand Island, NE 68802

Insurance Defense, Automobile, Product Liability, Workers' Compensation, Employment Practices Liability, Professional Malpractice, Fire, Premises Liability, Accident, Insurance Law, General Liability, Personal Injury, Professional Liability, Property and Casualty, Commercial and Personal Lines, Insurance Coverage Litigation, Trucking, Construction Defect, Automobile Liability, Commercial General Liability, Complex Litigation, Employment Law, Employment Litigation, Estate Litigation, Appellate

SEE COMPLETE LISTING UNDER GRAND ISLAND, NEBRASKA (96 MILES)

HOLDREGE † 5,495 Phelps Co.

Refer To

Leininger, Smith, Johnson, Baack, Placzek & Allen
104 North Wheeler Street
Grand Island, Nebraska 68801
 Telephone: 308-382-1930
 Fax: 308-382-5521

Mailing Address: P.O. Box 790, Grand Island, NE 68802

Insurance Defense, Automobile, Product Liability, Workers' Compensation, Employment Practices Liability, Professional Malpractice, Fire, Premises Liability, Accident, Insurance Law, General Liability, Personal Injury, Professional Liability, Property and Casualty, Commercial and Personal Lines, Insurance Coverage Litigation, Trucking, Construction Defect, Automobile Liability, Commercial General Liability, Complex Litigation, Employment Law, Employment Litigation, Estate Litigation, Appellate

SEE COMPLETE LISTING UNDER GRAND ISLAND, NEBRASKA (81 MILES)

KEARNEY † 30,787 Buffalo Co.

Refer To

Leininger, Smith, Johnson, Baack, Placzek & Allen
104 North Wheeler Street
Grand Island, Nebraska 68801
 Telephone: 308-382-1930
 Fax: 308-382-5521

Mailing Address: P.O. Box 790, Grand Island, NE 68802

Insurance Defense, Automobile, Product Liability, Workers' Compensation, Employment Practices Liability, Professional Malpractice, Fire, Premises Liability, Accident, Insurance Law, General Liability, Personal Injury, Professional Liability, Property and Casualty, Commercial and Personal Lines, Insurance Coverage Litigation, Trucking, Construction Defect, Automobile Liability, Commercial General Liability, Complex Litigation, Employment Law, Employment Litigation, Estate Litigation, Appellate

SEE COMPLETE LISTING UNDER GRAND ISLAND, NEBRASKA (50 MILES)

LEXINGTON † 10,230 Dawson Co.

Refer To

Leininger, Smith, Johnson, Baack, Placzek & Allen
104 North Wheeler Street
Grand Island, Nebraska 68801
 Telephone: 308-382-1930
 Fax: 308-382-5521

Mailing Address: P.O. Box 790, Grand Island, NE 68802

Insurance Defense, Automobile, Product Liability, Workers' Compensation, Employment Practices Liability, Professional Malpractice, Fire, Premises Liability, Accident, Insurance Law, General Liability, Personal Injury, Professional Liability, Property and Casualty, Commercial and Personal Lines, Insurance Coverage Litigation, Trucking, Construction Defect, Automobile Liability, Commercial General Liability, Complex Litigation, Employment Law, Employment Litigation, Estate Litigation, Appellate

SEE COMPLETE LISTING UNDER GRAND ISLAND, NEBRASKA (87 MILES)

LINCOLN † 258,379 Lancaster Co.

Cline Williams
Wright Johnson & Oldfather, L.L.P.

233 South 13th Street
1900 US Bank Building
Lincoln, Nebraska 68508
 Telephone: 402-474-6900
 Fax: 402-474-5393
 www.clinewilliams.com

(Omaha, NE Office*: One Pacific Place, Suite 600, 1125 South 103rd Street, 68124)
 (Tel: 402-397-1700)
 (Fax: 402-397-1806)
(Aurora, NE Office*: 1207 M Street, 68818, P.O. Box 510, 68818-0510)
 (Tel: 402-694-6314)
 (Fax: 402-694-6315)
(Scottsbluff, NE Office*: 416 Valley View Drive, Suite 304, 69361)
 (Tel: 308-635-1020)
 (Fax: 308-635-7010)
(Fort Collins, CO Office*: 330 South College Avenue, Suite 300, 80524)
 (Tel: 970-221-2637)
 (Fax: 970-221-2638)

Established: 1857

Casualty, Surety, Life Insurance, General Liability, Professional Liability, Property and Casualty, Medical Malpractice, Dental Malpractice

Firm Profile: Cline Williams Wright Johnson & Oldfather, L.L.P. is a Nebraska-based regional law firm. For more than 150 years, Cline Williams has had a tradition of representing clients in a professional and ethical manner, providing prompt cost-effective, quality representation in substantially all types of legal matters. From offices in Lincoln, Aurora, Omaha, Scottsbluff, Nebraska, and Fort Collins, Colorado, the firm represents insurance carriers,

NEBRASKA — LINCOLN

Cline Williams, Wright Johnson & Oldfather, L.L.P., Lincoln, NE (Continued)

self-insureds and individuals and businesses, including leading commercial, financial, service and industrial companies throughout Nebraska and the Midwest.

Insurance Clients

American National Property and Casualty Company
The Medical Protective Company
Minnesota Lawyers Mutual Insurance Company
Shelter Insurance Companies
State Farm Insurance Companies
Copic Insurance Company
GMAC Insurance
Midwest Medical Insurance Company
Preferred Professional Insurance Company
XL Design Professional

Insurance Practice Partners

Terry R. Wittler — 1952 — University of Nebraska, B.A., 1973; M.A., 1976; J.D., 1977 — Admitted to Bar, 1978, Nebraska; 2012, Colorado — E-mail: twittler@clinewilliams.com

Mark A. Christensen — 1958 — Doane College, B.A. (summa cum laude), 1981; University of Nebraska, J.D. (with distinction), 1984 — Admitted to Bar, 1984, Nebraska — Member American Board of Trial Advocates; American College of Trial Lawyers — E-mail: mchristensen@clinewilliams.com

Shawn D. Renner — 1959 — University of Nebraska, B.A., 1981; J.D. (with distinction), 1984 — Admitted to Bar, 1984, Nebraska — E-mail: srenner@clinewilliams.com

Susan Kubert Sapp — 1965 — University of Nebraska, B.S., 1986; J.D. (with high distinction), 1989 — Admitted to Bar, 1989, Nebraska; 2008, Iowa — E-mail: ssapp@clinewilliams.com

Kevin J. Schneider — 1963 — University of Nebraska, B.S.M.E., 1985; J.D. (with distinction), 1987 — Admitted to Bar, 1988, Texas; Nebraska — E-mail: kschneider@clinewilliams.com

Andrew D. Strotman — 1955 — Creighton University, B.A. (magna cum laude), 1978; J.D. (summa cum laude), 1986 — Admitted to Bar, 1986, Nebraska — E-mail: astrotman@clinewilliams.com

Andre R. Barry — 1972 — The University of Chicago, A.B., 1995; Harvard University, J.D. (cum laude), 1998 — Admitted to Bar, 1998, Illinois; 2002, Nebraska — E-mail: abarry@clinewilliams.com

Stanton N. Beeder — 1979 — University of Nebraska, B.J., 2001; J.D. (with distinction), 2004 — Admitted to Bar, 2004, Nebraska — E-mail: sbeeder@clinewilliams.com

Austin L. McKillip — 1979 — University of Nebraska, B.S.A.S. (with highest distinction), 2002; J.D. (with highest distinction), 2005 — Admitted to Bar, 2005, Nebraska — E-mail: amckillip@clinewilliams.com

Insurance Practice Associates

Michelle L. Sitorius — 1979 — University of Nebraska, B.A. (with high distinction), 2002; McGill University, M.A., 2005; University of Nebraska, J.D. (with distinction), 2009 — Admitted to Bar, 2009, Nebraska — E-mail: msitorius@clinewilliams.com

Coady H. Pruett — 1979 — California Polytechnic State University, B.S., 2002; University of Nebraska College of Law, J.D. (with high distinction), 2010 — Admitted to Bar, 2010, Colorado; Nebraska

Knudsen Law Firm

3800 VerMaas Place, Suite 200
Lincoln, Nebraska 68502
Telephone: 402-475-7011
Fax: 402-475-8912
Toll Free: 800-714-3439
www.knudsenlaw.com

Established: 1881

Knudsen Law Firm, Lincoln, NE (Continued)

Administrative Law, Agriculture, Alternative Dispute Resolution, Appellate Practice, Bankruptcy, Employment Law, Environmental Law, Health Care, Nursing Home Liability, Real Estate, Workers' Compensation, Mediation, Arbitration, Estate Planning, Litigation, Banking, Intellectual Property, Professional Liability, Tax Practice, Trial Advocacy, Financial Institution, Condemnation, Business & Commerce, Social Security Disability, Corporation Formation, Immigration Matters

Firm Profile: The Knudsen Law Firm is a full-service law firm with a singular focus on client satisfaction, achieved by resolving or preventing the challenges our clients face.

Insurance Clients

Catlin, Inc.
Creative Risk Solutions, Inc.
HCC Specialty
National Farmers Union Property & Casualty Company
Professional Indemnity Agency
Sedgwick CMS
Columbia Insurance Group
Gallagher Bassett Services, Inc.
Lancer Claims Services
New York Life Insurance Company
Safeco Insurance
Travelers

Non-Insurance Clients

Carter Feeders, Inc.
Snyder Industries, Inc.
Wells Fargo
Golden Living
Tenneco, Inc.

Members of the Firm

Richard C. Reier — University of Nebraska-Lincoln, B.A., 1971; M.B.A., 1972; J.D. (with distinction), 1975 — Phi Beta Kappa; Beta Gamma Sigman; Delta Theta Phi — Admitted to Bar, 1975, Nebraska — Practice Areas: Real Estate; Estate Planning; Intellectual Property; Banking; Business and Real Estate Transactions

Trev E. Peterson — University of Nebraska-Lincoln, B.A. (with high distinction), 1978; J.D. (with high distinction), 1981 — Phi Beta Kappa — Order of the Coif — Admitted to Bar, 1981, Nebraska — Fellow, Litigation Counsel of America; Super Lawyer Designation — Practice Areas: Appellate Practice; Bankruptcy; Intellectual Property; Banking; Agriculture

Shirley K. Williams — Kearney State College, B.S. (cum laude), 1980; University of Nebraska-Lincoln, J.D. (with distinction), 1984 — Order of the Coif — Admitted to Bar, 1984, Nebraska — Practice Areas: Administrative Law; Appellate Practice; Employment Law; Environmental Law; Mediation; Arbitration; Workers' Compensation

Jeanelle R. Lust — Managing Partner — Augustana College, B.A. (cum laude), 1991; Creighton University, J.D. (summa cum laude), 1994 — Admitted to Bar, 1994, South Dakota; Nebraska; 1995, Colorado — Co-Author: Nebraska Human Resources Manual; Model Policies & Forms for Nebraska Employers — Fellow, Litigation Counsel of America; Fellow, Nebraska State Bar Association; Super Lawyer Designation — Practice Areas: Administrative Law; Appellate Practice; Bankruptcy; Mediation; Arbitration

Kevin R. McManaman — University of Nebraska-Lincoln, B.A., 1990; Creighton University, J.D. (magna cum laude), 1994 — Admitted to Bar, 1994, Nebraska — Co-Author: Nebraska Human Resources Manual; Model Policies & Forms for Nebraska Employers — Super Lawyer Designation — Practice Areas: Administrative Law; Appellate Practice; Employment Law; Estate Planning; Mediation; Arbitration

Associates

Michael W. Khalili
Charles E. Wilbrand

Of Counsel

Michael P. Slattery
Richard R. Endacott
Richard A. Knudsen

Shively & Lannin, P.C., L.L.O.

4400 South 86th Street, Suite 100
Lincoln, Nebraska 68526
Telephone: 402-488-5044
Fax: 402-488-5110
E-Mail: rshively@shivelylaw.com
www.shivelylaw.com

Shively & Lannin, P.C., L.L.O., Lincoln, NE (Continued)

Established: 2002

Insurance Defense, Automobile, Homeowners, Commercial Law, Coverage Issues, General Liability, Property and Casualty, Agriculture, Self-Insured Defense, Mediation

Insurance Clients

Adventist Risk Management, Inc.
Auto-Owners Insurance Company
Bristol West Insurance Company
Cherokee Insurance Company
EMC Insurance Companies
Farmers Mutual Insurance Company of Nebraska
St. Paul Travelers
Atlantic Casualty Insurance Company
California Casualty Insurance Company
Farmers Insurance Group
League Association of Risk Management
West Bend Mutual Insurance Company

Non-Insurance Clients

Altec, Inc.
Equifunding, Inc.
PepsiCo, Inc.
Securitas Security Services USA, Inc.
Eaton Corporation
First National Acceptance Company
Waste Connections of Nebraska, Inc.

Partners

Robert W. Shively — 1959 — University of Nebraska-Lincoln, B.A., 1982; University of Nebraska College of Law, J.D., 1985 — Admitted to Bar, 1985, Nebraska; 1985, U.S. District Court, District of Nebraska; 2013, U.S. Court of Appeals, Eighth Circuit — Member American, Nebraska State and Lincoln (President, 2001-2002) Bar Associations; Defense Research Institute (State Representative, 1999-2003; Mid-Region Director 2010-2013); Nebraska Defense Counsel Association (Vice President, 2004-2006; President, 2006-2008); International Association of Defense Counsel; Federation of Defense and Corporate Counsel — Practice Areas: Mediation; Trial Practice — E-mail: rshively@shivelylaw.com

Robert S. Lannin — 1959 — University of Nebraska-Lincoln, B.A. (with distinction), 1981; University of Nebraska College of Law, J.D., 1984 — Admitted to Bar, 1984, Kansas; 1985, Nebraska; 1990, Missouri; 1985, U.S. District Court, District of Nebraska; 1987, U.S. Court of Appeals, Tenth Circuit; 1990, U.S. Supreme Court; 1998, U.S. Court of Appeals, Eighth Circuit — Member Nebraska State and Lincoln Bar Associations; Nebraska Defense Counsel Association (Board of Trustees, 2007-2010; Treasurer 2010-2012; Vice President, 2012-2013; President, 2013-2014); Defense Research Institute; American Board of Trial Advocates — Practice Areas: Litigation — E-mail: rlannin@shivelylaw.com

Associate

Ryan G. Norman — 1988 — University of Nebraska-Lincoln, B.J., 2010; University of Nebraska College of Law, J.D., 2013 — Admitted to Bar, 2013, Nebraska — Member Nebraska State and Lincoln Bar Associations; Nebraska Defense Counsel Association; Nebraska Association of Trial Attorneys — Practice Areas: Litigation — E-mail: rnorman@shivelylaw.com

MCCOOK † 7,698 Red Willow Co.

Refer To

Leininger, Smith, Johnson, Baack, Placzek & Allen
104 North Wheeler Street
Grand Island, Nebraska 68801
Telephone: 308-382-1930
Fax: 308-382-5521
Mailing Address: P.O. Box 790, Grand Island, NE 68802

Insurance Defense, Automobile, Product Liability, Workers' Compensation, Employment Practices Liability, Professional Malpractice, Fire, Premises Liability, Accident, Insurance Law, General Liability, Personal Injury, Professional Liability, Property and Casualty, Commercial and Personal Lines, Insurance Coverage Litigation, Trucking, Construction Defect, Automobile Liability, Commercial General Liability, Complex Litigation, Employment Law, Employment Litigation, Estate Litigation, Appellate

SEE COMPLETE LISTING UNDER GRAND ISLAND, NEBRASKA (153 MILES)

MINDEN † 2,923 Kearney Co.

Refer To

Leininger, Smith, Johnson, Baack, Placzek & Allen
104 North Wheeler Street
Grand Island, Nebraska 68801
Telephone: 308-382-1930
Fax: 308-382-5521
Mailing Address: P.O. Box 790, Grand Island, NE 68802

Insurance Defense, Automobile, Product Liability, Workers' Compensation, Employment Practices Liability, Professional Malpractice, Fire, Premises Liability, Accident, Insurance Law, General Liability, Personal Injury, Professional Liability, Property and Casualty, Commercial and Personal Lines, Insurance Coverage Litigation, Trucking, Construction Defect, Automobile Liability, Commercial General Liability, Complex Litigation, Employment Law, Employment Litigation, Estate Litigation, Appellate

SEE COMPLETE LISTING UNDER GRAND ISLAND, NEBRASKA (55 MILES)

NORTH PLATTE † 24,733 Lincoln Co.

Waite, McWha & Heng

116 North Dewey Street
North Platte, Nebraska 69101
Telephone: 308-532-2202
Fax: 308-532-2741
E-Mail: wmlf@nque.com
www.northplattelaw.com

Established: 1987

Insurance Defense, General Liability, Product Liability, Property Damage, Casualty, Automobile, Errors and Omissions, Workers' Compensation, Subrogation

Insurance Clients

AIG Life Insurance Company
American Mutual Liability Insurance Company
Amerisure Companies
CGU Hawkeye-Security Insurance Company
Empire Insurance Group
Federated Insurance Company
General Casualty Companies
John Deere Insurance Company
Minnesota Lawyers Mutual Insurance Company
National Farmers Union Standard Insurance Company
Royal Insurance Company of Canada
United Services Automobile Association (USAA)
Utica National Insurance Group
Zurich American Insurance Company
American Family Insurance Group
American States Insurance Company
CGU Group
CNA Insurance Companies
EMC Underwriters, Ltd.
Employers Mutual Companies
Gallagher Bassett Services, Inc.
Interstate Insurance Company
Michigan Mutual Insurance Company
National Casualty Company
National States Insurance Company
Nationwide Insurance
Scottsdale Insurance Company
Shelter Insurance Companies
Universal Underwriters Insurance Company
Viking Insurance Company of Wisconsin

Non-Insurance Clients

Coca-Cola Enterprises Inc.
Marten Transport, Ltd.
Con-Way Truckload, Inc.

Firm Members

Terrance O. Waite — 1952 — University of Nebraska-Lincoln, B.S.B.A., 1974; J.D., 1977 — Phi Alpha Delta — Omicron Delta Epsilon — Admitted to Bar, 1977, Nebraska; 1977, U.S. District Court, District of Nebraska; 1977, U.S. Court of Appeals, Eighth Circuit — Member Nebraska State Bar Association (Judicial Procedure Committee, 1991-1993; Workers' Compensation Section; Judiciary Committee, 1997-2000); Western Nebraska Bar Associaton (President, 1993-1994); Defense Research and Trial Lawyers Association; Nebraska Association of Trial Attorneys; Nebraska Defense Counsel Association — Appointed to Federal Practice Committee, District of Nebraska, (1989); Appointed, Supreme Court Committee on Minority and Justice Implementation; Arbitrator, National Arbitration Forum; Approved, Federal Court Mediator, 1995 — Practice Areas: Civil Litigation; Alternative Dispute Resolution

NEBRASKA

Waite, McWha & Heng, North Platte, NE (Continued)

Todd R. McWha — 1960 — University of Nebraska-Lincoln, B.S., 1983; J.D., 1989 — Admitted to Bar, 1989, Nebraska; U.S. District Court, District of Nebraska; U.S. Court of Appeals, Eighth Circuit — Member American Bar Association (Workers' Compensation and Civil Practice and Procedures); Nebraska State, Western Nebraska and Lincoln County (President, 2003) Bar Associations; Nebraska Association of Trial Attorneys; Defense Research Institute; Nebraska Defense Counsel Association — Appointed to Nebraska Federal Practice and Procedure Committee, 2003; Chairman, 2004 — Practice Areas: Civil Litigation

Patrick M. Heng — 1958 — University of Nebraska-Lincoln, B.S., 1981; University of Nebraska College of Law, J.D., 1984 — Admitted to Bar, 1984, Nebraska — Member Nebraska State, Lincoln County and Adams County Bar Associations — Practice Areas: Banking; Commercial Litigation; Municipal Law

Attorneys

Todd O. Engleman — 1974 — University of Nebraska at Kearney, B.S., 1998; Creighton University School of Law, J.D., 2001 — Admitted to Bar, 2001, Nebraska — Member Nebraska State Bar Association — Practice Areas: Employment Law; Environmental Law; Insurance Defense; Litigation; Personal Injury

Angela M. Franz — 1975 — Creighton University, B.A., 2002; Creighton University School of Law, J.D., 2012 — Admitted to Bar, 2012, Iowa; 2013, Nebraska; U.S. District Court, District of Nebraska — Member American, Nebraska State and Lincoln County Bar Associations — Practice Areas: Employment Law; Environmental Law; Insurance Defense; Litigation; Personal Injury

Lindsay E. Pedersen — Nebraska Wesleyan University, B.S., 2007; University of Nebraska College of Law, J.D., 2011 — Admitted to Bar, 2011, Nebraska; U.S. District Court, District of Nebraska — Member Nebraska State, Lincoln County and Omaha Bar Associations — Practice Areas: Employment Law; Environmental Law; Insurance Defense; Litigation; Personal Injury

(This firm is also listed in the Subrogation, Investigation and Adjustment section of this directory)

OMAHA † 390,007 Douglas Co.

Abrahams Kaslow & Cassman LLP

8712 West Dodge Road, Suite 300
Omaha, Nebraska 68114-3450
  Telephone: 402-392-1250
  Fax: 402-392-0816
  E-Mail: attorneys@akclaw.com
  www.akclaw.com

Established: 1944

Insurance Defense

Firm Profile: Abrahams Kaslow & Cassman LLP (AK&C) has over 100 years of collective litigation experience. In addition to its extensive commercial litigation practice, the firm has represented some of the largest insurance companies in the United States. AK&C has also defended numerous self-insured clients and is approved by carriers having excess liability coverage for clients with self-insured retentions. Our attorneys have defended cases for the Transit Authority for the City of Omaha d/b/a Metro Area Transit for over 25 years in the areas of general insurance defense, worker's compensation defense and employment defense.

AK&C's professional liability practice provides highly-skilled defense litigation, consulting and risk management services to both corporations and individuals. The firm's professional liability attorneys possess a thorough understanding of medical issues, JCAHO standards and state and federal regulations. While AK&C has a specialty in healthcare, the firm also does significant work defending real estate brokers and agents on issues of errors and omissions, and advising and defending employers in employment practice liability matters.

AK&C has a reputation for professionalism, efficiency and commitment to its clients.

OMAHA

Abrahams Kaslow & Cassman LLP, Omaha, NE (Continued)

Insurance Clients

AIG Insurance Company
American Claims Service
Atlantic Casualty Insurance Company
Continental Western Group
Fireman's Fund Insurance Company
Hartford Life Group Insurance
Interstate Insurance Group
Medicus Insurance Company
Mitsui Sumitomo Marine Management (USA), Inc.
Sedgwick CMS
Travelers Property Casualty Company of America
Alegent Health
American Claims Services, Inc.
Catholic Health Initiatives
Chartis Insurance
Employers Mutual Companies
First State Management Group, Inc.
The Hartford Steam Boiler Inspection and Insurance Company
Preferred Professional Insurance Company
Travelers
Travelers, Special Liability Group

Non-Insurance Clients

Baker's Supermarkets
Nebraska Methodist Health System d/b/a Nebraska Methodist Hospital, Physicians Clinic
Transit Authority for the City of Omaha d/b/a Metro
Kwik Shop
Premier Physician Services
Tenaska
Transgenomic, Inc.
The Weitz Company, L.L.C.

Partners

Harvey B. Cooper — 1947 — Temple University, B.A., 1969; Creighton University, J.D. (magna cum laude), 1976 — Admitted to Bar, 1976, Nebraska; 1976, U.S. District Court, District of Nebraska; 1976, U.S. Court of Appeals, Eighth Circuit — Member Nebraska State and Omaha Bar Associations — Nebraska-Iowa Wireless Association (Board Member, 2009-Present); Project Harmony (Board Member, 2010-Present); Beth El Synagogue (Former Director); Jewish Federation of Omaha (Former Director); NITA Trial School (Graduate) — Captain, U.S. Air Force — Practice Areas: Employment Law (Management Side); Commercial General Liability; Complex Litigation — E-mail: hcooper@akclaw.com

Timothy M. Kenny — Creighton University, J.D., 1973 — Admitted to Bar, 1974, Nebraska; U.S. District Court, District of Nebraska; U.S. Supreme Court; 1978, U.S. Court of Appeals, Eighth Circuit — Member Nebraska State Bar Association — Practice Areas: Municipal Law; Self-Insured Defense; Real Estate; Commercial General Liability; Insurance Defense; Workers' Compensation; Personal Injury; Public Entities; Tort Litigation — E-mail: tkenny@akclaw.com

Aaron D. Weiner — 1964 — Colorado College, B.A. (magna cum laude), 1986; University of Minnesota, J.D. (magna cum laude), 1989 — Admitted to Bar, 1989, Nebraska — Member Nebraska State and Omaha Bar Associations — Practice Areas: Commercial Litigation; Real Estate; Errors and Omissions; Mediation — E-mail: aweiner@akclaw.com

Jeffrey J. Blumel — 1963 — University of Nebraska-Lincoln, B.S.B.A., 1986; J.D., 1989 — Admitted to Bar, 1989, Nebraska; 2006, Kentucky; 1989, U.S. District Court, District of Nebraska — Member Nebraska State, Kentucky State and Omaha Bar Associations — Practice Areas: Insurance Defense; Premises Liability; Workers' Compensation; Civil Litigation — E-mail: jblumel@akclaw.com

Robert M. Schartz — University of Nebraska, B.S.B.A. (with honors), 1990; Creighton University School of Law, J.D., 1993 — Admitted to Bar, 1993, Nebraska; 2010, Iowa; 1993, U.S. District Court, District of Nebraska; 2011, U.S. District Court, Northern District of Iowa — Member American, Nebraska State, Iowa State and Omaha Bar Associations; Defense Research Institute (Former State Liasion, Medical Liability Section); Nebraska Defense Counsel Association — Assistant Public Defender, Douglas County (1993-1998) — Practice Areas: Insurance Defense; Medical Malpractice; Hospital Malpractice; Medical Negligence; Defense Litigation; Construction Litigation; Construction Defect; Litigation; Trial Practice — Tel: 402-392-1250 — E-mail: rschartz@akclaw.com

Associates

Nicole Seckman Jilek — University of Nebraska-Lincoln, B.S. (with distinction), 2004; University of Nebraska College of Law, J.D., 2007 — Admitted to Bar, 2007, Nebraska; U.S. District Court, District of Nebraska — Member Nebraska State and Omaha Bar Associations; Robert M. Spire Inns of Court — Practice Areas: Commercial Litigation; Professional Errors and Omissions; Professional Liability; Agent and Brokers Errors and Omissions; Agent/Broker Liability; Real Estate; Landlord and Tenant Law; Collections; Breach of Contract; Securities; Construction Defect — E-mail: njilek@akclaw.com

Abrahams Kaslow & Cassman LLP, Omaha, NE
(Continued)

Ryan M. Kunhart — Creighton University, B.A. (magna cum laude), 2007; Creighton University School of Law, J.D. (cum laude), 2011 — Deans Scholar; Phi Alpha Theta National History Honor Society; Certificate in Litigation; CALI Excellence for the Future Award Trial Practice — Admitted to Bar, 2011, Nebraska; U.S. District Court, District of Nebraska — Member Nebraska State and Omaha Bar Associations — Practice Areas: Employment Law (Management Side); Commercial General Liability; Municipal Law; Tort Litigation; Insurance Defense; Defense Litigation; Trial Practice; Construction Defect; Medical Negligence — E-mail: rkunhart@akclaw.com

Cline Williams
Wright Johnson & Oldfather, L.L.P.

One Pacific Place, Suite 600
1125 South 103rd Street
Omaha, Nebraska 68124
 Telephone: 402-397-1700
 Fax: 402-397-1806

(Lincoln, NE Office*: 233 South 13th Street, 1900 US Bank Building, 68508)
 (Tel: 402-474-6900)
 (Fax: 402-474-5393)
 (www.clinewilliams.com)
(Aurora, NE Office*: 1207 M Street, 68818, P.O. Box 510, 68818-0510)
 (Tel: 402-694-6314)
 (Fax: 402-694-6315)
(Scottsbluff, NE Office*: 416 Valley View Drive, Suite 304, 69361)
 (Tel: 308-635-1020)
 (Fax: 308-635-7010)
(Fort Collins, CO Office*: 330 South College Avenue, Suite 300, 80524)
 (Tel: 970-221-2637)
 (Fax: 970-221-2638)

Established: 1857

Casualty, Surety, Life Insurance, General Liability, Professional Liability, Property and Casualty, Medical Malpractice, Dental Malpractice

Insurance Practice Partners

James M. Bausch — 1944 — Creighton University, B.S.B.A., 1966; J.D., 1969; New York University, LL.M., 1973 — Admitted to Bar, 1969, Nebraska — Member American Board of Trial Advocates; Fellow, American College of Trial Lawyers — E-mail: jbausch@clinewilliams.com

John C. Hewitt — 1959 — Hastings College, B.A., 1982; University of Nebraska, J.D., 1985 — Admitted to Bar, 1985, Nebraska — E-mail: jhewitt@clinewilliams.com

Trenten P. Bausch — 1970 — Creighton University, B.A., 1992; J.D., 1995 — Admitted to Bar, 1995, Nebraska — E-mail: tbausch@clinewilliams.com

Rick Jeffries — 1968 — The University of Chicago, A.B., 1990; Creighton University, J.D. (cum laude), 1993 — Admitted to Bar, 1993, Nebraska — E-mail: rickjeffries@clinewilliams.com

Tara A. Stingley — 1979 — University of Nebraska, B.S. (summa cum laude), 2002; University of Nebraska College of Law, J.D. (with high distinction), 2005 — Admitted to Bar, 2005, Nebraska — E-mail: tstingley@clinewilliams.com

Insurance Practice Associate

Jonathan J. Papik — 1982 — Northwestern College, B.S. (summa cum laude), 2004; Harvard Law School, J.D. (magna cum laude), 2008 — Admitted to Bar, 2008, Nebraska — E-mail: jpapik@clinewilliams.com

(See listing under Lincoln, NE for additional information)

Engles, Ketcham, Olson & Keith, P.C.

1350 Woodmen Tower
1700 Farnam Street
Omaha, Nebraska 68102
 Telephone: 402-348-0900
 Fax: 402-348-0904
 E-Mail: mail@ekoklaw.com
 www.ekoklawfirm.com

(Council Bluffs, IA Office: 500 West Broadway, Suite 312, 51503)

Insurance Law, Negligence, Workers' Compensation, Personal Injury, General Civil Practice, Admiralty and Maritime Law, Appellate Practice, Bad Faith, Civil Litigation, Construction Law, Discrimination, Mediation, Mold and Mildew Claims, Premises Liability, Product Liability, Professional Negligence, Subrogation, Tort, Wrongful Death

Insurance Clients

ACE USA
Alpha Property & Casualty Insurance Company
American International Group
Associates Insurance Company
Berkley Risk & Insurance Services
Bituminous Insurance Company
Broadspire
CNA Insurance Company
Crum & Forster Insurance
Encompass Insurance
Financial Indemnity Company
FirstComp Insurance Company
Gallagher Bassett Services, Inc.
Golden Rule Insurance Company
Great American Insurance Company
Hartford Insurance Company
Infinity Insurance Company
Integrity Mutual Insurance Company
John Deere Insurance Company
Le Mars Insurance Company
Lumbermen's Underwriting Alliance
Minnesota Fire and Casualty Company
Nebraska Intergovernmental Risk Management Association (NIRMA)
Northwestern National Life Insurance Company
Progressive Insurance Company
Risk Services, Inc.
Safeco Insurance
Sedgwick CMS
State Farm Insurance Company
Switzerland General Insurance Company
United Heartland Inc
VELA Insurance Services (A Berkley Company)
Windsor Insurance Company
Zurich North America
Allied Insurance Company
American Income Life Insurance Company
Aon Risk Services, Inc. of Nebraska
Berkshire Hathaway Homestate Insurance Company
Catholic Mutual Insurance
Continental Insurance Company
EMC Insurance Companies
Federal Insurance Company
Fireman's Fund Insurance Company
General Casualty Company
Grange Insurance Association
GuideOne Insurance
Harleysville Insurance Company
The Hartford Steam Boiler Inspection and Insurance Company
Iowa Mutual Insurance Company
Kemper Auto and Home
Liberty Mutual Insurance Company
Markel Insurance Company
Metropolitan Property and Casualty Insurance Company
National Indemnity Company
Nebraska Property & Liability Insurance Guaranty Association
North River Insurance Company
Philadelphia Insurance Company
Prestige Casualty Company
QBE North America
RLI Insurance Company
SeaBright Insurance Company
State Auto Insurance Company
Stillwater Insurance Group, Inc.
Traders Insurance Company
Transportation Claims, Inc.
Unitrin Universal Companies
Viking Insurance Company of Wisconsin
Workmen's Auto Insurance Company

Non-Insurance Clients

Alexsis, Inc.
BFI Industries
Ciba-Geigy Corporation
State of Nebraska
Travelers Protective Association of America
Avis Rent-A-Car System, LLC
Boy Scouts of America
Lincoln Service Corporation
Swift Transportation Company, Inc.
Yellow Freight System

Firm Members

Albert M. Engles — 1947 — Creighton University, A.B., 1969; J.D., 1972 — Admitted to Bar, 1972, Nebraska; 1972, U.S. District Court, District of Nebraska; 1972, U.S. Court of Appeals, Eighth Circuit — Member American, Nebraska State and Omaha Bar Associations; Nebraska Association of Trial Attorneys; Nebraska Defense Counsel Association; Defense Research Institute — E-mail: bengles@ekoklaw.com

Engles, Ketcham, Olson & Keith, P.C., Omaha, NE
(Continued)

Dan H. Ketcham — 1962 — University of Nebraska, B.A., 1985; Creighton University, J.D., 1988 — Admitted to Bar, 1988, Arizona; 1989, Nebraska; 2000, Iowa; 1989, U.S. District Court, District of Nebraska; 2001, U.S. Court of Appeals, Eighth Circuit — Member Nebraska State and Omaha Bar Associations; State Bar of Arizona; Nebraska Association of Defense Attorneys; Nebraska Association of Trial Attorneys; Defense Research Institute; Iowa Trial Lawyers Association — Practice Areas: Civil Litigation; Insurance Defense; Product Liability; Professional Negligence — E-mail: dketcham@ekoklaw.com

Stephen G. Olson, II — 1964 — University of Nebraska-Lincoln, B.A., 1986; J.D., 1988 — Admitted to Bar, 1989, Nebraska; 1995, Iowa; 1989, U.S. District Court, District of Nebraska; 1995, U.S. District Court, Northern and Southern Districts of Iowa; 1995, U.S. Court of Appeals, Eighth Circuit; 1995, U.S. Supreme Court — Member American, Nebraska State, Iowa State and Omaha Bar Associations; Nebraska Association of Defense Attorneys; Claims & Litigation Management Alliance; Nebraska Association of Trial Attorneys; Nebraska Defense Counsel Association; Defense Research Institute; Iowa Trial Lawyers Association — Practice Areas: Civil Litigation; Commercial Litigation; Construction Law; Insurance Defense; Product Liability; Wrongful Death; Construction Defect; Construction Litigation; Nursing Home Liability; Professional Negligence; Trucking Liability; Transportation — E-mail: solson@ekoklaw.com

Robert S. Keith — 1970 — University of Nebraska-Lincoln, B.A., 1992; J.D. (cum laude), 1996 — Admitted to Bar, 1996, Nebraska — Member Nebraska State Bar Association; Nebraska Defense Counsel Association (Board of Directors); National Retail and Restaurant Defense Association; CLM; Association of Trial Lawyers of America; Defense Research Institute — Practice Areas: Civil Litigation; Construction Defect; Environmental Law; Insurance Defense; Litigation; Governmental Entity Defense — E-mail: rkeith@ekoklaw.com

Karen K. Bailey — 1974 — University of Nebraska at Kearney, B.S., 1997; University of Nebraska-Lincoln, J.D., 2004 — Admitted to Bar, 2004, Nebraska; 2009, Iowa; 2004, U.S. District Court, District of Nebraska — Member American, Nebraska State, Iowa State and Omaha Bar Associations; Nebraska Claims Association; Iowa-Nebraska International Association of Special Investigation Unit; Claims & Litigation Management Alliance; Defense Research Institute; Nebraska Defense Counsel Association; Nebraska Association of Trial Attorneys — Practice Areas: Civil Litigation; Insurance Coverage; Insurance Defense — E-mail: kbailey@ekoklaw.com

Jason A. Kidd — 1978 — University of Nebraska-Lincoln, B.S., 2000; Creighton University, J.D., 2004 — Admitted to Bar, 2004, Nebraska; 2010, Iowa; 2004, U.S. District Court, District of Nebraska — Member American and Nebraska State Bar Associations; Defense Research Institute — Practice Areas: Workers' Compensation — E-mail: jkidd@ekoklaw.com

L. Tyler Laflin — 1981 — University of Nebraska-Lincoln, B.S.B.A., 2003; Creighton University, J.D., 2006 — Admitted to Bar, 2006, Nebraska; 2007, Iowa; 2013, South Dakota — Member American, Nebraska State and Iowa State Bar Associations; The State Bar of South Dakota; National Retail and Restaurant Defense Association; Claims & Litigation Management Alliance; Iowa Association of Workers Compensation Lawyers — Practice Areas: Workers' Compensation — E-mail: llaflin@ekoklaw.com

Associates

Justin K. Burroughs — 1977 — University of Missouri-Columbia, B.A., 1999; J.D., 2002 — Admitted to Bar, 2002, Missouri; 2004, Illinois; 2008, Nebraska — Member Illinois State and Nebraska State Bar Associations; The Missouri Bar — E-mail: jburroughs@ekoklaw.com

Brynne E. Holsten — 1982 — University of Nebraska-Lincoln, B.A., 2005; J.D., 2008 — Admitted to Bar, 2008, Nebraska — Member American and Nebraska State Bar Associations; Nebraska Association of Trial Attorneys — E-mail: bholsten@ekoklaw.com

Michael L. Moran — 1983 — Creighton University, B.A., 2005; University of Nebraska-Lincoln, J.D., 2008 — Admitted to Bar, 2008, Iowa; Nebraska — Member Nebraska State and Iowa State Bar Associations — E-mail: mmoran@ekoklaw.com

Kristina J. Kamler — 1983 — University of Nebraska-Lincoln, B.J., 2004; Creighton University School of Law, J.D., 2008 — Admitted to Bar, 2008, Nebraska; Iowa — Member Nebraska State and Iowa State Bar Associations — E-mail: kkamler@ekoklaw.com

Elizabeth A. Smith — 1981 — Saint Louis University, B.A. (magna cum laude), 2003; J.D., 2007 — Admitted to Bar, 2007, Illinois; 2008, Nebraska — Member Nebraska State and Omaha Bar Associations — E-mail: esmith@ekoklaw.com

Engles, Ketcham, Olson & Keith, P.C., Omaha, NE
(Continued)

Angela D. Jensen-Blackford — 1984 — Creighton University, B.A./B.A. (cum laude), 2005; University of Nebraska College of Law, J.D., 2009 — Admitted to Bar, 2009, Iowa; 2010, Nebraska — Member Nebraska State, Iowa State, Omaha and Nebraska Womens Bar Associations — E-mail: ablackford@ekoklaw.com

James C. Boesen — Creighton University, B.A., 2008; University of Nebraska College of Law, J.D., 2011 — Admitted to Bar, 2011, Iowa; 2012, Nebraska — Member Nebraska State and Iowa State Bar Associations — E-mail: jboesen@ekoklaw.com

Garrett A. Lutovsky — 1986 — North Dakota State University, B.S. (summa cum laude), 2009; University of Nebraska College of Law, J.D. (with distinction), 2012 — Admitted to Bar, 2012, Iowa — Member Iowa State Bar Association — E-mail: glutovsky@ekoklaw.com

Katherine E. Fitzgerald — 1987 — Wayne State College, B.A. (summa cum laude), 2010; University of Nebraska-Lincoln, J.D., 2013 — Admitted to Bar, 2013, Nebraska — Member Nebraska State and Omaha Bar Associations — E-mail: kfitzgerald@ekoklaw.com

Kyle Seay — 1986 — Eastern Michigan University, B.S., 2008; Washington University in St. Louis, J.D., 2011 — Admitted to Bar, 2011, Illinois; 2013, Nebraska — Member Nebraska State Bar Association — E-mail: kseay@ekoklaw.com

Jennifer S. Schuelke — 1988 — The University of Iowa, B.A., 2007; Gonzaga University School of Law, J.D., 2014 — Admitted to Bar, 2014, Nebraska; Iowa — Member Nebraska State Bar Association — E-mail: jschuelke@ekoklaw.com

Philip Cusic — 1985 — Creighton University, B.A., 2007; Gonzaga University School of Law, J.D., 2014 — Admitted to Bar, 2014, Nebraska; Iowa — Member Nebraska State Bar Association — E-mail: pcusic@ekoklaw.com

(This firm is also listed in the Subrogation section of this directory)

Erickson & Sederstrom, P.C.
Regency Westpointe
10330 Regency Parkway Drive
Omaha, Nebraska 68114-3761
Telephone: 402-397-2200
Toll Free: 800-279-3756
www.eslaw.com

(Lincoln, NE Office: Cornhusker Plaza, Suite 400, 301 South 13th St., 68508)
(Tel: 402-476-1000)

Established: 1968

Insurance Defense, Automobile, Product Liability, Commercial Liability, Fire, Casualty, Life Insurance, Fidelity and Surety, Workers' Compensation, Professional Liability, Subrogation, Auto Racing and other Public Amusements

Insurance Clients

AIG
Cambridge Integrated Insurance Company
Capitol Indemnity Corporation
Church Mutual Insurance Company
Cornhusker Casualty Company
Essex Insurance Company
Gulf Insurance Company
Liberty International Underwriters
NAMIC Insurance Company, Inc.
Philadelphia Insurance Company
RLI Insurance Company
Sentry Insurance a Mutual Company
United States Liability Insurance Company
Zurich American Insurance Company
Ameriprise Auto & Home Insurance
CAMICO Mutual Insurance Company
Columbia Insurance Group
Economical Insurance Group
Great American AgriBusiness
James River Insurance Company
Liberty Mutual Insurance Company
National Indemnity Company
QBE North America
Secure Insurance, Inc.
Travelers Insurance Company
United National Insurance Company
XL Design Professional
Zurich North America

OMAHA   NEBRASKA

Erickson & Sederstrom, P.C., Omaha, NE   (Continued)

Attorneys

Thomas Culhane — 1947 — Creighton University, J.D., 1974 — Admitted to Bar, 1974, Nebraska; Iowa — Member Nebraska State Bar Association

Richard J. Gilloon — 1952 — Creighton University, J.D., 1977 — Admitted to Bar, 1977, Nebraska; 1987, Colorado — Member Nebraska State and Colorado Bar Associations

Jerald L. Rauterkus — 1952 — Creighton University, J.D., 1985 — Admitted to Bar, 1985, Nebraska; 1990, Colorado — Member Nebraska State and Colorado Bar Associations

Patrick R. Guinan — 1968 — University of Nebraska-Lincoln, J.D., 1993 — Admitted to Bar, 1993, Nebraska — Member Nebraska State Bar Association

Thomas J. Guilfoyle — 1940 — Creighton University, B.A., 1962; Creighton University School of Law, J.D., 1965 — Admitted to Bar, 1965, Nebraska; Colorado

Tiernan T. Siems — 1969 — University of Colorado at Boulder, B.A., 1992; Creighton University School of Law, J.D., 1997 — Admitted to Bar, 1997, Nebraska; 2003, Iowa — Member Iowa State, Nebraska State and Omaha Bar Associations

Matthew V. Rusch — 1974 — Creighton University, B.S.B.A. (cum laude), 1996; University of South Dakota, J.D., 1999 — Admitted to Bar, 1999, Nebraska; 2000, South Dakota — Member American and Nebraska State Bar Associations; State Bar of South Dakota

Heather B. Veik — 1980 — University of Nebraska, B.A., 2003; University of Nebraska College of Law, J.D., 2006 — Admitted to Bar, 2006, Nebraska — Member Nebraska State and Omaha Bar Associations

Matthew B. Reilly — 1983 — Creighton University, B.S.B.A., 2006; University of Nebraska College of Law, J.D. (with distinction), 2009 — Admitted to Bar, 2009, Nebraska — Member Nebraska State and Omaha Bar Associations

Sara A. Lamme — 1977 — Creighton University School of Law, J.D., 2003 — Admitted to Bar, 2003, Iowa; 2004, Nebraska — Member Nebraska State and Iowa State Bar Associations

Bonnie M. Boryca — 1983 — The University of Kansas School of Law, J.D., 2010 — Admitted to Bar, 2010, Kansas; 2012, Nebraska

Fitzgerald, Schorr, Barmettler & Brennan, P.C., L.L.O.

10050 Regency Circle, Suite 200
Omaha, Nebraska 68114
   Telephone: 402-342-1000
   Fax: 402-342-1025
   www.fitzlaw.com

Established: 1888

Automobile, Coverage Issues, ERISA, Employment Law, Intellectual Property, Personal Injury, Product Liability, Professional Liability, Property and Casualty, Municipal

Insurance Clients

AAA Automobile Club Insurance Company	AIG
Capitol Indemnity Corporation	All Risk Claims Service, Inc.
The Colony Group	CIGNA Property and Casualty Insurance Company
Colony Insurance Company	Connecticut General Life Insurance Company
Equitable General Insurance Company	Fremont Indemnity Company
Great American AgriBusiness	Home Insurance Company
John Deere Insurance Company	Lincoln General Insurance Company
Transamerica Group/AEGON USA, Inc.	Tudor Insurance Company
United Benefit Life Insurance Company	Western World Insurance Company
Zurich North America	

Non-Insurance Clients

The Goodyear Tire & Rubber Company	Intere Intermediaries, Inc.
	Novartis Crop Protection, Inc.

Fitzgerald, Schorr, Barmettler & Brennan, P.C., L.L.O., Omaha, NE   (Continued)

Principals

Gerald L. Friedrichsen — 1947 — The University of Iowa, B.B.A., 1970; Creighton University, J.D. (cum laude), 1977 — Admitted to Bar, 1979, Nebraska; U.S. Court of Appeals for the Federal, Fourth, Seventh, Eighth and Tenth Circuits; U.S. Supreme Court — Member American Bar Association (Litigation, Torts and Insurance Practice Sections); Nebraska State Bar Association (Co-Chair, Insurance Committee); Omaha Bar Association (President, Executive Council); Robert M. Spire Inns of Court; Nebraska Association of Defense Counsel; Fellow, Nebraska State Bar Foundation; Fellow, American College of Trial Lawyers — E-mail: gfriedrichsen@fitzlaw.com

Robert T. Cannella — 1948 — Creighton University, B.S.B.A., 1970; J.D. (cum laude), 1972 — Admitted to Bar, 1973, Nebraska; U.S. Court of Appeals, Eighth Circuit — Member Nebraska State Bar Association — Practice Areas: Employment Discrimination; Employment Law — E-mail: rcannella@fitzlaw.com

Andrew T. Schlosser — 1975 — Washington University, B.A. (with honors), 1997; Georgetown University, J.D., 2000 — Admitted to Bar, 2000, Nebraska — Member Nebraska State and Omaha Bar Associations; Nebraska Association of Trial Attorneys; Nebraska Defense Counsel Association — E-mail: aschlosser@fitzlaw.com

Of Counsel

Mark J. Daly — 1949 — University of Nebraska at Omaha, B.A., 1974; Creighton University School of Law, J.D., 1977 — Admitted to Bar, 1977, Nebraska; U.S. District Court, District of Nebraska; 1996, U.S. Court of Appeals, Eighth Circuit — Member Nebraska State and Omaha Bar Associations — E-mail: mdaly@fitzlaw.com

Gross & Welch P.C., L.L.O.

1500 Omaha Tower
2120 South 72nd Street
Omaha, Nebraska 68124
   Telephone: 402-392-1500
   Fax: 402-392-8101
   Toll Free: 866-503-9304
   E-Mail: info@grosswelch.com
   www.grosswelch.com

Established: 1927

Negligence, Automobile, Product Liability, Professional Liability, Fire, Workers' Compensation, Insurance Coverage, Subrogation, Construction, Business

Firm Profile: The law firm of Gross & Welch, P.C., L.L.O. was founded in 1927 by Daniel J. Gross and Harry L. Welch and consists of 24 attorneys. The primary area of practice is in the greater Omaha/Council Bluffs metropolitan area; however the firm handles cases in the entire State of Nebraska and Western Iowa. Specialized areas of litigation practice include professional malpractice, automobile cases, fire and explosion cases, workers' compensation, premises liability, products liability, insurance fraud and property cases, as well as general civil litigation.

The firm is committed to providing quality legal representation of insurance companies and their insureds.

Insurance Clients

AAA Automobile Club Insurance Company	ACUITY
American National Property and Casualty Company	Allied/Nationwide Insurance Company
Burlington Insurance Company	Auto-Owners Insurance Company
Cincinnati Insurance Company	Chartis Insurance
Employers Mutual Casualty Company	Columbia Insurance Company
Gallagher Bassett Insurance Company	Farm Bureau Insurance Company
Great West Casualty Company	Farmers Mutual Insurance Company of Nebraska
	Grain Dealers Mutual Insurance Company

NEBRASKA   OMAHA

Gross & Welch P.C., L.L.O., Omaha, NE   (Continued)

Grinnell Mutual Reinsurance Company
Horace Mann Insurance Company
Interstate Insurance Company
National Indemnity Company
Penn Millers Insurance Company
The St. Paul Companies
State Farm Insurance Companies
United Fire & Casualty Company
Zurich American Insurance Company

GuideOne Insurance
Heritage Insurance Group
Housing Authority Insurance, Inc.
Markel Insurance Company
Northwestern National Insurance Company
Shelter Mutual Insurance Company
Transport Insurance Company
Western World Insurance Group

Representative Clients

Cambridge Integrated Services
Hy-Vee, Inc.
PPG Industries, Inc.
Yellow Freight System

Clark Equipment Company
John Deere Company
Waste Management of Nebraska, Inc.

Shareholders

Thomas A. Grennan — Creighton University, B.A. (cum laude), 1975; J.D., 1978 — Admitted to Bar, 1978, Nebraska; 1978, U.S. District Court, District of Nebraska; 1979, U.S. Court of Appeals, Eighth Circuit; 1990, U.S. Supreme Court — E-mail: tgrennan@grosswelch.com

John W. Iliff — Hastings College, B.A., 1970; Boston University, M.E.D., 1975; Creighton University, J.D. (cum laude), 1983 — Admitted to Bar, 1983, Nebraska; 1983, U.S. District Court, District of Nebraska; 1986, U.S. Court of Appeals, Eighth Circuit; 1989, U.S. Supreme Court — E-mail: jiliff@grosswelch.com

Michael J. Mooney — Creighton University, B.A., 1959; J.D., 1963 — Admitted to Bar, 1963, Nebraska; 1963, U.S. District Court, District of Nebraska; 1999, U.S. District Court, District of Arizona — E-mail: mmooney@grosswelch.com

Christopher J. Tjaden — University of Notre Dame, B.A., 1983; Creighton University, J.D., 1986 — Admitted to Bar, 1986, Nebraska; 1987, Missouri; 1987, U.S. District Court, District of Nebraska — E-mail: ctjaden@grosswelch.com

John A. Svoboda — Creighton University, B.S. (magna cum laude), 1989; J.D., 1992 — Admitted to Bar, 1992, Nebraska; 1992, U.S. District Court, District of Nebraska; 2006, U.S. Court of Appeals, Eighth Circuit — E-mail: jsvoboda@grosswelch.com

Robert A. Mooney — University of Nebraska-Lincoln, B.A., 1994; University of Nebraska College of Law, J.D., 1997 — Admitted to Bar, 1997, Nebraska; 1999, U.S. District Court, District of Nebraska — E-mail: rmooney@grosswelch.com

Daniel P. Lenaghan — Saint Louis University, B.A., 2002; J.D., 2005 — Admitted to Bar, 2005, Nebraska; U.S. District Court, District of Nebraska — E-mail: dlenaghan@grosswelch.com

Andrew J. Wilson — Iowa State University, B.A./B.S.I.E., 1987; University of Nebraska College of Law, J.D., 1991 — Admitted to Bar, 1991, Nebraska; Iowa; U.S. District Court, District of Nebraska; 1992, U.S. District Court, Northern and Southern Districts of Iowa — E-mail: awilson@grosswelch.com

Associates

Adam Wachal — University of Nebraska, B.S.B.A., 2005; Creighton University School of Law, J.D., 2010 — Admitted to Bar, 2010, Nebraska; Iowa; U.S. District Court, Northern and Southern Districts of Iowa; 2011, U.S. District Court, District of Nebraska — E-mail: awachal@grosswelch.com

Abbie M. Schurman — Iowa State University, B.A. (magna cum laude), 2009; Creighton University School of Law, J.D. (magna cum laude), 2012 — Admitted to Bar, 2012, Nebraska; 2012, Iowa — Member Iowa State, Nebraska State and Omaha Bar Associations — E-mail: aschurman@grosswelch.com

Larry Roland — Marquette University, B.A., 1997; University of Nebraska at Omaha, M.B.A., 2009; Creighton University School of Law, J.D., 2013 — Admitted to Bar, 2013, Iowa; 2014, Nebraska — Member Iowa State, Nebraska State and Omaha Bar Associations — E-mail: lroland@grosswelch.com

(This firm is also listed in the Subrogation section of this directory)

Locher, Pavelka, Dostal, Braddy & Hammes, L.L.C.

200 The Omaha Club
2002 Douglas Street
Omaha, Nebraska 68102
   Telephone: 402-898-7000
   Fax: 402-898-7130
   Toll Free: 800-579-2240
   E-Mail: lpdbh@lpdbhlaw.com
   www.lpdbhlaw.com

(Locher Pavelka Dostal Braddy & Hammes, L.L.C.: 421 West Broadway, #401, Council Bluffs, IA, 51503)
(Tel: 712-256-5566)

Insurance Law, Negligence, Workers' Compensation, Personal Injury, General Civil Practice, Trial Practice, Insurance Defense, Admiralty and Maritime Law, Commercial Litigation, Insurance Fraud, Product Liability, Corporate Law, Subrogation, Commercial Fraud, Business Planning, Insurance Policy Interpretation, Law Enforcement Agency Representation

Firm Profile: Locher Pavelka Dostal Braddy & Hammes, LLC, is a general practice civil litigation law firm dedicated to providing our clients with reliable legal advice and aggressive trial advocacy. We offer our clients a broad range of legal experience and expertise in virtually all areas of civil law by combining traditional hard work with coordinated efforts across the firm's various specialization groups to serve our clients in an efficient, prompt and economical manner throughout the State and Federal Courts of Nebraska and Iowa.

Insurance Clients

Acceptance Indemnity Insurance Company
Allstate Insurance Company
American National Property and Casualty Company
Catlin Specialty Insurance Company
CNA Global Specialty Lines
CNA Standard Lines
Crum & Forster Insurance
Fidelity National Title Group
Gateway Insurance Company
Hanover Insurance Group
IAT Specialty
Liberty Mutual Insurance
Mutual of Omaha Group
Ohio Casualty Group
Pharmacists Mutual Insurance Company
Progressive Insurance Group
Royal Maccabees Life Insurance Company
SECURA Insurance Companies
Sedgwick Claims Management Services, Inc.
Swiss Re Life & Health America, Inc.
Universal Underwriters Insurance Company
Windsor Insurance Company

ACUITY
Allstate Indemnity Company
American Fire and Casualty Company
Berkley Risk Administrators Company, LLC
Chubb & Son, Inc.
CNA Insurance Company
Colonial Insurance Company
Deerbrook Insurance Company
First Americans Insurance Company
Hartford Insurance Company
Insurance Company of the West
Midwest Mutual Insurance Company
Old Republic National Title Insurance Company
Philadelphia Insurance Company
Reassure America Life Insurance Company
SECURA Insurance, A Mutual Company
Sentry Claims Services
Swiss Re
United States Fire Insurance Company
USAA Casualty Insurance Company
Yasuda Fire & Marine Insurance Company of America

Non-Insurance Clients

Carrier Corporation
J. C. Penney Company, Inc.
United Parcel Service, Inc.

Harrah's Entertainment, Inc.
Otis Elevator Company

Firm Members

Thomas M. Locher — 1952 — Creighton University, B.A., 1974; J.D., 1978 — Admitted to Bar, 1978, Nebraska; Iowa; U.S. District Court, District of Nebraska; U.S. Court of Appeals, Eighth Circuit; U.S. District Court, Northern and Southern Districts of Iowa — E-mail: tlocher@lpdbhlaw.com

Donald J. Pavelka, Jr. — 1957 — University of Nebraska at Omaha, B.A., 1980; Creighton University, J.D., 1984 — Admitted to Bar, 1984, Nebraska;

OMAHA   NEBRASKA

Locher, Pavelka, Dostal, Braddy & Hammes, L.L.C., Omaha, NE (Continued)

1993, Iowa; 1984, U.S. District Court, District of Nebraska; 1997, U.S. District Court, Northern and Southern Districts of Iowa; 2000, U.S. Court of Appeals, Eighth Circuit — E-mail: dpavelka@lpdbhlaw.com

Kevin J. Dostal — 1959 — University of Nebraska-Lincoln, B.S.B.A., 1981; Creighton University, J.D., 1984 — Admitted to Bar, 1984, Nebraska; U.S. District Court, District of Nebraska — Certified Public Accountant, 1985 — E-mail: kdostal@lpdbhlaw.com

Thomas M. Braddy — 1969 — Coe College, B.A., 1991; Creighton University, J.D. (cum laude), 1994 — Admitted to Bar, 1994, Nebraska; 2002, Iowa; 1994, U.S. District Court, District of Nebraska; U.S. Court of Appeals, Eighth Circuit; 2002, U.S. District Court, Northern and Southern Districts of Iowa — E-mail: tbraddy@lpdbhlaw.com

Matthew D. Hammes — 1971 — University of Nebraska-Lincoln, B.S., 1994; J.D. (with distinction), 1998 — Admitted to Bar, 1998, Nebraska; 1999, Iowa; 1998, U.S. District Court, District of Nebraska; 2002, U.S. District Court, Northern and Southern Districts of Iowa — E-mail: mhammes@lpdbhlaw.com

Gregory L. Galles — 1971 — Creighton University, B.A., 1995; The University of Iowa, J.D., 1998 — Admitted to Bar, 1998, Iowa; 1999, Nebraska; U.S. District Court, District of Nebraska; U.S. District Court, Southern District of Iowa — E-mail: ggalles@lpdbhlaw.com

Douglas W. Krenzer — 1971 — Colorado College, B.A., 1993; University of Nebraska, J.D., 1996 — Admitted to Bar, 1996, Nebraska; 2006, Iowa; 1996, U.S. District Court, District of Nebraska — E-mail: dkrenzer@lpdbhlaw.com

Matthew E. Eck — 1977 — Creighton University, B.S.B.A. (cum laude), 1999; J.D. (cum laude), 2001 — Admitted to Bar, 2001, Nebraska; 2004, Iowa; 2001, U.S. District Court, District of Nebraska; 2005, U.S. District Court, Northern and Southern Districts of Iowa — E-mail: meck@lpdbhlaw.com

Joel E. Feistner — 1972 — Colorado College, B.A., 1994; University of Nebraska, J.D., 1998 — Admitted to Bar, 1998, Nebraska; U.S. District Court, District of Nebraska — E-mail: jfeistner@lpdbhlaw.com

Ralph A. Froehlich — 1947 — United States Air Force Academy, B.S., 1969; Fletcher School of Law & Diplomacy, Tufts University, M.A., 1970; University of Nevada, J.D. (with distinction), 1991 — Admitted to Bar, 1992, Nebraska; U.S. District Court, District of Nebraska — Languages: German — E-mail: rfroehlich@lpdbhlaw.com

Joseph J. Kehm — 1972 — Drake University, B.A., 1995; University of Nebraska College of Law, J.D., 2002 — Law Clerk to Hon. John V. Hendry, Nebraska Supreme Court (2002-2003) — Admitted to Bar, 2002, Nebraska — E-mail: jkehm@lpdbhlaw.com

Amy M. Locher — 1985 — Creighton University, B.S., 2007; The University of Iowa College of Law, J.D., 2011 — Admitted to Bar, 2011, Iowa; 2012, Nebraska; U.S. District Court, District of Nebraska — E-mail: amylocher@lpdbhlaw.com

Kenneth M. Smith — 1988 — Creighton University, B.A., 2010; University of Nebraska College of Law, J.D., 2014 — Admitted to Bar, 2014, Nebraska — E-mail: ksmith@lpdbhlaw.com

McAnany, Van Cleave & Phillips, P.C.

10665 Bedford Avenue, Suite 101
Omaha, Nebraska 68134
  Telephone: 402-408-1340
  Fax: 402-493-0860
  www.mvplaw.com

(McAnany, Van Cleave & Phillips, P.A.*: 10 East Cambridge Circle Drive, Suite 300, Kansas City, KS, 66103)
  (Tel: 913-371-3838)
  (Fax: 913-371-4722)
(St. Louis, MO Office*: 505 North 7th Street, Suite 2100, 63101)
  (Tel: 314-621-1133)
  (Fax: 314-621-4405)
(Springfield, MO Office*: 4650 South National Avenue, Suite D-2, 65810)
  (Tel: 417-865-0007)
  (Fax: 417-865-0008)
(Tulsa, OK Office*: 2021 South Lewis, Suite 225, 74104)
  (Tel: 918-771-4465)

Established: 1901

McAnany, Van Cleave & Phillips, P.C., Omaha, NE (Continued)

Administrative Law, Antitrust, Bankruptcy, Business Law, Construction Law, Corporate Law, Creditor Rights, Directors and Officers Liability, Insurance Law, Labor and Employment, Land Use, Litigation, Municipal Law, Personal Injury, Product Liability, Professional Liability, Public Entities, Railroad Law, Real Estate, School Law, Transportation, Trial and Appellate Practice, Workers' Compensation

(See Kansas City, KS listing for additional information)

Morrow Willnauer Klosterman Church, LLC

1299 Farnam Street, Suite 250
Omaha, Nebraska 68102
  Telephone: 402-934-0100
  Fax: 402-330-1425
  E-Mail: kweston@mwklaw.com
  http://mwklaw.com

(Kansas City, MO Office*: 10401 Holmes Road, Suite 300, 64131)
  (Tel: 816-382-1382)
  (Fax: 816-382-1383)
(St. Louis, MO Office*: 500 North Broadway, Suite 1420, 63102)
  (Tel: 314-561-7300)
  (Fax: 314-875-9215)
  (mwklaw.com)

Automobile, Construction Liability, Coverage Analysis, Employment Law, Personal Injury, Premises Liability, Product Liability, Professional Liability, Public Entities, Transportation, Trucking Liability, Workers' Compensation

Firm Profile: At Morrow Willnauer Klosterman Church, LLC, the client relationship comes first. MWKC serves commercial, government, and individual clients' in civil litigation, workers' compensation and corporate law.

(See listing under Kansas City, MO for additional information)

Sodoro Daly Shomaker & Selde PC LLO

7000 Spring Street
Omaha, Nebraska 68106
  Toll Free: 888-476-3676
  Telephone: 402-397-6200
  Fax: 402-397-6290
  E-Mail: office@sodorolaw.com

Insurance Defense, Automobile Liability, General Liability, First Party Matters, Third Party, Property and Casualty, Professional Malpractice, Medical Malpractice, Legal Malpractice, Dental Malpractice, Insurance Coverage, Opinions, Workers' Compensation, Environmental Law, Toxic Torts, Product Liability, Excess and Reinsurance, Business Law, Insurance Litigation, Fidelity and Surety, Life Insurance, Accident and Health, Fire, Arson, Fraud, Construction Law, Governmental Liability, Law Enforcement Liability, Subrogation, Investigation and Adjustment, Intellectual Property, Transportation, Administrative Law, Regulatory and Compliance, Hospitals, Medical Liability

Insurance Clients

Adventist Risk Management, Inc.
Alexsis Risk Management Services, Inc.
Berkley Risk Services, LLC
CNA Insurance Companies
Columbia Insurance Group

AIG - Chartis
Allied Professionals Insurance Company
Brotherhood Mutual Insurance Company
Copic Insurance Company

Sodoro Daly Shomaker & Selde PC LLO, Omaha, NE
(Continued)

Crawford & Company
The Doctors Company
Excess Liability Fund
Fireman's Fund Insurance Company
GuideOne Insurance
Hartford Financial Products
Inservco Insurance Services, Inc.
Markel Shand, Inc.
MSIG Claims
National Chiropractic Mutual Insurance Company
OneBeacon Insurance Group
Professional Solutions Insurance Company
Select Medical Corp/Specialty Hospital/Omaha
Vanliner Insurance Company
Zurich
Darwin National Assurance Company
Fidelity National Insurance Company
Gallagher Bassett & Co.
Hamlin & Burton Liability Management
Lexington Insurance Company
Midwest Medical Insurance Company
National Union Fire Insurance Company
ProAssurance Group
The Redwoods Group
Sedgwick Caronia
Topa Insurance Company
Travelers
White Mountains Re Solutions LTD

Non-Insurance Clients

Avis Rent-A-Car System, LLC
Menards, Inc
Briggs & Stratton Corporation

Firm Members

Joseph S. Daly — 1944 — Creighton University, A.B., 1967; J.D., 1970 — Admitted to Bar, 1970, Nebraska — Member American, Nebraska State and Omaha Bar Associations; Fellow, Nebraska State Bar Foundation; American Inns of Court (Master of the Bench); Defense Counsel Association of Nebraska; American Board of Trial Advocates; International Society of Barristers; Defense Research Institute

John R. Sodoro — 1953 — Creighton University, B.A., 1975; J.D., 1978 — Admitted to Bar, 1978, Nebraska — Member American, Nebraska State and Omaha Bar Associations; Defense Counsel Association of Nebraska

Thomas J. Shomaker — 1948 — University of Minnesota, B.A., 1969; Creighton University, J.D., 1973 — Admitted to Bar, 1974, Nebraska — Member American, Nebraska State (Lifetime Fellow) and Omaha Bar Associations; Fellow, American College of Trial Lawyers; Defense Counsel Association of Nebraska

Ronald E. Frank — 1947 — University of Nebraska, B.A., 1970; J.D., 1973 — Admitted to Bar, 1973, Nebraska — Member American, Nebraska State, Iowa State and Omaha Bar Associations; Defense Counsel Association of Nebraska; Defense Research Institute

Robert F. Vacek — 1952 — University of Nebraska, B.S.B.A., 1976; Creighton University, J.D., 1979 — Admitted to Bar, 1979, Nebraska — Member American, Nebraska State and Omaha Bar Associations

William H. Selde — 1956 — Creighton University, B.S.B.A., 1984; J.D., 1987 — Admitted to Bar, 1987, Nebraska — Member American and Nebraska State Bar Associations; Association of Trial Lawyers of America; Nebraska Association of Trial Attorneys; Defense Counsel Association of Nebraska; Defense Research Institute

Allen J. Potts — 1953 — Creighton University, B.A., 1975; J.D., 1982 — Admitted to Bar, 1983, Nebraska — Member American, Nebraska State and Omaha Bar Associations; Defense Counsel Association of Nebraska

Mary M. Schott — Iowa State University, B.A.; University of South Dakota, J.D., 1996 — Admitted to Bar, 1996, Iowa; South Dakota; 1999, Nebraska — Member American, Nebraska State, Iowa State and Pottawattamie County Bar Associations

Associates

John P. Weis — 1963 — Creighton University, B.A., 1986; Creighton University School of Law, J.D., 1991 — Admitted to Bar, 1991, Nebraska; 2002, Wyoming — Member Nebraska State and Omaha Bar Associations; Wyoming State Bar; Nebraska Association of Defense Attorneys

Harry A. Hoch, III — 1981 — Creighton University, B.S.B.A., 2004; Creighton University School of Law, J.D., 2009 — Admitted to Bar, 2009, Nebraska — Member Nebraska State and Omaha Bar Associations

Timmermier, Gross & Prentiss
8712 West Dodge Road, #401
Omaha, Nebraska 68114
Telephone: 402-391-4600
Fax: 402-391-6221
E-Mail: tgp@tgplaw.com
www.tgplaw.com

Insurance Defense, Automobile, Commercial Law, General Liability, Product Liability, Workers' Compensation

Insurance Clients

ACE USA
American Family Insurance Company
FirstComp Insurance Company
Gallagher Bassett Services, Inc.
Kemper Insurance Companies
Liberty Mutual Insurance Company
Risk Enterprise Management, Ltd.
RSKCo
Travelers Insurance Companies
Zenith Insurance Company
Allstate Insurance Company
Broadspire, a Crawford Company
CIGNA Property and Casualty Insurance Company
Hartford Specialty Risk Services, Inc.
Mutual of Omaha Insurance Company
Sentry Insurance a Mutual Company

Non-Insurance Clients

Avaya, Inc.
Farmland Foods, Inc.
GatesMcDonald
Crawford & Company
Federal Express
Kawasaki Motors Corporation, U.S.A.

Partners

John R. Timmermier — 1945 — University of Nebraska-Lincoln, B.S., 1967; J.D., 1970 — Admitted to Bar, 1970, Nebraska; 1970, U.S. District Court, District of Nebraska — Member American Bar Association (Tort and Insurance Practice Section); Nebraska State Bar Association (Workers' Compensation Committee, 1992); Omaha Bar Association (Chairman Medical-Legal Section, 1987-1988); Federation of Insurance and Corporate Counsel (Committee on Workers' Compensation, 1980-1997); Nebraska Association of Trial Attorneys

Joseph F. Gross, Jr. — 1948 — Saint Mary's College, B.A., 1970; Saint Louis University, J.D., 1973 — Admitted to Bar, 1973, Missouri; 1976, Nebraska; 1973, U.S. Court of Appeals, Eighth Circuit; 1976, U.S. District Court, District of Nebraska — Member American (Litigation Section, 1973), Nebraska State and Omaha Bar Associations; Nebraska Association of Trial Attorneys; Association of Trial Lawyers of America

Paul F. Prentiss — 1956 — Trinity University, B.A., 1978; University of Nebraska-Lincoln, M.S., 1981; William Mitchell College of Law, J.D., 1986 — Admitted to Bar, 1986, Minnesota; 1987, Nebraska; 1995, Iowa; 1986, U.S. District Court, District of Minnesota; 1987, U.S. District Court, District of Nebraska; 1988, U.S. Court of Appeals, Eighth Circuit — Member American, Minnesota State, Nebraska State and Omaha Bar Associations

Associates

Jill Hamer Conway — 1979 — University of Nebraska at Omaha, B.S. (magna cum laude), 2000; University of Nebraska-Lincoln, J.D. (with distinction), 2005 — Admitted to Bar, 2005, Iowa; Nebraska

Christopher A. Sievers — 1977 — The University of Iowa, B.A., 1999; Creighton University School of Law, J.D., 2002 — Admitted to Bar, 2002, Nebraska; 2004, Iowa

SCOTTSBLUFF   NEBRASKA

ORD † 2,112 Valley Co.

Refer To

Leininger, Smith, Johnson, Baack, Placzek & Allen
104 North Wheeler Street
Grand Island, Nebraska 68801
  Telephone: 308-382-1930
  Fax: 308-382-5521

Mailing Address: P.O. Box 790, Grand Island, NE 68802

Insurance Defense, Automobile, Product Liability, Workers' Compensation, Employment Practices Liability, Professional Malpractice, Fire, Premises Liability, Accident, Insurance Law, General Liability, Personal Injury, Professional Liability, Property and Casualty, Commercial and Personal Lines, Insurance Coverage Litigation, Trucking, Construction Defect, Automobile Liability, Commercial General Liability, Complex Litigation, Employment Law, Employment Litigation, Estate Litigation, Appellate

SEE COMPLETE LISTING UNDER GRAND ISLAND, NEBRASKA (71 MILES)

PAPILLION † 18,894 Sarpy Co.

Adams & Sullivan, P.C., L.L.O.

1246 Golden Gate Drive, Suite 1
Papillion, Nebraska 68046
  Telephone: 402-339-9550
  Fax: 402-339-0401
  E-Mail: fett@adamsandsullivan.com
  www.adamsandsullivan.com

Established: 1951

Insurance Defense, Administrative Law, Business Law, Civil Litigation, Employment Law, Personal Injury, Real Estate, School Law, Workers' Compensation, Appellate Law, Estate, Family, Divorce, Corporate

Firm Profile: Adams & Sullivan, P.C., L.L.O. and its predecessors have been a renowned firm in the legal community since 1951. Our clients include businesses, school districts and political subdivisions. Our attorneys pride themselves on providing the most efficient and cost effective representation of our clients.

Insurance Clients

Creative Risk Solutions, Inc.	Diamond Insurance Company
Gallagher Bassett Services, Inc.	Paratransit Insurance Company
Travelers Insurance Companies	

Non-Insurance Clients

Bellevue Public Schools	Bellino Enterprises, Inc.
City of Bellevue	Exmark Manufacturing Company, Inc.
Flying J, Inc.	
Fundraising University, Inc.	Homestead Rehabilitation Center
Lancaster Manor	Marsh USA, Inc.
Reinke Manufacturing Company, Inc.	Shop KO, Inc.
	Valley View Assisted Living

Associate

Aimee C. Bataillon — Creighton University, B.A., 1997; Creighton University School of Law, J.D., 2001 — Admitted to Bar, 2001, Nebraska; U.S. District Court, District of Nebraska — Member Nebraska State Bar Association; Nebraska Association of Trial Attorneys — Practice Areas: Labor and Employment; Litigation

SCOTTSBLUFF 15,039 Scotts Bluff Co.

Cline Williams
Wright Johnson & Oldfather, L.L.P.

416 Valley View Drive
Suite 304
Scottsbluff, Nebraska 69361
  Telephone: 308-635-1020
  Fax: 308-635-7010

(Lincoln, NE Office*: 233 South 13th Street, 1900 US Bank Building, 68508)
  (Tel: 402-474-6900)
  (Fax: 402-474-5393)
  (www.clinewilliams.com)
(Omaha, NE Office*: One Pacific Place, Suite 600, 1125 South 103rd Street, 68124)
  (Tel: 402-397-1700)
  (Fax: 402-397-1806)
(Aurora, NE Office*: 1207 M Street, 68818, P.O. Box 510, 68818-0510)
  (Tel: 402-694-6314)
  (Fax: 402-694-6315)
(Fort Collins, CO Office*: 330 South College Avenue, Suite 300, 80524)
  (Tel: 970-221-2637)
  (Fax: 970-221-2638)

Casualty, Surety, Life Insurance, General Liability, Professional Liability, Property and Casualty, Medical Malpractice, Dental Malpractice

(See listing under Lincoln, NE for additional information)

Kovarik, Ellison & Mathis, P.C.

1715 11th Street
Gering, Nebraska 69341
  Telephone: 308-436-5297 (436-LAWS)
  Toll Free: 877-436-5291
  Fax: 308-436-2297
  E-Mail: gen@neblawyer.com
  www.neblawyer.com

Insurance Defense, Casualty, Workers' Compensation, Surety, Product Liability, Malpractice, Trial Practice, Subrogation, Personal Injury, Civil Trial Practice, Municipal Law, Commercial Litigation

Firm Profile: Kovarik, Ellison & Mathis, P.C. is a general practice firm with emphasis on personal injury, insurance defense, subrogation and commercial litigation throughout the entire state of Nebraska. The office is conveniently located directly across the street from the Scotts Bluff County Courthouse.

Insurance Clients

ACE American Insurance Company	Amerisafe Insurance Group
Church Mutual Insurance Company	Blue Cross Blue Shield of Nebraska
Continental Casualty Company	GEICO Insurance Companies
General Casualty Companies	Great West Casualty Company
League Association of Risk Management	National American Insurance Company
OneBeacon Insurance	Owner Operator Independent Driver Association
The Protective National Insurance Company of Omaha	Safeco Insurance
Sentry Insurance Company	Western World Insurance Company

Firm Members

Leland K. Kovarik — Nebraska Wesleyan University, B.A., 1960; University of Nebraska, J.D., 1966 — Admitted to Bar, 1966, Nebraska — Member American Board of Trial Advocates

James W. Ellison — University of Nebraska-Lincoln, B.A., 1972; J.D., 1975 — Admitted to Bar, 1976, Nebraska — Member Nebraska State and Scottsbluff

Kovarik, Ellison & Mathis, P.C., Scottsbluff, NE
(Continued)

County Bar Associations; Association of Defense Trial Attorneys; Nebraska Defense Counsel Association; International Association of Defense Counsel; Federation of Defense and Corporate Counsel

Associates

Audrey M. Elliott — University of Nebraska-Lincoln, B.A., 2003; Creighton University School of Law, J.D., 2006 — Admitted to Bar, 2006, Nebraska — Member Nebraska Association of Trial Attorneys

Mark L. Kovarik — University of Nebraska-Lincoln, B.A., 1994; Washburn University School of Law, J.D., 2005 — Admitted to Bar, 2006, Kansas

Matthew J. Turman — Nebraska Wesleyan University, B.A., 2006; University of Nebraska College of Law, J.D., 2010 — Admitted to Bar, 2010, Nebraska — Member Nebraska Association of Trial Attorneys

Simmons Olsen Law Firm, P.C.
Professional & Business Center
1502 Second Avenue
Scottsbluff, Nebraska 69361-3174
   Telephone: 308-632-3811
   Fax: 308-635-0907
   E-Mail: solsen@simmonsolsen.com
   www.simmonsolsen.com

Insurance Law

Insurance Clients

American Family Insurance Group
Columbia National Insurance Company
EMC Insurance Companies
Farmers Insurance Group
Farmers Mutual Insurance Company of Nebraska
Farmland Mutual Insurance Company
Iowa Mutual Insurance Company
Reliance Insurance Group
RSKCo
Tower Insurance Company of New York
Union Insurance Company
CNA Insurance Company
Continental Western Insurance Company
Farm Bureau Mutual Insurance Company
Farmers Union Co-Operative Insurance Company of Nebraska, Inc.
Horace Mann Insurance Company
National Farmers Union Standard Insurance Company
St. Paul Fire and Marine Insurance Company
Travelers Insurance Companies
United Fire & Casualty Company

Shareholders

Robert G. Simmons, Jr. — (1918-1998)

True R. (Ray) Ferguson — (1921-1997)

Howard P. Olsen, Jr. — 1943 — Loras College, B.A., 1965; Creighton University, J.D., 1968 — Admitted to Bar, 1968, Nebraska; 1989, Wyoming; 1968, U.S. District Court, District of Nebraska; 1968, U.S. Court of Appeals, Eighth and Tenth Circuits; 1968, U.S. Supreme Court — Member American, Nebraska State (Chairman, House of Delegates, 1989; President, 1996-1997), Western Nebraska, Wyoming State and Scotts Bluff County Bar Associations; American Trial Lawyers Association; Nebraska Association of Trial Attorneys — City Attorney, Scottsbluff 1989-present — U.S. Army, 1968-1970

John F. Simmons — 1947 — University of Nebraska, B.A. (with honors), 1969; University of Nebraska College of Law, J.D. (with honors), 1972 — Admitted to Bar, 1972, Nebraska; 1972, U.S. District Court, District of Nebraska — Member American, Nebraska State and Scotts Bluff County Bar Associations; Defense Research Institute; American Trial Lawyers Association; Nebraska Association of Trial Attorneys

Rick L. Ediger — 1952 — Nebraska Wesleyan University, B.S., 1974; University of Nebraska College of Law, J.D., 1976 — Admitted to Bar, 1977, Nebraska; 1977, U.S. District Court, District of Nebraska — Member Nebraska State, Western Nebraska and Scotts Bluff County Bar Associations

John A. Selzer — 1952 — University of Nebraska, B.S. (with high distinction), 1974; University of Nebraska College of Law, J.D. (with distinction), 1977 — Admitted to Bar, 1977, Nebraska; 1977, U.S. District Court, District of Nebraska — Member Nebraska State and Scotts Bluff County Bar Associations

James M. Carney — 1946 — Creighton University, B.S.B.A., 1969; J.D., 1972 — Admitted to Bar, 1972, Nebraska — Member American, Nebraska State, Western Nebraska and Scotts Bluff County Bar Associations

Simmons Olsen Law Firm, P.C., Scottsbluff, NE
(Continued)

Steven W. Olsen — 1958 — College of St. Thomas, B.A., 1980; Creighton University, J.D., 1983 — Admitted to Bar, 1983, Nebraska; 1983, U.S. District Court, District of Nebraska; 1983, U.S. Court of Appeals, Eighth Circuit; 1983, U.S. Supreme Court — Member American, Nebraska State, Scotts Bluff County and Western Nebraska Bar Associations; Defense Counsel Association of Nebraska; Nebraska Association of Trial Attorneys; American Trial Lawyers Association; Defense Research Institute

Kent A. Hadenfeldt — 1963 — Kearney State College, B.S., 1985; University of Nebraska-Lincoln, J.D., 1992 — Admitted to Bar, 1992, Nebraska — Member Nebraska State and Scottsbluff County Bar Associations

Associates

Andrea D. Miller — 1980 — University of Nebraska at Kearney, B.S. (magna cum laude), 2003; University of Nebraska, J.D., 2006 — Admitted to Bar, 2006, Nebraska

John L. Selzer — 1980 — University of Nebraska, B.S.B.A., 2002; University of Nebraska College of Law, J.D., 2005 — Admitted to Bar, 2005, Nebraska

Of Counsel

Stephanie E. Trumpp — 1976 — Kansas State University, B.A., 1998; University of Denver, J.D., 2001 — Admitted to Bar, 2001, Missouri; 2002, Kansas; 2003, Colorado; 2008, Nebraska

ST. PAUL † 2,290 Howard Co.

Refer To

Leininger, Smith, Johnson, Baack, Placzek & Allen
104 North Wheeler Street
Grand Island, Nebraska 68801
   Telephone: 308-382-1930
   Fax: 308-382-5521
Mailing Address: P.O. Box 790, Grand Island, NE 68802

Insurance Defense, Automobile, Product Liability, Workers' Compensation, Employment Practices Liability, Professional Malpractice, Fire, Premises Liability, Accident, Insurance Law, General Liability, Personal Injury, Professional Liability, Property and Casualty, Commercial and Personal Lines, Insurance Coverage Litigation, Trucking, Construction Defect, Automobile Liability, Commercial General Liability, Complex Litigation, Employment Law, Employment Litigation, Estate Litigation, Appellate

SEE COMPLETE LISTING UNDER GRAND ISLAND, NEBRASKA (25 MILES)

YORK † 7,766 York Co.

Refer To

Leininger, Smith, Johnson, Baack, Placzek & Allen
104 North Wheeler Street
Grand Island, Nebraska 68801
   Telephone: 308-382-1930
   Fax: 308-382-5521
Mailing Address: P.O. Box 790, Grand Island, NE 68802

Insurance Defense, Automobile, Product Liability, Workers' Compensation, Employment Practices Liability, Professional Malpractice, Fire, Premises Liability, Accident, Insurance Law, General Liability, Personal Injury, Professional Liability, Property and Casualty, Commercial and Personal Lines, Insurance Coverage Litigation, Trucking, Construction Defect, Automobile Liability, Commercial General Liability, Complex Litigation, Employment Law, Employment Litigation, Estate Litigation, Appellate

SEE COMPLETE LISTING UNDER GRAND ISLAND, NEBRASKA (49 MILES)

NEVADA

CAPITAL: CARSON CITY

COUNTIES AND COUNTY SEATS

County	County Seat
Churchill	Fallon
Clark	Las Vegas
Douglas	Minden
Elko	Elko
Esmeralda	Goldfield
Eureka	Eureka

County	County Seat
Humboldt	Winnemucca
Lander	Battle Mountain
Lincoln	Pioche
Lyon	Yerington
Mineral	Hawthorne
Nye	Tonopah

County	County Seat
Pershing	Lovelock
Storey	Virginia City
Washoe	Reno
White Pine	Ely

In the text that follows "†" indicates County Seats.

Our files contain additional verified data on the firms listed herein. This additional information is available on request.

A.M. BEST COMPANY

NEVADA

CARSON CITY † 55,274 Independent City

Refer To
Laxalt & Nomura, Ltd.
9600 Gateway Drive
Reno, Nevada 89521-8953
Telephone: 775-322-1170
Fax: 775-322-1865

Insurance Defense, Business Litigation, Product Liability, Construction Defect, Professional Liability, Insurance Coverage & Defense, Bad Faith, Asbestos Litigation, Medical Devices, Employment Law, Personal Injury, Land Use, Appeals

SEE COMPLETE LISTING UNDER RENO, NEVADA (25 MILES)

Refer To
Thorndal, Armstrong, Delk, Balkenbush & Eisinger
A Professional Corporation
6590 South McCarran Boulevard, Suite B
Reno, Nevada 89509-6112
Telephone: 775-786-2882
Fax: 775-786-8004

Insurance Law, Trial Practice

SEE COMPLETE LISTING UNDER RENO, NEVADA (25 MILES)

ELKO † 18,297 Elko Co.

Goicoechea, Di Grazia, Coyle & Stanton, Ltd.

530 Idaho Street
Elko, Nevada 89801
Telephone: 775-738-8091
Fax: 775-738-4220
E-Mail: gdclaws@frontiernet.net
www.elkolawyers.com

Established: 1976

Insurance Defense, Automobile, Trucks/Heavy Equipment, Bodily Injury, Property Damage, Cargo

Firm Profile: The law firm now known as Goicoechea, DiGrazia, Coyle & Stanton, Ltd. was established by Gary E. DiGrazia and Robert B. Goicoechea in 1976. Over the past 34 years of service to northern Nevada, the firm has engaged in many diverse practice areas, to include extensive litigation and trial practice, insurance defense, personal injury, business and corporate law, wills and estate planning, and municipal law. Working in both federal and state courts, the firm combines the experience and expertise of its attorneys to provide each of its clients with the best possible legal representation.

Insurance Clients

American Reliable Insurance Company
Bankers and Shippers Insurance Company
Great West Casualty Company
Hartford Insurance Company
Insurance Company of Florida
Reliable Life Insurance Company
St. Paul Fire and Marine Insurance Company
Transamerica Group/AEGON USA, Inc.
American States Insurance Company
CNA Insurance Company
Fireman's Fund Insurance Companies
Industrial Indemnity Company
Nationwide General Insurance Company
Superior National Insurance Company

Non-Insurance Clients

Alternative Service Concepts, LLC

Shareholders of Goicoechea, Di Grazia, Coyle & Stanton, Ltd.

Robert B. Goicoechea — 1945 — Loyola University, B.S., 1967; The University of Utah, J.D., 1970 — Phi Alpha Delta — Admitted to Bar, 1970, Utah; 1972, Nevada; 1974, U.S. Supreme Court; 1977, U.S. District Court, District of Nevada — Member American and Elko County Bar Associations; State Bar of Nevada; Utah State Bar

CARSON CITY

Goicoechea, Di Grazia, Coyle & Stanton, Ltd., Elko, NV (Continued)

Gary E. Di Grazia — 1943 — Georgetown University, B.S., 1965; University of the Pacific, McGeorge School of Law, J.D., 1974 — Admitted to Bar, 1974, Nevada; 1977, U.S. District Court, District of Nevada; 1995, U.S. Court of Appeals, Ninth Circuit; 2002, U.S. Court of Federal Claims — Member Elko County Bar Association; Nevada State Bar (Board of Bar Examiners 1982-1994); Association of Trial Lawyers of America; Nevada Trial Lawyers Association — 1st Lt., U.S. Army, 1966-1968 — Tel: 775-738-8091 — Fax: 775-738-4220 — E-mail: gdigrazia@frontiernet.net

Thomas J. Coyle, Jr. — 1963 — University of Nevada, Reno, B.A., 1987; University of Wyoming, J.D., 1990 — Phi Kappa Phi; Delta Theta Phi — Admitted to Bar, 1990, Nevada; 1990, U.S. District Court, District of Nevada — Member State Bar of Nevada; Elko County Bar Association

David M. Stanton — 1965 — South Dakota School of Mines & Technology, B.S. (with honors), 1988; University of South Dakota, J.D., 1991 — Admitted to Bar, 1991, Nevada; 1998, U.S. District Court, District of Nevada; 1999, U.S. Court of Appeals, Ninth Circuit; 2001, U.S. Supreme Court — Member State Bar of Nevada (Fee Dispute Committee); Elko County Bar Association; Nevada Supreme Court Bench-Bar Committee; Nevada Trial Lawyers Association — U.S. Army Judge Advocate Generals Corps, 1991-1997 — Languages: Spanish — Tel: 775-738-8091 — Fax: 775-738-4220 — E-mail: davidstanton@frontiernet.net

(This firm is also listed in the Subrogation section of this directory)

The following firms also service this area.

Laxalt & Nomura, Ltd.
9600 Gateway Drive
Reno, Nevada 89521-8953
Telephone: 775-322-1170
Fax: 775-322-1865

Insurance Defense, Business Litigation, Product Liability, Construction Defect, Professional Liability, Insurance Coverage & Defense, Bad Faith, Asbestos Litigation, Medical Devices, Employment Law, Personal Injury, Land Use, Appeals

SEE COMPLETE LISTING UNDER RENO, NEVADA (240 MILES)

Mills & Associates
3650 North Rancho Drive, Suite 114
Las Vegas, Nevada 89130
Telephone: 702-240-6060
Fax: 702-240-4267

Mailing Address: P.O. Box 570040, Las Vegas, NV 89157

Alternative Dispute Resolution, Arbitration, Automobile Liability, Bad Faith, Carrier Defense, Casualty Defense, Casualty Insurance Law, Civil Litigation, Commercial Vehicle, Common Carrier, Comprehensive General Liability, Coverage Analysis, Coverage Issues, Declaratory Judgments, Defense Litigation, Dispute Resolution, Examinations Under Oath, Excess and Surplus Lines, Excess and Umbrella, Extra-Contractual Liability, Extra-Contractual Litigation, First and Third Party Defense, First and Third Party Matters, Insurance Claim Analysis and Evaluation, Insurance Coverage Determination, Insurance Coverage Litigation, Insurance Defense, Insurance Fraud, Insurance Law, Insurance Litigation, Negligence, Opinions, Personal and Commercial Vehicle, Policy Construction and Interpretation, Primary and Excess Insurance, Product Liability, Property and Casualty, Self-Insured Defense, State and Federal Courts, Transportation, Truck Liability, Trucking, Trucking Law, Trucking Liability, Trucking Litigation, Trucks/Heavy Equipment, Uninsured and Underinsured Motorist, General and Commercial Insurance Coverage, Defense Practice

SEE COMPLETE LISTING UNDER LAS VEGAS, NEVADA (430 MILES)

LAKE TAHOE 25,000 Douglas Co.

Refer To
Laxalt & Nomura, Ltd.
9600 Gateway Drive
Reno, Nevada 89521-8953
Telephone: 775-322-1170
Fax: 775-322-1865

Insurance Defense, Business Litigation, Product Liability, Construction Defect, Professional Liability, Insurance Coverage & Defense, Bad Faith, Asbestos Litigation, Medical Devices, Employment Law, Personal Injury, Land Use, Appeals

SEE COMPLETE LISTING UNDER RENO, NEVADA (60 MILES)

LAS VEGAS † 583,756 Clark Co.

Atkin Winner & Sherrod
1117 South Rancho Drive
Las Vegas, Nevada 89102
Telephone: 702-243-7000
Fax: 702-243-7059
E-Mail: hr@awslawyers.com
www.awslawyers.com

Established: 2004

Automobile Liability, Civil Trial Practice, Bad Faith, Examinations Under Oath, Insurance Fraud, Insurance Coverage, Construction Defect, Workers' Compensation, Premises Liability, Public Liability, Appellate Practice, Civil Litigation

Insurance Clients

AAA Nevada Insurance Company
American Access Casualty Company
American Family Insurance Company
Civil Service Employees Group
CNA Insurance Company
Fred Loya Insurance
The Hartford
Lincoln General Insurance Company
Nationwide Mutual Insurance Company
Scottsdale Insurance Company
State Farm Fire and Casualty Company
Titan Insurance Company
Travelers Insurance Company
Western National Mutual Insurance Company
Allstate Property & Casualty Insurance Company
American Bankers Insurance Group
American National Property and Casualty Company
Farmers Insurance Group
Gallagher Bassett Services, Inc.
Horace Mann Insurance Company
Mercury Insurance Company
National Guaranty Insurance Company
Santa Fe Auto Insurance Company
Sedgwick Claims Management Services, Inc.
State Farm Mutual Automobile Insurance Company
21st Century Insurance Company
Young America Insurance Company

Non-Insurance Clients

Fraternal Order of Police - (FOP)
Sears Holdings Corporation
Kmart Corporation
Swift Transportation Company, Inc.

Partners and Members

Trevor L. Atkin — 1962 — Arizona State University, B.A., 1984; University of the Pacific, McGeorge School of Law, J.D., 1987 — Admitted to Bar, 1987, Nevada; U.S. District Court, District of Nevada; 1990, U.S. Supreme Court — Member State Bar of Nevada — E-mail: tatkin@awslawyers.com

Thomas E. Winner — 1966 — University of Nebraska, B.A. (with distinction), 1990; J.D., 1993 — Admitted to Bar, 1993, Nevada; U.S. District Court, District of Nevada; 1999, U.S. Court of Appeals, Ninth Circuit — Member State Bar of Nevada; Defense Research Institute — E-mail: twinner@awslawyers.com

Susan M. Sherrod — 1953 — Western Michigan University, B.A., 1975; Detroit College of Law, J.D., 1991 — Admitted to Bar, 1992, Michigan; 1994, Nevada; 1992, U.S. District Court, Eastern District of Michigan; 1994, U.S. District Court, District of Nevada — Member State Bar of Nevada; Defense Research Institute — E-mail: ssherrod@awslawyers.com

Christine M. Booze — 1964 — University of Oregon School of Law, J.D., 1999 — Admitted to Bar, 2001, Nevada; U.S. District Court, District of Nevada — Member State Bar of Nevada — E-mail: cbooze@awslawyers.com

Matthew J. Douglas — 1974 — University of Illinois at Urbana-Champaign, B.A., 1996; Chicago-Kent College of Law, J.D., 1999 — Admitted to Bar, 1999, Illinois; 2009, Nevada; 1999, U.S. District Court, Northern District of Illinois; 2009, U.S. District Court, District of Nevada — Member State Bar of Nevada — E-mail: mdouglas@awslawyers.com

Justin J. Zarcone — 1974 — University of Wisconsin-Milwaukee, B.S., 1997; Thomas M. Cooley Law School, J.D., 2001; University of San Diego School of Law, LL.M., 2002 — Admitted to Bar, 2001, California; 2003, Nevada; 2002, U.S. Tax Court; 2003, U.S. District Court, District of Nevada; 2004, U.S. Court of Appeals, Ninth Circuit — Member State Bar of Nevada — E-mail: jzarcone@awslawyers.com

Atkin Winner & Sherrod, Las Vegas, NV (Continued)

Associates

Nicholas L. Hamilton — 1979 — Texas Tech University, B.S., 2005; Drake University Law School, J.D., 2005 — Admitted to Bar, 2007, Texas; 2008, Nevada; 2009, U.S. District Court, District of Nevada — Member State Bar of Nevada — E-mail: nhamilton@awslawyers.com

Scott R. Pettitt — 1982 — Brigham Young University, B.A., 2006; University of Connecticut School of Law, J.D., 2009 — Admitted to Bar, 2009, Nevada; U.S. District Court, District of Nevada — Member State Bar of Nevada — E-mail: spettitt@awslawyers.com

Andrew D. Smith — 1973 — Weber State University, B.A., 1998; Washburn University School of Law, J.D., 2001 — Admitted to Bar, 2003, Utah; 2004, Nevada; 2003, U.S. District Court, District of Utah; 2004, U.S. District Court, District of Nevada — Member State Bar of Nevada; Utah State Bar — E-mail: asmith@awslawyers.com

Michael R. Smith — 1976 — Mississippi State University, B.S., 2001; Mississippi College School of Law, J.D., 2010 — Admitted to Bar, 2012, Nevada; U.S. District Court, District of Nevada — Member State Bar of Nevada — E-Mail: msmith@awslawyers.com

Steven P. Canfield — 1986 — Brigham Young University, B.A., 2009; University of Nebraska, J.D., 2012 — Admitted to Bar, 2012, Nevada; U.S. District Court, District of Nevada — Member State Bar of Nevada — E-mail: scanfield@awslawyers.com

Phil W. Su — 1980 — University of California, Berkeley, B.A., 2002; University of California, Hastings College of the Law, J.D., 2005 — Admitted to Bar, 2007, Nevada; 2007, California; 2012, North Carolina; 2007, U.S. District Court, District of Nevada — Member State Bar of Nevada; State Bar of California; North Carolina State Bar — E-mail: psu@awslawyers.com

Craig W. DuFord — 1984 — Fordham University, B.A., 2007; California Western School of Law, J.D., 2011 — Admitted to Bar, 2012, Nevada; U.S. District Court, District of Nevada; Supreme Court of Nevada — Member State Bar of Nevada — E-mail: cduford@awslawyers.com

Kelly E. DuFord — 1986 — University of San Diego, B.A., 2009; California Western School of Law, J.D., 2011 — Admitted to Bar, 2012, Nevada; 2013, California — E-mail: kduford@awslawyers.com

Christian A. Miles — 1986 — Brigham Young University, B.S., 2010; University of Cincinnati College of Law, J.D., 2013 — Admitted to Bar, 2013, Nevada; U.S. District Court, District of Nevada — E-mail: cmiles@awslawyers.com

J. Taylor Oblad — University of Nevada, B.A., 2005; California Western School of Law, J.D., 2008 — Admitted to Bar, Nevada; 2009, California — E-mail: joblad@awslawyers.com

Of Counsel

Bruce W. Kelley — 1964 — University of Nebraska, B.A., 1987; J.D., 1993 — Admitted to Bar, 1993, California; 2000, Nevada; U.S. District Court, District of Nevada — Member State Bar of Nevada — E-mail: bkelley@awslawyers.com

Kimberly L. Johnson — The Pennsylvania State University, B.A., 1999; New England School of Law, J.D., 2002 — Admitted to Bar, 2002, California; 2007, Nevada — E-mail: kjohnson@awslawyers.com

Backus · Carranza
3050 South Durango Drive
Las Vegas, Nevada 89117
Telephone: 702-872-5555
Fax: 702-872-5545
E-Mail: ecarranza@backuslaw.com
www.backuslaw.com

Established: 1997

General Defense, Professional Liability, Commercial General Liability, Employment Discrimination, Employment Practices Liability, Sexual Harassment, Wrongful Termination

Firm Profile: Backus Carranza was founded in 1997 with the goal of providing aggressive, cost-effective representation through the enhanced use of technology while affording clients the personal attention expected of a small law firm. Having succeeded in this goal, the firm's growing practice ranges from local representation of international corporations in multi-state complex

Backus · Carranza, Las Vegas, NV (Continued)

litigation to the defense of Nevada professionals and businesses against malpractice, products liability, construction defect and negligence claims.

Insurance Clients

AXA Corporate Solutions
Church Mutual Insurance Company
General Casualty Companies
Highlands Insurance Company
Kemper Insurance Company
Markel Insurance Company
Northwestern National Insurance Company
Reliant American Insurance Company
United Ohio Insurance Company
Vesta Fire Insurance Corporation
Canal Insurance Company
E & O Professionals
Great American Insurance Company
K & K Insurance Group, Inc.
NCMIC Insurance Company
Old Republic Title Insurance Group
Travelers Property Casualty Insurance Company
United States Liability Insurance Group

Non-Insurance Clients

Karol Western Corporation
Office Depot, Inc.
Star Transit, LLC
McDonald's Corporation
Star Limousine, LLC

Partners

Leland E. Backus — 1947 — College of Southern Utah; University of Nevada, Las Vegas, B.S., 1969; University of California, Los Angeles, J.D., 1972 — Admitted to Bar, 1972, California; 1973, Nevada; 1979, U.S. Supreme Court — Member American Bar Association (Construction Management, Defense/Build and Related Concepts Division); Clark County Bar Association (Sections: Litigation and Public Contracts; Forum Committee on the Construction Industry); State Bar of Nevada (Disciplinary Board, 1979-1987); State Bar of California; Eagle International Associates; American Health Lawyers Association

Edgar Carranza — 1969 — The University of Texas, B.A. (with honors), 1990; Arizona State University, J.D., 1994 — Admitted to Bar, 1996, Nevada; 1996, U.S. District Court, District of Nevada; 2000, U.S. Court of Appeals, Ninth Circuit; 2001, U.S. Supreme Court — Member American, Hispanic National, Latino and Clark County Bar Associations; Defense Research Institute (Sections: Food Liability Law; Employment Law) — Languages: Spanish

Jack P. Burden — 1970 — University of Nevada, B.A., 1993; Texas Southern University, J.D., 1998 — Admitted to Bar, 1999, Nevada; 1999, U.S. District Court, District of Nevada — Member State Bar of Nevada

Associates

Shea A. Backus — University of California, San Diego, B.S., 1998; Arizona State University, J.D. (with honors), 2003 — Admitted to Bar, 2003, Nevada; 2004, U.S. District Court, District of Nevada — Member Federal, Native American and Clark County Bar Associations

James J. Conway — 1977 — University of Nevada, Las Vegas, B.S. Business Admin., 2000; William S. Boyd School of Law, University of Nevada, Las Vegas, J.D., 2010 — Admitted to Bar, 2010, Nevada

Barron & Pruitt, LLP

3890 West Ann Road
North Las Vegas, Nevada 89031
   Telephone: 702-870-3940
   Fax: 702-870-3950
   E-Mail: bvhp@lvnvlaw.com
   www.barronpruitt.com

(Orem, UT Office*: 204 East 860 South, 84058-5013)
   (Tel: 801-802-6363)

Barron & Pruitt, LLP, Las Vegas, NV (Continued)

Appellate Practice, Asbestos Litigation, Automobile Liability, Bad Faith, Civil Litigation, Commercial Vehicle, Common Carrier, Complex Litigation, Construction Defect, Coverage Issues, Environmental Liability, Excess, First and Third Party Defense, Garage Liability, Insurance Coverage, Motor Carriers, Negligence, Personal Injury, Premises Liability, Primary and Excess Insurance, Product Liability, Professional Liability, Property Damage, Self-Insured Defense, Surety, Transportation, Trial and Appellate Practice, Trucks/Heavy Equipment, Uninsured and Underinsured Motorist, Wrongful Death

Firm Profile: Barron & Pruitt, LLP is a litigation-oriented firm that proudly serves the needs of the insurers, policy holders and business communities of Nevada and Utah. Our goal is simple: Form sound relationships with our clients and assist in managing their personal and business risks and liabilities.

Insurance Clients

AIG
American Equity Insurance Company
Chubb & Son, Inc.
Federated American Insurance Company
GAB Robins North America, Inc.
Golden Eagle Insurance Corporation
Hawkeye-Security Insurance Company
International Fidelity Insurance Company
Mitsui Sumitomo Insurance Group
Ohio Casualty Insurance Company
Peerless Insurance Company
USAA
Wausau General Insurance Company
Western Heritage Insurance Company
America First Insurance
Auto-Owners Insurance Company
Berkley Mid-Atlantic Insurance Company
Colorado Casualty Insurance Company
Fireman's Fund Insurance Company
Guaranty National Insurance Company
Hudson Insurance Company
Indiana Insurance Company
Lexington Insurance Company
Liberty Mutual Insurance Company
Nevada General Insurance Company
Underwriters at Lloyd's, London
U.S. Liability Insurance Company
Wells Fargo/Wachovia Insurance Services, Inc.
Zurich North America

Non-Insurance Clients

Black & Decker
Covanta Energy Corporation
Dover Corporation
Turner Construction Company
Yamaha Motor Corporation, U.S.A.
CCMSI
Crawford & Company
Escalera Landscaping, Inc.
The Whiting-Turner Contracting Company

Partners

David Barron — The University of Utah, B.S. (magna cum laude), 1977; University of the Pacific, McGeorge School of Law, J.D., 1980 — Admitted to Bar, 1981, California; 1981, Nevada; 1981, U.S. District Court, District of Nevada; 1983, U.S. District Court, Central District of California; 1990, U.S. Court of Appeals, Ninth Circuit; 1995, U.S. Supreme Court — Member American Bar Association; Association of Defense Counsel, Northern California; Association of Defense Counsel of Nevada; Defense Research Institute

William H. Pruitt — Brigham Young University, B.A., 1987; University of Idaho, J.D. (magna cum laude), 1990 — Admitted to Bar, 1991, Utah; 1998, Nevada; 1991, U.S. District Court, District of Utah; 1998, U.S. District Court, District of Nevada — Member American Bar Association; Utah State Bar; State Bar of Nevada; Defense Research Institute — Languages: Spanish

Peter Mazzeo — University of Bridgeport, B.S. (cum laude), 1983; Brooklyn Law School, J.D., 1988 — Admitted to Bar, 1989, New York; 2005, Nevada; 1989, U.S. District Court, Eastern and Southern Districts of New York

Associates

Joshua A. Sliker
Darren T. Rodriguez

Kent Law

9440 West Sahara Avenue, Suite 215
Las Vegas, Nevada 89117
   Telephone: 702-930-5368
   Fax: 775-324-9803
   E-Mail: skent@skentlaw.com
   www.skentlaw.com

(Reno, NV Office*: 201 West Liberty Street, Suite 320, 89501)
   (Tel: 775-324-9800)
   (Fax: 775-324-9803)

Established: 2010

Aviation, Bad Faith, Construction Defect, Insurance Defense, Insurance Coverage Litigation, Premises Liability, Real Estate, Securities, Trial and Appellate Practice, Truck, Bus, Marine, Civil Sexual Assault, Personal Injury Defense, Professional Liability (Civil Engineer, Structural Engineer, Real Estate Agent and Broker)

(See listing under Reno, NV for additional information)

Laxalt & Nomura, Ltd.

6720 Via Austi Parkway, Suite 430
Las Vegas, Nevada 89119
   Telephone: 725-388-1551
   Fax: 725-388-1559

(Reno, NV Office*: 9600 Gateway Drive, 89521-8953)
   (Tel: 775-322-1170)
   (Fax: 775-322-1865)
   (Emer/After Hrs: 775-786-3035)
   (Mobile: 775-762-8545)
   (E-Mail: dhayward@laxalt-nomura.com)
   (www.laxalt-nomura.com)

Established: 1986

Insurance Defense, Business Litigation, Product Liability, Construction Defect, Professional Liability, Insurance Coverage & Defense, Bad Faith, Asbestos Litigation, Medical Devices, Employment Law, Personal Injury, Land Use, Appeals

(See listing under Reno, NV for additional information)

Long Blumberg, LLP

7674 W. Lake Mead Boulevard, Suite 245
Las Vegas, Nevada 89128
   Telephone: 877-941-0090
   Fax: 877-941-0085
   www.longblumberg.com

Personal Injury, Construction Defect, Product Liability, Insurance Litigation, Asbestos, Subrogation, General Civil Litigation

Firm Profile: Over the past 25 years, Long Blumberg, LLP's experience and knowledge has given us the unique ability to skillfully handle a full range of extraordinary legal issues. We have dedicated ourselves to the highest level of legal representation and have consistently maintained a successful record.

(See listing under Walnut Creek, CA for additional information)

Mills & Associates

3650 North Rancho Drive, Suite 114
Las Vegas, Nevada 89130
   Telephone: 702-240-6060
   Fax: 702-240-4267
   E-Mail: mike@mcmillslaw.com
   www.NevadaInsuranceLaw.com
   www.NVCoverageLaw.com
   www.NVTruckingLaw.com

Established: 1997

Alternative Dispute Resolution, Arbitration, Automobile Liability, Bad Faith, Carrier Defense, Casualty Defense, Casualty Insurance Law, Civil Litigation, Commercial Vehicle, Common Carrier, Comprehensive General Liability, Coverage Analysis, Coverage Issues, Declaratory Judgments, Defense Litigation, Dispute Resolution, Examinations Under Oath, Excess and Surplus Lines, Excess and Umbrella, Extra-Contractual Liability, Extra-Contractual Litigation, First and Third Party Defense, First and Third Party Matters, Insurance Claim Analysis and Evaluation, Insurance Coverage Determination, Insurance Coverage Litigation, Insurance Defense, Insurance Fraud, Insurance Law, Insurance Litigation, Negligence, Opinions, Personal and Commercial Vehicle, Policy Construction and Interpretation, Primary and Excess Insurance, Product Liability, Property and Casualty, Self-Insured Defense, State and Federal Courts, Transportation, Truck Liability, Trucking, Trucking Law, Trucking Liability, Trucking Litigation, Trucks/Heavy Equipment, Uninsured and Underinsured Motorist, General and Commercial Insurance Coverage, Defense Practice

Firm Profile: Mills & Associates is a full service civil litigation coverage and defense firm. At Mills & Associates, we provide competent and cost effective legal counsel to all of our clients. The primary focus of our practice is coverage opinions, first-party claims/litigation and the defense of clients at the request of their insurance carriers. Our areas of emphasis also include defense of trucking, bodily injury, products liability, and professional malpractice. We are prepared to explore and exercise all options that may benefit the client, including settlement, mediation, arbitration, trial and appeal.

Counsel For

Acme Claims Service

Insurance Clients

Ameriprise Auto & Home Insurance	Dairyland Insurance Company
Global Hawk Insurance Company	FedEx Ground Risk Management
Grange Insurance Company	GoAuto Insurance
Great West Casualty Company	Great American Insurance Company
IDS Property Casualty Insurance Company	Infinity Insurance Company
National American Insurance Company	Littleton Group
National Unity Insurance Company	National Interstate Insurance Company
Sentry Insurance	Nevada General Insurance Company
State National Insurance Company, Inc.	USAA Insurance Company
Viking Insurance Company	Vanliner Insurance Company
Western National Mutual Insurance Company	Western General Insurance Company

Local Counsel For

Seyfarth Shaw

Partner

Michael C. Mills — 1956 — The University of Utah, J.D., 1983 — Admitted to Bar, 1983, Utah; 1988, Nevada; 1983, U.S. District Court, District of Utah; 1988, U.S. District Court, District of Nevada; 1988, U.S. Court of Appeals, Ninth Circuit; 2003, U.S. Supreme Court — Member State Bar of Nevada; Utah State Bar; Defense Research Institute (DRI); Nevada Motor Transport Association (General Counsel); Trucking Insurance Defense Association (TIDA); Utah Trucking Association — Judge Pro Tempore in the Nevada Short Trial Program — Certified Mediator; Certified Arbitrator (Nevada Court-Annexed Alternative Dispute Resolution Program) — U.S. Army

NEVADA / LAS VEGAS

Mills & Associates, Las Vegas, NV (Continued)

Judge Advocate Generals Corps.; Ret. Lt. Col., Nevada National Guard — Practice Areas: Trucking Liability; Insurance Coverage; Bad Faith; Insurance Defense; Product Liability; Personal Injury — E-mail: mike@mcmillslaw.com

Morales Fierro & Reeves

600 South Tonopah Drive, Suite 300
Las Vegas, Nevada 89106
   Telephone: 702-699-7822
   Fax: 702-699-9455

(Pleasant Hill, CA Office*: 2300 Contra Costa Boulevard, Suite 310, 94523)
   (Tel: 925-288-1776)
   (Fax: 925-288-1856)
   (E-Mail: LawOffice@mfrlegal.com)
   (www.mfrlegal.com)
(Phoenix, AZ Office: 3420 East Shea Boulevard, Suite 200, 85028)
   (Tel: 602-258-0755)
   (Fax: 602-258-0757)

Insurance Litigation, Coverage Analysis, Insurance Coverage, Bad Faith, Subrogation, Construction Defect, Workers' Compensation, Probate, Civil Trial Practice

Insurance Clients

ACE USA
HDI-Gerling America Insurance Company
Zurich North America
America First/One Beacon Insurance Company
Travelers Insurance Group

(See listing under Pleasant Hill, CA for additional information)

Murchison & Cumming, LLP

6900 Westcliff Drive, Suite 605
Las Vegas, Nevada 89145
   Telephone: 702-360-3956
   Fax: 702-360-3957

Civil Litigation, Business Transactions

(See listing under Los Angeles, CA for additional information)

Olson, Cannon, Gormley Angulo & Stoberski
A Professional Corporation

9950 West Cheyenne Avenue
Las Vegas, Nevada 89129-7544
   Telephone: 702-384-4012
   Fax: 702-383-0701
   www.ocgas.com

Established: 1960

Insurance Defense, Automobile, General Liability, Property Damage, Casualty, Errors and Omissions, Professional Liability, Medical Malpractice, Bodily Injury, Product Liability, Governmental Liability

Insurance Clients

Allianz Insurance Company
Allstate Reinsurance Company
American International Group, Inc.
American International Recovery, Inc.
Allstate Insurance Company
American Home Assurance Company
American Reliable Insurance Company

Olson, Cannon, Gormley Angulo & Stoberski, A Professional Corporation, Las Vegas, NV (Continued)

Amwest Surety Insurance Company
Bituminous Insurance Companies
California Casualty Insurance Company
Canal Insurance Company
CIGNA Insurance Company
Colonial Penn Insurance Company
Crum & Forster Insurance Group
The Doctors Company
Frontier Adjusters
Great American Insurance Company
The Hartford Insurance Group
Hawkeye-Security Insurance Company
Leader Insurance Company
Liberty Mutual Insurance Company
Maryland Casualty Company
Minnesota Life Insurance Company
Northbrook Property and Casualty Insurance Company
Occidental Fire & Casualty Company of North Carolina
Scott Wetzel Services, Inc.
Sentry Claims Services
Shand Morahan & Company, Inc.
Transport Insurance Company
Wausau General Insurance Company
Zurich Insurance Company
Associated Aviation Underwriters
Atlantic Casualty Insurance Company
California State Automobile Association
Chubb/Pacific Indemnity Company
CNA Insurance Company
Columbia Casualty Company
Custard Insurance Adjusters, Inc.
First State Insurance Company
GAB Robins North America, Inc.
Gresham Insurance Adjusters
Guaranty National Insurance Company
Home Insurance Company
Lancer Claims Services, Inc.
Lexington Insurance Company
Lincoln Insurance Group
Medical Insurance Exchange of California
Northbrook Excess & Surplus Insurance Company
Northland Insurance Company
Royal Insurance Company
Scottsdale Insurance Company
Self Insured Management Services, Inc.
Tokio Marine Management, Inc.
Travelers Property Casualty Corporation
Zurich American Insurance Group

Non-Insurance Clients

Albertsons, Inc.
Caesars Palace
Catholic Healthcare West
Clark County
General Star Manufacturing Company
London Agency, Inc.
McLarens Toplis North America, Inc.
The Salvation Army
Terra West Realty
University of Nevada, Las Vegas
Avis Rent-A-Car System, LLC
Carroon & Black
Chrysler Corporation
Crawford & Company
Honda North America, Inc.
Las Vegas Metropolitan Police Department
Michael Bland & Associates
Montevista Centre
State Farm Claims Office
University Medical Center
Value Rent-A-Car, Inc.

Firm Members

James R. Olson — 1948 — University of Nevada, B.S. (with high distinction), 1971; The University of Arizona, J.D. (with distinction), 1974 — Admitted to Bar, 1974, Nevada; 1975, U.S. District Court, District of Nevada; 1981, U.S. Court of Appeals, Ninth Circuit; 1982, U.S. Supreme Court — Member American College of Trial Lawyers; American Board of Trial Advocates

Walter R. Cannon — 1946 — California State University, Los Angeles, B.A. (magna cum laude), 1972; University of San Diego, J.D., 1975 — Admitted to Bar, 1975, California; 1976, Nevada; 1975, U.S. District Court, Central District of California; 1976, U.S. District Court, District of Nevada; 1977, U.S. Court of Appeals, Ninth Circuit; 1982, U.S. Supreme Court

John E. Gormley — 1949 — Susquehanna University, B.A., 1971; Duquesne University, J.D., 1974 — Admitted to Bar, 1974, Pennsylvania; 1979, Nevada; 1979, U.S. Court of Military Appeals; U.S. District Court, District of Nevada; U.S. Court of Appeals, Ninth Circuit

Peter M. Angulo — 1959 — Arizona State University, B.S., 1985; J. Reuben Clark Law School, Brigham Young University, J.D., 1989 — Admitted to Bar, 1989, Nevada; 1989, U.S. District Court, District of Nevada; 1989, U.S. Court of Appeals, Ninth Circuit

Michael E. Stoberski — 1966 — University of San Diego, B.A., 1988; J.D., 1991 — Admitted to Bar, 1991, California; 1992, Nevada; 1991, U.S. District Court, Southern District of California; 1991, U.S. Court of Appeals, Ninth Circuit; 1992, U.S. District Court, District of Nevada

Michael A. Federico — 1971 — University at Buffalo, B.S. (cum laude), 1993; M.B.A., 1995; University of Houston, J.D., 1996 — Admitted to Bar, 1996, Nevada; 1996, U.S. District Court, District of Nevada; 1998, U.S. Court of Appeals, Ninth Circuit — Member Clark County Bar Association; Italian American Lawyers Association

Thomas D. Dillard Jr. — 1969 — The University of Utah, B.S. (magna cum laude), 1994; J.D., 1997 — Admitted to Bar, 1997, Nevada; 1997, U.S. District Court, District of Nevada; 2002, U.S. Supreme Court — Member American and Clark County Bar Associations

LAS VEGAS / NEVADA

Olson, Cannon, Gormley Angulo & Stoberski, A Professional Corporation, Las Vegas, NV (Continued)

Max E. Corrick — 1972 — University of Virginia, B.A., 1994; Washington University, J.D., 1998 — Admitted to Bar, 1998, Nevada; 1998, U.S. District Court, District of Nevada — Member Clark County Bar Association; American Trial Lawyers Association; Nevada Trial Lawyers Association

Felicia Galati — 1966 — York University, B.A., 1987; The University of Western Ontario, LL.B., 1990 — Admitted to Bar, 1992, Ontario; 2000, Nevada; U.S. District Court, District of Nevada; U.S. Court of Appeals, Ninth Circuit — Member American and Clark County Bar Associations

Raymond E. McKay — William S. Boyd School of Law, University of Nevada, Las Vegas, J.D., 2003 — Admitted to Bar, 2003, Nevada; U.S. District Court, District of Nevada; 2004, U.S. Court of Appeals, Ninth Circuit — State Bar of Nevada Arbitrator and Mediator, Fee Dispute Arbitration Committee, (2006-present)

Associates

Christopher J. Richardson
Matthew A. Cavanaugh
Whitney L. Welch
Joslyn D. Shapiro
Brandon P. Smith
Stephanie Zinna

Of Counsel

Richard C. Maurer — (1944-2001)

William S. Boyd
George R. Lyles

Prince & Keating, LLP

9130 West Russell Road, Suite 200
Las Vegas, Nevada 89148
  Telephone: 702-228-6800
  Fax: 702-228-0443
  E-Mail: dprince@princekeating.com
  www.princekeating.com

Established: 2000

Automobile, Construction Defect, Environmental Law, Insurance Law, Premises Liability, Product Liability, Professional Negligence, Property and Casualty, Surety

Insurance Clients

Allstate Insurance Company
Contractors Liability Insurance Company, RRG
Esurance
Financial Pacific Insurance Company
Hanover Insurance Group
Kemper/Unitrin
Progressive Insurance Company
American National Property and Casualty Company
Encompass Insurance Company
Federated Service Insurance Company
First American Property & Casualty Insurance Company
Metropolitan Property and Casualty Insurance Company

Partners

Dennis M. Prince — 1967 — University of Nevada, Las Vegas, B.S. (with distinction), 1990; California Western School of Law, J.D. (magna cum laude), 1993 — Admitted to Bar, 1993, Nevada; U.S. District Court, District of Nevada; 2000, U.S. Court of Appeals, Ninth Circuit — Member American (Sections: Business Law, Litigation, Tort and Insurance) and Clark County Bar Associations; State Bar of Nevada; Nevada American Inn of Court; American Board of Trial Advocacy (ABOTA)

John T. Keating — 1970 — University of Nevada, Las Vegas, B.S., 1993; Creighton University, J.D., 1996 — Admitted to Bar, 1997, Nevada; U.S. District Court, District of Nevada — Member American (Young Lawers Division) and Clark County Bar Associations; State Bar of Nevada (Young Lawyers Division); American Board of Trial Advocacy (ABOTA)

Richard A. Englemann — 1961 — Southern Utah State College, B.S., 1988; Hamline University, J.D. (cum laude), 1999 — Admitted to Bar, 1999, Nevada; U.S. District Court, District of Nevada; 2000, U.S. Court of Appeals, Ninth Circuit — Member State Bar of Nevada; Clark County Bar Association; Nevada Trial Lawyers Association

Prince & Keating, LLP, Las Vegas, NV (Continued)

Associates

Garnet Beal — 1986 — New Mexico State University, B.S., 2009; Drake University Law School, J.D., 2012 — Admitted to Bar, 2012, Nevada; U.S. District Court, District of Nevada — Member State Bar of Nevada

Bryce B. Buckwalter — 1974 — University of Nevada, B.S.B.A., 1998; Whittier Law School, J.D., 2001 — Admitted to Bar, 2001, Nevada; 2002, Utah — Member State Bar of Nevada; Utah State Bar; Clark County Bar Association; American Trial Lawyers Association; Nevada Trial Lawyers Association

Ian C. Estrada — 1982 — University of California, Los Angeles, B.A. Political Science, 2006; Loyola Law School Los Angeles, J.D., 2009 — Admitted to Bar, 2009, California; 2012, Nevada

Michael Lafia — 1982 — Yale University, B.A., 2005; University of Nevada, Las Vegas, J.D., 2012 — Admitted to Bar, 2013, Nevada; U.S. District Court, District of Nevada — Member State Bar of Nevada; Nevada Society of Italian American Lawyers

Christina Mamer — University of Nevada, Las Vegas, B.A., 2008; J.D., 2012 — Admitted to Bar, 2013, Nevada; U.S. District Court, District of Nevada — Member State Bar of Nevada; Clark County Bar Association

Stephenson & Dickinson, P.C.

2820 West Charleston Boulevard, Suite 19
Las Vegas, Nevada 89102
  Telephone: 702-474-7229
  Fax: 702-474-7237
  Toll Free: 800-947-7229
  E-Mail: admin@sdlawoffice.net

Established: 1997

Insurance Defense, Product Liability, Coverage Issues, Bad Faith, Trucking Law, Transportation, Construction Defect, Premises Liability, Automobile

Insurance Clients

AAA Alaska Insurance Company
Affirmative Risk Management, Inc.
AXIS Insurance
Baldwin & Lyons, Inc.
Central Mutual Insurance Company
Claims Management Services, Inc.
Command Insurance Managers, Inc.
Crawford & Company
Deep South Insurance Services
Endurance Services, Ltd.
Financial Pacific Insurance Company
Gallagher Bassett Services, Inc.
Grocers Insurance Company
HDI-Gerling America Insurance Company
Interstate Insurance Group
Liberty Mutual Insurance Company
Mattei Insurance Services, Inc.
Midland Claims Administrators, Inc.
National Claims Management
National Transportation Adjusters, Inc.
Nevada Insurance Guaranty Association
Pinnacle Risk Management Services
Risk Enterprise Management, Ltd.
Scottsdale Insurance Company
Self Insured Management Services, Inc.
Specialty Claims, Incorporated
Specialty Claims Management, LLC
Transportation Claims, Inc.
21st Century Insurance Company
Administrative Claim Service
American Management Claims Administrators
Canal Insurance Company
Claims Control, Inc.
Colony Specialty
Commercial Truck Claims Management
Criterion Claim Solutions
Empire Insurance Group
Everest National Insurance Company
First Financial Insurance Company
General Security Insurance Company
Hudson Insurance Company
Indemnity Insurance Corporation
Lancer Insurance Company
LMS Risk Management Services
McLane Claims Management, Inc.
Milwaukee Insurance Company
National Casualty Company
National Interstate Insurance Company
Nationwide Insurance Enterprise
Nobel Insurance Services
Philadelphia Insurance Companies
Pioneer State Mutual Insurance Company
RLI Insurance Company
Sedgwick Claims Management Services, Inc.
SISCO Self Insured Services Company
TransGuard Insurance Company of America, Inc.
Travelers Property Casualty Insurance Company

Stephenson & Dickinson, P.C., Las Vegas, NV (Continued)

United Fire Group (FPIC West Coast Regional Office Branch)
Western Mutual Insurance Company
Westport Insurance Company
Vanliner Insurance Company
Western Heritage Insurance Company
Western National Insurance Group

Non-Insurance Clients

American Fence and Security Company, Inc.
Carrier Corporation
Commercial Truck Claims
Interstate Distributor Company
Interstate Management Group
National Food Processors Association
Pacific Coast Building Products
PFT Roberson
Specialty Moving Systems, Inc.
Truck Claims, Inc.
USF Bestway
Wal-Mart Transportation
Werner Company, Inc.
Werner Enterprises, Inc.
Atlas Van Lines, Inc.
Marie Callender's Pie Shops, Inc.
Caterpillar Inc.
Constitution State Service Company
Isis Unlimited, Inc.
North American Van Lines
PACCAR, Inc.
Penske Auto Centers, Inc.
R.D. Werner Company, Inc.
Transport Corporation of America, Inc.
Wal-Mart Stores, Inc.
Watkins Associated Companies (WACO)
Yellow Freight System

Principals and Shareholders

Marsha L. Stephenson — Eastern Montana College, B.A. (with honors), 1972; Montana State University, M.S., 1974; University of the Pacific, McGeorge School of Law, J.D. (with honors), 1983 — Order of the Coif — Admitted to Bar, 1983, California; 1997, Nevada; 1987, U.S. District Court, Central and Eastern Districts of California; 1997, U.S. District Court, District of Nevada — Member American (Construction Defect Committee) and Clark County Bar Associations; State Bar of Nevada; State Bar of California; Association of Defense Counsel, Nevada; National Board of Civil Trial Advocacy; American Board of Trial Advocates; Defense Research Institute — E-mail: mstephenson@sdlawoffice.net

Bruce Scott Dickinson — 1953 — The University of Arizona, B.A., 1975; J.D., 1979 — Note and Comment Editor, Arizona Law Review — Admitted to Bar, 1979, Arizona; 1980, Nevada; U.S. District Court, District of Nevada; 1981, U.S. Court of Appeals, Ninth Circuit — Member American Bar Association (Vice-Chair, Commercial Transportation Litigation Section, 1997-1998); State Bar of Nevada; State Bar of Arizona; Coalition of Food Industry Counsel; Trucking Industry Defense Association (Founding Member, 1993; Director, 1995-2004; President, 2001-2003); Product Liability Advisory Council; Master, American Inn of Court; Federation of Defense and Corporate Counsel; Defense Research Institute; Transportation Lawyers Association — E-mail: bdickinson@sdlawoffice.net

Associates

Michael Hottman — 1956 — Lewis Clark State University, B.S., 2001; William S. Boyd School of Law, University of Nevada, Las Vegas, J.D., 2004 — Admitted to Bar, 2005, Nevada; U.S. District Court, District of Nevada — Member American and Clark County Bar Associations — Practice Areas: Civil Litigation; Insurance Defense — E-mail: mhottman@sdlawoffice.net

Steven K. Gage II — Valparaiso School of Law, J.D., 2010 — Admitted to Bar, 2010, Nevada

Thorndal, Armstrong, Delk, Balkenbush & Eisinger
A Professional Corporation

1100 East Bridger Avenue
Las Vegas, Nevada 89101
Telephone: 702-366-0622
Fax: 702-366-0327
E-Mail: info@thorndal.com
www.thorndal.com

(Reno, NV Office*: 6590 South McCarran Boulevard, Suite B, 89509-6112)
(Tel: 775-786-2882)
(Fax: 775-786-8004)

Established: 1971

Insurance Law, Trial Practice

Thorndal, Armstrong, Delk, Balkenbush & Eisinger, A Professional Corporation, Las Vegas, NV (Continued)

Firm Profile: Founded in Las Vegas in 1971, the firm has grown from two lawyers to nearly thirty. It has expanded its statewide services with the opening of offices in Reno and Elko.

Insurance Clients

Chubb Group
First Mercury Insurance Company
Liberty Mutual
Nevada Public Agency Insurance Pool
United States Aviation Underwriters, Inc.
Zurich North America
Cincinnati Insurance Company
Gallagher Bassett Services, Inc.
Lloyd's of London
Travelers Insurance
United States Aircraft Insurance Group
U.S. Liability Insurance Company

Non-Insurance Clients

Boyd Gaming Corporation
Frias Transportation Management
Delta Air Lines, Inc.
Lowe's HIW, Inc.

Firm Members

John L. Thorndal — 1936 — The University of North Dakota, B.S.B.A., 1958; University of Denver, J.D., 1965 — Admitted to Bar, 1965, Colorado; 1967, Nevada; 1971, U.S. Supreme Court — Member Federal Bar Association (Vice President, 1978-1979); American and Clark County (President, 1976; Vice-President, 1974-1975; Treasurer, 1972-1974) Bar Associations; State Bar of Nevada (Civil Practice and Procedure Committee, 1978-1988); Defense Research Institute — Assistant U.S. Attorney, 1969-1970; Lawyer Delegate, Ninth Circuit Judicial Conference, 1984-1987 (Chairman, 1987) — Lt. Col., USAFR (Retired), JAG, Active Duty, 1958-1962 — E-mail: jthorndal@thorndal.com

James G. Armstrong — 1946 — The University of Iowa, B.A., 1968; University of Denver, J.D., 1970 — Admitted to Bar, 1971, Colorado; 1976, Nevada — Member State Bar of Nevada; Clark County Bar Association — USAF, Assistant Staff Judge Advocate, 1971-77 — E-mail: jarmstrong@thorndal.com

Craig R. Delk — 1953 — College of Idaho, B.A. (magna cum laude), 1976; Southwestern University School of Law, J.D. (Dean's List), 1979 — American Jurisprudence Award Recipient, in Corporations — Admitted to Bar, 1979, California; 1980, Nevada; 1980, U.S. District Court, District of Nevada; 1983, U.S. Court of Appeals, Ninth Circuit — Member The State Bar of California; State Bar of Nevada (Disciplinary Committee, 1983-88; Pro Bono Committee, 1985); Clark County Bar Association; Defense Research Institute — "Service of Process Under Hague Treaty", 1983; "Service of Process by Letters Rogatory", 1987; "The Insanity Defense", 1988 — E-mail: cdelk@thorndal.com

Stephen C. Balkenbush — 1952 — University of Colorado, B.S., 1975; California Western School of Law, J.D. (cum laude), 1978 — American Jurisprudence Award Recipient in Remedies and State and Local Taxation — California Western Law Review — Admitted to Bar, 1978, Nevada; 1984, U.S. Supreme Court — Member American and Washoe County Bar Associations; State Bar of Nevada; Association of Defense Counsel of Nevada; Defense Research Institute — Deputy Attorney General, 1978-1981; Chief Deputy District Attorney/County Counsel Douglas County, Nevada, 1981-1986 — U.S. Air Force, 1969-1972 — Resident Reno, NV Office — E-mail: sbalkenbush@thorndal.com

Paul F. Eisinger — 1957 — The University of Toledo, B.S., 1979; J.D., 1981 — Admitted to Bar, 1982, Nevada — Member American and Clark County Bar Associations; State Bar of Nevada; Defense Research Institute — E-mail: peisinger@thorndal.com

Charles L. Burcham — 1958 — California State University, B.A., 1981; University of Washington, J.D., 1985 — American Jurisprudence Award Recipient — Admitted to Bar, 1986, Nevada — Member State Bar of Nevada; Association of Defense Counsel of Nevada — Resident Reno, NV Office — E-mail: cburcham@thorndal.com

Brian K. Terry — 1953 — Brigham Young University, B.A., 1980; Northwestern School of Law of Lewis & Clark College, J.D., 1987 — Admitted to Bar, 1987, Nevada — Member American and Clark County Bar Associations; State Bar of Nevada — E-mail: bterry@thorndal.com

Brent T. Kolvet — 1950 — University of Nevada, Reno, B.A., 1972; University of the Pacific, McGeorge School of Law, J.D., 1976 — Admitted to Bar, 1976, Nevada — Member Washoe County Bar Association; State Bar of Nevada; Association of Defense Counsel of Nevada — District Attorney Douglas County, Nevada (1983-1991) — Resident Reno Office — E-mail: bkovet@thorndal.com

Thorndal, Armstrong, Delk, Balkenbush & Eisinger, A Professional Corporation, Las Vegas, NV (Continued)

Robert F. Balkenbush — 1954 — Eastern New Mexico University, B.S., 1977; California Western School of Law, J.D., 1980 — Admitted to Bar, 1980, Nevada; U.S. District Court, District of Nevada; U.S. Court of Appeals, Ninth Circuit — Member Washoe County Bar Association; Association of Defense Counsel of Nevada; Defense Research Institute — E-mail: rbalkenbush@thorndal.com

Philip Goodhart — 1965 — University of Alberta, B.C., 1987; University of San Diego, J.D., 1990 — Admitted to Bar, 1990, California; 1994, Nevada; 1990, U.S. District Court, Southern District of California; U.S. Court of Appeals, Ninth Circuit; 1994, U.S. District Court, District of Nevada — Member American, Clark County and San Diego County Bar Associations — E-mail: pgoodhart@thorndal.com

Christopher J. Curtis — 1963 — University of California, Los Angeles, B.A. (with honors), 1985; Loyola University, J.D., 1988 — Admitted to Bar, 1989, California; 1990, Nevada; 1990, U.S. District Court, Southern District of California; 1991, U.S. District Court, Central, Eastern and Northern Districts of California; U.S. Court of Appeals, Ninth Circuit; 1992, U.S. District Court, District of Nevada — Member American, Clark County and Los Angeles County Bar Associations; State Bar of Nevada; State Bar of California; Nevada Trial Lawyers Association; Defense Research Institute — E-mail: ccurtis@thorndal.com

Katherine F. Parks — 1972 — University of Nevada, Reno, B.S., 1995; California Western School of Law, J.D. (with honors), 1997 — Admitted to Bar, 1998, Nevada; 1999, California; 1998, U.S. District Court, District of Nevada — Member Washoe County Bar Association — Resident Reno Office — E-mail: kparks@thorndal.com

Deborah L. Elsasser — 1960 — University of Nebraska at Kearney, B.A. (cum laude), 1984; University of Nebraska-Lincoln, J.D. (with distinction), 1994 — Admitted to Bar, 1994, Nevada; U.S. District Court, District of Nevada — Member American and Clark County Bar Associations — E-mail: delsasser@thorndal.com

Kevin R. Diamond — 1968 — Loyola Marymount University, B.A. (cum laude), 1990; California Western School of Law, J.D. (cum laude), 1993 — Admitted to Bar, 1993, Nevada; U.S. District Court, District of Nevada — Member American and Clark County Bar Associations; State Bar of Nevada; Association of Trial Lawyers of America — E-mail: kdiamond@thorndal.com

Brian M. Brown — 1967 — San Diego State University, B.A., 1992; California Western School of Law, J.D., 1994 — Admitted to Bar, 1994, Nevada; 1995, U.S. District Court, District of Nevada; 1998, U.S. Court of Appeals, Ninth Circuit — Member American and Washoe County Bar Associations — U.S. Navy, 1988-1994 — Resident Reno Office — E-mail: bbrown@thorndal.com

Thierry V. Barkley — 1955 — University of California, Los Angeles, B.A., 1976; California Western School of Law, J.D., 1979 — Admitted to Bar, 1980, Nevada; 1981, U.S. District Court of Nevada; 1986, U.S. Supreme Court; 1990, U.S. Court of Appeals, Ninth Circuit — Member Washoe County Bar Association; State Bar of Nevada; Defense Research Institute — Resident Reno Office — E-mail: tbarkley@thorndal.com

Michael P. Lowry — 1982 — Drake University, B.A., 2003; J.D., 2007 — Admitted to Bar, 2007, Nevada; U.S. District Court of Nevada — Member Clark County Bar Association; State Bar of Nevada — E-mail: mlowry@thorndal.com

Kenneth R. Lund — 1978 — Brigham Young University, B.S., 2002; The University of Utah, S.J. Quinney College of Law, J.D., 2006 — Admitted to Bar, 2006, Nevada; 2008, Utah; U.S. District Court, District of Nevada — E-mail: krl@thorndal.com

John D. Hooks — 1977 — The George Washington University, B.A., 2000; University of Baltimore School of Law, J.D. (cum laude), 2003 — Admitted to Bar, 2003, Maryland; 2009, Nevada — Member Maryland State and Clark County Bar Associations; State Bar of Nevada — E-mail: jhooks@thorndal.com

Kevin A. Pick — 1984 — Wright State University, B.A. (Dean's List), 2006; Capital University Law School, J.D., 2009 — Admitted to Bar, 2010, Nevada — Member Washoe County Bar Association; Association of Defense Counsel of Nevada — Resident Reno Office — E-mail: kap@thorndal.com

Meghan M. Goodwin — 1983 — University of Nevada, Las Vegas, B.A., 2005; William S. Boyd School of Law, University of Nevada, Las Vegas, J.D., 2010 — Admitted to Bar, 2010, Nevada; 2011, U.S. District Court, District of Nevada — Member American and Clark County Bar Associations — E-mail: mgoodwin@thorndal.com

Gregory M. Schulman — 1969 — Columbia University, B.A., 1991; University of San Diego School of Law, J.D., 1994 — Admitted to Bar, 1994, California; 1995, Nevada; 2003, Arizona; 1994, U.S. District Court, Southern District of California; 1995, U.S. District Court, District of Nevada; 1996, U.S. Court of Appeals, Ninth Circuit — Member Clark County Bar Association — E-mail: gschulman@thorndal.com

Alexandra B. McLeod — 1978 — American University, B.A., 1999; University of the Pacific, McGeorge School of Law, J.D., 2002 — Admitted to Bar, 2002, Nevada; 2003, U.S. District Court, District of Nevada — Member Clark County Bar Association; Southern Nevada Association of Women Attorneys; Las Vegas Defense Lawyers — Languages: Spanish — Practice Areas: Insurance Defense; Civil Litigation — E-mail: abm@thorndal.com

Joseph E. Balkenbush — 1983 — University of Nevada, Reno, B.A., 2006; University of South Dakota School of Law, J.D., 2013 — Admitted to Bar, 2014, Nevada; U.S. District Court, District of Nevada — Member State Bar of Nevada; Washoe County Bar Association — E-mail: jeb@thorndal.com

Douglas J. Duesman — 1973 — St. Ambrose University, B.S., 1997; M.S., 2001; Drake University Law School, J.D., 2005 — Admitted to Bar, 2007, Nevada; U.S. District Court, District of Nevada; U.S. Court of Appeals, Ninth Circuit — Member State Bar of Nevada; Clark County Bar Association — E-mail: djd@thorndal.com

(Revisors of the Nevada Insurance Law Digest for this Publication)

The following firms also service this area.

Cooper Levenson, P.A.
1125 Atlantic Avenue, Third Floor
Atlantic City, New Jersey 08401
   Telephone: 609-344-3161
   Fax: 609-344-0939

Trial and Appellate Practice, State and Federal Courts, Negligence, Insurance Defense, Product Liability, Workers' Compensation, Environmental Law, Professional Liability, Employment Law, Dram Shop, Premises Liability, Mass Tort, Casino, Health/Hospital, Bedbug Liability Defense

SEE COMPLETE LISTING UNDER ATLANTIC CITY, NEW JERSEY

Laxalt & Nomura, Ltd.
9600 Gateway Drive
Reno, Nevada 89521-8953
   Telephone: 775-322-1170
   Fax: 775-322-1865

Insurance Defense, Business Litigation, Product Liability, Construction Defect, Professional Liability, Insurance Coverage & Defense, Bad Faith, Asbestos Litigation, Medical Devices, Employment Law, Personal Injury, Land Use, Appeals

SEE COMPLETE LISTING UNDER RENO, NEVADA (443 MILES)

RENO † 225,221 Washoe Co.

Erickson, Thorpe & Swainston, Ltd.
99 West Arroyo
Reno, Nevada 89509
   Telephone: 775-786-3930
   Fax: 775-786-4160
   E-Mail: etsreno@etsreno.com
   www.etsreno.com

Established: 1969

Litigation, Insurance Defense, Labor and Employment, Commercial Litigation, Product Liability, Personal Injury, Construction Defect, Professional Liability, Agent/Broker Liability, Architects and Engineers, Medical Liability, Legal, Pharmaceutical, Aviation, Transportation, Premises Liability, Civil Rights, Mediation, Alternative Dispute Resolution

Firm Profile: Erickson, Thorpe & Swainston, Ltd., was founded in Reno, Nevada, in 1969. For more than forty years, the Firm has efficiently and successfully represented its clients in state and federal courts in Nevada and

NEVADA

RENO

Erickson, Thorpe & Swainston, Ltd., Reno, NV
(Continued)

Northern California. As experienced trial and appellate attorneys, the Firm vigorously advocates its clients' interests while remaining committed to the principles of the highest legal ethics. The Firm provides the experience necessary to meet our client's expectations for an effective, efficient and timely resolution of their conflict issues. Our continuing success in this highly competitive profession demonstrates our widely recognized ability to deliver satisfaction and a positive outcome to those who give us their trust - our clients.

Insurance Clients

ACE Insurance Company
American Family Insurance
American Safety Insurance Company
Argonaut Insurance Company
Berkley Risk Administrators Company, LLC
Capitol Indemnity Corporation
Clarendon National Insurance Company
COUNTRY Insurance & Financial Services
ESIS Chicago Casualty Claims
Financial Pacific Insurance Company
First Mercury Insurance Company
Harco National Insurance Company
IAT Specialty
Kemper Insurance Companies
Lloyd's of London
Monticello Insurance Company
National Interstate Insurance Company
Nevada Public Agency Insurance Pool
Occidental Insurance Company
QBE North America
Royal Insurance Company
Sedgwick CMS
St. Paul Travelers Insurance Company
Ward North America, Inc.
Zurich American Insurance Company

Allstate Insurance Company
American National Property and Casualty Company
Ameriprise Insurance Company
Badger Mutual Insurance Company
Broadspire Services, Inc.
Capital Insurance Group
Claims Resource Management, Inc.
CNA Insurance Companies
Comstock Insurance Company
Criterion Claim Solutions
Deep South Insurance Services
Federated Insurance Company
Fireman's Fund Insurance Companies
Global Aerospace Underwriting Managers, Ltd.
Hartford Insurance Company
Jefferson Insurance Group
Liberty Mutual Insurance Company
Markel Corporation
National Fire and Marine Insurance Company
NCMIC Insurance Company
North American Risk Services
NovaPro Risk Solutions
OneBeacon Insurance Company
Resurgens Specialty Underwriting, Inc.
Shand Morahan & Company, Inc.
United Services Automobile Association (USAA)
Willis Administrative Services Corporation

Non-Insurance Clients

Accor Economy Lodging, Motel 6
Albertson's LLC
Associated Anesthesiologists of Reno
Bailey & McGah
Catholic Healthcare West
Club Cal-Neva
Diocese of Reno
Granite Construction
Johnny On The Spot, Inc.
Kingsbury General Improvement District
May Trucking Company
Regional Transportation Commission
Save Mart Supermarkets
7-Eleven, Inc.
Sierra Nevada Cardiology Associates
Smith's Food & Drug Centers
Truckee Meadows Water Authority
Western Village Inn and Casino
World of Toys
Young Electric Sign Company

Advantage Rent-A-Car
Alternative Service Concepts, LLC
Atlantic Companies
Avis Budget Group, Inc.
Bridgestone/Firestone, Inc.
City of Reno
Crete Carrier Corporation
Fortifiber Corporation
Jensen Enterprises, Inc. d/b/a Jensen Precast
Lennox International, Inc.
Lexus of Reno
Peppermill Casinos, Inc.
Reno Mazda Kia
Rheem Manufacturing Company
Sears Holdings Corporation
The Sherwin-Williams Company
Sigma Alpha Epsilon, National Fraternity
Toyota of Reno
United Rentals, Inc.
Woodgrain Millwork, Inc./Windsor Window & Doors

Firm Member

Thomas P. Beko — University of Nevada, Reno, B.A., 1982; University of the Pacific, McGeorge School of Law, J.D. (with honors), 1986 — Order of the Coif — Admitted to Bar, 1986, Nevada; 1987, California; 1989, U.S. Court of Appeals, Ninth Circuit; 1999, U.S. Supreme Court — Member American and Washoe County Bar Associations; State Bar of Nevada; State Bar of California; Association of Defense Counsel of Nevada; Defense Research Institute;

Erickson, Thorpe & Swainston, Ltd., Reno, NV
(Continued)

Nevada Trial Lawyers Association; Association of Defense Counsel, Northern California; American Board of Trial Advocates — Judge Pro Tempore, Nevada Short Trial Program; Nevada Superlawyers

Georgeson Angaran Chtd.

5450 Longley Lane
Reno, Nevada 89511
 Telephone: 775-827-6440
 Fax: 775-827-9256
 E-Mail: info@renotahoelaw.com
 www.renotahoelaw.com

Established: 1972

Insurance Defense, Trial Practice, Casualty, Fire, Negligence, Product Liability, Aviation, Professional Errors and Omissions, Employment Law, Commercial Litigation, Construction Defect, Medical Legal, Insurance Bad Faith, Dispute Resolution

Firm Profile: Georgeson Angaran focuses exclusively on providing defense oriented consultation and representation to employers, businesses and insurance companies in the areas of insurance defense, insurance bad faith, employment, construction defect, premises liability, product defect, professional liability, personal injury, corporate, real estate and commercial disputes and insurance law.

GA has successfully represented thousands of clients in Nevada and California, providing the highest quality legal representation in the most effective and cost efficient manner possible. Whether providing consultation services to identify problem areas and minimize your potential legal risks or defending your interests in court, GA emphasizes thorough, competent and efficient preparation to maximize your objectives and meet your particular needs.

Insurance Clients

American Economy Insurance Company
Armed Forces Insurance Exchange
Berkley Risk Services, LLC
Capitol Indemnity Corporation
CNA Insurance Companies
E & O Professionals
First National Insurance Company of America
GEICO General Insurance Company
General Casualty Insurance Company
Generali - US Branch
Gulf Insurance Group
Hanover Insurance Company
Houston General Insurance Company
Liberty Mutual Insurance Company
Markel American Insurance Company
North American Specialty Insurance Company
OneBeacon Insurance
Safeco Insurance Companies
Sentry Insurance a Mutual Company
Specialty Risk Services, Inc. (SRS)
United National Insurance Company
Universal Underwriters Insurance Company

American Reliable Insurance Company
Assurant Insurance Group
California State Automobile Association
Colorado Casualty Insurance Company
Gallagher Bassett Services, Inc.
GEICO Casualty Company
GEICO Indemnity Company
GEICO Insurance Companies
General Insurance Company of America
Government Employees Insurance Company
HDR Insurance Services
Interstate Insurance Group
Kemper Insurance Company
Lloyd's
Motorists Insurance Group
National Chiropractic Mutual Insurance Company
NovaPro Risk Solutions
Philadelphia Insurance Company
St. Paul Travelers
Sequoia Insurance Company
Shand Morahan & Company, Inc.
State Farm Insurance Companies
United States Liability Insurance Group
Wausau Insurance Companies
Western Heritage Insurance

Self-Insured Clients

Black & Decker (U.S.), Inc.
CNF/Con-way Inc.
Genermex
Honeywell International, Inc.
M. Scott Properties
Paragon Way, Inc.
Sierra Pacific Power Company

City of Reno
First Health Services Corporation
Golden Phoenix Minerals
Lithia Motors, Inc.
Nevada Public Agency Insurance Pool

Georgeson Angaran Chtd., Reno, NV (Continued)

Shareholders

Jack G. Angaran — 1945 — University of California, Santa Barbara, B.A., 1970; Mercer University, J.D., 1975 — Admitted to Bar, 1975, Georgia; 1982, Nevada; 1984, California; 1978, U.S. District Court, Southern District of Georgia; 1982, U.S. District Court, District of Nevada — Member State Bar of Nevada (State Chair, Fee Dispute Arbitrations, 1991-1996); State Bar of California; State Bar of Georgia; Washoe County Bar Association (President, 1993-1994); Association of Defense Counsel of Northern Nevada (President, 1987-1988); Association of Defense Counsel of Northern California and Nevada (Board of Directors, 1990-1991; 2000-2001); Volunteer Lawyers of Washoe County (President/Trustee, 1991-1993); Master, American Inns of Court; Western Trial Lawyers Association; American Board of Trial Advocates (President, Reno Chapter, 2005-2007; National ABOTA Director, 2008-2010); Defense Research Institute; American College of Trial Lawyers — Deputy District Attorney for Washoe County (1982-1984); Listed in Nevada/Mountain States Super Lawyers (2007-2009); Best Lawyers in America (Insurance Law, Litigation Real Estate, Litigation Construction) — E-mail: jack@renotahoelaw.com

Justin H. Pfrehm — 1975 — Oregon State University, B.S. (cum laude), 1996; Willamette University, J.D., 2000 — Admitted to Bar, 2001, Nevada; California; 2001, U.S. District Court, District of Nevada — Member State Bar of Nevada; Washoe County Bar Association; Association of Defense Counsel of Northern Nevada; Association of Defense Counsel, Northern California — Rising Star, Mountain States Super Lawyers (2009) — E-mail: justin@renotahoelaw.com

Ryan J. Mandell — 1976 — University of Nevada, B.A., 1999; Mercer University, J.D., 2002 — Law Clerk to Hon. Robert A. McQuaid, Jr., U.S. Magistrate Judge — Admitted to Bar, 2002, Nevada; 2002, U.S. District Court, District of Nevada — Member State Bar of Nevada; Washoe County Bar Association; Association of Defense Counsel of Northern Nevada; Association of Defense Counsel, Northern California — Rising Star, Mountain States Super Lawyers (2009) — E-mail: ryan@renotahoelaw.com

Associates

Mary-Ann S. LeBrun — 1986 — University of Nevada, Reno, B.A. Political Science (magna cum laude), 2008; Sandra Day O'Connor College of Law, Arizona State University, J.D. (cum laude), 2011 — Admitted to Bar, 2011, Nevada — Member State Bar of Nevada; Washoe County Bar Association; American Inns of Court

Andy Joy — 1986 — University of Nevada, Reno, B.A. (with distinction), 2007; Western State University College of Law, J.D., 2013 — Admitted to Bar, 2014, Nevada

Philip A. John — 1981 — California Polytechnic State University, B.A. Political Science (President's Honor Roll), 2003; University of San Francisco School of Law, J.D. (cum laude), 2007 — Admitted to Bar, 2007, California; Nevada — Member American and Clark County Bar Associations; State Bar of Nevada; State Bar of California — Rising Star, Mountain States Super Lawyers (2013)

Of Counsel

C. James Georgeson — 1942 — University of Nevada, B.S., 1965; University of California, Boalt Hall School of Law, J.D., 1968 — Beta Gamma Sigma, Omicron Delta Epsilon, Delta Signa Pi, Phi Alpha Delta — Law Clerk to Chief Justice Jon Collins, Nevada Supreme Court, 1968-1969 — Admitted to Bar, 1969, California; Nevada — Member American and Washoe County Bar Associations; State Bar of Nevada; State Bar of California; Fellow, American College of Trial Lawyers; American College of Trial Lawyers — Listed in The Best Lawyers in America; Listed in Nevada Super Lawyers (2007-2009) — E-mail: jim@renotahoelaw.com

Harold B. Thompson — 1948 — University of California, Santa Barbara, B.A. (with honors), 1970; University of California, Hastings College of the Law, J.D., 1974 — Law Clerk to Justice Cameron Batjer, Nevada Supreme Court, 1974-1975 — Admitted to Bar, 1974, California; 1975, Nevada — Member American and Washoe County (President, 1986-87) Bar Associations; State Bar of Nevada (Northern Nevada Disciplinary Board, 1988-); Association of Defense Counsel of Northern Nevada (President, 1991-1992); Association of Defense Counsel, Northern California; Defense Research Institute; American Judicature Society; Fellow, American College of Trial Lawyers — E-mail: harold@renotahoelaw.com

Kent Law

201 West Liberty Street, Suite 320
Reno, Nevada 89501
 Telephone: 775-324-9800
 Fax: 775-324-9803
 E-Mail: skent@skentlaw.com
 www.skentlaw.com

(Las Vegas, NV Office*: 9440 West Sahara Avenue, Suite 215, 89117)
 (Tel: 702-930-5368)
 (Fax: 775-324-9803)

Established: 2010

Aviation, Bad Faith, Construction Defect, Insurance Defense, Insurance Coverage Litigation, Personal Injury, Premises Liability, Professional Liability, Real Estate, Securities, Trial and Appellate Practice

Firm Profile: Stephen Kent is a defense trial lawyer with 33 years experience defending insureds for insurers, as well as self insureds, businesses, and individuals. In 2012 Mr. Kent obtained two defense verdicts for his clients in construction defect and premises liability jury trials. In 2013 Mr. Kent obtained a defense verdict after a 7 day jury trial for his defendant client, a civil engineer, in a construction defect case.

Insurance Clients

Avemco Insurance Company
Old United Casualty Company
QBE the Americas
U.S. Specialty Insurance Company
Western World Insurance Company

Chartis Aerospace Adjustment Services, Inc.
United States Aircraft Insurance Group

Non-Insurance Clients

The Hertz Corporation
Phoenix Aviation Managers, Inc.
Wal-Mart Stores, Inc.

Pella Corporation
Travelers Aviation
WinCo Foods, LLC

Stephen S. Kent — University of Nevada, B.A., 1975; University of the Pacific, McGeorge School of Law, J.D., 1980 — Admitted to Bar, 1980, Nevada; 1981, U.S. District Court, District of Nevada; 1986, U.S. Court of Appeals, Ninth Circuit; 2006, U.S. Supreme Court — Member American Bar Association (Sections: Litigation; Tort and Insurance Practice; Committees: Trial Techniques, Insurance Coverage and Business Torts); Washoe County Bar Association; State Bar of Nevada (Disciplinary Committee; Former Board Member, Young Lawyers Section; Former Member, Insurance and Fee Dispute Committees); Northern California-Nevada Association of Defense Counsel; International Association of Defense Counsel (Committees: Aviation; Life, Health and Accident Insurance; Casualty Insurance; Medical Malpractice); Fellow, Litigation Counsel of America; Reno Rotary; Reno Rodeo Association; Defense Research Institute — Certified Civil Trial Advocate, National Board of Trial Attorneys; Certified Civil Pretrial Practice Advocate, National Board of Civil Pretrial Practice Advocacy

Laxalt & Nomura, Ltd.

9600 Gateway Drive
Reno, Nevada 89521-8953
 Telephone: 775-322-1170
 Fax: 775-322-1865
 Emer/After Hrs: 775-786-3035
 Mobile: 775-762-8545
 E-Mail: dhayward@laxalt-nomura.com
 www.laxalt-nomura.com

(Las Vegas, NV Office*: 6720 Via Austi Parkway, Suite 430, 89119)
 (Tel: 725-388-1551)
 (Fax: 725-388-1559)

Established: 1986

Laxalt & Nomura, Ltd., Reno, NV (Continued)

Insurance Defense, Business Litigation, Product Liability, Construction Defect, Professional Liability, Insurance Coverage & Defense, Bad Faith, Asbestos Litigation, Medical Devices, Employment Law, Personal Injury, Land Use, Appeals

Firm Profile: Laxalt & Nomura, Ltd. is an AV-rated civil litigation law firm founded in 1986 by Bruce Laxalt and Don Nomura, two former Washoe County, Nevada, Chief Deputy District Attorneys. Our philosophy is to quickly determine each client's litigation objective, then work diligently to achieve that goal in an efficient and effective manner. Whether your case is resolved through mediation, motion practice, trial, or appeal, our team of attorneys has the skills and experience to provide you with the best possible legal representation at a reasonable cost.

We can provide state-wide legal services to our clients through our offices in Reno and Las Vegas.

Insurance Clients

- ACE USA
- AIG/American International Group
- American Specialty Insurance & Risk Services, Inc.
- Attorneys Liability Protection Society
- Chubb Group of Insurance Companies
- Commerce Insurance Company
- Fireman's Fund Insurance Company
- The Hartford Insurance Group
- Houston Casualty Company
- Lawyer's Protector Plan
- Markel Southwest Underwriters, Inc.
- National Fire and Marine Insurance Company
- Professionals Direct Insurance Company
- Safeco Insurance
- Seneca Insurance Company, Inc.
- Travelers Indemnity Company
- Admiral Insurance Company
- American Family Insurance
- American Trucking and Transportation Insurance Company
- Central Insurance Companies
- Church Mutual Insurance Company
- Citigroup/Travelers
- Farmers Insurance Group
- Gallagher Bassett Services, Inc.
- Great Northwest Insurance Company
- Interstate Insurance Group
- Markel Insurance Company
- MetLife Auto & Home
- Metropolitan Casualty Insurance Company
- Professional Indemnity Agency
- Ranger Insurance Company
- Royal Insurance Company
- The St. Paul Companies
- Sentry Insurance
- Travelers Insurance Companies

Non-Insurance Clients

- Aeolus Pharmaceuticals, Inc.
- Astra Pharmaceutical Products, Inc.
- Barr/Duramed Pharmaceuticals, Inc.
- Constitution State Services
- Golden Gaming, Inc.
- Merck & Company, Inc.
- Mountain Air Enterprises, Inc.
- Renown Health System
- St. Mary's Regional Medical Center
- Southwest Risk Services, Inc.
- Textron, Inc.
- WorthGroup Architects
- Altara
- Atlantis Hotel and Casino
- Bayer Corporation
- Caterpillar Inc.
- Deere & Company
- ITW Food Equipment Group
- Monitor Liability Managers, Inc.
- Pfizer, Inc.
- Reynen & Bardis Communities
- Signature Flight Support
- Southern Nevada Water Authority
- Terex Corporation
- Wells Fargo Bank

Shareholders

Robert Adair Dotson, III — Iowa State University, B.A., 1991; The University of Iowa, J.D. (with distinction), 1994 — Admitted to Bar, 1994, Iowa; Nevada; U.S. District Court, District of Nevada; U.S. Court of Appeals, Ninth Circuit — Member State Bar of Nevada (Alternative Dispute Resolution Section); Washoe County Bar Association (Officer, 2001-2007; President, 2006-2007) — Practice Areas: General Civil Litigation; Product Liability; Employment Litigation; Premises Liability; Commercial Litigation; Insurance Coverage Litigation; Appeals — E-mail: rdotson@laxalt-nomura.com

Steven E. Guinn — University of Nevada, B.S. (with distinction), 1986; Pepperdine University, J.D., 1989 — Admitted to Bar, 1989, California; 1994, Nevada; 1989, U.S. District Court, Central and Northern Districts of California; 1994, U.S. District Court, District of Nevada; U.S. Court of Appeals, Ninth Circuit — Member State Bar of Nevada; State Bar of California; Washoe County Bar Association — Practice Areas: Property Liability; Pharmaceutical; Medical Devices; General Defense — E-mail: sguinn@laxalt-nomura.com

Daniel T. Hayward — The University of Iowa; Iowa State University, B.A. (with distinction), 1991; The University of Iowa, J.D. (with high distinction), 1994 — Phi Kappa Phi — Admitted to Bar, 1994, Missouri; 1995, Kansas;

Laxalt & Nomura, Ltd., Reno, NV (Continued)

1996, Nevada; 1994, U.S. District Court, Western District of Missouri; 1995, U.S. District Court, District of Kansas; 1996, U.S. District Court, District of Nevada; 1996, U.S. Court of Appeals, Ninth Circuit — Member State Bar of Nevada; The Missouri Bar; Kansas Bar Association; Washoe County Bar Association; American Board of Trial Advocates; Defense Research Institute; Professional Liability Underwriting Society — Practice Areas: Legal Malpractice; Bad Faith; Product Liability; Business Litigation; Premises Liability; Professional Liability — E-mail: dhayward@laxalt-nomura.com

Jason W. Peak — University of Nevada, Reno, B.A., 1994; Willamette University, J.D., 1999 — Admitted to Bar, 1999, Nevada; 2000, California; 1999, U.S. District Court, District of Nevada; 2003, U.S. District Court, Eastern District of California — Member State Bar of Nevada; Washoe County Bar Association; Association of Defense Counsel; Defense Research Institute — Practice Areas: General Defense; Construction Defect; Product Liability; Personal Injury — E-mail: jpeak@laxalt-nomura.com

James E. Murphy — University of Illinois, B.A., 1997; University of Nevada, Las Vegas, M.A., 2000; William S. Boyd School of Law, University of Nevada, Las Vegas, J.D., 2003 — Admitted to Bar, 2003, Nevada; U.S. District Court, District of Nevada; 2009, U.S. Court of Appeals, Ninth Circuit; 2010, U.S. Supreme Court — Member American Bar Association; State Bar of Nevada — Practice Areas: General Defense; Automobile Liability; Premises Liability — E-mail: jmurphy@laxalt-nomura.com

Senior Attorneys

Holly Parker — University of Nevada, Reno, B.A., 2003; Thomas Jefferson School of Law, J.D. (magna cum laude), 2006 — Admitted to Bar, 2006, Nevada; U.S. District Court, District of Nevada — Member State Bar of Nevada; Washoe County Bar Association — Practice Areas: General Defense; Business Litigation; Construction Defect — E-mail: hparker@laxalt-nomura.com

Don Nomura — University of California, Los Angeles, B.A., 1971; Southwestern University, J.D., 1976 — Admitted to Bar, 1976, Nevada; 1978, U.S. District Court, District of Nevada; U.S. Court of Appeals, Ninth Circuit; Supreme Court of Nevada — Member State Bar of Nevada (Ethics Committee, 1986); Washoe County Bar Association; Association of Defense Counsel, Northern Nevada; Master, American Inns of Court; American Board of Trial Advocates (Associate); National District Attorneys Association; Defense Research Institute; Fellow, American College of Trial Lawyers — Practice Areas: Professional Malpractice; Civil Litigation; Medical Malpractice; Personal Injury — E-mail: dnomura@laxalt-nomura.com

Wayne A. Shaffer — University of Nevada, B.A., 1977; California Western School of Law, J.D. (magna cum laude), 1981 — Admitted to Bar, 1981, Nevada; 1982, California; 1983, U.S. District Court, District of Nevada; U.S. Court of Appeals, Ninth Circuit — Member American and Washoe County Bar Associations; State Bar of Nevada; State Bar of California; Master, American Inns of Court; Association of Trial Lawyers of America; Defense Research Institute; Association of Defense Trial Attorneys; Federation of Defense and Corporate Counsel — Practice Areas: Product Liability; Construction Defect; General Civil Litigation — E-mail: wshaffer@laxalt-nomura.com

Janice Hodge Jensen — Arizona State University, B.S. (cum laude), 1979; University of the Pacific, McGeorge School of Law, J.D., 1982 — Admitted to Bar, 1982, California; 1983, Nevada; 1983, U.S. District Court, District of Nevada; 1985, U.S. Court of Appeals, Ninth Circuit — Member State Bar of Nevada; State Bar of California; Washoe County Bar Association — Practice Areas: Professional Malpractice; Extra-Contractual Litigation — E-mail: jjensen@laxalt-nomura.com

Angela M. Bader — University of Nevada, Reno, B.S.B.A. (with high distinction), 1992; University of the Pacific, McGeorge School of Law, J.D. (with distinction), 1995 — Admitted to Bar, 1995, Nevada; 1996, California; 1995, U.S. District Court, District of Nevada; 2006, U.S. District Court, Central District of California — Member State Bar of California; State Bar of Nevada; Washoe County Bar Association; Association of Defense Counsel (President, 2003) — Practice Areas: General Defense; Product Liability; Premises Liability; Employment Litigation — E-mail: abader@laxalt-nomura.com

Madelyn Shipman — American University, B.A., 1964; Hamline University, J.D., 1977 — Admitted to Bar, 1977, Minnesota; 1983, Nevada; 1980, U.S. Supreme Court; 1983, U.S. District Court, District of Nevada — Member State Bar of Nevada; Washoe County Bar Association — Practice Areas: Administrative Law; Land Use; Water Law; Civil Rights; Employment Law

Lon Burke — Boise State University, B.S., 1991; The University of Iowa, J.D., 1994 — Admitted to Bar, 1994, Arizona; 1997, Nevada; 1998, Colorado; U.S. District Court, District of Arizona; U.S. District Court, District of Nevada; U.S. District Court, District of Colorado; U.S. Court of Appeals, Ninth Circuit — Member State Bar of Nevada — Practice Areas: General Defense;

Laxalt & Nomura, Ltd., Reno, NV (Continued)

Product Liability; Premises Liability; Professional Liability — E-mail: lburke@laxalt-nomura.com

Marshall S. Smith — University of Nevada, Las Vegas, M.A. (with honors), 1982; University of the Pacific, McGeorge School of Law, J.D., 1987 — Admitted to Bar, 1988, Nevada; 1989, U.S. District Court, District of Nevada; 1997, U.S. Court of Appeals, Ninth Circuit — Member State Bar of Nevada; Washoe County Bar Association — Practice Areas: Insurance Defense; Business Litigation; Construction Defect — E-mail: msmith@laxalt-nomura.com

Associates

Justin Vance — Brigham Young University, B.A., 2004; The University of Iowa College of Law, J.D., 2008 — Admitted to Bar, 2008, Nevada; U.S. District Court, District of Nevada — Member State Bar of Nevada; Washoe County Bar Association — Languages: Spanish — Practice Areas: General Defense; Construction Defect — E-mail: jvance@laxalt-nomura.com

Daniel C. Tetreault — William S. Boyd School of Law, University of Nevada, Las Vegas, J.D. (cum laude), 2008 — Admitted to Bar, 2009, Nevada; U.S. District Court, District of Nevada — Member State Bar of Nevada — Practice Areas: Insurance Defense; General Defense — E-mail: dtetreault@laxalt-nomura.com

Ryan Leary — University of Nevada, Reno, B.A., 2005; William S. Boyd School of Law, University of Nevada, Las Vegas, J.D. (magna cum laude), 2009 — Admitted to Bar, 2009, Nevada — Member American and Washoe County Bar Associations; State Bar of Nevada; American Inns of Court — Practice Areas: General Defense; Insurance Defense; Construction Defect — E-mail: rleary@laxalt-nomura.com

Marilee Breternitz — University of Nevada, Reno, B.A., 2008; University of the Pacific, McGeorge School of Law, J.D., 2011 — Admitted to Bar, 2011, California; 2012, Nevada; U.S. District Court, District of Nevada — Practice Areas: Litigation — E-mail: mbreternitz@laxalt-nomura.com

Thorndal, Armstrong, Delk, Balkenbush & Eisinger
A Professional Corporation

6590 South McCarran Boulevard, Suite B
Reno, Nevada 89509-6112
Telephone: 775-786-2882
Fax: 775-786-8004
E-Mail: info@thorndal.com
www.thorndal.com

(Las Vegas, NV Office*: 1100 East Bridger Avenue, 89101, P.O. Box 2070, 89125-2070)
(Tel: 702-366-0622)
(Fax: 702-366-0327)

Established: 1971

Insurance Law, Trial Practice

Stephen C. Balkenbush	Charles L. Burcham
Brent T. Kolvet	Robert F. Balkenbush
Katherine F. Parks	Brian M. Brown
Thierry V. Barkley	Brandon R. Price
Kevin A. Pick	Joseph E. Balkenbush

(See listing under Las Vegas, NV for additional information)

(Revisors of the Nevada Insurance Law Digest for this Publication)

The following firms also service this area.

Mills & Associates
3650 North Rancho Drive, Suite 114
Las Vegas, Nevada 89130
Telephone: 702-240-6060
Fax: 702-240-4267
Mailing Address: P.O. Box 570040, Las Vegas, NV 89157

Alternative Dispute Resolution, Arbitration, Automobile Liability, Bad Faith, Carrier Defense, Casualty Defense, Casualty Insurance Law, Civil Litigation, Commercial Vehicle, Common Carrier, Comprehensive General Liability, Coverage Analysis, Coverage Issues, Declaratory Judgments, Defense Litigation, Dispute Resolution, Examinations Under Oath, Excess and Surplus Lines, Excess and Umbrella, Extra-Contractual Liability, Extra-Contractual Litigation, First and Third Party Defense, First and Third Party Matters, Insurance Claim Analysis and Evaluation, Insurance Coverage Determination, Insurance Coverage Litigation, Insurance Defense, Insurance Fraud, Insurance Law, Insurance Litigation, Negligence, Opinions, Personal and Commercial Vehicle, Policy Construction and Interpretation, Primary and Excess Insurance, Product Liability, Property and Casualty, Self-Insured Defense, State and Federal Courts, Transportation, Truck Liability, Trucking, Trucking Law, Trucking Liability, Trucking Litigation, Trucks/Heavy Equipment, Uninsured and Underinsured Motorist, General and Commercial Insurance Coverage, Defense Practice

SEE COMPLETE LISTING UNDER LAS VEGAS, NEVADA (448 MILES)

NEW HAMPSHIRE

CAPITAL: CONCORD

COUNTIES AND COUNTY SEATS

County	County Seat
Belknap	Laconia
Carroll	Ossipee
Cheshire	Keene
Coos	Lancaster
Grafton	Woodsville
Hillsborough	Manchester and Nashua
Merrimack	Concord
Rockingham	Exeter
Strafford	Dover
Sullivan	Newport

In the text that follows "†" indicates County Seats.

Our files contain additional verified data on the firms listed herein. This additional information is available on request.

A.M. BEST COMPANY

NEW HAMPSHIRE — CONCORD

CONCORD † 42,695 Merrimack Co.

Mallory & Friedman, PLLC
3 North Spring Street, Suite 201
Concord, New Hampshire 03301
   Telephone: 603-228-2277
   Fax: 603-228-2275
   E-Mail: mark@malloryandfriedman.com
   www.malloryandfriedman.com

Established: 2001

Insurance Defense, Errors and Omissions, Insurance Coverage, Medical Malpractice, Premises Liability, Product Liability, Commercial Litigation, Lender Liability Defense, Litigation, Consultation, Motor Vehicle Accidents

Firm Profile: Mark Mallory and Chris Friedman bring more than 55 years of combined experience practicing exclusively in the civil litigation and insurance defense arena. Their wide-ranging experience includes representation of insureds, insurers and self-insured entities in complex litigation involving medical malpractice, product liability, construction accidents, wrongful death and other catastrophic injury claims, as well as in cases involving motor vehicle and premises liability accidents, and insurance coverage disputes.

The firm practices in the Superior Courts for all ten counties in the State of New Hampshire, as well as in the New Hampshire Supreme Court, the United States District Court for the District of New Hampshire and the First Circuit Court of Appeals. Mr. Mallory and Ms. Friedman have briefed or argued more than 30 New Hampshire Supreme Court and First Circuit appeals that have resulted in written opinions, many in the area of insurance coverage disputes.

The firm's attorneys offer private alternative dispute resolution services as well, enjoying an excellent reputation among both the plaintiff and defense bar as effective mediators and fair arbitrators.

Mallory and Friedman, PLLC is dedicated to affording the highest quality legal defense services, with the highest level of professionalism, personal attention and cost-consciousness.

Insurance Clients

AAA Automobile Club Inter-Insurance Exchange
Empire Fire and Marine Insurance Company
Hingham Group
Horace Mann Insurance Company
MMG Insurance Company
Patriot Insurance Company
Preferred Mutual Insurance Company
Safeco Insurance
State Farm Fire and Casualty Company
AXIS Insurance
Cincinnati Insurance Company
Hanover Insurance Company
The Hartford Financial Services Group, Inc.
Liberty Mutual Insurance Company
Mt. Washington Assurance Corp.
Plymouth Rock Assurance Corporation
Preferred Physicians Medical Risk Retention Group, Inc.
Vermont Mutual Insurance Company

Non-Insurance Clients

Nation Wide Ladder Company
The Provider Enterprises, Inc.
Toys "R" Us, Inc.
Peachtree Settlement Funding, JGWPT Holdings, LCC

Partners

Mark L. Mallory — 1953 — Middlebury College, B.A., 1975; University of Pennsylvania, J.D., 1980 — Admitted to Bar, 1980, New Hampshire; 1980, U.S. District Court, District of New Hampshire; 1982, U.S. Court of Appeals, First Circuit — Member American, New Hampshire and Manchester Bar Associations; Defense Research Institute — Practice Areas: Insurance Defense; Insurance Coverage Litigation; Medical Malpractice; Product Liability — E-mail: mark@malloryandfriedman.com

Christine Friedman — 1966 — The University of Maine, B.A., 1988; Franklin Pierce Law Center, J.D., 1991 — Admitted to Bar, 1991, New Hampshire; 1991, U.S. District Court, District of New Hampshire — Practice Areas: Insurance Defense; Medical Malpractice; Premises Liability; Product Liability; Commercial Litigation; Lender Liability Defense — E-mail: chris@malloryandfriedman.com

---

The following firms also service this area.

Desmarais, Ewing & Johnston, PLLC
175 Canal Street
Manchester, New Hampshire 03101
   Telephone: 603-623-5524
   Fax: 603-623-6383

Professional Liability, Insurance Coverage, Insurance Defense, Product Liability, Business Law, Civil Litigation, Personal Injury, Insurance Litigation, Construction Law

SEE COMPLETE LISTING UNDER MANCHESTER, NEW HAMPSHIRE (18 MILES)

Devine, Millimet & Branch, P.A.
111 Amherst Street
Manchester, New Hampshire 03101
   Telephone: 603-669-1000
   Fax: 603-669-8547

Insurance Defense, Automobile, Product Liability, Malpractice, Workers' Compensation, Environmental Law, Errors and Omissions, Surety, Professional Malpractice, Construction Law, Municipal Law, Insurance Coverage

SEE COMPLETE LISTING UNDER MANCHESTER, NEW HAMPSHIRE

Wadleigh, Starr & Peters, P.L.L.C.
95 Market Street
Manchester, New Hampshire 03101
   Telephone: 603-669-4140
   Fax: 603-669-6018

Fire, Casualty, Surety, Life Insurance, Medical Liability, Legal, Architects and Engineers, Engineers, Professional Malpractice, Product Liability, Arson, Hazardous Waste, Drug, Litigation, Subrogation, Defense Under All Lines, DES

SEE COMPLETE LISTING UNDER MANCHESTER, NEW HAMPSHIRE (18 MILES)

DOVER † 29,987 Strafford Co.

Refer To

Mallory & Friedman, PLLC
3 North Spring Street, Suite 201
Concord, New Hampshire 03301
   Telephone: 603-228-2277
   Fax: 603-228-2275

Insurance Defense, Errors and Omissions, Insurance Coverage, Medical Malpractice, Premises Liability, Product Liability, Commercial Litigation, Lender Liability Defense, Litigation, Consultation, Motor Vehicle Accidents

SEE COMPLETE LISTING UNDER CONCORD, NEW HAMPSHIRE (38 MILES)

MANCHESTER † 109,565 Hillsborough Co.

Bernard & Merrill, PLLC
814 Elm Street
Manchester, New Hampshire 03101
   Telephone: 603-622-8454
   Fax: 603-626-8490
   E-Mail: info@bernard-merrill.com
   www.bernard-merrill.com

Established: 1996

Workers' Compensation, Insurance Coverage, Personal Injury

Firm Profile: Bernard & Merrill, PLLC is committed to providing high quality legal representation in workers' compensation, personal injury and insurance matters. Our attorneys have experience before all New Hampshire State and Federal Courts, the Department of Labor, and the Workers' Compensation Appeals Board.

Our firm has maintained its edge in meeting the legal needs of the statewide business and insurance community by staying current with the latest developments in case law, legislation and regulations.

MANCHESTER   NEW HAMPSHIRE

Bernard & Merrill, PLLC, Manchester, NH   (Continued)

Bernard & Merrill, PLLC is a member of the National Workers' Compensation Defense Network and is AV® Preeminent™ Peer Review Rated through Martindale-Hubbell, the highest rating for legal ability and ethical standards.

Insurance Clients

AIM Insurance Company
Chubb Group of Insurance Companies
State Farm Fire and Casualty Company
Capitol Indemnity Corporation
Electric Insurance Company
Hanover Insurance Company
U.S. Liability Insurance Company

Non-Insurance Clients

Demoulas Super Markets, Inc.
Irving Oil Corporation
Local Government Workers' Compensation Fund
Shaw's Supermarkets
Sun Healthcare Group
Wentworth-Douglass Hospital
Granite State Workers' Compensation Manufacturers' Trust
Lumber Industries Self-Insured Group
Wal-Mart Stores, Inc.

Third Party Administrators

Cardinal Comp

Partners

Eric P. Bernard — 1953 — College of the Holy Cross, B.A., 1975; The Catholic University of America, Columbus School of Law, J.D., 1982 — Admitted to Bar, 1982, New Hampshire; 1982, U.S. District Court, District of New Hampshire — U.S. Navy 1971-1973 and 1976-1978 — Practice Areas: Insurance Coverage; Personal Injury; Workers' Compensation — E-mail: eric@bernard-merrill.com

Andrew A. Merrill — 1948 — Tufts University, B.A. (cum laude), 1971; Boston College Law School, J.D. (cum laude), 1980 — Admitted to Bar, 1980, New Hampshire; 1980, U.S. District Court, District of New Hampshire; 1980, U.S. Court of Appeals, First Circuit — Member New Hampshire Bar Association — Practice Areas: Personal Injury; Workers' Compensation — E-mail: andy@bernard-merrill.com

Kevin W. Stuart — 1971 — University of New Hampshire, B.A., 1993; M.P.A. (cum laude), 1995; Suffolk University Law School, J.D. (cum laude), 1999 — Admitted to Bar, 1999, New Hampshire; Maine; 1999, U.S. District Court, District of New Hampshire — Member New Hampshire Bar Association (Past-Chair, Workers' Compensation Section) — Practice Areas: Insurance Law; Personal Injury; Workers' Compensation — E-mail: kevin@bernard-merrill.com

Donna M. Daneke — 1962 — University of New Hampshire, B.A., 1984; University of New Hampshire School of Law, J.D., 1996 — Admitted to Bar, 1996, New Hampshire; 1996, U.S. District Court, District of New Hampshire — Member New Hampshire Bar Association — Practice Areas: Workers' Compensation — E-mail: ddaneke@bernard-merrill.com

Associates

Gary S. Harding — 1966 — University of Massachusetts Lowell, B.A., 1992; New England School of Law, J.D., 2001 — Admitted to Bar, 2001, Massachusetts; 2002, New Hampshire; 2001, U.S. District Court, District of Massachusetts; 2002, U.S. District Court, District of New Hampshire — Member New Hampshire and Massachusetts Bar Associations — U.S.M.C. — Practice Areas: Workers' Compensation; Insurance Coverage — E-mail: gary@bernard-merrill.com

Margaret P. Sack — 1960 — Saint Michael's College, B.A., 1982; New England School of Law, J.D. (cum laude), 1987 — Admitted to Bar, 1987, Maine; 2007, New Hampshire; 1987, U.S. District Court, District of Maine; 2007, U.S. District Court, District of New Hampshire — Member New Hampshire and Maine State Bar Associations — Practice Areas: Workers' Compensation — E-mail: meg@bernard-merrill.com

Merrick C. Weinstein — 1959 — State University of New York at Stony Brook, B.A. (cum laude), 1980; Boston University School of Law, J.D. (cum laude), 1983 — Admitted to Bar, 1983, New Hampshire; U.S. District Court, District of New Hampshire — Member New Hampshire and Manchester Bar Associations — Practice Areas: Insurance Law; Personal Injury; Workers' Compensation

Desmarais, Ewing & Johnston, PLLC

175 Canal Street
Manchester, New Hampshire 03101
   Telephone: 603-623-5524
   Fax: 603-623-6383
   E-Mail: desmaraisf@dejlawfirm.com
   www.dejlawfirm.com

Established: 2001

Professional Liability, Insurance Coverage, Insurance Defense, Product Liability, Business Law, Civil Litigation, Personal Injury, Insurance Litigation, Construction Law

Firm Profile: Desmarais, Ewing & Johnston, PLLC, is a New Hampshire trial law firm with seven trial attorneys dedicated to the representation of insurance carriers, their policyholders, and self-insureds. Its members have practiced in the trial and appellate courts in the State of New Hampshire. Clients include both regional and national insurance carriers whose policyholders range from individuals to multinational corporations. The firm's attorneys specialize in the defense of general liability claims, product liability actions, employment claims, directors and officer actions, professional malpractice claims, and insurance coverage matters.

Insurance Clients

Acadia Insurance Company
Andover Companies
Argonaut Insurance Company
Chubb Group
Commerce Insurance Company
Great American Insurance Company
Kemper Insurance Company
Merchants Insurance Company
Nationwide Insurance
Ohio Casualty Insurance Company
Patriot Insurance Company
State Farm Insurance Company
TIG Insurance Company
American Specialty Insurance Company
Atlantic Mutual Insurance Company
Gallagher Bassett Insurance Company
The Hartford
La Capitale Assurances Générale
Metropolitan Insurance Company
Nautilus Insurance Group
OneBeacon Insurance
Progressive Insurance Company
T.H.E. Insurance Company
Travelers Insurance Companies

Non-Insurance Clients

Albertsons, Inc.
Federal Express
Greyhound Lines, Inc.
Laidlaw, Inc.
McDonald's Corporation
Crawford & Company
Fun Festival
Guaranty Fund Management Services
Yellow Roadway Corporation

Partners

Fred J. Desmarais — 1950 — University of New Hampshire, B.A. (magna cum laude), 1972; University of Baltimore, J.D. (summa cum laude), 1976 — Admitted to Bar, 1976, New Hampshire; 1976, U.S. District Court, District of New Hampshire — Member American and New Hampshire Bar Associations; Defense Research Institute; Federation of Defense and Corporate Counsel — Editor, New Hampshire Product Liability Desk Reference Business Torts: A Fifty State Guide — Practice Areas: Commercial Litigation; Insurance Law; Product Liability; Professional Liability — Tel: 603-623-5524 — Fax: 603-623-6383 — E-mail: desmaraisf@dejlawfirm.com

Scott A. Ewing — 1957 — University of Rochester, B.A., 1983; The Catholic University of America, J.D., 1986 — Admitted to Bar, 1986, New Hampshire; 1986, U.S. District Court, District of New Hampshire — Member American and New Hampshire Bar Associations — Practice Areas: Insurance Law; Product Liability; Workers' Compensation — E-mail: ewings@dejlawfirm.com

David W. Johnston — 1962 — University of Vermont, B.A., 1984; Boston College Law School, J.D. (cum laude), 1992 — Notes & Comments Editor, Boston College International and Comparative Law Review — Admitted to Bar, 1992, New Hampshire; 2001, Massachusetts; 1992, U.S. District Court, District of New Hampshire; 2000, U.S. Court of Appeals, First Circuit — Member New Hampshire Bar Association; Defense Research Institute — Lieutenant, U.S. Navy — Practice Areas: Commercial Litigation; Insurance Coverage; Insurance Litigation — E-mail: johnstond@dejlawfirm.com

Associates

Debra L. Mayotte — 1965 — University of Lowell, B.S., 1987; New England School of Law, J.D., 1990 — Admitted to Bar, 1990, New Hampshire; 1991, Massachusetts; 1990, U.S. District Court, District of New Hampshire; 1991,

NEW HAMPSHIRE   MANCHESTER

Desmarais, Ewing & Johnston, PLLC, Manchester, NH (Continued)

U.S. District Court, District of Massachusetts; 2005, U.S. Supreme Court — Member New Hampshire Bar Association — Practice Areas: Insurance Coverage; Insurance Defense; Subrogation — E-mail: mayotted@dejlawfirm.com

Heather G. Silverstein — 1966 — University of Vermont, B.S., 1989; University of Maine School of Law, J.D. (cum laude), 1998 — Admitted to Bar, 1998, New Hampshire; 2000, U.S. District Court, District of New Hampshire — Member New Hampshire Bar Association — Reported Cases: Nilsson v. Bierman, 150 N.H. 393 (2004); MacDonald v. BMD Golf Association, Inc., 148 N.H. 582 (2002); In re Wingate, 149 N.H. 12 (2002); Appeal of Tim Calahan, Slipop. 2002 - 344, N.H. (2003). — Practice Areas: Insurance Defense; Personal Injury — E-mail: silversteinh@dejlawfirm.com

Emily M. Doherty — 1976 — University of New Hampshire, B.A., 1998; Quinnipiac University, J.D., 2002 — Admitted to Bar, 2003, New Hampshire; 2003, U.S. District Court, District of New Hampshire — Member American and New Hampshire Women's Bar Associations — Practice Areas: Civil Litigation; Insurance Coverage; Insurance Defense — E-mail: dohertye@dejlawfirm.com

Devine, Millimet & Branch, P.A.

111 Amherst Street
Manchester, New Hampshire 03101
   Telephone: 603-669-1000
   Fax: 603-669-8547
   E-Mail: firm-info@devinemillimet.com
   www.devinemillimet.com

(Concord, NH Office: 15 North Main Street, Suite 300, 03301)

Established: 1947

Insurance Defense, Automobile, Product Liability, Malpractice, Workers' Compensation, Environmental Law, Errors and Omissions, Surety, Professional Malpractice, Construction Law, Municipal Law, Insurance Coverage

Firm Profile: Established in 1947 Devine Millimet provides a wide range of corporate and litigation services with one of the largest and most diversified insurance defense practices in the region.

Insurance Clients

AIG	Liberty Mutual Insurance Company
Safety Insurance Company	

Shareholder

Andrew D. Dunn — 1949 — Columbia University, B.A., 1971; Duke University, J.D., 1974 — Admitted to Bar, 1974, New Hampshire — Member New Hampshire Bar Association (Editor: Insurance Law Section, Practice and Procedures Handbook, 1986-1990; Chairman, Professional Liability Insurance Committee, 1988-); American National Lawyers Insurance Reciprocal (Director) — State of New Hampshire, Legislative Task Force on Automobile Insurance (1990); Lawyer's Lawyer Award for Insurance Defense (1994) — Practice Areas: Civil Litigation; Insurance Law; Personal Injury — E-mail: adunn@devinemillimet.com

McDonough, O'Shaughnessy, Whaland & Meagher, PLLC

42 West Brook Street
Manchester, New Hampshire 03101
   Telephone: 603-669-8300
   Fax: 603-669-8517
   E-Mail: rmeagher@lawfirmnh.com
   www.lawfirmnh.com

Established: 1985

McDonough, O'Shaughnessy, Whaland & Meagher, PLLC, Manchester, NH (Continued)

Fire, Casualty, Surety, Life Insurance, Workers' Compensation, Automobile Liability, General Liability, Product Liability, Professional Malpractice, Public Liability, Governmental Liability, Civil Rights, Medical Malpractice

Insurance Clients

AAO Services, Inc.	ACE USA Claims
Burlington Insurance Company	Central Mutual Insurance Company
Covenant Insurance Company	Coverys
Crum & Forster Insurance Group	First Financial Insurance Company
First Mercury Insurance Company	Gallagher Bassett Services, Inc.
GMAC Insurance	Great West Casualty Company
Guilford Specialty Group, Inc.	Holyoke Mutual Insurance Company in Salem
Horace Mann Insurance Company	Medical Mutual Insurance Company of Maine
Lumber Insurance Companies	
MiddleOak	
National General Insurance Company	Norfolk and Dedham Mutual Fire Insurance Company
OMS National Insurance Company	Patriot Insurance Company
Preferred Mutual Insurance Company	

Non-Insurance Clients

City of Manchester	Exeter Hospital
Fluidmaster, Inc.	The Home Depot
Manchester School District	

Robert J. Meagher — **Managing Attorney** — 1956 — University of Massachusetts Amherst, B.A., 1980; University of New Hampshire School of Law, J.D., 1987 — Admitted to Bar, 1987, New Hampshire; 2008, Vermont; 1987, U.S. District Court, District of New Hampshire — Member American, New Hampshire, Vermont and Manchester Bar Associations; New Hampshire Trial Lawyers Association; Tri State Defense Lawyers Association; Association of Trial Lawyers of America — E-mail: Rmeagher@lawfirmnh.com

Robert G. Whaland — 1951 — The George Washington University, B.A., 1975; Franklin Pierce Law Center, J.D., 1979 — Admitted to Bar, 1979, New Hampshire; 1981, Florida; 1979, U.S. District Court, District of New Hampshire; 1980, U.S. Court of Appeals, First Circuit — Member New Hampshire Bar Association; The Florida Bar; Tri State Defense Lawyers Association; Association of Trial Lawyers of America; Defense Research Institute — E-mail: Rwhaland@lawfirmnh.com

Michael B. O'Shaughnessy — 1946 — Keene State College, A.B., 1969; Albany Law School, J.D., 1973 — Admitted to Bar, 1973, New Hampshire; U.S. District Court, District of New Hampshire — Member American, New Hampshire and Manchester Bar Associations; New Hampshire Trial Lawyers Association; International Association of Insurance Counsel; Northern New England Defense Counsel Association (President, 1998-1999); American Board of Trial Advocates; Association of Trial Lawyers of America; Federation of Defense and Corporate Counsel; Defense Research Institute

Wadleigh, Starr & Peters, P.L.L.C.

95 Market Street
Manchester, New Hampshire 03101
   Telephone: 603-669-4140
   Fax: 603-669-6018
   E-Mail: info@wadleighlaw.com
   www.wadleighlaw.com

Established: 1899

Fire, Casualty, Surety, Life Insurance, Medical Liability, Legal, Architects and Engineers, Engineers, Professional Malpractice, Product Liability, Arson, Hazardous Waste, Drug, Litigation, Subrogation, Defense Under All Lines, DES

Firm Profile: Since its inception in 1899, Wadleigh, Starr & Peters, P.L.L.C., has provided comprehensive legal services to the people of New Hampshire, and to companies nationwide. The firm currently has a staff of more than fifty experienced attorneys, paralegals, and support personnel.

MANCHESTER   NEW HAMPSHIRE

Wadleigh, Starr & Peters, P.L.L.C., Manchester, NH (Continued)

Wadleigh offers legal counsel in such areas as medical malpractice, professional liability, products liability, personal injury, insurance, construction, environmental, corporate, employment, land use planning, municipal law, education and other areas of general practice. The firm has an extensive and comprehensive commercial and real estate practice involving the representation of financial institutions, private lenders, real estate development firms, general contractors and business corporations, as well as individual investors. In addition, the firm offers services in tax, labor, civil rights, municipal and hospital, and represents clients in probate matters involving wills, estates and guardianships.

The firm is a member of ALFA International, the global legal network.

Insurance Clients

ACE USA
American Contractors Insurance Group
American States Insurance Company
Andover Companies
Chartis Insurance
CIGNA Insurance Company
CNA Insurance Companies
Electric Mutual Liability Insurance Company
Fireman's Fund Insurance Companies
GAINSCO, Inc.
Granite Shield Insurance Exchange
Interstate Insurance Group
Lawyers Title Insurance Corporation
Medical Professional Mutual Insurance Company
National Grange Mutual Insurance Company
OneBeacon Insurance Company
Peerless Insurance Company
Penn Mutual Insurance Company
Progressive Insurance Group
Republic Western Insurance Company
Scottsdale Insurance Company
Sedgwick James of New Hampshire, Inc.
Ticor Title Insurance Company
Travelers Property Casualty Insurance Company
United States Fidelity and Guaranty Company
Zurich U.S.
American Bankers Life Assurance Company of Florida
American Modern Home Insurance Company
American Trucking and Transportation Insurance Company
CNA HealthPro
Coverys
Fidelity National Title Insurance Company
Fitchburg Mutual Insurance Company
Gallagher Bassett Services, Inc.
Health Care Indemnity, Inc.
K & K Insurance Group, Inc.
Liberty Mutual Insurance Company
Medical Mutual Insurance Company of Maine
Metropolitan Life Insurance Company
New Hampshire Medical Malpractice Joint Underwriting Association
PRMS, Inc. - Professional Risk Management Services, Inc.
Risk Enterprise Management, Ltd.
The St. Paul/Travelers Companies, Inc.
Sentry Insurance Group
Shand Morahan & Company, Inc.
TIG Insurance Company
United Services Automobile Association (USAA)
Wausau General Insurance Company

Partners

William C. Tucker — 1944 — Yale University, B.A., 1966; Harvard Law School, J.D., 1969 — Admitted to Bar, 1969, New Hampshire — Member American and New Hampshire Bar Associations — E-mail: btucker@wadleighlaw.com

John E. Friberg — 1942 — Colby College, B.A., 1964; Boston University Law School, J.D., 1967 — Admitted to Bar, 1967, New Hampshire — Member American, New Hampshire and Manchester Bar Associations — E-mail: jfriberg@wadleighlaw.com

James C. Wheat — 1946 — University of Massachusetts, B.A., 1968; Boston University Law School, J.D., 1971 — Law Clerk, New Hampshire Supreme Court, 1971 — Admitted to Bar, 1971, Massachusetts; 1972, New Hampshire — Member American and New Hampshire Bar Associations; Defense Research Institute — E-mail: jwheat@wadleighlaw.com

Ronald J. Lajoie — 1952 — University of New Hampshire, B.A. (summa cum laude), 1974; Rutgers University, J.D., 1979 — Law Clerk, New Hampshire Supreme Court (1979-80) — Admitted to Bar, 1979, New Hampshire — Member American and New Hampshire Bar Associations; Association of Trial Lawyers of America; Defense Research Institute — E-mail: rlajoie@wadleighlaw.com

Jeffrey H. Karlin — 1954 — Boston College, B.A., 1976; J.D., 1982 — Admitted to Bar, 1982, New Hampshire — Member American, Massachusetts, New Hampshire and Manchester Bar Associations — E-mail: jkarlin@wadleighlaw.com

Wadleigh, Starr & Peters, P.L.L.C., Manchester, NH (Continued)

Donald J. Perrault — 1948 — Norwich University, B.A., 1970; Northeastern University School of Law, J.D., 1973 — Admitted to Bar, 1973, New Hampshire — Member American, New Hampshire and Merrimack County Bar Associations — Assistant Attorney General of New Hampshire, 1979-84 — E-mail: dperrault@wadleighlaw.com

Marc R. Scheer — 1952 — Tufts University, B.A., 1974; American University, Washington College of Law, J.D., 1977 — Admitted to Bar, 1977, New Hampshire; 1980, District of Columbia; 1981, U.S. Supreme Court — Assistant Attorney General, State of New Hampshire, 1979-85 — E-mail: mscheer@wadleighlaw.com

Gregory G. Peters — 1959 — Middlebury College, A.B., 1981; Boston University Law School, J.D., 1984 — Admitted to Bar, 1984, New Hampshire — Member New Hampshire Bar Association; New Hampshire Trial Lawyers Association — Author: "Reallocating Liability to Medical Staff Review Committee Members: A Response to the Hospital Corporate Liability Doctrine", American Journal of Law and Medicine, Vol. 10, No. 1, 115-138 (1984) — Associate Editor, American Journal of Law and Medicine (1983-84); — E-mail: gpeters@wadleighlaw.com

Robert E. Murphy, Jr. — 1952 — University of New Hampshire, B.S., 1974; University of Missouri, M.B.A., 1980; J.D., 1981 — Admitted to Bar, 1981, New Hampshire — E-mail: rmurphy@wadleighlaw.com

Dean B. Eggert — 1960 — Wheaton College, B.A. (with highest honors), 1982; University of California, Los Angeles, J.D., 1985 — Admitted to Bar, 1985, New Hampshire — E-mail: deggert@wadleighlaw.com

Michael R. Mortimer — 1960 — Williams College, B.A., 1982; Boston University, J.D. (cum laude), 1985 — Admitted to Bar, 1985, New Hampshire; 1986, Massachusetts — E-mail: mmortimer@wadleighlaw.com

Kathleen C. Peahl — 1962 — Boston College, B.A. (magna cum laude), 1984; J.D. (cum laude), 1989 — Admitted to Bar, 1989, New Hampshire; 1989, U.S. District Court, District of New Hampshire — Member American and New Hampshire Bar Associations — E-mail: kpeahl@wadleighlaw.com

Richard Thorner — 1964 — Dartmouth College, A.B. (cum laude), 1986; Boston University, J.D., 1989 — Admitted to Bar, 1989, New Hampshire; 1989, U.S. District Court, District of New Hampshire — Member New Hampshire Bar Association — E-mail: rthorner@wadleighlaw.com

Charles F. Cleary — 1964 — Colby College, B.A., 1986; Boston University, J.D., 1990 — Admitted to Bar, 1990, New Hampshire; 1990, U.S. District Court, District of New Hampshire — Member New Hampshire Bar Association — E-mail: ccleary@wadleighlaw.com

Christine A. Gordon — 1964 — Regis College, B.A. (cum laude), 1986; Boston University, J.D., 1993 — Admitted to Bar, 1993, New Hampshire; 1994, Massachusetts — E-mail: cgordon@wadleighlaw.com

Todd J. Hathaway — 1971 — University of Connecticut, J.D. (with honors), 1996 — Admitted to Bar, 1996, New Hampshire — E-mail: thathaway@wadleighlaw.com

Stephen J. Judge — 1949 — University of Maryland, B.A., 1976; Boston College Law School, J.D. (with honors), 1982 — Admitted to Bar, 1982, Massachusetts; 1983, New Hampshire; 1995, U.S. Court of Appeals, First Circuit; 1996, U.S. Supreme Court — U.S. Naval Reserve, 1971-1973 — E-mail: sjudge@wadleighlaw.com

Stephen L. Boyd — 1977 — Hofstra University, J.D., 2002 — Admitted to Bar, 2002, New Hampshire; 2011, Massachusetts — E-mail: sboyd@wadleighlaw.com

Alison M. Minutelli — 1979 — Brandeis University, B.A. (cum laude), 2002; Franklin Pierce Law Center, J.D., 2005 — Admitted to Bar, 2005, New Hampshire — E-mail: aminutelli@wadleighlaw.com

Michael J. Tierney — 1977 — Dartmouth College, A.B., 1999; University of Notre Dame Law School, J.D. (magna cum laude), 2005 — Admitted to Bar, 2005, New Hampshire; 2014, Vermont — E-mail: mtierney@wadleighlaw.com

James D. Kerouac — 1974 — University of New Hampshire, B.A./B.S. (magna cum laude), 1998; Boston University School of Law, J.D., 2001 — Admitted to Bar, 2001, New Hampshire; 2002, Maine; 2009, Massachusetts; 2012, Rhode Island — Member New Hampshire, Maine State, Massachusetts and Rhode Island Bar Associations — E-mail: jkerouac@wadleighlaw.com

Associates

Pierre A. Chabot — 1979 — Middlebury College, B.A. (magna cum laude), 2002; Hofstra University, J.D. (cum laude), 2008 — Admitted to Bar, 2008, New Hampshire — E-mail: pchabot@wadleighlaw.com

Joseph G. Mattson — 1982 — Plymouth State College, B.A. (summa cum laude), 2005; Franklin Pierce Law Center, J.D., 2009 — Admitted to Bar,

NEW HAMPSHIRE

Wadleigh, Starr & Peters, P.L.L.C., Manchester, NH (Continued)

2009, New Hampshire — Member New Hampshire Bar Association — E-mail: jmattson@wadleighlaw.com

Iris J. Lowery — College of the Atlantic, B.A., 2009; The George Washington University Law School, J.D., 2012 — Admitted to Bar, 2012, New Hampshire; 2012, Massachusetts — E-mail: ilowery@wadleighlaw.com

Emily G. Bolton — University of New Hampshire, B.A. (summa cum laude), 2007; University of Connecticut School of Law, J.D., 2012 — Admitted to Bar, 2012, New Hampshire; 2012, Massachusetts — E-mail: ebolton@wadleighlaw.com

Of Counsel

Eugene M. Van Loan, III — 1942 — Yale University, B.A., 1964; Harvard Law School, LL.B., 1967 — Admitted to Bar, 1967, New Hampshire — Member American, New Hampshire and Manchester Bar Associations — E-mail: evan@wadleighlaw.com

Kathleen N. Sullivan — 1954 — College of the Holy Cross, B.A., 1976; Cornell University, J.D., 1981 — Admitted to Bar, 1981, New Hampshire — Member New Hampshire and Manchester Bar Associations — E-mail: ksullivan@wadleighlaw.com

Jennifer L. St. Hilaire — Boston University Law School, J.D., 1995 — Admitted to Bar, 1995, New Hampshire — E-mail: jsthilaire@wadleighlaw.com

(Revisors of the New Hampshire Insurance Law Digest for this Publication)

NASHUA 86,494 Hillsborough Co.

Refer To

Coughlin Betke LLP
175 Federal Street
Boston, Massachusetts 02110
Telephone: 617-988-8050
Fax: 617-988-8005

Architects and Engineers, Casualty, Civil Rights, Construction Law, Contract Disputes, Creditor Rights, Employment Law, Environmental Law, Fire, Fraud, Insurance Coverage, Legal Malpractice, Personal Injury, Premises Liability, Product Liability, Professional Liability, Property Damage, Real Estate, Tort Litigation, Transportation

SEE COMPLETE LISTING UNDER BOSTON, MASSACHUSETTS (46 MILES)

Refer To

Desmarais, Ewing & Johnston, PLLC
175 Canal Street
Manchester, New Hampshire 03101
Telephone: 603-623-5524
Fax: 603-623-6383

Professional Liability, Insurance Coverage, Insurance Defense, Product Liability, Business Law, Civil Litigation, Personal Injury, Insurance Litigation, Construction Law

SEE COMPLETE LISTING UNDER MANCHESTER, NEW HAMPSHIRE (20 MILES)

Refer To

Mallory & Friedman, PLLC
3 North Spring Street, Suite 201
Concord, New Hampshire 03301
Telephone: 603-228-2277
Fax: 603-228-2275

Insurance Defense, Errors and Omissions, Insurance Coverage, Medical Malpractice, Premises Liability, Product Liability, Commercial Litigation, Lender Liability Defense, Litigation, Consultation, Motor Vehicle Accidents

SEE COMPLETE LISTING UNDER CONCORD, NEW HAMPSHIRE (35 MILES)

Refer To

Wadleigh, Starr & Peters, P.L.L.C.
95 Market Street
Manchester, New Hampshire 03101
Telephone: 603-669-4140
Fax: 603-669-6018

Fire, Casualty, Surety, Life Insurance, Medical Liability, Legal, Architects and Engineers, Engineers, Professional Malpractice, Product Liability, Arson, Hazardous Waste, Drug, Litigation, Subrogation, Defense Under All Lines, DES

SEE COMPLETE LISTING UNDER MANCHESTER, NEW HAMPSHIRE (20 MILES)

PORTSMOUTH 20779 Rockingham Co.

Refer To

Desmarais, Ewing & Johnston, PLLC
175 Canal Street
Manchester, New Hampshire 03101
Telephone: 603-623-5524
Fax: 603-623-6383

Professional Liability, Insurance Coverage, Insurance Defense, Product Liability, Business Law, Civil Litigation, Personal Injury, Insurance Litigation, Construction Law

SEE COMPLETE LISTING UNDER MANCHESTER, NEW HAMPSHIRE (45 MILES)

Refer To

Melick & Porter
1 Liberty Square
Boston, Massachusetts 02109
Telephone: 617-523-6200
Fax: 617-523-8130

Accountants, Administrative Law, Advertising Injury, Agent/Broker Liability, Appellate Practice, Architects and Engineers, Asbestos, Automobile, Bad Faith, Commercial Litigation, Complex Litigation, Construction Litigation, Dental Malpractice, Directors and Officers Liability, Employment Practices, Environmental Law, Fire, General Liability, Health Care, Hospitality, Insurance Coverage, Insurance Defense, Lead Paint, Legal Malpractice, Life Insurance, Liquor Liability, Medical Devices, Pharmaceutical, Pollution, Premises Liability, Product Liability, Professional Liability, Property and Casualty, Public Entities, Real Estate Agents & Brokers Liability, Restaurant Liability, State and Federal Courts, Toxic Torts, Transportation, Trucking, Workers' Compensation

SEE COMPLETE LISTING UNDER BOSTON, MASSACHUSETTS (56 MILES)

Refer To

Wadleigh, Starr & Peters, P.L.L.C.
95 Market Street
Manchester, New Hampshire 03101
Telephone: 603-669-4140
Fax: 603-669-6018

Fire, Casualty, Surety, Life Insurance, Medical Liability, Legal, Architects and Engineers, Engineers, Professional Malpractice, Product Liability, Arson, Hazardous Waste, Drug, Litigation, Subrogation, Defense Under All Lines, DES

SEE COMPLETE LISTING UNDER MANCHESTER, NEW HAMPSHIRE (45 MILES)

NEW JERSEY

CAPITAL: TRENTON

COUNTIES AND COUNTY SEATS

County	County Seat
Atlantic	Mays Landing
Bergen	Hackensack
Burlington	Mount Holly
Camden	Camden
Cape May	Cape May Court House
Cumberland	Bridgeton
Essex	Newark
Gloucester	Woodbury
Hudson	Jersey City
Hunterdon	Flemington
Mercer	Trenton
Middlesex	New Brunswick
Monmouth	Freehold
Morris	Morristown
Ocean	Toms River
Passaic	Paterson
Salem	Salem
Somerset	Somerville
Sussex	Newton
Union	Elizabeth
Warren	Belvidere

In the text that follows "†" indicates County Seats.

Our files contain additional verified data on the firms listed herein. This additional information is available on request.

A.M. BEST COMPANY

NEW JERSEY — ATLANTIC CITY

ATLANTIC CITY 39,558 Atlantic Co.

Cooper Levenson, P.A.

1125 Atlantic Avenue, Third Floor
Atlantic City, New Jersey 08401
Telephone: 609-344-3161
Fax: 609-344-0939
E-Mail: info@cooperlevenson.com
www.cooperlevenson.com

(Cherry Hill, NJ Office: Cherry Hill Plaza, Suite 205, 1415 Route 70 East, 08034)
(Tel: 856-795-9110)
(Fax: 856-795-8641)
(Las Vegas, NV Office: 6060 Elton Avenue, 89107-0126)
(Tel: 702-366-1125)
(Fax: 702-366-1857)

Established: 1957

Trial and Appellate Practice, State and Federal Courts, Negligence, Insurance Defense, Product Liability, Workers' Compensation, Environmental Law, Professional Liability, Employment Law, Dram Shop, Premises Liability, Mass Tort, Casino, Health/Hospital, Bedbug Liability Defense

Firm Profile: Full service firm with offices in NJ, PA, DE and Las Vegas, NV.

Representative Insurance Clients

ACE USA
AIG Claim Services, Inc.
Chartis
Crawford & Company
Donegal Mutual Insurance Company
Great American Insurance Company
Hertz Claim Management
International Marine Underwriters
Lloyd's
Millers Mutual Insurance Company
Palisades Safety and Insurance Association
Risk Enterprise Management, Ltd.
Sedgwick CMS
Specialty / Security Indemnity
XL Insurance/XL Environmental Inc.
Zurich American Insurance Company
AequiCap Claims Services
AIU Holdings, Inc.
CNA Insurance Companies
Deep South Insurance Services
ESIS
Gallagher Bassett Services, Inc.
Harleysville Insurance Company
The Hartford Insurance Group
Inservco Insurance Services, Inc.
Lexington Insurance Company
Majestic Insurance Company
National Indemnity Company
RCA Insurance Group
R.E.M., Inc.
Rockville Risk Management Associates, Inc.
Twin Lights Insurance Company
XL Select Professional
York Claims Service, Inc.
Zurich North America

Partners

Louis Niedelman — Temple University, B.A., 1966; Villanova University, J.D., 1969 — Admitted to Bar, 1969, New Jersey; 1969, U.S. District Court, District of New Jersey — Member New Jersey Defense Association; American Board of Trial Advocates; International Association of Defense Counsel — Certified by the Supreme Court of New Jersey as a Civil Trial Attorney — Practice Areas: Construction Defect; Construction Litigation; General Defense; Professional Malpractice — Tel: 609-572-7474 — E-mail: lniedelman@cooperlevenson.com

Russell L. Lichtenstein — Temple University, B.A., 1978; Western New England College School of Law, J.D., 1981 — Admitted to Bar, 1981, New Jersey; Pennsylvania; 1981, U.S. District Court, District of New Jersey; 1981, U.S. District Court, Eastern District of Pennsylvania — Member Association of Trial Lawyers of America — Certified by the Supreme Court of New Jersey as a Civil Trial Attorney — Practice Areas: Labor and Employment; Employment Law (Management Side); Employment Litigation — Tel: 609-572-7676 — E-mail: rlichtenstein@cooperlevenson.com

Kenneth J. Sylvester — Rutgers University, B.A., 1974; Temple University, J.D., 1978 — Admitted to Bar, 1982, New Jersey; 1982, U.S. District Court, District of New Jersey; 1982, U.S. Court of Appeals, Third Circuit — Practice

Cooper Levenson, P.A., Atlantic City, NJ (Continued)

Areas: Workers' Compensation — Tel: 856-857-5524 — E-mail: ksylvester@cooperlevenson.com

William J. Kohler — Rutgers University, B.S., 1978; Dickinson School of Law, J.D., 1986 — Admitted to Bar, 1986, New Jersey; 1986, Pennsylvania; 1986, U.S. District Court, District of New Jersey — Practice Areas: Amusements; Dram Shop; Liquor Liability; Automobile; Insurance Coverage; Premises Liability; Product Liability — Tel: 609-572-7404 — E-mail: wkohler@cooperlevenson.com

Joseph D. Deal — The Pennsylvania State University, B.A., 1983; Widener University School of Law, J.D., 1986 — Admitted to Bar, 1986, New Jersey; Pennsylvania; 1989, U.S. District Court, District of New Jersey; 1989, U.S. District Court, Eastern District of Pennsylvania; 1991, U.S. District Court, Western District of Pennsylvania — Practice Areas: Liquor Liability; Dram Shop; Legal Malpractice; Premises Liability; Product Liability — Tel: 856-857-5506 — E-mail: jdeal@cooperlevenson.com

James P. Paoli — Rutgers College, B.A., 1989; Widener University School of Law, J.D., 1992 — Admitted to Bar, 1992, New Jersey; Pennsylvania; 1992, U.S. District Court, District of New Jersey; 1993, U.S. District Court, Eastern District of Pennsylvania — Certified by the Supreme Court of New Jersey as a Workers Compensation Attorney — Practice Areas: Workers' Compensation — Tel: 856-857-5512 — E-mail: jpaoli@cooperlevenson.com

Jerry Busby — Brigham Young University, B.S., 1981; Arizona State University College of Law, J.D., 1984 — Admitted to Bar, 1984, Nevada — Member American Board of Trial Advocates; Federation of Defense and Corporate Counsel; Defense Research Institute — Practice Areas: Premises Liability; Automobile; Insurance Coverage; Product Liability; Professional Liability — Tel: 702-366-1125 — E-mail: jbusby@cooperlevenson.com

Carmelo T. Torraca — Villanova University, B.A., 1991; Widener University School of Law, J.D., 1995 — Admitted to Bar, 1996, New Jersey; Pennsylvania — Practice Areas: Construction Accidents; Commercial Vehicle; Self-Insured Defense; Legal Malpractice; Personal Injury; Premises Liability; Product Liability — Tel: 609-572-7520 — E-mail: ctorraca@cooperlevenson.com

Of Counsel

Brian D. Barr — Gettysburg College, B.A., 1986; Rutgers University, J.D. (with honors), 1989 — Admitted to Bar, 1989, New Jersey; Pennsylvania — Practice Areas: Insurance Coverage; Environmental Coverage; Toxic Torts; General Defense; Product Liability; Professional Malpractice — Tel: 856-857-5514 — E-mail: bbarr@cooperlevenson.com

---

The following firms also service this area.

Law Offices of Garrett L. Joest, L.L.C.

29 Hadley Avenue
Toms River, New Jersey 08753
Telephone: 732-505-0707
Fax: 732-505-1717

Insurance Defense, Insurance Coverage, Subrogation, Professional Malpractice, Personal Injury, Toxic Torts, Environmental Law, Asbestos Litigation

SEE COMPLETE LISTING UNDER TOMS RIVER, NEW JERSEY (51 MILES)

O'Connor Kimball LLP

51 Haddonfield Road, Suite 330
Cherry Hill, New Jersey 08002-4805
Telephone: 856-663-9292
Fax: 856-663-6566

General Civil Practice, Casualty, Product Liability, Employment Law, Construction Litigation, Real Estate, Environmental Law, Toxic Torts, Insurance Law, Excess, Professional Liability, Commercial Liability, Commercial Litigation, Workers' Compensation, Civil Rights, Real Estate and Small Business Development Transactions, Professional Liability Litigation

SEE COMPLETE LISTING UNDER CHERRY HILL, NEW JERSEY (53 MILES)

Powell, Birchmeier & Powell
1891 State Highway 50
Tuckahoe, New Jersey 08250
  Telephone: 609-628-3414
  Fax: 609-628-2966

Mailing Address: P.O. Box 582, Tuckahoe, NJ 08250-0582

General Civil Practice, Trial Practice, Insurance Defense, Negligence, Defense Litigation, Product Liability, Coverage Issues, Litigation, Workers' Compensation, Subrogation, Civil Rights, Governmental Liability, Medical Negligence, Wrongful Termination, General Chancery Practice, Section 1983 Litigation

SEE COMPLETE LISTING UNDER TUCKAHOE, NEW JERSEY (32 MILES)

AUDUBON 8,819 Camden Co.

Prutting & Lombardi

701 South White Horse Pike
Audubon, New Jersey 08106
  Telephone: 856-547-8404
  Fax: 856-547-0174
  E-Mail: esq@pruttinglaw.com
  www.pruttinglaw.com

Established: 1989

Insurance Defense, Negligence, Automobile, Premises Liability, Product Liability, Errors and Omissions, Coverage Issues, Commercial and Personal Lines, Workers' Compensation, Subrogation, State and Federal Courts, Garage Keepers, Defense of Automobile Dealership (All Aspects)

Firm Profile: Delaware Valley based civil litigation firm. Providing litigation and transactional services to its carrier and self-insured clientele. Practicing statewide in New Jersey, Philadelphia metro and Eastern Pennsylvania in state and federal courts.

Insurance Clients

Cambridge Integrated Services	Crawford & Company
Cumberland Insurance Group	Gallagher Bassett Services, Inc.
GMAC Insurance Group	Metropolitan Property and Casualty Insurance Company
Mount Vernon Fire Insurance Company	National Claims Management
National General Insurance Company	Nationwide Insurance
	Scottsdale Insurance Company
Titan Insurance Company	U.S. Liability Insurance Company

Non-Insurance Clients

BP Products North America, Inc.	Catelli Brothers, Inc.
Georgia-Pacific LLC	Limited Brands, Inc.
The Silvi Group Companies	Southwest Business Corporation

Partners

George A. Prutting, Jr. — 1959 — William Paterson College, B.A. (magna cum laude), 1981; Rutgers University-Camden, J.D., 1984 — Admitted to Bar, 1984, New Jersey; Pennsylvania; 1990, New York; 1984, U.S. District Court, District of New Jersey; 1984, U.S. District Court, Eastern District of Pennsylvania; 1984, U.S. Court of Appeals, Third Circuit; 1989, U.S. Supreme Court — Member American, New Jersey State, Pennsylvania, New York State and Camden County Bar Associations; New Jersey Defense Association — Author: "UIM Coverage," New Jersey Law Journal, November 1989; "Insurance Coverage for Environmental Claims," New Jersey Law Journal, July 1990

Marilou Lombardi — 1954 — Marietta College, B.A. (cum laude), 1976; Rutgers University-Camden, J.D., 1980 — Admitted to Bar, 1980, New Jersey; 1985, Pennsylvania; 1985, U.S. District Court, Eastern District of Pennsylvania; 1985, U.S. District Court, District of New Jersey; 1996, U.S. Court of Appeals, Third Circuit — Member New Jersey Defense Association (Board of Directors, 1991-1994)

Associates

Nicole P. Showers — York College of Pennsylvania, B.S., 2003; Widener University School of Law, J.D., 2007 — Admitted to Bar, 2007, New Jersey; Pennsylvania; U.S. District Court, District of New Jersey

Prutting & Lombardi, Audubon, NJ   (Continued)

Gregory J. Keresztury — 1983 — Ursinus College, B.A. (cum laude), 2005; Villanova University School of Law, J.D., 2008 — Admitted to Bar, 2008, Pennsylvania; 2009, New Jersey; U.S. District Court, District of New Jersey

BASKING RIDGE 3,060 Somerset Co.

Carroll McNulty & Kull LLC

120 Mountain View Boulevard
Basking Ridge, New Jersey 07920-3444
  Telephone: 908-848-6300
  Fax: 908-848-6310
  www.cmk.com

(New York, NY Office: 570 Lexington Avenue, 8th Floor, 10022)
  (Tel: 212-252-0004)
  (Fax: 212-252-0444)
(Philadelphia, PA Office: Two Liberty Place, 50 South 16th Street, Suite 2600, 19102)
  (Tel: 267-479-6700)
  (Fax: 267-479-6710)
(Chicago, IL Office: 100 North Riverside Plaza, 21st Floor, 60606)
  (Tel: 312-800-5000)
  (Fax: 312-800-5100)

Established: 1997

Insurance Coverage, Insurance Defense, General Liability, Automobile, Bodily Injury, Product Liability, Construction Law, Coverage Issues, Environmental Law, Premises Liability, Workers' Compensation, Subrogation, Admiralty and Maritime Law, Commercial Disputes, Construction and Surety, Intellectual Property Disputes and Counseling, Business Counseling, Employment

Firm Profile: Since our founding in 1997, we have worked to build a law firm that remains true to our guiding principles - elevate our clients above all other considerations through a diligent, effective and personal pursuit of their best interests.

Insurance Clients

CIGNA Property and Casualty Insurance Company	CNA Financial Corporation
	Crum & Forster Insurance
Fidelity and Deposit Company of Maryland	Selective Insurance Company of America
Travelers Indemnity Company	

Founding Members

Christopher R. Carroll — 1966 — St. Joseph's College, B.A., 1988; St. John's University, J.D., 1991 — Admitted to Bar, 1992, New York; 1994, New Jersey; 2008, Pennsylvania; 1994, U.S. District Court, District of New Jersey; 1996, U.S. District Court, Eastern and Southern Districts of New York; 1997, U.S. Court of Appeals, Fourth Circuit — Member American, New Jersey State and New York State Bar Associations — Author: "The Breadth of Section 514 of ERISA and the Preemptibility of State Antisubrogation Laws, " 5 St. John's Journal of Comm. 29 1990 — Editorial Advisory Board of Insurance Law and Litigation — Practice Areas: Commercial Transactions; Surety; Insurance Coverage — E-mail: ccarroll@cmk.com

Joseph P. McNulty — 1959 — Lafayette College, B.A., 1981; St. John's University, J.D., 1984 — Admitted to Bar, 1985, New Jersey; New York; 2009, Pennsylvania; 1985, U.S. District Court, District of New Jersey; 1991, U.S. District Court, Eastern and Southern Districts of New York — Member American, New Jersey State and New York State Bar Associations — Practice Areas: Surety; Insurance Defense — E-mail: jmcnulty@cmk.com

Gary S. Kull — 1959 — Lehigh University, B.A., 1983; University of Baltimore, J.D. (cum laude), 1987 — Admitted to Bar, 1987, New Jersey; 1987, U.S. District Court, District of New Jersey; 2008, U.S. District Court, Eastern District of Texas; 2011, U.S. District Court, Western District of Pennsylvania — Member National Coordinating Counsel — Practice Areas: Insurance Coverage; Land Use; Real Estate — E-mail: gkull@cmk.com

Carroll McNulty & Kull LLC, Basking Ridge, NJ
(Continued)

Members

Benjamin A. Blume — Knox College, B.A., 1985; Loyola University Chicago School of Law, J.D., 1989 — Admitted to Bar, 1989, Illinois; U.S. District Court, Eastern District of Wisconsin; U.S. District Court, Northern District of Illinois; U.S. Court of Appeals, Seventh Circuit; Supreme Court of Illinois — Practice Areas: Insurance Coverage; Insurance Defense; Reinsurance — Resident Chicago, IL Office — E-mail: bblume@cmk.com

Sean T. Burns — 1973 — Manhattan College, B.A., 1995; St. John's University, J.D., 1998 — Admitted to Bar, 1999, New York; 2004, U.S. District Court, Eastern and Southern Districts of New York; 2010, U.S. District Court, Northern District of New York — Practice Areas: Insurance Defense; Civil Litigation; Criminal Defense — Resident New York, NY Office — Tel: 212-252-0004 — Fax: 212-252-0444 — E-mail: sburns@cmk.com

Margaret F. Catalano — 1959 — Fairfield University, B.A. (cum laude), 1981; Seton Hall University, J.D. (cum laude), 1985 — Admitted to Bar, 1985, New Jersey; 1985, U.S. District Court, District of New Jersey — Tewksbury Education Foundation (Board of Directors); Somerset Hills YMCA Advisory Board — Practice Areas: Commercial Transactions; Surety; Insurance Coverage — E-mail: mcatalano@cmk.com

Martha E. Conlin — Saint Mary's College, B.A., 1993; Northwestern University School of Law, J.D., 1996 — Admitted to Bar, 1996, Illinois — Practice Areas: Insurance Coverage; Insurance Defense — E-mail: mconlin@cmk.com

Robert Coppersmith — Oberlin College, B.A., 1973; Boston University School of Law, J.D., 1978 — Admitted to Bar, 1979, New York; U.S. District Court, Southern District of New York — Practice Areas: Medical Malpractice Defense — Resident New York, NY Office — E-mail: rcoppersmith@cmk.com

Carlos del Carpio — Lewis University, B.A., 1982; Northwestern School of Law, J.D., 1985; Northwestern University, Kellogg School of Management, M.B.A., 2009 — Admitted to Bar, 1988, Illinois — Languages: Spanish — Practice Areas: Insurance Coverage; Commercial Litigation — Resident Chicago, IL Office — E-mail: cdelcarpio@cmk.com

Denise Marra DePekary — 1968 — Lafayette College, B.A., 1990; Benjamin N. Cardozo School of Law, Yeshiva University, J.D., 1993 — Admitted to Bar, 1993, New Jersey; 1994, New York — Practice Areas: Surety; Insurance Coverage; Insurance Defense; Workers' Compensation — E-mail: ddepekary@cmk.com

Mary E. Fechtig — Indiana University, B.S., 1988; Indiana University School of Law, J.D., 1991 — Admitted to Bar, 1991, Indiana; 1993, Illinois; 1998, District of Columbia; 2008, California (Inactive); U.S. Court of Appeals, Third Circuit — Practice Areas: Insurance Coverage; Appellate; Reinsurance — Resident Chicago, IL Office — E-mail: mfechtig@cmk.com

Barbara Finger — Union College at Schenectady, B.S., 1975; Hofstra University School of Law, J.D., 1979 — Admitted to Bar, 1980, New York; 1981, U.S. District Court, Eastern and Southern Districts of New York; 1982, U.S. Court of Appeals, Second Circuit — Practice Areas: Medical Malpractice Defense; Health Care — Resident New York, NY Office — E-mail: bfinger@cmk.com

Catherine J. Flynn — Saint Peter's College, B.S. (summa cum laude), 1983; Seton Hall University School of Law, J.D., 1986 — Admitted to Bar, 1987, New Jersey; U.S. District Court, District of New Jersey; 2012, U.S. Court of Appeals, Third Circuit — Member American, New Jersey State and Union County Bar Associations — Practice Areas: Medical Malpractice Defense; Health Care; Insurance Defense — E-mail: cflynn@cmk.com

Richard L. Furman — Hofstra University, B.A., 1967; State University of New York at Buffalo Law School, J.D., 1970 — Admitted to Bar, 1970, New York; 1971, U.S. Court of International Trade; 1977, U.S. District Court, Eastern and Southern Districts of New York; 1982, U.S. Court of Appeals for the Federal Circuit; 1992, U.S. District Court, Northern District of California; 1999, U.S. District Court, Northern District of New York; U.S. District Court, Eastern District of Michigan — Practice Areas: Admiralty and Maritime Law; Commercial Transactions; Aviation — Resident New York, NY Office — E-mail: rfurman@cmk.com

Kristin V. Gallagher — 1970 — Fairfield University, B.A., 1992; Seton Hall University, J.D., 1995 — Admitted to Bar, 1995, New Jersey; 1996, New York; 1996, U.S. District Court, District of New Jersey; 2010, U.S. District Court, Northern District of New York — Member New Jersey State and New York State Bar Associations; Justice Morris Pashman Inn of Court — Practice Areas: Surety; Insurance Coverage; Insurance Defense — E-mail: kgallagher@cmk.com

John P. Gilfillan — 1963 — Providence College, B.A., 1985; Seton Hall University, J.D., 1989 — Admitted to Bar, 1991, New Jersey; 1991, U.S. District Court, District of New Jersey; 1991, U.S. Court of Appeals, Fourth Circuit — Lay Board of Trustees of Delbarton School in Morristown, New Jersey — Languages: French — Practice Areas: General Defense; Product Liability — E-mail: jgilfillan@cmk.com

James J. Hickey — University of Dubuque, B.A., 1984; IIT, Chicago-Kent College of Law, J.D., 1988 — Admitted to Bar, 1988, Illinois; U.S. District Court, Northern District of Illinois; 1990, U.S. District Court, Central District of Illinois; 2000, U.S. District Court, Northern and Southern Districts of Indiana — Practice Areas: Insurance Coverage; Insurance Defense; Reinsurance — Resident Chicago, IL Office — E-mail: jhickey@cmk.com

James F. Kane — 1952 — Rutgers University, B.A., 1974; Fairleigh Dickinson University, M.B.A., 1977; Montclair State University, M.A., 2000; University of the Pacific, McGeorge School of Law, J.D., 1982 — Admitted to Bar, 1982, California; 1983, New Jersey; 1982, U.S. District Court, Eastern District of California; 1996, Supreme Court of New Jersey — Boy Scouts of America (Leader); Merit Badge Counselor, Morris-Sussex Council — Certified Civil Trial Attorney, 1993 — Practice Areas: Civil Litigation; Appellate Practice; Construction Defect; Product Liability; Professional Liability; Insurance Defense — E-mail: jkane@cmk.com

Daisy Khambatta — The University of Texas at Austin, B.S., 1996; South Texas College of Law, J.D., 2000 — Admitted to Bar, 2001, Illinois; Texas; U.S. District Court, Eastern District of Wisconsin; U.S. District Court, Northern District of Illinois; U.S. District Court, Southern District of Texas — Practice Areas: Insurance Coverage; Insurance Defense — Resident Chicago, IL Office — E-mail: dkhambatta@cmk.com

Elaine W. Klinger — American University, B.A. Political Science, 1988; Villanova University School of Law, J.D., 1991 — Admitted to Bar, 1991, Pennsylvania; New Jersey; U.S. District Court, District of New Jersey; U.S. District Court, Eastern District of Pennsylvania — Practice Areas: Insurance Coverage; Insurance Defense; Appellate; Employment — Resident Philadelphia, PA Office — E-mail: eklinger@cmk.com

David M. Kupfer — 1957 — Vanderbilt University, B.A., 1978; J.D., 1981 — Admitted to Bar, 1981, New Jersey; 1985, U.S. Supreme Court; 1997, U.S. Court of Appeals for the Federal Circuit; 2005, U.S. Court of Appeals, Third Circuit — Member American, New Jersey State and Union County Bar Associations — Practice Areas: Commercial Litigation; Insurance Coverage; Professional Liability — E-mail: dkupfer@cmk.com

John D. LaBarbera — University of Illinois at Chicago, B.A., 1991; Illinois Institute of Technology, Chicago-Kent College of Law, J.D., 2001 — Admitted to Bar, 2001, Illinois; 2001, U.S. District Court, Northern District of Illinois; 2003, U.S. Court of Appeals, Sixth and Seventh Circuits; 2007, U.S. District Court, Eastern District of Wisconsin; Supreme Court of Illinois — Practice Areas: Insurance Coverage; Insurance Defense; Reinsurance — Resident Chicago, IL Office — E-mail: jlabarbera@cmk.com

Matthew J. Lodge — 1965 — Kenyon College, B.A., 1988; Boston University, J.D., 1993 — Admitted to Bar, 1993, New Jersey; 1993, U.S. District Court, District of New Jersey — Practice Areas: Commercial Transactions; Insurance Defense; Real Estate — E-mail: mlodge@cmk.com

Ralph J. Luongo — Cornell University, B.A., 1980; Washington and Lee University School of Law, J.D., 1983 — Admitted to Bar, 1983, Pennsylvania; 1984, U.S. District Court, Eastern District of Pennsylvania; U.S. Court of Appeals, Third Circuit; 2000, U.S. District Court, Western District of Pennsylvania — Practice Areas: Insurance Coverage; Commercial Litigation — Resident Philadelphia, PA Office — E-mail: rluongo@cmk.com

Christopher H. Mansuy — 1946 — Penn State University, B.A., 1968; Temple University School of Law, J.D., 1974 — Admitted to Bar, 1974, Pennsylvania; 1975, New York; 1986, New Jersey; 1977, U.S. Court of Appeals, Second Circuit; 1980, U.S. Supreme Court; 1988, U.S. Court of Appeals, Third Circuit; 2001, U.S. Court of Appeals, Ninth Circuit; 2002, U.S. District Court, Eastern District of Pennsylvania — Member New Jersey State Bar Association; The Maritime Law Association of the United States — United States Naval Reserve — Practice Areas: Admiralty and Maritime Law; Arbitration; Commercial Law; International Law; Transportation — E-mail: cmansuy@cmk.com

Michael A. Moroney — Lafayette College, B.A. (cum laude), 1983; College of William & Mary, Marshall-Wythe School of Law, J.D., 1986 — Admitted to Bar, 1986, New Jersey; 1988, District of Columbia — Practice Areas: Medical Malpractice Defense; Health Care; Insurance Defense — E-mail: mmoroney@cmk.com

Bradley J. Mortensen — Harpur College, State University of New York at Binghamton, B.A., 1976; St. Johns University School of Law, J.D., 1981 — Admitted to Bar, 1982, New York; 1988, Pennsylvania; 1983, U.S. District Court, Northern District of New York; 1987, U.S. District Court, Eastern and Southern Districts of New York; 1995, U.S. District Court, Eastern District of

BASKING RIDGE   **NEW JERSEY**

Carroll McNulty & Kull LLC, Basking Ridge, NJ
(Continued)

Pennsylvania; 2010, U.S. District Court, Middle District of Pennsylvania — Practice Areas: Insurance Coverage; Insurance Defense; Reinsurance — Resident Philadelphia, PA Office — E-mail: bmortensen@cmk.com

Susan D. Noble — Suffolk Community College, A.A.S./RN, 1979; St. Joseph's College, B.S., 1988; Hofstra University School of Law, J.D., 1988 — Admitted to Bar, 1989, New York; U.S. District Court, Eastern and Southern Districts of New York — Practice Areas: Medical Malpractice Defense — Resident New York, NY Office — E-mail: snoble@cmk.com

Ann Odelson — 1970 — The Catholic University of America, B.A., 1992; City University of New York, J.D., 1997 — Admitted to Bar, 1997, New Jersey; 1998, New York; 2003, U.S. District Court, Eastern and Southern Districts of New York — Practice Areas: Insurance Coverage; Insurance Defense — Resident New York, NY Office — E-mail: aodelson@cmk.com

John A. Orzel — 1962 — Heidelberg College, B.A., 1984; Duquesne University, J.D., 1988; Tulane University, LL.M. (with distinction), 1989 — Admitted to Bar, 1989, New York; 1990, U.S. District Court, Eastern, Northern and Southern Districts of New York; U.S. Court of Appeals, Second and Fourth Circuits — Member The Maritime Law Association of the United States — Propeller Club of U.S. — Practice Areas: Admiralty and Maritime Law; Transportation — Resident New York, NY Office — E-mail: jorzel@cmk.com

Michael Osterman — Lehigh University, B.S. (with high honors), 1982; University of Pennsylvania Law School, J.D., 1985 — Admitted to Bar, 1985, New Jersey — Practice Areas: Commercial Transactions; Real Estate — E-mail: mosterman@cmk.com

Erik J. Pedersen — 1970 — State University of New York at Buffalo, B.A., 1994; Seton Hall University, J.D., 1997 — Admitted to Bar, 1997, New Jersey; 1999, New York; 1999, U.S. District Court, District of New Jersey; 2006, U.S. District Court, Eastern District of New York — Practice Areas: Surety; Insurance Defense; Workers' Compensation — Resident New York, NY Office — E-mail: epedersen@cmk.com

Cynthia Ruggerio — Fairfield University, B.S. Biology, 1984; Rutgers University School of Law-Camden, J.D., 1987 — Admitted to Bar, 1987, New Jersey; Pennsylvania; U.S. District Court, District of New Jersey; U.S. District Court, Eastern District of Pennsylvania; 1988, U.S. Court of Appeals, Third Circuit; 2010, U.S. Supreme Court — Practice Areas: Insurance Coverage; Insurance Defense; Commercial Transactions; Reinsurance — Resident Philadelphia, PA Office — E-mail: cruggerio@cmk.com

Michael R. Schneider — 1973 — New York University, B.S., 1995; Brooklyn Law School, J.D., 1998 — Admitted to Bar, 1999, New York; 2004, U.S. District Court, Eastern and Southern Districts of New York — Practice Areas: Insurance Defense; Real Estate; Workers' Compensation — Resident New York, NY Office — E-mail: mschneider@cmk.com

Heather E. Simpson — 1980 — University of Richmond, B.A. (cum laude), 2002; The George Washington University Law School, J.D. (with honors), 2005 — Admitted to Bar, 2005, New Jersey; 2007, New York; 2006, U.S. District Court, District of New Jersey; 2009, U.S. District Court, Southern District of New York — Practice Areas: Insurance Coverage; Insurance Defense — E-mail: hsimpson@cmk.com

Matthew T. Walsh — University of Illinois, B.S., 1985; University of San Diego School of Law, J.D., 1990 — Admitted to Bar, 1990, California; Illinois; U.S. District Court, Central and Southern Districts of California; U.S. District Court, Northern District of Illinois — Practice Areas: Insurance Coverage; Insurance Defense; Appellate — Resident Chicago, IL Office — E-mail: mwalsh@cmk.com

Frank J. Wenick — New York University, B.A., 1976; New York University School of Law, J.D., 1979 — Admitted to Bar, 1980, New York; U.S. District Court, Eastern and Southern Districts of New York; U.S. Court of Appeals, Second Circuit — Practice Areas: Appellate; Insurance Coverage; Medical Malpractice Defense — Resident New York, NY Office — E-mail: fwenick@cmk.com

Of Counsel

James J. Ross — 1948 — Brown University, A.B., 1970; Seton Hall University, J.D., 1977 — Admitted to Bar, 1978, New Jersey; U.S. District Court, District of New Jersey — Member American and New Jersey State Bar Associations; Morris Hills Regional Board of Education — Practice Areas: Alternative Dispute Resolution; Architects and Engineers; Professional Liability; Fidelity and Surety; Insurance Defense; Litigation — E-mail: jross@cmk.com

Michael J. Tricarico — State University of New York at Stony Brook, B.A., 1988; St. Johns University School of Law, J.D., 1991 — Admitted to Bar, 1991, Connecticut; 1992, New York; 1994, New Jersey; 1993, U.S. District Court, Eastern and Southern Districts of New York; 1994, U.S. District Court, District of New Jersey; 1996, U.S. Court of Appeals, Fourth Circuit; 2004, U.S. Court of Appeals for the District of Columbia and Second Circuits; U.S. Court of Appeals for the Armed Forces; U.S. Court of Federal Claims; Supreme Court of the United States; 2013, U.S. Court of Appeals, Eleventh Circuit — Practice Areas: Commercial Transactions; Insurance Coverage; Insurance Defense; Appellate — Resident New York, NY Office — E-mail: mtricarico@cmk.com

Associates

David P. Abatemarco — State University of New York at Binghamton, B.A., 1988; Touro College Jacob D. Fuchsberg Law Center, J.D., 1991 — Admitted to Bar, 1992, New York; Connecticut — Practice Areas: Insurance Defense — Resident New York, NY Office — E-mail: dabatemarco@cmk.com

Jillian G. Ackermann — 1984 — University of Virginia, B.A., 2006; Villanova University School of Law, J.D. (cum laude), 2009 — Judicial Law Clerk to Hon. William L'E. Wertheimer, J.S.C., Superior Court of New Jersey, Union County — Admitted to Bar, 2010, New Jersey; New York; U.S. District Court, District of New Jersey — Member American Bar Association — Practice Areas: Insurance Coverage; Insurance Defense — E-mail: jackermann@cmk.com

Carmen O. Barroso — Northeastern University, B.S. (magna cum laude, with honors), 1998; St. Johns University School of Law, J.D., 2001 — Admitted to Bar, 2002, New York; U.S. District Court, Southern District of New York — Languages: Spanish — Practice Areas: Medical Malpractice Defense — Resident New York, NY Office — E-mail: cbarroso@cmk.com

Elizabeth A. Bartman — Widener University, B.A. (summa cum laude), 2004; Villanova University School of Law, J.D., 2007 — Admitted to Bar, 2007, Pennsylvania; New Jersey; U.S. District Court, District of New Jersey; U.S. District Court, Eastern District of Pennsylvania; 2010, U.S. District Court, Middle District of Pennsylvania; 2012, U.S. District Court, Western District of Pennsylvania — Practice Areas: Insurance Coverage; Commercial Litigation — Resident Philadelphia, PA Office — E-mail: ebartman@cmk.com

Shaun I. Blick — 1977 — Temple University, B.A. (cum laude), 1999; Rutgers University School of Law, J.D., 2006 — Admitted to Bar, 2006, New Jersey; 2007, New York; 2006, U.S. District Court, District of New Jersey — Practice Areas: Commercial Litigation — E-mail: sblick@cmk.com

Sofya P. Borchard — Syracuse University, B.A. (cum laude), 2002; Albany Law School of Union University, J.D., 2005 — Admitted to Bar, 2006, New York; 2007, U.S. District Court, Eastern and Southern Districts of New York — Languages: Russian — Practice Areas: Medical Malpractice Defense — Resident New York, NY Office — E-mail: sborchard@cmk.com

James T. Byrnes IV — 1982 — The College of New Jersey, B.S. (cum laude), 2005; Pennsylvania State University-Dickinson School of Law, J.D. (cum laude), 2008 — Admitted to Bar, 2008, New Jersey; 2008, Pennsylvania — Practice Areas: Insurance Coverage; Insurance Defense — E-mail: jbyrnes@cmk.com

Kathryn A. Callahan — New York University, B.A., 2010; Rutgers University School of Law-Newark, J.D. (cum laude), 2013 — Admitted to Bar, 2013, New Jersey — Practice Areas: Insurance Coverage; Insurance Defense — E-mail: kcallahan@cmk.com

Eileen H. de Callies — 1969 — Hofstra University, B.A., 1991; Hofstra University School of Law, J.D., 1994 — Admitted to Bar, 1995, New York; 1997, U.S. District Court, Eastern and Southern Districts of New York; 2002, U.S. Court of Appeals, Sixth Circuit — Member New York State Bar Association — Practice Areas: Appellate Practice; Commercial Litigation; Insurance Coverage — Resident New York, NY Office — E-mail: edecallies@cmk.com

Bevin A. Carroll — 1986 — University of Illinois at Urbana-Champaign, B.A. Political Science, 2008; Chicago-Kent College of Law, J.D., 2012 — Admitted to Bar, 2012, Illinois — Practice Areas: Insurance Coverage; Insurance Defense — Resident Chicago, IL Office — E-mail: bcarroll@cmk.com

Theresa M. Carroll — Duke University, B.A. Political Science, 2007; Washington University in St. Louis School of Law, J.D. (cum laude), 2011 — Admitted to Bar, 2011, Missouri; 2012, Illinois; 2014, Pennsylvania; 2011, U.S. District Court, Eastern District of Missouri; 2011, U.S. Court of Appeals for the Federal and Eighth Circuits; 2012, U.S. District Court, Western District of Missouri; 2012, U.S. District Court, Southern District of Illinois — Practice Areas: Maritime Law; Commercial Litigation; Insurance Coverage; Insurance Defense — Resident Philadelphia Office — E-mail: tcarroll@cmk.com

Carol Lee Chevalier — Barnard College, B.A., 1985; New York Law School, J.D., 1988 — Admitted to Bar, 1989, New York; 1990, U.S. District Court,

NEW JERSEY

BASKING RIDGE

Carroll McNulty & Kull LLC, Basking Ridge, NJ (Continued)

Eastern and Southern Districts of New York — Languages: Spanish — Practice Areas: Insurance Defense — Resident New York, NY Office — E-mail: cchevalier@cmk.com

Teresa M. Cinnamond — 1968 — University of Richmond, B.A. (cum laude), 1990; Hofstra University School of Law, J.D. (with honors), 1993 — Admitted to Bar, 1994, New York; 1995, New Jersey; 1995, U.S. District Court, Eastern and Southern Districts of New York; 2005, U.S. District Court, District of New Jersey — Practice Areas: Insurance Coverage; Insurance Defense — E-mail: tcinnamond@cmk.com

Catherine De Angelis — 1975 — Seton Hall University, B.A., 1997; Touro College Jacob D. Fuchsberg Law Center, J.D., 2002 — Admitted to Bar, 2002, New Jersey; 2003, New York; 2002, U.S. District Court, District of New Jersey; 2011, U.S. District Court, Eastern and Southern Districts of New York — Practice Areas: Insurance Defense — E-mail: cdeangelis@cmk.com

Laura B. Dowgin — Colgate University, B.A., 2006; Seton Hall University School of Law, J.D. (magna cum laude), 2011 — Admitted to Bar, 2011, New Jersey; 2012, New York — Practice Areas: Insurance Coverage; Insurance Defense — Resident New York, NY Office — E-mail: ldowgin@cmk.com

Frank M. Falcone — 1984 — Lehigh University, B.A. (cum laude, Dean's List), 2007; Seton Hall University School of Law, J.D., 2010 — Delta Phi; Order of Omega (Greek Leadership Honors Society); Jon E. Krupnick Scholarship — Judicial Intern to The Hon. Madeline Cox Arleo, U.S. District Court of New Jersey — Defending Liberty, Pursuing Justice, The Lehigh Review, Vol. 15 (2007) 163-190 — Admitted to Bar, 2010, New Jersey; 2011, New York — Member Civil Litigation Clinic — Practice Areas: Insurance Coverage; Insurance Defense — E-mail: ffalcone@cmk.com

Dana E. Gambro — 1985 — Lafayette College, B.A. (magna cum laude), 2007; Tulane University Law School, J.D., 2012 — Admitted to Bar, 2013, New York — Practice Areas: Admiralty and Maritime Law; Insurance Coverage; Insurance Defense — Resident New York, NY Office — E-mail: dgambro@cmk.com

Mark F. Hamilton — 1968 — University of California, Santa Cruz, B.A., 1992; Rutgers University-Newark, J.D., 2008 — Admitted to Bar, 2008, New Jersey; 2009, New York — Practice Areas: Insurance Coverage; Insurance Defense

J. Christopher Henschel — Fairfield University, B.A. Political Science, 2010; B.A. International Relations, 2010; Seton Hall University School of Law, J.D., 2013 — Admitted to Bar, 2013, New Jersey — Practice Areas: Employment; Insurance Coverage; Insurance Defense; Workers' Compensation — E-mail: jhenschel@cmk.com

Katrine L. Hyde — 1983 — Stern College for Women; Sy Syms School of Business, B.S. (magna cum laude), 2005; Seton Hall University School of Law, J.D. (cum laude), 2008 — Admitted to Bar, 2008, New Jersey; 2009, New York — Languages: Russian — Practice Areas: Insurance Coverage; Insurance Defense — E-mail: khyde@cmk.com

Allison M. Kane — The Catholic University of America, B.A. (magna cum laude, Dean's List), 2007; Seton Hall University School of Law, J.D., 2011 — Admitted to Bar, 2011, New Jersey; 2012, New York — Practice Areas: Insurance Coverage; Insurance Defense — E-mail: akane@cmk.com

Nicole J. Kelly — 1983 — University of Wisconsin-Madison, B.A., 2005; University of Wisconsin Law School, J.D., 2008 — Admitted to Bar, 2008, Illinois; Wisconsin; U.S. District Court, Northern and Southern Districts of Illinois; U.S. District Court, Eastern and Western Districts of Wisconsin; U.S. District Court, Northern District of Indiana — Practice Areas: Reinsurance; Insurance Coverage — Resident Chicago, IL Office — E-mail: nkelly@cmk.com

Elizabeth S. Kelly — 1984 — University of Michigan, B.A., 2006; The University of Iowa College of Law, J.D., 2010 — Admitted to Bar, 2011, New York; Michigan — Practice Areas: Insurance Coverage; Insurance Defense — Resident New York Office — E-mail: ekelly@cmk.com

Sean Kennedy — 1988 — Seton Hall University, B.A. (cum laude), 2010; Seton Hall University School of Law, J.D., 2013 — Admitted to Bar, 2013, New Jersey; U.S. District Court, District of New Jersey — Member New Jersey State Bar Association — Practice Areas: Insurance Coverage; Insurance Defense — E-mail: skennedy@cmk.com

Joseph G. Kenny — St. John's University, B.A. (summa cum laude), 2009; Seton Hall University School of Law, J.D., 2013 — Admitted to Bar, 2013, New Jersey; 2014, New York; U.S. District Court, District of New Jersey — Practice Areas: Insurance Coverage — E-mail: jkenny@cmk.com

Michael S. Kerr — 1979 — University of South Carolina, B.A. (cum laude), 2002; Wake Forest University School of Law, J.D., 2008 — Admitted to Bar, 2008, New Jersey — Practice Areas: Insurance Coverage; Insurance Defense — E-mail: mkerr@cmk.com

Carroll McNulty & Kull LLC, Basking Ridge, NJ (Continued)

Kersten Kortbawi — 1981 — New York University, B.S. (cum laude), 2010; Rutgers University School of Law-Newark, J.D. (cum laude), 2013 — Admitted to Bar, 2013, New Jersey; 2014, New York; 2013, U.S. District Court, District of New Jersey — Member New Jersey State Bar Association — Practice Areas: Insurance Coverage; Insurance Defense — E-mail: kkortbawi@cmk.com

Andrew H. Lesnever — 1985 — University of Delaware, B.A., 2008; Rutgers University School of Law-Newark, J.D., 2011 — Admitted to Bar, 2011, New Jersey; 2012, New York — Practice Areas: Insurance Coverage; Insurance Defense — E-mail: alesnever@cmk.com

Katherine Lyons — Drew University, B.A. (summa cum laude), 1998; Wake Forest University School of Law, J.D., 2004 — Admitted to Bar, 2004, New Jersey; 2005, New York; 2004, U.S. District Court, District of New Jersey; 2006, U.S. Court of Appeals, Third Circuit — Practice Areas: Insurance Defense; Insurance Coverage; Health Care; Medical Malpractice Defense — E-mail: klyons@cmk.com

Gregory P. Markwell — University of Illinois-Urbana-Champaign, B.A., 2008; DePaul University College of Law, J.D., 2012 — Admitted to Bar, 2012, Illinois — Member Illinois State and Chicago Bar Associations — Practice Areas: Insurance Coverage; Insurance Defense — Resident Chicago, IL Office — E-mail: gmarkwell@cmk.com

Catherine A. Mirabel — The Hartt College of Music, Bach. Of Mus. (magna cum laude), 1982; St. Johns University School of Law, J.D., 1982 — Admitted to Bar, 1983, New York; U.S. District Court, Eastern District of New York — Practice Areas: Medical Malpractice Defense — Resident New York, NY Office — E-mail: cmirabel@cmk.com

Alexa J. Nasta — University of Rochester, B.A., 2001; Rutgers University School of Law-Camden, J.D., 2004 — Admitted to Bar, 2004, New Jersey; 2007, New York; 2005, U.S. District Court, District of New Jersey; 2010, U.S. Court of Appeals, Third Circuit — Author: "Through the Glass Darkly: Florida's Constitution May Not Protect the Privacy Rights of Nonpublic Employees' Personnel Records," 34 Rutgers L.J. 1293 (2004) — Practice Areas: Appellate Advocacy; Insurance Coverage — E-mail: anasta@cmk.com

Heather A. Novison — Penn State University, B.S. (cum laude), 2008; Brooklyn Law School, J.D. (cum laude), 2011 — Admitted to Bar, 2011, New Jersey; 2012, New York — Practice Areas: Insurance Coverage; Insurance Defense — Resident New York, NY Office — E-mail: hnovison@cmk.com

Jacob J. Palefski — 1981 — Yeshiva University, B.A. (magna cum laude), 2003; Benjamin N. Cardozo School of Law, J.D., 2006 — Admitted to Bar, 2007, New York; Massachusetts — Practice Areas: Insurance Coverage — Resident New York, NY Office — E-mail: jpalefski@cmk.com

Blake A. Palmer — 1981 — University of Rhode Island, B.A., 2003; Roger Williams University School of Law, J.D., 2006 — Admitted to Bar, 2007, New Jersey; 2007, New York; 2007, U.S. District Court, District of New Jersey — Practice Areas: Civil Litigation; Insurance Coverage; Insurance Defense — E-mail: bpalmer@cmk.com

Timothy B. Parlin — 1957 — Syracuse University, B.S., 1979; Northwestern University, M.S., 1980; Brooklyn Law School, J.D., 1987 — Admitted to Bar, 1989, New York; 2004, New Jersey; 2011, Pennsylvania; 1989, U.S. District Court, Eastern and Southern Districts of New York; 1991, U.S. Court of Appeals, Second Circuit; 1991, U.S. Supreme Court; 1992, U.S. Court of Appeals, Third Circuit — Practice Areas: Commercial Litigation; Insurance Coverage — E-mail: tparlin@cmk.com

Pasquale A. Pontoriero — 1980 — Drew University, B.A., 2002; Pace University School of Law, J.D., 2005 — Admitted to Bar, 2005, New Jersey; 2005, U.S. District Court, District of New Jersey — Practice Areas: Insurance Defense — E-mail: ppontoriero@cmk.com

Stefanie L. Rokosz — 1988 — University of South Carolina, B.A. (magna cum laude), 2010; Albany Law School, J.D. (cum laude), 2013 — Admitted to Bar, 2013, New Jersey; New York — Practice Areas: Health Care; Insurance Defense; Medical Malpractice Defense — E-mail: srokosz@cmk.com

Paul J. Rutigliano — Sacred Heart University, B.S. (cum laude), 2009; Pace University School of Law, J.D. (magna cum laude), 2013 — Admitted to Bar, 2013, New Jersey; 2014, New York — Practice Areas: Commercial Litigation; Insurance Coverage; Insurance Defense — Resident New York, NY Office — E-mail: prutigliano@cmk.com

Lindsay A. Sakal — 1982 — Tulane University, B.A. (cum laude), 2005; Tulane University Law School, J.D., 2009 — Law Clerk to Hon. Helen G. Berrigan, U.S. District Court of Eastern Louisiana (2007); Hon. Peter E. Doyne, A.J.S.C., Bergen County Superior Court (2009-2010) — Executive Board Member, Tulane Maritime Law Journal (2008); Tulane Juvenile Law Clinic (2008-2009) — Admitted to Bar, 2009, New Jersey; 2010, New York — Certificate in Admiralty & Maritime Law (2009) — Languages:

BRIDGETON   NEW JERSEY

Carroll McNulty & Kull LLC, Basking Ridge, NJ
(Continued)

Spanish — Practice Areas: Admiralty and Maritime Law; Civil Litigation; Insurance Coverage; Insurance Defense — Resident New York, NY Office — E-mail: lsakal@cmk.com

Christina R. Salem — The George Washington University, B.B.A. (magna cum laude), 2000; Fordham University School of Law, J.D., 2003 — Admitted to Bar, 2003, New Jersey; 2004, New York — Practice Areas: Professional Liability; Directors and Officers Liability; Insurance Coverage; Litigation — Resident New York, NY Office — E-mail: csalem@cmk.com

Anneliese Scott — College of William & Mary, B.A., 2001; Villanova University School of Law, J.D., 2004 — Admitted to Bar, 2004, Pennsylvania; New Jersey; U.S. District Court, District of New Jersey; 2005, U.S. District Court, Eastern District of Pennsylvania — Practice Areas: Insurance Coverage; Insurance Defense; Commercial Litigation; Employment; Workers' Compensation — Resident Philadelphia, PA Office — E-mail: ascott@cmk.com

Robert Seigal — 1978 — Binghamton University, B.A. (with honors), 2001; Benjamin N. Cardozo School of Law, J.D. (with honors), 2004 — Admitted to Bar, 2004, New Jersey; 2005, New York — Practice Areas: Insurance Defense — Resident New York, NY Office — E-mail: rseigal@cmk.com

Juliana B. Spitzer — 1981 — Seton Hall University, B.S. (summa cum laude), 2003; Seton Hall University School of Law, J.D., 2006 — Admitted to Bar, 2006, New Jersey; 2007, New York — "Rising Star" 2013 New Jersey Super Lawyers — Practice Areas: Health Care; Insurance Defense; Medical Malpractice Defense — E-mail: jspitzer@cmk.com

Dana L. Steinberg — 1980 — Williams College, B.A., 2002; Tulane University Law School, J.D., 2007; Tulane University Graduate School, M.A., 2007 — Admitted to Bar, 2008, New York; 2009, U.S. District Court, Eastern and Southern Districts of New York — Member New York State Bar Association; New York County Lawyers Association — Practice Areas: Insurance Defense — Resident New York, NY Office — E-mail: dsteinberg@cmk.com

Douglas J. Steinke — Johns Hopkins University, B.A., 1998; Columbia University, M.S., 1999; St. Johns University School of Law, J.D., 2005 — Admitted to Bar, 2006, New Jersey; U.S. District Court, Eastern, Southern and Western Districts of New York; U.S. Court of Appeals, Second Circuit; Supreme Court of the United States — Practice Areas: Insurance Coverage; Appellate; Commercial Litigation; Reinsurance — Resident New York, NY Office — E-mail: dsteinke@cmk.com

Beth A. Stroup — 1971 — Central Michigan University, B.S. Business Admin., 1994; DePaul University College of Law, J.D., 1998 — Admitted to Bar, 1998, Illinois; 2005, U.S. District Court, Northern District of Illinois — Member Chicago Bar Association — Practice Areas: Appellate; Commercial Litigation; Insurance Coverage; Insurance Defense — Resident Chicago, IL Office — E-mail: bstroup@cmk.com

Susan B. Thauer — Kenyon College, B.A., 1994; Villanova University School of Law, J.D., 2002 — Admitted to Bar, 2002, Pennsylvania; New Jersey; U.S. District Court, District of New Jersey; 2004, U.S. District Court, Eastern District of Pennsylvania — Member Pennsylvania and Philadelphia Bar Associations — Practice Areas: Insurance Coverage — Resident Philadelphia, PA Office — E-mail: sthauer@cmk.com

April T. Villaverde — 1979 — Rutgers University, Douglass College, B.A., 2001; Rutgers University School of Law-Newark, J.D., 2006 — Admitted to Bar, 2006, New Jersey; 2007, New York — Practice Areas: Insurance Coverage; Insurance Defense — E-mail: avillaverde@cmk.com

Nicholas A. Vytell — 1982 — Villanova University, B.A., 2005; Seton Hall University School of Law, J.D., 2008 — Law Clerk to the Hon. David H. Ironson, J.S.C. (2008-2009) — Admitted to Bar, 2008, New Jersey; 2008, U.S. District Court, District of New Jersey — Practice Areas: Insurance Coverage; Insurance Defense — E-mail: nvytell@cmk.com

Joshua C. Weisberg — 1979 — Yeshiva University, B.A. (magna cum laude), 2002; Fordham Law School, J.D., 2005 — Admitted to Bar, 2006, New York; 2006, Massachusetts; 2006, U.S. District Court, Eastern and Southern Districts of New York — Practice Areas: Commercial Litigation; Insurance Coverage; Insurance Regulation; Insurance Defense; Commercial Transactions — Resident New York, NY Office — E-mail: jweisberg@cmk.com

Joanna L. Young — 1971 — City College of the City University of New York, B.A. (magna cum laude), 1994; Pace University School of Law, J.D., 2001 — Admitted to Bar, 2002, New York; 2002, Massachusetts; 2002, U.S. District Court, Eastern and Southern Districts of New York — Practice Areas: Real Estate; Insurance Coverage — Resident New York, NY Office — E-mail: jyoung@cmk.com

Julie Zando-Dennis — 1961 — McGill University, B.A., 1984; Benjamin N. Cardozo School of Law, J.D., 2005 — Admitted to Bar, 2006, New Jersey; 2008, New York — Practice Areas: Appellate Practice; Insurance Coverage — E-mail: jzando@cmk.com

Carroll McNulty & Kull LLC, Basking Ridge, NJ
(Continued)

Anne K. Zangos — 1982 — Binghamton University, B.A., 2004; St. John's University School of Law, J.D., 2007 — Admitted to Bar, 2008, New York; 2009, U.S. District Court, Eastern and Southern Districts of New York — Languages: Greek — Practice Areas: Insurance Coverage; Reinsurance — Resident New York, NY Office — E-mail: azangos@cmk.com

BRIDGETON † 25,349 Cumberland Co.

Chance & McCann, L.L.C.

201 West Commerce Street
Bridgeton, New Jersey 08302
Telephone: 856-451-9100
Fax: 856-455-5227
E-Mail: chancemccann@chancemccann.com
www.chancemccann.com

(Woodstown, NJ Office: 84 East Grant Street, Suite 2, 08098, P.O. Box 10, 08098-0010)
(Tel: 856-769-9001)
(Fax: 856-769-9007)

Established: 1978

Insurance Defense, Property and Casualty, General Liability, Product Liability

Firm Profile: Our firm was founded in 1978 and has a continued heritage dating back to 1903 when Senator Albert Robeson McAllister began practicing law. Keron Chance, deceased, began practicing with Senator McAllister in 1938 and in 1978 joined his firm with Kevin P. McCann creating Chance & McCann.

Insurance Clients

Gloucester County Insurance Commission   Mid-Continent Insurance Company

Firm Managing Partner

Kevin P. McCann — 1947 — Monmouth University, B.A., 1970; Delaware Law School of Widener University, J.D., 1975; Temple University Beasley School of Law, LL.M., 1980 — Admitted to Bar, 1975, New Jersey; U.S. District Court, District of New Jersey; 1989, U.S. Court of Appeals, Third Circuit; 1998, U.S. District Court, Southern District of Texas — Member American, New Jersey State (President, 2012-2013) and Cumberland County Bar Associations; American Association for Justice

Associates

Shanna McCann — 1978 — Wake Forest University, B.A., 2000; Widener University School of Law, J.D., 2003 — Admitted to Bar, 2004, New Jersey; 2005, Pennsylvania; U.S. District Court, Eastern District of Pennsylvania

Beth White — 1981 — Rowan University, B.A., 2003; Fairleigh Dickinson University, Paralegal, 2005 — Admitted to Bar, 2008, New Jersey; 2011, U.S. District Court, District of New Jersey

Deana L. Walsh — 1965 — Widener University, B.A., 1987; Widener University School of Law, J.D., 1997 — Admitted to Bar, 1997, New Jersey; U.S. District Court, District of New Jersey

Matthew Weng — 1981 — Rutgers University-Camden, B.A., 2005; Rutgers University School of Law-Camden, J.D., 2008 — Admitted to Bar, 2009, New Jersey

NEW JERSEY
BURLINGTON

The following firms also service this area.

Powell, Birchmeier & Powell
1891 State Highway 50
Tuckahoe, New Jersey 08250
  Telephone: 609-628-3414
  Fax: 609-628-2966

Mailing Address: P.O. Box 582, Tuckahoe, NJ 08250-0582

General Civil Practice, Trial Practice, Insurance Defense, Negligence, Defense Litigation, Product Liability, Coverage Issues, Litigation, Workers' Compensation, Subrogation, Civil Rights, Governmental Liability, Medical Negligence, Wrongful Termination, General Chancery Practice, Section 1983 Litigation

SEE COMPLETE LISTING UNDER TUCKAHOE, NEW JERSEY (29 MILES)

BURLINGTON   9,920 Burlington Co.

Sobel Law Group LLC

6 Terry Lane, Suite 350
Burlington, New Jersey 08016
  Telephone: 856-673-0689
  E-Mail: bpevzner@sobellawgroup.com
  www.sobellawgroup.com

(Huntington, NY Office*: 464 New York Avenue, Suite 100, 11743)
  (Tel: 631-549-4677)
  (Fax: 631-549-0826)
  (E-Mail: csobel@sobellawgroup.com)
(New York, NY Office*: 30 Vesey Street, 8th Floor, 10007)
  (Tel: 212-216-0020)
  (E-Mail: csobel@sobellawgroup.com)

Amusements, Automobile, Bad Faith, Construction Law, Coverage Issues, Employment Law, Environmental Law, Equine Law, Fraud, Hospitality, Liquor Liability, Pharmaceutical, Premises Liability, Sports Law, Toxic Torts, Transportation, Trucking, Workers' Compensation

Firm Profile: Sobel Law Group, LLC successfully represents insurance carriers, self-insureds, municipalities and school districts, habitation companies, school and municipal bus companies, supermarket chains, "big box" retailers and construction companies in New York, New Jersey and Eastern Pennsylvania.

(See listing under Huntington, NY for additional information)

CAMDEN   † 77,344 Camden Co.

Refer To
Methfessel & Werbel
2025 Lincoln Highway, Suite 200
Edison, New Jersey 08817
  Telephone: 732-248-4200
  Fax: 732-248-2355

Mailing Address: P.O. Box 3012, Edison, NJ 08818-3012

Automobile Liability, Bad Faith, Carrier Defense, Casualty Defense, Civil Trial Practice, Comprehensive General Liability, Construction Litigation, Coverage Issues, Defense Litigation, Employment Practices Liability, Environmental Coverage, Environmental Liability, Examinations Under Oath, Excess and Umbrella, Insurance Coverage, Insurance Defense, Medical Liability, Premises Liability, Primary and Excess Insurance, Product Liability, Professional Malpractice, Property Liability, Public Entities, Toxic Torts, Uninsured and Underinsured Motorist, General Subrogation, Large Loss Subrogation Program

SEE COMPLETE LISTING UNDER EDISON, NEW JERSEY (69 MILES)

Refer To
O'Connor Kimball LLP
51 Haddonfield Road, Suite 330
Cherry Hill, New Jersey 08002-4805
  Telephone: 856-663-9292
  Fax: 856-663-6566

General Civil Practice, Casualty, Product Liability, Employment Law, Construction Litigation, Real Estate, Environmental Law, Toxic Torts, Insurance Law, Excess, Professional Liability, Commercial Liability, Commercial Litigation, Workers' Compensation, Civil Rights, Real Estate and Small Business Development Transactions, Professional Liability Litigation

SEE COMPLETE LISTING UNDER CHERRY HILL, NEW JERSEY (9 MILES)

Refer To
Powell, Birchmeier & Powell
1891 State Highway 50
Tuckahoe, New Jersey 08250
  Telephone: 609-628-3414
  Fax: 609-628-2966

Mailing Address: P.O. Box 582, Tuckahoe, NJ 08250-0582

General Civil Practice, Trial Practice, Insurance Defense, Negligence, Defense Litigation, Product Liability, Coverage Issues, Litigation, Workers' Compensation, Subrogation, Civil Rights, Governmental Liability, Medical Negligence, Wrongful Termination, General Chancery Practice, Section 1983 Litigation

SEE COMPLETE LISTING UNDER TUCKAHOE, NEW JERSEY (58 MILES)

CAPE MAY COURT HOUSE   † 5,338 Cape May Co.

Refer To
Powell, Birchmeier & Powell
1891 State Highway 50
Tuckahoe, New Jersey 08250
  Telephone: 609-628-3414
  Fax: 609-628-2966

Mailing Address: P.O. Box 582, Tuckahoe, NJ 08250-0582

General Civil Practice, Trial Practice, Insurance Defense, Negligence, Defense Litigation, Product Liability, Coverage Issues, Litigation, Workers' Compensation, Subrogation, Civil Rights, Governmental Liability, Medical Negligence, Wrongful Termination, General Chancery Practice, Section 1983 Litigation

SEE COMPLETE LISTING UNDER TUCKAHOE, NEW JERSEY (19 MILES)

CHERRY HILL   69,165 Camden Co.

Green, Lundgren & Ryan, P.C.

20 Brace Road, Suite 200
Cherry Hill, New Jersey 08034-2634
  Telephone: 856-428-5800
  Fax: 856-428-9802
  E-Mail: fxryan@glrlaw.com
  www.glrlaw.com

Established: 1978

Insurance Defense, Public Entities, General Liability, Automobile Tort, Property Damage, Personal Injury, Contract Disputes, Bad Faith, Land Use, Zoning, Extra-Contractual Claims, Coverage Litigation

Firm Profile: Founded in 1978, the attorneys of Green, Lundgren & Ryan are known for their outstanding credentials, professionalism and high ethical standards. For over 30 years we have taken great pride in promoting and protecting our clients' interests as formidable advocates in all types of civil proceedings.

Green, Lundgren & Ryan is client-centered and results oriented. We are committed to providing high quality legal services at competitive rates. We aggressively and efficiently represent individuals, businesses, insurance carriers and their insureds, self-insured entities, municipalities and corporations in federal and state courts, at both trial and appellate levels.

Our practice areas are broad and diverse, but concentrated sufficiently to offer specialized expertise to our clients. In the field of tort litigation, our attorneys

CHERRY HILL   NEW JERSEY

Green, Lundgren & Ryan, P.C., Cherry Hill, NJ
(Continued)

handle automobile, uninsured and underinsured motorist, premises liability, homeowners, product liability and environmental matters. We represent national insurers and individuals in matters of insurance coverage, fraud and bad faith litigation.

Insurance Clients

Allstate Insurance Company
Esurance Insurance Company
GEICO
Progressive Insurance Company
White Pine Insurance Company
Camden County Municipal Joint Insurance Fund
Mercury Insurance Group
Travelers Insurance Companies

Partners

Francis X. Ryan — 1953 — Saint Michael's College, B.A. (summa cum laude), 1975; Rutgers University School of Law-Camden, J.D. (with honors), 1978 — Admitted to Bar, 1978, New Jersey; 1978, U.S. District Court, District of New Jersey; 1980, U.S. Court of Appeals, Third Circuit — Member American, New Jersey State and Camden County Bar Associations; Defense Research Institute; New Jersey Defense Association — Practice Areas: Insurance Coverage Litigation; First and Third Party Matters; General Liability; Appellate Practice — E-mail: fxryan@glrlaw.com

Daniel J. DiStasi — 1954 — State University of New York, B.S., 1975; Rutgers University School of Law, J.D., 1979 — Admitted to Bar, 1979, New Jersey; U.S. District Court, District of New Jersey; 1983, U.S. Court of Appeals, Third Circuit; 1984, U.S. Supreme Court — Member New Jersey State (Civil Practice Section), Camden County and Burlington County (Bench-Bar Committee) Bar Associations; New Jersey Defense Association; Defense Research Institute — Practice Areas: General Civil Trial and Appellate Practice; Complex Litigation — E-mail: ddistasi@glrlaw.com

Charles F. Blumenstein, II — 1953 — Saint Joseph's University, B.A., 1975; Rutgers University School of Law, J.D., 1978 — Admitted to Bar, 1978, New Jersey; 1978, U.S. District Court, District of New Jersey; 1986, U.S. Court of Appeals, Third Circuit; 1988, U.S. Supreme Court — Member New Jersey State and Camden County Bar Associations; Defense Research Institute; New Jersey Defense Association — Practice Areas: General Civil Trial and Appellate Practice; Complex Litigation — E-mail: blumenst@glrlaw.com

James E. Mulroy — 1958 — Rutgers University, B.A., 1981; Valparaiso University, J.D., 1984 — Admitted to Bar, 1984, New Jersey; 1984, U.S. District Court, District of New Jersey; 1986, U.S. Court of Appeals, Third Circuit; 1987, U.S. Supreme Court — Member American, New Jersey State, Camden County and Burlington County Bar Associations; New Jersey School Board Association; New Jersey Defense Association; Defense Research Institute — Practice Areas: General Civil Trial and Appellate Practice; Complex Litigation — E-mail: jmulroy@glrlaw.com

Associate

Kristyn A. Holroyd — 1980 — University of Delaware, B.A., 2002; Rutgers University School of Law-Camden, J.D., 2006 — Law Clerk to Hon. Lee Laskin, J.S.C., 2006-2007 — Admitted to Bar, 2006, New Jersey; Pennsylvania — Practice Areas: Litigation; Property Damage; Personal Injury — E-mail: kah@glrlaw.com

Of Counsel

Peter P. Green — 1939 — Brown University, B.A. (with high honors), 1961; Yale University, J.D., 1964 — Admitted to Bar, 1965, New Jersey; 1965, U.S. District Court, District of New Jersey; 1980, U.S. Supreme Court — Member Burlington County and Camden County Bar Associations; New Jersey Defense Association — E-mail: pgreen@glrlaw.com

Marshall Dennehey Warner Coleman & Goggin

Woodland Falls Corporate Park
200 Lake Drive East, Suite 300
Cherry Hill, New Jersey 08002
  Telephone: 856-414-6000
  Fax: 856-414-6077
  www.marshalldennehey.com

Marshall Dennehey Warner Coleman & Goggin, Cherry Hill, NJ
(Continued)

(Philadelphia, PA Office*: 2000 Market Street, Suite 2300, 19103)
  (Tel: 215-575-2600)
  (Fax: 215-575-0856)
  (Toll Free: 800-220-3308)
  (E-Mail: marshalldennehey@mdwcg.com)
(Wilmington, DE Office*: Nemours Building, 1007 North Orange Street, Suite 600, 19801)
  (Tel: 302-552-4300)
  (Fax: 302-552-4340)
(Fort Lauderdale, FL Office*: 100 Northeast 3rd Avenue, Suite 1100, 33301)
  (Tel: 954-847-4920)
  (Fax: 954-627-6640)
(Jacksonville, FL Office*: 200 West Forsyth Street, Suite 1400, 32202)
  (Tel: 904-358-4200)
  (Fax: 904-355-0019)
(Orlando, FL Office*: Landmark Center One, 315 East Robinson Street, Suite 550, 32801-1948)
  (Tel: 407-420-4380)
  (Fax: 407-839-3008)
(Tampa, FL Office*: 201 East Kennedy Boulevard, Suite 1100, 33602)
  (Tel: 813-898-1800)
  (Fax: 813-221-5026)
(Roseland, NJ Office*: 425 Eagle Rock Avenue, Suite 302, 07068)
  (Tel: 973-618-4100)
  (Fax: 973-618-0685)
(New York, NY Office*: Wall Street Plaza, 88 Pine Street, 21st Floor, 10005-1801)
  (Tel: 212-376-6400)
  (Fax: 212-376-6490)
(Melville, NY Office*: 105 Maxess Road, Suite 303, 11747)
  (Tel: 631-232-6130)
  (Fax: 631-232-6184)
(Cincinnati, OH Office*: 312 Elm Street, Suite 1850, 45202)
  (Tel: 513-375-6800)
  (Fax: 513-372-6801)
(Cleveland, OH Office*: 127 Public Square, Suite 3510, 44114-1291)
  (Tel: 216-912-3800)
  (Fax: 216-344-9006)
(Allentown, PA Office*: 4905 West Tilghman Street, Suite 300, 18104)
  (Tel: 484-895-2300)
  (Fax: 484-895-2303)
(Doylestown, PA Office*: 10 North Main Street, 2nd Floor, 18901-4318)
  (Tel: 267-880-2020)
  (Fax: 215-348-5439)
(Erie, PA Office*: 717 State Street, Suite 701, 16501)
  (Tel: 814-480-7800)
  (Fax: 814-455-3603)
(Camp Hill, PA Office*(See Harrisburg listing): 100 Coporate Center Drive, Suite 201, 17011)
  (Tel: 717-651-3500)
  (Fax: 717-651-9630)
(King of Prussia, PA Office*: 620 Freedom Business Center, Suite 300, 19406)
  (Tel: 610-354-8250)
  (Fax: 610-354-8299)
(Pittsburgh, PA Office*: U.S. Steel Tower, Suite 2900, 600 Grant Street, 15219)
  (Tel: 412-803-1140)
  (Fax: 412-803-1188)
(Moosic, PA Office*(See Scranton listing): 50 Glenmaura National Boulevard, 18507)
  (Tel: 570-496-4600)
  (Fax: 570-496-0567)
(Rye Brook, NY Office*(See Westchester listing): 800 Westchester Avenue, Suite C-700, 10573)
  (Tel: 914-977-7300)
  (Fax: 914-977-7301)

Established: 1984

NEW JERSEY   CHERRY HILL

Marshall Dennehey Warner Coleman & Goggin, Cherry Hill, NJ *(Continued)*

Amusements, Sports and Recreation Liability, Asbestos and Mass Tort Litigation, Automobile Liability, Aviation and Complex Litigation, Construction Injury Litigation, Fraud/Special Investigation, General Liability, Hospitality and Liquor Liability, Maritime Litigation, Product Liability, Property Litigation, Retail Liability, Trucking & Transportation Liability, Appellate Advocacy and Post-Trial Practice, Architectural, Engineering and Construction Defect Litigation, Class Action Litigation, Commercial Litigation, Consumer and Credit Law, Employment Law, Environmental & Toxic Tort Litigation, Insurance Coverage/Bad Faith Litigation, Life, Health and Disability Litigation, Privacy and Data Security, Professional Liability, Public Entity and Civil Rights Litigation, Real Estate E&O Liability, School Leaders' Liability, Securities and Investment Professional Liability, Technology, Media and Intellectual Property Litigation, White Collar Crime, Birth Injury Litigation, Health Care Governmental Compliance, Health Care Liability, Health Law, Long-Term Care Liability, Medical Device and Pharmaceutical Liability, Medicare Set-Aside, Workers' Compensation

Firm Profile: Our firm established its first office in New Jersey in 1984. Since that time, this office has experienced consistent and, at times, quite dramatic growth. The Cherry Hill office is staffed by many long-time residents of New Jersey who handle professional liability, product liability, property and casualty, and workers' compensation litigation. The counties covered by this office include Mercer, Monmouth, Ocean, Burlington, Camden, Middlesex, Gloucester, Atlantic, Salem, Cumberland and Cape May.

Additional information regarding this office is available by contacting Richard Goldstein, Esquire, the managing attorney of this office, at (856) 414-6013 or rlgoldstein@mdwcg.com

Managing Shareholder

Richard L. Goldstein — **Supervisor, Professional Liability Practice Group, Southern NJ** — 1956 — Dickinson College, B.A. (cum laude), 1977; Villanova University School of Law, J.D., 1980 — New Jersey Super Lawyer (2005-2009, 2012-2013) — Villanova Law Review (1979-1980) — Admitted to Bar, 1982, New Jersey; U.S. District Court, District of New Jersey; U.S. Court of Appeals, Third Circuit; U.S. Supreme Court — Member New Jersey State and Camden County Bar Associations; New Jersey Defense Association — Author: "Rush v. Savchuk-Assertion of Quasi In Rem Jurisdiction under Rule of Seider v. Roth Held Violative of Due Process," 25 Vill. Law Review 811 (1980); Co-Author: "New Jersey Decides Key Areas of Coverage for Environmental Insurance," Defense Digest, Winter 1993, 1994; "New Jersey Finds Coverage For Environmental Claims For Groundwater Contamination," Defense Digest, Vol. 2, No. 9, 1996; "Architectural, Engineering & Construction Law Seminar," Employment Law section for CUH2A, Princeton Architectural Firm, May 2, 2002; Author: "Constitutional Torts Against Public Entities," Burlington County Joint Insurance Fund Presentation, July 12, 2002; Co-Author: "Employment Law Outline: Overview of Federal and NJ Statutes and Case Law," August 14, 2002; "Employment Law, Liability Risks and Ethics, Insurance Society of Philadelphia," New Jersey Employment Law Handbook (2002, 2003, 2004, 2006) — Reported Cases: Wade v. Armstrong World Industries, Inc., 746 F. Supp. 493 (D.N.J 1993); Civalier v. Estate of Trancicco, 138 N.J. 52 (1994); Carvalho v. Toll Bros., 278 N.J. Super. 451 (1995); Dombrowski v. City of Atlantic City, 308 N.J. Super. 459 (App. Div. 1998); Hurley v. Atlantic City Police Dept., 174 F. 3d 95 (3d Cir. 1999) — Certified Civil Trial Attorney, New Jersey Supreme Court — Practice Areas: Civil Rights; Employment Law (Management Side); Education Law; Municipal Law; Construction Law; Product Liability; Toxic Torts — E-mail: rlgoldstein@mdwcg.com

Special Counsel

Nancy L. Musser

Senior Counsel

Lary I. Zucker   John L. Slimm

Resident Shareholders

Dana C. Argeris   Matthew J. Behr
Lawrence B. Berg   Carolyn Kelly Bogart
Tracy L. Burnley   Sharon A. Campbell Suplee

Marshall Dennehey Warner Coleman & Goggin, Cherry Hill, NJ *(Continued)*

Barbara J. Davis   Robert J. Fitzgerald
James L. Johnson   Paul C. Johnson
Walter F. Kawalec, III   Walter J. Klekotka, Jr.
Peter A. Lentini   Diane Magram
Kevin M. McGoldrick   Kevin M. McKeon
Raymond J. Michaud   Lynne N. Nahmani
Kristy Olivo Salvitti   John H. Osorio
Jeffrey G. Rapattoni   Dante C. Rohr
Alicia M. Smith   Douglas D. Suplee
Arthur F. Wheeler   Lila Wynne

Resident Associates

David D. Blake   Kevin T. Bright
Ariel C. Brownstein   Matthew J. Burdalski
Michael G. Daly   George C. Deeney
Angela Y. DeMary   Susanne N. Finiello
Lisa L. Goldman   Michael A. Gorokhovich
Mari I. Grimes   Jammie N. Jackson
Edward M. Louka   Christopher J. Marcucci
Raymond J. Michaud   Kristy N. Olivo
Lisa M. Only   Kara A. Pullman
Dante C. Rohr   Matthew S. Rydzewski
Amy K. Sakowski   Ashley L. Toth
Rachael Snyder von Rhine   Jessica D. Wachstein
Jason S. Walker

(See listing under Philadelphia, PA for additional information)

Mayfield, Turner, O'Mara & Donnelly, P.C.

2201 Route 38, Suite 300
Cherry Hill, New Jersey 08002
  Telephone: 856-667-2600
  Fax: 856-667-8787
  www.mayfieldturner.com

(Philadelphia, PA Office: 1617 JFK Boulevard, Suite 932, 19103)
  (Tel: 215-564-0500)
  (Fax: 215-564-2212)

Insurance Defense, Bodily Injury, Property Damage, Toxic Torts, Product Liability, Environmental Law, Professional Liability, General Liability, Construction Law, Automobile, Property, Casualty, Medical Malpractice, Dental Malpractice, Employment Discrimination, Legal Malpractice, Carrier Defense, Construction Defect, Construction Litigation, Coverage Analysis, Employment Practices Liability, Self-Insured Defense, Truck Liability, Trucking Law, Appellate Practice, Elevators, Public Entity Tort Litigation

Firm Profile: At Mayfield, Turner, O'Mara & Donnelly, we provide the finest legal representation in a broad range of litigated matters in a variety of complex litigation and coverage matters throughout New Jersey and Eastern Pennsylvania including product liability, construction defects, environmental law, toxic torts and long-term exposure, medical, dental and other professional malpractice, public entity tort litigation, commercial litigation, employment law litigation, and appellate practice.

Insurance Clients

ACE USA   Admiral Insurance Company
American Alternative Insurance   American Home Assurance
  Corporation   Company
American Re-Insurance Company   Camden County Municipal Joint
Chubb/Federal Insurance Company   Insurance Fund
Coregis Insurance Company   Crawford & Company
Cumberland Insurance Group   Cunningham Lindsey U.S., Inc.
Diocesan Claims Service   First Trenton Indemnity Company
Gallagher Bassett Insurance   General Star Indemnity Company
  Company   Granite State Insurance Company
The Harleysville Insurance   Insurance Management Resources,
Knightbrook Insurance Company   L.P.
Lexington Insurance Company   Liberty Mutual Insurance Company
Medical Protective Insurance   Metropolitan Property and Casualty
  Services   Insurance Company

CHERRY HILL   NEW JERSEY

Mayfield, Turner, O'Mara & Donnelly, P.C., Cherry Hill, NJ (Continued)

Munich Reinsurance Company
Nautilus Insurance Group
Old Guard Insurance Company
Peerless Insurance Company
RSKCo
Scibal Associates, Inc.
SelecTech Claims
Selective Way Insurance Company
Travelers Insurance Companies
National Union Fire Insurance Company of Pittsburgh, PA
OneBeacon Insurance
Royal Specialty Underwriting, Inc.
The St. Paul Companies
Sedgwick Claims Management Services, Inc.
Summit Risk Services, Inc.
United Services Automobile Association (USAA)

Non-Insurance Clients

Boise Cascade, L.L.C.
Carrier Corporation
CVS Corporation
Dover Corporation
NORDYNE, Inc.
Otis Elevator Company
Riggs, Distler & Company, Inc.
Sikorsky Aircraft Corporation
Sysco Food Services of Philadelphia
Verizon New Jersey, Inc.
Whibco, Inc.
Boscov's Department Stores
Clayburn Construction Corporation
The Diocese of Camden
Essex Group, Inc.
OfficeMax Incorporated
Powermatic, Division of DeVlieg-Bullard, Inc.
State Industries, Inc.
Temple University
United Technologies Corporation
Verizon Wireless

Shareholders

John V. Petrycki, Jr. — 1969 — Gettysburg College, B.A. (with honors), 1991; Seton Hall University School of Law, J.D., 1994 — Admitted to Bar, 1994, Pennsylvania; 1995, New Jersey; U.S. District Court, District of New Jersey; 2008, U.S. Court of Appeals, Third Circuit; U.S. Supreme Court — Member New Jersey State and Camden County Bar Associations — E-mail: jpetrycki@mayfieldturner.com

David M. Mayfield — 1940 — United States Naval Academy, B.S., 1962; University of Connecticut, J.D., 1970 — Admitted to Bar, 1970, New Jersey; U.S. District Court, District of New Jersey; 1977, U.S. Supreme Court — Member American, New Jersey State and Camden County Bar Associations; New Jersey Defense Association; International Association of Defense Counsel; Defense Research Institute — E-mail: dmayfield@mayfieldturner.com

Directors/Shareholders

Linton W. Turner, Jr. — 1952 — Hamilton College, B.A., 1974; Suffolk University, J.D. (cum laude), 1978 — Law Clerk to Hon. J. Gilbert VanSciver, Jr., Superior Court, 1978-1979 — Admitted to Bar, 1978, Massachusetts; 1979, New Jersey; 1992, Pennsylvania; 1979, U.S. District Court, District of New Jersey; 1980, U.S. Court of Appeals, Third Circuit; 1983, U.S. Supreme Court — Member American, New Jersey State and Camden County Bar Associations; New Jersey Defense Association — E-mail: lturner@mayfieldturner.com

Michael J. O'Mara — 1956 — Rutgers University, B.A., 1978; University of Notre Dame, J.D., 1981 — Admitted to Bar, 1981, New Jersey; U.S. District Court, District of New Jersey; 1983, U.S. Court of Appeals, Third Circuit; 1986, U.S. Supreme Court — Member New Jersey State and Camden County Bar Associations; New Jersey Trial Lawyers Association; Defense Research Institute; New Jersey Defense Association — E-mail: momara@mayfieldturner.com

Francis X. Donnelly — 1957 — Loyola University New Orleans, B.A., 1979; Gonzaga University, J.D., 1983 — Law Clerk to Hon. E. Stevenson Fluharty, Superior Court of New Jersey, 1983-1984 — Admitted to Bar, 1983, New Jersey; U.S. District Court, District of New Jersey; 1985, U.S. Court of Appeals, Third Circuit — Member New Jersey State and Camden County Bar Associations; New Jersey Trial Lawyers Association; New Jersey Defense Association; Defense Research Institute — Certified Civil Trial Attorney by the Supreme Court of New Jersey — E-mail: fdonnelly@mayfieldturner.com

Officers

Tricia E. Habert — 1967 — Drew University, B.A., 1990; Dickinson School of Law, J.D., 1993 — Admitted to Bar, 1993, New Jersey; 1994, U.S. District Court, District of New Jersey — Member American, New Jersey State and Camden County Bar Associations; New Jersey Defense Association — E-mail: thabert@mayfieldturner.com

Christine D. McGuire — West Virginia University, B.A. (Phi Beta Kappa, summa cum laude), 1994; M.S.W., 1996; Villanova University School of Law, J.D., 1999 — Admitted to Bar, 1999, New Jersey; Pennsylvania; U.S. District Court, District of New Jersey — Member New Jersey State and Camden County Bar Associations — E-mail: cmcguire@mayfieldturner.com

Mayfield, Turner, O'Mara & Donnelly, P.C., Cherry Hill, NJ (Continued)

Karen A. Mascioli — 1964 — Rowan University, B.A., 2000; Rutgers University School of Law, J.D., 2003 — Admitted to Bar, 2003, New Jersey; Pennsylvania; U.S. District Court, District of New Jersey — Member American, New Jersey State and Camden County Bar Associations — E-mail: kmascioli@mayfieldturner.com

Associates

Robert J. Gillispie, Jr. — 1968 — University of Southern California, B.A., 1990; Rutgers University School of Law-Newark, J.D., 1996 — Law Clerk to Hon. Sybil R. Moses, A.J.S.C., Superior Court of New Jersey, Bergen County — Admitted to Bar, 1996, New Jersey; U.S. District Court, District of New Jersey; 2009, U.S. Court of Appeals, Third Circuit — Member New Jersey State and Camden County Bar Associations — E-mail: rgillispie@mayfieldturner.com

Joshua P. Locke — 1982 — University of Delaware, B.A. (cum laude), 2005; Rutgers University School of Law-Camden, J.D., 2008 — Law Clerk to the Hon. Anthony M. Pugliese, J.S.C., Camden County — Admitted to Bar, 2008, New Jersey; Pennsylvania; U.S. District Court, District of New Jersey — Member American, New Jersey State and Camden County Bar Associations — E-mail: jlocke@mayfieldturner.com

Katherine O. Mowll — 1982 — Rutgers College, B.A., 2004; Rutgers University School of Law-Camden, J.D., 2008 — Law Clerk to the Hon. James E. Rafferty, P.J.G.E., Gloucester, Salem and Cumberland Counties — Admitted to Bar, 2008, New Jersey; Pennsylvania; U.S. District Court, District of New Jersey; U.S. District Court, Eastern District of Pennsylvania — Member Pennsylvania, Camden County and Philadelphia County Bar Associations — Resident Philadelphia, PA Office — E-mail: kmowll@mayfieldturner.com

Zoe C. Elfenbein — 1984 — Emory University, B.A., 2006; Rutgers University School of Law-Camden, J.D., 2009 — Law Clerk to the Hon. David W. Morgan, J.S.C., Superior Court of New Jersey, Salem County — Admitted to Bar, 2010, New Jersey; Pennsylvania; U.S. District Court, Eastern District of Pennsylvania — Member American, New Jersey State, Pennsylvania State and Philadelphia Bar Associations — Resident Philadelphia, PA Office — E-mail: zelfenbein@mayfieldturner.com

Sara K. Saltsman — 1976 — Union College, B.A. (magna cum laude), 1998; Fordham University School of Law, J.D., 2001 — Admitted to Bar, 2002, New York; 2008, Pennsylvania; 2010, New Jersey — Member New Jersey State and Camden County Bar Associations — E-mail: ssaltsman@mayfieldturner.com

Christopher T. Chancler — 1983 — Boston College, B.A., 2005; Rutgers University School of Law-Camden, J.D., 2011 — Law Clerk to Hon. Deborah Silverman Katz, J.S.C., Superior Court of New Jersey, Camden County — Admitted to Bar, 2012, New Jersey; Pennsylvania; U.S. District Court, District of New Jersey — Member Camden County Bar Association — E-mail: cchancler@mayfieldturner.com

Andrew A. Keith — 1987 — Rutgers College, B.A. (magna cum laude), 2009; Rutgers University School of Law-Camden, J.D., 2012 — Admitted to Bar, 2012, New Jersey; Pennsylvania — E-mail: akeith@mayfieldturner.com

Mintzer Sarowitz Zeris Ledva & Meyers, LLP

2070 Springdale Road, Suite 400
Cherry Hill, New Jersey 08003
Telephone: 856-616-0700
Fax: 856-616-0776
www.Defensecounsel.com

(Additional Offices: Philadelphia, PA*; Miami, FL*; Hicksville, NY*; New York, NY*; Pittsburgh, PA*; Wilmington, DE*; Tampa, FL*; Wheeling, WV*)

Insurance Defense, Premises Liability, Product Liability, Environmental Law, Workers' Compensation, Coverage Issues, Asbestos Litigation, Medical Malpractice, Nursing Home Liability, Professional Liability, Trucking Law

Managing Partner

Kimberly A. Murphy

(See listing under Philadelphia, PA for additional information)

O'Connor Kimball LLP

51 Haddonfield Road, Suite 330
Cherry Hill, New Jersey 08002-4805
   Telephone: 856-663-9292
   Fax: 856-663-6566
   www.oconnorkimball.com

(Philadelphia, PA Office*: Two Penn Center Plaza, Suite 1100, 1500 John F. Kennedy Boulevard, 19102)
   (Tel: 215-564-0400)
   (Fax: 215-564-1973)

Established: 1987

General Civil Practice, Casualty, Product Liability, Employment Law, Construction Litigation, Real Estate, Environmental Law, Toxic Torts, Insurance Law, Excess, Professional Liability, Commercial Liability, Commercial Litigation, Workers' Compensation, Civil Rights, Real Estate and Small Business Development Transactions, Professional Liability Litigation

Partners

Michael P. O'Connor   Glen D. Kimball
Stephen E. Siegrist   Thomas J. Gregory
Martin J. McAndrew

(See listing under Philadelphia, PA for additional information)

The following firms also service this area.

Budd Larner, P.C.
150 John F. Kennedy Parkway
Short Hills, New Jersey 07078-2703
   Telephone: 973-379-4800
   Fax: 973-379-7734

General Practice, Insurance Law, Reinsurance
SEE COMPLETE LISTING UNDER SHORT HILLS, NEW JERSEY (82 MILES)

Law Offices of Glenn R. Cochran
812 State Road, Suite 120
Princeton, New Jersey 08540
   Telephone: 609-924-4011
   Fax: 609-924-5333
Mailing Address: P.O. Box 553, Princeton, NJ 08542

Insurance Defense, Trial Practice, Automobile, Professional Liability, Product Liability, Errors and Omissions, Liquor Liability, Commercial Liability, Subrogation, General
SEE COMPLETE LISTING UNDER PRINCETON, NEW JERSEY (33 MILES)

Cooper Levenson, P.A.
1125 Atlantic Avenue, Third Floor
Atlantic City, New Jersey 08401
   Telephone: 609-344-3161
   Fax: 609-344-0939

Trial and Appellate Practice, State and Federal Courts, Negligence, Insurance Defense, Product Liability, Workers' Compensation, Environmental Law, Professional Liability, Employment Law, Dram Shop, Premises Liability, Mass Tort, Casino, Health/Hospital, Bedbug Liability Defense
SEE COMPLETE LISTING UNDER ATLANTIC CITY, NEW JERSEY (60 MILES)

Law Office of John M. Palm, LLC
High Ridge Commons, Suite 101
200 Haddonfield-Berlin Road
Gibbsboro, New Jersey 08026
   Telephone: 856-783-5461
   Fax: 856-783-5464

Coverage Issues, General Liability, Premises Liability, Self-Insured Defense, Truck Liability, Sports Claims Defense, Automobile Negligence
SEE COMPLETE LISTING UNDER GIBBSBORO, NEW JERSEY (10 MILES)

EAST ORANGE 64,270 Essex Co.

Refer To
Philip M. Lustbader & David Lustbader, P.A.
615 West Mt. Pleasant Avenue
Livingston, New Jersey 07039
   Telephone: 973-740-1000
   Fax: 973-740-1520

Insurance Defense, Civil Trial Practice, Negligence, No-Fault, Uninsured and Underinsured Motorist, Product Liability, Workers' Compensation, Dental Malpractice, Medical Malpractice, Coverage Issues, Appellate Practice, Subrogation, Monitoring Litigation
SEE COMPLETE LISTING UNDER LIVINGSTON, NEW JERSEY (3 MILES)

EDISON 97,687 Middlesex Co.

Methfessel & Werbel

2025 Lincoln Highway, Suite 200
Edison, New Jersey 08817
   Telephone: 732-248-4200
   Fax: 732-248-2355
   E-Mail: mailbox@methwerb.com
   www.methwerb.com

(New York, NY Office*: 450 Seventh Avenue, Suite 1400, 10123)
   (Tel: 212-947-1999)
   (Fax: 212-947-3333)
(Wayne, PA Office*: 101 East Lancaster Avenue, Suite 304, 19087)
   (Tel: 610-902-0150)
   (Fax: 610-902-0152)

Established: 1972

Automobile Liability, Bad Faith, Carrier Defense, Casualty Defense, Civil Trial Practice, Comprehensive General Liability, Construction Litigation, Coverage Issues, Defense Litigation, Employment Practices Liability, Environmental Coverage, Environmental Liability, Examinations Under Oath, Excess and Umbrella, Insurance Coverage, Insurance Defense, Medical Liability, Premises Liability, Primary and Excess Insurance, Product Liability, Professional Malpractice, Property Liability, Public Entities, Toxic Torts, Uninsured and Underinsured Motorist, General Subrogation, Large Loss Subrogation Program

Firm Profile: Methfessel and Werbel was formed in 1972 exclusively to service the insurance industry. Our staff of 9 partners, 11 counsel, 28 associates and 45 support personnel is committed to providing the highest level of service possible. Our mission is to work as an extension of our clients to expeditiously achieve the most economically favorable resolution of claims on their behalf and on behalf of their insureds.

Insurance Clients

American Empire Surplus Lines Insurance Company
Chartis Insurance
Clarendon National Insurance Company
Erie Insurance Exchange
Essex Insurance Company
Franklin Mutual Insurance Company
Great American Insurance Company
GuideOne Insurance
Markel Corporation
Mercer Insurance Company
Municipal Excess Liability Joint Insurance Fund
Norfolk and Dedham Mutual Fire Insurance Company
Preferred Mutual Insurance Company
Quincy Mutual Fire Insurance Company
Andover Group
ARI Mutual Insurance Company
Chubb Group of Insurance Companies
The Cumberland Mutual Fire Insurance Company
Everest National Insurance Company
Gallagher Bassett Services, Inc.
Greater New York Mutual Insurance Company
Liberty Mutual Insurance Company
Meadowbrook Claims Service
Mercury Insurance Company
New Jersey School Boards Association
Peerless Insurance Company
Plymouth Rock Assurance Corporation
The Providence Mutual Fire Insurance Company
The Salem Group

FLEMINGTON   NEW JERSEY

Methfessel & Werbel, Edison, NJ   (Continued)

Specialty Risk Services, Inc. (SRS)
Tower Group Companies
Vermont Mutual Insurance Company
Summit Risk Services, Inc.
Travelers Insurance Companies

Non-Insurance Clients

AutoZone, Inc.

Partners

Edward L. Thornton — 1951 — Rider College, B.S., 1974; Seton Hall University, J.D., 1977 — Admitted to Bar, 1977, New Jersey — Certified Civil Trial Attorney, New Jersey Supreme Court

Joel N. Werbel — 1941 — Dartmouth College, B.A., 1963; Rutgers University, LL.B., 1966 — Admitted to Bar, 1965, New Jersey — Member Essex County Bar Association; New Jersey Defense Association

John Methfessel, Jr. — 1962 — University of Miami, B.B.A., 1983; Duke University, J.D., 1986 — Admitted to Bar, 1986, New Jersey; 1994, U.S. Supreme Court — Member New Jersey State Bar Association; New Jersey Defense Association; Defense Research Institute — Certified Civil Trial Attorney, New Jersey Supreme Court

Fredric P. Gallin — 1958 — Johns Hopkins University, B.A., 1979; Boston University, J.D., 1982; Pace University, LL.M., 1995 — Admitted to Bar, 1982, Massachusetts; 1983, New York; 1985, New Jersey; 1989, California — Member New Jersey State Bar Association; Defense Research Institute; New Jersey Defense Association — Certified Civil Trial Attorney by the New Jersey Supreme Court

Stephen R. Katzman — 1956 — Boston University, B.A. (cum laude), 1978; Loyola University, J.D., 1981 — Admitted to Bar, 1981, Louisiana; 1985, New Jersey; 1985, U.S. District Court, District of New Jersey; 1989, U.S. Court of Appeals, Third Circuit — Practice Areas: First Party Matters; Fraud; Insurance Defense; Product Liability; Property Damage

Eric L. Harrison — 1968 — Princeton University, B.A., 1990; Georgetown University, J.D., 1993 — Admitted to Bar, 1993, New Jersey

William S. Bloom — 1969 — University of Pennsylvania, B.S. (magna cum laude), 1991; Duke University, J.D., 1994 — Admitted to Bar, 1994, New Jersey

Matthew A. Werbel — 1971 — Franklin & Marshall College, B.A., 1994; Tulane University, J.D., 1998 — Admitted to Bar, 1998, New Jersey

Marc L. Dembling — Syracuse University, B.S., 1966; Rutgers University School of Law, J.D., 1969 — Admitted to Bar, 1969, New Jersey; 1981, New York; 1972, U.S. Supreme Court — Certified Civil Trial Attorney, New Jersey Supreme Court

Of Counsel

Donald L. Crowley
John Methfessel, Sr.

Counsel

Paul J. Endler, Jr.
Jared P. Kingsley
Charles T. McCook Jr.
Lori Brown Sternback
Gerald Kaplan
John R. Knodel
Gina M. Stanziale
Adam S. Weiss

Associates

Kegan S. Andeskie
Elizabeth C. Connelly
Edward D. Dembling
Michael Eatroff
James Foxen
Richard J. Isolde
Frank J. Keenan
Allison M. Koenke
Caitlin W. Lundquist
Raina Pitts
William J. Rada
Michael J. Raskys
Amanda Sawyer
Boris Shapiro
Lindsay A. Spero
Christopher P. Ward
Christian R. Baillie
Jacqueline Cuozzo
Michael V. DiGirolamo
Marco F. Ferreira
Jennifer Hermann
Maurice Jefferson
Leslie A. Koch
Vivian Lekkas
Richard Nelke
Matthew L. Rachmiel
Christen Rafuse
Nabila Saeed
Jared S. Schure
Mark A. Speed
Levi E. Updyke
Carrie G. Zalewski

(This firm is also listed in the Subrogation section of this directory)

ELIZABETH † 124,969 Union Co.

Refer To

Methfessel & Werbel
2025 Lincoln Highway, Suite 200
Edison, New Jersey 08817
Telephone: 732-248-4200
Fax: 732-248-2355

Mailing Address: P.O. Box 3012, Edison, NJ 08818-3012

Automobile Liability, Bad Faith, Carrier Defense, Casualty Defense, Civil Trial Practice, Comprehensive General Liability, Construction Litigation, Coverage Issues, Defense Litigation, Employment Practices Liability, Environmental Coverage, Environmental Liability, Examinations Under Oath, Excess and Umbrella, Insurance Coverage, Insurance Defense, Medical Liability, Premises Liability, Primary and Excess Insurance, Product Liability, Professional Malpractice, Property Liability, Public Entities, Toxic Torts, Uninsured and Underinsured Motorist, General Subrogation, Large Loss Subrogation Program

SEE COMPLETE LISTING UNDER EDISON, NEW JERSEY (19 MILES)

Refer To

Nowell Amoroso Klein Bierman, P.A.
155 Polifly Road
Hackensack, New Jersey 07601
Telephone: 201-343-5001
Toll Free: 800-246-0254
Fax: 201-343-5181

Insurance Defense, Bodily Injury, Asbestos Litigation, Environmental Law, Personal Liability, Automobile, Homeowners, Toxic Torts, Product Liability, Pollution, Property Damage

SEE COMPLETE LISTING UNDER HACKENSACK, NEW JERSEY (30 MILES)

Refer To

William J. Pollinger, P.A.
Claridge Plaza
302 Union Street
Hackensack, New Jersey 07601
Telephone: 201-487-5666
Fax: 201-487-6335

Insurance Defense, Product Liability, Automobile Liability, Negligence, Toxic Torts, Subrogation, Policy Construction and Interpretation, Insurance Coverage, Personal Injury

SEE COMPLETE LISTING UNDER HACKENSACK, NEW JERSEY (30 MILES)

FLEMINGTON † 4,581 Hunterdon Co.

Refer To

Methfessel & Werbel
2025 Lincoln Highway, Suite 200
Edison, New Jersey 08817
Telephone: 732-248-4200
Fax: 732-248-2355

Mailing Address: P.O. Box 3012, Edison, NJ 08818-3012

Automobile Liability, Bad Faith, Carrier Defense, Casualty Defense, Civil Trial Practice, Comprehensive General Liability, Construction Litigation, Coverage Issues, Defense Litigation, Employment Practices Liability, Environmental Coverage, Environmental Liability, Examinations Under Oath, Excess and Umbrella, Insurance Coverage, Insurance Defense, Medical Liability, Premises Liability, Primary and Excess Insurance, Product Liability, Professional Malpractice, Property Liability, Public Entities, Toxic Torts, Uninsured and Underinsured Motorist, General Subrogation, Large Loss Subrogation Program

SEE COMPLETE LISTING UNDER EDISON, NEW JERSEY (30 MILES)

Refer To

Nowell Amoroso Klein Bierman, P.A.
155 Polifly Road
Hackensack, New Jersey 07601
Telephone: 201-343-5001
Toll Free: 800-246-0254
Fax: 201-343-5181

Insurance Defense, Bodily Injury, Asbestos Litigation, Environmental Law, Personal Liability, Automobile, Homeowners, Toxic Torts, Product Liability, Pollution, Property Damage

SEE COMPLETE LISTING UNDER HACKENSACK, NEW JERSEY (60 MILES)

NEW JERSEY

FLORHAM PARK   11,696 Morris Co.

Hueston McNulty, P.C.
256 Columbia Turnpike, Suite 207
Florham Park, New Jersey 07932
   Telephone: 973-377-0200
   Fax: 973-377-6328
   Toll Free: 800-276-9982
   E-Mail: info@huestonmcnulty.com
   www.huestonmcnulty.com

(Toms River, NJ Office: Box 3473, 08756-3473)
   (Tel: 732-240-2300)
   (Fax: 732-341-7488)
   (Toll Free: 888-401-2300)
(New York, NY Office*: The Empire State Building, 350 Fifth Avenue, Suite 4810, 10118)
   (Tel: 973-377-0200)
   (Fax: 973-377-6328)
   (Toll Free: 800-276-9982)
(Blue Bell, PA Office: 450 Sentry Parkway, Suite 200, 19422)
   (Tel: 973-377-0200)
   (Fax: 973-377-6328)
   (Toll Free: 800-276-9982)

Established: 1972

Sports Claims Defense, Retail Liability, Directors and Officers Liability, Premises Liability, Automobile Liability, Insurance Coverage, Construction Defect, Municipal Law, Land Use, Real Estate, Alternative Dispute Resolution, Community Association Law

Firm Profile: Hueston McNulty, P.C. focuses its' practice as trial lawyers and counselors to community associations and in sport and recreational defense work for a number of insurers and their insureds. We represent ski areas, ski, bike and sporting goods manufacturers and retailers, amusement and water parks.

Insurance Clients

Travelers Insurance Company   United States Liability Insurance Group

Insurance Practice Group

Samuel J. McNulty — Ursinus College, B.A., 1986; Widener University School of Law, J.D., 1989 — Admitted to Bar, 1989, Pennsylvania; 1990, New Jersey; 1993, New York; U.S. District Court, Eastern District of Pennsylvania; U.S. District Court, District of New Jersey; U.S. Court of Appeals, Third Circuit — Member American, New Jersey State and Morris County Bar Associations; Association of Ski Defense Attorneys; College of Community Association Attorneys; New Jersey Defense Association — Certified Civil Trial Attorney by the Supreme Court of New Jersey

John J. Gaffney — State University of New York at Oneonta, B.S., 1982; New York Law School, J.D., 1991 — Admitted to Bar, 1992, New Jersey; New York; U.S. District Court, District of New Jersey; U.S. District Court, Eastern and Southern Districts of New York; U.S. Court of Appeals, Second Circuit — Member New Jersey State Bar Association; New Jersey Defense Association — Certified Civil Trial Attorney by the Supreme Court of New Jersey

Members

Robert J. Hueston   Samuel J. McNulty

Associates

John J. Gaffney   Edward J. Turro
Brian J. McIntyre   Donna B. Shaw

Of Counsel

Aimee H. McNulty   Hugh Emory
Carol A. Schrager   Stephen H. Shaw

FORT LEE   35,345 Bergen Co.

Kaufman, Semeraro & Leibman, LLC
Fort Lee Executive Park
Two Executive Drive, Suite 530
Fort Lee, New Jersey 07024
   Telephone: 201-947-8855
   Fax: 201-947-2402
   E-Mail: msemeraro@northjerseyattorneys.com
   www.northjerseyattorneys.com

Insurance Defense, Automobile, Commercial Litigation, Errors and Omissions, General Liability, Land Use, Personal Injury, Professional Liability, Public Entities, Real Estate, Trucking, Employment Law, Employment Liability

Firm Profile: Kaufman, Semeraro & Leibman, LLP is accomplished and respected in various legal practice areas. We apply the full benefits of our knowledge and experience to the determined pursuit of favorable outcomes for our clients, and are committed to protecting their interests.

Non-Insurance Clients

Borough of Ringwood   Century 21 Gemini, LLC Realty
Cushman & Wakefield   Langan Engineering and
Marathon National Bank   Environmental Services, Inc.
North Jersey Community Bank   Passaic Valley Sewerage
Prudential Gross & Jansen   Commission
Highlands Realty

Partners

Paul C. Kaufman — University of Wisconsin-Madison, B.A., 1970; New York Law School, J.D., 1973 — Admitted to Bar, 1974, New Jersey — Member American, New Jersey State and Bergen County Bar Associations — Practice Areas: Land Use; Real Estate; Corporate Law; Banking; Municipal Law; Employment Law

Mark J. Semeraro — **Department Head, Insurance Defense Group** — William Paterson College, B.A., 1989; University of Bridgeport School of Law, J.D., 1992 — Admitted to Bar, 1992, New Jersey; 1994, New York; 1992, U.S. District Court, District of New Jersey; U.S. Court of Appeals, Third Circuit — Member Bergen County Bar Association; Commerce and Industry Association of New Jersey; International Council of Shopping Centers — "AV Rated" by Martindale-Hubbell (2005-Present); "Top Bergen County Lawyer, 2012," 201 Magazine, April 2012; "Good Scout of the Year," Northern New Jersey Council, Boys Scouts of America (2008) — Practice Areas: Insurance Defense; Self-Insured Defense; Labor and Employment; Civil Rights; Commercial Litigation; Municipal Law; Land Use; Real Estate

Marc E. Leibman — Franklin & Marshall College, B.A., 1993; Seton Hall University School of Law, J.D., 1996 — Admitted to Bar, 1996, New Jersey; 2007, New York; 1996, U.S. District Court, District of New Jersey; U.S. Court of Appeals, Third Circuit; 2007, U.S. District Court, Eastern District of New York — Named Rising Star Criminal Attorney by New Jersey Monthly Magazine (2006-present) — Practice Areas: Land Use; Municipal Law; Criminal Law; Commercial Litigation; Real Estate

Associates

Jaime R. Placek   Deena B. Rosendahl
Justin D. Santagata   Bryan P. Regan
R. Scott Fahrney   Danielle M. Lamake

(This firm is also listed in the Subrogation section of this directory)

HACKENSACK
NEW JERSEY

FREEHOLD † 12,052 Monmouth Co.

Refer To
Law Offices of Glenn R. Cochran
812 State Road, Suite 120
Princeton, New Jersey 08540
  Telephone: 609-924-4011
  Fax: 609-924-5333

Mailing Address: P.O. Box 553, Princeton, NJ 08542

Insurance Defense, Trial Practice, Automobile, Professional Liability, Product Liability, Errors and Omissions, Liquor Liability, Commercial Liability, Subrogation, General

SEE COMPLETE LISTING UNDER PRINCETON, NEW JERSEY (35 MILES)

Refer To
Law Offices of Garrett L. Joest, L.L.C.
29 Hadley Avenue
Toms River, New Jersey 08753
  Telephone: 732-505-0707
  Fax: 732-505-1717

Insurance Defense, Insurance Coverage, Subrogation, Professional Malpractice, Personal Injury, Toxic Torts, Environmental Law, Asbestos Litigation

SEE COMPLETE LISTING UNDER TOMS RIVER, NEW JERSEY (24 MILES)

Refer To
Methfessel & Werbel
2025 Lincoln Highway, Suite 200
Edison, New Jersey 08817
  Telephone: 732-248-4200
  Fax: 732-248-2355

Mailing Address: P.O. Box 3012, Edison, NJ 08818-3012

Automobile Liability, Bad Faith, Carrier Defense, Casualty Defense, Civil Trial Practice, Comprehensive General Liability, Construction Litigation, Coverage Issues, Defense Litigation, Employment Practices Liability, Environmental Coverage, Environmental Liability, Examinations Under Oath, Excess and Umbrella, Insurance Coverage, Insurance Defense, Medical Liability, Premises Liability, Primary and Excess Insurance, Product Liability, Professional Malpractice, Property Liability, Public Entities, Toxic Torts, Uninsured and Underinsured Motorist, General Subrogation, Large Loss Subrogation Program

SEE COMPLETE LISTING UNDER EDISON, NEW JERSEY (24 MILES)

Refer To
Nowell Amoroso Klein Bierman, P.A.
155 Polifly Road
Hackensack, New Jersey 07601
  Telephone: 201-343-5001
  Toll Free: 800-246-0254
  Fax: 201-343-5181

Insurance Defense, Bodily Injury, Asbestos Litigation, Environmental Law, Personal Liability, Automobile, Homeowners, Toxic Torts, Product Liability, Pollution, Property Damage

SEE COMPLETE LISTING UNDER HACKENSACK, NEW JERSEY (53 MILES)

Refer To
Widman, Cooney, Wilson, McGann & Fitterer, L.L.C.
1803 Highway 35
Oakhurst, New Jersey 07755
  Telephone: 732-531-4141
  Fax: 732-531-7773

Insurance Defense, Casualty, Directors and Officers Liability, Employment Law, Automobile, Professional Negligence (Medical, Accountants and Attorneys, Insurance Agents, Realtors and Home Inspectors)

SEE COMPLETE LISTING UNDER OCEAN, NEW JERSEY (16 MILES)

GIBBSBORO 2,274 Camden Co.

Law Office of John M. Palm, LLC
High Ridge Commons, Suite 101
200 Haddonfield-Berlin Road
Gibbsboro, New Jersey 08026
  Telephone: 856-783-5461
  Fax: 856-783-5464
  E-Mail: palmlaw1@verizon.net

Coverage Issues, General Liability, Premises Liability, Self-Insured Defense, Truck Liability, Sports Claims Defense, Automobile Negligence

Firm Profile: Trial and appeal court defense of general liability, product liability, directors and officers, auto/truck accidents, construction, contract and declaratory judgment matters.

Insurance Clients

Auto Club South Insurance Company
National Continental Insurance Company

Camden County Municipal Joint Insurance Fund
State Farm Fire and Casualty Company

Non-Insurance Clients

Dollar-Thrifty Automotive Group, Inc.

ELCO Administrative Services

John M. Palm — 1948 — La Salle University, B.A., 1970; Temple University, J.D. (Dean's List), 1977 — Admitted to Bar, 1977, Pennsylvania; 1978, New Jersey; 1977, U.S. District Court, District of New Jersey; 1978, U.S. District Court, Eastern District of Pennsylvania; 1983, U.S. Supreme Court — Member New Jersey State and Camden County Bar Associations; New Jersey Defense Association — Certified Civil Trial Attorney by the New Jersey Supreme Court — Practice Areas: Insurance Defense; Premises Liability; Product Liability; Motor Vehicle

HACKENSACK † 43,010 Bergen Co.

Gallo Vitucci Klar LLP
1 University Plaza, Suite 306
Hackensack, New Jersey 07601
  Telephone: 201-343-1166
  www.gvlaw.com

(New York, NY Office*: 90 Broad Street, 3rd Floor, 10004)
  (Tel: 212-683-7100)
  (Fax: 212-683-5555)
(Irvington, NY Office: One Bridge Street, Suite 140, 10533)

Commercial Litigation, Construction Law, Dram Shop, Employment Law, Environmental Law, General Liability, Hospitality, Insurance Coverage, Maritime Law, Medical Malpractice, Municipal Liability, No-Fault, Personal Injury, Personal Injury Protection (PIP), Premises Liability, Product Liability, Professional Liability, School Law, Subrogation, Toxic Torts, Transportation, Trucking, Elevators and Escalator Liability, Restaurant Liability

(See listing under New York, NY for additional information)

Nicoletti Gonson Spinner LLP
One University Plaza, Suite 412
Hackensack, New Jersey 07601
  Telephone: 201-487-9400
  Fax: 201-487-9240

NEW JERSEY   **HACKENSACK**

Nicoletti Gonson Spinner LLP, Hackensack, NJ
(Continued)

(New York, NY Office*: 555 Fifth Avenue, 8th Floor, 10017)
  (Tel: 212-730-7750)
  (Fax: 212-730-7850)
  (E-Mail: fnicoletti@nicolettilaw.com)
  (www.nicolettilaw.com)

Insurance Law, Reinsurance, Coverage Analysis, Professional Liability, Product Liability, Excess and Surplus Lines, General Liability, Direct Defense

(See listing under New York, NY for additional information)

Nowell Amoroso Klein Bierman, P.A.

155 Polifly Road
Hackensack, New Jersey 07601
  Telephone: 201-343-5001
  Toll Free: 800-246-0254
  Fax: 201-343-5181
  E-Mail: info@nakblaw.com
  http://nakblaw.com

(New York, NY Office: 140 Broadway, 10005)
  (Tel: 212-858-7710)
  (Fax: 212-858-7750)

Established: 1989

Insurance Defense, Bodily Injury, Asbestos Litigation, Environmental Law, Personal Liability, Automobile, Homeowners, Toxic Torts, Product Liability, Pollution, Property Damage

Insurance Clients

ACE USA	American International Group, Inc.
Atlantic Mutual Insurance Company	Pennsylvania Counties Risk Pool
	Royal Insurance Company
St. Paul Insurance Company	Stonewall Insurance Company
TIG Insurance Company	Zurich American Insurance Group

Partners

Henry J. Amoroso — 1959 — Villanova University, B.S., 1981; Delaware Law School of Widener University, J.D., 1985 — Admitted to Bar, 1985, New Jersey; Pennsylvania — Member American, New Jersey State, Pennsylvania and Bergen County Bar Associations

Daniel C. Nowell — 1955 — University of Delaware, B.A., 1977; Delaware Law School of Widener University, J.D., 1981 — Admitted to Bar, 1981, New Jersey; Pennsylvania; 1981, U.S. District Court, District of New Jersey; 1984, U.S. Court of Appeals, Third Circuit; 1987, U.S. Supreme Court — Member American Bar Association (Sections: Tort and Insurance Practice, Natural Resources, Energy and Environmental Law); New Jersey State Bar Association (Product Liability, Toxic Tort Committee; Environmental Law Section); New Jersey Defense Association; Defense Research Institute

Herbert C. Klein — 1930 — Rutgers University, B.A. (cum laude), 1950; Harvard University, J.D., 1953; New York University, LL.M., 1958 — Admitted to Bar, 1953, District of Columbia; 1956, New Jersey — Member Essex County and Passaic County Bar Associations

William D. Bierman — 1942 — Rutgers University, A.B., 1964; J.D., 1967; New York University, LL.M., 1970 — Admitted to Bar, 1967, New Jersey; 1972, U.S. Court of Appeals, Second, Third and Fourth Circuits; 1972, U.S. Supreme Court — Member New Jersey State and Bergen County Bar Associations; New Jersey Trial Lawyers Association

Victor J. Herlinsky, Jr. — 1966 — Bucknell University, B.A., 1984; American University, Washington College of Law, J.D., 1988 — Admitted to Bar, 1991, New Jersey; 1992, New York; 1991, U.S. District Court, District of New Jersey; 1992, U.S. District Court, Southern District of New York — Member American, New Jersey State and Bergen County Bar Associations

Anthony Pantano — 1964 — Georgetown University, B.S., 1986; Villanova University School of Law, J.D., 1989; Villanova University, LL.M., 1994 — Admitted to Bar, 1989, New Jersey; Pennsylvania; 1994, New York

Linda Dunne — 1959 — Rutgers College, B.A., 1981; Nova University, J.D.,

Nowell Amoroso Klein Bierman, P.A., Hackensack, NJ
(Continued)

1985 — Admitted to Bar, 1986, New Jersey; 1986, U.S. District Court, District of New Jersey — Member New Jersey State Bar Association (Environmental Law); New Jersey Defense Association

David Edelberg — 1958 — Rutgers University, B.S., 1980; Brooklyn Law School, J.D., 1983 — Admitted to Bar, 1983, New Jersey; 1984, New York; 1983, U.S. District Court, District of New Jersey; 1987, U.S. District Court, Southern District of New York — Member American, New Jersey State, New York State and Bergen County Bar Associations

Michael J. Palma — 1956 — The Citadel, B.A., 1978; The Catholic University of America, Columbus School of Law, J.D., 1981 — Admitted to Bar, 1981, New Jersey; New York; 1981, U.S. District Court, District of New Jersey; 1982, U.S. Court of Military Review; U.S. District Court, Eastern and Southern Districts of New York; U.S. District Court, Eastern District of Pennsylvania; U.S. Court of Appeals, Third Circuit

Michael J. Noonan — 1949 — La Salle College, B.A., 1971; The John Marshall Law School, J.D., 1975 — Admitted to Bar, 1975, New Jersey; 1975, U.S. District Court, District of New Jersey

William C. Soukas — 1969 — Boston College, B.S. (cum laude), 1991; Seton Hall University School of Law, J.D., 1994 — Admitted to Bar, 1994, New Jersey; 1995, New York; 1994, U.S. District Court, District of New Jersey; 1998, U.S. District Court, Eastern and Southern Districts of New York

Bradley M. Wilson — 1949 — The University of Maine, B.A. (cum laude), 1976; Vermont Law School, J.D., 1979 — Admitted to Bar, 1979, Maine; 1981, New Jersey; 1979, U.S. District Court, District of Maine; 1981, U.S. District Court, District of New Jersey; 1981, U.S. Court of Appeals, Third Circuit; 1983, U.S. Supreme Court; 2003, U.S. District Court, Eastern and Southern Districts of New York — U.S. Army 1969-1972 (Three Bronze Stars, Two Army Commendation Medals)

Thomas C. Martin — 1972 — University of Maryland, B.A., 1994; Seton Hall University School of Law, J.D., 1997 — Admitted to Bar, 1997, New Jersey; 1997, U.S. District Court, District of New Jersey; 1997, U.S. Court of Appeals, Third Circuit

John R. Lloyd — Saint Joseph's University, B.A., 1977; University of Pennsylvania, M.S., 1987; Rutgers University School of Law, J.D., 1987 — Admitted to Bar, 1987, New Jersey; U.S. District Court, District of New Jersey; 1990, U.S. Supreme Court

Associates

Gregory K. Asadurian — 1972 — Montclair State University, B.A., 1995; Touro College Jacob D. Fuchsberg Law Center, J.D., 1999 — Admitted to Bar, 2000, New Jersey; 2000, U.S. District Court, District of New Jersey

Romal D. Bullock — Temple University, B.A., 1992; Rutgers University School of Law-Newark, J.D., 2003 — Admitted to Bar, 2003, New Jersey; U.S. District Court, District of New Jersey

Anthony Marchese — Rutgers University, B.A., 1995; Western New England College School of Law, J.D., 1998 — Admitted to Bar, 2003, New York; 2005, New Jersey; 2003, U.S. District Court, Eastern and Southern Districts of New York; 2004, U.S. District Court, Northern District of New York; 2005, U.S. District Court, District of New Jersey; 2006, U.S. Court of Appeals, Third Circuit

Yana Chechelnitsky — Montclair State University, B.A. (magna cum laude), 2001; Seton Hall University School of Law, J.D., 2005 — Admitted to Bar, 2005, New Jersey; 2006, New York; 2005, U.S. District Court, District of New Jersey — Languages: Russian, Ukrainian, Hebrew

Lisa J. Jurick — University of Virginia, B.A., 1984; Rutgers University School of Law-Newark, J.D., 2003 — Admitted to Bar, 2004, New Jersey; U.S. District Court, District of New Jersey

Of Counsel

Arthur Minuskin — 1924 — Harvard Law School, LL.B., 1948 — Admitted to Bar, 1949, New Jersey; 1949, U.S. District Court, District of New Jersey — Member American, New Jersey State, Bergen County and Passaic County Bar Associations; American Legion; Jewish War Veterans — Judge of the Superior Court of New Jersey, Bergen, Morris and Essex Counties 1977-2002

Karen A. Passaro — 1970 — Seton Hall University, B.A. (cum laude), 1992; M.B.A., 1993; J.D., 1996 — Admitted to Bar, 1996, New Jersey; 1996, U.S. District Court, District of New Jersey

Counsel

Rick A. Steinberg — Columbia University, B.A., 1982; Rutgers University, J.D., 1989 — Admitted to Bar, 1989, New Jersey; 2000, New York; 1989, U.S. District Court, District of New Jersey; U.S. District Court, Eastern, Northern, Southern and Western Districts of New York

HADDONFIELD — NEW JERSEY

Nowell Amoroso Klein Bierman, P.A., Hackensack, NJ
(Continued)

Joseph S. Sherman — Southwestern College, B.A., 1982; Wichita State University, M.S.; Washburn University School of Law, J.D., 1985 — Admitted to Bar, 1987, New Jersey; U.S. District Court, District of New Jersey

William J. Pollinger, P.A.

Claridge Plaza
302 Union Street
Hackensack, New Jersey 07601
Telephone: 201-487-5666
Fax: 201-487-6335
E-Mail: william.pollinger@verizon.net

Established: 1974

Insurance Defense, Product Liability, Automobile Liability, Negligence, Toxic Torts, Subrogation, Policy Construction and Interpretation, Insurance Coverage, Personal Injury

Insurance Clients

Countryway Insurance Company
Liberty Mutual Group
National General Insurance Company
United Services Automobile Association (USAA)
GMAC Insurance Group
Motors Insurance Corporation
Peerless Insurance Company
Tri-State Consumer Insurance Company

William J. Pollinger — 1944 — Rutgers University, B.A., 1966; American University, Washington College of Law, J.D., 1969 — Admitted to Bar, 1969, New Jersey; 1981, New York; 1969, U.S. District Court, District of New Jersey; 1981, U.S. Court of Appeals, Third Circuit; 1981, U.S. Supreme Court — Member New Jersey State and Bergen County Bar Associations; Bergen County District Ethics Committee, 1984-1988; Master, Justice Robert L. Clifford American Inn of Court; Defense Research Institute; Trial Attorneys of New Jersey — Certified Civil Trial Attorney by the Supreme Court of New Jersey — Practice Areas: Insurance Litigation

(This firm is also listed in the Subrogation section of this directory)

The following firms also service this area.

Buglione, Hutton & DeYoe, L.L.C.

401 Hamburg Turnpike, Suite 206
Wayne, New Jersey 07470
Telephone: 973-595-6300
Fax: 973-595-0146

Appellate Practice, Arbitration, Mediation and ADR, Construction Law, Environmental Law, Insurance Defense, Insurance and Re-Insurance, Labor and Employment Law, Litigation, Product Liability and Complex Tort Litigation, Sexual Abuse Defense, Subrogation and Recovery, Workers' Compensation

SEE COMPLETE LISTING UNDER WAYNE, NEW JERSEY (15 MILES)

Methfessel & Werbel

2025 Lincoln Highway, Suite 200
Edison, New Jersey 08817
Telephone: 732-248-4200
Fax: 732-248-2355

Mailing Address: P.O. Box 3012, Edison, NJ 08818-3012

Automobile Liability, Bad Faith, Carrier Defense, Casualty Defense, Civil Trial Practice, Comprehensive General Liability, Construction Litigation, Coverage Issues, Defense Litigation, Employment Practices Liability, Environmental Coverage, Environmental Liability, Examinations Under Oath, Excess and Umbrella, Insurance Coverage, Insurance Defense, Medical Liability, Premises Liability, Primary and Excess Insurance, Product Liability, Professional Malpractice, Property Liability, Public Entities, Toxic Torts, Uninsured and Underinsured Motorist, General Subrogation, Large Loss Subrogation Program

SEE COMPLETE LISTING UNDER EDISON, NEW JERSEY (38 MILES)

Shafer Glazer, LLP

90 John Street, Suite 701
New York, New York 10038
Telephone: 212-267-0011
Fax: 646-435-9434

Alternative Dispute Resolution, Appellate Practice, Automobile Liability, Business Law, Commercial Litigation, Directors and Officers Liability, Toxic Torts, General Liability, Insurance Coverage, Labor and Employment, Municipal Liability, Premises Liability, Product Liability, Professional Liability, Transportation, Trucking Industry Defense, Workers' Compensation, Security Company Liability, Cyber Liability and Data Privacy

SEE COMPLETE LISTING UNDER NEW YORK, NEW YORK (18 MILES)

HADDONFIELD 11,593 Camden Co.

Deasey, Mahoney & Valentini, LTD

80 Tanner Street
Haddonfield, New Jersey 08033
Telephone: 856-429-6331
Fax: 856-429-6562
www.dmvlawfirm.com

(Philadelphia, PA Office*: 1601 Market Street, Suite 3400, 19103)
 (Tel: 215-587-9400)
 (Fax: 215-587-9456)
 (E-Mail: dmvlawfirm@dmvlawfirm.com)
(Media, PA Office*: 103 Chesley Drive, Suite 101, 19063)
 (Tel: 610-892-2732)
 (Fax: 610-892-2926)

Product Liability, Professional Liability, Insurance Coverage, Bad Faith, Commercial Litigation, Construction Litigation, General Defense, Employment Practices Liability, Governmental Defense, Subrogation, Environmental/Toxic Defense, Environmental/Toxic Insurance Coverage, Admiralty

(See listing under Philadelphia, PA for additional information)

Dickie, McCamey & Chilcote, P.C.

41 South Haddon Avenue, Suite 5
Haddonfield, New Jersey 08033-1800
Telephone: 856-354-0192
Fax: 888-811-7144
Toll Free: 866-743-6334
E-Mail: info@dmclaw.com
www.dmclaw.com

(Additional Offices: Pittsburgh, PA*; Charlotte, NC*; Cleveland, OH*; Columbus, OH*; Camp Hill, PA*(See Harrisburg listing); Lancaster, SC*; Philadelphia, PA*; Cary, NC*(See Raleigh listing); Steubenville, OH*; Wheeling, WV*; Wilmington, DE*)

Established: 2000

Asbestos Litigation, Bad Faith, Captive Company Matters, Casualty, Commercial Litigation, Energy, Labor and Employment, Excess and Reinsurance, Extra-Contractual Litigation, Insurance Agents, Insurance Coverage, Insurance Coverage Litigation, Legal Malpractice, Medical Malpractice, Medicare Set-Aside Practice, Municipal Liability, Nursing Home Liability, Product Liability, Professional Liability, Property and Casualty, Surety, Transportation, Trucking, Uninsured and Underinsured Motorist, Workers' Compensation

Shareholders

Michael K. Willison — **Branch Office Shareholder-in-Charge** — University of Richmond, B.A., 1991; Widener University, J.D., 1995 — Admitted to

NEW JERSEY

Dickie, McCamey & Chilcote, P.C., Haddonfield, NJ (Continued)

Bar, 1995, Pennsylvania; 1996, New Jersey — E-mail: mwillison@dmclaw.com

William J. Smith

(See listing under Pittsburgh, PA for additional information)

Wilbraham, Lawler & Buba

24 Kings Highway West
Haddonfield, New Jersey 08033-2122
   Telephone: 856-795-4422
   Fax: 856-795-4699
   E-Mail: bbuba@wlbdeflaw.com
   www.wlbdeflaw.com

(Philadelphia, PA Office*: 1818 Market Street, Suite 3100, 19103-3631)
   (Tel: 215-564-4141)
   (Fax: 215-564-4385)
(Wilmington, DE Office*: 901 North Market Street, Suite 810, 19801-3090)
   (Tel: 302-421-9935)
   (Fax: 302-421-9955)
(Pittsburgh, PA Office*: 603 Stanwix Street, Two Gateway Center - 17 North, 15222)
   (Tel: 412-255-0500)
   (Fax: 412-255-0505)
(New York, NY Office*: 140 Broadway, 46th Floor, 10005-1101)
   (Tel: 212-858-7575)
   (Fax: 212-943-9246)

Appellate Practice, Asbestos Litigation, Civil Trial Practice, Commercial Litigation, Insurance Defense, Toxic Torts, Workers' Compensation, Product Liability Law

Insurance Clients

American International Adjustment Company
Lebanon Mutual Insurance Company
Harleysville Mutual Insurance Company
Millers Mutual Insurance Company

Non-Insurance Clients

CertainTeed Corporation
Envirosource

Partners

Edward J. Wilbraham — 1946 — University of Notre Dame, B.B.A., 1968; Villanova University School of Law, J.D., 1974 — Admitted to Bar, 1974, Pennsylvania; 1977, New Jersey; 1999, New York; 2002, West Virginia; 1977, U.S. District Court, Eastern District of Pennsylvania; 1989, U.S. District Court, Middle District of Pennsylvania; U.S. District Court, District of New Jersey; U.S. District Court, Northern District of Ohio; U.S. Court of Appeals, Third Circuit; 2002, U.S. District Court, Southern District of West Virginia — Member Defense Research Institute

Barbara J. Buba — 1957 — The University of North Carolina at Chapel Hill, B.S., 1979; Dickinson School of Law, J.D., 1982 — Admitted to Bar, 1982, Pennsylvania; 1992, New Jersey; 1999, New York; 2002, West Virginia; 1983, U.S. District Court, Eastern District of Pennsylvania; 1989, U.S. District Court, Middle District of Pennsylvania; 1992, U.S. District Court, District of New Jersey; 2002, U.S. District Court, Southern District of West Virginia — Tel: 215-972-2852

Michael J. Block — 1958 — Glassboro State College, B.A. (cum laude), 1980; Rutgers University School of Law, J.D., 1984 — Admitted to Bar, 1984, Pennsylvania; 1984, New Jersey; U.S. District Court, District of New Jersey; 1988, U.S. Court of Appeals, Third Circuit; U.S. Supreme Court; 1994, U.S. District Court, Eastern District of Pennsylvania

Associates

Mary S. Cook — 1950 — University of Minnesota, B.A., 1972; University of Minnesota Law School, J.D., 1975 — Admitted to Bar, 1975, Minnesota; 1980, New Jersey; 1986, Pennsylvania; 1975, U.S. District Court, District of

HOLMDEL

Wilbraham, Lawler & Buba, Haddonfield, NJ (Continued)

Minnesota; 1980, U.S. District Court, District of New Jersey; 1986, U.S. District Court, Eastern District of Pennsylvania

(See listing under Philadelphia, PA for additional information)

HOLMDEL   15,781 Monmouth Co.

White, Fleischner & Fino, LLP

Holmdel Corporate Plaza
2137 Route 35
Holmdel, New Jersey 07733
   Telephone: 732-530-7787
   Fax: 732-530-8552

(New York, NY Office*: 61 Broadway - 18th Floor, 10004)
   (Tel: 212-487-9700)
   (Fax: 212-487-9777)
   (E-Mail: INFO@WFF-law.com)
   (www.wff-law.com)
(Garden City, NY Office: 1527 Franklin Avenue, 11501)
   (Tel: 516-742-2750)
   (Fax: 516-742-4892)
(White Plains, NY Office: 303 Old Tarrytown Road, 10603)
   (Tel: 914-509-2910)
   (Fax: 914-997-0957)
(Philadelphia, PA Office: 1500 Market Street, 12th Floor, East Tower, 19102)
   (Tel: 215-665-5780)
   (Fax: 215-569-8228)
(Boca Raton, FL Office: 7777 Glades Road, Suite 100, 33434)
   (Tel: 561-241-6740)
   (Fax: 561-241-6741)
(London, United Kingdom Office: 8-9 Talbot Court, EC3V 0BP)
   (Tel: 011-44-170-247-3101)
   (Fax: 011-44-774-069-0915)

Insurance Defense, Defense Litigation, General Liability, Property, Malpractice, Product Liability, Subrogation, Coverage Analysis, Opinions, Excess and Reinsurance

Firm Profile: Established in 1976, White Fleischner & Fino, LLP has earned a reputation as a leading insurance coverage and defense law firm.

(See listing under New York, NY for additional information)

(This firm is also listed in the Subrogation section of this directory)

ISELIN   18,695 Middlesex Co.

Wright & O'Donnell, P.C.

33 Wood Avenue South, Suite 600
Iselin, New Jersey 08830
   Telephone: 732-452-9150
   Fax: 732-452-9151
   www.wright-odonnell.com

Insurance Coverage, Bad Faith, Trucking, Premises Liability, Product Liability, Subrogation

(See listing under Philadelphia, PA for additional information)

JERSEY CITY † 247,597 Hudson Co.

Marshall, Conway & Bradley, P.C.

One Exchange Place, Suite 1000
Jersey City, New Jersey 07302
  Telephone: 201-521-3170
  Fax: 201-521-3180

(New York, NY Office*: 45 Broadway, Suite 740, 10006)
  (Tel: 212-619-4444)
  (Fax: 212-962-2647)
  (E-Mail: mcw@mcwpc.com)
  (www.mcwpc.com)

Agent and Brokers Errors and Omissions, Alternative Dispute Resolution, Architects and Engineers, Bad Faith, Bodily Injury, Construction Liability, Directors and Officers Liability, Employment Practices Liability, Environmental Litigation, First Party Matters, Insurance Coverage, Liquor Liability, Motor Vehicle, Policy Construction and Interpretation, Pollution, Product Liability, Professional Liability, Regulatory and Compliance, State and Federal Courts, Toxic Torts, Trial and Appellate Practice, Reinsurance, Wrongful Death

Firm Member

Norman J. Golub — State University of New York at Binghamton, B.A. (Phi Beta Kappa), 1975; New York Law School, J.D., 1981 — Admitted to Bar, 1982, New York; 1994, New Jersey; 1982, U.S. District Court, Eastern and Southern Districts of New York; 1993, U.S. Court of Appeals, Sixth Circuit; 1994, U.S. District Court, District of New Jersey; 1998, U.S. Court of Appeals, Second and Third Circuits — Member New York State (Insurance, Negligence and Compensation Law Section) and New Jersey State Bar Associations (Insurance, Negligence and Compensation Law Section) — Practice Areas: Arbitration; Construction Accidents; Dram Shop; Mediation; Premises Liability; Property and Casualty

(See listing under New York, NY for additional information)

Molod Spitz & DeSantis, P.C.

35 Journal Square, Suite 1005
Jersey City, New Jersey 07306
  Telephone: 201-795-5400

(New York, NY Office*: 1430 Broadway, 21st Floor, 10018)
  (Tel: 212-869-3200)
  (Fax: 212-869-4242)
  (E-Mail: attorneys@molodspitz.com)
  (www.molodspitz.com)

General Practice, Trial Practice, Negligence, Fire, Casualty, Construction Law, Product Liability, Toxic Torts, Environmental Law, First Party Matters, Medical Malpractice, Subrogation

(See listing under New York, NY for additional information)

Suarez & Suarez

2016 Kennedy Boulevard
Jersey City, New Jersey 07305
  Telephone: 201-433-0778
  Fax: 201-433-4899
  E-Mail: msuarez@suarezandsuarez.com

Established: 1981

Insurance Defense, Professional Malpractice, Environmental Law, Professional Liability, Errors and Omissions, General Liability

---

Suarez & Suarez, Jersey City, NJ   (Continued)

Insurance Clients

ACE USA Specialty Claims
AIG - Chartis
Catlin, Inc.
Chubb Group of Insurance Companies
CNA Insurance Company
Employers Reinsurance Corporation
Lexington Insurance Company/AIG
RLI Insurance Company
Westport Insurance Company
Admiral Insurance Company
Beazley Insurance Company, Inc.
Certain Underwriters at Lloyd's, London
CNA/Continental Casualty Company
Gulf/Northland Insurance Company
Liberty International Underwriters
OneBeacon Professional Insurance
Swiss Re Group

Partners

David Suarez — (1926-2000)

Michael D. Suarez — 1952 — Albright College, B.A., 1973; Brooklyn Law School, J.D., 1976 — Admitted to Bar, 1976, New Jersey; 1976, U.S. District Court, District of New Jersey — Member Hudson County Bar Association

Joseph M. Suarez — 1958 — Albright College, B.A., 1979; Rutgers University School of Law-Newark, J.D., 1982 — Admitted to Bar, 1982, New Jersey; 1982, U.S. District Court, District of New Jersey; 1982, U.S. Court of Appeals, Third Circuit — Member Hudson County and Somerset County Bar Associations

Lisa Olshen Adelsohn — 1965 — State University of New York at Binghamton, B.A., 1987; The George Washington University, J.D., 1991 — Admitted to Bar, 1991, New Jersey; 1991, U.S. District Court, District of New Jersey — Member American and Hudson County Bar Associations

Associates

Anazette Ray — 1977 — Williams College, B.A., 1999; Villanova University School of Law, J.D., 2002 — Admitted to Bar, 2002, New Jersey; 2004, New York; 2002, U.S. District Court, District of New Jersey

David C. Rosciszewski — 1973 — Drew University, B.A., 1995; New York Law School, J.D., 1998 — Admitted to Bar, 1999, New York; 1999, New Jersey; U.S. District Court, District of New Jersey

Allan B. Thompson — Rutgers University School of Law-Camden, J.D., 2006 — Law Clerk to the Hon. Kyran Connor, J.S.C., Chancery Division Family Part, Superior Court of New Jersey — Admitted to Bar, 2006, New Jersey; 2007, Pennsylvania

Zarwin Baum DeVito Kaplan Schaer Toddy, P.C.

30 Montgomery Street, Suite 960
Jersey City, New Jersey 07302
  Telephone: 201-432-7840
  Fax: 201-432-3945
  www.zarwin.com

(Philadelphia, PA Office*: 1818 Market Street, 13th Floor, 19103-3638)
  (Tel: 215-569-2800)
  (Fax: 215-569-1606)
  (E-Mail: email@zarwin.com)
(Marlton, NJ Office*: Five Greentree Centre, Suite 303, 08053)
  (Tel: 856-810-3454)
  (Fax: 856-810-3494)
(Camp Hill, PA Office*(See Harrisburg listing): 3310 Market Street, Suite B, 2nd Floor Rear, 17011)
  (Tel: 717-695-4639)
  (Fax: 717-695-6036)

Insurance Defense, Automobile, General Liability, Product Liability, Professional Liability, Property and Casualty, Dram Shop, Coverage Issues, Workers' Compensation, Subrogation, Dental Malpractice, Commercial Vehicle, Truck Liability, Toxic Torts, Environmental Law, Employment Law

Shareholders

Gary A. DeVito — 1957 — University of Notre Dame, B.A., 1979; Temple University School of Law, J.D. (cum laude), 1982 — Admitted to Bar, 1982,

NEW JERSEY

Zarwin Baum DeVito Kaplan Schaer Toddy, P.C., Jersey City, NJ (Continued)

Pennsylvania; New Jersey; U.S. District Court, Eastern District of Pennsylvania; U.S. District Court, District of New Jersey; 1991, U.S. Court of Appeals, Third Circuit — Member Pennsylvania and Philadelphia Bar Associations

Mitchell S. Kaplan — 1957 — Temple University, B.B.A. (magna cum laude), 1979; Temple University School of Law, J.D., 1982 — Admitted to Bar, 1982, Pennsylvania; New Jersey; U.S. District Court, Eastern District of Pennsylvania; U.S. District Court, District of New Jersey; U.S. Court of Appeals, Third Circuit — Member Pennsylvania, New Jersey State and Philadelphia Bar Associations; Pennsylvania Defense Institute; Trucking Industry Defense Association

Theodore M. Schaer — 1960 — American University, B.S., 1982; Temple University School of Law, J.D., 1987 — Admitted to Bar, 1987, Pennsylvania; New Jersey; U.S. District Court, Eastern District of Pennsylvania; U.S. District Court, District of New Jersey; 1992, U.S. Court of Appeals, Third Circuit — Member American, Pennsylvania and Philadelphia Bar Associations; Trucking Industry Defense Association

Joseph M. Toddy — 1957 — University of Notre Dame, B.A., 1979; Delaware Law School of Widener University, J.D., 1984 — Admitted to Bar, 1984, Pennsylvania; 1998, New Jersey; 2002, New York; 1984, U.S. District Court, Eastern District of Pennsylvania; U.S. Court of Appeals, Third Circuit — Member American, New Jersey State, Pennsylvania and Philadelphia Bar Associations; Philadelphia Association of Defense Counsel; Defense Research Institute

Lisa Zinn Slotkin — 1969 — University of Maryland, B.S., 1991; Temple University Beasley School of Law, J.D., 1994 — Admitted to Bar, 1994, Pennsylvania; 1995, New Jersey; U.S. District Court, District of New Jersey; U.S. Court of Appeals, Third Circuit — Member Pennsylvania and Philadelphia Bar Associations

Michael Dankanich — 1959 — Temple University, B.A., 1984; Temple University Beasley School of Law, J.D., 1984 — Editor, Temple Law Review — Admitted to Bar, 1984, Pennsylvania; 1985, New Jersey; U.S. District Court, Eastern District of Pennsylvania; U.S. Supreme Court — Member Camden County and Philadelphia Bar Associations

Joseph W. Denneler, Jr. — 1969 — Rowan University, B.A., 1993; Rutgers University School of Law, J.D., 1998 — Admitted to Bar, 1998, Pennsylvania; New Jersey — Member Philadelphia Bar Association

Paul M. Schmidt — 1963 — Kent State University, B.S., 1986; Pace University School of Law, J.D., 1992 — Admitted to Bar, 1992, Colorado; 1998, Pennsylvania; U.S. District Court, District of Colorado; U.S. District Court, Eastern District of Pennsylvania — Member Delaware Valley Environmental American Inn of Court — Certificate of Environmental Law, Pace University, 1992 — Practice Areas: Environmental Law

Mark L. Freed — 1963 — Brandeis University, B.A. (cum laude), 1986; Villanova University School of Law, J.D., 1991 — Admitted to Bar, 1991, Pennsylvania; New Jersey; U.S. District Court, Eastern District of Pennsylvania; 1995, U.S. District Court, District of New Jersey; U.S. Court of Appeals, Third Circuit — Practice Areas: Environmental Law — E-mail: mfreed@langsamstevens.com

Jill Fisher — 1946 — The Pennsylvania State University, B.S., 1967; Temple University, M.A., 1978; Widener University School of Law, J.D., 1987 — Moot Court Honor Society — Admitted to Bar, 1987, Pennsylvania; New Jersey; U.S. District Court, District of New Jersey; U.S. District Court, Eastern District of Pennsylvania — Member Philadelphia Bar Association (Employment Law and Human Resources Sections); Society for Human Resource Management; Great Lehigh Valley Chamber of Commerce; National School and Community Corps

Timothy P. Mullin — 1971 — Saint Joseph's University, B.A., 1993; Widener University School of Law, J.D., 1998 — Judicial Internship, Chief Justice Norman E. Veasey, Delaware Supreme Court — Delaware Journal of Corporate Law — Admitted to Bar, 1998, Pennsylvania; New Jersey; U.S. District Court, District of New Jersey; U.S. District Court, Eastern District of Pennsylvania; U.S. Court of Appeals, Third Circuit

Associates

Noah Sinclair Shapiro — 1982 — Franklin & Marshall College, B.A., 2004; Temple University Beasley School of Law, J.D., 2007 — Admitted to Bar, 2007, Pennsylvania; New Jersey

Debra A. Goldstein — 1963 — Pace University, B.B.A., 1985; Pace University School of Law, LL.B., 1988 — Admitted to Bar, 1988, New Jersey; New York

Doris M. Aragon — 1972 — Rutgers University, B.A., 1994; Villanova University School of Law, J.D., 1997 — Admitted to Bar, 1998, Pennsylvania; New Jersey; 2000, U.S. District Court, Eastern District of Pennsylvania; U.S.

LIVINGSTON

Zarwin Baum DeVito Kaplan Schaer Toddy, P.C., Jersey City, NJ (Continued)

District Court, District of New Jersey — Member American Bar Association — Languages: Spanish, Portuguese

Manny J. Alvelo — 1977 — Wagner College, B.S., 1999; New York Law School, J.D., 2008 — Admitted to Bar, 2008, New Jersey; 2010, New York — Member Hudson County Bar Association

(See listing under Philadelphia, PA for additional information)

The following firms also service this area.

Methfessel & Werbel
2025 Lincoln Highway, Suite 200
Edison, New Jersey 08817
  Telephone: 732-248-4200
  Fax: 732-248-2355
Mailing Address: P.O. Box 3012, Edison, NJ 08818-3012

Automobile Liability, Bad Faith, Carrier Defense, Casualty Defense, Civil Trial Practice, Comprehensive General Liability, Construction Litigation, Coverage Issues, Defense Litigation, Employment Practices Liability, Environmental Coverage, Environmental Liability, Examinations Under Oath, Excess and Umbrella, Insurance Coverage, Insurance Defense, Medical Liability, Premises Liability, Primary and Excess Insurance, Product Liability, Professional Malpractice, Property Liability, Public Entities, Toxic Torts, Uninsured and Underinsured Motorist, General Subrogation, Large Loss Subrogation Program

SEE COMPLETE LISTING UNDER EDISON, NEW JERSEY (27 MILES)

Nowell Amoroso Klein Bierman, P.A.
155 Polifly Road
Hackensack, New Jersey 07601
  Telephone: 201-343-5001
  Toll Free: 800-246-0254
  Fax: 201-343-5181

Insurance Defense, Bodily Injury, Asbestos Litigation, Environmental Law, Personal Liability, Automobile, Homeowners, Toxic Torts, Product Liability, Pollution, Property Damage

SEE COMPLETE LISTING UNDER HACKENSACK, NEW JERSEY (20 MILES)

William J. Pollinger, P.A.
Claridge Plaza
302 Union Street
Hackensack, New Jersey 07601
  Telephone: 201-487-5666
  Fax: 201-487-6335

Insurance Defense, Product Liability, Automobile Liability, Negligence, Toxic Torts, Subrogation, Policy Construction and Interpretation, Insurance Coverage, Personal Injury

SEE COMPLETE LISTING UNDER HACKENSACK, NEW JERSEY (20 MILES)

LIVINGSTON   27,391 Essex Co.

Braff, Harris & Sukoneck
570 West Mt. Pleasant Avenue, Suite 200
Livingston, New Jersey 07039
  Telephone: 973-994-6677
  Fax: 973-994-1296
  E-Mail: bcharris@bhs-law.com
  www.bhs-law.com

Transportation, Employment Law, General Liability, Insurance Coverage, Governmental Liability, Municipal Liability, Product Liability, Professional Liability, Public Liability, Environmental Law, Toxic Torts, Workers' Compensation

Firm Profile: Braff, Harris, Sukoneck provides the insurance industry as well as publically and privately owned companies and individuals our team of highly qualified and experienced trial lawyers. We are dedicated to our client's interests, attentive to providing personalized service, and cost-effective time-proven results. Over the course of 76 years of providing defense to policy

LIVINGSTON   NEW JERSEY

Braff, Harris & Sukoneck, Livingston, NJ   (Continued)

holders in civil litigation, we have participated as trial lawyers in the most complex, highly publicized, and legally significant issues facing the insurance industry. Many of our cases have been considered by the New Jersey Supreme Court and have helped shape and formulate Tort Law in our state. In essence, Braff, Harris and Sukoneck seeks to protect the interests of our clients and enhance all client relationships, from the most recent to those which have spanned for generations. The breadth of our client base and the depth of experience of our attorneys allows the firm to anticipate areas of difficulty and handle all legal issues in a pragmatic, successful manner.

Insurance Clients

Argonaut Specialty Insurance
Church Mutual Insurance Company
Harco National Insurance Company
RLI Insurance Company
Tower Group Companies
Travelers Insurance Group
Chartis
General Star National Insurance Company
Lexington Insurance Company
Torus Insurance Group
Tower Risk Management
Western Litigation, Inc.

Non-Insurance Clients

Board of Education City of Newark
FOJP Service Corporation
Knight Transportation Company
Costco Wholesale Corporation
Greenman-Pedersen, Inc.
Performance Food Group

Partners

Brian C. Harris — 1941 — Boston University, B.S., 1963; Rutgers University, J.D., 1966 — Admitted to Bar, 1968, New Jersey; 1984, New York; U.S. District Court, District of New Jersey; U.S. Court of Appeals, Third Circuit; 1984, U.S. District Court, Southern District of New York; 1985, U.S. Court of Appeals, Second Circuit — Member American Bar Association (Sections: Employment Law, Tort and Insurance); New York State, New Jersey State (Insurance Committee) and Essex County Bar Associations; International Association of Defense Counsel (Vice Chair, Legal Malpractice Sub-Committee); Counsel for Litigation Management (Co-Chair, State of New Jersey); Transportation Defense Association; Defense Research Institute; New York State Trial Lawyers Association; Professional Liability Underwriting Society

Ira Sukoneck — 1947 — Northeastern University, B.S., 1969; Suffolk University Law School, J.D., 1972 — Admitted to Bar, 1972, Massachusetts; 1973, New Jersey; U.S. District Court, District of Massachusetts; U.S. District Court, District of New Jersey; 1978, U.S. Supreme Court — Member American and New Jersey State Bar Associations; New Jersey Workers' Compensation Association; American Society of Pharmacy Law; New Jersey Workers' Compensation Inn of Court (Founding Member and Master); American Trial Lawyers Association; New Jersey Defense Association — Certified Workers' Compensation Attorney by the Supreme Court of the State of New Jersey

Stephen L. Hopkins — 1947 — Trinity College, B.A., 1969; Boston University School of Law, J.D., 1973 — Admitted to Bar, 1973, Massachusetts; 1977, New Jersey; 1977, U.S. District Court, District of New Jersey — Member American Inns of Court, Essex County (Arthur T. Vanderbilt Chapter, 1991-1992; Master, 1993-1994) — Law Secretary to the Hon. Paul B. Thompson, J.C.C., 1977-1978 — Certified Civil Trial Attorney, Supreme Court of New Jersey, Board of Trial Certification

Keith Harris — 1967 — University of Maryland, B.A., 1989; University of San Diego School of Law, J.D., 1992 — Admitted to Bar, 1992, New Jersey; 1993, New York; U.S. District Court, District of New Jersey; 1993, U.S. District Court, Eastern District of New York — Member American, New Jersey State, New York State and Essex County Bar Associations; American Inns of Court (Arthur T. Vanderbilt Chapter); The Harmonie Group; National Association of Civil Defense Attorneys; Professional Liability Underwriting Society

Daniel A. Lynn — 1960 — Brandeis University, B.A. (with honors), 1982; Boston College Law School, J.D., 1985 — Admitted to Bar, 1985, New Jersey — Certified Workers' Compensation Attorney by the Supreme Court of the State of New Jersey

Andrew M. Lusskin — Monmouth University, B.S. (Dean's List), 1986; Rutgers University School of Law, J.D., 1989 — Admitted to Bar, 1989, New Jersey; U.S. District Court, District of New Jersey

Lawrence Berkeley — 1964 — Swarthmore College, B.A., 1987; New York University, J.D., 1990 — Admitted to Bar, 1990, Connecticut; 1991, New Jersey; New York — Certified Civil Trial Attorney by the Supreme Court of New Jersey

Senior Counsel

Gloria B. Cherry — Barnard College, B.A., 1956; Columbia Law School, LL.B., 1958 — Admitted to Bar, 1959, New York; 1978, New Jersey; U.S.

Braff, Harris & Sukoneck, Livingston, NJ   (Continued)

District Court, Eastern and Southern Districts of New York; U.S. District Court, District of New Jersey; U.S. Court of Appeals, Third Circuit; U.S. Supreme Court — Member New Jersey State Bar Association — Certified Civil Trial Attorney by the Supreme Court of New Jersey, Board on Trial Certification

Harold Jacobowitz — Herbert H. Lehman College of the City University of New York, B.A., 1972; Rutgers University, J.D., 1977 — Admitted to Bar, 1977, New York; U.S. District Court, Eastern and Southern Districts of New York

Adam J. Kipnis — Penn State University, B.A., 1996; Hofstra University School of Law, J.D., 1999 — Admitted to Bar, 2000, New Jersey; 2000, New York; 2007, Pennsylvania; 2011, Maryland

Kenneth Zaremba — 1965 — Rutgers College, B.A., 1987; Seton Hall University School of Law, J.D., 1990 — Admitted to Bar, 1990, New Jersey; 1992, Pennsylvania; 2011, New York — Member American, New Jersey State, Pennsylvania, New York State, Essex County and Philadelphia Bar Associations; New Jersey Defense Association — Reported Cases: Aquino v. State Farm, 348 NJ Super. 618 (App. Div. 2002) — Languages: English

Associates

Keith Kandel — Rutgers University, B.A., 1985; Widener University School of Law, J.D., 1993 — Admitted to Bar, 1994, New Jersey

Glenn Savarese — Rutgers University, B.A., 1993; New York Law School, J.D., 1996 — Admitted to Bar, 1996, New Jersey; New York; District of Columbia

Gwyneth K. Murray-Nolan — Villanova University School of Law, J.D., 1999 — Admitted to Bar, 2002, New Jersey; 2010, District of Columbia; New York

Alyse Berger Hielpern — Birmingham-Southern College, B.A. (Dean's List), 1997; Seton Hall University School of Law, J.D., 2000 — Admitted to Bar, 2000, New Jersey

Andrew L. Stern — Williams College, B.A., 1990; Pennsylvania State University-Dickinson School of Law, J.D., 1994 — Admitted to Bar, 1995, New Jersey; U.S. District Court, District of New Jersey

Daniel L. Maisel — The George Washington University, B.B.A., 1982; Benjamin N. Cardozo School of Law, J.D., 1989 — Admitted to Bar, 1989, New Jersey; U.S. District Court, District of New Jersey

Michael S. Goldenberg — University of Rhode Island, B.A., 2006; Pace University School of Law, J.D., 2009 — Admitted to Bar, 2009, New Jersey; 2010, New York

Philip H. Ziegler — Binghamton University, B.S., 1993; Hofstra University School of Law, J.D., 1996 — Admitted to Bar, 1996, New York; 1997, New Jersey; U.S. District Court, District of New Jersey; U.S. District Court, Eastern and Southern Districts of New York

Timothy R. Ryan — 1986 — Penn State University, B.S. (Dean's List), 2008; University of Miami School of Law, J.D. (cum laude), 2012 — Admitted to Bar, 2012, New Jersey; 2013, New York — Member New Jersey State, New York State and Middlesex County Bar Associations — Practice Areas: Commercial Litigation

Kenneth E. Sharperson Sr. — Hampton University, B.S., 1993; Rutgers University School of Law-Newark, J.D., 2001 — New Jersey Law Journal Top 40 (2009); New Jersey Monthly Magazine, Rising Star (2010) — Law Clerk to Hon. John E. Wallace, JAD - New Jersey Superior Court, Appellate Division — Rutgers Computer and Technology Law Journal — Admitted to Bar, 2002, New Jersey; 2003, New York; 2004, District of Columbia — Member American, National, New Jersey State and Garden State Bar Associations

Philip M. Lustbader & David Lustbader, P.A.

615 West Mt. Pleasant Avenue
Livingston, New Jersey 07039
Telephone: 973-740-1000
Fax: 973-740-1520
E-Mail: davidlustbader@lustbaderlaw.com
www.lustbaderlaw.com

Insurance Defense, Civil Trial Practice, Negligence, No-Fault, Uninsured and Underinsured Motorist, Product Liability, Workers' Compensation, Dental Malpractice, Medical Malpractice, Coverage Issues, Appellate Practice, Subrogation, Monitoring Litigation

NEW JERSEY

Philip M. Lustbader & David Lustbader, P.A., Livingston, NJ (Continued)

Insurance Clients

Claim & Risk Control, Inc.
General Accident Fire & Life Assurance Corporation
State Insurance Fund of New York
Eveready Insurance Company
Public Service Mutual Insurance Company

Partners

Philip M. Lustbader — Dana College, B.A., 1933; New Jersey Law School, LL.B., 1935 — Admitted to Bar, 1935, New Jersey; 1935, U.S. District Court, District of New Jersey; 1957, U.S. Supreme Court; 1958, U.S. Court of Appeals, Third Circuit — Member American, New Jersey State, Essex County and Hunterdon County Bar Associations; Fellow, American College of Trial Lawyers, 1972; New Jersey Defense Association; Federation of Insurance Counsel

David Lustbader — 1943 — Grinnell College, B.A., 1965; The George Washington University, J.D., 1968 — Admitted to Bar, 1968, New Jersey; 1969, District of Columbia; 1968, U.S. District Court, District of New Jersey; 1969, U.S. Court of Appeals for the District of Columbia Circuit — Member American, New Jersey State and Essex County Bar Associations; New Jersey Defense Association — Certified Civil Trial Attorney, 1982

Associates

John L. Riordan, Jr. — 1942 — University of Notre Dame, B.A., 1964; Seton Hall University, J.D., 1971 — Phi Alpha Delta — Admitted to Bar, 1972, New Jersey; 1972, U.S. District Court, District of New Jersey — Member American, New Jersey State and Essex County Bar Associations — Lt., U.S. Navy, 1964-1968

James S. Colavito — 1945 — Rutgers University, B.A., 1968; Fordham University, J.D., 1971 — Admitted to Bar, 1971, New Jersey; 1984, U.S. Court of Appeals, Third Circuit — Member Morris County Bar Association; Association of Trial Lawyers of America

(This firm is also listed in the Subrogation section of this directory)

MANALAPAN 33,423 Monmouth Co.

Law Offices of Kenneth L. Aron

151 Route 33 East, Suite 254
Manalapan, New Jersey 07726
Telephone: 732-414-2710
Fax: 732-414-2711

(New York, NY Office: 111 Broadway, Suite 1305, 10006)
 (Tel: 212-346-9200)
 (Fax: 212-346-9850)

Defense Litigation, Insurance Coverage, Property, Automobile Liability, General Liability, Fidelity and Surety, Subrogation

Insurance Clients

Erie Insurance Company
Shelter Insurance Companies
Trans Pacific Insurance Company
Flagship City Insurance Company
Tokio Marine and Fire Insurance Company, Ltd.

Firm Member

Kenneth L. Aron — 1958 — Brooklyn College, The City University of New York, B.A. (magna cum laude), 1980; New York Law School, J.D., 1983 — Phi Beta Kappa; Psi Chi; Phi Delta Phi — Law Clerk to U.S. Magistrate R.V. Washington (1983) — Admitted to Bar, 1983, New York; 1989, New Jersey; 1983, U.S. District Court, Eastern and Southern Districts of New York; 1988, U.S. Court of Appeals, Second Circuit; 1989, U.S. District Court, District of New Jersey; U.S. Supreme Court; 2002, U.S. District Court, Northern District of New York — Member American Bar Association (Fidelity and Surety Law Committee; Section on Tort and Insurance Practice, 1984-Present); New Jersey State, New York State, Monmouth County Bar and Brooklyn Bar Associations; New York County Lawyers Association — Practice Areas: Insurance Litigation; Coverage Issues; General Defense; Subrogation

---

Law Offices of Kenneth L. Aron, Manalapan, NJ (Continued)

Of Counsel

Andrea J. Baron — 1961 — Barnard College, B.A. (magna cum laude), 1983; New York University School of Law, J.D., 1986 — Phi Beta Kappa — Admitted to Bar, 1987, New York — Member New York City Bar Association

---

MANASQUAN 5,897 Monmouth Co.

Wolff, Helies, Spaeth & Lucas
A Professional Association

Valley Park Professional Center
2517 Highway 35, Building K, Suites 201-202
Manasquan, New Jersey 08736
 Telephone: 732-223-5100
 Fax: 732-223-5519
 www.wolffhelies.com

Established: 1977

Casualty

Insurance Clients

Chesterfield Services, Inc.
Gallagher Bassett Services, Inc.
Selective Insurance Company of America
Foremost Insurance Company
New Jersey Manufacturers Insurance Company

Non-Insurance Clients

New Jersey School Boards Association

Francis H. Wolff — (1915-1986)

Bruce E. Helies* — La Salle College, B.A., 1966; St. John's University, J.D., 1974 — Admitted to Bar, 1974, New Jersey — Certified Civil Trial Attorney

Peter H. Spaeth* — Wake Forest University, B.A., 1974; California Western School of Law, J.D., 1979 — Admitted to Bar, 1979, New Jersey — Certified Civil Trial Attorney

David G. Lucas, Jr.* — College of William & Mary, B.A., 1980; Rutgers University School of Law, J.D., 1983 — Admitted to Bar, 1983, New Jersey — Certified Civil Trial Attorney

(*Members of New Jersey State and Monmouth County Bar Associations; New Jersey Defense Association)

MARLTON 10,133 Burlington Co.

Cipriani & Werner, P.C.

155 Gaither Drive, Suite B
Mt. Laurel, New Jersey 08054
 Telephone: 856-761-3800
 Fax: 856-761-0726

(Pittsburgh, PA Office*: 650 Washington Road, Suite 700, 15228)
 (Tel: 412-563-2500)
 (Fax: 412-563-2080)
 (www.c-wlaw.com)
(Blue Bell, PA Office*(See Philadelphia listing): 450 Sentry Parkway, Suite 200, 19422)
 (Tel: 610-567-0700)
 (Fax: 610-567-0712)
(Lemoyne, PA Office*(See Harrisburg listing): 1011 Mumma Road, Suite 201, 17043)
 (Tel: 717-975-9600)
 (Fax: 717-975-3846)
(Scranton, PA Office*: 409 Lackawanna Avenue, Suite 402, 18503)
 (Tel: 570-347-0600)
 (Fax: 570-347-4018)

MARLTON　　　　　　　　　　　　　　　　　　　　　　　　　　　　　　　　　　　　　　　NEW JERSEY

Cipriani & Werner, P.C., Marlton, NJ　　　　(Continued)
(Wheeling, WV Office*: 1144 Market Street, Suite 300, 26003)
　(Tel: 304-232-3600)
　(Fax: 304-232-3601)
(Charleston, WV Office*: United Center, 400 Tracy Way, 25311)
　(Tel: 304-341-0500)
　(Fax: 304-341-0507)
(Wilmington, DE Office*: 1000 N. West Street, Suite 1200, 19801)
　(Tel: 302-401-1600)

Insurance Defense, General Liability, Product Liability, Professional Liability, Workers' Compensation, Transportation, First Party Matters, Coverage Analysis, Liquor Liability

Firm Profile: Cipriani & Werner, PC is a mid-Atlantic litigation law firm that is well established in the defense of businesses and insurers.

Partners/Shareholders

Gregory C. DiCarlo — Loyola College, B.A., 1993; Widener University, J.D., 1997 — Admitted to Bar, 1997, Pennsylvania; New Jersey; U.S. District Court, District of New Jersey — Member Camden County Bar Association; American Trial Lawyers Association — E-mail: gdicarlo@c-wlaw.com

Matthew K. Mitchell — Lafayette College, B.A., 1990; University of Miami, J.D. (cum laude), 1993 — Admitted to Bar, 1993, New Jersey; Florida — E-mail: mmitchell@c-wlaw.com

John J. Carvelli — East Stroudsburg University, B.S., 1999; Widener University, J.D., 2009 — Admitted to Bar, 2009, New Jersey — E-mail: jcarvelli@c-wlaw.com

Richard C. Bryan — Stockton State College, B.A., 1993; Widener University, J.D., 1997 — Admitted to Bar, 1998, New Jersey

Associates

Joseph Csipak — Kean College, B.A., 1988; Widener University, J.D., 1991 — Admitted to Bar, 1991, New Jersey — E-mail: jcsipak@c-wlaw.com

James J. Green — Rutgers College, B.A., 2004; Rutgers University-Camden, J.D., 2007 — Admitted to Bar, 2007, Pennsylvania — E-mail: jgreen@c-wlaw.com

Kenneth I. Zamrin — Rutgers University, B.A. (summa cum laude), 2005; Widener University, J.D., 2009 — Admitted to Bar, 2009, Pennsylvania; New Jersey — E-mail: kzamrin@c-wlaw.com

Steven D. Fairbank — Rowan University, B.A., 2005; Widener University, J.D., 2010 — Admitted to Bar, 2010, New Jersey; Pennsylvania — E-mail: sfairbank@c-wlaw.com

Marc R. Jones — Penn State University, B.A., 1994; Temple University School of Law, J.D., 2001 — Admitted to Bar, 2002, New Jersey — E-mail: mjones@c-wlaw.com

Alison Morrissey — Rutgers University-New Brunswick, B.A., 2000; Georgetown University, J.D., 2010 — Admitted to Bar, 2010, New Jersey; New York — E-mail: amorrissey@c-wlaw.com

Steven J. Lewis — Miami University, B.S. Business Admin., 1992; Widener University, J.D., 1995 — Admitted to Bar, 1995, New Jersey; Pennsylvania — E-mail: slewis@c-wlaw.com

Kendall J. Champion — Syracuse University, B.S., 2002; New York Law School, J.D., 2006 — Admitted to Bar, 2006, Pennsylvania; New Jersey

John N. Kaelin III — 1972 — Penn State University, B.A., 1994; Widener University School of Law, J.D., 1997 — Admitted to Bar, 1999, Pennsylvania; 2003, New Jersey

(See listing under Pittsburgh, PA for additional information)

Zarwin Baum DeVito Kaplan Schaer Toddy, P.C.
Five Greentree Centre, Suite 303
Marlton, New Jersey 08053
　Telephone: 856-810-3454
　Fax: 856-810-3494
　www.zarwin.com

Zarwin Baum DeVito Kaplan Schaer Toddy, P.C., Marlton, NJ　　　　(Continued)
(Philadelphia, PA Office*: 1818 Market Street, 13th Floor, 19103-3638)
　(Tel: 215-569-2800)
　(Fax: 215-569-1606)
　(E-Mail: email@zarwin.com)
(Jersey City, NJ Office*: 30 Montgomery Street, Suite 960, 07302)
　(Tel: 201-432-7840)
　(Fax: 201-432-3945)
(Camp Hill, PA Office*(See Harrisburg listing): 3310 Market Street, Suite B, 2nd Floor Rear, 17011)
　(Tel: 717-695-4639)
　(Fax: 717-695-6036)

Insurance Defense, Automobile, General Liability, Product Liability, Professional Liability, Property and Casualty, Dram Shop, Coverage Issues, Workers' Compensation, Subrogation, Dental Malpractice, Commercial Vehicle, Truck Liability, Toxic Torts, Environmental Law, Employment Law

Shareholders

Mitchell S. Kaplan — 1957 — Temple University, B.B.A. (magna cum laude), 1979; Temple University School of Law, J.D., 1982 — Admitted to Bar, 1982, Pennsylvania; New Jersey; U.S. District Court, Eastern District of Pennsylvania; U.S. District Court, District of New Jersey; U.S. Court of Appeals, Third Circuit — Member Pennsylvania, New Jersey State and Philadelphia Bar Associations; Pennsylvania Defense Institute; Trucking Industry Defense Association

Gary A. DeVito — 1957 — University of Notre Dame, B.A., 1979; Temple University School of Law, J.D. (cum laude), 1982 — Admitted to Bar, 1982, Pennsylvania; New Jersey; U.S. District Court, Eastern District of Pennsylvania; U.S. District Court, District of New Jersey; 1991, U.S. Court of Appeals, Third Circuit — Member Pennsylvania and Philadelphia Bar Associations

Theodore M. Schaer — 1960 — American University, B.S., 1982; Temple University School of Law, J.D., 1987 — Admitted to Bar, 1987, Pennsylvania; New Jersey; U.S. District Court, Eastern District of Pennsylvania; U.S. District Court, District of New Jersey; 1992, U.S. Court of Appeals, Third Circuit — Member American, Pennsylvania and Philadelphia Bar Associations; Trucking Industry Defense Association

Joseph M. Toddy — 1957 — University of Notre Dame, B.A., 1979; Delaware Law School of Widener University, J.D., 1984 — Admitted to Bar, 1984, Pennsylvania; 1998, New Jersey; 2002, New York; 1984, U.S. District Court, Eastern District of Pennsylvania; U.S. Court of Appeals, Third Circuit — Member American, New Jersey State, Pennsylvania and Philadelphia Bar Associations; Philadelphia Association of Defense Counsel; Defense Research Institute

Lisa Zinn Slotkin — 1969 — University of Maryland, B.S., 1991; Temple University Beasley School of Law, J.D., 1994 — Admitted to Bar, 1994, Pennsylvania; 1995, New Jersey; U.S. District Court, District of New Jersey; U.S. Court of Appeals, Third Circuit — Member Pennsylvania and Philadelphia Bar Associations

Michael Dankanich — 1959 — Temple University, B.A., 1984; Temple University Beasley School of Law, J.D., 1984 — Editor, Temple Law Review — Admitted to Bar, 1984, Pennsylvania; 1985, New Jersey; U.S. District Court, Eastern District of Pennsylvania; U.S. Supreme Court — Member Camden County and Philadelphia Bar Associations

Joseph W. Denneler, Jr. — 1969 — Rowan University, B.A., 1993; Rutgers University School of Law, J.D., 1998 — Admitted to Bar, 1998, Pennsylvania; New Jersey — Member Philadelphia Bar Association

Paul M. Schmidt — 1963 — Kent State University, B.S., 1986; Pace University School of Law, J.D., 1992 — Admitted to Bar, 1992, Colorado; 1998, Pennsylvania; 2001, Ohio; 2005, New Jersey; 1998, U.S. District Court, District of Colorado; U.S. District Court, Eastern District of Pennsylvania; U.S. Court of Appeals, Third Circuit — Member Philadelphia Bar Association — Certificate of Environmental Law, Pace University, 1992 — Practice Areas: Environmental Law

Mark L. Freed — 1963 — Brandeis University, B.A. (cum laude), 1986; Villanova University School of Law, J.D., 1991 — Associate Editor, Villanova Environmental Law Journal, 1990 — Admitted to Bar, 1991, Pennsylvania; New Jersey; U.S. District Court, Eastern District of Pennsylvania; 1995, U.S. District Court, District of New Jersey; U.S. Court of Appeals, Third Circuit — Member Pennsylvania Bar Association (Chair, Litigation Committee, Environmental, Mineral and Natural Resources Law Section) — Practice Areas: Environmental Law

NEW JERSEY

Zarwin Baum DeVito Kaplan Schaer Toddy, P.C., Marlton, NJ (Continued)

Jill Fisher — 1946 — The Pennsylvania State University, B.S., 1967; Temple University, M.A., 1978; Widener University School of Law, J.D., 1987 — Moot Court Honor Society — Admitted to Bar, 1987, Pennsylvania; New Jersey; U.S. District Court, District of New Jersey; U.S. District Court, Eastern District of Pennsylvania — Member Philadelphia Bar Association (Employment Law and Human Resources Sections); Society for Human Resource Management; Great Lehigh Valley Chamber of Commerce; National School and Community Corps

Timothy P. Mullin — Saint Joseph's University, B.A., 1993; Widener University School of Law, J.D., 1998 — Admitted to Bar, 1998, Pennsylvania; New Jersey

Associates

Noah Sinclair Shapiro — 1982 — Franklin & Marshall College, B.A., 2004; Temple University Beasley School of Law, J.D., 2007 — Admitted to Bar, 2007, Pennsylvania; New Jersey

Debra A. Goldstein — 1963 — Pace University, B.B.A., 1985; Pace University School of Law, LL.B., 1988 — Admitted to Bar, 1988, New Jersey; New York

Doris M. Aragon — 1972 — Rutgers University, B.A., 1994; Villanova University School of Law, J.D., 1997 — Admitted to Bar, 1998, Pennsylvania; New Jersey; 2000, U.S. District Court, Eastern District of Pennsylvania; U.S. District Court, District of New Jersey — Member American Bar Association — Languages: Spanish, Portuguese

Keith G. Gomer — University of Pittsburgh, B.S., 1988; Delaware Law School at Widener University, J.D., 1991 — Admitted to Bar, 1988, New Jersey; Pennsylvania; U.S. District Court, Eastern District of Pennsylvania

Michael R. Logue — 1968 — Widener University, B.A. (cum laude), 1991; Villanova University School of Law, J.D., 1994 — Pi Gamma Mu Honor Society; Admiral Herbert Leary Award for the Outstanding Graduating Government and Politics Major — Admitted to Bar, 1994, New Jersey; Pennsylvania

(See listing under Philadelphia, PA for additional information)

MILLBURN 19,765 Essex Co.

McDermott & McGee

75 Main Street
Millburn, New Jersey 07041
   Telephone: 973-467-8080
   Fax: 973-376-8669
   E-Mail: kjmcgee@mcdermottandmcgee.com
   www.mcdermottandmcgee.com

Commercial Liability, Automobile, Uninsured and Underinsured Motorist, Personal Injury Protection (PIP), Construction Accidents, Health Care, Medical Malpractice, Product Liability, Premises Liability, Public Entities, Wrongful Death, Appellate Practice, PIP Reimbursement

Insurance Clients

ACE Group Claims - SLA	Allstate Insurance Company
ARI Insurance Group	Cumberland Insurance Group
CURE Auto Insurance	Farmers Insurance Company of Flemington
Gallagher Bassett Insurance Services, Inc.	Greater New York Mutual Insurance Company
Hereford Insurance Company	Interboro Insurance Company
High Point Property and Casualty Insurance Company	Mercury Insurance Group
New Jersey Manufacturers Insurance Company	Progressive Insurance Company
Rider Insurance Company	Prudential Property and Casualty Insurance Company
Tokio Marine and Fire Insurance Company, Ltd.	Utica National Insurance Group
	Zurich American Insurance Group

Members

Richard P. Maggi — University of Notre Dame, B.A., 1973; Seton Hall University School of Law, J.D., 1976 — Admitted to Bar, 1976, New Jersey; U.S. District Court, District of New Jersey; U.S. Court of Appeals, Third Circuit — Member Union County Bar Association

McDermott & McGee, Millburn, NJ (Continued)

Thomas A. Wester — Seton Hall University, B.A. (magna cum laude), 1979; Seton Hall University School of Law, J.D. (cum laude), 1982 — Admitted to Bar, 1982, New Jersey; U.S. District Court, District of New Jersey; U.S. Court of Appeals, Third Circuit — Member New Jersey State and Essex County Bar Associations; American Board of Trial Advocates; New Jersey Defense Association

Richard M. Tango — Seton Hall University, B.S., 1980; Vermont Law School, J.D., 1983 — Admitted to Bar, 1984, New Jersey; U.S. District Court, District of New Jersey; U.S. Court of Appeals, Third Circuit — Member New Jersey State and Essex County Bar Associations; New Jersey Defense Association

John L. McDermott, Jr. — Lehigh University, B.S., 1979; Benjamin N. Cardozo School of Law, J.D. (cum laude), 1988 — Admitted to Bar, 1988, New Jersey; Pennsylvania; U.S. District Court, District of New Jersey; 2003, U.S. Court of Appeals, Third Circuit — Member New Jersey State and Essex County Bar Associations

A. Charles Lorenzo — University of Southern California, B.A., 1984; Seton Hall University School of Law, J.D., 1987 — Admitted to Bar, 1987, New Jersey; U.S. District Court, District of New Jersey; U.S. Court of Appeals, Third Circuit — Member New Jersey State and Essex County Bar Associations; New Jersey Defense Association

Kevin J. McGee — Fairfield University, B.A., 1987; University of Surrey; Seton Hall University School of Law, J.D., 1992 — Admitted to Bar, 1992, New Jersey; Pennsylvania; U.S. District Court, District of New Jersey; U.S. Court of Appeals, Third Circuit; U.S. Supreme Court — Member New Jersey State and Essex County Bar Associations; Insurance Council of New Jersey; American Board of Trial Advocates; Trial Attorneys of New Jersey; Defense Research Institute — Certified Civil Trial Attorney by the New Jersey Supreme Court

David J. Dickinson — United States Naval Academy, B.S., 1987; Temple University, J.D., 1990 — Admitted to Bar, 1990, New Jersey

MORRISTOWN † 18,411 Morris Co.

Bressler, Amery & Ross, PC

325 Columbia Turnpike, Suite 301
Florham Park, New Jersey 07932
   Telephone: 973-514-1200
   Fax: 973-514-1660
   E-Mail: srobshaw@bressler.com
   www.bressler.com

(New York, NY Office: 17 State Street, 34th Floor, 10004)
   (Tel: 212-425-9300)
   (Fax: 212-425-9337)
(Fort Lauderdale, FL Office: 200 East Las Olas Boulevard, Suite 1500, 33301)
   (Tel: 954-499-7979)
   (Fax: 954-499-7969)
(Birmingham, AL Office: 420 20th Street North, Suite 2200, 35203)
   (Tel: 205-719-0400)

Bankruptcy, Business Law, Civil Rights, Commercial Litigation, Construction Law, Corporate Law, Creditor's Rights, E-Discovery, Employee Benefits, Environmental Law, Errors and Omissions, Family Law, Health, Managed Care Liability, Insurance Agents, Insurance Coverage, Insurance Law, Insurance Litigation, Labor and Employment, Land Use, Legal Malpractice, Life Insurance, Personal Injury, Product Liability, Professional Liability, Real Estate, Regulatory and Compliance, Reinsurance, Securities, Toxic Torts, Trusts, Workers' Compensation, Franchise Law, Taxation

Representative Insurance Clients

CNA Insurance Companies	Horizon Blue Cross Blue Shield of New Jersey
New Jersey Life and Health Insurance Guaranty Association	Prudential Insurance Company of America
Underwriters at Lloyd's, London	
Zurich North America	

MORRISTOWN — NEW JERSEY

Bressler, Amery & Ross, PC, Morristown, NJ (Continued)

Firm Members

Cynthia J. Borrelli — Lehigh University, B.A., 1982; Seton Hall University, J.D., 1985 — Admitted to Bar, 1985, New Jersey; Pennsylvania; District of Columbia; New York; U.S. District Court, District of New Jersey; U.S. District Court, Eastern District of Pennsylvania; U.S. District Court, Southern District of New York; U.S. Court of Appeals for the District of Columbia Circuit — Member American, New Jersey State and Pennsylvania Bar Associations; National Conference of Guaranty Funds; Federation of Defense and Corporate Counsel; Federation of Regulatory Counsel — Co-Author: "Contingent Workers: Whose Employees are They Anyway?", NJBiz, Industry Insights, August 25, 2014 — E-mail: cborrelli@bressler.com

Harry M. Baumgartner — Rutgers University, B.A., 1980; Seton Hall University, J.D., 1990; Centenary College, M.B.A., 2005 — Admitted to Bar, 1990, New Jersey; U.S. District Court, District of New Jersey; U.S. Court of Appeals, Third Circuit; U.S. Supreme Court — Member American and New Jersey State Bar Associations; New Jersey Corporate Counsel Association; New Jersey Captive Insurance Association; Worrall F. Mountain American Inn of Court; Fellow, Council on Litigation Management; Council on Litigation Management; Defense Research Institute — E-mail: hbaumgartner@bressler.com

Diana C. Manning — Rutgers College, B.A., 1990; Rutgers University School of Law, J.D., 1993 — Admitted to Bar, 1993, New Jersey; New York; U.S. District Court, District of New Jersey; U.S. District Court, Southern District of New York; U.S. Court of Appeals, Second and Third Circuits; U.S. Supreme Court — Member American, New Jersey State and Morris County Bar Associations; Claims and Litigation Management Alliance; Trial Attorneys of New Jersey; Professional Liability Underwriting Society; New Jersey Defense Association; Defense Research Institute — E-mail: dmanning@bressler.com

Robert Novack — Rutgers University, B.A., 1975; University of Miami School of Law, J.D. (cum laude), 1978 — Admitted to Bar, 1979, New Jersey; New York; U.S. District Court, District of New Jersey; U.S. District Court, Eastern and Southern Districts of New York; U.S. Court of Appeals, Second and Third Circuits — Member Federal and New Jersey State Bar Associations — Supreme Court of New Jersey — E-mail: rnovack@bressler.com

Alex J. Sabo — University of South Florida, B.A., 1975; University of Dayton School of Law, J.D. (cum laude), 1978 — Admitted to Bar, 1978, Florida; U.S. District Court, Middle and Southern Districts of Florida; U.S. Court of Appeals, Eleventh Circuit — Member Florida Securities Dealers Association; Securities Industry and Financial Markets Association — E-mail: asabo@bressler.com

Angela M. Scafuri — Colgate University, B.A., 1996; Seton Hall University School of Law, J.D., 2000 — Admitted to Bar, 2000, New Jersey; U.S. District Court, District of New Jersey; U.S. District Court, Eastern, Northern and Southern Districts of New York; U.S. District Court, Western District of Michigan; U.S. Court of Appeals, Third Circuit — Member American and New Jersey State, Morris County and Somerset County Bar Associations; Association of the Federal Bar of the State of New Jersey; New Jersey Association of Professional Mediators; New Jersey Defense Association — Superior Court of New Jersey Civil Roster of Mediators — Languages: Italian, Spanish — E-mail: ascafuri@bressler.com

Susan Stryker — Rutgers College, B.A., 1982; Seton Hall University School of Law, J.D., 1985 — Admitted to Bar, 1985, New Jersey; U.S. District Court, District of New Jersey; U.S. Court of Appeals, Third Circuit; U.S. Supreme Court — Member American and New Jersey State Bar Associations; Association of Insurance Compliance Professionals; Insurance Federation of New York; Federation of Regulatory Counsel — E-mail: sstryker@bressler.com

Mark M. Tallmadge — University of Notre Dame, B.B.A., 1979; J.D., 1982 — Admitted to Bar, 1982, New Jersey; Illinois; U.S. District Court, District of New Jersey; U.S. District Court, Eastern and Southern Districts of New York; U.S. Court of Appeals, Second and Third Circuits — Member American, New Jersey State and Morris County Bar Associations; National Conference of Insurance Guaranty Funds; Professional Liability Underwriting Society; Defense Research Institute; New Jersey Defense Association — E-mail: mtallmadge@bressler.com

Samuel J. Thomas — Clark University, B.A., 1989; Rutgers University, J.D., 1992 — Admitted to Bar, 1992, Pennsylvania; New Jersey; New York; U.S. District Court, District of New Jersey; U.S. District Court, Eastern District of Pennsylvania; U.S. District Court, Eastern, Northern and Southern Districts of New York; U.S. District Court, Western District of Michigan; U.S. District Court, Western District of Arkansas; U.S. Supreme Court — Member Federal, American, New Jersey State and New York State Bar Associations; Association of the Federal Bar of the State of New Jersey; Defense Research Institute — E-mail: sthomas@bressler.com

Bressler, Amery & Ross, PC, Morristown, NJ (Continued)

Kenneth J. Cesta — Muhlenberg College, A.B., 1983; Quinnipiac University School of Law, J.D., 1986 — Admitted to Bar, 1986, New Jersey; 1986, U.S. District Court, District of New Jersey; 1996, U.S. Court of Appeals, Third Circuit; 2005, U.S. Court of Appeals, Fourth Circuit; 2010, U.S. District Court, Eastern District of Michigan — Practice Areas: Commercial Litigation; Insurance Litigation; Labor and Employment; Professional Liability — E-mail: kcesta@bressler.com

Douglas K. Eisenstein — University of Florida, B.A., 1992; Brooklyn Law School, J.D., 1995 — Admitted to Bar, 1996, New York; 1997, U.S. District Court, Eastern, Southern and Western Districts of New York — E-mail: deisenstein@bressler.com

MaryJane Dobbs — University of Dayton, B.A. (magna cum laude), 1986; Rutgers University School of Law-Newark, J.D., 1989 — Admitted to Bar, 1989, New Jersey; U.S. District Court, District of New Jersey; 2001, U.S. District Court, Southern District of New York — E-mail: mjdobbs@bressler.com

Colquhoun & Colquhoun
A Professional Corporation

165 South Street
Morristown, New Jersey 07960
Telephone: 973-540-0500, 973-540-0534
Fax: 973-540-0550
Add'l Tel: 973-540-0552, 973-540-0663

Carrier Defense, Automobile, General Liability, Product Liability, Fire, Workers' Compensation, Policy Construction and Interpretation, Administrative Law, Veterinary Medical Malpractice, Marine and Aircraft Defense, Branch Applications, Real Property

Insurance Clients

Andover Group
Atlantic Mutual Insurance Company
PMA Insurance Group
Safeco Insurance
The Salem Group

ARI Mutual Insurance Company
Carolina Casualty Insurance Company
Premier Claims Management Services, Inc.

Non-Insurance Clients

Fairleigh Dickinson University

Robert F. Colquhoun — Seton Hall University, B.S. (magna cum laude), 1949; Fordham Law School, LL.B., 1952; J.D., 1968 — Admitted to Bar, 1953, New Jersey; 1966, U.S. Supreme Court — Member American, New Jersey State (Ins. Chmn., Civ. Proc. Section, 1970; Executive Comm., Civ. Proc. Section, 1973-1976) and Morris County Bar Associations; New Jersey Trial Attorneys Association; Faculty of Seton Hall University School of Law (1953-1960); Master, Worrall F. Mountain American Inn of Court; New Jersey Defense Association

Kevin F. Colquhoun — King's College, B.A., 1975; Seton Hall University School of Law, J.D., 1978 — Admitted to Bar, 1978, New Jersey; 1980, Florida; 1992, Maine — Member American, New Jersey State, Maine State and Morris County Bar Associations; The Florida Bar; Master, Worrall F. Mountain American Inn of Court

Robert F. Colquhoun, II — King's College, B.A., 1975; Seton Hall University, J.D., 1980 — Admitted to Bar, 1980, New Jersey; 1983, Florida — Member American, New Jersey State and Morris County Bar Associations; The Florida Bar; Master, Worrall F. Mountain American Inn of Court — Law Secretary, New Jersey Superior Court, Appellate Div., 1980

Sean F. Colquhoun — Skidmore College, B.A., 1978; Seton Hall University, M.P.A., 1983; J.D., 1986 — Admitted to Bar, 1987, New Jersey — Member American, New Jersey State and Morris County Bar Associations; Barrister, Worrall F. Mountain Inn of Court

Moira E. Colquhoun — 1961 — Skidmore College, B.A., 1983; Boston College, M.A., 1986; Seton Hall University, J.D., 1989 — Admitted to Bar, 1989, New Jersey; 1991, Florida; 1992, Maine — Member American, New Jersey State, Maine State and Morris County Bar Associations; The Florida Bar; Barrister, Worrall F. Mountain American Inn of Court; New Jersey Defense Association

(This firm is also listed in the Subrogation section of this directory)

NEW JERSEY   MORRISTOWN

Gold, Albanese & Barletti

48 South Street
Morristown, New Jersey 07960-4136
 Telephone: 973-326-9099
 Fax: 973-326-9841
 E-Mail: main@goldandalbanese.com
 www.goldandalbanese.com

(Red Bank, NJ Office*: 58 Maple Avenue, 07701)
  (Tel: 732-936-9901)
  (Fax: 732-936-9904)
(Boston, MA Office*: 50 Congress Street, Suite 225, 02109)
  (Tel: 617-723-5118)
  (Fax: 617-367-8840)
(Massapequa, NY Office: 544 Broadway, Suite 200, 11758)
  (Tel: 516-541-0021)
  (Fax: 516-541-1964)

Automobile, Civil Rights, Comprehensive General Liability, Construction Litigation, Employment Discrimination, Environmental Law, Insurance Coverage, Intellectual Property, Medical Malpractice, Personal Injury, Pharmaceutical, Premises Liability, Product Liability, Professional Liability, Property Damage, Wrongful Death, Occupational Exposure, Insurance Fraud Investigation and Litigation, Commercial Trucking Litigation, Public Entity Tort Litigation

Insurance Clients

Admiral Insurance Company   Discover Re
Kemper Insurance Company

Non-Insurance Clients

Pep Boys, Inc.   Wakefern Food Corporation

Partners

Robert Francis Gold — Fordham University, B.A. (magna cum laude), 1976; Rutgers University School of Law, J.D., 1980 — Admitted to Bar, 1980, New Jersey; 1996, Massachusetts; 2003, New York; 1980, U.S. District Court, District of New Jersey; 1993, U.S. Court of Appeals, Third Circuit; 1998, U.S. District Court, District of Massachusetts; 1998, U.S. Court of Appeals, First Circuit; 1998, U.S. Supreme Court; 2003, U.S. District Court, Southern District of New York — Member American, New Jersey State, New York State, Massachusetts, Essex County, Morris County, Hudson County and Boston Bar Associations

Judy T. Albanese — Fairfield University, B.A., 1989; Widener University School of Law, J.D., 1992 — Admitted to Bar, 1992, New Jersey; 2000, Massachusetts — Member American, New Jersey State and Hudson County Bar Associations

James N. Barletti — Rutgers University, B.A., 1995; Seton Hall University, J.D., 1998 — Admitted to Bar, 1998, New Jersey — Member American, New Jersey State, Morris County and Hudson County Bar Associations

Anthony V. Locascio — Fairfield University, B.A., 1995; Seton Hall University School of Law, J.D., 1999 — Admitted to Bar, 1999, New Jersey

Associates

Christian Bruun — University of Delaware, B.A., 1995; Roger Williams University School of Law, J.D., 2001 — Admitted to Bar, 2002, New Jersey

Stefani Fields — Salem State College, B.S., 1996; Massachusetts School of Law, J.D., 2002 — Admitted to Bar, 2003, Massachusetts — Member Massachusetts and Essex County Bar Associations; Massachusetts Academy of Trial Attorneys

Sandra Clark — Fairleigh Dickinson University, Cert., 1997; Drew University, B.A., 1997; New York Law School, J.D., 2003 — Admitted to Bar, 2005, New Jersey — Languages: Spanish

Jacqueline Voronov — Penn State University, B.A., 2003; New England School of Law, J.D., 2006 — Admitted to Bar, 2006, Massachusetts; New

Gold, Albanese & Barletti, Morristown, NJ   (Continued)
Jersey — Member New Jersey State Bar Association — Tel: 973-326-9099 — Fax: 873-326-9841

Meredith Palumbo — Lafayette College, B.A., 2002; Seton Hall University School of Law, J.D., 2005 — Admitted to Bar, 2006, New Jersey; New York — Member New Jersey State and New York State Bar Associations — Tel: 732-936-9901 — Fax: 732-936-9904

Of Counsel

Philip Platzer — Touro College, B.A., 1976; St. John's University School of Law, J.D., 1979 — Admitted to Bar, 1983, New York — Member Federal, American and Nassau County Bar Associations; Society of Risk Management Consultant; CPCU Society

Graham Curtin
A Professional Association

4 Headquarters Plaza
Morristown, New Jersey 07960
 Telephone: 973-292-1700
 Fax: 973-292-1767
 E-Mail: mail@GrahamCurtin.com
 www.GrahamCurtin.com

Established: 1983

Appellate Practice, Arbitration, Automobile Liability, Construction Law, Coverage Issues, General Civil Practice, General Liability, Health Care, Insurance Defense, Intellectual Property, Internet Law, Labor and Employment, Mediation, Premises Liability, Product Liability, Professional Liability, Public Entities, Technology

Insurance Clients

AmTrust Group   Aspen Specialty Insurance
Berkshire Hathaway, Inc.   Company
CNA - New Jersey Professional   Crum & Forster/United States Fire
  Claims   Insurance Company
Employers Reinsurance   Everest National Insurance
  Corporation   Company
General Star Management   The Hartford
  Company   Hiscox Insurance Company
OneBeacon Insurance   Philadelphia Insurance Companies
SISCO RCM&D Self-Insured   Swiss Reinsurance Company
  Services Co., Inc.   Travelers
Westport Insurance Corporation   Zurich North America

Non-Insurance Clients

Mercedes-Benz USA, LLC   Samsung Electronics America, Inc.
Thorlabs, Inc.   Tommy Hilfiger

Partners

Thomas R. Curtin — 1943 — Fairfield University, A.B., 1965; University of Notre Dame, J.D., 1968 — Admitted to Bar, 1969, New Jersey; 1983, New York; 1969, U.S. District Court, District of New Jersey; 1981, U.S. Supreme Court; 1992, U.S. Court of Appeals, Third Circuit; 2004, U.S. Court of Appeals for the Federal Circuit — Member American Bar Association (New Jersey State Delegate and House of Delegates); New Jersey State and Morris County Bar Associations; The Association of the Federal Bar of the State of New Jersey (Trustee); U.S. District Court Historical Society for the District of New Jersey (Trustee); U.S. Court of Appeals for the Third Circuit Bar Association (Trustee); Legal Services of New Jersey (Trustee); U.S District Court, District of New Jersey (Chair, Lawyers Advisory Committee); Fellow, American Bar Foundation — E-mail: tcurtin@grahamcurtin.com

George C. Jones — 1952 — Yale University, A.B. (cum laude), 1974; Boston University, J.D. (cum laude), 1978 — Admitted to Bar, 1978, New Jersey; 1988, New York; 1978, U.S. District Court, District of New Jersey; 1983, U.S. Court of Appeals, Third Circuit; 1996, U.S. Court of Appeals for the Federal Circuit — Member American, New Jersey State, Essex County and Morris County Bar Associations — E-mail: gjones@grahamcurtin.com

Christopher J. Carey — 1956 — Fordham University, B.A., 1978; Seton Hall University, J.D., 1982 — Admitted to Bar, 1983, New Jersey; New York; U.S. District Court, District of New Jersey; U.S. District Court, Eastern District of New York; 1984, U.S. District Court, Northern, Southern and Western Districts of New York; 1989, U.S. Court of Appeals, Third Circuit; 1990, U.S. Supreme Court; 1997, U.S. District Court, District of Nevada; U.S.

MORRISTOWN   NEW JERSEY

Graham Curtin, A Professional Association, Morristown, NJ (Continued)

Court of Appeals, Ninth Circuit — Member American Bar Association (Standing Committee on Lawyers' Professional Liability); New Jersey State Bar Association (Chair, Malpractice Insurance Committee, 2004-2007); New York State, Essex County, Bergen County Bar Associations; Fellow, American Bar Foundation; American Board of Trial Advocates; Defense Research Institute; Professional Liability Underwriting Society — Reported Cases: Lanziano v. Cocoziello, 304 N.J. Super. 616, 701 A.2d 754 (1997); Dunn v. Borough of Mountainside, 301 N.J. Super. 262, 693 A.2d 1248 (1997); Hernandez v. Overlook Hosp., 293 N.J. Super. 260, 680 A.2d 765, N.J.Super.A.D. (1996); Olds v. Donnelly, 291 N.J. Super. 222, 677 A.2d 238 (1996); Tung v. Brian Park Homes, Inc., 287 N.J. Super. 232, 670 A.2d 1092 (1996); Cellucci v. Bronstein, 277 N.J. Super. 506, 649 A.2d 1333 (1994); Martin v. Home Ins. Co., 276 N.J. Super. 378, 648 A.2d 213 (1994); Circle Chevrolet Co. v. Giordano, Halleran & Ciesla, 274 N.J. Super. 405, 644 A.2d 626 (1994); Cooke v. Wilentz, Goldman & Spitzer, 261 N.J. Super. 391, 619 A.2d 222 (1992); Yelder v. Zuvich, 245 N.J. Super. 331, 585 A.2d 434 (1990); Alan J. Cornblatt, P.A. v. Barow, 153 N.J. 218, 708 A.2d 401 (1998); Olds v. Donnelly, 150 N.J. 424, 696 A.2d 633 (1997); Karpovich v. Barbarula, 150 N.J. 473, 696 A.2d 659 (1997); Hernandez v. Overlook Hosp., 149 N.J. 68, 692 A.2d 971 (1997); Circle Chevrolet Co. v. Giordano, Halleran & Ciesla, 142 N.J. 280, 662 A.2d 509 (1995); Manley v. Stark & Stark, P.C., Lexis 22088, (1999); Alampi v. Russo, 345 N.J.Super. 360, 785 A.2d 65 (N.J.Super.A.D., Nov. 29, 2001) (No. A-5594-99T2); Brach, Eichler, Rosenberg, Silver, Bernstein, Hammer & Gladstone, P.C. v. Ezekwo, 345 N.J.Super. 1, 783 A.2d 246 (N.J.Super.A.D., Oct. 22, 2001) (No. A-5887-99T5); Charter Oak Fire Ins. Co. v. State Farm Mut. Auto. Ins. Co., 344 N.J.Super. 408, 782 A.2d 452 (N.J.Super.A.D., Oct. 17, 2001) (No. A-3357-99T1); LaBracio Family Partnership v. 1239 Roosevelt Ave., Inc., 340 N.J.Super, 155, 773 A.2d 1209 (N.J.Super.A.D., May 01, 2001) (No. A-3078-99T5); NYLife Distributors, Inc. v. Adherence Group, Inc., 72 F.3d 371, 64 USLW 2405 (3rd Cir.(N.J.), Dec. 21, 1995) (NO. 94-5725); Moench v. Robertson, 62 F.3d. 553, 64 USLW 2164, 19 Employee Benefits Cas. 1713, Pens. Plan Guide (CCH) P 23911Z (3rd. Cir.(N.J.), Aug 10, 1995) (NO. 94-5637); U.S. Small Business Admin. v. Martignetti, 98 F.Supp.2d 587 (D.N.J., May 24, 2000) (NO. CIV. 99-2949 (DRD)); Provenzano v. Integrated Genetics, 66 F.Supp.2d 588 (D.N.J., Jun 30, 1999) (NO. CIV. A. 97-1460(MLC)); Provenzano v. Integrated Genetics, 22 F.Supp.2d 406 (D.N.J., Oct 13, 1998) (NO. CIV. A 97-1460(MLC)); RTC Mortg. Trust v. Fidelity Nat. Title Ins. Co., 16 F.Supp.2d 577 (D.N.J., Aug 14, 1998) (NO. CIV. A. 96-5874); Tennsco Corp. v. Estey Metal Products, Inc., 200 B.R. 542, 65 USLW 2304 (D.N.J., Sep 17, 1996) (NO. CIV. 96-1284 (GEB)); Carlyle Towers Condominium Ass'n., Inc. v. Crossland Sav., FSB, 944 F.Supp.341 (D.N.J., Jul 01, 1996) (NO. CIV. 95-6554); Siebuhr v. Booth Mem'l Hosp. 1999-08675, Supreme Court of New York Appellate Division, Second Department, 276 A.D.2d 617; 714 N.Y.S.2d 900; 2000 N.Y. App. Div, (Sept. 2000); Vastano v. Algeier, 178 N.J. 230; 837 A.2d 1081 (2003); Banco Popular North America v. Gandi, et al., 360 NJ Super 414, 424 (App. Div. 2003); GSC Partners CDO Fund v. Washington, 368 F.3d 228 (2004); Cherry Hill Manor Assocs., v. Faugno, 365 N.J. Super. 313; 839 A.2d 95 (2004); Puder v. Buechel, 2005 NJ Lexis 597 (June 7, 2005); Liberty Surplus Insurance Corporation, Inc. v. Nowell Amoroso, P.A., et al., 189 N.J. 436; 916 A.2d 440 (2007); Prospect Rehabilitation Services, Inc. v. Generoso Squitieri, Esq. 392 N.J. Super 157; 920 A.2d 135 (2007) — Certified Civil Trial Attorney by the Supreme Court of New Jersey; Certified Professional Liability Attorney by the American Bar Association Professional Liability Division; Certified Mediator — Tel: 973-401-7135 — E-mail: ccarey@grahamcurtin.com

Stephen V. Gimigliano — 1958 — Lehigh University, B.S. (summa cum laude), 1980; Boston College, J.D. (cum laude), 1983 — Admitted to Bar, 1983, New Jersey; 1987, New York; 1985, U.S. Court of Appeals for the District of Columbia Circuit; 1987, U.S. District Court, Eastern and Southern Districts of New York; 2007, U.S. Court of Appeals, Second Circuit; 2010, U.S. District Court, Northern District of New York; 2011, U.S. Court of Appeals, Third Circuit — Member American Bar Association; The Association of the Bar of the City of New York — Board of Editors, AmLaw's Insurance Coverage Law Bulletin — E-mail: sgimigliano@grahamcurtin.com

James J. O'Hara — 1956 — Fairfield University, B.A., 1978; Seton Hall University, J.D., 1985 — Admitted to Bar, 1986, New Jersey; U.S. District Court, District of New Jersey; 1998, U.S. Court of Appeals, Third Circuit — Member American, New Jersey State and Morris County Bar Associations; Defense Research Institute — E-mail: johara@grahamcurtin.com

Robert W. Mauriello, Jr. — 1969 — Rensselaer Polytechnic Institute, B.S. (magna cum laude), 1991; Columbia University, J.D., 1993 — Admitted to Bar, 1993, New Jersey; 1994, New York; 1993, U.S. District Court, District of New Jersey; 1996, U.S. Court of Appeals, Third Circuit; 2005, U.S.

Graham Curtin, A Professional Association, Morristown, NJ (Continued)

District Court, Southern District of New York; 2007, U.S. Court of Appeals, Second Circuit — Member American Bar Association — E-mail: rmauriello@grahamcurtin.com

David M. Blackwell — 1969 — The George Washington University, B.A., 1991; Seton Hall University, J.D., 1994 — Admitted to Bar, 1994, New Jersey; Pennsylvania; U.S. District Court, District of New Jersey; 2003, U.S. Court of Appeals, Third Circuit — Member American, New Jersey State and Morris County Bar Associations; District X Ethics Committee — E-mail: dblackwell@grahamcurtin.com

Patrick J. Galligan — 1969 — College of the Holy Cross, B.A., 1991; Seton Hall University, J.D., 1996 — Admitted to Bar, 1996, New Jersey; U.S. District Court, District of New Jersey; 2000, U.S. Court of Appeals, Third Circuit — Member American, New Jersey State and Morris County (Trustee) Bar Associations; Trial Attorneys of New Jersey (Member and Trustee) — E-mail: pgalligan@grahamcurtin.com

John Maloney — 1976 — The University of Chicago, A.B. (with honors), 1998; Boston College, J.D., 2001 — Admitted to Bar, 2001, New Jersey; 2003, District of Columbia; 2012, New York; 2001, U.S. District Court, District of New Jersey; 2008, U.S. Court of Appeals, Third Circuit; 2013, U.S. District Court, Southern District of New York — Member New Jersey State Bar Association — E-mail: jmaloney@grahamcurtin.com

Kathleen N. Fennelly — 1960 — Fairfield University, B.A. (magna cum laude), 1982; Seton Hall University, J.D. (cum laude), 1986 — Admitted to Bar, 1987, New Jersey; U.S. District Court, District of New Jersey; 1991, U.S. Court of Appeals, Third Circuit; 1997, U.S. Supreme Court — Member New Jersey State and Morris County Bar Associations; Association of the Federal Bar of the State of New Jersey — Reported Cases: Thiedemann v. Mercedes-Benz USA, 1983 N.J. 234 (2005) — E-mail: kfennelly@grahamcurtin.com

Adam J. Adrignolo — 1969 — Fairleigh Dickinson University, B.A. (summa cum laude), 1992; Seton Hall University School of Law, J.D. (cum laude), 1995 — Admitted to Bar, 1995, New Jersey; 1996, New York; 1997, District of Columbia; 1995, U.S. District Court, District of New Jersey; 1998, U.S. Court of Appeals, Third Circuit — Author: "Navigating the Channels for Due Process -Admiralty Rule C Arrests Without Minimum Contacts", 4 Seton Hall Const. L.J. 2 (1994) — Reported Cases: In Re U.S. Healthcare, 159 F.3rd 142 (3rd Cir. 1998) — E-mail: aadrignolo@grahamcurtin.com

Glen M. Diehl — 1957 — Rutgers University, B.S. Elec. Engr., 1980; Seton Hall University School of Law, J.D., 1986 — Admitted to Bar, 1986, New Jersey; 1987, U.S. Patent and Trademark Office; U.S. Court of Appeals, Third Circuit; U.S. Court of Appeal for the Federal Circuit — E-mail: gdiehl@grahamcurtin.com

Associates

Jennifer L. Schoenberg — 1980 — Cornell University, B.A., 2002; Seton Hall University School of Law, J.D., 2005 — Admitted to Bar, 2005, New Jersey; 2006, New York; 2005, U.S. District Court, District of New Jersey; 2007, U.S. District Court, Southern District of New York; 2012, U.S. Court of Appeals, Third Circuit; U.S. Supreme Court — Member American, New York State and Morris County Bar Associations — E-mail: jschoenberg@grahamcurtin.com

Kelley Hastie — Johnson & Wales University, B.S. (with honors), 2000; Seton Hall University School of Law, J.D., 2006 — Admitted to Bar, 2006, New Jersey; 2008, U.S. District Court, District of New Jersey — Member New Jersey State Bar Association — E-mail: khastie@grahamcurtin.com

Anthony Longo — 1980 — The Catholic University of America, B.A. (cum laude), 2003; Seton Hall University School of Law, J.D., 2006 — Admitted to Bar, 2006, New Jersey; U.S. District Court, District of New Jersey — E-mail: alongo@grahamcurtin.com

Megan Halverson Trexler — 1979 — Rutgers College, B.A., 2002; Rutgers University School of Law-Newark, J.D., 2007 — Admitted to Bar, 2007, New Jersey; 2009, New York; 2008, U.S. District Court, District of New Jersey; 2009, U.S. District Court, Southern District of New York — Member American and New Jersey State Bar Associations — E-mail: mtrexler@grahamcurtin.com

Brian B. McEvoy — 1978 — University of Notre Dame, B.A., 2000; Rutgers University School of Law-Newark, J.D., 2008 — Admitted to Bar, 2008, New Jersey; U.S. District Court, District of New Jersey — Member New Jersey State and Morris County Bar Associations — Armor Officer, U.S. Army — E-mail: bmcevoy@grahamcurtin.com

Caitlin M. Owens — 1985 — Bentley College, B.S. (cum laude), 2007; Seton Hall University School of Law, J.D., 2010 — Admitted to Bar, 2010, New Jersey; 2011, New York; 2010, U.S. District Court, District of New Jersey —

NEW JERSEY — MORRISTOWN

Graham Curtin, A Professional Association, Morristown, NJ (Continued)

Member American and New Jersey State Bar Associations — E-mail: cowens@grahamcurtin.com

Leah R. Bartlome — 1985 — American University, B.A., 2007; Seton Hall University School of Law, J.D., 2010 — Admitted to Bar, 2010, New Jersey; 2011, New York; 2010, U.S. District Court, District of New Jersey — Member New Jersey State, Morris County and Somerset County Bar Associations — E-mail: lbartlome@grahamcurtin.com

Jared J. Limbach — 1985 — University of Pennsylvania, B.A. (cum laude), 2007; Fordham University School of Law, J.D., 2010 — Admitted to Bar, 2010, New Jersey; 2011, New York; 2010, U.S. District Court, District of New Jersey; 2011, U.S. District Court, Southern District of New York — Member American, New Jersey State, New York State and Morris County Bar Associations — E-mail: jlimbach@grahamcurtin.com

Christopher Kim — 1982 — Columbia University, B.A., 2004; Seton Hall University School of Law, J.D. (cum laude), 2010 — Admitted to Bar, 2010, New Jersey; 2011, New York; 2010, U.S. District Court, District of New Jersey — Member American and New York State Bar Associations — E-mail: ckim@grahamcurtin.com

Joshua A. Druck — Johns Hopkins University, B.A., 2006; Duke Law School, J.D., 2010 — Admitted to Bar, 2010, New Jersey; New York; 2011, U.S. District Court, District of New Jersey — E-mail: jdruck@grahamcurtin.com

Theodore T. Reilly — 1984 — University of Delaware, B.A., 2006; Seton Hall University School of Law, J.D., 2011 — Admitted to Bar, 2011, New Jersey; 2013, New York; 2011, U.S. District Court, District of New Jersey — Member New Jersey State Bar Association — E-mail: treilly@grahamcurtin.com

Fonda J. Mazzillo — 1986 — Seton Hall University, B.A. (summa cum laude), 2007; Seton Hall University School of Law, J.D., 2011 — Admitted to Bar, 2012, New Jersey; New York; U.S. District Court, District of New Jersey — Member New Jersey State and Bergen County Bar Associations — E-mail: fmazzillo@grahamcurtin.com

Michelle M. O'Brien — Kings College, B.A. (magna cum laude), 2008; Seton Hall University School of Law, J.D., 2011 — Admitted to Bar, 2012, New Jersey; New York; U.S. District Court, District of New Jersey — Member New Jersey State and Middlesex County Bar Associations — E-mail: mobrien@grahamcurtin.com

Of Counsel

Charles Quinn — 1955 — Rutgers College, B.A. (with honors), 1977; Seton Hall University School of Law, J.D., 1981 — Admitted to Bar, 1981, New Jersey; 1990, New York; 1981, U.S. District Court, District of New Jersey; 1988, U.S. Court of Appeals, Third Circuit; 1989, U.S. Court of Appeals for the Federal Circuit; 1991, U.S. District Court, Eastern and Southern Districts of New York; 1997, U.S. Court of Appeals, Ninth Circuit; 2004, U.S. Court of Appeals, Second Circuit — Member New Jersey State Bar Association; New Jersey Intellectual Property Law Association; New York Intellectual Property Law Association — Author: "Depositions in Patent Cases," Patent Litigation Strategies Handbook (BNA 2000) (Chap. 11) — Reported Cases: Symbol, et al. v. Lemelson, 277 F.3d. 1361 (Fed. Cir. 2002); 301 F. Supp. 2d 1147 (D.Nev. 2004); 422 F.3d 1378 (Fed. Cir. 2005); Girl Scouts of the U.S. v. Steir, 102 Fed. Appx. 217 (2d Cir. 2004); Laitram Corp. v. NEC Corp., 952 F.2d 1357 (Fed. Circ. 1991); Hyundai v. U.S.I.T.C., 899 F.2d 1204 (Fed. Cir. 1990); Cognex Corp. v. Lemelson, 67 F. Supp. 2d (D. Mass. 1998) — E-mail: cquinn@grahamcurtin.com

Thomas J. Coffey — 1978 — University of Notre Dame, B.A. (cum laude), 2000; University of Notre Dame Law School, J.D., 2003 — Admitted to Bar, 2003, New Jersey; 2004, New York; 2003, U.S. District Court, District of New Jersey — Tel: tcoffey@grahamcurtin.com

William D. Tully, Jr. — 1976 — College of the Holy Cross, B.A., 1998; Rutgers University School of Law-Newark, J.D., 2002 — Admitted to Bar, 2002, New Jersey; U.S. District Court, District of New Jersey — Member Morris County Bar Association — E-mail: wtully@grahamcurtin.com

McElroy, Deutsch, Mulvaney & Carpenter, LLP

1300 Mount Kemble Avenue
Morristown, New Jersey 07962
Telephone: 973-993-8100
Fax: 973-425-0161
www.mdmc-law.com

McElroy, Deutsch, Mulvaney & Carpenter, LLP, Morristown, NJ (Continued)

(Greenwood Village, CO Office: 5600 South Quebec Street, Suite C100, 80111)
(Tel: 303-293-8800)
(Fax: 303-839-0036)
(Ridgewood, NJ Office: 40 West Ridgewood Avenue, 07450)
(Tel: 201-445-6722)
(Fax: 201-445-5376)
(New York, NY Office: Wall Street Plaza, 88 Pine Street, 10005)
(Tel: 212-483-9490)
(Fax: 212-483-9129)
(Newark, NJ Office: Three Gateway Center, 100 Mulberry Street, 07102-4079)
(Tel: 973-622-7711)
(Fax: 973-622-5314)
(Philadelphia, PA Office: 1617 JFK Boulevard, Suite 1500, 19103-1815)
(Tel: 215-557-2900)
(Fax: 215-557-2990, 215-557-2991)
(Hartford, CT Office: One State Street, 14th Floor, 06103-3102)
(Tel: 860-522-5175)
(Fax: 860-522-2796)
(Southport, CT Office: 30 Jelliff Lane, 06890)
(Tel: 203-319-4000)
(Fax: 203-259-0251)
(Boston, MA Office: One Financial Center, 15th Floor, 02111)
(Tel: 617-748-5500)
(Fax: 617-748-5555)
(Wilmington, DE Office: 300 Delaware Avenue, Suite 770, 19801)
(Tel: 302-300-4515)
(Fax: 302-654-4031)
(Tinton Falls, NJ Office: 4000 Route 66, 4th Floor, 07753)
(Tel: 732-733-6200)

Established: 1983

General Civil Practice, Administrative Law, Appellate Practice, Aviation, Business Law, Class Actions, Commercial Litigation, Construction Litigation, Corporate Law, Employee Benefits, Environmental Law, Errors and Omissions, Fidelity and Surety, Health Care, Hospitals, Insurance Defense, Intellectual Property, International Law, Labor and Employment, Personal Injury, Premises Liability, Product Liability, Professional Liability, Reinsurance, Toxic Torts, Municipal Law, Land Use, Real Estate, ERISA, Bankruptcy, Alternative Dispute Resolution, Renewable Energy, Insurance Services, Pharmaceutical and Related Services, Public Contracts, Government Agencies, Partnership Law, Hotels and Resorts Law, Wills and Estates, White Collar Criminal Defense, Tax, Immigration, Zoning, Unclaimed Property

Firm Profile: McElroy, Deutsch, Mulvaney & Carpenter, LLP is a national law firm with approximately 300 attorneys in eleven offices located in New Jersey, New York, Colorado, Connecticut, Pennsylvania, Massachusetts, and Delaware. We are uniquely positioned to represent Fortune 500 companies, middle market and smaller businesses, municipal and other public entities, as well as individual clients.

The Firm's growth has been built on a tradition of innovative thought and special attention to clients' needs and interests. In persistently challenging economic times, MDM&C will continue to deliver to clients an unusually competitive, realistic fee structure, combined with efficiencies in operations and client-first attorneys who are hands-on full-time practitioners producing effective solutions to client problems.

Insurance Clients

Harleysville Insurance Company   Liberty Mutual Insurance Company

Partners

Edward B. Deutsch — University of Rhode Island, B.S., 1968; Seton Hall University, J.D., 1971 — Admitted to Bar, 1971, New Jersey; 1993, U.S. District Court, District of New Jersey; 1995, U.S. District Court, Eastern District of Michigan; U.S. Supreme Court; 2000, U.S. Court of Appeals, Fourth Circuit — Certified Civil Trial Attorney, Supreme Court of New Jersey — Practice Areas: Commercial Litigation; Corporate Law; Mergers and Acquisitions

McElroy, Deutsch, Mulvaney & Carpenter, LLP, Morristown, NJ (Continued)

Robert J. Alter
Suzanne E. Baldasare
Jeffrey Bernstein
Thomas C. Bigosinski
James A. Budinetz
Anthony M. Carlino
John P. Cookson
Francis X. Dee
Edward J. De Pascale
Louis P. DiGiaimo
Colleen M. Duffy
Donna duBeth Gardiner
Peter A. Gaudioso
Robert W. Gifford
Gary S. Hammersmith
Stephen B. Hazard
Robert B. Hille
Eric J. Hughes
John Zen Jackson
Christopher H. Jones
Michael G. Keating
Randi F. Knepper
Walter R. Krzastek, Jr.
June Baker Laird
John P. Leonard
James Peter Lidon
Michael J. Marone
Andrew F. McBride III
Joseph J. McGlone
John C. McGuire
Kevin R. McNamara
Thomas B. Mitchell
Florina A. Moldovan
John W. Morris
William F. O'Connor, Jr.
James E. Patterson
John J. Peirano
Eric R. Perkins
H. James Pickerstein
Carol A. Pisano
Albert J. Pucciarelli
Michael Rato
David J. Reilly
J. Michael Riordan
Mark A. Rosen
Elliot Rothstein
Robert C. Scrivo
Robert C. Seiger, Jr.
Gary F. Sheldon
Walter W. Simmers
Craig J. Smith
Walter F. Timpone
Alfred A. Turco
Kevin B. Walker
Jane E. Young
H. George Avery
John P. Belardo
John P. Beyel
Gary D. Bressler
William A. Cambria
Craig J. Compoli, Jr.
John T. Coyne
Steven P. Del Mauro
Michael B. Devins
Robert P. Donovan
Kevin P. Galvin
James G. Gardner
Salvatore A. Giampiccolo
James G. Green Jr.
Charles J. Harriman
Keith R. Hemming
Frank Holahan
Thomas R. Hurd
Bernard E. Jacques
Lucille J. Karp
Barry D. Kleban
Peter L. Korn
Glendon L. Laird
Joseph P. LaSala
Thomas G. Librizzi
Kevin MacGillivray
Kristin B. Mayhew
Nancy McDonald
Thomas F. McGuane
Laurence M. McHeffey
Richard S. Mills
Louis A. Modugno
Victor M. Morales
James M. Mulvaney
George H. Parsells, III
Stephen F. Payerle
Louis R. Pepe
Jeffrey L. Pettit
Loren L. Pierce
Douglas M. Poulin
Joseph D. Rasnek
James D. Ray
Jane A. Rigby
James A. Robertson
David E. Rosengren
Adam R. Schwartz
Thomas P. Scrivo
Vimal K. Shah
William M. Shields
James R. Smart
John H. Suminski
Frank B. Tracy
Wendy Kennedy Venoit
Richard J. Williams, Jr.
Joshua A. Zielinski

Riker Danzig Scherer Hyland & Perretti LLP

Headquarters Plaza
1 Speedwell Avenue
Morristown, New Jersey 07962-1981
 Telephone: 973-538-0800
 Fax: 973-538-1984
 E-Mail: info@riker.com
 www.riker.com

(Trenton, NJ Office*: 50 West State Street, Suite 1010, 08608-1220)
 (Tel: 609-396-2121)
 (Fax: 609-396-4578)

Riker Danzig Scherer Hyland & Perretti LLP, Morristown, NJ (Continued)

(New York, NY Office: 500 Fifth Avenue, 10110)
 (Tel: 212-302-6574)
 (Fax: 212-302-6628)

Established: 1882

Administrative Law, Alternative Dispute Resolution, Appellate Practice, Civil Litigation, Civil Trial Practice, Commercial Litigation, Complex Litigation, Contract Disputes, Corporate Law, Deceptive Trade Practices, Declaratory Judgments, Defense Litigation, Directors and Officers Liability, Excess and Reinsurance, Fidelity and Surety, First Party Matters, Fraud, General Civil Practice, General Civil Trial and Appellate Practice, General Defense, General Practice, Health, Health Care, Hospitals, Insurance Corporate Practice, Insurance Coverage, Insurance Defense, Insurance Fraud, Insurance Law, Insurance Litigation, Insurance Regulation, International Law, Legislative Law, Litigation, Litigation and Counseling, Mediation, Mergers and Acquisitions, Opinions, Product Liability, Property and Casualty, Public Entities, Public Liability, Public Officials Liability, Punitive Damages, Regulatory and Compliance, Reinsurance, Self-Insured, State and Federal Courts, Surety, Surety Bonds, Title Insurance, Tort Litigation, Trial Practice, Trial and Appellate Practice

Firm Profile: Riker Danzig's Insurance Group draws on the combined resources of experienced litigators, governmental affairs attorneys and corporate attorneys to bring comprehensive understanding to matters on behalf of the insurance industry.

Insurance Clients

American Centennial Insurance Company
Chubb Group of Insurance Companies
Excess Insurance Company Limited
GLOBAL Reinsurance Corporation of America
Hudson Reinsurance Company, Ltd
The Philadelphia Contributionship Insurance Company
Toa Reinsurance Company of America
American Income Life Insurance Company
CIGNA Group
Crum & Forster Insurance Group
Gerling-Konzern Versicherung-Beteiligungs AG
The Harleysville Insurance
Harper Insurance Ltd.
Mitsui Sumitomo Marine Management (USA), Inc.
The Proformance Insurance Company

Partners

Shawn L. Kelly — 1952 — Duke University, A.B. (magna cum laude), 1974; Georgetown University, J.D., 1978 — Editor, The American Criminal Law Review, 1976-1978 — Admitted to Bar, 1978, New Jersey; 1978, U.S. District Court, District of New Jersey; 1978, U.S. Court of Appeals, Second and Third Circuits — Member Federation of Insurance and Corporate Counsel — Practice Areas: Arbitration; Insurance Coverage; Litigation; Reinsurance; International Law — E-mail: skelly@riker.com

Glenn A. Clark — 1954 — Seton Hall University, B.A. (summa cum laude), 1976; University of Notre Dame Law School, J.D. (magna cum laude), 1980 — Admitted to Bar, 1980, New Jersey; U.S. District Court, District of New Jersey — Practice Areas: Appellate Practice; Construction Law; Health Care; Insurance Law; Reinsurance; Intellectual Property; Labor and Employment; Litigation; Professional Malpractice — E-mail: gclark@riker.com

John M. Pellecchia — 1958 — Lafayette College, B.A., 1980; City of London Polytechnic Institute, 1979; Tulane University, J.D. (cum laude), 1983 — Admitted to Bar, 1983, New Jersey; 1983, U.S. District Court, District of New Jersey; 1994, U.S. Supreme Court — Member New Jersey Supreme Court (Tax Court Committee); State Law Resources, Inc. (Board of Directors) — Assistant Counsel to Hon. Thomas H. Kean, Governor of New Jersey, 1986-1988 — Practice Areas: Administrative Law; Alternative Dispute Resolution; Appellate Practice; Civil Litigation; Civil Trial Practice; Commercial Litigation; Complex Litigation; Contract Disputes; Corporate Law; Deceptive Trade Practices; Declaratory Judgments; Defense Litigation; Excess and Reinsurance; Fidelity and Surety; Fraud; General Civil Practice; General Civil Trial and Appellate Practice; General Defense; Insurance Defense; General Practice; Health; Health Care; Hospitals; Insurance Corporate Practice; Insurance Fraud; Insurance Law; Insurance Litigation; Insurance Regulation; Legislative Law; Litigation; Litigation and Counseling; Mediation; Mergers

NEW JERSEY — MORRISTOWN

Riker Danzig Scherer Hyland & Perretti LLP, Morristown, NJ (Continued)

and Acquisitions; Opinions; Product Liability; Property and Casualty; Public Entities; Public Liability; Public Officials Liability; Punitive Damages; Regulatory and Compliance; Reinsurance; Self-Insured; State and Federal Courts; Surety; Surety Bonds; Title Insurance; Tort Litigation; Trial and Appellate Practice; Trial Practice — E-mail: jpellecchia@riker.com

Glenn D. Curving — 1958 — Rutgers College, B.A. (with honors), 1980; Seton Hall University, J.D. (cum laude), 1983 — Admitted to Bar, 1983, New Jersey; 1983, U.S. District Court, District of New Jersey; 1994, U.S. Court of Appeals, Third Circuit — Practice Areas: Commercial Liability; Commercial Litigation; Insurance Law; Professional Liability — E-mail: gcurving@riker.com

Brian E. O'Donnell — 1963 — State University of New York at Albany, B.A. (cum laude), 1986; University of Notre Dame Law School, J.D., 1989 — Admitted to Bar, 1989, New Jersey; 1990, New York; 1989, U.S. District Court, District of New Jersey; 2000, U.S. District Court, Eastern and Southern Districts of New York; 2000, U.S. Court of Appeals, Third Circuit — Practice Areas: First and Third Party Defense; Insurance Coverage; Reinsurance; Alternative Dispute Resolution; Insurance Litigation — E-mail: bodonnell@riker.com

Mary Kathryn Roberts — 1965 — Boston College, B.A. (cum laude), 1988; American University, Washington College of Law, J.D., 1991 — Admitted to Bar, 1991, New Jersey; 1991, Pennsylvania; U.S. District Court, District of New Jersey — Member New Jersey State Bar Association (Banking Law Section); New Jersey Health Care Administration Board (Vice Chair) — Registered Governmental Affairs Agent, New Jersey Election Law Enforcement Commission — Practice Areas: Government Affairs; Insurance Regulation; Insurance Law; Health Care; Lobbying — Resident Trenton, NJ Office — Tel: 609-396-2121 — Fax: 609-396-4578 — E-mail: mroberts@riker.com

Lance J. Kalik — 1967 — Brandeis University, B.A., 1989; Rutgers University-Newark, J.D., 1994 — Admitted to Bar, 1994, New Jersey; Pennsylvania; U.S. District Court, District of New Jersey; U.S. District Court, Eastern and Southern Districts of New York; U.S. Court of Appeals, Third Circuit — Member New Jersey State Bar Association (Malpractice Insurance Committee); Professional Liability Underwriting Society — Practice Areas: Appellate Practice; Construction Law; Insurance Law; Litigation; Professional Malpractice; Reinsurance — E-mail: lkalik@riker.com

Mary Ellen Scalera — 1956 — University of Notre Dame, B.A., 1978; Seton Hall University School of Law, J.D., 1988 — Admitted to Bar, 1988, New Jersey; 1988, U.S. District Court, District of New Jersey — Editorial Board, Environmental Claims Journal — Practice Areas: Environmental Coverage; Insurance Coverage; Toxic Torts; Asbestos Litigation — E-mail: mscalera@riker.com

Caroline Brizzolara — 1956 — Rutgers University, B.A. (magna cum laude), 1979; Rutgers University School of Law-Newark, J.D., 1999 — Order of the Coif — Admitted to Bar, 1999, New Jersey; 1999, U.S. District Court, District of New Jersey — Member ARIAS U.S. (AIDA Reinsurance & Insurance Arbitration Society) — Practice Areas: Insurance Coverage; Insurance Law; Insurance Litigation; Litigation; Reinsurance — E-mail: cbrizzolara@riker.com

John R. Vales — 1972 — University of Notre Dame, B.A., 1994; University of Notre Dame Law School, J.D., 1997 — Admitted to Bar, 1997, Texas; 2001, New York; 2006, New Jersey; 2001, U.S. District Court, District of New Jersey; 2007, U.S. District Court, Eastern and Southern Districts of New York — Practice Areas: Litigation; Complex Litigation; Commercial Litigation; Insurance Coverage; Insurance Litigation; Defense Litigation; Reinsurance; First Party Matters; Tort Litigation; Fraud — E-mail: jvales@riker.com

Of Counsel

Sigrid S. Franzblau — 1947 — Barnard College, B.A., 1969; Rutgers University, J.D. (with honors), 1982 — Admitted to Bar, 1983, New Jersey; 1983, U.S. District Court, District of New Jersey; 1990, U.S. Court of Appeals, Third Circuit; 1995, U.S. Court of Appeals, Ninth Circuit — Practice Areas: Commercial Litigation; Trust and Estate Litigation — E-mail: sfranzblau@riker.com

Counsel

Anne M. Mohan — 1960 — University of Scranton, B.A. (magna cum laude), 1981; Seton Hall University School of Law, J.D. (cum laude), 1984 — Admitted to Bar, 1984, New Jersey; U.S. District Court, District of New Jersey; 1991, U.S. Court of Appeals, Third Circuit; U.S. Supreme Court — Member American and New Jersey State Bar Associations — Practice Areas: Insurance Litigation; Insurance Regulation; Reinsurance; Insurance Defense — E-mail: amohan@riker.com

Sullivan and Graber

60 Maple Avenue
Morristown, New Jersey 07960
  Telephone: 973-540-0877
  Fax: 973-540-8019
  E-Mail: ggraber@sullivangraberlaw.us
  www.sullivangraberlaw.com

(New York, NY Office*: 250 West 57th Street, 9th Floor, 10107) (Tel: 212-835-9462)

Alternative Dispute Resolution, Automobile, Arson, Bad Faith, Coverage Opinions, Declaratory Judgments, Dram Shop, Employment Practices Liability, Environmental Law, Errors and Omissions, Examinations Under Oath, Excess and Umbrella, First and Third Party Matters, Homeowners, Fraud, No-Fault, Personal Injury, Premises Liability, Product Liability, Professional Liability, Subrogation, Uninsured and Underinsured Motorist, Workers' Compensation, Wrongful Death, Insurance Fraud Investigations and Restitution Actions

Firm Profile: Sullivan and Graber serves as defense counsel to major national and international insurance companies doing business in New Jersey and New York. We offer our clients skilled, aggressive, responsive and efficient legal services in all areas of insurance law.

Insurance Clients

Allstate Insurance Company	Delta Dental of NJ
Encompass Insurance Company	Hanover Insurance Company
Kemper Services Group	MetLife Auto & Home
New Jersey Property-Liability	NJM Insurance Group
Insurance Guaranty Association	Selective Insurance Company
Unitrin Direct Insurance Company	

Members of the Firm

James F. Sullivan — College of the Holy Cross, A.B., 1972; Seton Hall University School of Law, J.D., 1975 — Admitted to Bar, 1975, New Jersey; U.S. District Court, District of New Jersey — Member New Jersey State and Morris County (Chairman, Civil Practice Committee) Bar Associations; Worrall F. Mountain American Inn of Court (Master) — Certified Civil Trial Attorney, Supreme Court of New Jersey Board on Trial Attorney Certification

Gordon S. Graber — University of Rochester, B.A. (with distinction), 1973; Rutgers University School of Law-Newark, J.D., 1977 — Law Secretary to New Jersey Superior Court Judge Joseph M. Thuring, 1977-1978 — Admitted to Bar, 1977, New Jersey; 1985, New York; 1977, U.S. District Court, District of New Jersey — Member American, New Jersey State, New York State and Morris County (Trustee, 2003-2007) Bar Associations; New Jersey Supreme Court District X (Chair, Ethics Committee, 1993-1994); American Immigration Lawyers Association; Morris County Bar Foundation (Trustee, 2010-Present) — Community Soup Kitchen of Morristown (Attorney-Trustee, 1990-1994); Morris County Organization for Hispanic Affairs (Trustee, 2004-Present); Morris County Assistant Prosecutor, 1978-1980 — Certified Civil Trial Attorney, New Jersey Supreme Court Board on Trial Certification; Approved R. 1:40 New Jersey Superior Court Mediator

Lee Scott Befeler — Bennington College, B.A., 1984; University of the Pacific, McGeorge School of Law, J.D., 1987 — Law Clerk, New Jersey Superior Court Judge Maurice J. Gallipoli, Law Division, Hudson County, 1987-1988 — Admitted to Bar, 1987, New Jersey; U.S. District Court, District of New Jersey — Member American (Member, Tort and Insurance Practice Section), New Jersey State and Morris County Bar Associations — Approved Mediator for Superior Court under R. 1:40

Keather M. Papa — University of Rochester, B.A. (cum laude), 2002; Syracuse University College of Law, J.D. (cum laude), 2006 — Law Clerk, New Jersey Superior Court the Honorable Ronald B. Sokalski, J.S.C., Law Division, Passaic County, 2006-2007 — Admitted to Bar, 2006, New Jersey; New York; U.S. District Court, District of New Jersey — Member New York State and New Jersey State Bar Associations

Christine C. Ryan — Rutgers College, B.A. (magna cum laude), 2001; Benjamin N. Cardozo School of Law, J.D., 2012 — Law Clerk to the Honorable Bruno Mongiardo, J.S.C., Superior Court of New Jersey, 2012-2013 — Admitted to Bar, 2012, New Jersey; New York

Rosa D. Forrester — Pace University, B.A. (cum laude), 2009; Seton Hall University School of Law, J.D., 2012 — Law Clerk to the Honorable James G.

NEW BRUNSWICK — NEW JERSEY

Sullivan and Graber, Morristown, NJ (Continued)

Troiano, J.S.C., Superior Court of New Jersey, 2012-2013 — Admitted to Bar, 2012, New Jersey; 2013, New York

Danyelle A. Halpern — American University, School of Public Affairs, B.A., 2008; Pace University School of Law, J.D., 2012 — Law Clerk to the Honorable Ronald L. Reisner, J.S.C., Superior Court of New Jersey, 2012-2013; Law Clerk to the Honorable Jerome St. John, J.A.D., Appellate Division, State of New Jersey, 2013-2014 — Admitted to Bar, 2013, New Jersey

The following firms also service this area.

Methfessel & Werbel
2025 Lincoln Highway, Suite 200
Edison, New Jersey 08817
  Telephone: 732-248-4200
  Fax: 732-248-2355

Mailing Address: P.O. Box 3012, Edison, NJ 08818-3012

Automobile Liability, Bad Faith, Carrier Defense, Casualty Defense, Civil Trial Practice, Comprehensive General Liability, Construction Litigation, Coverage Issues, Defense Litigation, Employment Practices Liability, Environmental Coverage, Environmental Liability, Examinations Under Oath, Excess and Umbrella, Insurance Coverage, Insurance Defense, Medical Liability, Premises Liability, Primary and Excess Insurance, Product Liability, Professional Malpractice, Property Liability, Public Entities, Toxic Torts, Uninsured and Underinsured Motorist, General Subrogation, Large Loss Subrogation Program

SEE COMPLETE LISTING UNDER EDISON, NEW JERSEY (31 MILES)

Nowell Amoroso Klein Bierman, P.A.
155 Polifly Road
Hackensack, New Jersey 07601
  Telephone: 201-343-5001
  Toll Free: 800-246-0254
  Fax: 201-343-5181

Insurance Defense, Bodily Injury, Asbestos Litigation, Environmental Law, Personal Liability, Automobile, Homeowners, Toxic Torts, Product Liability, Pollution, Property Damage

SEE COMPLETE LISTING UNDER HACKENSACK, NEW JERSEY (30 MILES)

MOUNT HOLLY † 10,639 Burlington Co.

Refer To
Law Offices of Glenn R. Cochran
812 State Road, Suite 120
Princeton, New Jersey 08540
  Telephone: 609-924-4011
  Fax: 609-924-5333

Mailing Address: P.O. Box 553, Princeton, NJ 08542

Insurance Defense, Trial Practice, Automobile, Professional Liability, Product Liability, Errors and Omissions, Liquor Liability, Commercial Liability, Subrogation, General

SEE COMPLETE LISTING UNDER PRINCETON, NEW JERSEY (25 MILES)

NEW BRUNSWICK † 55,181 Middlesex Co.

Busch and Busch, LLP

215 North Center Drive
North Brunswick, New Jersey 08902
  Telephone: 732-821-2300
  Fax: 732-821-5588
  E-Mail: lawyers@buschlaw.com
  www.buschlaw.com

Established: 1927

Errors and Omissions, Personal Injury, Defense Litigation, Asbestos Litigation, Public Entities

Insurance Clients

ACE Westchester Specialty Group
Chubb Group of Insurance Companies
Auto-Owners Insurance Company
Cincinnati Insurance Company
Federal Insurance Company

Busch and Busch, LLP, New Brunswick, NJ (Continued)

Helmsman Management Services, Inc.
Wisconsin Mutual Insurance Company
Pekin Insurance
Utica Mutual Insurance Company

Non-Insurance Clients

ESSCO Pumps & Controls
Maxon Corporation
Industrial Valve Sales & Service, Inc.

Partners

Bertram E. Busch — 1941 — Harvard University, B.A. (magna cum laude), 1962; Yale Law School, LL.B., 1965 — Admitted to Bar, 1965, New Jersey; 1965, U.S. District Court, District of New Jersey; 1996, U.S. Court of Appeals, Third Circuit — E-mail: beb@buschlaw.com

Mark N. Busch — 1942 — Rutgers University, A.B., 1964; Boston University, J.D., 1967 — Admitted to Bar, 1967, New Jersey; 1967, U.S. District Court, District of New Jersey; 1975, U.S. Court of Appeals, Third Circuit — Languages: French — E-mail: mnb@buschlaw.com

Ronald J. Busch — 1938 — Rutgers University, B.A., 1960; Vanderbilt University, LL.B., 1964 — Admitted to Bar, 1965, New Jersey — E-mail: rjb@buschlaw.com

Malcolm R. Busch — 1934 — Rutgers University, B.A. (magna cum laude), 1955; Yale Law School, LL.B., 1958 — Phi Beta Kappa; Order of the Coif — Admitted to Bar, 1958, New Jersey — E-mail: mrb@buschlaw.com

Leonard R. Busch — 1947 — Boston University, A.B., 1968; J.D., 1971 — Admitted to Bar, 1971, New Jersey; 1971, U.S. District Court, District of New Jersey — E-mail: lrb@buschlaw.com

Associate

Gregory A. Busch — 1971 — Lehigh University, B.A., 1993; Rutgers University, J.D., 1997 — Admitted to Bar, 1997, New Jersey — E-mail: gab@buschlaw.com

Counsel

Richard S. Cohen — 1934 — Princeton University, A.B. (cum laude), 1956; Yale Law School, LL.B. (cum laude), 1959 — Admitted to Bar, 1960, New Jersey; U.S. District Court, District of New Jersey — Practice Areas: Alternative Dispute Resolution — E-mail: adr@richardcohen.net

Sweet Pasquarelli, PC

17A Joyce Kilmer Avenue North
New Brunswick, New Jersey 08901
  Telephone: 732-249-7180
  Fax: 732-249-7705
  E-Mail: lawoffice@sweetpasquarelli.com
  www.sweetpasquarelli.com

Established: 1998

Insurance Defense, Coverage Issues, Property and Casualty, Subrogation, Personal Injury, Toxic Torts, Workers' Compensation, Construction Litigation, Asbestos Litigation

Insurance Clients

ACE Agribusiness
Chartis Insurance
Cumberland Insurance Group
Farmers Mutual Fire Insurance Company of Salem County
Global Indemnity (United American Insurance Group and Penn-America Insurance Company)
United Fire & Casualty Company
ACE Private Risk Services
CNA Insurance Companies
Farmers Insurance Company of Flemington
Franklin Mutual Insurance Company
Liberty Mutual Insurance Company
Philadelphia Insurance Company
Providence Mutual Group

Partners

Stephen G. Sweet — (1947-2010)

Anthony P. Pasquarelli — 1955 — Seton Hall University, B.S., 1977; J.D., 1981 — Admitted to Bar, 1981, New Jersey; U.S. District Court, District of New Jersey; 1985, U.S. Court of Appeals, Third Circuit — Member New Jersey State Bar Association (Insurance Section) — Reported Cases: Voorhees v. Preferred Mutual 128 N.J. 168 (1992); Pickett v. Lloyds 131 N.J. 457

Sweet Pasquarelli, PC, New Brunswick, NJ (Continued)

(1993); Trade Soft v. Franklin Mutual 329 N.J. Super 137 (App. Div. 2000) — Certified Civil Trial Attorney — Languages: Italian

Associates

Donald A. Mahoney — 1950 — The Catholic University of America, B.A., 1972; Loyola University, J.D., 1975 — Admitted to Bar, 1975, New Jersey; U.S. District Court, District of New Jersey — Member American, New Jersey State and Union County Bar Associations — Certified Civil Trial Attorney

Matthew G. Minor — 1982 — Rutgers University-New Brunswick, B.A., 2006; Rutgers University School of Law-Camden, J.D., 2010 — Admitted to Bar, 2010, New Jersey; 2010, Pennsylvania

William T. Hilliard — 1948 — Saint Peter's College, B.A., 1976; St. John's University School of Law, J.D., 1979 — Admitted to Bar, 1979, New Jersey; U.S. District Court, District of New Jersey — Member American Inns of Court

Kenneth C. Ho — 1980 — Rutgers University-New Brunswick, B.A., 2003; Rutgers University School of Law-Camden, J.D., 2006 — Admitted to Bar, 2007, New Jersey; U.S. District Court, District of New Jersey — Member Middlesex County Bar Association; Asian Pacific American Lawyers Association; New Jersey Defense Association — Languages: Mandarin Chinese

(This firm is also listed in the Subrogation section of this directory)

The following firms also service this area.

Law Offices of Glenn R. Cochran
812 State Road, Suite 120
Princeton, New Jersey 08540
 Telephone: 609-924-4011
 Fax: 609-924-5333

Mailing Address: P.O. Box 553, Princeton, NJ 08542

Insurance Defense, Trial Practice, Automobile, Professional Liability, Product Liability, Errors and Omissions, Liquor Liability, Commercial Liability, Subrogation, General

SEE COMPLETE LISTING UNDER PRINCETON, NEW JERSEY (15 MILES)

Methfessel & Werbel
2025 Lincoln Highway, Suite 200
Edison, New Jersey 08817
 Telephone: 732-248-4200
 Fax: 732-248-2355

Mailing Address: P.O. Box 3012, Edison, NJ 08818-3012

Automobile Liability, Bad Faith, Carrier Defense, Casualty Defense, Civil Trial Practice, Comprehensive General Liability, Construction Litigation, Coverage Issues, Defense Litigation, Employment Practices Liability, Environmental Coverage, Environmental Liability, Examinations Under Oath, Excess and Umbrella, Insurance Coverage, Insurance Defense, Medical Liability, Premises Liability, Primary and Excess Insurance, Product Liability, Professional Malpractice, Property Liability, Public Entities, Toxic Torts, Uninsured and Underinsured Motorist, General Subrogation, Large Loss Subrogation Program

SEE COMPLETE LISTING UNDER EDISON, NEW JERSEY (6 MILES)

Nowell Amoroso Klein Bierman, P.A.
155 Polifly Road
Hackensack, New Jersey 07601
 Telephone: 201-343-5001
 Toll Free: 800-246-0254
 Fax: 201-343-5181

Insurance Defense, Bodily Injury, Asbestos Litigation, Environmental Law, Personal Liability, Automobile, Homeowners, Toxic Torts, Product Liability, Pollution, Property Damage

SEE COMPLETE LISTING UNDER HACKENSACK, NEW JERSEY (38 MILES)

Law Offices of Michael E. Pressman
Warrenville Plaza, 31W
Mountain Boulevard
Warren, New Jersey 07059
 Telephone: 908-753-6661
 Fax: 908-755-5229; 212-480-2590
 Toll Free: 800-764-3030

Insurance Defense, Automobile, General Liability, Product Liability, Property and Casualty

SEE COMPLETE LISTING UNDER WARREN, NEW JERSEY (17 MILES)

Widman, Cooney, Wilson, McGann & Fitterer, L.L.C.
1803 Highway 35
Oakhurst, New Jersey 07755
 Telephone: 732-531-4141
 Fax: 732-531-7773

Insurance Defense, Casualty, Directors and Officers Liability, Employment Law, Automobile, Professional Negligence (Medical, Accountants and Attorneys, Insurance Agents, Realtors and Home Inspectors)

SEE COMPLETE LISTING UNDER OCEAN, NEW JERSEY (33 MILES)

NEWARK † 277,140 Essex Co.

Cottrell Solensky & Semple, P.A.
550 Broad Street
Suite 1000
Newark, New Jersey 07102-4599
 Telephone: 973-643-1400
 Fax: 973-643-1900
 E-Mail: fcottrell@css-legal.com
 www.css-legal.com

(Elmsford, NY Office: 5 West Main Street, Suite 201, 10523)
 (Tel: 914-592-1919)
 (Fax: 914-592-2987)

Established: 2003

Commercial Litigation, Environmental Law, Insurance Coverage, Insurance Defense, Negligence, Personal Injury, Product Liability, Toxic Torts, Transportation, Truck Liability, Wrongful Death

Firm Profile: The Law Office of Cottrell Solensky & Semple, P.A. provides high quality legal representation with a personal touch to each client, regardless of the legal issues they confront. Each case is as important to us as it is to the client. Every client receives the skills and personal attention of our top notch attorneys, dedicated to achieving the best results with an approach that is honest, thorough, and based on open communication.

Corporate Clients

Carlisle Carrier Corp.	J. C. Penney Company, Inc.
Kellermeyer Bergensons Services, LLC	Maersk, Inc.
Texas Roadhouse, Inc.	Starwood Hotels & Resorts Worldwide, Inc.
Wakefern Food Corporation	Wal-Mart Stores, Inc.

Insurance Clients

Canal Insurance Company	Carolina Casualty Insurance Company
Fidelity National Insurance Company	Housing Authority Risk Retention Group, Inc.
IAT Insurance Group	Maxum Specialty Insurance Group
Lancer Insurance Company	RLI Transportation
Nobel Insurance Company	
Sentry Insurance	

Third Party Administrators

Fleming & Hall, LTD	Gallagher Bassett Services, Inc.
Network Adjusters, Inc.	Sedgwick Claims Management Services, Inc.
York STB, Inc.	

Founder & Senior Managing Partner

Floyd G. Cottrell — 1958 — Fordham University, B.A., 1980; Fordham Law School, J.D., 1983 — Admitted to Bar, 1984, New York; 1985, New Jersey;

Cottrell Solensky & Semple, P.A., Newark, NJ
(Continued)

1984, U.S. District Court, Eastern and Southern Districts of New York; 1985, U.S. District Court, District of New Jersey; U.S. Court of Appeals, Second and Third Circuits; 2005, U.S. Supreme Court — Member American, New Jersey State, New York State and Essex County Bar Associations; National Retail and Restaurant Defense Association (Membership Committee 2013-); Claims & Litigation Management Alliance; Housing Authority Defense Association; Brennan-Vanderbilt Inns of Court (President, 2007-2008); Fellow, Litigation Counsel of America (LCA); New Jersey Defense Association; Trucking Industry Defense Association; Defense Research Institute — Certified Civil Trial Attorney, Supreme Court of New Jersey, Board of Trial Attorney Certification; Certified Civil Trial Specialist by the National Board of Trial Advocacy — Practice Areas: Insurance Defense; Trial and Appellate Practice; Insurance Coverage; Truck Liability; Automobile Liability; Product Liability; Premises Liability; Municipal Liability; Nursing Home Liability; Dram Shop; Wrongful Death; Retail Liability — Tel: 973-643-1400 x 13 — Fax: 973-643-1900 — E-mail: fcottrell@css-legal.com

Partners

Edward Solensky, Jr. — 1961 — Colby College, B.A. (magna cum laude), 1982; Syracuse University, J.D., 1985 — Admitted to Bar, 1985, New Jersey; U.S. District Court, District of New Jersey — Member New Jersey State and Morris County Bar Associations; American Society of Industrial Security; Claims & Litigation Management Alliance; National Retail and Restaurant Defense Association; New Jersey Defense Association; Defense Research Institute — Practice Areas: Insurance Defense; Premises Liability; Automobile Liability; Restaurant Liability; Retail Liability; Municipal Liability — Tel: 973-643-1400 x18 — E-mail: esolensky@css-legal.com

David A. Semple — University of Maryland, B.A., 1992; Seton Hall University School of Law, J.D., 1996 — Admitted to Bar, 1997, New Jersey; U.S. District Court, District of New Jersey; 2001, U.S. Court of Appeals, Third Circuit — Member New Jersey State Bar Association; Claims & Litigation Management Alliance; New Jersey Defense Association — Practice Areas: Employment Law; Litigation; Appeals; Premises Liability; Hospitality; Transportation; Personal Injury Protection (PIP); Trucking Law — Tel: 973-643-1400 x 11 — E-mail: dsemple@css-legal.com

Of Counsel

Lisa A. Perez — 1960 — College of Staten Island, City University of New York, B.A. (Dean's List), 1983; Benjamin N. Cardozo School of Law, Yeshiva University, J.D., 1986 — Admitted to Bar, 1986, New Jersey — Member Claims & Litigation Management Alliance; New Jersey Defense Association — Cranford Democratic Committee; City of Elizabeth Public Defender — Practice Areas: Insurance Defense; Municipal Liability; Municipal Litigation; Negligence; No-Fault; Subrogation; Premises Liability — Tel: 973-643-1400 x 12 — E-mail: lperez@css-legal.com

Associates

Annette J. Bertulfo — State University of New York at Binghamton, B.S., 2001; Pace University School of Law, J.D. (cum laude), 2007 — Admitted to Bar, 2007, New Jersey; 2008, New York — Member New York State Bar Association; Asian American Bar Association of New York — Practice Areas: Premises Liability; Automobile Liability; Municipal Liability; Commercial Vehicle

Amanda E. Miller — University of Connecticut at Storrs, B.A. (magna cum laude), 2008; Seton Hall University School of Law, J.D., 2011 — Law Clerk to Hon. Paul W. Armstrong, J.S.C., New Jersey Superior Court, Criminal Division (2011-2012) — Admitted to Bar, 2011, New Jersey; 2012, New York — Practice Areas: Premises Liability; Municipal Liability; Civil Rights Defense; Commercial Transportation Litigation

Podvey, Meanor, Catenacci, Hildner, Cocoziello & Chattman, P.C.

The Legal Center, 8th Floor
One Riverfront Plaza
Newark, New Jersey 07102-5497
 Telephone: 973-623-1000
 Fax: 973-623-9131
 www.podvey.com

(New York, NY Office: 570 Lexington Avenue, Suite 1600, 10022)
 (Tel: 212-432-7419)

Podvey, Meanor, Catenacci, Hildner, Cocoziello & Chattman, P.C., Newark, NJ
(Continued)

Insurance Law, Fire, Product Liability, Policy Construction and Interpretation, Appellate Practice, Insurance Fraud, Employment Practices, Casualty, Surety, Negligence, Trial Practice, Subrogation, Bad Faith

Firm Profile: Over its forty-year history, Podvey Meanor has earned a reputation for excellence and dedication to client service. The firm, with offices in Newark, New Jersey and New York City, specializes in insurance litigation and complex commercial litigation.

Insurance Clients

Affiliated FM Insurance Company
Factory Mutual Insurance Company
New Jersey Title Insurance Company
CNA
Fireman's Fund Insurance Company

Directors

Henry J. Catenacci — University of Notre Dame, J.D., 1969 — Admitted to Bar, 1969, New Jersey — New Jersey Super Lawyer (2009-present); Top Attorney in New Jersey (2011-present) — Practice Areas: Insurance Coverage; Subrogation; Complex Litigation; Commercial Litigation

Robert L. Podvey — New York University School of Law, J.D., 1964 — Admitted to Bar, 1965, New Jersey; District of Columbia — Designated New York and New Jersey Super Lawyer (2003 to present); Best Lawyers in America (2000-present) — Certified Trial Attorney (1982-present) — Practice Areas: Corporate Law; Business Law; Complex Litigation; Commercial Litigation; Insurance; Land Use; Construction Litigation; Banking

J. Barry Cocoziello — **Managing Director** — Rutgers University, J.D., 1976 — Admitted to Bar, 1976, New Jersey; 1978, Florida — Designated New York and New Jersey Super Lawyer (2004-present); Designated Leading Individual in Chambers USA America's Leading Lawyers for Business — Certified Trial Attorney, 1985 — Practice Areas: Complex Litigation; Commercial Litigation; Professional Liability; Insurance Fraud; Construction Litigation; Insurance Coverage; Subrogation; Personal Injury; Estate Litigation; Real Estate; Real Estate Litigation

H. Richard Chattman — Rutgers University, J.D. (with honors), 1975 — Admitted to Bar, 1977, New York; New Jersey — Practice Areas: Insurance Coverage; Subrogation

Marianne Tolomeo — Cornell University, J.D., 1986 — Admitted to Bar, 1987, New Jersey — Practice Areas: Complex Litigation; Commercial Litigation; Employment Law; Insurance Coverage; Subrogation

Gregory Miller — **Managing Director** — The University of Tulsa, J.D., 1995 — Admitted to Bar, 1995, Oklahoma; 1998, New Jersey; 2000, New York; District of Columbia — Designated as a New Jersey Super Lawyers Rising Star (2006-2009) — Practice Areas: Insurance Coverage; Subrogation; Complex Litigation; Commercial Litigation; Intellectual Property

Firm Members

Thomas V. Hildner — University of Virginia, LL.B., 1968 — Admitted to Bar, 1968, Virginia; 1969, New Jersey — Practice Areas: Alternative Dispute Resolution; Mediation; Family Law; Personal Injury; Complex Litigation; Commercial Litigation; Insurance Coverage; Subrogation; Product Liability; Professional Liability

Robert K. Scheinbaum — University of Pennsylvania Law School, J.D., 1994 — Admitted to Bar, 1994, New Jersey; 1996, New York; District of Columbia — Practice Areas: Complex Litigation; Commercial Litigation; Insurance Coverage; Subrogation; Bankruptcy; Creditor Rights

Lino Sciarretta — Pace University School of Law, J.D., 1997 — Admitted to Bar, 1997, New Jersey; New York — Practice Areas: Complex Litigation; Commercial Litigation; Insurance Coverage; Subrogation; Land Use; Insurance Fraud

Associates

Aaron Gould
Sarah C. Mitchell
Lainie Miller
Peter J. Mitchell

(This firm is also listed in the Subrogation section of this directory)

NEW JERSEY

NEWTON

The following firms also service this area.

Philip M. Lustbader & David Lustbader, P.A.
615 West Mt. Pleasant Avenue
Livingston, New Jersey 07039
 Telephone: 973-740-1000
 Fax: 973-740-1520

Insurance Defense, Civil Trial Practice, Negligence, No-Fault, Uninsured and Underinsured Motorist, Product Liability, Workers' Compensation, Dental Malpractice, Medical Malpractice, Coverage Issues, Appellate Practice, Subrogation, Monitoring Litigation

SEE COMPLETE LISTING UNDER LIVINGSTON, NEW JERSEY (11 MILES)

Nowell Amoroso Klein Bierman, P.A.
155 Polifly Road
Hackensack, New Jersey 07601
 Telephone: 201-343-5001
 Toll Free: 800-246-0254
 Fax: 201-343-5181

Insurance Defense, Bodily Injury, Asbestos Litigation, Environmental Law, Personal Liability, Automobile, Homeowners, Toxic Torts, Product Liability, Pollution, Property Damage

SEE COMPLETE LISTING UNDER HACKENSACK, NEW JERSEY (20 MILES)

William J. Pollinger, P.A.
Claridge Plaza
302 Union Street
Hackensack, New Jersey 07601
 Telephone: 201-487-5666
 Fax: 201-487-6335

Insurance Defense, Product Liability, Automobile Liability, Negligence, Toxic Torts, Subrogation, Policy Construction and Interpretation, Insurance Coverage, Personal Injury

SEE COMPLETE LISTING UNDER HACKENSACK, NEW JERSEY (20 MILES)

Law Offices of Michael E. Pressman
Warrenville Plaza, 31W
Mountain Boulevard
Warren, New Jersey 07059
 Telephone: 908-753-6661
 Fax: 908-755-5229; 212-480-2590
 Toll Free: 800-764-3030

Insurance Defense, Automobile, General Liability, Product Liability, Property and Casualty

SEE COMPLETE LISTING UNDER WARREN, NEW JERSEY (23 MILES)

NEWTON † 7,997 Sussex Co.

Refer To

Nowell Amoroso Klein Bierman, P.A.
155 Polifly Road
Hackensack, New Jersey 07601
 Telephone: 201-343-5001
 Toll Free: 800-246-0254
 Fax: 201-343-5181

Insurance Defense, Bodily Injury, Asbestos Litigation, Environmental Law, Personal Liability, Automobile, Homeowners, Toxic Torts, Product Liability, Pollution, Property Damage

SEE COMPLETE LISTING UNDER HACKENSACK, NEW JERSEY (52 MILES)

OCEAN 23,570 Monmouth Co.

Widman, Cooney, Wilson, McGann & Fitterer, L.L.C.
1803 Highway 35
Oakhurst, New Jersey 07755
 Telephone: 732-531-4141
 Fax: 732-531-7773
 E-Mail: generalmail@widmancooney.com
 www.widmancooney.com

Widman, Cooney, Wilson, McGann & Fitterer, L.L.C., Ocean, NJ *(Continued)*

Established: 1982

Insurance Defense, Casualty, Directors and Officers Liability, Employment Law, Automobile, Professional Negligence (Medical, Accountants and Attorneys, Insurance Agents, Realtors and Home Inspectors)

Insurance Clients

American Insurance Group
Fortress Insurance Company
Hanover Insurance Group
Kemper Insurance Company
Markel American Insurance Company
Oceanus Insurance Company
Princeton Insurance Company
Travelers Insurance Companies
United States Liability Insurance Group
CNA Insurance Company
Great American Insurance Group
Health Care Insurance Company
Lloyd's
Monmouth County Municipal Joint Insurance Fund
OMS National Insurance Company
TIG Specialty Insurance Company
United America Indemnity Group

Self-Insured Clients

JFK Health System
Robert Wood Johnson Health Network
Meridian Health System
Saint Peter's Healthcare System
St. Barnabas Healthcare System

Third Party Administrators

Cambridge Integrated Services
Certus Claims Administration, LLC
ProClaim America Incorporated
Sedgwick Claims Management Services, Inc.
Campania Management Company, Inc.
Gallagher Bassett Services, Inc.
Qual-Lynx

Firm Members

Douglas J. Widman — 1949 — Syracuse University, B.A. (cum laude), 1971; J.D., 1973 — Admitted to Bar, 1973, New Jersey; 1990, New York; 1973, U.S. District Court, District of New Jersey — Former Deputy Attorney General of New Jersey; Former Law Clerk to Superior Court; Arbitrator/Mediator — Practice Areas: Employment Law; General Liability; Professional Liability — E-mail: dwidman@widmancooney.com

Joseph K. Cooney — 1950 — University of Notre Dame, A.B. (magna cum laude), 1972; J.D., 1975 — Former Law Clerk to Superior Court Judge Thomas S. O'Brien, A.J.S.C. — Admitted to Bar, 1975, New Jersey — Member Diplomate, American Board of Trial Advocates; New Jersey Defense Association — Certified Civil Trial Attorney by the Supreme Court of New Jersey — Practice Areas: General Liability; Professional Liability — E-mail: jcooney@widmancooney.com

William E. Wilson — 1944 — Tulane University, B.A., 1966; Wake Forest University, J.D., 1969 — Admitted to Bar, 1969, New Jersey; 1969, U.S. Supreme Court — Practice Areas: Commercial General Liability — E-mail: wwilson@widmancooney.com

Michael E. McGann — 1961 — Fairfield University, B.S.B.M., 1983; Seton Hall University School of Law, J.D., 1986 — Admitted to Bar, 1986, New Jersey; U.S. District Court, District of New Jersey — Member Monmouth County Bar Association — Certified Civil Trial Attorney — Practice Areas: Professional Negligence — E-mail: mmcgann@widmancooney.com

Edmund F. Fitterer — Monmouth University, B.A., 1998; Seton Hall University School of Law, J.D., 2001 — Law Clerk to Superior Court Judge James N. Citta, J.S.C. Ocean County, New Jersey — Admitted to Bar, 2001, New Jersey; 2004, New York — Practice Areas: General Liability; Commercial Liability — E-mail: efitterer@widmancooney.com

Associates

Eileen W. McGann
Michael J. Kontos
Catherine M. Carton

PATERSON   NEW JERSEY

PARAMUS 26,342 Bergen Co.

Malapero Prisco Klauber & Licata LLP

61 South Paramus Road, Suite 280
Paramus, New Jersey 07652
   Telephone: 201-820-3488
   Fax: 201-820-3491
   http://www.malaperoprisco.com/nj

(Malapero & Prisco LLP*: 295 Madison Avenue, New York, NY, 10017)
   (Tel: 212-661-7300)
   (Fax: 212-661-7640)
   (E-Mail: defense@malaperoprisco.com)
   (www.malaperoprisco.com)

Insurance Defense, Insurance Coverage, Professional Liability, Subrogation, General Liability, Personal Injury, Construction Law, Labor and Employment, Insurance Law, Premises Liability, Motor Vehicle, Workers' Compensation, Property Damage, Product Liability, Appellate Practice, Alternative Dispute Resolution

Firm Profile: Malapero, Prisco, Klauber & Licata LLP provides litigation and related services to the insurance industry, third-party administrators, municipalities and self-insured entities. We strive to exceed our clients' expectations in every aspect of our representation by providing highly personalized legal services in partnership with our clients.

Insurance Clients

GAB Robins North America, Inc.
The Harleysville Insurance
St. Paul Travelers
Gallagher Bassett Services, Inc.
Liberty Mutual Insurance Company

Non-Insurance Clients

Turner Construction Company

Managing Partner

Thomas M. Licata — Pace University, B.A. (cum laude), 1984; Seton Hall University, J.D., 1987 — Outstanding Clinical Practitioner Award, 1987 — Admitted to Bar, 1987, New York; New Jersey; U.S. District Court, Eastern and Southern Districts of New York; U.S. District Court, District of New Jersey — Member Bergen County Bar Association — E-mail: tlicata@malaperoprisco.com

Partners

Raymond J. Malapero — 1955 — Fordham University, B.A. (cum laude), 1977; Fordham Law School, J.D., 1980 — Admitted to Bar, 1981, New York; New Jersey; U.S. District Court, Eastern and Southern Districts of New York — Member American, New York State, New Jersey State and Brooklyn Bar Associations; New York State Trial Lawyers Association — E-mail: rmalapero@malaperoprisco.com

Joseph J. Prisco, Jr. — 1959 — Fordham University, B.A., 1981; Pace University, J.D., 1984 — Admitted to Bar, 1985, New York; 1986, New Jersey; U.S. District Court, Eastern and Southern Districts of New York — Member New York State Bar Association; New York State Trial Lawyers Association — E-mail: jprisco@malaperoprisco.com

Andrew L. Klauber — 1957 — Franklin & Marshall College, B.A., 1979; Boston University School of Law, J.D., 1982 — Admitted to Bar, 1983, New York; New Jersey; U.S. District Court, District of New Jersey; U.S. District Court, Eastern and Southern Districts of New York — Member American Bar Association; Defense Association of New York (DANY); New York State Trial Lawyers Association — E-mail: aklauber@malaperoprisco.com

Associates

David T. Kuk — Rutgers University, B.A., 2001; Brooklyn Law School, J.D., 2005 — Admitted to Bar, 2006, New York; New Jersey; U.S. District Court, District of New Jersey — E-mail: defense@malaperoprisco.com

Grace E. Robol — College of New Jersey, B.A., 2006; California Western University, J.D., 2009 — Admitted to Bar, 2009, New Jersey — E-mail: defense@malaperoprisco.com

Evi Kallfa — Fordham University, B.A., 2009; Seton Hall University, J.D., 2012 — Admitted to Bar, 2013, New York; New Jersey — E-mail: defense@malaperoprisco.com

(See listing under New York, NY for additional information)

PASSAIC 69,781 Passaic Co.

Refer To
Buglione, Hutton & DeYoe, L.L.C.
401 Hamburg Turnpike, Suite 206
Wayne, New Jersey 07470
   Telephone: 973-595-6300
   Fax: 973-595-0146

Appellate Practice, Arbitration, Mediation and ADR, Construction Law, Environmental Law, Insurance Defense, Insurance and Re-Insurance, Labor and Employment Law, Litigation, Product Liability and Complex Tort Litigation, Sexual Abuse Defense, Subrogation and Recovery, Workers' Compensation

SEE COMPLETE LISTING UNDER WAYNE, NEW JERSEY (12 MILES)

PATERSON † 146,199 Passaic Co.

Refer To
Buglione, Hutton & DeYoe, L.L.C.
401 Hamburg Turnpike, Suite 206
Wayne, New Jersey 07470
   Telephone: 973-595-6300
   Fax: 973-595-0146

Appellate Practice, Arbitration, Mediation and ADR, Construction Law, Environmental Law, Insurance Defense, Insurance and Re-Insurance, Labor and Employment Law, Litigation, Product Liability and Complex Tort Litigation, Sexual Abuse Defense, Subrogation and Recovery, Workers' Compensation

SEE COMPLETE LISTING UNDER WAYNE, NEW JERSEY (8 MILES)

Refer To
Methfessel & Werbel
2025 Lincoln Highway, Suite 200
Edison, New Jersey 08817
   Telephone: 732-248-4200
   Fax: 732-248-2355

Mailing Address: P.O. Box 3012, Edison, NJ 08818-3012

Automobile Liability, Bad Faith, Carrier Defense, Casualty Defense, Civil Trial Practice, Comprehensive General Liability, Construction Litigation, Coverage Issues, Defense Litigation, Employment Practices Liability, Environmental Coverage, Environmental Liability, Examinations Under Oath, Excess and Umbrella, Insurance Coverage, Insurance Defense, Medical Liability, Premises Liability, Primary and Excess Insurance, Product Liability, Professional Malpractice, Property Liability, Public Entities, Toxic Torts, Uninsured and Underinsured Motorist, General Subrogation, Large Loss Subrogation Program

SEE COMPLETE LISTING UNDER EDISON, NEW JERSEY (32 MILES)

Refer To
Nowell Amoroso Klein Bierman, P.A.
155 Polifly Road
Hackensack, New Jersey 07601
   Telephone: 201-343-5001
   Toll Free: 800-246-0254
   Fax: 201-343-5181

Insurance Defense, Bodily Injury, Asbestos Litigation, Environmental Law, Personal Liability, Automobile, Homeowners, Toxic Torts, Product Liability, Pollution, Property Damage

SEE COMPLETE LISTING UNDER HACKENSACK, NEW JERSEY (10 MILES)

Refer To
William J. Pollinger, P.A.
Claridge Plaza
302 Union Street
Hackensack, New Jersey 07601
   Telephone: 201-487-5666
   Fax: 201-487-6335

Insurance Defense, Product Liability, Automobile Liability, Negligence, Toxic Torts, Subrogation, Policy Construction and Interpretation, Insurance Coverage, Personal Injury

SEE COMPLETE LISTING UNDER HACKENSACK, NEW JERSEY (10 MILES)

NEW JERSEY **PRINCETON**

PRINCETON 12,307 Mercer Co.

Law Offices of Glenn R. Cochran

812 State Road, Suite 120
Princeton, New Jersey 08540
   Telephone: 609-924-4011
   Fax: 609-924-5333

Established: 1984

Insurance Defense, Trial Practice, Automobile, Professional Liability, Product Liability, Errors and Omissions, Liquor Liability, Commercial Liability, Subrogation, General

Insurance Clients

Occidental Fire & Casualty   Penn Mutual Insurance Company
  Company of North Carolina

Non-Insurance Clients

Crawford & Company   IRISC, Inc.
Toll Brothers, Inc.

Glenn R. Cochran — 1955 — Drew University, A.B. (cum laude), 1977; Rutgers University, J.D., 1980 — Admitted to Bar, 1980, New Jersey; 1988, Pennsylvania; 1980, U.S. District Court, District of New Jersey; 1991, U.S. District Court, Eastern District of Pennsylvania — Member American, New Jersey State, Mercer County and Princeton Bar Associations; Defense Research Institute; New Jersey Defense Association

(This firm is also listed in the Subrogation section of this directory)

Fitzpatrick & Hunt, Tucker, Collier, Pagano, Aubert, LLP

Forrestal Village
116 Village Boulevard, Suite 200
Princeton, New Jersey 08540
   Telephone: 609-606-6940
   Fax: 609-606-6941
   www.fitzhunt.com

Alternative Dispute Resolution, Appellate Practice, Arbitration, Aviation, Class Actions, First and Third Party Defense, Insurance Litigation, International Law, Mediation, Product Liability, Reinsurance, Toxic Torts, Mass Disasters

Firm Profile: Fitzpatrick & Hunt specializes in products liability defense and claims prevention. Among the experienced product and services defense lawyers in our Firm are those with degrees and backgrounds in engineering and other technical fields. We provide advisory consultation to worldwide insurance markets and product manufacturers.

Equity Partner

Ralph V. Pagano — Stevens Institute of Technology, B.E., 1984; M.E., 1988; Fordham University School of Law, J.D., 1993; Temple University, LL.M., 1997 — Admitted to Bar, 1993, New York; New Jersey; Pennsylvania — Tel: 212-937-4004 — E-mail: ralph.pagano@fitzhunt.com

Partners

Tara E. Nicola — University of Connecticut, B.A., 2000; Seton Hall University School of Law, J.D. (cum laude), 2003 — Order of the Coif — Admitted to Bar, 2003, New Jersey; 2005, New York — Tel: 212-937-4026 — E-mail: tara.nicola@fitzhunt.com

Jason L. Vincent — University of Connecticut, B.A., 1993; Seton Hall University School of Law, J.D., 1996 — Admitted to Bar, 1996, New Jersey; 1997, New York; 1998, Connecticut — Tel: 212-937-4073 — E-mail: jason.vincent@fitzhunt.com

Fitzpatrick & Hunt, Tucker, Collier, Pagano, Aubert, LLP,
Princeton, NJ   **(Continued)**

Associate

Paul N. Bowles III

(See listing under New York, NY for additional information)

RED BANK 12,206 Monmouth Co.

Gold, Albanese & Barletti

58 Maple Avenue
Red Bank, New Jersey 07701
   Telephone: 732-936-9901
   Fax: 732-936-9904
   www.goldandalbanese.com

(Morristown, NJ Office*: 48 South Street, 07960-4136)
  (Tel: 973-326-9099)
  (Fax: 973-326-9841)
  (E-Mail: main@goldandalbanese.com)
(Boston, MA Office*: 50 Congress Street, Suite 225, 02109)
  (Tel: 617-723-5118)
  (Fax: 617-367-8840)
(Massapequa, NY Office: 544 Broadway, Suite 200, 11758)
  (Tel: 516-541-0021)
  (Fax: 516-541-1964)

Automobile, Civil Rights, Comprehensive General Liability, Construction Litigation, Employment Discrimination, Environmental Law, Insurance Coverage, Intellectual Property, Medical Malpractice, Personal Injury, Pharmaceutical, Premises Liability, Product Liability, Professional Liability, Property Damage, Wrongful Death, Occupational Exposure, Insurance Fraud Investigation and Litigation, Commercial Trucking Litigation, Public Entity Tort Litigation

(See listing under Morristown, NJ for additional information)

Traub Lieberman Straus & Shrewsberry LLP

322 Highway 35
Red Bank, New Jersey 07701
   Telephone: 732-985-1000
   Fax: 732-985-2000
   www.traublieberman.com

(Hawthorne, NY Office*: Mid-Westchester Executive Park, Seven Skyline Drive, 10532)
  (Tel: 914-347-2600)
  (Fax: 914-347-8898)
  (E-Mail: swolfe@traublieberman.com)
(St. Petersburg, FL Office*: 360 Central Avenue, 33701)
  (Tel: 727-898-8100)
  (Fax: 727-895-4838)
(Chicago, IL Office*: 303 West Madison, Suite 1200, 60606)
  (Tel: 312-332-3900)
  (Fax: 312-332-3908)
(Los Angeles, CA Office*: 626 Wilshire Boulevard, Suite 800, 90017)
  (Tel: 213-624-4500)
(London, United Kingdom Office*: Gallery 4, 12 Leadenhall Street, EC3V1LP)
  (Tel: +44 (0) 020 7816 5856)
(New York, NY Office*: 100 Park Avenue, 16th Floor, 10017)
  (Tel: 646-227-1700)

Established: 1996

ROSELAND   NEW JERSEY

Traub Lieberman Straus & Shrewsberry LLP, Red Bank, NJ (Continued)

Appellate Practice, Bad Faith, Extra-Contractual Litigation, Civil Rights, Complex Litigation, Construction Law, Coverage Issues, Environmental Law, General Liability, Insurance Coverage, Labor and Employment, Premises Liability, Product Liability, Professional Liability, Technology, Toxic Torts, Trucking Law, Transportation, Medical Malpractice

Founding Partner

Richard K. Traub — University of Miami, B.A., 1972; University of Miami School of Law, J.D. (cum laude), 1975 — Admitted to Bar, 1975, Florida; 1976, New Jersey; New York; U.S. District Court, District of New Jersey; 1979, U.S. Supreme Court; 1981, U.S. District Court, Eastern and Southern Districts of New York — Member Federation of Defense and Corporate Counsel (Vice-President and Member of Board of Directors; Past Chair, Technology Committee); USLAW Network (Vice Chair, Professional Liability Practice Group) — Dean of Curriculum, Litigation Management College — E-mail: rtraub@traublieberman.com

Partners

Aileen F. Droughton — Rutgers University, B.S., 1993; Fordham University School of Law, J.D., 1997 — Admitted to Bar, 1998, New Jersey; New York; U.S. District Court, District of New Jersey; U.S. District Court, Eastern and Southern Districts of New York — E-mail: adroughton@traublieberman.com

Stuart A. Panensky — Ithaca College, B.S., 2000; Syracuse University College of Law, J.D., 2003 — Admitted to Bar, 2003, New York; New Jersey; U.S. District Court, District of New Jersey — E-mail: spanensky@traublieberman.com

Senior Counsel

Richard J. Bortnick — Boston University, B.S. (summa cum laude), 1981; Villanova University School of Law, J.D. (cum laude), 1985 — Admitted to Bar, 1985, Pennsylvania; New York; New Jersey — E-mail: rbortnick@traublieberman.com

Associates

Claudia D. Condruz
Marta N. Kozlowska
Laura M. Faustino
Matthew Toto

(See listing under Hawthorne, NY for additional information)

ROSELAND 5,819 Essex Co.

Callahan & Fusco, LLC

103 Eishenhower Parkway, Suite 400
Roseland, New Jersey 07068
   Telephone: 973-618-9770
   Fax: 973-618-9772
   E-Mail: cfusco@callahanfusco.com
   www.callahanfusco.com

(New York, NY Office*: 40 Exchange Place, 18th Floor, 10005)
   (Tel: 212-448-9570)
   (Fax: 212-448-9772)
(Doylestown, PA Office: 196 West Ashland Street, 18901)
   (Tel: 267-895-1767)
   (Fax: 267-895-1768)

Insurance Defense, Casualty, Civil Litigation, Commercial Law, Construction Law, Contracts, Inland Marine, Insurance Law, Labor and Employment, Motor Carriers, Municipal Law, Personal Injury, Premises Liability, Product Liability, Public Entities, Reinsurance, Risk Management, School Law, Toxic Torts, Transportation, Workers' Compensation, Cargo Loss Defense

Firm Profile: Our Firm is built on our commitment to positive outcomes, strong negotiations and the proper advice at a reasonable cost.

Callahan & Fusco, LLC, Roseland, NJ (Continued)

The firm's transportation clients include motor, express carriers, carrier and transportation brokers. The firm's insurance clients include underwriters and adjusters of professional liability, inland marine, insureds assigned by Third-Party Administrators, motor vehicle, motor cargo, warehouse, casualty, construction, products liability, premises, general liability and reinsurance risks. The firm also represents construction companies as well as manufacturers and distributors of chemicals, metals, optical equipment, apparel and food products. In addition, the firm represents interests of public entities in all forms of litigation including labor issues, Civil Service issues, disciplinary hearings and Constitutional Law claims.

Insurance Clients

Acceptance Insurance Company
Berkley Risk & Praetorian Insurance Company
Montpelier US Insurance Company
QBE the Americas Group
Vela Insurance Services, Inc./Gemini Insurance Company

Admiral Insurance Company
Continental Western Group
LIG Insurance
North Pointe Insurance Company
Stonington Insurance Company
XL Insurance
Zurich American Insurance Company

Non-Insurance Clients

Aquacade Pool Building, Inc.
Criterion Claim Solutions
FedEx Corporation
FedEx Home Delivery
Insurance Services Network
Putnam County
Solera Construction, Inc./DCM Erectors, Inc.

Bravante Automatic Sprinkler Corporation
FedEx Ground
Forward Air, Inc.
Lorvin Steel Ltd.
Selco Manufacturing Corp.
Village of Mamaroneck

Partners

Beth A. Callahan — 1967 — The Catholic University of America, B.A., 1989; Seton Hall University, J.D., 1992 — Admitted to Bar, 1992, New Jersey; U.S. District Court, District of New Jersey — Member American, New Jersey State and Essex County (Chairperson, Rights of Persona with Disabilities Committee, 1992-1997) Bar Associations — E-mail: bcallahan@callahanfusco.com

Christopher G. Fusco — 1967 — The Catholic University of America, B.A., 1989; J.D., 1992 — Admitted to Bar, 1992, New York; New Jersey; Pennsylvania; U.S. District Court, Eastern, Northern and Southern Districts of New York; U.S. District Court, District of New Jersey; U.S. District Court, Eastern and Middle Districts of Pennsylvania — Member New York State Bar Association; The Association of the Bar of the City of New York (Construction Law Committee, 2000); Conference of Freight Counsel; Council of Litigation Management (CLM); Defense Research Institute — Legal Analyst for the MLB Network — Languages: Italian — Practice Areas: Transportation; General Liability; Employment Law; Civil Litigation; Construction Law; Product Liability; Insurance Coverage; Civil Rights; Civil Rights Defense — E-mail: cfusco@callahanfusco.com

Charles J. Reiter — 1966 — Emory University, B.A., 1988; J.D., 1991 — Admitted to Bar, 1992, New York; U.S. District Court, Eastern and Southern Districts of New York — Practice Areas: Toxic Torts; Transportation; Civil Litigation; Property Damage; Premises Liability; General Liability — E-mail: creiter@callahanfusco.com

Of Counsel

Catherine McGlone — 1967 — Seton Hall University, B.A. (magna cum laude), 1989; J.D., 1992 — Admitted to Bar, 1992, New Jersey; U.S. District Court, District of New Jersey; 2005, U.S. District Court, Eastern and Southern Districts of New York — Practice Areas: Insurance Defense; Premises Liability; Labor and Employment; Workers' Compensation; Contract Disputes; Mediation — E-mail: cmcglone@callahanfusco.com

Associates

William A. Sicheri — 1974 — Washington University, B.A., 1996; The George Washington University Law School, J.D., 2003 — Admitted to Bar, 2003, New Jersey; 2004, New York; 2003, U.S. District Court, District of New Jersey; 2004, U.S. District Court, Eastern and Southern Districts of New York — Member American, New Jersey State and New York State Bar Associations — Practice Areas: Personal Injury; Premises Liability; Municipal Law; Commercial Law; Commercial Vehicle; Contracts — E-mail: wsicheri@callahanfusco.com

Mitchell R. Ayes — 1981 — University of Maryland, College Park, B.S., 2003; Widener University School of Law, J.D., 2006 — Admitted to Bar, 2006,

Callahan & Fusco, LLC, Roseland, NJ (Continued)

New Jersey; 2007, New York; 2006, U.S. District Court, District of New Jersey; 2008, U.S. District Court, Eastern and Southern Districts of New York; 2013, U.S. District Court, Eastern District of Pennsylvania; Supreme Court of Pennsylvania — Practice Areas: Insurance Defense; Personal Injury; Premises Liability; General Liability; Civil Rights Defense; Construction Litigation; Dram Shop; Insurance Coverage; Lien Work, Defect and Delay Claims (Prosecution and Defense); Product Liability; Public Entities — E-mail: mayes@callahanfusco.com

Brian R. Masterson — 1981 — State University of New York at Oswego, B.A., 2003; University at Buffalo Law School, J.D., 2007 — Admitted to Bar, 2007, New Jersey; 2008, New York — Practice Areas: Civil Rights; Insurance Coverage; Insurance Defense; Personal Injury; Construction Law; Civil Litigation — E-mail: bmasterson@callahanfusco.com

Justin D. Berardo — 1980 — Providence College, B.A. (cum laude), 2003; Brooklyn Law School, J.D., 2009 — Admitted to Bar, 2010, New York; New Jersey; New Hampshire; U.S. District Court, District of New Jersey — E-mail: jberardo@callahanfusco.com

Mark P. Bradley — 1985 — Quinnipiac University (summa cum laude), 2007; Benjamin N. Cardozo School of Law, J.D., 2010 — Admitted to Bar, 2010, New Jersey; 2011, New York — E-mail: mbradley@callahanfusco.com

Lucinda J. McLaughlin — Brown University, B.A., 2002; Seton Hall University School of Law, J.D., 2007 — Admitted to Bar, 2007, New Jersey; 2008, New York — Practice Areas: Automotive Products Liability; Civil Litigation; Dram Shop; Dram Shop Liability; Fire Loss; Insurance; Insurance Claim Analysis and Evaluation; Insurance Defense; Insurance Litigation; Liquor Liability; Litigation; Municipal Liability; Municipal Litigation; Premise Litigation; Premises Liability; Product Liability Defense; Slip and Fall; Tort Claims Defense; Wrongful Death — E-mail: lmclaughlin@callahanfusco.com

Marshall Dennehey Warner Coleman & Goggin

425 Eagle Rock Avenue, Suite 302
Roseland, New Jersey 07068
Telephone: 973-618-4100
Fax: 973-618-0685
www.marshalldennehey.com

(Philadelphia, PA Office*: 2000 Market Street, Suite 2300, 19103)
 (Tel: 215-575-2600)
 (Fax: 215-575-0856)
 (Toll Free: 800-220-3308)
 (E-Mail: marshalldennehey@mdwcg.com)
(Wilmington, DE Office*: Nemours Building, 1007 North Orange Street, Suite 600, 19801)
 (Tel: 302-552-4300)
 (Fax: 302-552-4340)
(Fort Lauderdale, FL Office*: 100 Northeast 3rd Avenue, Suite 1100, 33301)
 (Tel: 954-847-4920)
 (Fax: 954-627-6640)
(Jacksonville, FL Office*: 200 West Forsyth Street, Suite 1400, 32202)
 (Tel: 904-358-4200)
 (Fax: 904-355-0019)
(Orlando, FL Office*: Landmark Center One, 315 East Robinson Street, Suite 550, 32801-1948)
 (Tel: 407-420-4380)
 (Fax: 407-839-3008)
(Tampa, FL Office*: 201 East Kennedy Boulevard, Suite 1100, 33602)
 (Tel: 813-898-1800)
 (Fax: 813-221-5026)
(Cherry Hill, NJ Office*: Woodland Falls Corporate Park, 200 Lake Drive East, Suite 300, 08002)
 (Tel: 856-414-6000)
 (Fax: 856-414-6077)
(New York, NY Office*: Wall Street Plaza, 88 Pine Street, 21st Floor, 10005-1801)
 (Tel: 212-376-6400)
 (Fax: 212-376-6490)

Marshall Dennehey Warner Coleman & Goggin, Roseland, NJ (Continued)

(Melville, NY Office*: 105 Maxess Road, Suite 303, 11747)
 (Tel: 631-232-6130)
 (Fax: 631-232-6184)
(Cincinnati, OH Office*: 312 Elm Street, Suite 1850, 45202)
 (Tel: 513-375-6800)
 (Fax: 513-372-6801)
(Cleveland, OH Office*: 127 Public Square, Suite 3510, 44114-1291)
 (Tel: 216-912-3800)
 (Fax: 216-344-9006)
(Allentown, PA Office*: 4905 West Tilghman Street, Suite 300, 18104)
 (Tel: 484-895-2300)
 (Fax: 484-895-2303)
(Doylestown, PA Office*: 10 North Main Street, 2nd Floor, 18901-4318)
 (Tel: 267-880-2020)
 (Fax: 215-348-5439)
(Erie, PA Office*: 717 State Street, Suite 701, 16501)
 (Tel: 814-480-7800)
 (Fax: 814-455-3603)
(Camp Hill, PA Office*(See Harrisburg listing): 100 Coporate Center Drive, Suite 201, 17011)
 (Tel: 717-651-3500)
 (Fax: 717-651-9630)
(King of Prussia, PA Office*: 620 Freedom Business Center, Suite 300, 19406)
 (Tel: 610-354-8250)
 (Fax: 610-354-8299)
(Pittsburgh, PA Office*: U.S. Steel Tower, Suite 2900, 600 Grant Street, 15219)
 (Tel: 412-803-1140)
 (Fax: 412-803-1188)
(Moosic, PA Office*(See Scranton listing): 50 Glenmaura National Boulevard, 18507)
 (Tel: 570-496-4600)
 (Fax: 570-496-0567)
(Rye Brook, NY Office*(See Westchester listing): 800 Westchester Avenue, Suite C-700, 10573)
 (Tel: 914-977-7300)
 (Fax: 914-977-7301)

Established: 1993

Amusements, Sports and Recreation Liability, Asbestos and Mass Tort Litigation, Automobile Liability, Aviation and Complex Litigation, Construction Injury Litigation, Fraud/Special Investigation, General Liability, Hospitality and Liquor Liability, Maritime Litigation, Product Liability, Property Litigation, Retail Liability, Trucking & Transportation Liability, Appellate Advocacy and Post-Trial Practice, Architectural, Engineering and Construction Defect Litigation, Class Action Litigation, Commercial Litigation, Consumer and Credit Law, Employment Law, Environmental & Toxic Tort Litigation, Insurance Coverage/Bad Faith Litigation, Life, Health and Disability Litigation, Privacy and Data Security, Professional Liability, Public Entity and Civil Rights Litigation, Real Estate E&O Liability, School Leaders' Liability, Securities and Investment Professional Liability, Technology, Media and Intellectual Property Litigation, White Collar Crime, Birth Injury Litigation, Health Care Governmental Compliance, Health Care Liability, Health Law, Long-Term Care Liability, Medical Device and Pharmaceutical Liability, Medicare Set-Aside, Workers' Compensation

Firm Profile: The Roseland, New Jersey office of Marshall Dennehey Warner Coleman & Goggin opened in February of 1993. Since that time, it has realized substantial growth in response to client demand for our professional services. Roseland is in Essex County, home to Newark, New Jersey's largest city, and is within 30 minutes of New York City. The office services the densely populated counties of the northern part of the state. The attorneys practicing in our Roseland office have easy access to all of the federal and state courts of Northern New Jersey, which counties include Bergen, Essex, Hudson, Hunterdon, Middlesex, Monmouth, Morris, Passaic, Somerset, Sussex, Union and Warren.

SHORT HILLS   NEW JERSEY

Marshall Dennehey Warner Coleman & Goggin, Roseland, NJ (Continued)

Additional informational regarding this office is available by contacting Joseph A. Manning, the managing attorney of this office, at (973) 618-4103 or jamanning@mdwcg.com

Managing Shareholders

Joseph A. Manning — Supervisor, Professional Liability Practice Group, Northern NJ — 1955 — Muhlenberg College, B.A. (cum laude), 1978; Villanova University, M.A. (magna cum laude), 1984; Villanova University School of Law, J.D., 1987 — New Jersey Super Lawyer (2006) — Admitted to Bar, 1987, Pennsylvania; 1993, New Jersey; U.S. District Court, Eastern District of Pennsylvania; U.S. District Court, District of New Jersey; U.S. Court of Appeals, Third Circuit — Member New Jersey State and Sussex County Bar Associations; National Association of College and University Attorneys; Sussex County Medical-Legal Society — Reported Cases: Kim v. Monmouth College, 320 N.J. Super. 157 — Seminars/Classes Taught: Villanova University, Adjunct Professor; Seton Hall University, Adjunct Professor; Litigation in the Medical Environment — Practice Areas: Professional Liability; Employment Law (Management Side); Construction Law; Personal Injury; Medical Malpractice — E-mail: jamanning@mdwcg.com

Matthew S. Schorr — Co-Chair Maritime Litigation Practice Group; Managing Attorney, Casualty Practice Group — 1966 — State University of New York at Albany, B.A. (cum laude, Dean's List), 1988; Fordham University School of Law, J.D., 1991 — Leonard F. Manning Scholar; New Jersey Super Lawyer (2011) — Admitted to Bar, 1991, New Jersey; 1992, New York; U.S. District Court, District of New Jersey; U.S. District Court, Eastern, Northern and Southern Districts of New York; U.S. Court of Appeals, Third Circuit — Member New Jersey State and New York State Bar Associations; The Maritime Law Association of the United States; Trial Attorneys of New Jersey; Association of Trial Lawyers of America — Seminars/Classes Taught: CLE Seminar: Settlements and Releases, June 5, 2009 — Certified Civil Trial Attorney, New Jersey Supreme Court (2005); Certified Proctor in Admiralty (1996) — Practice Areas: Premises Liability; Product Liability; Restaurant Liability; Admiralty and Maritime Law; Insurance Coverage; Subrogation; Retail Liability — E-mail: msschorr@mdwcg.com

Special Counsel

Timothy J. Jaeger

Senior Counsel

Christopher B. Block

Resident Shareholders

Dario J. Badalamenti	Gregory C. Bartley
Arthur D. Bromberg	Alicia L. Calaf
R. Scott Eichhorn	Robert T. Evers
Hillary A. Fraenkel	George P. Helfrich, Jr.
Rosalind B. Herschthal	Justin F. Johnson
Frank P. Leanza	Howard Mankoff
Patricia M. McDonagh	Bruce A. Seidman
Wendy H. Smith	Sunny Marie Sparano
Michael R. Speer	William F. Waldron, Jr.

Resident Associates

Ian J. Antonoff	Elizabeth A. Chang
Robert A. Diehl	Julie B. Dorfman
Ida M. Fuda	Ryan T. Gannon
Gabriella R. Garofalo-Johnson	Christopher J. Gonnella
Eric L. Grogan	Teagan S. Henwood
Julia A. Klubenspies	Perri Koll
Anna B. Krepps	Paul A. Lefebvre
Michael S. Levenson	John G. O'Brien
Rachel Ramsay-Lowe	Nicholas A. Rimassa
Pauline F. Tutelo	

(See listing under Philadelphia, PA for additional information)

The following firms also service this area.

Philip M. Lustbader & David Lustbader, P.A.
615 West Mt. Pleasant Avenue
Livingston, New Jersey 07039
Telephone: 973-740-1000
Fax: 973-740-1520

Insurance Defense, Civil Trial Practice, Negligence, No-Fault, Uninsured and Underinsured Motorist, Product Liability, Workers' Compensation, Dental Malpractice, Medical Malpractice, Coverage Issues, Appellate Practice, Subrogation, Monitoring Litigation

SEE COMPLETE LISTING UNDER LIVINGSTON, NEW JERSEY (2 MILES)

SALEM † 5,146 Salem Co.

Refer To

Powell, Birchmeier & Powell
1891 State Highway 50
Tuckahoe, New Jersey 08250
Telephone: 609-628-3414
Fax: 609-628-2966
Mailing Address: P.O. Box 582, Tuckahoe, NJ 08250-0582

General Civil Practice, Trial Practice, Insurance Defense, Negligence, Defense Litigation, Product Liability, Coverage Issues, Litigation, Workers' Compensation, Subrogation, Civil Rights, Governmental Liability, Medical Negligence, Wrongful Termination, General Chancery Practice, Section 1983 Litigation

SEE COMPLETE LISTING UNDER TUCKAHOE, NEW JERSEY (45 MILES)

SHORT HILLS 13,165 Essex Co.

Budd Larner, P.C.

150 John F. Kennedy Parkway
Short Hills, New Jersey 07078-2703
Telephone: 973-379-4800
Fax: 973-379-7734
E-Mail: info@buddlarner.com
www.buddlarner.com

(New York, NY Office: 260 Madison Avenue, 18th Floor, 10010)
 (Tel: 212-858-7503)
(Cherry Hill, NJ Office: Building B2, 3rd Floor, 923 Haddonfield Road, 08002)
 (Tel: 973-379-4800)
(Philadelphia, PA Office: 2 Penn Center, Suite 200, 15th & Market Streets, 19102)
 (Tel: 215-854-4051)

Established: 1934

General Practice, Insurance Law, Reinsurance

Insurance Clients

Aetna Casualty and Surety Company	AIG Domestic Claims, Inc.
American Druggists' Insurance Company	A.I. Management & Professional Liability Claim Adjusters
American Re-Insurance Company	American Home Assurance Company
Chartis Claims, Inc.	Continental Insurance Company
Employers Insurance Company of Wausau	Finnish-Marine Insurance Company, Ltd.
General Reinsurance Corporation	Hanover Insurance Company
Hartford Accident and Indemnity Company	Kemper Insurance Companies
Prudential Reinsurance Company	Protection Mutual Insurance Company
Reliance Insurance Company	Scottsdale Insurance Company
Sentry Insurance a Mutual Company	Southern Farm Bureau Casualty Insurance Company
Travelers Insurance Companies	

Non-Insurance Clients

American International Recovery, Inc.	Hyster Company
LMG Property	Johns Manville Corporation
Waste Management, Inc.	Machine Technology, Inc.

NEW JERSEY

Budd Larner, P.C., Short Hills, NJ (Continued)

Firm Members

David J. Novack — 1950 — Brown University, A.B., 1972; Seton Hall University, J.D., 1975 — Admitted to Bar, 1975, New Jersey; 1975, U.S. District Court, District of New Jersey; 2002, U.S. District Court, Southern District of New York — Member American, New Jersey State and Essex County Bar Associations; International Association of Defense Counsel — E-mail: dnovack@buddlarner.com

Joseph J. Schiavone — 1953 — College of William & Mary, B.A., 1975; University of Miami, J.D. (cum laude), 1978 — Admitted to Bar, 1978, Florida; 1980, New York; 1988, New Jersey; 1989, U.S. District Court, District of New Jersey; 1989, U.S. District Court, Eastern and Southern Districts of New York; 1989, U.S. Court of Appeals, Third, Fifth and Ninth Circuits — Member American, New Jersey State, New York State and New York County Bar Associations; Defense Research Institute — E-mail: jschiavone@buddlarner.com

Terence W. Camp — 1963 — Drew University, B.A., 1985; Dickinson School of Law, J.D., 1988 — Admitted to Bar, 1988, New Jersey; Pennsylvania — Member American, New Jersey State and Pennsylvania Bar Associations — E-mail: tcamp@buddlarner.com

Jeffrey S. Leonard — 1955 — Brandeis University, B.A., 1977; Boston University School of Law, J.D., 1980 — Admitted to Bar, 1981, New York; 1994, New Jersey — Member American Bar Association — E-mail: jleonard@buddlarner.com

Vincent J. Proto — 1965 — University of Notre Dame, B.A., 1987; Dickinson School of Law, J.D., 1990 — Admitted to Bar, 1990, New Jersey; Pennsylvania; 1997, New York — E-mail: vproto@buddlarner.com

Virginia A. Pallotto — University of Maryland, B.A., 1983; Delaware Law School of Widener University, J.D., 1986 — Admitted to Bar, 1986, New Jersey; Pennsylvania; 1986, U.S. District Court, District of New Jersey; 1987, U.S. District Court, Eastern District of Pennsylvania; 1993, U.S. Court of Appeals, Third Circuit — Member American Bar Association — E-mail: vpallotto@buddlarner.com

Mark D. Hoerrner — College of William & Mary, B.A., 1987; Boston College Law School, J.D., 1990 — Admitted to Bar, 1991, New Jersey; New York; U.S. District Court, District of New Jersey; U.S. District Court, Eastern and Southern Districts of New York — E-mail: mhoerrner@buddlarner.com

James F. Fitzsimmons
Sonya Longo
Peter J. Frazza
Mitchell Rait

Counsel

Christopher P. Anton

Associates

Philip S. Adelman
Lori Zeglarski
David I. Satine

The Peisner Girsh Group LLP

1 Short Hills Avenue
Short Hills, New Jersey 07078
Telephone: 212-964-0020
E-Mail: office@peisnerlaw.com
www.peisnerlaw.com

(New York, NY Office*: 225 Broadway, Suite 2199, 10007-3718)
(Tel: 212-964-0020)
(Fax: 212-964-0098)
(E-Mail: kpeisner@peisnerlaw.com)
(http://peisnerlawfirm.com/)

Amusements, Construction Accidents, Coverage Issues, Excess, Insurance Coverage, Insurance Defense, Intentional Torts, Liquor Liability, Malpractice, Municipal Liability, Premises Liability, Professional Negligence, Property Liability, Restaurant Liability, School Law, Slip and Fall, Tort Litigation, Trial and Appellate Practice, Wrongful Death, Negligent Security, Automobile Liability, Casualty Defense

(See listing under New York, NY for additional information)

SHREWSBURY

SHREWSBURY 3,809 Monmouth Co.

Borowsky & Borowsky, LLC

59 Avenue at the Common
Suites 101 & 102
Shrewsbury, New Jersey 07702
Telephone: 732-212-9400
Fax: 732-212-9445

(New York, NY Office: 30 Wall Street, 8th Floor, 10005-2205)
(Tel: 212-709-8369)

Appellate Practice, Construction Defect, Construction Liability, Environmental Law, Insurance Coverage, Policy Construction and Interpretation, Liability Defense, Insurance Liability

Insurance Clients

Liberty Mutual Group
Travelers Insurance Companies

Members

Frank E. Borowsky, Jr. — 1964 — Seton Hall University, B.A. (cum laude), 1986; Villanova University, J.D., 1989 — Admitted to Bar, 1989, New Jersey; Pennsylvania; 1989, U.S. District Court, District of New Jersey; 1990, U.S. Court of Appeals, Third Circuit; 2002, U.S. District Court, Southern District of New York — Member Defense Research Institute — Practice Areas: Insurance Coverage Litigation; Insurance Coverage Determination; Civil Litigation

Paula A. Borowsky — 1966 — Monmouth College, B.A. (summa cum laude), 1988; Seton Hall University, J.D., 1991 — Admitted to Bar, 1991, Pennsylvania; 1992, New Jersey; U.S. District Court, District of New Jersey — Languages: Italian

Associates

Keith C. Northridge — 1956 — Seton Hall University, B.A., 1978; M.A., 1981; Seton Hall University School of Law, J.D., 1996 — Admitted to Bar, 1996, New Jersey; 1997, New York; 2000, Massachusetts — Practice Areas: Civil Litigation; Insurance Defense

Michael A. Field — 1975 — Trenton State College, B.A. (magna cum laude), 1997; Rutgers University School of Law-Newark, J.D., 2001 — Admitted to Bar, 2002, New Jersey; 2004, New York — Practice Areas: Insurance Litigation; Civil Litigation; Insurance Defense

Erin M. McDevitt-Frantz — 1981 — Lake Forest College, B.A. (cum laude), 2003; Villanova University School of Law, J.D., 2006 — Admitted to Bar, 2007, Pennsylvania; New Jersey — Member American Bar Association — Practice Areas: Civil Litigation; Insurance Defense; Insurance Litigation

Stuart M. Berger — 1980 — University of Pennsylvania, B.A., 2002; Seton Hall University School of Law, J.D., 2005 — Admitted to Bar, 2006, New York; New Jersey; U.S. District Court, District of New Jersey; 2008, U.S. Court of Appeals, Third Circuit — Member New Jersey State, Mercer County and Ocean County Bar Associations — Practice Areas: Civil Litigation; Insurance Defense

Stephanie M. Hehman — University of Delaware, B.A. (with honors), 2006; Villanova Law School, J.D., 2010 — Admitted to Bar, 2010, New Jersey; Pennsylvania — Practice Areas: Civil Litigation; Insurance Coverage Litigation

SOMERVILLE † 12,098 Somerset Co.

Smith Mazure Director Wilkins Young & Yagerman, P.C.

92 East Main Street
Somerville, New Jersey 08876
Telephone: 908-393-7300
Fax: 908-231-1030
www.smithmazure.com

Smith Mazure Director Wilkins Young & Yagerman, P.C., Somerville, NJ (Continued)

(New York, NY Office*: 111 John Street, 10038)
  (Tel: 212-964-7400)
  (Fax: 212-374-1935)
  (E-Mail: contactus@smithmazure.com)
(Mineola, NY Office*: 200 Old Country Road, Suite 435, 11501)
  (Tel: 516-414-7400)
  (Fax: 516-294-7325)

Automobile, Transportation, Insurance Defense, Construction Law, Labor and Employment, Toxic Torts, Landowners Liability, Manufacturing, Hotels and Restaurants, Municipal Government, Land and Building Owners

(See listing under New York, NY for additional information)

(This firm is also listed in the Subrogation section of this directory)

The following firms also service this area.

Methfessel & Werbel
2025 Lincoln Highway, Suite 200
Edison, New Jersey 08817
  Telephone: 732-248-4200
  Fax: 732-248-2355

Mailing Address: P.O. Box 3012, Edison, NJ 08818-3012

Automobile Liability, Bad Faith, Carrier Defense, Casualty Defense, Civil Trial Practice, Comprehensive General Liability, Construction Litigation, Coverage Issues, Defense Litigation, Employment Practices Liability, Environmental Coverage, Environmental Liability, Examinations Under Oath, Excess and Umbrella, Insurance Coverage, Insurance Defense, Medical Liability, Premises Liability, Primary and Excess Insurance, Product Liability, Professional Malpractice, Property Liability, Public Entities, Toxic Torts, Uninsured and Underinsured Motorist, General Subrogation, Large Loss Subrogation Program

  SEE COMPLETE LISTING UNDER EDISON, NEW JERSEY (14 MILES)

Nowell Amoroso Klein Bierman, P.A.
155 Polifly Road
Hackensack, New Jersey 07601
  Telephone: 201-343-5001
  Toll Free: 800-246-0254
  Fax: 201-343-5181

Insurance Defense, Bodily Injury, Asbestos Litigation, Environmental Law, Personal Liability, Automobile, Homeowners, Toxic Torts, Product Liability, Pollution, Property Damage

  SEE COMPLETE LISTING UNDER HACKENSACK, NEW JERSEY (46 MILES)

SPARTA 8,930 Sussex Co.

Law Offices of John C. Lane
48 Woodport Road
Sparta, New Jersey 07871
  Telephone: 973-512-3244
  Fax: 973-512-3245
  E-Mail: law@jclane.com

(New York, NY Office*: PMB 46013, 140 Broadway, 46th Floor, 10005)
  (Tel: 212-363-8048)
  (Fax: 201-848-6808)

Law Offices of John C. Lane, Sparta, NJ (Continued)

Established: 1997

Insurance Defense, Automobile, Construction Law, Admiralty and Maritime Law, Environmental Law, Trucking Law, Transportation, Insurance Coverage, Commercial Law, General Liability, Professional Liability, Physical Damage, Cargo, Bodily Injury, Property Damage

Insurance Clients

Baldwin & Lyons Group
Canal Insurance Company
Cherokee Insurance Company
Criterion Claim Solutions
Daily Underwriters of America
Lexington Insurance Company
Maxum Specialty Insurance Group
National American Insurance Company
Protective Insurance Company
Sedgwick CMS
Water Quality Insurance Syndicate (WQIS)
XL Design Professional
Burlington Insurance Company
Captive Resources, LLC
Continental National Indemnity Company
Empire Fire and Marine Insurance Company
Motor Transport Underwriters, Inc.
Philadelphia Insurance Companies
Progressive Insurance Company
Seaboard Underwriters, Inc.
Through Transport Mutual Insurance Association
W.E. Love & Associates, Inc.
Zurich North America

Non-Insurance Clients

A.D. Transport Express, Inc.
Berger Transfer & Storage, Inc.
Captive-Aire Systems, Inc.
Con-way Transportation Services, Inc.
Dean Foods
Evergreen America Corporation
FedEx National LTL
Hamburg Sud North America, Inc.
Heartland Express, Inc.
Keen Transport, Inc.
Korea Express U.S.A., Inc.
Maersk Container Service Company, Inc.
MV Transportation, Inc.
National Carriers, Inc.
RoadLink USA, Inc.
Ruan Transportation Management Systems
Transact Corp.
Tyson Foods, Inc.
Wellington Financial Services, Inc.
Atlantic Container Line
BNSF Railway Company
Con-way Freight, Inc.
Con-Way Truckload, Inc.
Daily Express, Inc.
Emery Air Freight
Federal Express
Flexi-Van Leasing, Inc.
Hanjin Shipping Company, Ltd.
Interpool, Inc.
"K" Line America, Inc.
Kozy Heat Fireplaces
Maersk, Inc.
Mediterranean Shipping Company (USA)
RLI Transportation
Roadway Express, Inc.
Schneider National, Inc.
Trac Lease, Inc.
Triple Crown Services Company
USF Holland, Inc.
YRC Worldwide, Inc.

Partners

John C. Lane — 1946 — Virginia Military Institute, B.S. (with honors), 1968; Washington and Lee University, J.D., 1971 — Delta Theta Phi — Admitted to Bar, 1971, Virginia; 1972, New Jersey; 1975, New York; 1972, U.S. District Court, District of New Jersey; 1974, U.S. District Court, Eastern and Southern Districts of New York; 1975, U.S. Court of Appeals, Second Circuit; 1984, U.S. Court of Appeals, Third Circuit; 1998, U.S. District Court, Northern District of New York — Member American Bar Association (Tort and Insurance Practice Section; Committees: Construction, Transportation Litigation); New Jersey State (Insurance Section) and New York State (Tort and Insurance Section) Bar Associations; Virginia State Bar; Defense Research Institute (Regional Membership Chairman, Construction Law Committee; Committees: Insurance, Transportation, Construction); Transportation Lawyers Association; Trucking Industry Defense Association; The Maritime Law Association of the United States; New Jersey Defense Association — E-mail: jclane@jclane.com

Peter C. Bobchin — 1963 — Pace University, B.B.A., 1985; Ohio Northern University, Pettit College of Law, J.D., 1989 — Admitted to Bar, 1990, New Jersey; New York; 1990, U.S. District Court, District of New Jersey; 1992, U.S. District Court, Eastern District of New York; 1995, U.S. District Court, Southern District of New York — Member New Jersey Defense Association; Trucking Industry Defense Association — E-mail: pcbobchin@jclane.com

NEW JERSEY

SPRINGFIELD

SPRINGFIELD 14,429 Union Co.

Hardin, Kundla, McKeon & Poletto, P.A.

673 Morris Avenue
Springfield, New Jersey 07081
 Telephone: 973-912-5222
 Fax: 973-912-9212
 E-Mail: info@hkmpp.com
 http://www.hkmpp.com/

(New York, NY Office: 110 William Street, 10038)
 (Tel: 212-571-0111)
 (Fax: 212-571-1117)
(Allentown, PA Office: 311 Liberty Street, 18102)
 (Tel: 610-433-8400)
 (Fax: 610-433-0300)

Established: 1997

General Defense

Insurance Clients

AIG	Allstate Insurance Company
Bayside Casualty Insurance Company	Berkley Risk Services, LLC
	Carl Warren & Company
Chubb Group of Insurance Companies	Cincinnati Insurance Company
	CNA Insurance Companies
Crum & Forster Insurance	CURE Auto Insurance
Gallagher Bassett Services, Inc.	Great American Insurance Company
Health Care Insurance Exchange	
Hertz Claim Management	Highlands Insurance Company
Homestead Insurance Company	Meadowbrook Insurance Group
National Indemnity Company	Princeton Insurance Company
RiverStone Claims Management, LLC	Royal & SunAlliance Insurance Company
Seneca Insurance Company, Inc.	Travelers
Universal Underwriters Insurance Company	Utica Mutual Insurance Company

Non-Insurance Clients

Atlantic Health Systems, Inc.	Belden Wire & Cable Company
Christ Hospital	Conover Beyer Associates
Englewood Hospital and Medical Center, Inc.	Equipment Dealers Association
	The Hertz Corporation
John Deere Company	J.P. Bender & Associates, Inc.
J.R. Simplot Company	McDonald's Claim Center
Morristown Memorial Hospital	National Propane Corporation
Overlook Hospital	PACCAR, Inc.
Peterbilt and Kenworth Trucks	Shaklee Corporation
St. Barnabas Healthcare System	Suburban Propane
Tarmac America, Inc.	UniGroup, Inc./Mayflower Transit, LLC
United Chair Company, Inc.	
Volvo Cars of North America, Inc.	Volvo Trucks of North America, Inc.
Wayne General Hospital	

Partners

George R. Hardin — 1946 — Seton Hall University, B.A., 1968; J.D. (cum laude), 1974 — Admitted to Bar, 1974, New Jersey; 1981, New York; 1974, U.S. District Court, District of New Jersey; 1978, U.S. Court of Appeals, Second and Third Circuits; 1983, U.S. Supreme Court; 1990, U.S. District Court, Southern District of New York — Member American Bar Association (Tort and Insurance Practice Section); New Jersey State Bar Association (Appellate Practice Study Committee); Essex County Bar Association (Former Trustee); New Jersey Defense Association; Defense Research Institute — Martindale Hubbell AV Preeminent Rated — Certified Civil Trial Attorney — Practice Areas: Insurance Law; Product Liability; Toxic Torts; Mass Tort; Professional Liability; Construction Law; Alternative Dispute Resolution; Appeals; Litigation

Mark S. Kundla — 1956 — Seton Hall University, B.A. (cum laude), 1978; J.D. (cum laude), 1981 — Admitted to Bar, 1981, New Jersey; 1990, New York; 1983, U.S. Court of Appeals, Third Circuit — Member American and New Jersey State Bar Associations; LP Gas Defense Association; Defense Research Institute — Martindale Hubbell AV Preeminent Rated — Certified Civil Trial Attorney — Practice Areas: Product Liability; Fire & Explosion; Professional Liability; Transportation; Construction Law; Business Law; Commercial Law; General Defense Civil Litigation

Hardin, Kundla, McKeon & Poletto, P.A., Springfield, NJ (Continued)

John F. McKeon — 1958 — Muhlenberg College, B.A. (cum laude), 1980; Seton Hall University, J.D., 1983 — Admitted to Bar, 1983, New Jersey — Member American, Essex County and Union County Bar Associations — Martindale Hubbell AV Preeminent Rated — Certified Civil Trial Attorney — Practice Areas: Medical Malpractice; Health Care Liability; Negligence; Commercial Law; Human Services

Janet L. Poletto — 1955 — Bucknell University, B.A. (magna cum laude), 1976; Georgetown University Law Center, J.D., 1980 — Admitted to Bar, 1980, New Jersey — Member American Bar Association; New Jersey Defense Association — Martindale Hubbell AV Preeminent Rated — Certified Civil Trial Attorney — Practice Areas: Professional Liability; Medical Malpractice; Long-Term Care; Mass Tort; Toxic Torts; Insurance Law; Complex Litigation; Class Actions

Nicea J. D'Annunzio — 1962 — Fairleigh Dickinson University, B.S. (magna cum laude), 1982; Seton Hall University, J.D. (cum laude), 1985 — Phi Alpha Delta — Recipient, New Jersey State Bar Association Young Lawyers, Lawyer of the Year, Service to the Community Award (1990) — Judicial Law Clerk to Hon. Stanley G. Bedford, Superior Court of New Jersey, Essex County, 1985-1986 — Admitted to Bar, 1985, New Jersey; 1985, U.S. District Court, District of New Jersey — Member American, New Jersey State, Morris County and Essex County Bar Associations; New Jersey Defense Association — Who's Who in American Law; New Jersey Top Lawyers (2005, 2006); Martindale Hubbell AV Preeminent Rated — Practice Areas: Complex Litigation; Toxic Torts; Construction Litigation; Environmental Litigation; Product Liability; Asbestos Litigation

John S. Favate — 1960 — Saint Peter's College, B.A., 1982; University of Bridgeport, J.D., 1985 — Recipient, American Jurisprudence Award — Admitted to Bar, 1985, New Jersey; 1985, U.S. District Court, District of New Jersey; 1996, U.S. Court of Appeals, Third Circuit — Member American, New Jersey State and Essex County Bar Associations — Martindale Hubbell AV Preeminent Rated — Practice Areas: Litigation; Insurance Coverage; Employment Practices; Professional Liability

Patrick J. Clare — 1960 — Fordham University, B.A. (cum laude), 1982; Saint Louis University, J.D., 1986 — Admitted to Bar, 1986, New Jersey; 1986, U.S. District Court, District of New Jersey; 1989, U.S. Court of Appeals, Third Circuit — Member American and New Jersey State Bar Associations — Practice Areas: General Liability; Medical Malpractice; Hospital Malpractice; Criminal Defense; Health Care Liability

Paul Daly — 1968 — Rutgers College, B.A., 1990; J.D., 1995 — Admitted to Bar, 1995, New Jersey; 1995, U.S. District Court, District of New Jersey — Member New Jersey State Bar Association — Certified Civil Trial Attorney — Practice Areas: Product Liability; Fire; Complex Litigation; Professional Liability; Transportation; Construction Law; Business Law; Commercial Law; General Liability

Stephen J. Donahue — 1964 — Kean University, B.A., 1991; Seton Hall University, J.D., 1995 — Admitted to Bar, 1995, New York; 1996, New York; 1995, U.S. District Court, District of New Jersey; 1998, U.S. District Court, Eastern and Southern Districts of New York — Practice Areas: Civil Litigation; Commercial Litigation; General Civil Litigation; Personal Injury Litigation; Insurance Coverage

John R. Scott — 1964 — Lafayette College, B.A., 1986; Seton Hall University, J.D. (cum laude), 1989 — Admitted to Bar, 1989, New Jersey; U.S. District Court, District of New Jersey — Member New Jersey State and Morris County Bar Associations; New Jersey Trial Lawyers Association — Certified Civil Trial Attorney by the Supreme Court of New Jersey — Practice Areas: Personal Injury; Complex Litigation; Product Liability; Construction Litigation; Professional Liability; Insurance Coverage; Automobile Litigation; Premises Liability

Associates

Jeffrey H. Goldsmith	Eileen Bass Rudd
Patrick J. McCormick	Arthur A. Povelones, Jr.
Lilas Borsa	James P. McBarron
Cynthia Lee	Gary M. Sarno
Rosa M. Marques	Stephen P. Murray
John Grillos	Candice Huber Rienzo
Allyson N. Angelo	Brian C. Alfson
Daniel J. Garry	Jaclyn A. Martini
Robert E. Blanton Jr.	Henry T. LeFevre-Snee
Joseph A. DiPisa	James L. Fant
Rebecca Spatzner	Eileen P. Walsh
Erin E. Zecca	Kelly A. Samuels
David C. Blaxill	Eric Wagman
Nicole R. Fisher	Hunt S. Ricker

TOMS RIVER   NEW JERSEY

Hardin, Kundla, McKeon & Poletto, P.A., Springfield, NJ
(Continued)

James Yoo
Kyle E. Pozza
Eric John Meehan

(Revisors of the New Jersey Insurance Law Digest for this Publication)

Schechner Marcus LLP

155 Morris Avenue, Suite 203
Springfield, New Jersey 07081
 Telephone: 973-376-6200
 Fax: 973-376-5620
 E-Mail: shschechner@schechnerlaw.com
 www.schechnerlaw.com

Established: 1979

Insurance Defense, Civil Litigation, Negligence, Administrative Law, Professional Disciplinary Proceedings, Professional Liability Defense

Firm Profile: The law firm represents healthcare professionals in all aspects of health care practice, including defense of malpractice claims, before State Licensing Boards, insurance company audits, risk analysis and the purchase and sale of medical and dental practices.

Insurance Clients

The Dentists Insurance Company - TDIC	OMS National Insurance Company Princeton Insurance Company

Partners

Stephen H. Schechner — University of Bridgeport, B.A., 1967; Suffolk University, J.D., 1970; New York University, LL.M., 1976 — Admitted to Bar, 1970, New Jersey; U.S. District Court, District of New Jersey — Member Richard J. Hughes Inn of Court, Union County (Master, 1994-present) — Certified Civil Trial Attorney by the Supreme Court of New Jersey

Debra M. Marcus — Boston University, B.S., 1985; Benjamin N. Cardozo School of Law, J.D., 1988 — Admitted to Bar, 1989, New Jersey; U.S. District Court, District of New Jersey

Associate

Andrea Silverstein Glaser — University at Buffalo, B.A., 1997; Hofstra University School of Law, J.D., 2001 — Admitted to Bar, 2002, New Jersey; 2004, New York

SUMMIT 21,457 Union Co.

Brown Moskowitz & Kallen, P.C.

180 River Road, First Floor
Summit, New Jersey 07901
 Telephone: 973-376-0909
 Fax: 973-376-0903
 Emer/After Hrs: 201-755-6800
 E-Mail: agoldberger@bmk-law.com
 www.bmk-law.com
 www.RefLaw.com

Sports Claims Defense, Sports Law, Business Law, Commercial Litigation, Corporate Law, Sports Insurance Defense

Firm Profile: A nationally recognized authority on sports law and sports officiating, Alan Goldberger is frequently retained by insurance carriers and claims administrators to defend sports officials, coaches, camps, officials' associations and other sports industry insureds.

Insurance Clients

American Specialty Insurance Company	Employers Reinsurance Corporation
Markel Insurance Company	Westport Insurance Corporation

Brown Moskowitz & Kallen, P.C., Summit, NJ
(Continued)

Partner

Alan S. Goldberger — Franklin & Marshall College, A.B., 1971; Rutgers University School of Law-Camden, J.D., 1974 — Admitted to Bar, 1975, New Jersey; 1985, New York; 1999, Maryland — Member American Bar Association (Chair, Non-Profit Athletic and Recreation Associations Subcommittee); North Jersey Board of Approved Basketball Officials, Inc. (Past-President); Safety and Risk Management Council of AALF (Past-President) — Author: "Sports Officiating: A Legal Guide"; Co-Author: "Sport, Physical Activity and the Law"; Numerous Articles in Legal and Athletic Publications — Lecturer on Sports Law to Attorneys, Sports and Educational Organizations — E-mail: alan@RefLaw.com

TOMS RIVER † 88,791 Ocean Co.

Garvey, Ballou & Rogalski

204 Court House Lane
Toms River, New Jersey 08754
 Telephone: 732-341-1212
 Fax: 732-240-6704
 E-Mail: thefirm@courthouselane.com
 www.courthouselane.com

Established: 1993

General Practice, Insurance Law, Negligence, Municipal Law, Trial Practice, Appellate Practice

Insurance Clients

Allstate Insurance Company	Encompass Insurance Company
Farm Family Casualty Insurance Company	Gallagher Bassett Services, Inc. Harco National Insurance Company
High Point Insurance Company of America	Mercury Insurance Company
Penn-America Insurance Company	Penn Millers Insurance Company
Preserver Insurance Company	Princeton Insurance Company
Quincy Mutual Fire Insurance Company	Sedgwick Claims Service Center Sentry Insurance a Mutual Company
United National Group	

Non-Insurance Clients

Amerada Hess Corporation	Carl Warren & Company
Costco Wholesale Corporation	Ryder Truck Rental, Inc.
St. Barnabas Healthcare System	

Firm Members

Joseph J. Garvey — 1949 — Stevens Institute of Technology, B.Eng. (with honors), 1971; The Catholic University of America, J.D., 1976 — Admitted to Bar, 1976, New Jersey; 1977, District of Columbia — Certified Civil Trial Attorney, Supreme Court of New Jersey

Robert A. Ballou, Jr. — 1956 — Boston College, B.S., 1979; Seton Hall University, J.D., 1982 — Admitted to Bar, 1982, New Jersey; 1983, New York

Eleanore A. Rogalski — 1968 — Boston University, B.A. (cum laude), 1990; Rutgers University School of Law, J.D. (with honors), 1993 — Admitted to Bar, 1993, New Jersey; Pennsylvania — Certified Civil Trial Attorney

Law Offices of Garrett L. Joest, L.L.C.

29 Hadley Avenue
Toms River, New Jersey 08753
 Telephone: 732-505-0707
 Fax: 732-505-1717
 Mobile: 732-773-1216
 E-Mail: joestlaw@prodigy.net

Established: 1992

Insurance Defense, Insurance Coverage, Subrogation, Professional Malpractice, Personal Injury, Toxic Torts, Environmental Law, Asbestos Litigation

Law Offices of Garrett L. Joest, L.L.C., Toms River, NJ (Continued)

Firm Profile: Since its inception, the firm has placed a heavy emphasis on insurance coverage, both first and third party, and maintains a state-wide practice. The firm specializes in accounting malpractice, personal injury, toxic torts and asbestos defense. Garrett L. Joest, Esq. has been cited as environmental insurance coverage authority by the New Jersey Appellate Division in: *Broadwell Realty v. Fidelity*, 218 N.J. Super. 516, 534, 528 A.2d 85 (App. Div. 1987); and has reported cases of: *Finderne v. Barrett*, 355 N.J. Super. 197, 809 A.2d 857 (App. Div. 2002) (accounting malpractice); *Carfagno v. Aetna Cas. and Sur. Co.*, 770 F. Supp. 245 (D.N.J. 1991) (fire insurance coverage); *Meeker Sharkey v. National Union Fire Ins.*, 208 N.J. 354, 506 A.2d 19 (App. Div. 1986) (malpractice insurance coverage); and, *Twp. Jackson v. American Home Assurance Co.*, 186 N.J. Super. 156, 451 A2d. 990 (Law Div. 1982) (environmental insurance coverage).

Insurance Clients

AIG
CAMICO Mutual Insurance Company
Crum & Forster Insurance
Envision Claims Management Corporation
Fireman's Fund Insurance Companies
North American Specialty Insurance Company
PMA Insurance Group
Swiss Re Group
United States Fire Insurance Company
Assurance Company of America
CNA Global Specialty Lines
Commercial Underwriters Insurance Company
Farmers Insurance Company of Flemington
General Accident Insurance Company
North River Insurance Company
OneBeacon Insurance
The RiverStone Group
Underwriters Insurance Company
Zurich North America

Non-Insurance Clients

Cavell USA, Inc.

Garrett L. Joest III — 1948 — Fairleigh Dickinson University, B.A., 1971; Montclair State College, M.A., 1975; Seton Hall University, J.D., 1980 — Admitted to Bar, 1980, New Jersey; 1980, U.S. District Court, District of New Jersey; 1981, U.S. Court of Appeals, Third Circuit; 1985, U.S. Supreme Court — Member American and New Jersey State Bar Associations; Defense Research Institute; New Jersey Defense Association — Author: "Will Insurance Companies Clean the Augean Stables?" Insurance Counsel Journal, April 1983 — Adjunct Instructor, Ocean County College, Business Law I & II

Leyden, Capotorto, Ritacco & Corrigan, P.C.

250 Washington Street, Suite D
Toms River, New Jersey 08753
Telephone: 732-349-2443
Fax: 732-349-6917
E-Mail: afl@lawlcrc.com
www.lawlcrc.com

Established: 2010

Insurance Defense, Insurance Law, Personal Injury Protection (PIP), General Liability, Real Estate, Uninsured and Underinsured Motorist, Municipal Law, Trial and Appellate Practice

Firm Profile: Leyden, Capotorto, Ritacco & Corrigan was formed in May 2010. It is the successor corporation to the Lomell Law Firm and prior to that Lomell, Muccifori, Adler, Ravaschiere, Amabile & Pehlivanian. These firms have continuously served the community since 1957.

Insurance Clients

New Jersey Manufacturers Insurance Company
RLI/Mt. Hawley Insurance Company

Non-Insurance Clients

TTX Company

Leyden, Capotorto, Ritacco & Corrigan, P.C., Toms River, NJ (Continued)

Partners

Arthur F. Leyden, III — 1953 — Seton Hall University, B.A. (cum laude), 1975; Rutgers University, B.S., 1980; Seton Hall University School of Law, J.D., 1985 — Phi Alpha Delta — Admitted to Bar, 1985, New Jersey; 1985, U.S. District Court, District of New Jersey — Member American, New Jersey State and Ocean County (President, 2011-2012; Co-Chairperson, Civil Practice Committee; Co-Chair, Arbitration Committee) Bar Associations; The American Association of Nurse Attorneys; New Jersey Defense Association (Past-President; Past-Chairman of the Board); Defense Research Institute (NJDA State Representative, 2000-2003); New Jersey Defense Association; Trial Attorneys of New Jersey — District IIIA Ethics Committee Appointment (2000-2003); Instructor, New Jersey Defense Association Trial College; Instructor for Continuing Legal Education Courses including the Arbitrator Training Course; AV rated by Martindale-Hubbell; Recipient 2006 Ocean County Bar Association Professionalism Award; Recipient 2014 Ocean County Bar Association Achievement Award — Certified by the Supreme Court of New Jersey as a Civil Trial Attorney

Paul J. Capotorto — 1962 — Monmouth University, B.A., 1984; Western New England College School of Law, J.D., 1988 — Admitted to Bar, 1988, New Jersey; 1988, U.S. Court of Appeals, Third Circuit — Member American, New Jersey State and Ocean County Bar Associations; New Jersey Defense Association — Municipal Court Judge for Brielle, Manasquan and Sea Girt

Robert J. Ritacco — 1974 — William Paterson University, B.A., 1996; Seton Hall University, J.D., 2002 — Admitted to Bar, 2002, New Jersey; 2003, New York; 2002, U.S. District Court, District of New Jersey — Member American, New Jersey State, New York State and Ocean County Bar Associations; New Jersey Defense Association — Author: "Economic Duress and Anti-Competitive Practices - Coercive Tactics Utilized by the National Football League to Prevent Franchise Relocation", Seton Hall University School of Law Journal of Sport Law, 2002 — Mediator for the Ocean County Superior Court, Special Civil Part; District IIIA Ethics Committee Appointment (2010-2014); Community Medical Center Foundation Young Professional Advisory Council; Chairman, District IIIA Ethics Committee

Janet Kalapos Corrigan — 1961 — Rutgers University, B.A., 1983; Hofstra University, J.D., 1987 — Admitted to Bar, 1987, New Jersey — Member New Jersey State, Monmouth County and Ocean County Bar Associations; New Jersey Defense Association (Past Member, District IIIA Ethics Committee)

Associate

Jacqueline A. Chadwick — 1964 — Centenary College, B.S. (cum laude), 1986; Pennsylvania State University-Dickinson School of Law, J.D., 1990 — Admitted to Bar, 1990, Pennsylvania (Inactive); 2009, New Jersey — Member New Jersey State Bar Association (Young Lawyers Division)

In Memoriam

Leonard G. Lomell — (1920-2011)

Of Counsel

Dominic Ravaschiere — 1933 — Fordham University, LL.B., 1961 — Admitted to Bar, 1962, New Jersey; 1962, U.S. District Court, District of New Jersey; 1962, U.S. Supreme Court — Member American, New Jersey State and Ocean County Bar Associations

Francis E. Schachtele — 1948 — Seton Hall University, B.A. (cum laude), 1970; University of Notre Dame, J.D., 1975 — Admitted to Bar, 1976, New Jersey; U.S. District Court, District of New Jersey — Adjunct Professor, Mercer County College — Certified Civil Trial Attorney-New Jersey; Graduate, National Institute of Trial Advocacy Program (NITA)

(This firm is also listed in the Subrogation section of this directory)

TRENTON   NEW JERSEY

The following firms also service this area.

Law Offices of Glenn R. Cochran
812 State Road, Suite 120
Princeton, New Jersey 08540
   Telephone: 609-924-4011
   Fax: 609-924-5333
Mailing Address: P.O. Box 553, Princeton, NJ 08542

Insurance Defense, Trial Practice, Automobile, Professional Liability, Product Liability, Errors and Omissions, Liquor Liability, Commercial Liability, Subrogation, General

SEE COMPLETE LISTING UNDER PRINCETON, NEW JERSEY (40 MILES)

Methfessel & Werbel
2025 Lincoln Highway, Suite 200
Edison, New Jersey 08817
   Telephone: 732-248-4200
   Fax: 732-248-2355
Mailing Address: P.O. Box 3012, Edison, NJ 08818-3012

Automobile Liability, Bad Faith, Carrier Defense, Casualty Defense, Civil Trial Practice, Comprehensive General Liability, Construction Litigation, Coverage Issues, Defense Litigation, Employment Practices Liability, Environmental Coverage, Environmental Liability, Examinations Under Oath, Excess and Umbrella, Insurance Coverage, Insurance Defense, Medical Liability, Premises Liability, Primary and Excess Insurance, Product Liability, Professional Malpractice, Property Liability, Public Entities, Toxic Torts, Uninsured and Underinsured Motorist, General Subrogation, Large Loss Subrogation Program

SEE COMPLETE LISTING UNDER EDISON, NEW JERSEY (53 MILES)

Nowell Amoroso Klein Bierman, P.A.
155 Polifly Road
Hackensack, New Jersey 07601
   Telephone: 201-343-5001
   Toll Free: 800-246-0254
   Fax: 201-343-5181

Insurance Defense, Bodily Injury, Asbestos Litigation, Environmental Law, Personal Liability, Automobile, Homeowners, Toxic Torts, Product Liability, Pollution, Property Damage

SEE COMPLETE LISTING UNDER HACKENSACK, NEW JERSEY (76 MILES)

Powell, Birchmeier & Powell
1891 State Highway 50
Tuckahoe, New Jersey 08250
   Telephone: 609-628-3414
   Fax: 609-628-2966
Mailing Address: P.O. Box 582, Tuckahoe, NJ 08250-0582

General Civil Practice, Trial Practice, Insurance Defense, Negligence, Defense Litigation, Product Liability, Coverage Issues, Litigation, Workers' Compensation, Subrogation, Civil Rights, Governmental Liability, Medical Negligence, Wrongful Termination, General Chancery Practice, Section 1983 Litigation

SEE COMPLETE LISTING UNDER TUCKAHOE, NEW JERSEY (69 MILES)

Widman, Cooney, Wilson, McGann & Fitterer, L.L.C.
1803 Highway 35
Oakhurst, New Jersey 07755
   Telephone: 732-531-4141
   Fax: 732-531-7773

Insurance Defense, Casualty, Directors and Officers Liability, Employment Law, Automobile, Professional Negligence (Medical, Accountants and Attorneys, Insurance Agents, Realtors and Home Inspectors)

SEE COMPLETE LISTING UNDER OCEAN, NEW JERSEY (26 MILES)

TRENTON † 84,913 Mercer Co.

Barnaba & Marconi, LLP

315 Lowell Avenue
Trenton, New Jersey 08619
   Telephone: 609-584-1444
   Fax: 609-584-1555
   E-Mail: mbarnaba@barnaba-marconi.com
   www.barnaba-marconi.com

(Cherry Hill, NJ Office: 1913 Greentree Road, Suite A, 08003)
   (Tel: 609-489-0776)
(Philadelphia, PA Office: 19 South 21st Street, 19103)
   (Tel: 215-386-4136)

Established: 1996

Insurance Defense, General Liability, Litigation, Dram Shop, Product Liability, Premises Liability, Automobile, Workers' Compensation, Construction Liability, Insurance Law, Public Entities, Insurance Litigation, Truck Liability

Firm Profile: Barnaba & Marconi, LLP, with offices located in Mercer County, New Jersey, Camden County, New Jersey and Philadelphia County, Pennsylvania, is comprised of trial attorneys dedicated to providing the insurance and self-insured industry with the highest level of service and results. The firm has been aggressively providing its clients with high quality legal services in an efficient and professional manner from cases litigated in both Federal and State Courts throughout New Jersey and Pennsylvania. The firm's areas of practice include insurance defense, dram shop, general liability, product liability, premises liability, trucking litigation, workers' compensation, construction liability, insurance law and the defense of public entities. The firm handles matters for several Fortune 500 companies, small businesses, partnerships, individuals, insurance companies, third-party administrators and self-insureds. The goal of the firm is to obtain the best possible results for its clients in the most cost efficient manner. The firm also believes that an aggressive, tenacious and innovative approach to dispute resolution is in the client's best interest and that a results-oriented approach to litigation brings about resolutions of matters more quickly and efficiently.

Insurance Clients

All Risk Claims Service, Inc.	Chubb Services Corporation
Claims Administration Corporation	Essex Insurance Company
First Specialty Insurance Corporation	Gallagher Bassett Services, Inc.
	GMAC Insurance Group
Markel Insurance Company	National Interstate Insurance Company
The Peninsula Insurance Company	
T.H.E. Insurance Company	Xchanging Claims Services

Non-Insurance Clients

Payless ShoeSource   Ron Coleman & Associates, Ltd.
Township of Hamilton

Partners

Mario L. Barnaba — Villanova University, B.S. (cum laude), 1984; Seton Hall University School of Law, J.D., 1987 — Admitted to Bar, 1987, New Jersey; 1987, Pennsylvania; U.S. District Court, District of New Jersey; 1991, U.S. Court of Appeals, Third Circuit — Member American, New Jersey State, Camden County, Mercer County and Philadelphia Bar Associations; New Jersey Defense Association — E-mail: mbarnaba@barnaba-marconi.com

Dennis M. Marconi — Rutgers, The State University of New Jersey, B.A., 1985; J.D., 1988 — Admitted to Bar, 1988, New Jersey; Pennsylvania; 1988, U.S. District Court, District of New Jersey; 1989, U.S. District Court, Eastern District of Pennsylvania — Member New Jersey State, Burlington County and Camden County Bar Associations; New Jersey Defense Association; Trial Attorneys of New Jersey — Certified Civil Trial Attorney — E-mail: dmarconi@barnaba-marconi.com

Associates

Gary S. McDonald — University of Notre Dame, B.A. (magna cum laude), 1976; University of Pennsylvania, J.D., 1979 — Admitted to Bar, 1979, New Jersey; U.S. District Court, District of New Jersey; 1983, U.S. Court of Appeals, Third Circuit — Member New Jersey State and Gloucester County Bar

NEW JERSEY

Barnaba & Marconi, LLP, Trenton, NJ (Continued)

Associations; New Jersey Defense Association — E-mail: gmcdonald@barnaba-marconi.com

Charles C. Daley, Jr. — The Pennsylvania State University, B.S., 1977; Widener University School of Law, J.D., 1984 — Admitted to Bar, 1985, New Jersey; 1985, Pennsylvania — Member New Jersey State Bar Association; New Jersey Defense Association — Certified Civil Trial Attorney, New Jersey Supreme Court (1993-present) — E-mail: cdaley@barnaba-marconi.com

Michael C. Corcoran — Kings College, B.A., 1991; Widener University School of Law, J.D., 1997 — Admitted to Bar, 1997, New Jersey; 1997, Pennsylvania; U.S. District Court, District of New Jersey; U.S. District Court, Eastern District of Pennsylvania — Member American and New Jersey State Bar Associations; New Jersey Defense Association — E-mail: mcorcoran@barnaba-marconi.com

(This firm is also listed in the Subrogation section of this directory)

Riker Danzig Scherer Hyland & Perretti LLP

50 West State Street, Suite 1010
Trenton, New Jersey 08608-1220
Telephone: 609-396-2121
Fax: 609-396-4578
E-Mail: info@riker.com
www.riker.com

(Morristown, NJ Office*: Headquarters Plaza, 1 Speedwell Avenue, P.O. Box 1981, 07962-1981)
(Tel: 973-538-0800)
(Fax: 973-538-1984)
(New York, NY Office: 500 Fifth Avenue, 10110)
(Tel: 212-302-6574)
(Fax: 212-302-6628)

General Practice, Insurance Law, Reinsurance, Insurance Defense, Directors and Officers Liability, Product Liability, Administrative Law, Legislative Law, Regulatory and Compliance

Partner

Mary Kathryn Roberts — 1965 — Boston College, B.A. (cum laude), 1988; American University, Washington College of Law, J.D., 1991 — Admitted to Bar, 1991, New Jersey; 1991, Pennsylvania; U.S. District Court, District of New Jersey — Member New Jersey State Bar Association (Banking Law Section); New Jersey Health Care Administration Board (Vice Chair) — Registered Governmental Affairs Agent, New Jersey Election Law Enforcement Commission — Practice Areas: Government Affairs; Insurance Regulation; Insurance Law; Health Care; Lobbying — Resident Trenton, NJ Office — Tel: 609-396-2121 — Fax: 609-396-4578 — E-mail: mroberts@riker.com

(See listing under Morristown, NJ for additional information)

The following firms also service this area.

Law Offices of Glenn R. Cochran

812 State Road, Suite 120
Princeton, New Jersey 08540
Telephone: 609-924-4011
Fax: 609-924-5333
Mailing Address: P.O. Box 553, Princeton, NJ 08542

Insurance Defense, Trial Practice, Automobile, Professional Liability, Product Liability, Errors and Omissions, Liquor Liability, Commercial Liability, Subrogation, General

SEE COMPLETE LISTING UNDER PRINCETON, NEW JERSEY (12 MILES)

Methfessel & Werbel

2025 Lincoln Highway, Suite 200
Edison, New Jersey 08817
Telephone: 732-248-4200
Fax: 732-248-2355
Mailing Address: P.O. Box 3012, Edison, NJ 08818-3012

Automobile Liability, Bad Faith, Carrier Defense, Casualty Defense, Civil Trial Practice, Comprehensive General Liability, Construction Litigation, Coverage Issues, Defense Litigation, Employment Practices Liability, Environmental Coverage, Environmental Liability, Examinations Under Oath, Excess and Umbrella, Insurance Coverage, Insurance Defense, Medical Liability, Premises Liability, Primary and Excess Insurance, Product Liability, Professional Malpractice, Property Liability, Public Entities, Toxic Torts, Uninsured and Underinsured Motorist, General Subrogation, Large Loss Subrogation Program

SEE COMPLETE LISTING UNDER EDISON, NEW JERSEY (32 MILES)

Nowell Amoroso Klein Bierman, P.A.

155 Polifly Road
Hackensack, New Jersey 07601
Telephone: 201-343-5001
Toll Free: 800-246-0254
Fax: 201-343-5181

Insurance Defense, Bodily Injury, Asbestos Litigation, Environmental Law, Personal Liability, Automobile, Homeowners, Toxic Torts, Product Liability, Pollution, Property Damage

SEE COMPLETE LISTING UNDER HACKENSACK, NEW JERSEY (65 MILES)

O'Connor Kimball LLP

51 Haddonfield Road, Suite 330
Cherry Hill, New Jersey 08002-4805
Telephone: 856-663-9292
Fax: 856-663-6566

General Civil Practice, Casualty, Product Liability, Employment Law, Construction Litigation, Real Estate, Environmental Law, Toxic Torts, Insurance Law, Excess, Professional Liability, Commercial Liability, Commercial Litigation, Workers' Compensation, Civil Rights, Real Estate and Small Business Development Transactions, Professional Liability Litigation

SEE COMPLETE LISTING UNDER CHERRY HILL, NEW JERSEY (34 MILES)

Widman, Cooney, Wilson, McGann & Fitterer, L.L.C.

1803 Highway 35
Oakhurst, New Jersey 07755
Telephone: 732-531-4141
Fax: 732-531-7773

Insurance Defense, Casualty, Directors and Officers Liability, Employment Law, Automobile, Professional Negligence (Medical, Accountants and Attorneys, Insurance Agents, Realtors and Home Inspectors)

SEE COMPLETE LISTING UNDER OCEAN, NEW JERSEY (49 MILES)

TUCKAHOE 1,000 Cape May Co.

Powell, Birchmeier & Powell

1891 State Highway 50
Tuckahoe, New Jersey 08250
Telephone: 609-628-3414
Fax: 609-628-2966
E-Mail: powbirch@comcast.net
www.powbirch.com

(Woodbury, NJ Office*: 70 Euclid Street, 08096)
(Tel: 856-848-7091)

Established: 1982

General Civil Practice, Trial Practice, Insurance Defense, Negligence, Defense Litigation, Product Liability, Coverage Issues, Litigation, Workers' Compensation, Subrogation, Civil Rights, Governmental Liability, Medical Negligence, Wrongful Termination, General Chancery Practice, Section 1983 Litigation

Firm Profile: Since its inception, Powell, Birchmeier & Powell has placed its emphasis on defense, with a heavy concentration in negligence, civil rights and

VINELAND   NEW JERSEY

Powell, Birchmeier & Powell, Tuckahoe, NJ (Continued)

Section 1983 litigation. The firm is relatively modest in size, believing in a closely watched overhead, yet able to deliver quality legal services for its clients in a competitive market. With offices located in Tuckahoe, Cape May County and Woodbury, Gloucester County coupled with the geographical diversity of the members and associates, the firm is able to effectively and economically service its clients in the Southern New Jersey Counties of Burlington, Camden, Salem, Gloucester, Cumberland, Cape May, Atlantic and Ocean.

Insurance Clients

Allstate Insurance Company
Atlantic County Municipal Joint Insurance Fund
Camden County Municipal Joint Insurance Fund
Gloucester, Salem and Cumberland Counties Municipal Joint Insurance Fund
High Point Insurance Company of America
New Jersey Automobile Full Insurance Underwriting Association
State Farm Fire and Casualty Company
Summit Risk Services, Inc.
Tower Group Companies
Atlantic and Cape May Counties School Business Offices Joint Insurance Fund
Farmers' Mutual Fire Assurance Association of New Jersey
Gloucester, Salem, Cumberland School District Joint Insurance Fund
Municipal Excess Liability Joint Insurance Fund
New Jersey Property-Liability Insurance Guaranty Association
Plymouth Rock Assurance Corporation
State Farm Mutual Automobile Insurance Company
Utica Mutual Insurance Company

Non-Insurance Clients

City of Wildwood
County of Cape May
State of New Jersey
Western Litigation Specialists, Inc.
County of Atlantic
Public Service Electric & Gas Company

Partners

James R. Birchmeier — 1960 — Ursinus College, B.A., 1983; Ohio Northern University, J.D., 1986 — Admitted to Bar, 1986, New Jersey; Pennsylvania; 1986, U.S. District Court, District of New Jersey; U.S. Court of Appeals, Third Circuit; U.S. Supreme Court — Member American, New Jersey State, Atlantic County and Cape May County Bar Associations; Defense Research Institute; New Jersey Defense Association

Erin R. Thompson — 1964 — Indiana University, B.A., 1987; Ohio Northern University, J.D., 1990 — Admitted to Bar, 1990, New Jersey; 1990, U.S. District Court, District of New Jersey; U.S. Court of Appeals, Third Circuit; U.S. Supreme Court — Member New Jersey State and Cape May County Bar Associations; New Jersey Defense Association

Associates

Edward N. Romanik — 1958 — Dickinson College, B.A., 1981; Purdue University, M.A., 1983; Widener University, J.D., 1996 — Admitted to Bar, 1996, New Jersey; 1997, U.S. District Court, District of New Jersey — Member New Jersey State, Cape May County and Cumberland County Bar Associations; New Jersey Defense Association

Jennifer F. Torsiello — 1979 — The Richard Stockton College of New Jersey, B.A., 2002; Widener University School of Law, J.D., 2005 — Admitted to Bar, 2006, New Jersey; 2006, U.S. District Court, District of New Jersey — Member New Jersey State and Cape May County Bar Associations; New Jersey Defense Association

Of Counsel

Donald A. Powell — Retired — 1953 — University of Scranton, B.A., 1974; Rutgers University, J.D., 1977 — Admitted to Bar, 1977, New Jersey; 1977, U.S. District Court, District of New Jersey; U.S. Court of Appeals, Third Circuit; U.S. Supreme Court — Member American, New Jersey State, Gloucester County and Cape May County Bar Associations; New Jersey Defense Association; Defense Research Institute; American Arbitration Association

---

VINELAND 60,724 Cumberland Co.

Testa Heck Scrocca & Testa, PA

424 Landis Avenue
Vineland, New Jersey 08360
    Telephone: 856-691-2300
    Fax: 856-691-5655
    E-Mail: info@testalawyers.com
    www.testalawyers.com

Established: 1983

Defense Litigation, Trial Practice, Insurance Defense, Negligence, Casualty, Property, Automobile, General Liability, Product Liability, Medical Malpractice, Contractors Liability, Construction Liability, Bodily Injury, Workers' Compensation, Appellate Practice, Subrogation, Probate, Real Estate, Corporate Law, Commercial Law, Criminal Law, Construction Failure, Interpleader Actions, Construction and Design Professional Negligence, General Civil Practice and Litigation, State Government Law, Federal Practice, Insurance, Municipal Bonds, Zoning Law, Planning Law

Insurance Clients

Cumberland Insurance Group
Franklin Mutual Insurance Company
Farmers Mutual Fire Insurance Company of Salem County
Mercer Insurance Company

Non-Insurance Clients

Buena Borough Municipal Utilities Authority
Cumberland County College
Deerfield Township

Firm Members

Francis G. Basile — (1935-2005)

Renee E. Scrocca — (1959-2014)

Michael L. Testa — 1949 — Villanova University, B.A., 1971; J.D., 1975 — Admitted to Bar, 1975, New Jersey; 1975, U.S. District Court, District of New Jersey; 1975, U.S. Court of Appeals, Third Circuit; 1975, U.S. Supreme Court — Member American, New Jersey State and Cumberland County (Judicial and Prosecutorial Selection Committee) Bar Associations; New Jersey Association of Trial Lawyers of America (President, 1995-1996); Association of Criminal Defense Lawyers of New Jersey; American Arbitration Association; American Board of Trial Advocates — Certified Civil and Criminal Trial Attorney Supreme Court of New Jersey Board on Trial Attorney Certification; Certified in Civil Trial Advocacy by National Board on Trial Advocacy, May 12, 1989 — Practice Areas: Civil Litigation — E-mail: mtesta@testalawyers.com

Todd W. Heck — 1955 — Lehigh University, B.S. (with high honors), 1976; Villanova University, J.D., 1979; New York University, LL.M., 1983 — Admitted to Bar, 1979, Pennsylvania; 1980, New Jersey; 1990, New York; 1979, U.S. District Court, Eastern District of Pennsylvania; 1980, U.S. District Court, District of New Jersey; 1990, U.S. Tax Court; 1990, U.S. Claims Court; 1996, U.S. Court of Appeals, Third Circuit; 1996, U.S. Supreme Court — Member New Jersey State and Cumberland County Bar Associations — Practice Areas: Commercial Law; Commercial Litigation; Estate Planning; Real Estate; Land Use — E-mail: theck@testalawyers.com

Michael L. Testa, Jr. — 1976 — Villanova University, B.A., 1998; J.D., 2001; Temple University Beasley School of Law, LL.M. (Trial Advocacy), 2006 — Admitted to Bar, 2001, New Jersey; 2001, U.S. District Court, District of New Jersey — Member Cumberland County Bar Association (President, 2010-2011); New Jersey Association for Justice (Board of Governors) — Practice Areas: Civil Litigation — E-mail: mtestajr@testalawyers.com

Robert J. Casella — 1951 — University of Scranton, B.S., 1973; Delaware Law School at Widener University, J.D., 1976 — Admitted to Bar, 1977, New Jersey; 1977, U.S. District Court, District of New Jersey; 1989, U.S. Supreme Court — Member New Jersey State and Cumberland County Bar Associations — Practice Areas: Business Law; Real Estate; Probate — E-mail: rcasella@testalawyers.com

Justin R. White — 1979 — Rowan University, B.A., 2002; Rutgers University School of Law, J.D., 2005 — Admitted to Bar, 2005, New Jersey; 2006, Pennsylvania; U.S. District Court, District of New Jersey; U.S. District Court, Eastern District of Pennsylvania — Member American, New Jersey State and

NEW JERSEY   WARREN

Testa Heck Scrocca & Testa, PA, Vineland, NJ
(Continued)

Cumberland County Bar Associations — Practice Areas: Civil Litigation; Insurance Defense; Commercial Litigation — E-mail: jwhite@testalawyers.com

Sharon A. Ferrucci — 1957 — Boston College, B.A. (magna cum laude), 1979; Temple University School of Law, J.D., 1983 — Admitted to Bar, 1983, New Jersey; 1983, Pennsylvania; 1984, U.S. District Court, District of New Jersey — Member New Jersey State, Cumberland County, Gloucester County and Camden County Bar Associations — Court Approved Arbitrator and Mediator — Practice Areas: Insurance Defense; Workers' Compensation — E-mail: sferrucci@testalawyers.com

(This firm is also listed in the Subrogation section of this directory)

WARREN 1,000 Somerset Co.

Law Offices of Michael E. Pressman

Warrenville Plaza, 31W
Mountain Boulevard
Warren, New Jersey 07059
  Telephone: 908-753-6661
  Fax: 908-755-5229; 212-480-2590
  Toll Free: 800-764-3030
  E-Mail: mepressman@mepressman.com

(New York, NY Office*: 125 Maiden Lane-17th Floor, 10038)
  (Tel: 212-480-3030)
  (Fax: 212-480-2590)
  (Toll Free: 800-764-3030)
(Brooklyn, NY Office*: 26 Court Street, Suite 1700, 11242)
  (Tel: 718-237-4600)
  (Fax: 212-480-2590)
  (Toll Free: 800-764-3030)
(Garden City, NY Office*(See Long Island City listing): 114 Chestnut Street, 11530)
  (Fax: 212-480-2590)
  (Toll Free: 800-764-3030)

Established: 1984

Insurance Defense, Automobile, General Liability, Product Liability, Property and Casualty

(See Brooklyn and New York, NY listings for additional information)

WAYNE 54,069 Passaic Co.

Buglione, Hutton & DeYoe, L.L.C.

401 Hamburg Turnpike, Suite 206
Wayne, New Jersey 07470
  Telephone: 973-595-6300
  Fax: 973-595-0146
  E-Mail: abuglione@deyoe.com

Established: 1919

Appellate Practice, Arbitration, Mediation and ADR, Construction Law, Environmental Law, Insurance Defense, Insurance and Re-Insurance, Labor and Employment Law, Litigation, Product Liability and Complex Tort Litigation, Sexual Abuse Defense, Subrogation and Recovery, Workers' Compensation

Firm Profile: Buglione, Hutton & DeYoe, L.L.C., is a full service law firm, organized to provide a broad spectrum of quality services at competitive fees.

The firm's history dates back to 1919. We have built our growth on a foundation of diversified litigation, having handled virtually every type of civil case, from the most basic to the highly complex.

Buglione, Hutton & DeYoe, L.L.C., Wayne, NJ
(Continued)

Insurance Clients
Arbella Insurance Group

Non-Insurance Clients
Paterson Public School System

Firm Member

Albert C. Buglione — 1970 — Seton Hall University, B.A. (with honors), 1992; J.D., 1995 — Admitted to Bar, 1995, New Jersey — Member American, Essex County and Passaic County Bar Associations; New Jersey Defense Association

Associates
James M. LaBianca   Richard J. Turano

Of Counsel
Wood M. DeYoe   Hon. Anne Hutton, J.W.C., (Retired)

WEST ORANGE 44,943 Essex Co.

Sachs, Maitlin, Fleming & Greene

80 Main Street
West Orange, New Jersey 07052
  Telephone: 973-731-3400
  Fax: 973-731-2896
  E-Mail: smfglaw@aol.com

Established: 1933

Insurance Defense, Property and Casualty, Professional Liability, Automobile Liability, Insurance Coverage, Environmental Coverage, Litigation, Subrogation, Alternative Dispute Resolution, Product Liability, Appellate Practice

Firm Profile: The firm of Sachs, Maitlin, Fleming & Greene has serviced the insurance industry for over 70 years. We pride ourselves in providing quality legal representation with an emphasis on personal service to our clientele. We are particularly sensitive to our clients' needs in having a cost-efficient relationship with a focus on resolving matters quickly and efficiently. With over 70 years of experienced advocacy, in those circumstances where trials are necessary, our results are consistently successful.

Insurance Clients

Berkley Risk Administrators Company, LLC
Claims Service Bureau of New York
Greater New York Group
Health Care Insurance Company
National Casualty Company
ProMutual Group
Selective Insurance Company of America
Chubb Group of Insurance Companies
Crum & Forster Insurance
Farmers Insurance Group
Gulf Insurance Group
Montpelier US Insurance Company
Princeton Insurance Company
Scottsdale Insurance Company
Travelers Insurance Companies

Partners

Allan Maitlin — 1936 — Rutgers University, B.A., 1958; New York University, J.D., 1961 — Admitted to Bar, 1962, New Jersey; 1962, U.S. District Court, District of New Jersey; 1962, U.S. Court of Appeals, Third Circuit; 1962, U.S. Supreme Court; 1962, U.S. Court of Federal Claims — Member American, New Jersey State and Essex County Bar Associations — Practice Areas: Alternative Dispute Resolution; Insurance Coverage; Professional Liability

Raymond J. Fleming — 1948 — Seton Hall University, B.S., 1970; Rutgers University, J.D., 1973 — Admitted to Bar, 1973, New Jersey — Member New Jersey State Bar Association — Practice Areas: Medical Malpractice

Peter A. Greene — 1946 — Columbia University, B.A., 1968; M.S., 1969; Rutgers University, J.D., 1976 — Admitted to Bar, 1977, District of Columbia; New York; 1978, New Jersey; 1978, U.S. District Court, District of New Jersey — Member New York County Lawyers Association — U.S. Army, 1969-1971 — Practice Areas: Medical Malpractice; Product Liability

WESTFIELD   NEW JERSEY

Sachs, Maitlin, Fleming & Greene, West Orange, NJ
(Continued)

Harold D. Feuerstein — (1908-1967)
Marvin A. Sachs — (Retired)

Associates

David E. Maitlin — 1970 — Rutgers University, B.A., 1992; Boston University, J.D., 1995 — Admitted to Bar, 1996, New Jersey; New York — Member American, New Jersey State and Essex County Bar Associations — Practice Areas: Civil Litigation; Commercial Litigation

Christopher L. Klabonski — 1971 — Rutgers University, Rutgers College, B.A., 1996; Rutgers University-Newark, J.D., 1999 — Admitted to Bar, 1999, New Jersey; 2000, Pennsylvania; 1999, U.S. District Court, District of New Jersey — Practice Areas: Appellate Practice; Civil Litigation

Meghan E. Walsh — 1959 — University of Miami, B.A., 1981; Seton Hall University School of Law, J.D. (magna cum laude), 1988 — Admitted to Bar, 1988, New Jersey; Pennsylvania; U.S. District Court, District of New Jersey

Counsel

Glenn A. Farrell — 1963 — Syracuse University, B.S., 1985; Seton Hall University School of Law, J.D., 1988 — Admitted to Bar, 1988, New Jersey; 1989, New York; 1988, U.S. District Court, District of New Jersey; 1990, U.S. Court of Appeals, Third Circuit — Member New Jersey State Board of Medical Examiners — Practice Areas: General Liability; Product Liability

(This firm is also listed in the Subrogation section of this directory)

WESTFIELD 30,316 Union Co.

Lindabury, McCormick, Estabrook & Cooper, P.C.

53 Cardinal Drive
Westfield, New Jersey 07090
Telephone: 908-233-6800
Fax: 908-233-5078
E-Mail: info@lindabury.com
www.lindabury.com

(Summit, NJ Office: 480 Morris Avenue, 07901)
 (Tel: 908-273-1212)
 (Fax: 908-273-8922)
(Red Bank, NJ Office: 331 Newman Springs Road, Suite 225, 07701)
 (Tel: 732-741-7777)
 (Fax: 732-758-1879)
(New York, NY Office: 26 Broadway, Suite 2300, 10004)
 (Tel: 212-742-3390)
 (Fax: 212-269-5016)
(Philadelphia, PA Office: 1515 Market Street, 19102)
 (Tel: 215-854-4090)
 (Fax: 215-569-0216)

Established: 1954

General Practice, Insurance Law, General Liability, Employment Law, Employment Discrimination, Employment Practices Liability, Sexual Harassment, Wrongful Termination, Labor and Employment, Directors and Officers Liability, ERISA, Environmental Coverage, Environmental Law, Toxic Torts, Construction Law, Construction Litigation, Construction Defect, Subrogation, Architects and Engineers, Errors and Omissions, Agent and Brokers Errors and Omissions, Bad Faith, Punitive Damages, Coverage Issues, Opinions, Primary and Excess Insurance, Reinsurance, Fidelity, Surety, Health Care, Hospital Malpractice, Medical Malpractice, Professional Liability, School Law, Alternative Dispute Resolution, Asbestos Litigation, Insurance Defense, Automobile, Commercial Litigation, Product Liability, Mass Tort, Consumer Litigation

Firm Profile: Lindabury, McCormick, Estabrook & Cooper, P.C. is a premier corporate and commercial law firm that has been effectively handling insurance coverage and defense matters for our clients for 60 years. Our attorneys specialize in a wide variety of areas in the insurance practice and

Lindabury, McCormick, Estabrook & Cooper, P.C., Westfield, NJ
(Continued)

have extensive trial and appellate experience. We have several attorneys certified by the Supreme Court of New Jersey as trial attorneys, and considerable experience with the strategic use of alternative dispute resolution. Our responsiveness, responsible staffing and many years of delivering successful outcomes to our insurance clients make us a solid and reliable partner for insurance coverage and defense work.

Insurance Clients

Agricultural Excess and Surplus Insurance Company
AIU Insurance Company
American Alliance Insurance Company
American Home Assurance Company
American National Fire Insurance Company
Certain Underwriters at Lloyd's, London
Great American Insurance Company
Hartford Financial Products
Illinois National Insurance Company
National Union Fire Insurance Company of Pittsburgh, PA
Old Republic Insurance Company
Transport Insurance Company
Travelers Insurance Companies
Agricultural Insurance Company
AIG Claims, Inc.
Ambassador Insurance Company
American Alternative Insurance Corporation
American Modern Insurance Group, Inc.
Auto-Owners Insurance Company
The Beasley Group
Diploma Joint Insurance Fund
General Star Management Company
Hanover Insurance Company
The Hartford Financial Services Group, Inc.
Lexington Insurance Company
New Jersey Property-Liability Insurance Guaranty Association
Safeco/American States Insurance Company
Windsor Insurance Group

Non-Insurance Clients

Automobili Lamborghini, S.p.A.
BMW Financial Services NA, LLC
Matheson Tri-Gas
NOVAMEX
Volkswagen Group of America, Inc.
Bentley Motors, Inc.
BMW of North America, LLC
Nissan North America, Inc.
Rolls-Royce Motor Cars

Shareholders

Jay Lavroff — 1960 — Boston College, B.A. (cum laude), 1982; Seton Hall University, J.D., 1985 — Admitted to Bar, 1985, New Jersey; 1985, U.S. District Court, District of New Jersey; 2000, U.S. District Court, Western District of Pennsylvania; 2006, U.S. Supreme Court — Practice Areas: Asbestos Litigation; Construction Defect; Declaratory Judgments; Environmental Coverage; Insurance Coverage; Excess and Surplus Lines; General Liability; Opinions; Product Liability; Property and Casualty; Toxic Torts — E-mail: jlavroff@lindabury.com

Edward J. Frisch — 1943 — Saint Vincent College; Newark College of Engineering, B.S.M.E., 1971; Seton Hall University, J.D., 1976 — Admitted to Bar, 1976, New Jersey; 1976, U.S. District Court, District of New Jersey; 1977, U.S. Court of Appeals, Third Circuit; 1983, U.S. Supreme Court; 2007, U.S. Court of Appeals, Second Circuit — Practice Areas: Construction Defect; Construction Law; Fidelity and Surety; Surety — E-mail: efrisch@lindabury.com

John H. Schmidt, Jr. — 1952 — Rutgers College, B.A., 1973; Seton Hall University, J.D. (cum laude), 1977 — Admitted to Bar, 1977, New Jersey; 1977, U.S. District Court, District of New Jersey; 1979, U.S. Court of Appeals, Third Circuit; 1985, U.S. Supreme Court; 2005, U.S. District Court, Southern District of New York — The College of Labor and Employment Lawyers, 2007 — Certified by the Supreme Court of New Jersey as a Civil Trial Attorney — Practice Areas: Compensation; Employer Liability; Employment Practices Liability; Wrongful Termination; Employment Discrimination; Labor and Employment — E-mail: jschmidt@lindabury.com

James D. DeRose — 1946 — Wagner College, B.A., 1969; The Catholic University of America, J.D., 1978 — Admitted to Bar, 1978, New Jersey; U.S. District Court, District of New Jersey; U.S. Claims Court; 1981, U.S. Court of Appeals, Third Circuit; U.S. Supreme Court — Practice Areas: Automobile; Civil Litigation; Defense Litigation; Product Liability; Self-Insured Defense — E-mail: jderose@lindabury.com

Barry J. Donohue — 1945 — Saint Anselm College, A.B., 1967; The Catholic University of America, J.D., 1970 — Admitted to Bar, 1970, New Jersey; 1975, New York; 1975, U.S. Court of Appeals, Second Circuit; 1983, U.S. Court of Appeals, Third Circuit — Practice Areas: Construction Law; Construction Defect; Construction Liability; Construction Litigation; Surety — E-mail: bdonohue@lindabury.com

Lindabury, McCormick, Estabrook & Cooper, P.C., Westfield, NJ (Continued)

David R. Pierce — 1957 — Syracuse University, B.S. (magna cum laude), 1979; J.D. (magna cum laude), 1985 — Admitted to Bar, 1985, New Jersey; 1985, U.S. District Court, District of New Jersey; 1986, U.S. Court of Appeals, Third Circuit; 1993, U.S. Supreme Court — Practice Areas: Environmental Law; Environmental Litigation; Land Use; Real Estate; Commercial Litigation; Complex Litigation — E-mail: dpierce@lindabury.com

Anthony P. Sciarrillo — 1950 — Rutgers University, B.A., 1972; Montclair State College, M.A., 1975; Rutgers University, M.S., 1976; Seton Hall University, J.D., 1981; Ed.S., 2002; Ed.D., 2006 — Admitted to Bar, 1982, New Jersey; 1982, U.S. District Court, District of New Jersey — Practice Areas: Employment Practices Liability; Self-Insured Defense; School Law; Labor and Employment — E-mail: edlawgroup@lindabury.com

Eric B. Levine — 1970 — University of Massachusetts Amherst, B.B.A. (cum laude), 1992; Seton Hall University, J.D., 1995 — Admitted to Bar, 1995, New Jersey; 1995, U.S. District Court, District of New Jersey; 2006, U.S. Court of Appeals, Third Circuit — Practice Areas: Declaratory Judgments; Coverage Issues; Commercial Litigation; Real Estate — E-mail: elevine@lindabury.com

Greg K. Vitali — 1972 — Franklin & Marshall College, B.A., 1994; Seton Hall University School of Law, J.D. (cum laude), 1997 — Admitted to Bar, 1997, New Jersey; 1997, U.S. District Court, District of New Jersey; 2006, U.S. Court of Appeals, Third Circuit — Practice Areas: Construction Law; Commercial Litigation; Surety — E-mail: gvitali@lindabury.com

Jeffrey R. Merlino — 1970 — Montclair State University, B.S., 1995; Seton Hall University School of Law, J.D., 1997 — Admitted to Bar, 1997, New Jersey; 1997, U.S. District Court, District of New Jersey; 2002, New York; 2002, U.S. Court of Appeals, Third Circuit; 2003, U.S. District Court, Southern District of New York — Practice Areas: Personal Injury; Employer Liability; School Law; Subrogation; Wrongful Termination — E-mail: jmerlino@lindabury.com

Anne S. Burris — 1958 — Washington University, B.A., 1979; Northwestern University Medill School of Journalism, M.S.J., 1982; Seton Hall University School of Law, J.D., 1999 — Admitted to Bar, 1999, New Jersey; 2000, New York; 2006, Pennsylvania; 1999, U.S. District Court of New Jersey; 2009, U.S. District Court, Eastern District of Pennsylvania — Practice Areas: Automotive Products Liability; Commercial Litigation; Self-Insured Defense — E-mail: aburris@lindabury.com

Dennis McKeever — 1975 — Lafayette College, B.A., 1997; Seton Hall University School of Law, J.D., 2000 — Admitted to Bar, 2001, New Jersey — Practice Areas: Civil Litigation — E-mail: dmckeever@lindabury.com

Partners

Andrew J. Gibbs — University of Delaware, B.A., 1990; Widener University School of Law, J.D., 1995 — Admitted to Bar, 1995, New Jersey; 1996, U.S. District Court, District of New Jersey; 2004, U.S. District Court, Southern District of New York — Practice Areas: Accountants and Attorneys Liability; Agent/Broker Liability; Appellate Practice; Asbestos Litigation; Automobile Liability; Casualty Defense; Commercial Litigation; Complex Litigation; Construction Litigation; Environmental Litigation; General Liability; Hospital Malpractice; Insurance Coverage; Insurance Litigation; Litigation and Counseling; Mass Tort; Medical Negligence; Nursing Home Liability; Product Liability; Professional Negligence; Toxic Torts; Truck Liability; Wrongful Death — E-mail: agibbs@lindabury.com

Anthony J. La Russo — 1943 — Bucknell University, B.S., 1965; Villanova University, J.D., 1968 — Admitted to Bar, 1968, New Jersey; 1968, U.S. District Court, District of New Jersey; 1977, U.S. Court of Appeals, Third Circuit — Member New Jersey State Bar Association — Certified by the Supreme Court of New Jersey as a Civil Trial Attorney — Practice Areas: Litigation; Commercial Litigation; Real Estate; Title Insurance; Asbestos Litigation — E-mail: alarusso@lindabury.com

Bruce P. Ogden — 1953 — Stanford University, A.B., 1975; Rutgers University, J.D. (with honors), 1979 — Admitted to Bar, 1979, New Jersey; U.S. District Court, District of New Jersey; 1989, U.S. Court of Appeals, Third Circuit — Practice Areas: Construction Litigation; Hospitals; Trial and Appellate Practice — E-mail: bogden@lindabury.com

Steven Backfisch — 1955 — St. Bernard College, B.A. (summa cum laude), 1977; Seton Hall University, J.D. (cum laude), 1980 — Admitted to Bar, 1980, New Jersey; 1980, U.S. District Court, District of New Jersey; 1983, U.S. Court of Appeals, Third Circuit; 1989, U.S. Supreme Court — Master, Brennan Vanderbilt Inn of Court (President, 1999-2000) — Practice Areas: Employment Law; Personal Injury; Product Liability — E-mail: sbackfisch@lindabury.com

Kathleen M. Connelly — 1959 — Monmouth University, B.A. (cum laude), 1983; Rutgers University School of Law-Newark, J.D., 1990 — Admitted to Bar, 1990, New Jersey; 1991, New York; 1990, U.S. District Court, District of New Jersey — Practice Areas: Employer Liability; Sexual Harassment; Special Investigations; Wrongful Termination; Employment Discrimination; Wage and Hour Law — E-mail: kconnelly@lindabury.com

Of Counsel

John M. Boyle — 1929 — Rutgers University, B.A., 1952; J.D., 1954; University of Nevada Judicial College; Harvard Law School; The University of Kansas — Admitted to Bar, 1954, New Jersey; 1954, U.S. District Court, District of New Jersey; 1960, U.S. Supreme Court — Member International Society of Barristers — Fellow, American Bar Association; Presiding Judge, Equity Part, Chancery Division, Superior Court of New Jersey (1989-2002); Law Div. (1984-1989) — Practice Areas: Alternative Dispute Resolution; Arbitration; Mediation — E-mail: jboyle@lindabury.com

Scott M. Yaffe — 1956 — The University of Chicago, B.A., 1978; Benjamin N. Cardozo School of Law, J.D., 1982 — Admitted to Bar, 1984, New York; 1996, New Jersey; 1985, U.S. District Court, Eastern and Southern Districts of New York; 1985, U.S. District Court, District of New Jersey — Practice Areas: Construction Law — E-mail: syaffe@lindabury.com

WOODBURY † 10,174 Gloucester Co.

Powell, Birchmeier & Powell
70 Euclid Street
Woodbury, New Jersey 08096
Telephone: 856-848-7091
www.powbirch.com

(Tuckahoe, NJ Office*: 1891 State Highway 50, 08250, P.O. Box 582, 08250-0582)
(Tel: 609-628-3414)
(Fax: 609-628-2966)
(E-Mail: powbirch@comcast.net)

General Civil Practice, Trial Practice, Insurance Defense, Negligence, Defense Litigation, Product Liability, Coverage Issues, Litigation, Workers' Compensation, Subrogation, Civil Rights, Governmental Liability, Medical Negligence, Wrongful Termination, General Chancery Practice, Section 1983 Litigation

(See listing under Tuckahoe, NJ for additional information)

WOODSTOWN 3,505 Salem Co.

Refer To
Tighe & Cottrell, P.A.
One Customs House
704 King Street, Suite 500
Wilmington, Delaware 19801
Telephone: 302-658-6400
Fax: 302-658-9836
Mailing Address: P.O. Box 1031, Wilmington, DE 19899-1031

General Liability, Professional Liability, Construction Law, Coverage Issues, Litigation, Surety Bonds, Subrogation, Malpractice

SEE COMPLETE LISTING UNDER WILMINGTON, DELAWARE (17 MILES)

NEW MEXICO

CAPITAL: SANTA FE

COUNTIES AND COUNTY SEATS

County	County Seat	County	County Seat	County	County Seat
Bernalillo	Albuquerque	Harding	Mosquero	Roosevelt	Portales
Catron	Reserve	Hidalgo	Lordsburg	Sandoval	Bernalillo
Chaves	Roswell	Lea	Lovington	San Juan	Aztec
Cibola	Grants	Lincoln	Carrizozo	San Miguel	Las Vegas
Colfax	Raton	Los Alamos	Los Alamos	Santa Fe	Santa Fe
Curry	Clovis	Luna	Deming	Sierra	Truth or Consequences
De Baca	Fort Sumner	McKinley	Gallup	Socorro	Socorro
Dona Ana	Las Cruces	Mora	Mora	Taos	Taos
Eddy	Carlsbad	Otero	Alamogordo	Torrance	Estancia
Grant	Silver City	Quay	Tucumcari	Union	Clayton
Guadalupe	Santa Rosa	Rio Arriba	Tierra Amarilla	Valencia	Los Lunas

In the text that follows "†" indicates County Seats.

Our files contain additional verified data on the firms listed herein. This additional information is available on request.

A.M. BEST COMPANY

NEW MEXICO

ALAMOGORDO † 30,403 Otero Co.

Refer To

Atwood, Malone, Turner & Sabin, P.A.
400 North Pennsylvania Avenue, Suite 1100
Roswell, New Mexico 88201
  Telephone: 575-622-6221
  Fax: 575-624-2883
Mailing Address: P.O. Drawer 700, Roswell, NM 88202-0700

Insurance Defense, Casualty, Fire, Workers' Compensation, Life Insurance, Product Liability, Medical Malpractice, Professional Liability, Employment Law, Commercial Litigation

SEE COMPLETE LISTING UNDER ROSWELL, NEW MEXICO (123 MILES)

ALBUQUERQUE † 545,852 Bernalillo Co.

Butt, Thornton & Baehr, P.C.
Suite 300
4101 Indian School Road N.E.
Albuquerque, New Mexico 87110
  Telephone: 505-884-0777
  Fax: 505-889-8870
  www.btblaw.com

Established: 1959

Insurance Law, Casualty, Transportation, Automobile, Workers' Compensation, Professional Malpractice, Surety, Aviation, Product Liability, Environmental Law, Appellate Practice, Civil Rights, Commercial Litigation, Construction and Bond Claims, Government Entities

Firm Profile: Our practice is concentrated in defending claims in the areas of personal injury, aviation, products liability, insurance, workers' compensation, transportation, professional malpractice, construction and civil rights. In addition, our commercial section can meet your legal needs in the areas of banking, bonds, corporations, partnerships, mortgage financing, real estate, bankruptcy, wills, estate planning and related litigation since 1959.

Insurance Clients

American States Insurance Company
Chubb Group of Insurance Companies
CNA Insurance Companies
Colonial Insurance Company of California
E & O Professionals
First Colonial Insurance Company
GAB Robins North America, Inc.
Great American Insurance Company
Home Insurance Company
Insurance Company of North America
K & K Insurance Group, Inc.
Medical Claims Management Group
Northwestern National Insurance Company
Ohio Casualty Insurance Company
Progressive Insurance Company
Reliance Insurance Company
Royal Insurance Group
St. Paul Fire and Marine Insurance Company
Travelers Insurance Companies
United States Aviation Underwriters, Inc.
Wausau Insurance Companies
Western World Insurance Company
Associated Aviation Underwriters
Chrysler Insurance Company
CIGNA Property and Casualty Insurance Company
Colonial Insurance Company
Colorado Casualty Insurance Company
Fireman's Fund Insurance Company
General Accident Insurance Company
Guarantee Insurance Company
Horizon Health Care Corporation
Interstate Insurance Group
Kemper Insurance Companies
Liberty Mutual Insurance Company
The Medical Protective Company
Northland Insurance Company
Occidental Fire & Casualty Company of North Carolina
Progressive Casualty Insurance Company
Reliance National Insurance Company
Sentry Claims Services
Transamerica Insurance Company
United Pacific Insurance Company
Universal Underwriters Insurance Company
Western Insurance Group

Non-Insurance Clients

Alexsis, Inc.
Chrysler Corporation
American Suzuki Motor Corporation
Circle K Corporation
Equity General Agents, Inc.
Federal Express
FMC Corporation
Honda North America, Inc.
Michelin Tire Corporation
Mitsubishi Motors Corporation
Northern Telecom, Inc.
The Raymond Corporation
Circle K Stores, Inc., a division of Tosco Corp.
Ferrellgas
Ford Motor Company
Kawasaki Motors Corporation, U.S.A.
Navistar International Transportation Corporation

Shareholders

Carlos G. Martinez — 1947 — University of San Francisco, B.A., 1969; University of California, J.D., 1972 — Admitted to Bar, 1972, New Mexico; 1973, U.S. District Court, District of New Mexico; 1974, U.S. District Court, Western District of Texas; U.S. Court of Appeals, Fifth and Tenth Circuits; U.S. Court of International Trade; U.S. Court of Military Appeals — Member American and Albuquerque Bar Associations; State Bar of New Mexico; State Bar of Texas; Hispanic Bar Association; New Mexico Defense Lawyers Association (Workers' Compensation Newsletter Editor); New Mexico Workers' Compensation Association (Board Member) — New Mexico Workers' Compensation Manual — Board Certified, New Mexico Workers' Compensation Specialist — Practice Areas: Employment Litigation; General Liability; Workers' Compensation

Alfred L. Green, Jr. — 1947 — The University of New Mexico, B.A., 1969; University of Arkansas, M.S., 1972; The University of New Mexico, J.D., 1976 — Admitted to Bar, 1976, New Mexico; U.S. District Court, District of New Mexico; U.S. Court of Appeals, Tenth Circuit; U.S. Supreme Court; U.S. Court of Military Appeals — Member American and Albuquerque Bar Associations; State Bar of New Mexico; New Mexico Medical Review Commission; American Law Firm Association (Product Liability Section); Defense Research Institute; New Mexico Defense Lawyers Association — Past Litigation Director; AV Rated, Martindale-Hubbell — Practice Areas: Complex Litigation; Product Liability; Professional Liability

James H. Johansen — 1955 — New Mexico State University, B.B.A., 1977; The University of New Mexico, J.D., 1980 — Admitted to Bar, 1980, New Mexico; U.S. District Court, District of New Mexico; U.S. Court of Appeals, Tenth Circuit — Member American and Albuquerque Bar Associations; State Bar of New Mexico; New Mexico Defense Lawyers Association (President, 1995); Defense Research Institute (Seniro Advisor) — Senior Arbitrator, Better Business Bureau; AV Rated, Martindale-Hubbell — Practice Areas: Insurance Law; Bad Faith; Litigation

Rodney L. Schlagel — 1954 — University of Denver, B.A., 1976; J.D., 1979 — Admitted to Bar, 1979, Colorado; 1980, New Mexico; U.S. District Court, District of New Mexico; U.S. Court of Appeals, Tenth Circuit — Member American and Albuquerque Bar Associations; State Bar of New Mexico — President, Managing Partner — Practice Areas: Business Transactions; Commercial Transactions; Commercial Litigation; Business and Real Estate Transactions

Martin Diamond — 1945 — State University of New York at Buffalo, B.A., 1968; New York University, J.D., 1974 — Admitted to Bar, 1975, New York; 1978, New Mexico; U.S. District Court, District of New Mexico — Member State Bar of New Mexico; Albuquerque Bar Association; New Mexico Medical Review Commission; New Mexico Defense Lawyers Association; Defense Research Institute — Former Assistant District Attorney, Bronx County, New York; Former Assistant District Attorney, Bernalillo County, New Mexico; AV Rated, Martindale-Hubbell — Practice Areas: Construction Litigation; General Liability; Litigation; Trucking; Transportation

David N. Whitham — 1948 — The University of New Mexico, B.U.S., 1973; J.D., 1980 — Admitted to Bar, 1980, New Mexico; U.S. District Court, District of New Mexico — Member American and Albuquerque Bar Associations; State Bar of New Mexico; New Mexico Trial Lawyers Association; Association of Trial Lawyers of America; New Mexico Defense Lawyers Association; Defense Research Institute — AV Rated, Martindale-Hubbell — Practice Areas: Workers' Compensation; Employment Litigation; General Liability; Professional Liability

Emily A. Franke — 1955 — The University of New Mexico, B.A., 1977; M.B.A., 1981; J.D., 1985 — Admitted to Bar, 1985, New Mexico; U.S. District Court, District of New Mexico; U.S. Court of Appeals, Tenth Circuit; U.S. Supreme Court — Member American and Albuquerque Bar Associations; State Bar of New Mexico; New Mexico Review Commission; New Mexico Defense Lawyers Association; Defense Research Institute — Practice Areas: Alternative Dispute Resolution; Arbitration; Mediation; Tort Litigation

Glenna Hayes — 1946 — Eastern New Mexico University, B.S., 1971; M.Ed., 1979; The University of New Mexico, J.D., 1986 — Admitted to Bar, 1986,

ALBUQUERQUE

Butt, Thornton & Baehr, P.C., Albuquerque, NM
(Continued)

New Mexico; U.S. District Court, District of New Mexico; U.S. Court of Appeals, Tenth Circuit; Supreme Court of New Mexico — Member American and Albuquerque Bar Associations; State Bar of New Mexico; New Mexico Trial Lawyers Association; New Mexico Defense Lawyers Association; Defense Research Institute — Practice Areas: Workers' Compensation

Jane A. Laflin — 1957 — The University of New Mexico, B.S., 1980; J.D., 1987 — Admitted to Bar, 1987, New Mexico; U.S. District Court, District of New Mexico; U.S. Court of Appeals, Tenth Circuit — Member American and Albuquerque Bar Associations; State Bar of New Mexico; New Mexico Trial Lawyers Association; Women's Bar Association — Practice Areas: General Liability; Litigation; Product Liability; Workers' Compensation

Paul T. Yarbrough — Vice President — 1962 — The University of New Mexico, B.A., 1984; J.D., 1988 — Admitted to Bar, 1988, New Mexico; U.S. District Court, District of New Mexico; U.S. Court of Appeals, Tenth Circuit; Supreme Court of New Mexico — Member State Bar of New Mexico; Albuquerque Bar Association; Tenth Circuit Judicial Conference; New Mexico Defense Lawyers Association; Defense Research Institute; Transportation Lawyers Association; Trucking Industry Defense Association — AV Rated, Martindale-Hubbell — Practice Areas: Aviation; General Liability; Litigation; Sports Law; Trucking; Transportation

Michael P. Clemens — 1964 — University of Colorado at Denver, B.A., 1985; University of Denver, J.D., 1989 — Admitted to Bar, 1989, New Mexico; U.S. District Court, District of New Mexico; U.S. Court of Appeals, Tenth Circuit — Member American and Albuquerque Bar Associations; State Bar of New Mexico; Defense Research Institute; Federation of Defense and Corporate Counsel — Treasurer — Practice Areas: Civil Litigation; General Liability; Litigation; Insurance; Bad Faith; Errors and Omissions; Mediation

Agnes Fuentevilla Padilla — Secretary — 1966 — The University of New Mexico, B.A., 1988; J.D., 1992 — Admitted to Bar, 1992, New Mexico; U.S. District Court, District of New Mexico — Member American and Albuquerque Bar Associations; State Bar of New Mexico; New Mexico Trial Lawyers Association; New Mexico Women's Bar Association; American Law Firm Association; New Mexico Defense Lawyers Association; American Inns of Court — Certified Specialist, Employment and Labor Law — Languages: Spanish — Practice Areas: Employment Litigation; General Liability; Governmental Entity Defense; Civil Rights

Monica R. Garcia — Loyola Marymount University, B.B.A., 1991; The University of New Mexico, J.D., 1996 — Admitted to Bar, 1996, New Mexico; U.S. District Court, District of New Mexico — Member American Bar Association; Defense Research Institute; New Mexico Defense Lawyers Association — AV Rated, Martindale-Hubbell — Practice Areas: Employment Litigation; General Liability; Governmental Entity Defense; Civil Rights; Insurance Litigation; Bad Faith; Nursing Home Litigation; Product Liability; Retail Liability; Trucking; Transportation

S. Carolyn Ramos — 1971 — Middlebury College, B.A., 1993; The University of New Mexico, J.D., 2000 — Moot Court Team — Admitted to Bar, 2000, New Mexico; U.S. District Court, District of New Mexico; U.S. Court of Appeals, Tenth Circuit — Member American Bar Association; State Bar of New Mexico (Legal Panel, National Health Law); Hispanic National Bar Association — Languages: Spanish — Practice Areas: Medical Negligence; Trucking; Transportation; Product Liability; General Liability

W. Ann Maggiore — 1952 — The University of New Mexico, B.A., 1989; J.D., 1992 — Admitted to Bar, 1992, New Mexico; 1998, U.S. District Court, District of New Mexico; U.S. Court of Appeals, Tenth Circuit — Member State Bar of New Mexico (Board Member, Health Law Section); National Registry of Emergency Medical Technicians; National Association of EMS Physicians; Albuquerque Sexual Assualt Nurses Examiners (Board Member) — Practice Areas: Medical Negligence; Law Enforcement Liability; Governmental Entity Defense; Civil Rights

Raúl P. Sedillo — 1975 — New Mexico State University, B.C.J., 1999; The University of New Mexico, J.D., 2002 — Admitted to Bar, 2002, New Mexico; U.S. District Court, District of New Mexico; U.S. Court of Appeals, Tenth Circuit — Member State Bar of New Mexico; New Mexico Hispanic Bar Association (Young Lawyers Division); New Mexico Defense Lawyers Association (Trial Practice Board Member) — Practice Areas: Employment Litigation; Insurance Law; Bad Faith; General Liability; Governmental Entity Defense; Civil Rights; Professional Liability; Trucking; Transportation

Neil R. Blake — Colorado State University, B.A., 1987; The University of Arizona, J.D., 1991 — Admitted to Bar, 1991, New Mexico; 2005, Texas; 1991, U.S. District Court, District of New Mexico; U.S. Court of Appeals, Tenth Circuit — Member Albuquerque Bar Association; New Mexico Medical Review Commission; New Mexico Trial Lawyers Association; Association of

NEW MEXICO

Butt, Thornton & Baehr, P.C., Albuquerque, NM
(Continued)

Trial Lawyers of America — Practice Areas: Medical Malpractice; Professional Liability; Wrongful Death; Trucking; Transportation; Civil Litigation; General Liability

Paul R. Bishop — Purdue University, B.A. (distinguished graduate), 2002; The University of New Mexico, J.D., 2005 — Admitted to Bar, 2005, New Mexico

M. Scott Owen — 1979 — Michigan State University, B.S., 2002; Thomas M. Cooley Law School, J.D., 2006 — Admitted to Bar, 2006, New Mexico — Member State Bar of New Mexico

Associates

Phillip W. Cheves — Abilene Christian College, B.A., 1987; Pepperdine University, J.D., 1991 — Admitted to Bar, 1991, New Mexico; Texas; 2001, U.S. District Court, District of New Mexico; U.S. Supreme Court — Member State Bar of New Mexico; State Bar of Texas; Albuquerque Bar Association; New Mexico Defense Lawyers Association

Shawn Cummings — The University of New Mexico, B.A., 2004; J.D., 2008 — Admitted to Bar, 2008, New Mexico; U.S. District Court, District of New Mexico — Member State Bar of New Mexico; Albuquerque Bar Association; New Mexico Defense Lawyers Association

Candace J. Cavanaugh — The University of New Mexico, B.S., 1986; J.D., 1989 — Admitted to Bar, 1989, New Mexico; 2000, Colorado; 2009, U.S. District Court, District of New Mexico — Member State Bar of New Mexico; The Colorado Bar Association — Certified Equine Appraiser

Felicia C. Boyd — The University of New Mexico, J.D., 2005 — Admitted to Bar, 2005, New Mexico; 2005, U.S. District Court, District of New Mexico; U.S. Court of Appeals, Tenth Circuit — Member American and Albuquerque Bar Associations; State Bar of New Mexico; Defense Research Institute; New Mexico Defense Lawyers Association

Matthew A. Jones — 1977 — Brigham Young University, B.A., 2000; The University of New Mexico, M.S., 2003; J.D., 2010 — Admitted to Bar, 2010, New Mexico; U.S. District Court, District of New Mexico; U.S. Court of Appeals, Tenth Circuit — Member State Bar of New Mexico; J. Rueben Clark Law Society; Defense Research Institute

Geoffrey D. White — The University of New Mexico, B.A., 1992; J.D., 2009 — Admitted to Bar, 2009, New Mexico; U.S. District Court, District of New Mexico; U.S. Court of Appeals, Tenth Circuit — Member American Bar Association; Defense Research Institute; New Mexico Defense Lawyers Association

Scott E. Stromberg — The University of New Mexico, B.A. (summa cum laude), 2007; J.D., 2010 — Admitted to Bar, 2010, New Mexico; U.S. District Court, District of New Mexico; U.S. Court of Appeals, Tenth Circuit

Tobanna P. Barker — Seattle University, B.A., 2002; J.D., 2008 — Admitted to Bar, 2008, Washington; New Mexico; U.S. District Court, District of New Mexico — Member State Bar of New Mexico; Washington State and New Mexico Women's Bar Associations; New Mexico Defense Lawyers Association

Christopher Ryan   Brett Eaton

Of Counsel

Paul L. Butt — (1930-2009)

J. Duke Thornton — 1944 — The University of New Mexico, B.B.A., 1966; J.D., 1969 — Admitted to Bar, 1969, New Mexico; 1984, New York — Member American Bar Association; State Bar of New Mexico; American Board of Trial Advocates; Association for Transportation Law, Logistics and Policy; International Association of Insurance Counsel; Defense Research Institute — "Trial Handbook for New Mexico Lawyers," Lawyers Cooperative Publishing

Norman L. Gagne — 1943 — University of Colorado, B.A., 1966; The University of New Mexico, J.D., 1974 — Admitted to Bar, 1974, New Mexico; U.S. District Court, District of New Mexico; U.S. District Court, Western District of Texas; U.S. Court of Appeals, Fifth and Tenth Circuits; U.S. Court of Military Appeals — Member American and Albuquerque Bar Associations; State Bar of New Mexico; State Bar of Texas; Fellow, New Mexico Bar Foundation; Hispanic Bar Association; American Law Firm Association; New Mexico Defense Lawyers Association

Raymond A. Baehr — 1938 — Fairleigh Dickinson University, B.S., 1970; The University of New Mexico, J.D., 1973 — Admitted to Bar, 1973, New Mexico; 1985, New York; 1980, U.S. Supreme Court — Member American and Albuquerque Bar Associations; State Bar of New Mexico — Co-Editor, New Mexico Section, Cushman's Fifty State Construction Liens and Bond Claims, Wiley Publications

NEW MEXICO — ALBUQUERQUE

Butt, Thornton & Baehr, P.C., Albuquerque, NM (Continued)

Robert T. Booms — 1944 — Dartmouth College, A.B., 1966; University of Denver, J.D., 1970 — Admitted to Bar, 1970, Colorado; 1989, New Mexico; 1993, U.S. Supreme Court — Member New Mexico Supreme Court Rules of Evidence and Code of Conduct Committees; New Mexico Defense Lawyers Association; Defense Research Institute

Sherrill K. Filter — 1954 — William Woods College, B.A., 1975; University of Michigan, J.D., 1978 — Admitted to Bar, 1978, Michigan; 1984, New Mexico; U.S. District Court, Eastern District of Michigan; U.S. District Court, District of New Mexico — Member American and Albuquerque Bar Associations; State Bar of New Mexico; State Bar of Michigan

(Revisors of the New Mexico Insurance Law Digest for this Publication)

(This firm is also listed in the Subrogation section of this directory)

Civerolo, Gralow, Hill & Curtis
A Professional Association
20 First Plaza NW, Suite 500
Albuquerque, New Mexico 87102
Telephone: 505-842-8255
Fax: 505-764-6099
www.civerolo.com

Established: 1950

Civil Trial Practice, State and Federal Courts, Aviation, Civil Rights, Employment Law, Hospitals, Health Care, Insurance Defense, Risk Management, Professional Malpractice, Bad Faith, Insurance Coverage, Subrogation, Mediation/Settlement Facilitation, Trucking Claims Defense

Firm Profile: Founded in Albuquerque in 1950, Civerolo, Gralow, Hill & Curtis, P.A. is a civil litigation firm offering advice, counseling and, when necessary, trial and appellate representation.

The firm's attorneys and staff work together to provide effective management of our clients' cases, using up-to-date computerized word processing, data processing, conflict of interest searches, firm-wide calendaring and legal and technical research through national legal databases and internet resources.

Civerolo, Gralow, Hill & Curtis is committed to providing legal services promptly, competently and cost-effectively.

Insurance Clients

American Modern Home Insurance Company
Chubb & Son, Inc.
Deep South Insurance Services
Kmart Insurance Group
New Mexico Risk Management Division
Philadelphia Insurance Company
Titan Indemnity Company
United Services Automobile Association (USAA)
Carolina Casualty Insurance Company
Crum & Forster Insurance
The Hartford Insurance Group
National Interstate Insurance Company
OneBeacon Insurance
Risk Enterprise Management, Ltd.
United National Insurance Company

Non-Insurance Clients

Budget Rent-A-Car System, Inc.
Schneider National, Inc.

Richard C. Civerolo — (1917-2014)

Partner/Shareholder

Lawrence H. Hill — 1947 — The University of New Mexico, B.A. (magna cum laude), 1969; University of Connecticut, M.A., 1970; The University of Utah, J.D., 1973 — Admitted to Bar, 1973, New Mexico; U.S. District Court, District of New Mexico; U.S. Court of Appeals, Tenth Circuit — Member American and Albuquerque Bar Associations; State Bar of New Mexico (Committee on Trial Practice); American Board of Trial Advocates (President, 2005); New Mexico Defense Lawyers Association; Defense Research Institute — New Mexico Supreme Court Committee on Evidence, Medical Legal Panel Member — USAR, Judge Advocate, LTC (retired) — Practice Areas: Bad Faith; Insurance Coverage; Civil Litigation — E-mail: hilll@civerolo.com

Robert J. Curtis — 1959 — New Mexico State University, B.A., 1980; The University of New Mexico, J.D., 1986 — Admitted to Bar, 1986, New Mexico; 1987, U.S. Court of Appeals, Tenth Circuit; 1989, U.S. Supreme Court — Member New Mexico Rules of Evidence Committee; New Mexico Medical Review Committee; Fellow of Litigation Counsel of America; Defense Research Institute; Federation of Defense and Corporate Counsel — Practice Areas: Drug; Medical Devices; Medical Malpractice; Product Liability — E-mail: curtisr@civerolo.com

Lisa Entress Pullen — 1968 — College of William & Mary, B.S., 1988; J.D., 1991; Georgetown University, LL.M. (with distinction), 1992 — Admitted to Bar, 1991, Pennsylvania; 1992, New Mexico; 1993, U.S. District Court, District of New Mexico; U.S. Court of Appeals, Tenth Circuit — Member American and Albuquerque Bar Associations; State Bar of New Mexico; New Mexico Defense Lawyers Association; Defense Research Institute — Practice Areas: Employment Law; Product Liability; Insurance Coverage; Bad Faith — E-mail: pullenl@civerolo.com

Lance D. Richards — 1970 — The University of New Mexico, B.B.A., 1992; The University of Tulsa, J.D., 1995 — Admitted to Bar, 1996, Oklahoma; 1997, New Mexico; 1999, U.S. District Court, District of New Mexico; 2003, Acoma Pueblo Tribal Court — Member State Bar of New Mexico (Board Member, Trial Practice Section; Chairman, 2009); New Mexico Medical Review Commission; American Board of Trial Advocates (Treasurer, New Mexico Chapter); New Mexico Defense Lawyers Association; Trucking Industry Defense Association — Practice Areas: Insurance Defense; Trucking Law; Product Liability; Construction Law — E-mail: richardsl@civerolo.com

Megan Day Hill — 1974 — Bryn Mawr College, B.A., 1996; The University of New Mexico, J.D. (with honors), 1999 — Clerk to C. LeRoy Hansen, United States District Court for the District of New Mexico — New Mexico Law Review — Admitted to Bar, 1999, New Mexico; U.S. District Court, District of New Mexico; U.S. Court of Appeals, Tenth Circuit — Member American Bar Association; State Bar of New Mexico; National Transportation Safety Board Bar Association; Defense Research Institute — Practice Areas: Bad Faith; Trucking Law; Insurance Defense; Personal Injury — E-mail: hillm@civerolo.com

Associates

Justin Robbs — 1977 — Eastern New Mexico University, B.B.A., 1999; The University of New Mexico, J.D., 2011 — Admitted to Bar, 2012, New Mexico — E-mail: robbsj@civerolo.com

Joseph Reichert — 1952 — Tulane University, B.A., 1975; The University of New Mexico, J.D., 1978 — Admitted to Bar, 1978, New Mexico; U.S. District Court, District of New Mexico; 1988, U.S. Court of Appeals, Tenth Circuit; U.S. Supreme Court — Member American and Albuquerque Bar Associations; National Rifle Association — Languages: Spanish, German — Practice Areas: Workers' Compensation; Automobile Liability; Premises Liability; Appellate Practice — E-mail: reichertj@civerolo.com

David M. Wesner — 1967 — The University of New Mexico, B.A., 1995; J.D. (Dean's Honor Roll), 2002 — Thesis Honors — Admitted to Bar, 2002, New Mexico; 2006, U.S. District Court, District of New Mexico; 2009, U.S. Court of Appeals, Tenth Circuit — Member Albuquerque Bar Association; New Mexico Defense Lawyers Association — Practice Areas: Civil Litigation; Appeals; Insurance Coverage — E-mail: wesnerd@civerolo.com

Kerri L. Allensworth — 1970 — The University of New Mexico, J.D., 1993; J.D., 1996 — Admitted to Bar, 1996, New Mexico; 1997, U.S. District Court, District of New Mexico — Practice Areas: General Civil Litigation; Insurance Defense; Insurance Coverage — E-mail: allensworthk@civerolo.com

Of Counsel

M. Clea Gutterson — Northeastern University, B.A. (with high honors, Pi Sigma Alpha), 1982; Suffolk University, J.D., 1985 — Admitted to Bar, 1985, New Mexico; U.S. District Court, District of New Mexico; U.S. Court of Appeals, Tenth Circuit — Member American Bar Association (Tort and Insurance Practice Section); State Bar of New Mexico; New Mexico Defense Lawyers Association; Defense Research Institute — Languages: Portuguese — E-mail: guttersonc@civerolo.com

Special Counsel

Ellen M. Kelly — 1952 — The University of New Mexico, B.A., 1973; J.D. (Dean's Award), 1980; University of Washington, Master of Law, 1999 — Admitted to Bar, 1980, New Mexico; U.S. District Court, District of New Mexico; U.S. Court of Appeals, Tenth Circuit — Member State Bar of New

ALBUQUERQUE   NEW MEXICO

Civerolo, Gralow, Hill & Curtis, A Professional Association, Albuquerque, NM (Continued)

Mexico; Albuquerque Bar Association; New Mexico Medical Review Commission — Practice Areas: Insurance Defense — E-mail: kellye@civerolo.com

Kelly A. Genova, PC

916 Silver Avenue SW
Albuquerque, New Mexico 87102-3047
Telephone: 505-244-0547
Fax: 505-244-0557
E-Mail: KGenova@aol.com
www.KellyAGenovaPC.com

Established: 1992

Workers' Compensation, General Liability, Appellate Practice

Firm Profile: Kelly A. Genova has been recognized as a Specialist in Workers' Compensation Law by the New Mexico Board of Legal Specialization since 1992. As a sole proprietor, her practice is focused primarily on defense representation of employers and insurers. Ms. Genova graduated from St. John's College in 1982, and from the University of New Mexico School of Law in 1985. After practicing law with several firms, Ms. Genova opened her own law office in 1992, and became an attorney of Counsel to Civerolo, Gralow, Hill & Curtis, P.A. in 1999.

Insurance Clients

Adjusting Alternatives, LLC/Food Industry Self-Insurance Fund of New Mexico
Marriott Claims Service
Builders Trust of New Mexico
CCMSI
GAB Robins, Inc.
Sedgwick Claims Management Services, Inc.

Non-Insurance Clients

City of Albuquerque
Federal Express
San Juan County
State of New Mexico
Dollar General Corporation
New Mexico Association of Counties

Firm Member

Kelly A. Genova — 1960 — St. John's College, B.A., 1992; The University of New Mexico School of Law, J.D., 1985 — Admitted to Bar, 1985, New Mexico; 1987, Massachusetts; U.S. District Court, District of New Mexico; U.S. Court of Appeals, Tenth Circuit — Member State Bar of New Mexico; Massachusetts Bar Association — E-mail: KGenova@aol.com

Guebert Bruckner PC

6801 Jefferson Street NE, Suite 400
Albuquerque, New Mexico 87109
Telephone: 505-823-2300
Fax: 505-823-9600
E-Mail: kathleen@guebertlaw.com
www.guebertlaw.com

Bad Faith, Construction Defect, Insurance Coverage, Personal Injury, Product Liability, Wrongful Death

Firm Profile: Established in 1993, Guebert Bruckner P.C. is a civil trial litigation firm representing defendants in complex wrongful death, serious personal injury, and insurance litigation throughout the State of New Mexico. We are certified to practice in both State and Federal court and on the Navajo Nation.

Insurance Clients

State Farm Insurance Companies   Zurich North America

Partners/Shareholders

Terry R. Guebert — Southern Illinois University, B.A., 1973; Pepperdine University School of Law, J.D., 1976 — Admitted to Bar, 1976, California; 1982, New Mexico; 1997, Navajo Nation; U.S. District Court, District of New Mexico; U.S. Court of Military Appeals; U.S. Court of Appeals, Tenth Circuit —

Guebert Bruckner PC, Albuquerque, NM (Continued)

Member Fellow, American College of Trial Lawyers; American Board of Trial Advocates; Defense Research Institute; New Mexico Defense Lawyers Association — Southwest Super Lawyers, 2007-2012 — U.S. Air Force JAGC, 1977-1982; USAF Reserve, 1982-1987

Don Bruckner — Georgetown University, B.A. (cum laude), 1983; The University of New Mexico School of Law, J.D., 1986 — Admitted to Bar, 1986, New Mexico; 1990, Texas; 1987, U.S. Army Court of Military Review; 1989, U.S. Court of Military Appeals; U.S. District Court, District of New Mexico; U.S. Court of Appeals, Tenth Circuit — Member American Board of Trial Advocates; Defense Research Institute — Southwest Super Lawyers, 2010-2011 — U.S. Army JAGC, 1986-1991; Lieutenant Colonel, New Mexico Army National Guard, 1991-2003

Christopher J. DeLara — New Mexico State University, B.C.J., 1994; The University of New Mexico, M.P.A., 2000; The University of New Mexico School of Law, J.D., 2000 — Admitted to Bar, 2000, New Mexico; U.S. District Court, District of New Mexico; U.S. Court of Appeals, Tenth Circuit; 2004, Navajo Nation; 2013, U.S. District Court, District of Colorado — Member State Bar of New Mexico (Member, Young Lawyers Division; Board of Directors, 2002-2003); New Mexico Hispanic Bar Association; New Mexico Defense Lawyers Association; Defense Research Institute

Senior Attorney

Robert Gentile

Associates

Lawrence Junker   David C. Odegard
Rebecca A. Ralph   Jason A. Vigil

Keleher & McLeod, P.A.

201 3rd Street, N.W., 12th Floor
Albuquerque, New Mexico 87102-3382
Telephone: 505-346-4646
Fax: 505-346-1370
E-Mail: info@keleher-law.com
www.keleher-law.com

Established: 1915

Litigation, Insurance Defense, Aviation, Civil Rights, Construction Law, Environmental Law, Insurance Coverage, Medical Malpractice, Motor Vehicle, Premises Liability, Product Liability, Professional Liability, Property, Subrogation, Fidelity and Surety

Firm Profile: Keleher & McLeod is one of the oldest and largest firms in the state. The firm was founded in 1915 by W.A. Keleher. We are a particularly New Mexico firm, with more than half of our attorneys graduating from the University of New Mexico School of Law.

Insurance Clients

Allied Insurance Company
Ardent Health Services
Argo Pro
CNA
Developers Surety and Indemnity Company
Farmers Insurance
Great American Insurance Company
Liberty Mutual Insurance Company
National General Insurance Company
Oceanus Insurance Company
RLI Insurance Company
State Farm Insurance Companies
Titan Auto Insurance Claims
Travelers Bond & Financial Products
Westchester Fire Insurance Company
XL Insurance
American National Property and Casualty Company
Century Surety Company
Cress Insurance Consultants Inc
Employers Mutual Casualty Company
Fireman's Fund Insurance Company
Hudson Insurance Group
Metropolitan Property and Casualty Insurance Company
National Indemnity Company
Old Republic National Title Insurance Company
The Surety & Fidelity Association of America
Travelers Insurance Company
Tribal First/Alliant Specialty Insurance Services, Inc.
Westfield Group
Zurich

Non-Insurance Clients

Financial Resolutions, LLC   Fortegra Financial Corp
LifePoint Hospitals, Inc.   Presbyterian Healthcare Services

Keleher & McLeod, P.A., Albuquerque, NM (Continued)

Shareholders

S. Charles Archuleta — The University of New Mexico, B.S., 1986; Boston University, J.D., 1989 — Admitted to Bar, 1989, New Mexico; U.S. District Court, District of New Mexico; U.S. Court of Appeals, Tenth Circuit; Laguna Pueblo Tribal Court — Member State Bar of New Mexico (Employment Law Section); Albuquerque Bar Association; New Mexico Hispanic Bar; New Mexico Defense Lawyers Association — Practice Areas: Employment Law; Commercial Litigation; Business Law; Commercial Law; Insurance Defense

Arthur O. Beach — The University of New Mexico, B.B.A., 1967; J.D., 1970 — Admitted to Bar, 1970, New Mexico; 1971, U.S. Court of Appeals, Tenth Circuit; 1975, U.S. Supreme Court — Member American (Tort Trial and Insurance Practice Section) and Albuquerque Bar Associations; State Bar of New Mexico (Specialization Board, Unauthorized Practice of Law Committee, Dental-Legal Committee, New Mexico Medical Review Commission); New Mexico Bar Foundation — Practice Areas: Alternative Dispute Resolution; Civil Litigation; Complex Litigation; Insurance Defense; Professional Malpractice; Medical Malpractice

Mary Behm — University of Nevada, B.S./B.A., 1985; The University of New Mexico, J.D. (cum laude), 1999 — Order of the Coif — Admitted to Bar, 1999, New Mexico — Member American Bar Association; State Bar of New Mexico (Health Law Committee); New Mexico Women's Bar; New Mexico Defense Lawyers Association (Education Committee); Defense Research Institute — Practice Areas: Civil Litigation; Health Care; Insurance Law; Insurance Defense; Professional Malpractice

Ann Maloney Conway — University of Puget Sound, B.A. (cum laude), 1978; Eastern New Mexico University, M.A. (magna cum laude), 1980; University of Notre Dame, J.D., 1984 — Admitted to Bar, 1984, New Mexico; U.S. District Court, District of New Mexico; U.S. Court of Appeals, Tenth Circuit; U.S. Supreme Court — Member American (Tort Trial and Insurance Section; Fidelity and Surety Law, Insurance Coverage Litigation and Litigation Sub Committees) and Albuquerque (Past President) Bar Associations; Surety Claims Institute; New Mexico Defense Lawyers' Association (Director); Defense Research Institute — Practice Areas: Insurance Law; Class Actions; Fidelity and Surety; Arbitration; Mediation; Commercial Litigation; Civil Litigation; Employment Law

Jeffrey A. Dahl — The University of Utah, B.S. (magna cum laude), 1976; Brigham Young University, J.D. (cum laude), 1979 — Admitted to Bar, 1979, New Mexico; U.S. District Court, District of New Mexico; 1985, U.S. Court of Appeals, Tenth Circuit; 2006, U.S. Court of Appeals for the Federal Circuit — Member Federal and American Bar Association; State Bar of New Mexico — Practice Areas: Civil Litigation; Employment Law; Insurance Defense; Civil Rights; Commercial Litigation

Thomas F. Keleher — The University of New Mexico, B.S.C.E., 1964; J.D., 1974 — Admitted to Bar, 1974, New Mexico — Member American and Albuquerque Bar Associations; State Bar of New Mexico (Past Chair, Commercial Litigation and Antitrust Section); State Bar Medical-Legal Panel; American Arbitration Association Panel of Arbitrators — Practice Areas: Alternative Dispute Resolution; Business Law; Commercial Law; Construction Law; Construction Litigation; Real Estate Litigation; Insurance Defense; Professional Malpractice; Real Estate

Sean Olivas — University of California at Irvine, B.A. (magna cum laude), 1992; The University of New Mexico, J.D., 1995 — Admitted to Bar, 1995, New Mexico; U.S. District Court, District of New Mexico; U.S. Court of Appeals for the Federal and Tenth Circuits; U.S. Supreme Court — Member American and Albuquerque (Past President) Bar Associations; State Bar of New Mexico; New Mexico Defense Lawyers Association; American Law Institute — Practice Areas: Civil Rights; Employment Law; Commercial Litigation; Tort

Charles A. Pharris — The University of New Mexico, B.A., 1965; J.D., 1969 — Admitted to Bar, 1969, New Mexico; U.S. District Court, District of New Mexico — Member American (Litigation Section) and Albuquerque Bar Associations; State Bar of New Mexico; New Mexico Defense Lawyers Association — Practice Areas: Alternative Dispute Resolution; Commercial Litigation; Health Care; Insurance Defense; Product Liability; Legal Malpractice; Medical Malpractice; Professional Malpractice

David W. Peterson — Utah State University, B.A. (cum laude), 1988; M.A., 1990; The University of Utah, J.D., 1992 — Admitted to Bar, 1992, New Mexico — Member State Bar of New Mexico (Indian Law Section); New Mexico Defense Lawyers Association — Practice Areas: Appellate; Commercial Litigation; Employment Law; Insurance Defense; Product Liability; Tribal Law

Spencer Reid — University of the Pacific, 1972; University of California, Berkeley, B.A., 1974; The University of New Mexico, J.D., 1979 —

Keleher & McLeod, P.A., Albuquerque, NM (Continued)

Admitted to Bar, 1979, New Mexico; U.S. Court of Appeals, Tenth Circuit — Member Federal Bar Association; State Bar of New Mexico — 2012 New Mexico Lawyer of the Year (Estate Litigation); New Mexico Top 25 Lawyers — Practice Areas: Arbitration; Banking; Breach of Contract; Commercial Litigation; Real Estate; Title Insurance; Tort Litigation

Gary J. Van Luchene — Arizona State University, B.S., 1986; California Western University, J.D. (cum laude), 1993 — Executive Lead Articles Editor, California Western Law Review, 1992-1993 — Admitted to Bar, 1994, California; 1995, New Mexico, 1996, U.S. District Court, District of New Mexico; U.S. Court of Appeals, Tenth Circuit; 2003, U.S. Supreme Court — Member State Bar of New Mexico; New Mexico Defense Lawyers Association (Board of Directors); Defense Research Institute (Toxic Torts and Emvironmental Law Committee) — Practice Areas: Civil Litigation; Business Litigation; Commercial Litigation; Complex Litigation; Construction Law; Employment Law; Product Liability; Toxic Torts

Kurt Wihl — Swarthmore College, B.A., 1980; The University of New Mexico, J.D. (cum laude), 1984 — Order of the Coif; National Merit Scholar — Admitted to Bar, 1984, New Mexico — Languages: Spanish — Practice Areas: Civil Litigation; Civil Rights; Class Actions; Complex Litigation; Probate; Personal Injury; Real Estate Litigation

Kathleen M. Wilson — Saint Louis University, B.A. (cum laude), 1990; The University of New Mexico, J.D., 1997 — Admitted to Bar, 1997, New Mexico; U.S. District Court, District of New Mexico — Member State Bar of New Mexico (Medical Review Commission); Second Judicial District Court (Standing Committeeon Arbitration); New Mexico Defense Lawyers Association (President, 2006); Defense Research Institute — Practice Areas: Medical Malpractice; Health Care; Construction Defect; Insurance Defense; Premises Liability; Product Liability

Of Counsel

Michelle Lalley Blake — Regis College, B.S. (magna cum laude), 1987; The University of Arizona, J.D., 1991 — Admitted to Bar, 1991, New Mexico; U.S. District Court, District of New Mexico; U.S. Court of Appeals, Tenth Circuit — Member Albuquerque and Sandoval County Bar Associations; Second Judicial District Court Volunteer Mediator; New Mexico Medical Review Committee; New Mexico Defense Lawyers Association; Defense Research Institute — Practice Areas: Professional Liability; Medical Malpractice; Civil Rights; Civil Litigation

Robert J. Perovich — The University of New Mexico, B.S.C.E., 1975; J.D., 1980 — Admitted to Bar, 1980, New Mexico — Member State Bar of New Mexico; Albuquerque Bar Association; American Arbitration Association — Practice Areas: Alternative Dispute Resolution; Civil Litigation; Business Litigation; Commercial Litigation; Construction Law; Insurance Defense; Professional Malpractice

Maestas & Suggett, P.C.

Sun Valley Commercial Center
316 Osuna Road NE, Suite 103
Albuquerque, New Mexico 87107-5950
Telephone: 505-247-8100
Fax: 505-247-8125
E-Mail: paul@maestasandsuggett.com
www.maestasandsuggett.com

Established: 2005

Civil Litigation, Employment Law, Insurance Law, Personal Injury, Wrongful Death, Workers' Compensation, Construction Law, Surety, Toxic Torts

Firm Profile: At Maestas & Suggett, you will be personally helped by an attorney with over 20 years of experience in their respective field.

Insurance Clients

Adjusting Alternatives, LLC	Argonaut Insurance Company
CCMSI	Crawford & Company
Fireman's Fund Insurance Company	FirstComp Insurance Company
Gallagher Bassett Services, Inc.	Food Industry Self-Insurance Fund of New Mexico
Mountain States Insurance Group	State Farm Fire and Casualty Company

ALBUQUERQUE   NEW MEXICO

Maestas & Suggett, P.C., Albuquerque, NM (Continued)

Non-Insurance Clients

Honeywell International, Inc.
Jack B. Henderson Construction Company, Inc.
Miller Bonded, Inc.
Red River Ski Area, Inc.
Intel Corporation
Matrix Absence Management, Inc.
Mechanical Contractors Association of New Mexico, Inc.

Paul Maestas — 1959 — Oklahoma City University, B.A. (magna cum laude), 1980; University of California at Los Angeles School of the Law, J.D., 1983 — Admitted to Bar, 1983, New Mexico — Member American Bar Association (Sections on: Labor and Employment Law; Tort and Insurance Practice; Litigation; Appellate Practice); State Bar of New Mexico; New Mexico Workers' Compensation Association; New Mexico Defense Lawyers Association; Defense Research Institute — Languages: Spanish — E-mail: paul@maestasandsuggett.com

Wayne R. Suggett — 1964 — University of California, San Diego, B.A., 1988; Whittier Law School, J.D. (summa cum laude), 1992 — Magister, Phi Delta Phi — Law Clerk to the Honorable Juan G. Burciaga, Chief Judge, U.S. District Court, New Mexico, 1992-1994 — Member, Whittier Law Review — Admitted to Bar, 1992, California; 1994, New Mexico; 1995, Colorado; 1994, U.S. District Court, District of New Mexico; U.S. Court of Appeals, Tenth Circuit — Member American Bar Association; The Colorado Bar Association; State Bar of California; State Bar of New Mexico; New Mexico Trial Lawyers Association; Association of Trial Lawyers of America — Author: "The Summers Doctrine, McKennon and the Civil Rights Act of 1991: The Death or Resurrection of Peter Perfect?" New Mexico DLA Vol. 4 No. 2, Spring, 1995 — E-mail: wayne@maestasandsuggett.com

(This firm is also listed in the Subrogation section of this directory)

Law Offices of Bruce S. McDonald

211 Twelfth Street NW
Albuquerque, New Mexico 87102
  Telephone: 505-254-2854
  Fax: 505-254-2853
  Emer/After Hrs: 505-281-0196
  Mobile: 505-331-8318
  E-Mail: BSMlegal@aol.com

Established: 1994

Civil Trial Practice, Insurance Defense, Insurance Coverage, Personal Injury, Uninsured and Underinsured Motorist, Arbitration, Mediation

Firm Profile: The firm is committed to providing quality legal service to the insurance industry and their insureds. A broad range of experience in insurance defense has been developed and the firm is well positioned to meet the challenging demands of its clients.

The firm's goal is to facilitate a personal desire to deliver quality services as effectively as possible. The long standing relationships we have enjoyed with many of our clients is testament that the goal is being met. The challenge of the future is to continue this tradition.

We offer experience in all forums relating to litigation: mediations; arbitrations; administrative hearings and trials; bench trials and jury trials. In providing these services, we are constantly mindful of the needs of our clients and we are determined to fulfill their expectations.

Our commitment to offering dependable quality service has been demonstrated and it will remain our number one goal as the challenges of the future unfold. Martindale Hubbell AV rated firm.

Insurance Clients

American Reliable Insurance Company
Lancer Insurance Company
Sentry Insurance a Mutual Company
EMC Insurance Companies
Hallmark Insurance Company
Phoenix Indemnity Insurance Company

Law Offices of Bruce S. McDonald, Albuquerque, NM (Continued)

Firm Member

Bruce S. McDonald — 1957 — Texas Tech University, B.B.A., 1979; South Texas College of Law, J.D., 1989 — Admitted to Bar, 1989, New Mexico; 1990, Texas; U.S. Court of Appeals, Tenth Circuit — Member State Bar of Texas; State Bar of New Mexico; Albuquerque Bar Association (Member, Tort and Insurance Practice Section; Automobile Law Committee); Association of Trial Lawyers of America — Practice Areas: Civil Trial Practice; Insurance Defense; Insurance Coverage; Personal Injury; Uninsured and Underinsured Motorist; Arbitration; Mediation — E-mail: BSMlegal@aol.com

Firm Personnel

Lucinda R. Silva — 1971 — University of Southern California, B.A., 1993; The University of New Mexico School of Law, J.D. (cum laude), 1997 — Admitted to Bar, 1998, New Mexico; U.S. District Court, District of New Mexico; 2001, U.S. Court of Appeals, Tenth Circuit — Member State Bar of New Mexico — Practice Areas: Insurance Defense; Civil Litigation — E-mail: CindyBSMlegal@aol.com

Christian C. Doherty — 1960 — University of Lowell, B.S.M.E., 1983; University of Missouri-Columbia School of Law, J.D., 1991 — Admitted to Bar, 1991, New Mexico; 1994, U.S. District Court, District of New Mexico — Practice Areas: Civil Trial Practice; Insurance Defense — E-mail: ChrisBSMlegal@aol.com

Amanda R. Lucero — 1982 — The University of New Mexico, B.A. (magna cum laude), 2003; The University of New Mexico School of Law, J.D., 2006 — Admitted to Bar, 2006, New Mexico — Member Christian Legal Aid — Practice Areas: Personal Injury; Workers' Compensation — E-mail: AmandaBSMlegal@aol.com

Of Counsel

Tracy M. Jenks — 1958 — The University of Texas, B.A. (with high honors), 1980; The University of Texas School of Law, J.D., 1983 — Phi Beta Kappa — Admitted to Bar, 1983, New Mexico; U.S. District Court, District of New Mexico; U.S. Court of Appeals, Tenth Circuit; Supreme Court of New Mexico — Member State Bar of New Mexico — Practice Areas: Civil Trial Practice; Insurance Defense; Insurance Coverage; Personal Injury; Uninsured and Underinsured Motorist; Arbitration; Mediation; Trucking Litigation; Tort Litigation; Negligence; Nursing Home Litigation; Asbestos Litigation; Dram Shop — E-mail: TracyBSMlegal@aol.com

Ray, McChristian & Jeans, P.C.

6000 Uptown Boulevard NE, Suite 307
Albuquerque, New Mexico 87110
  Telephone: 505-855-6000
  Fax: 505-212-0140
  Mobile: 915-497-1244
  E-Mail: jray@rmjfirm.com
  www.rmjfirm.com

(El Paso, TX Office*: 5822 Cromo Drive, 79912)
  (Tel: 915-832-7200)
  (Fax: 915-832-7333)
  (Toll Free: 866-832-7200)
  (Mobile: 915-497-1244)
  (E-Mail: rmj@rmjfirm.com)
(San Antonio, TX Office*: 1250 NE Loop 410, Suite 700, 78209)
  (Tel: 210-341-3554)
  (Fax: 210-341-3557)
  (Toll Free: 866-832-7227)
  (Mobile: 915-497-1244)
  (E-Mail: rmj@rmjfirm.com)
(Fort Worth, TX Office*: 101 Summit Avenue, 76102)
  (Tel: 817-335-7201)
  (Fax: 817-335-7335)
  (Toll Free: 866-832-7247)
  (E-Mail: jmcchristian@rmjfirm.com)

Insurance Defense, Automobile, General Liability, Product Liability, Legal Malpractice, Workers' Compensation, Premises Liability, Bodily Injury, Medical Malpractice

NEW MEXICO / ALBUQUERQUE

Ray, McChristian & Jeans, P.C., Albuquerque, NM (Continued)

Shareholders

Jeff Ray — 1957 — The University of Texas at Austin, B.A. (with honors), 1979; St. Mary's University School of Law, J.D. (with honors), 1982 — Admitted to Bar, 1982, Texas; 1993, New Mexico; 1982, U.S. District Court, Southern and Western Districts of Texas; 1982, U.S. Court of Appeals, Fifth Circuit — Member American and El Paso Bar Associations; State Bar of Texas; State Bar of New Mexico; Texas Association of Defense Counsel; Texas Young Lawyers Association; Defense Research Institute — Board Certified, Personal Injury Trial Law, Texas Board of Legal Specialization — E-mail: jray@rmjfirm.com

Deena Buchanan Williams — 1973 — University of Pittsburgh, B.A. (summa cum laude), 1991; Georgetown University Law Center, J.D. (cum laude), 1998 — Admitted to Bar, 1998, New Mexico; 2000, New Jersey; 2000, Pennsylvania (Inactive); 2000, U.S. District Court, District of Pennsylvania; 2000, U.S. District Court, District of New Jersey; 2003, U.S. Court of Appeals, Third Circuit; 2008, U.S. District Court, District of New Mexico — Member American Bar Association (Litigation Section); Claims & Litigation Management Alliance; National Association of Professional Women; New Mexico Defense Lawyers Association — E-mail: dwilliams@rmjfirm.com

Shannon A. Parden — Michigan Technological University, B.A.; The University of New Mexico, J.D., 1990 — Admitted to Bar, 1990, New Mexico; 2000, Minnesota (Inactive); U.S. District Court, District of New Mexico; U.S. Court of Appeals, Tenth Circuit — Member American and Albuquerque Bar Associations; Claims & Litigation Management Alliance; New Mexico Defense Lawyers Association; Defense Research Institute — E-mail: sparden@rmjfirm.com

(See listing under El Paso, TX for additional information)

Scott & Kienzle, P.A.

1011 Las Lomas Road NE
Albuquerque, New Mexico 87102
Telephone: 505-246-8600
Fax: 505-246-8682
E-Mail: paul@kienzlelaw.com
www.kienzlelaw.com

Established: 1996

Commercial Litigation, Bankruptcy, Subrogation, Business Law, Commercial Law, Insurance, Civil Litigation, Indian Law, Insurance Defense

Firm Profile: Scott & Kienzle, P.A. is a litigation firm practicing in state, federal, and bankruptcy courts throughout New Mexico. The firm's clients range from large national financial institutions and insurance companies to local businesses.

Insurance Clients

The Cincinnati Insurance Companies
State Farm Insurance Companies

Non-Insurance Clients

Afni, Inc.

Attorneys

Paul M. Kienzle III — University of Illinois, J.D. (magna cum laude), 1992 — Admitted to Bar, 1992, Illinois; 1993, New Mexico; U.S. District Court, Northern District of Illinois; 1994, U.S. District Court, District of New Mexico; 1999, U.S. Court of Appeals, Tenth Circuit; U.S. Supreme Court; 2004, U.S. Court of Federal Claims; 2006, Navajo Nation — Practice Areas: Commercial Litigation; Civil Litigation; Collections; Business Law; Corporate Law; Subrogation; Indian Law; Insurance Defense

Duncan Scott — The University of Montana, J.D., 1982 — Admitted to Bar, 1982, Montana; 1985, Alaska; 1987, New Mexico; 1990, Colorado — Practice Areas: Commercial Law; Civil Litigation; Real Estate

Associate Attorneys

Paul W. Spear
Meagan A. Lopez

(This firm is also listed in the Subrogation section of this directory)

Stelzner, Winter, Warburton, Flores, Sanchez & Dawes, P.A.

302 8th Street NW, Suite 200
Albuquerque, New Mexico 87102
Telephone: 505-938-7770
Fax: 505-938-7781
E-Mail: rpw@stelznerlaw.com
www.stelznerlaw.com

(Jackson, WY Office*: 955 High Country Drive, 83001, P.O. Box 11246, 83002-1246)
(Tel: 307-739-2271)
(Fax: 307-739-2247)

Established: 2010

Alternative Dispute Resolution, Bad Faith, Civil Litigation, Commercial Litigation, Construction Litigation, Employment Law, Environmental Law, ERISA, Insurance Coverage, Motor Vehicle, Municipal Law, Personal Injury, Product Liability, Public Utilites, White Collar Crime

Insurance Clients

American Contractors Insurance Group
Chartis/Lexington Insurance Company
Catholic Mutual Relief Society of America
Golden Bear Management Corporation

Shareholders

Jaime Dawes — New Mexico State University, B.A. (with honors and distinction), 2000; The University of New Mexico School of Law, J.D. (summa cum laude), 2003 — Editor, National Resources Law Journal — Admitted to Bar, 2003, New Mexico; U.S. District Court, District of New Mexico; U.S. Court of Appeals, Tenth Circuit — E-mail: jd@stelznerlaw.com

Juan L. Flores — Del Mar College, A.A.S., 1983; New Mexico State University, B.A. (with honors), 1986; The University of New Mexico School of Law, J.D., 1990 — Admitted to Bar, 1990, New Mexico; U.S. District Court, District of New Mexico; 1995, U.S. Court of Appeals, Tenth Circuit — Member American and New Mexico Hispanic Bar Associations — Mr. Flore's practice focuses on trial work in the personal injury, products liability and contract areas. Mr. Flores has formal training in such diverse fields as fire fighting, plumbing, pipe fitting, welding and metal work, high pressure pipe welding, asbestos removal, carpentry, sheet metal work, automotive mechanics, and computer programming and systems design. Mr. Flores was born in Cd. Juarez, Chih. Mexico on July 7, 1958. He speaks, reads and writes the Spanish language. — E-mail: jflores@stelznerlaw.com

Sara N. Sanchez — Brown University, B.A. (cum laude), 1995; Harvard Law School, J.D. (magna cum laude), 2001 — Phi Beta Kappa — Admitted to Bar, 2001, District of Columbia; 2002, California; 2007, New Mexico; 2004, U.S. District Court, Central District of California; 2007, U.S. District Court, District of New Mexico; 2008, U.S. Court of Appeals, Tenth Circuit; 2010, U.S. Supreme Court — Practice Areas: Business Litigation; Criminal Defense; Employment Litigation — E-mail: ssanchez@stelznerlaw.com

Luis G. Stelzner — Georgetown University School of Foreign Service, B.S.F.S., 1964; University of California Davis School of Law, J.D., 1975 — Admitted to Bar, 1975, California; 1979, New Mexico; U.S. District Court, District of New Mexico; 1985, U.S. Court of Appeals, Tenth Circuit; 1988, U.S. Supreme Court — Best Lawyers in America; Southwest Super Lawyers; Top 25 Attorneys in New Mexico; AV Pre-eminent Attorney; Albuquerque 2012 Lawyer of the Year - Mediation — E-mail: lgs@stelznerlaw.com

Robert P. Warburton — University of Notre Dame, B.A. (cum laude), 1975; Georgetown University, M.A. (cum laude), 1977; The University of New Mexico School of Law, J.D. (cum laude), 1990 — Order of the Coif; Phi Kappa Phi — New Mexico Law Review, 1988-1990 — Admitted to Bar, 1990, New Mexico; 1998, Wyoming; 1991, U.S. District Court, District of New Mexico; 1998, U.S. Court of Appeals, Tenth Circuit; 1999, U.S. District Court, District of Wyoming; 2004, U.S. Supreme Court — Member New Mexico Trial Lawyers Association; Wyoming Trial Lawyers Association —

Stelzner, Winter, Warburton, Flores, Sanchez & Dawes, P.A., Albuquerque, NM (Continued)

Wall Street Journal Award; Best Lawyers in America — Practice Areas: Insurance Coverage; Bad Faith; Construction Defect; Architects and Engineers; Errors and Omissions; Complex Litigation; Class Actions — E-mail: rpw@stelznerlaw.com

Nann Winter — The University of New Mexico, B.B.A. (summa cum laude), 1981; The University of New Mexico School of Law, J.D., 1987 — Admitted to Bar, 1987, New Mexico; 1989, U.S. District Court, District of New Mexico; 2001, U.S. Court of Appeals, Fifth Circuit; 2003, U.S. Court of Appeals, Tenth Circuit; 2008, U.S. District Court, District of Colorado — New Mexico Board Certified Specialist Local Goverment LAw — E-mail: nwinter@stelznerlaw.com

Stiff, Keith & Garcia, LLC

400 Gold Avenue SW, Suite 1300
Albuquerque, New Mexico 87102
   Telephone: 505-243-5755
   Fax: 505-243-5855
   www.stifflaw.com

Established: 2000

Insurance Defense, Automobile Liability, Civil Rights, Premises Liability, Bad Faith, Product Liability, Employer Liability, Employment Discrimination, Employment Law, Employment Law (Management Side), Employment Practices Liability, Risk Management, School Law, Commercial Contract Litigation

Firm Profile: The New Mexico insurance defense attorneys at the law firm of Stiff, Keith & Garcia, L.L.C., provide effective and experienced legal defense for insurers, contractors, manufacturers, government entities, employers, and private individuals facing insurance and liability litigation. We provide small firm service with big firm capabilities, frequently representing large, nationally-recognized insurance companies.

Insurance Clients

Allstate Insurance Company	CCMSI
Clarendon National Insurance Company	Fred Loya Insurance
	MetLife Insurance Company
Safeco Insurance Companies	State Farm Insurance Company
Tudor Insurance Company	Western World Insurance Company

Owner and Principle Consultant

John S. Stiff — 1957 — Colorado College, B.A., 1978; Tulane University Law School, J.D., 1983 — Admitted to Bar, 1983, New Mexico; U.S. District Court, District of New Mexico; U.S. Court of Appeals, Tenth Circuit — Member American and Albuquerque Bar Associations; National Institute of Trial Lawyers; New Mexico Defense Lawyers Association; Defense Research Institute; Association of Trial Lawyers of America

Partners

Ann L. Keith — 1967 — The University of Arizona, B.A. (summa cum laude), 1989; Northern Arizona University, M.A. (with distinction), 1993; William & Mary School of Law, J.D., 2002 — Admitted to Bar, 2005, New Mexico; 2006, U.S. District Court, District of New Mexico

Arturo Ricardo Garcia — 1973 — The University of New Mexico, B.A., 2002; Gonzaga University School of Law, J.D., 2002 — Admitted to Bar, 2003, Washington; 2006, New Mexico; U.S. District Court, District of New Mexico — Member American Bar Association; National Hispanic Bar Association

Associates

Edward F. Snow — 1958 — The University of New Mexico, B.A., 1980; The University of New Mexico School of Law, J.D., 1983 — Admitted to Bar, 1983, New Mexico; U.S. District Court, District of New Mexico — Member New Mexico Trial Lawyers Association

Keith D. Drennan — 1985 — The University of Texas at Dallas, B.S. (cum laude), 2008; Texas Tech School of Law, J.D. (cum laude), 2012 — Admitted to Bar, 2012, New Mexico

---

The following firms also service this area.

Evans & Co.
2844 East Main, Suite 106, Box 280
Farmington, New Mexico 87401
   Telephone: 505-566-9400
   Fax: 877-585-1401
   Toll Free: 800-EVANSCO

Aviation, Comprehensive General Liability, Construction Law, Directors and Officers Liability, Employment Practices Liability, Energy, Environmental Law, Excess and Umbrella, Insurance Coverage, Insurance Defense, Motor Carriers, Oil and Gas, Product Liability, Professional Liability, Property and Casualty, Railroad Law, Toxic Torts

SEE COMPLETE LISTING UNDER FARMINGTON, NEW MEXICO (184 MILES)

ARTESIA 11,301 Eddy Co.

Refer To

Atwood, Malone, Turner & Sabin, P.A.
400 North Pennsylvania Avenue, Suite 1100
Roswell, New Mexico 88201
   Telephone: 575-622-6221
   Fax: 575-624-2883

Mailing Address: P.O. Drawer 700, Roswell, NM 88202-0700

Insurance Defense, Casualty, Fire, Workers' Compensation, Life Insurance, Product Liability, Medical Malpractice, Professional Liability, Employment Law, Commercial Litigation

SEE COMPLETE LISTING UNDER ROSWELL, NEW MEXICO (47 MILES)

CARLSBAD † 26,138 Eddy Co.

Refer To

Atwood, Malone, Turner & Sabin, P.A.
400 North Pennsylvania Avenue, Suite 1100
Roswell, New Mexico 88201
   Telephone: 575-622-6221
   Fax: 575-624-2883

Mailing Address: P.O. Drawer 700, Roswell, NM 88202-0700

Insurance Defense, Casualty, Fire, Workers' Compensation, Life Insurance, Product Liability, Medical Malpractice, Professional Liability, Employment Law, Commercial Litigation

SEE COMPLETE LISTING UNDER ROSWELL, NEW MEXICO (83 MILES)

Refer To

**Mounce, Green, Myers, Safi, Paxson & Galatzan
A Professional Corporation**
100 North Stanton, Suite 1000
El Paso, Texas 79901-1448
   Telephone: 915-532-2000
   Fax: 915-541-1526

Mailing Address: P.O. Box 1977, El Paso, TX 79999-1977

General Defense, General Liability, Casualty, Automobile, Surety, Fire, Workers' Compensation, Life Insurance, Accident and Health, Professional Liability, Construction Litigation, Asbestos Litigation, Trucking Law, Transportation, Premises Liability, Product Liability, Toxic Torts, Employer Liability, Governmental Liability, Municipal Liability, Coverage Questions

SEE COMPLETE LISTING UNDER EL PASO, TEXAS (155 MILES)

CARRIZOZO † 996 Lincoln Co.

Refer To

Atwood, Malone, Turner & Sabin, P.A.
400 North Pennsylvania Avenue, Suite 1100
Roswell, New Mexico 88201
   Telephone: 575-622-6221
   Fax: 575-624-2883

Mailing Address: P.O. Drawer 700, Roswell, NM 88202-0700

Insurance Defense, Casualty, Fire, Workers' Compensation, Life Insurance, Product Liability, Medical Malpractice, Professional Liability, Employment Law, Commercial Litigation

SEE COMPLETE LISTING UNDER ROSWELL, NEW MEXICO (96 MILES)

NEW MEXICO

CLOVIS † 37,775 Curry Co.

Refer To

Atwood, Malone, Turner & Sabin, P.A.
400 North Pennsylvania Avenue, Suite 1100
Roswell, New Mexico 88201
  Telephone: 575-622-6221
  Fax: 575-624-2883

Mailing Address: P.O. Drawer 700, Roswell, NM 88202-0700

Insurance Defense, Casualty, Fire, Workers' Compensation, Life Insurance, Product Liability, Medical Malpractice, Professional Liability, Employment Law, Commercial Litigation

SEE COMPLETE LISTING UNDER ROSWELL, NEW MEXICO (106 MILES)

DEMING † 14,855 Luna Co.

Refer To

Mounce, Green, Myers, Safi, Paxson & Galatzan
A Professional Corporation
100 North Stanton, Suite 1000
El Paso, Texas 79901-1448
  Telephone: 915-532-2000
  Fax: 915-541-1526

Mailing Address: P.O. Box 1977, El Paso, TX 79999-1977

General Defense, General Liability, Casualty, Automobile, Surety, Fire, Workers' Compensation, Life Insurance, Accident and Health, Professional Liability, Construction Litigation, Asbestos Litigation, Trucking Law, Transportation, Premises Liability, Product Liability, Toxic Torts, Employer Liability, Governmental Liability, Municipal Liability, Coverage Questions

SEE COMPLETE LISTING UNDER EL PASO, TEXAS (102 MILES)

FARMINGTON 45,877 San Juan Co.

Evans & Co.

2844 East Main, Suite 106, Box 280
Farmington, New Mexico 87401
  Telephone: 505-566-9400
  Fax: 877-585-1401
  Toll Free: 800-EVANSCO
  E-Mail: revans@evanslawfirm.com
  www.evanslawfirm.com

(Additional Offices: New Orleans, LA*; Durango, CO*; Greensboro, NC*; Katy, TX*(See Houston listing); Jackson, WY*)

Established: 1999

Aviation, Comprehensive General Liability, Construction Law, Directors and Officers Liability, Employment Practices Liability, Energy, Environmental Law, Excess and Umbrella, Insurance Coverage, Insurance Defense, Motor Carriers, Oil and Gas, Product Liability, Professional Liability, Property and Casualty, Railroad Law, Toxic Torts

Insurance Clients

Accident Insurance Company
AequiCap Claims Services
All Risk Claims Service, Inc.
American Family Insurance Company
American Hallmark Insurance Services, Inc.
American National Property and Casualty Company
Assicurazioni Generali S.p.A.
Atlantic Casualty Insurance Company
Bituminous Casualty Corporation
Canal Indemnity Company
Claims Management Corporation
CNA Insurance Company
Construction Insurance Company
COUNTRY Financial
ACE Westchester Specialty Group
Allianz Insurance Company
American Ambassador Casualty Company
American Fidelity Insurance Company
American Interstate Insurance Company
Anchor General Insurance Company
Atlantic Mutual Companies
Atlas Insurance Company
Boat/U.S. Marine Insurance
The Cincinnati Insurance Companies
Colony Insurance Group
Continental Western Group
Deep South Surplus, Inc.

Evans & Co., Farmington, NM (Continued)

Employers Insurance Company of Wausau
Erie Insurance Group
Farm Family Insurance Companies
General Security Insurance Company
H & W Insurance Services, Inc.
Liberty Insurance Services, Inc.
Meadowbrook Insurance Group
National Farmers Union Property & Casualty Company
Occidental Fire & Casualty Company of North Carolina
Penn National Insurance
Phoenix Indemnity Insurance Company
Professional Insurance Underwriters, Inc.
Shelter Insurance Companies
State National Companies, Inc.
Texas Select Lloyds Insurance Company
Transportation Casualty Insurance Company
Underwriters Indemnity Company
United Educators Insurance
United Fire & Casualty Company
United Specialty Insurance Company
Unitrin Property and Casualty Insurance Group
Virginia Mutual Insurance Company
XL Insurance
Employers Mutual Casualty Company
Essex Insurance Company
First Financial Insurance Company
Greenwich Insurance Company
GuideOne Insurance
Kiln Group
Markel Insurance Company
Mountain States Insurance Group
National Grange Mutual Insurance Company
Ocean Marine Indemnity Insurance Company
Phoenix Aviation Managers, Inc.
Preferred Contractors Insurance Company
St. Paul Fire and Marine Insurance Company
Southern Insurance Company
Texas All Risk General Agency, Inc.
T.H.E. Insurance Company
Transportation Claims, Inc.
Underwriters at Lloyd's, London
Underwriters Service Company, Inc.
United National Insurance Company
United States Liability Insurance Company
Universal Underwriters Insurance Company
Wilshire Insurance Company
Zurich North America

Non-Insurance Clients

High Country Transportation, Inc.
SAIA Motor Freight Line, Inc.
Jones Motor Group
United States Postal Service

Attorneys

Robert C. Evans — 1954 — Columbia University, B.A., 1975; University of Maryland, J.D. (with honors), 1980 — Admitted to Bar, 1980, Louisiana; Maryland; 1999, Colorado; 1980, U.S. District Court, Eastern, Middle and Western Districts of Louisiana; U.S. District Court, District of Maryland; U.S. Court of Appeals, Fifth Circuit; 1991, U.S. Court of Appeals, Eleventh Circuit — Member Louisiana State, Maryland State and New Orleans Bar Associations; The Colorado Bar Association; New Orleans Association of Defense Counsel; Louisiana Association of Defense Counsel; Lawyer-Pilots Bar Association; The Maritime Law Association of the United States; Defense Research Institute

Reagyn Germer — The University of Chicago, A.B., 1999; University of Colorado Law School, J.D., 2003 — Admitted to Bar, 2003, New Mexico — Member State Bar of New Mexico

Of Counsel

James Whitley — 1949 — University of Colorado, B.A., 1971; The University of New Mexico, J.D., 1978 — Admitted to Bar, 1978, New Mexico; 1998, Colorado; 1978, U.S. District Court, District of New Mexico; 1979, U.S. District Court, District of Colorado; U.S. Court of Appeals, Tenth Circuit — Member The Colorado, Southwest Colorado and San Juan County Bar Associations; State Bar of New Mexico

---

The following firms also service this area.

Butt, Thornton & Baehr, P.C.
Suite 300
4101 Indian School Road N.E.
Albuquerque, New Mexico 87110
  Telephone: 505-884-0777
  Fax: 505-889-8870

Mailing Address: P.O. Box 3170, Albuquerque, NM 87190

Insurance Law, Casualty, Transportation, Automobile, Workers' Compensation, Professional Malpractice, Surety, Aviation, Product Liability, Environmental Law, Appellate Practice, Civil Rights, Commercial Litigation, Construction and Bond Claims, Government Entities

SEE COMPLETE LISTING UNDER ALBUQUERQUE, NEW MEXICO (182 MILES)

LAS CRUCES   NEW MEXICO

HOBBS   34,122 Lea Co.

Refer To
Atwood, Malone, Turner & Sabin, P.A.
400 North Pennsylvania Avenue, Suite 1100
Roswell, New Mexico 88201
   Telephone: 575-622-6221
   Fax: 575-624-2883

Mailing Address: P.O. Drawer 700, Roswell, NM 88202-0700

Insurance Defense, Casualty, Fire, Workers' Compensation, Life Insurance, Product Liability, Medical Malpractice, Professional Liability, Employment Law, Commercial Litigation

SEE COMPLETE LISTING UNDER ROSWELL, NEW MEXICO (123 MILES)

Refer To
Butt, Thornton & Baehr, P.C.
Suite 300
4101 Indian School Road N.E.
Albuquerque, New Mexico 87110
   Telephone: 505-884-0777
   Fax: 505-889-8870

Mailing Address: P.O. Box 3170, Albuquerque, NM 87190

Insurance Law, Casualty, Transportation, Automobile, Workers' Compensation, Professional Malpractice, Surety, Aviation, Product Liability, Environmental Law, Appellate Practice, Civil Rights, Commercial Litigation, Construction and Bond Claims, Government Entities

SEE COMPLETE LISTING UNDER ALBUQUERQUE, NEW MEXICO (325 MILES)

Refer To
Mounce, Green, Myers, Safi, Paxson & Galatzan
A Professional Corporation
100 North Stanton, Suite 1000
El Paso, Texas 79901-1448
   Telephone: 915-532-2000
   Fax: 915-541-1526

Mailing Address: P.O. Box 1977, El Paso, TX 79999-1977

General Defense, General Liability, Casualty, Automobile, Surety, Fire, Workers' Compensation, Life Insurance, Accident and Health, Professional Liability, Construction Litigation, Asbestos Litigation, Trucking Law, Transportation, Premises Liability, Product Liability, Toxic Torts, Employer Liability, Governmental Liability, Municipal Liability, Coverage Questions

SEE COMPLETE LISTING UNDER EL PASO, TEXAS (225 MILES)

LAS CRUCES   † 97,618 Dona Ana Co.

Holt Mynatt Martinez PC
1660 Hickory Loop
Las Cruces, New Mexico 88005
   Telephone: 575-524-8812
   Fax: 575-524-0726
   E-Mail: btm@hbm-law.com
   www.hbm-law.com

Established: 1997

Alternative Dispute Resolution, Civil Rights, Construction Law, Employment Law, Insurance Defense, Law Enforcement Liability, Medical Malpractice, Premises Liability, Public Entities, Real Estate, Subrogation

Firm Profile: Here at Holt Mynatt Martinez, we take our commitment to our clients seriously. Our diverse and talented legal team provides legal expertise with depth and breadth.

We are proud of our innovative solutions, which are balanced with a seasoned and reprectful approach to process and procedure.

Insurance Guaranty Fund Clients

American National Property and Casualty Company	First American Title Insurance Company
The Hartford	New Mexico Association of Counties
Travelers	

Holt Mynatt Martinez PC, Las Cruces, NM   (Continued)
Directors

Damian L. Martinez — New Mexico Highlands University, B.S.W., 1998; St. Mary's University School of Law, J.D. (cum laude), 2001 — Admitted to Bar, 2001, New Mexico; 2002, U.S. Court of Appeals for the Armed Forces; U.S. Air Force Court of Criminal Appeals; 2005, U.S. District Court, District of New Mexico; 2007, U.S. District Court, District of Colorado; U.S. Court of Appeals, Tenth Circuit — Member State Bar of New Mexico — Leadership Las Cruces, 2006; Southwest Super Lawyer Rising Star, 2012; AV Rated, Martindale-Hubbell; Top 40 Lawyers Under 40, American Society of Legal Advocates — Captain, USAF Judge Advocate General Corps (2001-2005)

Blaine T. Mynatt — University of Washington, B.A., 1993; The University of New Mexico School of Law, J.D., 1997 — Admitted to Bar, 1997, New Mexico; 2002, U.S. District Court, District of New Mexico; 2006, U.S. District Court, District of Colorado; 2007, U.S. Court of Appeals, Tenth Circuit — Member American and Dona Ana County Bar Associations; State Bar of New Mexico; Fellow, Litigation Counsel of America — Board of Directors, University of New Mexico Law School Alumni; AV Rated, Martindale-Hubbell

Bradley A. Springer — Indiana University, Kelley School of Business, B.S., 2003; Indiana University School of Law, J.D., 2007 — Admitted to Bar, 2007, New Mexico; 2010, U.S. District Court, District of New Mexico; U.S. Court of Appeals, Tenth Circuit — Member State Bar of New Mexico

Senior Counsel

Matthew P. Holt	Stephen A. Hubert
David McNeil, Jr.	

Associates

Casey B. Fitch	John A. Frase
Edward Hernandez III	Benjamin J. Young

The following firms also service this area.

Atwood, Malone, Turner & Sabin, P.A.
400 North Pennsylvania Avenue, Suite 1100
Roswell, New Mexico 88201
   Telephone: 575-622-6221
   Fax: 575-624-2883

Mailing Address: P.O. Drawer 700, Roswell, NM 88202-0700

Insurance Defense, Casualty, Fire, Workers' Compensation, Life Insurance, Product Liability, Medical Malpractice, Professional Liability, Employment Law, Commercial Litigation

SEE COMPLETE LISTING UNDER ROSWELL, NEW MEXICO (191 MILES)

Butt, Thornton & Baehr, P.C.
Suite 300
4101 Indian School Road N.E.
Albuquerque, New Mexico 87110
   Telephone: 505-884-0777
   Fax: 505-889-8870

Mailing Address: P.O. Box 3170, Albuquerque, NM 87190

Insurance Law, Casualty, Transportation, Automobile, Workers' Compensation, Professional Malpractice, Surety, Aviation, Product Liability, Environmental Law, Appellate Practice, Civil Rights, Commercial Litigation, Construction and Bond Claims, Government Entities

SEE COMPLETE LISTING UNDER ALBUQUERQUE, NEW MEXICO (220 MILES)

Hicks & Llamas, P.C.
124 West Castellano Drive, Suite 100
El Paso, Texas 79912
   Telephone: 915-834-8400
   Fax: 915-587-8401
   Toll Free: 888-738-8401

Professional Liability, First Party Matters, Appellate Practice, Insurance Defense, Premises Liability, Medical Malpractice, General Liability, Product Liability, Workers' Compensation, Asbestos Litigation, Commercial Litigation, Labor and Employment, ERISA, Trucking Law, Transportation, Environmental Law, Civil Litigation, Civil Trial Practice, Nursing Home Liability, Self-Insured Defense, Administrative Disputes

SEE COMPLETE LISTING UNDER EL PASO, TEXAS (37 MILES)

NEW MEXICO

Mounce, Green, Myers, Safi, Paxson & Galatzan
A Professional Corporation
100 North Stanton, Suite 1000
El Paso, Texas 79901-1448
  Telephone: 915-532-2000
  Fax: 915-541-1526
Mailing Address: P.O. Box 1977, El Paso, TX 79999-1977

General Defense, General Liability, Casualty, Automobile, Surety, Fire, Workers' Compensation, Life Insurance, Accident and Health, Professional Liability, Construction Litigation, Asbestos Litigation, Trucking Law, Transportation, Premises Liability, Product Liability, Toxic Torts, Employer Liability, Governmental Liability, Municipal Liability, Coverage Questions

SEE COMPLETE LISTING UNDER EL PASO, TEXAS (46 MILES)

LOVINGTON † 11,009 Lea Co.

Refer To

Atwood, Malone, Turner & Sabin, P.A.
400 North Pennsylvania Avenue, Suite 1100
Roswell, New Mexico 88201
  Telephone: 575-622-6221
  Fax: 575-624-2883
Mailing Address: P.O. Drawer 700, Roswell, NM 88202-0700

Insurance Defense, Casualty, Fire, Workers' Compensation, Life Insurance, Product Liability, Medical Malpractice, Professional Liability, Employment Law, Commercial Litigation

SEE COMPLETE LISTING UNDER ROSWELL, NEW MEXICO (102 MILES)

PORTALES † 12,280 Roosevelt Co.

Refer To

Atwood, Malone, Turner & Sabin, P.A.
400 North Pennsylvania Avenue, Suite 1100
Roswell, New Mexico 88201
  Telephone: 575-622-6221
  Fax: 575-624-2883
Mailing Address: P.O. Drawer 700, Roswell, NM 88202-0700

Insurance Defense, Casualty, Fire, Workers' Compensation, Life Insurance, Product Liability, Medical Malpractice, Professional Liability, Employment Law, Commercial Litigation

SEE COMPLETE LISTING UNDER ROSWELL, NEW MEXICO (87 MILES)

ROSWELL † 48366 Chaves Co.

Atwood, Malone, Turner & Sabin, P.A.
400 North Pennsylvania Avenue, Suite 1100
Roswell, New Mexico 88201
  Telephone: 575-622-6221
  Fax: 575-624-2883
  E-Mail: atwood@atwoodmalone.com
  www.atwoodmalone.com

Established: 1937

Insurance Defense, Casualty, Fire, Workers' Compensation, Life Insurance, Product Liability, Medical Malpractice, Professional Liability, Employment Law, Commercial Litigation

Firm Profile: Atwood, Malone, Turner & Sabin, P.A. has an excellent reputation in litigation, natural resources, and general business representation. We have developed a broad based civil practice in the New Mexico state and federal courts and agencies, and see to provide the best legal services possible.

Insurance Clients

Allied World Assurance Company	American Hallmark Insurance Company of Texas
Amerisure Mutual Insurance Company	Berkley Select, LLC
Bituminous Insurance Companies	The Doctors Company
Farmers Alliance Mutual Insurance Company	Federated Insurance Company
Hallmark Insurance Company	Five Star Quality Care
	Kemper Insurance Companies

LOVINGTON

Atwood, Malone, Turner & Sabin, P.A., Roswell, NM
(Continued)

The Medical Protective Company	Mountain States Mutual Casualty Company
Nautilus Insurance Company	New Mexico Risk Management Division
New Mexico County Insurance Authority	Northland Insurance Company
New Mexico Self-Insurers Fund	Rice Insurance Services Company, LLC
Progressive Insurance Companies	State Farm Insurance Companies
Sentry Insurance a Mutual Company	Union Standard Insurance Group
Travelers Property Casualty Corporation	Western Litigation, Inc.

Shareholders

J. D. Atwood — (1883-1960)

Ross L. Malone — (1910-1974)

Charles F. Malone — (1923-1999)

Bob F. Turner — (Retired)

Robert E. Sabin — 1941 — University of Colorado, J.D., 1966 — Admitted to Bar, 1966, Colorado; 1967, New Mexico; 1966, U.S. District Court, District of Colorado; 1967, U.S. District Court, District of New Mexico; U.S. Court of Appeals, Tenth Circuit; 1974, U.S. Supreme Court — Member American Bar Association; State Bar of New Mexico; New Mexico Defense Lawyers Association (President, 1988-1989); Defense Research Institute (State Chair, 1991-1996); Federation of Defense and Corporate Counsel; Fellow, American College of Trial Lawyers — Practice Areas: Commercial Litigation; Personal Injury Litigation; Mediation — E-mail: rsabin@atwoodmalone.com

Lee M. Rogers, Jr. — 1958 — The University of Texas, J.D., 1983 — Admitted to Bar, 1983, New Mexico — Member American and Chaves County Bar Associations; State Bar of New Mexico; New Mexico Defense Lawyers Association (President, 2001); Defense Research Institute (New Mexico Representative, 2002-Present); Association of Defense Trial Attorneys — Practice Areas: Insurance Defense; Medical Malpractice Defense — E-mail: lrogers@atwoodmalone.com

Timothy A. Lucas — 1958 — The University of Oklahoma, J.D., 1983 — Admitted to Bar, 1983, New Mexico — Member State Bar of New Mexico; Chaves County Bar Association — Practice Areas: Workers' Compensation — E-mail: tlucas@atwoodmalone.com

Bryan D. Evans — 1964 — The University of New Mexico, J.D., 1990 — Admitted to Bar, 1990, New Mexico; U.S. District Court, District of New Mexico; U.S. Court of Appeals, Tenth Circuit — Member American and Chaves County Bar Associations; State Bar of New Mexico — Practice Areas: Employment Litigation; Insurance Defense — E-mail: bevans@atwoodmalone.com

Carla Ann Neusch Williams — 1977 — The University of Texas, J.D. (with honors), 2002 — Admitted to Bar, 2002, New Mexico; 2003, U.S. District Court, District of New Mexico; U.S. Court of Appeals, Tenth Circuit — Member State Bar of New Mexico; Chaves County Bar Association; New Mexico Defense Lawyers Association — Practice Areas: Employment Law; Insurance Defense; Professional Malpractice; Medical Malpractice Defense — E-mail: cwilliams@atwoodmalone.com

Cord D. Borner — 1975 — Texas Tech University, J.D. (cum laude), 2002 — Admitted to Bar, 2002, New Mexico; 2003, U.S. District Court, District of New Mexico; U.S. Court of Appeals, Tenth Circuit — Member American and Chaves County Bar Associations; State Bar of New Mexico; New Mexico Defense Lawyers Association — E-mail: cborner@atwoodmalone.com

Kay C. Jenkins — 1956 — New Mexico State University, A.D.N., 1977; B.S.N. (with highest honors), 1986; The University of Texas School of Law, J.D. (with honors), 1988 — Admitted to Bar, 1988, Texas; 1989, New Mexico; 1988, U.S. District Court, Western District of Texas; 1998, U.S. District Court, Northern District of Texas; 2004, U.S. District Court, District of New Mexico — Member State Bar of Texas; State Bar of New Mexico (Board of Directors, Health Law Section); Defense Research Institute; New Mexico Defense Lawyers Association; Texas Bar Foundation — Practice Areas: Medical Malpractice — E-mail: kjenkins@atwoodmalone.com

Barbara Smith Evans — 1975 — Washburn University, J.D. (magna cum laude), 2000 — Admitted to Bar, 2001, Kansas; 2002, Missouri; 2006, New Mexico; U.S. District Court, District of New Mexico; U.S. Court of Appeals, Tenth Circuit — Member State Bar of New Mexico (Board Member, Section on Employment and Labor Law); Chaves County Bar Association; New Mexico Defense Lawyers Association — Practice Areas: Employment Law; Insurance Defense — E-mail: bsmith@atwoodmalone.com

Associate

Aaron S. Holloman — 1984 — The University of New Mexico School of Law, J.D. (magna cum laude), 2011 — Admitted to Bar, 2011, New Mexico —

ROSWELL   NEW MEXICO

Atwood, Malone, Turner & Sabin, P.A., Roswell, NM
(Continued)

Member State Bar of New Mexico; Chaves County Bar Association; New Mexico Defense Lawyers Association — E-mail: aholloman@atwoodmalone.com

Hinkle, Hensley, Shanor & Martin, L.L.P.

400 Pennsylvania Avenue, Suite 640
Roswell, New Mexico 88201
Telephone: 575-622-6510
Fax: 575-623-9332
www.hinklelawfirm.com

(Santa Fe, NM Office*: 218 Montezuma, 87501, P.O. Box 2068, 87504)
  (Tel: 505-982-4554)
  (Fax: 505-982-8623)
(Midland, TX Office*: 508 West Wall, Suite 444, 79701, P.O. Box 3580, 79702)
  (Tel: 432-683-4691)
  (Fax: 432-683-6518)

Established: 1888

Insurance Law, Casualty, Fire, Automobile, Workers' Compensation, Malpractice, Product Liability, Surety, Aviation, Wrongful Death, Bad Faith, Directors and Officers Liability, Catastrophic Injury, Medical Malpractice

Insurance Clients

Advocate, MD
Federated Insurance Company
The Medical Protective Company
Texas Medical Liability Trust
American Physicians Insurance Company
Texas Liability Insurance Exchange

Non-Insurance Clients

ConocoPhillips
Pogo Producing Company
State of New Mexico, Risk Management Division
Devon Energy Corporation
Southwestern Public Service Company
State of New Mexico, Subsequent Injury Fund

Litigation Partners

Harold L. Hensley, Jr. — 1934 — Rice Institute, B.A., 1956; The University of Texas, LL.B., 1960 — Admitted to Bar, 1961, New Mexico; 2004, Texas — Member American, Midland County and Chaves County Bar Associations; State Bar of New Mexico; State Bar of Texas; American College of Trial Lawyers

Stuart D. Shanor — 1938 — Wittenberg College, A.B., 1959; University of Michigan, LL.B., 1962 — Admitted to Bar, 1962, Ohio; 1967, New Mexico — Member American, Ohio State and Chaves County Bar Associations; State Bar of New Mexico; American College of Trial Lawyers

Richard E. Olson — 1953 — The University of Mississippi, B.A., 1975; Southern Methodist University, J.D., 1978 — Admitted to Bar, 1978, New Mexico — Member American and Chaves County Bar Associations; State Bar of New Mexico; American College of Trial Lawyers; Defense Research Institute

Jeffrey L. Fornaciari — 1945 — University of Colorado, B.A., 1966; The University of New Mexico, J.D., 1970; The George Washington University, LL.M. (summa cum laude), 1971 — Admitted to Bar, 1970, New Mexico; 1971, District of Columbia — Member State Bar of New Mexico; The District of Columbia Bar

Albert L. Pitts — 1944 — Southern Methodist University; University of Illinois, B.A. (with distinction), 1971; Chicago-Kent College of Law, J.D., 1975 — Admitted to Bar, 1976, New Mexico — Member American and Chaves County Bar Associations; State Bar of New Mexico

Thomas M. Hnasko — 1957 — The University of North Dakota, B.A., 1979; J.D., 1982 — Admitted to Bar, 1982, New Mexico — Member American Bar Association; State Bar of New Mexico

Rebecca Nichols Johnson — 1959 — University of Pennsylvania, B.A. (cum laude), 1982; Washington and Lee University, J.D., 1985 — Admitted to Bar, 1985, New Mexico — Member American and Chaves County Bar Associations; State Bar of New Mexico

Hinkle, Hensley, Shanor & Martin, L.L.P., Roswell, NM
(Continued)

Andrew J. Cloutier — 1962 — University of Dallas, B.A. (cum laude), 1984; The University of Texas at Austin, J.D., 1987 — Admitted to Bar, 1987, Texas; 1988, New Mexico — Member American and Chaves County Bar Associations; State Bar of New Mexico; State Bar of Texas

Ellen Casey — 1952 — Manhattanville College, B.A., 1975; The University of New Mexico, J.D., 1985 — Admitted to Bar, 1985, New Mexico — Member American Bar Association; State Bar of New Mexico; New Mexico Women's Bar Association

S. Barry Paisner — 1955 — New York University, B.A., 1977; Northwestern School of Law of Lewis & Clark College, J.D., 1984 — Admitted to Bar, 1984, Arizona; 1985, New Mexico — Member American Bar Association; State Bar of New Mexico; State Bar of Arizona; Navajo Nation Bar

Max E. Wright — 1948 — The University of Texas at Austin, J.D., 1976 — Admitted to Bar, 1977, Texas; New Mexico — Member American and Midland County Bar Associations; Texas Association of Defense Counsel; Defense Research Institute; International Association of Defense Counsel

William Slattery — 1955 — University of California, Davis, B.A., 1978; Lewis & Clark Law School, J.D., 1981 — Admitted to Bar, 1982, New Mexico; U.S. District Court, District of New Mexico; U.S. Court of Appeals, Tenth Circuit — Member State Bar of New Mexico

David B. Lawrenz — 1961 — Amherst College, B.A. (magna cum laude), 1983; Columbia University School of International Affairs, M.A., 1986; University of Colorado at Boulder, J.D., 1991 — Admitted to Bar, 1991, Maryland; 1992, New Mexico; U.S. District Court, District of New Mexico; U.S. Court of Appeals, Tenth Circuit — Member State Bar of New Mexico

Dana Hardy — 1974 — Colorado State University (magna cum laude), 1996; The University of New Mexico, J.D. (magna cum laude), 2000 — Admitted to Bar, 2000, New Mexico; U.S. District Court, District of New Mexico; U.S. Court of Appeals, Tenth Circuit — Member State Bar of New Mexico

Steven S. Shanor — 1968 — Wittenberg University, B.A., 1990; University of Denver College of Law, J.D., 1993 — Admitted to Bar, 1993, New Mexico — Member State Bar of New Mexico (President 2010)

Nancy S. Cusack — 1952 — Southern Methodist University, B.S., 1974; J.D., 1976 — Admitted to Bar, 1976, Missouri; New Mexico

Gary Larson — Denison University, B.A., 1973; Indiana University, J.D., 1985 — Admitted to Bar, 1985, New Mexico

Lucas Williams — 1973 — The University of New Mexico, B.A., 1997; Pepperdine University, J.D., 2003 — Admitted to Bar, 2003, New Mexico — Member New Mexico Defense Lawyers Association; Defense Research Institute

Mary Baker — 1982 — Saint Mary's College, B.A. (summa cum laude), 2004; Texas Tech University, J.D. (cum laude), 2007 — Admitted to Bar, 2007, Texas

Chelsea Green — 1983 — New Mexico State University, B.S. (with high honors), 2005; Texas Tech University, J.D. (cum laude), 2008 — Admitted to Bar, 2008, New Mexico

Anna Brandl — University of Dallas, B.A. (summa cum laude), 2003; Texas Tech University, M.S., 2006; J.D. (summa cum laude), 2006 — Admitted to Bar, 2006, Texas

Attorneys with other Specialties

C.D. Martin
William B. Burford
Gregory J. Nibert
Jared Hembree
Zachary Taylor
Scott Morgan
John Shelton
Jared Ford
Julie Sakura
Taylor Spalla
T. Calder Ezzell, Jr.
Douglas L. Lunsford
James Bozarth
Mary Lynn Bogle
Jaclyn McLean
Parker Folse
Gareth Morton
Maryl McNally
Loren S. Foy

Sanders, Bruin, Coll & Worley, P.A.

701 West Country Club,
Roswell, New Mexico 88201
Telephone: 505-622-5440
Fax: 505-622-5853
www.sbcw-law.com

Established: 1946

NEW MEXICO

Sanders, Bruin, Coll & Worley, P.A., Roswell, NM
(Continued)

Insurance Defense, Automobile, General Liability, Bodily Injury, Property and Casualty, Workers' Compensation

Insurance Clients

Bituminous Insurance Companies
New Mexico Public Schools Insurance Authority
St. Paul Insurance Company
United Services Automobile Association (USAA)
GEICO General Insurance Company
Rockwood Casualty Insurance Company
United States Fidelity and Guaranty Company

Firm Members

Michael T. Worley — 1951 — Baylor University, B.A., 1973; J.D., 1975 — Admitted to Bar, 1975, Texas; New Mexico; 1977, U.S. District Court, District of New Mexico — Member State Bar of New Mexico; State Bar of Texas; Chaves County Bar Association; New Mexico Defense Lawyers Association; Defense Research Institute

Clay H. Paulos — 1964 — Texas A&M University, B.B.A., 1987; Texas Tech University, M.B.A., 1989; J.D., 1991 — Admitted to Bar, 1991, Texas; 1992, New Mexico; 1992, U.S. District Court, District of New Mexico; 1992, U.S. Court of Appeals, Tenth Circuit — Member American Bar Association

---

The following firms also service this area.

Butt, Thornton & Baehr, P.C.
Suite 300
4101 Indian School Road N.E.
Albuquerque, New Mexico 87110
  Telephone: 505-884-0777
  Fax: 505-889-8870

Mailing Address: P.O. Box 3170, Albuquerque, NM 87190

Insurance Law, Casualty, Transportation, Automobile, Workers' Compensation, Professional Malpractice, Surety, Aviation, Product Liability, Environmental Law, Appellate Practice, Civil Rights, Commercial Litigation, Construction and Bond Claims, Government Entities

SEE COMPLETE LISTING UNDER ALBUQUERQUE, NEW MEXICO (198 MILES)

RUIDOSO 8,029 Lincoln Co.

Refer To
Atwood, Malone, Turner & Sabin, P.A.
400 North Pennsylvania Avenue, Suite 1100
Roswell, New Mexico 88201
  Telephone: 575-622-6221
  Fax: 575-624-2883

Mailing Address: P.O. Drawer 700, Roswell, NM 88202-0700

Insurance Defense, Casualty, Fire, Workers' Compensation, Life Insurance, Product Liability, Medical Malpractice, Professional Liability, Employment Law, Commercial Litigation

SEE COMPLETE LISTING UNDER ROSWELL, NEW MEXICO (80 MILES)

SANTA FE † 67,947 Santa Fe Co.

Hinkle, Hensley, Shanor & Martin, L.L.P.
218 Montezuma
Santa Fe, New Mexico 87501
  Telephone: 505-982-4554
  Fax: 505-982-8623

(Roswell, NM Office*: 400 Pennsylvania Avenue, Suite 640, 88201)
  (Tel: 575-622-6510)
  (Fax: 575-623-9332)
  (www.hinklelawfirm.com)
(Midland, TX Office*: 508 West Wall, Suite 444, 79701, P.O. Box 3580, 79702)
  (Tel: 432-683-4691)
  (Fax: 432-683-6518)

Established: 1888

RUIDOSO

Hinkle, Hensley, Shanor & Martin, L.L.P., Santa Fe, NM
(Continued)

Insurance Law

Litigation Partners

Jeffrey L. Fornaciari — 1945 — University of Colorado, B.A., 1966; The University of New Mexico, J.D., 1970; The George Washington University, LL.M. (summa cum laude), 1971 — Admitted to Bar, 1970, New Mexico; 1971, District of Columbia — Member State Bar of New Mexico; The District of Columbia Bar

Thomas M. Hnasko — 1957 — The University of North Dakota, B.A., 1979; J.D., 1982 — Admitted to Bar, 1982, New Mexico — Member American Bar Association; State Bar of New Mexico

S. Barry Paisner — 1955 — New York University, B.A., 1977; Northwestern School of Law of Lewis & Clark College, J.D., 1984 — Admitted to Bar, 1984, Arizona; 1985, New Mexico — Member American Bar Association; State Bar of New Mexico; State Bar of Arizona; Navajo Nation Bar

Ellen S. Casey — Manhattanville College, B.A., 1975; The University of New Mexico, J.D., 1985 — Admitted to Bar, 1985, New Mexico — Member American Bar Association; State Bar of New Mexico; New Mexico Women's Bar Association

William Slattery — 1955 — University of California, Davis, B.A., 1978; Lewis & Clark Law School, J.D., 1981 — Admitted to Bar, 1982, New Mexico; U.S. District Court, District of New Mexico; U.S. Court of Appeals, Tenth Circuit — Member State Bar of New Mexico

David B. Lawrenz — 1961 — Amherst College, B.A. (magna cum laude), 1983; Columbia University School of International Affairs, M.A., 1986; University of Colorado at Boulder, J.D., 1991 — Admitted to Bar, 1991, Maryland; 1992, New Mexico; U.S. District Court, District of New Mexico; U.S. Court of Appeals, Tenth Circuit — Member State Bar of New Mexico

Dana Hardy — 1974 — Colorado State University (magna cum laude), 1996; The University of New Mexico, J.D. (magna cum laude), 2000 — Admitted to Bar, 2000, New Mexico; U.S. District Court, District of New Mexico; U.S. Court of Appeals, Tenth Circuit — Member State Bar of New Mexico

Nancy S. Cusack — 1952 — Southern Methodist University, B.S., 1974; J.D., 1976 — Admitted to Bar, 1976, New Mexico; Missouri

Gary Larson — Denison University, B.A., 1973; Indiana University, J.D., 1985 — Admitted to Bar, 1985, New Mexico

Litigation Associates

Zachary Taylor
Julie Sakura
Jaclyn McLean
Loren Foy

(See listing under Roswell, NM for additional information)

The following firms also service this area.

Butt, Thornton & Baehr, P.C.
Suite 300
4101 Indian School Road N.E.
Albuquerque, New Mexico 87110
  Telephone: 505-884-0777
  Fax: 505-889-8870

Mailing Address: P.O. Box 3170, Albuquerque, NM 87190

Insurance Law, Casualty, Transportation, Automobile, Workers' Compensation, Professional Malpractice, Surety, Aviation, Product Liability, Environmental Law, Appellate Practice, Civil Rights, Commercial Litigation, Construction and Bond Claims, Government Entities

SEE COMPLETE LISTING UNDER ALBUQUERQUE, NEW MEXICO (57 MILES)

VAUGHN

Evans & Co.
2844 East Main, Suite 106, Box 280
Farmington, New Mexico 87401
  Telephone: 505-566-9400
  Fax: 877-585-1401
  Toll Free: 800-EVANSCO

Aviation, Comprehensive General Liability, Construction Law, Directors and Officers Liability, Employment Practices Liability, Energy, Environmental Law, Excess and Umbrella, Insurance Coverage, Insurance Defense, Motor Carriers, Oil and Gas, Product Liability, Professional Liability, Property and Casualty, Railroad Law, Toxic Torts

SEE COMPLETE LISTING UNDER FARMINGTON, NEW MEXICO (210 MILES)

TAOS † 5,716 Taos Co.

Refer To
Evans & Co.
2844 East Main, Suite 106, Box 280
Farmington, New Mexico 87401
  Telephone: 505-566-9400
  Fax: 877-585-1401
  Toll Free: 800-EVANSCO

Aviation, Comprehensive General Liability, Construction Law, Directors and Officers Liability, Employment Practices Liability, Energy, Environmental Law, Excess and Umbrella, Insurance Coverage, Insurance Defense, Motor Carriers, Oil and Gas, Product Liability, Professional Liability, Property and Casualty, Railroad Law, Toxic Torts

SEE COMPLETE LISTING UNDER FARMINGTON, NEW MEXICO (204 MILES)

TATUM 798 Lea Co.

Refer To
Atwood, Malone, Turner & Sabin, P.A.
400 North Pennsylvania Avenue, Suite 1100
Roswell, New Mexico 88201
  Telephone: 575-622-6221
  Fax: 575-624-2883
Mailing Address: P.O. Drawer 700, Roswell, NM 88202-0700

Insurance Defense, Casualty, Fire, Workers' Compensation, Life Insurance, Product Liability, Medical Malpractice, Professional Liability, Employment Law, Commercial Litigation

SEE COMPLETE LISTING UNDER ROSWELL, NEW MEXICO (79 MILES)

VAUGHN 446 Guadalupe Co.

Refer To
Atwood, Malone, Turner & Sabin, P.A.
400 North Pennsylvania Avenue, Suite 1100
Roswell, New Mexico 88201
  Telephone: 575-622-6221
  Fax: 575-624-2883
Mailing Address: P.O. Drawer 700, Roswell, NM 88202-0700

Insurance Defense, Casualty, Fire, Workers' Compensation, Life Insurance, Product Liability, Medical Malpractice, Professional Liability, Employment Law, Commercial Litigation

SEE COMPLETE LISTING UNDER ROSWELL, NEW MEXICO (93 MILES)

NEW YORK

CAPITAL: ALBANY

COUNTIES AND COUNTY SEATS

County	County Seat	County	County Seat	County	County Seat
Albany	Albany	Herkimer	Herkimer	Richmond	St. George
Allegany	Belmont	Jefferson	Watertown	Rockland	New City
Bronx	Bronx	Kings	Brooklyn	St. Lawrence	Canton
Broome	Binghamton	Lewis	Lowville	Saratoga	Ballston Spa
Cattaraugus	Little Valley	Livingston	Geneseo	Schenectady	Schenectady
Cayuga	Auburn	Madison	Wampsville	Schoharie	Schoharie
Chautauqua	Mayville	Monroe	Rochester	Schuyler	Watkins Glen
Chemung	Elmira	Montgomery	Fonda	Seneca	Waterloo
Chenango	Norwich	Nassau	Mineola	Steuben	Bath
Clinton	Plattsburgh	New York	New York	Suffolk	Riverhead
Columbia	Hudson	Niagara	Lockport	Sullivan	Monticello
Cortland	Cortland	Oneida	Utica	Tioga	Owego
Delaware	Delhi	Onondaga	Syracuse	Tompkins	Ithaca
Dutchess	Poughkeepsie	Ontario	Canandaigua	Ulster	Kingston
Erie	Buffalo	Orange	Goshen	Warren	Lake George
Essex	Elizabethtown	Orleans	Albion	Washington	Hudson Falls
Franklin	Malone	Oswego	Oswego	Wayne	Lyons
Fulton	Johnstown	Otsego	Cooperstown	Westchester	White Plains
Genesee	Batavia	Putnam	Carmel	Wyoming	Warsaw
Greene	Catskill	Queens	Jamaica	Yates	Penn Yan
Hamilton	Lake Pleasant	Rensselaer	Troy		

In the text that follows "†" indicates County Seats.

Our files contain additional verified data on the firms listed herein. This additional information is available on request.

A.M. BEST COMPANY

NEW YORK

ALBANY

ALBANY † 97,856 Albany Co.

Bailey, Kelleher & Johnson, P.C.

Pine West Plaza 5, Suite 507
Washington Avenue Extension
Albany, New York 12205
 Telephone: 518-456-0082
 Fax: 518-456-4767
 E-Mail: jwbailey@bkjlaw.com
 www.bkjlaw.com

Established: 1980

Insurance Defense, Trial Practice, Product Liability, Municipal Law, Fire Loss, Premises Liability, Lead Paint, Homeowners, Slip and Fall, First and Third Party Defense, Police Liability Defense

Insurance Clients

Chubb Insurance Company	Gallagher Bassett Insurance Company
Kemper Auto and Home	
St. Paul Travelers	

Non-Insurance Clients

MTD Consumer Products Center	Network Adjusters, Inc.
Wal-Mart Stores, Inc.	

Shareholders

John W. Bailey — University at Albany, B.A. (cum laude), 1976; Albany Law School, J.D., 1979 — Admitted to Bar, 1980, New York; U.S. District Court, Northern District of New York; 1994, U.S. District Court, Southern District of New York; 1996, U.S. Court of Appeals, Second Circuit — Member American, New York State and Albany County Bar Associations; Defense Research Institute of Northeastern New York (Former President, 1991)

Nannette R. Kelleher — California State University, Humboldt, B.A., 1994; Albany Law School, J.D. (cum laude), 1997 — Admitted to Bar, 1998, New York; U.S. District Court, Northern, Southern and Western Districts of New York — Member Federal, New York State and Albany County Bar Associations; Capital District Women's Bar Association; Capital District Trial Lawyers Association

Thomas J. Johnson — Syracuse University, B.A. (magna cum laude), 1974; Georgetown University Law Center, J.D., 1977 — Admitted to Bar, 1978, New York; U.S. District Court, Eastern, Northern, Southern and Western Districts of New York — Member New York State and Albany County Bar Associations; Defense Research Institute of Northeastern New York (President, 2002); Defense Research Institute National

Vincent J. DeLeonardis — State University of New York at Albany, B.A., 1998; Albany Law School, J.D., 2001 — Admitted to Bar, 2002, New York; U.S. District Court, Northern and Western Districts of New York — Member American and New York State Bar Associations; Capital District Trial Lawyers Association; Association of Trial Lawyers of America

Associates

Crystal R. Peek	William T. Little
Marc J. Kaim	William C. Firth
Sara A. Ostrander	Ryan P. Bailey

Boeggeman, George & Corde, P.C.

39 North Pearl Street, Suite 501
Albany, New York 12207
 Telephone: 518-465-1100
 Fax: 518-465-1800
 E-Mail: boeggeman@bgclawfirm.com
 www.bgclawfirm.com

(White Plains, NY Office*: 1 Water Street, Suite 425, 10601)
 (Tel: 914-761-2252)
 (Fax: 914-761-5211)

Established: 1959

Boeggeman, George & Corde, P.C., Albany, NY (Continued)

Insurance Defense, Trial Practice, Automobile, Product Liability, Legal Malpractice, Medical Malpractice, Employment Law, Real Estate, Toxic Torts, Engineering Malpractice

Firm Profile: The BOEGGEMAN, GEORGE & CORDE law firm was founded in 1959 and has maintained its principal office in White Plains, New York since its inception. This firm also has an office in Albany. The practice focuses on trials and appeals in all courts throughout New York and Connecticut in such areas as products liability, toxic exposure, premises liability, municipal liability, motor vehicle accidents, lead poisoning, professional liability, labor law actions, asbestos claims, insurance coverage issues, sexual harassment and employment related litigation, environmental litigation, pharmaceutical malpractice, medical malpractice, insurance disclaimers, property damage including subrogation and general liability.

Insurance Clients

Broadspire	Crawford & Company
Gallagher Bassett Insurance Company	Lancer Insurance Company
New York Central Mutual Fire Insurance Company	Metropolitan Property and Casualty Insurance Company
State Farm Insurance Company	Selective Insurance Company of America
Summit Risk Services, Inc.	United Services Automobile Association (USAA)

Non-Insurance Clients

Adirondack Trailways	Akzo Nobel
Anheuser-Busch, Inc.	AT&T
Avis Rent-A-Car System, LLC	Eckerd Pharmacies
Electrolux North America	Fisher-Price, Inc.
Laidlaw Transit Services, Inc.	Lowe's Home Centers, Inc.
O'Brien & Gere Engineers, Inc.	

Partners

John E. Boeggeman — (1919-1993)

Richard G. Corde — 1959 — University of Delaware, B.S., 1981; University of Bridgeport School of Law, J.D., 1984 — Admitted to Bar, 1985, New York; Connecticut — Member American, New York State, Putnam County and Westchester County Bar Associations; Defense Association of New York (Board of Directors, 2000-2003); Federation of Defense and Corporate Counsel; Connecticut Trial Lawyers Association; Defense Research Institute — E-mail: rcorde@bgclawfirm.com

Robert S. Ondrovic — 1960 — Fordham University, B.A., 1982; Fordham University School of Law, J.D., 1985 — Admitted to Bar, 1985, New Jersey; 1986, New York — Member Westchester County Bar Association; New York County Lawyers Association — E-mail: rondrovic@bgclawfirm.com

Karen A. Jockimo — 1967 — Connecticut College, B.A. (magna cum laude), 1989; Pace University School of Law, J.D. (cum laude), 1993 — Admitted to Bar, 1994, New York; 1995, Connecticut — Member American and New York State Bar Associations; Westchester Womens Bar Association — E-mail: kjockimo@bgclawfirm.com

Paul A. Hurley — 1965 — Niagara University, B.S., 1987; St. John's University School of Law, J.D., 1990 — Admitted to Bar, 1991, New York — Member American, New York State and Rockland County Bar Associations — E-mail: phurley@bgclawfirm.com

Associates

Daniel E. O'Neill — 1957 — Hunter College of the City University of New York, B.A., 1987; Brooklyn Law School, J.D., 1993 — Admitted to Bar, 1993, New Jersey; 1994, New York; 1995, U.S. District Court, Eastern and Southern Districts of New York — E-mail: doneill@bgclawfirm.com

Michael F. McCusker — 1962 — University of Notre Dame, B.A., 1984; Pace University School of Law, J.D., 1987 — Admitted to Bar, 1987, Connecticut; 1988, New York; 1991, U.S. District Court, Southern District of New York — Member New York State and Connecticut Bar Associations — E-mail: mmccusker@bgclawfirm.com

Crystal Simpkin — 1985 — Florida Southern College, B.S., 2007; University of Miami School of Law, J.D. (cum laude), 2010 — Admitted to Bar, 2011, New York — Member New York State Bar Association — E-mail: csimpkin@bgclawfirm.com

Of Counsel

Joseph H. George — (Retired)

ALBANY   NEW YORK

Boeggeman, George & Corde, P.C., Albany, NY
(Continued)

Cynthia Dolan — 1968 — Pace University, B.A., 1991; M.S.T., 1992; Pace University School of Law, J.D., 1996 — Admitted to Bar, 1997, New York; Connecticut; 2000, U.S. District Court, Eastern, Northern, Southern and Western Districts of New York; U.S. Court of Appeals, Second Circuit — Member American Bar Association; Westchester Women's Bar Association; Women's Bar Association of Orange and Sullivan Counties — E-mail: cdolan@bgclawfirm.com

(See listing under White Plains, NY for additional information)

Burke, Scolamiero, Mortati & Hurd, LLP

7 Washington Square
Albany, New York 12212-5085
   Telephone: 518-862-1386
   Fax: 518-862-1393
   E-Mail: tom@bsmhlawfirm.com
   www.bsmhlawfirm.com

(Rome, NY Office: 107 West Liberty Street, 13440)
   (Tel: 315-336-3604)
   (Fax: 518-862-1386)
(Hudson, NY Office: 437 East Allen Street, 12534)
   (Tel: 518-671-6004)
   (Fax: 518-671-6008)

Established: 1993

Insurance Defense, Professional Malpractice, Medical Malpractice, Professional Liability, Construction Law, Labor and Employment, General Liability, Product Liability, Employer Liability, Automobile Liability, Civil Litigation, Commercial Litigation, Environmental Law, Toxic Torts, Personal Injury, Property and Casualty, Trial Practice, Professional Defense, Municipal Defense

Firm Profile: Burke, Scolamiero, Mortati & Hurd, LLP was originally founded in 1993 and since that time, clients have been our driving force. The firm's founders left leadership positions in larger firms to create a practice where the emphasis is on understanding and achieving our clients' objectives. Modern technology and a commitment to excellence enables us to control costs without sacrificing quality. Meeting clients' needs by finding innovative solutions is the essence of our practice.

Our practice focuses on the defense of civil litigation with primary emphasis in the areas of Medical and Professional Liability, Construction and Labor Law, Public Officials and Municipal Liability, Environmental and Toxic Torts, Product Liability Claims, Workers' Compensation and Commercial Litigation.

Insurance Clients

Acadia Insurance Company	Argonaut Insurance Company
Church Insurance Company	CNA Insurance Companies
Colony Insurance Company	Harleysville Insurance Company
The Hartford	Interstate Insurance Group
Medical Liability Mutual Insurance Company	Merastar Insurance Company
	Mercury Casualty Company
National Interstate Insurance Company	OneBeacon Insurance
	Philadelphia Insurance Company
Progressive Northern Insurance Company	Sentry Insurance
	Team Health
Travelers Insurance Companies	Zurich North America

Non-Insurance Clients

Albany Medical Center	Amsterdam Memorial Hospital
Barry, Bette & Led Duke Construction Company	Caronia Corporation
	Chenago Memorial Hospital
Claxton-Hepburn Medical Center	J.B. Hunt Transport Services, Inc.
LabOne, Inc.	LCA Vision/LASIK Plus
Northwest Toxicology, Inc.	Quest Diagnostics Incorporated
Rome Memorial Hospital	Saratoga County
Schenectady County	Schenectady Regional Orthopedics
Sports Physical Therapy of New York	United States Basketball League
	Warren County

Burke, Scolamiero, Mortati & Hurd, LLP, Albany, NY
(Continued)

Partners

Kevin P. Burke — 1963 — Siena College, B.A. (with honors), 1985; Albany Law School of Union University, J.D., 1988 — Admitted to Bar, 1989, New York; U.S. District Court, Northern and Southern Districts of New York; U.S. District Court, Eastern District of New York — Member American, New York State (Municipal Law and Insurance Law Sections) and Albany County Bar Associations; American Arbitration Association; Defense Research Institute; New York State Trial Lawyers Association — Practice Areas: Negligence; Labor and Employment; Professional Malpractice; Municipal Liability; Construction Law; Surety; Trial Practice; Medical Malpractice; Product Liability — E-mail: kevin@bsmhlawfirm.com

Peter M. Scolamiero — 1963 — State University of New York at Albany, B.A., 1985; Syracuse University College of Law, J.D., 1988 — Recipient: J.C. Penney Golden Rule Award; New York State Bar Association Pro-Bono Award — Admitted to Bar, 1989, New York; U.S. District Court, Northern District of New York; U.S. District Court, Eastern and Southern Districts of New York — Member New York State, Albany County and Saratoga County Bar Associations; New York State Trial Lawyers Association — Languages: Spanish — Practice Areas: Commercial General Liability; Construction Law; Negligence; Municipal Liability; Toxic Torts; Trial Practice; Medical Malpractice; Surety; Product Liability — E-mail: pete@bsmhlawfirm.com

Thomas J. Mortati — 1966 — Fordham University, B.A. (with honors), 1988; Albany Law School of Union University, J.D., 1991 — Phi Alpha Delta — Associate Editor, Albany Law Journal of Science and Technology — Admitted to Bar, 1991, Connecticut; 1992, New York; 1993, U.S. District Court, Eastern, Northern, Southern and Western Districts of New York; 1995, U.S. District Court, District of Connecticut; U.S. Court of Appeals, Eighth Circuit — Member American, New York State (Insurance, Negligence and Compensation Law Sections) and Albany County Bar Associations; Defense Research Institute — Practice Areas: Labor and Employment; Negligence; Medical Malpractice; Municipal Liability; Professional Malpractice; Public Officials Liability; Construction Law; Automobile Liability — E-mail: tom@bsmhlawfirm.com

Jeffrey Earl Hurd — 1967 — Wesleyan University, B.A., 1989; University of Cambridge School of Law, 1991; Hamline University School of Law, J.D. (with honors), 1992 — Admitted to Bar, 1993, Minnesota; 1994, New York; 1993, U.S. District Court, District of Minnesota; 1994, U.S. District Court, Eastern, Northern, Southern and Western Districts of New York; 1997, U.S. Court of Appeals, Second Circuit — Member New York State and Albany County Bar Associations — Practice Areas: Medical Malpractice; Municipal Liability; Civil Rights; Construction Law; Trial Practice; Automobile Liability — E-mail: jeff@bsmhlawfirm.com

Melissa J. Smallacombe — 1956 — State University of New York at New Paltz, B.S., 1980; Albany Law School of Union University, J.D., 1984 — Admitted to Bar, 1984, New York — Member Albany County Bar Association; Defense Research Institute — Practice Areas: Litigation; Personal Injury; Commercial and Personal Lines; Appellate Practice; Insurance Coverage — E-mail: melissa@bsmhlawfirm.com

Thomas J. Reilly — 1977 — Canisius College, B.A., 1999; Albany Law School, J.D., 2002 — Admitted to Bar, 2003, New York — Member American and New York State Bar Assocaitions — Practice Areas: Personal Injury; Medical Malpractice; Insurance Defense — E-mail: treilly@bsmhlawfirm.com

Thomas A. Cullen — 1964 — State University of New York at Purchase, B.A., 1987; St. John's University School of Law, J.D., 1996 — Admitted to Bar, 1997, New York — Member New York State Bar Association — Practice Areas: Medical Malpractice; Negligence; Automobile Liability; Professional Liability — E-mail: tcullen@bsmhlawfirm.com

Associates

Judith B. Aumand — 1981 — Elizabeth College, B.A., 2003; Albany Law School, J.D., 2006 — Admitted to Bar, 2007, New York — Member New York State and Albany County Bar Associations — Practice Areas: Personal Injury; Medical Malpractice; Insurance Defense — E-mail: judi@bsmhlawfirm.com

Megan B. Van Aken — 1972 — University of Hartford, B.S.B.A., 1994; Albany Law School of Union University, J.D., 1999 — Admitted to Bar, 2000, New York; U.S. District Court, Northern District of New York — Member American, New York State and Albany Bar Associations — Practice Areas: Trial Practice; Construction Law; Surety; Negligence; Professional Malpractice; Medical Malpractice; Product Liability; Municipal Liability — E-mail: megan@bsmhlawfirm.com

NEW YORK   ALBANY

Burke, Scolamiero, Morati & Hurd, LLP, Albany, NY
(Continued)

Sharon A. Siegel — 1962 — Cornell University, B.S., 1984; Brooklyn Law School, J.D., 1987 — Admitted to Bar, 1988, New York — Member New York State Bar Association; Capital District Women's Bar Association; New York Civil and Criminal Courts Bar Association — Practice Areas: Litigation; Personal Injury; Commercial and Personal Lines; Appellate Practice; Insurance Coverage — E-mail: sharon@bsmhlawfirm.com

Peter P. Balouskas — 1974 — La Salle University, B.A., 1996; Fordham University School of Law, J.D., 1999 — Phi Alpha Delta Pre-Law President (1995-1996) — Admitted to Bar, 1999, New Jersey; 2000, New York — Member Albany County Bar Association — Practice Areas: Medical Malpractice; Labor and Employment; Premises Liability; Motor Vehicle; Appellate Advocacy — E-mail: pbalouskas@bsmhlawfirm.com

Mark G. Mitchell — State University of New York at Geneseo, B.A. (summa cum laude), 2000; University of Wisconsin Law School, J.D. (magna cum laude), 2006 — Admitted to Bar, 2006, New York; New York — E-mail: mmitchwll@bsmhlawfirm.com

Amanda C. Sherman — Palm Beach Atlantic College, B.A., 2003; Albany Law School, J.D. (Pi Sigma Alpha), 2010 — Admitted to Bar, 2010, New York — Member American and New York State Bar Associations — E-mail: asherman@bsmhlawfirm.com

Donohue, Sabo, Varley & Huttner, LLP

120 Broadway, 2nd Floor
Albany, New York 12205
Telephone: 518-458-8922
Fax: 518-438-4349
www.dsvhlaw.com

Established: 1946

Insurance Defense, Product Liability, Professional Malpractice, Employment Law, Municipal Law

Firm Profile: Donohue, Sabo, Varley & Huttner, LLP has provided legal support for the insurance industry in the upstate New York region for well over 20 years. The firm specializes in all aspects of trial and appellate practice, including municipal law, products liability litigation, construction law, toxic tort defense (asbestos and latex litigation), and professional malpractice defense, including medical, legal and engineering malpractice.

The firm's location in Albany, NY makes us an ideal choice to service the three Courthouses in the Tri-City area: Albany, Schenectady and Rensselear County Supreme Courts. In addition, our central location permit us easy access to most upstate New York venues, including Dutchess, Columbia, Greene, Saratoga, Warren, Essex, Clinton, Fulton, Montgomery, Otsego and Franklin Counties.

The relatively small size of our firm assures that your case will receive the immediate attention every case deserves. Your case will be handled by one attorney, from beginning to end, so you can be assured that when you call us, an attorney knowledgeable about your case will be available with the answers you need. We pride ourselves on providing quality representation for our clients that is responsive and informed. From initial litigation plan to trial, Donohue, Sabo, Varley & Huttner, LLP is there when you need us.

Insurance Clients

Canal Insurance Company	CNA Insurance Companies
Coregis Group	Essex Insurance Company
K & K Insurance Group, Inc.	Shand Morahan & Company, Inc.
Tokio Marine Management, Inc.	Zurich American Insurance Company

Non-Insurance Clients

Burns International Services Corp.	Ladder Management Services
Village of Menands	Village of Waterford

Paul F. Donohue, Sr. — (Retired)
Robert J. Armstrong — (Retired)
Thomas J. Forrest — (Retired)

Donohue, Sabo, Varley & Huttner, LLP, Albany, NY
(Continued)

Firm Members

Fred J. Hutchison — State University of New York, Empire State College, B.A., 1981; Albany Law School of Union University, J.D., 1984 — Admitted to Bar, 1985, New York; 1985, U.S. District Court, Northern District of New York; 1985, U.S. Court of Appeals, Second Circuit — Member New York State Bar Association — Practice Areas: General Defense; Product Liability — E-mail: fhutchison@dsvhlaw.com

Bruce S. Huttner — State University of New York at Stony Brook, B.A. (with honors), 1981; Albany Law School of Union University, J.D., 1985 — Admitted to Bar, 1986, New York; 1986, U.S. District Court, Northern District of New York — Member American, New York State and Albany County Bar Associations; Defense Research Institute — Practice Areas: General Defense; Asbestos Litigation; Toxic Torts; Product Liability; Medical Malpractice — E-mail: bhuttner@dsvhlaw.com

Of Counsel

Alvin O. Sabo — Rutgers University, A.B., 1965; B.S.E.E., 1965; University of Michigan Law School, J.D., 1968 — Admitted to Bar, 1969, New York; U.S. District Court, Northern District of New York — Member New York State and Rensselaer County Bar Associations; Association of Trial Lawyers of America; International Association of Defense Counsel; American Board of Trial Advocates; Defense Research Institute — Former New York State Assistant Attorney General in charge of Contract Litigation (1969-1980) — Practice Areas: Defense Litigation; Professional Malpractice; Product Liability — E-mail: asabo@dsvhlaw.com

Kenneth G. Varley — Siena College, B.A., 1969; State University of New York at Albany, M.A., 1972; Albany Law School of Union University, J.D., 1977 — Admitted to Bar, 1978, New York; 1978, U.S. District Court, Northern District of New York; U.S. Court of Appeals, Second Circuit — Member New York State and Albany County Bar Associations; Defense Research Institute — Former New York State Court of Appeals Research Assistant (1977-1980) — Practice Areas: General Defense; Employment Law; Professional Malpractice — E-mail: kvarley@dsvhlaw.com

(This firm is also listed in the Subrogation section of this directory)

Gleason, Dunn, Walsh & O'Shea

40 Beaver Street
Albany, New York 12207
Telephone: 518-432-7511
Fax: 518-432-5221
E-Mail: tgleason@gdwo.net
www.gdwo.com

Established: 1988

Insurance Law, Administrative Law, Alternative Dispute Resolution, Appellate Practice, Business Formation, Commercial Litigation, Construction Litigation, Contracts, Health Care, Municipal Law, Education Law

Firm Profile: Gleason, Dunn, Walsh & O'Shea is committed to providing excellence in legal representation. We have the experience, knowledge and integrity to represent our clients in a competent, vigorous and professional manner. Client success is our mission, and we strive consistently to obtain practical cost-effective solutions.

Insurance Clients

Capital Area Schools Health Insurance Consortium	Dutchess Educational Health Insurance Consortium
New York Schools Insurance Reciprocal	New York State Public Schools Statewide Workers' Compensation Trust

Partners

Thomas F. Gleason — State University of New York at New Paltz, B.A., 1974; Albany Law School of Union University, J.D., 1978 — Albany Law Review, 1977-1978 — Admitted to Bar, 1978, New York; U.S. District Court, Northern District of New York; U.S. Court of Appeals, Second Circuit; U.S. Supreme Court — Member New York State and Albany County Bar

ALBANY   NEW YORK

Gleason, Dunn, Walsh & O'Shea, Albany, NY (Continued)

Associations; Advisory Committee on Civil Practice, 1986-Present; Subcommittees: Liability Insurance and Tort Law; Alternative Dispute Resolution; Appellate Jurisdiction; Collateral Source Rule; Costs and Disbursements (Chair); Criminal Contempt Law; Disclosure; Electronic Discovery (Chair); Evidence; Expansion of Offers to Compromise Provisions; Interest Rates on Judgments; Motion Practice; Periodic Payment of Judgments and Itemized Verdicts; Sanctions (Chair); Service of Process & Interlocutory Papers (Co-Chair); Statutes of Limitation; Technology; Tribal Court Judgments and Venue — Author: McKinney's Consolidated Laws of New York, Practice Commentaries CPLR 50-A, CPLR 50-B and CPLR 4111; Special Supplementary Practice Commentary on Electronic Filing CPLR 2103; Special Supplementary Practice Commentary on Electronic Filing CPLR 2101; Special Practice Commentary CPLR 5031; Practice Commentary CPLR Article 21 — Adjunct Professor of Insurance Law, Albany Law School, Albany, New York, 1981-2013; Columnist, New York Law Journal

Richard C. Reilly — St. Andrews University, College of the Holy Cross, B.A., 1994; Albany Law School of Union University, J.D. (magna cum laude), 2004 — Justinian Society — Editor in Chief, Albany Law Review, 2003-2004 — Admitted to Bar, 2004, New York; U.S. District Court, Eastern, Northern, Southern and Western Districts of New York; U.S. Court of Appeals, Second Circuit; U.S. Supreme Court — Member New York State and Albany County Bar Associations — Attorney, Village of Voorheesville, NY, Board of Trustees, Planning Commission and Zoning Board of Appeals; Past Member, New Scotland Town Board, New Scotland, NY

Napierski, VanDenburgh, Napierski, & O'Connor, LLP

296 Washington Avenue Extension, Ste 3
Albany, New York 12203
Telephone: 518-862-9292
Fax: 518-862-1519
Emer/After Hrs: 518-399-6361
E-Mail: info@nvnolaw.com
www.nvnolaw.com

Established: 2000

Civil Trial Practice, Insurance Defense, Appellate Practice, Automobile, Commercial Litigation, General Liability, Labor and Employment, Municipal Liability, Product Liability, Trial Practice, Accountants and Attorneys Liability, Coverage Issues, Directors and Officers Liability, Premises Liability, Asbestos Litigation, Automobile Liability, Automobile Tort, Construction Accidents, Construction Defect, Construction Liability, Professional Liability, Contractors Liability, Wrongful Termination, Subrogation, Medical Malpractice Defense

Firm Profile: After years of working in a large law firm environment, we wanted to create a firm that offered its clients the experience, technology and efficiency of a large firm and the tradition of service, responsiveness, accountability and customer satisfaction typically found in a small family business. We believe that our firm which opened on June 19, 2000, not only meets, but exceeds, that goal.

Our lawyers offer over 100 years of combined legal experience in State and Federal courtrooms throughout New York. Litigation is our primary focus and we concentrate our practice in the defense of professional liability claims (medical, legal, accounting, engineering and architectural); product liability defense; trucking and transportation liability; labor and employment law; the defense of municipalities in civil rights; lead paint and discrimination claims; and personal injury litigation. We are a dual resource to our clients. As trial attorneys, we are ready, willing and able to try even the most complex litigation to conclusion before judge or jury. As counselors at law, we assist our clients, both in resolving matters that should not be litigated and in preventing litigation before it starts.

Insurance Clients

Amica Mutual Insurance Company	Church Mutual Insurance Company
CNA PRO	Eastern Dentists Insurance Company
Farm Family Insurance Companies	
Lumber Insurance Company	Medical Liability Mutual Insurance Company
Motorists Insurance Company	
OneBeacon Insurance	St. Paul Insurance Company

Napierski, VanDenburgh, Napierski, & O'Connor, LLP, Albany, NY (Continued)

Selective Insurance Company of America	Travelers Insurance Companies
Zurich Insurance Company	Trident Insurance Company

Managing Partner

John W. VanDenburgh — 1959 — Siena College, B.A. (magna cum laude), 1984; Albany Law School of Union University, J.D., 1987 — Admitted to Bar, 1988, New York; U.S. District Court, Northern District of New York; 1993, U.S. District Court, Western District of New York; 2001, U.S. Supreme Court — Member Federal, American (Tort and Insurance Law Section) and New York State (Insurance, Negligence, Compensation Law and Employment Law Sections) Bar Associations; Albany County and Schenectady County Bar Associations; Defense Research Institute of Northeastern New York (Past President); Capital District Trial Lawyers Association; Defense Research Institute; New York State Trial Lawyers Association; Transportation Lawyers Association — Articles on Trial Tactics, Witness Preparation and the Doctrine of Informed Consent — Council on Litigation Management; Eagle International Associates Inc. (Member, Board of Directors); New York State Dental Society (Panel Counsel, Risk Management Presenter); Lecturer, Dental and Medical Societies on Risk Management and Liability Limitation; Martindale Hubbell AV-Preeminent, N.Y. State Super Lawyer; Listed in Best Lawyers' Best Attorneys in N.Y.

Partners

Eugene E. Napierski — 1944 — Siena College, B.A., 1965; Albany Law School of Union University, J.D. (cum laude), 1968 — Admitted to Bar, 1968, New York; U.S. District Court, Northern District of New York; 1974, U.S. Supreme Court — Member New York State and Albany County Bar Associations; Capital District Trial Lawyers Association; American College of Trial Lawyers; New York State Trial Lawyers Association; Defense Research Institute; American Arbitration Association; American Board of Trial Advocates

Eugene Daniel Napierski — 1966 — College of William & Mary, B.A., 1988; Albany Law School of Union University, J.D., 1991 — Admitted to Bar, 1992, New York; North Carolina; U.S. District Court, Northern District of New York — Member New York State Bar Association; North Carolina State Bar

Christine M. Napierski — 1964 — Syracuse University, B.A., 1986; Albany Law School of Union University, J.D., 1989 — Admitted to Bar, 1990, New York; 1992, U.S. District Court, Northern District of New York — Member New York State and Albany County Bar Associations; Capital District Trial Lawyers; Capital District Women's Bar Association; Defense Research Institute

Shawn F. Brousseau — 1969 — St. Lawrence University, B.A. (magna cum laude), 1991; Albany Law School of Union University, J.D., 1994 — Phi Beta Kappa — Admitted to Bar, 1995, New York; 1998, U.S. District Court, Northern District of New York; 2002, U.S. District Court, Southern and Western Districts of New York; U.S. Court of Appeals, Second Circuit; U.S. Supreme Court — Member American, New York State and Albany County Bar Associations; Capital District Trial Lawyers Association; Defense Research Institute — Contributor: Public Sector Labor & Employment Law, 2nd Edition

Kimberly E. Kenealy — 1957 — College of Saint Rose, B.A., 1980; Western New England College School of Law, J.D., 1996 — Admitted to Bar, 1997, New York; Massachusetts; U.S. District Court, Northern District of New York; U.S. Court of Appeals, Second Circuit — Member American, New York State, Schenectady County and Albany County Bar Associations; Capital District Women's Bar; Capital District Trial Lawyers Association; Council on Litigation Management; Eagle International Associates, Inc.; Defense Research Institute; New York State Trial Lawyers Association — Reported Cases: Matter of Tabrizi v Faxton-St. Luke's Health Care; 66 A.D.3d 1421;13 N.Y.3d 717, 922 N.E.2d 906; McLaughlin v Malone & Tate Bldrs., Inc., 13 AD3d 859, 861

Thomas J. O'Connor — 1941 — Fordham University, B.A., 1962; Albany Law School, J.D., 1968 — Admitted to Bar, 1968, New York; U.S. District Court, Northern District of New York; U.S. Court of Appeals, Second Circuit — Member American, New York State and Albany County Bar Associations; Capital District Trial Lawyers Association; Defense Research Institute

Mark J. Dolan — 1963 — State University of New York at New Paltz, B.A., 1986; University at Albany, M.A., 1991; Western New England College School of Law, J.D., 1994 — Admitted to Bar, 1994, Connecticut; 1995, New York; U.S. District Court, Northern and Southern Districts of New York — Member New York State and Albany County Bar Associations; Defense Research Institute — Coach, Albany Law School, National Trial Competition,

NEW YORK | ALBANY

Napierski, VanDenburgh, Napierski, & O'Connor, LLP, Albany, NY (Continued)

sponsored by The American College of Trial Lawyers, 2004-2008; Adjunct Professor of Law, Albany Law School 2009

Shawn T. Nash — 1973 — Northern Illinois University, B.S., 1997; Ohio Northern University, Pettit College of Law, J.D. (with high distinction), 1999 — Admitted to Bar, 2000, New York; 2001, Illinois; 2004, U.S. District Court, Northern District of New York; 2005, U.S. District Court, Southern District of New York; U.S. Court of Appeals, Second Circuit; U.S. Tax Court — Member American, New York State and Albany County Bar Associations; Defense Research Institute of Northeastern New York; Defense Research Institute; New York State Trial Lawyers Association

Associates

Christina D. Porter — 1967 — Oklahoma State University, B.A., 1989; Benjamin N. Cardozo School of Law, J.D. (cum laude), 1998 — Admitted to Bar, 1999, New York; U.S. District Court, Eastern and Southern Districts of New York; U.S. Supreme Court

Andrew S. Holland — 1980 — William Paterson University, B.A., 2002; Rutgers University School of Law, J.D., 2005 — Admitted to Bar, 2005, New York; 2005, New Jersey; 2006, U.S. District Court, Southern District of New York; 2007, U.S. District Court, Eastern and Northern Districts of New York; U.S. Court of Appeals, Second Circuit; 2010, U.S. Supreme Court; 2011, U.S. District Court, District of New Jersey; 2013, U.S. District Court, Western District of New York — Member New York State and Albany County Bar Associations; Capital District Trial Lawyers Association

Jennifer L. McGrath — 1982 — University of Massachusetts Amherst, B.A. (magna cum laude), 2005; Albany Law School of Union University, J.D., 2011 — Admitted to Bar, 2012, New York; 2013, U.S. District Court, Northern District of New York — Member New York State and Albany County Bar Associations; Capital District Women's Bar Association

(This firm is also listed in the Subrogation section of this directory)

O'Connor, O'Connor, Bresee & First, P.C.

20 Corporate Woods Boulevard, Fourth Floor
Albany, New York 12211
   Telephone: 518-465-0400
   Fax: 518-465-0015
   www.1stlaw.com

(Bennington, VT Office: 507 Main Street, 05201)
   (Tel: 802-440-1541)

Established: 1994

Insurance Defense, Professional Liability, General Liability, Product Liability, Employer Liability, Automobile, Premises Liability, Environmental Law, Toxic Torts, Mass Tort, Insurance Coverage, Extra-Contractual Litigation

Firm Profile: O'Connor, O'Connor, Bresee & First, P.C. is a dynamic litigation firm based in Albany, New York. Practicing throughout New York State and Vermont, the firm's highly dedicated men and women are committed to providing aggressive, attentive and cost-effective representation to their clients.

Insurance Clients

Acadia Insurance Company
Affinity Claims/Dentist's Advantage
Brotherhood Mutual Insurance Company
CNA Insurance Companies
Fireman's Fund Insurance Company
Great American Custom Insurance Services
Media/Professional Insurance
Mercury Insurance Group
National General Insurance
North American Specialty Insurance Company
Admiral Insurance Company
Ameriprise Auto & Home Insurance
Chubb Group of Insurance Companies
Farm Family Insurance Companies
Fortress Insurance Company
Gallagher Bassett Services, Inc.
K & K Insurance Group, Inc.
The Main Street America Group
Medmarc Insurance Group
Metropolitan Property and Casualty Insurance Company
Northland Insurance Company
OMS National Insurance Company

O'Connor, O'Connor, Bresee & First, P.C., Albany, NY (Continued)

Physicians Reciprocal Insurers
PRMS, Inc. - Professional Risk Management Services, Inc.
Selective Insurance Company of America
Travelers Insurance Companies
Podiatry Insurance Company of America (PICA)
Scottsdale Insurance Company
T.H.E. Insurance Company
TIG Specialty Insurance Solutions
Zurich North America

Non-Insurance Clients

AFPD - Administrators for the Professions of Delaware, Inc.
Wal-Mart Stores, Inc.

Partners

Terence P. O'Connor — 1958 — University of Copenhagen; St. Lawrence University, B.S. (magna cum laude), 1980; University of Notre Dame Law School, J.D., 1983 — Phi Beta Kappa, Omnicron Delta Kappa — Admitted to Bar, 1984, New York; U.S. District Court, Northern District of New York; 1985, U.S. Court of Appeals, Second Circuit — Member American, New York State and Albany County Bar Associations; Capital District Trial Lawyers Association; International Association of Defense Counsel; Defense Research Institute; Trucking Industry Defense Association — AV Rated, Martindale-Hubbell — Practice Areas: Professional Liability; Product Liability; General Liability; Commercial Litigation — E-mail: toconnor@oobf.com

Dianne C. Bresee — 1954 — Skidmore College, B.A., 1976; Albany Law School of Union University, J.D., 1979 — Phi Beta Kappa — Admitted to Bar, 1980, New York; U.S. District Court, Eastern, Northern, Southern and Western Districts of New York; U.S. Court of Appeals, Second Circuit — Member Federation of Defense and Corporate Counsel; Defense Research Institute — AV Rated, Martindale-Hubbell — Practice Areas: Insurance Coverage; Environmental Law; Mass Tort; Commercial Law; Toxic Torts — E-mail: bresee@oobf.com

Dennis A. First — 1953 — Vassar College; The Ohio State University, B.A. (with distinction), 1975; Albany Law School of Union University, J.D., 1978 — Law Clerk to Albany County Court (1978-1979) — Admitted to Bar, 1979, New York; U.S. District Court, Northern District of New York; U.S. Court of Appeals, Second Circuit — Member American Arbitration Association (Panel of Arbitrators); Defense Research Institute — AV Rated, Martindale-Hubbell — Practice Areas: Commercial Litigation; Medical Liability; Product Liability; Professional Liability; Environmental Law; Toxic Torts — E-mail: first@oobf.com

Michele M. Monserrate — 1964 — Georgetown University, B.A. (cum laude), 1986; Albany Law School of Union University, J.D. (cum laude), 1989 — Law Clerk to Honorable Howard A. Levine, Associate Justice, New York State Supreme Court (1990-1992) — Admitted to Bar, 1990, New York; Massachusetts; U.S. District Court, Northern District of New York; 1994, U.S. District Court, Southern District of New York; U.S. Court of Appeals, Second Circuit — Member New York State and Albany County Bar Associations; Capital District Women's Bar Association; Professional Liability Underwriting Society — AV Rated, Martindale-Hubbell; The Best Lawyers in America, Appellate Law — Practice Areas: Medical Liability; Professional Liability; Product Liability; Commercial Litigation — E-mail: monserrate@oobf.com

Justin O'C. Corcoran — 1968 — State University of New York at Binghamton, B.A., 1990; Albany Law School of Union University, J.D., 1994 — Albany Law Review — Admitted to Bar, 1995, New York; U.S. District Court, Northern District of New York; 1999, U.S. Court of Appeals, Second Circuit; 2000, U.S. District Court, Southern District of New York — AV Rated, Martindale-Hubbell — Practice Areas: Medical Liability; Product Liability; Professional Liability; Commercial Litigation — E-mail: corcoran@oobf.com

Michael P. Cavanagh — 1964 — State University of New York at Albany, B.A. (cum laude), 1986; Albany Law School of Union University, J.D. (cum laude), 1994 — Albany Law Review — Admitted to Bar, 1995, New York; U.S. District Court, Northern and Southern Districts of New York; U.S. District Court, District of Vermont — Member New York State and Albany County Bar Associations; Defense Research Institute — AV Rated, Martindale-Hubbell — Practice Areas: Professional Liability; Product Liability; Commercial Liability — E-mail: cavanagh@oobf.com

P. Baird Joslin — 1971 — University of Vermont, B.A., 1993; Albany Law School of Union University, J.D. (cum laude), 1997 — Justinian Society — Admitted to Bar, 1998, New York; U.S. District Court, Northern District of New York; U.S. Court of Appeals, Second Circuit — Member New York State and Albany County Bar Associations — AV Rated, Martindale-Hubbell — Practice Areas: Professional Liability; Environmental Law; Product Liability; Insurance Coverage — E-mail: joslin@oobf.com

ALBANY   NEW YORK

O'Connor, O'Connor, Bresee & First, P.C., Albany, NY
(Continued)

Maria Dracker Ascenzo — 1978 — Syracuse University, B.A., 2000; Albany Law School of Union University, J.D., 2003 — Admitted to Bar, 2004, New York; U.S. District Court, Northern District of New York — Member American, New York State, Onondaga and Albany County Bar Associations — Practice Areas: Professional Liability; Premises Liability; Motor Vehicle — E-mail: ascenzo@oobf.com

Danielle N. Meyers — 1980 — Hobart and William Smith Colleges, B.A., 2002; University at Buffalo Law School, J.D., 2005 — Admitted to Bar, 2006, New York — Member American, New York State, Albany County and Oneida County Bar Associations; Defense Research Institute — Practice Areas: Professional Liability; Product Liability; Environmental Liability; General Liability — E-mail: meyers@oobf.com

Anne M. Hurley — 1963 — State University of New York at Buffalo, B.A. (summa cum laude), 1985; State University of New York at Buffalo Law School, J.D., 1988 — Admitted to Bar, 1989, New York; U.S. District Court, Northern District of New York — Member New York State and Albany County Bar Associations; Capital District Women's Bar Association — Practice Areas: Insurance Law; Litigation — E-mail: hurley@oobf.com

Brian P. Krzykowski — Allegheny College, B.A., 1980; College of St. Rose, M.E.D., 2000; Albany Law School of Union University, J.D., 1983 — Kappa Delta Pi — Admitted to Bar, 1984, New York; U.S. District Court, Northern District of New York; 1988, U.S. District Court, Western District of New York — Member American, New York State, Albany County and Saratoga County Bar Associations; Capital District Trial Lawyers Association; Defense Research Institute — Practice Areas: Personal Injury; General Liability; Commercial Liability; Product Liability; Medical Malpractice; Automobile; Trucking; Professional Liability; Labor Law — E-mail: krzykowski@oobf.com

Associate

Margaret E. Dunham — Louisiana State University, B.S., 2005; Albany Law School of Union University, J.D. (cum laude), 2008 — Admitted to Bar, 2009, New York — Member New York State and Albany County Bar Associations — Practice Areas: Premises Liability; Professional Liability; General Practice; Insurance Defense; Personal Injury — E-mail: dunham@oobf.com

Lia B. Mitchell — State University of New York at Albany, B.A., 2002; Whittier Law School, J.D., 2005 — Admitted to Bar, 2005, California; 2007, New York — Member New York State and Albany County Bar Associations — E-mail: mitchell@oobf.com

Carol E. Crummey — Boston College, B.A. (Dean's List), 2008; Albany Law School of Union University, J.D. (Dean's List), 2013 — Admitted to Bar, 2014, New York; U.S. District Court, Northern District of New York — Member New York State and Albany County Bar Associations — E-mail: crummey@oobf.com

Roemer Wallens Gold & Mineaux LLP
13 Columbia Circle
Albany, New York 12203
Telephone: 518-464-1300
Fax: 518-464-1010
www.rwgmlaw.com

Established: 1995

Insurance Defense, General Liability, Product Liability, Commercial Liability, Aviation, Sports and Entertainment Liability, Specialty Casualty Losses

Insurance Clients

ACE USA	American Specialty Insurance Company
Atlantic Risk Management, Inc.	Burlington Insurance Company
Aviva Insurance Company of Canada	CalFarm Insurance Company
Claims Management Services, Inc.	Donegal Insurance Group
Hirsch Claims & Risk Services	Hudson Insurance Group
IFG Companies	K & K Insurance Group, Inc.
North American Risk Services	Philadelphia Indemnity Insurance Company
Royal Insurance Company of America	Summit Risk Services, Inc.
T.H.E. Insurance Company	Transamerica Group/AEGON USA, Inc.
Trident Insurance Services	
United Educators Insurance	Wells Fargo Insurance Services

Roemer Wallens Gold & Mineaux LLP, Albany, NY
(Continued)

Non-Insurance Clients

Acordia Resort Services	Albany County
Beech Aircraft Corporation	The Mattei Companies
The Richardson Group	Riverstone Resources
Willis of New Hampshire, Inc.	

Partner

Matthew James Kelly — 1954 — Cornell University, B.S., 1975; University at Buffalo Law School, J.D., 1979 — Admitted to Bar, 1980, New York; U.S. District Court, Northern District of New York; 1982, U.S. District Court, Eastern and Southern Districts of New York; 1989, U.S. Court of Appeals, Second Circuit; 1995, U.S. District Court, Western District of New York — Member New York State Bar Association (House of Delegates Member; Executive Committee Member-At-Large and Member, Insurance/Negligence Compensation Law Section); Albany County Bar Association (President, 1999); Defense Research Institute

Associates

Amanda Davis Twinam — 1978 — Wells College, B.A. (summa cum laude), 2000; Albany Law School, J.D. (magna cum laude), 2003 — Phi Beta Kappa — Admitted to Bar, 2004, New York; U.S. District Court, Northern District of New York — Member American and New York State Bar Associations

Earl T. Redding — 1978 — Gettysburg College, B.A., 2000; Albany Law School, J.D., 2003 — Admitted to Bar, 2004, New York — Member New York State Bar Association

Thuillez, Ford, Gold, Butler & Monroe, LLP
20 Corporate Woods Boulevard, 3rd Floor
Albany, New York 12211
Telephone: 518-455-9952
Fax: 518-462-4031
www.thuillezford.com

Casualty, Surety, Insurance Law, Product Liability, Medical Malpractice, Subrogation, Health, Commercial Litigation, Environmental Law, Insurance Defense, Appellate Practice, Medicare Audits, Professional Misconduct, Prisoner Litigation, Mental Health Law, Trucking Liability, Motor Vehicle Liability, Real Estate Transactions

Firm Profile: With a history dating back to the turn of the century the law firm of Thuillez, Ford, Gold, Butler & Monroe, LLP offers a broad range of legal services to our clients throughout New York State. Our firm's practice is dedicated to litigation with an emphasis in the areas of medical malpractice defense, insurance defense, health law, environmental and commercial litigation. We continue to build upon our heritage of providing the most effective and aggressive yet cost conscious legal representation to the insurance industry for the defense of medical malpractice, motor vehicle, trucking, prisoner rights and other personal injury claims. We believe we achieve the best results for our clients in any case by being ready and able to proceed to trial with one of our experienced trial attorneys.

Insurance Clients

Alterra Specialty	Blue Ridge Insurance Company
Chart Services, Inc.	Federated Insurance Company
General Casualty Company	Government Employees Insurance Company
Hartford Accident and Indemnity Company	Hudson Insurance Group
Medical Liability Mutual Insurance Company	Medical Mutual Liability Insurance Society of Maryland
OneBeacon Professional Insurance	PRMS, Inc. - Professional Risk Management Services, Inc.
Sentry Insurance	
Western Litigation, Inc.	

Non-Insurance Clients

Albany County	Corizon
Ellis Hospital	Gulf Stream Coach

Partners

Barry A. Gold — (1945-2002)

NEW YORK

Thuillez, Ford, Gold, Butler & Monroe, LLP, Albany, NY (Continued)

Donald P. Ford, Jr. — 1951 — Boston College, B.A., 1973; Albany Law School of Union University, J.D., 1976 — Admitted to Bar, 1977, New York; U.S. District Court, Northern District of New York; 1980, U.S. Court of Appeals, Second Circuit; 2008, U.S. District Court, Western District of New York; 2011, U.S. District Court, Southern District of New York — Member New York State (Insurance and Trial Lawyers Sections) and Albany County Bar Associations; Defense Research Institute of Northeastern New York

Karen A. Butler — 1951 — Vermont College, A.S., 1971; State University of New York, B.S.N., 1991; Albany Law School, J.D. (magna cum laude), 1995 — Admitted to Bar, 1996, New York; U.S. District Court, Northern District of New York; 1999, U.S. District Court, Southern District of New York; U.S. Court of Appeals, Second Circuit; U.S. Supreme Court — Member American, New York, Albany County and Saratoga County Bar Associations; American Association of Nurse Attorneys

Kelly M. Monroe — College of Saint Rose, B.A., 1999; Albany Law School, J.D., 2004 — Admitted to Bar, 2005, New York; U.S. District Court, Northern District of New York — Member New York State and Albany County Bar Associations

Special Counsel

Dale M. Thuillez — 1948 — Rensselaer Polytechnic Institute; Albany Law School of Union University, J.D., 1972 — Admitted to Bar, 1973, New York — Member New York State (Executive Committee, Trial Lawyers Section, Chairman, 1989-1990) and Albany County Bar Associations; Defense Research Institute of Northeastern New York (President, 1986); International Association of Defense Counsel — Adjunct Professor, Albany Law School

Associates

Andrew L. McNamara — 1985 — Albany State University, B.A. (summa cum laude), 2006; Albany Medical College, M.S., 2009; Albany Law School, J.D. (cum laude), 2009 — Admitted to Bar, 2010, New York; U.S. District Court, Northern District of New York; 2011, U.S. Court of Appeal for the Federal Circuit — Member New York State Bar Association

Molly C. Casey — 1984 — New York University, B.A. Political Science, 2006; Albany Law School, J.D., 2012 — Admitted to Bar, 2013, New York; U.S. District Court, Northern and Western Districts of New York — Member New York State and Albany County Bar Associations

Of Counsel

Daisy F. Paglia — 1979 — College of the Holy Cross, B.A. (summa cum laude), 2001; Albany Law School, J.D. (Valedictorian, summa cum laude), 2006 — Admitted to Bar, 2007, New York; U.S. District Court, Northern District of New York — Member New York State and Albany County Bar Associations

Towne, Ryan & Partners, P.C.

450 New Karner Road
Albany, New York 12205
 Telephone: 518-452-1800
 Fax: 518-452-6435
 E-Mail: albany@townelaw.com
 www.townelaw.com

Established: 2009

Business and Real Estate Transactions, Business Litigation, Civil Defense, Commercial Litigation, Construction Litigation, Daycare Liability, Employment Discrimination, Employment Law (Management Side), Estate Litigation, Garage Liability, General Defense Civil Litigation, Governmental Defense, Governmental Liability, Indian Law, Labor and Employment, Municipal Liability, Nursing Home Liability, Nursing Home Litigation, Police Liability Litigation, Premises Liability, Public Liability, Public Officials Defense, School Law, Self-Insured Defense, Slip and Fall, Tribal Law, Trust and Estate Litigation, Policy Liability Defense

Firm Profile: Towne, Ryan & Partners, P.C. is a NYS certified WBE, providing defense to insurance carriers and self-insured clients. The firm has argued cases in state, federal, trial and appellate courts on behalf of private and public organizations and their insurance carriers.

Towne, Ryan & Partners, P.C., Albany, NY (Continued)

Insurance Clients

Global Indemnity Group, Inc.
New York Municipal Insurance Reciprocal

Midrox Insurance Company
New York Schools Insurance Reciprocal

Non-Insurance Clients

City of Auburn
Stewart's Shops Corp.

City of Beacon

Principals

Claudia A. Ryan — LeMoyne University, B.A. (cum laude), 1976; Albany Law School of Union University, J.D., 1979 — Admitted to Bar, 1980, New York; U.S. District Court, Eastern, Northern and Southern Districts of New York — Member American, New York State (Executive Committee Member, Tort, Insurance and Compensation Law Section) and Albany County Bar Associations; New York Women's Bar Association; National Association of Dealer Counsel; Defense Research Institute

Elena DeFio Kean — College of St. Rose, B.A. (cum laude), 1989; Albany Law School of Union University, J.D., 1993 — Admitted to Bar, 1994, New York; U.S. District Court, Northern and Western Districts of New York; 1997, U.S. District Court, Southern District of New York; 2002, U.S. Court of Appeals, Second Circuit — Member New York State, Saratoga County and Albany County Bar Associations; National Association of Dealer Counsel; New York State Academy of Trial Lawyers

Susan F. Bartkowski — Wells College, B.A., 1987; Albany Law School of Union University, J.D., 1990 — Admitted to Bar, 1991, New York; U.S. District Court, Northern District of New York; 1997, U.S. District Court, Eastern and Southern Districts of New York; 1998, U.S. Court of Appeals, Second Circuit — Member New York State, Albany County and Saratoga County Bar Associations; National Association of Women in Construction; National Association of Dealer Counsel; Association of Trial Lawyers of America

James T. Towne, Jr. — University of Vermont, B.A., 1971; Albany Law School of Union University, J.D., 1975 — Admitted to Bar, 1976, New York; 1983, Vermont; 1976, U.S. District Court, Northern District of New York; 1983, U.S. District Court, District of Vermont; 1997, U.S. District Court, Eastern, Southern and Western Districts of New York; 1998, U.S. Court of Appeals, Second Circuit — Member American (Section of Trial Counsel, Corporate, Banking and Business Law), New York State and Vermont Bar Associations; Albany County, Saratoga County, Warren County and Rensselaer County Bar Associations; Federal Bar Council and Foundation; American Arbitration Association (1981-2000; Panel of Arbitrators, Commercial and Construction Panels); National Association of Dealer Counsel; New York State Trial Lawyers Association; Association of Trial Lawyers of America — Designated Arbitrator and Mediator and Early Neutral Evaluator, Dispute Resolution Program, U.S. District Court of the Northern District of New York

Associates

Caitlin A. Goetz
Dana K. Scalere
Sarah M. Hannah

Alexandra Bresee Morgen
Christopher W. Rust

Of Counsel

John F. Moore
Frank B. Williams

Michael Rhodes-Devey

The following firms also service this area.

Cook, Netter, Cloonan, Kurtz & Murphy, P.C.
85 Main Street
Kingston, New York 12401
 Telephone: 845-331-0702
 Fax: 845-331-1003
Mailing Address: P.O. Box 3939, Kingston, NY 12402

Business Transactions, Civil Litigation, Construction Accidents, Motor Vehicle, Municipal Law, Personal Injury, Premises Liability, Product Liability, Professional Liability, Public Entities, Real Estate, Sexual Harassment, State and Federal Courts, Title Insurance, Federal Civil Rights

SEE COMPLETE LISTING UNDER KINGSTON, NEW YORK (55 MILES)

BAY SHORE   NEW YORK

Hacker Murphy, LLP
7 Airport Park Boulevard
Latham, New York 12110
  Telephone: 518-783-3843
  Fax: 518-783-8101
  Toll Free: 800-213-3843

Self-Insured, Product Liability, Commercial Litigation, Corporate Law, Personal Injury, Labor and Employment

SEE COMPLETE LISTING UNDER LATHAM, NEW YORK (11 MILES)

ALBION † 6,056 Orleans Co.
Refer To
Barth Sullivan Behr
600 Convention Tower
43 Court Street
Buffalo, New York 14202
  Telephone: 716-856-1300
  Fax: 716-856-1494

Trial Practice, Appellate Practice, Alternative Dispute Resolution, Product Liability, Casualty, Fire, Professional Errors and Omissions, Coverage Issues, Insurance Fraud, Subrogation, Motor Vehicle, General Liability, Workers' Compensation, Premises Liability, Municipal Liability, Tractor-Trailer, Bad Faith

SEE COMPLETE LISTING UNDER BUFFALO, NEW YORK (58 MILES)

Refer To
Cohen & Lombardo, P.C.
343 Elmwood Avenue
Buffalo, New York 14222
  Telephone: 716-881-3010
  Fax: 716-881-2755
  Toll Free: 800-276-2640
Mailing Address: P.O. Box 5204, Buffalo, NY 14213-5204

Insurance Defense, Trial Practice, State and Federal Courts, Coverage Analysis, Litigation, Fire, Arson, Fraud, Property, Casualty, Surety, Marine, Employer Liability, Premises Liability, Product Liability, Environmental Law, Toxic Torts, Construction Law, Accident, Automobile, Professional Liability, Medical Malpractice, Subrogation, Advertising Injury, Errors and Omissions, Aviation, Bad Faith, Copyright and Trademark Law, Municipal Liability, Title Insurance, Niagara, Orleans, Monroe, Genesee, Livingston, Wyoming, Allegany, Cattaraugus and Chautauqua Counties

SEE COMPLETE LISTING UNDER BUFFALO, NEW YORK (55 MILES)

Refer To
Roach, Brown, McCarthy & Gruber, P.C.
1920 Liberty Building
424 Main Street
Buffalo, New York 14202-3511
  Telephone: 716-852-0400
  Fax: 716-852-2535

Insurance Defense, Trial and Appellate Practice, Medical Malpractice, Professional Malpractice, Product Liability, Construction Law, Sports and Entertainment Liability, Aviation, Fire, Excess, Coverage Issues

SEE COMPLETE LISTING UNDER BUFFALO, NEW YORK (53 MILES)

BATAVIA † 15,465 Genesee Co.
Refer To
Barth Sullivan Behr
600 Convention Tower
43 Court Street
Buffalo, New York 14202
  Telephone: 716-856-1300
  Fax: 716-856-1494

Trial Practice, Appellate Practice, Alternative Dispute Resolution, Product Liability, Casualty, Fire, Professional Errors and Omissions, Coverage Issues, Insurance Fraud, Subrogation, Motor Vehicle, General Liability, Workers' Compensation, Premises Liability, Municipal Liability, Tractor-Trailer, Bad Faith

SEE COMPLETE LISTING UNDER BUFFALO, NEW YORK (43 MILES)

Refer To
Cohen & Lombardo, P.C.
343 Elmwood Avenue
Buffalo, New York 14222
  Telephone: 716-881-3010
  Fax: 716-881-2755
  Toll Free: 800-276-2640
Mailing Address: P.O. Box 5204, Buffalo, NY 14213-5204

Insurance Defense, Trial Practice, State and Federal Courts, Coverage Analysis, Litigation, Fire, Arson, Fraud, Property, Casualty, Surety, Marine, Employer Liability, Premises Liability, Product Liability, Environmental Law, Toxic Torts, Construction Law, Accident, Automobile, Professional Liability, Medical Malpractice, Subrogation, Advertising Injury, Errors and Omissions, Aviation, Bad Faith, Copyright and Trademark Law, Municipal Liability, Title Insurance, Niagara, Orleans, Monroe, Genesee, Livingston, Wyoming, Allegany, Cattaraugus and Chautauqua Counties

SEE COMPLETE LISTING UNDER BUFFALO, NEW YORK (41 MILES)

Refer To
Roach, Brown, McCarthy & Gruber, P.C.
1920 Liberty Building
424 Main Street
Buffalo, New York 14202-3511
  Telephone: 716-852-0400
  Fax: 716-852-2535

Insurance Defense, Trial and Appellate Practice, Medical Malpractice, Professional Malpractice, Product Liability, Construction Law, Sports and Entertainment Liability, Aviation, Fire, Excess, Coverage Issues

SEE COMPLETE LISTING UNDER BUFFALO, NEW YORK (41 MILES)

BATH † 5,786 Steuben Co.
Refer To
Levene Gouldin & Thompson, LLP
450 Plaza Drive
Vestal, New York 13850
  Telephone: 607-763-9200
  Fax: 607-763-9211
Mailing Address: P.O. Box F 1706, Binghamton, NY 13902

Appeals, Arbitration, Mediation, Asbestos Litigation, Bad Faith, Construction Accidents, Dram Shop Liability, Liquor Liability, Fire Loss, Labor Law, Premises Liability, Product Liability, Property Claims, Sexual Harassment, Toxic Torts, Wrongful Death, Advocacy in Professional Discipline, Automobile, Motorcycle, Trucking Accidents, Contractual Indemnification, Defamation, Discrimination, Division of Human Rights/EEOC, Employment Law Violations, False Arrest/Constitutional Claims, Governmental Tort Liability, Infant Settlements, Insurance Coverage Disputes, Medical Malpractice Defense Matters, School District Liability, Um/Sum Claims

SEE COMPLETE LISTING UNDER BINGHAMTON, NEW YORK (97 MILES)

BAY SHORE   26,337 Suffolk Co.

Frenkel Lambert Weiss Weisman & Gordon, LLP
53 Gibson Street
Bay Shore, New York 11706
  Telephone: 631-969-7777
  Fax: 631-206-0540
  E-Mail: info@flwlaw.com
  www.flwlaw.com

(West Orange, NJ Office: 80 Main Street, Suite 460, 07052)
  (Tel: 973-325-6282)
  (Fax: 973-325-2264)
(New York, NY Office: One Whitehall Street, 20th Floor, 10004)
  (Tel: 212-344-3100)
  (Fax: 212-422-4047)
(Fort Lauderdale, FL Office: 440 North Andrews Avenue, 33301)
  (Tel: 954-522-3233)

NEW YORK
BAYSIDE

Frenkel Lambert Weiss Weisman & Gordon, LLP, Bay Shore, NY (Continued)

Insurance Coverage Litigation, Coverage Analysis, Fidelity and Surety, Insurance Defense, Subrogation, Construction Litigation, Premises Liability, Trucking Law, Product Liability, Motor Vehicle, ERISA, Negligent Security

Insurance Clients

Admiral Insurance Company
Crawford & Company
Safeco Insurance
York Claims Service, Inc.
AutoOne Insurance Company
Harleysville Insurance Company
Ward North America, Inc.

Non-Insurance Clients

GELCO

Firm Members

David Frenkel — New York Law School, J.D., 1990 — Admitted to Bar, 1992, New York; U.S. District Court, Eastern, Northern, Southern and Western Districts of New York — Member American, New York State and Suffolk County Bar Associations

Lisa K. Gordon — Touro College Jacob D. Fuchsberg Law Center, J.D., 1993 — Admitted to Bar, 1994, New York; U.S. District Court, Eastern, Northern, Southern and Western Districts of New York — Member New York State and Nassau County Bar Associations

Todd E. Weisman — Hofstra University School of Law, J.D., 1982 — Admitted to Bar, 1983, New York; 1984, U.S. District Court, Eastern and Southern Districts of New York — Member New York State, Nassau County and Suffolk County Bar Associations; Association of Trial Lawyers of America

Richard Lambert — New York Law School, J.D., 1990 — Admitted to Bar, 1990, New York

Arthur N. Lambert — Brooklyn Law School, J.D., 1968 — Admitted to Bar, 1968, New York — Member American and New York State Bar Associations; New York County Lawyers Association

Monroe Weiss — St. John's University School of Law, J.D., 1972 — Admitted to Bar, 1973, New York; 1974, Florida — Member American, New York State and New Jersey State Bar Associations; The Florida Bar; New York County Lawyers Association

Samuel J. Reichel — Benjamin N. Cardozo School of Law, Yeshiva University, J.D., 1992 — Admitted to Bar, 1993, New York

Associates

Alexander Iorio
Christie M. Bird
Dennis O'Neil Cowling
Dina L. Shuster
Edward Vincent
Howard Kleiman
Joseph F. Battista III
Matthew Stabile
Kathleen A. Casey
Kristin Farrell
Linda P. Manfredi
Margaret Tarab
Michelle Maccagnano
Michelle Stachura
Naser Selmanovic
Patricia Esdinsky
Robert Tremaroli
Seth Weinberg
Tim Seibold
Todd A. Schwartz
Barry Weiss
Daniel W. White
M. Diane Duszak
Dori L. Scovish
Eric M. Eusanio
Jennifer R. Brennan
Joseph Radano
Karen Sheehan
Matthew Stabile
Lawrence B. Lambert
Lucretia Pitts
Roxanne L. Jones
Victor B. Kao
Nancy Burlingame
Nicole Femminella
Andrew Stein
Roxanne Jones
Suly Espinoza
Timothy Riselvato
Todd C. Falasco

BAYSIDE 29,206 Queens Co.

Patterson and Sciarrino, L.L.P.

42-40 Bell Boulevard, Suite 606
Bayside, New York 11361
  Telephone: 718-631-4400
  Fax: 718-631-4440
  E-Mail: info@pslawny.com
  www.pslawny.com

General Liability, Trial and Appellate Practice, Municipal Liability, Product Liability, Insurance Law, Commercial Litigation

Firm Profile: Patterson & Sciarrino, L.L.P. is committed to be the best in our field, making the representation of our clients our highest priority. Our partners are seasoned trial lawyers with a combined total of 55 years legal experience. We represent insurers, self insured entities, third-party administrators and municipalities in State and Federal Courts throughout the New York metropolitan area.

Insurance Clients

Allstate Insurance Company
Park Insurance Company
State-Wide Insurance Company
Leading Insurance Group Insurance Co., Ltd.

Partners

Jerome Patterson — Albany State University, B.A., 1984; Lehman College of the City University of New York, M.S., 1986; New York Law School, J.D., 1991 — Admitted to Bar, 1992, New York; U.S. District Court, Eastern and Southern Districts of New York; 2003, U.S. Supreme Court — Member Queens County Bar Association; Queens County Asian Bar Association

Nicholas J. Sciarrino — Emory University, B.A., 1983; Loyola University School of Law, J.D., 1986 — Admitted to Bar, 1987, New York; U.S. District Court, Eastern and Southern Districts of New York; 1993, U.S. District Court, Northern District of New York; 1994, U.S. Court of Appeals, Second Circuit — Member New York State Trial Lawyers Association

---

BELMONT † 969 Allegany Co.

Refer To

Barth Sullivan Behr
600 Convention Tower
43 Court Street
Buffalo, New York 14202
  Telephone: 716-856-1300
  Fax: 716-856-1494

Trial Practice, Appellate Practice, Alternative Dispute Resolution, Product Liability, Casualty, Fire, Professional Errors and Omissions, Coverage Issues, Insurance Fraud, Subrogation, Motor Vehicle, General Liability, Workers' Compensation, Premises Liability, Municipal Liability, Tractor-Trailer, Bad Faith

SEE COMPLETE LISTING UNDER BUFFALO, NEW YORK (76 MILES)

Refer To

Cohen & Lombardo, P.C.
343 Elmwood Avenue
Buffalo, New York 14222
  Telephone: 716-881-3010
  Fax: 716-881-2755
  Toll Free: 800-276-2640

Mailing Address: P.O. Box 5204, Buffalo, NY 14213-5204

Insurance Defense, Trial Practice, State and Federal Courts, Coverage Analysis, Litigation, Fire, Arson, Fraud, Property, Casualty, Surety, Marine, Employer Liability, Premises Liability, Product Liability, Environmental Law, Toxic Torts, Construction Law, Accident, Automobile, Professional Liability, Medical Malpractice, Subrogation, Advertising Injury, Errors and Omissions, Aviation, Bad Faith, Copyright and Trademark Law, Municipal Liability, Title Insurance, Niagara, Orleans, Monroe, Genesee, Livingston, Wyoming, Allegany, Cattaraugus and Chautauqua Counties

SEE COMPLETE LISTING UNDER BUFFALO, NEW YORK (79 MILES)

BOHEMIA / NEW YORK

Refer To
Roach, Brown, McCarthy & Gruber, P.C.
1920 Liberty Building
424 Main Street
Buffalo, New York 14202-3511
   Telephone: 716-852-0400
   Fax: 716-852-2535

Insurance Defense, Trial and Appellate Practice, Medical Malpractice, Professional Malpractice, Product Liability, Construction Law, Sports and Entertainment Liability, Aviation, Fire, Excess, Coverage Issues

SEE COMPLETE LISTING UNDER BUFFALO, NEW YORK (77 MILES)

BINGHAMTON † 47,376 Broome Co.

Levene Gouldin & Thompson, LLP

450 Plaza Drive
Vestal, New York 13850
   Telephone: 607-763-9200
   Fax: 607-763-9211
   E-Mail: MLisi-Murray@lgtlegal.com
   http://www.lgtlegal.com

Established: 1927

Appeals, Arbitration, Mediation, Asbestos Litigation, Bad Faith, Construction Accidents, Dram Shop Liability, Liquor Liability, Fire Loss, Labor Law, Premises Liability, Product Liability, Property Claims, Sexual Harassment, Toxic Torts, Wrongful Death, Advocacy in Professional Discipline, Automobile, Motorcycle, Trucking Accidents, Contractual Indemnification, Defamation, Discrimination, Division of Human Rights/EEOC, Employment Law Violations, False Arrest/Constitutional Claims, Governmental Tort Liability, Infant Settlements, Insurance Coverage Disputes, Medical Malpractice Defense Matters, School District Liability, Um/Sum Claims

Firm Profile: Levene Gouldin & Thompson has long been a part of the Binghamton business and legal communities. The firm was founded in 1927 with the firm name changed to Levene Gouldin & Thompson in the 1950's. In 2000 the firm of Chernin & Gold joined Levene Gouldin & Thompson by way of merger. Both firms have historically been very strong in the litigation areas and over the years enjoyed excellent reputations with regards to insurance defence litigation.

Insurance Clients

American International Group, Inc.
Crum & Forster Insurance Group
Hospitals Insurance Company, Inc.
Liberty Mutual Insurance Company
OneBeacon Insurance Group
Progressive Insurance Group
United Services Automobile Association (USAA)
CNA Insurance Companies
Government Employees Insurance Company
Medical Liability Mutual Insurance Company
Travelers Insurance Companies

Partners

David M. Gouldin — Princeton University, A.B., 1963; Cornell University, LL.B., 1966 — Admitted to Bar, 1966, New York — Member New York State and Broome County (President 1989-1990) Bar Associations; Fellow, American College of Trial Lawyers — E-mail: dgouldin@lgtlegal.com

John J. Carlin — Cornell University, B.S., 1965; Georgetown University, J.D., 1968; New York University, LL.M., 1970 — Admitted to Bar, 1968, New York; 1968, U.S. District Court, Northern and Western Districts of New York — Member New York State and Broome County (President, 1993-1994) Bar Associations — E-mail: jcarlin@lgtlegal.com

John J. Pollock — University of Michigan, A.B., 1972; State University of New York at Binghamton, M.A., 1978; Syracuse University, J.D., 1982 — Admitted to Bar, 1983, New York — Member New York State and Broome County Bar Associations

Michael R. Wright — State University of New York at Buffalo, B.A., 1974; J.D., 1977 — Admitted to Bar, 1978, New York — Member American, New York State and Broome County Bar Associations

Levene Gouldin & Thompson, LLP, Binghamton, NY (Continued)

David F. McCarthy — Hamilton College, A.B., 1983; Boston College, J.D., 1986 — Admitted to Bar, 1987, New York — Member New York State and Broome County Bar Associations

Patricia M. Curtin — University of Toronto, University of St. Michael's College, B.A., 1979; State University of New York at Buffalo, J.D., 1983 — Admitted to Bar, 1984, New York — Member New York State and Broome County Bar Associations

Dorian D. Ames — Le Moyne College, B.A. (cum laude), 1978; Georgetown University, J.D., 1981 — Admitted to Bar, 1982, New York; 1993, Pennsylvania; 1982, U.S. District Court, Northern District of New York; 1987, U.S. District Court, Western District of New York — Member New York State and Pennsylvania Bar Associations

Robert G. Bullis — Hamilton College, B.A., 1968; Cornell University, J.D., 1976 — Admitted to Bar, 1977, New York; 1977, U.S. District Court, Northern District of New York — U.S. Air Force (1969-1973)

Cynthia Ann K. Manchester — State University of New York at Binghamton, B.S., 1987; Syracuse University, J.D., 1991 — Admitted to Bar, 1992, New York — Member New York State and Broome County Bar Associations

Maria E. Lisi-Murray — State University of New York at Binghamton, B.A., 1992; Syracuse University, J.D. (magna cum laude), 2002 — Admitted to Bar, 2003, New York; 2010, Pennsylvania; 2003, U.S. District Court, Northern and Western Districts of New York; 2006, U.S. Court of Appeals, Second Circuit; 2009, U.S. District Court, Southern District of New York; 2010, U.S. District Court, Middle District of Pennsylvania; 2010, U.S. Court of Appeals, Third Circuit — Member New York State, Broome County and Northern District of New York Bar Associations

Of Counsel

Sanford P. Tanenhaus — Cornell University, A.B., 1951; LL.B., 1953 — Admitted to Bar, 1953, New York — Member New York State and Broome County Bar Associations; American College of Trial Lawyers

---

The following firms also service this area.

Bailey, Kelleher & Johnson, P.C.
Pine West Plaza 5, Suite 507
Washington Avenue Extension
Albany, New York 12205
   Telephone: 518-456-0082
   Fax: 518-456-4767

Insurance Defense, Trial Practice, Product Liability, Municipal Law, Fire Loss, Premises Liability, Lead Paint, Homeowners, Slip and Fall, First and Third Party Defense, Police Liability Defense

SEE COMPLETE LISTING UNDER ALBANY, NEW YORK (134 MILES)

Smith, Sovik, Kendrick & Sugnet, P.C.
250 South Clinton Street, Suite 600
Syracuse, New York 13202
   Telephone: 315-474-2911
   Fax: 315-474-6015

Appellate Practice, Automobile, Commercial Litigation, Construction Law, Dental Malpractice, Labor and Employment, Medical Malpractice, Nursing Home Liability, Premises Liability, Product Liability, Professional Liability, Retail Liability, Subrogation, Toxic Torts, Trucking, Workers' Compensation, Wrongful Death

SEE COMPLETE LISTING UNDER SYRACUSE, NEW YORK (73 MILES)

BOHEMIA 10,180 Suffolk Co.

Mazzara & Small, P.C.

1698 Roosevelt Avenue
Bohemia, New York 11716
   Telephone: 631-360-0600
   Fax: 631-360-0669
   E-Mail: tmazzara@mazzarasmall.com
   www.mazzaraandsmall.com

Established: 2000

NEW YORK

Mazzara & Small, P.C., Bohemia, NY (Continued)

Personal Injury, Insurance Coverage, Construction Accidents, Product Liability, Wrongful Death, Appellate Practice

Firm Profile: Mazzara & Small, P.C. is a highly respected litigation firm that represents their clients with personal attention to their particular needs aggressively promptly and cost effectively. Our firm has a record of success at the trial and appellate levels in a wide variety of insurance defense matters.

Insurance Clients

Farm Family Casualty Ins. Co.

Non-Insurance Clients

Quintal Contracting Corp.	Campanelli Landscaping, Inc.
Robert Witcomb Landscaping, Inc.	Mark Joseph Contracting, Inc.

Members

Timothy F. Mazzara — Siena College, B.A., 1983; Western New England College School of Law, J.D., 1986 — Admitted to Bar, 1987, New York; Connecticut; U.S. District Court, Eastern, Northern and Southern Districts of New York — Member Suffolk County Bar Association (Co-Chair, Insurance Negligence and Compensation Defense Committee, 1998-2000) — Practice Areas: Personal Injury; Automobile Accidents; Medical Malpractice; Slip and Fall; Construction Accidents; Wrongful Death; Product Liability; Insurance; Appellate Practice

Kathy B. Small — State University of New York at Oneonta, B.S., 1984; Western New England College School of Law, J.D., 1987 — Admitted to Bar, 1987, Connecticut; 1988, New York — Member New York State and Suffolk County Bar Associations; Suffolk County Women's Bar Association (Member, Board of Directors); Claims and Litigation Management Alliance (CLM) — Practice Areas: Personal Injury; Automobile Accidents; Slip and Fall; Medical Malpractice; Construction Accidents; Wrongful Death

Drew W. Schirmer — State University of New York at Oneonta, B.A., 1983; Touro College Jacob D. Fuchsberg Law Center, J.D., 1990 — Admitted to Bar, 1991, New York; 1992, U.S. District Court, Eastern and Southern Districts of New York — Member Suffolk County Bar Association (Negligence-Defense Counsel Committee) — Practice Areas: Personal Injury; Insurance Defense; Construction Accidents; No-Fault; Motor Vehicle Accidents; Premises Accidents; Property Damage Matters; Insurance Coverage Disputes

Angela P. Pensabene — University of Delaware, B.S., 1994; Brooklyn Law School, J.D., 1997 — Admitted to Bar, 1997, New Jersey; 1998, New York; 1997, U.S. District Court, District of New Jersey; 1999, U.S. District Court, Eastern and Southern Districts of New York — Member New York State and Suffolk County Bar Associations — Practice Areas: Appellate Practice; Personal Injury; Insurance Defense; Premises Liability; Construction Accidents; Motor Vehicle Accidents

BRONX † 1,203,789 Bronx Co.

Refer To

Boeggeman, George & Corde, P.C.
1 Water Street, Suite 425
White Plains, New York 10601
　Telephone: 914-761-2252
　Fax: 914-761-5211

Insurance Defense, Trial Practice, Automobile, Product Liability, Legal Malpractice, Medical Malpractice, Employment Law, Real Estate, Toxic Torts, Engineering Malpractice

SEE COMPLETE LISTING UNDER WHITE PLAINS, NEW YORK (16 MILES)

Refer To

Connors & Connors, PC
766 Castleton Avenue
Staten Island, New York 10310-1700
　Telephone: 718-442-1700
　Fax: 718-442-1717

Insurance Defense, Commercial and Personal Lines, Self-Insured Defense, Trucking Law, Self-Retained Trucking Company Defense, Self-Retained Security Guard Companies, Self-Retained Retail Stores

SEE COMPLETE LISTING UNDER STATEN ISLAND, NEW YORK (37 MILES)

Refer To

Reardon & Sclafani, P.C.
220 White Plains Road
Tarrytown, New York 10591
　Telephone: 914-366-0201
　Fax: 914-366-0022

Insurance Law, Malpractice, Product Liability, General Liability, Motor Vehicle, Environmental Law, Trial Practice, Appellate Practice, State and Federal Courts

SEE COMPLETE LISTING UNDER TARRYTOWN, NEW YORK (19 MILES)

BROOKLYN † 2,602,012 Kings Co.

The Law Offices of Composto & Composto

142 Joralemon Street, 2nd Floor
Brooklyn, New York 11201
　Telephone: 718-875-5199
　Fax: 718-855-6866
　E-Mail: acomposto@compostolaw.com
　www.compostolaw.com

Established: 1932

General Liability, Defense Litigation, Personal Injury, Automobile, Homeowners, First Party Matters, Commercial Litigation, Toxic Torts, Lead Paint, Medical Malpractice, Property, Slip and Fall, Wrongful Death, Real Estate, Civil Litigation, Wills & Probate Administration

Firm Profile: Since 1932, The Law Offices of Composto & Composto and its predecessors have provided a broad range of legal services to private and business clients. Founded on tradition, skill and years of practical experience, we believe in building long-lasting relationships with our clients based upon trust, understanding and superior legal representation. We strive to be proactive and to bring each litigated matter to a prompt and final disposition.

Insurance Clients

Allstate Insurance Company	Country-Wide Insurance Company
General Casualty Insurance Company	New York State Insurance Department, Liquidation Bureau
Plymouth Rock Assurance Corporation	Prudential Property and Casualty Insurance Company

Partners

Andrea F. Composto — Albany Law School of Union University, J.D., 2002 — Admitted to Bar, 2003, New York; U.S. District Court, Eastern and Southern Districts of New York — New York State Certified Women Business Enterprise (WBE) — Practice Areas: Insurance Defense; Automobile Accidents; Personal Injury; Appellate Practice; Civil Litigation; Commercial Real Estate Law; General Civil Litigation; Premise Litigation; Real Estate; Wills

Frank A. Composto — St. John's University School of Law, J.D., 1972 — Admitted to Bar, 1972, New York; 1974, U.S. District Court, Eastern and Southern Districts of New York; 1994, U.S. Supreme Court — Capitan, United States Army Reserve (Infantry, 1970) — Practice Areas: Insurance Defense; Civil Litigation; First and Third Party Defense; Appellate Practice; Arbitration; Automobile; Business and Real Estate Transactions; Business Formation; General Civil Litigation; General Civil Trial and Appellate Practice; General Practice; Guardian and Conservatorships; Lead Paint; Medical Malpractice; No-Fault; Personal Injury; Premise Litigation; Probate; Real Estate; Slip and Fall; Trial and Appellate Practice; Wills

Associate Attorney

Diana E. Grangio — New York Law School, J.D., 2012 — Admitted to Bar, 2013, New York — Practice Areas: Insurance Defense; Automobile Litigation; Wills; Wills and Estate Litigation; Probate; Civil Litigation; General Practice

BROOKLYN   NEW YORK

The Law Offices of Composto & Composto, Brooklyn, NY (Continued)

Senior Counsel

David Greene — Fordham Law School, J.D., 1967 — Admitted to Bar, 1967, New York; District of Columbia; U.S. District Court, Eastern and Southern Districts of New York; U.S. Court of Appeals, Second Circuit; 1980, U.S. Supreme Court — Member American, New York State and Brooklyn Bar Associations; Jewish Lawyers Guild; Brooklyn Manhattan Trial Lawyers Association; Defense Association of New York; Defense Research Institute

Law Offices of Michael E. Pressman

26 Court Street, Suite 1700
Brooklyn, New York 11242
Telephone: 718-237-4600
Fax: 212-480-2590
Toll Free: 800-764-3030
E-Mail: mepressman@mepressman.com

(New York, NY Office*: 125 Maiden Lane-17th Floor, 10038)
  (Tel: 212-480-3030)
  (Fax: 212-480-2590)
  (Toll Free: 800-764-3030)
(Warren, NJ Office*: Warrenville Plaza, 31W, Mountain Boulevard, 07059)
  (Tel: 908-753-6661)
  (Fax: 908-755-5229; 212-480-2590)
  (Toll Free: 800-764-3030)
(Garden City, NY Office*(See Long Island City listing): 114 Chestnut Street, 11530)
  (Fax: 212-480-2590)
  (Toll Free: 800-764-3030)

Established: 1984

Insurance Defense, Automobile, General Liability, Product Liability, Property and Casualty

Insurance Clients

Alliance United Insurance Company
American Family Insurance Group
American Insurance Managers
Associated Mutual Insurance Cooperative
Central Mutual Insurance Company
Clermont Specialty Managers, Ltd.
FARA Insurance Services
Farm Bureau Insurance of Michigan
First State Insurance Company
General Star National Insurance Company
Indiana Farm Bureau
Leading Insurance Services, Inc.
Michigan Farm Bureau
Nebraska Farm Bureau
New York State Insurance Department
PSM Insurance Companies
RiverStone Claims Management, LLC
Virginia Farm Bureau Mutual Insurance Company
American Bankers Insurance Group
American Heartland Insurance Company
Assurant Insurance Group
CAA Insurance Company
Cincinnati Financial Corporation
Everest National Insurance Company
First Insurance Network, Inc.
First Judicial Claim Service Inc.
GAB Robins North America, Inc.
Georgia Farm Bureau Mutual Insurance Company
Kensington Insurance Company
Maya Assurance Company
Morstan General Agency, Inc.
New York Central Mutual Fire Insurance Company
North American Risk Services
QBE
United Automobile Insurance Company

Non-Insurance Clients

Central Parking Corporation
Papa John's International, Inc.
Office Depot, Inc.
The Shaw Group, Inc.

Senior Partner

Michael E. Pressman — 1950 — Clark University, B.A. (with high honors), 1972; Rutgers University School of Law, J.D., 1976 — Phi Beta Kappa — Admitted to Bar, 1976, Pennsylvania; 1977, New York; U.S. District Court, Eastern and Southern Districts of New York; U.S. Court of Appeals, Second Circuit — Member American and New York State Bar Associations (Lecturer); New York State Trial Lawyers Association (Lecturer); New York State Insurance Association (Lecturer); Association of Trial Lawyers of the

Law Offices of Michael E. Pressman, Brooklyn, NY (Continued)

City of New York (President); New York City Trial Lawyers (Board of Governors, Chairman of the Board, Judicial Screening Committee Brooklyn and Bronx); Defense Research Institute — New York State Judicial Selection Committee for Appointment of Supreme and Civil Court Judges for the City of New York (County of Kings and Bronx); Lawyer of the Year Award from UJA-Federation; Chair Person and Presenter of the Harlan Fiske Stone Award

Partners

Steven H. Cohen — 1956 — Adelphi University, B.S., 1979; Golden Gate University School of Law, J.D., 1982 — Admitted to Bar, 1985, New York; 1985, California — Member New York State Bar Association

Tod S. Fichtelberg — 1958 — State University of New York at Oswego, B.A., 1980; Vermont Law School, J.D., 1987 — Admitted to Bar, 1988, New York — Member New York State Bar Association; New York County Lawyers Association

Eric S. Fenyes — 1961 — Yeshiva University, B.A., 1984; Touro College Jacob D. Fuchsberg Law Center, J.D., 1987 — Admitted to Bar, 1988, New York — Member American Bar Association; New York County Lawyers Association

Seth I. Kudler — 1966 — American University, B.A., 1988; New York Law School, J.D., 1991 — Admitted to Bar, 1991, Connecticut; 1992, New York

Robert Baumgarten — 1959 — State University of New York at Stony Brook, B.A., 1981; New York Law School, J.D. (cum laude), 1984 — Admitted to Bar, 1985, New York; New Jersey; U.S. District Court, Eastern and Southern Districts of New York; U.S. District Court, District of New Jersey

Robert S. Bonelli — 1957 — Fordham University, B.A., 1979; Fordham University School of Law, J.D., 1983 — Admitted to Bar, 1985, New York — Languages: Spanish

Stuart B. Cholewa — 1978 — Syracuse University, B.S., 2000; University of Miami School of Law, J.D. (cum laude), 2003 — Admitted to Bar, 2004, New York

Steve D. Byoun — 1969 — Nyack College, B.A., 1994; Pace University School of Law, J.D., 1999 — Admitted to Bar, 2000, New York; New Jersey; 2001, U.S. District Court, Eastern and Southern Districts of New York

Associates

Allison B. Cennamo — 1980 — St. John's University, B.A., 2002; Touro College Jacob D. Fuchsberg Law Center, J.D., 2007 — Admitted to Bar, 2008, New York

Vanessa Turner Gottfried — 1987 — State University of New York at Binghamton, B.A. (Dean's List), 2009; Brooklyn Law School, J.D., 2012 — Pro Bono Award — Admitted to Bar, 2013, New York

Edward Robert Averbuch — 1982 — University of Connecticut, B.A., 2004; New York Law School, J.D., 2008 — Admitted to Bar, 2009, New York; Florida; U.S. District Court, Southern District of Florida; 2010, U.S. District Court, Eastern and Southern Districts of New York

Arthur G. Torkiver — 1988 — New York University, B.A., 2010; Brooklyn Law School, J.D., 2013 — Admitted to Bar, 2013, New York; New Jersey; 2014, U.S. District Court, Eastern and Southern Districts of New York — Languages: Russian

Jill Alexandra Farrington — 1984 — University of Dallas, B.A., 2006; St. Johns University School of Law, J.D., 2010 — Bureau of National Affairs Award for Excellence in Labor & Employment Law — Admitted to Bar, 2012, New York

(See listing under New York, NY for additional information)

The following firms also service this area.

Connors & Connors, PC

766 Castleton Avenue
Staten Island, New York 10310-1700
Telephone: 718-442-1700
Fax: 718-442-1717

Insurance Defense, Commercial and Personal Lines, Self-Insured Defense, Trucking Law, Self-Retained Trucking Company Defense, Self-Retained Security Guard Companies, Self-Retained Retail Stores

SEE COMPLETE LISTING UNDER STATEN ISLAND, NEW YORK (15 MILES)

NEW YORK — BUFFALO

Reardon & Sclafani, P.C.
220 White Plains Road
Tarrytown, New York 10591
  Telephone: 914-366-0201
  Fax: 914-366-0022

Insurance Law, Malpractice, Product Liability, General Liability, Motor Vehicle, Environmental Law, Trial Practice, Appellate Practice, State and Federal Courts

SEE COMPLETE LISTING UNDER TARRYTOWN, NEW YORK (34 MILES)

BUFFALO † 261,310 Erie Co.

Barth Sullivan Behr

600 Convention Tower
43 Court Street
Buffalo, New York 14202
  Telephone: 716-856-1300
  Fax: 716-856-1494
  www.barthbehr.com

(Syracuse, NY Office*: 224 Harrison Street, Suite 208, 13202)
  (Tel: 315-234-1864)
  (Fax: 315-410-1262)
  (E-Mail: lbehr@barthbehr.com)

Established: 1928

Trial Practice, Appellate Practice, Alternative Dispute Resolution, Product Liability, Casualty, Fire, Professional Errors and Omissions, Coverage Issues, Insurance Fraud, Subrogation, Motor Vehicle, General Liability, Workers' Compensation, Premises Liability, Municipal Liability, Tractor-Trailer, Bad Faith

Firm Profile: BARTH SULLIVAN BEHR since 1928 has successfully defended claims and suits in Western and Upstate/Central New York (COUNTIES: Albany, Allegany, Erie, Genesee, Jefferson, Livingston, Monroe, Niagara, Onondaga, Oswego, Otsego, St. Lawrence, Schuyler, Seneca, Steuben, Tompkins, Wayne, Wyoming, Yates), and in New York's Southern Tier (COUNTIES: Allegany, Cattaraugus, Chautauqua, Chemung). Our insurance coverage practice extends to the entire state, and we evaluate and litigate significant coverage disputes in other states as well. We are pleased to provide references upon request, from experienced claims executives with both major and regional carriers.

Insurance Clients

Amerisure Companies
Berkley Administrators
CNA Insurance Companies
Countryway Insurance Company
Dryden Mutual Insurance Company
Federated Mutual Insurance Company
Holyoke Mutual Insurance Company in Salem
J. C. Penney Casualty Insurance Company
Merchants Insurance Group
MetLife Auto & Home
Middlesex Mutual Assurance Company
North Country Insurance Company
Praetorian Insurance Company
R.C.A. Insurance Group
Safeco Insurance
Tower Risk Management
United Frontier Mutual Insurance Company
Wayne Cooperative Insurance Company
AutoOne Insurance Company
Claims Control Corporation
Community Mutual Insurance Company
Erie Insurance Exchange
Esurance Insurance Company
General Casualty Companies
Genesee Patrons' Co-Operative Insurance Company
The Infinity Group
Lancer Insurance Group
Material Damage Adjustment Corporation
Michigan Mutual Insurance Company
Midstate Mutual Insurance Company
Preferred Mutual Insurance Company
State Farm Insurance Companies
United Educators Insurance
United National Insurance Company

Non-Insurance Clients

Avis Rent-A-Car System, LLC
Dollar General Stores
Republic Financial Services, Inc.
Chesterfield Services, Inc.
ExxonMobil Corporation
The Salvation Army

Barth Sullivan Behr, Buffalo, NY (Continued)

Partners

Philip C. Barth, III — 1957 — State University of New York at Stony Brook, B.A., 1979; State University of New York at Buffalo, J.D., 1988 — Admitted to Bar, 1989, New York; U.S. District Court, Northern and Western Districts of New York — Member New York State and Erie County Bar Associations; Defense Research Institute; International Association of Defense Counsel

Laurence D. Behr — 1951 — State University of New York at Buffalo, B.A. (cum laude), 1974; J.D. (magna cum laude), 1981 — Confidential Law Clerk, U.S. District Court, Western District of New York (1981-1983) — Senior Editor, Buffalo Law Review — Admitted to Bar, 1982, New York; U.S. Court of Appeals, Second Circuit; U.S. District Court, Eastern, Northern, Southern and Western Districts of New York; 1987, U.S. Supreme Court — Member New York State and Erie County Bar Associations; National Lawyers Association; Defense Research Institute — "Bad Faith: 'Gross Disregard' Standard Confirmed and Applied by the New York State Court of Appeals," NYSBA/INCL Journal (June 1994); "Significant Recent Developments in the Law of 'Bad Faith' in New York," NYSBA/INCL Journal (June 1993) — Lecturer in numerous seminars on topics of insurance coverage and negligence law

Firm Members

Douglas P. Hamberger — 1954 — Canisius College, B.A., 1976; Miami University, J.D., 1979 — Admitted to Bar, 1980, Florida; 1982, New York; U.S. District Court, Western District of New York — Assistant District Attorney, 1982-1986; Trial Counsel, CGU Insurance, 1991- 2002; Senior Trial Counsel, Zurich Insurance, 2002-2007

J. William Savage — 1966 — University of Pittsburgh, J.D. (summa cum laude), 1996; Syracuse University, J.D., 1999 — Admitted to Bar, 2000, New York; U.S. District Court, Northern and Western Districts of New York — Member New York State and Onondaga County Bar Associations — Resident Syracuse, NY Office

David H. Walsh IV — 1954 — University of Rochester, B.S., 1977; Albany Law School of Union University, J.D. (cum laude), 1980 — Admitted to Bar, 1981, New York; U.S. District Court, Northern, Southern and Western Districts of New York; U.S. Court of Appeals, Second Circuit; U.S. Court of Federal Claims — Member New York State Bar Association — Assistant Corporation Counsel, City of Syracuse, 2002-2005 — Resident Syracuse, NY Office

James J. Greco — 1966 — Canisius College, B.A., 1984; University of Detroit School of Law, J.D., 1991 — Admitted to Bar, 1992, New York; U.S. District Court, Western District of New York; 1996, U.S. Bankruptcy Court — Member New York State and Erie County Bar Associations; Western New York Defense Trial Association

Alex M. Neurohr — 1989 — Nova Southeastern University, B.S. Business Admin. (cum laude), 2011; State University of New York at Buffalo Law School, J.D. (cum laude), 2014 — Recipient, Henry W. Box Scholarship — Senior Associate, Buffalo Intellectual Property Law Journal — Admitted to Bar, 2014, New York — Member Erie County Bar Association

Daniel K. Cartwright — 1985 — State University of New York at Buffalo, B.S. Business Admin., 2007; Florida International University College of Law, J.D. (cum laude), 2014 — Book Award: Torts; Dean's Scholars Scholarship; First Runner Up, 2013 National BLSA Internnational Law Negotiation Competition — Article/Comments Editor, Florida International University Law Review, 2013-2014 — Admitted to Bar, 2014, New York

Bouvier Partnership, LLP

Main Place Tower
350 Main Street, Suite 1400
Buffalo, New York 14202-3714
  Telephone: 716-856-1344
  Fax: 716-856-1369
  www.bouvierlaw.com

(East Aurora, NY Office: 359 Quaker Road, Route 20, 14052)
  (Tel: 716-652-9311)

Established: 1952

Appellate Practice, Product Liability, Insurance Coverage, Personal Injury, Automobile, Slip and Fall, Premises Liability, Commercial Litigation, Toxic Torts, Asbestos Litigation, Property Loss, Fire Loss, Nursing Home Liability

BUFFALO   NEW YORK

Bouvier Partnership, LLP, Buffalo, NY   (Continued)

Insurance Clients

A. Central Insurance Company
Argonaut Great Central Insurance Company
First Niagara Risk Management, Inc.
General Insurance Company
Grange Mutual Insurance Company
Home Indemnity Company
Kemper/Unitrin
Metropolitan Property and Casualty Insurance Company
New York Central Mutual Fire Insurance Company
Travelers Insurance
Trident Insurance Services
Arch Insurance Company
Auto-Owners Insurance Company
Erie and Niagara Insurance Association
Gallagher Bassett Services, Inc.
Genesee Patrons' Co-Operative Insurance Company
Home Insurance Company
Merchants Mutual Insurance Company
Motorists Insurance Company
Patriot National Insurance Group
State Farm Mutual Automobile Insurance Company
Zurich North America

Non-Insurance Clients

City of Lackawanna, New York
Town of Hamburg, New York
Town of Amherst, New York
Town of Tonawanda, New York

Partners

Peter J. Martin — 1939 — Georgetown University, B.S., 1961; State University of New York at Buffalo Law School, J.D., 1964; State University of New York at Buffalo, LL.B., 1964 — Admitted to Bar, 1964, New York; U.S. Tax Court — Member New York State and Erie County Bar Associations; American Arbitration Association — E-mail: pmartin@bouvierlaw.com

Dale A. Ehman — 1950 — State University of New York at Albany, B.S. (magna cum laude), 1972; State University of New York at Buffalo Law School, J.D., 1975 — Admitted to Bar, 1976, New York; U.S. District Court, Western District of New York — Member New York State and Erie County Bar Associations; Western New York Trial Lawyers Association (Board of Directors, 1990-1992); American Arbitration Association Board of Arbitrators — E-mail: dehman@bouvierlaw.com

George W. Collins, Jr. — 1951 — Grove City College, B.A., 1973; State University of New York at Buffalo Law School, J.D., 1984 — Admitted to Bar, 1985, New York; U.S. District Court, Western District of New York — Member Erie County Bar Association (Negligence Committee); Empire Mediation and Arbitration; Western New York Trial Lawyers Association; International Association of Defense Counsel — E-mail: gcollins@bouvierlaw.com

Paul F. Hammond — 1961 — State University of New York at Buffalo, B.S., 1984; Case Western Reserve University, 1985; State University of New York at Buffalo Law School, J.D., 1988 — Admitted to Bar, 1988, New York; 1989, U.S. District Court, Western District of New York — Member New York State (Trial Lawyers and T.I.C.L. Sections) and Erie County (Negligence Committee) Bar Associations; International Association of Defense Counsel Trial Academy; Western New York Trial Lawyers Association; Defense Research Institute — E-mail: pfhammond@bouvierlaw.com

Emilio Colaiacovo — 1975 — Mercyhurst College, B.A. (magna cum laude), 1998; State University of New York at Buffalo Law School, J.D., 2002 — Admitted to Bar, 2002, New York; U.S. District Court, Western District of New York — Member New York State and Erie County Bar Associations — E-mail: ecolaiac@bouvierlaw.com

Paula M. Eade Newcomb — St. Bonaventure University, B.A. (summa cum laude), 1987; State University of New York at Buffalo Law School, J.D. (cum laude), 1990 — Admitted to Bar, 1991, New York; U.S. District Court, Eastern, Northern, Southern and Western Districts of New York — Member New York State and Erie County Bar Associations — E-mail: pnewcomb@bouvierlaw.com

Special Counsel

Michael P. Caffery — 1951 — State University of New York at Fredonia, B.S. (cum laude), 1975; University of Toledo School of Law, J.D., 1978 — Admitted to Bar, 1978, New York — Member New York State, Erie County, and Chautauqua County Bar Associations; New York State Trial Lawyers Association — E-mail: mcaffery@bouvierlaw.com

Anthony J. Colucci, Jr. — Canisius College, B.S., 1955; State University of New York at Buffalo Law School, LL.B., 1958 — Admitted to Bar, 1958, New York; 1991, Pennsylvania; Florida; 1964, U.S. Supreme Court — Member New York State, Erie County and Palm Beach County Bar Associations; The Florida Bar; Catholic Lawyers Guild (Past President); Marshall Lawyers Club; State University of New York At Buffalo Law Alumni Association (Past President) — E-mail: acolucci@bouvierlaw.com

Roger T. Davison — State University of New York at Buffalo Law School, J.D., 1962 — Admitted to Bar, 1962, New York — Member New York State and Erie County Bar Associations; American Academy of Matrimonial Lawyers; Western New York Matrimonial Trial Lawyers Association; Law Guardian Panel — E-mail: rdavison@bouvierlaw.com

John P. DePaolo — 1961 — State University of New York at Buffalo, B.A., 1987; University of Dayton School of Law, J.D., 1990 — Admitted to Bar, 1990, Massachusetts; 1991, New York; U.S. District Court, District of Massachusetts; 2001, U.S. District Court, Western District of New York — Member New York State and Erie County Bar Associations; Western New York Defense Trial Lawyers Association — E-mail: jdepaolo@bouvierlaw.com

John F. Canale — 1922 — University at Buffalo Law School, LL.B., 1947 — Admitted to Bar, 1948, New York; 1950, U.S. District Court, Western District of New York — Member American, New York State and Erie County (Past Director) Bar Associations; Western New York Trial Lawyers Association (Past President); Fellow, American College of Trial Lawyers — E-mail: jcanale@bouvierlaw.com

Norman E.S. Greene — 1939 — University at Buffalo, B.A. (cum laude), 1962; Columbia Law School, LL.B., 1965; J.D., 1967 — Admitted to Bar, 1965, New York; 1969, U.S. District Court, Western District of New York; 1986, U.S. Court of Appeals, Second Circuit — Member American, New York State and Erie County Bar Associations; Western New York Trial Lawyers Association; American College of Trial Lawyers — Assistant United States Attorney, Western District of New York (1969-1973) — E-mail: ngreene@bouvierlaw.com

Kenneth A. Patricia — 1955 — University of Notre Dame, B.B.A. (cum laude), 1977; State University of New York at Buffalo, J.D., 1980 — Admitted to Bar, 1981, New York; 1983, Maryland — Member New York State, Maryland State and Erie County Bar Associations; American Board of Trial Advocates (Past President, Buffalo Chapter, 2005); New York State Trial Lawyers Association — Speaker, Trial Lawyer Seminars, Lorman Education Services — E-mail: kpatricia@bouvierlaw.com

Walter P. Seegert — St. Lawrence University, B.A., 1970; State University of New York at Buffalo Law School, J.D., 1973 — Admitted to Bar, 1973, New York; 1975, U.S. District Court, Western District of New York — Member New York State and Erie County Bar Associations — E-mail: wseegert@bouvierlaw.com

Associates

John P. Luhr — 1965 — University of Dayton, B.A., 1987; Albany Law School, J.D., 1990 — Admitted to Bar, 1991, New York; U.S. District Court, Western District of New York; U.S. Bankruptcy Court, Western District of New York — Member New York State Bar Association — E-mail: jluhr@bouvierlaw.com

Chad E. Murray — 1984 — Syracuse University, B.A., 2006; State University of New York at Buffalo Law School, J.D. (cum laude), 2009 — Admitted to Bar, 2010, New York; U.S. District Court, Western District of New York; U.S. Bankruptcy Court, Western District of New York — Member New York State and Erie County Bar Associations; New York State Defenders Association — E-mail: cmurray@bouvierlaw.com

Melissa H. Thore — 1976 — State University of New York at Buffalo, B.A., 1998; State University of New York at Buffalo Law School, J.D., 2001 — Admitted to Bar, 2002, New York — Member New York State and Erie County Bar Associations; Fourth Department Panel of Attorneys for the Child — E-mail: mthore@bouvierlaw.com

(This firm is also listed in the Subrogation section of this directory)

Chelus, Herdzik, Speyer & Monte, P.C.

438 Main Street, Tenth Floor
Buffalo, New York 14202
Telephone: 716-852-3600
Fax: 716-852-0038
E-Mail: mailbox@cheluslaw.com
www.cheluslaw.com

(Cheektowaga, NY Office: 2448 Union Road, 14227)
(Tel: 716-608-7664)

Established: 1896

Insurance Defense, Trial Practice, Fire, Casualty, Life Insurance, Accident and Health, Malpractice, Insurance Law, Product Liability, Workers' Compensation

NEW YORK — BUFFALO

Chelus, Herdzik, Speyer & Monte, P.C., Buffalo, NY (Continued)

Insurance Clients

ACE Private Risk Services
Amerisure Companies
Dryden Mutual Insurance Company
GEICO General Insurance Company
Harleysville Insurance Company
Maxum Specialty Insurance Group
Mercury Casualty Company
PMA Insurance Group
Restoration Risk Retention Group, Inc.
Trident Insurance Company
Zurich American Insurance Group
Allstate Insurance Company
The Cincinnati Companies
Erie Insurance Company
First Niagara Risk Management, Inc.
Hanover Insurance Group
Hastings Mutual Insurance Company
Northwestern National Insurance Company
Safe Auto Insurance Company
Sentry Insurance a Mutual Company

Non-Insurance Clients

Chesterfield Services, Inc.
Niagara Frontier Transportation Authority (NFTA)
Diocese of Buffalo
Town of Cheektowaga
Toys "R" Us, Inc.

Of Counsel

Michael F. Chelus — (Retired)

Members

Arthur A. Herdzik — 1950 — State University of New York at Buffalo, B.A. (magna cum laude), 1972; J.D., 1975 — Buffalo Law Review (Senior Editor, 1975) — Admitted to Bar, 1976, New York; 1978, U.S. District Court, Western District of New York; U.S. Federal Court — Member American, New York State and Erie County (Chairman, Negligence Committee, 1990 to 1993) Bar Associations; Defense Trial Lawyers Association of Western New York; Western New York Trial Lawyers Association; Defense Research Institute — Trial technique demonstration: "Masters in Trial," CLE program presented by the American Board of Trial Advocates and the Monroe County Bar Association, December 2004 at the Rochester Institute of Technology Inn and Conference Center, Henrietta, NY; Overall state-wide planning chair, course book contributor and lecturer: "The Basics of Trial Practice: After the Verdict - Remaining Issues, Decisions and Procedures," New York State Bar Association, 2000; Overall state-wide planning chair, course book contributor and lecturer: "The Basics of Discovery in New York - Statutes, Case Law and Practical Pointers," New York State Bar Association, 2000; Course book contributor and lecturer "Motor Vehicle Accidents," New York State Bar Association, 1998; Overall planning co-chair, course book contributor and lecturer: "Automobile Insurance Law and Practice," New York State Bar Association, 1996; Course book contributor and lecturer - Personal Injury Seminar, Erie County Bar Association, 1993; Course book contributor and lecturer: "Peoples Law School," Erie County Bar Association; Course book contributor and lecturer: "Law Day," Buffalo Claims Association; Course book contributor and lecturer: "Ethics and Civility in Litigation: Introductory Lessons for 21st Century Litigators," New York State Bar Association, 2006 & 2007 — Guest Appearance "The Law and You" radio program, WEBR Buffalo Public Radio — Counsel, Village of Lancaster, 1992-present; Village of Lancaster, New York, Prosecutor, 1983-1992; Village of Lancaster, New York Acting Village Justice, 1981-1983; Town of Lancaster, New York Board of Assessment Review, 1998-present — E-mail: aherdzik@cheluslaw.com

Thomas J. Speyer — 1960 — State University of New York at Buffalo, B.A., 1982; Detroit College of Law, J.D., 1985 — Admitted to Bar, 1986, New York; 1987, U.S. Bankruptcy Court; 1991, U.S. District Court, Western District of New York — Member New York State and Erie County Bar Associations; Western New York Trial Lawyers Association; Defense Research Institute — Author: "Federal Preemption of Vehicle and Traffic Law §388...and the Questions Remaining," Erie County Bar Journal, November 2005 — Classes/Seminars Taught: Adjunct Professor, University of Buffalo School of Law and Jurisprudence, Trial Technique Program — E-mail: tspeyer@cheluslaw.com

Rebecca E. Monte — 1960 — Rochester Institute of Technology, B.A., 1982; Washington and Lee University, J.D., 1985 — Admitted to Bar, 1985, Virginia; 1986, New York; 1991, U.S. District Court, Western District of New York; U.S. Federal Court; U.S. Bankruptcy Court, Western District of New York — Member New York State and Erie County Bar Associations; Annual Glaucoma Symposium (Member, Board of Directors); Cheektowaga Chamber of Commerce (Board of Directors, Chair-elect) — Fourth Judicial Department, Law Guardian Panel; Stewart Title Examing Counsel, Chicago Title Insurance Company; Classes/Seminars Taught: Speaker, "Elder Law Practice Post DRA," Erie Institute of Law, 2008; Course Book Contributor and Speaker, "Practicing Elder Law - Now that the Dust of the DRA has Settled," 2009; Speaker, "Practical Skills - Basic Elder Law Practice," New York State Bar Association CLE, 2009; Speaker, New York State Bar Association sponsored "Annual Decision-Making Day," 2005, 2006, 2010; Course Book Contributor and Speaker, "Elder Law and Middle Class Clients," Erie Institute of Law, 2004; Course Book Contributor and Speaker, "Estate Planning and Taxation," National Business Institute, 1995 — E-mail: rmonte@cheluslaw.com

Thomas P. Kawalec — 1970 — State University of New York at Buffalo, B.A., 1995; J.D., 1998 — Admitted to Bar, 1998, New York; 1998, U.S. District Court, Western District of New York; 2001, U.S. Bankruptcy Court; 2006, U.S. Supreme Court; 2007, U.S. Court of Appeals, Second Circuit; 2013, U.S. District Court, Northern District of New York — Member American, New York State and Erie County Bar Association; New York State Defender's Association; Defense Trial Lawyers Association; St. Thomas Moore Guild; Western New York Defense Trial Lawyers Association (Treasurer) — Author: Chapter 29 - "Fire Insurance and Property Insurance," in Insurance Law Practice, Second Edition, published by the New York State Bar Association, 2006 — Cheektowaga Chamber of Commerce; Charles Desmond Inns of Court (Director) — Languages: Polish — E-mail: tkawalec@cheluslaw.com

Kevin E. Loftus, Jr. — 1976 — Canisius College, B.A., 1998; State University of New York at Buffalo, J.D., 2002 — Admitted to Bar, 2003, New York; U.S. District Court, Western District of New York; U.S. Bankruptcy Court — Member New York State and Erie County (Negligence Committee, Young Lawyers Committee; Municipal Law Committee) Bar Associations; Defense Trial Lawyers of Western New York; Buffalo Claims Association; Western New York Trial Lawyers Association — Co-Authored: "Not for the Faint of Heart: Additional Personal Injury Protection (APIP) Benefits," New York State Bar Association Journal, Volume 78, 2006; "Conducting an Effective Cross-Examination in New York," Lorman Education Services, June, 2007 — E-mail: kloftus@cheluslaw.com

Associates

Michael J. Chmiel — 1972 — State University of New York at Buffalo, B.A., 1995; J.D. (cum laude), 1999 — Admitted to Bar, 2000, New York; 2002, U.S. District Court, Western District of New York; 2003, U.S. Bankruptcy Court; 2005, U.S. Supreme Court — Member New York State and Erie County (Criminal Law Committee) Bar Associations; Western New York Trial Lawyers Association; Defense Trial Lawyers Association; UB Law Alumni Association — Classes/Seminars Taught: "New Developments in Personal Injury Litigation - Healthcare Insurers' Right of Subrogation and Medicare Repayment Issues," for the Erie Institute of Law (Erie County Bar Association) May 26, 2010 — E-mail: mchmiel@cheluslaw.com

Michael M. Chelus — 1978 — The Pennsylvania State University, B.S., 2000; State University of New York at Buffalo, J.D., 2003 — Admitted to Bar, 2004, New York; U.S. District Court, Western District of New York; U.S. Bankruptcy Court, Western District of New York; 2007, U.S. Court of Appeals, Second Circuit; 2011, U.S. District Court, Northern District of New York — Member American, New York State and Erie County Bar Associations; Defense Trial Lawyers Association; Penn State Alumni Association (Alumni Recruitment Volunteer; Secretary, Western New York Chapter); Western New York Trial Lawyers Association — Author: Chapter 19, "Exceeding the No-Fault Threshold: Serious Injury," Insurance Law Practice, Second Edition, 2006 — Orchard Park High School Academy of Finance Advisory Board; Adjunct Professor, Bryant & Stratton College — Languages: Italian — E-mail: mmc@cheluslaw.com

Katy M. Hedges — 1980 — The University of Western Ontario, B.H.Sc., 2002; State University of New York at Buffalo, J.D., 2005 — Admitted to Bar, 2006, New York; 2008, U.S. District Court, Western District of New York; 2009, U.S. Bankruptcy Court, Western District of New York — Member American, New York State and Erie County Bar Associations; Western New York Defense Trial Lawyers Association; Women's Bar Association of the State of New York; Western New York Trial Lawyers Association — E-mail: khedges@cheluslaw.com

Katie L. Renda — 1981 — Niagara University, B.A. (Dean's List), 2003; University at Buffalo, J.D., 2011 — Admitted to Bar, 2012, New York; 2013, U.S. District Court, Western District of New York; U.S. Bankruptcy Court, Western District of New York — Member New York State and Erie County Bar Associations — E-mail: krenda@cheluslaw.com

Katelyn E. Dieffenderfer — 1987 — St. Bonaventure University, B.A. (magna cum laude), 2008; University at Buffalo, J.D. (magna cum laude), 2011 — Admitted to Bar, 2012, New York; 2013, U.S. District Court, Northern and Western Districts of New York; U.S. Bankruptcy Court, Western District of New York — Member American, New York State and Erie County Bar Associations — E-mail: KDieffenderfer@cheluslaw.com

Chelus, Herdzik, Speyer & Monte, P.C., Buffalo, NY
(Continued)

Leah A. Costanzo — 1986 — University at Buffalo, B.A., 2008; J.D., 2011 — Admitted to Bar, 2012, New York; 2013, U.S. Bankruptcy Court, Western District of New York; U.S. District Court, Western District of New York — Member New York State and Erie County Bar Associations; Women's Bar Association — New York Academy of Trial Lawyers; SUNY Buffalo Law Alumni Association — E-mail: lcostanzo@cheluslaw.com

Rebecca R. Josefiak — 1987 — Hobart and William Smith Colleges, B.A., 2009; University at Buffalo Law School, J.D., 2012 — Admitted to Bar, 2013, New York — Member New York State and Erie County Bar Associations; Erie County Federation of Republican Women; Daughters of the American Revolution — E-mail: rjosefiak@cheluslaw.com

Martha E. Donovan — Brown University, A.B., 2004; State University of New York at Buffalo, Ed.M., 2006; University at Buffalo, J.D. (cum laude), 2012 — Admitted to Bar, 2012, New Jersey; 2013, New York — Languages: Spanish — E-mail: mdonovan@cheluslaw.com

Christopher S. Safulko — 1984 — Canisius College, B.A., 2006; State University of New York at Buffalo, J.D. (cum laude), 2013 — Admitted to Bar, 2014, New York; U.S. District Court, Western District of New York — Member New York State and Erie County Bar Associations — Contributor to The Outpost: An Untold Story of American Valor by Jake Tapper, NY Times Bestseller — Mentor, City of Buffalo Veterans Treatment Court; IAVA; Team Rubicon; Team RWB; UB at Noon Speaker Series April 2013 — US Army, Captain, Afghanistan Veteran, Active 2006-2010, Reserve 2010-2013; The Bronze Star Medal; The Purple Heart — E-mail: csafulko@cheluslaw.com

Cohen & Lombardo, P.C.

343 Elmwood Avenue
Buffalo, New York 14222
Telephone: 716-881-3010
Fax: 716-881-2755
Toll Free: 800-276-2640
E-Mail: law@cohenlombardo.com
www.cohenlombardo.com

(Amherst, NY Office: 4140 Sheridan Drive, 14221)
(Tel: 716-881-3010)

Established: 1932

Insurance Defense, Trial Practice, State and Federal Courts, Coverage Analysis, Litigation, Fire, Arson, Fraud, Property, Casualty, Surety, Marine, Employer Liability, Premises Liability, Product Liability, Environmental Law, Toxic Torts, Construction Law, Accident, Automobile, Professional Liability, Medical Malpractice, Subrogation, Advertising Injury, Errors and Omissions, Aviation, Bad Faith, Copyright and Trademark Law, Municipal Liability, Title Insurance, Niagara, Orleans, Monroe, Genesee, Livingston, Wyoming, Allegany, Cattaraugus and Chautauqua Counties

Insurance Clients

Aegis Security Insurance Company
AIG Insurance Company
American International Group, Inc.
American International Insurance Company
Andover Companies
Bristol West Insurance Group
Central Mutual Insurance Company
Colonial Penn Insurance Company
Colony Insurance Company
Crawford & Company
Empire Insurance Group
General Accident Insurance Company
Greater New York Mutual Insurance Company
GuideOne Insurance
Guilford Specialty Group, Inc.
AIG Aviation, Inc.
Allegany Co-op Insurance Company
Amerisure Companies
Amica Mutual Insurance Company
Auto-Owners Insurance Company
Canal Insurance Company
Colonial Cooperative Insurance Company
Commercial Mutual Insurance Company
Erie Insurance Company
GMAC Insurance Group
Great American Insurance Company
Guaranty National Insurance Company
The Hartford Insurance Group
Hermitage Insurance Company
Lumbermens Mutual Casualty Company
Manufacturers and Merchants Mutual Insurance Company
Monarch Life Insurance Company
New Hampshire Insurance Company
New York Central Mutual Fire Insurance Company
Otsego Mutual Fire Insurance Company
Pennsylvania Lumbermens Mutual Insurance Company
Praetorian Insurance Company
The Providence Mutual Fire Insurance Company
Quincy Mutual Fire Insurance Company
Royal Specialty Underwriting, Inc.
Selective Insurance Company of America
U.S. Liability Insurance Company
Worcester Insurance Company
Indiana Lumbermens Mutual Insurance Company
Lumber Mutual Insurance Company
Midwest Mutual Insurance Company
New York Casualty Insurance Company
Norfolk and Dedham Mutual Fire Insurance Company
Pawtucket Insurance Company
Peerless Insurance Company
Pioneer Co-op Fire Insurance Company
Preferred Mutual Insurance Company
Providence Washington Insurance Company
Reliant Insurance Company
Security Mutual Insurance Company
Sterling Insurance Company
Western Surety Company

Non-Insurance Clients

Kmart Corporation
South Park Enterprises, Inc.

Firm Members

Richard N. Blewett — 1925 — Canisius College, B.A., 1948; University at Buffalo Law School, J.D., 1951 — Admitted to Bar, 1951, New York — Member American and New York State Bar Associations; Erie County Bar Association (Director, 1964-1967; President, 1985-1986); Western New York Trial Lawyers Association

Rocco Lucente, II — 1958 — Canisius College, B.S., 1980; Detroit College of Law, J.D., 1985 — Admitted to Bar, 1986, New York — Member American, New York State and Erie County Bar Associations

Stuart B. Shapiro — 1952 — State University of New York at Buffalo, B.A. (magna cum laude), 1975; State University of New York at Buffalo Law School, J.D., 1982 — Admitted to Bar, 1983, New York; Florida; 1984, U.S. District Court, Western District of New York; 1987, U.S. District Court, Northern District of New York; 1996, U.S. Supreme Court; 2000, U.S. Court of Appeals, Second Circuit; U.S. District Court, Eastern and Southern Districts of New York — Member Erie County Bar Association; American Arbitration Association (Panel of Arbitrators); Defense Research Institute — New York State Bar Association Handbook on Insurance Law

Katherine J. Bestine — 1962 — State University of New York at Buffalo, B.S., 1985; University of Dayton School of Law, J.D., 1989 — Admitted to Bar, 1990, New York; U.S. District Court, Western District of New York — Member New York State and Erie County Bar Associations; Women Lawyers of Western New York (President, 1999-2000); Women's Bar Association of the State of New York

Daniel J. Sperrazza — 1980 — State University of New York at Buffalo, B.S. (cum laude), 1983; State University of New York at Buffalo Law School, J.D., 1984 — Admitted to Bar, 1984, New York; 1991, U.S. District Court, Western District of New York — Member Erie County Bar Association

Daniel R. Connors — West Virginia University, B.A., 1996; State University of New York at Buffalo Law School, J.D., 1999 — Admitted to Bar, 2000, New York — Member New York State Bar Association

Associates

Jonathan D. Cox — 1962 — State University of New York at Buffalo, B.A., 1984; The University of Toledo College of Law, J.D., 1988 — Admitted to Bar, 1988, Illinois; 2002, New York; 2005, U.S. District Court, Western District of New York — Member New York State and Erie County Bar Associations

James Nash — 1978 — Northeastern University, B.S., 2001; Suffolk University Law School, J.D. (cum laude), 2004 — Phi Alpha Theta — Admitted to Bar, 2004, Massachusetts; 2005, New York; U.S. District Court, Western District of New York; 2008, U.S. District Court, District of Massachusetts — Member New York State and Erie County Bar Associations

Erin E. Cole — State University of New York at Oswego, B.A. (magna cum laude), 2005; State University of New York at Buffalo Law School, J.D. (cum laude), 2008 — Admitted to Bar, 2009, New York; 2011, U.S. District Court, Western District of New York

NEW YORK — BUFFALO

Cohen & Lombardo, P.C., Buffalo, NY (Continued)

Michele Schwach — State University of New York at Buffalo, B.A., 2005; State University of New York at Buffalo Law School, J.D., 2008 — Admitted to Bar, 2009, New York

Nicholas G. LoCicero — State University of New York at Brockport, B.S., 1999; State University of New York at Buffalo Law School, J.D., 2004 — Admitted to Bar, 2005, New York

Special Counsel

Anthony M. Nosek — 1947 — Canisius College, A.B., 1968; State University of New York at Buffalo Law School, J.D., 1971 — Admitted to Bar, 1972, New York — Member New York State and Erie County Bar Associations; Western New York Trial Lawyers Association

Of Counsel

Maryann Saccomando Freedman — 1934 — University at Buffalo Law School, J.D., 1958 — Admitted to Bar, 1959, New York; U.S. District Court, Western District of New York; U.S. Bankruptcy Court; 1963, U.S. Supreme Court — Member American Bar Association (House of Delegates, 1986 to Present); New York State Bar Association (President, 1987-1988); Erie County Bar Association (President, 1981-1982) — Board of Editors, New York State Bar Journal

Feldman Kieffer, LLP

The Dun Building, Suite 400
110 Pearl Street
Buffalo, New York 14202
  Telephone: 716-852-5875
  Fax: 716-852-4253
  E-Mail: mgrossman@feldmankieffer.com
  www.feldmankieffer.com

Established: 1993

Insurance Defense, General Liability, Professional Liability, Product Liability, Environmental Liability, Casualty

Insurance Clients

American International Group, Inc.	Liberty Mutual Group
Medical Liability Mutual Insurance Company	PICA Group
	Risk Enterprise Management, Ltd.
Travelers Insurance Companies	Utica Mutual Insurance Company

Partner

Andrew Feldman — 1943 — State University of New York at Buffalo, B.A., 1965; J.D., 1968 — Admitted to Bar, 1969, New York — Member International, American, New York State and Erie County Bar Associations; American Arbitration Association (Panel of Arbitrators); Western New York Trial Lawyers Association; International Association of Defense Counsel — Author: "Medical and Legal Dimensions", Management for Physicians — Lecturer, Niagara University, State University of New York at Buffalo and New York State Bar Association — E-mail: afeldman@feldmankieffer.com

Hagelin Kent LLC

135 Delaware Avenue, Suite 200
Buffalo, New York 14202
  Telephone: 716-849-3500
  Fax: 716-849-3501
  E-Mail: hagelin@hagelinkent.com
  hagelinkent.com

(Rochester, NY Office: The Powers Building, 16 West Main Street, Suite 700, 14614)
  (Tel: 585-325-9000)
  (Fax: 585-325-9007)
(Syracuse, NY Office: 1000 7th North Street, Suite 120, 13088)
  (Tel: 315-701-5768)
  (Fax: 315-701-5770)
(Garden City, NY Office: 1225 Franklin Avenue, Suite 325, 11530)
  (Tel: 516-240-8020)

Established: 1989

Hagelin Kent LLC, Buffalo, NY (Continued)

Automobile Liability, Municipal Liability, Premises Liability, Product Liability, Insurance Coverage, Malpractice, Appellate Practice, Arbitration

Firm Profile: When looking for trial counsel, please consider Hagelin Kent LLC. Our law practice is litigation intensive and results oriented. We are full time trial lawyers who know people and know the law. We have substantial experience in complex jury cases. Our rate of success is the envy of our peers.

Insurance Clients

AAA Insurance Exchange	Ameriprise Insurance Company
Global Liberty Insurance Company of New York	Park Insurance Company
	State Farm Insurance Company

Partners

Michael T. Hagelin — State University of New York at Buffalo, B.A., History, 1977; Pace University School of Law, J.D., 1980 — Admitted to Bar, 1982, New York; 1983, U.S. District Court, Western District of New York — Member New York State and Erie County (Negligence Committee) Bar Associations; Western New York Defense Lawyers Association — E-mail: hagelin@hagelinkent.com

Sean M. Spencer — Trinity College, B.A., 1999; University of Dayton School of Law, J.D., 2006 — Admitted to Bar, 2008, New York — Member American and Erie County Bar Associations — E-mail: spencer@hagelinkent.com

Of Counsel

Keith D. Miller	John H. Hagelin

Associates

Joseph A. Canepa	Brent C. Seymour
Ryan P. Heller	Benjamin R. Wolf

Roach, Brown, McCarthy & Gruber, P.C.

1920 Liberty Building
424 Main Street
Buffalo, New York 14202-3511
  Telephone: 716-852-0400
  Fax: 716-852-2535
  E-Mail: roachbrown@roachbrown.com
  www.roachbrown.com

Established: 1900

Insurance Defense, Trial and Appellate Practice, Medical Malpractice, Professional Malpractice, Product Liability, Construction Law, Sports and Entertainment Liability, Aviation, Fire, Excess, Coverage Issues

Firm Profile: Roach, Brown, McCarthy & Gruber, P.C. and its predecessor firms have been engaged in defense litigation for approximately 100 years. We have extensive experience and expertise in general liability matters, including automobile, falls, construction accidents, police and municipal liability, sports and products liability litigation. We have substantial expertise in malpractice (attorney, physician, and hospital) for both insured and un-insured clients and we represent medical professionals in disciplinary matters. We are also engaged in the representation of insurers in insurance coverage disputes, the defense of claims for employment discrimination, and various contractual matters. We practice primarily in Western New York State.

Insurance Clients

AAA Texas County Mutual Insurance Company	Academic Health Professionals Insurance Association
Caronia Corporation	Federated Insurance Companies
Gallagher Bassett Services, Inc.	HDI-Gerling America Insurance Company
Majestic Insurance Company	
Medical Liability Mutual Insurance Company	Medical Malpractice Insurance Company
North American Speciality Insurance (NAS)	OneBeacon Insurance
	ProClaim America Incorporated
Professional Risk Management	Sedgwick CMS
Travelers Property Casualty Corporation	Zurich Insurance Group

Roach, Brown, McCarthy & Gruber, P.C., Buffalo, NY
(Continued)

Non-Insurance Clients

Erie County Medical Center Corp.
Medical Society of the County of Erie
Sterris Corporation
Kaleida Health
Roswell Park Cancer Institute
State of New York

Partners

Joseph V. McCarthy — 1943 — St. Bonaventure University, B.S., 1965; The Catholic University of America, J.D., 1969 — Phi Alpha Delta — Confidential Clerk, U.S. District Court Judge, Western District of New York (1969-1971) — Admitted to Bar, 1970, New York; U.S. District Court, Western District of New York; 1993, U.S. District Court, Northern District of New York; 1998, U.S. Court of Appeals, Second Circuit — Member New York State Bar Association (Committee of Lawyers to Evaluate Action for Reform, 1995-1997; Committee on the CPLR, 1994-1996; Committee on Case Management, Fourth Judicial Department, 1995-1998; Committee on Merit Selection, 1992-1995; Executive Committee, 1997-2003); Erie County Bar Association (Director, 1988-1991; President-Elect, 1992-1993; Past President, 1993-1994; Chairman, Practice and Procedure Committee, 1984-1987; Board of Directors, Volunteer Lawyers Programs, 1992-1993); Eighth Judicial District Judicial Advisory Council (1993-1995); New York State Bar Foundation (Executive Committee 2011-Present); Erie County Bar Foundation (Board of Directors, President, 1994-2000; Committee on Standards and Goals of the Office of Court Administration, 1993-1996); Western New York Trial Lawyers Association (Director, 1985-1988); Western New York Defense Lawyers Association (Director, 1990-1993); Panel Member, American Arbitration Association; Malpractice Defense Lawyers Association; Chief Justice Judith Kaye's Committee on the Profession and the Courts (1993-2009); Fellow, American College of Trial Lawyers; American Board of Trial Advocates

J. Mark Gruber — 1954 — Villanova University, B.S. (cum laude), 1976; State University of New York at Buffalo, J.D., 1979 — Admitted to Bar, 1980, New York; 1981, U.S. District Court, Western District of New York; 1993, U.S. Court of Appeals, Second Circuit — Member Erie County Bar Association; New York State Magistrates Association; Erie County Magistrates Association; Chairman, Negligence Law Committee (1993-1995); Task Force on Court Facilities; Bench and Bar Committee; Committee on the Jury Project; Defense Trial Lawyers Association of Wester New York (Past President & Vice President); Western New York Trial Lawyers Association; Federation of Defense and Corporate Counsel — Town Justice for the Town of Tonawanda (2009-Present); Justice, Village of Kenmore, New York (1993-2009); Acting Justice, Village of Kenmore, New York (1983-1993)

John P. Danieu — 1965 — University of Rochester, B.A., 1988; State University of New York at Buffalo, J.D., 1991 — Admitted to Bar, 1992, New York; 1993, U.S. District Court, Western District of New York; 2000, U.S. Court of Appeals, Second Circuit — Member American and Erie County Bar Associations; Western New York Defense Lawyers Association; New York State Defenders Association

Gregory T. Miller — 1970 — Bowling Green State University, B.S., 1992; State University of New York at Buffalo, J.D., 1997 — Admitted to Bar, 1998, New York; U.S. District Court, Western District of New York — Member New York and Erie County Bar Associations

Elizabeth G. Adymy — 1964 — State University of New York at Buffalo, B.A. (magna cum laude, Phi Beta Kappa), 1987; J.D. (cum laude), 1993 — Admitted to Bar, 1994, New York — Member New York State Bar Association — Grader, for the New York State Board of Law Examiners

Joel J. Java, Jr. — 1973 — State University of New York at Albany, B.A. (summa cum laude), 1995; State University of New York at Buffalo, J.D. (magna cum laude), 1998 — Phi Beta Kappa — Admitted to Bar, 1999, New York; 2000, U.S. District Court, Western District of New York; U.S. Court of Appeals, Second Circuit — Member Erie County Bar Association; Defense Trial Lawyers Association (Current Secretary, Past Board Member); Western New York Trial Lawyers Association

Kevin Vasquez Hutcheson — 1977 — Niagara University, B.S. (magna cum laude), 1999; State University of New York at Buffalo, J.D., 2002 — Confidential Law Clerk Intern, Honorable John T. Curtin, United States Senior District Judge, Western District of New York, Summer 2001; Confidential Law Clerk Intern, Honorable Hugh B. Scott, United States Magistrate Judge, Western District of New York, 2001-2002 — Buffalo Law Review, 2000-2002, Publications Editor, 2001-2002; Buffalo Criminal Law Review, 2000-2002, Executive Editor, 2001-2002 — Admitted to Bar, 2003, New York; U.S. District Court, Western District of New York — Member Erie County and Niagara County Bar Associations; Western New York Defense

Roach, Brown, McCarthy & Gruber, P.C., Buffalo, NY
(Continued)

Lawyers Association; Western New York Trial Lawyers Association — Niagara University Adjunct Professor, 2008-Present; Niagara County Assigned Counsel and Conflict Defenders; UB Law Mentor Program

Associates

Kevin D. McCarthy — 1967 — St. Francis University, B.S. (magna cum laude, with honors), 1988; Syracuse University, J.D. (cum laude, Dean's List), 1994 — Admitted to Bar, 1992, U.S. Patent and Trademark Office; 1995, New York; 1996, District of Columbia (Inactive); Federal Circuit Court; 1997, U.S. District Court, Western District of New York — Member New York State and Erie County Bar Associations; Niagara Frontier Intellectual Property Association (Former President); American Intellectual Property Law Association

Matthew J. Batt — 1977 — Hamilton College, B.A., 1999; State University of New York at Buffalo, J.D., 2004 — Admitted to Bar, 2006, New York; U.S. District Court, Western District of New York — Member New York State and Erie County Bar Associations; Western New York Defense Trial Lawyers Association — Serve as Court-Appointed Attorney/Referee for Erie County; Lawyers for Learning Tutoring Program

Mark R. Affronti — 1983 — Elmira College, B.A. (magna cum laude), 2005; State University of New York at Buffalo, J.D. (cum laude), 2008 — Admitted to Bar, 2009, New York; U.S. District Court, Western District of New York

Adam P. Deisinger — 1985 — St. Bonaventure University, B.A. (cum laude), 2007; State University of New York at Buffalo, J.D., 2010 — Admitted to Bar, 2011, New York — Member American, New York State and Erie County Bar Associations

Kait R. Miceli — 1987 — State University of New York at Buffalo, B.A. (magna cum laude), 2009; J.D., 2013 — Admitted to Bar, 2014, New York

Kirstie A. Means — 1988 — Daemen College, B.A. (magna cum laude), 2009; State University of New York at Buffalo, J.D. (cum laude), 2013 — Admitted to Bar, 2014, New York

Special Counsel

Ruthanne Wannop — 1952 — State University of New York College at Brockport, B.S., 1974; State University of New York at Buffalo, J.D., 1995 — Admitted to Bar, 1996, New York; 1997, U.S. District Court, Western District of New York; 2010, U.S. Court of Appeals, Second Circuit — Member Erie County Bar Association

Of Counsel

T. Alan Brown — 1939 — John Carroll University, B.S., 1960; Fordham University, J.D., 1963 — Admitted to Bar, 1963, New York; 1964, U.S. District Court, Western District of New York — Member American, New York State and Erie County (Deputy Treasurer, 1999-2000; Treasurer, 2000-2001) Bar Associations; Erie County Bar Foundation (2003-2009; Vice-President, 2007-2008; President, 2008-2009); Western New York Trial Lawyers Association (Director, 1988-1991); Western New York Defense Lawyers Association; Panel Member, American Arbitration Association; U.S. Department of Veterans Affairs, Human Studies Subcommittee; Association of Defense Trial Attorneys; International Association of Defense Counsel; American Society of Law and Medicine — (Retired)

Sliwa & Lane

237 Main Street, Suite 840
Buffalo, New York 14203-2715
Telephone: 716-853-2050 Ext. 208
Fax: 716-853-2057
Mobile: 716-510-7352
E-Mail: KLane@Sliwa-Lane.com
www.Sliwa-Lane.com

Established: 1994

Insurance Defense, Bodily Injury, Casualty Defense, Examinations Under Oath, Mold and Mildew Claims, Product Liability, Premises Liability, Trial and Appellate Practice, Insurance Coverage (Initial analysis and related litigation), Defense of Public Entities (School Districts, Cities, Towns, etc.), Motor Vehicle Claims, Construction Site Claims

NEW YORK

Sliwa & Lane, Buffalo, NY (Continued)

Firm Profile: Sliwa & Lane focuses almost exclusively on the representation of self insurers, insurers and insureds. Our practice includes liability defense, coverage analysis and adjudication.

Insurance Clients

AIG Specialty Auto
GMAC Insurance
Lancer Insurance Company
Network Adjusters, Inc.
Crawford & Company
Housing Authority Insurance Group
Sterling Insurance Company

Non-Insurance Clients

Buffalo Municipal Housing Authority
National City Auto Leasing
New York State Dormitory Authority

Members

Kevin A. Lane — State University of New York College of Environmental Science & Forestry, B.S., 1978; New England School of Law, J.D. (magna cum laude), 1985 — Admitted to Bar, 1985, Massachusetts; 1986, New York; 1986, U.S. District Court, Western District of New York; 1987, U.S. District Court, Northern District of New York; 1990, U.S. District Court, Eastern District of New York; 1991, U.S. Supreme Court; 1997, U.S. District Court, Southern District of New York — Member American and New York State Bar Associations; Defense Research Institute — Practice Areas: Coverage Issues; Insurance Defense — Tel: 716-853-2050 Ext. 208 — E-mail: KLane@Sliwa-Lane.com

Stanley J. Sliwa — State University of New York at Fredonia, B.A. (summa cum laude), 1976; Rutgers University School of Law-Camden, J.D. (with honors), 1978 — Admitted to Bar, 1980, New York; 1980, U.S. District Court, Western District of New York; 1985, U.S. District Court, Eastern District of New York; 1995, U.S. District Court, Northern District of New York — Member New York State and Erie County Bar Associations; Defense Trial Lawyers Association of Western New York; Defense Research Institute — Tel: 716-853-2050 Ext. 211 — E-mail: StanSliwa@Sliwa-Lane.com

Smith, Sovik, Kendrick & Sugnet, P.C.

651 Delaware Avenue, Suite 144
Buffalo, New York 14202
Toll Free: 800-675-0011

(Syracuse, NY Office*: 250 South Clinton Street, Suite 600, 13202)
(Tel: 315-474-2911)
(Fax: 315-474-6015)
(E-Mail: firm@smithsovik.com)
(www.smithsovik.com)
(East Meadow, NY Office*(See Uniondale listing): The Financial Center at Mitchel Field, 90 Merrick Avenue Suite 500, 11554)
(Toll Free: 800-675-0011)

Appellate Practice, Automobile, Commercial Litigation, Construction Law, Dental Malpractice, Labor and Employment, Medical Malpractice, Nursing Home Liability, Premises Liability, Product Liability, Professional Liability, Retail Liability, Subrogation, Toxic Torts, Trucking, Workers' Compensation, Wrongful Death

(See listing under Syracuse, NY for additional information)

CARMEL † 3,395 Putnam Co.

Refer To

Boeggeman, George & Corde, P.C.
1 Water Street, Suite 425
White Plains, New York 10601
Telephone: 914-761-2252
Fax: 914-761-5211

Insurance Defense, Trial Practice, Automobile, Product Liability, Legal Malpractice, Medical Malpractice, Employment Law, Real Estate, Toxic Torts, Engineering Malpractice

SEE COMPLETE LISTING UNDER WHITE PLAINS, NEW YORK (31 MILES)

COBLESKILL 4,678 Schoharie Co.

Refer To

Towne, Ryan & Partners, P.C.
450 New Karner Road
Albany, New York 12205
Telephone: 518-452-1800
Fax: 518-452-6435

Mailing Address: P.O. Box 10572, Albany, NY 12212

Business and Real Estate Transactions, Business Litigation, Civil Defense, Commercial Litigation, Construction Litigation, Daycare Liability, Employment Discrimination, Employment Law (Management Side), Estate Litigation, Garage Liability, General Defense Civil Litigation, Governmental Defense, Governmental Liability, Indian Law, Labor and Employment, Municipal Liability, Nursing Home Liability, Nursing Home Litigation, Police Liability Litigation, Premises Liability, Public Liability, Public Officials Defense, School Law, Self-Insured Defense, Slip and Fall, Tribal Law, Trust and Estate Litigation, Policy Liability Defense

SEE COMPLETE LISTING UNDER ALBANY, NEW YORK (46 MILES)

COOPERSTOWN † 1,852 Otsego Co.

Refer To

Levene Gouldin & Thompson, LLP
450 Plaza Drive
Vestal, New York 13850
Telephone: 607-763-9200
Fax: 607-763-9211

Mailing Address: P.O. Box F 1706, Binghamton, NY 13902

Appeals, Arbitration, Mediation, Asbestos Litigation, Bad Faith, Construction Accidents, Dram Shop Liability, Liquor Liability, Fire Loss, Labor Law, Premises Liability, Product Liability, Property Claims, Sexual Harassment, Toxic Torts, Wrongful Death, Advocacy in Professional Discipline, Automobile, Motorcycle, Trucking Accidents, Contractual Indemnification, Defamation, Discrimination, Division of Human Rights/EEOC, Employment Law Violations, False Arrest/Constitutional Claims, Governmental Tort Liability, Infant Settlements, Insurance Coverage Disputes, Medical Malpractice Defense Matters, School District Liability, Um/Sum Claims

SEE COMPLETE LISTING UNDER BINGHAMTON, NEW YORK (82 MILES)

CORNING 11,183 Steuben Co.

Refer To

Levene Gouldin & Thompson, LLP
450 Plaza Drive
Vestal, New York 13850
Telephone: 607-763-9200
Fax: 607-763-9211

Mailing Address: P.O. Box F 1706, Binghamton, NY 13902

Appeals, Arbitration, Mediation, Asbestos Litigation, Bad Faith, Construction Accidents, Dram Shop Liability, Liquor Liability, Fire Loss, Labor Law, Premises Liability, Product Liability, Property Claims, Sexual Harassment, Toxic Torts, Wrongful Death, Advocacy in Professional Discipline, Automobile, Motorcycle, Trucking Accidents, Contractual Indemnification, Defamation, Discrimination, Division of Human Rights/EEOC, Employment Law Violations, False Arrest/Constitutional Claims, Governmental Tort Liability, Infant Settlements, Insurance Coverage Disputes, Medical Malpractice Defense Matters, School District Liability, Um/Sum Claims

SEE COMPLETE LISTING UNDER BINGHAMTON, NEW YORK (74 MILES)

ELMSFORD   NEW YORK

CORTLAND † 19,204 Cortland Co.
Refer To

Levene Gouldin & Thompson, LLP
450 Plaza Drive
Vestal, New York 13850
   Telephone: 607-763-9200
   Fax: 607-763-9211

Mailing Address: P.O. Box F 1706, Binghamton, NY 13902

Appeals, Arbitration, Mediation, Asbestos Litigation, Bad Faith, Construction Accidents, Dram Shop Liability, Liquor Liability, Fire Loss, Labor Law, Premises Liability, Product Liability, Property Claims, Sexual Harassment, Toxic Torts, Wrongful Death, Advocacy in Professional Discipline, Automobile, Motorcycle, Trucking Accidents, Contractual Indemnification, Defamation, Discrimination, Division of Human Rights/EEOC, Employment Law Violations, False Arrest/Constitutional Claims, Governmental Tort Liability, Infant Settlements, Insurance Coverage Disputes, Medical Malpractice Defense Matters, School District Liability, Um/Sum Claims

SEE COMPLETE LISTING UNDER BINGHAMTON, NEW YORK (42 MILES)

DELHI † 3,087 Delaware Co.
Refer To

Levene Gouldin & Thompson, LLP
450 Plaza Drive
Vestal, New York 13850
   Telephone: 607-763-9200
   Fax: 607-763-9211

Mailing Address: P.O. Box F 1706, Binghamton, NY 13902

Appeals, Arbitration, Mediation, Asbestos Litigation, Bad Faith, Construction Accidents, Dram Shop Liability, Liquor Liability, Fire Loss, Labor Law, Premises Liability, Product Liability, Property Claims, Sexual Harassment, Toxic Torts, Wrongful Death, Advocacy in Professional Discipline, Automobile, Motorcycle, Trucking Accidents, Contractual Indemnification, Defamation, Discrimination, Division of Human Rights/EEOC, Employment Law Violations, False Arrest/Constitutional Claims, Governmental Tort Liability, Infant Settlements, Insurance Coverage Disputes, Medical Malpractice Defense Matters, School District Liability, Um/Sum Claims

SEE COMPLETE LISTING UNDER BINGHAMTON, NEW YORK (68 MILES)

EAST AMHERST 17,991 Erie Co.

Schnitter Ciccarelli Mills, PLLC
8770 Transit Road, Suite 3
East Amherst, New York 14051
   Telephone: 716-639-7690
   Fax: 716-639-7317
   E-Mail: pciccarelli@scm-law.com
   www.scm-law.com

Insurance Defense, Insurance Coverage, Commercial Litigation, Employment Law, Personal Injury, Toxic Tort Defense, Small Business Consulting/Formation

Firm Profile: Schnitter Ciccarelli Mills provides exceptional representation to all our clients throughout New York State. Whether we handle routine matters in the most efficient and cost effective fashion, or try complex cases to verdict, we do not waiver in our uncompromising commitment to our clients.

Insurance Clients

Livingston Mutual Insurance Company
MetLife Auto & Home
Preferred Mutual Insurance Company
Merchants Mutual Insurance Company
New York Central Mutual Insurance Company
Utica National Insurance Company

Partners

Joseph M. Schnitter — State University of New York at Buffalo, B.A. (summa cum laude), 1976; J.D., 1979 — Admitted to Bar, 1980, New York; U.S. District Court, Western District of New York; U.S. Court of Appeals, Second Circuit

Patricia S. Ciccarelli — State University of New York at Binghamton, B.A., 1990; State University of New York at Buffalo, J.D., 1993 — Admitted to

Schnitter Ciccarelli Mills, PLLC, East Amherst, NY
(Continued)

Bar, 1993, Pennsylvania; 1994, New York; U.S. District Court, Western District of New York; U.S. Court of Appeals, Second Circuit

Ryan J. Mills — State University of New York at Buffalo, B.P.S. (cum laude), 2000; J.D., 2003 — Admitted to Bar, 2004, New York; U.S. District Court, Western District of New York; U.S. Court of Appeals, Second Circuit; U.S. Bankruptcy Court, Western District of New York

Counsel

Mary C. Fitzgerald

Associates

Carolyn M. Henry   Brittany A. Nasradinaj

ELMIRA † 29,200 Chemung Co.
Refer To

Levene Gouldin & Thompson, LLP
450 Plaza Drive
Vestal, New York 13850
   Telephone: 607-763-9200
   Fax: 607-763-9211

Mailing Address: P.O. Box F 1706, Binghamton, NY 13902

Appeals, Arbitration, Mediation, Asbestos Litigation, Bad Faith, Construction Accidents, Dram Shop Liability, Liquor Liability, Fire Loss, Labor Law, Premises Liability, Product Liability, Property Claims, Sexual Harassment, Toxic Torts, Wrongful Death, Advocacy in Professional Discipline, Automobile, Motorcycle, Trucking Accidents, Contractual Indemnification, Defamation, Discrimination, Division of Human Rights/EEOC, Employment Law Violations, False Arrest/Constitutional Claims, Governmental Tort Liability, Infant Settlements, Insurance Coverage Disputes, Medical Malpractice Defense Matters, School District Liability, Um/Sum Claims

SEE COMPLETE LISTING UNDER BINGHAMTON, NEW YORK (55 MILES)

ELMSFORD 4,664 Westchester Co.

Pillinger Miller Tarallo, LLP
570 Taxter Road, Suite 275
Elmsford, New York 10523
   Telephone: 914-703-6300
   Fax: 914-703-6688
   E-Mail: ntarallo@pmtlawfirm.com
   www.pmtlawfirm.com

(Syracuse, NY Office*: 507 Plum Street, Suite 120, 13204)
   (Tel: 315-295-3831)
   (Fax: 315-295-2575)
(New York, NY Office: 17 State Street, 15th Floor, 10004)
   (Tel: 212-461-6115)
   (Fax: 212-461-6116)
(Warren, NJ Office: 95 Mt. Bethel Road, 07059)
   (Tel: 908-757-8936)
   (Fax: 908-757-9609)
(Philadelphia, PA Office: 1800 John F. Kennedy Boulevard, 19103)
   (Tel: 215-789-6235)
   (Fax: 215-789-6236)

Construction Law, Labor and Employment, Premises Liability, Environmental Law, Toxic Torts, Product Liability, Automobile, No-Fault, Municipal Law, Personal Injury, Real Estate, Slip and Fall, Subrogation, Liquor Liability, Sports and Entertainment Liability

Insurance Clients

Arch Insurance Group
Broadspire
Burlington Insurance Company
Countrywide Insurance Group
The Hartford
Investors Underwriting Managers, Inc.
Nautilus Insurance Group
North American Insurance Company
AXA Insurance Company
Brownstone Agency
Chartis
Gallagher Bassett Services, Inc.
Hudson Insurance Company
Liberty Mutual Group
Metropolitan Life, Auto & Home Group
North Country Insurance Company
PMA Insurance Group

NEW YORK

GARDEN CITY

Pillinger Miller Tarallo, LLP, Elmsford, NY (Continued)

Republic Western Insurance Company
York Claims Service, Inc.
Scottsdale Insurance
XL Insurance Company, Ltd.
Zurich North America

Non-Insurance Clients

Coach USA
Old Republic Construction Program Group

Executive Partners

Marc H. Pillinger — Pace University, B.S., 1973; Brooklyn Law School, J.D., 1978 — Admitted to Bar, 1979, New York; U.S. District Court, Eastern and Southern Districts of New York — Member American and New York State Bar Associations; New York State Trial Lawyers Association — Languages: French — E-mail: mpillinger@pmtlawfirm.com

Jeffrey T. Miller — State University of New York at Buffalo, B.S. (cum laude), 1986; Hofstra University, J.D., 1989 — Admitted to Bar, 1990, New York; U.S. District Court, Southern District of New York; 1996, U.S. District Court, Eastern District of New York — Member American and New York State Bar Associations; New York State Trial Lawyers Association; New York County Lawyers Association; Defense Association of New York — E-mail: jmiller@pmtlawfirm.com

Nicholas Tarallo — Iona College, B.A. (magna cum laude), 1974; St. John's University, J.D., 1979 — Admitted to Bar, 1980, New York — Member New York State and Westchester County Bar Associaitons — E-mail: ntarallo@pmtlawfirm.com

Partners

Leslie G. Abele — Briar Cliff College, A.A., 1976; Mercy College, B.A., 1978; Pace University, J.D., 1983 — Admitted to Bar, 1984, New York — Member New York State and Westchester County Bar Associations — E-mail: labele@pmtlawfirm.com

Peter M. Dunne — Villanova University, B.A., 2001; Hofstra University, J.D., 2005 — Admitted to Bar, 2005, New York — E-mail: pdunne@pmtlawfirm.com

Edward C. Haynes — New York University, B.A., 1994; Fordham University, J.D., 1998 — Admitted to Bar, 1988, New York; U.S. District Court, Southern District of New York — Languages: Spanish, Italian, Greek — E-mail: ehaynes@pmtlawfirm.com

Jeffrey D. Schulman — University of Michigan, B.A., 1990; Hofstra University, J.D., 1993 — Admitted to Bar, 1994, New York; Florida — Member The Association of the Bar of the City of New York; New York County Lawyers Association — E-mail: jschulman@pmtlawfirm.com

Shawn M. Weakland — Rutgers University, B.S., 1991; New York Law School, J.D., 1996 — Admitted to Bar, 1996, New Jersey; 1999, New York — Member New Jersey State and New York State Bar Associations — E-mail: sweakland@pmtlawfirm.com

William Bryers — La Salle University, B.S., 1975; Seton Hall University, J.D., 1979 — Admitted to Bar, 1980, Pennsylvania; New Jersey — Member Philadelphia Bar Association; Defense Research Institute; American Arbitration Association — E-mail: wbryers@pmtlawfirm.com

Associates

Jeffrey D. Bollinger — University of Scranton, B.S., 2005; New York School of Law, J.D., 2008 — Admitted to Bar, 2009, New York; New Jersey — E-mail: jbollinger@pmtlawfirm.com

Lawrence J. Buchman — Springfield College, B.A. (magna cum laude), 1987; New York Law School, J.D., 1992 — Admitted to Bar, 1992, New Jersey; 1993, New York; 1995, District of Columbia — Member New York State, Nassau County and Queens County Bar Associations; New York State Trial Lawyers Association — E-mail: lbuchman@pmtlawfirm.com

J. McGarry Costello — Stonehill College, 1982; Fairfield University, B.A., 1984; Fordham University, J.D., 1988 — Admitted to Bar, 1991, New York; U.S. District Court, Eastern and Southern Districts of New York — Member New York State Bar Association — E-mail: jcostello@pmtlawfirm.com

Elizabeth L. Demler — Tulane University, B.A., 2003; Benjamin N. Cardozo School of Law, J.D., 2008 — Admitted to Bar, 2008, New York; U.S. District Court, Eastern and Southern Districts of New York — Member New York State Bar Association — E-mail: edemler@pmtlawfirm.com

Evan H. Echenthal — Long Island University, B.S., 1987; Thomas M. Cooley Law School, J.D., 1991 — Admitted to Bar, 1992, New Jersey; 1999, New York; U.S. District Court, Southern District of New York; 2001, U.S. Supreme Court — Member Westchester County Bar Association; New York County Lawyers Association — E-mail: eechenthal@pmtlawfirm.com

Pillinger Miller Tarallo, LLP, Elmsford, NY (Continued)

Kenneth A. Finder — Brown University, B.A., 1976; M.A., 1977; Hofstra University, J.D., 1980 — Admitted to Bar, 1981, New York; U.S. District Court, Eastern and Southern Districts of New York — Member New York State Bar Association — E-mail: kfinder@pmtlawfirm.com

Stephanie Gallo — The Pennsylvania State University, B.A., 1990; Thomas M. Cooley Law School, J.D., 1994 — Admitted to Bar, 1995, New York; 2000, New Jersey; 2003, U.S. District Court, Eastern and Southern Districts of New York — E-mail: sgallo@pmtlawfirm.com

Vanessa A. Gomez-Small — Iona College, B.A., 1993; Pace University, J.D., 1999 — Admitted to Bar, 1999, New York; New Jersey; Connecticut — E-mail: vgomezsmall@pmtlawfirm.com

Terri S. Hall — State University of New York at Binghamton, B.A., 1975; Pace University, J.D., 1990 — Judge Pace Law School Client Counseling Competition; Judge Pace Law School Moot Court Competition — Admitted to Bar, 1990, Connecticut; 1991, New York — Member New York State, Westchester County and Bronx Bar Associations; Westchester Women's Bar Associations — E-mail: thall@ptmtlawfirm.com

David E. Hoffberg — Emory University, B.A., 1989; Seton Hall University, J.D., 1992 — Admitted to Bar, 1993, New York — Member New York State and Rockland County Bar Associations; New York County Lawyers Association; New York State Trial Lawyers Association — E-mail: dhoffberg@pmtlawfirm.com

Alan L. Korzen — Pace University, J.D., 1989 — Admitted to Bar, 1989, Connecticut; 1990, New Jersey; 1991, New York; 1990, U.S. District Court, District of New Jersey; 1994, U.S. District Court, Southern District of New York; 1995, U.S. District Court, Eastern District of New York — Member New York State and New Jersey State Bar Associations — E-mail: akorzen@pmtlawfirm.com

Laurence McDonnell — Fordham University, B.A., 1984; St. John's University, J.D., 1988 — Admitted to Bar, 1988, New York; U.S. District Court, Eastern and Southern Districts of New York; U.S. Court of Appeals, Second Circuit; U.S. Supreme Court — E-mail: lmcdonnell@pmtlawfirm.com

Michael Neri — University of Houston, B.A., 2000; Thomas M. Cooley Law School, J.D., 2003 — Admitted to Bar, 2004, New York; U.S. District Court, Eastern and Southern Districts of New York — E-mail: mneri@pmtlawfirm.com

John Risi — Iona College, B.A., 1990; Fordham University, J.D., 1994 — Admitted to Bar, 1994, New York; Connecticut; U.S. District Court, Eastern and Southern Districts of New York; U.S. Court of Appeals, Second Circuit — E-mail: jrisi@pmtlawfirm.com

Neil T. Veilleux — Pace University, B.B.A., 1981; J.D., 1985 — Admitted to Bar, 1986, New York; U.S. District Court, Eastern and Southern Districts of New York — Member New York State and New York County Bar Associations — E-mail: nveilleux@pmtlawfirm.com

Of Counsel

Anthony M. Collura — New York University Stern School of Business, B.A., 1982; New York University, J.D., 1985 — Admitted to Bar, 1986, New York — Member New York State Bar Associaiton — E-mail: acollura@pmtlawfirm.com

(This firm is also listed in the Subrogation section of this directory)

GARDEN CITY 22,371 Nassau Co.

Cascone & Kluepfel, LLP

1399 Franklin Avenue, Suite 302
Garden City, New York 11530
  Telephone: 516-747-1990
  Fax: 516-747-1992
  www.cklaw.com

Insurance Defense, Negligence, Construction Accidents, Toxic Torts, Municipal Liability, Liquor Liability, Product Liability, Professional Malpractice, Insurance Coverage

Insurance Clients

Merchants Mutual Insurance Company
Selective Insurance Company of America
NOVA Casualty Company
Scottsdale Insurance Company

GOSHEN — NEW YORK

Cascone & Kluepfel, LLP, Garden City, NY   (Continued)

Non-Insurance Clients
Avis Budget Group, Inc.

Partners

Leonard M. Cascone — St. John's University, B.A. (summa cum laude), 1991; St. John's University School of Law, J.D., 1994 — Admitted to Bar, 1995, New York; U.S. District Court, Eastern and Southern Districts of New York — Member New York State, Nassau County and Suffolk County Bar Associations; Council on Litigation Management; Nassau-Suffolk Trial Lawyers Association; Defense Research Institute — E-mail: lcascone@cklaw.com

David F. Kluepfel — Ithaca College, B.S., 1990; Hofstra University School of Law, J.D., 1995 — Admitted to Bar, 1996, New York; U.S. District Court, Eastern and Southern Districts of New York — Member New York State and Nassau County Bar Associations; Suffolk County Bar Association (Insurance and Negligence Defense Counsel Subcommittee); Nassau-Suffolk Trial Lawyers Association; Defense Association of New York; Defense Research Institute — E-mail: dkluepfel@cklaw.com

Olympia Rubino — Hofstra University, B.A., 1996; Hofstra University School of Law, J.D., 1999 — Admitted to Bar, 1999, New York; U.S. District Court, Eastern and Southern Districts of New York — E-mail: orubino@cklaw.com

Andrew M. Lauri — Hofstra University, B.A., 1989; St. John's University School of Law, J.D., 1994 — Admitted to Bar, 1995, New York; 1998, U.S. District Court, Eastern and Southern Districts of New York — E-mail: alauri@cklaw.com

Associates

Ajay C. Bhavnani — University of Rochester, B.A., 1997; DePaul University College of Law, J.D., 2000 — Admitted to Bar, 2000, Illinois; 2006, New York — E-mail: abhavnani@cklaw.com

Howard R. Brandwein — University of Massachusetts, B.A., 1990; Brooklyn Law School, J.D., 1993 — Admitted to Bar, 1994, New York; U.S. District Court, Eastern and Southern Districts of New York — E-mail: hbrandwein@cklaw.com

Anthony J. Pagliuca — St. John's University, B.A., 1991; St. John's University School of Law, J.D., 1996 — Admitted to Bar, 1997, New York — E-mail: apagliuca@cklaw.com

Joseph A. Potenza — Binghamton University, B.A., 1996; St. John's University School of Law, J.D., 2004 — Admitted to Bar, 2006, New York — E-mail: jpotenza@cklaw.com

Kimberly A. von Arx — James Madison University, B.A., 2000; University of Maryland School of Law, J.D. (with honors), 2003 — Admitted to Bar, 2003, New York; 2004, U.S. District Court, Eastern and Southern Districts of New York — E-mail: kwolf@cklaw.com

Edgar R. White — St. John's University, B.A., 2003; University of South Carolina School of Law, J.D., 2009 — Admitted to Bar, 2009, New Jersey; 2010, New York; U.S. District Court, Eastern and Southern Districts of New York — E-mail: ewhite@cklaw.com

Paul J. Winterstein — University of Michigan, B.A., 2001; Hofstra University School of Law, J.D., 2005 — Admitted to Bar, 2006, New York; U.S. District Court, Eastern and Southern Districts of New York — E-mail: pwinterstein@cklaw.com

Maria Zouros — Hofstra University, B.A., 1993; Hofstra University School of Law, J.D., 1996 — Admitted to Bar, 1996, New York — E-mail: mzouros@cklaw.com

Ohrenstein & Brown, LLP

1305 Franklin Avenue, Suite 300
Garden City, New York 11530
Telephone: 516-873-6334
Fax: 516-873-8912
E-Mail: michael.brown@oandb.com
www.oandb.com

(New York, NY Office*: The Chrysler Building, 405 Lexington Avenue, 37th Floor, 10174)
   (Tel: 212-682-4500)
(West Caldwell, NJ Office: 1129 Bloomfield Avenue, Suite 214, 07006)
   (Tel: 973-882-8508)
   (Fax: 973-882-8717)

Ohrenstein & Brown, LLP, Garden City, NY   (Continued)

Agent/Broker Liability, Construction Litigation, Directors and Officers Liability, Employment Law, Environmental Law, Insurance Coverage, Municipal Liability, Product Liability, Professional Liability, Regulatory and Compliance, Reinsurance

Firm Profile: Ohrenstein & Brown is known for representing & advising insureds, industry trade groups, insurance brokers and insurance companies. Our meticulous understanding of multistate legislative and regulatory insurance has made us a trusted advisor to our clients in all aspects of the insurance industry.

Insurance Clients

American International Group, Inc. (AIG)	AmTrust Group
Arch Insurance Group	ARC Excess & Surplus LLC
Chubb Group of Insurance Companies	Baldwin & Lyons, Inc.
Foa & Son Corporation	The Distinguished Programs Group
HUB International Northeast, Ltd.	Federation of Jewish Philanthophies Service Corp.
Ironshore Insurance, Ltd.	Innovation Insurance Group, LLC
Public Service Mutual Insurance Company	Magna Carta Companies
Travelers Insurance Companies	RMS Insurance Brokerage, LLC
Waldorf & Associates	SterlingRisk
Zurich North America	U.S. Liability Insurance Company
	Wright Risk Management

Non-Insurance Clients

Combined Coordinating Council, Inc.	Community First Services, Inc.
The Pay-O-Matic Corp.	HNTB Corporation
Sackman Enterprises, Inc.	Richardson Brands Company
Tech-Clean Industries, Ltd.	Special Committee of the Board of Directors of Sino Gas International Holding Corp.
The Treeline Companies	

Partners

Michael D. Brown — Beloit College, B.A., 1967; New York University School of Law, J.D., 1970 — Admitted to Bar, 1971, New York; 1974, U.S. Supreme Court; 1975, U.S. District Court, Eastern and Southern Districts of New York; 1979, U.S. Court of Appeals, Second Circuit — Member Association of the Bar of the City of New York, Chairman of the Subcommittee on Insurance Demutualization

Manfred Ohrenstein — Brooklyn College, The City University of New York, B.A. (cum laude), 1948; Columbia Law School, J.D., 1951 — Harlan Fiske Stone Scholar — Admitted to Bar, 1951, New York; 1958, U.S. Court of Military Appeals; 1965, U.S. District Court, Southern District of New York; 1977, U.S. Court of Appeals, Second Circuit — Member Board of Directors, Insurance Federation of New York

Matthew Bryant — University of Oregon, B.A. (cum laude), 1998; The George Washington University Law School, J.D., 2002 — Admitted to Bar, 2003, New York; 2005, U.S. District Court, Eastern and Southern Districts of New York

Counsel

Rosario DeVito
Steven D. Dreyer

Brian M. Gerstein

GOSHEN † 5,454 Orange Co.

Refer To
Boeggeman, George & Corde, P.C.
1 Water Street, Suite 425
White Plains, New York 10601
   Telephone: 914-761-2252
   Fax: 914-761-5211

Insurance Defense, Trial Practice, Automobile, Product Liability, Legal Malpractice, Medical Malpractice, Employment Law, Real Estate, Toxic Torts, Engineering Malpractice

SEE COMPLETE LISTING UNDER WHITE PLAINS, NEW YORK (53 MILES)

NEW YORK

HAWTHORNE

Refer To

Collins, Fitzpatrick & Schoene, LLP
34 South Broadway, Suite 407
White Plains, New York 10601
Telephone: 914-437-8020
Fax: 914-437-8022

Appellate Practice, Architects and Engineers, Automobile, Dental Malpractice, Insurance Coverage, Legal Malpractice, Medical Malpractice, Municipal Liability, Premises Liability, Product Liability, Professional Malpractice, Real Estate

SEE COMPLETE LISTING UNDER WHITE PLAINS, NEW YORK (53 MILES)

Refer To

Drake, Loeb, Heller, Kennedy, Gogerty, Gaba & Rodd PLLC
555 Hudson Valley Avenue, Suite 100
New Windsor, New York 12553
Telephone: 845-561-0550
Fax: 845-561-1235

Appellate Practice, Americans with Disabilities Act, Automobile Liability, Carrier Defense, Civil Rights, Employment Discrimination, General Civil Trial and Appellate Practice, Medical Malpractice, Municipal Law, Product Liability, Professional Liability, School Law, Section 1983 Litigation

SEE COMPLETE LISTING UNDER NEW WINDSOR, NEW YORK

Refer To

LaRose & LaRose
510 Haight Avenue
Poughkeepsie, New York 12603
Telephone: 845-454-2001
Fax: 845-454-2535

Insurance Defense, Automobile, General Liability, Product Liability, Casualty, Medical Malpractice, Environmental Law

SEE COMPLETE LISTING UNDER POUGHKEEPSIE, NEW YORK (35 MILES)

Refer To

McCabe & Mack LLP
63 Washington Street
Poughkeepsie, New York 12601
Telephone: 845-486-6800
Fax: 845-486-7621

Mailing Address: P.O. Box 509, Poughkeepsie, NY 12602-0509

Insurance Defense, Negligence, Product Liability, General Liability, Municipal Liability, Casualty, Surety, Civil Rights, Subrogation, Environmental Law, Premises Liability, Labor Law

SEE COMPLETE LISTING UNDER POUGHKEEPSIE, NEW YORK (35 MILES)

HAWTHORNE 4,586 Westchester Co.

Traub Lieberman Straus & Shrewsberry LLP

Mid-Westchester Executive Park
Seven Skyline Drive
Hawthorne, New York 10532
Telephone: 914-347-2600
Fax: 914-347-8898
www.traublieberman.com
E-Mail: swolfe@traublieberman.com

(Red Bank, NJ Office*: 322 Highway 35, 07701)
(Tel: 732-985-1000)
(Fax: 732-985-2000)
(St. Petersburg, FL Office*: 360 Central Avenue, 33701)
(Tel: 727-898-8100)
(Fax: 727-895-4838)
(Chicago, IL Office*: 303 West Madison, Suite 1200, 60606)
(Tel: 312-332-3900)
(Fax: 312-332-3908)
(Los Angeles, CA Office*: 626 Wilshire Boulevard, Suite 800, 90017)
(Tel: 213-624-4500)
(London, United Kingdom Office*: Gallery 4, 12 Leadenhall Street, EC3V1LP)
(Tel: +44 (0) 020 7816 5856)

Traub Lieberman Straus & Shrewsberry LLP, Hawthorne, NY *(Continued)*

(New York, NY Office*: 100 Park Avenue, 16th Floor, 10017)
(Tel: 646-227-1700)

Established: 1996

Appellate Practice, Bad Faith, Extra-Contractual Litigation, Civil Rights, Complex Litigation, Construction Law, Environmental Law, General Liability, Insurance Coverage, Labor and Employment, Premises Liability, Product Liability, Professional Liability, Technology, Toxic Torts, Trucking Law, Transportation, Coverage Issues, Medical Malpractice

Firm Profile: TRAUB LIEBERMAN STRAUS & SHREWSBERRY LLP is a national mid-size firm providing all manner of legal services for the diverse needs of the insurance industry as well as counseling professionals and manufacturers, including policy drafting, litigation and counseling.

Members of the firm are active on many association committees which deal with issues relevant to the insurance industry, products liability, reinsurance, professional liability defense and counseling. We have also been privileged to participate in professional education panels on many occasions, have authored and published numerous papers on subjects of interest to (with an impact on) the insurance industry and its insureds.

Insurance Clients

ACE INA Group
ACE Westchester Specialty Group
Arch Insurance Company
AXIS Specialty Insurance Company
Catlin US
CPA Mutual Insurance Company of America, A RRG
Liberty International Insurance Company
Northwestern National Insurance Company
OneBeacon Insurance
RSUI Group, Inc.
Scottsdale Insurance Company
Zurich Insurance Group
ACE USA
American Safety Insurance Company
CAMICO Mutual Insurance Company
Century Surety Group
Crum & Forster Insurance Company
Markel Shand, Inc.
Mitsui Sumitomo Insurance Company of America
Old Republic Risk Management, Inc.
St. Paul Travelers Insurance Companies

Founding Partners

Meryl R. Lieberman — City College of New York School of Business, B.A. (magna cum laude), 1978; New York Law School, J.D. (magna cum laude), 1981 — Admitted to Bar, 1982, New York; 1991, U.S. District Court, Eastern and Southern Districts of New York; 1999, U.S. Court of Appeals, Fourth Circuit — Member American Bar Association; Professional Liability Underwriting Society; Westchester Women's Bar Association; USLAW Network; Association of Professional Insurance Women; Association of Trial Lawyers of America; Defense Research Institute — E-mail: mlieberman@traublieberman.com

Stephen D. Straus — Boston University, B.S.B.A., 1982; St. John's University School of Law, J.D., 1986 — Admitted to Bar, 1987, New York; U.S. District Court, Eastern and Southern Districts of New York; U.S. District Court, Eastern District of Wisconsin; U.S. Court of Appeals, Sixth and Seventh Circuits — Member American and New York State Bar Association; Association of the Bar of the City of New York; Professional Liability Underwriting Society; USLAW Network — E-mail: sstraus@traublieberman.com

Partners

Gerard Benvenuto — Lehigh University, B.A., 1989; University of Pennsylvania Law School, J.D., 1994 — Admitted to Bar, 1995, New York; 1996, U.S. District Court, Eastern and Southern Districts of New York — E-mail: gbenvenuto@traublieberman.com

Lisa J. Black — Binghamton State University, B.A., 1995; New York Law School, J.D., 1998 — Admitted to Bar, 1999, New York; U.S. District Court, Eastern and Southern Districts of New York; U.S. District Court, District of New Jersey — Member Federal Bar Council — E-mail: lblack@traublieberman.com

Megan E. Bronk — Hamilton College, B.A., 1997; Albany Law School, J.D., 2001 — Admitted to Bar, 2001, New Jersey; New York; Connecticut; U.S. District Court, Eastern and Southern Districts of New York — E-mail: mbronk@traublieberman.com

Traub Lieberman Straus & Shrewsberry LLP, Hawthorne, NY (Continued)

Mario Castellitto — Fordham University, B.S., 1989; Pace University School of Law, J.D. (cum laude), 1993 — Admitted to Bar, 1994, New York; U.S. District Court, Southern District of New York; 1995, U.S. District Court, Eastern District of New York — Member American and New York State Bar Associations; Association of the Bar of the City of New York — E-mail: mcastellitto@traublieberman.com

Jerri A. DeCamp — State University of New York at Binghamton, B.A. (with honors), 1999; Fordham University School of Law, J.D., 2002 — Admitted to Bar, 2002, Connecticut; 2003, New York; 2005, U.S. District Court, Eastern and Southern Districts of New York — E-mail: jdecamp@traublieberman.com

Daniel G. Ecker — Cornell University, B.A., 1993; Fordham University School of Law, J.D., 1996 — Admitted to Bar, 1997, New York; 2006, U.S. District Court, Southern District of New York; U.S. Court of Appeals, Second Circuit; 2009, U.S. District Court, Eastern District of New York — Member New York State and Westchester County Bar Associations; Justice Brandeis Westchester Law Society — E-mail: decker@traublieberman.com

Denis M. Farrell — Marist College, B.S., 1995; New York Law School, J.D., 2000 — Admitted to Bar, 2000, Connecticut; New York; U.S. District Court, Eastern District of New York; U.S. District Court, Southern District of New York — Member New York State Bar Association — E-mail: dfarrell@traublieberman.com

Copernicus T. Gaza — Rutgers University, B.A., 1990; New York Law School, J.D., 1995 — Chief Articles Editor, New York Law School Journal of Human Rights — Admitted to Bar, 1996, New Jersey; 2003, New York; 1997, U.S. District Court, District of New Jersey; 2003, U.S. District Court, Southern District of New York — E-mail: cgaza@traublieberman.com

Jonathan R. Harwood — University of Michigan, B.A., 1987; St. John's University School of Law, J.D., 1990 — Admitted to Bar, 1990, New York; 1993, U.S. District Court, Eastern and Southern Districts of New York — Member American Bar Association; Professional Liability Underwriters Society — E-mail: jharwood@traublieberman.com

Colleen E. Hastie — University of Michigan, B.A., 1999; Pace University School of Law, J.D., 2002 — Admitted to Bar, 2002, New York — Member New York State and New York County Bar Associations — E-mail: chastie@traublieberman.com

Adam Krauss — State University of New York at Brockport, B.S., 1985; St. John's University School of Law, J.D., 1989 — Admitted to Bar, 1989, New Jersey; 1990, New York; 1989, U.S. District Court, District of New Jersey — Member New York State Bar Association — E-mail: akrauss@traublieberman.com

Robert M. Leff — Pace University, B.S., 1990; Pace University School of Law, J.D. (cum laude), 1993 — Admitted to Bar, 1994, New York; U.S. District Court, Eastern and Southern Districts of New York — Member American, New York State and Westchester County Bar Associations — E-mail: rleff@traublieberman.com

Brian M. Margolies — Johns Hopkins University, B.A., 1995; Boston College Law School, J.D., 1998 — Admitted to Bar, 1999, Massachusetts; New York; U.S. District Court, Eastern and Southern Districts of New York — Member New York State Bar Association — E-mail: bmargolies@traublieberman.com

Robert S. Nobel — State University of New York at Binghamton, B.A., 1989; St. John's University School of Law, J.D. (cum laude), 1992 — Admitted to Bar, 1993, New York; U.S. District Court, Eastern and Southern Districts of New York — Member American Bar Association; USLAW Network — E-mail: rnobel@traublieberman.com

Hillary J. Raimondi — Binghamton University, B.A., 1990; Benjamin N. Cardozo School of Law, J.D., 1993 — Admitted to Bar, 1993, New York; U.S. District Court, Eastern and Southern Districts of New York; U.S. Court of Appeals for the District of Columbia and Second Circuits — Member American and New York State Bar Associations; Westchester Women's Bar Association (Employment Law Committee); Professional Liability Underwriting Society (Co-Chair); Defense Research Institute — E-mail: hraimondi@traublieberman.com

Richard J. Rogers — St. John's University, B.A., 1987; New York Law School, J.D., 1995 — Admitted to Bar, 1996, New York; 2001, U.S. District Court, Southern District of New York — Member American and New York State Bar Associations — E-mail: rrogers@traublieberman.com

Lisa M. Rolle — Fairleigh Dickinson University, B.A. (cum laude), 1991; Pace University School of Law, J.D., 1994 — Admitted to Bar, 1994, Connecticut; 1995, New York; U.S. District Court, Eastern and Southern Districts of New York; 2002, U.S. District Court, Northern District of New York — Member American and New York State Bar Associations — E-mail: lrolle@traublieberman.com

Christopher Russo — Bucknell University, B.A., 1998; New York Law School, J.D. (magna cum laude), 2001 — Admitted to Bar, 2001, New York; New Jersey; U.S. District Court, District of New Jersey; U.S. District Court, Southern District of New York — Member American and New York State Bar Associations; Professional Liability Underwriting Society — E-mail: crusso@traublieberman.com

Sheryl A. Sanford — John Jay College of Criminal Justice, B.S., 1998; Pace University School of Law, J.D. (cum laude), 2001 — Admitted to Bar, 2001, New York; U.S. District Court, Eastern and Southern Districts of New York — E-mail: ssanford@traublieberman.com

Lisa L. Shrewsberry — Central Connecticut State University, B.S. (cum laude), 1985; University of Connecticut School of Law, J.D., 1988 — Admitted to Bar, 1988, Connecticut; 1989, New York; 1993, U.S. Court of Appeals, Second Circuit; 1995, U.S. District Court, Eastern, Northern and Southern Districts of New York; U.S. Supreme Court — Member American Bar Association; Professional Liability Underwriting Society; Defense Research Institute — E-mail: lshrewsberry@traublieberman.com

Robert P. Siegel — State University of New York at Albany, B.A. (cum laude), 1977; Northwestern University, M.S., 1981; State University of New York at Buffalo Law School, J.D., 1981 — Admitted to Bar, 1982, New York; 1986, U.S. District Court, Eastern and Southern Districts of New York; 1988, U.S. Court of Appeals, Second Circuit — E-mail: rsiegel@traublieberman.com

Eric D. Suben — New York University, B.A. (cum laude), 1981; Tulane University Law School, J.D., 1993 — Admitted to Bar, 1993, New York; U.S. District Court, Eastern, Middle and Western Districts of Louisiana; U.S. District Court, Eastern, Southern and Western Districts of New York — E-mail: esuben@traublieberman.com

Richard K. Traub — University of Miami, B.A., 1972; University of Miami School of Law, J.D. (cum laude), 1975 — Admitted to Bar, 1975, Florida; 1976, New Jersey; New York; U.S. District Court, District of New Jersey; 1979, U.S. Supreme Court; 1981, U.S. District Court, Eastern and Southern Districts of New York — Member Federation of Defense and Corporate Counsel (Vice-President and Member of Board of Directors; Past Chair, Technology Committee); USLAW Network (Vice Chair, Professional Liability Practice Group) — Dean of Curriculum, Litigation Management College — E-mail: rtraub@traublieberman.com

Cheryl P. Vollweiler — Brandeis University, B.A., 1985; Hofstra University School of Law, J.D., 1988 — Admitted to Bar, 1989, New York; 1992, U.S. District Court, Eastern and Southern Districts of New York — Member American and New York State Bar Associations; Association of Professional Insurance Women; Financial Women's Association of New York; The International Alliance of Women — E-mail: cvollweiler@traublieberman.com

Dawn M. Warren — University of Delaware, B.S., 1996; Pace University School of Law, J.D., 2001 — Admitted to Bar, 2002, New York; U.S. District Court, Eastern and Southern Districts of New York — E-mail: dwarren@traublieberman.com

Special Counsel

Chang L. Kim — Northwestern School of Law, M.A./J.D., 2000 — Admitted to Bar, 2000, New York

Timothy G. McNamara — Binghamton University, B.A., 1981; Brooklyn Law School, J.D., 1984 — Admitted to Bar, 1984, New York — Member New York State and Rockland County Bar Associations — E-mail: tmcnamara@traublieberman.com

Associates

Andrew N. Adler	John W. Bieder
Christina M. Brescia	Jeffrey Briem
Chevon A. Brooks	J. Patrick Carley
Jamie R. Kuebler	Scott B. Ladanyi
Jennifer L. Lewkowski	James J. Lofrese
Jennifer M. Meyers	Brandon K. Mohr
Jeremy P. Monosov	Jennifer N. Netrosio
Nadia Niazi	Joseph Rapice
Evan B. Rudnicki	Meghan E. Ruesch
Nitin Sain	

NEW YORK

HICKSVILLE 41,547 Nassau Co.

Mintzer Sarowitz Zeris Ledva & Meyers, LLP

17 West John Street, Suite 200
Hicksville, New York 11801
  Telephone: 516-939-9200
  Fax: 516-939-9201
  www.Defensecounsel.com

(Additional Offices: Philadelphia, PA*; Miami, FL*; Cherry Hill, NJ*; New York, NY*; Pittsburgh, PA*; Wilmington, DE*; Tampa, FL*; Wheeling, WV*)

Insurance Defense, Premises Liability, Product Liability, Environmental Law, Workers' Compensation, Coverage Issues, Asbestos Litigation, Medical Malpractice, Nursing Home Liability, Professional Liability, Trucking Law

Managing Partner

Bradley J. Levien

(See listing under Philadelphia, PA for additional information)

HUNTINGTON 18,046 Suffolk Co.

Sobel Law Group LLC

464 New York Avenue, Suite 100
Huntington, New York 11743
  Telephone: 631-549-4677
  Fax: 631-549-0826
  E-Mail: csobel@sobellawgroup.com
  www.sobellawgroup.com

(New York, NY Office*: 30 Vesey Street, 8th Floor, 10007)
  (Tel: 212-216-0020)
(Burlington, NJ Office*: 6 Terry Lane, Suite 350, 08016)
  (Tel: 856-673-0689)
  (E-Mail: bpevzner@sobellawgroup.com)

Amusements, Automobile, Bad Faith, Construction Law, Coverage Issues, Employment Law, Environmental Law, Equine Law, Fraud, Hospitality, Liquor Liability, Pharmaceutical, Premises Liability, Sports Law, Toxic Torts, Transportation, Trucking, Workers' Compensation

Firm Profile: Sobel Law Group, LLC successfully represents insurance carriers, self-insureds, municipalities and school districts, habitation companies, school and municipal bus companies, supermarket chains, "big box" retailers and construction companies in New York, New Jersey and Eastern Pennsylvania.

Firm Members

Curtis Sobel — **Owner** — State University of New York at Albany, B.S., 1983; State University of New York at Buffalo Law School, J.D., 1986 — Admitted to Bar, 1986, New York; New Jersey; 2006, U.S. District Court, Eastern, Northern and Southern Districts of New York — Member New York State, Suffolk County and New York County Bar Associations; Nassau-Suffolk Trial Lawyers Association — E-mail: csobel@sobellawgroup.com

David M. Goldman — University of Maryland, B.S., 1989; Touro College Jacob D. Fuchsberg Law Center, J.D., 1995 — Admitted to Bar, 1996, New York; 2001, U.S. District Court, Eastern District of New York; 2011, U.S. District Court, Southern District of New York — E-mail: dgoldman@sobellawgroup.com

Bella I. Pevzner — John Jay College of Criminal Justice, B.A. (Dean's List), 2001; Brooklyn Law School, J.D., 2004 — Phi Eta Sigma National Honor Society — Admitted to Bar, 2004, New Jersey; 2005, New York; 2007, U.S. District Court, Southern District of New York; 2008, U.S. District Court,

Sobel Law Group LLC, Huntington, NY (Continued)

Eastern District of New York — Member New York County Bar Association — Languages: Russian — E-mail: bpevzner@sobellawgroup.com

Seth Rubine — University of Rhode Island, B.S., 1996; Thomas M. Cooley Law School, J.D., 1999 — Admitted to Bar, 2000, New Jersey; Pennsylvania; 2006, New York; 2002, U.S. District Court, Eastern District of Pennsylvania; U.S. District Court, Northern, Southern and Western Districts of New York — Member New York State and New York County Bar Associations — Languages: Russian — E-mail: srubine@sobellawgroup.com

Associates

Derek M. Zisser — Hofstra University, B.A., History, 2006; Touro College Jacob D. Fuchsberg Law Center, J.D., 2010 — Community Service Award, Touro College — Admitted to Bar, 2011, New York; 2012, New Jersey; 2011, U.S. District Court, Eastern and Southern Districts of New York; 2012, U.S. Court of Appeals, Second Circuit; 2014, U.S. District Court, District of New Jersey; U.S. District Court, Northern District of New York — Member New York State and New York County Bar Associations — Languages: Spanish, Hebrew — E-mail: dzisser@sobellawgroup.com

Aaron C. Gross — St. John's University, B.S., 1993; St. John's University School of Law, J.D., 1998 — Admitted to Bar, 1999, New York — E-mail: agross@sobellawgroup.com

Daniel P. Rocco — Stony Brook University, B.A. Political Science, 2009; St. John's University School of Law, J.D., 2013 — Admitted to Bar, 2014, New York — Member New York State Bar Association — E-mail: drocco@sobellawgroup.com

Nicole Licata-McCord — Binghamton University, B.A. (cum laude), 1998; Hofstra University School of Law, J.D., 2002 — Admitted to Bar, 2003, New York; 2006, U.S. District Court, Eastern and Southern Districts of New York — E-mail: rlicata@sobellawgroup.com

Michelle L. Meiselman — Stony Brook University, B.A. (Dean's List), 1996; Hofstra University School of Law, J.D., 1999 — Admitted to Bar, 2000, New York — E-mail: mmeiselman@sobellawgroup.com

Bradley K. Bettridge — West Virginia University, B.A. Political Science (cum laude), 2005; St. John's University School of Law, J.D., 2008 — Admitted to Bar, 2009, New York; 2013, U.S. District Court, Eastern and Southern Districts of New York — E-mail: bbettridge@sobellawgroup.com

Chelsea Swilling — University of Delaware, B.A. (with honors), 2008; Hofstra University School of Law, J.D., 2013 — Admitted to Bar, 2013, New York; New Jersey — Member New York State and Nassau County Bar Associations — E-mail: cswilling@sobellawgroup.com

Michael Lamendola — State University of New York at Geneseo, B.A., 2007; Hofstra University School of Law, J.D., 2011 — Admitted to Bar, 2012, New York; New Jersey — E-mail: mlamendola@sobellawgroup.com

ISLIP 18,689 Suffolk Co.

Law Offices of Richard A. Fogel, P.C.

389 Cedar Avenue
Islip, New York 11751-4627
  Telephone: 516-721-7161
  Mobile: 516-721-7161
  Fax: 631-650-5254
  E-Mail: rfogel@rfogellaw.com
  www.rfogellaw.com

Insurance Coverage, Environmental Law, Toxic Torts, Product Liability, Commercial Litigation, Medical Devices

Firm Profile: Mr. Fogel has an extensive science background with a Master's Degree in Marine Environmental Sciences and 20+ years experience with complex insurance disputes. He works closely with field experts to understand all aspects of your case and finds cost-effective ways to resolve your litigation and disputes.

Insurance Clients

GEICO
Medmarc Insurance Company
Sentry Insurance

Hastings Mutual Insurance Company
Travelers Insurance Company

JERICHO

Law Offices of Richard A. Fogel, P.C., Islip, NY
(Continued)

Firm Members

Richard A. Fogel — 1959 — Southampton College of LIU, B.S., 1980; State University of New York, Marine Science Research Center, M.S., 1982; Fordham University School of Law, J.D., 1987 — Admitted to Bar, 1987, New Jersey; 1988, New York; 1997, U.S. Supreme Court — Member Suffolk County Bar Association; Claims & Litigation Management Alliance; Babylon Environmental Conservation Commission (Former Chairman); Defense Research Institute — Adjunct Professor of Business Law and Litigation at Nassau Community College

The following firms also service this area.

Mazzara & Small, P.C.
1698 Roosevelt Avenue
Bohemia, New York 11716
Telephone: 631-360-0600
Fax: 631-360-0669

Personal Injury, Insurance Coverage, Construction Accidents, Product Liability, Wrongful Death, Appellate Practice

SEE COMPLETE LISTING UNDER BOHEMIA, NEW YORK (8 MILES)

ITHACA † 30,014 Tompkins Co.

Refer To

Levene Gouldin & Thompson, LLP
450 Plaza Drive
Vestal, New York 13850
Telephone: 607-763-9200
Fax: 607-763-9211

Mailing Address: P.O. Box F 1706, Binghamton, NY 13902

Appeals, Arbitration, Mediation, Asbestos Litigation, Bad Faith, Construction Accidents, Dram Shop Liability, Liquor Liability, Fire Loss, Labor Law, Premises Liability, Product Liability, Property Claims, Sexual Harassment, Toxic Torts, Wrongful Death, Advocacy in Professional Discipline, Automobile, Motorcycle, Trucking Accidents, Contractual Indemnification, Defamation, Discrimination, Division of Human Rights/EEOC, Employment Law Violations, False Arrest/Constitutional Claims, Governmental Tort Liability, Infant Settlements, Insurance Coverage Disputes, Medical Malpractice Defense Matters, School District Liability, Um/Sum Claims

SEE COMPLETE LISTING UNDER BINGHAMTON, NEW YORK (50 MILES)

JAMESTOWN 31,146 Chautauqua Co.

Refer To

Barth Sullivan Behr
600 Convention Tower
43 Court Street
Buffalo, New York 14202
Telephone: 716-856-1300
Fax: 716-856-1494

Trial Practice, Appellate Practice, Alternative Dispute Resolution, Product Liability, Casualty, Fire, Professional Errors and Omissions, Coverage Issues, Insurance Fraud, Subrogation, Motor Vehicle, General Liability, Workers' Compensation, Premises Liability, Municipal Liability, Tractor-Trailer, Bad Faith

SEE COMPLETE LISTING UNDER BUFFALO, NEW YORK (71 MILES)

NEW YORK

Refer To

Cohen & Lombardo, P.C.
343 Elmwood Avenue
Buffalo, New York 14222
Telephone: 716-881-3010
Fax: 716-881-2755
Toll Free: 800-276-2640

Mailing Address: P.O. Box 5204, Buffalo, NY 14213-5204

Insurance Defense, Trial Practice, State and Federal Courts, Coverage Analysis, Litigation, Fire, Arson, Fraud, Property, Casualty, Surety, Marine, Employer Liability, Premises Liability, Product Liability, Environmental Law, Toxic Torts, Construction Law, Accident, Automobile, Professional Liability, Medical Malpractice, Subrogation, Advertising Injury, Errors and Omissions, Aviation, Bad Faith, Copyright and Trademark Law, Municipal Liability, Title Insurance, Niagara, Orleans, Monroe, Genesee, Livingston, Wyoming, Allegany, Cattaraugus and Chautauqua Counties

SEE COMPLETE LISTING UNDER BUFFALO, NEW YORK (78 MILES)

Refer To

Roach, Brown, McCarthy & Gruber, P.C.
1920 Liberty Building
424 Main Street
Buffalo, New York 14202-3511
Telephone: 716-852-0400
Fax: 716-852-2535

Insurance Defense, Trial and Appellate Practice, Medical Malpractice, Professional Malpractice, Product Liability, Construction Law, Sports and Entertainment Liability, Aviation, Fire, Excess, Coverage Issues

SEE COMPLETE LISTING UNDER BUFFALO, NEW YORK (69 MILES)

JERICHO 13,567 Nassau Co.

Catalano Gallardo & Petropoulos, LLP

100 Jericho Quadrangle, Suite 326
Jericho, New York 11753
Telephone: 516-931-1800
Fax: 516-931-1033
E-Mail: rcatalano@cgpllp.com
www.cgpllp.com

Established: 2004

Automobile Liability, Bad Faith, Church Law, Commercial Litigation, Construction Liability, Coverage Analysis, Dental Malpractice, Directors and Officers Liability, Employment Practices Liability, Environmental Liability, General Liability, Hospital Malpractice, Insurance Coverage, Legal Malpractice, Mass Tort, Medical Devices, Medical Malpractice, Municipal Liability, Negligence, Nursing Home Liability, Personal Injury, Pharmaceutical, Premises Liability, Product Liability, Professional Malpractice, Religious Institutions, Restaurant Liability, School Law, Sexual Harassment, Toxic Torts, Trial and Appellate Practice, Wrongful Death

Firm Profile: Catalano Gallardo & Petropoulos, LLP is dedicated to providing the highest quality litigation and risk management services to the insurance industry and in the defense of professionals, directors and officers, corporations, manufacturing industries, construction companies, pharmaceutical and medical device companies, church and charitable institutions.

Insurance Clients

Church Mutual Insurance Company	CNA Global Specialty Lines
Fireman's Fund Specialty Insurance	Fortress Insurance Company
GuideOne Insurance	Great American Custom Insurance Services
Hamlin & Burton Liability Management	Hartford Insurance Company
Markel Corporation	Liberty International Underwriters
Medical Malpractice Insurance Pool	Medical Liability Mutual Insurance Company
Swiss Re America Holding Corporation	OMS National Insurance Company
	Utica National Insurance Company

NEW YORK

Catalano Gallardo & Petropoulos, LLP, Jericho, NY
(Continued)

Firm Members

Ralph A. Catalano — 1964 — Fordham University, B.A., 1986; Hofstra University School of Law, J.D., 1989 — Admitted to Bar, 1989, New York; New Jersey; U.S. District Court, Eastern and Southern Districts of New York; U.S. District Court, District of New Jersey; 1993, U.S. Court of Appeals, Second Circuit; 1994, U.S. Supreme Court — Member American, New York State and Nassau County Bar Associations; New York Medical Defense Bar Association; Defense Research Institute; Association of Trial Lawyers of America; Nassau-Suffolk Trial Lawyers Association — Practice Areas: Professional Liability; Product Liability; Negligence; Commercial Litigation; Discrimination; Appellate Practice; Insurance Law; Tort Litigation; Medical Malpractice; Church Law

Domingo R. Gallardo — 1963 — Fordham University, B.A., 1986; Hofstra University School of Law, J.D., 1989 — Admitted to Bar, 1990, New York; 1993, U.S. District Court, Southern District of New York; 1995, U.S. District Court, Eastern District of New York — Member American, New York State and Nassau County Bar Associations; New York Medical Defense Bar Association; Defense Research Institute; Association of Trial Lawyers of America; Nassau-Suffolk Trial Lawyers Association — U.S. Marine Corps Reserves, 1983-1987 — Languages: Spanish — Practice Areas: Professional Liability; Church Law; Medical Malpractice; Construction Litigation

Gary Petropoulos — 1960 — Trinity College, B.A., 1983; St. John's University School of Law, J.D., 1988; University of London, England, LL.M. (with merit), 1990 — Admitted to Bar, 1989, New York; U.S. District Court, Eastern and Southern Districts of New York — Member American, New York State and Nassau County Bar Associations; Nassau Suffolk Claim Managers' Council; Defense Research Institute; Professional Liability Underwriting Society — Languages: Greek, French — Practice Areas: Insurance Law; Insurance Litigation; Professional Liability; Church Law; Commercial Litigation; Appellate Practice; Legal Malpractice

Michele R. Levin — 1971 — Binghamton University, B.A. (cum laude), 1993; Hofstra University School of Law, J.D. (Dean's List), 1996 — Admitted to Bar, 1997, New York; 2004, U.S. District Court, Eastern and Southern Districts of New York — Member New York State and Nassau County Bar Associations; Defense Research Institute — Languages: French — Practice Areas: Medical Malpractice; Legal Malpractice; Nursing Home Liability; Employment Law; Church Law

Matthew K. Flanagan — 1967 — Fordham University, B.A., 1989; St. John's University School of Law, J.D., 1992 — Admitted to Bar, 1993, New York; U.S. District Court, Eastern and Southern Districts of New York; 1996, U.S. Court of Appeals, Second Circuit — Member American, New York State and Nassau County Bar Associations — Practice Areas: Professional Liability; Legal Malpractice; General Liability; Church Law

James P. Connors — 1974 — College of the Holy Cross, B.A., 1996; St. John's University School of Law, J.D. (Dean's List), 1999 — Admitted to Bar, 1999, Connecticut; 2000, New York; 2005, U.S. District Court, Eastern and Southern Districts of New York — Member American, New York State and Nassau County Bar Associations — Practice Areas: Professional Liability; Health Care Liability; Construction Law; Premises Liability; Personal Injury

June D. Reiter — College of the Holy Cross, B.A., 1999; Hofstra University School of Law, J.D., 2003 — Admitted to Bar, 2004, New York; U.S. District Court, Eastern and Southern Districts of New York — Member American, New York State and Nassau County Bar Associations — Practice Areas: Construction Law; Construction Defect; Property Defense; Medical Malpractice; Employment Law; Personal Injury

Karen Corbett — St. John's University, B.S., 1993; Brooklyn Law School, J.D., 1996 — Admitted to Bar, 1997, New York; U.S. District Court, Eastern and Southern Districts of New York — Member New York State and Nassau County Bar Associations; Queens County Women's Bar Association — Practice Areas: Professional Liability; Medical Malpractice Defense; Dental Malpractice; Nursing Home Liability; Construction Law; Premises Liability; Personal Injury

KINGSTON

KINGSTON † 23,893 Ulster Co.

Cook, Netter, Cloonan, Kurtz & Murphy, P.C.

85 Main Street
Kingston, New York 12401
Telephone: 845-331-0702
Fax: 845-331-1003
E-Mail: law@cookfirm.com
www.cookfirm.com

Established: 1905

Business Transactions, Civil Litigation, Construction Accidents, Motor Vehicle, Municipal Law, Personal Injury, Premises Liability, Product Liability, Professional Liability, Public Entities, Real Estate, Sexual Harassment, State and Federal Courts, Title Insurance, Federal Civil Rights

Firm Profile: Our firm is exceptionally experienced in trial law and approximately 80% of our practice involves civil trial work throughout the Hudson Valley and upstate New York. Our central location and familiarity with the local venues has permitted us to provide legal services to our clients throughout the Hudson Valley and New York State with a keen personal knowledge of local juries and adversaries, enabling us to obtain prompt resolution of legal matters.

Insurance Clients

Allstate Insurance Company
Assurant Specialty Property
Markel Insurance Company
Network Adjusters, Inc.
New York Mutual Underwriters
Sterling Insurance Company
Ulster County Insurance Department

Assurant Solutions
Gallagher Bassett Services, Inc.
Midwest Claims Service
New York Municipal Insurance Reciprocal
Trident Insurance

Non-Insurance Clients

Central Hudson Gas and Electric Corp.

City of Kingston

Firm Members

Robert E. Netter — 1942 — Siena College, B.A., 1964; Albany Law School of Union University, LL.B., 1967 — Admitted to Bar, 1967, New York — Member American, New York State and Ulster County Bar Associations

William N. Cloonan — 1946 — Marist College, B.A., 1968; Albany Law School of Union University, J.D., 1975 — Admitted to Bar, 1974, New York — Member American, New York State and Ulster County Bar Associations; Association of the Bar of the City of New York; Federation of Defense and Corporate Counsel; Defense Research Institute

Robert D. Cook — 1952 — College of the Holy Cross, B.A., 1974; Albany Law School of Union University, J.D., 1977 — Admitted to Bar, 1978, New York; 1978, U.S. District Court, Northern District of New York; 1994, U.S. District Court, Southern District of New York; U.S. Court of Appeals, Second Circuit; 2012, U.S. District Court, Eastern District of New York — Member New York State and Ulster County Bar Associations; Defense Research Institute

Eric M. Kurtz — 1960 — State University of New York at Albany, B.A. (cum laude), 1982; University at Buffalo Law School, J.D., 1985 — Admitted to Bar, 1986, New York; U.S. District Court, Northern District of New York; 1999, U.S. District Court, Southern District of New York; 2012, U.S. Court of Appeals, Second Circuit — Member New York State and Ulster County Bar Associations; Defense Research Institute

Thomas A. Murphy — 1960 — Siena College, B.A. (cum laude), 1982; Gonzaga University School of Law, J.D., 1986 — Admitted to Bar, 1987, New York — Member New York State and Ulster County Bar Associations

Michael T. Cook — 1971 — St. Bonaventure University, B.A., 1995; Albany Law School of Union University, J.D., 1998 — Admitted to Bar, 1999, New York; 2004, U.S. District Court, Northern District of New York; 2010, U.S. District Court, Southern District of New York — Member New York State and Ulster County Bar Associations

Cook, Netter, Cloonan, Kurtz & Murphy, P.C., Kingston, NY (Continued)

Associate Attorney

Kostas D. Leris — 1985 — Boston College, B.A., 2008; Albany Law School of Union University, J.D. (cum laude), 2013 — Admitted to Bar, 2014, New York; Massachusetts — Member American, New York State and Ulster County Bar Associations

---

The following firms also service this area.

Catania, Mahon, Milligram & Rider, PLLC
One Corwin Court
Newburgh, New York 12550
   Telephone: 845-565-1100
   Fax: 845-565-1999

Mailing Address: P.O. Box 1479, Newburgh, NY 12551

Insurance Defense, Insurance Coverage, School Law, Municipal Law, Construction Litigation

SEE COMPLETE LISTING UNDER NEWBURGH, NEW YORK (35 MILES)

LaRose & LaRose
510 Haight Avenue
Poughkeepsie, New York 12603
   Telephone: 845-454-2001
   Fax: 845-454-2535

Insurance Defense, Automobile, General Liability, Product Liability, Casualty, Medical Malpractice, Environmental Law

SEE COMPLETE LISTING UNDER POUGHKEEPSIE, NEW YORK (20 MILES)

McCabe & Mack LLP
63 Washington Street
Poughkeepsie, New York 12601
   Telephone: 845-486-6800
   Fax: 845-486-7621

Mailing Address: P.O. Box 509, Poughkeepsie, NY 12602-0509

Insurance Defense, Negligence, Product Liability, General Liability, Municipal Liability, Casualty, Surety, Civil Rights, Subrogation, Environmental Law, Premises Liability, Labor Law

SEE COMPLETE LISTING UNDER POUGHKEEPSIE, NEW YORK (20 MILES)

LAKE SUCCESS 2,934 Nassau Co.

Ivone, Devine & Jensen, LLP

2001 Marcus Avenue
Lake Success, New York 11042
   Telephone: 516-326-2400
   Fax: 516-352-4952
   E-Mail: idj@idjlaw.com

Established: 1984

Insurance Defense, General Liability, Personal Injury, Medical Malpractice

Firm Profile: Ivone, Devine & Jensen, LLP was formed in January of 1984 by Michael T. Ivone, Robert Devine and Richard C. Jensen. Each has extensive experience in the defense of negligence, products liability and medical malpractice actions. Briefly stated, we are a firm of ten lawyers who specialize in the defense of medical malpractice actions and other significant personal injury cases including automobile cases, general liability and construction cases, and products liability actions.

The firm is committed to provide the highest quality of legal representation to its clients in a timely, professional and cost-effective manner.

Insurance Clients

Affiliated Risk Control Administrators, Inc.
Employers Insurance Company of Wausau
Medical Liability Mutual Insurance Company
New York State Insurance Department, Liquidation Bureau
State Insurance Fund of New York
Zurich American Insurance Group
Medical Malpractice Insurance Association
Physicians Reciprocal Insurers
PRMS, Inc. - Professional Risk Management Services, Inc.

Partners

Michael T. Ivone — 1926 — Brooklyn College, B.A. (cum laude), 1956; New York University School of Law, LL.B., 1960 — Admitted to Bar, 1961, New York; 1969, U.S. District Court, Southern District of New York; 1970, U.S. District Court, Eastern District of New York — Member American, New York State and Suffolk County Bar Associations; Nassau-Suffolk Trial Lawyers Association

W. Robert Devine — 1939 — Georgetown University, A.B., 1961; J.D., 1964 — Admitted to Bar, 1965, New York; 1968, U.S. District Court, Eastern District of New York; 1978, U.S. District Court, Southern District of New York — Member New York State Bar Association

Richard C. Jensen — 1939 — Villanova University, B.S., 1961; Fordham University, LL.B., 1964 — Admitted to Bar, 1965, New York — Member American and New York State Bar Associations

Brian E. Lee — 1952 — Colgate University, A.B., 1974; Valparaiso University, J.D., 1976 — Admitted to Bar, 1977, New York; 1978, U.S. District Court, Eastern and Southern Districts of New York — Member American Bar Association (Tort and Insurance Practice Section); New York State Bar Association (Insurance, Negligence and Compensation Law Section); Christian Legal Society; New York County Lawyers Association

Associates

Deborah C. Sturm — 1975 — Albany Law School, J.D., 2000 — Admitted to Bar, 2001, New York

Anthony M. Maffia — 1977 — Albany Law School, J.D., 2002 — Admitted to Bar, 2003, New York

Mindy E. Plotkin — 1963 — University of Pennsylvania Law School, J.D., 2000 — Admitted to Bar, 2001, New York

---

LATHAM 10,131 Albany Co.

Hacker Murphy, LLP

7 Airport Park Boulevard
Latham, New York 12110
   Telephone: 518-783-3843
   Fax: 518-783-8101
   Toll Free: 800-213-3843
   E-Mail: jhacker@hackermurphy.com
   www.hackermurphy.com

Established: 1990

Self-Insured, Product Liability, Commercial Litigation, Corporate Law, Personal Injury, Labor and Employment

Non-Insurance Clients

Heritage Propane Partners, L.P.
Suburban Propane
Lennox International, Inc.

Partners

James E. Hacker — 1959 — Hamilton College, B.A., 1981; Albany Law School of Union University, J.D., 1984 — Admitted to Bar, 1985, New York; U.S. District Court, Northern and Southern Districts of New York; U.S. Court of Appeals, Second Circuit — Member American, New York State and Albany County Bar Associations; National Order of the Barristers; Inns of Court; Capital District Trial Lawyers Association (President, 2003); New York State Trial Lawyers Association; Association of Trial Lawyers of America; Defense Research Institute — Practice Areas: Litigation — E-mail: jhacker@hackermurphy.com

David R. Murphy — 1949 — Georgetown University, B.S.F.S., 1971; Albany Law School of Union University, J.D., 1975 — Admitted to Bar, 1976, New York; U.S. District Court, Northern District of New York; U.S. Court of Appeals, Second Circuit — Member American, New York State, Albany

NEW YORK   LITTLE VALLEY

Hacker Murphy, LLP, Latham, NY (Continued)

County, Saratoga County and Rensselaer County Bar Associations — Practice Areas: Litigation — E-mail: dmurphy@hackermurphy.com

Patrick L. Seely, Jr. — 1962 — College of the Holy Cross, A.B., 1984; Albany Law School of Union University, J.D. (magna cum laude), 1992 — Admitted to Bar, 1993, New York; Massachusetts; U.S. District Court, Northern District of New York — Member New York State and Albany County Bar Associations; Capital District Trial Lawyers Association — Practice Areas: Commercial Litigation

John F. Harwick — 1968 — Clark University, B.A., 1991; Albany Law School of Union University, J.D. (cum laude), 1995 — Admitted to Bar, 1996, New York; U.S. District Court, Northern and Southern Districts of New York — Member American, New York State and Albany County Bar Associations; Capital District Trial Lawyers Association — Practice Areas: Commercial Litigation; Tort Litigation

Associates

Cathy L. Drobny   Thomas J. Higgs
Ryan M. Finn

LITTLE VALLEY † 1,143 Cattaraugus Co.

Refer To

Barth Sullivan Behr
600 Convention Tower
43 Court Street
Buffalo, New York 14202
Telephone: 716-856-1300
Fax: 716-856-1494

Trial Practice, Appellate Practice, Alternative Dispute Resolution, Product Liability, Casualty, Fire, Professional Errors and Omissions, Coverage Issues, Insurance Fraud, Subrogation, Motor Vehicle, General Liability, Workers' Compensation, Premises Liability, Municipal Liability, Tractor-Trailer, Bad Faith

SEE COMPLETE LISTING UNDER BUFFALO, NEW YORK (58 MILES)

Refer To

Cohen & Lombardo, P.C.
343 Elmwood Avenue
Buffalo, New York 14222
Telephone: 716-881-3010
Fax: 716-881-2755
Toll Free: 800-276-2640
Mailing Address: P.O. Box 5204, Buffalo, NY 14213-5204

Insurance Defense, Trial Practice, State and Federal Courts, Coverage Analysis, Litigation, Fire, Arson, Fraud, Property, Casualty, Surety, Marine, Employer Liability, Premises Liability, Product Liability, Environmental Law, Toxic Torts, Construction Law, Accident, Automobile, Professional Liability, Medical Malpractice, Subrogation, Advertising Injury, Errors and Omissions, Aviation, Bad Faith, Copyright and Trademark Law, Municipal Liability, Title Insurance, Niagara, Orleans, Monroe, Genesee, Livingston, Wyoming, Allegany, Cattaraugus and Chautauqua Counties

SEE COMPLETE LISTING UNDER BUFFALO, NEW YORK (61 MILES)

Refer To

Roach, Brown, McCarthy & Gruber, P.C.
1920 Liberty Building
424 Main Street
Buffalo, New York 14202-3511
Telephone: 716-852-0400
Fax: 716-852-2535

Insurance Defense, Trial and Appellate Practice, Medical Malpractice, Professional Malpractice, Product Liability, Construction Law, Sports and Entertainment Liability, Aviation, Fire, Excess, Coverage Issues

SEE COMPLETE LISTING UNDER BUFFALO, NEW YORK (54 MILES)

LOCKPORT † 21,165 Niagara Co.

Refer To

Barth Sullivan Behr
600 Convention Tower
43 Court Street
Buffalo, New York 14202
Telephone: 716-856-1300
Fax: 716-856-1494

Trial Practice, Appellate Practice, Alternative Dispute Resolution, Product Liability, Casualty, Fire, Professional Errors and Omissions, Coverage Issues, Insurance Fraud, Subrogation, Motor Vehicle, General Liability, Workers' Compensation, Premises Liability, Municipal Liability, Tractor-Trailer, Bad Faith

SEE COMPLETE LISTING UNDER BUFFALO, NEW YORK (29 MILES)

Refer To

Cohen & Lombardo, P.C.
343 Elmwood Avenue
Buffalo, New York 14222
Telephone: 716-881-3010
Fax: 716-881-2755
Toll Free: 800-276-2640
Mailing Address: P.O. Box 5204, Buffalo, NY 14213-5204

Insurance Defense, Trial Practice, State and Federal Courts, Coverage Analysis, Litigation, Fire, Arson, Fraud, Property, Casualty, Surety, Marine, Employer Liability, Premises Liability, Product Liability, Environmental Law, Toxic Torts, Construction Law, Accident, Automobile, Professional Liability, Medical Malpractice, Subrogation, Advertising Injury, Errors and Omissions, Aviation, Bad Faith, Copyright and Trademark Law, Municipal Liability, Title Insurance, Niagara, Orleans, Monroe, Genesee, Livingston, Wyoming, Allegany, Cattaraugus and Chautauqua Counties

SEE COMPLETE LISTING UNDER BUFFALO, NEW YORK (28 MILES)

LONG ISLAND CITY 115,000 Queens Co.

Law Offices of Michael E. Pressman

114 Chestnut Street
Garden City, New York 11530
Fax: 212-480-2590
Toll Free: 800-764-3030
E-Mail: mepressman@mepressman.com

(New York, NY Office*: 125 Maiden Lane-17th Floor, 10038)
(Tel: 212-480-3030)
(Fax: 212-480-2590)
(Toll Free: 800-764-3030)
(Warren, NJ Office*: Warrenville Plaza, 31W, Mountain Boulevard, 07059)
(Tel: 908-753-6661)
(Fax: 908-755-5229; 212-480-2590)
(Toll Free: 800-764-3030)
(Brooklyn, NY Office*: 26 Court Street, Suite 1700, 11242)
(Tel: 718-237-4600)
(Fax: 212-480-2590)
(Toll Free: 800-764-3030)

Insurance Defense, Automobile, General Liability, Product Liability, Property and Casualty

(See Brooklyn and New York, NY listings for additional information)

MELVILLE   NEW YORK

LYONS † 3,619 Wayne Co.

Refer To

Barth Sullivan Behr
600 Convention Tower
43 Court Street
Buffalo, New York 14202
   Telephone: 716-856-1300
   Fax: 716-856-1494

Trial Practice, Appellate Practice, Alternative Dispute Resolution, Product Liability, Casualty, Fire, Professional Errors and Omissions, Coverage Issues, Insurance Fraud, Subrogation, Motor Vehicle, General Liability, Workers' Compensation, Premises Liability, Municipal Liability, Tractor-Trailer, Bad Faith

SEE COMPLETE LISTING UNDER BUFFALO, NEW YORK (113 MILES)

MAYVILLE † 1,711 Chautauqua Co.

Refer To

Cohen & Lombardo, P.C.
343 Elmwood Avenue
Buffalo, New York 14222
   Telephone: 716-881-3010
   Fax: 716-881-2755
   Toll Free: 800-276-2640

Mailing Address: P.O. Box 5204, Buffalo, NY 14213-5204

Insurance Defense, Trial Practice, State and Federal Courts, Coverage Analysis, Litigation, Fire, Arson, Fraud, Property, Casualty, Surety, Marine, Employer Liability, Premises Liability, Product Liability, Environmental Law, Toxic Torts, Construction Law, Accident, Automobile, Professional Liability, Medical Malpractice, Subrogation, Advertising Injury, Errors and Omissions, Aviation, Bad Faith, Copyright and Trademark Law, Municipal Liability, Title Insurance, Niagara, Orleans, Monroe, Genesee, Livingston, Wyoming, Allegany, Cattaraugus and Chautauqua Counties

SEE COMPLETE LISTING UNDER BUFFALO, NEW YORK (76 MILES)

Refer To

Roach, Brown, McCarthy & Gruber, P.C.
1920 Liberty Building
424 Main Street
Buffalo, New York 14202-3511
   Telephone: 716-852-0400
   Fax: 716-852-2535

Insurance Defense, Trial and Appellate Practice, Medical Malpractice, Professional Malpractice, Product Liability, Construction Law, Sports and Entertainment Liability, Aviation, Fire, Excess, Coverage Issues

SEE COMPLETE LISTING UNDER BUFFALO, NEW YORK (65 MILES)

MELVILLE   18,985 Suffolk Co.

Lawrence, Worden, Rainis & Bard, P.C.

225 Broad Hollow Road, Suite 105E
Melville, New York 11747
   Telephone: 631-694-0033
   Fax: 631-694-9331
   E-Mail: lkennedy@lwrlawyer.com
   www.lwrlawyer.com

Established: 1992

Insurance Litigation, Declaratory Judgments, Insurance Coverage, Bad Faith, Civil Litigation, Negligence, Construction Accidents, Environmental Liability, Fire, Mold and Mildew Claims, Pharmaceutical, Premises Liability, Product Liability, Property Damage, Professional Malpractice, Dental Malpractice, Hospital Malpractice, Medical Malpractice, Underinsured Motorist

Firm Profile: Lawrence, Worden, Rainis & Bard concentrates on the defense of high exposure damages cases. We are particularly known for developing comprehensive strategies focusing on medical causation, although the firm defends many different types of high exposure claims, including construction accidents, fire, explosion, products liability, premises liability, including lead paint and other toxic tort claims, auto liability as well as medical malpractice, legal malpractice, other professional liability, drug litigation and mass torts.

All partners have twenty plus years of experience and work together to recognize key issues early. The firm customizes its representation to the needs of the particular carrier/client. Good communication and compliance with guidelines is stressed. Accurate analysis, thorough preparation and aggressive action toward prompt resolution of lawsuits and claims is our goal.

Insurance Clients

Fireman's Fund Insurance Company
Travelers Casualty and Surety Company
The Hartford
Medical Liability Mutual Insurance Company
Zurich North America

Members

Roger B. Lawrence — Carnegie Mellon University, B.A., 1975; St. John's University School of Law, J.D., 1978 — Admitted to Bar, 1979, New York; U.S. District Court, Eastern and Southern Districts of New York; 1985, U.S. Court of Appeals, Second Circuit — Member American, Nassau County and Suffolk County Bar Associations; Defense Research Institute — E-mail: rlawrence@lwrlawyer.com

Robert P. Worden, Jr. — Hamilton College, A.B., 1976; University of Miami School of Law, J.D., 1980 — Admitted to Bar, 1980, New York; U.S. District Court, Eastern, Northern and Southern Districts of New York; U.S. Court of Appeals for the Federal Circuit; U.S. Court of Appeals for the Armed Forces; U.S. Court of Federal Claims; U.S. Supreme Court — Member New York State and Suffolk County Bar Associations; Defense Research Institute; Defense Association of New York; Nassau-Suffolk Trial Lawyers Association — E-mail: rworden@lwrlawyer.com

Matthew Rainis — University of Virginia, B.A., 1982; St. John's University School of Law, J.D., 1985 — Admitted to Bar, 1985, Connecticut; 1986, New York; U.S. District Court, Eastern and Southern Districts of New York — Member Nassau County and Suffolk County Bar Associations — E-mail: mrainis@lwrlawyer.com

Jeffrey Bard — University of Massachusetts Amherst, B.A., 1984; St. John's University School of Law, J.D., 1987 — Admitted to Bar, 1988, New York; 1992, Florida — Member American, Nassau County and Suffolk County Bar Associations — E-mail: jbard@lwrlawyer.com

Kathleen Fugelsang — State University of New York, B.A. (magna cum laude), 1981; Virginia Commonwealth University, M.S.W., 1985; University of Richmond, T.C. Williams School of Law, J.D., 1985 — Admitted to Bar, 1986, New York; U.S. District Court, Eastern and Southern Districts of New York; 1991, U.S. Court of Appeals for the Federal Circuit; U.S. Court of Federal Claims; U.S. Court of Appeals for the Armed Forces; U.S. Supreme Court — E-mail: kfugelsang@lwrlawyer.com

Margaret Herrmann — State University of New York at Albany, B.A., 1975; St. John's University School of Law, J.D., 1983 — Admitted to Bar, 1984, New York; 1985, U.S. District Court, Eastern District of New York; 1987, U.S. District Court, Southern District of New York; U.S. Court of Appeals, Second Circuit — E-mail: mherrmann@lwrlawyer.com

Mary Beth Reilly — St. John's University, B.S., 1986; St. John's University School of Law, J.D., 1989 — Admitted to Bar, 1989, New York; 1991, U.S. District Court, Eastern District of New York — Member Nassau County and Suffolk County Bar Associations — E-mail: mbreilly@lwrlawyer.com

Paul E. Hennings — Providence College, B.A., 1983; The Catholic University of America, Columbus School of Law, J.D., 1986 — Admitted to Bar, 1987, New York; 1989, U.S. District Court, Eastern and Southern Districts of New York — Member New York State Bar Association — E-mail: phennings@lwrlawyer.com

Gail J. McNally — Hofstra University, B.A., 1987; Touro College Jacob D. Fuchsberg Law Center, J.D., 1995 — Admitted to Bar, 1996, New York; 1997, U.S. District Court, Eastern and Southern Districts of New York — E-mail: gmcnally@lwrlawyer.com

Russell T. McHugh — New York University, B.A., 1983; American University, Washington College of Law, J.D., 1986 — Admitted to Bar, 1987, New York; U.S. District Court, Eastern and Southern Districts of New York — Member New York State Bar Association — E-mail: rmchugh@lwrlawyer.com

Lesley C. Siskind — Albany State University, B.A., 1988; University of Bridgeport School of Law, J.D., 1991 — Admitted to Bar, 1992, New York; Connecticut — Member New York State Trial Lawyers Association — E-mail: lsiskind@lwrlawyer.com

NEW YORK

Lawrence, Worden, Rainis & Bard, P.C., Melville, NY (Continued)

Associates

Leslie McHugh, R.N. — Union College, B.A., 1976; Brooklyn Law School, J.D., 1988 — Admitted to Bar, 1989, New York; U.S. District Court, Eastern, Southern and Western Districts of New York — Member New York State Bar Association — E-mail: lmchugh@lwrlawyer.com

Ilysa W. Cholewa — University of Massachusetts, B.A., 1999; Brooklyn Law School, J.D., 2002 — Admitted to Bar, 2002, New York; U.S. District Court, Eastern and Southern Districts of New York — E-mail: icholewa@lwrlawyer.com

Of Counsel

Karen J. Halpern, R.N. — State University of New York at Stony Brook, B.S., 1985; Touro College Jacob D. Fuchsberg Law Center, J.D., 1988; Duquesne University, M.S.N., 2003 — Admitted to Bar, 1988, New York; U.S. District Court, Eastern and Southern Districts of New York — Member New York State and Suffolk County Bar Associations; American Society for Healthcare Risk Management; International Association of Forensic Nurses; The American Association of Nurse Attorneys (NY Metropolitan Chapter, Board of Directors, Treasurer) — E-mail: khalpern@lwrlawyer.com

Marshall Dennehey Warner Coleman & Goggin

105 Maxess Road, Suite 303
Melville, New York 11747
    Telephone: 631-232-6130
    Fax: 631-232-6184
    www.marshalldennehey.com

(Philadelphia, PA Office*: 2000 Market Street, Suite 2300, 19103)
    (Tel: 215-575-2600)
    (Fax: 215-575-0856)
    (Toll Free: 800-220-3308)
    (E-Mail: marshalldennehey@mdwcg.com)
(Wilmington, DE Office*: Nemours Building, 1007 North Orange Street, Suite 600, 19801)
    (Tel: 302-552-4300)
    (Fax: 302-552-4340)
(Fort Lauderdale, FL Office*: 100 Northeast 3rd Avenue, Suite 1100, 33301)
    (Tel: 954-847-4920)
    (Fax: 954-627-6640)
(Jacksonville, FL Office*: 200 West Forsyth Street, Suite 1400, 32202)
    (Tel: 904-358-4200)
    (Fax: 904-355-0019)
(Orlando, FL Office*: Landmark Center One, 315 East Robinson Street, Suite 550, 32801-1948)
    (Tel: 407-420-4380)
    (Fax: 407-839-3008)
(Tampa, FL Office*: 201 East Kennedy Boulevard, Suite 1100, 33602)
    (Tel: 813-898-1800)
    (Fax: 813-221-5026)
(Cherry Hill, NJ Office*: Woodland Falls Corporate Park, 200 Lake Drive East, Suite 300, 08002)
    (Tel: 856-414-6000)
    (Fax: 856-414-6077)
(Roseland, NJ Office*: 425 Eagle Rock Avenue, Suite 302, 07068)
    (Tel: 973-618-4100)
    (Fax: 973-618-0685)
(New York, NY Office*: Wall Street Plaza, 88 Pine Street, 21st Floor, 10005-1801)
    (Tel: 212-376-6400)
    (Fax: 212-376-6490)
(Cincinnati, OH Office*: 312 Elm Street, Suite 1850, 45202)
    (Tel: 513-375-6800)
    (Fax: 513-372-6801)
(Cleveland, OH Office*: 127 Public Square, Suite 3510, 44114-1291)
    (Tel: 216-912-3800)
    (Fax: 216-344-9006)

MELVILLE

Marshall Dennehey Warner Coleman & Goggin, Melville, NY (Continued)

(Allentown, PA Office*: 4905 West Tilghman Street, Suite 300, 18104)
    (Tel: 484-895-2300)
    (Fax: 484-895-2303)
(Doylestown, PA Office*: 10 North Main Street, 2nd Floor, 18901-4318)
    (Tel: 267-880-2020)
    (Fax: 215-348-5439)
(Erie, PA Office*: 717 State Street, Suite 701, 16501)
    (Tel: 814-480-7800)
    (Fax: 814-455-3603)
(Camp Hill, PA Office*(See Harrisburg listing): 100 Coporate Center Drive, Suite 201, 17011)
    (Tel: 717-651-3500)
    (Fax: 717-651-9630)
(King of Prussia, PA Office*: 620 Freedom Business Center, Suite 300, 19406)
    (Tel: 610-354-8250)
    (Fax: 610-354-8299)
(Pittsburgh, PA Office*: U.S. Steel Tower, Suite 2900, 600 Grant Street, 15219)
    (Tel: 412-803-1140)
    (Fax: 412-803-1188)
(Moosic, PA Office*(See Scranton listing): 50 Glenmaura National Boulevard, 18507)
    (Tel: 570-496-4600)
    (Fax: 570-496-0567)
(Rye Brook, NY Office*(See Westchester listing): 800 Westchester Avenue, Suite C-700, 10573)
    (Tel: 914-977-7300)
    (Fax: 914-977-7301)

Amusements, Sports and Recreation Liability, Asbestos and Mass Tort Litigation, Automobile Liability, Aviation and Complex Litigation, Construction Injury Litigation, Fraud/Special Investigation, General Liability, Hospitality and Liquor Liability, Maritime Litigation, Product Liability, Property Litigation, Retail Liability, Trucking & Transportation Liability, Appellate Advocacy and Post-Trial Practice, Architectural, Engineering and Construction Defect Litigation, Class Action Litigation, Commercial Litigation, Consumer and Credit Law, Employment Law, Environmental & Toxic Tort Litigation, Insurance Coverage/Bad Faith Litigation, Life, Health and Disability Litigation, Privacy and Data Security, Professional Liability, Public Entity and Civil Rights Litigation, Real Estate E&O Liability, School Leaders' Liability, Securities and Investment Professional Liability, Technology, Media and Intellectual Property Litigation, White Collar Crime, Birth Injury Litigation, Health Care Governmental Compliance, Health Care Liability, Health Law, Long-Term Care Liability, Medical Device and Pharmaceutical Liability, Medicare Set-Aside, Workers' Compensation

Firm Profile: Marshall Dennehey Warner Coleman & Goggin established an office on Long Island in October 2011, first opening in Hauppauge and then relocating in 2014 to Melville to accommodate the firm's clients and growth. Located in the heart of Suffolk County, the office services its clients' needs throughout all of New York State.

Additional information regarding this office is available by contacting Anna M. DiLonardo, Esquire, the managing attorney of the office, at (631) 227-6346 or amdilonardo@mdwcg.com

Managing Shareholder

Anna M. DiLonardo — University of Cincinnati, B.B.A., 1985; University of Cincinnati College of Law, J.D., 1988 — Admitted to Bar, 1990, New York; 1991, U.S. District Court, Eastern, Northern and Southern Districts of New York — Practice Areas: Asbestos Litigation — E-mail: amdilonardo@mdwcg.com

Senior Counsel

James A. Gallagher   Kevin M. Ryan

Special Counsel

Colleen M. Cronin   Robert A. Faller

MIDDLETOWN   NEW YORK

Marshall Dennehey Warner Coleman & Goggin, Melville, NY (Continued)

Michael P. Kelly   Daniel W. Levin
Andrew M. Warshauer

Shareholders

Neil E. Higgins   William R. Pirk, Jr.

Associates

Jennifer M. Roberts   Noriel L. Sta. Maria

(See listing under Philadelphia, PA for additional information)

Speyer & Perlberg, LLP

115 Broadhollow Road, Suite 250
Melville, New York 11747
   Telephone: 631-673-6670
   Fax: 631-673-7073
   E-Mail: perlberg@speyerperlberg.com
   www.speyerperlberg.com

Established: 1960

First Party Property Defense, Fire, Inland Marine, General Liability, Product Liability, Subrogation, Commercial & Corporate Litigation

Firm Profile: The firm represents insurance companies in state and federal courts in New York City, Long Island, Westchester and northern New Jersey. The insurance practice is concentrated in coverage issues, fraud investigations and defense, property damage casualty defense and subrogation.

Insurance Clients

Admiral Insurance Company
CNA Insurance Companies
Fireman's Fund Insurance Company
The Hartford Insurance Group
Travelers Insurance Companies
Chubb Group
Farm Family Insurance Companies
Greater New York Mutual Insurance Company
New York Marine & General Insurance Company

Partners

Dennis M. Perlberg — Boston University, B.S., 1969; The Ohio State University, J.D. (cum laude), 1972 — Admitted to Bar, 1973, New York; 1973, U.S. District Court, Eastern and Southern Districts of New York; 1986, U.S. Court of Appeals, Second Circuit — E-mail: perlberg@speyerperlberg.com

Frank D. Platt — Rider University, B.A., 1966; Fordham University, J.D., 1969 — Admitted to Bar, 1969, New York

Counsel

Thomas E. Scott

Associates

Gina M. Fortunato   James M. O'Hara
Marie E. Garelle   Isaak Manashirov

MIDDLETOWN   28,086   Orange Co.

The Law Offices of Craig P. Curcio

384 Crystal Run Road, Suite 202
Middletown, New York 10941
   Telephone: 845-692-7000
   Fax: 845-692-7500
   E-Mail: curciolaw@frontiernet.net

Established: 1997

Professional Malpractice, Toxic Torts, Mass Tort, Product Liability, Inland Marine, General Liability, Insurance Law, Reinsurance

The Law Offices of Craig P. Curcio, Middletown, NY (Continued)

Insurance Clients

Amica Mutual Insurance Company
Cincinnati Insurance Company
Frankenmuth Mutual Insurance Company
Global Indemnity Group, Inc.
GuideOne Insurance
The Main Street America Group
Merchants Insurance Group
MetLife Auto & Home Group
NCMIC Insurance Company
Preferred Mutual Insurance Company
Security Mutual Insurance Company
Broadspire
First Financial Insurance Company
GEICO
General Star Management Company
Kemper Insurance Company
Meadowbrook Insurance Group
Mercury Insurance Company
Mutual Marine Office, Inc.
New York State Insurance Department, Liquidation Bureau
Progressive Insurance Company
Seneca Insurance Company, Inc.
Starr Indemnity & Liability Group

Non-Insurance Clients

Molins Corporation

Firm Member

Craig P. Curcio — 1960 — Manhattanville College, B.A. (cum laude), 1982; University of Colorado Law School, J.D., 1985 — Admitted to Bar, 1986, New York; U.S. District Court, Southern District of New York — Member American, New York State, Orange and Westchester County Bar Associations; New York State Trial Lawyers Institute — E-mail: curciolaw@frontiernet.net

Associates

Tony Semidey — 1968 — Herbert H. Lehman College of the City University of New York, B.S. (summa cum laude), 1994; New York Law School, J.D. (cum laude), 2001 — Phi Beta Kappa — Admitted to Bar, 2002, New York

Bryan R. Kaplan — 1971 — State University of New York at Buffalo, B.A., 1994; New York Law School, J.D., 1997 — Admitted to Bar, 1998, New York — Member New York State Bar Association

Douglas S. Goldberg — 1957 — Ramapo College of New Jersey, B.A., 1979; Hofstra University School of Law, J.D., 1982 — Admitted to Bar, 1984, New York — Member New York State, Orange and Bronx Counties Bar Associations

Kevin P. Ahrenholz — 1973 — College of the Holy Cross, B.A., 2003; Albany Law School, J.D., 2008 — Admitted to Bar, 2009, New York — Member American and New York State Bar Associations

Deborah J. Bookwalter — 1974 — Mount St. Mary's College, B.A., 2005; Pace University School of Law, J.D., 2009 — Admitted to Bar, 2010, New York — Member American and New York State Bar Association

Ryan Bannon — 1984 — University at Albany, B.S., 2006; Albany Law School, J.D., 2011 — Admitted to Bar, 2011, New Jersey; 2012, New York — Member New Jersey State Bar Association

MacVean, Lewis, Sherwin & McDermott, P.C.

34 Grove Street
Middletown, New York 10940
   Telephone: 845-343-3000
   Fax: 845-343-3866
   www.mlsmlaw.com

General Practice, Casualty, Life Insurance, Fire

Insurance Clients

Farm Family Insurance Companies
Government Employees Insurance Company
Travelers Insurance Companies
United Services Automobile Association (USAA)
Gallagher Bassett Services, Inc.
Lancer Insurance Company
New Jersey Manufacturers Insurance Company
Utica Mutual Insurance Company

Non-Insurance Clients

County of Orange   Orange and Rockland Utilities, Inc.

Partners

Kenneth A. MacVean — (1926-1999)

NEW YORK **MINEOLA**

MacVean, Lewis, Sherwin & McDermott, P.C., Middletown, NY (Continued)

Kermit W. Lewis — (1923-2002)

Paul T. McDermott — 1940 — Hamilton College, A.B., 1962; Cornell University, J.D., 1965 — Admitted to Bar, 1965, New York — Member New York State, Orange County and Middletown Bar Associations

Jeffrey D. Sherwin — 1948 — Bucknell University, A.B. (cum laude), 1971; Case Western Reserve University, J.D., 1974 — Admitted to Bar, 1974, Ohio; 1975, New York — Member American, New York State, Orange County and Middletown Bar Associations

Thomas P. Clarke — 1960 — Harvard University, A.B., 1982; St. John's University School of Law, J.D., 1987 — Admitted to Bar, 1988, New York — Member American, New York State, Orange County and Middletown Bar Associations

Kevin F. Preston — 1958 — Fordham University, B.A., 1980; J.D., 1985 — Admitted to Bar, 1986, New York; 1989, Pennsylvania; Michigan — Member American Bar Association, State Bar of Michigan

Associates

Ferol Reed-McDermott — 1968 — Pace University, B.A. (summa cum laude), 1990; Pace University School of Law, J.D., 1993 — Pace Law Review (1991-1993) — Admitted to Bar, 1994, New York; New Jersey — Member American and Rockland County Bar Associations

James V. Gavin — 1961 — Marist College, B.A. (cum laude), 1983; St. John's University School of Law, J.D., 1988 — Admitted to Bar, 1988, New York

Of Counsel

Louis H. Sherwin — 1917 — New York University, A.B., 1937; Harvard University, J.D., 1940 — Admitted to Bar, 1941, New York — Member New York State, Orange County and Middletown Bar Associations

John M. Clancy — 1951 — State University of New York College at Oneonta, B.A. (magna cum laude), 1974; New York Law School, J.D., 1983 — Admitted to Bar, 1984, New York — Member New York State and Orange County Bar Associations

---

The following firms also service this area.

Catania, Mahon, Milligram & Rider, PLLC
One Corwin Court
Newburgh, New York 12550
　Telephone: 845-565-1100
　Fax: 845-565-1999
Mailing Address: P.O. Box 1479, Newburgh, NY 12551

Insurance Defense, Insurance Coverage, School Law, Municipal Law, Construction Litigation

SEE COMPLETE LISTING UNDER NEWBURGH, NEW YORK (25 MILES)

MINEOLA † 18,799 Nassau Co.

Bee Ready Fishbein Hatter & Donovan, LLP

170 Old Country Road, Suite 200
Mineola, New York 11501
　Telephone: 516-746-5599
　Fax: 516-746-1045
　E-Mail: mail@beereadylaw.com
　www.beereadylaw.com

Established: 2001

Insurance Defense, Trial Practice, Appellate Practice

Firm Profile: Bee Ready Fishbein Hatter & Donovan, LLP was formed in 2001 with the merger of Bee Eisman & Ready and Hatter Donovan, LLP. The new firm provides our clients with attorneys having extensive trial experience, dedicated to serving our clients' needs with first-rate, cost-effective representation.

Insurance Clients

Allstate Insurance Company　　Amica Mutual Insurance Company

Bee Ready Fishbein Hatter & Donovan, LLP, Mineola, NY (Continued)

General Assurance Company
NAS Insurance Company
Prudential Insurance Company of America
St. Paul Fire and Marine Insurance Company
Liberty Mutual Insurance Company
Nationwide Insurance
Quincy Mutual Fire Insurance Company
State of New York Insurance Department Liquidation Bureau

Non-Insurance Clients

The New York Racing Association　　Triad Group, LLC

Firm Members

Peter A. Bee — 1952 — St. John's University, B.A., 1973; J.D., 1976 — Admitted to Bar, 1976, Florida; 1977, New York; 1977, U.S. District Court, Eastern and Southern Districts of New York — Member American, New York State and Nassau County Bar Associations; The Florida Bar

Richard Paul Ready — 1958 — Potsdam State College, B.A., 1982; St. John's University, J.D., 1987 — Admitted to Bar, 1988, New York; 1988, U.S. District Court, Eastern District of New York — Member American, New York State and Nassau County Bar Associations

Peter M. Fishbein — 1953 — C.W. Post College, B.S., 1976; Hofstra University, M.B.A., 1982; St. John's University, J.D. (cum laude), 1996 — Admitted to Bar, 1997, New York; 1997, U.S. District Court, Eastern District of New York — Member American and New York State Bar Associations

James R. Hatter — 1946 — C.W. Post College, B.A. (magna cum laude), 1972; Brooklyn Law School, J.D., 1975 — Admitted to Bar, 1976, New York; 1976, U.S. District Court, Eastern and Southern Districts of New York; 1995, U.S. Supreme Court — Member New York State Bar Association; Nassau County Bar Association (Chairman, Defendant's Round Table; Member, Grievance Committee; Vice Chair, Supreme Court Committee); Defense Association of New York; Defense Research Institute; Nassau-Suffolk Trial Lawyers Association

Kenneth A. Gray — 1968 — Hofstra University, B.S., 1990; New York Law School, J.D., 1993 — Admitted to Bar, 1994, New York; 1994, U.S. District Court, Eastern and Southern Districts of New York; 2006, U.S. Court of Appeals, Second Circuit — Member Nassau County Bar Association

Donald J. Farinacci — St. John's University, B.A., 1963; Fordham Law School, J.D., 1966 — Admitted to Bar, 1969, New York; 1970, U.S. Court of Appeals, Second Circuit — Member New York State, Nassau and Suffolk Counties Bar Associations

William DeWitt — 1973 — State University of New York at Stony Brook, B.A., 1996; Touro College Jacob D. Fuchsberg Law Center, J.D., 2000 — Admitted to Bar, 1973, New York

Associates

Angelo Bianco　　Michael Krall
Evelyn Gross　　Deanna Panico
Michael P. Siravo

Of Counsel

Thomas V. Pantelis

Gallagher, Walker, Bianco & Plastaras, LLP

98 Willis Avenue
Mineola, New York 11501
　Telephone: 516-248-2002
　Fax: 516-248-2394
　www.gwbplaw.com

Established: 1993

Insurance Defense, Medical Malpractice, Product Liability, Automobile, Premises Liability, Labor and Employment, Personal Injury, Commercial Litigation, Corporate Law, Elder Law, Real Estate

Insurance Clients

John Deere Insurance Company　　Medical Liability Mutual Insurance Company

MINEOLA   NEW YORK

Gallagher, Walker, Bianco & Plastaras, LLP, Mineola, NY (Continued)

Non-Insurance Clients

Costco Companies, Inc.   800-Flowers, Inc.

Partners

Robert J. Walker — 1954 — St. John's University, B.A., 1975; St. John's University School of Law, J.D. (with honors), 1978 — American Jurisprudence Award for Excellence in Criminal Procedure — Staff Member St. John's Law Review (1976-1977) — Admitted to Bar, 1979, New York; U.S. District Court, Eastern and Southern Districts of New York — Member New York State Bar Association (Special Committee on Medical Malpractice); Bar Association of Nassau County; Nassau-Suffolk Trial Lawyers Association — "Coverage Issues Relating to Premises Liability," 1996; "Application of Foreign Objects Discovery Rule Extended to Cause of Action in Negligence and Breach of Warranty," 51 St. John's Law Review 678, 1977 — Former Public Defender, Legal Aid Society — E-mail: rwalker@gwbplaw.com

Gerard M. Gallagher — 1952 — Georgetown University, B.A., 1975; St. John's University School of Law, J.D., 1978 — American Jurisprudence Award for Excellence in Contracts — Admitted to Bar, 1979, New York; U.S. District Court, Eastern and Southern Districts of New York — Member New York State and Queens County Bar Associations; Bar Association of Nassau County; Nassau-Suffolk Trial Lawyers Association — E-mail: ggallagher@gwbplaw.com

Dominic P. Bianco — 1952 — University of Notre Dame, B.A. (magna cum laude), 1974; New York University School of Law, J.D., 1977 — Admitted to Bar, 1978, New York; 1982, U.S. District Court, Eastern District of New York — Member New York State, Nassau County and Nassau-Suffolk Bar Associations — E-mail: dbianco@gwbplaw.com

Thomas E. Plastaras — 1957 — Ithaca College, B.A., 1979; California Western School of Law, J.D. (cum laude), 1982 — American Jurisprudence Award, Excellence in Insurance Law and Corporate Law — Admitted to Bar, 1982, California; 1983, New York; 1984, Minnesota; 1988, District of Columbia; 1982, U.S. District Court, Southern District of California; 1983, U.S. District Court, Eastern and Southern Districts of New York; 1988, U.S. Supreme Court — Member The State Bar of California; New York State and Suffolk County Bar Associations; New York State Trial Lawyers Association; Nassau/Suffolk Trial Lawyers Association — E-mail: tplastaras@gwbplaw.com

William P. Nolan — 1967 — Siena College, B.A., 1990; City University of New York, Law School at Queens College, J.D., 1994 — Admitted to Bar, 1995, New York — E-mail: wnolan@gwbplaw.com

John J. Kramer — 1976 — Iona College, B.A., 1998; Touro College Jacob D. Fuchsberg Law Center, J.D., 2001 — Admitted to Bar, 2002, New York — Member American and New York State Bar Associations — E-mail: jkramer@gwbplaw.com

Associates

Michael R. Walker — 1980 — University of Scranton, B.A., 2001; Touro College Jacob D. Fuchsberg Law Center, J.D., 2004 — Admitted to Bar, 2005, New York; 2008, U.S. District Court, Southern District of New York — Member New York State and Nassau County Bar Associations; Defense Research Institute — E-mail: mwalker@gwbplaw.com

Brian R. Kenney — 1977 — University of Scranton, B.S., 1999; Touro College Jacob D. Fuchsberg Law Center, J.D., 2009 — Admitted to Bar, 2010, New York; U.S. District Court, Eastern and Southern Districts of New York — Member New York State, Nassau County and Suffolk County Bar Associations; Defense Research Institute — E-mail: bkenney@gwbplaw.com

Kelly, Rode & Kelly, LLP

330 Old Country Road, Suite 305
Mineola, New York 11501
Telephone: 516-739-0400
Fax: 516-739-0434
Toll Free: 800-437-7737
E-Mail: info@krklaw.com
www.krklaw.com

(Riverhead, NY Office*: 218 Griffing Avenue, 11901)
 (Tel: 631-727-0110)
 (Toll Free: 800-437-7737)
 (Fax: 516-739-0434)

Kelly, Rode & Kelly, LLP, Mineola, NY (Continued)

Established: 1956

Medical Malpractice Defense, Hospital Malpractice, Nursing Home Litigation, Health Care Liability, Insurance Coverage & Defense, General Defense Civil Litigation, State and Federal Courts, Product Liability, Appellate Practice, Construction Accidents, Premises Liability, Trial and Coverage Opinions, Declaratory Judgments

Insurance Clients

Academic Health Professionals Insurance Association
Atlantic Mutual Insurance Company
Chubb Group of Insurance Companies
Hartford Life Insurance Company
Markel American Insurance Company
Medical Malpractice Insurance Pool
National Chiropractic Mutual Insurance Company
New York State Insurance Department, Liquidation Bureau
State Farm Fire and Casualty Company
United National Group
Virginia Farm Bureau Mutual Insurance Company
Allied Dealer Insurance Services
American Family Life Assurance Company of New York
Broadspire
Farm Bureau Mutual Insurance Company
Liberty Mutual Insurance Company
Medical Liability Mutual Insurance Company
Motorists Mutual Insurance Company
Nationwide Mutual Insurance Company
Philadelphia Insurance Companies
Physicians Reciprocal Insurers
State Farm Insurance Companies
Swiss Re America Group
Victoria Fire & Casualty Company

Non-Insurance Clients

Armco, Inc.
County of Suffolk
Electrolux Outdoor Products, Inc.
Honeywell, Inc.
New York Hospital Medical Center of Queens
North Shore-LIJ Health Systems
Royal-Liverpool Group
The Sherwin-Williams Company
Subaru of America, Inc.
Synergy Gas Corporation
Town of North Hempstead
Choice Hotels International
CVS Pharmacy, Inc.
Genway Corporation
MiniCo, Inc.
Northern Tool & Equipment Company
Richmond University Medical Center
State of New York, Office of the Comptroller - Division of Medical Malpractice

Partners

John D. Kelly — (1921-2000)

John Kenneth Rode — (Retired)

Shawn P. Kelly — 1952 — University of Notre Dame, B.B.A., 1974; St. John's University School of Law, J.D., 1977 — Admitted to Bar, 1978, New York; U.S. District Court, Eastern District of New York; 1979, U.S. District Court, Southern District of New York; U.S. Supreme Court; U.S. Claims Court; U.S. Court of Appeals, Armed Services — Member New York State, Suffolk County (Chair, Trial Lawyers Section) and Nassau County (Chair, Trial Lawyers Section, 2001-2002) Bar Associations; Fellow, American College of Trial Lawyers; Nassau-Suffolk Trial Lawyers Association (Member and Vice Chairman, Board of Directors, 1985-2002); New York State Medical Defense Bar Association; New York State Medical Malpractice Task Force (Subcommittee Member, 2007); National Institute of Trial Advocacy — Lecturer: New York State Bar Association; Practicing Law Institute; Nassau County Bar Association; Suffolk County Bar Association; Adjunct Faculty Member, Hofstra University School of Law; New York Metro Division Super Lawyers (2007-2014); Martindale-Hubbell Peer Review Rating AV Preeminent — Practice Areas: Medical Malpractice Defense; Hospital Malpractice; Insurance Coverage & Defense; Health Care Liability; Professional Malpractice; Insurance Defense; Civil Trial Practice; Product Liability; Personal Injury — E-mail: spkelly@krklaw.com

George J. Wilson — 1957 — Hofstra University, New College, B.A. (magna cum laude), 1979; St. John's University School of Law, J.D., 1984 — Admitted to Bar, 1985, New York; 1989, U.S. District Court, Eastern and Southern Districts of New York; 2003, U.S. District Court, Northern District of New York — Member New York State and Nassau County Bar Associations; Nassau-Suffolk Trial Lawyers Association — Martindale-Hubbell Peer Review Rating AV Preeminent — Practice Areas: Negligence; Medical Malpractice; Insurance Coverage; Product Liability — E-mail: gjwilson@krklaw.com

NEW YORK   MINEOLA

Kelly, Rode & Kelly, LLP, Mineola, NY   (Continued)

John W. Hoefling — 1948 — The Pennsylvania State University, B.A., 1970; Cumberland School of Law of Samford University, J.D., 1977 — Admitted to Bar, 1978, New York; U.S. District Court, Eastern and Southern Districts of New York; U.S. Court of Appeals, Second Circuit; 1992, U.S. Supreme Court; 2003, U.S. District Court, Northern District of New York — Member New York State and Nassau County Bar Associations; Nassau-Suffolk Trial Lawyers Association — Martindale-Hubbell Peer Review Rating AV Preeminent — Practice Areas: Insurance Coverage & Defense; Product Liability; Construction Accidents; Appellate Practice; Negligence — E-mail: jwhoefling@krklaw.com

Loris Zeppieri — 1973 — Adelphi University, B.S., 1994; St. John's University School of Law, J.D., 1997 — Admitted to Bar, 1998, New York — Member Nassau-Suffolk Trial Lawyers Association (Officer; PastTreasurer) — Languages: Italian, Spanish — Practice Areas: Negligence; Medical Malpractice; Insurance Coverage; Product Liability — E-mail: lzeppieri@krklaw.com

Eric B. Betron — 1977 — Washington University in St. Louis, B.S.B.A., 1999; Saint Louis University School of Law, J.D., 2002 — Admitted to Bar, 2002, New Jersey; 2003, New York; U.S. District Court, Eastern and Southern Districts of New York — Member American, New York State and Nassau County Bar Associations — Practice Areas: Medical Malpractice; Negligence; Product Liability; Appellate Practice; Insurance Coverage — E-mail: ebbetron@krklaw.com

Kevin E. Way — 1960 — Cathedral College of the Immaculate Conception, B.A. (cum laude), 1982; Hofstra University School of Law, J.D., 1985 — Admitted to Bar, 1986, New York; New Jersey (Inactive); 2004, U.S. District Court, Southern District of New York — Member New York State and Nassau County Bar Associations; Nassau-Suffolk Trial Lawyers Association — Martindale-Hubbell Peer Review Rating AV Preeminent — Practice Areas: Medical Malpractice; Insurance Defense — E-mail: keway@krklaw.com

Associates

Robert W. Corbin
Brian M. Dunphy
Peter D. Garone
Aryeh S. Klonsky
Colin J. McSherry
Michele A. Perlin
Steve K. F. Scott
Susan M. Ulrich
Barbara A. Dalton
Brian P. Flynn
Edward J. Kelly
Robert A. Koubek
John J. Morris
Colin Rathje
Sol Z. Sokel
Hilary M. Wissemann

Of Counsel

John J. Stewart, Jr.

(Also see listing under Riverhead, NY)

McCabe, Collins, McGeough & Fowler, LLP

346 Westbury Avenue
Carle Place, New York 11514
   Telephone: 516-741-6266
   Fax: 516-873-9496
   E-Mail: mail@mcmflaw.com
   www.mcmflaw.com

(Buffalo, NY Office: 651 Delaware Avenue, 14201)
   (Tel: 716-362-1207)
   (Fax: 516-873-9496)
(Albany, NY Office: 125 Wolf Road, Suite 201, 12205)
   (Tel: 518-709-3647)

Established: 1980

Asbestos Litigation, Automobile, Aviation, Casualty, Coverage Issues, Trial Practice, Appellate Practice, Subrogation, Product Liability, Insurance Law, Medical Malpractice, Municipal Liability, Professional Liability, Construction Accidents, Sports and Entertainment Liability, General Liability, Premises Liability, Food Poisoning, Toxic Chemicals, Matrimonial

McCabe, Collins, McGeough & Fowler, LLP, Mineola, NY   (Continued)

Insurance Clients

AIG Insurance Company
Amica Mutual Insurance Company
Andover Companies
Cardinal Claim Service, Inc.
Commerce Insurance Company
Cunningham Lindsey U.S., Inc.
EMC Insurance Company
ESIS
Esurance
First Niagara Risk Management, Inc.
General Insurance Company
GMAC Insurance Group
Gulf Insurance Company
Hallmark Specialty Underwriters, Inc.
Interboro Insurance Company
Mercury Insurance Company
National General Insurance Company
New York Central Mutual Fire Insurance Company
New York State Insurance Department, Liquidation Bureau
The Patrons Group
Pennsylvania Lumbermens Mutual Insurance Company
Quincy Mutual Fire Insurance Company
State Farm Mutual Automobile Insurance Company
Tower Insurance Company of New York
United States Liability Insurance Company
Ward North America, Inc.
American Insurance Group
AmTrust Group
AutoOne Insurance Company
Claims Service Bureau
Crawford & Company
Custard Insurance Adjusters, Inc.
Erie and Niagara Insurance Association
Farmers Insurance Company
Gallagher Bassett Services, Inc.
General Casualty Company
Global Indemnity Group
Greenville Casualty Insurance Company
Horace Mann Insurance Company
Integon Casualty Insurance Company
Narragansett Bay Insurance Company
Network Adjusters, Inc.
New York Municipal Insurance Reciprocal
North Carolina Farm Bureau Insurance Group
Pawtucket Insurance Company
Preferred Mutual Insurance Company
RCA Indemnity Corporation
Seneca Insurance Company, Inc.
State Insurance Fund of New York
TIG Insurance Company
United American Insurance Company
Waco Fire and Casualty Insurance Company

Non-Insurance Clients

Artis
Brownyard Group
County of Nassau
Dick's Sporting Goods, Inc.
George Weston Bakeries, Inc.
The Incorporated Village of Floral Park
Petro Oil Company
Sewanhaka Central High School
Town of Brookhaven
Barnes & Noble, Inc.
Coca-Cola Enterprises Inc.
County of Suffolk
Essential Services and Programs, Inc.
Long Island Rail Road
New York City Housing Authority
Rite Aid Corporation
Suffolk County Water Authority

Partners

Stephen M. McCabe — 1941 — Seton Hall University, B.A., 1962; Seton Hall University School of Law, J.D., 1965 — Admitted to Bar, 1966, New York; 1989, U.S. Court of Appeals, Second Circuit; U.S. District Court, Eastern and Southern Districts of New York; U.S. Supreme Court — Member American, New York State and Nassau County (Judiciary Committee) Bar Associations; The Brehon Law Society; Early Neutral Evaluator - U.S. Dsitrict Court, Eastern District of New York; International Association of Defense Counsel; Nassau-Suffolk Trial Lawyers Association; Defense Research Institute; Defense Association of New York

Brian J. McGeough — 1954 — State University of New York College at Oneonta, B.A. (magna cum laude), 1976; St. John's University School of Law, J.D., 1980 — Admitted to Bar, 1981, New York; 1984, U.S. District Court, Eastern and Southern Districts of New York — Member New York State and Nassau County Bar Associations; Nassau-Suffolk Trial Lawyers Association

David T. Fowler — 1955 — St. John's University, B.A. (cum laude), 1977; St. John's University School of Law, J.D., 1980 — Admitted to Bar, 1981, New York; U.S. District Court, Eastern and Southern Districts of New York — Member American, New York State and Nassau County Bar Associations; The Brehon Society; Nassau-Suffolk Trial Lawyers Association — Member, Board of Education, Floral Park-Bellerose School District; President, Sewanhaka Central High School District Board of Education

Patrick M. Murphy — 1957 — Fordham University, B.A., 1979; St. John's University School of Law, J.D., 1983 — Admitted to Bar, 1984, New York; 1985, Florida; New Jersey; U.S. District Court, Eastern and Southern Districts of New York; 1986, U.S. District Court, District of New Jersey; 1999, U.S. Court of Appeals, Second Circuit — Member New York State and

McCabe, Collins, McGeough & Fowler, LLP, Mineola, NY (Continued)

Nassau County (Member, Committee on Grievances) Bar Associations; The Florida Bar; Claims & Litigation Management Alliance

Thomas J. Nogan — 1960 — C.W. Post Campus of Long Island University, B.A., 1982; Tulsa University School of Law; Pace University School of Law, J.D., 1985 — Admitted to Bar, 1986, New York; 1988, U.S. District Court, Eastern and Southern Districts of New York — Member New York State Bar Association; Nassau County (Grievance and Supreme Court Committees) and Suffolk County Bar Associations; Nassau-Suffolk Trial Lawyers Association; American Trial Lawyers Association; New York State Trial Lawyers Association; Defense Research Institute — Supreme Court Mediator

Michael S. Levine — 1967 — Yeshiva University, B.A., 1988; Benjamin N. Cardozo School of Law, J.D., 1991 — Admitted to Bar, 1991, New Jersey; 1992, New York; 1991, U.S. District Court, District of New Jersey; U.S. District Court, Eastern District of New York — Member New York State Bar Association; Claims & Litigation Management Alliance; National Retail & Restaurant Defense Association; Trucking Industry Defense Association

Doron Rosenheck — 1956 — Queens College, B.S., 1979; St. John's University School of Law, J.D., 1982 — Admitted to Bar, 1984, New York; 1986, U.S. District Court, Eastern and Southern Districts of New York — Member New York State and Nassau County Bar Associations

John Joseph Connelly — 1970 — New York University, B.S., 1992; Brooklyn Law School, J.D., 1995 — Admitted to Bar, 1996, New York; U.S. District Court, Eastern and Southern Districts of New York — Member American, New York State and Brooklyn Bar Associations; New York State Trial Lawyers Association

Barry L. Manus — 1953 — Boston University, B.S., 1975; Nova University Law School, J.D., 1978 — Admitted to Bar, 1979, Florida; 1990, New York; U.S. District Court, Southern District of Florida; U.S. Court of Appeals, Fifth and Eleventh Circuits — Member New York State Bar Association; The Florida Bar

Michael L. Smar — 1973 — Hofstra University, B.A., 1996; Hofstra University School of Law, J.D., 2000 — Admitted to Bar, 2001, New York — Member American Bar Association; New York State Trial Lawyers Association

Of Counsel

Mark L. Weisenreder — 1945 — Ithaca College, B.M., 1967; St. John's University School of Law, J.D., 1974 — Admitted to Bar, 1974, New York; 1976, U.S. District Court, Eastern and Southern Districts of New York — Member New York State and Nassau County Bar Associations; Nassau-Suffolk Trial Lawyers Association

Associates

Teresa Campano — 1978 — Hofstra University, B.A., 2000; Hofstra University School of Law, J.D., 2003 — Admitted to Bar, 2004, New York; New Jersey; 2003, U.S. District Court, District of New Jersey; 2004, U.S. District Court, Eastern District of New York — Member New York State and Nassau County Bar Associations; Claims & Litigation Management Alliance

Jesse Lee Siegel — 1983 — Cornell University, A.B., 2005; University of Miami School of Law, J.D., 2008 — Admitted to Bar, 2009, New York — Member American and New York State Bar Associations

Allison Henig — 1984 — State University of New York at Cortland, B.S. (summa cum laude), 2005; Hofstra University School of Law, J.D., 2009 — Admitted to Bar, 2010, New York — Member American, New York State and Nassau County Bar Associations; Claims & Litigation Management Alliance

Tamara M. Harbold — 1966 — University of Rochester, B.A., 1988; University of Dayton School of Law, J.D., 1991 — Admitted to Bar, 1992, New York; 2009, Pennsylvania; 1992, U.S. District Court, Northern and Western Districts of New York — Member Buffalo Claims Association; Western New York Trial Lawyers Association — Former JAG for the NY Air National Guard/USAF, rank of Major, 1/24/94-11/30/2003 — Resident Buffalo, NY Office

Robert F. Barnashuk — 1982 — St. Bonaventure University, B.A. (cum laude), 2004; State University of New York at Buffalo Law School, J.D., 2007 — Admitted to Bar, 2008, New York; U.S. District Court, Western District of New York — Member American, New York State and Erie County Bar Associations; New York State Trial Lawyers Association — Resident Buffalo, NY Office

Michael J. Kelly — 1954 — Niagara University, B.S., 1976; St. John's University School of Law, J.D., 1979 — Admitted to Bar, 1980, New York; U.S. District Court, Eastern and Southern Districts of New York — Member New York State Bar Association; Association of Trial Lawyers of America; New

McCabe, Collins, McGeough & Fowler, LLP, Mineola, NY (Continued)

York State Trial Lawyers Association; Nassau-Suffolk Trial Lawyers Association — Volunteer Mediator for State Supreme Court ADR Program; Lecturer for New York State Association of Independent Adjusters

Christine M. Cusumano — 1986 — Fordham University, B.A., 2008; Touro College Jacob D. Fuchsberg Law Center, J.D., 2011 — Admitted to Bar, 2011, New Jersey; 2012, New York — Member New York State and Nassau County Bar Associations

James M. Hayes — 1953 — Manhattan College, B.S. (cum laude, Dean's List), 1975; St. John's University School of Law, J.D., 1981 — Admitted to Bar, 1982, New York; U.S. District Court, Eastern and Southern Districts of New York — Member Nassau County Bar Association

Frank J. Arneta — John Jay College of Criminal Justice, B.A., 1982; New York Law School, J.D., 1985 — Admitted to Bar, 1986, New York; New Jersey; U.S. District Court, District of New Jersey — Member New York State and Bronx County Bar Associations; New York State Trial Lawyers Association

Robert J. Passarelli — Fordham University, B.A., 1979; Hofstra University School of Law, J.D., 1982 — Admitted to Bar, 1982, New York; 1987, U.S. District Court, Eastern and Southern Districts of New York — Member Suffolk County Bar Association; New York State Academy of Trial Lawyers

George D. Argiriou — Fordham University, B.A., 1977; Fordham University School of Law, J.D., 1980 — Admitted to Bar, 1981, New York; 2009, U.S. District Court, Eastern District of New York — Member New York State Bar Association; Nassau-Suffolk Trial Lawyers Association

Arnie Wolsky — Syracuse University, B.A., 1979; Benjamin N. Cardozo School of Law, J.D., 1984 — Admitted to Bar, 1985, New York; U.S. District Court, Eastern and Southern Districts of New York

Purcell & Ingrao, P.C.

204 Willis Avenue
Mineola, New York 11501
Telephone: 516-248-6777
Fax: 516-248-2897
E-Mail: pilegal@purcell-ingrao.com

(Staten Island, NY Office: Suite 200, 811 Castleton Avenue, 10310)
(Tel: 718-727-2400)
(Fax: 718-420-9030)

Established: 1962

Insurance Defense, Commercial Litigation, Automobile, General Liability, Property and Casualty, Medical Malpractice, Professional Malpractice, Product Liability, Toxic Torts, Environmental Law, Coverage Issues

Insurance Clients

Claims Service Bureau
Gallagher Bassett Services, Inc.
Lancer Insurance Company
Monnex Insurance Management, Inc.
RCA Claim Service
Sedgwick Claims Management Services, Inc.
Everest National Insurance Company
Lexington Insurance Company
New York State Insurance Department, Liquidation Bureau
RLI Insurance Company
State Farm Insurance Company
York Claims Service, Inc.

Non-Insurance Clients

Alamo/Vanguard Car Rental Truck Claims, Inc.
Avis Corporation

Partners

Patrick J. Purcell — 1931 — Fordham University, B.S., 1953; New York Law School, LL.B., 1955 — Admitted to Bar, 1956, New York; 1960, U.S. Supreme Court — Member American, New York State, Nassau County, and Suffolk County Bar Associations; Nassau-Suffolk Trial Lawyers Association; New York State Trial Lawyers Association; Association of Defense Trial Attorneys

Joseph A. Ingrao — 1927 — St. John's University, B.B.A., 1950; LL.B., 1953 — Admitted to Bar, 1953, New York; 1963, U.S. Supreme Court — Member Nassau-Suffolk County Bar Association; Criminal Courts Bar Association of

NEW YORK

Purcell & Ingrao, P.C., Mineola, NY (Continued)

Suffolk County; Nassau-Suffolk Trial Lawyers Association; New York State Trial Lawyers Association — Resident Commack, NY Office

Lynn A. Ingrao — 1953 — State University of New York at Stony Brook, B.A., 1980; St. John's University School of Law, J.D., 1984 — Admitted to Bar, 1985, New York — Member American, New York State, and Suffolk County Bar Associations; Nassau-Suffolk Women's Bar Association

Terrance J. Ingrao — 1951 — Boston University, B.A., 1972; St. John's University School of Law, J.D., 1977 — Admitted to Bar, 1978, New York; 1978, U.S. District Court, Eastern and Southern Districts of New York; 1978, U.S. Court of Appeals, Second Circuit; 1978, U.S. Supreme Court — Member American Bar Association; Defense Research Institute; The Maritime Law Association of the United States; New York State Trial Lawyers Association; Association of Defense Trial Attorneys

Trial Counsel

George F. Sacco — 1951 — College of Holy Cross, St. John's College, B.A., 1973; St. John's University School of Law, J.D., 1977 — Admitted to Bar, 1978, New York; New Jersey — Member New York State and Richmond County Bar Associations; Columbian Lawyers Association of Brooklyn (Member and Past President)

Smith Mazure Director Wilkins Young & Yagerman, P.C.

200 Old Country Road, Suite 435
Mineola, New York 11501
   Telephone: 516-414-7400
   Fax: 516-294-7325
   www.smithmazure.com

(New York, NY Office*: 111 John Street, 10038)
   (Tel: 212-964-7400)
   (Fax: 212-374-1935)
   (E-Mail: contactus@smithmazure.com)
(Somerville, NJ Office*: 92 East Main Street, 08876)
   (Tel: 908-393-7300)
   (Fax: 908-231-1030)

Automobile, Transportation, Insurance Defense, Construction Law, Labor and Employment, Toxic Torts, Landowners Liability, Manufacturing, Hotels and Restaurants, Municipal Government, Land and Building Owners

(See listing under New York, NY for additional information)

(This firm is also listed in the Subrogation section of this directory)

The following firms also service this area.

Boeggeman, George & Corde, P.C.
1 Water Street, Suite 425
White Plains, New York 10601
   Telephone: 914-761-2252
   Fax: 914-761-5211

Insurance Defense, Trial Practice, Automobile, Product Liability, Legal Malpractice, Medical Malpractice, Employment Law, Real Estate, Toxic Torts, Engineering Malpractice

SEE COMPLETE LISTING UNDER WHITE PLAINS, NEW YORK (32 MILES)

Collins, Fitzpatrick & Schoene, LLP
34 South Broadway, Suite 407
White Plains, New York 10601
   Telephone: 914-437-8020
   Fax: 914-437-8022

Appellate Practice, Architects and Engineers, Automobile, Dental Malpractice, Insurance Coverage, Legal Malpractice, Medical Malpractice, Municipal Liability, Premises Liability, Product Liability, Professional Malpractice, Real Estate

SEE COMPLETE LISTING UNDER WHITE PLAINS, NEW YORK (32 MILES)

MONTICELLO

Ivone, Devine & Jensen, LLP
2001 Marcus Avenue
Lake Success, New York 11042
   Telephone: 516-326-2400
   Fax: 516-352-4952

Insurance Defense, General Liability, Personal Injury, Medical Malpractice

SEE COMPLETE LISTING UNDER LAKE SUCCESS, NEW YORK (6 MILES)

MONTICELLO † 6,726 Sullivan Co.

Stoloff & Silver, L.L.P.

26 Hamilton Avenue
Monticello, New York 12701
   Telephone: 845-794-4300
   Fax: 845-794-1371
   E-Mail: richard.stoloff@verizon.net

Established: 1995

Insurance Defense, Trial Practice, Casualty, Subrogation

Insurance Clients

Aegis Security Insurance Company
American Modern Home Insurance Company
Guarantee Insurance Company
Horizon Insurance Company
North American Risk Services
Old Republic Insurance Company
TIG Insurance Company
Alexsis Risk Management Services, Inc.
EMC Insurance Companies
Gulf Insurance Company
National Casualty Company
Northland Insurance Company
St. Paul Travelers
21st Century Insurance Company

Non-Insurance Clients

CrystalRun Healthcare
Kutsher's Country Club
Town of Mamakating
Woodstone Toronto Development, LLC
Irwin Siegel Agency, Inc.
Peck's Market, Inc.
Woodstone Lakes Development, LLC

Firm Members

Richard A. Stoloff — 1948 — City College of the City University of New York, B.A., 1969; Brooklyn Law School, J.D., 1973 — Admitted to Bar, 1974, New York; 1977, U.S. District Court, Southern District of New York; 1994, U.S. Court of Appeals, Second Circuit; 2000, U.S. District Court, Northern District of New York — Member American, New York State and Sullivan County (Director, 1981-1984; Vice President, 1990-1991; President, 1991-1992) Bar Associations; New York State Trial Lawyers Association

Gary D. Silver — 1960 — Brandeis University, B.A., 1981; Hofstra University School of Law, J.D. (with distinction), 1984 — Admitted to Bar, 1984, New York; 1987, U.S. District Court, Eastern and Southern Districts of New York; 2000, U.S. District Court, Northern District of New York — Member American, New York State and Sullivan County (Director, 1993-1995) Bar Associations

---

NEW CITY † 33,559 Rockland Co.

Refer To

Boeggeman, George & Corde, P.C.
1 Water Street, Suite 425
White Plains, New York 10601
   Telephone: 914-761-2252
   Fax: 914-761-5211

Insurance Defense, Trial Practice, Automobile, Product Liability, Legal Malpractice, Medical Malpractice, Employment Law, Real Estate, Toxic Torts, Engineering Malpractice

SEE COMPLETE LISTING UNDER WHITE PLAINS, NEW YORK (20 MILES)

NEW WINDSOR   NEW YORK

Refer To
Catania, Mahon, Milligram & Rider, PLLC
One Corwin Court
Newburgh, New York 12550
   Telephone: 845-565-1100
   Fax: 845-565-1999
Mailing Address: P.O. Box 1479, Newburgh, NY 12551

Insurance Defense, Insurance Coverage, School Law, Municipal Law, Construction Litigation

SEE COMPLETE LISTING UNDER NEWBURGH, NEW YORK (40 MILES)

Refer To
Collins, Fitzpatrick & Schoene, LLP
34 South Broadway, Suite 407
White Plains, New York 10601
   Telephone: 914-437-8020
   Fax: 914-437-8022

Appellate Practice, Architects and Engineers, Automobile, Dental Malpractice, Insurance Coverage, Legal Malpractice, Medical Malpractice, Municipal Liability, Premises Liability, Product Liability, Professional Malpractice, Real Estate

SEE COMPLETE LISTING UNDER WHITE PLAINS, NEW YORK (19 MILES)

NEW WINDSOR 8,922 Orange Co.

Drake, Loeb, Heller, Kennedy, Gogerty, Gaba & Rodd PLLC

555 Hudson Valley Avenue, Suite 100
New Windsor, New York 12553
   Telephone: 845-561-0550
   Fax: 845-561-1235
   E-Mail: arodd@drakeloeb.com
   www.drakeloeb.com

Appellate Practice, Americans with Disabilities Act, Automobile Liability, Carrier Defense, Civil Rights, Employment Discrimination, General Civil Trial and Appellate Practice, Medical Malpractice, Municipal Law, Product Liability, Professional Liability, School Law, Section 1983 Litigation

Firm Profile: Drake, Loeb, Heller, Kennedy, Gogerty, Gaba & Rodd PLLC is an AV-rated general practice law firm located in the Hudson Valley. Our insurance defense team handles a significant volume of cases for various carriers, mainly in the areas of school district liability, municipal liability and auto negligence.

Insurance Clients

AIG Domestic Claims, Inc.	Chicago Title Insurance Company
Gallagher Bassett Services, Inc.	Glatfelter Insurance Group
Harco National Insurance Company	New York Municipal Insurance Reciprocal
New York Schools Insurance Reciprocal	Physicians Reciprocal Insurers
Stewart Title Insurance Company	Selective Insurance Company of America
Travelers Insurance	Trident Insurance
Utica Mutual Insurance Company	

Non-Insurance Clients

Dutchess County Water & Wastewater Authority	Heritagenergy, Inc.
Orange County Chamber of Commerce, Inc.	Mettler Toledo, Inc.
	Orange Regional Medical Center
Sterling Forest, LLC	Related Companies
	Town of Cornwall

Partners

Richard J. Drake — (Retired)

James R. Loeb — Yale University, B.A., 1953; New York University, LL.B., 1958 — Admitted to Bar, 1958, New York; 1967, U.S. Supreme Court; 1970, U.S. Court of Appeals, Second Circuit; 1982, U.S. District Court, Eastern and Southern Districts of New York — Member American, New York State, and Orange County (President, 1975-1976) Bar Associations — Assistant Attorney, Orange County, New York, 1969-1970; Attorney: Cornwall, New York,

Drake, Loeb, Heller, Kennedy, Gogerty, Gaba & Rodd PLLC, New Windsor, NY   (Continued)

1963-Present; Monroe, New York, 1988-1990; Village of Walden, New York, 1987-1990; President, New York Association of Towns of the State of New York, 2002-2003; Speaker, Association of Towns of the State of New York Annual Meeting, 1975-Present; Former Member and President, Board of Trustees, St. Luke's Cornwall Hospital — U.S. Army 1953-1955 — E-mail: jloeb@drakeloeb.com

Glen L. Heller — State University of New York at Albany, B.A., 1981; Syracuse University, J.D., 1984; New York University, LL.M., 1985 — Admitted to Bar, 1985, New York; U.S. Tax Court; 1988, U.S. District Court, Eastern and Southern Districts of New York — Member New York State Bar Association (Elder Law Section, Trusts and Estates Section); Orange County Bar Association (Member, Elder Law Committee) — Hospice of Orange and Sullivan Counties (Treasurer, Past Chairman, Member, Board of Directors); St. Luke's Cornwall Hospital (Member); Hudson Valley Estate Planning Council (Member, Board of Directors); Boy Scout Troop and Pack 105 for Special Needs Children, Hudson Valley (Founder and Leader) — E-mail: gheller@drakeloeb.com

Marianna R. Kennedy — Mount Saint Mary College, B.S. (cum laude), 1987; Pace University, J.D. (magna cum laude), 1990 — Admitted to Bar, 1991, New York — Member New York State and Orange County Bar Associations — Member, Board of Directors, St. Luke's Cornwall Health System; Member, Board of Directors, Opera Company of the Highlands; Member, Board of Trustees, Mount Saint Mary College; Member, Board of Directors, The Greater Hudson Valley Family Health Center, Inc.; Member, Board of Directors, Ritz Theatre; Member, Board of Directors, Newburgh Ministry, Inc. — E-mail: mkennedy@drakeloeb.com

Gary J. Gogerty — Marist College, B.A. (cum laude), 1990; Quinnipiac College, J.D., 1994 — Admitted to Bar, 1994, Connecticut; 1995, New York; 1997, U.S. District Court, Southern District of New York — Member American, New York State and Orange County Bar Association; National Organization of Social Security Claimants Representatives; Hudson Valley Estate Planning Council — Accredited Attorney, Department of Veterans Affairs; Member, Membership Committee, Builders' Association of the Hudson Valley; Member, Board of Directors, Mid-Hudson Valley Mortgage Bankers' Association; Member, Board of Directors, Marlboro Yacht Club; Member, Board of Directors and Officer, Newburgh Preservation Association — E-mail: ggogerty@drakeloeb.com

Stephen J. Gaba — Fordham College, Fordham University, B.A., 1983; Albany Law School of Union University, J.D., 1987 — Admitted to Bar, 1988, New York; U.S. District Court, Northern and Southern Districts of New York; 1993, U.S. Court of Appeals, Second Circuit; U.S. Supreme Court; 1999, U.S. District Court, Eastern District of New York — Member New York State, Newburgh and Orange County Bar Associations — E-mail: sgaba@drakeloeb.com

Adam L. Rodd — State University of New York at Buffalo, B.S., 1984; The University of Toledo, J.D., 1987 — Admitted to Bar, 1987, Connecticut; 1988, New York; U.S. District Court, Eastern, Northern and Southern Districts of New York — Member New York State and Orange County Bar Associations — Member, Chairman, Board of Directors, Safe Harbors of the Hudson; Attorney, Town of Cornwall Zoning Board of Appeals; Town of Philipstown Zoning Board of Appeals — E-mail: arodd@drakeloeb.com

Dominic R. Cordisco — State University of New York at Plattsburgh, B.A., 1990; Fordham University, J.D., 1994 — Admitted to Bar, 1994, New Jersey; 1995, New York; U.S. District Court, Southern District of New York — Member New York State Bar Association (Environmental Law Section; Co-Chair, Standing Task Force on Mining, Oil & Gas Regulation, 2001-Present); Orange County Bar Association — 2012 Most Valuable Partner, Orange County Partnership; Past Region Three Attorney, New York State Department of Environmental Conservation; Co-Chair, Alliance for Balanced Growth; Board Member, Port Jervis Industrial Development Agency; Attorney, Town of New Windsor Planning Board — E-mail: dcordisco@drakeloeb.com

Timothy P. McElduff Jr. — Siena College, B.A., 1993; St. John's University, J.D., 1997 — Admitted to Bar, 1998, New York; New Jersey; U.S. District Court, Eastern, Northern, Southern and Western Districts of New York — Member New York State and Orange County Bar Associations — Town Justice, Town of Wawayanda; Vice-President, Orange County Magistrates Association; Member, Board of Directors, YMCA of Dutchess and Eastern Orange; Vice-President, Minisink Valley Little League — E-mail: tmcelduff@drakeloeb.com

Ralph L. Puglielle, Jr. — 1972 — State University of New York at New Paltz, B.A. (cum laude), 1994; Albany Law School, J.D. (cum laude), 1998 — Admitted to Bar, 1999, New York; 2001, District of Columbia; U.S. District Court, Northern and Southern Districts of New York; 2003, U.S. District

Drake, Loeb, Heller, Kennedy, Gogerty, Gaba & Rodd PLLC, New Windsor, NY (Continued)

Court, Eastern District of New York; 2006, U.S. Court of Appeals, Second Circuit; 2008, U.S. Supreme Court — Member New York State, Orange County, Ulster County and Dutchess County Bar Associations; Hudson Valley Bankruptcy Bar Association — Member, Board of Directors, Newburgh Community Improvement Corp.; Legal Counsel, Newburgh Chapter of UNICO National; Affiliated Attorney, Thomas More Law Center — E-mail: rpuglielle@drakeloeb.com

Associates

Nicholas A. Pascale — Colgate University, B.A. (cum laude), 1999; Emory University, J.D., 2002 — Admitted to Bar, 2003, New York; U.S. District Court, Northern and Southern Districts of New York — Member New York State and Orange County Bar Associations — E-mail: npascale@drakeloeb.com

Benjamin M. Wilkinson — University of Rochester, B.A. (cum laude), 2007; Pace University, J.D. (cum laude), 2010 — Admitted to Bar, 2011, New York; U.S. District Court, Southern District of New York — Member New York State Bar Association; Member, Orange County Chamber of Commerce Young Professionals — E-mail: bwilkinson@drakeloeb.com

Taylor M. Palmer — Wheaton College, B.A. (magna cum laude), 2007; Pace University, J.D. (cum laude), 2012 — Admitted to Bar, 2012, New York — Member New York State Bar Association; Member, Orange County Chamber of Commerce Young Professionals — E-mail: tpalmer@drakeloeb.com

Alana R. Bartley — College of Holy Cross, B.A. (Dean's List), 2007; University of Connecticut, J.D., 2010 — Admitted to Bar, 2010, New York; 2011, New Jersey; U.S. District Court, District of New Jersey; U.S. District Court, Northern and Southern Districts of New York — Member New York State Bar Association — E-mail: abartley@drakeloeb.com

Lisa M. Card — Harvard College, B.A. (cum laude), 2001; Harvard Law School, J.D. (cum laude), 2004 — Admitted to Bar, 2004, New York; U.S. District Court, Eastern, Northern and Southern Districts of New York; U.S. Court of Appeals, Second Circuit — Member New York State Bar Association — E-mail: lcard@drakeloeb.com

NEW YORK † 8,175,133 New York Co.

Armienti, DeBellis, Guglielmo & Rhoden, LLP

39 Broadway, Suite 520
New York, New York 10006
  Telephone: 212-809-7074
  Fax: 212-809-7713
  E-Mail: info@adgrlaw.com
  http://adgrlaw.com

(Mineola, NY Office: 170 Old Country Road, Suite 607, 11501)
  (Tel: 516-877-1202)
  (Fax: 516-877-8099)
  (www.adgrlaw.com)
(Teaneck, NJ Office: 375 Cedar Lane, 07666)
  (Tel: 201-222-8588)
  (www.adgrlaw.com)

Insurance Defense, Toxic Torts, General Liability, Product Liability, Medical Malpractice, Property Damage, Construction Liability, Municipal Liability, Automobile, Reinsurance, Litigation, Coverage Issues, Coverage Analysis, Examinations Under Oath, Insurance Coverage, Insurance Litigation, Municipal Law, No-Fault, Tort Litigation

Insurance Clients

Associated Mutual Insurance Cooperative
Claims Service Bureau of New York
F.A. Richard & Associates, Inc.
Kemper Auto and Home
The Main Street America Group
Navigators Insurance Company
New York State Insurance Department, Liquidation Bureau
Brownstone Agency
Catholic Mutual Group
Everest National Insurance Company
GAB Robins North America, Inc.
Liberty Mutual Insurance Company
National Grange Mutual Insurance Company
RLI Insurance Company/Mt. Hawley Insurance Company
Starr Indemnity & Liability Company
Unitrin, Inc.
Wausau General Insurance Company
Unitrin Auto & Home Insurance Company
Utica First Insurance Company
Willis of New York, Inc.
Zurich Insurance Company

Non-Insurance Clients

Bovis Lend Lease Holdings, Inc.
City of New York
MTA Bus Company
New York City Transit Authority
Skanska Koch
Bovis Lend Lease, Inc.
Metropolitan Transportation Authority
Riverbay Corporation

Firm Members

Michael Armienti — 1953 — Hofstra University, B.B.A. (with highest honors), 1975; Pace University School of Law, J.D., 1979 — Admitted to Bar, 1980, New York; 1982, Florida; 1980, U.S. District Court, Eastern and Southern Districts of New York — Member New York State and Bronx County Bar Associations; New York State Insurance Association; Risk and Insurance Management Society, Inc.; New York Claims Association; New York State Trial Lawyers Association; New York County Lawyers Association — E-mail: marmienti@adgrlaw.com

Silvana DeBellis — 1958 — Fordham University, B.A., 1979; New York Law School, J.D., 1984 — Admitted to Bar, 1985, New York; 1989, U.S. District Court, Eastern and Southern Districts of New York — Member Bronx County Bar Association; Metropolitan Women's Bar Association; New York Democratic Judicial Screening Committee;; New York Claims Association; New York County Lawyers Association — E-mail: sdebellis@adgrlaw.com

John M. Guglielmo — 1956 — Brooklyn College, The City University of New York, B.A. (magna cum laude), 1978; St. John's University School of Law, J.D., 1981 — Admitted to Bar, 1982, New York; U.S. District Court, Eastern District of New York; 1997, U.S. District Court, Southern District of New York — Member New York Insurance Association (Guest Lecturer, Education Committee) — E-mail: jguglielmo@adgrlaw.com

Horace O. K. Rhoden — 1962 — John Jay College of Criminal Justice, B.S. (magna cum laude), 1987; Howard University School of Law, J.D., 1998 — Admitted to Bar, 1999, New York; New Jersey — Member Metropolitan Black Bar Association (Co-chair of the Voting Rights Committee, 2005); New York County Lawyers Association — New York County Judicial Screening Panel (2005), Arbitrator, Civil Court of the City of New York, Kings County. — Lieutenant, Surface Warfare Officer, U.S. Navy (Persian Gulf Veteran) — E-mail: hrhoden@adgrlaw.com

Vanessa M. Corchia — 1959 — Pace University, B.A. (summa cum laude), 1981; Brooklyn Law School, J.D., 1984 — Admitted to Bar, 1985, New York; 1986, U.S. District Court, Eastern and Southern Districts of New York; 1988, U.S. Tax Court — E-mail: vcorchia@adgrlaw.com

Michael J. Pagliano — New York University, B.S., 1983; Hofstra University School of Law, J.D., 1986 — Admitted to Bar, 1987, New York; 1999, U.S. District Court, Eastern and Southern Districts of New York; U.S. Supreme Court — Member Columbia Lawyers of Nassau County, Inc.; Business Network International's Plainview Chapter (President); Business Network International's Garden City Chapter (President, 2004-2005); Northwest Suffolk Civil Coalition (Executive Board Member) — E-mail: mpagliano@adgrlaw.com

Associates

James J. Dunning
Harriet Wong
Daryl L. Parker
Jerry Granata
Ryan H. McAllister
Danielle L. Tabankin
Erin M. McGinnis
Susan D. Smodish
Dawn M. Miller
Michael L. Moriello
Matthew A. Windman
Gregory R. Picciano
Thomas J. Reape Jr.
Michelle S. Regan

Callahan & Fusco, LLC

40 Exchange Place, 18th Floor
New York, New York 10005
  Telephone: 212-448-9570
  Fax: 212-448-9772
  www.callahanfusco.com

NEW YORK

Callahan & Fusco, LLC, New York, NY (Continued)
(Roseland, NJ Office*: 103 Eishenhower Parkway, Suite 400, 07068)
 (Tel: 973-618-9770)
 (Fax: 973-618-9772)
 (E-Mail: cfusco@callahanfusco.com)
(Doylestown, PA Office: 196 West Ashland Street, 18901)
 (Tel: 267-895-1767)
 (Fax: 267-895-1768)

Insurance Defense, Cargo, Carrier Defense, Casualty, Civil Litigation, Commercial Law, Construction Law, Contracts, Inland Marine, Insurance Law, Labor and Employment, Motor Carriers, Municipal Law, Personal Injury, Premises Liability, Product Liability, Public Entities, Reinsurance, Risk Management, School Law, Toxic Torts, Transportation, Workers' Compensation

(See listing under Roseland, NJ for additional information)

Conway, Farrell, Curtin & Kelly, P.C.
48 Wall Street
New York, New York 10005
 Telephone: 212-785-2929
 Fax: 212-785-7229
 E-Mail: mail@conwayfarrell.com
 www.conwayfarrell.com

Trial and Appellate Practice, Labor and Employment, Construction Law, Real Estate, Insurance Coverage, Insurance Defense

Insurance Clients
QBE Insurance Company   Travelers Insurance Companies

Firm Members
Kevin J. Kelly — St. John's University, B.A., 1968; St. John's University School of Law, J.D., 1974 — Admitted to Bar, 1975, New York; U.S. District Court, Eastern and Southern Districts of New York; U.S. Court of Appeals, Second Circuit

Dorsey & Whitney LLP
CBS Black Rock Building
51 West 52nd Street
New York, New York 10019-6119
 Telephone: 212-415-9256
 Fax: 877-408-8286
 E-Mail: feeley.pat@dorsey.com
 www.dorsey.com/insurance

Insurance Law, Product Liability, Commercial Litigation, Appellate, Life, Disability, Energy Regulation, Environmental

Firm Profile: Our attorneys have extensive experience in the areas of insurance law and regulation, coverage counseling, and litigation. We have provided advice and represented clients in a variety of matters, including: property damage, business interruption, commercial general liability, errors and omissions liability and employment practices liability.

Insurance Clients
Employers Insurance Company of Wausau
Phoenix Life Insurance Company
The Guardian Life Insurance Company of America

Partner
Patrick J. Feeley — State University of New York at Oneonta, B.A., History (with high honors), 1977; Harvard Law School, J.D. (cum laude), 1986 —

Dorsey & Whitney LLP, New York, NY (Continued)
Admitted to Bar, 1986, New York — Member New York State Bar Association; Federation of Defense and Corporate Counsel; Defense Research Institute

Fitzpatrick & Hunt, Tucker, Collier, Pagano, Aubert, LLP
Tower 49
Twelve East 49th Street, 31st Floor
New York, New York 10017
 Telephone: 212-937-4000
 Fax: 212-937-4050
 E-Mail: info@fitzhunt.com
 www.fitzhunt.com

(Los Angeles, CA Office*: US Bank Tower, 633 West Fifth Street, 60th Floor, 90071)
 (Tel: 213-873-2100)
 (Fax: 213-873-2125)
(Princeton, NJ Office*: Forrestal Village, 116 Village Boulevard, Suite 200, 08540)
 (Tel: 609-606-6940)
 (Fax: 609-606-6941)

Alternative Dispute Resolution, Appellate Practice, Arbitration, Aviation, Class Actions, First and Third Party Defense, Insurance Litigation, International Law, Mediation, Product Liability, Reinsurance, Toxic Torts, Mass Disasters

Firm Profile: Fitzpatrick & Hunt specializes in products liability defense and claims prevention. Among the experienced product and services defense lawyers in our Firm are those with degrees and backgrounds in engineering and other technical fields. We provide advisory consultation to worldwide insurance markets and product manufacturers.

Insurance Clients
ACE
Aspen Insurance UK Limited
Marsh Inc.
XL London Market Ltd.
Allianz Global Corporate & Specialty
Talbot Underwriting Ltd.

Managing Partner
Garrett J. Fitzpatrick — University of Dayton, B.S., 1970; St. John's University School of Law, J.D., 1973 — Admitted to Bar, 1974, New York — Tel: 212-937-4002 — E-mail: garrett.fitzpatrick@fitzhunt.com

Equity Partners
Stephen Tucker — University of Florida College of Engineering, B.S. (with high honors), 1975; University of Florida College of Law, J.D., 1978 — Admitted to Bar, 1979, Georgia; 1981, New York — Tel: 212-937-4003 — E-mail: stephen.tucker@fitzhunt.com

Ralph V. Pagano — Stevens Institute of Technology, B.E., 1984; M.E., 1988; Fordham University School of Law, J.D., 1993; Temple University, LL.M., 1997 — Admitted to Bar, 1993, New York; New Jersey; Pennsylvania — Tel: 212-937-4004 — E-mail: ralph.pagano@fitzhunt.com

Partners
Roberta Miranda — Fordham University, B.A. (cum laude), 2001; Fordham University School of Law, J.D., 2004 — Admitted to Bar, 2005, New York — Tel: 212-937-4031 — E-mail: roberta.miranda@fitzhunt.com

Tara E. Nicola — University of Connecticut, B.A., 2000; Seton Hall University School of Law, J.D. (cum laude), 2003 — Order of the Coif — Admitted to Bar, 2003, New Jersey; 2005, New York — Tel: 212-937-4026 — E-mail: tara.nicola@fitzhunt.com

Thomas R. Pantino — Stevens Institute of Technology, B.E., 1984; St. John's University School of Law, J.D., 1992 — Admitted to Bar, 1993, New York — Tel: 212-937-4005 — E-mail: thomas.pantino@fitzhunt.com

Jason L. Vincent — University of Connecticut, B.A., 1993; Seton Hall University School of Law, J.D., 1996 — Admitted to Bar, 1996, New Jersey; 1997, New York; 1998, Connecticut — Tel: 212-937-4073 — E-mail: jason.vincent@fitzhunt.com

NEW YORK

Fitzpatrick & Hunt, Tucker, Collier, Pagano, Aubert, LLP, New York, NY (Continued)

Associates

Paul N. Bowles III
Nelson Camacho

French & Casey, LLP

29 Broadway, 27th Floor
New York, New York 10006
Telephone: 212-797-3544
Fax: 212-797-3545
Mobile: 917-837-0355
E-Mail: jfrench@frenchcasey.com
www.frenchcasey.com

(Douglaston, NY Office: 42-24 235th Street, 11363)
(Tel: 718-428-5292)
(Fax: 718-352-5706)

Insurance Defense, Product Liability, Construction Litigation, Employer Liability, Premises Liability, Negligence, Coverage Issues, Environmental Coverage, Subrogation, Professional Liability, Commercial Litigation, Railroad Litigation, Trusts and Estates, Probate Litigation

Insurance Clients

ACE USA
Associated Mutual Insurance Cooperative
Chubb Services Corporation
Claims Service Bureau of New York
Commercial Underwriters Insurance Company
Erie Insurance Group
Evanston Insurance Company
Generali - US Branch
Great American Custom Insurance Services
International Managers, Inc.
Lexington Insurance Company
Midland Claims Administrators, Inc.
Summit Underwriting Management, L.L.C.
U.S. Adjustment Corporation
UTC Risk Management Services, Inc.
American Specialty Insurance Services, Inc.
Chubb Insurance Company
Claims Administration Corporation
CNA Excess and Select
CNA Insurance Companies
Crawford & Company
Endurance U.S. Insurance Operations
Farmland Mutual Insurance Company
Great West Casualty Company
Gulf Insurance Group
K & K Insurance Group, Inc.
Liberty International Underwriters
NAS Insurance Group
Specialty Risk Services, Inc. (SRS)
United National Insurance Company
USF Insurance Company
Zurich American Insurance Group

Non-Insurance Clients

The Ameris Corporation
Gretchen Bellinger Inc
Morganti Group, Inc.
New York & Atlantic Railway
Procter & Gamble Company
The Children's Place
McLarens Young International
Navillus Construction Inc.
Nokia
The Salvation Army

Partners

Joseph A. French — 1956 — The University of North Carolina at Chapel Hill, B.A. (with highest honors), 1979; The Catholic University of America, Columbus School of Law, J.D., 1983 — Catholic University Law Review (1982-1983) — Admitted to Bar, 1984, New York; 1988, U.S. District Court, Eastern and Southern Districts of New York — Member New York State and Queens County Bar Associations; New York County Lawyers Association — Special Master, New York County Supreme Court (1989-Present) — E-mail: jfrench@frenchcasey.com

Moira E. Casey — 1957 — University of Vermont, B.A., 1979; The Catholic University of America, Columbus School of Law, J.D., 1983 — Production Editor, Catholic University Law Review (1981-1983) — Admitted to Bar, 1984, New York; 1988, U.S. District Court, Eastern and Southern Districts of New York — Member New York State Bar Association — E-mail: mcasey@frenchcasey.com

Susan A. Romano — 1971 — Villanova University, B.A. (with honors), 1993; Albany Law School of Union University, J.D., 1996 — Admitted to Bar, 1997, New York; 1998, U.S. District Court, Eastern and Southern Districts of New York — Member New York State Bar Association — E-mail: sromano@frenchcasey.com

French & Casey, LLP, New York, NY (Continued)

Douglas R. Rosenzweig — 1977 — University of Florida, B.A., 2000; University of North Carolina at Chapel Hill School of Law, J.D., 2003 — Admitted to Bar, 2004, New York; 2006, U.S. District Court, Eastern and Southern Districts of New York — Member New York County Lawyers Association; National Association of Railroad Trial Counsel — E-mail: drosenzweig@frenchcasey.com

Lance E. Benowitz — 1970 — Franklin & Marshall College, B.A., 1991; University of Southern California School of Law, J.D., 1994 — Admitted to Bar, 1995, California; 1996, New York — Member American and New York State Bar Associations — E-mail: lbenowitz@frenchcasey.com

Of Counsel

Barry Meade — 1953 — St. John's University, B.S., 1987; St. John's University School of Law, J.D., 1997 — Admitted to Bar, 1997, New Jersey; 1998, New York; 1997, U.S. District Court, Eastern and Southern Districts of New York; U.S. District Court, District of New Jersey — Member New York State Bar Association — E-mail: bmeade@frenchcasey.com

Associates

Jenna E. Elkind — 1982 — Barnard College, Columbia University, B.A. (cum laude), 2004; Boston University School of Law, J.D., 2007 — Admitted to Bar, 2008, New York; New Jersey; 2009, U.S. District Court, Eastern and Southern Districts of New York; U.S. District Court, District of New Jersey — Member New York State Bar Association; New York County Lawyers Association — Languages: Russian — E-mail: jelkind@frenchcasey.com

Ruth Kavanagh — 1980 — Seton Hall University, B.A. (magna cum laude), 2002; Seton Hall University School of Law, J.D., 2005 — Admitted to Bar, 2005, New Jersey; 2006, New York; 2005, U.S. District Court, District of New Jersey — Member New Jersey State Bar Association — E-mail: rkavanagh@frenchcasey.com

Karen M. Mahon — 1977 — Rider University, B.S., 2000; Seton Hall University School of Law, J.D., 2006 — Admitted to Bar, 2006, New Jersey; 2008, New York; 2009, U.S. District Court, District of New Jersey — Member New Jersey State and New York State Bar Associations — E-mail: kmahon@frenchcasey.com

Gallo Vitucci Klar LLP

90 Broad Street, 3rd Floor
New York, New York 10004
Telephone: 212-683-7100
Fax: 212-683-5555
www.gvlaw.com

(Hackensack, NJ Office*: 1 University Plaza, Suite 306, 07601)
(Tel: 201-343-1166)
(Irvington, NY Office: One Bridge Street, Suite 140, 10533)

Commercial Litigation, Construction Law, Dram Shop, Employment Law, Environmental Law, General Liability, Hospitality, Insurance Coverage, Maritime Law, Medical Malpractice, Municipal Liability, No-Fault, Personal Injury, Personal Injury Protection (PIP), Premises Liability, Product Liability, Professional Liability, School Law, Subrogation, Toxic Torts, Transportation, Trucking, Elevators and Escalator Liability, Restaurant Liability

Firm Profile: Gallo Vitucci Klar, LLP is a full service litigation firm having an extensive practice dedicated to providing experienced and innovative legal services to both long-term and new clients. Our firm consists of experienced trial and appellate attorneys that offer the highest quality legal representation in defending and counseling corporations and insurance companies.

Insurance Clients

Arch Insurance Group
Lancer Insurance Company
AXIS Insurance

Non-Insurance Clients

ABM Industries, Inc.
Coach USA

Senior Partners

Richard J. Gallo — Fordham University, B.A. (cum laude), 1989; St. John's University School of Law, J.D., 1992 — Admitted to Bar, 1993, New York; U.S. District Court, Eastern and Southern Districts of New York — Member

NEW YORK

Gallo Vitucci Klar LLP, New York, NY (Continued)

Council of Litigation Management (CLM); Torts, Insurance and Compensation Law (TICL) — Practice Areas: Transportation; Construction Law; Premises Liability; Insurance Coverage

Matthew J. Vitucci — St. John's University, B.A. (cum laude), 1984; St. John's University School of Law, J.D., 1987 — Admitted to Bar, 1987, New York; U.S. District Court, Eastern and Southern Districts of New York — Member New York State Bar Association; Member, Torts, Insurance & Compensation Law (TICL); Trucking Industry Defense Association — Practice Areas: Transportation

Howard P. Klar — Emory University, B.B.A. Accounting, 1986; Boston University School of Law, J.D., 1989 — Admitted to Bar, 1990, New York — Member Council of Litigation Management (CLM) — New York Super Lawyers, Insurance Defense, 2012, Metro Division — Practice Areas: Commercial Litigation; Insurance Coverage; Premises Liability; Construction Law; Transportation; Professional Liability; Product Liability

Partners

Howard L. Cogan
Jeffrey L. Richman
Kristen A. Murphy
Heather C. Ragone
Chad E. Sjoquist
Mary L. Maloney
Yolanda L. Ayala
Matthew P. Levy
Joseph F. Dunne
Stephen A. Denburg

Associates

Sae-Eun Ahn
Samantha Brooks
Jessica A. Clark
Laura M. Colatrella
Maria T. Ehrlich
Andrew N. Fluger
Terry Holmes-Nelson
Rick C. Kim
Thomas B. Lim
Daniel P. Mevorach
Kimberly A. Ricciardi
Alana J. Szemer
Alida Verdino
Sarah R. Allison
Jeremy B. Cantor
Rozaly Cohen
James V. Deegan
Maria Jorgelina Foglietta
Susan K. Hanley
Alex M. Howard
Andrea Klienman
Misty D. Marris
William Parra
Joseph Scarglato
Martha J. Vasquez
Cindy M. Yu

Of Counsel

Eliot R. Claus
Kalliopi P. Kousis
Steven DeMaggio
John T. Mahr

Gartner + Bloom, P.C.

801 Second Avenue, 15th Floor
New York, New York 10017
Telephone: 212-759-5800
Fax: 212-759-5842
www.gbglaw.com

(Springfield, NJ Office: 675 Morris Avenue, 07081)
(Tel: 973-921-0300)
(Fax: 973-921-0319)

Established: 1994

Insurance Defense, Trial Practice, General Liability, Environmental Liability, Property and Casualty, Workers' Compensation, Subrogation, Construction Defect, Insurance Coverage, Commercial Litigation, Commercial Auto Defense

Insurance Clients

Admiral Insurance Company
American Safety Insurance Holdings, Ltd.
Atlantic Mutual Companies
AXIS U.S. Insurance
Clarendon Insurance Group
C&S Specialty Underwriters
Farmers Mutual Insurance Company
First Mercury Insurance Company
Greater New York Mutual Insurance Company
American Claims Management, Inc.
American Safety Risk Retention Group, Inc.
Brownstone Agency
CNA Insurance Companies
Enstar (US) Inc.
Fireman's Fund Insurance Companies
Global Indemnity Group, Inc.
Harleysville Insurance Company
Knightbrook Insurance Company

Gartner + Bloom, P.C., New York, NY (Continued)

Legion/Villanova Insurance (In Liquidation)
Montpelier US Insurance Company
Mutual Marine Office, Inc.
National Indemnity Company
New York Property Insurance Underwriting Association
Preferred Contractors Insurance Company Risk Retention Group, LLC
State National Insurance Company, Inc.
West Coast Casualty Insurance
York Claims Service, Inc.
Markel Corporation Group
Midlands Claim Administrators, Inc.
National Claims Services, Inc.
Navigators Insurance Company
North American Risk Services
Praetorian Financial Group
Prime Specialty, Inc.
QBE the Americas
RiverStone Claims Management, LLC
Travelers Insurance Companies
XL Group
Zurich North America

Partners

Stuart F. Gartner — 1945 — Long Island University, B.A., 1967; State University of New York at Buffalo Law School, J.D., 1970 — Phi Alpha Theta — Admitted to Bar, 1971, New York; 1974, U.S. District Court, Southern District of New York — Member New York State Bar Association; American Trial Lawyers Association; New York State Trial Lawyers Association — E-mail: sgartner@gbglaw.com

Kenneth A. Bloom — 1956 — Cornell University, B.S., 1978; American University, Washington College of Law, J.D., 1981 — Admitted to Bar, 1981, District of Columbia; 1982, New York; 1990, Pennsylvania; 1983, U.S. District Court, Eastern and Southern Districts of New York; 1985, U.S. District Court, Eastern District of Michigan; U.S. Supreme Court; 1988, U.S. Court of Appeals, Second Circuit — Member American Bar Association (Tort and Insurance Practice Section; Alternate Dispute Resolution Section); New York State, Pennsylvania, and Brooklyn Bar Associations; District of Columbia Bar; New York State Former District Attorneys Association; New York County Lawyers Association — Assistant District Attorney, Kings County, New York (1981-1982) — Languages: Spanish, Hebrew — E-mail: kbloom@gbglaw.com

Arthur P. Xanthos — 1964 — Williams College, B.A., 1986; Fordham Law School, J.D., 1989 — Fordham Urban Law Journal (Managing Editor, 1988-1989) — Admitted to Bar, 1991, New York; New Jersey; U.S. District Court, District of New Jersey — "D&O Insurance: Disbursement of Insurance Money Covering an Insured's Legal Expenses as Incurred, " XVI Fordham Urban Law Journal III, cited in New York Law Journal (April, 1989) — Languages: French, Greek — E-mail: arthur@gbglaw.com

Christine M. Messina — 1972 — Boston University, B.A., 1994; St. John's University School of Law, J.D., 1997 — Judicial Law Clerk to the Hon. Marlene Lynch Ford, Superior Court of New Jersey; Ocean Vicinage (1997-1998) — Admitted to Bar, 1997, New Jersey; 1998, New York — Member New York State Bar Association; New York County Lawyers Association — New Jersey State Certified Mediator — E-mail: cmessina@gbglaw.com

Marc Shortino — 1972 — Rutgers University, B.A., 1994; Seton Hall University School of Law, J.D., 1998 — Judicial Law Clerk to the Honorable Stephen F. Smith, Superior Court of New Jersey, Civil Division, Morris Vicinage, 1998-1999 — Admitted to Bar, 1998, New Jersey; 1999, New York; 1998, U.S. District Court, District of New Jersey — Certified New Jersey State Mediator — E-mail: mshortino@gbglaw.com

Special Counsel

Douglas A. Gingold — 1966 — University of Delaware, B.A., 1988; New York Law School, J.D., 1991 — Admitted to Bar, 1991, New York; New Jersey; U.S. District Court, District of New Jersey; 1992, U.S. District Court, Eastern and Southern Districts of New York — E-mail: dgingold@gbglaw.com

Associates

Susan P. Mahon — 1958 — University of Delaware, B.A., 1980; Albany Law School of Union University, J.D., 1989 — Admitted to Bar, 1989, New Jersey; 1990, New York; 1991, U.S. District Court, Eastern and Southern Districts of New York; 2005, U.S. Court of Appeals, Third Circuit — Member New York State and New Jersey State Bar Associations; Maritime Law Association of the United States — E-mail: smahon@gbglaw.com

Alissa A. Mendys — 1978 — Boston College, B.A., 2000; Emory University School of Law, J.D., 2004 — Admitted to Bar, 2004, New Jersey; 2006, New York; 2004, U.S. District Court, District of New Jersey — E-mail: amendys@gbglaw.com

Of Counsel

Sharon Rosenthal — 1971 — Syracuse University, B.S., 1993; New York Law School, J.D., 1997 — Admitted to Bar, 1997, New Jersey; 1998, New York;

Gartner + Bloom, P.C., New York, NY (Continued)

U.S. District Court, Eastern and Southern Districts of New York — Member American and New York State Bar Associations; New York County Trial Lawyers Association; New York State Trial Lawyers Association

Goodman & Jacobs LLP

75 Broad Street, 30th Floor
New York, New York 10004-2415
Telephone: 212-385-1191
Fax: 646-559-6074
www.goodmanjacobs.com

Established: 1992

Insurance Coverage, Insurance Defense, Declaratory Judgments, Agent/Broker Liability, Bodily Injury, Toxic Torts, Reinsurance, Coverage Issues, Arbitration, Professional Liability, Directors and Officers Liability, Discrimination, Sexual Harassment, Employment Law, Appellate Practice

Firm Profile: Goodman & Jacobs LLP specializes in civil litigation, the defense of insureds and self-insureds, representation of insurance companies and reinsurance intermediaries in coverage, bad faith actions and arbitrations. In addition to representing numerous insurance companies, we represent a large real estate developer in all aspects of its litigation, a major university in tort, discrimination and insurance coverage actions, and several major insurance brokerage firms. The firm also represents individuals and corporations in coverage issues with insurers.

Insurance Clients

ACE Bermuda Insurance, Ltd.
American Country Insurance Company
Chubb Group of Insurance Companies
Everest National Insurance Company
Leone Claims Management, Inc.
Starr Indemnity & Liability Company
AIG Technical Services, Inc.
AON Corporation
Burlington Insurance Company
Cunningham Lindsey Claims Management, Inc.
First Financial Insurance Company
Frontier Insurance Company
MCIC Vermont, Inc.

Non-Insurance Clients

Columbia University
Lefrak Organization Inc.
The New York and Presbyterian Hospital
Extell Development Company
McNeil & Company, Inc.
Parc Vendome Condominiums
Ram Caterers of Flatbush, LLC

Partners

Judith F. Goodman — State University of New York at Binghamton, B.A., 1971; New York University, M.A., 1975; New York University School of Law, J.D., 1979 — Staff Member, Annual Survey of American Law (1977-1978) — Admitted to Bar, 1980, New York; U.S. District Court, Eastern and Southern Districts of New York; U.S. Court of Appeals, Second Circuit; U.S. Supreme Court — Member American Bar Association (TIPS Insurance Coverage Litigation Committee Annual Programs, Speaker 2006 and 2007, Chair, 2008); New York State Bar Association (Frequent Lecturer on Insurance Issues; Chair, "Personal Lines" CLE Program, 2002 (NYC); Statewide Chair, "Commercial Lines Insurance" CLE Program, 2004); New York County Lawyers Association (Vice-Chair, Tort Law Section, 1997-1998) — "Employees Lose Coverage for Negligent Supervision," New York Law Journal, August 25, 1997 (reprinted in Andrews Insurance Coverage Litigation Reporter, Employment Reported, Sexual Harassment Litigation Reporter); "Insurer's Right to Reimbursement for Defense Costs When There is No Defense Obligation," New York Law Journal, February 4, 1992; "First Amendment Protection Loses Ground," Leader's Product Liability Newsletter (co-authored), May 1985; "Training the Legal Assistant for Litigation Practice in a Large Firm," New York State Bar Journal, April 1985; "Television's Sex Crime: The Treatment of Women in Network Programming," New York Law Journal, May 11, 1978; "Attorney Malpractice: What it is, How it is Adjudicated and How Not to Do It," Co-author with Sue C. Jacobs; "New York and Delaware Business Entities," West 2001, chapter 33 "Insurance"; Transactional Lawyers Deskbook Advising Business Entities: West 2000, Chapter 8 "Reservation of Rights Waiver and Estoppel"; Law and Practice Insurance Coverage Litigation, West 1997, Chapter 33 "Insurance"; "Attorney Malpractice," The Brief, Winter 1998; Co-author with Sue C.

Goodman & Jacobs LLP, New York, NY (Continued)

Jacobs, "Law and Practice of Insurance Coverage Litigation," Chapter 8 Reservation of Rights, West, 2000 — Speaker: ABA Annual Meeting, 1995; Elected, "New York Super Lawyer," Insurance Coverage Specialty, 2006-2013; Appointed member Editorial Board, CGL Reporter, 2005-2007; Appointed Member Editorial Board of The Brief, published by the Tort and Insurance Practice Section of the ABA, 1987-1995; Appointee, TIPS Long Range Planning Committee, 1995-1998; Chair, Publication Sub-Committee, 1996-1998; Chair, TIPS Committee Coordinating Group, 1998, 1998; Editor-in-Chief, TortSource, 2003-2006 (ABA/TIPS publication); Member, TortSource Editorial Board, 2000-2003; Member, ABA/TIPS Publication Editorial Board (2006-Present); Member, ABA/TIPS Continuing Legal Education Board (2006-Present); Chair, ABA/TIPS Insurance Coverage Litigation Committee Annual Program (2008)

Sue C. Jacobs — Hunter College, B.A. (cum laude, with honors), 1960; American University, M.A. (with honors), 1967; Pace University, J.D., 1979 — Admitted to Bar, 1980, New York; U.S. District Court, Southern District of New York; 1985, U.S. Court of Appeals, Third Circuit; 1992, U.S. District Court, Eastern District of New York; 1996, U.S. Court of Appeals, Second Circuit — Member American Bar Association (Litigation Section, Torts and Insurance Practice Coverage Section); New York State Bar Association (Committee on Association Insurance, 2003-Present; Chair, Personal Lines CLE Program, 2005); New York County Lawyers' Association (Board of Directors, 1995-Present; Executive Committee, 1997-Present, Treasurer, 2002-2003; Chair, Insurance Comm — Columnist, Professional Liability, New York Law Journal, 1993-Present; Co-Author (with Judith F. Goodman): "Insurance", Transactional Lawyer's Deskbook: Advising Business Entities (West Publishing Co., 2001); Chapter 33, The New York and Delaware Business Entities: Choice, Information, Operations, Financing and Acquisitions (West Publishing Co., 1997); Law and Practice of Insurance Coverage Litigation, Chapter 8 "Reservation of Rights, Waiver and Estoppel" (West Publishing Co., 2000); Co-Author (with Judith F. Goodman): "Attorney Malpractice," The Brief (Winter, 1998); Co-Author: "Attorney Malpractice: What it is and How to Avoid It"; Co-Author: "Liability Insurance Coverage Principles," ALI-ABA; Lecturer and Author: "Attorney-Malpractice" 1998, 1999; "The Duty to Defend" - 14th, 13th Annual Insurance, Excess and Reinsurance Coverage Disputes Seminar, 1997, 1996 PLI; Lecturer, and Co-Author, "Professional Liability Coverage Issues" - 11th Annual Insurance, Excess and Reinsurance Coverage Disputes Seminar, 1994 PLI; Resource Materials - Civil Practice and Litigation in Federal and State Courts, Third and Fourth Editions; "The Attorney's Duty to Non-Clients" appeared in the Spring 1997 Quality Assurance Review, published by Minet; Contributor: Insurance Excess and Reinsurance Coverage Disputes, rev. ed. 1983, 1986, 1987, ed.; Author and Panelist: "Legal and Accounting Malpractice Litigation", Continuing Legal Education, Satellite Network, 1993 — Lecturer, New York County Lawyers' Association, Solo and Small Firm Seminar, Annual Program, 2000-2009; Lecturer, American Medical Women's Association, 2013; Lecturer, New York State Bar Association Insurance CLE Program, 2004-2007; Lecturer, Association of the Bar of the City of New York, Insurance Coverage, 2001, 2003; Practicing Law Institute; Guardian, Family Court, Westchester County, New York, 1980-1984; Arbitrator, Civil Court, City of New York, 1985-Present; Winner, President's Medal, New York Young Lawyers' Association, 2013; American College of Coverage and Extracontractual Counsel

Lester Chanin — Hunter College, B.A., 1984; Rutgers University School of Law, J.D., 1990 — Admitted to Bar, 1990, New Jersey; 1992, New York; 1990, U.S. District Court, District of New Jersey; 1993, U.S. District Court, Southern District of New York — Member New York County Lawyers Association — Co-Author: "The Surety's Rights of Assignment and Power of Attorney Under General Indemnity Agreements", 31 Tort and Insurance Law Journal 17 (1995)

Thomas J. Cirone — Hamilton College, B.A. (magna cum laude), 1987; University of Miami, J.D. (cum laude), 1990 — Admitted to Bar, 1991, New York; 1995, U.S. District Court, Eastern and Southern Districts of New York; 1998, U.S. Court of Appeals, Second Circuit — Member New York County Lawyers Association (Co-Chair, Lawyers Professional Liability Committee, 2002) — New York Metro Super Lawyers for General Litigation, Insurance Coverage and Personal Injury Defense, 2011, 2013

Associate

Howard M. Wagner — University of Maryland, College Park, B.A., 1994; Boston University School of Law, J.D., 1997 — G. Joseph Tauro Scholar — Admitted to Bar, 1999, New York — Contributor, Professional Liability, New York Law Journal, 2012-Present

Gruvman, Giordano & Glaws, LLP

61 Broadway, Suite 2715
New York, New York 10006
Telephone: 212-269-2353
Fax: 212-269-2354
E-Mail: info@g3law.com
www.g3law.com

Established: 2002

Insurance Defense, Litigation, Coverage Issues, Professional Liability, Medical Liability, Product Liability, Toxic Torts, Construction Liability, Appellate Practice, Trial Practice, Municipal Liability

Insurance Clients

Ag Workers Mutual Auto Insurance Company
CNA Insurance Company
International Managers, Inc.
Lloyd's
NAS Insurance Group
St. Paul Travelers
Sedgwick CMS
Zurich North America
Broadspire
Cambridge Integrated Services
ESIS
Lexington Insurance Company/AIG
New York State Insurance Department, Liquidation Bureau
SUA Insurance Company

Non-Insurance Clients

Johnson & Johnson
Kraft Foods, Inc.
Total Safety Consulting, LLC
Kohl's Department Stores, Inc.
New York City Transit Authority
Walgreen Co.

Members

Paul S. Gruvman — 1964 — State University of New York at Stony Brook, B.A., 1986; Rutgers University School of Law-Camden, J.D., 1989 — Admitted to Bar, 1989, New Jersey; 1990, New York; 1989, U.S. District Court, District of New Jersey; 1996, U.S. District Court, Eastern and Southern Districts of New York — Member American, New York State and Brooklyn Bar Associations; Defense Research Institute; Defense Association of New York — Languages: Spanish

Louis P. Giordano — 1968 — State University of New York at Binghamton, B.A., 1990; Brooklyn Law School, J.D., 1993 — Admitted to Bar, 1994, New York; 2000, U.S. District Court, Eastern and Southern Districts of New York — Member Brooklyn Bar Association

Charles T. Glaws — 1961 — Tulane University, B.A., 1983; Tufts University, M.A., 1985; Brooklyn Law School, J.D., 1991 — Admitted to Bar, 1992, New York; 1995, U.S. District Court, Eastern and Southern Districts of New York; 2000, U.S. Court of Appeals, Second Circuit; U.S. Supreme Court — Member Brooklyn Bar Association; New York County Lawyers Association

Gwertzman, Lefkowitz & Burman

80 Broad Street, 16th Floor
New York, New York 10004
Telephone: 212-968-1001
Fax: 212-344-4140
E-Mail: postmaster@gwertzmanlaw.com

Insurance Defense, Insurance Law, Trial Practice, Appellate Practice, Fire, Inland Marine, Subrogation, Investigations

Insurance Clients

Adriatic Insurance Company
American Home Assurance Company
CNA Insurance Companies
Commerce and Industry Insurance Company
General Star Management Company
Greater New York Group
Kemper Insurance Companies
Lexington Insurance Company
Lloyds New York Insurance Company
Allianz Insurance Company
American International Group, Inc.
American Motorists Insurance Company
CUMIS Insurance Society, Inc.
Generali Group
Government Employees Insurance Company
Insurance Company of the State of Pennsylvania
Liberty Mutual Insurance Company
Maryland Commercial Insurance Group

Gwertzman, Lefkowitz & Burman, New York, NY
(Continued)

National Grange Mutual Insurance Company
Old Republic Surety Company
PEMCO Mutual Insurance Company
Preferred Risk Mutual Insurance Company
St. Paul Coverage Group
Underwriters at Lloyd's, London
National Union Fire Insurance Company
Patrons Mutual Insurance Company of Connecticut
Preferred Mutual Insurance Company
Providence Washington Insurance Company
Utica First Insurance Company

Non-Insurance Clients

Essential Services and Programs, Inc.
IRM Services, Inc.

Firm Members

Max J. Gwertzman — (1906-1987)

Ellen Lefkowitz — 1949 — Brooklyn College, B.A., 1971; New York Law School, J.D., 1976 — Admitted to Bar, 1977, New York; 1977, U.S. District Court, Eastern and Southern Districts of New York — Member New York State Bar Association; New York County Lawyers Association

Roberta Burman — 1947 — Queens College of the City University of New York, B.A., 1969; New York Law School, J.D., 1979 — Admitted to Bar, 1979, New York; 1979, U.S. District Court, Eastern and Southern Districts of New York — Member New York State Bar Association; New York County Lawyers Association

(This firm is also listed in the Subrogation section of this directory)

Hill, Betts & Nash, LLP

1 World Financial Center
200 Liberty Street, 26th Floor
New York, New York 10281
Telephone: 212-839-7000
Fax: 212-466-0514
Mobile: 917-864-9673
www.hillbetts.com

(Fort Lauderdale, FL Office*: 1515 SE 17th Street, Suite A115, 33316)
 (Tel: 954-522-2271)
 (Fax: 954-522-2355)

Established: 1898

Insurance Defense, Personal Injury, Premises Liability, Jones Act, Longshore and Harbor Workers' Compensation, Construction Law, Product Liability, Property Damage, Environmental Law, Inland and Ocean Marine, Coverage Issues, Reinsurance, Subrogation, Fidelity and Surety, General Passenger Claim Defense, Cruise Passenger

Insurance Clients

A. Bilbrough & Co. Ltd.
Allianz Global Corporate & Specialty
Charles Taylor P&I Management
Gard AS
Gard (North America) Inc.
Shipowners Claims Bureau, Inc.
Steamship Mutual Underwriting Association Limited
AI Marine Adjusters, Inc.
Berkley Offshore Underwriting Managers, LLC
Chubb & Son, a division of Federal Insurance Company
Liberty International Underwriters
Skuld
XL Insurance

Non-Insurance Clients

Liberty Maritime Corporation
Royal Caribbean Cruises, Ltd.
SEACOR Holdings, Inc.
The Vane Brothers Company
McAllister Towing & Transportation Co., Inc.
Sealift, Inc.

Principals

Mark M. Jaffe — 1941 — The Wharton School of the University of Pennsylvania, B.S.Ec., 1962; Columbia Law School, J.D., 1965 — Admitted to Bar, 1965, New Jersey; 1968, Louisiana; 1970, New York; U.S. District Court, Eastern and Southern Districts of New York; U.S. District Court, Eastern District of Louisiana; U.S. Court of Appeals, Second and Eleventh Circuits; U.S.

Hill, Betts & Nash, LLP, New York, NY (Continued)

Court of Military Appeals; U.S. Supreme Court — Member American, New York State, New Jersey State and Louisiana State Bar Associations; Association of the Bar of the City of New York; The Maritime Law Association of the United States — E-mail: mjaffe@hillbetts.com

Gregory W. O'Neill — 1945 — Fordham University, B.A., 1967; Fordham University School of Law, J.D., 1972 — Admitted to Bar, 1973, New York — Member New York State Bar Association; The Maritime Law Association of the United States — Languages: French — E-mail: goneill@hillbetts.com

Partners

James D. Kleiner — 1950 — University of Paris - Sorbonne, Certificat de Langue Francaise, 1970; The London School of Economics and Political Science, LL.B. (with honors), 1973; University of London, England, LL.M., 1975 — Admitted to Bar, 1974, England; Wales; 1979, New York; U.S. District Court, Eastern, Northern, Southern and Western Districts of New York — Member American Bar Association; Association of the Bar of the City of New York (Committee on Admiralty, 1984-1987); Maritime Law Association of the United States (Committee on Intergovernmental Organizations); Association of Average Adjusters; American Arbitration Association (Commercial Panel of Arbitrators) — Languages: Spanish, French — E-mail: jkleiner@hillbetts.com

Gordon S. Arnott — 1954 — United States Merchant Marine Academy, B.S. (cum laude), 1977; Syracuse University College of Law, J.D. (magna cum laude), 1985 — Admitted to Bar, 1986, New York; Pennsylvania; New Jersey; U.S. District Court, Eastern and Southern Districts of New York; 1995, U.S. Court of Appeals, First Circuit; U.S. Supreme Court — Member Maritime Law Association of the United States — E-mail: garnott@hillbetts.com

Mary T. Reilly — 1951 — University of Denver; Queens College of the City University of New York, B.A. (cum laude), 1973; Brooklyn Law School, J.D., 1977 — Admitted to Bar, 1978, New York; U.S. District Court, Eastern, Northern and Southern Districts of New York; 1985, U.S. Court of Appeals, Second Circuit — Member Association of the Bar of the City of New York; Maritime Law Association of the United States; Women's International Shipping and Trading Association — E-mail: mreilly@hillbetts.com

Elizabeth McCoy — 1960 — The University of Chicago, B.A. (with honors), 1982; Seton Hall University, M.B.A. (with honors), 2002; University of Michigan Law School, J.D., 1986 — Admitted to Bar, 1986, Michigan; 1988, New York; 1993, U.S. District Court, Eastern and Southern Districts of New York — Member New York County Lawyers Association — E-mail: emccoy@hillbetts.com

James E. Forde — United States Merchant Marine Academy, B.S., 1988; City University of New York, Law School at Queens College, J.D., 1992 — Admitted to Bar, 1993, New York; 1994, District of Columbia — Member Maritime Law Association — E-mail: jforde@hillbetts.com

Thomas M. Rittweger — United States Merchant Marine Academy, B.S., 1986; Hofstra University School of Law, J.D., 1992 — Managing Editior, Hofstra Labor Law Journal, 1991 - 1992 — Admitted to Bar, 1992, New Jersey; 1993, New York — Member American Bar Association; New York County Lawyers Association — USNR (Ret.), Lieutenant — E-mail: trittweger@hillbetts.com

Of Counsel

Terence Gargan — 1934 — State University of New York Maritime College, B.M.E., 1958; New York University, M.E., 1964; New York Law School, J.D., 1969 — Admitted to Bar, 1969, New York; Florida; U.S. Virgin Islands; 1971, U.S. District Court, Eastern and Southern Districts of New York; 1984, U.S. Supreme Court — Member The Florida Bar; Virgin Islands Bar Association; Maritime Law Association — U.S. Coast Guard Chief Engineer's License — U.S. Naval Reserves, Retired Lieutenant (20 years) — E-mail: tgargan@hillbetts.com

Michael J. Ryan — 1931 — Saint Peter's College, A.B., 1953; University of Michigan Law School, LL.B., 1958 — Phi Alpha Delta — Admitted to Bar, 1959, Illinois; Michigan; 1963, New York; 1962, U.S. District Court, Northern District of Illinois; 1963, U.S. District Court, Eastern and Southern Districts of New York; 1965, U.S. Court of Appeals, Second Circuit; 1983, U.S. Supreme Court; 1990, U.S. Court of Appeals, Third Circuit; 1992, U.S. Court of Appeals, Ninth Circuit — Member American Bar Association; Maritime Law Association of the United States; Comite Maritime Internationale — Col., U.S. Marine Corps Reserve (ret) — E-mail: mryan@hillbetts.com

Counsel

Christine F. Reidy — 1962 — Albany State University, B.A. (magna cum laude), 1982; Pennsylvania State University-Dickinson School of Law, J.D.,

Hill, Betts & Nash, LLP, New York, NY (Continued)

1987 — Admitted to Bar, 1988, New York — Member American (International Law Section) and New York State Bar Associations — E-mail: creidy@hillbetts.com

Ella W. Dodson — 1955 — Washington University in St. Louis, B.A., 1977; Chicago-Kent College of Law, J.D. (with high honors), 1984; Columbia University of Law, LL.M., 1986 — Admitted to Bar, 1986, New York; 2001, New Jersey — E-mail: edodson@hillbetts.com

Associates

Boriana Farrar — University of Sofia, LL.B., 2000; University of San Diego School of Law, LL.M., 2002; Tulane University Law School, LL.M., 2005 — Admitted to Bar, 2007, New York — E-mail: bfarrar@hillbetts.com

Andrew J. High — Johns Hopkins University, B.A., 2004; University of Miami School of Law, J.D., 2007 — Admitted to Bar, 2007, Florida; 2009, District of Columbia — E-mail: ahigh@hillbetts.com

Kenneth F. McGinis — 1970 — State University of New York College at Purchase, B.A. (Departmental Honors), 1995; Pace University School of Law, J.D. (Departmental Honors), 2005 — Admitted to Bar, 2005, New York; U.S. District Court, Eastern and Southern Districts of New York — E-mail: kmcginis@hillbetts.com

Brooke Shapiro — 1986 — University of Michigan - Ann Arbor, B.A. (with honors), 2008; St. John's University School of Law, J.D., 2011 — Admitted to Bar, 2011, New Jersey; 2012, New York; 2011, U.S. District Court, District of New Jersey — E-mail: bshapiro@hillbetts.com

Hoffman Roth & Matlin, L.L.P.

505 8th Avenue, Suite 1704
New York, New York 10018
Telephone: 212-964-1890
Fax: 212-964-4306
E-Mail: info@hrmnylaw.com
www.hrmnylaw.com

Premises Liability, Automobile, Municipal Liability, Product Liability, Liquor Liability, Insurance Coverage, Malpractice, Construction, Recreation Liability

Insurance Clients

Associated Mutual Insurance Cooperative	Berkley Custom Insurance Managers
Chartis Insurance	Colony Specialty
Endurance U.S. Insurance Operations	FARA - A York Company
HUB International Northeast, Ltd.	Fulmont Mutual Insurance Company
Merchants Insurance Group	Utica First Insurance Company

Non-Insurance Clients

Everest Scaffolding, Inc.	Rockledge Scaffold Corp.
Whitestar Consulting & Contracting, Inc.	

Firm Members

Barry M. Hoffman — State University of New York at Albany, B.A. (magna cum laude), 1974; Albany Law School of Union University, J.D., 1977 — Admitted to Bar, 1978, New York; U.S. District Court, Eastern and Southern Districts of New York — Member Bronx County Bar Association; New York County Lawyers Association — E-mail: bhoffman@hrmnylaw.com

James A. Roth — Brown University, A.B., 1978; New York Law School, J.D., 1981 — Admitted to Bar, 1982, New York; 1989, U.S. District Court, Eastern and Southern Districts of New York — Member New York State Bar Association; New York County Lawyers Association; New York State Trial Lawyers Association; Defense Association of New York — E-mail: jroth@hrmnylaw.com

William S. Matlin — University of Massachusetts Amherst, B.A., 1992; Benjamin N. Cardozo School of Law, J.D., 1997 — Admitted to Bar, 1998, New York; 2001, U.S. District Court, Eastern District of New York; 2005, U.S. District Court, Southern District of New York; 2009, U.S. Court of Appeals, Second Circuit — Member New York State Bar Association; New York State Trial Lawyers Association — E-mail: wmatlin@hrmnylaw.com

Associates

Joshua R. Hoffman	Danielle L. Olverd

Hueston McNulty, P.C.

The Empire State Building
350 Fifth Avenue, Suite 4810
New York, New York 10118
 Telephone: 973-377-0200
 Fax: 973-377-6328
 Toll Free: 800-276-9982
 www.huestonmcnulty.com

(Florham Park, NJ Office*: 256 Columbia Turnpike, Suite 207, 07932)
 (Tel: 973-377-0200)
 (Fax: 973-377-6328)
 (Toll Free: 800-276-9982)
 (E-Mail: info@huestonmcnulty.com)
(Toms River, NJ Office: Box 3473, 08756-3473)
 (Tel: 732-240-2300)
 (Fax: 732-341-7488)
 (Toll Free: 888-401-2300)
(Blue Bell, PA Office: 450 Sentry Parkway, Suite 200, 19422)
 (Tel: 973-377-0200)
 (Fax: 973-377-6328)
 (Toll Free: 800-276-9982)

Sports Claims Defense, Retail Liability, Directors and Officers Liability, Premises Liability, Automobile Liability, Insurance Coverage, Construction Defect, Municipal Law, Land Use, Real Estate, Alternative Dispute Resolution, Community Association Law

Firm Profile: Hueston McNulty, P.C. focuses its' practice as trial lawyers and counselors to community associations and in sport and recreational defense work for a number of insurers and their insureds. We represent ski areas, ski, bike and sporting goods manufacturers and retailers, amusement and water parks.

(See listing under Florham Park, NJ for additional information)

Jones Morrison, LLP

60 East 42nd Street, 40th Floor
New York, New York 10165
 Telephone: 212-759-2500
 www.jonesmorrisonlaw.com
 E-Mail: info@jonesmorrisonlaw.com

(Scarsdale, NY Office*(See White Plains listing): 670 White Plains Road, Penthouse, 10583)
 (Tel: 914-472-2300)
 (Fax: 914-472-2312)
(Stamford, CT Office*: 60 Long Ridge Road, Suite 202, 06902)
 (Tel: 203-965-7700)

Alternative Dispute Resolution, Architects and Engineers, Asbestos, Bad Faith, Bankruptcy, Business Law, Commercial Litigation, Construction Law, Creditor's Rights, Coverage Analysis, Directors and Officers Liability, Environmental Law, Errors and Omissions, Labor and Employment, Medical Malpractice, Motor Vehicle, Municipal Liability, Premises Liability, Product Liability, Professional Liability, Property Damage

Insurance Clients

Everest National Insurance Company	GEICO
Markel Insurance Company	The Hartford
Sompo Japan Insurance Company of America	Selective Insurance Company of America
	Travelers Indemnity Company

Jones Morrison, LLP, New York, NY (Continued)

Managing Partner

Stephen J. Jones — Williams College, B.A., 1987; Fordham University School of Law, J.D., 1993 — Admitted to Bar, 1994, New York; U.S. District Court, Eastern and Southern Districts of New York; U.S. Supreme Court — Member The Business Council of Westchester (Chairman of the Board; Executive Committee Member); United Way of Westchester and Putnam (Director); Westchester-Putnam Council of the Boys Scouts of America (Director, Executive Committee Member); Westchester County Industrial Development Agency (Board Member); Legal Services of the Hudson Valley (Past Director); Justice Court for the Village of Tarrytown, New York State Unified Court System (Past Justice); Westchester-Putnam Fordham Law Alumni (Past President); The Williams Club of New York (Past Board of Governors) — Eagle Scout — Practice Areas: Corporate Law; Commercial Transactions; Litigation; Real Estate

Partner

Steven T. Sledzik — Georgetown University, B.A., 1984; Georgetown University Law Center, J.D., 1990 — Admitted to Bar, 1990, Connecticut; 1992, New York; U.S. District Court, District of Connecticut; U.S. District Court, Eastern and Southern Districts of New York; U.S. Court of Appeals, Second Circuit — Member New York State and New York City Bar Associations; Federal Bar Council — Former Board of Director President of the non-profit children's theater company, Westco Productions; Provided pro bono services for New York City's Volunteer Lawyers for the Arts — Practice Areas: Employment Litigation; Commercial Litigation; Civil Rights; Contract Disputes; Complex Litigation

(See listing under White Plains, NY for additional information)

Kennedy Lillis Schmidt & English

75 Maiden Lane, Suite 402
New York, New York 10038-4816
 Telephone: 212-430-0800
 Fax: 212-430-0810
 E-Mail: info@klselaw.com
 www.klselaw.com

Established: 1986

Marine, Insurance Coverage, Transportation, Energy, Cargo, Aviation, Inland Marine

Insurance Clients

Chartis Marine Adjusters, Inc.	The St. Paul/Travelers Companies, Inc.

Partners

John T. Lillis, Jr. — St. John's University School of Law, J.D., 1976 — Admitted to Bar, 1976, New Jersey; 1977, New York — Tel: 212-430-0801 — E-mail: jlillis@klselaw.com

Charles E. Schmidt — Fordham University School of Law, J.D., 1975 — Admitted to Bar, 1976, New York — Tel: 212-430-0802 — E-mail: cschmidt@klselaw.com

Counsel

Craig S. English — University of San Francisco School of Law, J.D., 1975 — Admitted to Bar, 1976, California; 1978, New York — Tel: 212-430-0803 — E-mail: cenglish@klselaw.com

Krez & Flores, LLP

225 Broadway
New York, New York 10007
 Telephone: 212-266-0400
 Fax: 212-724-0011
 E-Mail: mail@krezflores.com
 www.krezflores.com

NEW YORK

Krez & Flores, LLP, New York, NY (Continued)

Personal Injury, Insurance Coverage, Trial and Appellate Practice, Transportation, Federal Employer Liability Claims (FELA), Labor Law (§§240, 241)

Firm Profile: We are a certified minority owned, AV rated insurance defense firm specializing in the defense of high exposure personal injury cases in difficult venues in the New York Metropolitan area.

Insurance Clients

American International Group | Liberty Mutual Insurance Company

Non-Insurance Clients

Metropolitan Transportation Authority | New York City Housing Authority
Verizon, Inc.

Firm Members

Paul A. Krez — Fordham University, B.A., 1972; Brooklyn Law School, J.D., 1977 — Admitted to Bar, 1978, New York; 1979, U.S. District Court, Eastern and Southern Districts of New York; 1983, U.S. District Court, Northern and Western Districts of New York; U.S. District Court, District of Connecticut; U.S. Court of Appeals, Second Circuit; 1984, U.S. Supreme Court — Languages: Spanish — E-mail: pkrez@krezflores.com

Edward A. Flores — Yale University, B.S., 1980; Rutgers University School of Law, J.D., 1984 — Admitted to Bar, 1984, New York; 1991, U.S. District Court, Eastern and Southern Districts of New York — Languages: Spanish — E-mail: eflores@krezflores.com

Junior Partners

Edwin H. Knauer — Hunter College, B.A., 1968; Fordham University School of Law, J.D., 1971 — Admitted to Bar, 1971, New York; 1986, New Jersey; 1972, U.S. District Court, Eastern and Southern Districts of New York; 1986, U.S. District Court, District of New Jersey — First Lieutenant, U.S. Army Reserves

Joseph M. Hiraoka, Jr. — University of California, Riverside, B.A./B.S., 1988; New York Law School, J.D., 1991 — Admitted to Bar, 1992, New York; U.S. District Court, Eastern District of New York

William J. Blumenschein — Dartmouth College, B.A., 1963; Georgetown University Law Center, J.D., 1972; Vrije Universiteit Brussel, LL.M., 1974 — Admitted to Bar, 1975, New York; 2006, Vermont; 1975, U.S. District Court, Eastern and Southern Districts of New York; 1977, U.S. Court of Appeals, Second Circuit; 1988, U.S. Court of Appeals, Eleventh Circuit — Lieutenant, U.S. Naval Reserve (Active Duty-Vietnam & Washington, D.C., 1964-1968) — Languages: German

Associates

N. Jeffrey Brown — Ohio University, B.A., 1979; University of Toledo School of Law, J.D., 1982 — Admitted to Bar, 1983, Ohio; 1984, New York; U.S. District Court, Eastern and Southern Districts of New York; 1993, U.S. Court of Appeals, Second Circuit; 1994, U.S. District Court, District of New Jersey

Alexandra Vandoros — City University of New York, B.A. (cum laude), 1995; University of Miami School of Law, J.D. (cum laude), 1998 — Admitted to Bar, 1999, New York; 1999, U.S. District Court, Eastern and Southern Districts of New York; 2007, U.S. Court of Appeals, Second Circuit — Languages: Greek

Karen S. Drotzer — State University of New York at Stony Brook, B.A., 1978; Brooklyn Law School, J.D., 1983 — Admitted to Bar, 1984, New York; 1993, U.S. District Court, Eastern and Southern Districts of New York; 1995, U.S. Tax Court

Virginia Gillikin — Providence College, B.A. (Dean's List), 1974; Columbia University, M.A./M.Ed, 1976; Brooklyn Law School, J.D., 1982 — Admitted to Bar, 1983, New York; 1988, U.S. District Court, Eastern and Southern Districts of New York

Law Offices of Charles E. Kutner, LLP

950 Third Avenue, 11th Floor
New York, New York 10022-2775
Telephone: 212-308-0210
Fax: 212-308-0213

Established: 2001

Law Offices of Charles E. Kutner, LLP, New York, NY (Continued)

Medical Malpractice, Dental Malpractice, Litigation, Professional Liability, Product Liability, Administrative Law, Commercial Litigation

Firm Profile: The Firm concentrates primarily in the defense of complex professional liability claims against physicians, hospitals, nurses, certified nurse midwives, nurse practitioners, physician assistants and dentists. The Firm also handles legal malpractice and general liability claims as well as premises liability and insurance litigation.

Insurance Clients

Medical Liability Mutual Insurance Company | Physicians Reciprocal Insurers

Partners

Charles E. Kutner — 1950 — Adelphi University, B.A., 1972; University of New Haven, M.P.A., 1978; Albany Law School of Union University, J.D., 1981 — Admitted to Bar, 1982, New York; 1982, U.S. District Court, Eastern and Southern Districts of New York; 1982, U.S. Court of Appeals, Second Circuit

Cheryl Zimmerli | Bruce R. Friedrich

Associates

Carlie E. Parsoff | Katelin Foley
Christine M. Nash

Law Offices of John C. Lane

PMB 46013
140 Broadway, 46th Floor
New York, New York 10005
Telephone: 212-363-8048
Fax: 201-848-6808
E-Mail: law@jclane.com

(Sparta, NJ Office*: 48 Woodport Road, 07871)
(Tel: 973-512-3244)
(Fax: 973-512-3245)

Insurance Defense, Automobile, Construction Law, Admiralty and Maritime Law, Environmental Law, Trucking Law, Transportation, Insurance Coverage, Commercial Law, General Liability, Professional Liability, Physical Damage, Cargo, Bodily Injury, Property Damage

(See listing under Sparta, NJ for additional information)

Locke Lord LLP

Three World Financial Center, Floor 20
New York, New York 10281
Telephone: 212-415-8600
Fax: 212-303-2754
www.lockelord.com

(Chicago, IL Office*: 111 South Wacker Drive, 60606-4410)
(Tel: 312-443-0700)
(Fax: 312-443-0336)
(Atlanta, GA Office*: Terminus 200, Suite 1200, 3333 Piedmont Road NE, 30305)
(Tel: 404-870-4600)
(Fax: 404-872-5547)
(Austin, TX Office*: 600 Congress Avenue, Suite 2200, 78701-2748)
(Tel: 512-305-4700)
(Fax: 512-305-4800)
(Dallas, TX Office*: 2200 Ross Avenue, Suite 2200, 75201)
(Tel: 214-740-8000)
(Fax: 214-740-8800)

NEW YORK

Locke Lord LLP, New York, NY (Continued)

(Houston, TX Office*: 2800 JPMorgan Chase Tower, 600 Travis, 77002-3095)
 (Tel: 713-226-1200)
 (Fax: 713-223-3717)
(London, United Kingdom Office*: 201 Bishopsgate, DX 567 London/City, EC2M 3AB)
 (Tel: +44 (0) 20 7861 9000 (Int'l))
 (Tel: 011 44 207861 9000 (US))
 (Fax: +44 (0) 20 7785 6869 201 (Bishopsgate))
(Los Angeles, CA Office*: 300 South Grand Avenue, Suite 2600, 90071-3119)
 (Tel: 213-485-1500)
 (Fax: 213-485-1200)
(New Orleans, LA Office*: 601 Poydras, Suite 2660, 70130)
 (Tel: 504-558-5100)
 (Fax: 504-558-5200)
(Sacramento, CA Office: 500 Capitol Mall, Suite 1800, 95814)
 (Tel: 916-554-0240)
 (Fax: 916-554-5440)
(San Francisco, CA Office*: 44 Montgomery Street, Suite 2400, 94104)
 (Tel: 415-318-8810)
 (Fax: 415-676-5816)
(Washington, DC Office*: 701 8th Street, N.W., Suite 700, 20001)
 (Tel: 202-521-4100)
 (Fax: 202-521-4200)
(Hong Kong, China-PRC Office: 21/F Bank of China Tower, 1 Garden Road, Central)
 (Tel: +852 3465 0600)
 (Fax: +852 3014 0991)

Antitrust, Arbitration, Aviation, Business Law, Class Actions, Construction Law, Corporate Law, Directors and Officers Liability, Employee Benefits, Environmental Law, Health Care, Insurance Law, Intellectual Property, Labor and Employment, Land Use, Admiralty and Maritime Law, Mergers and Acquisitions, Product Liability, Railroad Law, Regulatory and Compliance, Reinsurance, Securities, Technology, Transportation, Appellate, Long Term Care

Partners

Joseph N. Froehlich — Fairfield University, B.A. (magna cum laude), 1993; The University of North Carolina School of Law, J.D. (with honors), 1996 — Admitted to Bar, 1996, New Jersey; 1997, New York; 1998, U.S. District Court, Eastern District of New York; 2002, U.S. Supreme Court — Member American Bar Association — Practice Areas: Insurance Law; Reinsurance; Business Law

Kenneth J. Gormley — Fordham University, B.A., 1991; Fordham University School of Law, J.D., 1994 — Admitted to Bar, 1995, New Jersey; New York; U.S. District Court, Eastern, Northern and Southern Districts of New York; U.S. Court of Appeals, Second Circuit; U.S. Supreme Court — Practice Areas: Aviation; Product Liability

Robert A. Romano — 1951 — Harvard College, B.A. (cum laude), 1973; New York University School of Law, J.D., 1978 — Admitted to Bar, 1979, New York — Languages: Italian, Portuguese, Spanish — Practice Areas: Corporate Law; Insurance Law; Regulatory and Compliance

Steven Schwartz — Princeton University, A.B. (cum laude), 1981; Columbia University of Law, J.D., 1984 — Harlan Fiske Stone Scholar — Admitted to Bar, 1984, New York — Member American Bar Association; The Association of the Bar of the City of New York — Practice Areas: Insurance; International Law; Reinsurance

Kevin J. Walsh — University of Virginia School of Law, J.D., 1974 — Admitted to Bar, 1975, New York — Practice Areas: Business Law; Reinsurance

Rachel B. Coan — Smith College, A.B., 1977; Rutgers University School of Law, J.D., 1984 — Admitted to Bar, 1985, New York

Of Counsel

Karen S. Deibert

Associate

Sarah M. Chen

(See listing under Chicago, IL for additional information)

London Fischer LLP

59 Maiden Lane, 39th Floor Reception
New York, New York 10038
 Telephone: 212-972-1000
 Fax: 212-972-1030
 E-Mail: VPetrungaro@LondonFischer.com
 www.londonfischer.com

(Irvine, CA Office*: 2505 McCabe Way, Suite 100, 92614)
 (Tel: 949-252-0550)
 (Fax: 949-252-0553)
 (E-Mail: REndres@LondonFischer.com)
(Woodland Hills, CA Office*: 21550 Oxnard Street, 3rd Floor, 91367)
 (Tel: (818) 224-6068)
 (Fax: (818) 224-6061)
 (E-Mail: DLeMontree@LondonFischer.com)
 (www.LondonFischer.com)

Established: 1991

Construction Law, Professional Liability, Admiralty and Maritime Law, Civil Rights, Commercial Litigation, Directors and Officers Liability, Employment Law, Environmental Law, Fidelity and Surety, Insurance Coverage, Insurance Regulation, Marine Insurance, Mass Tort, Municipal Liability, Product Liability, Property Loss, Reinsurance, Subrogation, Toxic Torts, Transportation, Trucking Law, Employment Litigation and Counseling, Catastrophic Loss Investigations and Litigation, National Appellate Practice, National Trial Practice, Professional Contracts and Disputes

Firm Profile: London Fischer is a litigation and business law firm that provides counsel and advisory services for the insurance, construction and manufacturing industries. With offices in New York and California, we provide nationwide service for many of the world's most prestigious insurance groups and corporations.

Insurance Clients

Academic Health Professionals Insurance Association
Berkley Specialty Underwriting Managers, LLC
CNA
Colony Specialty
Fireman's Fund Insurance Company
Ironshore Insurance Services, LLP
MidStates Reinsurance Corporation
North American Specialty Insurance Company
QBE North America
Swiss Re Underwriters
Travelers Property Casualty Corporation
ACE North American Claims
Allied North America
Catlin, Inc.
Chubb Group of Insurance Companies
Electric Insurance Company
Great American Insurance Group
Hartford Insurance Company
Liberty Mutual Insurance Company
New York State Insurance Fund
OneBeacon Insurance
Protective Insurance Company
RPC Insurance Agency, LLC
Tokio Marine Claims Service, Inc.
Zurich North America

Non-Insurance Clients

Alfa Laval, Inc.
Home Box Office, Inc.
Milstein Properties Corporation
Skanska U.S.A. Civil Inc.
Time Warner, Inc.
The Walt Disney Company
EMCOR Group
Makita USA, Inc.
The Related Companies, L.P.
Time Warner Cable
Turner Construction Company

Retired

James L. Fischer — Member American Bar Association (Member, Sections on Local Government, Tort and Insurance Law and Litigation); New York State (Member, Sections on Insurance, Negligence and Compensation Law and Trial Lawyers), and Westchester County Bar Associations; Association of the Bar of the City of New York — "Minimum Contacts, Shaffer's Unified Jurisdictional Test," 12 Valp. Law Review 25

Partner

Bernard London — 1950 — New York University, B.S., 1972; The College of Insurance, St. John's University, 1973; St. John's University School of Law, J.D., 1977 — Admitted to Bar, 1978, New York; U.S. District Court, Eastern,

NEW YORK

London Fischer LLP, New York, NY (Continued)

Northern, Southern and Western Districts of New York; U.S. Court of Appeals, Second Circuit; U.S. Court of Federal Claims — Member New York State Bar Association (Committees on Professional Liability, Reinsurance and Litigation); Defense Research Institute — Author and Lecturer on Construction and Insurance Law; Author of Municipal Zoning Codes, Professional Liability Insurance and Construction Law — Trustee, Village of Lloyd Harbor, 1999; Police Commissioner, Village of Lloyd Harbor; Selected for inclusion in the New York Super Lawyers list, 2009, 2010, 2011, 2012, 2013 and 2014 — E-mail: BLondon@LondonFischer.com

Daniel Zemann, Jr. — 1953 — Fairleigh Dickinson University, B.A., 1975; South Texas College of Law, J.D., 1983 — Admitted to Bar, 1983, Texas; 1987, New York; 1983, U.S. Court of Appeals, Fifth Circuit; U.S. District Court, Eastern and Southern Districts of Texas; 1991, U.S. District Court, Eastern and Southern Districts of New York; 1997, U.S. Court of Appeals, Second Circuit — Member New York State Bar Association; State Bar of Texas — Practice Areas: Construction Litigation; Insurance Coverage; General Liability; Professional Liability; Trial and Appellate Practice; Construction Claims; Construction Defect; Product Liability Defense — E-mail: DZemann@LondonFischer.com

Richard S. Endres — 1963 — State University of New York at Albany, B.S., 1985; California Western School of Law, J.D. (magna cum laude), 1989 — Admitted to Bar, 1989, California; 1990, New York; 1989, U.S. District Court, Southern District of California; 1990, U.S. District Court, Eastern and Southern Districts of New York; 2003, U.S. District Court, Central and Northern Districts of California; U.S. Court of Appeals, Ninth Circuit — Member New York State Bar Association (Sections on Product Liability, Torts and Insurance, Construction, Trial Lawyers); State Bar of California (Sections on Product Liability, Torts and Insurance, Construction, Business Litigation); Los Angeles County and Orange County Bar Associations; Professional Liability Underwriting Society — Practice Areas: Advertising Injury; Agent/Broker Liability; Bad Faith; Bodily Injury; Carrier Defense; Casualty Insurance Law; Catastrophic Injury; Commercial Insurance; Comprehensive General Liability; Construction Accidents; Coverage Analysis; Declaratory Judgments; Directors and Officers Liability; Errors and Omissions; Excess and Surplus Lines; Excess and Umbrella; Extra-Contractual Liability; Extra-Contractual Litigation; Fire Loss; Insurance Coverage Litigation; Insurance Defense; Medical Product Liability; Premises Liability; Product Liability; Professional Errors and Omissions; Property and Casualty; Property Damage; Risk Management — E-mail: REndres@LondonFischer.com

John E. Sparling — 1962 — St. Joseph's College, B.A., 1984; Hofstra University School of Law, J.D., 1987 — Hofstra Law Review, Staff Writer, 1985-1986, Assistant Editor, 1986-1987 — Admitted to Bar, 1988, New York; New York for Multiple Pro Hac Vice Admissions; 1988, U.S. District Court, Eastern, Northern, Southern and Western Districts of New York — Member American Bar Association (Committees on Litigation, Tort and Insurance Practice and Real Property, Probate and Trust Law); New York State Bar Association; Council on Litigation Management (Frequent Lecturer and Education Committee Member); New York County Lawyers Association — Reported Cases: Burack v. Tower Ins. Co. of New York, 12 A.D.3d 167, 784 N.Y.S.2d 53; Owusu v. Hearst Communications, Inc., 52 A.D.3d 285, 860 N.Y.S.2d 38; Harsch v. City of New York, 78 A.D.3d 781, 910 N.Y.S.2d 540; Mahoney v. Turner Const. Co., 61 A.D.3d 101, 872 N.Y.S.2d 433; Gropper v. St. Luke's Hospital Center, 234 A.D.2d 171, 651 N.Y.S.2d 469; Guiga v. JLS Construction Co., 255 A.D.2d 244, 685 N.Y.S.2d 1; Jani v. City of New York, 284 A.D.2d 304,725 N.Y.S.2d 388; Isola v. JWP Forest Electric Corp., 262 A.D.2d 95, 691 N.Y.S.2d 492; Ilardi v. Inte-Fac Corp., 290 A.D.2d 490, 736 N.Y.S.2d 401; Juliano v. Prudential Securities Incorporated, 287 A.D.2d 260, 731 N.Y.S.2d 142; Bachrow v. Turner Construction Company, 46 A.D.3d 388, 848 N.Y.S.2d 86; Miranda v. City of New York, 281 A.D.2d 403, 721 N.Y.S.2d 391; Yofi Book Publishing, Inc. v. Wil-Brook Realty Corp., 287 A.D.2d 712, 732 N.Y.S.2d 238; Longwood Central School District v. American Employers Insurance Company, 35 A.D.3d 550, 827 N.Y.S.2d 194; Smolik v. Turner Construction Company, 48 A.D.3d 452, 851 N.Y.S.2d 616; Gonzalez v. Turner Construction Company, 29 A.D.3d 630, 815 N.Y.S.2d 179; Schalansky v. McSpedon, 236 A.D.2d 461, 654 N.Y.S.2d 584; Wojcik v. 42nd Street Development Project, Inc., 386 F. Supp.2d 442, So. Dist. N.Y. 2005— Appointed "Steering Committee Counsel" in the mass tort litigation entitled: In Re World Trade Center Disaster Site Litigation, with over 10,000 plaintiffs surrounding the clean-up of the 9/11 disaster in 2001; Lecturer, Council on Litigation Management in New Orleans (Topic: Litigation Management - Protecting Catastrophic Losses with Appropriate Investigation and Experts); Lecturer, Ace North America in Jersey City, NJ (Topic: Key Coverage Issues: Property); World Trade Center Clean-Up/Air Inhalation Litigation - Played critical role along with the WTC Captive and the entire WTC defense team in ultimately facilitating the execution of the global $712 million settlement agreement that included the overwhelming majority of the police officer, firefighter, sanitation and construction worker debris removal and recovery plaintiffs in the WTC Disaster Site litigation; Worked closely with Turner, lobbyists and Congress to effectuate the recent passage of the 9/11 Health and Compensation Act (the so-called Zadroga Bill) that reopens the Victim's Compensation Fund with an additional $2.3 billion in compensation for economic losses and injuries and establishes a 5 year $4.3 billion program to provide medical monitoring/screening to eligible responders and community members and also providing clients with a limitation on liability for the remaining lawsuits that did not enter into the settlement and future cases that are filed. Represents Insurance Brokers, Insurance Carriers and Insureds in complex insurance coverage and litigation matters; consultation in regulatory, insurance policy drafting and interpretation issues, insurance program recommendations and consultation; handled insurance coverage actions and policy interpretation for over twenty years. — Practice Areas: Construction Litigation; General Liability; Insurance Coverage; Insurance Defense; Product Liability; Trial and Appellate Practice; Contract Disputes; Employment Discrimination; Mass Tort; Premises Liability; Property Damage; Toxic Torts; Construction Accidents; Construction Defect; Fire and Water Subrogation — E-mail: JSparling@LondonFischer.com

James Walsh — 1967 — Fordham University, B.A. (magna cum laude), 1989; University of Pennsylvania Law School, J.D., 1992 — Admitted to Bar, 1993, New York; U.S. District Court, Eastern and Southern Districts of New York — Reported Cases: Klewinowski v. City of New York, 103 A.D.3d 547, 959 N.Y.S.2d 493 (1st Dep't 2013); In re Ancillary Receivership of Reliance Insurance Company. O'Brien & Gere Technical Services, Inc. v. New York Liquidation Bureau (Reliance Insurance Company in Liquidation) 81 A.D.3d 533, 918 N.Y.S.2d 25 (1st Dep't 2011); In the Matter of Continental Casualty Company v. Tibor Lecei, 47 A.D.3d 509, 850 N.Y.S.2d 76 (1st Dep't 2008); Romang v. Welsbach Electric Corp., 47 A.D.3d 789 (2d Dep't 2008); Travelers Indemnity Co. v. Bally Total Fitness Holding Corp., 448 F.Supp.2d 976 (N.D. Ill. 2006); Mickey's Rides-N-More Inc. v. Anthony Viscuso Brokerage Inc., 17 A.D.3d 308, 792 N.Y.S.2d 750 (2d Dep't 2005); Gannon v. JWP Forest Electric Corp., 275 A.D.2d 231, 712 N.Y.S.2d 494 (1st Dep't 2000) — Practice Areas: Construction Litigation; Insurance Coverage; Insurance Defense; Professional Liability; Directors and Officers Liability; Reinsurance; Errors and Omissions; Arbitration; General Liability — E-mail: JWalsh@LondonFischer.com

Anthony F. Tagliagambe — 1953 — Columbia University, B.A. (cum laude), 1975; Albany Law School of Union University, J.D., 1978 — Admitted to Bar, 1979, New York; U.S. District Court, Eastern and Southern Districts of New York — Member New York State Bar Association; Federation of Defense and Corporate Counsel (Elected Member, Chairman of the Premises and Security Liability Section) — Author: "Defendant's Strategies for Summation in a Labor Law Case," NYSBA CLE, December 2011; "Cross-Examination of the Liability Expert," NYSBA CLE Construction Site Accidents, December 2009; "Food for Thought: Defending the Food Purveyor When the Meal Turns Bad," Federation of Defense and Corporate Counsel Quarterly, Fall 2008; "An Employee By Any Other Name is Still An Employee: Determining Employment Status Under New York Law," New York State Bar Journal, February 1992 — Reported Cases: Mas v. Two Bridges, 75 N.Y.2d 680, 55 N.Y.S.2d 669, 554 N.E.2d 1257; Abbadessa v. Sprint, 291 A.D.2d 363, 736 N.Y.S.2d 881 (Mem), 2002 N.Y. Slip Op. 01067 N.Y.A.D. 2 Dept. Feb. 4, 2002; Allen v. Village of Farmingdale, 282 A.D.2d 485, 723 N.Y.S.2d 219 2001 N.Y. Slip Op. 02991, N.Y.A.D. 2 Dept. Apr. 09, 2001; Colon v. BIC USA, Inc., 199 F. Supp. 2d 53, So. Dist. N.Y. 2001; Uzdavines v. Metropolitan Baseball Club Inc., 115 Misc. 2d 343, 454 N.Y.S.2d 238, N.Y. City Civ. Ct., August 25, 1982 — Lecturer, New York State Bar Association, New York City Bar, Practicing Law Institute, Federation of Defense and Corporate Counsel (Topics: Cross Exam of Experts, Defending Product Liability Actions, Defending Construction Cases, Handling Catastrophic Injury Cases, Litigating Food Safety Cases); Selected for inclusion in the New York Super Lawyers list, 2007, 2008, 2009, 2010, 2011, 2012, 2013 and 2014 — Practice Areas: Construction Litigation; Product Liability; Negligence; Medical Malpractice; Municipal Liability — E-mail: ATagliagambe@LondonFischer.com

Clifford B. Aaron — 1958 — Franklin & Marshall College, B.A. (cum laude), 1980; Villanova University School of Law, J.D., 1983 — Admitted to Bar, 1984, New York; 2010, Tennessee; U.S. District Court, Eastern, Southern and Western Districts of New York — Member American Bar Association; New York County Lawyers Association (Treasurer, Product Liability Subcommittee of Tort Division); Defense Research Institute — Assistant District Attorney, Bronx County, New York, 1983-1988; Adjunct Professor, New York Law School, 1992-1995; Lecturer, DRI Electronic Discovery Abuse, 1999, San Francisco, CA; Lecturer, New York County Lawyers Association Continuing Legal Education (2004-Present); DRI Steering Committee on Trial Tactics; DRI Mock Trial Faculty and Participant (2014), Miami, FL; Selected for inclusion in the New York Super Lawyers list, 2009, 2010, 2011,

NEW YORK

London Fischer LLP, New York, NY (Continued)

2012, 2013 and 2014 — Practice Areas: Product Liability; General Liability; Insurance Defense; Catastrophic Injury — E-mail: CAaron@LondonFischer.com

Virginia Goodman Futterman — 1957 — Marymount College, B.A. (magna cum laude), 1979; St. John's University School of Law, J.D., 1982 — Admitted to Bar, 1983, New York; U.S. District Court, Eastern, Northern, Southern and Western Districts of New York — Member New York State Bar Association; Defense Research Institute — Mediator, Eastern and Southern Districts of New York — Practice Areas: Defense Litigation; Product Liability; Personal Injury; Premises Liability; Construction Litigation; Asbestos Litigation; Employment Discrimination — E-mail: VFutterman@LondonFischer.com

Brian A. Kalman — 1968 — State University of New York at Binghamton, B.A. (with honors), 1990; Boston University School of Law, J.D., 1993 — Admitted to Bar, 1993, New Jersey; 1994, New York; 1995, U.S. District Court, Eastern and Southern Districts of New York; 1999, U.S. District Court, Northern District of New York; 2006, U.S. District Court, Western District of New York — Reported Cases: UTC Fire & Security Americas Corp. v. NCS Power, Inc. 844 F.Supp. 2d 366 (S.D.N.Y. 2012), Auriemma v. Biltmore Theatre 82 A.D. 3d 1, 917 N.Y.S.2d 130 (1st Dept. 2011), Gayle v. National Railroad Passenger Corp. 701 F.Supp. 2d 556 (S.D.N.Y. 2010), Astudillo v. City of New York, 71 A.D. 3d 709, 895 N.Y.S.2d 731 (2d Dep't 2010), Mann v. Dambrosio, 58 A.D.3d 701, 873 N.Y.S.2d 317 (2d Dep't 2009); Heimbuch v. Grumman Corp. 51 A.D.3d 865, 858 N.Y.S.2d 378 (2d Dep't 2008); Meza v. Consolidated Edison Co. of New York, 50 A.D.3d 452, 854 N.Y.S.2d 646 (1st Dep't 2008); Seabury v. County of Dutchess, 38 A.D.3d 752, 832 N.Y.S.2d 269 (2d Dep't 2007); Singh v. Kolcas, 283 A.D.2d 350, 725 N.Y.S.2d 37 (1st Dep't 2001) — Selected for inclusion in the New York Super Lawyers list, 2009, 2010, 2011, 2012, 2013 and 2014; Lecturer, New York County Lawyers Association Continuing Education, 2012-Present — Practice Areas: Product Liability; Construction Law; General Liability — E-mail: BKalman@LondonFischer.com

Spiro K. Bantis — 1960 — New York University, B.A., 1982; Temple University Beasley School of Law, J.D., 1985 — Admitted to Bar, 1986, New York; U.S. District Court, Eastern and Southern Districts of New York — Member Bar Association of the City of New York — General Counsel, Gulf Insurance Company (Retired); Board Member, Insurance Federation of New York; Board Member, Atrium Insurance Corporation — Certified Arbitrator - ARIAS-US — Practice Areas: Insurance Corporate Practice; Insurance Coverage; Insurance Law; Insurance Regulation — E-mail: SBantis@LondonFischer.com

Perry I. Kreidman — Colgate University, B.S. (cum laude), 1973; New York University School of Law, J.D., 1976 — Admitted to Bar, 1977, New York — Member American Bar Association — Lectured and written on insurance and reinsurance coverage and claims in the U.S., Bermuda, and England — Practice Areas: Insurance Coverage; Reinsurance; Litigation; Arbitration; Professional Liability; Architects and Engineers; Directors and Officers Liability — E-mail: PKreidman@LondonFischer.com

Michael J. Carro — 1960 — Queens College, B.A., 1983; Pace University School of Law, J.D., 1987 — Phi Alpha Delta — Admitted to Bar, 1988, New York; 1989, U.S. District Court, Eastern and Southern Districts of New York — Member New York State Bar Association — Practice Areas: Personal Injury; Labor and Employment; Medical Malpractice; Premises Liability; Product Liability; Toxic Torts — E-mail: MCarro@LondonFischer.com

Matthew K. Finkelstein — 1970 — Franklin & Marshall College, B.A., 1991; St. Johns University School of Law, J.D. (cum laude), 1996 — Admitted to Bar, 1998, New York; 2000, U.S. District Court, Eastern and Southern Districts of New York; 2009, U.S. Court of Appeals, Second Circuit — Member New York State Bar Association — Practice Areas: Construction Accidents; Construction Defect; General Liability; Motor Vehicle; Premises Liability; Product Liability; Professional Liability — E-mail: MFinkelstein@LondonFischer.com

Christopher Ruggiero — 1979 — Manhattanville College, B.A. (summa cum laude), 2001; Brooklyn Law School, J.D. (Dean's List), 2004 — Brooklyn Journal of International Law, Staff Writer 2002-2003, Notes and Comments Editor, 2003-2004 — Admitted to Bar, 2005, New York; District of Columbia; U.S. District Court, Eastern and Southern Districts of New York — Member New York State Bar Association; Claims and Litigation Management Alliance; New York County Lawyers Association — Reported Cases: In Re World Trade Center Disaster Site Litigation; Baumann v. Metropolitan Life Ins. Co., 17 A.D.3d 260, 793 N.Y.S.2d 410 (1st Dep't 2005); Mayo v. Metropolitan Opera Ass'n, Inc., 108 A.D.422 (1st Dep't 2013) — Practice Areas: Automobile; Construction Litigation; Insurance Coverage; Mass Tort; Premises Liability; Property Damage — Tel: CRuggiero@LondonFischer.com

London Fischer LLP, New York, NY (Continued)

Daniel W. London — 1979 — University of Pennsylvania, B.A., 2001; Brooklyn Law School, J.D., 2005 — Admitted to Bar, 2005, New Jersey; 2006, New York; 2005, U.S. District Court, District of New Jersey; U.S. District Court, Eastern and Southern Districts of New York — Practice Areas: Commercial Litigation; Insurance Coverage; Insurance Law; Insurance Regulation — E-mail: DLondon@LondonFischer.com

James T. H. Deaver — 1961 — The Wharton School of the University of Pennsylvania, B.S., 1985; Temple University School of Law, J.D. (cum laude), 1991; New York University School of Law, LL.M., 1992 — Admitted to Bar, 1993, New York; U.S. District Court, Eastern and Southern Districts of New York — Reported Cases: Representative Cases: Appalachian Ins. Co. v. General Electric Co., 796 N.Y.S.2d 609 (N.Y. App. Div. 1st Dep't, 2005); Bridgestone/Firestone North American Tire, LLC v. Sompo Japan Ins. Co. of America, Civ. Ac. No. 3-02-1117 (M.D.Tenn)(case filed 2002) — Practice Areas: Insurance Coverage Litigation — E-mail: JDeaver@LondonFischer.com

Darren Le Montree — 1972 — University of California, Los Angeles, B.A. Political Science, 1994; Southwestern University School of Law, J.D. (cum laude), 1998 — Admitted to Bar, 1998, California; U.S. District Court, Central, Eastern, Northern and Southern Districts of California — Member Los Angeles County Bar Assocation — Reported Cases: Feldman v. Illinois Union Ins. Co., 198 Cal.App. 4th 1495 (2011) — Practice Areas: Commercial Litigation; Employment Litigation; Insurance Coverage; Professional Liability — E-mail: DLemontree@LondonFischer.com

(Associates not listed)
(Revisors of the New York Insurance Law Digest for this Publication)

(This firm is also listed in the Subrogation, Investigation and Adjustment section of this directory)

Malapero & Prisco LLP

295 Madison Avenue
New York, New York 10017
   Telephone: 212-661-7300
   Fax: 212-661-7640
   E-Mail: defense@malaperoprisco.com
   www.malaperoprisco.com

(Malapero Prisco Klauber & Licata LLP*: 61 South Paramus Road, Suite 280, Paramus, NJ, 07652)
(Tel: 201-820-3488)
(Fax: 201-820-3491)
(http://www.malaperoprisco.com/nj)

Established: 1990

Insurance Defense, Insurance Coverage, Professional Liability, Subrogation, General Liability, Personal Injury, Construction Law, Labor and Employment, Insurance Law, Premises Liability, Motor Vehicle, Workers' Compensation, Property Damage, Product Liability, Appellate Practice, Alternative Dispute Resolution

Firm Profile: Malapero & Prisco specializes in providing litigation and related services to the insurance industry. Our partners each have over twenty-five years of litigation experience. As a foundation to building a successful relationship with its insurance carriers, third party administrators and clients, we are dedicated to the early formulation of a defense strategy in concert with the client and in maintaining close communication with the claims professional. This allows the client to quickly and reliably identify those cases which would benefit from an early resolution and to control litigation costs.

Malapero & Prisco have trial experience in the five counties of New York, as well as Nassau County, Suffolk County, Westchester County, Rockland County, Putnam County, Dutchess County and Orange County, the Federal Courts for the Southern and Eastern Districts of New York, and the State and Federal Courts of New Jersey.

Insurance Clients

GAB Robins North America, Inc.	Gallagher Bassett Services, Inc.
The Harleysville Insurance	Liberty Mutual Insurance Company
St. Paul Travelers	

NEW YORK

Malapero & Prisco LLP, New York, NY (Continued)

Non-Insurance Clients

Turner Construction Company

Partners

Raymond J. Malapero — 1955 — Fordham University, B.A. (cum laude), 1977; Fordham Law School, J.D., 1980 — Admitted to Bar, 1981, New York; New Jersey; U.S. District Court, Eastern and Southern Districts of New York — Member American, New York State, New Jersey State and Brooklyn Bar Associations; New York State Trial Lawyers Association — E-mail: rmalapero@malaperoprisco.com

Joseph J. Prisco, Jr. — 1959 — Fordham University, B.A., 1981; Pace University, J.D., 1984 — Admitted to Bar, 1985, New York; 1986, New Jersey; U.S. District Court, Eastern and Southern Districts of New York — Member New York State Bar Association; New York State Trial Lawyers Association — E-mail: jprisco@malaperoprisco.com

Andrew L. Klauber — 1957 — Franklin & Marshall College, B.A., 1979; Boston University School of Law, J.D., 1982 — Admitted to Bar, 1983, New York; New Jersey; U.S. District Court, District of New Jersey; U.S. District Court, Eastern and Southern Districts of New York — Member American Bar Association; Defense Association of New York (DANY); New York State Trial Lawyers Association — E-mail: aklauber@malaperoprisco.com

George L. Mahoney — 1964 — Manhattan College, B.A., 1986; Tulane University Law School, J.D., 1993 — Admitted to Bar, 1994, New York; 1995, U.S. District Court, Eastern and Southern Districts of New York — E-mail: gmahoney@malaperoprisco.com

Frank J. Lombardo — 1960 — St. John's University, B.A., 1983; Thomas M. Cooley Law School, J.D., 1987 — Admitted to Bar, 1987, New York; U.S. District Court, Eastern and Southern Districts of New York — Member Brooklyn Manhattan Trial Lawyers Association (President); New York City Trial Lawyers Association — E-mail: flombardo@malaperoprisco.com

Glenn E. Richardson — 1952 — Temple University, B.A., 1975; Temple University Beasley School of Law, J.D., 1978 — Admitted to Bar, 1978, Pennsylvania; 1980, New York — Member New York County Lawyers Association — E-mail: defense@malaperoprisco.com

Keith J. Norton — John Jay College of Criminal Justice, M.A., 2001; Queens College of the City University of New York, J.D., 2002 — Admitted to Bar, 2002, New York; New Jersey — E-mail: defense@malaperoprisco.com

Of Counsel

Thomas M. Licata — Pace University, B.A. (cum laude), 1984; Seton Hall University, J.D., 1987 — Outstanding Clinical Practitioner Award, 1987 — Admitted to Bar, 1987, New York; New Jersey; U.S. District Court, Eastern and Southern Districts of New York; U.S. District Court, District of New Jersey — Member Bergen County Bar Association — E-mail: tlicata@malaperoprisco.com

Associates

Youngmin Oh Campbell — State University of New York at Buffalo, B.S., 1996; Albany Law School, J.D., 1999 — Admitted to Bar, 2003, New York — E-mail: defense@malaperoprisco.com

Cynthia P. Camacho — Le Moyne College, B.S., 1995; Albany Law School, J.D., 1998 — Admitted to Bar, 1998, New York — E-mail: defense@malaperoprisco.com

Mark A. Bethmann — Hofstra University, B.A., 1987; St. John's University School of Law, J.D., 1990 — Admitted to Bar, 1990, Connecticut — E-mail: defense@malaperoprisco.com

John J. Peplinski — State University of New York at New Paltz, B.A., 1984; Boston University School of Law, J.D., 1992 — Admitted to Bar, 1992, New York — E-mail: defense@malaperoprisco.com

Jeffrey N. Rejan — Columbia College, Columbia University, A.B., 1977; Boston University School of Law, J.D., 1980 — Admitted to Bar, 1980, New York — E-mail: defense@malaperoprisco.com

Odessa Kennedy — Brooklyn College, B.A., 1994; St. John's University School of Law, J.D., 1997 — Admitted to Bar, 1997, New York — E-mail: defense@malaperoprisco.com

David Allweiss — State University of New York at Oswego, B.A., 1994; Touro College Jacob D. Fuchsberg Law Center, J.D., 1999 — Admitted to Bar, 1999, New York; New Jersey — E-mail: defense@malaperoprisco.com

Robert L. Emmons — Fordham University, B.A., 1977; Fordham University School of Law, J.D., 1980 — Admitted to Bar, 1980, New York — E-mail: defense@malaperoprisco.com

Malapero & Prisco LLP, New York, NY (Continued)

Rhonda D. Thompson — John Jay College of Criminal Justice, B.S., 1981; Rutgers University School of Law, J.D., 1993 — Admitted to Bar, 1993, New York; New Jersey; North Carolina — E-mail: defense@malaperoprisco.com

Michael N. Lopez — State University of New York at New Paltz, B.A., 2006; Hofstra University, J.D., 2012 — Admitted to Bar, 2013, New York — E-mail: defense@malaperoprisco.com

Michael J. Snizek — Fairfield University, B.A., 1998; Wake Forest University, J.D., 2005 — Admitted to Bar, 2011, New York — E-mail: defense@malaperoprisco.com

Joseph V. McBride — Niagara University, B.S., 1991; St. John's University, J.D., 1995 — Admitted to Bar, 1996, New York — E-mail: defense@malaperoprisco.com

Jana B. Sperry — The University of Georgia, B.A., 1996; Brooklyn Law School, J.D., 2000 — Admitted to Bar, 2001, New York; 2004, North Carolina; 2006, New Jersey — E-mail: defense@malaperoprisco.com

Frank D. Thompson — Franklin & Marshall College, B.A., 2000; Widener University, J.D., 2003 — Admitted to Bar, 2003, New York; 2004, New Jersey; Connecticut; Pennsylvania; 2005, Maryland — E-mail: defense@malaperoprisco.com

Toni N. Guarino — St. John's University, B.A., 2008; New York Law School, J.D., 2013 — Admitted to Bar, 2013, New York — E-mail: defense@malaperoprisco.com

Bari M. Lewis — Binghamton University, B.A., 1983; The University of North Carolina at Chapel Hill, J.D., 1986 — Admitted to Bar, 1987, New York — E-mail: defense@malaperoprisco.com

William B. Cunningham — Brooklyn College, B.A., 1979; Fordham University, J.D., 1982 — Admitted to Bar, 1983, New York — E-mail: defense@malaperoprisco.com

Amanda N. Prescott — University at Albany, State University of New York, B.A., 2008; City University of New York, J.D., 2012 — Admitted to Bar, 2013, New York — E-mail: defense@malaperoprisco.com

Thomas J. Keevins — Loyola University Maryland, B.A., 1997; St. John's University, J.D., 2000 — Admitted to Bar, 2000, New York; U.S. District Court, Southern District of New York — E-mail: defense@malaperoprisco.com

Costas Cyprus — Fordham University, B.A., 2005; St. John's University, J.D., 2009 — Admitted to Bar, 2010, New York; U.S. District Court, Eastern and Southern Districts of New York — E-mail: defense@malaperoprisco.com

Rikki L. Davidoff — Florida Atlantic University, B.A., 2010; Chicago-Kent College of Law, J.D., 2013 — Admitted to Bar, 2013, New Jersey — E-mail: defense@malaperoprisco.com

Clinton S. Hein — Northern Arizona University, B.S., 1988; Golden Gate University, J.D., 1996 — Admitted to Bar, 1997, California; New York — E-mail: defense@malaperoprisco.com

Denise A. Palmeri — Brooklyn College, B.A., 1989; Touro College Jacob D. Fuchsberg Law Center, J.D., 1993 — Admitted to Bar, 1993, New York — E-mail: defense@malaperoprisco.com

Marshall, Conway & Bradley, P.C.

45 Broadway, Suite 740
New York, New York 10006
Telephone: 212-619-4444
Fax: 212-962-2647
E-Mail: mcw@mcwpc.com
www.mcwpc.com

(Jersey City, NJ Office*: One Exchange Place, Suite 1000, 07302)
(Tel: 201-521-3170)
(Fax: 201-521-3180)

Agent and Brokers Errors and Omissions, Alternative Dispute Resolution, Architects and Engineers, Bad Faith, Bodily Injury, Construction Liability, Directors and Officers Liability, Employment Practices Liability, Environmental Litigation, First Party Matters, Insurance Coverage, Liquor Liability, Motor Vehicle, Policy Construction and Interpretation, Pollution, Product Liability, Professional Liability, Regulatory and Compliance, State and Federal Courts, Toxic Torts, Trial and Appellate Practice, Reinsurance, Wrongful Death

NEW YORK

Marshall, Conway & Bradley, P.C., New York, NY
(Continued)

Firm Profile: Marshall, Conway & Bradley P.C. is one of the leading insurance defense law firms in New York and New Jersey. Our firm predominantly represents national and multi-national insurance companies as well as self-insured corporations that are domiciled throughout the United States and London.

Insurance Clients

- American Access Casualty Company
- AXA Insurance Company
- First State Management Group, Inc.
- Genesis Underwriting Management Company
- National Indemnity Company
- New York State Insurance Department, Liquidation Bureau
- Philadelphia Indemnity Insurance Company
- Royal & SunAlliance Insurance Company
- Superior Insurance Company
- Torus Insurance Group
- Tower Risk Management
- United National Insurance Company
- U.S. Underwriters Insurance Company
- AXA Corporate Solutions
- AXA France Assurance
- Chubb Services Corporation
- General Star Management Company
- Grange Insurance Group
- Mount Vernon Fire Insurance Company
- Pennsylvania Lumbermens Mutual Insurance Company
- Progressive Casualty Insurance Company
- Seneca Insurance Company, Inc.
- State Farm Fire and Casualty Company
- Tower Insurance Company of New York
- United States Liability Insurance Company
- Utica First Insurance Company

Non-Insurance Clients

ICON Health & Fitness, Inc.

Firm Members

Jeffrey A. Marshall — State University of New York at Stony Brook, B.A., 1973; New England School of Law, J.D., 1976 — Admitted to Bar, 1977, New York; 1980, U.S. District Court, Eastern and Southern Districts of New York; 1998, U.S. Supreme Court — Member American Bar Association (Tort and Insurance Practice Section); New York State Bar Association (Insurance, Negligence and Compensation Section); Defense Research Institute; American Board of Trial Advocates — AV Rated; Super Lawyers, 2010 — Practice Areas: Arbitration; Construction Accidents; Dram Shop; Mediation; Premises Liability; Property and Casualty

Robert J. Conway — Fordham University, B.A., 1973; Albany Law School of Union University, J.D., 1976 — Admitted to Bar, 1977, New York; 1978, U.S. District Court, Eastern and Southern Districts of New York — Member American Bar Association (Tort and Insurance Practice Section); New York State (Insurance Negligence and Compensation Section) and Nassau County Bar Associations; Defense Research Institute; American Arbitration Association; American Board of Trial Advocates — Super Lawyers 2010 — Practice Areas: Arbitration; Asbestos; Construction Accidents; Dram Shop; Lead Paint; Mediation; Mold Litigation; Premises Liability; Property and Casualty

Christopher T. Bradley — Manhattan College, B.A. (Dean's List), 1974; St. John's University, M.A., 1982; St. John's University School of Law, J.D., 1984 — Admitted to Bar, 1985, New York; 1992, U.S. District Court, Southern District of New York; 1995, U.S. District Court, Eastern District of New York; 2006, U.S. Court of Appeals, Second Circuit; 2010, U.S. District Court, Northern District of New York — Member New York State Bar Association (Torts and Insurance Practice Section); The Association of the Bar of the City of New York; Claims & Litigation Management Alliance; Defense Research Institute — Practice Areas: Insurance Coverage; Professional Liability; Bad Faith; Environmental Law; Regulatory and Compliance; Arbitration; Construction Accidents; Mediation; Property and Casualty

Michael Gollub — Allegheny College, B.S., 1991; Hofstra University School of Law, J.D., 1994; The George Washington University, LL.M., 1996 — Admitted to Bar, 1994, Connecticut; 1995, New York — Member Federal, American and New York State Bar Associations; New York County Lawyers Association; Defense Research Institute — Practice Areas: Class Actions; Construction Litigation; Fraud; Mass Tort

Amy Weissman — Lafayette College, B.A., 1999; New York Law School, J.D., 2002 — Admitted to Bar, 2002, New Jersey; 2003, New York; 2005, U.S. District Court, Eastern and Southern Districts of New York — Member New York State Bar Association — Practice Areas: Arbitration; Construction Accidents; Dram Shop; Mediation; Premises Liability; Property and Casualty

Of Counsel

John Szewczuk

Marshall, Conway & Bradley, P.C., New York, NY
(Continued)

Associates

- Stacey H. Snyder
- Guy P. Dauerty
- Allison J. Seidman
- Thomas J. Nemia
- Brian L. Greben
- Steven M. Ziolkowski
- Marci D. Mitkoff
- Adam J. Golub
- Lauren Turkel
- Leonard Silverman
- William J. Edwins
- David A. Richman

Marshall Dennehey Warner Coleman & Goggin

Wall Street Plaza
88 Pine Street, 21st Floor
New York, New York 10005-1801
   Telephone: 212-376-6400
   Fax: 212-376-6490
   www.marshalldennehey.com

(Philadelphia, PA Office*: 2000 Market Street, Suite 2300, 19103)
   (Tel: 215-575-2600)
   (Fax: 215-575-0856)
   (Toll Free: 800-220-3308)
   (E-Mail: marshalldennehey@mdwcg.com)
(Wilmington, DE Office*: Nemours Building, 1007 North Orange Street, Suite 600, 19801)
   (Tel: 302-552-4300)
   (Fax: 302-552-4340)
(Fort Lauderdale, FL Office*: 100 Northeast 3rd Avenue, Suite 1100, 33301)
   (Tel: 954-847-4920)
   (Fax: 954-627-6640)
(Jacksonville, FL Office*: 200 West Forsyth Street, Suite 1400, 32202)
   (Tel: 904-358-4200)
   (Fax: 904-355-0019)
(Orlando, FL Office*: Landmark Center One, 315 East Robinson Street, Suite 550, 32801-1948)
   (Tel: 407-420-4380)
   (Fax: 407-839-3008)
(Tampa, FL Office*: 201 East Kennedy Boulevard, Suite 1100, 33602)
   (Tel: 813-898-1800)
   (Fax: 813-221-5026)
(Cherry Hill, NJ Office*: Woodland Falls Corporate Park, 200 Lake Drive East, Suite 300, 08002)
   (Tel: 856-414-6000)
   (Fax: 856-414-6077)
(Roseland, NJ Office*: 425 Eagle Rock Avenue, Suite 302, 07068)
   (Tel: 973-618-4100)
   (Fax: 973-618-0685)
(Melville, NY Office*: 105 Maxess Road, Suite 303, 11747)
   (Tel: 631-232-6130)
   (Fax: 631-232-6184)
(Cincinnati, OH Office*: 312 Elm Street, Suite 1850, 45202)
   (Tel: 513-375-6800)
   (Fax: 513-372-6801)
(Cleveland, OH Office*: 127 Public Square, Suite 3510, 44114-1291)
   (Tel: 216-912-3800)
   (Fax: 216-344-9006)
(Allentown, PA Office*: 4905 West Tilghman Street, Suite 300, 18104)
   (Tel: 484-895-2300)
   (Fax: 484-895-2303)
(Doylestown, PA Office*: 10 North Main Street, 2nd Floor, 18901-4318)
   (Tel: 267-880-2020)
   (Fax: 215-348-5439)
(Erie, PA Office*: 717 State Street, Suite 701, 16501)
   (Tel: 814-480-7800)
   (Fax: 814-455-3603)
(Camp Hill, PA Office*(See Harrisburg listing): 100 Coporate Center Drive, Suite 201, 17011)
   (Tel: 717-651-3500)
   (Fax: 717-651-9630)

NEW YORK

Marshall Dennehey Warner Coleman & Goggin, New York, NY (Continued)

(King of Prussia, PA Office*: 620 Freedom Business Center, Suite 300, 19406)
 (Tel: 610-354-8250)
 (Fax: 610-354-8299)
(Pittsburgh, PA Office*: U.S. Steel Tower, Suite 2900, 600 Grant Street, 15219)
 (Tel: 412-803-1140)
 (Fax: 412-803-1188)
(Moosic, PA Office*(See Scranton listing): 50 Glenmaura National Boulevard, 18507)
 (Tel: 570-496-4600)
 (Fax: 570-496-0567)
(Rye Brook, NY Office*(See Westchester listing): 800 Westchester Avenue, Suite C-700, 10573)
 (Tel: 914-977-7300)
 (Fax: 914-977-7301)

Established: 2010

Amusements, Sports and Recreation Liability, Asbestos and Mass Tort Litigation, Automobile Liability, Aviation and Complex Litigation, Construction Injury Litigation, Fraud/Special Investigation, General Liability, Hospitality and Liquor Liability, Maritime Litigation, Product Liability, Property Litigation, Retail Liability, Trucking & Transportation Liability, Appellate Advocacy and Post-Trial Practice, Architectural, Engineering and Construction Defect Litigation, Class Action Litigation, Commercial Litigation, Consumer and Credit Law, Employment Law, Environmental & Toxic Tort Litigation, Insurance Coverage/Bad Faith Litigation, Life, Health and Disability Litigation, Privacy and Data Security, Professional Liability, Public Entity and Civil Rights Litigation, Real Estate E&O Liability, School Leaders' Liability, Securities and Investment Professional Liability, Technology, Media and Intellectual Property Litigation, White Collar Crime, Birth Injury Litigation, Health Care Governmental Compliance, Health Care Liability, Health Law, Long-Term Care Liability, Medical Device and Pharmaceutical Liability, Medicare Set-Aside, Workers' Compensation

Firm Profile: Marshall Dennehey Warner Coleman & Goggin's New York City office is located in Manhattan's Financial District. The office is close to the City's Supreme and Civil Courts.

The home of many renowned business institutions, such as The New York Stock Exchange, the City also boasts the presence of some of the world's finest museums, theaters, universities, sport venues, hotels and restaurants.

Additional information regarding this office is available by contacting Jeffrey J. Imeri, Esquire, at (212) 376-6408 or jjimeri@mdwcg.com

Managing Shareholder

Jeffrey J. Imeri — 1960 — Queens College of the City University of New York, B.A., 1982; M.S., 1985; New York Law School, J.D. (cum laude) 1989 — Admitted to Bar, 1990, New York; 1991, U.S. District Court, Eastern and Southern Districts of New York; 2006, U.S. Court of Appeals, Second Circuit — Seminars/Classes Taught: Numerous training seminars for insurance company claim professionals nationwide with respect to proper claim handling, discovery, litigation and the avoidance of bad faith claims — Practice Areas: Insurance Coverage; Bad Faith; Professional Liability; Legal Malpractice; Medical Malpractice; Premises Liability; Motor Vehicle; Product Liability; Personal Injury; Environmental Law; Toxic Torts; Reinsurance; Errors and Omissions; Directors and Officers Liability — E-mail: jimeri@mdwcg.com

Senior Counsel

James A. Gallagher　　　　　Thomas G. Vaughan

Of Counsel

William R. Connor, III　　　　John K. McElligott
James J. Ruddy

Marshall Dennehey Warner Coleman & Goggin, New York, NY (Continued)

Resident Shareholders

Steven M. Christman　　　　Daniel G. McDermott
Edward C. Radzik

Resident Associates

Adam C. Calvert　　　　　　John T. Cofresi
Christopher DiCicco　　　　Michael P. Gallagher
Jay A. Hamad　　　　　　　Nadira Kirkland
R. David Lane　　　　　　　Matthew T. Loesberg
Jillian M. Mark　　　　　　　Lori J. Quinn
Sholom P. Wohlgelernter

(See listing under Philadelphia, PA for additional information)

McAloon & Friedman, P.C.

123 William Street, Floor 25
New York, New York 10038-3804
 Telephone: 212-732-8700
 Fax: 212-227-2903
 E-Mail: tedrosenzweig@mcf-esq.com

Established: 1946

Medical Malpractice, Health Care, Hospital Malpractice, Trial and Appellate Practice, Dental Malpractice, Regulatory and Compliance, Medical Litigation

Firm Profile: McAloon & Friedman is dedicated to serving the legal needs of health care professionals and institutions in the New York area. The firm has provided a full range of legal services and advice related to the practice of medicine for more than 60 years.

Insurance Clients

Allied World Assurance Company
Combined Coordinating Council, Inc.
Hospitals Insurance Company, Inc.
Medical Liability Mutual Insurance Company
Physicians Reciprocal Insurers
CHG Healthcare Services, Inc.
Federation of Jewish Philanthophies Service Corp.
Interstate Insurance Company
Medical Malpractice Insurance Pool of New York State
Uni-Ter Underwriting Management Corporation

Non-Insurance Clients

Continuum Health Partners, Inc.
The New York Presbyterian Hospital
New York City Health & Hospitals Corp.
Planned Parenthood Federation of America, Inc.

Partners

Stanley B. Friedman — Vanderbilt University; New York University, B.A., 1952; LL.B., 1954 — Admitted to Bar, 1955, New York; 1978, Florida — Member American Board of Professional Liability Attorneys; American Board of Trial Advocates

Theodore B. Rosenzweig　　Gary A. Greenfield
Brendan J. Lantier　　　　　Lawrence W. Mumm
Laura R. Shapiro　　　　　Stephen S. York
Wayne M. Roth　　　　　　Lisa B. Goldstein
Adam R. Goldsmith　　　　Charles K. Faillace
Gillian A. Fisher　　　　　　Corey L. Wishner
Linda P. McMillan　　　　　Kenneth Fox
Matthew L. Prisco　　　　　Jayne Jahre
Gina B. DiFolco　　　　　　David Bohrer

Senior Counsel

Kenneth P. Starace　　　　Lawrence Burnett

NEW YORK

Mendes & Mount, LLP

750 Seventh Avenue
New York, New York 10019-6829
   Telephone: 212-261-8000
   Fax: 212-261-8750
   E-Mail: info@mendes.com
   www.mendes.com

Established: 1916

Insurance Law, Excess, Reinsurance, Medical Malpractice, Legal Malpractice, Product Liability, Professional Liability, Admiralty and Maritime Law, Aviation, Casualty, Inland Marine, Trial Practice, Appellate Practice, Utilities

Firm Profile: With offices in New York, New Jersey and Los Angeles, Mendes & Mount, LLP serves the insurance and reinsurance industry throughout the United States. Founded early in the 20th Century, the Firm has grown to its current size through careful attention to the needs of its clients and awareness of the forces and emerging trends driving their industry. The attorneys at Mendes & Mount, LLP counsel their clients in insurance and reinsurance areas such as professional liability, directors' and officers' liability, aviation, comprehensive general liability, medical malpractice and property coverage. Clients of the Firm consistently benefit from an institutional body of knowledge that helps them craft innovative solutions to the underwriting and claims challenges encountered in today's marketplace.

A significant component of the Firm's practice involves the litigation and arbitration of insurance and reinsurance coverage disputes. Appearing before state and federal courts throughout the United States, the attorneys of the Firm have represented insurers in all manner of coverage disputes, including asbestos, pollution, property, professional liability and aviation claims. In arbitration, Mendes & Mount, LLP attorneys have represented reinsurers and cedents in long-tail and current year coverage disputes. In addition to coverage proceedings, the Firm's attorneys also act as defense counsel in such matters as aviation product claims and asbestos disputes.

Insurance Clients

ACE Global Markets Limited (UK)
Global Aerospace Underwriting Managers, Ltd.
Axis Re
Swiss Re Financial Services Business Group

Partners

Matthew B. Anderson — 1970 — Western Washington State College, B.S., 1993; Northwestern School of Law of Lewis & Clark College, J.D., 1996 — Admitted to Bar, 1996, Washington; 1999, New York — E-mail: matthew.anderson@mendes.com

SoJin Bae — 1973 — Cornell University, B.A., 1996; Fordham University School of Law, J.D., 2001 — Admitted to Bar, 2002, New York — E-mail: sojin.bae@mendes.com

Heather K. Calvano — 1974 — Hofstra University, B.A., 1995; Hofstra University School of Law, J.D., 1998 — Admitted to Bar, 1999, New York — E-mail: heather.calvano@mendes.com

Mary Ann D'Amato — 1950 — Fordham University, B.A., 1972; St. John's University School of Law, J.D., 1975 — Admitted to Bar, 1976, New York — E-mail: maryann.damato@mendes.com

Patrick J. Donohue — 1965 — Bucknell University, B.A., 1987; M.A., 1991; University of Pittsburgh School of Law, J.D., 1994 — Admitted to Bar, 1995, New York — E-mail: patrick.donohue@mendes.com

Robert M. Flannery — 1957 — Boston College, A.B. (cum laude), 1979; Fordham University School of Law, J.D., 1982 — Admitted to Bar, 1984, New York — E-mail: robert.flannery@mendes.com

Michael A. Fleming — 1968 — Rensselaer Polytechnic Institute, B.S.I.E., 1991; Brooklyn Law School, J.D., 1998 — Admitted to Bar, 1999, New York — E-mail: michael.fleming@mendes.com

Kevin G. Flynn — 1964 — St. John's University, B.S., 1986; St. John's University School of Law, J.D., 1989 — Admitted to Bar, 1990, New York — E-mail: kevin.flynn@mendes.com

William H. Jeberg — 1976 — State University of New York at Binghamton, B.A., 1998; St. John's University School of Law, J.D., 2001 — Admitted to Bar, 2002, New York — E-mail: william.jeberg@mendes.com

Eileen T. McCabe — 1960 — Gettysburg College, B.A. (magna cum laude),

Mendes & Mount, LLP, New York, NY (Continued)

1982; Washington and Lee University School of Law, J.D., 1985 — Admitted to Bar, 1985, Virginia; 1988, New York — E-mail: eileen.mccabe@mendes.com

Richard C. Milazzo — 1955 — Manhattan College, B.A. (summa cum laude), 1977; Brooklyn Law School, J.D., 1980 — Admitted to Bar, 1981, New York — E-mail: richard.milazzo@mendes.com

Michael E. Morley — 1963 — East Carolina University, B.S., 1985; Syracuse University College of Law, J.D., 1989 — Admitted to Bar, 1989, Connecticut; 1990, New York — E-mail: michael.morley@mendes.com

Edward T. Smith — 1972 — Binghamton University, B.S. Mech. Engr., 1994; Fordham Law School, J.D., 1997 — Admitted to Bar, 1998, New York — E-mail: edward.smith@mendes.com

Anthony P. Spain — 1957 — Manhattan College, B.A. (cum laude), 1979; Fordham University School of Law, J.D., 1983 — Admitted to Bar, 1984, New York — E-mail: anthony.spain@mendes.com

Michelle Szalai — 1978 — University of Pennsylvania, B.A., 2000; St. Johns University School of Law, J.D., 2003 — Admitted to Bar, 2004, New York — E-mail: michelle.szalai@mendes.com

Raymond R. Trismen — 1958 — Fairfield University, B.S. (cum laude), 1980; Fordham University School of Law, J.D., 1983 — Admitted to Bar, 1984, New York — E-mail: raymond.trismen@mendes.com

Arthur J. Washington — 1952 — Northwestern University, B.A., 1973; Northwestern University School of Law, J.D., 1976 — Admitted to Bar, 1978, New York — E-mail: arthur.washington@mendes.com

Of Counsel

John G. McAndrews — 1949 — State University of New York at Stony Brook; Fordham University, B.S., 1971; New York University School of Law, J.D., 1974 — Admitted to Bar, 1975, New York — E-mail: john.mcandrews@mendes.com

Thomas J. Quinn — 1946 — Villanova University; Seton Hall University, B.A., 1968; Fordham University School of Law, J.D., 1976 — Admitted to Bar, 1976, New Jersey; 1977, New York — E-mail: thomas.quinn@mendes.com

Methfessel & Werbel

450 Seventh Avenue, Suite 1400
New York, New York 10123
   Telephone: 212-947-1999
   Fax: 212-947-3333
   www.methwerb.com

(Edison, NJ Office*: 2025 Lincoln Highway, Suite 200, 08817, P.O. Box 3012, 08818-3012)
   (Tel: 732-248-4200)
   (Fax: 732-248-2355)
   (E-Mail: mailbox@methwerb.com)
(Wayne, PA Office*: 101 East Lancaster Avenue, Suite 304, 19087)
   (Tel: 610-902-0150)
   (Fax: 610-902-0152)

Automobile Liability, Bad Faith, Carrier Defense, Casualty Defense, Casualty Insurance Law, Civil Rights, Civil Trial Practice, Comprehensive General Liability, Construction Litigation, Coverage Analysis, Coverage Issues, Defense Litigation, Employment Practices Liability, Environmental Coverage, Environmental Liability, Examinations Under Oath, Excess and Umbrella, Insurance Coverage, Insurance Defense, Medical Liability, Premises Liability, Primary and Excess Insurance, Product Liability, Professional Malpractice, Property Liability, Public Entities, Toxic Torts, Uninsured and Underinsured Motorist

(See listing under Edison, NJ for additional information)

(This firm is also listed in the Subrogation section of this directory)

NEW YORK

Mintzer Sarowitz Zeris Ledva & Meyers, LLP

39 Broadway, Suite 950
New York, New York 10006
   Telephone: 212-968-8300
   Fax: 212-968-9840
   www.Defensecounsel.com

(Additional Offices: Philadelphia, PA*; Miami, FL*; Cherry Hill, NJ*; Hicksville, NY*; Pittsburgh, PA*; Wilmington, DE*; Tampa, FL*; Wheeling, WV*)

Insurance Defense, Premises Liability, Product Liability, Environmental Law, Workers' Compensation, Coverage Issues, Asbestos Litigation, Medical Malpractice, Nursing Home Liability, Professional Liability, Trucking Law

Managing Partner

Richard A. Gash

(See listing under Philadelphia, PA for additional information)

Molod Spitz & DeSantis, P.C.

1430 Broadway, 21st Floor
New York, New York 10018
   Telephone: 212-869-3200
   Fax: 212-869-4242
   E-Mail: attorneys@molodspitz.com
   www.molodspitz.com

(Jersey City, NJ Office*: 35 Journal Square, Suite 1005, 07306)
   (Tel: 201-795-5400)

General Practice, Trial Practice, Negligence, Fire, Casualty, Construction Law, Product Liability, Toxic Torts, Environmental Law, First Party Matters, Medical Malpractice, Subrogation

Firm Profile: Molod Spitz & DeSantis, P.C. offers a full range of legal services to the risk industry including defense of individuals, corporations, and insureds in many areas of third party litigation. We assume an aggressive defense posture, pursuing discovery early in order to define the parameters of every case on which we serve. To contain the economic impact of litigation, we balance the cost of defense against all possible outcomes, and constantly update our clients.

The lawyers on the Molod Spitz & DeSantis staff are experienced litigators who have handled trials of cases with significant exposure in all types of civil litigation including automobile accidents, construction accidents, premises liability, lead paint litigation, security claims, product liability, fire related cases, first party coverage questions, first party claims, and error and omission in the brokerage, agent and legal areas, medical malpractice and workplace claims such as harassment and discrimination.

Our clients include prominent insurance companies, self-insureds, major consumer product companies and retail chains, trucking and leasing companies, and numerous uninsured defendants.

Insurance Clients

Church Mutual Insurance Company
Colony Insurance Company
Global Indemnity Group, Inc.
GuideOne Insurance
Nationwide Mutual Insurance Company
Philadelphia Insurance Companies
United Educators Insurance
Clermont Specialty Managers, Ltd.
Federated Mutual Insurance Company
Magna Carta Companies
Navigators Management Company
Park Insurance Company
TransGuard Insurance Company of America, Inc.

Non-Insurance Clients

Mendon Leasing Corporation
Target Corporation
Yeshiva University
New York Institute of Technology
Veolia Transportation, Inc.

Molod Spitz & DeSantis, P.C., New York, NY (Continued)

Partners

Frederick M. Molod — 1930 — Brooklyn Law School, LL.B., 1951; LL.M., 1952 — Admitted to Bar, 1951, New York; 1952, U.S. District Court, Eastern and Southern Districts of New York; 1998, U.S. Supreme Court — Member Association of Trial Lawyers of the City of New York; Federation of Insurance and Corporate Counsel; The Harmonie Group; New York State Trial Lawyers Association; New York County Lawyers Association; American Board of Trial Advocates; Defense Research Institute — E-mail: fmolod@molodspitz.com

Alice Spitz — 1956 — University of Maryland, B.A., 1978; Benjamin N. Cardozo School of Law, J.D., 1981 — Admitted to Bar, 1983, New York; U.S. District Court, Southern District of New York; 1985, U.S. District Court, Eastern District of New York; 2011, U.S. District Court, Northern District of New York — Member American and New York State Bar Associations; New York County Trial Lawyers Association; National Association of Insurance Women; The Harmonie Group; International Association of Defense Counsel; Defense Research Institute; American Board of Trial Advocates — E-mail: aspitz@molodspitz.com

Salvatore J. DeSantis — 1960 — State University of New York at Binghamton, 1982; St. John's University School of Law, J.D., 1985 — Admitted to Bar, 1985, New Jersey; 1986, New York; 1985, U.S. District Court, District of New Jersey; 1986, U.S. District Court, Eastern and Southern Districts of New York — Member New York State Bar Association (Tort and Insurance Practice and Compensation Law Sections); New York State Trial Lawyers Association; Defense Research Institute; Federation of Defense and Corporate Counsel — Resident New York, NY and Jersey City, NJ Office — E-mail: sdesantis@molodspitz.com

Julie E. Molod — 1970 — State University of New York at Binghamton, B.A., 1991; Brooklyn Law School, J.D., 1994 — Admitted to Bar, 1994, New Jersey; 1995, New York; U.S. District Court, Eastern and Southern Districts of New York — Member American and New York State Bar Associations — Resident New York, NY and Jersey City, NJ Office — E-mail: jmolod@molodspitz.com

David B. Owens — 1962 — Queens College of the City University of New York, B.A., 1984; Brooklyn Law School, J.D., 1987 — Admitted to Bar, 1987, New York; 1988, New Jersey; U.S. District Court, District of New Jersey — Resident Nerw York, NY and Jersey City, NJ Office — E-mail: dowens@molodspitz.com

Sean P. King — 1966 — Boston University School of Law, B.A./J.D., 1990 — Admitted to Bar, 1990, Massachusetts; 1993, New York; 2010, New Jersey; 1992, U.S. District Court, District of Massachusetts; U.S. Court of Appeals, First Circuit; 2006, U.S. District Court, Eastern and Southern Districts of New York; U.S. Court of Appeals, Second Circuit; 2010, U.S. District Court, District of New Jersey — Resident New York, NY and Jersey City, NJ Office — E-mail: sking@molodspitz.com

Teresa Gruber — 1971 — Indiana University, B.A., 1993; Pace University School of Law, J.D., 1996 — Admitted to Bar, 1997, Connecticut; 1998, New York; 2001, U.S. District Court, Eastern and Southern Districts of New York — E-mail: tgruber@molodspitz.com

Associates

Andrew B. Small — Tufts University, B.S., 1981; Marquette University Law School, J.D., 1986 — Thomas More Scholar — Admitted to Bar, 1986, Connecticut; 1987, New York; U.S. District Court, Eastern and Southern Districts of New York — E-mail: asmall@molodspitz.com

Carl S. Young — 1937 — Brooklyn College, The City University of New York, B.S., 1961; Brooklyn Law School, LL.B., 1964 — Admitted to Bar, 1965, New York — E-mail: cyoung@molodspitz.com

Christina Romanelli — 1986 — Marist College, B.A., 2008; New York Law School, J.D., 2011 — Admitted to Bar, 2011, New York; New Jersey — Resident New York, NY and Jersey City, NJ Office — E-mail: cromanelli@molodspitz.com

Christopher M. Coleman — 1971 — University of Maryland, B.A., 1994; New England School of Law, J.D., 1998 — Admitted to Bar, 1998, Maryland; 2001, District of Columbia; 2007, New York; 2001, U.S. District Court for the District of Columbia; 2003, U.S. District Court, District of Maryland; 2007, U.S. District Court, Southern District of New York; 2008, U.S. District Court, Eastern District of New York — E-mail: ccoleman@molodspitz.com

Oisin Lambe — 1983 — University College Dublin, B.B.A./LL.B., 2006; University of California at Los Angeles School of the Law, LL.M., 2008 — Admitted to Bar, 2007, New York; 2013, U.S. District Court, Eastern and Southern Districts of New York — Member Irish American Bar Association of New York (Director, 2013); National Association of Subrogation Professionals — E-mail: olambe@molodspitz.com

NEW YORK

Molod Spitz & DeSantis, P.C., New York, NY (Continued)

Robert A. Von Hagen — 1984 — Loyola University, B.A., 2006; St. John's University School of Law, J.D., 2011 — Admitted to Bar, 2012, New York; Florida — E-mail: rvonhagen@molodspitz.com

Ross Weaver — 1948 — Alfred University, B.A., 1970; St. John's University School of Law, J.D., 1973 — Admitted to Bar, 1974, New York; 1976, U.S. District Court, Eastern and Southern Districts of New York; 1984, U.S. Court of Appeals, Second Circuit — E-mail: rweaver@molodspitz.com

Of Counsel

Marcy Sonneborn — 1952 — Cornell University, B.S., 1973; New York Law School, J.D. (cum laude), 1978 — Admitted to Bar, 1979, New York; 2011, U.S. Court of Appeals, Second Circuit — E-mail: msonneborn@molodspitz.com

(This firm is also listed in the Subrogation section of this directory)

Newman Myers Kreines Gross Harris, P.C.

40 Wall Street, 26th Floor
New York, New York 10005
Telephone: 212-619-4350
Fax: 212-619-3622
E-Mail: lawfirm@nmkgh.com
www.nmkgh.com

Established: 1970

Trial Practice, Commercial Law, Property and Casualty, Insurance Law, Insurance Coverage, Employment Law, Appellate Practice, Cargo, Construction Law, Architects and Engineers, General Liability, Drug, Medical Devices, Professional Liability, Admiralty and Maritime Law, Truck Liability, Environmental Law, Toxic Torts, Fidelity and Surety, Public Authority Liability

Firm Profile: Our practice is dedicated to the representation of corporations, insurance companies, public authorities and municipalities in the defense and prosecution of their interests in both state and federal courts in New York and New Jersey; our firm's practice involves statewide litigation in all counties in both New York and New Jersey.

Insurance Clients

ACE USA
Allied World Assurance Company
AON Corporation
Berkshire Hathaway Specialty Insurance
Chartis Insurance
Chubb Group of Insurance Companies
Daily Underwriters of America
ESIS
Landmark Insurance Company
Lexington Insurance Company
Liberty Mutual
Metropolitan Life Insurance Company
RLI Insurance Company
St. Paul Travelers
Sedgwick Claims Management Services, Inc.
Unigard Insurance Company
XL Design Professional
Zurich American Insurance Company
AIG Property Casualty
American International Group, Inc.
Arch Insurance Group
Broadspire
Carolina Casualty Insurance Company
Crawford & Company
Crum & Forster Insurance Group
Endurance Services, Ltd.
Illinois National Insurance Company
Liberty International Underwriters
Markel Corporation
Nautilus Insurance Group
QBE the Americas Group
Rockville Risk Management Associates, Inc.
TransGlobal Adjusting Corp.
Travelers Insurance
Wells Fargo Insurance Services
York Risk Services Group, Inc.
Zurich North America

Non-Insurance Clients

Altria Group, Inc.
Cablevision Industries
The City University of New York
Columbia University
The Dormitory Authority of the State of New York
FedEx Freight East
Forest City Ratner Companies
The Brickman Group, Ltd.
Cable Vision Systems Corporation
Civetta Cousins JV
Daily Express, Inc.
Dragados USA
Federal Express
Forest City Enterprises, Inc.
General Growth Properties, Inc.

Newman Myers Kreines Gross Harris, P.C., New York, NY (Continued)

Home Box Office, Inc.
The Hunt Corporation
Lend Lease Americas, Inc.
Lend Lease (US) Construction Holdings, Inc.
Lend Lease (US) Public Partnerships, LLC
New York City Housing Authority
New York One News/NYC All News Channel, Inc.
Schiavone Construction Co., LLC
Schwan's Home Services
State University of New York
Stevens Transport, Inc.
Sun Company
Time Warner Cable
Turner Broadcasting Corporation
The Howard Hughes Corporation
John P. Picone Inc.
Lend Lease Interiors, Inc.
Lend Lease (US) Construction, Inc.
Lend Lease (US) Construction LMB, Inc.
Metropolitan Transportation Authority
Paragon Communications/Paragon Cable - Manhattan
The Schwan Food Company
Starwood Hotels & Resorts Worldwide, Inc.
SulzerMedica - USA, Inc.
Time, Inc.
Time Warner, Inc.
Zale Corporation

Partners

Jan Kevin Myers — 1955 — State University of New York at Albany, B.A. (cum laude), 1977; Syracuse University College of Law, J.D., 1980 — Admitted to Bar, 1984, New York; 1985, U.S. District Court, Eastern and Southern Districts of New York; 2001, U.S. Supreme Court — Member American and New York State Bar Associations; New York Building Congress; American Institute of Architects; The Associated General Contractors of America; Defense Research Institute — Practice Areas: Construction Law; Professional Liability; Premises Liability; Personal Injury; Property and Casualty; Environmental Law; Product Liability; Toxic Torts — E-mail: jmyers@nmkgh.com

Charles W. Kreines — 1958 — New York University, B.A. (cum laude), 1980; Fordham Law School, J.D., 1983 — Admitted to Bar, 1984, New York; U.S. District Court, Eastern and Southern Districts of New York — Member New York State and Brooklyn Bar Associations; Defense Association of New York; Defense Research Institute — Practice Areas: Personal Injury; Premises Liability; Automobile; Construction Law — E-mail: ckreines@nmkgh.com

Olivia M. Gross — 1959 — Brooklyn College, The City University of New York, B.A. (magna cum laude), 1981; Pace University School of Law, J.D. (cum laude), 1985 — Admitted to Bar, 1986, New York; U.S. District Court, Eastern and Southern Districts of New York — Member New York State Bar Association; New York County Lawyers Association (Torts and Insurance Sections); Professional Women in Construction — Practice Areas: Personal Injury; Trucking Law; Premises Liability; Commercial Law; Construction Law; Insurance Coverage — E-mail: ogross@nmkgh.com

Ian F. Harris — 1959 — State University of New York at Binghamton, B.S., 1981; Emory University School of Law, J.D., 1984 — Admitted to Bar, 1985, New York; U.S. District Court, Eastern and Southern Districts of New York — Member New York State and Westchester County Bar Associations; New York Building Congress; Defense Research Institute — Practice Areas: Construction Law; Premises Liability; Personal Injury; Employment Law; Commercial Law — E-mail: iharris@nmkgh.com

Stephen N. Shapiro — 1947 — Fairleigh Dickinson University, B.A., 1969; Syracuse University College of Law, J.D., 1972 — Admitted to Bar, 1973, New York; U.S. District Court, Eastern District of New York; U.S. Court of Appeals, Second Circuit — E-mail: sshapiro@nmkgh.com

Charles Dewey Cole, Jr. — 1952 — Columbia College, A.B., 1974; The University of Texas at Austin, M.L.I.S., 1982; St. John's University School of Law, J.D., 1979; New York University School of Law, LL.M., 1988; Pace University School of Law, LL.M. (Environmental Law), 1993; Temple University, LL.M. (Trial Advocacy), 1999; The Nottingham Trent University, LL.M. (Advanced Litigation), 2003 — Law Clerk to Chief Justice Judge Joe J. Fisher, U.S. District Court, Eastern District of Texas, 1979-1982; Judge Thomas M. Reavley, U.S. Court of Appeals, Fifth Circuit, 1981-1982 — Admitted to Bar, 1980, New York; Texas; 1986, New Jersey; 1988, District of Columbia; 1995, England; Wales (Solicitor); 2002, England; Wales (Solicitor-Advocate (Civil Proceedings)) — Member New York State Bar Association; The District of Columbia Bar; State Bar of Texas; New York County Lawyers Association — E-mail: dcole@nmkgh.com

Associates

Abraham A. Friedman — 1955 — New York University, B.A. (magna cum laude), 1976; New York University School of Law, J.D., 1979 — Admitted to Bar, 1980, New York; 1994, U.S. District Court, Eastern and Southern Districts of New York; U.S. Supreme Court — E-mail: afriedman@nmkgh.com

NEW YORK

Newman Myers Kreines Gross Harris, P.C., New York, NY (Continued)

Janine Silver — 1956 — University of California, B.A., 1979; St. John's University School of Law, J.D., 1983 — Admitted to Bar, 1984, New York — E-mail: jsilver@nmkgh.com

Richard E. Schmedake — 1965 — State University of New York at New Paltz, B.A., 1993; Brooklyn Law School, J.D., 1998 — Admitted to Bar, 1998, New York; 2003, U.S. District Court, Eastern and Southern Districts of New York — E-mail: rschmedake@nmkgh.com

Adrienne Yaron — 1967 — Columbia University, B.S. (cum laude), 1995; Whittier Law School, J.D. (summa cum laude), 2003 — Admitted to Bar, 2004, New York — E-mail: ayaron@nmkgh.com

Luis G. Sabillon — 1977 — Binghamton University, B.A., 1999; Syracuse University College of Law, J.D., 2002 — Admitted to Bar, 2004, New York; New Jersey — Languages: Spanish — E-mail: lsabillon@nmkgh.com

Michael J. Winter — 1978 — New York University, B.A., 2001; New York Law School, J.D., 2005 — Admitted to Bar, 2006, New York — E-mail: mwinter@nmkgh.com

Patrick M. Caruana — 1979 — University of Southern Maine, B.A., 2002; Touro College Jacob D. Fuchsberg Law Center, J.D. (cum laude), 2006 — Admitted to Bar, 2006, New Jersey; 2007, New York; 2008, U.S. District Court, Eastern and Southern Districts of New York; 2009, U.S. District Court, District of New Jersey — E-mail: pcaruana@nmkgh.com

Suzanne S. Swanson — 1983 — University of Michigan, B.A., 2005; Wayne State University Law School, J.D., 2009 — Admitted to Bar, 2010, New York; Michigan — E-mail: sswanson@nmkgh.com

Andrew Metzar — 1980 — State University of New York at Geneseo, B.A. (cum laude), 2002; New York Law School, J.D., 2009 — Admitted to Bar, 2010, New York — E-mail: ametzar@nmkgh.com

Marc Borden — 1983 — Rutgers College, B.A., 2006; Seton Hall University School of Law, J.D., 2013 — Admitted to Bar, 2013, New Jersey; 2014, New York — E-mail: mborden@nmkgh.com

Nicoletti Gonson Spinner LLP

555 Fifth Avenue, 8th Floor
New York, New York 10017
Telephone: 212-730-7750
Fax: 212-730-7850
E-Mail: fnicoletti@nicolettilaw.com
www.nicolettilaw.com

(Hackensack, NJ Office*: One University Plaza, Suite 412, 07601)
(Tel: 201-487-9400)
(Fax: 201-487-9240)

Established: 1995

Insurance Law, Reinsurance, Coverage Analysis, Product Liability, Excess and Surplus Lines, General Liability, Professional Indemnity, Direct Defense

Insurance Clients

Allied Professionals Insurance Company
Arch Insurance Group
Aspen Specialty Insurance Company
AXA Reinsurance Company
Berkley Custom Insurance Services, LLC
First Excess & Reinsurance Corporation
Fulmont Mutual Insurance Company
HCC Public Risk Claim Service, Inc.
Liberty International Underwriters
Magna Carta Companies
NAS Insurance Group
New York Mutual Underwriters
ProSight Specialty Insurance Company
Allied World Assurance Company
American Service Insurance Company
AXA Liabilities Managers, Inc. (USA)
Axis Re
Clermont Specialty Managers, Ltd.
Endurance U.S. Insurance Operations
First Mercury Insurance Company
Great American Custom Insurance Services
HCC Specialty
Ironshore Environmental
Liberty Mutual Group
Markel Underwriting Managers, Inc.
OneBeacon Insurance
QBE Reinsurance Corporation
Rockhill Insurance Company

Nicoletti Gonson Spinner LLP, New York, NY (Continued)

ROM Reinsurance Management Company
Starr Indemnity & Liability Company
Swiss Re Underwriters
United National Group
Utica First Insurance Company
Westport Insurance Company
Scottsdale Insurance Company
Security Mutual Insurance Company
Swiss Reinsurance Company
Tokio Marine Management, Inc.
United States Liability Insurance Group
Wuerttembergische Versicherungs AG

Non-Insurance Clients

U-Haul International, Inc.

Partners

Frank M. Nicoletti — 1944 — Syracuse University, B.A., 1966; Suffolk University Law School, J.D., 1970 — Admitted to Bar, 1972, New York; 1973, U.S. District Court, Eastern and Southern Districts of New York; 1975, U.S. Court of Appeals, Second Circuit; U.S. Supreme Court; 1993, U.S. District Court, Northern District of New York; 2004, U.S. District Court for the District of Columbia — Member International, American and New York State Bar Associations; The Association of the Bar of the City of New York; Columbian Lawyers Association of New York; International Association of Claim Professionals; ARIAS; New York County Lawyers Association; Defense Association of New York; Defense Research Institute — General Counsel, ROM Reinsurance Management Company (1986-Present); General Counsel, IACP (2006-2012); IACP Meritorious Service Award, 2009

Benjamin N. Gonson — 1959 — University of Maryland, B.A., 1981; Inter American University Law School, J.D., 1986 — Admitted to Bar, 1987, New York; 1988, U.S. District Court, Northern and Southern Districts of New York — Member American and New York State Bar Associations; The Association of the Bar of the City of New York (Tort Committee); New York County Trial Lawyers Association

Marina A. Spinner — 1967 — Barnard College, B.A., 1988; Pace University School of Law, J.D., 1994 — Admitted to Bar, 1994, New Jersey; 1995, New York; 1994, U.S. District Court, District of New Jersey — Member American Bar Association

Joseph J. Gulino — 1958 — St. Mary of the Plains College, B.A., 1980; California Western School of Law, J.D., 1983 — National Trial Team, California Western School of Law — Admitted to Bar, 1984, New York; 1985, New Jersey; 1984, U.S. District Court, Eastern and Southern Districts of New York; 1985, U.S. District Court, District of New Jersey — Member New York State Bar Association; New York County Lawyers Association

Kevin M. Ryan — 1963 — University of Virginia, B.A. (with high distinction), 1985; Boston College Law School, J.D., 1988 — Admitted to Bar, 1989, New York; 1991, U.S. District Court, Eastern and Southern Districts of New York — Member New York County Lawyers Association; Defense Association of New York

Kevin Pinter — 1965 — Binghamton University, B.S., 1987; Brooklyn Law School, J.D. (Dean's List), 1990 — Admitted to Bar, 1991, New York; New Jersey; U.S. District Court, Eastern, Northern and Southern Districts of New York; U.S. District Court, District of New Jersey — Member New York State Bar Association; Defense Association of New York — Languages: Spanish

Gary R. Greenman — 1951 — Queens College of the City University of New York, B.A., 1973; St. John's University School of Law, J.D., 1981 — Admitted to Bar, 1982, New York; U.S. District Court, Eastern and Southern Districts of New York; U.S. Court of Appeals, Second Circuit; U.S. Supreme Court

Junior Partners

Michael S. Brown — 1968 — University of Maryland, B.A., 1990; New York Law School, J.D., 1993 — Admitted to Bar, 1994, New York; Connecticut; 1996, District of Columbia; U.S. District Court, Eastern and Southern Districts of New York — Member New York State Bar Association

Edward S. Benson — 1963 — College of Law, London, England, 1985; University College London, LL.B., 1984 — Admitted to Bar, 1993, New York; U.S. District Court, Eastern and Southern Districts of New York — Member The Law Society of England and Wales

Elana Maureen Schachner — 1972 — Tel Aviv University, LL.B., 1998 — Admitted to Bar, 1998, Israel; 1999, New York

Angela A. Lainhart — 1964 — State University of New York at Binghamton, B.A., 1986; St. John's University School of Law, J.D., 1991 — Admitted to Bar, 1992, New York; 1998, New Jersey; 1992, U.S. District Court, Eastern and Southern Districts of New York; U.S. Court of Appeals, Second

NEW YORK

Nicoletti Gonson Spinner LLP, New York, NY (Continued)

Circuit — Member New York State Bar Association; New York County Lawyers Association

Associates

Laura M. Mattera — 1954 — State University of New York at Stony Brook, B.A., 1975; Fordham Law School, J.D., 1978 — Admitted to Bar, 1979, New York; U.S. District Court, Eastern and Southern Districts of New York

Jamie T. Packer — 1970 — State University of New York at Albany, B.A., 1992; Whittier Law School, J.D., 1995 — Admitted to Bar, 1995, New Jersey; 1996, New York; 2000, U.S. District Court, Eastern and Southern Districts of New York — Member New York State Bar Association

Melissa Jacobs — 1970 — Cornell University, B.A. (Dean's List), 1992; Georgia State University College of Law, J.D., 1998 — Admitted to Bar, 1999, New York — Member New York State Trial Lawyers Association — Languages: French

Valerie Rivera — 1968 — John Jay College of Criminal Justice, B.A., 1992; Quinnipiac College School of Law, J.D., 2000 — Admitted to Bar, 2000, New York; 2002, U.S. District Court, Eastern and Southern Districts of New York — Member New York State Trial Lawyers Association — Languages: Spanish

Christine Vetter — 1978 — The Pennsylvania State University, B.A. (Dean's List), 2001; University at Buffalo Law School, J.D., 2004 — Admitted to Bar, 2005, New York — Member New York State Bar Association

Kevin S. Locke — 1970 — State University of New York at Albany, B.S., 1992; Touro College Jacob D. Fuchsberg Law Center, J.D., 1995 — Moot Court Board — Admitted to Bar, 1996, New York

Jason I. Gomes — Hofstra University, B.A., 2000; Hofstra University School of Law, J.D., 2004 — Admitted to Bar, 2005, New York; 2011, U.S. District Court, Eastern and Southern Districts of New York — Member New York State Bar Association; New York State Trial Lawyers Association

Aaliyah C. Shorte — 1976 — State University of New York at Albany, B.A. (Dean's List), 1998; Pace University School of Law, J.D., 2002 — Member, Grand Moot Court Team — Admitted to Bar, 2004, New York — Member New York State Bar Association; New York State Trial Lawyers Association

Sean O. Edwards — Cornell University, B.S., 1996; Northeastern University School of Law, J.D., 1999 — Admitted to Bar, 2001, New York; 2002, U.S. District Court, Eastern and Southern Districts of New York

Rachel E. Katz — 1979 — Washington University in St. Louis, B.S., 2001; New York University, M.A., 2005; Case Western Reserve University School of Law, J.D., 2008 — Admitted to Bar, 2008, New Jersey; 2009, New York; Connecticut; U.S. District Court, Eastern and Southern Districts of New York; 2011, U.S. District Court, District of Connecticut

Kenneth Kim — 1977 — University of California, Los Angeles, B.A., 1999; University of San Diego School of Law, J.D., 2002 — Admitted to Bar, 2002, California; 2008, New York

Frank G. DiSpirito — 1984 — University of Tampa, B.A. (cum laude), 2005; New York Law School, J.D. (cum laude), 2009 — Admitted to Bar, 2010, New York; New Jersey

Dana M. Catanzaro — Fairfield University, B.A. (cum laude), 2006; New York Law School, J.D. (cum laude), 2009 — Admitted to Bar, 2009, New Jersey; 2010, New York; 2009, U.S. District Court, District of New Jersey; 2010, U.S. District Court, Eastern and Southern Districts of New York

Ohrenstein & Brown, LLP

The Chrysler Building
405 Lexington Avenue, 37th Floor
New York, New York 10174
   Telephone: 212-682-4500
   www.oandb.com

(Garden City, NY Office*: 1305 Franklin Avenue, Suite 300, 11530)
   (Tel: 516-873-6334)
   (Fax: 516-873-8912)
   (E-Mail: michael.brown@oandb.com)
(West Caldwell, NJ Office: 1129 Bloomfield Avenue, Suite 214, 07006)
   (Tel: 973-882-8508)
   (Fax: 973-882-8717)

Ohrenstein & Brown, LLP, New York, NY (Continued)

Agent/Broker Liability, Construction Litigation, Directors and Officers Liability, Employment Law, Environmental Law, Insurance Coverage, Municipal Liability, Product Liability, Professional Liability, Regulatory and Compliance, Reinsurance

Firm Profile: Ohrenstein & Brown is known for representing & advising insureds, industry trade groups, insurance brokers and insurance companies. Our meticulous understanding of multistate legislative and regulatory insurance has made us a trusted advisor to our clients in all aspects of the insurance industry.

(See listing under Garden City, NY for additional information)

The Peisner Girsh Group LLP

225 Broadway, Suite 2199
New York, New York 10007-3718
   Telephone: 212-964-0020
   Fax: 212-964-0098
   E-Mail: kpeisner@peisnerlaw.com
   http://peisnerlawfirm.com/

(Short Hills, NJ Office*: 1 Short Hills Avenue, 07078, 225 Broadway, Suite 2199, 10007)
   (Tel: 212-964-0020)
   (E-Mail: office@peisnerlaw.com)
   (www.peisnerlaw.com)

Amusements, Construction Accidents, Coverage Issues, Excess, Insurance Coverage, Insurance Defense, Intentional Torts, Liquor Liability, Malpractice, Municipal Liability, Premises Liability, Professional Negligence, Property Liability, Restaurant Liability, School Law, Slip and Fall, Tort Litigation, Trial and Appellate Practice, Wrongful Death, Negligent Security, Automobile Liability, Casualty Defense

Firm Profile: We are a tort litigation firm known for integrity, tenacity, successful resolution of cases, and superb service at reasonable fees. Diverse in gender (majority female ownership), and ethnicity, we are Martindale-Hubbell AV rated for highest in legal ability and ethical standards.

We specialize in litigation involving premises liability, labor law, negligent security, assaults, amusements, school liability, restaurant liability, food poisoning, Dram Shop, intentional torts, and subrogation. We have a reputation for consistant success at trial and mediation. We handle our own appeals.

Representative Insurance Clients

Magna Carta Companies	QBE Insurance Company
Rockville Risk Management Associates, Inc.	

Partners

Kathi Peisner — University of Michigan, B.A., 1975; New York Law School, J.D. (cum laude), 1980 — Admitted to Bar, 1981, New York; 1983, U.S. District Court, Eastern and Southern Districts of New York — Member New York State Bar Association; International Association of Claims Professionals (Past Presenter); The Council on Litigation Management (Nominated Member) — E-mail: kpeisner@peisnerlaw.com

Larisa Girsh — Temple University, B.A. (cum laude), 1996; Touro College Jacob D. Fuchsberg Law Center, J.D., 1999 — Admitted to Bar, 2000, New York; New Jersey — Member American and New York State Bar Associations; The Association of Professional Insurance Women — Languages: Russian — E-mail: lgirsh@peisnerlaw.com

Senior Attorneys

Allen H. Gueldenzopf — University of Wisconsin, B.A. (with honors), 1975; New York Law School, J.D., 1979 — Admitted to Bar, 1980, New York; 1982, U.S. District Court, Eastern and Southern Districts of New York — Member New York County Lawyers Association — E-mail: agueldenzopf@peisnerlaw.com

NEW YORK

The Peisner Girsh Group LLP, New York, NY (Continued)

Gerald G. Cowen — Wagner College, B.A., 1975; St. John's University School of Law, J.D., 1978 — Admitted to Bar, 1978, New York; U.S. District Court, Eastern and Southern Districts of New York — E-mail: gcowen@peisnerlaw.com

Of Counsel

Matthew E. Schaefer   Brian King

Law Offices of Michael E. Pressman

125 Maiden Lane-17th Floor
New York, New York 10038
    Telephone: 212-480-3030
    Fax: 212-480-2590
    Toll Free: 800-764-3030
    E-Mail: mepressman@mepressman.com

(Warren, NJ Office*: Warrenville Plaza, 31W, Mountain Boulevard, 07059)
    (Tel: 908-753-6661)
    (Fax: 908-755-5229; 212-480-2590)
    (Toll Free: 800-764-3030)
(Brooklyn, NY Office*: 26 Court Street, Suite 1700, 11242)
    (Tel: 718-237-4600)
    (Fax: 212-480-2590)
    (Toll Free: 800-764-3030)
(Garden City, NY Office*(See Long Island City listing): 114 Chestnut Street, 11530)
    (Fax: 212-480-2590)
    (Toll Free: 800-764-3030)

Established: 1984

Insurance Defense, Automobile, General Liability, Product Liability, Property and Casualty

Insurance Clients

Alliance United Insurance Company
American Family Insurance Group
American Insurance Managers
Associated Mutual Insurance Cooperative
Central Mutual Insurance Company
Clermont Specialty Managers, Ltd.
FARA Insurance Services
Farm Bureau Insurance of Michigan
First State Insurance Company
General Star National Insurance Company
Indiana Farm Bureau
Leading Insurance Services, Inc.
Michigan Farm Bureau
Nebraska Farm Bureau
New York State Insurance Department
PSM Insurance Companies
RiverStone Claims Management, LLC
Virginia Farm Bureau Mutual Insurance Company
American Bankers Insurance Group
American Heartland Insurance Company
Assurant Insurance Group
CAA Insurance Company
Cincinnati Financial Corporation
Everest National Insurance Company
First Insurance Network, Inc.
First Judicial Claim Service Inc.
GAB Robins North America, Inc.
Georgia Farm Bureau Mutual Insurance Company
Kensington Insurance Company
Maya Assurance Company
Morstan General Agency, Inc.
New York Central Mutual Fire Insurance Company
North American Risk Services
QBE
United Automobile Insurance Company

Non-Insurance Clients

Central Parking Corporation
Papa John's International, Inc.
Office Depot, Inc.
The Shaw Group, Inc.

Senior Partner

Michael E. Pressman — 1950 — Clark University, B.A. (with high honors), 1972; Rutgers University School of Law, J.D., 1976 — Phi Beta Kappa — Admitted to Bar, 1976, Pennsylvania; 1977, New York; U.S. District Court, Eastern and Southern Districts of New York; U.S. Court of Appeals, Second Circuit — Member American and New York State Bar Associations (Lecturer); New York State Trial Lawyers Association (Lecturer); New York State Insurance Association (Lecturer); Association of Trial Lawyers of the

Law Offices of Michael E. Pressman, New York, NY (Continued)

City of New York (President); New York City Trial Lawyers (Board of Governors, Chairman of the Board, Judicial Screening Committee Brooklyn and Bronx); Defense Research Institute — New York State Judicial Selection Committee for Appointment of Supreme and Civil Court Judges for the City of New York (County of Kings and Bronx); Lawyer of the Year Award from UJA-Federation; Chair Person and Presenter of the Harlan Fiske Stone Award

Partners

Steven H. Cohen — 1956 — Adelphi University, B.S., 1979; Golden Gate University School of Law, J.D., 1982 — Admitted to Bar, 1985, New York; California — Member New York State Bar Association

Eric S. Fenyes — 1961 — Yeshiva University, B.A., 1984; Touro College Jacob D. Fuchsberg Law Center, J.D., 1987 — Admitted to Bar, 1988, New York — Member American Bar Association; New York County Lawyers Association

Tod S. Fichtelberg — 1958 — State University of New York at Oswego, B.A., 1980; Vermont Law School, J.D., 1987 — Admitted to Bar, 1988, New York — Member New York State Bar Association; New York County Lawyers Association

Seth I. Kudler — 1966 — American University, B.A., 1988; New York Law School, J.D., 1991 — Admitted to Bar, 1991, Connecticut; 1992, New York

Robert Baumgarten — 1959 — State University of New York at Stony Brook, B.A., 1981; New York Law School, J.D. (cum laude), 1984 — Admitted to Bar, 1985, New York; New Jersey; U.S. District Court, Eastern and Southern Districts of New York; U.S. District Court, District of New Jersey

Robert S. Bonelli — 1957 — Fordham University, B.A., 1979; Fordham University School of Law, J.D., 1983 — Admitted to Bar, 1985, New York — Languages: Spanish

Stuart B. Cholewa — 1978 — Syracuse University, B.S., 2000; University of Miami School of Law, J.D. (cum laude), 2003 — Admitted to Bar, 2004, New York

Steve D. Byoun — 1969 — Nyack College, B.A., 1994; Pace University School of Law, J.D., 1999 — Admitted to Bar, 2000, New York; New Jersey; 2001, U.S. District Court, Eastern and Southern Districts of New York

Associates

Alison B. Cennamo — 1980 — St. John's University, B.A., 2002; Touro College Jacob D. Fuchsberg Law Center, J.D., 2007 — Admitted to Bar, 2008, New York

Vanessa Turner Gottfried — 1987 — State University of New York at Binghamton, B.A. (Dean's List), 2009; Brooklyn Law School, J.D., 2012 — Pro Bono Award — Admitted to Bar, 2013, New York

Edward Robert Averbuch — 1982 — University of Connecticut, B.A., 2004; New York Law School, J.D., 2008 — Admitted to Bar, 2009, New York; Florida; U.S. District Court, Southern District of Florida; 2010, U.S. District Court, Eastern and Southern Districts of New York

Arthur G. Torkiver — 1988 — New York University, B.A., 2010; Brooklyn Law School, J.D., 2013 — Admitted to Bar, 2013, New York; New Jersey; 2014, U.S. District Court, Eastern and Southern Districts of New York — Languages: Russian

Jill Alexandra Farrington — 1984 — University of Dallas, B.A., 2006; St. Johns University School of Law, J.D., 2010 — Bureau of National Affairs Award for Excellence in Labor & Employment Law — Admitted to Bar, 2012, New York

Ropers, Majeski, Kohn & Bentley
A Professional Corporation

750 Third Avenue, 25th Floor
New York, New York 10017
    Telephone: 212-668-5927
    Fax: 212-668-5929
    www.rmkb.com

(Redwood City, CA Office*: 1001 Marshall Street, Suite 500, 94063)
    (Tel: 650-364-8200)
    (Fax: 650-780-1701)
(Los Angeles, CA Office*: 515 South Flower Street, Suite 1100, 90071)
    (Tel: 213-312-2000)
    (Fax: 213-312-2001)

Ropers, Majeski, Kohn & Bentley, A Professional Corporation, New York, NY (Continued)

(San Francisco, CA Office*: 150 Spear Street, Suite 850, 94105)
 (Tel: 415-543-4800)
 (Fax: 415-972-6301)
(San Jose, CA Office*: 50 West San Fernando Street, Suite 1400, 95113)
 (Tel: 408-287-6262)
 (Fax: 408-918-4501)
(Boston, MA Office*: Ten Post Office Square, 8th Floor South, 02109)
 (Tel: 617-850-9087)
 (Fax: 617-850-9088)

Established: 1950

Antitrust, Appellate Practice, Business Litigation, Commercial Litigation, Civil Rights, Class Actions, Complex Litigation, Construction Law, Corporate Law, Elder Abuse, Employment Law, Entertainment Law, Environmental Law, ERISA, Estate Planning, Governmental Entity Defense, Health Care, Intellectual Property, International Law, Mergers and Acquisitions, Personal Injury, Premises Liability, Product Liability, Professional Liability, Real Estate, Toxic Torts, Asset Protection, Banking/Consumer Credit, Catastrophic Injury, Cost Control, Elder Rights, Fee Disputes, Insurance Services, IT and Business Process Outsourcing, Litigation Management, Non-Profit, Proposition 65, Special Education Law, Taxation, Wealth Management

Partners

Andrew L. Margulis — 1963 — Cornell University, B.S., 1965; St. John's University School of Law, J.D., 1988 — Member, St. John's Law Review — Admitted to Bar, 1988, Connecticut; 1989, New York; U.S. District Court, Eastern and Southern Districts of New York; U.S. Court of Appeals, Second and Fifth Circuits — Member New York State Bar Association — Author: "Discovering Justice in Toxic Tort Litigation: CPLR 214-c," 61 St. John's Law Review 262 — Reported Cases: Voluntary Hospitals of America v. National Union, et al., 859 F.Supp. 260 (N.D. Tex) — Practice Areas: Business Litigation; Commercial Litigation; Fidelity; Surety; Employment Litigation; Dispute Resolution; Insurance Litigation; Intellectual Property; Professional Liability; Directors and Officers Liability; Antitrust

Geoffrey W. Heineman — 1958 — New York University, B.A., 1980; St. John's University School of Law, J.D., 1983; New York University School of Law, LL.M., 1988 — Admitted to Bar, 1984, New York; U.S. District Court, Southern District of New York; U.S. Court of Appeals, Second Circuit; U.S. Supreme Court — Member New York State Bar Association; Professional Liability Underwriting Society — Practice Areas: Business Litigation; Commercial Litigation; Employment Litigation; Dispute Resolution; ERISA; Insurance Litigation; Professional Liability

Jung H. Park — 1973 — State University of New York at Binghamton, B.A. (cum laude), 1995; Boston University School of Law, J.D., 1998 — Admitted to Bar, 1999, New York; 2000, California; New Jersey; U.S. District Court, Central, Eastern, Northern and Southern Districts of California; 2007, U.S. District Court, Eastern and Southern Districts of New York — Member National Asian Pacific American Bar Association; National Association Insurance Women — Practice Areas: Business Litigation; Commercial Litigation; Construction Litigation; Professional Liability; Class Actions; Insurance Litigation; Antitrust

Eric C. Weissman — 1977 — Indiana University, B.S., 1999; New York Law School, J.D., 2002 — Admitted to Bar, 2002, New Jersey; 2003, New York; 2002, U.S. District Court, District of New Jersey; 2003, U.S. District Court, Eastern and Southern Districts of New York; U.S. District Court, District of Colorado; U.S. Court of Appeals, Third Circuit — Practice Areas: Business Litigation; Commercial Litigation; Professional Liability; Insurance Litigation; Directors and Officers Liability

Blaise U. Chow — 1975 — University of Rochester, B.A., 1997; Brooklyn Law School, J.D., 2000 — Admitted to Bar, 2000, New York; U.S. District Court, Eastern and Southern Districts of New York — Languages: Cantonese — Practice Areas: Insurance Litigation

Amber W. Locklear — 1979 — University of North Carolina at Asheville, B.A., 2001; Brooklyn College Law School, J.D. (cum laude), 2005 — Admitted to Bar, 2006, New York — Practice Areas: Business Litigation; Commercial Litigation; Employment Litigation; Dispute Resolution; Insurance Litigation; Professional Liability

J. Patrick Geraghty — 1969 — Boston University, B.A., 1991; Seton Hall University School of Law, J.D., 1995 — Admitted to Bar, 1996, New Jersey;

Ropers, Majeski, Kohn & Bentley, A Professional Corporation, New York, NY (Continued)

New York — Member Maritime Law Association — Author: "Every Seafarer Has a Primary Duty That May Provide the Basis of a Defense in a Personal Injury Action," Journal of Law and Commerce, 29 J.L. & COM. 25 (Fall 2010) — Practice Areas: Admiralty and Maritime Law; Business Litigation; Commercial Litigation; Insurance Litigation

Scott W. Bermack — 1964 — Brandeis University, B.A., 1986; American University, Washington College of Law, J.D., 1989 — Admitted to Bar, 1989, New Jersey; 1990, New York; 1991, District of Columbia; U.S. District Court, District of New Jersey; U.S. District Court, Eastern and Southern Districts of New York; Supreme Court of the United States — Member New York State Bar Association; Risk Insurance Management Society; Council on Litigation Management (Chair, New York Labor Law Subcommittee of the Construction Committee); National Retail Restaurant Defense Association (Board of Directors) — Practice Areas: Construction Litigation; Insurance Litigation; Business Litigation; Commercial Litigation; Professional Liability; Catastrophic Injury; Personal Injury; Medical Malpractice; Premises Liability; Product Liability; Toxic Torts

Associates

Diane Fazzolari
Samantha Aster
Michelle L. Gordon

Kirsten M. Lee
Lisa M. Fitzgerald

Of Counsel

Jennifer A. Lowitt — Lehigh University, B.A., 1990; Hofstra University School of Law, J.D., 1993 — Admitted to Bar, 1994, New York — Practice Areas: Insurance Coverage

Robert A. Suarez — 1965 — Rutgers University, B.A., 1988; Temple University School of Law, J.D., 1992 — Admitted to Bar, 1993, New Jersey; 1998, New York; U.S. District Court, District of New Jersey — Member New York State, New Jersey State and Bergen County Bar Associations; Maritime Law Association; Connecticut Maritime Association — Practice Areas: Admiralty and Maritime Law; Business Litigation; Commercial Litigation; Insurance Litigation

(See listing under Redwood City, CA for additional information)

Russo & Toner, LLP

33 Whitehall Street, 16th Floor
New York, New York 10004
 Telephone: 212-482-0001
 Fax: 212-482-0002
 E-Mail: (1stinitiallastname)@russotoner.com
 www.russotoner.com

(Edison, NJ Office: 1024 Amboy Avenue, 08837)
 (Tel: 973-533-4494)
(Trevose, PA Office*: One Neshaminy Interplex, Suite 305, 19053)
 (Tel: 215-874-6816)
(Hartford, CT Office: 100 Pearl Street, 06103)
 (Tel: 860-986-7845)
(Stamford, CT Office: One Stamford Plaza, 263 Tresser Boulevard, 06901)
 (Tel: 203-883-0800)

Established: 1996

Insurance Defense, Automobile, Product Liability, Medical Malpractice, Premises Liability, Professional Liability, Insurance Coverage, Trial Practice, Appellate Practice, Bodily Injury, Property Damage, Toxic Torts, Health, Life Insurance, General Liability, Lead Paint, Subrogation, Errors and Omissions, Construction Litigation, Directors and Officers Liability, Dram Shop Liability, Group Benefits, Coverage Questions, Chemical Exposure

Firm Profile: RUSSO & TONER, LLP is a civil litigation firm which focuses its practice on the defense of insurance companies, insureds and self-insured entities from liability arising out of property, casualty and professional liablity claims pending in both state and federal court.

NEW YORK

Russo & Toner, LLP, New York, NY (Continued)

The firm's primary practice areas include: general liability; auto liability; construction accident cases; complex tort (lead paint, asbestos, mold exposure, etc.); products liability; health, disability and life insurance; ERISA; medical malpractice; errors and ommissions; directors and officers insurance coverage disputes; and appeals.

RUSSO & TONER, LLP was founded in New York City in 1996 by experienced trial attorneys premised upon the promise of delivering results, not merely a defense. The firm is committed to providing the best defense possible with integrity and purpose. It is this commitment which gives us a competitive edge enabling us to consistently achieve our client's goals - whether by trial, settlement, appeal or alternative dispute resolution.

We invite you to browse the RUSSO & TONER, LLP website to learn more about the firm, our attorneys, and the legal services we provide.

Insurance Clients

Academic Health Professionals Insurance Association
AmTrust North America
Arch Insurance Group
Brownstone Agency
The Hartford Insurance Group
Navigators Management Company
North Sea Insurance Company
Park Insurance Company
RLI/Mt. Hawley Insurance Company
Utica Mutual Insurance Company
ACE USA
American Transit Insurance Company
Avalon Bay Communities, Inc.
CIGNA Insurance Company
Liberty Mutual Group
New York Central Mutual Fire Insurance Company
Pure Insurance
RLI Corp.
Travelers Insurance Company

Members of the Firm

Alan Russo — 1955 — American University, B.A. (with honors), 1977; Villanova University School of Law, J.D., 1980 — Admitted to Bar, 1980, Pennsylvania; 1981, New York; 1990, New Jersey; 1991, U.S. District Court, Eastern and Southern Districts of New York; U.S. District Court, District of New Jersey — Member Defense Association of New York — E-mail: arusso@russotoner.com

Stephen B. Toner — 1956 — University of Massachusetts Amherst, B.S., 1978; University of London, England, 1979; University of Hong Kong, 1980; New England School of Law, J.D., 1983 — Admitted to Bar, 1984, Massachusetts; 1986, New York; 2009, Connecticut; 1984, U.S. District Court, District of Massachusetts; 1985, U.S. Court of Appeals, First and Second Circuits; 1987, U.S. District Court, Eastern and Southern Districts of New York; 1989, U.S. Supreme Court — Member American Bar Association; Insurance Federation of New York; New York State Trial Lawyers Association; Defense Research Institute — Certified, Civil Trial Specialist, National Board of Trial Advocacy (NBTA) — E-mail: s.toner@russotoner.com

Partners

Kevin G. Horbatiuk — 1957 — Fordham University, B.A. (summa cum laude), 1978; Fordham University School of Law, J.D., 1981 — Admitted to Bar, 1982, New York; 1985, U.S. District Court, Eastern and Southern Districts of New York; 1993, U.S. Supreme Court; 1994, U.S. District Court, Northern District of New York; 2000, U.S. District Court, Western District of New York; U.S. Court of Appeals, Second Circuit — Member American Bar Association; Defense Research Institute (Life Health and Disability Committee); New York State Trial Lawyers Association; New York County Lawyers Association — E-mail: khorbatiuk@russotoner.com

David Gould — 1964 — University of Wisconsin-Madison, B.A., 1986; Pace University School of Law, J.D., 1991 — Admitted to Bar, 1992, New York; 1998, U.S. District Court, Eastern and Southern Districts of New York — Member American Bar Association; New York State Trial Lawyers Association — Languages: Spanish — E-mail: dgould@russotoner.com

John J. Komar — 1954 — State University of New York at Purchase, B.A., 1980; University of Massachusetts, M.A., 1982; Pace University School of Law, J.D., 1988 — Admitted to Bar, 1988, New York; 1991, U.S. District Court, Southern District of New York; 1997, U.S. Supreme Court — Member New York State Bar Association — E-mail: jkomar@russotoner.com

Theresa Villani — 1955 — State University of New York at Stony Brook, B.A., 1977; St. John's University School of Law, J.D., 1980 — Admitted to Bar, 1981, New York; 1982, U.S. District Court, Eastern and Southern Districts of New York — E-mail: tvillani@russotoner.com

Of Counsel

Michael J. Sweeney — 1959 — Fordham University, B.A., 1981; Stanford University, M.A., 1982; Rutgers University School of Law-Camden, J.D.,

Russo & Toner, LLP, New York, NY (Continued)

1991 — Admitted to Bar, 1992, New York; New Jersey; Pennsylvania — Languages: Spanish — E-mail: msweeney@russotoner.com

Judith H. Maxwell — 1947 — Cornell University, B.S., 1968; St. Johns University School of Law, J.D., 1998 — Admitted to Bar, 1999, New York — E-mail: jmaxwell@russotoner.com

Senior Associates

Marie A. Castronuovo — 1960 — St. John's University, B.S., 1982; Gonzaga University School of Law, J.D., 1986 — Admitted to Bar, 1987, New York — E-mail: mcastronuovo@russotoner.com

Lee-David Weiner — 1980 — University at Albany, B.A. (summa cum laude), 2002; University of Miami School of Law, J.D., 2005 — Admitted to Bar, 2006, New York — E-mail: lweiner@russotoner.com

Cecil E. Floyd — 1954 — Colby College, B.A., 1976; American University, Washington College of Law, J.D., 1981 — Admitted to Bar, 1984, New York; 1990, Connecticut; 1984, U.S. District Court, Eastern and Southern Districts of New York — E-mail: cfloyd@russotoner.com

Steven Balson-Cohen — 1957 — Yeshiva College, B.A., 1979; Benjamin N. Cardozo School of Law, Yeshiva University, J.D., 1982 — Admitted to Bar, 1985, New York; U.S. District Court, Eastern, Northern, Southern and Western Districts of New York; 1990, U.S. Court of Appeals, Second, Third and Fourth Circuits — Languages: Hebrew — E-mail: sbalson-cohen@russotoner.com

Steven R. Dyki — 1974 — Central Michigan University, B.S., 1996; DePaul University College of Law, J.D. (Dean's Scholar), 1999 — Admitted to Bar, 1999, Illinois; 2006, New York; 2012, U.S. District Court, Eastern and Southern Districts of New York — E-mail: sdyki@russotoner.com

Charles B. Stokes — 1955 — Temple University, B.A. (magna cum laude), 1977; Villanova University School of Law, J.D., 1980 — Admitted to Bar, 1980, Pennsylvania; 1981, U.S. District Court, Eastern District of Pennsylvania; 2001, U.S. Court of Appeals, Third Circuit; 2008, U.S. District Court, Middle District of Pennsylvania — Resident Bristol, PA Office — E-mail: cstokes@russotoner.com

John W. Magrino — 1968 — Pace University, B.A., 1990; St. John's University School of Law, J.D., 1994 — Admitted to Bar, 1997, New Jersey; 2005, New York; District of Columbia; 1997, U.S. District Court, District of New Jersey; 2006, U.S. District Court, Eastern and Southern Districts of New York — E-mail: jmagrino@russotoner.com

Associates

Marcin J. Kurzatkowski — 1984 — New York University, B.A., 2006; St. John's University School of Law, J.D., 2009 — Admitted to Bar, 2010, New York — Languages: Polish — E-mail: mkurzatkowski@russotoner.com

Andrew Teig — 1986 — The George Washington University, B.A., Business Administration, 2008; Touro College Jacob D. Fuchsberg Law Center, J.D., 2011 — Admitted to Bar, 2012, New York; New Jersey — E-mail: ateig@russotoner.com

Alexandra L. Alvarez — 1984 — Fordham University, B.A. (Dean's List), 2006; Fordham University School of Law, J.D., 2011 — Admitted to Bar, 2011, New Jersey; 2012, New York — Languages: French — E-mail: aalvarez@russotoner.com

Andrew C. Wiener — 1962 — American University, B.A., 1985; London School of Economics, M.S., 1988; Golden Gate University School of Law, J.D., 1992 — Admitted to Bar, 1993, California; 1996, New York; 1993, U.S. District Court, Northern District of California; U.S. District Court, Central and Southern Districts of New York; U.S. Court of Appeals, Ninth Circuit; 2007, U.S. District Court, Eastern District of New York — Member New York State Bar Association — E-mail: awiener@russotoner.com

Lauren Garvey — 1984 — Barnard College, B.A. Accounting (cum laude), 2008; DePaul University College of Law, J.D., 2012 — Admitted to Bar, 2012, Illinois; 2014, New York — Member Womens Bar Association of the State of New York — Languages: French — E-mail: lgarvey@russotoner.com

Saretsky Katz Dranoff & Glass, L.L.P.

475 Park Avenue South
New York, New York 10016
Telephone: 212-973-9797
Fax: 212-973-0939
E-Mail: info@skdglaw.com
www.skdglaw.com

NEW YORK

Saretsky Katz Dranoff & Glass, L.L.P., New York, NY (Continued)

(Piermont, NY Office: 450 Piermont Avenue, 10968)
 (Tel: 845-398-3030)
 (Fax: 845-398-6019)

Established: 1994

Insurance Coverage, Litigation, Excess and Reinsurance, Bad Faith, Policy Construction and Interpretation, Captive Company Matters, Insurance Fraud, Insurance Defense, Professional Liability, Tort Litigation, Defense Litigation, Appellate Practice, Personal Injury, Property Damage, Civil Rights, Municipal Liability, Primary and Excess Insurance, Reinsurance, Automobile Liability, Insurance Litigation, Directors and Officers Liability, Employment Practices Liability

Insurance Clients

Crum & Forster	Hereford Insurance Company
New York Central Mutual Fire Insurance Company	Seneca Insurance Company, Inc.
	State Farm Mutual Automobile Insurance Company

Non-Insurance Clients

Combined Coordinating Council, Inc.	FOJP Service Corporation
	The Metropolitan Museum of Art

Partners

Barry G. Saretsky — 1947 — Brooklyn College, The City University of New York, B.A., 1968; Rutgers University School of Law, J.D. (with honors), 1973 — Admitted to Bar, 1974, New York; 1976, U.S. District Court, Eastern and Southern Districts of New York; 1988, U.S. Court of Appeals, Second Circuit; 1989, U.S. Supreme Court; 1992, U.S. Court of Appeals, Third Circuit; 2005, U.S. District Court, Western District of New York — Member American Bar Association (Member, Insurance Practice Section, Insurance Coverage Litigation Committee); New York State Bar Association (Member, Torts, Insurance and Compensation Law, Commercial and Federal Litigation Sections; Member, Reinsurance and Insurance Coverage Disputes Committee); Defense Research Institute — General Editor, Lawyers Cooperative Publishing, New York Litigation Forms — E-mail: bsaretsky@skdglaw.com

Alan G. Katz — 1957 — University of Maryland, B.S., 1979; New England School of Law, J.D. (cum laude), 1982 — Admitted to Bar, 1983, New York; U.S. District Court, Eastern and Southern Districts of New York; 2005, U.S. District Court, Western District of New York — Member New York State Bar Association — General Editor, Lawyers Cooperative Publishing, New York Litigation Forms — E-mail: akatz@skdglaw.com

Eric Dranoff — 1959 — American University, B.S.B.A. (cum laude), 1981; Albany Law School of Union University, J.D. (cum laude), 1984 — Phi Kappa Pi; Justinian Honor Society — Admitted to Bar, 1985, New York; 1989, U.S. District Court, Eastern and Southern Districts of New York; 2005, U.S. District Court, Western District of New York — Member New York State Bar Association (Vice Chair, Torts, Insurance and Compensation Law, Automobile Liability Committee; Member, Torts, Insurance and Compensation Law Professional Liability Committee; Editor, Automobile Liability Newsletter); National Association of Home Builders Legal Action Network for Developmental Strategies; Lawyers Cooperative Publishing, New York Advisory Board (1993-Present), Vice Chairperson and Treasurer, County of Rockland Industrial Developement Agency (1995); Program Chair, New York State Bar Association TICL Fall Meeting (2000) — Legal Writing Instructor, Albany Law School (1983-1984); Member, Executive Committee, Albany Law School Moot Court Board (1983-1984); General Editor, Lawyers Cooperative Publishing, New York Litigation Forms (February, 1996); Lecturer: "Financing Alternatives, The Role of the Industrial Development Agency" (November, 1996); Lecturer: "Traditional and Emerging Programs for Financing Economic Development", Rockland Economic Development Corporation's Connections (1996 Conference, New York State Bar Association Fall Meeting, 1999); Lecturer: "Dealing with Prosperity, How the Deal was Done", 1998; Lecturer, No Fault Updates, New York State Bar Association Torts Insurance Compensation Law Section Fall Meeting, 1999; Case Studies on Insurance Practice, New York State Bar Association Torts Insurance Compensation Law Section, Winter Meeting, 2002; Advertising Injury, New York State Bar Association Torts Insurance Compensation Law Section, Fall Meeting, 2001 — E-mail: edranoff@skdglaw.com

Howard J. Newman — 1950 — New York Institute of Technology, B.S. (magna cum laude), 1972; Brooklyn Law School, J.D., 1975 — Admitted to Bar, 1976, New York; 1978, U.S. District Court, Southern District of New York; 1989, U.S. District Court, Eastern District of New York; 1993, U.S. District Court, Northern District of New York; U.S. Court of Appeals, Second Circuit — Member New York State Bar Association (Torts, Insurance and Compensation Law Section; Committee on Professional Liability; Committee on Ethics) — "Limiting Lenders' Lead Paint Liability", The Banking Law Journal (January, 1998); "Liability for In Utero Injuries", New York Law Journal (August, 1994); "Statute of Limitation in Child Sex Abuse Cases", New York Law Journal (May, 1993); "Ensuring Notice to Insurers", Directorship (March, 1993); "Collateral Estoppel Effect of Administrative Hearings", New York Law Journal (July, 1992); "A Legal Status Problem for Distributors", Marketing Management; "A Warning About Product Dangers", Marketing Law — E-mail: hnewman@skdglaw.com

Marsha Weinstein — 1953 — Hamilton College, B.A., 1979; Benjamin N. Cardozo School of Law, J.D., 1982 — Admitted to Bar, 1983, New York; 1984, U.S. District Court, Eastern and Southern Districts of New York — Member New York State and Queens County Bar Associations; Women's Bar Association of the State of New York; National Association of Insurance Women — E-mail: mweinstein@skdglaw.com

Allen L. Sheridan — 1959 — Adelphi University, B.A. (with honors), 1981; State University of New York at Buffalo Law School, J.D. (with honors), 1984 — Admitted to Bar, 1985, New York; U.S. District Court, Eastern and Southern Districts of New York — E-mail: asheridan@skdglaw.com

Patrick J. Dellay — 1960 — University of California, Berkeley, B.A., 1982; Brooklyn Law School, J.D., 1989 — Admitted to Bar, 1990, New York; U.S. District Court, Eastern and Southern Districts of New York; 2005, U.S. Court of Appeals, Second Circuit — Member American Bar Association; Association of the Bar of the City of New York — E-mail: pdellay@skdglaw.com

Robert B. Weissman — 1968 — University of Rochester, B.A. (cum laude), 1990; Northeastern University School of Law, J.D., 1993 — Admitted to Bar, 1994, New York; 1996, District of Columbia; 2006, U.S. District Court, Eastern and Southern Districts of New York — Member New York State Bar Association — E-mail: rweissman@skdglaw.com

Of Counsel

Gary J. Levy — 1951 — University of Rochester, B.A., 1973; Simon Graduate School of Business, University of Rochester, M.B.A., 1974; Brooklyn Law School, J.D., 1977 — Admitted to Bar, 1978, New York; U.S. District Court, Eastern and Southern Districts of New York; 1981, U.S. Tax Court — E-mail: glevy@skdglaw.com

Sheri A. Yodowitz — 1957 — State University of New York College at Oneonta, B.A., 1978; Pace University School of Law, J.D., 1982 — Admitted to Bar, 1983, New York — Member The Association of Collaborative Lawyers of Rockland/Westchester — E-mail: syodowitz@skdglaw.com

Robert Yodowitz — 1953 — State University of New York at Oneonta, B.A., 1975; State University of New York at Albany, M.P.A., 1977; Pace University School of Law, J.D., 1983 — Admitted to Bar, 1983, New York; 1984, U.S. District Court, Eastern and Southern Districts of New York — E-mail: ryodowitz@skdglaw.com

C. Scott Vanderhoef — Alfred University, B.A., 1971; Teachers College, Columbia University, M.A., 1972; Pace University School of Law, J.D., 1981 — Admitted to Bar, 1982, New York; U.S. District Court, Eastern and Southern Districts of New York — E-mail: svanderhoef@skdglaw.com

Cary Maynard — State University of New York at Albany, B.A. (summa cum laude, Phi Beta Kappa), 1976; St. John's University School of Law, J.D., 1979 — Admitted to Bar, 1980, New York; U.S. District Court, Eastern and Southern Districts of New York — E-mail: cmaynard@skdglaw.com

Associates

Sue J. Park — 1976 — Barnard College, B.A., 1998; University of Pennsylvania Law School, J.D., 2003 — Admitted to Bar, 2004, New York — E-mail: spark@skdglaw.com

Jeanne M. Lane — 1986 — College of William & Mary, B.A., 2008; State University of New York at Buffalo Law School, J.D., 2011 — Admitted to Bar, 2012, New York — E-mail: jlane@skdglaw.com

Shafer Glazer, LLP

90 John Street, Suite 701
New York, New York 10038
Telephone: 212-267-0011
Fax: 646-435-9434
E-Mail: HShafer@ShaferGlazer.com
www.ShaferGlazer.com

Established: 2005

Alternative Dispute Resolution, Appellate Practice, Automobile Liability, Business Law, Commercial Litigation, Directors and Officers Liability, Toxic Torts, General Liability, Insurance Coverage, Labor and Employment, Municipal Liability, Premises Liability, Product Liability, Professional Liability, Transportation, Trucking Industry Defense, Workers' Compensation, Security Company Liability, Cyber Liability and Data Privacy

Firm Profile: Shafer Glazer strives to provide the best defense possible, while working within company guidelines and maintaining a cost conscious attitude towards defense - without sacrificing quality. Our lawyers work in and out of the courtroom to achieve positive results, believing that a good legal defense requires careful analysis and direction from start to finish. All matters are then evaluated at appropriate junctures of the litigation, so that resolution can be considered at each step of the way. We maintain close contact with company representatives to make sure that our plan is your plan.

Insurance Clients

GAB Robins North America, Inc.
Travelers Insurance Companies
RBC General Insurance Company
Zurich American Insurance Company

Non-Insurance Clients

AlliedBarton Security Services

Partners

Howard S. Shafer — Rutgers University, B.A., 1986; Brooklyn Law School, J.D., 1989 — Admitted to Bar, 1989, New York; 2006, New Jersey; 1990, U.S. District Court, Eastern and Southern Districts of New York; 2006, U.S. District Court, District of New Jersey — Member New York State Bar Association (Chair, Corporate Counsel Section; Member, Sections on: Labor and Employment Law; Torts, Insurance and Compensation Law); Professional Liability Underwriting Society — Court Appointment: Arbitrator, New York City Civil Court, New York County

David A. Glazer — Duke University, A.B., 1992; Brooklyn Law School, J.D., 1995 — Admitted to Bar, 1996, New York; 2006, New Jersey; 1996, U.S. District Court, Eastern and Southern Districts of New York — Member New York State Bar Association (Editor, Torts Insurance and Compensation Law Journal; Executive Committee Member, Torts Insurance and Compensation Law Section)

Timothy M. Wenk — Baruch College, City University of New York, B.A. (cum laude), 1997; Brooklyn Law School, J.D., 2000 — Admitted to Bar, 2001, New York; New Jersey; U.S. District Court, Eastern and Southern Districts of New York; U.S. District Court, District of New Jersey — Member New York State Bar Association

Associates

Mika M. Mooney
Karen Schnur
Tara A. Johnson
Nicole M. Snyder
Brian S. Nache

Of Counsel

Yanai Z. Siegel

Smith Mazure Director Wilkins Young & Yagerman, P.C.

111 John Street
New York, New York 10038
Telephone: 212-964-7400
Fax: 212-374-1935
E-Mail: contactus@smithmazure.com
www.smithmazure.com

(Somerville, NJ Office*: 92 East Main Street, 08876)
  (Tel: 908-393-7300)
  (Fax: 908-231-1030)
(Mineola, NY Office*: 200 Old Country Road, Suite 435, 11501)
  (Tel: 516-414-7400)
  (Fax: 516-294-7325)

Automobile, Transportation, Labor and Employment, Environmental Law, Construction Law, Municipal Liability, Insurance Litigation, Alternative Dispute Resolution, Appellate Practice, Construction Accidents, Construction Defect, Garage Liability, Lead Paint, Toxic Torts, Premises Liability, Property Liability, Product Liability, Directors and Officers Liability, Errors and Omissions, Civil Rights Litigation, Claims Management, Discrimination Litigation, Excess Risk Claims, Insurance Coverage Litigation, Large Property Loss, Maritime Law, No-Fault/Uninsured Motorist Coverage, Security Liability, Subrogation Litigation

Firm Profile: Smith Mazure Director Wilkins Young and Yagerman, P.C., is a liability defense firm that is dedicated to the needs of its diverse client-base. For more than half of a century, the Firm has provided expert counsel for multiple industry segments, and has achieved a success rate envied by competitors and revered by plaintiff counsel.

Insurance Clients

AIG Construction Risk Management Group
Cambridge Integrated Services
Claims Control, Inc.
CNA Insurance Companies
CSC Insurance Services
ECS Claims Administrators, Inc.
Encompass Insurance
Florists' Mutual Insurance Company
Gallagher Bassett Services, Inc.
Hertz Claim Management
Insurance Company of the State of Pennsylvania
Material Damage Adjustment Corporation
North American Specialty Insurance Company
Pacesetter Adjustment Company
Philadelphia Insurance Company
PMA Insurance Group
Risk Management Planning Group, Inc.
SCOR Reinsurance Company
Specialty Claims Management, LLC
World Wide Claims Management
Zurich American Insurance Group
AIG Risk Management, Inc.
Automobile Club Insurance Company
Claims Service Bureau
Crawford & Company
Cunningham Lindsey Claims Management, Inc.
Fireman's Fund Insurance Companies
GAB Robins North America, Inc.
HDI-Gerling America Insurance Company
John Deere Insurance Company
K & K Insurance Agency
MetLife Auto & Home
New Jersey Automobile Full Insurance Underwriting Association
Pennsylvania National Mutual Casualty Insurance Company
Prudential Property and Casualty Insurance Company
St. Paul Fire and Marine Insurance Company
Specialty Risk Services, Inc. (SRS)
Ward North America, Inc.
York Claims Service, Inc.

Non-Insurance Clients

AXIA Services, Inc.
Essential Services and Programs, Inc.
Long Island Rail Road
McLarens Toplis North America, Inc.
Metro-North Railroad
New York City Housing Authority
New York City Transit Authority
Rental Adjusting Services
SpectaGuard Integrated Asset Protection
Willis Administrative Services Corporation
Blackmoor Group, Inc.
The Hertz Corporation
Kemper Environmental Ltd.
Market Transition Facility of New Jersey
McNeil & Company, Inc.
Metropolitan Transportation Authority
Recumar, Inc.
SelecTech Claims
Sterling Administrative Services, Inc.

NEW YORK

Smith Mazure Director Wilkins Young & Yagerman, P.C., New York, NY (Continued)

Senior Members

David E. Mazure — 1939 — Brooklyn College, The City University of New York, B.A., 1960; Brooklyn Law School, LL.B., 1963 — Admitted to Bar, 1963, New York — Member New York State Bar Association; The Association of the Bar of the City of New York; Association of Trial Lawyers of the City of New York (President, 1982-1983; Permanent Member, Board of Directors); New York State Trial Lawyers Association — E-mail: dmazure@smithmazure.com

J. Jay Young — 1955 — Rutgers University, B.A., 1977; New York Law School, J.D., 1980 — Omicron Delta Kappa — Admitted to Bar, 1980, New Jersey; 1981, New York — Member New York State Bar Association; Defense Association of New York (Board of Directors); Association of Trial Lawyers of the City of New York; New York County Lawyers Association — Author: "Vicarious Liability of Rental Firms Preempted by Federal Law"; "Limiting Your Exposure After an Accident"; "The End of 'Open and Obvious' Defense"; "Defending Against Mold-Related Personal Injury Actions" — E-mail: jyoung@smithmazure.com

Mark S. Yagerman — 1954 — Brooklyn College, The City University of New York, B.A., 1976; Benjamin N. Cardozo School of Law, J.D., 1979 — Admitted to Bar, 1980, New York — Member New York State Bar Association; Defense Research Institute; New York State Trial Lawyers Association — Author: "Indemnification and Article 16: In for a Penny or Pound?"; "Got Mold"; "Objections: Practical Evidencel A Civil Case Primer New York State Bar Association"; "Disclosure of an Informant's Identity at Suppression Hearings and at Trials"; "The Use of Non-Lawyer Judges in New York State Criminal Proceedings"; "How Obamacare May Limit Projected Expenses in Personal Injury Life Case," Published by Cardozo Law — Executive Member, Cardozo Alumni Association — E-mail: myagerman@smithmazure.com

Corey A. Tavel — 1965 — Hofstra University, B.A., 1987; Touro College Jacob D. Fuchsberg Law Center, J.D., 1991 — Admitted to Bar, 1991, New York; Connecticut; 1992, U.S. District Court, Eastern and Southern Districts of New York — Author: "Vicarious Liability of Rental Firms Preempted by Federal Law"; "Limiting Your Exposure After an Accident"; "Defending Against Mold-Related Personal Injury Actions"; "Court Clarifies Vicious Propensitites in Dog Behaviors"; "NVLAJoins Coalition to Fight LVL"; "Lesser Vicatious Liability" — E-mail: ctavel@smithmazure.com

Members

Michael K. Berman — 1955 — State University of New York College at Oneonta, B.A., 1977; Southwestern University School of Law, J.D., 1981 — Admitted to Bar, 1981, New York — Member New York State Bar Association

Thomas Bizzaro — Hofstra University, B.B.A., 1995; St. Johns University School of Law, J.D., 1999 — Admitted to Bar, 2000, New York; 2001, U.S. District Court, Eastern and Southern Districts of New York — Member Nassau County Bar Association

Ann P. Eccher — 1973 — Adelphi University, B.A. (cum laude), 1995; Hofstra University School of Law, J.D., 1998 — Admitted to Bar, 1999, New York — Member New York State Bar Association

Andrew J. Funk — 1966 — Muhlenberg College, B.A., 1988; Brooklyn Law School, J.D., 1991 — Admitted to Bar, 1991, New York; Connecticut; 1992, District of Columbia — Member American and New York State Bar Associations

Anna A. Higgins — Florida State University, B.A., 1994; St. Thomas University School of Law, J.D., 1999 — Admitted to Bar, 2000, Florida; 2003, New York — Member New York State Bar Association; The Florida Bar

Mark D. Levi — 1951 — Case Western Reserve University, B.A., 1973; Western New England College School of Law, J.D., 1976 — Admitted to Bar, 1977, New York — Member American Bar Association; American Trial Lawyers Association

Christopher W. McKenna — Stockton State College, B.A., 1988; Seton Hall University School of Law, J.D., 1995 — Admitted to Bar, 1995, New Jersey — Member New Jersey State Bar Associaiton

Angela Lurie Milch — 1965 — American University, B.A., 1987; New York Law School, J.D. (cum laude), 1994 — Admitted to Bar, 1994, New Jersey; 1995, New York — Member American and New York State Bar Associations

Robert J. Paliseno — St. John's University, B.A., 1997; Brooklyn Law School,

Smith Mazure Director Wilkins Young & Yagerman, P.C., New York, NY (Continued)

J.D., 2000 — Admitted to Bar, 2000, New Jersey; 2001, New York — Member New York State Bar Association; New York State Trial Lawyers Association

Catherine J. Poissant — State University of New York at Stony Brook, B.A., 2001; Hofstra University School of Law, J.D., 2004 — Admitted to Bar, 2005, New York — Member New York State Bar Association; New York State Trial Lawyers Association

J. Kevin Reilly — 1952 — Fairfield University, B.A., 1974; St. Mary's University; University of London, England, J.D., 1977 — Admitted to Bar, 1983, New York — Member New York State Bar Association

Joel M. Simon — 1961 — State University of New York at Albany, B.A., 1983; New York Law School, J.D., 1986 — Admitted to Bar, 1986, New York; New Jersey; Florida — Member American and New York State Bar Associations

Lesley C. Siskind — State University of New York at Albany, B.A., 1988; University of Bridgeport School of Law, J.D., 1991 — Admitted to Bar, 1992, New York; Connecticut — Member New York State Trial Lawyers Association

Howard J. Snyder — 1971 — State University of New York at Albany, B.A., 1993; Albany Law School, J.D., 1996 — Admitted to Bar, 1997, New York — Member New York State Bar Association

Daniel Y. Sohnen — Queens College, B.A., 2003; Touro College Jacob D. Fuchsberg Law Center, J.D., 2007 — Admitted to Bar, 2008, New York; U.S. District Court, Eastern and Southern Districts of New York — Member American and New York State Bar Associations; New York County Lawyers Association

Mark A. Taustine — State University of New York at Geneseo, B.A., 1991; New York Law School, J.D., 1999 — Admitted to Bar, 2000, New York; New Jersey

Constantine G. Vlavianos — 1960 — Fordham University, B.A., 1982; Pace University School of Law, J.D., 1986 — Admitted to Bar, 1986, New York; Connecticut — Member American and New York State Bar Associations

Evan D. Yagerman — Indiana University, B.A., 2003; New York University, Paralegal, 2005; Benjamin N. Cardozo School of Law, J.D., 2008 — Admitted to Bar, 2008, New York; 2009, U.S. District Court, Eastern and Southern Districts of New York — Member New York County Lawyers Association

Associates

Max Bookman — University of Vermont, B.A., 2010; Benjamin N. Cardozo School of Law, J.D., 2013 — Admitted to Bar, 2014, New York

David A. Bourgeois — Syracuse University, B.S., 1989; New England School of Law, J.D., 1992 — Admitted to Bar, 1993, New York; Massachusetts; 1994, U.S. District Court, Eastern and Southern Districts of New York

Megan Boyar — University of Florida, B.S. (magna cum laude), 2009; Benjamin N. Cardozo School of Law, J.D., 2012 — Admitted to Bar, 2012, New York

Louise M. Cherkis — State University of New York at Binghamton, B.A., 1977; Benjamin N. Cardozo School of Law, J.D., 1982 — Admitted to Bar, 1983, New Jersey; 1984, New York; 1988, U.S. District Court, Eastern and Southern Districts of New York; 1995, U.S. Supreme Court; 2006, U.S. Court of International Trade — Member Association of the Bar of the City of New York; Defense Research Institute

Gamaliel B. Delgado — University of Massachusetts, B.A. (cum laude), 2003; Rutgers University School of Law, J.D., 2006 — Admitted to Bar, 2006, New Jersey; 2007, New York; 2014, U.S. District Court, District of New Jersey; U.S. District Court, Eastern and Southern Districts of New York — Member Hispanic National Bar Association (Deputy Regional President, New York); Association of Latin American Law Students; Association of Black Law Students

Jonathan Flamhaft — State University of New York at Stony Brook, B.A., 1988; Quinnipiac College School of Law, J.D., 1992 — Admitted to Bar, 1993, New York — Member New York State Bar Association; Association of the Bar of the City of New York

Michael V. Kuntz — University of Detroit, B.A., 2003; Hofstra University School of Law, J.D., 2008 — Admitted to Bar, 2009, New York — Member New York County Lawyers Association; Nassau County Criminal Courts Bar Association

Stacy I. Malinow — State University of New York at Albany, B.A., 1991; New York Law School, J.D. (cum laude), 1994 — Admitted to Bar, 1994, Connecticut; 1995, New York; 2001, Florida; 1996, U.S. District Court, Eastern and Southern Districts of New York; 2001, U.S. Supreme Court — Member New York State Bar Association

Smith Mazure Director Wilkins Young & Yagerman, P.C., New York, NY (Continued)

Matthew E. Markoff — Binghamton University, B.A. (cum laude), 2004; Touro College Jacob D. Fuchsberg Law Center, J.D. (summa cum laude), 2008 — Admitted to Bar, 2008, Connecticut; 2009, New York; U.S. District Court, Eastern and Southern Districts of New York — Member New York City and Suffolk County Bar Associations

Stephen J. Molinelli — 1967 — Villanova University, B.S. (with honors), 1989; St. John's University School of Law, J.D., 1992 — Admitted to Bar, 1992, New Jersey; 1993, New York — Member New York State Bar Association

Steven M. Pardalis — Ramapo College of New Jersey, B.A. (summa cum laude), 2009; Seton Hall University School of Law, J.D., 2012 — Admitted to Bar, 2013, New Jersey — Resident Somerville, NJ Office

Christopher L. Parisi — Rutgers University, B.A. (Dean's Honor List), 2007; New England School of Law, J.D. (Dean's Honor List), 2012 — Admitted to Bar, 2012, New York — Member American and New York State Bar Associations; Rutgers Alumni Association

Steven D. Phillips — Tufts University, B.A. (cum laude), 1976; The Ohio State University Moritz College of Law, J.D., 1979 — Admitted to Bar, 1989, Pennsylvania; 1999, New York

Marcia Raicus — 1957 — University of Rochester, B.A., 1978; Boston University School of Law, J.D., 1981 — Admitted to Bar, 1983, New York; 1984, U.S. District Court, Eastern and Southern Districts of New York — Member American and New York State Bar Associations; New York State Trial Lawyers Association

Shannon L. Saks — American University, B.A., 1999; Brooklyn Law School, J.D., 2002 — Admitted to Bar, 2003, New York; U.S. District Court, Eastern and Southern Districts of New York

Ivan C. Torres — St. John's University, B.S. (magna cum laude), 2002; Hofstra University School of Law, J.D., 2005 — Admitted to Bar, 2006, New York

Irina Yakhnis — The University of Kansas, B.S./B.A., 2009; Benjamin N. Cardozo School of Law, J.D., 2012 — Admitted to Bar, 2012, New Jersey; 2013, New York — Benjamin N. Cardozo School of Law Alumni

(This firm is also listed in the Subrogation section of this directory)

Sobel Law Group LLC

30 Vesey Street, 8th Floor
New York, New York 10007
Telephone: 212-216-0020
E-Mail: csobel@sobellawgroup.com
www.sobellawgroup.com

(Huntington, NY Office*: 464 New York Avenue, Suite 100, 11743)
 (Tel: 631-549-4677)
 (Fax: 631-549-0826)
(Burlington, NJ Office*: 6 Terry Lane, Suite 350, 08016)
 (Tel: 856-673-0689)
 (E-Mail: bpevzner@sobellawgroup.com)

Amusements, Automobile, Bad Faith, Construction Law, Coverage Issues, Employment Law, Environmental Law, Equine Law, Fraud, Hospitality, Liquor Liability, Pharmaceutical, Premises Liability, Sports Law, Toxic Torts, Transportation, Trucking, Workers' Compensation

Firm Profile: Sobel Law Group, LLC successfully represents insurance carriers, self-insureds, municipalities and school districts, habitation companies, school and municipal bus companies, supermarket chains, "big box" retailers and construction companies in New York, New Jersey and Eastern Pennsylvania.

(See listing under Huntington, NY for additional information)

Stern & Montana, LLP

115 Broadway
New York, New York 10006
Telephone: 212-532-8100
Fax: 212-532-7271
E-Mail: Info@stern-montana.com
www.stern-montana.com

Insurance Fraud

Insurance Clients

Allstate Insurance Company
Encompass Insurance
Erie Insurance Company
Liberty Mutual Insurance
Selective Insurance Company of America
American Transit Insurance Company
GEICO
Nationwide Insurance

Partners

Robert A. Stern — 1962 — Adelphi University, B.S. (with honors), 1984; New York Law School, J.D., 1988 — Admitted to Bar, 1989, New York; Connecticut; 1998, U.S. District Court, Eastern and Southern Districts of New York — Member The Association of the Bar of the City of New York; New York Court Lawyers Association; Instructor: International Association of Special Investigation Unit (1995-1999); New Jersey Special Investigators Association (1996, 1997, 1998-2001); Counsel to New York Alliance Against Insurance Fraud — "Insurance Investigation and The Right to Privacy," Mealey's Litigation Reports (July 31, 1996); "Retrospective Premium Clauses Create Wave of Litigation," New York Law Journal (December 8, 1994); "What Insurers Need to Know About Investigating Claims," New York Law Journal (July 28, 1995); "Retrospective Premium Policies and The Emergence of a New Burden For Workers' Compensation Insurers," Mealey's Litigation Reports (June 9, 1994); "Tackling Fraud is Logical, Effective Way to Increase Profits," Business Insurance (June 20, 1994); "For the Insurance Industry, The Question is Which Way to Turn," SIU Awareness (December, 1995); "Identifying Patterns of Medical Provider Fraud," FraudReport.com (December 1999); "Investigating Claims and The Right to Privacy," SIU Awareness (December 1999); "Take the Money and Run: The Fraud Crisis in New York's No-Fault System," New York Law Journal (October 2003); Co-Author: "Like Client, Like Attorney; Partners In Organized Crime," SIU Awareness (September 2002); "The Truth About EUOs and Their Use in Third Party Claims," SIU Awareness (September 1999); "Identify Patterns of Medical Provider Fraud Through Data Base Graphic Pattern," FraudReport.com (December 31, 1999) — Practice Areas: Insurance Fraud; Bad Faith; Coverage Issues

Richard Montana — 1960 — University of Pennsylvania, B.A., 1982; New York Law School, J.D. (cum laude), 1988 — Admitted to Bar, 1989, New York; 1998, U.S. District Court, Eastern and Southern Districts of New York — Member The Association of the Bar of the City of New York

Sandra P. Burgos — 1972 — Barry University, B.S., 1993; University of Miami School of Law, J.D., 1997 — Admitted to Bar, 1998, New York; Florida — Languages: Spanish

Associates

Alexis Angell — The University of Texas at Austin, B.B.A., 2007; Benjamin N. Cardozo School of Law, J.D., 2010 — Admitted to Bar, 2010, New Jersey; 2011, New York — E-mail: a.angell@stern-montana.com

Daniel Beatty — American University, B.A., 2007; Temple University Beasley School of Law, J.D., 2010 — Admitted to Bar, 2011, New York — E-mail: d.beatty@stern-montana.com

Elizabeth Caldwell — McGill University, B.A., 2008; Tulane University Law School, J.D., 2011 — Admitted to Bar, 2012, New York — E-mail: e.caldwell@stern-montana.com

Soraya Campbell — Baruch College, City University of New York, B.B.A., 1991; Pace University School of Law, J.D., 1996 — Admitted to Bar, 1996, New York; 1997, Connecticut; 1996, U.S. District Court, Eastern District of New York — E-mail: s.campbell@stern-montana.com

Jenntyng Chern — Brandeis University, B.A., 2006; Seton Hall University School of Law, J.D., 2009 — Admitted to Bar, 2010, New Jersey; 2011, New York — E-mail: j.chern@stern-montana.com

Dionne Fabiatos — Hobart and William Smith Colleges, B.A., 2006; New York Law School, J.D., 2010 — Admitted to Bar, 2011, New York — E-mail: d.fabiatos@stern-montana.com

NEW YORK

Stern & Montana, LLP, New York, NY (Continued)

Jacqueline Figueroa — Florida State University, B.S., 2003; Florida State University College of Law, J.D., 2010 — Admitted to Bar, 2011, Florida; New York — E-mail: j.figueroa@stern-montana.com

Allison J. Kamensky — State University of New York at Albany, B.A.; Brooklyn Law School, J.D., 2003 — Admitted to Bar, 2003, New York — E-mail: a.kamensky@stern-montana.com

Tina Karkera — University of Florida, B.A., 2001; American University, Washington College of Law, J.D., 2004 — Admitted to Bar, 2004, Connecticut; 2005, District of Columbia; New York; 2007, Pennsylvania — E-mail: t.karkera@stern-montana.com

Benjamin Khabie — New York University, B.A., 2000; University of Miami School of Law, J.D., 2005 — Admitted to Bar, 2008, New York — E-mail: b.khabie@stern-montana.com

Christopher Kupka — Cornell University, A.B., 2007; University of Pennsylvania Law School, J.D., 2010 — Admitted to Bar, 2011, New York — E-mail: c.kupka@stern-montana.com

James Landivar — The University of North Carolina at Chapel Hill, B.A., 2003; Northeastern University School of Law, J.D., 2006 — Admitted to Bar, 2007, Massachusetts; 2008, New York — E-mail: j.landivar@stern-montana.com

Daniel Marvin — Hofstra University, B.A. (with honors), 1997; Hofstra University School of Law, J.D., 2001 — Admitted to Bar, 2001, New York — E-mail: d.marvin@stern-montana.com

Jennifer McDonald — Siena College, B.A., 2007; Union Graduate College, M.B.A., 2008; Albany Law School, J.D., 2011 — Admitted to Bar, 2012, New York — E-mail: j.mcdonald@stern-montana.com

James McKenney — Saint Anselm College, B.A., 1994; New York Law School, J.D., 2000 — Admitted to Bar, 2000, New York — E-mail: j.mckenney@stern-montana.com

Robin Pass — 1965 — University of Illinois, B.A., 1987; Chicago-Kent College of Law, J.D., 1991 — Admitted to Bar, 1991, Illinois; 2004, Florida; 1991, U.S. District Court, Northern District of Illinois; 1995, U.S. District Court, Central District of Illinois; 2005, U.S. District Court, Southern District of Florida — E-mail: r.pass@stern-montana.com

Dayna R. Steinberger — University of Maryland, College Park, B.A. (Dean's List), 2000; Hofstra University School of Law, J.D., 2003 — Admitted to Bar, 2003, New York — E-mail: d.steinberger@stern-montana.com

Danielle Tabankin — Iona College, B.A., 2008; Albany Law School of Union University, J.D., 2011 — Admitted to Bar, 2012, New York — E-mail: d.tabankin@stern-montana.com

Sullivan and Graber

250 West 57th Street, 9th Floor
New York, New York 10107
  Telephone: 212-835-9462

(Morristown, NJ Office*: 60 Maple Avenue, 07960, P.O. Box 912, 07963-0912)
  (Tel: 973-540-0877)
  (Fax: 973-540-8019)
  (E-Mail: ggraber@sullivangraberlaw.us)
  (www.sullivangraberlaw.com)

Alternative Dispute Resolution, Automobile, Arson, Bad Faith, Coverage Opinions, Declaratory Judgments, Dram Shop, Employment Practices Liability, Environmental Law, Errors and Omissions, Examinations Under Oath, Excess and Umbrella, First and Third Party Matters, Homeowners, Fraud, No-Fault, Personal Injury, Premises Liability, Product Liability, Professional Liability, Subrogation, Uninsured and Underinsured Motorist, Workers' Compensation, Wrongful Death, Insurance Fraud Investigations and Restitution Actions

Firm Profile: Sullivan and Graber serves as defense counsel to major national and international insurance companies doing business in New Jersey and New York. We offer our clients skilled, aggressive, responsive and efficient legal services in all areas of insurance law.

(See listing under Morristown, NJ for additional information)

Swartz Law Offices

475 Park Avenue South, Floor 27
New York, New York 10016-6901
  Telephone: 212-725-7070
  Fax: 212-725-1803
  E-Mail: gnswartz@attorneyswartz.com
  www.attorneyswartz.com

Established: 1994

Insurance Defense, General Liability, Bodily Injury, Product Liability, Personal Injury, Property Damage

Insurance Clients

ACE/ESIS
Travelers Property Casualty Insurance Company

AIG Domestic Claims, Inc.

Non-Insurance Clients

Edward R. Reilly & Co., Inc.
Flexcon Industries, Inc.
Hasbro, Inc.
Invensys Energy Management
Nidec Minster Corporation
Viking Range, LLC

Federal-Mogul Corporation
Fujitec America, Inc.
Herman Miller, Inc.
Kellogg Company
Philips Electronics, N.A.
W.W. Grainger, Inc.

Firm Member

Gerald Neal Swartz — 1948 — Rensselaer Polytechnic Institute, B.S., 1970; Albany Law School of Union University, J.D. (cum laude), 1975 — Justinian Society — Admitted to Bar, 1976, New York; U.S. District Court, Northern District of New York; 1978, U.S. District Court, Eastern and Southern Districts of New York; 1979, U.S. Court of Appeals, Second Circuit; 1980, U.S. Supreme Court — Member American (Torts and Insurance Practice Section) and New York State Bar Associations; Society of Automotive Engineers

Traub Lieberman Straus & Shrewsberry LLP

100 Park Avenue, 16th Floor
New York, New York 10017
  Telephone: 646-227-1700
  www.traublieberman.com

(Hawthorne, NY Office*: Mid-Westchester Executive Park, Seven Skyline Drive, 10532)
  (Tel: 914-347-2600)
  (Fax: 914-347-8898)
  (E-Mail: swolfe@traublieberman.com)
(Red Bank, NJ Office*: 322 Highway 35, 07701)
  (Tel: 732-985-1000)
  (Fax: 732-985-2000)
(St. Petersburg, FL Office*: 360 Central Avenue, 33701)
  (Tel: 727-898-8100)
  (Fax: 727-895-4838)
(Chicago, IL Office*: 303 West Madison, Suite 1200, 60606)
  (Tel: 312-332-3900)
  (Fax: 312-332-3908)
(Los Angeles, CA Office*: 626 Wilshire Boulevard, Suite 800, 90017)
  (Tel: 213-624-4500)
(London, United Kingdom Office*: Gallery 4, 12 Leadenhall Street, EC3V1LP)
  (Tel: +44 (0) 020 7816 5856)

Appellate Practice, Bad Faith, Extra-Contractual Litigation, Civil Rights, Complex Litigation, Construction Law, Environmental Law, General Liability, Insurance Coverage, Labor and Employment, Premises Liability, Product Liability, Professional Liability, Technology, Toxic Torts, Trucking Law, Transportation, Coverage Issues, Medical Malpractice

NEW YORK

Wade Clark Mulcahy

111 Broadway
New York, New York 10006
  Telephone: 212-267-1900
  Fax: 212-267-9470
  www.wcmlaw.com

(Springfield, NJ Office: 955 South Springfield Avenue, Suite 100, 07081)
  (Tel: 973-258-1700)
  (Fax: 973-258-17408)

(Philadelphia, PA Office: 1515 Market Street, Suite 2050, 19102)
  (Tel: 267-239-5526)
  (Fax: 267-565-1236)

Established: 1994

Insurance Defense, Insurance Law, Defense Litigation, Personal Injury, Product Liability, Reinsurance, Professional Malpractice, Subrogation, Investigation and Adjustment, Insurance Coverage, Premises Liability, Property and Jewelers Block

Insurance Clients

ACE Private Risk Services
All American Adjusters, Inc.
Boat/U.S. Marine Insurance
CNA Insurance Companies
First Specialty Insurance Corporation
Jewelers Mutual Insurance Company
Lloyd's of London Underwriters
Mitsui Marine Claims Service Corporation
Nautilus Insurance Group
Safeco Insurance Companies
Sphere Drake Insurance Limited
AIG - Private Client Group
American Claims Services, Inc.
Burlington Insurance Company
Coregis Group
GRE Insurance Group
Hanover Insurance Company
Lexington Insurance Company
Liberty Mutual Insurance Company
Markel Insurance Company
Monroe Guaranty Insurance Company
Reliance National Insurance Company
Tower Insurance Company of New York

Non-Insurance Clients

Honeywell, Inc.
Marriott International, Inc.
Nordstrom, Inc.
Wachovia Bank, N.A.
IRISC, Inc.
New York University
Sodexo USA

Partners

Dennis M. Wade — Hobart College, B.A. (magna cum laude), 1974; Fordham University School of Law, J.D., 1978 — Phi Beta Kappa — Admitted to Bar, 1979, New York; 1985, New Jersey; 1980, U.S. District Court, Eastern and Southern Districts of New York; 1985, U.S. District Court, District of New Jersey; U.S. Court of Appeals, Second and Third Circuits; U.S. Supreme Court — Member American, New York State (Insurance Committee, 1985-Present), and New Jersey State Bar Associations; The Association of the Bar of the City of New York; New York County Lawyers Association (Insurance Committee, 1986-Present); New York County Trial Lawyers Association; Defense Research Institute

Paul F. Clark — Fairfield University, B.A. (cum laude), 1980; St. John's University School of Law, J.D., 1984 — Moot Court Board — Admitted to Bar, 1984, New Jersey; 1985, New York; 1984, U.S. District Court, District of New Jersey; 1987, U.S. District Court, Eastern and Southern Districts of New York; 1990, U.S. District Court, Northern District of New York; U.S. Court of Appeals, Third Circuit — Member American, New Jersey State and New York State Bar Associations; New York County Lawyers Association; New York State Trial Lawyers Association — "Reversible Error - Opening and Closing Statements", New York State Trial Lawyers Quarterly, Vol. 9, #2 (Summer, 1988); "Into The Wild: A Review of the Recreational Use Statue", New York State Bar Journal, Vol. 70, #5 (1998); "Discovery of Experts Under CPLR 3101 (d)(1) and Fed. R.C.V.p. 216 (6)(14): A Comparative Analysis", Insurance, Negligence and Compensation Law Journal, New York State Bar Association (1987) — Lecturer, New York State Bar Association, Product Liability Seminar (Fall, 1999)

John Mulcahy — Tufts University, B.A. (cum laude), 1972; Georgetown University Law Center, J.D., 1977 — Admitted to Bar, 1978, Massachusetts; 1979, New York; 1980, U.S. District Court, Southern District of New York; 1985, U.S. Court of Appeals, Second Circuit; U.S. Supreme Court; 1990, U.S. District Court, Eastern District of New York

Wade Clark Mulcahy, New York, NY (Continued)

Nicole Y. Brown — State University of New York at Albany, B.A., 1995; St. John's University School of Law, J.D., 1998 — Admitted to Bar, 1998, New Jersey; 1999, New York; U.S. District Court, Eastern and Southern Districts of New York

Robert J. Cosgrove — Georgetown University, B.S.F.S., 1996; Fordham Law School, J.D., 1999 — Admitted to Bar, 2000, New York; 2003, U.S. District Court, Eastern and Southern Districts of New York — Member Regis Bar Association; New York County Lawyers Association — Resident Philadelphia, PA Office

Michael A. Bono — Villanova University, B.S.B.A., 1992; Fordham Law School, J.D., 1995 — Admitted to Bar, 1996, New York; 2005, New Jersey; 2004, U.S. District Court, Eastern and Southern Districts of New York — Member New York State Bar Association

Denise F. Ricci — Saint Mary's College, B.A., 1979; University of Notre Dame Law School, J.D., 1982 — Admitted to Bar, 1982, New Jersey; U.S. District Court, District of New Jersey — Resident Mountainside, NJ Office

Cheryl D. Fuchs — Brooklyn College, B.A. (summa cum laude), 2002; Benjamin N. Cardozo School of Law, Yeshiva University, J.D., 2005 — Jacob Burns Medal; Moot Court Honor Society — Admitted to Bar, 2005, New Jersey; 2006, New York; 2005, U.S. District Court, District of New Jersey — Member New York State and New York City Bar Associations

Brian D. Gibbons — Boston College, B.A., 2000; St. John's University School of Law, J.D., 2003 — Admitted to Bar, 2004, New York

Counsel

Vincent F. Terrasi — University of Southern California, B.A. Political Science, 1991; New York Law School, J.D., 1995 — American Jurisprudence Award, Legal Writing and Research — Admitted to Bar, 1998, Connecticut; 1999, New York; 2005, U.S. District Court, Southern District of New York

Associates

Alison M. Weintraub — Cornell University, B.S., 2005; St. John's University School of Law, J.D. (cum laude), 2008 — Recipient, Florence M. Glaser Scholarship for Excellence in Legal Writing; Recipient, American Bar Association/Bureau of National Affairs Award for Excellence in the Study of Labor and Employment Law — Member, American Bankruptcy Institute Law Review — Admitted to Bar, 2008, New Jersey; 2009, New York; 2008, U.S. District Court, District of New Jersey

Heather L. Aquino — William Paterson University, B.A., 2004; St. John's University School of Law, J.D., 2008 — Admitted to Bar, 2008, New Jersey; 2009, New York — Resident Mountainside, NJ Office

Georgia Stagias — New York University, B.A., 2006; Fordham University School of Law, J.D., 2009 — Admitted to Bar, 2009, New Jersey; 2010, New York

Gabriel Darwick — University of Maryland, B.A. (Dean's List), 2005; Benjamin N. Cardozo School of Law, J.D., 2009 — Admitted to Bar, 2010, New York; U.S. District Court, Southern District of New York — Member New York State Bar Association

Remy L. Cahn — Washington University in St. Louis, B.A., 2007; Fordham University School of Law, J.D., 2010 — Sigma Delta Tau; Paul Fuller Scholar — Admitted to Bar, 2010, Pennsylvania; New Jersey; 2001, U.S. District Court, Eastern District of Pennsylvania — Member American Bar Association — Resident Philadelphia, PA Office

Steven M. Kaye, Jr. — College of the Holy Cross, B.A. (cum laude), 2006; Brooklyn Law School, J.D. (cum laude), 2009 — Admitted to Bar, 2009, Connecticut; 2010, New York

Colleen Hayes — Villanova University, B.A., 2003; Villanova University School of Law, J.D. (magna cum laude), 2011 — Order of The Coif — Admitted to Bar, 2011, Pennsylvania; 2012, U.S. District Court, Eastern District of Pennsylvania — Member Philadelphia Association of Defense Counsel — Resident Philadelphia, PA Office

Johan A. Obregon — St. John's University, B.A., 2006; St. Johns University School of Law, J.D., 2009 — Admitted to Bar, 2010, New York; New Jersey; 2012, U.S. District Court, District of New Jersey — Member American and New York State Bar Associations — Languages: Spanish

Emily Kidder — Plymouth State College, B.A., 2002; New England School of Law, J.D., 2009 — Admitted to Bar, 2009, Massachusetts; 2011, New Jersey — Resident Mountainside, NJ Office

Michael A. Gauvin — Providence College, B.A., 1999; University of Notre Dame Law School, J.D., 2003 — Admitted to Bar, 2004, New York; 2007, Rhode Island; 2008, Massachusetts; 2005, U.S. District Court, Southern District of New York; 2006, U.S. District Court, Eastern District of New York;

NEW YORK

Wade Clark Mulcahy, New York, NY   (Continued)

2008, U.S. District Court, District of Rhode Island; 2013, U.S. District Court, District of Massachusetts

Anne C. Henry — Binghamton University, B.A. (magna cum laude), 2007; Benjamin N. Cardozo School of Law, J.D., 2011 — Phi Betta Kappa — Associate Editor, Cardozo Law Review — Admitted to Bar, 2012, New York; U.S. District Court, Southern District of New York

Adam J. Gomez — Wesleyan University, B.A., 2010; Temple University Beasley School of Law, J.D. (cum laude), 2013 — Admitted to Bar, 2013, Pennsylvania; 2014, U.S. District Court, Eastern District of Pennsylvania — Member Philadelphia Association of Defense Counsel — Languages: Spanish — Resident Philadelphia, PA Office

James Rogers — East Carolina University, B.A., 1991; City College of the City University of New York, M.A., 2004; Nova Southeastern University, Shepard Broad Law Center, J.D. (cum laude), 2010 — Admitted to Bar, 2010, Florida; 2012, New York

Eric Clendening — Cornell University, B.A. (magna cum laude), 2010; Washington University School of Law, J.D. (cum laude), 2013 — Admitted to Bar, 2013, Pennsylvania; 2014, U.S. District Court, Eastern and Western Districts of Pennsylvania — Member Philadelphia Association of Defense Counsel — Resident Philadelphia, PA Office

Steve J. Kim — University of Rochester, B.A., 2009; Syracuse University College of Law, J.D. (Dean's List), 2012 — Admitted to Bar, 2013, New Jersey; 2014, New York — Languages: Korean — Resident Springfield, NJ Office

Sheri M. Flannery — University of Scranton, B.A. (summa cum laude), 2009; Villanova University School of Law, J.D. (cum laude), 2013 — Admitted to Bar, 2013, Pennsylvania; New Jersey; 2014, U.S. District Court, Eastern District of Pennsylvania — Member Pennsylvania Bar Association; Philadelphia Association of Defense Counsel — Resident Philadelphia, PA Office

Jeremy Seeman — Colgate University, B.A., 2005; St. John's University School of Law, J.D., 2012 — Admitted to Bar, 2013, New York

Moya O'Connor — Georgetown University, B.A. (Dean's List), 2006; Brooklyn Law School, J.D., 2009 — Admitted to Bar, 2010, New York; 2013, U.S. District Court, Eastern and Southern Districts of New York — Member New York City and New York County Bar Associations; Metropolitan Black Bar Association

Bryan Lipsky — Columbia University, B.A., 2005; The Jewish Theological Seminary, B.A. (cum laude), 2005; Fordham University School of Law, J.D., 2008 — Admitted to Bar, 2008, New Jersey; 2009, New York; 2008, U.S. District Court, District of New Jersey; 2013, U.S. District Court, Southern District of New York

Betsy K. Silverstine — Florida State University, B.S., 2003; University of Miami School of Law, J.D., 2006 — Admitted to Bar, 2006, Florida; 2007, New York; U.S. District Court, Southern District of New York; 2013, U.S. District Court, Eastern, Northern and Western Districts of New York

Maria J. Foglietta — University of Houston, B.A. Political Science (magna cum laude), 2005; Brooklyn Law School, J.D., 2008 — Admitted to Bar, 2009, New York; New Jersey; U.S. District Court, Eastern, Southern and Western Districts of New York; 2012, U.S. Court of Appeals, Second Circuit — Member Maritime Lawyers Association — Languages: Spanish

(This firm is also listed in the Subrogation section of this directory)

Wechsler & Cohen, LLP

17 State Street, 15th Floor
New York, New York 10004
  Telephone: 212-847-7900
  Fax: 212-847-7955
  E-Mail: mcohen@wechco.com
  www.wechco.com

Insurance Defense, Insurance Coverage, Reinsurance, Agent and Brokers Errors and Omissions, Arson, Product Liability, Commercial General Liability, Commercial Litigation, Construction Liability, Construction Litigation, Environmental Coverage, Examinations Under Oath, Extra-Contractual Litigation, First Party Matters, First and Third Party Defense, Fraud

Firm Profile: Wechsler & Cohen, LLP, offers a broad range of litigation, arbitration, negotiation, and other legal services. Our commitment to clients combines the highest professional standards with personalized attention, flexibility, and responsiveness. For this reason, our practice continues to grow,

Wechsler & Cohen, LLP, New York, NY   (Continued)

our client relationships continue to mature, and our client base continues to expand.

The Firm's practice covers a broad range involving litigation and arbitration, insurance, reinsurance, employment, real estate and land use, securities, corporate, and general business matters. Our experience and ability to provide superior legal services at reasonable rates sets us apart from other firms and enables us to represent high profile and other clients in complex matters as well as in more ordinary transactions and litigations.

Insurance Clients

AIG	American States Insurance Company
Argonaut Insurance Company	
Chartis	CNA Insurance Company
CNA MCU	Commonwealth Insurance Company
Hanover Insurance Company	
HealthCare Subrogation Group, LLC	Hudson Insurance Group
	Insurance Corporation of New York
Lexington Insurance Company	
Mitsui Sumitomo Insurance Group	MSI Claims (USA), Inc.
National Union Fire Insurance Company	Safeco Insurance
	SCOR Reinsurance Company
Sompo Japan Insurance Company of America	Trenwick America Reinsurance Corporation
Wilton Re Services, Inc.	

Non-Insurance Clients

Mack-Cali Realty Corp.   SL Green Realty Corp.

Partners

David B. Wechsler — 1958 — State University of New York at Albany, B.A. (magna cum laude), 1980; Boston University School of Law, J.D. (magna cum laude), 1983 — Admitted to Bar, 1984, New York; U.S. District Court, Eastern and Southern Districts of New York; U.S. Court of Appeals, First, Second, Third and Fifth Circuits

Mitchell S. Cohen — 1959 — State University of New York at Albany, B.A. (cum laude), 1981; Boston University School of Law, J.D., 1984 — Admitted to Bar, 1985, New York; U.S. District Court, Eastern and Southern Districts of New York; 1990, U.S. Court of Appeals, Second Circuit; 1997, U.S. Court of Appeals, Third Circuit; 2006, U.S. Supreme Court — Member New York State Bar Association

James F. X. Hiler — 1955 — Fordham University, B.A. (In Corsu Honorum), 1977; Fordham Law School, J.D., 1981 — Fordham Law Review, 1980-1981 — Admitted to Bar, 1982, New York; U.S. District Court, Eastern and Southern Districts of New York; 1983, U.S. District Court, Northern District of New York; 1988, U.S. Court of Appeals, Second Circuit — Member American and New York State Bar Association

Todd A. Gutfleisch — 1966 — Stevens Institute of Technology, B.E., 1988; Benjamin N. Cardozo School of Law, J.D. (cum laude), 1994 — Admitted to Bar, 1994, New Jersey; 1995, New York; U.S. District Court, Eastern and Southern Districts of New York; 2000, U.S. Court of Appeals, Second Circuit; 2001, U.S. District Court, Western District of New York; 2007, U.S. Supreme Court

Counsel

Debora A. Pitman — 1951 — Adelphi University, B.S., 1973; M.A., 1975; New York Law School, J.D. (cum laude), 1985 — Admitted to Bar, 1985, Connecticut; 1986, New York; 1996, U.S. District Court, Eastern and Southern Districts of New York; 1999, U.S. Court of Appeals, Second Circuit

Kim Lauren Michael — 1977 — Cornell University, B.S., 1999; New York University School of Law, J.D., 2003 — Admitted to Bar, 2003, New York; U.S. District Court, Southern District of New York — Member Association of the Bar of the City of New York

Of Counsel

Leonard B. Pack — Columbia University, B.A., 1966; M.A., 1970; Columbia University of Law, J.D., 1970 — Admitted to Bar, 1970, New York; U.S. District Court, Eastern and Southern Districts of New York; U.S. Supreme Court

Associates

Dylan Murphy — 1977 — College of the Holy Cross, B.A., 1999; Fordham University School of Law, J.D., 2004 — Admitted to Bar, 2005, New York; New Jersey; 2007, U.S. District Court, Eastern and Southern Districts of New York

NEW YORK

Wechsler & Cohen, LLP, New York, NY (Continued)

Daniel B. Grossman — 1986 — University of Michigan, B.A., 2008; Rutgers University School of Law, J.D., 2011 — Admitted to Bar, 2011, New Jersey; 2012, New York; U.S. District Court, District of New Jersey; 2013, U.S. District Court, Eastern and Southern Districts of New York

White, Fleischner & Fino, LLP

61 Broadway - 18th Floor
New York, New York 10004
Telephone: 212-487-9700
Fax: 212-487-9777
E-Mail: INFO@WFF-law.com
www.wff-law.com

(Holmdel, NJ Office*: Holmdel Corporate Plaza, 2137 Route 35, 07733)
 (Tel: 732-530-7787)
 (Fax: 732-530-8552)
(Garden City, NY Office: 1527 Franklin Avenue, 11501)
 (Tel: 516-742-2750)
 (Fax: 516-742-4892)
(White Plains, NY Office: 303 Old Tarrytown Road, 10603)
 (Tel: 914-509-2910)
 (Fax: 914-997-0957)
(Philadelphia, PA Office: 1500 Market Street, 12th Floor, East Tower, 19102)
 (Tel: 215-665-5780)
 (Fax: 215-569-8228)
(Boca Raton, FL Office: 7777 Glades Road, Suite 100, 33434)
 (Tel: 561-241-6740)
 (Fax: 561-241-6741)
(London, United Kingdom Office: 8-9 Talbot Court, EC3V 0BP)
 (Tel: 011-44-170-247-3101)
 (Fax: 011-44-774-069-0915)

Established: 1976

Insurance Defense, Defense Litigation, Property, General Liability, Malpractice, Product Liability, Coverage Analysis, Opinions, Excess and Reinsurance, Subrogation, Professional Errors and Omissions

Firm Profile: Established in 1976, White Fleischner & Fino, LLP has earned a reputation as a leading insurance coverage and defense law firm.

Insurance Clients

Acceptance Insurance Company
Chartis Insurance Group
Commonwealth Insurance Company
Essex Insurance Company
Fireman's Fund Insurance Company
Grange Insurance Group
HDI-Gerling America Insurance Company
Interstate Fire & Casualty Company
QBE Insurance Group Limited
State Farm Insurance Company
Underwriters at Lloyd's, London
Zurich Insurance Group
AIU Insurance Company
CNA Insurance Companies
Crawford & Company
Empire Fire and Marine Insurance Company
Frontier Insurance Company
Gallagher Bassett Services, Inc.
The Hartford Insurance Group
International Risk Management Group
Lancer Insurance Company
Prudential Property and Casualty Insurance Company
State-Wide Insurance Company
WNC First Insurance Services

Non-Insurance Clients

Avis Rent-A-Car System, LLC
CJW & Associates
Divine Brothers Company
Island Construction Company
McLarens Young International
Sodexho Marriott
VeriClaim, Inc.
Budget Rent-A-Car Corporation
Cunningham Lindsey U.S., Inc.
GAB Robins, Inc.
Marriott International, Inc.
Raphael & Associates
Starwood Hotels & Resorts Worldwide, Inc.

Partners

Paul A. Fino, Jr. — Georgetown University, B.A., 1966; Fordham Law School, J.D., 1969 — Admitted to Bar, 1970, New York; 1982, U.S. District Court, Eastern and Southern Districts of New York; 1992, U.S. District Court, Western District of New York — Member New York State, Bronx County, Nassau County, Kings County and Westchester Bar Associations; The Association of

White, Fleischner & Fino, LLP, New York, NY (Continued)

Trial Lawyers of the City of New York; American Subrogation Attorneys; New York City Trial Lawyers Association (Past-President) — Lecturer on Wrongful Death at New York State Trial Lawyers Institute

Benjamin A. Fleischner — Columbia College, Columbia University, B.A., 1975; New York Law School, J.D., 1978 — Admitted to Bar, 1979, New York; 1985, New Jersey; 1979, U.S. District Court, Eastern, Southern and Western Districts of New York; 1985, U.S. District Court, District of New Jersey; U.S. Court of Appeals, Second, Third and Fifth Circuits; U.S. Supreme Court — Conference Chairman and Speaker, American Conference Institute; New York Super Lawyer, Insurance — Practice Areas: Defense Litigation; Insurance Coverage

Sheri Holland — Trenton State College, B.A., 1984; Rutgers University School of Law, J.D., 1987 — Admitted to Bar, 1989, New York; New Jersey; U.S. District Court, District of New Jersey; 1994, U.S. District Court, Southern District of New York — Member Black Prosecutors Association; New York County Lawyers Association — Assistant District Attorney, New York County (1987-1994)

Wendy K. Cardali — State University of New York at Stony Brook, B.A., 1986; St. John's University School of Law, J.D., 1990 — Admitted to Bar, 1990, Connecticut; 1991, New York; 1994, U.S. District Court, Eastern and Southern Districts of New York — Member New York State Bar Association; New York County Lawyers Association; New York State Trial Lawyers Association

Daniel M. Stewart — Drew University, B.A., 1991; New York Law School, J.D., 1996 — Managing Editor, New York Law School Journal of Human Rights — Admitted to Bar, 1997, New York; New Jersey — Member New York County Lawyers Association

Gregory S. Pennington — Villanova University, B.A., 1992; Roger Williams University School of Law, J.D., 1997 — Admitted to Bar, 1997, New York; New Jersey; U.S. District Court, District of New Jersey

Patti F. Potash — American University School of Government and Public Administration, B.A., 1977; Washington University School of Law, J.D., 1981 — Admitted to Bar, 1981, California; 1983, New York — Member Metropolitan Women's Bar Association; New York County Lawyers Association; New York State Trial Lawyers Association

Deanna E. Hazen — University of Michigan, B.B.A., 1981; University of Detroit School of Law, J.D., 1984 — Admitted to Bar, 1984, Michigan; 1992, Law Society of Upper Canada; 1995, New York; 1984, U.S. District Court, Eastern and Western Districts of Michigan; U.S. District Court, Eastern and Southern Districts of New York; U.S. Court of Appeals for the Federal and Sixth Circuits; 1995, U.S. Court of International Trade — Member American and New York State Bar Association; Association of Trial Lawyers of the City of New York; New York County Lawyers Association

Nancy D. Lyness — Dartmouth College, B.A., 1987; Brooklyn Law School, J.D., 1993 — Admitted to Bar, 1994, New York

Gil M. Coogler — Washington & Jefferson College, B.A. (cum laude), 1978; Washington University School of Law, J.D., 1981 — Admitted to Bar, 1981, Pennsylvania; 1988, California; 1999, New York; 1981, U.S. District Court, Western District of Pennsylvania; U.S. Court of Appeals, Third Circuit; 1988, U.S. District Court, Central, Eastern and Northern Districts of California; U.S. Court of Appeals, Ninth Circuit; 1999, U.S. District Court, Southern District of New York — Member New York State Bar Association

Jonathan S. Chernow — Tufts University, B.A. (cum laude), 1990; Brooklyn Law School, J.D., 1995 — Admitted to Bar, 1997, New York; 1999, U.S. District Court, Eastern District of New York — Former Assistant District Attorney, Kings County

Evan A. Richman — Yeshiva University, B.A. (magna cum laude), 1995; Benjamin N. Cardozo School of Law, Yeshiva University, J.D., 1998 — Notes and Comments Editor, Cardoza's Arts and Entertainment Law Journal; Author: "Deception in Political Advertising: The Clash between the First Amendment and Defamation Law 16", Cadias Arts and End. L.J., 667 (1998) — Admitted to Bar, 1998, New York

Jared T. Greisman — Rollins College, B.A., 1992; Cornell University Law School, J.D., 1997 — Admitted to Bar, 1998, New Jersey; 1999, New York — Member New York State and New Jersey State Bar Associations; The Association of the Bar of the City of New York

Adam P. Stark — Rutgers College, B.A., 1994; Rutgers University School of Law-Camden, J.D., 1997 — Admitted to Bar, 1998, New Jersey; 1999, New York; 1998, U.S. District Court, District of New Jersey

Gregg D. Minkin — Muhlenberg College, B.A., 1989; Albany Law School of Union University, J.D. (cum laude), 1993 — Admitted to Bar, 1992, New York; U.S. District Court, Eastern, Northern and Southern Districts of New York; U.S. Court of Appeals, Second Circuit — Resident White Plains, NY Office

NEW YORK

White, Fleischner & Fino, LLP, New York, NY (Continued)

Counsel Emeritus

Allan P. White — New York University, B.A., 1963; New York University School of Law, J.D., 1967 — Admitted to Bar, 1969, New York; 1972, U.S. District Court, Southern District of New York — Member New York State Bar Association; The Association of Trial Lawyers of the City of New York (Board of Directors); Loss Executives Association; Professional Liability Underwriting Society (Board of Directors); American Judges Association (Small Claims Court Arbitrator, 1978); New York State Trial Lawyers Association; New York County Lawyers Association — Lecturer to Company Claim Department, Agents and Adjuster Groups on Defense Litigation and Trial Preparation, Workshop Panelist, Property Loss Research Bureau

Of Counsel

Alisa Dultz — Cornell University, B.S., 1983; St. John's University School of Law, J.D. (magna cum laude), 1990 — Admitted to Bar, 1991, New York; Connecticut; 1992, U.S. District Court, Eastern and Southern Districts of New York; 1997, U.S. District Court, District of Connecticut — Practice Areas: Litigation — E-mail: adultz@wff-law.com

Ann Marie Petrey — New York University, B.A., 1980; Brooklyn Law School, J.D., 1983 — Brooklyn Law Review — Admitted to Bar, 1984, New York; 1987, New Jersey; 1984, U.S. District Court, Eastern and Southern Districts of New York; U.S. District Court, District of New Jersey — Member Brooklyn Bar Association; Association of Professional Insurance Women

Renee S. Schwartz — Case Western Reserve University, B.A. (magna cum laude), 1972; Temple University Beasley School of Law, J.D., 1975; New York University School of Law, LL.M., 1985 — Phi Beta Kappa — Admitted to Bar, 1975, Pennsylvania; 1980, New York — Member New York State Bar Association — Senior Law Examiner for the New York State Board of Law Examiners (1989 to present) — Languages: French

Walter Williamson — Cornell University, B.A. (with honors), 1960; New York University School of Medicine, M.D., 1964; Columbia Law School, J.D., 1973 — Admitted to Bar, 1974, New York; 1977, U.S. District Court, Eastern and Southern Districts of New York — Member American and New York State Bar Associations; New York County Lawyers Association

Mitchell L. Shadowitz — Hebrew University; Concordia University, B.A., 1981; California Western School of Law, J.D., 1984 — Admitted to Bar, 1985, New York; 1991, Florida; 1988, U.S. District Court, Southern District of New York; 1990, U.S. District Court, Eastern District of New York; 1993, U.S. District Court, Southern District of Florida; 1998, U.S. District Court, Middle District of Florida — Member American and New York State Bar Associations; The Florida Bar — Languages: French, Hebrew — Resident Boca Raton, FL Office

Beth Shadowitz — University of Florida, B.S., 1981; California Western School of Law, J.D., 1984 — Admitted to Bar, 1985, New York; 1992, Florida; 1987, U.S. District Court, Eastern and Southern Districts of New York; 1993, U.S. District Court, Southern District of Florida — Resident Boca Raton, FL Office

William M. Billings — Fordham University, B.A., 1978; St. John's University School of Law, J.D., 1981 — Admitted to Bar, 1982, New York; 1985, U.S. District Court, Eastern and Southern Districts of New York; 1987, U.S. Court of Appeals, Second Circuit; 1991, U.S. Court of Appeals, Ninth Circuit; U.S. Supreme Court; 1992, U.S. District Court, Northern District of California

Dharman P. Niles — St. Olaf College, B.A., 1992; American University, Washington College of Law, J.D., 1995 — Admitted to Bar, 1998, New York; Connecticut; 2000, U.S. District Court, Southern District of New York; U.S. District Court, District of Connecticut

Mirna M. Santiago — New York University, B.A., 1992; State University of New York at Buffalo Law School, J.D., 1995 — Admitted to Bar, 1996, New York; U.S. District Court, Western District of New York; 1997, U.S. District Court, Eastern and Southern Districts of New York — Member New York State Bar Association — Languages: Spanish, Garifuna

Eric B. Schoenfeld — University of Pittsburgh, B.A., 1969; New York Law School, J.D., 1972 — Admitted to Bar, 1973, New York; 1985, New Jersey — Former Insurance Counsel, Kennedy International Airport Cogeneration Partners; Former Litigation Counsel, United States Tennis Assoiacation Arthur Ashe Tennis Stadium Construction Project; Counsel to the Insurers, General Motors Transportation Program, Port to Port, Worldwide

Sharon Moreland — Cornell University, B.A. (cum laude), 1991; Boston University School of Law, J.D., 1994 — Admitted to Bar, 1994, Massachusetts; 1996, New Jersey; New York; 1997, U.S. District Court, District of New Jersey; U.S. District Court, Eastern and Southern Districts of New York

Brian M. Thorn — Rutgers University, B.S., 1996; Benjamin N. Cardozo School of Law, J.D., 1999 — Admitted to Bar, 1999, New York; New Jersey; U.S. District Court, District of New Jersey — Member American, New Jersey State and Monmouth County Bar Associations

Shelly K. Werbel — Pratt Institute, B.A., 1986; Benjamin N. Cardozo School of Law, J.D. (cum laude), 1989 — Admitted to Bar, 1989, New York; 1990, New Jersey; U.S. District Court, Eastern and Southern Districts of New York; U.S. District Court, District of New Jersey

Stuart G. Glass — Clark University, B.A., 1992; New York Law School, J.D., 1997 — Admitted to Bar, 1998, New York; U.S. District Court, Eastern and Southern Districts of New York — Resident Garden City, NY Office

Associates

Jason Steinberg — Union College, B.A., 2000; Brooklyn Law School, J.D., 2003 — Admitted to Bar, 2003, New York; Connecticut; U.S. District Court, Eastern and Southern Districts of New York

Jennifer L. Coviello — State University of New York at Albany, B.A., 1996; New York Law School, J.D., 1999 — Executive Articles Editor, New York Law School Journal of International and Comparative Law — Admitted to Bar, 2000, New York; Connecticut; 2001, U.S. District Court, Eastern and Southern Districts of New York — Member The Association of the Bar of the City of New York

Marisa Okun — The Pennsylvania State University, B.A. (Dean's List, Golden Key Honor Society), 2001; New York Law School, J.D. (cum laude), 2004 — Associate Editor, New York Law Review — Admitted to Bar, 2005, New York — Member New York County Lawyers Association

Nathan Losman — State University of New York at Binghamton, B.A. (with honors), 1982; Emory University School of Law, J.D., 1985 — Admitted to Bar, 1986, New York; 1994, New Jersey; 2003, District of Columbia; Texas; 2005, Massachusetts; 1988, U.S. District Court, Eastern and Southern Districts of New York — Member New York State Bar Association

Michael F. Daly — Fordham College, Fordham University, B.A. (cum laude), 1999; Oxford University, Blackfriars Hall, 1998; Emory University School of Law, J.D., 2003 — Admitted to Bar, 2005, New York; U.S. District Court, Eastern and Southern Districts of New York — Member New York State Bar Association; New York County Lawyers Association — Languages: Spanish

Craig Rokuson — Cornell University, B.S., 2003; St. John's University School of Law, J.D. (cum laude), 2006 — Admitted to Bar, 2006, New Jersey; 2007, New York — Member American Bar Association

Eric R. Leibowitz — Cornell University, B.A., 1999; Brooklyn Law School, J.D. (magna cum laude), 2005 — Admitted to Bar, 2005, New York; 2009, U.S. District Court, Southern District of New York — Member New York City Bar Association

Maria DellaRatta — New York University, B.A., 1988; Brooklyn Law School, J.D., 1994 — Admitted to Bar, 1996, New York; U.S. District Court, Eastern District of New York

James P. Ricciardi, Jr. — Monmouth University, B.A. (cum laude), 2005; Widener University School of Law, J.D., 2008 — Admitted to Bar, 2008, New Jersey; Pennsylvania; U.S. District Court, District of New Jersey; 2010, U.S. Court of Appeals, Third Circuit — Member Pennsylvania and Monmouth County Bar Associations

Nicholas L. Paone — Columbia University, B.A., 1983; Villanova University School of Law, J.D., 1987 — Admitted to Bar, 1987, Pennsylvania; New Jersey; 1993, New York; 1987, U.S. District Court, District of New Jersey; U.S. District Court, Eastern District of Pennsylvania; 1993, U.S. District Court, Eastern and Southern Districts of New York

Janet P. Ford — Barnard College; Columbia University, A.B. (cum laude), 1994; University of California, Berkeley, M.S.W. (with honors); Benjamin N. Cardozo School of Law, Yeshiva University, J.D. (cum laude), 1997 — Pro Se Law Clerk, U.S. Court of Appeals, Second Circuit — Articles Editor, Benjamin N. Cardozo Women's Law Journal — Admitted to Bar, 1998, New York; 2002, U.S. District Court, Eastern and Southern Districts of New York

Joseph M. Glatstein — Brooklyn College, B.A. (magna cum laude), 1976; Benjamin N. Cardozo School of Law, Yeshiva University, J.D., 1979 — Moot Court — Admitted to Bar, 1980, New York; U.S. District Court, Eastern and Southern Districts of New York; U.S. Court of Appeals, Second Circuit — Member New York County Lawyers Association

Jennifer Mindlin — Emory University, B.A. (summa cum laude), 2009; Fordham University School of Law, J.D. (cum laude), 2012 — Admitted to Bar, 2013, New York; U.S. District Court, Southern District of New York

Matthew I. Toker — University of Delaware, B.A., 2006; Touro College Jacob D. Fuchsberg Law Center, J.D. (Dean's List), 2009 — CALI Award — Admitted to Bar, 2009, New Jersey; 2010, New York

NEW YORK

White, Fleischner & Fino, LLP, New York, NY (Continued)

Laura R. Fleischner — Emory University, B.A., 2003; Brooklyn Law School, J.D. (cum laude), 2008 — Admitted to Bar, 2009, New York; New Jersey; U.S. District Court, Eastern and Southern Districts of New York

Kirsten J. Orr — New York University, B.A. (cum laude), 2008; New York Law School, J.D., 2011 — Admitted to Bar, 2011, New Jersey; 2012, New York — Resident Holmdel, NJ Office

Victoriya V. Baranchuk — Brooklyn College, B.A., 2008; Touro College Jacob D. Fuchsberg Law Center, J.D. (magna cum laude), 2013 — Admitted to Bar, 2014, New York — Resident Garden City, NY Office

Robert M. Drucker — University of Wisconsin, B.A., 1998; Hofstra University School of Law, J.D., 2001 — Admitted to Bar, 2002, New York; U.S. District Court, Eastern and Southern Districts of New York

(This firm is also listed in the Subrogation section of this directory)

Wilbraham, Lawler & Buba

140 Broadway, 46th Floor
New York, New York 10005-1101
  Telephone: 212-858-7575
  Fax: 212-943-9246
  E-Mail: bbuba@wlbdeflaw.com
  www.wlbdeflaw.com

(Philadelphia, PA Office*: 1818 Market Street, Suite 3100, 19103-3631)
  (Tel: 215-564-4141)
  (Fax: 215-564-4385)
(Wilmington, DE Office*: 901 North Market Street, Suite 810, 19801-3090)
  (Tel: 302-421-9935)
  (Fax: 302-421-9955)
(Haddonfield, NJ Office*: 24 Kings Highway West, 08033-2122)
  (Tel: 856-795-4422)
  (Fax: 856-795-4699)
(Pittsburgh, PA Office*: 603 Stanwix Street, Two Gateway Center - 17 North, 15222)
  (Tel: 412-255-0500)
  (Fax: 412-255-0505)

Appellate Practice, Asbestos Litigation, Civil Trial Practice, Commercial Litigation, Insurance Defense, Toxic Torts, Workers' Compensation, Product Liability Law

Partners

Edward J. Wilbraham — 1946 — University of Notre Dame, B.B.A., 1968; Villanova University School of Law, J.D., 1974 — Admitted to Bar, 1974, Pennsylvania; 1977, New Jersey; 1999, New York; 2002, West Virginia; 1977, U.S. District Court, Eastern District of Pennsylvania; 1989, U.S. District Court, Middle District of Pennsylvania; U.S. District Court, District of New Jersey; U.S. District Court, Northern District of Ohio; U.S. Court of Appeals, Third Circuit; 2002, U.S. District Court, Southern District of West Virginia — Member Defense Research Institute

Robert B. Lawler — 1938 — Columbia University, B.A., 1969; Villanova University School of Law, J.D., 1972 — Admitted to Bar, 1972, Pennsylvania; 1992, New Jersey; 1999, New York; 1980, U.S. District Court, Eastern District of Pennsylvania; 1981, U.S. Supreme Court; 1989, U.S. District Court, Middle District of Pennsylvania; 1992, U.S. District Court, District of New Jersey — Tel: 215-972-2812

Barbara J. Buba — 1957 — The University of North Carolina at Chapel Hill, B.S., 1979; Dickinson School of Law, J.D., 1982 — Admitted to Bar, 1982, Pennsylvania; 1992, New Jersey; 1999, New York; 1983, U.S. District Court, Eastern District of Pennsylvania; 1989, U.S. District Court, Middle District of Pennsylvania; 1992, U.S. District Court, District of New Jersey

John S. Howarth — 1967 — University of Notre Dame, B.A., 1989; Rutgers University School of Law, J.D., 1992 — Admitted to Bar, 1992, Pennsylvania; New Jersey; 2000, New York; 1992, U.S. District Court, District of New Jersey; 1994, U.S. District Court, Eastern District of Pennsylvania

Edward J. Stolarski — 1955 — Mercyhurst College, B.A., 1977; M.S., 1981; Widener University School of Law, J.D., 1984 — Admitted to Bar, 1984, Pennsylvania; New Jersey; 2003, New York; 1984, U.S. District Court, Eastern District of Pennsylvania; U.S. District Court, District of New Jersey; U.S.

Wilbraham, Lawler & Buba, New York, NY (Continued)

Court of Appeals, Third Circuit; 2003, U.S. District Court, Southern District of New York — Tel: 215-972-2856

(See listing under Philadelphia, PA for additional information)

The following firms also service this area.

Law Offices of Kenneth L. Aron
151 Route 33 East, Suite 254
Manalapan, New Jersey 07726
  Telephone: 732-414-2710
  Fax: 732-414-2711

Defense Litigation, Insurance Coverage, Property, Automobile Liability, General Liability, Fidelity and Surety, Subrogation

SEE COMPLETE LISTING UNDER MANALAPAN, NEW JERSEY (44 MILES)

Boeggeman, George & Corde, P.C.
1 Water Street, Suite 425
White Plains, New York 10601
  Telephone: 914-761-2252
  Fax: 914-761-5211

Insurance Defense, Trial Practice, Automobile, Product Liability, Legal Malpractice, Medical Malpractice, Employment Law, Real Estate, Toxic Torts, Engineering Malpractice

SEE COMPLETE LISTING UNDER WHITE PLAINS, NEW YORK (20 MILES)

Budd Larner, P.C.
150 John F. Kennedy Parkway
Short Hills, New Jersey 07078-2703
  Telephone: 973-379-4800
  Fax: 973-379-7734

General Practice, Insurance Law, Reinsurance

SEE COMPLETE LISTING UNDER SHORT HILLS, NEW JERSEY (43 MILES)

Connors & Connors, PC
766 Castleton Avenue
Staten Island, New York 10310-1700
  Telephone: 718-442-1700
  Fax: 718-442-1717

Insurance Defense, Commercial and Personal Lines, Self-Insured Defense, Trucking Law, Self-Retained Trucking Company Defense, Self-Retained Security Guard Companies, Self-Retained Retail Stores

SEE COMPLETE LISTING UNDER STATEN ISLAND, NEW YORK (26 MILES)

Hardin, Kundla, McKeon & Poletto, P.A.
673 Morris Avenue
Springfield, New Jersey 07081
  Telephone: 973-912-5222
  Fax: 973-912-9212
Mailing Address: P.O. Box 730, Springfield, NJ 07081

General Defense

SEE COMPLETE LISTING UNDER SPRINGFIELD, NEW JERSEY (21 MILES)

McCabe, Collins, McGeough & Fowler, LLP
346 Westbury Avenue
Carle Place, New York 11514
  Telephone: 516-741-6266
  Fax: 516-873-9496
Mailing Address: P.O. Box 9000, Carle Place, NY 11514

Asbestos Litigation, Automobile, Aviation, Casualty, Coverage Issues, Trial Practice, Appellate Practice, Subrogation, Product Liability, Insurance Law, Medical Malpractice, Municipal Liability, Professional Liability, Construction Accidents, Sports and Entertainment Liability, General Liability, Premises Liability, Food Poisoning, Toxic Chemicals, Matrimonial

SEE COMPLETE LISTING UNDER MINEOLA, NEW YORK (20 MILES)

NEWBURGH   NEW YORK

Reardon & Sclafani, P.C.
220 White Plains Road
Tarrytown, New York 10591
  Telephone: 914-366-0201
  Fax: 914-366-0022

Insurance Law, Malpractice, Product Liability, General Liability, Motor Vehicle, Environmental Law, Trial Practice, Appellate Practice, State and Federal Courts

SEE COMPLETE LISTING UNDER TARRYTOWN, NEW YORK (30 MILES)

The Law Office of Lawrence N. Rogak, LLC
3355 Lawson Boulevard
Oceanside, New York 11572
  Telephone: 516-763-2996
  Fax: 516-763-2998

Insurance Defense, Coverage Issues, Automobile, Product Liability, Subrogation, General Liability, Uninsured and Underinsured Motorist, Property and Casualty, Investigation and Adjustment, Bodily Injury, Pollution, Garage Liability, Special Concentration in New York No-Fault Procedure and Defense

SEE COMPLETE LISTING UNDER OCEANSIDE, NEW YORK (21 MILES)

NEWBURGH 28,866 Orange Co.

Catania, Mahon, Milligram & Rider, PLLC

One Corwin Court
Newburgh, New York 12550
  Telephone: 845-565-1100
  Fax: 845-565-1999
  E-Mail: cmmr@cmmrlegal.com
  www.cmmrlegal.com

(Chestnut Ridge, NY Office: 100 Red Schoolhouse Road, Suite C-12, 10977)
(Fishkill, NY Office: 703 Route 9, 12524)
  (Tel: 845-231-1403)
  (Fax: 845-897-2160)

Established: 1972

Insurance Defense, Insurance Coverage, School Law, Municipal Law, Construction Litigation

Firm Profile: Catania, Mahon, Milligram & Rider, PLLC, offers personalized legal services backed by the resources and proficiency of one of the largest general practice law firms in the Hudson Valley. We seek the highest level of client satisfaction while fulfilling the legal and business goals of our clients.

Insurance Clients

Armed Forces Insurance Exchange	CNA Insurance Company
Fireman's Fund Insurance Company	GAB Robins, Inc.
INS Insurance, Inc.	Gallagher Bassett Services, Inc.
Medical Liability Mutual Insurance Company	Liberty Mutual Group
New York Schools Insurance Reciprocal	New York Municipal Insurance Reciprocal
Penn Millers Insurance Company	Ophthalmic Mutual Insurance Company
Royal Insurance Company	Physicians Reciprocal Insurers
	St. Paul Travelers

Non-Insurance Clients

Correctional Medical Services, Inc.	NETREX Claims
Schneider National Carriers, Inc.	Wal-Mart Stores, Inc.

Members

Joseph A. Catania, Jr. — 1950 — Boston College, B.A., 1972; Albany Law School of Union University, J.D., 1977 — Admitted to Bar, 1978, New York; 1982, U.S. Supreme Court — Member New York State, Orange County and Newburgh Bar Associations; American Arbitration Association Construction Industry Panel of Neutrals; New York State Trial Lawyers Association; Association of Trial Lawyers of America — Certified Civil Trial Advocate, National Board of Trial Advocacy — E-mail: jcatania@cmmrlegal.com

Catania, Mahon, Milligram & Rider, PLLC, Newburgh, NY (Continued)

Richard M. Mahon, II — 1959 — Cornell University, A.B., 1981; Boston College Law School, J.D., 1985 — Admitted to Bar, 1986, District of Columbia; 1987, New York — Member New York State, Orange County and Newburgh Bar Associations; The District of Columbia Bar — E-mail: rmahon@cmmrlegal.com

Steven I. Milligram — 1953 — State University of New York at Buffalo, B.A., 1976; Pace University School of Law, J.D., 1981 — Admitted to Bar, 1982, New York; 1983, New Jersey — Member New York State, Orange County and Newburgh Bar Associations; New York State Trial Lawyers Association — E-mail: smilligram@cmmrlegal.com

Michelle F. Rider — 1966 — St. Bonaventure University, B.A. (summa cum laude), 1988; Albany Law School of Union University, J.D. (cum laude), 1995 — Admitted to Bar, 1996, Florida; New York — Member American and New York State Bar Associations; The Florida Bar; American Institute of Certified Public Accountants; American Bar Foundation — E-mail: mrider@cmmrlegal.com

Paul S. Ernenwein — State University of New York at Albany, B.A., 1991; Western New England College School of Law, J.D., 1995 — Admitted to Bar, 1996, New York — Member American, New York State and Orange County Bar Associations — E-mail: pernenwein@cmmrlegal.com

Hobart J. Simpson — State University of New York at New Paltz, B.A. (magna cum laude), 1997; Albany Law School, J.D., 2000 — Admitted to Bar, 2001, New York — Member New York State and Orange County Bar Associations — E-mail: hsimpson@cmmrlegal.com

Julia Goings-Perrot — 1969 — Grinnell College, B.A., 1991; The University of Iowa College of Law, J.D. (with distinction), 1997 — Admitted to Bar, 1998, New York — Member New York State, Orange County and Dutchess County Bar Associations; American Health Lawyers Association — Languages: French — E-mail: jgoings-perrot@cmmrlegal.com

Michael E. Catania — University of Delaware, B.A., 2003; Albany Law School of Union University, J.D. (magna cum laude), 2006 — Admitted to Bar, 2006, Massachusetts; 2007, New York; North Carolina; New Jersey; 2008, Connecticut — E-mail: mcatania@cmmrlegal.com

Joseph McKay — Pace University, B.B.A., 1986; Touro College Jacob D. Fuchsberg Law Center, J.D., 1991 — Admitted to Bar, 1992, New York — Member New York State and Orange County Bar Associations — E-mail: jmckay@cmmrlegal.com

Associates

Mark L. Schuh — State University of New York at Albany, B.A., 1990; Pace University School of Law, J.D. (cum laude), 2000 — Admitted to Bar, 2000, New York — E-mail: mschuh@cmmrlegal.com

Daniel F. Sullivan — 1958 — St. Francis College, B.S., 1985; St. John's University School of Law, J.D., 1990 — Admitted to Bar, 1991, New York — Member New York State Bar Association — E-mail: dsullivan@cmmrlegal.com

Holly L. Reinhardt — 1975 — University of Massachusetts, B.A., 1997; Hofstra University School of Law, J.D., 2000 — Admitted to Bar, 2000, New Jersey; 2009, New York — Member New York State, New Jersey State and Orange County Bar Associations — E-mail: hreinhardt@cmmrlegal.com

Rebecca Baldwin Mantello — St. Lawrence University, B.S. (magna cum laude), 2002; Albany Law School, J.D. (magna cum laude), 2007 — Admitted to Bar, 2007, Connecticut; 2008, New York — Member New York State and Orange County Bar Associations — E-mail: rmantello@cmmrlegal.com

Ari Bauer — State University of New York at Albany, B.S. (cum laude), 2004; Fordham University School of Law, J.D., 2008 — Admitted to Bar, 2010, New York — E-mail: abauer@cmmrlegal.com

Eric Ossentjuk — Dominican College, B.A. (cum laude), 1998; Pace University School of Law, J.D., 2001 — Admitted to Bar, 2002, New Jersey; 2003, New York — Member New York State and Orange County Bar Associations; Women's Bar Association of Orange and Sullivan Counties — E-mail: eossentjuk@cmmrlegal.com

Sarita Bhandarkar — Tufts University, B.A. (cum laude), 1999; William & Mary School of Law, J.D., 2002; New York Law School, LL.M. Taxation — Admitted to Bar, 2003, New York — Member New York State and Orange County Bar Associations; Women's Bar Association of Orange and Sullivan Counties; Hudson Valley Estate Planning Council — E-mail: sbhandarkar@cmmrlegal.com

Seamus P. Weir — State University of New York at Binghamton, B.A., 2003; St. Johns University School of Law, J.D., 2006 — Admitted to Bar, 2008, New York; 2012, U.S. District Court, Eastern and Southern Districts of New York — Member New York State and Orange County Bar Associations — E-mail: sweir@cmmrlegal.com

NEW YORK

Catania, Mahon, Milligram & Rider, PLLC, Newburgh, NY (Continued)

Lia E. Fierro — Hofstra University, B.A. (magna cum laude), 2006; Boston University School of Law, J.D., 2010 — Member, American Journal of Law & Medicine — Admitted to Bar, 2011, Massachusetts; 2012, New York — Member New York State and Boston Bar Associations; Women's Bar Association of Orange and Sullivan Counties — E-mail: lfierro@cmmrlegal.com

Michael R. Frascarelli — Cornell University, B.A., 2004; Albany Law School, J.D., 2012 — Admitted to Bar, 2012, New York; 2013, New Jersey — E-mail: mfrascarelli@cmmrlegal.com

David A. Rosenberg — New York University, B.A. Economics, 2003; New York Law School, J.D., 2013 — Admitted to Bar, 2013, New York; New Jersey — E-mail: drosenberg@cmmrlegal.com

Special Counsel

Jay F. Jason — 1952 — Duke University, A.B., 1973; Boston University School of Law, J.D., 1976; New York University, M.S., 2005 — Admitted to Bar, 1977, Massachusetts; 1980, New York; 1981, U.S. Court of Appeals, Second Circuit; 1996, U.S. Supreme Court — E-mail: jjason@cmmrlegal.com

Robert E. DiNardo — Fordham University, B.A., 1966; New York Law School, J.D. (cum laude), 1970 — Admitted to Bar, 1971, District of Columbia; 1972, New York; U.S. District Court, Eastern, Northern and Southern Districts of New York; U.S. Court of Appeals, Second Circuit — Member New York State (Employment Law Section; Business Law Section) and Orange County (President, 1991-1992) Bar Associations — E-mail: rdinardo@cmmrlegal.com

---

The following firms also service this area.

Cook, Netter, Cloonan, Kurtz & Murphy, P.C.
85 Main Street
Kingston, New York 12401
Telephone: 845-331-0702
Fax: 845-331-1003
Mailing Address: P.O. Box 3939, Kingston, NY 12402

Business Transactions, Civil Litigation, Construction Accidents, Motor Vehicle, Municipal Law, Personal Injury, Premises Liability, Product Liability, Professional Liability, Public Entities, Real Estate, Sexual Harassment, State and Federal Courts, Title Insurance, Federal Civil Rights

SEE COMPLETE LISTING UNDER KINGSTON, NEW YORK (39 MILES)

Drake, Loeb, Heller, Kennedy, Gogerty, Gaba & Rodd PLLC
555 Hudson Valley Avenue, Suite 100
New Windsor, New York 12553
Telephone: 845-561-0550
Fax: 845-561-1235

Appellate Practice, Americans with Disabilities Act, Automobile Liability, Carrier Defense, Civil Rights, Employment Discrimination, General Civil Trial and Appellate Practice, Medical Malpractice, Municipal Law, Product Liability, Professional Liability, School Law, Section 1983 Litigation

SEE COMPLETE LISTING UNDER NEW WINDSOR, NEW YORK

NIAGARA FALLS 50,193 Niagara Co.

Refer To
Barth Sullivan Behr
600 Convention Tower
43 Court Street
Buffalo, New York 14202
Telephone: 716-856-1300
Fax: 716-856-1494

Trial Practice, Appellate Practice, Alternative Dispute Resolution, Product Liability, Casualty, Fire, Professional Errors and Omissions, Coverage Issues, Insurance Fraud, Subrogation, Motor Vehicle, General Liability, Workers' Compensation, Premises Liability, Municipal Liability, Tractor-Trailer, Bad Faith

SEE COMPLETE LISTING UNDER BUFFALO, NEW YORK (21 MILES)

NIAGARA FALLS

Refer To
Cohen & Lombardo, P.C.
343 Elmwood Avenue
Buffalo, New York 14222
Telephone: 716-881-3010
Fax: 716-881-2755
Toll Free: 800-276-2640
Mailing Address: P.O. Box 5204, Buffalo, NY 14213-5204

Insurance Defense, Trial Practice, State and Federal Courts, Coverage Analysis, Litigation, Fire, Arson, Fraud, Property, Casualty, Surety, Marine, Employer Liability, Premises Liability, Product Liability, Environmental Law, Toxic Torts, Construction Law, Accident, Automobile, Professional Liability, Medical Malpractice, Subrogation, Advertising Injury, Errors and Omissions, Aviation, Bad Faith, Copyright and Trademark Law, Municipal Liability, Title Insurance, Niagara, Orleans, Monroe, Genesee, Livingston, Wyoming, Allegany, Cattaraugus and Chautauqua Counties

SEE COMPLETE LISTING UNDER BUFFALO, NEW YORK (19 MILES)

Refer To
Roach, Brown, McCarthy & Gruber, P.C.
1920 Liberty Building
424 Main Street
Buffalo, New York 14202-3511
Telephone: 716-852-0400
Fax: 716-852-2535

Insurance Defense, Trial and Appellate Practice, Medical Malpractice, Professional Malpractice, Product Liability, Construction Law, Sports and Entertainment Liability, Aviation, Fire, Excess, Coverage Issues

SEE COMPLETE LISTING UNDER BUFFALO, NEW YORK (25 MILES)

NORWICH † 7,190 Chenango Co.

Refer To
Levene Gouldin & Thompson, LLP
450 Plaza Drive
Vestal, New York 13850
Telephone: 607-763-9200
Fax: 607-763-9211
Mailing Address: P.O. Box F 1706, Binghamton, NY 13902

Appeals, Arbitration, Mediation, Asbestos Litigation, Bad Faith, Construction Accidents, Dram Shop Liability, Liquor Liability, Fire Loss, Labor Law, Premises Liability, Product Liability, Property Claims, Sexual Harassment, Toxic Torts, Wrongful Death, Advocacy in Professional Discipline, Automobile, Motorcycle, Trucking Accidents, Contractual Indemnification, Defamation, Discrimination, Division of Human Rights/EEOC, Employment Law Violations, False Arrest/Constitutional Claims, Governmental Tort Liability, Infant Settlements, Insurance Coverage Disputes, Medical Malpractice Defense Matters, School District Liability, Um/Sum Claims

SEE COMPLETE LISTING UNDER BINGHAMTON, NEW YORK (40 MILES)

OCEANSIDE 32,109 Nassau Co.

The Law Office of Lawrence N. Rogak, LLC
3355 Lawson Boulevard
Oceanside, New York 11572
Telephone: 516-763-2996
Fax: 516-763-2998
Emer/After Hrs: 516-322-2470
E-Mail: insurancelawyer@yahoo.com
www.rogak.com

Established: 1994

Insurance Defense, Coverage Issues, Automobile, Product Liability, Subrogation, General Liability, Uninsured and Underinsured Motorist, Property and Casualty, Investigation and Adjustment, Bodily Injury, Pollution, Garage Liability, Special Concentration in New York No-Fault Procedure and Defense

ONEONTA NEW YORK

The Law Office of Lawrence N. Rogak, LLC, Oceanside, NY (Continued)

Firm Profile: Lawrence N. Rogak LLC is dedicated solely to the representation of insurers and self-insured corporations in matters pertaining to liability and coverage. This firm researches and writes more articles on insurance law than all the other insurance defense firms in New York combined. Lawrence N. Rogak is the author of "Rogak's New York No-Fault Law & Practice", the first comprehensive guide ever published on this subject, and "Rogak's New York Insurance & Negligence Law" [James Publishing, 1999], the most comprehensive "desk book" ever written on the subject. The firm also publishes a daily newsletter, "The Rogak Report," which is available at groups.yahoo.com/groups/TheRogakReport. This blog reviews the latest insurance/negligence case law and developments. We also publish a New York PIP newsletter at groups.yahoo.com/group/NewYorkPIP.

Our enormous research and writing output directly benefits our clients in that, what other law firms have to look up, we already know. Therefore not only are we armed with superior knowledge, but our clients need pay for only a small fraction of the legal research for which other law firms must charge.

In addition to general liability, auto liability and coverage litigation, the firm also has a major specialty in no-fault defense. According to analyses performed by some of our clients, our firm brings lawsuits to a conclusion faster and for less money than any other law firm they have used.

Insurance Clients

Adirondack Insurance Exchange
Cambridge Integrated Services
Commercial Mutual Insurance Company
Corporate Claims Service, Inc.
Gallagher Bassett Services, Inc.
Hartford Insurance Company
Lancer Insurance Company
Merchants Insurance Group
New Jersey Skylands Insurance Company
NOVA Casualty Company
Occidental Fire & Casualty Company
Preserver Insurance Company
Prime Insurance Syndicate, Inc.
Security Mutual Insurance Company
Unitrin Direct Insurance Company
Unitrin, Inc.
Amica Mutual Insurance Company
Chartis Insurance
Community Mutual Insurance Company
ELCO Administrative Services
GuideOne Insurance
Infinity Insurance Company
Long Island Insurance Company
Motor Vehicle Accident Indemnification Corporation
New York Central Mutual Fire Insurance Company
OneBeacon Insurance
Pennsylvania Lumbermens Mutual Insurance Company
Protective Insurance Company
State Farm Insurance Company
Tower Insurance Company of New York
Western Continent Claims Association

Partner

Lawrence N. Rogak — 1957 — University of Miami, B.A., 1978; Brooklyn Law School, J.D., 1981 — Admitted to Bar, 1982, New York; 1992, Colorado; 1985, U.S. District Court, Southern District of New York; 1988, U.S. District Court, Eastern District of New York — Member Brooklyn Bar Association (Ethics Committee, 1985) — "One City's Successful Move to Self-Insurance," Risk Management Magazine (December, 1989); "Transferring Liability: One City's Experience," New York Law Journal (February 1, 1991); "Workers Comp Act: Ramifications for General Liability Defense," New York Law Journal (April 9, 1997); "Priority of Coverage in Garage Liability Policies," New York Law Journal (May 30, 1997); "Terminating Assigned Risk Auto Policies," New York Law Journal (April 24, 1998); "Rogak's New York Insurance & Negligence Law," [James Publishing 1999]; Columnist, "Claims Magazine"; Columnist, "Insurance Advocate"; "Rogak's New York No-Fault Law & Practice" (1Universe, 2007; Updates 2009,2011)

Associates

Renee Breitner — 1950 — Hofstra University, B.A., 1972; Touro College Jacob D. Fuchsberg Law Center, J.D., 1989 — American Jurisprudence Award — Admitted to Bar, 1989, New York; New Jersey; 1990, Florida; Colorado; 1996, U.S. District Court, Eastern and Southern Districts of New York — Member Nassau County Bar Association

David A. Gierasch — 1978 — Binghamton University, B.A., 2000; Hofstra University School of Law, J.D., 2004 — Admitted to Bar, 2005, New York

OLEAN 14,452 Cattaraugus Co.

Refer To
Barth Sullivan Behr
600 Convention Tower
43 Court Street
Buffalo, New York 14202
Telephone: 716-856-1300
Fax: 716-856-1494

Trial Practice, Appellate Practice, Alternative Dispute Resolution, Product Liability, Casualty, Fire, Professional Errors and Omissions, Coverage Issues, Insurance Fraud, Subrogation, Motor Vehicle, General Liability, Workers' Compensation, Premises Liability, Municipal Liability, Tractor-Trailer, Bad Faith

SEE COMPLETE LISTING UNDER BUFFALO, NEW YORK (74 MILES)

Refer To
Cohen & Lombardo, P.C.
343 Elmwood Avenue
Buffalo, New York 14222
Telephone: 716-881-3010
Fax: 716-881-2755
Toll Free: 800-276-2640

Mailing Address: P.O. Box 5204, Buffalo, NY 14213-5204

Insurance Defense, Trial Practice, State and Federal Courts, Coverage Analysis, Litigation, Fire, Arson, Fraud, Property, Casualty, Surety, Marine, Employer Liability, Premises Liability, Product Liability, Environmental Law, Toxic Torts, Construction Law, Accident, Automobile, Professional Liability, Medical Malpractice, Subrogation, Advertising Injury, Errors and Omissions, Aviation, Bad Faith, Copyright and Trademark Law, Municipal Liability, Title Insurance, Niagara, Orleans, Monroe, Genesee, Livingston, Wyoming, Allegany, Cattaraugus and Chautauqua Counties

SEE COMPLETE LISTING UNDER BUFFALO, NEW YORK (78 MILES)

Refer To
Roach, Brown, McCarthy & Gruber, P.C.
1920 Liberty Building
424 Main Street
Buffalo, New York 14202-3511
Telephone: 716-852-0400
Fax: 716-852-2535

Insurance Defense, Trial and Appellate Practice, Medical Malpractice, Professional Malpractice, Product Liability, Construction Law, Sports and Entertainment Liability, Aviation, Fire, Excess, Coverage Issues

SEE COMPLETE LISTING UNDER BUFFALO, NEW YORK (73 MILES)

ONEONTA 13,901 Otsego Co.

Refer To
Levene Gouldin & Thompson, LLP
450 Plaza Drive
Vestal, New York 13850
Telephone: 607-763-9200
Fax: 607-763-9211

Mailing Address: P.O. Box F 1706, Binghamton, NY 13902

Appeals, Arbitration, Mediation, Asbestos Litigation, Bad Faith, Construction Accidents, Dram Shop Liability, Liquor Liability, Fire Loss, Labor Law, Premises Liability, Product Liability, Property Claims, Sexual Harassment, Toxic Torts, Wrongful Death, Advocacy in Professional Discipline, Automobile, Motorcycle, Trucking Accidents, Contractual Indemnification, Defamation, Discrimination, Division of Human Rights/EEOC, Employment Law Violations, False Arrest/Constitutional Claims, Governmental Tort Liability, Infant Settlements, Insurance Coverage Disputes, Medical Malpractice Defense Matters, School District Liability, Um/Sum Claims

SEE COMPLETE LISTING UNDER BINGHAMTON, NEW YORK (60 MILES)

NEW YORK — OWEGO

OWEGO † 3,896 Tioga Co.

Refer To

Levene Gouldin & Thompson, LLP
450 Plaza Drive
Vestal, New York 13850
   Telephone: 607-763-9200
   Fax: 607-763-9211
Mailing Address: P.O. Box F 1706, Binghamton, NY 13902

Appeals, Arbitration, Mediation, Asbestos Litigation, Bad Faith, Construction Accidents, Dram Shop Liability, Liquor Liability, Fire Loss, Labor Law, Premises Liability, Product Liability, Property Claims, Sexual Harassment, Toxic Torts, Wrongful Death, Advocacy in Professional Discipline, Automobile, Motorcycle, Trucking Accidents, Contractual Indemnification, Defamation, Discrimination, Division of Human Rights/EEOC, Employment Law Violations, False Arrest/Constitutional Claims, Governmental Tort Liability, Infant Settlements, Insurance Coverage Disputes, Medical Malpractice Defense Matters, School District Liability, Um/Sum Claims

SEE COMPLETE LISTING UNDER BINGHAMTON, NEW YORK (21 MILES)

POUGHKEEPSIE † 32,736 Dutchess Co.

LaRose & LaRose

510 Haight Avenue
Poughkeepsie, New York 12603
   Telephone: 845-454-2001
   Fax: 845-454-2535
   E-Mail: laroseandlarose@gmail.com

Established: 1996

Insurance Defense, Automobile, General Liability, Product Liability, Casualty, Medical Malpractice, Environmental Law

Firm Profile: Founding member, Keith LaRose, has provided legal services to insurance companies for 30 years. We provide general defense services as well as handle subrogation matters. All appeals are done in-house.

Insurance Clients

Acceptance Risk Managers, Inc.
American Family Insurance Group
Capital Mutual Insurance Company
Glatfelter Claims Management, Inc.
RSA Surplus Lines Insurance Services, Inc.
UTC Risk Management Services, Inc.
Admiral Insurance Company
Associated Mutual Insurance Cooperative
Midrox Insurance Company
Preferred Mutual Insurance Company
Travelers Insurance Company, Environmental
Utica National Insurance Group

Partners

Keith V. LaRose — 1953 — Northwestern University, B.S., 1975; Syracuse University, J.D. (magna cum laude), 1978 — Admitted to Bar, 1979, New York; 1979, U.S. District Court, Eastern, Northern and Southern Districts of New York — Member Dutchess County Bar Association; Mid-Hudson Claims Association; Association of Trial Lawyers of America; New York State Trial Lawyers Association

Shelly-Ann LaRose — 1953 — State University of New York at Stony Brook, B.A., 1974; Pace University School of Law, J.D., 1981 — Admitted to Bar, 1981, New York; 1981, U.S. District Court, Eastern and Southern Districts of New York; 1982, U.S. District Court, Northern District of New York

McCabe & Mack LLP

63 Washington Street
Poughkeepsie, New York 12601
   Telephone: 845-486-6800
   Fax: 845-486-7621
   E-Mail: info@mccm.com
   www.mccm.com

Established: 1896

McCabe & Mack LLP, Poughkeepsie, NY   (Continued)

Insurance Defense, Negligence, Product Liability, General Liability, Municipal Liability, Casualty, Surety, Civil Rights, Subrogation, Environmental Law, Premises Liability, Labor Law

Insurance Clients

A. Central Insurance Company
Community Mutual Insurance Company
HCC Public Risk Claim Service, Inc.
New York Central Mutual Fire Insurance Company
Sterling Insurance Company
United Services Automobile Association (USAA)
U.S. Specialty Insurance Company
Amica Mutual Insurance Company
Eastern Mutual Insurance Company
Hertz Claim Management
Integrity Administrators
New York Municipal Insurance Reciprocal
Trident Insurance Services/Argonaut Insurance Company

Non-Insurance Clients

Central Hudson Gas and Electric Corp.
City of Poughkeepsie
County of Orange
City of Newburgh
City of Peekskill
County of Dutchess
Town of Poughkeepsie

Partners

David L. Posner — 1949 — Union College, B.A., 1971; New York Law School, J.D., 1975 — Admitted to Bar, 1976, New York — Member New York State, Dutchess County and Westchester County Bar Associations; New York State Trial Lawyers Association; American Board of Trial Advocates — AV Rating by Martindale Hubbell; New York Super Lawyers - Upstate, 2007-Present — E-mail: dposner@mccm.com

Scott D. Bergin — 1960 — Hamilton College, B.A., 1982; Albany Law School of Union University, J.D., 1985 — Admitted to Bar, 1985, Connecticut; 1986, New York — Member New York State and Dutchess County Bar Associations; New York State Trial Lawyers Association; Association of Defense Trial Attorneys — AV Rating by Martindale Hubbell; New York Super Lawyers - Upstate, 2009-Present — E-mail: sbergin@mccm.com

Matthew V. Mirabile — 1967 — Pace University, B.A., 1990; Pace University School of Law, J.D., 1992 — Admitted to Bar, 1993, New York — Member American, New York State, Dutchess County and Westchester County Bar Associations — BV Rating by Martindale Hubbell — E-mail: mmirabile@mccm.com

Kimberly Hunt Lee — 1975 — Siena College, B.A., 1996; Albany Law School of Union University, J.D., 1999 — Admitted to Bar, 2000, New York — Member New York State and Dutchess County Bar Associations; Mid-Hudson Women's Bar Association — BV Rating by Martindale Hubbell; Super Lawyers - 2013 Upstate New York Rising Star — E-mail: klee@mccm.com

Associates

Betsy N. Garrison — 1982 — State University of New York at Albany, B.A. (cum laude), 2003; Albany Law School, J.D., 2005 — Admitted to Bar, 2006, New York — Member New York State and Dutchess County Bar Associations; Mid-Hudson Women's Bar Association — E-mail: bgarrison@mccm.com

Daniel C. Stafford — 1981 — Texas A&M University, B.A., 2004; The John Marshall Law School, J.D., 2008 — Admitted to Bar, 2009, Georgia; 2012, New York — Member New York State and Dutchess County Bar Associations — E-mail: dstafford@mccm.com

Christina M. Piracci — 1981 — Alfred University, B.A. (cum laude), 2003; St. John's University School of Law, J.D., 2009 — Pi Gamma Mu; Pi Gamma Alpha — Admitted to Bar, 2009, New York — Member New York State and Dutchess County Bar Associations; Mid-Hudson Women's Bar Association — E-mail: cpiracci@mccm.com

(This firm is also listed in the Subrogation section of this directory)

RIVERHEAD — NEW YORK

The following firms also service this area.

Boeggeman, George & Corde, P.C.
1 Water Street, Suite 425
White Plains, New York 10601
   Telephone: 914-761-2252
   Fax: 914-761-5211

Insurance Defense, Trial Practice, Automobile, Product Liability, Legal Malpractice, Medical Malpractice, Employment Law, Real Estate, Toxic Torts, Engineering Malpractice

SEE COMPLETE LISTING UNDER WHITE PLAINS, NEW YORK (56 MILES)

Catania, Mahon, Milligram & Rider, PLLC
One Corwin Court
Newburgh, New York 12550
   Telephone: 845-565-1100
   Fax: 845-565-1999

Mailing Address: P.O. Box 1479, Newburgh, NY 12551

Insurance Defense, Insurance Coverage, School Law, Municipal Law, Construction Litigation

SEE COMPLETE LISTING UNDER NEWBURGH, NEW YORK (20 MILES)

Collins, Fitzpatrick & Schoene, LLP
34 South Broadway, Suite 407
White Plains, New York 10601
   Telephone: 914-437-8020
   Fax: 914-437-8022

Appellate Practice, Architects and Engineers, Automobile, Dental Malpractice, Insurance Coverage, Legal Malpractice, Medical Malpractice, Municipal Liability, Premises Liability, Product Liability, Professional Malpractice, Real Estate

SEE COMPLETE LISTING UNDER WHITE PLAINS, NEW YORK (64 MILES)

Cook, Netter, Cloonan, Kurtz & Murphy, P.C.
85 Main Street
Kingston, New York 12401
   Telephone: 845-331-0702
   Fax: 845-331-1003

Mailing Address: P.O. Box 3939, Kingston, NY 12402

Business Transactions, Civil Litigation, Construction Accidents, Motor Vehicle, Municipal Law, Personal Injury, Premises Liability, Product Liability, Professional Liability, Public Entities, Real Estate, Sexual Harassment, State and Federal Courts, Title Insurance, Federal Civil Rights

SEE COMPLETE LISTING UNDER KINGSTON, NEW YORK (21 MILES)

Towne, Ryan & Partners, P.C.
450 New Karner Road
Albany, New York 12205
   Telephone: 518-452-1800
   Fax: 518-452-6435

Mailing Address: P.O. Box 10572, Albany, NY 12212

Business and Real Estate Transactions, Business Litigation, Civil Defense, Commercial Litigation, Construction Litigation, Daycare Liability, Employment Discrimination, Employment Law (Management Side), Estate Litigation, Garage Liability, General Defense Civil Litigation, Governmental Defense, Governmental Liability, Indian Law, Labor and Employment, Municipal Liability, Nursing Home Liability, Nursing Home Litigation, Police Liability Litigation, Premises Liability, Public Liability, Public Officials Defense, School Law, Self-Insured Defense, Slip and Fall, Tribal Law, Trust and Estate Litigation, Policy Liability Defense

SEE COMPLETE LISTING UNDER ALBANY, NEW YORK (80 MILES)

QUEENS   1,951,598 Queens Co.

Refer To
Connors & Connors, PC
766 Castleton Avenue
Staten Island, New York 10310-1700
   Telephone: 718-442-1700
   Fax: 718-442-1717

Insurance Defense, Commercial and Personal Lines, Self-Insured Defense, Trucking Law, Self-Retained Trucking Company Defense, Self-Retained Security Guard Companies, Self-Retained Retail Stores

SEE COMPLETE LISTING UNDER STATEN ISLAND, NEW YORK (27 MILES)

RENSSELAER   9,392 Rensselaer Co.

Refer To
Boeggeman, George & Corde, P.C.
39 North Pearl Street, Suite 501
Albany, New York 12207
   Telephone: 518-465-1100
   Fax: 518-465-1800

Insurance Defense, Trial Practice, Automobile, Product Liability, Legal Malpractice, Medical Malpractice, Employment Law, Real Estate, Toxic Torts, Engineering Malpractice

SEE COMPLETE LISTING UNDER ALBANY, NEW YORK (2 MILES)

RIVERHEAD   † 13,299 Suffolk Co.

Kelly, Rode & Kelly, LLP

218 Griffing Avenue
Riverhead, New York 11901
   Telephone: 631-727-0110
   Toll Free: 800-437-7737
   Fax: 516-739-0434
   E-Mail: info@krklaw.com
   www.krklaw.com

(Mineola, NY Office*: 330 Old Country Road, Suite 305, 11501)
   (Tel: 516-739-0400)
   (Fax: 516-739-0434)
   (Toll Free: 800-437-7737)

Established: 1956

Medical Malpractice Defense, Hospital Malpractice, Nursing Home Litigation, Health Care Liability, Insurance Coverage & Defense, General Defense Civil Litigation, State and Federal Courts, Product Liability, Appellate Practice, Construction Accidents, Premises Liability, Trial and Coverage Opinions, Declaratory Judgments

Insurance Clients

Academic Health Professionals Insurance Association
Atlantic Mutual Insurance Company
Chubb Group of Insurance Companies
Hartford Life Insurance Company
Markel American Insurance Company
Medical Malpractice Insurance Pool
National Chiropractic Mutual Insurance Company
New York State Insurance Department, Liquidation Bureau
Physicians Reciprocal Insurers
State Farm Insurance Companies
Swiss Re America Group
Victoria Fire & Casualty Company

Allied Dealer Insurance Services
American Family Life Assurance Company of New York
Broadspire
Farm Bureau Mutual Insurance Company
Liberty Mutual Insurance Company
Medical Liability Mutual Insurance Company
Motorists Mutual Insurance Company
Nationwide Mutual Insurance Company
PHF Life Insurance Company
Philadelphia Insurance Companies
State Farm Fire and Casualty Company
United National Group
Virginia Farm Bureau Mutual Insurance Company

Non-Insurance Clients

Armco, Inc.   Choice Hotels International

NEW YORK

Kelly, Rode & Kelly, LLP, Riverhead, NY (Continued)

County of Suffolk
Electrolux Outdoor Products, Inc.
Honeywell, Inc.
New York Hospital Medical Center of Queens
North Shore-LIJ Health Systems
Royal-Liverpool Group
The Sherwin-Williams Company
Subaru of America, Inc.
Synergy Gas Corporation
Town of North Hempstead
CVS Pharmacy, Inc.
Genway Corporation
MiniCo, Inc.
Northern Tool & Equipment Company
Richmond University Medical Center
State of New York, Office of the Comptroller - Division of Medical Malpractice

Partners

John D. Kelly — (1921-2000)

John Kenneth Rode — (Retired)

Shawn P. Kelly — 1952 — University of Notre Dame, B.B.A., 1974; St. John's University School of Law, J.D., 1977 — Admitted to Bar, 1978, New York; U.S. District Court, Eastern District of New York; 1979, U.S. District Court, Southern District of New York; U.S. Supreme Court; U.S. Claims Court; U.S. Court of Appeals, Armed Services — Member New York State, Suffolk County (Chair, Trial Lawyers Section) and Nassau County (Chair, Trial Lawyers Section, 2001-2002) Bar Associations; Fellow, American College of Trial Lawyers; Nassau-Suffolk Trial Lawyers Association (Member and Vice Chairman, Board of Directors, 1985-2002); New York State Medical Defense Bar Association; New York State Medical Malpractice Task Force (Subcommittee Member, 2007); National Institute of Trial Advocacy — Lecturer: New York State Bar Association; Practicing Law Institute; Nassau County Bar Association; Suffolk County Bar Association; Adjunct Faculty Member, Hofstra University School of Law; New York Metro Division Super Lawyers (2007-2014); Martindale-Hubbell Peer Review Rating AV Preeminent — Practice Areas: Medical Malpractice Defense; Hospital Malpractice; Insurance Coverage & Defense; Health Care Liability; Professional Malpractice; Insurance Defense; Civil Trial Practice; Product Liability; Personal Injury — E-mail: spkelly@krklaw.com

George J. Wilson — 1957 — Hofstra University, New College, B.A. (magna cum laude), 1979; St. John's University School of Law, J.D., 1984 — Admitted to Bar, 1985, New York; 1989, U.S. District Court, Eastern and Southern Districts of New York; 2003, U.S. District Court, Northern District of New York — Member New York State and Nassau County Bar Associations; Nassau-Suffolk Trial Lawyers Association — Martindale-Hubbell Peer Review Rating AV Preeminent — Practice Areas: Negligence; Medical Malpractice; Insurance Coverage; Product Liability — E-mail: gjwilson@krklaw.com

John W. Hoefling — 1948 — The Pennsylvania State University, B.A., 1970; Cumberland School of Law of Samford University, J.D., 1977 — Admitted to Bar, 1978, New York; U.S. District Court, Eastern and Southern Districts of New York; U.S. Court of Appeals, Second Circuit; 1992, U.S. Supreme Court; 2003, U.S. District Court, Northern District of New York — Member New York State and Nassau County Bar Associations; Nassau-Suffolk Trial Lawyers Association — Martindale-Hubbell Peer Review Rating AV Preeminent — Practice Areas: Insurance Coverage & Defense; Product Liability; Construction Accidents; Appellate Practice; Negligence — E-mail: jwhoefling@krklaw.com

Loris Zeppieri — 1973 — Adelphi University, B.S., 1994; St. John's University School of Law, J.D., 1997 — Admitted to Bar, 1998, New York — Member Nassau-Suffolk Trial Lawyers Association (Officer; PastTreasurer) — Languages: Italian, Spanish — Practice Areas: Negligence; Medical Malpractice; Insurance Coverage; Product Liability — E-mail: lzeppieri@krklaw.com

Eric B. Betron — 1977 — Washington University in St. Louis, B.S.B.A., 1999; Saint Louis University School of Law, J.D., 2002 — Admitted to Bar, 2002, New Jersey; 2003, New York; U.S. District Court, Eastern and Southern Districts of New York — Member American, New York State and Nassau County Bar Associations — Practice Areas: Medical Malpractice; Negligence; Product Liability; Appellate Practice; Insurance Coverage — E-mail: ebbetron@krklaw.com

Kevin E. Way — 1960 — Cathedral College of the Immaculate Conception, B.A. (cum laude), 1982; Hofstra University School of Law, J.D., 1985 — Admitted to Bar, 1986, New York; New Jersey (Inactive); 2004, U.S. District Court, Southern District of New York — Member New York State and Nassau County Bar Associations; Nassau-Suffolk Trial Lawyers Association — Martindale-Hubbell Peer Review Rating AV Preeminent — Practice Areas: Medical Malpractice; Insurance Defense — E-mail: keway@krklaw.com

ROCHESTER

Kelly, Rode & Kelly, LLP, Riverhead, NY (Continued)

Associates

Robert W. Corbin
Brian M. Dunphy
Peter D. Garone
Aryeh S. Klonsky
Colin J. McSherry
Michele A. Perlin
Steve K. F. Scott
Susan M. Ulrich
Barbara A. Dalton
Brian P. Flynn
Edward J. Kelly
Robert A. Koubek
John J. Morris
Colin Rathje
Sol Z. Sokel
Hilary M. Wissemann

Of Counsel

John J. Stewart, Jr.

(Also see listing under Mineola, NY)

The following firms also service this area.

Boeggeman, George & Corde, P.C.
1 Water Street, Suite 425
White Plains, New York 10601
   Telephone: 914-761-2252
   Fax: 914-761-5211

Insurance Defense, Trial Practice, Automobile, Product Liability, Legal Malpractice, Medical Malpractice, Employment Law, Real Estate, Toxic Torts, Engineering Malpractice

SEE COMPLETE LISTING UNDER WHITE PLAINS, NEW YORK (85 MILES)

McCabe, Collins, McGeough & Fowler, LLP
346 Westbury Avenue
Carle Place, New York 11514
   Telephone: 516-741-6266
   Fax: 516-873-9496

Mailing Address: P.O. Box 9000, Carle Place, NY 11514

Asbestos Litigation, Automobile, Aviation, Casualty, Coverage Issues, Trial Practice, Appellate Practice, Subrogation, Product Liability, Insurance Law, Medical Malpractice, Municipal Liability, Professional Liability, Construction Accidents, Sports and Entertainment Liability, General Liability, Premises Liability, Food Poisoning, Toxic Chemicals, Matrimonial

SEE COMPLETE LISTING UNDER MINEOLA, NEW YORK (56 MILES)

ROCHESTER † 210,565 Monroe Co.

Chamberlain D'Amanda

1600 Crossroads Building
Two State Street
Rochester, New York 14614-1397
   Telephone: 585-232-3730
   Fax: 585-232-3882
   E-Mail: kdumitrescu@cdog.com
   www.cdog.com

Established: 1879

Insurance Defense, Automobile, Casualty, Product Liability, Fire, Subrogation, Municipal Liability, Aviation

Firm Profile: Chamberlain D'Amanda is a full-service law firm with headquarters in Rochester, New York. For more than 130 years, we have represented a wide of variety of businesses, individuals, and labor groups throughout the region and nationally.

Insurance Clients

American International Group
Frankenmuth Financial Group
Lexington Insurance Company
New York State Insurance Department
United Services Automobile Association (USAA)
Argonaut Insurance Company
Gallagher Bassett Services, Inc.
Livingston Mutual Insurance Company
Trident Insurance Services
York Claims Service, Inc.

ROCHESTER NEW YORK

Chamberlain D'Amanda, Rochester, NY (Continued)

Non-Insurance Clients

Avis Rent-A-Car System, LLC
Hyatt Corporation
The Hertz Corporation

Members

Henry R. Ippolito — 1942 — Syracuse University, A.B. (cum laude), 1964; Cornell University Law School, J.D. (with distinction), 1967 — Order of the Coif (Cornell) — Admitted to Bar, 1967, New York — Member American Bar Association; New York State Bar Association (House of Delegates, 1987-1989); Monroe County Bar Association (Trustee, 1982-1983; 1986-1989; President, 1987-1988) — Lt. JAG(C), USN, 1968-1971 — E-mail: hippolito@cdog.com

J. Michael Wood — 1967 — Cornell University, B.A. (with distinction), 1989; Albany Law School of Union University, J.D. (summa cum laude), 1994 — Associate Editor, Albany Law Review, 1992-1994 — Admitted to Bar, 1995, New York; U.S. District Court, Northern and Western Districts of New York; 1999, U.S. Court of Appeals, Second Circuit — Member New York State Bar Association; Monroe County Bar Association (Academy of Law Executive Board, 1998-1999; Chair, Young Lawyers Section, 1999-2000; Litigation Section Executive Council, 1998-2002); Wayne County Bar Association — E-mail: mwood@cdog.com

Connors & Corcoran PLLC

45 Exchange Street
Times Square Building, Suite 250
Rochester, New York 14614
  Telephone: 585-232-5885
  Fax: 585-546-3631
  E-Mail: law@connorscorcoran.com
  www.connorscorcoran.com

Established: 1928

Architects and Engineers, Construction Accidents, Disability, Labor and Employment, Estate Litigation, Life Insurance

Firm Profile: Certified woman-owned firm handling labor law, construction, retail, hospitality, life, health, disability, and estates. Staff includes mechanical engineer and registered nurse.

Insurance Clients

Gallagher Bassett Services, Inc.
New York State Secretary of
  Financial Services, Liquidation
  Bureau
GEICO

Firm Member

Eileen E. Buholtz — Eastman School of Music, University of Rochester, B.M., 1973; Syracuse University, J.D., 1979 — Admitted to Bar, 1980, New York; U.S. District Court, Northern and Western Districts of New York; U.S. Court of Appeals, Second Circuit — Member American, New York State and Monroe County Bar Associations; Women's Bar Association of State of New York; Defense Research Institute — Women Business Enterprise (New York Contract System; Women Business Enterprise National Council)

Of Counsel

Denine K. Carr
Odette J. Belton

Osborn, Reed & Burke, LLP

45 Exchange Boulevard
Rochester, New York 14614
  Telephone: 585-454-6480
  Fax: 585-232-4877
  E-Mail: ccc@orblaw.com
  www.osbornreed.com

Osborn, Reed & Burke, LLP, Rochester, NY (Continued)

Asbestos, Automobile, Civil Rights, Commercial and Personal Lines, Hospitals, Insurance Coverage, Labor and Employment, Lead Paint, Mass Tort, Medical Malpractice, Personal Injury, Premises Liability, Product Liability, Property Damage, School Law

Firm Profile: Osborn, Reed & Burke, LLP has a strong reputation in the legal representation of hospitals, insurance companies, municipalities, school districts, and self insured companies. With our diversity and competive size, we provide a wide range of services with personal attention at a reasonable cost.

Insurance Clients

Cincinnati Insurance Company
Liberty Mutual Insurance
Farm Family Casualty Insurance
  Company

Partners

John C. Osborn — (1923-2013)

James A. Reed, Jr. — (1930-2008)

Christian C. Casini — Monroe County Community College, A.S., 1990; State University of New York at Buffalo, B.A. (summa cum laude), 1992; J.D., 1995 — New York State Sheriff's Association Award, 1990; Judge Matthew J. Jasen Appellate Practice Award, 1995; Western New York Trial Lawyers Association Robert J. Connelly Award for Excellence in Trial Advocacy, 1995 — Admitted to Bar, 1995, New York; U.S. District Court, Northern and Western Districts of New York; U.S. Court of Appeals for the Federal Circuit — Member New York State and Monrow County Bar Associations — Super Lawyers® 2012-2014 — E-mail: ccasini@orblaw.com

Aimée L. Lafever Koch — St. Bonaventure University, B.A. (magna cum laude), 1992; State University of New York at Buffalo, J.D., 1995 — Admitted to Bar, 1996, New York — Member American, New York State and Monroe County Bar Associations; Greater Rochester Association of Women Attorneys (Judicial Committee Member); Federal Employees Parents Association (President) — E-mail: alafeverkoch@orblaw.com

Jeffrey P. DiPalma — University of Rochester, B.A. (cum laude), 1991; Albany Law School of Union University, J.D. (cum laude), 1995 — Admitted to Bar, 1995, Massachusetts; 1996, New York — Member New York State and Monroe County Bar Associations — E-mail: jdipalma@orblaw.com

Jennifer M. Schwartzott — Ithaca College, B.A. (magna cum laude), 1998; University of Maryland, J.D. (with honors), 2001 — Admitted to Bar, 2001, Maryland; 2004, District of Columbia; 2010, New York; 2001, U.S. District Court, District of Maryland; 2008, District of Columbia Court of Appeals; 2009, U.S. District Court for the District of Columbia — Member New York State, Maryland State and Monroe County Bar Associations; The District of Columbia Bar; Greater Rochester Association for Women Attorneys — E-mail: jschwartzott@orblaw.com

Of Counsel

David W. Lippitt
Michael A. Reddy

Associates

L. Damien Costanza
Casey P. Acker
Jennifer B. Tarolli
Claire F. Galbraith

Trevett, Cristo, Salzer & Andolina, P.C.

2 State Street, Suite 1000
Rochester, New York 14614
  Telephone: 585-454-2181
  Fax: 585-454-4026
  E-Mail: lcristo@trevettlaw.com
  www.trevettlaw.com

General Practice, Premises Liability, Fire, Casualty, Surety, Malpractice, Aviation, Construction Litigation, Product Liability, Directors and Officers Liability, Environmental Law, Toxic Torts, Municipal Law

Firm Profile: The firm of Trevett, Cristo, Salzer & Andolina was originally formed in 1926 as Brown & Zurett in Rochester, New York. It was one of three affiliated firms in upstate New York formed primarily to serve the legal needs of major insurance carriers. The firm consists of 20 partners and 4

NEW YORK

ROCHESTER

Trevett, Cristo, Salzer & Andolina, P.C., Rochester, NY (Continued)

associates. Our goal has been to provide cost effective legal services to all of our clients. The firm also practices real estate; wills and estate administration; corporate organization; limited liability companies; sole proprietorship and taxation; environmental; and matrimonial and family law.

The firm's alumni include judges of the New York State Appellate Court, State Supreme Court and the City Court of Rochester as well as chairmen of the insurance defense sections of the State Bar and Presidencies of the local County Bars.

Insurance Clients

Erie Insurance Company
Travelers Insurance Group

Partners

Louis B. Cristo — 1959 — University of Rochester, B.A., 1981; Albany Law School of Union University, J.D., 1984 — Admitted to Bar, 1985, New York; 1989, Florida; U.S. District Court, Northern and Western Districts of New York — Member American, New York State (Former Chairman, Torts, Insurance and Compensation Law Section) and Monroe County Bar Associations

Lawrence J. Andolina — 1948 — Boston College, B.A., 1970; Albany Law School of Union University, J.D., 1974 — Admitted to Bar, 1975, New York — Member New York and Monroe County (President and Board of Trustees) Bar Associations

Clark J. Zimmermann, Jr. — 1963 — St. John Fisher College, B.A., 1985; Western New England College School of Law, J.D., 1991 — Admitted to Bar, 1992, New York — Member Monroe County Bar Association

Valerie L. Barbic — Union College, B.A., 1988; New England School of Law, J.D., 1991 — Admitted to Bar, 1992, New York; 2000, U.S. District Court, Western District of New York; 2003, U.S. District Court, Northern District of New York — Member Monroe County Bar Association

Melanie S. Wolk — 1974 — Manhattanville College, B.S. (with honors), 1995; Pace University School of Law, J.D., 1998 — Admitted to Bar, 1999, New York; U.S. District Court, Eastern, Southern and Western Districts of New York — Member New York State and Monroe County Bar Associations; Greater Rochester Association for Women Attorneys

Daniel P. DeBolt — 1978 — Cornell University, B.A., 2000; Georgetown University Law Center, J.D. (cum laude), 2003 — Admitted to Bar, 2004, New York; 2006, U.S. District Court, Northern and Western Districts of New York; 2009, U.S. Court of Appeals, Second Circuit — Member Monroe County Bar Association

Eric Dolan — 1977 — State University of New York at Albany, B.A. Political Science (cum laude), 1999; Albany Law School, J.D., 2003 — Admitted to Bar, 2002, New York; 2003, U.S. District Court, Western District of New York; 2013, U.S. District Court, Northern District of New York — Member New York State and Monroe County Bar Associations

Underberg & Kessler LLP

300 Bausch & Lomb Place
Rochester, New York 14604
Telephone: 585-258-2800
Fax: 585-258-2821
E-Mail: info@underbergkessler.com
www.underbergkessler.com

(Buffalo, NY Office: 50 Fountain Plaza, Suite 320, 14202)
(Tel: 716-848-9000)
(Fax: 716-847-6004)
(Canandaigua, NY Office: 23 Sly Street, 14424)
(Tel: 585-919-0009)
(Fax: 585-394-1614)

Established: 1926

Underberg & Kessler LLP, Rochester, NY (Continued)

General Civil Practice, Trial and Appellate Practice, Insurance Defense, Complex Litigation, Product Liability, Professional Liability, Fire, Casualty, Surety, Employment Law, Americans with Disabilities Act, Copyright and Trademark Law, Intellectual Property, Environmental Law, Mold and Mildew Claims, Toxic Torts, Asbestos Litigation, Construction Law, Drug, Health Care, Medical Devices, Construction Accidents, Contract Disputes, Insurance Coverage, Medical Malpractice, Alternative Dispute Resolution, Arbitration, Nursing Home Defense, EMT Defense Litigation

Firm Profile: Underberg & Kessler LLP is a full service law firm with offices in Rochester, Buffalo, Canandaigua, Newark & Geneseo, NY. The firm has been serving its business and individual clients for more than 85 years with practice groups in banking, business and corporate, creditors' rights, employment law, environmental law, estates & trusts, health care, intellectual property, litigation, municipal, real estate and tax.

Insurance Clients

Admiral Insurance Company
Chubb Group of Insurance Companies
CNA Global Specialty Lines
CNA HealthPro
Coverys
Crum & Forster
Employers Reinsurance Corporation
GAB Robins North America, Inc.
Glatfelter Claims Management, Inc.
HealthCap Risk Management and Liability Insurance
Kemper Insurance Companies
Massachusetts Mutual Life Insurance Company
Medical Malpractice Insurance Pool of New York State
ProClaim America Incorporated
Reliance Insurance Company
Resolute Management, Inc. NE
The RiverStone Group
Travelers Insurance
American Specialty Claims Service
Cincinnati Insurance Company
CNA Environmental & Mass Torts Claims
CNA Insurance Company
Crawford Company
Darwin Allied World National Assurance Company
Essex Insurance Company
General Star
Hanover Insurance Company
The Hartford Life Insurance Company
Hudson Insurance Group
Lumbermens Mutual Group
Media/Professional Insurance
Medical Liability Mutual Insurance Company
OneBeacon Insurance Group
Professional Risk Management Services, Inc.
Resolute Management Inc NW
Sentry Insurance
York Risk Services Group, Inc.

Non-Insurance Clients

Coach USA
Hamlin & Burton Liability Management

Litigation Members

Paul V. Nunes — 1952 — Durham University, England, 1973; College of the Holy Cross, B.A., 1974; Syracuse University College of Law, J.D., 1977 — Admitted to Bar, 1978, New York; 1980, U.S. District Court, Western District of New York; 1982, U.S. District Court, Eastern and Southern Districts of New York; 1990, U.S. District Court, Northern District of New York — Member American Bar Association; Rochester Claims Association; Risk and Insurance Management Society (RIMS) — Certified Federal Court Mediator — E-mail: pnunes@underbergkessler.com

Paul F. Keneally — 1967 — Amherst College, B.A., 1989; Fordham Law School, J.D. (cum laude), 1993 — Admitted to Bar, 1994, New York; U.S. District Court, Eastern and Southern Districts of New York; 1996, U.S. District Court, Northern and Western Districts of New York; U.S. District Court, Central District of Illinois — Member American Bar Association — E-mail: pkeneally@underbergkessler.com

Margaret E. Somerset — 1964 — Providence College, B.A., 1986; Syracuse University College of Law, J.D. (cum laude), 1989 — Admitted to Bar, 1990, New York; 1992, U.S. District Court, Northern and Western Districts of New York; 1999, U.S. Supreme Court — Member New York State Academy of Trial Lawyers — E-mail: msomerset@underbergkessler.com

Litigation Associates

Colin D. Ramsey — 1977 — Hamilton College, B.A., 1999; Syracuse University College of Law, J.D., 2002 — Pi Sigma Alpha; Order of the Barristers; National Moot Court Team — Admitted to Bar, 2003, New York; U.S. District Court, Western District of New York — E-mail: cramsey@underbergkessler.com

Jennifer S. Castaldo — 1976 — State University of New York at Buffalo, B.A., 1999; State University of New York at Buffalo Law School, J.D. (cum laude),

SCHENECTADY — NEW YORK

Underberg & Kessler LLP, Rochester, NY (Continued)

2008 — Admitted to Bar, 2008, New York — E-mail: jcastaldo@underbergkessler.com

Senior Counsel

Ronald G. Hull — 1953 — La Salle College, B.A. (magna cum laude), 1975; Trinity College, Dublin, 1975-1976; Syracuse University College of Law, J.D./M.P.A. (summa cum laude), 1979 — Admitted to Bar, 1980, New York — E-mail: rhull@underbergkessler.com

David H. Fitch — 1970 — Virginia Polytechnic Institute and State University, B.S., 1992; State University of New York at Buffalo Law School, J.D., 1997 — Admitted to Bar, 1998, New York — E-mail: dfitch@underbergkessler.com

(All Attorneys are Members of the New York State and Local County Bar Associations)

The following firms also service this area.

Barth Sullivan Behr
600 Convention Tower
43 Court Street
Buffalo, New York 14202
   Telephone: 716-856-1300
   Fax: 716-856-1494

Trial Practice, Appellate Practice, Alternative Dispute Resolution, Product Liability, Casualty, Fire, Professional Errors and Omissions, Coverage Issues, Insurance Fraud, Subrogation, Motor Vehicle, General Liability, Workers' Compensation, Premises Liability, Municipal Liability, Tractor-Trailer, Bad Faith

SEE COMPLETE LISTING UNDER BUFFALO, NEW YORK (76 MILES)

Roach, Brown, McCarthy & Gruber, P.C.
1920 Liberty Building
424 Main Street
Buffalo, New York 14202-3511
   Telephone: 716-852-0400
   Fax: 716-852-2535

Insurance Defense, Trial and Appellate Practice, Medical Malpractice, Professional Malpractice, Product Liability, Construction Law, Sports and Entertainment Liability, Aviation, Fire, Excess, Coverage Issues

SEE COMPLETE LISTING UNDER BUFFALO, NEW YORK (75 MILES)

Smith, Sovik, Kendrick & Sugnet, P.C.
250 South Clinton Street, Suite 600
Syracuse, New York 13202
   Telephone: 315-474-2911
   Fax: 315-474-6015

Appellate Practice, Automobile, Commercial Litigation, Construction Law, Dental Malpractice, Labor and Employment, Medical Malpractice, Nursing Home Liability, Premises Liability, Product Liability, Professional Liability, Retail Liability, Subrogation, Toxic Torts, Trucking, Workers' Compensation, Wrongful Death

SEE COMPLETE LISTING UNDER SYRACUSE, NEW YORK (88 MILES)

SARATOGA SPRINGS 26,586 Saratoga Co.

Refer To
Bailey, Kelleher & Johnson, P.C.
Pine West Plaza 5, Suite 507
Washington Avenue Extension
Albany, New York 12205
   Telephone: 518-456-0082
   Fax: 518-456-4767

Insurance Defense, Trial Practice, Product Liability, Municipal Law, Fire Loss, Premises Liability, Lead Paint, Homeowners, Slip and Fall, First and Third Party Defense, Police Liability Defense

SEE COMPLETE LISTING UNDER ALBANY, NEW YORK (29 MILES)

Refer To
Donohue, Sabo, Varley & Huttner, LLP
120 Broadway, 2nd Floor
Albany, New York 12205
   Telephone: 518-458-8922
   Fax: 518-438-4349

Mailing Address: P.O. Box 15056, Albany, NY 12212-5056

Insurance Defense, Product Liability, Professional Malpractice, Employment Law, Municipal Law

SEE COMPLETE LISTING UNDER ALBANY, NEW YORK (34 MILES)

Refer To
Towne, Ryan & Partners, P.C.
450 New Karner Road
Albany, New York 12205
   Telephone: 518-452-1800
   Fax: 518-452-6435

Mailing Address: P.O. Box 10572, Albany, NY 12212

Business and Real Estate Transactions, Business Litigation, Civil Defense, Commercial Litigation, Construction Litigation, Daycare Liability, Employment Discrimination, Employment Law (Management Side), Estate Litigation, Garage Liability, General Defense Civil Litigation, Governmental Defense, Governmental Liability, Indian Law, Labor and Employment, Municipal Liability, Nursing Home Liability, Nursing Home Litigation, Police Liability Litigation, Premises Liability, Public Liability, Public Officials Defense, School Law, Self-Insured Defense, Slip and Fall, Tribal Law, Trust and Estate Litigation, Policy Liability Defense

SEE COMPLETE LISTING UNDER ALBANY, NEW YORK (32 MILES)

SCHENECTADY † 66,135 Schenectady Co.

Refer To
Bailey, Kelleher & Johnson, P.C.
Pine West Plaza 5, Suite 507
Washington Avenue Extension
Albany, New York 12205
   Telephone: 518-456-0082
   Fax: 518-456-4767

Insurance Defense, Trial Practice, Product Liability, Municipal Law, Fire Loss, Premises Liability, Lead Paint, Homeowners, Slip and Fall, First and Third Party Defense, Police Liability Defense

SEE COMPLETE LISTING UNDER ALBANY, NEW YORK (13 MILES)

Refer To
Boeggeman, George & Corde, P.C.
39 North Pearl Street, Suite 501
Albany, New York 12207
   Telephone: 518-465-1100
   Fax: 518-465-1800

Insurance Defense, Trial Practice, Automobile, Product Liability, Legal Malpractice, Medical Malpractice, Employment Law, Real Estate, Toxic Torts, Engineering Malpractice

SEE COMPLETE LISTING UNDER ALBANY, NEW YORK (18 MILES)

Refer To
Donohue, Sabo, Varley & Huttner, LLP
120 Broadway, 2nd Floor
Albany, New York 12205
   Telephone: 518-458-8922
   Fax: 518-438-4349

Mailing Address: P.O. Box 15056, Albany, NY 12212-5056

Insurance Defense, Product Liability, Professional Malpractice, Employment Law, Municipal Law

SEE COMPLETE LISTING UNDER ALBANY, NEW YORK (15 MILES)

NEW YORK   SEAFORD

Refer To
Napierski, VanDenburgh, Napierski, & O'Connor, LLP
296 Washington Avenue Extension, Ste 3
Albany, New York 12203
   Telephone: 518-862-9292
   Fax: 518-862-1519

Civil Trial Practice, Insurance Defense, Appellate Practice, Automobile, Commercial Litigation, General Liability, Labor and Employment, Municipal Liability, Product Liability, Trial Practice, Accountants and Attorneys Liability, Coverage Issues, Directors and Officers Liability, Premises Liability, Asbestos Litigation, Automobile Liability, Automobile Tort, Construction Accidents, Construction Defect, Construction Liability, Professional Liability, Contractors Liability, Wrongful Termination, Subrogation, Medical Malpractice Defense

SEE COMPLETE LISTING UNDER ALBANY, NEW YORK (15 MILES)

SEAFORD   15,294 Nassau Co.

Kerley, Walsh, Matera & Cinquemani, P.C.

2174 Jackson Avenue
Seaford, New York 11783-2608
   Telephone: 516-409-6200
   Fax: 516-409-8288
   E-Mail: @kerleywalsh.com
   www.kerleywalsh.com

Established: 1987

Insurance Defense, Civil Litigation, Tort, Personal Injury, Medical Malpractice, Trusts, Estate Planning, Real Estate

Firm Profile: Kerley, Walsh, Matera and Cinquemani, P.C. specializes in personal injury and medical malpractice defense litigation for insurance carriers and self-insureds in New York City, Long Island and Westchester County. We also have a Trusts & Estates division, which handles wills, trusts, estate planning, guardianships, commercial and residential real estates, and various other matters.

Insurance Clients

Academic Health Professionals Insurance Association
Physicians Reciprocal Insurers
Medical Liability Mutual Insurance Company
Utica Mutual Insurance Company

Partners

Brian P. Kerley — 1957 — St. John's University, B.A., 1979; New York Law School, J.D. (cum laude), 1982 — Admitted to Bar, 1983, New York; U.S. Court of Appeals for the Federal Circuit; U.S. Court of International Trade; 1984, U.S. District Court, Eastern District of New York — E-mail: bkerley@kerleywalsh.com

Jeffrey G. Walsh — 1959 — Manhattan College, B.S. (magna cum laude), 1981; St. John's University School of Law, J.D. (with honors), 1984 — Admitted to Bar, 1985, New York; U.S. District Court, Eastern and Southern Districts of New York — Member National Board of Trial Attorneys (Board Certified, Civil Trial Advocacy) — E-mail: jwalsh@kerleywalsh.com

Glenn Joseph Matera — 1959 — State University of New York at Oswego, B.A. (cum laude), 1981; St. John's University School of Law, J.D., 1984 — Admitted to Bar, 1985, New York; U.S. District Court, Eastern and Southern Districts of New York — E-mail: gmatera@kerleywalsh.com

Rosemary Cinquemani — 1959 — Adelphi University, B.A. (cum laude), 1981; St. John's University School of Law, J.D., 1984 — Admitted to Bar, 1985, New York; U.S. District Court, Eastern and Southern Districts of New York — E-mail: rcinquemani@kerleywalsh.com

Jeffrey M. DiLuccio — 1965 — St. John's University, B.S., 1987; Hofstra University School of Law, J.D., 1991 — Admitted to Bar, 1992, New York; 1996, U.S. District Court, Eastern and Southern Districts of New York — E-mail: jdiluccio@kerleywalsh.com

Kathleen Lindsay — 1961 — Molloy College, B.S., 1983; Touro College Jacob D. Fuchsberg Law Center, J.D., 1993 — Sigma Theta Tau — Admitted to Bar, 1994, New York — E-mail: klindsay@kerleywalsh.com

Patrick J. Shelley — 1977 — Fordham University, B.A., 1999; St. John's University School of Law, J.D., 2002 — Admitted to Bar, 2003, New York — E-mail: pshelley@kerleywalsh.com

Kerley, Walsh, Matera & Cinquemani, P.C., Seaford, NY (Continued)

Stephen Rach, II — 1976 — Indiana University, B.A., 1998; St. John's University School of Law, J.D., 2002 — Admitted to Bar, 2003, New York — E-mail: srach@kerleywalsh.com

James P. Cronin — 1965 — St. John's University, B.A., 1986; St. John's University School of Law, J.D., 1990 — Admitted to Bar, 1991, New York — E-mail: jcronin@kerleywalsh.com

Robert K. Lapping — 1951 — Fairfield University, B.A., 1973; St. John's University School of Law, J.D., 1976 — Admitted to Bar, 1977, New York — E-mail: rlapping@kerleywalsh.com

Lauren B. Bristol — 1962 — C.W. Post Campus of Long Island University, B.A. (magna cum laude), 1983; Hofstra University School of Law, J.D. (with honors), 1986 — Admitted to Bar, 1987, New York; 1989, U.S. District Court, Eastern and Southern Districts of New York — E-mail: lbristol@kerleywalsh.com

Richard J. Hull — 1956 — Seton Hall University School of Law, J.D., 1984 — Admitted to Bar, 1985, New Jersey — E-mail: rhull@kerleywalsh.com

Associates

Kerri E. Levy — 1970 — State University of New York at Albany, B.A., 1992; Benjamin N. Cardozo School of Law, J.D., 1995 — Admitted to Bar, 1996, New York; New Jersey — E-mail: klevy@kerleywalsh.com

Timothy D. Cameron — 1976 — State University of New York at Stony Brook, B.A., 2001; Hofstra University School of Law, J.D., 2004 — Admitted to Bar, 2005, New York — E-mail: tcameron@kerleywalsh.com

Timothy M. Shelley — 1979 — Villanova University, B.A., 2002; St. John's University School of Law, J.D., 2005 — Admitted to Bar, 2006, New York — E-mail: tshelley@kerleywalsh.com

Gerilynn F. Falasco — 1976 — State University of New York at Stony Brook, B.A., 1999; Hofstra University School of Law, J.D., 2004 — Admitted to Bar, 2005, New York; U.S. District Court, Eastern District of New York — Languages: Spanish — E-mail: gfalasco@kerleywalsh.com

Brett J. Milgrim — 1983 — New York University, B.A., 2005; Hofstra University School of Law, J.D., 2008 — Admitted to Bar, 2009, New York — E-mail: bmilgrim@kerleywalsh.com

Argiro Drakos — 1983 — Hofstra University, B.A., 2004; Hofstra University School of Law, J.D., 2008 — Admitted to Bar, 2009, New York — E-mail: adrakos@kerleywalsh.com

Stephanie A. Johnston — 1983 — American University, B.A., 2005; Hofstra University School of Law, J.D., 2009 — Admitted to Bar, 2010, New York — E-mail: sjohnston@kerleywalsh.com

Farije Freilich — 1982 — St. John's University, B.A., 2004; Touro College Jacob D. Fuchsberg Law Center, J.D., 2009 — Admitted to Bar, 2010, New York — E-mail: ffreilich@kerleywalsh.com

Angela Mastrantonio — 1988 — Hofstra University, B.A., 2009; Hofstra University School of Law, J.D., 2011 — Admitted to Bar, 2011, New Jersey; 2012, New York — E-mail: amastrantonio@kerleywalsh.com

Sean Donovan — 1971 — Trinity College, B.A., 1994; St. John's University School of Law, J.D., 2002 — Admitted to Bar, 2002, New York — E-mail: sdonovan@kerleywalsh.com

Mary M. Holupka — Queens College of the City University of New York, B.A., 2009; St. John's University School of Law, J.D., 2013 — Admitted to Bar, 2013, New York — E-mail: mholupka@kerleywalsh.com

STATEN ISLAND   352,121 Richmond Co.

Connors & Connors, PC

766 Castleton Avenue
Staten Island, New York 10310-1700
   Telephone: 718-442-1700
   Fax: 718-442-1717
   E-Mail: jpc@connorslaw.com
   www.connorslaw.com

(Long Branch, NJ Office: Morris Brook Commons, Suite 6, 422 Morris Avenue, 07740)
(New York, NY Office: 17 Battery Place, 10004)

Established: 1955

SYRACUSE   NEW YORK

Connors & Connors, PC, Staten Island, NY   (Continued)

Insurance Defense, Commercial and Personal Lines, Self-Insured Defense, Trucking Law, Self-Retained Trucking Company Defense, Self-Retained Security Guard Companies, Self-Retained Retail Stores

Firm Profile: Founded in 1955 by John P. Connors, the firm was originally located in Manhattan. From 1955 to 1980, John P. Connors, P.C. represented litigants in thousands of personal injury cases throughout the City of New York. In 1980, the firm constructed its own professional office building and moved to its present location. Since then, the firm has expanded both its client lists and fields of expertise. At present, the firm represents numerous clients as attorneys of record and trial counsel in the City of New York and Northern New Jersey. We pride ourselves on our ability to thoroughly analyze issues presented and develop a litigation strategy which reflects our clients' goals and objectives.

Insurance Clients

Allstate Insurance Company
Gallagher Bassett Services, Inc.
Kemper Insurance Company
Liberty Mutual Insurance Company
New Jersey Manufacturers Insurance Company
Public Service Mutual Insurance Company
Broadspire
GEICO General Insurance Company
Motor Vehicle Accident Indemnification Corporation
Peerless Insurance Company
St. Paul Travelers
Sedgwick Claims Management Services, Inc.

Non-Insurance Clients

Pinkerton's, Inc.
Target Stores
Wells Fargo Bank
Ryder System, Inc.
Unilever United States, Inc.

Partners

John P. Connors — (1927-2003)

John P. Connors, Jr. — 1956 — Georgetown University, B.A., 1978; J.D., 1981 — Admitted to Bar, 1982, New York; 1983, District of Columbia; 1984, New Jersey — Member American Bar Association; New York State Bar Association(Chair, Trial Lawyers Section; Chairman, Committee on Alternative Dispute Resolution); Richmond County Bar Association (Chairman, Continuing Legal Education Committee; President Elect) — Board of Directors: St. Vincent's Medical Center, 1994-present; St. Elizabeth Ann Rehabilitation Center, 1994-present; St. Vincent's Services, 1999-present; Board of Directors, Norte Dame Academy Board of Trustees

Senior Associates

Harold J. Siegel — 1937 — The Citadel, B.A., 1959; St. John's University, LL.B., 1962 — Admitted to Bar, 1963, New York — Member American and Richmond County Bar Associations; Staten Island Trial Lawyers Association (Past President)

Susan E. O'Shaughnessy — 1966 — State University of New York at Binghamton, B.A., 1988; Albany Law School of Union University, J.D., 1991 — Admitted to Bar, 1991, Connecticut; 1992, New York; 1992, New Jersey — Member American, New York State, Richmond County and Staten Island Bar Associations

Michael B. Kelly — 1964 — Denison University, B.A.; St. John's University, J.D., 1990 — Admitted to Bar, 1990, New York

Robert J. Pfuhler — 1969 — New York University, B.A., 1991; Fordham Law School, J.D., 1994 — Admitted to Bar, 1994, New Jersey; 1995, New York; U.S. District Court, Eastern and Southern Districts of New York — Member American, New York State, Richmond County and Staten Island Bar Associations

Associates

Louis J. Rasso — 1972 — John Jay College of Criminal Justice, B.S. (magna cum laude), 1995; Brooklyn Law School, J.D., 1999 — Admitted to Bar, 2001, New York

Timothy M. O'Donovan — 1968 — St. John's University, B.A. (magna cum laude), 1990; St. John's University School of Law, J.D., 1993 — Admitted to Bar, 1993, New Jersey; 1994, New York; 1993, U.S. District Court, District of New Jersey; 1997, U.S. District Court, Eastern and Southern Districts of New York

Richard A. Waldron — 1964 — St. John's University, B.A., 1987; New York Law School, J.D., 1997 — Admitted to Bar, 2001, New York — Member New York State Bar Association; New York State Trial Lawyers Association

---

SYRACUSE † 145,170 Onondaga Co.

Barth Sullivan Behr

224 Harrison Street, Suite 208
Syracuse, New York 13202
  Telephone: 315-234-1864
  Fax: 315-410-1262
  E-Mail: lbehr@barthbehr.com
  www.barthbehr.com

(Buffalo, NY Office*: 600 Convention Tower, 43 Court Street, 14202)
  (Tel: 716-856-1300)
  (Fax: 716-856-1494)

Established: 1928

Trial Practice, Appellate Practice, Alternative Dispute Resolution, Product Liability, Casualty, Fire, Professional Errors and Omissions, Coverage Issues, Insurance Fraud, Subrogation, Motor Vehicle, General Liability, Workers' Compensation, Premises Liability, Municipal Liability, Tractor-Trailer, Bad Faith

Firm Members & Associates

Philip C. Barth, III
J. William Savage
Laurence D. Behr
David H. Walsh IV

(See listing under Buffalo, NY for additional information)

Pillinger Miller Tarallo, LLP

507 Plum Street, Suite 120
Syracuse, New York 13204
  Telephone: 315-295-3831
  Fax: 315-295-2575
  www.pmtlawfirm.com

(Additional Offices: Elmsford, NY*; New York, NY; Warren, NJ; Philadelphia, PA)

Construction Law, Labor and Employment, Premises Liability, Environmental Law, Toxic Torts, Product Liability, Automobile, No-Fault, Municipal Law, General Liability, Insurance Defense

---

Jeffrey D. Schulman — 1968 — University of Michigan, B.A., 1990; Hofstra University School of Law, J.D., 1993 — Admitted to Bar, 1994, New York; Florida — Member The Association of the Bar of the City of New York; New York County Lawyers Association — E-mail: jschulman@pmtlawfirm.com

(See listing under Elmsford, NY for additional information)

(This firm is also listed in the Subrogation section of this directory)

Smith, Sovik, Kendrick & Sugnet, P.C.

250 South Clinton Street, Suite 600
Syracuse, New York 13202
  Telephone: 315-474-2911
  Fax: 315-474-6015
  E-Mail: firm@smithsovik.com
  www.smithsovik.com

(East Meadow, NY Office*(See Uniondale listing): The Financial Center at Mitchel Field, 90 Merrick Avenue Suite 500, 11554)
  (Toll Free: 800-675-0011)
(Buffalo, NY Office*: 651 Delaware Avenue, Suite 144, 14202)
  (Toll Free: 800-675-0011)

NEW YORK

Smith, Sovik, Kendrick & Sugnet, P.C., Syracuse, NY (Continued)

Appellate Practice, Automobile, Commercial Litigation, Construction Law, Dental Malpractice, Labor and Employment, Medical Malpractice, Nursing Home Liability, Premises Liability, Product Liability, Professional Liability, Retail Liability, Subrogation, Toxic Torts, Trucking, Workers' Compensation, Wrongful Death

Firm Profile: Smith, Sovik, Kendrick & Sugnet, P.C. is one of the premier litigation firms in New York State. We have a reputation for the most effective, intelligent, hard-nosed and successful trial attorneys in the area, and aggressively and cost-effectively obtaining the very best results for our clients.

Insurance Clients

Acadia Insurance Company
Admiral Insurance Company
Allstate Insurance Company
Atlantic Risk Management, Inc.
CNA Insurance Companies
Crum & Forster Insurance Company
Encompass Insurance
Essex Insurance Company
GAB Robins North America, Inc.
GMAC Insurance
Guthrie Healthcare System
Harco National Insurance Company
KFC Risk Management
Liberty Mutual Group
Maxum Specialty Insurance Group
Medical Malpractice Insurance Plan of NY
National Chiropractic Mutual Insurance Company
Nationwide Insurance
Navigators Insurance Company
OneBeacon Insurance
Pinnacle Risk Management Services
Praetorian Insurance Company
PRMS, Inc. - Professional Risk Management Services, Inc.
RLI
RLI Transportation
Scottsdale Insurance Company
Travelers Insurance Companies
United Services Automobile Association (USAA)
Vermont Mutual Insurance Company
W.R. Berkley
York Claims Service, Inc.
ACE USA
AIG
Arrowhead Claims Management
Chubb Group of Insurance Companies
ECS Claims Administrators, Inc.
EMP Management Group
Erie Insurance Group
Evanston Insurance Company
Gallagher Bassett Services, Inc.
Greenlight RE
Hanover Insurance Company
Hartford Financial Products
Kemper Insurance Companies
Liberty International Underwriters
Markel Shand, Inc.
Medical Liability Mutual Insurance Company
The Medical Protective Company
National Grange Mutual Insurance Company
Nautilus Insurance Company
Northland Insurance Company
Philadelphia Insurance Company
PMA Companies, Inc.
Podiatry Insurance Company of America (PICA)
QBE North America
RiverStone Claims Management, LLC
Safeco Insurance
Specialty Risk Services, Inc. (SRS)
United Educators Insurance
Unitrin Business Insurance
Vanliner Insurance Company
Worcester Insurance Company
Worldwide Insurance Group
XL Insurance
Zurich Insurance Company

Non-Insurance Clients

AutoZone, Inc.
Carrols Restaurant Group, Inc.
Coyote Logistics LLC
Crouse Hospital
Darden Restaurants
Emery Worldwide
Estes Express Lines
Freightliner, LLC
Golub Corporation
The Heil Company
Jefferson Smurfit Corporation
Knight Transportation Company
The Manitowoc Company, Inc.
McLarens Toplis North America, Inc.
Oshkosh Truck Corporation
Pep Boys, Inc.
Rite Aid Corporation
Square D Company
Swift Transportation Company, Inc.
Werner Enterprises, Inc.
Yale Materials Handling Corporation
Budget Rent-A-Car Corporation
Consolidated Freightway Corporation
Daewoo Heavy Industries
Delta International Machinery Corporation
Federal Express Corporation
Genuine Parts Company
Greyhound Lines, Inc.
HMC Corporation
Johnson Controls, Inc.
Laidlaw Transit Services, Inc.
McLane Company, Inc.
New York State Dental Society
Old Dominion Freight Line, Inc.
Pacer International, Inc.
Pharmacia & Upjoin Company
Scott Wetzel Services, Inc.
Stevens Transport, Inc.
Taco Bell Corporation
UPS Freight
Willis Administrative Services Corporation
Yellow Freight System

SYRACUSE

Smith, Sovik, Kendrick & Sugnet, P.C., Syracuse, NY (Continued)

Managing Partner

Kevin E. Hulslander — Dartmouth College, A.D. (cum laude, with distinction), 1982; Boston University, J.D., 1986 — Admitted to Bar, 1986, Massachusetts; 1987, New York — Member International Association of Defense Counsel; Transportation Lawyers Association; Defense Research Institute; Trucking Industry Defense Association

Partners

Laurence F. Sovik — University of Notre Dame, A.B., 1954; Syracuse University, LL.B., 1957 — Admitted to Bar, 1957, New York — Member Fellow, American College of Trial Lawyers

James D. Lantier — Boston College, B.A. (cum laude), 1969; Syracuse University, J.D., 1973 — Admitted to Bar, 1974, New York — Member Defense Research Institute

Michael P. Ringwood — 1953 — Marquette University, B.A., 1975; Syracuse University, J.D., 1979 — Admitted to Bar, 1980, New York

Eric G. Johnson — Colgate University, B.A. (cum laude), 1983; College of William & Mary, J.D., 1986 — Admitted to Bar, 1987, New York

Steven W. Williams — State University of New York College at Cortland, B.A., 1990; California Western University, J.D., 1990 — Admitted to Bar, 1990, California; 1994, New York — United States Navy Reserves, Judge Advocate General's Corps (1990-1995)

James W. Cunningham — Le Moyne College, B.S., 1990; Syracuse University, J.D., 1994 — Admitted to Bar, 1995, New York — Member Trucking Industry Defense Association

Edward J. Smith — St. Lawrence University, B.A., 1986; Boston University, J.D., 1990 — Admitted to Bar, 1991, New York

Brandon R. King — State University of New York at Oswego, B.A. (cum laude), 1992; Albany Law School of Union University, J.D., 1995 — Admitted to Bar, 1996, New York — Member Defense Research Institute

Robert P. Cahalan — St. Lawrence University, B.A., 1990; Syracuse University, J.D., 1995 — Admitted to Bar, 1996, New York; U.S. District Court, Northern District of New York

Kristin L. Norfleet — University of Rochester, B.A., 1996; Case Western Reserve University, M.A./J.D., 1999 — Admitted to Bar, 2000, New York

Kristen M. Benson — State University of New York College at Brockport, B.A., 1995; Albany Law School of Union University, J.D., 2000 — Admitted to Bar, 2001, New York

David A. D'Agostino — University of Pittsburgh, B.A., 1996; Syracuse University, J.D., 2000 — Admitted to Bar, 2001, New York

Daniel R. Ryan — Siena College, B.A. (cum laude), 1996; Albany Law School of Union University, J.D., 1999 — Admitted to Bar, 2000, New York

Kenneth T. Boyd — State University of New York at Binghamton, B.A. (cum laude), 1982; American University, J.D., 1988 — Admitted to Bar, 1988, New York — Resident East Meadow, NY Office

Anthony R. Brighton — The University of Iowa, B.A., 1992; The University of Iowa College of Law, J.D. (with special honors), 1996 — Admitted to Bar, 1996, New York

Karen Guyder Felter — Boston University, B.A., 1989; Albany Law School of Union University, J.D., 1992 — Admitted to Bar, 1993, New York

Thomas J. Cannavo — Canisius College, B.A., 1990; State University of New York at Buffalo Law School, J.D., 1993 — Admitted to Bar, 1994, New York — Member Western New York Trial Lawyers Association — Resident Buffalo, NY Office

Attorney

Victor L. Prial
John D. Goldman
Aaron M. Schiffrick
Karen J. Krogman
Shane P. Simon

Kristen L. Wilson
Brady J. O'Malley
Phillip D. Dysert
Christopher F. DeFrancesco

TROY **NEW YORK**

The following firms also service this area.

Cook, Netter, Cloonan, Kurtz & Murphy, P.C.
85 Main Street
Kingston, New York 12401
  Telephone: 845-331-0702
  Fax: 845-331-1003
Mailing Address: P.O. Box 3939, Kingston, NY 12402

Business Transactions, Civil Litigation, Construction Accidents, Motor Vehicle, Municipal Law, Personal Injury, Premises Liability, Product Liability, Professional Liability, Public Entities, Real Estate, Sexual Harassment, State and Federal Courts, Title Insurance, Federal Civil Rights

SEE COMPLETE LISTING UNDER KINGSTON, NEW YORK (196 MILES)

TARRYTOWN 11,277 Westchester Co.

Reardon & Sclafani, P.C.
220 White Plains Road
Tarrytown, New York 10591
  Telephone: 914-366-0201
  Fax: 914-366-0022
  E-Mail: sclafanimv@msn.com

Established: 1974

Insurance Law, Malpractice, Product Liability, General Liability, Motor Vehicle, Environmental Law, Trial Practice, Appellate Practice, State and Federal Courts

Insurance Clients

Acceptance Insurance Company
Alexander Hamilton Life Insurance Company of America
American National Property and Casualty Company
Claims America, Inc.
COUNTRY Mutual Insurance Company
Homesite Insurance Company
Horace Mann Insurance Company
Insurance Company of North America
Motorists Mutual Insurance Company
Redland Insurance Company
Self-Insurers Service, Inc.
Teacher's Insurance Plan of New Jersey
Agricultural Excess and Surplus Insurance Company
American Hardware Mutual Insurance Company
CIGNA Group
Colonial Penn Insurance Company
Crawford & Company
Employers Self-Insurance Service, Inc.
The Infinity Group
Lancer Insurance Company
Liberty Mutual Insurance Company
New York State Insurance Department
Risk Retention Services, Inc.
Sompo Japan Insurance Company of America
Yasuda Fire & Marine Insurance Company of America

Non-Insurance Clients

Avis Budget Car Rental, LLC
Borden, Inc.
Budget Rent-A-Car System, Inc.
Constitution State Service Company
Dollar Rent A Car Systems, Inc.
El Fenix de Puerto Rico
Hamilton Beach/Proctor-Silex, Inc.
Ladder Management Services
Mendon Leasing Corporation
Pfizer, Inc.
Ryder Truck Rental, Inc.
Avis Rent-A-Car System, LLC
Bradlees, Inc.
Burger King Corporation
Dean Foods
DHL Airways, Inc.
Eastman Kodak Company
ELRAC, Inc.
INAPRO
Melville Corporation
Orion Capital Companies
PHH Fleetamerica Corporation
York STB, Inc.

Firm Members

Michael V. Sclafani — 1959 — Fairleigh Dickinson University, B.S., 1981; Gonzaga University School of Law, J.D., 1985 — Admitted to Bar, 1986, New York; U.S. District Court, Eastern and Southern Districts of New York; 1989, U.S. Court of Appeals, Second Circuit; 1996, U.S. District Court, Northern District of New York; 1999, U.S. District Court, Western District of New York; U.S. Supreme Court — Member American, New York State and Bronx County Bar Associations; Defense Association of New York; Defense Research Institute

Reardon & Sclafani, P.C., Tarrytown, NY (Continued)

Vincent M. Sclafani — 1926 — St. Francis College, B.A., 1950; Fordham Law School, LL.B., 1953 — Admitted to Bar, 1953, New York; U.S. District Court, Eastern and Southern Districts of New York — Member New York State and Bronx County Bar Associations; Insurance Management Institute; Defense Association of New York

Nicholas J. Accurso — State University of New York at Purchase, B.S., 1985; Pace University School of Law, J.D., 1988 — Admitted to Bar, 1988, New York; U.S. District Court, Eastern and Southern Districts of New York

Edward D. Schmitt — State University of New York College at Cortland, B.A., 1988; California Western School of Law, J.D., 1992 — Admitted to Bar, 1992, New York; California; 2005, U.S. District Court, Eastern and Southern Districts of New York

TROY † 50,129 Rensselaer Co.

Stockton, Barker & Mead, LLP
433 River Street, Suite 6002
Troy, New York 12180
  Telephone: 518-435-1919
  Fax: 518-435-1939
  E-Mail: mmead@sbmfirm.com
  www.sbmfirm.com

Established: 1994

Insurance Defense, Workers' Compensation, Personal Injury, Defense Litigation, Product Liability

Firm Profile: Stockton, Barker & Mead, LLP was founded in 1994 by Robert Stockton, Christopher Barker and Matthew Mead. The firm provides high quality, cost effective legal service to business and insurance clients throughout New York State. Our firm represents and advises clients in the areas of Insurance Defense, Workers' Compensation, Personal Injury, Defense Litigation and Product Liability. Our attorneys represent clients in every level of state and federal courts and before various administrative agencies. Our attorneys are committed to solving and preventing problems for our clients. We pride ourselves on partnering with our clients in setting and achieving their goals. We utilize technology and cost-effective methods to provide services in a timely, client-oriented manner. Our approach focuses on the goals of our clients, and we are committed to prompt and effective communication with our clients and colleagues. Our dedication to quality, understanding of the law, professionalism and integrity are the foundation of our long-standing client relationships.

Insurance Clients

CNA Insurance Company
Saratoga County Self Insurance

Non-Insurance Clients

First Cardinal Corp.
RMSCO, Inc.
Golub Corporation

Partners

Robert S. Stockton — 1947 — Canisius College, B.S. (cum laude), 1969; Albany Law School of Union University, J.D., 1972 — Admitted to Bar, 1973, New York; U.S. District Court, Northern District of New York — Member American, New York State, Albany County and Saratoga Bar Associations

Christopher L. Barker — 1956 — State University of New York, B.A. (cum laude), 1978; Albany Law School of Union University, J.D., 1982 — Admitted to Bar, 1983, New York — Member New York State Bar Association

Matthew R. Mead — 1960 — Le Moyne College, B.A., 1982; Albany Law School of Union University, J.D., 1985 — Admitted to Bar, 1987, New York; U.S. District Court, Northern District of New York — Member American Bar Association (Litigation Law Practice Management Section); New York State and Albany County Bar Associations; Association of Trial Lawyers of America — Lecturer, New York Workers' Compensation Law Issues, Albany County Bar Association — Arbitrator, U.S. District Court, Northern District of New York and American Arbitration Association

Mederic J. Ethier — 1967 — Le Moyne College, B.S., 1989; Albany Law School of Union University, J.D., 1992 — Admitted to Bar, 1993, New York — Member American and Schenectady County Bar Associations

William M. Pausley — 1967 — Le Moyne College, B.A., 1990; Albany Law School of Union University, J.D., 1993 — Admitted to Bar, 1994, New

NEW YORK

Stockton, Barker & Mead, LLP, Troy, NY (Continued)

York — Member American, New York State and Schenectady County Bar Associations

John B. Paniccia — 1967 — State University of New York at Brockport, B.A., 1990; Thomas M. Cooley Law School, J.D., 1996 — Admitted to Bar, 1996, New Jersey; 1997, New York — Member New York State, Albany County and New York County Bar Associations

Associates

Shawn Yerdon — 1975 — Ashland University, B.S., 1996; Albany Law School, J.D., 2000 — Admitted to Bar, 2001, New York; U.S. District Court, Northern District of New York

Oleg Tsyn — 1976 — Drew University, B.A., 1998; Albany Law School, J.D., 2001 — Admitted to Bar, 2002, New York — Languages: Russian

Michael G. Jones — 1976 — The University of North Carolina at Chapel Hill, B.S., 1998; Albany Law School of Union University, J.D., 2005 — Admitted to Bar, 2006, New York

Of Counsel

Leith Carole Ramsey — 1962 — State University of New York College at Cortland, B.A., 1984; Western New England College School of Law, J.D., 1988 — Admitted to Bar, 1989, New York; 1990, U.S. District Court, Northern District of New York — Member New York State Bar Association (Insurance, Negligence and Compensation Law Section); Schenectady County Bar Association; Association of Trial Lawyers of America

---

The following firms also service this area.

Bailey, Kelleher & Johnson, P.C.
Pine West Plaza 5, Suite 507
Washington Avenue Extension
Albany, New York 12205
Telephone: 518-456-0082
Fax: 518-456-4767

Insurance Defense, Trial Practice, Product Liability, Municipal Law, Fire Loss, Premises Liability, Lead Paint, Homeowners, Slip and Fall, First and Third Party Defense, Police Liability Defense

SEE COMPLETE LISTING UNDER ALBANY, NEW YORK (11 MILES)

Boeggeman, George & Corde, P.C.
39 North Pearl Street, Suite 501
Albany, New York 12207
Telephone: 518-465-1100
Fax: 518-465-1800

Insurance Defense, Trial Practice, Automobile, Product Liability, Legal Malpractice, Medical Malpractice, Employment Law, Real Estate, Toxic Torts, Engineering Malpractice

SEE COMPLETE LISTING UNDER ALBANY, NEW YORK (8 MILES)

Donohue, Sabo, Varley & Huttner, LLP
120 Broadway, 2nd Floor
Albany, New York 12205
Telephone: 518-458-8922
Fax: 518-438-4349

Mailing Address: P.O. Box 15056, Albany, NY 12212-5056

Insurance Defense, Product Liability, Professional Malpractice, Employment Law, Municipal Law

SEE COMPLETE LISTING UNDER ALBANY, NEW YORK (8 MILES)

Napierski, VanDenburgh, Napierski, & O'Connor, LLP
296 Washington Avenue Extension, Ste 3
Albany, New York 12203
Telephone: 518-862-9292
Fax: 518-862-1519

Civil Trial Practice, Insurance Defense, Appellate Practice, Automobile, Commercial Litigation, General Liability, Labor and Employment, Municipal Liability, Product Liability, Trial Practice, Accountants and Attorneys Liability, Coverage Issues, Directors and Officers Liability, Premises Liability, Asbestos Litigation, Automobile Liability, Automobile Tort, Construction Accidents, Construction Defect, Construction Liability, Professional Liability, Contractors Liability, Wrongful Termination, Subrogation, Medical Malpractice Defense

SEE COMPLETE LISTING UNDER ALBANY, NEW YORK (8 MILES)

UNIONDALE

UNIONDALE 24,759 Nassau Co.

Congdon Flaherty O'Callaghan Reid Donlon Travis & Fishlinger

333 Earle Ovington Boulevard, Suite 502
Uniondale, New York 11553-3625
Telephone: 516-542-5900
Fax: 516-542-5912
E-Mail: Cschnepp@cfolegal.com
www.cfolegal.com

Established: 1975

Insurance Defense, Subrogation

Insurance Clients

California Casualty Management Company
Crawford & Company
Liberty Mutual Insurance Company
MetLife Auto & Home
New York Municipal Insurance Reciprocal
New York State Insurance Department, Liquidation Bureau
Sedgwick CMS
Tower Risk Management
The Wright Insurance Companies
Century Insurance Group
Chubb Services Corporation
Kemper Insurance Company
The Main Street America Group
New York Central Mutual Fire Insurance Company
New York Schools Insurance Reciprocal
Peerless Insurance Company
State Insurance Fund of New York
Western World Insurance Group

Non-Insurance Clients

Interstate Brands Company
New York City Housing Authority

Founder

Alan E. Congdon — (1932-1989)

Partners

Michael S. Congdon — 1951 — Hofstra University, B.A., 1974; Pace University School of Law, J.D., 1982 — Admitted to Bar, 1983, New York; U.S. District Court, Eastern and Southern Districts of New York — Member New York State Bar Association

Edward J. Donlon — 1941 — St. John's University, B.A., 1964; Saint Louis University School of Law, J.D., 1967 — Admitted to Bar, 1968, New York; U.S. District Court, Eastern and Southern Districts of New York; U.S. Supreme Court; U.S. Court of Military Appeals — Member New York State Trial Lawyers Association

Laura A. Endrizzi — 1962 — Fordham University, B.A., 1984; St. John's University School of Law, J.D., 1987 — Admitted to Bar, 1987, New York; 1997, U.S. District Court, Eastern and Southern Districts of New York; U.S. Supreme Court

Thomas M. Evans — 1964 — St. John's University, B.A., 1985; St. John's University School of Law, J.D., 1988 — Admitted to Bar, 1988, New York — Member New York State and Nassau County Bar Associations

William J. Fishlinger — 1944 — University of Maryland, B.A., 1971; St. John's University School of Law, J.D., 1987 — Admitted to Bar, 1988, New York; U.S. District Court, Eastern District of New York — Member American, New York State and Nassau County Bar Associations; Defense Research Institute

John P. Flaherty — 1948 — Hofstra University, B.A. (cum laude), 1969; Fordham Law School, J.D., 1972; Columbia University Law Masters Program — Fordham Law Review — Admitted to Bar, 1972, Hawaii; 1973, New York; U.S. District Court, District of Hawaii; U.S. District Court, Eastern District of New York; U.S. Court of Appeals, Second and Ninth Circuits; U.S. Supreme Court; U.S. Court of Military Appeals — Member Hawaii State, Nassau County and Suffolk County Bar Associations; Association of Trial Lawyers of America; Nassau-Suffolk Trial Lawyers Association

Christine Gasser — 1953 — Fordham University, B.A. (magna cum laude), 1974; M.S., 1978; St. John's University School of Law, J.D. (cum laude), 1987 — Editor, St. John's Law Review — Admitted to Bar, 1988, New York; U.S. District Court, Eastern and Southern Districts of New York; U.S. Court of Appeals, Second Circuit — Member American Bar Association

James J. Leyden, Jr. — 1946 — State University of New York College at Cortland, B.A., 1967; Adelphi University, M.A., 1970; New York Law

UNIONDALE   NEW YORK

Congdon Flaherty O'Callaghan Reid Donlon Travis & Fishlinger, Uniondale, NY (Continued)

School, J.D. (magna cum laude), 1977 — Admitted to Bar, 1978, New York; 1979, U.S. District Court, Eastern and Southern Districts of New York — Member New York State and Suffolk County Bar Associations; Brehon Society; Nassau-Suffolk Trial Lawyers Association

Jane M. O'Callaghan — 1966 — Regis College, B.A., 1988; St. John's University School of Law, J.D., 1994 — Admitted to Bar, 1994, Connecticut; 1995, New York; U.S. District Court, Eastern District of New York — Member American, New York State and Nassau County Bar Associations

Lawrence H. Reid, Jr. — 1946 — Hofstra University, B.A., 1968; St. John's University School of Law, J.D., 1971 — Admitted to Bar, 1972, New York; U.S. District Court, Eastern, Northern and Southern Districts of New York — Member New York State and Nassau County Bar Associations; Defense Research Institute; Nassau-Suffolk Trial Lawyers Association

Charles M. Schnepp, Jr. — 1951 — Dowling College, B.B.A., 1973; St. John's University School of Law, J.D., 1983 — Admitted to Bar, 1984, New York; U.S. District Court, Eastern and Southern Districts of New York; 1989, U.S. District Court, Northern District of New York; U.S. Court of Appeals, Second Circuit — Member New York State and Suffolk County Bar Associations; Defense Research Institute

Francis X. Schroeder — 1959 — Villanova University, B.S., 1981; Villanova University School of Law, J.D., 1989 — Admitted to Bar, 1990, New York; 1995, U.S. District Court, Eastern District of New York; 2006, U.S. District Court, Southern District of New York — Member Nassau County Bar Association; Nassau-Suffolk Trial Lawyers Association

Kathy A. Schulze-Leyden — 1960 — Adelphi University, B.S.N., 1982; University of Missouri-Kansas City School of Law, J.D., 1989 — Admitted to Bar, 1989, Missouri; 1990, New York — Member American Bar Association — Registered Nurse, New York State

Francis A. Travis — 1947 — Boston College, B.A., 1969; Vermont Law School, J.D., 1979 — Editor, Vermont Law Review — Admitted to Bar, 1980, New York; U.S. Court of Appeals, Second Circuit; U.S. Supreme Court; U.S. District Court, Eastern and Southern Districts of New York; U.S. Court of Military Appeals — Member New York State and Nassau Bar Associations; Nassau-Suffolk Trial Lawyers Association; New York State Trial Lawyers Association; Association of Trial Lawyers of America

Associates

Avis Spencer Decaire — 1974 — Siena College, B.A., 1996; Albany Law School of Union University, J.D., 1999 — Admitted to Bar, 2000, New York; U.S. District Court, Northern District of New York — Member New York State Bar Association

James V. Derenze — 1959 — Adelphi University, B.A., 1982; Hofstra University School of Law, J.D., 1988 — Admitted to Bar, 1988, New York

Kathleen D. Foley — 1963 — Hofstra University, B.A., 1985; St. John's University School of Law, J.D., 1992 — Editor, St. John's Law Review — Admitted to Bar, 1992, Connecticut; 1993, New York; U.S. District Court, Eastern and Southern Districts of New York; 1994, U.S. Court of Appeals, Second Circuit — Member New York State and Nassau County Bar Associations

Robert T. Krause — 1948 — St. John's University, B.S., 1970; St. John's University School of Law, J.D., 1973 — Admitted to Bar, 1974, New York; 1980, Massachusetts; 1975, U.S. District Court, Eastern and Southern Districts of New York

Heather J. Mondelli — 1975 — Boston College, B.A., 1997; Santa Clara University School of Law, J.D., 2000 — Admitted to Bar, 2001, Connecticut; New York; 2004, U.S. District Court, Eastern and Southern Districts of New York — Member New York State and Nassau County Bar Associations; American Trial Lawyers Association

Richard J. Nicolello — 1960 — St. John's University, B.A. (magna cum laude), 1982; Fordham Law School, J.D., 1985 — Admitted to Bar, 1986, New York; 1987, U.S. District Court, Eastern and Southern Districts of New York — Member New York State and Nassau County Bar Associations; Columbian Lawyers Association; New York State Association of School Attorneys; Education Law Committee of Nassau Bar; Nassau County Legislature

Paula Pavlides — 1970 — Loyola College, B.A., 1992; St. John's University School of Law, J.D., 1995 — Admitted to Bar, 1996, New York; New Jersey; U.S. District Court, Eastern and Southern Districts of New York — Member Queens County Bar Association

Lynne B. Prommersberger — 1956 — New York Institute of Technology, B.S., 1978; Touro College Jacob D. Fuchsberg Law Center, J.D., 1991 — Admitted to Bar, 1992, New York; U.S. District Court, Eastern and Southern Districts of New York — Member American, New York State and Nassau County Bar Associations

Congdon Flaherty O'Callaghan Reid Donlon Travis & Fishlinger, Uniondale, NY (Continued)

Michael T. Reagan — 1966 — State University of New York at Stony Brook, B.A. Political Science, 1997; Fordham Law School, J.D., 1999 — Admitted to Bar, 1999, New York

Of Counsel

Warren J. Finnell — 1930 — Harvard College, B.A., 1952; Harvard Law School, J.D., 1955 — Admitted to Bar, 1958, New York — Member New York State and Nassau County Bar Associations

Richard M. O'Callaghan — (Retired)

(This firm is also listed in the Subrogation section of this directory)

Rivkin Radler LLP

926 RXR Plaza
Uniondale, New York 11556-0111
  Telephone: 516-357-3000
  Fax: 516-357-3333
  www.rivkinradler.com

(New York, NY Office: 555 Madison Avenue, 10022-3338)
  (Tel: 212-455-9555)
  (Fax: 212-687-9044)
(Hackensack, NJ Office: Court Plaza South, 21 Main Street, 07601)
  (Tel: 201-287-2460)
  (Fax: 201-489-0495)

Established: 1953

General Civil Practice, Trial Practice, Appellate Practice, State and Federal Courts, Casualty, Professional Malpractice, Product Liability, Insurance Coverage, Toxic Torts, Antitrust, Environmental Law, Corporate Law, Securities, Employment Law, Medical Liability, Technology, Labor and Employment, Business Law

Insurance Clients

AEGIS Insurance Services, Inc.	Aetna Life and Casualty Company
AIG National Insurance Company, Inc.	Allstate Insurance Company
	Central Mutual Insurance Company
CGU Insurance Company	Chubb Group of Insurance Companies
CNA Insurance Company	Fireman's Fund Insurance Companies
Coregis Group	
GEICO General Insurance Company	General Accident Insurance Company
Hanover Insurance Company	Interstate National Corporation
The Hartford Insurance Group	Medical Liability Mutual Insurance Company
Lexington Insurance Company	
Metropolitan Property and Casualty Insurance Company	Physicians Reciprocal Insurers
Royal Insurance Company	Safeco Insurance
Sentry Insurance a Mutual Company	State Farm Insurance Company
Zurich American Insurance Group	Travelers Property Casualty Insurance Company

Non-Insurance Clients

Chase Manhattan Bank	Citibank, N.A.
Copesan Services	Enterprise Rent-A-Car Company
L.I. Power Authority	Pall Corporation
Town of Hempstead	Underwriters Laboratories, Inc.

Firm Members

Brian Ade — 1954 — Rutgers University, B.A., 1976; Western New England College, J.D., 1980 — Admitted to Bar, 1980, New Jersey; U.S. District Court, District of New Jersey; U.S. District Court, Eastern, Northern and Southern Districts of New York

James W. Aiosa — City University of New York, B.A. (summa cum laude), 1989; New York University, J.D., 1992 — Admitted to Bar, 1992, New York

Todd Belous — 1965 — State University of New York at Binghamton, B.A.; Syracuse University, J.D., 1991 — Admitted to Bar, 1991, New York

Bruce A. Bendix — 1958 — Hofstra University, B.B.A., 1980; St. John's University, J.D., 1983 — Admitted to Bar, 1984, New York; 1986, U.S. District Court, Eastern and Southern Districts of New York

NEW YORK

UNIONDALE

Rivkin Radler LLP, Uniondale, NY (Continued)

Stuart M. Bodoff — 1972 — Yeshiva University, B.A. (magna cum laude), 1993; Fordham University, J.D. (cum laude), 1996 — Admitted to Bar, 1997, New York; 1998, New Jersey; 2001, U.S. District Court, Eastern and Southern Districts of New York

Michael E. Buckley — University of Notre Dame, B.A. (with honors), 1981; Villanova University, J.D., 1984 — Admitted to Bar, 1984, New Jersey; Pennsylvania; 1990, New York

David M. Cassidy — 1954 — State University of New York at Stony Brook, B.A., 1981; St. John's University, J.D., 1985 — Admitted to Bar, 1985, New York; U.S. District Court, Eastern District of New York

George Choriatis — Hofstra University, B.A. (with honors), 1998; J.D. (with honors), 2001 — Admitted to Bar, 2002, New York

Brian S. Conneely — 1952 — Duke University, B.A., 1974; Hofstra University, J.D. (cum laude), 1977 — Admitted to Bar, 1978, New York; U.S. District Court, Eastern and Southern Districts of New York; U.S. District Court, Eastern District of Virginia; U.S. Court of Appeals, Second and Fourth Circuits

Peter C. Contino — 1952 — Franklin & Marshall College, B.S., 1974; New England School of Law, J.D. (cum laude), 1977 — Admitted to Bar, 1978, New York; 1979, U.S. District Court, Eastern and Southern Districts of New York

William Cornachio — 1951 — Colgate University, B.A., 1973; Fordham University, J.D., 1997 — Admitted to Bar, 1978, New York; 1979, District of Columbia; U.S. District Court, Eastern and Southern Districts of New York

George K. DeHaven — 1954 — St. John's University, B.A., 1976; New York Law School, J.D., 1981 — Admitted to Bar, 1982, New York; U.S. District Court, Southern District of New York; 1984, U.S. District Court, Eastern District of New York

Janice DiGennaro — 1958 — Queens College of the City University of New York, B.A. (cum laude), 1980; State University of New York at Buffalo, J.D. (cum laude), 1983 — Admitted to Bar, 1984, New York; 1987, U.S. District Court, Eastern and Southern Districts of New York

John K. Diviney — Cornell University School of Industrial and Labor Relations, B.A., 1983; St. John's University, J.D., 1985 — Admitted to Bar, 1986, New York

Alan C. Eagle — 1961 — C.W. Post College, B.A., 1983; St. John's University, J.D., 1986 — Admitted to Bar, 1986, New York

Glenn Egor — State University of New York at Oswego, B.A. (magna cum laude), 1991; Hofstra University, J.D., 1994 — Admitted to Bar, 1995, New York; U.S. District Court, Eastern, Northern and Southern Districts of New York

Scott Eisenmesser — 1961 — Emory University, B.B.A., 1983; Baruch College, City University of New York, M.B.A., 1998; University of Bridgeport, J.D., 1987 — Admitted to Bar, 1987, Connecticut; 1988, New York — Certified Public Accountant

Joanne M. Engeldrum — 1971 — Wesleyan University, B.A., 1994; St. John's University, J.D., 1997 — Admitted to Bar, 1997, New York

Harvey Epstein — 1962 — State University of New York at Buffalo, B.S. (cum laude), 1983; Fordham University, J.D., 1986 — Admitted to Bar, 1987, New York

Richard S. Feldman — 1951 — State University of New York at Binghamton, B.A. (cum laude), 1973; State University of New York at Buffalo, J.D., 1976 — Admitted to Bar, 1977, New York; 1978, District of Columbia; 1977, U.S. District Court, Eastern and Southern Districts of New York; 1985, U.S. Supreme Court

Anthony R. Gambardella — 1954 — St. John's University, B.A. (summa cum laude), 1976; J.D., 1979 — Admitted to Bar, 1980, New York; U.S. District Court, Eastern and Southern Districts of New York; U.S. Court of Appeals, Second Circuit

Max Gershenoff — The University of Georgia, A.B., 2003; Benjamin N. Cardozo School of Law, J.D., 2006 — Admitted to Bar, 2007, New York; U.S. District Court, Eastern District of New York

Frank J. Giliberti — 1953 — C.W. Post Campus of Long Island University, B.A. (magna cum laude), 1975; Pace University, J.D., 1981 — Admitted to Bar, 1982, New York; 1983, U.S. District Court, Eastern and Southern Districts of New York; 1993, U.S. District Court, Northern District of New York

Erez Glambosky — State University of New York at Binghamton, B.A. (cum laude), 1997; Hofstra University, J.D., 2000 — Admitted to Bar, 2000, New Jersey; 2001, New York; U.S. District Court, Eastern and Southern Districts of New York

Stuart I. Gordon — 1957 — The George Washington University, B.A., 1979; St. John's University, J.D., 1982 — Admitted to Bar, 1983, New York; U.S.

Rivkin Radler LLP, Uniondale, NY (Continued)

District Court, Eastern and Southern Districts of New York; 1991, U.S. Court of Appeals, Second Circuit

M. Paul Gorfinkel — 1954 — Yeshiva University, B.A., 1975; New York Law School, J.D., 1978 — Admitted to Bar, 1979, New York

Jeffrey Greener — 1962 — State University of New York at Albany, B.A. (magna cum laude), 1984; The George Washington University, J.D., 1987 — Admitted to Bar, 1987, New York; Connecticut; 1990, U.S. Tax Court

David M. Grill — State University of New York at Binghamton, B.A., 1989; Brooklyn Law School, J.D., 1992 — Dean's Merit Scholar — Admitted to Bar, 1993, New York; New Jersey

Keith S. Grover — 1969 — State University of New York at Stony Brook, B.S., 1991; Touro College, J.D., 1994 — Admitted to Bar, 1994, New Jersey; 1995, New York

Walter J. Gumersell — 1955 — St. John's University, B.A. (summa cum laude), 1976; Hofstra University, J.D., 1979; New York University, LL.M., 1986 — Moot Court Honors Award — Admitted to Bar, 1980, New York; 1982, U.S. District Court, Eastern District of New York; 1983, U.S. District Court, Southern District of New York; 1984, U.S. Supreme Court; 1985, U.S. Court of Appeals, Second Circuit

Michael J. Jones — Rutgers University, B.A., 1981; Villanova University, J.D., 1984 — Admitted to Bar, 1985, New Jersey; 2011, New York; Pennsylvania

George D. Kappus — 1945 — Harvard College, A.B., 1967; Boston College, J.D., 1971 — Admitted to Bar, 1974, New York; 1984, Michigan; 1974, U.S. District Court, Southern District of New York

Jay D. Kenigsberg — University of Rochester, B.A., 1985; State University of New York at Buffalo, J.D., 1988 — Admitted to Bar, 1988, New York; 1990, U.S. District Court, Eastern and Southern Districts of New York

Cheryl F. Korman — State University of New York at Albany, B.S., 1988; St. John's University, J.D., 1991 — Admitted to Bar, 1991, New York; New Jersey

Yaron Kornblum — Brooklyn College, B.A. (summa cum laude), 1990; Hofstra University, J.D., 1993 — Admitted to Bar, 1993, New York; 1994, U.S. District Court, Eastern and Southern Districts of New York

Michael A. Kotula — 1965 — Emory University, B.A., 1987; The George Washington University, J.D., 1990 — Admitted to Bar, 1990, New Jersey; 1991, District of Columbia; 1995, New York; 1990, U.S. District Court, District of New Jersey; 1991, U.S. District Court for the District of Columbia; 1992, U.S. Court of Appeals, Third Circuit

Evan H. Krinick — 1961 — Union College, B.A., 1983; Albany Law School of Union University, J.D., 1985 — Admitted to Bar, 1985, New York; 1988, U.S. District Court, Eastern and Southern Districts of New York; U.S. Court of Appeals, Second Circuit; 1991, U.S. Supreme Court

Christopher J. Kutner — State University of New York at Stony Brook, B.E.M.E., 1987; St. John's University School of Law, J.D., 1990 — Admitted to Bar, 1990, New York; Connecticut; U.S. District Court, Eastern and Southern Districts of New York — Member American and New York State Bar Associations

Anthony J. LaPorta — 1968 — Lafayette College, B.A., 1990; St. John's University, J.D., 1993 — Admitted to Bar, 1993, New Jersey; 1994, New York

Carol A. Lastorino — 1965 — State University of New York at Stony Brook, B.A., 1987; Hofstra University, J.D., 1991 — Admitted to Bar, 1992, New York; 1995, Georgia

Barry I. Levy — 1966 — The Ohio State University, B.A. (cum laude), 1988; J.D. (with honors), 1991 — Admitted to Bar, 1992, New York; U.S. District Court, Eastern and Southern Districts of New York; 1994, U.S. Court of Appeals, Second Circuit

Lawrence A. Levy — 1958 — State University of New York at Stony Brook, B.A., 1980; St. John's University, J.D., 1985 — Admitted to Bar, 1986, New York; U.S. District Court, Eastern and Southern Districts of New York

Shari C. Lewis — 1957 — State University of New York at Buffalo, B.A., 1978; J.D., 1981 — Admitted to Bar, 1983, New York; 1986, U.S. District Court, Eastern and Southern Districts of New York

Paul V. Majkowski — 1966 — New York University, B.A., 1991; St. John's University, J.D., 1994 — Admitted to Bar, 1995, New York; New Jersey; U.S. District Court, Eastern and Southern Districts of New York

Benjamin P. Malerba — 1973 — State University of New York at Stony Brook, B.A., 1998; Hofstra University, M.B.A.; J.D., 2001 — Admitted to Bar, 2002, New York; U.S. District Court, Eastern and Southern Districts of New York

David A. Manko — 1969 — Purdue University, B.A., 1991; California Western University, J.D., 1993 — Admitted to Bar, 1994, California; 1995, New York

Rivkin Radler LLP, Uniondale, NY (Continued)

John M. McFaul — State University of New York at New Paltz, B.A. (cum laude), 1972; Brooklyn Law School, J.D., 1975 — Admitted to Bar, 1976, New York; U.S. District Court, Eastern and Southern Districts of New York; U.S. Court of Appeals, Second Circuit

Peter P. McNamara — 1955 — St. John's University, B.S., 1977; J.D., 1981 — Admitted to Bar, 1982, New York; U.S. District Court, Eastern and Southern Districts of New York

Howard M. Merkrebs — 1955 — State University of New York at Stony Brook, B.A., 1976; Hofstra University, M.B.A., 1984; New York Law School, J.D., 1991 — Admitted to Bar, 1991, New York; 1992, U.S. District Court, Eastern and Southern Districts of New York

Joseph Monteleone — St. John's University, B.A., 1977; New York Law School, J.D., 1980 — Admitted to Bar, 1980, New York; New Jersey

Michael Mule — 1970 — Boston College, B.A. (magna cum laude), 1991; Fordham University, J.D. (with honors), 1995 — Order of the Coif — Admitted to Bar, 1996, New York; New Jersey; Connecticut; Massachusetts; U.S. District Court, Eastern and Southern Districts of New York; U.S. District Court, District of New Jersey; U.S. Court of Appeals, Second Circuit

Anne M. Murray — 1967 — Boston College, B.A., 1989; Suffolk University, J.D., 1992 — Admitted to Bar, 1993, New York; U.S. District Court, Eastern District of New York

Kenneth A. Novikoff — 1964 — Dartmouth College, B.A., 1986; American University, Washington College of Law, J.D. (cum laude), 1990 — Admitted to Bar, 1991, New York; 1992, U.S. District Court, Eastern District of New York; 1993, U.S. Court of Appeals, Second Circuit

Albert W. Petraglia — 1946 — Pratt Institute, B.S., 1969; St. John's University, J.D., 1973 — Admitted to Bar, 1974, New York

Joseph K. Poe — 1971 — University of Notre Dame, B.A., 1994; Hofstra University, J.D., 1997 — Admitted to Bar, 1998, New York; U.S. District Court, Eastern and Southern Districts of New York

Frank Raia — Providence College, B.A.; Southwestern University, J.D., 1987 — Admitted to Bar, 1987, New York

David Richman — 1954 — State University of New York at Buffalo, B.A., 1976; New York University, M.P.A., 1978; New York Law School, J.D., 1982 — Admitted to Bar, 1983, New York; 1984, U.S. District Court, Eastern and Southern Districts of New York

Pia E. Riverso — Manhattan College, B.S.B.A. (summa cum laude), 1982; St. John's University, J.D., 1985 — Admitted to Bar, 1986, New York

John L. Rivkin — 1955 — Union College, B.A. (summa cum laude), 1978; University of Virginia, J.D., 1981 — Admitted to Bar, 1982, New York; 1983, Florida; 1985, District of Columbia; 1982, U.S. District Court, Eastern and Southern Districts of New York; 1985, U.S. Supreme Court

John Robertelli — Montclair State College, B.S., 1986; DePaul University, J.D., 1989 — Admitted to Bar, 1990, New Jersey; U.S. District Court, District of New Jersey; U.S. Court of Appeals, Third Circuit

Alan S. Rutkin — 1958 — Union College, B.A., 1980; Boston University, J.D., 1983 — Admitted to Bar, 1984, New York

William M. Savino — 1949 — Villanova University, B.S., 1971; Fordham University, J.D., 1974 — Admitted to Bar, 1975, New York; U.S. District Court, Eastern and Southern Districts of New York; 1978, U.S. Court of Appeals, Second Circuit; 1980, U.S. Supreme Court

Evan R. Schieber — State University of New York at Binghamton, B.A., 1989; Brooklyn Law School, J.D., 1992 — Admitted to Bar, 1992, New York; New Jersey; U.S. District Court, Eastern and Southern Districts of New York

Brian S. Schlosser — 1975 — State University of New York at Oswego, B.S.; Touro College, J.D., 2001 — Admitted to Bar, 2001, New York; U.S. District Court, Eastern District of New York

Laura Shockley — State University of New York at Stony Brook, B.A., 1998; Fordham University, J.D., 2001 — Admitted to Bar, 2002, New York; U.S. District Court, Eastern and Southern Districts of New York

Michael A. Sirignano — 1963 — State University of New York at Albany, B.A. (magna cum laude), 1985; Fordham University, J.D., 1988 — Admitted to Bar, 1989, New York

Stephen J. Smirti, Jr. — 1950 — New York University, B.A., 1972; St. John's University, J.D., 1976 — Admitted to Bar, 1976, District of Columbia; 1977, New York; U.S. District Court, Eastern and Southern Districts of New York; 1979, U.S. Court of Appeals, Second Circuit; 1980, U.S. Supreme Court

Eric S. Strober — 1970 — Syracuse University, B.A., 1992; Brooklyn Law School, J.D., 1995 — Admitted to Bar, 1996, New York; U.S. District Court, Eastern and Southern Districts of New York

Joshua M. Tare — City University of New York, B.A., 1998; New York Law School, J.D., 2001 — Admitted to Bar, 2001, New York; New Jersey

Rivkin Radler LLP, Uniondale, NY (Continued)

Norman L. Tolle — 1948 — State University of New York at Stony Brook, B.A. (cum laude), 1969; New York University, J.D., 1972 — Admitted to Bar, 1973, New York; 1974, U.S. District Court, Eastern and Southern Districts of New York; 1975, U.S. Court of Appeals, Second Circuit; 1983, U.S. District Court, Northern District of Texas; U.S. Court of Appeals, Fifth Circuit; 1986, U.S. District Court, Eastern District of Michigan; U.S. Court of Appeals, Eleventh Circuit

Michael Troisi — 1960 — University of Hartford, B.A., 1982; Temple University, J.D., 1985 — Admitted to Bar, 1986, New York; 1988, U.S. District Court, Eastern and Southern Districts of New York; 2004, U.S. District Court, Eastern District of Wisconsin

Robert Tugander — 1967 — State University of New York at Stony Brook, B.A., 1989; Hofstra University, J.D., 1992 — Admitted to Bar, 1993, New York

Frank A. Valverde — Queens College, B.A., 1998; New York Law School, J.D. (cum laude), 2001 — Admitted to Bar, 2002, New York; U.S. District Court, Eastern and Southern Districts of New York

Michael P. Versichelli — Hofstra University, B.A. (magna cum laude), 1989; Fordham University, J.D. (cum laude), 1993 — Phi Beta Kappa — Admitted to Bar, 1994, New York

Stephen B. Weissman — 1950 — Northwestern University, B.A., 1972; Columbia University, J.D., 1975 — Admitted to Bar, 1976, New York

Michael P. Welch — Syracuse University, B.A. (magna cum laude), 1998; Brooklyn Law School, J.D. (magna cum laude), 2001 — Admitted to Bar, 2002, New York

David S. Wilck — State University of New York at Binghamton, B.A., 1990; Touro College, J.D. (cum laude), 1993 — Admitted to Bar, 1993, New Jersey; 1994, New York

Steven M. Zuckermann — 1970 — State University of New York at Albany, B.A., 1992; St. John's University, J.D., 1996 — Admitted to Bar, 1997, New York

Of Counsel

Robert Aurigema — 1947 — Fordham University, B.A. (Dean's List), 1969; J.D. (summa cum laude), 1972 — Admitted to Bar, 1973, New York; U.S. District Court, Western District of New York; 1975, U.S. District Court, Eastern District of New York

Michael A. L. Balboni — Adelphi University, B.A., 1982; St. John's University, J.D., 1985 — Admitted to Bar, 1985, New York

Louis D'Amaro — 1961 — State University of New York at Stony Brook, B.A., 1983; St. John's University, J.D., 1986 — Admitted to Bar, 1987, New York

Claudia Hinrichsen — State University of New York at Geneseo, B.A. (magna cum laude), 1987; Hofstra University, J.D. (with distinction), 1990 — Admitted to Bar, 1990, New York

Geoffrey R. Kaiser — University of Virginia, B.A. (with honors, Phi Beta Kappa), 1985; New York University, J.D., 1988 — Admitted to Bar, 1988, New York

Charles Pendola — St. John's University, B.B.A., 1966; John Jay College of Criminal Justice of the City University of New York, M.P.A., 1971; C.W. Post Campus of Long Island University, M.P.S., 1976; Touro College, J.D., 2002 — Admitted to Bar, 2003, New York

Associates

Dominic Anamdi	Brian Bank
Christopher Barbarello	Michelle Bholan
Merril C. Biscone	Sandra Buchanan
Jacqueline Bushwack	Justin A. Calabrese
Michael Cannata	Gina Dolan
Patricia E. Doran	Jeannine Farino
Christopher J. Fichtl	Andrew Firkins
Carlie Fitapelli	Kerry Flynn
Avigael Fyman	Joseph Fusco
Dana Gold	Ryan Goldberg
Seth Goldberg	Gaddi Goren
Scott R. Green	Janice Greenberg
David Guadagnoli	Jason Gurdus
Lawrence Han	Tamika Hardy
Karen C. Higgins	Jeremy Honig
Monica Kashyap	Matthew Lampert
Francis J. Leddy III	Robert Maloney
Henry Mascia	Sean McAloon
Karin M. McCarthy	Michael McIsaac

NEW YORK

Rivkin Radler LLP, Uniondale, NY (Continued)

Christopher Miehl
Frank Misiti
Marilyn Oppedisano
John Panagopoulos
Sarah B. Rebosa
Andrea Sacks
Shana Slawitsky
Joseph Sulzbach
Clara Villarreal
John J. Vobis
Richard Yam
Susan Miller
Gregory Mitchell
Julie Ovicher
Alexander Pappas
Jason M. Romeo
Michael B. Schnepper
Matthew V. Spero
Frank Tiscione
Laura Villeck
Amy S. Wiedmann

Smith, Sovik, Kendrick & Sugnet, P.C.

The Financial Center at Mitchel Field
90 Merrick Avenue Suite 500
East Meadow, New York 11554
  Toll Free: 800-675-0011

(Syracuse, NY Office*: 250 South Clinton Street, Suite 600, 13202)
  (Tel: 315-474-2911)
  (Fax: 315-474-6015)
  (E-Mail: firm@smithsovik.com)
  (www.smithsovik.com)
(Buffalo, NY Office*: 651 Delaware Avenue, Suite 144, 14202)
  (Toll Free: 800-675-0011)

Appellate Practice, Automobile, Commercial Litigation, Construction Law, Dental Malpractice, Labor and Employment, Medical Malpractice, Nursing Home Liability, Premises Liability, Product Liability, Professional Liability, Retail Liability, Subrogation, Toxic Torts, Trucking, Workers' Compensation, Wrongful Death

(See listing under Syracuse, NY for additional information)

UTICA † 62,235 Oneida Co.

Refer To

Bailey, Kelleher & Johnson, P.C.
Pine West Plaza 5, Suite 507
Washington Avenue Extension
Albany, New York 12205
  Telephone: 518-456-0082
  Fax: 518-456-4767

Insurance Defense, Trial Practice, Product Liability, Municipal Law, Fire Loss, Premises Liability, Lead Paint, Homeowners, Slip and Fall, First and Third Party Defense, Police Liability Defense

SEE COMPLETE LISTING UNDER ALBANY, NEW YORK (89 MILES)

Refer To

Smith, Sovik, Kendrick & Sugnet, P.C.
250 South Clinton Street, Suite 600
Syracuse, New York 13202
  Telephone: 315-474-2911
  Fax: 315-474-6015

Appellate Practice, Automobile, Commercial Litigation, Construction Law, Dental Malpractice, Labor and Employment, Medical Malpractice, Nursing Home Liability, Premises Liability, Product Liability, Professional Liability, Retail Liability, Subrogation, Toxic Torts, Trucking, Workers' Compensation, Wrongful Death

SEE COMPLETE LISTING UNDER SYRACUSE, NEW YORK (49 MILES)

WARSAW † 3,473 Wyoming Co.

Refer To

Cohen & Lombardo, P.C.
343 Elmwood Avenue
Buffalo, New York 14222
  Telephone: 716-881-3010
  Fax: 716-881-2755
  Toll Free: 800-276-2640

Mailing Address: P.O. Box 5204, Buffalo, NY 14213-5204

Insurance Defense, Trial Practice, State and Federal Courts, Coverage Analysis, Litigation, Fire, Arson, Fraud, Property, Casualty, Surety, Marine, Employer Liability, Premises Liability, Product Liability, Environmental Law, Toxic Torts, Construction Law, Accident, Automobile, Professional Liability, Medical Malpractice, Subrogation, Advertising Injury, Errors and Omissions, Aviation, Bad Faith, Copyright and Trademark Law, Municipal Liability, Title Insurance, Niagara, Orleans, Monroe, Genesee, Livingston, Wyoming, Allegany, Cattaraugus and Chautauqua Counties

SEE COMPLETE LISTING UNDER BUFFALO, NEW YORK (48 MILES)

Refer To

Roach, Brown, McCarthy & Gruber, P.C.
1920 Liberty Building
424 Main Street
Buffalo, New York 14202-3511
  Telephone: 716-852-0400
  Fax: 716-852-2535

Insurance Defense, Trial and Appellate Practice, Medical Malpractice, Professional Malpractice, Product Liability, Construction Law, Sports and Entertainment Liability, Aviation, Fire, Excess, Coverage Issues

SEE COMPLETE LISTING UNDER BUFFALO, NEW YORK (42 MILES)

WATERTOWN † 27,023 Jefferson Co.

Refer To

Smith, Sovik, Kendrick & Sugnet, P.C.
250 South Clinton Street, Suite 600
Syracuse, New York 13202
  Telephone: 315-474-2911
  Fax: 315-474-6015

Appellate Practice, Automobile, Commercial Litigation, Construction Law, Dental Malpractice, Labor and Employment, Medical Malpractice, Nursing Home Liability, Premises Liability, Product Liability, Professional Liability, Retail Liability, Subrogation, Toxic Torts, Trucking, Workers' Compensation, Wrongful Death

SEE COMPLETE LISTING UNDER SYRACUSE, NEW YORK (70 MILES)

WESTCHESTER 1,203,789 New York Co.

Marshall Dennehey Warner Coleman & Goggin

800 Westchester Avenue, Suite C-700
Rye Brook, New York 10573
  Telephone: 914-977-7300
  Fax: 914-977-7301
  www.marshalldennehey.com

(Philadelphia, PA Office*: 2000 Market Street, Suite 2300, 19103)
  (Tel: 215-575-2600)
  (Fax: 215-575-0856)
  (Toll Free: 800-220-3308)
  (E-Mail: marshalldennehey@mdwcg.com)
(Wilmington, DE Office*: Nemours Building, 1007 North Orange Street, Suite 600, 19801)
  (Tel: 302-552-4300)
  (Fax: 302-552-4340)
(Fort Lauderdale, FL Office*: 100 Northeast 3rd Avenue, Suite 1100, 33301)
  (Tel: 954-847-4920)
  (Fax: 954-627-6640)
(Jacksonville, FL Office*: 200 West Forsyth Street, Suite 1400, 32202)
  (Tel: 904-358-4200)
  (Fax: 904-355-0019)

WESTCHESTER

NEW YORK

Marshall Dennehey Warner Coleman & Goggin, Westchester, NY (Continued)

(Orlando, FL Office*: Landmark Center One, 315 East Robinson Street, Suite 550, 32801-1948)
(Tel: 407-420-4380)
(Fax: 407-839-3008)
(Tampa, FL Office*: 201 East Kennedy Boulevard, Suite 1100, 33602)
(Tel: 813-898-1800)
(Fax: 813-221-5026)
(Cherry Hill, NJ Office*: Woodland Falls Corporate Park, 200 Lake Drive East, Suite 300, 08002)
(Tel: 856-414-6000)
(Fax: 856-414-6077)
(Roseland, NJ Office*: 425 Eagle Rock Avenue, Suite 302, 07068)
(Tel: 973-618-4100)
(Fax: 973-618-0685)
(New York, NY Office*: Wall Street Plaza, 88 Pine Street, 21st Floor, 10005-1801)
(Tel: 212-376-6400)
(Fax: 212-376-6490)
(Melville, NY Office*: 105 Maxess Road, Suite 303, 11747)
(Tel: 631-232-6130)
(Fax: 631-232-6184)
(Cincinnati, OH Office*: 312 Elm Street, Suite 1850, 45202)
(Tel: 513-375-6800)
(Fax: 513-372-6801)
(Cleveland, OH Office*: 127 Public Square, Suite 3510, 44114-1291)
(Tel: 216-912-3800)
(Fax: 216-344-9006)
(Allentown, PA Office*: 4905 West Tilghman Street, Suite 300, 18104)
(Tel: 484-895-2300)
(Fax: 484-895-2303)
(Doylestown, PA Office*: 10 North Main Street, 2nd Floor, 18901-4318)
(Tel: 267-880-2020)
(Fax: 215-348-5439)
(Erie, PA Office*: 717 State Street, Suite 701, 16501)
(Tel: 814-480-7800)
(Fax: 814-455-3603)
(Camp Hill, PA Office*(See Harrisburg listing): 100 Coporate Center Drive, Suite 201, 17011)
(Tel: 717-651-3500)
(Fax: 717-651-9630)
(King of Prussia, PA Office*: 620 Freedom Business Center, Suite 300, 19406)
(Tel: 610-354-8250)
(Fax: 610-354-8299)
(Pittsburgh, PA Office*: U.S. Steel Tower, Suite 2900, 600 Grant Street, 15219)
(Tel: 412-803-1140)
(Fax: 412-803-1188)
(Moosic, PA Office*(See Scranton listing): 50 Glenmaura National Boulevard, 18507)
(Tel: 570-496-4600)
(Fax: 570-496-0567)

Amusements, Sports and Recreation Liability, Asbestos and Mass Tort Litigation, Automobile Liability, Aviation and Complex Litigation, Construction Injury Litigation, Fraud/Special Investigation, General Liability, Hospitality and Liquor Liability, Maritime Litigation, Product Liability, Property Litigation, Retail Liability, Trucking & Transportation Liability, Appellate Advocacy and Post-Trial Practice, Architectural, Engineering and Construction Defect Litigation, Class Action Litigation, Commercial Litigation, Consumer and Credit Law, Employment Law, Environmental & Toxic Tort Litigation, Insurance Coverage/Bad Faith Litigation, Life, Health and Disability Litigation, Privacy and Data Security, Professional Liability, Public Entity and Civil Rights Litigation, Real Estate E&O Liability, School Leaders' Liability, Securities and Investment Professional Liability, Technology, Media and Intellectual Property Litigation, White Collar Crime, Birth Injury Litigation, Health Care Governmental Compliance, Health Care Liability, Health Law, Long-Term Care Liability, Medical Device and Pharmaceutical Liability, Medicare Set-Aside, Workers' Compensation

Marshall Dennehey Warner Coleman & Goggin, Westchester, NY (Continued)

Firm Profile: Marshall Dennehey opened its 20th office, and third in New York State, in July 2014 in Westchester County, New York. Located in Rye Brook, in what is arguably the region's most recognized corporate landmark office building at 800 Westchester Avenue (white-domed, post-modern design originally built as General Foods' worldwide headquarters), the new location complements and expands upon the firm's existing offerings in Manhattan and Melville, Long Island.

Marshall Dennehey's expansion in New York is precipitated by the considerable growth in Westchester and the surrounding community as a regional commercial center over the past few decades. The county serves as a vibrant cross-section of business operations for numerous companies headquartered in Manhattan and across the Northeast corridor.

Additional information about the Westchester office is available by contacting Jim Connors, managing attorney of this office, at (914) 977-7310 or jpconnors@mdwcg.com

Managing Shareholder

James P. Connors — Managing Attorney — Herbert H. Lehman College of the City University of New York, B.A., 1974; New York Law School, J.D. (cum laude), 1977; New York University School of Law, LL.M., 1985 — New York Metro Area Super Lawyers, 2006, 2010-2011 — Admitted to Bar, 1978, New York; 1988, Pennsylvania; 1978, U.S. District Court, Eastern, Southern and Western Districts of New York; U.S. Court of Appeals for the District of Columbia Circuit; 2004, U.S. Supreme Court — Member American Bar Association (Sections on Litigation and Tort and Insurance Practice); New Yorkl State Bar Association (Committee on Aviation Law, Insurance Negligence and Compensation Law Section and Trial Lawyers Section); Defense Association of New York; New York County Lawyers Association — Author: "Assumption of Risk: New Thinking on Old Concept," New York Law Journal, p. 1, August 15, 1997; "Workers' Compensation Reform Legislation," New York State Bar Journal, Vol. 69, No. 1, January 1997; "Medical Malpractice Remifications of President Clinton's Health Security Act," ABA, Torts and Insurance Practice Section, Trial Techniques Committee, p. 4, Spring, 1994; "Medical Malpractice Effects of Clinton's HAS," New York Law Journal, p. 1, February 25, 1994; "Assault on an Effective Way to Expose Fraud," New York Law Journal, p. 1, December 1, 1993; "Department Dispute: Let's Go to the Video Tape," New York State Bar Journal, p. 42, July/August 1992; "Edmonson v. Leesville Concrete Co.: Effect on the Civil Jury Selection Process." New York Law Journal, p. 1, August 9, 1991; "Marte v. W.O. Hickok: Should We Fear Flying Horses? - Discoverability of Video Tapes," New York Law Journal, August 7, 1990, p. 1, col. 1, republished INCL Journal, Vol. 19, No. 2, December 1990, p. 44; "Impact of Mandatory Periodic Payment of Judgments," New York Law Journal, August 16, 1988, p. 1, col. L; "Pandora's Box Opened in Expansion of Recovery for Emotional Distress," New York Law Journal, August 4, 1987, p. 1, col. L; "An Analysis of New York's Medical Malpractice Reform," New York Law Journal, August 15, 1986, p. 1, col. L; "New York's Controversial Medical Malpractice Bill," New York State Law Journal, Vol, 58, No. 2, February 1986; Medical-Legal Forum, Medical Malpractice Reform Laws," Manhattan Medicine, Vol. 4, No. 1, November 1985; "Hospital Liability," Medical Trial Technique Quarterly, Spring 1984, pg. 393; "The Bad Faith Action—Insurers' Nettlesome Problem," New York Law Journal, September 20, 1983, p. 1, col. 1; "Hospital Liability, Treatment of the Institution, Past Present and Future," The Nassau Lawyer, Vol. 29, 1981; "Should Physicians Have the Right to Approve Insurance Settlements for Alleged Malpractice/Point-Counterpoint," Law, Medicine, and Health Care, October 1981; "The Expanding Parameters of Hospital Liability," New York Law Journal, April 21, 1981, p. 1, col. 1; "Opinoin Evidence: It's Time to Change Rule on Admissibility," New York Law Journal, January 13, 1981, p. 1, col. 1 — Seminars/Classes Taught: Hyatt Security Seminar, New York, 1994, 1992; Defending Catastrophic Injury Cases, CIGNA Senior Attorney Training Program, January 1992; Malpractice in Ophthalmology, American Academy of Ophthalmology, co-presented with Vivien Boniuk, M.D., J.D, Annual Conference, New Orleans, November 1986; Dallas, October 1987; Las Vegas, October 1988; New Orleans, October 1989; and Atlanta, October 1990; The New York State Medical Malpractice Reform Act of 1985, Association of Hospital Risk Managers, presented at Mount Sinai Hospital, November 1985; Hospital Liability Seminar, New York Law Journal, July 1985; Medical Malpractice: Its Avoidance Through Foresight, Bellevue Hospital, September 1984; Workshop in Medical Malpractice, Law & Medicine, New York University School of Law, Graduate Division, and New York University School of Medicine, August 1982 — FAA Licensed Pilot — Practice Areas: Premises Liability; Aviation; Complex Litigation; Product Liability; Health Care Liability; Professional

NEW YORK

WHITE PLAINS

Marshall Dennehey Warner Coleman & Goggin, Westchester, NY *(Continued)*

Liability; Employment Law; Negligent Security — E-mail: jpconnors@mdwcg.com

Special Counsel

Angela M. Evangelista

Shareholders

Daniel S. Corde Charles T. Gura

(See listing under Philadelphia, PA for additional information)

(Revisors of the Pennsylvania Insurance Law Digest for this Publication)

WHITE PLAINS † 56,853 Westchester Co.

Boeggeman, George & Corde, P.C.

1 Water Street, Suite 425
White Plains, New York 10601
Telephone: 914-761-2252
Fax: 914-761-5211
E-Mail: boeggeman@bgclawfirm.com
www.bgclawfirm.com

(Albany, NY Office*: 39 North Pearl Street, Suite 501, 12207)
(Tel: 518-465-1100)
(Fax: 518-465-1800)

Established: 1959

Insurance Defense, Trial Practice, Automobile, Product Liability, Legal Malpractice, Medical Malpractice, Employment Law, Real Estate, Toxic Torts, Engineering Malpractice

Firm Profile: The BOEGGEMAN, GEORGE & CORDE law firm was founded in 1959 and has maintained its principal office in White Plains, New York since its inception. This firm also has an office in Albany. The practice focuses on trials and appeals in all courts throughout New York and Connecticut in such areas as products liability, toxic exposure, premises liability, municipal liability, motor vehicle accidents, lead poisoning, professional liability, labor law actions, asbestos claims, insurance coverage issues, sexual harassment and employment related litigation, environmental litigation, pharmaceutical malpractice, medical malpractice, insurance disclaimers, property damage including subrogation and general liability.

Insurance Clients

Broadspire
Gallagher Bassett Insurance Company
New York Central Mutual Fire Insurance Company
State Farm Insurance Company
Summit Risk Services, Inc.
Crawford & Company
Lancer Insurance Company
Metropolitan Property and Casualty Insurance Company
Selective Insurance Company of America
United Services Automobile Association (USAA)

Non-Insurance Clients

Adirondack Trailways
Anheuser-Busch, Inc.
Avis Rent-A-Car System, LLC
Electrolux North America
Laidlaw Transit Services, Inc.
O'Brien & Gere Engineers, Inc.
Akzo Nobel
AT&T
Eckerd Pharmacies
Fisher-Price, Inc.
Lowe's Home Centers, Inc.

Partners

John E. Boeggeman — (1919-1993)

Richard G. Corde — 1959 — University of Delaware, B.S., 1981; University of Bridgeport School of Law, J.D., 1984 — Admitted to Bar, 1985, New York; Connecticut — Member American, New York State, Putnam County and Westchester County Bar Associations; Defense Association of New York (Board of Directors, 2000-2003); Federation of Defense and Corporate Counsel; Connecticut Trial Lawyers Association; Defense Research Institute — E-mail: rcorde@bgclawfirm.com

Boeggeman, George & Corde, P.C., White Plains, NY *(Continued)*

Robert S. Ondrovic — 1960 — Fordham University, B.A., 1982; Fordham University School of Law, J.D., 1985 — Admitted to Bar, 1985, New Jersey; 1986, New York; U.S. District Court, District of New Jersey; 1989, U.S. District Court, Central and Southern Districts of New York; U.S. Court of Appeals, Second Circuit; 1990, U.S. Supreme Court — Member Westchester County Bar Association; New York County Lawyers Association — E-mail: rondrovic@bgclawfirm.com

Karen A. Jockimo — 1967 — Connecticut College, B.A. (magna cum laude), 1989; Pace University School of Law, J.D. (cum laude), 1993 — Admitted to Bar, 1994, New York; 1995, Connecticut — Member American and New York State Bar Associations; Westchester Womens Bar Association — E-mail: kjockimo@bgclawfirm.com

Paul A. Hurley — 1965 — Niagara University, B.S., 1987; St. John's University School of Law, J.D., 1990 — Admitted to Bar, 1991, New York — Member American, New York State and Rockland County Bar Associations — E-mail: phurley@bgclawfirm.com

Associates

Daniel E. O'Neill — 1957 — Hunter College of the City University of New York, B.A., 1987; Brooklyn Law School, J.D., 1993 — Admitted to Bar, 1993, New Jersey; 1994, New York; 1995, U.S. District Court, Eastern and Southern Districts of New York — E-mail: doneill@bgclawfirm.com

Michael F. McCusker — 1962 — University of Notre Dame, B.A., 1984; Pace University School of Law, J.D., 1987 — Admitted to Bar, 1987, Connecticut; 1988, New York; 1991, U.S. District Court, Southern District of New York — Member New York State and Connecticut Bar Associations — E-mail: mmccusker@bgclawfirm.com

Crystal Simpkin — 1985 — Florida Southern College, B.S., 2007; University of Miami School of Law, J.D. (cum laude), 2010 — Admitted to Bar, 2011, New York — Member New York State Bar Association — E-mail: csimpkin@bgclawfirm.com

Of Counsel

Joseph H. George — (Retired)

Cynthia Dolan — 1968 — Pace University, B.A., 1991; M.S.T., 1992; Pace University School of Law, J.D., 1996 — Admitted to Bar, 1997, New York; Connecticut; 2000, U.S. District Court, Eastern, Northern, Southern and Western Districts of New York; U.S. Court of Appeals, Second Circuit — Member American Bar Association; Westchester Women's Bar Association; Women's Bar Association of Orange and Sullivan Counties — E-mail: cdolan@bgclawfirm.com

Thomas M. Bona, P.C.

12 Water Street
White Plains, New York 10601
Telephone: 914-428-1438
Fax: 914-428-1413
E-Mail: tmbona@bonapc.net
www.thomasmbonapc.com

(Newburgh, NY Office: 84 Plattekill Turnpike, 12550)
(Tel: 914-562-5910)
(Uniondale, NY Office: PMB # 4002, 50 Charles Lindbergh Boulevard, Suite 4, 11553)
(Tel: 516-227-1040)

Established: 1988

Insurance Defense, Automobile, General Liability

Firm Profile: The firm consists of 9 attorneys and 4 paralegals. The firm is committed to providing excellent representation while controlling defense costs by eliminating work which is not necessary to the proper defense of the action.

Insurance Clients

Amica Mutual Insurance Company
Carl Warren & Company
Community Association Underwriters of America, Inc.
Eastern Mutual Insurance Company
Andover Companies
The Colony Group
Crawford & Company
Donegal Mutual Insurance Company
Erie Insurance Company

WHITE PLAINS   NEW YORK

Thomas M. Bona, P.C., White Plains, NY (Continued)

Essex Insurance Company
Hess Insurance Company
Holyoke Mutual Insurance Company in Salem
New York Mutual Underwriters
Rockville Risk Management Associates, Inc.
State of New York Insurance Department Liquidation Bureau
Great American Insurance Company
Liberty Mutual Insurance Company
MetLife Auto & Home
Penn Millers Insurance Company
Safeco Insurance
Specialty Insurance
Universal Underwriters Insurance Company

Non-Insurance Clients

New York Metropolitan Transit Authority
Village of Pelham Manor

Firm Member

Thomas M. Bona — 1955 — Colgate University, A.B., 1977; St. John's University, M.B.A., 1979; St. John's University School of Law, J.D., 1982 — Admitted to Bar, 1983, New York; 1984, U.S. District Court, Eastern and Southern Districts of New York; 2003, U.S. District Court, Northern District of New York; 2004, U.S. District Court, Western District of New York — Member American, New York State and Westchester County Bar Associations

Associates

Anthony M. Napoli — 1962 — Fordham University, B.A., 1984; St. John's University School of Law, J.D., 1988 — Admitted to Bar, 1989, New York; 1995, U.S. District Court, Eastern and Southern Districts of New York; 2004, U.S. District Court, Western District of New York; 2005, U.S. District Court, Northern District of New York

James C. Miller — 1952 — City College of the City University of New York, B.A., 1970; New York University, M.A., 1975; Brooklyn Law School, J.D., 1984 — Admitted to Bar, 1985, New York; 1989, U.S. District Court, Eastern and Southern Districts of New York; 2004, U.S. District Court, Western District of New York; 2005, U.S. District Court, Northern District of New York

Michael Kestenbaum — 1958 — University of Bridgeport, B.A., 1983; University of Bridgeport School of Law, J.D., 1986 — Admitted to Bar, 1987, New York; U.S. District Court, Eastern and Southern Districts of New York

Kimberly C. Sheehan — 1959 — State University of New York at Binghamton, Harpur College, B.A., 1981; State University of New York at Buffalo Law School, J.D., 1984 — Admitted to Bar, 1985, New York; 1987, U.S. District Court, Eastern and Southern Districts of New York

Debra C. Salvi — 1968 — Bloomsburg University of Pennsylvania, B.A., 1990; Widener University School of Law, J.D., 1997 — Admitted to Bar, 1997, Pennsylvania; New Jersey; 1999, New York

Elliot Gaztambide Jr. — 1969 — State University of New York at Albany, B.A., 1991; St. John's University School of Law, J.D., 1994 — Admitted to Bar, 1995, New York; U.S. District Court, Eastern and Southern Districts of New York

Michael A. Flake — 1972 — Ball State University, B.S., 1994; Brooklyn College Law School, J.D., 2002 — Admitted to Bar, 2003, New York; 2004, U.S. District Court, Eastern and Southern Districts of New York

Stephanie Bellantoni — 1970 — St. John's University School of Law, J.D. (Dean's List), 1995 — Admitted to Bar, 1996, New York

Collins, Fitzpatrick & Schoene, LLP

34 South Broadway, Suite 407
White Plains, New York 10601
   Telephone: 914-437-8020
   Fax: 914-437-8022
   E-Mail: cfs@cfsllp-law.com
   www.cfsllp-law.com

Established: 2011

Appellate Practice, Architects and Engineers, Automobile, Dental Malpractice, Insurance Coverage, Legal Malpractice, Medical Malpractice, Municipal Liability, Premises Liability, Product Liability, Professional Malpractice, Real Estate

Firm Profile: Our hardworking New York law firm is dedicated to helping insurers protect their exposure and advising businesses about their insurance coverage status. The firm's lawyers take a meticulous approach to the analysis of every insurance claim, providing thoughtful coverage opinions and tenacious litigation. Our attention to detail is the hallmark of our strategy for addressing coverage issues and the successful defense of filed claims.

Insurance Clients

Allstate Insurance Company
Encompass Insurance
American Claims Service, Inc.
Eveready Insurance Company

Non-Insurance Clients

Mount Vernon Urban Renewal Agency
St. Joseph's Medical Center

Partners

Charles A. Collins, Jr. — New York University, B.A. (Phi Beta Kappa), 1972; Fordham University School of Law, J.D., 1975 — New York University Founders Day Award for Scholastic Excellence — Admitted to Bar, 1976, New York; 1980, U.S. District Court, Eastern and Southern Districts of New York — Member New York State and Westchester County Bar Associations — Chairman, Town of Mount Pleasant Zoning Board

Kevin P. Fitzpatrick — College of the Holy Cross, B.A., 1988; St. John's University School of Law, J.D., 1992 — Member, St. John's Journal of Legal Commentary, 1990-1991 — Admitted to Bar, 1992, New Jersey; 1993, New York; U.S. District Court, Eastern and Southern Districts of New York — Member New York State Bar Association

Ralph F. Schoene — Manhattan College, B.S., 1975; New York Law School, J.D., 1978 — Admitted to Bar, 1978, Connecticut; 1979, New York; Illinois; 1978, U.S. District Court, Southern District of Illinois; 1980, U.S. District Court, Eastern and Southern Districts of New York; U.S. Court of Appeals, Second Circuit — Member Westchester County Bar Association

Jones Morrison, LLP

670 White Plains Road, Penthouse
Scarsdale, New York 10583
   Telephone: 914-472-2300
   Fax: 914-472-2312
   E-Mail: info@jonesmorrisonlaw.com
   www.jonesmorrisonlaw.com

(Stamford, CT Office*: 60 Long Ridge Road, Suite 202, 06902)
   (Tel: 203-965-7700)
(New York, NY Office*: 60 East 42nd Street, 40th Floor, 10165)
   (Tel: 212-759-2500)

Established: 2001

Alternative Dispute Resolution, Architects and Engineers, Asbestos, Bad Faith, Bankruptcy, Business Law, Commercial Litigation, Construction Law, Creditor's Rights, Coverage Analysis, Directors and Officers Liability, Environmental Law, Errors and Omissions, Labor and Employment, Medical Malpractice, Motor Vehicle, Municipal Liability, Premises Liability, Product Liability, Professional Liability, Property Damage

Firm Profile: Jones Morrison, LLP was founded to serve the legal needs of our clients in an efficient, coordinated, full service and first quality manner. We believe that we can only meet our clients' objectives by the efforts of dedicated attorneys committed to being leaders in their disciplines.

Insurance Clients

Everest National Insurance Company
Markel Insurance Company
Sompo Japan Insurance Company of America
GEICO
The Hartford
Selective Insurance Company of America
Travelers Indemnity Company

Managing Partner

Stephen J. Jones — Williams College, B.A., 1987; Fordham University School of Law, J.D., 1993 — Admitted to Bar, 1994, New York; U.S. District Court,

Jones Morrison, LLP, White Plains, NY (Continued)

Eastern and Southern Districts of New York; U.S. Supreme Court — Member The Business Council of Westchester (Chairman of the Board; Executive Committee Member); United Way of Westchester and Putnam (Director); Westchester-Putnam Council of the Boys Scouts of America (Director, Executive Committee Member); Westchester County Industrial Development Agency (Board Member); Legal Services of the Hudson Valley (Past Director); Justice Court for the Village of Tarrytown, New York State Unified Court System (Past Justice); Westchester-Putnam Fordham Law Alumni (Past President); The Williams Club of New York (Past Board of Governors) — Eagle Scout — Practice Areas: Corporate Law; Commercial Transactions; Litigation; Real Estate

Partners

Daniel W. Morrison — Haverford College, B.A., 1980; Fordham University School of Law, J.D., 1984 — Admitted to Bar, 1985, New York; Connecticut; U.S. District Court, Eastern, Northern, Southern and Western Districts of New York; U.S. Supreme Court — Member American and New York State (Co-Chair, Environmental Insurance Committee) Bar Associations; Claims & Litigation Management Alliance; American Corporate Counsel Association; Westchest-Putman Fordham Law Alumni Association (Past President) — Practice Areas: Insurance Law; Product Liability; Professional Liability; Environmental Law; Construction Law; Commercial Litigation; Corporate Litigation; Real Estate; Bad Faith

Clifford I. Bass — Tufts University, B.A. (magna cum laude), 1974; Albany Law School of Union University, J.D., 1978 — Admitted to Bar, 1978, New York; U.S. District Court, Eastern and Southern Districts of New York — Member New York State and Westchester County Bar Associations; Insurance Broker's Association of New York; Defense Association of New York — Practice Areas: Tort Litigation; Insurance Coverage; Trial and Appellate Practice; Premises Liability; Product Liability; Professional Liability; Construction Accidents; Automobile Liability

Steven T. Sledzik — Georgetown University, B.A., 1984; Georgetown University Law Center, J.D., 1990 — Admitted to Bar, 1990, Connecticut; 1992, New York; U.S. District Court, District of Connecticut; U.S. District Court, Eastern and Southern Districts of New York; U.S. Court of Appeals, Second Circuit — Member New York State and New York City Bar Associations; Federal Bar Council — Former Board of Director President of the non-profit children's theater company, Westco Productions; Provided pro bono services for New York City's Volunteer Lawyers for the Arts — Practice Areas: Employment Litigation; Commercial Litigation; Civil Rights; Contract Disputes; Complex Litigation

Attorneys

Marcy Blake — Columbia University School of Engineering and Applied Science, B.S., 1978; M.S., 1980; Pace University School of Law, J.D. (summa cum laude), 1993 — Admitted to Bar, 1994, New York; U.S. District Court, Southern District of New York — Member Westchester County Bar Association — Practice Areas: Commercial Litigation; Contracts; Labor and Employment; Premises Liability; Product Liability

Stefano F. Costa — University of Michigan, B.A., 2000; Fordham University School of Law, J.D., 2008 — Admitted to Bar, 2008, Connecticut; 2010, New York; 2013, U.S. District Court, Southern District of New York

Pino & Associates, LLP
Attorneys and Counsellors at Law

Westchester Financial Center
50 Main Street
White Plains, New York 10606
Telephone: 914-946-0600
Fax: 914-946-0650
E-Mail: rpino@pinolaw.com
www.pinolaw.com

Established: 1992

Pino & Associates, LLP, Attorneys and Counsellors at Law, White Plains, NY (Continued)

Insurance Defense, General Liability, Product Liability, Railroad Law, Property Damage, Bodily Injury, Arbitration, Alternative Dispute Resolution, Aviation, Construction Litigation, Employment Law, Environmental Law, Toxic Torts, Municipal Law, Professional Liability (Non-Medical) Defense, Premises Liability, Dram Shop Liability, Liquor Liability, Reinsurance, Insurance Coverage, Complex Litigation, Subrogation, Aerospace Litigation, Export Compliance

Firm Profile: Pino & Associates, LLP is a White Plains, New York-based law firm focusing on all facets of civil and commercial litigation. Our seasoned litigators achieve timely and cost-effective solutions to our clients' legal and business needs. We have the breadth and depth of experience to handle the most demanding and complex litigation and arbitration.

Insurance Clients

ACE USA Aerospace	Aerospace Claims Management Group
Amica Mutual Insurance Company	Assicurazioni Generali S.p.A.
Arch Insurance Group	AXA Space, Inc.
Assurances Generales de France IART	AXIS Insurance
Brit Space Consortium	Chartis Global Recovery Services
Chubb Insurance Company	Generali Global Risk
Generali - US Branch	Global Aerospace, Inc.
Global Aerospace Underwriting Managers, Ltd.	Hannover Re
Hiscox Syndicates Limited	The Hiscox ATMT Space Consortium 9221
La Reunion Francaise	Muenchener Rueckversicherungs - Gesellschaft
Munich Reinsurance Company	
SCOR Global P&C	SCOR Re Companies
Starr Aviation Agency, Inc.	State Auto Insurance Companies
Tokio Marine & Nichido Fire Insurance Co., Ltd	Underwriters at Lloyd's Catlin Syndicate
Underwriters at Lloyd's Liberty Syndicates	Underwriters at Lloyd's Watkins Syndicate
United States Aviation Underwriters, Inc.	United States Liability Insurance Group
Winterthur International America Insurance Company	XL Aerospace
	Zurich North America

Non-Insurance Clients

AgustaWestland Philadelphia Corporation	AgustaWestland SpA
Black & Decker (U.S.), Inc.	Barcelo Hotels & Resorts
Christian Brothers Risk Pooling Trust	Charlotte Adjusting, Inc.
	Colt Manufacturing, Inc.
Danieli & C. S.p.A.	Danieli Corporation
De'Longi America, Inc.	DeLonghi, S.p.A.
Honeywell, Inc.	Gateway, Inc.
Jack in the Box, Inc.	International Lifestyles, Inc.
Marx Realty & Improvement Co., Inc.	The Macerich Company
Midland Credit Management, Inc.	MEASAT Satellite Systems Sdn. Bhd.
	Zero Motorcycles, Inc.

Firm Members

Rudolph V. Pino, Jr. — 1951 — Fairfield University, B.A., 1973; New York Law School, J.D., 1977 — Admitted to Bar, 1978, New York; U.S. District Court, Eastern District of New York; U.S. Supreme Court; 1979, U.S. District Court, Southern District of New York — E-mail: RPino@pinolaw.com

Thomas E. Healy — 1964 — Cornell University, B.S., 1986; Fordham Law School, J.D., 1990 — Admitted to Bar, 1991, New York; Connecticut; 1992, U.S. District Court, Eastern and Southern Districts of New York; 1996, U.S. Supreme Court; 1997, U.S. District Court, Northern District of New York; 1999, U.S. Court of Appeals, Fourth Circuit; 2002, U.S. Court of Appeals, Second Circuit; 2006, U.S. District Court, Western District of New York — E-mail: THealy@pinolaw.com

Richard T. Petrillo — 1968 — Princeton University, A.B., 1990; Fordham Law School, J.D., 1993 — Admitted to Bar, 1994, New York; 1999, U.S. District Court, Eastern and Southern Districts of New York — Assistant District Attorney, Bronx County (1993-1999) — E-mail: RPetrillo@pinolaw.com

Brian W. Colistra — 1969 — Canisius College, B.A., 1991; New York Law School, J.D., 1995 — Admitted to Bar, 1998, New York; U.S. District Court, Eastern, Northern, Southern and Western Districts of New York — E-mail: BColistra@pinolaw.com

John M. Socolow — 1961 — University of Pennsylvania, B.A., 1983; Fordham Law School, J.D., 1986 — Admitted to Bar, 1986, Massachusetts; 1987, New

Pino & Associates, LLP, Attorneys and Counsellors at Law, White Plains, NY (Continued)

York; 1987, U.S. District Court, Eastern and Southern Districts of New York; 1998, U.S. District Court, Western District of New York; 2008, U.S. Court of Appeals, Fifth Circuit; 2009, U.S. District Court, District of Connecticut; 2009, U.S. Court of Appeals, Second Circuit — Languages: Spanish — E-mail: JSocolow@pinolaw.com

Of Counsel

Matthew D. Kennedy — 1972 — Georgetown University, B.A., 1996; Brooklyn Law School, J.D., 2002 — Admitted to Bar, 2002, New York; 2005, U.S. District Court, Southern District of New York; 2009, U.S. District Court, Northern District of New York; 2011, U.S. District Court, Eastern District of New York; 2013, U.S. District Court, Western District of Michigan — Languages: Spanish — E-mail: MKennedy@pinolaw.com

Associates

Marc A. Rousseau — 1969 — Messiah College, B.S., 1991; Hofstra University School of Law, J.D., 1996 — Admitted to Bar, 1996, Connecticut; 1997, New York; U.S. District Court, Eastern, Northern, Southern and Western Districts of New York — E-mail: MRousseau@pinolaw.com

Brian P. Mitchell — 1978 — Fordham University, B.A., 2002; Universidad Iberoamericana; St. John's University School of Law, J.D., 2007 — Admitted to Bar, 2007, New Jersey; 2008, New York; 2009, District of Columbia; 2007, U.S. District Court, District of New Jersey; 2008, U.S. District Court, Eastern and Southern Districts of New York; 2009, U.S. District Court, Northern District of New York — E-mail: BMitchell@pinolaw.com

William Salerno — 1965 — State University of New York at Albany, B.A., 1987; Pace University School of Law, J.D., 2009 — Admitted to Bar, 2009, New Jersey; 2010, New York; 2009, U.S. District Court, District of New Jersey; 2010, U.S. District Court, Eastern and Southern Districts of New York — E-mail: WSalerno@pinolaw.com

Neha M. Chaubey — 1985 — Nagpur University, LL.B., 2008; Widener University School of Law, LL.M., 2010 — Admitted to Bar, 2008, Bar Council of Maharashtra and Goa, India; 2012, New York — Languages: Hindi, Marathi — E-mail: NChaubey@pinolaw.com

(This firm is also listed in the Subrogation section of this directory)

Wilson, Bave, Conboy, Cozza & Couzens, P.C.

Two William Street, 5th Floor
White Plains, New York 10601
Telephone: 914-686-9010
Fax: 914-686-0873
E-Mail: wbccc@wbccc.com
www.wbccc.com

Established: 1947

Casualty Insurance Law, Automobile Liability, Civil Litigation, Defense Litigation, Employer Liability, Employment Discrimination, Hospital Malpractice, Insurance Coverage, Insurance Defense, Malpractice, Medical Malpractice, Municipal Liability, Negligence, Premises Liability, Product Liability, Tort Litigation, Trial Practice

Firm Profile: Welcome to Wilson, Bave, Conboy, Cozza & Couzens, P.C., with offices at Two William Street, White Plains New York. Founded in Yonkers, NY in 1947 by the late William H. Bave, Sr. and Donald C. Wilson, Wilson, Bave, Conboy, Cozza & Couzens, P.C. is one of the premier personal injury defense firms in the New York metropolitan area with a proven record of success. The attorneys of Wilson, Bave, Conboy, Cozza & Couzens, P.C. have significant courtroom experience in defending personal injury and wrongful death claims in a broad spectrum of areas including automobile accidents, construction accidents, product liability, premises liability, medical malpractice and other tort claims, as well as coverage issues.

The firm handles matters in Westchester, Rockland, Putnam, Dutchess, Orange and Ulster counties, as well as in the five boroughs of New York, in both State and Federal Courts.

Wilson, Bave, Conboy, Cozza & Couzens, P.C. is dedicated to providing quality legal services. The firm's use of technology, including effective case,

Wilson, Bave, Conboy, Cozza & Couzens, P.C., White Plains, NY (Continued)

time and billing management software, and internet based legal research and docket management, enhances the attorneys' effectiveness and efficiency, as well as their communication with clients.

Insurance Clients

HCC Insurance Company
Metropolitan Property and Casualty Insurance Company
Specialty Insurance Company
State Farm Mutual Automobile Insurance Company
Medical Liability Mutual Insurance Company
QBE Insurance (International) Ltd.
Starr Indemnity & Liability Company

Non-Insurance Clients

City of Mount Vernon
City of Peekskill
County of Westchester
Westchester County Health Care Corporation
City of New Rochelle
City of Yonkers
Ryder Truck Rental, Inc.

Firm Members

Donald C. Wilson — (1917-1994)

William H. Bave — (1919-1991)

R. Kevin Conboy — (1946-2007)

William H. Bave, Jr. — 1948 — Providence College, B.A., 1970; Fordham University, J.D., 1973 — Admitted to Bar, 1974, New York; 1975, U.S. District Court, Eastern and Southern Districts of New York — Member New York State and Westchester County Bar Associations; International Association of Defense Counsel; Fellow, American College of Trial Lawyers — Assistant District Attorney, Westchester County (1973-1978)

Michael J. Cozza — 1952 — Iona College, B.A., 1974; Fordham University, J.D., 1978 — Admitted to Bar, 1979, New York; U.S. District Court, Eastern and Southern Districts of New York — Member New York State and Westchester County Bar Associations

John C. Couzens, Jr. — 1951 — Georgetown University, B.S.B.A., 1973; Fordham University, J.D., 1976 — Admitted to Bar, 1977, New York; 1979, U.S. District Court, Southern District of New York — Member New York State and Westchester County Bar Associations — General Counsel, Yonkers Board of Education (1980-1983)

Associates

Alexandra C. Karamitsos — 1968 — Fordham University, B.A. (cum laude), 1989; J.D., 1992 — Admitted to Bar, 1992, Connecticut; 1993, New York — Member New York State, Connecticut and Westchester County Bar Associations — Languages: Greek

James A. Rogers — 1971 — Fordham University, B.A., 1993; Long Island University, M.B.A., 2001; Quinnipiac University, J.D., 1999 — Admitted to Bar, 2000, New York; U.S. District Court, Eastern and Southern Districts of New York — Member New York State and Westchester County Bar Associations — Languages: Spanish

Robert J. Gironda — 1961 — State University of New York at Westchester, A.A.S. (summa cum laude), 1996; Mercy College, B.S. (summa cum laude), 1998; Pace University, J.D. (cum laude), 2001 — Admitted to Bar, 2001, Connecticut; 2002, New York — Member American, New York State and New York County Bar Associations; American Trial Lawyers Association

Claudine L. Weis — 1970 — Pace University, B.A., 1995; J.D., 1998 — Admitted to Bar, 1998, New York; U.S. District Court, Southern District of New York; 2001, U.S. District Court, Northern District of New York — Member New York State and Westchester County Bar Associations

Donna Cook — 1984 — Cazenovia College, B.S. (summa cum laude), 2006; Pace University, J.D. (cum laude), 2009 — Admitted to Bar, 2009, Connecticut; 2010, New York; U.S. District Court, Eastern and Southern Districts of New York — Member American, New York State and Westchester County Bar Associations — Languages: Spanish

NEW YORK

WHITE PLAINS

The following firms also service this area.

Catania, Mahon, Milligram & Rider, PLLC
One Corwin Court
Newburgh, New York 12550
  Telephone: 845-565-1100
  Fax: 845-565-1999

Mailing Address: P.O. Box 1479, Newburgh, NY 12551

Insurance Defense, Insurance Coverage, School Law, Municipal Law, Construction Litigation

SEE COMPLETE LISTING UNDER NEWBURGH, NEW YORK (50 MILES)

Cook, Netter, Cloonan, Kurtz & Murphy, P.C.
85 Main Street
Kingston, New York 12401
  Telephone: 845-331-0702
  Fax: 845-331-1003

Mailing Address: P.O. Box 3939, Kingston, NY 12402

Business Transactions, Civil Litigation, Construction Accidents, Motor Vehicle, Municipal Law, Personal Injury, Premises Liability, Product Liability, Professional Liability, Public Entities, Real Estate, Sexual Harassment, State and Federal Courts, Title Insurance, Federal Civil Rights

SEE COMPLETE LISTING UNDER KINGSTON, NEW YORK (88 MILES)

McCabe & Mack LLP
63 Washington Street
Poughkeepsie, New York 12601
  Telephone: 845-486-6800
  Fax: 845-486-7621

Mailing Address: P.O. Box 509, Poughkeepsie, NY 12602-0509

Insurance Defense, Negligence, Product Liability, General Liability, Municipal Liability, Casualty, Surety, Civil Rights, Subrogation, Environmental Law, Premises Liability, Labor Law

SEE COMPLETE LISTING UNDER POUGHKEEPSIE, NEW YORK (56 MILES)

NORTH CAROLINA

CAPITAL: RALEIGH

COUNTIES AND COUNTY SEATS

County	County Seat	County	County Seat	County	County Seat
Alamance	Graham	Franklin	Louisburg	Pamlico	Bayboro
Alexander	Taylorsville	Gaston	Gastonia	Pasquotank	Elizabeth City
Alleghany	Sparta	Gates	Gatesville	Pender	Burgaw
Anson	Wadesboro	Graham	Robbinsville	Perquinans	Hertford
Ashe	Jefferson	Granville	Oxford	Person	Roxboro
Avery	Newland	Greene	Snowhill	Pitt	Greenville
Beaufort	Washington	Guilford	Greensboro	Polk	Columbus
Bertie	Windsor	Halifax	Halifax	Randolph	Asheboro
Bladen	Elizabethtown	Harnett	Lillington	Richmond	Rockingham
Brunswick	Southport	Haywood	Waynesville	Robeson	Lumberton
Buncombe	Asheville	Henderson	Hendersonville	Rockingham	Wentworth
Burke	Morganton	Hertford	Winton	Rowan	Salisbury
Cabarras	Concord	Hoke	Raeford	Rutherford	Rutherfordton
Caldwell	Lenoir	Hyde	Swanquarter	Sampson	Clinton
Camden	Camden	Iredell	Statesville	Scotland	Laurinburg
Carteret	Beaufort	Jackson	Sylva	Stanly	Albemarle
Caswell	Yanceyville	Johnston	Smithfield	Stokes	Danbury
Catawba	Newton	Jones	Trenton	Surry	Dobson
Chatham	Pittsboro	Lee	Sanford	Swain	Bryson City
Cherokee	Murphy	Lenoir	Kinston	Transylvania	Brevard
Chowan	Edenton	Lincoln	Lincolnton	Tyrrell	Columbia
Clay	Hayesville	Macon	Franklin	Union	Monroe
Cleveland	Shelby	Madison	Marshall	Vance	Henderson
Columbus	Whiteville	Martin	Williamston	Wake	Raleigh
Craven	New Bern	McDowell	Marion	Warren	Warrenton
Cumberland	Fayetteville	Mecklenburg	Charlotte	Washington	Plymouth
Currituck	Currituck	Mitchell	Bakersville	Watauga	Boone
Dare	Manteo	Montgomery	Troy	Wayne	Goldsboro
Davidson	Lexington	Moore	Carthage	Wilkes	Wilkesboro
Davie	Mocksville	Nash	Nashville	Wilson	Wilson
Duplin	Kenansville	New Hanover	Wilmington	Yadkin	Yadkinville
Durham	Durham	Northhampton	Jackson	Yancey	Burnsville
Edgecombe	Tarboro	Onslow	Jacksonville		
Forsyth	Winston-Salem	Orange	Hillsborough		

In the text that follows "†" indicates County Seats.

Our files contain additional verified data on the firms listed herein. This additional information is available on request.

A.M. BEST COMPANY

NORTH CAROLINA

ASHEBORO

ASHEBORO † 25,012 Randolph Co.

Refer To

Henson & Talley, L.L.P.
Suite 600 Piedmont Building
114 North Elm Street
Greensboro, North Carolina 27401
  Telephone: 336-275-0587
  Fax: 336-273-2585

Mailing Address: P.O. Box 3525, Greensboro, NC 27402-3525

Trial and Appellate Practice, State and Federal Courts, Insurance Defense, Automobile, Trucking Law, Workers' Compensation, Construction Law, Professional Malpractice, Product Liability, Fire, Insurance Coverage, Subrogation

SEE COMPLETE LISTING UNDER GREENSBORO, NORTH CAROLINA (31 MILES)

ASHEVILLE † 83,393 Buncombe Co.

Leake & Stokes

501 BB&T Building
Asheville, North Carolina 28801
  Telephone: 828-253-3661

(Marshall, NC Office*: Main Street, P.O. Box 451, 28753)
  (Tel: 828-649-3883)

Established: 1974

Insurance Defense, Automobile, General Liability, Product Liability, Fire, Casualty, Medical Malpractice, Workers' Compensation, Subrogation

Insurance Clients

Atlantic Casualty Insurance Company
Burlington Insurance Company
CNA Insurance Company
Maryland Casualty Company
Providian Auto & Home Insurance Company
Southern Heritage Insurance Company
United States Fidelity and Guaranty Company
Bankers and Shippers Insurance Company of New York
Casualty Insurance Consultants
Foremost Insurance Company
Progressive Insurance Company
St. Paul Insurance Company
Seaboard Underwriters, Inc.
Titan Insurance Company
United States Aviation Underwriters, Inc.

Non-Insurance Clients

Bekins Van Lines
French Broad Electric Membership Corporation
Delta Air Lines, Inc.
Graward General Companies
Hot Springs Health Program

Partners

A. E. Leake — (1911-1992)

Robert E. Harrell — (1925-2000)

Larry B. Leake — 1950 — The University of North Carolina, B.A., 1972; J.D., 1974 — Phi Beta Kappa — Admitted to Bar, 1974, North Carolina — Member American and Buncombe County Bar Associations; North Carolina State Bar; North Carolina Association of Defense Attorneys; Defense Research Institute

Jamie Allen Stokes — 1979 — The University of North Carolina at Chapel Hill, B.A., 2002; J.D., 2005 — Admitted to Bar, 2005, North Carolina — Member North Carolina Bar Association; Twenty-Eighth Judicial District Bar Association

(This firm is also listed in the Subrogation section of this directory)

The following firms also service this area.

Bennett & Guthrie, P.LL.C.
1560 Westbrook Plaza Drive
Winston-Salem, North Carolina 27103
  Telephone: 336-765-3121
  Fax: 336-765-8622

Alternative Dispute Resolution, Asbestos Litigation, Automobile Litigation, Carrier Defense, Civil Litigation, Commercial Litigation, Construction Law, Coverage Issues, Employment Law, General Defense Civil Litigation, General Liability, Health Care Liability, Hospital Malpractice, Insurance Coverage, Insurance Defense, Insurance Litigation, Mediation, Medical Malpractice Defense, Premises Liability, Product Liability, Product Liability Defense, Professional Liability, Professional Liability (Non-Medical) Defense, Self-Insured Defense, Trial and Appellate Practice, Trucking Litigation, Wrongful Death

SEE COMPLETE LISTING UNDER WINSTON-SALEM, NORTH CAROLINA (143 MILES)

Evans & Co.
101 West Friendly Avenue, Suite 500
Greensboro, North Carolina 27401
  Telephone: 336-275-1400
  Fax: 336-275-1401
  Toll Free: 800-EVANSCO

Admiralty and Maritime Law, Aviation, Comprehensive General Liability, Construction Law, Directors and Officers Liability, Employment Practices Liability, Energy, Environmental Law, Excess and Umbrella, Insurance Coverage, Insurance Defense, Motor Carriers, Oil and Gas, Product Liability, Professional Liability, Property and Casualty, Railroad Law, Toxic Torts

SEE COMPLETE LISTING UNDER GREENSBORO, NORTH CAROLINA (166 MILES)

Vernis & Bowling of Charlotte, PLLC
4701 Hedgemore Drive, Suite 812
Charlotte, North Carolina 28209
  Telephone: 704-910-8162
  Fax: 704-910-8163

Civil Litigation, Insurance Law, Workers' Compensation, Premises Liability, Labor and Employment, Civil Rights, Commercial Litigation, Automobile Liability, Complex Litigation, Product Liability, Directors and Officers Liability, Errors and Omissions, Construction Law, Construction Defect, Environmental Liability, Personal and Commercial Vehicle, Appellate Practice, Admiralty and Maritime Law, Real Estate, Family Law, Elder Law, Personal Injury Protection (PIP)

SEE COMPLETE LISTING UNDER CHARLOTTE, NORTH CAROLINA (131 MILES)

BEAUFORT † 4,039 Carteret Co.

Refer To

Crossley McIntosh Collier Hanley & Edes, PLLC
5002 Randall Parkway
Wilmington, North Carolina 28403
  Telephone: 910-762-9711
  Fax: 910-256-0310
  Toll Free: 800-499-9711

Insurance Defense, Automobile, General Liability, Product Liability, Professional Malpractice, Casualty, Personal Injury, Municipal Liability, First Party Matters, Workers' Compensation, Admiralty and Maritime Law, Subrogation, Investigations, Construction Law, Pre-Suit

SEE COMPLETE LISTING UNDER WILMINGTON, NORTH CAROLINA (127 MILES)

Refer To

Wallace, Morris, Barwick, Landis & Stroud, P.A.
131 South Queen Street
Kinston, North Carolina 28502-3557
  Telephone: 252-523-2000
  Fax: 252-523-0408
  Toll Free: 888-523-3557

Mailing Address: P.O. Box 3557, Kinston, NC 28502-3557

Insurance Law, Automobile Tort, Fire, Casualty, Defense Litigation, Construction Defect

SEE COMPLETE LISTING UNDER KINSTON, NORTH CAROLINA (75 MILES)

BOLIVIA 143 Brunswick Co.
Refer To
Crossley McIntosh Collier Hanley & Edes, PLLC
5002 Randall Parkway
Wilmington, North Carolina 28403
  Telephone: 910-762-9711
  Fax: 910-256-0310
  Toll Free: 800-499-9711

Insurance Defense, Automobile, General Liability, Product Liability, Professional Malpractice, Casualty, Personal Injury, Municipal Liability, First Party Matters, Workers' Compensation, Admiralty and Maritime Law, Subrogation, Investigations, Construction Law, Pre-Suit

SEE COMPLETE LISTING UNDER WILMINGTON, NORTH CAROLINA (22 MILES)

BOONE † 17,122 Watauga Co.
Refer To
Bennett & Guthrie, P.L.L.C.
1560 Westbrook Plaza Drive
Winston-Salem, North Carolina 27103
  Telephone: 336-765-3121
  Fax: 336-765-8622

Alternative Dispute Resolution, Asbestos Litigation, Automobile Litigation, Carrier Defense, Civil Litigation, Commercial Litigation, Construction Law, Coverage Issues, Employment Law, General Defense Civil Litigation, General Liability, Health Care Liability, Hospital Malpractice, Insurance Coverage, Insurance Defense, Insurance Litigation, Mediation, Medical Malpractice Defense, Premises Liability, Product Liability, Product Liability Defense, Professional Liability, Professional Liability (Non-Medical) Defense, Self-Insured Defense, Trial and Appellate Practice, Trucking Litigation, Wrongful Death

SEE COMPLETE LISTING UNDER WINSTON-SALEM, NORTH CAROLINA (82 MILES)

BURGAW † 3,872 Pender Co.
Refer To
Crossley McIntosh Collier Hanley & Edes, PLLC
5002 Randall Parkway
Wilmington, North Carolina 28403
  Telephone: 910-762-9711
  Fax: 910-256-0310
  Toll Free: 800-499-9711

Insurance Defense, Automobile, General Liability, Product Liability, Professional Malpractice, Casualty, Personal Injury, Municipal Liability, First Party Matters, Workers' Compensation, Admiralty and Maritime Law, Subrogation, Investigations, Construction Law, Pre-Suit

SEE COMPLETE LISTING UNDER WILMINGTON, NORTH CAROLINA (26 MILES)

BURLINGTON 49,963 Alamance Co.
Refer To
Henson & Talley, L.L.P.
Suite 600 Piedmont Building
114 North Elm Street
Greensboro, North Carolina 27401
  Telephone: 336-275-0587
  Fax: 336-273-2585
Mailing Address: P.O. Box 3525, Greensboro, NC 27402-3525

Trial and Appellate Practice, State and Federal Courts, Insurance Defense, Automobile, Trucking Law, Workers' Compensation, Construction Law, Professional Malpractice, Product Liability, Fire, Insurance Coverage, Subrogation

SEE COMPLETE LISTING UNDER GREENSBORO, NORTH CAROLINA (22 MILES)

CAMDEN † 599 Camden Co.
Refer To
Hornthal, Riley, Ellis and Maland, L.L.P.
301 East Main Street
Elizabeth City, North Carolina 27909
  Telephone: 252-335-0871
  Fax: 252-335-4223

Insurance Defense, Automobile, Homeowners, Property Damage, Coverage Issues, Product Liability, Professional Liability

SEE COMPLETE LISTING UNDER ELIZABETH CITY, NORTH CAROLINA (5 MILES)

CHAPEL HILL 57,233 Orange Co.
Refer To
Bailey & Dixon, L.L.P.
434 Fayetteville Street, Suite 2500
Raleigh, North Carolina 27601
  Telephone: 919-828-0731
  Fax: 919-828-6592
Mailing Address: P.O. Box 1351, Raleigh, NC 27602-1351

General Defense, Litigation, Automobile, Construction Defect, Governmental Liability, Product Liability, General Liability, Civil Rights, Employment Law, Sexual Harassment, Environmental Law, Drug, Medical Devices, Arson, Fraud, Legal Malpractice, Life and Health, Workers' Compensation, Insurance Coverage, Bad Faith, Nursing Home Liability, Excess and Reinsurance, Regulatory and Compliance, Trial Practice, State and Federal Courts, Administrative Law, Corporate Law, Insurance Defense, Medical Malpractice, Mergers and Acquisitions, Professional Liability, Real Estate, OSHA, Government Liability, Unfair Claim/Trade Practice Defense Litigation

SEE COMPLETE LISTING UNDER RALEIGH, NORTH CAROLINA (33 MILES)

CHARLOTTE † 731,424 Mecklenburg Co.

Allen, Kopet & Associates, PLLC
3 Coliseum Centre
2550 West Tyvola Road, Suite 175
Charlotte, North Carolina 28217
  Telephone: 704-644-0925
  Fax: 704-831-8030

(See listing under Chattanooga, TN for additional information)

Clawson & Staubes, LLC
756 Tyvola Road, Suite 130
Charlotte, North Carolina 28217
  Telephone: 800-774-8242
  Fax: 704-522-9033
  www.clawsonandstaubes.com

(Charleston, SC Office*: 126 Seven Farms Drive, Suite 200, 29492)
  (Tel: 800-774-8242)
  (Fax: 843-722-2867)
(Greenville, SC Office*: 223 West Stone Avenue, Suite 100, 29609)
  (Tel: 800-774-8242)
  (Fax: 864-232-2921)
(Columbia, SC Office*: 1612 Marion Street, Suite 200, 29201)
  (Tel: 800-774-8242)
  (Fax: 843-722-2867)

Insurance Defense, Trial and Appellate Practice, Automobile, Commercial Liability, General Liability, Product Liability, Life and Health, Construction Liability

Firm Profile: Clawson and Staubes, LLC has been providing clients with quality legal services for 40 years.

Firm Members

Ronnie F. Craig — 1959 — St. Andrews Presbyterian College, B.A., 1982; University of Arkansas at Little Rock, J.D., 1986 — Admitted to Bar, 1986,

NORTH CAROLINA — CHARLOTTE

Clawson & Staubes, LLC, Charlotte, NC (Continued)

Arkansas; 1991, South Carolina; 1987, U.S. Court of Military Appeals — Member Federal, American and Arkansas Bar Associations; South Carolina Bar; Association of Trial Lawyers of America — Special Assistant, United States Attorney (1990-1991) — Practice Areas: Insurance Law — E-mail: rcraig@clawsonandstaubes.com

Andrew J. Santaniello — 1970 — The University of North Carolina, B.A., 1991; Wake Forest University, J.D., 1996 — Admitted to Bar, 1996, North Carolina — Member North Carolna and Mecklenburg County Bar Associations; North Carolina Association of Defense Attorneys — Practice Areas: Personal Injury; Insurance Law — E-mail: andys@clawsonandstaubes.com

(See listing under Charleston, SC for additional information)

Dickie, McCamey & Chilcote, P.C.

2115 Rexford Road, Suite 210
Charlotte, North Carolina 28211-5453
Telephone: 704-998-5184
Fax: 888-811-7144
Toll Free: 800-634-8441
E-Mail: info@dmclaw.com
www.dmclaw.com

(Additional Offices: Pittsburgh, PA*; Cleveland, OH*; Columbus, OH*; Haddonfield, NJ*; Camp Hill, PA*(See Harrisburg listing); Lancaster, SC*; Philadelphia, PA*; Cary, NC*(See Raleigh listing); Steubenville, OH*; Wheeling, WV*; Wilmington, DE*)

Established: 2003

Asbestos Litigation, Bad Faith, Captive Company Matters, Casualty, Commercial Litigation, Energy, Labor and Employment, Excess and Reinsurance, Extra-Contractual Litigation, Insurance Agents, Insurance Coverage, Insurance Coverage Litigation, Legal Malpractice, Medical Malpractice, Medicare Set-Aside Practice, Municipal Liability, Nursing Home Liability, Product Liability, Professional Liability, Property and Casualty, Surety, Transportation, Trucking, Uninsured and Underinsured Motorist, Workers' Compensation

Shareholders

Susan H. Briggs — Branch Office Shareholder-in-Charge — The University of North Carolina at Chapel Hill, B.A., 1991; J.D., 1994 — Admitted to Bar, 1994, North Carolina — E-mail: sbriggs@dmclaw.com

John T. Holden

(See listing under Pittsburgh, PA for additional information)

Thomas D. Garlitz, PLLC

Suite 930, The Johnston Building
212 South Tryon Street
Charlotte, North Carolina 28281
Telephone: 704-372-1282
Fax: 704-372-1621
E-Mail: tgarlitz@gwattorneys.com
www.gwattorneys.com

General Civil Trial and Appellate Practice, Life and Health, Accident, Property and Casualty, Environmental Law, Transportation

Thomas D. Garlitz, PLLC, Charlotte, NC (Continued)

Insurance Clients

The Hartford
New York Life Insurance Company
Shenandoah Life Insurance Company
USAble Life
Lincoln National Life Insurance Company
Pan-American Life Insurance Company
Transamerica Occidental Life Insurance Company

Firm Member

Thomas D. Garlitz — 1953 — The University of North Carolina, A.B., 1975; J.D. (with honors), 1978 — Admitted to Bar, 1978, North Carolina — E-mail: tgarlitz@gwattorneys.com

Golding Holden & Pope, L.L.P.

6701 Carmel Road, Suite 105
Charlotte, North Carolina 28226
Telephone: 704-374-1600
Fax: 704-759-8966
E-Mail: jdavis@ghplaw.net
www.ghplaw.net

Professional Liability, Product Liability, Automobile Liability, Premises Liability, Construction Law, Workers' Compensation, Criminal Law

Firm Profile: Golding Holden & Pope, L.L.P. has been providing service to the insurance industry for more than 60 years. We concentrate in the investigation and defense of liability and first party claims throughout North Carolina. Our mission is to achieve the most favorable resolution of claims or litigation.

Insurance Clients

AIG Insurance Company
Auto-Owners Insurance Company
Brownyard Claims Management, Inc.
Discovery Insurance Company
National General Insurance Company
American National Property and Casualty Companies
Builders Mutual Insurance Company
Farmers Insurance Exchange
State Farm Insurance Companies
Travelers

Non-Insurance Clients

Harris Teeter, Inc.
SGL Carbon

Partners

C. Byron Holden — Yale University, B.A., 1972; Wake Forest University School of Law, J.D., 1975 — Admitted to Bar, 1975, North Carolina

James W. Pope — The University of North Carolina, B.A., 1977; University of South Carolina School of Law, J.D., 1981 — Admitted to Bar, 1981, North Carolina; South Carolina

Robert J. Aylward — State University of New York College at Oneonta, B.A., 1983; Webster University, M.A., 1986; Touro College Jacob D. Fuchsberg Law Center, J.D., 1992 — Admitted to Bar, 1993, New York; North Carolina

Edward A. Sweeney — Kennesaw State University, B.A., 2001; Wake Forest University School of Law, J.D., 2004 — Admitted to Bar, 2004, North Carolina

Associates

C. Preston Armstrong, IV — Appalachian State University, B.A., 1999; Michigan State University School of Law, J.D. (cum laude), 2002 — Admitted to Bar, 2002, North Carolina

Brooks T. Pope — The University of North Carolina at Chapel Hill, B.A. (with distinction), 2008; The University of North Carolina School of Law, J.D., 2012 — Admitted to Bar, 2012, North Carolina

Of Counsel

John G. Golding — Williams College, B.A., 1950; The University of North Carolina School of Law, J.D., 1953 — Admitted to Bar, 1953, North Carolina

COLUMBIA   NORTH CAROLINA

Vernis & Bowling of Charlotte, PLLC
4701 Hedgemore Drive, Suite 812
Charlotte, North Carolina 28209
  Telephone: 704-910-8162
  Fax: 704-910-8163
  www.national-law.com

Established: 1970

Civil Litigation, Insurance Law, Workers' Compensation, Premises Liability, Labor and Employment, Civil Rights, Commercial Litigation, Automobile Liability, Complex Litigation, Product Liability, Directors and Officers Liability, Errors and Omissions, Construction Law, Construction Defect, Environmental Liability, Personal and Commercial Vehicle, Appellate Practice, Admiralty and Maritime Law, Real Estate, Family Law, Elder Law, Personal Injury Protection (PIP)

Firm Members

Robert G. Lewis   Tonya N. Tackett
Thomas Nance

(See listing under Miami, FL for additional information)

York Williams, L.L.P.
1915 Rexford Road, Suite 200
Charlotte, North Carolina 28211
  Telephone: 704-375-4480
  Fax: 704-375-6895
  E-Mail: firm@yorkwilliamslaw.com
  www.yorkwilliamslaw.com

Established: 1994

Business Law, Civil Litigation, Insurance Defense, Bodily Injury, Property Damage, General Liability, Product Liability, First Party Matters, Coverage Issues, Public Liability, Trucking Law, Transportation, Health Care, Alternative Dispute Resolution

Firm Profile: York Williams' promises implicit honesty and integrity to our clients, whose reputation guides our practice. Firm members belong to the North Carolina and Mecklenburg County Bar Associations, the North Carolina State Bar, the North Carolina Association of Defense Attorneys, and the Defense Research Institute.

Insurance Clients

Allstate Insurance Company
Berkley Risk Administrators Company, LLC
GEICO Insurance Companies
The Hartford
Kemper/Unitrin
Nautilus Insurance Group
Republic Services, Inc.
State Farm Insurance Companies
The Travelers Companies, Inc.
United Services Automobile Association (USAA)

Argo Group US
Chartis Insurance
Erie Insurance Group
Harford Mutual Insurance Company
Liberty Mutual Group
QBE Insurance Group Limited
Shelter Insurance Companies
TransGuard Insurance Company of America, Inc.
Universal Insurance Company

Non-Insurance Clients

J.B. Hunt Transport, Inc.   USA Truck, Inc.

Partners

Gregory C. York — 1956 — The University of North Carolina at Chapel Hill, B.A. (with honors), 1978; University of North Carolina at Chapel Hill School of Law, J.D., 1981 — Phi Delta Phi — Admitted to Bar, 1981, North Carolina; 1985, U.S. District Court, Eastern and Western Districts of North Carolina; 1986, U.S. District Court, Middle District of North Carolina — Member North Carolina State Bar; Federal, North Carolina and Mecklenburg

York Williams, L.L.P., Charlotte, NC   (Continued)
County Bar Associations; North Carolina Association of Defense Attorneys; Defense Research Institute

Thomas E. Williams — 1957 — Appalachian State University, B.A. (cum laude), 1979; Wake Forest University School of Law, J.D., 1982 — Admitted to Bar, 1982, North Carolina; 1983, U.S. District Court, Western District of North Carolina; 1984, U.S. Court of Appeals, Fourth Circuit — Member North Carolina State Bar; North Carolina and Mecklenburg County Bar Associations; North Carolina Association of Defense Attorneys

Robyn M. Buckley — 1973 — West Virginia University, B.S., 1995; West Virginia University College of Law, J.D., 2000 — Admitted to Bar, 2000, North Carolina; U.S. District Court, Western District of North Carolina — Member North Carolina State Bar; North Carolina and Mecklenburg County Bar Associations; North Carolina Association of Defense Attorneys

Associates

Steven A. Lucente — 1983 — North Carolina State University, B.A., 2005; Elon University School of Law, J.D., 2009 — Admitted to Bar, 2009, North Carolina — Member North Carolina State Bar; North Carolina and Mecklenburg County Bar Associations; North Carolina Association of Defense Attorneys

Martá P. Brown — 1983 — North Carolina State University, B.A., 2006; University of North Carolina at Chapel Hill School of Law, J.D., 2009 — Admitted to Bar, 2009, North Carolina — Member North Carolina State Bar; North Carolina and Mecklenburg County Bar Associations; North Carolina Association of Defense Attorneys

Jacob M. Gehron — 1979 — The University of Tennessee, B.A. (cum laude), 2001; Campbell University Norman Adrian Wiggins School of Law, J.D., 2008 — Admitted to Bar, 2008, North Carolina — Member North Carolina State Bar; North Carolina and Mecklenburg County Bar Associations; North Carolina Association of Defense Attorneys

---

The following firms also service this area.

Bennett & Guthrie, P.L.L.C.
1560 Westbrook Plaza Drive
Winston-Salem, North Carolina 27103
  Telephone: 336-765-3121
  Fax: 336-765-8622

Alternative Dispute Resolution, Asbestos Litigation, Automobile Litigation, Carrier Defense, Civil Litigation, Commercial Litigation, Construction Law, Coverage Issues, Employment Law, General Defense Civil Litigation, General Liability, Health Care Liability, Hospital Malpractice, Insurance Coverage, Insurance Defense, Insurance Litigation, Mediation, Medical Malpractice Defense, Premises Liability, Product Liability, Product Liability Defense, Professional Liability, Professional Liability (Non-Medical) Defense, Self-Insured Defense, Trial and Appellate Practice, Trucking Litigation, Wrongful Death

SEE COMPLETE LISTING UNDER WINSTON-SALEM, NORTH CAROLINA (81 MILES)

Evans & Co.
101 West Friendly Avenue, Suite 500
Greensboro, North Carolina 27401
  Telephone: 336-275-1400
  Fax: 336-275-1401
  Toll Free: 800-EVANSCO

Admiralty and Maritime Law, Aviation, Comprehensive General Liability, Construction Law, Directors and Officers Liability, Employment Practices Liability, Energy, Environmental Law, Excess and Umbrella, Insurance Coverage, Insurance Defense, Motor Carriers, Oil and Gas, Product Liability, Professional Liability, Property and Casualty, Railroad Law, Toxic Torts

SEE COMPLETE LISTING UNDER GREENSBORO, NORTH CAROLINA (96 MILES)

COLUMBIA † 891 Tyrrell Co.
Refer To

Hornthal, Riley, Ellis and Maland, L.L.P.
301 East Main Street
Elizabeth City, North Carolina 27909
  Telephone: 252-335-0871
  Fax: 252-335-4223

Insurance Defense, Automobile, Homeowners, Property Damage, Coverage Issues, Product Liability, Professional Liability

SEE COMPLETE LISTING UNDER ELIZABETH CITY, NORTH CAROLINA (53 MILES)

NORTH CAROLINA

CONCORD

CONCORD † 79,066 Cabarrus Co.

Refer To

Vernis & Bowling of Charlotte, PLLC
4701 Hedgemore Drive, Suite 812
Charlotte, North Carolina 28209
 Telephone: 704-910-8162
 Fax: 704-910-8163

Civil Litigation, Insurance Law, Workers' Compensation, Premises Liability, Labor and Employment, Civil Rights, Commercial Litigation, Automobile Liability, Complex Litigation, Product Liability, Directors and Officers Liability, Errors and Omissions, Construction Law, Construction Defect, Environmental Liability, Personal and Commercial Vehicle, Appellate Practice, Admiralty and Maritime Law, Real Estate, Family Law, Elder Law, Personal Injury Protection (PIP)

SEE COMPLETE LISTING UNDER CHARLOTTE, NORTH CAROLINA (28 MILES)

CURRITUCK † 100 Currituck Co.

Refer To

Hornthal, Riley, Ellis and Maland, L.L.P.
301 East Main Street
Elizabeth City, North Carolina 27909
 Telephone: 252-335-0871
 Fax: 252-335-4223

Insurance Defense, Automobile, Homeowners, Property Damage, Coverage Issues, Product Liability, Professional Liability

SEE COMPLETE LISTING UNDER ELIZABETH CITY, NORTH CAROLINA (18 MILES)

DURHAM † 228,330 Durham Co.

Haywood, Denny & Miller, L.L.P.

3511 Shannon Road, Suite 140
Durham, North Carolina 27707
 Telephone: 919-403-0000
 Fax: 919-403-0001
 E-Mail: hdmllp@hdmllp.com
 www.hdmllp.com

Established: 1955

Insurance Law, Litigation, Corporate Law, Business Law, Governmental Affairs

Insurance Clients

Brotherhood Mutual Insurance Company
Sentry Select Insurance Company
State Farm Mutual Automobile Insurance Company
Lititz Mutual Insurance Company
North Carolina Farm Bureau Mutual Insurance Company
Teachers Insurance and Annuity Association of America

Non-Insurance Clients

Carolina Canners, Inc.
North Carolina Railroad Company
Pepsi Cola Bottling Company of Rocboro, NC, Inc.
FedEx Ground Package System, Inc.
Walgreen Co.

Partners

Egbert L. Haywood — (1911-1985)

Emery B. Denny, Jr. — (1924-1982)

George W. Miller, Jr. — 1930 — The University of North Carolina, B.S., 1954; LL.B., 1957 — Admitted to Bar, 1957, North Carolina; U.S. District Court, Eastern, Middle and Western Districts of North Carolina; U.S. Court of Appeals, Fourth Circuit; U.S. Supreme Court — Member American, North Carolina and Durham County Bar Associations; American College of Trial Lawyers; International Association of Defense Counsel — North Carolina General Assembly (1971 to 2000) — Practice Areas: Business Law; Corporate Law; Government Affairs — E-mail: gwmjr@hdmllp.com

Kevin W. Butterfield — 1957 — Kalamazoo College, B.A., 1979; University of Minnesota, M.A., 1981; The University of North Carolina, J.D., 1986 — Admitted to Bar, 1986, North Carolina; 1987, U.S. District Court, Eastern

Haywood, Denny & Miller, L.L.P., Durham, NC
(Continued)

and Middle Districts of North Carolina — Member North Carolina and Durham County Bar Associations; North Carolina State Bar — E-mail: kwbutterfield@hdmllp.com

Robert E. Levin — 1961 — North Carolina State University, B.A. (cum laude), 1983; The University of North Carolina at Chapel Hill, J.D., 1986 — Admitted to Bar, 1986, North Carolina; 1988, U.S. District Court, Middle District of North Carolina; 1989, U.S. District Court, Eastern District of North Carolina; 1997, U.S. Court of Appeals, Fourth Circuit — Member North Carolina and Durham County Bar Associations; North Carolina Association of Defense Attorneys; Defense Research Institute — E-mail: rlevin@hdmllp.com

John R. Kincaid — 1965 — The University of North Carolina at Chapel Hill, B.A., 1987; The University of North Carolina, J.D. (with honors), 1991 — Admitted to Bar, 1991, North Carolina; 1992, U.S. District Court, Eastern and Middle Districts of North Carolina — Member North Carolina and Durham County Bar Associations; North Carolina State Bar — E-mail: jrk@hdmllp.com

George Washington Miller, III — 1965 — The University of North Carolina at Chapel Hill, B.A., 1990; Campbell University, J.D., 1996 — Phi Alpha Delta — Admitted to Bar, 1996, North Carolina; 1997, U.S. District Court, Eastern, Middle and Western Districts of North Carolina — Member American, North Carolina and Durham County Bar Associations; North Carolina State Bar; North Carolina Association of Defense Attorneys; Defense Research Institute — E-mail: gwm3@hdmllp.com

(This firm is also listed in the Subrogation section of this directory)

The following firms also service this area.

Bailey & Dixon, L.L.P.
434 Fayetteville Street, Suite 2500
Raleigh, North Carolina 27601
 Telephone: 919-828-0731
 Fax: 919-828-6592

Mailing Address: P.O. Box 1351, Raleigh, NC 27602-1351

General Defense, Litigation, Automobile, Construction Defect, Governmental Liability, Product Liability, General Liability, Civil Rights, Employment Law, Sexual Harassment, Environmental Law, Drug, Medical Devices, Arson, Fraud, Legal Malpractice, Life and Health, Workers' Compensation, Insurance Coverage, Bad Faith, Nursing Home Liability, Excess and Reinsurance, Regulatory and Compliance, Trial Practice, State and Federal Courts, Administrative Law, Corporate Law, Insurance Defense, Medical Malpractice, Mergers and Acquisitions, Professional Liability, Real Estate, OSHA, Government Liability, Unfair Claim/Trade Practice Defense Litigation

SEE COMPLETE LISTING UNDER RALEIGH, NORTH CAROLINA (29 MILES)

EDENTON † 5,004 Chowan Co.

Refer To

Hornthal, Riley, Ellis and Maland, L.L.P.
301 East Main Street
Elizabeth City, North Carolina 27909
 Telephone: 252-335-0871
 Fax: 252-335-4223

Insurance Defense, Automobile, Homeowners, Property Damage, Coverage Issues, Product Liability, Professional Liability

SEE COMPLETE LISTING UNDER ELIZABETH CITY, NORTH CAROLINA (29 MILES)

ELIZABETH CITY † 18,683 Pasquotank Co.

Hornthal, Riley, Ellis and Maland, L.L.P.

301 East Main Street
Elizabeth City, North Carolina 27909
 Telephone: 252-335-0871
 Fax: 252-335-4223
 E-Mail: hrem@hrem.com
 www.hrem.com

(Nags Head, NC Office: 2502 South Croatan Highway, 27959)
 (Tel: 252-441-0871)
 (Fax: 252-441-8822)

FAYETTEVILLE   NORTH CAROLINA

Hornthal, Riley, Ellis and Maland, L.L.P., Elizabeth City, NC (Continued)

(Columbia, NC Office: 211 West Main Street, P.O. Box 510, 27925)
(Tel: 252-796-8561)
(Fax: 252-796-1083)

Established: 1985

Insurance Defense, Automobile, Homeowners, Property Damage, Coverage Issues, Product Liability, Professional Liability

Insurance Clients

Admiral Insurance Company	American Hardware Mutual Insurance Company
Buckeye Union Insurance Company	Canal Insurance Company
Castle Insurance Company	Chubb Group of Insurance Companies
Continental Insurance Company	Dairyland Insurance Company
Continental National American Group	Employers Insurance Company of Wausau
Employers Mutual Companies	GAB Robins North America, Inc.
Federated Insurance Company	GMAC Insurance
General Reinsurance Corporation	Grain Dealers Mutual Insurance Company
Government Employees Insurance Company	Horace Mann Insurance Company
Harleysville Mutual Insurance Company	Indiana Lumbermens Mutual Insurance Company
Kemper Insurance Companies	Michigan Mutual Liability Company
Keystone Insurance Company	New Jersey Manufacturers Insurance Company
National Grange Mutual Insurance Company	North Carolina Hospital Reciprocal Insurance Exchange
North Carolina Farm Bureau Mutual Insurance Company	North Carolina League of Municipalities
North Carolina Insurance Guaranty Association	Progressive Insurance Company
Pennsylvania Lumbermens Mutual Insurance Company	Reliance Insurance Company
Prudential Property and Casualty Insurance Company	Sentry Insurance Group
State Farm Fire and Casualty Company	State Farm Mutual Automobile Insurance Company
Transamerica Insurance Company	Unigard Insurance Group
Unisun Insurance Company	United States Casualty Company
Universal Insurance Company	Universal Underwriters Insurance Company
Virginia Farm Bureau Mutual Insurance Company	Virginia Mutual Insurance Company
Zurich American Insurance Company	

Partners

L. P. Hornthal Jr. — 1936 — The University of North Carolina, A.B., 1958; LL.B., 1963 — Admitted to Bar, 1963, North Carolina — Member North Carolina Bar Association (President, 1996-1997); North Carolina Association of Defense Attorneys (President, 1984-1985); International Association of Defense Counsel; Association of Insurance Attorneys; Fellow, American College of Trial Lawyers

M. H. Hood Ellis — 1949 — North Carolina State University, B.S., 1972; Wake Forest University, J.D., 1975 — Admitted to Bar, 1975, North Carolina — Member North Carolina Bar Association; North Carolina Association of Defense Attorneys

Donald C. Prentiss — 1955 — Wake Forest University, B.A., 1977; J.D., 1981 — Admitted to Bar, 1981, North Carolina — Member North Carolina Bar Association; North Carolina Association of Defense Attorneys (Board of Directors, 1997-Present); Defense Research Institute

Robert B. Hobbs, Jr. — 1960 — The University of North Carolina at Chapel Hill, B.A., 1983; Campbell University, J.D., 1986 — Admitted to Bar, 1986, North Carolina — Member North Carolina Bar Association

John D. Leidy — 1962 — Denison University, B.A., 1984; The University of North Carolina, J.D., 1987 — Admitted to Bar, 1987, North Carolina — Member North Carolina Bar Association; North Carolina Association of Defense Attorneys

L. Phillip Hornthal III — 1967 — The University of North Carolina at Chapel Hill, B.A., 1989; Campbell University, J.D., 1993 — Admitted to Bar, 1993, North Carolina — Member North Carolina Bar Association; North Carolina Association of Defense Attorneys; Defense Research Institute

W. Brock Mitchell — 1973 — College of Charleston, B.A., 1996; Mississippi College, J.D., 2000; University of Denver, LL.M., 2001 — Admitted to Bar, 2002, North Carolina — Member North Carolina Bar Association

Hornthal, Riley, Ellis and Maland, L.L.P., Elizabeth City, NC (Continued)

David C. Gadd — 1977 — North Carolina State University, B.S., 2000; Florida State University, J.D., 2004 — Admitted to Bar, 2004, North Carolina — Member North Carolina Bar Association; North Carolina Association of Defense Attorneys

Benjamin M. Gallop — 1976 — North Carolina State University, B.S., 2000; Campbell University, J.D. (cum laude), 2005 — Admitted to Bar, 2005, North Carolina; U.S. District Court, Eastern District of North Carolina — Member American and North Carolina Bar Association; North Carolina State Bar

Of Counsel

Charles W. Ogletree — 1939 — The University of North Carolina at Chapel Hill, A.B., 1962; J.D., 1965 — Admitted to Bar, 1965, North Carolina — Member North Carolina Bar Association

Retired

J. Fred Riley — 1938 — Wake Forest University, A.B., 1960; The University of North Carolina, J.D., 1967 — Admitted to Bar, 1967, North Carolina

Thomas L. White, Jr. — 1938 — The University of North Carolina, A.B., 1960; J.D., 1970 — Admitted to Bar, 1970, North Carolina

(Attorneys are Members of American and North Carolina Bar Associations)

The following firms also service this area.

Crossley McIntosh Collier Hanley & Edes, PLLC
5002 Randall Parkway
Wilmington, North Carolina 28403
Telephone: 910-762-9711
Fax: 910-256-0310
Toll Free: 800-499-9711

Insurance Defense, Automobile, General Liability, Product Liability, Professional Malpractice, Casualty, Personal Injury, Municipal Liability, First Party Matters, Workers' Compensation, Admiralty and Maritime Law, Subrogation, Investigations, Construction Law, Pre-Suit

SEE COMPLETE LISTING UNDER WILMINGTON, NORTH CAROLINA (210 MILES)

ELIZABETHTOWN † 3,583 Bladen Co.

Refer To

Crossley McIntosh Collier Hanley & Edes, PLLC
5002 Randall Parkway
Wilmington, North Carolina 28403
Telephone: 910-762-9711
Fax: 910-256-0310
Toll Free: 800-499-9711

Insurance Defense, Automobile, General Liability, Product Liability, Professional Malpractice, Casualty, Personal Injury, Municipal Liability, First Party Matters, Workers' Compensation, Admiralty and Maritime Law, Subrogation, Investigations, Construction Law, Pre-Suit

SEE COMPLETE LISTING UNDER WILMINGTON, NORTH CAROLINA (50 MILES)

FAYETTEVILLE † 200,564 Cumberland Co.

Anderson, Johnson, Lawrence & Butler, L.L.P.

109 Green Street, Suite 204
Fayetteville, North Carolina 28301
Telephone: 910-483-1171
Fax: 910-483-5005
E-Mail: AJLB@andersonjohnson.com
www.andersonjohnson.com

Established: 1954

Anderson, Johnson, Lawrence & Butler, L.L.P., Fayetteville, NC (Continued)

Alternative Dispute Resolution, Appellate Advocacy, Automobile, Commercial Litigation, Construction Law, Contract Disputes, Environmental Litigation, Governmental Liability, Homeowners, Insurance Coverage, Legal Malpractice, Medical Malpractice, Nursing Home Liability, Premises Liability, Product Liability, Subrogation, Truck Liability, Workers' Compensation

Firm Profile: The law firm of Anderson, Johnson, Lawrence & Butler, L.L.P. has a strong tradition for almost 60 years of representing insurance clients and has expanded through the years to provide high quality, aggressive trial work on complex matters to clients in a broad spectrum of insurance coverage issues. Our experience exceeds firms of far greater size and has earned us the reputation as one of the most effective, efficient firms in the region. Our attorneys are admitted and have appeared in all North Carolina State and Federal Courts and The United States Court of Appeals for the Fourth Circuit in Richmond, Virginia.

Insurance Clients

Allstate Insurance Company
Amerisure Companies
Auto-Owners Insurance Company
Canal Insurance Company
The Cincinnati Insurance Companies
EMC Insurance Companies
Erie Insurance Group
GMAC Insurance
Government Employees Insurance Company
John Hancock Property and Casualty Insurance Company
Nationwide Mutual Insurance Company
North Carolina Grange Mutual Insurance Company
Peerless Insurance Company
Republic Claims Service
Royal Insurance Company of America
Scottsdale Insurance Company
State Auto Insurance Companies
American Modern Insurance Group, Inc.
Builders Mutual Insurance Company
CNA Insurance Company
CUMIS Insurance Society, Inc.
Equitable Life Insurance Company
Fireman's Fund Insurance Company
Integon Casualty Insurance Company
National Casualty Insurance Company
North Carolina Farm Bureau Mutual Insurance Company
Occidental Fire & Casualty Company of North Carolina
PRMS, Inc. - Professional Risk Management Services, Inc.
Safeco Insurance
St. Paul Insurance Company
The Seibels Bruce Group, Inc.
Vanliner Insurance Company

Partners

Henry L. Anderson — (1911-1986)

Lee Best Johnson — The University of North Carolina, B.S., 1969; Cumberland School of Law of Samford University, J.D., 1974 — Delta Theta Phi, (Vice Dean, 1972-1973; Dean, 1973-1974) — Admitted to Bar, 1974, North Carolina; 1975, U.S. District Court, Eastern District of North Carolina — Member American, North Carolina and Cumberland County (President, 2004-2005) Bar Associations; North Carolina State Bar; American Counsel Association; American Bar Endowment; North Carolina Association of Defense Attorneys; Defense Research Institute — Assistant District Attorney, Twelfth Judicial District, North Carolina (1975)

John Huske Anderson, II — North Carolina State University, B.S., 1968; Wake Forest University School of Law, J.D. (cum laude), 1975 — Phi Delta Phi Legal Fraternity — Admitted to Bar, 1975, North Carolina; 1977, U.S. District Court, Eastern District of North Carolina — Member Federal, American, North Carolina and Cumberland County Bar Associations; North Carolina State Bar; Association of Defense Trial Attorneys; North Carolina Association of Defense Attorneys; Defense Research Institute — Assistant District Attorney, Twelfth Judicial District, Cumberland County (1975-1976) — AOC Certified Mediator

Steven C. Lawrence — East Carolina University; The University of North Carolina, B.A., 1981; Campbell University School of Law, J.D., 1984 — Phi Alpha Delta — Admitted to Bar, 1984, North Carolina; 1985, U.S. District Court, Eastern District of North Carolina; 1989, U.S. Court of Appeals, Fourth Circuit; 1991, U.S. Supreme Court; 1998, U.S. District Court, Middle District of North Carolina — Member North Carolina and Cumberland County Bar Associations; North Carolina State Bar; North Carolina Association of Defense Attorneys

J. Stewart Butler, III — The University of North Carolina, B.A., 1979; North Carolina Central University School of Law, J.D., 1985 — Phi Delta Phi Legal Fraternity — Admitted to Bar, 1985, North Carolina; 1986, U.S. District Court, Eastern District of North Carolina; 2000, U.S. District Court, Middle District of North Carolina — Member North Carolina and Cumberland

Anderson, Johnson, Lawrence & Butler, L.L.P., Fayetteville, NC (Continued)

County Bar Associations; North Carolina State Bar; North Carolina Association of Defense Attorneys — Assistant District Attorney, Twelfth Judicial District (1986)

Associates

Stacey E. Tally — University of Virginia, B.A. (with distinction), 2005; Charleston School of Law, J.D. (magna cum laude, Dean's List), 2009 — Phi Delta Phi — Law Clerk to the Honorable Cheri L. Beasley, N.C. Court of Appeals (2010-2011) — Articles Editor, Charleston Law Review — Admitted to Bar, 2009, North Carolina — Member North Carolina and Cumberland County (Young Lawyers' Division, Treasurer, 2012) Bar Associations; North Carolina State Bar; Defense Research Institute; North Carolina Association of Defense Attorneys — Languages: Spanish

Lee B. Johnson, Jr. — East Carolina University, B.S. (Dean's List), 2010; Cumberland School of Law at Samford University, J.D. (Dean's List), 2013 — Admitted to Bar, 2013, North Carolina — Member North Carolina and Cumberland County Bar Associations; Defense Research Institute; North Carolina Association of Defense Attorneys

Murray, Craven & Inman, L.L.P.

2517 Raeford Road
Fayetteville, North Carolina 28305
Telephone: 910-483-4990
Fax: 910-483-6822

Insurance Defense, General Liability, Automobile Liability, Life and Health, Casualty, Trial Practice, Appellate Practice

Insurance Clients

Guaranty National Insurance Company
Nationwide Mutual Insurance Company
Royal & SunAlliance USA
State Farm Mutual Automobile Insurance Company
Metropolitan Life Insurance Company
North Carolina Farm Bureau Mutual Insurance Company
State Farm Fire and Casualty Company

Firm Members

Ocie F. Murray, Jr. — 1941 — Elon College, A.B., 1964; College of William & Mary, J.D., 1967; Georgetown University, LL.M., 1969 — Admitted to Bar, 1967, Virginia; 1971, North Carolina; U.S. District Court, Middle District of North Carolina; U.S. Supreme Court; 1972, U.S. District Court, Eastern District of North Carolina — Member American, North Carolina and Virginia Bar Associations

Richard T. Craven — 1953 — The University of North Carolina, B.A., 1975; Cumberland School of Law of Samford University, J.D., 1979 — Admitted to Bar, 1979, North Carolina; U.S. District Court, Eastern District of North Carolina; 1985, U.S. Court of Appeals, Fourth Circuit; 1986, U.S. Supreme Court — Member American, North Carolina and Cumberland County (President, 2005-2006) Bar Associations; Cumberland County Young Lawyers Association (President, 1986-1987) — Assistant District Attorney, Twelfth Judicial District of North Carolina (1980-1981)

Stephen G. Inman — 1947 — The University of North Carolina, A.B., 1969; Medical College of Virginia, D.D.S., 1973; Campbell University School of Law, J.D. (cum laude), 1988 — Admitted to Bar, 1988, North Carolina; U.S. District Court, Eastern District of North Carolina — Member American, North Carolina and Cumberland County Bar Associations

GOLDSBORO

The following firms also service this area.

Bailey & Dixon, L.L.P.
434 Fayetteville Street, Suite 2500
Raleigh, North Carolina 27601
  Telephone: 919-828-0731
  Fax: 919-828-6592
Mailing Address: P.O. Box 1351, Raleigh, NC 27602-1351

General Defense, Litigation, Automobile, Construction Defect, Governmental Liability, Product Liability, General Liability, Civil Rights, Employment Law, Sexual Harassment, Environmental Law, Drug, Medical Devices, Arson, Fraud, Legal Malpractice, Life and Health, Workers' Compensation, Insurance Coverage, Bad Faith, Nursing Home Liability, Excess and Reinsurance, Regulatory and Compliance, Trial Practice, State and Federal Courts, Administrative Law, Corporate Law, Insurance Defense, Medical Malpractice, Mergers and Acquisitions, Professional Liability, Real Estate, OSHA, Government Liability, Unfair Claim/Trade Practice Defense Litigation

SEE COMPLETE LISTING UNDER RALEIGH, NORTH CAROLINA (62 MILES)

Crossley McIntosh Collier Hanley & Edes, PLLC
5002 Randall Parkway
Wilmington, North Carolina 28403
  Telephone: 910-762-9711
  Fax: 910-256-0310
  Toll Free: 800-499-9711

Insurance Defense, Automobile, General Liability, Product Liability, Professional Malpractice, Casualty, Personal Injury, Municipal Liability, First Party Matters, Workers' Compensation, Admiralty and Maritime Law, Subrogation, Investigations, Construction Law, Pre-Suit

SEE COMPLETE LISTING UNDER WILMINGTON, NORTH CAROLINA (87 MILES)

GASTONIA † 71,741 Gaston Co.

Refer To
Vernis & Bowling of Charlotte, PLLC
4701 Hedgemore Drive, Suite 812
Charlotte, North Carolina 28209
  Telephone: 704-910-8162
  Fax: 704-910-8163

Civil Litigation, Insurance Law, Workers' Compensation, Premises Liability, Labor and Employment, Civil Rights, Commercial Litigation, Automobile Liability, Complex Litigation, Product Liability, Directors and Officers Liability, Errors and Omissions, Construction Law, Construction Defect, Environmental Liability, Personal and Commercial Vehicle, Appellate Practice, Admiralty and Maritime Law, Real Estate, Family Law, Elder Law, Personal Injury Protection (PIP)

SEE COMPLETE LISTING UNDER CHARLOTTE, NORTH CAROLINA (27 MILES)

GATESVILLE † 321 Gates Co.

Refer To
Hornthal, Riley, Ellis and Maland, L.L.P.
301 East Main Street
Elizabeth City, North Carolina 27909
  Telephone: 252-335-0871
  Fax: 252-335-4223

Insurance Defense, Automobile, Homeowners, Property Damage, Coverage Issues, Product Liability, Professional Liability

SEE COMPLETE LISTING UNDER ELIZABETH CITY, NORTH CAROLINA (30 MILES)

GOLDSBORO † 36,437 Wayne Co.

Walker, Allen, Grice, Ammons & Foy, L.L.P.

1407 West Grantham Street
Goldsboro, North Carolina 27530
  Telephone: 919-734-6565
  Fax: 919-734-6720
  www.nctrialattorneys.com

Established: 1985

Walker, Allen, Grice, Ammons & Foy, L.L.P., Goldsboro, NC (Continued)

Automobile Liability, Commercial General Liability, Health Care Liability, Insurance Coverage & Defense, Medical Malpractice, Nursing Home Liability

Insurance Clients

Alfa Alliance Insurance Corporation
Farm Bureau Insurance of N.C. Inc.
Medical Security Insurance Company
Progressive Insurance Company
State Farm Mutual Automobile Insurance Company
Allstate Insurance Company
EMC Insurance Companies
Medical Mutual Insurance Company
National General Insurance Company
Sentry Insurance Group
Strickland Insurance Group
Travelers

Partners

Robert D. Walker, Jr. — 1949 — North Carolina State University, B.A., 1971; Wake Forest University School of Law, J.D., 1974 — Admitted to Bar, 1974, North Carolina; U.S. Court of Appeals, Fourth Circuit; 1978, U.S. Supreme Court — Member North Carolina Bar Association; North Carolina State Bar; North Carolina Association of Defense Attorneys; Defense Research Institute — Named in The Best Lawyers of America publication; Recognized as Legal Elite in Business North Carolina publication (Top Vote Getter 2008, Ligitation) — E-mail: bob@nctrialattorneys.com

Jerry A. Allen, Jr. — 1962 — Mount Olive College, A.A./A.S., 1983; The University of North Carolina at Chapel Hill, B.A., 1986; Campbell University School of Law, J.D., 1989 — Admitted to Bar, 1989, North Carolina; U.S. District Court, Eastern and Western Districts of North Carolina; 1990, U.S. Court of Claims — Member North Carolina Bar Association; North Carolina Association of Defense Attorneys — North Carolina Legal Elite, Business North Carolina (Litigation); The Best Lawyers in America (Medical Malpractice Law, Defendants; Personal Injury Litigation); AV Preeminent Rating, Martindale-Hubbel; North Carolina Super Lawyers; Top Attorneys in North Carolina, Charlotte Magazine; North Carolina's Top Rated Lawyers, National Law Journal & Martindale-Hubbell — Practice Areas: Civil Litigation; Insurance Defense; Medical Malpractice Defense — E-mail: jerry@nctrialattorneys.com

O. Drew Grice, Jr. — 1969 — Hampden-Sydney College, B.A., 1991; Cumberland School of Law of Samford University, J.D., 1995 — Admitted to Bar, 1995, North Carolina; U.S. District Court, Eastern District of North Carolina — Member North Carolina and Wayne County Bar Associations; North Carolina Association of Defense Attorneys; Defense Research Institute — Recognized as Legal Elite in Business North Carolina publication — E-mail: drew@nctrialattorneys.com

Jeffrey T. Ammons — 1970 — University of South Carolina, B.A., 1992; Campbell University, Norman Adrian Wiggins School of Law, J.D., 1996 — Admitted to Bar, 1996, North Carolina; South Carolina — Member American, North Carolina and Wayne County Bar Associations; Defense Research Institute; North Carolina Association of Defense Attorneys — North Carolina Legal Elite, 2008; North Carolina Super Lawyers, 2010; The Best Lawyers in America, 2013 & 2014; North Carolina Insurance Crime Information Exchange Member — E-mail: jeff@nctrialattorneys.com

Louis F. Foy, III (Trey) — 1974 — Elon College, B.S. (cum laude), 1996; Campbell University School of Law, J.D., 2000 — Admitted to Bar, 2000, North Carolina; U.S. District Court, Eastern District of North Carolina — Member North Carolina Bar Association; North Carolina Association of Defense Attorneys — E-mail: trey@nctrialattorneys.com

Amanda M. Wells — 1980 — East Carolina University, B.A. (magna cum laude), 2002; North Carolina Central University School of Law, J.D., 2005 — Admitted to Bar, 2005, North Carolina; U.S. District Court, Eastern District of North Carolina — Member North Carolina and Wayne County Bar Associations; North Carolina Association of Defense Attorneys — North Carolina Insurance Crime Information Exchange Member — E-mail: amanda@nctrialattorneys.com

Associates

Jackie S. Houser — 1962 — Mount Olive College, B.S. (summa cum laude), 2002; Liberty University School of Law, J.D., 2009 — Admitted to Bar, 2009, North Carolina — Member North Carolina and Wayne County Bar Associations; North Carolina Association of Defense Attorneys — E-mail: jackie@nctrialattorneys.com

Ashley H. Rodriguez — 1986 — University of North Carolina Wilmington, B.A., 2008; Campbell University Norman Adrian Wiggins School of Law,

Walker, Allen, Grice, Ammons & Foy, L.L.P., Goldsboro, NC (Continued)

J.D., 2011 — Admitted to Bar, 2011, North Carolina — Member North Carolina and Wayne County Bar Associations — E-mail: ashley@nctrialattorneys.com

Alexandra L. Couch — 1988 — Duke University, B.A., 2010; Campbell University, Norman Adrian Wiggins School of Law, J.D., 2013 — Admitted to Bar, 2013, North Carolina — E-mail: alexandra@nctrialattorneys.com

GRAHAM † 14,153 Alamance Co.

Refer To
Henson & Talley, L.L.P.
Suite 600 Piedmont Building
114 North Elm Street
Greensboro, North Carolina 27401
Telephone: 336-275-0587
Fax: 336-273-2585

Mailing Address: P.O. Box 3525, Greensboro, NC 27402-3525

Trial and Appellate Practice, State and Federal Courts, Insurance Defense, Automobile, Trucking Law, Workers' Compensation, Construction Law, Professional Malpractice, Product Liability, Fire, Insurance Coverage, Subrogation

SEE COMPLETE LISTING UNDER GREENSBORO, NORTH CAROLINA (23 MILES)

GREENSBORO † 269,666 Guilford Co.

Brotherton Ford Berry & Weaver, PLLC

127 North Greene Street, Fourth Floor
Greensboro, North Carolina 27401
Telephone: 336-346-1116
Fax: 336-346-1117
E-Mail: brotherton@brothertonford.com
www.brothertonford.com

Established: 2004

Appellate, Employment Law, Insurance Defense, Medical Malpractice Defense, Workers' Compensation, Commercial General Liability, Professional Negligence, Business Litigation, Commercial Litigation, Transportation, Trucking, Insurance Law, Property and Casualty, Professional Licensing Boards

Firm Profile: At Brotherton Ford Berry & Weaver, we share a passion to provide quality legal services with measurable results. Together, we wield over 90 years of legal experience. We provide our clients with aggressive and effective representation throughout North Carolina. At Brotherton Ford Berry & Weaver, we take pride in our reputation for successful settlements and jury verdicts. We strive to exceed client expectations and build professional relationships rooted in integrity, character and reliability. We serve as advisers and advocates for a distinguished roster of clients that includes local, national and international organizations in such fields as insurance, health care, manufacturing, trucking, retail sales, and finance.

Our practice covers a range of services for professional clients, the insurance industry, businesses and individuals.

Our offices are centrally located in Greensboro, North Carolina, which allows us to serve clients across the state. Throughout North Carolina, we are concerned professionals delivering excellent results.

Insurance Clients

Auto-Owners Insurance Company
Kemper Auto and Home
The Hartford
Sedgwick Claims Management Services, Inc.

Non-Insurance Clients

Corizon Health, Inc.
Wake Forest Baptist Medical Center

Brotherton Ford Berry & Weaver, PLLC, Greensboro, NC (Continued)

Firm Members

Joseph F. Brotherton — 1954 — The University of North Carolina, B.A., 1976; J.D., 1979 — Phi Beta Kappa — Admitted to Bar, 1979, North Carolina; U.S. District Court, Middle District of North Carolina — Member American, North Carolina and Greensboro Bar Associations; North Carolina State Bar; North Carolina Association of Defense Attorneys — Practice Areas: Insurance Litigation; Insurance Coverage Litigation; Workers' Compensation; Business Law; Corporate Litigation — E-mail: brotherton@brothertonford.com

Robert A. Ford — 1955 — Washington and Lee University, B.A. (magna cum laude), 1977; Wake Forest University, J.D. (magna cum laude), 1984 — Phi Beta Kappa — Wake Forest Law Review, 1982-1984 — Admitted to Bar, 1984, North Carolina; U.S. District Court, Eastern, Middle and Western Districts of North Carolina; U.S. Court of Appeals, Fourth Circuit — Member American, North Carolina and Greensboro Bar Associations; North Carolina State Bar; North Carolina Association of Defense Attorneys; Defense Research Institute — U.S. Army, 1977-1981 — Practice Areas: Employment Litigation; Professional Malpractice; Commercial Litigation; Medical Malpractice; Professional Licensure — E-mail: ford@brothertonford.com

Demetrius W. Berry — 1972 — Campbell University, B.A. (summa cum laude), 1994; The University of North Carolina at Chapel Hill, J.D., 1997 — Phi Kappa Phi — Admitted to Bar, 1997, North Carolina; U.S. District Court, Middle and Western Districts of North Carolina; U.S. Court of Appeals, Fourth Circuit — Member American, North Carolina and Greensboro Bar Associations; North Carolina State Bar; North Carolina Association of Defense Attorneys (Board of Directors, 2004-2007) — Practice Areas: Workers' Compensation; General Liability; Medical Malpractice; Civil Litigation — E-mail: berry@brothertonford.com

Steven P. Weaver — 1976 — The University of North Carolina at Chapel Hill, B.A. (with highest distinction), 1999; J.D., 2002 — Phi Beta Kappa — Admitted to Bar, 2002, North Carolina; U.S. District Court, Middle District of North Carolina; 2003, U.S. Court of Appeals, Fourth Circuit; 2005, U.S. District Court, Eastern District of North Carolina; 2007, U.S. District Court, Western District of North Carolina; 2009, U.S. Supreme Court — Member American, North Carolina and Greensboro Bar Associations; North Carolina State Bar; North Carolina Association of Defense Attorneys; Defense Research Institute — Practice Areas: Insurance Defense; Insurance Coverage; Medical Malpractice Defense; Civil Rights Defense; Appellate — E-mail: weaver@brothertonford.com

Evans & Co.

101 West Friendly Avenue, Suite 500
Greensboro, North Carolina 27401
Telephone: 336-275-1400
Fax: 336-275-1401
Toll Free: 800-EVANSCO
E-Mail: rmciver@evanslawfirm.com
www.evanslawfirm.com

(Additional Offices: New Orleans, LA*; Durango, CO*; Katy, TX*(See Houston listing); Farmington, NM*; Jackson, WY*)

Established: 1983

Admiralty and Maritime Law, Aviation, Comprehensive General Liability, Construction Law, Directors and Officers Liability, Employment Practices Liability, Energy, Environmental Law, Excess and Umbrella, Insurance Coverage, Insurance Defense, Motor Carriers, Oil and Gas, Product Liability, Professional Liability, Property and Casualty, Railroad Law, Toxic Torts

Insurance Clients

Accident Insurance Company
AequiCap Claims Services
ACE Westchester Specialty Group
Allianz Insurance Company

GREENSBORO   NORTH CAROLINA

Evans & Co., Greensboro, NC   (Continued)

All Risk Claims Service, Inc.
American Family Insurance Company
American Hallmark Insurance Services, Inc.
American National Property and Casualty Company
Assicurazioni Generali S.p.A.
Atlantic Casualty Insurance Company
Bituminous Casualty Corporation
Canal Indemnity Company
Claims Management Corporation
CNA Insurance Companies
Colony Insurance Group
Continental Western Group
Deep South Surplus, Inc.
Employers Mutual Casualty Company
Essex Insurance Company
First Financial Insurance Company
Greenwich Insurance Company
GuideOne Insurance
Kiln Group
Markel Insurance Company
Mountain States Insurance Group
National Grange Mutual Insurance Company
Ocean Marine Indemnity Insurance Company
Phoenix Aviation Managers, Inc.
Preferred Contractors Insurance Company
St. Paul Fire and Marine Insurance Company
Southern Insurance Company
Texas All Risk General Agency, Inc.
T.H.E. Insurance Company
Transportation Claims, Inc.
Underwriters at Lloyd's, London
Underwriters Service Company, Inc.
United National Insurance Company
United States Liability Insurance Company
Universal Underwriters Insurance Company
Wilshire Insurance Company
Zurich North America

American Ambassador Casualty Company
American Fidelity Insurance Company
American Interstate Insurance Company
Anchor General Insurance Company
Atlantic Mutual Companies
Atlas Insurance Company
Boat/U.S. Marine Insurance
The Cincinnati Insurance Companies
CNA Insurance Company
Construction Insurance Company
COUNTRY Financial
Employers Insurance Company of Wausau
Erie Insurance Group
Farm Family Insurance Companies
General Security Insurance Company
H & W Insurance Services, Inc.
Liberty Insurance Services, Inc.
Meadowbrook Insurance Group
National Farmers Union Property & Casualty Company
Occidental Fire & Casualty Company of North Carolina
Penn National Insurance
Phoenix Indemnity Insurance Company
Professional Insurance Underwriters, Inc.
Shelter Insurance Companies
State National Companies, Inc.
Texas Select Lloyds Insurance Company
Transportation Casualty Insurance Company
Underwriters Indemnity Company
United Educators Insurance
United Fire & Casualty Company
United Specialty Insurance Company
Unitrin Property and Casualty Insurance Group
Virginia Mutual Insurance Company
XL Insurance

Non-Insurance Clients

High Country Transportation, Inc.
SAIA Motor Freight Line, Inc.
Jones Motor Group
United States Postal Service

Attorneys

Robert C. Evans — 1954 — Columbia University, B.A., 1975; University of Maryland, J.D. (with honors), 1980 — Admitted to Bar, 1980, Louisiana; Maryland; 1999, Colorado; 1980, U.S. District Court, Eastern, Middle and Western Districts of Maryland; 1980, U.S. Court of Appeals, Fifth Circuit; 1991, U.S. Court of Appeals, Eleventh Circuit — Member Louisiana State, Maryland State and New Orleans Bar Associations; The Colorado Bar Association; New Orleans Association of Defense Counsel; Louisiana Association of Defense Counsel; Lawyer-Pilots Bar Association; The Maritime Law Association of the United States; Defense Research Institute

Robert G. McIver — 1952 — Harvard College, B.A. (cum laude), 1975; Trinity College, Dublin, 1976; University of Virginia, J.D., 1980 — Admitted to Bar, 1981, Louisiana; 1986, North Carolina; 1982, U.S. District Court, Eastern District of Louisiana; 1982, U.S. Court of Appeals, Fifth Circuit; 1985, U.S. District Court, Western District of Louisiana; 1986, U.S. District Court, Eastern and Middle Districts of North Carolina; U.S. Court of Appeals, Fourth Circuit — Member American and North Carolina Bar Associations — Board Certified Mediator

Jeffery M. Davis — Clemson University, B.A., 2000; The University of North Carolina at Chapel Hill, J.D., 2003 — Admitted to Bar, 2003, North Carolina — Member North Carolina Bar Association

Henson & Talley, L.L.P.

Suite 600 Piedmont Building
114 North Elm Street
Greensboro, North Carolina 27401
Telephone: 336-275-0587
Fax: 336-273-2585
www.hensonlawyers.com

Established: 1968

Trial and Appellate Practice, State and Federal Courts, Insurance Defense, Automobile, Trucking Law, Workers' Compensation, Construction Law, Professional Malpractice, Product Liability, Fire, Insurance Coverage, Subrogation

Insurance Clients

Baldwin & Lyons, Inc.
Canal Insurance Company
Carolina Farmers Mutual Insurance Company
Discovery Insurance Company
GEICO Insurance Companies
Harco National Insurance Company
Protective Insurance Company
Sedgwick Claims Management Services, Inc.

Builders Mutual Insurance Company
Colony Insurance Company
Cottingham & Butler Claims Services, Inc.
Grange Mutual Casualty Company
Midwestern Insurance Alliance
North Carolina Farm Bureau Mutual Insurance Company

Non-Insurance Clients

Epes Transport System, Inc.
MGM Transport Corporation
Sears Holdings Corporation
Kmart Corporation
Old Dominion Freight Line, Inc.

Partners

Perry C. Henson — (1922-2003)

Perry C. Henson, Jr. — 1952 — The University of North Carolina at Chapel Hill, B.A., 1974; J.D., 1977 — Admitted to Bar, 1977, North Carolina; U.S. District Court, Eastern, Middle and Western Districts of North Carolina; U.S. Court of Appeals, Fourth Circuit; U.S. Supreme Court — Member American, North Carolina and Greensboro Bar Associations; International Association of Defense Counsel; North Carolina Association of Defense Attorneys; Defense Research Institute — E-mail: phenson@hensonlawyers.com

Karen Strom Talley — 1977 — The University of North Carolina at Greensboro, B.A. (cum laude), 1999; The University of North Carolina at Chapel Hill, J.D. (with honors), 2002 — Admitted to Bar, 2002, North Carolina; U.S. District Court, Eastern, Middle and Western Districts of North Carolina; U.S. Court of Appeals, Fourth Circuit — Member American, North Carolina and Greensboro Bar Associations; Guilford County Association of Women Attorneys; North Carolina Association of Women Attorneys; Guilford Inn of Court; North Carolina Association of Defense Attorneys — E-mail: ktalley@hensonlawyers.com

Associate

Heather Nicolini Wade — 1984 — High Point University, B.A., 2006; Elon University, J.D., 2009 — Admitted to Bar, 2009, North Carolina; U.S. District Court, Middle District of North Carolina — Member American, North Carolina and Greensboro Bar Associations; North Carolina Association of Defense Attorneys — E-mail: hwade@hensonlawyers.com

(This firm is also listed in the Subrogation section of this directory)

Pinto Coates Kyre & Bowers, PLLC

3203 Brassfield Road
Greensboro, North Carolina 27410
Telephone: 336-282-8848
Fax: 336-282-8409
E-Mail: rpinto@pckb-law.com
www.pckb-law.com

Established: 1994

NORTH CAROLINA

Pinto Coates Kyre & Bowers, PLLC, Greensboro, NC (Continued)

Insurance Defense, Civil Litigation, Automobile, Product Liability, Commercial Law, Workers' Compensation, Insurance Coverage, Premises Liability, General Liability, Construction Litigation, Bad Faith

Firm Profile: Pinto Coates Kyre & Bowers is a civil litigation law firm that practices statewide, regularly handling cases in many counties of North Carolina, as well as in all of the federal courts in the state, and including appeals to the N.C. appellate courts and the U.S. Fourth Circuit Court of Appeals.

Insurance Clients

Central Mutual Insurance Company
General Casualty Insurance Company
Harleysville Mutual Insurance Company
North Carolina Farm Bureau Mutual Insurance Company
QBE Regional Insurance
GEICO
Global Indemnity Insurance Company
Grain Dealers Mutual Insurance Company
The Main Street America Group
Pennsylvania National Mutual Casualty Insurance Company
State Farm Insurance Company

Non-Insurance Clients

Georgia-Pacific LLC
Lowe's Companies, Inc.

Partners

Richard L. Pinto — 1955 — Wake Forest University, B.A. (cum laude), 1977; J.D., 1980 — Phi Alpha Theta; Kappa Sigma — Admitted to Bar, 1980, North Carolina; U.S. District Court, Middle District of North Carolina; 1981, U.S. District Court, Eastern District of North Carolina; 2005, U.S. District Court, Western District of North Carolina; 2009, U.S. Supreme Court — Member North Carolina and Greensboro Bar Associations; North Carolina State Bar; Claim and Litigation Management Alliance; North Carolina Association of Defense Attorneys; Defense Research Institute; Federation of Defense and Corporate Counsel — Practice Areas: Litigation; Mediation — E-mail: rpinto@pckb-law.com

Paul D. Coates — 1956 — The University of North Carolina at Greensboro, B.S. (magna cum laude), 1978; The University of North Carolina at Chapel Hill, J.D., 1981 — Admitted to Bar, 1981, North Carolina; U.S. District Court, Middle District of North Carolina; 1995, U.S. Court of Appeals, Fourth Circuit; 2007, U.S. District Court, Eastern and Western Districts of North Carolina; 2009, U.S. Supreme Court — Member American, North Carolina and Greensboro Bar Associations; North Carolina State Bar; North Carolina Advocates for Justice; American Association for Justice — Practice Areas: Litigation — E-mail: pcoates@pckb-law.com

Kenneth Kyre, Jr. — 1951 — Shenandoah University, A.A. (summa cum laude), 1972; St. Andrews Presbyterian College, B.A. (with high honors), 1974; Wake Forest University, J.D. (cum laude), 1977 — Law Clerk to U.S. District Judge Hiram H. Ward, U.S. District Court, Middle District of North Carolina (1977-1979) — Wake Forest Law Review, Member (1975-1976); Research Editor (1976-1977) — Admitted to Bar, 1977, North Carolina; 1979, U.S. District Court, Eastern and Middle Districts of North Carolina; 1980, U.S. Court of Appeals, Fourth Circuit; 1981, U.S. Supreme Court; 1983, U.S. District Court, Western District of North Carolina — Member North Carolina and Greensboro Bar Associations; North Carolina Association of Defense Attorneys (President, 2007-2008); Defense Research Institute — Practice Areas: Litigation; Mediation — E-mail: kkyre@pckb-law.com

Deborah J. Bowers — 1952 — The University of Texas, B.A., 1974; University of Houston, J.D. (cum laude), 1980 — Order of the Barons; Phi Delta Phi — International Law Journal (1978-1980) — Admitted to Bar, 1980, Texas; 1981, New Jersey; 1998, North Carolina; 1981, U.S. District Court, District of New Jersey; 2000, U.S. District Court, Middle District of North Carolina; 2001, U.S. District Court, Eastern and Western Districts of North Carolina; 2009, U.S. Supreme Court — Member American, North Carolina and Greensboro Bar Associations; North Carolina State Bar; State Bar of Texas; North Carolina Association of Defense Attorneys — Practice Areas: Litigation; Mediation — E-mail: dbowers@pckb-law.com

G. Clark Hering, IV — 1962 — Wake Forest University, B.A., 1985; Dickinson College, J.D., 1992 — Admitted to Bar, 1992, Delaware; 1995, North Carolina; 1993, U.S. District Court, District of Delaware; 1996, U.S. District Court, Middle District of North Carolina; 1997, U.S. District Court, Western District of North Carolina — Member North Carolina and Greensboro Bar Associations; North Carolina Association of Defense Attorneys — Certified Mediator — Practice Areas: Litigation; Mediation — E-mail: chering@pckb-law.com

Pinto Coates Kyre & Bowers, PLLC, Greensboro, NC (Continued)

Jonathan P. Ward — 1979 — The University of North Carolina at Chapel Hill, B.A. (Phi Beta Kappa), 2001; The University of North Carolina, J.D. (with honors), 2007 — Admitted to Bar, 2007, North Carolina; U.S. District Court, Middle District of North Carolina; 2008, U.S. District Court, Eastern and Western Districts of North Carolina — Member North Carolina and Greensboro Bar Associations — Practice Areas: Litigation — E-mail: jward@pckb-law.com

Associates

Lenneka H. Feliciano — 1982 — North Carolina State University, B.A. (cum laude), 2004; Elon University, J.D., 2011 — Admitted to Bar, 2011, North Carolina; U.S. District Court, Middle District of North Carolina; 2012, U.S. District Court, Eastern District of North Carolina — Member North Carolina State Bar; North Carolina and Greensboro Bar Associaitons; North Carolina Association of Defense Attorneys — Moot Court Board (2009-2011) — Practice Areas: Litigation — E-mail: nfeliciano@pckb-law.com

Adam L. White — 1984 — University of Wisconsin-Madison, B.A. Political Science, 2007; Wake Forest University, J.D. (cum laude), 2013 — Admitted to Bar, 2013, North Carolina; U.S. District Court, Middle District of North Carolina — Member North Carolina State Bar — E-mail: awhite@pckb-law.com

Danielle N. Godfrey — 1988 — University of Virginia, B.A. (with distinction), 2010; Wake Forest University, J.D., 2013 — Admitted to Bar, 2013, North Carolina; U.S. District Court, Middle District of North Carolina — E-mail: dgodfrey@pckb-law.com

(This firm is also listed in the Subrogation section of this directory)

The following firms also service this area.

Bennett & Guthrie, P.L.L.C.
1560 Westbrook Plaza Drive
Winston-Salem, North Carolina 27103
 Telephone: 336-765-3121
 Fax: 336-765-8622

Alternative Dispute Resolution, Asbestos Litigation, Automobile Litigation, Carrier Defense, Civil Litigation, Commercial Litigation, Construction Law, Coverage Issues, Employment Law, General Defense Civil Litigation, General Liability, Health Care Liability, Hospital Malpractice, Insurance Coverage, Insurance Defense, Insurance Litigation, Mediation, Medical Malpractice Defense, Premises Liability, Product Liability, Product Liability Defense, Professional Liability, Professional Liability (Non-Medical) Defense, Self-Insured Defense, Trial and Appellate Practice, Trucking Litigation, Wrongful Death

SEE COMPLETE LISTING UNDER WINSTON-SALEM, NORTH CAROLINA (29 MILES)

Vernis & Bowling of Charlotte, PLLC
4701 Hedgemore Drive, Suite 812
Charlotte, North Carolina 28209
 Telephone: 704-910-8162
 Fax: 704-910-8163

Civil Litigation, Insurance Law, Workers' Compensation, Premises Liability, Labor and Employment, Civil Rights, Commercial Litigation, Automobile Liability, Complex Litigation, Product Liability, Directors and Officers Liability, Errors and Omissions, Construction Law, Construction Defect, Environmental Liability, Personal and Commercial Vehicle, Appellate Practice, Admiralty and Maritime Law, Real Estate, Family Law, Elder Law, Personal Injury Protection (PIP)

SEE COMPLETE LISTING UNDER CHARLOTTE, NORTH CAROLINA (100 MILES)

GREENVILLE † 84,554 Pitt Co.
Refer To
Crossley McIntosh Collier Hanley & Edes, PLLC
5002 Randall Parkway
Wilmington, North Carolina 28403
 Telephone: 910-762-9711
 Fax: 910-256-0310
 Toll Free: 800-499-9711

Insurance Defense, Automobile, General Liability, Product Liability, Professional Malpractice, Casualty, Personal Injury, Municipal Liability, First Party Matters, Workers' Compensation, Admiralty and Maritime Law, Subrogation, Investigations, Construction Law, Pre-Suit

SEE COMPLETE LISTING UNDER WILMINGTON, NORTH CAROLINA (118 MILES)

Refer To
Wallace, Morris, Barwick, Landis & Stroud, P.A.
131 South Queen Street
Kinston, North Carolina 28502-3557
 Telephone: 252-523-2000
 Fax: 252-523-0408
 Toll Free: 888-523-3557
Mailing Address: P.O. Box 3557, Kinston, NC 28502-3557

Insurance Law, Automobile Tort, Fire, Casualty, Defense Litigation, Construction Defect

SEE COMPLETE LISTING UNDER KINSTON, NORTH CAROLINA (28 MILES)

HENDERSON † 15,368 Vance Co.
Refer To
Bailey & Dixon, L.L.P.
434 Fayetteville Street, Suite 2500
Raleigh, North Carolina 27601
 Telephone: 919-828-0731
 Fax: 919-828-6592
Mailing Address: P.O. Box 1351, Raleigh, NC 27602-1351

General Defense, Litigation, Automobile, Construction Defect, Governmental Liability, Product Liability, General Liability, Civil Rights, Employment Law, Sexual Harassment, Environmental Law, Drug, Medical Devices, Arson, Fraud, Legal Malpractice, Life and Health, Workers' Compensation, Insurance Coverage, Bad Faith, Nursing Home Liability, Excess and Reinsurance, Regulatory and Compliance, Trial Practice, State and Federal Courts, Administrative Law, Corporate Law, Insurance Defense, Medical Malpractice, Mergers and Acquisitions, Professional Liability, Real Estate, OSHA, Government Liability, Unfair Claim/Trade Practice Defense Litigation

SEE COMPLETE LISTING UNDER RALEIGH, NORTH CAROLINA (45 MILES)

HENDERSONVILLE † 13,137 Henderson Co.
Refer To
Vernis & Bowling of Charlotte, PLLC
4701 Hedgemore Drive, Suite 812
Charlotte, North Carolina 28209
 Telephone: 704-910-8162
 Fax: 704-910-8163

Civil Litigation, Insurance Law, Workers' Compensation, Premises Liability, Labor and Employment, Civil Rights, Commercial Litigation, Automobile Liability, Complex Litigation, Product Liability, Directors and Officers Liability, Errors and Omissions, Construction Law, Construction Defect, Environmental Liability, Personal and Commercial Vehicle, Appellate Practice, Admiralty and Maritime Law, Real Estate, Family Law, Elder Law, Personal Injury Protection (PIP)

SEE COMPLETE LISTING UNDER CHARLOTTE, NORTH CAROLINA (108 MILES)

HERTFORD † 2,143 Perquimans Co.
Refer To
Hornthal, Riley, Ellis and Maland, L.L.P.
301 East Main Street
Elizabeth City, North Carolina 27909
 Telephone: 252-335-0871
 Fax: 252-335-4223

Insurance Defense, Automobile, Homeowners, Property Damage, Coverage Issues, Product Liability, Professional Liability

SEE COMPLETE LISTING UNDER ELIZABETH CITY, NORTH CAROLINA (17 MILES)

HIGH POINT 104,371 Guilford Co.
Refer To
Henson & Talley, L.L.P.
Suite 600 Piedmont Building
114 North Elm Street
Greensboro, North Carolina 27401
 Telephone: 336-275-0587
 Fax: 336-273-2585
Mailing Address: P.O. Box 3525, Greensboro, NC 27402-3525

Trial and Appellate Practice, State and Federal Courts, Insurance Defense, Automobile, Trucking Law, Workers' Compensation, Construction Law, Professional Malpractice, Product Liability, Fire, Insurance Coverage, Subrogation

SEE COMPLETE LISTING UNDER GREENSBORO, NORTH CAROLINA (20 MILES)

HILLSBOROUGH † 6,087 Orange Co.
Refer To
Henson & Talley, L.L.P.
Suite 600 Piedmont Building
114 North Elm Street
Greensboro, North Carolina 27401
 Telephone: 336-275-0587
 Fax: 336-273-2585
Mailing Address: P.O. Box 3525, Greensboro, NC 27402-3525

Trial and Appellate Practice, State and Federal Courts, Insurance Defense, Automobile, Trucking Law, Workers' Compensation, Construction Law, Professional Malpractice, Product Liability, Fire, Insurance Coverage, Subrogation

SEE COMPLETE LISTING UNDER GREENSBORO, NORTH CAROLINA (42 MILES)

JACKSONVILLE † 70,145 Onslow Co.
Refer To
Crossley McIntosh Collier Hanley & Edes, PLLC
5002 Randall Parkway
Wilmington, North Carolina 28403
 Telephone: 910-762-9711
 Fax: 910-256-0310
 Toll Free: 800-499-9711

Insurance Defense, Automobile, General Liability, Product Liability, Professional Malpractice, Casualty, Personal Injury, Municipal Liability, First Party Matters, Workers' Compensation, Admiralty and Maritime Law, Subrogation, Investigations, Construction Law, Pre-Suit

SEE COMPLETE LISTING UNDER WILMINGTON, NORTH CAROLINA (51 MILES)

Refer To
Wallace, Morris, Barwick, Landis & Stroud, P.A.
131 South Queen Street
Kinston, North Carolina 28502-3557
 Telephone: 252-523-2000
 Fax: 252-523-0408
 Toll Free: 888-523-3557
Mailing Address: P.O. Box 3557, Kinston, NC 28502-3557

Insurance Law, Automobile Tort, Fire, Casualty, Defense Litigation, Construction Defect

SEE COMPLETE LISTING UNDER KINSTON, NORTH CAROLINA (44 MILES)

KENANSVILLE † 855 Duplin Co.
Refer To
Crossley McIntosh Collier Hanley & Edes, PLLC
5002 Randall Parkway
Wilmington, North Carolina 28403
 Telephone: 910-762-9711
 Fax: 910-256-0310
 Toll Free: 800-499-9711

Insurance Defense, Automobile, General Liability, Product Liability, Professional Malpractice, Casualty, Personal Injury, Municipal Liability, First Party Matters, Workers' Compensation, Admiralty and Maritime Law, Subrogation, Investigations, Construction Law, Pre-Suit

SEE COMPLETE LISTING UNDER WILMINGTON, NORTH CAROLINA (58 MILES)

NORTH CAROLINA — KINSTON

KINSTON † 21,677 Lenoir Co.

Wallace, Morris, Barwick, Landis & Stroud, P.A.

131 South Queen Street
Kinston, North Carolina 28502-3557
Telephone: 252-523-2000
Fax: 252-523-0408
Toll Free: 888-523-3557
E-Mail: sls@wmblawyers.com
www.wmblawyers.com

Established: 1919

Insurance Law, Automobile Tort, Fire, Casualty, Defense Litigation, Construction Defect

Firm Profile: Nothing affects the quality of legal service more than the quality of lawyers. Good academic credentials as well as the abilities to listen, assess, and communicate are the common traits of the attorneys of Wallace, Morris, Barwick, Landis & Stroud, P.A.

Insurance Clients

Alfa Alliance Insurance Corporation
Carolina Casualty Insurance Company
CIGNA Group
Colonial Insurance Company
Employers Mutual Casualty Company
Federated Mutual Insurance Company
Grain Dealers Mutual Insurance Company
Indiana Lumbermens Mutual Insurance Company
National General Insurance Company
Nationwide Insurance Companies
North Carolina Farm Bureau Mutual Insurance Company
Progressive Insurance Company
Royal Insurance Group
State Farm Insurance Companies
United Services Automobile Association (USAA)
Zurich
Allstate Insurance Company
Builders Mutual Insurance Company
CGU Southeast
Cincinnati Insurance Company
Empire Fire and Marine Insurance Company
Farmers Insurance Group
Foremost Insurance Company
Glatfelter Insurance Group
Harleysville Insurance Company
Horace Mann Insurance Company
Liberty Mutual Insurance Company
Mutual of Omaha Insurance Company
National Grange Mutual Insurance Company
Ohio Casualty Group
Penn National Insurance
QBE Insurance Group
Security Insurance Group
Travelers Indemnity Company
Utica Mutual Insurance Company
XL Select Professional

Firm Members

Thomas H. Morris — 1936 — Wake Forest University, B.A., 1958; J.D., 1963 — Admitted to Bar, 1963, North Carolina; U.S. District Court, Eastern District of North Carolina; 1975, U.S. Court of Appeals, Fourth Circuit; 2001, U.S. Supreme Court — Member American, North Carolina (Board of Governors, 1980-1981) and Lenoir County Bar Associations; North Carolina State Bar; Eastern North Carolina Inn of Court (Master); North Carolina Association of Defense Attorneys — North Carolina Certified Superior Court Mediator

P.C. Barwick, Jr. — 1937 — Wake Forest University, B.A., 1959; LL.B., 1960 — Admitted to Bar, 1961, North Carolina; U.S. District Court, Eastern District of North Carolina; 1966, U.S. Court of Appeals, Fourth Circuit; 1996, U.S. Supreme Court — Member North Carolina and Lenoir County Bar Associations; North Carolina State Bar (Councilor, 1989-1994); Eastern North Carolina Inn of Court (Master); North Carolina Association of Defense Attorneys — North Carolina Certified Superior Court Mediator

Richard F. Landis, II — 1948 — Catawba College, A.B., 1970; Wake Forest University, J.D., 1973 — Admitted to Bar, 1973, North Carolina — Member American, North Carolina and Lenoir County Bar Associations; North Carolina State Bar

Stuart L. Stroud — 1967 — The University of North Carolina at Chapel Hill, B.A., 1989; Campbell University, J.D., 1992 — Admitted to Bar, 1992, North Carolina; 1995, U.S. District Court, Eastern District of North Carolina — Member North Carolina and Lenoir County Bar Associations; North Carolina State Bar; Eastern North Carolina Inn of Court; North Carolina Association of Defense Attorneys — Certified Superior Court Mediator

Wallace, Morris, Barwick, Landis & Stroud, P.A., Kinston, NC (Continued)

Kimberly Connor Benton — 1977 — DePauw University, B.A. (cum laude), 1999; Valparaiso University, J.D. (magna cum laude), 2002 — Phi Delta Phi — Admitted to Bar, 2002, North Carolina — Member North Carolina and Lenoir County Bar Associations; North Carolina Association of Women Attorneys

Associate

Donald K. Phillips — 1972 — The University of North Carolina at Chapel Hill, B.A., 1994; Widener University, J.D., 1999 — Editor-in-Chief, Widener University Law Review — Admitted to Bar, 1999, North Carolina; 2009, U.S. District Court, Eastern District of North Carolina — Member North Carolina and Lenoir County Bar Associations; North Carolina State Bar; Eighth Judicial District Bar; North Carolina Association of Defense Attorneys

LEXINGTON † 18,931 Davidson Co.

Refer To

Henson & Talley, L.L.P.

Suite 600 Piedmont Building
114 North Elm Street
Greensboro, North Carolina 27401
Telephone: 336-275-0587
Fax: 336-273-2585

Mailing Address: P.O. Box 3525, Greensboro, NC 27402-3525

Trial and Appellate Practice, State and Federal Courts, Insurance Defense, Automobile, Trucking Law, Workers' Compensation, Construction Law, Professional Malpractice, Product Liability, Fire, Insurance Coverage, Subrogation

SEE COMPLETE LISTING UNDER GREENSBORO, NORTH CAROLINA (36 MILES)

LILLINGTON † 3,194 Harnett Co.

Refer To

Bailey & Dixon, L.L.P.

434 Fayetteville Street, Suite 2500
Raleigh, North Carolina 27601
Telephone: 919-828-0731
Fax: 919-828-6592

Mailing Address: P.O. Box 1351, Raleigh, NC 27602-1351

General Defense, Litigation, Automobile, Construction Defect, Governmental Liability, Product Liability, General Liability, Civil Rights, Employment Law, Sexual Harassment, Environmental Law, Drug, Medical Devices, Arson, Fraud, Legal Malpractice, Life and Health, Workers' Compensation, Insurance Coverage, Bad Faith, Nursing Home Liability, Excess and Reinsurance, Regulatory and Compliance, Trial Practice, State and Federal Courts, Administrative Law, Corporate Law, Insurance Defense, Medical Malpractice, Mergers and Acquisitions, Professional Liability, Real Estate, OSHA, Government Liability, Unfair Claim/Trade Practice Defense Litigation

SEE COMPLETE LISTING UNDER RALEIGH, NORTH CAROLINA (32 MILES)

LOUISBURG † 3,359 Franklin Co.

Refer To

Bailey & Dixon, L.L.P.

434 Fayetteville Street, Suite 2500
Raleigh, North Carolina 27601
Telephone: 919-828-0731
Fax: 919-828-6592

Mailing Address: P.O. Box 1351, Raleigh, NC 27602-1351

General Defense, Litigation, Automobile, Construction Defect, Governmental Liability, Product Liability, General Liability, Civil Rights, Employment Law, Sexual Harassment, Environmental Law, Drug, Medical Devices, Arson, Fraud, Legal Malpractice, Life and Health, Workers' Compensation, Insurance Coverage, Bad Faith, Nursing Home Liability, Excess and Reinsurance, Regulatory and Compliance, Trial Practice, State and Federal Courts, Administrative Law, Corporate Law, Insurance Defense, Medical Malpractice, Mergers and Acquisitions, Professional Liability, Real Estate, OSHA, Government Liability, Unfair Claim/Trade Practice Defense Litigation

SEE COMPLETE LISTING UNDER RALEIGH, NORTH CAROLINA (32 MILES)

RALEIGH   NORTH CAROLINA

LUMBERTON † 21,542 Robeson Co.

Refer To

Crossley McIntosh Collier Hanley & Edes, PLLC
5002 Randall Parkway
Wilmington, North Carolina 28403
   Telephone: 910-762-9711
   Fax: 910-256-0310
   Toll Free: 800-499-9711

Insurance Defense, Automobile, General Liability, Product Liability, Professional Malpractice, Casualty, Personal Injury, Municipal Liability, First Party Matters, Workers' Compensation, Admiralty and Maritime Law, Subrogation, Investigations, Construction Law, Pre-Suit

SEE COMPLETE LISTING UNDER WILMINGTON, NORTH CAROLINA (78 MILES)

MANTEO † 1,434 Dare Co.

Refer To

Hornthal, Riley, Ellis and Maland, L.L.P.
301 East Main Street
Elizabeth City, North Carolina 27909
   Telephone: 252-335-0871
   Fax: 252-335-4223

Insurance Defense, Automobile, Homeowners, Property Damage, Coverage Issues, Product Liability, Professional Liability

SEE COMPLETE LISTING UNDER ELIZABETH CITY, NORTH CAROLINA (65 MILES)

MARSHALL † 872 Madison Co.

Leake & Stokes
Main Street
Marshall, North Carolina 28753
   Telephone: 828-649-3883

(Asheville, NC Office*: 501 BB&T Building, 28801)
   (Tel: 828-253-3661)

Established: 1974

Insurance Defense, Automobile, General Liability, Product Liability, Fire, Casualty, Medical Malpractice, Workers' Compensation, Subrogation

(See listing under Asheville, NC for additional information)

NEW BERN † 29,524 Craven Co.

Refer To

Crossley McIntosh Collier Hanley & Edes, PLLC
5002 Randall Parkway
Wilmington, North Carolina 28403
   Telephone: 910-762-9711
   Fax: 910-256-0310
   Toll Free: 800-499-9711

Insurance Defense, Automobile, General Liability, Product Liability, Professional Malpractice, Casualty, Personal Injury, Municipal Liability, First Party Matters, Workers' Compensation, Admiralty and Maritime Law, Subrogation, Investigations, Construction Law, Pre-Suit

SEE COMPLETE LISTING UNDER WILMINGTON, NORTH CAROLINA (176 MILES)

Refer To

Wallace, Morris, Barwick, Landis & Stroud, P.A.
131 South Queen Street
Kinston, North Carolina 28502-3557
   Telephone: 252-523-2000
   Fax: 252-523-0408
   Toll Free: 888-523-3557

Mailing Address: P.O. Box 3557, Kinston, NC 28502-3557

Insurance Law, Automobile Tort, Fire, Casualty, Defense Litigation, Construction Defect

SEE COMPLETE LISTING UNDER KINSTON, NORTH CAROLINA (35 MILES)

PITTSBORO † 3,743 Chatham Co.

Refer To

Bailey & Dixon, L.L.P.
434 Fayetteville Street, Suite 2500
Raleigh, North Carolina 27601
   Telephone: 919-828-0731
   Fax: 919-828-6592

Mailing Address: P.O. Box 1351, Raleigh, NC 27602-1351

General Defense, Litigation, Automobile, Construction Defect, Governmental Liability, Product Liability, General Liability, Civil Rights, Employment Law, Sexual Harassment, Environmental Law, Drug, Medical Devices, Arson, Fraud, Legal Malpractice, Life and Health, Workers' Compensation, Insurance Coverage, Bad Faith, Nursing Home Liability, Excess and Reinsurance, Regulatory and Compliance, Trial Practice, State and Federal Courts, Administrative Law, Corporate Law, Insurance Defense, Medical Malpractice, Mergers and Acquisitions, Professional Liability, Real Estate, OSHA, Government Liability, Unfair Claim/Trade Practice Defense Litigation

SEE COMPLETE LISTING UNDER RALEIGH, NORTH CAROLINA (34 MILES)

PLYMOUTH † 3,878 Washington Co.

Refer To

Hornthal, Riley, Ellis and Maland, L.L.P.
301 East Main Street
Elizabeth City, North Carolina 27909
   Telephone: 252-335-0871
   Fax: 252-335-4223

Insurance Defense, Automobile, Homeowners, Property Damage, Coverage Issues, Product Liability, Professional Liability

SEE COMPLETE LISTING UNDER ELIZABETH CITY, NORTH CAROLINA (52 MILES)

RALEIGH † 403,892 Wake Co.

Allen, Kopet & Associates, PLLC
2501 Blue Ridge Road, Suite 250
Raleigh, North Carolina 27607
   Telephone: 919-341-4463
   Fax: 919-827-8981

(See listing under Chattanooga, TN for additional information)

Bailey & Dixon, L.L.P.
434 Fayetteville Street, Suite 2500
Raleigh, North Carolina 27601
   Telephone: 919-828-0731
   Fax: 919-828-6592
   www.bdixon.com

Established: 1916

General Defense, Litigation, Automobile, Construction Defect, Governmental Liability, Product Liability, General Liability, Civil Rights, Employment Law, Sexual Harassment, Environmental Law, Drug, Medical Devices, Arson, Fraud, Legal Malpractice, Life and Health, Workers' Compensation, Insurance Coverage, Bad Faith, Nursing Home Liability, Excess and Reinsurance, Regulatory and Compliance, Trial Practice, State and Federal Courts, Administrative Law, Corporate Law, Insurance Defense, Medical Malpractice, Mergers and Acquisitions, Professional Liability, Real Estate, OSHA, Government Liability, Unfair Claim/Trade Practice Defense Litigation

Insurance Clients

Admiral Insurance Company	Aetna Casualty and Surety Company
AIG Insurance Company	
Allied Insurance Company	American Insurance Association (AIA)
Amerisure Companies	
Burlington Insurance Group	Cambridge Integrated Services

NORTH CAROLINA

RALEIGH

Bailey & Dixon, L.L.P., Raleigh, NC (Continued)

Colonial Insurance Company
Employers Casualty Company
GAB Robins North America, Inc.
Great-West Life Assurance Company
Jefferson-Pilot Life Insurance Company
Liberty Mutual Insurance
Markel American Insurance Company
National Indemnity Company
Nationwide Mutual Fire Insurance Company
Ohio Casualty Group
Philadelphia Insurance Company
Scottsdale Insurance Company
Southern Pilot Insurance Company
State Auto Insurance Companies
State Farm Insurance Companies
Tower Hill Insurance Company
Direct Insurance Company
Erie Insurance Group
Great American Insurance Company
The Hartford Insurance Group
Lawyers Mutual Liability Insurance Company of North Carolina
Mid-Atlantic Insurance Services of North Carolina, LLC
Nationwide Life Insurance Company
Nationwide Mutual Insurance Company
Safeco Insurance
Sedgwick CMS
Specialty Claims Management, LLC
Titan Insurance Company
Zurich American Insurance Group

Non-Insurance Clients

Inter Local Risk Financing Fund of North Carolina
North Carolina League of Municipalities Risk Management Services

Firm Members

Ralph McDonald — 1940 — The University of North Carolina, A.B., 1961; LL.B., 1964 — Admitted to Bar, 1964, North Carolina; U.S. District Court, Eastern and Middle Districts of North Carolina; U.S. Court of Appeals, Fourth Circuit; U.S. Supreme Court — Member American, North Carolina and Wake County Bar Associations — Practice Areas: Administrative Law; Transportation — E-mail: rmcdonald@bdixon.com

David S. Coats — 1962 — Guilford College, B.S., 1984; Wake Forest University, J.D., 1988 — Admitted to Bar, 1988, North Carolina; U.S. District Court, Eastern, Middle and Western Districts of North Carolina; U.S. Court of Appeals, Fourth Circuit — Member American, North Carolina and Wake County Bar Associations — Listed in: North Carolina Business Magazine's Legal Elite, North Carolina Super Lawyers, The Best Lawyers in America; Fellow, Litigation Counsel of America and Your House Counsel — Practice Areas: Construction Law; Appellate Practice; Insurance Coverage; Insurance Defense; Commercial Litigation — E-mail: dcoats@bdixon.com

David S. Wisz — 1969 — St. Bonaventure University, B.B.A. (magna cum laude), 1991; University of Kentucky, J.D. (with high distinction), 1994 — Admitted to Bar, 1994, Kentucky; 1996, North Carolina; 1994, U.S. Court of Appeals, Sixth Circuit; 1994, U.S. District Court, Eastern District of Kentucky; U.S. District Court, Eastern District of North Carolina; U.S. Court of Appeals, Fourth Circuit; U.S. Supreme Court — Member American, Kentucky, Louisville State, North Carolina and Wake County Bar Associations — Practice Areas: Civil Litigation; Insurance Law; Negligence; Premises Liability; Tort; Litigation; Construction Law — E-mail: dwisz@bdixon.com

Robert H. Merritt, Jr. — 1948 — The University of North Carolina at Chapel Hill, B.A., 1971; Southern Methodist University, J.D., 1974; LL.M., 1976 — Admitted to Bar, 1974, Texas; 1977, North Carolina; 1978, U.S. District Court, Middle District of North Carolina; 1979, U.S. District Court, Eastern District of North Carolina; 1980, U.S. District Court, Western District of North Carolina; 1981, U.S. Court of Appeals, Fourth Circuit — Member American and North Carolina Bar Associations — Member, Legislative Study Committee on Revenue Laws, 1979-1984 — Practice Areas: Business Law; Commercial Litigation — E-mail: rmerritt@bdixon.com

G. Lawrence Reeves, Jr. — 1952 — The University of North Carolina at Chapel Hill, B.S., 1975; J.D., 1978 — Admitted to Bar, 1978, North Carolina; U.S. District Court, Eastern, Middle and Western Districts of North Carolina; U.S. Supreme Court — Member North Carolina and Wake County Bar Associations — Attorney General's Office (Appellate Section, Assistant Attorney General) — Practice Areas: Insurance Defense; Personal Injury; Workers' Compensation; Professional Malpractice; Medical Malpractice; Coverage Issues — E-mail: lreeves@bdixon.com

Michael L. Weisel — 1957 — Guilford College, B.S., 1977; North Carolina State University, M.A., 2003; Campbell University, J.D., 1980 — Admitted to Bar, 1980, North Carolina; U.S. District Court, Eastern District of North Carolina; U.S. Supreme Court — Member North Carolina and Wake County Bar Associations — Practice Areas: Administrative Law; Corporate Law; Real Estate — E-mail: mlweisel@bdixon.com

Philip A. Collins — 1964 — The University of North Carolina at Chapel Hill, B.A., 1986; North Carolina State University, M.A., 1996; The University of North Carolina at Chapel Hill, J.D. (with honors), 2000 — Admitted to Bar, 2000, North Carolina; U.S. District Court, Eastern District of North

Bailey & Dixon, L.L.P., Raleigh, NC (Continued)

Carolina — Member North Carolina Bar Association; North Carolina Association of Defense Attorneys — Practice Areas: Civil Litigation; Insurance Coverage; Personal Injury; Professional Malpractice; Appellate Practice — E-mail: pcollins@bdixon.com

Of Counsel

Charles F. McDarris — 1963 — Presbyterian College, B.S., 1985; Wake Forest University, J.D., 1990 — Admitted to Bar, 1991, North Carolina; 1996, U.S. District Court, Eastern District of North Carolina; 1998, U.S. Court of Appeals, Fourth Circuit; 1998, U.S. Supreme Court — Member North Carolina and Wake County Bar Associations; Tenth Judicial Bar — Practice Areas: Administrative Law; Municipal Law; Litigation — E-mail: cmcdarris@bdixon.com

J. Heydt Philbeck — 1967 — Elon University, B.A. (magna cum laude), 1989; Valparaiso University, J.D., 1992 — Admitted to Bar, 1992, North Carolina; U.S. District Court, Eastern, Middle and Western Districts of North Carolina; U.S. Court of Appeals, Fourth Circuit; U.S. Court of International Trade; U.S. Supreme Court — Member North Carolina and Wake County Bar Associations; North Carolina Academy of Trial Lawyers; Braxton Craven American Inn of Court (Barrister); Association of Trial Lawyers of America; National Institute of Trial Advocacy — Practice Areas: Trial Practice; Litigation; Civil Rights; Discrimination; Business Law; Contracts; Employment Law — E-mail: hphilbeck@bdixon.com

Jeffrey P. Gray — 1959 — Western Carolina University, B.S., 1981; Campbell University, J.D., 1985 — Admitted to Bar, 1985, North Carolina; U.S. District Court, Eastern, Middle and Western Districts of North Carolina; U.S. Court of Appeals, Fourth Circuit; U.S. Supreme Court — Member North Carolina State Bar; North Carolina and Wake County Bar Associations; Tenth Judicial District Bar — Practice Areas: Administrative Law; Appellate Practice; Business Law; Civil Litigation; Eminent Domain; Lobbying; Real Estate — E-mail: jgray@bdixon.xom

Sabra J. Faires — Davidson College, B.A. (Phi Beta Kappa), 1977; The University of North Carolina at Chapel Hill, J.D. (with honors), 1980 — Admitted to Bar, 1980, North Carolina — Member North Carolona State Bar; Wake County Bar Association (Sections on Administrative Law; Government & Public Sector) — Practice Areas: Administrative Law; Regulatory and Compliance; Business Law; Corporate Law; Employment Law; Government Affairs; Municipal Law — E-mail: sfaires@bdixon.com

William R. Gilkeson, Jr. — Rhodes College, B.A., 1969; The University of North Carolina at Chapel Hill, J.D., 1985 — Admitted to Bar, 1985, North Carolina — Practice Areas: Administrative Law; Regulatory and Compliance; Employment Law; Government Affairs — E-mail: wgilkeson@bdixon.com

Associates

John T. Crook — 1981 — North Carolina State University, B.A. (magna cum laude), 2003; Campbell University, J.D., 2006 — Admitted to Bar, 2006, North Carolina — Member American, North Carolina and Wake County Bar Associations — Practice Areas: Civil Litigation; Personal Injury; Professional Liability — E-mail: jtcrook@bdixon.com

Adam N. Olls — 1983 — The University of North Carolina, Kenan-Flagler Business School, B.S.B.A., 2005; The University of North Carolina, J.D. (with honors), 2008 — William Richardson Davie Scholar — Admitted to Bar, 2008, North Carolina — Member American, North Carolina and Wake County Bar Associations; Tenth Judicial District Bar — Practice Areas: Business Law; Corporate Law; Administrative Law; Real Estate — E-mail: aolls@bdixon.com

Mollie M. Livingston — 1984 — Meredith College, B.A. (cum laude), 2006; Campbell University, J.D., 2009 — Admitted to Bar, 2009, North Carolina — Member American, North Carolina and Wake County Bar Associations — Practice Areas: Civil Litigation; Insurance Defense; Insurance Law; Litigation — E-mail: mlivingston@bdixon.com

Jeffrey D. McKinney — 1984 — Davidson College, B.A., 2006; Wake Forest University, J.D., 2009 — Admitted to Bar, 2009, North Carolina — Member American, North Carolina and Wake County Bar Associations — Practice Areas: Administrative Law; Business Law; Corporate Law — E-mail: jmckinney@bdixon.com

Allison Pope Cooper — 1980 — Virginia Tech, B.A. (magna cum laude), 2002; Campbell University, J.D., 2005 — Admitted to Bar, 2005, North Carolina — Member North Carolina and Wake County Bar Associations; First and Tenth Judicial Districts Bar Associations; North Carolina Association of Women Attorneys — Practice Areas: Administrative Law; Eminent Domain; Estate Planning; Municipal Law; Real Estate; Corporate Law; Civil Trial Practice; Lobbying — E-mail: acooper@bdixon.com

RALEIGH   NORTH CAROLINA

Bailey & Dixon, L.L.P., Raleigh, NC   (Continued)

Daniel M. Nunn — 1978 — Duke University, B.A., 2001; University of Miami School of Law, J.D., 2010 — Admitted to Bar, 2011, North Carolina — Member American, North Carolina and Wake County Bar Associations; Tenth Judicial District Car — Practice Areas: Civil Litigation — E-mail: dnunn@bdixon.com

(Revisors of the North Carolina Insurance Law Digest for this Publication)

(This firm is also listed in the Regulatory and Compliance section of this directory)

Cranfill Sumner & Hartzog LLP

5420 Wade Park Boulevard, Suite 300
Raleigh, North Carolina 27607
   Telephone: 919-828-5100
   Fax: 919-828-2277
   E-Mail: bpennell@cshlaw.com
   www.cshlaw.com

(Charlotte, NC Office: 2907 Providence Road, Suite 200, 28211, P.O. Box 30787, 28230)
   (Tel: 704-332-8300)
   (Fax: 704-332-9994)
(Wilmington, NC Office: 1209 Culbreth Drive, Suite 200, 28405)
   (Tel: 910-509-9778)
   (Fax: 910-509-9676)

Established: 1992

Appellate, Commercial Litigation, Construction Law, Dram Shop, Liquor Liability, Environmental Law, Toxic Torts, Fire, Arson, Insurance Coverage, Labor and Employment, Medical Malpractice, Motor Vehicle, Premises Liability, Product Liability, Professional Liability, Trucking, Commercial Vehicle, Workers' Compensation, Environmental Law, Food Liability Law, Municipal & Police Law

Insurance Clients

CNA Insurance Company	The Hartford
Liberty Mutual Group	Nautilus Insurance Group
Penn National Insurance Company	Zurich North America

Managing Partner

Dan M. Hartzog — The University of North Carolina, B.A., 1969; J.D., 1972 — Admitted to Bar, 1973, North Carolina — Member North Carolina (Member, Litigation Section) and Wake County (Secretary, 1979-1984; Board of Directors, 1984-1986) Bar Associations; North Carolina Association of Defense Attorneys; Defense Research Institute; American Board of Trial Advocates — DRC Certified Mediator

Dickie, McCamey & Chilcote, P.C.

8000 Regency Parkway, Suite 485
Cary, North Carolina 27518-8580
   Telephone: 919-337-4644
   Fax: 888-811-7144
   Toll Free: 855-288-0277
   E-Mail: info@dmclaw.com
   www.dmclaw.com

(Additional Offices: Pittsburgh, PA*; Charlotte, NC*; Cleveland, OH*; Columbus, OH*; Haddonfield, NJ*; Camp Hill, PA*(See Harrisburg listing); Lancaster, SC*; Philadelphia, PA*; Steubenville, OH*; Wheeling, WV*; Wilmington, DE*)

Established: 2011

Dickie, McCamey & Chilcote, P.C., Raleigh, NC   (Continued)

Asbestos Litigation, Bad Faith, Captive Company Matters, Casualty, Commercial Litigation, Energy, Labor and Employment, Excess and Reinsurance, Extra-Contractual Litigation, Insurance Agents, Insurance Coverage, Insurance Coverage Litigation, Legal Malpractice, Medical Malpractice, Medicare Set-Aside Practice, Municipal Liability, Nursing Home Liability, Product Liability, Professional Liability, Property and Casualty, Surety, Transportation, Trucking, Uninsured and Underinsured Motorist, Workers' Compensation

Shareholder

Michael W. Ballance — Branch Office Shareholder-in-Charge — North Carolina State University, B.A. (magna cum laude), 1992; The University of North Carolina at Chapel Hill, J.D. (with honors), 1996 — Admitted to Bar, 1996, North Carolina

(See listing under Pittsburgh, PA for additional information)

Manning, Fulton & Skinner, P.A.

3605 Glenwood Avenue, Suite 500
Raleigh, North Carolina 27612
   Telephone: 919-787-8880
   Fax: 919-325-4618
   E-Mail: inquiry@manningfulton.com
   www.manningfulton.com

Established: 1954

Commercial Litigation, Insurance Defense, Professional Negligence, Employment Litigation, Real Estate Litigation, Construction Litigation

Firm Profile: Manning Fulton's Insurance Defense team is experienced in handling a wide variety of claims and litigation. Retained by top carriers to defend clients in federal and state courts in all districts of North Carolina, our Professional Liability Defense Group has been approved as panel counsel for many carriers to defend attorneys, health care providers, architects, engineers, dentists, accountants, directors and officers, real estate brokers and agents and financial planners under their E&O policies. Our insurance defense attorneys stay current on new coverage areas, such as Cyber Liability, so that we can be prepared to defend clients against claims as new legal issue areas like breach of data and privacy become more prevalent.

Manning Fulton also has particular expertise representing insurance professionals, including brokers, agents, third party administrators and adjusters in thousands of disputes and lawsuits covering: professional negligence, breach of contract, unfair trade practices, ERISA violations, breach of fiduciary duty, fraud, failure to procure insurance, misrepresentation of incorrect advice, unauthorized binding of coverage, improper conduct relating to premium finance loans, mishandling of claims, lien priority disputes, deed reformation actions, boundary line disputes, undisclosed/missing heirs disputes, inheritance disputes and forgery actions. The firm's extensive representation of insurance company clients has given us great insight and knowledge that benefits our corporate clients in their questions about claims, disputes or coverage issues.

Insurance Clients

Allied Insurance Company	Allstate Insurance Company
AmRisc, LP	Broadspire Services, Inc.
Certain Underwriters at Lloyd's	Chicago National Title Insurance Company
Chubb Specialty Insurance	
Custard Insurance Adjusters, Inc.	Delta Dental
Employers Reinsurance Corporation	Fidelity National Title Insurance Company
First Mercury Insurance Company	General Star
Greenville Casualty Insurance Company	Hanover Insurance Group
	Hiscox, Ltd.

NORTH CAROLINA — RALEIGH

Manning, Fulton & Skinner, P.A., Raleigh, NC (Continued)

Houston Casualty Company
Kemper Insurance Companies
Lawyers Mutual Insurance Company
MAG Mutual Insurance Company
Monitor Liability Managers, LLC
North American Claims Control
North Carolina Self-Insurance Security Association
Professional Indemnity Agency
State National Companies, Inc.
Travelers Insurance Companies
XL Insurance
Insurance Federation of North Carolina
Lawyers Title Insurance Corporation
Medical Mutual Insurance Company
North American Specialty Claims
Old Republic National Title Insurance Company
Sagicor Claims Management, Inc.
Swiss Reinsurance Company
Westport Insurance Corporation

Firm Members

Michael T. Medford — The University of North Carolina, B.A., 1973; Columbia University, J.D., 1976 — Admitted to Bar, 1976, North Carolina; U.S. District Court, Eastern, Middle and Western Districts of North Carolina; U.S. Court of Appeals, Fourth Circuit; U.S. Supreme Court — Member Fellow, Litigation Counsel of America; Federal Bar Advisory Council (1993-1996) — Practice Areas: Insurance Coverage; Insurance Defense; Professional Liability; Commercial Litigation

Michael S. Harrell — Old Dominion University, B.A., 1985; Wake Forest University, M.A., 1987; University of Virginia, J.D., 1999 — Admitted to Bar, 1990, North Carolina; U.S. District Court, Eastern and Middle Districts of North Carolina — Practice Areas: Insurance Defense; Commercial Litigation; Family Law

William C. Smith, Jr. — The University of North Carolina at Chapel Hill, B.A., 1983; J.D., 1987 — Admitted to Bar, 1987, North Carolina; U.S. District Court, Eastern and Middle Districts of North Carolina — Practice Areas: Professional Liability; Insurance Defense; Bankruptcy; Creditor's Rights

Robert Shields — The University of North Carolina, B.A., 1978; J.D., 1981 — Admitted to Bar, 1981, North Carolina; U.S. District Court, Eastern District of North Carolina — Member Defense Research Institute; North Carolina Association of Defense Attorneys — Practice Areas: Professional Liability; Commercial Litigation

Judson A. Welborn — The University of North Carolina, B.A., 1995; Campbell University, J.D., 1998 — Admitted to Bar, 1998, North Carolina; U.S. District Court, Eastern, Middle and Western Districts of North Carolina; U.S. Court of Appeals, Fourth Circuit — Member North Carolina Land Title Association — Practice Areas: Real Estate Litigation; Construction Litigation; Business Litigation

William S. Cherry, III — North Carolina State University, B.A., 1994; Campbell University, J.D., 2005 — Admitted to Bar, 2005, North Carolina; U.S. District Court, Eastern, Middle and Western Districts of North Carolina — Practice Areas: Insurance Litigation; Commercial Litigation; Employment Litigation

John B. McMillan — The University of North Carolina, B.A., 1964; The University of North Carolina at Chapel Hill, J.D., 1967 — Admitted to Bar, 1967, North Carolina — Practice Areas: Government Affairs; Litigation; Eminent Domain; Appellate

Associates

J. Whitfield Gibson — The University of North Carolina at Chapel Hill, B.A., 2005; Campbell University, J.D. (cum laude), 2010 — Admitted to Bar, 2010, North Carolina; U.S. District Court, Middle and Western Districts of North Carolina — Practice Areas: Professional Liability; Commercial Litigation; Estate Litigation

Natalie M. Rice — The University of North Carolina, B.A. (with distinction), 2004; Campbell University, J.D., 2011 — Admitted to Bar, 2011, North Carolina; U.S. District Court, Eastern, Middle and Western Districts of North Carolina — Member Defense Research Institute; North Carolina Association of Defense Attorneys — Practice Areas: Real Estate Litigation; Professional Liability; Insurance Litigation; Commercial Litigation

Millberg Gordon Stewart PLLC

1101 Haynes Street, Suite 104
Raleigh, North Carolina 27604
Telephone: 919-836-0090
Fax: 919-836-8027
Toll Free: 888-878-5104
E-Mail: mgsfirm@mgsattorneys.com
www.mgsattorneys.com

Millberg Gordon Stewart PLLC, Raleigh, NC (Continued)

Product Liability, Toxic Torts, Professional Liability, Civil Trial Practice, Civil Litigation, Insurance Coverage, Construction Law, Wrongful Death, Catastrophic Injury, Railroad Law, Trucking Law, Environmental Law, Energy, Premises Liability, Employment Litigation, Commercial Litigation, Class Actions, Utilities

Firm Profile: Since 1994, Millberg Gordon Stewart PLLC has built a reputation for handling its clients' legal affairs with skill & vigor. The firm's attorneys are experienced trial lawyers who regularly defend & try cases for target defendants, often against the best attorneys the plaintiffs' bar has to offer.

Insurance Clients

Broadspire

Non-Insurance Clients

Caterpillar Inc.
Duke Energy Corp.
Norfolk Southern Corporation
RailAmerica, Inc.
CSX Transportation Inc.
National Railroad Passenger Corporation (AMTRAK)
SPX Corporation

Firm Members

John C. Millberg — Bowling Green State University, B.A. (cum laude), 1977; Wake Forest University School of Law, J.D., 1980 — Admitted to Bar, 1980, Texas; 1986, North Carolina; 2000, South Carolina; U.S. District Court, Eastern and Southern Districts of Texas; U.S. District Court, Eastern, Middle and Western Districts of North Carolina; U.S. District Court, District of South Carolina; U.S. Court of Appeals, Fourth, Fifth and Eleventh Circuits — Member North Carolina Bar Association; State Bar of Texas; South Carolina Bar; Transportation Research Board; North Carolina Association of Defense Attorneys; National Association of Railroad Trial Counsel

Frank J. Gordon — North Carolina State University, B.S.Ch.E., 1985; Wake Forest University School of Law, J.D., 1988 — Law Clerk to Honorable Frank W. Bullock, Jr., U.S. District Judge, Middle District of North Carolina — Wake Forest University Law Review, 1986-1988 — Admitted to Bar, 1988, North Carolina; 2003, South Carolina; U.S. District Court, Eastern, Middle and Western Districts of North Carolina; U.S. Court of Appeals, Fourth Circuit; U.S. Supreme Court — Member North Carolina Bar Association; North Carolina Trucking Association; National Association of Railroad Trial Counsel; North Carolina Association of Defense Attorneys; Defense Research Institute

William W. Stewart, Jr. — Mississippi College, B.S., 1987; Mississippi College School of Law, J.D. (with distinction), 1993 — Law Clerk to Honorable Franklin T. Dupree, Jr., Senior U.S. District Judge, Eastern District of North Carolina — Managing Editor, Mississippi College Law Review, 1992-1993 — Admitted to Bar, 1994, North Carolina; 2004, South Carolina; U.S. District Court, Eastern and Middle Districts of North Carolina — Member American, North Carolina and Wake County Bar Associations; South Carolina Bar; North Carolina Trucking Association; Railroad Association of North Carolina; National Association of Railroad Trial Counsel; Defense Research Institute; North Carolina Association of Defense Attorneys

Associates

Meredith E. Woods — The University of Tennessee, B.A., 2002; University of North Carolina at Chapel Hill School of Law, J.D., 2008 — Admitted to Bar, 2008, North Carolina; 2009, South Carolina; U.S. District Court, Eastern, Middle and Western Districts of North Carolina; U.S. District Court, District of South Carolina — Member North Carolina State Bar; South Carolina Bar; Wake County Bar Association; Tenth Judicial District Bar Association

Tyler Brooks — Wake Forest University, B.A. (summa cum laude, with honors), 2003; Vanderbilt University Law School, J.D., 2006 — Admitted to Bar, 2007, Tennessee; North Carolina; South Carolina; U.S. District Court, Eastern, Middle and Western Districts of North Carolina; U.S. Court of Appeals for the Federal, Fourth and Sixth Circuits — Member Federal, American, North Carolina and Wake County Bar Associations; Tenth Judicial District Bar Association

Julie O. Yates — The University of North Carolina at Chapel Hill, B.A., 2008; Campbell University Norman Adrian Wiggins School of Law, J.D., 2012 — Admitted to Bar, 2012, North Carolina; South Carolina; U.S. District Court, Eastern, Middle and Western Districts of North Carolina — Member American, North Carolina and Wake County Bar Associations

RALEIGH   NORTH CAROLINA

Patterson Dilthey LLP
4101 Lake Boone Trail, Suite 514
Raleigh, North Carolina 27607
   Telephone: 919-821-4020
   Fax: 919-829-0055
   E-Mail: cderrenbacher@pattersondilthey.com
   www.pattersondilthey.com

Administrative Law, Automobile Liability, Bad Faith, Commercial Litigation, Construction Defect, Construction Law, Employment Law, Extra-Contractual Litigation, Indian Law, Insurance Coverage, Medical Malpractice, Motor Vehicle, Personal Injury, Premises Liability, Product Liability, Property Damage, Professional Malpractice, Truck Liability, Workers' Compensation, Wrongful Death

Firm Profile: Patterson Dilthey, LLP, is known for exceptional representation of clients and trial success. The firm understands the significance a reputation has for any business. They utilize teamwork, attention to detail, and thorough trial preparation to ensure the professional standing of clients is maintained for the duration of litigation, and after.

Insurance Clients

American Home Assurance Company	Ameriprise Auto & Home Insurance
AMEX Assurance Company	Broadspire
Crawford & Company	EMC Insurance Company
Firemen's Insurance Company of Washington, D.C.	Gallagher Bassett Services, Inc.
Liberty Mutual Insurance Company	Lawyers Mutual Insurance Company
Montgomery Insurance	Philadelphia Insurance Company
State Farm Insurance Company	Union Insurance Company
Universal Underwriters Insurance Company	W.R. Berkley Corporation/Mid-Atlantic Group
Zurich	

Non-Insurance Clients

Asplundh Tree Expert Company	Baker Furniture Company
Dolgencorp, Inc.	Dollar General Stores
Erwin Oil Company, Inc.	Food Lion, LLC
Kohler Company	Lumbee Tribe of North Carolina
Macy's Corporate Services	McKee Foods Corporation
Red Star Fuel Oil Company, Inc.	Universal Forest Products, Inc.

Retired

Grady S. Patterson, Jr. — Wake Forest University, B.A., 1946; J.D., 1950 — Admitted to Bar, 1950, North Carolina — (Retired)

Partners

Ronald C. Dilthey — Wake Forest College, B.S., 1957; LL.B., 1960 — Admitted to Bar, 1960, North Carolina — Member American and Wake County Bar Associations; North Carolina Bar Association (Lecturer, Annual Practical Skills Course, 1969-1995; Chairman, Committee on Medico-Legal Liaison, 1976-1979; Member, Board of Governors, 1982-1985; Chairman, Litigation Section, 1983-1984; Chairman, Administration of Justice Study Committee, 1992-1993; Chairman, Administration of Justice Study Task Force, 1993-1996; Vice President, 1996-1998); Fellow, American College of Trial Lawyers

Phillip J. Anthony — The University of Akron, B.A., 1981; Webster University, M.A., 1988; Campbell University, J.D., 1992 — Admitted to Bar, 1992, North Carolina; U.S. District Court, Eastern District of North Carolina; U.S. Court of Appeals, Fourth Circuit — Member North Carolina and Wake County Bar Associations; Defense Research Institute

Christopher J. Derrenbacher — East Carolina University, B.A., 1994; Campbell University, J.D. (cum laude), 1998 — Admitted to Bar, 1998, North Carolina; U.S. District Court, Eastern, Middle and Western Districts of North Carolina — Member North Carolina (Litigation Section) and Wake County Bar Associations; North Carolina Association of Defense Attorneys; Defense Research Institute

Julie L. Bell — The University of North Carolina at Greensboro, B.A., 1989; The University of North Carolina at Chapel Hill, J.D., 1992 — Admitted to Bar, 1992, North Carolina; 1997, U.S. District Court, Eastern District of North Carolina; 2000, U.S. District Court, Middle and Western Districts of

Patterson Dilthey LLP, Raleigh, NC   **(Continued)**

North Carolina — Member North Carolina and Wake County Bar Associations; Capital City Lawyers Association; North Carolina Association of Defense Attorneys

Associates

Kristy G. Shotwell — North Carolina State University, B.A. (magna cum laude), 2000; North Carolina Central University, J.D. (magna cum laude), 2003 — Admitted to Bar, 2003, North Carolina — Member North Carolina and Wake County (Member, 10th Judicial District) Bar Associations; North Carolina State Bar

Eric Sauls — University of North Carolina Wilmington, B.S., 2005; Campbell University, J.D., 2008 — Admitted to Bar, 2008, North Carolina — Member North Carolina (Member, Young Lawyers Division) and Wake County Bar Associations; North Carolina Tenth Judicial District Bar Association; North Carolina Association of Defense Attorneys

Of Counsel

Kristen L. Harris — The University of North Carolina at Chapel Hill, B.A., 1996; Wake Forest University, J.D., 2003 — Admitted to Bar, 2003, North Carolina; U.S. District Court, Eastern, Middle and Western Districts of North Carolina — Member North Carolina and Wake County Bar Associations; North Carolina Tenth Judicial District Bar Association

Scott J. Lasso — The University of Mississippi, B.B.A., 1989; Wake Forest University, J.D., 1992 — Admitted to Bar, 1992, North Carolina — Member North Carolina State Bar; North Carolina Tenth Judicial District Bar Association

Phelps Dunbar LLP
4140 Parklake Avenue, Suite 100
Raleigh, North Carolina 27612-3723
   Telephone: 919-789-5300
   Fax: 919-789-5301
   E-Mail: info@phelps.com
   www.phelpsdunbar.com

(New Orleans, LA Office*: Canal Place, 365 Canal Street, Suite 2000, 70130-6534)
   (Tel: 504-566-1311)
   (Fax: 504-568-9130)
(Baton Rouge, LA Office*: II City Plaza, 400 Convention Street, Suite 1100, 70802-5618, P.O. Box 4412, 70821-4412)
   (Tel: 225-346-0285)
   (Fax: 225-381-9197)
(Jackson, MS Office*: 4270 I-55 North, 39211-6391, P.O. Box 16114, 39236-6114)
   (Tel: 601-352-2300)
   (Fax: 601-360-9777)
(Tupelo, MS Office*: One Mississippi Plaza, 201 South Spring Street, Seventh Floor, 38804, P.O. Box 1220, 38802-1220)
   (Tel: 662-842-7907)
   (Fax: 662-842-3873)
(Gulfport, MS Office*: NorthCourt One, 2304 19th Street, Suite 300, 39501)
   (Tel: 228-679-1130)
   (Fax: 228-679-1131)
(Houston, TX Office*: One Allen Center, 500 Dallas Street, Suite 1300, 77002)
   (Tel: 713-626-1386)
   (Fax: 713-626-1388)
(Tampa, FL Office*: 100 South Ashley Drive, Suite 1900, 33602-5311)
   (Tel: 813-472-7550)
   (Fax: 813-472-7570)
(Mobile, AL Office*: 2 North Royal Street, 36602, P.O. Box 2727, 36652-2727)
   (Tel: 251-432-4481)
   (Fax: 251-433-1820)
(London, United Kingdom Office*: Lloyd's, Suite 725, Level 7, 1 Lime Street, EC3M 7DQ)
   (Tel: 011-44-207-929-4765)
   (Fax: 011-44-207-929-0046)

NORTH CAROLINA — RALEIGH

Phelps Dunbar LLP, Raleigh, NC (Continued)

(Southlake, TX Office*(See Dallas listing): 115 Grand Avenue, Suite 222, 76092)
(Tel: 817-488-3134)
(Fax: 817-488-3214)

Insurance Law

Insurance Clients

Acceptance Casualty Insurance Company
Aegis Janson Green Insurance Services Inc.
AIG Columbus
Alabama Municipal Insurance Corporation
AmTrust Underwriters, Inc.
Arch Insurance Company (Europe) Ltd.
Aspen Insurance UK Limited
Associated Aviation Underwriters
Bankers Insurance Group
Berkley Select, LLC
Bluebonnet Life Insurance Company
Britannia Steam Ship Insurance Association Ltd.
CNA
Commercial Union Insurance Company
Companion Property and Casualty Group
ELCO Administrative Services
Endurance Services, Ltd.
Erie Insurance Company
Evanston Insurance Company
Fidelity National Financial
First Premium Insurance Group, Inc.
GE Insurance Solutions
General & Cologne Life Reinsurance of America
General Star Indemnity Company
Glencoe Group
Global Special Risks, Inc.
Great American Insurance Companies
Gulf Insurance Group
The Hartford Insurance Group
Homesite Group, Inc.
ICAT Boulder Claims
Infinity Insurance Company
Lexington Insurance Company
Liberty Mutual Group
Louisiana Farm Bureau Mutual Insurance Company
Louisiana Workers' Compensation Corporation
Markel
MetLife Auto & Home
NAS Insurance Group
Nautilus Insurance Company
Old American Insurance Company
Pharmacists Mutual Insurance Company
RenaissanceRe
RLI Insurance Company
Royal & SunAlliance
SCOR Global P&C
Sedgwick Claims Management Services, Inc.
SR International Business Insurance Company, Ltd.
Steamship Mutual Underwriting Association Limited
Torus
Underwriters at Lloyd's, London
Unitrin Business Insurance
Vesta Eiendom AS
Western Heritage Insurance Company
Westport Insurance Corporation
XL Insurance Group
ACE Group of Insurance and Reinsurance Companies
Aetna Insurance Company
AFLAC - American Family Life Assurance Company of
Allstate Insurance Company
American Family Life Assurance Company of Columbus
Argonaut Insurance Company
Aspen Insurance
Aspen Re
AXIS Insurance
Beazley Group
Bituminous Insurance Company
Blue Cross & Blue Shield of Mississippi
Chartis Insurance
Chubb Group of Insurance Companies
Commonwealth Insurance Company
Cotton States Insurance
Criterion Claim Solutions
Employers Reinsurance Corporation
Esurance Insurance Company
Farmers Insurance Group
Fireman's Fund Insurance Company
Foremost Insurance Company
General American Life Insurance Company
General Reinsurance Corporation
General Star Management Company
Golden Rule Insurance Company
Great Southern Life Insurance Company
Hanover Insurance Group
Hermitage Insurance Company
Houston Casualty Company
Indian Harbor Insurance Company
Ironshore Insurance, Ltd.
Liberty International Underwriters
Life Insurance Company of Alabama
Louisiana Health Insurance Association
Lyndon Property Insurance Company
Munich-American Risk Partners
Nationwide Insurance
The Navigators Group, Inc.
OneBeacon Insurance Group
Prime Syndicate
QBE
Republic Western Insurance Company
St. Paul Travelers
Scottsdale Insurance Company
Sentry Insurance
Southern Farm Bureau Casualty Insurance Company
State National Insurance Company, Inc.
Terra Nova Insurance Company Limited
United States Fidelity and Guaranty Company
Victoria Insurance Group
West of England Ship Owners Mutual Insurance Association (Luxembourg)
Zurich

Phelps Dunbar LLP, Raleigh, NC (Continued)

Member of the Firm

Kevin O'Brien — Florida State University, B.S. (magna cum laude), 1997; Florida State University College of Law, J.D. (Order of the Coif), 2001 — Admitted to Bar, 2001, Florida; North Carolina; South Carolina; U.S. District Court, Middle, Northern and Southern Districts of Florida; U.S. District Court, Eastern, Middle and Western Districts of North Carolina; U.S. District Court, District of South Carolina; U.S. Court of Appeals, Fourth and Eleventh Circuits — Member The Florida, North Carolina State and South Carolina Bars; Wake County and Tenth Judicial District Bar Associations

(See listing under New Orleans, LA for additional information)

Ragsdale Liggett PLLC

2840 Plaza Place, Suite 400
Raleigh, North Carolina 27612
Telephone: 919-787-5200
Fax: 919-783-8991
E-Mail: gstrickland@rl-law.com
www.rl-law.com

Established: 1972

Civil Litigation, Corporate Law, Commercial Real Estate Law, Insurance Defense, Insurance Regulatory Law, Residential Real Estate

Firm Profile: Our lawyers are among the most experienced in North Carolina in all aspects of insurance law. While a substantial portion of our practice arises from the representation of insurers and insureds in all types of litigation, we also have the most experienced insurance regulatory lawyers in the state. Ragsdale Liggett provides a full range of services to the insurance industry.

The firm's civil litigation experience is wide-ranging and we routinely handle sophisticated, complex litigation with exceptional results. In the corporate and business arena, we represent both large and small companies and provide representation including entity selection and formation, daily business counsel, mergers and acquisitions, work-outs and dissolution, Our team of commercial and residential real estate lawyers is unmatched by any firm in the state.

Insurance Clients

Acceptance Casualty Insurance Company
AMEX Assurance Company
Builders Mutual Insurance Company
Chartis Insurance
Chubb Group of Insurance Companies
Fidelity National Title Insurance Company
Harco National Insurance Company
Lawyers Title Insurance Corporation
National Interstate Insurance Company
PICA Group
Strickland Insurance Group
TransGuard Insurance Company of America, Inc.
United American Insurance Company
Wilshire Insurance Company
World Insurance Company
Acceptance Indemnity Insurance Company
Atlantic Casualty Insurance Company
Catlin Insurance Company, Inc.
Chicago Title Insurance Company
Cincinnati Insurance Company
Commercial Alliance Insurance Company
General Reinsurance Corporation
Hudson Insurance Group
Investors Title Insurance Company
Liberty Mutual Group
Lloyd's America Inc
Occidental Fire & Casualty Company of North Carolina
Service Insurance Company
Terra Insurance Company (A Risk Retention Group)
Travelers Indemnity Insurance Company
Unity Mutual Life Insurance Company
XL Design Professional

Non-Insurance Clients

North Carolina Surplus Lines Association

Managing Partner

David K. Liggett — The University of North Carolina, B.A., 1988; J.D., 1995 — Admitted to Bar, 1995, North Carolina — Member North Carolina Surplus Lines Association (General Counsel); Federation of Regulatory Counsel (Director, Secretary) — E-mail: dliggett@rl-law.com

Ragsdale Liggett PLLC, Raleigh, NC (Continued)

Founding Partner

George R. Ragsdale — The University of North Carolina, B.A., 1958; J.D., 1961 — Admitted to Bar, 1962, North Carolina — E-mail: gragsdale@rl-law.com

Frank R. Liggett III — The University of North Carolina, B.A., 1963; J.D., 1969 — Admitted to Bar, 1966, North Carolina — Member Federation of Regulatory Counsel (Former Chairman) — E-mail: fliggett@rl-law.com

Partners

Mary Hulett — Stanford University, B.A., 1963; The George Washington University, J.D., 1977 — Admitted to Bar, 1977, Virginia; District of Columbia; 1980, California; 2000, North Carolina — E-mail: mhulett@rl-law.com

John M. Nunnally — North Carolina State University, B.A., 1988; Campbell University, J.D., 1992 — Admitted to Bar, 1992, North Carolina — E-mail: jnunnally@rl-law.com

Dorothy B. Burch — Meredith College, B.A., 1987; The University of North Carolina, J.D., 1991 — Admitted to Bar, 1991, North Carolina — E-mail: dburch@rl-law.com

Melissa Dewey Brumback — The University of North Carolina, B.A., 1994; The University of North Carolina at Chapel Hill, J.D., 1998 — Admitted to Bar, 1998, North Carolina — E-mail: mbrumback@rl-law.com

Sandra W. Mitterling — The University of North Carolina, B.A., 1988; J.D., 1991 — Admitted to Bar, 1995, North Carolina — E-mail: smitterling@rl-law.com

William W. Pollock — Wake Forest University, B.A., 1984; University of South Carolina, J.D., 1987 — Admitted to Bar, 1987, Pennsylvania; 1988, District of Columbia; 1992, North Carolina — E-mail: bpollock@rl-law.com

Ashley Huffstetler Campbell — The University of North Carolina, B.A., 1999; J.D., 2003 — Admitted to Bar, 2003, North Carolina — E-mail: acampbell@rl-law.com

Mary M. Webb — The University of North Carolina at Chapel Hill, B.A., 1988; Campbell University, J.D., 1992 — Admitted to Bar, 1992, North Carolina — E-mail: mwebb@rl-law.com

Associates

Amie C. Sivon — Wake Forest University, B.A., 1998; The University of North Carolina, J.D., 2005 — Admitted to Bar, 2005, North Carolina — E-mail: asivon@rl-law.com

Angela M. Allen — Wake Forest University, B.A., 2002; J.D., 2006 — Admitted to Bar, 2006, Florida; 2008, North Carolina — E-mail: aallen@rl-law.com

John Bowen "Bo" Walker — Wake Forest University, B.S., 2002; J.D., 2006 — Admitted to Bar, 2006, South Carolina; 2007, North Carolina — E-mail: bwalker@rl-law.com

Edward E. Coleman — University of Virginia, B.A., 2004; Campbell University, J.D., 2007 — Admitted to Bar, 2007, Virginia; 2011, North Carolina — E-mail: ecoleman@rl-law.com

(This firm is also listed in the Regulatory and Compliance section of this directory)

Stuart Law Firm, PLLC

1033 Wade Avenue, Suite 202
Raleigh, North Carolina 27605
Telephone: 919-787-6050
Fax: 919-787-9988
E-Mail: jstuart@stuartlawfirm.com
www.stuartlawfirm.com

Regulatory and Compliance, Workers' Compensation, Construction Liability, Mold Litigation, Intellectual Property, Alternative Dispute Resolution

Firm Profile: As general counsel to three North Carolina property and casualty insurers, with client service areas extending into Tennessee, South Carolina, Virginia, Georgia, Mississippi, Maryland and the District of Columbia, Stuart Law Firm, PLLC provides a unique perspective in representing insurers in regulatory matters and in the defense of workers

Stuart Law Firm, PLLC, Raleigh, NC (Continued)

compensation and general liability claims. Our mediators also use this experience in mediating a wide range of insurance disputes for non-clients. The firm's thirty years of representing the home building and general contracting industries has resulted in both experience and expertise in construction claims, including mold, chinese drywall and construction practices litigation. Our work defending self-insured medical centers gives us particular insight in issues arising from the health care industry. In the regulatory arena, the firm has successfully organized four North Carolina domestic insurers, the admission of North Carolina insurers in Tennessee, South Carolina, Virginia, Georgia, Mississippi, Maryland and the District of Columbia as well as the admission of out-of-state insurers in North Carolina.

Stuart Law Firm, PLLC, represents companies in regulatory matters and defends workers' compensation and general liability matters. The Firm's extensive work defending builders and property owners has resulted in particular emphasis in construction defects, product liability, copyright infringement (building plans), chinese drywall, mold and environmental compliance cases.

Insurance Clients

Amerisafe Insurance Group
Builders Premier Insurance Company
Forestry Mutual Insurance Company
Builders Mutual Insurance Company
Carolinas Roofing and Sheet Metal Contractors Association Inc.
North Carolina Self-Insurance Security Association

Non-Insurance Clients

North Carolina Home Builders Association

Self-Insured Clients

Duke University   High Point Regional Health System

Firm Members

James L. Stuart — 1950 — Duke University, B.S.E. (with distinction), 1971; The George Washington University Law School, J.D. (with honors), 1975 — Admitted to Bar, 1975, North Carolina; 1988, District of Columbia; 2001, Tennessee; 1980, U.S. Supreme Court — Member American, North Carolina and Wake County Bar Associations — Adjunct Instructor, University of North Carolina School of Law, 1983-1984; Research Assistant and Professional Staff Member, United States Senate Judiciary Subcommittees on Constitutional Rights and Separation of Powers, Senator Sam J. Ervin, Jr., Staff, 1972-1974; Assistant Attorney General, State of North Carolina, 1975-1980

Catherine R. Stuart — 1955 — The University of North Carolina at Chapel Hill, B.A., 1977; Tulane University Law School, J.D., 1981 — Senior Fellow — Law Clerk to the Honorable Franklin T. Dupree, U.S. District Court, Eastern District of North Carolina, 1981-1983 — Admitted to Bar, 1982, North Carolina; 1986, U.S. District Court, Eastern, Middle and Western Districts of North Carolina; U.S. Court of Appeals, Fourth Circuit; U.S. Supreme Court — Member American, North Carolina and Wake County Bar Associations — Assistant Attorney General, North Carolina Department of Justice, 1984-1986; Adjunct Instructor, School of Law, University of North Carolina at Chapel Hill, 1983-1984; General Counsel, Local Organizing Committee, U.S. Olympic Festival, 1986-1987 — Certified Superior Court Mediator, North Carolina Dispute Resolution Commission

Theresa S. Dew — 1975 — Campbell University, B.A. (summa cum laude), 1997; The University of North Carolina School of Law, J.D. (with honors), 2000 — Phi Delta Phi — Admitted to Bar, 2000, North Carolina; 2001, South Carolina — Member American and North Carolina (Business Section) Bar Associations; South Carolina Bar

Associates

Susan J. Vanderweert — 1957 — University of Minnesota Duluth, B.A., 1979; Duke University, M.A., 1999; University of North Carolina at Chapel Hill School of Law, J.D., 2002 — Admitted to Bar, 2002, North Carolina — Member North Carolina and Wake County Bar Associations; North Carolina Association of Defense Attorneys

C. Carr Taylor — Rice University, B.A., 2007; Northwestern University School of Law, J.D., 2012 — Admitted to Bar, 2012, Florida; 2013, North Carolina; U.S. District Court, Eastern District of North Carolina — Member American, North Carolina and Wake County Bar Associations — Languages: Spanish

(This firm is also listed in the Regulatory and Compliance, Subrogation section of this directory)

Yates, McLamb & Weyher, L.L.P.

One Bank of America Plaza
421 Fayetteville Street, Suite 1200
Raleigh, North Carolina 27601
　　Telephone: 919-835-0900
　　Fax: 919-835-0910
　　E-Mail: denglish@ymwlaw.com
　　www.ymwlaw.com

Commercial & Business Litigation, Healthcare, Insurance Defense & Coverage Litigation, Civil Litigation, Construction Law, Professional Licensing & Government Oversignt, Toxic Tort & Class Action Litigation, Appellate Representation, Mediation & Alternative Dispute Resolution

Firm Profile: We are proud of the history of our firm and the reputation we have built with our clients and in the legal community. It is a reputation based on listening to our clients' needs and representing them with pragmatism, efficency, creativitiy, and professionalism.

Insurance Clients

CNA
MAG Mutual Insurance Company
Medical Mutual Insurance Company
Metropolitan Property and Casualty Insurance Company
State Farm Mutual Automobile Insurance Company
Zurich U.S.
Lawyers Mutual Liability Insurance Company of North Carolina
The Medical Protective Company
Philadelphia Insurance Company
Preferred Physicians Medical Risk Retention Group, Inc.
Travelers Property Casualty Corporation

Non-Insurance Clients

CVS Pharmacy, Inc.
Nash Health Care Systems
WakeMed
Duke University Health System
Pitt County Memorial Hospital

Managing Partners

Dan J. McLamb — The University of North Carolina at Chapel Hill, A.B., 1971; J.D. (with honors), 1974 — Admitted to Bar, 1974, North Carolina — E-mail: dmclamb@ymwlaw.com

Rodney E. Pettey — Bob Jones University, B.S., 1987; Wake Forest University, J.D. (cum laude), 1990 — Admitted to Bar, 1990, North Carolina — E-mail: rpettey@ymwlaw.com

Barry S. Cobb — The University of North Carolina at Chapel Hill, B.S. (with honors), 1989; J.D. (with honors), 1992 — Admitted to Bar, 1992, North Carolina — E-mail: bcobb@ymwlaw.com

Partners

Barbara B. Weyher
John T. Honeycutt
Ryan M. Shuirman
Sean T. Partrick
Maria P. Wood
Brian M. Williams
David M. Fothergill
John W. Minier
Erin McNeil Young
Shirley Maring Pruitt
Jennifer Maldonado
Kathrine E. Fisher
Samuel G. Thompson, Jr.
Dr. Lori A. Meyerhoffer

Young Moore and Henderson P.A.

3101 Glenwood Avenue, Suite 200
Raleigh, North Carolina 27612
　　Telephone: 919-782-6860
　　Fax: 919-782-6753
　　www.youngmoorelaw.com

Established: 1952

Young Moore and Henderson P.A., Raleigh, NC
(Continued)

Accident and Health, Administrative Law, Alternative Dispute Resolution, Business Law, Construction Law, Disability, Employment Law, Environmental Law, Governmental Liability, Insurance Coverage, Insurance Defense, Insurance Law, Insurance Litigation, Insurance Regulation, Labor and Employment, Life Insurance, Medical Malpractice, Nursing Home Liability, Premises Liability, Product Liability, Professional Liability, Reinsurance, Retail Liability, Truck Liability, Workers' Compensation

Firm Profile: Young Moore and Henderson, P.A. has been a vital part of the legal profession in North Carolina for more than eighty years. We have made and continue to make significant contributions of leadership to our profession, the administration of justice and civic improvement. Our dedication to professional excellence, integrity and service has earned us the confidence, respect and cooperation of both the bench and bar. This dedication and our reputation allow us to represent our clients effectively in diverse areas of practice and in all courts and administrative agencies throughout the state.

Insurance Clients

Auto-Owners Insurance Company
Federated Rural Electric Insurance Exchange
Lawyers Mutual Liability Insurance Company of North Carolina
North Carolina Farm Bureau Mutual Insurance Company
North Carolina Reinsurance Facility
OneBeacon Insurance
Republic Western Insurance Company
Fairmont Specialty Group
Fidelity and Guaranty Life Insurance Company
Medical Mutual Insurance Company
Montgomery Insurance Companies
North Carolina Joint Underwriting Assn./North Carolina Insurance Underwriting Assn.
OMS National Insurance Company
Progressive Insurance Company
State Farm Insurance Company

Non-Insurance Clients

North Carolina Rate Bureau

Firm Members

Charles H. Young, Sr. — (1915-2011)

Joseph C. Moore, Jr. — (1919-1988)

Charles H. Young, Jr. — (1947-1992)

B. T. Henderson, II — (1928-2000)

John N. Fountain — 1944 — Duke University, B.A., 1965; Wake Forest University, J.D., 1968 — Admitted to Bar, 1968, North Carolina — N.C.D.R.C. Certified Mediator

William M. Trott — 1946 — The University of North Carolina, A.B., 1968; J.D., 1971; The George Washington University, LL.M., 1975 — Admitted to Bar, 1971, North Carolina — Member American, North Carolina and Wake County Bar Associations; North Carolina State Bar

R. Michael Strickland — 1947 — Duke University, A.B., 1969; Wake Forest University, J.D., 1972 — Admitted to Bar, 1972, North Carolina

Robert C. Paschal — 1951 — The University of North Carolina, B.A., 1975; Duke University, J.D., 1978 — Admitted to Bar, 1978, North Carolina

Walter E. Brock, Jr. — 1952 — The University of North Carolina, B.A., 1975; J.D., 1978 — Admitted to Bar, 1978, North Carolina; U.S. Court of Appeals, Fourth Circuit; U.S. District Court, Eastern, Middle and Western Districts of North Carolina

Joseph W. Williford — 1956 — Wake Forest University, B.A., 1978; J.D., 1981 — Admitted to Bar, 1981, North Carolina; U.S. District Court, Eastern, Middle and Western Districts of North Carolina; U.S. Court of Appeals, Fourth Circuit

Rudy L. Ogburn — 1956 — Wake Forest University, B.A., 1979; J.D., 1982 — Admitted to Bar, 1982, North Carolina — Certified Specialist: Estate Planning and Probate Law, North Carolina State Bar

Marvin Mitchel Spivey, Jr. — 1958 — The University of North Carolina, B.A., 1980; J.D., 1983 — Admitted to Bar, 1983, North Carolina

David M. Duke — 1958 — College of William & Mary, B.A., 1981; Wake Forest University, J.D., 1984 — Admitted to Bar, 1984, North Carolina; U.S. District Court, Eastern, Middle and Western Districts of North Carolina; U.S. Court of Appeals, Fourth Circuit

Joe E. Austin, Jr. — 1965 — Davidson College, A.B., 1986; Wake Forest University, J.D., 1989 — Admitted to Bar, 1989, North Carolina — Certified

RALEIGH

Young Moore and Henderson P.A., Raleigh, NC
(Continued)

Specialist: Workers Compensation Law, North Carolina State Bar; N.C.D.R.C. Certified Mediator

Donna R. Rutala — 1957 — The University of North Carolina at Chapel Hill, B.S.N., 1980; North Carolina Central University, J.D., 1989 — Admitted to Bar, 1989, North Carolina; U.S. District Court, Eastern and Middle Districts of North Carolina — Registered Nurse, North Carolina, 1980

Dana H. Hoffman — 1965 — The University of North Carolina at Chapel Hill, B.A., 1987; Wake Forest University, J.D., 1990 — Admitted to Bar, 1990, North Carolina; U.S. District Court, Eastern, Middle and Western Districts of North Carolina; U.S. Court of Appeals, Fourth Circuit

Glenn C. Raynor — 1965 — The University of North Carolina at Chapel Hill, B.S., 1987; J.D., 1991 — Admitted to Bar, 1991, North Carolina; U.S. District Court, Eastern, Middle and Western Districts of North Carolina

Jay P. Tobin — 1964 — The University of North Carolina, B.A., 1986; J.D., 1991 — Admitted to Bar, 1991, North Carolina; 1992, U.S. District Court, Eastern, Middle and Western Districts of North Carolina

Christopher A. Page — 1966 — Duke University, B.A. (summa cum laude), 1989; Yale University, J.D., 1992 — Admitted to Bar, 1995, North Carolina; U.S. District Court, Eastern, Middle and Western Districts of North Carolina; U.S. Court of Appeals, Fourth Circuit

Brian O. Beverly — 1968 — The University of North Carolina, B.A., 1992; North Carolina Central University, J.D., 1995 — Admitted to Bar, 1995, North Carolina; U.S. District Court, Eastern, Middle and Western Districts of North Carolina; U.S. Court of Appeals, Fourth Circuit — N.C.D.R.C. Certified Mediator

Jeffrey T. Linder — 1969 — University of California, B.A., 1992; The University of North Carolina, J.D. (with honors), 1995 — Admitted to Bar, 1995, North Carolina

Dawn D. Raynor — 1970 — Mary Washington College, B.A. (magna cum laude), 1992; Wake Forest University, J.D., 1995 — Admitted to Bar, 1995, North Carolina; 1996, U.S. District Court, Eastern, Middle and Western Districts of North Carolina

Reed N. Fountain — 1970 — Duke University, B.A., 1993; The University of North Carolina, J.D., 1997 — Admitted to Bar, 1996, North Carolina; U.S. District Court, Eastern, Middle and Western Districts of North Carolina; U.S. Court of Appeals, Fourth Circuit — N.C.D.R.C. Certified Mediator

Robert C. deRosset — 1969 — The University of North Carolina, B.A., 1991; University of South Carolina, J.D., 1996 — Admitted to Bar, 1996, South Carolina; 2001, North Carolina; U.S. District Court, Eastern, Middle and Western Districts of North Carolina — N.C.D.R.C. Certified Mediator — United States Peace Corps, 1998-2000

Alexander R. Atchison — 1972 — The University of North Carolina, B.A., 1995; Cumberland University, J.D., 1998 — Admitted to Bar, 1998, North Carolina — Certified Specialist: Estate Planning and Probate Law, North Carolina State Bar

Elizabeth P. McCullough — 1974 — Davidson College, B.A. (with honors), 1996; Wake Forest University, J.D. (with honors), 1999 — Admitted to Bar, 1999, Virginia; 2005, North Carolina; U.S. District Court, Eastern, Middle and Western Districts of North Carolina; U.S. District Court, Eastern and Western Districts of Virginia; U.S. Court of Appeals, Fourth Circuit

Zachary C. Bolen — 1973 — The University of North Carolina, B.A., 1995; Campbell University, Norman Adrian Wiggins School of Law, J.D., 2000 — Admitted to Bar, 2000, North Carolina

Matthew J. Gray — 1976 — North Carolina State University, B.S., 1998; Wake Forest University, J.D., 2003 — Admitted to Bar, 2003, North Carolina; U.S. District Court, Eastern District of North Carolina

Angela F. Craddock — 1978 — The University of North Carolina at Chapel Hill, B.A. (with honors), 2001; J.D. (with honors), 2004 — Admitted to Bar, 2004, North Carolina

Shannon S. Frankel — 1978 — Duke University, B.A., 2000; College of William & Mary, J.D., 2005 — Admitted to Bar, 2005, North Carolina; U.S. District Court, Eastern, Middle and Western Districts of North Carolina

Kelly S. Brown — University of Virginia, B.A. (with distinction), 2001; College of William & Mary, J.D., 2005 — Admitted to Bar, 2005, Texas; 2008, North Carolina

Julia E. Dixon — Meredith College, B.A., 1991; The University of North Carolina at Chapel Hill, J.D., 2001 — Admitted to Bar, 2001, North Carolina

Of Counsel

Robert M. Clay — The University of North Carolina at Chapel Hill, A.B., 1959; J.D., 1961 — Admitted to Bar, 1961, North Carolina

NORTH CAROLINA

Young Moore and Henderson P.A., Raleigh, NC
(Continued)

Mary B. Wells — University of Florida, B.S., 1986; Villanova University, J.D., 1989 — Admitted to Bar, 1990, Florida; 1993, North Carolina

Associates

Josephine R. Darden — 1952 — The University of North Carolina, B.A., 1974; University of Virginia, M.A., 1976; Boston College, J.D., 1985 — Admitted to Bar, 1985, North Carolina

Michael S. Rainey — North Carolina State University, B.S. (magna cum laude), 2004; Campbell University, J.D. (cum laude), 2007 — Admitted to Bar, 2007, North Carolina

Patrick M. Aul — The University of North Carolina at Chapel Hill, B.A. (with distinction), 2006; The University of North Carolina, J.D. (with honors), 2009 — Admitted to Bar, 2009, North Carolina; U.S. District Court, Eastern, Middle and Western Districts of North Carolina

Andrew P. Flynt — 1984 — North Carolina State University, B.S. (summa cum laude), 2007; The University of North Carolina, J.D. (with honors), 2010 — Admitted to Bar, 2010, North Carolina; U.S. District Court, Eastern and Middle Districts of North Carolina

Michelle A. Greene — 1983 — The University of North Carolina at Chapel Hill, B.A., 2005; The University of North Carolina, J.D., 2010 — Admitted to Bar, 2010, North Carolina; U.S. District Court, Eastern District of North Carolina

Lori M. Allen — 1985 — The University of North Carolina at Chapel Hill, B.A. (with highest distinction), 2007; The University of North Carolina, J.D., 2010 — Admitted to Bar, 2010, North Carolina; U.S. District Court, Eastern District of North Carolina

Stephen A. Brown — The University of North Carolina at Greensboro, B.A./B.M., 2005; The University of North Carolina, J.D., 2008 — Admitted to Bar, 2008, North Carolina; U.S. Tax Court

David A. Senter, Jr. — Wake Forest University, B.A., 2007; J.D., 2012 — Admitted to Bar, 2012, North Carolina; U.S. District Court, Eastern District of North Carolina — Member North Carolina and Wake County Bar Associations

Brodie D. Erwin — Appalachian State University, B.S. (with honors), 2009; Wake Forest University, J.D., 2012 — Admitted to Bar, 2012, North Carolina; U.S. District Court, Eastern District of North Carolina — Member North Carolina and Wake County Bar Associations

Adam C. Stacy — Virginia Polytechnic Institute and State University, B.S., 2001; The University of Akron, J.D. (with high honors), 2005 — Admitted to Bar, 2005, Ohio; 2006, West Virginia; 2012, North Carolina; U.S. District Court, Eastern District of North Carolina; U.S. Court of Appeals, Sixth Circuit — Member North Carolina and Wake Forest Bar Associations

Chadwick I. McCullen — The University of North Carolina at Chapel Hill, B.A., 2005; Charleston School of Law, J.D. (with honors), 2008; University of Florida, M.L.T., 2009 — Admitted to Bar, 2008, North Carolina

Retired

J. Clark Brewer   William P. Daniell

The following firms also service this area.

Anderson, Johnson, Lawrence & Butler, L.L.P.
109 Green Street, Suite 204
Fayetteville, North Carolina 28301
Telephone: 910-483-1171
Fax: 910-483-5005

Mailing Address: P.O. Drawer 2737, Fayetteville, NC 28302-2737

Alternative Dispute Resolution, Appellate Advocacy, Automobile, Commercial Litigation, Construction Law, Contract Disputes, Environmental Litigation, Governmental Liability, Homeowners, Insurance Coverage, Legal Malpractice, Medical Malpractice, Nursing Home Liability, Premises Liability, Product Liability, Subrogation, Truck Liability, Workers' Compensation

SEE COMPLETE LISTING UNDER FAYETTEVILLE, NORTH CAROLINA (65 MILES)

NORTH CAROLINA

Bennett & Guthrie, P.L.L.C.
1560 Westbrook Plaza Drive
Winston-Salem, North Carolina 27103
   Telephone: 336-765-3121
   Fax: 336-765-8622

Alternative Dispute Resolution, Asbestos Litigation, Automobile Litigation, Carrier Defense, Civil Litigation, Commercial Litigation, Construction Law, Coverage Issues, Employment Law, General Defense Civil Litigation, General Liability, Health Care Liability, Hospital Malpractice, Insurance Coverage, Insurance Defense, Insurance Litigation, Mediation, Medical Malpractice Defense, Premises Liability, Product Liability, Product Liability Defense, Professional Liability, Professional Liability (Non-Medical) Defense, Self-Insured Defense, Trial and Appellate Practice, Trucking Litigation, Wrongful Death

SEE COMPLETE LISTING UNDER WINSTON-SALEM, NORTH CAROLINA (102 MILES)

Evans & Co.
101 West Friendly Avenue, Suite 500
Greensboro, North Carolina 27401
   Telephone: 336-275-1400
   Fax: 336-275-1401
   Toll Free: 800-EVANSCO

Admiralty and Maritime Law, Aviation, Comprehensive General Liability, Construction Law, Directors and Officers Liability, Employment Practices Liability, Energy, Environmental Law, Excess and Umbrella, Insurance Coverage, Insurance Defense, Motor Carriers, Oil and Gas, Product Liability, Professional Liability, Property and Casualty, Railroad Law, Toxic Torts

SEE COMPLETE LISTING UNDER GREENSBORO, NORTH CAROLINA (71 MILES)

Vernis & Bowling of Charlotte, PLLC
4701 Hedgemore Drive, Suite 812
Charlotte, North Carolina 28209
   Telephone: 704-910-8162
   Fax: 704-910-8163

Civil Litigation, Insurance Law, Workers' Compensation, Premises Liability, Labor and Employment, Civil Rights, Commercial Litigation, Automobile Liability, Complex Litigation, Product Liability, Directors and Officers Liability, Errors and Omissions, Construction Law, Construction Defect, Environmental Liability, Personal and Commercial Vehicle, Appellate Practice, Admiralty and Maritime Law, Real Estate, Family Law, Elder Law, Personal Injury Protection (PIP)

SEE COMPLETE LISTING UNDER CHARLOTTE, NORTH CAROLINA (161 MILES)

REIDSVILLE   14,520 Rockingham Co.
Refer To

Henson & Talley, L.L.P.
Suite 600 Piedmont Building
114 North Elm Street
Greensboro, North Carolina 27401
   Telephone: 336-275-0587
   Fax: 336-273-2585

Mailing Address: P.O. Box 3525, Greensboro, NC 27402-3525

Trial and Appellate Practice, State and Federal Courts, Insurance Defense, Automobile, Trucking Law, Workers' Compensation, Construction Law, Professional Malpractice, Product Liability, Fire, Insurance Coverage, Subrogation

SEE COMPLETE LISTING UNDER GREENSBORO, NORTH CAROLINA (24 MILES)

SALISBURY   † 33,662 Rowan Co.
Refer To

Vernis & Bowling of Charlotte, PLLC
4701 Hedgemore Drive, Suite 812
Charlotte, North Carolina 28209
   Telephone: 704-910-8162
   Fax: 704-910-8163

Civil Litigation, Insurance Law, Workers' Compensation, Premises Liability, Labor and Employment, Civil Rights, Commercial Litigation, Automobile Liability, Complex Litigation, Product Liability, Directors and Officers Liability, Errors and Omissions, Construction Law, Construction Defect, Environmental Liability, Personal and Commercial Vehicle, Appellate Practice, Admiralty and Maritime Law, Real Estate, Family Law, Elder Law, Personal Injury Protection (PIP)

SEE COMPLETE LISTING UNDER CHARLOTTE, NORTH CAROLINA (48 MILES)

REIDSVILLE

SANFORD   † 28,094 Lee Co.
Refer To

Bailey & Dixon, L.L.P.
434 Fayetteville Street, Suite 2500
Raleigh, North Carolina 27601
   Telephone: 919-828-0731
   Fax: 919-828-6592

Mailing Address: P.O. Box 1351, Raleigh, NC 27602-1351

General Defense, Litigation, Automobile, Construction Defect, Governmental Liability, Product Liability, General Liability, Civil Rights, Employment Law, Sexual Harassment, Environmental Law, Drug, Medical Devices, Arson, Fraud, Legal Malpractice, Life and Health, Workers' Compensation, Insurance Coverage, Bad Faith, Nursing Home Liability, Excess and Reinsurance, Regulatory and Compliance, Trial Practice, State and Federal Courts, Administrative Law, Corporate Law, Insurance Defense, Medical Malpractice, Mergers and Acquisitions, Professional Liability, Real Estate, OSHA, Government Liability, Unfair Claim/Trade Practice Defense Litigation

SEE COMPLETE LISTING UNDER RALEIGH, NORTH CAROLINA (43 MILES)

SMITHFIELD   † 10,966 Johnston Co.
Refer To

Bailey & Dixon, L.L.P.
434 Fayetteville Street, Suite 2500
Raleigh, North Carolina 27601
   Telephone: 919-828-0731
   Fax: 919-828-6592

Mailing Address: P.O. Box 1351, Raleigh, NC 27602-1351

General Defense, Litigation, Automobile, Construction Defect, Governmental Liability, Product Liability, General Liability, Civil Rights, Employment Law, Sexual Harassment, Environmental Law, Drug, Medical Devices, Arson, Fraud, Legal Malpractice, Life and Health, Workers' Compensation, Insurance Coverage, Bad Faith, Nursing Home Liability, Excess and Reinsurance, Regulatory and Compliance, Trial Practice, State and Federal Courts, Administrative Law, Corporate Law, Insurance Defense, Medical Malpractice, Mergers and Acquisitions, Professional Liability, Real Estate, OSHA, Government Liability, Unfair Claim/Trade Practice Defense Litigation

SEE COMPLETE LISTING UNDER RALEIGH, NORTH CAROLINA (29 MILES)

Refer To

Crossley McIntosh Collier Hanley & Edes, PLLC
5002 Randall Parkway
Wilmington, North Carolina 28403
   Telephone: 910-762-9711
   Fax: 910-256-0310
   Toll Free: 800-499-9711

Insurance Defense, Automobile, General Liability, Product Liability, Professional Malpractice, Casualty, Personal Injury, Municipal Liability, First Party Matters, Workers' Compensation, Admiralty and Maritime Law, Subrogation, Investigations, Construction Law, Pre-Suit

SEE COMPLETE LISTING UNDER WILMINGTON, NORTH CAROLINA (114 MILES)

STATESVILLE   † 24,532 Iredell Co.
Refer To

Vernis & Bowling of Charlotte, PLLC
4701 Hedgemore Drive, Suite 812
Charlotte, North Carolina 28209
   Telephone: 704-910-8162
   Fax: 704-910-8163

Civil Litigation, Insurance Law, Workers' Compensation, Premises Liability, Labor and Employment, Civil Rights, Commercial Litigation, Automobile Liability, Complex Litigation, Product Liability, Directors and Officers Liability, Errors and Omissions, Construction Law, Construction Defect, Environmental Liability, Personal and Commercial Vehicle, Appellate Practice, Admiralty and Maritime Law, Real Estate, Family Law, Elder Law, Personal Injury Protection (PIP)

SEE COMPLETE LISTING UNDER CHARLOTTE, NORTH CAROLINA (51 MILES)

WILMINGTON   NORTH CAROLINA

WAYNESVILLE † 9,869 Haywood Co.

Refer To

Vernis & Bowling of Charlotte, PLLC
4701 Hedgemore Drive, Suite 812
Charlotte, North Carolina 28209
   Telephone: 704-910-8162
   Fax: 704-910-8163

Civil Litigation, Insurance Law, Workers' Compensation, Premises Liability, Labor and Employment, Civil Rights, Commercial Litigation, Automobile Liability, Complex Litigation, Product Liability, Directors and Officers Liability, Errors and Omissions, Construction Law, Construction Defect, Environmental Liability, Personal and Commercial Vehicle, Appellate Practice, Admiralty and Maritime Law, Real Estate, Family Law, Elder Law, Personal Injury Protection (PIP)

SEE COMPLETE LISTING UNDER CHARLOTTE, NORTH CAROLINA (152 MILES)

WHITEVILLE † 5,394 Columbus Co.

Refer To

Crossley McIntosh Collier Hanley & Edes, PLLC
5002 Randall Parkway
Wilmington, North Carolina 28403
   Telephone: 910-762-9711
   Fax: 910-256-0310
   Toll Free: 800-499-9711

Insurance Defense, Automobile, General Liability, Product Liability, Professional Malpractice, Casualty, Personal Injury, Municipal Liability, First Party Matters, Workers' Compensation, Admiralty and Maritime Law, Subrogation, Investigations, Construction Law, Pre-Suit

SEE COMPLETE LISTING UNDER WILMINGTON, NORTH CAROLINA (48 MILES)

WILMINGTON † 106,476 New Hanover Co.

Crossley McIntosh Collier Hanley & Edes, PLLC

5002 Randall Parkway
Wilmington, North Carolina 28403
   Telephone: 910-762-9711
   Fax: 910-256-0310
   Toll Free: 800-499-9711
   E-Mail: reception@cmclawfirm.com
   www.cmclawfirm.com

Established: 1949

Insurance Defense, Automobile, General Liability, Product Liability, Professional Malpractice, Casualty, Personal Injury, Municipal Liability, First Party Matters, Workers' Compensation, Admiralty and Maritime Law, Subrogation, Investigations, Construction Law, Pre-Suit

Insurance Clients

AIG
Arcadian Risk Managers
CNA Insurance Company
Federated Insurance Company
GAB Robins North America, Inc.
Great American Insurance Company
Horace Mann Insurance Company
Metropolitan Property and Casualty Insurance Company
North Carolina League of Municipalities
State Auto Insurance Company
Western Surety Company
Allstate Insurance Company
Atlantic Casualty Insurance Company
Fireman's Fund Insurance Company
Harleysville Mutual Insurance Company
Lloyd's
North Carolina Farm Bureau Mutual Insurance Company
St. Paul Fire and Marine Insurance Company
State Farm Group
Zurich U.S.

Firm Members

Douglas F. McIntosh — 1959 — Oakland University, B.S., 1981; Campbell University, J.D., 1984 — Campbell Scholar — Admitted to Bar, 1984, North Carolina; 1987, U.S. District Court, Eastern, Middle and Western Districts of North Carolina; 1990, U.S. Court of Appeals, Fourth Circuit; 1991, U.S. Supreme Court — Member North Carolina and New Hanover County Bar Associations; North Carolina Association of Defense Attorneys; Defense Research Institute — Certified Mediator and Arbitrator — Practice Areas: Professional Liability; Product Liability; Personal Injury; Admiralty and Maritime Law; Automobile Liability; Trucking Law; Premises Liability — E-mail: douglasm@cmclawfirm.com

Clay A. Collier — 1959 — The University of North Carolina at Chapel Hill, A.B., 1982; Campbell University, J.D., 1985 — Admitted to Bar, 1986, North Carolina; 1987, U.S. District Court, Eastern District of North Carolina; U.S. Court of Appeals, Fourth Circuit — Member American, North Carolina and New Hanover County Bar Associations; North Carolina Association of Defense Attorneys; Defense Research Institute — E-mail: clayc@cmclawfirm.com

Andrew J. Hanley — 1963 — Cornell University, B.A., 1985; Tulane University, J.D. (cum laude), 1991 — Admitted to Bar, 1991, Texas; 1997, North Carolina; 1991, U.S. District Court, Eastern and Southern Districts of Texas; 1997, U.S. District Court, Eastern, Middle and Western Districts of North Carolina — Member Fifth Circuit Bar Association; Southeastern Admiralty Law Institute; The Maritime Law Association of the United States — E-mail: andrewh@cmclawfirm.com

Brian E. Edes — 1971 — University of North Carolina Wilmington, B.A., 1995; Campbell University, J.D., 1998 — Admitted to Bar, 1998, North Carolina; 1998, U.S. District Court, Eastern District of North Carolina; 2000, U.S. District Court, Western District of North Carolina; 2004, U.S. Court of Appeals, Fourth Circuit — Member North Carolina State Bar; North Carolina and New Hanover County Bar Associations; Defense Research Institute; North Carolina Association of Defense Attorneys — E-mail: briane@cmclawfirm.com

Norwood P. Blanchard, III — 1968 — East Carolina University, B.S./B.A., 1993; Duke University, J.D., 1999 — Admitted to Bar, 1999, North Carolina — Member North Carolina and New Hanover County Bar Associations; North Carolina Association of Defense Attorneys — Practice Areas: Civil Litigation; Municipal Law; Employment Law — E-mail: norwood@cmclawfirm.com

Associate Attorneys

Jarrett W. McGowan — 1981 — University of North Carolina Wilmington, B.S., 2004; Campbell University, J.D., 2009 — Admitted to Bar, 2009, North Carolina — Member North Carolina and New Hanover County Bar Associations; North Carolina Association of Defense Attorneys — Practice Areas: Civil Litigation; Municipal Law; Employment Law — E-mail: jarrettm@cmclawfirm.com

Andrew D. Penny — 1986 — University of North Carolina Wilmington, B.A. Political Science, 2010; Elon University, J.D., 2013 — Admitted to Bar, 2014, North Carolina; U.S. District Court, Eastern District of North Carolina — Member North Carolina and New Hanover County Bar Associations — Practice Areas: Civil Litigation — E-mail: andrewp@cmclawfirm.com

Ennis, Baynard, Morton & Medlin, P.A.

105 Burke Avenue, Suite E
Wilmington, North Carolina 28403
   Telephone: 910-256-3992
   Fax: 910-256-3578
   E-Mail: e-b@ennis-baynard.com
   www.ebmmlawfirm.com

Established: 1999

Insurance Defense, Litigation, Arson, Fraud, Examinations Under Oath, Property, Casualty, Automobile, Personal Injury, Premises Liability, Coverage Issues, Opinions, Subrogation, Product Liability, Workers' Compensation, Admiralty and Maritime Law, Trial Practice, State and Federal Courts

Insurance Clients

Allstate Insurance Company
Arch Insurance Company
Bankers Insurance Company
Essex Insurance Company
The Hartford
American Empire Insurance Company
Discovery Insurance Company
Esurance
The Horace Mann Companies

NORTH CAROLINA

Ennis, Baynard, Morton & Medlin, P.A., Wilmington, NC (Continued)

Insurance Management Solutions Corporation
Midland Claims Administrators, Inc.
North Carolina Farm Bureau Mutual Insurance Company
Progressive Insurance
Scottsdale Insurance Company
The Seibels Bruce Group, Inc.
Sentry Insurance a Mutual Company
State Farm Insurance Company
VFIS Claims Management
Liberty Mutual Insurance Company
Markel Southwest Underwriters, Inc.
Montgomery Mutual Insurance Company
Penn-America Insurance Company
Providence Washington Insurance Companies
Selective Insurance Company of America
Southern Insurance Underwriters
Universal Insurance Company

Non-Insurance Clients

Arbitration Forums, Inc.
Sears, Roebuck and Co.
Woodard Forest Imports
Brownyard Group
Terminix

Firm Members

Donald W. Ennis — 1960 — North Carolina State University, B.S. (cum laude), 1982; Campbell University School of Law, J.D., 1986 — Phi Alpha Delta; Trial Advocacy Team — Admitted to Bar, 1986, North Carolina; U.S. District Court, Eastern and Middle Districts of North Carolina — Member American Bar Associations (Litigation, Tort and Insurance Law Sections); North Carolina and New Hanover County Bar Associations; North Caorlina State Bar; North Carolina Association of Defense Attorneys; Defense Research Institute — Practice Areas: Defense Litigation — E-mail: don.ennis@ennis-baynard.com

Stephen C. Baynard — 1968 — The University of North Carolina at Chapel Hill, B.A., 1990; Campbell University School of Law, J.D., 1993 — Phi Alpha Delta Justice 1993 — AV Preeminent Rating — Admitted to Bar, 1993, North Carolina; 1994, U.S. District Court, Eastern District of North Carolina; 2000, U.S. District Court, Middle District of North Carolina — Member American, North Carolina and New Hanover County Bar Associations; North Carolina Association of Defense Attorneys (Young Lawyers Committee, President, 2003-2005; Chair, General Liability Section, 2006-Present; Vice-Chair); 5th Judicial District Bar (President, 2005); North Carolina Conference of Bar Presidents (Executive Committee, 2006-Present); Chief Justice's Commission on Professionalism (Judicial Response Committee, 2007-Present); Defense Research Institute — Reported Cases: Robinson v. Leach, 514 S.E.2d 567 (1999); 350 N.C. 835, 539 S.E.2d 293, (1999); Moore v. Cincinnati Ins., 147 N.C. App. 761, 556 S.E.2d 682(2001); Wolfson v. Cox, 164 N.C.App. 601, 596 S.E.2d 473 (2004); Parker v. Willis, 606 S.E.2d 184, N.C. App., (2004); 359 N.C. 411, 612 S.E.2d 322, N.C., (2005); Smith v. Murrell, 605, S.E.2d 742, (2004); Hailey v. Terminix Co. of North Carolina, Inc., WL 1892559, 646 S.E.2d 443 (2007); Moore v Rhodes 190 N.C.App. 822, 662 S.E.2d 36 (2008); Hewett v. Weisser, 364 N.C. 129, 695 S.E.2d 759 (2009); Kelly v. Shoaf 718 SE2d 423 (2011); Spooner v. Clemmons, 718 SE2d 423 (2011), review denied 722 SE2d 788 (2012). — Practice Areas: Civil Litigation — E-mail: sbaynard@ennis-baynard.com

Dan Morton — 1960 — Duke University, B.A., 1982; The University of North Carolina at Chapel Hill, J.D., 1985 — Admitted to Bar, 1985, North Carolina; Superior Court of North Carolina; Supreme Court of North Carolina; U.S. District Court, Eastern, Middle and Western Districts of North Carolina; U.S. Court of Appeals, Fourth Circuit — Member North Carolina Association of Defense Attorneys; Defense Research Institute; National Institute of Trial Advocacy — E-mail: dmorton@ennis-baynard.com

Ronald D. Medlin Jr. — 1977 — Appalachian State University, B.S./B.A. (cum laude), 2000; The University of North Carolina at Chapel Hill, J.D., 2003 — Admitted to Bar, 2003, North Carolina; Superior Court of North Carolina; Supreme Court of North Carolina; U.S. District Court, Eastern District of North Carolina — Member North Carolina Association of Defense Attorneys — E-mail: rmedlin@ennis-baynard.com

(This firm is also listed in the Subrogation section of this directory)

WILSON

The following firms also service this area.

Anderson, Johnson, Lawrence & Butler, L.L.P.
109 Green Street, Suite 204
Fayetteville, North Carolina 28301
 Telephone: 910-483-1171
 Fax: 910-483-5005

Mailing Address: P.O. Drawer 2737, Fayetteville, NC 28302-2737

Alternative Dispute Resolution, Appellate Advocacy, Automobile, Commercial Litigation, Construction Law, Contract Disputes, Environmental Litigation, Governmental Liability, Homeowners, Insurance Coverage, Legal Malpractice, Medical Malpractice, Nursing Home Liability, Premises Liability, Product Liability, Subrogation, Truck Liability, Workers' Compensation

SEE COMPLETE LISTING UNDER FAYETTEVILLE, NORTH CAROLINA (91 MILES)

Bennett & Guthrie, P.L.L.C.
1560 Westbrook Plaza Drive
Winston-Salem, North Carolina 27103
 Telephone: 336-765-3121
 Fax: 336-765-8622

Alternative Dispute Resolution, Asbestos Litigation, Automobile Litigation, Carrier Defense, Civil Litigation, Commercial Litigation, Construction Law, Coverage Issues, Employment Law, General Defense Civil Litigation, General Liability, Health Care Liability, Hospital Malpractice, Insurance Coverage, Insurance Defense, Insurance Litigation, Mediation, Medical Malpractice Defense, Premises Liability, Product Liability, Product Liability Defense, Professional Liability, Professional Liability (Non-Medical) Defense, Self-Insured Defense, Trial and Appellate Practice, Trucking Litigation, Wrongful Death

SEE COMPLETE LISTING UNDER WINSTON-SALEM, NORTH CAROLINA (240 MILES)

Vernis & Bowling of Charlotte, PLLC
4701 Hedgemore Drive, Suite 812
Charlotte, North Carolina 28209
 Telephone: 704-910-8162
 Fax: 704-910-8163

Civil Litigation, Insurance Law, Workers' Compensation, Premises Liability, Labor and Employment, Civil Rights, Commercial Litigation, Automobile Liability, Complex Litigation, Product Liability, Directors and Officers Liability, Errors and Omissions, Construction Law, Construction Defect, Environmental Liability, Personal and Commercial Vehicle, Appellate Practice, Admiralty and Maritime Law, Real Estate, Family Law, Elder Law, Personal Injury Protection (PIP)

SEE COMPLETE LISTING UNDER CHARLOTTE, NORTH CAROLINA (202 MILES)

WILSON † 49,167 Wilson Co.

Refer To

Bailey & Dixon, L.L.P.
434 Fayetteville Street, Suite 2500
Raleigh, North Carolina 27601
 Telephone: 919-828-0731
 Fax: 919-828-6592

Mailing Address: P.O. Box 1351, Raleigh, NC 27602-1351

General Defense, Litigation, Automobile, Construction Defect, Governmental Liability, Product Liability, General Liability, Civil Rights, Employment Law, Sexual Harassment, Environmental Law, Drug, Medical Devices, Arson, Fraud, Legal Malpractice, Life and Health, Workers' Compensation, Insurance Coverage, Bad Faith, Nursing Home Liability, Excess and Reinsurance, Regulatory and Compliance, Trial Practice, State and Federal Courts, Administrative Law, Corporate Law, Insurance Defense, Medical Malpractice, Mergers and Acquisitions, Professional Liability, Real Estate, OSHA, Government Liability, Unfair Claim/Trade Practice Defense Litigation

SEE COMPLETE LISTING UNDER RALEIGH, NORTH CAROLINA (48 MILES)

WINSTON-SALEM

NORTH CAROLINA

WINDSOR † 3,630 Bertie Co.

Refer To

Hornthal, Riley, Ellis and Maland, L.L.P.
301 East Main Street
Elizabeth City, North Carolina 27909
Telephone: 252-335-0871
Fax: 252-335-4223

Insurance Defense, Automobile, Homeowners, Property Damage, Coverage Issues, Product Liability, Professional Liability

SEE COMPLETE LISTING UNDER ELIZABETH CITY, NORTH CAROLINA (52 MILES)

WINSTON-SALEM † 229,617 Forsyth Co.

Bennett & Guthrie, P.L.L.C.

1560 Westbrook Plaza Drive
Winston-Salem, North Carolina 27103
Telephone: 336-765-3121
Fax: 336-765-8622
E-Mail: rbennett@bennett-guthrie.com
www.bennett-guthrie.com

Established: 1995

Alternative Dispute Resolution, Asbestos Litigation, Automobile Litigation, Carrier Defense, Civil Litigation, Commercial Litigation, Construction Law, Coverage Issues, Employment Law, General Defense Civil Litigation, General Liability, Health Care Liability, Hospital Malpractice, Insurance Coverage, Insurance Defense, Insurance Litigation, Mediation, Medical Malpractice Defense, Premises Liability, Product Liability, Product Liability Defense, Professional Liability, Professional Liability (Non-Medical) Defense, Self-Insured Defense, Trial and Appellate Practice, Trucking Litigation, Wrongful Death

Firm Profile: The firm's attorneys practice in the North Carolina state and federal courts at both the trial and appellate levels and are frequently called upon by attorneys from other states to serve as local counsel for their clients. The firm is devoted to aggressively representing its clients and to achieving the best possible results while, at the same time, keeping clients well-informed and involved in the decision-making process.

All attorneys in the firm are members of the North Carolina Association of Defense Attorneys. Richard V. Bennett is a past President of that organization. All attorneys in the firm are members of the Defense Research Institute.

Insurance Clients

American Home Assurance Company
Canal Insurance Company
Great West Casualty Company
Liberty Mutual Insurance Company
MAG Mutual Insurance Company
North American Risk Services
North Carolina Farm Bureau Insurance Group
Universal Underwriters Group
U.S. Liability Insurance Company
Western Litigation Specialists, Inc.
Atlantic Mutual Insurance Company
Colony Insurance Company
Hartford Casualty Insurance Company
National General Insurance Company
State Farm Insurance Company
Swiss Re Life & Health America, Inc.
Western Heritage Insurance Company

Non-Insurance Clients

Bayada Nurses, Inc.
Novant Health
Select Specialty Hospital - Winston-Salem, Inc.
Hospice of Winston-Salem/North Carolina Inc.
Wake Forest Baptist Health

Partners

Richard V. Bennett — Wake Forest University, B.A., 1968; Wake Forest University School of Law, J.D. (cum laude), 1974 — Robert Elster Award for Professional Excellence, N.C. Association of Defense Attorneys — Law Clerk to Honorable Hiram H. Ward, U.S. District Court Judge, Middle District of North Carolina (1974-1976) — Board of Editors, Wake Forest Law Review (1973-1974) — Admitted to Bar, 1974, North Carolina; U.S. District Court, Eastern, Middle and Western Districts of North Carolina; U.S. Court of Appeals, Fourth Circuit; U.S. Supreme Court — Member North Carolina State Bar (Councilor, 1995-2001); North Carolina (Chair, Bench Bar Liaison Committee, 2006-2008) and Forsyth County Bar Associations; Defense Research Institute (North Carolina State Representative, 2001-2003); North Carolina Association of Defense Attorneys (Board of Directors, 1991-2001; Secretary-Treasurer, 1992-1994; Secretary, 1995-1996; Executive Vice President, 1997-1998; President-Elect, 1998-1999; President, 1999-2000); Fourth Circuit Judicial Conference (Permanent Member); Joseph Branch Inn of Court (2001-Present) — Martindale-Hubble Rating "AV" 27 consecutive years; Best Lawyers in America, 2001-2014; North Carolina Legal Elite-Litigation, 2006-2014; North Carolina Super Lawyers, 2007-2014 — Certified Superior Court Mediator — E-mail: rbennett@bennett-guthrie.com

Rodney A. Guthrie — Stetson University, B.A. (cum laude), 1974; Wake Forest University School of Law, J.D., 1980 — Admitted to Bar, 1980, North Carolina; U.S. District Court, Eastern, Middle and Western Districts of North Carolina; U.S. Court of Appeals, Fourth Circuit — Member North Carolina Bar Association; Claims and Litigation Management Alliance; Defense Research Institute; North Carolina Association of Defense Attorneys — Martindale-Hubble Rating "AV"; Best Lawyers in America, 2013 — Certified Superior Court Mediator — E-mail: rguthrie@bennett-guthrie.com

Roberta King Latham — Wake Forest University, B.A. (cum laude), 1997; Wake Forest University School of Law, J.D., 2002 — Wake Forest Law Review — Admitted to Bar, 2003, North Carolina; U.S. District Court, Eastern, Middle and Western Districts of North Carolina — Member North Carolina Bar Association (Young Lawyers Division, Chair, 2010-2011); North Carolina Association of Defense Attorneys (Board of Directors, 2011-2014; Young Lawyers Committee, Chair, 2009-2010); Defense Research Institute — Martindale-Hubble Rating "AV"; Super Lawyers Civil Litigation Defense, 2014; Super Lawyers, Rising Stars, Civil Litigation Defense, 2011, 2012, 2013; Business North Carolina Legal Elite, Young Guns, 2011, 2012; Women Extraordinaire Recipient, Business Leader Media, 2010; Charles F. Blanchard Outstanding Young Lawyer Award of the Year (2007-2008); Wake Forest Moot Court Board — E-mail: rlatham@bennett-guthrie.com

Joshua H. Bennett — Davidson College, B.A., 2000; The University of North Carolina School of Law, J.D., 2004 — Admitted to Bar, 2004, North Carolina; U.S. District Court, Eastern, Middle and Western Districts of North Carolina — Member North Carolina Bar Association; 21st Judicial District (Forsyth County, Ethics and Grievance Committee Member 2009-2012, Chair 2012, Executive Committee Member, 2011-2014); North Carolina Association of Defense Attorneys; Defense Research Institute — North Carolina Super Lawyers, Rising Stars, 2012- 2014 — E-mail: jbennett@bennett-guthrie.com

Of Counsel

Kimberly S. Shipley — University of Richmond, B.A., 2001; Wake Forest University School of Law, J.D., 2004 — Admitted to Bar, 2005, North Carolina; U.S. District Court, Middle District of North Carolina — E-mail: kshipley@bennett-guthrie.com

The following firms also service this area.

Henson & Talley, L.L.P.
Suite 600 Piedmont Building
114 North Elm Street
Greensboro, North Carolina 27401
Telephone: 336-275-0587
Fax: 336-273-2585

Mailing Address: P.O. Box 3525, Greensboro, NC 27402-3525

Trial and Appellate Practice, State and Federal Courts, Insurance Defense, Automobile, Trucking Law, Workers' Compensation, Construction Law, Professional Malpractice, Product Liability, Fire, Insurance Coverage, Subrogation

SEE COMPLETE LISTING UNDER GREENSBORO, NORTH CAROLINA (29 MILES)

NORTH CAROLINA

Vernis & Bowling of Charlotte, PLLC
4701 Hedgemore Drive, Suite 812
Charlotte, North Carolina 28209
   Telephone: 704-910-8162
   Fax: 704-910-8163

Civil Litigation, Insurance Law, Workers' Compensation, Premises Liability, Labor and Employment, Civil Rights, Commercial Litigation, Automobile Liability, Complex Litigation, Product Liability, Directors and Officers Liability, Errors and Omissions, Construction Law, Construction Defect, Environmental Liability, Personal and Commercial Vehicle, Appellate Practice, Admiralty and Maritime Law, Real Estate, Family Law, Elder Law, Personal Injury Protection (PIP)

SEE COMPLETE LISTING UNDER CHARLOTTE, NORTH CAROLINA (88 MILES)

WINTON † 769 Hertford Co.

Refer To

Hornthal, Riley, Ellis and Maland, L.L.P.
301 East Main Street
Elizabeth City, North Carolina 27909
   Telephone: 252-335-0871
   Fax: 252-335-4223

Insurance Defense, Automobile, Homeowners, Property Damage, Coverage Issues, Product Liability, Professional Liability

SEE COMPLETE LISTING UNDER ELIZABETH CITY, NORTH CAROLINA (50 MILES)

YANCEYVILLE † 2,039 Caswell Co.

Refer To

Henson & Talley, L.L.P.
Suite 600 Piedmont Building
114 North Elm Street
Greensboro, North Carolina 27401
   Telephone: 336-275-0587
   Fax: 336-273-2585

Mailing Address: P.O. Box 3525, Greensboro, NC 27402-3525

Trial and Appellate Practice, State and Federal Courts, Insurance Defense, Automobile, Trucking Law, Workers' Compensation, Construction Law, Professional Malpractice, Product Liability, Fire, Insurance Coverage, Subrogation

SEE COMPLETE LISTING UNDER GREENSBORO, NORTH CAROLINA (39 MILES)

NORTH DAKOTA

CAPITAL: BISMARCK

COUNTIES AND COUNTY SEATS

County	County Seat	County	County Seat	County	County Seat
Adams	Hettinger	Grant	Carson	Ransom	Lisbon
Barnes	Valley City	Griggs	Cooperstown	Renville	Mohall
Benson	Minnewaukan	Hettinger	Mott	Richland	Wahpeton
Billings	Medora	Kidder	Steele	Rolette	Rolla
Bottineau	Bottineau	La Moure	La Moure	Sargent	Forman
Bowman	Bowman	Logan	Napoleon	Sheridan	McClusky
Burke	Bowbells	McHenry	Towner	Sioux	Fort Yates
Burleigh	Bismarck	McIntosh	Ashley	Slope	Amidon
Cass	Fargo	McKenzie	Watford City	Stark	Dickinson
Cavalier	Langdon	McLean	Washburn	Steele	Finley
Dickey	Ellendale	Mercer	Stanton	Stutsman	Jamestown
Divide	Crosby	Morton	Mandan	Towner	Cando
Dunn	Manning	Mountrail	Stanley	Traill	Hillsboro
Eddy	New Rockford	Nelson	Lakota	Walsh	Grafton
Emmons	Linton	Oliver	Center	Ward	Minot
Foster	Carrington	Pembina	Cavalier	Wells	Fessenden
Golden Valley	Beach	Pierce	Rugby	Williams	Williston
Grand Forks	Grand Forks	Ramsey	Devils Lake		

In the text that follows "†" indicates County Seats.

Our files contain additional verified data on the firms listed herein. This additional information is available on request.

A.M. BEST COMPANY

NORTH DAKOTA

BELCOURT 2,078 Rolette Co.

Refer To

Traynor Law Firm, PC
509 Fifth Street NE, Suite 1
Devils Lake, North Dakota 58301
   Telephone: 701-662-4077
   Fax: 701-662-7537
   Toll Free: 877-872-9667

Mailing Address: P.O. Box 838, Devils Lake, ND 58301-0838

Oil and Gas, Business Litigation, General Liability, Trucking, Transportation, Product Liability, Insurance Coverage, Bad Faith, ERISA, Employment Practices Liability, Directors and Officers Liability, Professional Negligence, Nursing Home Liability, Environmental Law, Toxic Torts, Agriculture, Construction Law, Real Estate, Government Affairs, Appellate Practice

SEE COMPLETE LISTING UNDER DEVILS LAKE, NORTH DAKOTA (83 MILES)

BEULAH 3,121 Mercer Co.

Refer To

Ebeltoft . Sickler . Lawyers PLLC
2272 8th Street West
Dickinson, North Dakota 58601
   Telephone: 701-225-LAWS (5297)
   Fax: 701-225-9650

Real Estate, Mineral and Environmental, Organizational, Alternatives to Litigation, Personal Planning, Litigation Solutions, Business Solutions

SEE COMPLETE LISTING UNDER DICKINSON, NORTH DAKOTA (78 MILES)

BISMARCK † 61,272 Burleigh Co.

Crowley Fleck PLLP

100 West Broadway, Suite 250
Bismarck, North Dakota 58501
   Telephone: 701-223-6585
   Fax: 701-222-4853
   www.crowleyfleck.com

(Billings, MT Office*: 500 Transwestern Plaza II, 490 North 31st Street, 59101-1288)
   (Tel: 406-252-3441)
   (Fax: 406-256-8526, 406-259-4159, 406-256-0277)
   (E-Mail: jkresslein@crowleyfleck.com)
(Bozeman, MT Office*: 45 Discovery Drive, 59718-6957)
   (Tel: 406-556-1430)
   (Fax: 406-556-1433)
(Butte, MT Office*: Thornton Building, 65 East Broadway, Suite 503, 59701)
   (Tel: 406-533-6892)
   (Fax: 406-533-6830)
(Helena, MT Office*: 900 North Last Chance Gulch, Suite 200, 59601)
   (Tel: 406-449-4165)
   (Fax: 406-449-5149)
(Kalispell, MT Office*: 1667 Whitefish Stage Road, Suite 101, 59901-4835)
   (Tel: 406-752-6644)
   (Fax: 406-752-5108)
(Missoula, MT Office*: 305 South 4th Street East, Suite 100, 59801-2701)
   (Tel: 406-523-3600)
   (Fax: 406-523-3636)
(Williston, ND Office*: 1331 9th Avenue NW, 2nd Floor, 58801, P.O. Box 1206, 58802-1206)
   (Tel: 701-572-2200)
   (Fax: 701-572-7072)
(Casper, WY Office*: 152 North Durbin Street, Suite 220, 82601)
   (Tel: 307-265-2279)
   (Fax: 307-265-2307)
(Cheyenne, WY Office*: 237 Storey Boulevard, Suite 110, 82009)
   (Tel: 307-426-4100)
   (Fax: 307-426-4099)
(Sheridan, WY Office*: 101 West Brundage Street, 82801)
   (Tel: 307-673-3000)
   (Fax: 307-672-1732)

Crowley Fleck PLLP, Bismarck, ND (Continued)

Civil Litigation, Trial and Appellate Practice, Product Liability, Personal Injury, Construction Law, Design Professionals, Malpractice, Wrongful Termination, Employer Liability, Medical Negligence, Legal, Professional Negligence, Insurance Coverage, Bad Faith, Agent/Broker Liability, Workers' Compensation, Oil and Gas, Environmental Law

Litigation Partner

Michael C. Waller — 1957 — The University of North Dakota, B.S. (cum laude), 1980; University of Idaho College of Law, J.D. (cum laude) 1985 — Admitted to Bar, 1985, Montana; 1991, North Dakota; 1986, U.S. District Court, District of Montana; 1987, U.S. Court of Appeals, Eighth Circuit; 1991, U.S. District Court, District of North Dakota

Partners

Brian Bjella
Shane A. Hanson
Blaine Johnson
John W. Morrison

Craig B. Burns
Kenneth G. Hedge
Tim D. Lervick
Craig C. Smith

Associates

Kimberly Backman
Paul Forster

Stephanie Dassinger
Amy Oster

Of Counsel

Malcolm Brown

Gary R. Wolberg

(See listing under Billings, MT for additional information)

(Revisors of the North Dakota Insurance Law Digest for this Publication)

Vogel Law Firm

200 North 3rd Street, Suite 201
Bismarck, North Dakota 58501-4012
   Telephone: 701-258-7899
   Toll Free: 877-629-0705
   Fax: 701-258-9705
   E-Mail: vogellaw@vogellaw.com
   www.vogellaw.com

(Fargo, ND Office*: 218 NP Avenue, 58102-6983, P.O. Box 1389, 58107-1389)
   (Tel: 701-237-6983)
   (Fax: 701-237-0847)
   (Toll Free: 800-677-5027)

Insurance Defense

(See listing under Fargo, ND for additional information)

The following firms also service this area.

Ebeltoft . Sickler . Lawyers PLLC
2272 8th Street West
Dickinson, North Dakota 58601
   Telephone: 701-225-LAWS (5297)
   Fax: 701-225-9650

Real Estate, Mineral and Environmental, Organizational, Alternatives to Litigation, Personal Planning, Litigation Solutions, Business Solutions

SEE COMPLETE LISTING UNDER DICKINSON, NORTH DAKOTA (100 MILES)

DICKINSON   NORTH DAKOTA

Flom Law Office, P.A.
1703 32nd Avenue South
Fargo, North Dakota 58103-5936
   Telephone: 701-280-2300
   Fax: 701-280-1880

Insurance Defense, Trial and Appellate Practice, State and Federal Courts, Medical Malpractice, Professional Malpractice, Civil Rights, Construction Law, Product Liability, Casualty, Fire, Automobile Liability, Asbestos Litigation, Toxic Substances, Pollution, No-Fault, Coverage Issues, Liquor Liability, Automobile, Premises Liability, Commercial Litigation, Subrogation, Environmental Law, Employment Law, Governmental Liability, Municipal Liability, Errors and Omissions, Health

SEE COMPLETE LISTING UNDER FARGO, NORTH DAKOTA (193 MILES)

Swanson & Warcup, Ltd.
1397 Library Circle, Suite 202
Grand Forks, North Dakota 58201
   Telephone: 701-772-3407
   Fax: 701-772-3833

Mailing Address: P.O. Box 12909, Grand Forks, ND 58208-2909

Insurance Defense, Casualty, Fire, Automobile, Product Liability, Professional Liability, Negligence, Governmental Liability, Coverage Issues, Insurance Litigation, Dram Shop, Construction Law

SEE COMPLETE LISTING UNDER GRAND FORKS, NORTH DAKOTA (250 MILES)

Traynor Law Firm, PC
701 4th Avenue NE
Minot, North Dakota 58703
   Telephone: 701-838-4077
   Fax: 701-662-7537
   Toll Free: 877-872-9667

Oil and Gas, Business Litigation, General Liability, Trucking, Transportation, Product Liability, Insurance Coverage, Bad Faith, ERISA, Employment Practices Liability, Directors and Officers Liability, Professional Negligence, Nursing Home Liability, Environmental Law, Toxic Torts, Agriculture, Construction Law, Real Estate, Government Affairs, Appellate Practice

SEE COMPLETE LISTING UNDER MINOT, NORTH DAKOTA (110 MILES)

DEVILS LAKE † 7,141 Ramsey Co.

Traynor Law Firm, PC
509 Fifth Street NE, Suite 1
Devils Lake, North Dakota 58301
   Telephone: 701-662-4077
   Fax: 701-662-7537
   Toll Free: 877-872-9667
   E-Mail: dantraynor@traynorlaw.com
   www.traynorlaw.com

(Minot, ND Office*: 701 4th Avenue NE, 58703)
   (Tel: 701-838-4077)
   (Fax: 701-662-7537)
   (Toll Free: 877-872-9667)

Established: 1897

Oil and Gas, Business Litigation, General Liability, Trucking, Transportation, Product Liability, Insurance Coverage, Bad Faith, ERISA, Employment Practices Liability, Directors and Officers Liability, Professional Negligence, Nursing Home Liability, Environmental Law, Toxic Torts, Agriculture, Construction Law, Real Estate, Government Affairs, Appellate Practice

Firm Profile: From our founding in 1897, the Traynor Law Firm has been known for its extraordinary success in the courtrooms of North Dakota and for its innovative client service.

Insurance Clients

American Trucking and Transportation Insurance Company	Arch Insurance Group
CNA	Capitol Indemnity Corporation
Dakota Fire Insurance Company	Chartis Claims, Inc.
	Crawford Technical Services
	EMC Insurance Companies

Traynor Law Firm, PC, Devils Lake, ND   (Continued)

Farmers Alliance Mutual Insurance Company	GMAC Insurance
Grinnell Mutual Reinsurance Company	Great West Casualty Company
National Indemnity Company	Hawkeye-Security Insurance Company
North Star Mutual Insurance Company	National Interstate Insurance Company
Rice Insurance Services Company, LLC	OneBeacon Insurance
State Auto Insurance Companies	Riverport Insurance Company
W.R. Berkley Corporation	Scottsdale Insurance Company
	Wells Fargo

Partners

Daniel M. Traynor — The University of North Dakota, B.A., 1994; The University of North Dakota School of Law, J.D. (with distinction), 1997 — Order of the Coif — Admitted to Bar, 1997, North Dakota; Minnesota; U.S. District Court, District of North Dakota; 1998, Spirit Lake Tribal Court; Turtle Mountain Tribal Court; Three Affiliated Tribes Tribal Court — Member American Bar Association; State Bar Association of North Dakota; North Dakota Defense Lawyers Association; Defense Research Institute; American Law Institute — Practice Areas: Insurance Defense; Insurance Coverage; Coverage Analysis; Business Litigation; Government Affairs; Personal Injury; Tribal Law; Election Law — E-mail: dantraynor@traynorlaw.com

J. Thomas Traynor, Jr. — The University of North Dakota, B.A. (cum laude), 1977; The University of North Dakota School of Law, J.D., 1980 — Phi Delta Phi — Case Comment Editor, University of North Dakota Law Review, 1979-1980 — Admitted to Bar, 1980, North Dakota; U.S. District Court, District of North Dakota — Member State Bar Association of North Dakota; Lake Region Bar Association (Past President) — City Attorney, Devils Lake, North Dakota, 1993-Present; Municipal Judge, 1983-1984 — Practice Areas: Business and Real Estate Transactions; Municipal Law; Title Insurance; Estate Planning; Wills; Trusts.— E-mail: tomtraynor@traynorlaw.com

Associate

Michael P. Hurly — North Dakota State University, B.A., 2000; The University of North Dakota School of Law, J.D., 2005 — Law Clerk, Hon. Joe L. Hegel and Hon. Gary L. Gay, 16 Montana Judicial District — Admitted to Bar, 2007, North Dakota — Member American and Lake Region (President) Bar Associations; State Bar Association of North Dakota — City Prosecutor, City of Devils Lake — Practice Areas: Automobile; Professional Malpractice; Business Litigation; Estate Planning; Probate; Family Law; Municipal Law; Civil Litigation — E-mail: mikehurly@traynorlaw.com

Of Counsel

John T. Traynor

The following firms also service this area.

Swanson & Warcup, Ltd.
1397 Library Circle, Suite 202
Grand Forks, North Dakota 58201
   Telephone: 701-772-3407
   Fax: 701-772-3833

Mailing Address: P.O. Box 12909, Grand Forks, ND 58208-2909

Insurance Defense, Casualty, Fire, Automobile, Product Liability, Professional Liability, Negligence, Governmental Liability, Coverage Issues, Insurance Litigation, Dram Shop, Construction Law

SEE COMPLETE LISTING UNDER GRAND FORKS, NORTH DAKOTA (89 MILES)

DICKINSON † 17,787 Stark Co.

Ebeltoft . Sickler . Lawyers PLLC
2272 8th Street West
Dickinson, North Dakota 58601
   Telephone: 701-225-LAWS (5297)
   Fax: 701-225-9650
   www.ndlaw.com

Real Estate, Mineral and Environmental, Organizational, Alternatives to Litigation, Personal Planning, Litigation Solutions, Business Solutions

NORTH DAKOTA — FARGO

Ebeltoft . Sickler . Lawyers PLLC, Dickinson, ND
(Continued)

Firm Profile: Focused expertise, personal service, second-to-none accessibility to your lawyers, and teamwork in legal problem solving serve as our collective driving vision. A balance of experienced lawyers and young professionals ensures a mix of worldviews, educational backgrounds and practice interests.

Insurance Clients

Aetna Insurance Company
Allstate Insurance Company
American Hardware Mutual Insurance Company
Arch Insurance Company
Austin Mutual Insurance Company
Berkley Oil & Gas Specialty Services, LLC
Catholic Health Initiatives
Center Mutual Insurance Company
CNA Insurance Company
Commercial Union Insurance Company
Employers Mutual Companies
Farmland Mutual Insurance Company
Fireman's Fund Insurance Company
Government Employees Insurance Company
Great West Casualty Company
Guaranty National Group
The Hartford Insurance Group
Highlands Insurance Group
Horace Mann Insurance Group
Liberty Mutual Insurance Company
Milbank Insurance Company
National Health Insurance Company
Nodak Mutual Insurance Company
North Dakota Insurance Reserve Fund
Preferred Professional Insurance Company
RSUI Group, Inc.
Seaworthy Insurance Company
State Farm Group
Travelers Insurance Companies
Union Standard Insurance Company
United States Fidelity and Guaranty Company
Western National Insurance Group
Zurich American Insurance Company
Allied Group
American Family Insurance Group
American Modern Home Insurance Company
Arch Insurance Group
AXA Assurances, Inc.
Bituminous Insurance Companies
Boat/U.S. Marine Insurance
CBCS
Chubb Group of Insurance Companies
CUMIS Insurance Society, Inc.
Dakota Fire Insurance Company
Farmers Alliance Mutual Insurance Company
Federated Insurance Company
First Mercury Insurance Company
Gallagher Bassett Services, Inc.
Great American Insurance Company
Grinnell Mutual Reinsurance Company
Hawkeye-Security Insurance Company
Lexington Insurance Company
Mid-Continent Group
National Farmers Union Casualty Group
Nationwide Group
Northbridge Insurance
Northwest G. F. Mutual Insurance Company
Ranger Insurance Company
RLI Insurance Company
The St. Paul Companies
Sentry Claims Services
Sunshine Insurance Company
Tri-State Insurance Company of Minnesota
United Fire & Casualty Company
Utica Mutual Insurance Company
Wausau Insurance Companies
Westfield Insurance Company

Firm Members

Paul F. Ebeltoft — 1949 — The George Washington University Law School, J.D., 1976 — Admitted to Bar, 1976, North Dakota — E-mail: pebeltoft@ndlaw.com

Randall N. Sickler — 1963 — The University of North Dakota School of Law, J.D., 1989 — Admitted to Bar, 1989, Colorado; 1993, North Dakota; 2009, South Dakota — E-mail: rsickler@ndlaw.com

Jennifer D. Grosz — 1981 — University of Nebraska College of Law, J.D., 2005 — Admitted to Bar, 2005, North Dakota; 2008, Montana — Languages: Spanish — E-mail: jgrosz@ndlaw.com

Nathan M. Bouray — 1980 — University of Nebraska College of Law, J.D., 2005 — Admitted to Bar, 2005, Nebraska; 2007, North Dakota — E-mail: nbouray@ndlaw.com

Associates

Courtney Presthus — 1985 — The University of North Dakota, J.D., 2010 — Admitted to Bar, 2010, North Dakota — E-mail: cpresthus@ndlaw.com

Bekki W. Grant — 1983 — Gonzaga University School of Law, J.D. (cum laude), 2009 — Admitted to Bar, 2009, Montana; 2011, North Dakota — E-mail: bgrant@ndlaw.com

Nicholas A. Grant — 1983 — Gonzaga University School of Law, J.D. (summa cum laude), 2010 — Admitted to Bar, 2010, Montana; 2011, Oregon (Inactive); 2012, North Dakota — E-mail: ngrant@ndlaw.com

Ebeltoft . Sickler . Lawyers PLLC, Dickinson, ND
(Continued)

Peter D. Morowski — 1984 — Gonzaga University School of Law, J.D., 2010 — Admitted to Bar, 2011, Texas; 2013, North Dakota — E-mail: pmorowski@ndlaw.com

---

The following firms also service this area.

Swanson & Warcup, Ltd.
1397 Library Circle, Suite 202
Grand Forks, North Dakota 58201
Telephone: 701-772-3407
Fax: 701-772-3833

Mailing Address: P.O. Box 12909, Grand Forks, ND 58208-2909

Insurance Defense, Casualty, Fire, Automobile, Product Liability, Professional Liability, Negligence, Governmental Liability, Coverage Issues, Insurance Litigation, Dram Shop, Construction Law

SEE COMPLETE LISTING UNDER GRAND FORKS, NORTH DAKOTA (346 MILES)

FARGO † 105,549 Cass Co.

Flom Law Office, P.A.

1703 32nd Avenue South
Fargo, North Dakota 58103-5936
Telephone: 701-280-2300
Fax: 701-280-1880
E-Mail: joel@flowlaw.com
www.flomlaw.com

Established: 1986

Insurance Defense, Trial and Appellate Practice, State and Federal Courts, Medical Malpractice, Professional Malpractice, Civil Rights, Construction Law, Product Liability, Casualty, Fire, Automobile Liability, Asbestos Litigation, Toxic Substances, Pollution, No-Fault, Coverage Issues, Liquor Liability, Automobile, Premises Liability, Commercial Litigation, Subrogation, Environmental Law, Employment Law, Governmental Liability, Municipal Liability, Errors and Omissions, Health

Firm Profile: Flom Law Office, P.A., was established for the purpose of concentrating in civil litigation. The firm's primary emphasis is representing insurance companies and their insureds in all areas of modern day tort and contract claims. With more than 25 years of experience in insurance defense, the firm does trial and appellate work in both Minnesota and North Dakota. The firm also handles commercial and business law for select clients.

Insurance Clients

ACUITY
American Reliable Insurance Company
Center Mutual Insurance Company
Chartis Insurance
Commercial Union Insurance Company
Diamond State Insurance Company
Farmers Home Group
First Specialty Insurance Corporation
Gallagher Bassett Services, Inc.
Great American Insurance Company
Illinois Casualty Company
Imperial Fire and Casualty Insurance Company
Liberty Mutual Insurance
The Medical Protective Company
National Farmers Union Standard Insurance Company
North American Specialty Insurance Company
Principal Casualty Insurance Company
Admiral Insurance Company
Arch Insurance Company
Atlantic Mutual Insurance Company
CNA Insurance Company
Continental Insurance Company
Continental Insurance HealthCare
Essex Insurance Company
Federated Mutual Insurance Company
GAB Robins North America, Inc.
Gateway Insurance Company
Hartford Insurance Company
Hawkeye-Security Insurance Company
IMT Insurance Company
Indiana Lumbermens Mutual Insurance Company
Midwest Medical Insurance Company
Nodak Mutual Insurance Company
Northland Insurance Company
Preferred Risk Group
Reliance Insurance Company
Reliance National Risk Specialists

FARGO NORTH DAKOTA

Flom Law Office, P.A., Fargo, ND (Continued)

Rice Insurance Services Company, LLC
Scottsdale Insurance Company
State Auto Insurance Company
Transco Insurance Services
Travelers Property Casualty Corporation
Zurich North America
Royal Insurance Company
Safeco Insurance
Shand Morahan & Company, Inc.
Swiss Reinsurance America Corporation
Tri-State, Ltd.
United National Insurance Company

Non-Insurance Clients

Adjusting Services Unlimited
Aid Association for Lutherans
CBS Corporation
Jerguson Gage & Valve
Rheem Manufacturing Company
UB West Virginia, Inc. f/k/a Union Boiler Co.
Adjustment Services, Inc.
Borg-Warner Automotive, Inc.
Honeywell, Inc.
Lowe's Companies, Inc.
Sepco Corporation
Wachovia Bank, N.A.

Shareholder

Joel A. Flom — 1953 — University of Minnesota, B.A., 1975; William Mitchell College of Law, J.D., 1981 — Admitted to Bar, 1981, Minnesota; 1987, North Dakota; 1981, U.S. District Court, District of Minnesota; 1986, U.S. Court of Appeals, Eighth Circuit; 1987, U.S. District Court, District of North Dakota — Member Minnesota State, 7th District, Clay County and Cass County Bar Associations; State Bar Association of North Dakota; Minnesota Defense Lawyers Association; North Dakota Defense Lawyers Association; Defense Research Institute — Certified Civil Trial Specialist — Practice Areas: Insurance Defense; Medical Malpractice; Personal Injury; Product Liability; Environmental Coverage; Liquor Liability; Appellate Practice; Errors and Omissions; Professional Liability; Construction Law; Insurance Coverage; Asbestos Litigation; Toxic Substances; Commercial Litigation — E-mail: joel@flomlaw.com

Associates

Zachary C. Burmeister — 1982 — Bemidji State University, B.S., 2006; Hamline University School of Law, J.D., 2009 — Admitted to Bar, 2009, Minnesota; 2013, North Dakota; U.S. District Court, District of North Dakota — Member Minnesota State, 7th District, Clay County and Cass County Bar Associations; State Bar Association of North Dakota — Practice Areas: Civil Litigation; Insurance Defense

Rachel E. Hoffman — University of St. Thomas, B.A., 2008; The University of North Dakota School of Law, J.D., 2012 — Admitted to Bar, 2012, North Dakota; 2014, Minnesota; 2013, U.S. District Court, District of North Dakota — Member State Bar Association of North Dakota; Minnesota State, 7th District, Clay County and Cass County Bar Associations — Practice Areas: Civil Litigation; Subrogation; Asbestos Litigation — E-mail: rachel@flomlaw.com

Nilles Law Firm

201 North Fifth Street
Fargo, North Dakota 58102
Telephone: 701-237-5544
Fax: 701-280-0762
E-Mail: mkemmer@nilleslaw.com
www.nilleslaw.com

Established: 1920

Fire, Casualty, Surety, Life and Health, Investigation and Adjustment

Firm Profile: The Nilles Law Firm has been handling insurance matters since the early 1920's. We represent many insurance companies in a wide variety of matters. Our insurance department is committed to handling all insurance matters efficiently and effectively. We want our insurance clients to be fully satisfied with our services.

Our insurance practice covers all areas of insurance - Property and Casualty, Commercial and Personal Lines, Life Insurance, Health and Accident, Construction and Fidelity Bonds, Officers and Directors Liability, Professional Liability and Errors and Omissions, Reinsurance and other lines of insurance.

Nilles Law Firm, Fargo, ND (Continued)

Our major area of emphasis is insurance defense of first party and third party claims and insurance coverage law. However, our attorneys have each developed specialized areas of insurance practice, thereby adding to our effectiveness. They specialize in automobile insurance law, property claims, premise liability claims, product liability, arson defense, insurance subrogation, professional liability law, employment law, construction litigation, aviation and crop litigation, and toxic torts litigation. We also handle workers compensation claims for the North Dakota Workers' Compensation Bureau.

Insurance Clients

AAA Michigan
AIG Aviation, Inc.
Auto-Owners Insurance Company
Employers Reinsurance Corporation
Founders Insurance Company
Liberty Mutual Insurance Company
Nodak Mutual Insurance Company
Philadelphia Insurance Company
Progressive Insurance Company
Safeco Insurance
The St. Paul/Travelers Companies, Inc.
State Farm General Insurance Company
United States Aviation Underwriters, Inc.
ACUITY
Argonaut Insurance Company
EMC Insurance Companies
Farmers Insurance Group
Fireman's Fund Insurance Companies
Mendota Insurance Company
North Star Mutual Insurance Company
Rice Insurance Services Company, LLC
SECURA Insurance Companies
State Farm Fire and Casualty Company
United Fire & Casualty Company
Zurich American Insurance Company

Retired

Russell F. Freeman

Timothy Q. Davies

E. Thomas Conmy, III

Duane H. Ilvedson

Shareholders

Stephen W. Plambeck — 1950 — The George Washington University, B.A., 1972; J.D., 1975 — Admitted to Bar, 1975, North Dakota — Member Defense Research Institute; American College of Trial Lawyers; International Society of Barristers — Practice Areas: Class Actions; Product Liability; Railroad Law — E-mail: splambeck@nilleslaw.com

Gregory B. Selbo — 1950 — Southern Methodist University, B.B.A., 1972; The University of North Dakota, J.D., 1975 — Admitted to Bar, 1975, North Dakota — Practice Areas: Business Law; Real Estate; Estate Planning; Probate — E-mail: gselbo@nilleslaw.com

William P. Harrie — 1960 — The University of North Dakota, B.S.B.A., 1982; J.D. (with distinction), 1986 — Admitted to Bar, 1986, North Dakota; Minnesota — Member North Dakota Defense Lawyers Association; Defense Research Institute — Practice Areas: Insurance Defense; Insurance Coverage; Product Liability; Civil Litigation; Commercial Litigation — E-mail: wharrie@nilleslaw.com

Mark R. Hanson — 1964 — Valley City State College, B.S. (cum laude), 1986; The University of North Dakota, J.D. (with distinction), 1989 — Admitted to Bar, 1989, North Dakota; South Dakota — Practice Areas: Commercial Litigation; Insurance Defense; Insurance Coverage — E-mail: mhanson@nilleslaw.com

Douglas W. Gigler — 1959 — Mayville State University, B.S., 1988; The University of North Dakota, J.D., 1992 — Admitted to Bar, 1992, North Dakota — Practice Areas: Construction Litigation; Bonds; Employment Law; Insurance Coverage; Insurance Defense — E-mail: dgigler@nilleslaw.com

Andrew L.B. Noah — 1967 — The University of North Dakota, B.A.A. (summa cum laude), 1989; J.D. (with distinction), 1993 — Admitted to Bar, 1993, North Dakota — Practice Areas: Business Law; Real Estate — E-mail: anoah@nilleslaw.com

Jacqueline S. Anderson — 1962 — Moorhead State College, B.A. (summa cum laude), 1992; The University of North Dakota, J.D. (with distinction), 1995 — Admitted to Bar, 1995, North Dakota; Minnesota — Practice Areas: Workers' Compensation; Employment Law; Litigation — E-mail: janderson@nilleslaw.com

Shanon M. Gregor — 1970 — North Dakota State University, B.A. (with honors), 1992; The University of North Dakota, J.D. (with distinction), 1998 — Admitted to Bar, 1999, Minnesota — Practice Areas: Insurance Law; Civil Litigation; Workers' Compensation — E-mail: sgregor@nilleslaw.com

Mark R. Western — 1978 — Concordia College, B.A., 2000; The University of North Dakota, J.D. (with distinction), 2007 — Order of Barristers; Order of

Nilles Law Firm, Fargo, ND (Continued)

the Coif — Admitted to Bar, 2007, North Dakota; 2008, Minnesota; U.S. District Court, District of North Dakota — Member American and Cass County Bar Associations; State Bar Associaiton of North Dakota; Ronald N. Davies Inns of Court — Practice Areas: Civil Litigation; Insurance Law — E-mail: mwestern@nilleslaw.com

Associates

Ryan C. McCamy — 1982 — North Dakota State University, B.S. (with honors), 2004; The University of North Dakota, J.D. (with distinction), 2009 — Admitted to Bar, 2009, North Dakota; U.S. District Court, District of North Dakota — Member American and Cass County Bar Associations; Ronald Davies Inns of Court — Practice Areas: Insurance Defense; Insurance Coverage; Construction Law — E-mail: rmccamy@nilleslaw.com

Charlotte J. Skar — 1984 — The University of North Dakota, B.A., 2007; J.D. (with distinction), 2010 — Order of the Coif — Admitted to Bar, 2010, North Dakota; 2012, Minnesota — Member North Dakota Defense Lawyers Association — E-mail: cskar@nilleslaw.com

Benjamin J. Williams — 1984 — Concordia College, B.A., 2008; The University of North Dakota, J.D. (with distinction), 2011 — Order of the Coif — North Dakota Bar Foundation Best Law Review (2010) — Admitted to Bar, 2011, North Dakota — E-mail: bwilliams@nilleslaw.com

Justin G. Hughes — 1985 — The University of North Dakota, B.S., 2008; J.D. (with distinction), 2011 — Admitted to Bar, 2011, North Dakota — E-mail: jhughes@nilleslaw.com

Patrick T. Dixon — 1978 — Kansas State University, M.A., 2004; The University of North Dakota, J.D., 2007 — Admitted to Bar, 2008, North Dakota — E-mail: pdixon@nilleslaw.com

William J. Behrmann — 1987 — The University of North Dakota, B.A., Business Administration, 2009; J.D. (cum laude), 2013 — Admitted to Bar, 2013, North Dakota; U.S. District Court, District of North Dakota — Member State Bar of North Dakota; Cass County Bar Association; Inns of Court — E-mail: wbehrmann@nilleslaw.com

Michael P. Carlson — 1985 — The University of North Dakota, B.A./B.S., 2010; J.D. (with distinction), 2013 — Admitted to Bar, 2014, North Dakota — E-mail: mcarlson@nilleslaw.com

(All Attorneys are Members of the American and Cass County Bar Associations and State Bar Association of North Dakota)

Serkland Law Firm

10 Roberts Street N
Fargo, North Dakota 58102
Telephone: 701-232-8957
Fax: 701-237-4049
E-Mail: firm@serklandlaw.com
www.serklandlaw.com

Established: 1888

Alternative Dispute Resolution, Bad Faith, Commercial Law, Coverage Issues, Declaratory Judgments, Errors and Omissions, First and Third Party Defense, Homeowners, No-Fault, Professional Malpractice, Property, Uninsured and Underinsured Motorist

Firm Profile: Well-known throughout the local community for excellence in the practice of insurance defense, The Serkland Law Firm represents and advises many large insurance companies in North Dakota and Minnesota. In addition, we consult with and advise other attorneys on matters of North Dakoka insurance law.

Insurance Clients

ACE North American
Attorneys Liability Protection Society
CHG Healthcare
Chubb Insurance Company
Firemen's Insurance Company of Newark, New Jersey
The Guardian Life Insurance Company of America
Liberty Mutual Insurance Company
AIG
Bankers Life and Casualty Company
Chicago Title Insurance Company
Empire Insurance Company
First National Insurance Company of America
The Hartford Insurance Group
Houston General Insurance Company

Serkland Law Firm, Fargo, ND (Continued)

Lloyd's of London
Minnesota Lawyers Mutual Insurance Company
North Dakota Insurance Reserve Fund
Prudential Insurance Company of America
Travelers
Wausau General Insurance Company
Massachusetts Mutual Life Insurance Company
New York Life Insurance Company
Ohio Casualty Group
Safeco Select Markets
St. Paul Fire and Marine Insurance Company
Western Surety Company

Insurance Litigation Partners

Ronald H. McLean — University of Wisconsin, B.A. (with honors), 1972; The University of North Dakota, J.D., 1975 — Senior Editor, University of North Dakota Law Review (1974-1975) — Admitted to Bar, 1975, North Dakota; 1983, Minnesota — Member American Bar Association (Litigation, Tort and Insurance Practice Law and Class Actions and Derivative Suits Sections); State Bar Association of North Dakota (Chairman, North Dakota Supreme Court, Pattern Jury Insurance Commission, 1990, 1993; Joint Legal Services to the Poor Committee, 1987-1991; North Dakota Supreme County Joint Procedures Committee, 1985-2005; Board of Directors, Legal Assistance for North Dakota, 1983-1990; President, 1989-1990); Minnesota State and Cass County Bar Association; Attorneys Liability Protection Society (Chairman of the Board of Directors, 1997-2006); Fellow, American College of Trial Lawyers (State Chair); Fellow, International Society of Barristers; Norwegian Consul for North Dakota; Defense Research Institute; North Dakota Defense Lawyers Association — Author: "Admissibility of Polygraph Evidence," North Dakota Law Review (1975) — Norwegian Consul for North Dakota — Practice Areas: Class Actions; Commercial Law; Insurance Litigation; Negligence; Personal Injury; Professional Malpractice

Jane L. Dynes — Concordia College, B.A. (summa cum laude), 1982; The University of North Dakota, J.D., 1987 — Admitted to Bar, 1987, North Dakota; 1990, Minnesota; 1989, U.S. District Court, District of North Dakota; 1996, U.S. District Court, District of Minnesota — Member American and Cass County Bar Associations; State Bar Association of North Dakota — Practice Areas: Litigation; Insurance Defense; Product Liability; Class Actions; Employment Law

Joseph A. Wetch, Jr. — The University of North Dakota, B.A. (magna cum laude), 1998; J.D. (with distinction), 2001 — Admitted to Bar, 2001, North Dakota; 2002, Minnesota; 2001, U.S. District Court, District of North Dakota; 2004, Turtle Mountain Tribal Court — Member American, Minnesota State and Cass County Bar Associations; State Bar Association of North Dakota; North Dakota Defense Lawyers Association; Association of Trial Lawyers of America — "Constitutional Law - First Amendment - Commercial Speech: Broadcasters Come Up All 7'S: Advertising of Casinos and Gambling," 76 NDLR 161 — U.S. Army Reserves, 1985-1987; U.S. Army, 1987-1995 — Practice Areas: Class Actions; Medical Malpractice; Insurance Defense; Personal Injury; Product Liability

Associate

Peter Zuger — University of Mary, B.S. (cum laude), 2003; The University of North Dakota, J.D. (with distinction), 2008 — Admitted to Bar, 2008, North Dakota; Minnesota; U.S. District Court, District of North Dakota; U.S. District Court, District of Minnesota; U.S. Court of Appeals, Eighth Circuit — Member Minnesota State and Cass County Bar Associations; State Bar Association of North Dakota; Pattern Jury Instruction Commission — Author: "COVENANTS AGAINST COMPETITION IN FRANCHISE AGREEMENTS," ABA Forum on Franchising, at 433-38 (Michael R. Gray and Natalma M. McKnew, eds., 3d ed. 2012). — Rising Star, Great Plains Super Lawyers, 2013 — Practice Areas: Commercial Litigation; Construction Litigation; Corporate Law; Product Liability; Insurance Defense; Professional Malpractice; Personal Injury; Employment Litigation

Vogel Law Firm

218 NP Avenue
Fargo, North Dakota 58102-6983
Telephone: 701-237-6983
Fax: 701-237-0847
Toll Free: 800-677-5027
E-Mail: vogellaw@vogellaw.com
www.vogellaw.com

CINCINNATI   OHIO

Lindhorst & Dreidame Co., L.P.A., Cincinnati, OH
(Continued)

Transport Insurance Company
Unitrin Insurance Company
Universal Underwriters Group
Western World Insurance Company
Zurich Insurance Company
United Southern Assurance Company
Vanliner Insurance Company
Zurich American Insurance Company

Non-Insurance Clients

America Wide Administrators
Dollar-Thrifty Automotive Group, Inc.
The Hertz Corporation
Norfolk Southern Corporation
Roadway Services, Inc.
CSX Corporation
Enterprise Rent-A-Car Company
Greyhound Lines, Inc.
Joseph Auto Group
Pepsi-Cola Bottlers, Inc.

Shareholders

James L. O'Connell — 1931 — Xavier University, H.A.B. (magna cum laude), 1953; University of Cincinnati College of Law, LL.B., 1958 — Order of the Coif — Admitted to Bar, 1958, Ohio — Member Federal, Ohio State and Cincinnati Bar Associations; Advocate, American Board of Trial Advocates; Ohio Association of Civil Trial Attorneys; National Association of Railroad Trial Counsel; Fellow, American College of Trial Lawyers

Jay R. Langenbahn — 1950 — University of Kentucky, B.S., 1972; Salmon P. Chase College of Law, J.D., 1976 — Admitted to Bar, 1976, Ohio; 1983, Kentucky — Member Ohio State, Kentucky, Northern Kentucky and Cincinnati Bar Associations; Ohio Association of Civil Trial Attorneys — E-mail: jlangenbahn@lindhorstlaw.com

James H. Smith III — 1950 — Kenyon College, A.B., 1972; The University of Toledo, J.D. (cum laude), 1975; New York University, LL.M., 1976 — Admitted to Bar, 1975, Ohio — Member Ohio State and Cincinnati Bar Associations — E-mail: jsmith@lindhorstlaw.com

Michael F. Lyon — 1947 — Xavier University, B.A., 1969; Salmon P. Chase College of Law, J.D., 1975 — Admitted to Bar, 1975, Ohio — Member Federal, American, Ohio State and Cincinnati Bar Associations; Advocate, American Board of Trial Advocates — E-mail: mlyon@lindhorstlaw.com

Thomas E. Martin — 1954 — Wittenberg University, B.A. (cum laude), 1976; University of Cincinnati College of Law, J.D., 1979 — Order of the Coif — Admitted to Bar, 1979, Ohio — Member American, Ohio State and Cincinnati Bar Associations — E-mail: tmartin@lindhorstlaw.com

James F. Brockman — 1952 — University of Cincinnati, B.S., 1975; Rutgers University, M.A., 1977; University of Cincinnati College of Law, J.D., 1981 — Admitted to Bar, 1981, Ohio; U.S. District Court, Eastern District of Kentucky; U.S. District Court, Southern District of Ohio — Member Ohio State and Cincinnati Bar Associations; Ohio Association of Civil Trial Attorneys; National Association of Railroad Trial Counsel; American Board of Trial Advocates — E-mail: jbrockman@lindhorstlaw.com

Barry F. Fagel — 1965 — Xavier University, B.S.B.A., 1987; University of Cincinnati College of Law, J.D., 1991 — Admitted to Bar, 1991, Kentucky; 1992, Ohio — Member American, Ohio State, Kentucky, Northern Kentucky and Cincinnati Bar Associations — E-mail: bfagel@lindhorstlaw.com

Michelle L. Clemons — 1970 — University of South Florida, B.S., 1992; Capital University, J.D./LL.M., 1997 — Admitted to Bar, 1997, Ohio — Member Ohio State and Cincinnati Bar Associations — E-mail: mclemons@lindhorstlaw.com

Bradley D. McPeek — 1973 — University of Notre Dame, B.A., 1995; University of Cincinnati College of Law, J.D., 1999 — Admitted to Bar, 1999, Ohio — Member American, Ohio State and Cincinnati Bar Associations — E-mail: bmcpeek@lindhorstlaw.com

David E. Williamson — 1973 — Hanover College, B.A., 1995; Salmon P. Chase College of Law, J.D., 1999 — Admitted to Bar, 1999, Ohio — Member Ohio State and Cincinnati Bar Associations — E-mail: dwilliamson@lindhorstlaw.com

Laurie A. McCluskey — University of Cincinnati, B.S.N., 1996; Salmon P. Chase College of Law, J.D., 2002 — Admitted to Bar, 2002, Ohio — Member Ohio State and Cincinnati Bar Associations — E-mail: lmccluskey@lindhorstlaw.com

Associate

Matthew A. Mikhail

Marshall Dennehey Warner Coleman & Goggin
312 Elm Street, Suite 1850
Cincinnati, Ohio 45202
  Telephone: 513-375-6800
  Fax: 513-372-6801
  www.marshalldennehey.com

(Philadelphia, PA Office*: 2000 Market Street, Suite 2300, 19103)
  (Tel: 215-575-2600)
  (Fax: 215-575-0856)
  (Toll Free: 800-220-3308)
  (E-Mail: marshalldennehey@mdwcg.com)
(Wilmington, DE Office*: Nemours Building, 1007 North Orange Street, Suite 600, 19801)
  (Tel: 302-552-4300)
  (Fax: 302-552-4340)
(Fort Lauderdale, FL Office*: 100 Northeast 3rd Avenue, Suite 1100, 33301)
  (Tel: 954-847-4920)
  (Fax: 954-627-6640)
(Jacksonville, FL Office*: 200 West Forsyth Street, Suite 1400, 32202)
  (Tel: 904-358-4200)
  (Fax: 904-355-0019)
(Orlando, FL Office*: Landmark Center One, 315 East Robinson Street, Suite 550, 32801-1948)
  (Tel: 407-420-4380)
  (Fax: 407-839-3008)
(Tampa, FL Office*: 201 East Kennedy Boulevard, Suite 1100, 33602)
  (Tel: 813-898-1800)
  (Fax: 813-221-5026)
(Cherry Hill, NJ Office*: Woodland Falls Corporate Park, 200 Lake Drive East, Suite 300, 08002)
  (Tel: 856-414-6000)
  (Fax: 856-414-6077)
(Roseland, NJ Office*: 425 Eagle Rock Avenue, Suite 302, 07068)
  (Tel: 973-618-4100)
  (Fax: 973-618-0685)
(New York, NY Office*: Wall Street Plaza, 88 Pine Street, 21st Floor, 10005-1801)
  (Tel: 212-376-6400)
  (Fax: 212-376-6490)
(Melville, NY Office*: 105 Maxess Road, Suite 303, 11747)
  (Tel: 631-232-6130)
  (Fax: 631-232-6184)
(Cleveland, OH Office*: 127 Public Square, Suite 3510, 44114-1291)
  (Tel: 216-912-3800)
  (Fax: 216-344-9006)
(Allentown, PA Office*: 4905 West Tilghman Street, Suite 300, 18104)
  (Tel: 484-895-2300)
  (Fax: 484-895-2303)
(Doylestown, PA Office*: 10 North Main Street, 2nd Floor, 18901-4318)
  (Tel: 267-880-2020)
  (Fax: 215-348-5439)
(Erie, PA Office*: 717 State Street, Suite 701, 16501)
  (Tel: 814-480-7800)
  (Fax: 814-455-3603)
(Camp Hill, PA Office*(See Harrisburg listing): 100 Coporate Center Drive, Suite 201, 17011)
  (Tel: 717-651-3500)
  (Fax: 717-651-9630)
(King of Prussia, PA Office*: 620 Freedom Business Center, Suite 300, 19406)
  (Tel: 610-354-8250)
  (Fax: 610-354-8299)
(Pittsburgh, PA Office*: U.S. Steel Tower, Suite 2900, 600 Grant Street, 15219)
  (Tel: 412-803-1140)
  (Fax: 412-803-1188)

OHIO

CINCINNATI

Marshall Dennehey Warner Coleman & Goggin, Cincinnati, OH (Continued)

(Moosic, PA Office*(See Scranton listing): 50 Glenmaura National Boulevard, 18507)
(Tel: 570-496-4600)
(Fax: 570-496-0567)
(Rye Brook, NY Office*(See Westchester listing): 800 Westchester Avenue, Suite C-700, 10573)
(Tel: 914-977-7300)
(Fax: 914-977-7301)

Established: 1962

Amusements, Sports and Recreation Liability, Asbestos and Mass Tort Litigation, Automobile Liability, Aviation and Complex Litigation, Construction Injury Litigation, Fraud/Special Investigation, General Liability, Hospitality and Liquor Liability, Maritime Litigation, Product Liability, Property Litigation, Retail Liability, Trucking & Transportation Liability, Appellate Advocacy and Post-Trial Practice, Architectural, Engineering and Construction Defect Litigation, Class Action Litigation, Commercial Litigation, Consumer and Credit Law, Employment Law, Environmental & Toxic Tort Litigation, Insurance Coverage/Bad Faith Litigation, Life, Health and Disability Litigation, Privacy and Data Security, Professional Liability, Public Entity and Civil Rights Litigation, Real Estate E&O Liability, School Leaders' Liability, Securities and Investment Professional Liability, Technology, Media and Intellectual Property Litigation, White Collar Crime, Birth Injury Litigation, Health Care Governmental Compliance, Health Care Liability, Health Law, Long-Term Care Liability, Medical Device and Pharmaceutical Liability, Medicare Set-Aside, Workers' Compensation

Firm Profile: From Fountain Square in Cincinnati to historic Public Square in Cleveland, Marshall Dennehey's Ohio lawyers represent insurance carriers and other clients throughout the state of Ohio and beyond. The Cincinnati office is located downtown, right along the Ohio River bordering Kentucky, and serves the needs of clients in the greater Cincinnati region and throughout all of southwestern Ohio.

For additional information regarding the Cincinnati office, please feel free to contact its managing attorney Samuel Casolari, Jr. at (513) 372-6802 or sgcasolari@mdwcg.com

Managing Shareholder

Samuel G. Casolari, Jr. — Managing Attorney — 1961 — Grove City College, B.A. (cum laude), 1983; The University of Akron School of Law, J.D., 1986 — Admitted to Bar, 1986, Ohio; U.S. District Court, Northern District of Ohio; 1987, U.S. Court of Appeals, Sixth Circuit; 2004, U.S. District Court, Southern District of Ohio — Member Ohio State Bar Association (Committee on Judicial Administration and Legal Reform) — Author: "Open, Obvious, & Ohio," Defense Digest, Vol. 16, No. 2, June, 2010; "Two Bites At The Apple," Defense Digest, Vol. 16, No. 2, June, 2010; "Ohio Supreme Court Limits Damages," Defense Digest, Vol. 14, No. 3, September, 2008; "Doing Buiness in Ohio - Some Good News For Pennsylvania Employer," Defense Digest, Vol. 12, No. 3, September, 2006; "Ohio's Continued Tort Reform Adventure: Caps, Seatbelts, Collateral Source, and More," Defense Digest, Vol. 11, No. 3, September, 2005; "Insurer's Beware! Watch Out For Those Assignments When Settling Claims!," Defense Digest, Vol. 11, No. 3, September, 2005; "When An Expert Cannot Be An Expert," Defense Digest, Vol. 10, No. 4, December, 2004; "Intentional Torts and Coverage For Workplace Torts In Ohio," Defense Digest, Vol. 9, No. 4, December, 2003; "The Trend In Construing The Ohio Employer Intentional Tort Exception - A Consistent, Workable Standard Or Confusing, Expansive Quandry?," Defense Digest, Vol. 9, No. 4, December, 2003; "What Goes Around Comes Around: An Ohio Court Allows Evidence Against Plaintiff's Doctor," Defense Digest, Vol. 7, No. 4, August, 2001; "All In The Family - Ohio Recognizes The Right Of Adult Emancipated Children To Recover For Loss Of Parental Consortium," Defense Digest, Vol. 7, No. 3, June, 2001; "When A Picture May Not Be Worth A Thousand Words - Photographic Evidence In Low-Impact Collisions In Ohio," Defense Digest, Vol. 7, No. 2, April, 2001; "Ohio Enters Uncharted Waters," Defense Digest, Vol. 6, No. 6, December, 2000; Co-Author: "Civil Rule 35 Examinations, Law Office Practice Series," Ohio - Chapter Contribution — Reported Cases: Criss v. Springfield Tp., 538 N.E.2d 406 (Ohio 1989); Criss v. Springfield Township, 566 N.E.2d 1232 (Ohio 1991); Forste v. Oakview Construction, Inc., 5516 (Ohio 2009);

Marshall Dennehey Warner Coleman & Goggin, Cincinnati, OH (Continued)

McGee v. Lowe's Home CTRS., 4981 (Ohio 2007); O'Brien v. Bob Evans Farms, Inc., 6948 (Ohio 2004); Davidson v. Forshaw Distribution, Inc., 2869 (Ohio 2004); Ruvolo Homovich, 5852 (Ohio 2002); Budich v. Reece, 2008-Ohio-3630, 2008-Ohio App., LEXIS 3070, (July 23, 2008); Aldridge v. Reckart Equipment Co., 2006-Ohio-4964, 2006-Ohio App. LEXIS 4904, CCH Prod. Liab. Rep. P17579, discretionary appeal not allowed by Aldridge v. Reckart Equipment Co., 2007-Ohio-3699, 2007-Ohio LEXIS 1803, (Ohio, July 25, 2007); Caldwell v. Petersburg Stone Co., 2005-Ohio-6793, 2005-Ohio App. LEXIS 6119, (December 16, 2005); McGuinea v. Ganley Nissan, Inc., 2005-Ohio-6239, 2005-Ohio App. LEXIS 5629, (November 23, 2005); Timothy M. Johnson v. Tim Hundley, 2005-Ohio-6812, 2003-Ohio App. LEXIS 6161, (December 17, 2003); Conese v. Nichols, 131 Ohio App. 3d 308; 722 N.E. 2d 541, 1998 Ohio-App. LEXIS 965, 26 Media L. Rep. 1907, (March 13, 1998) — Seminars/Classes Taught: Paralegal Studies, Adjunct Instructor, College of Mt. St. Joseph, Cincinnati, Ohio, 1995-1999 — Practice Areas: Automobile Liability; Appellate; Asbestos Litigation; Product Liability; Premises Liability; Trucking; Transportation — E-mail: sgcasolari@mdwcg.com

Resident Shareholder

Ray C. Freudiger — University of Cincinnati, B.A., 1982; University of Cincinnati College of Law, J.D., 1991 — Admitted to Bar, 1991, Ohio; U.S. District Court, Southern District of Ohio — Member Ohio State (Education Law Committee), Cincinnati and Dayton (Civil Trial Practice Committee) Bar Associations; Ohio Association of Civil Trial Attorneys (Alternative Dispute Resolution Committee); Education Law Association; Defense Research Institute — E-mail: rcfreudiger@mdwcg.com

Resident Associate

Laura I. Hillerich

(See listing under Philadelphia, PA for additional information)

Reminger Co., L.P.A.

525 Vine Street, Suite 1700
Cincinnati, Ohio 45202
Telephone: 513-721-1311
Fax: 513-721-2553
www.reminger.com

(Cleveland, OH Office*: 101 West Prospect Avenue, Suite 1400, 44115-1093)
(Tel: 216-687-1311)
(Fax: 216-687-1841)
(Columbus, OH Office*: Capitol Square Office Building, 65 East State Street, 4th Floor, 43215)
(Tel: 614-228-1311)
(Fax: 614-232-2410)
(Indianapolis, IN Office*: 3925 River Crossing Parkway, Suite 280, 46240)
(Tel: 317-663-8570)
(Fax: 317-663-8580)

Trial Practice, State and Federal Courts, Insurance Law, Malpractice, Self-Insured, Risk Management, Transportation, Product Liability, Errors and Omissions, Civil Rights, Investigation and Adjustment

Robert Hojnoski — Gannon University, B.S. (cum laude), 1995; University of Dayton School of Law, J.D., 1998 — Admitted to Bar, 1998, Ohio; 1999, Kentucky — E-mail: rhojnoski@reminger.com

(See listing under Cleveland, OH for additional information)

CLEVELAND   OHIO

Rendigs, Fry, Kiely & Dennis, L.L.P.

600 Vine Street, Suite 2650
Cincinnati, Ohio 45202
 Telephone: 513-381-9200
 Fax: 513-381-9206
 E-Mail: info@rendigs.com
 www.rendigs.com

Established: 1946

Insurance Defense, State and Federal Courts, Automobile, Product Liability, Admiralty and Maritime Law, Architects and Engineers, Civil Rights, Commercial Litigation, Construction Litigation, Employment Law, Environmental Law, Medical Malpractice, Mold and Mildew Claims, Municipal Law, Nursing Home Liability, Personal Injury, Premises Liability, Professional Liability, Legal Malpractice

Firm Profile: Rendigs, Fry, Kiely & Dennis LLP, a 2014 U.S. News & World Report Best Law Firm, offers legal counsel and litigation services with a strong emphasis on client service and responsiveness.

Insurance Clients

ACE USA
American Commerce Insurance Company
American Management Insurance
Chubb & Son, Inc.
CNA Insurance Company
Crawford & Company
Federated Mutual Insurance Company
Gallagher Bassett Services, Inc.
Glatfelter Claims Management, Inc.
Great Central Insurance Company
Harco National Insurance Company
Homesite Insurance Company
Liberty Mutual Insurance Company
Lincoln General Insurance Company
Motorists Mutual Insurance Company
Ohio Mutual Insurance Company
Pekin Insurance
Sentry Claims Services
Sentry Insurance Group
State Farm Fire and Casualty Company
Travelers Insurance Companies
Western Reserve Group
Zurich North America Specialty Claims
Admiral Insurance Company
American International Adjustment Company
Chartis Insurance
The Cincinnati Insurance Companies
Empire Fire and Marine Insurance Company
Fireman's Fund Insurance Companies
Grange Mutual Insurance Company
Great American Insurance Company
HDI-Gerling America Insurance Company
Indiana Lumbermens Mutual Insurance Company
The Medical Protective Company
Mid-Continent Casualty Company
North American Risk Services
Ohio Insurance Guaranty Association
Royal & SunAlliance Insurance Company
Standard Mutual Insurance Company
Sumitomo Marine and Fire Insurance Company, Ltd.
Westport Insurance

Partner

Donald C. Adams, Jr. — University of Cincinnati College of Law, J.D., 1982 — Admitted to Bar, 1982, Ohio; 1991, Kentucky

J. Jeffrey Albrinck — University of Toledo School of Law, J.D., 1987 — Admitted to Bar, 1987, Ohio; 2001, Kentucky

Robert F. Brown — The Ohio State University Moritz College of Law, J.D., 1988 — Admitted to Bar, 1988, Ohio; 1995, Kentucky

Karen A. Carroll — University of Cincinnati College of Law, J.D., 1987 — Admitted to Bar, 1987, Ohio; 1994, Kentucky

Thomas M. Evans — University of Cincinnati College of Law, J.D., 1985 — Admitted to Bar, 1986, Ohio

Michael P. Foley — Ohio Northern University, Pettit College of Law, J.D., 1992 — Admitted to Bar, 1993, Ohio; 1995, Kentucky

Felix J. Gora — University of Cincinnati College of Law, J.D., 1980 — Admitted to Bar, 1980, Ohio; 1991, Kentucky

Steven D. Hengehold — University of Cincinnati College of Law, J.D., 1985 — Admitted to Bar, 1985, Ohio

Jeffrey M. Hines — Salmon P. Chase College of Law, J.D., 1998 — Admitted to Bar, 1999, Ohio

Rendigs, Fry, Kiely & Dennis, L.L.P., Cincinnati, OH
(Continued)

Paul W. McCartney — The Ohio State University Moritz College of Law, J.D., 1988 — Admitted to Bar, 1988, Ohio

John F. McLaughlin — Georgetown University Law Center, J.D., 1987 — Admitted to Bar, 1987, Virginia; 1988, Massachusetts; 1989, Kentucky; 1991, Ohio; Florida

Peter L. Ney — University of Cincinnati College of Law, J.D., 1987 — Admitted to Bar, 1987, Ohio; 1993, Kentucky

Arthur E. Phelps, Jr. — Case Western Reserve University School of Law, J.D., 1985 — Admitted to Bar, 1985, Ohio; Kentucky

Jonathan P. Saxton — University of Cincinnati College of Law, J.D., 1989 — Admitted to Bar, 1989, Ohio; 1996, Kentucky; 2005, West Virginia

Leonard A. Weakley, Jr. — Salmon P. Chase College of Law, J.D., 1977 — Admitted to Bar, 1977, Ohio; 1978, Kentucky

Wilson G. Weisenfelder, Jr. — Salmon P. Chase College of Law, J.D., 1985 — Admitted to Bar, 1985, Ohio

Chad E. Willits — University of Cincinnati College of Law, J.D., 1996 — Admitted to Bar, 1996, Ohio; 1999, Indiana

Of Counsel

Donyetta D. Bailey — Capital University Law School, J.D., 2000 — Admitted to Bar, 2000, Ohio; 2005, New York

James J. Englert — University of Cincinnati College of Law, J.D., 1990 — Admitted to Bar, 1990, Ohio; 1992, Kentucky

W. Roger Fry — Salmon P. Chase College of Law, J.D., 1966 — Admitted to Bar, 1966, Ohio; 1990, Kentucky

Edward R. Goldman — Salmon P. Chase College of Law, J.D., 1973 — Admitted to Bar, 1973, Ohio

David Winchester Peck — Salmon P. Chase College of Law, J.D., 1966 — Admitted to Bar, 1966, Ohio; 1989, Kentucky

Anthony J. Perfilio — University of Pittsburgh School of Law, J.D., 1973 — Admitted to Bar, 1973, Pennsylvania; 1980, Ohio

Paul F. Wenker — Georgetown University Law Center, J.D., 1967 — Admitted to Bar, 1967, Ohio

Associates

Michael J. Chapman
William H. Fry
Monica H. McPeek
C. Jessica Pratt
Ryan J. Dwyer
Kandyce K. Lykins
Aaron M. Monk
W. Jonathan Sweeten

CLEVELAND † 396,815 Cuyahoga Co.

Bonezzi Switzer Polito & Hupp Co. L.P.A.

1300 East 9th Street, Suite 1950
Cleveland, Ohio 44114-1501
 Telephone: 216-875-2767
 Fax: 216-875-1570
 Toll Free: 800-875-2767
 E-Mail: jvanwagner@bsphlaw.com
 www.bsphlaw.com

(Cincinnati, OH Office*: 201 East Fifth Street, Suite 1900, 45202)
 (Tel: 513-766-9444)
 (Fax: 513-766-9301)
 (E-Mail: pmccartney@bsphlaw.com)
(St. Petersburg, FL Office*: City Center, 100 2nd Avenue South, Suite 502-S, 33701-4313)
 (Tel: 727-826-0909)
 (Fax: 727-826-0914)
 (E-Mail: wbonezzi@bsphlaw.com)

Established: 1998

Bonezzi Switzer Polito & Hupp Co. L.P.A., Cleveland, OH (Continued)

Appellate Practice, Arbitration, Catastrophic Injury, Civil Rights Defense, Class Actions, Commercial Litigation, Directors and Officers Liability, Employment Law, Environmental Law, Errors and Omissions, Insurance Defense, Long-Term Care, Medical Malpractice, Mediation, Nursing Home Liability, Premises Liability, Product Liability, Professional Liability, Toxic Torts, Insurance Defense, Assisted Living

Firm Profile: Bonezzi Switzer Polito & Hupp Co. L.P.A. is a full-service civil defense trial firm with offices in Ohio and Florida. Our firm represents a diverse clientele across a number of different practice areas.

To achieve successful results in complex litigation, a client needs more than just the facts on their side. They need experienced counsel who can investigate the evidence and persuasively present this evidence to a judge and jury. A client needs lawyers who fully comprehend exactly how to prepare a case to achieve favorable results at every stage. A client needs lawyers with a record of success in trial. You will find these lawyers at BSPH.

We understand that case preparation is essential to successfully defend against a lawsuit or claim. Our innovations in defending medical malpractice and toxic torts claims have been recognized by other practitioners and are now the standard in the industry. We maintain databases of renowned expert witnesses in a broad spectrum of disciplines and specialties. Very few law firms of our size nationwide can match our experience in the courtroom.

At BSPH, we employ a team approach. Our lawyers can always turn to experienced nurses, paralegals and other staff to fully serve the needs of our clients. As advocates, we believe strongly in offering our objective analysis of the case at early stages and take great pride in offering effective, efficient representation designed to achieve the best results.

Insurance Clients

Altercare of Ohio
Beazley Group
CORSA
GuideOne
Kaiser Foundation Health Plan of Ohio
Medical Protective Insurance Services
The Northern Group
ProAssurance Company
Sedgwick Claims Management Services, Inc.
Westfield Group
Avalon Claims Management, LLC
Berkley Risk Administrators Company, LLC
Healthcare Underwriters Group Mutual of Ohio
Maxum Insurance Company
Munich Reinsurance America, Inc.
Nationwide Insurance
OneBeacon Professional Insurance
Rockhill Insurance Company
Western World Insurance Company

Shareholders

William D. Bonezzi — Bowling Green State University, B.S., 1970; Cleveland State University, Cleveland-Marshall College of Law, J.D., 1973 — Admitted to Bar, 1973, Ohio; 2011, Florida; 1976, U.S. District Court, Northern District of Ohio; 2009, U.S. District Court, Southern District of Ohio; 2011, U.S. District Court, Middle District of Florida — Member The Florida Bar; Ohio State, St. Petersburg and Clearwater Bar Associations — Ohio Super Lawyers, 2007-2014; The Best Lawyers in America, 2007-2015; AV Rated, Martindale-Hubbell — U.S. Marine Corps, Rank E-4 — Practice Areas: Commercial Litigation; Environmental Law; Insurance Defense; Long-Term Care; Medical Malpractice Defense; Nursing Home Defense; Premises Liability; Product Liability Defense; Professional Negligence; Toxic Torts; Workers' Compensation — Resident St. Petersburg, FL Office — Tel: 727-826-0909 ext. 102 — Fax: 727-826-0914 — E-mail: wbonezzi@bsphlaw.com

Steven J. Hupp — John Carroll University, B.A., 1985; Cleveland-Marshall College of Law, J.D., 1988 — Admitted to Bar, 1988, Ohio; 1990, U.S. District Court, Northern District of Ohio; 1992, U.S. Court of Appeals, Sixth Circuit; 2001, U.S. Supreme Court — Member Ohio State Bar Association — Ohio Super Lawyer, 2008-2014; AV Rated, Martindale-Hubbell — Practice Areas: Appellate Practice; Directors and Officers Liability; Errors and Omissions; Hospital Malpractice; Long-Term Care; Medical Malpractice; Nursing Home Liability — Tel: 216-875-2060 — E-mail: shupp@bsphlaw.com

Kevin O. Kadlec — Cleveland State University, B.A., 1978; Cleveland-Marshall College of Law, J.D., 1987 — Admitted to Bar, 1987, Ohio; 1988, U.S. District Court, Northern District of Ohio; 1991, U.S. Court of Appeals, Sixth Circuit — Member Ohio State and Cleveland Bar Associations — Practice Areas: Asbestos Litigation; Insurance Defense; Medical Malpractice Defense; Motor Vehicle; Premises Liability; Product Liability Defense; Toxic Torts — Tel: 216-875-2069 — E-mail: kkadlec@bsphlaw.com

Ronald A. Margolis — University of Cincinnati, B.A., 1979; Cleveland-Marshall College of Law, J.D., 1982 — Admitted to Bar, 1983, Ohio; U.S. District Court, Northern District of Ohio; 2007, U.S. District Court, Southern District of Ohio — Ohio Super Lawyer, 2011-2014 — Practice Areas: Class Actions; Commercial Litigation; Medical Liability; Pharmaceutical — Tel: 216-875-2068 — E-mail: rmargolis@bsphlaw.com

Paul W. McCartney — Kenyon College, B.A., 1984; The Ohio State University Moritz College of Law, J.D., 1988 — Admitted to Bar, 1988, Ohio — Practice Areas: Nursing Home Defense; Medical Malpractice Defense — Tel: 513-766-9444 — E-mail: pmccartney@bsphlaw.com

Bret C. Perry — Bowling Green State University, B.S., 1997; Cleveland-Marshall College of Law, J.D., 2000 — Admitted to Bar, 2001, Ohio; 2003, U.S. District Court, Northern District of Ohio; 2008, U.S. Court of Appeals, Sixth Circuit; 2009, U.S. District Court, Southern District of Ohio — Member American and Ohio State Bar Associations; Association of Defense Trial Attorneys — Ohio Super Lawyer Rising Star, 2009-2014 — U.S. Navy Veteran, Desert Shield and Desert Storm — Practice Areas: Appellate Practice; Hospital Malpractice; Insurance Defense; Long-Term Care; Medical Malpractice Defense; Nursing Home Liability; Professional Liability; Risk Management — Tel: 216-875-2056 — E-mail: bperry@bsphlaw.com

John S. Polito — Xavier University, B.A., 1974; Cleveland-Marshall College of Law, J.D., 1977 — Admitted to Bar, 1977, Ohio; 1978, U.S. District Court, Northern District of Ohio; 1980, U.S. Court of Appeals, Sixth Circuit — Member American and Ohio State Bar Associations; Cleveland Association of Civil Trial Attorneys; Defense Research Institute — Ohio Super Lawyer, 2010-2014; The Best Lawyers in America, 2008-2015; AV Rated, Martindale-Hubbell — Practice Areas: Asbestos Litigation; Insurance Defense; Medical Malpractice Defense; Motor Vehicle; Premises Liability; Product Liability; Toxic Torts — Tel: 216-875-2070 — E-mail: jpolito@bsphlaw.com

Donald J. Richardson — Oberlin College, B.A., 1989; University of Pennsylvania, M.G.A., 1992; Case Western Reserve University School of Law, J.D., 1997 — Admitted to Bar, 1997, Ohio; U.S. District Court, Northern District of Ohio; 2003, U.S. District Court, Southern District of Ohio — Member Ohio State and Cleveland Bar Associations; Defense Research Institute; Cleveland Association of Civil Trial Attorneys — Ohio Super Lawyer, 2011-2014 — Practice Areas: Automobile Liability; Legal Malpractice; Medical Devices; Medical Malpractice Defense; Nursing Home Liability; Pharmaceutical; Premises Liability; Product Liability Defense; Toxic Torts — Tel: 216-875-2063 — E-mail: drichardson@bsphlaw.com

Beth A. Sebaugh — Ohio University, B.S.E., 1976; Cleveland-Marshall College of Law, J.D., 1980 — Admitted to Bar, 1980, Ohio; 1981, U.S. District Court, Northern District of Ohio; 1982, U.S. Court of Appeals, Sixth Circuit; 1993, U.S. Supreme Court; 2005, U.S. District Court, Southern District of Ohio — Member Ohio State and Cleveland Bar Associations; Defense Research Institute — AV Rated, Martindale-Hubbell; Ohio Super Lawyer, 2007, 2013, 2014; Super Lawyer in the Corporate Counsel Edition, 2008 — Practice Areas: Administrative Law; Civil Litigation; Employment Law; Medical Malpractice Defense; Personal Injury; Product Liability Defense; Professional Negligence; School Law; Toxic Torts — Tel: 216-875-2062 — E-mail: bsebaugh@bsphlaw.com

Donald H. Switzer — Texas A&M University, B.A., 1972; University of Virginia School of Law, J.D., 1978 — Admitted to Bar, 1978, Ohio; 1979, U.S. District Court, Northern District of Ohio — Member Ohio State Bar Association; Ohio Association of Civil Trial Attorneys — Ohio Super Lawyer, 2008-2014; The Best Lawyers in America, 2009-2015; AV Rated, Martindale-Hubbell — U.S. Army, Captain — Practice Areas: Contract Disputes; Hospital Malpractice; Medical Malpractice Defense; Personal Injury; Premises Liability; Toxic Torts — Tel: 216-875-2065 — Fax: 876-875-1570 — E-mail: dswitzer@bsphlaw.com

Jeffrey W. Van Wagner — John Carroll University, B.A., 1976; Case Western Reserve University School of Law, J.D. (Order of the Coif), 1979 — Admitted to Bar, 1979, Ohio; 1980, U.S. District Court, Northern District of Ohio; 1986, U.S. Court of Appeals, Sixth Circuit; 1993, U.S. Court of Appeals, Fifth Circuit; 2003, U.S. District Court, Southern District of Ohio — Member American, Ohio State and Cleveland Metropolitan Bar Associations; Defense Research Institute — Ohio Super Lawyer, 2007-2014; Cleveland Top 50 and Ohio Top 100 Super Lawyer, 2012, 2013; The Best Lawyers in America, 2013-2015; AV Rated, Martindale-Hubbell — Practice Areas: Liability Defense; Medical Malpractice Defense; Negligence; Nursing Home Liability;

CLEVELAND   OHIO

Bonezzi Switzer Polito & Hupp Co. L.P.A., Cleveland, OH (Continued)

Product Liability; Professional Liability — Tel: 216-875-2061 — E-mail: jvanwagner@bsphlaw.com

Associates

Jennifer R. Becker — University of Dayton, B.S., 1998; Cleveland-Marshall College of Law, J.D., 2003 — Admitted to Bar, 2006, Ohio; 2008, U.S. District Court, Northern District of Ohio — Ohio Super Lawyers Rising Star, 2012-2014 — Practice Areas: Appellate Practice; Insurance Defense; Medical Malpractice Defense; Nursing Home Defense; Personal Injury Defense; Product Liability Defense; Professional Liability — Tel: 216-875-2073 — E-mail: jbecker@bsphlaw.com

Brian F. Lange — Miami University, B.S., 2003; The Ohio State University Moritz College of Law, J.D., 2006 — Admitted to Bar, 2006, Ohio; 2009, U.S. District Court, Northern District of Ohio — Ohio Super Lawyers Rising Star, 2014 — Practice Areas: Appellate Practice; Employment Defense; Medical Malpractice Defense; Nursing Home Litigation; Personal Injury Defense — Tel: 216-875-2057 — E-mail: blange@bsphlaw.com

Christopher F. Mars — Ohio University, B.A., 2008; Cleveland-Marshall College of Law, J.D., 2013 — Admitted to Bar, 2014, Ohio — Practice Areas: Asbestos Litigation; Employment Defense; Long-Term Care; Medical Malpractice Defense; Nursing Home Defense — Tel: 216-875-2064 — E-mail: cmars@bsphlaw.com

Jason A. Paskan — Ohio University, B.A., 2006; Cleveland-Marshall College of Law, J.D., 2009 — Admitted to Bar, 2009, Ohio; 2010, U.S. District Court, Northern District of Ohio — Member Lake County Bar Association — Ohio Super Lawyers Rising Star, 2013-2014 — Practice Areas: Appellate Practice; Asbestos Litigation; Employment Law; Medical Malpractice Defense; Nursing Home Defense; Personal Injury Defense — Tel: 216-875-2059 — E-mail: jpaskan@bsphlaw.com

Geoffrey W. Vance — Clearwater Christian College, B.A., 2010; Stetson University College of Law, J.D., 2013 — Admitted to Bar, 2013, Florida — Practice Areas: Medical Malpractice Defense; Nursing Home Defense; Long-Term Care; Environmental Liability; Workers' Compensation — Tel: 727-826-0909 — E-mail: gvance@bsphlaw.com

Britton, Smith, Peters & Kalail Co., L.P.A.

3 Summit Park Drive, Suite 400
Cleveland, Ohio 44131
Telephone: 216-503-5055
Fax: 216-503-5065
www.ohioedlaw.com

School Law, Civil Rights, Employment Discrimination, Personal Injury, Workers' Compensation, Labor and Employment, Trial and Appellate Practice, General Defense

Firm Profile: Britton, Smith, Peters & Kalail Co., L.P.A., located in Cleveland, Ohio, is a law firm devoted exclusively to the representation of Ohio school boards across the entire state. The Firm is founded upon the experience of its attorneys, who regularly respond to the needs of school board clients, whether through direct representation or through appointment by insurance carriers to defend boards in civil actions in state and federal court. Firm lawyers adhere to the philosophy that sound legal representation is provided not only by responding to emergent matters faced by school boards, but also by assisting boards to reduce the risk of future problems. An in-depth understanding of the legal issues impacting education is pivotal to effective representation of school boards in every area of the law and the Firm's concentration in the practice has enabled its attorneys to develop that understanding.

Insurance Clients

Allied World National Assurance Company	Hylant Group
Ohio Casualty Insurance Company	Indiana Insurance Company
Trident Insurance	SORSA
	Wright Risk Management America (WRM America)

Managing Partners

John E. Britton — 1955 — Valparaiso University, B.A., 1978; The University of Toledo, J.D., 1981 — Admitted to Bar, 1981, Ohio; U.S. District Court, Northern District of Ohio; U.S. Court of Appeals, Sixth Circuit — Member

Britton, Smith, Peters & Kalail Co., L.P.A., Cleveland, OH (Continued)

Ohio State and Akron Bar Associations; Ohio Council of School Board Attorneys; National School Boards Association's Council of School Attorneys; Education Law Association — Tel: 216-503-5060 — E-mail: jbritton@ohioedlaw.com

Scott C. Peters — 1967 — Kenyon College, B.A. (cum laude), 1989; Case Western Reserve University, J.D., 1992 — Admitted to Bar, 1992, Ohio; U.S. District Court, Northern District of Ohio; U.S. Court of Appeals, Sixth Circuit; 2006, U.S. Supreme Court; 2007, U.S. District Court, Southern District of Ohio — Member American, Ohio State and Cleveland Metropolitan Bar Associations; Ohio Council of School Board Attorneys; Education Law Association; National School Boards Association's Council of School Attorneys; Defense Research Institute — Tel: 216-503-5080 — E-mail: speters@ohioedlaw.com

Karrie M. Kalail — 1963 — Ohio University, B.A. (cum laude), 1985; The University of Akron, J.D., 1988 — Admitted to Bar, 1988, Ohio; U.S. District Court, Northern and Southern Districts of Ohio — Member Ohio State and Akron Bar Associations; Ohio Council of School Board Attorneys; National School Boards Association's Council of School Attorneys — Tel: 216-503-5070 — E-mail: kkalail@ohioedlaw.com

Krista K. Keim — 1971 — Miami University, B.A., 1993; Case Western Reserve University, J.D., 1996 — Admitted to Bar, 1996, Ohio; U.S. District Court, Northern District of Ohio; U.S. Court of Appeals, Sixth Circuit; 2004, U.S. District Court, Southern District of Ohio — Member Ohio State and Cleveland Metropolitan Bar Associations; Ohio Council of School Board Attorneys; National School Boards Association's Council of School Attorneys — Tel: 216-503-5075 — E-mail: kkeim@ohioedlaw.com

Sherrie Clayborne Massey — 1969 — The College of Wooster, B.A., 1992; The Ohio State University, J.D., 1995 — Admitted to Bar, 1996, Ohio; 1999, District of Columbia; 2002, U.S. District Court, Northern District of Ohio; U.S. Court of Appeals, Sixth Circuit — Member Ohio State and Cleveland Metropolitan Bar Associations; The District of Columbia Bar; Ohio Council of School Board Attorneys — Tel: 216-503-5085 — E-mail: smassey@ohioedlaw.com

Kathryn I. Perrico — 1976 — Kent State University, B.A. (summa cum laude), 1998; The University of Akron, J.D., 2003 — Admitted to Bar, 2003, Ohio; U.S. District Court, Northern District of Ohio; 2004, U.S. Court of Appeals, Sixth Circuit; 2008, U.S. District Court, Southern District of Ohio — Member Ohio State and Cleveland Metropolitan Bar Associations; Ohio Council of School Board Attorneys — Tel: 216-503-5062 — E-mail: kperrico@ohioedlaw.com

Of Counsel

David K. Smith — 1947 — Case Western Reserve University, B.A., 1969; Cleveland State University, M.Ed., 1979; Cleveland-Marshall College of Law, J.D. (magna cum laude), 1984 — Admitted to Bar, 1984, Ohio; U.S. District Court, Northern District of Ohio; 1989, U.S. Court of Appeals, Sixth Circuit; 2004, U.S. District Court, Southern District of Ohio; 2006, U.S. Supreme Court — Member American, Ohio State and Cleveland Metropolitan Bar Associations; Ohio Council of School Board Attorneys; Education Law Association; National School Boards Association's Council of School Attorneys; Defense Research Institute; Ohio Association of Civil Trial Attorneys — Tel: 216-503-5090 — E-mail: dsmith@ohioedlaw.com

Associates

Giselle S. Spencer — University of Michigan, B.A., 1983; Ohio Northern University, J.D., 1986 — Admitted to Bar, 1986, Ohio; U.S. District Court, Southern District of Ohio; 1988, U.S. Court of Appeals, Sixth Circuit; 2011, U.S. District Court, Northern District of Ohio — Member National and Cleveland Metropolitan Bar Associations; Norman S. Minor Bar Association; Thurgood Marshall Law Society; National School Boards Association's Council of School Attorneys; Ohio Council of School Board Attorneys — Tel: 216-503-5093 — E-mail: gspencer@ohioedlaw.com

David S. Hirt — 1965 — Kent State University, B.S., 1986; Indiana University, M.S., 1988; J.D., 1994 — Admitted to Bar, 1994, Ohio; 2002, U.S. District Court, Northern District of Ohio; 2003, U.S. Court of Appeals, Sixth Circuit; 2008, U.S. District Court, Southern District of Ohio — Member Ohio State and Portage County Bar Associations; Ohio Council of School Board Attorneys — Tel: 216-503-5082 — E-mail: dhirt@ohioedlaw.com

Lindsay F. Gingo — 1982 — The Ohio State University, B.A. (cum laude, with honors), 2004; Chicago-Kent College of Law, J.D. (with honors), 2008 — Admitted to Bar, 2008, Ohio; U.S. District Court, Northern District of Ohio; 2009, U.S. District Court, Southern District of Ohio; U.S. Court of Appeals, Sixth Circuit — Member Ohio State and Cleveland Metropolitan Bar

Britton, Smith, Peters & Kalail Co., L.P.A., Cleveland, OH (Continued)

Associations; Ohio Council of School Board Attorneys; National School Boards Association's Council of School Board Attorneys; Defense Research Institute; National Institute of Trial Advocacy — Tel: 216-503-5058 — E-mail: lgingo@ohioedlaw.com

Paul J. Deegan — 1981 — Cleveland State University, B.A., 2005; Cleveland-Marshall College of Law, J.D., 2009 — Admitted to Bar, 2009, Ohio; 2010, U.S. District Court, Northern District of Ohio; U.S. Court of Appeals, Sixth Circuit; 2011, U.S. District Court, Southern District of Ohio — Member American, Ohio State and Cleveland Metropolitan Bar Associations; Ohio Council of School Board Attorneys; National Institute of Trial Advocacy — Tel: 216-503-5072 — E-mail: pdeegan@ohioedlaw.com

Miriam Pearlmutter — 1975 — Barnard College, Columbia University, B.A., 1998; Tufts University, M.S.Ed., 2005; The Ohio State University, J.D. (with honors), 2011 — Admitted to Bar, 2011, Ohio; U.S. District Court, Northern District of Ohio — Member Ohio State and Cleveland Metropolitan Bar Associations; Ohio Council of School Board Attorneys — Tel: 216-503-5068 — E-mail: mpearlmutter@ohioedlaw.com

Megan Bair Zidian — 1985 — The Ohio State University, B.A. (cum laude), 2007; The University of Akron, J.D., 2011 — Admitted to Bar, 2011, Ohio; U.S. District Court, Northern District of Ohio; 2012, U.S. Court of Appeals, Sixth Circuit — Member Ohio State Bar Association; Ohio Council of School Board Attorneys — Tel: 216-503-5088 — E-mail: mzidian@ohioedlaw.com

Sarah E. Kutscher — 1985 — Northwestern University, B.S. (cum laude), 2007; DePaul University, J.D. (magna cum laude), 2012 — Admitted to Bar, 2012, Ohio; 2013, U.S. District Court, Northern and Southern Districts of Ohio; U.S. Court of Appeals, Sixth Circuit — Member Ohio State, Cleveland Metropolitan and Westshore Bar Associations; Ohio Council of School Board Attorneys — Tel: 216-503-5063 — E-mail: skutscher@ohioedlaw.com

Davis & Young

1200 Fifth Third Center
600 Superior Avenue, East
Cleveland, Ohio 44114
  Telephone: 216-348-1700
  Fax: 216-621-0602
  E-Mail: atty@davisyoung.com
  www.davisyoung.com

(Akron, OH Office: One Cascade Plaza, Suite 800, 44308)
  (Tel: 330-376-1717)
  (Fax: 330-376-1797)
(Dublin, OH Office: 655 Metro Place South, Suite 200, 43017)
  (Tel: 614-901-9600)
  (Fax: 614-901-2723)
(Youngstown/Warren, Ohio: Governor Insurance Building, 972 Youngstown-Kingsville Road, Suite G, Vienna, OH, 44473)
  (Tel: 330-539-6111)
  (Fax: 330-539-6303)
(Mansfield, OH Office: 24 West Third Street, Suite 204, 44902)
  (Tel: 419-522-6242)
  (Fax: 419-525-0258)

Established: 1922

Trial and Appellate Practice, State and Federal Courts, Insurance Law, Environmental Law, Toxic Torts, Product Liability, Medical Malpractice, Legal, Litigation, Personal Injury, Legal Malpractice, Municipal Liability, Civil Rights, Employment Practices Liability, Commercial Liability, Complex Mass Torts

Firm Profile: With a rich history since 1922, Davis & Young is headquartered in Cleveland, Ohio with offices in Akron, Columbus, and the Youngstown/Warren area.

From its founding by a pair of law school classmates in 1922, Davis & Young has provided the highest quality legal representation to individuals and businesses throughout the region and nation. Over these many decades, our core emphasis has continued to be providing clients with superior litigation and appellate representation. As a result, our attorneys are widely recognized as some of the finest in these fields. While our expertise permits us to provide high quality litigation and appellate representation for any need, our experience is unparalleled in certain specialties, including: general liability and personal injury, professional liability (including legal and medical malpractice), employer intentional tort, toxic tort, products liability, insurance coverage (including bad faith and extra-contractual exposure), construction defect, complex litigation and class actions.

Our success representing clients in litigation has caused many of them to ask us to protect their interests before litigation ever arises. In response to this demand, our attorneys bring their considerable talents, experience and energy to such areas as risk management counseling, insurance coverage and alternative dispute resolution ("ADR"). Today, our attorneys are leaders in these fields as well.

In addition to individuals and professionals, our clients include businesses and entities from throughout the region and nation, including insurers, manufacturers, retailers, hospitals, service providers, small businesses and local governments. Each client represents a valued relationship. Each client has come to know and appreciate our dedication to those relationships and the principles upon which we foster those relationships: integrity, tradition and responsiveness.

Insurance Clients

Central Mutual Insurance Company	Cincinnati Insurance Company
CNA Insurance Company	Erie Insurance Company
The Hartford	Kaiser Foundation Health Plan of Ohio
Motorists Mutual Insurance Company	Progressive Casualty Insurance Company
St. Paul Fire and Casualty Insurance Company	State Farm Fire and Casualty Company
State Farm Insurance Company	Travelers Indemnity Company
State Farm Mutual Automobile Insurance Company	Westfield Companies

Non-Insurance Clients

Avis Rent-A-Car System, LLC   Sysco Corporation
University Hospitals of Cleveland

In Memoriam

Rees H. Davis, Sr. — (1892-1965)
Fred J. Young — (1889-1946)

Managing Partner

Thomas W. Wright — 1959 — Ohio University, A.B. (summa cum laude), 1981; Case Western Reserve University School of Law, J.D., 1984; Ohio University, M.B.A., 2013 — Phi Beta Kappa — Admitted to Bar, 1984, Ohio — Member Ohio State, Cuyahoga County, Lake County, Cleveland and Akron Bar Associations; Cleveland Association of Civil Trial Attorneys; Defense Research Institute — E-mail: twright@davisyoung.com

Partners/Shareholders

C. Richard McDonald — 1948 — DePauw University, B.A., 1970; Case Western Reserve University School of Law, J.D., 1973 — Editor, Case Western Reserve Law Review (1972-1973) — Admitted to Bar, 1973, Ohio — Member Ohio State, Cleveland and Akron Bar Associations; Ohio Association of Civil Trial Attorneys; Defense Research Institute — E-mail: rmcdonald@davisyoung.com

Paul D. Eklund — 1952 — Miami University, A.B., 1975; Case Western Reserve University School of Law, J.D., 1978 — Admitted to Bar, 1978, Ohio — Member American Bar Association (Sections of Tort and Insurance Practice and Litigation); Ohio State and Cleveland Bar Associations; Cleveland Association of Civil Attorneys (President, 1994-1995); Ohio Association of Civil Trial Attorneys; Defense Research Institute — Assistant Attorney General of Ohio (1978-1979) — E-mail: peklund@davisyoung.com

Jan L. Roller — 1954 — Denison University, B.A. (cum laude), 1976; Case Western Reserve University School of Law, J.D., 1979 — Admitted to Bar, 1980, Massachusetts; 1983, Ohio — Member Ohio State and Cleveland Bar Associations; Ohio Women's Bar Association; Master Bencher of the Judge John M. Manos Inn of Court; Fellow of the International Society of Barristers; Cleveland Association of Civil Trial Attorneys; Defense Research Institute — Life Delegate, Judicial Conference of the Eighth Judicial District — E-mail: jroller@davisyoung.com

David J. Fagnilli — 1958 — Southern California College, B.A., 1980; Cleveland-Marshall College of Law, J.D., 1986 — Admitted to Bar, 1986, Ohio — Member American Bar Association (Tort and Insurance Practice and Litigation Sections); Ohio State, Lake County and Cleveland Bar Associations; Justinian Forum; Midwest Environmental Claims Association; Ohio Association

CLEVELAND   OHIO

Davis & Young, Cleveland, OH   (Continued)

of Civil Trial Attorneys; Cleveland Association of Civil Trial Attorneys; Defense Research Institute — Life Delegate, Eighth Judicial Conference — E-mail: dfagnilli@davisyoung.com

Gregory H. Collins — 1963 — Hiram College, B.A., 1985; Case Western Reserve University School of Law, J.D., 1988 — Admitted to Bar, 1988, Ohio — Member American, Ohio State and Cleveland Bar Associations; Ohio Association of Civil Trial Attorneys; Cleveland Association of Civil Trial Attorneys; Defense Research Institute — E-mail: gcollins@davisyoung.com

Patrick F. Roche — 1949 — Hofstra University, B.B.A., 1972; Cleveland-Marshall College of Law, J.D., 1976 — Admitted to Bar, 1976, Ohio — Member Ohio State Bar Association; Defense Research Institute — Assistant Cuyahoga County Prosecutor (1976-1980); Chief Trial Counsel, City of Cleveland Prosecutor (1980-1984); Chief Police Prosecutor, City of Cleveland (1984-1986) — E-mail: proche@davisyoung.com

David G. Utley — 1962 — Kent State University, B.A., 1984; Case Western Reserve University School of Law, J.D., 1987 — Admitted to Bar, 1987, Ohio — Member Ohio State and Cleveland Bar Associations — E-mail: dutley@davisyoung.com

Dennis R. Fogarty — 1965 — John Carroll University, B.A., 1987; Cleveland-Marshall College of Law, J.D., 1991 — Admitted to Bar, 1991, Ohio — Member Ohio State and Cleveland Bar Associations; Cleveland Association of Civil Trial Attorneys; Defense Research and Trial Lawyers Association — E-mail: dfogarty@davisyoung.com

Ann Marie O'Brien — 1965 — Hiram College, B.A., 1987; Kent State University Honors College, 1987; The University of Akron School of Law, J.D., 1991 — Admitted to Bar, 1991, Ohio; U.S. District Court, Northern District of Ohio; U.S. Court of Appeals, Sixth Circuit; 2011, U.S. District Court, Southern District of Ohio; U.S. Supreme Court of Ohio — Member American, Ohio State, Portage County and Akron County Bar Associations; Ohio Academy of Trial Lawyers; Defense Research Institute — E-mail: aobrien@davisyoung.com

William Jack Meola — 1959 — Miami University, B.A., 1981; Case Western Reserve University School of Law, J.D., 1984 — Admitted to Bar, 1984, Ohio; 1986, U.S. District Court, Northern District of Ohio — Member American, Ohio State and Trumbull County Bar Associations; Defense Research Institute; Ohio Association of Civil Trial Attorneys — E-mail: jmeola@davisyoung.com

Richard M. Garner — 1968 — The Ohio State University, B.A., 1990; The Ohio State University Moritz College of Law, J.D., 1993 — Admitted to Bar, 1993, Ohio — Member Ohio State and Cleveland Bar Associations; National Lawyers Association; Federalist Society — Served as a Prosecutor and as a Magistrate in Delaware County, Ohio; Instructor for Court and Law Enforcement Personnel on Civil and Criminal Procedure and Constitutional Law; Developed the course currently use by the State of Ohio to train bailiffs and court security personnel on execution of process in civil proceedings — E-mail: rgarner@davisyoung.com

Patrick M. Roche — 1973 — University of Dayton, B.S., 1995; Cleveland-Marshall College of Law, J.D., 1999 — Admitted to Bar, 1999, Ohio — Member Ohio State and Cleveland Bar Associations — E-mail: patr@davisyoung.com

Partners

Ronald J. Ziehm — 1965 — Bowling Green State University, B.S., 1988; Cleveland-Marshall College of Law, J.D., 1991 — Admitted to Bar, 1991, Ohio — Member Ohio State, Cleveland and Medina Bar Associations — E-mail: rziehm@davisyoung.com

James P. Salamone — 1972 — Cleveland State University, B.A., 1995; Cleveland-Marshall College of Law, J.D., 2000 — Admitted to Bar, 2000, Ohio — Member Lake County Board of Arbitration — Staff Attorney , Lake County Court of Common Pleas (2000-2002) — E-mail: jsalamone@davisyoung.com

Shannon M. Fogarty — 1980 — Bowling Green State University, B.A. (cum laude), 2001; Case Western Reserve University School of Law, J.D., 2004 — Admitted to Bar, 2004, Ohio — Member Ohio State and Cleveland Metropolitan Bar Associations — E-mail: sfogarty@davisyoung.com

Brian J. Bradigan — 1951 — Grove City College, B.A., 1978; Buffalo State University, M.A.; Capital University Law School, J.D., 1981 — Admitted to Bar, 1981, Ohio; U.S. District Court, Northern and Southern Districts of Ohio; U.S. Court of Appeals, Sixth Circuit; U.S. Bankruptcy Court; U.S. Supreme Court of Ohio — Member Ohio State and Columbus Bar Associations; Defense Research Institute; International Association of Defense Counsel; Ohio Association of Civil Trial Attorneys; American Board of Trial Advocates — E-mail: bbradigan@davisyoung.com

Davis & Young, Cleveland, OH   (Continued)

David W. Orlandini — 1970 — Alma College, B.A., 1991; Capital University Law School, J.D., 1995 — Admitted to Bar, 1995, Ohio; U.S. District Court, Southern District of Ohio; 1996, U.S. Court of Appeals, Sixth Circuit — Member Ohio State (Board of Governors, Litigation Section) and Columbus (Real Property Section) Bar Associations; Defense Research Institute (Product Liability Committee); Ohio Association of Civil Trial Attorneys — E-mail: dorlandini@davisyoung.com

Beverly A. Adams — 1976 — Baldwin-Wallace College, B.A. (magna cum laude), 1998; Cleveland State University, M.B.A., 2001; Cleveland-Marshall College of Law, J.D., 2001 — Admitted to Bar, 2002, Ohio; 2005, U.S. District Court, Northern District of Ohio — Member Ohio State, Cuyahoga County and Cleveland Bar Associations — Staff Attorney for Judge Janet R. Burnside, Cuyahoga County Common Pleas Court, 2003-2005 — E-mail: badams@davisyoung.com

Margo S. Meola — 1969 — John Carroll University, B.A., 1991; Ohio Northern University, Pettit College of Law, J.D., 1995 — Admitted to Bar, 1995, Ohio; 1998, U.S. District Court, Northern District of Ohio; 2009, Supreme Court of the United States — Member American, Ohio State, Trumbull County and Mahoning County Bar Associations; Ohio Women's Bar Association; Ohio Association of Civil Trial Attorneys — E-mail: mmeola@davisyoung.com

Megan D. Stricker — 1981 — Mount Union College, B.A. (summa cum laude), 2003; The University of Akron School of Law, J.D. (cum laude), 2006 — Admitted to Bar, 2006, Ohio — Member Ohio State and Cleveland Metropolitan Bar Associations — E-mail: mstricker@davisyoung.com

Kenneth R. Beddow — 1956 — Bowling Green State University, B.S., 1978; University of Toledo School of Law, J.D., 1981 — Admitted to Bar, 1981, Ohio; 1982, U.S. District Court, Northern District of Ohio; 1987, U.S. Court of Appeals, Sixth Circuit — Member American, Ohio State and Richland County Bar Associations; Ohio Association of Civil Trial Attorneys; Defense Research Institute — E-mail: kbeddow@davisyoung.com

Associates

Jennifer S. Carlozzi — 1973 — Canisius College, B.A., 1995; Cleveland-Marshall College of Law, J.D., 2000 — Admitted to Bar, 2000, Ohio; 2002, Florida — Member Ohio State and Cuyahoga County Bar Associations; The Florida Bar — Arbitrator, Cuyahoga County Court of Common Pleas, Alternative Dispute Resolution Department — E-mail: jcarlozzi@davisyoung.com

Sunny L. Horacek — 1986 — The Ohio State University, B.A. (cum laude), 2009; The Ohio State University Moritz College of Law, J.D., 2012 — Admitted to Bar, 2012, Ohio — Member Ohio State Bar Association — Languages: French — E-mail: shoracek@davisyoung.com

Erica M. Skelly — 1985 — The University of Akron, B.A., 2008; The University of Akron School of Law, J.D., 2012 — Phi Delta Phi International Legal Honor Society — Admitted to Bar, 2012, Ohio — Member Ohio State and Akron Bar Associations — E-mail: eskelly@davisyoung.com

Gary Safir — 1988 — Michigan State University, B.A., 2010; Case Western Reserve University School of Law, J.D., 2013 — Admitted to Bar, 2013, Ohio — Member American and Ohio State Bar Associations; Ohio Association of Civil Trial Attorneys — Languages: French

Matthew P. Baringer — 1981 — The Ohio State University, B.A. (cum laude, with honors), 2003; Cleveland State University, Cleveland-Marshall College of Law, J.D. (cum laude), 2007 — Admitted to Bar, 2007, Ohio — Member Ohio State and Cleveland Metropolitan Bar Associations — Staff Attorney for Judge Timothy P. McCormick of the Cuyahoga County Court of Common Pleas — E-mail: mbaringer@davisyoung.com

Deanna K. Richards — 1988 — State University of New York at Geneseo, B.A. (cum laude), 2010; Case Western Reserve University School of Law, J.D. (cum laude), 2013 — Admitted to Bar, 2013, Ohio — Member Ohio State and Cleveland Metropolitan Bar Associations — Order of Barristers; Paul J. Hergenroeder Award for Trial Tactics; Anderson Publishing Company Book Award in Contracts — Languages: French — E-mail: drichards@davisyoung.com

Counsel Emeritus

Martin J. Murphy — 1937 — John Carroll University, B.S.S., 1960; Case Western Reserve University, LL.B., 1963 — Admitted to Bar, 1963, Ohio — Member American Bar Association (Sections of Tort and Insurance Practice and Litigation); Ohio State and Cuyahoga County Bar Associations; Cleveland Association of Civil Trial Attorneys (President, 1983-1984); Fellow, American College of Trial Lawyers (State Committee, 1994-1998); International Academy of Trial Lawyers; Ohio Association of Civil Trial Attorneys;

Gallagher Sharp, Cleveland, OH (Continued)

Michigan — Member Ohio State, Toledo and Cleveland Bar Associations; State Bar of Michigan; Ohio's Women's Bar Association; Fellow, Litigation Council of America; National Association of Railroad Trial Counsel; Defense Research Institute; Ohio Association of Civil Trial Attorneys; Cleveland Association of Civil Trial Attorneys

Daniel J. Michalec — 1946 — Kent State University, B.S., 1968; The University of Akron, M.S., 1981; J.D., 1989 — Admitted to Bar, 1989, Ohio — Member Ohio State, Akron and Medina Bar Associations

Colleen A. Mountcastle — 1972 — University of Dayton, B.A., 1995; Case Western Reserve University, J.D., 1998 — Admitted to Bar, 1998, Ohio — Member Ohio State and Cleveland Bar Associations; Judicial Conference of the Eighth Appellate District; William K. Thomas Inn of Court; Ohio Association of Civil Trial Attorneys; Defense Research Institute — Certified Appellate Law Specialist, Ohio State Bar Association

John T. Murphy — 1956 — Miami University, B.S., 1978; Cleveland-Marshall College of Law, J.D., 1990 — Admitted to Bar, 1990, Ohio — Member Ohio State Bar Association — Chartered Property Casualty Underwriter Society, Cleveland Chapter

Gary L. Nicholson — 1959 — The Ohio State University, B.A., 1980; The University of Toledo, J.D., 1983 — Admitted to Bar, 1984, Ohio — Member Defense Research Institute; Ohio Association of Civil Trial Attorneys

Scott A. Norcross — Miami University, B.A., 1997; The University of Toledo College of Law, J.D., 2000 — Admitted to Bar, 2001, Ohio; U.S. Court of Appeals, Sixth Circuit; U.S. District Court, Northern District of Ohio — Member Ohio State and Cleveland Metropolitan Bar Associations

Matthew T. Norman — Bowling Green State University, B.S. (cum laude), 1995; Cleveland-Marshall College of Law, J.D. (cum laude), 1999 — Admitted to Bar, 1999, Ohio — Member Ohio State Bar Association

Holly Olarczuk-Smith — 1974 — Pennsylvania State University, The Behrend College, B.A., 1986; Cleveland-Marshall College of Law, J.D., 2000 — Admitted to Bar, 2000, Ohio — Member Ohio State Bar Associaiton

Joseph W. Pappalardo — 1955 — Case Western Reserve University, B.A., 1977; The Ohio State University, J.D., 1980 — Admitted to Bar, 1980, Ohio — Member John M. Manos Inn of Court; Ohio Trucking Association; Cleveland Association of Civil Trial Attorneys; Defense Research Institute; Trucking Industry Defense Association; Transportation Lawyers Association

Alan M. Petrov — 1949 — Rutgers University, A.B., 1971; Case Western Reserve University, J.D., 1974 — Admitted to Bar, 1974, Ohio — Member American (Standing Committee on Professional Liability), Ohio State and Cleveland Bar Associations; International Association of Defense Counsel; Defense Research Institute

Michael J. Pike — 1973 — Fairfield University, B.S., 1997; Case Western Reserve University, J.D., 2001 — Admitted to Bar, 2001, Ohio; 2008, Michigan — Member Ohio State Bar Association; State Bar of Michigan; Defense Research Institute; Ohio Association of Civil Trial Attorneys

Richard C.O. Rezie — State University of New York College at Oneonta, B.A. (magna cum laude), 1996; Case Western Reserve University, J.D. (magna cum laude), 1999 — Admitted to Bar, 1999, Ohio — Member Ohio State and Ukranian American Bar Associations

Jay C. Rice — 1954 — Case Western Reserve University, B.A./M.A., 1976; J.D., 1979 — Admitted to Bar, 1979, Ohio — Member Ohio State Bar Association; Ohio Association of Civil Trial Attorneys; Cleveland Association of Civil Trial Attorneys

Theresa A. Richthammer — 1972 — Michigan State University, B.A., 1994; Cleveland-Marshall College of Law, J.D., 1997 — Admitted to Bar, 1997, Ohio — Member Ohio State Bar Association

Timothy P. Roth — 1969 — Fordham University, B.A., 1991; Case Western Reserve University, J.D., 1994 — Admitted to Bar, 1994, Ohio — Member Ohio State Bar Association; Transportation Lawyers Association; Trucking Industry Defense Association

Monica A. Sansalone — 1970 — Loyola University Chicago, B.A. (with honors), 1992; Cleveland-Marshall College of Law, J.D. (cum laude), 1995 — Admitted to Bar, 1995, Ohio — Member American, Ohio State and Cleveland Bar Associaitons; Commission on Professionalism of the Supreme Court of Ohio; Defense Research Institute

Joseph J. Santoro — 1971 — John Carroll University, B.S., 1994; The University of Toledo, J.D. (cum laude), 1997 — Admitted to Bar, 1997, Ohio; 2007, Michigan — Member Ohio State Bar Association; State Bar of Michigan; National Association of Railroad Trial Counsel

P. Kohl Schneider — 1967 — University of Notre Dame, B.S., 1989; Cleveland-Marshall College of Law, J.D., 1992 — Admitted to Bar, 1992, Ohio — Member Ohio State Bar Association; Defense Research Institute; Cleveland

Gallagher Sharp, Cleveland, OH (Continued)

Association of Civil Trial Attorneys; Professional Liability Underwriting Society

John Travis — 1952 — The Ohio State University, B.S., 1973; J.D., 1976 — Admitted to Bar, 1976, Ohio — Member American, Ohio State and Cleveland Bar Associations; Defense Research Institute; Federation of Defense and Corporate Counsel

James T. Tyminski, Jr. — 1969 — John Carroll University, B.A., 1991; Cleveland-Marshall College of Law, J.D., 1998 — Admitted to Bar, 1999, Ohio; U.S. District Court, Northern District of Ohio — Member Ohio State and Geauga County Bar Associations; Polish American Attorneys Association; Transportation Lawyers Association; Trucking Industry Defense Association

Deborah W. Yue — 1966 — Carnegie Mellon University, B.S., 1989; Cleveland-Marshall College of Law, J.D., 1994 — Admitted to Bar, 1994, Ohio; 1995, U.S. District Court, Northern District of Ohio — Member Ohio State, Cleveland and Cleveland Metropolitan (Trustee) Bar Associations; Asian American Bar Association; Cleveland Claims Association

Staff Attorney

Jamie Manning — 1951 — University of Southern California, B.A. (with honors), 1972; University of San Francisco, J.D., 1977; University of Washington, 1977 — Admitted to Bar, 1980, Ohio; U.S. District Court, Northern District of Ohio — Member Ohio State Bar Association

Of Counsel

William H. Fulton

Retired

Thomas E. Betz
Burt J. Fulton
Forrest A. Norman
Alton L. Stephens
James F. Sweeney

Edward J. Cass
James G. Gowan
James L. Ryhal, Jr.
George W. Stuhldreher

Associates

Markus E. Apelis — Ohio University, B.S.J. (magna cum laude), 2004; B.A. (magna cum laude), 2005; Case Western Reserve University, J.D. (magna cum laude), 2008 — Admitted to Bar, 2008, Ohio — Member Ohio State and Cleveland Metropolitan Bar Associations

Hannah M. Klang — Western Michigan University, B.S. (summa cum laude), 2009; Cleveland-Marshall College of Law, J.D. (magna cum laude), 2013 — Admitted to Bar, 2013, Ohio — Member Ohio State Bar Association

Shane A. Lawson — Bowling Green State University, B.S. (cum laude), 2006; Case Western Reserve University, J.D. (magna cum laude), 2010 — Admitted to Bar, 2010, Ohio

Kevin R. Marchaza — Ohio University, B.A. (cum laude), 2007; Cleveland-Marshall College of Law, J.D. (cum laude), 2011 — Admitted to Bar, 2011, Ohio — Member Ohio State and Cleveland Metropolitan Bar Associations

Justin L. Monday — Vanderbilt University, B.A., 2004; Cleveland-Marshall College of Law, J.D., 2011 — Admitted to Bar, 2011, Ohio; U.S. District Court, Northern District of Ohio — Member American, Ohio State and Cleveland Metropolitan Bar Associations — Volunteer Magistrate, Cuyahoga County Juvenile Diversion Program; Deputy Finance Director, U.S. Senator Sherrod Brown, D-Ohio (2005-2006)

Catherine Peters — Georgetown University, B.A., 2000; Case Western Reserve University, J.D. (cum laude), 2004 — Admitted to Bar, 2004, Ohio; 2005, U.S. District Court, Northern District of Ohio — Member American and Ohio State Bar Associations

Jamie A. Price — 1984 — Northwestern University, B.A. (with honors), 2005; Case Western Reserve University, J.D., 2008 — Admitted to Bar, 2008, Ohio — Member Ohio State and Cleveland Metropolitan Bar Associations

Roxanne S. Rahamim — Miami University, B.A. (cum laude), 2010; Cleveland-Marshall College of Law, J.D. (cum laude), 2013 — Admitted to Bar, 2013, Ohio — Member Ohio State Bar Association

Adam P. Sadowski — The University of Toledo, B.A. (cum laude), 2006; J.D. (cum laude), 2009 — Admitted to Bar, 2009, Ohio; 2010, Michigan — Member American, Ohio State, Toledo and Detroit Bar Associations; State Bar of Michigan

Melanie R. Shaerban — John Carroll University, B.A., 2005; Cleveland-Marshall College of Law, J.D., 2008 — Admitted to Bar, 2008, Ohio; U.S. Court of Appeals, Sixth Circuit; U.S. District Court, Northern District of Ohio; U.S. District Court, Southern District of Ohio — Member Ohio Association of Civil Trial Attorneys; Cleveland Association of Civil Trial Attorneys

CLEVELAND   OHIO

Gallagher Sharp, Cleveland, OH (Continued)

Stephen D. Strang — Miami University, B.A., 2003; Case Western Reserve University, J.D. (cum laude), 2009 — Admitted to Bar, 2009, Ohio — Member Federal (Northern District of Ohio Chapter), Ohio State and Cleveland Metropolitan Bar Associations

Mark M. Turner — 1966 — Case Western Reserve University, B.A., 1990; Canisius College, M.B.A., 1995; The Ohio State University, J.D., 2002 — Admitted to Bar, 2002, Ohio; U.S. District Court, Northern District of Ohio — Member Ohio State Bar Association; Cleveland Association of Civil Trial Attorneys; Defense Research Institute

Erik J. Wineland — The University of Findlay, B.S. (with honors), 1992; The University of Toledo, J.D., 1999 — Admitted to Bar, 2000, Ohio; 2001, Michigan — Member Ohio and Toledo Bar Associations; State Bar of Michigan; National Association of Retail Collection Attorneys

Glowacki & Imbrigiotta, LPA

7550 Lucerne Drive, Suite 408
Middleburg Heights, Ohio 44130
   Telephone: 440-243-2727
   Fax: 440-243-2636
   E-Mail: mail@glowacki-associates.com
   www.glowimbro.com

Insurance Defense, Automobile, General Liability, Property and Casualty, Subrogation

Insurance Clients

Acuity/Heritage Insurance Company	CIGNA Property and Casualty Insurance Company
Encompass Insurance	Esurance
FCCI Insurance Company	Fortis Health
Highlands Insurance Group	Indiana Insurance Company
Metropolitan Property and Casualty Insurance Company	Mid-Continent Insurance Company
	Ohio Mutual Insurance Group
OneBeacon Insurance Company	Safe Auto Insurance Company
Safeco Insurance	Selective Insurance Company of America
State Automobile Insurance Association	Utica National Insurance Group

Non-Insurance Clients

Yellow Roadway Corporation

Firm Members

James L. Glowacki — 1950 — Kent State University, B.A. (cum laude), 1973; Cleveland-Marshall College of Law, J.D., 1980 — Admitted to Bar, 1980, Ohio; 1981, U.S. District Court, Northern District of Ohio — Member Ohio State and Cleveland Metropolitan Bar Associations

James J. Imbrigiotta — 1962 — Capital University, B.A. (cum laude), 1985; Cleveland-Marshall College of Law, J.D., 1988 — Admitted to Bar, 1988, Ohio; U.S. District Court, Northern District of Ohio; 1990, Supreme Court of Ohio; 2008, U.S. Court of Appeals, Sixth Circuit — Member Ohio State and Cleveland Metropolitan Bar Associations; Ohio Association of Civil Trial Attorneys; Defense Research Institute

Associates

William H. Kotar — 1968 — The University of Akron, B.S., 1994; Cleveland-Marshall College of Law, J.D., 2000 — Admitted to Bar, 2001, Ohio — Member Ohio State Bar Association — U.S. Army

Stephen B. Doucette — 1967 — The Ohio State University, B.A., 1989; Cleveland-Marshall College of Law, J.D., 1993 — Admitted to Bar, 1993, Ohio; 1995, U.S. District Court, Northern District of Ohio; 2003, U.S. Court of Appeals, Sixth Circuit — Member Ohio State and Cleveland Metropolitan Bar Associations

(This firm is also listed in the Subrogation section of this directory)

Hermann Cahn & Schneider LLP

1301 East Ninth Street, Suite 500
Cleveland, Ohio 44114
   Telephone: 216-781-5515
   Fax: 216-781-1030

Hermann Cahn & Schneider LLP, Cleveland, OH (Continued)

Insurance Defense, Fire, Product Liability, Casualty, Toxic Torts, Trucking Industry Defense, Trucking Liability

Insurance Clients

ACUITY Group	Hastings Mutual Insurance Company
Motorists Mutual Insurance Company	

Transportation Clients

Con-Way Truckload, Inc.	FedEx

Partners

Hunter S. Havens — 1968 — The University of Texas, B.B.A., 1989; Case Western Reserve University School of Law, J.D., 1994 — Admitted to Bar, 1994, Ohio

Peter J. Krembs   Hugh Berkson
Jeffrey S. Moeller

Associate

Terese M. Fennell

Marshall Dennehey Warner Coleman & Goggin

127 Public Square, Suite 3510
Cleveland, Ohio 44114-1291
   Telephone: 216-912-3800
   Fax: 216-344-9006
   www.marshalldennehey.com

(Philadelphia, PA Office*: 2000 Market Street, Suite 2300, 19103)
   (Tel: 215-575-2600)
   (Fax: 215-575-0856)
   (Toll Free: 800-220-3308)
   (E-Mail: marshalldennehey@mdwcg.com)
(Wilmington, DE Office*: Nemours Building, 1007 North Orange Street, Suite 600, 19801)
   (Tel: 302-552-4300)
   (Fax: 302-552-4340)
(Fort Lauderdale, FL Office*: 100 Northeast 3rd Avenue, Suite 1100, 33301)
   (Tel: 954-847-4920)
   (Fax: 954-627-6640)
(Jacksonville, FL Office*: 200 West Forsyth Street, Suite 1400, 32202)
   (Tel: 904-358-4200)
   (Fax: 904-355-0019)
(Orlando, FL Office*: Landmark Center One, 315 East Robinson Street, Suite 550, 32801-1948)
   (Tel: 407-420-4380)
   (Fax: 407-839-3008)
(Tampa, FL Office*: 201 East Kennedy Boulevard, Suite 1100, 33602)
   (Tel: 813-898-1800)
   (Fax: 813-221-5026)
(Cherry Hill, NJ Office*: Woodland Falls Corporate Park, 200 Lake Drive East, Suite 300, 08002)
   (Tel: 856-414-6000)
   (Fax: 856-414-6077)
(Roseland, NJ Office*: 425 Eagle Rock Avenue, Suite 302, 07068)
   (Tel: 973-618-4100)
   (Fax: 973-618-0685)
(New York, NY Office*: Wall Street Plaza, 88 Pine Street, 21st Floor, 10005-1801)
   (Tel: 212-376-6400)
   (Fax: 212-376-6490)
(Melville, NY Office*: 105 Maxess Road, Suite 303, 11747)
   (Tel: 631-232-6130)
   (Fax: 631-232-6184)

OHIO   CLEVELAND

Marshall Dennehey Warner Coleman & Goggin, Cleveland, OH (Continued)

(Cincinnati, OH Office*: 312 Elm Street, Suite 1850, 45202)
 (Tel: 513-375-6800)
 (Fax: 513-372-6801)
(Allentown, PA Office*: 4905 West Tilghman Street, Suite 300, 18104)
 (Tel: 484-895-2300)
 (Fax: 484-895-2303)
(Doylestown, PA Office*: 10 North Main Street, 2nd Floor, 18901-4318)
 (Tel: 267-880-2020)
 (Fax: 215-348-5439)
(Erie, PA Office*: 717 State Street, Suite 701, 16501)
 (Tel: 814-480-7800)
 (Fax: 814-455-3603)
(Camp Hill, PA Office*(See Harrisburg listing): 100 Coporate Center Drive, Suite 201, 17011)
 (Tel: 717-651-3500)
 (Fax: 717-651-9630)
(King of Prussia, PA Office*: 620 Freedom Business Center, Suite 300, 19406)
 (Tel: 610-354-8250)
 (Fax: 610-354-8299)
(Pittsburgh, PA Office*: U.S. Steel Tower, Suite 2900, 600 Grant Street, 15219)
 (Tel: 412-803-1140)
 (Fax: 412-803-1188)
(Moosic, PA Office*(See Scranton listing): 50 Glenmaura National Boulevard, 18507)
 (Tel: 570-496-4600)
 (Fax: 570-496-0567)
(Rye Brook, NY Office*(See Westchester listing): 800 Westchester Avenue, Suite C-700, 10573)
 (Tel: 914-977-7300)
 (Fax: 914-977-7301)

Established: 1999

Amusements, Sports and Recreation Liability, Asbestos and Mass Tort Litigation, Automobile Liability, Aviation and Complex Litigation, Construction Injury Litigation, Fraud/Special Investigation, General Liability, Hospitality and Liquor Liability, Maritime Litigation, Product Liability, Property Litigation, Retail Liability, Trucking & Transportation Liability, Appellate Advocacy and Post-Trial Practice, Architectural, Engineering and Construction Defect Litigation, Class Action Litigation, Commercial Litigation, Consumer and Credit Law, Employment Law, Environmental & Toxic Tort Litigation, Insurance Coverage/Bad Faith Litigation, Life, Health and Disability Litigation, Privacy and Data Security, Professional Liability, Public Entity and Civil Rights Litigation, Real Estate E&O Liability, School Leaders' Liability, Securities and Investment Professional Liability, Technology, Media and Intellectual Property Litigation, White Collar Crime, Birth Injury Litigation, Health Care Governmental Compliance, Health Care Liability, Health Law, Long-Term Care Liability, Medical Device and Pharmaceutical Liability, Medicare Set-Aside, Workers' Compensation

Firm Profile: Located on historic Public Square, overlooking Lake Erie, Marshall Dennehey's Cleveland office provides legal representation to insurance carriers and other clients throughout the state and beyond.

The office handles cases in both state and federal courts in the majority of counties and all major cities in Ohio, as does our Cincinnati office. In every stage of litigation, from the taking and defending of depositions to trying cases to verdict, our lawyers take seriously the interests of clients and customers in the practical and efficient resolution of claims.

For additional information regarding the Cleveland office, please feel free to contact the office's managing attorney, Leslie M. Jenny, Esquire, at (216) 912-3805 or lmjenny@mdwcg.com

Managing Shareholder

Leslie M. Jenny — Baldwin-Wallace College, B.A. (cum laude), 1993; Cleveland-Marshall College of Law, J.D., 1996 — Ohio Super Lawyer Rising Star, 2011-2012; Claims & Litigation Management Alliance — Admitted to Bar,

Marshall Dennehey Warner Coleman & Goggin, Cleveland, OH (Continued)

1996, Ohio; 2008, U.S. District Court, Northern District of Ohio — Member Ohio State and Cleveland Metropolitan Bar Associations; American Society for Healthcare Risk Management — Seminars/Classes Taught: Review of Claims and Other Legal Actions Involving Unprofessional Behavior by Physicians and Staff, Risk Management/Patient Safety Seminars for 2012, Lexington Insurance Company/Chartis, 2012 — Practice Areas: Medical Malpractice; Long-Term Care; Medical Devices; Pharmaceutical — E-mail: lmjenny@mdwcg.com

Resident Shareholder

Andrew M. Wargo

Resident Associates

Jason P. Ferrante   Beau D. Hollowell

(See listing under Philadelphia, PA for additional information)

Mazanec, Raskin & Ryder Co., L.P.A.

100 Franklin's Row
34305 Solon Road
Cleveland, Ohio 44139
 Telephone: 440-248-7906
 Fax: 440-248-8861
 www.mrrlaw.com

(Columbus, OH Office*: 175 South 3rd Street, Suite 1000, 43215)
 (Tel: 614-228-5931)
 (Fax: 614-228-5934)

Established: 1980

Insurance Defense, Automobile, Commercial Law, Product Liability, Property and Casualty, Medical Malpractice, Professional Malpractice, Dram Shop, Municipal Liability, Public Officials Liability, Law Enforcement Liability, Civil Rights, Fidelity and Surety, Environmental Law, Toxic Torts, General Practice

Firm Profile: Founded in Cleveland, Ohio in 1980, Mazanec, Raskin & Ryder Co., L.P.A. is a mid-size regional law firm with 30 attorneys serving clients throughout the State of Ohio from offices located in Cleveland and Columbus. The firm provides insurance defense, municipal law, business and employment law, and general litigation services to regional and national industry leaders, organizations and individuals. The firm has built its reputation and practice by providing uncompromising legal representation that exceeds the objectives and expectations of its clients. For more information, visit our website.

Insurance Clients

ACE USA	AIG
Alfa Vision Insurance Corp.	American Family Insurance
American Indemnity Company	American Modern Insurance Group, Inc.
American National Property and Casualty Company	Broadspire
Capitol Indemnity Corporation	Century Surety Company
CNA Insurance Companies	Continental Western Insurance Company
County Risk Sharing Authority (CORSA)	Crawford & Company
EMC Insurance Company	Empire Fire and Marine Insurance Company
Fireman's Fund Insurance Company	First Mercury Insurance Company
Frankenmuth Mutual Insurance Company	Freedom Specialty Insurance Company
GAB Robins, Inc.	GAINSCO, Inc.
Gallagher Bassett Services, Inc.	General Star Management Company
German Mutual Insurance Company	GMAC Insurance
Great American Insurance Company	Great Midwest Insurance Company
Great-West Life and Annuity Insurance Company	Great West Casualty Company
	Hamilton Mutual Insurance Company
Houston Casualty Company	IAT Specialty

CLEVELAND   OHIO

Mazanec, Raskin & Ryder Co., L.P.A., Cleveland, OH
(Continued)

Illinois Insurance Exchange
Lexington Insurance Company
Midwest Claims Service
National Casualty Company
National Interstate Insurance Company
NCMIC Insurance Company
Northland Insurance Company
Ohio Casualty Group
Philadelphia Insurance Company
Professional Claims Managers, Inc.
Progressive Casualty Insurance Company
Republic Insurance Company
RiverStone Claims Management, LLC
Selective Insurance Company of America
Summit Risk Services, Inc.
Trident Insurance
United States Liability Insurance Group
Windsor Insurance Company
York Claims Service, Inc.
Indiana Insurance Company
Liberty Mutual Insurance Company
Monitor Liability Managers, Inc.
National Indemnity Company
Nationwide Insurance
Nautilus Insurance Company
New Hampshire Insurance Company
OneBeacon Insurance
Pioneer Claims Management, Inc.
Professional Indemnity Agency
Public Entity Risk Services
Republic-Franklin Insurance Company
Scottsdale Insurance Company
Sedgwick Claims Management
Sentry Insurance Company
Specialty Risk Services
Travelers Insurance Companies
United America Indemnity Group
Utica Mutual Insurance Company
Western Heritage Insurance Company
Zurich American Insurance Company

Non-Insurance Clients

American Custom Insurance Services, Inc.
Cover X Corporation
Hilton Hotels Corporation
Specialty Risk Portfolio Services, Inc.
Classic Syndicate, Inc.
Covenant Transport, Inc.
Forest City Enterprises, Inc.
Quality Carriers, Inc.
Tyson Foods, Inc.

Firm Members

Thomas S. Mazanec — 1949 — Xavier University, B.S.B.A., 1971; Cleveland-Marshall College of Law, J.D., 1976 — Admitted to Bar, 1976, Ohio; U.S. District Court, Southern District of Ohio; 1980, U.S. District Court, Northern District of Ohio; 1981, U.S. Supreme Court; 1986, U.S. Court of Appeals, Sixth Circuit — Member American, Ohio State and Cleveland Bar Associations; Cleveland Association of Civil Trial Attorneys; Defense Research Institute — Practice Areas: Automobile; Commercial Vehicle; Business Law; Construction Litigation; General Liability; Insurance Coverage; Bad Faith; Liquor Liability; Product Liability; Medical Malpractice; Professional Liability

Todd M. Raskin — 1950 — Kent State University, B.S., 1972; Cleveland-Marshall College of Law, J.D., 1979 — Admitted to Bar, 1980, Ohio; U.S. District Court, Northern District of Ohio; 1985, U.S. Supreme Court; 1988, U.S. District Court, Eastern District of Michigan; U.S. District Court, Western District of Pennsylvania; U.S. Court of Appeals, Third and Sixth Circuits — Member American, Ohio State and Cleveland Bar Associations; Federation of Defense and Corporate Counsel; Defense Research Institute; Cleveland Association of Civil Trial Attorneys; Ohio Association of Civil Trial Attorneys — Practice Areas: Civil Rights; Governmental Liability; Labor and Employment; Municipal Law; Directors and Officers Liability; Insurance Coverage; Bad Faith

Edward M. Ryder — 1948 — Cleveland State University, B.A., 1970; Cleveland-Marshall College of Law, J.D., 1977 — Admitted to Bar, 1977, Ohio; U.S. District Court, Northern District of Ohio; 1984, U.S. Supreme Court; 1988, U.S. Court of Appeals, Sixth Circuit; 1996, U.S. District Court, Southern District of Ohio — Member Ohio State and Cleveland Bar Associations; Ohio Association of Civil Trial Attorneys — Ohio House of Representatives (1971-1972) — Practice Areas: Automobile; Commercial Vehicle; General Liability; Product Liability; Construction Litigation; Errors and Omissions; Professional Liability

John T. McLandrich — 1957 — John Carroll University, B.S., 1979; Case Western Reserve University School of Law, J.D., 1983 — Admitted to Bar, 1983, Ohio; 1988, U.S. District Court, Northern District of Ohio; U.S. Supreme Court; 1989, U.S. Court of Appeals, Sixth Circuit; U.S. District Court, Southern District of Ohio — Member Ohio State Bar Association; Defense Research Institute — Practice Areas: Appellate Practice; Civil Rights; Governmental Liability; Municipal Law; Business Law; Real Estate; Directors and Officers Liability; Professional Liability

James A. Climer — 1954 — Miami University, B.A., 1977; The University of Toledo College of Law, J.D., 1980 — Admitted to Bar, 1980, Ohio; 1981, U.S. District Court, Northern and Southern Districts of Ohio; 1990, U.S. Court of Appeals, Sixth Circuit — Member Federal, Ohio State and Parma Bar Associations; Cuyahoga County Law Directors Association; Defense Research Institute; Ohio Association of Civil Trial Attorneys — Practice Areas: Business Law; Real Estate; Labor and Employment; Municipal Law; Civil Rights; Governmental Liability; General Liability

Joseph F. Nicholas, Jr. — 1961 — University of Dayton, B.A. (cum laude), 1983; Cleveland-Marshall College of Law, J.D., 1986 — Admitted to Bar, 1987, Ohio; 1991, U.S. District Court, Northern District of Ohio; 1995, U.S. Court of Appeals, Sixth Circuit — Member Ohio State, Lake County and Cleveland Bar Associations — Practice Areas: Automobile; Commercial Vehicle; Errors and Omissions; Professional Liability; General Liability; Insurance Coverage; Bad Faith

Patrick W. Winslow — 1953 — The Wharton School of the University of Pennsylvania, B.S., 1974; Cleveland State University, Cleveland-Marshall College of Law, J.D., 1977 — Admitted to Bar, 1977, Ohio; 1982, U.S. District Court, Northern District of Ohio; U.S. Tax Court; 1984, U.S. Court of Appeals, Sixth Circuit — Member Ohio State and Cleveland Bar Associations — Certified Public Accountant — Practice Areas: Business Law

Carl E. Cormany — 1954 — Miami University, A.B. (cum laude), 1977; University of Michigan Law School, J.D., 1980 — Phi Beta Kappa — Admitted to Bar, 1980, Ohio; 1983, U.S. District Court, Northern District of Ohio; 1985, U.S. Court of Appeals, Sixth Circuit; 1986, U.S. Court of Appeals, Seventh Circuit; 2007, U.S. Supreme Court — Member Federal and Ohio State (Litigation and Labor and Employment Law Sections) Bar Associations — Practice Areas: Civil Rights; Governmental Liability; Municipal Law; Labor and Employment

Jeffrey T. Kay — 1972 — Ashland University, B.S. (magna cum laude), 1993; Cleveland State University, Cleveland-Marshall College of Law, J.D., 1997 — Admitted to Bar, 1998, Ohio; 1999, U.S. District Court, Northern and Southern Districts of Ohio; U.S. Court of Appeals, Sixth Circuit — Member American and Ohio State Bar Associations — Practice Areas: Appellate Practice; Labor and Employment; Insurance Coverage; Bad Faith; Civil Rights; Governmental Liability; General Liability; Municipal Law

George V. Pilat — 1962 — Ohio Wesleyan University, B.A., 1984; Case Western Reserve University School of Law, J.D., 1987 — Admitted to Bar, 1988, Ohio; U.S. District Court, Northern District of Ohio; 1989, U.S. Court of Appeals, Sixth Circuit; 1994, U.S. Court of Appeal for the Federal Circuit; 2002, U.S. Court of Appeals, Seventh Circuit — Member Cleveland Metropolitan Bar Association — Practice Areas: Insurance Defense; Insurance Agents; Insurance Coverage Litigation; Commercial Litigation; Contracts; Employment Litigation

Frank Scialdone — 1970 — Nazareth College of Rochester, B.A., 1994; Cleveland-Marshall College of Law, J.D. (magna cum laude), 2002 — Admitted to Bar, 2002, Ohio; U.S. District Court, Northern District of Ohio; 2003, U.S. Court of Appeals, Sixth Circuit; 2005, U.S. District Court, Southern District of Ohio; 2006, U.S. Supreme Court — Member American, Ohio State and Cleveland Bar Associations; Ohio Association of Civil Trial Attorneys; Defense Research Institute — Certified Specialist in Appellate Law, Ohio State Bar Association — Practice Areas: Appellate Practice; Labor and Employment; Municipal Law; Civil Rights; Governmental Liability; General Liability; Professional Liability

Robert F. Cathcart — 1970 — University of Nevada, Reno, B.A., 1995; Case Western Reserve University School of Law, J.D., 1999 — Admitted to Bar, 1999, Ohio; 2000, U.S. District Court, Northern District of Ohio; U.S. Court of Appeals, Sixth Circuit — Member Ohio State Bar Association — Practice Areas: Civil Rights; Governmental Liability; Municipal Law; Labor and Employment

Thomas F. Naughton — 1966 — The Ohio State University, B.A., 1989; Michigan State University College of Law, J.D. (cum laude, with honors), 1994 — Admitted to Bar, 1994, Michigan; 2000, Ohio; 2004, U.S. District Court, Northern District of Ohio; 2005, U.S. District Court, Eastern District of Michigan — Member Ohio State Bar Association; State Bar of Michigan — Practice Areas: Construction Litigation; Errors and Omissions; General Liability; Insurance Coverage; Bad Faith; Product Liability; Professional Liability

Neil S. Sarkar — 1971 — The University of Chicago, B.A. (with honors), 1993; Case Western Reserve University School of Law, J.D., 1997 — Admitted to Bar, 1997, Ohio; 2001, U.S. District Court, Northern and Southern Districts of Ohio — Member Ohio State Bar Association — Practice Areas: Labor and Employment

Associates

Tami Z. Hannon — 1980 — Geneva College, B.S. (magna cum laude), 2002; The University of Akron School of Law, J.D. (magna cum laude), 2005 — Admitted to Bar, 2005, Ohio; 2008, U.S. District Court, Northern District of Ohio; 2010, U.S. District Court, Southern District of Ohio — Practice Areas:

OHIO   CLEVELAND

Mazanec, Raskin & Ryder Co., L.P.A., Cleveland, OH (Continued)

Civil Rights; Governmental Liability; General Liability; Labor and Employment

Mary Beth Klemencic — 1961 — David N. Meyers College, B.S. (summa cum laude), 2001; Cleveland State University, Cleveland-Marshall College of Law, J.D., 2006 — Admitted to Bar, 2006, Ohio — Member Ohio State, Lake County and Cleveland Bar Associations — Practice Areas: Automobile; Commercial Vehicle; General Liability; Construction Litigation; Liquor Liability

John D. Pinzone — 1976 — The Ohio State University, B.S., 1999; Cleveland-Marshall College of Law, J.D. (cum laude), 2002 — Admitted to Bar, 2002, Ohio; 2006, U.S. District Court, Northern District of Ohio — Member Ohio State Bar Association — Practice Areas: Labor and Employment; Municipal Law

Elaine Tso — 1975 — Massachusetts Institute of Technology, B.S., 2003; The University of Akron School of Law, J.D., 2006 — Admitted to Bar, 2006, Ohio; 2009, U.S. District Court, Northern District of Ohio — Member American, Ohio State and Cleveland Metropolitan Bar Associations; Asian Services in Action, Inc. (Board Member, 2008-Present); Asian American Bar Association of Ohio; National Asian Pacific American Bar Association — Practice Areas: Appellate Practice; Product Liability; General Liability; Professional Liability

Cara M. Wright — 1983 — University of Cincinnati, B.A. (summa cum laude), 2005; University of Cincinnati College of Law, J.D., 2008 — Admitted to Bar, 2009, Ohio; U.S. District Court, Northern District of Ohio; 2010, U.S. District Court, Southern District of Ohio; U.S. District Court, Eastern District of Michigan; U.S. Court of Appeals, Sixth Circuit — Member Ohio State and Akron Bar Associations — Practice Areas: Civil Rights; Governmental Liability; Labor and Employment; Municipal Law

David M. Smith — 1979 — Heidelberg College, B.S., 2002; Cleveland-Marshall College of Law, J.D., 2005 — Admitted to Bar, 2005, Ohio; 2010, U.S. District Court, Northern District of Ohio — Member American and Ohio State Bar Associations — Practice Areas: Civil Rights; Governmental Liability; Labor and Employment; General Liability

Terence L. Williams — 1981 — Miami University, B.A., 2003; University of Dayton School of Law, J.D., 2006 — Western Golf Association Evans Scholarship — Admitted to Bar, 2006, Ohio; 2011, U.S. District Court, Southern District of Ohio — Member Ohio State and Dayton Bar Associations — Practice Areas: General Liability

Michael P. Byrne — 1986 — Elon University, B.A., 2007; Capital University Law School, J.D., 2012 — Admitted to Bar, 2012, Ohio — Practice Areas: Insurance Defense; Automobile; Trucking; Construction Litigation; General Liability; Professional Liability

Michael R. Trivisonno — 1986 — The University of Toledo, B.A., 2008; Cleveland-Marshall College of Law, J.D. (cum laude), 2012 — Admitted to Bar, 2013, Ohio — Practice Areas: Insurance Defense; Civil Rights; Municipal Law

Kyle B. Melling — 1985 — Miami University, B.S., 2007; Cleveland-Marshall College of Law, J.D., 2013 — Admitted to Bar, 2013, Ohio — Member Cleveland Metropolitan Bar Association — Practice Areas: Insurance Defense; Civil Rights Defense; General Liability; Governmental Liability; Municipal Law

McNeal, Schick, Archibald & Biro Co., L.P.A.

Van Sweringen Arcade
123 West Prospect Avenue, Suite 250
Cleveland, Ohio 44115
 Telephone: 216-621-9870
 Fax: 216-522-1112
 www.msablaw.com
 E-Mail: msab@apk.net

Established: 1934

Insurance Defense, Trial and Appellate Practice, State and Federal Courts, Casualty, Product Liability, Malpractice, Environmental Law, Toxic Substances

Firm Profile: McNeal, Schick, Archibald & Biro Co., L.P.A., is a Legal Professional Association whose members have provided litigation services for insurance companies and corporate clients for over 75 years. The firm

McNeal, Schick, Archibald & Biro Co., L.P.A., Cleveland, OH (Continued)

specializes in defense litigation, and also provides legal advice on insurance matters and commercial and corporate matters. It has a support staff of paralegals and legal assistants. The firm's practice is in the State of Ohio, primarily in the northern one-half of the State.

Highest AV Rating from Martindale-Hubbell

Insurance Clients

AAA Michigan
Auto-Owners Insurance Company
CNA Insurance Companies
Everest National Insurance Company
Pekin Insurance
West Bend Mutual Insurance Company
Allstate Insurance Company
Church Mutual Insurance Company
Electric Insurance Company
Great West Casualty Company
Hudson Insurance Group
RLI Insurance Company
XL Insurance

Non-Insurance Clients

Phelps Dunbar, LLP

Firm Members

Harley J. McNeal — (1911-1996)

Albert J. Biro — (1926-1995)

Thomas Schick — (1923-1997)

Robert D. Archibald — 1931 — The College of Wooster, A.B., 1953; Youngstown State University; Western Reserve University, J.D., 1956 — Phi Delta Phi — Admitted to Bar, 1956, Ohio — Member American, Ohio State and Cleveland Metropolitan (Trustee, 1979-1982) Bar Associations; Fellow, American College of Trial Lawyers — Author: "Military Jurisdiction over Discharged Serviceman", Seven Western Reserve Law Review 191 (1955); Editorial Board, Western Reserve Law Review (1955-1956) — Highest AV Rating from Martindale-Hubbell — E-mail: arch@msablaw.com — (Retired)

Paul W. Ziegler — 1946 — Georgetown University, A.B., 1968; J.D., 1971 — Admitted to Bar, 1971, Ohio; 1982, District of Columbia; 1973, U.S. District Court, Northern District of Ohio — Member Ohio State and Cleveland Metropolitan (Trustee, 1993-1996) Bar Associations; District of Columbia Bar; Life Member, Judicial Conference for the Eighth Judicial District; Ohio Association of Civil Trial Attorneys; Cleveland Association of Civil Trial Attorneys; Association of Defense Trial Attorneys — Highest AV Rating from Martindale-Hubbell — E-mail: ziggy@msablaw.com

Fredric E. Kramer — 1937 — John Carroll University, B.S.S., 1959; University of Detroit; Case Western Reserve University, LL.B., 1962 — Admitted to Bar, 1962, Ohio; 1964, U.S. District Court, Northern District of Ohio; 1980, U.S. Supreme Court; 1982, U.S. Court of Appeals, Sixth Circuit — Member Ohio State (Council of Delegates, 1997-Present) and Cleveland Metropolitan (Trustee, 1987-1990) Bar Associations; Life Member, Judicial Conference for the Eighth Judicial District; Master Bencher, William K. Thomas Inns of Court — Highest AV Rating from Martindale-Hubbell — E-mail: kramer@msablaw.com

John C. Cubar — 1952 — Miami University, A.B., 1974; Cleveland State University, J.D., 1978 — Admitted to Bar, 1978, Ohio; 1979, U.S. District Court, Northern District of Ohio; 1980, U.S. Court of Appeals, Sixth Circuit; 1987, U.S. Supreme Court — Member Ohio State Bar Association; Cleveland Association of Civil Trial Attorneys — Highest AV Rating from Martindale-Hubbell — E-mail: jcc@msablaw.com

Marilyn J. Singer — 1955 — Bryn Mawr College, A.B., 1976; Case Western Reserve University, J.D., 1979 — Admitted to Bar, 1979, Ohio; 1980, U.S. District Court, Northern District of Ohio; 1984, U.S. Court of Appeals, Sixth Circuit — Member Ohio State and Cleveland Metropolitan Bar Associations — Highest AV Rating from Martindale-Hubbell — E-mail: mjs@msablaw.com

Brian T. Winchester — 1971 — Xavier University, B.A., 1993; Cleveland-Marshall College of Law, J.D., 1997 — Admitted to Bar, 1998, Ohio; 1999, U.S. District Court, Northern District of Ohio; 2003, U.S. Court of Appeals, Sixth Circuit; 2005, U.S. District Court, Southern District of Ohio — Member Ohio State and Cleveland Metropolitan Bar Associations; William K. Thomas American Inns of Court; Cleveland Association of Civil Trial Attorneys — Highest AV Rating from Martindale-Hubbell — E-mail: btw@msablaw.com

CLEVELAND   OHIO

McNeal, Schick, Archibald & Biro Co., L.P.A., Cleveland, OH (Continued)

Associate

Patrick J. Gump — 1980 — Kent State University, B.A. Political Science, 2002; Cleveland State University, J.D., 2006 — Admitted to Bar, 2010, Ohio; 2013, U.S. District Court, Northern District of Ohio — Member Cleveland Metropolitan Bar Association — E-mail: pgump@msablaw.com

Reminger Co., L.P.A.

101 West Prospect Avenue, Suite 1400
Cleveland, Ohio 44115-1093
  Telephone: 216-687-1311
  Fax: 216-687-1841
  www.reminger.com

(Cincinnati, OH Office*: 525 Vine Street, Suite 1700, 45202)
  (Tel: 513-721-1311)
  (Fax: 513-721-2553)
(Columbus, OH Office*: Capitol Square Office Building, 65 East State Street, 4th Floor, 43215)
  (Tel: 614-228-1311)
  (Fax: 614-232-2410)
(Indianapolis, IN Office*: 3925 River Crossing Parkway, Suite 280, 46240)
  (Tel: 317-663-8570)
  (Fax: 317-663-8580)

Established: 1958

Trial Practice, State and Federal Courts, Self-Insured, Risk Management, Transportation, Product Liability, Errors and Omissions, Civil Rights, Investigation and Adjustment, Excess and Surplus Lines, Medical Malpractice, Appellate Practice, Commercial Litigation, Premises Liability, Construction Defect, Construction Law, Construction Liability, Construction Litigation, Corporate Law, Coverage Analysis, Coverage Issues, Dental Malpractice, Directors and Officers Liability, Employment Law, Employment Practices Liability, Engineering and Construction, Environmental Coverage, Environmental Law, Environmental Liability, General Civil Trial and Appellate Practice, General Defense, General Liability, Health Care, Insurance Coverage, Legal Malpractice, Mass Tort, Mediation, Medical Devices, Medical Liability, Municipal Liability, Nursing Home Liability, Pharmaceutical, Professional Errors and Omissions, Professional Liability, Professional Liability (Non-Medical) Defense, Public Liability, Real Estate, Toxic Torts, Trial and Appellate Practice, Workers' Compensation

Insurance Clients

ACE USA
American National Property and Casualty Company
Broadspire
Chartis
Cincinnati Insurance Company
CNA
The Doctors Company
Fortress Insurance Company
Great West Casualty Company
National Indemnity Company
OMSNIC
Penn National Insurance
ProClaim America Incorporated
Scottsdale Insurance Company
Travelers Insurance
United America Insurance Group
Zurich North America
Allianz SE
American Specialty Insurance & Risk Services, Inc.
Carolina Casualty Insurance Company
Clarendon National Insurance Company
Fireman's Fund Specialty Group
Gallagher Bassett Services, Inc.
The Medical Protective Company
Ohio Casualty Company
OneBeacon Insurance
Philadelphia Insurance Company
QBE
Tokio Marine & Nichido Fire Insurance Co., Ltd
U.S. Liability Insurance Company

Non-Insurance Clients

Akron General Medical Center
Catholic Diocese of Cleveland
The Cleveland Plain Dealer
FedEx Corporation
HCR Manor Care, Inc.
Hyundai Motor America
America Honda Motor Co., Inc.
Cleveland Clinic Foundation
Dolgencorp, Inc.
Genuine Parts Company
Howard Hanna Real Estate Services

Reminger Co., L.P.A., Cleveland, OH (Continued)

J.B. Hunt Transport, Inc.
Kindred Healthcare
Macy's
Marriott International, Inc.
Nordstrom, Inc.
Rockies Express Pipeline, LLC
Swift Transportation Corporation
University Hospitals
Volvo Cars of North America, Inc.
Kia Motors America, Inc.
Lincoln Electric Company
Marathon Oil Corporation
Mercedes-Benz USA, LLC
North American Van Lines
Starbucks Corporation
Team Health
Volkswagen Group of America, Inc.

Managing Partner

Stephen Walters — Cleveland State University, B.A. (cum laude), 1980; Cleveland-Marshall College of Law, J.D., 1983 — Admitted to Bar, 1983, Ohio — Member Federation of Defense and Corporate Counsel — Practice Areas: Construction Liability; Governmental Liability; Medical Malpractice; Professional Liability; Public Liability — E-mail: swalters@reminger.com

Smith Marshall, LLP

815 Superior Avenue, Suite 1425
Cleveland, Ohio 44114
  Telephone: 216-781-4994
  Fax: 216-781-9448
  E-Mail: law@smithmarshall.com
  www.smithmarshall.com

Established: 1953

Insurance Defense, Architects and Engineers, Asbestos Litigation, Automobile, Bad Faith, Business Law, Construction Law, Coverage Issues, Discrimination, Employer Liability, Environmental Law, Errors and Omissions, Fidelity and Surety, Fire, Governmental Liability, Intentional Torts, Malpractice, Premises Liability, Product Liability, Professional Negligence, Property, Toxic Torts, Trial and Appellate Practice, Civil Rights

Firm Profile: For more than fifty years, Smith Marshall, LLP has offered "big-firm" expertise and support in a small firm setting where the representation provided is efficient, result-oriented and personal.

Insurance Clients

Capitol Indemnity Corporation
Discover Re
DPIC Companies, Inc.
Federated Insurance Company
GAB Robins North America, Inc.
Hallmark Financial Group
Magna Carta Companies
MetLife Auto & Home
Old National Bancorp/JWF Specialty Co., Inc.
Permanent General Assurance Corporation
RCA Insurance Group
Risk Administration and Management Company
Victoria Fire & Casualty Company
Zurich American Insurance Group
Chubb Group of Insurance Companies
Employers Mutual Companies
Fireman's Fund Insurance Company
The Hartford Insurance Group
Merastar Insurance Company
Monroe Guaranty Insurance Company
Pennsylvania National Mutual Casualty Insurance Company
Prudential Property and Casualty Insurance Company
Specialty Risk Services, Inc. (SRS)
State Automobile Mutual Insurance Company

Local Counsel For

Polaris Industries, Inc.

Regional Counsel For

ABM Industries, Inc.
OneSource Facility Services, Inc.
Coach USA
Schindler Elevator Corporation

Richard C. Green — (1910-1967)
John M. Cronquist — (1931-1993)
Jack F. Smith — (1923-1997)
Frederick P. Vergon, Jr. — (1944-2008)

Partners

Wentworth J. Marshall, Jr. — 1931 — Williams College, B.A., 1953; Case Western Reserve University, LL.B., 1956 — Admitted to Bar, 1956, Ohio —

Smith Marshall, LLP, Cleveland, OH (Continued)

Member Cleveland Metropolitan Bar Association — E-mail: wjm@smithmarshall.com

Philip J. Weaver, Jr. — 1947 — Wittenberg University, A.B., 1969; The Ohio State University, J.D. (cum laude), 1974 — Admitted to Bar, 1974, Ohio; 1976, U.S. District Court, Northern District of Ohio; 1983, U.S. Court of Appeals, Sixth Circuit; 1990, U.S. District Court, Middle District of Louisiana; 1992, U.S. District Court, Eastern District of Michigan; 1999, U.S. District Court, District of Colorado — Member American, Ohio State, and Cleveland Metropolitan Bar Associations; Harold F. Burton Inn of Court; Ohio Association of Civil Trial Attorneys; Cleveland Association of Civil Trial Attorneys; Defense Research Institute — E-mail: pjw@smithmarshall.com

R. Eric Smearman — 1968 — John Carroll University, B.A., 1990; Case Western Reserve University, J.D. (cum laude), 1993 — Admitted to Bar, 1993, Ohio; U.S. District Court, Northern District of Ohio; 1999, U.S. District Court, District of Colorado — Member American, Ohio State, Lake County and Cleveland Metropolitan Bar Associations; Ohio Association of Civil Trial Attorneys; Defense Research Institute — E-mail: res@smithmarshall.com

Associate

Eric K. Grinnell — 1987 — The College of Wooster, B.A. (cum laude), 2009; Cleveland State University, J.D. (cum laude), 2012 — Admitted to Bar, 2012, Ohio; 2014, U.S. District Court, Northern District of Ohio — Member Federal, American, Ohio State and Cleveland Metropolitan Bar Associations; Ohio Association of Civil Trial Attorneys — E-mail: ekg@smithmarshall.com

The following firms also service this area.

Carr Law Office, LLC

5824 Akron-Cleveland Road, Suite A
Hudson, Ohio 44236
Telephone: 330-655-1662
Fax: 330-653-5469

Insurance Coverage, Insurance Defense, Bad Faith, Bodily Injury, Wrongful Death, Civil Litigation, Appeals, Advertising Injury, Appellate, Appellate Advocacy, Appellate Practice, Automobile, Automobile Liability, Automobile Tort, Breach of Contract, Business Litigation, Casualty, Casualty Defense, Casualty Insurance Law, Catastrophic Injury, Civil Defense, Civil Trial Practice, Class Actions, Commercial and Personal Lines, Commercial General Liability, Commercial Insurance, Commercial Law, Commercial Liability, Commercial Lines, Commercial Litigation, Commercial Vehicle, Comprehensive General Liability, Consumer Law, Contract Disputes, Coverage Analysis, Coverage Issues, Declaratory Judgments, Defense Litigation, Errors and Omissions, Examinations Under Oath, Excess, Excess and Reinsurance, Excess and Umbrella, Extra-Contractual Liability, Extra-Contractual Litigation, Fraud, General Civil Trial and Appellate Practice, Homeowners, Insurance Agents, Insurance Claim Analysis and Evaluation, Insurance Coverage Determination, Insurance Coverage Litigation, Insurance Fraud, Insurance Law, Insurance Litigation, Legal, Legal Malpractice, Litigation, Malpractice, Motor Vehicle, Negligence, Non-Subscriber Litigation and Defense, Opinions, Personal and Commercial Vehicle, Personal Injury, Personal Liability, Personal Lines, Policy Construction and Interpretation, Premises Liability, Primary and Excess Insurance, Product Liability, Professional Errors and Omissions, Professional Liability, Professional Liability (Non-Medical) Defense, Professional Malpractice, Professional Negligence, Property, Property and Casualty, Property Damage, Property Defense, Property Liability, Property Loss, Real Estate Errors and Omissions, Real Estate Litigation, Restaurant Liability, Retail Liability, Risk Management, Self-Insured, Self-Insured Defense, Slip and Fall, State and Federal Courts, Tort, Tort Liability, Tort Litigation, Trial and Appellate Practice, Trial Practice, Underwriting, Uninsured and Underinsured Motorist

SEE COMPLETE LISTING UNDER AKRON, OHIO

Ritter, Robinson, McCready & James, Ltd.

1850 National City Bank Building
405 Madison Avenue
Toledo, Ohio 43604-1294
Telephone: 419-241-3213
Fax: 419-241-4925

Insurance Defense, Trial and Appellate Practice, Negligence, Product Liability, Premises Liability, Construction Defect, Animal Law, Arson, Insurance Fraud, Automobile Liability, Bad Faith, Truck Liability, Insurance Coverage, Employment Law, Subrogation, Municipal Law

SEE COMPLETE LISTING UNDER TOLEDO, OHIO (116 MILES)

COLUMBUS † 787,033 Franklin Co.

Dickie, McCamey & Chilcote, P.C.

2109 Stella Court
Columbus, Ohio 43215-1032
Telephone: 614-258-6000
Fax: 888-811-7144
Toll Free: 866-226-9645
E-Mail: info@dmclaw.com
www.dmclaw.com

(Additional Offices: Pittsburgh, PA*; Charlotte, NC*; Cleveland, OH*; Haddonfield, NJ*; Camp Hill, PA*(See Harrisburg listing); Lancaster, SC*; Philadelphia, PA*; Cary, NC*(See Raleigh listing); Steubenville, OH*; Wheeling, WV*; Wilmington, DE*)

Established: 2010

Asbestos Litigation, Bad Faith, Captive Company Matters, Casualty, Commercial Litigation, Energy, Labor and Employment, Excess and Reinsurance, Extra-Contractual Litigation, Insurance Agents, Insurance Coverage, Insurance Coverage Litigation, Legal Malpractice, Medical Malpractice, Medicare Set-Aside Practice, Municipal Liability, Nursing Home Liability, Product Liability, Professional Liability, Property and Casualty, Surety, Transportation, Trucking, Uninsured and Underinsured Motorist, Workers' Compensation

Shareholder

Joseph J. Golian — **Branch Office Shareholder-in-Charge** — Washington & Jefferson College, B.A., 1982; Capital University, J.D., 1985 — Admitted to Bar, 1985, Ohio — E-mail: jgolian@dmclaw.com

R. Leland Evans

(See listing under Pittsburgh, PA for additional information)

Freund, Freeze & Arnold, A Legal Professional Association

Capital Square Office Building
65 East State Street, Suite 800
Columbus, Ohio 43215-4247
Telephone: 614-827-7300
Telephone: 877-FFA-1LAW
E-Mail: ffalawco@ffalaw.com
www.ffalaw.com

Established: 1984

Members

Sandra R. McIntosh — Capital University Law School, J.D. (cum laude), 2004 — Admitted to Bar, 2004, Ohio

Mark L. Schumacher — The University of Toledo College of Law, J.D., 1981 — Admitted to Bar, 1981, Ohio

Mazanec, Raskin & Ryder Co., L.P.A.

175 South 3rd Street, Suite 1000
Columbus, Ohio 43215
Telephone: 614-228-5931
Fax: 614-228-5934
www.mrrlaw.com

COLUMBUS   OHIO

Mazanec, Raskin & Ryder Co., L.P.A., Columbus, OH
(Continued)

(Cleveland, OH Office*: 100 Franklin's Row, 34305 Solon Road, 44139)
   (Tel: 440-248-7906)
   (Fax: 440-248-8861)

Insurance Defense, Automobile, Commercial Law, Product Liability, Property and Casualty, Medical Malpractice, Professional Malpractice, Dram Shop, Municipal Liability, Public Officials Liability, Law Enforcement Liability, Civil Rights, Fidelity and Surety, Environmental Law, Toxic Torts, General Practice

Insurance Clients

Acceptance Insurance Company
AIG
Allstate Insurance Company
American Family Insurance
American Indemnity Company
American National Property and Casualty Company
Capitol Indemnity Corporation
CNA Insurance Companies
County Risk Sharing Authority (CORSA)
EMC Insurance Company
Fireman's Fund Insurance Company
Frankenmuth Mutual Insurance Company
GAB Robins, Inc.
Gallagher Bassett Services, Inc.
German Mutual Insurance Company
Great American Insurance Company
Great-West Life and Annuity Insurance Company
Houston Casualty Company
Illinois Insurance Exchange
Lancer Insurance Company
Liberty Mutual Insurance Company
Monitor Liability Managers, Inc.
National Indemnity Company
Nationwide Insurance
NCMIC Insurance Company
Northland Insurance Company
Ohio Casualty Group
Philadelphia Insurance Company
Professional Claims Managers, Inc.
Progressive Casualty Insurance Company
Republic Insurance Company
Safe Auto Insurance Company
Selective Insurance Company of America
Summit Risk Services, Inc.
Travelers Insurance Companies
United America Indemnity Group
Utica Mutual Insurance Company
Western Heritage Insurance Company
Zurich American Insurance Company

ACE USA
Alfa Vision Insurance Corp.
American Custom Insurance Services, Inc.
American Modern Insurance Group, Inc.
Broadspire
Century Surety Company
Continental Western Insurance Company
Crawford & Company
Empire Fire and Marine Insurance Company
First Mercury Insurance Company
Freedom Specialty Insurance Company
GAINSCO, Inc.
General Star Management Company
GMAC Insurance
Great Midwest Insurance Company
Great West Casualty Company
Hamilton Mutual Insurance Company
IAT Specialty
Indiana Insurance Company
Lexington Insurance Company
Midwest Claims Service
National Casualty Company
National Interstate Insurance Company
New Hampshire Insurance Company
OneBeacon Insurance
Pioneer Claims Management, Inc.
Professional Indemnity Agency
Public Entity Risk Services
Republic-Franklin Insurance Company
Scottsdale Insurance Company
Specialty Risk Services
State Farm Fire and Casualty Company
Trident Insurance
United States Liability Insurance Group
Windsor Insurance Company
York Claims Service, Inc.

Non-Insurance Clients

Central Ohio Transit Authority
Covenant Transport, Inc.
Forest City Enterprises, Inc.
Quality Carriers, Inc.
Tyson Foods, Inc.

Classic Syndicate, Inc.
Cover X Corporation
Hilton Hotels Corporation
Specialty Risk Portfolio Services, Inc.

Firm Members

Robert H. Stoffers — 1957 — Otterbein College, B.A., 1979; The University of Toledo College of Law, J.D., 1982 — Admitted to Bar, 1982, Ohio; 1989, Illinois; 1985, U.S. District Court, Northern District of Ohio; 1989, U.S. District Court, Southern District of Ohio; 1994, U.S. Court of Appeals, Sixth Circuit; U.S. Supreme Court — Member American, Ohio State and Cleveland Bar Associations; Defense Research Institute; Ohio Association of Civil Trial Attorneys — Practice Areas: Civil Rights; Construction Litigation; Employment Law; Insurance Coverage; Motor Vehicle; Premises Liability; Product Liability; Professional Negligence

Mazanec, Raskin & Ryder Co., L.P.A., Columbus, OH
(Continued)

David K. Frank — Miami University, B.A. (cum laude), 1971; The Ohio State University, M.A., 1974; The Ohio State University Moritz College of Law, J.D., 1974 — Phi Beta Kappa; American Jurisprudence Award — Admitted to Bar, 1974, Ohio; 1975, U.S. Court of Military Appeals; U.S. District Court, Southern District of Ohio; 1983, U.S. Supreme Court; 1986, U.S. Court of Appeals, Sixth Circuit; 2002, U.S. Court of Veterans Appeals — Member Ohio State and Columbus Bar Associations — Practice Areas: Appellate Practice; General Liability; Professional Liability

Douglas C. Boatright — 1957 — The University of Akron, B.S./B.A., 1981; A.A.S., 1984; The University of Akron School of Law, J.D., 1989 — Admitted to Bar, 1989, Ohio; 1997, Pennsylvania; 1999, West Virginia; 1990, U.S. District Court, Northern and Southern Districts of Ohio; U.S. Court of Appeals, Sixth Circuit; 1994, U.S. Supreme Court; 1999, U.S. District Court, Southern District of West Virginia; 2001, U.S. District Court, Northern District of West Virginia — Member Ohio State and Columbus Bar Associations

Michael S. Loughry — 1969 — The University of Texas at Austin, B.A., 1991; Capital University Law School, J.D., 2001 — Admitted to Bar, 2001, Ohio; 2002, U.S. District Court, Southern District of Ohio; U.S. Court of Appeals, Sixth Circuit; 2004, U.S. District Court, Northern District of Ohio — Member Federal, American and Ohio State Bar Associations; Columbus Bar Association (Certified Grievance Committee, 2009-Present; Federal Courts Committee Co-Chair, 2006-2008; Barrister Leader Program, 2002-2003; Planning Committee, 2003-2004) — Practice Areas: Appellate Practice; Automobile; Commercial Vehicle; Civil Rights; Governmental Liability; General Liability; Labor and Employment; Liquor Liability; Municipal Law; Product Liability; Professional Liability

Jeffery S. Maynard — 1968 — The Ohio State University, B.A., 1995; Capital University Law School, J.D. (magna cum laude), 2001 — Admitted to Bar, 2001, Ohio; U.S. District Court, Northern and Southern Districts of Ohio — Practice Areas: Construction Litigation; Errors and Omissions; General Liability; Insurance Coverage; Bad Faith; Product Liability

Associate

Jason R. Deschler — 1980 — The Ohio State University, B.S., 2003; Capital University Law School, J.D., 2006 — Admitted to Bar, 2006, Ohio; 2007, U.S. District Court, Southern District of Ohio; 2008, U.S. Court of Appeals, Sixth Circuit — Member American, Ohio and Columbus Bar Associations — Practice Areas: Civil Rights; Governmental Liability; Construction Litigation; General Liability; Labor and Employment; Professional Liability

(See listing under Cleveland, OH for additional information)

Reminger Co., L.P.A.

Capitol Square Office Building
65 East State Street, 4th Floor
Columbus, Ohio 43215
   Telephone: 614-228-1311
   Fax: 614-232-2410
   www.reminger.com

(Cleveland, OH Office*: 101 West Prospect Avenue, Suite 1400, 44115-1093)
   (Tel: 216-687-1311)
   (Fax: 216-687-1841)
(Cincinnati, OH Office*: 525 Vine Street, Suite 1700, 45202)
   (Tel: 513-721-1311)
   (Fax: 513-721-2553)
(Indianapolis, IN Office*: 3925 River Crossing Parkway, Suite 280, 46240)
   (Tel: 317-663-8570)
   (Fax: 317-663-8580)

Trial Practice, State and Federal Courts, Insurance Law, Malpractice, Self-Insured, Risk Management, Transportation, Product Liability, Errors and Omissions, Civil Rights, Investigation and Adjustment

OHIO   COLUMBUS

Reminger Co., L.P.A., Columbus, OH   (Continued)

Ronald A. Fresco — The Ohio State University, B.A., 1989; Capital University Law School, J.D., 1992 — Admitted to Bar, 1992, Ohio — E-mail: rfresco@reminger.com

(See listing under Cleveland, OH for additional information)

Steptoe & Johnson PLLC

Huntington Center
41 South High Street, Suite 2200
Columbus, Ohio 43215
    Telephone: 614-221-5100
    Fax: 614-221-0952
    E-Mail: lyle.brown@steptoe-johnson.com
    www.steptoe-johnson.com

Established: 1913

Professional Malpractice, Toxic Torts, Employment Practices Liability, Commercial Litigation, Insurance First Party/Bad Faith/Coverage/Fraud, General Civil Litigation Defense

Resident Partner

Lyle B. Brown

(See listing under Bridgeport, WV for additional information)

(This firm is also listed in the Investigation and Adjustment section of this directory)

Vorys, Sater, Seymour and Pease LLP

52 East Gay Street
Columbus, Ohio 43215
    Telephone: 614-464-6400
    Fax: 614-464-6350
    E-Mail: info@vorys.com
    www.vorys.com

(Washington, DC Office: Suite 900, 1909 K Street NW, 20006-1152)
    (Tel: 202-467-8800)
    (Fax: 202-467-8900)
(Cincinnati, OH Office: 301 East Fourth Street, Suite 3500, Great American Tower, 45202)
    (Tel: 513-723-4000)
    (Fax: 513-723-4056)
(Cleveland, OH Office: 2100 One Cleveland Center, 1375 East Ninth Street, 44114-1724)
    (Tel: 216-479-6100)
    (Fax: 216-479-6060)
(Akron, OH Office: 106 South Main Street, Suite 1100, 44308)
    (Tel: 330-208-1000)
    (Fax: 330-208-1001)
(Houston, TX Office: 700 Louisiana Street, Suite 4100, 77002)
    (Tel: 713-588-7000)
    (Fax: 713-588-7050)

Established: 1909

Vorys, Sater, Seymour and Pease LLP, Columbus, OH (Continued)

Insurance Defense, Antitrust, Directors and Officers Liability, Employment Practices Liability, Environmental Law, Health, Legal Malpractice, Malpractice, Medical Malpractice, Product Liability, Professional Malpractice, Toxic Torts, Workers' Compensation, Life Insurance, Property and Casualty, Government Affairs, Insurance Law, Insurance Litigation, Reinsurance, Administrative Law, Mergers and Acquisitions, Regulatory Compliance, Health Insuring Corporations, Sales Practices Claims and Coverage Issues, Formation and Financing, Market Conduct, Financial Examinations and Financial Issues, Surplus Lines, Rate, Form and Rule Filings, Portfolio Transfers, Assumptions, Agent and Agency Matters, Market Expansion and Withdraw, Self-Insurance

Firm Profile: Vorys has nearly 375 attorneys in six offices in Columbus, Cincinnati, Cleveland and Akron, Ohio; Washington, D.C.; and Houston, Texas and currently ranks as one of the 200 largest U.S. law firms according to American Lawyer.

We handle the organization, capitalization, and restructuring of insurance companies and agencies, as well as mergers, mutual-to-stock conversions, and conversions to mutual holding companies. We assist in obtaining the admissions of domestic companies to other states and of foreign companies to Ohio, and secure regulatory approvals of insurance policies & forms. We aid in the negotiation of insurance and reinsurance contracts and the licensing and management of agents/brokers. We provide counsel to reinsurance companies, captive insurers, and risk retention groups, and represent trade associations and organizations involved in insurance education. We often advise clients on insurance issues that arise in connection with commercial, real estate, employment, governance, and transactional matters.

Insurance Clients

Delta Dental Plan of Ohio   Grange Mutual Casualty Company

Partners

Roger E. Lautzenhiser — Stanford University, A.B. (Phi Beta Kappa), 1976; University of California, Los Angeles School of Law, J.D., 1979 — Admitted to Bar, 1979, Ohio — Practice Areas: Corporate Law; Insurance

Thomas E. Szykowny — Denison University, B.A. (summa cum laude), 1979; The Ohio State University Moritz College of Law, J.D., 1982 — Admitted to Bar, 1982, Ohio — Member American, Ohio State and Columbus Bar Associations — Practice Areas: Insurance; Corporate Law

Shawn M. Flahive — University of Notre Dame, B.A. (with high honors), 1981; Georgetown University Law Center, J.D. (cum laude), 1984 — Admitted to Bar, 1984, Ohio — Practice Areas: Insurance; Corporate Law

Robert N. Webner — The Ohio State University, B.A., 1980; Georgetown University Law Center, J.D. (magna cum laude), 1985 — Admitted to Bar, 1985, Ohio — Member Columbus Bar Association; Association of Defense Trial Attorneys; Defense Research Institute — Practice Areas: Insurance; Litigation

Glenn V. Whitaker — Denison University, B.A. (magna cum laude), 1969; The George Washington University Law School, J.D. (cum laude), 1972 — Admitted to Bar, 1972, Maryland; 1973, District of Columbia; 1980, Ohio — Practice Areas: Insurance; Insurance Litigation; Litigation

Robert C. Mitchell — Denison University, B.A., 1978; University of Cincinnati College of Law, J.D., 1981 — Admitted to Bar, 1981, Indiana; 1990, Ohio — Practice Areas: Insurance; Litigation

Senior Attorneys

Gregory J. Zelasko — Mount Union College, B.S. (cum laude), 1978; Capital University Law School, J.D., 1981 — Admitted to Bar, 1981, Ohio — Member Columbus Bar Association — Practice Areas: Insurance; Corporate Law

Anthony Spina — The University of Akron, B.S., 1995; Capital University Law School, J.D. (cum laude), 1998 — Admitted to Bar, 1998, Ohio — Member American and Ohio State Bar Associations — Practice Areas: Insurance; Corporate Law

(This firm is also listed in the Regulatory and Compliance section of this directory)

DAYTON   OHIO

Williams & Petro Co., LLC

338 South High Street
Columbus, Ohio 43215
   Telephone: 614-224-0531
   Fax: 614-224-0553
   E-Mail: jpetro@wplaw.org

(Independence, OH Office: 5005 Rockside Road, Suite 600, 44131)
   (Tel: 216-573-3710)
(Cincinnati, OH Office: 9435 Waterstone Boulevard, Suite 140, 45249)
   (Tel: 513-444-2189)

Established: 1998

First and Third Party Defense, Automobile, General Liability, Professional Malpractice, Errors and Omissions, Fidelity and Surety, Bad Faith, Construction Litigation, Employment Law, Dram Shop, Municipal Liability

Firm Profile: Richard A. Williams and John P. Petro founded Williams and Petro Co., LLC in June 1998 to provide outstanding civil litigation services to their clients at a reasonable cost. Founded on the principle that value is a measure of integrity, intellect and effort, the firm has grown to include four associates and a dedicated support staff. As a group, the attorneys of Williams & Petro combine legal knowledge, professional acumen, hard work, and a commitment to our clients as a means of maximizing value and results at every stage of litigation. Significant experience at all trial and appellate levels in the Federal and State courts of Ohio and familiarity with local practices enable us to guide, advise and assist our clients at every stage of litigation.

Insurance Clients

ACE INA Group	AIG Technical Services, Inc.
American Safety Insurance Company	Century Surety Company
CNA Surety Corporation	Cincinnati Insurance Company
Continental Western Insurance Company	Community Association Undewriters of America, Inc.
EMC Insurance Companies	CORSA
Farmers Insurance Company	Erie Insurance Company
Founders Insurance Company	Farmers Relief Mutual Association
Hamilton Mutual Insurance Company	Frankenmuth Mutual Insurance Company
The Hartford	Harleysville Insurance Company
Interstate Insurance Company	Horace Mann Insurance Group
Liberty Bond Services	Kemper Insurance Company
Mid-State Surety Corporation	Merchants Insurance Company
North Pointe Insurance Company	NAS Surety Group
Old Republic Surety Company	Ohio Mutual Insurance Group
Preferred Mutual Insurance Company	Pekin Insurance
RLI Surety	QBE Insurance Company
Safe Auto Insurance Company	Republic-Franklin Insurance Company
Selective Insurance Company of America	St. Paul Surety
Travelers Insurance	State Auto Insurance Company
Utica Mutual Insurance Company	State Farm Insurance Company
XL Surety	Unitrin Insurance Company
	Westfield Companies
	York Insurance Company

Non-Insurance Clients

National American Corporation

Partners

Richard A. Williams — 1957 — Miami University, B.S., 1979; The University of Toledo College of Law, J.D., 1982 — Admitted to Bar, 1982, Ohio; 1986, U.S. District Court, Northern District of Ohio; U.S. Court of Appeals, Sixth Circuit; 1991, U.S. District Court, Southern District of Ohio; 1994, U.S. Supreme Court — Member Ohio State and Columbus Bar Associations

John P. Petro — 1967 — Miami University, B.A. (cum laude), 1989; The Ohio State University Moritz College of Law, J.D., 1992 — Phi Beta Kappa — Admitted to Bar, 1992, Ohio; 1993, U.S. District Court, Southern District of Ohio — Member American, Ohio State and Columbus Bar Associations

Josh L. Schoenberger — The University of Findlay, B.A. (cum laude), 2001; The Ohio State University Moritz College of Law, J.D., 2004 — Admitted to Bar, 2004, Ohio — Member Ohio State and Columbus Bar Associations

Williams & Petro Co., LLC, Columbus, OH (Continued)

Associates

Lorree L. Dendis — 1974 — William Smith College, B.A. (summa cum laude), 1996; The Ohio State University Moritz College of Law, J.D., 2000 — Phi Beta Kappa; Omicron Delta Epsilon — Admitted to Bar, 2000, Ohio; U.S. District Court, Northern District of Ohio; 2001, U.S. District Court, Southern District of Ohio; U.S. Court of Appeals, Sixth Circuit — Member American, Ohio State and Columbus Bar Associations; Franklin American Inn of Court

Susan S. R. Petro — 1964 — The Ohio State University, B.A. (cum laude), 1987; University of North Carolina at Chapel Hill School of Law, J.D., 1990 — Admitted to Bar, 1990, Ohio

Of Counsel

John J. Petro — 1937 — The Ohio State University, B.A., 1959; The Ohio State University Moritz College of Law, J.D., 1962 — Phi Delta Phi — Admitted to Bar, 1962, Ohio — Member American, Ohio State and Columbus Bar Associations; Federation of Insurance and Corporate Counsel

The following firms also service this area.

Ritter, Robinson, McCready & James, Ltd.
1850 National City Bank Building
405 Madison Avenue
Toledo, Ohio 43604-1294
   Telephone: 419-241-3213
   Fax: 419-241-4925

Insurance Defense, Trial and Appellate Practice, Negligence, Product Liability, Premises Liability, Construction Defect, Animal Law, Arson, Insurance Fraud, Automobile Liability, Bad Faith, Truck Liability, Insurance Coverage, Employment Law, Subrogation, Municipal Law

SEE COMPLETE LISTING UNDER TOLEDO, OHIO (143 MILES)

DAYTON † 14,1527 Montgomery Co.

Freund, Freeze & Arnold, A Legal Professional Association

One South Main Street - Suite 1800
Dayton, Ohio 45402-2017
   Telephone: 937-222-2424
   Fax: 937-222-5369
   Toll Free: 877-FFA-1LAW
   E-Mail: ffalawda@ffalaw.com
   www.ffalaw.com

(Cincinnati, OH Office*: Fourth and Walnut Centre, 105 East Fourth Street, Suite 1400, 45202-4035)
   (Tel: 513-665-3500)
   (Tel: 877-FFA-1LAW)
   (E-Mail: ffalawci@ffalaw.com)
(Columbus, OH Office*: Capital Square Office Building, 65 East State Street, Suite 800, 43215-4247)
   (Tel: 614-827-7300)
   (Tel: 877-FFA-1LAW)
   (E-Mail: ffalawco@ffalaw.com)
(Ft Mitchell, KY Office*(See Fort Mitchell listing): Chamber Office Park, 2400 Chamber Center Drive, Suite 200, 41017)
   (Tel: 859-292-2088)
   (Toll Free: 877-FFA-1LAW)
   (E-Mail: ffalawky@ffalaw.com)
   (www.ffalawky.com)

Established: 1984

Product Liability, Professional Malpractice, Life and Health, Automobile, Bodily Injury, Errors and Omissions, Property Damage, Bad Faith, Insurance Coverage

Firm Profile: Freund, Freeze & Arnold's strength is grounded in more than 50 attorneys and legal professionals, who bring diverse backgrounds, deep experience and expertise in business, commercial, government, medical,

OHIO   DAYTON

Freund, Freeze & Arnold, A Legal Professional Association, Dayton, OH   (Continued)

insurance, employment, environmental, construction and other litigation-related matters.

Insurance Clients

Auto-Owners Insurance Company
CNA Insurance Company
Farmers Insurance Group
The Hartford
Kemper Insurance Companies
Liberty Mutual Group
MetLife Auto & Home
Ohio Mutual Insurance Group
Safeco Insurance
Shelby/Vesta Insurance Companies
Superior Insurance Company
Cincinnati Insurance Company
Erie Insurance Company
Gallagher Bassett Services, Inc.
Indiana Insurance Company
Leader Insurance Company
The Medical Protective Company
OHIC Insurance Company
Royal & SunAlliance USA
The St. Paul Companies
State Auto Insurance Company

Non-Insurance Clients

The Children's Medical Center
Dayton Power and Light Company
Miami Valley Hospital
City of Dayton
Good Samaritan Hospital
University of Cincinnati

Firm Members

Stephen V. Freeze — Case Western Reserve University, J.D., 1974 — Admitted to Bar, 1974, Ohio; 1991, Kentucky — Member Ohio State, Butler County and Dayton Bar Associations; Ohio Association of Civil Trial Attorneys (Vice-President, 2004-2005, President, 2006)

Kevin C. Connell — West Virginia University, J.D., 1994 — Admitted to Bar, 1994, Ohio

Green & Green, Lawyers

109 North Main Street
800 Performance Place
Dayton, Ohio 45402-1290
   Telephone: 937-224-3333
   Fax: 937-224-4311
   E-Mail: info@green-law.com
   www.green-law.com

Established: 1976

Casualty, Product Liability, Malpractice, Surety, Fire, Life Insurance, Accident and Health, Toxic Torts, Trial and Appellate Practice, State and Federal Courts, Specialty Insurance and Defense Practice

Firm Profile: Green & Green, Lawyers located in Dayton Ohio is a leading provider of general and complex multi-party litigation services in Southern Ohio and Northern Kentucky. We focus on commercial litigation, personal injury and property damage litigation as well as civil rights, labor relations, insurance and employment issues. Our clients include individuals, businesses and municipalities as both plaintiffs and defendants.

Green & Green attorneys regularly appear in the state and federal trial appellate courts of our practice area. Green & Green, Lawyers assists clients in the following areas: auto accidents, civil rights litigation, commercial litigation, employment, insurance, labor relations, medical malpractice, municipal liability litigation.

Insurance Clients

Auto-Owners Group
Cincinnati Insurance Company
Frankenmuth Mutual Insurance Company
Zurich American Insurance Company
Celina Mutual Insurance Company
Empire Insurance Group
Liberty Mutual Insurance Company
Midwest Insurance Company

Firm Members

F. Thomas Green — (1923-1998)

Thomas M. Green — 1951 — Kenyon College, A.B., 1973; The Ohio State University, J.D., 1976 — Admitted to Bar, 1976, Ohio — Member American, Ohio State and Dayton Bar Associations; Ohio Academy of Trial Lawyers; International Association of Defense Counsel; Ohio Association of Civil

Green & Green, Lawyers, Dayton, OH   (Continued)

Trial Attorneys; American Trial Lawyers Association; Defense Research Institute — Reported Cases: McClain v. Northwest Cmty. Corr. Ctr. Judicial Corr. Bd., No. 05-3154, U.S. Ct. App. 6th Cir., 06a008p.06, 440 F.3d 320; 2006 U.S. App. LEXIS 5570; FED App. 0086P (6th Cir.); 97 Fair Empl. Prac. Cas. (BNA) 1148, February 2, 2006; Cantrell v. GAF Corp., Nos. 89-3221/3231, U.S. Ct. App. 6th Cir., 999 F.2d 1007; 1993 U.S. App. LEXIS 18806; 26 Fed. R. Serv. 3d (Callaghan) 608; CCH Prod. Liab. Rep. P13,580, June 10, 1993; Greyhound Food Management, Inc. v. Dayton, No. 87-3396, U.S. Ct. App. 6th Cir., 852 F.2d 866; 1988 U.S. App. LEXIS 10025, March 18, 1988; Yung v. Raymark Industries, Inc., No. 85-3301, U.S. Ct. App. 6th Cir., 789 F.2d 397; 1986 U.S. App. LEXIS 24717; 4 Fed. R. Serv. 3d (Callaghan); CCH Prod. Liab. Rep. P10,976, February 6, 1986; Lynch v. Johns-Manville Sales Corp., Nos. 83-3118, 83-3119, 83-3120, 83-3121, 83-3122, 83-3123, 83-3124, 83-3125, 83-3126, 83-3127, U.S. Ct. App. 6th Cir., 710 F.2d 1194; 1983 U.S. App. LEXIS 26148; Bankr. L. Rep. (CCH) P69,317; 8 Collier Bankr. Cas. 2d (MB) 1301; 10 Bankr. Ct. Dec. 1282, May 24, 1983; Lynch v. Johns-Manville Sales Corp., Nos. 82-8413, 83-8418, 82-8426, 82-8428, 82-8429, 82-8430, 82-8431, 82-8432, 82-8435, U.S. Ct. App. 6th Cir., 701 F.2d 42; 1983 U.S. App. LEXIS 30295, February 22, 1983; Lynch v. Johns-Manvill Sales Corp., No. 82-3724, U.S. Ct. App. 6th Cir., 701 F.2d 44; 1983 U.S. App. LEXIS 30297, February 22, 1983 — E-mail: tmgreen@green-law.com

Peter F. von Meister — 1947 — Knox College, B.A., 1969; University of Cincinnati, J.D., 1972 — Admitted to Bar, 1972, Ohio — Member American, Ohio State and Dayton Bar Associations; District of Columbia Bar; Virginia State Bar; Virginia Trial Lawyers Association — E-mail: pfvmeister@green-law.com

Jane M. Lynch — 1955 — Wright State University, B.A., 1979; University of Dayton, J.D. (cum laude), 1982 — Admitted to Bar, 1982, Ohio — Member American, Ohio State and Dayton Bar Associations; Defense Research Institute; Ohio Association of Civil Trial Attorneys — E-mail: jmlynch@green-law.com

Erin B. Moore — 1968 — Indiana University, B.A. (with high distinction), 1989; The Ohio State University, J.D. (with honors), 1993 — Admitted to Bar, 1993, Ohio — Member American, Ohio State, Toledo and Dayton Bar Associations — E-mail: ebmoore@green-law.com

Jared A. Wagner — 1978 — Ohio Northern University, B.A. (with high distinction), 2000; College of William & Mary, J.D., 2003 — Admitted to Bar, 2003, Ohio — Member Ohio State and Dayton Bar Associations — E-mail: jawagner@green-law.com

Associate

Robert W. Young — 1968 — The Ohio State University, B.A., 1992; Capital University, J.D., 1995 — Admitted to Bar, 1995, Ohio — Member Ohio State and Dayton Bar Associations — E-mail: rwyoung@green-law.com

Young & Alexander Co., L.P.A.

130 West Second Street, Suite 1500
Dayton, Ohio 45402
   Telephone: 937-224-9291
   Fax: 937-224-8977
   E-Mail: cklipfer@yandalaw.com
   www.yandalaw.com

(Cincinnati, OH Office: One Sheakley Way, Suite 125, 45246)
   (Tel: 513-326-5555)
   (Fax: 513-326-5550)

Personal Injury, Fire, Product Liability, Professional Liability, Fraud, Property Damage, Coverage Issues, Uninsured and Underinsured Motorist, Construction Claims, Homeowners, Automobile, Premises Liability, Employment Law, Appellate Practice, Toxic Torts, Asbestos, Mold Litigation, Subrogation

Firm Profile: Y&A defends self-insured companies and insurance companies against liability and coverage claims in state and federal courts. We conduct arbitrations, mediations, and provide timely research and opinion letters. We litigate in Ohio, Indiana and Kentucky, and all federal courts in those States.

Insurance Clients

Central Mutual Insurance Company
State Farm Insurance Company

HAMILTON   OHIO

Young & Alexander Co., L.P.A., Dayton, OH (Continued)

Firm Members

Steven O. Dean — Ohio Northern University, B.A. (with high distinction), 1980; J.D. (with high distinction), 1983 — Admitted to Bar, 1983, Ohio — Member American, Ohio State and Dayton Bar Associations; National Society of Professional Insurance Investigators; Ohio Association of Civil Trial Attorneys — E-mail: sdean@yandalaw.com

Thomas P. Erven — Miami University, B.A. (cum laude), 1980; The Ohio State University, J.D., 1983 — Admitted to Bar, 1983, Ohio; 1997, Kentucky; 1983, U.S. District Court, Southern District of Ohio; 1997, U.S. District Court, Northern District of Ohio — Member Butler County Bar Association (Co-Chair, Civil Litigation Committee; Member, ADR Committee); Ohio Association of Civil Trial Attorneys (Board of Directors; Chairperson, ADR Committee); Defense Research Institute — E-mail: terven@yandalaw.com

Jonathon L. Beck — Marquette University, B.A., 1999; University of Dayton, J.D., 2002 — Admitted to Bar, 2002, Florida; 2003, Ohio; U.S. District Court, Southern District of Ohio; 2004, U.S. District Court, Northern District of Ohio; 2005, U.S. Court of Appeals, Sixth Circuit — Member Ohio State and Dayton (Chairman, Attorney Grievance and Discipline Committee) Bar Associations; The Florida Bar; National Association of Subrogation Professionals; Ohio Association of Civil Trial Attorneys — 2010 Outstanding Young Lawyer Award, Ohio Association of Civil Trial Attorneys; 2014 Super Lawyer (Litigation); Martindale Hubbel AV Rated — E-mail: jbeck@yandalaw.com

Associates

Natalie M. E. Wais   Michael V. Porter

The following firms also service this area.

Ritter, Robinson, McCready & James, Ltd.
1850 National City Bank Building
405 Madison Avenue
Toledo, Ohio 43604-1294
   Telephone: 419-241-3213
   Fax: 419-241-4925

Insurance Defense, Trial and Appellate Practice, Negligence, Product Liability, Premises Liability, Construction Defect, Animal Law, Arson, Insurance Fraud, Automobile Liability, Bad Faith, Truck Liability, Insurance Coverage, Employment Law, Subrogation, Municipal Law

SEE COMPLETE LISTING UNDER TOLEDO, OHIO (149 MILES)

DELAWARE † 34,753 Delaware Co.

Refer To

Mazanec, Raskin & Ryder Co., L.P.A.
175 South 3rd Street, Suite 1000
Columbus, Ohio 43215
   Telephone: 614-228-5931
   Fax: 614-228-5934

Insurance Defense, Automobile, Commercial Law, Product Liability, Property and Casualty, Medical Malpractice, Professional Malpractice, Dram Shop, Municipal Liability, Public Officials Liability, Law Enforcement Liability, Civil Rights, Fidelity and Surety, Environmental Law, Toxic Torts, General Practice

SEE COMPLETE LISTING UNDER COLUMBUS, OHIO (25 MILES)

EATON † 8,407 Preble Co.

Refer To

Green & Green, Lawyers
109 North Main Street
800 Performance Place
Dayton, Ohio 45402-1290
   Telephone: 937-224-3333
   Fax: 937-224-4311

Casualty, Product Liability, Malpractice, Surety, Fire, Life Insurance, Accident and Health, Toxic Torts, Trial and Appellate Practice, State and Federal Courts, Specialty Insurance and Defense Practice

SEE COMPLETE LISTING UNDER DAYTON, OHIO (25 MILES)

ELYRIA † 54,533 Lorain Co.

Refer To

Roderick Linton Belfance, LLP
50 South Main Street, Suite 10
Akron, Ohio 44308-1828
   Telephone: 330-434-3000
   Fax: 330-434-9220

Insurance Defense, Trial Practice, Legal Malpractice, Medical Malpractice, Product Liability, Professional Liability, Toxic Torts, Property Damage, Bodily Injury, Errors and Omissions, Life Insurance, Coverage Issues

SEE COMPLETE LISTING UNDER AKRON, OHIO (52 MILES)

GALLIPOLIS † 3,641 Gallia Co.

Refer To

Jenkins Fenstermaker, PLLC
325 8th Street
Huntington, West Virginia 25701
   Telephone: 304-523-2100
   Fax: 304-523-2347, 304-523-9279
   Toll Free: 800-982-3476

Mailing Address: P.O. Box 2688, Huntington, WV 25726

Civil Litigation, State and Federal Courts, Mediation, Arbitration, Trial Practice, Appellate Practice, Commercial Litigation, Personal Injury, Product Liability, Medical Malpractice, Professional Malpractice, Toxic Torts, Construction Litigation, Insurance Defense, Insurance Coverage, ERISA, Workers' Compensation, Employment Law, Administrative Law, Labor and Employment Law, Automobile Warranty, Labor Negotiations, Counseling, Warranty Litigation

SEE COMPLETE LISTING UNDER HUNTINGTON, WEST VIRGINIA (45 MILES)

GREENVILLE † 13,227 Darke Co.

Refer To

Green & Green, Lawyers
109 North Main Street
800 Performance Place
Dayton, Ohio 45402-1290
   Telephone: 937-224-3333
   Fax: 937-224-4311

Casualty, Product Liability, Malpractice, Surety, Fire, Life Insurance, Accident and Health, Toxic Torts, Trial and Appellate Practice, State and Federal Courts, Specialty Insurance and Defense Practice

SEE COMPLETE LISTING UNDER DAYTON, OHIO (37 MILES)

HAMILTON † 62,477 Butler Co.

McGowan & Jacobs, LLC

246 High Street
Hamilton, Ohio 45011
   Telephone: 513-844-2000
   Fax: 513-868-1190
   E-Mail: MichaelJacobs@jcmcgowan.com
   www.mcgowanandjacobs.com

Appellate Practice, Architects and Engineers, Automobile Liability, Civil Rights, Construction Law, Coverage Issues, Dental Malpractice, Errors and Omissions, Fire Loss, Insurance Defense, Governmental Liability, Insurance Fraud, Intellectual Property, Medical Devices, Medical Malpractice, Personal Injury, Product Liability, Professional Malpractice, Property and Casualty, School Law, Special Investigative Unit Claims, Trial Practice

Insurance Clients

Allstate Indemnity Company
Everest National Insurance Company
Indiana Insurance Company
The Medical Protective Company
Personal Service Insurance Company
Cincinnati Equitable Insurance Company
Globe American Casualty Company
Ohio Bar Liability Insurance Company
Safe Auto Insurance Company

OHIO

McGowan & Jacobs, LLC, Hamilton, OH (Continued)

State Automobile Mutual Insurance Company

Zurich American Insurance Company

Non-Insurance Clients

CORSA

Members

Jack C. McGowan — Miami University; University of Cincinnati, B.S.M.E., 1970; The George Washington University Law School, J.D. (cum laude), 1974 — Pi Tau Sigma — Admitted to Bar, 1974, Ohio; 1975, U.S. District Court, Southern District of Ohio; 1978, U.S. Supreme Court — Member Ohio State Bar Association; Defense Research Institute; Ohio Association of Civil Trial Attorneys; American Board of Trial Advocates — E-mail: jcm@jcmcgowan.com

Michael E. Jacobs — University of Cincinnati, B.Arch., 1993; Southwestern University School of Law, J.D., 1995 — Admitted to Bar, 1996, Kentucky; 1997, Ohio; 2001, Indiana — Member American Institute of Architects; National Society of Professional Insurance Investigators — E-mail: michaeljacobs@jcmcgowan.com

The following firms also service this area.

Albert T. Brown, Jr.
13 East Court Street, Fourth Floor
Cincinnati, Ohio 45202-1156
Telephone: 513-621-2825
Fax: 513-621-2823
Toll Free: 877-621-2825

General Defense, Product Liability, Bonds, Fire, Aviation

SEE COMPLETE LISTING UNDER CINCINNATI, OHIO (22 MILES)

Green & Green, Lawyers
109 North Main Street
800 Performance Place
Dayton, Ohio 45402-1290
Telephone: 937-224-3333
Fax: 937-224-4311

Casualty, Product Liability, Malpractice, Surety, Fire, Life Insurance, Accident and Health, Toxic Torts, Trial and Appellate Practice, State and Federal Courts, Specialty Insurance and Defense Practice

SEE COMPLETE LISTING UNDER DAYTON, OHIO (37 MILES)

IRONTON † 11,129 Lawrence Co.

Refer To

Jenkins Fenstermaker, PLLC
325 8th Street
Huntington, West Virginia 25701
Telephone: 304-523-2100
Fax: 304-523-2347, 304-523-9279
Toll Free: 800-982-3476

Mailing Address: P.O. Box 2688, Huntington, WV 25726

Civil Litigation, State and Federal Courts, Mediation, Arbitration, Trial Practice, Appellate Practice, Commercial Litigation, Personal Injury, Product Liability, Medical Malpractice, Professional Malpractice, Toxic Torts, Construction Litigation, Insurance Defense, Insurance Coverage, ERISA, Workers' Compensation, Employment Law, Administrative Law, Labor and Employment Law, Automobile Warranty, Labor Negotiations, Counseling, Warranty Litigation

SEE COMPLETE LISTING UNDER HUNTINGTON, WEST VIRGINIA (20 MILES)

LANCASTER † 38,780 Fairfield Co.

Refer To

Mazanec, Raskin & Ryder Co., L.P.A.
175 South 3rd Street, Suite 1000
Columbus, Ohio 43215
Telephone: 614-228-5931
Fax: 614-228-5934

Insurance Defense, Automobile, Commercial Law, Product Liability, Property and Casualty, Medical Malpractice, Professional Malpractice, Dram Shop, Municipal Liability, Public Officials Liability, Law Enforcement Liability, Civil Rights, Fidelity and Surety, Environmental Law, Toxic Torts, General Practice

SEE COMPLETE LISTING UNDER COLUMBUS, OHIO (20 MILES)

LEBANON † 20,033 Warren Co.

Refer To

Albert T. Brown, Jr.
13 East Court Street, Fourth Floor
Cincinnati, Ohio 45202-1156
Telephone: 513-621-2825
Fax: 513-621-2823
Toll Free: 877-621-2825

General Defense, Product Liability, Bonds, Fire, Aviation

SEE COMPLETE LISTING UNDER CINCINNATI, OHIO (31 MILES)

Refer To

Green & Green, Lawyers
109 North Main Street
800 Performance Place
Dayton, Ohio 45402-1290
Telephone: 937-224-3333
Fax: 937-224-4311

Casualty, Product Liability, Malpractice, Surety, Fire, Life Insurance, Accident and Health, Toxic Torts, Trial and Appellate Practice, State and Federal Courts, Specialty Insurance and Defense Practice

SEE COMPLETE LISTING UNDER DAYTON, OHIO (26 MILES)

LIMA † 38,771 Allen Co.

Refer To

Ritter, Robinson, McCready & James, Ltd.
1850 National City Bank Building
405 Madison Avenue
Toledo, Ohio 43604-1294
Telephone: 419-241-3213
Fax: 419-241-4925

Insurance Defense, Trial and Appellate Practice, Negligence, Product Liability, Premises Liability, Construction Defect, Animal Law, Arson, Insurance Fraud, Automobile Liability, Bad Faith, Truck Liability, Insurance Coverage, Employment Law, Subrogation, Municipal Law

SEE COMPLETE LISTING UNDER TOLEDO, OHIO (77 MILES)

LISBON † 2,821 Columbiana Co.

Refer To

Baker, Dublikar, Beck, Wiley & Mathews
400 South Main Street
North Canton, Ohio 44720
Telephone: 330-499-6000
Fax: 330-499-6423

Insurance Defense, Trial Practice, Governmental Liability, Professional Liability, Product Liability, Automobile Liability, Negligence, Casualty, Property Damage, Errors and Omissions

SEE COMPLETE LISTING UNDER CANTON, OHIO (46 MILES)

SPRINGFIELD   OHIO

LORAIN   64,097 Lorain Co.
Refer To
Mazanec, Raskin & Ryder Co., L.P.A.
100 Franklin's Row
34305 Solon Road
Cleveland, Ohio 44139
   Telephone: 440-248-7906
   Fax: 440-248-8861

Insurance Defense, Automobile, Commercial Law, Product Liability, Property and Casualty, Medical Malpractice, Professional Malpractice, Dram Shop, Municipal Liability, Public Officials Liability, Law Enforcement Liability, Civil Rights, Fidelity and Surety, Environmental Law, Toxic Torts, General Practice

SEE COMPLETE LISTING UNDER CLEVELAND, OHIO (28 MILES)

MANSFIELD   † 47,821 Richland Co.
Refer To
Carr Law Office, LLC
5824 Akron-Cleveland Road, Suite A
Hudson, Ohio 44236
   Telephone: 330-655-1662
   Fax: 330-653-5469

Insurance Coverage, Insurance Defense, Bad Faith, Bodily Injury, Wrongful Death, Civil Litigation, Appeals, Advertising Injury, Appellate, Appellate Advocacy, Appellate Practice, Automobile, Automobile Liability, Automobile Tort, Breach of Contract, Business Litigation, Casualty, Casualty Defense, Casualty Insurance Law, Catastrophic Injury, Civil Defense, Civil Trial Practice, Class Actions, Commercial and Personal Lines, Commercial General Liability, Commercial Insurance, Commercial Law, Commercial Liability, Commercial Lines, Commercial Litigation, Commercial Vehicle, Comprehensive General Liability, Consumer Law, Contract Disputes, Coverage Analysis, Coverage Issues, Declaratory Judgments, Defense Litigation, Errors and Omissions, Examinations Under Oath, Excess, Excess and Reinsurance, Excess and Umbrella, Extra-Contractual Liability, Extra-Contractual Litigation, Fraud, General Civil Trial and Appellate Practice, Homeowners, Insurance Agents, Insurance Claim Analysis and Evaluation, Insurance Coverage Determination, Insurance Coverage Litigation, Insurance Fraud, Insurance Law, Insurance Litigation, Legal, Legal Malpractice, Litigation, Malpractice, Motor Vehicle, Negligence, Non-Subscriber Litigation and Defense, Opinions, Personal and Commercial Vehicle, Personal Injury, Personal Liability, Personal Lines, Policy Construction and Interpretation, Premises Liability, Primary and Excess Insurance, Product Liability, Professional Errors and Omissions, Professional Liability, Professional Liability (Non-Medical) Defense, Professional Malpractice, Professional Negligence, Property, Property and Casualty, Property Damage, Property Defense, Property Liability, Property Loss, Real Estate Errors and Omissions, Real Estate Litigation, Restaurant Liability, Retail Liability, Risk Management, Self-Insured, Self-Insured Defense, Slip and Fall, State and Federal Courts, Tort, Tort Liability, Tort Litigation, Trial and Appellate Practice, Trial Practice, Underwriting, Uninsured and Underinsured Motorist

SEE COMPLETE LISTING UNDER AKRON, OHIO (72 MILES)

Refer To
Ritter, Robinson, McCready & James, Ltd.
1850 National City Bank Building
405 Madison Avenue
Toledo, Ohio 43604-1294
   Telephone: 419-241-3213
   Fax: 419-241-4925

Insurance Defense, Trial and Appellate Practice, Negligence, Product Liability, Premises Liability, Construction Defect, Animal Law, Arson, Insurance Fraud, Automobile Liability, Bad Faith, Truck Liability, Insurance Coverage, Employment Law, Subrogation, Municipal Law

SEE COMPLETE LISTING UNDER TOLEDO, OHIO (105 MILES)

MEDINA   † 26,678 Medina Co.
Refer To
Mazanec, Raskin & Ryder Co., L.P.A.
100 Franklin's Row
34305 Solon Road
Cleveland, Ohio 44139
   Telephone: 440-248-7906
   Fax: 440-248-8861

Insurance Defense, Automobile, Commercial Law, Product Liability, Property and Casualty, Medical Malpractice, Professional Malpractice, Dram Shop, Municipal Liability, Public Officials Liability, Law Enforcement Liability, Civil Rights, Fidelity and Surety, Environmental Law, Toxic Torts, General Practice

SEE COMPLETE LISTING UNDER CLEVELAND, OHIO (29 MILES)

Refer To
Roderick Linton Belfance, LLP
50 South Main Street, Suite 10
Akron, Ohio 44308-1828
   Telephone: 330-434-3000
   Fax: 330-434-9220

Insurance Defense, Trial Practice, Legal Malpractice, Medical Malpractice, Product Liability, Professional Liability, Toxic Torts, Property Damage, Bodily Injury, Errors and Omissions, Life Insurance, Coverage Issues

SEE COMPLETE LISTING UNDER AKRON, OHIO (22 MILES)

NEW PHILADELPHIA   † 17,288 Tuscarawas Co.
Refer To
Baker, Dublikar, Beck, Wiley & Mathews
400 South Main Street
North Canton, Ohio 44720
   Telephone: 330-499-6000
   Fax: 330-499-6423

Insurance Defense, Trial Practice, Governmental Liability, Professional Liability, Product Liability, Automobile Liability, Negligence, Casualty, Property Damage, Errors and Omissions

SEE COMPLETE LISTING UNDER CANTON, OHIO (35 MILES)

NEWARK   † 47,573 Licking Co.
Refer To
Mazanec, Raskin & Ryder Co., L.P.A.
175 South 3rd Street, Suite 1000
Columbus, Ohio 43215
   Telephone: 614-228-5931
   Fax: 614-228-5934

Insurance Defense, Automobile, Commercial Law, Product Liability, Property and Casualty, Medical Malpractice, Professional Malpractice, Dram Shop, Municipal Liability, Public Officials Liability, Law Enforcement Liability, Civil Rights, Fidelity and Surety, Environmental Law, Toxic Torts, General Practice

SEE COMPLETE LISTING UNDER COLUMBUS, OHIO (25 MILES)

RAVENNA   † 11,724 Portage Co.
Refer To
Roderick Linton Belfance, LLP
50 South Main Street, Suite 10
Akron, Ohio 44308-1828
   Telephone: 330-434-3000
   Fax: 330-434-9220

Insurance Defense, Trial Practice, Legal Malpractice, Medical Malpractice, Product Liability, Professional Liability, Toxic Torts, Property Damage, Bodily Injury, Errors and Omissions, Life Insurance, Coverage Issues

SEE COMPLETE LISTING UNDER AKRON, OHIO (20 MILES)

SPRINGFIELD   † 60,608 Clark Co.
Refer To
Green & Green, Lawyers
109 North Main Street
800 Performance Place
Dayton, Ohio 45402-1290
   Telephone: 937-224-3333
   Fax: 937-224-4311

Casualty, Product Liability, Malpractice, Surety, Fire, Life Insurance, Accident and Health, Toxic Torts, Trial and Appellate Practice, State and Federal Courts, Specialty Insurance and Defense Practice

SEE COMPLETE LISTING UNDER DAYTON, OHIO (25 MILES)

OHIO

ST. CLAIRSVILLE † 5,184 Belmont Co.

Refer To

McDermott & Bonenberger, P.L.L.C.
53 Washington Avenue
Wheeling, West Virginia 26003
Telephone: 304-242-3220
Fax: 304-242-2907

Insurance Defense, Bad Faith, Litigation, Complex Litigation
SEE COMPLETE LISTING UNDER WHEELING, WEST VIRGINIA (11 MILES)

STEUBENVILLE † 18,659 Jefferson Co.

Dickie, McCamey & Chilcote, P.C.

401 Market Street, Suite 401
Steubenville, Ohio 43952-2846
Telephone: 740-284-1682
Fax: 888-811-7144
Toll Free: 888-277-3518
E-Mail: info@dmclaw.com
www.dmclaw.com

(Additional Offices: Pittsburgh, PA*; Charlotte, NC*; Cleveland, OH*; Columbus, OH*; Haddonfield, NJ*; Camp Hill, PA*(See Harrisburg listing); Lancaster, SC*; Philadelphia, PA*; Cary, NC*(See Raleigh listing); Wheeling, WV*; Wilmington, DE*)

Asbestos Litigation, Bad Faith, Captive Company Matters, Casualty, Commercial Litigation, Energy, Labor and Employment, Excess and Reinsurance, Extra-Contractual Litigation, Insurance Agents, Insurance Coverage, Insurance Coverage Litigation, Legal Malpractice, Medical Malpractice, Medicare Set-Aside Practice, Municipal Liability, Nursing Home Liability, Product Liability, Professional Liability, Property and Casualty, Surety, Transportation, Trucking, Uninsured and Underinsured Motorist, Workers' Compensation

Shareholder

Melvin F. O'Brien — Branch Office Shareholder-in-Charge — Bowling Green State University, B.S.B.A., 1988; Cleveland-Marshall College of Law, J.D., 1994 — Admitted to Bar, 1994, Ohio; 1995, West Virginia — E-mail: mobrien@dmclaw.com

(See listing under Pittsburgh, PA for additional information)

TOLEDO † 287,208 Lucas Co.

Bahret & Associates Co., L.P.A.

7050 Spring Meadows West
Holland, Ohio 43528
Telephone: 419-861-7800
Fax: 419-861-7808
E-Mail: rbahret@bahret-law.com

Established: 1988

Civil Litigation, Insurance Defense, Subrogation, Automobile Liability, General Liability, Personal Injury, Bodily Injury, Property Damage, Errors and Omissions, Declaratory Judgments, Medical Malpractice, Defense Litigation, Fraud, Coverage Issues, Aviation

Insurance Clients

AIG Specialty Auto
AOPA Insurance Company
Auto-Owners Insurance Company
Century Surety Company
American Modern Home Insurance Company
Baldwin & Lyons, Inc.
Cincinnati Insurance Company

Bahret & Associates Co., L.P.A., Toledo, OH (Continued)

CNA Insurance Company
Frankenmuth Mutual Insurance Company
German Mutual Insurance Company
Lightning Rod Mutual Insurance Company
Motorists Mutual Insurance Company
Progressive Insurance Company
Specialty Risk Services, Inc. (SRS)
State Auto Insurance Company
U.S. Aviation Underwriters
Westfield Companies
Continental Western Insurance Company
General Casualty Insurance Company
Liberty Mutual Insurance Company
Michigan Millers Mutual Insurance Company
Permanent General Assurance Corporation
Selective Insurance Company of America
Titan Insurance Company
Western Reserve Group
Windsor Group

Non-Insurance Clients

GLA Water Management Company
Wylie & Sons Landscaping
Welded Construction, L.P.

Partner

Robert J. Bahret — 1953 — University of Cincinnati, B.A., 1975; The University of Toledo, J.D., 1979 — Admitted to Bar, 1980, Ohio; 1982, Michigan; U.S. District Court, Northern District of Ohio; U.S. Court of Appeals, Sixth Circuit — Member Ohio State and Toledo Bar Associations; State Bar of Michigan; Toledo Claims Association; Ohio Association of Civil Trial Attorneys; Defense Research Institute — Board Certified Civil Trial Specialist by National Board of Trial Advocacy — Practice Areas: Civil Litigation; Insurance Defense; Aviation — E-mail: rbahret@bahret-law.com

Associates

Andrew J. Ayers — 1952 — Hillsdale College, B.A., 1975; The University of Toledo, J.D., 1978 — Admitted to Bar, 1979, Ohio; U.S. District Court, Northern District of Ohio; U.S. Court of Appeals, Sixth Circuit — Member American, Ohio State and Toledo Bar Associations; Ohio Association of Civil Trial Attorneys; Defense Research Institute — Practice Areas: Civil Litigation; Personal Injury; Insurance Defense; Corporate Law — E-mail: aayers@bahret-law.com

Christine M. Gaynor — 1967 — The University of Toledo, B.S., 1990; Louisiana State University, J.D., 1994 — Admitted to Bar, 1996, Ohio; U.S. District Court, Northern District of Ohio — Member Toledo Bar Association — Practice Areas: Civil Litigation; Insurance Defense; Personal Injury — E-mail: cgaynor@bahret-law.com

Paralegal

Denise M. Schmidt

Ritter, Robinson, McCready & James, Ltd.

1850 National City Bank Building
405 Madison Avenue
Toledo, Ohio 43604-1294
Telephone: 419-241-3213
Fax: 419-241-4925
E-Mail: james@rrmj.com
www.rrmjlaw.com

Insurance Defense, Trial and Appellate Practice, Negligence, Product Liability, Premises Liability, Construction Defect, Animal Law, Arson, Insurance Fraud, Automobile Liability, Bad Faith, Truck Liability, Insurance Coverage, Employment Law, Subrogation, Municipal Law

Insurance Clients

ACUITY
Celina Insurance Group
EMC Insurance Company
Safe Auto Insurance Company
State Farm Insurance Company
Westfield Insurance Company
Auto-Owners Insurance Company
Cincinnati Insurance Company
Gallagher Bassett Services, Inc.
State Auto Insurance Companies
United Ohio Insurance Company

Partners

Timothy C. James — 1954 — Miami University, B.A. (cum laude), 1977; The Ohio State University, J.D. (Phi Beta Kappa), 1980 — Admitted to Bar, 1980, Ohio; 1981, U.S. District Court, Northern District of Ohio — Member American, Ohio State and Toledo Bar Associations; Ohio Association of Civil Trial

Ritter, Robinson, McCready & James, Ltd., Toledo, OH (Continued)

Attorneys; Defense Research Institute — Legal Seminar Instructor on Civil Litigation and Trial Practice

Mark P. Seitzinger — 1963 — Kent State University, B.A. (summa cum laude), 1985; The Ohio State University, J.D. (Phi Beta Kappa), 1988 — Admitted to Bar, 1989, Ohio; 1990, U.S. District Court, Northern District of Ohio — Member Ohio State and Toledo Bar Associations; Ohio Association of Civil Trial Attorneys

Associates

Shannon Julienne George — 1970 — Hillsdale College, B.A. (cum laude), 1980; The University of Toledo, J.D., 1993; M.A., 1995 — Admitted to Bar, 1994, Michigan; 1997, Ohio — Member Ohio State and Toledo Bar Associations; State Bar of Michigan — Instructor, Department of Philosophy, University of Toledo (1995-1996)

Van P. Andres — 1963 — The Ohio State University, B.A., 1985; The University of Toledo, J.D., 1988 — Admitted to Bar, 1989, Ohio; 1990, U.S. District Court, Northern District of Ohio — Member Ohio State and Toledo Bar Associations

Lorri J. Britsch — Millikin University, B.A., 1993; Capital University, J.D., 1996 — Admitted to Bar, 1997, Ohio — Member Ohio State and Toledo Bar Associations

Brad A. Everhardt — 1973 — Bowling Green State University, B.A., 1998; The University of Toledo, J.D., 2000 — Delta Theta Phi — Technical Editor, University of Toledo Law Review, 1999-2000 — Admitted to Bar, 2001, Ohio; Indiana; 2002, Michigan; U.S. District Court, Northern and Southern Districts of Indiana — Member Ohio State, Indiana State and LaGrange County (Vice-President) Bar Associations; State Bar of Michigan — Languages: Spanish

Law Offices of Ward, Anderson, Porritt & Bryant, PLC

5757 Park Center Court
Toledo, Ohio 43615
   Telephone: 419-841-7211
   Fax: 419-843-9850
   E-Mail: ohio@wardanderson.com
   www.wardanderson.com

(Bloomfield Hills, MI Office*: 4190 Telegraph Road, Suite 2300, 48302)
   (Tel: 248-593-1440)
   (Fax: 248-593-7920)
   (E-Mail: firm@wardanderson.com)

Established: 1991

Insurance Defense, Property and Casualty, Arson, Transportation, Liquor Liability, General Liability, Professional Malpractice, Errors and Omissions, Automobile, Product Liability, Discrimination, Coverage Issues, Truck Liability, Trucking Law

Resident Partner

Russell W. Porritt II

(See listing under Bloomfield Hills, MI for additional information)

TROY † 25,058 Miami Co.
Refer To

Green & Green, Lawyers
109 North Main Street
800 Performance Place
Dayton, Ohio 45402-1290
   Telephone: 937-224-3333
   Fax: 937-224-4311

Casualty, Product Liability, Malpractice, Surety, Fire, Life Insurance, Accident and Health, Toxic Torts, Trial and Appellate Practice, State and Federal Courts, Specialty Insurance and Defense Practice

SEE COMPLETE LISTING UNDER DAYTON, OHIO (22 MILES)

URBANA † 11,793 Champaign Co.
Refer To

Green & Green, Lawyers
109 North Main Street
800 Performance Place
Dayton, Ohio 45402-1290
   Telephone: 937-224-3333
   Fax: 937-224-4311

Casualty, Product Liability, Malpractice, Surety, Fire, Life Insurance, Accident and Health, Toxic Torts, Trial and Appellate Practice, State and Federal Courts, Specialty Insurance and Defense Practice

SEE COMPLETE LISTING UNDER DAYTON, OHIO (40 MILES)

WESTERVILLE 36,120 Delaware and Franklin Cos.

Alber Crafton, PSC

501 West Schrock Road, Suite 104
Westerville, Ohio 43081-3360
   Telephone: 614-890-5632
   Fax: 614-890-5638

(Prospect, KY Office*(See Louisville listing): 9418 Norton Commons Boulevard, Suite 200, 40059)
   (Tel: 502-815-5000)
   (Fax: 502-815-5005)
   (E-Mail: lhutchens@albercrafton.com)
   (www.albercrafton.com)
(Troy, MI Office*: 2301 West Big Beaver Road, Suite 300, 48084)
   (Tel: 248-822-6190)
   (Fax: 248-822-6191)
   (www.albercrafton.com)
(Oklahoma: P.O. Box 14517, Tulsa, OK, 74159)
   (Tel: 918-935-3459)

Fidelity and Surety, Insurance Defense, Investigations, Defense Litigation, Construction Law

(See listing under Louisville, KY for additional information)

WILMINGTON † 12,520 Clinton Co.
Refer To

Green & Green, Lawyers
109 North Main Street
800 Performance Place
Dayton, Ohio 45402-1290
   Telephone: 937-224-3333
   Fax: 937-224-4311

Casualty, Product Liability, Malpractice, Surety, Fire, Life Insurance, Accident and Health, Toxic Torts, Trial and Appellate Practice, State and Federal Courts, Specialty Insurance and Defense Practice

SEE COMPLETE LISTING UNDER DAYTON, OHIO (35 MILES)

WOOSTER † 26,119 Wayne Co.
Refer To

Baker, Dublikar, Beck, Wiley & Mathews
400 South Main Street
North Canton, Ohio 44720
   Telephone: 330-499-6000
   Fax: 330-499-6423

Insurance Defense, Trial Practice, Governmental Liability, Professional Liability, Product Liability, Automobile Liability, Negligence, Casualty, Property Damage, Errors and Omissions

SEE COMPLETE LISTING UNDER CANTON, OHIO (41 MILES)

OHIO

XENIA † 25,719 Greene Co.

Refer To

Green & Green, Lawyers
109 North Main Street
800 Performance Place
Dayton, Ohio 45402-1290
   Telephone: 937-224-3333
   Fax: 937-224-4311

Casualty, Product Liability, Malpractice, Surety, Fire, Life Insurance, Accident and Health, Toxic Torts, Trial and Appellate Practice, State and Federal Courts, Specialty Insurance and Defense Practice

SEE COMPLETE LISTING UNDER DAYTON, OHIO (18 MILES)

YOUNGSTOWN † 66,982 Mahoning Co.

Melnick & Melnick

PNC Building
16 Wick Avenue, Suite 504
Youngstown, Ohio 44503
   Telephone: 330-744-8973
   Fax: 330-744-0302
   E-Mail: AAMRRM@AOL.COM

Insurance Defense, Trial Practice, Subrogation, Civil Litigation, Appellate Practice

Insurance Clients

Brotherhood Mutual Insurance
   Company

Non-Insurance Clients

Ryder Truck Rental, Inc.

Partners

Arseny A. Melnick — (1925-2001)

Robert R. Melnick — 1956 — Ohio Northern University, Pettit College of Law, J.D., 1981 — Admitted to Bar, 1983, Ohio — Member Ohio State and Mahoning County Bar Associations — Judge Advocate General Corps Reserves, Lt. Colonel, USAR

XENIA

The following firms also service this area.

Carr Law Office, LLC
5824 Akron-Cleveland Road, Suite A
Hudson, Ohio 44236
   Telephone: 330-655-1662
   Fax: 330-653-5469

Insurance Coverage, Insurance Defense, Bad Faith, Bodily Injury, Wrongful Death, Civil Litigation, Appeals, Advertising Injury, Appellate, Appellate Advocacy, Appellate Practice, Automobile, Automobile Liability, Automobile Tort, Breach of Contract, Business Litigation, Casualty, Casualty Defense, Casualty Insurance Law, Catastrophic Injury, Civil Defense, Civil Trial Practice, Class Actions, Commercial and Personal Lines, Commercial General Liability, Commercial Insurance, Commercial Law, Commercial Liability, Commercial Lines, Commercial Litigation, Commercial Vehicle, Comprehensive General Liability, Consumer Law, Contract Disputes, Coverage Analysis, Coverage Issues, Declaratory Judgments, Defense Litigation, Errors and Omissions, Examinations Under Oath, Excess, Excess and Reinsurance, Excess and Umbrella, Extra-Contractual Liability, Extra-Contractual Litigation, Fraud, General Civil Trial and Appellate Practice, Homeowners, Insurance Agents, Insurance Claim Analysis and Evaluation, Insurance Coverage Determination, Insurance Coverage Litigation, Insurance Fraud, Insurance Law, Insurance Litigation, Legal, Legal Malpractice, Litigation, Malpractice, Motor Vehicle, Negligence, Non-Subscriber Litigation and Defense, Opinions, Personal and Commercial Vehicle, Personal Injury, Personal Liability, Personal Lines, Policy Construction and Interpretation, Premises Liability, Primary and Excess Insurance, Product Liability, Professional Errors and Omissions, Professional Liability, Professional Liability (Non-Medical) Defense, Professional Malpractice, Professional Negligence, Property, Property and Casualty, Property Damage, Property Defense, Property Liability, Property Loss, Real Estate Errors and Omissions, Real Estate Litigation, Restaurant Liability, Retail Liability, Risk Management, Self-Insured, Self-Insured Defense, Slip and Fall, State and Federal Courts, Tort, Tort Liability, Tort Litigation, Trial and Appellate Practice, Trial Practice, Underwriting, Uninsured and Underinsured Motorist

SEE COMPLETE LISTING UNDER AKRON, OHIO (49 MILES)

OKLAHOMA

CAPITAL: OKLAHOMA CITY

COUNTIES AND COUNTY SEATS

County	County Seat	County	County Seat	County	County Seat
Adair	Stilwell	Grant	Medford	Nowata	Nowata
Alfalfa	Cherokee	Greer	Mangum	Okfuskee	Okemah
Atoka	Atoka	Harmon	Hollis	Oklahoma	Oklahoma City
Beaver	Beaver	Harper	Buffalo	Okmulgee	Okmulgee
Beckham	Sayre	Haskell	Stigler	Osage	Pawhuska
Blaine	Watonga	Hughes	Holdenville	Ottawa	Miami
Bryan	Durant	Jackson	Altus	Pawnee	Pawnee
Caddo	Anadarko	Jefferson	Waurika	Payne	Stillwater
Canadian	El Reno	Johnston	Tishomingo	Pittsburg	McAlester
Carter	Ardmore	Kay	Newkirk	Pontotoc	Ada
Cherokee	Tahlequah	Kingfisher	Kingfisher	Pottawatomie	Shawnee
Choctaw	Hugo	Kiowa	Hobart	Pushmataha	Antlers
Cimarron	Boise City	Latimer	Wilburton	Roger Mills	Cheyenne
Cleveland	Norman	Le Flore	Poteau	Rogers	Claremore
Coal	Coalgate	Lincoln	Chandler	Seminole	Wewoka
Comanche	Lawton	Logan	Guthrie	Sequoyah	Sallisaw
Cotton	Walters	Love	Marietta	Stephens	Duncan
Craig	Vinita	Major	Fairview	Texas	Guymon
Creek	Sapulpa	Marshall	Madill	Tillman	Frederick
Custer	Arapaho	Mayes	Pryor	Tulsa	Tulsa
Delaware	Jay	McClain	Purcell	Wagoner	Wagoner
Dewey	Taloga	McCurtain	Idabel	Washington	Bartlesville
Ellis	Arnett	McIntosh	Eufaula	Washita	Cordell
Garfield	Enid	Murray	Sulphur	Woods	Alva
Garvin	Pauls Valley	Muskogee	Muskogee	Woodward	Woodward
Grady	Chickasha	Noble	Perry		

In the text that follows "†" indicates County Seats.

Our files contain additional verified data on the firms listed herein. This additional information is available on request.

A.M. BEST COMPANY

OKLAHOMA

ADA † 16,810 Pontotoc Co.

Refer To

Fischl, Culp, McMillin, Chaffin, Bahner & Long, L.L.P.
100 E Street, S.W.
Ardmore, Oklahoma 73401
   Telephone: 580-223-4321
   Fax: 580-226-4795

Mailing Address: P.O. Box 1766, Ardmore, OK 73402-1766

Insurance Defense, Trial Practice, Automobile, Product Liability, General Liability, Property and Casualty, Bad Faith

SEE COMPLETE LISTING UNDER ARDMORE, OKLAHOMA (70 MILES)

ARDMORE † 24,283 Carter Co.

Fischl, Culp, McMillin, Chaffin, Bahner & Long, L.L.P.
100 E Street, S.W.
Ardmore, Oklahoma 73401
   Telephone: 580-223-4321
   Fax: 580-226-4795
   E-Mail: bbahner@fischlculplaw.com

Established: 1952

Insurance Defense, Trial Practice, Automobile, Product Liability, General Liability, Property and Casualty, Bad Faith

Firm Profile: Fischl, Culp has been continuously listed in Best's Directory since 1955. We continue our tradition of zealously representing our clients.

Insurance Clients

Allstate Insurance Company
Employers Mutual Companies
Grain Dealers Mutual Insurance Company
NAU Country Insurance Company
Oklahoma Property and Casualty Insurance Company
Worldwide Insurance Group
Charter Insurance Group
Federated Mutual Insurance Company
National American Insurance Company
Shelter Insurance Companies
United Services Automobile Association (USAA)

Non-Insurance Clients

Elmbrook Properties, Inc.
Noble Energy, Inc.
Homeland Stores, Inc.

Partners

Louis A. Fischl — (1893-1973)

Joseph M. Culp — (1914-1997)

F. Lovell McMillin — (Retired)

Donald J. Chaffin — 1952 — Oklahoma State University, B.A., 1974; The University of Oklahoma, J.D., 1977 — Admitted to Bar, 1977, Oklahoma — Member Oklahoma and Carter County (President, 1979) Bar Associations; Oklahoma Association of Defense Counsel

S. Brent Bahner — 1957 — Baylor University, B.A., 1979; The University of Oklahoma, J.D., 1982 — Admitted to Bar, 1982, Oklahoma; 1982, U.S. District Court, Western District of Oklahoma; 1986, U.S. District Court, Eastern District of Oklahoma; 1998, U.S. District Court, Northern District of Oklahoma; 2001, U.S. District Court, Eastern District of Texas — Member Oklahoma and Carter County Bar Associations; Oklahoma Association of Defense Counsel (Board of Directors, 1988-1994, 2001-present); American Board of Trial Advocates (Associate); Association of Defense Trial Attorneys; Defense Research Institute

Robert D. Long — 1952 — The University of Oklahoma, B.S., 1974; J.D., 1978 — Admitted to Bar, 1978, Oklahoma — Member Oklahoma and Carter County Bar Associations

The following firms also service this area.

Frailey, Chaffin, Cordell, Perryman, Sterkel, McCalla & Brown, L.L.P.
201 North Fourth Street
Chickasha, Oklahoma 73023
   Telephone: 405-224-0237
   Fax: 405-222-2319

Mailing Address: P.O. Box 533, Chickasha, OK 73018

Administrative Law, Agriculture, Business Law, Civil Litigation, Commercial Transactions, Energy, Fire, Governmental Liability, Insurance Coverage, Insurance Defense, Municipal Law, Negligence, Oil and Gas, Premises Liability, Product Liability, Tort Litigation

SEE COMPLETE LISTING UNDER CHICKASHA, OKLAHOMA (91 MILES)

ATOKA † 3,107 Atoka Co.

Refer To

Fischl, Culp, McMillin, Chaffin, Bahner & Long, L.L.P.
100 E Street, S.W.
Ardmore, Oklahoma 73401
   Telephone: 580-223-4321
   Fax: 580-226-4795

Mailing Address: P.O. Box 1766, Ardmore, OK 73402-1766

Insurance Defense, Trial Practice, Automobile, Product Liability, General Liability, Property and Casualty, Bad Faith

SEE COMPLETE LISTING UNDER ARDMORE, OKLAHOMA (70 MILES)

CHICKASHA † 16,036 Grady Co.

Frailey, Chaffin, Cordell, Perryman, Sterkel, McCalla & Brown, L.L.P.
201 North Fourth Street
Chickasha, Oklahoma 73023
   Telephone: 405-224-0237
   Fax: 405-222-2319
   www.fccpsm.com
   E-Mail: jbrown@fccpsm.com

Administrative Law, Agriculture, Business Law, Civil Litigation, Commercial Transactions, Energy, Fire, Governmental Liability, Insurance Coverage, Insurance Defense, Municipal Law, Negligence, Oil and Gas, Premises Liability, Product Liability, Tort Litigation

Firm Profile: The insurance defense and subrogation attorneys at Frailey, Chaffin, Cordell, Perryman, Sterkel, McCalle & Brown LLP have years of experience providing legal representation to insurance companies' insureds in all types of tort litigation and coverage disputes in state and federal courts throughout Oklahoma.

Insurance Clients

Argonaut Insurance Company
Mid-Continent Casualty Company
Trident Insurance Company
Chubb Insurance Company
Music Insurance Company

Non-Insurance Clients

Masco Corporation
Oxy Inc.

Partners

F. Thomas Cordell, Jr. — 1954 — Oklahoma State University, B.A., 1972; University of Idaho College of Law, J.D., 1979 — Admitted to Bar, 1979, Oklahoma; U.S. District Court, Eastern and Western Districts of Oklahoma; 2009, U.S. District Court, Northern District of Oklahoma — Member American and Oklahoma Bar Associations; Federation of Defense and Corporate Counsel (President, 2010); Oklahoma Association of Defense Counsel (President, 1988) — Maurice Merrill Award (1982); Defense Research Institute Exceptional Performance Award (1988); Defense Research Institute State Chairman (1990-1994) — E-mail: tcordell@fccpsm.com

Jeromy E. Brown — Bethany College, B.A., 1994; Oklahoma City University School of Law, J.D. (cum laude), 1998 — Phi Delta Phi Honorary

EDMOND

Frailey, Chaffin, Cordell, Perryman, Sterkel, McCalla & Brown, L.L.P., Chickasha, OK (Continued)

Fraternity — Admitted to Bar, 1997, Oklahoma; U.S. District Court, Eastern, Northern and Western Districts of Oklahoma — Member American, Oklahoma and Grady County Bar Associations; Oklahoma Association of Defense Counsel (Vice-President, Chair of Oil & Gas Committee, 2007-Present); Defense Research Institute — E-mail: jbrown@fccpsm.com

Michael R. Chaffin — Southwestern University, B.S., 1969; The University of Oklahoma College of Law, J.D., 1971 — Admitted to Bar, 1972, Oklahoma; U.S. District Court, Eastern and Western Districts of Oklahoma; U.S. Court of Appeals, Tenth Circuit — Member American and Oklahoma Bar Associations; Oklahoma Association of Defense Counsel (Vice President, 1988) — Assistant District Attorney, Grady and Caddo Counties, 1972-1978; Assistant District Judge, Grady County, 1979 — E-mail: mchaffin@fccpsm.com

Associates

Kristan Bolding   Amy J. Stuart

(This firm is also listed in the Subrogation section of this directory)

DUNCAN † 23,431 Stephens Co.

Ellis, Buckholts & Hicks

Patterson Building
929 West Willow
Duncan, Oklahoma 73533-4921
   Telephone: 580-252-3240
   Fax: 580-252-9596
   E-Mail: elb@texhoma.net

Insurance Defense, Automobile, General Liability, Bodily Injury, Property Damage, Personal Injury, Commercial Liability

Insurance Clients

Clarendon National Insurance Company
Oklahoma Farmers Union Mutual Insurance Company
Equity Fire and Casualty Insurance Company
Republic Casualty Company
Scottsdale Insurance Company

Non-Insurance Clients

Silvey Companies

Partners

Thomas T. Ellis — 1950 — The University of Oklahoma, B.A., 1971; J.D., 1975 — Admitted to Bar, 1975, Oklahoma; 1975, U.S. District Court, Western District of Oklahoma — Member American, Oklahoma and Stephens County (President, 1981) Bar Associations; Oklahoma Association of Defense Counsel; Defense Research Institute

Phillip H. Leonard — 1939 — The University of Oklahoma, B.A., 1961; LL.B. 1963 — Admitted to Bar, 1963, Oklahoma; 1978, U.S. District Court, Western District of Oklahoma — Member Oklahoma and Stephens County Bar Associations

E. J. Buckholts II — 1952 — The University of Oklahoma, B.B.A., 1975; Oklahoma City University, J.D., 1979 — Admitted to Bar, 1979, Oklahoma — Member American, Oklahoma and Stephens County Bar Associations

The following firms also service this area.

Fischl, Culp, McMillin, Chaffin, Bahner & Long, L.L.P.

100 E Street, S.W.
Ardmore, Oklahoma 73401
   Telephone: 580-223-4321
   Fax: 580-226-4795
Mailing Address: P.O. Box 1766, Ardmore, OK 73402-1766

Insurance Defense, Trial Practice, Automobile, Product Liability, General Liability, Property and Casualty, Bad Faith

SEE COMPLETE LISTING UNDER ARDMORE, OKLAHOMA (70 MILES)

DURANT † 15,856 Bryan Co.

Refer To

Fischl, Culp, McMillin, Chaffin, Bahner & Long, L.L.P.

100 E Street, S.W.
Ardmore, Oklahoma 73401
   Telephone: 580-223-4321
   Fax: 580-226-4795
Mailing Address: P.O. Box 1766, Ardmore, OK 73402-1766

Insurance Defense, Trial Practice, Automobile, Product Liability, General Liability, Property and Casualty, Bad Faith

SEE COMPLETE LISTING UNDER ARDMORE, OKLAHOMA (50 MILES)

EDMOND 81,405 Oklahoma Co.

Nelson Terry Morton DeWitt Paruolo & Wood

3540 South Boulevard, Suite 300
Edmond, Oklahoma 73013
   Telephone: 405-705-3600
   Fax: 405-705-2573
   E-Mail: Tom@ntmdlaw.com
   www.ntmdlaw.com

Accident, Alternative Dispute Resolution, Appellate Practice, Arbitration, Bad Faith, Bodily Injury, Breach of Contract, Business Law, Civil Litigation, Class Actions, Commercial and Personal Lines, Commercial Vehicle, Common Carrier, Complex Litigation, Construction Law, Consumer Law, Contractors Liability, Contracts, Coverage Analysis, Declaratory Judgments, Directors and Officers Liability, Excess, Extra-Contractual Litigation, Fire, First and Third Party Defense, Homeowners, Insurance Corporate Practice, Insurance Coverage, Insurance Law, Insurance Policy Enforcement, Legal Malpractice, Mediation, Medical Devices, Motor Carriers, Motor Vehicle, Negligence, Nursing Home Liability, Personal and Commercial Vehicle, Personal Injury, Personal Liability, Personal Lines, Policy Construction and Interpretation, Premises Liability, Product Liability, Professional Errors and Omissions, Professional Liability, Property, Slip and Fall, Tort Liability, Tort Litigation, Trial and Appellate Practice, Truck Liability, Uninsured and Underinsured Motorist, Wrongful Death

Firm Profile: Nelson Terry Morton DeWitt Paruolo & Wood has developed a broad base of experience in multiple areas of civil trial practice. Our attorneys have tried, mediated, arbitrated and otherwise resolved civil litigation matters for their clients throughout Oklahoma and other states.

Insurance Clients

Berkley Oil & Gas Specialty Services, LLC
Markel Insurance Company
Northland Insurance Company
Phoenix Insurance Company
St. Paul Fire and Marine Insurance Company
Catholic Mutual Insurance
Charter Oak Fire Insurance Company
Oklahoma Attorneys Mutual Insurance Company
Standard Fire Insurance Company
Travelers Insurance Company

Non-Insurance Clients

Archdiocese of Oklahoma City
Duit Construction Company, Inc.
TTK Construction Co., Inc.
The Boldt Company
Greyhound Lines, Inc.

Partners

Robert W. Nelson — 1956 — East Central University, B.S., 1977; The University of Oklahoma College of Law, J.D., 1979 — Admitted to Bar, 1980, Oklahoma; U.S. District Court, Eastern, Northern and Western Districts of Oklahoma — Member Oklahoma, Oklahoma County and Canadian County Bar Associations; American Board of Trial Advocates; Fellow, American College of Trial Lawyers — Oklahoma Super Lawyer; Best Lawyers in America — Practice Areas: Insurance Defense; Product Liability; Personal Injury — E-mail: rnelson@ntmdlaw.com

OKLAHOMA

Nelson Terry Morton DeWitt Paruolo & Wood, Edmond, OK (Continued)

Douglas A. Terry — 1967 — Northeastern State University, B.A. (summa cum laude), 1990; The University of Oklahoma College of Law, J.D. (with honors), 1993 — University of Oklahoma Law Review — Admitted to Bar, 1993, Oklahoma; 2009, Arkansas; 1993, U.S. District Court, Eastern, Northern and Western Districts of Oklahoma; 2009, U.S. District Court, Eastern and Western Districts of Arkansas — Member American, Oklahoma, Arkansas and Oklahoma County Bar Associations; Oklahoma Association for Justice — Practice Areas: Class Actions; Bad Faith; Insurance Coverage; Personal Injury — E-mail: terry@ntmdlaw.com

Derrick Lee Morton — 1973 — Texas Tech University, B.B.A., 1996; The University of Oklahoma College of Law, J.D., 1999 — Admitted to Bar, 1999, Oklahoma; 2009, Arkansas; 1999, U.S. District Court, Western District of Oklahoma; 2000, U.S. District Court, Northern District of Oklahoma; 2001, U.S. District Court, Eastern District of Oklahoma; 2009, U.S. District Court, Eastern and Western Districts of Arkansas — Member American, Oklahoma and Oklahoma County Bar Associations; Oklahoma Association for Justice — Practice Areas: Class Actions; Insurance Litigation; Personal Injury — E-mail: morton@ntmdlaw.com

Derrick T. DeWitt — 1973 — Oklahoma State University, B.A., 1995; Oklahoma City University School of Law, J.D. (cum laude), 1998 — Admitted to Bar, 1998, Oklahoma; U.S. District Court, Eastern, Northern and Western Districts of Oklahoma; 1999, U.S. Court of Appeals, Tenth Circuit; 2012, U.S. Court of Appeals, Seventh Circuit — Member Oklahoma and Oklahoma County Bar Associations; Defense Research Institute; Oklahoma Association of Defense Counsel — Practice Areas: Litigation; Insurance Coverage; Bad Faith; Tort; Trucking; Consumer Law; Product Liability; Business Litigation — E-mail: dewitt@ntmdlaw.com

Thomas A. Paruolo — 1974 — Baylor University, B.A. Political Science, 1996; Syracuse University College of Law, J.D. (cum laude), 1999 — Admitted to Bar, 1999, Oklahoma; U.S. District Court, Eastern, Northern and Western Districts of Oklahoma — Member Oklahoma Bar Association; Oklahoma Association of Defense Counsel; Defense Research Institute — Practice Areas: Insurance Defense; Insurance Coverage; Bad Faith; Civil Litigation — E-mail: tom@ntmdlaw.com

Guy R. Wood — 1968 — Cameron University, B.B.A. (with high honors), 1993; The University of Oklahoma College of Law, J.D., 1993 — Admitted to Bar, 1993, Oklahoma; 1997, U.S. District Court, Western District of Oklahoma; 1998, U.S. District Court, Northern District of Oklahoma; 2003, U.S. District Court, Eastern District of Oklahoma — Member Oklahoma and Oklahoma County Bar Associations — E-mail: guywood@ntmdlaw.com

EL RENO † 16,749 Canadian Co.

Refer To

Bass Law
Suite 700, 201 Robert S. Kerr
Oklahoma City, Oklahoma 73102
 Telephone: 405-262-4040
 Fax: 405-262-4058

Life and Health, Property and Casualty, Disability, Long-Term Care, Automobile, Business Law, General Liability, Uninsured and Underinsured Motorist, Insurance Coverage, Oil and Gas

SEE COMPLETE LISTING UNDER OKLAHOMA CITY, OKLAHOMA (28 MILES)

Refer To

Wheatley, Segler, Osby & Miller, LLC
501 West Main Street
Yukon, Oklahoma 73099
 Telephone: 405-354-5276
 Fax: 405-350-0537

Mailing Address: P.O. Box 850126, Yukon, OK 73085

Insurance Defense, General Liability, Trucking Law, Product Liability, Subrogation, Life and Health, Business Law

SEE COMPLETE LISTING UNDER YUKON, OKLAHOMA (10 MILES)

ENID † 49,379 Garfield Co.

Refer To

Frailey, Chaffin, Cordell, Perryman, Sterkel, McCalla & Brown, L.L.P.
201 North Fourth Street
Chickasha, Oklahoma 73023
 Telephone: 405-224-0237
 Fax: 405-222-2319

Mailing Address: P.O. Box 533, Chickasha, OK 73018

Administrative Law, Agriculture, Business Law, Civil Litigation, Commercial Transactions, Energy, Fire, Governmental Liability, Insurance Coverage, Insurance Defense, Municipal Law, Negligence, Oil and Gas, Premises Liability, Product Liability, Tort Litigation

SEE COMPLETE LISTING UNDER CHICKASHA, OKLAHOMA (98 MILES)

MADILL † 3,770 Marshall Co.

Refer To

Fischl, Culp, McMillin, Chaffin, Bahner & Long, L.L.P.
100 E Street, S.W.
Ardmore, Oklahoma 73401
 Telephone: 580-223-4321
 Fax: 580-226-4795

Mailing Address: P.O. Box 1766, Ardmore, OK 73402-1766

Insurance Defense, Trial Practice, Automobile, Product Liability, General Liability, Property and Casualty, Bad Faith

SEE COMPLETE LISTING UNDER ARDMORE, OKLAHOMA (25 MILES)

MARIETTA † 2,445 Love Co.

Refer To

Fischl, Culp, McMillin, Chaffin, Bahner & Long, L.L.P.
100 E Street, S.W.
Ardmore, Oklahoma 73401
 Telephone: 580-223-4321
 Fax: 580-226-4795

Mailing Address: P.O. Box 1766, Ardmore, OK 73402-1766

Insurance Defense, Trial Practice, Automobile, Product Liability, General Liability, Property and Casualty, Bad Faith

SEE COMPLETE LISTING UNDER ARDMORE, OKLAHOMA (20 MILES)

MUSKOGEE † 39,223 Muskogee Co.

Refer To

Daily & Woods, P.L.L.C.
58 South Sixth
Fort Smith, Arkansas 72901
 Telephone: 479-782-0361
 Fax: 479-782-6160

Mailing Address: P.O. Box 1446, Fort Smith, AR 72902

Insurance Defense

SEE COMPLETE LISTING UNDER FORT SMITH, ARKANSAS (80 MILES)

NORMAN † 110,925 Cleveland Co.

Barnum & Clinton, PLLC

1011 24th Avenue, N.W.
Norman, Oklahoma 73069
 Telephone: 405-579-7300
 Fax: 405-579-0140

Workers' Compensation, Premises Liability, Automobile Liability, Business Litigation, Business Transactions, Commercial Law, Commercial Litigation, Employer Liability, Employment Law, Employment Litigation, General Civil Litigation, General Defense, Occupational Accident

Firm Profile: Barnum & Clinton PLLC is a boutique style firm handling business related litigation matters. Our primary focus is on employment

OKLAHOMA CITY

Barnum & Clinton, PLLC, Norman, OK (Continued)

liability and workers' compensation defense, commercial liability defense, general defense and business law. We also provide general legal services for our clients. Our clients appreciate the business-focused attention we provide them in their legal matters. We are known for our aggressive handling of our litigation assignments.

Insurance Clients

Gallagher Bassett Services, Inc.
Old Glory Insurance Company

Non-Insurance Clients

City of Mustang
Evans & Associates Enterprises, Inc.
Georg Fischer Central Plastics, LLC
Hillcrest Healthcare System
Mazzio's Corporation
Stillwater Medical Center
Claims Administrative Services, Inc.
Gentiva Health Services, Inc.
Great Plains Coca-Cola Corporation
Mathis Brothers Furniture, LLC
McCurtain Memorial Hospital

Partners

Cathy C. Barnum — 1955 — The University of Oklahoma, B.A., 1978; The University of Oklahoma College of Law, J.D. (with honors), 1980 — Admitted to Bar, 1981, Oklahoma; 1982, Texas (Inactive); 1983, U.S. District Court, Western District of Oklahoma; U.S. Court of Appeals, Tenth Circuit; 1987, U.S. District Court, Eastern District of Oklahoma; 1988, U.S. District Court, Northern District of Oklahoma; U.S. District Court, Eastern District of Arkansas — Member American, Oklahoma and Cleveland County Bar Associations; State Bar of Texas; Oklahoma Self Insured's Association — Practice Areas: Business Law; Business Litigation; Civil Litigation; Civil Trial Practice; Commercial Litigation; Comprehensive General Liability; Copyright and Trademark Law; Defense Litigation; Employer Liability; Employment Law; Employment Litigation; General Civil Practice; General Defense; Insurance Defense; Self-Insured Defense; Workers' Compensation — E-mail: cbarnum@coxinet.net

Robert M. Clinton — 1951 — The University of Oklahoma, B.A., 1973; M.B.A., 1979; The University of Oklahoma College of Law, J.D., 1979 — Admitted to Bar, 1979, Oklahoma — Member Oklahoma Bar Association; Oklahoma Society of Certified Public Accountants; Institute of Management Accountants; The American Institute of Certified Public Accountants

Associates

Donald R. Lindauer, II — 1957 — Tulane University, B.A., 1979; Oklahoma City University School of Law, J.D., 1982 — Admitted to Bar, 1982, Oklahoma — E-mail: dlindauer@coxinet.net

Kelley A. Bodell — 1986 — The University of Oklahoma, B.A., 2008; Washington and Lee University School of Law, J.D., 2011 — Admitted to Bar, 2011, Oklahoma — E-mail: kbodell@coxinet.net

---

The following firms also service this area.

Frailey, Chaffin, Cordell, Perryman, Sterkel, McCalla & Brown, L.L.P.

201 North Fourth Street
Chickasha, Oklahoma 73023
Telephone: 405-224-0237
Fax: 405-222-2319
Mailing Address: P.O. Box 533, Chickasha, OK 73018

Administrative Law, Agriculture, Business Law, Civil Litigation, Commercial Transactions, Energy, Fire, Governmental Liability, Insurance Coverage, Insurance Defense, Municipal Law, Negligence, Oil and Gas, Premises Liability, Product Liability, Tort Litigation

SEE COMPLETE LISTING UNDER CHICKASHA, OKLAHOMA (35 MILES)

OKLAHOMA CITY † 579,999 Oklahoma Co.

Abowitz, Timberlake & Dahnke, P.C.

105 North Hudson, 10th Floor
Oklahoma City, Oklahoma 73102
Telephone: 405-236-4645
Fax: 405-239-2843
E-Mail: accounting@abowitzlaw.com
www.abowitzlaw.com

Established: 1978

Antitrust, Business Litigation, Civil Litigation, Commercial Litigation, Employment Law, Extra-Contractual Litigation, First and Third Party Defense, Insurance Coverage, Product Liability, Professional Liability, Securities, Transportation

Firm Profile: Abowitz, Timberlake & Dahnke, P.C. is a professional corporation engaged in civil trial and appellate practice in all state and federal courts, including general tort and business litigation, products liability, insurance, professional liability, employment, transportation, antitrust, securities, legal ethics and licensure.

Insurance Clients

ACCC Insurance Company
Affirmative Risk Management, Inc.
Atain Specialty Insurance Company
CapSpecialty
Century Surety Company
Certain Underwriters at Lloyd's, London
Detroit Stoker Company
Farmers Insurance Group
Fireman's Fund Insurance Company
The Hanover American Insurance Company
Kemper - A Unitrin Business
Meadowbrook Insurance Group
Oklahoma Attorneys Mutual Insurance Company
RiverStone Claims Management, LLC
State National Insurance Co.
Travelers Insurance Company
United States Liability Insurance Group
Admiral Insurance Company
American Safety Casualty Insurance Company
Capitol Indemnity Corporation
Carolina Casualty Insurance Company
The Cincinnati Insurance Companies
Everest National Insurance Company
Gibson & Associates
Great American Insurance Group
Jaeger Haines, Inc.
Johnson Claim Service, Inc.
Liberty Mutual Insurance Company
Midway Insurance Management International, Inc.
OneBeacon Insurance Company
Seneca Insurance Company
Starr Insurance Holdings, Inc.
TCS-One Insurance Group
Travelers Insurance - Hartford
Wesco Insurance
York Risk Service Group, Inc.

Non-Insurance Clients

Airgo Systems
American Biomedical Group, Inc.
Best Well Services
Hercules, Inc.
MasterCard
MV Purchasing
Standard Testing and Engineering Company
Sulzer Pumps, Inc.
Altec, Inc.
Belger Cartage Service, Inc.
CBS Corporation
Keen Energy Services
Medtronic Sofamor Danek, Inc.
Novartis Pharmaceuticals Corporation
Stroud Safety, Inc.
Utility Trailer Manufacturing Company

Director

Murray E. Abowitz — 1941 — University of Pennsylvania, B.S., 1965; Seton Hall University School of Law, LL.B., 1971 — Admitted to Bar, 1971, Oklahoma; U.S. District Court, Eastern, Northern and Western Districts of Oklahoma; U.S. District Court, District of Arizona; U.S. District Court, Eastern District of Texas; U.S. District Court, Eastern and Southern Districts of New York; U.S. District Court, Eastern District of Louisiana; U.S. District Court, Eastern District of Missouri; U.S. District Court, District of Nebraska; U.S. District Court, Eastern District of Pennsylvania; Superior Court of the State of California, Orange County; Supreme Court of Iowa; U.S. Court of Appeals, Tenth Circuit; U.S. District Court, Northern District of Ohio; U.S. Supreme Court — Member Oklahoma Bar Association; Luther Bohanon American Inn of Court XXIII (Emeritus Master of the Bench); Oklahoma

OKLAHOMA

Abowitz, Timberlake & Dahnke, P.C., Oklahoma City, OK (Continued)

Lawyers of Children; Federation of Defense and Corporate Counsel; Trial Attorneys of America; American Board of Trial Advocates; American College of Trial Lawyers — E-mail: mea@abowitzlaw.com

Directors/Shareholders

Sarah J. Timberlake — 1954 — The University of Oklahoma, B.A. (Phi Beta Kappa), 1976; The University of Oklahoma College of Law, J.D., 1980 — Admitted to Bar, 1980, Oklahoma; U.S. District Court, Eastern, Northern and Western Districts of Oklahoma; U.S. Court of Appeals, Tenth Circuit; U.S. Supreme Court — Member Oklahoma and Oklahoma County Bar Associations; American Inn of Court XXIII; Federation of Defense and Corporate Counsel (Board of Directors); Oklahoma Association of Defense Counsel (Past President); Defense Research Institute — E-mail: sjt@abowitzlaw.com

George W. Dahnke — 1940 — Westminster College, B.A., 1962; Northwestern University School of Law, J.D., 1965 — Admitted to Bar, 1965, Oklahoma; U.S. District Court, Eastern, Northern and Western Districts of Oklahoma; U.S. Court of Appeals, Tenth Circuit; U.S. Supreme Court — Member American, Oklahoma and Oklahoma County Bar Associations; Luther Bohanon Inn of Court XXII; Oklahoma Association of Defense Counsel — Muscogee (Creek) Nation Tribal Courts — E-mail: gwd@abowitzlaw.com

Of Counsel

William C. McAlister — 1938 — The University of Oklahoma, B.S., 1961; Oklahoma City University School of Law, J.D., 1969 — Admitted to Bar, 1969, Oklahoma; U.S. District Court, Eastern, Northern and Western Districts of Oklahoma; U.S. District Court, Northern District of Texas; U.S. Court of Appeals, Fifth, Tenth and Eleventh Circuits; U.S. Supreme Court — Member Oklahoma and Oklahoma County Bar Associations; American Arbitration Association Panel of Neutrals; Oklahoma Association of Defense Counsel; Defense Research Institute — E-mail: wcm@abowitzlaw.com

William P. Tunell Jr — 1970 — University of Pennsylvania, B.A. Political Science, 1992; University of Notre Dame Law School, J.D./M.B.A., 1996 — Admitted to Bar, 1996, Oklahoma; U.S. District Court, District of Oklahoma; U.S. District Court, Eastern and Northern Districts of Oklahoma; U.S. Court of Appeals, Tenth Circuit — E-mail: wpt@abowitzlaw.com

Associates

John D. Cowan — 1973 — Oklahoma University, B.F.A., 1995; Oklahoma City University School of Law, J.D. (cum laude), 2013 — Admitted to Bar, 2013, Oklahoma; U.S. District Court, Eastern and Western Districts of Oklahoma — Member Oklahoma and Oklahoma County Bar Associations — E-mail: jdc@abowitzlaw.com

April B. Eberle — 1974 — Oklahoma City University, B.A. Political Science (with honors), 1996; Oklahoma City University School of Law, J.D. (summa cum laude), 1999 — Admitted to Bar, 1999, Oklahoma; U.S. District Court, Western District of Oklahoma — Member Oklahoma and Oklahoma County Bar Associations — E-mail: abe@abowitzlaw.com

Nicolas D. Grimwood — 1986 — College of the Ozarks, B.A., 2008; Oklahoma City University School of Law, J.D., 2014 — Admitted to Bar, 2014, Oklahoma; U.S. District Court, Eastern and Western Districts of Oklahoma — Member Oklahoma and Oklahoma County Bar Associations — E-mail: ndg@abowitzlaw.com

Bass Law

Suite 700, 201 Robert S. Kerr
Oklahoma City, Oklahoma 73102
Telephone: 405-262-4040
Fax: 405-262-4058
E-Mail: gabe@basslaw.net
www.basslaw.net

(El Reno, OK Office: 104 North Rock Island, P.O. Box 157, 73036)
(Tel: 405-262-4040)
(Fax: 405-262-4058)

Life and Health, Property and Casualty, Disability, Long-Term Care, Automobile, Business Law, General Liability, Uninsured and Underinsured Motorist, Insurance Coverage, Oil and Gas

Firm Profile: With a reputation for quality, expertise and results dating back to our founding in 1934, Bass Law is a business, litigation and estates law firm focused on the needs of business leaders. We work with clients who seek sophisticated solutions and a high level of attention to their individual needs.

Insurance Clients

MDOW Insurance

Oklahoma Attorneys Mutual Insurance Company

Managing Partner

A, Gabriel "Gabe" Bass — The University of Oklahoma Price College of Business, B.B.A., 1998; The University of Oklahoma, M.S., 2003; The University of Oklahoma College of Law, J.D., 2003 — Admitted to Bar, 2003, Oklahoma; U.S. District Court, Eastern and Western Districts of Oklahoma; U.S. Bankruptcy Court, Western District of Oklahoma; U.S. Supreme Court — Member American Bar Association (Vice-Chair, TIPS Trial Techniques Committee (2008-2011); TIPS Leadership Academy (2008); Oklahoma, Canadian County (President, 2010) and Oklahoma County Bar Associations; Oklahoma Bar Foundation (Trustee, 2010-Present) — E-mail: gabe@basslaw.net

Senior Partner

John A. "Andy" Bass

Of Counsel

James C. Bass

Tony Van Eck

Attorneys

Joseph P. Weaver, Jr.
Justin D. Meek
Kevin Cunningham
Lori Smith
Sarah Moore

Ryan L. Dean
Dustin L. Compton
Benjamin Grubb
Matt Von Tungeln
Colin Barrett

Bullard & Associates, P.C.

312 N.W. 13th Street
Oklahoma City, Oklahoma 73103-3730
Telephone: 405-604-5000
Fax: 405-604-5005
E-Mail: mail@bullard-associates.com

Established: 1992

Insurance Defense, Workers' Compensation, Comprehensive General Liability, Coverage Issues, Personal Injury, Employment Law, Environmental Coverage

Insurance Clients

ACE/USA Insurance Company
Claim Indemnity Services, Inc.
Commercial Union Insurance Company
Electric Insurance Company
Fireman's Fund Insurance Company
Hartford Specialty Risk Services, Inc.
Sentry Insurance a Mutual Company

AIG International Insurance Group
CNA Insurance Company
CompSource Oklahoma
Crawford & Company
Farmers Insurance Group
GAB Robins North America, Inc.
Gallagher Bassett Services, Inc.
The MEGA Life and Health Insurance Company

Non-Insurance Clients

Albertsons, Inc.
Kwikset
Remington Park

Grace Living Centers
Mercury Marine, Inc.
Rollins Protective Services

Partners

Donald A. Bullard — 1959 — Southwestern Oklahoma State University, B.S., 1981; The University of Oklahoma, J.D., 1984 — Admitted to Bar, 1984, Oklahoma; 1984, U.S. District Court, Western District of Oklahoma — Member American Bar Association (Labor and Employment, Litigation, Tort and Insurance Practice); Oklahoma and Oklahoma County Bar Associations; Defense Research Institute; Oklahoma Association of Defense Counsel — Instructor: "Nuts and Bolts of Workers' Compensation", Seminar (May 6, 1994); "Basic Primer of Workers' Compensation", Seminar (March 10,

OKLAHOMA CITY

Bullard & Associates, P.C., Oklahoma City, OK (Continued)

1995); "Statutory and Judicial Update of the Workers' Compensation Court", Continuing Education Courses for Adjusters (February 16, 1996); "Oklahoma Workers' Compensation-An Introduction to the Advanced Perspective" (August 8 and 11, 1997); "Nuts & Bolts of Workers' Compensation" (December 4, 1997); "Oklahoma Workers' Compensation" (November 19-20, 1998); "Oklahoma Workers' Compensation-A Comprehensive Review" (November 18-19, 1999); "Oklahoma Workers' Compensation - Major Changes in the Law Effecting Claims Handling & Reserving" (November 16-17, 2000) — E-mail: don@bullard-associates.com

Associates

H. Lee Endicott, III — 1959 — Oklahoma State University, B.S., 1981; The University of Oklahoma, J.D., 1984 — Admitted to Bar, 1984, Oklahoma; 1984, U.S. District Court, Eastern, Northern and Western Districts of Oklahoma; U.S. Court of Appeals, Tenth Circuit; 1996, U.S. Court of Appeals, Fifth Circuit; U.S. Supreme Court — Member American, Oklahoma and Oklahoma County Bar Associations — E-mail: lee@bullard-associates.com

Robert C. Simpson — 1972 — University of San Francisco, B.A., 1995; The University of Oklahoma, J.D., 2001 — Phi Delta Phi — Admitted to Bar, 2001, Oklahoma — Member American and Oklahoma Bar Associations — E-mail: Robbie@Bullard-Associates.com

Elizabeth Honeywell Gray — 1957 — Southeastern Oklahoma State University, B.A., 1979; Oklahoma City University, J.D., 1982 — Admitted to Bar, 1982, Oklahoma; 1997, U.S. District Court, Western District of Oklahoma — Practice Areas: Workers' Compensation; Insurance Defense — E-mail: Elizabeth@Bullard-Associates.com

Michael T. Egan — 1958 — The University of Oklahoma, B.A., 1980; Oklahoma City University, J.D., 1984 — Admitted to Bar, 1984, Oklahoma — Member Oklahoma Bar Association (Workers' Compensation Section) — E-mail: Mike@Bullard-Associates.com

James Leo Gaston, Jr. — 1954 — Temple University, B.A., 1976; Oklahoma City University School of Law, J.D., 1979 — Admitted to Bar, 1979, Oklahoma; 1981, U.S. District Court, Western District of Oklahoma — Member Oklahoma and Oklahoma County Bar Associations — E-mail: James@Bullard-Associates.com

R. Dale Kimsey — 1960 — Oklahoma State University, B.A., 1982; The University of Oklahoma, J.D., 1986 — Admitted to Bar, 1986, Oklahoma; 1986, U.S. District Court, Western District of Oklahoma — Member American Bar Association (Labor & Employment, Tort & Insurance Practice Section); Oklahoma and Oklahoma County Bar Associations; Oklahoma Association of Defense Counsel — E-mail: Dale@Bullard-Associates.com

Julie Thompson Weller — 1974 — Midwestern State University, B.S., 1997; Oklahoma City University, J.D., 2001 — Admitted to Bar, 2001, Oklahoma; U.S. District Court, Western District of Oklahoma — Member American Bar Association — E-mail: Julie@Bullard-Associates.com

Sarah C. Bullard — 1982 — East Central University, B.A., 2004; Oklahoma City University, J.D., 2006 — Admitted to Bar, 2007, Oklahoma; U.S. District Court, Western District of Oklahoma — Member Oklahoma Bar Association (Workers' Compensation Section; Young Lawyers Division) — E-mail: SarahB@Bullard-Associates.com

(This firm is also listed in the Subrogation section of this directory)

Cathcart & Dooley
A Professional Corporation

Cornett Building
2807 North Classen Boulevard
Oklahoma City, Oklahoma 73106
   Telephone: 405-524-1110
   Fax: 405-524-4143
   E-Mail: bcathcart@cathcartdooley.com
   E-Mail: cdooley@cathcartdooley.com
   www.cathcartdooley.com

Insurance Law, Property, Fire, Casualty, Subrogation, Investigation and Adjustment

OKLAHOMA

Cathcart & Dooley, A Professional Corporation, Oklahoma City, OK (Continued)

Insurance Clients

Allstate Insurance Company
American National Property and Casualty Company
Chubb Group of Insurance Companies
Foremost Insurance Company
Guaranty National Insurance Company
Hanover Insurance Company
Le Mars Insurance Company
Lexington Insurance Company
Nodak Mutual Insurance Company
North Star Mutual Insurance Company
Prudential Property and Casualty Insurance Company
Shelter Mutual Insurance Company
State and County Mutual Fire Insurance Company
State Farm Mutual Automobile Insurance Company
Wellington Insurance Company
American Modern Insurance Group, Inc.
Atlanta Casualty Company
Essex Insurance Company
Farmers Insurance Company
Great American Property & Casualty Group
GuideOne Insurance
Hartford Casualty Insurance Company
National Lloyds Insurance Company
Oklahoma Farm Bureau Mutual Insurance Company
Republic Insurance Company
St. Paul Fire and Marine Insurance Company
State Farm Fire and Casualty Company
United Services Automobile Association (USAA)
Westfield Insurance Company

Firm Members

William R. Cathcart — 1945 — Roanoke College, B.A., 1967; Oklahoma City University, J.D., 1971 — Admitted to Bar, 1971, Oklahoma; U.S. District Court, Eastern, Northern and Western Districts of Oklahoma; U.S. Court of Appeals, Tenth Circuit; 2004, U.S. Supreme Court — Member American, Oklahoma, and Oklahoma County Bar Associations; Oklahoma Association of Defense Counsel; Defense Research Institute

Cary D. Dooley — 1963 — Baylor University, B.A., 1985; The University of Oklahoma, J.D., 1988 — Admitted to Bar, 1988, Oklahoma; U.S. District Court, Eastern, Northern and Western Districts of Oklahoma — Member Oklahoma and Oklahoma County Bar Associations

Virginia Cathcart Holleman — 1966 — The University of Oklahoma, B.B.A., 1989; J.D., 1993 — Admitted to Bar, 1993, Oklahoma; U.S. District Court, Eastern, Northern and Western Districts of Oklahoma; U.S. Court of Appeals, Tenth Circuit; 2004, U.S. Supreme Court — Member Federal, Oklahoma and Oklahoma County Bar Associations

Associates

Jason E. Marshall — 1983 — University of Central Oklahoma, B.A., 2007; Oklahoma City University, J.D., 2010 — Admitted to Bar, 2010, Oklahoma; U.S. District Court, Eastern, Northern and Western Districts of Oklahoma — Member Oklahoma and Oklahoma County Bar Associations

Jarrett A. Wilson — 1981 — Texas State University, B.A., 2009; Oklahoma City University School of Law, J.D., 2012 — Admitted to Bar, 2012, Oklahoma; Arkansas; U.S. District Court, Eastern and Western Districts of Arkansas; U.S. District Court, Western District of Oklahoma — Member Oklahoma and Oklahoma County Bar Associations

(This firm is also listed in the Subrogation section of this directory)

Cheek Law Firm, P.L.L.C.
F/K/A Cheek, Cheek & Cheek

Law Center Building
311 North Harvey Avenue
Oklahoma City, Oklahoma 73102
   Telephone: (405) 272-0621
   Fax: (405) 232-1707
   E-Mail: tcheek@cheeklaw.com
   www.cheeklawfirm.com

Established: 1943

OKLAHOMA — OKLAHOMA CITY

Cheek Law Firm, P.L.L.C., F/K/A Cheek, Cheek & Cheek, Oklahoma City, OK (Continued)

Insurance Defense, Insurance Coverage, Appellate Practice, State and Federal Courts, Amusements, Arbitration, Automobile, Aviation, Bad Faith, Business Litigation, Civil Litigation, Construction Defect, Employment Law, Mass Tort, Motor Carriers, Opinions, Personal Injury, Premises Liability, Product Liability, Real Estate, Subrogation, Toxic Torts, Trucking Litigation, Boat Accident Litigation, Motorcycle Accident Litigation, Swimming Pool Accident Litigation

Firm Profile: Formerly known as Cheek, Cheek & Cheek, Cheek Law Firm, P.L.L.C. has an aggressive civil practice in all Oklahoma state and federal courts. The firm is listed in the Bar Register of Preeminent Lawyers under Insurance Defense, and represents clients in a wide variety of cases.

Insurance Clients

Aegis Security Insurance Company
American International Group, Inc.
American Reliable Insurance Company
Atlantic Casualty Insurance Company
Carolina Casualty Insurance Company
Chicago Insurance Company
Cincinnati Insurance Company
Crum & Forster Insurance
First State Insurance Company
General Reinsurance Corporation
General Star Management Company
Grange Insurance Group
Great West Casualty Company
Harbor Insurance Company
Homestead Insurance Company
Markel Insurance Companies
Markel Service, Incorporated
Merastar Insurance Company
Motorists Mutual Insurance Company
National Fire and Casualty Company
Nationwide Insurance
North Star Mutual Insurance Company
The Republic Group
State National Insurance Company, Inc.
21st Century Insurance Company
Universal Casualty Company
Universal Underwriters Insurance Company
American Equity Insurance Company
American Southern Insurance Company
Balboa Insurance Company
California State Automobile Association
Central National Insurance Company of Omaha
Country-Wide Insurance Company
Diamond State Insurance Company
Fort Dearborn Life Insurance Company
Government Employees Insurance Company
Great American Custom Insurance Services
Highlands Insurance Company
Lloyd's
Markel Insurance Company
Markel Southwest Underwriters, Inc.
Motors Insurance Corporation
National Casualty Company
National Security Group, Inc.
National Union Fire Insurance Company
Old Republic Insurance Company
Protective Insurance Company
Safeco Insurance
Time Insurance Company n.k.a. Assurant Health
Unionamerica Insurance Company Limited
Voyager Indemnity Insurance Company

Non-Insurance Clients

Chef's Requested Foods, Inc.
Government Employees Finance Company
McKesson Corporation
Shadid Brothers
USA Inc.
Warren Properties, Inc.
Corporation Guaranty and Trust
Hewlett-Packard Company
Home Owners Warranty Corporation
Tom Vorderlandwehr, Inc., Tuscany Homes

Firm Members

Alex Cheek — (1916-1996)

William C. Cheek — (1923-1997)

John D. Cheek — (1920-2010)

Tim N. Cheek — Whitworth College, B.A. (cum laude), 1981; The University of Oklahoma, M.B.A., 1985; J.D., 1985 — Admitted to Bar, 1985, Oklahoma; U.S. District Court, Eastern, Northern, and Western Districts of Oklahoma; U.S. Court of Appeals, Tenth Circuit; Supreme Court of Oklahoma — Member Oklahoma Bar Association; U.S. District Courts of Oklahoma; Oklahoma Association of Defense Counsel — Practice Areas: Insurance Defense; Civil Defense; Product Liability; Medical Malpractice Defense; Insurance Coverage; Bad Faith; Civil Litigation; Appeals; Motor Carriers — E-mail: tcheek@cheeklaw.com

D. Todd Riddles — Oklahoma State University, B.S., 1990; The University of Oklahoma, M.B.A., 1994; J.D., 1994 — Admitted to Bar, 1994, Oklahoma; Supreme Court of Oklahoma; U.S. District Court, Eastern, Northern, and Western Districts of Oklahoma; U.S. Court of Appeals, Tenth Circuit; U.S. Supreme Court — Member Federal, American and Oklahoma Bar Associations; Oklahoma Association of Defense Counsel — Practice Areas: Construction Defect; Real Estate; Business Litigation; Personal Injury; Insurance Defense; Insurance Coverage Determination; Bad Faith; Medical Malpractice; Professional Liability; Motor Carriers — E-mail: triddles@cheeklaw.com

Associates

Greg Winningham — Metropolitan State College of Denver, B.A., 2004; Oklahoma City University, J.D., 2008 — Phi Delta Pi Legal Fraternity — Admitted to Bar, 2009, Oklahoma; Supreme Court of Oklahoma; U.S. District Court, Eastern, Northern, and Western Districts of Oklahoma — Member Oklahoma Bar Association; Oklahoma County Bar Association; American Bar Association; Oklahoma Association of Defense Counsel; American Association for Justice — U.S. Navy, Hospital Corpsman, Chief Petty Officer, Active Duty 1991-1997; Navy Reserve 1998-Present; U.S.S. America, 1995-1996; Deployed in support of Operation Iraqi Freedom, 2004; Deployed in support of Operation Enduring Freedom, 2013 — Practice Areas: Insurance Defense; Bad Faith; Coverage Issues; Product Liability; Construction Defect; Personal Injury — E-mail: gwinningham@cheeklaw.com

Tyler J. Coble — Missouri Southern State University, B.S. (summa cum laude), 2005; Oklahoma University, J.D. (with distinction), 2010 — Phi Delta Phi Legal Fraternity — Note Editor, American Indian Law Review (2009-2010) — Admitted to Bar, 2010, Missouri; Oklahoma; Supreme Court of Missouri; Supreme Court of Oklahoma; U.S. District Court, Eastern, Northern, and Western Districts of Oklahoma; U.S. Court of Appeals, Tenth Circuit — Member Oklahoma Bar Association; Missouri Bar Association; Oklahoma County Bar Association — Practice Areas: Insurance Coverage & Defense; Bad Faith; Civil Litigation; Personal Injury; Uninsured and Underinsured Motorist — E-mail: tcoble@cheeklaw.com

Durbin, Larimore & Bialick

920 North Harvey
Oklahoma City, Oklahoma 73102-2610
Telephone: 405-235-9584
Fax: 405-235-0551
E-Mail: dlb@dlb.net
www.dlb.net

Established: 1983

General Civil Practice, Litigation, Personal Injury, Insurance Law, Fire, Property and Casualty, Product Liability, Defense Litigation, Corporate Law, Toxic Torts, Federal and State

Insurance Clients

AAA Insurance
ACE North American Claims
ACE USA
Allianz
American Farmers & Ranchers Mutual Insurance Company
Amerisure Insurance Company
Arch Insurance Group
Atlas Insurance Company
Bituminous Insurance Companies
Casualty Corporation of America
CBCS
Columbia Insurance Group
Crawford & Company
Equity Insurance Company
GAB Robins North America, Inc.
Great Central Insurance Company
Hallmark Insurance Company
Harbor Insurance Company
Hudiburg Auto Group
Mid-Continent Casualty Company
National American Insurance Company
PacifiCare of Oklahoma, Inc.
The Plus Companies, Inc.
Shelter Insurance Companies
ACE American Insurance Company
Aetna Insurance Company
Allstate Insurance Company
American Fidelity Insurance Company
Amica Mutual Insurance Company
Argo Select
Benchmark Insurance Company
Brotherhood Mutual Insurance Company
CNA Insurance Company
Continental Loss Adjusting Services
Erie Insurance Company
GHS Property and Casualty Insurance Company
Hanover Insurance Company
The Hartford Insurance Group
Kansas City Fire and Marine Insurance Company
Nationwide Insurance
Oklahoma Farm Bureau Mutual Insurance Company
Sedgwick Claims Management Services, Inc.

OKLAHOMA CITY

Durbin, Larimore & Bialick, Oklahoma City, OK
(Continued)

Statewide Claims Service
USAA
Zurich North America
Union Mutual Insurance Company
Westchester Fire Insurance Company

Non-Insurance Clients

Blue Bell Creameries, LP
CRST International, Inc.
Davita, Inc.
Dollar Tree Stores, Inc.
Fleming Guardian Group
HAC, Inc.
J.B. Hunt Transport Services, Inc.
Love's Travel Stops & Country Stores, Inc.
Musket Corporation
Pilot Flying J
The Stanley Works
Yellow Cab

Braum's Ice Cream and Dairy Stores
Dillard's, Inc.
Federal Express
Gemini Motor Transport, LP
Hobby Lobby Stores, Inc.
Kindred Healthcare
Mardel, Inc.
Moore Group, Inc.
Old Navy, Inc.
7-Eleven, Inc.
Werner Enterprises, Inc.

Founding Partners

Gerald E. Durbin, II — 1944 — The University of Oklahoma, B.B.A., 1968; The University of Oklahoma College of Law, J.D., 1971 — Phi Alpha Delta — Admitted to Bar, 1971, Oklahoma; U.S. District Court, Eastern, Northern and Western Districts of Oklahoma; U.S. Court of Appeals, Tenth Circuit; U.S. Supreme Court — Member American, Oklahoma and Oklahoma County (Board of Directors; President, 2001-2002) Bar Association; Oklahoma Association of Defense Counsel; Fellow, American College of Trial Lawyers — The Best Lawyers in America (2006-2007, 2011-2012); Top 50 Oklahoma Super Lawyers, PI General: Plaintiff, Oklahoma Magazine (2006-2014); Lecturer on Trial Tactics, Bad Faith, Medical Malpractice — Practice Areas: Litigation; Appeals; Insurance; Medical Malpractice; Motor Vehicle; Nursing Home Litigation; Personal Injury; Product Liability; Professional Malpractice — E-mail: gdurbin@dlb.net

James K. Larimore — 1949 — The University of Oklahoma, B.A. (with distinction), 1971; The University of Oklahoma College of Law, J.D. (with special distinction), 1974 — Phi Delta Phi — Order of the Coif — Editor, Oklahoma Law Review, 1973-1974 — Admitted to Bar, 1974, Oklahoma; U.S. District Court, Eastern, Northern and Western Districts of Oklahoma; U.S. Court of Appeals, Tenth Circuit; U.S. Supreme Court — Member American, Oklahoma and Oklahoma County Bar Associations; American Association of Justice — The Best Lawyers of America (2006-2007, 2011-2012); Oklahoma Super Lawyers, Business/Corporate, Oklahoma Magazine (2006-2014) — Practice Areas: Business Litigation; Commercial Litigation; Real Estate; Probate; Estate Litigation; Trusts; Wills — E-mail: jlarimore@dlb.net

Mark E. Bialick — 1956 — The University of Oklahoma, B.A., 1978; The University of Oklahoma College of Law, J.D., 1981 — Editor, Oklahoma Law Review (1979-1981) — Admitted to Bar, 1981, Oklahoma; U.S. District Court, Eastern, Northern and Western Districts of Oklahoma; U.S. Court of Appeals, Tenth Circuit; U.S. Supreme Court — Member American, Oklahoma and Oklahoma County Bar Associations; Defense Research Institute; Fellow, American College of Trial Lawyers — The Best Lawyers in American (2005-2007, 2011-2012); Top 10 Oklahoma Super Lawyers, PI General: Plaintiff, Oklahoma Magazine (2006-2014); Top 50 Oklahoma Super Lawyers, PI General: Plaintiff, Oklahoma Magazine (2014); Listed in Chambers USA (2013) — Practice Areas: Insurance Law; Litigation; Appeals; Personal Injury; Product Liability — E-mail: mbialick@dlb.net

Managing Partner

David B. Donchin — 1959 — The University of Oklahoma, B.A., 1981; The University of Oklahoma College of Law, J.D., 1984 — Phi Alpha Delta — Admitted to Bar, 1984, Oklahoma; U.S. District Court, Eastern, Northern and Western Districts of Oklahoma; U.S. Court of Appeals, Tenth Circuit; U.S. Supreme Court — Member Oklahoma and Oklahoma County (Board of Directors, 1989-1991, 2011-2013; Vice President, 1991-1992) Bar Associations; Oklahoma Association of Defense Counsel; Fellow, American College of Trial Lawyers — Top 10 Oklahoma Super Lawyers, PI General: Defense, Oklahoma Magazine (2014); Top 50 Oklahoma Super Lawyers, PI General: Defense, Oklahoma Magazine (2010-2014); Oklahoma Super Lawyers, Oklahoma Magazine (2006-2013) — Practice Areas: Employment Law; Insurance; Mass Tort; Medical Malpractice; Motor Vehicle; Personal Liability; Product Liability; Toxic Torts — E-mail: ddonchin@dlb.net

Partners

Hilary S. Allen — 1970 — The University of Oklahoma, B.A., 1993; The University of Oklahoma College of Law, J.D., 1996 — Admitted to Bar, 1996, Oklahoma; U.S. District Court, Eastern, Northern and Western Districts of Oklahoma; U.S. Court of Appeals, Tenth Circuit — Member Oklahoma and Oklahoma County Bar Associations; America Inn of the Court (William F. Holloway, Jr.) — Oklahoma Super Lawyers "Rising Star," Oklahoma Magazine (2010); Lecturer on: Insurance Law, Damages, Bad Faith — Practice Areas: Civil Rights; Contracts; Discrimination; Employment Law; Insurance Law; Litigation; Appeals; Medical Malpractice; Motor Vehicle; Nursing Home Litigation; Personal Injury; Product Liability; Sexual Harassment; Toxic Torts — E-mail: hallen@dlb.net

Micheal L. Darrah — 1951 — Central State University, B.A., 1974; Oklahoma City University School of Law, J.D., 1977 — Delta Theta Phi — Admitted to Bar, 1977, Oklahoma; U.S. District Court, Eastern, Northern and Western Districts of Oklahoma; U.S. Court of Appeals, Tenth Circuit; U.S. Supreme Court — Member Oklahoma and Oklahoma County Bar Associations; Independent Petroleum Association; America Inn of Court (Masters of the Bench); Oklahoma Association of Defense Counsel; Defense Research Institute; American Board of Trial Advocates — Lecturer on: Oil & Gas, Environmental; Oklahoma Super Lawyers, Energy & Resources, Oklahoma Magazine (2014) — Practice Areas: Eminent Domain; Environmental Law; Insurance; Litigation; Appeals; Personal Injury; Product Liability; Toxic Torts; Mass Tort — E-mail: mdarrah@dlb.net

R. Ryan Deligans — 1977 — New Mexico State University, B.S., 1999; The University of Oklahoma College of Law, J.D., 2003 — Admitted to Bar, 2003, Oklahoma; U.S. District Court, Eastern, Northern and Western Districts of Oklahoma; U.S. Court of Appeals, Tenth Circuit — Member Oklahoma and Oklahoma County Bar Associations; American Inns of Court — Oklahoma Super Lawyers "Rising Star", Oklahoma Magazine (2008-2011); Oklahoma Super Lawyers, Civil Litigation: Defense, Oklahoma Magazine (2014) — Practice Areas: Insurance; Litigation; Appeals; Toxic Torts; Personal Injury; Product Liability; Trucking; Pharmaceutical — E-mail: rdeligans@dlb.net

Katherine Taylor Loy — 1967 — The University of Oklahoma, B.B.A. (with distinction), 1989; The University of Oklahoma College of Law, J.D. (with honors), 1992 — Order of the Coif — Admitted to Bar, 1992, Oklahoma; U.S. District Court, Eastern, Northern and Western Districts of Oklahoma; U.S. Court of Appeals, Tenth Circuit; U.S. Supreme Court — Member Oklahoma and Oklahoma County Bar Associations — Lecturer on: Insurance Law, Bad Faith, Uninsured Motorist; Oklahoma Super Lawyers, Oklahoma Magazine (2014) — Practice Areas: Employment Law; Entertainment Law; Sports Law; Environmental Law; Insurance Law; Litigation; Appeals; Personal Injury; Product Liability — E-mail: kloy@dlb.net

Glen Mullins — 1948 — The University of Oklahoma, B.A., 1970; The University of Oklahoma College of Law, J.D., 1976 — Admitted to Bar, 1976, Oklahoma; U.S. District Court, Eastern, Northern and Western Districts of Oklahoma; U.S. Court of Appeals, Tenth Circuit — Member American, Oklahoma and Oklahoma County Bar Associations; Defense Research Institute — Oklahoma Super Lawyers, Oklahoma Magazine (2009-2011); Oklahoma Super Lawyers, PI General: Defense, Oklahoma Magazine (2014); Lecturer on: Bad Faith, Nursing Home Litigation, Health Insurance, Trial Pratice (Expert Witness Presentation) — United States Army, Vietnam Veteran — Practice Areas: Insurance Law; Litigation; Appeals; Motor Vehicle; Nursing Home Litigation; Personal Injury — E-mail: gmullius@dlb.com

E. Edd Pritchett, Jr. — 1969 — Oklahoma State University, B.A., 1992; The University of Oklahoma College of Law, J.D., 1995 — Phi Delta Phi — Order of the Coif — Admitted to Bar, 1995, Oklahoma; 1996, U.S. District Court, Northern and Western Districts of Oklahoma — Member Oklahoma and Oklahoma County Bar Associations — Oklahoma Super Lawyers "Rising Star", Oklahoma Magazine (2008) — Practice Areas: Civil Litigation; Eminent Domain; Insurance Defense; Oil and Gas — E-mail: epritchett@dlb.net

Jennifer K. Christian — 1981 — The University of Oklahoma, B.A. (with distinction), 2003; The University of Oklahoma College of Law, J.D. (summa cum laude), 2007 — Phi Delta Phi — Phi Kappa Phi Honor Society — Editor-in-Chief, Oklahoma City University Law Review, 2007 — Admitted to Bar, 2007, Oklahoma; U.S. District Court, Eastern, Northern and Western Districts of Oklahoma; U.S. Court of Appeals, Tenth Circuit — Member American, Oklahoma and Oklahoma County Bar Associations — Oklahoma Super Lawyers "Rising Star", Business Litigation, Oklahoma Magazine (2011, 2014) — E-mail: jchristian@dlb.net

Associates

Andrew M. Gunn — 1976 — The University of Oklahoma, B.B.A., 1998; The University of Oklahoma College of Law, J.D., 2002 — Admitted to Bar, 2002, Texas; Oklahoma; U.S. District Court, Western District of Oklahoma — Member Oklahoma Bar Association; State Bar of Texas — Oklahoma

OKLAHOMA

OKLAHOMA CITY

Durbin, Larimore & Bialick, Oklahoma City, OK (Continued)

Super Lawyers "Rising Star", Oklahoma Magazine (2010) — Practice Areas: Insurance Litigation; Personal Injury; Bad Faith; Construction Litigation; Appeals; Toxic Torts; Product Liability; Trucking; Pharmaceutical — E-mail: agunn@dlb.net

Thomas R. Kendrick — 1971 — University of Central Oklahoma, B.S., 1995; Oklahoma City University School of Law, J.D., 1998 — Admitted to Bar, 1998, Oklahoma — Member Oklahoma and Oklahoma County Bar Associations; Oklahoma Criminal Defense Lawyers Association; Defense Research Institute — Practice Areas: Insurance Defense; Litigation; Appeals; Motor Vehicle; Personal Injury; Product Liability; Environmental Law; Insurance; Toxic Torts — E-mail: tkendrick@dlb.net

Timothy L. Martin — 1947 — The University of Oklahoma, B.B.A., 1971; Oklahoma City University School of Law, J.D., 1983 — Phi Delta Phi — Notes Editor, Oklahoma City University Law Review — Admitted to Bar, 1983, Oklahoma; U.S. District Court, Eastern, Northern and Western Districts of Oklahoma; U.S. Court of Appeals, Tenth Circuit — Member American, Oklahoma and Oklahoma County Bar Associations; Defense Research Institute — Oklahoma Super Lawyers, Oklahoma Magazine (2008-2011); The Best Lawyers in America (2012) — Practice Areas: Insurance Defense; Litigation; Appeals; Motor Vehicle; Personal Injury; Product Liability; Environmental Law; Insurance; Toxic Torts — E-mail: tmartin@dlb.net

Kaci L. Trojan — 1983 — Oklahoma State University, B.S., 2006; The University of Oklahoma College of Law, J.D. (with distinction), 2009 — Pi Beta Phi; Phi Kappa Phi — Regent's Distinguished Scholar, 2006 — Admitted to Bar, 2009, Oklahoma; U.S. District Court, Northern and Western Districts of Oklahoma; U.S. Court of Appeals, Tenth Circuit — Member Oklahoma and Oklahoma County Bar Associations; Oklahoma Lawyers for Children; American Inns of Court — Lecturer on: Legislative Update, Tort Reform, Insurance Claims Handling, The Demise of Parret; Oklahoma Super Lawyers "Rising Star", Civil Litigation: Defense, Oklahoma Magazine (2014) — Practice Areas: Litigation; Personal Injury — E-mail: ktrojan@dlb.net

Bryan T. Gordon — 1984 — Duke University, B.A., 2007; The University of Oklahoma College of Law, J.D., 2011 — Admitted to Bar, 2011, Oklahoma; U.S. District Court, Western District of Oklahoma — Member Oklahoma and Oklahoma County Bar Associations — Practice Areas: Civil Litigation; Personal Injury; Insurance Law; Product Liability; Motor Vehicle — E-mail: bgordon@dlb.net

Lane R. Neal — 1982 — The University of Oklahoma, B.B.A., 2004; The University of Oklahoma College of Law, J.D., 2008 — Sigma Alpha Epsilon — Admitted to Bar, 2008, Oklahoma; U.S. District Court, Northern and Western Districts of Oklahoma — Member Oklahoma and Oklahoma County Bar Associations — Practice Areas: Civil Litigation; Insurance Law; Motor Vehicle; Personal Injury; Product Liability — E-mail: lneal@dlb.net

Gregory P. Chansolme — 1982 — The University of Oklahoma, B.A., 2005; The University of Oklahoma College of Law, J.D./M.B.A., 2009 — Admitted to Bar, 2005, Oklahoma; U.S. District Court, Western District of Oklahoma — Member Oklahoma and Oklahoma County Bar Associations — Practice Areas: Banking; Business Law; Business Formation; Business Transactions; Contracts; Estate Planning; Probate; Real Estate; Trusts; Wills — E-mail: gchansolme@dlb.net

Of Counsel

Stephen A. Sherman — 1953 — University of Michigan, B.G.S. (with high distinction), 1975; Santa Clara University School of Law, J.D./M.B.A., 1979 — Admitted to Bar, 1980, Oklahoma; U.S. District Court, Eastern, Northern, and Western Districts of Oklahoma; U.S. Court of Appeals, Tenth Circuit; U.S. Tax Court; U.S. Supreme Court — Practice Areas: Real Estate; Banking; Business Litigation; Business Law; Business Formation; Business Transactions; Commercial Law; Commercial Litigation; Contracts — E-mail: ssherman@dlb.net

GableGotwals

Fifteenth Floor, One Leadership Square
211 North Robinson
Oklahoma City, Oklahoma 73102-7101
Telephone: 405-235-5500
Fax: 405-235-2875
E-Mail: info@gablelaw.com
www.gablelaw.com

GableGotwals, Oklahoma City, OK (Continued)

(Tulsa, OK Office*: 1100 ONEOK Plaza, 100 West Fifth Street, 74103-4217)
(Tel: 918-595-4800)
(Fax: 918-595-4990)

Administrative Law, Alternative Dispute Resolution, Appellate Practice, Aviation, Bad Faith, Breach of Contract, Class Actions, Construction Law, Energy, Environmental Law, Entertainment Law, Health Care, Intellectual Property, Insurance Coverage, Labor and Employment, Mergers and Acquisitions, Oil and Gas, Product Liability, Professional Liability, Governmental Relations

Firm Profile: Established in 1919, GableGotwals is a full-service law firm that provides high quality legal services through 90+ highly experienced litigators and transactional attorneys who represent a diversified client base across the nation. Though Oklahoma-based, our connections and reach are global.

Insurance Clients

Aetna Health Inc.
Hartford Life and Accident Insurance Company
Metropolitan Life Insurance Company
The Principal Financial Group
Principal Life Insurance Company
Colony Insurance Company
John Hancock Life Insurance Company
Ohio National Financial Services
The Northwestern Mutual Life Insurance Company

Insurance Practice Members

Dale Cottingham — Oklahoma Baptist University, B.A., 1979; Southern Methodist University, J.D., 1982 — Admitted to Bar, 1982, Oklahoma, 2008, Texas — Member American and Oklahoma Bar Associations; State Bar of Texas; Oklahoma City Mineral Lawyers Society — Best Lawyers, Lawyer of the Year in Energy Law 2014, Lawyer of the Year in Water Law 2012; Chambers USA; AV Preeminent Martindale-Hubbell Lawyer Rating

Sidney G. Dunagan — The University of Tulsa, B.A., 1964; The University of Tulsa College of Law, J.D., 1967 — Admitted to Bar, 1968, Oklahoma — Member American, Oklahoma, Oklahoma County and Tulsa County Bar Associations; American College of Trial Lawyers — Oklahoma Super Lawyers; Best Lawyers in America, Lawyer of the Year 2013; AV Preminent Martindale-Hubbell Lawyer Rating; Chambers USA

David L. Kearney — The University of Oklahoma, B.B.A., 1982; J.D., 1985 — Admitted to Bar, 1985, Oklahoma — Member American, Oklahoma and Oklahoma County Bar Associations — Super Lawyers; AV Preeminent Lawyer Rating

Leslie L. Lynch — Oklahoma Baptist University, B.B.A., 1987; Oklahoma City University, J.D., 1993 — Admitted to Bar, 1993, Oklahoma; 2006, Nebraska — Member Oklahoma and Oklahoma County Bar Associations; American Inns of Court, Robert J. Turner Chapter — Best Lawyers in America; Super Lawyers

Leasa M. Stewart — The University of Oklahoma, B.S., 1988; Georgetown University Law Center, J.D., 1991 — Admitted to Bar, 1991, Oklahoma; 1999, Texas — Member American, Oklahoma and Oklahoma County Bar Associations; State Bar of Texas; Defense Research Institute — AV Preeminent Martindale-Hubbell Lawyers Rating; Super Lawyers

Amy M. Stipe — The University of Oklahoma, B.A., 1995; J.D., 1999 — Admitted to Bar, 1999, Oklahoma — Member American, Oklahoma and Oklahoma County Bar Associations; American Inns of Court, William J. Holloway, Jr. Chapter; Fellow, Oklahoma Bar Foundation; Oklahoma City Mineral Lawyers Society; Fellow, American Bar Foundation — AV Preeminent Martindale-Hubbell Lawyer Rating; Best Lawyers in America; Super Lawyers Rising Stars

Of Counsel

Jeffrey A. Curran

(See listing under Tulsa, OK for additional information)

OKLAHOMA CITY

Hiltgen & Brewer, P.C.

9505 North Kelley Avenue
Oklahoma City, Oklahoma 73131
   Telephone: 405-605-9000
   Fax: 405-605-9010
   www.hiltgenbrewer.com

Established: 1996

Insurance Defense, Civil Litigation, Special Investigations, Examinations Under Oath, Medical Liability, Managed Care Liability, Tort Litigation, Contracts, Workers' Compensation, Subrogation, Product Liability, Premises Liability, Employment Law, Transportation, Railroad Law, Vicarious Liability, Warranty Law, Pharmacy Negligence

Insurance Clients

Allstate Insurance Company	American Agency System, Inc.
AXIS Insurance	Clarendon National Insurance Company
CNA Excess and Select	ESIS
E & O Professionals	Fireman's Fund Insurance Company
Farmland Mutual Insurance Company	Millers Insurance Group
Harco National Insurance Company	Pennsylvania Lumbermens Mutual Insurance Company
Sagamore Insurance Company	

Shareholders

Cary E. Hiltgen — 1954 — Hutchinson Community Junior College, A.A., 1974; Northwest Missouri State University, B.S., 1976; Oklahoma City University, J.D., 1980 — Admitted to Bar, 1981, Oklahoma; U.S. District Court, Eastern, Northern and Western Districts of Oklahoma; U.S. Court of Appeals, Tenth Circuit; 1993, U.S. District Court, District of Arizona; 1994, U.S. District Court, District of Nebraska; 1995, U.S. District Court, Central District of Illinois; U.S. Court of Appeals, Third, Seventh, Eighth and Ninth Circuits; 1996, U.S. District Court, Western District of New York; U.S. District Court, Central District of Utah; 2004, U.S. Supreme Court — Member American, Oklahoma and Oklahoma County Bar Associations; Coalition of Food Industry Counsel; Defense Research Institute (Past President, 2011; Past Chair, Product Liability Committee, Law Institutes); Product Liability Advisory Counsel; Trucking Industry Defense Association; International Association of Defense Counsel — E-mail: Cehiltgen@hiltgenbrewer.com

Michael W. Brewer — 1960 — The University of Oklahoma, B.S.M.E., 1982; J.D., 1986 — Phi Delta Phi; Recipient, American Jurisprudence Award in Anti-Trust Law — Admitted to Bar, 1986, Oklahoma; U.S. District Court, Eastern, Northern and Western Districts of Oklahoma; U.S. Court of Appeals, Tenth Circuit — Member American, Oklahoma and Oklahoma County (Board of Directors) Bar Associations; Federation of Defense and Insurance Counsel; Defense Research Institute (Past Chairman of Insurance Roundtable, Product Liability Committee, Representative to Diversity Committee, Past Chairman, Technology Section); Early Neutral Evaluation Panel for Western District of Oklahoma; Oklahoma Association of Defense Counsel (Past President); William J. Holloway Jr. American Inns of Court (Barrister, 1993-1996); Transportation Lawyers Association — "Workers' Compensation: Erosion of the Exclusive Remedy Provision", Oklahoma Law Review, Vol. 38-3 (Fall, 1985) — Arbitration Panel, Arbitration Forum; — E-mail: Mwbrewer@hiltgenbrewer.com

Director

Brock C. Bowers — 1969 — The University of Oklahoma, B.A., 1991; J.D. (with honors), 1994 — Phi Beta Kappa — Admitted to Bar, 1994, Oklahoma; 1995, U.S. District Court, Eastern and Western Districts of Oklahoma; 1996, U.S. Court of Appeals, Tenth Circuit — Member American, Oklahoma and Oklahoma County Bar Associations; Defense Research Institute; Oklahoma Association of Defense Counsel — E-mail: Bcbowers@hiltgenbrewer.com

Associates

Norman Lemonik — 1954 — Syracuse University, B.S., 1976; New York University, J.D., 1980 — Admitted to Bar, 1980, Michigan; Oklahoma; 1991, U.S. Court of Appeals, Tenth Circuit; 1994, U.S. District Court, Northern District of Oklahoma — Member American and Oklahoma Bar Associations; Defense Research Institute; Oklahoma Association of Defense Counsel — E-mail: Nlemonik@hiltgenbrewer.com

OKLAHOMA

Hiltgen & Brewer, P.C., Oklahoma City, OK (Continued)

Scott C. Sublett — 1952 — University of Colorado, B.S., 1975; The University of Tulsa, J.D. (with honors), 1979 — Admitted to Bar, 1979, Oklahoma; 1980, U.S. District Court, Northern District of Oklahoma; 1982, U.S. District Court, Western District of Oklahoma; 1989, U.S. Court of Appeals, Tenth Circuit; 1999, U.S. District Court, Eastern District of Oklahoma; U.S. Court of Appeals, Ninth Circuit — Member Oklahoma Bar Association; Defense Research Institute; Oklahoma Association of Defense Counsel — E-mail: Ssublett@hiltgenbrewer.com

Jeffrey C. Grotta — 1961 — The University of Oklahoma, B.A., 1986; J.D. (Dean's List), 1993 — American Indian Law Review — Admitted to Bar, 1993, Oklahoma; 1994, U.S. District Court, Eastern, Northern and Western Districts of Oklahoma — Member Oklahoma and Oklahoma County Bar Associations; Oklahoma Association of Defense Counsel; Defense Research Institute — E-mail: Jcgrotta@hiltgenbrewer.com

Lance C. Cook — 1979 — Emory University, B.A., 2002; Oklahoma City University, J.D. (Phi Delta Kappa), 2006 — Admitted to Bar, 2006, Oklahoma; U.S. District Court, Western District of Oklahoma — Member Oklahoma and Oklahoma County Bar Associations; Oklahoma Association of Defense Counsel; Defense Research Institute — E-mail: Lcook@hiltgenbrewer.com

Jennifer Ahrend — 1981 — The University of Oklahoma (distinguished graduate), 2004; J.D. (Dean's List), 2009 — Admitted to Bar, 2009, Oklahoma — Member Oklahoma and Oklahoma County Bar Associations — Languages: Mandarin Chinese — E-mail: Jahrend@hiltgenbrewer.com

Katie R. McCune — 1981 — University of Central Oklahoma, B.A., 2007; Oklahoma City University, J.D., 2012 — Admitted to Bar, 2013, Oklahoma; U.S. District Court, Northern and Western Districts of Oklahoma — Member Defense Research Institute — E-mail: Kmccune@hiltgenbrewer.com

Of Counsel

J. Randy Baker — 1955 — Oklahoma State University, B.S., 1977; Oklahoma City University, J.D. (with honors), 1980 — Admitted to Bar, 1980, Oklahoma; U.S. District Court, Eastern, Northern and Western Districts of Oklahoma; U.S. Court of Appeals, Tenth Circuit; U.S. Supreme Court — Member American, Oklahoma and Oklahoma County Bar Associations; Defense Research Institute; Oklahoma Association of Defense Counsel — Administrative Law Judge, Oklahoma Department of Labor — E-mail: Rbaker@hiltgenbrewer.com

(This firm is also listed in the Subrogation section of this directory)

Jennings Teague

204 North Robinson, Suite 1000
Oklahoma City, Oklahoma 73102
   Telephone: 405-609-6000
   Fax: 405-609-6501
   E-Mail: sglenn@jenningsteague.com
   www.jenningsteague.com

Established: 2000

Insurance Defense, Transportation, Bad Faith, Class Actions, Product Liability, Personal Injury, Employment Law, Civil Rights, Civil Litigation

Firm Profile: The lawyers of Jennings Teague represent domestic and international manufacturers and insurers in product liability litigation, negligence and other general liability litigation, transportation cases, insurance matters including bad faith claims, employment law, commercial litigation and provide defense for local and national fraternal organizations.

Jennings Teague focuses on high-stakes, complex litigation, efficiently and capably handling cases in district and appellate courts. The firm provides professional service to its clients with aggressive claim investigation, thorough case preparation, excellence in oral and written advocacy and persuasive trial presentation. Our attorneys serve their local, national and international clients in the state of Oklahoma and in courts throughout the United States.

The firm employs an experienced staff and utilizes its investigators, experts and consultants to provide a team approach to litigation. Contact Jennings Teague to learn more about how we can provide legal services to your company.

OKLAHOMA

OKLAHOMA CITY

Jennings Teague, Oklahoma City, OK (Continued)

Insurance Clients

Claim Management, Inc.
GuideOne Insurance
Shelter Insurance Companies
State Auto Insurance Company
Tokio Marine Claims Service, Inc.
Cunningham Lindsey U.S., Inc.
Royal & SunAlliance
Specialty Claims Management, LLC

Non-Insurance Clients

Briggs & Stratton Corporation
Freightliner, LLC
International Truck & Engine Corp.
Toyota Motor Sales, U.S.A., Inc.
Caterpillar Inc.
Hyundai Motor America
PACCAR, Inc.
Winnebago Industries, Inc.

Firm Members

James A. Jennings, III — 1949 — Oklahoma State University, B.A., 1971; The University of Oklahoma, J.D., 1974 — Phi Delta Phi — Admitted to Bar, 1974, Oklahoma; U.S. District Court, Eastern, Northern and Western Districts of Oklahoma; U.S. Court of Appeals, Tenth Circuit; U.S. Supreme Court — Member American, Oklahoma and Oklahoma County Bar Associations; Product Liability Advisory Council; Litigation Counsel of America; Oklahoma Attorneys Mutual Insurance Company (Board of Directors); Bank2 (Board of Directors); Defense Research Institute; International Association of Defense Counsel; American Board of Trial Advocates — Practice Areas: Product Liability; Bad Faith; Insurance Defense; Commercial Litigation; Environmental Law; Toxic Torts — E-mail: jaj@jctokc.com

J. Derrick Teague — 1967 — Oklahoma State University, B.S., 1990; Oklahoma City University, J.D., 1993 — Admitted to Bar, 1993, Oklahoma; U.S. District Court, Eastern, Northern and Western Districts of Oklahoma; U.S. Court of Appeals, Tenth Circuit — Member American, Oklahoma and Oklahoma County Bar Associations; Defense Research Institute — Practice Areas: Product Liability; Insurance Defense; Bad Faith; Workers' Compensation; Civil Litigation; Transportation — E-mail: dteague@jenningsteague.com

Linda G. Kaufmann — 1964 — The University of Oklahoma, B.S., 1988; Oklahoma City University, J.D., 1991 — Phi Delta Phi — Editor-In-Chief, Oklahoma City University Law Review (1990-1991) — Admitted to Bar, 1991, Oklahoma; U.S. District Court, Eastern, Northern and Western Districts of Oklahoma; U.S. Court of Appeals, Tenth Circuit — Member Oklahoma and Oklahoma County Bar Associations — Practice Areas: Product Liability; Insurance Defense; Civil Litigation; Appellate Practice — E-mail: lkaufmann@jenningsteague.com

W. Brett Willis — 1968 — Oklahoma University, B.B.A., 1990; J.D., 1993 — Admitted to Bar, 1993, Oklahoma; U.S. District Court, Eastern, Northern and Western Districts of Oklahoma; U.S. Court of Appeals, Tenth Circuit — Member Oklahoma and Oklahoma County Bar Associations; American Inns of Court — Practice Areas: Complex Litigation; Product Liability; Bad Faith — E-mail: wwillis@jenningsteague.com

Associates

Marty R. Skrapka — 1982 — The University of Oklahoma, B.S. (summa cum laude), 2004; J.D. (with distinction), 2007 — Managing Editor, Oklahoma Law Review (2006-2007) — Admitted to Bar, 2007, Oklahoma; U.S. District Court, Northern and Western Districts of Oklahoma — Member Oklahoma and Oklahoma County Bar Associations — Practice Areas: Product Liability; Insurance Defense; Bad Faith; Civil Litigation; Transportation — E-mail: mskrapka@jenningsteague.com

Haylie D. Treas — 1986 — Louisiana College, B.A. (magna cum laude), 2007; Oklahoma University, J.D., 2010 — Admitted to Bar, 2010, Oklahoma; 2011, U.S. District Court, Western District of Oklahoma — Member Oklahoma and Oklahoma County Bar Associations — Practice Areas: Product Liability; Insurance Defense; Civil Litigation; Commercial Litigation — E-mail: htreas@jenningsteague.com

Laura Eakens — 1979 — Oklahoma Baptist University, B.A., 2001; The University of Tulsa, Jur., 2004 — Admitted to Bar, 2004, Oklahoma; 2005, U.S. District Court, Eastern, Northern, and Western Districts of Oklahoma; U.S. Court of Appeals for the Federal and Tenth Circuits — Member Oklahoma County and Tulsa County Bar Associations — Practice Areas: Product Liability; Transportation; Insurance Defense; Employment Law — E-mail: leakens@jenningsteague.com

Johnston Legal Group PC

300 North Walker Avenue
Oklahoma City, Oklahoma 73102
Telephone: 405-232-5300
Fax: 405-232-5301

(Fort Worth, TX Office*: Dispute Management Center, 4200 Airport Freeway, 76117-6262)
(Tel: 817-820-0825)
(Fax: 817-820-0830)
(Toll Free: 800-771-6946)
(E-Mail: johnston@johnstonlegalgroup.com)
(www.johnstonlegalgroup.com)
(Houston, TX Office*: 7838 Hillmont Street, 77040)
(Tel: 713-830-4816)
(Fax: 713-830-4815)
(San Antonio, TX Office*: 206 East Locust Street, 78212)
(Tel: 210-734-3311)
(Fax: 210-734-3341)
(Lubbock, TX Office: 1014 Broadway, 79401)
(Tel: 806-281-0825)
(Fax: 806-281-0830)

Property, Third Party, Product Liability, Subrogation

(See listing under Fort Worth, TX for additional information)

Kerr, Irvine, Rhodes & Ables

201 Robert S. Kerr Avenue, Suite 600
Oklahoma City, Oklahoma 73102
Telephone: 405-272-9221
Fax: 405-236-3121
E-Mail: aables@kiralaw.com
www.kiralaw.com

Established: 1955

Insurance Defense, Insurance Regulation, Litigation, Life Insurance, Accident and Health, Property and Casualty

Firm Profile: The firm was established in 1955 as Kerr, Conn & Davis and in 1972, Robert S. Kerr, Jr., Francis S. Irvine and Horace G. Rhodes joined together to create the present firm. In 1985, J. Angela Ables, former Deputy Insurance Commissioner, joined the firm. In 1989 the name was changed to Kerr, Irvine, Rhodes & Ables. The firm consists of four partners, two associates and one "of counsel" attorney. All aspects of insurance law are provided by the firm including administrative, regulatory, defense, policy review and reinsurance contract services. Insurance coverage issues are handled by J. Angela Ables and environmental law issues are handled by R. Tom Lay.

Insurance Clients

Allstate Insurance Company
Association of Oklahoma Life Insurance Companies
Blue Cross and Blue Shield of Oklahoma
Globe Life and Accident Insurance Company
Leaders Life Insurance Company
Mission Life Insurance Company
Munich American Reassurance Company
Pre-Paid Legal Casualty, Inc.
Property Casualty Insurers Association of America
American Fidelity Assurance Company
Assured Guaranty Corp.
Financial Security Assurance of Oklahoma, Inc.
Great-West Life Assurance Company
LifeShield National Insurance Company
NAC Reinsurance Corporation
Oklahoma Life and Health Insurance Guaranty Association
Wellington Insurance Company

Partners

Horace G. Rhodes — 1927 — The University of Oklahoma, B.S., 1950; LL.B., 1955 — Admitted to Bar, 1955, Oklahoma; 1981, U.S. District Court, Western District of Oklahoma; 1985, U.S. Court of Appeals, Tenth Circuit; U.S.

OKLAHOMA CITY

Kerr, Irvine, Rhodes & Ables, Oklahoma City, OK (Continued)

Supreme Court — Member American (International Law), Oklahoma and Oklahoma County Bar Associations; Federation of Regulatory Counsel — E-mail: buhohgr@aol.com

J. Angela Ables — 1950 — East Central Oklahoma State University, B.A. (with honors), 1972; Oklahoma City University, J.D., 1975 — Admitted to Bar, 1976, Oklahoma; U.S. District Court, Northern District of Oklahoma; 1978, U.S. Court of Appeals, Tenth Circuit; 1981, U.S. District Court, Western District of Oklahoma; 1984, U.S. Supreme Court; 1998, U.S. District Court, Eastern District of Oklahoma — Member American Bar Association (Tort and Insurance Practice, Administrative Law); Oklahoma Bar Association (Vice Chairman, Group Insurance Committee, 1996-1998, 2001, Chairman 1998-2001, 2002-2007); Oklahoma County Bar Association (Law Day Committee, Chairman, 1994; Fee Grievance Committee); Federation of Regulatory Counsel (1988-Present; Board of Directors, 1995-2000; Vice Chairman, 1997; Chairman, 1998); Oklahoma Association of Defense Counsel — Board of Directors, Oklahoma Attorneys Mutual Insurance Company — E-mail: aables@kiralaw.com

James W. Rhodes — 1958 — Wesleyan University, B.A., 1980; The University of Oklahoma, J.D., 1984 — Admitted to Bar, 1984, Oklahoma; U.S. District Court, Western District of Oklahoma; 1986, U.S. Court of Appeals, Tenth Circuit; 1989, U.S. Supreme Court — Member American, Oklahoma and Oklahoma County Bar Associations — E-mail: oklhiga@aol.com

R. Thomas Lay — 1948 — Oklahoma State University, B.S., 1970; Oklahoma City University, J.D., 1973 — Admitted to Bar, 1973, Oklahoma; U.S. District Court, Western District of Oklahoma; U.S. Supreme Court — Member American, Oklahoma and Oklahoma County Bar Associations — E-mail: rtl@kiralaw.com

Associates

Johnny R. Blassingame — 1980 — Texas Tech University, B.A. (cum laude), 2002; The University of Oklahoma, J.D., 2006 — Admitted to Bar, 2006, Oklahoma; U.S. District Court, Western District of Oklahoma — Member American, Oklahoma and Oklahoma County Bar Associations — E-mail: jblassingame@kiralaw.com

Andrew G. Hill — Oklahoma State University, B.A., 2008; The University of Oklahoma, J.D., 2011 — Admitted to Bar, 2011, Oklahoma; Supreme Court of Oklahoma — Member American, Oklahoma and Oklahoma County Bar Associations — E-mail: ahill@kiralaw.com

(This firm is also listed in the Regulatory and Compliance section of this directory)

Monnet, Hayes, Bullis, Thompson & Edwards

120 North Robinson, Suite 1719 West
Oklahoma City, Oklahoma 73102
Telephone: 405-232-5481
Fax: 405-235-9159
Toll Free: 877-232-5481
E-Mail: office@monnethayes.com

Established: 1946

Insurance Defense, Casualty, Property, Product Liability, Surety, Life Insurance, Accident and Health

Insurance Clients

American Insurance Group
Globe Life and Accident Insurance Company
Travelers Insurance Companies
Fireman's Fund Insurance Company
Hartford Insurance Company
Wausau General Insurance Company

Non-Insurance Clients

Citation Oil & Gas Corp.
J. Walter Duncan Oil Company, LLC
Natural Gas Pipe Line Company of America
XTO Energy, Inc.
JPMorgan Chase Bank, N.A.
Lance Ruffel Oil & Gas Corporation
Oklahoma National Stockyards
OXY USA, Inc.

Monnet, Hayes, Bullis, Thompson & Edwards, Oklahoma City, OK (Continued)

Partners

Claude Monnet — (1899-1980)
Lynn J. Bullis, Jr. — (1910-1984)
Coleman Hayes — (1903-1985)
Russell F. Thompson — (1920-1985)
John T. Edwards — (1927-2012)
James M. Peters — 1939 — Oklahoma State University, B.A., 1962; The University of Oklahoma, J.D., 1965 — Admitted to Bar, 1965, Oklahoma
James S. Drennan — 1950 — Oklahoma State University, B.S., 1972; M.S., 1974; The University of Oklahoma, J.D., 1977 — Admitted to Bar, 1977, Oklahoma
Gayle Freeman Cook — 1949 — The University of Oklahoma, B.S., 1971; M.Ed., 1972; Oklahoma City University, J.D., 1974 — Admitted to Bar, 1975, Oklahoma
Sarah Lynn Stuhr — 1956 — The University of Tulsa, B.A., 1978; The University of Oklahoma, J.D., 1981 — Admitted to Bar, 1981, Oklahoma
Robert C. Smith, Jr. — 1950 — The University of North Carolina, B.S., 1976; Oklahoma City University, J.D., 1980 — Admitted to Bar, 1980, Oklahoma
Michael S. Peters — 1966 — Westminster College, B.A., 1989; Oklahoma City University, J.D., 1992 — Admitted to Bar, 1992, Oklahoma
Robert A. French — 1959 — The University of Oklahoma, B.A. (with honors), 1984; M.A. (with highest honors), 1988; J.D., 1993 — Admitted to Bar, 1993, Oklahoma

Walker, Ferguson & Ferguson

Ferguson Law Building
941 East Britton Road
Oklahoma City, Oklahoma 73114
Telephone: 405-843-8855
Fax: 405-843-8934
E-Mail: tferg@wffatty.com

Established: 1974

Insurance Defense, Automobile, Product Liability, Bad Faith, Workers' Compensation, Employment Law, Bodily Injury, Uninsured and Underinsured Motorist, General Liability, Subrogation, Truck Liability

Insurance Clients

American Home Shield
The Cincinnati Insurance Companies
Essex Insurance Company
Markel American Insurance Company
Oklahoma Municipal Assurance Group
Tokio Marine Management, Inc.
Argonaut Great Central Insurance Company
Employers Mutual Companies
Goodville Mutual Casualty Company
National Security Fire and Casualty
Pharmacists Mutual Insurance Company

Non-Insurance Clients

Jack Cooper Transport
Unit Parts, Inc.
Loomis Armored U.S., Inc.
Yellow Freight System

Partners

Thomas G. Ferguson, Jr. — 1948 — Virginia Military Institute, B.A., 1970; Washington and Lee University, J.D., 1973 — Phi Delta Phi — Admitted to Bar, 1973, Virginia; 1977, West Virginia; 1979, Oklahoma; 1976, U.S. Tax Court; 1979, U.S. District Court, Eastern, Northern and Western Districts of Oklahoma; U.S. Court of Appeals, Tenth Circuit; U.S. Supreme Court — Member American, Oklahoma, Virginia, West Virginia and Oklahoma County Bar Associations; Virginia State Bar; West Virginia State Bar; Defense Research Institute — LTC, JAGC, U.S. Army, 1973-1977; U.S. Army Reserve, Retired
James C. Ferguson — 1951 — Washington and Lee University, B.S., 1974; Oklahoma University, M.A., 1978; J.D., 1985 — Admitted to Bar, 1985, Oklahoma; U.S. District Court, Western District of Oklahoma — Member

OKLAHOMA

Walker, Ferguson & Ferguson, Oklahoma City, OK (Continued)

American, Oklahoma and Oklahoma County (Workers' Compensation Section) Bar Associations — U.S. Army FA, 1974-1981; COL., Oklahoma Army National Guard, Retired

James E. Walker — 1944 — Oklahoma University, B.B.A., 1967; J.D., 1974 — Phi Alpha Delta — Admitted to Bar, 1974, Oklahoma; U.S. District Court, Eastern, Northern and Western Districts of Oklahoma; U.S. Court of Appeals, Tenth Circuit; U.S. Tax Court — Member American, Oklahoma and Oklahoma County Bar Associations — U.S. Army, 1967-1970, 1974-1976; Brigadier General, Oklahoma Army National Guard, Retired

Associates

Jon L. Derouen, Jr. — 1970 — Texas A&M University, B.A., 1993; Oklahoma City University, J.D., 1998 — Admitted to Bar, 1998, Oklahoma; U.S. District Court, Western District of Oklahoma; 1999, U.S. District Court, Eastern District of Oklahoma — Member American, Oklahoma and Oklahoma County Bar Associations; Oklahoma Workers' Compensation Defense Council

Of Counsel

Bruce W. Winston — 1947 — The University of Oklahoma, B.B.A., 1970; Oklahoma City University, J.D., 1973 — Phi Delta Phi — Admitted to Bar, 1973, Oklahoma; U.S. District Court, Western District of Oklahoma; 1975, U.S. District Court, Eastern District of Oklahoma; 1979, U.S. District Court, Eastern and Northern Districts of Oklahoma; U.S. Court of Appeals, Tenth Circuit — Member American, Oklahoma and Oklahoma County Bar Associations; Oklahoma Association of Defense Counsel; International Association of Defense Counsel; Defense Research Institute

Welch & Smith, P.C.

6440 Avondale Drive, Suite 206
Oklahoma City, Oklahoma 73116
Telephone: 405-286-0801
Fax: 405-286-0301
E-Mail: mwelch@welchsmith.com

Established: 1995

Insurance Coverage, Bad Faith, Errors and Omissions, Tort Litigation

Insurance Clients

American Farmers & Ranchers Mutual Insurance Company
Grain Dealers Mutual Insurance Company
Hanover Insurance Group
Markel Corporation
American Interstate Insurance Company
Great American Insurance Company
The Main Street America Group
Oklahoma Attorneys Mutual Insurance Company

Non-Insurance Clients

Avis Rent-A-Car System, LLC
Tractor Supply Co.

Firm Members

Mort G. Welch — 1950 — The University of Oklahoma, B.A. (with special distinction), 1972; The University of Texas at Austin, J.D., 1975 — Phi Beta Kappa — Admitted to Bar, 1975, Texas; 1976, Oklahoma; 1977, U.S. District Court, Western District of Oklahoma; U.S. Court of Appeals, Tenth Circuit; 1979, U.S. District Court, Northern District of Oklahoma; 1999, U.S. Supreme Court — Member American (Tort and Insurance Practice Section), Oklahoma and Oklahoma County Bar Associations; International Association of Defense Counsel; Defense Research Institute — "Allocation of Fault - Identifying All Angles," Oklahoma Bar Association CLE, February (1989); "Replacement Cost Property Insurance Coverage Without Replacement," The Conference on Consumer Finance Law (December, 1996); "Identifying and Using Insurance Coverages - Commercial Liability" Oklahoma Bar Association CLE (February, 1990); "Documenting the Agreement," Oklahoma Bar Association CLE (December, 1991; February, 1995); "There Are Many People Who Want Your Client's UM Money: Pitfalls in the Settlement of UM Claims" Oklahoma Bar Association CLE (October 2009); Program Chair, "What the Other UM Seminars Didn't Tell You: How To Settle and (If All Else Fails) Try UM Cases" Oklahoma Bar Association, CLE (October 2009);

OKLAHOMA CITY

Welch & Smith, P.C., Oklahoma City, OK (Continued)

"Substantial Certainty Tort Claims By Injured Employees Against Their Employers: What Workers Compensation Professionals Should Know," 11th Annual Spring Insurance Update Seminar (April, 2010); "Basic Elements of Auto Liability Coverage and Case Law Restrictions, What Must be Proved to Prevail on a UM Claim, The Interface Between Auto Liability and UM Coverages when the Claim's Value Potentially Exceeds the Liability Coverage Limit, Last Minute Continuing Legal Education," (Leflore County Bar Ass'n. Dec. 16, 2010) — Reported Cases: Akin v. Ashland Chem. Co., 156 F.3d 1030 (10th Cir. 1998), cert. den'd 526 U.S. 1112 (1999); Alea London Ltd. v. Canal Club, Inc., 231 P.3d 157 (Okla. Civ. App. 2009); American Farmers & Ranchers Mutual Insurance Company v. Shelter Mutual Insurance Company, 267 P.3d 147 (Okla. Civ. App 2011); American Interstate Ins. Co. v. Wilson Paving & Excavating, Inc., 2009 WL 3427992 (N.D. Okla.), 2010 WL 2624133 (N.D. Okla.); Angelo v. Armstrong World Industries, 11 F.3d 957 (10th Cir. 1993); Barnard v. Sutton, 321 P.3d 999 (Okla. Civ. App. 2013); Beeman v. Manville Corp. Asbestos Disease Compensation Fund, 496 N.W.2d 247 (Iowa 1993); Bristol v. Fibreboard Corp., 789 F.2d 846 (10th Cir. 1986); Case v. Fibreboard Corp., 743 P.2d 1062 (Okla. 1987); Cofer v. Morton, 784 P.2d 67 (Okla. 1989); Coleman v. Turpen, 697 F.2d 1341 (10th Cir. 1982), app. after remand 827 F.2d 667 (10th Cir. 1987); Condray v. Unum Life Ins. Co. of Am., 2009 WL 1312515 (W.D. Okla.); Employers Ins. Co. of Wausau v. Midwest Towers, Inc. 2011 WL 5117610 (W.D. Okla.); Fisher v. Owens Corning Fiberglass Corp., 868 F.2d 1175 (10th Cir. 1989); Fleming v. Hall, 638 P.2d 1115 (Okla. 1981); Gonzalez v. Dub Ross Co., Inc., 224 P.3d 1283 (Okla. Civ. App. 2009); Grain Dealers Mut. Ins. Co. v. Farmers All. Mut. Ins. Co., 298 F.3d 1178 (10th Cir. 2002); GuideOne Mutual Ins. Co. v. The Shore Ins. Agy., 259 P.3d 864 (Okla. Civ. App. 2011); Hanover Am. Ins. Co. v. Saul, 2013 WL 812353, 2013 WL 4542284 (W.D. Okla.); Horace Mann Ins. Co. v. Johnson, 953 F.2d 575 (10th Cir. 1991); Huff v. Fibreboard Corp., 836 F.2d 473 (10th Cir. 1987); Kerr-McGee Corporation v. Admiral Ins. Co., 905 P.2d 760 (Okla. 1995); Lindsey v. Dayton-Hudson Corp., 592 F.2d 1118 (10th Cir.) cert. den'd 444 U.S. 856 (1979); Livengood v. Thedford, 681 F.Supp. 695 (W.D. Okla. 1988); Mulford v. Neal, 264 P.3d 1173 (Okla. 2011); Oklahoma Farmers Union Mut. Ins. Co. v. John Deere Ins. Co., 967 P.2d 479 (Okla. Civ. App. 1998); O'Rear v. American Gen. Assur. Co., 2010 WL 2594748 (W.D. Okla.); Poteau Ford Mercury, Inc. v. Zurich American Ins. Co., 2009 WL 9508739 (Okla. Civ. App.); Ray v. Oklahoma Heritage Home Care, Inc., 2013 WL 2368808 (W.D. Okla.); Republic Underwriters Ins. Co. v. Moore, 2010 WL 4365566 (N.D. Ok.), 493 Fed. Appx. 907 (10th Cir. 2012); Sargent v. Central Nat'l Bk. & T. Co. of Enid, Oklahoma, 809 P.2d 1298 (Okla. 1991); Short v. Oklahoma Farmers Union, 619 P.2d 588 (Okla. 1980); Snethen v. Oklahoma State Union of the Farmers' Educational and Cooperative Union of America, 664 P.2d 377 (Okla. 1982); State Farm Mut. Ins. Co. v. Schwartz, 933 F.2d 848 (10th Cir. 1991) (amicus curiae); Takagi v. Wilson Foods Corp., 662 P.2d 308 (Okla. 1983); Tax Investments Concepts, Inc. v. McLaughlin, 670 P.2d 981 (Okla. 1982); Thiry v. Armstrong World Indus., 661 P.2d 515 (Okla. 1983); Timberlake Const. Co. v. U.S.F. & G. Co., 71 F.3d 335 (10th Cir. 1995); Trinity Univ. Ins. Co. v. Broussard, 932 F.Supp. 1307 (N.D. Okla. 1996); Vilsick v. Fibreboard Corp., 861 S.W.2d 659 (Mo. App. 1993); Wever v. State ex rel. Dept. of Human Services, 839 P.2d 672 (Okla. Civ. App. 1990); Wilson & Co. v. Reed, 603 P.2d 1172 (Okla. Civ. App. 1979); Wilson Foods Corp. v. Noble, 613 P.2d 485 (Okla. Civ. App. 1980); Wilson Foods Corp. v. Porter, 612 P.2d 261 (Okla. 1980). — Oklahoma Superlawyers 2009-2014 — E-mail: mwelch@welchsmith.com

Sherry L. Smith — 1956 — Oklahoma City University, B.A. (magna cum laude), 1981; The University of Oklahoma, J.D., 1984 — Jessup Moot Court — Admitted to Bar, 1984, Oklahoma; U.S. District Court, Western District of Oklahoma; 1985, U.S. District Court, Eastern District of Oklahoma; 1986, U.S. Court of Appeals, Tenth Circuit — Member American Bar Association (Law Practice Management and Tort and Insurance Practice Sections); Oklahoma and Oklahoma County Bar Associations; Oklahoma Association of Defense Counsel — Reported Cases: Barnard v. Sutton, 321 P.3d 999 (Okla. Civ. App. 2013); Cimarron Pipeline Constr. v. U.S.F. & G. Co., 848 P.2d 1161 (Okla. 1983); Employers Ins. Co. of Wausau v. Midwest Towers, Inc. 2011 WL 5117610 (W.D. Okla.); Macy v. Oklahoma City School District, 961 P.2d 804 (Okla. 1998); Grain Dealers Mut. Ins. Co. v. Farmers All. Mut. Ins. Co., 298 F.3d 1179 (10th Cir. 2002); Ray v. Oklahoma Heritage Home Care, Inc., 2013 WL 2368808 (W.D. Okla.). — E-mail: ssmith@welchsmith.com

SULPHUR

Wheeler, Wheeler, Morgan, Faulkner & Brown

1900 NW Expressway, Suite 450
Oklahoma City, Oklahoma 73118-1849
   Telephone: 405-840-5151
   Fax: 405-840-5183

Established: 1957

Trial Practice, Personal Injury, Workers' Compensation, Insurance Defense, Business Law, Commercial Litigation, State and Federal Courts, Litigation, Real Estate

Insurance Clients

CNA Global Specialty Lines	The Hartford
The Infinity Group	Titan Insurance Company
United Home Insurance Company	Unitrin Specialty Insurance
Victoria Insurance Company	

Firm Member

Joe D. Wheeler, Jr. — 1948 — Oklahoma City University, B.A., 1971; Oklahoma City University School of Law, J.D., 1975 — Phi Delta Phi — Admitted to Bar, 1975, Oklahoma — Member Oklahoma and Oklahoma County Bar Associations; Oklahoma Association of Defense Counsel — Tel: 405-840-5151 ext. 134 — E-mail: jwheeler@50pennlaw.com, sjsmith@50pennlaw.com

---

The following firms also service this area.

Barnum & Clinton, PLLC

1011 24th Avenue, N.W.
Norman, Oklahoma 73069
   Telephone: 405-579-7300
   Fax: 405-579-0140

Mailing Address: P.O. Box 720298, Norman, OK 73070

Workers' Compensation, Premises Liability, Automobile Liability, Business Litigation, Business Transactions, Commercial Law, Commercial Litigation, Employer Liability, Employment Law, Employment Litigation, General Civil Litigation, General Defense, Occupational Accident

SEE COMPLETE LISTING UNDER NORMAN, OKLAHOMA (20 MILES)

Frailey, Chaffin, Cordell, Perryman, Sterkel, McCalla & Brown, L.L.P.

201 North Fourth Street
Chickasha, Oklahoma 73023
   Telephone: 405-224-0237
   Fax: 405-222-2319

Mailing Address: P.O. Box 533, Chickasha, OK 73018

Administrative Law, Agriculture, Business Law, Civil Litigation, Commercial Transactions, Energy, Fire, Governmental Liability, Insurance Coverage, Insurance Defense, Municipal Law, Negligence, Oil and Gas, Premises Liability, Product Liability, Tort Litigation

SEE COMPLETE LISTING UNDER CHICKASHA, OKLAHOMA (43 MILES)

Wheatley, Segler, Osby & Miller, LLC

501 West Main Street
Yukon, Oklahoma 73099
   Telephone: 405-354-5276
   Fax: 405-350-0537

Mailing Address: P.O. Box 850126, Yukon, OK 73085

Insurance Defense, General Liability, Trucking Law, Product Liability, Subrogation, Life and Health, Business Law

SEE COMPLETE LISTING UNDER YUKON, OKLAHOMA (10 MILES)

PAULS VALLEY † 6,187 Garvin Co.

Refer To

Fischl, Culp, McMillin, Chaffin, Bahner & Long, L.L.P.

100 E Street, S.W.
Ardmore, Oklahoma 73401
   Telephone: 580-223-4321
   Fax: 580-226-4795

Mailing Address: P.O. Box 1766, Ardmore, OK 73402-1766

Insurance Defense, Trial Practice, Automobile, Product Liability, General Liability, Property and Casualty, Bad Faith

SEE COMPLETE LISTING UNDER ARDMORE, OKLAHOMA (45 MILES)

POTEAU † 8,520 Le Flore Co.

Refer To

Smith, Cohen & Horan, PLC

1206 Garrison Avenue
Fort Smith, Arkansas 72901
   Telephone: 479-782-1001
   Fax: 479-782-1279

Mailing Address: P.O. Box 10205, Fort Smith, AR 72917-0205

Insurance Defense, Automobile Liability, Transportation, Product Liability, Subrogation, Employment Law, Environmental Law, General and Product Liability

SEE COMPLETE LISTING UNDER FORT SMITH, ARKANSAS (44 MILES)

SALLISAW † 8,880 Sequoyah Co.

Refer To

Daily & Woods, P.L.L.C.

58 South Sixth
Fort Smith, Arkansas 72901
   Telephone: 479-782-0361
   Fax: 479-782-6160

Mailing Address: P.O. Box 1446, Fort Smith, AR 72902

Insurance Defense

SEE COMPLETE LISTING UNDER FORT SMITH, ARKANSAS (24 MILES)

Refer To

Smith, Cohen & Horan, PLC

1206 Garrison Avenue
Fort Smith, Arkansas 72901
   Telephone: 479-782-1001
   Fax: 479-782-1279

Mailing Address: P.O. Box 10205, Fort Smith, AR 72917-0205

Insurance Defense, Automobile Liability, Transportation, Product Liability, Subrogation, Employment Law, Environmental Law, General and Product Liability

SEE COMPLETE LISTING UNDER FORT SMITH, ARKANSAS (24 MILES)

SULPHUR † 4,929 Murray Co.

Refer To

Fischl, Culp, McMillin, Chaffin, Bahner & Long, L.L.P.

100 E Street, S.W.
Ardmore, Oklahoma 73401
   Telephone: 580-223-4321
   Fax: 580-226-4795

Mailing Address: P.O. Box 1766, Ardmore, OK 73402-1766

Insurance Defense, Trial Practice, Automobile, Product Liability, General Liability, Property and Casualty, Bad Faith

SEE COMPLETE LISTING UNDER ARDMORE, OKLAHOMA (35 MILES)

OKLAHOMA

TISHOMINGO † 3,034 Johnston Co.

Refer To

Fischl, Culp, McMillin, Chaffin, Bahner & Long, L.L.P.
100 E Street, S.W.
Ardmore, Oklahoma 73401
  Telephone: 580-223-4321
  Fax: 580-226-4795

Mailing Address: P.O. Box 1766, Ardmore, OK 73402-1766

Insurance Defense, Trial Practice, Automobile, Product Liability, General Liability, Property and Casualty, Bad Faith

SEE COMPLETE LISTING UNDER ARDMORE, OKLAHOMA (30 MILES)

TULSA † 391,906 Tulsa Co.

Atkinson, Haskins, Nellis, Brittingham, Gladd & Fiasco

1500 Park Centre
525 South Main Street
Tulsa, Oklahoma 74103-4524
  Telephone: 918-582-8877
  Fax: 918-585-8096
  E-Mail: ahnmail@ahn-law.com
  www.ahn-law.com

Established: 1962

General Civil Practice, Insurance Law, Trial Practice, Appellate Practice, Negligence, Product Liability, Medical Malpractice, Legal Malpractice, Aviation, Oil and Gas, Commercial Litigation, Workers' Compensation, Environmental Law, Civil Rights, Employment Law, Pharmaceutical, Construction Litigation, Indian Law, Gaming Law, Broker-Dealer Disputes

Insurance Clients

Allstate Insurance Company
Chartis Insurance
Crum & Forster Insurance
Hartford Insurance Company
Liberty Mutual Insurance Company
National American Insurance Company
Northbrook Property and Casualty Insurance Company
Physicians Liability Insurance Company
State Farm Mutual Automobile Insurance Company
United Services Automobile Association (USAA)
American National Property and Casualty Company
Goodville Mutual Casualty Company
The Medical Protective Company
Nationwide Insurance
NCMIC Insurance Group
Oklahoma Attorneys Mutual Insurance Company
State Farm Fire and Casualty Company
Tribal First
Underwriters at Lloyd's, London
Utica Mutual Insurance Company

Non-Insurance Clients

Bank of Commerce
Grand River Dam Authority
Matrix Service Company
Muscogee (Creek) Nation Office of Public Gaming
Boy Scouts of America
Ion Laboratories, Inc.
Muscogee (Creek) Nation
Singer Brothers, LLC
YRC, Inc.

Partners

Michael P. Atkinson — 1946 — The University of Oklahoma, B.A., 1968; The University of Oklahoma College of Law, J.D., 1972; The University of Texas School of Law, LL.M., 1975 — Admitted to Bar, 1972, Oklahoma — Member Oklahoma and Tulsa County Bar Associations; Diplomate, American Board of Trial Advocates; Master Emeritus, American Inns of Court; Fellow, American College of Trial Lawyers; Fellow, International Academy of Trial Lawyers — Listed in The Best Lawyers in America and Oklahoma Super Lawyers — E-mail: matkinson@ahn-law.com

Walter D. Haskins — 1956 — Drury College, B.A. (magna cum laude), 1977; The University of Kansas School of Law, J.D., 1980 — Pi Kappa Delta, Sigma Phi Epsilon, Omicron Delta Kappa — Admitted to Bar, 1980, Oklahoma; U.S. District Court, Eastern, Northern and Western Districts of Oklahoma; 1981, U.S. Court of Appeals, Tenth Circuit; 1988, U.S. Supreme Court; 1990, U.S. District Court, Eastern and Western Districts of

Atkinson, Haskins, Nellis, Brittingham, Gladd & Fiasco, Tulsa, OK
(Continued)

Arkansas — Member Oklahoma Bar Association; Advocate, American Board of Trial Advocates; United States District Court for the Northern District of Oklahoma Criminal Justice Act Panel; Lawyer-Pilots Bar Association; Oklahoma Association of Defense Counsel; International Association of Defense Counsel — Elected to The Best Lawyers in America, Oklahoma SuperLawyers; Multi-million dollar Advocates Forum; Oklahoma Association for Justice — E-mail: whaskins@ahn-law.com

Gregory D. Nellis — 1955 — Southwestern Oklahoma State University, B.A. (magna cum laude), 1976; The University of Oklahoma College of Law, J.D., 1980 — Phi Delta Phi — Admitted to Bar, 1980, Oklahoma; 1981, U.S. District Court, Eastern, Northern and Western Districts of Oklahoma; U.S. Court of Appeals, Tenth Circuit; U.S. Supreme Court — Member American, Oklahoma and Tulsa County Bar Associations; International Association of Defense Counsel; Oklahoma Association of Defense Counsel; Defense Research and Trial Lawyers Association; American Board of Trial Advocates; Defense Research Institute — E-mail: gnellis@ahn-law.com

Galen L. Brittingham — 1954 — Southwest Missouri State University, B.S., 1976; Central Missouri State University, M.S., 1983; Washburn University School of Law, J.D. (with honors), 1987 — Admitted to Bar, 1987, Oklahoma; U.S. District Court, Northern District of Oklahoma; U.S. Court of Appeals, Tenth Circuit — Member Oklahoma and Tulsa County Bar Associations — E-mail: gbrittingham@ahn-law.com

John S. Gladd — 1961 — Oklahoma State University, B.S., 1983; The University of Tulsa College of Law, J.D., 1987 — Phi Alpha Delta — Admitted to Bar, 1987, Oklahoma; 1988, U.S. District Court, Eastern, Northern and Western Districts of Oklahoma; U.S. Court of Appeals, Tenth Circuit — Member American, Oklahoma, Tulsa County and Tulsa Bar Associations; Defense Counsel Trial Academy; Oklahoma Association of Defense Counsel; Defense Research Institute — Oklahoma Super Lawyers (2006-2012); Super Lawyers Corporate (2007-2012) — E-mail: jgladd@ahn-law.com

William A. Fiasco — 1961 — The University of Oklahoma, B.A., 1983; The University of Oklahoma College of Law, J.D., 1988 — Admitted to Bar, 1988, Oklahoma; U.S. District Court, Eastern, Northern and Western Districts of Oklahoma — Member American, Oklahoma and Tulsa County Bar Associations; Oklahoma Association of Defense Counsel; Defense Research Institute; American Board of Trial Advocates — Oklahoma SuperLawyers (2006-2013) — E-mail: wfiasco@ahn-law.com

James N. Edmonds — 1961 — The University of Kansas, B.A., 1987; M.A., 1990; The University of Kansas School of Law, J.D., 1993 — Admitted to Bar, 1993, Oklahoma; U.S. District Court, Eastern, Northern and Western Districts of Oklahoma; U.S. Court of Appeals, Tenth Circuit — Member American, Oklahoma and Tulsa County Bar Associations; Defense Research Institute — E-mail: jedmonds@ahn-law.com

Mark W. Maguire — 1963 — Oklahoma State University, B.S., 1986; The University of Oklahoma College of Law, J.D., 1989 — Omicron Delta Kappa, Blue Key — Admitted to Bar, 1989, Oklahoma; U.S. District Court, Eastern, Northern and Western Districts of Oklahoma — Member American, Oklahoma and Tulsa County Bar Associations; Defense Counsel Trial Academy; American Board of Trial Advocates; Oklahoma Association of Defense Counsel; Defense Research Institute; American Inns of Court — E-mail: mmaguire@ahn-law.com

Jennifer R. Annis — 1972 — The University of Oklahoma, B.A., 1994; The University of Oklahoma College of Law, J.D., 1998 — American Jurisprudence Award, Disability Law and Trial Techniques — Admitted to Bar, 1998, Oklahoma; U.S. District Court, Eastern, Northern and Western Districts of Oklahoma — Member American, Oklahoma and Tulsa County Bar Associations; Defense Research Institute; Oklahoma Association of Defense Counsel — E-mail: jannis@ahn-law.com

Andrew Jayne — 1976 — Westminster College, B.A., 1999; The University of Oklahoma College of Law, J.D., 2002 — Admitted to Bar, 2002, Oklahoma; 2003, U.S. District Court, Eastern, Northern and Western Districts of Oklahoma — Member Oklahoma and Tulsa County Bar Associations — E-mail: ajayne@ahn-law.com

Carol J. Allen — 1965 — Northeastern State University, B.S. (summa cum laude), 1995; The University of Tulsa College of Law, J.D., 1998 — Admitted to Bar, 1999, Oklahoma; U.S. District Court, Northern District of Oklahoma; 2000, U.S. District Court, Eastern District of Oklahoma; U.S. Court of Appeals, Tenth Circuit; 2001, U.S. District Court, Western District of Oklahoma — Member Oklahoma, Tulsa County and Muscogee (Creek) Nation Bar Associations — AV Rated, Martindale-Hubbell — E-mail: callen@ahn-law.com

Martha J. Phillips — 1949 — Oklahoma State University, B.S., 1971; The University of Tulsa College of Law, J.D., 1986 — Delta Theta Phi — Admitted to Bar, 1986, Oklahoma; U.S. District Court, Eastern, Northern and Western

TULSA

Atkinson, Haskins, Nellis, Brittingham, Gladd & Fiasco, (Continued)
Tulsa, OK

Districts of Oklahoma; U.S. Court of Appeals, Tenth Circuit — Member American, Oklahoma and Tulsa County Bar Associations; Defense Research Institute — E-mail: mphillips@ahn-law.com

Marthanda J. Beckworth — 1949 — Northeastern Oklahoma State University, B.A. (with honors), 1971; The University of Tulsa College of Law, J.D. (with honors), 1983 — Admitted to Bar, 1983, Oklahoma; U.S. District Court, Eastern and Northern Districts of Oklahoma; U.S. Court of Appeals, Tenth Circuit; U.S. Supreme Court — Member American, Oklahoma and Tulsa County Bar Associations — E-mail: mbeckworth@ahn-law.com

Andrew G. Wakeman — 1975 — University of South Alabama, B.A., 1998; M.P.A., 2002; The University of Tulsa College of Law, J.D., 2002 — Phi Delta Phi — Admitted to Bar, 2006, Oklahoma; U.S. District Court, Eastern and Northern Districts of Oklahoma — Member American, Oklahoma and Tulsa County Bar Associations — E-mail: awakeman@ahn-law.com

Associates

Meredith D. Lindaman — 1983 — Oklahoma State University, B.S., 2005; University of Tulsa College of Law, J.D., 2008 — CALI Award, Excellence in Evidence; Order of the Barristers — Admitted to Bar, 2008, Oklahoma; U.S. District Court, Eastern, Northern and Western Districts of Oklahoma — Member Oklahoma Bar Association; American Health Lawyers Association; Defense Research Institute; Oklahoma Association of Defense Counsel — Certificate in Health Law — E-mail: mlindaman@ahn-law.com

Keith B. Bartsch — 1960 — The Citadel, B.S. (Departmental Honors), 1982; Webster University, M.A., 1990; University of Tulsa College of Law, J.D. (with honors), 2008 — Phi Alpha Delta — CALI Award, Insurance Law and Selling and Leasing; Scott A. Sanditen Memorial Award; Martin H. Belsky Award, Public Interest Law; University of Tulsa Marcy Lawless Service Award; Merit Scholarship — University of Tulsa Law Review — Admitted to Bar, 2008, Oklahoma; U.S. District Court, Eastern, Northern and Western Districts of Oklahoma; Muscogee (Creek) Nation Courts; Chickasaw Nation Tribal Court; Cherokee Nation Tribal Courts; Choctaw Tribal Court — Member Oklahoma and Tulsa County Bar Associations; Oklahoma Indian Bar Association; Fellow, Oklahoma Bar Foundation — Certificate in Native American Law — E-mail: kbartsch@ahn-law.com

J. Andrew Brown — 1977 — Northeastern State University, B.B.A. (magna cum laude), 2002; The University of Tulsa College of Law, J.D., 2009 — Phi Delta Phi — Senior Articles Editor, Tulsa Journal of Comparative and International Law — Admitted to Bar, 2009, Oklahoma; U.S. District Court, Eastern, Northern and Western Districts of Oklahoma; Cherokee Nation Tribal Courts; U.S. Court of Appeals, Tenth Circuit — Member American, Oklahoma and Tulsa County Bar Associations; Tulsa County Bench and Bar Committee — E-mail: jbrown@ahn-law.com

Jennifer Ary — 1983 — The University of Oklahoma, B.A. (summa cum laude), 2005; The University of Oklahoma College of Law, J.D. (with honors), 2009 — Phi Delta Phi; Comfort Scholar; A.L. Jeffrey Municipal Law Award; Order of the Coif — University of Oklahoma Law Review — Admitted to Bar, 2009, Oklahoma; U.S. District Court, Eastern, Northern and Western Districts of Oklahoma; 2011, U.S. Court of Appeals, Tenth Circuit — Member Oklahoma and Tulsa County Bar Associations — E-mail: jary@ahn-law.com

Rachel A. Hubner — 1987 — Drury University, B.A. (magna cum laude), 2009; University of Tulsa College of Law, J.D. (Dean's Honors), 2012 — The Tulsa Law Review, Editor, Outstanding Editor (2011-2012) — Admitted to Bar, 2012, Oklahoma; U.S. District Court, Northern District of Oklahoma — Member Student Bar Association (Vice President; Director of the Board of Advocates) — E-mail: rhubner@ahn-law.com

Rachael F. Hughes — 1986 — Oklahoma State University, B.A., 2008; Tulsa University School of Law, J.D. (with highest honors), 2013 — CALI awards in Constitutional Law; Order of the Curule Chair — Editor in Chief, Tulsa Law Review — Admitted to Bar, 2013, Oklahoma; U.S. District Court, Northern and Western Districts of Oklahoma — Member American and Oklahoma Bar Associations — Author: "Changes in Oklahoma Campaign Finance: The Rise in Corporate Influence and the Need for Disclosure," Tulsa Law Review, 2013 — E-mail: rhughes@ahn-law.com

Of Counsel

K. Clark Phipps — 1957 — The University of Oklahoma, B.S., 1980; Tulane University Law School, J.D. (cum laude), 1986 — Admitted to Bar, 1986, Oklahoma; 1995, Texas; 1986, U.S. District Court, Eastern, Northern and Western Districts of Oklahoma; U.S. Court of Appeals, Tenth Circuit — Member American, Oklahoma and Tulsa County Bar Associations; State Bar of Texas; American Board of Trial Advocates (Past President); Defense Counsel Trial Academy; Oklahoma Association of Defense Counsel; International Association of Defense Counsel; Defense Research Institute — E-mail: cphipps@ahn-law.com

Best & Sharp

Williams Tower I
One West Third Street, Suite 900
Tulsa, Oklahoma 74103
Telephone: 918-582-1234
Fax: 918-585-9447
www.bestsharp.com

Established: 1988

Trial Practice, Insurance Defense, Medical Malpractice, Negligence, Product Liability, General Liability, Labor and Employment, Civil Rights, Appellate Practice

Insurance Clients

Admiral Insurance Company
Alliance of Nonprofits for Insurance
American Physicians Insurance Company
API
Beazley Group
CNA HealthPro
Erie Insurance Group
Hiscox USA
The Medical Protective Company
Mt. Hawley Insurance Company
North Star Mutual Insurance Company
Ophthalmic Mutual Insurance Company
Physicians Liability Insurance Company
Prudential Insurance Company of America
St. Paul Travelers
Supermarket Insurance Group
Trident Insurance Services

AFLAC, Inc.
Allied World National Assurance Company
American Specialty Insurance & Risk Services, Inc.
Assurant Solutions
Church Mutual Insurance Company
The Doctors Company
Gallagher Bassett Services, Inc.
LaFarge North America, Inc.
Moose International & Fraternal Insurance
Oceanus Insurance Company
Oklahoma Municipal Assurance Group
Penn Treaty Network America Insurance Company
ProAssurance Professional Liability Group
QBE Insurance Corporation
Sedgwick CMS
Travelers
Verus Underwriting Managers, LLC

Non-Insurance Clients

Brookdale Living Centers
Cunningham Lindsey Claims Services
Gateway Mortgage Corporation
Gateway Risk Services, Inc.
Triad Eye Medical Center

Corrections Corporation of America
Eastern Oklahoma Orthopedic Center
Schindler Elevator Corporation
Tulsa Surgical Arts

Partners

Timothy G. Best — 1960 — Oklahoma State University, B.S., 1982; The University of Tulsa, J.D., 1988 — Admitted to Bar, 1988, Oklahoma; U.S. District Court, Eastern, Northern and Western Districts of Oklahoma — E-mail: tbest@bestsharp.com

Thomas A. LeBlanc — 1965 — Louisiana State University, B.A., 1987; University of Maryland, J.D., 1991 — Admitted to Bar, 1991, Oklahoma; 1992, U.S. Court of Appeals, Tenth Circuit; 1996, U.S. Court of Appeals, Eighth Circuit; U.S. District Court, Eastern, Northern and Western Districts of Oklahoma — Member Academy of Correctional Health Professionals; Defense Research Institute — E-mail: tleblanc@bestsharp.com

Sean H. McKee — 1965 — Graceland College, B.S., 1987; The University of Tulsa, J.D., 1990 — Admitted to Bar, 1990, Oklahoma; 1991, U.S. District Court, Eastern and Northern Districts of Oklahoma; U.S. Court of Appeals, Tenth Circuit; 1994, U.S. Supreme Court — E-mail: smckee@bestsharp.com

Matthew B. Free — 1973 — Oklahoma State University, B.S. (with honors), 1995; The University of Oklahoma, J.D. (with honors), 1998 — Admitted to Bar, 1998, Oklahoma; U.S. District Court, Eastern and Northern Districts of Oklahoma — E-mail: mfree@bestsharp.com

OKLAHOMA

TULSA

Buckman & Gray
A Professional Corporation
10108 East 79th Street
Tulsa, Oklahoma 74133
Telephone: 918-587-1525
Fax: 918-587-1535
E-Mail: sbuckman@buckmangray.com
www.buckmangray.com

Insurance Law, Agent and Brokers Errors and Omissions, Arson, Builders Risk, Cargo, Casualty, Commercial General Liability, Common Carrier, Complex Litigation, Construction Law, Construction Litigation, Coverage Issues, Declaratory Judgments, Employment Practices Liability, Errors and Omissions, Examinations Under Oath, Extra-Contractual Litigation, Fire, Inland Marine, Motor Carriers, Professional Errors and Omissions, Professional Negligence, State and Federal Courts, Transportation, Trucks/Heavy Equipment, Uninsured and Underinsured Motorist

Insurance Clients

ALEA London Ltd
American General Life and Accident Insurance Company
American Southern Insurance Company
Atlantic Insurance Company
Central Insurance Companies
Gulf Life Insurance Company
Le Mars Insurance Company
National American Insurance Company
St. Paul Reinsurance Company Limited
Sentry Insurance a Mutual Company
Underwriters at Lloyd's, London
Unionamerica Insurance Company Limited
United Fire & Casualty Company
American Bankers Insurance Group
American Safety Insurance Company
Associates Insurance Company
Atlas Insurance Company
Gulf Insurance Company
The Hartford
Mendota Insurance Company
Northland Insurance Company
OneBeacon Insurance
St. Paul Travelers
Select Insurance Company
State Auto Insurance Company
Terra Nova Insurance Company Limited
United Automobile Insurance Company

Partners

Steven V. Buckman — 1960 — Oklahoma State University, B.S., 1981; Oklahoma City University, J.D., 1984 — Admitted to Bar, 1984, Oklahoma; 1985, Texas; 2007, Arkansas; 1988, U.S. District Court, Eastern, Northern and Western Districts of Oklahoma; U.S. Court of Appeals, Tenth Circuit; U.S. Supreme Court — Member Oklahoma, Arkansas and Tulsa County Bar Associations; State Bar of Texas; Defense Research Institute — E-mail: sbuckman@buckmangray.com

Kristina L. Gray — 1982 — Texas Tech University, B.S. (summa cum laude), 2004; Oklahoma University, J.D. (with distinction), 2007 — Phi Kappa Phi — Recipient: American Jurisprudence Award Legal Research; American Jurisprudence Award Complex Litigation — Admitted to Bar, 2007, Oklahoma; 2008, U.S. District Court, Eastern and Northern Districts of Oklahoma — Member American and Oklahoma Bar Associations — E-mail: kgray@buckmangray.com

GableGotwals
1100 ONEOK Plaza
100 West Fifth Street
Tulsa, Oklahoma 74103-4217
Telephone: 918-595-4800
Fax: 918-595-4990
E-Mail: info@gablelaw.com
www.gablelaw.com

(Oklahoma City, OK Office*: Fifteenth Floor, One Leadership Square, 211 North Robinson, 73102-7101)
(Tel: 405-235-5500)
(Fax: 405-235-2875)

GableGotwals, Tulsa, OK (Continued)

Administrative Law, Alternative Dispute Resolution, Appellate Practice, Aviation, Bad Faith, Breach of Contract, Class Actions, Construction Law, Energy, Environmental Law, Entertainment Law, Health Care, Intellectual Property, Insurance Coverage, Labor and Employment, Mergers and Acquisitions, Oil and Gas, Product Liability, Professional Liability, Governmental Relations

Firm Profile: Established in 1919, GableGotwals is a full-service law firm that provides high quality legal services through 90+ highly experienced litigators and transactional attorneys who represent a diversified client base across the nation. Though Oklahoma-based, our connections and reach are global.

Insurance Clients

Aetna Health Inc.
Colony Insurance Company
John Hancock Life Insurance Company
The Northwestern Mutual Life Insurance Company
Principal Life Insurance Company
Travelers Indemnity Group
Aetna Life Insurance Company
Hartford Life and Accident Insurance Company
Metropolitan Life Insurance Company
Ohio National Financial Services
Prudential Insurance Company of America

Insurance Practice Members

David L. Bryant — The University of Oklahoma, B.A., 1977; The University of Texas, J.D., 1981 — Admitted to Bar, 1981, Oklahoma; 2012, Texas — Member American, Oklahoma and Tulsa County Bar Associations; American Inns of Court, Robert D. Hudson Chapter; American College of Trial Lawyers — Oklahoma Super Lawyers; Best Lawyers in America, Lawyer of the year 2014; Chambers USA; AV Preeminent Martindale-Hubbell Lawyer Rating

Timothy A. Carney — Southwest Missouri State University, B.S., 1983; The University of Tulsa, J.D. (with honors), 1986 — Order of the Curule, Chair — Admitted to Bar, 1986, Oklahoma — Member American, Oklahoma and Tulsa County Bar Associations; Oklahoma Association of Defense Counsel — Oklahoma Super Lawyers; Best Lawyers in America, Tulsa Insurance Lawyer of the Year 2011; AV Preeminent Martindale-Hubbell Rating

Erin K. Dailey — The University of Oklahoma, B.A. (summa cum laude, with honors), 2000; The University of Tulsa, J.D. (with highest honors), 2004 — Order of the Curule, Chair — Admitted to Bar, 2004, Oklahoma — Member American, Oklahoma and Tulsa County Bar Associations; American Inns of Court; Oklahoma Association of Defense Counsel — Oklahoma Super Lawyers' Rising Star

Renée DeMoss — Oklahoma City University, B.A. (summa cum laude), 1980; The University of Oklahoma, J.D. (with honors), 1984 — Order of the Coif; Order of the Barrister — Articles Editor, Oklahoma Law Review — Admitted to Bar, 1984, Oklahoma — Member American, Oklahoma and Tulsa County Bar Associations; American Bar Foundation; Defense Research Institute — Oklahoma Super Lawyers; AV Preeminent Martindale-Hubbell Lawyer Rating

Craig A. Fitzgerald — Oklahoma Christian College, B.S., 1989; Vanderbilt University, J.D., 1992 — Admitted to Bar, 1992, Oklahoma — Member American, Oklahoma and Tulsa County Bar Associations; American Inns of Court, Hudson-Hall-Wheaton Chapter, Master — Oklahoma Super Lawyer; Best Lawyer in America; AV Preeminent Martindale-Hubbell Lawyer Rating

Oliver S. Howard — Oklahoma Christian College, B.A., 1967; Abilene Christian University, M.A., 1970; Hebrew Union College, Ph.D., 1978; University of Cincinnati, J.D., 1979 — Order of the Coif — University of Cincinnati Law Review — Admitted to Bar, 1979, Oklahoma — Member American, Oklahoma and Tulsa County Bar Associations; American Inns of Court, Council Oak/Johnson-Sontag Chapter; American College of Trial Lawyers; Fellow, American Bar Foundation; Fellow, International Academy of Trial Lawyers — Oklahoma Super Lawyers; Best Lawyers in America, Lawyer of the Year 2012 and 2014; AV Preeminent Martindale-Hubbell Lawyer Rating; Chambers USA

David E. Keglovits — University of Notre Dame, B.S., 1985; The University of Texas, J.D., 1990 — Admitted to Bar, 1990, Oklahoma — Member American (Forum on Construction Industry), Oklahoma and Tulsa County Bar Associations; Energy Bar Association; Litigation Counsel of America — Oklahoma Super Lawyers; Best Lawyers in America, Lawyer of the Year 2013; AV Preeminent Martindale-Hubbell Lawyer Rating

David B. McKinney — Rice University, B.S., 1974; Columbia University, J.D., 1975 — State Scholar - Top 10% — Admitted to Bar, 1975, Oklahoma —

TULSA

GableGotwals, Tulsa, OK (Continued)

Member Oklahoma and Tulsa County Bar Associations; National Association of College and University Attorneys; American Health Lawyers Association — Best Lawyers in America, Lawyer of the Year 2012; Oklahoma Super Lawyers; AV Preeminent Martindale-Hubbell Lawyer Rating

Ronald N. Ricketts — The University of Oklahoma, B.A., 1965; The University of Tulsa, J.D., 1968 — Admitted to Bar, 1969, Oklahoma — Member American, Oklahoma and Tulsa County Bar Associations; Fellow, Academy of Court Appointed Masters; American Inns of Court, Hudson-Hall-Wheaton Chapter — Oklahoma Super Lawyers; Best Lawyers in America; AV Preeminent Martindale-Hubbell Lawyer Rating

John Henry Rule — Oklahoma City University, B.S., 1972; The University of Texas, J.D., 1977; Virginia Theological Seminary, M.Div., 2005 — Order of the Coif — Admitted to Bar, 1977, Oklahoma — Member American, Oklahoma and Tulsa County Bar Associations; American Inns of Court, Hudson-Hall-Wheaton Chapter — Best Lawyers in America; AV Preeminent Martindale-Hubbell Lawyer Rating

Lisa T. Silvestri — The University of Texas at Austin, B.A., 1992; The University of Texas, J.D., 1996 — Staff Member, The Review of Litigation — Admitted to Bar, 1996, Texas; 2001, Oklahoma — Member American, Oklahoma, and Tulsa County Bar Association; State Bar of Texas — Oklahoma Super Lawyers; Best Lawyers in America

Mia Vahlberg — The University of Oklahoma, B.B.A., 1979; The University of Tulsa, J.D., 2004 — Order of Curule, Chair — University of Tulsa Law Review — Admitted to Bar, 2004, Oklahoma — Member American, Oklahoma and Tulsa County Bar Associations; Defense Research Institute — Oklahoma Super Lawyers; Best Lawyers in America

Of Counsel

Dennis C. Cameron

Gibbs Armstrong Borochoff Mullican & Hart, P.C.

601 South Boulder Avenue, Suite 500
Tulsa, Oklahoma 74119
  Telephone: 918-587-3939
  Fax: 918-582-5504
  Toll Free: 888-587-3939
  E-Mail: office@gabmh.com
  www.gabmh.com

Established: 2001

Insurance Defense, Railroad Law, Nursing Home Litigation, Bad Faith, Medical Malpractice, Environmental Liability, Federal Employer Liability Claims (FELA)

Firm Profile: We offer more than fifty years of diverse trial experience in civil litigation, with our primary focus on insurance and railroad defense matters. The firm tries lawsuits throughout Oklahoma and Arkansas, as well as practicing before the U.S. Supreme and U.S. Appeals Courts. The firm enjoys a reputation for a personalized, responsive, and cost-conscious practice that serves as the cornerstone of its commitment to build and maintain long-term attorney-client relationships.

Insurance Clients

Brotherhood Mutual Insurance Company
Equity Insurance Company
Gulf Insurance Group
Philadelphia Insurance Company
U.S. Risk Insurance Company
Colony Insurance Company
EMC Insurance Companies
GuideOne Insurance
OneBeacon Insurance
Sun Healthcare Group
Western Heritage Insurance Company

Non-Insurance Clients

Baptist Village Retirement Communities of OK
Sand Springs Railway Company
Watco Companies, LLC
Burlington Northern Santa Fe Railway
Union Pacific Railroad Company

Shareholders

George Gibbs — Southern Baptist College, A.A., 1974; Southern Baptist University, B.A., 1976; Southern Baptist Theological Seminary, M.A., 1980;

Gibbs Armstrong Borochoff Mullican & Hart, P.C., Tulsa, OK (Continued)

Oklahoma City University School of Law, J.D., 1986 — Admitted to Bar, 1986, Oklahoma; 1987, Arkansas; U.S. District Court, Eastern, Northern and Western Districts of Oklahoma; U.S. District Court, Eastern and Northern Districts of Arkansas; U.S. Court of Appeals, Eighth and Tenth Circuits — Member Oklahoma, Arkansas and Tulsa County Bar Associations; ; Oklahoma Association of Defense Counsel; Association of Trial Lawyers of America; National Association of Railroad Trial Counsel

Tom L. Armstrong — University of California, Santa Barbara, B.A., 1968; University of California, Berkeley Boalt Hall School of Law, J.D., 1971 — Phi Beta Kappa — Admitted to Bar, 1971, Oklahoma; 1972, California; 1971, U.S. District Court, Western District of Oklahoma; 1973, U.S. Court of Appeals, Tenth Circuit; 1975, U.S. District Court, Eastern District of Oklahoma; 1976, U.S. District Court, Northern District of Oklahoma; 1979, U.S. Supreme Court; 1981, U.S. District Court, Northern District of Texas — Member American, Oklahoma and Tulsa County Bar Associations; State Bar of California; National Association of Railroad Trial Counsel

Douglas M. Borochoff — The University of Oklahoma, B.A., 1986; The University of Tulsa College of Law, J.D., 1990 — Phi Alpha Delta — Admitted to Bar, 1990, Oklahoma; 1990, U.S. District Court, Northern District of Oklahoma; 1992, U.S. District Court, Eastern District of Oklahoma; 1997, U.S. Court of Appeals, Tenth Circuit — Member Oklahoma and Tulsa County Bar Associations; Oklahoma Association of Defense Counsel; National Association of Railroad Trial Counsel

George R. Mullican — Northeastern Oklahoma State University, B.B.A. (cum laude), 1992; The University of Oklahoma College of Law, J.D. (with honors), 1995 — University of Oklahoma Law Review — Admitted to Bar, 1995, Oklahoma; 2000, U.S. District Court, Eastern, Northern and Western Districts of Oklahoma; U.S. Court of Appeals, Tenth Circuit — Member Oklahoma and Tulsa County Bar Associations; National Association of Railroad Trial Counsel — Capt., U.S. Army JAGC (1995-1999)

Robert D. Hart — Northeastern Oklahoma State University, B.B.A. (cum laude), 1992; The University of Oklahoma College of Law, J.D. (with distinction), 1995 — Alpha Chi; Pho Theta Sigma — Admitted to Bar, 1995, Oklahoma; U.S. District Court, Eastern, Northern and Western Districts of Oklahoma; 2000, U.S. Court of Appeals, Eighth and Tenth Circuits — Member Oklahoma and Tulsa County Bar Associations; National Association of Railroad Trial Counsel

Christopher D. Wolek — Tulane University, B.S. (cum laude), 1992; The University of Oklahoma College of Law, J.D. (with distinction), 1995 — Admitted to Bar, 1995, Texas; 2002, Oklahoma; 1995, U.S. District Court, Northern District of Texas; 1997, U.S. Court of Appeals, Fifth Circuit; 2003, U.S. District Court, Eastern, Northern and Western Districts of Oklahoma; U.S. Court of Appeals, Eighth Circuit; 2005, U.S. Court of Appeals, Tenth Circuit — Member Oklahoma Bar Association; State of Texas Bar Association; National Association of Railroad Trial Counsel

Associates

Diane M. Black
Jared A. DeSilvey
Steven O. Kuperman
Jamie A. Rogers
Eddie L. Carr
Kevin S. Hoskins
Charles A. McSoud
Michael P. Womack

Hall, Estill, Hardwick, Gable, Golden & Nelson, P.C.

320 South Boston Avenue, Suite 200
Tulsa, Oklahoma 74103
  Telephone: 918-594-0400
  Fax: 918-594-0505
  E-Mail: firminformation@hallestill.com
  www.hallestill.com

(Fayetteville, AR Office: 75 North East Avenue, Suite 402, 72701-5388)
  (Tel: 479-973-5200)
  (Fax: 479-973-0520)
(Oklahoma City, OK Office: Chase Tower, 100 North Broadway, Suite 2900, 73102-8865)
  (Tel: 405-553-2828)
  (Fax: 405-553-2855)

OKLAHOMA

Hall, Estill, Hardwick, Gable, Golden & Nelson, P.C., Tulsa, OK
(Continued)

Established: 1967

Civil Trial Practice, Bad Faith, Construction Litigation, Employment Law (Management Side), First and Third Party Defense, Nursing Home Liability

Firm Profile: One of Oklahoma's largest and most trusted law firms since 1967, Hall Estill delivers powerful results to its clients regionally, nationally and internationally. With a client-first mentality that provides friendly, attentive client service, the firm delivers results through creative, cost-effective solutions. Hall Estill attorneys represent clients from Fortune 500 corporations and medium-sized companies, to non-profit organizations, emerging businesses and individuals. Hall Estill attorneys are leaders in their respective fields and in their communities; regularly publishing and lecturing in their areas of expertise, continuing to build on the firm's reputation of excellence. Hall Estill in nationally recognized and highly respected for a wide range of experience and depth of legal knowledge.

Insurance Clients

Aetna Life Insurance Company
Allied Group Insurance
American Family Insurance Group
American Guarantee and Liability Insurance Company
Arch Insurance Company
Bankers Life and Casualty Company
Chubb & Son, a division of Federal Insurance Company
CUNA Mutual Group
Employers Insurance Company of Wausau
Fireman's Fund Insurance Company
The Hartford
Hartford Casualty Insurance Company
Jefferson/Allianz Global Assistance
Kemper Insurance Company
Medmarc, Inc.
Mutual of Omaha Insurance Company
Oklahoma Municipal Assurance Group
The Republic Group
Safeco Insurance
Sedgwick Claims Management Services, Inc.
Trinity Universal Insurance Company
AIG Technical Services, Inc.
Allied World National Assurance Company
American International Companies
Aon Risk Services, Inc.
AXIS Pro
Chubb Group of Insurance Companies
Colonial Life and Accident Insurance Company
Empire Fire and Marine Insurance Company
Federated Insurance Company
First Assurance Unsecured
Great American Custom Insurance Services
Houston Casualty Company
Indiana Lumbermens Mutual Insurance Company
Kansas City Life Insurance Company
Mid-Continent Casualty Company
North American Risk Services
Oklahoma Attorneys Mutual Insurance Company
Old Republic Insurance Company
RLI Insurance Company
St. Paul Travelers
Stewart Title Guaranty Company
Travelers
U.S. Specialty Insurance Company
Zurich American Insurance Company

Non-Insurance Clients

Coventry Health Care, Inc.

Firm Members

Mark K. Blongewicz — University of Nebraska, B.S., 1977; Duke University, J.D., 1980 — Admitted to Bar, 1980, Oklahoma; 1985, Nebraska — Member Oklahoma and Tulsa County Bar Associations; Defense Research Institute — E-mail: mblongewicz@hallestill.com
Larry G. Ball — Resident Oklahoma City, OK Office — E-mail: lball@hallestill.com
Steven A. Broussard — E-mail: sbroussard@hallestill.com
Margaret Mary Clarke — E-mail: mclarke@hallestill.com
J. Patrick Cremin — E-mail: pcremin@hallestill.com
Angelyn L. Dale — E-mail: adale@hallestill.com
Seth Aaron Day — Resident Oklahoma City, OK Office — E-mail: sday@hallestill.com
Theodore Q. Eliot — E-mail: teliot@hallestill.com
Jon A. Epstein — Resident Oklahoma City, OK Office — E-mail: jepstein@hallestill.com
Robert P. Fitz-Patrick — E-mail: rfitzpatrick@hallestill.com
Susanna M. Gattoni — E-mail: sgattoni@hallestill.com
Trent A. Gudgel — E-mail: tgudgel@hallestill.com

Hall, Estill, Hardwick, Gable, Golden & Nelson, P.C., Tulsa, OK
(Continued)

Bonnie N. Hackler — E-mail: bhackler@hallestill.com
John F. Heil, III — E-mail: jheil@hallestill.com
Curtis E. Hogue — Resident Fayetteville, AR Office — E-mail: chogue@hallestill.com
Christian S. Huckaby — Resident Oklahoma City, OK Office — E-mail: chuckaby@hallestill.com
Anthony J. Jorgenson — Resident Oklahoma City, OK Office — E-mail: ajorgenson@hallestill.com
Michael T. Keester — E-mail: mkeester@hallestill.com
Michael J. Lissau — E-mail: mlissau@hallestill.com
Robert D. Looney, Jr. — Resident Oklahoma City, OK Office — E-mail: rlooney@hallestill.com
James C. Milton — E-mail: jmilton@hallestill.com
Elisabeth E. Muckala — Resident Oklahoma City, OK Office — E-mail: emuckala@hallestill.com
Robert D. Nelon — Resident Oklahoma City, OK Office — E-mail: bnelon@hallestill.com
Bryan J. Nowlin — E-mail: bnowlin@hallestill.com
James J. Proszek — E-mail: jproszek@hallestill.com
James M. Reed — E-mail: jreed@hallestill.com
Robert K. Rhoads — Resident Fayetteville, AR Office — E-mail: rrhoads@hallestill.com
Michael E. Smith — Resident Oklahoma City, OK Office — E-mail: mesmith@hallestill.com
Elaine R. Turner — Resident Oklahoma City, OK Office — E-mail: eturner@hallestill.com
D. Kenyon Williams, Jr. — E-mail: kwilliams@hallestill.com

Associates

Conor Cleary
Travis Cushman
Stephanie T. Gentry
Kelly Comarda
Kristen Evans
Nathaniel Haskins

Johnson & Jones, P.C.

2200 Bank of America Center
15 West Sixth Street
Tulsa, Oklahoma 74119
Telephone: 918-584-6644
Fax: 888-789-0940
E-Mail: cdavis@johnson-jones.com
www.johnson-jones.com

Established: 1994

Insurance Defense, Commercial Litigation, Civil Litigation, Employment Law, Oil and Gas, Product Liability, Breach of Contract, Alternative Dispute Resolution, Construction Law, First and Third Party Matters, Uninsured and Underinsured Motorist, Business Law, Intellectual Property

Firm Profile: The firm is an established, highly respected mid-size law firm in Eastern Oklahoma, known for its blue-chip clients and high level of professional service. The firm's litigation talents have achieved successful results in over half of Oklahoma's 77 counties, Indian Tribal Courts, all Oklahoma federal courts, the 10th Circuit Court of Appeals, and the Federal Circuit Court of Appeals. All of the firm's shareholders are AV rated and are frequently voted as Oklahoma Super Lawyers.

Insurance Clients

ACE USA/ESIS, Inc.
American International Group
Chubb Group of Insurance Companies
The United Methodist Property and Casualty Trust
American Farmers & Ranchers Mutual Insurance Company
Glatfelter Insurance Group
Shelter Insurance Companies
Zurich North America

TULSA

Johnson & Jones, P.C., Tulsa, OK (Continued)

Partner/Shareholder

J. Christopher Davis — 1965 — Oral Roberts University, B.A., 1989; M.A., 1991; M.Ed., 1992; The University of Oklahoma College of Law, J.D., 1995 — Order of Barristers; National Moot Court Team; National Trial Team; Jessup International Moot Court Team; Super Lawyer, 2008-2014, Martindale-Hubbell AV rating — Law Clerk to U.S. District Judge Jimm Larry Hendren, U.S. District Court, Western District of Arkansas, 1995-1996 — Assistant Note Editor, American Indian Law Review — Admitted to Bar, 1995, Oklahoma; 1996, U.S. District Court, Eastern, Northern and Western Districts of Oklahoma; 1997, U.S. Court of Appeals, Tenth Circuit — Member Federal, American, Oklahoma and Tulsa County (Chairman, Litigation Section) Bar Associations; Muscogee Creek Nation Tribal Bar Association; Defense Research Institute; Oklahoma Association of Defense Counsel; American Inns of Court; Federation of Defense and Corporate Counsel — Author: "Indemnity and Contribution Law in Oklahoma," Oklahoma Bar Journal Vol. 84-No. 2, 1/12/2013 — Tulsa Area Human Resource Managers; Recipient, Teaching Fellowship for Legal Research and Writing Program, 1993-1995; Adjunct Settlement Judge, U.S. District Court, Northern District of Oklahoma; Former Federal Law Clerk with over 25 complex trials to verdict — Practice Areas: Business Litigation; Insurance Defense; Product Liability; Employment Law; Construction Accidents; Complex Litigation; Intellectual Property; Trucking Industry Defense; Subrogation — E-mail: cdavis@johnson-jones.com

E. Andrew Johnson — 1969 — Oklahoma State University, B.S., 1991; The University of Oklahoma College of Law, J.D. (with honors), 1995 — Admitted to Bar, 1995, Oklahoma — E-mail: ajohnson@johnson-jones.com

Paul D. Kingsolver — 1958 — The University of Tulsa, B.S., 1980; The University of Tulsa College of Law, J.D., 1983 — Law Clerk to the Honorable Roy W. Harper, U.S.District Court, St. Louis, MO., 1983-1984 — Admitted to Bar, 1983, Oklahoma; 1984, Missouri; U.S. Tax Court — E-mail: pkingsolver@johnson-jones.com

Whitney M. Eschenheimer — 1970 — The University of Kansas, B.A. (cum laude, with distinction), 1992; The University of Oklahoma College of Law, J.D. (with distinction), 1996 — Admitted to Bar, 1996, Oklahoma; U.S. District Court, Eastern, Northern and Western Districts of Oklahoma — Member Oklahoma (Work Life Balance Committee) and Tulsa County (Litigation Committee; TCBA Mentor) Bar Associations; Oklahoma Association of Defense Counsel; Defense Research Institute — Author: "Fraud or Misrepresentation: Does It Matter What It's Called," Oklahoma Claims Association; "Why You Should Read the Policy, the UM Statute, and the Cases: Duties Owed by Insurers in Processing UM Claims," Oklahoma Bar Association - Rising Star - Super Lawyers, 2008, 2010 — Practice Areas: Insurance Law; Insurance Defense; Transportation; Insurance Claim Analysis and Evaluation; Employment Litigation; Legal Malpractice — E-mail: weschenheimer@johnson-jones.com

Of Counsel

Stephanie D. Phipps — 1970 — Oklahoma State University, B.S., 1992; The University of Oklahoma College of Law, J.D., 1995 — Admitted to Bar, 1995, Oklahoma; 1999, Texas; Federal Circuit Court — Member Oklahoma Bar Association; State Bar of Texas — E-mail: sphipps@johnson-jones.com

Senior Associates

Jonathan D. Cartledge — 1976 — Oral Roberts University, B.A. (summa cum laude), 1998; University of Tulsa College of Law, J.D. (summa cum laude), 2001 — Recipient, George and Jean Price Award for Excellence in Research and Writing; Outstanding First Year Student Award; ABA/BNA Award for Excellence in the Study of Labor and Employment Law; CALI Awards for academic excellence in the following subjects: Legal Research and Writing, Civil Procedure, Introduction to Alternative Dispute Resolution, Administrative Law, and Federal Income Taxation — Admitted to Bar, 2001, Oklahoma; U.S. District Court, Eastern, Northern and Western Districts of Oklahoma — "Oklahoma Voids General Contractor's "own negligence" Provisions in General-Sub Contracts," DRI - The Critical Path, Spring, 2007 — Order of the Curule Chair; Chief Justice of the University of Tulsa College of Law Supreme Court — E-mail: jcartledge@johnson-jones.com

Trevor L. Hughes — 1982 — St. Cloud State University, B.A. (cum laude), 2003; Hamline University School of Law, J.D. (Dean's List), 2006 — Giles Rich IP Moot Court — Hamline University Law Review — Admitted to Bar, 2006, Oklahoma; 2008, U.S. District Court, Eastern District of Oklahoma — Member Oklahoma Bar Association (Committee for Law Schools) — Super Lawyers Rising Stars, 2013 — E-mail: thughes@johnson-jones.com

OKLAHOMA

Johnson & Jones, P.C., Tulsa, OK (Continued)

Associates

Kari Deckard — Oklahoma State University, B.S. (magna cum laude), 2004; The University of Tulsa College of Law, J.D. (with honors), 2008 — Order of the Curule Chair; CALI Awards in Civil Procedure I and II, and Legal Writing — Energy Law Journal, Senior Staff — Admitted to Bar, 2008, Texas; 2010, Oklahoma; 2011, U.S. District Court, Northern and Western Districts of Oklahoma — Member American and Oklahoma Bar Associations; State Bar of Texas — Super Lawyers Rising Stars, 2013 — Languages: French — E-mail: kstaats@johnson-jones.com

Gauri D. Nautiyal — 1987 — The University of Tulsa, B.A. (with distinction), 2009; Oklahoma University, J.D. (dean's list, President's List), 2013 — Admitted to Bar, 2013, Oklahoma — Member Oklahoma Bar Association — Super Lawyers Rising Stars, 2013 — E-mail: gnautiyal@johnson-jones.com

All attorneys are members of the Oklahoma and Tulsa County Bar Associations.

McAnany, Van Cleave & Phillips, P.C.

2021 South Lewis, Suite 225
Tulsa, Oklahoma 74104
Telephone: 918-771-4465
www.mvplaw.com

(McAnany, Van Cleave & Phillips, P.A.*: 10 East Cambridge Circle Drive, Suite 300, Kansas City, KS, 66103)
 (Tel: 913-371-3838)
 (Fax: 913-371-4722)
(St. Louis, MO Office*: 505 North 7th Street, Suite 2100, 63101)
 (Tel: 314-621-1133)
 (Fax: 314-621-4405)
(Springfield, MO Office*: 4650 South National Avenue, Suite D-2, 65810)
 (Tel: 417-865-0007)
 (Fax: 417-865-0008)
(Omaha, NE Office*: 10665 Bedford Avenue, Suite 101, 68134)
 (Tel: 402-408-1340)
 (Fax: 402-493-0860)

Established: 1901

Administrative Law, Antitrust, Bankruptcy, Business Law, Construction Law, Corporate Law, Creditor Rights, Directors and Officers Liability, Insurance Law, Labor and Employment, Land Use, Litigation, Municipal Law, Personal Injury, Product Liability, Professional Liability, Public Entities, Railroad Law, Real Estate, School Law, Transportation, Trial and Appellate Practice, Workers' Compensation

McAtee Law Office
R. Jay McAtee

1115 South Cincinnati
Tulsa, Oklahoma 74119
Telephone: 918-746-4332
Fax: 918-746-4334
Emer/After Hrs: 918-633-8051
E-Mail: jmcatee@mcateelawoffice.com
www.mcateelawoffice.com

Established: 2001

Workers' Compensation, Insurance Defense, Subrogation, Employment Law

Insurance Clients

Chubb Group
Consolidated Benefits Resources, LLC
TRISTAR Risk Management

CompSource Oklahoma
Gallagher Bassett Services, Inc.
Lumbermen's Underwriting Alliance

OKLAHOMA — TULSA

McAtee Law Office, R. Jay McAtee, Tulsa, OK (Continued)

Non-Insurance Clients

Becco Contractors, Inc.
OK Foods
John Christner Trucking
RPCS, Inc.

Firm Member

R. Jay McAtee — 1956 — Oklahoma State University, B.A., 1980; The University of Tulsa, J.D., 1983 — Admitted to Bar, 1983, Oklahoma; 1983, U.S. District Court, Northern District of Oklahoma; 2012, Cherokee Nation Tribal Courts; 2013, Muscogee (Creek) Nation Courts — Member Oklahoma and Tulsa County Bar Associations; Oklahoma Association of Defense Counsel; Defense Research Institute — E-mail: jmcatee@mcateelawoffice.com

McDaniel Acord, PLLC

9343 East 95th Court
Tulsa, Oklahoma 74133
Telephone: 918-382-9200
Fax: 918-382-9282
E-Mail: smcdaniel@ok-counsel.com
www.ok-counsel.com

Established: 2007

Construction Law, Environmental Law, Product Liability, Professional Liability, Transportation, Toxic Torts, Commercial Litigation, Torts, Design Professional Liability

Firm Profile: Our Focus Areas of Practice are: Design Professionals liability, construction defects, environmental claims, toxic torts and general commercial litigation.

Our highly-motivated group of professionals prides itself on client service and maximizing client outcomes. Our dedication to this goal has earned us a reputation for zealous, ethical representation that achieves results. Our track record includes successful outcomes in state and federal courts throughout Oklahoma and western Arkansas.

Insurance Clients

Beazley Group
Fireman's Fund Insurance Company
National American Insurance Company
Xchanging
Cambridge Integrated Services
Integrated Risk Management
Lexington Insurance Company
North American Risk Services
Travelers Insurance Companies
XL Insurance

Non-Insurance Clients

Ardent Health Services
Champion Enterprises, Inc.
HKS Architects, Inc.
Peterson Farms, Inc.
BP America, Inc.
CITGO Petroleum Corporation
NTA, Inc.
Residential Warranty Corporation

Regional Counsel For

4Front Engineered Solutions, Inc.
Tyson Foods, Inc.
Gulf Stream Coach
URS Corporation

Members

A. Scott McDaniel — 1958 — North Carolina State University, B.S., 1981; University of Tulsa College of Law, J.D. (with highest honors), 1995 — Order of the Curule Chair; Gable Gotwals 1L Student of the Year, Merit Scholar — Managing Editor, Tulsa Law Journal, 1994-1995; Currently serves as Construction and Real Estate Editor for the Journal of American Law. — Admitted to Bar, 1995, Oklahoma; 2005, Arkansas; 1995, U.S. District Court, Eastern, Northern and Western Districts of Oklahoma; 2001, U.S. Court of Appeals, Tenth Circuit; 2002, U.S. Supreme Court; 2009, U.S. Court of Federal Claims; 2012, U.S. District Court, Eastern and Western Districts of Arkansas; 2013, Cherokee Nation Tribal Courts — Member Federal, Oklahoma and Tulsa County Bar Associations; Professional Liability Defense Federation; Claims and Litigation Management Alliance; Defense Research Institute; Transportation Lawyers Association; Professional Liability Underwriting Society — Author: "The Good, the Bad, and the Unqualified: The Public Interest and the Unregulated Practice of General Contracting in Oklahoma," 20 Tulsa Law Journal 799 (1994); "Oklahoma Lien Law," Construction Publications, Inc., www.lienlawonline.com, 2007-2014; "Compliance with Statutes and Regulations: No Safe Harbor Against Liability for Common-Law Negligence," Proceedings of the Third International Petroleum Environmental Conference, 1996 — Reported Cases: Thompson v. Cendant Corp., 130 F.Supp.2d 1255 (N.D. OK 2001); City of Tulsa v. Tyson Foods, et al., 258 F.Supp.2d 1263 (N.D. OK 2003); Holder v. Gold Fields Mining Corp. et al., 239 F.R.D. 652 (N.D. OK 2005); Emmitt v Dickey, 188 Fed. Appx. 681 (10th Cir. 2006); Spencer v Wal-Mart Stores, Inc., 203 Fed. Appx 193 (10th Cir. 2006); B.H. v. Gold Fields Mining Corp, et al., 506 F.Supp.2d 792 (N.D. OK 2007); Green v. Alpharma, et al., 284 SW3d 29 (Ark. 2008); Oklahoma v. Tyson, et al., 258 F.R.D. 472 (N.D. OK 2009); Attorney General of Oklahoma v. Tyson, et al., 565 F.3d 769, (10th Cir. 2009); Green v George's Farms, Inc., 2011 Ark. 70, S.W.3d (Ark. 2011) — Adjunct Settlement Judge; 2008 Tulsa County Bar Association Leadership in the Law Award; 2012 John 3:16 Mission Geisinger Award; Graduate Leadership Oklahoma Class XXVII — Registered Professional Engineer (Oklahoma, 1992, Retired; North Carolina, 1985, Retired); Certified Mediator; Institute for Conflict Management, Mediation Certificate, 2004 — Practice Areas: Architects and Engineers; Commercial Litigation; Construction Litigation; Design Professionals; Engineering and Construction; Environmental and Toxic Injury; Environmental Liability; Environmental Litigation; Insurance Defense

Stacy L. Acord — 1974 — Oklahoma State University, B.A., 1996; The University of Oklahoma College of Law, J.D., 2000 — Phi Delta Phi — Leadership Jenks, 2013-2014; Oklahoma Bar Association Leadership Academy, 2010; Recipient of "The Journal Records" Achievers Under 40 Award, 2008; The Council Oak American Inn of Court, 2002-2005; Luther Bohannon American Inn of Court, 1999-2000 — Admitted to Bar, 2000, Oklahoma; 2008, Arkansas; 2000, U.S. District Court, Eastern, Northern and Western Districts of Oklahoma; U.S. Court of Appeals, Tenth Circuit; 2012, U.S. District Court, Eastern and Western Districts of Arkansas — Member American, Oklahoma and Tulsa County Bar Associations; Oklahoma Association of Defense Counsel (Board of Directors, 2005-2007); Resonance Center for Women (Legal Counsel; Board of Directors, 2007-2011); Claims & Litigation Management Alliance; Defense Research Institute; Transportation Lawyers Association — Co-Author of CLM Oklahoma Claims Handling Guide — Reported Cases: B.H. v. Gold Fields Mining Corp., 506 F.Supp.2d 792 (N.D.Okla. 2007); Holder v. Gold Fields Mining Corp., 239 F.R.D. 652 (N.D.Okla. 2005) — Super Lawyers Rising Star, 2010, 2011, 2012 and 2013 — Practice Areas: Insurance Defense; Product Liability; Business Litigation; Adoption; Family Law

Associates

Andrew M. Conway — 1983 — The University of Tulsa, B.S.B.A. (cum laude), 2006; University of Tulsa College of Law, J.D. (with honors), 2009 — Phi Delta Phi; Order of the Barristers — Articles Editor, Energy Law Journal, 2008-2009 — Admitted to Bar, 2009, Oklahoma; 2010, U.S. District Court, Eastern, Northern and Western Districts of Oklahoma — Member American, Oklahoma and Tulsa County Bar Associations; American Inns of Court

Miranda R. Russell — 1985 — The University of Science and Arts of Oklahoma, B.A. (cum laude), 2007; The University of Oklahoma College of Law, J.D. (with honors), 2010 — Order of the Solicitors; Academic Achievement Award in Civil Pretrail Litigation — Oklahoma Law Review — Admitted to Bar, 2010, Oklahoma; 2012, U.S. District Court, Eastern and Northern Districts of Oklahoma; 2012, U.S. District Court, Western District of Michigan; 2013, Cherokee Nation Tribal Courts — Member Tulsa County Bar Association — Oklahoma Law Review National Trial Competition; Super Lawyers Rising Star, 2014

Perrine, Redemann, Berry, Taylor & Sloan PLLC

1800 South Baltimore Avenue, Suite 900
Tulsa, Oklahoma 74119
Telephone: 918-382-1400
Fax: 918-382-1499
www.pmrlaw.net

Established: 2002

Workers' Compensation, Insurance Defense, Bad Faith, Asbestos Litigation, Toxic Torts, Product Liability, Employment Law

TULSA

Perrine, Redemann, Berry, Taylor & Sloan PLLC, Tulsa, OK (Continued)

Firm Profile: The firm was established in 2002 by a highly experienced group of litigation attorneys who have focused in complex civil cases and workers compensation. Personal contact, efficiency through technology and trial experience are the firm's hall marks. The firm represents international as well as domestic clients.

Insurance Clients

AIG
Gallagher Bassett Insurance Company
Zurich Specialties London Limited
ESIS/ACE INA Group
Travelers Insurance
Zurich North America

Non-Insurance Clients

Bechtel
Manhattan Construction
The Sherwin-Williams Company
Linde Processing
The Shaw Group, Inc.
Target Corporation

William D. Perrine — 1951 — The University of Oklahoma, B.S., 1977; The University of Tulsa, J.D., 1986 — Delta Theta Phi; Order of the Curcule Chair — Staff Member, Tulsa Law Journal, 1985-1986 — Admitted to Bar, 1986, Oklahoma; U.S. District Court, Eastern, Northern and Western Districts of Oklahoma; U.S. Court of Appeals, Tenth Circuit — Member Oklahoma and Tulsa County Bar Associations; Fellow, Oklahoma Bar Foundation; Oklahoma Association of Defense Counsel; Defense Research Institute — United States Army — E-mail: wperrine@pmrlaw.net

Robert P. Redemann — 1951 — University of Wisconsin-Madison, B.S., 1973; The University of Tulsa, J.D., 1978 — Staff Member, Tulsa Law Journal, 1976-1978 — Admitted to Bar, 1978, Oklahoma; 1978, Wisconsin; U.S. District Court, Northern District of Oklahoma; 1982, U.S. Court of Appeals, Tenth Circuit; 1985, U.S. District Court, Eastern District of Oklahoma; 1990, U.S. District Court, Western District of Oklahoma; 1998, U.S. Supreme Court — Member American (Member, Tort and Insurance Practice Section, 1984), Oklahoma and Tulsa County Bar Associations; State Bar of Wisconsin; American Inns of Court, Hudson-Hall-Wheaton Chapter; Defense Research Institute; Oklahoma Association of Defense Counsel — "The Evolution of PRP Standing Under the Comprehensive Environmental Response, Compensation, and Liability Act of 1980," 21 Wm. & Mary Env. & Policy L. Rev. 300 (1997); "Duty to Defend" chapter, Law and Practice of Insurance Coverage Litigation; " 'Cafe FRCP': A Defense Attorney's View on the Amendments to the Discovery Rules," TortSource, Vo. 2 No. 3 (Spring 2000); "General Electric v. Joiner and Kumho Tire v. Carmichael: The Ipse Dixit Twins," The Brief, Vol. 28, No. 4 (Summer 1999) — Reported Cases: Sun Co., Inc. (R&M) & Texaxo Inc. v. Browning-Ferris Industries, Inc., 124 F.3d 1187 (10th Cir. 1997); Quinton v. Farmland Industries, In., 928 F.2d 335 (10th Cir. 1991); Robinson v. Audi NSU Union Aktiengesellschaft, 739 F.2d 1481 (10th Cir. 1984); Timmons v. Royal Globe Ins., 653 P.2d 907 (Okla. 1982) — Adjunct Settlement Judge for United States District Court for the Northern District of Oklahoma; Former Editor in Chief, "The Brief" — Practice Areas: Civil Litigation; Asbestos Litigation; Toxic Torts; Insurance Law; Product Liability; Employment Law — E-mail: rredemann@pmrlaw.net

Kevin D. Berry — 1961 — University of Missouri, B.A., 1983; The University of Tulsa, J.D., 1986 — Delta Theta Phi — Staff Member, Tulsa Law Journal, 1985-1986 — Admitted to Bar, 1986, Oklahoma; U.S. District Court, Eastern, Northern and Western Districts of Oklahoma; U.S. Court of Appeals, Tenth Circuit — Member American Bar Association; Oklahoma Bar Association (Board of Governors and Secretary/Treasurer, Workers' Compensation Section, 1994-1996); Tulsa County Bar Association (Member, Workers Compensation Section); Fellow, Oklahoma Bar Foundation — Practice Areas: Workers' Compensation; Civil Litigation; Insurance Defense — E-mail: kberry@pmrlaw.net

Catherine C. Taylor — 1961 — The University of Oklahoma, B.A., 1983; The University of Tulsa, J.D., 1990 — Phi Alpha Delta (Historian, 1988-1989; Vice Justice, 1989-1990); Member, Board of Advocates, 1988-1989 — Staff Member, Tulsa Law Journal, 1988-1990 — Admitted to Bar, 1990, Oklahoma; U.S. District Court, Eastern, Northern and Western Districts of Oklahoma; U.S. Court of Appeals, Tenth Circuit — Member American Bar Association; Oklahoma Bar Association (Member, Public Information Committee, 1993; Secretary, Workers' Compensation Section, 1998-1999; President, 1999-2000); Tulsa County Bar Association; American Inns of Court, W. Lee Jackson Chapter; Oklahoma Association of Defense Counsel — Practice Areas: Workers' Compensation; Employment Law; Insurance Defense — E-mail: ctaylor@pmrlaw.net

Perrine, Redemann, Berry, Taylor & Sloan PLLC, Tulsa, OK (Continued)

Jennifer A. Sloan — The University of Tulsa, B.A. (cum laude), 1999; J.D. (with highest honors), 2003 — CALI Award for Excellence in Evidence and Constitutional Law — Admitted to Bar, 2003, Oklahoma; 2004, U.S. District Court, Eastern, Northern and Western Districts of Oklahoma; U.S. Court of Appeals, Tenth Circuit — Member American, Oklahoma and Tulsa County (Board Member, Workers' Compensation Section) Bar Associations — Languages: French — Practice Areas: Workers' Compensation; Administrative Law; Employment Law — E-mail: jsloan@pmrlaw.net

Reagan M. Fort — Oklahoma State University, B.S. (magna cum laude), 2002; University of Arkansas, J.D. (cum laude), 2005 — Admitted to Bar, 2005, Oklahoma; U.S. District Court, Eastern, Northern and Western Districts of Oklahoma; U.S. Court of Appeals, Tenth Circuit; U.S. Supreme Court — Practice Areas: Litigation; Bad Faith; Primary and Excess Insurance; Employment Law — E-mail: rmadison@pmrlaw.net

David J. L. Frette — The Ohio State University, B.A., 1992; The University of Oklahoma, J.D., 1995 — Admitted to Bar, 1995, Oklahoma; 1996, Missouri; 1998, U.S. District Court, Northern District of Oklahoma — Member Oklahoma Bar Association (Workers' Compensation Section); The Missouri Bar — Practice Areas: Workers' Compensation; Appellate Practice; Insurance Coverage; Subrogation — E-mail: dfrette@pmrlaw.net

Lindsey E. Grisamer — The University of Texas at Austin, B.A., 2008; The University of Tulsa, J.D., 2011 — Articles Editor, Energy Law Journal — Admitted to Bar, 2011, Texas; 2012, Oklahoma — Member American, Oklahoma and Tulsa County Bar Associations; State Bar of Texas — Practice Areas: Insurance Defense; Workers' Compensation — E-mail: lgrisamer@pmrlaw.net

(This firm is also listed in the Subrogation section of this directory)

Rhodes, Hieronymus, Jones, Tucker & Gable, PLLC

Williams Center Tower II
Two West 2nd Street, Suite 1000
Tulsa, Oklahoma 74103-3131
Telephone: 918-582-1173
Fax: 918-592-3390
E-Mail: jhtucker@rhodesokla.com
www.rhodesokla.com

Established: 1931

Trial and Appellate Practice, Insurance Defense, Extra-Contractual Liability Insurance Defense

Firm Profile: Rhodes Hieronymus, founded in 1931, is a civil trial and appellate law firm. We represent insurers, manufacturers, employers, transportation companies, professionals, and health care providers throughout Oklahoma and other states. We use technology and our data management system to properly and successfully manage files to and through trial and appeal. As our primary practice is a trial practice, our system enables us to be very competitive while providing excellent representation.

Insurance Clients

ACE USA
American Farmers & Ranchers Mutual Insurance Company
Atlantic Mutual Companies
Chartis Insurance
CNA Surety Corporation
Colony Specialty
Fidelity & Deposit Group
Granite State Insurance Company
Hanover Insurance Company
Lancer Claims Services, Inc.
Lexington Insurance Company
Medmarc, Inc.
National Union Fire Insurance Company
Pacific Indemnity Company
Protective Insurance Company
Republic Insurance Company
AIG Companies
Arch Insurance Group
Argo Pro
Catlin, Inc.
Chubb Group of Insurance Companies
Federal Insurance Company
Global Aerospace Underwriting Managers, Ltd.
HDI-Gerling Industrie Versicherung AG
LVL Claims Services, LLC
Mercury Insurance Group
Oklahoma Farm Bureau Mutual Insurance Company
Physicians Specialty Ltd Risk Retention Group
RLI Transportation

OKLAHOMA

Rhodes, Hieronymus, Jones, Tucker & Gable, PLLC, Tulsa, OK (Continued)

St. Paul Travelers
United Automobile Insurance Company
Utica National Insurance Company
XL Insurance Company, Ltd.
Tokio Marine and Fire Insurance Company, Ltd.
Universal Underwriters Insurance Company
Zurich North America

Non-Insurance Clients

Air Products and Chemicals, Inc.
Cargill, Inc.
Coca-Cola North America Group
Con-way Freight, Inc.
Deere & Company
ENGlobal Engineering, Inc.
Koch Trucking, Inc.
PPG Industries, Inc.
QuikTrip Corporation
SCI
Sunoco, Inc.
Trek Bicycle Corporation
XTO Energy, Inc.
APAC-Central, a division of Ashland Oil
Community Newspaper Holdings, Inc.
DIRECTV, LLC
FlightSafety International
PPG Industries, Inc.
SAIA Motor Freight Line, Inc.
Sears Holdings Management Corporation
Waste Connections, Inc.

Partners

E. D. Hieronymus — (1908-1994)

George W. Gable — (1918-2000)

Bert M. Jones — (1932-2012)

John H. Tucker — 1942 — The University of Oklahoma, B.A., 1964; J.D., 1966 — Admitted to Bar, 1966, Oklahoma — Member American, Oklahoma and Tulsa County Bar Associations; Fellow, American and Oklahoma Bar Foundations; Oklahoma Judicial Nominating Commission; American College of Trial Lawyers; American Board of Trial Advocates; American Inns of Court; Fellow, International Academy of Trial Lawyers — E-mail: jhtucker@rhodesokla.com

Chris L. Rhodes, III
Dan S. Folluo
Kerry R. Lewis
Theresa N. Hill
William T. McKee
Jo Anne Deaton
Colin H. Tucker
Nathan E. Clark
Randall E. Long

Of Counsel

Larry D. Henry
James D. Johnson

Associates

Carlye O. Jimerson
Denelda L. Richardson
J. Brian Brandes
Lindsay J. McDowell
Rachel M. Lee
Stephen L. Kirschner

Richards & Connor, PLLP

12th Floor, Park Centre Building
525 South Main Street
Tulsa, Oklahoma 74103-4509
Telephone: 918-585-2394
Fax: 918-585-1449
E-Mail: info@richardsconnor.com
www.richardsconnor.com

Established: 1997

Insurance Defense, Insurance Law, Coverage Issues, Extra-Contractual Litigation, Medical Malpractice, Product Liability, Defense Litigation, Errors and Omissions, General Liability, Bad Faith, Automobile, Casualty, Professional Liability, Premises Liability, Commercial Litigation, Business Law, Employment Law, Construction Law, Liquor Liability, Directors and Officers Liability

Firm Profile: Richards & Connor is devoted to providing the highest quality legal services to its clients in the business community and the insurance industry. Whether involving litigation or transactional matters, the attorneys of Richards & Connor have broad experience in the representation of local businesses to multinationals. Its highly experienced and respected trial lawyers are supported by associates skilled in litigation support, and its trial resume of over 350 jury trials to verdict includes a multitude of cases involving commercial, insurance, medical, personal injury, and criminal matters. Its

Richards & Connor, PLLP, Tulsa, OK (Continued)

transactional lawyers bring a broad knowledge of the practical concerns of businesses through a depth of industry experience.

Insurance Clients

Admiral Insurance Company
American Commerce Insurance Company
American Modern Home Insurance Company
Arch Insurance Company
Bituminous Insurance Company
EMC Insurance Company
Gateway Insurance Company
Great American Insurance Company
HomeFirst Agency, Inc.
Lloyd's Underwriters
The Medical Protective Company
Olympia Risk Retention Group, Inc.
ProPoint Claim Services, LLC
RSA Surplus Lines Insurance Services, Inc.
United States Aviation Underwriters, Inc.
Western National Mutual Ins. Co.
American Bankers Insurance Company of Florida
American Family Insurance Group
American National Property and Casualty Company
Atain Insurance Companies
Capitol Indemnity Corporation
Fireman's Fund Insurance Company
Hanover Insurance Group
The Hartford Insurance Group
James River Insurance Company
Meadowbrook Insurance Company
NCMIC Insurance Company
OneBeacon Insurance
Physicians Liability Insurance Company
Specialty Risk Services, Inc. (SRS)
State Auto Insurance Companies
United States Liability Insurance Company

Non-Insurance Clients

Bristol-Myers Squibb Company
Continuous Care Centers
DHL Express (USA), Inc.
Rental Service Corporation
St. John Medical Center, Inc.
Subway
Target Corporation
City of Tulsa
DEUTZ Corporation
Mazzio's Corporation
Res-Care, Inc.
SecurCare Properties
Sunshine Homes, Inc.

Firm Members

Phil R. Richards — 1958 — The University of Oklahoma, B.A., 1980; J.D., 1983 — Phi Alpha Delta; Recipient, American Jurisprudence Award — Admitted to Bar, 1983, Oklahoma; 1984, U.S. District Court, Northern District of Oklahoma; 1985, U.S. District Court, Western District of Oklahoma; 1986, U.S. District Court, Eastern District of Oklahoma; U.S. Court of Appeals, Tenth Circuit; 1998, U.S. Supreme Court — Member Oklahoma and Tulsa County Bar Associations; Oklahoma Association of Defense Counsel (President, 2004); American College of Coverage and Extracontractual Counsel; Defense Research Institute; Federation of Defense and Corporate Counsel; American Inns of Court; American College of Trial Lawyers — District Attorneys Office, Stephens and Grady Counties (1982-1984); Top 10 Oklahoma Super Lawyer — Practice Areas: Insurance Law; Civil Litigation — E-mail: prichards@richardsconnor.com

James W. Connor, Jr. — 1961 — The University of Tulsa, B.S.B.A., 1984; J.D., 1987 — Delta Theta Phi — Law Clerk to Honorable Layn R. Phillips, U.S. District Judge, Western District of Oklahoma (1987-1988) — Admitted to Bar, 1987, Oklahoma; U.S. District Court, Eastern, Northern and Western Districts of Oklahoma; 1988, U.S. Court of Appeals, Tenth Circuit — Member Tulsa County Bar Association; Fellow, American College of Trial Lawyers — Practice Areas: Medical Malpractice Defense; Civil Litigation — E-mail: jconnor@richardsconnor.com

Associates

Mary Elizabeth Nesser — 1981 — The University of Oklahoma, B.A./B.A. (magna cum laude, Phi Beta Kappa), 2005; J.D., 2008 — Order of the Barrister; University of Oklahoma Letzeiser Award — Managing Editor, American Indian Law Review — Admitted to Bar, 2008, Oklahoma; 2009, U.S. District Court, Eastern, Northern and Western Districts of Oklahoma — Member American, Oklahoma and Tulsa County Bar Associations; Defense Research Institute; Oklahoma Association of Defense Counsel — Oklahoma Super Lawyers Rising Star — Languages: Spanish — Practice Areas: Medical Malpractice Defense; Civil Litigation — E-mail: mnesser@richardsconnor.com

Randy J. Lewin — 1951 — The University of Texas, B.S., 1972; J.D., 1975 — Admitted to Bar, 1975, Texas; 1994, Oklahoma; 2012, U.S. District Court, Eastern, Northern and Western Districts of Oklahoma; U.S. Court of Appeals, Tenth Circuit — Member Oklahoma Bar Association; State Bar of Texas — Practice Areas: Civil Litigation — E-mail: rlewin@richardsconnor.com

Jessica N. Battson — 1985 — California State University, Dominguez Hills, B.A. (with honors), 2007; The University of Tulsa, J.D. (with honors), 2009 — Admitted to Bar, 2010, Oklahoma; U.S. District Court, Eastern, Northern and Western Districts of Oklahoma; Supreme Court of Oklahoma — Member

OKLAHOMA

TULSA

Richards & Connor, PLLP, Tulsa, OK (Continued)

Oklahoma and Tulsa County Bar Associations; American Inns of Court, Hudson Hall Wheaton Chapter — Practice Areas: Civil Litigation — E-mail: jbattson@richardsconnor.com

Brett E. Gray — 1973 — The University of Oklahoma, B.A., 2004; J.D., 2007 — Admitted to Bar, 2007, Oklahoma; U.S. District Court, Eastern, Northern and Western Districts of Oklahoma; U.S. Court of Appeals, Tenth Circuit — Member Federal, American, Oklahoma, Tulsa County and Muscogee (Creek) Nation Bar Associations — Practice Areas: Civil Litigation; Insurance Defense; Bad Faith — E-mail: bgray@richardsconnor.com

Grant T. Lloyd — 1982 — Oklahoma State University, B.A., 2004; The University of Tulsa, J.D., 2007 — Admitted to Bar, 2007, Oklahoma; U.S. District Court, Eastern, Northern, and Western Districts of Oklahoma; Supreme Court of Oklahoma — Member Oklahoma and Tulsa County Bar Associations — Practice Areas: Civil Litigation; Family Law — E-mail: glloyd@richardsconnor.com

Lauren N. Chandler — 1982 — Northeastern State University, B.A. Political Science (cum laude), 2003; The University of Tulsa, J.D., 2005 — Admitted to Bar, 2006, Oklahoma; U.S. District Court, Eastern, Northern and Western Districts of Oklahoma; Supreme Court of Oklahoma — Member Oklahoma and Tulsa County Bar Associations — Practice Areas: Civil Litigation — E-mail: lchandler@richardsconnor.com

Mariann M. Atkins — 1985 — The University of Oklahoma, B.A. (summa cum laude), 2007; The University of Tulsa, J.D. (with honors), 2011 — Admitted to Bar, 2011, Oklahoma; U.S. District Court, Eastern, Northern and Western Districts of Oklahoma — Member Oklahoma and Tulsa County Bar Associations — Practice Areas: Insurance Defense; Bad Faith; Insurance Coverage Litigation — E-mail: matkins@richardsconnor.com

Christopher U. Brecht — 1984 — Oklahoma State University, B.A., 2006; The University of Tulsa, J.D., 2009 — Admitted to Bar, 2009, Oklahoma — Member Oklahoma and Tulsa County Bar Associations — Practice Areas: Insurance Coverage; Bad Faith; Criminal Defense; Family Law — E-mail: cbrecht@richardsconnor.com

Anthony D. Mann — 1980 — The University of Iowa, B.A., 2003; The University of Tulsa, J.D. (with honors), 2011 — Admitted to Bar, 2011, Oklahoma — Member Oklahoma Bar Association — Practice Areas: Insurance Coverage Litigation; Bad Faith; Insurance Defense — E-mail: amann@richardsconnor.com

Adam L. Wilson — 1977 — Oklahoma State University, B.S.Ed., 2000; The University of Oklahoma, J.D., 2010 — Admitted to Bar, 2010, Oklahoma; U.S. District Court, Eastern, Northern and Western Districts of Oklahoma; U.S. Court of Appeals, Tenth Circuit — Member Oklahoma Bar Association — Practice Areas: Insurance Coverage — E-mail: awilson@richardsconnor.com

Colby C. Pearce — 1986 — University of Arkansas, B.S. Business Admin. (cum laude), 2008; The University of Oklahoma, J.D., 2011 — Admitted to Bar, 2011, Oklahoma; U.S. District Court, Eastern and Northern Districts of Oklahoma — Member Oklahoma and Tulsa County Bar Associations — Practice Areas: Insurance Coverage Litigation; Insurance Defense; Bad Faith — E-mail: cpearce@richardsconnor.com

Nicole D. Herron — 1984 — Oklahoma State University, B.S. Business Admin., 2007; The University of Oklahoma, J.D., 2010 — Admitted to Bar, 2010, Oklahoma — Member Oklahoma Bar Association — Practice Areas: Insurance Coverage Litigation; Insurance Defense — E-mail: nherron@richardsconnor.com

Matthew S. Saint — 1966 — Oklahoma State University, B.A. Political Science, 2010; The University of Tulsa, J.D., 2013 — Admitted to Bar, 2014, Oklahoma — Member Oklahoma and Tulsa County Bar Associations; American Inns of Court — Practice Areas: Insurance Defense; Bad Faith; Insurance Coverage — E-mail: msaint@richardsconnor.com

Stephen G. Layman — 1977 — Colorado College, B.A., 2000; The University of Tulsa, J.D., 2008 — Admitted to Bar, 2009, Oklahoma; U.S. District Court, Northern District of Oklahoma; 2010, U.S. District Court, Western District of Oklahoma; 2012, U.S. Court of Appeals, Tenth Circuit; 2013, U.S. District Court, Eastern District of Oklahoma — Member Oklahoma and Tulsa County Bar Associations; American Inns of Court — Practice Areas: Medical Malpractice Defense; General Civil Litigation; Criminal Defense — E-mail: slayman@richardsconnor.com

Of Counsel

Lawrence R. Murphy Jr. — 1972 — Saint Anselm College, B.A., 1994; The University of Tulsa, J.D., 1997 — Admitted to Bar, 1997, Oklahoma — Member Oklahoma Bar Association; Claims and Litigation Management Alliance; Litigation Counsel of America — Practice Areas: Insurance Coverage; Bad Faith; Class Actions — E-mail: lmurphy@richardsconnor.com

---

Savage Baum & Glass

401 South Boston Avenue, Suite 2300
Tulsa, Oklahoma 74103
Telephone: 918-938-7944
Fax: 918-938-7966
E-Mail: jglass@savagebaumglass.com
www.savagebaumglass.com

Civil Litigation, Excess and Surplus Lines, Extra-Contractual Litigation, Health Care, Insurance Coverage, Professional Liability

Firm Profile: The attorneys of Savage Baum & Glass have over 70 years of combined legal expertise. The firm is committed to meeting their client's legal needs in an effective, efficient and professional manner. Our clients' rights and interests will be aggressively protected and advocated throughout the legal process.

Insurance Clients

James River Insurance Company
United States Liability Insurance Company
GEICO

Partners

R. Scott Savage — Oklahoma University, B.A. (President's Honor Roll), 1975; J.D. (Dean's List), 1978 — Admitted to Bar, 1978, Oklahoma; U.S. District Court, Eastern, Northern and Western Districts of Oklahoma; U.S. Court of Appeals, Tenth Circuit — Member Oklahoma and Tulsa County Bar Associations; Oklahoma Attorneys Mutual (Board of Directors); American Inns of Court — Adjunct Settlement Judge, U.S. District Court, Northern District of Oklahoma

Jeffrey C. Baum — The University of Oklahoma, B.A., 1992; J.D., 1995 — Admitted to Bar, 1996, Oklahoma; U.S. District Court, Eastern, Northern and Western Districts of Oklahoma; U.S. Court of Appeals, Tenth Circuit; U.S. Supreme Court — Member Oklahoma and Tulsa County (Board of Directors, 2002) Bar Associations; Oklahoma Association of Defense Counsel; Defense Research Institute; American Inns of Court

Jason Lee Glass — Southern Methodist University, B.A./B.B.A. (magna cum laude), 1993; The University of Texas at Austin, J.D., 1997 — Admitted to Bar, 1997, Oklahoma; U.S. District Court, Eastern, Northern and Western Districts of Oklahoma; U.S. Court of Appeals, Tenth Circuit; U.S. Supreme Court — Member Oklahoma and Tulsa County Bar Associations; Oklahoma Association of Defense Counsel (Officer, Board Member); Community Food Bank of Eastern Oklahoma (Board Member); Defense Research Institute

---

Secrest, Hill, Butler & Secrest, P.C.

7134 South Yale, Suite 900
Tulsa, Oklahoma 74136
Telephone: 918-494-5905
Fax: 918-494-2847
E-Mail: wmhill@secresthill.com
www.secresthill.com

Established: 1984

Insurance Defense, General Liability, Automobile Liability, Medical Malpractice, Dental Malpractice, Professional Liability, Product Liability, Environmental Law, Workers' Compensation, Bad Faith, Extra-Contractual Litigation, Trucking Law, Aviation, Medical Devices, Nursing Home Liability, Accountant Malpractice, Employment Law, Construction Defect, Architects and Engineers Malpractice

Firm Profile: Since its formation, the philosophy of Secrest, Hill, Butler & Secrest has been to provide exceptional, aggressive and ethical legal representation to its clients in the civil judicial system. There are three principles underlying our philosophy.

First, the firm is committed to providing personalized service to our clients, always keeping them informed as to the status of their cases. Dialogue is constantly promoted between the firm and our clients, focusing upon their personal involvement in the legal process.

Secrest, Hill, Butler & Secrest, P.C., Tulsa, OK (Continued)

Second, we endeavor to perform only truly productive and meaningful discovery. Through such discovery, we seek to bring legal matters to an early resolution if possible, and if not, thoroughly and aggressively prepare them for successful resolution at trial.

Third, in representing our clients, we are committed to maintaining the ethical standards of our profession, as officers of the court. This includes providing exceptional legal services at fair and reasonable rates.

Although Secrest, Hill, Butler & Secrest has historically provided legal counsel to named defendants through assignments from insurance carriers, and continues to do so, the changing insurance climate has resulted in many corporations and companies becoming self-insured. As a result, a growing percentage of our legal services are provided directly to named defendants. Additionally, we have extensive experience in representing insurers directly in coverage and extra-contractual disputes with their policyholders.

Insurance Clients

Allied Fidelity Insurance Company
American Continental Insurance Company
Burlington Insurance Company
Canal Insurance Company
Century Insurance Group
Chubb Group of Insurance Companies
CNA Insurance Companies
ESIS Insurance Services
Fortress Insurance Company
GEICO Insurance Companies
Great West Casualty Company
GuideOne Insurance
Liberty Mutual Insurance Company
National American Insurance Company
North American Specialty Insurance Company
Philadelphia Indemnity Insurance Company
Progressive Group
ProSight Specialty Insurance Company
Safeco/American States Insurance Company
Shand Morahan & Company, Inc.
Stonecreek Specialty
Travelers Insurance Companies
Western Heritage Insurance
Alterra Specialty Insurance Company
Brotherhood Mutual Insurance Company
Catlin Specialty Insurance Company
Cincinnati Equitable Insurance Company
Darwin Professional Underwriters, Inc.
Gallagher Bassett Services, Inc.
Great American Insurance Company
Legion Insurance Company
Mid-Continent Casualty Company
North American Physicians Insurance Risk Retention Group
OMS National Insurance Company
Pennsylvania Lumbermens Mutual Insurance Company
Podiatry Insurance Company of America (PICA)
Reliance National Insurance Company
St. Paul Insurance Company
Scottsdale Insurance Company
State Volunteer Mutual Insurance Company
United National Group
Zurich U.S.

Non-Insurance Clients

Alexsis, Inc.
Avis Rent-A-Car System, LLC
Community Health Systems, Inc.
Flying J, Inc.
HoganTaylor, LLP
Koch Industries, Inc.
Parke-Davis
Raytheon Company
Sears, Roebuck and Co.
AutoZone, Inc.
Cessna Aircraft Company
Contract Freighters, Inc.
Freightliner, LLC
Kentucky Fried Chicken Corporation
Pepsi-Cola Company
SAIA Motor Freight Line, Inc.
Warner-Lambert Company

Partners/Shareholders

James K. Secrest, II — 1947 — The University of Tulsa, B.S.B.A., 1969; J.D., 1972 — Admitted to Bar, 1972, Oklahoma; Supreme Court of Oklahoma; 1979, U.S. District Court, Eastern, Northern and Western Districts of Oklahoma; U.S. Court of Appeals, Tenth Circuit; U.S. Supreme Court — Member Federal and Tulsa County Bar Associations; Oklahoma Association of Defense Counsel (President, 1986; President Elect, 1985; Secretary-Treasure, 1982-1985; Board of Directors, 1980-1982); Fellow, American College of Trial Lawyers; The American Board of Trial Advocates (Charter Member; Past President, Oklahoma Chapter); American Arbitration Association (Commercial Panel); International Association of Defense Counsel; American Inns of Court; Fellow, International Academy of Trial Lawyers — E-mail: jsecrest@secresthill.com

W. Michael Hill — 1947 — Baylor University, B.A., 1969; The University of Tulsa, J.D., 1973 — Admitted to Bar, 1974, Oklahoma; 1976, U.S. District Court, Eastern, Northern and Western Districts of Oklahoma; U.S. Court of Appeals, Eighth and Tenth Circuits; 1979, U.S. Supreme Court — Member American, Oklahoma and Tulsa County Bar Associations; Oklahoma Association of Defense Counsel (Board of Directors, 1985-1988; Vice President, 1989); American Board of Trial Advocates (Charter Member); Federation of Defense and Corporate Counsel; American Inns of Court; Defense Research Institute — E-mail: wmhill@secresthill.com

Roger N. Butler, Jr. — 1964 — The University of Oklahoma, B.A., 1986; J.D., 1989 — Admitted to Bar, 1989, Oklahoma; 1993, Arkansas; 1989, U.S. District Court, Northern District of Oklahoma; 1990, U.S. District Court, Eastern District of Oklahoma; 1992, U.S. District Court, Western District of Oklahoma; 1993, U.S. District Court, Eastern and Western Districts of Arkansas; U.S. Court of Appeals, Tenth Circuit; 1995, U.S. Court of Appeals, Eighth Circuit — Member Arkansas, Oklahoma and Tulsa County Bar Associations; Oklahoma Association of Defense Counsel (Board of Directors, 2006-2009; Vice-President, 2006; President Elect, 2007; President, 2008; Past President, 2009); Defense Research Institute (Professionalism Committee, 2007-2009); International Association of Defense Counsel — "Piercing Workers' Compensation Exclusivity Through the Independent Legal Relationship Doctrine", 61 Oklahoma Bar Journal 3436, 12-29-90 — E-mail: rbutler@secresthill.com

James Keith Secrest, III — 1972 — Oklahoma State University, B.S., 1996; The University of Tulsa, J.D., 2000 — Admitted to Bar, 2000, Oklahoma; U.S. District Court, Eastern, Northern and Western Districts of Oklahoma — Member American and Oklahoma Bar Associations; Trial Lawyers Bar Association; Oklahoma Association of Defense Counsel; Defense Research Institute; International Association of Defense Counsel — E-mail: jsecrest3@secresthill.com

Partners

Edward J. Main — 1947 — The University of Tulsa, B.A., 1969; Southern Illinois University Carbondale, M.A., 1974; Ph.D., 1982; The University of Tulsa, J.D. (with honors), 1986 — Admitted to Bar, 1986, Oklahoma; U.S. District Court, Eastern, Northern and Western Districts of Oklahoma; U.S. Court of Appeals, Eighth and Tenth Circuits; U.S. Supreme Court — Member American, Oklahoma and Tulsa County Bar Associations; Oklahoma Association of Defense Counsel — "Bad Faith After Badillo", 77 Oklahoma Bar Journal 149 (January 14, 2006); "The Perfect(ed) Appeal", 75 Oklahoma Bar Journal 749 (March 13, 2004); "Who Owns a Nursing Facility?", 75 Oklahoma Bar Journal 111 (January 17, 2004); "The Current State of Landowner Liability in Oklahoma", 63 Oklahoma Bar Journal 2723, (September 30, 1992); "Bad Faith in the Workers' Compensation Context: A Cause in Search of an Action", 30 Tulsa Law Journal 507 (1995); "The Relevance of a Biological Definition of Life to Fundamental Rights", 6 Medicine and Law 189 (1987); "The Neglected Prong of the Miller Test for Obscenity: Serious Literary, Artistic, Political or Scientific Value", 11 Southern Illinois University Law Journal 1159 (1987); "Removal, Remand and Review of 'Bad Faith' Workers' Compensation Claims", 13 Thomas M. Cooley Law Review 121 (1996) — E-mail: emain@secresthill.com

Tara Perkinson — 1975 — University of Arkansas, B.A., 1998; J.D., 2001 — Admitted to Bar, 2001, Oklahoma; 2005, U.S. District Court, Northern and Western Districts of Oklahoma — E-mail: tperkinson@secresthill.com

Associates

Jennifer L. Struble — 1971 — Oklahoma State University, B.S., 1993; The University of Oklahoma, M.P.A., 1995; The University of Tulsa, J.D. (with honors), 2003 — Admitted to Bar, 2003, Oklahoma; U.S. District Court, Eastern, Northern and Western Districts of Oklahoma; 2004, U.S. District Court, District of Colorado; U.S. Court of Appeals, Tenth Circuit; 2012, U.S. Supreme Court — Member Oklahoma and Tulsa County Bar Associations; Defense Research Institute; Oklahoma Association of Defense Counsel — Reported Cases: Southern Hospitality, Inc. v. Zurich, 393 F.3d 1137 (10th Circuit 2004); Larry Snyder and Company v. Miller, 648 F.3d 1156 (10th Cir. 2011). — E-mail: jstruble@secresthill.com

Eric L. Clark — 1973 — The University of Oklahoma, B.A., 1997; Texas A&M University, J.D., 2008 — Admitted to Bar, 2008, Oklahoma; U.S. District Court, Eastern and Northern Districts of Oklahoma; U.S. District Court, Western District of Oklahoma; Chickasaw Nation Tribal Court — Member Oklahoma and Tulsa County Bar Associations; National Conference of Law Reviews (Board of Director, 2008-2013); Oklahoma Association of Defense Counsel — Super Lawyers Rising Star, 2014 — E-mail: eclark@secresthill.com

Seth A. Caywood — 1984 — The University of Tulsa, B.Mus., 2007; J.D., 2011 — Admitted to Bar, 2011, Oklahoma; 2012, U.S. District Court, Eastern, Northern, and Western Districts of Oklahoma; Cherokee Nation Tribal Courts — Member American, Oklahoma and Tulsa County Bar Associations;

TULSA

Secrest, Hill, Butler & Secrest, P.C., Tulsa, OK (Continued)

Defense Research Institute; Oklahoma Association of Defense Counsel — E-mail: scaywood@secresthill.com

James L. Colvin III — 1980 — The University of Georgia, B.A., 2002; The University of Tulsa, J.D., 2004 — Admitted to Bar, 2005, Oklahoma; 2010, Utah; 2005, U.S. District Court, Eastern, Northern and Western Districts of Oklahoma; 2010, U.S. District Court, District of Utah — Member Oklahoma and Tulsa County Bar Associations; Utah State Bar; American Inns of Court; Defense Research Institute; Oklahoma Association of Defense Counsel — E-mail: jcolvin@secresthill.com

Jeffrey Fields — 1971 — Eastern Kentucky University, B.S. (Dean's List), 1992; The University of Tulsa, J.D., 1999 — Admitted to Bar, 2000, Oklahoma; U.S. District Court, Eastern, Northern and Western Districts of Oklahoma; U.S. Court of Appeals, Tenth Circuit — Member Oklahoma Bar Association — E-mail: jfields@secresthill.com

Diane M. Black — 1968 — The University of Tulsa, B.A./B.A., 1994; J.D., 1999 — Admitted to Bar, 2000, Oklahoma; U.S. District Court, Eastern and Northern Districts of Oklahoma; 2001, U.S. District Court, Western District of Oklahoma; 2006, U.S. Court of Appeals, Tenth Circuit — Member Oklahoma and Tulsa County Bar Associations; Oklahoma Association of Defense Counsel — E-mail: dblack@secresthill.com

Eddie L. Carr — 1961 — Central State University, B.S.P.S., 1984; Oklahoma City University, J.D., 1988 — Admitted to Bar, 1989, Oklahoma; U.S. District Court, Eastern, Northern and Western Districts of Oklahoma — E-mail: ecarr@secresthill.com

Smiling, Wangsgard, Smiling & Burgess

9175 South Yale Avenue, Suite 300
Tulsa, Oklahoma 74137
Telephone: 918-477-7500
Fax: 918-477-7510
E-Mail: slf@smilinglaw.com
www.smilinglaw.com

Established: 2000

Insurance Defense, State and Federal Courts, First and Third Party Defense, Product Liability, Medical Malpractice, Legal Malpractice, Hospitals, Nursing Home Liability, Health Care, Civil Rights, Employment Law, Workers' Compensation, Premises Liability, Subrogation, Environmental Law, Transportation, Common Carrier, Arson, Property and Casualty, Commercial Litigation, Mediation, Arbitration, Construction Law, Adoption, Trucking, Criminal Law, Business Planning

Insurance Clients

American Premier Insurance Company
Columbia Insurance Company
Farmers Insurance Company
Farmers Insurance Exchange
Markel Insurance Company
Mid-Century Insurance Company
Nationwide Insurance
Republic Insurance Company
Shelter Life Insurance Company
Truck Insurance Exchange
Zurich Insurance Company
Atlanta Casualty Company
Burlington Insurance Company
Employers Mutual Insurance Company
Fulcrum Insurance Company
Mercury Insurance Company
Mountain Insurance Agency, Inc.
Nautilus Insurance Company
St. Paul Reinsurance Company Limited
Universal Underwriters Insurance Company

Non-Insurance Clients

Covenant Transport, Inc.

Firm Members

A. Mark Smiling — 1958 — Lee College, B.S., 1980; O.W. Coburn School of Law, Oral Roberts University, J.D., 1983 — Admitted to Bar, 1984, Oklahoma; 1998, North Carolina; 2004, Missouri — Member Oklahoma and Tulsa County Bar Associations; Oklahoma Association of Defense Counsel (Vice President, 1991; Board of Directors); Diplomat, American Board of Trial Advocates; National Association of Subrogation Professionals; Defense Research Institute; International Association of Defense Counsel; Federation of Defense and Corporate Counsel — Selected Best Lawyers in America; Super Lawyers, Oklahoma; Tulsa Top Lawyers — E-mail: msmiling@smilinglaw.com

Smiling, Wangsgard, Smiling & Burgess, Tulsa, OK (Continued)

Gentry M. Smiling — 1986 — Oklahoma State University, B.A., 2009; The University of Oklahoma College of Law, J.D., 2012 — Admitted to Bar, 2012, Oklahoma; U.S. District Court, Northern and Western Districts of Oklahoma; 2013, U.S. District Court, Eastern District of Oklahoma — Member Oklahoma and Tulsa County Bar Associations — E-mail: gsmiling@smilinglaw.com

Stephan A. Wangsgard — 1967 — Arizona State University, B.A., 1993; University of Tulsa College of Law, J.D., 1996 — Admitted to Bar, 1996, Oklahoma; 2000, U.S. District Court, Northern District of Oklahoma; 2002, U.S. District Court, Eastern District of Oklahoma — Member Oklahoma and Tulsa County Bar Associations — E-mail: swangsgard@smilinglaw.com

Shena E. Burgess — 1975 — Catawba College, B.A., 1997; University of Tulsa College of Law, J.D., 2000 — Admitted to Bar, 2000, Oklahoma; U.S. District Court, Eastern, Northern and Western Districts of Oklahoma — Member Tulsa County Bar Association; Oklahoma Criminal Defense Lawyers Association; Tulsa County Defense Lawyers Association — E-mail: sburgess@smilinglaw.com

Stauffer & Nathan, P.C.

5705 East 71st Street, Suite 150
Tulsa, Oklahoma 74136
Telephone: 918-592-7070
Fax: 918-592-7071
E-Mail: jnathan@staufferlaw.com
www.staufferlaw.com

Established: 1990

Insurance Coverage, Insurance Defense, Product Liability, Personal Injury, Commercial Litigation, Civil Litigation

Firm Profile: Since 1990, Stauffer & Nathan have been providing their clients with excellent quality legal services at a reasonable price. The firm handles and tries insurance coverage issues, bad faith claims, complex personal injury cases, and products liability claims. Personal, professional service is the key to our success, and we prove it every day by winning our clients' cases.

Insurance Clients

Casualty Corporation of America
Mt. Hawley Insurance Company
Sedgwick CMS
State Farm Fire and Casualty Company
West Bend Mutual Insurance Company
MetLife Auto & Home
RLI Insurance Company
Shelter Mutual Insurance Company
State Farm Mutual Automobile Insurance Company

Non-Insurance Clients

Hickok-Dible Companies

Firm Members

Neal E. Stauffer — 1956 — The University of Oklahoma, B.B.A., 1979; J.D., 1989 — Admitted to Bar, 1989, Oklahoma; U.S. District Court, Eastern, Northern and Western Districts of Oklahoma; U.S. Court of Appeals, Tenth Circuit — Member American, Oklahoma and Tulsa County Bar Associations; International Association of Special Investigation Units (IASIU)

Jody R. Nathan — 1957 — Reed College, B.A., 1979; The University of Oklahoma, J.D., 1986 — Admitted to Bar, 1986, Oklahoma; 2007, Arkansas; 2010, Missouri; 1986, U.S. District Court, Eastern, Northern and Western Districts of Oklahoma; U.S. Court of Appeals, Eighth and Tenth Circuits; 1993, U.S. Supreme Court — Member American, Oklahoma and Tulsa County Bar Associations; Tenth Circuit Judicial Conference; Oklahoma Association of Defense Counsel

Associates

Nathaniel Guy Parrilli — 1975 — University of Illinois, B.A., 1997; The University of Tulsa, J.D., 2000 — Admitted to Bar, 2000, Oklahoma; U.S. District Court, Eastern and Northern Districts of Oklahoma

Timothy P. Clancy — 1958 — University of Arkansas, B.S.B.A., 1980; The University of Tulsa, J.D., 1990 — Admitted to Bar, 1990, Oklahoma; U.S. District Court, Eastern, Northern and Western Districts of Oklahoma

Jessica L. Tait — 1977 — The University of Tulsa, B.A. (Phi Beta Kappa, magna cum laude), 2001; J.D. (magna cum laude), 2011 — Admitted to Bar,

OKLAHOMA

Stauffer & Nathan, P.C., Tulsa, OK (Continued)

2011, Oklahoma; U.S. District Court, Eastern District of Oklahoma; 2014, U.S. District Court, Northern and Western Districts of Oklahoma; U.S. Court of Appeals, Eighth and Tenth Circuits — Member American, Oklahoma and Tulsa County Bar Associations

Of Counsel

Lawrence (Larry) W. Zeringue — 1946 — The University of Iowa, B.S., 1971; The University of Tulsa, J.D., 1974 — Phi Delta Phi — Admitted to Bar, 1975, Iowa; 1978, Oklahoma; U.S. District Court, Eastern, Northern and Western Districts of Oklahoma; U.S. Court of Appeals, Tenth Circuit; 1979, U.S. Supreme Court — Member American, Oklahoma and Tulsa County Bar Associations; Council Oak/Johnson-Sontag Chapter, American Inns of Court (Master of the Bar) — Tulsa's Top Lawyers, 2011, 2012; Oklahoma's Top Rated Lawyers, 2012

The following firms also service this area.

Barnum & Clinton, PLLC
1011 24th Avenue, N.W.
Norman, Oklahoma 73069
 Telephone: 405-579-7300
 Fax: 405-579-0140

Mailing Address: P.O. Box 720298, Norman, OK 73070

Workers' Compensation, Premises Liability, Automobile Liability, Business Litigation, Business Transactions, Commercial Law, Commercial Litigation, Employer Liability, Employment Law, Employment Litigation, General Civil Litigation, General Defense, Occupational Accident

SEE COMPLETE LISTING UNDER NORMAN, OKLAHOMA (123 MILES)

Frailey, Chaffin, Cordell, Perryman, Sterkel, McCalla & Brown, L.L.P.
201 North Fourth Street
Chickasha, Oklahoma 73023
 Telephone: 405-224-0237
 Fax: 405-222-2319

Mailing Address: P.O. Box 533, Chickasha, OK 73018

Administrative Law, Agriculture, Business Law, Civil Litigation, Commercial Transactions, Energy, Fire, Governmental Liability, Insurance Coverage, Insurance Defense, Municipal Law, Negligence, Oil and Gas, Premises Liability, Product Liability, Tort Litigation

SEE COMPLETE LISTING UNDER CHICKASHA, OKLAHOMA (148 MILES)

WAURIKA † 2,064 Jefferson Co.

Refer To

Fischl, Culp, McMillin, Chaffin, Bahner & Long, L.L.P.
100 E Street, S.W.
Ardmore, Oklahoma 73401
 Telephone: 580-223-4321
 Fax: 580-226-4795

Mailing Address: P.O. Box 1766, Ardmore, OK 73402-1766

Insurance Defense, Trial Practice, Automobile, Product Liability, General Liability, Property and Casualty, Bad Faith

SEE COMPLETE LISTING UNDER ARDMORE, OKLAHOMA (55 MILES)

WOODWARD † 12,051 Woodward Co.

Refer To

Frailey, Chaffin, Cordell, Perryman, Sterkel, McCalla & Brown, L.L.P.
201 North Fourth Street
Chickasha, Oklahoma 73023
 Telephone: 405-224-0237
 Fax: 405-222-2319

Mailing Address: P.O. Box 533, Chickasha, OK 73018

Administrative Law, Agriculture, Business Law, Civil Litigation, Commercial Transactions, Energy, Fire, Governmental Liability, Insurance Coverage, Insurance Defense, Municipal Law, Negligence, Oil and Gas, Premises Liability, Product Liability, Tort Litigation

SEE COMPLETE LISTING UNDER CHICKASHA, OKLAHOMA (148 MILES)

YUKON 22,709 Canadian Co.

Wheatley, Segler, Osby & Miller, LLC

501 West Main Street
Yukon, Oklahoma 73099
 Telephone: 405-354-5276
 Fax: 405-350-0537
 E-Mail: mwyukonlaw@swbell.net

Established: 1960

Insurance Defense, General Liability, Trucking Law, Product Liability, Subrogation, Life and Health, Business Law

Insurance Clients

County Claims of Oklahoma, Inc.
Liberty International Underwriters
National American Insurance Company
Sedgwick CMS
Union Fidelity Life Insurance Company
Fairmont Specialty Group
Lombard Canada
Old Republic Insurance Company
Royal Surplus Lines Insurance Company

Partners

Matt L. Wheatley — 1959 — Oklahoma State University, B.S., 1982; The University of Oklahoma, J.D., 1991 — Admitted to Bar, 1991, Oklahoma; U.S. District Court, Eastern, Northern, and Western Districts of Oklahoma; U.S. Court of Appeals, Tenth Circuit — Member Oklahoma Association of Defense Counsel — E-mail: mwyukonlaw@swbell.net

Michael D. Segler — 1958 — The University of Oklahoma, B.B.A., 1981; J.D., 1984 — Admitted to Bar, 1984, Oklahoma; U.S. District Court, Eastern, Northern, and Western Districts of Oklahoma — Yukon City Attorney (1994 to Present) — E-mail: msyukonlaw@swbell.net

Associates

Mark W. Osby — 1968 — The University of Oklahoma, B.A., 1991; Oklahoma City University, J.D., 1994 — Admitted to Bar, 1994, Oklahoma; U.S. District Court, Western District of Oklahoma — E-mail: moyukonlaw@swbell.net

Jonathan E. Miller — 1959 — Oklahoma State University, B.S., 1981; The University of Oklahoma, J.D. (with honors), 1984 — Admitted to Bar, 1984, Oklahoma; U.S. District Court, Eastern and Western Districts of Oklahoma; 2003, U.S. Supreme Court — E-mail: jemyukonlaw@swbell.net